THE NEW INTERNATIONAL
WEBSTER'S
DICTIONARY
& THESAURUS
OF THE ENGLISH LANGUAGE

INTERNATIONAL
ENCYCLOPEDIC EDITION

TRIDENT PRESS
INTERNATIONAL
2002 EDITION

TRIDENT PRESS INTERNATIONAL
Copyright © 2002

Dictionary Portion: pages 1-1150
Copyright © 1992-2002
by Typhoon International

derived from
Funk & Wagnalls
New Comprehensive International Dictionary
of the English Language

2002 PRINTING

ISBN 1-888777-85-0 Jacketed Std.
ISBN 1-582794-41-3 Jacketed Intl.
ISBN 1-582793-17-4 Jacketed U.S.A.
ISBN 1-888777-86-0 Padded
Printed in Canada

Contents

Explanatory Notes

See pronunciation key on page i x

Syllabication — **Car·bo·run·dum** (kär'bə·run'dəm) *n.* An abrasive of silicon carbide: ⌊a trade name.⌋

Pronunciation —

Trade name — **-cidal** *combining form⌋* Killing; able to kill: *homicidal.* [<L *caedere* kill]

Combining form — **Col·o·ra·do** (kol'ə·rä'dō, -rad'ō) A western State of the United States; 103,967 square miles; capital, Denver; entered the Union Aug. 1, 1876: nicknamed *Centennial State:*

Geographic entry —

Abbreviation — abbr. *Colo.⌋*

com- *prefix⌋* With; together: *combine, compare.* Also: *co-* before *gn, h,* and vowels; *col-* before *l,* as in *collide; con-* before *c, d, f, g, j, n, q, s, t, v,* as in *concur, confluence, connect, conspire; cor-* before *r,* as in *correspond.* [<L *com- < cum* with]

Prefix —

Cross-reference — **craal** (kräl) ⌊See KRAAL.⌋

Part of speech — **crab¹** (krab) *n.⌋* **1** Any of various species of ten-footed crustaceans of the suborder *Brachyura* in the order *Decapoda,* characterized by a small abdomen folded under the body, a flattened carapace, and short antennae. They can walk in any direction without turning, but usually move sideways. **2** The hermit crab. **3** The horseshoe crab. **4** A

Taxonomic classification — crab louse, ⌊*Phthirus pubis.*⌋ **5** *Aeron.* The lateral slant in an airplane needed to maintain a flight line in a cross-wind. **6** A form of windlass. **7** *pl.* The lowest throw of a pair of

Idiomatic phrase — dice.⌋ **— to catch a crab⌋** In rowing, to sink an oar blade too deeply; also, to miss the water entirely or skim the surface in making a stroke, and thus fall backward. — *v.* **crabbed, crab·bing** *v.i.* **1** To take or fish for crabs.

Usage label — **2** ⌊*U.S. Colloq.*⌋ To back out: to *crab* out of an agreement. **3** *Naut.* To drift sideways, as a

Field label — ship. — *v.t.* **4** ⌊*Aeron.*⌋ To head (an airplane) across a contrary wind so as to compensate for drift. [OE *crabba.* Akin to CRAB³.]

Homograph — **crab²** (krab) *n.* **1** A crab apple. **2** A crab-apple tree. **3** An ill-tempered, surly, or querulous person. — *v.* **crabbed, crab·bing** *v.i.* **1** *Colloq.* To disparage; belittle; complain about. **2**

Illustrative example — *Colloq.* To ruin or spoil: ⌊*He crabbed* the entire act.⌋ **3** *Obs.* To make surly or sour; irritate. **4** *Brit. Dial.* To cudgel or beat, as with a crabstick. — *v.i.* **5** To be ill-tempered. [? <Scand. Cf. dial. Sw. *scrabba* wild apple.]

Inflected forms — **crab³** (krab) *v.i.* ⌊**crabbed, crab·bing**⌋ To seize each other fiercely, as hawks when fighting; claw. [<MDu. *crabben* scratch. Akin to CRAB¹.]

Crab A constellation and sign of the Zodiac; Cancer.

Phrasal entry — **crab angle⌋** The angle between the direction of movement . of an airplane, rocket, or guided missile and the direction in which the nose points, resembling . . .

Variant — **crab apple** A kind of small, sour apple: ⌊also called *crab.*⌋

Hyphenation — **deep·seat·ed⌋** (dēp'sē'tid) *adj.* So far in as to be ineradicable or almost ineradicable: said of emotions, diseases, etc.

Deep South The southernmost parts of Alabama, Georgia, Louisiana, and Mississippi, conventionally regarded as typifying Southern culture and traditions.

deer (dir) *n. pl.* **deer 1** A ruminant (family *Cervidae*) having deciduous antlers, usually in the male only, as the moose, elk, and reindeer.

Popularly, *deer* is used mainly of the smaller species. ⌊◆ Collateral adjective: *cervine.*⌋ See — Collateral adjective
FALLOW DEER, VENISON. **2** A deerlike animal. **3** Formerly, any quadruped; a wild animal. ⌊◆ Homophone: *dear.*⌋ [OE *dēor* beast] — Homophone

deer·fly (dir'flī') *n.* ⌊*pl.* **·flies**⌋ A bloodsucking — Inflected form
fly (genus *Chrysops*), similar to a horsefly but smaller and with banded wings. For illustration see INSECTS (injurious).

di·eth·y·lene glycol (dī·eth'ə·lēn) *Chem.* An organic compound, ⌊O(CH₂CH₂OH)₂,⌋ used as — Chemical formula
an anti-freeze mixture and as an agent in many chemical processes for the . . . .

di·eth·yl·stil·bes·trol (dī·eth'əl·stil·bes'trōl) *n. Biochem.* ⌊Stilbestrol.⌋ — Cross-reference

di·e·ti·tian (dī'ə·tish'ən) *n.* One skilled in the principles of dietetics and in their practical application in health and disease. ⌊Also **di·e· — Variants
tet·ist** (dī'ə·tet'ist), **di·e·ti'cian.**⌋

Dieu vous garde (dyœ' vōō' gärd') ⌊*French*⌋ — Foreign language label
God protect you.

⌊**Diez** (dēts), **Friedrich Christian,**⌋ 1794-1876, — Biographic entry
German philologist.

dif·fer (dif'ər) *v.i.* **1** To be unlike in quality, degree, form, etc.: ⌊often with *from.*⌋ **2** To disagree; dissent: ⌊often with *with.*⌋ **3** To quarrel: ⌊sometimes with *over* or *about.*⌋ [< — Usage notes
OF *differer* <L *differre* <*dis-* apart + *ferre* carry. Doublet of DEFER¹.]

dif·fer·ence (dif'ər·əns, dif'rəns) *n.* **1** The state or quality of being other or unlike, or that in which two things are unlike; . . . . **8** *Her.* A device in blazons to distinguish persons bearing the same arms. — *v.t.* **·enced, ·enc·ing** ⌊**1**⌋ To make or mark as different; — Definition numbers
distinguish; discriminate. ⌊**2**⌋ *Her.* To add a mark of difference to.

⌊*Synonyms (noun):*⌋ contrariety, contrast, disagreement, discrepancy, discrimination, disparity, dissimilarity, dissimilitude, distinction, divergence, diversity, inconsistency, inequality, unlikeness, variation. A *difference* is in the things compared; . . . .*Diversity* involves more than two objects; *variation* is a *difference* in the condition or action . of the same object at different times. ⌊*Antonyms:* — Antonyms
agreement, consonance, harmony, identity, likeness, resemblance, sameness, similarity, uniformity, unity.

dif·fer·ent (dif'ər·ənt, dif'rənt) *adj.* **1** Not the same; distinct; other: ⌊A *different* clerk is there now.⌋ **2** Marked by a difference; completely — Illustrative example
or partly unlike; dissimilar. **3** Unusual. See synonyms under CONTRARY. [<F *différent* <L *differens, -entis,* ppr. of *differre.* See DIFFER.⌋ **— dif'fer·ent·ly** *adv.* **— dif'fer·ent-** — Run-on entries
ness *n.*⌋ ⌊◆ **different from, than, to**⌋ In American — Usage note
usage, *from* is established as the idiomatic preposition to follow *different;* when, however, a clause follows the connective, *than* is gaining increasing acceptance: a result *different than* (= *from that which* or *from what*) had been expected. This last is established British usage, which also accepts *to* . . . .

⌊**-dom** *suffix of nouns*⌋ **1** State or condition of — Suffix
being: *freedom.* **2** Rank of; domain of: *kingdom.* **3** The totality of those having a certain rank, state or condition: *Christendom.* ⌊⌊OE — Etymology
-dōm < dōm state⌋⌋

v

Syllabication   Division of words into syllables — as an indication of the points at which a word may be broken at the end of a line — is indicated by a centered dot (·) in the main bold-faced entries, as **ad·jec·ti·val**. In the secondary entries (run-on derivatives and variant forms) the centered dot is eliminated wherever the primary and secondary syllable stresses are marked, as in **ad′jec·ti′val·ly**. In hyphened compounds the hyphen takes the place of a centered dot. Phrasal entries of two or more words are not syllabified when each element is entered elsewhere, as in **caballine fountain.**

Pronunciations   The pronunciation is shown in parentheses immediately following the bold-faced entry, as **di·chot·o·my** (dī·kot′ə·mē). When more than one pronunciation is recorded, the first given is usually the most widely used wherever it has been possible to determine extent of usage; often, however, usage may be almost equally divided. The order of the pronunciations is not intended to be an indication of preference; all pronunciations shown are valid for educated American speech.

The syllabication of the pronunciations follows, in general, the syllabic breaks heard in speech, rather than the conventional division of the bold-faced entry, as **bod·ing** (bō′ding), **grat·er** (grā′tər), **ju·di·cial** (jōō·dish′əl), **an·es·the·tize** (ə·nes′thə·tīz).

When a variant pronunciation differs merely in part from the first pronunciation recorded, only the differing syllable or syllables are shown, provided that there is no possibility of misinterpretation, as **eq·ua·bil·i·ty** (ek′wə·bil′ə·tē, ē′kwə-). Phrasal entries (those which consist of two or more words) are not pronounced if the individual elements are separately entered in proper alphabetic place.

Parts of speech   These are shown in italics following the pronunciation for main entries, and are abbreviated as follows: *n.* (noun), *v.* (verb), *pron.* (pronoun), *adj.* (adjective), *adv.* (adverb), *prep.* (preposition), *conj.* (conjunction), *interj.* (interjection). When more than one part of speech is entered under a main entry, the additional designations are run in and preceded by a bold-faced dash, as **cor·ner** (kôr′nər) *n. . . . — v.t. . . . . —v.i. . . . . —adj. . . . .* Verbs used transitively are identified as *v.t.,* those intransitively as *v.i.;* those used both transitively and intransitively in all senses are designated *v.t. & v.i.*

Inflected forms   These include the past tense, past participle, and present participle of verbs, the plural of nouns, and the comparative and superlative of adjectives and adverbs. The inflected forms are entered wherever there is some irregularity in spelling or form. They are shown in boldface type, with syllabication, immediately after the part of speech designation. Only the syllable affected is shown, provided there is no ambiguity possible, as **com·pute** (kəm·pyōōt′) *v.t.* **·put·ed, ·put·ing.** An inflected form that requires pronunciation or is alphabetically distant from the main entry may also be separately entered and pronounced in its proper vocabulary place.

Principal parts of verbs The order in which the principal parts are shown is past tense, past participle, and present participle, as **come** (kum) *v.* **came, come, com·ing.** Where the past tense and past participle are identical, only two forms are entered, as **bake** (bāk) *v.* **baked, bak·ing.** When alternative forms are given, the first form indicated is usually the one preferred, as **grov·el** (gruv′əl, grov′-) *v.i.* **grov·eled** or **grov·elled, grov·el·ing** or **grov·el·ling.** Variant forms not in the standard vocabulary are shown in parentheses and labeled, as **drink** (dringk) *v.* **drank** (*Obs.* **drunk**), **drunk** (*Obs.* **drunk·en**), **drink·ing.** Principal parts entirely regular in formation — those that add –*ed* and –*ing* directly to the infinitive without spelling modification — are not shown.

Plural of nouns Irregular forms are here preceded by the designation *pl.,* as **a·lum·nus** (ə·lum′nəs) *n. pl.* **·ni** (-nī); **co·dex** (kō′deks) *n. pl.* **co·di·ces** (kō′də·sēz, kod′ə-); **deer** (dir) *n. pl.* **deer.** When alternative plurals are given, the first shown is the preferred form, as **buf·fa·lo**

(buf′ə·lō) *n. pl.* **·loes** or **·los; chrys·a·lis** (kris′ə·lis) *n. pl.* **chrys·a·lis·es** or **chry·sal·i·des** (kri·sal′ə·dēz).   Words that have different plural forms for specific senses are shown as follows:

an·ten·na (an·ten′ə) *n. pl.* **an·ten·nae** (an·ten′ē) *for def.* **1, an·ten·nas** *for def.* **2. 1** *Entomol.* One of the paired, lateral, movable, jointed appendages on the head of an insect or other arthropod. **2** *Telecom.* A system of wires upheld in a vertical or horizontal position by a mast or tower, for transmitting or receiving electromagnetic waves in wireless telegraphy, telephony, and radio. . . . .

Comparison of adjectives and adverbs The comparatives and superlatives of adjectives and adverbs are shown immediately after the part of speech when there is some spelling modification or a complete change of form, as **mer·ry** (mer′ē) *adj.* **·ri·er, ·ri·est; bad**[1] (bad) *adj.* **worse, worst; well**[2] (wel) *adv.* **bet·ter, best.**

Definition numbers   In entries for words having several senses, the order in which the definitions appear is, wherever possible, that of frequency of use, rather than semantic evolution. Each such definition is distinguished by a bold-faced number, the numbering starting anew after each part-of-speech designation when it is followed by more than one sense. Closely related meanings, especially those within a specific field or area of study, are defined under the same number and set apart by small bold-faced letters.

bol·ster (bōl′stər) *n.* **1** A long, narrow pillow as wide as a bed. **2** A pad used as a support or . . . . **3** Anything shaped like . . . . **4** *Archit.* **a** The lateral part of the volute of an Ionic capital. **b** A crosspiece of an arch centering . . . . **5** *Mech.* A steel block . . . . *—v.t.* **1** To support with a pillow. **2** To prop up . . . . **3** To furnish with padding. . . .

Restrictive labels   Entries or particular senses of words and terms having restricted application are variously labeled according to: (1) usage level, as *Slang, Colloq.* (colloquial), *Dial.* (dialectal), *Poetic,* etc.; (2) localization, as *U.S.* (United States), *Brit.* (British), *Austral.* (Australian), *Scot.* (Scottish English), etc.; (3) field or subject, as *Astron.* (astronomy), *Geom.* (geometry), *Mining* (mining), *Naut.* (nautical), *Surg.* (surgery), etc.; (4) language of origin, as *Afrikaans, French, German, Latin,* etc.

These labels serve as a guide in the ready identification of special aspects of a word or term as a whole or of one or more of its parts. The usage labels qualify a word in terms of its relationship to standard English; the localized area designations identify the geographical region of the English-speaking world in which a word has originated or where it has particular application; the subject labels indicate that a word or definition has a specialized use in some field of work or study; and the foreign language labels reflect the fact that a word or phrase, although used in English speech and writing, has not yet undergone the process of Anglicization of pronunciation, meaning, or usage, and is still felt to be foreign (these foreign terms are usually italicized in writing).

Restrictive labels that apply to only one sense of a word are entered after the definition number, as:

beat (bēt) *v.* . . . . **9** *Music* To mark or measure with or as with a baton: to *beat* time. **13** *Colloq.* To baffle; perplex: It *beats* me. **14** *Slang* To defraud; swindle. . . . . **20** *Physics* To alternate in intensity so as to pulsate . . . . **24** *Naut.* To work against contrary winds or currents by tacking.

Labels entered immediately after the part of speech designation apply to all the senses for that part of speech; those shown directly after the pronunciation and before the first part-of-speech designation refer to the entire entry, as:

hal·i·dom (hal′ə·dəm) *n. Archaic* **1** Holiness. **2** A holy relic. **3** A holy place; sanctuary. . . .
grouch (grouch) *U.S. Colloq. v.i.* To grumble; be surly or discontented. *— n.* **1** A discontented, grumbling person. **2** A grumbling, sulky mood. . . . .
A complete list of the label abbreviations used in this dictionary will be found on page xx.

Variant forms   In the case of words having more than one approved spelling (as *esthetic, aesthetic; center, centre*), the main entry is made under what is considered to be the form in more general use in the United States. The alternate form is cross-referred when it is not within close range of the alphabetic position of the main entry, and is also shown in italic type at the end of the main entry or after all the definitions for a particular part of speech to which it applies. Variant forms that do not require cross-reference are shown in the same position in the main entry but in boldface type with syllabication, stress marks, and, when necessary, pronunciation. A variant that applies to but one of several senses of a word is attached with a colon to the definition to which it pertains.

bach·e·lor (bach′ə·lər, bach′lər) *n.* . . . . **3** A young knight serving under another's banner: also **bach′e·lor-at-arms′.** . . . . **5** A young male fur seal kept from the breeding grounds by the older males: also called *holluschick.* . . . .

Forms that have some restricted usage are labeled accordingly, as **hon·or** . . . Also *Brit.* **hon′our.**

Phrasal entries   Numerous phrases are entered and defined in the vocabulary section of this book in alphabetic place according to the first word of the phrase, as **bird of paradise, earth inductor, free verse, right of search.** In many other instances, however, it has been more expedient to enter and define such phrases under the main element. Thus, *Old English* and *Middle English* are run in as subordinate entries under **English,** preceded by a heavy dash; *alternating current, direct current,* and *eddy current* are entered and defined under **current.** All such entries are cross-referred in alphabetic place.

In some entries, particularly those for plants and animals, varying combinations of the word being defined are given within the main entry in boldface type and not entered in alphabetic place, as **leop·ard** · · · **2** Any similar cat, such as the **American leopard** or jaguar, the **hunting leopard** or cheetah, the **snow leopard** or ounce.

Encyclopedic entries A similar device has been employed where it has been advisable to bring together in one place as much logically related information as possible. Certain groups of terms are fully treated in an alphabetic boldface listing under the primary word common to each group. This treatment points up significant relationships between terms, facilitates comparison and selection of the term desired, and allows for the presentation of a range of information ordinarily characteristic of encyclopedias. For example, the entry for **time** contains a listing, with full definitions, of the various classifications from *astronomical time* through *zone time.* Similar listings have been included under the following entries: *angle, calendar, court, cross, current (ocean currents), diamond, fraction, glass, law, number, school, spaniel,* and *terrier.* All terms so entered are separately cross-referred.

Idiomatic phrases   Often a main-entry word, when in conjunction with various prepositions, adverbs, adjectives, etc., will form a phrase distinct in sense from the meaning of the combined elements. Such idiomatic phrases are shown in smaller boldface type within the entry for the principal word in the phrase; they are preceded by a heavy dash, and follow all the definitions for the particular part of speech involved. Thus, under the verb **carry** will be found subordinate entries for the phrases *carry arms, carry away, carry off, carry on,* etc.; under the entry for the noun **hand** such phrases as *at first hand, by hand, to have one's hands full,*

add,āce,câre,pälm; end,ēven; it,īce; odd,ōpen,ôrder; tŏŏk,pōōl; up,bûrn; ə = a in *above,* e in *sıcken,* i in *clarity,* o in *melon,* u in *focus;* yōō = u in *fuse;* oi,oil; ou,pout; ch,check; g,go; ng,ring; th,thin; th,this; zh,vision. Foreign sounds á,œ,ü,kh,ń; and ◆: see page xx. < from; + plus; ? possibly.

to lend a hand, etc., are set apart and defined in detail.

Collateral adjectives   Because of the grafting of Norman French and late Renaissance Latin idioms on early English we find a good many English nouns which have adjectives closely connected with them in sense but not in form, such as *brachial* with *arm, cervical* with *neck, lacustrine* with *lake, hibernal* with *winter, diurnal* with *day, reticular* with *net,* and the like. Such adjectives which, through a collateral line of meaning, have come to express certain special adjectival senses, are, of course, listed in their regular alphabetic place, but, as a convenience for those who do not know or cannot recall them, a large number of such functionally related adjectives have been entered with their associated nouns, attached to the particular meaning of the noun to which they apply, in the form ◆ Collateral adjective: *brachial.*

Homophones   Words identical in sound but different in spelling and meaning, such as the groups *altar / alter, filter / philter, hail / hale, principal / principle, right / rite / write,* and several hundred others, often lead to confusion in the writing of English. A large number of these have been listed just before the etymology of every relevant entry, in the form ◆ Homophone: *altar.* No entries have been made for such groups as *horse / hoarse, burrow / burro* which, because of variant pronunciations, are homophonic for some speakers but not for others.

Etymologies   The etymologies are shown in brackets after the definitions and before the run-on derivatives. The following examples show the manner of entry and the use of cross-references: (1) **spe·cial** . . . [<OF *especial* <L *specialis* < *species* kind, species]; the etymology is to be read: derived from (<) the Old French (OF) word *especial* from the Latin (L) word *specialis* which in turn is from Latin *species* meaning "kind, species"; (2) **arroyo** . . . [<Sp.]; here the reading is to be: derived from (<) a Spanish (Sp.) word of the same form and meaning; (3) **has·sle** . . . [? <HAGGLE + TUSSLE]; this etymology is to be read: perhaps (?) derived from (<) a blending of "haggle" and (+) "tussle," the small capital letters indicating that the etymologies of these words will be found under their main entries; (4) **de·cep·tion** . . . [<L *deceptio, -onis* < *decipere.* See DECEIVE.]; (5) **bul·wark** . . . [<MHG *bolwerc.* Akin to BOULEVARD.]; (6) **a·dult** . . . [<L *adultus,* pp. of *adolescere* grow up < *ad-* + *alescere* grow. Related to ADOLESCENT.]; (7) **jour·nal** . . . [<OF <L *diurnalis.* Doublet of DIURNAL.]

Cross-references In (4), "See" directs attention to the etymology under "deceive" for further information; in (5), "Akin to" points to the fact that "boulevard" and "bulwark" are cognate words; in (6), "Related to" indicates that these words derive from different recorded stems of the same word; in (7), "Doublet of" marks the fact that "journal" and "diurnal" are ultimately derived from the same Latin word, but have come into English by different paths, in this case, the former through Old French and the latter directly from Latin.

For the complete list of the abbreviations which are used in the etymologies in this work, see page xx.

Run-on entries   Words that are actually or ostensibly derived from other words by the addition or replacement of a suffix, and whose sense can be inferred from the meaning of the main word, are run on, in smaller boldface type, at the end of the appropriate main entries. The run-on entries are preceded by a heavy dash and followed by a part-of-speech designation. They are syllabified and stressed, and, when necessary, a full or partial pronunciation is indicated, as **in·sip·id** (in·sip′id) *adj.* . . . — **in·si·pid·i·ty** (in′si·pid′ə·tē), **in·sip′id·ness** *n.* — **in·sip′id·ly** *adv.*

Usage notes   Points of grammar and idiom., when an integral part of definition, are included, following a colon, after the particular sense of a word to which they apply, as **anx·ious** . . . **3** Intent; eagerly desirous; solicitous: with *for* or the infinitive with *to: anxious* for success; *anxious* to succeed . . .

More extensive notes consisting of supplementary information on grammar, accepted usage, the relative status of variant forms, etc., are entered at the end of the relevant entries and prefaced with the symbol ◆. (See **any-one, Asiatic, can, have.**)

Synonyms and antonyms   Extended discussions of the differentiation in shades of meaning within a group of related words, or in some cases simple lists of synonyms, are given at the end of relevant entries in paragraphed form after the run-on derivatives. Lists of antonyms are often added as well to point up further distinctions in meaning.

Alphabetization   All entries in this dictionary (general vocabulary, affixes, geographical and biographical entries, foreign words and phrases, etc.) are in one alphabetic list, with the exception of an extended list of abbreviations given, for the sake of ready reference, in one section at the back of the book. Thus, the entry for **ampere** (the electrical unit) immediately precedes that for **André Marie Ampère,** for whom it was named; the entry for **Bridge of Sighs** precedes **Bridgeport** and follows **bridge-head;** the prefix **pro-** is entered immediately after the word **pro** (a professional) and before the word **proa** (a sailing vessel).

Hyphens   The hyphen used in the spelling of hyphemes (hyphened words) in this dictionary is printed with extra length to distinguish it as a spelling characteristic, as **cap-a–pie, battle–scarred.** This lengthened hyphen is also used in the entries for prefixes, suffixes, and combining forms, as **un–, –less, hydro–.** The standard hyphen is utilized at the ends of lines to indicate syllabic breaks in words ordinarily written solid, as *com-prehensive,* while the lengthened hyphen is retained for the end-of-line breaks in hyphemes.

Homographs   These words, which are identical in spelling but differ in meaning and origin (and often in pronunciation), are separately entered and differentiated by the following superior figure, as **bushel¹** (measure), **bushel²** (mend); **pink¹** (color), **pink²** (stab), **pink³** (sailing vessel), **pink⁴** (fade). The numbering also serves to simplify cross-reference to such words.

Cross-references   Cross-references are directions to see another entry for additional information. They direct the reader from a variant spelling, inflected form, subentry, etc., to a main entry. The entry to be sought is generally indicated in small capital letters, as **car·a·cul** . . . See KARAKUL; **aes·thete** . . . , **aes·thet·ic** . . . See ESTHETE, etc.; **cor·po·ra** . . . Plural of CORPUS; **Old English** See under ENGLISH.

Sometimes a cross-reference is made to a homograph entry or to a particular definition or part of speech of the main entry, as

flied (flīd) Past tense and past participle of FLY¹ (def. 7).

taps (taps) See TAP² (*n.* def. 3).

Some entries are defined by citing another form, as

se·pi·o·lite . . . *n.* Meerschaum.

This is a type of cross-reference. Complete information will be found under the word or term used in the definition.

See the note on **Etymologies,** for the system of cross-referring there used.

Prefixes, suffixes, and combining forms These are entered and defined in regular alphabetic order. The prefix is followed by the lengthened hyphen, the suffix preceded by it, as **anti–** *prefix;* **–ical** *suffix.*

Similarly, the combining form is followed or preceded by the lengthened hyphen depending on its position in combination, as **proto–** *combining form;* **–cide** *combining form.*

Word lists   The meaning of many combinations of words (hyphemes, solidemes, and two-word phrases) is easily deduced by combining the senses of their component parts. Such self-explaining compounds have been entered in list form under the first element — that is, under prefixes (**bi–, co–, non–, re–,** etc.) combining forms (**auto–, counter–, mid–,** etc.), and words (**corn, heart, man, peace,** etc.). These lists serve

to indicate the preferred form of a compound — whether written solid, with a hyphen, or as a two–word phrase. The listings are not intended to be all-inclusive; most of the prefixes and combining forms so entered combine freely in English in the formation of new compounds based on existing forms.

Chemical formulas   As an integral part of the definitions of the large number of chemical substances listed in this dictionary, the reader will find the formulas which, in the chemist's shorthand, indicate what constituents enter into a compound, and in what proportions. These formulas, though usually of the simple empirical type, help to prevent confusion in the identification of hundreds of the substances used in medicine, industry, and the arts, and are particularly useful in recognizing distinctions between the two broad fields of inorganic and organic chemicals.

Taxonomic classification   Essential technical information regarding the many plants and animals described under their common names is provided by the listing, usually in italic type enclosed in parentheses, of one or more of the principal taxonomic categories — phylum or division, class, order, family, genus, and species — by which they are correctly identified in botanical and zoological usage. This information, checked against the latest and most reliable sources, is especially useful in showing relationships between seemingly very different types and in discriminating within and between deceptively similar groups, such as toads and frogs, spruce and hemlock, and moths and butterflies.

Trade names   Of the thousands of words used to identify trademarked or proprietary articles, drugs, processes, and services, a generous number have been entered and defined in this book because of their wide public acceptance. In every such case the word is entered as though it were a proper name: that is, with an initial capital letter, and the added notation, "a trade name" or — chiefly for the pharmaceutical products — "a proprietary name (or brand) . . ." This technique is employed to alert the reader to the commercial status of a word and, by implication, to caution him against employing it in a generic sense that might involve him in legal difficulties with those claiming a prescriptive or legal right to its use. This treatment of proprietary names is in no sense to be interpreted as establishing a formal status within the meaning of any of the various statutes involving the protection and use of trade names, registered or otherwise.

Illustrations, maps, and tables   The illustrations in this book — all of them carefully prepared line drawings — have been selected with the emphasis on their explanatory value rather than their pictorial or decorative effect. They often include informative captions, and are intended to supplement the definitions.

A certain number of geographic entries are accompanied by small, precise spot maps which show at a glance just how a given place, region, lake, island, or other feature is related to its immediate surroundings — as under *Congo* (river system), *English Channel, Holy Roman Empire, Suez.*

For a selected group of entries supplementary information has been provided in the form of charts and tables, as for foreign alphabets (see **alphabet**), the geological time scale (see **geology**), chemical elements (see **periodic table**), the major wars of history (see **war**), constellations, clouds, the endocrine glands, etc.

Abbreviations   The abbreviations used in the body of this book (in labeling within entries, in etymologies, etc.) will be found listed on page xx. Where abbreviations of main-entry words are entered, they are shown at the end of the entry, as Abbr. *B.A., A.B.* (Bachelor of Arts); Abbr. *AWOL, awol, A.W.O.L., a.w.o.l.* (absent without leave); Abbr. *Dan.* (Danish). Biblical references are to the King James Bible and indicate book, chapter, and verse, in that order, as *Matt.* v 3–12. An extended list of standard abbreviations will be found at the end of the dictionary, following the vocabulary section.

TABLE OF ENGLISH SPELLINGS

FOLLOWING is a list of words exemplifying the possible spellings for the sounds of English. The sounds represented by these spellings are shown in the pronunciation symbols used in this dictionary, followed by their equivalents in the International Phonetic Alphabet.

a	æ	c*a*t, pl*ai*d, c*a*lf, l*au*gh
ā	eɪ,e	m*a*te, b*ai*t, g*ao*l, g*au*ge, p*ay*, st*ea*k, sk*ei*n, w*eigh*, pr*ey*
â(r)	ɛ,ɛr	d*a*re, f*ai*r, pr*ay*er, wh*e*re, b*ea*r, th*ei*r
ä	ɑ	d*a*rt, *a*h, c*a*lf, l*au*gh, s*e*rgeant, h*ea*rt
b	b	*b*oy, ru*bb*er
ch	tʃ	*ch*ip, ba*tch*, righ*t*eous, bas*ti*on, struc*tu*re
d	d	*d*ay, la*dd*er, calle*d*
e	ɛ	m*a*ny, *ae*sthete, s*ai*d, s*ay*s, b*e*t, st*ea*dy, h*ei*fer, l*eo*pard, fr*ie*nd, f*oe*tid
ē	i	C*ae*sar, qu*ay*, sc*e*ne, m*ea*t, s*ee*, s*ei*ze, p*eo*ple, k*ey*, rav*i*ne, gr*ie*f, ph*oe*be
f	f	*f*ake, *c*offin, cou*gh*, hal*f*, *ph*ase
g	g	*g*ate, be*gg*ar, *gh*oul, *gu*ard, va*gue*
h	h	*h*ot, *wh*om
hw	hw,ʍ	*wh*ale
i	ɪ	pr*e*tty, b*ee*n, t*i*n, s*ie*ve, w*o*men, b*u*sy, g*ui*lt, l*y*nch
ī	aɪ	*ai*sle, *ay*e, sl*eigh*t, *eye*, d*i*me, p*ie*, s*igh*, gu*i*le, b*uy*, *try*, l*ye*
j	dʒ	*e*dge, sol*d*ier, mo*d*ulate, ra*ge*, exa*gg*erate, *j*oy
k	k	*c*an, a*cc*ost, sa*cch*arine, *ch*ord, ta*ck*, a*cq*uit, *k*ing, ta*lk*, li*qu*or
l	l	*l*et, ga*ll*
m	m	dra*chm*, phle*gm*, pa*l*m, *m*ake, li*mb*, gra*mm*ar, conde*mn*
n	n	*gn*ome, *kn*ow, *mn*emonic, *n*ote, ba*nn*er, *pn*eumatic
ng	ŋ	si*nk*, ri*ng*, meri*ngue*
o	ɑ,ɒ	w*a*tch, p*o*t
ō	ou,o	b*eau*, y*eo*man, s*ew*, *o*ver, s*oa*p, r*oe*, *oh*, br*oo*ch, s*ou*l, th*ough*, gr*ow*
ô	ɔ	b*a*ll, b*a*lk, f*au*lt, d*aw*n, c*o*rd, br*oa*d, *ough*t
oi	ɔɪ	p*oi*son, t*oy*
ou	aʊ	*ou*t, b*ough*, c*ow*
o͞o	u	rh*eu*m, dr*ew*, m*o*ve, can*oe*, m*oo*d, gr*ou*p, thr*ough*, fl*u*ke, s*ue*, fr*ui*t
o͝o	ʊ	w*o*lf, f*oo*t, c*ou*ld, p*u*ll
p	p	ma*p*, ha*pp*en
r	r	*r*ose, *rh*ubarb, ma*rr*y, dia*rrh*ea, w*r*iggle
s	s	*c*ite, di*c*e, p*s*yche, *s*aw, *sc*ene, *sch*ism, ma*ss*
sh	ʃ	o*c*ean, *ch*ivalry, vi*ci*ous, *p*shaw, *s*ure, *sch*ist, pre*sc*ience, nau*s*eous, *sh*all, pen*s*ion, ti*ss*ue, fi*ss*ion, po*ti*on
t	t	walk*ed*, though*t*, *phth*isic, *p*tarmigan, *t*one, *Th*omas, bu*tt*er
th	θ	*th*ick
th	ð	*th*is, ba*the*
u	ʌ	s*o*me, d*oe*s, bl*oo*d, y*ou*ng, s*u*n
yo͞o	ju,ɪu	b*eau*ty, *eu*logy, q*ueue*, p*ew*, *ewe*, ad*ieu*, v*iew*, f*u*se, c*ue*, y*ou*th, *yu*le
û(r)	ɜr,ɝ	y*ea*rn, f*e*rn, *e*rr, g*i*rl, w*o*rm, j*ou*rnal, b*u*rn, gu*e*rdon, m*y*rtle
v	v	o*f*, Ste*ph*en, *v*ise, fli*vv*er
w	w	*ch*oir, q*u*ilt, *w*ill
y	j	on*i*on, hallelu*j*ah, *y*et
z	z	wa*s*, di*s*cern, *s*cissors, *x*ylophone, *z*oo, mu*zz*le
zh	ʒ	rou*g*e, plea*s*ure, inci*s*ion, sei*z*ure, gla*z*ier
ə	ə	*a*bove, fount*ai*n, dark*e*n, clar*i*ty, parl*ia*ment, cann*o*n, porp*oi*se, vici*ou*s, loc*u*s
ər	ər,ɚ	mort*ar*, broth*er*, elix*ir*, don*or*, glam*our*, aug*ur*, nat*u*re, zeph*yr*

SPELLING:
Plurals and Participles

BASICALLY, plurals in English are formed by the addition of -*s* or -*es* (depending on the preceding sound) to the complete word; past participles are formed by the addition of -*ed,* and present participles by adding -*ing.* There are, however, many exceptions. In this book, all such exceptions (the "irregular" inflected forms) are indicated within the entry, in boldface immediately following the part–of–speech label.

fly (flī) *n. pl.* **flies** . . .
sheep (shēp) *n. pl.* **sheep** . . .
cal·ci·fy (kal′sə·fī) *v.t. & v.i.* **·fied, ·fy·ing** . . .
go (gō) *v.i.* **went, gone, go·ing** . . .

Some rules for the spelling of these forms (with the exception of nouns which form their plurals by some internal change and the so–called strong verbs) are listed below:

PLURALS

1. Nouns ending in *y* preceded by a consonant change *y* to *i* and add -*es.*

baby babies   story stories

2. Nouns ending in *y* preceded by a vowel add -*s* without change.

chimney chimneys   valley valleys

Note, however, that *money* may have either form in the plural — *moneys, monies.*

3. Some nouns ending in *f* or *fe* change this to *v* and add -*es.*
knife knives   shelf shelves
BUT: roof roofs   safe safes
Note: Some words may have alternate plural forms.

scarf scarfs or scarves

4. Most words ending in *o* form a plural in -*os.*
cameo cameos   folio folios   halo halos
A few words ending in *o* (*echo, hero, Negro,* etc.) form the plural only in -*oes* (*echoes, heroes, Negroes*), but many others in this category have alternative plurals in both forms.

buffalo   buffalos or buffaloes
mosquito   mosquitos or mosquitoes
volcano   volcanoes or volcanos

PAST AND PRESENT PARTICIPLES

1. The final consonant is doubled for monosyllables or words accented on the final syllable when they end in a *single* consonant preceded by a *single* vowel.

control, controlled, controlling
hop, hopped, hopping
occur, occurred, occurring
quit, quitted, quitting (*Note: a u following
q is not to be counted as an additional vowel.*)
BUT: help, helped, helping (*two consonants*)
seed, seeded, seeding (*two vowels*)

Some words *not* accented on the final syllable have a variant participial form with a doubled consonant; the single consonant form is preferred in the United States.

travel, traveled or travelled, traveling or travelling
worship, worshiped or worshipped, worshiping or worshipping

2. Words ending in silent or mute *e* drop the *e* before -*ed* and -*ing,* unless it is needed to avoid confusion with another word.

change, changed, changing   love, loved, loving
singe, singed, singeing   dye, dyed, dyeing

3. Verbs ending in *ie* usually change this to *y* before adding -*ing.*

die, died, dying   lie, lied, lying

4. Verbs ending in *c* add a *k* before -*ed* and -*ing.*
mimic, mimicked, mimicking
picnic, picnicked, picnicking

PRONUNCIATION KEY

The primary stress mark (′) is placed after the syllable bearing the heavier stress or accent; the secondary stress mark (′) follows a syllable having a somewhat lighter stress, as in **com·men·da·tion** (kom′ən·dā′shən).

a	add, map	f	fit, half	n	nice, tin	p	pit, stop	u	up, done	ə	the schwa, an un-
ā	ace, rate	g	go, log	ng	ring, song	r	run, poor	û(r)	urn, term		stressed vowel
â(r)	care, air	h	hope, hate			s	see, pass	yōō	use, few		representing the
ä	palm, father	i	it, give	o	odd, hot	sh	sure, rush				sound of
b	bat, rub	ī	ice, write	ō	open, so	t	talk, sit	v	vain, eve		*a* in *above*
ch	check, catch			ô	order, jaw	th	thin, both	w	win, away		*e* in *sicken*
d	dog, rod	j	joy, ledge	oi	oil, boy	th	this, bathe	y	yet, yearn		*i* in *clarity*
		k	cool, take	ou	out, now			z	zest, muse		*o* in *melon*
e	end, pet	l	look, rule	ōō	pool, food			zh	vision, pleasure		*u* in *focus*
ē	even, tree	m	move, seem	ŏŏ	took, full						

FOREIGN SOUNDS

à   as in French *ami, patte*. This is a vowel midway in quality between (a) and (ä).

œ   as in French *peu*, German *schön*. Round the lips for (ō) and pronounce (ā).

ü   as in French *vue*, German *grün*. Round the lips for (ōō) and pronounce (ē).

kh   as in German *ach*, Scottish, *loch*. Pronounce a strongly aspirated (h) with the tongue in position for (k) as in *cool* or *keep*.

n   This symbol indicates that the preceding vowel is nasal. The nasal vowels in French are œn (*brun*), an (*main*), än (*chambre*), ôn (*dont*). This symbol indicates that a

preceding (l) or (r) is voiceless, as in French *débâcle* (dā·bä′kl′) or *fiacre* (fyà′kr′), or that a preceding (y) is pronounced consonantly in a separate syllable followed by a slight schwa sound, as in French *fille* (fē′y′).

Note on the accentuation of foreign words: Many languages do not employ stress in the manner of English; only an approximation can be given of the actual situa-

tion in such languages. As it is not possible to reproduce the tones of Chinese in a work of this kind, Chinese names have been here recorded with primary stress on each syllable and may be so pronounced. Japanese and Korean have been shown without stress and may be pronounced with a level accent throughout. French words are shown conventionally with a primary stress on the last syllable; however, this stress tends to be evenly divided among the syllables (except for those that are completely unstressed), with slightly more force and higher pitch on the last syllable.

ABBREVIATIONS USED IN THIS WORK

abbr.	abbreviation(s)	Ezek.	Ezekiel	Mech.	Mechanics	Philos.	Philosophy
A.D.	year of our Lord	F, Fr.	French	Med.	Medicine, Me-	Phonet.	Phonetics
adj.	adjective	fem.	feminine		dieval	Phot.	Photography
adv.	adverb	freq.	frequentative	Med. Gk.	Medieval Greek	Physiol.	Physiology
Aeron.	Aeronautics	G, Ger.	German		(600–1500)	pl.	plural
AF	Anglo-French	Gal.	Galatians	Med. L	Medieval Latin	pp.	past participle
Agric.	Agriculture	Gen.	Genesis		(600–1500)	ppr.	present participle
Alg.	Algebra	Geog.	Geography	Metall.	Metallurgy	prep.	preposition
alter.	alteration	Geol.	Geology	Meteorol.	Meteorology	prob.	probably
Am. Ind.	American Indian	Geom.	Geometry	MF	Middle French	pron.	pronoun
Anat.	Anatomy	Gk.	Greek (Homer—		(1400–1600)	Prov.	Proverbs
Anthropol.	Anthropology		A.D. 200)	MHG	Middle High	Ps., Psa.	Psalms
appar.	apparently	Gmc.	Germanic		German (1100	Psychoanal.	Psychoanalysis
Archeol.	Archeology	Govt.	Government		–1450)	Psychol.	Psychology
Archit.	Architecture	Gram.	Grammar	Mic.	Micah	pt.	preterit
assoc.	association	Hab.	Habakkuk	Mil.	Military	ref.	reference
Astron.	Astronomy	Hag.	Haggai	MLG	Middle Low	Rev.	Revelation
aug.	augmentative	Heb.	Hebrews		German (1100	Rom.	Romans
Austral.	Australian	Her.	Heraldry		–1450)	Sam., Saml.	Samuel
Bacteriol.	Bacteriology	HG	High German	n.	noun	Scand.	Scandinavian
B.C.	Before Christ	Hind.	Hindustani	Nah.	Nahum	Scot.	Scottish
Biochem.	Biochemistry	Hos.	Hosea	Naut.	Nautical	SE	Southeast
Biol.	Biology	Icel.	Icelandic	Nav.	Naval	sing.	singular
Bot.	Botany	Illit.	Illiterate	N. Am. Ind.	North American	Skt.	Sanskrit
Brit.	British	imit.	imitative		Indian	Sociol.	Sociology
c.	century	infl.	influence, influ-	NE	Northeast	S. of Sol.	Song of Solomon
Can.	Canadian		enced	Neh.	Nehemiah	S. Am. Ind.	South American
cf.	compare	intens.	intensive	neut.	neuter		Indian
Chem.	Chemistry	interj.	interjection	NL	New Latin (after	Sp.	Spanish
Chron.	Chronicles	Is., Isa.	Isaiah		1500)	Stat.	Statistics
Col.	Colossians	Ital.	Italian	Norw.	Norwegian	superl.	superlative
Colloq.	Colloquial	Jas.	James	Num., Numb.	Numbers	Surg.	Surgery
compar.	comparative	Jer.	Jeremiah	NW	Northwest	Sw.	Swedish
conj.	conjunction	Jon.	Jonah	O	Old	SW	Southwest
Cor.	Corinthians	Josh.	Joshua	Ob., Obad.	Obadiah	Technol.	Technology
Dan.	Daniel, Danish	Judg.	Judges	Obs.	Obsolete	Telecom.	Telecommunica-
def.	definition	L, Lat.	Latin (Classical,	OE	Old English (be-		tion
Dent.	Dentistry		80 B.C.–A.D. 200)		fore 1150)	Theol.	Theology
Deut.	Deuteronomy	Lam.	Lamentations	OF	Old French (be-	Thess.	Thessalonians
Dial.	Dialect, Dialectal	Lev., Levit.	Leviticus		fore 1400)	Tim.	Timothy
dim.	diminutive	LG	Low German	OHG	Old High Ger-	Tit.	Titus
Du.	Dutch	LGk.	Late Greek (200–		man (before	trans.	translation
E	English		600)		1100)	Trig.	Trigonometry
Eccl.	Ecclesiastical	Ling.	Linguistics	ON	Old Norse (be-	ult.	ultimate, ulti-
Eccles.	Ecclesiastes	lit.	literally		fore 1500)		mately
Ecclus.	Ecclesiasticus	LL	Late Latin (200–	orig.	original, origi-	U.S.	United States
Ecol.	Ecology		600)		nally	v.	verb
Econ.	Economics	M	Middle	Ornithol.	Ornithology	var.	variant
Electr.	Electricity	Mal.	Malachi	OS	Old Saxon (be-	v.i.	verb intransitive
Engin.	Engineering	masc.	masculine		fore 1100)	v.t.	verb transitive
Entomol.	Entomology	Math.	Mathematics	Paleontol.	Paleontology	WGmc.	West Germanic
Eph.	Ephesians	Matt.	Matthew	Pet.	Peter	Zech.	Zechariah
esp.	especially	MDu.	Middle Dutch	Pg.	Portuguese	Zeph.	Zephaniah
Esth.	Esther	ME	Middle English	Phil.	Philippians	Zool.	Zoology
Ex., Exod.	Exodus		(1150–1500)	Philem.	Philemon		

◆ Usage note;   Homophone;   Collateral adjective   < from   + plus   ? possibly

A

a, A (ā) *n. pl.* **a's, A's** or **As, aes** (āz) **1** The first letter of the English alphabet: from Phoenician *aleph*, through the Hebrew *aleph*, Greek *alpha*, and Roman *A*. **2** Any sound of the letter *a*. See ALPHABET. — *symbol* **1** Primacy in class or order: grade *A* beef. **2** A substitute for the numeral 1: section *A*. **3** *Music* **a** One of a series of tones, the sixth in the natural diatonic scale of C, or the first note in the related minor scale. **b** A standard for tuning instruments: the pitch of this tone. **c** The written note representing this tone. **d** The scale built upon A. **3** *Chem.* Argon (symbol A).

a¹ (ə, *stressed* ā) *indefinite article* or *adj.* In each; to each; for each: twice *a* year; one dollar *a* bushel: equivalent to *per.* ◆ **a, per** *A* is preferred to *per*, except where *per* is required in business and statistical writing. [OE *an, on* in, on, at; orig. a prep.]

a² (ə, *stressed* ā) *indefinite article* or *adj.* One; any; some; each: before a vowel, *an*. See AN, ARTICLE.

Special uses: before plural nouns with *few, great many*, or *good many*; with *on, at*, or *of*, denoting oneness, sameness: birds of *a* feather; before proper names referring to the qualities or character of an individual: He is *a* Hercules in strength [Reduced form of AN used before consonant sounds]

◆ **a, an** *A* is used before a word beginning with a consonant sound, now including *h* when pronounced: *a* history, *a* hotel (*Brit.* often *an* hotel). Before an unaccented syllable beginning with *h* some writers prefer the older usage: *an* historical novel, *an* hysterical cry. *An* is used before a word beginning with a vowel sound, including one which is pronounced though not written: *an* X-ray, *an* n-dimensional figure.

a³ (ā, ô, ə) *v. Brit. Dial.* Have.

a⁴ (ā, ô, ə) *pron. Brit. Dial.* He, she, it, they: an unstressed form.

a-¹ *prefix* On; in; at: *aboard, asleep, agog, agoing.* [OE *an, on* in, on, at]

a-² *prefix* Used as an intensive or without added meaning: *arise, abide.* [OE *ā-*]

a-³ *prefix* Of; from: *athirst, akin, anew.* [OE *of* off, of]

a-⁴ *prefix* **1** Without; not: *achromatic.* **2** Apart from; unconcerned with: *amoral.* See note under ALPHA PRIVATIVE. [Reduced form of AN- used before consonant sounds]

a-⁵ Reduced var. of AB- before *m, p*, and *v*.

a-⁶ Reduced var. of AD- before *sc, sp*, and *st*.

a·a (ä′ä′) *n.* A brittle, scoriaceous substance consisting of sand, earth, stones, and melted lava, cooled and broken up. [<Hawaiian]

Aar (är) The longest river that is entirely in Switzerland, flowing 183 miles to the Rhine. Also **Aa·re** (ä′rə).

aard·vark (ärd′-värk′) *n.* A burrowing, ant-eating African mammal (genus *Orycteropus*) about the size of the pig, with long protrusile, sticky tongue to which the ants adhere, and strong, digging forefeet; an ant bear. [<Afri-

AARDVARK

kaans <Du. *aarde* earth + *vark* pig]

aard·wolf (ärd′woolf′) *n.* A hyenalike, nocturnal, carnivorous mammal (*Proteles cristata*) of southern and eastern Africa, living chiefly on carrion and termites. [<Afrikaans <Du. *aarde* earth + *wolf* wolf]

aas·vo·gel (äs′fō′gəl) *n.* A vulture. [<Afrikaans]

Ab (ab, äb) A Hebrew month. The 9th day of Ab is a fast day to commemorate the destruction of Jerusalem and the Temple, 586 B.C. and A.D. 70. The 15th day is a secular festival. See CALENDAR (Hebrew).

ab-¹ *prefix* Off; from; away: *absolve, abduct, abrogate.* Also: *a-* before *m, p, v*, as in *avocation*; *abs-* before *c, t*, as in *abscess, abstract.* [<L <*ab* from]

ab-² Assimilated var. of AD-.

ab·a·ca (ab′ə·kä, ä′bə·kä′) *n.* **1** A banana plant (*Musa textilis*) of the Philippine Islands. **2** The inner fiber of this plant, used for cordage. Also **ab′a·ka.** [<Tagalog]

ab·a·cis·cus (ab′ə·sis′kəs) *n.* **1** A square tile in a mosaic floor or pavement. **2** *Obs.* An abacus. [<L <Gk. *abakiskos*, dim. of *abax* a slab]

ab·a·cist (ab′ə·sist) *n.* One who uses an abacus.

a·back (ə·bak′) *adv.* So as to be pressed backward, as sails; backward; aloof. — **taken aback 1** *Naut.* Caught by a sudden change of wind so as to reverse the sails. **2** Disconcerted, as by a sudden check. [OE *on bæc* to or on the back]

ab·a·cus (ab′ə·kəs) *n. pl.* **cus·es** or **·ci** (-sī) **1** An ancient calculating device with counters sliding on wires or in grooves. **2** *Archit.* A slab forming the top of a capital. For illustration see CAPITAL. [<L <Gk. *abax* counting table]

A·ba·dan (ä′bä·dän′, ab′ə·dän′) Chief town on **Abadan Island** in the Shatt-al-Arab delta of SW Iran: oil refining and shipping center.

A·bad·don (ə·bad′ən) In the Old Testament: **1** The bottomless pit; hell; the place of destruction. **2** The angel of the bottomless pit; Apollyon. [<Hebrew *ăbaddōn* destruction]

(the abacus illustration)

ABACUS (*def.* 1)

a·baft (ə·baft′, ə·bäft′) *adv. Naut.* Toward the stern; back; behind. — *prep.* Further aft than; astern of: *abaft* the mainmast. [OE *on be·æftan* <*on* on, at + *be* about + *æftan*, adv., behind, back]

ab·a·lo·ne (ab′ə·lō′nē) *n.* A shellfish (genus *Haliotis*) having a perforated ear-shaped shell lined with mother-of-pearl, which is used for inlaying, making buttons, beads, etc. Its meat is used for food. [<Sp.]

ab·am·pere (ab·am′pir) *n.* The cgs electromagnetic unit of current, equal to 10 absolute amperes. [<AB(SOLUTE) + AMPERE]

a·ban·don (ə·ban′dən) *v.t.* **1** To give up wholly; desert; forsake, as an effort or attempt. **2** To surrender or give over: with *to*: He *abandoned* his share to his partner. **3** To yield (oneself) without restraint, as to a feeling or pastime. — *n.* **1** Utter surrender to one's feelings or natural impulses. **2** Freedom

[<OF *abandoner* <*a bandon* under one's own control] — **a·ban′don·a·ble** *adj.* — **a·ban′don·er** *n.* — **a·ban′don·ment** *n.*

Synonyms (*verb*): abdicate, abjure, cease, cede, desert, discontinue, forgo, forsake, forswear, leave, quit, recant, relinquish, renounce, repudiate, resign, retract, surrender, vacate. *Abandon* denotes the complete and final giving up, letting go, or withdrawal from persons or things of any kind; *abdicate* and *resign* apply to office, authority, or power; *cede* to territorial possessions; *surrender* especially to military force, and more generally to any demand, claim, passion, etc. *Quit* carries an idea of suddenness or abruptness not necessarily implied in *abandon*, and may not have the same suggestion of finality. *Relinquish* commonly implies reluctance; the creditor *relinquishes* his claim. *Abandon* implies previous association with responsibility for or control of; *forsake* implies previous association with inclination or attachment; a man may *abandon* or *forsake* home or friends; he *abandons* an enterprise. *Forsake*, like *abandon*, may be used either in the favorable or unfavorable sense; *desert* is commonly unfavorable, except when used of localities; as, "The *Deserted* Village"; a soldier *deserts* his post. While a monarch *abdicates*, a president or other elected or appointed officer *resigns*. See also RENOUNCE. *Antonyms*: adopt, advocate, assert, cherish, claim, court, defend, favor, haunt, hold, keep, maintain, occupy, prosecute, protect, pursue, retain, seek, support, undertake, uphold, vindicate.

a·ban·doned (ə·ban′dənd) *adj.* **1** Deserted; left behind; forsaken. **2** Unrestrained; without moderation. **3** Given over to dissolute practices; profligate; shameless. See synonyms under ADDICTED, BAD.

a·base (ə·bās′) *v.t.* **a·based, a·bas·ing 1** To lower in position, rank, prestige, or estimation; cast down; humble. **2** *Obs.* To reduce in value, as coin; debase. [<OF *abaissier* <*a* to + *baissier* to lower <L *ad-* + LL *bassus* low] — **a·bas·ed·ly** (ə·bā′sid·lē) *adv.* — **a·bas′ed·ness** *n.* — **a·bas′er** *n.* — **a·base′ment** *n.*

Synonyms: debase, degrade, depress, discredit, disgrace, dishonor, humble, humiliate, lower, reduce, sink. *Abase* generally refers to outward conditions, *debase* to quality or character: The coinage is *debased* by excess of alloy, the man by vice. *Humble* refers chiefly to the feelings, *humiliate* to outward conditions. To *disgrace* is chiefly applied to deserved moral odium: he *disgraced* himself by his conduct. To *dishonor* a person is to deprive him of honor that should or might be given. To *discredit* one is to injure his reputation. *Degrade* may refer to station, but is now chiefly used of character: drunkenness is a *degrading* vice.

a·bash (ə·bash′) *v.t.* To deprive of self-possession; disconcert; make ashamed or confused. [<OF *esbaïss-*, stem of *esbaïr* astonish] — **a·bash·ed·ly** (ə·bash′id·lē) *adv.* — **a·bash′ment** *n.*

Synonyms: bewilder, chagrin, confound, confuse, daunt, discompose, disconcert, dishearten, embarrass, humble, humiliate, mortify, overawe, shame. Any sense of inferiority *abashes*, with or without the sense of wrong. The poor are *abashed* at the splendor of wealth, the ignorant at the learning of the scholar. To *confuse* is to bring into

---

add,āce,câre,pälm; end,ēven; it,īce; odd,ōpen,ôrder; tōōk,pōōl; up,bûrn; ə = a in *above*, e in *sicken*, i in *clarity*, o in *melon*, u in *focus*; yōō = u in *fuse*; oi,oil; ou,pout; ch,check; g,go; ng,ring; th,thin; ŧħ,this; zh,vision. Foreign sounds à,œ,ü,kh,ṅ; and ◆: see page xx. < from; + plus; ? possibly.

a state of mental bewilderment; to *confound* is to overwhelm the mental faculties; to *daunt* is to subject to a certain degree of fear. Conf'ision generally refers to the intellect, embarrassment to the feelings. A witness may be *embarrassed* by annoying remarks or questions so as to become *confused* in statements. To *mortify* a person is to bring upon him a painful sense of humiliation: The parent is *mortified* by the child's rudeness, the child *abashed* at the parent's reproof. The *embarrassed* speaker finds it difficult to proceed. The mob is *overawed* by the military, the hypocrite *shamed* by exposure.

a·bate (ə·bāt') *v.* **a·bat·ed, a·bat·ing** *v.t.* **1** To make less; reduce in size, number, degree, amount, importance, speed, or force. **2** To deduct, as part of a payment. **3** *Law* To do away with; annul. —*v.i.* **4** To become less, as in strength or degree. **5** *Law* To fail; become void. [< OF *abatre* beat down < *a-* to (< L *ad-*) + *batre* beat < L *batuere*] —**a·bat·a·ble** (ə·bā'tə·bəl) *adj.* —**a·bat·er** (ə·bā'tər) *n.*

Synonyms: decline, decrease, diminish, ebb, lessen, lower, mitigate, moderate, reduce, relax, subside. See ABOLISH, ALLAY, ALLEVIATE. *Antonyms:* aggravate, augment, enhance, increase, intensify.

a·bate·ment (ə·bāt'mənt) *n.* **1** An abating or the amount abated. **2** *Law* A doing away with; annulment.

A battery *Electr.* A battery that supplies the power for the filaments of a vacuum tube.

ab·at·toir (ab'ə·twär') *n.* A slaughter house. [< F]

ab·ax·i·al (ab·ak'sē·əl) *adj.* Situated or facing away from the axis. [< AB-¹ + AXIAL]

abb (ab) *n.* In weaving, the warp or the yarn for it. [OE *āweb*]

Ab·ba (ab'ə) *n.* **1** Father: a title used with the names of patriarchs and bishops in the Syrian, the Coptic, and the Ethiopian churches. **2** God: a form of address used in the New Testament: *Mark* xiv 36. [< Aramaic]

ab·ba·cy (ab'ə·sē) *n. pl.* **·cies** The office, term of office, dignity, or jurisdiction of an abbot. [< LL *abbatia* < L *abbas* ABBOT]

ab·ba·tial (ə·bā'shəl) *adj.* Of or pertaining to an abbot or an abbey. Also **ab·bat·i·cal** (ə·bat'i·kəl).

ab·bé (ab'ā, *Fr.* á·bā') *n.* **1** A title of respect in France given to a priest or any person entitled to wear ecclesiastical dress. **2** An abbot. [< F]

ab·bess (ab'is) *n.* A woman superior of a community of nuns connected with an abbey. [< OF *abbesse* < LL *abbatissa* < L *abbas* ABBOT]

Ab·be·ville (ab'ə·vil, *Fr.* áb·vēl') A town in northern France.

Ab·be·vil·li·an (ab'ə·vil'ē·ən) *adj. Anthropo* Designating a culture stage of the Lower Paleolithic period, represented by crude handaxes of the core type: with the Clactonian it comprises most of the stage formerly known as the Chellean. [from *Abbeville*, France, where artifacts were found]

ab·bey (ab'ē) *n. pl.* **ab·beys 1** The monastic establishment of a society of monks under the jurisdiction of an abbot or of nuns under an abbess. **2** The buildings of such a society; its monastery or convent. **3** The church attached to a monastery or convent. See synonyms under CLOISTER. [< OF *abaie* < LL *abbatia* < L *abbas* ABBOT]

ab·bot (ab'ət) *n.* The superior of a community of monks connected with an abbey. [OE *abbod* < L < Gk. *abbas* < Aramaic *abba* father] —**ab'bot·cy,** *ab'bot·ship n.*

ab·bre·vi·ate (ə·brē'vē·āt) *v.t.* **·at·ed, ·at·ing 1** To condense or make briefer. **2** To shorten, as a word or expression, especially by omission or contraction: Mistress is *abbreviated* to Mrs. [< L *abbreviatus*, pp. of *abbreviare* < *ad-* to + *breviare* shorten < *brevis* short. Doublet of ABRIDGE.] —**ab·bre'vi·a·tor** *n.*

Synonyms: abridge, compress, condense, contract, curtail, epitomize, prune, reduce, shorten. Compare ABBREVIATION, ABRIDGMENT. *Antonyms:* amplify, enlarge, expand, extend, lengthen.

ab·bre·vi·a·tion (ə·brē'vē·ā'shən) *n.* **1** A shortened form or contraction, as of a word or phrase; abridgment. **2** A making shorter or the state of being shortened. **3** *Music* A notation indicating repeated notes, chords, etc., by a single symbol.

Synonyms: abridgment, abstract, compendium, condensation, contraction, curtailment, epitome, reduction, shortening, summary. An *abbreviation* is a shortening by any method; a *contraction* is a *reduction* of size by the drawing together of the parts. A *contraction* of a word is made by omitting certain letters or syllables and bringing together the first and last letters or elements; a *contraction* is an *abbreviation*, but an *abbreviation* is not necessarily a *contraction*. *Rec't* for receipt, *mdse.* for merchandise, and *Dr.* for debtor are *contractions* and also *abbreviations; Am.* for American is an *abbreviation,* but not a *contraction. Abbreviation* and *contraction* are used of words and phrases, *abridgment* of books, paragraphs, sentences, etc. See ABRIDGMENT. *Antonyms:* amplification, dilation, dilution, elongation, enlargement, expansion, expatiation, explication, extension, prolongation.

ABBREVIATION (def. 3)

ABC (ā'bē·sē') *pl.* **ABC's 1** The alphabet: usually plural. **2** The rudiments, elements, or basic facts (of a subject). **3** *Obs.* A primer.

ab·cou·lomb (ab'kōo'lom') *n.* The cgs electromagnetic unit of charge, equal to 10 absolute coulombs. [< AB(SOLUTE) + COULOMB]

Abd- A word element meaning "servant," "slave," used as a prefix before names for the Deity to form proper names in Semitic languages; as, *Abdallah* servant of God.

ab·di·cate (ab'də·kāt) *v.* **·cat·ed, ·cat·ing** *v.t.* To give up formally; renounce, as claims to or possession of a throne, power, or rights. —*v.i.* To renounce a throne, power, or rights: His subjects forced the king to *abdicate.* See synonyms under ABANDON. [< L *abdicatus*, pp. of *abdicare* < *ab-* away + *dicare* proclaim] —**ab·di·ca·ble** (ab'di·kə·bəl) *adj.* —**ab'di·ca'tion** *n.* —**ab'di·ca'tive** *adj.* —**ab'di·ca'tor** *n.*

ab·do·men (ab'də·mən, ab·dō'mən) *n.* **1** In mammals, the visceral cavity between the diaphragm and the pelvic floor; the belly: in human anatomy often restricted to the cavity above the true pelvis. **2** In vertebrates other than mammals, the region or cavity that contains the viscera. **3** *Entomol.* The hindmost of the main divisions of the arthropod body. [< L]

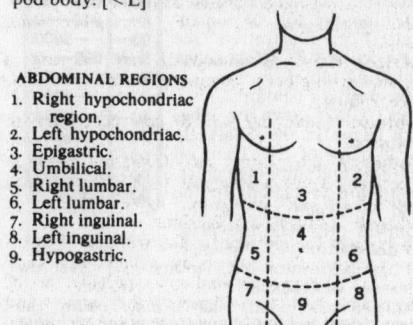

ABDOMINAL REGIONS
1. Right hypochondriac region.
2. Left hypochondriac.
3. Epigastric.
4. Umbilical.
5. Right lumbar.
6. Left lumbar.
7. Right inguinal.
8. Left inguinal.
9. Hypogastric.

ab·dom·i·nal (ab·dom'ə·nəl) *adj.* Of, pertaining to, or situated on or in the abdomen. —**ab·dom'i·nal·ly** *adv.*

ab·dom·i·nous (ab·dom'ə·nəs) *adj.* Big-bellied.

ab·duce (ab·dōos', -dyōos') *v.t. Physiol.* To draw or lead away, as by muscular action. [< L *abducere.* See ABDUCT.] —**ab·du'cent** *adj.*

ab·duct (ab·dukt') *v.t.* **1** To carry away wrongfully, as by force or fraud; kidnap. **2** *Physiol.* To draw aside or away from the original position. [< L *abductus*, pp. of *abducere* < *ab-* away + *ducere* lead] —**ab·duc'tion** *n.*

Abe (āb) Diminutive of ABRAHAM or ABRAM.

a·beam (ə·bēm') *adj. & adv.* At right angles to the line of a vessel's keel; opposite the waist of a ship.

a·be·ce·dar·i·an (ā'bē·sē·dâr'ē·ən) *adj.* **1** Pertaining to or formed by the alphabet; alphabetically arranged. **2** Pertaining to a learner of the alphabet; rudimentary; ignorant. —*n.* **1** A teacher of

the alphabet or one who is learning it. **2** A novice; beginner. Also **a·be·ce·da·ry** (ā'bē·sē'dar·ē). [< Med.L *abecedarius*]

A·bel (ā'bəl) A masculine personal name. [< L < Gk. *Abel* < Hebrew *Hebel*, lit., breath] — **Abel** Second son of Adam. *Gen.* iv 2.

Ab·e·lard (ab'ə·lärd), **Pierre,** 1079–1142, French scholastic philosopher; husband of Héloïse. Also **Ab'ai·lard.**

a·bele (ə·bēl', ā'bəl) *n.* The white poplar (*Populus alba*). [< Du. *abeel* < OF *abel* < LL *albellus*, dim. of L *albus* white]

a·be·li·a (ə·bēl'ē·ə, -lyə) *n.* A shrub having small glossy leaves and bell-like flowers ranging from pink to white.

Ab·er·deen (ab'ər·dēn') A county in NE Scotland; 1,972 square miles; county town, Aberdeen. Also **Ab'er·deen'shire.**

Aberdeen An·gus (ang'gəs) A breed of hornless black cattle of Scottish origin.

ab·er·rance (ab·er'əns) *n.* A wandering from the right way; deviation from the path of rectitude. Also **ab·er'ran·cy.**

ab·er·rant (ab·er'ənt) *adj.* **1** Straying from the right way or usual course; wandering. **2** Varying from type; abnormal; exceptional. [< L *aberrans, -antis*, ppr. of *aberrare* < *ab-* from + *errare* wander]

ab·er·ra·tion (ab'ə·rā'shən) *n.* **1** Deviation from a right, customary, prescribed, or natural course or condition; wandering; error. **2** Partial mental derangement. **3** *Optics* The failure of a lens or mirror to bring all light rays to the same focus: called **chromatic aberration** when due to different refrangibility of light of different colors, and **spherical aberration** when due to the form of lens or mirror. **4** *Astron.* An apparent displacement of a heavenly body, due to the effect of relative motion upon the light coming from it. **5** An abnormal structure; a deviation from a standard type: a chromosomal *aberration.* [< L *aberratio, -onis* < *aberrare.* See ABERRANT.]

a·bet (ə·bet') *v.t.* **a·bet·ted, a·bet·ting** To encourage and support, especially wrong-doing or a wrongdoer; instigate; countenance. [< OF *abeter* incite, arouse < *a-* to (< L *ad-*) + *beter* tease, bait < ON *beita* cause to bite] —**a·bet'ment, a·bet'tal** *n.*

Synonyms: aid, assist, countenance, embolden, encourage, help, incite, instigate, promote, sanction, support, uphold. *Abet* and *instigate* are used almost without exception in a bad sense; one may *incite* either to good or evil. One *incites* or *instigates* to the doing of something not yet done, or to increased activity or further advance in the doing of it; one *abets* by giving sympathy, countenance, or substantial aid to the doing of that which is already projected or in process of commission. See AID. *Antonyms:* baffle, confound, counteract, denounce, deter, disapprove, disconcert, discourage, dissuade, frustrate, hinder, impede, obstruct.

a·bet·tor (ə·bet'ər) *n.* One who abets. See synonyms under ACCESSORY. Also **a·bet'ter.**

a·bey·ance (ə·bā'əns) *n.* **1** Suspension or temporary inaction. **2** *Law* An undetermined condition, as of an estate awaiting an owner. Also **a·bey'an·cy.** [< AF *abeiance* < OF *beer* gape < LL *badare*] —**a·bey'ant** *adj.*

ab·far·ad (ab·far'əd, -ad) *n.* The cgs electromagnetic unit of capacitance, equal to 1 abcoulomb per abvolt, or 1,000,000,000 farads. [< AB (SOLUTE) + FARAD]

ab·hen·ry (ab·hen'rē) *n.* The cgs electromagnetic unit of inductance, equal to 10⁻⁹ henry. [< AB(SOLUTE) + HENRY]

ab·he·sive (ab·hē'siv) *adj.* Not sticking to another material.

ab·hom·i·na·ble (ab·hom'ə·nə·bəl) *adj. Obs.* Abominable: a spelling commonly used until the 17th century.

ab·hor (ab·hôr') *v.t.* **ab·horred, ab·hor·ring** To regard with repugnance; feel horror of; detest; loathe. [< L *abhorrere* < *ab-* from + *horrere* shrink] —**ab·hor'rer** *n.*

Synonyms: abominate, despise, detest, dislike, hate, loathe, scorn, shun. *Abhor* is stronger than *despise,* implying a shuddering recoil, especially a moral recoil. *Detest* expresses indignation, with something of contempt. *Loathe* implies disgust, physical or moral. We *abhor* a traitor, *despise* a coward, *detest* a liar. We *dislike* an uncivil person.

We *abhor* cruelty, *hate* tyranny. Compare ABOMINATION. Antonyms: admire, approve, covet, crave, desire, enjoy, esteem, like, love, relish.

ab·hor·rence (ab-hôr′əns, -hor′-) *n.* The act of abhorring, or that which is abhorred. See synonyms under ABOMINATION, ANTIPATHY, HATRED.

ab·hor·rent (ab-hôr′ənt, -hor′-) *adj.* 1 Detestable or horrible: with *to.* 2 Feeling abhorrence. —**ab·hor′rent·ly** *adv.*

a·bi·dal (ə-bīd′l) *n.* 1 Abidance. 2 Abode.

a·bi·dance (ə-bīd′ns) *n.* 1 An abiding; dwelling. 2 Continuance; adherence to or an abiding by (rules, methods, etc.).

a·bide (ə-bīd′) *v.* **a·bode** or **a·bid·ed, a·bid·ing** *v.i.* 1 To continue in a place; stay. 2 To have one's abode; dwell; reside. 3 To continue in some condition or state; remain faithful or unchanging. — *v.t.* 4 To look for; wait for: to *abide* the event. 5 To await expectantly or defiantly. 6 To endure; put up with. —**to abide by** 1 To behave in accordance with; be faithful to, as a promise or rule. 2 To accept the consequences of; submit to. [OE *abidan*] —**a·bid′er** *n.* —**a·bid′ing** *adj.* —**a·bid′ing·ly** *adv.*

Synonyms: anticipate, await, bear, bide, continue, dwell, endure, expect, inhabit, live, lodge, remain, reside, rest, sojourn, stand, stay, stop, tarry, tolerate, wait, watch. To *abide* is to remain continuously without limit of time unless expressed by the text. *Lodge, sojourn, stay, tarry,* and *wait,* always imply a limited time; *lodge,* to pass the night; *sojourn,* to *remain* temporarily; *live, dwell, reside,* to have a permanent home. *Reside* is a word of more dignity than *live or dwell. Stop,* in the sense of *stay or sojourn,* is colloquial. Compare ENDURE, REST. Antonyms: abandon, avoid, depart, forfeit, forfend, journey, migrate, move, proceed, reject, resist, shun.

Ab·i·djan (ab′i-jän′) A port in west Africa, capital of the Ivory Coast Republic.

ab·i·et·ic acid (ab′ē-et′ik) *Chem.* An acid, $C_{20}H_{30}O_2$, isolated from pine rosin in the form of a slightly yellow crystalline powder; it is used in lacquers, varnishes, soaps, and driers. [< L *abies* fir]

ab·i·gail (ab′ə-gāl) *n.* A lady's maid: from a character in Beaumont and Fletcher's *The Scornful Lady.*

A·bi·jah (ə-bī′jə) King of Judah. I *Kings* xiv 1. [< Hebrew, whose father is Jehovah]

a·bil·i·ty (ə-bil′ə-tē) *n. pl.* **·ties** 1 The state of being able; physical, mental, legal, or financial power to do. 2 *pl.* Talents. 3 *Psychol.* That which a person can actually do on the basis of present development and training. [< OF *ablete* < L *habilitas* < *habilis.* See ABLE.]

Synonyms: aptitude, capability, capacity, cleverness, competence, competency, dexterity, efficiency, expertness, faculty, power, qualification, readiness, skill, talent. *Ability* includes every form of *power. Capacity* is power to receive. *Dexterity* and *skill* are readiness and facility in action, having a special end, and are largely acquired. *Efficiency* brings all one's *ability* to bear promptly on the thing to be done. Compare POWER. Antonyms: awkwardness, imbecility, inability, incapacity, incompetency, inefficiency, stupidity.

A·bim·e·lech (ə-bim′ə-lek) Son of Gideon; king of Shechem. *Judges* viii 31.

ab in·i·ti·o (ab i·nish′ē·ō) *Latin* From the beginning.

ab in·tra (ab in′trə) *Latin* From within.

ab·i·o·gen·e·sis (ab′ē-ō-jen′ə-sis) *n.* The springing up of living from non-living matter; especially, the old doctrine of the generation of new organisms from putrid and decomposing organic matter; spontaneous generation. Compare BIOGENESIS. [< A.[4] + BIO- + GENESIS] —**ab·i·o·ge·net·ic** (ab′ē-ō-jə-net′ik) or **·i·cal** *adj.* —**ab·i·oge·nist** (ab′ē-oj′ə-nist) *n.*

ab·i·o·sis (ab′ē-ō′sis) *n.* Absence of life; a lifeless state. [< Gk. *abios* lifeless] —**ab·i·ot·ic** (ab′ē-ot′ik) *adj.*

ab·i·ot·ro·phy (ab′ē-ot′rə-fē) *n.* Premature or abnormal degeneration or wasting away of the body. [< A.[4] + BIO- + -TROPHY]

ab·ir·ri·tant (ab·ir′ə-tənt) *n.* A soothing agent; a medicine that eases irritation. —*adj.* Relieving irritation; soothing.

ab·ir·ri·tate (ab·ir′ə-tāt) *v.t.* **·tat·ed, ·tat·ing** To di-

minish sensibility in; relieve irritation in. — **ab·ir′ri·ta′·tion** *n.*

juring or state of being abjured; repudiation.

ab·jure (ab-joor′) *v.t.* **ab·jured, ab·jur·ing** 1 To renounce under oath; forswear. 2 To retract or recant, as an opinion; repudiate; abandon. See synonyms under ABANDON, RENOUNCE. [< L *abjurare* deny on oath < *ab-* away + *jurare* swear] —**ab·jur·a·to·ry** (ab-joor′ə·tôr′ē, -tō′rē) *adj.* —**ab·jur′er** *n.*

ab·lac·ta·tion (ab′lak-tā′shən) *n.* The act or process of weaning from the breast. [< L *ablactatus,* pp. of *ablactare* wean < *ab-* away + *lactare* suckle < *lac* milk]

ab·late (ab-lāt′) *v.t.* **·lat·ed, ·lat·ing** 1 To remove, as by cutting away, eroding, etc. 2 To undergo ablation.

ab·la·tion (ab-lā′shən) *n.* 1 The surgical removal of tissues or organs from the body. 2 *Geol.* The wearing away of rocks. 3 *Aerospace* The disintegration of part of the nose cone on a missile or spacecraft when it reenters the atmosphere. [< L *ablatio, -onis* a carrying away < *ablatus,* pp. of *auferre* < *ab-* away + *ferre* carry]

ab·la·ti·tious (ab′lə-tish′əs) *adj.* Tending to lessen or take away; diminishing. [< L *ablatus* carried away. See ABLATION.]

ablative absolute In Latin grammar, the construction in the ablative case of a noun and participle, a noun and an adjective, or two nouns, constituting an adverbial phrase which stands apart in syntax from the rest of the sentence; as, *sole oriente,* nox fugit (*the sun rising,* night flees).

ab·laut (äb′lout, ab′-; *Ger.* äp′lout) *n.* The change of one root vowel into another to show a variation of tense, part of speech, or meaning, as in *swim, swam, swum.* Compare UMLAUT. [< G < *ab* off + *laut* sound]

a·blaze (ə-blāz′) *adj. & adv.* On fire; in a blaze; hence, in a glow of excitement; zealous; ardent.

a·ble (ā′bəl) *adj.* **a·bler** (ā′blər), **a·blest** (ā′blist) 1 Having adequate power; competent; qualified. 2 Having superior abilities; capable. See synonyms under ADEQUATE, CLEVER, COMPETENT, GOOD, SAGACIOUS. [< OF *hable* able < L *habilis* manageable, suitable, fit < *habere* have, hold]

-able *suffix* 1 Given to; tending to; like to: *peaceable, changeable.* 2 Fit to; able to; capable of; worthy of: *eatable, salable, solvable.* Also spelled *-ble, -ible. -ible* is used to form words from Latin verbs of the third and fourth conjugations (ending in *-ere, -ire*) as *edible* from *edere, audible* from *audire.* The *-able* ending, originally used to form adjectives from Latin verbs of the first conjugation, as *disputable, estimable,* etc., is now extended in English to form adjectives from native verbs, nouns, and phrases, as *answerable, plowable, get-at-able,* etc. [< F < L *-abilis, -ibilis, -bilis*]

a·ble-bod·ied (ā′bəl·bod′ēd) *adj.* Having a sound strong body; competent for physical service; robust.

a·bloom (ə-bloom′) *adj. & adv.* Blooming; in blossom.

ab·lu·ent (ab′loo-ənt) *adj.* Cleansing. —*n.* A cleansing agent; a detergent. [< L *abluens, -entis,* ppr. of *abluere* < *ab-* away + *luere* wash]

a·blush (ə-blush′) *adj.* Blushing.

ab·lu·tion (ab-loo′shən) *n.* 1 A washing or cleansing, especially of the body; a bath. 2 A ceremonial or symbolic washing; especially, in the Roman Catholic Church, the wine and water used to remove any trace of the eucharistic elements from the chalice and the priest's fingers after communion. 3 The washing of the hands of the priest before, during, and after the celebration of the Mass. 4 In the Greek Church, the public washing of persons seven days after their baptism. 5 Any liquid used in washing or cleansing. [< L *ablutio, -onis* < *abluere* wash away. See ABLUENT.] —**ab·lu′tion·ar·y** *adj.*

a·bly (ā′blē) *adv.* With ability; capably.

-ably *suffix* Like; in the manner of: *peaceably:* used to form adverbs from adjectives ending in *-able.*

ab·mho (ab′mō) *n.* The cgs electromagnetic unit of conductance, equal to a current in a conductor of one abampere when the potential difference between the ends of the conductor is one abvolt. [< AB(SOLUTE) + MHO]

ab·ne·gate (ab′nə·gāt) *v.t.* **·gat·ed, ·gat·ing** To

deny to oneself, as a right or privilege; renounce. [< L *abnegatus,* pp. of *abnegare* < *ab-* away + *negare* deny] —**ab′ne·ga·tor** *n.*

ab·ne·ga·tion (ab′nə-gā′shən) *n.* Renunciation; denial; self-denial.

ab·net (ab′net) *n.* A long girdle or sash, usually of linen, worn around the body by ancient Jewish priests. [< Hebrew]

ab·nor·mal (ab-nôr′məl) *adj.* Not according to rule; different from the usual or average; hence, unnatural; irregular. See synonyms under IRREGULAR. [Earlier *anormal* < F < Med.L *anormalus,* alter. of *anomalus* < Gk. *anōmalos* irregular; re-formed on Latin *ab* away, from] —**ab·nor′mal·ly** *adv.*

ab·nor·mal·i·ty (ab′nôr-mal′ə-tē) *n. pl.* **·ties** 1 Irregularity. 2 That which is abnormal.

ab·nor·mi·ty (ab-nôr′mə-tē) *n. pl.* **·ties** An irregularity; malformation; a monstrosity. [< L *abnormitas, -tatis* < *abnormis* irregular < *ab-* from + *norma* rule]

a·board (ə-bôrd′, ə-bōrd′) *adv.* 1 On board; into, in, or on a conveyance. 2 Alongside; on one side. —**all aboard!** Get on board or in!: a warning to passengers that their conveyance is about to start. —*prep.* 1 On board of; upon or within, as a conveyance: *aboard* the train. 2 Across or alongside of.

a·bode[1] (ə-bōd′) *n.* 1 A place of abiding; dwelling; home. 2 The state or act of abiding; sojourn; stay. See synonyms under HOME, HOUSE. —*v.* Past tense and past participle of ABIDE. [OE *abad*]

a·bode[2] (ə-bōd′) *Obs. v.t. & v.i.* **a·bod·ed, a·bod·ing** To forebode; be ominous. —*n.* An omen. Also *Obs.* **a·bode′ment** *n.* [ME *abeden* announce, OE *abeodan*]

ab·ohm (ab-ōm′) *n.* The cgs electromagnetic unit of resistance, equal to one millionth of an ohm. [< AB(SOLUTE) + OHM]

a·bol·ish (ə-bol′ish) *v.t.* To do away with; put an end to; annul; destroy. [< F *aboliss-,* stem of *abolir* < L *abolescere* decay, vanish, inceptive of *abolere* destroy] —**a·bol′ish·a·ble** *adj.* —**a·bol′ish·er** *n.* —**a·bol′ish·ment** *n.*

Synonyms: abate, abrogate, annihilate, annul, destroy, end, eradicate, exterminate, extirpate, nullify, obliterate, overthrow, prohibit, remove, repeal, reverse, revoke, subvert, supplant, suppress, terminate. *Abolish* is now used only of institutions, customs, and conditions, especially those wide-spread and long-existing; as, to *abolish* poverty. A building that is burned to the ground is said to be *destroyed* by fire. *Annihilate* signifies to put absolutely out of existence. Matter is never *annihilated,* but only changes its form. *Abolish* is not said of laws. There we use *repeal, abrogate, nullify,* etc.; *repeal* by the enacting body, *nullify* by revolutionary proceedings; a later statute *abrogates,* any earlier law with which it conflicts. An appellate court may *reverse* or set aside the decision of an inferior court. *Overthrow* may be used in either a good or a bad sense; *suppress* is commonly in a good, *subvert* always in a bad sense; as to *subvert* our liberties; to *suppress* a rebellion. The law *prohibits* what may never have existed; it *abolishes* an existing evil. We *abate* a nuisance, *terminate* a controversy. Compare CANCEL, DEMOLISH, EXTERMINATE. Antonyms: authorize, cherish, confirm, continue, enact, establish, institute, introduce, legalize, promote, reinstate, renew, repair, restore, revive, support, sustain.

ab·o·li·tion (ab′ə-lish′ən) *n.* The act of abolishing; extinction; the state or fact of being abolished; specifically, the abolishing of slavery in the United States. [< L *abolitio, -onis* < *abolere* destroy] —**ab′o·li′tion·al** *adj.*

ab·o·li·tion·ar·y (ab′ə-lish′ən·er′ē) *adj.* Destructive; subversive.

ab·o·li·tion·ism (ab′ə-lish′ən·iz′əm) *n.* The principles of those who opposed slavery in the United States. —**ab′o·li′tion·ist** *n.*

A-bomb (ā′bom′) See ATOMIC BOMB under BOMB.

a·bom·i·na·ble (ə-bom′ə-nə-bəl) *adj.* Very hateful; loathsome; detestable; horrible. See synonyms under BAD, CRIMINAL. [< OF < L *abominabilis* < *abominari.* See ABOMINATE.] **a·bom′i·na·bly** *adv.*

a·bom·i·nate (ə-bom′ə-nāt) *v.t.* **·nat·ed, ·nat·ing** 1 To regard with horror or loathing; abhor. 2 To

---

add, āce, câre, pälm; end, ēven; it, īce; odd, ōpen, ôrder; took, pool; up, bûrn; ə = a in *above,* e in *sicken,* i in *clarity,* o in *melon,* u in *focus;* yoo = u in *fuse,* oi, oil; ou, pout; ch, check; g, go; ng, ring; th, thin; ŧh, this; zh, vision. Foreign sounds á, œ, ü, kh, ń; and ✦: see page xx. < from; + plus; ? possibly.

dislike strongly. See synonyms under ABHOR. [< L *abominatus*, pp. of *abominari* abhor as an ill omen < *ab-* off + *omen* omen] — **a·bom′i·na′tor** *n*.

a·bom·i·na·tion (ə·bom′ə·nā′shən) *n*. **1** Strong aversion or loathing; extreme disgust and hatred. **2** Anything that excites disgust, hatred, or loathing; any detestable act or practice; anything vile or shamefully wicked.
Synonyms: abhorrence, abuse, annoyance, aversion, crime, curse, detestation, disgust, evil, execration, hatred, horror, iniquity, nuisance, offense, plague, shame, villainy, wickedness. *Abomination* was originally applied to anything held in religious or ceremonial *aversion* or *abhorrence*. The word is now oftener applied to the object of such *aversion* or *abhorrence* than to the state of mind that so regards it; in common use *abomination* signifies something loathed, or that deserves to be. A toad is to many an object of *disgust*; a foul sewer is an *abomination*. *Antonyms:* affection, appreciation, approval, benefit, blessing, delight, desire, enjoyment, esteem, gratification, joy.

ab·o·rig·i·nal (ab′ə·rij′ə·nəl) *adj*. **1** Of or pertaining to the aborigines. **2** Native to the soil; indigenous; primitive. —*n*. **1** *pl*. **·nes** (-nēz) *Austral*. An Australian aborigine. **2** An original inhabitant. —**ab′o·rig′i·nal·ly** *adv*.

ab·o·rig·i·ne (ab′ə·rij′ə·nē) *n*. **1** One of the original native inhabitants of a country. **2** *pl*. Flora and fauna indigenous to a geographical area. [< L *aborigines* earliest inhabitants < *ab origine* from the beginning]

a·bort (ə·bôrt′) *v.i.* **1** To bring forth young prematurely; miscarry. **2** *Biol*. To fail of complete development. **3** *Mil*. To fail to carry out a mission. —*v.t.* **4** To cause to have a miscarriage. **5** To bring to a premature or unsuccessful conclusion. [< L *abortus*, pp. of *aboriri* miscarry < *ab-* off, away + *oriri* arise, be born]

a·bor·ti·cide (ə·bôr′tə·sīd) *n*. **1** The intentional destruction of the fetus in the womb. **2** An agent for killing the fetus. [< L *abortus* (see ABORT) + -CIDE]

a·bor·ti·fa·cient (ə·bôr′tə·fā′shənt) *adj*. Causing abortion. —*n*. Anything used to cause abortion. [< L *abortus* (see ABORT) + -*i-* + -FACIENT]

a·bor·tion (ə·bôr′shən) *n*. **1** The expulsion of a fetus prematurely, when non-viable; miscarriage. **2** A miscarriage produced artificially. **3** The defective result of a premature birth; a monstrosity. **4** *Biol*. Partial or complete arrest of development, as of an embryo. **5** Failure of anything to progress or develop normally or as expected. [< L *abortio*, *-onis* < *aboriri*. See ABORT.] — **a·bor′tion·al** *adj*.

a·bor·tion·ist (ə·bôr′shən·ist) *n*. One who causes abortion.

a·bor·tive (ə·bôr′tiv) *adj*. **1** Brought forth or born prematurely. **2** Imperfectly developed. **3** Rudimentary, as an organ or stamen. **4** Coming to naught; failing, as an effort. **5** Causing abortion. **6** *Med*. Shortened in its course: an *abortive* fever. See synonyms under USELESS, VAIN. — **a·bor′tive·ly** *adv*. —**a·bor′tive·ness** *n*.

a·bor·tus (ə·bôr′təs) *n. pl.* **·tus·es** An aborted fetus, or any product of an abortion.

a·bound (ə·bound′) *v.i.* **1** To be in abundance; be plentiful. **2** To have plenty of; be rich in: with *in*: The book *abounds* in humorous incidents. **3** To be full of; teem: with *with*: The lakes *abound* with fish. See synonyms under FLOW. Compare AMPLE. [< OF *abunder* < L *abundare* overflow < *ab-* from + *undare* flow in waves < *unda* wave]

a·bout (ə·bout′) *adv*. **1** Around the outside; on every side: Blessings compass thee *about*. **2** Almost; approximately: in *about* an hour. **3** Around, in revolution or rotation: turn and turn *about*. **4** In any direction; toward any, every, or the opposite side: to look or move *about*. **5** Here and there, as without direction: to wander *about*. —*prep*. **1** On the outside or on every side of; encircling: walls *about* the city. **2** Here and there in; to and fro upon: lambs running *about* the fields. **3** Somewhere near or within; on some side of: Stay *about* the house today. **4** Attached to as an attribute: an aura of sanctity *about* him. **5** Approximating to; not far from, as in quantity or time: leaving *about* midnight; troops numbering *about* four thousand. **6** Engaged in; concerned with: Go on *about* your

business; He goes *about* his work skilfully. **7** In reference to; concerning: a book *about* Napoleon. **8** In possession of; at hand: I do not have the money *about* me. See synonyms under AT. [OE *onbūtan*, *ābūtan*]

a·bout-face (ə·bout′fās′) *n*. **1** *Mil*. A drill movement and command for pivoting about to face in exactly the opposite direction. **2** Any turning around or reversal, as of opinion or point of view, especially if sudden. —*v.i.* (ə·bout′fās′) **-faced, -fac·ing 1** To perform an about-face. **2** To change one's opinions, ways, etc.

about-ship (ə·bout′ship′) *v.i.* **-shipped, -ship·ping** *Naut*. To change a ship's course by going on the opposite tack.

a·bove (ə·buv′) *adv*. **1** Vertically up or in a higher place; overhead; on the upper side. **2** Superior in rank or position. **3** In a previous or an earlier place: in the paragraph *above*. **4** In heaven. —*adj*. Given, said, placed, etc., in what is above; preceding. —*n*. That which precedes or is just before; something above. —*prep*. **1** Vertically over; higher than; rising beyond: books piled *above* one another; mountains towering *above* the plain. **2** *Geog*. Farther north than: *above* the fortieth parallel. **3** Exceeding a specific period; more than: a show lasting *above* three hours. **4** More than; in excess of: He ran *above* 500 yards. **5** Surpassing in volume, clearness, or intensity: a voice heard *above* the din. **6** Surpassing in authority, quality, or power: a moral law *above* the civil law. **6** Beyond the reach or influence of: conduct *above* suspicion. [OE *abufen*]

a·bove-board (ə·buv′bôrd′, -bōrd′) *adj. & adv*. In open sight; hence, without concealment, fraud, or trickery; honest. See synonyms under CANDID.

a·bove-ground (ə·buv′ground′) *adj. & adv*. **1** Above the surface of the ground: *aboveground* nuclear testing. **2** In the open; not secret. **3** Not buried; alive.

a·bove-men·tioned (ə·buv′men′shənd) *adj*. mentioned before: the *abovementioned* data.

ab·ra·ca·dab·ra (ab′rə·kə·dab′rə) *n*. A cabalistic word written in triangular form, anciently used as a preventive or curative charm; a spell; hence, any jargon of conjuring or nonsensical words. [< L]

a·brade (ə·brād′) *v.t.* **a·brad·ed, a·brad·ing** To rub or wear off by friction; scrape away. [< L *abradere* < *ab-* away + *radere* scrape] — **a·bra′dant** *adj. & n*. —**a·brad′er** *n*.

a·bran·chi·al (ə·brang′kē·əl, ā-) *adj*. Without gills. Also **a·bran·chi·ate** (ə·brang′kē·it, -āt, ā-), **a·bran·chi·ous** (ə·brang′kē·əs, ā-). [< A-⁴ without + Gk. *branchia* gills]

a·bra·sion (ə·brā′zhən) *n*. **1** The act or result of abrading. **2** *Geol*. A wearing away, as of rocks by glaciers. **3** An abraded place. See synonyms under FRICTION. [< L *abrasio*, *-onis* < *abradere*. See ABRADE.]

a·bra·sive (ə·brā′siv, -ziv) *adj*. Abrading or tending to abrade. —*n*. An abrading substance.

ab·re·ac·tion (ab′rē·ak′shən) *n. Psychoanal*. The releasing of pent-up emotion or disagreeable memories by reliving them through words, feelings, or actions: a form of catharsis. [< AB-¹ from + REACTION, after G *abreagierung*]

a·breast (ə·brest′) *adv*. Side by side and equally advanced. —**abreast of** (or **with**) Side by side with; not behind or ahead of.

a·bri (ə·brē′, *Fr.* á·brē′) *n. pl.* **a·bris** (ə·brēz′, *Fr.* á·brē′) A refuge or shelter; specifically, a dugout or an air-raid shelter. [< F]

a·bridge (ə·brij′) *v.t.* **a·bridged, a·bridg·ing 1** To give the substance of in fewer words; condense; epitomize. **2** To shorten, as in time. **3** To curtail or lessen, as rights. **4** To deprive; stint, as a person of privileges: with *of*. See synonyms under ABBREVIATE, RESTRAIN, RETRENCH. [< OF *abregier* < L *abbreviare*. Doublet of ABBREVIATE.]

a·bridg·ment (ə·brij′mənt) *n*. **1** The act of abridging; the state of being abridged. **2** Something that has been abridged; an epitome or abstract. **3** *Obs*. That which causes time to pass quickly. Also **a·bridge′ment**.
Synonyms: abbreviation, abstract, analysis, compend, compendium, conspectus, digest, epitome, outline, *précis*, summary, synopsis. An *abridgment* gives the most important portions of a work substantially as they stand. An *out-*

line or *synopsis* is a kind of sketch closely following the plan. An *abstract*, *digest* or *précis* is an independent statement of what a book or an article contains, the *abstract* closely following the main heads, the *digest* or *précis* giving the substance with careful consideration of all. An *analysis* draws out the chief thoughts or arguments, expressed or implied. An *epitome*, *compend*, or *compendium* is a condensed view of a subject, whether derived from a previous publication or not. See ABBREVIATION. *Antonyms:* amplification, expansion, paraphrase.

a·brim (ə·brim′) *adj*. Brimming: eyes *abrim* with tears.

a·broach (ə·brōch′) *adj. & adv*. In a condition to let out the liquor; on tap; in circulation; astir. [< A-¹ on + BROACH]

a·broad (ə·brôd′) *adv*. **1** Out of one's home or abode; out of doors. **2** Out of one's own country; in or into foreign lands. **3** Broadly; widely; at large; in circulation. **4** Wide of the mark; astray. [ME *abrood*. See A-¹ and BROAD.]

ab·ro·gate (ab′rə·gāt) *v.t.* **·gat·ed, ·gat·ing** To annul by authority, as a law; abolish; repeal. See synonyms under ABOLISH, ANNUL, CANCEL. [< L *abrogatus*, pp. of *abrogare* < *ab-* away + *rogare* ask, propose] —**ab·ro·ga·ble** (ab′rə·gə·bəl) *adj*. —**ab′ro·ga·tive** *adj*. —**ab′ro·ga′tor** *n*.

ab·ro·ga·tion (ab′rə·gā′shən) *n*. The act or process of abrogating; authoritative repeal.

a·brupt (ə·brupt′) *adj*. **1** Beginning, ending, or changing suddenly; broken off. **2** Unceremonious; sudden, as a departure. **3** Changing subject suddenly; unconnected, as style. **4** Steep, as a cliff. See synonyms under BLUFF², STEEP¹. [< L *abruptus*, pp. of *abrumpere* < *ab-* off + *rumpere* break] —**a·brup′tion** *n*. **a·brupt′ly** *adv*. —**a·brupt′ness** *n*.

A·bruz·zi (ä·brōōt′sē) A region of central Italy on the Adriatic, including the most rugged part of the Apennines.

abs- Var. of AB-.

ab·scess (ab′ses) *n*. A collection of pus in a body cavity formed by tissue disintegration; it may be caused by bacteria and is often accompanied by painful inflammation. —*v.i.* to form an abscess. [< L *abscessus* < *abscedere* go away < *ab-* away + *cedere* go; with ref. to the flowing of humors into the area] —**ab′scessed** *adj*.

ab·scind (ab·sind′) *v.t.* To cut off. [< L *abscindere* < *ab-* off + *scindere* cut]

ab·scis·sa (ab·sis′ə) *n. pl.* **ab·scis·sas** or **ab·scis·sae** (-ē) The distance of any point from the vertical Y-axis of ordinates in a two-dimensional system of reference, measured on a line parallel to the horizontal X-axis of abscissas. [< L (*linea*) *abscissa* (line) cut off, fem. of *abscissus*, pp. of *abscindere*. See ABSCIND.]

ABSCISSA
AB: X-axis. AC: Y-axis. df or Ae: abscissa of point f.

ab·scond (ab·skond′) *v.i.* To depart suddenly and secretly; to escape and hide oneself. See synonyms under ESCAPE. [< L *abscondere* < *ab-* away + *condere* store] —**ab·scon′dence** *n*. —**ab·scond′er** *n*.

ab·sence (ab′səns) *n*. **1** The state, fact, or time of not being present. **2** Lack; want. **3** Mental abstraction; lack of attention. See synonyms under WANT. [< F < L *absentia* < *absens*. See ABSENT.]

ab·sent (ab′sənt) *adj*. **1** Not present. **2** Lacking; missing; nonexistent: In some fishes the ribs are *absent*. **3** Inattentive; absent-minded. See synonyms under INATTENTIVE. —*v.t.* (ab·sent′) To take or keep (oneself) away; not be present. [< L *absens*, *-entis*, pp. of *abesse* < *ab-* away + *esse* be] —**ab·sen·ta·tion** (ab′sən·tā′shən) *n*. — **ab·sent′er** *n*. —**ab′sent·ly** *adv*. —**ab′sent·ness** *n*.

ab·sen·tee (ab′sən·tē′) *n*. One who is absent, as from a job. —*adj*. **1** Relating to one who is temporarily absent: an *absentee* voter. **2** Nonresident: an *absentee* landlord. —**ab′sen·tee′ism** *n*.

ab·sent-mind·ed (ab′sənt·mīn′did) *adj*. Lacking in attention to immediate demands or business because of preoccupation. See synonyms under ABSTRACTED. —**ab′sent-mind′ed·ly** *adv*. — **ab′sent-mind′ed·ness** *n*.

ab·sinthe (ab′sinth) *n*. **1** Wormwood or absinthium. **2** A green, bitter, alcoholic liqueur having the flavor of licorice, made from oils of wormwood and other aromatics. Also **ab'sinth.** [< F < L *absinthium* wormwood < Gk. *apsinthion*] — **ab·sin'thi·al, ab·sin'thi·an** *adj.*

ab·so·lute (ab'sə-lōōt) *adj.* **1** Free from restriction or relation; unlimited; independent; unconditional: an *absolute* monarchy. **2** Complete; perfect. **3** Unadulterated; pure. **4** Positive; entire; total; unquestionable. **5** *Gram.* **a** Free from the usual relations of syntax or construction with other words in the sentence, as *It being late* in *It being late, we started home.* **b** Of a transitive verb, having no object expressed and, hence, functioning as intransitive, as *He writes well.* **c** Of an adjective standing without a noun, as *Only the brave deserve the fair.* **6** *Physics* Not dependent on any arbitrary standard; non-relative; specifically determined or measured only by the fundamental notions of space, mass, and time: *absolute* measurement; also, relating to the absolute-temperature scale: 15° *absolute.* —*n.* That which is absolute or perfect. —**the Absolute** The ultimate basis of all thought, reasoning, or being; God. [< L *absolutus,* pp. of *absolvere.* See ABSOLVE.] —**ab'so·lute'ness** *n.*

Synonyms (adj.): arbitrary, autocratic, despotic, infinite, perfect, pure, supreme, tyrannical, unconditional, unequivocal. As used of human authorities, *absolute* signifies free from limitation by other authority and *supreme* exalted over all other; as, an *absolute* monarch, the *supreme* court. As *absolute* power in human hands is usually abused, the unfavorable meaning of the word predominates. *Autocratic* power is *absolute* power self-established and self-maintained. *Despotic* is commonly applied to a masterful or severe use of power, which is expressed more decidedly by *tyrannical. Arbitrary* may be used in good sense; as, the pronunciation of proper names is *arbitrary;* but the bad sense is the prevailing one; as, an *arbitrary* proceeding, *arbitrary* power. Compare ARBITRARY, FLAT¹, IMPERIOUS, INFINITE, PERFECT. *Antonyms:* accountable, conditional, conditioned, constitutional, limited, responsible, restrained.

absolute alcohol Ethyl alcohol containing not more than 1 percent alcohol.

ab·so·lute·ly (ab'sə-lōōt'lē, *emphatic* ab'sə-lōōt'lē) *adv.* **1** Completely; unconditionally. **2** *Colloq.* Positively. **3** *Gram.* So as not to take an object: to use a verb *absolutely.*

absolute pitch 1 The pitch of a musical tone determined by the number of its vibrations per second in relation to the frequency of a basic or standard tone (usually middle C). **2** The inherent ability to discriminate very minute differences in pitch. Also called *perfect pitch.*

absolute temperature Temperature reckoned from absolute zero.

absolute zero That temperature at which a body would be wholly deprived of heat, and at which a perfect gas would exert no pressure: equivalent to about −273°C., −459°F., or −219° Réaumur.

ab·so·lu·tion (ab'sə-lōō'shən) *n.* **1** An absolving, or a being absolved; forgiveness. **2** In the Roman Catholic Church, the act of a priest in pronouncing the remission of sin, its eternal punishment, or the canonical penalties attached to it; the act of releasing from censure without the sacrament of penance; or a solemn rite performed at the end of a requiem mass. **3** In other churches, the declaration or imploring of God's forgiveness by a priest or minister; also, the forgiveness itself. [< L *absolutio, -onis* < *absolvere.* See ABSOLVE.]

ab·so·lu·tism (ab'sə-lōō-tiz'əm) *n.* **1** The doctrine or practice of unlimited authority and control; despotism; predestination. **2** Absoluteness; positiveness. —**ab'so·lu'tist** *n.* —**ab'so·lu·tis'tic** *adj.*

ab·sol·u·to·ry (ab·sol'yə-tôr'ē, -tō'rē) *adj.* Having power to absolve; absolving. [< L *absolutorius* < *absolvere.* See ABSOLVE.]

ab·solve (ab·solv', -zolv') *v.t.* **ab·solved, ab·solv·ing 1** To pronounce free from the penalties or consequences of an action: His excuses do not *absolve* him from blame. **2** To acquit, as of guilt or complicity. **3** To release from an obligation, li-

ability, or promise. **4** *Eccl.* To grant a remission of sin, its punishment, or the canonical penance attached to it; pardon. [< L *absolvere* < *ab-* from + *solvere* loose. Doublet of ASSOIL.] — **ab·solv'a·ble** *adj.* —**ab·sol'vent** *adj. & n.* — **ab·solv'er** *n.*

Synonyms: acquit, clear, discharge, exculpate, exempt, exonerate, forgive, free, justify, liberate, pardon, release. To *absolve,* in the strict sense, is to *set free* from any bond. One may be *absolved* from a promise by a breach of faith on the part of one to whom the promise was made. To *absolve* from sins is formally to remit their condemnation and penalty. To *acquit* of sin or crime is to *free* from the accusation of it; the innocent are rightfully *acquitted;* the guilty may be mercifully *absolved.* Compare JUSTIFY, PARDON. *Antonyms:* accuse, bind, charge, compel, condemn, convict, impeach, inculpate, obligate, oblige.

ab·so·nant (ab'sə-nənt) *adj.* Discordant; unreasonable. [< AB-¹ + L *sonans.* See SONANT.]

ab·sorb (ab·sôrb', -zôrb') *v.t.* **1** To drink in or suck up, as through or into pores: A sponge *absorbs* water. **2** To engross completely; occupy wholly: Study *absorbs* him. **3** *Physics, Chem.* To take up or in by chemical or molecular action, as gases, heat, liquid, light, etc.: distinguished from *adsorb.* **4** To assimilate, as in the processes of nutrition and growth. **5** To take in and incorporate so as to swallow up identity or individuality: The city *absorbs* the suburbs. **6** To receive the force or action of; intercept: A spring *absorbs* a jar or jolt. **7** To take up entirely by purchase or use, as an issue of bonds or the output of a factory. [< L *absorbere* < *ab-* from + *sorbere* suck in] — **ab·sorb'a·bil'i·ty** *n.* —**ab·sorb'a·ble** *adj.* —**ab·sorb'ing** *adj.* —**ab·sorb'ing·ly** *adv.*

ab·sorbed (ab·sôrbd', -zôrbd') *adj.* **1** Deeply engrossed; rapt. **2** Sucked up or sunken in, as paint on a porous surface. See synonyms under ABSTRACTED. —**ab·sorb·ed·ly** (ab·sôr'·bid·lē, -zôr'-) *adv.* —**ab·sorb'ed·ness** *n.*

ab·sor·bent (ab·sôr'bənt, -zôr'-) *adj.* Absorbing or tending to absorb. —*n.* A substance, duct, etc., that absorbs. [< L *absorbens, -entis,* ppr. of *absorbere.* See ABSORB.] —**ab·sor'ben·cy** *n.*

ab·sorb·er (ab·sôr'bər, -zôr'-) *n.* **1** One who or that which absorbs. **2** *Mech.* A part, as in a caloric engine, having the function of absorbing heat and giving it out later; a regenerator. **3** In an automobile spring, a device for absorbing the shock or jar of a machine in motion; a shock absorber.

ab·sorp·tance (ab·sôrp'təns, -zôrp'-) *n.* The ratio of the light absorbed by a body to the light that enters it.

ab·sorp·tion (ab·sôrp'shən, -zôrp'-) *n.* **1** The act of absorbing or the condition of being absorbed. **2** *Physics* **a** The process by which a liquid or gas is taken into the interstices of a porous substance and held there. **b** The transformation of any emission as it passes through a material substance. **3** Engrossment of the mind; preoccupation. **4** Assimilation, as by incorporation or by the digestive process. —**ab·sorp'tive** *adj.* **ab·sorp'tive·ness, ab·sorp·tiv'i·ty** *n.* [< L *absorptio, -onis* < *absorbere.* See ABSORB.]

ab·stain (ab·stān') *v.i.* To keep oneself back; refrain voluntarily: with *from.* See synonyms under CEASE, REFRAIN¹. [< L *abstenir* < L *abstinere* < *ab-* from + *tenere* hold]

ab·ste·mi·ous (ab·stē'mē·əs) *adj.* **1** Eating and drinking sparingly. **2** Characterized by or spent in abstinence; avoiding excess; self-denying; temperate. See synonyms under SOBER. [< L *abstemius* temperate < *ab-* from + root of *temetum* intoxicating drink] —**ab·ste'mi·ous·ly** *adv.* — **ab·ste'mi·ous·ness** *n.*

ab·sten·tion (ab·sten'shən) *n.* A refraining or abstaining. [< L *abstentio, -onis* < *abstinere.* See ABSTAIN.] —**ab·sten'tious** *adj.*

ab·sti·nence (ab'stə-nəns) *n.* The act or practice of abstaining; forbearing voluntarily, especially from intoxicating drinks; self-denial. [< F < L *abstinentia* < *abstinere.* See ABSTAIN.]

ab·sti·nent (ab'stə-nənt) *adj.* Abstemious. See synonyms under SOBER. —**ab'sti·nent·ly** *adv.*

ab·stract (ab·strakt', ab'strakt) *adj.* **1** Considered apart from the concrete; general, as opposed to particular. **2** Theoretical; ideal, as opposed to practical. **3** Considered or expressed without reference to particular example, as numbers, attributes, or qualities: 8 is an *abstract* number; Redness and valor are *abstract* nouns. **4** Withdrawn from contemplation of present objects; abstracted. **5** *Philos.* Dissociated from closely applied perceptions or ideas: *abstract* truth. **6** In art, generalized or universal, as opposed to concrete, specific, or representational; tending away from the realistic or literal. —*n.* (ab'strakt) **1** A summary or epitome. **2** *Law* A compendium. **3** *Logic* An abstract idea or term. **4** *Gram.* An abstract noun. See under NOUN. **5** In pharmacy, the preparation of a drug in powder form. See synonyms under ABBREVIATION, ABRIDGMENT. —**in the abstract** Apart from concrete relation or embodiment; in its general reference or meaning; abstractly. —*v.t.* (ab·strakt') **1** To take away; remove. **2** To take away secretly; purloin. **3** To withdraw or disengage (the attention, interest, etc.). **4** To consider apart from particular or material instances; form a general notion of: to *abstract* the idea of humanity from a crowd of men. **5** (ab'strakt) To make an abstract of, as a book or treatise; summarize; abridge. [< L *abstractus,* pp. of *abstrahere* < *ab-* away + *trahere* draw] —**ab·stract'er** *n.* —**ab·stract'ly** *adv.* —**ab·stract'ness** *n.*

Synonyms (verb): detach, disengage, divide, draw, purloin, remove, separate, steal, withdraw. The central idea of *withdrawing* makes *abstract* in common speech a euphemism for *purloin, steal.* In mental processes, we *separate* some one element from all that does not necessarily belong to it, *abstract* it, and view it alone. The mind is *abstracted* when it is *withdrawn* from all other subjects and concentrated upon one. *Antonyms:* add, increase, insert, interpose, restore, unite.

ab·stract·ed (ab·strak'tid) *adj.* **1** Absent-minded. **2** Separated from all else; apart; abstruse. —**ab·stract'ed·ly** *adv.* —**ab·stract'ed·ness** *n.*

Synonyms: absent, absent-minded, absorbed, heedless, inattentive, oblivious, preoccupied. As regards mental action, *absorbed, abstracted,* and *preoccupied* refer to the cause, *absent* or *absent-minded* to the effect. The man *absorbed* in one thing will appear *absent* in others. The *absent-minded* man is *oblivious* of ordinary matters, because his thoughts are elsewhere. One who is *preoccupied* is intensely busy in thought; one may be *absent-minded* simply through inattention, with fitful and aimless wandering of thought. Compare ABSTRACT. *Antonyms:* alert, attentive, ready.

ab·strac·tion (ab·strak'shən) *n.* **1** State of being abstracted; an abstracting. **2** An abstract idea; a theory. **3** Separation; removal; theft. **4** Absence of mind; preoccupation. **5** Seclusion of life, as by a hermit; withdrawal from worldly objects. **6** The quality that makes a work of art generalized or universal, as distinguished from literal or concrete, present in varying degrees in widely differing art forms. **7** An art form or a work of art in which the qualities are either predominantly or totally abstract: opposed to *naturalism, realism.* Compare NON-OBJECTIVE ART. [< L *abstractio, -onis* < *abstrahere.* See ABSTRACT.]

ab·strac·tive (ab·strak'tiv) *adj.* Of, pertaining to, or tending to abstraction; having the power of abstraction; epitomizing. —**ab·strac'tive·ly** *adv.* —**ab·strac'tive·ness** *n.*

ab·struse (ab·strōōs') *adj.* **1** Hard to understand. **2** *Obs.* Hidden; concealed. See synonyms under COMPLEX, MYSTERIOUS, OBSCURE. [< L *abstrusus,* pp. of *abstrudere* < *ab-* away + *trudere* thrust] —**ab·struse'ly** *adv.* —**ab·struse'ness** *n.*

ab·surd (ab·sûrd', -zûrd') *adj.* Opposed to manifest reason or truth; irrational; preposterous; ridiculous. —*n.* a literary and philosophical term suggesting the illogicality or pointlessness of the human condition from an existential point of view. [< F < L *absurdus* out of tune, incongruous, senseless < *ab-* completely + *surdus* deaf] —**ab·surd′·ly** *adv.* —**ab·surd′ness** *n.*

Synonyms: anomalous, foolish, incorrect, irrational, ludicrous, mistaken, monstrous, nonsensical, paradoxical, preposterous, ridiculous, senseless, stupid, unreasonable, wild. That is *absurd* which is contrary to the first principles of reasoning; as, that a part should be greater than the whole is *absurd*. A *paradoxical* statement appears at first thought contradictory or *absurd*, while it may be really true. Anything is *irrational* when clearly contrary to sound reason, *foolish* when contrary to practical good sense, *unreasonable* when there seems a perverse bias or an intent to go wrong. *Monstrous* and *preposterous* refer to what is overwhelmingly *absurd*. The *ridiculous* or the *nonsensical* is worthy only to be laughed at. Compare INCONGRUOUS. *Antonyms:* consistent, demonstrable, established, incontestable, incontrovertible, indisputable, indubitable, logical, rational, reasonable, sagacious, sensible, sound, substantial, true, undeniable, unquestionable, wise.

ab·surd·i·ty (ab·sûr′də·tē, ·zûr′-) *n. pl.* **·ties 1** The quality of being absurd. **2** Something absurd.

a·bu·li·a (ə·boo̅′lē·ə, ə·byoo̅′-) *n. Psychiatry* A form of mental derangement in which the will power is lost or impaired: also **aboulia.** [< *NL* < *Gk. aboulia* < *a-* without + *boulē* will] —**a·bu′lic** *adj.*

a·bun·dance (ə·bun′dəns) *n.* A plentiful supply; a great quantity or number; copiousness; plenty. See synonyms under COMFORT. [< *OF* < *L abundantia* < *abundans.* See ABUNDANT.]

a·bun·dant (ə·bun′dənt) *adj.* Affording a plentiful supply; abounding; ample; copious. See synonyms under AMPLE. [< *OF* < *L abundans, -antis,* ppr. of *abundare.* See ABOUND.] —**a·bun′dant·ly** *adv.*

a·buse (ə·byoo̅z′) *v.t.* **a·bused, a·bus·ing 1** use improperly or injuriously; misuse. **2** To hurt by treating wrongly; injure: to *abuse* friendship. **3** To speak in coarse or bad terms of; revile; malign. **4** *Obs.* To deceive. —*n.* (ə·byoos′) **1** Improper or injurious use; perversion; misuse. **2** Ill–treatment; cruel treatment; injury. **3** Vicious conduct, practice, or act. **4** Vituperation; slander. See synonyms under ABOMINATION, OUTRAGE. [< *F abuser* < *L abusus,* pp. of *abuti* misuse < *ab-* away + *uti* use] —**a·bus′er** *n.*

Synonyms (verb): damage, defame, defile, harm, ill–treat, ill–use, injure, malign, maltreat, misemploy, misuse, molest, oppress, persecute, pervert, pollute, prostitute, ravish, reproach, revile, ruin, slander, victimize, vilify, violate, vituperate, wrong. *Abuse* covers all unreasonable or improper use or treatment by word or act. A tenant does not *abuse* rented property by reasonable wear, even if that may *damage* the property and *injure* its sale; he may *abuse* it by needless defacement or neglect. *Defame, malign, revile, slander, vilify,* and *vituperate* are used always in a bad sense. One may be justly *reproached.* To *persecute* one is to *ill–treat* him for opinion's sake, commonly for religious belief; to *oppress* is generally for political or pecuniary motives. *Misemploy, misuse,* and *pervert* are commonly applied to objects rather than to persons. Compare POLLUTE. *Antonyms:* applaud, benefit, cherish, conserve, consider, eulogize, extol, favor, laud, panegyrize, praise, protect, respect, shield, sustain, uphold, vindicate.

A·bu Sim·bel (ä′boo̅ sim′bel) Site of ancient rock temples on the west bank of the Nile in southern Egypt: also *Ipsambul.*

a·bu·sive (ə·byoo̅′siv) *adj.* **1** Of the nature of or characterized by abuse; harsh; vituperative. **2** Using wrongly or improperly; misapplying. —**a·bu′sive·ly** *adv.* —**a·bu′sive·ness** *n.*

a·but (ə·but′) *v.* **a·but·ted, a·but·ting** *v.i.* To

ABU SIMBEL
Colossal statues
of Rameses II.

touch, join, or cause to adjoin or touch at the end or side; border: with *on, upon,* or *against.* —*v.t.* To border on; end at: This building *abuts* the park. See synonyms under ADJACENT. [< *OF abouter* border on (< *a-* to + *bout* end); infl. by *OF abuter* touch with an end (< *a-* to + *but* end)] —**a·but′ter** *n.* —**a·but′ting** *adj.*

a·but·ment (ə·but′mənt) *n.* **1** The act of abutting. **2** That which abuts, or the place which is abutted upon. **3** A supporting or buttressing structure, as at the end of a bridge or wall; also, that part of an arch that takes the thrust or strain. For illustration see ARCH. **4** *Mil.* The block at the rear end of a gun which receives the rearward pressure of explosion or detonation.

a·but·tal (ə·but′l) *n.* **1** An abutting or abutment. **2** An abutting part; a boundary.

a·by (ə·bī′) *v.t.* **a·bought** *Obs.* **1** To pay the penalty for. **2** To endure; suffer, as a fate. Also **a·bye′.** [OE *ābycgan* pay for]

a·bysm (ə·biz′əm) *n.* An abyss; an unfathomable depth. [< *OF abisme* < *L abyssus* ABYSS]

a·bys·mal (ə·biz′məl) *adj.* Unfathomable; hence, extreme: an *abysmal* ignorance. —**a·bys′mal·ly** *adv.*

a·byss (ə·bis′) *n.* **1** A bottomless gulf. **2** Hell. **3** Any vast depth; hence, a great moral or intellectual depth: an *abyss* of degradation and humiliation. **4** The lowest depths of the sea. [< *L abyssus* < *a-* without + *byssos* bottom]

a·bys·sal (ə·bis′əl) *adj.* **1** Pertaining to an abyss. **2** Designating those ocean depths beyond the continental shelf. Also **a·bys′sic.** (ə·bis′ik).

Ab·ys·sin·i·a (ab′ə·sin′ē·ə) Ethiopia. —**Ab′·ys·sin·i·an** *adj. & n.*

Abyssinian cat Any of a breed of medium-sized cats with long, tapering tails, small paws, and short, silky hair with dark-colored tips.

ac- Assimilated var. of AD-.

-ac *suffix* **1** Having; affected by: *demoniac.* **2** Pertaining to; of: *cardiac.* [< *Gk. -akos* or *L -acus* or *F -aque*]

Ac *Chem.* Actinium (symbol Ac).

a·ca·cia (ə·kā′shə) *n.* **1** Any of a large genus (*Acacia*) of flowering trees and shrubs of the bean family found in the tropics and warm temperate regions, especially the green wattle acacia (*A. decurrens*) of Australia. **2** The common locust tree. **3** Gum arabic or gummy exudation of certain acacias. [< *L* < *Gk. akakia* a thorny tree of Egypt < *akē* point]

ac·a·dem·i·a (ak′ə·dē′mē·ə) *n. Often cap.* Academic institutions collectively; the academic world. [< *L.* See ACADEMY.]

ac·a·dem·ic (ak′ə·dem′ik) *adj.* **1** Pertaining to an academy, college, or university; scholarly. **2** Classical and literary rather than practical; formal or theoretical, as opposed to practical. **3** According to scholastic rules or usage; conventional; traditional. Also **ac′a·dem′i·cal.** —*n.* **1** A college or university student. **2** A member of a learned society. [< *L academicus* < *academia.* See ACADEMY.] —**ac′a·dem′i·cal·ly** *adv.*

ac·a·dem·i·cals (ak′ə·dem′i·kəlz) *n. pl.* The prescribed dress of an academy, college, etc.; cap and gown.

a·cad·e·mi·cian (ə·kad′ə·mish′ən, ak′ə·də-) *n.* A member of an academy of art, science, or literature.

ac·a·dem·i·cism (ak′ə·dem′ə·siz′əm) *n.* **1** The state or quality of being academic in style or procedure. **2** Pedantic formalism, as in art or literature. Also **a·cad·e·mism** (ə·kad′ə·miz′əm).

a·cad·e·my (ə·kad′ə·mē) *n. pl.* **·mies 1** A school, especially one intermediate between a common school and a college. **2** A learned society for the advancement of arts or sciences. [< *F académie* < *L academia* < *Gk. akadēmeia* the grove of *Akadēmos* where Plato taught] —**ac′a·dem′ic** *adj. & n.*

Academy Award One of the awards made annually by the Academy of Motion Picture Arts and Sciences.

a·can·thine (ə·kan′thin) *adj.* **1** Pertaining to or like an acanthus. **2** Decorated with the acanthus leaf.

acantho- *combining form* Thorn or thorny; spine, point, prickle: *acanthocephalan.* Also, before vowels, **acanth-,** as in *acanthoid.* [< *Gk. akantha* thorn]

a·can·tho·ceph·a·lan (ə·kan′thō·sef′ə·lən) *n.* Any of a phylum (*Acanthocephala*) of worms parasitic when adult in the intestines of fishes and other vertebrates, having a proboscis covered with hooks. Also **a·can′tho·ceph′a·lid.** [< ACANTHO- + *Gk. kephalē* head]

a·can·thoid (ə·kan′thoid) *adj.* Spiny.

a·can·thus (ə·kan′thəs) *n. pl.* **·thus·es** or **·thi** (-thī) **1** Any plant of the genus *Acanthus* having large spinous leaves: common in the Mediterranean region. **2** A conventionalized architectural and decorative representation of its leaf, characteristic of the Corinthian capital. Also **acanthus leaf.** [< *Gk. akanthos* < *akē* thorn]

ACANTHUS *(def. 2)*

a cap·pel·la (ä′ kə·pel′ə, *Ital.* ä′ käp·pel′lä) *Music* **1** In chapel or church style, *i.e.,* sung without instrumental accompaniment. **2** In church time, *i.e.,* with four half notes in each bar. [< *Ital.* < *L ad* according to + *cappella* chapel]

a ca·pric·cio (ä′ kä·prēt′chō) *Music* At the performer's pleasure as to tempo and expression; capriciously. [< *Ital.*]

A·ca·pul·co (ä′kä·pool′kō) A port and resort city of SW Mexico on the Pacific.

ac·a·rid (ak′ə·rid) *n.* Any of an order (*Acarina*) of arachnids, including the mites and ticks. —*adj.* Of or pertaining to the acarids. [Gk. *akari* mite]

ac·a·roid (ak′ə·roid) *adj.* Of or like the acarids; mitelike. [< *Gk. akari* mite, + -OID]

a·car·pel·ous (ā·kär′pəl·əs) *adj. Bot.* Having no carpels. Also **a·car′pel·lous.**

a·car·pous (ā·kär′pəs) *adj. Bot.* Not bearing fruit. [< A.⁴ without + *Gk. karpos* fruit]

ac·a·rus ak′ər·əs) *n. pl.* **·a·ri** (-ə·rī) Any of the numerous mites of the genus *Acarus.* [< *Gk. akari* mite]

a·cat·a·lec·tic (ā·kat′ə·lek′tik) *adj.* Metrically complete; not catalectic; having the required number of feet or of syllables, especially in the last foot. —*n.* A full or metrically complete verse.

a·cau·date (ā·kô′dāt) *adj. Zool.* Having no tail; tailless. Also **a·cau′dal.** [< A.⁴ not + CAUDATE]

ac·au·les·cence (ak′ô·les′əns) *n. Bot.* Absence, real or apparent, of the stem. —**ac′au·les′cent,** *adj.*

a·caus·al (ā kôz′əl) *adj.* not causal; not having to do with cause and effect.

ac·cede (ak·sēd′) *v.i.* **ac·ced·ed, ac·ced·ing 1** To give one's consent or adherence; agree; assent: with *to.* **2** To come into or enter upon an office or dignity: with *to.* See synonyms under AGREE, ASSENT. [< *L accedere* < *ad-* to + *cedere* yield, go]

ac·ced·ence (ak·sē′dəns) *n.* The act of acceding; agreeing to.

ac·cel·er·an·do (ak·sel′ə·ran′dō; *Ital.* ät·che′le·rän′dō) *adj. & adv. Music* With gradual quickening of the time. [< *Ital.*]

ac·cel·er·ant (ak·sel′ər·ənt) *adj.* Accelerating; hastening. —*n.* That which accelerates.

ac·cel·er·ate (ak·sel′ə·rāt) *v.* **·at·ed, ·at·ing** *v.t.* **1** To cause to act or move faster; increase the speed of. **2** *Physics* To increase the rate of change of (the linear or angular velocity of a body). **3** To hasten the natural or usual course of: to *accelerate* combustion. **4** To cause to happen ahead of time. —*v.i.* **5** To move or become faster; to increase in speed. See synonyms under QUICKEN. [< *L acceleratus,* pp. of *accelerare* < *ad-* to + *celerare* hasten < *celer* quick] —**ac·cel·er·a·ble** (ak·sel′ər·ə·bəl) *adj.*

ac·cel·er·a·tion (ak·sel′ə·rā′shən) *n.* **1** The act of accelerating, or the process of being accelerated; a quickening, as of progress, action, functional activity, etc. **2** The rate at which the speed of a body increases. **3** *Physics* The rate at which the velocity of a body increases per unit of time: used also of decrease of velocity, which is expressed as a **negative acceleration.**

acceleration of gravity An increase in the velocity of a body due to the force of gravity. At sea level it is about 32.17 feet per second per second.

ac·cel·er·a·tive (ak·sel′ə·rā′tiv) *adj.* Of, pertaining to, or causing acceleration; tending to accelerate. Also **ac·cel·er·a·to·ry.**

ac·cel·er·a·tor (ak·sel′ə·rā′tər) *n.* **1** One who or that which accelerates. **2** *Phot.* Any chemical or device for hastening the appearance or development of the picture on an exposed sensitized plate or print. **3** *Mech.* A device for increasing the speed of a machine. **4** *Chem.* A substance or agent which quickens the speed of a chemical reaction; a catalyst. **5** *Physiol.* A muscle or nerve which acts to increase the speed of a function. **6** *Physics* Any of various devices for accelerating the velocity of subatomic particles by subjecting them to the force of a synchronized electromagnetic field, as a cyclotron or synchrotron.

ac·cent (ak′sent) *n.* **1** A stress of voice on a particular syllable in pronouncing a word. **2** A mark used to indicate such stress: known as **primary** (noting the chief stress) and **secondary** (noting weaker stress on some other syllable or syllables) accents. In ə·brē′vē·ā′·shən, the primary accent is on the fourth syllable, and the secondary accent is on the second syllable. **3** One of three marks, used chiefly in the Romance languages, to indicate the quality of a vowel or diphthong: acute (′), grave (`), and circumflex (^) accents. **4** *Music* Stress of voice or instrument. **5** A modulation of the voice; mode of utterance; pronounciation. **6** *pl.* Speech. **7** *Math.* A mark or marks to distinguish the value or order of similar symbols: a′ (a prime), a″ (a second), a‴ (a third), etc.; also to denote minutes and seconds in geometry, trigonometry, etc.: ′ = minutes, ″ = seconds. **8** In mensuration, a similar mark or marks to denote feet and inches, as ′ = feet; ″ = inches. **9** In prosody, the stress determining the rhythm of poetry; ictus. —*v.t.* (ak′sent, ak·sent′) **1** To speak or pronounce with an accent; stress. **2** To write or print with a mark indicating accent or stress. **3** To call attention to; accentuate. [< L *accentus,* lit., song added to speech (a trans. of Gk. *prosōidia* PROSODY) < *ad-* to + *cantus* a singing < *canere* sing]

ac·cen·tu·al (ak·sen′chōō·əl) *adj.* Of, pertaining to, having, or made by accent. —**ac·cen′tu·al·ly** *adv.*

ac·cen·tu·ate (ak·sen′chōō·āt) *v.t.* **·at·ed, ·at·ing** **1** To strengthen or heighten the effect of; emphasize. **2** To speak or pronounce with an accent. **3** To write or print with a mark indicating accent. [< Med.L *accentuatus,* pp. of *accentuare* < L *accentus* ACCENT] —**ac·cen′tu·a′tion** *n.*

ac·cept (ak·sept′) *v.t.* **1** To take when offered; receive with favor or willingness, as a gift. **2** To give an affirmative answer to: to *accept* an invitation, an offer of marriage, etc. **3** To agree to; admit: to *accept* an apology. **4** To take with good grace; submit to: to *accept* the inevitable. **5** To agree to pay, as a draft. **6** To believe in: to *accept* Christianity. **7** *Law* To acknowledge as valid or received: He *accepted* the subpoena. —*v.i.* **8** To agree or promise to fulfil an engagement; receive favorably. See synonyms under ACKNOWLEDGE, AGREE, ASSENT, ASSUME, CONFESS, RATIFY. [< L *acceptare,* freq. of *accipere* take < *ad-* to + *capere* take] —**ac·cept′er** *n.*

ac·cept·a·ble (ak·sep′tə·bəl) *adj.* **1** That is worthy of being accepted or capable of acceptance; pleasing; welcome. **2** Tolerable; detrimental, though not judged to require corrective measures: *acceptable* air pollution. See synonyms under AGREEABLE, DELIGHTFUL. —**ac·cept′a·ble·ness, ac·cept′a·bil·i·ty** *n.* —**ac·cept′a·bly** *adv.*

ac·cep·tance (ak·sep′təns) *n.* **1** The act of accepting; state of being accepted or acceptable; also, consent to receive. **2** An agreement to pay a bill of exchange, draft, order, or the like, according to its terms; also, the paper itself when endorsed accepted." **3** *Law* Any form or act by which one positively or constructively acknowledges the validity or sufficiency of an act done by another, agrees to the terms of a contract, or the like. Also **ac·cep′tan·cy.**

ac·cep·tant (ak·sep′tənt) *adj.* Ready or willing to accept; receptive.

ac·cep·ta·tion (ak′sep·tā′shən) *n.* **1** The accepted meaning of a word or expression; general interpretation. **2** The state of being accepted or acceptable.

ac·cept·ed (ak·sep′tid) *adj.* Commonly recognized, believed, or approved; popular.

ac·cess (ak′ses) *n.* **1** The act, opportunity, or means of approaching; admittance; approach; passage; path. **2** Increase; addition; accession: an *access* of territory. **3** An attack, as of disease; a fit of passion or zeal; outburst. **4** *Eccl.* Approach to God: *access* by faith (*Rom.* v 2): used especially in the titles of certain prayers. See synonyms under ENTRANCE, INCREASE. [< L *accessus* an approach < *accedere.* See ACCEDE.

ac·ces·sa·ry (ak·ses′ər·ē) *adj., n. pl.* **·ries** *Law* Accessory. ◆ **accessary, accessory** The earlier form is *accessary* (see -ARY¹), now retained primarily in legal usage. Later, the adjective was refashioned to *accessory* (on analogy with *promissory, amatory, illusory,* etc.), which also influenced the form of the noun. The two spellings are now practically interchangeable, although *accessory* is supplanting the other in both common and legal usage.

ac·ces·si·ble (ak·ses′ə·bəl) *adj.* **1** Easy of access. **2** That can be approached. **3** Attainable; that can be obtained. **4** Open to the influence of: with *to:* His heart is *accessible* to pity. See synonyms under FRIENDLY. —**ac·ces·si·bil′i·ty** *n.* —**ac·ces′si·bly** *adv.*

ac·ces·sion (ak·sesh′ən) *n.* **1** One who or that which is added; addition. **2** Attainment, as of office; succession to a throne; induction or elevation. **3** Access; admittance; approach: the *accession* of light. **4** Assent; agreement; consent. **5** *Law* The acquisition of property of a concomitant nature by virtue of the ownership of the principal, to which it is accessory as an incident. **6** A beginning, increase, or paroxysm, of disease, anger, folly, etc. See ACCESS. —*v.t.* To record, as additions to a library or museum. [< L *accessio, -onis* < *accedere.* See ACCEDE.] —**ac·ces′sion·al** *adj.*

Synonyms (noun): addition, arrival augmentation, enlargement, extension, inauguration, increase, influx. See ENTRANCE.

ac·ces·so·ry (ak·ses′ər·ē) *n. pl.* **·ries** **1** A person or thing that aids subordinately; an adjunct; appurtenance; accompaniment. **2** *pl.* Such items of apparel as complete an outfit, as gloves, a scarf, hat, or handbag. **3** *Law* A person who, even if not present, is concerned, either before or after, in the perpetration of a felony below the crime of treason. See also note under ACCESSARY. —*adj.* **1** Aiding the principal design, or assisting subordinately the chief agent, as in the commission of a crime. **2** Contributory; supplemental; additional: *accessory* nerves. Also *accessary.* [< L *accessorius* < *accessus,* pp. of *accedere.* See ACCEDE.] —**ac·ces′so·ri·ly** *adv.* —**ac·ces′so·ri·ness** *n.*

Synonyms (noun): abetter or abettor, accomplice, ally, assistant, associate, attendant, coadjutor, colleague, companion, confederate, follower, helper, henchman, participator, partner, retainer.

ac·ci·dence (ak′sə·dəns) *n.* **1** *Gram.* That part of grammar that treats of the accidents or inflections of words. **2** A book dealing with the rudiments of grammar. **3** The rudiments or elements of any art or science. [< *accidents,* pl. of ACCIDENT (def. 3)]

ac·ci·dent (ak′sə·dənt) *n.* **1** Anything that happens by chance; anything occurring unexpectedly, undesignedly, or without known or assignable cause; a contingency; especially, any unpleasant or unfortunate occurrence involving injury, loss, suffering, or death; a casualty; mishap. **2** Any non-essential circumstance or attribute. **3** *Gram.* An inflection, as of case, gender, number, etc. **4** *Logic* Any feature, element, or accompaniment of an object not essential to the conception of it. [< L *accidens, -entis,* ppr. of *accidere* happen < *ad-* upon + *cadere* fall]

Synonyms: adventure, calamity, casualty, chance, contingency, disaster, fortuity, hap, happening, hazard, incident, misadventure, misfortune, mishap, possibility. An *accident* is that which happens without anyone's direct intention; a *chance* that which happens without any known cause. An *incident* is viewed as occur-

ring in the regular course of things, but subordinate to the main purpose, or aside from the main design. *Fortune* and *chance* are nearly equivalent, but *chance* can be used of human effort and endeavor as *fortune* cannot be; we say there is one *chance* in a thousand"; as personified, we speak of fickle *Fortune,* blind *Chance.* Since the unintended is often the undesirable, *accident* tends to signify some *calamity* or *disaster,* but we may speak of a fortunate or happy *accident.* An *adventure* is that which may turn out ill, a *misadventure* that which does turn out ill. A slight disturbing *accident* is a *mishap.* Compare CATASTROPHE, EVENT, HAZARD.

ac·ci·den·tal (ak′sə·den′təl) *adj.* **1** Happening or coming by chance or without design; casual; fortuitous; taking place unexpectedly, unintentionally, or out of the usual course. **2** Non-essential; subordinate; incidental: said of any attribute or feature not entering into the very nature of a thing. **3** *Music* Pertaining to or indicating a sharp, natural, flat, etc., elsewhere than in the signature. —*n.* **1** A casual, incidental, or non-essential feature or property. **2** *Music* A sharp, flat, or natural elsewhere than in the signature. There are five *accidentals* or signs of chromatic alteration to show that the notes to which they are applied have to be raised or lowered a semitone or a tone: the sharp, double-sharp, flat, double-flat, and the natural. —**ac′ci·den′tal·ness** *n.*

ac·ci·den·tal·ly (ak′sə·den′təl·ē) *adv.* **1** By accident or chance; unintentionally; casually. **2** As an accidental or subsidiary feature or effect; incidentally.

ac·ci·dent·ed (ak′sə·den′tid) *adj.* Marked by undulations in the surface: an *accidented* field.

ac·claim (ə·klām′) *v.t.* **1** To proclaim by acclamation; hail as: to *acclaim* him victor. **2** To shout approval of; show enthusiasm for. **3** To shout; call out: *acclaim* one's sorrow. —*v.i.* **4** To applaud; shout approval. —*n.* Applause; pronouncement. See synonyms under APPLAUSE. [< L *acclamare* < *ad-* to + *clamare* shout] —**ac·claim′a·ble** *adj.* —**ac·claim′er** *n.*

ac·cla·ma·tion (ak′lə·mā′shən) *n.* **1** The act of acclaiming; that which is expressed in the act; a shout, as of applause. **2** A loud and general viva-voce vote of approval, as in public assembly. **3** In the Roman Catholic Church, the elevation to an ecclesiastical dignity by the unanimous voice of the electors, without voting: one of the ways of electing a pope. **4** *Music* The responsive chant in antiphonal singing. **5** *Archeol.* A short inscription containing a wish or injunction, found on tombs, amultes, etc.; also, a representation, in sculpture or on a medal, of persons expressing joy or approval. See synonyms under APPLAUSE. [< L *acclamatio, -onis* < *acclamare.* See ACCLAIM.]

ac·clam·a·to·ry (ə·klam′ə·tôr′ē, -tō′rē) *adj.* Relating to or expressing joy and acclamation.

ac·cli·mate (ə·klī′mit, ak′lə·māt) *v.t. & v.i.* **·mat·ed, ·mat·ing** To adapt or become adapted to a foreign climate or new environment: said of persons, plants, or animals; acclimatize. [< F *acclimater* < *à* to (< L *ad-*) + *climat* CLIMATE] —**ac·cli·ma·ta·ble** (ə·klī′mə·tə·bəl) *adj.* —**ac·cli·ma·tion** (ak′lə·mā′shən), **ac·cli·ma·ta·tion** (ə·klī′mə·tā′shən) *n.*

ac·cliv·ous (ə·klī′vəs) *adj.* Sloping upward. Also **ac·cliv·i·tous** (ə·kliv′ə·təs).

ac·co·lade (ak′ə·lād′, -läd′) *n.* **1** *Music* A vertical brace or heavy bar. **2** *Archit.* A curved ornamental molding. **3** The salutation, at first an embrace, later a light blow with a sword, in conferring knighthood; hence, an honor conferred. [< F < Ital. *accollata* < *accollare* embrace about the neck < L *ad* to + *collum* neck]

ACCOLADE *(def. 2)*

ac·com·mo·date (ə·kom′ə·dāt) v. **·dat·ed, ·dat·ing** v.t. **1** To do a favor for; oblige; help. **2** To provide for; give lodging to. **3** To be suitable for; to contain comfortably: The hall *accommodates* large numbers. **4** To adapt or modify; adjust: He *accommodated* his needs to our capacity to fulfil them. **5** To reconcile or settle, as conflicting opinions. —v.i. **6** To be or become adjusted or conformed, as the eye to distance. [< L *accommodatus*, pp. of *accommodare* < *ad-* to + *commodare* make fit, suit < *com-* with + *modus* measure] —ac·com′mo·da′tive adj. —ac·com′mo·da′tive·ness n.
  Synonyms: adapt, adjust, entertain, fit, furnish, harmonize, lodge, oblige, receive, reconcile, serve, suit, supply. See ADAPT, ADJUST.
ac·com·mo·dat·ing (ə·kom′ə·dā′ting) adj. Disposed to accommodate; obliging. —ac·com′mo·dat′ing·ly adv.
ac·com·mo·da·tion (ə·kom′ə·dā′shən) n. **1** The act of accommodating, or the state of being accommodated; adjustment; adaptation. **2** A convenience; entertainment; specifically, lodging, board, etc. **3** A loan or other help or favor; specifically, an accommodation bill. **4** Obligingness. **5** An accommodation train. **6** The adjustment of the eye to vision at different distances.
ac·com·pa·ni·ment (ə·kum′pə·ni·mənt, ə·kump′ni-) n. **1** Anything that accompanies. **2** *Music* A subordinate part, vocal or instrumental, accompanying, enriching, or supporting a leading part. See synonyms under APPENDAGE, CIRCUMSTANCE.
ac·com·pa·nist (ə·kum′pə·nist, ə·kump′nist) n. A musician who plays or sings the accompaniment.
ac·com·pa·ny (ə·kum′pə·nē) v.t. **·nied, ·ny·ing 1** To go with; attend; escort. **2** To be or occur with; coexist with: Weakness often *accompanies* disease. **3** To supplement with: He *accompanied* his insults with blows. **4** To play a musical accompaniment to or for. See synonyms under FOLLOW. [< F *accompagner* < *à* to + *compagne* COMPANION] —ac·com′pa·ni·er n.
ac·com·plice (ə·kom′plis) n. **1** An associate in wrong or crime, whether as principal or accessory. **2** *Obs.* One who cooperates; an associate. See synonyms under ABETTOR, ACCESSORY. [< *a*, indefinite article + F *complice* accomplice < LL *complex* accomplice. See COMPLEX.]
ac·com·plish (ə·kom′plish) v.t. **1** To bring to pass; perform; effect. **2** To bring to completion; finish. **3** *Obs.* To make complete; perfect, as in external acquirements or mental polish. [< OF *acompliss-*, stem of *acomplir* < LL *accomplere* < L *ad-* to + *complere* fill up, complete] —ac·com′plish·a·ble adj. —ac·com′plish·er n.
  Synonyms: achieve, complete, consummate, discharge, do, effect, execute, finish, fulfil, perform, realize. *Perform* and *accomplish* both imply working toward the end; but *perform* always allows a possibility of not attaining, while *accomplish* carries the thought of full completion. See ATTAIN, EFFECT.
ac·com·plished (ə·kom′plisht) adj. **1** Proficient; polite; polished; having accomplishments. **2** Completed; consummated. See synonyms under POLITE.
ac·com·plish·ment (ə·kom′plish·mənt) n. **1** An accomplishment; fulfilment; performance; completion. **2** An acquirement or attainment that tends to perfect or equip in character, manners, or person. See synonyms under ACT, ATTAINMENT, END.
ac·cord (ə·kôrd′) v.t. **1** To render as due; grant; concede: to *accord* merited honor. **2** To bring into agreement; make harmonize or correspond, as opinions. **3** To reconcile; literally, to bring heart to heart, as former enemies. —v.i. **4** To agree; harmonize: Those colors *accord* well together. See synonyms under AGREE, ASSENT. —n. **1** Harmony, especially of sounds; agreement. **2** Spontaneous impulse; choice: of one's own *accord.* **3** A settlement of any difference; reconciliation; specifically, an agreement between governments. See synonyms under HARMONY. [< OF *acorder* < LL *accordare* be of one mind, agree < L *ad-* to + *cor* heart] —ac·cord′a·ble adj. —ac·cord′er n.
ac·cord·ance (ə·kôr′dəns) n. Agreement; conformity. See synonyms under HARMONY.

ac·cord·ant (ə·kôr′dənt) adj. Consonant; agreeing; corresponding. —ac·cord′ant·ly adv.
ac·cord·ing (ə·kôr′ding) adj. Being in accordance or agreement; harmonizing. —adv. Agreeably; conformably; just.
ac·cord·ing·ly (ə·kôr′ding·lē) adv. In a conformable manner; suitably; consequently. See synonyms under CONSEQUENTLY, HENCE, THEREFORE, WHEREFORE.
ac·cor·di·on (ə·kôr′dē·ən) n. A portable free-reed musical wind-instrument with from 5 to 50 keys, the air for which is furnished by a bellows alternately pulled apart and pressed together by the performer. [< Ital. *accordare* accord, harmonize] —ac·cor′di·on·ist n.
ac·cost (ə·kôst′, ə·kost′) v.t. **1** To speak to first; address; greet. **2** To approach for sexual purposes; proposition. See synonyms under ADDRESS. —n. Manner or act of addressing; greeting. [< F *accoster* < LL *accostare* be side to side < L *ad-* to + *costa* rib]
ac·count (ə·kount′) v.t. **1** To hold to be; consider; estimate. —v.i. **2** To provide a reckoning, as of funds paid or received: with *to* or *with* (someone) *for* (something). **3** To give a rational explanation; refer to some cause or natural law: with *for.* **4** To be responsible; answer: with *for.* **5** To cause death, capture, or incapacitation: with *for.* See synonyms under CALCULATE. —n. **1** A record of a transaction; reckoning; computation. **2** Any narrative, statement, report, or description; notice; explanation. **3** The act or time of rendering a reckoning; judgment. **4** Consideration, as of value; importance; concern; estimation; esteem. **5** A record of debits and credits, receipts and expenditures; any methodical enumeration, score, or reckoning: to render an *account*, charge to one's *account*, an *account* at a bank. See synonyms under HISTORY, REASON, REPORT. —**on account of** Because of; for the sake of. [< OF *aconter* < LL *accomptare* < L *ad-* to + *computare* COUNT]
ac·count·a·ble (ə·koun′tə·bəl) adj. **1** Liable to be called to account; responsible. **2** Capable of being accounted for or explained. —ac·count′a·bil′i·ty n. —ac·count′a·bly adv.
ac·count·an·cy (ə·koun′tən·sē) n. The work, art, or business of an accountant.
ac·count·ant (ə·koun′tənt) n. **1** One whose business is to keep or examine books, as of a mercantile or banking house or in a public office. **2** One who keeps, examines, or is skilled in accounts. **3** One who is accountable or responsible.
ac·count·ing (ə·koun′ting) n. The art or system of recording, classifying, and summarizing commercial transactions in monetary terms. Compare BOOKKEEPING.
ac·cou·ter (ə·kōō′tər) v.t. **·tered** or **·tred** (-tərd), **·ter·ing** or **·tring** To furnish with dress or trappings; equip, as for military service. Also **ac·cou′tre.** [< F *accoutrer*; ult. origin uncertain]
ac·cou·ter·ment (ə·kōō′tər·mənt) n. **1** Equipment; apparel; dress; trappings: chiefly used in plural; also, the act of accoutering. **2** *Mil.* The equipment of a soldier other than arms and dress. Also **ac·cou′tre·ment.** See synonyms under CAPARISON.
Ac·cra (ak′rə) A port on the Gulf of Guinea, capital of Ghana: also *Akkra.*
ac·cred·it (ə·kred′it) v.t. **1** To furnish or send with credentials, as an ambassador; authorize. **2** To vouch for officially; certify as fulfilling requirements. **3** To enter on the credit side of the ledger; give credit for. **4** To attribute to: with *with:* He *accredited* his foes with as much wit as his friends. **5** To accept as true; believe. **6** To confer acceptance or favor on: His actions do not tend to *accredit* his words. [< F *accréditer* < *à* to (< L *ad-*) + *crédit* CREDIT]
ac·cred·i·ta·tion (ə·kred′ə·tā′shən) n. *U.S.* The grant to an academic institution, by an accrediting body, of status indicating valuation of its course credits and degrees as in accord with the standards set by the accrediting body.
ac·crete (ə·krēt′) v. **ac·cret·ed, ac·cret·ing** v.i. **1** To grow together or be united by adhesion: with *to.* **2** To increase by a series of additions. —v.t. **3** To cause to grow together or be added: with *to:* The student should *accrete* discretion to his other quali-

ties of mind. —adj. **1** Formed or marked by accretions. **2** *Bot.* Grown together: said of parts normally separate. [< L *accretus*, pp. of *accrescere*. See ACCRESCE.]
ac·cre·tion (ə·krē′shən) n. **1** Growth or formation by external additions; increase by adhesion or inclusion; an accumulation or external addition; matter added. **2** *Pathol.* Abnormal adhesion or growing together.
ac·cru·al (ə·krōō′əl) n. **1** The act of accruing; increase. **2** The amount of increase. Also **ac·crue′ment.**
ac·crue (ə·krōō′) v.i. **·crued, ·cru·ing 1** To come as a natural result or increment, as by growth: with *to.* **2** To arise from, accession, or advantage; accumulate, as the interest on money: with *from.* **3** *Law* To become established as a permanent right. —n. A loop or false mesh in network which increases the number of meshes in a given row. [< obs. n. *accrue* an accession < F *accrû*, pp. of *accroître* increase < L *accrescere*. See ACCRESCE.]
ac·cum·bent (ə·kum′bənt) adj. **1** Lying down; recumbent. **2** *Bot.* Lying against something, as a cotyledon against a radicle. [< L *accumbens, -entis*, ppr. of *accumbere* lie down] —ac·cum′ben·cy n.
ac·cu·mu·late (ə·kyōōm′yə·lāt) v. **·lat·ed, ·lat·ing** v.t. **1** To heap or pile up; amass; collect. —v.i. **2** To become greater in quantity or number; increase. [< L *accumulatus*, pp. of *accumulare* < *ad-* to + *cumulare* heap < *cumulus* a heap] —ac·cu·mu·la·ble (ə·kyōōm′yə·lə·bəl) adj.
ac·cu·mu·la·tion (ə·kyōōm′yə·lā′shən) n. **1** An amassing; increase; a collected mass. **2** A surplus accumulated in excess of all liabilities and credited to the active capital of a corporation. **3** *Geol.* The underground movement of oil and gas into porous rock formations, where large reserves may collect.
ac·cu·mu·la·tive (ə·kyōōm′yə·lā′tiv) adj. Serving or tending to accumulate; characterized by accumulation; given to amassing; cumulative; collective. —ac·cu′mu·la·tive·ly adv. —ac·cu′mu·la′tive·ness n.
ac·cu·mu·la·tor (ə·kyōōm′yə·lā′tər) n. **1** A person or thing that accumulates. **2** A power-storing hydraulic apparatus. **3** *Electr.* A storage battery or cell utilizing the energy of reversible chemical reactions. **4** A Leyden jar, or a condenser. **5** A resilient insert in a trace or in a chain or rope used in dredging, to prevent parting by too sudden strain.
ac·cu·ra·cy (ak′yər·ə·sē) n. The quality of being accurate; exactness; precision; correctness.
ac·cu·rate (ak′yər·it) adj. Conforming exactly to truth or to a standard; without error; precise; exact; correct. See synonyms under CORRECT, JUST, PARTICULAR, PRECISE. [< L *accuratus* done with care, pp. of *accurare* take care of < *ad-* to + *cura* care] —ac′cu·rate·ly adv. —ac′cu·rate·ness n.
ac·curs·ed (ə·kûr′sid, ə·kûrst′) adj. **1** Doomed to, deserving, or causing a curse. **2** Cursed; detestable; miserable. Also **ac·curst′.** —ac·curs′ed·ly adv. —ac·curs′ed·ness n.
ac·cu·sa·tion (ak′yōō·zā′shən) n. **1** A charge of crime or misconduct; an indictment. **2** The act of accusing; arraignment. **3** The crime or act with which one is charged. Also **ac·cu·sal** (ə·kyōō′zəl). —ac·cu·sa·to·ry (ə·kyōō′zə·tôr′ē·tō′rē) adj.
ac·cu·sa·tive (ə·kyōō′zə·tiv) *Gram.* adj. Denoting, in inflected languages, the relation of the direct object of a verb or preposition, or the goal toward which an action is directed; objective. Also **ac·cu·sa·ti·val** (ə·kyōō′zə·tī′vəl). —n. **1** The case of Latin and Greek nouns corresponding to the English objective. **2** A word in this case. [< L *accusativus*, trans. of Gk. (*ptōsis*) *aitiatikē* (the case) of accusing or pertaining to that which is caused < *aitiatos* produced by a cause] —ac·cu′sa·tive·ly adv.
ac·cu·sa·to·ri·al (ə·kyōō′zə·tôr′ē·əl, -tō′rē·əl) adj. Pertaining to an accuser.
ac·cuse (ə·kyōōz′) v. **ac·cused, ac·cus·ing** v.t. **1** To charge with fault or error; blame; censure. **2** To bring charges against, as of a crime or an offense: with *of.* —v.i. **3** To make accusation; utter charges. See synonyms under ARRAIGN, BLAME.

[< OF *acuser* < L *accusare* call to account < *ad-* to + *causa* cause, lawsuit] **—ac·cus′er** *n.* **—ac·cus′ing·ly** *adv.*

ac·cused (ə-kyōozd′) *n. Law* The defendant or defendants in a criminal case: The judge ordered the *accused* to be brought before him.

ac·cus·tom (ə-kus′təm) *v.t.* To make familiar by use; habituate or inure, as oneself: with *to.* [< OF *acostumer* < a- to (< L *ad-*) + *costume* CUSTOM]

ac·cus·tomed (ə-kus′təmd) *adj.* **1** Habitual; usual: his *accustomed* haunts. **2** Used; in the habit: with the infinitive or *to:* He is *accustomed* to rising early. See synonyms under ADDICTED, HABITUAL, USUAL.

ac·cus·tom·ize (ə-kus′təm-īz) *v.t.* & *v.i.* **·ized, ·iz·ing** To adapt or become adapted to the conditions and requirements of a new environment. **—ac·cus′tom·i·za′tion** *n.*

ace (ās) *n.* **1** A single spot, as on a playing card or die; a card or side of a die so marked. **2** A very small amount, distance, or degree; a unit; particle. **3** Something excellent or first-rate; hence, one who excels in any field. **4** A military aviator who has destroyed five or more enemy aircraft. **5** In tennis and similar games, a point won by a single stroke, as upon the service. **—within an ace** Within a hair's breadth; on the very point or verge. **—v.t. aced** (āst), **ac·ing 1** To score a point against in a single stroke, as upon the service in tennis. **2** *Slang* To get the better of, as by a timely move or act. [< OF *as* < L *as* unity, unit]

a·ce·di·a (ə-sē′dē-ə) *n.* **1** Listlessness; mental depression. **2** Sloth, the fourth of the seven deadly sins. Also *accidie.* [< LL < Gk. *akēdia* < *a-* without + *kēdos* care]

a·cel·lu·lar (ā′sel′yə-lər) *adj.* Lacking cells; not composed of cells.

a·cen·tric (ā-sen′trik) *adj.* Without a center; not in, or directed from, a center. **—n.** *Genetics* A fragment of a chromosome without a centromere.

-aceous *suffix* Of the nature of; belonging or pertaining to; like: *cretaceous* chalky: *herbaceous* herblike: used in botany and zoology to form adjectives corresponding to nouns in *-acea, -aceae.* [< L *-aceus* of the nature of]

a·ceph·a·lous (ā-sef′ə-ləs) *adj.* **1** Headless. **2** *Zool.* Without a clearly defined head, as certain mollusks. **3** Having no ruler. **4** Lacking proper beginning, as a line of verse. [< L *acephalus* < Gk. *akephalos* headless < *a-* without + *kephalē* head]

ac·e·rate (as′ə-rāt) *adj. Bot.* Acerose. Also **ac′e·rat′ed.**

a·cerb (ə-sûrb′) *adj.* Sour and astringent; harsh; sharp. See synonyms under BITTER. [< L *acerbus* < *acer* sharp] Also **a·cerb′ic.**

ac·er·bate (as′ər-bāt) *v.t.* **·bat·ed, ·bat·ing 1** To make sour; embitter. **2** To irritate; exasperate.

a·cer·bi·ty (ə-sûr′bə-tē) *n. pl.* **·ties 1** Sourness; bitterness, or astringency of flavor, as that of unripe fruit. **2** Severity, as of temper, etc.; harshness; sharpness. See synonyms under ACRIMONY. Also **a·cer·bi·tude** (ə-sûr′bə-tōod, -tyōod) [< F *acerbité* < L *acerbitas, -tatis* < *acerbus* sharp]

a·cer·ic (a-ser′ik) *adj.* Pertaining to the maple. [< NL *acericus* < L *acer* maple]

ac·e·rose[1] (as′ə-rōs) *adj. Bot.* Needle-shaped, like pine leaves. [< L *acerosus* ACEROSE[2]; later erroneously derived from L *acus* needle]

ac·e·rose[2] (as′ə-rōs) *adj.* Like chaff. [< L *acerosus* < *acus* chaff]

a·cer·vate (ə-sûr′vit, -vāt, as′ər-vāt) *adj. Bot.* Massed or heaped together; growing compactly in clusters. [< L *acervatus,* pp. of *acervare* heap up < *acervus* heap] **—a·cer′vate·ly** *adv.*

a·cer·vu·lus (ə-sûr′vyōo-ləs) *n. pl.* **·li** (-lī) *Bot.* An open, saucer-shaped, non-sexual, spore-producing fruit body, appearing in some parasitic, imperfectly known fungi. [< NL, dim. of L *acervus* heap]

a·ces·cent (ə-ses′ənt) *adj.* Becoming or tending to become sour; slightly sour. **—n.** That which is slightly sour. [< L *acescens, -entis,* ppr. of *acescere* become sour]

acet- Var. of ACETO-.

ac·e·tab·u·lum (as′ə-tab′yə-ləm) *n. pl.* **·la** (-lə) **1** *Anat.* The socket in the hip in which the head of the femur rests and revolves. **2** A sucker, as on a tapeworm, leech, or other invertebrate. **3** Any of the depressions in an insect's exoskeleton into which a leg fits. [< L, a small vinegar cup < *acetum* vinegar]

ac·e·ta·min·o·phen (as′ə-tə-min′ə-fən) *n.* A synthetic crystalline compound, $C_8H_9NO_2$, used in chemical synthesis and in medicine as an analgesic and antipyretic drug.

ac·e·tate (as′ə-tāt) *n.* **1** A salt or ester of acetic acid. **2** A fiber formed of partially hydrolyzed cellulose *acétate,* used in the textile industry. Also called *acetate rayon.*

a·ce·tic (ə-sē′tik, ə-set′ik) *adj.* Pertaining to or like vinegar; sour. [< L *acetum* vinegar]

acetic acid A colorless, pungent liquid or deliquescent crystalline solid acid, $C_2H_4O_2$, used industrially and constituting in dilute solution the chief component of vinegar.

a·cet·i·fy (ə-set′ə-fī) *v.* **·fied, ·fy·ing** *v.t.* To convert into acid or vinegar. **—v.i.** To become acid or vinegar. **—a·cet′i·fi·ca′tion** *n.* **—a·cet′i·fi′er** *n.*

aceto- *combining form* Of, pertaining to, or from acetic acid or acetyl. Also, before vowels, *acet.* [< L *acetum* vinegar]

ac·e·tous (as′ə-təs) *adj.* **1** Of, pertaining to, or producing vinegar or acetic acid. **2** Tasting like vinegar; sour. See synonyms under BITTER. Also **ac·e·tose** (as′ə-tōs). **—ac·e·tos·i·ty** (as′ə-tos′ə-tē) *n.*

a·ce·tum (ə-sē′təm) *n.* Vinegar. [< L]

ac·e·tyl·cho·line (as′ə-til-kō′lēn, -kol′in) *n.* A compound, $C_7H_{17}O_3N$, released at certain nerve endings where it facilitates transmission of autonomous nerve impulses, and also present in many tissues and species of organisms, including ergot, from which it is obtained for medical uses.

a·cet·y·lene (ə-set′ə-lēn) *n.* A colorless flammable, gaseous hydrocarbon, C_2H_2, obtainable by the action of water on calcium carbide, and used in organic syntheses and as a fuel for welding, cutting metals, etc. [< ACETYL + -ENE]

acetylene series The series of alkynes, of which the simplest member is acetylene.

ac·e·tyl·sal·i·cyl·ic acid (as′ə-til-sal′ə-sil′ik, ə-sē′təl-) Aspirin.

ache (āk) *v.i.* **ached** (ākt), **ach·ing 1** To suffer dull, continued pain; be in pain or distress. **2** *Colloq.* To yearn; be eager; followed by *for* or the infinitive. [Orig. *ake,* OE *acan*; present spelling due to infl. of the n.] **—n.** A local, dull, and protracted pain. See synonyms under AGONY. [OE *œce* < the v.; pron. before 1700 (āch), present pron. due to infl. of the v.] **—ach′er** *n.* **—ach′ing** *adj.* & *n.* **—ach′ing·ly** *adv.*

a·chene (ā-kēn′) *n. Bot.* A small, dry, indehiscent pericarp containing one seed, as in the dandelion, buttercup, etc.: also spelled *akene.* Also **a·che·ni·um** (ā-kē′nē-əm) *pl.* **·ni·a** (-nē-ə). [< NL *achenium* < A.[4] not + Gk. *chainein* gape, recoil] **—a·che′ni·al** *adj.*

A·cher·nar (ā′kər-när) One of the 20 brightest stars, 0.60 magnitude; Alpha in the constellation Eridanus. See STAR. [< Arabic *ākhir al-nahr* end of the river]

Ach·e·ron (ak′ə-ron) **1** In Greek and Roman mythology, the river of woe, one of the five rivers surrounding Hades, across which Charon ferried the dead. **2** Hades.

A·cheu·le·an (ə-shōo′lē-ən) *adj. Anthropol.* Describing a culture stage following the second glacial epoch of the Pleistocene and noted chiefly for a superior working of stone implements and weapons. Also **A·cheu′li·an.** [from *St. Acheul,* France, where artifacts were found]

a·chieve (ə-chēv′), *v.* **a·chieved, a·chiev·ing** *v.t.* **1** To accomplish; finish successfully. **2** To win or attain, as by effort, skill, or perseverance; He *achieved* a position of eminence. **—v.i. 3** To ac-

complish something; to attain an object. See synonyms under ACCOMPLISH, ATTAIN, EFFECT, GAIN, GET, SUCCEED. [< OF *achever* < *a chief (venir)* (come) to a head, finish < LL *ad caput (venire)*] **—a·chiev′a·ble** *adj.* **—a·chiev′er** *n.*

a·chieve·ment (ə-chēv′mənt) *n.* **1** An achieving or accomplishing attainment. **2** A thing achieved; a noteworthy and successful action or a distinguished feat. **3** *Her.* An escutcheon. See synonyms under ACT, CAREER, END, VICTORY, WORK.

achievement test *Psychol.* A test for measuring an individual's progress in the mastery of a subject to be learned. Compare INTELLIGENCE TEST.

Ach·il·le·an (ak′ə-lē′ən) *adj.* Of or like Achilles; all but invulnerable; wrathful; valiant; swift.

A·chil·les (ə-kil′ēz) In the *Iliad,* the son of Peleus and Thetis, foremost Greek hero of the Trojan War who killed Hector and was killed by the arrow Paris shot into his right heel, the only vulnerable spot on his body.

Achilles' heel A vulnerable point.

Achilles' tendon The large tendon for the superficial muscles of the calf of the leg, attached to the bone of the heel.

ach·ro·mat·ic (ak′rə-mat′ik) *adj.* **1** *Optics* Free from color or iridescence; transmitting light without showing or separating it into its constituent colors, as a lens. **2** *Biol.* Resisting the usual staining agents; also, containing achromatin. **3** *Music* Unmodulated; without accidentals. [< Gk. *achrōmatos* < *a-* without + *chrōma* color] **—ach′ro·mat′i·cal·ly** *adv.* **—a·chro·ma·tism** (ə-krō′mə-tiz′əm), **a·chro·ma·tic·i·ty** (ə-krō′mə-tis′ə-ətē) *n.*

a·chro·ma·tin (ə-krō′mə-tin) *n.* The substance in the cell nucleus which does not readily take color from basic stains.

a·chro·ma·tize (ə-krō′mə-tīz) *v.t.* **·tized, ·tiz·ing** To make achromatic.

a·chro·ma·top·si·a (ə-krō′mə-top′sē-ə) *n.* Total lack of color vision. [< Gk. *achrōmatos* without color + *opsis* sight]

a·chro·ma·tous (ə-krō′mə-təs) *adj.* Having less than the normal color; colorless.

a·chro·mic (ə-krō′mik) *adj.* Colorless. Also **a·chro′mous.**

a·cic·u·la (ə-sik′yə-lə) *n. pl.* **·lae** (-lē) **1** A slender needlelike process; a bristle or prickle, as on a plant or animal. **2** A needle-shaped body, as some crystals. [< L, dim. of *acus* needle] **—a·cic′u·lar, a·cic′u·late** (-lit, -lāt), **a·cic′u·lat′ed** *adj.*

ac·id (as′id) *adj.* **1** Sharp and biting to the taste, as vinegar; sour. **2** Pertaining to, yielding, like, or reacting like, an acid. **3** Acidic. **4** Sharp-tempered; biting. **—n. 1** Any sour substance. **2a** Any of a class of compounds that in aqueous solution turns blue litmus red and reacts with bases and with certain metals to form salts. **b** A compound that dissociates in water to yield hydrogen ions. **c** A compound that dissociates in a solvent to produce the positive ion of the solvent. **d** A molecule or ion that can attach itself to another molecule or ion by a covalent bond with an unshared pair of electrons. See synonyms under BITTER. [< L *acidus* sharp, sour] **—ac′id·ly** *adv.* **—ac′id·ness** *n.*

ac·id—fast (as′id-fast′, -fäst′) *adj.* Not readily decolorized by acids when stained: said of bacteria, epithelial tissue, etc.

ac·id—form·ing (as′id-fôr′ming) *adj.* Pertaining to or designating foods which in metabolism yield a large acid residue.

a·cid·ic (ə-sid′ik) *adj.* **1** Acid; having properties of an acid. **2** Forming an acid as a result of a chemical or metabolic process; acid-forming.

a·cid·i·fy (ə-sid′ə-fī) *v.* **·fied, ·fy·ing** *v.t.* **1** To render acid. **2** To change into an acid. **—v.i. 3** To become acid. **—a·cid′i·fi′a·ble** *adj.* **—a·cid′i·fi·ca′tion** *n.* **—a·cid′i·fi′er** *n.*

ac·i·dim·e·ter (as′ə-dim′ə-tər) *n.* Any apparatus or device for estimating or measuring the amount of acid in a sample. See HYDROMETER. **—ac·i·di·met·ric** (as′ə-di-met′rik), **ac′i·di·met′ri·cal** *adj.* **—ac′i·di·met′ry** *n.*

a·cid·i·ty (ə·sid′ə·tē) *n.* **1** The state or quality of being acid. **2** Degree of acid strength. **3** Hyperacidity.

ac·id·o·phil (a·sid′ə·fil) *n.* Any acidophilic substance, organism, or tissue. Also **ac·id·o·phile**.

ac·i·doph·i·lic (as′ə·dof′ə·lik) *adj.* **1** Having an affinity for acid stains. **2** Having a preference for an acid environment.

ac·i·doph·i·lus milk (as′ə·dof′ə·ləs) Milk that has been fermented by certain bacteria *(Lactobacillus acidophilus)* to improve its qualities as an intestinal tonic.

ac·i·do·sis (as′ə·dō′sis) *n.* An abnormal condition of depleted alkaline reserves in the blood and other body fluids. —**as·i·dot·ic** *adj.*

acid rain Atmospheric precipitation with a pH of 5.6 or lower due to dissolved air pollutants such as oxides of nitrogen and sulfur.

acid rock A kind of rock-and-roll music with sound and lyrics which suggest drug-taking or psychedelic experiences.

acid test A definite test of value, quality, truth, virtue, etc.: from the alchemists' method of testing metals after attempting transmutation to gold.

a·cid·u·late (ə·sij′ōō·lāt) *v.t.* **·lat·ed, ·lat·ing** To make somewhat acid or sour. —**a·cid′u·la′tion** *n.*

a·cid·u·lous (ə·sij′ōō·ləs) *adj.* Slightly acid; subacid; sour. Also **a·cid′u·lent.** See synonyms under BITTER. [< L *acidulus* slightly sour, dim. of *acidus* sour]

ac·i·er·ate (as′ē·ə·rāt) *v.t.* **·at·ed, ·at·ing** To turn into steel. [< F *acier* steel] —**ac′i·er·a′tion** *n.*

ac·i·form (as′ə·fôrm) *adj.* Needle-shaped. [< L *acus* needle + -FORM]

ac·i·nar (as′ə·nər) *adj.* Pertaining to, constituting an acinus.

a·cin·i·form (ə·sin′ə·fôrm) *adj.* **1** Having a clustered structure like a bunch of grapes. **2** Like a grape. [< L *acinus* grape + -FORM]

ac·i·nus (as′ə·nəs) *n. pl.* **·ni** (-nī) **1** *Bot.* One of the drupelets of an aggregate baccate fruit, as a raspberry; also, a grape seed. **2** A berry, as a grape, growing in bunches; a bunch of such berries. **3** *Anat.* The terminal division of the secreting portion of a racemose gland. [< L, ape]

-acious *suffix of adjectives* Abounding in; characterized by; given to: *pugnacious, vivacious.* [< L *-ax, -acis* + -OUS]

-acity *suffix* Quality or state of: *tenacity, pugnacity:* used to form abstract nouns corresponding to adjectives in *-acious.* [< L *-acitas, -acitatis*]

ack-ack (ak′ak′) *n. Slang* Anti-aircraft fire. [British radio operator's code for A.A. (anti-aircraft)]

ac·knowl·edge (ak·nol′ij) *v.* **·edged, ·edg·ing** *v.t.* **1** To own or admit as true; confess: He *acknowledged* his ignorance. **2** To recognize as or avow to be: The savages *acknowledged* the idol as their god. **3** To declare or admit the authority of, as a claim or right. **4** *Law* To assent to the validity of; certify: He *acknowledged* the service of a writ. **5** To own or admit as implying obligation or incurring responsibility: He *acknowledged* his debts to all his creditors. **6** To show appreciation of; thank for: She *acknowledged* the favor graciously. **7** To report and respond to the receipt or arrival of: His secretary *acknowledged* our letter. —*v.i.* **8** In card games, to respond to a partner's bid so as to indicate a weak hand. [Earlier *aknowledge* < obs. *aknow* admit, confess (OE *oncnāwan*) + *knowledge,* v., admit] —**ac·knowl′edge·a·ble** *adj.* —**ac·knowl′edg·er** *n.*

Synonyms: accept, admit, avow, certify, concede, confess, endorse, grant, own, profess, recognize. See AVOW, CONFESS. *Antonyms:* deny, disavow, disclaim, disown, repudiate.

ac·knowl·edg·ment (ak·nol′ij·mənt) *n.* **1** The act of acknowledging; avowal; confession; recognition; report or admission of receipt. **2** *Law* A formal declaration before competent authority, or the official certificate of such declaration. Also *Brit.* **ac·knowl′edge·ment.** See synonyms under APOLOGY.

ac·me (ak′mē) *n.* The highest point, or summit; perfection; climax. [< Gk. *akmē* point]

ac·ne (ak′nē) *n.* A chronic skin affliction seen chiefly in adolescents and characterized by inflammation of the sebaceous glands and hair

follicles and the development of blackheads and pimples on the face, chest, and back. —**ac·need** *adj.* [? Alter. of Gk. *akmē* point]

ac·node (ak′nōd) *n. Math.* A point outside a curve whose coordinates satisfy the equation of the curve; a conjugate point. [< L *acus* needle + NODE]

a·cock (ə·kok′) *adj.* **1** In cocked fashion or position. **2** Alert; vigilant. —*adv.* In a cocked manner or position: He set his hat *acock.*

ac·o·nite (ak′ə·nīt) *n.* **1** The monkshood or any of the generally poisonous plants of the genus *Aconitum.* Also **ac′o·ni′tum. 2** A very toxic drug obtained from the root of *Aconitum napellus.* [< F *aconit* < L *aconitum* < Gk. *akoniton*]

a·corn (ā′kôrn, ā′kərn) *n.* **1** The fruit of the oak, a one-seeded nut, fixed in a woody cup. **2** *Aeron.* A special type of fitting used to prevent

ACORNS
a. Red oak. *b.* Scarlet oak. *c.* Pin oak.
d. Black oak. *e.* White oak.

abrasion of intersecting wires in the cross-bracing of an aircraft. [OE *æcern*]

acorn squash A variety of winter squash of acornlike shape having a dark green, ridged rind and yellow flesh.

acorn tube A small thermionic radio tube for use at high frequencies. Also *Brit.* **acorn valve.**

a·cot·y·le·don (ā′kot·ə·lē′dən) *n. Bot.* A plant without cotyledons or seed lobes. [< A.[4] without + COTYLEDON] —**a′cot·y·le′do·nous** *adj.*

a·cou·me·ter (ə·kōō′mi·tər, ə·kou′-) *n.* An instrument for testing the delicacy of the sense of hearing. [< Gk. *akouein* hear + -METER]

a·cous·tic (ə·kōōs′tik, ə·kous′-) *adj.* **1** Pertaining to the act or sense of hearing, the science of sound, or the sound heard. **2** Designed to deaden, enhance, or otherwise modify sound. **3** Having no electronic amplification, as a musical instrument. Also **a·cous′ti·cal.** [< F *acoustique* < Gk. *akoustikos* pertaining to hearing < *akouein* hear] —**a·cous′ti·cal·ly** *adv.*

acoustic distortion The discrepancy between the acoustic values of sounds as transmitted over a telecommunication system and as received by the listener.

a·cous·tics (ə·kōōs′tiks, ə·kous′-) *n.* **1** That branch of physics which treats of the phenomena and laws of sound: construed as singular. **2** The sound-producing qualities of an auditorium: construed as plural. See -ICS.

ac·quaint (ə·kwānt′) *v.t.* **1** To make familiar or conversant with *with: Acquaint* yourself with the court routine. **2** To cause to know; inform: with *with:* He *acquainted* his son with the circumstances of his birth. [< OF *acointer* < LL *adcognitare* make known < L *ad-* to + *cognitus,* pp. of *cognoscere* know < *com-* with + *gnoscere* come to know]

ac·quain·tance (ə·kwān′təns) *n.* **1** Knowledge of any person or thing. **2** A person or persons with whom one is acquainted. —**ac·quain′tance·ship** *n.*

Synonyms: association, companionship, experience, familiarity, fellowship, friendship, intimacy, knowledge. *Acquaintance* between persons is mutual, assuming that each knows the other. *Acquaintance* is less than *familiarity* or *intimacy;* it does not involve *friendship,* for one may be well acquainted with an enemy. *Fellowship* involves not merely *acquaintance* and *companionship,* but sympathy as well. Compare FRIENDSHIP, LOVE. As regards studies, pursuits, etc., *acquaintance* is less than *familiarity,* which supposes minute *knowledge* of particulars, arising often from long *experience* or *association.* *Antonyms:* ignorance, ignoring, inexperience, unfamiliarity.

ac·quaint·ed (ə·kwān′tid) *adj.* Having acquaintance; having personal knowledge of: with *with.*

ac·quest (ə·kwest′) *n.* **1** An act of acquiring; also, the thing acquired. **2** *Law* Property acquired by means other than inheritance, as by gift or purchase. [< MF < LL *acquistum* for L *acquisitum* < *acquirere.* See ACQUIRE.]

ac·qui·esce (ak′wē·es′) *v.i.* **esced (-est′), esc·ing** To consent or concur tacitly; assent; comply; with *in* (formerly with *to*): The candidate *acquiesced* in all his party's plans. See synonyms under AGREE, ASSENT. [< MF *acquiescer* < L *acquiescere* < *ad-* to + *quiescere* rest] —**ac′qui·es′cent** *adj.* —**ac′qui·esc′ing·ly** *adv.*

ac·qui·es·cence (ak′wē·es′əns) *n.* Quiet submission; passive consent: with *in* (formerly with *to*). Also **ac′qui·es′cen·cy.**

ac·quire (ə·kwīr′) *v.t.* **·quired, ·quir·ing 1** To obtain or receive by one's endeavor or purchase. **2** To get as one's own; gain. See synonyms under ATTAIN, GAIN, GET, LEARN. [< L *acquirere* < *ad-* to + *quaerere* seek] —**ac·quir′a·ble** *adj.* —**ac·quir′er** *n.*

acquired immunodeficiency syndrome A virulent disease of irregular distribution and unknown cause in which a deficient immune system is manifested in infections by any of various pathogens and/or in certain forms of cancer. Also **AIDS.**

ac·quire·ment (ə·kwīr′mənt) *n.* **1** The act of acquiring. **2** An acquired power or attainment. See synonyms under ATTAINMENT.

ac·qui·si·tion (ak′wə·zish′ən) *n.* **1** The act of acquiring. **2** Anything gained or won; a power or possession. See synonyms under ATTAINMENT. [< L *acquisitio, -onis* < *acquirere.* See ACQUIRE.]

ac·quis·i·tive (ə·kwiz′ə·tiv) *adj.* Able or inclined to acquire, as money or property. —**ac·quis′i·tive·ly** *adv.* —**ac·quis′i·tive·ness** *n.*

ac·quit (ə·kwit′) *v.t.* **ac·quit·ted, ac·quit·ting 1** To free or clear, as from an accusation; declare innocent; exonerate. **2** To relieve, as of an obligation; absolve: Your generosity *acquits* you of all further duties toward me. **3** To repay or return, as a favor; discharge, as a debt. **4** To conduct (oneself); perform one's part: He *acquitted* himself like a man. See synonyms under ABSOLVE, JUSTIFY, PARDON. [< OF *aquiter* < L *ad-* to + *quietare* settle, quiet] —**ac·quit′ter** *n.*

ac·quit·tal (ə·kwit′l) *n.* **1** The act of acquitting, or the state of being acquitted or found innocent of a charge or accusation. **2** The performance of a duty. Also **ac·quit′ment.**

ac·quit·tance (ə·kwit′ns) *n.* Release or discharge, as from indebtedness; satisfaction of indebtedness or obligation; a receipt; an acquittal.

a·cra·si·a (ə·krā′zhē·ə) *n.* Extreme lack of self-control. [< Med.L < Gk. *akrasia* bad mixture < *akratos* unmixed (of drinks), intemperate]

a·cre (ā′kər) *n.* **1** A measure of land, commonly 160 square rods; also 43,560 square feet, 4,840 square yards, or 0.404 hectare. The Scottish acre contains about 6,150 square yards and the Irish acre, 7,840. **2** A field. **3** *pl.* Lands. —**God's acre** A churchyard or burial ground. [OE *æcer* field]

a·cre·age (ā′kər·ij) *n.* Area in acres; acres collectively.

a·cred (ā′kərd) *adj.* Comprising or owning many acres of land.

a·cre·foot (ā′kər·fōōt′) *n.* The amount of water required to cover one level acre to a depth of 1 foot; 43,560 cubic feet: used by irrigation engineers.

ac·rid (ak′rid) *adj.* Of a cutting, burning taste or odor; pungent. See synonyms under BITTER. [< L *acer, acris;* infl. by *acid*] —**ac′rid·ly** *adv.* —**ac′rid·ness** *n.*

a·crid·i·ty (ə·krid′ə·tē) *n.* The quality of being acrid; acrimony of speech or temper.

ac·ri·mo·ni·ous (ak′rə·mō′nē·əs) *adj.* Full of bitterness; sarcastic; caustic; sharp. See synonyms under BITTER, MOROSE. —**ac′ri·mo′ni·ous·ly** *adv.* —**ac′ri·mo′ni·ous·ness** *n.*

ac·ri·mo·ny (ak′rə·mō′nē) *n. pl.* **·nies** Sharpness or bitterness of speech or temper; acridity. [< L *acrimonia* < *acer* sharp]

acro- *combining form* **1** At the top; highest; topped with; at the tip or end of: *acrogen.* **2** *Med.* Pertaining to the extremities: *acromegaly.* [< Gk.

akros at the top or end]

ac·ro·bat (ak′rə-bat) *n.* **1** One who is skilled in feats requiring muscular coordination, as in tight-rope walking, tumbling, trapeze performing, etc.; a gymnast. **2** One who makes surprising political or other changes. [< F *acrobate* < Gk. *akrobatos* walking on tiptoe < *akros* tip + *bainein* walk, go] —**ac·ro·bat′ic** or **·i·cal** *adj.* —**ac′ro·bat′i·cal·ly** *adv.*

ac·ro·cen·tric (ak′rō-sen′trik) *adj.* Having the centromere located close to one end: said of a chromosome.

ac·ro·gen (ak′rə-jən) *n. Bot.* An organism growing at the apex only, as ferns, mosses, etc. [< ACRO- + -GEN]

ac·ro·gen·ic (ak′rə-jen′ik) *adj. Bot.* Growing at the apex, as certain cryptogams and zoophytes; also, of or pertaining to an acrogen. Also **a·crog·e·nous** (ə-kroj′ə-nəs). —**a·crog′e·nous·ly** *adv.*

ac·ro·lith (ak′rə-lith) *n.* A statue with stone head and extremities, the trunk being usually of wood and draped. [< ACRO- + -LITH¹] —**a·crol·i·than** (ə-krol′ə-thən), **ac′ro·lith′ic** *adj.*

ac·ro·log·ic (ak′rə-loj′ik) *adj.* Relating to or based on initials. [< ACRO- + Gk. *logos* word]

ac·ro·meg·a·ly (ak′rō-meg′ə-lē) *n.* A chronic disorder due to oversecretion of pituitary growth hormone, characterized by enlargement of the face, extremities, and viscera, including both soft and bony tissue. [< F *acromégalie* < Gk. *akros* ACRO- + *megas, megalon* big] —**ac·ro·me·gal·ic** (ak′rō-mi-gal′ik) *adj.*

ac·ro·nym (ak′rə-nim) *n.* A word formed by the combining of initial letters (*Eniac, Unesco*) or syllables and letters (*radar* and *sonar*) of a series of words or a compound term. [< ACRO- + -nym name, as in HOMONYM]

ac·ro·pho·bi·a (ak′rə-fō′bē-ə) *n.* Dread stimulated by being at a great height: also called *hypsophobia.*

a·crop·o·lis (ə-krop′ə-lis) *n.* The citadel of an ancient Greek city, especially **the Acropolis,** that of Athens. [< Gk. *akropolis* < *akros* top, highest part + *polis* city]

ac·ro·some (ak′rə-sōm) *n.* A tiny structure at the front of a sperm cell. [< ACRO- + Gk. *soma* body]

ac·ro·spire (ak′rə-spīr) *n. Bot.* The first sprout from a germinating seed of grain. [< ACRO- + Gk. *speira* anything twisted]

a·cross (ə-krôs′, ə-kros′) *adv.* **1** From one side to the other. **2** On or at the other side. **3** Crosswise; crossed; as arms. —*prep.* **1** On or from the other side of; beyond; over: the music from *across* the street. **2** Through or over the surface of: riding *across* the field; A tree fell *across* the road. [< A-¹ on, in + CROSS]

a·cros·tic (ə-krôs′tik, ə-kros′-) *n.* A poem or other composition in which initial or other letters, taken in order, form a word or phrase. [< L *acrostichis* < Gk. *akrostichis* < *akros* end + *stichos* line of verse] —**a·cros′ti·cal·ly** *adv.*

a·cryl·ic (ə-kril′ik) *adj.* Designating an acid, C₃H₄O₂, having a sharp, acrid odor, prepared from acrolein or from certain derivatives of propionic acid, used in making commercial transparent resins and plastics. —*n.* **1** A paint having a base of acrylic resin. **2** A painting made with such a paint. **3** Acrylic resin. **4** Acrylic fiber. [< ACR(OLEIN) + -YL + -IC]

act (akt) *v.t.* **1** To play the part of; impersonate, as in a drama: She *acted* Juliet well. **2** To perform on the stage, as a play: The company *acted* most of Shakespeare's works. **3** To perform as if on a stage; feign the character of: Don't *act* the martyr. **4** To behave as suitable to: *Act* your age. **5** *Obs.* To actuate. —*v.i.* **5** To behave or conduct oneself: He knows how to *act* in society. **6** To carry out a purpose or function; perform: The brake refused to *act.* **7** To carry out a purpose or function in a particular way: with *as:* The test *acted* as a check. **8** To put forth power; produce an effect: often with *on:* The poison *acted* on his stomach at once. **9** To serve temporarily or as a

substitute, as in some office or capacity: with *for:* The corporal *acted* for his commanding officer. **10** To perform on or as on the stage: She *acts* for a living. **11** To pretend; play a part so as to appear: She concealed her real feelings and *acted* friendly. **12** To serve for theatrical performance or use: This scene *acts* well. —**to act on** (or **upon**) To order one's conduct in accordance with; obey: to *act on* someone's advice. —**to act up** *Colloq.* To behave mischievously; appear troublesome. [< L *actus*, pp. of *agere* do, infl. in development by the n.] —*n.* **1** The exertion of power, bodily or mental; something done; a deed. **2** A section of a drama; the largest division of a play or opera. **3** An enactment or edict; a formal transaction, as of a legislative body. **4** A formal written statement. **5** The performance of a natural function or process. [< L *actus* a doing, and *actum* a thing done < *agere* do]

Synonyms (noun): accomplishment, achievement, action, consummation, deed, doing, effect, execution, exercise, exertion, exploit, feat, motion, movement, operation, performance, proceeding, transaction, work. *Act* is single, individual, momentary; *action* a complex of *acts,* or a process, state, or habit of exerting power. *Act* and *deed* are both used for the thing done, but *act* refers to the power put forth, *deed* to the result accomplished. *Deed* is commonly used of great, notable, and impressive *acts,* as are *achievement, exploit,* and *feat.* A *feat* exhibits strength, skill, personal power, whether mental or physical; as, a *feat* of arms, a *feat* of memory. *Achievement* is the doing of something great and noteworthy; an *exploit* is brilliant, but its effect may be transient; an *achievement* is solid, and its effect enduring. See EXERCISE, MOTION. *Antonyms:* cessation, deliberation, endurance, immobility, inaction, inactivity, inertia, passion (in philosophic sense), quiescence, quiet, repose, rest, suffering, suspension.

ac·ta (ak′tə) *n.* Acts; especially, proceedings or minutes of proceedings kept on record in a court. [< L, pl. of *actum* a thing done]

act·a·ble (ak′tə-bəl) *adj.* That can be acted, as a role in a play. —**act′a·bil′i·ty** *n.*

Ac·tae·on (ak-tē′ən) In Greek mythology, a hunter who surprised Diana bathing and was turned by her into a stag and killed by his own dogs. Also **Ac·tæ′on.**

Ac·te (ak′tē) See AKTI.

ACTH A hormone that is secreted by the anterior lobe of the pituitary gland and that stimulates the secretion of cortisone and other hormones by the cortex of the adrenal glands. [< *a(dreno)c(ortico)t(ropic) h(ormone)*]

ac·tin (ak′tin) *n.* A protein component of muscle fibrils that interacts with myosin in muscular contraction.

ac·ti·nal (ak′tə-nəl, ak-tī′-) *adj. Zool.* **1** Bearing tentacles or rays. **2** Of or pertaining to the tentacle-bearing oral region of certain radially symmetrical animals, as the sea anemone.

act·ing (ak′ting) *adj.* **1** Operating or officiating, especially in place of another: *acting* secretary. **2** Functioning; in working order. **3** Containing directions for actors: the *acting* script. —*n.* **1** Performance, especially of a part in a play. **2** Pretense or simulation.

ac·tin·i·a (ak-tin′ē-ə) *n. pl.* **·i·ae** (-i-ē) or **·i·as** A sea anemone. [< NL < Gk. *aktis, aktinos* ray] —**ac·tin′i·an** *adj. & n.*

ac·tin·ic (ak-tin′ik) *adj.* **1** Pertaining to actinism. **2** Potent to effect chemical changes by radiant energy. —**ac·tin′i·cal·ly** *adv.*

actinic rays Radiation in the violet and ultraviolet part of the spectrum capable of effecting chemical changes, as in photography.

ac·tin·i·form (ak-tin′ə-fôrm) *adj.* Having a radiate form, as actinia.

ac·tin·ism (ak′tin-iz′əm) *n.* **1** The property of electromagnetic radiation, especially in the violet and ultra-violet range, of effecting chemical change. **2** The production of such change. [< ACTIN(O)- + -ISM]

ac·tin·i·um (ak-tin′ē-əm) *n.* A short-lived radioactive element (symbol Ac, atomic number 89),

occurring naturally in uranium and radium ores and produced synthetically in nuclear reactors, the most stable isotope having an atomic mass of 227 and a half-life of 21.6 years. See PERIODIC TABLE.

actino- *combining form* **1** Pertaining to a radiate structure or the presence of tentacles: *actinozoan.* **2** Pertaining to the action of light or other electromagnetic radiation: *actinograph.* Also **actin-, actini-.** [< Gk. *aktis, aktinos* ray]

ac·ti·nol·o·gy (ak′ti·nol′ə·jē) *n.* The science of the chemical action of light.

ac·ti·no·my·cete (ak′ti·nō·mī·sēt′) *n.* Any of an order (Actinomycetales) of filamentous or rod-shaped bacteria, including many animal and plant pathogens as well as saprophytes in soil, water, and decaying organic matter. —**ac·ti·no·my·cet·ous** *adj.*

ac·ti·no·my·co·sis (ak′ti·nō·mī·kō′sis) *n.* An infectious disease of cattle, hogs, and occasionally humans, caused by an actinomycete (*Actinomyces bovis*) and characterized by tumors about the jaws and neck: also called *lumpy jaw.* —**ac·ti·no·my·cot′ic** (-kot′ik) *adj.*

ac·ti·non (ak′ti·non) *n.* An isotope of radon emanating from actinium, having mass number 219 and a half-life of nearly four seconds.

ac·tin·o·ther·a·py (ak′tin·ō·ther′ə·pē) *n.* Radiotherapy.

ac·tin·o·u·ra·ni·um (ak′tin·ō·yŏŏq·rā′nē·əm) *n.* The uranium isotope of mass 238.

ac·tion (ak′shən) *n.* **1** The putting forth or exerting of power; an acting, doing, or working; operation; activity. **2** The performance by any organ of its proper function: The *action* of the heart was normal. **3** The movement of the parts or mechanism of something: the *action* of the engine. **4** The result of putting forth power; the thing done; especially, any act of volition; deed: the rational *actions* of men. **5** In literature, the connected series of events on which the interest depends. **6** A military conflict; battle: a general *action.* **7** *Rel.* A devotional exercise or religious function. **8** *Law* The lawful demand of one's right through judicial proceedings; a judicial proceeding for the enforcement of rights, the redress of wrongs, or the punishment of public offenses. **9** In sculpture or painting, gesture or attitude represented as expressing passion or sentiment. **10** *Physics* A magnitude describing the condition of any dynamic system, expressible as twice the mean kinetic energy of the system during a given interval, multiplied by the duration of the interval. **11** *Slang* Lively or exciting social activity; excitement: where the *action* is. **12** *Slang* Money wagered; betting. See synonyms under ACT, BATTLE, BEHAVIOR, EXERCISE, MOTION, OPERATION, TRANSACTION, WORK. [< F < L *actio, -onis* < *agere* do]

ac·tion·a·ble (ak′shən·ə·bəl) *adj.* Affording ground for prosecution, as a trespass or a libel. —**ac′tion·a·bly** *adv.*

ac·ti·vate (ak′tə·vāt) *v.t.* **·vat·ed, ·vat·ing** **1** To make active. **2** To put into or make capable of action, as a military unit. **3** To make radioactive. **4** To promote or hasten chemical reactivity, as by heat or other agency. **5** To purify sewage by aeration or other means of facilitating bacterial action. —**ac′ti·va′tion** *n.*

ac·ti·va·tor (ak′tə·vā′tər) *n.* **1** *Biochem.* A substance that renders active an enzyme that is secreted in an inactive form. **2** *Chem.* A catalyst.

ac·tive (ak′tiv) *adj.* **1** Abounding in action; agile; lively; quick; brisk; busy. **2** *Gram.* **a** Designating a voice of the verb which indicates that the subject of the sentence is performing the action, as *fires* is in the active voice in *The soldier fires the gun:* opposed to *passive* **b** Describing verbs expressing action as distinguished from being and state, as *run, hit, jump.* **3** Being in or pertaining to a state of action: opposed to *quiescent, extinct,* or *latent:* an *active* volcano. **4** Causing or promoting action, or manifested in action; practical. **5** Bearing interest; also, consisting of cash or of property easily exchanged for cash. **6** Radioactive. —*n. Gram.* The active voice. [< F *actif*, fem. *active* < L *activus* < *agere* do] —**ac·tive·ly** *adv.* —**ac·tive·ness** *n.*

Synonyms: agile, alert, brisk, bustling, busy, diligent, energetic, expeditious, industrious, lively, mobile, nimble, prompt, quick, ready, restless, sprightly, spry, supple, vigorous. *Active* refers to both quickness and constancy of action; in the former sense it is allied with *agile, alert, brisk,* etc.; in the latter, with *busy, diligent, industrious.* The *active* enjoy employment, the *busy* are actually employed, the *diligent* and the *industrious* are habitually *busy.* The *restless* are *active* from inability to keep quiet; their activity may be without purpose, or out of all proportion to the purpose contemplated. The *officious* are undesirably *active* in the affairs of others. Compare ALERT, ALIVE, BUSY, MEDDLESOME. *Antonyms:* dull, heavy, idle, inactive, indolent, inert, lazy, quiescent, quiet, slow, sluggish, stupid.

ac·tiv·i·ty (ak·tiv′ə·tē) *n. pl.* **·ties 1** The state or quality of being active; action; vigorous movement; active force or operation. **2** *Mech.* Mechanical work done in a unit of time. **3** *Physics* **a** The degree of emission from a radioactive substance in terms of observed effects. **b** The excitability of a gas subject to ionization. **4** *Optics* Capacity of a substance to rotate the plane of polarized light to left or right, measured by a polariscope. See synonyms under EXERCISE.

Act of Congress A bill which has passed both houses of the United States Congress and has become law either with or without the approval of the President, in accordance with the provisions of the Constitution.

act of God *Law* An inevitable event occurring by reason of the operations of nature unmixed with human agency or human negligence.

act of war An act of armed aggression by a nation without a formal declaration of war.

ac·tor (ak′tər) *n.* **1** One who acts; specifically, a player on the stage, motion pictures, etc. **2** Any doer. See synonyms under AGENT, CAUSE. [< L, a doer < *agere* do]

ac·tress (ak′tris) *n.* A woman who acts, as on the stage, in television, motion pictures, etc.

ac·tu·al (ak′chōō·əl) *adj.* **1** Existing in fact; real. **2** Being in existence or action now; existent; present. See synonyms under SURE. —*n.* **1** Something real or actually existing; a reality. **2** In finance, actual assets or receipts. **3** A drama based on actual persons or events; especially, such a story adapted to television presentation. [< F *actuel* < LL *actualis* < L *actus* a doing. See ACT.]

ac·tu·al·i·ty (ak′chōō·al′ə·tē) *n. pl.* **·ties 1** The quality of being actual; reality; realism. **2** A documentary film or broadcast.

ac·tu·al·ize (ak′chōō·əl·īz) *v.t.* **·ized, ·iz·ing 1** To make real; realize in action, as a possibility. **2** To make seem real; describe or represent realistically. —**ac′tu·al·i·za′tion** *n.*

ac·tu·al·ly (ak′chōō·əl·ē) *adv.* In act or fact; as a matter of fact; in reality; really; truly.

ac·tu·ar·y (ak′chōō·er′ē) *n. pl.* **·ar·ies** One who specializes in the mathematics of insurance, mortality rates, and the like; especially, the official statistician of an insurance company, who calculates and states risks, premiums, etc. [< L *actuarius* clerk < *actus.* See ACT.] —**ac·tu·ar·i·al** (ak′chōō·âr′ē·əl) *adj.* —**ac·tu·ar′i·al·ly** *adv.*

ac·tu·ate (ak′chōō·āt) *v.t.* **·at·ed, ·at·ing 1** To move to action; impel, as a mechanism. **2** To incite or influence, as the will: He was *actuated* by motives of kindness. [< Med.L *actuatus*, pp. of *actuare* < L *actus* a doing. See ACT.] —**ac′tu·a′tion** *n.*

Synonyms: activate, compel, dispose, draw, drive, excite, impel, incite, incline, induce, influence, lead, move, persuade, prompt, stir, urge. One is *urged* from without, *actuated* or *impelled* from within. See INFLUENCE. *Antonyms:* deter, dissuade, hinder, restrain.

ac·tu·a·tor (ak′chōō·ā′tər) *n.* **1** One who or that which actuates. **2** The mechanism which releases the trigger of an automatic weapon.

acu- *combining form* Needle; point. [< L *acus*]

ac·u·ate (ak′yōō·it, -āt) *adj.* Pointed; sharp.

a·cu·i·ty (ə·kyōō′ə·tē) *n.* Acuteness; sharpness.

[< MF *acuité* < Med.L *acuitas* < L *acus* needle]

a·cu·le·ate (ə·kyōō′lē·it, -āt) *adj.* **1** Armed with a sting. **2** *Bot.* Provided with prickles; prickly. [< L *aculeatus* < *aculeus*, dim. of *acus* needle]

a·cu·le·o·late (ə·kyōō′lē·ə·lit) *adj. Bot.* Provided with very tiny prickles.

a·cu·men (ə·kyōō′mən) *n.* Quickness of insight or discernment; keenness of intellect. [< L, point, sharpness (of the mind) < *acuere* sharpen]

Synonyms: acuteness, cleverness, discernment, insight, keenness, perception, perspicacity, sagacity, sharpness, shrewdness. *Sharpness, acuteness,* and *insight,* however keen, and *perception,* however deep, fall short of the meaning of *acumen,* which belongs to an astute and discriminating mind. *Cleverness* is a practical aptitude for study or learning. *Perspicacity* is the power to see clearly and quickly through that which is difficult or involved. Compare SAGACIOUS. *Antonyms:* dullness, obtuseness, stupidity.

a·cu·mi·nate (ə·kyōō′mə·nāt) *v.t.* **·nat·ed, ·nat·ing** To sharpen; make pointed. —*adj.* (ə·kyōō′mə·nit, -nāt) Ending in a long tapering point, as a leaf, feather, fin, etc. Compare ACUTE, and see illustration under LEAF. [< L *acuminatus*, pp. of *acuminare* point < *acumen.* See ACUMEN.] —**a·cu′mi·na′tion** *n.*

a·cu·mi·nous (ə·kyōō′mə·nəs) *adj.* Having acumen.

ac·u·punc·ture (ak′yōō·pungk′chər) *n.* A traditional Chinese treatment for pain or disease in which numerous long, fine needles are inserted at predetermined points on the body. [< ACU- + PUNCTURE]

ac·u·punc·tur·ist (ak′yōō·pungk′chər·ist) *n.* One who practices acupuncture.

a·cute (ə·kyōōt′) *adj.* **1** Keenly discerning or sensitive: an *acute* thinker. **2** Keenly discerning or sensitive: *acute* hearing. **3** Affecting keenly; poignant; intense. **4** Of rapid onset and short duration: an *acute* illness. **5** *Music* Shrill; high. **6** Threatening; critical: an *acute* shortage of water. [< L *acutus*, pp. of *acuere* sharpen] —**a·cute′ly** *adv.* —**a·cute′ness** *n.*

Synonyms: astute, cunning, discerning, intelligent, keen, penetrating, perspicacious, piercing, pointed, sagacious, sharp, shrewd, subtile, subtle. See ASTUTE, SAGACIOUS. *Antonyms:* blunt, chronic, dull, grave, heavy, obtuse, stolid, stupid.

acute accent See under ACCENT.

acute angle See under ANGLE.

-acy *suffix of nouns* Forming nouns of quality, state or condition from adjectives in *-acious,* and nouns and adjectives in *-ate: fallacy, celibacy, curacy.* [< F *-atie* < L *-acia, -atia* < Gk. *-ateia*; or directly < L or < Gk.]

a·cy·clic (ə·sī′klik, ə·sik′lik) *adj.* **1** *Bot.* Arranged in spirals rather than whorls. **2** *Chem.* Having atoms in the molecule connected in an open chain rather than a ring.

ad[1] (ad) *n. Colloq.* An advertisement.

ad[2] (ad) *prep. Latin* To; toward; as to.

ad- *prefix* To; toward; near: *adhere, advert, adrenal*; often, in English, without perceptible force. Also: *a-* before *sc, sp, st,* as in *ascribe; ab-* before *b,* as in *abbreviate; ac-* before *c, q,* as in *acquire; af-* before *f,* as in *afferent; ag-* before *g,* as in *agglutinate; al-* before *l,* as in *allude; an-* before *n,* as in *annex; ap-* before *p,* as in *append; ar-* before *r,* as in *arrive; as-* before *s,* as in *associate; at-* before *t,* as in *attract.* [< L *ad-* < *ad* to]

-ad[1] *suffix* Of or pertaining to; used to form: **1** Collective numerals: *triad.* **2** Names of poems: *Iliad, Dunciad.* **3** *Bot.* Names of some plants: *cycad.* [< Gk. *-as, -ados*]

-ad[2] *suffix of adverbs Anat., Zool.* To; toward; in the direction of: *dorsad,* toward the back. [< L *ad* to, toward]

ad·age (ad′ij) *n.* A saying that has obtained credit or force by long use; a proverb. [< F < L *adagium* < *ad-* to + root of *aio* I say]

Synonyms: aphorism, apothegm, axiom, byword, dictum, maxim, motto, precept, proverb, saw, saying. See PROVERB.

a·da·gio (ə·dä′jō, -zhē·ō) *Music adj.* Slow: faster than *largo* but slower than *andante.* —*n.* A mus-

ical composition, movement, etc. in adagio time. —*adv.* Slowly. [< Ital. *adagio,* lit., at ease]

Ad·am (ad′əm) A masculine personal name. [< Hebrew, man]

—**Adam** The first man, progenitor of the human race, *Gen.* ii 7. Hence, mankind collectively. — **the old Adam** Unregenerate or depraved human nature. —**A·dam·ic** (ə·dam′ik) *adj.*

ad·a·mant (ad′ə·mant, -mənt) *n.* **1** A very hard imaginary mineral. **2** Formerly, the diamond or lodestone. **3** *Archaic* Exceeding hardness; impenetrability. —*adj.* Immovable; unyielding. [< OF *adamaunt* < L *adamas, -antis* the hardest metal (here, unyielding) < Gk. *adamas* < *a-* not + *damaein* conquer. Doublet of DIAMOND.]

ad·a·man·tine (ad′ə·man′tin, -tēn, -tīn) *adj.* **1** Made of or like adamant; of impenetrable hardness. **2** Having a diamondlike luster. Also **ad·a·man·te·an** (ad′ə·man·tē′ən).

Ad·ams (ad′əmz) A prominent Massachusetts family, including **John,** 1735–1826, second president of the United States 1797–1801; his son **John Quincy,** 1767–1848, sixth president of the United States 1825–29; **Charles Francis,** 1807–86, son of John Quincy, diplomat; **Henry Brooks,** 1838–1918, son of Charles Francis, author; **Samuel,** 1722–1803, cousin of John, patriot, signer of Declaration of Independence.

Adam's apple *Anat.* The prominence made by the thyroid cartilage on the front of the human throat, conspicuous in males.

a·dapt (ə·dapt′) *v.t.* **1** To make suitable, as by remodeling: with *for:* to *adapt* a novel for the theater. **2** To modify (oneself) to conform to a situation or environment. —*v.i.* **3** To become adjusted to a circumstance or environment: with *to:* Some plants *adapt* well to high altitudes. [< F *adapter* < L *adaptare* < *ad-* to + *aptare* fit]

Synonyms: accommodate, adjust, arrange, attune, conform, fashion, fit, harmonize, prepare, proportion, set, suit. *Fit* and *adapt* refer to the bringing about of agreement; *fit* applies especially to original purpose; as, the key is *fitted* to the lock; *adapt* often applies to the securing of agreement by partial change; a novel is *adapted* for the stage by changing it from the narrative to the dramatic form. *Adjust* refers chiefly to relative position; the parts of a typewriter, already *fitted* and *adapted* to each other, must be *adjusted* for perfect alinement. To *suit* is to make one thing or person in all respects agreeable to another. *Conform* implies external agreement, as of a glacier to a rock surface, or of dissenters to an established church. *Accommodate* implies some concession or yielding to secure harmony; as, to *accommodate* oneself to circumstances. *Arrange* refers to position and order, commonly of detached objects; as, to *arrange* the furniture of a room, or the heads of a discourse. See ACCOMMODATE. Compare SET.

a·dapt·a·ble (ə·dap′tə·bəl) *adj.* Capable of being adapted. —**a·dapt′a·bil′i·ty, a·dapt′a·ble·ness** *n.*

ad·ap·ta·tion (ad′əp·tā′shən) *n.* **1** The act of adapting or fitting one thing to another; the state of being suited or fitted. **2** The process of adapting or adjusting to new conditions. **3** Anything adapted. **4** *Biol.* An advantageous conformation of an organism to changes in its environment. **5** *Physiol.* The change in the response of an organ of sense due to prolonged or repeated stimulation. —**ad′ap·ta′tion·al** *adj.* —**ad′ap·ta′tion·al·ly** *adv.*

a·dapt·er (ə·dap′tər) *n.* **1** A person or thing that adapts. **2** *Mech.* Any device that serves to connect or fit together two parts of an apparatus, or to permit the use of an apparatus for a purpose for which it was not intended. **3** A device for converting available electric current to a form required to power a given device. Also **a·dap′tor.**

a·dap·tive (ə·dap′tiv) *adj.* Capable of, pertaining to, fit for, or manifesting adaptation. — **a·dap′tive·ly** *adv.* —**a·dap′tive·ness** *n.*

A·dar (ə·där′, ä′där) A Hebrew month. See CALENDAR (Hebrew).

ad·ax·i·al (ad·ak′sē·əl) *adj.* Toward or beside the axis of an organism or an organ.

a·days (ə·dāz′) *adv.* By day; on each day; during the day: now only in *nowadays.*

add (ad) *v.t.* **1** To join or unite, so as to increase the importance, size, quantity or number: to *add* more weight to his load; *add* insult to injury. **2** To find the sum of, as a column of figures; unite in a total. **3** To say or write further. —*v.i.* **4** To produce an increase in: with *to*: His new duties *added* to his worries. **5** To perform the arithmetical process of addition. —**to add up 1** To accumulate to a total. **2** *Colloq.* To make sense. [< L *addere* < *ad-* to + *dare* give] —**add′a·bil′i·ty, add′i·bil′i·ty** *n.* —**add′a·ble, add′i·ble** *adj.*

Synonyms: adjoin, affix, amplify, annex, append, attach, augment, enlarge, extend, increase, subjoin. To *add* is to *increase* by *adjoining* or *uniting:* in distinction from *multiply*, which is to *increase* by repeating. To *augment* a thing is to *increase* it by any means, but this word chiefly indicates an extension of volume. We may *enlarge* a house, a farm, or an empire, *extend* influence or dominion, *augment* a stream, power, or influence, *attach* or *annex* a building to one that it *adjoins*, or *annex* a territory, *affix* a seal or a signature, *attach* a condition to a promise. A speaker may *amplify* a discourse by a fuller treatment throughout than was originally planned, or he may *append* or *subjoin* certain remarks without change of what has gone before. *Antonyms:* abstract, deduct, diminish, dissever, lessen, reduce, remove, subtract, withdraw.

Ad·dams (ad′əmz), **Jane**, 1860–1935, U.S. social worker.

ad·dax (ad′aks) *n.* A North African and Arabian antelope (*Addax nasomaculata*) with shaggy hair on the throat and forehead, long and twisted horns, a white spot on the face, and a whitish body. [< L < native African word]

ADDAX
(3 feet high at shoulder;
3 to 4 feet long)

ad·dend (ad′end, ə·dend′) *n. Math.* A quantity or number which is to be united in one sum with another quantity or number called the *augend.* [See ADDENDUM]

ad·den·dum (ə·den′dəm) *n. pl.* **-da** (-də) **1** A thing added, or to be added. **2** *Mech.* The radial distance between the pitch circle and the outer ends of the teeth on a geared wheel; also, the part of a tooth outside the pitch circle. See synonyms under APPENDAGE, INCREASE. [< L neut. gerundive of *addere* add]

ad·der[1] (ad′ər) *n.* **1** A viper, especially the common European viper (*Vipera berus*), about two feet long, of a brownish color variegated with black. **2** One of various other snakes, as the harmless puff adder of the United States. [OE *nædre* (a *nadder* in ME becoming an *adder*)]

ad·der[2] (ad′ər) *n.* **1** A person or thing that adds. **2** An adding machine.

ad·der's-tongue (ad′ərz·tung′) *n.* **1** A cosmopolitan fern (genus *Ophio-glossum*), so named from the form of its spore-bearing spike. **2** Any of various flowering plants, as the dog's-tooth violet.

ADDER'S-TONGUE
(def. 2)

ad·dict (ə·dikt′) *v.t.* **1** To apply or devote (oneself) persistently or habitually: with *to.* **2** To cause to pursue or practice continuously: with *to*: This task *addicted* him to obscure research. —*n.* (ad′ikt) One who is habituated to some practice such as using alcohol or drugs. [< L *addictus*, pp. of *addicere* assign, devote to < *ad-* to + *dicere* say]

ad·dict·ed (ə·dik′tid) *adj.* Accustomed; inclined to the pursuit, practice, or taking of anything: *addicted* to drugs.

Synonyms: abandoned, accustomed, attached, devoted, disposed, given, habituated, inclined,

predisposed, prone, wedded. One is *addicted* to that which he has allowed to gain a strong, habitual, and enduring hold upon action, inclination, or involuntary tendency. A man may be *accustomed* to labor, *attached* to his profession, *devoted* to his religion, *given* to study or to gluttony (in the bad sense). One *inclined* to luxury may become *habituated* to poverty. One is *wedded* to that which has become a second nature, as to science or to art. *Prone* is used only in a bad sense, and generally of natural tendencies; as, our hearts are *prone* to evil. *Abandoned* tells of acquired viciousness to which one has surrendered himself. *Addicted* is used in a good or, more frequently, a bad sense; *devoted*, chiefly in the good sense; as, a mother's *devoted* affection. *Antonyms:* averse, disinclined, indisposed, unaccustomed.

ad·dic·tion (ə·dik′shən) *n.* **1** Habitual inclination; bent. **2** A condition of compulsive psychological or physiological dependence on a drug.

ad·dic·tive (ə·dik′tiv) *adj.* Of, pertaining to, or causing addiction; habit-forming.

Ad·dis A·ba·ba (ä′dis ä′bə·bä, ad′is ab′ə·bə) The capital of Ethiopia. Also **A′dis A′ba·ba.**

ad·dit·a·ment (ə·dit′ə·mənt) *n.* A thing added; addition. Also **ad·dit′i·ment.** [< L *additamentum*]

ad·di·tion (ə·dish′ən) *n.* **1** The act of adding, or that which is added; an increase; annex; accession. **2** *Music* A dot at the right of a musical note, lengthening it one half. **3** *Law* A title or mark of designation attached to a man's name. **4** *Her.* Augmentation. **5** *Math.* The uniting of two or more arithmetical or algebraic quantities in one sum, indicated by the plus sign (+). See synonyms under ACCESSION, APPENDAGE, INCREASE. [< F < L *additio, -onis* < *addere.* See ADD.]

ad·di·tion·al (ə·dish′ən·əl) *adj.* Being in addition, supplementary. —*n.* An addition. —**ad·di′tion·al·ly** *adv.*

ad·di·tive (ad′ə·tiv) *n.* An extra ingredient added in small quantity to a product for the purpose of altering or improving some characteristic, such as stability, flavor, performance, cost, or the like. —*adj.* That is to be added; serving or tending to increase. [< L *additivus* < *addere.* See ADD.] —**ad′di·tive·ly** *adv.*

ad·dle (ad′l) *v.* **ad·dled, ad·dling** *v.i.* **1** To become spoiled, as eggs. **2** To become muddled or mixed up, as a discourse. —*v.t.* **3** To cause to spoil. **4** To cause to become confused. —*adj.* **1** Spoiled, as eggs; rotten. **2** Confused; mixed up, as discourse: now generally in compounds: *addle-pated.* [OE *adela* liquid filth]

ad·dle-brained (ad′l·brānd′) *adj.* Confused; mixed up. Also **ad′dle-head′ed, ad′dle-pat′ed, ad′dle-wit′ted.**

add-on (ad′on′, -ôn′) —*n.* An additional or added sum, quantity, or item. —*adj.* Additional; accessory: *add-on* units for air conditioning.

ad·dress (ə·dres′) *v.t.* **ad·dressed, ad·dress·ing 1** To speak to; accost: He *addressed* the bystanders fiercely. **2** To deliver a set discourse to: The president *addressed* the council every third week. **3** To direct, as spoken or written words, to the attention of: with *to*: He *addressed* his prayers to his God. **4** To devote the energy or force of (oneself): with *to*: He *addressed* himself to the task. **5** To superscribe or mark with a destination, as a letter. **6** To consign, as a cargo to a merchant. **7** To aim or direct, as a ball by a golf club. **8** To pay court to, as a lover; woo. —*n.* (ə·dres′, *esp. for* **2** *and* **3** ad′res) **1** A set or formal discourse; a speaking to or accosting; an appeal; application; petition. **2** The writing on an envelope, etc. directing something to a person or place. **3** The name, place, residence, etc. of a person. **4** Consignment, as of a vessel or cargo. **5** The manner of a person; delivery; bearing. **6** *Chiefly pl.* Any courteous or devoted attention; wooing. **7** Skilful conduct or action; adroitness; tact. **8** *Electronics* A particular location in the memory or storage element of a computer, as indicated by a number or other symbol. **9** *Obs.* Preparation or that

which is prepared. [< OF *adresser* < VL *addrictiare, addirectiare* < L *ad-* to + *directus* straight] —**ad·dress·er, ad·dress·or** *n.*

Synonyms (verb): accost, apostrophize, appeal, approach, court, greet, hail, inscribe, salute, woo. To *accost* is to speak first to; *greet* is not so distinctly limited; to *salute* is to *greet* with special token of respect; to *hail* is to *greet* in a loud-voiced and commonly hearty and joyous way. *Address* is slightly more formal than *accost* or *greet*, though it may often be interchanged with them. One may *address* another at considerable length in a speech or in writing; he *accosts* orally and briefly. *Antonyms:* avoid, cut, elude, ignore, overlook, pass, shun.

Synonyms (noun): adroitness, courtesy, dexterity, discretion, ingenuity, manners, politeness, readiness, speech, tact. *Address*, as here considered, is a general power to direct to the matter in hand whatever qualities are most needed for it at the moment. It includes *adroitness* and *discretion* to know what to do or say and what to avoid; *ingenuity* to devise; *readiness* to speak or act; the *dexterity* that comes of practice; and *tact*, which is the power of fine touch as applied to human character and feeling. *Courtesy* and *politeness* are indispensable elements of good *address.* Compare SPEECH. *Antonyms:* awkwardness, boorishness, clownishness, clumsiness, fatuity, folly, rudeness, stupidity, unmannerliness, unwisdom.

ad·dress·ee (ad′res·ē′, ə·dres′ē′). *n.* One who is addressed.

ad·duce (ə·dōōs′, ə·dyōōs′) *v.t.* **ad·duced, ad·duc·ing** To bring forward for proof or consideration, as an example; cite; allege. See synonyms under ALLEGE. [< L *adducere* < *ad-* to + *ducere* lead] —**ad·duce′a·ble, ad·duc′i·ble** *adj.*

ad·du·cent (ə·dōō′sənt, ə·dyōō′-) *adj.* Drawing together; adducting.

ad·duct (ə·dukt′) *v.t. Physiol.* To draw toward the axis: said of muscles. [< L *adductus*, pp. of *adducere.* See ADDUCE.] —**ad·duc′tion** *n.*

ad·duc·tive (ə·duk′tiv) *adj.* **1** Adducing. **2** Tending to adduct.

ad·duc·tor (ə·duk′tər) *n.* An adducting muscle.

-ade[1] *suffix of nouns* **1** Act or action: *cannonade.* **2** A person or group concerned in an action or process: *cavalcade.* **3** Product of an action or process: *lemonade.* [< F *-ade* < Provençal, Pg., or Sp. *-ada* or Ital. *-ata* < L *-ata*, fem. pp. ending]

-ade[2] *suffix of nouns* Relating to; pertaining to: *decade.* The more common English form of this suffix is *-ad.* See *-*AD[1]. [< F *-ade* < Gk. *-ados*]

a·deem (ə·dēm′) *v.t.* **1** To take away. **2** *Law* To revoke, as the bequest of a legacy. [< L *adimere* < *ad-* to (oneself) + *emere* take]

Ad·e·laide (ad′ə·lād) The capital of South Australia.

a·del·phous (ə·del′fəs) *adj. Bot.* Having stamens with clustered or coalescent filaments: used mainly as a suffix. [< Gk. *adelphos* brother]

a·demp·tion (ə·demp′shən) *n. Law* Disposal by a testator in his lifetime of specific property bequeathed in his will so that the bequest is adeemed. [< L *ademptio, -onis* < *adimere.* See ADEEM.]

A·den (äd′n, ād′n) A former British colony at the sw tip of the Arabian peninsula, now a part of Yemen; principal city **Aden**, pop. about 100,000.

Aden, Gulf of A western inlet of the Arabian Sea, between Yemen and Somalia.

A·den·i (ä′den·ē) *n. pl.* **A·den·is** A native or inhabitant of Aden. —*adj.* Of or pertaining to Aden. Also **A·den·ese** (ä′dən·ēz′, -ēs′, ä′dən-).

ad·e·noid (ad′ə·noid) *adj.* Of or like a gland; glandular: also **ad′e·noi′dal.** —*n. Usually pl.* An enlarged mass of lymphoid tissue in the nasopharynx, in severe cases obstructing breathing and speech. [< ADEN(O)- + -OID]

a·dept (ə·dept′) *adj.* Highly skilful; proficient. —**ad·ept** (ad′ept, ə·dept′) *n.* **1** One fully skilled in any art; an expert. **2** *Archaic* An alchemist who professed to have discovered how to convert base metals into gold. [< L *adeptus* having attained, pp. of *adipisci* attain < *ad-* to + *apisci* get] —**a·dept′ly** *adv.* —**a·dept′ness** *n.*

ad·e·quate (ad′ə·kwit) *adj.* **1** Equal to what is required; suitable to the case or occasion; fully sufficient. **2** Equal in size, extent, value, etc. [< L *adaequatus*, pp. of *adaequare* < *ad-* to + *aequus* equal] —**ad·e·qua·cy** (ad′ə·kwə·sē), **ad′e·quate·ness** *n.* —**ad′e·quate·ly** *adv.*
Synonyms: commensurate, enough, equal, fit, fitting, plentiful, satisfactory, sufficient. *Adequate, commensurate, enough,* and *sufficient* signify *equal* to some given occasion or work. *Commensurate* is the more precise and learned word, signifying that which exactly measures the matter in question. Work is *satisfactory* if it satisfies those for whom it is done, while it may be very poor work judged by some higher standard. Compare AMPLE, COMPETENT. *Antonyms:* inadequate, insufficient, unequal, unfit, unsatisfactory.

ad ex·tre·mum (ad eks·trē′məm) *Latin* To the extreme; finally.

ad·fect·ed (ad·fek′tid) *adj. Math.* Containing different powers of an unknown quantity. [Specialized var. of AFFECTED]

ad fin. At, to, or toward the end (L *ad finem*)

ad fi·nem (ad fī′nem) *Latin* To the end.

ad·here (ad·hir′) *v.i.* **ad·hered, ad·her·ing 1** To stick fast or together. **2** To be attached or devoted, as a follower or disciple, to a party or faith: with *to*. **3** To follow closely or without deviation: with *to*: He *adhered* to the plan. **4** *Obs.* To be consistent, as an alibi. [< L *adhaerere* < *ad-* to + *haerere* stick]

ad·her·ence (ad·hir′əns) *n.* The act or state of adhering; attachment; adhesion. Also **ad·her′en·cy.** See synonyms under ATTACHMENT.

ad·her·ent (ad·hir′ənt) *adj.* **1** Clinging or sticking fast. **2** *Bot.* Adnate; grown together. —*n.* One who is devoted or attached, as to a cause or leader; a follower: also **ad·her′er.** —**ad·her′ent·ly** *adv.*
Synonyms (noun): aid, aider, ally, backer, disciple, follower, partisan, supporter. An *adherent* is one who is devoted or attached to a person, party, principle, cause, creed, or the like. *Allies* may differ on every point except the specific ground of union. *Allies* are regarded as equals; *adherents* and *disciples* are followers. *Partisan* has the narrow sense of adherence to a party. One may be an *adherent* or *supporter* of a party and not a *partisan. Backer* usually indicates a financial *supporter.* Compare ACCESSORY. *Antonyms:* adversary, antagonist, betrayer, deserter, enemy, hater, opponent, renegade, traitor.

ad·he·sion (ad·hē′zhən) *n.* **1** The act of adhering; the state of being attached; adherence. **2** Assent; concurrence. **3** Close connection, as of ideas. **4** *Physics* The binding force exerted by molecules of unlike substances when brought in contact, as wood and glue. **5** The union of normally separate tissues in the body by proliferating fibrous tissue. See synonyms under ATTACHMENT. [< F *adhésion* < L *adhaesio, -onis* < *adhaerere.* See ADHERE.]

ad·he·sive (ad·hē′siv) *adj.* **1** Having the quality of adhering; tending or causing to adhere; sticky; clinging. **2** Prepared to adhere; gummed. —*n.* A substance that causes adhesion. —**ad·he′sive·ly** *adv.* —**ad·he′sive·ness** *n.*
Synonyms (adj.): cohesive, glutinous, gummy, sticking, sticky, viscid, viscous. *Adhesive* is the scientific, *sticky* the popular word. That which is *adhesive* tends to join itself to the surface of any other body with which it is placed in contact; *cohesive* expresses the tendency of particles of the same substance to hold together. *Antonyms:* free, inadhesive, loose, separable.

ad·hib·it (ad·hib′it) *v.t.* **1** To let in; admit, as to a court of law. **2** To affix; fasten, as a label. **3** To apply; administer, as a medicine. [< L *adhibitus,* pp. of *adhibere* hold towards, apply to < *ad-* to + *habere* have, hold] —**ad·hi·bi′tion** (ad′hi·bish′ən) *n.*

ad hoc (ad hok′) *Latin* With respect to this (particular thing); up to this time.

ad hom·i·nem (ad hom′ə·nem) *Latin* To the man; to one's individual passions and prejudices.

a·dieu (ə·dōō′, ə·dyōō′; *Fr.* à·dyœ′) *n. pl.* **a·dieus,** *Fr.* **a·dieux** (à·dyœ′) A farewell. —*interj.* Good-by; farewell: literally, "to God (I

commend you)." See synonyms under FAREWELL. [< F *à* to + *dieu* God]

ad in·fi·ni·tum (ad in′fə·nī′təm) To infinity; hence, limitlessly. [< L]

ad in·ter·im (ad in′tər·im) Meanwhile; in the meantime. [< L]

a·di·os (ä′dē·ōs′, ad′ē·ōs′; *Sp.* ä·dyōs′) *interj.* Farewell: good-by: literally, "to God (I commend you)." [< Sp. < *a* to + *dios* God]

ad·i·pose (ad′ə·pōs) *adj.* Of or pertaining to fat; fatty. See synonyms under CORPULENT. [< NL *adiposus* < L *adeps* fat] —**ad′i·pose′ness, ad·i·pos·i·ty** (ad′ə·pos′ə·tē) *n.*

adipose tissue A type of connective tissue containing many cells specialized for storing fat.

ad·it (ad′it) *n.* **1** An approach; entrance; passage. **2** A nearly horizontal entrance to a mine. **3** Access; admission. See synonyms under ENTRANCE. [< L *aditus,* pp. of *adire* approach < *ad-* to + *ire* go]

ad·ja·cen·cy (ə·jā′sən·sē) *n. pl.* **·cies** That which is contiguous or adjacent; contiguity. Also **ad·ja′cence.**

ad·ja·cent (ə·jā′sənt) *adj.* Lying near or close at hand; adjoining, contiguous. [< L *adjacens, -entis,* ppr. of *adjacere* < *ad-* near + *jacere* lie] —**ad·ja′cent·ly** *adv.*
Synonyms: abutting, adjoining, attached, beside, bordering, close, conterminous, contiguous, near, neighboring, next, nigh. *Adjacent* farms may not be connected; if *adjoining,* they meet at the boundary line. *Conterminous* would imply that their dimensions were exactly equal on the side where they adjoin. *Contiguous* may be used for either *adjacent* or *adjoining. Near* is a relative word, places being called *near* upon the railroad which would elsewhere be deemed remote. *Neighboring* always implies such proximity that the inhabitants may be neighbors. *Next* views some object as the nearest of several or many. *Antonyms:* detached, disconnected, disjoined, distant, remote, separate.

adjacent angle See under ANGLE.

ad·jec·ti·val (aj′ik·tī′vəl, aj′ik·ti·vəl) *adj.* **1** Pertaining to or like an adjective. **2** Used as an adjective. —*n.* A word or group of words used as an adjective. —**ad′jec·ti′val·ly** *adv.*

ad·jec·tive (aj′ik·tiv) *n.* **1** *Gram.* A word used to limit or qualify a noun: one of the eight traditional parts of speech. **2** A dependent or corollary. —*adj.* **1** Pertaining to an adjective. **2** *Gram.* Depending upon or standing in adjunct relation to a noun. **3** Of the nature of an adjunct; dependent; procedural: *adjective* law. **4** *Chem.* Requiring the use of a mordant, as in dyeing. [< L *adjectivus* that is added < *adjicere* add to < *ad-* to + *jacere* throw] —**ad′jec·tive·ly** *adv.*

ad·join (ə·join′) *v.t.* **1** To be next to; border upon. **2** *Obs.* To join to; append; unite: with *to.* —*v.i.* **3** To lie close together; be in contact. See synonyms under ADD. [< OF *ajoindre* < L *adjungere* < *ad-* to + *jungere* join]

ad·join·ing (ə·joi′ning) *adj.* Lying next; bordering; contiguous. See synonyms under ADJACENT.

ad·journ (ə·jûrn′) *v.t.* **1** To put off to another day or place, as a meeting or session; postpone. **2** To put off to the next session, as the decision of a council. —*v.i.* **3** To postpone or suspend proceedings for a specified time: The court *adjourned* for three days. **4** *Colloq.* To move or go to another place: Shall we *adjourn* to the porch? See synonyms under PROCRASTINATE, POSTPONE. [< OF *ajorner, ajurner* < LL *adjurnare* set a day < L *ad-* to + *diurnus* daily < *dies* day]

ad·journ·ment (ə·jûrn′mənt) *n.* The act of adjourning, or the period for which anything is adjourned; postponement.

ad·judge (ə·juj′) *v.t.* **1** To determine or decide judicially, as a case. **2** To pronounce or order by law: His testimony was *adjudged* perjury. **3** To condemn or sentence: with *to*: The defendant was *adjudged* to imprisonment. **4** To award by law, as damages. **5** *Obs.* To regard or consider. [< OF *ajugier* < L *adjudicare* < *ad-* to + *judicare* judge. Doublet of ADJUDICATE.]

ad·ju·di·cate (ə·jōō′də·kāt) *v.* **·cat·ed, ·cat·ing** *v.t.* **1** To determine judicially; settle; adjudge. —*v.i.* **2** To act as a judge. [< L *adjudicatus,* pp. of *adjudicare.* Doublet of ADJUDGE.] —**ad·ju′di·ca′tor** *n.*

ad·ju·di·ca·tion (ə·jōō′də·kā′shən) *n.* The act or process of adjudicating or adjudging; judicial decision.

ad·junct (aj′ungkt) *adj.* Joined subordinately; auxiliary. —*n.* **1** Something connected subordinately; an auxiliary. **2** A person associated with another person in an auxiliary or subordinate relation; a helper; associate; assistant. **3** *Gram.* A word or words added to define, limit, qualify, or modify other words. **4** *Logic* Any non-essential quality of a thing, as distinguished from its essence or substance. See synonyms under APPENDAGE, HELP. [< L *adjunctus,* pp. of *adjungere.* See ADJOIN.]

ad·junc·tive (ə·jungk′tiv) *adj.* Constituting or contributing to form an adjunct. —**ad·junc′tive·ly** *adv.*

ad·ju·ra·tion (aj′ōō·rā′shən) *n.* The act of adjuring; a solemn oath.

ad·jur·a·to·ry (ə·jōōr′ə·tôr′ē, -tō′rē) *adj.* Of, pertaining to, or containing an adjuration or command.

ad·jure (ə·jōōr′) *v.t.* **ad·jured, ad·jur·ing 1** To charge or entreat solemnly, as under oath or penalty. **2** To appeal to earnestly. [< L *adjurare* < *ad-* to + *jurare* swear] —**ad·jur′er, ad·ju′ror** *n.*

ad·just (ə·just′) *v.t.* **1** To arrange so as to fit or match; make correspond, as to a standard. **2** To harmonize or compose, as differences. **3** To arrange in order; systematize. **4** To regulate or make accurate, as a compass. **5** To make allowance for elevation and deflection, as of a gun in firing. **6** To determine an amount to be paid, as in settling an insurance claim. —*v.i.* **7** To adapt oneself; conform, as to a new environment. See synonyms under ACCOMMODATE, ADAPT, PREPARE, REGULATE, SET, SETTLE. [< OF *ajouster* < L *ad-* to + *juxta* near; refashioned on F *juste* right < L *justus*] —**ad·just′a·ble** *adj.* —**ad·just′er, ad·jus′tor** *n.* —**ad·jus′tive** *adj.*

ad·just·ment (ə·just′mənt) *n.* **1** The act, process, means, or result of adjusting; regulation; arrangement; settlement. **2** *Mech.* **a** An instrument or means whereby something may be adjusted; that which regulates; as, the *adjustments* of a watch, telescope, or microscope. **b** A device, as a screw or wedge, for raising or adjusting a part so as to take up wear or lost motion. **3** The determining of the just amount of insurance payable for losses, as in fire or shipping; also, of the just amount payable for the failure of an article to fulfil a guarantee made of its reasonable wear and use.

ad·ju·vant (aj′ə·vənt) *adj.* Assisting; helpful. —*n.* **1** A helper. **2** Any substance that heightens the action of an antigen or a drug. [< L *adjuvans, -antis,* ppr. of *adjuvare.* See AID.]

ad·lib (ad′lib′) *v.t. & v.i.* **·libbed, ·lib·bing** *Colloq.* To improvise, as words, gestures, or music not called for in the original script or score. —*adj.* Made up on the spot: *adlib* comments. —*adv.* On the spur of the moment: to dictate *adlib.* [< AD LIBITUM]

ad lib·i·tum (ad lib′ə·təm) *Latin* **1** At will; as one pleases. **2** *Music* Freely: a direction indicating that a section or passage may be omitted or varied as the performer wishes.

ad li·tem (ad lī′təm) *Latin* For the particular suit or action.

ad·min·is·ter (ad·min′is·tər) *v.t.* **1** To have the charge or direction of; manage. **2** To supply or provide with; apply, as medicine or treatment. **3** To inflict; mete out; dispense, as punishment or the sacraments. **4** *Law* To settle by testamentary or official appointment; act as executor of, as an estate. **5** To tender, as an oath. —*v.i.* **6** To contribute toward an end; minister: with *to.* **7** To carry out the functions of an administrator. See synonyms under EXECUTE. [< OF *aministrer* (F *administrer*) < L *administrare* minister to < *ad-* to + *ministrare* serve] —**ad·min·is·te·ri·al** (ad·min′is·tir′ē·əl) *adj.* —**ad·min·is·tra·ble** (ad·min′is·trə·bəl) *adj.*

ad·min·is·trant (ad·min′is·trənt) *adj.* Managing affairs; executive. —*n.* One who administers.

ad·min·is·trate (ad·min′is·trāt) *v.t.* **·trat·ed, ·trat·ing** To administer.

ad·min·is·tra·tion (ad·min′is·trā′shən) *n.* **1** The act of administering, or the state of being administered; management of public affairs. **2** The government as existing, or the persons collectively who compose it, especially its executive department; also, the official tenure of such government. **3** *Law* The legal management and settlement of the estate of a deceased person, as by an executor, or of a minor, lunatic, or one otherwise incompetent, as by a trustee or administrator.

ad·min·is·tra·tive (ad·min'is·trā'tiv) *adj.* Pertaining to administration; executive. **—ad·min'is·tra'tive·ly** *adv.*

ad·min·is·tra·tor (ad·min'is·trā'tər) *n.* **1** One who administers something. **2** *Law* One commissioned by a competent court to administer upon the personal property of a deceased person. [< L] **—ad·min'is·tra'tor·ship** *n.*

ad·mi·ra·ble (ad'mər·ə·bəl) *adj.* **1** Worthy of admiration; excellent. **2** Wonderful; praiseworthy. See synonyms under EXCELLENT, GOOD. [< L *admirabilis* < *admirari*. See ADMIRE.] **—ad'mi·ra·ble·ness, ad'mi·ra·bil'i·ty** *n.* **—ad'mi·ra·bly** *adv.*

ad·mi·ral (ad'mər·əl) *n.* **1** A naval officer of the highest rank, in the United States Navy equivalent in rank to a general in the United States Army; also, loosely, a rear admiral in the United States Navy, and a rear admiral or vice admiral in other navies. **2** The flagship of a fleet. **3** Any of various showy butterflies of Europe and North America, such as the red admiral (*Vanessa atalanta*), and the white admiral (*Limenitis sybilla*). **—rear admiral** A naval officer ranking next below a vice admiral: in the United States Navy, equivalent in rank to a major general. **— vice admiral** A naval officer ranking next below an admiral: in the United States Navy, equivalent in rank to a lieutenant general. See table under GRADE. [< OF *amiral, admiral* < Arabic *amīr-al* commander of the (as in *amīr-al-bahr* commander of the sea); influenced by L *admirabilis* admirable]

INSIGNIA–U.S.N.
a. Rear Admiral.
b. Vice Admiral.
c. Admiral.
d. Admiral of the Fleet.

ad·mi·ral·ship (ad'mər·əl·ship') *n.* The office or rank of an admiral.

Ad·mi·ral·ty (ad'mər·əl·tē) *n. pl.* **·ties** A department of the British government having supreme charge of naval affairs; the Board of Admiralty; also the building in London which houses the Board of Admiralty.

ad·mi·ral·ty (ad'mər·əl·tē) *n.* **1** The office or functions of an admiral. **2** The branch of jurisprudence or of the judiciary that takes cognizance of maritime affairs, civil and criminal.

admiralty law The code or system of law and procedure relating to maritime affairs; maritime law.

ad·mi·ra·tion (ad'mə·rā'shən) *n.* **1** Wonder combined with approbation in view of anything rare, great, excellent, beautiful, sublime; hence, pleased and gratified observation and contemplation. **2** That which is admired or excites pleased approval; anything marvelous or prodigious. **3** *Obs.* Wonder. See synonyms under AMAZEMENT.

ad·mire (ad·mīr') *v.* **ad·mired, ad·mir·ing** *v.t.* **1** To regard with wonder, pleasure, and approbation. **2** To have respect or esteem for. **3** *Obs.* To wonder or marvel at. —*v.i.* **4** To feel or express admiration. **5** *U.S. Dial.* To wish or desire: with *to*: I would *admire* to go to your party. [< L *admirari* < *ad-* at + *mirari* wonder] **—ad·mir'er** *n.* **—ad·mir'ing** *adj.* **—ad·mir'ing·ly** *adv.*

Synonyms: adore, applaud, approve, enjoy, esteem, extol, honor, love, respect, revere, venerate. We *admire* beauty in nature and art, *enjoy* books or society. We *approve* what is excellent, *applaud* heroic deeds, *esteem* the good, *love* our friends. We *honor* and *respect* noble character wherever found; we *revere* and *venerate* it in the

aged. We *extol* or *adore* the goodness, majesty, and power of God. *Antonyms*: abhor, abominate, contemn, despise, detest, dislike, execrate, hate, ridicule, scorn.

ad·mis·si·ble (ad·mis'ə·bəl) *adj.* **1** Such as may be admitted; allowable, as proof. **2** Worthy of being considered, as an idea. **—ad·mis'si·bil'i·ty, ad·mis'si·ble·ness** *n.* **—ad·mis'si·bly** *adv.*

ad·mis·sion (ad·mish'ən) *n.* **1** The act of admitting, or the state of being admitted; entrance. **2** A conceding, or that which is conceded; acknowledging or confessing: an *admission* of guilt. **3** The price charged or paid to be admitted; entrance fee. **4** *Rel.* A formal act, by ecclesiastical authority, admitting a candidate to a benefice or church. **5** *Mech.* **a** Entrance of steam or other motive fluid into a cylinder. **b** The point in the stroke or rotation at which such entrance takes place. **c** The period between entrance of motive force and expansion or exhaust thereof. See synonyms under BELIEF, ENTRANCE¹. [< L *admissio, -onis* < *admissus*, pp. of *admittere*. See ADMIT.]

ad·mis·sive (ad·mis'iv) *adj.* Characterized by, tending to, implying, or granting admission. Also **ad·mis·so·ry** (ad·mis'ər·ē).

ad·mit (ad·mit') *v.* **ad·mit·ted, ad·mit·ting** *v.t.* **1** To allow to enter; grant entrance to: to *admit* visitors to a house. **2** To be the means or channel of admission to; let in: This key will *admit* you. **3** To have room for; contain: The port *admits* only two ships at once. **4** To leave room for; permit: His impatience *admits* no delay. **5** To concede or grant, as the truth of an argument. **6** To acknowledge or avow: He *admitted* his part in the conspiracy. **7** To allow to join or become associated with; consider as entitled to the privileges of: to *admit* a person to the bar as an attorney. —*v.i.* **8** To give scope or warrant: with *of*: This problem *admits* of several solutions. **9** To afford entrance; open on: with *to*: This gate *admits* to the garden. [< L *admittere* < *ad-* to + *mittere* send, let go] **—ad·mit'ta·ble, ad·mit'ti·ble** *adj.*

ad·mit·tance (ad·mit'ns) *n.* **1** The act of admitting, or the state or fact of being admitted; entrance; right or permission to enter; actual entrance; admission. **2** *Electr.* The reciprocal of the impedance of an alternating-current circuit. **3** In English law, the last stage, or perfection, of copyhold assurances of title. See synonyms under ACCESS, ENTRANCE¹.

ad·mit·ta·tur (ad'mi·tā'tər) *n.* A certificate of admission granted by some colleges. [< L, let him be admitted]

ad·mit·ted (ad·mit'id) *adj.* Accepted as valid or true; acknowledged; conceded. See synonyms under AUTHENTIC.

ad·mit·ted·ly (ad·mit'id·lē) *adv.* Confessedly.

ad·mix (ad·miks') *v.t.* **ad·mixed** or **ad·mixt, ad·mix·ing** To mingle or mix with something else. [Back formation from ME *admixt* mixed with < L *admixtus*, pp. of *admiscere* < *ad-* to + *miscere* mix]

ad·mix·ture (ad·miks'chər) *n.* **1** That which is formed by admixing; a mixture. **2** The ingredient added to the principal substance in forming a mixture. **3** The act of mingling or mixing, or the state of being mixed. See synonyms under ALLOY. [< L *admixtus*, pp. of *admiscere* mix with. See ADMIX.]

ad·mon·ish (ad·mon'ish) *v.t.* **1** To advise of a fault; administer mild reproof to. **2** To caution against danger or error; warn, as of something to be avoided: The gallows *admonished* the citizens against a life of crime. **3** To charge authoritatively; exhort; urge: He *admonished* me to follow him. [< OF *amonester* < LL *admonestare* < L *admonere* < *ad-* to + *monere* warn] **—ad·mon'ish·er** *n.*

ad·mo·ni·tion (ad'mə·nish'ən) *n.* The act of admonishing; gentle reproof. Also **ad·mon'ish·ment.** [< L *admonitio, -onis* < *admonere*. See ADMONISH.]

ad·mon·i·tor (ad·mon'ə·tər) *n.* One who admonishes; a monitor. [< L]

ad·mon·i·to·ry (ad·mon'ə·tôr·ē, -tō·rē) *adj.* Giving admonition. Also **ad·mon'i·tive.**

ad nau·se·am (ad nô'shē·am, -sē-) *Latin* To the

degree of disgust; so as to nauseate or produce disgust.

ad·noun (ad'noun) *n. Gram.* An adjective; especially, an adjective used as a noun. [< AD-, NOUN; modeled on *adverb*] **—ad·nom·i·nal** (ad·nom'ə·nəl) *adj.*

a·do (ə·dōō') *n.* Unnecessary activity; bustle; fuss; trouble. [ME *at do*, northern dial. form for the infinitive *to do*]

a·do·be (ə·dō'bē) *n.* **1** A sun-dried brick or a structure of such material. **2** The mixed earth or sandy, calcareous clay of which such bricks are made. **3** A brick of clay material with which pulverized ore may be combined. **4** *U.S. Dial.* A Mexican silver dollar. —*adj.* Composed of adobe: often used figuratively to denote things made in Mexico. [< Sp. < Arabic *at-tub* the brick]

ad·o·les·cence (ad'ə·les'əns) *n.* **1** The process of growing up. **2** The state or period of growth from the onset of puberty to the stage of adult development. Also **ad'o·les'cen·cy.**

ad·o·les·cent (ad'ə·les'ənt) *adj.* **1** Approaching adult development. **2** Characteristic of or pertaining to youth. —*n.* A person in the period of adolescence. [< L *adolescens, -entis*, ppr. of *adolescere* grow up. See ADULT.]

A·don·is (ə·don'is, ə·dō'nis) **1** In Greek mythology, a youth beloved by Venus for his beauty: killed by a wild boar. **2** Any youth of rare beauty.

a·dopt (ə·dopt') *v.t.* **1** To take into a new relationship; accept and treat as a member of one's family. **2** To take into one's family or as one's child by legal measures. **3** To take and make as one's own, as a course of action. **4** To take up from someone else and use as one's own, as a phrase, practice, or creed. **5** To vote to accept, as a motion or committee report See synonyms under EMBRACE. [< F *adopter* < L *adoptare* < *ad-* to + *optare* choose] **—a·dopt'er** *n.*

a·dopt·ee (ə·dop'tē') *n.* One who is adopted.

a·dop·tion (ə·dop'shən) *n.* **1** The act of adopting, or the condition of being adopted. **2** The legal act whereby an adult person takes a minor into the relation of a child. **3** The acceptance of a word unchanged in form from a foreign language. **4** The receiving into a clan or tribe of one from outside, and treating him as one of the same blood.

a·dop·tive (ə·dop'tiv) *adj.* Pertaining or tending to adoption; characterized by adoption. **—a·dop'tive·ly** *adv.*

a·dor·a·ble (ə·dôr'ə·bəl, ə·dōr'-) *adj.* **1** Worthy of adoration. **2** Worthy of or calling forth devoted affection or attachment. **—a·dor·a·bil'i·ty, a·dor'a·ble·ness** *n.* **—a·dor'a·bly** *adv.*

ad·o·ra·tion (ad'ə·rā'shən) *n.* **1** The act of adoring; worship of God or reverence of the divine. **2** An emotion composed of profound admiration, utmost love, and devotion. **3** Formerly, a method of electing a pope by an act of homage from two thirds of the cardinals present, now, the homage given by the cardinals after his election. **4** A representation of homage to or worship of a person or object, especially of a divine person, as the infant Jesus. See synonyms under PRAYER, REVERENCE, VENERATION. [< F < L *adoratio, -onis* < *adorare*. See ADORE.]

a·dore (ə·dôr', ə·dōr') *v.* **a·dored, a·dor·ing** *v.t.* **1** To render divine honor to; worship as divine. **2** To love or honor with intense devotion. **3** *Colloq.* To like especially. —*v.i.* **4** To worship. See synonyms under ADMIRE, PRAISE, VENERATE. [< F *adorer* < L *adorare* < *ad-* to + *orare* speak, pray] **—a·dor'er** *n.* **—a·dor'ing** *adj.*

a·dorn (ə·dôrn') *v.t.* **1** To be an ornament to; increase the beauty of. **2** To furnish or decorate with ornaments. [< F *adorner* < L *adornare* < *ad-* to + *ornare* furnish, deck out] **—a·dorn'ing** *adj. & n.* **—a·dorn'ment** *n.*

Synonyms: beautify, bedeck, decorate, embellish, garnish, gild, illustrate, ornament. An author *embellishes* his narrative with fine descriptions, the artist *illustrates* it with beautiful engravings, the binder *gilds* and *decorates* the volume. A feast is *garnished* with flowers. *Deck* and *bedeck* are commonly said of apparel. To *ornament* is to add outward embellishment. *Adorn* is more lofty and spiritual, referring to a beauty which is not material and cannot be put on by ornaments or decorations. See GARNISH. *Antonyms*: deface, deform, disfigure, mar, spoil.

ADP Symbol for adenosine diphosphate.

ad pa·tres (ad pä′trēz) *Latin* Dead; literally, to his fathers.

ad·press (ad·pres′) *v.t.* To press close to. [< L *adpressus*, pp. of *adprimere* < *ad-* to + *premere* press]

ad quem (ad kwem′) *Latin* At or to which.

ad ref·er·en·dum (ad ref′ə·ren′dəm) *Latin* For further consideration.

ad rem (ad rem′) *Latin* To the point; direct; pertinent.

ad·re·nal (ə·drē′nəl) *adj.* 1 Near the kidneys. 2 Of or from the adrenal glands. —*n.* Either of the adrenal glands. [< AD- + L *renes* kidneys]

adrenal gland Either of the two endocrine glands located on the upper end of each kidney and consisting of a medulla, which secretes epinephrine and norepinephrine, and a cortex, which secretes various steroidal hormones. Also called *suprarenal gland*.

ad·ren·a·lin (ə·dren′ə·lin) *n.* 1 *Brit.* Epinephrine. 2 An internal stimulant popularly adduced as the initiator of energetic reactions to danger, challenge, etc. Also **ad·ren·a·line**.

ad·ren·er·gic (ad′rə·nėr′gik) *adj.* 1 Having chemical activity similar to that of epinephrine or related substances. 2 Stimulating the release of epinephrine or similar hormones.

ad·re·no·cor·ti·cal (ə·drē′nō·kôr′tə·kəl) *adj.* Pertaining to or secreted by the cortex of the adrenal gland.

A·dri·at·ic (ā′drē·at′ik) *adj.* Of or pertaining to the Adriatic Sea or to the inhabitants of its coastal regions.

Adriatic race See DINARIC RACE.

Adriatic Sea An arm of the Mediterranean Sea, east of Italy; 500 miles long.

a·drift (ə·drift′) *adv. & adj.* In a drifting state; drifting.

a·droit (ə·droit′) *adj.* Skilful in emergencies; dexterous; expert. See synonyms under CLEVER. [< F < *à* to (< L *ad-*) + *droit* right < L *directus*] —**a·droit′ly** *adv.* —**a·droit′ness** *n.*

ad·sci·ti·tious (ad′sə·tish′əs) *adj.* Supplemental; adventitious; added from without; not essential. [< L *adscitus*, pp. of *adsciscere* admit, accept < *ad-* to + *sciscere* acknowledge]

ad·sorb (ad·sôrb′, -zôrb′) *v.t. Chem.* To condense and hold by adsorption: distinguished from *absorb*. [< AD- + L *sorbere* suck in] —**ad·sor′bent** *n.*

ad·sorp·tion (ad·sôrp′shən, -zôrp′-) *n.* The retention of molecules or ions of a gas or liquid on the surface of a different substance. [< ADSORB; modeled on *absorption*] —**ad·sorp′tive** *adj.*

ad·sum (ad′sum) *Latin* I am present: an answer to a roll call.

ad sum·mum (ad sum′əm) *Latin* To the highest point or amount.

ad·u·la·res·cence (aj′ə·lə·res′əns) *n.* The peculiar sheen of the ordinary moonstone. [< ADULARIA + -ESCENCE]

ad·u·lar·i·a (aj′ə·lâr′ē·ə) *n. Mineral.* A transparent or translucent form of orthoclase; moonstone. [from Mt. *Adula*, in Switzerland]

ad·u·late (aj′ə·lāt) *v.t.* **·lat·ed**, **·lat·ing** To flatter servilely; praise extravagantly. [< L *adulatus*, pp. of *adulari* fawn] —**ad′u·la′tor** *n.*

ad·u·la·tion (aj′ə·lā′shən) *n.* Servile flattery; extravagant and hypocritical praise; fulsome compliment.

ad·u·la·to·ry (aj′ə·lə·tôr′ē, -tō′rē) *adj.* Obsequiously flattering.

a·dult (ə·dult′, ad′ult) *n.* 1 A person who has attained the age of maturity or legal majority. 2 *Biol.* A fully developed animal or plant. —*adj.* 1 Grown-up; full-grown. 2 Of an adult person. 2 Of or for grown-up persons: *adult* behavior, *adult* education. [< L *adultus*, pp. of *adolescere* grow up < *ad-* to + *alescere* grow. Related to ADOLESCENT.] —**a·dult′ness** *n.*

a·dul·ter·ant (ə·dul′tər·ənt) *n.* An adulterating substance. See synonyms under ALLOY.

a·dul·ter·ate (ə·dul′tər·āt) *v.t.* **·at·ed**, **·at·ing** To make impure or inferior by admixture of other or baser ingredients; corrupt. —*adj.* (ə·dul′tər·it) 1 Adulterated; corrupted; debased; spurious. 2 Adulterous. [< L *adulteratus*, pp. of *adulterare* corrupt < *ad-* + *alter* other, different] —**a·dul′ter·a′tion** *n.* —**a·dul′ter·a′tor** *n.*

a·dul·ter·ine (ə·dul′tər·in, -īn) *adj.* 1 Originating in, or pertaining to, adultery: *adulterine* children. 2 Unauthorized; spurious.

a·dul·ter·ous (ə·dul′tər·əs) *adj.* Of, pertaining to, or given to adultery; illicit. —**a·dul′ter·ous·ly** *adv.*

a·dul·ter·y (ə·dul′tər·ē) *n. pl.* **·ter·ies** 1 The sexual intercourse of two persons, either of whom is married to a third person; unchastity; unfaithfulness. 2 Any lewdness or unchastity of act or thought, as in violation of the divine commandments. *Matt.* v 27, 28. 3 *Eccl.* A marriage not approved by ecclesiastical authority. [< L *adulterium*] —**a·dul′ter·er** *n.* —**a·dul′ter·ess** *n. fem.*

a·dult·hood (ə·dult′hood) *n.* The state of being an adult.

ad·um·brate (ad·um′brāt) *v.t.* **·brat·ed**, **·brat·ing** 1 To represent the mere shadow of; to outline sketchily. 2 To foreshadow; prefigure. 3 To shade or overshadow; darken. [< L *adumbratus*, pp. of *adumbrare* < *ad-* to + *umbrare* shade < *umbra* shade]

ad·um·bra·tion (ad′əm·brā′shən) *n.* 1 A slight sketch. 2 A foreshadowing. 3 An overshadowing; obscuration.

ad·um·bra·tive (ad·um′brə·tiv) *adj.* Faintly indicative.

a·dust (ə·dust′) *adj.* 1 Burning; hot; seared. 2 Browned; sunburnt. 3 Parched and dry; formerly said of the body or blood. 4 Melancholy; gloomy. [< L *adustus*, pp. of *adurere* burn up < *ad-* to + *urere* burn]

ad·vance (ad·vans′, -väns′) *v.* **ad·vanced**, **ad·vanc·ing** *v.t.* 1 To cause to go forward or upward; move forward in position or place. 2 To put in a better or more advantageous situation. 3 To further; promote: to *advance* the progress of science. 4 To make occur earlier; accelerate. 5 To offer; propose: to *advance* a suggestion. 6 To raise in rate or price: to *advance* a discount to five per cent. 7 To pay, as money or interest, before legally due. 8 To lend: Can you *advance* me some money? 9 *Law* To provide, as financial support, for children, especially before the distribution of an estate. —*v.i.* 10 To move or go forward: The armies *advance* on all fronts. 11 To make progress; rise or improve: The stock market *advanced* three points. See synonyms under ACCELERATE, AMEND, FLOURISH, INCREASE, PROMOTE, SERVE. —*adj.* Of, pertaining to, or being an advance; being before in time or place: an *advance* payment. —*n.* 1 The act of advancing, or the state of being advanced; forward movement; progress; improvement; also, an increase or rise, as of prices. 2 One who or that which is at the head; the foremost part. 3 Anything supplied or paid beforehand; also, the act of so supplying or paying. 4 An act of personal approach; overture; proposal: His *advances* were rejected. 5 The place at the front, or in the lead. 6 *Naut.* The distance made by a vessel in the line of a previous course after putting down the helm, as for a tack: distinguished from *transfer*. 7 In fencing, a swift, short step forward with the right foot, promptly followed by the left, in such a manner as to enable the fencer to retain his balance and be in readiness for parry, etc. See synonyms under PROGRESS. [ME *avancen* < OF *avancier* < L *ab-* away + *ante* before; the initial *a-* was later altered to *ad-* as if from L *ad-* to, toward] —**in advance** 1 In front. 2 Before due; beforehand. —**ad·vanc′er** *n.*

ad·vanced (ad·vanst′, -vänst′) *adj.* 1 Being ranged at the front, or in advance of others, as in progress or thought: *advanced* ideas. 2 Having arrived at a somewhat late or forward stage, as of life, time, etc.: an *advanced* age.

ad·vance·ment (ad·vans′mənt, -väns′-) *n.* 1 The act of advancing, or the state of being advanced; progression; furtherance; promotion; preferment; uplift: the *advancement* of knowledge. 2 A payment of money before it is due.

ad·vanc·ing (ad·vans′ing, -väns′-) *adj.* Forward-moving; increasing; progressive. —**ad·vanc′ing·ly** *adv.*

ad·van·tage (ad·van′tij, -vän′-) *n.* 1 Anything favorable to success; superiority; favoring circumstance. 2 Gain or benefit; profit. See synonyms under PROFIT, RIGHT, UTILITY, VICTORY. —**to advantage** So as to reveal the best of or bring about the best results. —*v.t.* **·taged**, **·tag·ing** To give advantage or profit to; be a benefit or service to. [< OF *avantage* < *avant* before < L *ab ante* from before. See ADVANCE.]

ad·van·ta·geous (ad′vən·tā′jəs) *adj.* Affording advantage; profitable; favorable; beneficial. See synonyms under EXPEDIENT, GOOD. —**ad′van·ta′geous·ly** *adv.* —**ad′van·ta′geous·ness** *n.*

ad·vent (ad′vent) *n.* A coming or arrival, as of any important event or person. [< L *adventus*, pp. of *advenire* < *ad-* to + *venire* come]

Ad·vent (ad′vent) *n.* 1 The birth of Christ. 2 The second coming of Christ. 3 The season including the four Sundays before Christmas.

ad·ven·ti·ti·a (ad′ven·tish′ē·ə) *n.* The outermost covering of an organ or a blood vessel, composed of extrinsic connective tissue. —**ad′ven·ti′tial** *adj.*

ad·ven·ti·tious (ad′ven·tish′əs) *adj.* 1 Not inherent; extrinsic; accidental; casual. 2 Accidental; acquired, not inherited. 3 *Biol.* **a** Occurring in an unusual location: an *adventitious* root. **b** Adventitial. **c** Adventive. [< L *adventicius* coming from abroad, foreign. See ADVENT.] —**ad′ven·ti′tious·ly** *adv.* —**ad′ven·ti′tious·ness** *n.*

ad·ven·tive (ad·ven′tiv) *adj. Biol.* Exotic; not firmly established in a new environment. —*n.* An adventive organism.

Advent Sunday The Sunday nearest to St. Andrew's Day, the last day of November.

ad·ven·ture (ad·ven′chər) *v.* **·tured**, **·tur·ing** *v.t.* 1 To venture upon; take the chance of. 2 To risk the loss of; imperil. —*v.i.* 3 To run risks. 4 To venture upon daring or dangerous undertakings. —*n.* 1 A hazardous or exciting experience; daring feat. 2 A commercial venture; speculation. 3 *Obs.* Danger; hazard; chance; fortune. See synonyms under ACCIDENT. [< OF *aventure* < L *adventura (res)* (a thing) about to happen < *advenire*. See ADVENT.]

ad·ven·tur·er (ad·ven′chər·ər) *n.* A seeker of adventures or fortune in new fields or by questionable means.

ad·ven·tur·ous (ad·ven′chər·əs) *adj.* 1 Disposed to seek adventures or take risks; venturesome. Also **ad·ven′ture·some** (-səm). 2 Attended with risk; hazardous. See synonyms under BRAVE. —**ad·ven′tur·ous·ly** *adv.* —**ad·ven′tur·ous·ness** *n.*

ad·verb (ad′vûrb) *n.* 1 Any of a class of words used to modify the meaning of a verb, adjective, or other adverb, in regard to time, place, manner, means, cause, degree, etc.: one of the eight traditional parts of speech. 2 Any word or phrase having this function. [< L *adverbium* < *ad-* to + *verbum* verb]

ad·ver·bi·al (ad·vûr′bē·əl) *adj.* Of, pertaining to, containing, used like an adverb, or tending to use adverbs. —**ad·ver′bi·al·i·ty** (ad·vûr′bē·al′ə·tē) *n.* —**ad·ver′bi·al·ly** *adv.*

ad·ver·sar·y (ad′vər·ser′ē) *n. pl.* **·sar·ies** One actively hostile; an opponent; enemy. See synonyms under ANTAGONIST, ENEMY. —**the Adversary** Satan. [< L *adversarius*, lit., one turned towards < *adversus*. See ADVERSE.]

ad·ver·sa·tive (ad·vûr′sə·tiv) *adj.* Expressing opposition or antithesis. —*n.* An antithetic word or proposition. —**ad·ver′sa·tive·ly** *adv.*

ad·verse (ad·vûrs′, ad′vûrs) *adj.* 1 Opposing or opposed; antagonistic; also, unpropitious; detrimental. 2 *Bot.* Turned toward the stem or main axis. 3 Opposite. See synonyms under INIMICAL. [< L *adversus* turned against, pp. of *advertere* < *ad-* to + *vertere* turn] —**ad·verse′ly** *adv.* —**ad·verse′ness** *n.*

ad·ver·si·ty (ad·vûr′sə·tē) *n. pl.* **·ties** A condition of hardship or affliction; misfortune; calamity. See synonyms under CATASTROPHE, MISFORTUNE. [< OF *aversite* < L *adversitas* < *adversus*. See ADVERSE.]

ad·vert (ad·vûrt′) *v.i.* To turn the attention; take notice; refer: with *to*. See synonyms under ALLUDE. [< L *advertere* < *ad-* to + *vertere* turn] —**ad·ver′tence**, **ad·ver′ten·cy** *n.*

ad·ver·tent (ad·vûr′tənt) *adj.* Giving attention;

heedful. —**ad·ver'tent·ly** *adv.*

ad·ver·tise (ad'vər·tīz, ad'vər·tīz') *v.* **·tised**, **·tis·ing** *v.t.* **1** To make known by public notice; to proclaim the qualities of, as by publication or broadcasting, generally in order to sell. **2** *Obs.* To notify or warn. —*v.i.* **3** To inquire by public notice, as in a newspaper: with *for:* to *advertise* for a house. **4** To distribute or publish advertisements: The company *advertised* widely in national magazines. See synonyms under AN-NOUNCE, INFORM, PUBLISH. Also **ad'ver·tize**. [< MF *advertiss-*, stem of *advertir* warn, give notice to < L *advertere*. See ADVERT.] —**ad'ver·tis'er** *n.*

ad·ver·tise·ment (ad'vər·tīz'mənt, ad·vûr'tis·mənt, -tiz-) *n.* **1** A public notice, as in a newspaper or on a radio or television program. **2** A giving notice; notification; information. Also **ad'ver·tize'ment.**

ad·ver·tis·ing (ad'vər·tī'zing) *n.* **1** Any system or method of attracting public notice to an event to be attended, or the desirability of commercial products for sale; promotion; also, advertisements collectively. **2** The business of writing and publicizing advertisements; promoting. Also **ad'ver·tiz'ing.**

ad·ver·tor·i·al (ad·vər·tôr'ē·əl; -tō'rē-) *n.* An editorial that includes elements of a commercial advertising message. [Blend of ADVERT(ISING) + (EDIT)ORIAL]

ad·vice (ad·vīs') *n.* **1** Encouragement or dissuasion; counsel; suggestion. **2** *Often pl.* Information; notification. **3** *Obs.* Deliberation; forethought; hence, opinion. See synonyms under COUNSEL. [< OF *avis* view, opinion < L *ad-* to + *visum,* pp. of *videre* see]

ad·vis·a·ble (ad·vī'zə·bəl) *adj.* Proper to be advised or recommended; expedient. —**ad·vis'a·bil'i·ty, ad·vis'a·ble·ness** *n.* —**ad·vis'a·bly** *adv.*

ad·vise (ad·vīz') *v.* **ad·vised, ad·vis·ing** *v.t.* **1** To give advice to; counsel. **2** To recommend: to *advise* a course of action. **3** To notify; inform, as of a transaction. **4** *Obs.* To consider; observe. —*v.i.* **5** To take counsel: with *with:* He *advised* with his lawyer. **6** To give advice. See synonyms under ADMONISH, INFORM[1]. [< OF *aviser* < *avis.* See ADVICE.]

ad·vised (ad·vīzd') *adj.* **1** Done with advice or counsel, or with deliberation and forethought; intended; deliberate; prudent. **2** Counseled. **3** Informed. See synonyms under CONSCIOUS.

ad·vis·ed·ly (ad·vī'zid·lē) *adv.* With forethought or advice; not hastily.

ad·vise·ment (ad·vīz'mənt) *n.* Consultation; deliberation.

ad·vis·er (ad·vī'zər) *n.* One who advises; specifically, a teacher in a school or college to whom certain students are assigned for periodic counsel. Also **ad·vi'sor.**

ad·vi·so·ry (ad·vī'zər·ē) *adj.* Having power to advise; containing or given as advice; not mandatory. —*n.* **1** A bulletin or report that advises about certain developments: a weather *advisory.* **2** A recommendation.

ad·vo·ca·cy (ad'və·kə·sē) *n.* The act of advocating or pleading a cause; a vindication; defense.

ad·vo·cate (ad'və·kāt) *v.t.* **·cat·ed, ·cat·ing** To speak or write in favor of; defend; recommend. [< *n.*] —*n.* (ad'və·kit, -kāt) One who pleads the cause of another; an intercessor; defender; counselor. See synonyms under PLEAD. [< OF *avocat* < L *advocatus* one summoned to another < *advocare* < *ad-* to + *vocare* call] —**ad'vo·ca'tor** *n.* —**ad·voc·a·to·ry** (ad·vok'ə·tôr'ē, -tō'rē) *adj.*

ad·y·tum (ad'ə·təm) *n. pl.* **·ta** (-tə) **1** An inner or secret shrine in some ancient places of worship. **2** Hence, a sanctum. [< L < Gk. *adyton,* neut. of *adytos* not to be entered < *a- no* + *dyein* enter]

adze (adz) *n.* A hand cutting tool having its blade at right angles with its handle and usually curved: used for dressing timber, etc. —*v.t.* **adzed, adz·ing** To hew or dress with an adze. Also **adz.** [OE *adesa*]

ADZES
a. Sculptor's. *b.* Cooper's.
c. Carpenter's.

---

ae- For words not found here, see under E-.

æ 1 A digraph of Latin origin, equivalent to Greek *ai:* sometimes retained in the spelling of Greek and Latin proper names and used in certain scientific terms. **2** A digraph in Old English, symbolizing the sound of *a* in *hat.* Also printed as **ae.**

Ae·ae·a (ē·ē'ə) A legendary island between Italy and Sicily, mentioned in the *Odyssey* as the home of Circe. Also **Æ·æ'a.** —**Ae·ae'an** *adj.*

Ae·ge·an (i·jē'ən) *adj.* Of or pertaining to the Aegean Islands or the Aegean Sea; specifically, of or pertaining to the ancient civilization of this region: also *Egean.* Also **Æ·ge'an.**

Aegean Islands The islands of Asia Minor north of the Dodecanese Islands, comprising an administrative division of Greece; 1,506 square miles; capital, Mytilene, on Lesbos.

Aegean Sea An arm of the Mediterranean Sea between Greece and Asia Minor.

Ae·geus (ē'jōōs, ē'jē·əs) In Greek mythology, a king of Athens, father of Theseus. Also **Æ'geus.**

Ae·gid·i·us (ē·jid'i·ē·əs) Latin form of GILES. Also **Æ·gid'i·us.**

Æ·gir (ē'jər, ā'jər) The Norse god of the sea. Also **Æ'ger.** [< ON]

ae·gis (ē'jis) *n.* **1** In Greek mythology, an attribute of Zeus used in various forms by several other gods, as Athena's goatskin cloak bearing Medusa's head. **2** Any shield or defensive armor. **3** A protecting influence or power; sponsorship: also spelled *egis.* Also **æ'gis.**

Ae·ne·as (i·nē'əs) In Greek and Roman legend, a Trojan, son of Anchises and Venus, hero of the *Aeneid:* after the sack of Troy he wandered for seven years before reaching Latium where he founded the city of Lavinium. See ASCANIUS, DIDO. Also **Æ·ne'as.**

Ae·ne·id (i·nē'id) *n.* A Latin epic poem by Vergil narrating the adventures of Aeneas. Also **Æ·ne'id.**

aer- Var. of AERO-.

aer·ate (âr'āt, ā'ə·rāt) *v.t.* **·at·ed, ·at·ing 1** To supply or charge with air or gas. **2** To purify by exposure to air. **3** To oxygenate, as blood. [< AER- + -ATE[2]] —**aer·a'tion** *n.*

aer·a·tor (âr'ā·tər, ā'ə·rā'tər) *n.* **1** An apparatus for charging liquids with gas under pressure. **2** A device for supplying a stream of gas or air, as for fumigating, destroying fungi, etc.

aeri- Var. of AERO-.

aer·i·al (âr'ē·əl, ā·ir'ē·əl) *adj.* **1** Of or in the air. **2** Like air; atmospheric. **3** *Bot.* Growing or living in the air and not in the soil or in water. **4** Airy; insubstantial; spiritual. **5** Existing or performed in the air. **6** Of, by, or for aircraft: *aerial* bombardment. See synonyms under AIRY. —*n.* (âr'ē·əl) An antenna, as in television and radio. [< L *aerius* airy < *aer* air] —**aer'i·al·ly** *adv.*

aer·i·al·ist (âr'ē·əl·ist, ā·ir'ē·əl-) *n.* One who performs feats of skill in the air, as a tightrope walker, trapeze artist, etc.

aer·i·al·i·ty (âr'ē·əl'ə·tē, ā·ir'ē-) *n.* Tenuity, or want of substance; airiness.

aer·ie (âr'ē, ir'ē) *n.* **1** The nest of a predatory bird, as the eagle, on a crag. **2** The brood or young of such a bird. Also spelled *aery, eyry, eyrie.* [< Med.L *aeria* < OF *aire,* ? < L *area* open space] —**aer'ied** *adj.*

aer·if·er·ous (âr·if'ər·əs, ā'ə·rif'-) *adj.* Containing or conveying air. [< AERI- + -FEROUS]

aer·i·fi·ca·tion (âr'ə·fi·kā'shən, ā'ə·rə-) *n.* **1** The act or process of converting into air, gas, or vapor; the process of becoming air, gas, or vapor. **2** Purification by exposure to air; aeration. Also **aer'i·fac'tion.**

aer·i·form (âr'ə·fôrm, ā'ə·rə·fôrm') *adj.* Like air; gaseous; unsubstantial; intangible.

aer·i·fy (âr'ə·fī, ā'ə·rə·fī) *v.t.* **·fied, ·fy·ing 1** To aerate. **2** To change into a gaseous form.

---

aero- *combining form* **1** Air; of the air: *aerobiology.* **2** Of aircraft or flying: *aeromarine.* **3** Gas; of gases: *aerogen.* Also *aer-, aeri-.* [< Gk. *aēr* air]

aer·o·al·ler·gen (âr'ō·al'ər·jən, ā'ər·ō-) *n.* An airborne substance that is capable of producing an allergenic response in a sensitized subject. —**aer'o·al·ler·gen'ic** *adj.*

aer·o·bal·lis·tics (âr'ō·bə·lis'tiks, ā'ər·ō-) *n.* The ballistics of missiles dropped, launched, or fired from aircraft in flight. —**aer'o·bal·lis'tic** *adj.*

aer·o·bat·ics (âr'ə·bat'iks, ā'ər·ō-) *n.* Aerial maneuvers which are not necessary to normal flight voluntarily performed in aircraft; trick or stunt flying. [< AERO- + (ACRO)BATICS]

aer·obe (âr'ōb, ā'ər·ōb) *n.* A microorganism that can live only in the presence of free oxygen: opposed to *anaerobe.* [< AERO- + Gk. *bios* life]

aer·o·bic (âr·ō'bik, ā·ə·rō'-) *adj.* **1** Living in air. **2** Pertaining to aerobics. —**aer·o'bi·cal·ly** *adv.*

aer·o·bics (âr·ō'biks, ā'ər·ō-) *n. pl.* A system of calisthenics and other strenuous physical activities designed to improve the functioning of the lungs and heart by speeding up oxygen consumption and circulation.

aer·o·dy·nam·ics (âr'ō·dī·nam'iks, ā'ər·ō-) *n.* The branch of physics that treats of the laws of motion of gases, especially atmospheric, under the influence of gravity and other mechanical forces, and of the mechanical effects produced by such motion. —**aer'o·dy·nam'ic** *adj.*

aer·om·e·try (âr·om'ə·trē, ā·ə·rom'-) *n.* The science of weighing and measuring air and other gases. —**aer·o·met·ric** (âr'ə·met'rik, ā'ər·ə-) *adj.*

aer·o·naut (âr'ə·nôt, ā'ər·ō-) *n.* **1** One who navigates the air; a balloonist or aviator. **2** A space traveler. [< F *aéronaute* < Gk. *aēr* air + *nautēs* sailor]

aer·o·nau·tic (âr'ə·nô'tik, ā'ər·ō-) *adj.* **1** Pertaining to, floating in, or navigating the air. **2** Pertaining to aeronautics. Also **aer·o·nau'ti·cal.**

aer·o·nau·tics (âr'ə·nô'tiks, ā'ər·ō-) *n.* **1** The science or art of navigating aircraft. **2** That branch of engineering which deals with the design, construction, operation, and performance characteristics of aircraft.

aer·on·o·my (âr·on'ə·mē, ā'ər·on'-) *n.* The scientific study of the physics and chemistry of the earth or other orbiting body. —**aer'o·nom'·i·cal** *adj.*

aer·o·pha·gi·a (âr'ə·fā'jē·ə, ā'ər·ə-) *n. Med.* The swallowing of air.

aer·o·pho·bi·a (âr'ə·fō'bē·ə, ā'ər·ə-) *n.* **1** A morbid fear of fresh air and of airborne infection. **2** A morbid fear of flying. **3** *Biol.* Movement of an organism away from air or oxygen.

aer·o·phys·ics (âr'ō·fiz'iks, ā'ər·ō-) *n.* Physical science considered with reference to the design, construction, and operation of aircraft, rockets, guided missiles, etc.: the physics of aeronautics and aviation.

aer·o·sid·er·ite (âr'ō·sid'ə·rīt, ā'ər·ō-) *n.* A meteorite of which iron is the chief constituent.

aer·o·sid·er·o·lite (âr'ō·sid'ər·ə·līt', ā'ər·ō-) *n.* A meteorite that is both metallic and stony.

aer·o·sol (âr'ə·sōl, -sol, ā'ər·ə-) *n.* **1** A colloidal dispersion of solid or liquid particles in a gaseous medium. **2** A substance packaged under pressure along with a volatile propellant which, upon release through a nozzle, disperses fine particles of the substance in the air. —*adj.* Pertaining to, resembling, dispensing, or dispensed as an aerosol. Also **aer'o·sol'ic.** [< AERO- + SOL(UTION)]

aer·o·space (âr'ō·spās, ā'ər·ō-) *n.* **1** The earth's atmosphere and outer space, considered as a single region in the operation of rockets, guided missiles, and spacecraft. **2** The study and investigation of this region, especially with reference to space travel.

aer·o·sphere (âr'ə·sfir, ā'ər·ə-) *n.* The entire atmosphere considered as a single gaseous shell surrounding the earth.

aer·o·stat (âr'ə·stat, ā'ər·ə-) *n.* Any aircraft which is lighter than air, as a balloon or dirigible. [< F *aérostat* < Gk *aēr* air + *statos* standing]

---

add,āce,câre,pälm; end,ēven; it,īce; odd,ōpen,ôrder; tŏŏk,pōŏl; up,bûrn; ə = a in *above,* e in *sicken,* i in *clarity,* o in *melon,* u in *focus* ; yōō = u in *fuse,* oi,oil; ou,pout; ch,check; g,go; ng,ring; th,thin; th,this; zh,vision. Foreign sounds â,œ,ü,kh,ṅ; and ♦: see page xx. < from; + plus; ? possibly.

—**aer·o·stat·ic** or **·i·cal** *adj.*

aer·o·stat·ics (âr'ə-stat'iks, ā'ər-ə-) *n.* **1** The branch of physics that treats of the mechanical properties of air and gases not in motion. **2** The art and science of operating lighter-than-air aircraft, as balloons and dirigibles: distinguished from *aviation.*

aer·o·sta·tion (âr'ə-stā'shən, ā'ər-ə-) *n.* **1** The art of raising and supporting bodies, as balloons, by means of fluids lighter than air: opposed to *aviation.* **2** *Obs.* Aerostatics. Compare AEROSTATICS.

aer·o·ther·mo·dy·nam·ics (âr'ō-thûr'mō-dī-nam'iks, ā'ər-ō-) *n.* The branch of thermodynamics that deals with the relations between heat and mechanical energy in gases, especially in their applications to changes induced by the motions of bodies in the medium.

aer·y[1] (âr'ē, ā'ər-ē) *adj.* Airy; aerial.

aer·y[2] (âr'ē, ir'ē) See AERIE.

Aes·chy·le·an (es'kə-lē'ən) *adj.* Similar to, or in the style of, the tragedies of Aeschylus; hence, majestic; stately. Also **Æs'chy·le'an.**

Aes·chy·lus (es'kə-ləs), 525–456 B.C., Greek tragic dramatist. Also **Æs'chy·lus.**

Ae·sop (ē'səp, ē'sop) Greek author of fables, sixth century B.C. Also **Æ'sop.**

aes·thete (es'thēt), **aes·thet·ic** (es·thet'ik) See ESTHETE, etc.

af- Assimilated var. of AD-.

a·far (ə-fär') *adv.* At, from, or to a distance; remotely. [< A-[1] on + FAR]

a·feard (ə-fird') *adj. Dial.* Afraid; fearful. Also **a·feared'.**

a·fe·brile (ā-fē'brəl, ā-feb'rəl) *adj.* Free from fever.

af·fa·ble (af'ə-bəl) *adj.* **1** Easy and courteous in manner; approachable. **2** Benign; mild. See synonyms under BLAND, FRIENDLY. [< F < L *affabilis,* lit., able to be spoken to < *affari* < *ad-* to + *fari* speak] —**af'fa·bil'i·ty, af'fa·ble·ness** *n.* —**af'fa·bly** *adv.*

af·fair (ə-fâr') *n.* **1** Anything done or to be done; business; concern: often in plural. **2** An unimportant event, as a skirmish; matter; thing. **3** A vague or indefinite object or fact: The first ship was a rude *affair.* **4** See LOVE AFFAIR. See synonyms under BATTLE, BUSINESS, TRANSACTION. [< OF *afaire* < *a faire* to do < L *ad* to + *facere* do]

af·fect[1] (ə-fekt') *v.t.* **1** To act upon or have an effect upon; impress; influence. **2** To touch or move emotionally. **3** To attack or attaint: A disease *affects* the body. See synonyms under CONCERN, INFLUENCE. Compare EFFECT. — *n.* **1** (af'ekt) *Psychol.* **a** That which tends to arouse emotion rather than to stimulate thought or perception. **b** The diffuse mental condition thus produced. **c** The fundamental controlling element in an emotional state. **2** *Obs.* Inward disposition; inclination. [< L *afficere* influence, attack < *ad-* to + *facere* do; def 1 of noun < G *affekt*]

af·fect[2] (ə-fekt') *v.t.* **1** To have a liking for; show a preference for; fancy: to *affect* large hats. **2** To imitate or counterfeit for effect; make a show of one's liking or aptitude for: to *affect* a British accent; to *affect* omniscience. **3** To tend toward naturally; haunt; frequent: said of animals and plants. **4** *Obs.* To aim at; to aspire for or to. See synonyms under ASSUME, LIKE, PRETEND. [< F *affecter* < L *affectare* aim at, freq. of *afficere.* See AFFECT[1].]

af·fec·ta·tion (af'ek·tā'shən) *n.* **1** A studied pretense; shallow display: with *of:* an *affectation* of wealth. **2** Artificiality of manner or behavior; affectedness. See synonyms under HYPOCRISY, PRETENSE. [< L *affectatio, -onis* < *affectare.* See AFFECT[2].]

af·fect·ed[1] (ə-fek'tid) *adj.* **1** Acted upon, as by a drug. **2** Moved emotionally; influenced. **3** Attacked, as by disease; diseased. **4** *Math.* Adfected. [pp. of AFFECT[1]]

af·fect·ed[2] (ə-fek'tid) *adj.* **1** Assumed falsely or in outward semblance only; showing affectation. **2** Having a liking, inclination, or affection; inclined. **3** Fondly cherished; loved; frequented. See synonyms under FACTITIOUS, SQUEAMISH. [pp. of AFFECT[2]] —**af·fect'ed·ly** *adv.* —**af·fect'ed·ness** *n.*

af·fect·ing[1] (ə-fek'ting) *adj.* Having power to

move the feelings; pathetic. —**af·fect'ing·ly** *adv.*

af·fect·ing[2] (ə-fek'ting) *adj. Obs.* **1** Showing love. **2** Pretending; falsely displaying.

af·fec·tion (ə-fek'shən) *n.* **1** Often *pl.* Good disposition, as towards another; fond attachment; kind feelings: usually distinguished from *love* as less powerful or intense. **2** Often *pl.* A mental state brought about by any influence; an emotion or feeling: to influence men by playing on their *affections.* **3** An abnormal state of the body; disease. **4** The act of affecting or influencing or the state of being influenced. **5** A property or attribute: Thought is said to be an *affection* of matter. **6** *Psychol.* Conscious perception of feeling or emotion: distinguished from *cognition.* **7** *Obs.* Constitutional inclination; tendency. See synonyms under ATTACHMENT, FRIENDSHIP, LOVE, INFLUENCE, DISEASE.

af·fec·tion·al (ə-fek'shən·əl) *adj.* Of or pertaining to affections. —**af·fec'tion·al·ly** *adv.*

af·fec·tion·ate (ə-fek'shən·it) *adj.* **1** Having or expressing love; loving; fond. **2** *Obs.* Favorably inclined. See synonyms under FRIENDLY. —**af·fec'tion·ate·ly** *adv.* —**af·fec'tion·ate·ness** *n.*

af·fec·tive (ə-fek'tiv) *adj.* **1** Pertaining to or exciting affection; emotional or stirring emotion. **2** *Psychol.* Pertaining to or arising from feeling or emotional reactions rather than from thought.

af·fec·tiv·i·ty (af'ek·tiv'ə·tē) *n. Psychol.* The relative intensity of response to a feeling or emotion.

af·fect·less (ə-fekt'lis) *adj.* Unfeeling; unemotional. —**af·fect'less·ly** *adv.* —**af·fect'less·ness** *n.*

af·fer·ent (af'ər·ənt) *adj.* Conducting inward, or toward the center: said of those nerve processes which transmit sensory stimuli from receptor organs to the central nervous system: opposed to *efferent.* [< L *afferens, -entis,* ppr. of *afferre* < *ad-* to + *ferre* bear]

af·fi·ance (ə-fī'əns) *v.t.* **·anced, ·anc·ing 1** To promise in marriage; betroth. **2** *Archaic* To pledge. —*n.* **1** A betrothal; pledge of faith. **2** *Obs.* Confidence. [< OF *afiancer* < *afiance* trust, confidence < *after* trust < Med.L *affidare* < L *ad-* to + *fidus* faithful]

af·fi·da·vit (af'ə·dā'vit) *n.* **1** A voluntary sworn declaration, in writing, made before competent authority. **2** Any solemn or formal declaration. [< Med.L, he has stated on oath, perfect tense of *affidare.* See AFFIANCE.]

af·fil·i·ate (ə-fil'ē-āt) *v.* **·at·ed, ·at·ing** *v.t.* **1** To associate or unite, as a member or branch to a larger or principal body: with *to* or *with.* **2** To join or associate (oneself): with *with.* **3** To receive as a child; adopt. **4** To fix the legal paternity of. **5** To determine relations of, as the sources or branches of a field of study. —*v.i.* **6** To associate or ally oneself: with *with.* —*adj.* Affiliated. —*n.* Something affiliated. [< L *affiliatus,* pp. of *affiliare* adopt < *ad-* to + *filius* son]

af·fil·i·a·tion (ə-fil'ē·ā'shən) *n.* **1** The act of affiliating, or the state of being affiliated; association; friendly relationship; connection; adoption. **2** Combination; union.

af·fine (ə-fīn') *n. Obs.* **1** A relative by marriage. **2** A kinsman. [< F *affin* < L *affinis.* See AFFINITY.]

af·fined (ə-fīnd') *adj.* **1** Joined by artificial ties; allied; related by marriage. **2** *Obs.* Under obligation, due to some close relation. [< F *affiné* related < *affin.* See AFFINE.]

af·fin·i·ty (ə-fin'ə·tē) *n. pl.* **·ties 1** Any natural drawing or inclination; close relation or agreement. **2** *Biol.* A structural or physiologic likeness in different organisms indicative of a common origin. **3** Structural likenesses indicating a common origin, as in languages. **4** *Chem.* The force of attraction by which differing chemical elements unite to form compounds. **5** Connection through certain relations formed, as by church or state; especially, relationship through marriage (as opposed to blood relationship). **6** A Platonic or spiritual attraction held to exist between certain persons, especially between those of opposite sexes; also, the person exerting such attraction. [< L *affinitas, -tatis* < *affinis* adjacent, related < *ad-* to + *finis* end]

Synonyms: alliance, analogy, birth, blood, consanguinity, descent, family, kin, kind, kindred, race, relationship. *Kind* is broader than *kin,* denoting the most general *relationship,* as one of

the whole human species in man*kind,* human*kind,* etc.; *kin* and *kindred* denote direct *relationship* that can be traced through either blood or marriage, especially the former; either of these words may signify collectively all persons of the same blood or members of the same family, relatives or relations. *Affinity* is *relationship* by marriage, *consanguinity* is *relationship* by blood. *Antonyms:* See ANTIPATHY.

af·firm (ə-fûrm') *v.t.* **1** To declare or state positively; assert and maintain to be true; aver. **2** To confirm or ratify, as a judgment or law. —*v.i.* **3** *Law* To make a formal judicial declaration, but not under oath. [< OF *afermer* < L *affirmare* < *ad-* to + *firmare* make firm < *firmus* strong] —**af·firm'a·ble** *adj.* —**af·firm'a·bly** *adv.* —**af·firm'ance** *n.* —**af·firm'ant** *adj. & n.* —**af·firm'er** *n.*

Synonyms: assert, asseverate, aver, declare, depose, endorse, maintain, predicate, propound, protest, state, swear, tell, testify. *Affirm* has less of egotism than *assert,* more solemnity than *declare,* and more composure than *asseverate,* which is to *assert* emphatically. In legal usage, *affirm* differs from *swear* in not invoking the name of God. See ALLEGE, ASSERT, STATE. *Antonyms:* contradict, deny, dispute, gainsay, negative, oppose, refute.

af·fir·ma·tion (af'ər·mā'shən) *n.* **1** The act of affirming, or that which is affirmed. **2** A declaration; statement; predication. **3** A solemn declaration made before a competent officer, in place of a judicial oath. **4** Confirmation; ratification. See synonyms under TESTIMONY.

af·firm·a·tive (ə-fûr'mə·tiv) *adj.* **1** Characterized by affirmation; asserting that the fact is so; ratifying; confirmative. **2** *Math.* Positive; affirmative quantity. Also **af·firm·a·to·ry** (ə-fûr'mə·tôr'ē, -tō're). —*n.* **1** A word or expression of affirmation or assent; that which affirms or asserts: to answer in the *affirmative.* **2** That side in a debate which affirms the proposition debated.

af·firm·a·tive·ly (ə-fûr'mə·tiv·lē) *adv.* In an affirmative manner; positively; on the affirmative side.

af·fix (ə-fiks') *v.t.* **1** To fix or attach; fasten, as a seal; append, as a signature at the end of a document. **2** To connect with or lay upon, as blame, responsibility, etc. See synonyms under ADD. — *n.* (af'iks) **1** That which is attached, appended, or added. **2** *Ling.* A prefix, suffix, or infix. [< L *affixus,* pp. of *affigere* < *ad-* to + *figere* fasten]

af·flict (ə-flikt') *v.t.* **1** To distress with continued suffering; trouble. **2** *Obs.* To cast down; overthrow. See synonyms under CHASTEN, HURT. [< obs. afflict, adj., afflicted < L *afflictus,* pp. of *affligere* dash against, strike down < *ad-* to + *fligere* dash, strike]

af·flic·tion (ə-flik'shən) *n.* **1** The state of being afflicted; sore distress of body or mind. **2** That which causes great suffering or distress; misfortune; calamity. See synonyms under GRIEF, MISFORTUNE.

af·flic·tive (ə-flik'tiv) *adj.* Causing or involving pain or distress; grievous. See synonyms under TROUBLESOME. —**af·flic'tive·ly** *adv.*

af·flu·ence (af'lōō·əns) *n.* **1** A profuse or abundant supply, as of riches; wealth; abundance; opulence. **2** A flowing toward; concourse. [< F < L *affluentia* < *affluere.* See AFFLUENT.]

af·flu·ent (af'lōō·ənt) *adj.* **1** Abounding; abundant. **2** Wealthy; opulent. **3** Flowing freely; fluent. See synonyms under AMPLE. —*n.* A stream that flows into another; a tributary. [< L *affluens, -entis,* ppr. of *affluere* < *ad-* to + *fluere* flow] —**af'flu·ent·ly** *adv.*

af·flux (af'luks) *n.* A flowing toward a point, as blood to a tissue or organ; congestion. Also **af·flux'ion.** [< Med.L *affluxus* < *affluere.* See AFFLUENT.]

af·force (ə-fôrs', ə-fōrs') *v.t.* **af·forced, af·forc·ing** To reinforce, as a jury by the addition of new members. [< OF *aforcer* < L *ex* out + *fortis* strong] —**af·force'ment** *n.*

af·ford (ə-fôrd', ə-fōrd') *v.t.* **1** To have sufficient means for; be able to meet the expense of: Can you *afford* to go to Europe? **2** To incur without detriment: He can *afford* to suffer now. **3** To produce or furnish, as in behalf of; confer, as pleasure or profit: It *affords* me great delight to tell you this. [OE *geforthian* further, promote] —**af·ford'a·ble** *adj.*

af·fran·chise (ə·fran′chīz) *v.t.* **·chised, ·chis·ing** To enfranchise; liberate. [< F *affranchiss*-, stem of *affranchir* < *à* to + *franchir* free. See FRAN-CHISE.]

af·fray (ə·frā′) *n.* **1** A public brawl or fight; a disturbance of the peace. **2** *Law* The fighting in public of two or more persons in a manner that will naturally produce terror in others. See synonyms under ALTERCATION, QUARREL. —*v.t.* *Archaic* To cause to feel sudden fear; terrify; startle. [< OF *effrei, esfrei,* ult. < L *ex*- out + a Gmc. word for "peace" (cf. OHG *fridu*)]

af·fri·cate (af′ri·kit) *n.* *Phonet.* A complex sound consisting of a stop followed by the fricative release of breath at the point of contact, as *ch* (t + sh) in *church.* [< L *affricatus,* pp. of *affricare* < *ad*- against + *fricare* rub] —**af·fric·a·tive** (ə·frik′ə·tiv) *adj., n.*

af·fright (ə·frīt′) *Obs. v.t.* To strike with sudden fear; frighten. See synonyms under FRIGHTEN. —*n.* Sudden fear; also, a cause of terror. See synonyms under ALARM, FEAR, FRIGHT. [OE *āfyrhtan*] —**af·fright′ment** *n.*

af·front (ə·frunt′) *v.t.* **1** To insult openly; treat with insolence; offend by word or act. **2** To confront in defiance; accost. **3** *Archaic* To front in position; face toward. —*n.* **1** An open insult or indignity. **2** *Obs.* A meeting. See synonyms under OUTRAGE. [< OF *afronter* strike on the forehead < LL *affrontare* strike against < L *ad*- to + *frons* forehead] —**af·front′er** *n.* —**af·fron′tive** *adj.*

Synonyms (verb) : aggravate, annoy, displease, exasperate, insult, irritate, offend, provoke, tease, vex, wound. *Aggravate* in the sense of *offend* is not in approved use. To *provoke,* literally to call out or challenge, is to begin a contest; one *provokes* another to violence. To *affront* is to offer some defiant offense or indignity, as it were to one's face. Compare PIQUE¹. *Antonyms* : conciliate, content, gratify, honor, please.

af·fuse (ə·fyo͞oz′) *v.t.* **af·fused, af·fus·ing** *Archaic.* To pour on, as water. [< L *affusus,* pp. of *affundere* < *ad*-to + *fundere* pour]

af·fu·sion (ə·fyo͞o′zhən) *n.* A pouring on or into; a sprinkling, as in baptism.

af·ghan (af′gən, -gan) *n.* A soft wool coverlet, knitted or crocheted, often in many-colored geometrical patterns.

Af·ghan (af′gən, -gan) *n.* **1** A native of Afghanistan. **2** The dominant language of Afghanistan: also called *Pushtu.* **3** An Afghan hound. —*adj.* Of or pertaining to Afghanistan, its inhabitants, or their language.

Af·ghan·i·stan (af·gan′ə·stan) An independent country of south central Asia; 250,000 square miles; capital, Kabul.

a·fi·cio·na·do (ə·fish′ə·nä′dō, ə·fis′ē-, ə·fē′sē·ə-, *Sp.* ä·fē·thyō·nä′thō, -fē·syō-) *n. pl.* **·dos** (-dōz, *Sp.* -thōs) An avid follower or fan, as of a sport or activity; devotee: an *aficionado* of horse racing. [< Sp.]

a·field (ə·fēld′) *adv.* **1** In or to the field; abroad. **2** Off the track; astray.

a·fire (ə·fir′) *adv. & adj.* On fire.

a·flame (ə·flām′) *adv. & adj.* Flaming; glowing.

af·la·tox·in (af′lə·tok′sən) *n.* Any of several toxic carcinogens produced by certain strains of a fungus (*Aspergillus flavus*) growing on peanuts, corn, beans, etc.

AFL-CIO A United States labor organization with a membership of 16 million workers, created in 1955 as a result of a merger between the *American Federation of Labor* and the *Congress of Industrial Organizations.*

a·float (ə·flōt′) *adv. & adj.* **1** Floating on the surface of a liquid or a body of water. **2** Not aground or ashore. **2** In motion or circulation, as a rumor. **3** Adrift; unfixed. **4** Overflowed; flooded, as the deck of a ship.

a·foot (ə·fo͝ot′) *adv.* **1** On foot. **2** Able to walk. **3** In motion or progress; on the move; astir. [ME *on fot*]

a·fore (ə·fôr′, ə·fōr′) *adv., prep., & conj.* Before. [OE *onforan,* blended with *æt-foran* before. See ON, AT, and FORE.]

a·fore·hand (ə·fôr′hand′, ə·fōr′-) *adv. & adj.* Beforehand; prepared; supplied with what is needed for the future.

a·fore·said (ə·fôr′sed′, ə·fōr′-) *adj.* Said or mentioned before.

a·fore·thought (ə·fôr′thôt′, ə·fōr′-) *adj.* Intended; devised, contrived, or planned beforehand; premeditated. —*n.* Premeditation.

a·fore·time (ə·fôr′tīm′, ə·fōr′-) *adv.* At a previous time; formerly.

a·foul (ə·foul′) *adv. & adj.* In entanglement or collision; entangled. —**to run (or fall) afoul of** To become entangled with; get into difficulties with.

a·fraid (ə·frād′) *adj.* Filled with fear or apprehension; apprehensive; fearful. [Orig. pp. of AFFRAY]

A–frame (ā′frām′) *n.* A framework in the shape of the letter A, as that supporting a slanted roof.

a·fresh (ə·fresh′) *adv.* Once more; anew; again: We started *afresh.*

Af·ri·ca (af′ri·kə) *n.* The second largest continent, located in the eastern hemisphere south of Europe and joined to Asia by the Sinai peninsula; 11,500,000 square miles.

Af·ri·can (af′ri·kən) *adj.* Of or pertaining to Africa, to North (ancient) Africa, or to the black race, including the Negroes and Negritic groups of Africa. —*n.* **1** A native or naturalized inhabitant of Africa. **2** One of the African races; Negro.

African American *n.* An American of black African descent.

Af·ri·kaans (af′ri·käns′, -känz′) *n.* A South African language which developed from the speech of the 17th century Dutch settlers in this region, containing many words of English, French, and Malay origin: also called *Taal, South African Dutch, Cape Dutch.*

Afro- *combining form* Africa; African. [< L *Afer* an African]

aft (aft, äft) *adj.* Of or near the stern, or rear, of a vessel. —*adv.* Toward the rear; astern. [OE *æftan* behind]

af·ter (af′tər, äf′-) *adj.* **1** *Naut.* Farther aft; toward the stern. **2** Following in time or place; subsequent; later. —*adv.* **1** At a later time. **2** In the rear; behind. —*prep.* **1** In the rear of; farther back than; following: The prisoners followed *after* the soldiers. **2** Subsequently to; at a later period than: His will was read *after* his death. **3** In succession to; following repeatedly: the same routine day *after* day. **4** As a result of; subsequently to and because of: *After* their quarrel they decided to separate. **5** Notwithstanding; subsequently to and in spite of: *After* the best endeavors, one may fail. **6** Next below in order or importance: This man comes right *after* the king in power. **7** In search or pursuit of: to strive *after* wisdom. **8** According to the nature, wishes, or customs of; in conformity with: a man *after* my own heart. **9** In imitation of; in the manner of: a painting *after* Vermeer. **10** In honor, remembrance, or observance of: I was named *after* Lincoln. **11** In relation to; concerning: to inquire *after* someone's health. —*conj.* Following the time that: *After* I went home, I went to bed. [OE *æfter* behind]

af·ter·birth (af′tər·bûrth′, äf′-) *n.* The placenta and fetal membranes expelled from the uterus following delivery of mammalian offspring.

af·ter·burn·er (af′tər·bûr′nər, äf′-) *n. Aeron.* A device for injecting extra fuel into the exhaust system of a jet engine as a means of increasing the thrust.

af·ter·ef·fect (af′tər·ə·fekt′, äf′-) *n.* **1** An effect succeeding its cause after an interval. **2** A result following the initial effects of an agent, as a drug, X-rays, etc.

af·ter·glow (af′tər·glō′, äf′-) *n.* **1** A glow after a light has disappeared, as in metals cooling after being heated to incandescence or in the western sky after sunset. **2** The luminosity of a rarefied gas after the passage of an electric charge through it. **3** An agreeable feeling occurring after a pleasant or profitable experience.

af·ter·im·age (af′tər·im′ij, äf′-) *n.* **1** *Psychol.* The persistence of a visual sensation after the direct stimulus has been withdrawn from the retina. Also called *photogene.* **2** A similar effect of other senses.

af·ter·life (af′tər·līf′, äf′-) *n.* Life after death.

af·ter·math (af′tər·math, äf′-) *n.* **1** Results; consequences; especially, ill consequences. **2** *Agric.* The second grass crop of the season, after the first has been cut for hay; a second mowing. [< AFTER + MATH¹]

af·ter·most (af′tər·mōst, äf′-) *adj.* **1** *Naut.* Nearest the stern: also **aft′most. 2** Last.

af·ter·noon (af′tər·no͞on′, äf′-) *n.* That part of the day between noon and sunset; hence, the closing part: the *afternoon* of life. —*adj.* Of, for, or occurring in the afternoon.

af·ter·taste (af′tər·tāst′, äf′-) *n.* A taste persisting in the mouth, as after a meal.

af·ter·thought (af′tər·thôt′, äf′-) *n.* **1** A later or more deliberate thought, as after decision or action. **2** A thought occurring too late to affect action in the matter to which it refers.

af·ter·time (af′tər·tīm′, äf′-) *n.* Time following the present; the future.

af·ter·ward (af′tər·wərd, äf′-) *adv.* In time following; subsequently. Also **af′ter·wards.** [OE *æfterweard*]

af·ter·world (af′tər·wûrld′, äf′-) *n.* The future world; also, the world after death.

a·gain (ə·gen′, *esp. Brit.* ə·gān′) *adv.* **1** At a second or another time; once more; anew; afresh: to bring a subject to life *again.* **2** Once repeated: half as much *again.* **3** To the same place or over the same course; back, as in a previous condition: Here we are *again!* **4** In correspondence with something previous or preceding; in reply; in return: The valley echoed *again* to the sound of horns. **5** In the next place; further; moreover: *Again,* since the weather is uncertain, I may not be able to come. **6** On the other hand; from another point of view. [OE *ongegn*]

a·gainst (ə·genst′, *esp. Brit.* ə·gānst′) *prep.* **1** In contact with and pressing upon: leaning *against* the wall. **2** In collision with: The ship was dashed *against* the rocks. **3** In front of; directly opposite: *against* the background of the sky. **4** In anticipation of; in preparation for: to be ready *against* the third day; to hoard wealth *against* old age. **5** In opposition to; contrary to: *against* my wishes. **6** In hostility to: fighting *against* the invader. **7** To the debit of: Charge it *against* my account. **8** In comparison with; contrasted with: my word *against* his. [OE *ongegn* + *-es,* adverbial genitive suffix + inorganic *-t*]

A·ga Khan (ä′gə kän′) A hereditary Mohammedan title passing to the heads of families descended from Ali.
—**Aga Khan III,** 1877–1957, leader of Ismaelian Mohammedans, succeeding his father, Aga Khan II, in 1885.

Ag·a·mem·non (ag′ə·mem′non, -nən) In Greek legend, king of Mycenae, brother of Menelaus and father of Orestes, Electra, and Iphigenia: chief of the Greek army in the Trojan war, he was killed on his return by his wife Clytemnestra and her lover Aegisthus.

a·gape¹ (ə·gāp′, ə·gap′) *adv. & adj.* In a gaping state; gaping.

ag·a·pe² (ag′ə·pē) *n. pl.* **·pae** (-pē) The social meal or love feast of the primitive Christians which usually accompanied the Eucharist. [< Gk. *agapē* love]

a·gar (ä′gär, ā′gər, ä′gär) *n.* A gelatinous substance obtained from certain red algae and used as a gelling material in culture media and in the food industry. Also **a·gar-a·gar.** [< Malay *agar-agar*]

ag·ate (ag′it) *n.* **1** A variegated waxy quartz or chalcedony, SiO₂, in which the colors are usually in bands. **2** A child's playing marble. **3** *Printing* 5 1/2 point type. See TYPOGRAPHY. **4** Any of several instruments, as the drawplate of gold-wire drawers. **5** *Obs.* A very diminutive person; in allusion to the figures cut upon agates for rings. [< F < L *achates* < Gk. *achatēs* < *Achatēs,* a river in Sicily]

a·gaze (ə·gāz′) *adv.* In the posture or attitude of gazing.

age (āj) *n.* **1** The entire period of life or existence, as of a person, thing, nation, etc. **2** The period or stage of life as measured by the time already or previously passed. **3** The closing period of life; decline of life; the state of being old. **4** Any period of life that fits or unfits for any function, office, duty, etc.; specifically, that time of life at which one legally becomes mature, independent, and age responsible, usually 21 years; majority: used especially in the phrase **of age. 5** Any period of life naturally distinct; stage of life. **6** Any great and distinct period of time in the history of man, of the earth, etc.; era; epoch; generation. **7** A century. **8** A long time; protracted period: *He has been gone an age.* **9** In poker, the eldest hand. **10** *Psychol.* The physical and mental development of a person, measured in years, in relation to the normal physical and mental development of an average child. —*v.* **aged, ag·ing** or **age·ing** *v.t.* **1** To make or cause to grow old. **2** In dyeing, to fix and distribute the mordant in, as fabric, by exposure to air or chemicals. —*v.i.* **3** To assume or show some characteristics of age; ripen: *Tobacco ages in storing.* [< OF *aage* < L *aetas* age, a span of life]

-age *suffix of nouns* **1** Collection or aggregate of: *baggage, leafage.* **2** Condition, office, service, or other relation or connection of: *drayage; pilgrimage.* [< OF < L *-aticum*, neut. adj. suffix]

a·ged (ā′jid *for defs.* 1, 2, 4; ājd *for def.* 3) *adj.* **1** Advanced in years; very old. **2** Of, like, or characteristic of old age. **3** Of or at the age of: a child, *aged* five. **4** *Geol.* Nearing base level reduction: said of configuration of ground. See synonyms under ANCIENT. —**a′ged·ly** *adv.* — **a′ged·ness** *n.*

a·gee (ə·jē′) *adv. & adj.* Awry; askew. [< A-¹ + GEE²]

age·ing (ā′jing) See AGING.

age·ism (ā′jiz·əm) *n.* Discrimination or prejudice, esp. as directed against elderly people. — **age′ist** *n., adj.*

age·less (āj′lis) *adj.* **1** Not seeming to grow old. **2** Having no limits of duration.

age·long (āj′lông′, -long′) *adj.* Lasting a long time; everlasting: *agelong myths.*

a·gen·cy (ā′jən·sē) *n. pl.* **·cies 1** Active power or operation; activity. **2** Means; instrumentality. **3** The relation of an agent to his principal. **4** The business, office, or place of business, of an agent. **5** Any establishment where business is done for others. See synonyms under OPERATION. [< L *agentia* < *agere* do]

a·gen·da (ə·jen′də) *n. pl. of agendum* A record of things to be done, as items of business; a memorandum; specifically, a program of business to be done or papers to be read at a meeting: *What's on the agenda for today?*

a·gent (ā′jənt) *n.* **1** One who or that which acts or has power to act; an efficient cause of anything; actor; doer. **2** One who or that which acts for another; a factor; steward; deputy. **3** Any force or substance having power to effect a material change in bodies, as a chemical, drug, or earth movement. **4** A means by which something is done. **5** One who transacts business for another: *a literary agent.* **6** A traveling salesman or canvasser. —*adj. Obs.* Acting: opposed to *passive.* [< L *agens, agentis*, ppr. of *agere* do]

Synonyms (noun): actor, cause, doer, factor, instrument, means, mover, operator, performer, promoter. In strict philosophical usage, the prime *mover* or *doer* of an act is the *agent.* Thus we speak of man as a free *agent.* But in common usage, especially in business, an *agent* is not the prime *actor*, but only an *instrument* or *factor*, acting under orders or instructions. Compare CAUSE. *Antonyms:* chief, inventor, originator, principal.

a·gent pro·vo·ca·teur (ā·zhän′ prô·vô·kä·tœr′) *pl.* **a·gents pro·vo·ca·teurs** (ā·zhän′ prô·vô·kä·tœr′) *French* A secret agent implanted in an organization, as a trade union or political party, to incite its members to actions or declarations that will incur penalties or punishment.

age-old (āj′ōld′) *adj.* Extremely old; ancient: *age-old traditions.*

ag·er (ā′jər) *n.* **1** That which promotes age or produces an effect of age. **2** A boxlike vessel in which fabrics are treated with steam or ammonia fumes to fix the colors.

a·geu·si·a (ə·gyōō′sē·ə) *n.* Loss or impairment of the sense of taste. Also **a·geus·ti·a** (ə·gyōōs′tē·ə). [< NL < Gk. *a-* without + *geusis* taste] — **a·geu′sic** *adj.*

ag·ger (aj′ər) *n.* **1** A mound or heap; an earthwork; especially, in ancient Rome, the rampart of a fortified camp; a bank against a wall that overtops the defenses. **2** A military road. [< L]

ag·glom·er·ate (ə·glom′ə·rāt) *v.t. & v.i.* **·at·ed, ·at·ing** To gather, form, or grow into a ball or rounded mass. —*adj.* (ə·glom′ər·it, -ə·rāt) Gathered into a mass or heap; clustered densely. —*n.* (ə·glom′ər·it, -ə·rāt) **1** A heap or mass of things thrown together indiscriminately. **2** *Geol.* An unstratified mass of compacted volcanic debris with fragments of all sizes. [< L *agglomeratus*, pp. of *agglomerare* < *ad-* to + *glomerare* gather into a ball < *glomus* ball] —**ag·glom·er·at·ic**, **ag·glom′er·a′tive** *adj.*

ag·glom·er·a·tion (ə·glom′ə·rā′shən) *n.* **1** The process of agglomerating. **2** The state or condition of being agglomerated. **3** A jumbled heap or mass.

ag·glu·ti·nant (ə·glōō′tə·nənt) *adj.* Tending to cause adhesion; sticky. —*n.* An adhesive substance.

ag·glu·ti·nate (ə·glōō′tə·nāt) *v.t. & v.i.* **·nat·ed, ·nat·ing 1** To unite, as with glue; join by adhesion. **2** *Ling.* To form (words) by agglutination. **3** To mass together, as living cells or bacteria, by agglutination. —*adj.* (ə·glōō′tə·nit, -nāt) Joined by adhesion. [< L *agglutinatus*, pp. of *agglutinare* glue to < *ag-* to + *glutinare* < *gluten* glue]

ag·glu·ti·na·tion (ə·glōō′tə·nā′shən) *n.* **1** Adhesion of distinct parts; a mass formed by adhesion. **2** *Ling.* In some languages, a combination of word elements without change of form or meaning to form new compound word elements. **3** The clumping together of particles, as red blood cells, bacteria, etc., suspended in blood serum or other medium.

ag·gran·dize (ə·gran′dīz, ag′rən·dīz) *v.t.* **·dized, ·diz·ing 1** To make great or greater; increase. **2** To increase the power or rank of (oneself): to *aggrandize* oneself at another's expense. **3** To make appear greater; exalt. [< F *agrandiss-*, stem of *agrandir* < L *ad-* to + *grandire* make great] — **ag·gran·dize·ment** (ə·gran′diz·mənt) *n.* — **ag·gran′diz·er** *n.*

ag·gra·vate (ag′rə·vāt) *v.t.* **·vat·ed, ·vat·ing 1** To make worse; increase, intensify, as an offense. **2** To make heavier or more burdensome, as a duty. **3** *Colloq.* To provoke or exasperate; arouse to anger. [< L *aggravatus*, pp. of *aggravare* make heavy or burdensome < *ad-* to + *gravare* make heavy < *gravis* heavy. Doublet of AGGRIEVE.] — **ag′gra·vat′ing** *adj.* —**ag′gra·vat′ing·ly** *adv.* — **ag′gra·va′tive** *adj.*

Synonyms: affront, enhance, heighten, increase, intensify, magnify. *Enhance* and *magnify* are most often used in the lofty and good sense; as, to *enhance* the glory of God; "I *magnify* mine office," *Rom.* xi 13. *Aggravate* is used always in the bad sense meaning to make worse what is already bad; as, to *aggravate* a fever or an enmity. See AFFRONT, INCREASE. *Antonyms:* alleviate, assuage, attenuate, diminish, lessen, palliate, reduce, soften.

ag·gra·va·tion (ag′rə·vā′shən) *n.* **1** A making heavier or worse or the state of being aggravated. **2** Some extrinsic circumstance considered as increasing the atrocity of a crime. **3** *Colloq.* Exasperation; irritation.

ag·gre·gate (ag′rə·gāt) *v.t.* **·gat·ed, ·gat·ing 1** To bring or gather together, as into a mass, sum, or body; collect; mass. **2** To amount to; form a total of. See synonyms under AMASS. —*adj.* (ag′rə·git) **1** Collected into a sum, mass, or total; gathered into a whole; formed by collection; collective. **2** *Bot.* **a** Crowded close together in a dense cluster, as a flower head. **b** Formed of a coherent mass of drupelets, as a fruit. **3** *Geol.* Composed of distinct minerals separable by mechanical means, as granite. —*n.* (ag′rə·git) **1** The entire number, sum, mass, or quantity of something; amount; total, collection. **2** Material for making concrete. —**in the aggregate** Collectively; as a whole. [< L *aggregatus*, pp. of *aggregare*, lit., bring to the flock < *ad-* to + *gregare* collect < *grex* flock] — **ag′gre·ga′tive** *adj.* —**ag′gre·ga′tor** *n.*

Synonyms (noun): agglomeration, aggregation, amount, collection, entirety, heap, mass, sum, total, totality, whole. An *aggregate* of financial items is an *amount*, *sum*, or *total.* An *aggregate* or *aggregation* of material objects is a *collection*, *mass*, or *whole*; an *agglomeration* is a heterogeneous *mass. Collection* points rather to the differ-

ences, *mass* to the unity. We say a *collection* of minerals, a *mass* of rock. The result of multiplication is a product, the result of addition a *sum*, *total*, or *aggregate.*

ag·gre·ga·tion (ag′rə·gā′shən) *n.* **1** A collection into a whole; a mass; aggregate; whole. **2** The act of aggregating, or the state of being aggregated.

ag·gress (ə·gres′) *v.i.* To undertake an attack; begin a quarrel. [< L *aggressus*, pp. of *aggredi* approach, attack < *ad-* to + *gradi* step, go < *gradus* a step]

ag·gres·sion (ə·gresh′ən) *n.* **1** An unprovoked attack; encroachment. **2** Habitual aggressive action or practices. **3** *Psychoanal.* A primary instinct, generally associated with emotional states, to carry out action in a forceful way.

Synonyms: assault, attack, encroachment, incursion, intrusion, invasion, onslaught, trespass. An *attack* may be by word; an *aggression* is always by deed. An *assault* may be upon the person, an *aggression* is upon rights, possessions, etc. An *invasion* of a nation's territories is an act of *aggression*; an *intrusion* upon a neighboring estate is a *trespass. Onslaught* signifies intensely violent *assault*, as by an army or a desperado, yet it is sometimes used of violent speech. *Antonyms:* defense, repulsion, resistance, retreat.

ag·gres·sive (ə·gres′iv) *adj.* **1** Disposed to begin an attack or encroachment. **2** Disposed to vigorous activity; assertive. —**ag·gres′sive·ly** *adv.* — **ag·gres′sive·ness** *n.*

ag·gres·sor (ə·gres′ər) *n.* One who commits an aggression or begins a quarrel.

ag·grieve (ə·grēv′) *v.t.* **ag·grieved, ag·griev·ing 1** To cause sorrow to; distress or afflict. **2** To give cause for just complaint, as by injustice. See synonyms under ABUSE. [< OF *agrever* < L *aggravare.* Doublet of AGGRAVATE.]

ag·grieved (ə·grēvd′) *adj.* **1** Subjected to illtreatment; feeling an injury or injustice. **2** Injured, as by legal decision adversely infringing upon one's rights. —**ag·griev·ed·ness** (ə·grēv′id·nis) *n.*

a·ghast (ə·gast′, ə·gäst′) *adj.* Struck dumb with horror. [pp. of obs. *agast* frighten, OE *ā-* A-¹ + *gǣstan* terrify; spelling infl. by *ghost*]

ag·ile (aj′əl, aj′il) *adj.* **1** Able to move or act quickly and easily; active; nimble. **2** Characterized by quickness of perception or response; alert: an *agile* mind. See synonyms under ACTIVE, NIMBLE. [< F < L *agilis* < *agere* do, move] —**ag′ile·ly** *adv.* —**ag′ile·ness** *n.*

a·gil·i·ty (ə·jil′ə·tē) *n.* Quickness and readiness in movement or mind; nimbleness. [< F *agilité* < L *agilitas* < *agilis.* See AGILE.]

ag·ing (ā′jing) *n.* **1** The process of acquiring characteristics of age. **2** *Biol.* The progressive breakdown of an organism or any of its parts through the cumulative effects of irreversible physicochemical changes acting over a period of time. **3** The effects of time on the properties of materials or substances. **4** Any means for obtaining such effects artificially, as the weathering of clay for bricks, or the acid treatment of bronze to obtain a patina. **5** *Metall.* A change in the properties of certain metals, as hardness and tensile strength, caused by heat treatment and cold working. **6** A method of steaming fabrics to develop and fix the colors. Also spelled *ageing.*

ag·i·tate (aj′ə·tāt) *v.* **·tat·ed, ·tat·ing** *v.t.* **1** To shake or move irregularly. **2** To set or keep moving, as a fan. **3** To excite or endeavor to excite, as a crowd; perturb. **4** To discuss publicly and incessantly, as a controversial question. **5** *Archaic* To revolve in the mind; plan. —*v.i.* **6** To keep a subject or cause under continuous discussion, in order to excite public interest. [< L *agitatus*, pp. of *agitare* set in motion, freq. of *agere* move]

ag·i·ta·tion (aj′ə·tā′shən) *n.* **1** Violent motion. **2** Open, active discussion; urgent consideration. **3** Strong or tumultuous emotion. See synonyms under TUMULT.

a·gi·ta·to (ä′jē·tä′tō) *adj. & adv. Music* Stirring, restless; agitated: a direction in musical execution. [< Ital.]

ag·i·ta·tor (aj′ə·tā′tər) *n.* One who or that which agitates; specifically, one who promotes social change.

ag·it·prop (aj′it·prop′) *n.* **1** Communist political propaganda, as in a play, film, etc. **2** Any political propaganda. —*adj.* Pertaining to or of the nature of agitprop. [< Russ., Communist Party agency for agitation and propaganda]

a·glow (ə·glō′) *adv. & adj.* In a glow; glowing.

ag·mi·nate (ag′mə·nit, -nāt) *adj.* Grouped in clusters. Also **ag′mi·nat·ed.** [< L *agmen, agminis* troop, crowd + -ATE¹]

ag·nate (ag′nāt) *adj.* **1** Related on the male or the father's side. **2** Akin; similar. —*n.* A relative in the male line only. Compare COGNATE. ENATE. [< F *agnat* < L *agnatus* a relation (on the father's side), orig., added by birth, pp. of *agnasci* be born in addition to < *ad-* to + *nasci* be born] — **ag·nat·ic** (ag·nat′ik) *adj.* —**ag·nat′i·cal·ly** *adv.*

ag·na·tion (ag·nā′shən) *n.*

ag·no·si·a (ag·nō′sē·ə) *n.* Impairment or loss of the ability to recognize or interpret sensory perceptions of familiar persons or things. [< NL < Gk. *a-* without + *gnōsis* knowing, knowledge] —**ag·no′sic** *adj.*

ag·nos·tic (ag·nos′tik) *adj.* Professing ignorance or the inability to know, especially in religion. —*n.* One who holds the theory of agnosticism. See synonyms under SKEPTIC. [< Gk. *agnōstos* unknowing, unknown < *a-* not + *gignōskein* know]

ag·nos·ti·cism (ag·nos′tə·siz′əm) *n.* **1** The doctrine of nescience, or the theory which maintains that man cannot have, and has not, any real or valid knowledge, but can know only impressions. **2** The theory that first truths, substance, cause, the human soul, and a First Cause, can neither be proved nor disproved, and must remain unknown or unknowable. **3** *Theol.* The theory that God is unknown or unknowable: distinguished from *atheism.*

ag·nus (ag′nəs) *n. pl.* **ag·ni** (ag′nī) The lamb as a Christian emblem; an Agnus Dei. [< L, lamb]

Ag·nus De·i (ag′nəs dē′ī, dā′ē) **1** *Eccl.* A figure of a lamb, as an emblem of Christ, often bearing a cross and banner. **2** In the Roman Catholic Church, a medallion or cake of wax stamped with this emblem and blessed by the Pope. **3** *Eccl.* **a** A prayer in the mass, beginning with the words *Agnus Dei.* **b** In Anglican and some other churches, a translation of this prayer, beginning "O Lamb of God." **4** A musical setting for this prayer. **5** In the Greek Church, a cloth bearing the figure of a lamb, used to cover the elements of the Eucharist. [< LL, Lamb of God. See *John* i 29.]

a·go (ə·gō′) *adv.* In the past; in time gone by; since. —*adj.* Gone by; past. [OE *āgān* past, gone away]

a·gog (ə·gog′) *adv. & adj.* In a state of eager curiosity; excited with interest or expectation. [< MF *en gogues* in a merry mood]

-agog *combining form* Leading, promoting, or inciting: *demagog, pedagog.* Also **-agogue.** [< Gk. *agōgos* leading]

a·gone (ə·gôn′, ə·gon′) *adj. & adv. Obs.* Ago.

a·gon·ic (ə·gon′ik) *adj.* Having or forming no angle. [< Gk. *agōnos* < *a-* without + *gōnia* angle]

ag·o·nis·tics (ag′ə·nis′tiks) *n.* The art or science of athletic contests.

ag·o·nize (ag′ə·nīz) *v.* **·nized, ·niz·ing** *v.i.* **1** To be in or suffer extreme pain or anguish. **2** To make convulsive efforts, as in wrestling; strive. —*v.t.* **3** To subject to agony; torture. [< F *agoniser* < Med.L *agonizare* < Gk. *agōnizesthai* contend, strive < *agōn* contest]

ag·o·ny (ag′ə·nē) *n. pl.* **·nies 1** Intense suffering of body or mind; anguish; struggle. **2** Violent or very earnest contest or striving. **3** The suffering or struggle that precedes death. [< L *agonia* < Gk. *agōnia* < *agōn* contest]

Synonyms: ache, anguish, distress, pain, pang, paroxysm, suffering, throe, torment, torture. *Agony* and *anguish* express the uttermost *pain* or *suffering* of body or mind; *agony* that with which the sufferer struggles; *anguish,* that by which he is crushed. Compare AFFLICTION, GRIEF.

a·go·ra (ag′ər·ə) *n. pl.* **ag·o·rae** (-ər·ē) or **ag·o·ras 1** In ancient Greece, a popular assembly for political or other purposes. **2** A place of popular assembly; especially, the market place. [< Gk.]

ag·o·ra·pho·bi·a (ag′ər·ə·fō′bē·ə) *n.* Morbid fear of open spaces; fear of exposure to unidentified dangers.

a·graffe (ə·graf′) *n.* **1** A hook or clasp; especially, an ornamental clasp used on armor or for fastening rich clothing. **2** A builders' cramp iron. Also **a·grafe′.** [< F]

a·graph·i·a (ā·graf′ē·ə) *n.* A partial or total loss of the ability to write. [< NL < Gk. *a-* without + *graphein* write] —**a·graph′ic** *adj.*

a·grar·i·an (ə·grâr′ē·ən) *adj.* **1** Pertaining to land or its tenure or to a general distribution of lands. **2** Organizing or furthering agricultural interests and aid to farmers: an *agrarian* investment. —*n.* One who advocates agrarianism. [< L *agrarius* < *ager* field]

a·grar·i·an·ism (ə·grâr′ē·ən·iz′əm) *n.* **1** The theory or practice of equal distribution of lands. **2** Agitation or political dissension with the view of redistributing tenure of lands or of equalizing farm income, especially by the use of government controls.

a·gree (ə·grē′) *v.* **a·greed, a·gree·ing** *v.i.* **1** To give consent; accede: with *to.* **2** To come into or be in harmony. **3** To be of one mind; concur: with *with.* **4** To come to terms, as in the details of a transaction: with *about* or *on.* **5** To be acceptable or favorable; suit: with *with:* This food does not *agree* with him. **6** To conform or match, as scales of measurement. **7** *Gram.* To correspond in person, number, case, or gender. —*v.t.* **8** To grant as a concession: with a noun clause: I *agree* that the choice is difficult, but you must choose. [< OF *agreer* < *a gre* to one's liking < L *ad* to + *gratus* pleasing]

Synonyms: accede, accept, accord, acquiesce, admit, approve, assent, coincide, combine, comply, concur, consent, harmonize. *Agree* is the most general term of this group; to *concur* is to *agree* in general; to *coincide* is to *agree* in every particular. One *accepts* another's terms, *complies* with his wishes, *admits* his statement, *approves* his plan, *conforms* to his views of doctrine or duty, *accedes* or *consents* to his proposal. *Accede* expresses the more formal agreement, *consent* the more complete. One may silently *acquiesce* in that which does not meet his views, but which he does not care to contest. See ASSENT. *Antonyms:* contend, contradict, decline, demur, deny, differ, disagree, dispute, dissent, oppose, protest, refuse.

a·gree·a·ble (ə·grē′ə·bəl) *adj.* **1** Agreeing with or suited to the mind or senses; pleasurable; especially, of persons, giving pleasure by manner, bearing, or conversation. **2** Naturally or logically corresponding; suitable; correspondent; conformable: a truth *agreeable* to human reason. **3** Ready to agree; favorably inclined; giving assent; willing. **4** Being in accordance or conformity; conforming. —**a·gree′a·bil′i·ty, a·gree′a·ble·ness** *n.* —**a·gree′a·bly** *adv.*

Synonyms: acceptable, amiable, comfortable, delightful, good, grateful, gratifying, pleasant, pleasing, welcome. See AMIABLE. *Antonyms:* disagreeable, hateful, obnoxious, offensive.

a·greed (ə·grēd′) *adj.* **1** Brought into or being in harmony; united. **2** Settled by consent, bargain, or contract. **3** Admitted or conceded; granted.

a·gree·ment (ə·grē′mənt) *n.* **1** The act of coming into accord, or the state of being in accord; conformity. **2** An arrangement or understanding between two or more parties as to a course of action; a covenant, or treaty. **3** *Law* A contract. See synonyms under CONTRACT, HARMONY. **4** *Gram.* concord (def. 3).

a·gres·tial (ə·gres′chəl) *adj.* Growing wild on cultivated ground, as weeds. Also **a·gres·tal** (ə·gres′təl).

a·gres·tic (ə·gres′tik) *adj.* Rural; unpolished. Also **a·gres′ti·cal.** [< L *agrestis* < *ager* field]

ag·ri·bus·i·ness (ag′rə·biz′nis, -niz) *n.* All those commercial activities associated with agriculture, including the production, processing, and distribution of farm products and the manufacture of farm equipment. [< AGRI-(CULTURE) + BUSINESS]

ag·ri·cul·ture (ag′rə·kul′chər) *n.* **1** The cultivation of the soil; the raising of food crops, breeding and raising of livestock, etc.; tillage; farming. **2** The science that treats of the cultivation of the soil. —**Department of Agriculture** An executive department of the U.S. government since 1889 (originally established 1862), headed by the Sec-

retary of Agriculture, that acquires and diffuses information on agricultural subjects and administers laws to protect the farmer and consuming public. [< F < L *agricultura* < *ager* field + *cultura* cultivation] —**ag·ri·cul′tur·al** *adj.* —**ag′ri·cul′tur·al·ly** *adv.*

Synonyms: cultivation, culture, farming, floriculture, gardening, horticulture, husbandry, tillage. *Agriculture* is the generic term, including the science, the art, and the process of supplying human wants by raising the products of the soil, and by the associated industries; *farming* is the practice of *agriculture* as a business. We speak of the science of *agriculture,* the business of *farming:* scientific *agriculture* may be wholly in books; scientific *farming* is practiced upon the land.

agro- *combining form* Of or pertaining to fields or agriculture: *agronomy.* [< *agros* field]

ag·ro·ma·ni·a (ag′rō·mā′nē·ə) *n.* A morbid desire to live in open country, and especially in solitude.

ag·ro·nom·ic (ag′rə·nom′ik) *adj.* Of or pertaining to agronomy or agronomics. Also **agro·nom′i·cal.**

ag·ro·nom·ics (ag′rə·nom′iks) *n.* **1** In political economy, the science that treats of the distribution and management of land, especially as a source of the wealth of a nation. **2** Agronomy.

a·gron·o·my (ə·gron′ə·mē) *n.* The application of scientific principles to the cultivation of land; scientific husbandry, especially in production of field crops. —**a·gron′o·mist** *n.* [< Gk. *agronomos* an overseer of lands < *agros* field + *nemein* distribute, manage]

Synonyms: agriculture. *Agronomy* differs from *agriculture* in that it is concerned only with crop-production, while *agriculture* includes the improvement and care of animals and their products.

a·ground (ə·ground′) *adv. & adj.* On the shore or bottom, as a vessel; stranded.

a·gue (ā′gyōō) *n.* **1** *Pathol.* A periodic malarial fever; intermittent fever; chills and fever. **2** A chill or paroxysm of violent shivering. [< OF < L (*febris*) *acuta* an acute fever]

a·gu·ish (ā′gyōō·ish) *adj.* Like, producing, or tending to produce ague; chilly; subject to ague. —**a′gu·ish·ly** *adv.* —**a′gu·ish·ness** *n.*

ah (ä) *interj.* An exclamation expressive of various emotions, as surprise, triumph, satisfaction, contempt, compassion, or complaint.

a·ha (ä′hä) *n.* A sunk fence; a ha-ha.

a·ha² (ä·hä′) *interj.* An exclamation expressing surprise, triumph, or mockery.

a·head (ə·hed′) *adv.* **1** At the head or front. **2** In advance. **3** Onward; forward: He pressed *ahead.* **4** Without restraint; headlong. —**ahead of** In advance of, as in time, rank, achievement, etc. —**to get ahead** To make one's way socially, financially, etc. [< A-¹ + HEAD]

a·hem (ə·hem′) *interj.* An exclamation to attract attention.

a·him·sa (ə·him′sä) *n.* The doctrine that all life is sacred, exemplified in the Jainist, Brahman, and Buddhist philosophies by strict non-violence to all living things. [< Skt. *ahimsā* non-injury]

a·his·tor·i·cal (ā′his·tôr′ə·kəl, -tər′-) *adj.* Not historical; without regard for history.

a·hold¹ (ə·hōld′) *adv.* Close to the wind: to lay a ship *ahold.*

a·hold² (ə·hōld) *U.S. Dialect* A hold (of): to get *ahold* of one's arm.

a·hoy (ə·hoi′) *interj.* Ho there! a call used in hailing: ship *ahoy!* [Var. of HOY]

aid (ād) *v.t. & v.i.* To render assistance (to); help; succor. —*n.* **1** The act or result of helping or succoring, or the means employed; cooperation; assistance. **2** A person or thing that affords assistance; a helper; assistant; aide-de-camp. **3** *Law* A remedy; correction; also, a subsidy. **4** In medieval law, a pecuniary contribution by a feudal vassal to his lord, limited by Magna Carta to three special occasions. See synonyms under ADHERENT, AUXILIARY, HELP, SUBSIDY. [< OF *aider* < L

Synonyms (verb): abet, assist, befriend, cooperate, encourage, foster, help, second, serve, succor, support, sustain, uphold. *Help* expresses greater dependence and deeper need than *aid*. To *aid* is to *second* another's own exertions, but may fall short of the meaning of *help*. In law, to *aid* or *abet* makes one a principal. (Compare synonyms for ACCESSORY). To *cooperate* or *collaborate* implies complete or approximate equality, *collaborate* being used chiefly of literary or scientific work; to *assist* implies a subordinate and secondary relation. One *assists* a fallen friend to rise; he *cooperates* with him in helping others. We *encourage* the timid or despondent, *succor* those in danger, *support* the weak, *uphold* those who else might be shaken or cast down. Compare ABET, ACCESSORY, PROMOTE. *Antonyms:* counteract, discourage, hinder, obstruct, oppose, resist, thwart, withstand.

A·ï·da (ä·ē′də) The heroine and title of an opera (1871) by Giuseppe Verdi.

aid·ance (ād′ns) *n.* The act of aiding; assistance; help. —**aid′ant** *adj.*

aide (ād) *n.* **1** An officer of the personal staff of the head of a government. **2** An aide-de-camp. **3** A naval officer assisting a superior officer. [< F, assistant]

aide-de-camp (ād′də-kamp′) *n. pl.* **aides-de-camp** An officer of the personal staff of a general, who transmits his orders, bears confidential relationship to him, and attends to matters of etiquette and protocol. Also **aid-de-camp, aide.** [< F *aide de camp*, lit., field assistant]

AIDS (ādz) Acquired immunodeficiency syndrome.

ai·guille (ā·gwēl′, ā′gwēl) *n.* **1** *Geol.* A sharp rocky mountain peak, as those of the Italian Alps near Mont Blanc. **2** A slender rock-perforating drill. [< F, needle]

ail (āl) *v.t.* To cause uneasiness or pain to; trouble; make ill. —*v.i.* To be somewhat ill; feel pain. ◆ Homophone: *ale.* [OE *eglan*] —**ail′ing** *adj.*

ail·ment (āl′mənt) *n.* Indisposition of body or mind; slight illness.

ai·lu·ro·phile (ā·loor′ə·fīl) *n.* A person who likes cats.

ai·lu·ro·pho·bi·a (ā·loor′ə·fō′bē·ə) *n.* Morbid fear of cats. Also called *galeophobia, gatophobia.* [< Gk. *ailouros* cat + -PHOBIA]

aim (ām) *v.t.* **1** To direct, as a missile, blow, weapon, word, or act, toward or against something or person; point or level: to *aim* a gun at a man; to *aim* a speech at an offender. —*v.i.* **2** To have a purpose; endeavor earnestly: with the infinitive: to *aim* to please. **3** To direct a missile, weapon, etc.: We *aimed* and fired. —*n.* **1** The act of aiming, directing, or pointing a weapon, missile, remark, etc., at anything. **2** The line of direction of anything aimed. **3** The object or point aimed at or to be aimed at; a mark or target. **4** Design; purpose. **5** Conjecture; guess. [< OF *aesmer* < *a-* to (< L *ad-*) + *esmer* < L *aestimare* estimate]

Synonyms (noun): aspiration, design, determination, direction, end, endeavor, goal, inclination, intent, intention, mark, object, purpose, reason, tendency. The *aim* is the direction in which one shoots, or that which is aimed at. The *mark* is that at which one shoots; the *goal,* that toward which one moves or works. All indicate the direction of *endeavor.* The *end* is the point at which one expects or hopes to close his labors; the *object,* that which he would grasp as the reward of his labors. *Aspiration, design, endeavor, purpose,* referring to the mental acts by which the *aim* is attained, are often used as interchangeable with *aim.* Compare AMBITION, DESIGN, DIRECTION, PURPOSE. *Antonyms:* aimlessness, avoidance, carelessness, heedlessness, neglect, negligence, oversight, purposelessness, thoughtlessness.

aim·less (ām′lis) *adj.* Wanting in aim or purpose. —**aim′less·ly** *adv.* —**aim′less·ness** *n.*

ain't (ānt) *Illit. & Dial.* Am not; also used for *are not, is not, has not,* and *have not.*
◆ **ain't, aren't I** *Ain't* is used in dialog representing uneducated or homely speech. The emergence of the ungrammatical but idiomatic *aren't I* as a genteel substitute for *ain't I* shows the need for a colloquial contraction for *am not.* This need has not removed the stigma from *ain't,* though until a century ago it was good colloquial English and is still so considered by some in Scotland.

air (âr) *n.* **1** The atmosphere of the earth, consisting of a mixture of gases containing approximately 79 percent nitrogen, 19 percent oxygen, and small amounts of other gases including carbon dioxide, hydrogen, helium, argon, and methane. **2** The open space around and above the earth. **3** An atmospheric movement or current; breeze; wind. **4** Utterance abroad; publicity: to give *air* to one's views. **5** The medium through which radio waves are transmitted; airways. **6** The representation of atmosphere in painting; atmospheric perspective. **7** Something light and ethereal; wind. **8** Peculiar or characteristic appearance; mien; manner. **9** Assumed manner; affectation: to put on *airs.* **10** *Music* A melody as contrasted with a harmony; tune; especially, the leading or soprano part in a harmonized piece. **11** *Obs.* Breath. **12** *Obs.* Secret intelligence; private information. See synonyms under TUNE, WIND. —**in the air 1** Prevalent; abroad, as gossip; astir; in the making, as plans. **2** Without foundation in fact; unformed: The project is still *in the air.* **3** Excited; mentally upset. —**on the air** Broadcasting by radio; being broadcast. —*v.t.* **1** To expose to the air; admit air into so as to purify or dry; ventilate. **2** To make public; show off; display; exhibit. **3** *Colloq.* To broadcast by radio or television. ◆ Homophone: *heir.* [< OF < L *aer* < Gk. *aer* air, mist]

Synonyms (noun): appearance, bearing, behavior, carriage, demeanor, deportment, expression, fashion, look, manner, mien, port, pretense, sort, style, way. *Air* is that combination of qualities which makes the entire impression we receive in a person's presence; we say he has the *air* of a scholar, or the *air* of a villain. *Appearance* refers more to the dress and other externals. *Expression* and *look* especially refer to the face. *Expression* is oftenest applied to that which is habitual; as, a pleasant *expression; look* may be momentary; as, a *look* of dismay passed over his face. We may, however, speak of the *look* or *looks* as indicating all that we look at; as, he had the *look* of an adventurer. *Bearing* indicates often the expression of feeling or state of mind through bodily pose; as, a noble *bearing; port,* practically identical in meaning with *bearing,* is more exclusively a literary word. *Carriage,* the manner of holding the body, as in walking, is more completely physical than *bearing. Mien* is closely synonymous with *air,* but is a somewhat stilted or literary usage. Compare BEHAVIOR, PRETENSE.

air·bag (âr′bag′) *n.* An automatically inflatable safety device installed beneath the dashboard of an automobile and designed to cushion passengers in case of a collision.

air bladder 1 An air-filled sac situated under the spinal column of most fishes and serving as a hydrostatic device. Also called *swim bladder.* **2** Any sac filled with air or gas, as the flotation devices on bladderwrack and other seaweeds.

air·borne (âr′bôrn′, -bōrn′) *adj.* **1** Transported in aircraft; specifically, designating specialized units of infantry or parachute troops so carried. **2** Aloft; no longer in contact with the ground. **3** Transported by air currents, as pollen, dust, etc.

air brake A brake operated by compressed air.

air·bra·sive (âr′brā′siv, -ziv) *adj.* Of or pertaining to a method of drilling teeth by means of a finely powdered abrasive pinpointed against the surface in a minute, controlled jet of air or other gas under high pressure.

air·brush (âr′brush′) *n.* An implement for spraying liquids by compressed air, especially one used by commercial artists and photographers for coating surfaces with a film of color.

air·burst (âr′bûrst′) *n.* An explosion in the air, as of a bomb or projectile.

air carrier An aircraft that carries freight.

air·con·di·tion (âr′kən·dish′ən) *v.t.* To equip with or ventilate by air-conditioning. —**air′·con·di′tioned** *adj.*

air·con·di·tion·ing (âr′kən·dish′ən·ing) *n.* A system for treating air in buildings, dwellings, and other enclosed structures so as to maintain those conditions of temperature, humidity, and purity which are best adapted to technical operations, industrial processes, and personal comfort.

air·craft (âr′kraft′, -kräft′) *n.* Any form of craft designed for flight through or navigation in the air, as airplanes, dirigibles, balloons, helicopters, kites, and gliders.

aircraft carrier A large ship designed to carry aircraft, with a level upper flight deck usually extending beyond the bow and stern, serving as a mobile air base at sea: also called *flattop.*

air·drop (âr′drop′) *n.* Personnel, food, equipment, and other supplies dropped by parachute from an aircraft. —*v.t. & v.i.* **·dropped, ·drop·ping** To drop (personnel, supplies, etc.) by parachute from an aircraft.

air·field (âr′fēld′) *n.* An airport; specifically, the field or course of an airport.

air·flow (âr′flō′) *n.* **1** A flow of air. **2** The air currents developed by the motion of an automobile, aircraft, etc.

air·foil (âr′foil′) *n. Aeron.* A winglike surface designed to provide the maximum aerodynamic advantage for an airplane in flight.

air force The air arm of a country's defense forces. —**United States Air Force** The air force of the United States administered by the Department of the Air Force under the Department of Defense; established in 1947 and organized in 1951 to consist of the Regular Air Force, the Air Force Reserve, and the Air National Guard of the United States. Until 1947 it was part of the Army, under the title of the United States Army Air Force. See ROYAL AIR FORCE, ROYAL CANADIAN AIR FORCE, ROYAL AUSTRALIAN AIR FORCE.

air gun A gun impelling a missile by compressed air.

air·head (âr′hed′) *n.* **1** A position established in enemy territory that can be supplied and reinforced by air. **2** *Slang* A brainless person.

air·hole (âr′hōl′) *n.* **1** A hole containing, or made by or for, gas or air. **2** A flaw in a casting. **3** An opening in the ice over a body of water. **4** *Aeron.* An air pocket. Also **air hole.**

air·i·ly (âr′ə·lē) *adv.* **1** In a light or airy manner; delicately. **2** In light spirits; jauntily; gaily.

air·i·ness (âr′ē·nis) *n.* The quality of being airy.

air·ing (âr′ing) *n.* **1** An exposure to the air, as for drying. **2** Public exposure or discussion. **3** Exercise in the air.

air·less (âr′lis) *adj.* Destitute of air or of fresh air.

air·lift (âr′lift′) *n.* **1** The operation of transporting foodstuffs and other commodities into Berlin by airplane during the land blockade imposed by the U.S.S.R. in 1948. **2** Any similar operation for any purpose. **3** The load carried by such a transport method. —*v.t. & v.i.* To transport (food and supplies) by airplane, especially during a land blockade.

air·line (âr′līn′) *n.* **1** The shortest distance between two points on the earth's surface. **2** A regular route traveled by aircraft carrying freight and passengers. **3** The business organization operating such a transport system. **4** A direct railroad route.

air·lin·er (âr′lī′nər) *n.* A large, passenger aircraft operated by an airline.

air·lock (âr′lok′) *n.* **1** An airtight antechamber, as of a submarine caisson, for graduating the air pressure.

air mail 1 Mail carried by airplane. **2** A system of carrying mail by airplane; particularly, a postal system in charge of forwarding of mail by aircraft. —**air′-mail′, air′mail′** *adj.*

air·plane (âr′plān′) *n.* A heavier-than-air flying craft, supported by aerodynamic forces acting upon fixed wings, and kept in flight by propellers or jet propulsion.

air pollution The contamination of the air, esp. by industrial waste gases, fuel exhaust, or smoke.

air·port (âr′pôrt′, -pōrt′) *n.* A field laid out as a base for aircraft, including all structures and appurtenances necessary for operation, housing, storage, repair, and maintenance: also called *airdrome.*

air·post (âr′pōst′) *n.* Air mail.

air pump A pump for exhausting, compressing, or transmitting air.

air raid An attack by military aircraft, especially bombers in mass formation.

air-raid shelter A place set aside and equipped for the protection of people during an air raid.

air sac 1 *Ornithol.* One of the membranous sacs filled with air in different parts of the body in birds, often extending through the bones and communicating with the lungs. 2 *Entomol.* Any of the large, thin-walled structures connected to the tracheal system in some insects. 3 An alveolus of the lungs.

air·ship (âr′ship′) *n.* 1 An aircraft, generally of large size, mechanically propelled and depending upon gases for flotation; a dirigible balloon. 2 Loosely, an airplane.

air·sick·ness (âr′sik′nis) Motion sickness experienced while flying. —**air′sick** *adj.*

air·space (âr′spās′) *n.* 1 The atmosphere. 2 That portion of the atmosphere overlying a designated geographical area, considered as subject to territorial jurisdiction or international law in respect to its use by aircraft, guided missiles, rockets, etc.

AIRPLANE SHOWING FUNCTIONAL PARTS
A. Four-passenger light plane.
B. Helicopter. *C.* Turbojet.

air speed The speed of an airplane with relation to the air: distinguished from *ground speed.*

air·spring (âr′spring′) *n.* A device for resisting sudden pressure by the elasticity of compressed air.

air·stream (âr′strē′) *n.* A current or flow of air, especially one set up by the propeller or propellers of an aircraft.

air·strip (âr′strip′) *n.* A makeshift airfield, usually prepared from prefabricated materials for temporary use, as for landing fighter planes: also called *fighter strip.*

air·tight (âr′tīt′) *adj.* 1 Not allowing air to escape or enter. 2 Hence, having no weak places; flawless: an *airtight* argument.

air·way (âr′wā′) *n.* 1 Any passageway for air, as the windpipe, a ventilator shaft, etc. 2 *Aeron.* A specific route of travel selected for aircraft. 3 *pl. U.S. Colloq.* Channels for radio or television broadcasting.

air·wor·thi·ness (âr′wûr′thē·nis) *n.* 1 Fitness for flight. 2 The status of one who has met certain requirements for flying an airplane.

air·wor·thy (âr′wûr′thē) *adj.* Being in fit condition for flight.

air·y (âr′ē) *adj.* **air·i·er, air·i·est** 1 Of or pertaining to the air; in the air. 2 Open to or pervaded by the free air; breezy: an *airy* retreat. 3 Like or of the nature of air; as light as air; hence, immaterial; delicate; graceful; ethereal; buoyant: an *airy* evening dress, *airy* music, *airy* nothings. 4 Without reality, or dealing in unreal things or fancies; visionary; speculative. 5 Putting on airs; affected. 6 Light or quick of mood; vivacious; gay. 7 In painting, having transparent atmospheric effect. 8 Pertaining to the soul; spiritual.

Synonyms: aerial, animated, ethereal, fairylike, frolicsome, gay, joyous, light, lively, sprightly. *Aerial* and *airy* both signify of or belonging to the air, but *airy* describes that which seems as if made of air; we speak of *airy* shapes where we could not well say *aerial; ethereal* describes its objects as belonging to the upper air, the pure ether, and so, often, heavenly. *Sprightly,* spiritlike, refers to light, free, cheerful activity of mind and body. That which is *lively* or *animated* may be agreeable or the reverse; as, an *animated* discussion; a *lively* company. *Antonyms:* clumsy, heavy, inert, ponderous, slow.

aisle (īl) *n.* 1 A passageway, as in a church, theater, or other audience-room, by which the pews or seats may be reached or the room traversed. 2 Originally, a lateral division or wing of a church, flanking the main structure or nave, from which it usually is divided by a range of columns or piers. 3 Any similar wing or passage, as in a forest. ◆ Homophone: *isle.* [< OF *aile, ele* wing (of a building) < L *ala* wing; spelling infl. by *isle*]

aisled (īld) *adj.* 1 Provided with aisles. 2 Placed in an aisle.

a·jar[1] (ə·jär′) *adv. & adj.* Partly open, as a door. [ME *a-* on + *char,* OE *cerr* turn]

a·jar[2] (ə·jär′) *adv. & adj.* In a jarring or discordant condition; wanting in harmony. [< A-[1] + JAR[2]]

a·kim·bo (ə·kim′bō) *adv.* With the hands on hips and the elbows outward. [ME *in kene bowe* in a sharp bow]

a·kin (ə·kin′) *adj. & adv.* 1 Of the same kin; related by blood. 2 Of similar nature or qualities. See synonyms under ALIKE. [< A-[2] + KIN]

ak·i·ne·sis (ak′ə·nē′sis) *n.* 1 Impairment or loss of motor function. 2 Immobility due to any cause. Also **ak·i·ne·si·a** (ak′ə·nē′sē·ə). [< NL < Gk. *a-* without + *kinēsis* motion]—**ak′i·ne′sic** *adj.*

al-[1] *prefix* The: Arabic definite article, as in *Al-koran, algebra.*

al-[2] Assimilated var. of AD-.

-al[1] *suffix of adjectives and nouns* Of or pertaining to; characterized by; connected with: *personal, musical;* also in some nouns that were originally adjectives: *animal, rival.* [< L *-alis*]

-al[2] *suffix of nouns* The act of doing or the state of suffering that which is expressed by the verb stem: *betrayal, refusal.* [< OF *-aille* < L *-alia,* neut. pl. of *-alis*]

-al[3] *suffix Chem.* Denoting a compound having the properties of or derived from an aldehyde: *chloral.* [< AL(DEHYDE)]

a·la (ā′lə) *n. pl.* **a·lae** (ā′lē) *Biol.* Any wing or winglike structure, as one of the lateral projections of the nose, one of the two side petals of a papilionaceous flower, a projection found on certain seeds, etc. [< L, wing]

à la (ä′lä, ä′lə; *Fr.* à là) **1** After the manner of: hair dressed *à la* Pompadour. **2** In Cooking, as done in; according to or prepared after the manner of: lobster *à la* Newburg. Also **a la.** [< F]

Al·a·bam·a (al′ə·bam′ə) A State in the SE United States, bordering on the Gulf of Mexico; 51,609 square miles; capital, Montgomery; entered the Union Dec. 14, 1819; nickname, *Cotton State;* abbr. **AL** —**Al·a·bam·i·an** (al′ə·bam′ē·ən), **Al′a·bam′an** *adj. & n.*

al·a·bas·ter (al′ə·bas′tər, -bäs′-) *n.* 1 A white or delicately tinted fine-grained gypsum. 2 A dense, translucent variety of calcite, sometimes banded like marble. —*adj.* Made of or like alabaster; smooth and white. [< L < Gk. *alabast(r)os* an alabaster box, ? from the name of a town in Egypt] —**al′a·bas′trine** (-trin) *adj.*

a·lack (ə·lak′) *interj. Archaic* An exclamation of regret or sorrow. Also **a·lack·a·day** (ə·lak′ə·dā′). [< *ah* oh + *lack* failure, disgrace]

a·lac·ri·ty (ə·lak′rə·tē) *n.* Cheerful willingness and promptitude; facility. [< L *alacritas, -tatis* < *alacer* lively] —**a·lac′ri·tous** *adj.*

A·lad·din (ə·lad′n) A boy in the *Arabian Nights* who is able to cause one jinni to appear and do his bidding whenever he rubs a magic lamp, and another whenever he rubs a magic ring.

a·la·li·a (ə·lā′lē·ə) *n.* Inability to speak, whether due to impairment or paralysis of the organs of speech or to brain damage. [< Gk. *a-* without + *lalia* talking] —**a·la′lic** *adj.*

al·a·me·da (al′ə·mē′də, -mā′-) *n. SW U.S.* A shaded walk: so called because generally planted with *alamos* or poplar trees. [< Sp. < *álamo* poplar]

al·a·mo (al′ə·mō, ä′lə·mō) *n. pl.* **-mos** Any of various species of cottonwood. [< Sp.]

Al·a·mo (al′ə·mō) A Franciscan mission building, San Antonio, Texas; besieged and taken by Mexicans, 1836. —**Remember the Alamo!** A rallying cry for United States forces in the Mexican War (1848).

à la mode (ä′ lə mōd′, al′ə mōd′) **1** Literally, according to the mode; in the fashion. **2** Served with ice cream: pie *à la mode.* [< F]

a·lar (ā′lər) *adj.* Pertaining to an ala or wing; wing-shaped. [< L *alaris* < *ala* wing]

a·larm (ə·lärm′) *n.* 1 Sudden fear or apprehension arousing to defense or escape. 2 Any sound or signal to apprise of danger or arouse from sleep. 3 A mechanism, as of a clock, giving such signal. 4 A call to arms, to meet danger. 5 *Obs.* A sudden attack. —*v.t.* 1 To strike with sudden fear. 2 To arouse to a sense of danger; give warning to. See synonyms under FRIGHTEN. [< OF *alarme* < Ital. *all' arme* to arms] —**a·larm′a·ble** *adj.*

Synonyms (noun): affright, apprehension, consternation, dismay, disquiet, dread, fear, fright, panic, terror, timidity. *Alarm,* according to its derivation, is a sudden arousal to meet and repel danger and may be quite consistent with true courage. *Apprehension, disquiet,* and *dread* are in anticipation of danger; *consternation, dismay,* and *terror* are overwhelming *fear,* generally in the actual presence of that which is terrible. Compare FEAR. *Antonyms:* assurance, calmness, confidence, repose, security.

alarm clock A clock fitted with a bell which rings when a trip is sprung as the hands reach a predetermined hour.

a·larm·ing (ə·lär′ming) *adj.* Exciting alarm; causing fear and apprehension; disturbing: an *alarming* symptom. —**a·larm′ing·ly** *adv.*

a·larm·ist (ə·lär′mist) *n.* 1 One who needlessly excites or tries to excite alarm. 2 One who is easily or overeasily alarmed. —**a·larm′ism** *n.*

a·lar·um (ə·lar′əm, ə·lär′əm) *n. Obs.* An alarm.

a·la·ry (ā′lər·ē, al′ə·rē) *adj.* Pertaining to alae or wings; wing-shaped. [< L *alarius* < *ala* wing]

a·las (ə·las′, ə·läs′) *interj.* An exclamation of disappointment, regret, sorrow, etc. [< OF *a* ah! + *las* wretched < L *lassus* weary]

A·las·ka (ə·las′kə) A State of the United States in NW North America, including the Aleutian Islands and the Alexander Archipelago; 586,400 square miles; capital, Juneau; entered the Union Jan. 3, 1959; —**A·las′kan** *adj. & n.*

Alaska, Gulf of A broad northern inlet of the Pacific on the south coast of Alaska between Alaska Peninsula and the Alexander Archipelago.

a·late (ā′lāt) *adj.* Having wings or structures resembling wings. Also **a′lat·ed.** [< L *alatus* < *ala* wing]

a·la·tion (ā·lā′shən) *n.* 1 The condition of being winged. 2 *Entomol.* The way in which an insect's wings are arranged.

alb (alb) *n. Eccl.* A white linen vestment, reaching to the ankles, close-sleeved and girded at the waist, worn over the cassock and amice. [OE *albe* < L *alba (vestis)* white garment)]

ALB
As worn by
a priest.

al·ba[1] (al′bə) *n. Physiol.* The white substance of the central nervous system. [< NL < L, white]

al·ba[2] (äl′bə, al′bə) *n.* A short, formal lyric in Provençal troubadour literature, originally evoked by the necessity for lovers to separate when a watchman announced the dawn; aubade. [< Provençal, dawn]

al·ba·core (al′bə·kôr, -kōr) *n. pl.* **-core** or **-cores** Any of various large scombroid fishes, especially a commercially important food and game fish (*Thunnus alalunga*) having very long pectoral fins. [< Pg. *albacor* < Arabic *al* the + *bukr*

young camel]

Al·ba·ni·a (al-bā′nē-ə, -bān′yə) A Balkan republic south of Yugoslavia; 10,629 square miles; capital, Tirana. *Albanian* **Shqip·ni** (shkyip-nē′).

Al·ba·ni·an (al-bā′nē-ən, -bān′yən) *adj.* Of or pertaining to Albania, its people, or their language. —*n.* **1** A native or inhabitant of Albania. **2** The language of Albania, belonging to the Albanian subfamily of Indo-European languages.

Al·ba·ny (ôl′bə-nē) The capital of New York, a port on the Hudson River.

al·ba·tross (al′bə-trôs, -tros) *n. pl.* **·tross·es** or **·tross** Any of a small family (Diomedeidae) of large web-footed sea birds with long, narrow wings and hooked beaks, confined mostly to the Southern Hemisphere. [Orig. *alcatras* frigate bird < Pg. *alcatraz* pelican < Arabic *al-ghaṭṭas* a sea eagle]

albatross cloth A smooth-faced woolen textile fabric of medium weight.

ALBATROSS

al·be·it (ôl-bē′it) *conj.* Even though; even if; notwithstanding; although. [ME *al be it* although it be]

al·ber·ca (äl-ber′kə) *n. SW U.S.* A pond; pool; also, a sink to carry off waste or dirty water. [< Sp.]

Al·ber·ta (al-bûr′tə) A province in western Canada; 255,285 square miles; capital, Edmonton.

al·bin·ism (al′bə-niz′əm) *n.* **1** An abnormal condition in human beings characterized by a genetically determined lack of pigment in certain cells of the skin, hair, and eyes, and giving a very white or pale appearance. **2** Deficient pigmentation in an animal or plant. **3** The state or condition of being an albino. —**al·bin·ic** (al-bin′ik) *adj.*

al·bi·no (al-bī′nō) *n. pl.* **·nos** A person, animal, or plant lacking normal pigmentation. [< Pg. < *albo* < L *albus* white]

Al·bi·on (al′bē-ən) England: an ancient name now generally only in literary use. [< L]

al·bum (al′bəm) *n.* **1** A book for holding photographs or the like. **2** A blank book for registering names or preserving autographs, stamps, poetical selections, etc. **3** A printed compilation. **4** A single long-playing phonograph record. **5** A set of phonograph records or tape recordings. [< L, white tablet]

al·bu·men (al-byōō′mən) *n.* **1** The white of an egg. **2** *Bot.* The nutritive material that fills the space in a seed between the embryo and the seed coats; endosperm or perisperm. **3** Albumin. [< L, white of an egg < *albus* white]

al·bu·min (al-byōō′mən) *n.* Any of a group of simple proteins which are common in plant and animal tissues and which are soluble in water and coagulable by heat. [< F *albumine* < L *albumen, -inis.* See ALBUMEN.]

al·bu·min·ize (al-byōō′mən-īz) *v.t.* **·ized, ·iz·ing 1** To convert into albumin. **2** To coat or saturate with albumin. Also spelled *albumenize.* —**al·bu′min·i·za′tion** *n.* —**al·bu′min·iz′er** *n.*

Al·bu·quer·que (al′bə-kûr′kē) A resort city on the Rio Grande in NW New Mexico.

Al·ca·traz (al′kə-traz) A small island in San Francisco Bay, California; former site of a Federal prison.

al·che·mist (al′kə-mist) *n.* One skilled in or practicing alchemy.

al·che·mis·tic (al′kə-mis′tik) *adj.* Of or pertaining to alchemy or alchemists; practicing alchemy. Also **al′che·mis′ti·cal.**

al·che·mize (al′kə-mīz) *v.t.* **·mized, ·miz·ing** To transmute by or as by alchemy.

al·che·my (al′kə-mē) *n.* **1** An ancient quasi-magical art through which practitioners sought a formula to cure any disease, confer eternal youth, and transmute base metals into gold. **2** Any cunning, mysterious, or preternatural process of changing the structure or appearance of things. [< OF *alkemie* < Med.L *alchimia* < Arabic *al-kimiyā* < L Gk. *chēmeia* transmutation of metals, later prob. confused with *chymeia* pouring, infusion < *cheein* pour] —**al·chem·ic** (al-kem′ik) *adj.* —**al·chem′i·cal·ly** *adv.*

al·co·hol (al′kə-hôl, -hol) *n.* **1** A colorless, volatile, inflammable liquid, C_2H_5OH, produced commercially by the fermentation of cereal grains, molasses, and fruits, widely used as a solvent in industry and medicine, and as the intoxicating principle in beer, wine, and distilled liquor. Also called *ethanol, ethyl alcohol, grain alcohol.* **2** Any of a group of organic compounds containing one or more functional hydroxyl (OH) groups. **3** Any liquor containing ethyl alcohol. [< Med.L, orig., fine powder < Arabic *al-koh′l* the powdered antimony]

al·co·hol·ic (al′kə-hôl′ik, -hol′-) *adj.* **1** Of, pertaining to, or containing alcohol. **2** Produced by alcohol: an *alcoholic* stupor. **3** Afflicted with alcoholism. —*n.* One who consumes alcohol compulsively. —**al·co·hol′i·cal·ly** *adv.*

al·co·hol·ic·i·ty (al′kə-hol′ə-tē, -hol-) *n.* The quality of being alcoholic; alcoholic strength: the *alcoholicity* of a wine.

al·co·hol·ism (al′kə-hôl′iz-əm, -hol′-) *n.* Compulsive and habitual consumption of alcohol accompanied by varying degrees of deterioration, especially of the nervous and digestive systems.

al·co·hol·y·sis (al′kə-hôl′ə-sis, -hol-) *n.* A decomposing by the action of alcohol.

al·co·sol (al′kə-sôl, -sol) *n.* An alcoholic colloidal solution.

al·cove (al′kōv) *n.* **1** A recess connected with or at the side of a larger room, as to contain a bed. **2** Any embowered or secluded spot. **3** A niche in the face of a cliff or the wall of a building. [< F *alcôve* < Sp. *alcoba* < Arabic *al-qobbah* the vaulted chamber]

Al·deb·a·ran (al-deb′ə-rən) A red star, Alpha in the constellation Taurus; one of the 20 brightest stars, 1.06 magnitude. See STAR. [< Arabic *al-dabarān* the follower (i.e., of the Pleiades)]

al den·te (äl-den′tā) *Ital.* Cooked so as to be chewy; firm to the tooth.

al·der (ôl′dər) *n.* **1** Any of a genus (Alnus) of catkin-bearing shrubs and trees usually growing in moist areas in the Northern Hemisphere. **2** Any of various unrelated species resembling *Alnus* species. [OE *alor*]

al·der·man (ôl′dər-mən) *n. pl.* **·men 1** A member of a municipal legislative body, who usually also exercises certain judicial functions. **2** In England and Ireland, a member of the higher branch of a town council, as in a borough, whose office corresponds to that of the *bailie* in Scotland. [OE *ealdorman* head man] —**al′der·man·cy** (-mən-sē), **al′der·man·ship** *n.*—**al′der·man′ic** (-man′ik) *adj.*

ale (āl) *n.* **1** A beverage made from a fermented infusion of malt, usually flavored with hops: ale resembles beer but generally has more body. **2** An English rural ale-drinking festival. ◆ Homophone: *ail.* [OE *ealu*]

a·le·a·tor·ic (ā′lē-ə-tôr′ik, -tōr′-) *adj. Music* Made up of chance or random elements: *aleatoric* melodies.

a·le·a·to·ry (ā′lē-ə-tôr′ē, -tōr′ē) *adj.* **1** Of or pertaining to gambling or luck. **2** Dependent upon contingency. [< L *aleatorius* < *aleator* gambler < *alea* a die, chance]

ale·house (āl′hous′) *n.* A place where ale is sold to the public.

a·lem·bic (ə-lem′bik) *n.* **1** An apparatus of glass or metal formerly used in distilling. **2** Anything that tests, purifies, or transforms. [< OF *alambic* < L *alambicus* < Arabic *al-anbīq* the still < Gk. *ambix* a cup]

a·lert (ə-lûrt′) *adj.* **1** Keenly watchful; on the look-out; ready for sudden action; vigilant. **2** Lively; nimble. —*n.* **1** A warning against sudden attack; especially, a signal to prepare for an air raid or gas attack. **2** An alert attitude; guard; the period of preparedness for defense. **3** *Aeron.* The condition of an airplane which is manned and equipped to make a sortie. —**on the alert** On the look-out; ready. —*v.t.* To prepare for action; warn, as of a threatened attack or raid. [< F *alerte* < Ital. *all′erta* on the watch] —**a·lert′ly** *adv.* —**a·lert′ness** *n.*

Synonyms (adj.): active, alive, brisk, bustling, nimble, prepared, prompt, ready, vigilant, watchful, wide-awake. *Alert, ready,* and *wide-*

awake refer to a watchful promptness for action. *Ready* suggests preparation; the wandering Indian is *alert,* the trained soldier is *ready. Ready* expresses more life and vigor than *prepared.* The gun is *prepared;* the man is *ready. Prompt* expresses readiness for appointment or demand at the required moment. The good general is *ready* for emergencies, *alert* to perceive opportunity or peril, *prompt* to seize occasion. Compare ACTIVE, ALIVE, NIMBLE. *Antonyms*: drowsy, dull, heavy, inactive, slow, sluggish, stupid.

-ales *suffix Bot.* A feminine plural used to form the scientific names of plant orders. [< L, pl. of -ALIS]

Al·e·ut (al′ē-ōōt) *n. pl.* **Al·e·uts** or **Al·e·ut 1** A native of the Aleutian Islands belonging to either of two Eskimoan tribes called *Unungun.* **2** A subfamily of the Eskimo-Aleut family of languages, comprising the Aleutian Island dialects. —**A·leu·tian** (ə-lōō′shən), **A·leu′tic** *adj.*

A·leu·tian Islands (ə-lōō′shən) A chain of volcanic islands, extending some 1,100 miles from the tip of the Alaska Peninsula between the North Pacific and the Bering Sea. Also **A·leu′tians.**

Aleutian Range A mountain range of SW Alaska, extending along the Alaska Peninsula and continued by the Aleutian Islands.

ale·wife (āl′wīf′) *n. pl.* **·wives** A small North American anadromous fish of the herring family (*Pomolobus pseudoharengus*). [? < Am. Ind.]

Al·ex·an·der (al′ig-zan′dər, -zän′-; *Du., Ger.* ä′lek-sän′dər) A masculine personal name. —**Alexander the Great,** 356–323 B.C., king of Macedon 336–323, conqueror of Asia.

A·lex·an·dri·a (al′ig-zan′drē-ə, -zän′-) The chief port and ancient capital of Egypt. *Arabic* **Al Is·kan·da·ri·ya** (al is-kan-da-rē′yə).

A·lex·an·dri·an (al′ig-zan′drē-ən, -zän′-) *adj.* **1** Of or pertaining to Alexander the Great, his reign, or his conquests. **2** Of or pertaining to the Alexandrian school or its influence. **3** In prosody, Alexandrine. —*n.* **1** A native or inhabitant of Alexandria. **2** In prosody, an Alexandrine verse.

a·lex·i·a (ə-lek′sē-ə) *n.* Loss of ability to grasp the significance of written or printed matter. Also called *word blindness.* [< NL < Gk. *a-* without + *lexis* speech < *legein* speak]

al·fal·fa (al-fal′fə) *n.* A perennial leguminous herb (*Medicago sativa*) having deep roots, compound pinnate leaves, and clusters of small purple flowers, widely grown for fodder. Also called *lucerne, purple medic.* [< Sp. < Arabic *al-faṣfaṣah* the best kind of fodder]

al·for·ja (al-fôr′jə, *Sp.* äl-fôr′hä) *n.* **1** A leather pouch; saddle bag. **2** A cheek pouch, especially of the baboon. [< Sp. < Arabic *al-khorj*]

Al·fred (al′frid; *Dan.* äl′frid; *Du., Ger.* äl′fret; *Fr.* àl·fred′) A masculine personal name. —**Alfred the Great,** 849–901, king of the West Saxons; defeated the Danish invaders, built the first English navy, and is known as the father of English prose literature.

al·fres·co (al-fres′kō) *adv.* In the open air. —*adj.* Occurring outdoors, as a meal. Also **al fresco.** [< Ital.]

al·gae (al′jē) *n. pl.* A large group of primitive, mostly aquatic, chlorophyll-bearing plants lacking specialized tissues and organs such as roots, stems, leaves, and flowers, and including forms ranging from giant seaweeds to single-celled diatoms and pond scums. [< L, seaweed] —**al·gal**

(al′gəl) adj.

Al·gar·ve (äl·gär′və) The southernmost province of Portugal; 1,958 square miles; capital, Faro; formerly a Moorish kingdom.

al·ge·bra (al′jə·brə) n. 1 The branch of mathematics which treats of quantity and number in the abstract, and in which calculations are performed by means of letters and symbols: it includes the solution of equations of any degree. 2 A treatise on this subject. [< Ital. < Arabic *al-jebr* the reunion of broken parts, bone-setting]

al·ge·bra·ic (al′jə·brā′ik) adj. Pertaining to algebra. Also **al′ge·bra′i·cal.** —**al′ge·bra′i·cal·ly** adv.

al·ge·don·ic (al′jə·don′ik) adj. Characterized by or relating to the agreeable and the disagreeable. [< Gk. *algos* pain + *hēdonikos* pleasurable]

al·ge·don·ics (al′jə·don′iks) n. Psychol. The study of pain and pleasure in relation to human life.

Al·ge·ri·a (al·jir′ē·ə) A republic in NW Africa, formerly a dependency of France; 919,352 square miles; capital, Algiers. French **Al·gé·rie** (àl·zhā·rē′). —**Al·ge′ri·an** adj. & n.

Al·ge·rine (al′jə·rēn′) n. 1 An inhabitant or native of Algeria, especially a native Berber, Arab, or Moor; an Algerian. 2 A pirate.

al·ge·si·a (al·jē′zē·ə) n. Sensitiveness to pain. [< Gk. *algos* pain]

al·get·ic (al·jet′ik) adj. Relating to or causing pain. [< Gk. *algein* feel pain]

-algia suffix Pain or disease of: *neuralgia*. [< Gk. *algos* pain]

al·gid (al′jid) adj. Cold; chilly: the *algid* stage of ague. [< F *algide* < L *algidus* cold < *algere* be cold] —**al·gid′i·ty** n.

Al·giers (al·jirz′) The capital of Algeria, a major port on the Mediterranean.

Al·gon·ki·an (al·gong′kē·ən) adj. 1 Geol. Of, pertaining to, or characterized by a series of rock strata between the Archaean and the Cambrian; Proterozoic. 2 Former spelling of ALGONQUIAN.

Al·gon·qui·an (al·gong′kē·ən, -kwē·ən) n. 1 A large linguistic stock of North American Indians, formerly inhabiting the territory from Hudson Bay south to North Carolina and Tennessee, east of the Mississippi, including the Algonquin, Arapaho, Blackfoot, Cheyenne, Cree, Ojibwa, Micmac, Sauk, Delaware, Massachuset, and Shawnee tribes. 2 A member of one of the tribes belonging to this stock. —adj. Of or pertaining to the Algonquian family.

Al·gon·quin (al·gong′kin, -kwin) n. 1 A member of certain Algonquian tribes formerly inhabiting territory near the mouth of the Ottawa river, and of certain other tribes north of the St. Lawrence river. 2 The language spoken by these tribes, belonging to the East Central subfamily of Algonquian Indian languages. Also **Al·gon·kin** (al·gong′kin).

al·go·pho·bi·a (al′gə·fō′bē·ə) n. Psychiatry A morbid fear of pain. [< Gk. *algos* pain + -PHOBIA] —**al′go·pho′bic** adj.

al·gor (al′gôr) n. Pathol. Cold; chilliness; especially, an abnormal coldness, as in the early stages of a fever. [< L]

al·go·rism (al′gə·riz′əm) n. 1 The Arabic or decimal system of numeration. 2 Any method of computation using Arabic notation. 3 Arithmetic. Also **al·go·rithm** (al′gə·rith′əm). [< OF *algorisme* < Med.L *algorismus* < Arabic *al-Khowārazmī*, lit., the native of Khwārazm (Khiva), surname of a 9th cent. Arab mathematician]

a·li·as (ā′lē·əs) n. pl. **a·li·as·es** 1 An assumed name. 2 Law A second writ to the same effect as

a former one, issued after the first has failed. —adv. Otherwise called; called by an assumed name. [< L, at another time or place]

A·li (ä′lē), 600?–661, son-in-law and adopted son of Mohammed; fourth Arabian calif.

A·li Ba·ba (ä′lē bä′bä) In the *Arabian Nights*, the hero of the tale *Ali Baba and the Forty Thieves*, who gains entrance to a robbers' cave by crying out the magic words "Open sesame."

al·i·bi (al′ə·bī) n. 1 A form of defense by which the accused, in order to establish his innocence, undertakes to show that he was elsewhere when the crime was committed: He had a perfect *alibi*. 2 Colloq. Any excuse; especially, a poor and flimsy excuse. —v.i. Colloq. To make excuses for oneself. [< L, elsewhere]

al·i·bil·i·ty (al′ə·bil′ə·tē) n. Nutritive quality or value.

al·i·ble (al′ə·bəl) adj. Nourishing; nutritive. [< L *alibilis* < *alere* nourish]

al·i·dade (al′i·dād) n. 1 An auxiliary circle, frame, or movable arm, carrying microscopes or verniers, for reading the divisions of a graduated circle or arc. 2 A theodolite having such an arm. Also **al·i·dad** (al′i·dad). [< F < Med.L *alhidada* < Arabic *al-'idādah* the revolving radius of a graduated circle]

al·ien (āl′yən, ā′lē·ən) adj. 1 Of another country; foreign. 2 Of foreign character; not similar; incongruous; inconsistent; also, unsympathetic. —n. 1 An unnaturalized foreign resident. 2 One of another race. 3 One estranged or excluded. 4 Bot. A plant native to one region maintaining itself under conditions prevailing in another. —v.t. 1 To transfer to another, as property. 2 To estrange. [< L *alienus* belonging to another]

Synonyms (adj.): conflicting, contradictory, contrary, contrasted, distant, foreign, hostile, opposed, remote, strange, unconnected, unlike. *Foreign* refers to difference of birth, *alien* to difference of allegiance. In their figurative use, that is *foreign* which is *remote*, *unlike*, or *unconnected*; that is *alien* which is *conflicting*, *hostile*, or *opposed*. *Antonyms*: akin, appropriate, apropos, essential, germane, pertinent, proper, relevant.

Synonyms (noun): foreigner, stranger. A naturalized citizen is not an *alien*, even if a *foreigner* by birth, and perhaps a *stranger* in the place where he resides. A person of foreign birth not naturalized is an *alien*, though he may have been long resident in the country, and ceased to be a stranger. He is an *alien* in one country if his allegiance is to another. *Antonyms*: citizen, countryman, native.

al·ien·a·ble (āl′yən·ə·bəl, ā′lē·ən-) adj. That can be made over or transferred, as property to the ownership of another. —**al′ien·a·bil′i·ty** n.

al·ien·ate (āl′yən·āt, ā′lē·ən-) v.t. **·at·ed, ·at·ing** 1 To make indifferent or unfriendly; estrange: to *alienate* a friend. 2 To cause to feel estranged or withdrawn from society. 3 To make over; transfer, as property to the ownership of another. 4 To turn away, as affection or interest. —**al′ien·a′tor** n.

al·ien·a·tion (āl′yən·ā′shən, ā′lē·ən-) n. 1 The act of alienating, or the state of being alienated. 2 An anxious or resentful feeling of not belonging to or having a fit place in society. 3 An abnormal condition of indifference to or estrangement from others. 4 Law The transfer of property, or title, to another.

al·ien·ist (āl′yən·ist, ā′lē·ən-) n. One skilled in the study or treatment of mental disorders: term used chiefly in medical jurisprudence. [< F *aliéniste*, ult. < L *alienus* foreign, strange]

a·lif (ä′lif) n. The first letter in the Arabic alphabet.

al·i·form (al′ə·fôrm, ā′lə·fôrm) adj. Wing-shaped; alar. [< L *ala* a wing + -FORM]

a·light[1] (ə·līt′) v.i. **a·light·ed** or **a·lit, a·light·ing** 1 To descend and come to rest; settle, as after flight. 2 To dismount, as from a horse or vehicle. 3 To come or fall upon by accident: with *on* or *upon*. [< OE *ālīhtan* < *ā-* out, off + *līhtan* alight, orig., make light]

a·light[2] (ə·līt′) adj. & adv. Lighted; lighted up; on fire; kindled. [ME *aliht*, pp. of *alihten* light up]

a·lign (ə·līn′) v.t. To arrange or place in a line; bring into line. —v.i. To fall into line. Also spelled *aline*. [< F *aligner* < *a-* to (< L *ad-*) + *ligne* line < L *linea*] —**a·lign′ment** n.

a·like (ə·līk′) adj. Having resemblance; like one another; resembling, wholly or in part. —adv. In like manner. [OE *gelic, onlic*] —**a·like′ness** n.

Synonyms (adj.): akin, analogous, equal, equivalent, homogeneous, identical, kindred, like, resembling, similar, synonymous, uniform. Two or more objects are *alike* when each resembles the other or others; by modifiers *alike* may be made to express more or less resemblance; as, these houses are somewhat (that is, partially) *alike*; or, exactly (that is, in all respects) *alike*; or *alike* in color or structure. Substances are *homogeneous* which are made up of elements of the same kind, or which are the same in structure. To say "this is the *identical* man" is to say not merely that he is *similar* to the one in mind, but that he is the very *same* person. Things are *analogous* when they are *similar* in idea, plan, use, or character, but perhaps quite unlike in appearance; as, the gills of fishes are said to be *analogous* to the lungs in terrestrial animals. Compare IDENTICAL. *Antonyms*: different, dissimilar, distinct, heterogeneous, unlike.

al·i·ment (al′ə·mənt) n. Food; nutriment; sustenance. See synonyms under FOOD. —v.t. To furnish with food; nourish. [< L *alimentum* < *alere* nourish] —**al·i·men·tal** (al′ə·men′təl) adj. —**al′i·men′tal·ly** adv.

al·i·men·ta·ry (al′ə·men′tər·ē) adj. Supplying nourishment; connected with the function of nutrition.

alimentary canal The continuous digestive tube leading from the mouth through the esophagus, stomach, and intestines, having muscular walls which absorb nutrients and by peristalsis propel waste material to be discharged at the anus.

al·i·men·ta·tion (al′ə·men·tā′shən) n. 1 The act or process of supplying nutrition. 2 The act, process, or capacity of receiving nourishment or being nourished. 3 Maintenance; support.

al·i·men·ta·tive (al′ə·men′tə·tiv) adj. Of or pertaining to alimentation; nutritive.

al·i·mo·ny (al′ə·mō′nē) n. 1 Law The allowance made to a woman by order of court, from her husband's estate or income, for her maintenance after her divorce or legal separation from him, or during a suit therefor. The allowance made during suit is called **alimony pendente lite.** 2 Maintenance; means of living or sustenance. [< L *alimonia* food, support < *alere* nourish]

a·line (ə·līn′) v. **a·lined, a·lin·ing** v.t. To arrange or place in a line; bring into line. —v.i. To fall into line. Also spelled *align*. [< F *aligner* < *a-* to (< L *ad-*) + *ligne* line < L *linea*]

a·line·ment (ə·līn′mənt) n. 1 Position or place in line; formation in line. 2 A straight line through two or more points. 3 Eng. The ground plan, as of a railroad. Also spelled *alignment*.

al·i·ped (al′ə·ped) adj. Having winglike membranes connecting the digits and the front and hind feet on each side, as a bat. —n. An aliped animal; a bat. [< L *alipes, -pedis* wing-footed < *ala* wing + *pes* foot]

al·i·quant (al′ə·kwənt) adj. Contained in another number, but with remainder. [< L *aliquantus* some, somewhat < *alius* other + *quantus* how large, how much]

al·i·quot (al′ə·kwət) adj. Contained in another quantity an exact number of times. —n. A small aliquot portion of a measured volume or weight of a substance taken as a sample representing the whole. [< L *aliquot* < *alius* other + *quot* how many]

a·list (ə·list′) adv. & adj. In a canted or inclined position; listed over.

a·lit (ə·lit′) Past tense and past participle of ALIGHT[1].

a·live (ə·līv′) adj. 1 In a living state, or a state in which the organs perform their functions; having life: said of organisms: opposed to *dead*. 2 In ac-

add,āce,câre,pälm; end,ēven; it,īce; odd,ōpen,ôrder; took,pool; up,bûrn; ə = a in *above*, e in *sicken*, i in *clarity*, o in *melon*, u in *focus*; yōō = u in *fuse*, oi,oil; ou,pout; ch,check; g,go; ng,ring; th,thin; th,this; zh,vision. Foreign sounds à,œ,ü,kh,ṅ; and ♦: see page xx. < from; + plus; ? possibly.

tion, motion, or existence; in force, or operation; in full vigor. **3** In lively action; in an animated state; sprightly: *alive* with enthusiasm. **4** In a condition of attentiveness, sensitiveness, or susceptibility; open to impressions. **5** Abounding in life or living things, or in evidences of life: The hive was *alive* with bees. [OE *on life* in life] *Synonyms*: active, alert, animate, animated, breathing, brisk, existent, existing, live, lively, living, quick, subsisting, vivacious. *Alive* applies to all degrees of life, from that which shows one to be barely *existing* or *existent* as a living thing, as when we say he is barely *alive*, to that which implies the utmost of vitality and power. So the word *quick*, which began by signifying "having life," is now mostly applied to energy of life as shown in swiftness of action. *Breathing* is capable of like contrast. We say of a dying man, "he is still *breathing*"; or we speak of a *breathing* statue, where we mean having, or seeming to have breath and life. Compare ACTIVE, ALERT, NIMBLE. *Antonyms*: dead, deceased, defunct, dispirited, dull, inanimate, lifeless, spiritless.

al·ka·les·cen·cy (al′kə-les′ən-sē) *n.* A tendency to become alkaline; slight alkalinity. Also **al′ka·les′cence.**

al·ka·les·cent (al′kə-les′ənt) *adj.* Becoming or tending to become alkaline. —*n.* An alkalescent compound.

al·ka·li (al′kə-lī) *n. pl.* **·lis** or **·lies 1** *Chem.* A compound of hydrogen and oxygen with any one of the elements lithium, sodium, potassium, rubidium, and cesium, or the ammonium radical, characterized by great solubility in water and capability of neutralizing acids and of turning red litmus paper blue. **2** Anything that will neutralize an acid, as lime, magnesia, etc. **3** Sodium carbonate. **4** Mineral matter, not including sodium chloride, found in natural waters and in soils. [< MF *alcali* < Arabic *al-qalīy* the ashes of saltwort]

al·kal·ic (al-kal′ik) *adj.* Containing or characterized by a considerable amount of the alkaline bases, especially soda and potash.

al·ka·li·fy (al′kə-lə-fī, al-kal′ə-fī) *v.t. & v.i.* **·fied, ·fy·ing** To change into or become alkaline or an alkali.

alkali metals Any of the metallic elements of group Ia of the periodic table, including lithium, sodium, potassium, rubidium, cesium, and francium.

al·ka·line (al′kə-līn, -lin) *adj.* **1** Of, pertaining to, or having the characteristics of an alkali; containing or produced by an alkali. **2** Having a pH greater than 7.

al·ka·lin·i·ty (al′kə-lin′ə-tē) *n.* The state or quality of being alkaline.

al·ka·lize (al′kə-līz) *v.t. & v.i.* **·lized, ·liz·ing** To convert into or become alkali or alkaline. —**al′ka·li·za′tion** *n.*

al·ka·loid (al′kə-loid) *n.* Any of various nitrogenous bases of vegetable origin, usually having a toxic effect on animals, as strychnine, nicotine, or cocaine. —**al′ka·loi′dal** *adj.*

al·ka·lo·sis (al′kə-lō′sis) *n.* A higher concentration than normal of carbonate in body fluids.

all (ôl) *adj.* **1** The entire substance or extent of: *all* Europe; *all* wisdom. **2** The entire number of; the individual components of, without exception: to be known to *all* men. **3** The greatest possible: in *all* haste. **4** Any whatever: beyond *all* doubt. **5** Every: used in phrases with *manner, sorts,* and *kinds: all* manner of men. **6** Nothing except: He was *all* skin and bones. See synonyms under EVERY. —*n.* **1** Everything that one has; entire interest or possession: to give one's *all.* **2** Whole being; totality. —*pron.* **1** Everyone: *All* are condemned. **2** Each one: When he questioned his students, *all* were ready with an answer. **3** Everything: *All* is in readiness. **4** Every part, as of a whole: *All* of it is gone. ◆ Homophone, *awl.* [OE] —**above all** Primarily; of the first importance. —**after all 1** On the other hand. **2** In the long run; in spite of everything. —**all in all 1** All things considered; taken as a whole. —**at all. 1** In any way: I can't come *at all.* **2** To any degree or extent; no luck *at all.* —**for all** To the degree that: *For all* I care, you can go without me. —**for all of** (me, you, him, her, or us) As for: You can leave now, *for all of* me. —**in all** Including everything; all told. —**onceand for all** Once and no more; finally. —

adv. **1** Wholly; entirely: fallen *all* to bits; running*all* the way; traveling *all* through the night. **2** Exclusively; only: That portion is *all* three *all.* —**all along** All the time: I knew it *all along.* —**all but 1** Almost; on the verge of: I was *all but* exhausted by my trip. **2** Every one except: He took *all but* six. —**all in** *Colloq.* Wearied, as from exertion. —**all of** No less than; quite: It's *all of* ten miles. —**all out** Making every effort: They went *all out* for victory. —**all over 1** Finished; past and gone: The love affair is *all over* between us. **2** Everywhere; in all parts: He's been *all over.* **3** Typically; in every way: That's George *all over.* —**all the** (**better, more,** etc.) So much the (better, more, etc.) —**all up with** *Colloq.* Ended; without power to continue: It's *all up with* him.

all·es·the·sia (al′ak·is·thē′zhə, -zhē-ə) *n.* A tactile sensation localized elsewhere than at the point of stimulation. Also *allesthesia.* [< Gk. *allachē* elsewhere + *aisthēsis* feeling]

Al·lah (al′ə, ä′lə) In the Moslem religion, the one supreme being; God. [< Arabic]

al·lan·toid (ə-lan′toid) *adj.* **1** Sausage-shaped. **2** Resembling or possessing an allantois. Also **al·lan·toi·dal** (al′ən-toi′dəl). [Gk. *allantoeidēs* < *allas* sausage + *eidos* form]

al·lan·to·is (ə-lan′tō·is) *n.* A membranous, fluid-filled sac that develops from the hindgut in the embryos of reptiles, birds, and mammals. [< NL < *allantoides* < GK. See ALLANTOID.] —**al·lan·to·ic** (al′ən-tō′ik) *adj.*

al·lay (ə-lā′) *v.t.* **al·layed, al·lay·ing 1** To lessen the violence or reduce the intensity of. **2** To lay to rest, as fears; pacify; calm. [OE *ālecgan* < *ā-* away + *lecgan* lay] —**al·lay′er** *n.* *Synonyms*: abate, alleviate, appease, assuage, calm, compose, lessen, lighten, mitigate, moderate, mollify, pacify, palliate, quiet, reduce, relieve, soften, soothe, still, tranquilize. We *allay* suffering by using means to *soothe* and *tranquilize* the sufferer; we *alleviate* suffering by doing something toward removal of the cause. *Pacify* and *appease* signify to bring to peace; to *mollify* is to soften; to *mitigate* is to make mild; we *mollify* a temper, *mitigate* rage or pain. To *calm, quiet,* or *tranquilize* is to make still; *compose,* to adjust to a calm and settled condition; to *soothe* is to bring to pleased quietude. We *allay* excitement, *calm* agitation, *compose* our feelings, *pacify* the quarrelsome, *quiet* the clamorous, *soothe* grief or distress. Compare ALLEVIATE. *Antonyms*: agitate, arouse, excite, fan, kindle, provoke, rouse, stir.

al·le·ga·tion (al′ə-gā′shən) *n.* **1** The act of alleging. **2** That which is alleged; a formal assertion. **3** Something alleged without proof. **4** *Law* The assertion of a party to a suit, which he undertakes to prove. [< L *allegatio, -onis* < *allegare* send a message < *ad-* to + *legare* commission]

al·lege (ə-lej′) *v.t.* **al·leged, al·leg·ing 1** To assert to be true without proving; affirm. **2** To plead as an excuse, in support of or in opposition to a claim or accusation. **3** *Archaic* To cite or quote. [< AF *alegier,* OF *esligier* < L *ex-* out + *litigare* sue; infl. by L *allegare* (see ALLEGATION) and *lex* law] —**al·lege′a·ble** *adj.* —**al·leged′** *adj.* —**al·leg′er** *n.* *Synonyms*: adduce, advance, affirm, assert, asseverate, assign, aver, cite, claim, declare, introduce, maintain, offer, plead, produce, say, state. To *allege* is formally to state as true, without proving. *Adduce* is a secondary word; nothing can be *adduced* in evidence until something has been *stated* or *alleged,* which the evidence is to sustain. An *alleged* fact stands open to question or doubt. When an *alleged* criminal is brought to trial, the counsel on either side are accustomed to *advance* a theory, and *adduce* the strongest possible evidence in its support; they will *produce* documents and witnesses, *cite* precedents, *assign* reasons, *introduce* suggestions, *offer* pleas. The accused will usually *assert* his innocence. Compare STATE. *Antonyms*: see AFFIRM.

al·leg·ed·ly (ə-lej′id-lē) *adv.* According to allegation.

al·le·giance (ə-lē′jəns) *n.* **1** Fidelity, or an obligation of fidelity, to a government from a citizen, to a superior, or to a principle. **2** The obligation of fidelity in general. **3** *Archaic* The duty and obligation of a vassal holding lands by fealty to the

superior lord. [ME *alegeaunce* < *a-* to (< L *ad-*) + OF *ligeance* < *liege.* See LIEGE.] *Synonyms*: devotion, faithfulness, fealty, fidelity, homage, loyalty, obedience, subjection. The feudal uses of these words have mostly passed away with the state of society that gave them birth; but their origin still colors their present meaning. A patriotic American feels an enthusiastic *loyalty* to the Republic; he takes an oath of *allegiance* to the government, but his *loyalty* will lead him to do more than mere *allegiance* could demand; he pays *homage* to God or to those principles of right that are supreme; he acknowledges the duty of *obedience* to all rightful authority; he resents the idea of *subjection.* *Fealty,* except in poetic style, has given place to *faithfulness* or *fidelity.* *Antonyms*: disaffection, disloyalty, rebellion, sedition, treason.

al·le·giant (ə-lē′jənt) *adj. Obs.* Loyal; faithful.

al·le·gor·ic (al′ə-gôr′ik, -gor′-) *adj.* Pertaining to, appearing in, or containing allegory; figurative. Also **al′le·gor′i·cal.** —**al′le·gor′i·cal·ly** *adv.* —**al′le·gor′i·cal·ness** *n.*

al·le·go·rist (al′ə-gôr′ist, -gō′rist, al′ə-gər-ist) *n.* One who composes or uses allegories.—**al′le·go·ris′tic** *adj.*

al·le·go·rize (al′ə-gə-rīz) *v.* **·rized, ·riz·ing** *v.t.* **1** To turn into an allegory; relate in the manner of an allegory. **2** To explain or interpret as an allegory. —*v.i.* **3** To make or use allegory. —**al′le·go·ri·za·tion** (al′ə-gôr′ə-zā′shən, -gor′-) *n.* —**al′le·go·riz′er** *n.*

al·le·go·ry (al′ə-gôr′ē, -gō′rē) *n. pl.* **·ries 1** The setting forth of a subject or the telling of a story in figurative or symbolic language requiring interpretation; especially, a narrative veiling a moral by symbolic devices, such as personification, metaphor, etc. **2** Any subject or story so presented. **3** Loosely, any symbolic representation in literature or art; an emblem. [< L *allegoria* < Gk. *allēgoria,* lit., a speaking otherwise < *allos* other + *agoreuein* speak in public assembly < *agora* forum] *Synonyms*: fable, fiction, illustration, metaphor, parable, simile, story. The *allegory, parable,* or *fable* tells its story as if true, leaving the reader or hearer to discover its fictitious character and learn its lesson. The word *fiction* is applied almost exclusively to novels, short stories, or romances. An *allegory* or *parable* is a moral or religious tale, of which the moral lesson is the substance and all descriptions and incidents but accessories; the *parable* is generally briefer and less adorned than the *allegory.* A *fable* is generally brief, representing animals as the speakers and actors, and conveying some lesson of practical wisdom or shrewdness. Compare SIMILE, STORY. *Antonyms*: chronicle, fact, history, narrative, record.

al·le·gret·to (al′ə-gret′ō, *Ital.* ä′lä-gret′tō) *adj. & adv. Music* Rather fast: faster than *andante* but slower than *allegro.* —*n. pl.* **·tos** A movement in allegretto time. [< Ital.]

al·le·gro (ə-lā′grō, ə-leg′rō; *Ital.* äl-lā′grō) *adj. & adv. Music* Quick; lively: faster than *allegretto* but slower than *presto.* —*n. pl.* **·gros** A musical composition, movement, etc., in such tempo. [< Ital.]

al·lele (ə-lēl′) *n. Genetics* An allelomorph.

al·le·lo·morph (ə-lē′lə-môrf, ə-lel′ə-) *n. Genetics* In Mendel's law, one of a pair of contrasted characters which become segregated in the formation of reproductive cells. [< Gk. *allēlōn* of one another + *morphē* form] —**al·le·lo·mor′phic** *adj.* —**al·le′lo·mor′phism** *n.*

al·le·lu·ia (al′ə-lōō′yə) *n. & interj.* Hallelujah. Also **al′le·lu′iah.** [< L. See HALLELUJAH.] —**al·le·lu·iat·ic** (al′ə-lōō-yat′ik) *adj.*

al·ler·gen (al′ər-jən) *n.* Any substance capable of producing allergy. —**al·ler·gen·ic** (al′ər-jen′-ik) *adj.*

al·ler·gic (ə-lûr′jik) *adj.* **1** Characteristic of or pertaining to allergy. **2** Highly susceptible to. **3** *Colloq.* Having an aversion to.

al·ler·gist (al′ər-jist) *n.* A specialist in the treatment of allergies.

al·ler·gy (al′ər-jē) *n. pl.* **·gies 1** A condition of exaggerated sensibility, as manifested by various physiologic reactions to an environmental substance or sensory stimulus that produces no reaction in nonsensitive individuals. **2** Anaphylaxis. [< NL *allergia* < Gk. *allos* other + *ergon* work]

al·le·vi·ate (ə·lē′vē·āt) *v.t.* **·at·ed, ·at·ing** To make lighter or easier to bear; relieve, as pain; mitigate. [< L *alleviatus*, pp. of *alleviare* < *ad-* to + *levis* light]

Synonyms: abate, allay, assuage, lessen, lighten, mitigate, moderate, reduce, relieve, remove, soften. *Alleviate* is less than *relieve; relieve*, ordinarily, less than *remove. Assuage* is to sweeten; *mitigate*, to make milder; *moderate*, to bring within measure; *abate*, to beat down and so make less. We *abate* a fever; *lessen* anxiety; *moderate* passions or desires; *lighten* burdens; *mitigate* or *alleviate* pain; *reduce* inflammation; *soften, assuage*, or *moderate* grief; we *lighten* or *mitigate* punishments; we *relieve* suffering. Compare ALLAY. *Antonyms*: aggravate, augment, embitter, enhance, heighten, increase, intensify, magnify. —**al·le′vi·a′tion** *n.* —**al·le′·vi·a′tor** *n.*

al·le·vi·a·tive (ə·lē′vē·ā′tiv, ə·lē′vē·ə·tiv) *adj.* Tending to alleviate. Also **al·le·vi·a·to·ry** (ə·lē′·vē·ə·tôr′ē, -tō′rē). —*n.* Anything that alleviates.

al·ley[1] (al′ē) *n.* **1** A narrow passageway, street, path, or walk; especially, a narrow way behind city buildings, running parallel to a street. **2** A long narrow space for bowling, or the building containing it. See synonyms under WAY. [< OF *alee* a going, passage < *aler* go, ? < L *ambulare*]

al·ley[2] (al′ē) *n.* A large playing marble. [< ALABASTER]

alley cat A cat which forages for food in alleys, etc.

al·leyed (al′ēd) *adj.* Having an alley or alleys; having the form or nature of an alley.

al·ley·way (al′ē·wā′) *n.* A short or narrow passageway between buildings.

al·li·ance (ə·lī′əns) *n.* **1** A formal treaty or agreement between states or other parties. **2** The union so formed; any intimate relationship. [< OF *aliance* (MF *alliance*) < L *alligantia* < *alligare*. See ALLY.]

Synonyms: affinity, coalition, compact, confederacy, confederation, federation, fusion, kin, league, partnership, union. Commonly, *alliance* is a connection formed by treaty between sovereign states for mutual aid in war; *partnership* is a mercantile word. We speak of an alliance *with* a neighboring people; *against* the common enemy; *for* offense and defense; alliance *of, between,* or *among* nations. *Coalition* is oftenest used of political parties; *fusion* is now the more common word in this sense. In a *confederacy* or *confederation* there is an attempt to unite separate states in a general government without surrender of sovereignty. *Union* makes the separate states substantially one. *Federation* is a poetic and rhetorical word expressing something of the same thought. The United States is a federal *union*. See ASSOCIATION. *Antonyms*: antagonism, discord, disunion, divorce, enmity, hostility, schism, secession, separation, war.

al·lied (ə·līd′) *adj.* **1** United, confederated, or leagued. **2** Morphologically, genetically, or otherwise related.

al·li·ga·tion (al′ə·gā′shən) *n.* Formerly, the method of finding or rule for finding the relation between the prices of the ingredients in a mixture, their proportions, quality, and the price of the mixture. In **alligation alternate** the proportion is required, the other two quantities being given: in **alligation medial** the cost of the mixture is required. [< L *alligatio, -onis* < *alligare* < *ad-* to + *ligare* bind]

al·li·ga·tor (al′ə·gā′tər) *n.* **1** Either of two species of large, crocodilian reptiles (genus *Alligator*), found only in rivers and swamps of the southern United States and in the Yangtze River in China, having a shorter, blunter head than the crocodile and no lower teeth protruding when the jaw is closed. **2** Any crocodilian. **3** Leather made from the hide of an alligator. **4** A machine for squeezing ore, etc. [Earlier *alligarta* < Sp. *el lagarto* the lizard < L *lacertus*]

ALLIGATOR
(Length up to 18 feet)

al·li·sion (ə·lizh′ən) *n. Naut.* The act of a vessel's striking or dashing against another: distinguished from *collision*. [< L *allisio, -onis* < *allidere* < *ad-* against + *laedere* strike violently]

al·lit·er·ate (ə·lit′ə·rāt) *v.* **·at·ed, ·at·ing** *v.i.* **1** To speak alliteratively; use alliteration, as in the writing of verse. **2** To constitute alliteration: These two lines of verse *alliterate.* —*v.t.* **3** To make alliterative: to *alliterate* verses. [< AL-[2] to + L *littera* a letter (of the alphabet)]

al·lit·er·a·tion (ə·lit′ə·rā′shən) *n.* **1** The use or repetition of a succession of words with same initial letter or sound: Langland uses *alliteration* in his line "A fair field full of folk." —**al·lit·er·a·tive** (ə·lit′ə·rā′tiv, -ər·ə·tiv) *adj.* —**al·lit′er·a′tive·ly** *adv.* —**al·lit′er·a′tive·ness** *n.*

allo- *combining form* **1** Other; alien: *allotheism,* worship of strange gods. **2** Variant; different: *allogeneic,* differing genetically. [< Gk. *allos* other]

al·lo·cate (al′ə·kāt) *v.t.* **·cat·ed, ·cat·ing 1** To set apart for a special purpose, as funds. **2** To apportion; assign, as a share or in shares. **3** To locate or localize, as a person or event. [< Med.L *allocatus*, pp. of *allocare* < L *ad-* to + *locare* place < *locus* a place] —**al·lo·ca·ble** (al′ə·kə·bəl) *adj.*

al·lo·ca·tion (al′ə·kā′shən) *n.* **1** An allocating or being allocated. **2** Something allocated.

al·lo·cu·tion (al′ə·kyōō′shən) *n.* A formal, official, or authoritative exhortation or address. [< L *allocutio, -onis* < *alloqui* < *ad-* to + *loqui* speak]

al·log·a·my (ə·log′ə·mē) *n. Bot.* Fecundation of a flower by pollen from another flower of the same species; cross-fertilization: opposed to *autogamy.* [< ALLO- + Gk. *gamos* marriage]—**al·log′a·mous** *adj.*

al·lo·ge·ne·ic (al′ə·jə·nē′ik) *adj.* Differing genetically to the extent of having the potential to initiate an immune reaction. Also **al·lo·gen·ic** (al′ə·jen′ik) *adj.*

al·lo·graft (al′ə·graft, -gräft) *n.* A graft of tissue from a donor who differs genetically but is of the same species as the recipient; homograft.

al·lom·e·try (ə·lom′ə·trē) *n.* The relative changes in dimension of organs and parts of the body during development and growth of the organism as a whole. —**al·lo·met·ric** (al′ə·met′rik) *adj.*

al·lo·path·ic (al′ə·path′ik) *adj.* Pertaining to, favoring, or practicing allopathy. —**al′lo·path′i·cal·ly** *adv.*

al·lop·a·thy (ə·lop′ə·thē) *n. Med.* The system of remedial treatment in which it is sought to cure a disease by producing a condition different from or incompatible with the effects of the disease: opposed to *homeopathy.* [< ALLO- + Gk. *pathos* suffering] —**al·lop′a·thist,** **al·lo·path** (al′ə·path) *n.*

al·lo·phone (al′ə·fōn) *n. Phonet.* Any of the nondistinctive variants of a phoneme: The velar (k) of *coop* and the palatal (k) of *keep* are allophones of the phoneme /k/. [< ALLO- + Gk. *phōnē* a sound, voice]

al·lo·some (al′ə·sōm) *n.* **1** Sex chromosome. **2** Any aberrant chromosome. [< ALLO- + Gk. *sōma* body]

al·lot (ə·lot′) *v.t.* **al·lot·ted, al·lot·ting 1** To assign by lot; distribute so that the recipients have no choice: to *allot* duties. **2** To apportion or assign, as to a special function, person, or place: with *to:* to *allot* ten years to the acquisition of knowledge. [< OF *aloter* < *a-* to (< L *ad-*) + *lot.* See LOT.]

Synonyms: appoint, apportion, assign, award, destine, distribute, divide, give, grant, select. *Allot* applies to the giving of a definite thing; a portion or extent of time or space is *allotted. Appoint* may be used of time, space, or person; as the *appointed* day; the *appointed* place; an officer was *appointed* to this station. *Destine* fixes or assumes to fix what is considerably in the future; as, he *destines* his son to follow his own profession. *Assign* is rarely used of time, but rather of places, persons, or things. That which is *allotted, appointed,* or *assigned* is more or less arbitrary; that which is *awarded* is the due return for something the receiver has done, and he has right and claim to it, as, the medal was *awarded* for valor. *Antonyms*: appropriate, confiscate, deny, refuse, resume, retain, seize, withhold.

al·lot·ment (ə·lot′mənt) *n.* **1** The act of allotting or that which is allotted. **2** *U.S. Mil.* A portion of one's pay assigned to a member of the family. **3** A plot of land. **4** Destiny.

al·lo·trope (al′ə·trōp) *n.* One of the forms assumed by an allotropic substance: The diamond is an *allotrope* of carbon.

al·lo·trop·ic (al′ə·trop′ik) *adj.* Of, pertaining to, or having the property of allotropy: Ozone is an *allotropic* form of oxygen. Also **al′lo·trop′i·cal.** —**al′lo·trop′i·cal·ly** *adv.*

al·lot·ro·pism (ə·lot′rə·piz′əm) *n.* Allotropy.

al·lot·ro·py (ə·lot′rə·pē) *n.* The property shown by certain elements of having more than one physical form, usually due to different groupings of atoms stable under different conditions, especially different temperatures. [< Gk. *allotropia* variation < *allos* other + *tropos* turn, manner]

al·low (ə·lou′) *v.t.* **1** To put no obstacle in the way of; permit to occur or do: Children are *allowed* in the park; He *allowed* the flowers to wither. **2** To admit; grant, as something claimed; acknowledge as true or valid: I *allow* her ability, but not her right to exercise it. **3** To make an addition, deduction, or concession of, as for a consideration not formally appearing in the reckoning: to *allow* three pounds extra for waste; to *allow* customers a month to pay. **4** To grant; allot, as a share or portion: The emperor *allowed* him one hundred pounds a year. **5** *U.S. Dial.* To maintain; declare. **6** *Archaic* Approve; sanction. —*v.i.* **7** To permit the occurrence or realization of: with *of*: Your remark *allows* of several interpretations. **8** To bear in mind as a modifying or extenuating circumstance; make due allowance for: with *for*: to *allow* for traffic conditions in getting to the train on time. [< OF *alouer* place, use, assign < Med.L *allocare* (see ALLOCATE) and OF *alouer, aloer* approve < L *allaudare* extol < *ad-* to + *laudare* praise] —**al·lowed′** *adj.*

Synonyms: admit, concede, confess, endure, grant, let, permit, sanction, suffer, tolerate, yield. We *allow* that which we do not attempt to hinder; we *permit* that to which we give express authorization; we *concede* a right; *grant* a request; *permit* an inspection of accounts; *sanction* a marriage; *tolerate* the rudeness of a well-meaning clerk; *submit* to a surgical operation; *yield* to a demand or necessity against our wish or will. *Suffer*, in the sense of mild concession, is now becoming rare. Compare PERMISSION. *Antonyms*: deny, disallow, disapprove, forbid, protest, refuse, reject, resist, withstand. See synonyms for PROHIBIT.

al·low·a·ble (ə·lou′ə·bəl) *adj.* That can be allowed; permissible; admissible. —**al·low′a·ble·ness** *n.* —**al·low′a·bly** *adv.*

al·low·ance (ə·lou′əns) *n.* **1** An allowing or being allowed. **2** That which is allowed. **3** A limited amount or portion, as of an income or food, granted at regular intervals. **4** A sum or item put to one's credit in a transaction, as in consideration of the exchange of the used article or a purchase in volume; discount: The dealer will give you an *allowance* on your old car. **5** A difference permitted in excess or abatement, as of a specification: to make *allowances* for haste. **6** *Obs.* Acknowledgment. See synonyms under PERMISSION, SALARY, SUBSIDY. —*v.t.* **·anced, ·anc·ing 1** To put on an allowance; limit to a regular amount. **2** To supply in limited or meager quantities.

al·low·ed·ly (ə·lou′id·lē) *adv.* By general allowance or admission; admittedly.

al·loy (al′oi, ə·loi′) *n.* Any of numerous substances having metallic properties and consisting of two or more elements of which at least one is a metal. **2** Anything that reduces purity. —*v.t.* (ə·loi′) **1** To reduce the purity of, as a metal, by mixing with an alloy. **2** To combine (substances) to form an alloy. **3** To modify or debase, as by mixture with something inferior. —*v.i.* To become a constituent of an alloy: Carbon *alloys* with iron to form steel. [< F *aloi,* OF *alei* < *aleier* combine < L *alligare ad-* to + *ligare* bind]

Synonyms (noun): admixture, adulteration, debasement, deterioration. *Adulteration, debase-*

ment, and *deterioration* are always used in the bad sense; *admixture* is neutral, and may be good or bad; *alloy* is commonly good in the literal sense, as for giving hardness to coin, etc. An excess of *alloy* virtually amounts to *adulteration*; but *adulteration* is commonly restricted to articles used for food, drink, medicine, and kindred uses.

all right 1 Satisfactory: His work is *all right.* **2** Correct, as a result in addition. **3** Uninjured; not hurt: Were you *all right* after your fall? **4** Certainly; without a doubt: I'll be there *all right!* **5** Yes: usually in answer to a question: May I leave now? *All right.* See ALRIGHT.

all·seed (ôl′sēd′) *n.* Any of various small many-seeded plants, as knotgrass, goosefoot, flaxwort, etc.

all·spice (ôl′spīs′) *n.* **1** The aromatic dried berry of a West Indian tree; the pimento. **2** The sharply flavored, fragrant spice made from it. [So called because thought to combine the flavors of several spices]

al·lude (ə·lood′) *v.i.* **al·lud·ed, al·lud·ing** To refer without express mention; make indirect or casual reference: with *to.* [< L *alludere* play with, joke < *ad-* to + *ludere* play]

Synonyms: advert, hint, imply, indicate, insinuate, intimate, mention, point, refer, signify, suggest. *Allude* is erroneously used in the general sense of *mention* or *speak of.* We *allude* to a matter slightly, in passing; we *advert* to it when we turn from our path to treat it; we *refer* to it by any clear utterance or expression. One may *hint* at a thing in a friendly way, but what is *insinuated* is always unfavorable, generally both hostile and cowardly. One may *indicate* his wishes, *intimate* his plans, *imply* his opinion, *signify* his will, *suggest* a course of action. Compare SUGGESTION.

al·lure (ə·loor′) *v.t. & v.i.* **al·lured, al·lur·ing** To draw with or as with a lure; attract or exercise attraction; entice. *—n.* That which allures; allurement. [< OF *alurer, aleurrer* < *a-* to (< L *ad-*)+ *leurre* lure. See LURE.] **—al·lur′er** *n.*

Synonyms (verb): attract, cajole, captivate, coax, decoy, draw, entice, inveigle, lure, seduce, tempt, win. One may *attract* without intent. One may *allure* to evil, but ordinarily to good. *Lure* is more akin to the physical nature and commonly used in an unfavorable sense. To *tempt* is to endeavor to lead one wrong; to *seduce* is to succeed in *winning* one from good to ill. *Win* may be used in a good sense, in which it surpasses the highest sense of *allure,* because it succeeds in that which *allure* attempts. *Coax* expresses the attraction of the person, not of the thing. A man may be *coaxed* to that which is by no means *alluring. Cajole* and *decoy* carry the idea of deceiving and ensnaring. To *inveigle* is to lead one blindly, as into folly or wrong. See DRAW, PERSUADE. *Antonyms:* chill, damp, deter, dissuade, repel, warn.

al·lure·ment (ə·loor′mənt) *n.* **1** Enticement; fascination; attraction. **2** A charm or bait. **3** The act of alluring, as by some charm or bait.

al·lur·ing (ə·loor′ing) *adj.* That draws as with a lure; attractive; fascinating. **—al·lur′ing·ly** *adv.* **—al·lur′ing·ness** *n.*

al·lu·sion (ə·loo′zhən) *n.* **1** An alluding; indirect reference; suggestion. **2** A figure of speech consisting of a passing, but significant, reference to a well-known person, place, event etc. [< L *allusio, -onis* < *allusus,* pp. of *alludere.* See ALLUDE.]

al·lu·sive (ə·loo′siv) *adj.* Having allusion to; suggestive; figurative. **—al·lu′sive·ly** *adv.* **—al·lu′sive·ness** *n.*

al·lu·vi·al (ə·loo′vē·əl) *adj.* Pertaining to or composed of alluvium. *—n.* Alluvium.

al·lu·vi·on (ə·loo′vē·ən) *n.* **1** A flood deposit of earth; alluvium. **2** Inundation; flood. **3** The wash or flow of waves against the shore or banks. **4** *Law* The gradual increase of land by the action of flowing water. **5** *Geol.* A downpour of volcanic cinder mud. [< F < L *alluvio, -onis* < *alluere* < *ad-* to + *luere* wash]

al·lu·vi·um (ə·loo′vē·əm) *n. pl.* **·vi·a** (-vē·ə) or **·vi·ums** *Geol.* Deposits, as of sand or mud, transported and laid down by flowing water in river beds, flood-plains, lakes, and estuaries. [< L]

al·ly (ə·lī′) *v.* **al·lied, al·ly·ing** *v.t.* To unite or combine in an affinity, marriage, or association, by relationship, similarity of structure, treaty, or compact: generally in the passive with *to* or *with,* or used reflexively: The minister hoped to *ally* France with Spain against England; He *allied* himself with all liberal thinkers. *—v.i.* To enter into alliance; become allied. *—n.* (al′ī, ə·lī′) *pl.* **al·lies 1** A person or thing connected with another, usually in some relation of helpfulness or kinship; a state, sovereign, or chief leagued with another, as by treaty or common action. **2** Any friendly associate or helper. **3** An organism or substance associated with another by similarity of structure or properties. See synonyms under ACCESSORY, ADHERENT, ASSOCIATE, AUXILIARY. **—the Allies 1** The twenty-seven nations allied against the Central Powers in World War I; specifically, Russia, France, Great Britain, Italy, and Japan, adhering to the Declaration of London; the **Allied and Associated Powers** included twenty-two other nations, co-belligerent but not adhering to the Declaration. **2** The nations and governments-in-exile known as the United Nations in World War II. [< OF *alier* < L *alligare* < *ad-* to + *ligare* bind]

al·ma ma·ter (al′mə mä′tər, al′mə mā′tər, äl′mə mā′tər) The institution of learning which one has attended. [< L, fostering mother]

al·ma·nac (ôl′mə·nak) *n.* A yearly calendar giving the days of the week and month through the year, with weather forecasts, astronomical information, times of high and low tides, and other tabulated data. [< Med.L < Sp. < Arabic *al-manākh*]

al·me·mar (al·mē′mär) *n.* In a Jewish synagog, the platform from which the Pentateuch and the Prophets are read. [< Arabic *al-minbar* the pulpit]

al·might·y (ôl·mī′tē) *adj.* **1** Able to do all things; omnipotent. **2** Great; remarkable. *—adv. Slang* Exceedingly: *almighty* mad. **—the Almighty** God; the Supreme Being. [OE *ealmihtig* < *eal* all + *mihtig* mighty] **—al·might′i·ly** *adv.* **—al·might′i·ness** *n.*

al·mond (ä′mənd, am′ənd) *n.* **1** A small rosaceous tree (*Prunus amygdalus*) widely cultivated in warm temperate regions. **2** The nutlike edible seed of this tree. **3** Anything having a flattened oval shape resembling the almond seed. **4** A pale brown, the color of an almond shell. [< OF *almande, amande* < L *amygdala* < Gk. *amygdalē*]

al·mon·er (al′mən·ər, ä′mən-) *n.* An official dispenser of alms; formerly, a household chaplain, as of a prince. Also **alm·ner** (alm′·nər, äm′nər). [< OF *almosnier* < LL *eleemosynarius* pertaining to alms < L *eleemosyna* alms. See ALMS.]

al·mon·ry (al′mən·rē, ä′mən-) *n. pl.* **·ries** The residence of an almoner; a place where alms are dispensed.

al·most (ôl′mōst, ôl·mōst′) *adv.* Approximately; very nearly; all but. *—adj.* not quite: to have *almost* nothing. [OE *ealmǣst.* See ALL, MOST.]

alms (ämz) *n. sing. & pl.* A gift or gifts for the poor; charitable offerings; charity. Some self-explaining compounds have *alms* as their first element: **almsgiver, almsgiving, almsmoney,** etc. Collateral adjective: *eleemosynary.* [OE *ælmesse* < L *eleemosyna* alms < Gk. *eleēmosynē* < *eleos* pity]

alms·deed (ämz′dēd′) *n.* An act of charity.

alms·house (ämz′hous′) *n.* **1** A house where paupers are supported; a poorhouse. **2** In England, a house where deserving poor people are supported by charity, generally on a charitable foundation.

alms·man (ämz′mən) *n. pl.* **·men** (-mən) **1** One supported by charity. **2** *Obs.* A giver of alms. **—alms′wom′an** *n. fem.*

al·oe (al′ō) *n. pl.* **·oes 1** Any member of a genus (*Aloe*) of Old World plants of the lily family, some species of which furnish a drug, and others valuable fiber. **2** *pl. (construed as singular)* A bitter cathartic obtained from the juice of certain species of aloe. **3** *pl. (construed as singular)* Agalloch. [OE *aluwe* < L *aloe* < Gk. *aloē*]**—al·o·et·ic** (al·ō·et′ik) *adj.*

a·loft (ə·lôft′, ə·loft′) *adv.* **1** In or to a high or higher place; on high; high up. **2** *Naut.* At or to the higher parts of a ship's rigging. [< ON *a lopt* in (the) air]

a·lo·ha (ə·lō′ə, ä·lō′hä) *n. Hawaiian* Love: used also as a salutation and a farewell.

a·lone (ə·lōn′) *adv. & adj.* **1** Without company; solitary. **2** Without equal; unique; unparalleled. **3** Excluding all others; solely; only. [ME *al one* all alone]

a·long (ə·lông′, ə·long′) *adv.* **1** Over, through, or following the length of in time or space; lengthwise. **2** Progressively onward in the course of motion. **3** In company or association: with *with*: I came *along* with my cousins. **4** Together; side by side: The donkey came *along* all the way. **5** Advanced in age or duration: well *along* in years. **—all along** The whole time; from the outset. **—along with** As well as; in addition to. **—right along** Continuously. **—to get along 1** To manage in spite of difficulties. **2** To go away: Get along with you! **3** To exist together in harmony: Her cat and dog *get along* very well. *—prep.* **1** In the line of; through or over the length of: The ship sailed *along* the coast. **2** At points throughout or over the length of: Trees are planted *along* the road. **3** During the course of; throughout: *along* the track of centuries. [OE *andlang*]

a·long·shore (ə·lông′shôr′, ə·long′-, -shōr′) *adv.* Along the shore, either on the water or on the land.

a·long·side (ə·lông′sīd′, ə·long′-) *adv.* Close to or along the side. *—prep.* Side by side with; at the side of.

a·loof (ə·loof′) *adj.* Distant, especially in manner or interest; not in sympathy with or desiring to associate with others. *—adv.* At a distance; apart: to stand, keep, or hold *aloof.* [< A-¹ + *loof* < Du. *loef* LUFF] **—a·loof′ly** *adv.*

al·o·pe·ci·a (al′ə·pē′shē·ə, -sē·ə) *n.* Loss of hair; partial or total baldness. [< L, baldness, fox mange < Gk. *alōpekia* < *alōpex* fox]

a·loud (ə·loud′) *adv.* Loudly or audibly.

a·low¹ (ə·lō′) *adv.* In or to a lower position; below: opposed to *aloft.*

alp (alp) *n.* **1** Any peak of the Alps. **2** An alpine pasture. **3** A lofty mountain. [< L *Alpes* the Alps]

al·pac·a (al·pak′ə) *n.* **1** A domesticated ruminant (*Lama pacos*) of South America related to the guanaco and llama. **2** Its long, silky wool. **3** Cloth made from the wool of the alpaca. **4** A glossy, usually black fabric made of various fiber combinations other than alpaca wool. [< Sp. < Arabic *al* the + Peruvian *paco* name of the animal]

ALPACA
(About 3½ feet high at the shoulder)

al·pen·glow (al′pən·glō′) *n.* **1** The rosy light of the rising or setting sun, seen on the Alps or other mountains. **2** The reappearance of the sunset colors on a mountain summit after the original colors have faded. **3** A similar phenomenon preceding the regular sunrise coloration. [Trans. of G *Alpenglühen*]

al·pen·stock (al′pən·stok′) *n.* A long, iron-pointed staff, used by mountain-climbers. [< G, lit., alps stick]

al·pes·trine (al·pes′trin) *adj.* **1** Of, pertaining to, or growing on mountain heights below the limit of forest growth. **2** Subalpine. [< L *alpestris* < L *Alpes* Alps]

al·pha (al′fə) *n.* **1** The first letter and vowel in the Greek alphabet (A, α); corresponding to English a. As a numeral it denotes 1. **2** The beginning or first of anything. **—the alpha and omega** Both the first and the last; beginning and end; the sum total: used of Christ. *Rev.* i 8. *—adj.* **1** Designating the first in order of importance or discovery: *alpha* test. **2** *Chem.* Denoting a carbon atom next to a designated carbon in an organic molecule. **3** *Physics* Denoting the first of a series of radiations or emissions arranged in order of increasing frequency: *alpha* rays, *alpha* particle. [< Gk. < Hebrew *aleph* ox]

Al·pha (al′fə) *n. Astron.* The principal or brightest star in a constellation.

al·pha·bet (al′fə·bet) *n.* **1** The letters that form the elements of written language, in order as fixed by usage: in English, 26 in number. **2** Any system of characters or symbols representing the simple sounds of speech. See TABLE OF FOREIGN ALPHABETS on next page. **3** The simplest elements or rudiments of anything. —*v.t.* To alphabetize. [< L *alphabetum* < Gk. *alpha* a + *bēta* b]

al·pha·bet·ic (al'fə·bet'ik) *adj.* **1** Pertaining to, having, or expressed by an alphabet. **2** Arranged in the order of the alphabet. Also **al'pha·bet'i·cal.** —**al'pha·bet'i·cal·ly** *adv.*

al·pha·bet·ize (al'fə·bə·tīz') *v.t.* **·ized, ·iz·ing 1** To put in alphabetical order. **2** To express by or furnish with an alphabet or alphabetic symbols. — **al·pha·bet·i·za·tion** (al'fə·bet'ə·zā'shən) *n.* —**al'pha·bet·iz'er** *n.*

al·pha·nu·mer·ic (al'fə·nōō·mer'ik, -nyōō-) *adj.* Able to use both letters and numbers: an *alphanumeric* computer.

alpha particle *Physics* The positively charged nucleus of the helium atom (H⁴), consisting of two protons and two neutrons; it is a product of disintegration of various isotopes of both natural and artificial radioactive elements.

alpha ray *Physics* A stream of alpha particles, emitted with an initial velocity and over a mean range varying with the source and method of production.

alp-horn (alp'hôrn') *n.* A slightly curved, very sonorous horn, made of wood and from 7 to 12 feet long, used by cowherds in the Alps and formerly by Swiss soldiers: also *alpenhorn.* [< Gk. *alpenhorn* horn of the Alps]

Al·pine (al'pīn, -pin) *adj.* **1** Pertaining to or characteristic of the Alps. **2** Designating a European racial stock found in the Alps and adjacent districts, and marked by medium height, broad short skull and face, and brunette coloring. [< L *Alpinus*]

al·pine (al'pīn, -pin) *adj.* **1** Like an alp or mountain; lofty and towering: alpine *terrian.* **2** Occurring in regions above the timberline in mountains or tundra. —*n.* A plant native to treeless tundra or mountain tops.

habiting or growing in mountain regions above the limits of forest growth.

al·pi·nist (al'pə·nist) *n.* A climber of alps; a mountaineer. —**al'pi·nism** *n.*

Alps (alps) A mountain system of southern Europe, extending 680 miles from the Mediterranean coast of southern France to the Adriatic coast of Yugoslavia, separating the Po valley of northern Italy from the lowlands of France, Germany, and the Danubian plain; highest peak, 15,781 feet.

al·read·y (ôl·red'ē) *adv.* Before or by this time or the time mentioned; even now. [< ALL + READY]

al·right (ôl·rīt') All right: a spelling not yet considered acceptable.

Al·sace (al·sās', al'sas; *Fr.* àl·zás') A region and former province of France along the Rhine bor-

TABLE OF FOREIGN ALPHABETS

(1) ARABIC			(2) HEBREW			(3) GREEK			(4) RUSSIAN			(5) GERMAN		
ا	alif	—¹	א	aleph	—⁶	A α	alpha	ä	А а		ä	𝔄 α		ä
ب	ba	b	ב,בּ	beth	b, v	B β	beta	b	Б б		b	𝔄 ä		e
ت	ta	t	ג,ג	gimel	g, gh²	Γ γ	gamma	g	В в		v	𝔅 b		b
ث	sa	th	ד,ד	daleth	d, ~~th~~	Δ δ	delta	d	Г г		g	ℭ c		k, ts, s
ج	jim	j	ה,ה	he	h	E ε	epsilon	e	Д д		d	𝔇 d		d
ح	ha	h	ה	he	h	Z ζ	zeta	z	Е е		e, ye	𝔈 e		e, ā
خ	kha	kh	ו	vav	v	H η	eta	ā	Ж ж		zh	𝔉 f		f
د	dal	d	ז	zayin	z	Θ θ	theta	th⁹	З з		z	𝔊 g		g
ذ	zal	~~th~~	ח	heth	kh	I ι	iota	ē	И и		ē, yē	𝔥 h		h
ر	ra	r	ט	teth	t	K κ	kappa	k	Й й		e¹²	𝔦 i		i, ē
ز	za	z	י	yod	y	Λ λ	lambda	l	К к		k	𝔧 j		y
س	sin	s	כ,ך,כּ	kaph	k⁵, kh	M μ	mu	m	Л л		l	𝔏 l		l
ش	shin	sh	ל	lamed	l	N ν	nu	n	М м		m	𝔐 m		m
ص	sad	s	מ,ם	mem	m	Ξ ξ	xi	ks	Н н		n	𝔑 n		n
ض	dad	d	נ,ן	nun	n	O o	omicron	o	О о		ô, o	𝔬 o		ŏ, ō
ط	ta	t	ס	samek	s	Π π	pi	p	П п		p	𝔓 p		p
ظ	za	z	ע	ayin	—⁷	P ρ	rho	r	Р р		r	𝔔(u) q(u)		k(v)
ع	ain	—²	פ,ף,פּ	pe	p, f	Σ σ, ς⁹	sigma	s	С с		s	𝔯 r		r
غ	ghain	gh³	צ,ץ	sade	s	T τ	tau	t	Т т		t	𝔖 ſ, ß⁸		s, z
ف	fa	f	ק	koph	k⁶	Y υ	upsilon	ü, ōō	У у		ōō	𝔗 t		t
ق	qaf	k⁴	ר	resh	r	Φ φ	phi	f¹⁰	Ф ф		f	𝔲 u		ōō, ōō
ك	kaf	k⁵	שׂ,שׁ	sin, shin	s, sh	X χ	chi	kh¹¹	Х х		kh	𝔳 v		f
ل	lam	l	ת,ת	tav	t, th	Ψ ψ	psi	ps	Ц ц		ts	𝔴 w		v
م	mim	m				Ω ω	omega	ō	Ч ч		ch	𝔵 x		ks
ن	nun	n							Ш ш		sh	𝔶 y		ē, ü
ه	ha	h							Щ щ		shch	𝔷 z		ts
و	waw	w							Ъ ъ		—¹³			
ي	ya	y							Ы ы		œ			
									Ь ь		—¹⁴			
									Э э		e			
									Ю ю		yōō			
									Я я		yä			

In each column the characters of the alphabet are given first, followed by the names of the characters in Arabic, Hebrew, and Greek. The last row in each column shows the approximate English sound represented by each character. Columns 3, 4, and 5 show the upper- and lower-case forms. The Arabic characters are given in their final, unconnected forms. The German style of letter, called *fraktur*, has, since the 1880's, been gradually replaced in German printing by the Latin letter.

¹ Functions as the bearer of hamza (the glottal stop), or as a lengthener of short *a*. ² A voiced pharyngeal fricative. ³ A voiced velar fricative. ⁴ A uvular stop. ⁵ A voiceless velar stop. ⁶ A glottal stop, now usually silent, or pronounced according to the accompanying vowel points. ⁷ A pharyngeal fricative, now usually silent, or pronounced according to the accompanying vowel points. ⁸ The alternate form is restricted to the ends of words. ⁹, ¹⁰, ¹¹ In classical Greek these were pronounced as aspirated stops similar to the sounds in foot*h*ill, ha*ph*azard, and bloc*kh*ouse.

¹² Appears only as the second vowel in a diphthong. ¹³ Formerly, a sign of non-palatalization of consonants at the ends of words; since 1918, used only between two syllables to indicate that they are separately pronounced. ¹⁴ A sign of palatalization of a preceding consonant.

der of Germany: ancient **Al·sa·tia** (al-sā'shə): German *Elass.*

Al·sa·tia (al-sā'shə) A section of London, formerly a sanctuary for insolvent debtors and criminals: also called *Whitefriars.* [< Med.L < G *Elsass,* lit., foreign settlement]

Al·sa·tian (al-sā'shən) *adj.* **1** Of or pertaining to Alsace. **2** Of or pertaining to Alsatia. —*n.* **1** A native or inhabitant of Alsace. **2** A resident of Alsatia; hence, a debtor or criminal in sanctuary. **3** A German shepherd.

al·so (ôl'sō) *adv. & conj.* **1** As something further tending in the same direction; besides; in addition: They *also* serve who only stand and wait. **2** In like manner; likewise: to provide for the pupils and *also* for the teachers. [OE *alswā, ealswā* all (wholly) so.]

Al·ta·mi·ra (äl'tä-mē'rä) A cave near Santander, in Spain, noted for the early Stone Age drawings on its walls.

ALTAMIRA
A cave drawing.

al·tar (ôl'tər) *n.* **1** Any raised place or structure on which sacrifices may be offered or incense burned as an act of worship. **2** *Eccl.* The structure of wood or stone on which the elements are consecrated in the Eucharist; the communion table. **—to lead to the altar** To marry. ◆ Homophone: *alter.* [OE < L *altare* high altar < *altus* high]

al·tar-piece (ôl'tər-pēs') *n.* A painting, mosaic, or bas-relief over and behind the altar; a reredos.

alt·az·i·muth (alt-az'ə-məth) *n. Astron.* An instrument with two graduated circles, one vertical and one horizontal, for measuring the altitude and azimuth of celestial bodies.

al·ter (ôl'tər) *v.t.* **1** To cause to be different; change; modify; transform. **2** To castrate or spay. —*v.i.* **3** To become different; change, as in character or appearance. See synonyms under CHANGE. ◆ Homophone: *altar.* [< MF *altérer* < Med.L *alterare* < L *alter* other]

al·ter·a·bil·i·ty (ôl'tər-ə-bil'ə-tē) *n.* Liability to or capacity for change.

al·ter·a·ble (ôl'tər-ə-bəl) *adj.* Capable of alteration. **—al·ter·a·bil·i·ty** (ôl'tər-ə-bil'ə-tē), **al'ter·a·ble·ness** *n.* **—al'ter·a·bly** *adv.*

al·ter·a·tion (ôl'tə-rā'shən) *n.* **1** The act or result of altering; or the state of being altered; modification; change. **2** *Geol.* Any change in the composition or texture of a rock occurring subsequent to its formation but not due to a cementing or induration of its original constituents. —*adj.* Of or pertaining to a geological alteration: an *alteration* product. See synonyms under CHANGE.

al·ter·a·tive (ôl'tə-rā'tiv) *adj.* **1** Tending to produce change. **2** *Med.* Tending to change gradually the bodily condition to a normal state. —*n.* An alterative medicine or treatment. Also **al·ter·ant** (ôl'tər-ənt).

al·ter·cate (ôl'tər-kāt, al'-) *v.i.* **·cat·ed, ·cat·ing** To dispute vehemently; wrangle. [< L *altercatus,* pp. of *altercari* < *alter* other]

al·ter·ca·tion (ôl'tər-kā'shən, al'-) *n.* Angry controversy; disputing; wrangling.
Synonyms: affray, brawl, broil, contention, controversy, debate, discussion, disputation, dispute, dissension, disturbance, fracas, quarrel, wrangle, wrangling. *Dispute* is preferably used of rights and claims; as, the title or the will is in *dispute; debate* and *discussion* refer rather to abstract matters, and may be entirely amicable. *Disputation* has a touch of bitterness. *Altercation, contention, controversy,* and *wrangle* are all words signifying more or less of ill-feeling; so is *dispute* in common speech; as, a sharp *dispute. Contention* and *controversy* are capable of a good sense in the learned or elevated style. See QUARREL. *Antonyms:* agreement, concord, consonance, harmony, unanimity, unity.

al·ter e·go (ôl'tər ē'gō, al'tər eg'ō) **1** Another self; a double. **2** An intimate friend. [< L, lit., other I]

al·ter·nate (ôl'tər-nāt, al'-) *v.* **·nat·ed, ·nat·ing** *v.t.* **1** To arrange, use, or perform in alternation. **2** To cause to succeed and be succeeded by continuously: with *by* or *with:* to *alternate* a passive with an active style. —*v.i.* **3** To occur or appear alternately. **4** To take turns: to *alternate* on a job. **5** To pass from one thing or condition to an-

other and back again repeatedly: Cycles of depression and inflation *alternate.* **6** *Electr.* To change from the positive to the negative direction and back rapidly; vibrate; pulsate. —*adj.* (ôl'tər-nit, al'-) **1** Existing, occurring, or following by turns; reciprocal. **2** Referring or pertaining to every other (of a series). **3** Alternative: an *alternate* method. **4** *Bot.* **a** Placed singly at regular intervals on opposite sides of the stem, as leaves. **b** Disposed by turn among other parts, as stamens opposite the intervals between petals. —*n.* (ôl'tər-nit, al'-) A substitute or second; especially, one substituting for another in the performance of a duty or in the filling of a position; a second choice. [< L *alternatus,* pp. of *alternare* < *alternus* every second one < *alter* other] —**al'ter·nate·ness** *n.*

al·ter·nate·ly (ôl'tər-nit-lē, al'-) *adv.* In alternate order or position; by turns.

al·ter·na·tion (ôl'tər-nā'shən, al'-) *n.* Occurrence or action of two things or series of things in turn; passage from one place, state, or condition to another and back again: *alternation* between day and night.

al·ter·na·tive (ôl-tûr'nə-tiv, al-) *adj.* **1** Affording a choice between two things. **2** Of or pertaining to alternation; implying or involving an alternative: *alternative* conjunctions. —*n.* **1** Something that may or must be instead of something else; a choice between two things: used sometimes, loosely, of more than two. **2** One of the things to be chosen. **—al·ter'na·tive·ly** *adv.* **—al·ter'na·tive·ness** *n.*
Synonyms: choice, election, option, pick, preference, resource. A *choice* may be among many things; an *alternative* is in the strictest sense of *choice* between two things, but the usage is often extended to more than two. *Option* is the right or privilege of choosing; *choice* may be either the right to choose, the act of choosing, or the thing chosen. A *choice, pick, election,* or *preference* is that which suits one best; an *alternative* is that to which one is restricted; a *resource,* that to which one is glad to betake oneself. *Antonyms:* compulsion, necessity.

al·ter·na·tor (ôl'tər-nā'tər, al'-) *n.* **1** One who or that which alternates. **2** *Electr.* A dynamo giving an alternating current. Also **al'ter·nat'er.**

alt·horn (alt'hôrn') *n.* A wind instrument of the saxhorn class: used by military bands. [< ALT + HORN]

al·though (ôl-thō') *conj.* Admitting or granting that; though: *Although* I believe the contrary, I accept your explanation. Also **al·tho'.** [< ALL + THOUGH]

alti- *combining from* High: *altiscope.* Also *alto-.* [< L *altus* high]

al·ti·pla·no (äl'ti-plä'nō) *n.* High upland plateaus, especially in Andean countries. [< Sp. < Latin *altus* high + *planus* level]

al·tis·o·nant (al-tis'ə-nənt) *adj.* High-sounding; pompous.

al·ti·tude (al'tə-tōōd; -tyōōd) *n.* **1** Vertical elevation above any given point, especially above mean sea level; height. **2** *Astron.* Angular elevation above the horizon. **3** *Geom.* The vertical distance from the base of a figure to its highest point. **4** A high or the highest point. See synonyms under HEIGHT. [< L *altitudo* < *altus* high]

altitude sickness A syndrome of varying severity due to inadequate atmospheric oxygen at the low barometric pressures obtaining at high altitudes and including hyperventilation, dizziness, nausea, etc.

al·ti·tu·di·nal (al'tə-tōō'də-nəl, -tyōō'-) *adj.* Relating to altitude.

al·to (al'tō) *adj.* Sounding or ranging between tenor and treble. —*n. pl.* **·tos 1** The lowest female voice; contralto. **2** The highest male voice, or countertenor. **3** A singer who has an alto voice. **4** A tenor violin. **5** An althorn. [< Ital. < L *altus* high]

alto- See ALTI-.

al·to·geth·er (ôl'tə-geth'ər, ôl'tə-geth'ər) *n.* A whole; also, the general effect; tout ensemble. **—in the altogether** *Colloq.* In the nude. —*adv.* **1** Completely; wholly; entirely. **2** With everything included; in all; all told. [< ALL + TOGETHER]

al·to-re·lie·vo (al'tō-ri-lē'vō) *n. pl.* **·vos** High relief; sculptured or carved work in which the carving, figures, etc., stand out very strongly from the background: contrasted with *bas-relief.* See RELIEF. [< Ital.]

al·tri·cial (al-trish'əl) *adj.* Having young that hatch in a naked and helpless state requiring

care by one or both parent birds. Compare *precocial.* [< L *altrices,* pl. of *altrix* a nurse + -IAL]

al·tru·ism (al'trōō·iz'əm) *n.* **1** Devotion to the interests of others; disinterested benevolence: opposed to *egoism.* **2** *Biol.* Consistent behavior by individual organisms that tends to decrease the total reproductive output of the individual while enhancing that of other members of the group or species. [< F *altruisme,* ult. < L *alter* other]

al·tru·ist (al'trōō·ist) *n.* One devoted to or professing altruism.

al·tru·is·tic (al'trōō·is'tik) *adj.* Pertaining to altruism or altruists. **—al'tru·is'ti·cal·ly** *adv.*

al·u·del (al'yə·del) *n. Chem.* One of a series of pear-shaped vessels of glass or earthenware fitted one into another and used for condensation, as in subliming mercury. [< F < Sp. < Arabic *al-uthāl* the utensil]

al·u·la (al'yə·lə) *n. pl.* **·lae** (lē) **1** *Ornithol.* A tuft of feathers on that part of a bird's wing homologous to the thumb. Also called *bastard wing.* **2** *Entomol.* A membranous lobe separated from the wing base in certain flies. [< NL, dim. of L *ala* wing] **—al'u·lar** *adj.*

a·lu·mi·nize (ə·lōō'mə·nīz) *v.t.* **·nized, ·niz·ing** To cover with a film or coat of aluminum or an aluminum compound.

a·lu·mi·num (ə·lōō'mə·nəm) *n.* An abundant metallic element (symbol Al, atomic number 13) found only in combination, chiefly with oxygen, and having the useful properties of lightness and resistance to oxidation. Also *Brit.* **al·u·min·i·um** (al'yə·min'ē·əm). See PERIODIC TABLE. [< NL < L *alumen, -minis* alum] **—a·lu'mi·nous** *adj.*

a·lum·na (ə·lum'nə) *n. pl.* **·nae** (-nē) A female graduate of a college or school. [< L, fem. of *alumnus*]

a·lum·nus (ə·lum'nəs) *n. pl.* **·ni** (-nī) **1** A male graduate of a college or school. **2** Originally, any pupil. [< L, foster son, pupil < *alere* nourish]

al·ve·o·lus (al·vē'ə·ləs) *n. pl.* **·li** (-lī) **1** A minute air sac at the end of each bronchiole in the lungs. **2** A tooth socket. **3** An acinus in a racemose gland. **4** One of the cells of a honeycomb. [< L, dim. of *alveus* a hollow]

al·vine (al'vin, -vīn) *adj.* Pertaining to the abdomen and the intestines. [< L *alvus* belly]

al·ways (ôl'wiz, -wāz) *adv.* **1** Perpetually; for all time; ceaselessly. **2** At every time; on all occasions: opposed to *sometimes.* Also *Archaic* or *Poetic* **al·way** (ôl'wā). [< ALL + WAY + adverbial genitive ending -s]

am (am, *unstressed* əm) Present tense, first person singular, of BE. [OE *eom, am*]

am·a·bil·i·ty (am'ə·bil'ə·tē) *n.* Lovableness. [< L *amabilitas, -tatis* < *amabilis* lovely]

a·main (ə·mān') *adv.* Vehemently; forcibly; exceedingly; without delay; at full speed. [< A-¹ + MAIN¹ strength]

a·mal·gam (ə·mal'gəm) *n.* **1** An alloy of mercury and one or more metals. **2** Any mixture or combination of two or more bodies, substances, or things. [< MF *amalgame* < Med.L *amalgama* < Arabic *al-malgham* < Gk. *malagma* an emollient < *malassein* soften]

a·mal·gam·a·ble (ə·mal'gə·mə·bəl) *adj.* Capable of forming an amalgam.

a·mal·ga·mate (ə·mal'gə·māt) *v.t. & v.i.* **·mat·ed, ·mat·ing 1** To form an amalgam; unite in an alloy with mercury, as a metal. **2** To unite or combine: The four parts of the original are *amalgamated* into two. See synonyms under MIX, UNITE. **— a·mal·ga·ma·tive** (ə·mal'gə·mā'tiv) *adj.* **— a·mal·ga·ma·tor** (ə·mal'gə·mā'tər) *n.*

a·mal·ga·ma·tion (ə·mal'gə·mā'shən) *n.* **1** The forming of an amalgam. **2** A mingling of racial or ethnic stocks. **3** The removal of metals from their ores by treatment with mercury. **4** A substance formed by mixture.

a·man·u·en·sis (ə·man'yōō·en'sis) *n. pl.* **·ses** (-sēz) One who copies manuscript or takes dictation; a secretary. [< L < *a-* (*ab-*) from + *manus* hand]

a·mass (ə·mas') *v.t.* To heap up; accumulate, especially as wealth or possessions for oneself. [< OF *amasser* < *a-* to (< L *ad-*) + *masser* pile up < L *massa* mass] **—a·mass'a·ble** *adj.* **—a·mass'er** *n.* **—a·mass'ment** *n.*
Synonyms: accumulate, aggregate, collect, gather. To *amass* is to bring together materials

that make a mass, a great bulk or quantity, *ac-cumulate* being commonly applied to the more gradual, *amass* to the more rapid gathering of money or materials. We say interest is *accumulated* rather than is *amassed;* a fortune may be rapidly *amassed* by shrewd speculations. *Aggregate* is now most commonly used of numbers and amounts; as, the expenses will *aggregate* a round million. Compare AGGREGATE. *n. Antonyms:* disperse, dissipate, divide, parcel, portion, scatter, spend, squander, waste.

am·a·teur (am′ə-chŏŏr, -tŏŏr, -tyŏŏr, am′ə-tûr′) *adj.* **1** Pertaining to or done by an amateur. **2** Composed of amateurs: an *amateur* cast. **3** Not expert or professional. —*n.* **1** One who practices an art or science, not professionally, but for his own pleasure. **2** An athlete who has not engaged in contests for money, or used any athletic art as a means of livelihood. **3** One who does something without professional skill or ease. [< F < L *amator* lover < *amare* love]—**am′a·teur·ism** *n.*

Synonyms (noun): connoisseur, critic, dilettante, novice, tyro. Etymologically, the *amateur* is one who loves, the *connoisseur* one who knows. The *amateur* practices to some extent that in regard to which he may not be well informed; the *connoisseur* is well informed in regard to that which he may not practice at all. *Dilettante,* which had originally the sense of *amateur,* has come to denote one who is superficial, pretentious, and affected, whether in theory or practice.

am·a·teur·ish (am′ə-chŏŏr′ish, -tŏŏr′-, -tyŏŏr′-, -tûr′-) *adj.* Lacking the skill or perfection of an expert or professional. —**am′a·teur′ish·ly** *adv.* —**am′a·teur′ish·ness** *n.*

am·a·tive (am′ə-tiv) *adj.* Pertaining to sexual love; amorous. [< L *amatus,* pp. of *amare* love] —**am′a·tive·ly** *adv.*

am·a·tive·ness (am′ə-tiv-nis) *n.* The propensity to love or to sexual passion.

am·a·to·ry (am′ə-tôr′ē, -tō′rē) *adj.* Characterized by or designed to excite love; expressing or given to sexual love; erotic, as a poem. Also **am′a·to′ri·al.** [< L *amatorius* < *amare* love]

am·au·ro·sis (am′ô-rō′sis) *n.* Total or partial loss of sight without apparent organic defect. [< Gk. *amaurōsis* < *amauros* dark] —**am·au·rot·ic** (am′ô-rot′ik) *adj.*

a·maze (ə-māz′) *v.t.* **a·mazed, a·maz·ing** **1** To overwhelm, as by wonder or surprise; astonish greatly. **2** *Obs.* To puzzle; bewilder. [OE *āmasian*]—**a·mazed′** *adj.* —**a·maz·ed·ly** (ə-mā′zid·lē) *adv.* —**a·maz′ed·ness** *n.*

a·maze·ment (ə-māz′mənt) *n.* **1** Wonder; surprise; astonishment. **2** *Obs.* Stupefaction; frenzy; dementia. Also *Archaic* **a·maze′.**

Synonyms: admiration, astonishment, awe, bewilderment, confusion, consternation, perplexity, surprise, wonder. *Amazement* and *astonishment* both express the momentary overwhelming of the mind by that which is beyond expectation. *Awe* is the yielding of the mind to something supremely grand in character or formidable in power, and ranges from apprehension or dread to reverent worship. *Surprise* lies midway between *astonishment* and *amazement,* and usually concerns slighter matters. *Consternation* adds terror to *astonishment* or *amazement.* Compare PERPLEXITY. *Antonyms:* anticipation, calmness, composure, coolness, expectation, indifference, preparation, self-possession, steadiness.

a·maz·ing (ə-mā′zing) *adj.* Causing amazement; astonishing; wonderful. See synonyms under EXTRAORDINARY. —**a·maz′ing·ly** *adv.*

Am·a·zon (am′ə-zon, -zən) *n.* **1** In Greek mythology, one of a race of female warriors, said to have lived in Scythia, near the Black Sea. **2** A female warrior. **3** Any large, strong or athletic woman or girl. Also **am′a·zon** *n.* [< L < Gk. *Amazōn;* derived by the Greeks as < *a-* without + *mazos* breast, because of the fable that they cut off the right breast to facilitate the use of the bow]

Am·a·zon (am′ə-zon, -zən) A river in South

America, carrying the largest volume of water

of any in the world and flowing about 3,300 miles from the Andes through northern Brazil to the Atlantic. *Spanish & Portuvese* **A·ma·zo·nas** (*Sp.* ä·mä·sō′näs, *Pg.* ä·mə·zō′nəs).

Am·a·zo·ni·an (am′ə-zō′nē-ən) *adj.* **1** Pertaining to the Amazons; warlike; masculine: said of women. **2** Pertaining to the Amazon River. —*n.* An Amazon.

am·bage (am′bij) *n. pl.* **am·bag·es** (am′bə-jiz, *Lat.* am·bä′jēz) **1** A winding or circuitous path. **2** *Usually pl.* An indirect method of proceeding. [< OF *ambages* < L *ambi-* around + *agere* go] —**am·ba·gious** (am·bā′jəs) *adj.* —**am·ba′gious·ly** *adv.* —**am·ba′gious·ness** *n.*

am·bas·sa·dor (am·bas′ə·dər, -dôr) *n.* **1** An accredited diplomatic agent of the highest rank, appointed as the representative of one government or state to another (**ambassador extraordinary and plenipotentiary**) or to represent a government or state at a particular function, as the wedding of a king (**ambassador extraordinary on special mission**). **2** Any personal representative or messenger. Also **embassador.** See synonyms under HERALD. —**ambassador-at-large** An ambassador accredited to no specific country or government. —**goodwill ambassador** Any person traveling in a foreign country to promote friendly relations and understanding. [< F *ambassadeur* < Ital. *ambasciatore*] —**am·bas·sa·do·ri·al** (am·bas′ə·dôr′ē·əl, -dō′rē-) *adj.* —**am·bas′sa·dor·ship** *n.*

am·bas·sa·dress (am·bas′ə·dris) *n.* **1** A woman ambassador. **2** The wife of an ambassador.

am·ber (am′bər) *n.* **1** A translucent yellow to reddish brown fossil resin of an extinct coniferous tree, used mainly as an ornament. **2** Anything the color of amber. **3** An amber-colored light used to produce the effect of sunlight, as on a stage. —*v.t.* **1** To encase or preserve in amber. **2** To give an amber color to. —*adj.* Pertaining to, like, or of the color of amber. [< F *ambre* < Arabic *'anbar* ambergris]

ambi- *combining form* Both: *ambidextrous.* [< L *ambo* both]

am·bi·ance (am′bē·əns) *n.* Ambience. [< F]

am·bi·dex·ter (am′bə·dek′stər) *adj.* Ambidextrous. —*n.* **1** One who uses both hands equally well. **2** A double-dealer; hypocrite. [< Med. L < L *ambo* both + *dexter* right (hand)] —**am′bi·dex′tral** (-dek′strəl) *adj.*

am·bi·dex·ter·i·ty (am′bə·dek·ster′ə·tē) *n.* **1** The state or quality of being ambidextrous. **2** Duplicity; trickery.

am·bi·dex·trous (am′bə·dek′strəs) *adj.* **1** Able to use both hands equally well. **2** Very dexterous or skilful. **3** Dissembling; double-dealing. —**am′bi·dex′trous·ly** *adv.* —**am′bi·dex′trous·ness** *n.*

am·bi·ence (am′bē·əns) *n.* The environment or pervading atmosphere of a place, situation, etc. Also *ench* **am·bi·ance** (*äṅ·*be·ans′). [< L *ambiens* AMBIENT]

am·bi·ent (am′bē·ənt) *adj.* **1** Surrounding; encircling; encompassing. **2** Circulating. —*n.* Anything that encompasses. [< L *ambiens, -entis,* ppr. of *ambire* < *ambi-* around + *ire* go]

am·bi·gu·i·ty (am′bə·gyōō′ə·tē) *n. pl.* **·ties** **1** The quality of being ambiguous; doubtfulness. **2** An expression or statement that can be variously interpreted.

am·big·u·ous (am·big′yōō·əs) *adj.* **1** Capable of being understood in more senses than one; having a double meaning; equivocal. **2** Doubtful or

uncertain: a liquid of *ambiguous* nature. **3** Obscure, indistinct, as shadows. See synonyms under EQUIVOCAL, OBSCURE. [< L *ambiguus* < *ambigere* wander about < *ambi-* around + *agere* go] —**am·big′u·ous·ly** *adv.* —**am·big′u·ous·ness** *n.*

am·bit (am′bit) *n.* **1** That which bounds; a boundary. **2** Circumference; circuit. **3** Extent or sphere, as of actions or words; scope. [< L *ambitus* circuit < *ambire.* See AMBIENT.]

am·bi·tion (am·bish′ən) *n.* **1** Eager or inordinate desire, as for power, wealth, or distinction. **2** A strong desire to achieve something considered great or good: with *of* or the infinitive. **3** An object so desired or striven for. **4** *Obs.* A canvassing for an office or the like. —*v.t.* To desire and seek eagerly. [< L *ambitio, -onis* a going about (to solicit votes) < *ambire.* See AMBIENT.] —**am·bi′tion·less** *adj.*

Synonyms (noun): aspiration, competition, emulation, opposition, rivalry. *Aspiration* is the desire for excellence, pure and simple. *Ambition,* literally a going around to solicit votes, has primary reference to the award or approval of others, and is the eager desire for power, fame, or something deemed great and eminent. *Emulation* is not so much to win any excellence or success for itself as to equal or surpass other persons. Compare EMULATION. *Antonyms:* carelessness, contentment, humility, indifference, satisfaction.

am·bi·tious (am·bish′əs) *adj.* **1** Actuated or characterized by ambition. **2** Greatly desiring; eager for: with *of* or the infinitive. **3** Aspiring, as to a high or imposing position. —**am·bi′tious·ly** *adv.* —**am·bi′tious·ness** *n.*

am·biv·a·lence (am·biv′ə·ləns) *n. Psychol.* The state of being ambivalent.

am·biv·a·lent (am·biv′ə·lənt) *adj.* **1** Uncertain or subject to change, especially because affected by contradictory emotions or ideas: an *ambivalent* attitude. **2** *Psychol.* Experiencing contradictory and opposing emotions toward the same person at the same time, especially love and hate. [< AMBI- + L *valens, -entis,* ppr. of *valere* be strong, be worth]

am·ble (am′bəl) *v.i.* **am·bled** (-bəld), **am·bling** **1** To move, as a horse, by lifting the two feet on one side together, alternately with the two feet on the other. **2** To move with an easy, swaying motion resembling this gait; proceed leisurely. —*n.* **1** The single-foot. **2** An ambling movement, like that of a horse. [< OF *ambler* < L *ambulare* walk] —**am′bling·ly** *adv.*

am·bler (am′blər) *n.* One that ambles, especially an ambling horse.

am·broid (am′broid) *n.* A reconstructed or imitation amber consisting of fragments of amber and sometimes other resins united by pressure and heat. Also *amberoid.*

am·bro·sia (am·brō′zhə, -zhē·ə) *n.* **1** The food of the gods, giving immortality. **2** Hence, any very delicious food or drink. **3** A richly perfumed salve or unguent. **4** *Bot.* Any of a genus (*Ambrosia*) of coarse herbs, weedy composite herbs comprising the ragweeds. [< L < Gk. *ambrosia* < *ambrotos* immortal < *a-* not + *brotos* mortal]

am·bro·si·a·ceous (am·brō·zē·ā′shəs) *adj.* Belonging to the genus *Ambrosia,* comprising weedy herbs of the composite family, as the ragweeds.

AMBROSIA (def. 4)
(3 to 6 feet high)

am·bro·sial (am·brō′zhəl, -zhē·əl) *adj.* **1** Of or like ambrosia; fragrant; delicious. **2** Worthy of the gods; heavenly. Also **am·bro·sian** (am·brō′zhən, -zhē·ən). —**am·bro′sial·ly** *adv.*

am·bry (am′brē) *n. pl.* **·bries** **1** A depository for goods, food, or money; pantry; cupboard; closet. **2** *Eccl.* A closet near the altar for the sacred vessels. **3** *Obs.* A library. Also **am·ber·y** (am′bər·ē). [ME *almarie, amerie, ambrie* < L *armarium* a chest, orig., a place for storing arms]

ambs·ace (āmz′ās′, amz′-) *n.* **1** Both aces, the lowest throw at dice. **2** Bad luck; misfortune. **3** Worthlessness; that which is next to nothing. [< OF *ambes as* < L *ambas as* double ace]

am·bu·cy·cle (am′byə·sī′kəl) *n.* A small ambulance attached like a side-car to a motorcycle. [<AMBU(LANCE) + (MOTOR)CYCLE]

am·bu·lance (am′byə·ləns) *n.* **1** A covered vehicle for conveying the sick and wounded. **2** A moving or field hospital. **3** A boat or airplane for conveying sick and wounded personnel. [<F <(*hôpital) ambulant* walking (hospital) <L *ambulare* walk]

am·bu·lant (am′byə·lənt) *adj.* Walking or moving about from place to place; shifting. [<L *ambulans, -antis,* ppr. of *ambulare* walk]

am·bu·late (am′byə·lāt) *v.i.* **·lat·ed, ·lat·ing** To walk about; move from place to place. [<L *ambulatus,* pp. of *ambulare* walk] **—am′bu·la′tion** *n.* **—am·bu·la·tive** (am′byə·lā′tiv, -lə·tiv) *adj.*

am·bu·la·to·ry (am′byə·lə·tôr′ē, -tō′rē) *adj.* **1** Pertaining to or for walking or walkers. **2** Able to walk, as an invalid. **3** Shifting; not fixed or stationary. **4** *Law* Alterable, as a writ or pleading until filed, or a will at any time during the testator's life. **—n. pl. ·ries** A place, as a corridor, for walking.

am·bus·cade (am′bəs·kād′) *n.* **1** The act of hiding, or the state of being hidden, to surprise adversaries. **2** The place of hiding, or persons hidden; an ambush. **—v.t. & v.i. ·cad·ed, ·cad·ing** To ambush. Also *Archaic* **am·bus·ca·do** (am′bəs·kā′dō). [<F *embuscade* <Ital. *imboscata* an ambush <*imboscare.* See AMBUSH.] **—am′bus·cad′er** *n.*

am·bush (am′bŏŏsh) *n.* **1** The act or condition of lying in wait to surprise or attack an enemy. **2** The hiding place or the persons hidden. Also **am′bush·ment. —v.t. & v.i. 1** To hide in order to attack unexpectedly. **2** To attack from a hidden place; waylay. [<OF *embusche* <*embuschier* <Ital. *imboscare* place in a bush, set an ambush <L *in-* in + *boscus* a wood] **—am′bush·er** *n.*

a·me·ba (ə·mē′bə) *n. pl.* **·bas** or **·bae** (-bē) Any of various naked protozoans of the genus *Amoeba* and other genera in the order Amoebidae, typically of indefinite shape, moving and feeding by the action of pseudopodia, and reproducing by fission. Also *amoeba.* [<NL <Gk. *amoibē* change] **—a·me′bic** *adj.*

AMEBA

am·e·be·an (am′ə·bē′ən) *adj.* Alternately or reciprocally responsive: also spelled *amoebaean, amoebean.* [<L *amoebaeum (carmen)* <Gk. *(asma) amoibaion* responsive (song) <*amoibē* change]

am·e·bi·a·sis (am′ə·bī′ə·sis) *n.* Infection by a parasitic ameba, especially *Entamoeba histolytica,* usually manifested by severe intestinal symptoms. Also *amoebiasis.* [<NL <AMEBA + -IASIS]

amebic dysentery Severe amebiasis involving ulceration and bleeding of the colon and painful diarrhea.

a·meer (ə·mir′) *n.* **1** The sovereign of Afghanistan. **2** A Mohammedan prince or governor. Also **a·mir′.** [<Arabic *amīr* ruler]

a·mel·io·rate (ə·mēl′yə·rāt) *v.t. & v.i.* **·rat·ed, ·rat·ing** To make or become better; meliorate; improve. See synonyms under AMEND. [<F *améliorer* <L *ad-* to + *meliorare* to better <*melior* better] **—a·mel·io·ra·ble** (ə·mēl′yə·rə·bəl) *adj.* **—a·mel′io·rant** (-rənt) *n.* **—a·mel·io·ra·tive** (ə·mēl′yə·rā′tiv, -rə·tiv) *adj.* **—a·mel′io·ra′tor** *n.*

a·mel·io·ra·tion (ə·mēl′yə·rā′shən) *n.* The act, process, or result of ameliorating, or the state of being ameliorated; improvement.

a·men (ā′men′, ä′-) *interj.* So it is; so be it. **—n. 1** The word *amen* at the end of a prayer or hymn, meaning *so be it.* **2** Any expression of hearty assent or conviction. **3** A concluding act or word; termination. **—v.t.** To say amen to; express hearty concurrence in or approval of. **2** To say or write that last word of; make an end of. **—adv. Obs.** Verily; truly. [<L <Gk. <Hebrew *āmēn* verily]

a·me·na·ble (ə·mē′nə·bəl, ə·men′ə-) *adj.* **1** Liable to be called to account; responsible to authority. **2** Submissive; tractable. **3** Capable of being tested or judged by rule or law. See synonyms under DOCILE. [<F *amener* bring to <*a-* to (<L *ad-*) + *mener* lead <L *minare* drive with threats) <*minari* threaten] **—a·me′na·bil′i·ty, a·me′na·ble·ness** *n.* **—a·me′na·bly** *adv.*

a·mend (ə·mend′) *v.t.* **1** To change for the better; improve. **2** To free from faults; correct; reform. **3** To change or alter by authority: to *amend* a bill. **4** *Obs.* To mend or repair. **—v.i. 5** To become better in conduct. [<OF *amender* <L *emendare* to free from faults <*ex-* from + *mendum* fault] **—a·mend′a·ble** *adj.* **—a·mend′a·ble·ness** *n.* **—a·mend′er** *n.*

Synonyms: advance, ameliorate, better, cleanse, correct, emend, improve, meliorate, mend, mitigate, purify, reclaim, rectify, reform, repair. To *amend* is to change for the better by removing faults, errors, or defects; it always refers to that which at some point falls short of a standard of excellence. *Advance, better,* and *improve* may refer either to what is quite imperfect or to what has reached a high degree of excellence. We *correct* evils, *reform* abuses, *rectify* incidental conditions of evil or error; we *ameliorate* poverty and misery, which we cannot wholly remove. We *mend* a tool, *repair* a building, *correct* proof; we *amend* character or conduct that is faulty, or a statement or law that is defective. Compare ALLAY, ALLEVIATE, EMEND. *Antonyms:* aggravate, blemish, corrupt, debase, depress, deteriorate, harm, impair, injure, mar, spoil, tarnish, vitiate.

a·mend·a·to·ry (ə·men′də·tôr′ē, -tō′rē) *adj.* Tending to amend; corrective.

a·mende (ə·mend′, *Fr.* ả·mäṅd′) *n.* A reparation or recantation. [<F]

a·mend·ment (ə·mend′mənt) *n.* **1** Change for the better. **2** A removal of faults; correction. **3** The changing, as of a law, bill, or motion. **4** The statement of such a change, as in a clause or paragraph.

a·mends (ə·mendz′) *n. pl.* Reparation, as in satisfaction or compensation for loss, damage, or injury. See synonyms under RECOMPENSE. [<OF *amendes,* pl. of *amende* a fine <*amender.* See AMEND.]

a·men·i·ty (ə·men′ə·tē) *n. pl.* **·ties 1** Agreeableness; pleasantness. **2** *pl.* Agreeable features or aspects, as of a place or scene. **3** *Often pl.* Any of the pleasant acts and courtesies of polite behavior. [<L *amoenitas, -tatis* <*amoenus* pleasant]

a·men·or·rhe·a (ā·men′ə·rē′ə) *n.* Abnormal suppression or absence of menstruation. [<NL <Gk. *a-* not + *mēn* month + *rheein* flow] **—a·men′or·rhe′ic, a·men′or·rhoe′ic** *adj.*

am·ent (am′ənt, ā′mənt) *n.* A catkin. [<L *amentum* a thong]

a·men·tia (ā·men′shə, -shē·ə) *n.* **1** Congenital lack of normal mental development; feeblemindedness. **2** Temporary insanity. [<L <*a-* (*ab-*) away + *mens* mind]

Am·er·a·sian (am′ər·ā′zhən) *adj.* Having both American and Asian parentage. **—n.** A person of American and Asian parentage.

a·merce (ə·mûrs′) *v.t.* **a·merced, a·merc·ing 1** To punish by an assessment or fine. **2** To punish, as by deprivation. [<AF *amercier* to fine <*a merci* at the mercy of] **—a·merce′a·ble** *adj.* **—a·merce′ment** *n.* **—a·merc′er** *n.*

A·mer·i·ca (ə·mer′ə·kə) **1** The lands in the Western Hemisphere; specifically, either of the two continents, North America or South America. Also **the Americas. 2** The United States of America.

America A popular patriotic hymn written by S. F. Smith; also, the tune to which it is sung, that of the English "God Save the King."

A·mer·i·can (ə·mer′ə·kən) *adj.* **1** Pertaining to the continent or people of North or South America, or of the Western Hemisphere. **2** Pertaining to the United States of America, its history, government, people, etc. **—n. 1** A citizen of the United States. **2** The English language as spoken and written in the United States; American English. **3** An inhabitant of America.

A·mer·i·ca·na (ə·mer′ə·kä′nə, -kan′ə, -kā′nə) *n. pl.* Things American, collectively; any collection of American literary papers, sayings, or other data, especially relating to American history and traditions.

American Indian A member of one of the aboriginal races of America.

A·mer·i·can·ism (ə·mer′ə·kən·iz′əm) *n.* **1** A word, phrase, usage, or a trait, custom, or tradition peculiar to the people of the United States or to some of them. **2** Attachment to America or its institutions, traditions, and way of life.

A·mer·i·can·ist (ə·mer′ə·kən·ist) *n.* One who makes a special study of subjects pertaining to America, as its history, geography, or resources.

American Samoa See SAMOA.

am·er·i·ci·um (am′ə·rish′ē·əm) *n.* A transuranium element (symbol Am, atomic number 95) produced in nuclear reactors by neutron bombardment of plutonium, the most stable isotope having mass number 243 and a half-life of 7370 years. See PERIODIC TABLE. [<NL, after *America*]

Am·er·in·di·an (am′ə·rin′dē·ən) *adj.* Of or pertaining to the American Indians or the Eskimos, individually or collectively. Also **Am′er·in′dic. —n.** An American Indian or Eskimo. Also **Am·er·ind** (am′ə·rind). [<AMER(ICAN) + INDIAN]

ames·ace (āmz′ās′) See AMBSACE.

am·e·thyst (am′ə·thist) *n.* A violet to purple gemstone consisting of either quartz or corundum. **2** A violet to purple color. **—adj.** Violet or purple. [<OF *ametiste* <L *amethystus* <Gk. *amethystos* not drunken <*a-* not + *methystos* drunken <*methy* wine; from the ancient belief that a wearer of the stone would be unaffected by wine]

a·mi·a·bil·i·ty (ā′mē·ə·bil′ə·tē) *n.* Sweetness of disposition; lovableness. Also **a′mi·a·ble·ness.**

a·mi·a·ble (ā′mē·ə·bəl) *adj.* **1** Pleasing in disposition, kind-hearted. **2** Free from irritation; friendly: an *amiable* rivalry. [<OF <L *amicabilis* friendly <*amicus* friend. Doublet of AMICABLE.] **—a′mi·a·bly** *adv.*

Synonyms: agreeable, attractive, benignant, charming, engaging, gentle, good-natured, kind, lovable, lovely, loving, pleasant, pleasing, sweet, winning, winsome. *Amiable* combines the senses of *lovable* or *lovely* and *loving; amiable* is a higher and stronger word than *good-natured* or *agreeable. Lovely* is often applied to externals; as, a *lovely* face. *Amiable* denotes a disposition desirous to cheer, please, and make happy. A selfish man of the world may have the art to be *agreeable;* a handsome, brilliant, and witty person may be *charming* or even *attractive,* while by no means *amiable. Antonyms:* acrimonious, churlish, crabbed, cruel, crusty, disagreeable, dogged, gruff, hateful, ill-conditioned, ill-humored, ill-natured, ill-tempered, morose, sour, sullen, surly, unamiable.

am·i·ca·ble (am′i·kə·bəl) *adj.* Showing or promoting good will; friendly; peaceable. [<L *amicabilis* <*amicus* friend. Doublet of AMIABLE.] **—am·i·ca·bil·i·ty** (am′i·kə·bil′ə·tē), **am′i·ca·ble·ness** *n.* **—am′i·ca·bly** *adv.*

Synonyms: cordial, favorable, friendly, hearty, kind, neighborly, sociable. The Anglo-Saxon *friendly* is stronger than the Latin *amicable;* that which is *amicable* may be merely formal; that which is *friendly* is from the heart. *Antonyms:* adverse, antagonistic, hostile, unfriendly.

a·mid (ə·mid′) *prep.* **1** In the midst of; among: He continued working *amid* the clamor of the crowd. **2** Mingled with or surrounded by: villages *amid* the woodlands. Also *amidst.* [OE *amiddan,* for *on middan* in the middle]

Synonyms: amidst, among, amongst, between, betwixt. *Amid* or *amidst* denotes surrounded by; *among* or *amongst,* mingled with. *Between* is said of two persons or objects, or of two groups of persons or objects. *Amid* denotes mere position; *among,* some active relation, as of companionship, hostility, etc. We say *among* (never *amid*) friends, or *among* (sometimes *amid*) enemies. *Antonyms:* beyond, outside, without.

a·mid·most (ə·mid′mōst′) *adv.* In the very middle. **—prep.** In the center of.

a·mid·ships (ə·mid′ships) *adv. Naut.* Halfway between stem and stern of a ship.

a·midst (ə·midst′) *prep.* Amid. [ME *amidde* + adverbial genitive suffix *-s* + inorganic *t*]

-amine *combining form Chem.* Used to denote an amine: *methylamine.*

a·mi·no (ə·mē′nō, am′ə·nō) *adj.* Containing the NH₂ group attached to a nonacid radical. [< AMINE]

amino- *combining form* Indicating a compound containing the group NH₂ attached to a nonacid radical.

amino acid Any of a group of some 80 organic compounds which contain one or more basic amino and acid carboxyl groups and which in some cases polymerize to form peptides and proteins.

Am·ish (am′ish, ä′mish) *adj.* Relating to or designating the adherents of Jacob Ammann, a 17th century Mennonite. —*n. pl.* A sect of Mennonites, founded by Jacob Ammann: also spelled *Omish.*

a·miss (ə·mis′) *adj.* Out of order or relation; wrong; improper: used predicatively: Something is *amiss.* —*adv.* 1 Improperly. 2 Erroneously. 3 Defectively. —**to take amiss** To take offense at; feel resentment toward. [ME *amis* < *a-* at + *mis* miss²]

a·mi·to·sis (am′ə·tō′sis) *n.* Cell division by simple fission of the nucleus and cytoplasm without the formation and splitting of chromosomes. [< NL < A-⁴ without + MITOSIS] —**am·i·tot·ic** (am′ə·tot′ik) *adj.* —**am′i·tot′i·cal·ly** *adv.*

am·i·ty (am′ə·tē) *n. pl.* **·ties** Peaceful relations; mutual good will; friendship. See synonyms under FRIENDSHIP, HARMONY. [< MF *amitié*, ult. < L *amicus* friend]

Am·man (äm′män) The capital of Jordan.

am·mo·nia (ə·mōn′yə, ə·mō′nē·ə) *n.* 1 A colorless, pungent gas, NH₃, readily soluble in water to form an alkaline solution, produced in the decomposition of many organic nitrogenous compounds. 2 Ammonium hydroxide. [< SAL AMMONIAC]

am·mo·ni·ac¹ (ə·mō′nē·ak) *adj.* Of, containing, or resembling ammonia. Also **am·mo·ni·a·cal** (am′ə·nī′ə·kəl).

am·mo·ni·ac² (ə·mō′nē·ak) *n.* A gum resin obtained from an umbelliferous plant (*Dorema acconiacum*) of Asia. Also called *gum ammoniac.* [< F < L *ammoniacum* < Gk. *ammōniakon,* a resinous gum said to come from a plant growing near the temple of *Ammon* in Libya]

am·mo·ni·ate (ə·mō′nē·āt) *v.t.* **·at·ed, ·at·ing** To treat or combine with ammonia. —*n.* (ə·mō′nē·it) A compound containing ammonia. —**am·mo′ni·a′tion** *n.*

am·mon·i·fi·ca·tion (ə·mon′ə·fi·kā′shən) *n.* 1 The addition of ammonia or ammonium salts, as in the form of fertilizer added to the soil. 2 The stage in the nitrogen cycle in which nitrogenous compounds are decomposed to form ammonia by the action of bacteria, fungi, etc.

am·mon·i·fy (ə·mon′ə·fī) *v.t. & v.i.* **·fied, ·fy·ing** To bring about or undergo ammonification.

am·mon·ite¹ (am′ən·īt) *n.* Any of various flat spiral shells of an extinct order (Ammonoidea) of cephalopods that flourished in the Mesozoic era. Also **am′·mon·oid.** [< L *cornu Ammonis* horn of Ammon]

AMMONITE
(European)

am·mo·ni·um (ə·mō′nē·əm) *n. Chem.* The univalent radical NH₄, which in compounds formed from ammonia acts as an alkali metal. [< NL < AMMONIA]

am·mu·ni·tion (am′yə·nish′ən) *n.* 1 *Mil.* Any one of various articles used in the discharge of firearms and ordnance, as cartridges, shells, shot, rockets, primers, fuses, grenades, and chemicals. 2 Any resources for attack or defense. —*v.t.* To supply with ammunition. [< MF *amunition,* for *munition* (la munition taken as *l'amunition*) < L *munitio, -onis* < *munire* fortify]

am·ne·sia (am·nē′zhə, -zhē·ə) *n.* Loss or impairment of memory; morbid forgetfulness. [< NL < Gk. *amnēsia* forgetfulness < *a-* not + *mnasthai* remember] —**am·ne·sic** (am·nē′sik, -zik) *adj.*

am·ne·si·ac (am·nē′zhē·ak, -zē-) *n.* One suffering from amnesia. —*adj.* Pertaining to or causing loss of memory.

am·nes·tic (am·nes′tik) *n.* Any agent that produces amnesia. —*adj.* Amnesiac.

am·nes·ty (am′nəs·tē) *n. pl.* **·ties** 1 An official act of oblivion or pardon on the part of a government, absolving without trial all offenders or groups of offenders. 2 Intentional forgetfulness or overlooking, especially of wrongdoing. —*v.t.* **·tied, ·ty·ing** To pardon; grant amnesty to. [< F *amnestie* < L *amnestia* < Gk. *amnēstia* < *a-* not + *mnasthai* remember]

am·ni·o·cen·te·sis (am′nē·ō·sen·tē′sis) *n.* The sampling of amniotic fluid of a pregnant woman, as to detect chromosomal anomalies or to determine the sex of the fetus. [< AMNION + Gk. *kentein* to prick]

am·ni·on (am′nē·ən) *n. pl.* **·ni·ons** or **·ni·a** (-nē·ə) A tough, membranous, fluid-containing sac enclosing the embryo of birds, reptiles, and mammals. [< Gk. *amnion* the fetal envelope, dim. of *amnos* lamb] —**am·ni·on·ic** (am′nē·on′ik), **am·ni·ot·ic** (am′nē·ot′ik) *adj.*

am·ni·ote (am′nē·ōt) *n.* Any member of the three classes of animals (Reptilia, Aves, and Mammalia) in which the embryo is protected by an amnion. —*adj.* Of or pertaining to amniotes.

a·mock, a·mok (ə·muk′, ə·mok′), **a·moke** (ə·mōk′), etc. See AMUCK.

a·moe·ba (ə·mē′bə), **a·moe·bic** (ə·mē′bik), **a·moe·boid** (ə·mē′boid), etc. See AMEBA, etc.

among (ə·mung′) *prep.* 1 In the midst of: a house *among* the trees. 2 Mingled with; included within a mass or multitude: He was just one *among* hundreds. 3 In the class, group, number, or company of: one example *among* many. 4 In association with; connected with: Some truth may be found *among* many errors. 5 Shared by; affecting all of: money divided *among* the poor. 6 According to the customs of; in the country or time of: usage *among* educated people; a practice *among* the French. Also **amongst.** See synonyms under AMID, BETWEEN. [OE *on gemong* in the crowd]

a·mor·al (ā·môr′əl, ā·mor′əl) *adj.* 1 Not subject to or concerned with moral or ethical judgment or distinctions. 2 Lacking a sense of right or wrong; lacking moral responsibility. [< A-⁴ not + MORAL] —**a·mo·ral·i·ty** (ā′mə·ral′ə·tē) *n.* —**a·mor′al·ly** *adv.*

am·o·ret·to (am′ə·ret′ō) *n. pl.* **·ret·ti** (-ret′ē) A cupid. [< Ital., dim of *amore* love < L *amor*]

a·mo·ri·no (ä′mō·rē′nō) *n.* **·ni** (-nē) An amoretto.

am·o·rist (am′ə·rist) *n.* 1 A lover; one given to amours. 2 One who writes about romantic love. —**am′o·ris′tic** *adj.*

a·mo·ro·so (ä′mō·rō′sō) *adj. Music* Tender. —*adv. Music* Tenderly. —*n. pl.* **·si** (-sē) A gallant; lover. [< Ital., amorous]

am·o·rous (am′ə·rəs) *adj.* 1 Having a propensity for falling in love; influenced by sexual affection or appetite; loving; ardent in affection. 2 Of or pertaining to love; showing, springing from, or exciting to love or sexual desire. 3 In love; enamored: usually with *of.* [< OF < LL *amorosus* < L *amor* love] —**am′orous·ly** *adv.* —**am′o·rous·ness** *n.*

a·mor pa·tri·ae (ā′môr pā′tri·ē) *Latin* Love of native country; patriotism.

a·mor·phism (ə·môr′fiz·əm) *n.* The state or quality of being amorphous.

a·mor·phous (ə·môr′fəs) *adj.* 1 Without definite form or shape; structureless. 2 *Geol.* Found or occurring in masses lacking definite stratification. 3 Anomalous; unorganized. 4 Having no apparent fine structure; not crystalline. [< Gk. *amorphos* < *a-* without + *morphē* form] —**a·mor′phous·ly** *adv.* —**a·mor′phous·ness** *n.*

am·or·ti·za·tion (am′ər·tə·zā′shən, ə·môr′tə·zā′shən) *n.* 1 An amortizing or being amortized. 2 The sum of money set aside or devoted to amortizing a debt.

am·or·tize (am′ər·tīz, ə·môr′tīz) *v.t.* **·tized, ·tiz·ing** 1 To extinguish, as a debt or liability, by payments to a sinking fund or creditor. 2 *Law* To sell and convey, as land, to a corporation having perpetual succession; alienate in mortmain. Also *Brit.* **am′or·tise.** [< OF *amortiss-,* stem of *amortir* extinguish, sell in mortmain < L *ad-* to + *mors, mortis* death] —**am·or·tiz·a·ble** (am′ər·tīz′ə·bəl, ə·môr′tiz·ə·bəl) *adj.*

a·mor·tize·ment (ə·môr′tiz·mənt) *n.* 1 Amortization. 2 *Archaic* The finishing portion at the top of any part of a structure.

a·mount (ə·mount′) *n.* 1 A sum total; aggregate. 2 The value of the principal with the interest upon it, as in a loan. 3 The entire significance, value, or effect. 4 Quantity: a considerable *amount* of discussion. See synonyms under AGGREGATE. [< *v.*] —*v.i.* 1 To rise in number of quantity so as to reach: with *to:* This bill *amounts* to ten dollars. 2 To be equivalent in effect or importance: He doesn't *amount* to a row of beans. [< OF *amonter* < *amont* upward < *a mont* to the mountain < L *ad* to + *mons, montis* mountain]

a·mour (ə·moor′) *n.* A love affair; intrigue. [< F]

amp (amp) *n. Colloq.* 1 Ampere. 2 An electrically amplified guitar.

am·pere (am′pir, am·pir′) *n. Electr.* The practical unit of electric-current strength; such a current as would be given with an electromotive force of one volt through a wire having a resistance of one ohm. —**international ampere** The current which on passing through a silver-nitrate solution will deposit silver at the rate of 0.001118 gram a second. [after A. M. *Ampère*]

am·per·sand (am′pər·sand, am′pər·sand′) *n.* The character (& or &) meaning *and.* [< *and per se and,* lit., & by itself = and]

am·phet·a·mine (am·fet′ə·mēn, -min) *n.* — 1 A colorless liquid, C₉H₁₃N, used as a stimulant of the central nervous system. 2 any of the various crystalline compounds of amphetamine used as drugs. [< *a(lpha)-m(ethyl)-ph(enyl)-et(hyl)-amine*]

amphi- *prefix* 1 On both or all sides; at both ends: *amphicoelous.* 2 Around: *amphigean.* 3 Of both kinds; in two ways: *amphibious.* [< Gk. < *amphi* around]

am·phib·i·an (am·fib′ē·ən) *n. pl.* **·bi·ans** or **·bi·a** (def. 1) 1 Any of a class (*Amphibia*) of cold-blooded vertebrate organisms with smooth, moist skin, whose life cycle typically comprises tadpoles which hatch from eggs as aquatic, gilled, limbless forms and which metamorphose into terrestrial air-breathing adults with four limbs, as frogs, toads, newts, salamanders, etc. 2 Any amphibious organism. 3 An airplane constructed to rise from and alight on either land or water. 4 A craft capable of self-propulsion upon land and upon water. —*adj.* Amphibious.

am·phib·i·ol·o·gy (am·fib′ē·ol′ə·jē) *n. pl.* **·gies** 1 The scientific study of amphibians. 2 A treatise relating to this subject.

am·phib·i·ot·ic (am·fib′ē·ot′ik, am′fə·bī·ot′ik) *adj.* Having a life cycle with successive aquatic and terrestrial cycles.

am·phib·i·ous (am·fib′ē·əs) *adj.* 1 Living or adapted to life on land or in water. 2 Capable of operating on land or water: an *amphibious* tank. 3 Capable of operating on water and in the air: an *amphibious* airplane. 4 Of a mixed nature; connected with two ranks, classes, etc. [< Gk. *amphibios* having a double life < *amphi-* of two kinds + *bios* life] —**am·phib′i·ous·ly** *adv.* —**am·phib′i·ous·ness** *n.*

am·phi·bol·ic (am′fə·bol′ik) *adj.* Pertaining to or like amphiboly; ambiguous. Also **am·phib·o·lous** (am·fib′ə·ləs).

am·phi·bol·o·gy (am′fə·bol′ə·jē) *n. pl.* **·gies** An ambiguous phrase or sentence; ambiguity. [< F *amphibologie* < LL *amphibologia,* for L *amphibolia* < Gk. *amphibolia* ambiguity < *amphiballein,* see AMPHIBOLE.] —**am·phib·o·log·i·cal** (am·fib′ə·loj′i·kəl) *adj.*

am·phib·o·ly (am·fib′ə·lē) *n. pl.* **·lies** An ambiguous construction of language; a group of words admitting of two meanings. [< L *amphibolia.* See AMPHIBOLOGY.]

am·phi·brach (am′fə·brak) *n.* In prosody, a metrical foot, consisting of a long or accented syllable between two short or unaccented ones (‿ – ‿). [< L *amphibrachys* < Gk. < *amphi-* at both ends + *brachys* short]

am·phi·chro·ic (am'fə·krō'ik) *adj.* Exhibiting either of two colors, as certain substances when subjected to tests with acids or alkalis. Also **am·phi·chro·mat·ic** (am'fə·krō·mat'ik). [< AMPHI- + Gk. *chroa* color]

am·phi·ge·an (am'fə·jē'ən) *adj. Bot.* Extending around the globe in nearly the same latitude, as certain species of plants. [< AMPHI- + Gk. *gē* earth]

am·phi·gen·e·sis (am'fə·jen'ə·sis) *n.* **1** *Biol.* The merging of two gametes to form a fertilized cell or zygote. **2** *Psychol.* Sexual response of a predominantly homosexual person in regard to members of the opposite sex. —**am·phi·gen·ic** (am'fə·jen'ik) *adj.*

am·phi·go·ry (am'fə·gôr'ē, -gō'rē) *n. pl.* **·ries** A meaningless rigmarole with a semblance of sense; a burlesque, as one written in nonsensical verse. Also **am·phi·gou·ri** (am'fə·gōō'rē) *pl.* **·ris** (-rēz). [< F *amphigouri*; ult. origin unknown] —**am·phi·gor·ic** (am'fə·gôr'ik, -gor'-) *adj.*

am·phim·a·cer (am·fim'ə·sər) In prosody, a metrical foot consisting of one short or unaccented syllable between two long or accented ones (- ˘ -): opposed to *amphibrach.* Also called *cretic.* [< L *amphimacrus* < Gk. *amphimakros* < *amphi-* on both sides + *makros* long]

am·phis·bae·na (am'fis·bē'nə) *n.* **1** A mythical serpent having a head at each end of the body and moving in either direction. **2** *Zool.* A tropical, legless lizard (family *Amphisbaenidae*) having head and tail much alike. [< L < Gk. *amphisbaina* < *amphis,* amphi- at both ends + *bainein* go] —**am·phis·bae·nic** *adj.*

am·phi·sty·lar (am'fə·stī'lər) *adj. Archit.* With columns at each end or on each side. [< AMPHI- + Gk. *stylos* pillar]

am·phi·the·a·ter (am'fə·thē'ə·tər) *n.* **1** An edifice of elliptical shape, constructed about a central open space or arena, with tiers of seats sloping upward. **2** Any structure of similar shape, as a natural area or theater having slopes or tiers of seats entirely surrounding a central space. **3** The place where a spectacle or battle takes place; scene of action. Also **am'phi·the·a·tre.** [< L *amphitheatrum* < Gk. *amphitheatron* < *amphi-* around + *theatron* theater]

am·phi·the·at·ri·cal (am'fə·thē·at'ri·kəl) *adj.* Of, pertaining to, resembling, or performed in an amphitheater. Also **am·phi·the·a·tral** (am'fə ·thē'ə·trəl), **am·phi·the·at·ric** (am'fə·thē·at'rik). —**am'phi·the·at'ri·cal·ly** *adv.*

am·pho·ra (am'fə·rə) *n. pl.* **·rae** (-rē) In ancient Greece, a tall, two-handled earthenware jar for wine or oil, narrow at the neck and the base. [< L < Gk. *amphoreus* < *amphi-* on both sides + *phoreus* bearer < *pherein* bear] —**am'pho·ral** *adj.*

AMPHORAE

am·phor·ic (am·fôr'ik, -for'-) *adj.* **1** Having a sound like that made by blowing into the mouth of an amphora. **2** Amphoral.

am·pho·ter·ic (am'fə·ter'ik) *adj.* Capable of reacting chemically as either an acid or a base. [< Gk. *amphoteros* both]

am·pi·cil·lin (am'pə·sil'ən) *n.* A kind of penicillin that is especially effective against Gram-negative bacteria

am·ple (am'pəl) *adj.* **1** Of great dimensions or capacity; large; great in amount of degree. **2** More than enough; abundant; liberal. **3** Fully sufficient to meet all needs or requirements; adequate. [< F < L *amplus* large, abundant] —**am'ple·ness** *n.*

Synonyms: abundant, affluent, bountiful, complete, copious, enough, full, large, liberal, plenteous, plentiful, sufficient. That is *enough* which just meets a given demand; that is *ample* which gives a safe, but not a large, margin beyond; that is *abundant, affluent, bountiful, liberal, plentiful,* which is largely in excess of manifest need. Compare ENOUGH, LARGE, PLENTIFUL. *Antonyms:* deficient, inadequate, insufficient, niggardly, scant, small, stingy.

am·pli·a·tive (am'plē·ā'tiv) *adj.* Supplementing; adding to.

am·pli·fi·ca·tion (am'plə·fi·kā'shən) *n.* **1** An amplifying or being amplified; augmentation; addition. **2** An extended statement; the matter added

to amplify a subject; details. **3** *Electr.* An increase in the voltage or power of an electric current. See synonyms under INCREASE.

am·pli·fi·er (am'plə·fī'ər) *n.* **1** One who or that which amplifies or increases. **2** A megaphonelike device for increasing the volume of sound. **3** *Electr.* A device for increasing the intensity of electric impulses by the control of power supplied by a local source, usually by means of vacuum tubes or dynamos. **4** A loudspeaker.

am·pli·fy (am'plə·fī) *v.* **·fied, ·fy·ing** *v.t.* **1** To enlarge or increase in scope, significance, or power. **2** To add to so as to make more complete, as by illustrations. **3** To exaggerate; magnify. **4** *Electr.* To increase the strength or amplitude of, as electromagnetic impulses. —*v.i.* **5** To make additional remarks; expatiate. [< F *amplifier* < L *amplificare* < *amplus* large + *facere* make] —**am·pli·fi·ca·tive** (am'plə·fi·kā'tiv, am·plif'i·kə·tiv), **am·plif·i·ca·to·ry** (am·plif'i·kə·tôr'ē, -tō'rē) *adj.*

Synonyms: augment, develop, dilate, enlarge, expand, expatiate, extend, increase, unfold, widen. *Amplify* is now chiefly applied to discourse or writing, signifying to make fuller in statement, as by stating fully what was before only implied, or by adding illustrations to make the meaning more readily apprehended, etc. We may *develop* a thought, *expand* an illustration, *extend* a discussion, *expatiate* on a hobby, *dilate* on some theme or incident, *enlarge* a volume, *unfold* a scheme, *widen* the range of treatment. Compare ADD. *Antonyms:* abbreviate, abridge, amputate, compress, condense, curtail, delete, epitomize, reduce, retrench, shorten, summarize, contract, tighten.

am·pli·tude (am'plə·tōōd, -tyōōd) *n.* **1** Greatness of extent; largeness; breadth; the state or quality of being ample: the *amplitude* of the oceans. **2** Fullness or completeness; abundance or richness: the *amplitude* of life. **3** Broad range or scope, as of mental capacity: an *amplitude* of talent. **4** *Astron.* The arc of the horizon between true east and west and the center of the sun, moon, or any star at its rising or setting. **5** *Physics* The extent of the swing of a vibrating body on each side of the mean position. **6** *Electr.* The peak value attained by an alternating current during one complete cycle. [< L *amplitudo* < *amplus* large]

am·ply (am'plē) *adv.* In an ample manner; largely; liberally; sufficiently.

am·poule (am·pōōl) *n. Med.* A small, hermetically sealed vial, usually made of glass, containing a medicament for injection or other use. Also **am·pule** (am'pyōōl), **am·pul** (am'pul). [< F < L *ampulla* ampulla (def. 3)]

am·pul·la (am·pul'ə) *n. pl.* **am·pul·lae** (-pul'ē) **1** *Eccl.* A flask for holding the consecrated oil used in confirmation, ordination, and extreme unction; specifically, that used in England at the consecration of kings. **2** The cruet used for the wine or water at mass. **3** An ancient Roman bottle or vase with a slender neck and flattened mouth, used to hold perfumes and oils and for carrying wine. **4** *Anat.* A small sac or dilated segment of a tube or gland. [< L, dim. of *amphora* jar] —**am·pul'lar** *adj.*

am·pu·tate (am'pyōō·tāt) *v.t.* **·tat·ed, ·tat·ing** **1** *Surg.* To remove by cutting, as a limb; cut off the whole or a part of. **2** To reduce; prune: to *amputate* funds for a project. [< L *amputatus,* pp. of *amputare* < *ambi-* around + *putare* trim, prune] —**am'pu·ta'tion** *n.* —**am'pu·ta'tor** *n.*

am·pu·tee (am'pyōō·tē') *n.* One who has had a limb or limbs removed by amputation.

am·ri·ta (um·rē'tə) *n.* In Hindu mythology: **1** The ambrosia of immortality, sometimes represented as the fruit of a tree or the cream of the ocean churned by the gods. **2** Immortality. Also **am·ree'ta.** [< Skt. *amrta*]

Am·ster·dam (am'stər·dam) A port on the Zuider Zee; constitutional capital and largest city of the Netherlands.

a·muck (ə·muk') *adj.* Possessed with murderous frenzy. —*adv.* In a violent or frenzied manner. —**to run amuck** To run about attacking everybody one meets. Also spelled *amock, amok, amoke.* [< Malay *amoq* engaging furiously in battle]

am·u·let (am'yə·lit) *n.* Anything worn about one's person to protect from witchcraft, accident, or ill luck; a charm. See synonyms under TALISMAN. [< L *amuletum* charm]

a·muse (ə·myōōz') *v.t.* **a·mused, a·mus·ing** **1**

To occupy pleasingly; entertain; divert: to *amuse* oneself by playing the guitar. **2** To cause to laugh or smile, as with pleasure. **3** *Archaic* To beguile; delude. [< F *amuser* < *à* at (< L *ad-*) + OF *muser* stare] —**a·mus'a·ble** *adj.* —**a·mus'er** *n.*

a·muse·ment (ə·myōōz'mənt) *n.* **1** The state of being amused; the feeling of delight or joy, as in some diversion: **2** That which amuses, as an entertainment, game, or spectacle. See synonyms under COMFORT, ENTERTAINMENT, FROLIC, SPORT.

a·mus·ing (ə·myōō'zing) *adj.* **1** Entertaining or diverting. **2** Arousing laughter.

a·mu·sive (ə·myōō'ziv, -siv) *adj.* Having power to amuse; amusing.

amylo- *combining form* **1** Of starch: *amyloplast.* **2** Of amyl. Also, before vowels, **amyl-.** [def. 1 < AMYLUM; def. 2 < AMYL]

am·y·loid (am'ə·loid) *n.* **1** *Bot.* A gummy or starchlike substance formed in woody tissues in the process of lignification. **2** *Pathol.* Waxy matter formed in certain diseased tissues of the body, but not chemically related to starch. —*adj.* Like or containing starch. —**am'y·loi'dal** *adj.*

am·y·lum (am'ə·ləm) *n.* Starch. [< L < Gk. *amylon* starch]

an¹ (an, *unstressed* ən) *indefinite article & adj.* **1** Each or any. **2** One; one kind of; one single. Used like the article *a,* but before words beginning with a vowel sound; as, *an* acorn, *an* honest man. **3** For each: The price is a dollar *an* apple. [OE *an* one]

an² (an, *unstressed* ən) *conj. Archaic* And, especially in the sense *and if,* or *if:* often written **an'.** See AND.

an-¹ *prefix* Without; not: *anacid, anarchy.* Also, before consonants except *h,* **a-** (called *alpha privative*). [< Gk.]

an-² Var. of ANA-.

an-³ Assimilated var. of AD-.

-an *suffix* Used to form adjectives and nouns denoting connection with a country, person, group, doctrine, etc., as follows: **1** Pertaining to; belonging to: *human, sylvan.* **2** Originating in; living in: *Italian.* **3** Adhering to; following: *Lutheran.* [< L -*anus*]

a·na¹ (ā'nə, ä'nə) *n.* **1** A collection of notes, sketches, or scraps of literature bearing on some particular person, place, or subject. **2** The information in such a collection. See -ANA.

an·a² (an'ə) *adv. Med.* Of each a like amount: used in prescriptions. [< Gk. *ana* throughout]

ana- *prefix* **1** Up; upward: *andromorous.* **2** Back; backward: *anapest.* **3** Anew: sometimes capable of being rendered *re-,* as *anabaptism,* rebaptism. **4** Throughout; thoroughly: *analysis.* Also, before vowels or *h,* **an-,** as in *anode.* [< Gk. < *ana* on]

-ana *suffix* Pertaining to: added to the names of notable persons, places, etc., to indicate a collection of materials, such as writings or anecdotes, about the subject: *Americana, Johnsoniana.* Also **-iana.** [< L, neut. pl. of -*anus.* See-AN]

an·a·bi·o·sis (an'ə·bī·ō'sis) *n.* A suspension of animation susceptible of resuscitation. [< NL < ANA- + Gk. *bios* life]

an·a·bi·ot·ic (an'ə·bī·ot'ik) *adj.* Lifeless, but capable of resuscitation.

an·a·bol·ic steroid (an'ə·bol'ik) Any of various synthetic drugs that stimulate the development of large and strong muscles.

a·nab·o·lism (ə·nab'ə·liz'əm) *n.* The phase of metabolism in which large and complex compounds are built up from smaller, simpler compounds. [< Gk. *anabolē* a heaping up < *ana-* up + *bolē* a stroke] —**an·a·bol·ic** (an'ə·bol'ik) *adj.*

an·a·ca·thar·sis (an'ə·kə·thär'sis) *n. Med.* **1** Regurgitation; vomiting. **2** Expectoration. [< NL < Gk. *anakatharsis* < *ana-* up + *katharsis* purification]

a·nach·o·rism (ə·nak'ə·riz'əm) *n.* Something foreign to a country or unsuited to local conditions; a geographical error: compare with *anachronism.* [< ANA- + Gk. *chōros* country, place]

a·nach·ro·nism (ə·nak'rə·niz'əm) *n.* **1** A chronological error. **2** Something occurring or represented as occurring out of its proper time. [< F *anachronisme* < L *anachronismus* < Gk. *anachronismos* < *anachronizein* refer to a wrong time < *ana-* against + *chronos* time] —**an·a·chron·ic**

(an'ə·kron'ik), **a·nach·ro·nis'·ti·cal, a·nach'ro·nous** adj.

an·ac·id (an·as'id) adj. Med. Lacking the normal degree of acidity: said especially of gastric secretions. —**an·a·cid·i·ty** (an'ə·sid'·ə·tē) n.

a·nac·la·sis (ə·nak'lə·sis) n. In prosody, the exchange of place of a short syllable with a preceding long one; thus, ˘˘‒‿ for ‒‿˘˘. [< NL < Gk. anaklasis < anaklaein bend back < ana- back + klaein break]

an·a·clas·tic (an'ə·klas'tik) adj. 1 Optics Pertaining to refraction or bending; caused by or causing refraction. 2 In prosody, characterized by anaclasis.

an·a·co·lu·thon (an'ə·kə·lōō'thon) n. pl. ·thons or ·tha (-thə) 1 Violation of grammatical sequence, as for the sake of energy or to express strong emotion. 2 An instance of this; a sentence in which anacoluthon occurs. [< Gk. anakolouthos lacking sequence < an- not + akolouthos following] —**an'a·co·lu'thic** adj.

an·a·con·da (an'ə·kon'də) n. 1 A very large nonvenomous, semiaquatic snake, Eunectes murinus, of tropical South America, which crushes its prey in its coils. 2 Any of very large constrictors. [Origin unknown]

an·a·cru·sis (an'ə·krōō'sis) n. 1 In prosody, one or more unemphatic introductory syllables in a line of verse that would properly begin with a stressed syllable. 2 Music An upbeat. [< NL < Gk. anakrousis < anakrouein push back < ana- back + krouein strike] —**an·a·crus·tic** (an'ə·krus'tik) adj.

an·a·dem (an'ə·dem) n. A wreath for the head; garland; fillet. [< L anadema < Gk. anadēma < anadein wreathe < ana- up + dein bind]

an·a·di·plo·sis (an'ə·di·plō'sis) n. Rhetorical repetition, in which the ending of a sentence, line, or clause is repeated and emphasized at the beginning of the next. [< L < Gk. anadiplōsis < ana- again + diploein to double < diploos double]

an·aer·obe (an·âr'ōb, an·ā'ə·rōb) n. A microorganism that thrives in the absence of free oxygen. [< AN-¹ without + AERO- + Gk. bios life]

an·aer·o·bic (an'âr·ō'bik, -ob'ik, an'ā·ə·rō'bik, -rob'ik) adj. Living or functioning in the absence of free oxygen: anaerobic bacteria. 2 Containing no uncombined oxygen: an anaerobic environment. —**an'aer·o'bi·cal·ly** adv.

an·aes·the·sia (an'is·thē'zhə, -zhē·ə), **an·aes·thet·ic** (an'is·thet'ik), etc. See ANESTHESIA, etc.

an·a·glyph (an'ə·glif) n. 1 An ornament in low relief, as a cameo. 2 Optics A stereoscopic picture of an object produced in two colors, red and green, and from two angles, as from the right and the left eye: used to determine abnormal binocular vision. [< Gk. anaglyphē < ana- up + glyphein carve]

an·a·go·ge (an'ə·gō'jē) n. Spiritual or mystical significance or interpretation of words, especially of the Scriptures. [< NL < Gk. anagōgē a leading up < ana- up + agein lead]

an·a·gram (an'ə·gram) n. 1 A word or phrase formed by transposing the letters of another word or phrase. 2 pl. A game in which the players make words by transposing or adding letters. [< NL anagramma < Gk. ana- anew + gramma a letter < graphein write] —**an·a·gram·mat·ic** (an'ə·grə·mat'ik) or **·i·cal** adj. —**an'a·gram·mat'i·cal·ly** adv.

an·a·gram·ma·tize (an'ə·gram'ə·tīz) v.t. ·tized, ·tiz·ing To arrange as an anagram.

a·nal (ā'nəl) adj. 1 a Of, pertaining to, or situated in the region of the anus. b Situated near the anus. 2 Psychoanal. a Of or relating to the second stage of psychosexual development of the child in which interest in excretion is dominant. b Of, pertaining to, or characterized by qualities in the adult, as orderliness or an inclination to hoard, regarded as typifying this stage of development. Compare GENITAL, ORAL.

an·a·lect (an'ə·lekt) n. pl. **an·a·lec·ta** (an'ə·lek'tə) or **·lects** A selection or fragment from a literary work or group of works: usually in the plural. [< L analecta, pl. < Gk. analekta < analegein collect < ana- up + legein gather] —**an'a·lec'tic** adj.

an·al·ge·si·a (an'əl·jē'zē·ə, -sē·ə) n. Insensibility to pain without loss of consciousness. [< NL < Gk. analgēsia < an- without + algos pain]

an·al·ge·sic (an'əl·jē'zik, -sik) n. A drug that prevents or relieves pain. —adj. Pertaining to or promoting analgesia.

an·a·log (an'ə·lôg, -log) n. 1 Anything analogous to something else. 2 Biol. An organ analogous to one in another species or group: distinguished from homolog. Also **an'a·logue.** [< F analogue < L analogus. See ANALOGY.]

an·a·log·i·cal (an'ə·loj'i·kəl) adj. Pertaining to, containing, or based on analogy. Also **an'a·log'ic.** —**an'a·log'i·cal·ly** adv.

a·nal·o·gist (ə·nal'ə·jist) n. One who uses or reasons from analogy.

a·nal·o·gize (ə·nal'ə·jīz) v. ·gized, ·giz·ing v.i. To use or reason by analogy. —v.t. To show to be analogous.

a·nal·o·gous (ə·nal'ə·gəs) adj. 1 Resembling in certain respects. 2 Biol. Having a similar function but different in origin and structure, as the wings of birds and insects. See synonyms under ALIKE. —**a·nal'o·gous·ly** adv. —**a·nal'o·gous·ness** n.

a·nal·o·gy (ə·nal'ə·jē) n. pl. ·gies 1 Resemblance of properties or relations; similarity without identity. 2 Any similarity or agreement. 3 Biol. A similarity in function and superficial appearance, but not in origin: opposed to homology. 4 Logic Reasoning in which from certain observed and known relations or parallel resemblances others are inferred; reasoning that proceeds from the individual or particular to a coordinate individual or particular, thus involving both induction and deduction. 5 Ling. The formative process by which words take on inflections or constructions that are imitative of more familiar words and existing patterns without having undergone the same true linguistic development; as, the past tense of climb changed from the strong form clomb to the weak form climbed on analogy with the weak verbs. [< F analogie < L analogia < Gk. analogia < analogos proportionate, conformable < ana- according to + logos proportion]

Synonyms: coincidence, comparison, likeness, parity, proportion, relation, resemblance, semblance, similarity, simile, similitude. Analogy is specifically a resemblance of relations; a resemblance that may be reasoned from, so that from the likeness in certain respects we may infer that other and perhaps deeper relations exist. Parity of reasoning is said of an argument equally conclusive on subjects not strictly analogous. Coincidence is complete agreement in some one or more respects. Similitude is a rhetorical comparison of one thing to another with which it has some points in common. Resemblance and similarity are external or superficial, and may involve no deeper relation. Compare ALLEGORY. Antonyms: disagreement, disproportion, dissimiliarity, incongruity, unlikeness.

an·al·pha·bet·ic (an·al'fə·bet'ik) adj. & n. Illiterate.

a·nal·y·sand (ə·nal'ə·sand) n. Psychoanal. The person who is being analyzed.

an·a·lyse (an'ə·līz) British spelling of ANALYZE.

a·nal·y·sis (ə·nal'ə·sis) n. pl. ·ses (-sēz) 1 The resolution of a whole into its parts or elements: opposed to synthesis. 2 A statement of the results of this; logical synopsis. 3 A method of determining or describing the nature of a thing by resolving it into its parts: to study literature by the analysis of texts. 4 Math. a The process of resolving a problem into its first elements. b The investigation of the relations of variable or indeterminate quantities by means of symbols, including some branches of algebra and the differential and integral calculus. 5 Chem. a The identification of constituents of a compound, solution, mixture, or the like. See qualitative analysis. b The determination of the quantity or proportion of such constituents. See quantitative analysis. c A statement of the results of an analysis. 6 Psychoanalysis. See synonyms under ABRIDGMENT. Compare SYNTHESIS. [< Med.L < Gk. analysis

< ana- throughout + lysis a loosing < lyein to loose]

an·a·lyst (an'ə·list) n. 1 One who analyzes or is skilled in analysis. 2 A psychoanalyst. ♦ Homophone: annalist.

an·a·lyt·ic (an'ə·lit'ik) adj. 1 Pertaining to, skilled in, or proceeding by analysis. 2 Resolving into constituent parts or first principles. 3 Ling. Describing a language, such as Modern English, that expresses grammatical relationships and the modification of word meanings by means of particles, auxiliaries, etc., rather than by inflection: opposed to synthetic or inflectional. Also **an'a·lyt'i·cal.** —**an'a·lyt'i·cal·ly** adv.

an·a·lyt·ics (an'ə·lit'iks) n. 1 The science or use of analysis. 2 The part of logic concerned with analysis.

an·a·lyze (an'ə·līz) v.t. ·lyzed, ·lyz·ing 1 To resolve into constituent parts or elements. 2 To make an analysis of, as a chemical compound or a mathematical problem. 3 Gram. To separate (a sentence) into its grammatical elements. 4 To examine minutely or critically, as a text. Also Brit. **an'a·lyse.** [< F analyser < analyse < Med. L analyses. See ANALYSIS.] —**an'a·lyz'a·ble** adj. —**an'a·ly·za'tion** n. —**an'a·lyz'er** n.

an·am·ne·sis (an'am·nē'sis) n. pl. ·ses (·sēz) 1 Psychol. A reproducing in memory; recollection. 2 The complete medical history of a patient as obtained from all available sources. [< Gk. anamnēsis < ana- back + mimnēskein call to mind]

an·am·nes·tic (an'am·nes'tik) adj. 1 Stimulating the faculty of memory. 2 Pertaining to anamnesis.

an·a·mor·phism (an'ə·môr'fiz·əm) n. 1 Distortion of shape. 2 Biol. Anamorphosis. [< ANA- up + Gk. morphē form]

an·a·nym (an'ə·nim) n. A pseudonym consisting of a name written backwards, as Niamert for Tremain. [< Gk. ana- back + onoma, onyma name]

an·a·pest (an'ə·pest) n. 1 In prosody, a metrical foot consisting of two short or unaccented syllables followed by one long or accented syllable. 2 A line of verse made up of or characterized by such feet. Also **an'a·paest.** [< L anapaestus < Gk. anapaistos < ana- back + paiein strike] —**an'a·pes'tic** or **·ti·cal, an'a·paes'tic** or **·ti·cal** adj.

an·a·phase (an'ə·fāz) n. Biol. The stage of mitosis or meiosis in which the corresponding parts of the divided chromosomes move to opposite poles of the spindle. **an'a·pha'sic** adj. [ANA- up + PHASE]

a·naph·o·ra (ə·naf'ə·rə) n. The rhetorical device of repeating a word or phrase in the beginning of several successive verses, clauses, or sentences. [< L < Gk. anaphora < ana- back + pherein carry]

an·aph·ro·dis·i·a (an·af'rə·diz'ē·ə) n. Absence or impairment of sexual desire. [< NL < AN-¹ without + Gk. aphrodisia sexual pleasure < Aphroditē, the goddess of love]

an·aph·ro·dis·i·ac (an·af'rə·diz'ē·ak) adj. Of, pertaining to, or tending to produce anaphrodisia. —n. An anaphordisiac agent or treatment.

an·a·phy·lax·is (an'ə·fə·lak'sis) n. Hypersensitivity to a foreign protein following injection of a small sensitizing dose. Also called allergy. [< NL < ANA- + (PRO)PHYLAXIS] —**an'a·phy·lac'tic** (-lak'tik) adj.

an·a·plas·tic (an'ə·plas'tik) adj. 1 Surg. Restoring lost or absent parts, as by transplanting tissue. 2 Biol. Of or pertaining to anaplasia.

an·a·plas·ty (an'ə·plas'tē) n. Plastic surgery. [< NL < Gk. anaplastos < ana- anew + plassein form]

an·ar·chic (an·är'kik) adj. 1 Pertaining to or like anarchy. 2 Advocating anarchy. 3 Inducing anarchy; lawless. Also **an·ar'chi·cal.** —**an·ar'chi·cal·ly** adv.

an·ar·chism (an'ər·kiz'əm) n. 1 The theory that all forms of government are incompatible with individual and social liberty and should be abolished. 2 The methods, especially terroristic ones, of anarchists. —**philosophic anarchism** The advocacy of voluntary cooperation and mutual aid as a substitute for the coercive power of the state.

an·ar·chist (an′ər·kist) *n.* **1** One who believes in and advocates anarchism. **2** One who encourages or furthers anarchy. Also **an·arch** (an′ärk). —**an′ar·chis′tic** *adj.*

an·ar·chy (an′ər·kē) *n.* **1** Absence of government. **2** Lawless confusion and political disorder. **3** General disorder. See synonyms under DISORDER, REVOLUTION. [< Gk. *anarchia* < *anarchos* without a leader < *an-* without + *archos* leader, chief]

an·ar·throus (an-är′thrəs) *adj.* **1** *Gram.* Used without the article: said of some Greek nouns in certain cases. **2** *Zool.* Lacking distinct joints. [< Gk. *anarthros* unjointed < *an-* without + *arthron* joint]

an·as·tig·mat·ic (an·as′tig·mat′ik) *adj. Optics* **1** Not astigmatic; specifically, corrected for astigmatism, as a lens. **2** Pertaining to a compound photographic lens, each element of which is adapted to correct the astigmatism of the other. [< AN-¹ + ASTIGMATIC]

a·nas·to·mose (ə-nas′tə-mōz) *v.* **·mosed, ·mos·ing** *v.t.* To create an anastomosis. —*v.i.* To be connected by one or more anastomoses.

a·nas·to·mo·sis (ə-nas′tə-mō′sis) *n. pl.* **·ses** (-sēz) A natural or artificial connection, interlacing, or union of parts or branches of a system of blood vessels, leaf veins, rivers, or the like. Also called *inosculation.* [< NL < Gk. *anastomōsis* opening < *ana-* again + *stoma* mouth] —**a·nas′to·mot′ic** (-mot′ik) *adj.*

a·nas·tro·phe (ə-nas′trə-fē) *n.* In rhetoric, the inversion of the natural or usual order of words, as "homeward directly he went." Also **a·nas′tro·phy.** [< Gk. *anastrophē* < *ana strephein* < *ana-* back + *strephein* turn]

a·nath·e·ma (ə-nath′ə-mə) *n. pl.* **·mas** or **·ma·ta** (-mətə) **1** A formal ecclesiastical ban or curse, excommunicating a person or damning something, as a book or heresy. **2** Any curse or imprecation. **3** A person or thing excommunicated or damned. **4** A person or thing greatly disliked or detested. See synonyms under IMPRECATION. [< L < Gk. *anathema* a thing devoted (to evil) < *anatithenai* dedicate < *ana-* up + *tithenai* set, place]

a·nath·e·ma·tize (ə-nath′ə-mə-tīz) *v.* **·tized, ·tiz·ing** *v.t.* To pronounce an anathema against. —*v.i.* To utter or express anathemas. —**a·nath′e·ma·ti·za′tion** *n.*

an·a·tom·i·cal (an′ə-tom′i·kəl) *adj.* **1** Pertaining to the structure of an organism. **2** Structural, especially as distinguished from functional. Also **an′a·tom′ic.** —**an′a·tom′i·cal·ly** *adv.*

a·nat·o·mist (ə-nat′ə-mist) *n.* One skilled in or a student of anatomy; a dissector.

a·nat·o·mize (ə-nat′ə-mīz) *v.t.* **·mized, ·miz·ing 1** To dissect an animal or plant for the purpose of investigating the structure, position, and interrelationships of its parts. **2** To examine critically or minutely; analyze. —**a·nat′o·mi·za′tion** *n.*

a·nat·o·my (ə-nat′ə-mē) *n. pl.* **·mies 1** The science of the structure of organisms, as of the human body, and of the interrelations of their parts. **2** The art or practice of dissection in order to investigate the structure, position, and interrelationship of organs. **3** A textbook or treatise dealing with the art or practice of dissection. **4** A skeleton. **5** An anatomical model, showing the structure, position, and interrelationship of organs. **6** Any kind of analysis or close examination. [< F *anatomie* < L *anatomia* < Gk. *anatomia,* earlier *anatomē* dissection < *anatemnein* cut up < *ana-* up + *temnein* cut]

-ance *suffix of nouns* Forming nouns of action, quality, state, or condition from adjectives in *-ant,* and also directly from verbs, as in abundance, resistance, forbearance. Compare -ANCY. [< F *-ance* < L *-antia, -entia,* a suffix used to form nouns from present participles; or directly from Latin]

♦ **-ance, -ence** The modern spelling of words in this group is unpredictable. The confusion arose originally in borrowings from Old French (*resistance, assistance*) where *-ance* had come to represent Latin *-entia,* as well as *-antia.* Since 1500,

however, some of these have been altered back to *-ence* on the Latin model, as in the case of *dependence,* earlier *dependance.* Later Latin borrowings in French and in English (through French or directly from Latin) discriminate between *-ance* and *-ence* according to the vowel of the Latin original.

an·ces·tor (an′ses·tər) *n.* **1** One from whom descent is derived; especially, such person further back in the line than a grandparent; forefather; progenitor; forebear. **2** *Law* One who precedes another in the line of legal inheritance, whether or not a direct progenitor: correlative of *heir.* **3** *Biol.* An actual or hypothetical organism from which subsequent types have developed; a prototype. [< OF *ancestre* < L *antecessor* < *antecedere* < *ante-* before + *cedere* go]

an·ces·tral (an·ses′trəl) *adj.* Of, pertaining to, or inherited from an ancestor. —**an·ces′tral·ly** *adv.*

an·ces·try (an′ses·trē) *n. pl.* **·tries 1** The line or body of ancestors; ancestors collectively. **2** Descent; ancestral lineage. **3** Noble or worthy lineage.

an·chor¹ (ang′kər) *n.* **1** A heavy implement, usually of iron or steel and having a long shank and two or more hooks or flukes that grip the sea bottom: used for holding fast a vessel by means of a connecting cable. **2** Any similar object used in such a manner for such a purpose. **3** Anything that makes stable or secure; anything depended on for support or security. **4** A military base from which an army operates. —**at anchor** Anchored, as a ship. —**to cast** (or **drop**) **anchor** To put down the anchor in order to hold fast a vessel. —**to ride at anchor** To be anchored, as a ship. —**to weigh anchor** To take up the anchor so as to sail away. —*v.t.* **1** To secure or make secure by an anchor. **2** To fix firmly. —*v.i.* **3** To come to anchor; lie at anchor, as a ship. **4** To become fixed; to hold oneself fast, as to a place. [OE *ancor* < L *ancora* < Gk. *ankyra*]

ANCHORS
1. Fluke 2. Mushroom
3. Grapnel
r. Ring *e.* Eye *h.* Hoops
st. Stock *sh.* Shank *b.* Bills
or pees *f.* Flukes or palms
a. Arms *c.* Crown

an·chor² (ang′kər) *n.* An anchorite.

an·chor·age (ang′kər·ij) *n.* **1** A place fit for or used for anchoring. **2** A coming to or lying at anchor. **3** That to which something is anchored; a means of support or security. **4** The fee charged for anchoring or the right to anchor, as in a harbor.

An·chor·age (ang′kər·ij) A southern Alaskan port, the largest city in Alaska.

an·cho·rite (ang′kə·rīt) *n.* **1** One who has withdrawn from the world; a religious recluse; hermit. Also **an′cho·ret** (-rit, -ret). [< L *anachoreta* < Gk. *anachōrētēs* < *anachōreein* retire, retreat < *ana-* back + *chōreein* withdraw] —**an′cho·rit′ic** (-rit′ik) *adj.*

an·chor·less (ang′kər·lis) *adj.* **1** Without an anchor. **2** Not settled or stable; drifting; insecure; without roots.

anchor man 1 An athlete, as in a relay race, who competes last for his team. **2** A television or radio broadcaster who coordinates the coverage of an event or program.

an·cho·vy (an′chō·vē, -chə·vē, an·chō′vē) *n. pl.* **·vies** Any of several very small, herring-like marine fishes (family Engraulidae) including some of commercial value as food or as a source of fishmeal. [< Sp., Pg. *anchova,* ? < Basque *anchua* < *antzua* dry]

an·chy·lose (ang′kə·lōs) *v.* **·losed, ·los·ing** To ankylose.

an·chy·lo·sis (ang′kə·lō′sis) *n.* Ankylosis.

an·cient¹ (ān′shənt) *adj.* **1** Existing or occurring in times long gone by, especially before the fall of the Roman Empire of the West, in 476: opposed to *modern: ancient* history, *ancient* authors. **2** Belonging to or having existed from a remote antiquity; of great age: *ancient* relics. **3** *Archaic* Venerable; sage. —*n.* **1** One who lived in ancient times. **2** An ancient or venerable per-

son. —**the ancients 1** The ancient Greeks, Romans, Hebrews, or other civilized nations of antiquity. **2** The ancient authors of Greece and Rome. [< OF *ancien,* ult. ·< L *ante* before] —**an′cient·ness** *n.*

Synonyms (adj.): aged, antiquated, antique, gray, hoary, immemorial, old, olden, time-honored, time-worn, venerable. *Ancient,* from the French, is the more stately; *old,* from the Anglo-Saxon, the more familiar word. *Venerable* expresses the involuntary reverence that we yield to the majestic and the long-enduring. See ANTIQUE, OLD. *Antonyms:* fresh, modern, new, novel, recent.

an·cient² (ān′shənt) *n.* An ensign, standard, or flag. **2** A flag standard-bearer. [Alter. of ENSIGN]

an·cient·ly (ān′shənt·lē) *adv.* In the distant past; of old.

an·cil·lar·y (an′sə·ler′ē) *adj.* **1** Subordinate. **2** Auxiliary; serving to help. [< L *ancillaris* < *ancilla* maid]

-ancy *suffix of nouns* A modern variant of -ANCE: *infancy, vacancy:* used to form new words expressing quality, state, or condition, or to refashion older nouns of quality in *-ance,* the latter being largely reserved for nouns of action: *constancy.* [< L *-antia*]

and (and, *unstressed* ənd, ən) *conj.* **1** Also; added to; as well as: a particle denoting addition, emphasis, or union, used as a connective between words, phrases, clauses, and sentences: shoes *and* ships *and* sealing wax; walking miles *and* miles; a horse both swift *and* strong. **2** As a result or consequence: Speak one word *and* you are a dead man! **3** To: in idiomatic use with *come, go, try,* etc.: Try *and* stop me; Come *and* see us; Go *and* find the answer. **4** *Archaic* Then: *And* she answered unto him. **5** *Obs.* If; in addition. See synonyms under BUT¹. [OE]

an·dan·te (an-dän′tē, än-dän′tä) *adj. & adv. Music* Moderately slowly; slower than allegretto but faster than larghetto. —*n. Music* in andante tempo. [< Ital., lit., walking]

an·dan·ti·no (an′dän·tē′nō, än′dän-) *adj. & adv. Music* Slightly quicker than andante: originally, slower than andante, but now generally meaning not so slow as andante. —*n. Music* in andantino tempo. [< Ital., dim. of *andante*]

An·de·an (an-dē′ən, an′dē·ən) *adj.* Of or pertaining to the Andes Mountains.

An·der·sen (an′dər·sən), **Hans Christian,** 1805–75, Danish writer of fairy tales.

An·des (an′dēz) A mountain range in western South America, extending over 4,000 miles from Venezuela southward to Tierra del Fuego; highest peak, Aconcagua, 22,835 feet. *Spanish* **Los An·des** (lōs än′dās).

and·i·ron (and′ī′ərn) *n.* One of two iron, steel, etc., supports for wood to be burned in an open fireplace. Also called *firedog.* [< OF *andier;* infl. by IRON]

and/or Either *and* or *or,* according to the meaning intended: Place bills *and/or* coins in this container: a business and legal usage.

An·dor·ra (an-dôr′ə, -dor′ə) A republic between France and Spain, subject to the joint suzerainty of the president of France and the Bishop of Urgel, Spain; 191 square miles; capital, Andorra la Vella.

andr- *combining form* Variant of ANDRO-.

andro- *combining form* **1** Human: *androcephalous.* **2** Male; masculine: *andromorphous.* **3** *Bot.* Stamen; anther: *androecium.* [< Gk. *anēr, andros* man]

an·dro·cen·trism (an′drə·sen′triz·əm) *n.* Preoccupation with men and the activities of men to the exclusion of women in human affairs. —**an·dro·cen·tric** (an′drə·sen′trik) *adj.*

an·dro·ceph·a·lous (an′drə·sef′ə·ləs) *adj.* Having a human head, especially when joined to the body of an animal, as the Egyptian sphinx. [< ANDRO- + Gk. *kephalē* head]

an·droc·ra·cy (an·drok′rə·sē) *n.* The rule of males; male supremacy. [< Greek *anēr, andros* man + *kratos* rule] —**an·dro·crat·ic** (an′drə·krat′ik) *adj.*

an·dro·gen (an′drə·jən) *n.* Any of various steroid hormones produced in the testes and the adrenal cortex which affect the development of masculine sexual characteristics.—**an·dro·gen·ic** (an′drə·jen′ik) *adj.*

an·drog·en·ize (an·droj′ə·nīz) *v.* **ized, ·iz·ing.** To effect the development of masculine characteristics in, as by treatment with androgens. — **an′dro·gen·i·za′tion** *n.*

an·drog·e·nous (an-droj′ə-nəs) *adj.* Pertaining to or characterized by the production of male offspring.

an·dro·gyne (an′drə-jin, -jīn) *n.* **1** A hermaphrodite. **2** *Bot.* An androgynous plant. [< MF < L *androgynus* < Gk. *androgynos* having the characteristics of both sexes < *anēr, andros* man + *gynē* woman]

an·drog·y·noid (an-droj′ə-noid) *adj.* Designating a male with hermaphroditic characteristics. [< ANDRO- + Gk. *gynē* woman]

an·drog·y·nous (an-droj′ə-nəs) *adj.* **1** Uniting the characteristics of both sexes; hermaphrodite. **2** *Bot.* Having the male and female flowers in the same cluster. **3** Undifferentiated as to sex, as in dress, bearing, etc.; unisex. Also **an·drog·y·nal** (an-droj′ə-nəl), **an·dro·gyn·ic** (an′drə-jin′ik).

an·drog·y·ny (an-droj′ə-nē) *n.* Hermaphroditism.

an·droid (an′droid) *adj.* Having a human shape. —*n.* An automaton made to simulate a human being; a humanoid robot. [< NL *androides* < Gk. *androeidēs* manlike]

an·drol·o·gy (an-drol′ə-jē) *n.* The study of the male reproductive system and the disorders peculiar to it. —**an·drol′o·gist** *n.*

an·dro·mor·phous (an′drə-môr′fəs) *adj.* Having masculine shape or appearance. [< ANDRO- + Gk. *morphē* form]

an·dro·sphinx (an′drə-sfingks′) *n.* A sphinx with a man's head and a lion's body. See SPHINX.

-androus *suffix* **1** *Bot.* Having a stamen or stamens: *monandrous, diandrous.* **2** Pertaining to men: *polyandrous.* [< Gk. *anēr, andros* man]

-ane[1] *suffix* Used primarily to differentiate words that have a corresponding form in -AN, as *human, humane.* [< L *-anus*]

-ane[2] *suffix Chem.* Denoting an open-chain saturated hydrocarbon compound of the methane series: *pentane.* [An arbitrary formation]

a·near (ə-nir′) *v., adv. & prep. Poetic* or *Archaic* Near.

an·ec·do·ta (an′ik-dō′tə) *n. pl.* Unpublished historical details.

an·ec·dot·age (an′ik-dō′tij) *n.* **1** Anecdotes collectively. **2** *Colloq.* Old age: humorously considered the age for anecdotes.

an·ec·do·tal (an′ik-dōt′l) *adj.* Pertaining to, characterized by, or consisting of anecdotes. — **an′ec·do′tal·ly** *adv.*

an·ec·dote (an′ik-dōt) *n.* A brief account of some incident; a short narrative of an interesting or entertaining nature. See synonyms under STORY. [< Med.L *anecdota* < Gk. *anekdota,* neut. pl. of *anekdotos* unpublished < *an-* not + *ekdotos* published < *ekdidonai* give out, publish < *ek-* out + *didonai* give]

an·ec·dot·ic (an′ik-dot′ik) *adj.* **1** Anecdotal. **2** Habitually telling or given to anecdotes. Also **an′ec·dot′i·cal.** —**an′ec·dot′i·cal·ly** *adv.*

an·ec·dot·ist (an′ik-dō′tist) *n.* One who collects, publishes, or is given to telling anecdotes.

an·e·cho·ic (an′e-kō′ik) *adj.* **1** Without echoes. **2** Completely devoid of sound-wave reverberations: applied especially to researches in the problems of sound and acoustics.

an·e·lec·tric (an′ə-lek′trik) *adj.* Non-electric. —*n. Obs.* A non-electric substance.

a·ne·mi·a (ə-nē′mē-ə) *n.* A general or local deficiency in the amount or quality of red blood corpuscles or of hemoglobin in the blood or of both. Also spelled **anaemia.** [< NL < Gk. *anaimia* < *an-* without + *haima* blood]

a·ne·mic (ə-nē′mik) *adj.* **1** Of, having, or characterized by anemia. **2** Pale; without strength or vigor. Also spelled **anaemic.**

anemo- *combining form* Wind: *anemometer.* [< Gk. *anemos*]

an·e·mo·met·ro·graph (an′ə-mō-met′rə-graf, -gräf) *n. Meteorol.* An anemograph, especially one that records both force and direction.

an·e·mom·e·try (an′ə-mom′ə-trē) *n. Meteorol.* The act or art of determining the velocity, force, and direction of the winds.

an·e·moph·i·ly (an′ə-mof′ə-lē) *n.* Pollination by the wind.

an·en·ce·phal·ic (an-en′sə-fal′ik) *adj.* Lacking a brain. —*n.* A fetus with a rudimentary brain or none. [< Gk. *an-* without + *enkephalos* brain]

a·nent (ə-nent′) *prep.* **1** *Archaic & Scot.* Concerning; in regard to. **2** *Obs.* On a line with. **3** *Obs.* Facing toward. [OE *onefen, onemn* near to + in-organic *-t*]

an·er·gy (an′ər-jē) *n.* **1** Lack of energy; inactivity. **2** Absent or reduced sensitivity to a specific allergen or antigen. [< NL *anergia* < Gk. *an-* without + *ergon* work] —**an·er·gic** (an-ûr′jik) *adj.*

an·es·the·sia (an′is-thē′zhə, -zhē-ə) *n.* **1** Partial or total loss of physical sensation, particularly of touch, due to disease or psychic disturbances. **2** Local or general insensibility to pain induced by the injection of an anesthetic drug, or the inhaling of an anesthetic gas. Also **an·es·the·sis** (an′is-thē′sis): also spelled *anaesthesia* [< NL < Gk. *anaisthēsia* insensibility < *an-* without + *aisthēsis* sensation]

an·es·the·si·ol·o·gy (an′is-thē′zē-ol′ə-jē) *n.* The branch of medicine that deals with the study and administration of anesthetics. Also spelled *anaesthesiology.* —**an′es·the′si·ol′o·gist** *n.*

an·es·thet·ic (an′is-thet′ik) *adj.* **1** Pertaining to or like anesthesia. **2** Producing anesthesia; making insensible to pain. —*n.* A drug or gas that causes unconsciousness or deadens sensation, as morphine, ether, chloroform, etc. Also spelled *anaesthetic.*

an·es·the·tist (ə-nes′thə-tist) *n.* A person trained to administer anesthetics: also spelled *anaesthetist.*

an·es·the·tize (ə-nes′thə-tīz) *v.t.* **·tized, ·tiz·ing** To induce anesthesia in; to render insensible, especially to pain: also spelled *anaesthetize.* — **an·es·the·ti·za·tion** (ə-nes′thə-tə-zā′shən, an′is-thet′ə-) *n.*

an·es·trus (an-es′trəs) *n.* The interval of sexual quiescence between successive periods of estrus. —**an·es·trous** *adj.*

an·eu·rysm (an′yə-riz′əm) *n.* A blood-filled, pulsating sac due to a localized abnormal dilatation of the wall of an artery. Also spelled **an′eu·rism.** [< Gk. *aneurysma* < *ana-* up + *eurys* wide] — **an·eu·rys·mal** (an′yə-riz′məl) or **·ris′mal** *adj.*

a·new (ə-nōō′, ə-nyōō′) *adv.* **1** As a new act; in a new way. **2** Again; over again in a different way.

an·frac·tu·os·i·ty (an-frak′chōō-os′ə-tē) *n. pl.* **·ties 1** The state or quality of being anfractuous. **2** A tortuous channel, depression, or process.

an·frac·tu·ous (an-frak′chōō-əs) *adj.* Tortuous; having many winding passages or grooves; sinuous. [< L *anfractuosus* < *anfractus* a winding < *an- (ambi-)* around + *frangere* break]

an·ga·ry (ang′gə-rē) *n.* In international law, the right of a warring nation, in case of need, to seize and use, or to destroy, neutral property, especially ships, the exercise of this right being subject to claim for compensation. Also **an·gar·i·a** (ang-gâr′ē-ə). [< F *angarie* < L *angaria* forced service to a lord < Gk. *angaros* courier]

an·gel (ān′jəl) *n.* **1** *Theol.* One of an order of spiritual beings endowed with immortality, attendant upon the Deity; a heavenly guardian, ministering spirit, or messenger. **2** A fallen spiritual being, also immortal. **3** In traditional and popular thought, the glorified spirit of a deceased person. **4** A pastor or bishop. *Rev.* ii 1. **5** A person of real or fancied angelic qualities. **6** In Christian Science, a message from Truth and Love; the inspiration of goodness, purity, and immortality, counteracting all evil, sensuality, and mortality. **7** A conventional representation of an angel, usually a youthful winged human figure in white robes with a halo. **8** A former English gold coin with the archangel Michael shown on it. **9** A guardian spirit or attendant. **10** *Colloq.* The financial backer of a play or of any enterprise. — *adj.* Angelic. [OE *engel* < L *angelus* < Gk. *angelos* messenger]

an·gel·ic (an-jel′ik) *adj.* **1** Pertaining to, of, or consisting of angels; celestial. **2** Like an angel; pure; beautiful; saintly. Also **an·gel′i·cal.** [< L *angelicus* < Gk. *angelikos* < *angelos* messenger] —**an·gel′i·cal·ly** *adv.*

an·gel·ol·o·gy (ān′jəl-ol′ə-jē) *n.* The doctrine concerning angels; the branch of theology that treats of angels. —**an·gel·o·log·ic** (ān′jəl-ə-loj′ik) or **·log′i·cal** *adj.*

an·ge·lus (an′jə-ləs) *n.* **1** In the Roman Catholic Church, a prayer said to commemorate the Annunciation: named from its first word. **2** A bell rung at morning, noon, and night as a call to recite this prayer: also called **angelus bell.** Also **An′ge·lus.** [< L]

an·ger (ang′gər) *n.* Violent vindictive passion; sudden and strong displeasure, as a result of injury, opposition, or mistreatment; wrath; ire. — *v.t.* **1** To make angry; enrage. **2** *Dial.* To inflame; make painful. See synonyms under INCENSE[1]. [< ON *angr* grief]

Synonyms (noun): animosity, choler, displeasure, exasperation, fury, hatred, impatience, indignation, ire, irritation, offense, passion, rage, resentment, temper, wrath. *Anger* is sharp, sudden, and, like all violent passions, necessarily brief. *Resentment* (a feeling back or feeling over again) is persistent brooding over injuries. *Rage* drives one beyond the bounds of prudence or discretion: *fury* is stronger yet, and sweeps one away into uncontrollable violence. *Anger* is personal and usually selfish. *Wrath* is deeper, more enduring than *anger,* and may be vengeful. *Indignation* is impersonal and unselfish *displeasure* at unworthy acts (L *indigna*), that is, at wrong as wrong. Pure *indignation* is not followed by regret, and is often a duty. See HATRED. *Antonyms:* forbearance, gentleness, long-suffering, patience, peace, peaceableness, peacefulness, self-control.

an·gi·na (an-jī′nə, an′jə-nə) *n.* **1** Any disease characterized by spasmodic suffocating pain, as quinsy, croup, etc. **2** Angina pectoris. [< L, quinsy < *angere* choke] —**an·gi′nal** *adj.* — **an·gi·nose** (an′jə-nōs) *adj.*

angina pec·to·ris (pek′tə-ris) Paroxysmal pain below the sternum and sometimes extending to the left shoulder and arm, due to inadequate blood and oxygen supplied to the heart. [< NL, angina of the chest]

angio- *combining form* **1** *Bot.* Seed vessel: *angiosperm.* **2** *Med.* Blood vessel; lymph vessel: *angiology.* Also, before vowels, **angi-.** [< Gk. *angeion* case, vessel, capsule]

an·gi·o·car·di·og·ra·phy (an′jē-ō-kär′dē-og′rə-fē) *n.* Radiography of the heart and connecting blood vessels of the chest following injection of a substance opaque to radiation. —**an′gi·o·car′di·o·graph′ic** *adj.*

an·gi·o·car·pous (an′jē-ə-kär′pəs) *adj. Bot.* **1** Having the fruit covered by a distinct envelope. **2** Having the fruit-bearing surface disposed inside the tissue of the sporocarp, as certain fungi, or lining the interior of cavities, as certain lichens. Also **an′gi·o·car′pic.** —**an·gi·o·car·py** (an′jē-ō-kär′pē) *n.*

an·gi·o·ma (an′jē-ō′mə) *n. pl.* **·mas** or **·ma·ta** (-mə-tə) A tumor consisting of blood vessels and/or lymph vessels. [< NL < ANGI(O)- + -OMA] —**an·gi·om·a·tous** (an′jē-om′ə-təs) *adj.*

an·gi·o·sperm (an′jē-ə-spûrm′) *n.* Any plant of a division (Magnoliophyta, formerly Angiospermae) of vascular seed plants in which the ovules are enclosed in an ovary. Also called *flowering plant.* **an′gi·o·sper′mous** *adj.*

an·gle[1] (ang′gəl) *v.i.* **an·gled, an·gling 1** To fish with a hook and line. **2** To try to get slyly or artfully: with *for.* [< *n.*] —*n. Obs.* A fish hook; fishing tackle. [OE *angel* fish hook]

an·gle[2] (ang′gəl) *n.* **1** *Geom.* **a** The figure formed by the meeting of two lines or of two or more surfaces; corner; point. **b** The figure,

PLANE ANGLES

concept, or relation of two straight lines (sides) emanating from one point (the vertex). **c** The figure formed by the intersection of two straight lines or of two or more planes. See list of geometric angles below. **2** A secluded place resembling a corner; nook. **3** The point of view or aspect from which any object, question, or situation may be regarded. **—critical angle 1** The least angle of incidence at which a ray is totally reflected. **2** *Aeron.* The angle of attack at which the airflow striking the under surface of an airplane changes abruptly, causing similar changes in lift and drag. **—gliding angle** *Aeron.* The angle the flight path of an airplane makes with the horizontal when flying in still air under the influence of gravity alone. **—v. an·gled, an·gling** *v.t.* **1** To move or turn at an angle or by angles: to *angle* a ball to avoid a hazard. **2** *Colloq.* To impart a particular bias or interpretation, as to a story or report. **—v.i. 3** To proceed or turn itself at an angle or by angles: The road *angled* up the hill. [< F < L *angulus* a corner, angle]

PRINCIPAL GEOMETRIC ANGLES
—acute angle An angle less than a right angle.
—adjacent angle An angle having a common side with another angle and the same vertex.
—alternate angle Either of two non-adjacent interior or exterior angles formed on opposite sides of a line which crosses two other lines.
—central angle An angle whose vertex is the center of a circle and whose sides are radii.
—complementary angle One of two angles whose sum is a right angle.
—conjugate angle Either of two angles whose sum is a perigon.
—dihedral angle The relation of two intersecting planes, as measured by the difference in direction of perpendiculars to them.
—exterior angle 1 Any of four angles formed on the outside of two straight lines cut by a third line. **2** The angle formed between any side of a polygon and the extension of an adjacent side.
—interior angle 1 One of the four angles formed between two straight lines cut by a third line. **2** The angle formed in the interior of a polygon by two adjacent sides.
—obtuse angle An angle greater than a right angle.
—plane angle An angle made by lines lying in one plane.
—reflex angle An angle greater than a straight angle.
—right angle An angle whose sides are perpendicular to each other; an angle of 90°.
—solid angle The angle formed at the vertex of a cone or subtended at the point of intersection of three or more planes; equal to 4π steradians.
—spherical angle The angle formed at the intersection of two great circles on a sphere: its value is a measure of the difference in direction of the arcs of the intersecting circles.
—straight angle An angle of 180°, generated by two straight lines extending in opposite directions from the vertex.
—supplementary angle One of two angles whose sum is a straight angle.
an·gled (ang'gəld) *adj.* **1** Having angles. **2** Set or placed at an angle.
an·gler (ang'glər) *n.* **1** One of a family (*Lophiidae*) of fishes having a wide, froglike mouth and antennalike filaments attached to the head with which it angles for its prey: also called *frogfish.* **2** One who fishes with rod, hook, and line.
an·gle·worm (ang'gəl·wûrm') *n.* An earthworm commonly used as bait in angling.
An·gli·a (ang'glē·ə) The Latin name for ENGLAND.
An·glic (ang'glik) *n.* A simplified form of English evolved for use as an auxiliary international language by R. E. Zachrisson, 1880–1937, Swedish linguist. **—adj.** Anglian.
An·gli·can (ang'glə·kən) *adj.* **1** Pertaining to the Church of England, the churches derived from it, or the High-Church party in any of these. **2** Pertaining to England or that which is English. **—n.** A member of the Church of England or of any church derived from it; also, a High-Churchman. [< Med.L

Anglicanus < *Anglicus* English < L *Angli* the Angles, the English]
An·gli·ce (ang'glə·sē) *adv.* In English; according to the usage of the English language: Napoli, *Anglice* Naples. [< Med.L]
An·gli·cism (ang'glə·siz'əm) *n.* **1** Any word, phrase, or idiom peculiarly English. **2** A word, phrase, or sense used in England, but not in accepted use in the United States; a Briticism. **3** Any trait or usage peculiarly English. **4** The state or quality of being English.
An·gli·cist (ang'glə·sist) *n.* An authority on or student of English language and literature.
An·gli·ci·za·tion (ang'glə·sə·zā'shən, -sī·zā'shən) *n.* **1** The act of making or becoming English in quality, character, or form. **2** The result or effect of Anglicizing.
An·gli·cize (ang'glə·sīz) *v.* **·cized, ·ciz·ing** *v.t.* To give an English form, style, or idiom to. **—v.i.** To acquire some English trait or peculiarity; become like the English. Also *Brit.* **An'gli·cise.**
An·gli·form (ang'glə·fôrm) *adj.* Having English form.
An·gli·fy (ang'glə·fī) *v.t. & v.i.* **·fied, ·fy·ing** To Anglicize.
an·gling (ang'gling) *n.* The act or art of fishing with a hook, line, and rod.
An·glist (ang'glist) *n.* An authority on England.
Anglo– *combining form* English; English and: used in various adjectives and nouns indicating relations of language, interests, etc., between the countries concerned or natives of them: *Anglo-Asiatic, Anglo-Irish.* [< L *Anglus* an Angle, an Englishman]
An·glo (ang'glō) *n. pl.* **·glos** *U.S.* An Anglo-American, especially as distinguished from a Mexican-American.
An·glo–A·mer·i·can (ang'glō·ə·mer'ə·kən) *adj.* **1** Of or pertaining to England and America or the relations of the peoples of the two countries: *Anglo–American* trade. **2** Of or pertaining to the English people who have settled in America. **—n.** A native of England or a descendant of a native of England who has settled in the United States or in America.
An·glo·ma·ni·a (ang'glō·mā'nē·ə) *n.* Overfondness for or imitation of English manners, speech, institutions, or customs. **—An'glo·ma'ni·ac** (-ak) *n.*
An·glo·phile (ang'glə·fīl, -fil) *n.* A lover of England or its people, customs, institutions, or manners. **—adj.** Of or like Anglophiles. Also **An'glo·phil** (-fil).
An·glo–Sax·on (ang'glō·sak'sən) *n.* **1** A member of one of the Germanic tribes (Angles, Saxons, and Jutes) that conquered Britain in the fifth and sixth centuries. **2** A member of the nation descended from these peoples which dominated England until the Norman Conquest. **3** Their West Germanic language; Old English. **4** Any one of English nationality or descent. **5** *Colloq.* Simple, pithy, unadorned English, free of scholarly borrowings or circumlocutions: the native element in the language being considered more forceful and direct. **6** *Colloq.* The short, vulgar words of the language, as used for their pungency. **7** Loosely, the modern English language. **—adj.** Of or pertaining to the Anglo-Saxons, their language, customs, or descendants. **—An'glo–Sax'on·ism** *n.*
An·go·la (ang·gō'lə) A Portuguese overseas province in western Africa; 481,351 square miles; capital, Loanda: also *Portuguese West Africa.*
An·go·ra (ang·gôr'ə, -gō'rə) *n.* **1** An Angora goat. **2** The long, silky hair of this goat: when manufactured, often called *mohair.* **3** An imitation of Angora cloth made of rabbit hair. **4** A shawl, cloth, etc., made of Angora material or its imitations. **5** An Angora cat.
an·gry (ang'grē) *adj.* **an·gri·er, an·gri·est 1** Feeling, showing, or excited by anger; indignant. **2** Showing signs of anger; appearing to threaten: *angry* skies. **3** Badly inflamed: an *angry* sore. **—an·gri·ly** (ang'grə·lē) *adv.* **—an·gri·ness** *n.*
angst (ängst) *n.* Anxiety; dread. [< G]
ang·strom (ang'strəm) *n.* A unit for the measurement of wavelength, equal to a hundred millionth of a centimeter, or 0.003937 millionths of an inch. Also **angstrom unit.** [after A. J. *Ångström*]

an·gui·form (ang'gwə·fôrm) *adj.* Shaped like a snake. [< L *anguis* snake + -FORM]
An·guil·la (ang·gwil'ə) See ST. CHRISTOPHER, NEVIS AND ANGUILLA.
an·guil·li·form (ang·gwil'ə·fôrm) *adj.* Having the form of an eel. [< L *anguilla* eel + -FORM]
an·guine (ang'gwin) *adj.* Of, pertaining to, or like a snake. [< L *anguinus* < *anguis* snake]
an·guish (ang'gwish) *n.* Excruciating mental or bodily pain; agony; torture. See synonyms under AGONY, ANXIETY. **—v.t. & v.i.** To affect or suffer with anguish, difficulty. [OF *anguisse* < L *angustia* tightness, difficulty < *angustus* narrow, tight]
an·gu·lar (ang'gyə·lər) *adj.* **1** Having, forming, or constituting an angle or angles; sharp-cornered; pointed. **2** Measured by an angle: *angular* motion. **3** Pertaining to angles. **4** Bony; gaunt and with little flesh, so as to be awkward or ungraceful. **5** Of a crabbed or unaccommodating disposition. [< L *angularis* < *angulus* corner, angle] **—an'gu·lar·ly** *adv.*
an·gu·lar·i·ty (ang'gyə·lar'ə·tē) *n. pl.* **·ties 1** The state or condition of being angular. **2** *pl.* Angular outlines or corners. Also **an'gu·lar·ness.**
an·gu·late (ang'gyə·lit, -lāt) *adj.* Having angles; angular: used chiefly in botany: *angulate* leaves. Also **an'gu·lat·ed.** **—v.t. & v.i. ·lat·ed, ·lat·ing** To make or become angular. [< L *angulatus*, pp. of *angulare* make angular < *angulus* corner, angle] **—an'gu·late·ly** *adv.*
an·gu·la·tion (ang'gyə·lā'shən) *n.* **1** The making of angles. **2** An angular formation or position.
an·gus·tate (ang·gus'tāt) *adj.* Compressed; narrowed. [< L *angustatus*, pp. of *angustare* narrow < *angustus* narrow]
an·he·la·tion (an'hi·lā'shən) *n. Pathol.* Shortness of breath; difficult respiration; dyspnoea. [< F *anhélation* < L *anhelatio, -onis* < *anhelare* pant]
an·he·lous (an·hē'ləs) *adj.* Short-breathed; panting.
an·hi·dro·sis (an'hi·drō'sis) *n. Pathol.* Partial or complete lack of perspiration. Also **an·i·dro·sis** (an'i·drō'sis). [< NL < Gk. *an-* without + *hidrōs* perspiration] **—an·hi·drot·ic** (an'hi·drot'ik) *adj.*
an·hy·drate (an·hī'drāt) *v.t.* **·drat·ed, ·drat·ing** To dehydrate.
an·hy·drous (an·hī'drəs) *adj. Chem.* Pertaining to or designating a compound which has no water in its composition, especially one having no water of crystallization. [< Gk. *anydros* waterless < *an-* without + *hydōr* water]
a·nigh (ə·nī') *adv. & prep.* Near; nigh; nigh to.
a·night (ə·nīt') *adv.* At night; nightly. Also **a·nights'.**
an·ile (an'īl, ā'nīl, an'il) *adj.* Like an old woman; weak or feeble-minded. [< L *anilis* < *anus* old woman] **—a·nil·i·ty** (ə·nil'ə·tē) *n.*
an·i·mad·ver·sion (an'ə·mad·vûr'zhən, -shən) *n.* Criticism or censure; a censorious comment or reflection: with *on* or *upon.* [< L *animadversio, -onis* < *animadvertere.* See ANIMADVERT.] **—an'i·mad·ver'sive** (-siv) *adj.* **—an'i·mad·ver'sive·ness** *n.*
Synonyms: aspersion, blame, censure, chiding, comment, criticism, disapproval, rebuke, reflection, reprehension, reproof. *Comment* and *criticism* may be favorable as well as censorious; they imply no superiority or authority on the part of him who utters them; nor do *reflection* and *reprehension*, which are simply turning the mind back upon what is disapproved. *Reprehension* is calm and just, and with good intent; it is therefore a serious matter, however mild, and is capable 'of great force, as expressed in the phrase severe *reprehension. Reflection* is often from mere ill feeling, and is likely to be more personal and less impartial than *reprehension;* we often speak of unkind or unjust *reflections. Rebuke,* literally a stopping of the mouth, is administered to a forward or hasty person; *reproof* is administered to one intentionally or deliberately wrong; both words imply authority in the reprover. *Antonyms:* approbation, approval, commendation, encomium, eulogy, panegyric, praise.
an·i·mad·vert (an'ə·mad·vûrt') *v.i.* **1** To comment critically, usually in an adverse sense: with *upon.* **2** *Obs.* To notice. [< L *animadvertere* take notice of < *animus* mind + *advertere* turn to. See ADVERT.]

an·i·mal (an′ə·məl) *n.* **1** A sentient living organism typically endowed with voluntary motion and sensation: distinguished from *plant.* **2** Any such creature as distinguished from man; a beast or brute. **3** A debased and bestial human being. **4** *pl.* Domestic quadrupeds. **5** Any creature but a bird, fish, or insect. —*adj.* **1** Of or pertaining to animals. **2** Bestial.

Synonyms (noun): beast, brute, fauna. An *animal* is a sentient being, distinct from inanimate matter and from vegetable life on the one side and from purely mental and spiritual existence on the other. Man is properly classified as an *animal,* but to call any individual man an *animal* is to imply that the animal nature has undue supremacy. The *brute* is the *animal* viewed as dull to all finer feeling; the *beast* is looked upon as a being of appetites. *Creature* is a word of wide signification, including inanimate objects, plants, animals, angels, or men as *divinely* created. The *animals* of a region are collectively called its *fauna.* Antonyms: angel, man, matter, mind, mineral, soul, spirit, vegetable.

an·i·mal·cu·la (an′ə·mal′kyə·lə) Plural of ANI-MALCULUM.

an·i·mal·cule (an′ə·mal′kyool) *n.* **1** A microscopic, usu. motile organism, as a paramecium, ameba, etc. **2** *Obs.* Any small animal, as a gnat. [< L *animalculum,* dim. of *animal* animal] **an′i·mal′cu·lar** (-kyə·lər) *adj.*

an·i·mal·cu·lism (an′ə·mal′kyə·liz′əm) *n.* An old biological theory that animalcules are the cause or source of vital phenomena and also of disease.

an·i·mal·cu·lum (an′ə·mal′kyə·ləm) *n.* *pl.* **·la** (-lə) An animalcule.

an·i·mal·ism (an′ə·məl·iz′əm) *n.* **1** The state or condition of mere animals; the state of being actuated by sensual appetites only. **2** The belief or doctrine that man is entirely animal, having no soul or spirit.

an·i·mal·ist (an′ə·məl·ist) *n.* **1** An adherent to the doctrine of animalism. **2** A painter or sculptor of animals. —**an′i·mal·is′tic** *adj.*

an·i·mal·i·ty (an′ə·mal′ə·tē) *n.* **1** The animal qualities. **2** Animal life; the animal kingdom. **3** The merely animal nature, as distinguished from the moral and spiritual.

an·i·mal·i·za·tion (an′ə·məl·ə·zā′shən, -ī·zā′-) *n.* **1** The act of animalizing, or the state of being animalized. **2** *Ecol.* The number and kinds of animals, as horses, cattle, etc., in a country or district.

an·i·mal·ize (an′ə·məl·īz′) *v.t.* **·ized, ·iz·ing 1** To render brutal; sensualize. **2** To change into animal matter, especially by digestive assimilation. **3** *Obs.* To give animal form to.

animal kingdom One of the three great divisions of nature, embracing all animal organisms: contrasted with the *mineral* and *vegetable kingdoms;* also, all animals, collectively.

an·i·mal·ly (an′ə·məl·ē) *adv.* **1** In an animal manner; with respect to the body; corporally, as distinguished from mentally. **2** With respect to the animal or animal spirits; physically, as distinguished from spiritually.

animal magnetism 1 Mesmerism. **2** Magnetic personal qualities. **3** Sensualism: usually with opprobrious implications.

an·i·mate (an′ə·māt) *v.t.* **·mat·ed, ·mat·ing 1** To impart life to; make alive. **2** To move to action; incite; inspire: What motives *animated* him? **3** To produce activity or energy in: The wind *animated* the flags. See synonyms under ENCOURAGE, STIMULATE, STIR[1]. —*adj.* (an′ə·mit) **1** Possessing animal life; living. **2** Vivacious; lively. Also **an′i·mat′ed.** See synonyms under AIRY, ALIVE, EAGER, SANGUINE, VIVID. [< L *animatus,* pp. of *animare* to fill with breath, make alive < *anima* breath, soul] —**an′i·mat′ed·ly** *adv.*

an·i·mat·ing (an′ə·māt′ing) *adj.* Imparting life or animation; inspiring. —**an′i·mat′ing·ly** *adv.*

an·i·ma·tion (an′ə·mā′shən) *n.* **1** The act of imparting or the state of possessing life. **2** The state of being animated; liveliness; vivacity. **3** The process and technique of preparing the set of drawings to be filmed and exhibited as an animated cartoon. See synonyms under WARMTH.

an·i·ma·tive (an′ə·mā′tiv) *adj.* Enlivening; inspiring.

an·i·ma·tor (an′ə·mā′tər) *n.* **1** One who or that which animates. **2** An artist who prepares a given set of drawings to be filmed as an animated cartoon.

an·i·mism (an′ə·miz′əm) *n.* **1** The doctrine that the phenomena of animal life are produced by a soul or spiritual force distinct from matter. **2** The belief in the existence of spirit or soul, as distinct from matter. **3** The doctrine that inanimate objects and natural phenomena possess a personal life or soul. [< L *anima* soul] —**an′i·mist** *n.* —**an′i·mis′tic** *adj.*

an·i·mos·i·ty (an′ə·mos′ə·tē) *n.* *pl.* **·ties** Active and vehement enmity; hatred; ill will. See synonyms under ANGER, ENMITY, FEUD[1], HATRED, HOSTILITY. [< L *animositas, -tatis* high spirit, boldness < *animus* soul, mind, spirit]

an·i·mus (an′ə·məs) *n.* **1** Hostile feeling or intent; animosity. **2** The animating thought or purpose; disposition; temper. **3** Purpose; intention. [< L]

an·ise (an′is) *n.* **1** A small South European and North African plant (*Pimpinella anisum*) that furnishes aniseed. **2** Aniseed. Compare DILL. [< OF *anis* < L *anisum* < Gk. *anison*]

an·i·seed (an′i·sēd′) *n.* The fragrant seed of the anise plant, used in cookery and medicine.

an·i·sette (an′ə·zet′, -set′) *n.* A cordial made from or flavored with aniseed. [< F]

aniso- *combining form* Unequal; dissimilar: *anisogamy.* See ISO-. [< Gk. *anisos* unequal]

an·i·sog·a·my (an′i·sog′ə·mē) *n.* *Biol.* A union of gametes similar in general type but unequal in size: opposed to *isogamy.* —**an′i·sog′a·mous** *adj.*

an·i·so·mer·ic (an·ī′sə·mer′ik) *adj.* *Chem.* Composed of the same elements but in different proportions: opposed to *isomeric.*

An·ka·ra (äng′kə·rə, ang′-) The capital of Turkey since 1923, located in central Anatolia: ancient *Ancyra:* formerly *Angora.*

An·ka·ra·tra Highlands (äng′kä·rä′trä) A mountainous region of central Madagascar; highest point, 8,552 feet.

an·ker (ang′kər) *n.* A liquid measure of about 10 gallons. [< Du.]

ankh (angk) *n.* In Egyptian art and mythology, a tau cross having a looped top: an emblem of generation; the ansate cross. For illustration see under CROSS. [< Egyptian *ānkh* life, soul]

an·kle (ang′kəl) *n.* *Anat.* **1** The joint connecting the foot and the leg. **2** The part of the leg between the foot and the calf near the ankle joint. [Prob. < ON, replacing OE *anclēow*]

an·kle·bone (ang′kəl·bōn′) *n.* *Anat.* The talus or astragalus. Also **ankle bone.**

an·klet (ang′klit) *n.* **1** An ornament or fetter for the ankle. **2** A short sock reaching just above the ankle.

an·kus (ang′kəs, -kəsh) *n.* An elephant goad consisting of a sharp spike and hook set on a short staff. Also **an·kush** (ang′kəsh). [< Hind.]

an·ky·lose (ang′kə·lōs) *v.t.* & *v.i.* **·losed, ·los·ing** To unite or join by ankylosis: also spelled *anchylose.*

an·ky·lo·sis (ang′kə·lō′sis) *n.* **1** *Anat.* The knitting together or consolidation of two bones or parts of bones. **2** *Pathol.* The abnormal adhesion of bones, especially those forming a joint; stiffening of a joint. Also spelled *anchylosis.* [< NL < Gk. *ankylōsis* < *ankylos* crooked] —**an′ky·lot′ic** (-lot′ik) *adj.*

an·lace (an′lis) *n.* A broad two-edged dagger or short sword. Also **an′las.** [< OF *alenas, alenaz* dagger < *alesne* awl < Gmc.]

an·nal (an′əl) *n.* The record of a single year; an item or entry in a book of annals.

an·nal·ist (an′əl·ist) *n.* A writer of annals; a historian. ◆Homophone: *analyst.* —**an′nal·is′tic** *adj.*

an·nals (an′əlz) *n.* *pl.* **1** A record of events in

their chronological order, year by year. **2** A narrative of events in which the order of time, rather than the causal relation, is followed or made prominent; chronicles. **3** A periodical publication of discoveries, transactions, etc. **4** History or records in general: the *annals* of crime. **5** In the Roman Catholic Church, masses said at stated intervals during the year. See synonyms under HISTORY. [< L *annales (libri)* yearly (record), chronicles < *annus* year]

An·nap·o·lis (ə·nap′ə·lis) The capital of Maryland; seat of the United States Naval Academy.

Anne (an, *Fr.* än) A feminine personal name. See ANN.
—**Anne,** 1665–1714, English queen; last of the Stuarts.
—**Anne of Austria,** 1601–66, consort of Louis XIII of France; regent 1643–61 for her son, Louis XIV.
—**Anne of Bohemia,** 1366–94, wife of Richard II of England.
—**Anne Boleyn** See BOLEYN.
—**Anne of Cleves** (klēvz), 1515–57, fourth wife of Henry VIII.
—**Anne of Denmark,** 1574–1619, wife of James I of England.

an·neal (ə·nēl′) *v.t.* **1** To render tough, as something formerly brittle, by heating and then slowly cooling. **2** To toughen; render enduring, as the will. **3** *Archaic* To fix in place by heating and then cooling, as colors or enamel. [OE *ancǣlan* burn]

an·nec·tent (ə·nek′tənt) *adj.* Connecting; joining on. [< L *annectens, -entis,* ppr. of *annectere.* See ANNEX.]

an·ne·lid (an′ə·lid) *n.* *Zool.* Any of a phylum (*Annelida*) of segmented invertebrates, including the earthworms, leeches, marine worms, etc. —*adj.* Of or pertaining to this phylum. [< NL < F *annélide < anneler* arrange in rings < OF *annel* a ring < L *annellus* for *anellus,* dim. of *anulus* a ring]

an·nex (ə·neks′) *v.t.* **1** To add or append, as an additional or minor part, to existing possessions; affix. **2** To attach, as an attribute, condition, or consequence: What punishment is *annexed* to vice? **3** *Archaic:* To join; unite. —*n.* (an′eks) **1** An addition to a building; also, a nearby building used in addition to the main building. **2** A supplementary service or department. **3** An addition to a document; addendum. **4** *Mil.* An appendix to a combat order specifying the details prescribed in a given field or subject: an artillery *annex.* [< F *annexer* < L *annexus,* pp. of *annectere* tie together < *ad-* to + *nectere* tie] —**an·nex′a·ble** *adj.* —**an·nex′ive** *adj.*

an·nex·a·tion (an′ek·sā′shən) *n.* **1** An annexing or being annexed. **2** That which is annexed. **3** The permanent incorporation of newly acquired territory with the national domain. Also **an·nex′ment.**

an·ni·hi·late (ə·nī′ə·lāt) *v.t.* **·lat·ed, ·lat·ing 1** To destroy absolutely. **2** To annul; abolish; make void. See synonyms under ABOLISH, EXTERMINATE. [< L *annihilatus,* pp. of *annihilare < ad- + nihil* nothing] —**an·ni·hi·la·ble** (ə·nī′ə·lə·bəl) *adj.* —**an·ni′hi·la′tor** *n.*

an·ni·hi·la·tion (ə·nī′ə·lā′shən) *n.* An annihilating or being annihilated; extinction.

an·ni·hi·la·tion·ism (ə·nī′ə·lā′shən·iz′əm) *n.* *Theol.* The doctrine that the finally impenitent will be totally annihilated after death.

an·ni·hi·la·tion·ist (ə·nī′ə·lā′shən·ist) *n.* A believer in annihilation or annihilationism.

an·ni·hi·la·tive (ə·nī′ə·lā′tiv) *adj.* Tending to annihilate. Also **an·ni·hi·la·to·ry** (ə·nī′ə·lə·tôr′ē, -tō′rē).

an·ni·ver·sa·ry (an′ə·vûr′sər·ē) *n.* *pl.* **·ries 1** A day separated by a year or by an exact number of years from some past event. **2** A commemorative observance or celebration on such occasion. Wedding anniversaries are popularly named from the character of the presents regarded as appropriate to their celebration: **paper anniversary** (1st), **wooden anniversary** (5th), **tin anniversary** (10th), **crystal anniversary** (15th), **china anniversary** (20th), **silver anniversary** (25th), **golden anniversary** (50th), **diamond anniversary** (60th and 75th). —*adj.* **1** Recurring annually or at the same date every year. **2** Pertaining to or occurring on an anniversary. [< L *anniversarius* < *annus* year + *versus*, pp. of *vertere* turn]

an·no Dom·i·ni (an'ō dom'ə·nī) *Latin* In the year of our Lord or of the Christian era: abbr. *A.D.*

an·no mun·di (an'ō mun'dī) *Latin* In the year of the world: used in chronology, with the suppositious date of creation at 4004 B.C.

an·no·tate (an'ō·tāt) *v.t.* **-tat·ed, -tat·ing** To make explanatory or critical notes on or upon; to provide a commentary for, as a text. [< L *annotatus*, pp. of *annotare* < *ad-* to + *notare* note, mark < *nota* a mark] —**an'no·ta·tor** *n.*

an·no·ta·tion (an'ō·tā'shən) *n.* **1** An annotating or being annotated. **2** A critical or explanatory note; a comment.

an·no·ta·tive (an'ō·tā'tiv) *adj.* Of or marked by annotations. Also **an·no·ta·to·ry** (ə·nō'tə·tôr'ē, -tō'rē).

an·nounce (ə·nouns') *v.t.* **an·nounced, an·nounc·ing 1** To make known publicly or officially; proclaim; publish. **2** To give notice of the approach or appearance of, as by a signal. **3** To make known to the senses: A roar *announced* the presence of the avalanche. **4** To serve as the announcer for, as a radio program. [< OF *anoncier* < L *annuntiare* < *ad-* to + *nuntiare* report < *nuntius* messenger]

Synonyms: advertise, communicate, declare, enunciate, herald, notify, proclaim, promulgate, propound, publish, report, reveal, speak. *Announce* is chiefly anticipatory; we *announce* a forthcoming book, a guest when he arrives. We *advertise* our business, *communicate* our intentions, *enunciate* our views; we *notify* an individual of a matter. We *propound* a question or an argument, *promulgate* the views of a sect or party. We *report* an interview, *reveal* a secret, *herald* the coming of some great event. *Declare* has often been an authoritative force; to *declare* war is to cause war to be. We *declare* war, *proclaim* peace. *Antonyms:* bury, conceal, hide, hush, secrete, suppress, withhold.

an·nounce·ment (ə·nouns'mənt) *n.* **1** An announcing or being announced. **2** That which is announced. **3** A printed declaration or publication.

an·nounc·er (ə·noun'sər) *n.* **1** One who announces. **2** A person who identifies the station from which a radio or television program is broadcast, introduces the performers and the program, etc.

an·noy (ə·noi') *v.t.* **1** To be troublesome to; bother; irritate. **2** To do harm to or injure continuously or by repeated acts: Guerrilla fire *annoyed* the regiment. See synonyms under AFFRONT, HARASS. —*n.* *Obs.* Annoyance. [< OF *anuier, anoier* < L *in odio* in hatred] —**an·noy'er** *n.*

an·noy·ance (ə·noi'əns) *n.* **1** An annoying or being annoyed. **2** One who or that which annoys. See synonyms under ABOMINATION.

an·noy·ing (ə·noi'ing) *adj.* Vexatious, troublesome. See synonyms under TROUBLESOME. —**an·noy'ing·ly** *adv.* —**an·noy'ing·ness** *n.*

an·nu·al (an'yōō·əl) *adj.* **1** Returning, performed, or occurring every year. **2** Pertaining to the year; reckoned by the year. **3** *Bot.* Lasting or living only one year. —*n.* **1** A book or pamphlet issued once a year. **2** *Bot.* A plant living for a single year or season. **3** In the Roman Catholic Church, a yearly mass for a deceased person; also, the offering made for it. **4** *Archaic* A yearly payment. [< OF *annuel* < L *annualis* yearly < *annus* year]

an·nu·al·ly (an'yōō·əl·ē) *adv.* Year by year; yearly.

an·nu·i·tant (ə·nōō'ə·tənt, ə·nyōō'-) *n.* One receiving, or entitled to receive, an annuity.

an·nu·it coep·tis (an'yōō·it sep'tis) *Latin* He (God) has favored our undertakings: motto on the reverse of the great seal of the United States.

an·nu·i·ty (ə·nōō'ə·tē, ə·nyōō'-) *n.* *pl.* **·ties 1** An annual allowance or income; also, the right to receive such an allowance or the duty of paying it. **2** The return from an investment of capital, with interest, in a series of yearly payments; especially, an agreed amount paid by an insurance company at stated intervals, usually monthly, in consideration of either a single premium or premiums paid over a period of years. [< F *annuité* < Med.L *annuitas, -tatis* < L *annus* year]

an·nul (ə·nul') *v.t.* **an·nulled, an·nul·ling 1** To destroy the force of; declare void or invalid, as a law. **2** To reduce to nothing; extinguish: One loyalty may *annul* another in the mind. **3** To put an end or stop to, as a practice. [< OF *anuller* < LL *annullare* < L *ad-* to + *nullus* none] —**an·nul'la·ble** *adj.*

Synonyms: abolish, abrogate, cancel, destroy, extinguish, nullify, obliterate, quash, repeal, rescind, revoke. See ABOLISH, CANCEL. *Antonyms:* confirm, enact, establish, institute, maintain, preserve, sustain, uphold.

an·nu·lar (an'yə·lər) *adj.* **1** Pertaining to or formed like a ring; ring-shaped. **2** Marked with rings. [< L *annularis* < *annulus, anulus* ring] —**an'nu·lar·ly** *adv.*

annular eclipse *Astron.* A solar eclipse in which a narrow circular strip of the sun is visible beyond the dark mass of the moon.

an·nu·late (an'yə·lit, -lāt) *adj.* Furnished with rings; ringed. Also **an'nu·lat·ed.**

an·nu·la·tion (an'yə·lā'shən) *n.* **1** The act of forming rings. **2** A ringlike formation or segment, as in an annelid.

an·nu·let (an'yə·lit) *n.* **1** A small ring. **2** *Archit.* A small projecting circular molding, specifically, around the capital of a pillar. [< L *annulus* a ring + -ET]

an·nul·ment (ə·nul'mənt) *n.* **1** An annulling or being annulled. **2** An invalidation, as of a marriage.

an·nu·lus (an'yə·ləs) *n.* *pl.* **·li** (-lī) or **·lus·es 1** A ringlike body or figure. **2** *Geom.* The area between the circumferences of two concentric circles. **3** *Astron.* The thin, visible edge of the sun's disk as it appears around the body of the moon in an annular eclipse. [< L, a ring]

an·nun·ci·ate (ə·nun'shē·āt, -sē-) *v.t.* **·at·ed, ·at·ing** To announce. [< L *annuntiatus*, pp. of *annuntiare*. See ANNOUNCE.]

an·nun·ci·a·tion (ə·nun'sē·ā'shən, -shē-) *n.* **1** The act of announcing, or that which is announced; a proclamation.

An·nun·ci·a·tion (ə·nun'sē·ā'shən, -shē-) *n.* **1** The announcement of the Incarnation to the Virgin by an angel. *Luke* i 28–38. **2** The festival (March 25) commemorating this event.

an·nun·ci·a·tor (ə·nun'shē·ā'tər, -sē-) *n.* **1** A person or thing that announces. **2** An electrical indicator that shows a number or name when a bell is rung.

an·o·dal (an·ō'dəl) *adj.* Pertaining to an anode.

an·ode (an'ōd) *n.* *Electr.* The electrode through which current enters a non-metallic conductor and toward which electrons or anions flow from the cathode. It is positive for an electrolytic bath or vacuum tube, negative for a voltaic cell. [< Gk. *anodos* a way up < *ana-* up + *hodos* road, way]

an·od·ic (an·od'ik) *adj.* **1** Pertaining to an anode. **2** Proceeding upward.

an·o·dize (an'ə·dīz) *v.t.* **·dized, ·diz·ing** To oxidize or coat the surface of (a metal) by making it the anode of an electrolytic bath containing sodium phosphate or other suitable electrolyte.

an·o·dyne (an'ə·din) *adj.* Having power to allay pain; soothing. —*n.* Any drug that relieves pain or soothes. [< L *anodynus* < Gk. *anōdynos* < *an-* without + *odynē* pain]

a·noint (ə·noint') *v.t.* **1** To smear with oil or any soft substance; pour or rub oil upon; apply ointment to. **2** To put oil on as a sign of consecration, as in a religious ceremony. [< OF *enoint*, pp. of *enoindre* < L *inungere* < *in-* on + *ungere* smear] —**a·noint'er** *n.* —**a·noint'ment** *n.*

a·nom·a·lism (ə·nom'ə·liz'əm) *n.* **1** That which is anomalous; an anomaly. **2** *Rare* The state or fact of being anomalous.

a·nom·a·lous (ə·nom'ə·ləs) *adj.* Deviating from the common rule; irregular; exceptional; abnormal. See synonyms under ABSURD, IRREGULAR, ODD. [< L *anomalus* < Gk. *anōmalos* < *an-* not + *homalos* even < *homos* same]—**a·nom'a·lous·ly** *adv.* —**a·nom'a·lous·ness** *n.*

a·nom·a·ly (ə·nom'ə·lē) *n.* *pl.* **·lies 1** Deviation from rule, type, or form; irregularity; anything abnormal. **2** *Astron.* **a** The angular distance of a planet from its perihelion, as seen from the sun. **b** The angle which measures apparent irregularities in the movement of a planet. [< L *anomalia* < Gk. *anōmalia* < *anōmalos*. See ANOMALOUS.]

a·nom·a·lis·tic (ə·nom'ə·lis'tik) or **·ti·cal** *adj.*

an·o·mie (an'ə·mē) *n.* An anxious awareness that

the prevailing values of society have little or no personal relevance to one's condition; also, a condition of society characterized by the relative absence of norms or moral standards. [< F < Gk. *anomia* lawlessness < *a-* without (See A.⁴) + *nomos* law] —**a·nom·ic** (ə·nom'ik) *adj.*

a·non (ə·non') *Archaic adv.* **1** In a little while; soon; presently. **2** Immediately. **3** At another time; again. —**ever and anon** Now and again. —*interj.* At once! [OE *on an* in one]

Anon. Abbreviation for ANONYMOUS.

an·o·nym (an'ə·nim) *n.* **1** An anonymous person or writer. **2** A pseudonym.

a·non·y·mous (ə·non'ə·məs) *adj.* Having no acknowledged name; bearing no name; of unknown authorship or agency. [< Gk. *anōnymos* < *an-* without + *onoma, onyma* name] —**a·no·nym·i·ty** (an'ə·nim'ə·tē), **a·non'y·mous·ness** *n.* —**a·non'y·mous·ly** *adv.*

a·no·rak (ä'nə·räk) *n.* A warm, hooded jacket, worn in arctic climates. [< Eskimo *anoraq*]

an·o·rec·tic (an'ə·rek'tik) *n.* A person having anorexia. —*adj.* of or pertaining to anorexia.

an·o·rex·i·a (an'ə·rek'sē·ə) *n.* Absence of appetite, especially when accompanied by emotional stress and resulting in malnutrition and emaciation. Also **anorexia nervosa.** [< NL < Gk. *anorexia* < *an-* without + *orexis* appetite]

an·o·rex·ic (an'ə·rek'sik) *adj.* Avoiding food; suffering from anorexia. —*n.* An anorexic person.

an·or·tho·scope (an·ôr'thə·skōp) *n.* An instrument by which distorted figures drawn on one of two revolving disks can be seen as normal images through slits in the other. [< AN-¹ + ORTHO- + -SCOPE]

an·os·mi·a (an·oz'mē·ə, -os'-) *n.* *Pathol.* Loss of the sense of smell. [< NL < Gk. *an-* without + *osmē* smell] —**an·os'mic** *adj.*

an·oth·er (ə·nuth'ər) *adj. & pron.* **1** Not the same; distinct; different: often used as the correlative of *one*: One man's meat is *another* man's poison. **2** Different in character while of the same or similar substance: From that time I became *another* man. **3** Different in substance while of the same or similar character. **4** A further; an additional; one more. ◆ *Another* was originally written as two words, *an other.* As a pronoun its plural is *others.*

an·ox·e·mi·a (an'ok·sē'mē·ə) *n.* *Pathol.* Lack of oxygen in the blood. [< NL < AN-¹ + OX(YGEN) + -EMIA] —**an'ox·e'mic** *adj.*

an·ox·i·a (an·ok'sē·ə) *n.* *Pathol.* Oxygen deficiency; any condition characterized by defective or insufficient oxidation of the body tissues. [< AN-¹ + OX(YGEN) + -IA] —**an·ox'ic** *adj.*

an·sa (an'sə) *n.* *pl.* **·sae** (-sē) **1** *pl. Astron.* The apparent ends of Saturn's rings, which, seen obliquely, seem to project from the sides of the planet like handles. **2** A handle, as of a pitcher. [< L, a handle]

an·sate (an'sāt) *adj.* Having a handle. Also **an'sat·ed.** [< L *ansatus* < *ansa* handle]

An·ser (an'sər) *n.* **1** *Ornithol.* A genus of birds typical of *Anserinae*, a subfamily including the geese. **2** *Astron.* A small star in the constellation of the Fox and Goose (Vulpecula cum Ansere). See CONSTELLATION. [< L, goose]

an·ser·ine (an'sə·rin, -sər·in) *adj.* **1** Pertaining to a goose; gooselike, as the human skin when chilled. **2** Silly; stupid. **3** Pertaining or belonging to the subfamily *Anserinae* of birds; the geese. Also **an'ser·ous.** —*n.* An organic substance, $C_{10}H_{16}O_3N_4$, obtained from the muscles of birds, fishes, and reptiles. [< L *anserinus* < *anser* a goose]

an·swer (an'sər, än'-) *v.i.* **1** To reply or respond, as by words or actions. **2** To serve the purpose; prove successful: This solution *answers* best. **3** To be responsible or accountable: with *for*. I will *answer* for his honesty. **4** To correspond or match, as in appearance: with *to*: This man *answers* to your description. —*v.t.* **5** To speak, write, or act in response or reply to: to *answer* a letter. **6** To be sufficient for; satisfy: This rod *answers* the purpose. **7** To pay for; discharge, as a debt or liability: to *answer* damages. **8** To conform or correspond to; match: to *answer* a description. **9** *Law* To reply favorably to, as a petition or petitioner. —**to answer back** To reply emphatically or rudely; talk back, as in contradiction. —*n.* **1** A reply, especially one that is definite and final. **2** Any action in return or in kind; retaliation. **3** The result of a calculation or solution of a problem in mathematics. **4** *Law* The written defense of a defendant in an action to charges filed against him by the plaintiff in which he sets up matters of *fact* as defense in contradistinction to a *demurrer*. **5** *Music* The restatement of a musical theme or phrase by a different voice or instrument. [OE *andswerian*] —**an'swer·er** *n.*

Synonyms (noun): rejoinder, repartee, reply, response, retort. Anything said or done in return for some word, action, or suggestion of another may be called an *answer*, as the blow of an angry man, the movement of a bolt in a lock, an echo, etc. A *reply* is an unfolding, and ordinarily implies thought and intelligence. An *answer* to a charge or an argument effectually meets or disposes of it, as a *reply* may not do. See RESPONSE.

an·swer·a·ble (an'sər-ə-bəl, än'-) *adj.* **1** Liable to be called to account (*for* anything or *to* someone); responsible. **2** Requiring or admitting of answer; also, obligated to answer. **3** Corresponding; adequate; suitable. —**an'swer·a·ble·ness** *n.* —**an'swer·a·bly** *adv.*

ant (ant) *n.* A small social hymenopterous insect (family *Formicidae*); an emmet. The communities of ants are made up of winged males, females winged till after pairing, and wingless neuters or workers. For illustration see under INSECT (injurious). [OE *ǣmete*]

an't (ant, änt, änt) **1** Are not. **2** *Brit.* Am not. **3** *Illit. & Dial.* Is not; has not; have not.

ant- Var. of ANTI-.

-ant *suffix* **1** In the act or process of doing (what is denoted by the stem): used to form adjectives with nearly the meaning of the present participle: *militant, litigant,* etc. **2** One who or that which does (what is indicated by the stem): forming nouns of participial origin: *servant* one who serves. [< F *-ant* < L *-ans (-antis), -ens(-entis),* present participial suffixes]

an·ta (an'tə) *n. pl.* **·tae** (-tē) *Archit.* A pilaster, especially when forming the termination of a side wall continued beyond a transverse wall, or when placed on a wall to form a range of columns. [< L]

ant·ac·id (ant·as'id) *n. Med.* An alkaline remedy for stomach acidity. —*adj.* Correcting acidity. Also **an'ti·ac'id.**

an·tag·o·nism (an-tag'ə-niz'əm) *n.* Mutual resistance; opposition; hostility. See synonyms under ANTIPATHY, ENMITY. [< Gk. *antagōnisma < antagōnizesthai.* See ANTAGONIZE.]

an·tag·o·nist (an-tag'ə-nist) *n.* **1** An adversary; opponent. See synonyms under ENEMY. **2** Any agent having an effect contrary to that of a similar agent, as a drug, muscle, hormone, etc.

an·tag·o·nis·tic (an-tag'ə-nis'tik) *adj.* Opposed; hostile. Also **an·tag·o·nis'ti·cal.** See synonyms under CONTRARY, INIMICAL. —**an·tag·o·nis'ti·cal·ly** *adv.*

an·tag·o·nize (an-tag'ə-nīz) *v.* **·nized, ·niz·ing** *v.t.* **1** To oppose, contend with, or struggle against. **2** To make unfriendly; to make an antagonist of. **3** To counteract; neutralize, as a force or action. —*v.i.* **4** To act antagonistically. See synonyms under CONTEND. [< Gk. *antagōnizesthai* struggle against < *anti-* against + *agōnizesthai* struggle, strive]

ant·al·gic (ant·al'jik) *adj.* Tending to alleviate pain. —*n.* An anodyne. [< ANT- + Gk. *algos* pain]

ant·al·ka·li (ant·al'kə-lī) *n. pl.* **·lis** or **·lies** Any substance able to neutralize alkalis, or counteract an alkaline tendency in the system. [< ANT- + ALKALI] —**ant·al'ka·line** (-līn, -lin) *adj. & n.*

ant·arc·tic (ant·ärk'tik, -är'tik) *adj.* Pertaining to or designating the South Pole or the regions near it. [< L *antarcticus* < Gk. *antarktikos* southern < *anti-* opposite + *arktos* the Bear (a northern constellation), the north]

Ant·arc·ti·ca (ant·ärk'tə-kə, -är'-) A continent surrounding the South Pole of the earth, extending at certain points north of the antarctic circle and almost entirely covered by a vast ice sheet; over 5,000,000 square miles. Also **Antarc·tic Continent.**

Antarctic Circle The boundary of the South Frigid Zone, 23°30' from the South Pole, including most of Antarctica.

Antarctic Ocean The ocean within the Antarctic Circle and bordering Antarctica.

Antarctic Zone The region, including most of Antarctica, enclosed by the Antarctic Circle.

An·tar·es (an-târ'ēz) A giant red star, Alpha in the constellation Scorpio; one of the 20 brightest stars, 1.22 magnitude. [< Gk. *Antarēs < anti-* similar to + *Arēs* Mars; with ref. to its color]

ant bear **1** The giant ant-eater (*Myrmecophaga jubata*), a large edentate mammal of tropical America that feeds wholly or chiefly on ants; it has a long snout, protrusible tongue, powerful digging claws, and a shaggy, black-banded coat. **2** The aardvark.

ant bird Any of numerous small birds of the family *Formicariidae*, of South America, which feed upon ants. Also called **ant'-catch'er.**

ant cow An aphid insect kept by ants as a source of food. The aphids yield a honeylike fluid on being stroked on the abdomen by the antennae of the ants.

an·te (an'tē) *v.t.* & *v.i.* **an·teed** or **an·ted, an·te·ing** **1** In poker, to put up, as a stake, before the cards are dealt. **2** *Slang* To pay (one's share). —**to ante up** *Slang* To ante. —*n.* **1** The stake put up in a game of poker. **2** A stake put up after the cards are dealt, but before drawing new ones. [< L, before]

ante- *prefix* **1** Before in time or order: *antenatal.* **2** Before in position; in front of: *antechamber.* [< L *ante* before]

an·te·a (an'tē-ə) *adv. Law Latin* Formerly; heretofore.

ant·eat·er *n.* **1** The ant bear. **2** One of several other mammals that feed partly on ants, as the tamandua, echidna, or aardvark. **3** An ant bird.

THE GIANT ANT-EATER
(8 feet long over-all;
2 feet tall)

an·te·bel·lum (an'tē-bel'əm) *adj.* Of the time before the war, especially, before the Civil War in the United States. [< L *ante bellum* before the war]

an·te·bra·chi·um (an'tē-brā'kē-əm) *n. pl.* **·chi·a** (-kē-ə) *Anat.* The forearm. [< NL < ANTE- + L *brachium* arm]

an·te·cede (an'tə-sēd') *v.t.* & *v.i.* **·ced·ed, ·ced·ing** To go or come before, as in rank, place, or time; precede. [< L *antecedere < ante* before + *cedere* go]

an·te·ce·dence (an'tə-sēd'ns) *n.* **1** Precedence; going before; priority. **2** *Astron.* The apparent retrograde motion of a planet. Also **an'te·ce'den·cy.**

an·te·ce·dent (an'tə-sēd'nt) *adj.* **1** Going before; prior in time, place, or order; preceding; anterior: often with *to.* **2** *Geol.* Having a course across a fold or fault of the earth's surface: contrasted with *consequent.* —*n.* **1** One who or that which precedes or goes before. **2** *Gram.* The word, phrase, or clause to which a pronoun, especially a relative pronoun, refers. **3** *pl.* The facts, collectively, that have gone before in the history of a person or thing; also, ancestry. **4** *Math.* The first term of a ratio; in a proportion, the first and third terms. **5** *Logic* That upon which something else is based. See synonyms under CAUSE, PRECEDENT. [< L *antecedens, -entis,* ppr. of *antecedere.* See ANTECEDE.]—**an'te·ce'dent·ly** *adv.*

Synonyms (adj.): anterior, earlier, foregoing, former, introductory, precedent, preceding, preliminary, previous, prior. When used simply of time, *antecedent* and *previous* refer to that which happens at any prior time; *preceding* to that which is immediately or next before. See PREVIOUS. *Antonyms:* consequent, following, later, posterior, subsequent, succeeding.

an·te·ces·sor (an'tə-ses'ər) *n.* One who precedes or goes before; a leader; pioneer. [< L *antecedere.* See ANTECEDE.]

an·te·cham·ber (an'ti-chām'bər) *n.* A room serving as an entranceway to another apartment.

an·te·chap·el (an'tē-chap'əl) *n.* The portion of a chapel outside of the rood screen; a vestibule or narthex.

an·te·choir (an'ti-kwīr') *n.* A portion of a chapel set apart just in front of the choir, enclosed, or partially enclosed, by a screen.

an·te·date (an'ti·dāt' *v.t.* **·dat·ed, ·dat·ing 1** To assign to a date earlier than the actual one, as a document; date back. **2** To be or occur earlier than; precede. **3** To cause to happen at or return to an earlier date; accelerate.

an·te·di·lu·vi·an (an'ti·di·lōō've·ən) *adj.* **1** Pertaining to the times, events, etc., before the Flood. **2** Antiquated; primitive. —*n.* **1** A person, animal, or plant that lived before the Flood. **2** An old or old-fashioned person. [< ANTE- + L *diluvium* deluge]

an·te·fix (an'ti·fiks) *n. pl.* **·fix·es** or **·fix·a** (-fik'sə) *Archit.* An upright ornament at the eaves of a tiled roof, to hide the joints between two adjacent rows of tiles, or at the edge of a frieze; sometimes also at the ridge, forming part of a cresting. [< L *antefixus.* See ANTE- and FIX.] —**an'te·fix'al** *adj.*

ANTEFIX

an·te·lope (an'tə·lōp) *n. pl.* **·lope** or **·lopes 1** Any one of various Old World hollow-horned ruminants of the family *Bovidae*, including the gazelle, chamois, gnu, etc. **2** The hide of such an animal. **3** *U.S.* The pronghorn. [< OF *antelop* < Med.L *antalopus* < LGk. *antholops*]

an·te·me·rid·i·an (an'ti·mə·rid'ē·ən) *adj.* Before noon; between midnight and the next noon.

an·te me·rid·i·em (an'tē mə·rid'ē·em) *Latin* Before the sun reaches the meridian, counted from the preceding midnight; before noon. Abbr. *a.m.* or *A.M.*

an·te·mun·dane (an'ti·mun'dān) *adj.* Pertaining to, existing, or occurring before the world's creation. [< ANTE- + L *mundus* world]

an·te·na·tal (an'ti·nāt'l) *adj.* Occurring or existing before birth; pertaining to conditions before birth.

an·ten·na (an·ten'ə) *n. pl.* **an·ten·nae** (an·ten'ē) for def. **1**, **an·ten·nas** for def. **2**. **1** *Entomol.* One of the paired, lateral, movable, jointed appendages on the head of an insect or other arthropod. **2** *Telecom.* A system of wires upheld in a vertical or horizontal position by a mast or tower, for transmitting or receiving electromagnetic waves in wireless telegraphy, telephony, and radio. —**cage antenna** A radio antenna consisting of several wires arranged in parallel around a series of loops between two uprights and converging at each end. [< NL < L, a yard on which a sail is spread]

an·te·nup·tial (an'ti·nup'shəl, -chəl) *adj.* Previous to marriage; occurring or being before marriage.

an·te·pas·chal (an'ti·pas'kəl) *adj.* Occurring before the Passover or Easter.

an·te·past (an'ti·past, -päst) *n.* **1** Foretaste. **2** *Obs.* An appetizer. See synonyms under ANTICIPATION. [< ANTE- + L *pastus* food]

an·te·pen·di·um (an'ti·pen'dē·əm) *n. pl.* **·di·a** (-dē-ə) A covering, usually embroidered, for the front of the altar. [< Med.L < L *ante* before + *pendere* hang]

an·te·pe·nult (an'ti·pē'nult, -pi·nult') *n.* The last syllable but two of a word. Also **an·te·pe·nul·ti·ma** (an'ti·pi·nul'tə·mə).

an·te·pe·nul·ti·mate (an'ti·pi·nul'tə·mit) *adj.* Pertaining to the last but two of any series. —*n.* The antepenult.

an·te·pran·di·al (an'ti·pran'dē·əl) *adj.* Occurring or being before dinner.

an·te·ri·or (an·tir'ē·ər) *adj.* **1** Antecedent in time; prior; earlier: ages *anterior* to the Flood. **2** Farther front or forward, in space: an *anterior* cavity. **3** *Biol.* Situated in front: opposed to *posterior,* in the lower animals, relatively near the head; in man, toward the ventral side of the body. **4** *Bot.* Turned away from the main axis or stem, as the side of a leaf or flower; lower. [< L, compar. of *ante* before] —**an·te'ri·or·ly** *adv.*

Synonyms: former, forward, front, prior. *Anterior* is employed chiefly with reference to place.

Prior bears exclusive reference to time. *Former* is used of time, or of position in written or printed matter, not of space in general. Compare ANTE- CEDENT, PREVIOUS. *Antonyms:* after, hind, hinder, hindmost, later, latter, posterior, subsequent, succeeding.

antero- *combining form* Anterior; placed in front. [< L *anterus* (assumed form)]

an·ter·o·in·fe·ri·or (an'tər-ō-in-fir'ē-ər) *adj.* Situated in front and below.

an·te·room (an'ti-rōōm', -rŏŏm') *n.* A waiting-room; antechamber.

an·ter·o·pos·te·ri·or (an'tər-ō-pos-tir'ē-ər) *adj.* **1** Of or pertaining to the front and rear; extending from front to rear. **2** Median.

an·te·type (an'ti-tīp') *n.* A preceding type; prototype.

an·te·ver·sion (an'ti-vûr'zhən, -shən) *n.* *Pathol.* A turning or tipping forward, as of the uterus.

an·te·vert (an'ti-vûrt') *v.t. Pathol.* To displace by turning or tipping forward, as an internal organ. [< L *antevertere* < *ante* before + *vertere* turn]

anth- Var. of ANTI-.

ant·he·li·on (ant-hē'lē-ən, an-thē'-) *n. pl.* **·li·a** (-lē-ə) *Astron.* A faint glory or series of diffraction rings about the shadow of an object cast by a low sun upon a cloud or fog bank; a mock sun. [< NL < Gk. *anthēlion* < *anti-* against + *hēlios* sun]

ant·he·lix (ant-hē'liks, an-thē'-) *n. pl.* **ant·hel·i·ces** (ant-hel'ə-sēz, an-thel'-) *Anat.* The inner curved ridge on the cartilage of the external ear: also *antihelix*. [< ANT- + HELIX]

an·them (an'thəm) *n.* **1** A musical composition, usually set to words from the Bible. **2** A joyous or triumphal song or hymn, or the music to which it is set. —*v.t.* To celebrate with, or sing as, an anthem. [OE *antefn* < LL *antiphona* < Gk. *antiphōna*, lit., things sounding in response < *anti-* against + *phōnē* voice. Doublet of ANTIPHON.]

an·the·mi·on (an-thē'mē·on) *n. pl.* **·mi·a** (-mē-ə) The honeysuckle or palm-leaf pattern in decorative designs: common in Greek art. [< Gk., flower]

an·ther (an'thər) *n. Bot.* The pollen-bearing part of a stamen. [< F *anthère* < L *anthera*, a medicine obtained from flowers < Gk. *anthēra*, fem. of *anthēros* flowery < *anthos* flower]

ANTHEMION

antho- *combining form* Flower: *anthophorous*. [< Gk. *anthos* a flower]

an·tho·ceph·a·lous (an'thō-sef'ə-ləs) *adj.* Having a head like a flower. [< ANTHO- + Gk. *kephalē* head]

an·thoid (an'thoid) *adj.* Like a flower.

an·thol·o·gize (an·thol'ə-jīz) *v.* **·gized, ·giz·ing** *v.i.* To make an anthology or anthologies. —*v.t.* To put into an anthology or make an anthology of.

an·thol·o·gy (an·thol'ə·jē) *n. pl.* **·gies** A collection of choice or representative literary extracts. [< L *anthologia* < Gk. *anthologia* a garland, collection of poems < *anthos* flower + *legein* gather] **—an·tho·log·i·cal** (an'thə·loj'i·kəl) *adj.* **— an·thol'o·gist** *n.*

an·tho·phore (an'thə·fôr, -fōr) *n. Bot.* A stipe formed by the prolongation of an internode between the calyx and the corolla.

an·thoph·o·rous (an·thof'ər·əs) *adj.* Flowerbearing. [< Gk. *anthophoros* < *anthos* flower + *pherein* bear]

an·tho·tax·y (an'thə·tak'sē) *n. Bot.* The arrangement of flowers on the axis of inflorescence. [< ANTHO- + Gk. *taxis* arrangement]

an·tho·zo·oid (an'thə·zō'oid) *n.* An individual polyp in a compound colony.

an·thra·cene (an'thrə·sēn) *n. Chem.* A blue fluorescent crystalline compound, $C_{14}H_{10}$, obtained in the last products of coal-tar distillation and used largely in the manufacture of alizarin and related dyes. [< Gk. *anthrax, -akos* coal + -ENE]

an·thra·cite (an'thrə·sīt) *n.* Mineral coal of nearly pure carbon which burns slowly and with little flame; hard coal. [< L *anthracites* < Gk. *anthrakitēs* coallike < *anthrax* coal] **— an·thra·cit·ic** (an'thrə·sit'ik) *adj.*

an·thrac·nose (an·thrak'nōs) *n.* A destructive disease of plants usually manifested by sharply defined discolored spots and caused by various fungi. [< Gk. *anthrax, -akos* coal, carbuncle +

nosos disease]

an·thra·coid (an'thrə·koid) *adj.* **1** Resembling anthrax. **2** Like the precious carbuncle or like carbon.

sēz) **1** A carbuncle. **2** *Pathol.* An infectious and malignant febrile disease of man and some animals, caused by *Bacillus anthracis*, often with carbuncular swellings; splenic fever. **3** A bacillus found in the blood of those affected with splenic fever. **4** A gem stone of the ancients: probably the carbuncle. [< Gk., coal, carbuncle]

an·throp·ic (an·throp'ik) *adj.* Pertaining to the human species or the period of its existence. Also **an·throp'i·cal.**

anthropo- *combining form* Man; human: *anthropometry.* Also, before vowels, **anthrop-**, as in *anthropoid.* [< Gk. *anthrōpos* man]

an·thro·po·cen·tric (an'thrə·pō·sen'trik) *adj.* **1** Centering in man; regarding man as the central fact or final aim and end of the universe, or of any system: an *anthropocentric* philosophy. **2** Based on comparison with man: *anthropocentric* analysis of animal instincts.

an·thro·pog·e·ny (an'thrə·poj'ə·nē) *n.* The branch of anthropology that treats of the origin and development of man, either individually (ontogeny) or ethnically (phylogeny). See ANTHRO- POLOGY. Also **an·thro·po·gen·e·sis** (an'thrə· pō·jen'ə·sis).

an·thro·pog·ra·phy (an'thrə·pog'rə·fē) *n.* The branch of anthropology that treats of the geographic distribution, variations, and peculiarities of the human race or its component parts; descriptive anthropology.

an·thro·poid (an'thrə·poid) *adj.* **1** Like a human being in form or other characteristics; manlike: said of the highest apes, as the gorilla, chimpanzee, and orang. **2** *Zool.* Of or pertaining to a suborder of primate mammals, including man, apes, and monkeys (*Anthropoidea*). Also **an'thro·poid'al.** —*n.* An anthropoid ape.

an·thro·pol·o·gy (an'thrə·pol'ə·jē) *n.* **1** The science of man in his physical, social, material, and cultural development, including the study of his origins, evolution, geographic distribution, ethnology, and communal forms. **2** The detailed study of the customs, beliefs, folkways, and superstitions of an ethnic group, especially on a comparative basis. **—an·thro·po·log·i·cal** (an'thrə· pə·loj'i·kəl) or **·log'ic** *adj.* **—an'thro· po·log'i·cal·ly** *adv.* **—an'thro·pol'o·gist** *n.*

an·thro·pom·e·try (an'thrə·pom'ə·trē) *n.* The science and technique of human measurements, specifically of anatomical and physiological features; also, the analysis and interpretation of the data so obtained. **—an·thro·po·met·ric** (an'thrə· pō·met'rik) or **·met'ri·cal** *adj.*

an·thro·po·mor·phic (an'thrə·pō·môr'fik) *adj.* Of or pertaining to anthropomorphism; having human form or human characteristics; manshaped.

an·thro·po·mor·phism (an'thrə·pō·môr'fiz·əm) *n.* The ascription of human attributes, feelings, conduct, or characteristics to God or any spiritual being, or to the powers of nature, etc. — **an'thro·po·mor'phist** *n.*

an·thro·po·mor·phize (an'thrə·pō·môr'fīz) *v.t. & v.i.* **·phized, ·phiz·ing** To endow (gods or natural objects) with human characteristics or qualities.

an·thro·po·mor·pho·sis (an'thrə·pō·môr'fə·sis) *n.* Transformation into human shape.

an·thro·po·mor·phous (an'thrə·pō·môr'fəs) *adj.* Having or resembling human form.

an·thro·pon·o·my (an'thrə·pon'ə·mē) *n.* The science of the laws that regulate the development of man in relation to environment and to other organisms. Also **an'thro·po·nom'ics**(-pō·nom'·iks). **—an'thro·po·nom'i·cal** *adj.*

an·thro·pop·a·thism (an'thrə·pop'ə·thiz'əm) *n.* **1** Anthropopathy. **2** An expression used in anthropopathy.

an·thro·pop·a·thy (an'thrə·pop'ə·thē) *n.* The attributing of human emotions, passions, suffering, etc., to God or to gods. [< Med. L *anthropopathia* < Gk. *anthrōpopatheia* humanity < *anthrōpos* man + *pathos* feeling]

an·thro·poph·a·gi (an'thrə·pof'ə·jī) *n. pl. sing.* **a·gus** (-ə·gəs) Eaters of human flesh; cannibals. [< L, pl. of *anthropophagus* < Gk. *anthrōpoph- agos* < *anthrōpos* man + *phagein* eat]

an·thro·po·phag·ic (an'thrə·pō·faj'ik) *adj.* Pertaining to the anthropophagi; man-eating. Also

an·thro·po·phag·i·cal.

an·thro·poph·a·gite (an'thrə·pof'ə·jīt) *n.* A cannibal. Also **an'thro·poph'a·gist.**

an·thro·poph·a·gous (an'thrə·pof'ə·gəs) *adj.* Cannibalistic.

an·thro·poph·a·gy (an'thrə·pof'ə·jē) *n.* The eating of human flesh; cannibalism.

an·thro·po·zo·ic (an'thrə·pō·zō'ik) *adj. Geol.* Characterized by the existence of man: applied to the Quaternary period.

an·thu·ri·um (an·thŏŏr'ē·əm) *n.* Any of a genus (*Anthurium*) of tropical American perennials of the arum family, with heart-shaped or lobed leaves and densely flowered spathes. [< NL < Gk. *anthos* flower + *oura* tail]

an·ti (an'ti, an'tē) *n. pl.* **·tis** *Colloq.* One opposed to any proposed or enacted policy.

anti- *prefix*
1 Against; opposed to:
    anti-abrasion   antileveling
2 Opposite to; reverse:
    anticyclic   antilogic
    antihero   antipole
3 Rivaling; spurious:
    anti-Caesar   anti-king
    anticritic   anti-Messiah
    anti-emperor   antiprophet
4 *Med.* Counteracting; curative; neutralizing:
    antimycotic   antityphoid
    antinarcotic   antivirus
Anti- usually changes to *ant-* before words beginning with a vowel, as in *antacid*, and to *anth-* before the aspirate in words of Greek formation or analogy, as *anthelmintic*. [< Gk. < *anti* against]

an·ti·aer·i·al (an'tē·âr'ē·əl, -ā·ir'ē·əl) *adj.* Opposing attack from the air, as by parachute or glider troops.

an·ti·air·craft (an'tē·âr'kraft', -âr'kräft') *adj.* Opposed to or directed against aircraft: said especially of a type of gun or defense.

anti-aircraft artillery Fixed or mobile equipment used to spot, illuminate, and shoot at enemy aircraft, including sound locators, radar, searchlights, guns, etc.

an·ti·ar (an'tē·är) *n.* **1** The upas tree. **2** The acrid, virulent poison found in the gum of this tree, the glucoside antiarin, $C_{27}H_{42}O_{10}$· $4H_2O$, used as an arrow poison [< Javanese *antjar*]

an·ti·bi·o·sis (an'ti·bī·ō'sis) *n.* The condition of associated organisms in which one is detrimental to the other; antipathy.

an·ti·bi·ot·ic (an'ti·bī·ot'ik) *n.* **1** That which is antagonistic toward or destructive of life. **2** *Biochem.* **a** Any of a large class of substances produced by various micro-organisms and fungi that have the power of arresting the growth of other micro-organisms or of destroying them: some, as penicillin and streptomycin, are of value in the treatment of certain infectious diseases. **b** A chemical having similar properties produced by higher plants, some animals, and synthetically.

an·ti·bod·y (an'ti·bod'ē) *n. pl.* **·bod·ies** A globulin formed in the body in response to a foreign substance, as a protein or polysaccharide, and serving to neutralize the foreign substance.

an·tic (an'tik) *n.* **1** A prank; caper. **2** A clown; buffoon. **3** A grotesque figure or play. —*adj.* Odd; fantastic; ludicrous; incongruous. —*v.i.* **an·ticked, an·tick·ing** To play the clown; perform antics. Also *Obs.* **an'tick.** [< Ital. *antico* old (but used in the sense of grotesque) < L *antiquus.* Doublet of ANTIQUE.] **—an'tic·ly** *adv.*

an·ti·cat·a·lyst (an'ti·kat'ə·list) *n. Chem.* A catalyst which stops or retards a chemical reaction; a negative catalyst.

an·ti·cath·ode (an'ti·kath'ōd) *n.* The electrode in a vacuum or X-ray tube which receives and reflects the rays emitted from the cathode.

An·ti·christ (an'ti·krīst') *n.* Any opponent or enemy of Christ, whether a person or a power; specifically, a great enthroned antagonist, foretold in the Scriptures, who, as some have understood, is to precede the second coming of Christ: by some considered as evil personified. See I *John* ii 18.

an·ti·christ (an'ti·krīst') *n.* **1** A false claimant of the attributes and characteristics of Christ. **2** A denier or opponent of Christ or Christianity. — **an·ti·chris·tian** (an'ti·kris'chən) *adj.*

an·tic·i·pant (an·tis'ə·pənt) *adj.* Coming or acting in advance; anticipating; expectant. —*n.* One who anticipates or expects.

an·tic·i·pate (an·tis′ə·pāt) *v.t.* **·pat·ed, ·pat·ing** **1** To experience or realize beforehand; expect; foresee: to *anticipate* a successful season. **2** To act or arrive sooner than. **3** To act or arrive sooner than so as to prevent; forestall: to *anticipate* an opponent's tactics. **4** To foresee and fulfil beforehand, as expectations. **5** To take or make use of beforehand, as income not yet available. **6** To discharge, as a debt or liability before it is due. **7** To cause to happen earlier; accelerate. [< L *anticipatus,* pp. of *anticipare* < *ante-* before + *capere* take] **—an·tic′i·pa′tor** *n.*

Synonyms: abide, apprehend, expect, forecast, foretaste, hope. We *expect* that which we have good reason to believe will happen. We *hope* for that which we much desire and somewhat expect. We *apprehend* what we both *expect* and fear. *Anticipate* is commonly used now, like *foretaste,* of that which we *expect* both with confidence and pleasure. In this use it is a stronger word than *hope;* I *hope* for a visit from my friend; I *expect* it when he writes that he is coming; and as the time draws near I *anticipate* it with pleasure. Compare ABIDE, PREVENT. *Antonyms:* distrust, doubt, dread, fear, recall, recollect, remember.

an·tic·i·pa·tion (an·tis′ə·pā′shən) *n.* **1** The act of anticipating; especially, a foreseeing or foretaste; expectation. **2** An instinctive prevision. **3** *Music* The introduction of a note

ANTICIPATION *(def. 3)*

before its expected place in the harmony.

Synonyms: antepast, apprehension, expectancy, expectation, foreboding, forecast, foresight, foretaste, forethought, hope, presentiment, prevision. *Expectation* may be either of good or evil; *presentiment* almost always, *apprehension* and *foreboding* always, of evil; *anticipation* and *antepast,* commonly of good. Thus, we speak of the pleasures of *anticipation.* A *foretaste* may be of good or evil, and is more than imaginary; it is a part actually received in advance. *Foresight* and *forethought* prevent future evil and secure future good by timely looking forward, and acting upon what is foreseen. Compare ANTICIPATE. *Antonyms:* astonishment, consummation, despair, doubt, dread, enjoyment, fear, realization, surprise, wonder.

an·tic·i·pa·tive (an·tis′ə·pā′tiv) *adj.* Anticipating; having the nature, quality, or habit of anticipation. **—an·tic′i·pa′tive·ly** *adv.*

an·tic·i·pa·to·ry (an·tis′ə·pə·tôr′ē, -tō′rē) *adj.* Pertaining to, showing, or embodying anticipation. **—an·tic′i·pa·to′ri·ly** *adv.*

an·ti·clas·tic (an′ti·klas′tik) *adj. Math.* Having opposite curvature in different directions; convex in one direction and concave in another. Compare SYNCLASTIC. [< ANTI- + Gk. *klastos* broken < *klaein* break]

an·ti·cler·i·cal (an′ti·kler′i·kəl) *adj.* Opposed to clerical influence; specifically, opposed to the Roman Catholic Church.

an·ti·cli·max (an′ti·klī′maks) *n.* **1** A real, apparent, or ludicrous decrease in the importance or impressiveness of what is said: opposed to *climax.* **2** Any sudden descent or fall contrasted with a previous rise. **—an′ti·cli·mac′tic** (-klī·mak′tik) *adj.*

an·ti·cli·nal (an′ti·klī′nəl) *adj. Geol.* Forming a bend with the convex side upward, as a rock stratum or group of strata: also **an′ti·clin′ic** (-klin′ik). **—***n.* An anticlinal line, fold, or disposition of strata; a saddleback: also **an′ti·cline.** See SYNCLINAL. [< ANTI- + Gk. *klinein* slope]

an·ti·co·her·er (an′ti·kō·hir′ər) *n. Electr.* A wave-sensitive device which differs from the coherer in that its resistance increases, instead of decreases, under the action of electromagnetic waves. See DE-COHERER.

an·ti·cos·mon (an′ti·koz′mon) *n. Physics* The supposed fundamental particle from which the anticosmos developed, characterized by a nucleonic charge opposite to that of the cosmon.

an·ti·cos·mos (an′ti·koz′məs) *n. Physics* A cosmos composed entirely of antimatter and supposed to have been formed by the splitting of the universon into two distinct parts existing independently of each other in a condition of metastable equilibrium.

an·ti·cy·clone (an′ti·sī′klōn) *n. Meteorol.* An atmospheric condition of high central pressure relative to the surrounding area, with horizontal spiral currents flowing clockwise in the northern hemisphere, counterclockwise in the southern; also, the region subject to this condition.

an·ti·cy·clon·ic (an′ti·sī·klon′ik) *adj.* **1** Of or pertaining to an anticyclone. **2** Opposed to the cyclonic theory in meteorology.

an·ti·dote (an′ti·dōt) *n.* Anything that will counteract or remove the effects of poison, disease, or any evil. [< L *antidotum* < Gk. *antidoton* < *antidotos* given against < *anti-* against + *didonai* give] **—an′ti·do′tal** *adj.* **—an′ti·do′tal·ly** *adv.*

an·ti·drom·ic (an′ti·drom′ik) *adj. Physiol.* Denoting a movement or course opposed to the normal, as of a nerve impulse. [< ANTI- + Gk. *dromos* a running]

an·ti·en·er·gis·tic (an′tē·en′ər·jis′tik) *adj.* Resisting applied energy: contrasted with *synergistic.*

An·tie·tam (an·tē′tam) A village near Sharpsburg in western Maryland at the mouth of Antietam Creek; site of the fiercest day's battle of the Civil War, September 17, 1862.

an·ti·fe·brile (an′ti·fē′brəl, -feb′rəl) *adj.* Having the power to allay fever; antipyretic. **—***n.* An antifebrile agent.

an·ti·fed·er·al (an′ti·fed′ər·əl, -fed′rəl) *adj.* Opposed to federalism: capitalized when used historically to mean opposed to the adoption of the U.S. Constitution in 1787–89.

an·ti·fed·er·al·ism (an′ti·fed′ər·əl·iz′əm, -fed′rəl-) *n.* Opposition to federalism, especially to the Federal party. **—an′ti·fed′er·al·ist** *n.*

An·ti·fed·er·al·ist (an′ti·fed′ər·əl·ist, -fed′rəl-) *n.* A member of the political party that opposed the ratification of the U.S. Constitution. After it was ratified, the Antifederalists, led by Jefferson, opposed any extension of the powers of the Federal government.

an·ti·freeze (an′ti·frēz′) *n.* A liquid of low freezing point, added to or substituted for the cooling agent in combustion-engine radiators, to prevent freezing.

an·ti·fric·tion (an′ti·frik′shən) *adj.* Lessening or tending to lessen friction, as by lubricants or rollers. **—***n.* **1** A lubricant. **2** A roller or other device for lessening friction. **—antifriction metal** Any alloy having a low coefficient of friction: used for bearing-surfaces.

an·ti·gen (an′tə·jən) *n.* Any of several substances, such as toxins, enzymes, proteins, which, injected into an organism, cause the development of antibodies. Also **an′ti·gene** (-jēn). **—an·ti·gen·ic** (an′tə·jen′ik) *adj.*

An·tig·o·ne (an·tig′ə·nē) In Greek legend, a daughter of Oedipus and Jocasta who accompanied her blinded father into exile and later was sentenced to death by her uncle Creon for illegally burying her brother Polynices.

An·ti·gua (an·tē′gwə, -gə) A presidency of the Leeward Islands, comprising the island of Antigua (108 square miles) and its dependencies: Barbuda; 62 square miles; and Redonda; 1/2 square mile; capital, St. John's, on Antigua.

Antigua Guatemala A resort city in south central Guatemala; former capital of Guatemala. Also **Antigua.**

an·ti·he·lix (an′ti·hē′liks) See ANTHELIX.

an·ti·his·ta·mine (an′ti·his′tə·mēn, -min) *n. Med.* Any of certain drugs which neutralize the vasoconstrictor action of histamine in the body: used especially in the treatment of allergic conditions, as hay fever, asthma, etc., and of the common cold. **—an′ti·his′ta·min′ic** (-min′ik) *adj.*

an·ti·ic·er (an′tē·ī′sər) *n. Aeron.* A device for preventing the formation of ice on airplane wings and other exposed surfaces by the use of a spray delivering warm air or a special liquid preparation. Compare DE-ICER.

an·ti·ke·to·gen·e·sis (an′ti·kē′tə·jen′ə·sis) *n. Biochem.* The reduction or prevention of ketosis

by the oxidation of sugar or allied substances in the body.

an·ti·knock (an′ti·nok′) *adj.* Tending to prevent detonation or pinging in an internal-combustion engine. **—***n.* Any agent, as tetraethyllead, having antiknock properties.

an·ti·le·gal·ist (an′ti·lē′gəl·ist) *n.* One who repudiates law as the guide of human conduct.

an·ti·lip·oid (an′ti·lip′oid) *n.* An antibody which reacts with fatlike substances.

an·ti·lith·ic (an′ti·lith′ik) *Med. adj.* Efficacious against stones or calculi. **—***n.* An agent which prevents or destroys urinary calculi. [< ANTI- + Gk. *lithos* stone]

An·til·les (an·til′ēz) The islands of the West Indies, except the Bahamas; divided into the **Greater Antilles:** Cuba, Hispaniola, Jamaica, and Puerto Rico; and the **Lesser Antilles:** Trinidad, the Leeward and Windward Islands, Barbados, and other islands: also *Caribbees.*

an·ti·log·a·rithm (an′ti·lôg′ə·rith′əm, -log′-) *n. Math.* The number corresponding to a given logarithm.

an·til·o·gous (an·til′ə·gəs) *adj. Physics* Designating that pole of a pyro-electric crystal which is negative while the crystal is being heated and positive as it cools. Compare ANALOGOUS. [< Gk. *antilogos* contradictory < *anti-* against + *legein* speak]

an·til·o·gy (an·til′ə·jē) *n. pl.* **·gies** Inconsistency in terms or ideas; contradiction.

an·ti·ma·cas·sar (an′ti·mə·kas′ər) *n.* A covering to prevent the soiling of the backs of chairs or sofas by contact with the hair; a tidy. [< ANTI- + MACASSAR (OIL)]

an·ti·mask (an′ti·mask′, -mäsk′) *n.* A grotesque interlude between the acts of a mask, often burlesquing it: also called *antic mask.* Also **an′ti·masque′.**

an·ti·mat·ter (an′ti·mat′ər) *n. Physics* Matter composed of antiparticles.

an·ti·mere (an′tə·mir) *n. Biol.* A part symmetrical with, or corresponding to, a part on the opposite side of the main axis; an opposite, symmetrical, or homotypic part, as an arm of a starfish, or the right or left half of a bilaterally symmetrical animal: also called *actinomere.* [< ANTI- + Gk. *meros* part] **—an·ti·mer·ic** (an′tə·mer′ik) *adj.* **—an·tim·er·ism** (an·tim′ə·riz′əm) *n.*

an·ti·mol·e·cule (an′ti·mol′ə·kyōol) *n.* A molecule of antimatter.

an·ti·mo·nar·chic (an′ti·mə·när′kik) *adj.* Opposed to monarchism. Also **an′ti·mo·nar′chi·cal.**

an·ti·mo·ni·al (an′tē·mō′nē·əl) *adj.* Of or containing antimony. **—***n.* A medicine, one of whose ingredients is antimony.

an·ti·mon·ic (an′tə·mō′nik, -mon′ik) *adj.* Of, pertaining to, or containing antimony, especially when combined in its higher or pentad valence: *antimonic* sulfide, Sb_2S_5.

an·ti·mo·nous (an′tə·mō′nəs) *adj.* Of, pertaining to, or containing antimony, especially in its lower valence: *antimonous* oxide, Sb_4O_6. Also **an′ti·mo′ni·ous.**

an·ti·mo·ny (an′tə·mō′nē) *n.* A silver-white, brittle, flaky metallic element (symbol Sb, atomic number 51), sometimes found native, used chiefly in alloys. See PERIODIC TABLE. ◆ Collateral adjective: *stibial.* [< Med.L *antimonium,* ? < Arabic]

an·ti·mu·ta·gen (an′ti·myōō′tə·jən) *n.* A chemical regarded as having the property of inhibiting or decreasing the hereditary variability of micro-organisms and germ cells. [< ANTI- + L *mutare* alter + -GEN] **— an′ti·mu′ta·gen′ic** (-myōō′tə·jen′ik) *adj.*

an·ti·neu·tron (an′ti·nōō′tron, -nyōō′-) *n. Physics* An antiparticle having the same mass as a neutron, but having a reversed magnetic moment of equal magnitude.

an·ti·no·mi·an (an′ti·nō′mē·ən) *n. Theol.* One holding that faith frees the Christian from the obligations of the moral law. **—** *adj.* Of or pertaining to this doctrine. **— an′ti·no′mi·an·ism** *n.*

an·tin·o·my (an·tin′ə·mē) *n. pl.* **·mies** **1** Self-contradiction in a law; opposition of one law or rule to another. **2** Irreconcilability of seemingly necessary inferences or conclusions; paradox. [< L *antinomia* < Gk. *antinomia* < *anti-* against + *nomos* law]

---

add,āce,câre,pälm; end,ēven; it,īce; odd,ōpen,ôrder; tŏŏk,pōōl; up,bûrn; ə = a in *above,* e in *sicken,* i in *clarity,* o in *melon,* u in *focus;* yōō = u in *fuse,* oi,oil; ou,pout; ch,check; g,go; ng,ring; th,thin; ŧħ,this; zh,vision. Foreign sounds å,œ,ü,kh,ṅ; and ◆: see page xx. < from; + plus; ? possibly.

An·ti·och (an′tē·ok) An ancient city on the Orontes in southern Turkey; former capital of Syria: Arabic and Turkish *Antakiya* or *Antakya,* Roman *Caesarea.*

An·ti·o·pe (an·tī′ə·pē) **1** In Greek mythology, a maiden loved by Zeus in the form of a satyr, to whom she bore two sons, Amphion and Zethus. **2** Hippolyta, queen of the Amazons.

an·ti·par·ti·cle (an′ti·pär′ti·kəl) *n. Physics* An elementary particle, as a positron, antiproton, antineutron, etc., equal in mass to another elementary particle, as an electron, proton, neutron, etc., but opposite to it in charge and in magnetic properties. Contact between a particle and its opposite results in mutual annihilation and the release of energy.

an·ti·pas·to (än′tē·päs′tō) *n.* A course of smoked or salted meat, fish, vegetables, etc., served as an appetizer. [<Ital. < *anti-* before (<L *ante*) + *pasto* food <L *pastus*]

an·tip·a·thet·ic (an·tip′ə·thet′ik, an′ti·pə-) *adj.* Having antipathy; naturally repugnant or opposed. Also **an·tip′a·thet′i·cal. — an·tip′a·thet′i·cal·ly** *adv.*

an·tip·a·thy (an·tip′ə·thē) *n. pl.* **·thies 1** An instinctive feeling of aversion or dislike. **2** One who or that which excites aversion. [<Gk. *antipatheia* < *anti-* against + *pathein* feel, suffer] *Synonyms*: abhorrence, antagonism, aversion, detestation, disgust, dislike, distaste, hatred, hostility, loathing, opposition, repugnance, uncongeniality. *Antipathy, repugnance,* and *uncongeniality* are instinctive; other forms of *dislike* may be acquired or cherished for cause. Compare ACRIMONY, ANGER, HATRED. *Antonyms*: affinity, agreement, attraction, congeniality, harmony, kindliness, partiality, predilection, regard, sympathy.

an·ti·per·son·nel (an′ti·pûr′sə·nel′) *adj. Mil.* Designating weapons, such as bombs, mines, etc., which are employed against individuals rather than against defenses or mechanized equipment.

an·ti·per·spi·rant (an′ti·pûr′spə·rənt) *n.* A preparation which acts to diminish or prevent perspiration: an astringent applied to the skin.

an·ti·phlo·gis·tic (an′ti·flō·jis′tik) *Med. adj.* Capable of reducing inflammation. — *n.* A remedy for inflammation.

an·ti·phon (an′tə·fon) *n.* **1** A verse of a psalm or hymn said or chanted in response to another. **2** A composition consisting of passages for alternate singing or chanting. **3** A versicle chanted before, and often after, a psalm or canticle, and varying with the church season or feast. [<LL *antiphona* <Gk. *antiphona.* Doublet of ANTHEM.] — **an′ti·phon′ic** or **·i·cal** *adj.*

an·tiph·o·nal (an·tif′ə·nəl) *adj.* Of or pertaining to an antiphon. — *n.* An antiphonary. — **an·tiph′o·nal·ly** *adv.*

an·tiph·o·nar·y (an·tif′ə·ner′ē) *n. pl.* **·nar·ies** A book of antiphons. Also **an·tiph′o·nar** (-nər). — *adj.* Of or pertaining to a book of antiphons.

an·tiph·o·ny (an·tif′ə·nē) *n. pl.* **·nies 1** An anthem or other composition to be sung antiphonally. **2** Antiphonal singing. **3** In ancient Greek music, accompaniment in the octave.

an·tiph·ra·sis (an·tif′rə·sis) *n. pl.* **·ses** (-sēz) The use of a term in a sense opposite to its meaning; irony. [<L <Gk. *antiphrasis* < *anti-* against + *phrazein* express by antithesis < *anti-* against + *phrazein* speak]

an·tip·o·dal (an·tip′ə·dəl) *adj.* **1** Pertaining to or situated on the opposite side of the earth. **2** Diametrically opposed. Also **an·tip·o·de·an** (an·tip′ə·dē′ən).

an·ti·pode (an′ti·pōd) *n.* An exact opposite.

an·tip·o·des (an·tip′ə·dēz) *n. pl.* **1** A place or region on the opposite side of the earth, or its inhabitants. **2** Any person or thing diametrically opposed to another, or at the opposite extreme from another. [<L <Gk. *antipodes,* pl. of *antipous* having the feet opposite < *anti-* opposite + *pous* foot]

an·ti·pope (an′ti·pōp′) *n.* A usurping pope or one not canonically elected.

an·ti·pro·ton (an′ti·prō′ton) *n. Physics* An antiparticle having the same mass as the proton, an equal but opposite charge, and a reversed magnetic moment of equal magnitude; its collision with a proton or neutron results in the liberation of energy equivalent to both particles.

an·ti·py·ret·ic (an′ti·pī·ret′ik) *Med. adj.* Preventive or alleviative of fever. — *n.* A medicine to allay fever. [<ANTI- + Gk. *pyretos* fever]

an·ti·py·rine (an′ti·pī′rin, -rēn) *n.* A white crystalline compound, $C_{11}H_{12}N_2O$, used in medicine as an antipyretic. Also **an′ti·py′rin** (-rin).

an·ti·quar·i·an (an′ti·kwâr′ē·ən) *adj.* Pertaining to antiquity or to the knowledge of or collecting of antiquities. — *n.* An antiquary. — **an′ti·quar′i·an·ism** *n.*

an·ti·quar·y (an′ti·kwer′ē) *n. pl.* **·quar·ies** One who collects, examines, deals in, or studies ancient objects; one versed in ancient things, as relics, monuments, old manuscripts, etc. [<L *antiquarius* < *antiquus* ancient]

an·ti·quate (an′ti·kwāt) *v.t.* **·quat·ed, ·quat·ing 1** To make old, out of date, or obsolete. **2** To cause to look antique; give an old-fashioned air or style to. — **an′ti·qua′tion** *n.*

an·ti·quat·ed (an′ti·kwā′tid) *adj.* **1** Out of date; old-fashioned; obsolete. **2** Ancient; superannuated. See synonyms under ANCIENT, ANTIQUE.

an·tique (an·tēk′) *adj.* **1** Of, pertaining to, or having come down from ancient times. **2** In the style of ancient times. **3** Old; old-fashioned. **4** Pertaining or belonging to ancient Greece or Rome. — *n.* **1** The style of ancient art, or a specimen of it. **2** Any ancient object, as a piece of furniture, glass, etc. **3** A Roman-faced type with all the lines of nearly the same thickness. — *v.t.* **an·tiqued, an·ti·quing** To make seemingly old; give the appearance of antiquity to. [<F <L *antiquus* ancient < *ante* before. Doublet of ANTIC.] — **an·tique′ly** *adv.* — **an·tique′ness** *n.* *Synonyms (adj.)*: ancient, antiquated, old-fashioned, quaint, superannuated. *Antique* refers to an *ancient, antiquated* to a discarded style. The *antique* is that which is either *ancient* in fact or *ancient* in style. The *antiquated* is not so much out of date as out of vogue. *Old-fashioned* may be used approvingly or contemptuously. In the latter case it becomes a synonym for *antiquated;* in the good sense it approaches the meaning of *antique,* but indicates less duration. *Quaint* combines the idea of age with a pleasing oddity. The *antiquated* person is out of style and out of sympathy with the present generation by reason of age; the *superannuated* person is incapacitated for present activities by reason of age. Compare ANCIENT, OLD. *Antonyms*: fashionable, fresh, modern, modish, new, recent, stylish.

an·tiq·ui·ty (an·tik′wə·tē) *n. pl.* **·ties 1** The state or quality of being ancient. **2** Ancient times, people, or civilization. **3** Anything belonging to ancient times.

an·ti·re·mon·strant (an′ti·ri·mon′strənt) *n.* An opponent of remonstrance. — *adj.* Opposed to remonstrance.

An·ti·re·mon·strant (an′ti·ri·mon′strənt) *n.* A Dutch Calvinist who opposed the Arminian Remonstrance. — *adj.* Pertaining to such opposition.

an·ti·sab·ba·tar·i·an (an′ti·sab′ə·târ′ē·ən) *adj.* Of or pertaining to one who opposes the observance of the Sabbath. — *n.* One who denies the moral obligation to observe the Sabbath, or opposes its strict or puritanical observance.

an·tis·cians (an·tish′ənz) *n. pl.* Dwellers on the same meridian on opposite sides of the equator, whose shadows at noon fall in opposite directions. Also **an·tis·ci·i** (an·tish′ē·ī). [<L *antiscii* <Gk. *antiskioi* < *anti-* opposite + *skia* shadow]

an·ti·Sem·i·tism (an′ti·sem′ə·tiz′əm) *n.* Opposition to, prejudice or discrimination against, or intolerance of Jews, Jewish culture, etc. — **an′ti·Sem′ite** *n.* — **an′ti·Se·mit′ic** (-sə·mit′ik) *adj.* — **an′ti·Se·mit′i·cal·ly** *adv.*

an·ti·sep·sis (an′tə·sep′sis) *n.* **1** The condition in or method by which a substance, or organism, is kept sterile against the growth of pathogenic or putrefactive bacteria. **2** Listerism. [<NL <ANTI- + Gk. *sēpsis* putrefaction]

an·ti·sep·tic (an′tə·sep′tik) *adj.* **1** Of, pertaining to, or used in antisepsis. **2** Preventing or counteracting putrefaction, etc. Also **an′ti·sep′ti·cal.** — *n.* Any substance having antiseptic qualities, as solutions of carbolic acid and of corrosive sublimate. — **an′ti·sep′ti·cal·ly** *adv.* — **an′ti·sep′ti·cism** (-sep′tə·siz′əm) *n.*

an·ti·sep·ti·cize (an′tə·sep′tə·sīz) *v.t.* **·cized, ·ciz·ing** To render antiseptic; treat by the application of antiseptics.

an·ti·se·rum (an′ti·sir′əm) *n.* A serum which contains antibodies, the injection of which into the blood stream provides immunity from specific diseases.

an·ti·so·cial (an′ti·sō′shəl) *adj.* **1** Averse to social intercourse or society. **2** Opposed to treating society as a unit; anarchistic. **3** Obstructive or disruptive of social good.

an·ti·so·cial·ist (an′ti·sō′shəl·ist) *n.* One hostile to socialistic teachings. — **an′ti·so′cial·is′tic** *adj.*

an·ti·so·lar (an′tī·sō′lər) *adj.* **1** Situated or occurring at a point in the heavens 180 degrees from the sun in azimuth. **2** Diametrically opposite the sun, as the center of a rainbow.

an·ti·spas·mod·ic (an′ti·spaz·mod′ik) *adj.* Relieving or checking spasms. — *n.* An antispasmodic preparation, as ammonia, camphor, etc.

an·tis·tro·phe (an·tis′trə·fē) *n.* **1** In ancient Greek poetry, the verses sung by the chorus in a play while returning from left to right, in answer to the previous strophe. **2** In classical prosody, the lines of an ode comprising a stanza and alternating with the strophe. **3** The second of two alternating metrical systems in a poem. [<Gk. *antistrophē* < *antistrephein* turn against < *anti-* against, opposite + *strephein* turn] — **an·ti·stroph·ic** (an′ti·strof′ik) *adj.*

an·ti·te·tan·ic (an′tī·te·tan′ik) *Med. adj.* Relieving or preventing tetanus. — *n.* A remedy for tetanus.

an·ti·the·ism (an′ti·thē′iz·əm) *n.* **1** Opposition to belief in God. **2** In philosophy and religion, opposition to theism.

an·tith·e·sis (an·tith′ə·sis) *n. pl.* **·ses** (-sēz) **1** The balancing of contrasted words or ideas against each other. **2** The direct contrary; a strong contrast. [<L <Gk. < *antitithenai* oppose < *anti-* against + *tithenai* place]

an·ti·thet·i·cal (an′tə·thet′i·kəl) *adj.* Directly opposed; strongly contrasted. Also **an′ti·thet′ic.** — **an′ti·thet′i·cal·ly** *adv.*

an·ti·tox·in (an′ti·tok′sin) *n.* A substance, usually a protein, formed in the living tissues of a plant or animal, which neutralizes the bacterial poison that produced it. Also **an′ti·tox′ine** (-tok′sin, -sēn) — **an′ti·tox′ic** *adj.*

an·ti·trade (an′ti·trād′) *Meteorol. n.* One of the upper air currents in the tropics, moving contrary to the trade winds. — *adj.* Pertaining to or designating such an air current.

an·tit·ra·gus (an·tit′rə·gəs) *n. pl.* **·gi** (-jī) *Anat.* The conical eminence behind the opening of the ear. [<ANTI- + TRAGUS]

an·ti·Trin·i·tar·i·an (an′ti·trin′ə·târ′ē·ən) *adj. Theol.* Opposing the doctrine of the Trinity. — *n.* One who opposes the doctrine of the Trinity.

an·ti·trust (an′ti·trust′) *adj.* Pertaining to the regulation of or opposition to trusts, cartels, pools, monopolies, and other organizations and practices in restraint of trade.

an·ti·twi·light (an′ti·twī′līt) *n. Meteorol.* A pink or purplish light sometimes seen after sunset or before sunrise in the part of the sky opposite the sun.

an·ti·type (an′ti·tīp′) *n.* **1** That which a type or symbol represents; the original of a type. **2** A person or event in the New Testament prefigured by one in the Old. [<Gk. *antitypos* < *anti-* corresponding to, against + *typos* stamp, type] — **an·ti·ty·pal** (an′ti·tī′pəl), **an·ti·typ·ic** (an′ti·tip′ik) or **·i·cal** *adj.*

an·ti·ven·in (an′ti·ven′in) *n.* **1** The active principle of a serum which protects animals against snake poison or venom. **2** The serum. Also **an·ti·ven·ene, an·ti·ven·ine** (an′ti·ven′ēn, -və·nēn′). [<ANTI- + L *venenum* poison]

an·ti·vi·ral (an′ti·vī′rəl) *adj.* **1** Injurious to or destructive of viruses. **2** Counteracting a virus, as certain drugs.

an·ti·vi·rot·ic (an′ti·vī·rot′ik) *n.* A substance which destroys viruses or inhibits their development. — *adj.* Antiviral.

an·ti·world (an′ti·wûrld′) *n. Physics* A hypothetical world or universe composed only of

Antonio de Se·dil·la (thä sä·thē′lyä) 1748–1829, Spanish Capuchin priest in New Orleans, accused of trying to introduce the Inquisition: called *Père Antoine.*

An·to·ni·us (*Ger.* än·tō′nē·ŏŏs, *Lat.* an·tō′nē·əs) German and Latin form of ANTHONY.

an·to·no·ma·sia (an'tə·nō·mā'zhə, -zhē·ə) *n.* **1** The substitution of a title or epithet for a proper name, as *his Honor,* for a judge. **2** The use of the name of a representative individual for a class, as a *Cicero,* for an orator. [< L < Gk. < *antonomazein* name instead < *anti-* instead of + *onoma* name]

An·to·ny (an'tə·nē)
— **Antony, Mark,** 83–30 B.C., Roman general and triumvir: also *Marcus Antonius.*

an·to·nym (an'tə·nim) *n.* A word directly opposed to another in meaning: contrasted with *synonym.* [< Gk. *antōnymia* < *anti-* opposite + *onoma, onyma* name]

an·tre (an'tər) *n. Obs.* A cavern. [< F < L *antrum* < Gk. *antron* cave]

an·trorse (an·trôrs') *adj. Biol.* Directed forward or upward, as the short feathers hiding the nostrils in corvine birds. [< NL *antrorsus* < ANTERO- + L *versus,* pp. of *vertere* turn] — **an·trorse'ly** *adv.*

an·trum (an'trəm) *n. pl.* **·tra** (-trə) *Anat.* A cavity, usually in a bone. [< L < Gk. *antron* cave]

antrum of High·more (hī'môr, -mōr) *Anat.* A cavity in the upper jaw opening into the nose. [after Nathaniel *Highmore,* 1613–85, English anatomist]

an·trus·tion (an·trus'chən) *n.* A vassal follower and companion of the early Frankish princes. Compare THANE. [< F < Med. L *antrustio, -onis* < OHG *trōst* trust, protection] — **an·trus'tion·ship** *n.*

Ant·werp (ant'wûrp) A port on the Scheldt in northern Belgium: French *Anvers.* Flemish **Ant·wer·pen** (änt'ver·pən).

A·nu (ä'nōō) In Babylonian mythology, the sky god.

A·nu·bis (ə·nōō'bis, ə·nyōō'-) In Egyptian mythology, the jackal-headed conductor of the dead to judgment: identified with the Greek *Hermes.*

ANUBIS

A·nu·ra·dha·pu·ra (ə·nōō'rä·də·pōōr'ə) A Buddhist pilgrimage center in north central Ceylon; former capital of Ceylon.

a·nu·ran (ə·nōōr'ən, ə·nyōōr'-) *adj. & n. Zool.* Salientian. [< AN-¹ without + Gk. *oura* tail] — **a·nu'rous** *adj.*

an·u·re·sis (an'yōō·rē'sis) *n.* Anury. — **an'u·ret'ic** (-ret'ik) *adj.*

an·u·ry (an'yōō·rē) *n. Pathol.* Suppression or defective excretion of the urine. Also **a·nu·ri·a** (ə·nōōr'ē·ə, ə·nyōōr'-). [< NL *anuria* < Gk. *an-* without + *ouron* urine] — **a·nu·ric** (ə·nōōr'·ik, ə·nyōōr'-) *adj.*

a·nus (ä'nəs) *n. Anat.* The opening at the lower extremity of the alimentary canal. [< L, orig. a ring]

An·vers (äṅ·vâr') The French name for ANTWERP.

an·vil (an'vil) *n.* **1** A heavy block of iron or steel on which metal may be forged. **2** Anything similar to an anvil, as the lower contact of a telegraph key, etc. **3** *Anat.* The incus of the inner ear. **4** That part of the primer in a cartridge or shell which receives the impact of the firing pin and detonates the charge. **5** *Mech.* The fixed element of a measuring device, as in calipers. — *v.t. & v.i.* **an·viled** or **·villed, an·vil·ing** or **·vil·ling** To work at or shape on an anvil. [OE *anfilte*]

DOUBLE–BEAK ANVIL
a. Rounded beak. *b.* Flat beak. *c.* Cutter, or chisel hole.

an·vil·top (an'vil·top') *n. Meteorol.* A large, dense, anvil-shaped mass of cloud usually formed at the top of a cumulonimbus cloud preceding heavy showers or thunderstorms; incus (def. 2). For illustration see CLOUD.

anx·i·e·ty (ang·zī'ə·tē) *n. pl.* **·ties** **1** Disturbance of mind regarding some uncertain event; misgiving; worry. **2** Strained or solicitous desire, as for some object or purpose; eagerness. [< L *anxietas, -tatis* < *anxius.* See ANXIOUS.]

Synonyms: anguish, apprehension, care, concern, disquiet, disturbance, dread, fear, foreboding, fretfulness, fretting, misgiving, perplexity, solicitude, trouble, worry. *Anxiety* refers to some future event, always suggesting hopeful possibility, and thus differing from *apprehension, fear, dread, foreboding, terror,* all of which may be quite despairing. *Worry* is a more petty, restless, and manifest *anxiety*; *anxiety* may be quiet and silent; *worry* is communicated to all around. *Solicitude* is a milder *anxiety. Fretting* or *fretfulness* is a weak complaining without thought of accomplishing or changing anything, but merely as a relief to one's own *disquiet. Perplexity* often involves *anxiety,* but may be quite free from it. One feels anxiety *for* a friend's return; anxiety *about, for, in regard to,* or *concerning* the future. *Antonyms:* apathy, assurance, calmness, carelessness, confidence, ease, lightheartedness, nonchalance, satisfaction, tranquillity.

anx·ious (angk'shəs, ang'-) *adj.* **1** Troubled in mind respecting some uncertain matter; having anxiety: often with *about, at,* or *over: anxious* about health; *anxious* at the delay; *anxious* over her safety. **2** Fraught with or causing anxiety; worrying; distressing: an *anxious* matter. **3** Intent; eagerly desirous; solicitous: with *for* or the infinitive with *to: anxious* for success; *anxious* to succeed. See synonyms under EAGER. [< L *anxius* < *angere* choke, distress] — **anx'ious·ly** *adv.* — **anx'ious·ness** *n.*

an·y (en'ē) *adj.* **1** One (person, thing, or part) indefinitely and indifferently; a; an; some; no matter what: at *any* price. **2** Some (individuals) of a number, class, or total. See synonyms under EVERY. — *pron.* One or more persons, things, or portions out of a number. — *adv.* Somewhat; in the least; at all: doing *any* better today. ◆ *Any,* in colloquial negative and interrogative sentences, is used absolutely to mean noticeably, at all: Did you hurt yourself *any?* [OE *ænig* < *ān* one]

an·y·bod·y (en'i·bod'ē, -bud'ē) *pron.* Any person whatever; anyone. — *n. pl.* **·bod·ies** **1** Any common or ordinary person. **2** A person of prestige or importance: He isn't *anybody.*

an·y·how (en'i·hou') *adv.* **1** In any way whatever; by any means. **2** Notwithstanding; in any case: *Anyhow,* we did the best we could. **3** Carelessly.

any more **1** Anything added: Do not give me *any more.* **2** Now; from now on: He's not welcome *any more.*

any more than With more reason or likelihood than: I couldn't do that *any more than* I could fly.

an·y·one (en'i·wun', -wən) *pron.* Any person. ◆ **any one, anyone** *Any one* is used to distinguish one person from others in the same group or class: *Any one* of these men may be guilty. *Anyone* (indefinite pronoun) means any person at all: Can *anyone* identify the culprit?

an·y·thing (en'i·thing') *pron.* Any thing, event, or matter of any sort. — *n.* A thing of any kind. — *adv. Archaic* To any degree; in any way.

anything but By no means; far from: *anything but* safe.

an·y·way (en'i·wā') *adv.* **1** No matter what happens; in any event. **2** Nevertheless; anyhow. **3** Carelessly; haphazardly.

an·y·ways (en'i·wāz') *adv. Dial.* In any way; at all.

an·y·where (en'i·hwâr') *adv.* In, at, or to any place whatever.

an·y·wise (en'i·wīz') *adv.* In any manner.

An·zac (an'zak) *adj.* Pertaining to the *A*ustralian and *N*ew *Z*ealand *A*rmy *C*orps during World War I. — *n.* **1** A member of this army corps. **2** Any soldier from Australia or New Zealand.

An·zi·o (an'zē·ō, *Ital.* än'tsyō) A town on the west coast of Italy south of Rome; site of Allied beachhead in the invasion of Italy, World War II, January, 1944.

A-OK (ā'ō·kā') *adj. Colloq.* Perfectly all right; just fine. Also **A'-o·kay'.**

A-one (ā'wun') *n.* **1** First or highest class: said of a vessel to denote condition of its hull and equipment. Written **A-1.** **2** *Colloq.* Excellent; first-rate; superior.

a·o·rist (ā'ə·rist) *n.* A tense of Greek verbs simply expressing past action without further limitation as to completion, continuance, or repetition. Abbr. *aor.* [< Gk. *aoristos* indefinite < *a-* without + *horos* boundary]

a·o·ris·tic (ā'ə·ris'tik) *adj.* **1** Relating to the aorist tense. **2** Indefinite; undefined.

a·or·ta (ā·ôr'tə) *n. pl.* **·tas** or **·tae** (-tē) *Anat.* The great artery springing from the left ventricle of the heart and forming the main arterial trunk which distributes blood to all of the body except the lungs. [< NL < Gk. *aortē* < *aeirein* raise, heave] — **a·or'tal, a·or'tic** *adj.*

a·ou·dad (ä'ōō-dad) *n.* The bearded argali (genus *Ammotragus*), a wild sheep of North Africa: also spelled *audad.* [< F < Berber *audad*]

ap-¹ Assimilated var. of AD-.

ap-² Var. of APO-.

a·pace (ə·pās') *adv.* Rapidly; fast. [< A-¹ on + PACE]

A·pach·e (ə·pach'ē) *n. pl.* **A·pach·es** or **A·pach·e** One of a tribe of fierce North American Indians of Athapascan stock.

a·pache (ə·päsh', ə·pash'; *Fr.* á·pásh') *n.* One of a band of lawless persons formerly frequenting the streets of Paris by night. [< F < *Apache*]

Apache State Nickname of ARIZONA.

ap·a·go·ge (ap'ə·gō'jē) *n.* **1** *Math.* The use of one proposition already demonstrated to prove another. **2** *Logic* Establishment of a thesis by showing its contrary to be absurd. [< Gk. *apagōgē* a leading away < *apagein* < *apo-* away + *agein* lead] — **ap'a·gog'ic** (-goj'ik) or **·i·cal** *adj.*

a·pa·re·jo (ä'pä·rā'hō) *n. pl.* **·jos** (-hōz) *SW U.S.* A type of packsaddle with stuffed leather cushions. [< Sp.]

a·part (ə·pärt') *adv.* **1** So as to be separated in space or time, or from companionship, sympathy, or the like; aside. **2** So as to be isolated or separated for use of purpose. **3** So as to be independent logically or in thought. **4** Part from part; in pieces or to pieces; asunder. [< F *à part* < L *ad* to + *pars, partis* part]

a·part·heid (ə·pärt'hīt, -hāt) *n.* Racial segregation in the Republic of South Africa, especially as supported by law as an instrument of government policy. [< Afrikaans, apartness]

a·part·ment (ə·pärt'mənt) *n.* **1** A room or suite of rooms. **2** One of several similar suites of rooms in one building, equipped for housekeeping; a flat. [< F *appartement* < Ital. *appartamento,* ult. < L *ad* to + *pars, partis* part]

apartment house A multiple-dwelling building divided into a number of apartments.

a·pas·ti·a (ə·pas'tē·ə) *n. Psychiatry* Morbid abstention from food. [< Gk.] — **a·pas'tic** *adj.*

ap·as·tron (ap·as'tron) *n. Astron.* That point in the orbit of either member of a double star when the stars are at maximum distance from each other: opposed to *periastron.* [< AP- away from + Gk. *astron* star]

ap·a·tet·ic (ap'ə·tet'ik) *adj. Zool.* Having natural camouflage of imitative coloration or form. [< Gk. *apatētikos* deceiving < *apatē* deceit]

ap·a·thet·ic (ap'ə·thet'ik) *adj.* **1** Without emotion or feeling. **2** Indifferent; unconcerned; stolid. Also **ap'a·thet'i·cal.** — **ap'a·thet'i·cal·ly** *adv.*

ap·a·thy (ap'ə·thē) *n. pl.* **·thies** **1** Lack of feeling, emotion, or sensation; insensibility. **2** Indifference; lack of interest. [< L *apathia* < Gk. *apatheia* < *a-* without + *pathos* feeling < *pathein* feel]

Synonyms: calmness, composure, immobility, impassibility, indifference, insensibility, lethargy, phlegm, quietness, quietude, sluggishness, stillness, stoicism, tranquillity, unconcern, unfeelingness. *Composure* results ordinarily from force of will, or from perfect confidence in one's own resources. *Indifference* is a want of interest; *insensibility* is a want of feeling; *unconcern* has reference to consequences. *Stoicism* is an intentional suppression of feeling and deadening of sensibilities, while *apathy* is involuntary, denoting a simple absence of emotion. Compare CALM. REST. STUPOR. *Antonyms:* agitation, alarm, anxiety, care, distress, disturbance, eagerness, emotion, excitement, feeling, frenzy, fury, passion, sensibility, sensitiveness, storm, susceptibility, sympathy, turbulence, vehemence, violence.

ap·a·tite (ap′ə·tīt) *n. Mineral.* A hexagonal, usually brown or green calcium phosphate of chlorine or fluorine. [< Gk. *apatē* deceit + -ITE¹; because it was mistaken for other minerals]

ape (āp) *n.* **1** A large, tailless, Old World primate, as a gorilla or chimpanzee. **2** Loosely, any monkey. **3** A mimic. —*v.t.* **aped, ap·ing** To imitate; mimic. See synonyms under IMITATE. [OE *apa*]

a·peak (ə·pēk′) *adv. Naut.* In or nearly in a vertical position, as an anchor.

ape man Any of various primates resembling man, as Pithecanthropus.

Ap·en·nines (ap′ə·nīnz) A mountain range constituting most of the Italian peninsula south of the Po valley; highest peak, 9,560 feet.

a·pep·si·a (ā·pep′sē·ə, ə-) *n. Med.* Lack of capacity to digest. Also **a·pep′sy.** [< NL < Gk. *a-* not + *peptein* digest] —**a·pep′tic** (-tik) *adj.*

a·per·çu (à·per·sü′) *n. pl.* **a·per·çus** (-sü′) *French* **1** A glance. **2** An insight or perception. **3** An outline or conspectus.

a·pe·ri·ent (ə·pir′ē·ənt) *Med. adj.* Tending mildly to stimulate the action of the bowels; laxative. —*n.* A gently purgative remedy. Also **a·per·i·tive** (ə·per′ə·tiv). [< L *aperiens, -entis,* ppr. of *aperire* open]

a·pe·ri·od·ic (ā′pir·ē·od′ik) *adj.* **1** *Pathol.* Not manifesting periodicity, as some diseases. **2** *Physics* **a** Without cyclic vibrations; not periodic. **b** Pertaining to any vibrating system whose oscillations are reduced or eliminated by sufficient damping, as the pointer of an indicating device which comes to a full stop without terminal vibration.

aperiodic antenna A radio antenna responding with a high degree of constancy to a wide range of frequencies.

aperiodic compass A magnetic compass whose needle assumes its final position in one movement and without any further fluctuation.

a·pe·ri·o·dic·i·ty (ā·pir′ē·ə·dis′ə·tē) *n.* Aperiodic condition.

a·pé·ri·tif (à·pā·rē·tēf′) *n. French* A drink of alcoholic liquor or wine taken as an appetizer.

a·pert (ə·pûrt′) *adj. Archaic* Open; undisguised. [< OF < L *apertus,* pp. of *aperire* open] —**a·pert′ly** *adv.* —**a·pert′ness** *n.*

ap·er·ture (ap′ər·chŏŏr, -chər) *n.* **1** An open passage; orifice; hole; cleft. **2** An opening, often adjustable in diameter, through which light enters the lens of a camera or other optical instrument. See synonyms under HOLE. [< L *apertura < apertus,* pp. of *aperire* open] —**ap′er·tur·al** *adj.* —**ap′er·tured** *adj.*

ap·er·y (ā′pər·ē) *n. pl.* **·er·ies** The act of aping; mimicry.

a·pet·al·ous (ā·pet′əl·əs) *adj. Bot.* **1** Without petals. **2** Pertaining to the *Apetalae,* a division of plants in which the flowers are without petals.

a·pex (ā′peks) *n. pl.* **a·pex·es** or **ap·i·ces** (ap′ə·sēz, ā′pə-) **1** The highest point; tip; top. **2** *Geom.* The vertex (of an angle). **3** Climax. **4** *Phonet.* The tip of the tongue. [< L]

aph- Var. of APO-.

a·pha·gi·a (ə·fā′jē·ə) *n. Pathol.* Loss of the power to swallow. [< NL < Gk. *a-* not + *phagein* eat]

a·pha·ki·a (ə·fā′kē·ə) *n. Pathol.* A condition of the eye marked by absence of the lens. Also **a·pha′ci·a.** [< NL < Gk. *a-* without + *phakē* lentil, lens of the eye]

a·phan·i·sis (ə·fan′ə·sis) *n. Psychoanal.* The fear of losing sexual potency. [< Gk., obliteration < *aphanizein* make unseen, destroy < *a-* not + *phainein* show]

aph·a·nite (af′ə·nīt) *n. Mineral.* A dense, fine-grained diabase with a compact texture. [< Gk. *aphanēs* unseen + -ITE¹; so called because its grains are invisible to the naked eye] —**aph′-a·nit′ic** (-nit′ik) *adj.*

a·pha·sia (ə·fā′zhə, -zhē·ə) *n.* Partial or total loss of the ability to articulate or understand language due to damage to the cerebral cortex. See

[< NL < Gk. *aphasia < aphatos* speechless < *a-* not + *phanai* speak] —**a·pha·sic** (ə·fā′zik, -sik), **a·pha·si·ac** (ə·fā′·zē·ak) *adj. & n.*

a·phe·li·on (ə·fē′lē·ən). *n. pl.* **·li·ons** or **·li·a** (-lē·ə). *Astron.* The point in an orbit of a planet or comet, farthest from the sun: opposed to *perihelion.* [< APH-(APO-) away from + Gk. *hēlios* sun] —**a·phe′li·an** (-ən) *adj.*

APHELION
P. Perihelion. S. Sun.
A. Aphelion.

a·phe·li·o·trop·ic (ə·fē′lē·ə·trop′ik) *adj.* Turning away from the source of light; having negative heliotropism. [< APH- (APO-) + HELIOTROPIC] —**a·phe′-li·o·trop′i·cal·ly** *adv.* —**a·phe·li·ot·ro·pism** (ə·fē′lē·ot′rə·piz′əm) *n.*

a·phe·mi·a (ə·fē′mē·ə) *n. Pathol.* A form of aphasia characterized by inability to name objects by speech, while retaining power to name them by writing. See SPEECH DISORDER. [< NL < Gk. *a-* without + *phēmē* voice] —**a·phem·ic** (ə·fem′ik) *adj.*

a·phen·go·scope (ə·feng′gə·skōp) *n.* A epidiascope. [< Gk. *aphengēs* without light (< *a-* without + *phengos* light) + -SCOPE]

a·pher·e·sis (ə·fer′ə·sis) *n.* The dropping of an unaccented syllable or sound from the beginning of a word, as in *squire* for *esquire:* opposite of *apocope.* Also **a·phaer′e·sis.** [< L *aphaeresis* < Gk. *aphairesis < aphairein* take away < *apo-* away + *hairein* take] —**aph·e·ret·ic** (af′ə·ret′ik) *adj.*

aph·e·sis (af′ə·sis) *n.* The gradual, developmental loss of a short or unaccented vowel at the beginning of a word, as in *mend* for *amend:* a form of apheresis. [< NL < Gk., a letting go < *aphienai < apo-* from + *hienai* send] —**a·phet·ic** (ə·fet′ik) *adj.*

a·phid (ā′fid, af′id) *n.* Any of a family (*Aphididae*) of numerous, small, juice-sucking insects, injurious to plants; a plant louse. [< APHIS]

a·phis (ā′fis, af′is) *n. pl.* **aph·i·des** (af′ə·dēz) A member of a genus (*Aphis*) especially injurious to fruits and vegetables. [< NL; origin uncertain]

aph·lo·gis·tic (af′lō·jis′tik, ā′flō-) *adj.* Flameless; giving light by incandescence, as a lamp. [< Gk. *aphlogistos* not flammable]

a·pho·ni·a (ə·fō′nē·ə, ā-) *n. Pathol.* Loss of voice, especially when due to organic or structural causes; hoarseness. [< NL < Gk. *aphōnia < a-* without + *phōnē* voice]

a·phon·ic (ə·fon′ik, ā-) *adj.* **1** *Pathol.* Affected with or characterized by aphonia. **2** *Phonet.* **a** Not representing a sound; lacking pronunciation. **b** Voiceless.

aph·o·rism (af′ə·riz′əm) *n.* **1** A brief, sententious statement of a truth or principle. **2** A proverb; maxim; precept. See synonyms under ADAGE. [< F *aphorisme* < Med. L *aphorismus* < Gk. *aphorismos* definition < *aphorizein* mark off, define < *apo-* from + *horizein* divide < *horos* boundary]

aph·o·ris·mic (af′ə·riz′mik) *adj.* Having the form of an aphorism; containing or abounding in aphorisms. Also —**aph·o·ris·mat·ic** (af′ə·riz·mat′ik).

aph·o·rist (af′ə·rist) *n.* A maker or user of aphorisms. —**aph′o·ris′tic** or **·ti·cal** *adj.* —**aph′o·ris′ti·cal·ly** *adv.*

aph·o·rize (af′ə·rīz) *v.i.* **·rized, ·riz·ing** To write or speak in aphorisms.

a·pho·tic (ā·fō′tik) *adj.* Without light; dark. [< Gk. *aphōs, aphōtos < a-* without + *phōs* light]

aph·ro·dis·i·a (af′rə·diz′ē·ə) *n. Pathol.* Excessive sexual desire.

aph·ro·dis·i·ac (af′rə·diz′ē·ak) *adj.* Arousing or increasing sexual desire or potency. —*n.* An aphrodisiac drug, food, etc. [< Gk. *aphrodisiakos < Aphroditē* goddess of love]

Aph·ro·di·te (af′rə·dī′tē) In Greek mythology, the daughter of Zeus and Dione, the goddess of love and beauty, said to have been born from the foam of the sea: identified with the Phoenician *Astarte* and the Roman *Venus.* [< Gk. *Aphroditē* the foam-born]

aph·ro·di·te (af′rə·dī′tē) *n.* A brilliantly colored butterfly (*Argynnis aphrodite*) of the United States.

aph·tha (af′thə) *n. pl.* **·thae** (-thē) *Pathol.* A small vesicle or speck, appearing in the mouth or stomach, caused by a fungous parasite. [< L < Gk.] —**aph′thous** *adj.*

aph·thoid (af′thoid) *adj.* Having the nature of or like an aphtha.

aph·tho·sis (af·thō′sis) *n. Pathol.* Any morbid condition marked by the presence of aphthae.

a·phyl·lous (ə·fil′əs, ā-) *adj. Bot.* Without leaves. Also **a·phyl·lose** (ə·fil′ōs, ā-). [< Gk. *aphyllos < a-* without + *phyllon* leaf]

a·phyl·ly (ə·fil′ē, ā-) *n. Bot.* Leaflessness.

a·pi·an (ā′pē·ən) *adj.* Of or pertaining to bees.

a·pi·ar·i·an (ā′pē·âr′ē·ən) *adj.* Of or relating to bees or the keeping of bees. —*n.* An apiarist.

a·pi·a·rist (ā′pē·ə·rist) *n.* A beekeeper.

a·pi·a·ry (ā′pē·er′ē) *n. pl.* **·ar·ies** **1** A place where bees are kept. **2** A set of hives, bees, and equipment. [< L *apiarium < apis* bee]

ap·i·cal (ap′i·kəl, ā′pi-) *adj.* **1** Situated at or belonging to the apex or top, as of a conical figure. **2** *Phonet.* Describing those consonants produced with the tip of the tongue, as (t), (d), and (s). Also **a·pi·cial** (ə·pish′əl). [< L *apex, apicis* tip]

apical cell *Bot.* In many cryptogamous plants, the cell which terminates the apex of roots and stems.

ap·i·ces (ap′ə·sēz, ā′pə-) A plural of APEX.

a·pi·cul·ture (ā′pi·kul′chər) *n.* Beekeeping. [< L *apis* bee + CULTURE] —**a′pi·cul′tur·ist** *n.*

a·pic·u·lus (ə·pik′yə·ləs) *n. pl.* **·li** (-lī) *Bot.* The point terminating a leaf. [< NL, dim. of L *apex* tip] —**a·pic′u·late** (-lit, -lāt) *adj.*

a·piece (ə·pēs′) *adv.* For each person or thing; to each one; each.

à pied (à pyě′) *French* On foot.

a·pi·ol·o·gy (ā′pē·ol′ə·jē) *n.* The study of bees. [< L *apis* bee + -(O)LOGY]

A·pis (ā′pis) A sacred bull worshiped by the ancient Egyptians. See SERAPIS.

ap·ish (ā′pish) *adj.* Like an ape; servilely imitative; foolish and tricky. —**ap′ish·ly** *adv.* —**ap′ish·ness** *n.*

A·pi·um (ā′pē·əm, ap′ē·əm) *n.* A genus of umbeliferous succulent herbs; celery. [< L, parsley]

a·piv·o·rous (ā·piv′ər·əs) *adj. Zool.* Bee-eating. [< L *apis* bee + -VOROUS]

a·pla·cen·tal (ā′plə·sen′təl, ap′lə-) *adj. Zool.* Without a placenta; implacental, as the monotremes and marsupials.

ap·la·nat·ic (ap′lə·nat′ik) *adj. Optics* Free from spherical or chromatic aberration. [< A-⁴ not + *planatikos* wandering]

a·pla·sia (ə·plā′zhə, -zhē·ə) *n. Pathol.* **1** Partial or complete failure of tissue to grow. **2** Arrested development of parts of the body; congenital atrophy. [< NL < Gk. *a-* without + *plasis* a molding]

a·plas·tic (ā·plas′tik) *adj. Pathol.* Lacking the power of normal growth.

a·plomb (ə·plom′, *Fr.* à·plôn′) *n.* Assurance; self-confidence. [< F, perpendicularity, assurance < *à* according to + *plomb* plummet]

ap·noe·a (ap·nē′ə) *n. Pathol.* Suspension of respiration, partial or entire; suffocation. Also **ap·ne′a.** [< NL < Gk. *apnoia < a-* without + *pnoiē, pnoē* breath] —**ap·noe′al, ap·noe′ic** *adj.*

A·po (ä′pō), **Mount** A volcano in SE Mindanao; highest peak in the Philippines; 9,690 feet.

apo- *prefix* **1** Off; from; away: *apostasy.* **2** *Chem.* Used to indicate a derived compound: *apomorphine.* Also: ap- before vowels, as in *apagoge;* aph- before an aspirate, as in *aphelion.* [< Gk. < *apo* from, off]

a·poc·a·lypse (ə·pok′ə·lips) *n.* A prophecy or disclosure; any remarkable revelation. [< L *apocalypsis < Gk. apokalypsis < apokalyptein* disclose < *apo-* from + *kalyptein* cover] —**a·poc′-a·lyp′tic** (-lip′tik) or **·ti·cal** —**a·poc′-a·lyp′ti·cal·ly** *adv.*

A·poc·a·lypse (ə·pok′ə·lips) The book of Revelation, the last book of the New Testament.

ap·o·carp (ap′ə·kärp) *n. Bot.* A gynoecium having separate carpels, as the distinct ovaries of the crowfoot family. [< APO- distinct + Gk. *karpos* fruit] —**ap′o·car′pous** *adj.*

ap·o·chro·mat·ic (ap′ə·krō·mat′ik) *adj. Optics* More exactly achromatic than an ordinary achromatic lens. —**ap′o·chro′ma·tism** (-krō′mə·tiz′əm) *n.*

a·poc·o·pate (ə·pok′ə·pāt) *v.t.* **·pat·ed, ·pat·ing** To shorten by apocope. Also **a·poc′o·pat·ed** (-pā′tid). —**a·poc′o·pa′tion** *n.*

a·poc·o·pe (ə·pok′ə·pē) *n.* A cutting off or elision

of the last sound or syllable of a word. [<Gk. *apokopē* <*apokoptein* cut off <*apo-* off + *koptein* cut]

ap·o·crus·tic (ap′ə·krus′tik) *adj.* Having the power to repel; astringent. [<NL *apocrusticus* <Gk. *apokroustikos* <*apokrouein* beat off, repel]

A·poc·ry·pha (ə·pok′rə·fə) *n. pl.* **1** Fourteen books of the Septuagint in the Vulgate but not in the canonical Hebrew Scriptures nor in the Authorized Version. **2** One of the various collections of unauthenticated writings that abounded in the first and second centuries, proposed as additions to, but not admitted to the New Testament Gospels. [<LL, neut. pl. of *apocryphus* <Gk. *apokryphos* hidden <*apokryptein* <*apo-* away + *kryptein* hide] — **A·poc′ry·phal** *adj.*

a·poc·ry·phal (ə·pok′rə·fəl) *adj.* Of doubtful authenticity; spurious. —**a·poc′ry·phal·ly** *adv.* —**a·poc′ry·phal·ness** *n.*

a·poc·y·na·ceous (ə·pos′ə·nā′shəs) *adj. Bot.* Belonging to the dogbane family of herbaceous or woody plants (*Apocynaceae*), mainly tropical, with milky, mostly acrid juice and simple leaves, as Indian hemp, oleander, and periwinkle. [<NL *Apocynaceae* <Gk. *apokynon* dogbane <*apo-* from + *kyōn* dog]

a·poc·y·nin (ə·pos′ə·nin) *n. Chem.* An organic compound, $C_9H_{10}O_3$, forming one of the active principles of hemp dogbane. [<APOCYN(UM) + -IN]

A·poc·y·num (ə·pos′ə·nəm) *n.* Any of a genus of perennial herbs with a tough, fibrous bark and a milky juice, whose roots have medicinal qualities. [<NL, dogbane <Gk. *apo-* away + *kyōn, kynos* a dog]

ap·od (ap′əd) *n. Zool.* An animal without feet. Also **ap·o·dan** (ap′ə·dən). [<Gk. *apous, apodos* footless <*a-* without + *pous* foot]

ap·o·dac·tyl·ic (ap′ō·dak·til′ik) *adj. Pathol.* Without the use of the fingers. [<Gk. *apo-* away + *dactylos* a finger]

ap·o·dal (ap′ə·dəl) *adj. Zool.* **1** Without ventral fins. **2** Of or relating to an animal lacking distinct footlike appendages. **3** Of or relating to an order (*Apoda*) of holothurians without ambulacral feet.

ap·o·deic·tic (ap′ə·dīk′tik) *adj.* Apodictic. Also **ap′o·deic′ti·cal.** —**ap′o·deic′ti·cal·ly** *adv.*

ap·o·dic·tic (ap′ə·dik′tik) *adj.* Clearly demonstrable; indisputable. Also **ap′o·dic′ti·cal.** [<L *apodicticus* <Gk. *apodeiktikos* <*apodeiknynai* show by argument <*apo-* from + *deiknynai* show] —**ap′o·dic′ti·cal·ly** *adv.*

a·pod·o·sis (ə·pod′ə·sis) *n. pl.* **·ses** (-sēz) The conclusion in a conditional sentence; also, the clause expressing result in a sentence not conditional. [<Gk., a giving back <*apo-* back + *didonai* give]

a·pog·a·my (ə·pog′ə·mē) *n.* **1** *Bot.* **a** Absence of the sexual function in plants. **b** The development of the mature plant from the prothallium without intervention of sexual organs, as in certain of the higher cryptogams. **2** *Biol.* In evolution, the mating and interbreeding of segregated groups that do not differ significantly in character from other groups of their kind. [<APO- + Gk. *gamos* marriage] —**ap·o·gam·ic** (ap′ə·gam′ik) *adj.* — **a·pog′a·mous** *adj.*

ap·o·gee (ap′ə·jē) *n.* **1** *Astron.* The point in the orbit of the moon or of an artificial satellite where it is farthest from the earth; opposed to *perigee.* **2** The highest point; climax. [<F *apogée* <Gk. *apogaiou* <*apogaion* <*apo-* away from + *gē, gaia* earth] —**ap·o·ge·al** (ap′ə·jē′əl), **ap′o·ge′an** *adj.*

APOGEE
P. Perigee. *E.* Earth.
A. Apogee.

ap·o·ge·ot·ro·pism (ap′ō·jē·ot′rə·piz′əm) *n. Bot.* The tendency to grow away from the earth, in opposition to gravitation, as plant stems and tree trunks; negative geotropism: also called *ageotropism.* [<APO- + GEOTRO-

---

PISM] —**ap·o·ge·o·trop·ic** (ap′ō·jē′ə·trop′ik) *adj.*

à point (à pwan′) *French* To the point; exactly; just enough.

A·pol·lo (ə·pol′ō) **1** In Greek and Roman mythology, the god of music, poetry, prophecy, and medicine; the type of manly youth and beauty, later identified with *Helios.* **2** Any handsome young man. [<L <Gk. *Apollōn*]

Ap·ol·lo·ni·a (ap′ə·lō′nē·ə) An ancient port of western Cyrenaica on the Mediterranean.

A·pol·lo·ni·us Rho·di·us (ap′.ə·lō′nē·əs rō′dē·əs), late third to early second century B.C., Greek poet and grammarian.

APOLLO
After the Apollo Belvedere in the Vatican.

A·pol·los (ə·pol′əs) First century Alexandrian Jew who continued the work of St. Paul at Corinth and Ephesus. *Acts* xviii 24.

A·pol·lyon (ə·pol′yən) The angel of the bottomless pit. *Rev.* ix 11. See also ABADDON. [<Gk. *apollyōn* destroying <*apollyein* destroy completely]

ap·o·log (ap′ə·lôg, -log) *n.* A fable or moral tale. Also **ap′o·logue.** See synonyms under FICTION. [<L *apologus* <Gk. *apologos* <*apo-* from + *logos* speech]

ap·ol·o·get·ic (ə·pol′ə·jet′ik) *adj.* **1** Of the nature of an apology; excusing. **2** Defending or explaining. Also **a·pol′o·get′i·cal.** — *n.* An apology or defense. [<F *apologétique* <L *apologeticus* <Gk. *apologētikos* <*apologia* a speech in defense. See APOLOGY.] —**a·pol′o·get′i·cal·ly** *adv.*

ap·ol·o·get·ics (ə·pol′ə·jet′iks) *n.* That branch of theology which deals with the defensive facts and proofs of Christianity.

ap·o·lo·gi·a (ap′ə·lō′jē·ə) *n.* A justification or defense. [<L <Gk.]

a·pol·o·gist (ə·pol′ə·jist) *n.* One who argues in defense of any person or cause.

a·pol·o·gize (ə·pol′ə·jīz) *v.i.* **·gized, ·giz·ing** **1** To offer or make excuse; acknowledge, with regret, any fault or offense. **2** To make a justification or formal defense in speech or writing. —**a·pol′o·giz′er** *n.*

a·pol·o·gy (ə·pol′ə·jē) *n. pl.* **·gies** **1** A formal acknowledgment, as of error, offense, or incivility. **2** Originally, a justification or defense. **3** A poor substitute. [<L *apologia* <Gk. *apologia* a speech in defense <*apo-* from + *logos* speech]

Synonyms: acknowledgment, confession, defense, exculpation, excuse, justification, plea, vindication. According to its present meaning, he who offers an *apology* admits himself, at least technically and seemingly, in the wrong. An *excuse* for a fault is an attempt at partial justification; as, one alleges haste as an *excuse* for carelessness. *Acknowledgment* is neutral, and may be either of fact, duty, obligation, etc., or of error or fault. *Confession* is a full *acknowledgment* of wrong, generally of a grave wrong, with or without *apology* or *excuse.* Compare CONFESS, DEFENSE. *Antonyms:* accusation, censure, charge, complaint, condemnation, imputation, injury, insult, offense, wrong.

ap·o·mix·is (ap′ə·mik′sis) *n.* **1** *Biol.* Parthenogenesis. **2** *Bot.* Reproduction from cells other than ovules. [<NL <APO- from + Gk. *mixis* a mingling] —**ap′o·mic′tic** (-mik′-tik) *adj.*

ap·o·mor·phine (ap′ə·môr′fēn, -fin) *n. Med.* A crystalline alkaloid, $C_{17}H_{17}O_2N$, obtained from morphine by removing one molecule of water: used as an emetic and expectorant.

ap·o·neu·ro·sis (ap′ə·no̅o̅·rō′sis, -nyo̅o̅-) *n. pl.* **·ses** (-sēz) *Anat.* The white fibrous tissue investing or forming the end or attachment of certain muscles. [<Gk. *aponeurōsis* <*apo-* from + *neuron* a nerve] —**ap′o·neu·rot′ic** (-rot′ik) *adj.*

ap·o·pemp·tic (ap′ə·pemp′tik) *adj.* Bidding farewell; valedictory. — *n.* A farewell hymn or ode. [<Gk. *apopemptikos* <*apopempein* send away <*apo-* away + *pempein* send]

ap·o·pet·al·ous (ap′ə·pet′əl-əs) *adj. Bot.* Polypetalous; having separated petals.

---

a·poph·a·sis (ə·pof′ə·sis) *n.* A mentioning of something by denying that it will be mentioned. *Example:* I will not remind you of the following instance of his heroism. [<NL <Gk. *apophasis* denial <*apophanai* speak out, deny <*apo-* away + *phanai* speak]

ap·o·phthegm (ap′ə·them), etc. See APOTHEGM, etc.

a·poph·y·ge (ə·pof′ə·jē) *n. Archit.* **1** A concave curve in a column where the shaft rises from the base or joins the capital. **2** A hollow molding immediately below the echinus of some Doric capitals. [<Gk. *apophygē* escape <*apopheugein* flee away <*apo-* away + *pheugein* flee]

a·poph·yl·lite (ə·pof′ə·līt, ap′ə·fil′īt) *n. Chem.* A white, crystalline silicate of calcium and hydrogen, sometimes containing potassium and·calcium. [<APO- + Gk. *phyllon* leaf +-ITE[1]]

ap·o·phyl·lous (ap′ə·fil′əs) *adj. Bot.* Composed of distinct floral leaves: said of a perianth. [<APO- + Gk. *phyllon* leaf]

a·poph·y·sis (ə·pof′ə·sis) *n. pl.* **·ses** (-sēz) **1** *Anat.* A bony protuberance, as of a vertebra. **2** *Zool.* In arthropods, any hardened process of the body wall. **3** *Geol.* A branching offshoot from an intrusion of igneous rock. [<NL <Gk. *apophysis* branch, offshoot <*apo-* from + *phyein* grow]

ap·o·plec·tic (ap′ə·plek′tik) *adj.* Pertaining to, affected with, or tending toward apoplexy. Also **ap′o·plec′ti·cal.** — *n.* A person subject to apoplexy.

ap·o·plex (ap′ə·pleks) *v.t. Obs.* To strike with apoplexy.

ap·o·plex·y (ap′ə·plek′sē) *n. Pathol.* **1** Sudden loss or diminution of sensation and of the power of voluntary motion, due to an acute vascular lesion of the brain, as from hemorrhage; a stroke of paralysis. **2** A sudden discharge of blood within an organ. [<OF *apoplexie* <L *apoplexia* <Gk. *apoplēxia* <*apoplēssein* disable by a stroke <*apo-* from, off + *plēssein* strike]

a·port (ə·pôrt′, ə·pōrt′) *adv. Naut.* On or toward the left or port side of a ship.

ap·o·sep·al·ous (ap′ə·sep′əl-əs) *adj. Bot.* Polysepalous.

ap·o·si·o·pe·sis (ap′ə·sī′ə·pē′sis) *n.* A sudden interruption of a thought in the middle of a sentence, as if the speaker or writer were unable or unwilling to continue. *Example:* When I perceived the delights of paradise— but who could describe them? [<L <Gk. *aposiōpēsis* <*aposiōpaein* <*apo-* from + *siōpaein* be silent] —**ap′o·si′o·pet′ic** (-pet′ik) *adj.*

a·pos·po·ry (ə·pos′pər·ē) *n. Bot.* **1** A loss of the sporogenous function. **2** The development of a new organism from or near the spore–producing organ without the intervention of spores, as in some ferns. [<APO- + SPORE] —**a·pos′po·rous** *adj.*

a·pos·ta·sy (ə·pos′tə·sē) *n. pl.* **·sies** Desertion of one's faith, religion, party, or principles. Also **a·pos′ta·cy.** [<L *apostasia* <Gk. *apostasia* a standing off, desertion <*apo-* away + *stasis* a standing]

a·pos·tate (ə·pos′tāt, -tit) *adj.* Guilty of apostasy; false. — *n.* One who apostatizes.

a·pos·ta·tize (ə·pos′tə·tīz) *v.i.* **·tized, ·tiz·ing** To forsake one's faith or principles.

ap·o·stem (ap′ə·stem) *n. Pathol.* An abscess. Also **ap′o·steme** (-stēm). [<Gk. *apostēma* separation (i.e., of pus) <*apostēnai* stand off <*apo-* from + *stēnai* stand]

a·pos·te·mate (ə·pos′tə·māt) *v.i.* **·mat·ed, ·mat·ing** *Obs.* To form an abscess.

a pos·te·ri·o·ri (ā′ pos·tir′ē·ôr′ī, -ō′rī) **1** Reasoning from facts to principles or from effect to cause: opposed to *a priori.* **2** Inductive; empirical. [<L, from what comes after]

a·pos·til (ə·pos′til) *n.* A marginal note; annotation. Also **a·pos′tille.** [<F *apostille*]

a·pos·tle (ə·pos′əl) *n.* **1** One of the twelve disciples originally commissioned by Christ to preach the gospel (*Matt.* x 2–4); later also denoting Matthias, who replaced Judas Iscariot (*Acts* i 26), and Paul (*Rom.* i 1). **2** One of a class of missionaries or preachers in the early church (I *Cor.* xii 28). **3** A Christian missionary who first evangelizes a nation or place. **4** The earliest or foremost advocate of a cause. **5** In the Mormon

---

Church, one of the twelve members of the church's administrative council. See PRESIDENCY (def. 4). [OE *apostol* <L *apostolus* <Gk. *apostolos* one sent forth, a messenger < *apostellein* < *apo-* from + *stellein* send] **—a·pos'tle·ship, a·pos·to·late** (ə·pos'tə·lit, -lāt) *n.*

Apostles' Creed A traditional and still widely accepted Christian confession of faith, beginning "I believe in God the Father Almighty": originally attributed to the twelve apostles, but now assigned to the fourth or fifth century.

ap·os·tol·ic (ap'ə·stol'ik) *adj.* **1** Of or pertaining to an apostle, the apostles, or their times. **2** According to the doctrine or practice of the apostles. **3** *Often cap.* Papal. Also **ap'os·tol'i·cal. — ap'os·tol'i·cism** (-ə·siz'-əm) *n.* **— ap·os·to·lic·i·ty** (ə·pos'tə·lis'ə·tē) *n.*

Apostolic Constitutions A fourth century collection of writings on ecclesiastical matters, claiming apostolic authorship, its final section comprising a collection of 85 regulations on church discipline and worship, the **Apostolic Canons.**

Apostolic Fathers 1 A group of early Christian writers, including Clement of Rome, Ignatius, Polycarp, and others who were younger contemporaries of the apostles. **2** An ancient collection of writings attributed to them.

Ap·os·tol·i·ci (ap'ə·stol'ə·sī) *n. pl.* **1** A third century Gnostic sect practicing a strict asceticism for which they claimed apostolic precedent. **2** A similar German sect of the 12th century. **3** An Italian sect of the 13th and 14th centuries which advocated absolute poverty and attacked the worldliness of the church. **4** An Anabaptist sect which practiced ceremonially the washing of feet. [<L, apostolic < *apostolus* APOSTLE]

apostolic see Any church or bishopric originally founded by an apostle.

Apostolic See 1 The Church of Rome, regarded as having been founded by St. Peter. **2** The papacy.

apostolic succession The regular and uninterrupted transmission of spiritual authority from the apostles, claimed for their bishops by the Anglican, Greek, Roman Catholic, and some other churches.

a·pos·tro·phe¹ (ə·pos'trə·fē) *n.* **1** A symbol (') above the line, to mark the omission of a letter or letters from a word, to indicate the possessive case, the end of a quotation, or the plural of figures or letters. **2** The omission so indicated. [<F <L *apostrophus* <Gk. *apostrophos*] **— ap·os·troph·ic** (ap'ə·strof'ik) *adj.*

a·pos·tro·phe² (ə·pos'trə·fē) *n.* **1** A digression from a discourse; specifically, a turning aside, as from an audience, to speak to an imaginary or absent person, an attribute, or the Deity. **2** *Bot.* The arrangement of chlorophyll granules (as on the lateral walls of leaf cells) when exposed to strong light: opposed to *epistrophe.* [<L <Gk. *apostrophē* a turning away < *apostrephein* < *apo-* from + *strephein* turn] **— ap·os·troph·ic** (ap'ə·strof'ik) *adj.*

a·pos·tro·phize¹ (ə·pos'trə·fīz) *v.i.* **·phized, ·phiz·ing** To use the apostrophe; shorten a word by omission.

a·pos·tro·phize² (ə·pos'trə·fīz) *v.t. & v.i.* **·phized, ·phiz·ing** To address by or in a rhetorical apostrophe; to speak or write an apostrophe. See synonyms under ADDRESS.

apothecaries' measure A system of liquid measure used in pharmacy. Units and values as used in the United States are as follows:

60 minims	=	1 fluid dram
8 fluid drams	=	1 fluid ounce
4 fluid ounces	=	1 gill
4 gills	=	1 pint
2 pints	=	1 quart
4 quarts	=	1 gallon

a·poth·e·car·y (ə·poth'ə·ker'ē) *n. pl.* **·car·ies** One who keeps drugs for sale and puts up prescriptions; a druggist; pharmacist. [<LL *apothecarius* storekeeper <L *apotheca* storehouse <Gk. *apothēkē* < *apotithenai* put away < *apo-* away + *tithenai* put]

ap·o·the·ci·um (ap'ə·thē'shē·əm, -sē·əm) *n. pl.* **·ci·a** (-shē·ə, -sē·ə) *Bot.* An open, more or less cup-shaped fruit body in which the asci-bearing layer lies exposed during the maturing of the asci; an ascocarp. Also **ap·o·the·ce** (ap'ə·thē'sē, ap'ə·thēs). [<NL <Gk. *apothēkē*

storehouse] **— ap'o·the'cial** (-shəl) *adj.*

ap·o·thegm (ap'ə·them) *n.* A terse, instructive, practical saying; a sententious maxim: also spelled *apophthegm.* See synonyms under ADAGE. [<Gk. *apophthegma* a thing uttered, a terse saying < *apophthengesthai* < *apo-* from + *phthengesthai* speak, utter] **— ap·o·theg·mat·ic** (ap'ə·theg·mat'ik) or **·i·cal** *adj.*

ap·o·them (ap'ə·them) *n. Geom.* The perpendicular from the center to any side of a regular polygon. [<APO- + Gk. *thema* that which is placed < *tithenai* place]

a·poth·e·o·sis (ə·poth'ē·ō'sis, ap'ə·thē'ə·sis) *n. pl.* **·ses** (-sēz) **1** Exaltation to divine honors; deification. **2** Supreme exaltation of any person, principle, etc., as if to divine honor. [<L <Gk. *apotheōsis* < *apo-* from + *theos* a god]

a·poth·e·o·size (ə·poth'ē·ə·sīz', ap'ə·thē'ə·sīz) *v.t.* **·sized, ·siz·ing 1** To deify. **2** To glorify.

ap·o·tro·pa·ism (ap'ə·trō·pā'iz·əm) *n.* In folklore, the warding off of evil by incantations or ritual acts. [<Gk. *apotropaios* averting evil < *apo-* away + *trepein* turn]

ap·pal (ə·pôl') *v.t.* **ap·palled, ap·pal·ling** To fill with dismay or horror; terrify; shock. Also **ap·pall'.** See synonyms under FRIGHTEN. [<OF *apallir* become or make pale < *a-* to (<L *ad-*) + *pale* pale <L *pallidus.* See PALE, PALLID.]

Ap·pa·la·chi·an (ap'ə·lā'chē·ən, -chən, -lach'ən) *adj.* Of or pertaining to the Appalachian Mountains.

Appalachian Mountains A mountain system of eastern North America extending from Quebec to Alabama; highest peak, 6,684 feet.

Appalachian tea 1 The leaves of either of two shrubs, the inkberry and the withe rod, used for tea in some localities of the United States. **2** Either of these two plants.

Appalachian Trail A footpath for hikers, extending 2,050 miles along the crests of the Appalachian system from Maine to Georgia.

ap·pal·ling (ə·pô'ling) *adj.* Causing or apt to cause dismay or terror. **— ap·pall'ing·ly** *adv.*

ap·pa·loo·sa (ap'əloo'sə) *n. Often cap.* One of a breed of Western saddle horses having a characteristically mottled appearance. [Prob. after *Palouse* Indians of the northwest]

ap·pa·nage (ap'ə·nij) *n.* **1** A dependent territory or property. **2** A natural accompaniment, attribute, or endowment. **3** A portion of land assigned by a king for support of his younger sons; the public allowance to the prince of a reigning house: also *apanage.* [<F *apanage* <OF *apaner* nourish <L *ad-* to + *panis* bread]

ap·pa·ra·tus (ap'ə·rā'təs, -rat'əs) *n. pl.* **·tus** or (rarely) **·tus·es 1** A complex device or machine for a particular purpose: an X-ray *apparatus.* **2** An integrated assembly of tools, appliances, instruments, etc., operating to achieve a specified result. **3** *Physiol.* Those organs and parts of the body by means of which natural processes are carried on: digestive *apparatus.* **4** *L,* preparation < *apparare* make ready < *ad-* to + *parare* prepare]

ap·par·el (ə·par'əl) *n.* **1** Raiment; clothing. **2** *Eccl.* Any oblong piece of embroidery ornamenting the alb and amice. **3** Things provided for special use; arrangements or furnishings, especially for a ship or a house. See synonyms under DRESS. **— v.t. ·eled** or **·elled, ·el·ing** or **·el·ling 1** To clothe; dress. **2** *Archaic* To deck or equip. [<OF *apareil* preparation, provision < *apareiller* prepare, ult. <L *ad-* to + *par* equal]

ap·par·ent (ə·par'ənt, ə·pâr'-) *adj.* **1** Clearly perceived or perceivable; clear; evident; obvious; manifest; also, visible. **2** Seeming, in distinction from real or true. [<OF *aparant,* ppr. of *aparoir* appear <L *apparere.* See APPEAR.] **— ap·par'en·cy** *n.*

Synonyms: likely, presumable, probable, seeming. The *apparent* is that which appears, either that which is manifest, visible, certain, or that which is merely in seeming; as, the *apparent* motion of the sun around the earth. *Apparent* indicates less assurance than *probable* and more than *seeming.* See EVIDENT. *Antonyms:* doubtful, dubious, improbable, unimaginable, unlikely.

ap·par·ent·ly (ə·par'ənt·lē, ə·pâr'-) *adv.* Obviously or seemingly. Abbr. *appar.*

ap·pa·ri·tion (ap'ə·rish'ən) *n.* **1** A specter; phantom; ghost. **2** Any appearance, especially if remarkable; a phenomenon. **3** The

act of appearing, or the state of being visible. **4** *Astron.* The period for most favorable observation of a planet, comet, or other heavenly body. [<MF <L *apparitio, -onis* < *apparere.* See APPEAR.] **— ap'pa·ri'tion·al** *adj.*

ap·par·i·tor (ə·par'ə·tər, ə·pâr'-) *n.* **1** Formerly, an official of a civil court. **2** In ecclesiastical law, an official who serves summonses and executes the processes of an ecclesiastical court. **3** *Brit.* The beadle of a university. [<L < *apparere* appear]

ap·par·te·ment (à·pàrt·män') *French* Living quarters; an apartment.

ap·peach (ə·pēch') *v.t. Obs.* To impeach; accuse. [ME *apechen,* var. of *empechen* <OF *empechier.* See IMPEACH.]

ap·peal (ə·pēl') *n.* **1** An earnest entreaty for aid, sympathy, or the like; prayer; supplication. **2** A quality or manner which elicits sympathy or attraction. **3** A resort to some higher power or final means, for sanction, proof, or aid. **4** *Law* **a** The carrying of a cause from a lower to a higher tribunal for a rehearing (see COURT OF APPEALS under COURT). **b** The right to do this. **c** A request to do this. **d** A case so carried. **4** In old English law, the accusation of a criminal by an accomplice. **5** In any parliamentary body, a reference to the house of a disputed decision made by the chairman. See synonyms under ADDRESS, PLEA, SUIT. **— v.t. 1** *Law* To refer or remove, as a case, to a higher court. **2** *Archaic* To challenge. **— v.i. 3** To make an earnest supplication or request, as for sympathy, corroboration, or aid. **4** To awaken a favorable response; be interesting: Does this idea *appeal* to you? **5** *Law* To remove a case, or request that a case be moved, to a higher court. **6** To resort or have recourse: with *to:* to *appeal* to reason to solve a difficulty. [<OF *apeler* <L *appellare* accost, call upon, var. of *appellere* < *ad-* to + *pellere* drive] **— ap·peal'a·ble** *adj.* **— ap·peal'er** *n.* **— ap·peal'ing·ly** *adv.*

ap·pear (ə·pir') *v.i.* **1** To come forth into view or public notice; become visible, plain, public, or certain. **2** To be visible. **3** To be published, as a book or other writing. **4** To seem, or seem likely. **5** *Law* To come into court in person or by attorney, and submit or object to its jurisdiction in a given cause. [<OF *aparoir* <L *apparere* < *ad-* to + *parere* come forth, appear]

ap·pear·ance (ə·pir'əns) *n.* **1** External show or aspect. **2** That which appears or seems; semblance. **3** *pl.* Circumstances or indications collectively. **4** A becoming manifest or public; advent; publication. **5** A coming formally into court. **6** A phenomenon. See synonyms under AIR¹, MANNER.

ap·pease (ə·pēz') *v.t.* **ap·peased, ap·peas·ing 1** To reduce or bring to peace; placate; soothe, as by making concessions or yielding to demands. **2** To bribe, as an aggressor nation, with territorial or political concessions in order to avoid war or a break in diplomatic relations. **3** To satisfy or allay: *Appease* your hunger with this bread. See synonyms under ALLAY. [<OF *apaisier* < *a-* to (<L *ad-*) + *pais* peace <L *pax*] **— ap·peas'a·ble** *adj.* **— ap·peas'a·bly** *adv.* **— ap·peas'er** *n.* **— ap·peas'ing·ly** *adv.* **— ap·pea·sive** (ə·pē'siv) *adj.*

ap·pease·ment (ə·pēz'mənt) *n.* **1** The act of placating or pacifying. **2** The policy of making territorial or other concessions to potential aggressors in order to maintain peace.

ap·pel (à·pel') *n.* **1** In fencing, a feint, often accompanied by a stamp of the foot, to procure an opening. **2** In diplomatic correspondence, the salutation of the person addressed, as Sire, Excellency, etc. [<F, lit., a call]

ap·pel·la·ble (ə·pel'ə·bəl) *adj.* Appealable. **— ap·pel'la·bil'i·ty, ap·pel·lan·cy** (ə·pel'ən·sē) *n.*

ap·pel·lant (ə·pel'ənt) *adj. Law* Of or pertaining to an appeal; appellate. **— n.** One who appeals, in any sense.

ap·pel·late (ə·pel'it) *adj. Law* Pertaining to or having jurisdiction of appeals: an *appellate* court. [<L *appellatus,* pp. of *appellare.* See APPEAL.]

ap·pel·la·tion (ap'ə·lā'shən) *n.* **1** A name or title. **2** The act of calling or naming. See synonyms under NAME.

ap·pel·la·tive (ə·pel'ə·tiv) *adj.* **1** Serving to designate or name. **2** Denoting a class, as common nouns. — *n.* **1** A title; appellation. **2** A common noun. — **ap·pel′la·tive·ly** *adv.* — **ap·pel′la·tive·ness** *n.*

ap·pel·la·to·ry (ə·pel′ə·tôr′ē, -tō′rē) *adj.* Containing an appeal.

ap·pel·lee (ap′ə·lē′) *n. Law* One against whom an appeal is taken; a defendant. [<F *appelé,* pp. of *appeler* appeal]

ap·pel·lor (ə·pel′ôr, ap′ə·lôr′) *n.* In old English law, a confessed criminal who accused an accomplice. [<AF *apelour,* OF *apeleor* <L *appellator* one who appeals < *appellare.* See APPEAL.]

ap·pend (ə·pend′) *v.t.* **1** To add, as something subordinate or supplemental. **2** To hang or attach: to *append* a seal. See synonyms under ADD. [<L *appendere* < *ad-* to + *pendere* hang]

ap·pend·age (ə·pen′dij) *n.* **1** Anything appended; a subordinate addition or adjunct: a mere *appendage.* **2** *Biol.* **a** Any part joined to or diverging from the axial trunk or from any adjunct of it. **b** A subordinate or subsidiary part, as a limb, tail, leaf, hair, etc.

Synonyms: accessory, accompaniment, addendum, addition, adjunct, appendix, appurtenance, attachment, auxiliary, concomitant, extension, increase, supplement. An *adjunct* constitutes no real part of the thing or system to which it is joined; an *appendage* is commonly a real, but not an essential or necessary, part of that with which it is connected; an *appurtenance* belongs subordinately to something by which it is employed, especially as an instrument to accomplish some purpose. An *attachment* in machinery is some mechanism that can be brought into optional connection with the principal movement; a hemmer is an *attachment* of a sewing machine. An *extension,* as of a railroad or of a franchise, adds to something already existing. See SUPPLEMENT.

ap·pen·dant (ə·pen′dənt) *adj.* **1** Hanging; attached; adjunct. **2** Associated with in a subordinate capacity. **3** Related by cause or purpose; consequent. **4** *Law* Belonging to a land grant or tenure as an added but lesser right. — *n. Law* A subsidiary right attached to one more important. Also **ap·pen′dent.**

ap·pen·dec·to·my (ap′ən·dek′tə·mē) *n. pl.* **·mies** *Surg.* The excision of the vermiform appendix. Also **ap·pen·di·cec·to·my** (ə·pen′də·sek′tə·mē). [<APPENDIX + -ECTOMY]

ap·pen·di·ceal (ap′ən·dish′əl, ə·pen′də·sē′əl) *adj. Anat.* Of or relating to the vermiform appendix.

ap·pen·di·ces (ə·pen′də·sēz) A plural of APPENDIX.

ap·pen·di·ci·tis (ə·pen′də·sī′tis) *n. Pathol.* Inflammation of the vermiform appendix.

ap·pen·di·cle (ə·pen′di·kəl) *n.* A small appendage. [<L *appendicula,* dim. of *appendix*]

ap·pen·dic·u·lar (ap′ən·dik′yə·lər) *adj.* **1** Of, pertaining to, or being an appendage or appendicle; appendiculate. **2** *Anat.* Of or pertaining to the limbs or appendages.

ap·pen·dic·u·late (ap′ən·dik′yə·lit, -lāt) *adj.* **1** Having appendages, as a leaf. **2** Of the nature of or forming an appendage.

ap·pen·dix (ə·pen′diks) *n. pl.* **·dix·es** or **·di·ces** (-də·sēz) **1** An addition or appendage, as of supplementary matter at the end of a book. **2** An appendage. **3** *Anat.* **a** The vermiform appendix. **b** A process or projection; an outgrowth or prolongation. **4** *Aeron.* A large tube hanging from a spherical balloon, through which the gas passes in or out. [<L, an appendage < *appendere.* See APPEND.]

Synonyms: addendum, addition, supplement. We add an *appendix* to a book, as a dictionary, to contain names, dates, lists, etc., which would encumber the text; we add a *supplement* to supply omissions, as, for instance, to bring it up to date. An *addition* might be matter interwoven in the body of the work, an index, plates, editorial notes, etc., which might be valuable *additions,* but are not within the meaning of *appendix* or *supplement.* See APPENDAGE.

ap·per·ceive (ap′ər·sēv′) *v.t.* **·ceived, ·ceiv·ing** *Psychol.* To perceive with conscious attention, integrating new experiences, concepts, ideas, etc., with the old. [<F *apercevoir* <L *ad-* to + *percipere.* See PERCEIVE.]

ap·per·cep·tion (ap′ər·sep′shən) *n.* **1** *Psychol.* **a** That kind of perception in which the mind is conscious of the act of perceiving. **b** The adding of other mental acts to perception proper, as interpretation, recognition, and classification. **c** An act of voluntary consciousness accompanied by self-consciousness; also, the coalescence of part of a new idea with an old one by modification. **2** The powers of intellect involved in the acquisition, conservation, and elaboration of knowledge; the understanding. [<F *aperception* <*apercevoir.* See APPERCEIVE.] — **ap′per·cep′tive** *adj.*

ap·per·son·a·tion (ə·pûr′sə·nā′shən) *n. Psychiatry* The compulsive identification with or impersonation of another person: noted in many mental disorders, especially dementia precox.

ap·per·tain (ap′ər·tān′) *v.i.* To pertain or belong as by custom, function, nature, right, or fitness; relate: with *to.* See synonyms under PERTAIN. [<OF *apertenir* <LL *appertinere* < *ad-* to + *pertinere.* See PERTAIN.]

ap·pe·tence (ap′ə·təns) **1** Strong craving or propensity. **2** Instinct or tendency: the *appetence* of ducks for water. **3** *Chem.* Affinity, as in atoms and molecules. Also **ap′pe·ten·cy.** See synonyms under APPETITE, DESIRE. [<L *appetentia* < *appetere.* See APPETITE.] — **ap′pe·tent** *adj.*

ap·pe·tite (ap′ə·tīt) *n.* **1** A desire for food or drink. **2** A craving or desire; strong liking. [<OF *appetit* <L *appetitus* < *appetere* strive for < *ad-* to + *petere* seek] — **ap′pe·ti·tive** *adj.*

Synonyms: appetence, craving, desire, disposition, impulse, inclination, liking, longing, lust, passion, proclivity, proneness, propensity, relish, thirst, zest. *Appetite* is used only of the demands of the physical system, unless otherwise expressly stated, as when we say an *appetite* for knowledge; *passion* includes all excitable impulses of our nature, as anger, fear, love, hatred, etc. *Appetite* is thus more animal than *passion;* we say an *appetite* for food, a *passion* for fame. Compare DESIRE. *Antonyms:* antipathy, aversion, detestation, disgust, dislike, disrelish, distaste, hatred, indifference, loathing, repugnance, repulsion. Compare ANTIPATHY.

ap·pe·tize (ap′ə·tīz) *v.t.* **·tized, ·tiz·ing** *Rare* To excite appetite or hunger in.

ap·pe·tiz·er (ap′ə·tī′zər) *n.* Anything that excites appetite or gives relish; specifically, food or drink served before a meal to stimulate the appetite. Also *Brit.* **ap′pe·tis′er.**

ap·pe·tiz·ing (ap′ə·tī′zing) *adj.* Giving relish; tempting to the appetite. Also *Brit.* **ap′pe·tis′ing.** — **ap′pe·tiz′ing·ly** *adv.*

ap·plaud (ə·plôd′) *v.t. & v.i.* **1** To express approval, as of a performer, particularly by clapping the hands. **2** To commend; praise in an audible or visible manner. See synonyms under ADMIRE, PRAISE. [<L *applaudere* < *ad-* to + *plaudere* clap hands, strike] — **ap·plaud′er** *n.* — **ap·plaud′ing·ly** *adv.*

ap·plause (ə·plôz′) *n.* Acclamation; approval; praise; especially as shown by clapping the hands, shouting, etc. [<L *applausus,* pp. of *applaudere.* See APPLAUD.] — **ap·plau·sive** (ə·plô′siv) *adj.* — **ap·plau′sive·ly** *adv.*

Synonyms: acclaim, acclamation, cheering, cheers, eulogy, laudation, plaudit, praise. *Praise* is the expressed and hearty approval of an individual, or of a number or multitude, one by one; *applause,* the spontaneous outburst of many at once. *Applause* is expressed in any way, by clapping of hands, etc., as well as by the voice; *acclamation* is strictly by the voice alone. *Acclaim* is the more poetic term for *acclamation,* commonly understood in a loftier sense. *Plaudit* is a shout of *applause,* and is commonly used in the plural. See EULOGY, PRAISE. *Antonyms:* denunciation, derision, hissing, obloquy, scorn, vituperation.

ap·ple (ap′əl) *n.* **1** The fleshy edible fruit or pome of any variety of a widely distributed tree (*Malus malus*) of the rose family, usually of a roundish or conical shape with a depression at each end. **2** The similar fruit of several allied species of *Malus,* as *M. prunifolia* and *M. baccata,* the Siberian crab apple, and *M. coronaria,* the American crab apple. **3** A tree of any one of the species bearing apples as its natural fruit. **4** One of several fruits or plants with little or no resemblance to the apple: May *apple,* love *apple,* oak *apple,* etc. **5** In the Bible, the apple proper; also, a citron, apricot, pear, quince, or other fruit. [OE *æppel*]

apple green A clear, light yellowish green.

ap·ple·jack (ap′əl·jak′) *n.* Brandy made from fermented cider.

ap·ple·john (ap′əl·jon′) *n. Obs.* A variety of apple considered to taste best when shriveled: said to ripen about St. John's Day: also called *John apple.*

apple of discord In Greek mythology, the golden apple inscribed "for the fairest," thrown among the gods by Eris; claimed by Hera, Aphrodite, and Athena, it was awarded by Paris to Aphrodite after she promised him Helen, fairest of women.

apple of the eye 1 The pupil of the eye. **2** Something precious.

apple polisher *U.S. Slang* One who seeks favor by obsequious behavior, flattery, etc.

ap·ple·sauce (ap′əl·sôs′) *n.* **1** Apples stewed to a pulp. **2** *U.S. Slang* Nonsense; bunk.

Ap·ple·seed (ap′əl·sēd), **Johnny** Nickname of John Chapman, 1775?-1847, American pioneer, famous for distributing seeds to establish orchards in the Middle West.

ap·pli·ance (ə·plī′əns) *n.* **1** Something applied to effect a result; a machine or device; an instrument. **2** *Rare* An applying or being applied. **3** *Obs.* Compliance.

ap·pli·ca·ble (ap′li·kə·bəl) *adj.* Capable of or suitable for application; relevant; fitting. [<L *applicare* apply + -ABLE] — **ap′pli·ca·bil′i·ty, ap′pli·ca·ble·ness** *n.* — **ap′pli·ca·bly** *adv.*

ap·pli·cant (ap′li·kənt) *n.* One who applies, as for a position; a candidate.

ap·pli·ca·tion (ap′li·kā′shən) *n.* **1** The act of applying. **2** That which is applied, as a remedial agent. **3** That by which one applies; especially, a formal written request or demand; a requisition; request. **4** Appropriation to a particular use. **5** The testing or carrying into effect of a general law, truth, or precept by bringing it into relation with practical affairs; also, the capacity of being thus used. **6** The act, habit, or faculty of close and continuous attention. **7** The denoting or extending of a term, or the presenting of a proposition in a manner that combines logical strength with correctness of form. See synonyms under EXERCISE, INDUSTRY. [<L *applicatio, -onis* a joining to < *applicare.* See APPLY.]

ap·pli·ca·tive (ap′li·kā′tiv) *adj.* Applying or capable of being applied; pertaining to application; applicatory; practical.

ap·pli·ca·tor (ap′li·kā′tər) *n.* An instrument or utensil for applying medication, etc., in the form of liquids or pastes.

ap·pli·ca·to·ry (ap′li·kə·tôr′ē, -tō′rē) *adj.* **1** Fit for application. **2** Making application; practical.

ap·plied (ə·plīd′) *adj.* **1** Put in practice; utilized: opposed to *abstract* or *pure: applied* science. **2** Dealing with certain data or problems in a practical manner as opposed to a merely theoretical one: *applied* ethics.

ap·pli·er (ə·plī′ər) *n.* A person or thing that applies.

ap·pli·qué (ap′li·kā′) *adj.* Applied: said of ornaments, as in needlework, wood, metal, etc., cut out from one material and fastened to the surface of another. — *n.* Decoration or ornaments so applied. — *v.t.* **·quéd** (-kād′), **·qué·ing** (-kā′ing) To sew or decorate by sewing, as ornaments of one material to the surface of another. [<F]

ap·ply (ə·plī′) *v.* **ap·plied, ap·ply·ing** *v.t.* **1** To bring into contact with something; attach, as surfaces. **2** To devote or put to a particular use: to *apply* steam to navigation. **3** To connect, as an epithet, with a particular person or thing. **4** To give (oneself) wholly to; devote: to *apply* oneself to study. — *v.i.* **5** To make a request or petition; ask: with *for:* to *apply* for a position. **6** To have reference or appropriate relation; belong naturally: Your orders don't *apply* in an emergency. [<OF *aplier* <L *applicare* join to < *ad-* to

+ *plicare* fold]

ap·pog·gia·tu·ra (ə-poj′ə-tŏŏr′ə, -tyŏŏr′ə; *Ital*. äp·pôd′jä·tŏŏ′rä) *n. Music* An ornament consisting of a single note preceding another note. [<Ital. < *appoggiare* lean upon, rest]

ap·point (ə-point′) *v.t.* **1** To name or select, as a person for a position, a time and place for an act or meeting, etc. **2** To ordain, as by decree; command; prescribe: These laws are *appointed* by God. **3** To fit out; equip; furnish: used chiefly in the past participle: a *well-appointed* yacht. **4** *Law* To establish as a trustee or guardian. See synonyms under ALLOT, APPORTION, INSTITUTE, SET. [<OF *apointer* arrange, settle <LL *appunctare* <L *ad-* to + *punctum* a point]

ap·point·ee (ə·poin′tē′) *n.* One appointed to an office or position.

ap·point·ment (ə·point′mənt) *n.* **1** An appointing or being appointed; position or service to which one is or may be appointed; station; office. **2** An agreement, as for meeting at a given time; an engagement. **3** Something agreed upon; direction; decree. **4** Anything for use or adornment; equipment. **5** *Law* A power or right to control or designate the disposition of property. **6** *Obs.* Preparation.

Ap·po·mat·tox (ap′ə·mat′əks) A village and county in central Virginia. At **Appomattox Court House**, established in 1940 as a national monument, Lee surrendered to Grant, April 9, 1865, virtually ending the Civil War.

Appomattox River A river of central Virginia, flowing east 137 miles to the James River.

ap·por·tion (ə·pôr′shən, ə·pōr′-) *v.t.* To divide and assign proportionally; allot. [<OF *apportionner* <LL *apportionare* <L *ad-* to + *portio, -onis* portion]

Synonyms: allot, appoint, appropriate, assign, deal, dispense, distribute, divide, grant, share. To *allot* or *assign* may be to make an arbitrary division; the same is true of *distribute* or *divide*. That which is *apportioned* is given by some fixed rule, which is meant to be uniform and fair. To *dispense* is to give out freely; as, the sun *dispenses* light and heat. One may *apportion* what he only holds in trust; he *shares* what is his own. Compare ALLOT. *Antonyms:* collect, consolidate, receive, retain.

ap·por·tion·ment (ə·pôr′shən·mənt, ə·pōr′-) *n.* **1** An apportioning or being apportioned; any proportional division or allotment. **2** *U.S.* The decision by law as to the number of representatives that a state may have in the Federal House of Representatives, or that a county or other political subdivision may have in a state legislature.

ap·pose (ə·pōz′) *v.t.* **ap·posed, ap·pos·ing** **1** To apply or put, as one thing to another: with *to*: *appose* a seal to a document. **2** To arrange side by side. [<F *apposer* <a- to (<L *ad-*) + *poser* put. See POSE¹.] — **ap·pos′a·ble** *adj.*

ap·po·site (ap′ə·zit) *adj.* **1** Fit for or well adapted to the purpose; appropriate; pertinent; relevant: an *apposite* simile. **2** Placed or being in apposition; apposed. [<L *appositus*, pp. of *apponere* put near to < *ad-* to + *ponere* put] — **ap′po·site·ly** *adv.* — **ap′po·site·ness** *n.*

ap·po·si·tion (ap′ə·zish′ən) *n.* **1** *Gram.* The placing of one substantive beside another to add to or explain the first, as in *John, president* of the class. **2** A placing or being in immediate connection; application; addition. **3** *Biol.* Growth or increase by juxtaposition, as of tissue. — **ap′po·si′tion·al** *adj.* — **ap′po·si′tion·al·ly** *adv.*

ap·pos·i·tive (ə·poz′ə·tiv) *adj.* In or pertaining to a state of apposition. — *n.* A word or phrase in apposition. — **ap·pos′i·tive·ly** *adv.*

ap·prais·al (ə·prā′zəl) *n.* An appraising; official valuation. Also **ap·praise′ment**.

ap·praise (ə·prāz′) *v.t.* **ap·praised, ap·prais·ing** **1** To make an official valuation of; set a price or value on, especially by authority of law or agreement of interested parties. **2** To estimate the amount, quality, or worth of; judge. [<AP-¹ + PRAISE] — **ap·prais′a·ble** *adj.* — **ap·prais′er** *n.*

ap·pre·ci·a·ble (ə·prē′shē·ə·bəl, -shə·bəl) *adj.* Capable of being valued or estimated. — **ap·pre′ci·a·bly** *adv.*

ap·pre·ci·ate (ə·prē′shē·āt) *v.* **·at·ed, ·at·ing** *v.t.* **1** To form an estimate of, as to quality, etc. **2** To estimate correctly or adequately. **3** To consider highly; be keenly aware of or sensitive

to. **4** To show gratitude for. **5** To raise or increase the price or value of. — *v.i.* **6** To rise in value. [<L *appretiatus*, pp. of *appretiare* appraise < *ad-* to + *pretium* price]

Synonyms: esteem, estimate, prize, value. A jeweler *estimates* an old ring as worth so much cash; the owner may *value* it beyond price, as a family heirloom, or he may *prize* it as the gift of an *esteemed* friend, without *appreciating* its commercial value. *Antonyms:* depreciate, despise, flout, misjudge, scorn, undervalue.

ap·pre·ci·a·tion (ə·prē′shē·ā′shən) *n.* **1** An appreciating; true or adequate estimation or recognition. **2** Increase in value.

ap·pre·ci·a·tive (ə·prē′shē·ā′tiv, -shə·tiv) *adj.* Capable of showing appreciation; manifesting appreciation. — **ap·pre′ci·a·tive·ly** *adv.* — **ap·pre′ci·a·tive·ness** *n.*

ap·pre·ci·a·tor (ə·prē′shē·ā′tər) *n.* **1** One who appreciates. **2** An apparatus by means of which the proportion of gluten in flour is determined.

ap·pre·ci·a·to·ry (ə·prē′shē·ə·tôr′ē, -tō′rē, -shə-) *adj.* Appreciative. — **ap·pre′ci·a·to′ri·ly** *adv.*

ap·pre·hend (ap′ri·hend′) *v.t.* **1** To lay hold of or grasp mentally; grasp a truth or statement; perceive. **2** To expect with anxious foreboding; look forward with fear or anxiety. **3** To arrest; seize in the name of the law. **4** *Obs.* To take hold of. [<L *apprehendere* < *ad-*to + *prehendere* seize] — **ap′pre·hend′er** *n.*

Synonyms: anticipate, arrest, catch, comprehend, conceive, grasp, imagine, know, perceive, understand. In strictness we *perceive* only what is presented through the senses. We *apprehend* what is presented to the mind by any means whatever. A child can *apprehend* the distinction between right and wrong, yet the philosopher cannot *comprehend* it in its fulness. Compare ALARM, IDEA. *Antonyms:* ignore, lose, misapprehend, miss, misunderstand, overlook.

ap·pre·hen·si·ble (ap′ri·hen′sə·bəl) *adj.* Capable of being apprehended. — **ap′pre·hen′si·bil′i·ty** *n.*

ap·pre·hen·sion (ap′ri·hen′shən) *n.* **1** Distrust or dread concerning the future; foreboding; misgiving; presentiment. **2** The power of apprehending; cognition; conception. **3** An estimate; idea; opinion. **4** Legal arrest. See synonyms under ALARM, ANTICIPATION, ANXIETY, FEAR, IDEA, KNOWLEDGE, UNDERSTANDING. [<L *apprehensio, -onis* < *apprehendere*. See APPREHEND.]

ap·pre·hen·sive (ap′ri·hen′siv) *adj.* **1** Anticipative of evil; anxious; fearful; suspicious. **2** Quick to apprehend. **3** Responsive to sense impressions. **4** Having cognizance; conscious. — **ap′pre·hen′sive·ly** *adv.* — **ap′pre·hen′sive·ness** *n.*

ap·pren·tice (ə·pren′tis) *n.* **1** One who is bound by a legal agreement to serve another for an agreed period of time in order to learn a trade or business. **2** Any learner or beginner. — *v.t.* **·ticed, ·tic·ing** To bind or take on as an apprentice. [<OF *aprentis* <*aprendre* teach <L *apprehendere* comprehend. See APPREHEND.] — **ap·pren′tice·ship** *n.*

ap·pressed (ə·prest′) *adj. Bot.* Pressed or applied closely against something, as leaves against a stem. [<L *appressus*, pp. of *apprimere* <*ad-* to + *premere* press]

ap·pres·sor (ə·pres′ər) *n. Bot.* The expansion at the tip of the hyphae of certain parasitic fungi, by means of which they fasten on to the host. Also **ap·pres·so·ri·um** (ap′rə·sôr′ē·əm, -sō′rē-).

ap·prise (ə·prīz′) *v.t.* **ap·prised, ap·pris·ing** To notify, as of an event; inform: also spelled *apprize*. See synonyms under INFORM. [<F *appris*, pp. of *apprendre* teach, inform <L *apprehendere*. See APPREHEND.] — **ap·prise′ment** *n.* — **ap·pris′er** *n.*

ap·prize¹ (ə·prīz′) *v.t.* **ap·prized, ap·priz·ing** Appraise. Also **ap·prise′**.

ap·prize² (ə·prīz′) *v.t.* **ap·prized, ap·priz·ing** Apprise. — **ap·prize′ment** *n.* — **ap·priz′er** *n.*

ap·proach (ə·prōch′) *v.i.* **1** To come near or nearer in time or space. — *v.t.* **2** To come or cause to come near or nearer to. **3** To make advances to; offer a solicitation, proposal, or bribe to. **4** To come close to; almost reach; approximate: to *approach* a solution; to *approach* Bluebeard in cruelty. — *n.* **1** The act of approaching; a coming nearer. **2** Nearness; approximation. **3** Opportunity, means,

or way of approaching; access. **4** Advances, as to acquaintance, etc.; also, the manner in which any advance is made: a kindly *approach*. **5** In golf, the stroke made after the tee shot, which lands the player's ball on the putting green. **6** *pl. Mil.* Constructed works, trenches, etc., by which besiegers attack a fortified position. See synonyms under APPROXIMATION. [<OF *aprochier* <LL *appropiare* <L *ad-* to + *prope* near] — **ap·proach′a·ble·ness** *n.* — **ap·proach′a·ble** *adj.*

ap·pro·bate (ap′rə·bāt) *v.t.* **·bat·ed, ·bat·ing** **1** To approve. **2** To sanction formally or officially. See synonyms under PRAISE. [<L *approbatus*, pp. of *approbare*. See APPROVE.]

ap·pro·ba·tion (ap′rə·bā′shən) *n.* **1** The act of approving; approval; commendation. **2** *Eccl.* **a** Papal official approval of a religious order. **b** A bishop's official approval of a priest as confessor. **3** *Obs.* Proof; probation. See synonyms under PRAISE.

ap·pro·ba·tive (ap′rə·bā′tiv) *adj.* Expressing or implying approbation. Also **ap·pro·ba·to·ry** (ə·prō′bə·tôr′ē, -tō′rē). — **ap′pro·ba′tive·ness** *n.*

ap·pro·pri·a·ble (ə·prō′prē·ə·bəl) *adj.* That can be appropriated.

ap·pro·pri·ate (ə·prō′prē·it) *adj.* Suitable for or belonging to the person, circumstance, or place; fit; proper; relevant. — *v.t.* (ə·prō′prē·āt) **·at·ed, ·at·ing** **1** To set apart for a particular use. **2** To take for one's own use. See synonyms under ABSTRACT, APPORTION, ASSUME. [<L *appropriatus*, pp. of *appropriare* <*ad-* to + *proprius* one's own] — **ap·pro′pri·ate·ly** *adv.* — **ap·pro′pri·ate·ness** *n.* — **ap·pro′pri·a′tive** *adj.* — **ap·pro′pri·a′tor** *n.*

Synonyms (adj.): adapted, apt, becoming, befitting, congruous, fit, meet, pertinent, proper, suitable. *Antonyms:* inappropriate, incongruous, irrelevant, unfit, unsuitable.

ap·pro·pri·a·tion (ə·prō′prē·ā′shən) *n.* **1** Something, as money, appropriated, or set apart, as by a legislature, for a special use. **2** An appropriating or being appropriated.

ap·prov·al (ə·prōō′vəl) *n.* **1** An approving or being approved; approbation. **2** Official consent; sanction. **3** Favorable opinion; praise; commendation. See synonyms under PRAISE. — **on approval** For (a customer's) examination without obligation to purchase.

ap·prove¹ (ə·prōōv′) *v.* **ap·proved, ap·prov·ing** *v.t.* **1** To regard as worthy, proper, or right; be favorably disposed toward. **2** To confirm formally or authoritatively; sanction; ratify. **3** To show or prove (oneself) worthy of approval. **4** *Obs.* To prove by trial; test. — *v.i.* **5** To show or state approval: with *of*: He *approved* of my desire. See synonyms under ADMIRE, AGREE, ASSENT, JUSTIFY, LIKE, PRAISE, RATIFY. [<OF *aprover* <L *approbare* <*ad-* to + *probare* approve, prove <*probus* good] — **ap·prov′a·ble** *adj.* — **ap·prov′er** *n.* — **ap·prov′ing·ly** *adv.*

ap·prove² (ə·prōōv′) *v.t. Law* To turn to one's profit; appropriate, as waste or common land. [<OF *approuer* profit <*a* to + *pro* profit]

ap·prox·i·mal (ə·prok′sə·məl) *adj. Anat.* Close together: said of the surfaces of teeth.

ap·prox·i·mate (ə·prok′sə·mit) *adj.* **1** Nearly, but not exactly, accurate or complete. **2** Near. — *v.* (ə·prok′sə·māt) **·mat·ed, ·mat·ing** *v.t.* **1** To bring close to or cause to approach closely, as in time, space, or condition, without exact coincidence. **2** *Math.* To calculate a value progressively closer to exactitude: to *approximate* the square root of 6. — *v.i.* **3** To come near or close; be similar: That watch isn't the same as mine, but it *approximates.* [<L *approximatus*, pp. of *approximare* come near <*ad-* to + *proximus*, superl. of *prope* near] — **ap·prox′i·mate·ly** *adj.*

ap·prox·i·ma·tion (ə·prok′sə·mā′shən) *n.* **1** The act or process of approximating. **2** *Math.* A result sufficiently exact for a specified purpose.

Synonyms: approach, contiguity, likeness, nearness, neighborhood, propinquity, resemblance, similarity. *Approximation* expresses as near an approach to accuracy and certainty as the conditions in any given case make possible. *Resemblance* and *similarity* may be but superficial and apparent; *approximation* is real. *Approach* is a relative term, indicating that one has come nearer than before; *approximation* brings one really near. *Nearness, neighborhood,* and *propinquity* are commonly used of place; *approximation,* of mathematical calculations and abstract reasoning; we speak of *approach* to the shore, *nearness* to the town, *approximation* to the truth. *Antonyms*: difference, distance, error, remoteness, unlikeness, variation.

ap·prox·i·ma·tive (ə·prok′sə·mā′tiv, -mə·tiv) *adj*. Approaching almost to, but not quite; obtained by or involving approximation; approximate. —**ap·prox′i·ma′tive·ly** *adv*.

ap·pulse (ə·puls′) *n. Astron.* The approach of a heavenly body toward the meridian. [< L *appulsus* < *appellere* drive to < *ad-* to + *pellere* drive] —**ap·pul′sive** (-siv) *adj*.

ap·pul·sion (ə·pul′shən) *n*. The act of striking against.

ap·pur·te·nance (ə·pûr′tə·nəns) *n*. Something belonging or attached to something else as an accessory or adjunct. See synonyms under APPENDAGE. [< AF *apurtenance*, OF *apertenance* < L *appertinere*. See APPERTAIN.]

ap·pur·te·nant (ə·pûr′tə·nənt) *adj*. Appertaining or belonging, as by right; accessory. — *n*. An appurtenance.

a·pri·cot (ā′pri·kot, ap′ri·kot) *n*. 1 A fruit (genus *Prunus*) of the rose family, intermediate between the peach and the plum. 2 The tree bearing this fruit. 3 A reddish-yellow color. [Earlier *apricock* (prob. directly < Pg.), *abricot* < F *abricot* < Pg. *albricoque* or Sp. *albaricoque* < Arabic *al-barqūq* < Med. Gk. *praikokion* < L *praecoquus* early ripe < *prae-* before + *coquere* cook]

A·pril (ā′prəl) The fourth month of the year, containing 30 days. [< L *Aprilis*]

April fool The subject of a practical joke on April 1, known as **April** (or **All**) **Fools' Day**.

a pri·o·ri (ā′ prī·ô′rī, ä′ prē·ôr′ē) 1 *Logic* Proceeding, as an argument, from cause to effect, or from an assumption to its logical conclusion: opposed to *a posteriori*. 2 Prior to, and thus independent of, experience; innate. 3 Previous to, or with insufficient, examination. See TRANSCENDENTAL. [< L, from what is before]

a·pri·or·i·ty (ā′prī·ôr′ə·tē, -or′-) *n*. The quality of being a priori, or not derived from experience.

a·pron (ā′prən, ā′pərn) *n*. 1 A covering to protect or adorn the front of a person's clothes, or any similar covering. 2 A part of the dress of a bishop or of the regalia of Masonic orders or other societies. 3 *Mech.* a Any of various overlapping pieces protecting parts of machines. b An endless band, as of cloth or leather, usually inclined, for conducting loose moving material, as grain in a separator. 4 *Eng.* a The platform or sill at the entrance to a dock. b The platform below a dam or in a sluiceway, or hinged to the river side of a fishing float. 5 *Geol.* A sheet of sand or gravel lying for some distance in front of the terminal moraines of a glacier. 6 *Aeron.* A hard-surfaced area in front of and around a hangar or aircraft shelter, to facilitate the handling of aircraft. 7 The part of a theater stage in front of the curtain. 8 *Mil.* a A movable screen of camouflage material, used to conceal artillery. b A network of barbed wire surrounding a post or stake in an entanglement. 9 A band of leather composing that part of an Oxford shoe which extends from the shank up and over the instep. — *v.t.* To cover or furnish with or as with an apron. [< OF *naperon*, dim. of *nape* cloth < L *mappa* cloth, napkin; in ME *a napron* became *an apron*] —**a′pron·like′** *adj*.

ap·ro·pos (ap′rə·pō′) *adj*. 1 Suited to the time, place, or occasion; pertinent; opportune: an *apropos* remark. —*adv.* 1 With reference or regard; in respect; as suggested by: with *of*: *apropos* of spring. 2 To the purpose; at the proper time; in the proper way; pertinently; appropriately: He spoke quite *apropos*. 3 By the way; incidentally: used to introduce a remark or observation. [< F *à propos* < *à* to < *propos* purpose]

apse (aps) *n. Archit.* 1 An extending portion of an edifice, from the interior a recess and from the exterior a projection, usually semicircular with a half dome. 2 The eastern or altar end of a church. [< L *apsis* arch < Gk. *hapsis* a fastening, loop, wheel < *haptein* fasten]

ap·si·dal (ap′sə·dəl) *adj*. Of, pertaining to, like, or having an apse, apses, or apsides.

ap·sis (ap′sis) *n. pl.* **ap·si·des** (ap′sə·dēz) 1 *Astron.*

A point of an eccentric orbit that is nearest to or farthest from the center of attraction, as the aphelion or perihelion of a planet. 2 *Geom.* The line joining these points to form the major axis of an ellipse. 3 An apse. 4 A reliquary. [< L. See APSE.]

apt (apt) *adj*. 1 Having a natural or habitual tendency; liable; likely. 2 Quick to learn; skilful. 3 Pertinent; apposite. [< L *aptus* fitted, suited] —**apt′ly** *adv.* —**apt′ness** *n*.

Synonyms: liable, likely. *Apt* inclines toward the meaning of *likely* and suggests an inherent inclination or ability. The distinction between *likely* and *liable* is that *likely* looks upon the probable event as favorable, *liable* as unfavorable; *likely* to succeed; *liable* to fail. See APPROPRIATE, CLEVER, LIKELY, SAGACIOUS.

Ap·ter·a (ap′tər·ə) *n. pl.* An order of small, primitive, wingless insects, formerly inclusive of many species now assigned to other orders. [< NL < Gk. *apteros* wingless < *a-* without + *pteron* wing]

ap·ter·al (ap′tər·əl) *adj*. 1 *Entomol.* Apterous. 2 *Archit.* Having no lateral ranges of columns, as a temple.

ap·ter·ous (ap′tər·əs) *adj*. 1 *Entomol.* Lacking wings, as the silverfish and other thysanurans. 2 *Bot.* Having no winglike expansions, as on a petiole or stem.

ap·ter·yx (ap′tər·iks) *n*. A New Zealand bird (genus *Apteryx*) with undeveloped wings, now nearly extinct. See KIWI. [< NL < Gk. *a-* without + *pteryx* wing] —**ap·ter·yg·i·al** (ap′tə·rij′ē·əl) *adj*.

ap·ti·tude (ap′tə·tōod, -tyōod) *n*. 1 Natural or acquired adaptation, bent, or gift: an *aptitude* for being a gracious host. 2 General fitness. 3 Quickness of understanding; readiness: an *aptitude* for spelling. Also **apt′ness.** See synonyms under ABILITY, DEXTERITY. [< F < LL *aptitudo* < L *aptus* fitted, suited. Doublet of ATTITUDE.]

aptitude test *Psychol.* A test designed to indicate the ability or fitness of an individual to engage successfully in any of a number of specialized activities.

Ap·u·lei·us (ap′yə·lē′əs), **Lucius**, second century Roman satirist and philosopher.

A·pu·lia (ə·pyōō′lyə) A region of SE Italy; 7,469 square miles. *Italian* **Pu·glia** (pōō′lyä).

aq·ua (ak′wə· ā′kwə) *n. pl. for def.* 1 **aq·uae** (ak′wē, ā′kwē) or **aq·uas**, *for def.* 2 **aq·uas** 1 Water. 2 A light bluish-green color; aquamarine. —*adj.* Light bluish-green. [< L]

aq·ua·cul·ture (ak′wə·kul′chər) *n*. The growing of plants or animals, especially fish or shellfish, in a body of water.

aqua for·tis (fôr′tis) Commercial nitric acid. Also **aq′ua·for′tis** *n*. [< L, strong water]

Aq·ua·lung (ak′wə·lung′) *n*. An underwater breathing apparatus or scuba: a trade name. Also **aq′ua·lung′.**

aq·ua·ma·rine (ak′wə·mə·rēn′) *n*. 1 A sea-green variety of precious beryl. 2 A bluish-green color. —*adj.* Bluish-green. [< L *aqua marina* sea water]

aq·ua·naut (ak′wə·nôt) *n*. One who explores or performs tasks underwater and is trained and equipped to live underwater over a period of time. [< L *aqua* water + -*naut* (< Gk. *nautēs* sailor), on analogy with *aeronaut, astronaut*]

aq·ua·plane (ak′wə·plān′) *n*. A board on which one stands while being towed over water by a motorboat. —*v.i.* -**planed,** -**plan·ing** To ride on aquaplane.

aq·ua·relle (ak′wə·rel′) *n*. A kind of painting in transparent water colors. [< F < Ital. *acquerella* water color, dim. of *acqua* water < L *aqua*] —**aq′ua·rel′list** *n*.

a·quar·i·um (ə·kwâr′ē·əm) *n. pl.* **a·quar·i·ums** or **a·quar·i·a** (ə·kwâr′ē·ə) 1 A tank, pond, or the like for the exhibition or study of aquatic animals or plants. 2 A public building containing such an exhibition. [< L, neut. sing. of *aquarius* pertaining to water < *aqua* water]

A·quar·i·us (ə·kwâr′ē·əs) 1 The eleventh sign of the zodiac, the Water-bearer. 2 A constellation of the zodiac. See CONSTELLATION. [< L]

a·quat·ic (ə·kwat′ik, ə·kwot′-) *adj*. Pertaining to, living or growing in, or adapted to water. Also **a·quat′i·cal.** — *n*. 1 An aquatic animal or plant. 2

pl. Aquatic sports, as boating, etc. [< L *aquaticus* < *aqua* water]

aq·ua·tint (ak′wə·tint′) *n*. A form of engraving differing from an etching in that spaces instead of, or as well as, lines are bitten in by acid to give the effect of washes or tints in monochrome; also, an engraving printed from a plate so prepared. [< F *aquatinte* < Ital. *acqua tinta* dyed water < L *aqua tincta*]

a·qua·vit (ä′kwə·vēt) *n*. A Scandinavian liquor distilled from a grain or potato mash and flavored with caraway seed. Also **ak·va·vit** (äk′vä·vēt).

aqua vi·tae (vī′tē) 1 Alcohol. 2 Distilled spirits; whisky; brandy. [< L, water of life]

aq·ue·duct (ak′wə·dukt) *n*. 1 A water-conduit, particularly one for supplying a community from a distance. 2 A structure supporting a canal carried across a river or over low ground. 3 *Anat.* Any of several canals through which body liquids are conducted: the Fallopian *aqueduct*. [< L *aquaeductus* < *aqua* water + *ductus*, pp. of *ducere* lead]

a·que·ous (ā′kwē·əs, ak′wē-) *adj*. Pertaining to, made with, formed by, or containing water; watery.

aqueous humor *Physiol.* A clear, limpid, alkaline fluid that fills the anterior chamber of the eye from the cornea to the crystalline lens.

aqueous tension *Physics* The partial pressure due to the water vapor mixed with a gas measured over water. It is definite for each temperature.

aqui- *combining form* Water: *aquiferous*. [< L *aqua*]

aq·ui·cul·ture (ak′wi·kul′chər, ā′kwi-) *n*. Aquaculture.

aq·ui·fer (ak′wə·fər) *n. Geol.* Any water-bearing formation or group of formations, especially one that supplies ground water, wells, or springs.

a·quif·er·ous (ə·kwif′ər·əs) *adj*. Conveying or supplying water or watery fluid.

aq·ui·form (ak′wə·fôrm, ā′kwə-) *adj*. Like water; liquid.

aq·ui·fuge (ak′wə·fyōoj) *n. Geol.* A rock formation or structure which will neither absorb nor transmit water. [< AQUI- + L *fugere* flee]

A·qui·nas (ə·kwī′nəs), **Saint Thomas,** 1225?-1274, Italian Dominican monk and theologian.

Aq·ui·taine (ak′wə·tān′) A region of SW France; formerly a duchy, an independent kingdom, and the province of Guienne. Ancient **Aq·ui·ta·ni·a** (ak′wə·tā′nē·ə).

a·quose (ā′kwōs, ə·kwōs′) *adj*. Aqueous; watery.

a·quos·i·ty (ə·kwos′ə·tē) *n*. Moistness; wateriness.

ar (är) See ARE[2].

Ar *Chem.* Argon (symbol Ar).

ar- Assimilated var. of AD-.

-ar[1] *suffix* 1 Pertaining to; like: *regular, singular.* 2 The person or thing pertaining to: *scholar.* [ME -*er* < OF -*er*, F -*aire*, -*ier* < L -*aris* (in nouns -*are*), used for -*alis* when preceded by *l*]

-ar[2] *suffix* A form of -ARY, -ER[2]: refashioned in imitation of -AR[1]: *vicar*, ME *vicary, viker.*

-ar[3] *suffix* A form of -ER[1]: refashioned in imitation of -AR[2]: *pedlar.*

Ar·ab (ar′əb) *n*. 1 A native or inhabitant of Arabia. 2 One of a Semitic people inhabiting Arabia from ancient times, commonly the nomadic Bedouins: now scattered and admixed with various other native peoples. 3 A horse of a graceful, intelligent breed originally native to Arabia. 4 A homeless street wanderer, especially a child; a street Arab. —*adj.* Arabian.

ar·a·besque (ar′ə·besk′) *n*.
1 An ornament or design, as those used in Arabian or Moorish architecture, employing patterns of intertwined scrollwork, conventionalized leaves or flowers, etc., painted or sculptured in low relief. 2 In ballet, a position in which the dancer extends one leg straight backward,

ARABESQUE

one arm forward, and the other arm backward. **3** *Music* A short, lively composition in rondo form. —*adj.* Relating to, executed in, or resembling arabesque; fanciful; ornamental. Also **ar′a·besk′**. [<F <Ital. *arabesco* <*Arabo* Arab]

A·ra·bi·a (ə·rā′bē·ə) A peninsula of SW Asia, between the Red Sea and the Persian Gulf; 1,000,000 square miles; anciently divided into **Arabia De·ser·ta** (di·zûr′tə), northern Arabia, **Arabia Fe·lix** (fē′liks), generally restricted to Yemen, and **Arabia Pe·trae·a** (pe·trē′ə), NW Arabia.

A·ra·bi·an (ə·rā′bē·ən) *adj.* Of or pertaining to Arabia or the Arabs. —*n.* **1** A native or inhabitant of Arabia. **2** An Arab (def. 3).

Arabian Desert 1 The desert in eastern Egypt between the Nile and the Gulf of Suez. **2** Popularly, the desert in northern Arabia.

Arabian Nights A collection of stories from Arabia, India, Persia, etc., dating from the tenth century A.D.: also called *The Thousand and One Nights.*

Arabian Sea A broad arm of the Indian Ocean, between Arabia and India.

Ar·a·bic (ar′ə·bik) *adj.* Of or pertaining to Arabia, the Arabs, their language, culture, etc. —*n.* The Southwest Semitic language of the Arabians, now widely spread among Moslem nations.

Arabic numerals The figures 1, 2, 3, 4, 5, 6, 7, 8, 9, and the zero (0). See NUMERAL.

ar·a·ble (ar′ə·bəl) *adj.* Capable of being plowed or cultivated. —*n.* Land fit for cultivation. [<L *arabilis* <*arare* plow] —**ar′a·bil′i·ty** *n.*

Arab League A confederation, established 1945, of the states of Iraq, Jordan (then *Trans-Jordan*), Lebanon, Saudi Arabia, the United Arab Republic (then *Egypt* and *Syria*), and Yemen; joined by 1959 by Libya, Morocco, Sudan, and Tunisia, and in 1961 by Kuwait.

Ar·a·by (ar′ə·bē) *Archaic* or *Poetic* Arabia.

a·ra·ceous (ə·rā′shəs) *adj.* Belonging to the arum family (*Araceae*) of plants, mainly tropical, and bearing flowers on a spadix which is usually surrounded by a spathe. [<AR(UM) + -ACEOUS]

A·rach·ne (ə·rak′nē) In Greek mythology, a Lydian girl who challenged Athena to a weaving contest and was changed by the goddess into a spider. [<L <Gk. *Arachnē* <*arachnē* spider]

a·rach·nid (ə·rak′nid) *n.* Any of a class (*Arachnida*) of arthropods, embracing the spiders, scorpions, harvestmen, mites, etc. [<NL *Arachnida* <Gk. *arachnē* spider] —**a·rach·ni·dan** (ə·rak′nə·dən) *adj.* & *n.*

a·rach·noid (ə·rak′noid) *adj.* **1** Like a spider's web; thin and fine. **2** Of or pertaining to the arachnoid membrane or to the *Arachnida.* **3** *Bot.* Composed of slender entangled hairs; cobwebby. —*n.* One of the *Arachnida.* [<Gk. *arachnē* spider + -OID]

Ar·a·gon (ar′ə·gon) A region of NE Spain; 18,382 square miles; formerly an independent kingdom. *Spanish* **A·ra·gón** (ä′rä·gōn′).

Ar·a·go·nese (ar′ə·gə·nēz′, -nēs′) *adj.* Of or pertaining to Aragon, its people, or their language. —*n. pl.* **·nese 1** A native or inhabitant of Aragon. **2** The dialect of Spanish spoken in Aragon.

Ar·al Sea A salt inland sea, bordered by Kazakhstan and Uzbekistan in Asia; one of the world's largest inland seas; 74,635 square miles. Also **Lake of Aral.**

Ar·am (âr′əm), **Eugene,** 1704–59, English philologist; executed for murder.

Ar·am (âr′əm) The Biblical name of an ancient country of SW Asia, generally identified with Syria. Also **Ar·a·me·a** (ar′ə·mē′ə).

Ar·a·ma·ic (ar′ə·mā′ik) *n.* **1** Any of a group of Northwest Semitic languages, embracing Biblical Aramaic (erroneously, Chaldee), Syriac, etc. **2** The language of the Jews in Palestine after the captivity and that spoken by Christ and his disciples. Also **Aramean.** —*adj.* Aramean.

Ar·a·me·an (ar′ə·mē′ən) *adj.* Of or pertaining to ancient Aram or Aramea, or its peoples, languages, etc. —*n.* **1** An inhabitant of Aram. **2** The Aramaic language, especially in the broad sense. See ARAMAIC. Also **Ar·a·mae′an.**

A·ra·ne·ae (ə·rā′ni·ē) *n. pl.* An order of arachnids; the spiders. [<L *aranea* spider]

a·ra·ne·ous (ə·rā′nē·əs) *adj.* Made up of or covered with slender tangled hairs; cobwebby. Also **a·ra′ne·ose** (-ōs).

A·rap·a·ho (ə·rap′ə·hō) *n. pl.* **·ho** or **·hoes** An Indian of a nomadic tribe of Algonquian stock. Also **A·rap′a·hoe.**

Ar·a·rat (ar′ə·rat), **Mount** The highest peak in eastern Turkey; 16,945 feet; traditional resting place of Noah's ark. *Gen* viii 4. *Turkish* **Ağ·ri Da·ği** (ä·ri′ dä·i′).

A·ra·wak (ä′rä·wäk) *n.* Arawakan.

A·ra·wa·kan (ä′rä·wä′kən) *n.* **1** The most widely spread South American Indian linguistic stock, found from the headwaters of the Paraguay River, in southern Bolivia, to the northernmost part of the South American continent, and throughout the Antilles. **2** A member of any of the tribes speaking these languages. Also *Arawak.* —*adj.* Of or pertaining to this linguistic stock.

ar·ba·lest (är′bə·list) *n.* A medieval crossbow requiring a mechanical appliance to bend it.

ARBALEST
With windlass for winding back bowstring.

Also **ar′ba·list.** [<OF *arbaleste* <L *arcuballista* <*arcus* a bow + *ballista.* See BALLISTA.] —**ar′ba·lest′er** *n.*

ar·bi·ter (är′bə·tər) *n.* **1** A chosen or appointed judge or umpire, as between parties in a dispute. **2** One who has matters under his sole control; an absolute and final judge. See synonyms under JUDGE. [<L, one who goes to see, a witness, judge <*ad-* to + *bitere, betere* go]

ar·bi·tra·ble (är′bə·trə·bəl) *adj.* Subject to, capable of, or suitable for arbitration.

ar·bi·trage (är′bə·trij, är′bə·träzh′) *n.* **1** The simultaneous buying and selling of the same thing, as stocks or bonds, in different markets, in order to profit by the difference between the prices ruling in such markets. **2** Arbitration. [<F <*arbitrer* arbitrate] —**ar·bi·trag·ist** (är′bə·trə·jist) *n.*

ar·bi·tral (är′bə·trəl) *adj.* Pertaining to an arbitrator or arbitration; subject to arbitration.

ar·bi·tra·ment (är·bit′rə·mənt) *n.* **1** The act of deciding by arbitration, or the decision of an arbitrator; an award. **2** Absolute and final decision by any power or authority to which a contest has been or may be appealed; also, the power or right to make such decision. Also **ar·bit′re·ment.** [<OF *arbitrement* <*arbitrer.* See ARBITRATE.]

ar·bi·trar·y (är′bə·trer′ē) *adj.* **1** Based on mere opinion or prejudice; capricious. **2** Absolute; despotic. **3** *Law* Not determined by statute; discretionary. [<L *arbitrarius* <*arbiter.* See ARBITER.] —**ar′bi·trar′i·ly** *adv.* —**ar′bi·trar′i·ness** *n.*

Synonyms: absolute, despotic, dictatorial, domineering, harsh, imperious, irresponsible, overbearing, peremptory, tyrannical, tyrannous. See ABSOLUTE, IMPERIOUS. *Antonyms:* constitutional, equitable, free, lenient, limited, mild, obliging, restrained, restricted.

ar·bi·trate (är′bə·trāt) *v.t.* & *v.i.* **·trat·ed, ·trat·ing 1** To submit to or settle by arbitration. **2** To act as judge or arbitrator, as for a case. [<L *arbitratus*, pp. of *arbitrari* <*arbiter.* See ARBITER.] —**ar′bi·tra′tive** *adj.*

ar·bi·tra·tion (är′bə·trā′shən) *n.* The hearing and settlement of a dispute between two parties by the decision of a third party or court to which the matter is referred by the contestants as a means of avoiding war, a strike, a lawsuit, etc. See CONCILIATION,

MEDIATION.

ar·bi·tra·tor (är′bə·trā′tər) *n.* **1** A person chosen by agreement of parties to decide a dispute between them. **2** One empowered to decide a matter; an arbiter. See synonyms under JUDGE. [<L]

ar·bor[1] (är′bər) *n.* **1** A bower, as of latticework, supporting vines or trees; a place shaded by trees. **2** *Obs.* An orchard. Also *Brit.* **ar′bour.** [Earlier *erber, herber* <AF, var. of OF *erbier, herbier* <L *herbarium* a collection of herbs <*herba* grass, herb]

ar·bor[2] (är′bər) *n. pl.* **ar·bo·res** (är′bər·ēz) *for defs.* 1 and 3, **ar·bors** *for def.* 2. **1** A tree: used chiefly in botanical names. **2** *Mech.* **a** A shaft, mandrel, spindle, or axle, as of a circular saw, lathe, or watch wheel. **b** A principal support of a machine. **3** A pictured genealogical tree. [<L, tree]

ar·bo·re·al (är·bôr′ē·əl, -bō′rē-) *adj.* **1** Of or pertaining to a tree or trees; arborescent. **2** Living or situated among trees.

ar·bo·re·ous (är·bôr′ē·əs, -bō′rē-) *adj.* **1** Of the nature of or like a tree. **2** Forming a tree trunk, as distinguished from a shrub. **3** Having many trees; wooded.

ar·bo·res·cent (är′bə·res′ənt) *adj.* Treelike in character, appearance, or size; branching. —**ar′bo·res′cence** *n.*

ar·bo·re·tum (är′bə·rē′təm) *n. pl.* **·tums** or **·ta** (-tə) A botanical garden exhibiting trees for their scientific interest and educational value, and in association with appropriate wildlife features. [<L <*arbor* tree]

arbori- *combining form* Tree: *arboriform.* [<L *arbor* tree]

ar·bo·ri·cul·ture (är′bə·ri·kul′chər) *n.* The cultivation of trees or shrubs. —**ar′bo·ri·cul′tur·al** *adj.* —**ar′bo·ri·cul′tur·ist** *n.*

ar·bo·ri·form (är′ber·ə·fôrm, är·bôr′ə-, är·bor′ə-) *adj.* Formed like a tree.

ar·bor·i·za·tion (är′bər·ə·zā′shən, -i·zā′-) *n.* The formation of a treelike arrangement or figure, as in some minerals and fossils.

ar·bor·ous (är′bər·əs) *adj.* Of, pertaining to, or formed by trees.

arc (ärk) *n.* **1** Anything in the shape of an arch, of a curve, or of a part of a circle; a bow; arch. **2** *Geom.* A part of any algebraic curve, especially of a circle. **3** *Electr.* The bow of flame occurring in an arc light. **4** *Astron.* A part of the apparent path of a heavenly body. —*v.i.* **arcked** or **arced** (ärkt), **arck·ing** or **arc·ing** (är′king) *Electr.* To form a voltaic arc. ◆ Homophone: *ark.* [<L *arcus* bow, arch. Doublet of ARCH[1].]

ar·cade (är·kād′) *n.* **1** *Archit.* **a** A vaulted roof. **b** An ornamental series or range of arches with their supporting columns or piers, standing against the face of a wall (**blind arcade**) or free, as a support of a ceiling, roof, etc. **2** A roofed passageway or street, especially one having shops, etc., opening from it. **3** An avenue of trees, statues, etc. —*v.t.* **·cad·ed, ·cad·ing** To furnish with or form into an arcade or arcades. [<F <Med.L *arcata* <L *arcus* bow, arch]

Ar·ca·di·a (är·kā′dē·ə) **1** A nome of central Peloponnesus, Greece, traditionally associated with the pastoral pursuits of its ancient inhabitants. **2** Hence, any region of ideal rustic simplicity and contentment. *Modern Greek* **Ar·ka·dhi·a** (är·kä·thē′ä).

Ar·ca·di·an (är·kā′dē·ən) *adj.* **1** Of or pertaining to Arcadia. **2** Ideally rural or simple; pastoral. —*n.* **1** A native of or dweller in Arcadia. **2** One with simple, pastoral tastes.

Ar·ca·dy (är′kə·dē) *Archaic* or *Poetic* Arcadia.

ar·cane (är·kān′) *adj.* Secret; hidden. [<L *arcanus.* See ARCANUM.]

ar·ca·num (är·kā′nəm) *n. pl.* **·na** (-nə) **1** An inner secret or mystery. **2** One of the great secrets of nature which the alchemists sought to discover. **3** A secret remedy; an elixir. [<L, neut. of *arcanus* hidden <*arca* chest]

ar·ca·ture (är′kə·chŏŏr) *n.* **1** A small arcade formed by a series of little arches. **2** A blind arcade, used merely for ornament.

arc-bou·tant (ár·bŏŏ·tän′) *n. pl.* **arcs-bou·tants** (är·bŏŏ·tän′) *French* An arched buttress.

arch[1] (ärch) *n.* **1** A curved structure spanning an opening, formed of wedge-shaped parts resting on supports at the two extremities. **2** Any similar structure or object; an archway.

TYPES OF ARCHES

3 The form of an arch; a bowlike curve. **4** *Mech.* The height within the curve of an arched body, as through the central portion of a leaf spring. **5** *Aeron.* **a** The curve of a surface from front to rear. **b** A curved wing tip. **6** *Anat.* A curved or archlike part: the dental arch. **7** One of the major patterns into which all fingerprints are divided: subclassed as *plain, tented,* and *exceptional.* —*v.t.* **1** To cause to form an arch or arches. **2** To furnish with an arch or arches. **3** To span; extend over, as an arch. —*v.i.* **4** To form an arch or arches. [< OF *arche* < Med. L. *arca* < L *arcus* bow, arch. Doublet of ARC.]

arch² (ärch) *adj.* **1** Cunning; roguish; sly; coy. **2** Most eminent; chief. [< ARCH-] —**arch′ly** *adv.* —**arch′ness** *n.*

arch- *prefix* **1** Chief; principal: *archchancellor.* **2** Very great; extreme: *archknave.* Also *archi-,* as in *archidiaconal.* [OE *arce-, erce-* < L *arch-, arche-, archi-* < Gk. *archos* ruler]

Ar·chae·an (är·kē′ən) See ARCHEAN.

archaeo- See ARCHEO-.

ar·chae·ol·o·gy (är′kē·ol′ə·jē), etc. See AR-CHEOLOGY, etc.

ar·chae·op·ter·yx (är′kē·op′tər·iks) *n.* A representative of a genus (*Archaeopteryx*) of fossil reptilian birds of the Upper Jurassic period, combining reptilian and avian characteristics. Also **ar′che·op′ter·yx.** [< NL < ARCHAEO- + Gk. *pteryx* wing]

ar·cha·ic (är·kā′ik) *adj.* **1** Belonging to a former period; no longer in use; antiquated. **2** Characterizing a word, an inflectional form, or a phrase found only in the older literature and in the Bible, but no longer in current use. Also **ar·cha′i·cal.** [< Gk. *archaikos* < *archaios* ancient]

ar·cha·ism (är′kē·iz′əm, -kā-) *n.* **1** An archaic word, idiom, or expression. **2** Archaic style or usage.

ar·cha·ist (är′kē·ist, -kā-) *n.* **1** One who uses or affects archaisms or the archaic. **2** One who studies antiquities; an archeologist.

ar·cha·is·tic (är′kē·is′tik, -kā-) *adj.* Of, pertaining to, or imitating the archaic; inclined to, characterized by, or affecting archaism.

ar·cha·ize (är′kē·īz, -kā-) *v.* **·ized, ·iz·ing** *v.t.* To make archaic or archaistic. —*v.i.* To use archaisms. Also *Brit.* **ar′cha·ise.** —**ar′cha·iz′er** *n.*

arch·an·gel (ärk′ān′jəl) *n.* **1** An angel of highest rank; in Christian legend one of seven, in the Koran one of four, chief angels. **2** The garden angelica. —**the Archangel** In Christian legend, usually Michael. [< L *archangelus* < Gk. *archangelos* < *arch-* chief + *angelos* angel] — **arch·an·gel·ic** (ärk′an·jel′ik) or **·i·cal** *adj.*

arch·bish·op (ärch′bish′əp) *n.* The chief bishop of an ecclesiastical province.

arch·bish·op·ric (ärch′bish′əp·rik) *n.* **1** The office, rank, term of office, or jurisdiction of an archbishop. **2** The ecclesiastical province over which an archbishop has jurisdiction.

arch·dea·con (ärch′dē′kən) *n. Eccl.* A church official who administers the property, temporal affairs, missionary work, etc., of a diocese under powers delegated from the bishop: chiefly an Anglican usage.

arch·dea·con·ate (ärch′dē′kən·it) *n.* The jurisdiction of an archdeacon.

arch·dea·con·ry (ärch′dē′kən·rē) *n. pl.* **·ries 1** The title, office, or dignity of an archdeacon. **2** An archdeacon's residence. Also **arch′dea′-con·ship.**

arch·di·o·cese (ärch′dī′ə·sēs, -sis) *n.* The diocese or jurisdiction of an archbishop.

arch·du·cal (ärch′doo′kəl, -dyoo′-) *adj.* Of or pertaining to an archduke or an archduchy.

arch·duch·ess (ärch′duch′is) *n.* **1** A princess of the former imperial family of Austria. **2** The wife or widow of an archduke.

arch·duch·y (ärch′duch′ē) *n. pl.* **·duch·ies** The territory ruled by an archduke. Also **arch′-duke′dom.**

arch·duke (ärch′dook′, -dyook′) *n.* A chief duke, especially a prince of the former imperial family of Austria.

Ar·che·an (är·kē′ən) *adj. Geol.* Pertaining to a rock group associated with the Archeozoic era of earth's history, consisting of the oldest stratified rocks, predominantly igneous and without fossil remains. Also **Ar·chae′an.** [< Gk. *archaios* ancient < *archē* beginning]

arched (ärcht) *adj.* **1** Having the form of an arch; characterized by arches. **2** Covered or furnished with arches.

arch-en·e·my (ärch′en′ə·mē) *n. pl.* **·mies 1** Satan. **2** The principal enemy.

ar·chen·ter·on (är·ken′tər·on) *n. Biol.* The primitive enteron or alimentary cavity. [< ARCH(I)- + Gk. *enteron* intestine] —**ar·chen·ter·ic** (är′ken·ter′ik) *adj.*

archeo- *combining form* Ancient: *Archeozoic.* Also *archaeo-* [< Gk. *archaios* ancient]

ar·che·o·as·tron·o·my (är′kē·ō·ə·stron′ə·mē) *n.* The astronomy of ancient cultures as deduced from archeological evidence.

ar·che·ol·o·gy (är′kē·ol′ə·jē) *n.* The science or study of history from the evidence of the relics and remains of early human cultures as discovered chiefly by systematic excavations: also spelled *archaeology.* —**ar·che·o·log·i·cal** (är′kē·ə·loj′i·kəl) or **·log′ic** *adj.* —**ar′che·ol′o·gist** (-jist) *n.*

ar·che·op·ter·yx (är′kē·op′tər·iks) See ARCHAE-OPTERYX.

Ar·che·o·zo·ic (är′kē·ə·zō′ik) *n. Geol.* The oldest of the eras making up the geological record. See chart under GEOLOGY. —*adj.* Belonging to or indicating this era. Also spelled *Archaeozoic* [< ARCHEO- + Gk. *zōon* animal]

arch·er (är′chər) *n.* One who shoots with a bow and arrow. [< OF *archier* < L *arcarius* bowman < *arcus* bow]

Arch·er (är′chər) The tenth sign of the zodiac. See SAGITTARIUS.

arch·er·fish (är′chər·fish′) *n. pl.* **·fish** or **·fish·es** A percomorph fish (*Toxotes jaculator*) of India and Polynesia, with the ability to shoot drops of water to bring down its insect prey.

arch·er·y (är′chər·ē) *n.* **1** The art or sport of shooting with the bow and arrows. **2** The weapons and outfit of the archer. **3** Archers collectively.

ar·che·type (är′kə·tīp) *n.* An original or standard pattern or model; a prototype. See synonyms under EXAMPLE, IDEA, IDEAL, MODEL. [< L *archetypum* < Gk. *archetypon* pattern, model < *arche-* first + *typos* stamp, pattern] —**ar′che·typ′al** or **ar′che·typ′ic** (-tip′ik) or **·i·cal** *adj.*

arch·fiend (ärch′fēnd′) *n.* A chief fiend; specifically, Satan.

archi- *prefix* **1** Var. of ARCH-. **2** *Biol.* Original; primitive: *archiblast.* [See ARCH-]

ar·chi·blast (är′kə·blast) *n. Biol.* **1** The primitive portion of the blastoderm or germinal disk. **2** The epiblast. [< ARCHI- + Gk. *blastos* germ]

ar·chi·di·ac·o·nal (är′ki·dī·ak′ə·nəl) *adj.* Pertaining to an archdeacon or an archdeaconry.

ar·chi·di·ac·o·nate (är′ki·dī·ak′ə·nāt) *n.* The office of an archdeacon.

ar·chi·e·pis·co·pa·cy (är′kē·i·pis′kə·pə·sē) *n. pl.* **·cies** The rank and rule of an archbishop. Also **ar′chi·e·pis′co·pate** (-pāt).

ar·chi·e·pis·co·pal (är′kē·i·pis′kə·pəl) *adj.* Of or pertaining to an archbishop, his office, or residence.

ar·chi·mage (är′kə·māj) *n.* **1** A chief magician; great wizard. **2** The chief priest of the Persian fire-worshipers. Also **ar·chi·ma·gus** (är′kə·mā′gəs). [< ARCHI- + Gk. *magos* magician]

Ar·chi·me·de·an (är′kə·mē′dē·ən, -mə·dē′ən) *adj.* Of, discovered by, or pertaining to Archimedes.

Archimedean screw *Mech.* A spiral conduit about an inclined axis, for raising liquid by rotation. Also **Ar·chimedes′ screw.**

ARCHIMEDEAN SCREW

Ar·chi·me·des (är′kə·mē′dēz), 287?–212 B.C., Greek mathematician; born in Sicily.

ar·chi·mime (är′kə·mīm) *n.* In ancient Rome, the actor who impersonated the leading roles of satirical dramas.

arch·ing (är′ching) *n.* **1** An arch or series of arches. **2** The building of arches. **3** Any curve.

ar·chi·pel·a·go (är′kə·pel′ə·gō) *n. pl.* **·goes** or **·gos** A sea studded with many islands, or the islands collectively. [< Ital. *arcipelago,* ult. < Gk. *archi-* chief + *pelagos* sea; with ref. to the Aegean Sea] —**ar·chi·pe·lag·ic** (är′kə·pə·laj′ik) *adj.*

Ar·chi·pel·a·go (är′kə·pel′ə·gō) The ancient name for the AEGEAN SEA.

ar·chi·tect (är′kə·tekt) *n.* **1** One whose profession is to design and draw up the plans for buildings, etc., and supervise their construction. **2** One who devises, plans, or creates anything. [< L *architectus* < Gk. *architektōn* < *archi-* chief + *tektōn* worker]

ar·chi·tec·ton·ic (är′kə·tek·ton′ik) *adj.* **1** Pertaining to architecture; constructive. **2** *Philos.* Relating to the scientific classification of knowledge. Also **ar′chi·tec·ton′i·cal.** [< L *architectonicus* < Gk. *architektonikos* < *architektōn.* See ARCHITECT.]

ar·chi·tec·ton·ics (är′kə·tek·ton′iks) *n. pl.* (construed as singular) **1** The science of architecture. **2** *Philos.* The scientific arrangement and construction of systems of knowledge. **3** Structural design, as in works of music or art.

ar·chi·tec·ture (är′kə·tek′chər) *n.* **1** The science, art, or profession of designing and constructing buildings or other structures. **2** A style or system of building: Gothic *architecture.* **3** Construction or structure generally; any ordered arrangement of the parts of a system: the *architecture* of the universe. **4** A building, or buildings collectively. [< F < L *architectura* < *architectus.* See ARCHITECT.] —**ar′chi·tec′tur·al** *adj.* —**ar′-chi·tec′tur·al·ly** *adv.*

ar·chi·trave (är′kə·trāv) *n. Archit.* **1** A chief beam; that part of an entablature which rests upon the column heads and supports the frieze. See illustration under ENTABLATURE. **2** A molded ornament, as of an arch; the archivolt, or the ornament skirting the head and sides of a door or window. [< F < Ital. < *archi-* chief (< Gk.) + *trave* beam < L *trabs*]

ar·chi·val (är·kī′vəl) *adj.* Of, pertaining to, or contained in archives.

ar·chives (är′kīvz) *n. pl.* **1** A place where public records and historical documents are kept. **2** Public records, documents, etc., as kept in such a depository. See synonyms under HISTORY. [< F *archives,* pl. of *archif* < L *archivum* < Gk. *archeion* a public office < *archē* government]

ar·chi·vist (är′kə·vist) *n.* A keeper of archives.

ar·chiv·ol·o·gy (är′kiv·ol′ə·jē) *n.* The science of maintaining and cataloging public documents. —**ar′chiv·ol′o·gist** *n.*

ar·chi·volt (är′kə·vōlt) *n. Archit.* **1** An ornamental molding following the outer curve of an arch. **2** An arch considered as supporting superincumbent weight. Also **ar′chi·vault** (-vôlt). [< Ital. *archivolto* an arched vault]

arch·let (ärch′lit) *n.* A little arch.

ar·chon (är′kon) *n.* **1** One of the nine chief magistrates of ancient Athens. **2** One of various magistrates or other officials in the Byzantine empire and modern Greece. **3** Any ruler or supreme commander. [< Gk. *archōn* < *archein* rule]

---

add,āce,câre,pälm; end,ēven; it,īce; odd,ōpen,ôrder; took,pool; up,bûrn; ə = a in *above,* e in *sicken,* i in *clarity,* o in *melon,* u in *focus* ; yoo = u in *fuse,* oi,oil; ou,pout; ch,check; g,go; ng,ring; th,thin; th,this; zh,vision. Foreign sounds à,œ,ü,kh,ṅ; and ✦: see page xx. < *from* ; + *plus* ; ? *possibly.*

ar·chon·ship (är'kon·ship) *n.* The office or official term of an archon. Also **ar·chon·tate** (är'kən·tāt).

arch·priest (ärch'prēst') *n.* **1** Formerly, the chief or senior priest of a cathedral chapter, serving as assistant to a bishop: later called a *dean.* **2** A rural dean. **3** A papal delegate appointed in 1598 as superior of Roman Catholic clergy in England: succeeded in 1623 by a vicar apostolic. —**arch'priest'hood, arch'priest'ship** *n.*

arch·way (ärch'wā') *n.* An entrance or passage under an arch.

-archy *combining form* Rule; government: *heptarchy,* government by seven. [<Gk. *-archia* < *archos* ruler]

ar·ci·form (är'sə·fôrm) *adj.* Shaped like an arc or bow. [<L *arcus* bow + -FORM]

arc light A lamp in which light of high intensity is produced between two adjacent electrodes connected with a powerful source of electricity. Also **arc lamp.**

ar·co·graph (är'kə·graf, -gräf) *n.* An instrument for drawing curves without striking them from a center point. [<L *arcus* arc + -GRAPH]

Arc·tal·pine (ärk·tal'pin) *adj.* **1** *Geog.* Of or pertaining to northern regions beyond the limits of tree growth; also, to mountain heights above the timber line. **2** *Ecol.* Designating those plant and animal forms which live beyond or above the limits of tree growth.

arc·tic (ärk'tik, är'tik) *adj.* **1** Pertaining to, suitable for, or characteristic of the North Pole or the regions, etc., near it. **2** Extremely cold; frigid. —*n.* **1** The region around the North Pole. **2** The Arctic Circle. **3** *pl. U.S.* Warm, waterproof overshoes. [Earlier *artik* <OF *artique* <L *articus, arcticus* <Gk. *arktikos* of the Bear (the northern constellation *Ursa Major*), northern < *arktos* bear]

Arctic Archipelago A north Canadian island group in the Arctic Ocean, comprising most of Franklin District, Northwest Territories. Also **Arctic Islands.**

Arctic Circle The boundary of the North Frigid Zone, 23° 28′ from the North Pole.

Arctic Ocean An almost landlocked sea north of the Arctic Circle and surrounding the North Pole; 5,440,000 square miles.

Arc·tu·rus (ärk·tŏor'əs, -tyŏor'-) One of the 20 brightest stars, 0.24 magnitude and of an orange color; Alpha in the constellation Boötes. See STAR. [<L <Gk. *Arktouros* guardian of the bear < *arktos* a bear + *ouros* a guard]

ar·cu·ate (är'kyŏo·it, -āt) *adj.* Bent or curved like a bow; arched. Also **ar'cu·at·ed.** [<L *arcuatus,* pp. of *arcuare* curve like a bow < *arcus* a bow]

ar·cu·a·tion (är'kyŏo·ā'shən) *n.* **1** The act of curving or bending, or the state of being bent. **2** *Archit.* The use of arches; arched work.

ar·cus (är'kəs) *n. Meteorol.* A cloud resembling an arch: seen usually in cumulonimbus clouds. [<L, arch]

-ard *suffix of nouns* One who does something to excess or who is to be disparaged: *drunkard, coward;* sometimes changed to -*art: braggart.* [<OF -*ard,* -*art* <G -*hard,* -*hart* hardy]

ar·den·cy (är'dən·sē) *n.* The quality of being ardent; ardor; intensity; warmth.

ar·dent (är'dənt) *adj.* **1** Vehement in emotion or action; passionate; zealous; intense. **2** Red; glowing; flashing. **3** On fire; burning. [<L *ardens, -entis,* ppr. of *ardere* burn] —**ar'dent·ly** *adv.* —**ar'dent·ness** *n.*

Synonyms: burning, eager, excitable, fervent, fervid, fierce, fiery, glowing, hot, impassioned, inflammable, intense, keen, longing, passionate, sanguine, vehement. See EAGER[1]. *Antonyms:* apathetic, calm, cold, cool, dispassionate, frigid, icy, indifferent, listless, phlegmatic, stolid, stony.

ardent spirits Alcoholic distilled liquors.

ar·dor (är'dər) *n.* **1** Warmth or intensity of passion or affection; eagerness; vehemence; zeal. **2** Great heat, as of fire, sun, or fever. Also *Brit.* **ar'dour.** See synonyms under ENTHUSIASM, WARMTH. [<L *ardor* < *ardere* burn]

ar·du·ous (är'jŏo·əs) *adj.* **1** Involving great labor, hardship, or difficulty; difficult. **2** Toiling strenuously; energetic. **3** Steep; hard to climb or surmount. [<L *arduus* steep] —**ar'du·ous·ly** *adv.* —**ar'du·ous·ness** *n.*

Synonyms: difficult, exhausting, hard, laborious, onerous, severe, toilsome, trying. *Hard* may

be active or passive; a thing may be *hard* to do or *hard* to bear. *Arduous* is always active. That which is *difficult* may require labor, or simply skill and address, as a *difficult* problem or puzzle. That which is *arduous* always requires persevering toil. *Antonyms:* easy, facile, light, pleasant, slight, trifling, trivial.

are[1] (är) *v.* First, second, and third person plural, present indicative, of the verb BE; also used as second person singular. [OE (Northumbrian) *aron*]

are[2] (âr, är) *n.* A measure of area in the metric system comprising a square dekameter or one hundred square meters. See METRIC SYSTEM. [<F <L *area.* Doublet of AREA.]

ar·e·a (âr'ē·ə) *n. pl.* **ar·e·as;** *for def. 6,* often **ar·e·ae** (âr'ē·ē) **1** Any open space. **2** A tract or portion of the earth's surface; region. **3** Superficial extent; total outside surface. See SQUARE MEASURE. **4** A yard of a building; areaway. **5** Figuratively, the extent of anything; scope. **6** *Anat.* A section of the cerebral cortex with a specific motor or sensory function. [<L, an open space of level ground. Doublet of ARE[2].] —**ar'e·al** *adj.*

area code A three-digit number that identifies one of the telephone areas into which the United States is divided.

ar·e·a·way (âr'ē·ə·wā') *n.* **1** A small sunken court before basement windows or passageway to a basement door. **2** A passageway, as from one building or part of a building to another.

ar·e·ic (ar'ē·ik) *adj. Geog.* Pertaining to or designating a region of the earth contributing little or no surface drainage, as the Sahara. [<L *arere* be dry]

a·re·na (ə·rē'nə) *n.* **1** The central space for contestants in a Roman amphitheater. **2** Any place like this: The football players came into the *arena.* **3** A sphere of action or contest. [<L, sand, sandy place]

ar·e·na·ceous (ar'ə·nā'shəs) *adj.* **1** Pertaining to or like sand. **2** Full of or growing in sand; sandy. [<L *arenaceus* < *arena* sand]

arena theater A stage in the center of a room or auditorium, surrounded by seats and with out proscenium: also called *theater-in-the-round, central staging.*

ar·e·nic·o·lous (ar'ə·nik'ə·ləs) *adj.* Living in sand. [<L *arena* sand + *colere* dwell]

aren't (ärnt) A contraction of *are not.* ◆ **Aren't I?** is condoned as a genteel colloquial substitute for the illiterate *Ain't I?,* though it is at variance with grammar.

areo- *combining form* Mars: *areography.* [<Gk. *Arēs*]

ar·e·o·cen·tric (âr'ē·ō·sen'trik) *adj.* Having reference to the planet Mars as a center or origin.

ar·e·og·ra·phy (âr'ē·og'rə·fē) *n.* A description of the physical features of the planet Mars.

a·re·o·la (ə·rē'ə·lə) *n. pl.* **·lae** (-lē) or **·las 1** *Bot.* A small space or interstice in a network of veins or vessels, as on leaves. **2** *Anat.* The colored circle about a nipple or about a vesicle; a depressed spot. Also **ar·e·ole** (âr'ē·ōl). [<L, dim. of *area* open space] —**a·re'o·lar** *adj.*

areolar tissue *Anat.* Connective tissue composed of loose meshes of fibers enclosing irregular cavities; cellular tissue.

a·re·o·late (ə·rē'ə·lit, -lāt) *adj.* Marked off into areolae. Also **a·re'o·lat·ed.**

a·re·o·la·tion (ə·rē'ə·lā'shən) *n.* **1** The state of being areolate. **2** The arrangement of areolae. **3** A space containing areolae.

ar·e·ol·o·gy (âr'ē·ol'ə·jē) *n.* The scientific study of the planet Mars in all its aspects.

Ar·e·op·a·gite (ar'ē·op'ə·jīt, -gīt) *n.* A member of the court of the Areopagus.

Ar·e·op·a·gus (ar'ē·op'ə·gəs) A hill NW of the Acropolis on which the highest court of ancient Athens held its sessions; hence, the court itself. [<L <Gk. *Areiopagos* < *Arēs* Mars + *pagos* hill]

Ar·es (âr'ēz) In Greek mythology, the god of war: identified with the Roman *Mars.*

a·rête (ə·rāt') *n. Geog.* A sharp mountain spur or ridge. [<F <L *arista* awn of wheat, fishbone]

ar·gent (är'jənt) *n.* **1** *Her.* The white color of armorial bearings, symbolic of purity, innocence, etc. **2** Silver. **3** Silvery quality or color; whiteness. —*adj.* Like or made of silver; white; silvery: also **ar·gen·tal** (är·jen'təl). [<F <L *argentum* silver] —**ar·gen·te·ous** (är·jen'tē·əs).

ar·gen·tan (är'jən·tən) *n.* German silver. [<L *argentum* silver]

ar·gen·tate (är'jən·tāt) *adj.* Silvery or shining

white.

ar·gen·ta·tion (är'jən·tā'shən) *n.* A coating or plating with silver.

ar·gen·tic (är·jen'tik) *adj.* Containing or pertaining to silver, especially in its higher valence or ordinary proportion: *argentic* chloride, AgCl.

ar·gen·tif·er·ous (är'jən·tif'ər·əs) *adj.* Containing or producing silver: *argentiferous* ore.

Ar·gen·ti·na (är'jən·tē'nə) A republic of southern South America between the Andes and the Atlantic; 1,073,699 square miles; capital, Buenos Aires. Also **Argentine Republic** or **the Argentine.**

ar·gen·tine (är'jən·tin, -tīn) *n.* **1** Silver-white metal. **2** A precipitate of tin and zinc. **3** A pearly calcite. **4** The silvery substance obtained from fish scales and used in making artificial pearls. **5** Silver. —*adj.* Silvery. [<F *argentin* < <*argentum* silver]

Ar·gen·tine (är'jən·tēn, -tīn) *adj.* Of or pertaining to Argentina. —*n.* A native or citizen of Argentina. —**Ar·gen·tin·an** (är'jən·tin'·ē·ən) *n.*

ar·gil (är'jil) *n.* **1** Potters' clay; white clay. **2** Aluminite. [<F *argile* <L *argilla* white clay <Gk. *argilla* < *argos* white] —**ar·gil·lif·er·ous** (är'jə·lif'ər·əs) *adj.*

ar·gil·la·ceous (är'jə·lā'shəs) *adj.* Containing, consisting of, or like clay; clayey.

ar·gil·lite (är'jə·līt) *n.* An argillaceous sedimentary rock, with or without slaty cleavage; mudrock: sometimes called *pelite* [<L *argilla* white clay + -ITE[1]]

ar·gil·lous (är·jil'əs) *adj.* Argillaceous; clayey.

ar·gi·nine (är'jə·nēn, -nin, -nīn) *n.* One of the amino acids essential to nutrition, $C_6H_{14}O_2N_4$, obtained from animal and vegetable proteins by hydrolysis or bacterial action. [<L *argentum* silver + -INE[2]]

Ar·gi·nu·sae (är'jə·nŏo'sē, -nyŏo'-) The ancient name of three islands between Lesbos and Asia Minor; site of a naval battle in which the Athenians defeated the Spartans in 406 B.C. Also **Ar'gi·nu'sæ.**

Ar·give (är'jiv, -giv) *adj.* **1** Of or pertaining to Argos or Argolis. **2** Greek. —*n.* **1** An inhabitant of Argos or Argolis. **2** A Greek, as in Homer.

ar·gle (är'gəl) *v.i. Scot.* To wrangle; argue. Also **ar'gle-bar'gle.**

Ar·go (är'gō) **1** In Greek legend, the ship in which Jason and the Argonauts sailed for the Golden Fleece. **2** *Astron.* A large southern constellation, the Ship, now generally divided into four parts.

ar·gol (är'gəl) *n.* Crude cream of tartar: the base of tartaric acid: also spelled *argal.* [ME *argoile;* origin unknown]

Ar·go·lis (är'gə·lis) A region of Greece in the NE Peloponnesus around the city of Argos, bordering on the **Gulf of Argolis,** an inlet of the Aegean.

ar·gon (är'gon) *n.* An inert gaseous element (symbol Ar, atomic number 18), constituting about 0.94% of the atmosphere. See PERIODIC TABLE. [<NL <Gk., neuter of *argos* idle, inert]

ar·go·naut (är'gə·nôt) *n. Zool.* The paper nautilus.

Ar·go·naut (är'gə·nôt) *n.* **1** In Greek legend, one who sailed with Jason in the ship Argo to find the Golden Fleece. **2** A gold-seeker who went to California in 1849. [<L *Argonauta* <Gk. *Argonautēs* <*Argo,* the ship + *nautēs* sailor] —**ar'go·nau'tic** *adj.*

Ar·gos (är'gos, -gəs) A city of NE Peloponnesus, traditionally the oldest city in Greece.

ar·go·sy (är'gə·sē) *n. pl.* **·sies 1** A large merchant ship. **2** A fleet of merchant vessels. [Earlier *ragusy* < *Ragusa,* Italian port which carried on extensive trade with England in the 16th C.]

ar·got (är'gō, -gət) *n.* **1** The secret language of the underworld. **2** The phraseology peculiar to any class or group. [<F] —**ar·got·ic** (är·got'ik) *adj.*

ar·gue (är'gyŏo) *v.* **ar·gued, ar·gu·ing** *v.i.* **1** To urge reasons to support or contest a measure or opinion; reason. **2** To dispute or quarrel: Are you trying to *argue* with me? **3** To reason in opposition; raise objections: Don't stand there *arguing*—do as I say! —*v.t.* **4** To urge reasons for or against; discuss, as a proposal. **5** To contend or maintain, as by giving reasons: to *argue* that all men are equal. **6** To prove or indicate, as from evidence: His manner of speaking *argued* a good education. **7** To influence or convince, as by argument: to *argue* someone into buying a house. [< OF *arguer* < L *argutare*, freq. of *arguere* make clear, prove] —**ar·gu·a·ble** *adj.* —**ar·gu·er** *n.*

Synonyms: debate, demonstrate, discuss, dispute, prove, question, reason. To *argue* is to show the reasons for or against, so as to make a matter clear by reasoning; to *discuss* is to shake a matter apart for examination or analysis: One may *argue* or *discuss* a matter by himself; or with advocates, to make all clear; or with opponents, to *prove* his position and answer objections. We *argue* a case, *dispute* a bill. One side may do all the *arguing*, in *debating* both sides take part. See DISPUTE, PLEAD, REASON.

ar·gu·fy (är'gyə·fī) *v.* ·**fied**, ·**fy·ing** *Colloq.* or *Dial.*—*v.t.* **1** To worry with arguing. —*v.i.* **2** To signify. **3** To argue, especially obstinately or merely for the sake of the argument. [< ARGUE + -FY]

ar·gu·ment (är'gyə·mənt) *n.* **1** A reason offered for or against something. **2** Something offered in proof; evidence. **3** A process of reasoning to establish or refute a position by the use of evidence; demonstration. **4** A contest in reasoning; debate; discussion. **5** *Logic* The middle term of a syllogism. **6** The plot or gist of a literary work. **7** *Stat.* A number given on the margin of a table to facilitate finding any of the included values. **8** *Math.* An independent variable from which another quantity can be deduced or on which its calculation depends. **9** *Obs.* The subject matter of a discourse or discussion; theme. See synonyms under REASON, REASONING. [< F < L *argumentum* < *arguere* make clear, prove]

ar·gu·men·ta·tion (är'gyə·men·tā'shən) *n.* **1** The methodical or logical setting forth of premises and the drawing of conclusions therefrom. **2** Interchange of argument; discussion; debate. **3** A sequence of arguments; process of reasoning.

ar·gu·men·ta·tive (är'gyə·men'tə·tiv) *adj.* Pertaining to, consisting of, or marked by argument; given to argumentation: an *argumentative* style. —**ar'gu·men'ta·tive·ly** *adv.* —**ar'gu·men'ta·tive·ness** *n.*

Ar·gus (är'gəs) In Greek mythology, a giant with a hundred eyes: killed by Hermes, after which his eyes were put into the peacock's tail.

Ar·gus-eyed (är'gəs·īd') *adj.* Sharp-sighted; vigilant.

ar·gute (är·gyōōt') *adj.* **1** Quick or subtle; sharp; shrewd. **2** Shrill of sound. **3** *Bot.* Sharp-toothed, as a serrate leaf. [< L *argutus*, pp. of *arguere* make clear, prove]

Ar·gyle plaid (är'gīl) Plaid design of solid blocks or diamonds overlaid by a contrasting plaid. [from the tartan of the clan Campbell of *Argyll*]

Ar·gyll (är·gīl') A country of western Scotland; 3,110 square miles. Also **Ar·gyll·shire** (är·gīl'·shir).

a·ri·a (ä'rē·ə, âr'ē·ə) *n.* **1** An air; melody. **2** An elaborate solo for single voice, as in an opera or oratorio, often with instrumental accompaniment. [< Ital. < L *aer* air]

-aria *suffix* Used in forming new Latin names, especially in zoological and botanical classifications. [< NL < L *-arius*]

Ar·i·ad·ne (ar'ē·ad'nē) In Greek mythology, the daughter of Minos and Pasiphae, who gave Theseus the thread by which he found his way out of the Labyrinth: when he fled Crete, Theseus took her with him, but later abandoned her on Naxos.

Ar·i·an (âr'ē·ən) *adj.* Of or pertaining to Arius or Arianism. —*n.* A believer in Arianism.

-arian *suffix* Used in forming adjectives and adjectival nouns denoting occupation, age, sect, beliefs, etc.: *nonagenarian*, *predestinarian*. [< L *-arius*-ary + *-anus*-an]

Ar·i·an·ism (âr'ē·ən·iz'əm) *n.* The doctrines of Arius (fourth century) and his followers, denying that Christ is one substance with the Father.

ar·id (ar'id) *adj.* **1** Parched with heat; dry. **2** Unfruitful; barren. **3** Without interest; dull. **4** Profitless. [< L *aridus* < *arere* be dry] —**a·rid·i·ty** (ə·rid'ə·tē), **ar'id·ness** *n.* —**ar'id·ly** *adv.*

ar·i·el (âr'ē·əl) *n.* An African gazelle (*Gazella dama*). Also **ariel gazelle.** [< Arabic *aryal*]

Ar·i·el (âr'ē·əl) A masculine personal name. [< Hebrew, lion of God]
—**Ariel** In medieval folklore, a spirit of the air.
—**Ariel** In Shakespeare's *Tempest*, an airy spirit employed by Prospero.

Ar·i·el (âr'ē·əl) The inner satellite of Uranus.

Ar·ies (âr'ēz, âr'ē·iz) **1** *Astron.* A constellation, the Ram. **2** In astrology, the first sign of the zodiac, which the sun enters on or about March 21st, the vernal equinox. See CONSTELLATION. [< L, the Ram]

ar·i·et·ta (ar'ē·et'ə) *n.* A short aria. Also **ar·i·ette** (ar'ē·et'). [< Ital.]

a·right (ə·rīt') *adv.* In a right way; correctly; rightly; exactly.

A·ri·ka·ra (ə·rē'kər·ə) *n.* A member of a North American Indian tribe of Caddoan linguistic stock, formerly inhabiting the Dakotas.

ar·il (ar'il) *n.* *Bot.* An accessory covering of a seed, orginating at or around the funiculus. [< NL < Med. L *arilli* dried grapes] —**ar·il·late** (ar'ə·lāt), **ar'il·lat'ed** *adj.*

Ar·i·ma·the·a (ar'ə·mə·thē'ə) A town of ancient Palestine, the home of Joseph, a disciple of Jesus, *Matt.* xxvii 57. Also **Ar'i·ma·thae'a.** —**Ar'·i·ma·the'an** *adj.*

ar·i·ose (ar'ē·ōs, ar'ē·ōs') *adj.* *Music* Characteristic of a melody; songlike. [< Ital. *arioso* < *aria* air]

a·ri·o·so (ä·ryō'sō) *adj.* & *adv.* *Music* Of the nature or in the manner of both recitative and aria: said of a passage of dramatic or declamatory character emphasized by the libretto. [< Ital.]

-arious *suffix of adjectives* Connected with; pertaining to: *gregarious*. [< L *-arius*-ary + -OUS]

a·rise (ə·rīz') *v.i.* **a·rose** (ə·rōz), **a·ris·en** (ə·riz'·ən), **a·ris·ing** **1** To get up, as from a prone position. **2** To rise; ascend, as the sun above the horizon. **3** To spring forth; originate, as a river from its source. **4** To be born; come into being; appear. **5** *Poetic* To revive from death. [OE *ārisan* < *ā-* up + *rīsan* rise]

aristo- *combining form* Best, finest: *aristocracy*. [< Gk. *aristos*]

ar·is·toc·ra·cy (ar'is·tok'rə·sē) *n. pl.* ·**cies** **1** A hereditary nobility or privileged class, preeminent by birth or privilege and having prescriptive rank and rights. **2** The chief persons of a country; hence, any group preeminent in any way, as by virtue of wealth, talent, etc. **3** A state ruled by its best citizens. **4** The ruling class in such a state. [< L *aristocratia* < Gk. *aristokratia* < *aristos* best + *kratein* rule]

a·ris·to·crat (ə·ris'tə·krat, ar'is·tə·krat') *n.* **1** A member of an aristocracy. **2** A proud and exclusive person. **3** One who prefers an aristocratic form of government. —**a·ris'to·crat'ic** or ·**i·cal** *adj.* —**a·ris'to·crat'i·cal·ly** *adv.*

Ar·is·to·te·li·an (ar'is·tə·tē'lē·ən, -tə·tēl'yən, ə·ris'tə-) *adj.* Pertaining to or characteristic of Aristotle or his philosophy. —*n.* An adherent of Aristotle or of Aristotelianism.

Ar·is·to·te·li·an·ism (ar'is·tə·tē'lē·ən·iz'əm, -tēl'yən-, ə·ris'tə-) *n.* The philosophy or doctrines of Aristotle, especially as distinguished from Platonism by empirical or deductive reasoning.

Aristotelian logic 1 The deductive logic of Aristotle, characterized by the syllogism. **2** Logic considered from the standpoint of the form, rather than the content, of propositions.

Ar·is·tot·le (ar'is·tot'l), 384–322 B.C., Greek philosopher; pupil of Plato.

Aristotle's lantern *Zool.* The skeleton of the mouth parts of a sea urchin.

ar·ith·man·cy (ar'ith·man'sē) *n.* Divination by numbers. [< Gk. *arithmos* number + *manteia* divination]

a·rith·me·tic (ə·rith'mə·tik) *n.* **1** The science of numbers and of computing with numbers under the four operations of addition, subtraction, multiplication, and division. **2** A treatise upon this science. —**ar·ith·met·ic** (ar'ith·met'ik) *adj.* Of or pertaining to arithmetic: also **ar·ith·met'i·cal.** [< L *arithmetica* < Gk. *(hē) arithmetikē (technē)* (the) counting (art) < *arithmeein* count, number < *arithmos* number] —**ar'ith·met'i·cal·ly** *adv.*

a·rith·me·ti·cian (ə·rith'mə·tish'ən, ar'ith-) *n.* One who uses or is skilled in arithmetic.

ar·ith·met·ic mean (ar'ith·met'ik) The sum of a group of measures, observations, magnitudes, scores, etc., divided by the total number of items in the group.

ar·ith·met·ic progression (ar'ith·met'ik) A sequence of terms such that each except the first differs from the preceding one by a constant quantity, either plus or minus, as 2, 4, 6, 8. See GEOMETRIC PROGRESSION. Also **arithmetical progression, arithmetic series, arithmetic sequence.**

a·rith·mo·ma·ni·a (ə·rith'mō·mā'nē·ə, -mān'yə) *n.* The impulse or desire to count everything. [< NL < Gk. *arithmos* number + -MANIA]

ar·ith·mom·e·ter (ar'ith·mom'ə·tər) *n.* A calculating machine.

-arium *suffix of nouns* **1** A place for: *herbarium*. **2** Connected with: *honorarium*. [< L < *-arius*. See -ARY.]

A·ri·us (ə·rī'əs, âr'ē·əs), 280?–336, Greek theologian; patriarch of Alexandria. See ARIANISM.

a ri·ve·der·ci (ä rē·vä·dâr'chē) *Italian* Until we meet again; so long.

Ar·i·zo·na (ar'ə·zō'nə) A State of the SW United States, bordering on Mexico; 113,909 square miles; capital, Phoenix; entered the Union Feb. 14, 1912: nickname *Apache State*: abbr. AZ —**Ar'i·zo'nan, Ar'i·zo'ni·an** (-nē·ən) *adj.* & *n.*

ark (ärk) *n.* **1** The ship of Noah (*Gen.* vi 14–22). **2** The chest containing the tables of the law (*Ex.* xxv 10): also called the **ark of the covenant. 3** The papyrus cradle of Moses (*Ex.* ii 3). **4** A flat–bottomed freight boat or scow; also, a large farm wagon. **5** *Dial.* A coffer, chest, or bin. ◆ Homophone: *arc.* [OE *arc* < L *arca* chest]

Ar·kan·san (är·kan'zən) *n.* A native or inhabitant of Arkansas.

Ar·kan·sas (är'kən·sô) **1** A State of the south central United States, just west of the Mississippi River; 53,102 square miles; capital, Little Rock; entered the Union June 15, 1836: nickname *Wonder State* or *Bear State*: abbr. AR **2** See QUAPAW.

Ar·kan·sas River (är'kən·sô, är·kan'zəs) A river rising in the Rocky Mountains of central Colorado and flowing SE 1,450 miles to the Mississippi in Arkansas.

arles (ärlz) *n.* *Brit. Dial.* **1** Money given in confirmation of a bargain: also **arles'–pen'ny. 2** An earnest or foretaste.

Arles (ärlz, *Fr.* ärl) A city in SE France; site of Roman ruins. Ancient **Ar·e·las** (ar'ə·las).

Ar·ling·ton (är'ling·tən) An urban county of NE Virginia on the Potomac River opposite Washington, D.C.; site of a national cemetery containing the tomb of the Unknown Soldier.

arm[1] (ärm) *n.* **1** *Anat.* **a** The upper limb of the human body, from the shoulder to the hand or wrist. **b** The part from the shoulder joint to the elbow joint. **2** The fore limb of vertebrates other than man. ◆ Collateral adjective: *brachial*. **3** An armlike part or appendage. **4** The part in contact with the human arm: *arm* of a chair. **5** Anything branching out like an arm from the main body, or set apart or considered as a distinct part or branch; a subdivision: an *arm* of the sea. **6** *Naut.* **a** One of the projecting members of an anchor, ending in a fluke. **b** An end of a spar. **7** Strength to accomplish or aid; might: the *arm* of the law. —**arm in arm** With arms enlaced, as two persons walking together. —**at arm's length** At a distance, so as to keep from being friendly or intimate. —**with open arms** Cordially; warmly. [OE *arm, earm*]

arm[2] (ärm) *n.* **1** A weapon. **2** A distinct branch of the naval or military service: the air arm. —v.t. **1** To supply with instruments of warfare; equip, as with weapons or tools. **2** To make secure, as with a protective covering. —v.i. **3** To supply or equip oneself with weapons or other defensive means. **4** To supply oneself with the means necessary for an undertaking. [See ARMS]

ar·ma·da (är·mä′də, -mā′-) *n.* A fleet of war-vessels. —**the Armada** The fleet sent against England by Spain in 1588. It was defeated by the English navy and almost entirely destroyed by storms: also called **Invincible Armada, Spanish Armada.** [<Sp. <L *armata* <*armare* arm. Doublet of ARMY.]

ar·ma·dil·lo (är′mə· dil′ō) *n. pl.* **·los** An American burrowing nocturnal mammal (family *Dasypodidae*) of the Edentate order, having an armorlike covering of jointed plates; especially, the nine-banded armadillo *(Dasypus novemcinctus)* of Mexico and Texas. [<Sp., dim. of *armado* armed <L *armatus,* pp. of *armare* arm]

ARMADILLO
(1 1/2 feet from head to tail;
tail about 1 foot)

Ar·ma·ged·don (är′mə·ged′n) **1** In Biblical prophecy, the scene of a great battle between the forces of good and evil, to occur at the end of the world. *Rev.* xvi 16. **2** Any great or decisive conflict. [<LL *Armagedon* <Gk. *Armageddon,* prob. <Hebrew *Megiddon* the plain of Megiddo, a perennial battlefield]

Ar·ma·gnac (är·mä·nyák′) *n.* Brandy distilled from wine in the Armagnac region of SW France.

ar·ma·ment (är′mə·mənt) *n.* **1** A land or naval force. **2** The guns, munitions, and other military equipment of a fortification, military unit, airplane, vehicle, or vessel. **3** Equipment or the act of arming or equipping for war or battle. **4** The body of naval, air, and ground forces equipped for war, engaged in an expedition, or present in a given command area. **5** The aggregate of a nation's organized war power. See synonyms under ARMY. [<L *armamenta* implements, ship's tackle <*armare* arm]

ar·ma·ture (är′mə·choor) *n.* **1** A piece of soft iron joining the poles of a magnet to prevent the loss of magnetic power. **2** *Electr.* **a** In a dynamo or motor, the cylindrical, laminated iron core carrying the coils of insulated wire to be revolved through the magnetic field. **b** The part of a relay, as a buzzer or bell, that vibrates when activated by a magnetic field. **3** *Biol.* **a** Protective covering for defense or offense, as the shells of animals, prickles on plants, etc. **b** A set of organs: the gastric *armature.* **4** *Archit.* Framing used to stiffen or brace. **5** In sculpture, a framework to support the clay or other substance used in modeling. **6** Arms; armor. —v.t. **·tured, ·tur·ing** To furnish or provide with an armature. [<F <L *armatura* armor <*armare* arm. Doublet of ARMOR.]

arm·band (ärm′band′) *n.* A brassard. Also **arm band.**

arm·chair (ärm′chār′) *n.* A chair with side supports for the arms or elbows.

armed (ärmd) *adj.* Equipped with arms; provided with or bearing weapons.

armed forces The combined military and naval forces of a nation; in the United States, the Army, Navy, Air Force, Marine Corps, and Coast Guard.

Ar·me·ni·a (är·mē′nē·ə, -mēn′yə) **1** A former kingdom in NE Asia Minor; generally understood to include eastern Turkey and the Armenian S.S.R. **2** A constituent republic **(Armenian S.S.R.)** of Transcaucasian U.S.S.R.; 11,500 square miles; capital, Erivan. *Armenian* **Ha·yas·dan** (hä′yäs·tän′, -dän′).

Ar·me·ni·an (är·mē′nē·ən, -mēn′yən) *adj.* Of or pertaining to the country, people, or language of Armenia. —*n.* **1** A native of Armenia. **2** The language of Armenia, belonging to the Armenian subfamily of Indo-European languages.

arm·er (är′mər) *n.* One who arms.

ar·met (är′met) *n.* A light steel helmet of the 15th and 16th centuries, with vizor and neckguard. [<F <OF *armette,* dim. of *arme* arm²]

arm·ful (ärm′fool′) *n. pl.* **·fuls** That which is

held, or as much as can be held, in the arm or arms.

arm·hole (ärm′hōl′) *n.* An opening for the arm in a garment.

ar·mi·ger (är′mə·jər) *n.* **1** An armorbearer attending a knight; a squire. **2** A person entitled to bear heraldic arms. Also **ar·mig·e·ro** (är·mij′ə·rō). [<L <*arma* weapons + *gerere* bear]

ar·mil·lar·y (är′mə·ler′ē, är·mil′ə·rē) *adj.* Pertaining to or consisting of a ring or rings. [< L *armilla* arm ring, bracelet]

armillary sphere *Astron.* An arrangement of concentric rings in the form of a skeleton sphere, representing the relative positions of the ecliptic and other celestial circles.

arm·ing (är′ming) *n.* **1** The act of supplying with or taking arms. **2** That with which anything is armed. **3** *Naut.* Tallow on a sounding plummet to bring up matter from sea bottom. **4** *Her.* A coat of arms.

ar·mi·stice (är′mə·stis) *n.* A temporary cessation, by mutual agreement, of hostilities; a truce. [<F <L *arma* arms + *stare* stand still]

arm·let (ärm′lit) *n.* **1** A little arm, as of the sea. **2** An ornamental band worn around the upper arm. **3** A small, short sleeve. **4** *Archaic* A piece of armor for the arm.

ar·moire (är·mwär′) *n.* A large, movable, often ornate cabinet or cupboard; ambry. [<F <OF *aumoire* <L *armarium* a chest, orig., a place for storing arms]

ar·mor (är′mər) *n.* **1** A defensive covering, as of mail for a warrior, or of metallic plates for a war vessel, a tank, a deep-sea diver's suit, etc. **2** The aggregate of armored assault vehicles available to a military command. **3** *Biol.* The protective covering of various animals, as turtles, armadillos, and some fishes. See synonyms under ARMS. —v.t. & v.i. To furnish with or put on armor. Also *Brit.* **ar′mour.** [< OF *armeüre* <L *armatura.* Doublet of ARMATURE.]

ar·mor·bear·er (är′mər·bâr′ər) *n.* One bearing the arms of a warrior; a squire; armiger.

ar·mor–clad (är′mər·klad′) *adj.* Covered or plated with armor.

ar·mored (är′mərd) *adj.* **1** Protected by armor, as an automobile, a cruiser, or train. **2** Equipped with armored vehicles, as a military unit. Also *Brit.* **ar′moured.**

armored car 1 *Mil.* A motor vehicle protected by armor plate and used for reconnaissance, carrying ammunition or personnel, or as a self-propelled mount for machine-guns, anti-aircraft artillery, etc. **2** A small truck or other vehicle protected by light armor plate, used for transporting money, etc.

ar·mor·er (är′mər·ər) *n.* **1** A maker, repairer, or custodian of arms or armor. **2** A manufacturer of arms. **3** *Mil.* An enlisted man in charge of the repair, maintenance, and supply of small arms. Also *Brit.* **ar′mour·er.**

ar·mo·ri·al (är·môr′ē·əl, -mō′rē-) *adj.* Pertaining to heraldry or heraldic arms. —*n.* A treatise on heraldry.

armor plate A protective covering of special high carbon steel alloy containing variable proportions of nickel, chrome, and manganese, forged under great pressure and given a hard surface. —**ar′mor–plat′ed** *adj.*

ar·mor·y¹ (är′mər·ē) *n. pl.* **·mor·ies 1** A place for the safekeeping of arms. **2** A building for the use of a body of militia, including general storage for arms and equipment, drill-rooms, etc. **3** *U.S.* A factory for making firearms. **4** *Archaic* Arms collectively; armor. **5** *Archaic* The craft or trade of the armorer. Also *Brit.* **ar′mour·y.** [Prob. <ARMOR]

ar·mor·y² (är′mər·ē) *n. Archaic* **1** Armorial bearings; heraldic arms. **2** Heraldry; the science of blazoning arms. [<OF *armoirie* <*armoier* blazoner <*armoier* blazon, publish a coat of arms]

ar·mour (är′mər) *etc.* See ARMOR, etc.

arms (ärmz) *n. pl.* **1** Weapons collectively. **2** Warfare. **3** The official insignia or device of a state, person, or family. **4** Heraldic symbols. —**small arms** Firearms of small caliber, carried by hand, as pistols, rifles, machine-guns, etc. —**to arms!** Arm yourselves! Make ready for battle! —**to bear arms 1** To be provided with arms. **2** To serve as a member of the armed forces. —**under arms** Provided with weapons; ready for war. —**up in arms** Aroused and ready to fight. [<F *armes* <L *arma* weapons]

Synonyms: armor; weapons. *Arms* are imple-

ments of attack; *armor* is a defensive covering. Any vessel provided with cannon is an *armed* vessel; an *armored* ship is steel-clad. Anything that can be wielded in fight may be a *weapon; arms* are especially made and designed for conflict.

Arm·strong (ärm′strông, -strong), **Edwin Howard,** 1890–1954, U.S. electrical engineer. —**Neil Alden,** born 1930, U.S. astronaut; first man to walk on the moon, July 20, 1969.

ar·mure (är′myŏor) *n.* A twilled fabric woven in ridges to resemble chain mail. [<F <OF *armeüre.* See ARMOR.]

ar·my (är′mē) *n. pl.* **ar·mies 1** A large organized body of men armed for military service on land. **2** The largest organized autonomous unit of the U.S. land forces, consisting of a headquarters, a variable number of corps, and auxiliary troops and trains: also called **field army. 3** Any large, united body: an *army* of ants. **4** A host. — **United States Army 1** The U.S. land military forces administered by the Department of the Army under the Department of Defense and including the Regular Army, the Army Reserve, and the National Guard of the United States. **2** Loosely, the Regular Army. [< OF *armee* <L *armata.* Doublet of ARMADA.]

Synonyms: armament, force, forces, host, legions, military, multitude, phalanx, soldiers, soldiery, troops. *Host* is used for any vast and orderly assemblage; as, the stars are called the heavenly *host. Multitude* expresses number without order or organization. Organization and unity rather than numbers are the essentials of an *army. Legion* and *phalanx* are applied by a kind of poetic license to modern *forces;* the plural *legions* is preferred to the singular. Any organized body of men by whom law is executed is a *force.*

Ar·my (är′mē) *n.* The total military land forces of a specified country, exclusive in some countries of the air forces: the British *Army,* the French *Army,* the American *Army,* etc.

Arn·hem (ärn′hem) The capital of Gilderland province on the lower Rhine, eastern Netherlands. *German* **Arn·heim** (ärn′him).

Arn·hem Land (är′nəm) A coastal region of Northern Territory, Australia; designated as an aboriginal reservation in 1931; about 31,200 square miles.

ar·ni·ca (är′ni·kə) *n.* **1** Any of a genus *(Arnica)* of widely distributed herbaceous perennials of the composite family, especially the common European arnica *(A. montana).* **2** A tincture prepared from the flower heads and roots of this herb, extensively used for sprains and bruises. [<NL]

Arnold, Benedict, 1741–1801, American Revolutionary general who became a traitor. —**Sir Edwin,** 1832–1904, English poet and Orientalist. —**Henry Harky,** 1886–1950, commanding general of United States Army Air Forces in World War II. —**Matthew,** 1822–88, English poet and critic. —**Thomas,** 1795–1842, English educator, father of preceding.

ar·oid (âr′oid) *adj.* Araceous. Also **a·roi·de·ous** (ə·roi′dē·əs). —*n.* Any araceous plant. [< AR(UM) + -OID]

a·roint (ə·roint′) *v.i. Archaic* Avaunt! Begone!: used in the imperative, with reflexive *thee* or *ye.* Also **a·roynt′.** [Origin uncertain]

a·ro·ma (ə·rō′mə) *n.* **1** Fragrance, as from plants; agreeable odor. **2** Characteristic quality or style. [< L < Gk. *arōma* spice] —**a·ro·ma·tous** (ə·rō′mə·təs) *adj.*

ar·o·mat·ic (ar′ə·mat′ik) *adj.* **1** Having an aroma; fragrant; spicy. **2** *Chem.* Pertaining to a group of hydrocarbon compounds of the closed-ring formation and derived chiefly from benzene, as naphthalene: distinguished from *aliphatic.* Also **ar·o·mat′i·cal.** —*n.* **1** Any vegetable or drug of agreeable odor. **2** An aromatic chemical compound. —**ar·o·mat′i·cal·ly** *adv.*

a·ro·ma·tic·i·ty (ə·rō′mə·tis′ə·tē) *n. Chem.* The aromatic character of certain hydrocarbons as determined by their molecular structure rather than by their smell.

a·ro·ma·tize (ə·rō′mə·tīz) *v.t.* **·tized, ·tiz·ing 1** To make fragrant or aromatic. **2** *Chem.* To convert (an aliphatic hydrocarbon) into one of the aromatic group.

a·rose (ə·rōz′) Past tense of ARISE.

a·round (ə·round′) *adv.* **1** So as to encompass or encircle all sides; in various directions. **2** So as to face the opposite way or different ways succes-

sively. **3** *U.S.* From place to place; here and there: to walk *around*. **4** *U.S. Colloq.* Nearby; in the vicinity: Wait *around* until I call. **5** In or to a particular place: Come *around* to see us again. **6** *U.S. Colloq.* Approximately; about: *around* fifty dollars. **—to come around 1** To revive; regain consciousness. **2** To become convinced, as of an opinion. **—to get around 1** To coax; wheedle; cajole. **2** To overcome; as an obstacle; hence, to evade or circumvent, as a law or rule. **—to get around to** To give attention to or accomplish: He'll *get around to* it in time. **—to have been around** *Colloq.* To be experienced in the ways of the world. **—prep. 1** About the circuit of; encircling: to travel *around* the world. **2** In all or many directions about: a field of force *around* either magnetic pole. **3** On the other side of; to be reached or found by passing to the left or right of: the church *around* the corner. **4** Here and there in; in the region of; in various parts of: He wandered *around* the city. **5** Somewhere near or within: You'll find me *around* the house. **6** Approximately: The train leaves *around* midnight. [< A-¹ on + ROUND]
a·rous·al (ə·rou′zəl) *n.* An arousing; awakening.
a·rouse (ə·rouz′) *v.* **a·roused, a·rous·ing** *v.t.* **1** To stir up, as from sleep; awaken. **2** To excite, as to a state of high emotion; animate. —*v.i.* **3** To arouse oneself. See synonyms under ENCOURAGE, STIR. [< ROUSE, on analogy with *arise*]
a·row (ə·rō′) *adv.* In a row.
ar·peg·gi·o (är·pej′ē·ō, -pej′ō) *n. pl.* **·gi·os** *Music* **1** The sounding or playing of the notes of a chord in rapid succession instead of simultaneously, as in playing the harp. **2** A chord so played. [< Ital. < *arpeggiare* play on a harp < *arpa* a harp]

ARPEGGIO

ar·peg·gi·oed (är·pej′ē·ōd) *adj.* Sounded in the manner of an arpeggio.
ar·pent (är′pənt, *Fr.* år·pän′) *n.* An old French measure of land, equivalent to about an acre: still used in Louisiana and in Quebec. Also **ar·pen** (är′pən). [< F]
ar·rack (ar′ək) *n.* A strong Oriental liquor distilled from rice, molasses, etc. [< Arabic '*araq* sweat, juice]
ar·raign (ə·rān′) *v.t.* **1** *Law* To call into court and cause to answer to an indictment. **2** To call upon for an answer; accuse. —*n.* Accusation; indictment. [< AF *arainer*, OF *araisnier* < LL *arrationare* call to account < L *ad-* to + *ratio* reason] —**ar·raign′ment** *n.*
Synonyms (verb): accuse, censure, charge, cite, impeach, indict, summon. One may *charge* another with any fault, great or trifling, privately or publicly, formally or informally. *Accuse* suggests more of the formal and criminal. *Indict* and *arraign* apply strictly to judicial proceedings; an alleged criminal is *indicted* by the grand jury and *arraigned* before the court. *Censure* carries the idea of fault but not of crime; it may be private and individual, or public and official. A judge, a president, or other officer of high rank may be *impeached* before the appropriate tribunal for high crimes; the veracity of a witness may be *impeached* by damaging evidence. One is *arraigned at the bar, before* the tribunal, *of* or *for* a crime, *on* or *upon* an indictment. *Antonyms:* acquit, condone, discharge, excuse, exonerate, forgive, overlook, pardon, release.
Ar·ran (ar′ən) An island in the Firth of Clyde, Buteshire, Scotland; 166 square miles.
ar·range (ə·rānj′) *v.* **ar·ranged, ar·rang·ing** *v.t.* **1** To put in definite or proper order. **2** To adjust, as a conflict or dispute; settle. **3** To change or adapt, as a musical composition for other instruments or voices than those originally intended. —*v.i.* **4** To come to an agreement or understanding: often with *with*. **5** To see about the details; make plans: I was late, but he *arranged* accordingly. See synonyms under ADAPT, ADJUST, CLASSIFY, PREPARE, RANGE, REGULATE, SET,

SETTLE. [< OF *arangier* < *a-* to (< L *ad-*) + *rangier* put in order < *rang* rank¹. See RANK¹.]
ar·range·ment (ə·rānj′mənt) *n.* **1** An arranging or that which is arranged; disposition; order. **2** A preparation, measure, or plan. **3** Settlement, as of a dispute; adjustment. **4** The style in which something is arranged, as a stage scene or combination of colors; a system of parts arranged: the *arrangement* of a library or museum. **5** *Music* **a** The adaptation of a composition to other voices or instruments than those for which it was originally composed. **b** The composition so adapted.
ar·rant (ar′ənt) *adj.* **1** Notoriously bad; unmitigated. **2** *Obs.* Wandering about. [Var. of ERRANT] —**ar′rant·ly** *adv.*
ar·ras (ar′əs) *n.* **1** A tapestry. **2** A hanging for the walls of a room, especially one made of tapestry. [from *Arras*, France]
ar·ra·sene (ar′ə·sēn′) *n.* An embroidery material of wool or silk. [< ARRAS]
ar·ras·tre (ä·räs′trä) *n.* **1** A crude apparatus for grinding and mixing ores. **2** In the Philippine Islands, lighterage, storage, and haulage, as of cargo. Also **ar·ras·tra** (ä·räs′trə). [< Sp.]
ar·ray (ə·rā′) *n.* **1** Regular or proper order; arrangement, as for a battle, display, etc. **2** The persons or things arrayed, especially a military force. **3** Clothing; fine dress. **4** An orderly arrangement, as of brilliant objects, or a series of values in a statistical table. **5** In English history, the arming of militia: commission of *array*. —*v.t.* **1** To draw up in order of battle, as troops; set in order. **2** To adorn; dress, as for display. See synonyms under DRESS. [< AF *arai*, OF *arei* < *a-* to (< L *ad-*) + *rei* order < Gmc.]
ar·ray·al (ə·rā′əl) *n.* **1** The act or process of arraying; mustering of a force. **2** Anything arrayed; an array.
ar·rear·age (ə·rir′ij) *n.* **1** The state of being in arrears. **2** The amount in arrears. **3** *Rare* A thing kept in reserve.
ar·rear (ə·rir′) *n.* **1** The state of being behind or behindhand, as with obligations, business, etc. **2** *Usually pl.* That which is behindhand; a part, as of a debt, overdue and unpaid. **—in arrears** (or **arrear**) Behind in meeting payment, fulfilling an obligation, etc. [< OF *arere* < L *ad-* to + *retro* backward]
ar·rest (ə·rest′) *v.t.* **1** To stop suddenly; check, as the course, movement, or development of. **2** To take into custody by legal authority. **3** To attract and fix, as the attention; engage. —*n.* **1** An arresting or being arrested; especially, seizure by legal authority. **2** A device for arresting motion, as in a machine. [< OF *arester* < LL *arrestare* < L *ad-* + *restare* stop, remain]
Synonyms (verb): apprehend, capture, catch, delay, hold, obstruct, restrain, secure, seize, stop. *Antonyms:* discharge, dismiss, free, liberate, release.
ar·rest·er (ə·res′tər) *n.* **1** One who or that which arrests. **2** In Scots law, one who makes an arrestment.
ar·rest·ing (ə·res′ting) *adj.* Notable; compelling attention.
ar·rest·ment (ə·rest′mənt) *n.* **1** A stoppage, as of growth. **2** In Scots law, an attachment or garnishment of property or credits in the hands of a third party.
ar·rhi·zal (ə·rī′zəl) *adj.* Rootless. Also **ar·rhi·zous** (-zəs). [< Gk. *arrhizos* < *a-* without + *rhiza* a root]
ar·rhyth·mi·a (ə·rith′mē·ə, ə·rith′-) *n. Pathol.* Irregularity of the heart or pulse. [< NL < Gk. *arrhythmia* lack of rhythm < *a-* without + *rhythmos* measure] —**ar·rhyth·mic** (ə·rith′mik, ə·rith′-) *adj.*
ar·ri·ère (ar′ē·âr, ə·rir′) *n.* The rear: often used adjectively in the sense of dependent or subordinate: *arrière*-vassal. [< F. See ARREAR.]
ar·ri·ère-ban (ar′ē·âr·ban′, *Fr.* å·ryâr·bän′) *n.* **1** In the Middle Ages, the edict of a king summoning his vassals to military service. **2** The vassals thus summoned. [< F, ult. < OHG *hari, heri* army + *ban* edict]
ar·rière-guard (ə·rir′gärd′) *n.* Rear guard. Also

French **ar·rière-garde** (å·ryâr·gård′).
ar·ris (ar′is) *n. Archit.* The sharp edge or ridge formed by the meeting of two surfaces, especially the sharp ridge between two channels of a Doric column. Also **ar′is.** [< OF *areste* < L *arista* awn, fishbone. Doublet of ARISTA.]
ar·ri·val (ə·rī′vəl) *n.* **1** The act of arriving. **2** One who or that which arrives or has arrived. See synonyms under ACCESSION.
ar·rive (ə·rīv′) *v.i.* **ar·rived, ar·riv·ing 1** To reach or come to a destination or place. **2** To come at length, by any stage or process: often with *at*: to *arrive* at an idea, fatherhood, etc. **3** To attain the circumstances of success or fame in the world. [< OF *ariver* < LL *arripare* come to shore < L *ad-* to + *ripa* shore]
Synonyms: attain, come, enter, land, reach. See ATTAIN. *Antonyms:* depart, embark, go, leave, start.
ar·ri·viste (å·rē·vēst′) *n. French* A social climber or careerist.
ar·ro·gance (ar′ə·gəns) *n.* The quality or state of being arrogant; haughtiness; overbearing pride. Also **ar′ro·gan·cy.** [< OF < L *arrogantia.* See ARROGANT.]
Synonyms: assumption, assurance, disdain, haughtiness, insolence, presumption, pride, superciliousness, vanity. *Arrogance* claims much for itself and concedes little to others. *Pride* is an absorbing sense of one's own greatness. *Disdain* sees contemptuously the inferiority of others to oneself. *Presumption* claims place or privilege above one's right. *Assumption* quietly takes for granted superiority and privilege which others might or might not concede. *Vanity* intensely craves admiration and applause. *Superciliousness* silently manifests mingled *haughtiness* and *disdain. Insolence* is open and rude expression of contempt and hostility, generally from an inferior to a superior, as from a clerk to a customer. See ASSURANCE, IMPERTINENCE.
ar·ro·gant (ar′ə·gənt) *adj.* **1** Unduly or excessively proud; overbearing; haughty. **2** Characterized by or due to arrogance: *arrogant* proposals. See synonyms under DOGMATIC, IMPERIOUS. [< OF < L *arrogans, -antis,* ppr. of *arrogare.* See ARROGATE.] —**ar′ro·gant·ly** *adv.*
ar·ro·gate (ar′ə·gāt) *v.t.* **·gat·ed, ·gat·ing 1** To claim, demand, or take unreasonably or presumptuously; assume; usurp. **2** To attribute or ascribe without reason: to *arrogate* a privilege. See synonyms under ASSUME. [< L *arrogatus,* pp. of *arrogare* claim for oneself < *ad-* to + *rogare* ask] —**ar′ro·ga′tion** *n.*
ar·ron·disse·ment (å·rôn·dēs·män′) *n. pl.* **·ments** (-män′) *French* **1** The chief subdivision of a French department. **2** A district: Paris is divided into 20 arrondissements.
ar·row (ar′ō) *n.* **1** A straight, slender shaft generally feathered at one end and with a pointed head at the other, to be shot from a bow. **2** Anything resembling an arrow in shape, function, speed, etc. **3** A sign or figure in the shape of an arrow, used to indicate directions, as on maps, charts, etc. ♦Collateral adjective: *sagittal.* [OE *earh, arwe*]
ar·row·head (ar′ō·hed′) *n.* **1** The sharp-pointed head of an arrow. **2** Something resembling an arrowhead, as a mark used to point direction, etc. **3** *Archit.* The dart or tongue of an egg-and-dart molding. **4** *Bot.* Any aquatic plant of the genus *Sagittaria,* of the water-plantain family (*Alismaceae*), with arrow-shaped leaves. —**ar′row·head′ed** *adj.*
ar·row·root (ar′ō·root′, -root′) *n.* **1** A nutritious starch obtained from the rhizomes of a tropical American plant (*Maranta arundinacea*). **2** The plant. **3** A similar starchy product from other tropical plants.
ar·row·y (ar′ō·ē) *adj.* **1** Resembling an arrow or arrows in shape, appearance, or motion; swift; sharp; darting. **2** Full of or abounding in arrows.
ar·roy·o (ə·roi′ō) *n. pl.* **·os** (-ōz) *SW U.S.* **1** The steep-sided, flat channel of an intermittent stream. **2** The stream itself. **3** A deep, dry gulch. [< Sp.]
ar·se·nal (är′sə·nəl) *n.* A public repository or

manufactory of arms and munitions of war. [< Ital. *arsenale* < Arabic *dār aṣ-ṣinā'ah* workshop]

ar·se·nate (är'sə·nāt, -nit) *n. Chem.* A salt of arsenic acid containing the trivalent radical AsO₄. Also **ar·se·ni·ate** (är·sē'nē·āt, -it).

ar·se·nic (är'sə·nik) *n.* **1** A poisonous element (symbol As, atomic number 33), existing in several allotropic forms, commonly as a gray, very brittle, crystalline, semimetallic substance. See PERIODIC TABLE. **2** A tasteless, poisonous compound, arsenic trioxide, As₂O₃, used in agricultural pesticides. **3** White arsenic or arsenic trioxide, As₂O₃, a tasteless, poisonous compound. —**ar·sen·ic** (är·sen'ik) *adj.* Arsenical. [< OF < L *arsenicum* < Gk. *arsenikon* yellow orpiment]

ar·sen·i·cal (är·sen'i·kəl) *adj.* Of, pertaining to, or containing arsenic. —*n.* Any preparation of arsenic used as an insecticide or drug.

ar·se·nous (är'sə·nəs) *adj.* Of, pertaining to, or containing arsenic, especially when combined in its triad valence: *arsenous* oxide, As₂O₃; *arsenous* sulfide, As₂S₃. Also **ar·se·ni·ous** (är·sē'nē·əs).

ars gra·ti·a ar·tis (ärz grä'shē·ə är'tis) *Latin* Art for art's sake.

ar·sine (är·sēn', är'sēn, är'sin) *n.* **1** A poisonous, inflammable, gaseous compound, AsH₃, with a nauseous odor, used as an agent of chemical warfare in shells, etc. **2** Any of various derivatives of this compound in which the hydrogen atom is replaced by a radical. [< ARS(ENIC) + -INE²]

ar·sis (är'sis) *n. pl.* **·ses** (-sēz) **1** In prosody: **a** The syllable that receives the ictus or stress of voice. **b** The stress itself. **c** In the original Greek usage, the raising of the foot in beating time, and hence the metrically unaccented part of the foot: the reverse of modern usage. **2** *Music* The unaccented part of a bar. [< L < Gk. *arsis* a lifting, raising < *airein* raise]

ars lon·ga, vi·ta bre·vis (ärz lông'gə vī'tə brev'is) *Latin* Art (is) long, life short.

ar·son (är'sən) *n. Law* The malicious burning of a dwelling or other structure belonging to another; also the similar burning of other property, including one's own, when insured, with the intent to defraud the insurers. [< OF < LL *arsio, -onis* a burning < L *arsus*, pp. of *ardere* burn]

ars po·et·i·ca (ärz pō·et'i·kə) *Latin* The art of poetry.

art¹ (ärt) *n.* **1** The skilful, systematic arrangement or adaptation of means for the attainment of some end, especially by human endeavor as opposed to natural forces. **2** The practical application of knowledge or natural ability; skilled workmanship; mastery; dexterity. **3** A set or system of rules, principles, etc., devised for procuring some scientific, esthetic, or practical result, as by exercise; a branch of learning to be studied in order to be applied. **4 a** The application, or the principles of application, of skill, knowledge, etc., in a creative effort to produce works that have form or beauty, esthetic expression of feeling, etc., as in music, painting, sculpture, literature, architecture, and the dance. **b** Any particular branch of this, especially painting, drawing, etc. **c** The works thus created; statues; paintings; etc. **5** *Usually pl.* Any of certain branches of academic learning, as rhetoric, grammar, music, mathematics, etc.; the liberal arts, especially as distinguished from the sciences. **6** An illustration, as in a magazine or newspaper. **7** Craft; cunning; artfulness. **8** *Usually pl.* Stratagem; wiles; tricks. **9** An organized body of men trained in some trade or vocation; guild. —**fine arts** Those arts considered purely esthetic or expressive, as distinguished from the "useful arts": painting, drawing, sculpture, ceramics, architecture, literature, music, and the dance. —**household arts** The duties involved in managing a household. —**industrial arts** The technical skills used in industry, especially as subjects of study in schools. —**liberal arts** The course of study, including literature, philosophy, languages, history, etc., distinguished from professional or technical subjects, offered by an academic college: also called *arts*: a translation of Latin *artes liberales*, arts suitable for *liberi*, or free men. [< OF < L *ars, artis* skill]

Synonyms: address, aptitude, artifice, business,

ness, cleverness, dexterity, esthetics, ingenuity, knack, science, skill, tact. In the highest sense, *art* has no synonym. The term *esthetics* denotes the theory of the beautiful which furnishes the basis of *art*. For subordinate senses, see ARTIFICE, BUSINESS. For the distinction between *science* and *art*, see synonyms for SCIENCE.

art² (ärt) Archaic or poetic second person singular present tense of BE: used with *thou*.

art de·co (ärt de'kō) A style of decorative design characterized by ornamentals, geometrical forms, asymmetry, and bold colors. Also **Art De'co**.

ar·te·ri·al (är·tir'ē·əl) *adj.* **1** Pertaining to, like, or contained or carried in the arteries or an artery. **2** *Physiol.* Pertaining to the blood which has undergone aeration in the lungs, distinguished by its bright red color. **3** Resembling an artery in having a main channel and a system of secondary branches: an *arterial* highway.

ar·te·ri·al·ize (är·tir'ē·əl·īz) *v.t.* **·ized**, **·iz·ing** *Physiol.* To convert venous blood into arterial blood by oxygenation during its passage through the lungs in respiration. Also *Brit.* **ar·te'ri·al·ise'**. —**ar·te'ri·al·i·za'tion** *n.*

arterio— *combining form* Artery. [< Gk. *artēria*]

ar·te·ri·og·ra·phy (är·tir'ē·ogr'ə·fē) *n.* **1** The anatomy, description, etc., of the arteries or the arterial system. **2** The production of graphic representations of the action and state of the pulse.

ar·te·ri·ol·o·gy (är·tir'ē·ol'ə·jē) *n.* **1** The scientific study of the arteries in health and disease. **2** A treatise on the subject.

ar·te·ri·o·scle·ro·sis (är·tir'ē·ō·sklə·rō'sis) *n. Pathol.* The thickening and hardening of the walls of an artery, with impairment of blood circulation, as in old age. [< NL < ARTERIO- + SCLEROSIS] —**ar·te'ri·o·scle·rot'ic** (-rot'ik) *adj.*

ar·te·ri·ot·o·my (är·tir'ē·ot'ə·mē) *n.* **1** Dissection of arteries. **2** Any cutting or opening of an artery, as for letting blood.

ar·te·ri·tis (är·tə·rī'tis) *n. Pathol.* Inflammation of an artery or of its external coat.

ar·ter·y (är'tər·ē) *n. pl.* **·ter·ies** **1** *Anat.* Any of a large number of muscular vessels conveying blood away from the heart to every part of the body. **2** Any principal channel in a communication or transportation network. —*v.t.* **·ter·ied**, **·ter·y·ing** To supply with or as if with arteries; flow through, like an artery: Rivers *artery* the land. [< L *arteria* artery, windpipe < Gk. *artēria*]

ar·te·sian well (är·tē'zhən) A well bored down to a water-bearing stratum between impermeable strata, from a surface lower than the source of the water supply, so that the water pressure is great enough to force a flow of water out at the surface. [< F *artésien*, from *Artois*, town in France]

art·ful (ärt'fəl) *adj.* **1** Crafty; cunning; tricky. **2** Artificial; imitative. **3** Skilful; ingenious. See synonyms under INSIDIOUS. —**art'ful·ly** *adv.* —**art'ful·ness** *n.*

ar·thral·gia (ar·thral'jə) *n. Pathol.* Neuralgic pain in a joint. —**ar·thral'gic** (-jik) *adj.*

ar·thrit·ic (är·thrit'ik) *adj.* Pertaining to, having, or affected by arthritis.

ar·thri·tis (är·thrī'tis) *n. Pathol.* Inflammation of a joint. [< L < Gk. *arthritis* < *arthron* joint]

arthro— *combining form* Joint: *arthrography*. Also, before vowels, **arthr—**, as in *arthralgia*. [< Gk. *arthron*]

ar·throc·a·ce (är·throk'ə·sē) *n.* **1** Disease of the joints, characterized by caries or dead bone. **2** An endemic disease that attacks very young animals, as calves, colts, etc. [< ARTHRO- + Gk. *kakē* illness]

ar·throd·e·sis (är·throd'ə·sis) *n. Surg.* The operation of fusing of the surfaces of joints; artificial ankylosis. [< NL < ARTHRO- + Gk. *desis* a joining]

ar·throg·ra·phy (är·throg'rə·fē) *n.* A scientific description of the joints.

ar·thro·mere (är'thrə·mir) *n. Zool.* Any typical segment in the body of an articulate invertebrate. [< ARTHRO- + -MERE]

ar·throp·a·thy (är·throp'ə·thē) *n.* Any disease of the joints.

ar·thro·plas·ty (är'thrə·plas'tē) *n. Surg.* A plastic operation on a joint or the formation of an artificial joint. —**ar'thro·plas'tic** *adj.*

ar·thro·pod (är'thrə·pod) *n. Zool.* Any of a

large phylum (*Arthropoda*) of invertebrate animals characterized by jointed legs, chitinous exoskeletons, and segmented body parts, including insects, spiders, and crabs. —*adj.* Of or pertaining to the *Arthropoda*. [< ARTHRO- + Gk. *pous, podos* foot] —**ar·throp·o·dous** (är·throp'ə·dəs), **ar·throp'o·dal** *adj.*

ar·thro·sis (är·thrō'sis) *n. pl.* **·ses** (-sēz) **1** Articulation; connection of parts by joints. **2** *Pathol.* A degenerative condition of the joints.

ar·thro·spore (är'thrə·spôr, -spōr) *n.* **1** *Bot.* One of a series of spores in some algae and fungi, formed by fission and resembling a string of beads. **2** *Bacteriol.* An isolated vegetative cell in a resting state. —**ar'thro·spor'ic** (-spôr'ik, -spor'ik), **ar·thros·po·rous** (ar·thros'pə·rəs) *adj.*

Ar·thur (är'thər, *Fr.* àr·tür') A masculine personal name. Also *Lat.* **Ar·thu·rus** (är·tŏŏr'əs). —**Arthur** A legendary British king of the sixth century A.D., hero of the Round Table and subject of many romances. [? < Celtic, high admirable]

Ar·thur (är'thər), **Chester Alan**, 1830–86, president of the United States 1881–85, following the assassination of President Garfield.

ARTESIAN WELL
THROUGH GEOLOGICAL STRATA
A. Water level. *B.* Artesian well. *C.* Ordinary well.

Ar·thu·ri·an (är·thŏŏr'ē·ən) *adj.* Of or pertaining to King Arthur and his knights. See ROUND TABLE.

ar·ti·choke (är'tə·chōk) *n.* **1** A thistlelike garden plant (*Cynara scolymus*). **2** Its succulent flower head, used as a vegetable. **3** The Jerusalem artichoke. [< Ital. *articiocco* < Arabic *al-kharshūf*]

ar·ti·cle (är'ti·kəl) *n.* **1** A particular object or substance; a material thing or class of things: an *article* of food; an *article* for sale. **2** A literary composition forming an independent part of a publication: an *article* in a newspaper. **3** A definite division; a distinct proposition, statement, or stipulation in a series of such, as in a constitution, an impeachment, or a treaty. **4** A complete item of religious belief; a point of doctrine, especially when forming a part of a statement of religious beliefs: the Thirty-nine *Articles*. **5** *Gram.* One of a class of auxiliary words inserted before a noun or a word used as a noun, or, in some languages, prefixed or suffixed to it, to limit or modify it in some way; as, English *a, an* (indefinite *article*) and *the* (definite *article*). **6** A definite part, as of a system; item; point. **7** *Archaic* A point of time; exact instant: the *article* of death. —*v.* **·cled**, **·cling** *v.t.* **1** To bind by a written contract, as to an attorney for instruction in law; especially, to bind to service: to *article* a seaman for a voyage. **2** To set forth in articles; specify. **3** To charge specifically; accuse by formal articles. —*v.i.* **4** To make accusations: with *against*. [< F < L *articulus*, dim. of *artus* a joint]

ar·tic·u·lar (är·tik'yə·lər) *adj.* Pertaining to a joint or the joints.

ar·tic·u·late (är·tik'yə·lit) *adj.* **1** Jointed; segmented. **2** Particularized in articles; specific; distinct. **3** Divided into consecutive syllables so as to form speech. **4** Able to speak, especially to speak well or clearly. **5** Arranged with coherence; interrelated. Also **ar·tic'u·lat·ed** (-lā'tid). —*v.* (är·tik'yə·lāt) **·lat·ed**, **·lat·ing** *v.t.* **1** To utter distinctly, enunciate. **2** To give utterance to; express in words: to *articulate* your wrongs. **3** *Phonet.* To produce, as a speech sound, by the movement of the organs of speech. **4** To joint together; unite by joints. — *v.i.* **5** To speak distinctly. **6** *Phonet.* To produce a speech sound. **7** *Anat.* To form a joint: used with *with*. **8** *Obs.* To make terms. See synonyms under SPEAK. [<L *articulatus*, pp. of *articulare* divide into joints, utter distinctly < *articulus* ARTICLE.] — **ar·tic′u·late·ly** *adv.*

ar·tic·u·la·tion (är·tik′yə·lā′shən) *n.* **1** A jointing or being jointed together; also the manner or method of this. **2** A joint between two bones. **3** *Anat.* The union forming a joint, as of bones. **4** The utterance of articulate sounds; enunciation. **5** A speech sound, especially a consonant. **6** *Phonet.* The movements of the organs of speech in producing an articulate sound. **7** *Bot.* **a** A joint between two separable parts, as a leaf and a stem. **b** A node or the space between two nodes. — **ar·tic·u·la·to·ry** (är·tik′yə·lə·tôr′ē, -tō′rē) *adj.*

ar·tic·u·la·tor (är·tik′yə·lā′tər) *n.* **1** One who or that which articulates. **2** *Dent.* A device to secure proper articulation. **3** *Phonet.* A movable organ of speech, as the tongue.

ar·ti·fact (är′tə·fakt) *n.* **1** Anything made by human work or art. **2** *Biol.* A structure or appearance which is not normally present in a cell or tissue but is produced by artificial means. Also **ar′te·fact.** [<L *ars, artis* art, skill + *factus,* pp. of *facere* make]

ar·ti·fice (är′tə·fis) *n.* **1** Subtle or deceptive craft; trickery. **2** Skill; ingenuity. **3** An ingenious expedient; stratagem; maneuver. [<F <L *artificium* handicraft, skill < *ars* art + *facere* make]
Synonyms: art, blind, cheat, contrivance, craft, cunning, device, dodge, finesse, fraud, guile, imposture, invention, machination, maneuver, ruse, strategem, subterfuge, trick, wile. An *artifice, contrivance,* or *device* may be either good or bad. An *artifice* is a carefully and delicately prepared *contrivance* for doing indirectly what one could not well do directly. A *device* is something studied out for promoting an end, as in a mechanism. *Finesse* is especially subtle *contrivance,* delicate *artifice,* whether for good or evil. A *cheat* is a mean advantage in a bargain; a *fraud,* any form of covert robbery or injury. *Imposture* is a deceitful *contrivance* for securing charity, credit, or consideration. A *strategem* or *maneuver* may be good or bad. A *wile* is often but not necessarily evil. A *trick* is commonly low, injurious, and malicious, but the word is used playfully with less than its full meaning. A *ruse* or a *blind* may be quite innocent and harmless. *Antonyms:* artlessness, candor, fairness, frankness, guilelessness, honesty, ingenuousness, innocence, openness, simplicity, sincerity, truth.

ar·tif·i·cer (är·tif′ə·sər) *n.* **1** One who constructs with skill; a craftsman. **2** *Mil.* A worker in an artillery laboratory. **3** A skilful designer; an inventor.

ar·ti·fi·cial (är′tə·fish′əl) *adj.* **1** Produced by human art rather than by nature. **2** Made in imitation of or as a substitute for something natural: an *artificial* leg. **3** Not genuine or natural; affected. See synonyms under FACTITIOUS. [<L *artificialis* < *artificium.* See ARTIFICE.] — **ar′ti·fi′cial·ly** *adv.* — **ar′ti·fi′cial·ness** *n.*

artificial horizon 1 *Aeron.* An instrument like a gyroscope, providing a surface always parallel to the true horizon and indicating the deviations of an aircraft from level flight. **2** *Astron.* A level reflector, as a surface of mercury, used to determine the altitude of celestial bodies.

artificial insemination Impregnation of the female with semen from the male without direct sexual contact: also called *eutelegenesis.*

ar·ti·fi·ci·al·i·ty (är′tə·fish′ē·al′ə·tē) *n.* *pl.* **·ties 1** The character, fact, or state of being artificial. **2** Something artificial.

ar·til·ler·y (är·til′ə·rē) *n.* **1** Guns of larger caliber than machine-guns: usually classified according to caliber as *light, medium,* and *heavy.* **2** Military units armed with such guns. **3** Branches of the United States Army composed of such units: Field *Artillery,* Coast

Artillery Corps. **4** *U.S. Colloq.* Any small firearm. **5** The science of gunnery. **6** *Obs.* Implements of war. [<OF *artillerie* < *artiller* fortify]

ar·til·ler·y·man (är·til′ə·rē·mən) *n.* *pl.* **·men** (-mən) **1** One who studies artillery. **2** A soldier in the artillery. Also **ar·til′ler·ist.**

ar·ti·o·dac·tyl (är′tē·ō·dak′təl)· *n.* A member of a mammalian order or suborder (*Artiodactyla*) of ungulate quadrupeds with two or four equal-hoofed digits to each foot, including the ruminants, hogs, etc. — *adj.* Of or pertaining to the *Artiodactyla;* having two or four digits to each foot. [<NL <Gk. *artios* even + *daktylos* finger, toe] — **ar′ti·o·dac′ty·lous** (-ləs) *adj.*

ar·ti·san (är′tə·zən) *n.* A trained or skilled workman; superior mechanic. [<F <Ital. *artigiano,* ult. <L *ars* art]

art·ist (är′tist) *n.* **1** One who is skilled in or who makes a profession of any of the fine arts. **2** Any professional public performer, as an actor, singer, etc. **3** One who does anything particularly well, as with a feeling for form, effect, etc. [<F *artiste* <Ital. *artista* <L *ars* art]
Synonyms: artificer, artisan, mechanic, operative, workman. The work of the *artist* is creative; that of the *artisan* mechanical. The *artificer* is between the two, putting more thought, intelligence, and taste into his work than the *artisan,* but less of the idealizing, creative power than the *artist.* The man who constructs anything by mere routine and rule is a *mechanic.* The man whose work involves thought, skill, and constructive power is an *artificer.* Those who operate machinery which is nearly automatic are *operators* or *operatives.*

ar·tiste (är·tēst′) *n.* A professional dancer, singer, or entertainer. [<F]

ar·tis·tic (är·tis′tik) *adj.* **1** Of or pertaining to art or artists. **2** Conforming or conformable to the principles of art; tastefully executed. **3** Fond of or sensitive to art. Also **ar·tis′ti·cal.** — **ar·tis′ti·cal·ly** *adv.*

art·ist·ry (är′tis·trē) *n.* **1** The pursuits or occupation of an artist. **2** Artistic characteristics or ability.

Ar·ti·um Bac·ca·lau·re·us (är′shē·əm bak′ə·lô′rē·əs) *Latin* Bachelor of Arts. Abbr. *A.B.* or *B.A.*

Ar·ti·um Ma·gis·ter (är′shē·əm mə·jis′tər) *Latin* Master of Arts. Abbr. *A.M.* or *M.A.*

art·less (ärt′lis) *adj.* **1** Without craft or deceit; unaffected. **2** Natural; simple. **3** Without art or skill; clumsy. **4** Without taste; ignorant. See synonyms under CANDID, INNOCENT, RUSTIC. — **art′less·ly** *adv.* — **art′less·ness** *n.*

Art Nou·veau (ärt noō·vō′, *Fr.* àr noō·vō′) A style of art and design of the late 19th and early 20th centuries characterized by curved and twisting shapes often representing natural objects. [<F, lit., new art]

art·work (ärt′wûrk′) *n.* Illustrations, calligraphy, or other decorative elements accompanying printed text.

art·y (är′tē) *adj.* Pretending to be artistic; ostentatiously claiming artistic worth. — **art′i·ness** *n.*

A·ru·ba (ä·roō′bə) An island in the western group of the Netherlands West Indies; 69 square miles.

ar·um (âr′əm) *n.* **1** Any of a genus (*Arum*) of araceous Old World herbs, especially the cuckoo pint. **2** One of various related plants, as the calla lily. [<L <Gk. *aron*]

a·run·di·na·ceous (ə·run′də·nā′shəs) *adj.* *Bot.* Pertaining to a reed or reeds; reedlike. [<L *arundinaceus* < *arundo* reed]

ar·un·din·e·ous (ar′ən·din′ē·əs) *adj.* *Bot.* Abounding in or like reeds; reedy.

ar·y (âr′ē) *adj.* *Dial.* Any; opposite of *nary.*

-ary¹ *suffix of adjectives and nouns* **1** Connected with or pertaining to what is expressed in the root word: *elementary, honorary, secondary.* **2** A person employed as or engaged in: *apothecary, antiquary, secretary.* **3** A thing connected with or a place dedicated to: *dictionary, diary, sanctuary.* [<L *-arius, -arium*]

-ary² *suffix of adjectives* Of or pertaining to; belonging to: *military, salutary.* See -AR¹. [<L *-aris*]

Ar·y·an (âr′ē·ən, ar′-, är′yən) *n.* **1** A member or descendant of a prehistoric people who spoke Indo-European. **2** In Nazi ideology, a Caucasian gentile, especially one of Nordic stock. **3** *Ling.* **a** The Indo-Iranian subfamily of Indo-European. **b** A former name for the parent language of the Indo-European family. — *adj.* **1** Of or pertaining to the Aryans or their languages. **2** In Nazi ideology, of or pertaining to Caucasian gentiles. Also spelled *Arian.* [<Skt. *ārya* noble]

as¹ (az, *unstressed* əz) *adv.* **1** To the same extent or degree; equally: Do I look *as* pretty? **2** For instance; thus: to release, *as* prisoners, from confinement. —*conj.* **1** To the same extent, degree, or amount: Such a man *as* he cannot fail. **2** To the degree in which; in proportion to which: He became gentler *as* he grew older. **3** In the manner of; in the way that: Do *as* I tell you. **4** At the same time that; while: They sang *as* we left. **5** Because; considering that: *As* the weather was bad, the game was postponed. **6** However; though: Bad *as* it was, it might have been worse. See synonyms under BECAUSE. —*pron.* Who, which, or that, after *such, many,* and *same:* Such people *as* like sports will enjoy the game; He lost the same kind of pen *as* you have; As many *as* are here will receive tickets. [ME *as, als, alse,* OE *ealswā* entirely so, just as. See ALSO.] **—as . . . as** A correlative construction that indicates identity or equality of two things: *as* much *as, as* good *as.* — **as for** Concerning; in the case of. **—as if.** As it would if. Also **as though. —as is** *Colloq.* Just as it is; not guaranteed perfect: said of an article or commodity somewhat shopworn or damaged. — **as it were** So to speak; in a manner; in some sort. **—as to** Concerning. **—as well** Besides. **—as well as** Equally; just as much; in addition to. **—as yet** Up to the present time; hitherto; so far.

as² (as) *n. pl.* **as·ses** (as′iz) **1** An early Roman coin of copper or copper alloy: originally weighing about a pound. **2** An ancient Roman unit of weight of about one pound. [<L]

As *Chem.* Arsenic (symbol As).

as- Assimilated var. of AD-.

A·sa·ma (ä·sä·mä) The highest and most violent of Japan's active volcanos, on central Honshu island; 8,200 feet.

as·bes·tos (as·bes′təs, az-) *n.* **1** A white or lightgray mineral, obtained chiefly from actinolite and amphibole, occurring in long slender needles or fibrous masses which may be woven or shaped into acid-resisting, nonconducting, and fireproof articles: also called *earthflax, mountain cork.* **2** A fireproof curtain, as in a theater. —*adj.* Pertaining to, containing, or made of asbestos. Also **as·bes′tus.** [<L <Gk., unquenchable < *a-* not + *sbennynai* quench; orig. applied to quicklime] **—as·bes·ti·form** (as·bes′tə·fôrm, az-) *adj.* — **as·bes·tine** (as·bes′tin, az-), **as·bes′tic** *adj.*

as·bes·to·sis (as′bes·tō′sis, az′-) *n. Pathol.* Pneumoconiosis caused by inhaling particles of asbestos.

as·ca·rid (as′kə·rid) *n. Zool.* A nematode worm of the genus *Ascaris,* as a roundworm or pinworm. [<Gk. *askaris, -idos* worm in the intestines]

as·cend (ə·send′) *v.i.* **1** To go or move upward; rise. **2** To rise by degrees, as from particulars to generals, from the present to the past, from the lower to the higher notes of a musical scale, etc. **3** To lie along an ascending slope: The path *ascends* sharply here. —*v.t.* **4** To move or slope upward on: to *ascend* a mountain. [<L *ascendere* < *ad-* to + *scandere* climb] **—as·cend′a·ble** or **·i·ble** *adj.*

as·cen·dence (ə·sen′dəns) *n.* Ascendency. Also **as·cen′dance.**

as·cen·den·cy (ə·sen′dən·sē) *n.* The quality, fact, or state of being in the ascendent; domination; sway. Also **as·cen′dan·cy.**

as·cen·dent (ə·sen′dənt) *adj.* **1** Ascending; rising. **2** Superior; dominant. **3** *Astron.* Coming to or above the horizon. **4** *Bot.* Ascending. See synonyms under PREDOMINANT. —*n.* **1** A position of supreme power; preeminence; domination. **2** In astrology: **a** The point of the ecliptic that is rising above the eastern horizon at any instant. **b**

Horoscope. **3** *Rare* An ancestor: opposed to *descendant*. Also **as·cen'dant. —to be in the ascendent** To approach or occupy a predominating position; have controlling power, fame, influence, etc.

as·cend·er (ə-sen'dər) *n.* **1** One who or that which ascends. **2** *Printing* **a** The part of a letter that reaches into the top of the body of the type. **b** Any of such letters, as *b, d, h,* etc.

as·cend·ing (ə-sen'ding) *adj.* **1** Rising or. directed upward. **2** *Bot.* Slanting or curving upward.

as·cen·sion (ə-sen'shən) *n.* **1** The act of ascending. **2** *Astron.* The elevating or rising of a star above the horizon in the celestial sphere. **—the Ascension** *Theol.* The bodily ascent of Christ into heaven after the Resurrection, commemorated on **Ascension Day** (also *Holy Thursday*), the fortieth day after Easter. [< L *ascensio, -onis* < *ascendere.* See ASCEND.] **—as·cen'sion·al** *adj.*

As·cen·sion (ə-sen'shən) **1** A British island in the South Atlantic, administered with St. Helena; 34 square miles. **2** A former name for PONAPE.

as·cen·sion·ist (ə-sen'shən·ist) *n.* One who makes ascensions, as a balloonist or a mountaineer.

as·cen·sive (ə-sen'siv) *adj.* **1** Tending upward. **2** Causing to rise. [< L *ascensus,* pp. of *ascendere.* See ASCEND.]

as·cent (ə-sent') *n.* **1** The act of ascending or going up; a rising or soaring. **2** The act of climbing or traveling up, as a mountain. **3** The method or way of ascending; that by which one ascends, as the upward slope of a hill. **4** The amount or degree of upward slope: an *ascent* of 30°. **5** A rise in state, rank, or station; advancement, as in esteem or succession. **6** *Rare* A going back in time or genealogy. ◆ Homophone: *assent.* [< ASCEND, on analogy with *descent*.]

as·cer·tain (as'ər·tān') *v.t.* **1** To learn with certainty about; find out. **2** *Obs.* To make certain; determine; define. See synonyms under DISCOVER, KNOW. [< OF *acertener* <a- to (<L *ad-*) + *certain.* See CERTAIN.] **—as'cer·tain'·a·ble** *adj.* **—as'cer·tain'a·ble·ness** *n.* **—as'cer·tain'a·bly** *adv.* **—as'cer·tain'ment** *n.*

as·cet·ic (ə-set'ik) *n.* **1** Originally, in the early church, one who renounced social life and comfort for solitude, self-mortification, and religious devotion; a hermit; recluse. **2** Hence, one who leads a very austere and self-denying life. *—adj.* Given to severe self-denial and austerity; practicing rigid abstinence and devotion. Also **as·cet'i·cal.** [< Gk. *askētikos* exercised, industrious, athletic < *askētēs* one who exercises (selfdenial), a monk < *askeein* exercise] **—as·cet'i·cal·ly** *adv.*

as·cet·i·cism (ə-set'ə·siz'əm) *n.* **1** Ascetic belief and conduct. **2** The belief that one can attain to a high intellectual or spiritual level through solitude, mortification of the flesh, and devotional contemplation.

as·cians (ash'yənz) *n. pl.* Shadowless men: applied to inhabitants of the torrid zone, who twice in the year cast no shadow at noon. Also **as·ci·i** (ash'ē·ī). [< L *ascius* < Gk. *askios* without shadow < *a-* without + *skia* shadow]

a·scor·bic (ə-skôr'bik) See ANTISCORBUTIC.

ascorbic acid The scurvy-preventing vitamin C, a white, odorless, crystalline compound, $C_6H_8O_6$, present in citrus and other fresh fruits, tomatoes, potatoes, and green leafy vegetables, and also made synthetically from glucose.

as·co·spore (as'kə·spôr, -spōr) *n. Bot.* A spore developed within an ascus. **—as·cos·po·rous** (as·kos'pə·rəs), **as·co·spor·ic** (as'kə·spôr'ik, -spor'-) *adj.*

as·cot (as'kət, -kot) *n.* A kind of scarf or necktie, knotted so that the broad ends are laid one across the other. [from *Ascot*]

As·cot (as'kət, -kot) A village in Berkshire, England, near Windsor; site of annual races instituted in 1711.

as·cribe (ə-skrīb') *v.t.* **as·cribed, as·crib·ing** **1** To refer, as to a cause or source; attribute; impute. **2** To consider or declare as belonging or being due or appropriate; assign as a quality or attribute. See synonyms under ATTRIBUTE. [< L *ascribere* < *ad-* to + *scribere* write] **—as·crib·a·ble** (ə-skrī'bə·bəl) *adj.*

as·crip·tion (ə-skrip'shən) *n.* **1** An ascribing or being ascribed. **2** An expression ascribing, or

that which is ascribed. **3** A text or sentence ascribing praise and glory to the Almighty. [< L *ascriptio, -onis* < *ascribere.* See ASCRIBE.]

as·cus (as'kəs) *n. pl.* **as·ci** (as'ī) *Bot.* A large cell or spore case in ascomycetous fungi and lichens. [< NL < Gk. *askos* bag, wine-skin]

as·dic (az'dik) *n.* A hydrophone, operating through the reflection of sound waves under water. Also **AS'DIC.** [< A(LLIED) S(UBMARINE) D(ETECTION) I(NVESTIGATION) C(OMMITTEE)]

-ase *suffix Chem.* Used in naming enzymes, chiefly of vegetable origin: sometimes added to a part or the whole of the name of the compound which the enzyme decomposes: *amylase, casease,* etc. [< (DIAST)ASE]

a·sea (ə-sē') *adv.* To or toward the sea; at sea.

a·se·mi·a (ə-sē'mē·ə) *n. Psychiatry* Loss of power to understand signs of communication. [< NL < A.⁴ without + Gk. *sēma* sign]

a·sep·sis (ə-sep'sis, ā-) *n. Med.* **1** Absence of or freedom from putrefactive infection. **2** The prevention of septic infection by the use of sterilized instruments, dressings, etc.

a·sep·tic (ə-sep'tik, ā-) *adj.* **1** Exempt from septic or blood poisoning conditions and from pathogenic micro-organisms. **2** Characterizing processes tending to remove such conditions. **3** Free from disease germs or tendency to putrefaction. *—n.* An aseptic preparation. **—a·sep'ti·cal·ly** *adv.*

a·sep·ti·cism (ə-sep'tə·siz'əm, ā-) *n.* The theory and practice of aseptic surgery.

a·sep·ti·cize (ə-sep'tə·sīz, ā-) *v.t.* **·cized, ·ciz·ing** To make aseptic.

a·sex·u·al (ā-sek'shōō·əl) *adj. Biol.* **1** Having no distinct sexual organs; without sex. **2** Occurring or performed without commerce of the sexes; agamic: *asexual* methods of reproduction. **—a·sex·u·al·i·ty** (ā-sek'shōō·al'ə·tē) *n.* **—a·sex'u·al·ly** *adv.*

a·sex·u·al·i·za·tion (ā-sek'shōō·əl·ə·zā'shən, -ī·zā'-) *n.* The act of unsexing, as by castration.

As·gard (as'gärd, äs'-) In Norse mythology, the home of the Æsir; the residence of heroes slain in battle. See BIFROST. Also **As·garth** (äs'gärth), **As·gar·dhr** (äs'gär'thr').

ash¹ (ash) *n.* **1** The powdery, whitish-gray residue of a substance that has been burnt. See ASHES. **2** *Geol.* Comminuted lava as ejected by a volcano. [OE *asce, æsce*]

ash² (ash) *n.* **1** Any of a widely distributed genus (*Fraxinus*) of trees of the olive family, as the American white ash (*F. alba*) and the European ash (*F. excelsior*). **2** Its light, tough, elastic wood. *—adj.* Made of ash wood. [OE *æsc*]

a·shamed (ə-shāmd') *adj.* **1** Feeling shame; confused by consciousness of fault or impropriety; abashed. **2** Deterred by fear of shame; reluctant. [Orig. pp. of obs. v. *ashame* to shame or feel shame] **—a·sham·ed·ly** (ə-shā'·mid·lē) *adv.* **—a·sham·ed·ness** *n.*

A·shan·ti (ə-shan'tē, ə-shän'-) **1** A former native kingdom and British protectorate in western Africa, included since 1957 in Ghana. **2** A native of this region. **3** The Sudanic language spoken there: also called *Twi.* Also **A·shan'tee.**

ash·cake (ash'kāk) *n.* A cake, especially cornbread, baked in hot ashes.

ash·can (ash'kan) *n.* **1** A large can or metal receptacle for cinders and ashes. **2** *U.S. Slang* A depth bomb.

ash·en¹ (ash'ən) *adj.* Of, pertaining to, or like ashes: pale in color; gray.

ash·en² (ash'ən) *adj.* Pertaining to or made of the wood of the ash tree.

ash·er·y (ash'ər·ē) *n. pl.* **·er·ies** **1** A place of deposit for ashes. **2** A place where potash is made.

ash·es (ash'iz) *n. pl.* **1** The grayish-white, powdery particles, often intermixed with charred fragments, remaining after something has been burned. **2** The remains of the human body after cremation. **3** Any dead body; corpse. **4** Remains or ruins, as after destruction. **5 The Ashes** A symbol of victory in international cricket matches between Australia and England. See ASH¹.

Ashe·ville (ash'vil) A resort city of western North Carolina.

a·shine (ə-shīn') *adv.* Luminously. *—adj.* Shining.

Ash·ke·lon (ash'kə·lon) An ancient city on the Mediterranean coast of southern Palestine: also *Ascalon, Askalon.*

Ash·ke·naz·im (ash'kə·naz'im, äsh'kə·nä'zim) *n. pl.* The Jews settled in northern and central Europe: distinguished from the *Sephardim.* [< Hebrew] **—Ash'ke·naz'ic** *adj.*

ash·lar (ash'lər) *n.* **1** In masonry, a rough-hewn block of stone. **2** A thin, dressed, squared stone, used for facing a wall. **3** Masonwork made of either kind of ashlar. Also **ash'ler.** [< OF *aiseler* < L *axilla,* dim. of *axis* board, plank]

ash·lar·ing (ash'lər·ing) *n.* **1** In carpentry, upright wooden plaster studs running from the floor of a garret to the rafters. **2** Ashlar masonry. Also **ash'ler·ing.**

ash·man (ash'man) *n. pl.* **·men** (-men') A man who collects and removes ashes.

a·shore (ə-shôr', ə-shōr') *adv.* **1** To or on the shore. **2** On land; aground.

ash·ram (äsh'rəm) *n.* **1** In India, a Hindu hermitage or religious retreat. **2** A religious commune. **3** A commune of hippies. [< Skt. *āśrama* < *ā* toward + *śrama* exertion]

Ash·to·reth (ash'tə·reth) An ancient Phoenician and Syrian goddess of love and fertility: identified with *Astarte.*

ash·tray (ash'trā) *n.* A receptacle for the ashes and butts of cigars, cigarettes, and pipes. Also **ash tray.**

A·shur (ä'shōōr, ash'ər) See ASSYRIA.

A·shur·ba·ni·pal (ä'shoor·bä'ni·päl) Assyrian king 668–625 B.C.: known as *Sardanapalus.*

Ash Wednesday The first day of Lent: from the sprinkling of ashes on the heads of penitents.

ash·y (ash'ē) *adj.* **ash·i·er, ash·i·est** **1** Of, pertaining to, or like ashes; ash-covered. **2** Ash-colored; ashen.

A·sia (ā'zhə, ā'shə) The world's largest continent, bounded by Europe and the Pacific, Arctic, and Indian Oceans; 16,900,000 square miles.

Asia Minor The peninsula of extreme western Asia between the Black and the Mediterranean Seas, comprising most of Turkey in Asia: also *Anatolia.*

A·sian (ā'zhən, ā'shən) *adj.* Of, pertaining to, or characteristic of Asia or its peoples. *—n.* A native or inhabitant of Asia.

A·si·at·ic (ā'zhē·at'ik, ā'shē-) *adj. & n.* Asian. ◆ Especially in the ethnic sense *Asian* is now preferred to *Asiatic,* because of the supposed derogatory implications of the latter term.

Asiatic beetle A scarabaeid beetle (*Anomala orientalis*) destructive of sugarcane and grass roots, introduced from Japan into Hawaii and the NE United States.

a·side (ə-sīd') *adv.* **1** On or to one side; apart; away. **2** Out of thought or use. **3** Away from the general company; in seclusion: He drew his friend *aside* to speak more intimately. **4** Away from one's person; down: He cast his weapon *aside.* **5** In reserve: Keep some *aside* for me. **—aside from 1** Excepting. **2** *U.S.* Apart from. **—to set aside** *Law* To declare of no authority, as a verdict, judgment, etc. *—n.* Something spoken privately, as a remark or speech by an actor supposed to be heard by the audience but not by the other actors. [< A.¹ on + SIDE]

as·i·nine (as'ə·nīn) *adj.* Pertaining to or like an ass, characterized as a stupid, silly animal. [< L *asininus* < *asinus* ass] **—as'i·nine'ly** *adv.* **—as·i·nin·i·ty** (as'ə·nin'ə·tē) *n.*

A·sir (ä·sir') A mountainous region in western Arabia on the Red Sea between Hejaz and Yemen.

ask (ask, äsk) *v.t.* **1** To put a question to: Don't *ask* me. **2** To put a question about; inquire after: to *ask* someone the time. **3** To make a request for; solicit: to *ask* advice. **4** To need or require: This job *asks* more of me than I can give. **5** To state the price of; demand: They are *asking* three dollars a plate. **6** To invite: Were many guests *asked*? **7** *Archaic* To publish or proclaim, as the banns of marriage in a church. *—v.i.* **8** To make inquiries with *for, after,* or *about.* **9** To make a request: How often must I *ask*? [OE *āscian*] **—ask'er** *n.* **—ask'ing** *n.*

Synonyms: beg, beseech, crave, demand, entreat, implore, petition, plead, pray, request, require, solicit, supplicate. One *asks* what he feels that he may fairly claim and reasonably expect; he *begs* for that to which he advances no claim but pity. *Entreat* implies a special earnestness of asking, and *beseech,* a still added and more humble intensity. To *supplicate* is to *ask,* as it were, on bended knees; to *implore,* with the added force of tears. *Crave* and *request* are somewhat formal terms; *crave* has almost disappeared from conversation. *Pray* is now used chiefly of address to the Supreme Being; *petition* is used of written request to persons in authority. *Beg* and *pray* are often used in polite forms of slight request; *beseech* was formerly so used. Compare DEMAND, INQUIRE. *Antonyms:* claim, command, deny, enforce, exact, extort, insist, refuse.

a·skance (ə·skans′) *adv.* **1** With a side glance; sidewise. **2** Disdainfully; distrustfully. Also **a·skant′.** [Origin unknown]

a·skew (ə·skyōō′) *adj.* Oblique. —*adv.* In an oblique position or manner; to one side. [< A-¹ on + SKEW]

a·slant (ə·slant′, ə·slänt′) *adj.* Slanting; oblique. —*adv.* In a slanting direction or position; obliquely. —*prep.* Across or over in a slanting direction or position; athwart.

a·sleep (ə·slēp′) *adj.* **1** In a state of sleep; sleeping. **2** Dormant; inactive. **3** Benumbed. **4** Dead. —*adv.* Into a sleeping condition: to fall *asleep.*

a·slope (ə·slōp′) *adj.* Sloping. —*adv.* In a sloping position.

a·so·cial (ā·sō′shəl) *adj.* **1** Avoiding society; not gregarious. **2** Regardless of one's fellow beings; self-centered.

a·so·ma·tous (ā·sō′mə·təs, ə-) *adj.* Not having bodily form; disembodied; incorporeal. [< L *asomatus,* < Gk. *asōmatos* < *a-* without + *sōma* body]

A·so·san (ä·sō·sän) A group of five extinct volcanic cones on central Kyushu island, Japan; 5,223 feet; world's largest crater, 10 by 15 miles. Also **Mount A·so** (ä′sō).

asp¹ (asp) *n.* **1** The common European viper. **2** The haje. **3** The uraeus. [< OF *aspe* < L *aspis* < Gk.]

asp² (asp) *n.* The aspen.

as·par·a·gus (ə·spar′ə·gəs) *n.* **1** The succulent edible shoots of a cultivated variety of a perennial herb *(Asparagus officinalis)* of the lily family. **2** Any plant of this genus. [< L < Gk. *asparagos, aspharogos*]

asparagus beetle A beetle *(Crioceris asparagi)* harmful to asparagus shoots. See illustration under INSECT. (injurious).

as·par·tame (as·pär′tām) *n.* A synthetic combination of the amino acids aspartic acid and phenylalanine, used as a sweetener in foods.

as·par·tic acid (as·pär′tik) A white crystalline amino acid, $C_4H_7O_4N$, found in plant and animal proteins. [< ASPARAGUS]

as·pect (as′pekt) *n.* **1** The look a person has; expression of countenance. **2** Appearance presented to the eye by something; look. **3** Appearance presented to the mind by circumstances, etc.; interpretation. **4** A looking or facing in a given direction. **5** The side or surface facing in a certain direction. **6** In astrology: **a** Any configuration of the planets. **b** The supposed resulting influence of this for good or evil. **7** *Gram.* A categorizing of the verb indicating, primarily, the nature of the action performed in regard to the passage of time, as in English *he ran* (perfective), *he was running* (imperfective or durative), and, in certain languages, the manner in which the action is performed, the intent of the subject, etc., as in Hebrew *'ākhal* he eats, *'ikkēl* he eats greedily. Aspect is shown in the various languages by means of auxiliaries, affixes, root changes, etc. **8** *Obs.* A look; glance. See synonyms under MANNER. [< L *aspectus,* pp. of *aspicere* look at < *ad-* at + *specere* look]

asp·en (as′pən) *n.* Any of several kinds of poplar of North America or Europe with leaves that tremble in the slightest breeze, especially the *quaking* aspen *(Populus tremuloides)* of North America: also *asp.* —*adj.* Of, like, or pertaining to the aspen; hence, shaking; tremulous. [OE *æspe*]

As·pen (as′pən) A resort and cultural center in west central Colorado.

as·per·ate (as′pə·rāt) *v.t.* ·at·ed, ·at·ing To make harsh or uneven, as in sound or contour. [< L *asperatus,* pp. of *asperare* roughen

< *asper* rough]

as·per·ges (ə·spûr′jēz) *n.* **1** A short service before the high mass on Sundays during which the celebrant sprinkles the altar and congregation with holy water. **2** An anthem, beginning "Asperges me", sung during this service. [< L, thou shalt sprinkle]

as·per·gill (as′pər·jil) *n.* In the Roman Catholic Church, a brush or other instrument used for sprinkling holy water: also *aspergillum.* See ASPERSORIUM. [< LL *aspergillum* < L *aspergere.* See ASPERSE.]

ASPERGILL

as·per·gil·lo·sis (as·pûr′jə·lō′sis) *n.* An infectious disease of animals and man, caused by any fungus of the genus *Aspergillus.*

as·per·gil·lum (as′pər·jil′əm) *n. pl.* ·gil·la (-jil′ə) or ·gil·lums Aspergill.

as·per·gil·lus (as′pər·jil′əs) *n. pl.* ·gil·li (-jil′ī) *Bot.* Any of a genus *(Aspergillus)* of fungi belonging to the *Ascomycetes,* including the common mold fungus found on decaying vegetables, jellies, etc. [< NL; so named because of its resemblance to the ASPERGILL]

as·per·i·ty (as·per′ə·tē) *n. pl.* ·ties **1** Roughness or harshness, as of surface, sound, style, etc. **2** Something uneven, harsh, or rough. **3** Bitterness or sharpness of temper; harsh feelings. See synonyms under ACRIMONY. [< OF *asprete* < L *asperitas, -tatis* roughness < *asper* rough]

a·sper·mous (ā·spûr′məs) *adj. Bot.* Without seeds. Also **a·sper·ma·tous** (ā·spûr′mə·təs). [< Gk. *aspermos* < *a-* without + *sperma* seed]

as·perse (ə·spûrs′) *v.t.* **as·persed** (ə·spûrst′), **as·pers·ing 1** To spread false charges against; slander. **2** To besprinkle; bespatter. [< L *aspersus,* pp. of *aspergere* sprinkle on < *ad-* to + *spargere* sprinkle] —**as·pers′er, as·per′sor** *n.* —**as·per′sive** (-siv) *adj.*

Synonyms: backbite, calumniate, decry, defame, depreciate, disparage, libel, malign, revile, slander, traduce, vilify. To *asperse* is to bespatter with injurious charges; to *defame* is to assail one's good name; to *malign* is to circulate studied and malicious attacks upon character; to *traduce* is to exhibit real or assumed traits in an odious light. *Antonyms:* defend, eulogize, extol, laud, praise.

as·per·sion (ə·spûr′zhən, -shən) *n.* **1** A slandering. **2** Slander; a slanderous report or charge. See synonyms under SCANDAL. **3** Sprinkling; specifically, baptism by sprinkling.

as·per·so·ri·um (as′pər·sôr′ē·əm, -sō′rē-) *n. pl.* ·so·ri·a (-sôr′ē·ə, -sō′rē·ə) or ·so·ri·ums **1** A font for holy water. **2** An aspergill. Also **as·per·so·ry** (as·pûr′sə·rē). [< LL < L *aspersus.* See ASPERSE.]

as·phalt (as′fôlt, -falt) *n.* **1** A bituminous, solid, brownish–black, odorous combustible mixture of different hydrocarbons occurring in superficial deposits in various parts of the world and also obtained as a residue in the refining of petroleum; mineral pitch. **2** A mixture of this with sand or gravel, used for paving, etc. Also **as·phal·tum** (as·fal′təm), **as·phal′tus.** —*v.t.* To pave or cover with asphalt. [< LL *asphaltum* < Gk. *asphaltos,* ? < Semitic] —**as·phal·tic** (as·fôl′tik, -fal′-) *adj.*

as·pho·del (as′fə·del) *n.* **1** A plant (genus *Asphodelus*) of the lily family, bearing white or yellow flowers. **2** Any one of certain somewhat similar plants. [< L *asphodelus* < Gk. *asphodelos.* Doublet of DAFFODIL.]

as·phyx·i·a (as·fik′sē·ə) *n. Pathol.* A condition, characterized by loss of consciousness, caused by too little oxygen and too much carbon dioxide in the blood, generally as a result of suffocation. Also **as·phyx·y** (as·fik′sē). [< NL < Gk. *asphyxia* < *a-* not + *sphyzein* beat] —**as·phyx′i·al** *adj.*

as·phyx·i·ant (as·fik′sē·ənt) *adj.* Producing or tending to produce asphyxia. —*n.* An asphyxiant agent or condition.

as·phyx·i·ate (as·fik′sē·āt) *v.* ·at·ed, ·at·ing *v.t.* **1** To cause asphyxia in. **2** To suffocate, as by drowning or causing to breathe noxious gases. —*v.i.* To undergo asphyxia. —*as-*

phyx′i·a′tion *n.* —as·phyx′i·a′tor *n.*

as·pic¹ (as′pik) *n. Poetic* The asp. Also **as′pis.** [< F < L *aspis*]

as·pic² (as′pik) *n.* The spike lavender. See under LAVENDER. [< F < Provençal *espic* < L *spica* spike, ear of corn]

as·pic³ (as′pik) *n.* A savory jelly of meat juice or vegetable juices, served as a relish or mold for meat, vegetables, etc. [< F; ult. origin uncertain]

as·pi·dis·tra (as′pə·dis′trə) *n.* Any of a small genus *(Aspidistra)* of smooth, stemless, Chinese and Japanese herbs of the lily family, with large, glossy, evergreen leaves: widely cultivated as a house plant. [< NL < Gk. *aspis, aspidos* shield + *astron* star]

as·pir·ant (ə·spīr′ənt, as′pər·ənt) *n.* One who aspires, as after honors or place; a candidate. —*adj.* Aspiring.

as·pi·rate (as′pə·rāt) *v.t.* ·rat·ed, ·rat·ing **1** *Phonet.* **a** To utter with a breathing or as if preceded by the letter *h.* **b** In the articulation of a stop consonant, to follow with an explosive release of breath, as (p), (t), and (k) when in initial position. **2** *Med.* To draw out, as gas or fluid, from a vessel or cavity. —*n.* (as′pər·it) *Phonet.* **a** The glottal fricative represented in English and many other languages by the letter *h.* **b** The sudden expulsion of breath in the release of a stop consonant before a vowel, as after the (p) in *pat.* **2** The rough breathing in Greek or the symbol (′) indicating it. **3** Any consonant pronounced with a puff of breath. —*adj.* (as′pər·it) *Phonet.* Uttered with an aspirate or strong *h* sound: also **as′pi·rat′ed.** [< L *aspiratus,* pp. of *aspirare.* See ASPIRE.]

as·pi·ra·tion (as′pə·rā′shən) *n.* **1** The act of aspiring; exalted desire; high ambition. **2** The act or effect of aspirating; a breath. **3** *Med.* The use of an aspirator for remedial purposes. **4** *Phonet.* **a** The pronunciation of a consonant with an aspirate. **b** An aspirate. See synonyms under AIM, AMBITION, DESIRE.

as·pi·ra·tor (as′pə·rā′tər) *n.* **1** An appliance for producing a suction current of air or other gas. **2** *Med.* A device for drawing off fluid matter or gases from the body by suction.

as·pi·ra·to·ry (ə·spīr′ə·tôr′ē, -tō′rē) *adj.* Of, pertaining to, or adapted for breathing or suction.

as·pire (ə·spīr′) *v.i.* **as·pired, as·pir·ing 1** To have an earnest desire or ambition, as for something high and good: with *to.* **2** To long for; seek after: with *after.* **3** *Obs.* To reach or rise upward. [< L *aspirare* breathe on, attempt to reach < *ad-* to + *spirare* breathe] —**as·pir′ing** *adj.* —**as·pir′er** *n.*

as·pi·rin (as′pər·in) *n.* A white crystalline compound, the acetyl derivative of salicylic acid, $C_9H_8O_4$, having antipyretic and antirheumatic properties. [< A(CETYL) + SPIR- (AEIC ACID), former name of salicylic acid, + -IN]

a·squint (ə·skwint′) *adj. & adv.* With sidelong glance. [< A-¹ on + SQUINT (of uncertain origin)]

ass¹ (as) *n.* **1** A long-eared equine quadruped *(Equus asinus)* smaller than the ordinary horse. **2** The Mongolian onager. **3** An obstinate or stupid person. [OE *assa,* ? < OIrish *assan* < L *asinus*]

ass² (äs) *n. Scot.* Ashes: also spelled *aise.*

ass³ (as) *n. Slang* The buttocks: usually considered vulgar. [ME *ars* < OE *ærs, ears*]

as·sa·gai (as′ə·gī) *n.* **1** A light spear, used by

ASSAGAI

Zulus, Kafirs, etc. **2** The assagai tree. —*v.t.* To pierce with an assagai. Also *assegai.* [< Sp. *azagaya* or Pg. *azagaia* < Arabic *az-zaghāyah* < *al* the + *zaghāyah* spear < native Berber word]

assagai tree A South African tree *(Curtisia faginea)* of the dogwood family, used for making spears.

as·sai¹ (ä·sä′ē) *n.* **1** A palm of the genus *Euterpe,* especially *E. edulis,* bearing a purple, fleshy fruit. **2** A drink made from this fruit. [< Pg. *assahy* < Tupian]

---

add,āce,câre,pälm; end,ēven; it,īce; odd,ōpen,ôrder; tōōk,pōōl; up,bûrn; ə = a in *above,* e in *sicken,* i in *clarity,* o in *melon,* u in *focus;* yōō = u in *fuse,* oi,oil; ou,pout; ch,check; g,go; ng,ring; th,thin; t̷h,this; zh,vision. Foreign sounds à,œ,ü,kh,ṅ; and ◆: see page xx. <from; + plus; ? possibly.

as·sai² (äs·sä′ē) *adv. Music* Very: Adagio *assai* means very slowly. [<Ital.]

as·sail (ə·sāl′) *v.t.* **1** To attack violently, as by force, argument, or censure; assault. **2** To approach, as a difficulty, with the intention of mastering. See synonyms under ATTACK. [<OF *asalir, asaillir* <LL *adsalire* leap upon <L *ad-* to + *salire* leap] — **as·sail′a·ble** *adj.* — **as·sail′a·ble·ness** *n.* — **as·sail′er** *n.*

as·sail·ant (ə·sā′lənt) *adj.* Attacking; hostile. — *n.* One who assails.

as·sas·sin (ə·sas′in) *n.* **1** One who kills, tries to kill, secretly or treacherously. **2** One who undertakes to commit murder, particularly of a political figure, for a reward.

as·sas·si·nate (ə·sas′ə·nāt) *v.t.* **·nat·ed, ·nat·ing 1** To kill by secret or surprise assault. **2** To destroy or wound by treachery, as a reputation. See synonyms under KILL. — **as·sas′si·na′tion** *n.* — **as·sas′si·na′tor** *n.*

as·sault (ə·sôlt′) *n.* **1** Any violent attack, as an act, speech, or writing assailing a person or institution. **2** *Law* An unlawful attempt or offer to do bodily injury to another: distinguished from *battery*. **3** A rape. **4** *Mil.* A violent attack by troops, as upon a fortified place. See synonyms under AGGRESSION, ATTACK. — *v.t. & v.i.* To attack with violence; make an assault (upon). [<OF *asaut* <L *ad-* to + *salire* leap] — **as·sault′er** *n.*

assault and battery *Law* The carrying out of an assault with force and violence; a beating.

as·say (ə·sā′, as′ā) *n.* **1** The chemical analysis or testing of an alloy or ore, to ascertain the ingredients and their proportions. **2** The substance to be so examined. **3** The result of such a test. **4** Any examination or testing. **5** *Obs.* Attempt; trial. — *v.t.* (ə·sā′) **1** To subject to chemical analysis; make an assay of. **2** To prove; test. **3** *Obs.* To attempt. — *v.i.* **4** To show by analysis a certain value or proportion, as of a precious metal: to *assay* low in platinum. [<OF *assai*, var. of *essai* trial <L *exagium* a weighing < *exigere* prove < *ex-* out + *agere* drive, do. Doublet of ESSAY.] — **as·say′er** *n.*

as·sem·blage (ə·sem′blij, *for def.* 4, *also* Fr. à·säN·blàzh′) *n.* **1** An assembling or being assembled. **2** Any gathering of persons or things; collection; assembly. **3** A fitting together, as parts of a machine. **4** A work of art created by assembling materials and objects; also, the technique of making such works. See synonyms under ASSEMBLY, COMPANY. [<F]

as·sem·ble (ə·sem′bəl) *v.t. & v.i.* **·bled, ·bling 1** To collect or convene; come together; congregate, as a group or meeting. **2** To fit or join together, as the parts of a mechanism. See synonyms under CONVOKE. [<OF *as(s)embler* <L *assimulare* <*ad-* to + *simul* together] — **as·sem′bler** *n.*

as·sem·bly (ə·sem′blē) *n. pl.* **·blies 1** An assembling or being assembled. **2** A number of persons met together for a common purpose. **3** The act or process of fitting together the parts of a machine, etc., especially where such parts are machine-made in great numbers so as to be interchangeable. **4** A unit made up of such parts. **5** The parts themselves, before or after being fitted together. **6** *Mil.* The signal calling troops to form ranks. [<OF *as(s)emblee* <*as(s)embler*. See ASSEMBLE.]

Synonyms: assemblage, collection, company, conclave, concourse, conference, congregation, convention, convocation, crowd, gathering, group, host, meeting, multitude. An *assemblage* may be of persons or of objects and is promiscuous and unorganized, an *assembly* is always of persons and is organized and united in some common purpose.

assembly line An arrangement of machines and workers in a factory, as along a moving track or belt, so that a number of specialized operations may be performed on a unit of work as it passes from one to another.

as·sent (ə·sent′) *v.i.* To express agreement, as with an abstract proposition; acquiesce; concur: usually with *to*. — *n.* **1** Mental concurrence or agreement. **2** Consent of will; acquiescence. ◆ Homophone: *ascent.* [<OF *as(s)enter* <L *assentare*, freq. of *assentire* <*ad-* to + *sentire* feel] — **as·sent′er** *n.*

Synonyms (verb): accede, accept, accord, acquiesce, admit, agree, approve, coincide, concur, consent, ratify, sustain, uphold. To

assent is an act of the understanding; to *consent*, of the will. *Assent* is sometimes used for a mild or formal *consent*. See BELIEF. *Antonyms:* contradict, demur, deny, differ, disagree, disavow, disclaim, dissent, object, protest, question, refuse.

as·sen·ta·tion (as′en·tā′shən) *n.* Obsequious assent, as to the opinions of another.

as·sert (ə·sûrt′) *v.t.* **1** To state positively; affirm; declare. **2** To maintain as a right or claim, as by words or force. **3** To insist on the recognition of (oneself): He *asserted* himself at the conference. [<L *assertus*, pp. of *asserere* bind to, claim <*ad-* to + *serere* bind] — **as·sert′er, as·ser′tor** *n.*

Synonyms: affirm, allege, asseverate, aver, avouch, avow, claim, declare, maintain, pronounce, protest, say, state, tell. One may *assert* himself, his right, his belief, etc. *Assert* is controversial; *affirm, state,* and *tell* are simply declarative. See AFFIRM, ALLEGE. *Antonyms:* contradict, contravene, controvert, deny, disprove, dispute, gainsay, oppose, repudiate, retract, waive.

as·ser·tion (ə·sûr′shən) *n.* **1** The act of asserting. **2** A positive declaration without attempt at proof. **3** Insistence upon a right or claim. See synonyms under ASSURANCE.

as·ser·tive (ə·sûr′tiv) *adj.* **1** Of, pertaining to, or characterized by assertion. **2** Characterized by excessive assertion; overly insistent. — **as·ser′tive·ly** *adv.* — **as·ser′tive·ness** *n.*

as·ser·to·ry (ə·sûr′tər·ē) *adj.* Tending to assert.

as·sess (ə·ses′) *v.t.* **1** To charge with a tax, fine, or other payment, as a person or property. **2** To determine the amount of, as a tax or other fine on a person or property. **3** To value, as property, for taxation. **4** To take stock of; evaluate: to *assess* the situation. See synonyms under TAX. [<OF *assesser* <LL *assessare* fix a tax <L *assidere* sit by (as a judge in court) <*ad-* to + *sedere* sit] — **as·sess′a·ble** *adj.*

as·sess·ment (ə·ses′mənt) *n.* **1** An assessing. **2** Apportionment or amount assessed. **3** The valuation of property for taxation.

as·ses·sor (ə·ses′ər) *n.* **1** One who makes assessments, as for taxation. **2** A specialist assisting a judge. **3** Any adviser or assistant. [<L, lit., one who sits beside, an assistant judge (in LL, an assessor of taxes) <*assidere*. See ASSESS.] — **as·ses·so·ri·al** (as′ə·sôr′ē·əl, -sō′rē-) *adj.*

as·set (as′et) *n.* **1** An item of property. **2** A person, thing, or quality regarded as useful or valuable: Her intelligence is an *asset.*

as·sets (as′ets) *n. pl.* **1** *Law* The property of a deceased person that is convertible into money and held for the payment of debts or legacies. **2** All the property, real and personal, of a person, of a corporation, or of a partnership, which is or may be chargeable with the debts or legacies of such parties or persons. **3** In accounting, the entries in a balance sheet showing all the property or resources of a person or business, as accounts receivable, inventory, deferred charges, and plant: opposed to *liabilities.* — **liquid assets** Such securities and assets as can be realized immediately. — **working assets** Non-permanent convertible invested funds. [<AF *asetz*, OF *asez* enough <L *ad-* to + *satis* enough]

as·sev·er·ate (ə·sev′ə·rāt) *v.t.* **·at·ed, ·at·ing** To affirm or aver emphatically or solemnly. See synonyms under AFFIRM, ALLEGE, ASSERT. [<L *asseveratus*, pp. of *asseverare* <*ad-* to + *severus* serious] — **as·sev′er·a′tion** *n.*

as·sib·i·late (ə·sib′ə·lāt) *v.t.* **·lat·ed, ·lat·ing** To utter with a sibilant or hissing sound; change into· a sibilant. [<L *assibilatus*, pp. of *assibilare* <*ad-* to + *sibilare* hiss] — **as·sib′i·la′tion** *n.*

as·si·du·i·ty (as′ə·doo′ə·tē, -dyoo′-) *n. pl.* **·ties 1** Close and continuous application or effort. **2** *Usually pl.* Faithful personal attentions; carefulness; watchfulness. See synonyms under INDUSTRY.

as·sid·u·ous (ə·sij′oo·əs) *adj.* **1** Devoted or constant, as a person. **2** Unremitting; persistent, as an action. See synonyms under BUSY, INDUSTRIOUS. [<L *assiduus* <*assidere* sit by <*ad-* to + *sedere* sit] — **as·sid′u·ous·ly** *adv.* — **as·sid′u·ous·ness** *n.*

as·sign (ə·sīn′) *v.t.* **1** To set apart, as for a particular function; designate. **2** To appoint or station: to *assign* a soldier to a post. **3** To

allot: to *assign* a share to a participant. **4** To ascribe or attribute: to *assign* a date to an event. **5** *Law* To make over or transfer, as personal property, to another. **6** *Mil.* To allocate, as personnel, units or materiel, to a military unit as an integral unit thereof: distinguished from *attach.* See synonyms under ALLEGE, ALLOT, APPORTION, ATTRIBUTE, COMMIT, SET. — *n. Law* Usually *pl.* Assignee. [<OF *as(s)igner* <L *assignare* <*ad-* to + *signare* make a sign <*signum* sign]

as·sign·a·ble (ə·sī′nə·bəl) *adj.* **1** Capable of being assigned or allotted. **2** Legally transferable. **3** Attributable: Volcanoes are *assignable* to these geographical conditions. — **as·sign′a·bil′i·ty** *n.* — **as·sign′a·bly** *adv.*

as·sig·na·tion (as′ig·nā′shən) *n.* **1** An assigning or being assigned. **2** Something assigned; assignment. **3** An appointment for meeting, especially a secret or illicit one as made by lovers. **4** *Law* An assignment. [<OF *assignacion* <L *assignatio, -onis* < *assignare.* See ASSIGN.]

as·sign·ee (ə·sī′nē′, as′ə·nē′) *n.* **1** *Law* A person to whom property, rights, or powers are transferred by another. **2** *Obs.* An agent or trustee.

as·sign·ment (ə·sīn′mənt) *n.* **1** An assigning or being assigned. **2** Anything assigned, as a lesson or task. **3** *Law* **a** The transfer of a claim, right, or property or the instrument or writing of transfer. **b** The claim, right, or property transferred.

as·sign·or (ə·sī′nôr′, as′ə·nôr′) *n. Law* One who assigns or makes an assignment of any property, right, or interest. Also **as·sign·er** (ə·sī′nər).

as·sim·i·la·ble (ə·sim′ə·lə·bəl) *adj.* Capable of being assimilated. — **as·sim′i·la·bil′i·ty** *n.*

as·sim·i·late (ə·sim′ə·lāt) *v.* **·lat·ed, ·lat·ing** *v.t.* **1** *Physiol.* To take up and incorporate, as food. **2** To make into a homogeneous part, as of a substance or system. **3** To make alike or similar; cause to resemble: to *assimilate* British law to the laws of Scotland. **4** *Phonet.* To cause (a sound) to undergo assimilation. — *v.i.* **5** To become alike or similar. **6** To become absorbed or assimilated. See synonyms under COMPARE. [<L *assimilatus*, pp. of *assimilare* <*ad-* to + *similare* make like <*similis* like]

as·sim·i·la·tion (ə·sim′ə·lā′shən) *n.* **1** The act or process of assimilating. **2** *Physiol.* The transformation of digested nutriment into an integral and homogeneous part of the solids or fluids of the organism. **3** *Bot.* The starch-making function of plants. Compare ANABOLISM. **4** *Phonet.* The process whereby a sound is changed or modified to cause it to approach, or become identical with, a neighboring sound, as in the pronunciation (hôrsh′shōō′) for horseshoe. **5** *Psychol.* The process by which all new experience, when received into consciousness, is modified so as to be incorporated with the results of previous conscious processes. **6** *Sociol.* The acceptance by one social group or community of cultural traits normally associated with another.

as·sim·i·la·tive (ə·sim′ə·lā′tiv) *adj.* Assimilating; characterized by or tending to assimilation. Also **as·sim·i·la·to·ry** (ə·sim′ə·lə·tôr·ē, -tō′rē).

As·sin·i·boin (ə·sin′ə·boin) *n. pl.* **·boins** or **·boin 1** A member of a tribe of North American Indians of Siouan stock, formerly inhabiting parts of Montana, North Dakota, and Saskatchewan. **2** The language of this tribe.

As·sin·i·boine (ə·sin′ə·boin) **1** A river in eastern Saskatchewan, Canada, flowing SE 600 miles to Red River at Winnipeg. **2** A mountain of the Canadian Rockies, in Banff National Park; 11,870 feet.

As·si·si (ə·sē′zē, *Ital.* äs·sē′zē) A town in Umbria, central Italy; birthplace of St. Francis.

as·sist (ə·sist′) *v.t.* **1** To give succor or support to; render help or service to; relieve. **2** To act as subordinate or deputy to. — *v.i.* **3** To give help or support. **4** In baseball, to aid a teammate or partner in a play. — **to assist at** To be present at (a ceremony, entertainment, etc.). — *n.* In baseball, a play that helps to put out a runner. See synonyms under ABET, AID, HELP, SERVE. [<F *assister* <L *assistere* <*ad-* to + *sistere* cause to stand]

—as·sist′er, as·sis′tor *n.*

as·sis·tance (ə-sis′təns) *n.* Help; aid; support; relief. See synonyms under HELP.

as·sis·tant (ə-sis′tənt) *adj.* **1** Holding a subordinate or auxiliary place, office, or rank. **2** Affording aid; assisting. —*n.* One who or that which assists; a deputy or subordinate; helper. See synonyms under ACCESSORY, AUXILIARY.

as·so·ci·a·ble (ə-sō′shē-ə-bəl, -shə-bəl) *adj.* Capable of being associated, connected, or joined. —as·so′ci·a·bil′i·ty *n.*

as·so·ci·ate (ə-sō′shē-it, -āt) *n.* **1** A companion; one who is habitually or frequently in the company or society of another. **2** A partner; one who is connected with another, as in some business, act, interest, office, or position. **3** Anything that habitually or frequently accompanies or is associated with something else; a concomitant. **4** One admitted to partial membership in an association, society, or institution. **5** In some educational institutions, one who has finished a course shorter than that set for a degree: an *associate* in arts. —*adj.* **1** Joined with another or others; united; allied; existing or occurring together; concomitant. **2** Having subordinate or secondary status or privileges: an *associate* professor; also, entitled to a limited or specified participation, as in rights, privileges, and functions: an *associate* member of a society. —*v.* (ə-sō′shē-āt) ·at·ed, ·at·ing *v.t.* **1** To bring into company or relation; combine together. **2** To unite (oneself) with another or others, as in friendship or partnership. **3** To connect mentally: to *associate* poetry with madness. —*v.i.* **4** To join or be in company or relation: with *with:* She *associates* chiefly with musicians. **5** To unite, as nations in a league; combine. See synonyms under ATTRIBUTE, MIX, UNITE. [<L *associatus,* pp. of *associare* join to < *ad-* to + *sociare* join < *socius* ally]

Synonyms (noun): ally, chum, coadjutor, colleague, companion, comrade, consort, fellow, friend, helpmate, mate, partner, peer. An *associate,* as used officially, implies a chief, leader, or principal, to whom the *associate* is not fully equal in rank. *Associate* is popularly used for mere friendly relations, but oftener implies some work, enterprise, or pursuit in which the associated persons unite. We rarely speak of *associates* in crime or wrong, using *confederates* or *accomplices* instead. *Companion* gives itself with equal readiness to the good or the evil sense. *Peer* implies equality rather than companionship; as, a jury of his *peers.* *Comrade* expresses more fellowship and good feeling than *companion.* *Consort* is a word of equality and dignity, as applied especially to the marriage relation. Compare ACCESSORY, ACQUAINTANCE, FRIENDSHIP. *Antonyms:* antagonist, enemy, foe, hinderer, opponent, opposer, rival, stranger.

as·so·ci·a·tion (ə-sō′sē-ā′shən, -shē-) *n.* **1** An associating or the act of associating. **2** The state of being associated; fellowship; companionship. **3** A body of persons associated for some common purpose; corporation; society; partnership. **4** *U.S.* An organized, unchartered body of persons analogous to but distinguished legally from a corporation. **5** *Chem.* An aggregate, as of molecules: $(H_2O)_2$ is an *association* of two molecules of water. **6** *Ecol.* A grouping of many plant species over a wide area, sharing a common habitat and similar geographic conditions: a forest *association.* **7** *Psychol.* **a** The connection or relation of ideas, feelings, etc., with each other, with objects suggesting them, or with subjects of thought, by means of which their succession in the mind is determined. **b** The process of establishing such a connection. **8** *Brit.* Association football. —as·so′ci·a′tion·al *adj.*

Synonyms: alliance, club, community, companionship, company, confederacy, confederation, conjunction, connection, corporation, familiarity, federation, fellowship, fraternity, friendship, lodge, partnership, society, union. We speak of an *alliance* of nations, a *club* of pleasure-seekers, a *community* of Shakers, a *company* of soldiers or of friends, a con-

federacy, confederation, federation, or *union* of states, a *partnership, corporation,* or *company* in business, a *conjunction* of planets, a religious, literary, or scientific *association* or *society.* See ACQUAINTANCE, ALLIANCE, ASSOCIATE, CLASS, FRIENDSHIP, INTERCOURSE. *Antonyms:* disconnection, disunion, independence, isolation, separateness, separation, severance, solitude.

association football Soccer.

as·so·ci·a·tive (ə-sō′shē-ā′tiv, -shē-ə-) *adj.* **1** Of, pertaining to, or characterized by association. **2** Causing association. —as·so′ci·a′tive·ly *adv.*

as·so·nance (as′ə-nəns) *n.* **1** Resemblance in sound; specifically, in prosody, correspondence of the accented vowels, but not of the consonants, as in *main, came.* **2** Rough likeness; approximation. [<F <L *assonans,* ppr. of *assonare* sound to, respond to < *ad-* to + *sonare* sound] —as′so·nant *adj. & n.*

as·sort (ə-sôrt′) *v.t.* **1** To distribute into groups or classes according to kinds; classify. **2** To furnish, as a warehouse, with a variety of goods, etc. —*v.i.* **3** To fall into groups or classes of the same kind. **4** To associate; consort: with ·*with.* [<OF *assorter* < *a-* to (<L *ad-*) + *sorte* sort <L *sors* lot] —as·sort·a·tive (ə-sôr′tə·tiv) *adj.*

as·sort·ed (ə-sôr′tid) *adj.* **1** Consisting of or arranged in various sorts or kinds; varied; miscellaneous. **2** Sorted out; classified. **3** Matched; suited.

as·sort·ment (ə-sôrt′mənt) *n.* **1** The act of assorting or a being assorted; classification. **2** A collection or group of various things; miscellany.

as·suage (ə-swāj′) *v.* as·suaged, as·suag·ing *v.t.* **1·** To make less harsh or violent; soothe; calm, as an excited person. **2** To alleviate; allay, as feelings. —*v.i.* **3** *Obs.* To grow less; abate; subside. Also *Obs.* as·swage′. See synonyms under ALLAY, ALLEVIATE. [<OF *as-(s)ouagier,* ult. <L *ad-* to + *suavis* sweet] —as·suage′ment *n.*

as·sua·sive (ə-swā′siv) *adj.* Soothing; alleviating. —*n.* An alleviative.

as·sume (ə-sōōm′) *v.t.* as·sumed, as·sum·ing **1** To take up or adopt, as a style of dress, aspect, or character: to *assume* a haughty mien. **2** To undertake, as an office or duty. **3** To arrogate to oneself; usurp, as powers of state. **4** To take for granted; suppose to be a fact: to *assume* the sun will shine tomorrow. **5** To affect; pretend to have. [<L *assumere* take up, adopt < *ad-* to + *sumere* take] —as·sum·a·ble (ə-sōō′mə·bəl) *adj.*

Synonyms: accept, affect, appropriate, arrogate, claim, feign, postulate, presume, pretend, take, usurp. The distinctive idea of *assume* is to *take* by one's own independent volition, whether well or ill, rightfully or wrongfully. One may *accept* an obligation or *assume* an authority that properly belongs to him; if he *assumes* what does not belong to him, he is said to *arrogate* or *usurp* it. A man may *usurp* the substance of *power* in the most unpretending way; what he *arrogates* to himself he *assumes* with a haughty and overbearing manner. If he *takes* to himself the credit and appearance of qualities he does not possess, he is said to *affect* or *feign,* or to *pretend* to, the character he thus *assumes.* What a debater *postulates* he openly states and *takes* for granted without proof; what he *assumes* he may *take* for granted without mention. What a man *claims* he asserts his right to *take;* what he *assumes* he *takes.* See PRETEND. *Antonyms:* see synonyms for RENOUNCE.

as·sumed (ə-sōōmd′) *adj.* **1** Taken for granted. **2** Pretended; fictitious.

as·sum·ing (ə-sōō′ming) *adj.* Presumptuous; arrogant.

as·sump·sit (ə-sump′sit) *n. Law* **1** A promise or contract not under seal. **2** An action to enforce this, or to recover damages for a breach of this. [<L, he undertook]

as·sump·tion (ə-sump′shən) *n.* **1** An assuming, or that which is assumed. **2** A taking for granted; supposition. **3** Presumption; arrogance. **4** *Logic* A minor premise. See synonyms under ARROGANCE, ASSURANCE, PRE-

TENSE. — the Assumption **1** *Theol.* The doctrine that the Virgin Mary was bodily taken up into heaven at her death. **2** A church feast, observed on August 15, commemorating this event. [<L *assumptio, -onis* < *sumere.* See ASSUME.]

as·sump·tive (ə-sump′tiv) *adj.* **1** Characterized by assumption. **2** That can be assumed. **3** Presumptuous. —as·sump′tive·ly *adv.*

as·sur·ance (ə-shoor′əns) *n.* **1** The act of assuring; a being assured. **2** A positive or encouraging declaration. **3** Full confidence; undoubting conviction. **4** Self-confidence; firmness of mind. **5** Boldness; effrontery. **6** *Brit.* Insurance.

Synonyms: arrogance, assertion, assumption, boldness, confidence, effrontery, impudence, presumption, self-assertion, self-confidence, self-reliance, trust. *Confidence* is founded upon reasons; *assurance* is largely a matter of feeling. In the bad sense, *assurance* is a vicious courage, with belief of one's ability to outwit or defy others; it is less gross than *impudence,* which is (according to its etymology) a shameless *boldness.* *Assurance* appears in act or manner; *impudence,* in speech. *Effrontery* is *impudence* defiantly displayed. Compare BELIEF, CERTAINTY, EFFRONTERY, FAITH, IMPUDENCE, PRIDE. *Antonyms:* bashfulness, confusion, consternation, dismay, distrust, doubt, hesitancy, misgiving, shyness, timidity.

as·sure (ə-shoor′) *v.t.* as·sured, as·sur·ing **1** To make sure or secure; establish against change: His poems *assured* his immortality. **2** To give confidence to; convince: His success *assured* him of the validity of his mission. **3** To offer assurances concerning; guarantee, as something risky. **4** To promise confidently: He *assured* his friends he would return. **5** To insure. See synonyms under CONFIRM. [<OF *aseurer* <LL *assecurare* <L *ad-* to + *securus* safe] —as·sur′a·ble *adj.*

as·sured (ə-shoord′) *adj.* **1** Made certain; undoubted; sure. **2** Self-possessed; confident. **3** Insured. See synonyms under CONSCIOUS, SECURE, SURE. —*n.* An insured person or persons. —as·sur·ed·ly (ə-shoor′id·lē) *adv.* —as·sur′ed·ness *n.*

as·sur·er (ə-shoor′ər) *n.* **1** One who or that which assures. **2** *Brit.* An insurance underwriter. Also as·sur′or.

as·sur·gent (ə-sûr′jənt) *adj.* **1** Rising or tending to rise. **2** *Her.* Rising out of the sea. **3** *Bot.* Curving upward. [<L *assurgens, -entis.* ppr. of *assurgere* <L *ad-* to + *surgere* rise] —as·sur′gen·cy *n.*

As·syr·i·a (ə-sir′ē-ə)
An ancient empire of western Asia: capital, Nineveh. Also *Ashur, Asshur.*

As·syr·i·an (ə-sir′ē-ən) *adj.* Of, pertaining to, or characteristic of Assyria or its people. —*n.* **1** A native of Assyria or the Assyrian empire. **2** The Semitic language spoken by the Assyrians.

a·stat·ic (ā-stat′ik, ə-) *adj.* **1** *Physics* Being in neutral equilibrium; having no tendency toward any change of position. **2** Unsteady. —a·stat′i·cal·ly *adv.* —a·stat·i·cism (ā-stat′ə· siz′əm, ə-) *n.*

as·ter (as′tər) *n.* **1** Any of a large genus *(Aster)* of plants of the composite family, having alternate leaves, and flowers with white, purple, or blue rays and yellow disk. **2** One of various allied plants, as the China aster. **3** *Biol.* The star-shaped figure appearing in the cytoplasm of a cell during mitosis and associated with the centrosome and spindle fibers. See OVUM. [<L <Gk. *astēr* star]

aster- *combining form* Star: *asteroid.* Also **asteri-, astero-.** [<Gk. *astēr*]

-aster *suffix* A contemptuous diminutive: *poetaster, criticaster.* [<L *-aster,* dim. *suffix*]

as·te·ri·a (as·tir′ē·ə) *n.* Any gemstone which when properly cut exhibits asterism. [<L, a precious stone <Gk. *asterios* starry]

as·te·ri·at·ed (as·tir′ē·ā′tid) *adj.* **1** Grouped like stars. **2** Radiating, as the rays of a star. **3** *Mineral.* Exhibiting asterism, as certain sapphires.

as·ter·isk (as′tər·isk) *n.* **1** *Printing* A starlike figure (*) used to indicate omissions, footnotes, references, etc. **2** Anything shaped like a star. —*v.t.* To mark with an asterisk. [< L *asteriscus* < Gk. *asteriskos,* dim. of *astēr* star]

as·ter·ism (as′tə·riz′əm) *n.* **1** *Printing* **a** A group of asterisks (***, ****). **b** A group of three asterisks set in front of a passage in the form of a triangle to call attention to it. **2** *Astron.* **a** A cluster of stars. **b** A constellation. **3** *Mineral.* The property of some crystals of showing a starlike figure by reflected or transmitted light.

a·stern (ə·stûrn′) *adv. Naut.* **1** In or at the stern. **2** In the rear; at any point behind a vessel. **3** To the rear; backward.

a·ster·nal (ā·stûr′nəl) *adj. Anat.* **1** Not attached to the sternum. **2** Not having a sternum.

as·ter·oid (as′tə·roid) *adj.* **1** Star-shaped. **2** *Bot.* Pertaining to or like an aster. —*n.* **1** *Astron.* Any of several hundred small planets between Mars and Jupiter: also called *planetoid.* **2** *Zool.* A starfish. —**as′ter·oi′dal** *adj.*

as·the·ni·a (as·thē′nē·ə, as′thə·nī′ə) *n. Pathol.* General debility; lack of bodily strength; weakness. Also **as·the·ny** (as′thə·nē). [< NL < Gk. *astheneia* < *a-* without + *sthenos* strength]

as·then·ic (as·then′ik) *n.* **1** One who is physically weak or undeveloped. **2** *Anthropol.* One who is characterized by a lean, generally tall figure, and light muscular development. —*adj.* **1** Of or pertaining too an asthenic person or type. **2** Of, pertaining to, or characterized by asthenia. Also **as·then′i·cal** *adj.*

asth·ma (az′mə, as′-) *n. Pathol.* A chronic respiratory disorder characterized by recurrent paroxysmal coughing, and a sense of constriction due to spasmodic contraction of the bronchi. [< Gk., a panting < *azein* breathe hard]

asth·mat·ic (az·mat′ik, as-) *adj.* Of, pertaining to, or affected with asthma. Also **asth·mat′i·cal.** —*n.* A person suffering from or subject to asthma. —**asth·mat′i·cal·ly** *adv.*

a·stig·ma·tism (ə·stig′mə·tiz′əm) *n.* A structural defect of the eye or a lens such that the rays of light from an object do not converge to a focus, thus causing imperfect vision or images. [< A.⁴ without + Gk. *stigma* mark]

as·tig·mat·ic (as′tig·mat′ik) *adj.* **1** Of, having, or characterized by astigmatism. **2** Correcting astigmatism.

a·stir (ə·stûr′) *adv. & adj.* Stirring; moving about.

a·stom·a·tous (ā·stom′ə·təs, ā·stō′mə-) *adj. Biol.* Without a mouth or breathing pores. Also **as·to·mous** (as′tə·məs). [< A.⁴ without + Gk. *stoma, stomatos* mouth]

a·ston·ish (ə·ston′ish) *v.t.* **1** To affect with wonder and surprise; amaze; confound. **2** *Obs.* To stun or paralyze, as by a shock. [< OF *estoner* < L *ex-* out + *tonare* thunder] —**a·ston′ish·er** *n.* —**a·ston′ish·ing** *adj.* —**a·ston′ish·ing·ly** *adv.*

a·ston·ish·ment (ə·ston′ish·mənt) *n.* **1** An act of astonishing or the state of being astonished; surprise; amazement. **2** An object or cause of such emotion. See synonyms under AMAZEMENT, PERPLEXITY.

a·ston·y (ə·ston′ē) *v.t.* **a·ston·ied, a·ston·y·ing** *Obs.* **1** To astound; astonish. **2** To stun. [See ASTONISH.] —**a·ston′ied** *adj.*

a·stound (ə·stound′) *v.t.* To overwhelm or shock with wonder or surprise; confound. —*adj. Obs.* Amazed; astonished. [ME *astoned* stunned, pp. of *astonien* < OF *estoner.* See ASTONISH.]

as·tra·dle (ə·strad′l) *adv. & adj.* In a straddling position; astride.

as·tra·gal (as′trə·gəl) *n.* **1** *Archit.* A small convex molding in the form of a string of beads. **2** *Anat.* The ankle bone or tarsus. **3** *pl.* Dice: originally made from such bones. [< L *astragalus* < Gk. *astragalos*]

as·trag·a·lus (as·trag′ə·ləs) *n. pl.* **·li** (-lī) *Anat.* The proximal bone of the foot, as in man or other vertebrates; talus; anklebone. [< L < Gk. *astragalos*] —**as·trag′a·lar** (-lər) *adj.*

as·tral (as′trəl) *adj.* **1** Of, pertaining to, coming from, or like the stars; starry. **2** *Biol.* Of, pertaining to, or exhibiting an aster: an *astral* phase. **3** In alchemy, susceptible to influences from the stars: *astral* gold. **4** In theosophy, pertaining to or consisting of a supersensible substance supposed to pervade all space and to be refined beyond the tangible world. —*n.* **1** An astral body. **2** An astral lamp. [< LL *astralis* < L *astrum* star < Gk. *astron*] —**as′tral·ly** *adv.*

astral body 1 Any fantasmal appearance of the human body. **2** In theosophy, a counterpart of the human body, composed of astral substance, accompanying it in life, and surviving its death.

a·strand (ə·strand′) *adv. & adj.* Aground; stranded.

as·tra·pho·bi·a (as′trə·fō′bē·ə) *n.* Morbid fear of thunder and lightning. Also **as·tra·po·pho·bi·a** (as′trə·pə·fō′bē·ə). [< NL < Gk. *astrapē* lightning + -PHOBIA]

a·stray (ə·strā′) *adv. & adj.* Away from the right path; wandering in or into error or evil. [< OF *estraie,* pp. of *estraier* < L *extra-* beyond + *vagare* wander]

as·trict (ə·strikt′) *v.t.* **1** To bind; restrict; limit. **2** To bind by moral or legal obligation, as an inheritance. [< L *astrictus,* pp. of *astringere.* See ASTRINGE.] —**as·tric′tion** *n.*

as·tric·tive (ə·strik′tiv) *adj.* **1** Astringent; styptic. **2** *Obs.* Restrictive; obligatory. —*n.* An astringent. —**as·tric′tive·ly** *adv.* —**as·tric′tive·ness** *n.*

a·stride (ə·strīd′) *adv. & adj.* **1** With one leg on each side. **2** With the legs far apart. —*prep.* With one leg on each side of: *astride* a horse.

as·tringe (ə·strinj′) *v.t.* **as·tringed, as·tring·ing** To bind or draw together; compress; constrict. [< L *astringere* < *ad-* to + *stringere* bind fast]

as·trin·gent (ə·strin′jənt) *adj.* **1** *Med.* Tending to contract or draw together organic tissues; binding; styptic. **2** Harsh; stern; austere. —*n.* An astringent substance, as alum, tannin, etc. [< L *astringens, -entis,* ppr. of *astringere.* See ASTRINGE.] —**as·trin′gen·cy** *n.* —**as·trin′gent·ly** *adv.*

astro- *combining form* Star: *astrometry.* [< Gk. *astron* star]

as·tro·cyte (as′trə·sīt) *n. Biol.* **1** A star-shaped cell, as of the neuroglia. **2** A bone corpuscle; osteoblast.

as·tro·dome (as′trə·dōm) *n.* A transparent domelike structure incorporated in some aircraft to facilitate observation of celestial bodies.

as·tro·ga·tion (as′trə·gā′shən) *n.* In space travel, navigation by the stars. [< ASTRO- + (NAVI)GATION] —**as′tro·ga′tor** *n.*

as·tro·labe (as′trə·lāb) *n.* An instrument formerly used for obtaining the altitudes of planets and stars. [< OF *astrelabe* < Med.L *astrolabium* < Gk. *astrolabon,* orig., star-taking < *astron* star + *lambanein* take]

as·trol·o·ger (ə·strol′ə·jər) *n.* **1** One who studies astrology. **2** *Obs.* An astronomer.

as·trol·o·gy (ə·strol′ə·jē) *n.* **1** Originally, the practical application of astronomy to human uses. **2** The study professing to fortell the future and interpret the influence of the heavenly bodies upon the destinies of men. [< L *astrologia* < Gk. *astrologia* < *astron* star + *logos* discourse < *legein* speak] —**as·tro·log·ic** (as′trə·loj′ik) or **·i·cal, as·trol′o·gous** (-gəs) *adj.* —**as′tro·log′i·cal·ly** *adv.*

as·trom·e·try (ə·strom′ə·trē) *n.* That branch of astronomy which determines the apparent positions, motions, and magnitudes of the heavenly bodies.

as·tro·naut (as′trə·nôt) *n.* One who travels in space. [< ASTRO- + (aero)naut]

as·tro·nau·tics (as′trə·nô′tiks) *n.* The science of space travel.

as·tro·nav·i·ga·tion (as′trō·nav′ə·gā′shən) *n.* That part of navigation in which position is determined by observation of celestial bodies; nautical astonomy. —**as′tro·nav′i·ga′tor** *n.*

as·tron·o·mer (ə·stron′ə·mər) *n.* One learned or expert in astronomy; a skilled observer of the heavenly bodies.

as·tro·nom·ic (as′trə·nom′ik) *adj.* **1** Of or pertaining to astronomy. **2** Enormously or inconceivably large, like the quantities used in astronomy. Also **as′tro·nom′i·cal.** —**as′tro·nom′i·cal·ly** *adv.*

astronomical unit A space unit for expressing the distances of the stars, equal to the mean distance of the earth from the sun. Compare PARSEC.

astronomical year See under YEAR.

as·tron·o·my (ə·stron′ə·mē) *n.* **1** The science that treats of the heavenly bodies, their motions, magnitudes, distances, and physical constitution. **2** A treatise on this science. [< OF *astronomie* < L *astronomia* < Gk. *astronomia* < *astron* star + *nomos* law < *nemein* distribute, arrange]

as·tro·phys·ics (as′trō·fiz′iks) *n.* That branch of astronomy which treats of the physical constitution and properties of the heavenly bodies, especially as revealed by spectrum analysis. —**as′tro·phys′i·cal** *adj.* —**as′tro·phys·i·cist** (as′trō·fiz′ə·sist) *n.*

as·tute (ə·stoot′, ə·styoot′) *adj.* Keen in discernment; acute; shrewd; sagacious; cunning. Also **as·tu·cious** (ə·stoo′shəs, ə·styoo′-), **as·tu′tious.** [< L *astutus* < *astus* cunning] —**as·tute′ly** *adv.* —**as·tute′ness** *n.*

Synonyms: acute, clear-sighted, crafty, cunning, discerning, discriminating, keen, knowing, penetrating, penetrative, perspicacious, sagacious, sharp, shrewd, subtile, subtle. *Acute* suggests the sharpness of the needle's point; *keen* the sharpness of the cutting edge. The *astute* mind adds to *acuteness* and *keenness* an element of cunning or finesse. *Knowing* has often a slightly invidious sense. See ACUTE, INTELLIGENT, KNOWING. *Antonyms:* blind, dull, idiotic, imbecile, shallow, short-sighted, stolid, stupid, undiscerning, unintelligent.

A·sun·ción (ä·sōōn·syôn′) The capital of Paraguay and principal port on the Parauay River.

a·sun·der (ə·sun′dər) *adv.* **1** In or into a different place or direction. **2** Apart; into pieces. —*adj.* Separated; apart. [OE *on sundran.* See SUNDER.]

As·wan (äs·wän′) A city on the Nile in southern Egypt; site of the **Aswan Dam** (1 1/4 miles long; 176 feet high): also *Assouan, Assuan:* ancient *Syene.*

a·swim (ə·swim′) *adv. & adj.* Afloat; swimming.

a·swoon (ə·swōōn′) *adv. & adj.* In a swooning state.

a·syl·lab·ic (ā′si·lab′ik) *adj.* Not syllabic.

a·sy·lum (ə·sī′ləm) *n. pl.* **·lums** or **·la** (-lə) **1** An institution for the care of some class of afflicted, unfortunate, aged, or destitute persons; a retreat. **2** A place of refuge; retreat; shelter. **3** An inviolable shelter from arrest or punishment, as a temple or church in ancient times. **4** The protection afforded by a sanctuary or refuge. See synonyms under REFUGE. —**right of asylum** In international law: **1** The right to protection from arrest, subject to the will of the official in charge, enjoyed by a person who takes refuge in a foreign embassy or ministry or on a foreign warship. **2** The right to sanctuary enjoyed by troops or naval vessels taking refuge in neutral territory or waters. **3** Formerly, the right to shelter from extradition granted a political refugee in a foreign country. [< L < Gk. *asylon* < *a-* without + *sylon* right of seizure]

a·sym·met·ric (ā′si·met′rik, as′i-) *adj.* **1** Not symmetrical. **2** *Chem.* Designating an atom with optical activity, each of whose valences is held by a different atom or radical. Also **a′sym·met′ri·cal.** —**a′sym·met′ri·cal·ly** *adv.*

a·sym·me·try (ā·sim′ə·trē) *n.* Lack of symmetry or proportion. [< Gk. *asymmetria* < *a-* without + *symmetria* symmetry]

a·symp·to·mat·ic (ā′simp·tə·mat′ik) *adj.* Without symptoms: an *asymptomatic* patient.

as·ymp·tote (as′im·tōt) *n. Math.* A straight line which an indefinitely extended curve continually approaches as a limit. [< Gk. *asymptōtos* not falling together < *a-* not + *syn-* together + *piptein* fall] —**as′ymp·tot′ic** (-tot′ik) or **·i·cal** *adj.* —**as′ymp·tot′i·cal·ly** *adv.*

a·syn·chro·nism (ā·sing′krə·niz′əm) *n.* Lack of synchronism, or coincidence in time. —**a·syn′chro·nous** (-nəs) *adj.*

as·yn·det·ic (as′in·det′ik) *adj.* **1** Of or pertaining to asyndeton. **2** Without cross-references: said of a library catalog. —**as′yn·det′i·cal·ly** *adv.*

a·syn·de·ton (ə·sin′də·ton) *n.* In rhetoric, the omission of conjunctions between parts of a sentence, as "On your mark, get set, go!" Compare POLYSYNDETON. [< L < Gk. *asyndeton* < *a-* not + *syn-* together + *deein* bind]

a·syn·tac·tic (ā′sin·tak′tik) *adj.* Not according to syntax; ungrammatical.

at (at, *unstressed* ət) *prep.* **1** In the exact position of: the point *at* the center of the circle. **2** On or near the coming of: the train leaving *at* two; a man *at* sixty. **3** During the course or lapse of: *At* the moment the matter is uncertain. **4** In contact with; on; upon: *at* the bottom of the sea. **5** To or toward: Look *at* that sunset! **6** Through; by way of: smoke coming out *at* the windows. **7** Within the limits of; present in: to be *at* the ball grounds. **8** Engaged or occupied in: to be *at* work. **9** Attending: He was *at* the party. **10** In the state or condition of: a nation *at* war. **11** In the region or vicinity of; in proximity to: The car is *at* the door. **12** Viewed from; with an interval of: a target *at* sixty paces. **13** Having reference to: He winced *at* the thought. **14** In the manner of: *at* a trot. **15** In pursuit or quest of; in the direction of: to catch *at* straws. **16** Dependent upon: to be *at* an enemy's mercy. **17** According to: Proceed *at* your discretion. **18** To the extent of; amounting to: paying interest *at* two per cent; pencils *at* a dime apiece. [OE *æt*]
   Synonyms: about, by, during, in, near, on, to, toward, with, within. As regards place, *at* is not used with names of countries; we say *in* England, *in* France, etc.; with names of cities and towns we use *at* when we think merely of the local or geographical point; when we think of inclusive space, we employ *in;* as, we arrived *at* Liverpool; there are few rich men *in* this village. As regards time, *at* is used of a point of time, as of the hour, minute, or second; as, the train leaves *at* 10:30 a.m.; *at* is also used of indefinite divisions of time involving some duration; as, *at* morning, noon, or night; to lie awake *at* night. We say *at* the hour, *on* the day, *in* the year. *On* with certain divisions of time has a special precision, signifying exactly *at*, neither before nor after; as, the train leaves *on* the hour.
At *Chem.* Astatine (symbol At).
at- Assimilated var. of AD-.
at·a·bal (at′ə·bal) *n.* A Moorish tabor or kettledrum. [< Sp. < Arabic *at-tabl* the drum]
A·ta·ca·ma Desert (ä′tä·kä′mä) An arid region of northern Chile, rich in natural nitrate deposits, extending 600 miles south from the border of Peru.
a·tac·a·mite (ə·tak′ə·mīt) *n.* A dark-green basic chloride of copper, crystallizing in the orthorhombic system. [from Atacama Desert]
a·ta·jo (ä·tä′hō) *n. SW U.S.* **1** A string of mules. **2** A cross-path shortening a road. [< Sp. *hatajo*]
At·a·lan·ta (at′ə·lan′tə) In Greek mythology, a maiden who agreed to marry any suitor who could outrun her, the losers being put to death. She was won by Hippomenes, who outwitted her by dropping three golden apples which she paused to pick up allowing him to outrun her.
at·a·rac·tic (at′ə·rak′tik) *adj.* **1** Conducive to peace of mind. **2** *Med.* Having the power to tranquilize and to lessen nervous tension: said of certain drugs, as reserpine. Also **at′a·rax′ic** (-rak′sik). [< NL < Gk. *ataraktos* untroubled < *atarakteein* be calm. See ATARAXIA.]
at·a·rax·i·a (at′ə·rak′sē·ə) *n.* Freedom from anxiety; peace of mind. Also **at′a·rax·y** (at′ə·rak′sē). [< NL < Gk. *ataraxia* < *atarakteein* be calm < *a-* not + *tarattein* disturb, trouble]
a·taunt (ə·tônt′) *adv. Naut.* **1** With all sails set; in full-rigged condition. **2** In order; shipshape. [< F *autant* as much (as possible)]
at·a·vism (at′ə·viz′əm) *n.* **1** Reversion to an earlier or primitive type. **2** *Biol.* Reversion. [< F *atavisme* < L *atavus* ancestor < *at-* beyond + *avus* grandfather] —**a·tav·ic** (ə·tav′ik) *adj.* — **at′a·vist** *n.* —**at′a·vis′tic** *adj.*
a·tax·i·a (ə·tak′sē·ə) *n. Pathol.* **1** Irregularity in muscular action through failure of muscular coordination. **2** Locomotor ataxia. Also **a·tax·y** (ə·tak′sē). [< NL < Gk. *ataxia* lack of order < *a-* not + *tattein* arrange]
a·tax·ic (ə·tak′sik) *adj.* Characteristic of or caused by ataxia. —*n.* One afflicted with ataxia.
a·tax·it·ic (ā′tak·sit′ik) *adj. Geol.* Of or pertaining to ore deposits occurring in unstratified form: opposed to *eutaxitic.*
ate[1] (āt, *chiefly Brit.* et) Past tense of EAT.

a·te[2] (ā′tē) *n.* In ancient Greek culture, the fatal and reckless blindness inciting men to crime. [< GK. *atē*]
-ate[1] *suffix* Forming: **1** Participial adjectives equivalent to those in *-ated: desolate, separate.* **2** Adjectives from nouns with the meaning "possessing or characterized by": *caudate, foliate.* **3** Verbs, originally from stems of Latin verbs of the first conjugation, and, by analogy, extended to other stems: *fascinate, assassinate.* **4** *Chem.* Verbs with the meaning "combine or treat with": *chlorinate.* [< L *-atus,* pp. ending of 1st conjugation verbs]
-ate[2] *suffix* Forming: **1** Nouns denoting office, function, or agent: *magistrate.* **2** Nouns denoting the object or result of an action: *mandate.* [< L *-atus,* suffix of nouns]
-ate[3] *suffix Chem.* Used to form the names of salts and esters derived from acids whose names end in *-ic: carbonate, nitrate.* [< L *-atum,* neut. of *-atus* -ATE[1]]
a·tech·nic (ā·tek′nik) *adj.* Without technical knowledge. [< Gk. *atechnos* unskilled < *a-* without + *technē* skill]
at·el·ier (at′əl·yā, Fr. à·tə·lyā′) *n.* A workshop, especially of an artist; studio. [< F, orig., pile of chips < OF *astele* chip < LL *astella* < L *astula* chip. splinter]
a tem·po (ä tem′pō) *Music* In the regular time; resuming the rate of speed originally indicated. [< Ital.]
a·tem·po·ral (ā·tem′pə·rəl) *adj.* Timeless; outside of or apart from time.
ath·a·na·sia (ath′ə·nā′zhə, -zhē·ə) *n.* Deathlessness; immortality. Also **a·than·a·sy** (ə·than′ə·sē). [< Gk. < *a-* without + *thanatos* death]
Ath·a·pas·can (ath′ə·pas′kən) *n.* **1** A large North American Indian linguistic stock, including languages of Alaska and NW Canada, the Pacific coast (especially in Oregon and California), and the Apache and Navaho tribes of the southern SW United States. **2** A member of a tribe speaking these languages. Also **Athabascan.**
a·thart (ə·thôrt′) *adv. & prep.* Athwart. Also **a·thort′.**
a·the·ism (ā′thē·iz′əm) *n.* **1** The belief that there is no God. **2** The disbelief in the existence of God. **3** Godlessness in life or conduct. [< F *athéisme* < Gk. *atheos* < *a-* without + *theos* god]
a·the·ist (ā′thē·ist) *n.* One who denies or disbelieves in the existence of God. See synonyms under SKEPTIC.
a·the·is·tic (ā′thē·is′tik) *adj.* **1** Of or pertaining to atheism or atheists. **2** Given to atheism; godless. Also **a′the·is′ti·cal.** —**a′the·is′ti·cal·ly** *adv.*
ath·el·ing (ath′ə·ling) *n. Archaic* **1** A crown prince. **2** Any member of a noble family. Also spelled *ætheling.* [OE *ætheling* < *æthelu* noble ancestry]
a·the·mat·ic (ā′thē·mat′ik) *adj. Ling.* Not attached to or not constituting a stem.
A·the·na (ə·thē′nə) In Greek mythology, the goddess of wisdom, war, and patroness of arts and crafts: identified with the Roman *Minerva.* Also **A·the·ne** (ə·thē′·nē). [< Gk. *Athēnē*]
ath·e·ne·um (ath′ə·nē′əm) *n.* **1** A literary club, academy, or other institution for the promotion of learning. **2** A reading room, library, etc. Also **ath′e·nae′um.**
Ath·e·ne·um (ath′ə·nē′əm) *n.* **1** The temple of Athena at Athens. **2** An academy founded by Hadrian at Rome for the promotion of learning. Also **Ath′e·nae′um.** [< L < Gk. *Athenaion*]
A·the·ni·an (ə·thē′nē·ən) *adj.* Of or pertaining to Athens, or to its art or culture. —*n.* A native or citizen of Athens.
Ath·ens (ath′ənz) An ancient city in Attica and the present capital of Greece. *Greek* **A·the·nai,** **A·thi·nai** (ä·the′ne).

ATHENA
After a gold and ivory statuette: possibly by Phidias.

a·ther·man·cy (ā·thûr′mən·sē) *n.* The state or quality of being athermanous.
a·ther·ma·nous (ā·thûr′mə·nəs) *adj.* Impervious to radiant heat. [< A.-[4] without + Gk. *thermainein* heat < *thermos* hot]
ath·er·o·ma (ath′ə·rō′mə) *n. Pathol.* **1** A sebaceous cyst. **2** Arteriosclerosis accompanied by pronounced degenerative changes. [< L < Gk. *atherōma* < *athērē* gruel; with ref. to the encysted matter]
ath·er·o·scle·ro·sis (ath′ər·ō·sklə·rō′sis) *n. Pathol.* Hardening of the arteries, accompanied by degenerative tissue changes in the arterial walls. [< NL < Gk. *athērē* gruel + *sklēros* hard]
ath·e·to·sis (ath′ə·tō′sis) *n. Pathol.* A derangement of the nervous system, in which the hands and feet, especially the fingers and toes, keep moving or twitching. [< Gk. *athetos* without position, unfixed < *a-* not + *tithenai* place]
a·thirst (ə·thûrst′) *adj.* **1** Wanting water; thirsty. **2** Keenly desirous; longing. [OE *ofthyrsted,* pp. of *ofthyrstan* < *of-,* intensive + *thyrstan* thirst]
ath·lete (ath′lēt) *n.* **1** One trained in acts or feats of physical strength and agility, as rowing, wrestling, etc. **2** In classical antiquity, a contestant in the public games. [< L *athleta* < Gk. *athlētēs* a contestant in the games < *athleein* contend for a prize < *athlos* a contest < *athlon* a prize]
athlete's foot Ringworm of the foot, caused by a parasitic fungus; dermophytosis.
ath·let·ic (ath·let′ik) *adj.* **1** Of, pertaining to, or like an athlete. **2** Strong; vigorous; muscular. — **ath·let′i·cal·ly** *adv.* —**ath·let′i·cism** (ath·let′ə·siz′əm) *n.*
ath·let·ics (ath·let′iks) *n. pl.* **1** Athletic games and exercises collectively. **2** A system of athletic training: usually construed as singular.
a·thrill (ə·thril′) *adj.* Thrilled.
a·thwart (ə·thwôrt′) *adv.* **1** From side to side; across. **2** So as to thwart; perversely. —*prep.* **1** Across the course of; from side to side of: The ship sailed *athwart* our course. **2** Contrary to; in opposition to: His action went *athwart* our plans. [< A.-[1] on + THWART]
-atic *suffix* Of; of the kind of: used in adjectives of Latin or Greek origin: *erratic.* [< F *-atique* or < L *-aticus* < Gk. *-atikos*]
a·tilt (ə·tilt′) *adv. & adj.* **1** In a tilted manner; tilted up. **2** Like one tilting or making a lance thrust; hence, in spirited opposition.
at·i·my (at′ə·mē) *n.* Public dishonor or disgrace; deprivation of civic rights. [< Gk. *atimia* < *a-* without + *timē* honor]
-ation *suffix of nouns* **1** Action or process of: *creation.* **2** Condition or quality of: *affectation.* **3** Result of: *reformation.* Also *-ion, -tion.* ◆ **-ation** was originally found in English nouns borrowed from Latin, and is now used by analogy to form nouns on any stem, as in *starvation, thunderation.* [< F *-ation* or L *-atio, -ationis* < *-atus* -ATE[1] + *-io* -ION]
a·tip·toe (ə·tip′tō′) *adv.* On the tips of the toes.
A·ti·tlán (ä′tē·tlän′) **1** A town in SW Guatemala, on the south shore of **Lake Atitlán** (53 square miles). **2** An inactive volcano near Lake Atitlán; 11,565 feet.
-ative *suffix* Denoting relation, tendency, or characteristic: *tentative, remunerative, laxative.* [< F *-atif,* masc., *-ative,* fem. or < L *-ativus*]
At·ka (at′kə) The largest island of the Andreanof group in the Aleutian Islands.
At·lan·ta (at·lan′tə) A city in NW central Georgia; the state capital.
At·lan·te·an (at′lan·tē′ən) *adj.* **1** Pertaining to Atlas. **2** Pertaining to Atlantis. Also **At·lan·ti·an** (at·lan′tē·ən).
at·lan·tes (at·lan′tēz) *n. pl. Archit.* Male human figures, used in place of columns or pilasters. [< L < Gk. *Atlantes,* pl. of *Atlas*]
At·lan·tic (at·lan′tik) *adj.* **1** Of, near, in, or pertaining to the Atlantic Ocean. **2** Pertaining to or derived from Mount Atlas or the Atlas Mountains in NW Africa. —*n.* The Atlantic Ocean. [< L *Atlanticus* < Gk. *Atlantikos* pertaining to Atlas]
Atlantic City A resort city on the Atlantic coast of SE New Jersey.
Atlantic Ocean The world's second largest ocean, extending from the Arctic to the Antarctic regions between the Americas and Europe

and Africa; 31,500,000 square miles; divided by the equator into the **North Atlantic Ocean** and the **South Atlantic Ocean.**

At·lan·ti·des (at-lan'tə-dēz) *n. pl.* **1** The children of Atlas: the Pleiades, the Hesperides, etc. **2** The inhabitants of Atlantis.

At·lan·tis (at-lan'tis) A legendary island described by Plato as a center of civilization that was engulfed by the sea.

at·las (at'ləs) *n.* **1** A volume of maps usually bound together. **2** Hence, any bound collection of plates or engravings showing systematically the development of a subject, or any work producing such effect by tabular arrangement. **3** A large size of paper, 26 by 33 (34) inches. **4** *Anat.* The first cervical vertebra: so called after Atlas, who bore the world on his shoulders. **5** *Archit.* Any of the Atlantes. [def. 1 < ATLAS; because some early collections of maps contained a picture of Atlas supporting the heavens]

At·las (at'ləs) **1** In Greek mythology, a Titan supporting the pillars of heaven on his shoulders. **2** Anyone bearing a great burden. **3** An intercontinental ballistic missile of the U.S. Air Force. [< L < Gk. *Atlas* < *tlaein* bear]

at·latl (ät'lät·l) *n.* A throwing stick used to hurl a spear or harpoon at birds or aquatic animals. [< Nahuatl]

at·man (ät'mən) *n.* In Hinduism, the soul, or selfhood; the spark in man emanating from divinity. —**Atman** The supreme soul from which all individual souls are derived and to which they return. [< Skt.]

atmo- *combining form* Vapor: *atmometer.* [< Gk. *atmos*]

at·mol·o·gy (at-mol'ə-jē) *n.* The science that treats of the laws of aqueous vapor. — **at·mo·log·ic** (at'mə-loj'ik) or **·i·cal** *adj.* — **at·mol·o·gist** *n.*

at·mol·y·sis (at-mol'ə-sis *n.* The act or process of partially separating mixtures of gases into their ingredients by virtue of their different diffusibility through porous substances. [< ATMO- + Gk. *lysis* a loosing]

at·mo·lyze (at'mə-līz) *v.t.* **·lyzed, ·lyz·ing** To separate by atmolysis. Also *Brit.* **at'mo·lyse.** — **at'mo·ly·za'tion** *n.* —**at'mo·lyz'er** *n.*

at·mos·phere (at'məs·fir) *n.* **1** The mass or body of gases that surrounds the earth or any heavenly body. **2** The particular climatic condition of any place or region regarded as dependent on the air. **3** Any surrounding or pervasive element or influence: an *atmosphere* of gloom. **4** The prevailing tone of a poem, novel, painting, etc. **5** *Colloq.* An indefinable aura regarded as especially characteristic: This café has *atmosphere.* **6** *Physics* A conventional unit of pressure, the equivalent of the weight of a column of mercury 1 centimeter in diameter and 29.92 inches high at sea level, at a temperature of 0° C.: one atmosphere equals a pressure of 14.69 pounds per square inch. [< NL *atmosphaera* < Gk. *atmos* vapor + *sphaira* sphere]

at·mos·pher·ic (at'məs·fer'ik) *adj.* **1** Pertaining or belonging to or existing in atmosphere. **2** Dependent on, caused by, or resulting from the atmosphere. **3** Giving or creating atmosphere: *atmospheric* music. Also **at'mos·pher'i·cal.** See STATIC. —**at'mos·pher'i·cal·ly** *adv.*

at·mos·pher·ics (at'məs·fer'iks) *n.* Atmospheric conditions due to electromagnetic disturbances, especially as they affect radio transmission: also called *sferics, spherics.*

a·to·le (ä·tō'lä) *n.* *SW U.S.* Cornmeal mush. [< Sp. < Nahuatl]

at·oll (at'ôl, -ol, ə·tol') *n.* A ring-shaped coral island and its associated reef, nearly or quite enclosing a lagoon. [< Malayalam *adal* closing, uniting]

ATOLL
a. Islets. *b.* Barrier reef *c.* Fringing reef. *d.* Lagoon *e.* Passage.

at·om (at'əm) *n.* **1** *Chem.* The smallest part of an element capable of existing alone or in combination and which cannot be changed or destroyed in any chemical reaction: an *atom* of sulfur, carbon, etc.: distinguished from

molecule. **2** *Physics* The electrically neutral combination of a nucleus and its complement of electrons to form a relatively stable, distinguishable unit, regarded as a unitary system. **3** A hypothetical entity admitting of no division into smaller parts. **4** An exceedingly small quantity or particle; iota. [< L *atomus* < Gk. *atomos* indivisible < *a-* not + *temnein* cut]

a·tom·ic (ə-tom'ik) *adj.* **1** Of or pertaining to an atom or atoms: also **a·tom'i·cal. 2** Very minute; infinitesimal. **3** Of, characterized by or employing atomic energy: an *atomic* power plant. — **a·tom'i·cal·ly** *adv.*

atomic bomb See under BOMB. Also **atom bomb.**

atomic clock A high-precision instrument for the measurement of time by a constant frequency associated with a selected line in the spectrum of ammonia gas or other suitable vibrator.

atomic energy The energy contained within the nucleus of the atom; especially, such energy when made available for human use by controlled nuclear fission or thermonuclear reactions.

at·o·mic·i·ty (at'ə-mis'ə·tē) *n.* *Chem.* **1** The number of atoms in a molecule. **2** Valence. **3** In the molecule of a compound, the number of replaceable atoms or groups.

atomic number *Physics* A number which represents the unit positive charges (protons) in the atomic nucleus of each element and corresponds to the number of extra-nuclear electrons. Hydrogen is assigned an atomic number of 1; on this basis, carbon is 6, oxygen 8, iron 26, gold 79, etc.

atomic theory 1 *Chem.* The doctrine that elements unite with one another, atom by atom, and in definite simple proportions by weight. **2** *Physics* The concept that all bulk matter is composed of atoms, and that the properties of matter are ultimately to be understood in terms of the properties and interactions of the component atoms.

atomic weight *Chem.* **a** Since 1961, the weight of an atom of an element relative to that of an atom of carbon, taken as 12.01115. **b** Formerly, the weight of an atom of an element relative to that of an atom of oxygen, taken as 16.

at·om·ize (at'əm·īz) *v.t.* **·ized, ·iz·ing 1** To reduce to or separate into atoms; pulverize. **2** To spray or reduce to a spray, as by an atomizer. Also *Brit.* **at'om·ise.** —**at'om·i·za'tion** *n.*

at·om·iz·er (at'əm·ī'zər) *n.* **1** An apparatus for reducing a liquid, especially medicine or perfume, to a spray.

at·om·me·ter (at'əm·mē'tər) *n.* The angstrom unit.

a·to·nal (ā·tō'nəl) *adj.* *Music* Without tonality; lacking key. —**a·to'nal·ly** *adv.*

a·to·nal·ism (ā·tō'nəl·iz'əm) *n.* The theory of atonally composed music. —**a·to'nal·is'tic** *adj.*

a·to·nal·i·ty (ā'tō·nal'ə·tē) *n.* *Music* Lack of tonality; absence of key.

a·tone (ə-tōn') *v.* **a·toned, a·ton·ing** *v.i.* **1** To make an expiation, as for sin or a sinner; make amends, reparation, or satisfaction. **2** *Obs.* To be at one, agree. —*v.t.* **3** *Rare* To expiate. **4** *Obs.* To propitiate; reconcile. [< earlier adverbial phrase *at one* in accord, short for *to set at one,* i.e., reconcile] —**a·ton'a·ble, a·tone'a·ble** *adj.* —**a·ton'er** *n.*

a·tone·ment (ə-tōn'mənt) *n.* **1** Satisfaction, reparation, or expiation made for wrong or injury; amends. **2** *Theol.* Usually *cap.* **a** The redemptive work of Christ. **b** The reconciliation between God and man effected by Christ's life, passion, and death. **3** In Christian Science, the exemplification of man's unity with God, whereby man reflects divine Truth, Life, and Love. **4** *Obs.* Reconciliation.

a·ton·ic (ə-ton'ik, ā-) *adj.* **1** Not accented, as a word or syllable. **2** Lacking tone or vigor. —*n.* An unaccented syllable or word. [< Gk. *atonos* slack < *a-* not + *teinein* stretch]

at·o·ny (at'ə-nē) *n.* **1** *Pathol.* Want of tone or power; abnormal relaxation, as of a muscle. **2** Lack of stress, as in a syllable. [< Gk. *atonia* slackness < *a-* not + *teinein* stretch]

a·top (ə-top') *adv. & adj.* On or at the top. — *prep.* On the top of.

-atory *suffix of adjectives* Of or pertaining to;

producing or produced by; of the nature of; expressing: *exclamatory.* [< L *-atorius* adj. suffix]

at·ra·bil·ious (at'rə·bil'yəs) *adj.* Disposed to hypochondria; melancholy; splenetic. Also **at'ra·bil'i·ar** (-bil'ē·ər) [< L *atra bilis* black bile, a trans. of Gk. *melancholia.* See MELANCHOLY.] — **at'ra·bil'ious·ness** *n.*

at·ra·men·tal (at'rə·men'təl) *adj.* Of the nature of ink; inklike; inky. Also **at'ra·men'tous.** [< L *atramentum* ink < *ater* black]

a·tre·ol (ā'trē·ōl, -ol) *n.* An aqueous solution of ammonium salts derived from organic acids, obtained as a black sirupy liquid, and used as a mild antiseptic. [< L *ater, atri* black + -OL]

a·tri·al (ā'trē·əl) *adj.* Of or pertaining to an atrium.

at·ri·cho·sis (at'ri·kō'sis) *n.* *Pathol.* Loss of or failure to develop hair. [< NL < Gk. *atrichos* hairless (< *a-* without + *thrix* hair) + -OSIS]

at·ri·chous (at'ri·kəs) *adj.* *Biol.* Destitute of cilia.

a·tri·o·ven·tric·u·lar (ā'trē·ō·ven·trik'yə·lər) *adj.* Pertaining to the auricles and ventricles of the heart.

a·trip (ə-trip') *adv. & adj.* *Naut.* **1** In a position for motion; just started from the bottom, as an anchor. **2** Properly hoisted and ready for trimming: said of a sail or a yard. **3** Freed from the fid and ready for lowering: said of a topmast. [< A-¹ on + TRIP]

a·tri·um (ā'trē·əm) *n. pl.* **a·tri·a** (ā'trē·ə) **1** The entrance hall or central open court of an ancient Roman house. **2** A court or hall. **3** *Anat.* One of the upper chambers of the heart through which venous blood is transmitted to the ventricles: also called *auricle.* **4** *Zool.* A cavity or sac. — **atrium of infection** *Med.* Any opening affording bacterial infection. [< L (def. 1)]

a·tro·cious (ə-trō'shəs) *adj.* **1** Outrageously wicked, criminal, vile, or cruel; heinous. **2** *Colloq.* Very bad or in bad taste: an *atrocious* remark. See synonyms under BARBAROUS, FLAGRANT, INFAMOUS. [< L *atrox, atrocis* harsh, cruel < *ater* black] —**a·tro'cious·ly** *adv.* —**a·tro'cious·ness** *n.*

a·troc·i·ty (ə-tros'ə·tē) *n. pl.* **·ties 1** The state or quality of being atrocious. **2** An atrocious deed or act; cruelty or wickedness. **3** *Colloq.* A bad piece of work; something in very bad taste. [< L *atrocitas, -tatis* cruelty < *atrox.* See ATROCIOUS.]

at·ro·phied (at'rə·fēd) *adj.* Wasted away; withered.

at·ro·phy (at'rə·fē) *n. pl.* **·phies** *Pathol.* **1** A wasting or withering of the body or any of its parts. **2** A stoppage of growth or development, as of a part. —*v.* **·phied, ·phy·ing** *v.t.* To cause to waste away or wither; affect with atrophy. —*v.i.* To waste away; wither. [< F *atrophie* < L *atrophia* < Gk. *atrophia* < *a-* not+ *trephein* nourish] — **a·troph·ic** (ə-trof'ik), **at·ro·phous** (at'rə·fəs) *adj.*

at·ro·pine (at'rə·pēn, -pin) *n.* A crystalline, bitter, poisonous alkaloid, $C_{17}H_{23}O_3N$, found in the deadly nightshade and in the seeds of the thorn apple or jimsonweed: used in medicine as an antispasmodic and having the power of enlarging the pupil of the eye. Also **at'ro·pin** (-pin). [< NL *Atropa* the genus of belladonna < Gk. *Atropos.* See ATROPOS]

at·ro·pism (at'rə·piz'əm) *n.* A morbid state produced by overdoses of atropine.

At·ro·pos (at'rə·pos) One of the three Fates. [< Gk., inflexible < *a-* not + *trepein* turn]

at·ro·pous (at'rə·pəs) *adj.* *Bot.* Not inverted; erect, as an ovule. [< Gk. *atropos.* See ATROPOS.]

at·tac·ca (ät·täk'kä) *Music* Continue without pause. [< Ital.]

at·tach (ə-tach') *v.t.* **1** To make fast to something; affix; fasten on. **2** To connect or join on as a part of something: He *attached* himself to the expedition. **3** To add or append, as a word or signature. **4** To attribute; add as appropriate to: to *attach* great importance to the outcome of an event. **5** *Law* To secure for legal jurisdiction; seize or arrest by legal process: to *attach* an employee's salary. **6** *Mil.* To allocate, as personnel, units, or materiel, to a military organization temporarily or as a non-integral part: The regiment *attached* a medical officer. **7** *Obs.* To seize. — *v.i.* **8** To be united in sympathy or affection: with *to:* to be *attached* to someone out of sympathy. **9** To belong, as a quality or circumstance; be incidental to: with *to:* Much interest *attaches* to this opinion. See synonyms under ADD, UNITE. [<OF *atachier* <*a-* to (<L *ad-*) + *tache* nail <Gmc. Related to ATTACK.] — **at·tach′a·ble** *adj.*

at·ta·ché (at′ə·shā′, *esp. Brit.* ə·tash′ā) *n.* A person regularly and officially attached to a diplomatic mission or staff: military *attaché*, naval *attaché*. [<F, pp. of *attacher* attach]

at·tach·ment (ə·tach′mənt) *n.* **1** An attaching or a being attached; adherence; affection. **2** That by which, or the point at which, anything is attached; a bond; band; tie. **3** Affection; devoted regard. **4** An appendage or adjunct. **5** *Law* **a** Seizure of a person or property. **b** The writ commanding this.

Synonyms: adherence, adhesion, affection, devotion, esteem, estimation, friendship, inclination, love, regard, tenderness, union. An *attachment* is an affection that binds a person to another person or thing; we speak of a man's *adherence* to his purpose, his *adhesion* to his party, or to anything to which he clings tenaciously, but with no special tenderness; of his *attachment* to his church, to the old homestead, or to any persons or objects that he may hold dear. *Inclination* expresses simply a tendency, which may be good or bad, yielded to or overcome; as, an *inclination* to study. *Regard* is more distant than *affection* or *attachment*, but closer and warmer than *esteem*; we speak of high esteem, kind *regard*. Compare ACQUAINTANCE, APPENDAGE, FRIENDSHIP, LOVE, UNION. *Antonyms:* alienation, animosity, antipathy, aversion, coolness, dislike, distance, divorce, enmity, estrangement, indifference, opposition, repugnance, separation, severance.

at·tack (ə·tak′) *v.t.* **1** To set upon suddenly; begin battle or conflict with. **2** To assail with hostile words; criticize, censure. **3** To begin work on; set about, as an undertaking, with the intention of completing. **4** To begin to affect seriously or injuriously; seize: Acid *attacks* metal; Disease *attacks* a person. — *v.i.* **5** To make an attack; begin battle: The enemy *attacked* at dawn. — *n.* **1** The act of assaulting: with *on* or *upon.* **2** The first movement toward any undertaking. **3** Any hostile, offensive part or action, as with troops. **4** A seizure, as by disease. **5** *Music* The manner of beginning a phrase or passage with decision and spirit. [<F *attaquer* <Ital. *attaccare*, ult. <same source as ATTACH]

Synonyms (verb): assail, assault, beleaguer, beset, besiege, charge, combat, encounter, invade. To *attack* is to begin hostilities of any kind. *Assail* and *assault*, while of the same original etymology, have diverged in meaning, so that *assault* alone retains the meaning of direct personal violence. One may *assail* another with reproaches; he *assaults* him with a blow, a brandished weapon, etc. To *encounter* is to meet face to face, and may be said either of the *attacking* or of the resisting force or person, or of both. *Antonyms:* aid, befriend, cover, defend, preserve, protect, resist, shelter, shield, support, sustain, uphold, withstand.

Synonyms (noun): aggression, assault, encroachment, incursion, infringement, intrusion, invasion, onset, onslaught, trespass. An *attack* may be by word; an *aggression* is always by deed, upon rights, possessions, etc. An *invasion* of a nation's territories is an act of *aggression*; an *intrusion* upon a neighboring estate is a *trespass. Onslaught* signifies intensely violent *assault*, as by an army or a desperado, but it is sometimes used of violent speech. See AGGRESSION. *Antonyms:* defense, repulsion, resistance, retreat, submission, surrender.

at·tain (ə·tān′) *v.t.* **1** To achieve, accomplish or gain, as a desired purpose or state. **2** To come to, as in time; arrive at: He *attained* a ripe old age. — **to attain to** To arrive at with effort; succeed in reaching: Few men have *attained* to power such as his. [<OF *ataindre* <L *attingere* reach <*ad-* to + *tangere* touch] — **at·tain·a·ble** (ə·tā′nə·bəl) *adj.* That can be attained; practicable; feasible. — **at·tain′a·bil′·i·ty, at·tain′a·ble·ness** *n.*

at·tain·der (ə·tān′dər) *n.* **1** The loss of all civil rights of a person, as one dead in law, upon the pronouncing of sentence of death or of outlawry against him for a capital of-

fense. **2** *Obs.* Dishonor. — **bill of attainder** A legal act making certain crimes punishable by attainder. [<OF *ataindre* attain, strike, accuse; infl. in meaning by F *taindre* stain]

at·tain·ment (ə·tān′mənt) *n.* **1** The act of attaining. **2** That which is attained; an acquisition, as of skill.

Synonyms: accomplishment, acquirement, acquisition. These words are oftenest used in the plural. *Accomplishments* are showy, graceful, pleasing; *acquirements* are substantial and useful; *attainments* are lofty and ennobling. *Acquisitions*, unless otherwise expressly stated, are understood to be of money or property. Compare WISDOM.

at·taint (ə·tānt′) *v.t.* **1** To inflict attainder upon; condemn. **2** To disgrace; taint; sully. **3** To touch or affect, as disease. **4** *Obs.* To accuse: with *of.* **5** *Obs.* To touch; hit, as in tilting. — *n.* **1** Imputation; stigma. **2** Attainder. [<OF *ataint*, pp. of *ataindre.* See ATTAIN.]

at·tain·ture (ə·tān′chər) *n. Obs.* **1** Imputation of dishonor. **2** Attainder.

at·tar (at′ər) *n.* The fragrant essential oil extracted from the petals of flowers, especially roses: also called *ottar.* [<Persian *′aṭar* <Arabic *′iṭr* perfume]

at·tem·per (ə·tem′pər) *v.t.* **1** To reduce or modify by or as by mixture. **2** To modify the temperature of. **3** To moderate or appease, as excited feelings. **4** To adapt (oneself) so as to harmonize. **5** *Obs.* To control; regulate. [<OF *atemprer* <L *attemperare* adjust <*ad-* to + *temperare* regulate]

at·tempt (ə·tempt′) *v.t.* **1** To make an effort or trial to perform or get; endeavor to effect; try. **2** *Archaic* To try to overcome, master, win, seduce, or take by force; attack; assault: to *attempt* the life of someone. **3** *Archaic* To attract by allurements; tempt. See synonyms under ENDEAVOR. — *n.* **1** A putting forth of effort; a trial; endeavor; essay. **2** An attack. See synonyms under ENDEAVOR. [<OF *attenter, attempter* <L *attentare, attemptare* try <*ad-* toward + *tentare, temptare*, freq. of *tendere* stretch] — **at·tempt′a·ble** *adj.* — **at·tempt′a·bil′i·ty** *n.*

at·tend (ə·tend′) *v.t.* **1** To wait upon; minister to; visit or care for professionally. **2** To be present at or in, as a meeting. **3** To follow as a result. **4** To accompany. **5** *Archaic* To give heed; listen. **6** *Archaic* To await. See synonyms under FOLLOW, LISTEN, SERVE. [<OF *atendre* wait, expect <L *attendere* give heed to, consider <*ad-* toward + *tendere* stretch]

at·ten·dance (ə·ten′dəns) *n.* **1** An attending. **2** Those who attend; an audience or congregation; retinue. [<OF *atendance* <*atendre.* See ATTEND.]

at·ten·dant (ə·ten′dənt) *n.* **1** One who attends, especially as a servant; also, one who is present at a ceremony. **2** A concomitant; consequent. — *adj.* Following or accompanying; waiting upon.

at·tent (ə·tent′) *adj. Archaic* Eagerly attentive; intent. [<L *attentus*, pp. of *attendere.* See ATTEND.]

at·ten·tion (ə·ten′shən) *n.* **1** The act or faculty of attending. **2** Active consciousness; the power or faculty of mental concentration. **3** An act of courtesy or gallantry. **4** Practical consideration; care. **5** *Mil.* The prescribed position of readiness to obey orders; also, the order to assume this position. See synonyms under CARE, INDUSTRY. [<L *attentio, -onis* <*attendere.* See ATTEND.]

at·ten·tive (ə·ten′tiv) *adj.* **1** Of, pertaining to, giving, or showing attention; observant; thoughtful. **2** Courteous; gallant; polite. See synonyms under OBSEQUIOUS, THOUGHTFUL. — **at·ten′tive·ly** *adv.* — **at·ten′tive·ness** *n.*

at·ten·u·ant (ə·ten′yo͞o·ənt) *adj.* Making thin; diluting. — *n.* A medicine that dilutes the body fluids or thins the blood. [<L *attenuans, -antis*, ppr. of *attenuare.* See ATTENUATE.]

at·ten·u·ate (ə·ten′yo͞o·āt) *v.* **·at·ed, ·at·ing** *v.t.* **1** To make thin, small, or fine; draw out, as a wire. **2** To reduce in value, quantity, size, or strength; weaken; impair. **3** To reduce in density; rarefy, as a liquid or gas. **4** *Bacteriol.* To weaken the virulence of a micro-organism. — *v.i.* **5** To become thin, weak, rarefied, etc.

— *adj.* (ə·ten′yo͞o·it) **1** Made thin; slender; rarefied; diluted. **2** *Bot.* Slender and tapering; narrow. [<L *attenuatus*, pp. of *attenuare* weaken <*ad-* + *tenuare* make thin <*tenuis* thin]

at·ten·u·a·tion (ə·ten′yo͞o·ā′shən) *n.* **1** The act or process of attenuating, or the state of being attenuated. **2** *Bacteriol.* Reduction of the virulence of micro-organisms by repeated cultivation in artificial media, exposure to light, etc.

at·test (ə·test′) *v.t.* **1** To confirm as accurate, true, or genuine; vouch for. **2** To certify, as by signature or oath. **3** To be proof of: His many works *attest* his industry. **4** To put upon oath. — *v.i.* **5** To bear witness; testify: with *to.* — *n.* One who or that which certifies or confirms; attestation. [<F *attester* <L *attestari* confirm <*ad-* to + *testari* bear witness]

at·tes·ta·tion (at′es·tā′shən) *n.* **1** A presenting (of something) as testimony. **2** Testimony; something presented as evidence.

at·tic (at′ik) *n.* **1** A half-story next the roof; a garret. **2** A low, decorative wall or structure, in classical style, above a cornice or entablature. [<F *attique*, orig. Athenian; from the false supposition that the attic was of Athenian origin]

At·tic (at′ik) *adj.* **1** Of or pertaining to Attica in ancient Greece. **2** Of, characteristic of, or pertaining to Athens; Athenian; characteristic of the Athenians; pertaining to the language, literature, art, or literary style of the Athenians. **3** Graceful; delicate; refined: *Attic* wit. — *n.* The dialect of Attica, closely related to Ionic, representing ancient Greek in its most refined form as used by Aeschylus, Sophocles, Euripides, and most of the great Greek writers. [<L *Atticus* <Gk. *Attikos* Athenian <*Attikē* Attica]

At·ti·ca (at′i·kə) A nome of east central Greece; 1,310 square miles; capital, Athens; formerly an ancient kingdom and republic of Greece.

At·ti·la (at′ə·lə), 406?–453, king of the Huns: called "the scourge of God."

at·tire (ə·tīr′) *v.t.* **at·tired, at·tir·ing** **1** To dress; array; adorn. **2** *Obs.* To equip. — *n.* **1** Dress or clothing; apparel; garments; costume; adornment. **2** *Her.* Antlers or horns, as of a stag. See synonyms under DRESS. [<OF *atirer* arrange, adorn <*a-* in (<L *ad-*) + *tire* row, order (of uncertain origin)]

at·tire·ment (ə·tīr′mənt) *n.* Apparel; garb; attire.

At·tis (at′is) In classical mythology, a vegetation god worshiped with the Great Mother: an annual spring festival commemorated his death and resurrection. Also *Atys.*

at·ti·tude (at′ə·to͞od, -tyo͞od) *n.* **1** Position of the body, as suggesting some thought, feeling, or action. **2** State of mind, behavior, or conduct regarding some matter, as indicating opinion or purpose. **3** *Aeron.* The position of an airplane with reference to some plane, as the earth or the horizon; tilt or tip. **4** *Med.* The position of the fetus in the womb. [<F <Ital. *attitudine* <LL *aptitudo* fitness <L *aptus* fitted, suited. Doublet of APTITUDE.] — **at·ti·tu·di·nal** (at′ə·to͞o′də·nəl, -tyo͞o′-) *adj.*

Synonyms: pose, position, posture. A *posture* is assumed without any special reference to expression of feeling; *attitude* is the *position* appropriate to the expression of some feeling, whether consciously or unconsciously assumed. A *pose* is a *position* studied for artistic effect or considered with reference to such effect.

at·tor·ney (ə·tûr′nē) *n.* **1** A person empowered by another to act in his stead; especially, one legally qualified to prosecute and defend actions in a court of law; an attorney at law; a lawyer. **2** *Obs.* An agent. — **by attorney** By proxy. — **power of attorney** Legal written authority to transact business for another. — **prosecuting attorney** *U.S.* The law officer empowered to act in behalf of the government, whether state, county, or national, in prosecutions for penal offenses: also called **district attorney.** [<OF *atorné*, pp. of *atorner.* See ATTORN.] — **at·tor′·ney·ship** *n.*

attorney at law An attorney who is qualified to

prosecute and defend actions in a court of law: also called *public attorney.*

attorney general *pl.* **attorneys general, attorney generals** The chief law officer of a government.

Attorney General *U.S.* A cabinet officer who heads the Department of Justice and is chief legal adviser to the President.

at·tract (ə-trakt′) *v.t.* **1** To draw to or cause to come near by some physical force, as magnetism, and without apparent mechanical connection. **2** To draw, as the admiration or attention of, by some winning influence; allure; entice. See synonyms under ALLURE, DRAW, INTEREST. [< L *attractus,* pp. of *attrahere* < *ad-* toward + *trahere* draw, drag] —**at·tract′a·ble** *adj.* —**at·tract′a·ble·ness, at·tract′a·bil′i·ty** *n.* —**at·tract′er, at·trac′tor** *n.*

at·trac·tile (ə-trak′təl) *adj.* Having power to attract.

at·trac·tion (ə-trak′shən) *n.* **1** The act or process of attracting, or that which attracts. **2** A physical force which, exerted between or among bodies, tends to make them approach each other or prevents their separating. Compare REPULSION. **3** Anything pleasing or alluring. See synonyms under INCLINATION, LOVE.

at·trac·tive (ə-trak′tiv) *adj.* Having the power or quality of attracting; drawing; pleasing; winning. See synonyms under AMIABLE, BEAUTIFUL, PLEASANT. —**at·trac′tive·ly** *adv.* —**at·trac′tive·ness** *n.*

at·tra·hent (at′rə-hənt) *adj.* **1** Drawing to or toward something. **2** *Anat.* Drawing a part forward. —*n.* **1** An external application that draws fluids to the place where it is applied. **2** A muscle that acts by drawing forward. [< L *attrahens, -entis,* ppr. of *attrahere.* See ATTRACT.]

at·trib·ute (ə-trib′yoot) *v.t.* **·ut·ed, ·ut·ing** To consider or ascribe as belonging to, resulting from, owing to, or caused by; assign; refer: to *attribute* the invention of music to Orpheus; to *attribute* wisdom to gray hair.

—**at·tri·bute** (at′rə-byoot) *n.* **1** That which is assigned or ascribed; a characteristic. **2** *Gram.* An adjective or its equivalent. **3** In art and mythology, a distinctive mark or symbol. [< L *attributus,* pp. of *attribuere* bestow, assign < *ad-* to + *tribuere* allot, give over] —**at·trib′u·ta·ble** *adj.*

Synonyms (verb): ascribe, assign, associate, charge, connect, impute, refer. We may *attribute* to a person either that which belongs to him or that which we merely suppose to be his. Where we are quite sure, we simply *refer* a matter to the cause or class to which it belongs or *ascribe* to one what is surely his, etc. We *associate* things which may have no necessary or causal relations; as, we may *associate* the striking of a clock with the serving of dinner. We *charge* a person with what we deem blameworthy. We may *impute* good or evil, but more commonly evil. *Antonyms:* deny, disconnect, dissociate, separate, sever, sunder. ·

Synonyms (noun): property, quality. A *quality* denotes what a thing really is in some one respect; an *attribute* is what we conceive a thing to be in some one respect; thus, while *attribute* may, *quality* must, express something of the real nature of that to which it is ascribed; we speak of the *attributes* of God, the *qualities* of matter. A *property* is what belongs especially to one thing as its own peculiar possession, in distinction from all other things; when we speak of the *qualities* or the *properties* of matter, *quality* is the more general, *property* the more limited term. Compare CHARACTERISTIC, EMBLEM, FIGURE. *Antonyms:* being, essence, nature, substance.

at·tri·bu·tion (at′rə-byoo′shən) *n.* **1** An attributing or being attributed. **2** An ascribed characteristic or quality; attribute.

at·trib·u·tive (ə-trib′yə-tiv) *adj.* **1** Pertaining to or of the nature of an attribute; expressing or assigning an attribute. **2** So ascribed, as a work of art: That canvas is an *attributive* Vermeer. **3** *Gram.* Expressing an attribute; in English, designating an adjective or its equivalent which stands before the noun it modifies, as opposed to a predicate adjective which follows a linking verb; as, in the expression "a silver watch," silver is an *attributive* adjective. —*n. Gram.* An attributive word. —**at·trib′u·tive·ly** *adv.* —

at·trib′u·tive·ness *n.*

at·trite (ə-trit′) *adj.* **1** Worn down by rubbing or friction. **2** *Theol.* Having attrition. Also **at·trit·ed** (ə-trit′id). [< L *attritus,* pp. of *atterere.* See ATTRITION.]

at·tri·tion (ə-trish′ən) *n.* **1** A rubbing out or grinding down, as by friction. **2** A gradual wearing down or weakening: a war of *attrition.* **3** *Theol.* Repentance for sin, arising from inferior motives; imperfect contrition (see under CONTRITION). [< L *attritio, -onis* rubbing, friction < *atterere* rub away < *ad-* to, against + *terere* rub]

At·tu (at′too) The westernmost island of the Aleutians, largest of the Near Islands.

at·tune (ə-toon′, ə-tyoon′) *v.t.* **at·tuned, at·tuning 1** To bring into accord with; harmonize. **2** To adjust to the right pitch, as a musical instrument; tune. See synonyms under ADAPT. [< AD- + TUNE]

a·twain (ə-twān′) *adv.* In two; asunder. [< A-¹ on + TWAIN]

a·typ·ic (ā-tip′ik) *adj.* Not typical; without typical character; differing from the type; irregular. Also **a·typ′i·cal.** —**a·typ′i·cal·ly** *adv.*

Au *Chem.* Gold (symbol Au).

au·burn (ô′bûrn) *adj.* Reddish-brown: *auburn* hair. —*n.* An auburn color; a reddish-brown. [< OF *auborne, alborne* < LL *alburnus* whitish < L *albus* white; infl. in meaning by ME *brun* brown]

Auck·land (ôk′lənd) A chief port and former capital of New Zealand, on North Island.

auc·tion (ôk′shən) *n.* **1** A public sale of property in which the price offered for individual items is increased by bids, until the highest bidder becomes the purchaser. **2** The bidding in bridge. **3** Auction bridge (see under BRIDGE²). —*v.t.* To sell by or at auction. —**to auction off** To sell by or at auction. [< L *auctio, -onis* an increase, a public sale (with increasing bids) < *augere* increase]

auc·tion·eer (ôk′shən·ir′) *n.* One who conducts an auction, usually as a business. —*v.t.* To sell by auction.

au·da·cious (ô-dā′shəs) *adj.* **1** Having or exhibiting an unabashed or fearless spirit; defiant of ordinary restraint, as of law or decorum. **2** Presumptuous; shameless; insolent. [< F *audacieux* < L *audacia.* See AUDACITY.] —**au·da′cious·ly** *adv.* —**au·da′cious·ness** *n.*

au·dac·i·ty (ô-das′ə-tē) *n. pl.* **·ties 1** The quality or state of being audacious. **2** An audacious act, remark, etc. See synonyms under EFFRONTERY, TEMERITY. [< L *audacia* boldness < *audax* bold, rash < *audere* dare]

au·di·bil·i·ty (ô′də·bil′ə·tē) *n.* **1** Ability to be heard. **2** *Telecom.* The ratio of the strength of a transmitted signal to that of a barely audible signal.

au·di·ble (ô′də·bəl) *adj.* Perceptible by the ear; loud enough to be heard. [< Med. L *audibilis* < L *audire* hear] —**au′di·ble·ness** *n.* —**au′di·bly** *adv.*

au·di·ence (ô′dē·əns) *n.* **1** An assembly gathered to hear and see, as at a concert. **2** Those who are reached by a book, television program, etc. **3** The act of hearing; attention. **4** A formal hearing, interview, or conference. **5** Opportunity to be heard. [< OF < L *audientia* a hearing < *audire* hear]

au·di·ent (ô′dē·ənt) *adj.* Listening; hearing. [< L *audiens, -entis,* ppr. of *audire* hear]

au·dile (ô′dil, ô′dil) *n. Psychol.* An individual having a tendency to form mental images derived from auditory sensations. —*adj.* Auditory. [< L *audire* hear + -ILE]

au·di·o (ô′dē·ō) *adj. Telecom.* **1** Of or pertaining to characteristics associated with sound waves. **2** Designating devices used in transmission or reception of sound waves: in television, distinguished from *video.* [< L *audire* hear]

audio- *combining form* Pertaining to hearing: *audiogram.* Also **audi-.** [< L *audire* hear]

au·di·o·cas·sette (ô′dē·ō·kə·set′; -ka·set′) *n. Electronics.* A cassette for the storage of audio material.

au·di·o·com·mu·ni·ca·tion (ô′dē·ō·kə·myoo′nə·kā′shən) *n.* **1** Vocal communication. **2** Any form of communication which utilizes electroacoustic methods in the transmission, recording, and amplification of sound waves.

au·di·o·vis·u·al (ô′dē·ō·vizh′oo·əl) *adj.* Pertaining

to forms of instruction and entertainment other than books, as radio, television, motion pictures, photographs, recordings, etc.: *audiovisual* aids.

au·dit (ô′dit) *v.t.* **1** To examine, adjust, and certify, as accounts. **2** To attend as a listener: to *audit* a course in college. [< *n.*] —*n.* **1** An examination of an accounting document and of the evidence in support of its correctness. **2** A calling to account. **3** A settlement of accounts. **4** A balance sheet. **5** *Obs.* A hearing. [< L *auditus* a hearing < *audire* hear]

au·di·tion (ô·dish′ən) *n.* **1** The act or sense of hearing. **2** An audience or hearing; especially, a trial test or hearing, as of an actor or singer —*v.t.* To try out, as an actor or singer for a special role. —*v.i.* To demonstrate one's ability or talent when applying for an acting or singing job. [< L *auditio, -onis* a hearing < *audire* hear]

au·di·tor (ô′də·tər) *n.* **1** One who audits accounts. **2** One who listens; a hearer. **3** One who audits classes. —**au′di·tress** *n. fem.*

au·di·to·ri·um (ô′də·tôr′ē·əm), -tō′rē·əm *n. pl.* **·to·ri·ums** or **·to·ri·a** (-tôr′ē·ə, -tō′rē·ə) **1** The room or part of a building, as a church, theater, etc., occupied by the audience. **2** A building for concerts, public meetings, etc. [< L, lecture room, courtroom, orig. neut. of *auditorius.* See AUDITORY.]

au·di·to·ry (ô′də·tôr′ē, -tō′rē) *adj.* Of or pertaining to hearing or the organs or sense of hearing. —*n. pl.* **·ries 1** An assembly of hearers; an audience. **2** An auditorium, particularly the nave of a church. [< L *auditorius* < *audire* hear] —**au′di·to′ri·ly** *adv.*

auditory canal *Anat.* The passage leading from the auricle to the tympanic membrane. See illustration under EAR.

au·gen (ou′gən) *n. pl. Geol.* A rock formation which contains packed masses of eye-shaped particles. [< G, eyes]

au·gend (ô′jend) *n. Math.* A quantity or number to which another is to be added. See ADDEND. [< L *augendum,* neut. gerundive of *augere* increase]

au·ger (ô′gər) *n.* **1** A large tool with a spiral groove for boring holes in wood, etc. **2** An earth-boring tool. ◆Homophone: *augur.* [OE *nafugār,* lit., nave-borer < *nafu* nave of a wheel + *gār* borer, spear (a *nauger* in ME becoming an *auger*)]

Au·ghra·bies Falls (ô·khrä′bēs, ō·grä′-) A waterfall in the Orange River, in northwest Cape Province, Union of South Africa; 480 feet: also *King George's Falls.*

AUGERS
a. Twisted.   *b.* Posthole.   *c.* Ship.   *d.* Chuck-shanked.   *e.* Gimlet.   *f.* Expanding.

aught¹ (ôt) *n.* Anything; any part or item. —*adv.* By any chance; at all; in any respect. Also spelled *ought.* ◆Homophone: *ought.* [OE *āwiht* < *ā* ever + *wiht* thing]

aught² (ôt) *n.* The figure 0; cipher; a naught; nothing. ◆Homophone: *ought.* [*a naught* taken as an *aught*]

aug·ment (ôg·ment′) *v.t.* **1** To make greater, as in size, number, or amount; enlarge; intensify. **2** In Greek and Sanskrit grammar, to add the augment to. —*v.i.* To become greater, as in size, number, or amount. See synonyms under ADD, INCREASE. —*n.* (ôg′ment) **1** Increase; enlargement. **2** In Greek and Sanskrit grammar, a vowel prefixed to a verb, or a lengthening of the initial vowel, to indicate past time. [< F *augmenter* < L *augmentare* < *augmentum* an increase < *augere* increase] —**aug·ment′a·ble** *adj.* —**aug·ment′er** *n.*

aug·men·ta·tion (ôg′men·tā′shən) *n.* **1** An augmenting or being augmented. **2** The result of augmenting; enlargement; increase; an addition. **2** *Music* The repetition of a theme in notes of twice the time value of those first used; opposite of *diminution.* See synonyms under ACCESSION, INCREASE.

aug·men·ta·tive (ôg·men′tə·tiv) *adj.* **1** Having the quality or power of augmenting. **2** *Gram.* Denoting greater size or intensity, as the suffix -*agne* in French *montagne* a mountain (from *mont* a hill). — *n. Gram.* An augmentative form. Also **aug·men'tive.** Abbr. *aug.*

aug·men·ted (ôg·men'tid) *adj. Music* Increased by a half step more than the corresponding major interval.

aug·men·tor (ôg·men'tər) *n. Aeron.* A duct for increasing the thrust of a jet engine by forcing the air-fuel mixture through a narrowed channel just behind the exit nozzle.

au gra·tin (ō grät'n, grat'n; *Fr.* ōgrá·taṅ') Sprinkled with bread crumbs or grated cheese and baked until brown. [< F]

au·gur (ô'gər) *n.* 1 A religious official of ancient Rome whose duty it was to foretell future events by interpreting omens, such as the flights of birds, and to give advice on public affairs accordingly. 2 Hence, a prophet; soothsayer. Also *Obs.* **au'gur·er.** — *v.t.* 1 To predict; divine; prognosticate from or as from signs and omens; also, to conjecture from indications. 2 To betoken; portend; to be an omen of. — *v.i.* 3 To conjecture from signs and omens. 4 To be an augury or omen. ◆ Homophone: *auger*. [< L *augur* < *avis* bird + -*gar* (? akin to *garrire* talk, interpret)]
Synonyms (verb): betoken, bode, forbode, forecast, foretell, foretoken, portend, predict, presage, prognosticate, prophesy. Persons only *divine, forecast, foretell, predict,* or *prophesy;* things only *betoken, foretoken,* or *portend;* either persons or things *augur, bode, forebode, presage,* or *prognosticate.* As regards the outcome, *bode, forebode,* and *portend* always refer to evil or misfortune; the other words are neutral, applying equally to good or ill. One may *augur* or *divine* from indications too slight to be explained; to *forecast* always denotes calculation. See PROPHESY. *Antonyms:* assure, demonstrate, determine, establish, insure, prove, warrant.

au·gu·ral (ô'gyə·rəl) *adj.* Of or pertaining to augurs or auguries.

au·gu·ry (ô'gyə·rē) *n. pl.* **·ries** 1 The art or practice of foretelling by signs or omens; divination. 2 A portent or omen; presage. 3 The rite or ceremony conducted by an augur.

au·gust (ô·gust') *adj.* 1 Majestic; grand; imposing. 2 Of high birth or rank; venerable; eminent. See Synonyms under AWFUL, GRAND, KINGLY. [< L *augustus* < *augere* increase, exalt] — **au·gust'ly** *adv.* — **au·gust'ness** *n.*

Au·gust (ô'gəst) The eighth month of the year, containing 31 days. [< L, after AUGUSTUS CAESAR]

Au·gus·tan (ô·gus'tən) *adj.* 1 Of or pertaining to the emperor Augustus or to his times. 2 Pertaining to any era which resembles that of Augustus in refinement and taste. 3 Classical; refined. 4 Pertaining to Augsburg. — *n.* A writer or artist of an Augustan age.

Au·gus·tine (ô'gəs·tēn, ô·gus'tin) A masculine personal name. Also **Au·gus·tin** (ô·gus'tən; *Fr.* ō·güs·taṅ', *Ger.* ou'gōō·stēn), *Lat.* **Au·gus·ti·nus** (ô'gəs·tī'nəs). [< L, venerable]
— **Augustine, Saint,** 354–430, bishop of Hippo and a father of the church. — **Augustine, Saint,** died 604?, brought Christianity to England: also known as *Saint Austin.*

Au·gus·tin·i·an (ô'gəs·tin'ē·ən) *adj.* 1 Of or pertaining to St. Augustine or his doctrines. 2 Belonging to a monastic order named after St. Augustine or following his rule. — *n.* 1 A disciple of St. Augustine. 2 A member of any of the mendicant monastic orders named after St. Augustine: also **Au·gus·tin** (ô·gus'tin). — **Au'gus·tin'i·an·ism, Au·gus'tin·ism** *n.*

Au·gus·tus (ô·gus'təs) A masculine personal name. Also *Fr.* **Au·guste** (ō·güst'). [< L, venerable]
— **Augustus Caesar,** 63 B.C.–A.D. 14, Gaius Julius Caesar Octavianus, the first Roman emperor 27 B.C.–A.D. 14: before 27 B.C. called *Octavian.*

au jus (ō zhü') *French* Served with its natural juice or gravy: said of meats.

Auld Horn·ie (hôr'nē) *Scot.* The devil.

auld lang syne (ôld' lang sīn', zīn') *Scot.* Literally, old long since; hence, long ago.

au·lic (ô'lik) *adj.* Pertaining to a royal court. [< F *aulique* < L *aulicus* < Gk. *aulikos* < *aulē*

a court]

au na·tu·rel (ō nà·tü·rel') *French* 1 Ungarnished; plainly cooked, as food. 2 In the nude.

aunt (ant, änt) *n.* 1 The sister of one's father or mother, or the wife of one's uncle. 2 An elderly woman: familiar or affectionate use. [< OF *aunte, ante* < L *amita* paternal aunt]

aunt·y (an'tē, än'-) *n.* A familiar, diminutive form of AUNT. Also **aunt'ie.**

au pair (ō pâr) *Chiefly Brit.* 1 An arrangement whereby one receives room and board in a foreign household in exchange for doing certain chores, as housekeeping and the care of children: often used attributively: *au pair girls.* 2 *Colloq.* A girl participating in such an arrangement. [< F, lit., at par]

au·ra (ôr'ə) *n. pl.* **au·ras** or **au·rae** (ôr'ē) 1 An invisible emanation or exhalation. 2 A distinctive air or quality enveloping or characterizing a person or thing: an *aura* of wealth. 3 A gentle breeze. 4 *Electr.* **a** *Obs.* A subtile fluid supposed to surround an electrified body. **b** The current of air caused by a convective discharge from a sharp point. 5 *Pathol.* The sensory, motor, or psychic manifestations preceding an epileptic attack or other paroxysm. 6 In psychic research, the hypothetical emanations from living organisms. [< L, breeze < Gk. *aurē* breath]

au·ral¹ (ôr'əl) *adj.* Pertaining to the ear or the sense of hearing; auricular. [< L *auris* ear + -AL]

au·ral² (ôr'əl) *adj.* Pertaining to an aura.

au·rate¹ (ôr'āt) *adj.* Having ears or earlike expansions. Also **au'rat·ed.** [< L *auris* ear + -ATE¹]

au·rate² (ôr'āt) *n.* A salt of auric acid, containing the trivalent radical AuO_3: ammonium *aurate* (fulminating gold). [< AUR(IC ACID) + -ATE³]

au·re·ate (ôr'ē·it) *adj.* Of the color of gold; golden. [< LL *aureatus* < L *aureus* < *aurum* gold]
man emperor 161–180, and Stoic philosopher: full name: *Marcus Aurelius Antoninus.*

au·re·o·la (ô·rē'ə·lə) *n.* 1 In art, a radiance enveloping the whole figure or head of Christ or any sanctified being; a glory; halo; aureole. 2 A radiance, or something resembling or likened to it. 3 In the Roman Catholic Church, a reward added to the essential bliss of heaven for spiritual victories achieved on earth. [< L < *aureolus* golden, dim. of *aureus* < *aurum* gold]

au·re·ole (ôr'ē·ōl) *n.* 1 *Astron.* The corona of the sun; a halo surrounding the image of a brilliant body as seen in a telescope. 2 An aureola. [< L *aureolus.* See AUREOLA]

au re·voir (ō rə·vwär') *French* Good-by; till we meet again; literally, to the seeing again.

au·ric (ôr'ik) *adj.* Of, pertaining to, or containing gold, especially when combined in its highest or triad valency: *auric* chloride, $AuCl_3$. [< L *aurum* gold]

au·ri·cle (ôr'i·kəl) *n.* 1 *Anat.* **a** An atrium of the heart. **b** An auricular appendix. **c** The external ear; pinna. 2 An ear or ear-shaped appendage or part. 3 An ear trumpet. [< L *auricula,* dim. of *auris* ear] — **au'ri·cled** *adj.*

au·ric·u·lar (ô·rik'yə·lər) *adj.* 1 Of or pertaining to the ear or the sense of hearing. 2 Intended for or perceived by the ear; audible; confidential. 3 Ear-shaped. 4 Of or pertaining to an auricle. — *n. Ornithol.* One of the feathers overlying the ear: usually in the plural.

au·ric·u·late (ô·rik'yə·lit, -lāt) *adj.* 1 Having ear-shaped appendages or projections. 2 *Bot.* Having rounded projections at the base, as a leaf. 3 Like an ear. Also **au·ric'u·lat·ed.** — **au·ric'u·late·ly** *adv.*

au·rif·er·ous (ô·rif'ər·əs) *adj.* Containing gold. [< L *aurifer* < *aurum* gold + *ferre* bear] — **au·rif'er·ous·ly** *adv.*

au·ri·form (ôr'ə·fôrm) *adj.* Shaped like or resembling an ear; ear-shaped. [< L *auris* ear + -FORM]

Au·rig·na·cian (ôr'ig·nā'shən) *adj. Anthropol.* Of or pertaining to an Upper Paleolithic culture appearing toward the end of the Pleistocene. It is associated with the rise of Cro-Magnon man in western Europe and is

characterized by implements of flint, bone, and horn, delicately modeled ivory figurines, and early examples of cave painting. [from *Aurignac,* town in Haute-Garonne, France, where the relics were discovered]

au·ri·scope (ôr'ə·skōp) *n.* An instrument for examining the ear. — **au·ris·co·py** (ô·ris'kə·pē) *n.*

au·rochs (ôr'oks) *n.* The extinct European bison; urus. [< G *auerochs* < OHG *ūrohso* < *ūr* the urus + *ohso* ox]

au·ro·ra (ô·rôr'ə, ô·rō'rə) *n.* 1 The dawn. 2 The early stage or development of anything. 3 *Meteorol.* A luminous, sometimes richly colored display of arcs, bands, streamers, etc., occasionally seen in the skies of high northern and southern latitudes: it is caused by electrical disturbances in the atmosphere: also **au·ro·ra po·la·ris** (pə·lâr'is). [< L, dawn]

Au·ro·ra (ô·rôr'ə, ô·rō'rə) In Roman mythology, the goddess of the dawn: identified with the Greek *Eos.*

aurora aus·tra·lis (ôs·trā'lis) *Meteorol.* The aurora as seen in far southern latitudes: also called *southern lights.* [< NL, southern aurora < L *auster* south wind]

aurora bo·re·al·is (bôr'ē·al'is, -ā'lis, bō'rē-) *Meteorol.* The aurora as seen in the high northern latitudes: also called *northern lights.* [< NL, northern aurora < Gk. *boreas* north wind]

au·ro·ral (ô·rôr'əl, ô·rō'rəl) *adj.* 1 Pertaining to or like the dawn; dawning; roseate. 2 Of, like, or caused by an aurora: an *auroral* display. Also **au·ro·re·an** (ô·rôr'ē·ən, ô·rō'rē-), **au·ro'ric.** — **au·ro'ral·ly** *adv.*

au·rous (ôr'əs) *adj.* Of, pertaining to, or containing gold, especially in its monad valency: *aurous* chloride, AuCl. See AURIC. [< L *aurum* gold]

au·rum (ôr'əm) *n.* Gold. [< L]

Au·schwitz (ou'shvits) The German name for Oświecim, a city in SW Poland; site of a German extermination camp in which about 4,000,000 victims, mostly Jews, were slaughtered during World War II.

aus·cul·tate (ôs'kəl·tāt) *v.t. & v.i.* **·tat·ed, ·tat·ing** *Med.* To examine by auscultation. [< L *auscultatus,* pp. of *auscultare* listen, give ear to] — **aus·cul·ta·tive** (ôs·kul'tə·tiv) *adj.*

aus·cul·ta·tion (ôs'kəl·tā'shən) *n.* 1 *Med.* The act, art, or process of listening, as with a stethoscope, for sounds produced in the chest, abdomen, etc., to determine any abnormal condition. 2 A listening.

aus·cul·ta·tor (ôs'kəl·tā'tər) *n.* 1 One skilled in or practicing auscultation. 2 A stethoscope. 3 One who listens. — **aus·cul·ta·to·ry** (ôs·kul'tə·tôr'ē, -tō'rē) *adj.*

aus·pex (ôs'peks) *n. pl.* **aus·pi·ces** (ôs'pə·sēz) An augur, soothsayer, or diviner of ancient Rome; especially, one who observed and interpreted the omens connected with the flight, singing, cries, or feeding, etc., of birds; a bird-viewer. [< L *auspex* < *avis* bird + *specere* look at, observe]

aus·pi·cate (ôs'pi·kāt) *v.t.* To initiate or begin, especially under favorable circumstances, as with a ceremony calculated to insure good luck. [< L *auspicatus,* pp. of *auspicari* take omens, begin < *auspex.* See AUSPEX.]

aus·pice (ôs'pis) *n. pl.* **aus·pi·ces** (ôs'pə·sēz) 1 *Usually pl.* Favoring influence or guidance; patronage. 2 An augury, omen, or sign, especially when taken from meteorological phenomena, the movements of birds, etc. 3 The observation of such omens, etc. [< F < L *auspicium* < *auspex.* See AUSPEX.]

aus·pi·cial (ôs·pish'əl) *adj.* 1 Pertaining to augury. 2 Auspicious.

aus·pi·cious (ôs·pish'əs) *adj.* 1 Of good omen; propitious. 2 Successful; prosperous; fortunate. — **aus·pi'cious·ly** *adv.* — **aus·pi'cious·ness** *n.*
Synonyms: encouraging, favorable, fortunate, happy, hopeful, lucky, opportune, promising, propitious, prosperous, successful. See PROPITIOUS. *Antonyms:* baleful, discouraging, hopeless, inauspicious, unfavorable, unpromising, unpropitious.

Aus·ten (ôs'tən), **Jane,** 1775–1817, English novelist.

aus·tere (ô·stir′) *adj.* **1** Severe, grave, or stern, as in aspect, disposition, judgment, or conduct. **2** Morally strict; abstemious; ascetic. **3** Sour and astringent. **4** Severely simple; unadorned. [< OF < L *austerus* < Gk. *austeros* harsh, bitter < *auein* dry] **—aus·tere′ly** *adv.*
Synonyms: hard, harsh, morose, relentless, rigid, rigorous, severe, stern, strict, unrelenting, unyielding. The *austere* person is severely simple or temperate, *strict* in self-restraint or discipline, and similarly *unrelenting* toward others. We speak of *austere* morality, *rigid* rules, *rigorous* discipline, *stern* commands, *severe* punishment, *harsh* speech or a *harsh* voice, *hard* requirements, *strict* injunctions, and *strict* obedience. *Strict* discipline holds one exactly and unflinchingly to the rule; *rigorous* discipline punishes severely any infraction of it.
aus·ter·i·ty (ô·ster′ə·tē) *n. pl.* **·ties 1** Gravity or rigor in attitude or conduct toward others. **2** Severe self-restraint. **3** Rigid economy in expenditure. **4** *pl.* Austere acts or practices. Also **aus·tere′ness.**
Aus·tin (ôs′tən) A city on the Colorado River; the capital of Texas.
aus·tral (ôs′trəl, os′-) *adj.* Southern; torrid. [< L *australis* southern < *auster* south wind]

Aus·tral·a·sia (ôs′trəl·ā′zhə, -ā′shə, os′-) The islands of the South Pacific, including Australia, New Zealand, New Guinea, and adjacent islands; sometimes applied to all of Oceania. **—Aus′tral·a′sian** *adj. & n.*
Aus·tra·lia (ô·strāl′yə, o-) An island continent SE of Asia, comprising the **Commonwealth of Australia,** a self-governing member of the Commonwealth of Nations, consisting of a union of six states and two territories together with its dependencies; 2,948,366 square miles; capital, Canberra.
Australia Day An Australian holiday, January 26th, commemorating the landing of the British in 1788. Also *Anniversary Day.*
Aus·tra·lian (ô·strāl′yən, o-) *n.* **1** A native or naturalized inhabitant of Australia. **2** One of the Australian aborigines. **3** Any of the aboriginal languages of Australia. *—adj.* Designating a zoogeographical region including Australia, New Guinea and adjacent islands, New Zealand, and Polynesia.
Australian Alps A mountain range in SE New South Wales and eastern Victoria, Australia; highest peak, 7,316 feet.
Australian English The English language as spoken and written in Australia: sometimes called *Austral English.*
Aus·tra·lian·ism (ô·strāl′yən·iz′əm, o-) *n.* **1** A trait, custom, or tradition of Australia or Australians. **2** A word, phrase, or usage characteristic of Australian English. **3** Devotion to Australia, its institutions, etc.
Aus·tra·lo·pi·the·cus (ô·strā′lō·pi·thē′kəs) *n.* A genus of small-brained primates of the Pliocene and early Pleistocene, first identified from a fossil juvenile skull found in 1924 at Taungs, South Africa; subsequent remains confirm its position as a transitional form between ape and man. Also called *Taungs skull.* **—Aus·tra′lo·pi·the′cine** (-thē′sīn, -sin) *adj.* [< NL < L *australis* southern + Gk. *pithēkos* ape]
Aus·tri·a (ôs′trē·ə) A federal republic of central Europe; 32,375 square miles; capital Vienna; German *Österreich.* **—Aus′tri·an** *adj. & n.*
Austro- *combining form* **1** Austrian: *Austro-Hungarian.* **2** Australian: *Austro-Malayan.*
Aus·tro·A·si·at·ic (ôs′trō·ā′zhē·at′ik, -ā′shē-) A family of languages of SE Asia, including the Mon-Khmer and Munda subfamilies. *—adj.* Of or pertaining to this linguistic family.
Aus·tro·Hun·gar·i·an (ôs′trō·hung·gâr′ē·ən)

adj. Of or pertaining to Austria-Hungary.
Aus·tro·Ma·lay·an (ôs′trō·mə·lā′ən) *adj.* Of or pertaining to the Papuan subregion north of Australia, including islands from San Cristobal to Celebes.
Aus·tro·ne·sia (ôs′trō·nē′zhə, -shə) The islands of Indonesia, Melanesia, Micronesia, and Polynesia.
Aus·tro·ne·sian (ôs′trō·nē′zhən, -shən) *adj.* Of or pertaining to Austronesia, its inhabitants, or their languages. *—n.* A family of languages spoken throughout the Pacific in an area roughly bounded by Madagascar to the west, Easter Island to the east, Formosa to the north, and New Zealand to the south, but excluding Australia, Tasmania, and a large part of New Guinea. The Austronesian family is divided linguistically into three subfamilies: Indonesian or Malayan, Oceanic (including the Melanesian and Micronesian languages), and Polynesian. Also *Malayo-Polynesian.*
aut- Var. of AUTO-[1].
au·ta·coid (ô′tə·koid) *n.* Hormone. [< AUT- + Gk. *akos* remedy + -OID]
au·tar·chy (ô′tär·kē) *n.* **1** Absolute rule or sovereignty or a country under such rule; unrestricted power; autocracy. **2** Self-government. **3** Autarky. [< Gk. *autarchos* absolute ruler < *autos* self + *archein* rule] **—au·tar′chic** (ô·tär′kik) or **·chi·cal** *adj.*
au·tar·ky (ô′tär·kē) *n.* National economic self-sufficiency; a policy of establishing independence of imports from other countries: also *autarchy.* [< Gk. *autarkeia* self-sufficiency < *autos* self + *arkeein* suffice] **—au·tar·ki·cal** (ô·tär′ki·kəl) *adj.*
au·te·col·o·gy (ô′tē·kol′ə·jē) *n.* The ecology of individual organisms: distinguished from *synecology.*
au·teur (ō·tœr′) *n.* A film director whose work is the product of personal vision and total production control. [< F, lit., author]
au·then·tic (ô·then′tik) *adj.* **1** According with the facts; authoritative; trustworthy; reliable. **2** Of undisputed origin; genuine. **3** *Law* Duly executed before the proper officer. Also **au·then′ti·cal.** [< OF *autentique* < L *authenticus* < Gk. *authentikos* < *authentēs* the doer of a deed] **—au·then′ti·cal·ly** *adv.*
Synonyms: accepted, accredited, authoritative, authorized, certain, current, genuine, legitimate, original, real, received, sure, true, trustworthy, veritable. *Antonyms:* apocryphal, baseless, counterfeit, disputed, exploded, fabulous, false, fictitious, spurious, unauthorized.
au·then·ti·cate (ô·then′ti·kāt) *v.t.* **·cat·ed, ·cat·ing 1** To make genuine, credible, or authoritative. **2** To give legal force or validity to. **3** To establish or certify, as a book or painting, to be the work of a certain person. **—au·then′ti·ca′tion** *n.*
au·then·ti·ca·tor (ô·then′ti·kā′tər) *n.* **1** One who or that which authenticates. **2** *Telecom.* A code signal transmitted with a radio message as a proof of genuineness.
au·then·tic·i·ty (ô′thən·tis′ə·tē) *n.* The state or quality of being authentic, authoritative, or genuine. Also **au·then′tic·ness.**
au·thor (ô′thər) *n.* **1** An originator; first cause; creator. **2** The original writer, as of a book; also, one who makes literary compositions his profession. **3** An author's writings collectively. See synonyms under CAUSE. *—v.t. Informal* To be the author of; write. [< OF *autor* < L *auctor* originator, producer < *augere* increase] **—au′thor·ess** *n. fem.* **—au·tho·ri·al** (ô·thôr′ē·əl, ô·thō′rē-) *adj.*
au·thor·i·tar·i·an (ə·thôr′ə·târ′ē·ən, ə·thor′-) *adj.* Encouraging and upholding authority against individual freedom; specifically, relating to a type of government in which the individual and his rights are subordinated to interests of state. *—n.* A defender of the principle of authority or of a type of government organized on an authoritarian basis. **—au·thor′i·tar′i·an·ism** *n.*
au·thor·i·ta·tive (ə·thôr′ə·tā′tiv, ə·thor′-) *adj.* **1** Possessing or proceeding from proper authority; duly sanctioned. **2** Exercising authority; positive; commanding; dictatorial. See synonyms under ABSOLUTE, AUTHENTIC, DOGMATIC, IMPERIOUS. **—au·thor′i·ta·tive·ly** *adv.* **—au·thor′i·ta·tive·ness** *n.*
au·thor·i·ty (ə·thôr′ə·tē, ə·thor′-) *n. pl.* **·ties 1**

The right to command and to enforce obedience; the right to act officially. **2** Personal power that commands influence, respect, or confidence. **3** The person or persons in whom government or command is vested: often in the plural. **4** That which is or may be appealed to in support of action or belief, as an author, volume, etc. **5** An authoritative opinion, decision, or precedent. See synonyms under INFLUENCE, PERMISSION, PRECEDENT. [< F *autorité* < L *auctoritas, -tatis* power, authority < *augere* increase]
au·thor·i·za·tion (ô′thər·ə·zā′shən) *n.* **1** The act of conferring legality. **2** Formal legal power; sanction.
au·thor·ize (ô′thər·īz) *v.t.* **·ized, ·iz·ing 1** To confer authority upon; empower; commission. **2** To warrant; justify. **3** To sanction; approve. **4** *Obs.* To vouch for. See JUSTIFY. **—au′thor·iz′er** *n.*
au·thor·ized (ô′thər·izd) *adj.* **1** Endowed with authority; accepted as authoritative. **2** Formally or legally sanctioned.
au·thor·ship (ô′thər·ship) *n.* **1** The profession or occupation of an author. **2** Origin or source.
au·tism (ô′tiz·əm) *n. Psychol.* A tendency to morbid daydreaming and introspection uninfluenced by objective norms and realities. [< AUT- + -ISM] **—au·tis·tic** (ô·tis′tik) *adj.*
au·to (ô′tō) *U.S. Colloq. n.* An automobile. *—v.i.* To ride in or travel by an automobile.
auto-[1] *combining form* **1** Arising from some process or action within the object; not induced by any stimulus from without; as in:

autoagglutination	autofecundation
autocombustible	autohybridization
autoelectrolysis	autoinduction
autoelectrolytic	autoinhibitive
autoexcitation	autoluminescence
autoretardation	autosepticemia
autorhythmic	autosymbolic

2 Acting, acted, or directed upon the self; as in:

autoanalysis	autoimmunity
autoanalytic	autolavage

Also, before vowels, *aut-,* as in *autism.* [< Gk. *autos* self]
auto-[2] *combining form* Self-propelled: *auto-boat.* [< *automobile*]
au·to·bi·og·ra·phy (ô′tə·bī·og′rə·fē, -bē·og′-) *n. pl.* **·phies** The story of one's life written by oneself. See synonyms under HISTORY. **—au′to·bi·og′ra·pher** *n.* **—au·to·bi·o·graph·ic** (ô′tə·bī′ə·graf′ik) or **·i·cal** *adj.* **—au·to·bi′o·graph′i·cal·ly** *adv.*
au·to·chrome (ô′tə·krōm) *n.* A single plate for three-color photography.
au·toch·thon (ô·tok′thən) *n. pl.* **·thons** or **·tho·nes** (-thə·nēz) **1** Originally, one sprung from the earth itself. **2** *pl.* The aboriginal inhabitants. **3** *Ecol.* An indigenous animal or plant. [< Gk. *autochthīn* indigenous < *autos* self + *chthīn* earth, land]
au·toch·thon·ism (ô·tok′thən·iz′əm) *n.* Origin from the soil of a country; origination in or primitive occupation of a region. Also **au·toch·tho·ny** (ô·tok′thə·nē).
au·toch·tho·nous (ô·tok′thə·nəs) *adj.* **1** Sprung from the soil; native to a place; indigenous; aboriginal. **2** *Geol.* Of or pertaining to rocks which, with their constituents, have been formed *in situ,* as rock salt, stalactites, etc. Also **au·toch′tho·nal, au·toch·thon·ic** (ô·tok·thon′ik). **—au·toch′tho·nous·ly** *adv.*
au·to·clave (ô′tə·klāv) *n.* **1** A strong gastight vessel in which chemical reactions can be effected under pressure. **2** An enclosed chamber for the sterilization of drugs, vaccines, instruments, etc., under specified pressure. **3** A steamtight cooking utensil; a pressure cooker. [< F *auto-* AUTO-[1] + L *clavis* a key]
au·toc·ra·cy (ô·tok′rə·sē) *n.* **1** Absolute government by an individual; rule or authority of an autocrat. **2** A state ruled by an autocrat. **3** Complete power or dominance over others.
au·to·crat (ô′tə·krat) *n.* **1** A supreme ruler of unrestricted power. **2** One exercising unlimited power over others. **3** An arrogant, dictatorial person. [< F *autocrate* < Gk. *autokratēs* self-ruling, independent < *autos* self + *kratos* power] **—au·to·crat′ic** or **·i·cal** *adj.* **—au·to·crat′i·cal·ly** *adv.*

au·to·da·fé (ô'tō·də·fā', ou'-) *n. pl.* **au·tos·da·fé** (ô'tōz-, ou'tōz-) The public announcement and execution of the sentence of the Inquisition, with the attendant ceremonies, as the burning of heretics at the stake, etc. Also *Spanish* **au·to de fe** (ou'tō dā fā'). [< Pg., lit., act of the faith]

au·toe·cious (ô·tē'shəs) *adj. Bot.* 1 Having male and female reproductive organs on the same plant, as certain mosses. 2 Completing the whole development on a single host, as seen in certain rust fungi and other parasites: opposed to *heteroecious.* [< AUTO·¹ + Gk. *oikos* dwelling]

au·toe·cism (ô·tē'siz·əm) *n.* The condition of being autoecious.

au·to·er·o·tism (ô'tō·er'ə·tiz'əm) *n.* 1 *Psychoanal.* Sexual impulses taking one's own body as their object, without association with or stimulus from another person. 2 Masturbation. Also **au·to·e·rot·i·cism** (ô'tō·i·rot'ə·siz'·əm). [< AUTO·¹ + Gk. *erōs, erotos* love] — **au·to·e·rot·ic** (ô'tō·i·rot'ik) *adj.*

au·tog·a·mous (ô·tog'ə·məs) *adj. Bot.* Self-fertilized; capable of self-fertilization: said of certain flowers.

au·tog·a·my (ô·tog'ə·mē) *n.* 1 *Biol.* Self-fertilization; fecundation of a flower by its own pollen. 2 *Biol.* The union of closely related cells or of nuclei within a cell; karyogamy. [< AUTO·¹ + Gk. *gameein* marry]

au·to·gen·e·sis (ô'tō·jen'ə·sis) *n. Biol.* Spontaneous formation of a tissue or organism.

au·to·ge·net·ic (ô'tō·jə·net'ik) *adj.* 1 Of or pertaining to autogenesis. 2 *Geog.* Of, pertaining to, regulated by, or indicating a self-established system of drainage. — **au·to·ge·net'i·cal·ly** *adv.*

au·tog·e·nous (ô·toj'ə·nəs) *adj.* 1 Self-produced or independent. 2 *Physiol.* Developed within the body, as new tissue or skeletal parts. 3 *Mech.* Designating a process of soldering by means of a hydrogen flame. Also **au·to·gen·ic** (ô'tō·jen'ik). [< Gk. *autogenēs* self-produced]

au·to·graft (ô'tō·graft', -gräft) *n.* A mass of tissue transplanted from one site to another on the same organism. — *v.t.* To transplant (tissue) in making an autograft.

au·to·graph (ô'tə·graf, -gräf) *n.* 1 One's own handwriting or signature. 2 Something in one's own handwriting; a manuscript in an author's handwriting. — *v.t.* 1 To write one's name in or affix one's signature to. 2 To write in one's own handwriting. — *adj.* Written by one's own hand, as a will. [< L *autographum,* orig. neut. of *autographus* < Gk. *autographos* written with one's own hand < *autos* self + *graphein* write]

au·to·graph·ic (ô'tə·graf'ik) *adj.* 1 Of the nature of or like an autograph. 2 Written in one's own or the author's handwriting. 3 In telegraphy, recording or transmitting in facsimile. Also **au'to·graph'i·cal.** — **au·to·graph'·i·cal·ly** *adv.*

au·tog·ra·phy (ô·tog'rə·fē) *n.* 1 The writing of a document in one's own handwriting. 2 Autographs collectively. 3 One's own handwriting. 4 Facsimile reproduction.

au·to·harp (ô'tō·härp) *n.* A musical instrument resembling a zither, but having a piano scale and an arrangement of dampers enabling the player to produce the correct chords easily.

au·to·hyp·no·sis (ô'tō·hip·nō'sis) *n.* The state or condition of self-hypnotism.

au·to·im·mune (ô''tō·i·myoōn') *adj.* Caused by antibodies that operate against the body's own tissues: *autoimmune* diseases. — **au'to·im·mu'ni·ty** *n.*

au·to·in·fec·tion (ô'tō·in·fek'shən) *n. Pathol.* Infection due to agents or toxins generated in the body, as the infection causing peritonitis when perforation of the intestine occurs.

au·to·in·oc·u·la·tion (ô'tō·in·ok'yə·lā'shən) *n.* 1 Inoculation with a virus or other morbid matter already present in one's own body. 2 The spreading of infection from a center to other portions of the same body.

au·to·ki·net·ic (ô'tō·ki·net'ik, -kī-) *adj.* Self-moving. [< Gk. *autokinētos* self-moved < *autos* self + *kineein* move]

au·tol·y·sis (ô·tol'ə·sis) *n. Biochem.* The disintegration of cells and tissues after death by the action of enzymes already present: distinguished from *heterolysis.* 2 *Physiol.* Self-digestion of organic material. [< NL < AUTO·¹ + Gk. *lysis* dissolution < *lyein* loosen, dissolve] — **au·to·lyt·ic** (ô'tə·lit'ik) *adj.*

au·to·mat (ô'tə·mat) *n.* 1 An automatic device: applied to various articles, as a camera shutter, etc. 2 *U.S.* A restaurant in which food is automatically made available from a receptacle when money is deposited in a slot alongside.

au·to·mat·a·ble (ô'tə·mat'ə·bəl) *adj.* Suitable for or capable of automation: an *automatable* production process.

au·to·mate (ô'tə·māt) *v.* **·mat·ed, ·mat·ing** *v.t.* To adapt, as a machine, factory, or process, for automation. — *v.i.* To install or convert to automation equipment.

au·to·mat·ic (ô'tə·mat'ik) *adj.* 1 Self-moving, self-regulating, or self-acting. 2 Acting mechanically. 3 *Psychol.* Done from force of habit or without volition. 4 *Physiol.* Independent of the will, as a reflex action. 5 *Mech.* Having a self-acting mechanism by which certain operations are performed under predetermined conditions: an *automatic* pilot. Also **au'to·mat'i·cal, au·tom·a·tous** (ô·tom'ə·təs). — *n.* A self-acting machine, device, or weapon. See synonyms under SPONTANEOUS. [< Gk. *automatos* acting of oneself. See AUTOMATON.] — **au'to·mat'i·cal·ly** *adv.*

au·tom·a·tic·i·ty (ô·tom'ə·tis'ə·tē) *n.* State or condition of being automatic.

automatic pilot *Aeron.* An automatic-control mechanism operating on the gyroscope principle: designed to keep an aircraft in level flight and on an even course: also called *gyro pilot, robot pilot.*

au·to·ma·tion (ô'tə·mā'shən) *n. Technol.* 1 The automatic transfer of one unit of a complex industrial assembly to a succession of self-acting machines each of which completes a specified stage in the total manufacturing process from crude material to finished product. 2 The application of fully automatic procedures in the efficient performance and control of operations involving a sequence of complex, standardized, or repetitive processes on a large scale. 3 The theory, art, and technique of converting a mechanical process to maximum automatic operation, especially by the use of electronic control mechanisms and electronic computers for the rapid organizing and processing of data in a wide range of technical, industrial, and business information. [< AUTOM(ATIC) + (OPER)ATION]

au·tom·a·tism (ô·tom'ə·tiz'əm) *n.* 1 The state or quality of being automatic; automatic action. 2 *Philos.* The theory that consciousness does not control one's actions but is only a by-product of physiological changes. 3 *Physiol.* The functioning or power of functioning of muscular or other processes in response to external stimuli but independent of conscious control, as winking. 4 *Biol.* Spontaneous activity of cells and tissues, as the beating of a heart freed from its nervous connections. 5 *Psychol.* **a** A condition in which actions are performed without the conscious knowledge or will of the subject. **b** Any such action. 6 Suspension of the conscious mind in order to release for expression the repressed ideas and images of the subconscious, as practiced by surrealist artists and writers. — **au·tom'a·tist** *n.*

au·tom·a·tize (ô·tom'ə·tīz) *v.t.* **·tized, ·tiz·ing** 1 To render automatic. 2 To reduce to an automaton.

au·tom·a·ton (ô·tom'ə·ton, -tən) *n. pl.* **·tons** or **·ta** (-tə) 1 A contrivance or apparatus that appears to function of itself by the action of a concealed mechanism. 2 Any living being whose actions are or appear to be involuntary or mechanical. 3 Anything capable of spontaneous movement or action. [< Gk. *automaton,* neut. of *automatos* acting of oneself, independent]

au·to·mo·bile (ô'tə·mə·bēl', ô'tə·mə·bēl', ô'tə·mō'bēl) *n.* A self-propelled vehicle; specifically, one driven by an internal-combustion engine or storage battery and independent of rails or tracks; a motorcar. — *v.i.* **·biled, bil·ing** To ride in or drive an automobile. — *adj.* (ô'tə·mō'bil) 1 Self-propelling. 2 Of or for automobiles. [< F]

au·to·mo·bil·ism (ô'tə·mə·bēl'iz·əm, -mō'bil·iz'əm) *n.* The practice of using motorcars; also, the acts and methods of those who use them. — **au·to·mo·bil·ist** (ô'tə·mə·bēl'ist, -mō'bil·ist) *n.*

au·to·mo·tive (ô'tə·mō'tiv) *adj.* 1 Self-propelling. 2 Of or for automobiles: *automotive* parts.

au·to·nom·ic (ô'tə·nom'ik) *adj.* 1 Autonomous. 2 *Biol.* Spontaneous: said of functions in plants and animals produced by inherent conditions. Also **au'to·nom'i·cal.** — **au'to·nom'i·cal·ly** *adv.*

au·ton·o·mous (ô·ton'ə·məs) *adj.* 1 Independent; self-governing. 2 Of or pertaining to an autonomy. 3 *Biol.* Independent of any other organism. 4 *Bot.* Autonomic. [< Gk. *autonomos* independent < *autos* self + *nomos* law, rule] — **au·ton'o·mous·ly** *adv.*

au·ton·o·my (ô·ton'ə·mē) *n. pl.* **·mies** 1 The condition or quality of being autonomous; especially the power or right of self-government. 2 A self-governing community or local group in a particular sphere, as in religion, education, etc. 3 Self-determination, as of the will. [< Gk. *autonomia* independence < *autonomos.* See AUTONOMOUS.] — **au·ton'o·mist** *n.*

au·to·pho·bi·a (ô'tə·fō'bē·ə) *n.* Morbid fear of oneself or of being alone: also called *eremophobia, monophobia.* — **au·to·pho·bic** (ô'tə·fō'bik, -fob'ik) *adj.*

au·top·sy (ô'top·sē, ô'təp-) *n. pl.* **·sies** 1 Postmortem examination of a human body, especially to determine the cause of death for medical or legal purposes. Compare BIOPSY.] 2 The act of seeing with one's own eyes. [< NL *autopsia* < Gk. *autopsia* a seeing for oneself < *autos* self + *opsis* a seeing]

au·top·tic (ô·top'tik) *adj.* 1 Seen with one's own eyes. 2 Of or as of an eyewitness. Also **au·top'ti·cal.**

au·to·some (ô'tə·sōm) *n. Biol.* Any chromosome other than those which determine the sex of an organism. [< AUTO·¹ + (CHROMO)SOME] — **au'to·so'mal** *adj.*

au·to·sta·bil·i·ty (ô'tō·stə·bil'ə·tē) *n.* Stability owing to innate qualities, or to automatic machinery.

au·tot·o·my (ô·tot'ə·mē) *n. Zool.* The spontaneous shedding of a part of an organism from the whole, as in starfish, salamanders, and crabs. [< AUTO·¹ + Gk. *tomē* a cutting < *temnein* cut]

au·to·tox·e·mi·a (ô'tō·tok·sē'mē·ə) *n.* The poisoning of self from noxious secretions of one's own body; autointoxication. Also **au'to·tox·ae'mi·a, au·to·tox·i·co·sis** (ô'tō·tok'si·kō'sis).

au·to·tox·in (ô'tō·tok'sin) *n.* Any toxin produced by changes of tissue within an organism.

au·to·tox·is (ô'tō·tok'sis) *n.* Autotoxemia. Also **au·to·tox·i·ca·tion** (ô'tō·tok'si·kā'shən). — **au'to·tox'ic** *adj.*

au·to·trans·form·er (ô'tō·trans·fôr'mər) *n. Electr.* An automatic compensator used with alternating-current motors, in which the motor is fed from different points in an impedance coil placed across the supply circuits; a compensator.

au·to·troph·ic (ô'tə·trof'ik) *adj. Bot.* Self-nourishing: said of green plants that make their own food by photosynthesis, and of bacteria which can grow without organic carbon and nitrogen. [< AUTO·¹ + Gk. *trophē* food < *trephein* nourish]

au·tot·ro·pism (ô·tot'rə·piz'əm) *n. Bot.* The tendency of the organs of a plant, uninfluenced from without, to grow in straight lines. [< AUTO·¹ + Gk. *tropē* a turning < *trepein* turn] — **au·to·trop·ic** (ô'tə·trop'ik) *adj.*

au·to·type (ô'tə·tīp) *n.* 1 A photographic process by which pictures are produced in monochrome in a carbon pigment. 2 The print so produced. 3 A facsimile. — **au·to·typ·ic** (ô'tə·tip'ik) *adj.*

au·to·ty·pog·ra·phy (ô'tō·tī·pog'rə·fē) *n.* The art or process of drawing on gelatin, with a special ink, relief designs which are then transferred by pressure to soft metal plates from which copies may be printed.

au·to·ty·py (ô′tə·tī′pē) *n.* Reproduction by the autotype process.

au·tox·i·da·tion (ô·tok′sə·dā′shən) *n. Chem.* 1 Oxidation of a substance or compound on exposure to air. 2 Oxidation occurring only in the presence of a second substance which serves to complete the reaction.

au·tumn (ô′təm) *n.* 1 The third season of the year; in the northern hemisphere, September, October and November: often called *fall.* 2 A time of maturity and incipient decline. — *adj.* Autumnal. [Earlier *autumpne* <OF *autompne* <L *autumnus*; ult. origin uncertain]

au·tum·nal (ô·tum′nəl) *adj.* 1 Of, pertaining to, or like autumn; ripening or harvested in autumn. 2 Past maturity; denoting a later period of life; declining. — **au·tum′nal·ly** *adv.*

aux·il·ia·ry (ôg·zil′yər·ē, -zil′ər-) *adj.* 1 Giving or furnishing aid. 2 Subsidiary; accessory. — *n. pl.* **·ries** 1 One who or that which aids or helps; assistant; associate. 2 *Gram.* **a** A verb that helps to express the tense, mood, voice, or aspect of another verb, as *have* in "We *have* gone," *may* in "I *may* leave tomorrow": also called *helping verb.* Also **auxiliary verb. b** A word which functions as a subordinate element in a sentence and is fully meaningful only in association with the main words, as a preposition or conjunction. 3 *pl.* Foreign troops associated with those of a nation at war. 4 An auxiliary vessel. [<L *auxiliarius* <*auxilium* a help <*augere* increase]
Synonyms (noun): accessory, aid, ally, assistant, coadjutor, confederate, helper, mercenary, promoter, subordinate. *Allies* unite as equals; *auxiliaries,* in military usage, are troops of one nation uniting with the armies, and acting under the orders, of another. *Mercenaries* serve only for pay; *auxiliaries* often for reasons of state, policy, or patriotism as well. Compare ACCESSORY, APPENDAGE. *Antonyms*: antagonist, hinderer, opponent.

aux·i·mone (ôk′si·mōn) *n. Biochem.* One of several plant foods, analogous to vitamins, minute quantities of which are sufficient for plant nutrition. [<Gk. *auximos* assisting growth]

aux·in (ôk′sin) *n. Bot.* Any of a group of plant hormones which in minute quantities act to promote or modify the growth of plants, as in root and bud formation, stem curvature, and leaf drop. [<Gk. *auxein* increase + -IN]

aux·o·chrome (ôk′sə·krōm) *n. Chem.* Any of certain radicals which will convert a chromophore into an acidic or basic dye suitable for use in textile fabrics. [<Gk. *auxein* increase + -CHROME]

a·vail (ə·vāl′) *n.* 1 Utility for a purpose; benefit; good. 2 *pl.* Proceeds. See synonyms under PROFIT, UTILITY. — *v.t.* To assist or aid; profit. — *v.i.* To be of value or advantage; suffice. — **to avail oneself of** To take advantage of; utilize. [<OF *a-* to (<L *ad-*) + *valoir* <L *valere* be strong] — **a·vail′ing** *adj.* — **a·vail′ing·ly** *adv.*

a·vail·a·ble (ə·vāl′lə·bəl) *adj.* 1 Capable of being used advantageously; usable; profitable; at one's disposal, as funds. 2 Of adequate power for a result; effectual; valid. — **a·vail′a·bil′i·ty, a·vail′a·ble·ness** *n.* — **a·vail′·a·bly** *adv.*

av·a·lanche (av′ə·lanch, -länch) *n.* 1 The fall of a mass of snow or ice down a mountain slope. 2 The mass so falling. 3 Something like an avalanche, as in power, destructiveness, etc. — *v.i.* To fall or slide like an avalanche. — *v.t.* To fall or come down upon like an avalanche. [<F <dial. F (Swiss) *lavenche* (of uncertain origin); infl. by OF *avaler* descend <*a val* to the valley <L *ad vallem*]

Av·a·lon (av′ə·lon) In Arthurian legend, the island tomb of King Arthur: generally identified with Glastonbury.

a·vant (ə·vänt′, *Fr.* à·vän′) Before; forward: the first element in some compounds from the French. [<F *avant* before <LL *abante* <L *ab* from, + *ante* before]

a·vant–garde (à·vän·gàrd′) Vanguard: applied to the group of those who support or further the most recent trends or ideas in a movement. — *adj.* Of or pertaining to this group. [<F, lit., advance guard]

av·a·rice (av′ə·ris) *n.* Passion for riches; covetousness; greed. [<OF <L *avaritia* <*avarus* greedy <*avere* desire, crave]

av·a·ri·cious (av′ə·rish′əs) *adj.* Greedy of gain; grasping; miserly. — **av′a·ri′cious·ly** *adv.* — **av′a·ri′cious·ness** *n.*
Synonyms: close, covetous, greedy, miserly, niggardly, parsimonious, penurious, rapacious, sordid, stingy. The *avaricious* man desires both to get and to keep; the *covetous* man to get something away from its possessor; *miserly* and *niggardly* persons seek to gain by mean and petty savings; the *miserly* by stinting themselves, the *niggardly* by stinting others. *Parsimonious* and *penurious* may apply to one's outlay either for himself or for others; in the latter use, they are somewhat less harsh and reproachful terms than *niggardly*. *Greedy* and *stingy* are used not only of money, but often of other things, as food, etc. The *greedy* child tries to get everything for himself; the *stingy* child, to keep others from getting what he has. *Antonyms*: bountiful, free, generous, liberal, munificent, prodigal, wasteful.

a·vast (ə·vast′, ə·väst′) *interj. Naut.* Stop! hold! cease! [<Du. *hou′ vast, houd vast* hold fast]

av·a·tar (av′ə·tär′) *n.* In Hindu mythology, the incarnation of a god. 2 Any concrete manifestation. [<Skt. *avatāra* descent]

a·vaunt (ə·vônt′, ə·vänt′) *interj. Archaic* Begone! away! [<OF *avant* forward <LL *abante* <*ab* from + *ante* before]

a·ve (ä′vē, ä′vā) *interj.* 1 Hail! 2 Farewell! — *n.* The salutation *ave*. [<L, hail or farewell]

A·ve (ä′vē, ä′vä) *n.* 1 A prayer of invocation to the Virgin Mary: also called *Ave Maria.* 2 The time when the Ave Maria is to be said, marked by the ringing of the Ave bell. Compare ANGELUS. 3 The small beads on a rosary, used to number the Aves repeated.

A·ve Ma·ri·a (ä′vä mə·rē′ə, ä′vē) A Catholic prayer to the Virgin Mary, consisting of Biblical salutations (*Luke* i 28, 42) and a plea for her intercession. Also **A·ve Mar·y** (ä′vē mâr′ē). [<L, Hail Mary]

a·venge (ə·venj′) *v.t.* **a·venged, a·veng·ing** 1 To take vengeance or exact exemplary punishment for, as in behalf of a person or persons. 2 To inflict revenge upon, as for an act or insult. — *v.i.* 3 To take vengeance. [<OF *avengier* <*a-* to (<L *ad-*) + *vengier* punish <L *vindicare* avenge] — **a·veng′er** *n.* — **a·veng′ing** *adj.* — **a·veng′ing·ly** *adv.*
Synonyms: punish, retaliate, revenge, vindicate, visit. To *avenge* is to *visit* some offense with fitting punishment; to *revenge* is to inflict harm or suffering upon another through personal anger and resentment. See REVENGE. *Antonyms*: see synonyms for PARDON.

a·ven·tu·rine (ə·ven′chər·in) *n.* 1 An opaque, brown glass, flecked with fine metal particles. 2 A variety of quartz or feldspar containing shining particles, usually of mica or hematite: also called *sunstone.* Also **a·ven′tu·rin.** [<F <Ital. *avventurina* <*avventura* chance; def. 1 so called from its accidental discovery]

av·e·nue (av′ə·nyōō, -nōō) *n.* 1 A broad thoroughfare. 2 A way of approach, as to a building, bordered with trees or statues. 3 A mode of access. See synonyms under WAY. [<F *avenue,* orig. fem. pp. of *avenir* approach <L *advenire* <*ad-* toward + *venire* come]

a·ver (ə·vûr′) *v.t.* **a·verred, a·ver·ring** 1 To declare confidently as fact; affirm. 2 *Law* To assert formally; prove or justify (a plea). See synonyms under AFFIRM, ALLEGE, ASSERT, AVOW. [<OF *averer* confirm <L *ad-* to + *verus* true] — **a·ver′ment** *n.* — **a·ver′ra·ble** *adj.*

av·er·age (av′rij, av′ər·ij) *n.* 1 *Math.* **a** The quotient of any sum divided by the number of its terms; the arithmetic mean. **b** A number representing an array of values of which it is a function. 2 The ordinary rank, degree, or amount; general type. 3 In marine law: **a** The loss arising by damage to a ship or cargo. **b** The proportion of such loss falling to a single person in an equitable distribution among those interested. — *adj.* 1 Obtained by calculating the mean of several. 2 Medium; ordinary. — *v.* **·aged, ·ag·ing** *v.t.* 1 To fix or calculate as the mean. 2 To amount to or obtain an average of: He *averages* three dollars profit every hour. 3 To apportion on the average. — *v.i.* 4 To be or amount to an average. [<F *avarie* damage to a ship or its cargo (see *n.*

def. 3) <Ital. *avaria;* ult. origin uncertain] — **av′er·age·ly** *adv.*

a·verse (ə·vûrs′) *adj.* 1 Opposed; unfavorable; reluctant: with *to.* 2 *Bot.* Turned away from the main axis: opposed to *adverse.* See synonyms under INIMICAL. [<L *aversus,* pp. of *avertere* turn aside. See AVERT.] — **a·verse′ly** *adv.* — **a·verse′ness** *n.*

a·ver·sion (ə·vûr′zhən, -shən) *n.* 1 Extreme dislike; opposition; antipathy. 2 That to which one is averse. See synonyms under ABOMINATION, ANTIPATHY, HATRED.

a·vert (ə·vûrt′) *v.t.* 1 To turn or direct away or aside from, as one's regard. 2 To prevent or ward off, as a danger. See synonyms under AVOID. [<OF *avertir* <L *avertere* turn aside <*ab-* away + *vertere* turn] — **a·vert′ed·ly** *adv.* — **a·vert′i·ble, a·vert′a·ble** *adj.*

A·ves (ā′vēz) *n. pl.* A class of the vertebrates which comprises the birds. See BIRD. [<L, pl. of *avis* bird]

a·vi·an (ā′vē·ən) *adj.* Pertaining to birds. Also **a·vic·u·lar** (ə·vik′yə·lər). — *n.* A bird. [<L *avis* bird]

a·vi·ar·y (ā′vē·er′ē) *n. pl.* **·ar·ies** An enclosure or large cage for live birds. [<L *aviarium* <*avis* bird] — **a·vi·a·rist** (ā′vē·er′ist, -ər·ist) *n.*

a·vi·ate (ā′vē·āt, av′ē-) *v.i.* **·at·ed, ·at·ing** To operate an aircraft. [Back formation <AVIATION]

a·vi·a·tion (ā′vē·ā′shən, av′ē-) *n.* 1 The act, science, or art of flying heavier-than-air aircraft. 2 The aircraft flown. [<F <L *avis* bird]

a·vi·a·tor (ā′vē·ā′tər, av′ē-) *n.* One who flies airplanes and other heavier-than-air aircraft; a pilot. — **a·vi·a·tress** (-tris) or **a·vi·a·trix** (ā′vē·ā′triks, av′ē-) *n. fem.*

Av·i·cen·na (av′ə·sen′ə), 980–1037, Arab physician and philosopher. Arabic **ibn-Sina** (ib′ən·sē′nä).

a·vi·cul·ture (ā′vi·kul′chər, av′i-) *n.* The rearing of birds. [<L *avis* bird + CULTURE]

av·id (av′id) *adj.* Very desirous; eager; greedy. [<L *avidus* <*avere* crave] — **av′id·ly** *adv.*

a·vid·i·ty (ə·vid′ə·tē) *n.* 1 Extreme eagerness; greediness. 2 *Chem.* Affinity.

a·vi·fau·na (ā′və·fô′nə) *n. Ecol.* The birds of a given region: also called *ornis.* [<L *avis* bird + FAUNA] — **a′vi·fau′nal** *adj.*

av·i·ga·tion (av′ə·gā′shən) *n.* The handling and guidance of aircraft in the air. [<AVI(ATION) + (NAVI)GATION]

A·vi·gnon (à·vē·nyôn′) A city in SE France on the Rhone; papal seat, 1309–77.

a·vi·on·ics (ā′vē·on′iks, av′ē-) *n.* The study of the applications of electricity and electronics to aviation. [<AVI(ATION ELECTR)ONICS] — **a′vi·on′ic** *adj.*

a·vi·so (ə·vī′zo) *n. pl.* **·sos** 1 Advice; information. 2 A dispatch boat. [<Sp., information, advice]

av·o·ca·do (av′ə·kä′dō, ä′və-) *n. pl.* **·dos** 1 A tropical American evergreen tree *(Persea americana)* having leathery leaves and bearing large pear-shaped drupes with a dark leathery rind and bland, buttery flesh. 2 The edible fruit for which this tree is commercially cultivated. Also called *alligator pear.* [<Sp., alter. of AGUACATE <Nahuatl *ahuacatl*]

av·o·ca·tion (av′ə·kā′shən) *n.* 1 A casual or transient occupation; diversion; hobby. 2 One's business or vocation: now rarely used, to avoid confusion with def. 1. 3 *Obs.* A calling away; withdrawal. See synonyms under HOBBY. [<L *avocatio, -onis* a calling away, diversion <*ab-* away + *vocare* call]

a·vo·ca·to·ry (ə·vok′ə·tôr′ē, -tō′rē) *adj.* Recalling; calling away or back: Letters *avocatory* are used by a sovereign to recall his citizens from a state with which he is at war.

av·o·cet (av′ə·set) *n.* A long-legged shore bird (genus *Recurvirostra*) having webbed feet and slender up-curved bill. Also **av′o·set.** [<F *avocette* <Ital. *avocetta*]

A·vo·ga·dro (ä′vō·gä′drō), Amedeo, 1776–1856, Conte di Quaregna, Italian physicist.

Avogadro number The actual number of molecules in one gram-molecule or the actual number of atoms in one gram-atom of an element or any pure substance. This number is 6.023×10^{23}. Also **Avogadro's constant.**

Avogadro's hypothesis or **rule** The rule that equal volumes of all gases, at the same temperature and pressure, contain the same number of molecules.

a·void (ə·void′) *v.t.* **1** To keep away or at a distance from; shun; evade, as an unpleasant duty. **2** *Law* To make void. **3** *Obs.* To void; empty. See synonyms under ESCAPE. [< AF *avoider*, OF *esvuidier* empty < *es-* out (< L *ex-*) + *vuidier* < L *viduare* empty, deprive] —**a·void′a·ble** *adj.* — **a·void′a·bly** *adv.* —**a·void′er** *n.*

a·void·ance (ə·void′ns) *n.* **1** The act of avoiding. **2** *Law* Annulment; a making void.

av·oir·du·pois (av′ər·də·poiz′) *n.* **1** The ordinary system of weights of the United States and Great Britain in which 16 ounces avoirdupois make a pound. See under WEIGHT. **2** *Colloq.* Weight; corpulence: a facetious use. [< OF *avoir de pois* goods of (i.e., sold by) weight < L *habere* have + *de* of + *pensum* weight]

A·von (ā′vən, av′ən) **1** A river in England, flowing SE 96 miles from Northampton past Stratford to the Severn at Tewksbury. **2** Any of several other rivers in England, Scotland, and Wales.

a·vouch (ə·vouch′) *v.t.* **1** To vouch for; guarantee. **2** To affirm positively; proclaim. **3** To acknowledge; avow. See synonyms under ASSERT, AVOW. [< OF *avochier* affirm < L *advocare* call to one's aid, summon < *ad-* to + *vocare* call]

a·vow (ə·vou′) *v.t.* To declare openly, as facts; own or confess frankly; acknowledge: to *avow* oneself a conspirator. [< OF *avouer* < L *advocare* summon (< *ad-* to + *vocare* call) or LL *advotare* bind by oath < *ad-* to + *votare* freq. of *vovere* vow] —**a·vow′a·ble** *adj.* —**a·vow′a·ble·ness** *n.* —**a·vow′a·bly** *adv.* —**a·vow′er** *n.*

Synonyms: acknowledge, admit, aver, avouch, confess, declare, own, proclaim, profess, protest, testify, witness. To *avow* is to declare boldly and openly, commonly as something one is ready to justify, maintain, or defend against challenge or opposition. A man *acknowledges* another's claim or his own promise; he *admits* an opponent's advantage or his own error; he *declares* either what he has seen or experienced or what he has received from another; he *avers* what he is sure of from his own knowledge or consciousness; he *avows* openly a belief or intention that he has silently held. Compare ACKNOWLEDGE, AFFIRM, ALLEGE, ASSERT, CONFESS, STATE. *Antonyms:* contradict, deny, disavow, disclaim, disown, ignore, repudiate.

a·vow·al (ə·vou′əl) *n.* Open declaration; frank admission or acknowledgment. See synonyms under BELIEF.

a·vowed (ə·voud′) *adj.* Openly acknowledged; plainly declared. See synonyms under OSTENSIBLE. —**a·vow·ed·ly** (ə·vou′id·lē) *adj.* —**a·vow′ed·ness** *n.*

a·vulse (ə·vuls′) *v.t.* To remove forcibly; tear away. [< L *avulsus*, pp. of *aveller* < *ab-* away + *vellere* pull]

a·vul·sion (ə·vul′shən) *n.* **1** A pulling off or tearing away; forcible separation. **2** That which is torn away. **3** *Law* A sudden removal of the soil from the estate of one and its deposit upon or adjunction to the land of another by the violent action of water. The land thus torn away continues to be vested in the original owner. [< L *avulsio, -onis* < *avellere*. See AVULSE.]

a·wait (ə·wāt′) *v.t.* **1** To wait for; expect. **2** To be ready or in store for. See synonyms under ABIDE. [< OF *awaitier* watch for < *a-* to (< L *ad-*) + *waitier* watch < OHG *wahtēn* watch]

a·wake (ə·wāk′) *adj.* Not asleep; alert; vigilant. —*v.* **a·woke** or **a·waked** (ə·wākt′), **a·waked** or **a·woke**, **a·wak·ing** *v.t.* **1** To arouse from sleep. **2** To stir up; excite. —*v.i.* **3** To cease to sleep; become awake. **4** To become alert or aroused. See note under WAKE¹. [< OE *onwæcnan* rise from sleep < *on-* A-¹ + *wæcnan* rise and *āwacian* arise < *ā-* A-² + *wacian* watch]

a·wak·en (ə·wā′kən) *v.t. & v.i.* To awake. See note under WAKE¹. See synonyms under STIR. [< OE *onwæcnan* arise < *on-* A¹ + *wæcnan* rise] —**a·wak′en·er** *n.*

a·wak·en·ing (ə·wā′kən·ing) *adj.* Stirring; exciting. —*n.* **1** The act of waking. **2** An arousing of attention or interest; revival.

a·ward (ə·wôrd′) *v.t.* **1** To adjudge as due, as by legal decisions. **2** To bestow as the result of a contest or examination, as a prize. See synonyms under ALLOT. —*n.* **1** A decision, as by a judge, umpire, or arbitrator. **2** The document containing it. **3** That which is awarded. **4** A badge, medal, citation, or the like, given for meritorious service, as to a soldier. [< AF *awarder*, OF *esguarder* observe, examine < *es-* out (< L *ex-*) + *guarder* watch < Gmc.] —**a·ward′a·ble** *adj.* —**a·ward′er** *n.*

a·ware (ə·wâr′) *adj.* Possessing knowledge (of some fact or action); conscious; cognizant. See synonyms under CONSCIOUS, SURE. [< OE *gewær* watchful] —**a·ware′ness** *n.*

a·wash (ə·wosh′, ə·wôsh′) *adv. & adj.* **1** Level with or just above the surface of the water. **2** Tossed or washed about by waves. **3** Covered or overflowed with water.

A·wash (ä′wäsh) A river in eastern Ethiopia, flowing 500 miles NE to Lake Abbé: formerly *Hawash.*

a·way (ə·wā′) *adv.* **1** From a given place; off. **2** Far; at or to a distance. **3** In another direction; aside. **4** Out of existence; at an end. **5** On and on continuously: to peg *away* at a task. **6** From one's keeping, attention, or possession. **7** At once, without hesitation: Fire *away!* —**to do** (or **make**) **away with 1** To get rid of. **2** To kill. —*adj.* **1** Absent. **2** At a distance. —*interj.* Begone! [OE *on weg* on (one's) way]

awe¹ (ô) *v.t.* **awed, aw·ing** or **awe·ing** To impress with reverential fear. —*n.* **1** Reverential fear; dread mingled with veneration. **2** *Obs.* Overawing influence. **3** *Obs.* Dread; terror. See synonyms under AMAZEMENT, FEAR, REVERENCE, VENERATION. [< ON *agi* fear]

awe² (ô) *v.t. Scot.* To owe.

a·weigh (ə·wā′) *adv. Naut.* Hanging with the flukes just clear of the bottom so that the vessel is free to move: said of an anchor.

awe·less (ô′lis) *adj.* Without fear; fearless. Also **aw′less.**

awe·some (ô′səm) *adj.* **1** Inspiring awe. **2** Characterized by or expressing awe; reverential. —**awe′some·ly** *adv.* —**awe′some·ness** *n.*

aw·ful (ô′fəl) *adj.* **1** Inspiring or suited to inspire awe; majestically or solemnly impressive. **2** Inspiring fear; terrible; dreadful. **3** *Colloq.* Exceedingly bad, monotonous, or unpleasant; ugly. **4** *Colloq.* Exceedingly great. **5** Filled with awe; reverential. Also *Scot.* **aw·fu'** (ô′fōō). —**aw′ful·ness** *n.*

Synonyms: alarming, appalling, august, dire, direful, dread, dreadful, fearful, frightful, grand, horrible, imposing, majestic, noble, portentous, shocking, solemn, stately, terrible, terrific. In careful speech *awful* should not be used of things which are merely disagreeable or annoying, nor of all that are *alarming* and *terrible*, but only of such as bring a solemn awe upon the soul, as in the presence of a superior power; as, the *awful* hush before a battle. We speak of an *exalted* station, a *grand* mountain, an *imposing* presence, a *majestic* cathedral, a *noble* mien, a *solemn* litany, a *stately* march, an *august* assembly. See FRIGHTFUL, GRAND. *Antonyms:* base, beggarly, commonplace, contemptible, despicable, humble, inferior, lowly, mean, paltry, undignified, vulgar.

aw·ful·ly (ô′fəl·ē) *adv.* **1** In an awful manner. **2** (ô′flē) *Colloq.* Excessively; very: *awfully* rich.

a·while (ə·hwīl′) *adv.* For a brief time. [OE *āne hwīle* a while]

a·whirl (ə·hwûrl′) *adj. & adv.* In a whirl; whirling.

awk·ward (ôk′wərd) *adj.* **1** Ungraceful in bearing. **2** Unskilful in action; bungling. **3** Embarrassing or perplexing. **4** Difficult or dangerous to deal with, as an opponent. **5** Inconvenient for use; uncomfortable. **6** *Obs.* Perverse; untoward. [< ON *afug* turned the wrong way + -WARD] —**awk′ward·ly** *adv.* —**awk′ward·ness** *n.*

Synonyms: boorish, bungling, clownish, clumsy, gawky, maladroit, uncouth, ungainly, unhandy, unskilful. *Awkward* is *offward*, turned the wrong way; it was anciently used

of a back-handed blow in battle, of squinting eyes, etc. *Clumsy* originally signified benumbed, stiffened with cold; as, *clumsy* fingers, *clumsy* limbs. Thus, *awkward* primarily refers to action, *clumsy* to condition. See RUSTIC. *Antonyms:* adroit, clever, dexterous, handy, skilful.

awl (ôl) *n.* A pointed steel instrument for making small holes. ◆ Homophone: *all.* [OE *æl, awel*]

awl·wort (ôl′wûrt′) *n.* A small stemless aquatic plant (*Subularia aquatica*) of the mustard family (*Brassicaceae*) having awl-shaped leaves.

awn (ôn) *n. Bot.* A bristlelike appendage of certain grasses; beard, as of wheat or rye. [< ON *ögn* chaff] —**awned** (ônd) *adj.* —**awn′less** *adj.* —**awn′y,** *Scot.* **awn′ie** *adj.*

awn·ing (ô′ning) *n.* **1** A rooflike cover, as of canvas, for protection from sun or rain. **2** A shelter resembling this. [Origin unknown]

a·woke (ə·wōk′) Past tense of AWAKE.

AWOL (*as an acronym pronounced* ā′wôl) *Mil.* Absent or absence without leave. Also **awol, A.W.O.L., a.w.o.l.**

a·wry (ə·rī′) *adj. & adv.* **1** Toward one side; crooked; distorted; obliquely. **2** Out of the right course; erroneously; perversely. [< A-¹ on + WRY]

ax¹ (aks) *n. pl.* **ax·es 1** A tool with a bladed head mounted on a handle, used for chopping, hewing, etc. **2** An ax-hammer. See also ICE AX. —*v.t.* To cut, shape, trim, or fashion with an ax. —**to have an ax to grind** *Colloq.* To have a private purpose or interest to pursue. Also **axe.** [OE *æx, eax*] —**ax′like′** *adj.*

ax² (aks) *v.t. & v.i. Scot.* To ask.

ax·ham·mer (aks′ham′ər) *n.* A stonecutter's tool with cutting edges at either end of the head, or one cutting edge and one hammer face. —**ax′-ham′mered** *adj.*

ax·i·al (ak′sē·əl) *adj.* **1** Of, pertaining to, or constituting an axis. **2** On or along an axis.

axial cable *Aeron.* A wire running through the axis of a rigid airship from bow to stern.

ax·il (ak′sil) *n. Bot.* **1** The cavity or angle formed by the junction of the upper side of a leafstalk, branch, etc., with a stem or branch. **2** *Anat.* The axilla. [< L *axilla* armpit]

ax·ile (ak′sil, -sīl) *adj.* Of, pertaining to, or situated in, or in the line of, an axis.

ax·il·la (ak·sil′ə) *n. pl.* **ax·il·lae** (-sil′ē) **1** The armpit. **2** An axil. [< L]

ax·il·lar (ak′sə·lər) *adj.* Axillary. —*n. Ornithol.* One of the relatively long, stiff feathers on the undersurface of the wing of a bird.

ax·il·lar·y (ak′sə·ler′ē) *adj.* **1** *Bot.* Of, pertaining to, or situated in an axil or axilla: *axillary* buds. **2** *Anat.* Attached to a joint. —*n. pl.* **·lar·ies** An axillar.

ax·i·ol·o·gy (aks′ē·ol′ə·jē) *n. Philos.* The theory or study of values or of the nature of value. [< Gk. *axios* worthy + -LOGY]

ax·i·om (ak′sē·əm) *n.* **1** A self-evident or universally recognized truth. **2** An established principle or rule. **3** *Logic & Math.* A proposition assumed to be true without proof. [< F *axiome* < L *axioma* < Gk. *axiôma* a thing thought worthy, a self-evident thing < *axioein* think worthy < *axios* worthy]

Synonym: truism. Both the *axiom* and the *truism* are instantly seen to be true, and need no proof; but in an *axiom* there is progress of thought, while the *truism* simply says what is too manifest to need saying. Hence the *axiom* is valuable and useful, while the *truism* is weak and flat. Compare ADAGE, PROVERB. *Antonyms:* absurdity, contradiction, demonstration, nonsense, paradox, sophism.

ax·i·o·mat·ic (ak′sē·ə·mat′ik) *adj.* **1** Of, pertaining to, or resembling an axiom; self-evident. **2** Full of axioms; aphoristic, as a literary style. Also **ax′i·o·mat′i·cal.** —**ax′i·o·mat′i·cal·ly** *adv.*

ax·is¹ (ak′sis) *n. pl.* **ax·es** (ak′sēz) **1** A line around which a turning body revolves or may be supposed to revolve. **2** *Geom.* **a** One of the principal lines through the center of a plane or solid figure, especially the longest or shortest, or a line as to which the plane figure or solid is symmetrical. **b** A fixed line along which distances are measured or to which positions are referred. **3** An imaginary line through the center of a drawing or sculpture for purposes of measurement or reference. **4** The central line about which parts of a body are symmetrically arranged. **5** *Bot.* The central body, part, line, or longitudinal support on, along, or above which organs or other parts are arranged. **6** *Anat.* **a** A short arterial trunk from which several nearly equal branches radiate. **b** The second cervical vertebra, or the large, blunt, toothlike odontoid process which surmounts it and forms a pivot on which the atlas and head turn. **7** One of the lines of reference meeting at the center of a crystal, and determining to which system it belongs. **8** *Geol.* The dominant central section of a mountain chain, or the line tracing the crest throughout its length. **9** *Aeron.* One of the three axes of an aircraft. **10** An affiliation or coalition of two or more nations to promote and insure mutual interest, cooperation, and solidarity of front in their relations with foreign powers; also, the nations so affiliated. [< L, axis, axle]

ax·is² (ak′sis) *n.* A small deer (genus *Axis*) of southern Asia, having the body spotted with white. Also **axis deer.** [< L]

Ax·is (ak′sis) *n.* A coalition which developed from the Rome-Berlin Axis of 1936 and ultimately included Germany, Italy, Japan, Rumania, Bulgaria, Hungary, and others: opposed to the Allied and associated powers in World War II. Also **Axis Powers.**

ax·le (ak′səl) *n.* **1** A crossbar supporting a vehicle, and on or with which its wheel or wheels turn: also called **ax′le·tree′.** **2** A shaft or spindle on which a wheel is mounted and on or with which it turns. [ME *axel* in *axeltre* axletree < ON *öxultrē* < *öxull* axle + *trē* tree, bar] — **ax′led** *adj.*

ax·man (aks′mən) *n. pl.* **·men** (-mən) One who wields an ax; a woodman. Also **axe′man.**

ax·o·lotl (ak′sə·lotl′) *n.* A North American tailed amphibian (genus *Ambystoma*), as *A. mexicanum* of Mexican lakes and marshes, which retains its external gills, and breeds in a larval state. [< Sp. < Nahuatl, lit., servant of water]

MEXICAN AXOLOTL
(From 6-9 inches long)

ax·on (ak′son) *n.* **1** *Zool.* The body axis of a vertebrate. **2** *Anat.* The axis-cylinder process of a nerve cell, usually carrying impulses away from the cells. See DENDRITE, NEURON. Also **ax·one** (ak′sōn). [< NL < Gk. *axōn* axis]

ax·seed (aks′sēd′) *n.* An Old World perennial crownvetch (*Coronilla varia*) with odd-pinnate leaves, and pink or white flowers, cultivated in the United States. [< AX + SEED; from the shape of the pods]

aye¹ (ī) *n.* An affirmative vote or voter. —*adv.* Yes; yea. Also *ay.* ◆ Homophone: *eye.*

aye² (ā) See AY¹.

aye-aye (ī′ī′) *n.* A nocturnal arboreal lemur (genus *Daubentonia*) of Madagascar, about the size of a cat and having rodentlike teeth. [< F < Malagasy *aiay*; so called from its cry]

A·ye·sha (ä′i·shä) See AISHA.

a·yin (ä′yēn) The sixteenth Hebrew letter. See ALPHABET.

Ay·ma·ra (ī′mä·rä′) *n.* One of a tribe of South American Indians, of highly developed pre-In-

can culture, at the Aymaran linguistic stock: formerly occupying nearly all of Bolivia and Peru, and still comprising three-fourths of the population of Bolivia.

Ay·ma·ran (ī′mä·rän′) *adj.* Of or pertaining to a large and important linguistic stock of South American Indians inhabiting Bolivia and Peru.—*n.* The family of languages spoken by the Aymaran tribes: now largely superseded by Quechua.

a·zal·ea (ə·zāl′yə) *n.* A flowering shrub of the heath family (genus *Rhododendron*, formerly *Azalea*), especially the flame azalea (*R. calendulaceum*) with showy scarlet or orange flowers. [< NL < Gk. *azalea*, fem. of *azaleos* dry < *azein* parch, dry up; from its preference for dry soil]

a·zan (ä·zän′) *n. Arabic* In Moslem countries, the muezzin's call to prayer, usually given from the minaret of a mosque five times a day; also, the time spent in these prayers.

a·zed·a·rach (ə·zed′ə·rak) *n.* **1** A large ornamental Eastern tree (*Melia azedarach*) of Asia and tropical America, with bipinnate leaves and panicles of lilac-colored flowers, succeeded by yellowish drupes: also called *Chinaberry tree, hagbush, pride of China.* **2** The bark from the roots of this tree, used as a cathartic, emetic, or vermifuge. [< F *azédarac*, ult. < Persian *āzād dirakht* noble tree]

A·zer·bai·jan (ä′zər·bī·jän′, az′ər-) **1** A constituent republic of the southern U.S.S.R., west of the Caspian Sea; 33,100 square miles; capital, Baku. Also **A′zer·bai·dzhan′.** Officially **Azerbaijan Soviet Socialist Republic.** **2** A former province of NW Iran between Turkey and the Caspian Sea; 41,000 square miles; chief city, Tabriz.

A·zer·bai·ja·ni (ä′zər·bī·jä′nē, az′ər-) *n. pl.* **·ni** or **·nis** (-nēz) **1** A native or inhabitant of Azerbaijan. **2** The Turkic language of these people.

A·zil·ian (ə·zil′yən) *adj. Anthropol.* Designating a subdivision of Mesolithic culture associated with artifacts found in the **Mas d'A·zil** (mäs dä·zēl′), a village of southern France.

az·i·muth (az′ə·məth) *n.* **1** *Astron.* The arc of the horizon that a vertical plane passing through a heavenly body makes with the meridian of the place of observation. **2** *Mil.* **a** Direction to right or left of a horizontal plane. **b** That element in the movement of a bomb or guided missile to the right or left of its downward course: distinguished from *range.* [< F *azimut* < Arabic *assumūt* the ways, pl. of *samt* way] —**az·i·muth·al** (az′ə·muth′əl) *adj.* — **az′i·muth·al·ly** *adv.*

az·ine (az′ēn, -in) *n. Chem.* One of a class of nitrogenous heterocyclic compounds arranged in a six-membered ring, identified by the number of nitrogen atoms, as *diazine, triazine,* etc. [< AZ- + -INE²]

az·o (az′ō, ā′zō) *adj. Chem.* Containing nitrogen: an *azo* compound, *azo* dye. [< AZOTE]

azo- *combining form Chem.* Indicating the pres-

AZIMUTH
PO. Observation point. *A.* Altitude. *AW* Azimuth west. *W.* West. *E.* East. *NH.* North horizon. *Z.* Zenith. *S.* Star.

ence of nitrogen, especially in those organic compounds in which two atoms of nitrogen are connected with two similar radicals of the benzene series: *azobenzene,* C_6H_5N: NC_6H_5. Also, before vowels, *az-,* as in *azine.* [< AZOTE]

azo dye Any of an important class of coaltar dyes containing the azo radical N:N.

a·zo·ic (ə·zō′ik) *adj. Geol.* Of or pertaining to those periods on earth before life appeared; without organic remains. [< Gk. *azōos* lifeless < *a-* without + *zōē* life]

az·ole (az′ōl, ə·zōl′) *n. Chem.* Pyrrole. [< AZ(o)- + -OLE¹]

az·on (az′on) *n.* A type of bomb equipped with control surfaces in the tail to permit radio guidance in azimuth only. [< *az(imuth) on(ly)*]

a·zon·ic (ā·zon′ik) *adj.* Not peculiar to any zone or region; not local.

A·zores (ə·zôrz′, ā′zôrz) Three island groups west of Portugal, divided into three Portuguese districts: *Angra do Heroísmo, Horta,* and *Ponta Delgada;* total area, 888 square miles. *Portuguese* **A·ço·res** (ə·sō′rēsh).

az·ote (az′ōt, ə·zōt′) *n.* Nitrogen: former name. [< F < Gk. *a-* not + *zōein* live; so called by Lavoisier from its inability to support life] — **az·ot·ed** (az′ō·tid, ə·zō′tid) *adj.*

az·oth (az′oth) *n.* **1** Mercury: the name given by the alchemists. **2** The universal remedy of Paracelsus. [< Arabic *az-zāūq* the quicksilver]

a·zot·ic (ə·zot′ik) *adj.* Of, pertaining to, or containing azote or nitrogen.

az·o·tize (az′ə·tīz) *v.t.* **·tized, ·tiz·ing** To nitrogenize.

A·zov (ä·zôf′), **Sea of** A northern arm of the Black Sea in southern U.S.S.R.; 14,000 square miles. Also **Az·of′.**

Az·ra·el (az′rē·əl) In the Moslem and ancient Jewish mythology, the angel who separates the soul from the body at death. [< Hebrew, help of God]

Az·tec (az′tek) *n.* **1** One of tribe of Mexican Indians of Nahuatlan stock, founders of the Mexican Empire which was at its height when Cortés invaded the country in 1519. **2** Any of the Uto-Aztecan dialects spoken by the Aztecs; Nahuatl. —*adj.* Of or pertaining to the Aztec Indians, their language, culture, or empire: also **Az·tec·an** (az′tek·ən).

az·ure (azh′ər, ā′zhər) *adj.* **1** Like the blue of the sky; sky-blue. **2** Like the clear sky; cloudless; spotless. —*n.* **1** A clear sky-blue color or pigment. **2** *Poetic* The sky. **3** *Her.* Blue: represented in engraving by parallel horizontal lines. [< OF *azur* < Arabic *al-lāzward* < Persian *lazhward* lapis lazuli]

az·u·rite (azh′ə·rīt) *n.* **1** A vitreous, monoclinic, azure blue, basic copper carbonate: also called *blue bice.* **2** A gemstone.

a·zy·go·spore (ə·zī′gə·spôr, -spōr) *n. Bot.* A spore parthenogenetically formed in certain fungi, and resembling a zygospore. Also **a·zy′·go·sperm.**

az·y·gous (az′i·gəs) *adj. Biol.* Having no mate; occurring singly; not paired. [< Gk. *azygos* unpaired < *a-* without + *zygon* a yoke]

az·yme (az′īm, -im) *n.* Unleavened bread. Also **az·ym** (az′im). [< Gk. *azymos* unleavened < *a-* without + *zymē* leaven] —**a·zym·ic** (ə·zim′ik), **az·y·mous** (az′ə·məs) *adj.*

az·zi·mi·na (äd′zē·mē′nä) *n. Italian* Elaborate, metallic decoration in damask patterns.

B

b, B (bē) *n. pl.* **b's, B's** or **Bs, bs, bees** (bēz) **1** The second letter of the English alphabet: from Phoenician *beth,* through Greek *beta,* Roman *B.* **2** The sound of the letter *b,* the voiced bilabial stop. See ALPHABET. —*symbol* **1** *Music* **a** One of a series of tones, the seventh in the natural diatonic scale of C. **b** The pitch of this tone or the written note representing it. **c** A scale built

upon B. **2** *Chem.* Boron (symbol B).

ba (bä) *n.* In Egyptian mythology, the soul, believed to depart from the body at death and expected to return to it: represented by a bird with a human head. [< Egyptian]

Ba *Chem.* Barium (symbol Ba).

ba' (bä, bô) *n. Scot.* A ball.

baa (bä, ba) *v.i.* **baaed, baa·ing** To bleat, as a

sheep. —*n.* The bleat, as of a sheep. [Imit.]

Ba·al (bā′əl, bäl) *n. pl.* **Ba·al·im** (bā′əl·im) **1** Any of several ancient Semitic gods of fertility and flocks; a sun god. **2** An idol or false god. [< Hebrew *Ba'al* lord] —**Ba′al·ish** *adj.*

Baal·bek (bäl′bek) A tourist center in central Lebanon; site of ancient Phoenician temple to Baal: Greek *Heliopolis.*

Ba·al·ist (bā′əl·ist) *n.* **1** A worshiper of Baal. **2** A worshiper of idols. Also **Ba′al·ite** (-īt). — **Ba′al·ism** *n.*

Baan (bän) See PAAN.

Bab (bäb) *n.* The title of the founder of Babism.

Bab (bab) Diminutive of BARBARA.

ba·ba (bä′bä) *n.* A cake made with yeast and steeped in rum. Also *French* **ba·ba au rhum** (bá·bá′ ō rôm′). [< F, prob. < Polish *baba* grandmother]

Ba·bar (bä′bər) See BABER.

ba·bas·su (bä′bə·sōō′) *n.* **1** A Brazilian palm tree (*Orbignya martiana*) bearing nuts yielding an oil used in making margarine, soap, etc. **2** The oil from this tree: also called **babassu oil**. [< native Brazilian name]

bab·bitt (bab′it) *v.t.* To line, bush, fill, or face with Babbitt metal. —*n.* Babbitt metal.

Bab·bitt (bab′it) *n.* A type of conventional American businessman, ambitious in his business, but otherwise provincial, mediocre, and smug: from George *Babbitt*, a character in Sinclair Lewis's novel *Babbitt* (1922).

bab·ble (bab′əl) *n.* **1** A murmuring or rippling sound, as of a stream. **2** Prattle, as of an infant. **3** A confusion of sounds, as of a crowd. **4** *Telecom.* The confused sound of cross-talk from a number of interfering radio channels. —*v.* **bab·bled, bab·bling** *v.t.* **1** To utter unintelligibly. **2** To blurt out; tell thoughtlessly or foolishly. —*v.i.* **3** To utter inarticulate sounds or meaningless noises, as a baby or idiot. **4** To murmur, as a brook. **5** To talk unwisely or foolishly. [ME *babelen*]—**bab′ble·ment** *n.*—**bab′bler** *n.*

Synonyms (verb): blab, blurt, cackle, chat, chatter, gabble, gossip, jabber, murmur, palaver, prate, prattle, tattle, twaddle. Most of these words are onomatopoetic. The *cackle* of a hen, the *gabble* of a goose, the *chatter* of a magpie, the *babble* of a running stream, as applied to human speech, indicate a rapid succession of what are to the listener meaningless sounds. *Blab* and *blurt* refer to the letting out of what the lips can no longer keep in. To *chat* is to talk in an easy, pleasant way, not without sense, but without special purpose; to *prattle* is to talk freely and artlessly, as children. To *prate* is to talk idly, presumptuously, or foolishly, but not necessarily incoherently. To *jabber* is to utter a rapid succession of unintelligible sounds, generally more noisy than *chattering*. To *gossip* is to talk of petty personal matters. To *twaddle* is to talk feeble nonsense. To *murmur* is to utter suppressed or even inarticulate sounds, suggesting the notes of a dove, or the sound of a running stream. Compare SPEAK.

babe (bāb) *n.* **1** An infant; baby. **2** *U.S. Colloq.* An artless person; one lacking experience, sophistication, or guile. **3** *U.S. Slang* A girl. [ME; of uncertain origin]

ba·bel (bā′bəl, bab′əl) *n.* A confusion of many voices or languages; tumult. Also **Ba′bel.**

Ba·bel (bā′bəl, bab′əl) An ancient city in Shinar. —**Tower of Babel 1** A tower built by the descendants of Noah in Babel and intended to reach to heaven: God punished the builders for their presumption by confusing their language, preventing them from understanding each other and from completing the tower *Gen.* xi 9. **2** Any impractical scheme or structure; a visionary project.

Bab-el-Man·deb (bäb′el-män′deb) A strait between the Red Sea and the Gulf of Aden; 17 miles wide.

Ba·ber (bä′bər), 1483–1530, founder of the Great Mogul dynasty in India: real name Zahir ed-Din Mohammed: also spelled *Babar, Babur.*

Ba·bi (bä′bē) *n.* An adherent of Babism.

ba·bies′-breath (bā′bēz·breth) *n.* Baby's-breath.

ba·biche (bá·bēsh′) *n.* *Canadian* Rawhide thongs or lacings. [< Can. F]

bab·i·ru·sa (bab′ə·rōō′sə, bäb′ə-) *n.* A wild hog (*Babirussa babirussa*) of SE Asia and the East Indies. The lower canines of the male pierce the upper lips and curve backwards. Also **babi·rous′sa, bab′i·rus′sa.** [< Malay *bābi* hog + *rūsa* deer]

Ba·bism (bä′biz·əm) *n.* The principles and practices of the Babis, a pantheistic Persian sect founded in 1844 by the Bab, Mirza Ali Mohammed ibn Radhik, 1824–50. Its philosophy recognizes the equality of the sexes and forbids polygamy, drinking, and mendicancy. [< Persian *bāb* gate] —**Ba·bite** (bä′bīt), **Ba′·bist** *adj. & n.*

Ba·bol (bä·bôl′) A city in northern Iran near the Caspian Sea: formerly *Barfrush.* Also **Ba·bul** (bä·bōōl′).

ba·boon (ba·bōōn′) *n.* A large, terrestrial monkey (*Papio* and related genera) of Africa and Asia, having front and back legs of nearly equal length, doglike muzzle, large bare callosities on the buttocks, and usually a short tail. [< OF *babuin*] —**ba·boon′ish** *adj.*

BABOON
(About 30 inches high at the shoulder)

ba·boon·er·y (ba·bōō′nər·ē) *n.* Baboonish antics or behavior.

ba·bu (bä′bōō) *n.* **1** A Hindu gentleman: a polite form of address, equivalent to *sir* or *Mr.* **2** In India, a native merchant or clerk who can write English. **3** A native of India with a smattering of English education: a derogatory term. Also **ba′boo.** [< Hind. *bābū*, a term of respect] —**ba′bu·ism** *n.*

ba·bul (bä·bōōl′) *n.* **1** An acacia (*Acacia arabica*) yielding a hard and heavy wood, and a gum used as a substitute for gum arabic. **2** The bark or gum of this acacia. Also **ba·bool′.** [< Hind., the acacia tree]

Ba·bur (bä′bər) See BABER.

ba·bush·ka (bə·bōōsh′kə) *n.* A woman's scarf, often made or folded in a triangular shape, worn as a hood with the ends tying under the chin. [< Russian, grandmother]

ba·by (bā′bē) *n. pl.* **ba·bies 1** A very young child of either sex; an infant. **2** The youngest or smallest member of a family or group. **3** One who has the appearance, behavior, or disposition of a young child, especially one with little courage or fortitude. **4** *Slang* A girl. **5** Any young animal. **6** *Obs.* A doll or puppet. —*adj.* **1** For a baby: *baby* shoes. **2** Childish; infantile: *baby* ways. **3** Small; diminutive; miniature. —*v.t.* **ba·bied, ba·by·ing** To treat as a baby; play tenderly with; pamper. —**ba′by·hood** *n.* — **ba′by·like** *adj.* [ME *baby*, dim. of *babe* BABE]

ba·by-blue-eyes (bā′bē·blōō′īz′) *n.* Any of several annual plants (genus *Nemophila*, especially *N. menzies* of the Pacific Coast) with alternate leaves and showy sky-blue flowers: also called *blueball.* Also **baby blue-eyes.**

ba·by·ish (bā′bē·ish) *adj.* Childish; infantile. See synonyms under CHILDISH. —**ba′by·ish·ly** *adv.* —**ba′by·ish·ness** *n.*

Bab·y·lon (bab′ə·lən, -lon) **1** An ancient city of Mesopotamia on the Euphrates, capital of Babylonia from about 2100 B.C.; celebrated as a seat of wealth, luxury, and vice. **2** Any city or place of great wealth, luxury, or vice. **3** Any place of captivity: in allusion to the *Babylonian captivity.* —**Bab′y·lon′ic** (-lon′ik), **Bab′y·lo′nish** (-lō′nish) *adj.*

Bab·y·lo·ni·a (bab′ə·lō′nē·ə) An ancient empire of Mesopotamia; capital, Babylon; surrendered to Persia 538 B.C.

Bab·y·lo·ni·an (bab′ə·lō′nē·ən) *adj.* **1** Of, like, or pertaining to ancient Babylon or Babylonia. **2** Wicked; luxurious. —*n.* **1** A native or inhabitant of Babylonia. **2** The Semitic language of ancient Babylonia, belonging to the Akkadian group.

ba·by's-breath (bā′bēz·breth′) *n.* **1** An Old World perennial (*Gypsophila paniculata*) with numerous clusters of small, white or pink, fragrant flowers. **2** Any of certain other fragrant herbs, as the naturalized wild madder of the eastern United States: also spelled *babies′ -breath.* Also **ba′by's-breath′.**

ba·by-sit (bā′bē·sit′) *v.* **-sat, -sit·ting** To act as a baby sitter.

baby sitter (bā′bē sit′ər) *n.* A person employed to take care of young children during the hours when the parents are absent.

Ba·car·di (bə·kär′dē) *n.* A kind of Cuban rum. [after *Bacardi*, the original distillers]

bac·ca·lau·re·ate (bak′ə·lôr′ē·it) *n.* **1** The degree of bachelor of arts, bachelor of science, etc. **2** A sermon or address to a graduating class at commencement: also **baccalaureate sermon.** [< Med. L *baccalaureatus* < *baccalaureus*, var. of *baccalarius* a young farmer, ? < LL *bacca* cow; infl. in form by *bacca lauri* laurel berry. See BACHELOR]

bac·ca·rat (bak′ə·rä′, bak′ə·rä) *n.* A card game of chance. The winnings are decided by comparison of hands with that of the banker. Also **bac′ca·ra′.** [< F *baccara*, a game of cards]

bac·cate (bak′āt) *adj. Bot.* **1** Like a berry. **2** Bearing berries. Also **bac′cat·ed.** [< L *baccatus* < *bacca* berry]

Bac·chae (bak′ē) **1** In Greek mythology, the female companions of Bacchus or Dionysus in his travels through the East. **2** Women taking part in the Dionysian celebrations. Also **Bac′chæ.**

bac·cha·nal (bak′ə·nəl) *n.* **1** A votary of Bacchus; hence, a drunken reveler. **2** *pl.* Bacchanalia. **3** A drunken revel; orgy. —*adj.* Bacchanalian. [< L *bacchanalis* of Bacchus < *Bacchus* god of wine]

bac·cha·na·li·a (bak′ə·nā′lē·ə, -nāl′yə) *n. pl.* Drunken revelries; orgies.

Bac·cha·na·li·a (bak′ə·nā′lē·ə, -nāl′yə) *n. pl.* An ancient Roman festival in honor of Bacchus.

bac·cha·na·li·an (bak′ə·nā′lē·ən, -nāl′yən) *adj.* Of, pertaining to, or indulging in orgies; carousing; uproariously drunk. —**bac′cha·na′·li·an·ism** *n.*

bac·chant (bak′ənt) *n. pl.* **bac·chants** or **bac·chan·tes** (bə·kan′tēz) A votary of Bacchus; hence, a carouser; bacchanal. —*adj.* Given to drunkenness. [< L *bacchans, -antis* ppr. of *bacchari* celebrate the festival of Bacchus, carouse]

bac·chan·te (bə·kan′tē, bə·kant′, bak′ənt) *n.* A female votary of Bacchus.

bac·chic (bak′ik) *adj.* Riotous; orgiastic; drunken. Also **bac′chi·cal.**

Bac·chic (bak′ik) *adj.* Of, pertaining to, or like Bacchus or his rites.

Bac·chus (bak′əs) In Roman mythology, the god of wine and revelry: identified with the Greek *Dionysus.*

bac·cif·er·ous (bak·sif′ər·əs) *adj. Bot.* Bearing or yielding berries. [< L *baccifer* bearing berries < *bacca* berry + *ferre* bear]

bac·ci·form (bak′sə·fôrm) *adj.* Berry-shaped. [< NL *bacciformis* berry-formed < *bacca* berry + -FORM]

bac·civ·o·rous (bak·siv′ər·əs) *adj. Zool.* Feeding on berries. [< L *bacca* berry + *vorare* eat]

Bach (bäkh) A family of German musicians and composers, of whom the best known are **Johann Sebastian,** 1685–1750, and his sons, **Karl Philipp Emanuel,** 1714–88 and **Johann Christian,** 1735–82.

bach·e·lor (bach′ə·lər, bach′lər) *n.* **1** An unmarried man. **2** One who has taken his first university or college degree. **3** A young knight serving under another's banner: also **bach′e·lor-at-arms′.** **4** A fresh-water fish, the crappie. **5** A young male fur seal kept from the breeding grounds by the older males: also called *holluschick.* [< OF *bacheler* < Med. L *baccalaris*; origin and meaning uncertain] —**bach′e·lor·hood** *n.* — **bach′e·lor·ship** *n.*

Bachelor of Arts 1 A degree given by a college or university to a person who has completed a four-year course or its equivalent in the humanities. **2** A person who has received this degree. Abbr. *B.A., A.B.*

Bachelor of Science 1 A degree given by a college or university to a person who has completed a four-year course or its equivalent, majoring in science rather than the humanities. **2** A person who has received this degree. Abbr. *B.S., B.Sc.*

bach·e·lor's-but·ton (bach′ə·lərz·but′n, bach′lərz-) *n.* Any of several plants with button-shaped flowers or flower heads, especially certain species of the genus *Centaurea*, as the cornflower (*C. cyanus*).

bac·il·lar·y (bas′ə·ler′ē) *adj.* **1** Rod-shaped: also **ba·cil·li·form** (bə·sil′ə·fôrm). **2** Pertaining to, characterized by, or due to bacilli: also **ba·cil·lar** (bə·sil′ər, bas′ə·lər).

ba·cil·lo·my·cin (bə·sil′ō·mī′sin) *n.* An antibiotic

---

add, āce, câre, pälm; end, ēven; it, īce; odd, ōpen, ôrder; tōōk, pōōl; up, bûrn; ə = a in *above*, e in *sicken*, i in *clarity*, o in *melon*, u in *focus*; yōō = u in *fuse*, oi, oil; ou, pout; ch, check; g, go; ng, ring; th, thin; th, this; zh, vision. Foreign sounds á, œ, ü, kh, ṅ; and •: see page xx. < from; + plus; ? possibly.

isolated from a soil organism (*Bacillus subtilis*); it has a strong action against fungi, especially those causing athlete's foot. [< BACILLUS + Gk. *mykēs* fungus + -IN]

ba·cil·lus (bə·sil′əs) *n. pl.* **ba·cil·li** (-sil′ī) **1** Any of a large and numerous class of straight, rod-shaped bacteria having both beneficial and pathogenic effects: distinguished from *coccus* and *spirillum* types. **2** Any of a family (*Bacillaceae*) of straight, rod-shaped, aerobic, spore-forming bacteria, occurring singly or in chains. **3** Loosely, a bacterium. For illustration see BACTERIA. [< NL < *bacillum*, dim. of *baculus* a stick]

bac·i·tra·cin (bas′ə·trā′sin) *n.* An antibiotic produced from a bacillus, used in the treatment of some bacterial skin infections.

back¹ (bak) *n.* **1** The part of the body nearest the spine; in man the hinder, in quadrupeds the upper part, extending from the neck to the base of the spine. ◆ Collateral adjective: *dorsal, fergal.* **2** The backbone. **3** The rear or posterior part: Sit in the *back* of the car. **4** The farther or other side; the part away from the beholder: the *back* of the door. **5** The part which comes behind or is opposite to the part used in the ordinary movements of a thing: the *back* of a knife, the *back* of the hand. **6** The part of the leaves of a book sewed together into the binding; also, the part of the binding around this part. **7** The lining attached to the unexposed side of a thing, as for reinforcement. **8** In football, a member of the offensive or defensive backfield. **9** The ridge of a hill. **10** *Phonet.* The part of the tongue directly behind the front and below the velum. **—at one's back** Following closely. **—behind one's back 1** Secretly. **2** Treacherously. **—in back of** *Colloq.* Behind; to the rear of. **—to be (flat) on one's back** To be helplessly ill. **—to get (or put) one's back up** To become (or make) angry or obstinate. **—to put one's back into** To exert all the physical strength of which one is capable. **—to turn one's back on** To show contempt or ill feeling toward by turning away from or ignoring. **—with one's back to the wall** Cornered; having no issue save by fighting one's way out. **—v.t. 1** To cause to move or go backwards; force to the rear: often with *up.* **2** To form the back of; supply with a back. **3** To strengthen at the back. **4** To support, assist, or uphold; be in favor of: often with *up.* **5** To support financially. **6** To bet on the success or chances of. **7** To mount, sit, or ride on the back of, as a horse. **8** To write on the back of; address or endorse, as a check. **—v.i. 9** To move or go backward: often with *up.* **10** To shift counterclockwise: said of the wind: opposed to *veer.* **—to back and fill 1** *Naut.* To keep (a vessel) in midchannel by alternately filling and spilling the sails, so as to be advanced by the current alone. **2** To be irresolute; vacillate. **—to back down** To withdraw from a position, abandon a claim, etc. **—to back off** To retreat, as from contact. **—to back out** To withdraw from or refuse to carry out an engagement or contest. **—to back water 1** To retard the progress or reverse the motion of a vessel by reversing the action of the oars or of the propelling machinery. **2** To withdraw from a position; retract, as a claim. **—adj. 1** In the rear; behind: a *back* room. **2** Distant; remote: the *back* country. **3** Of or for a date earlier than the present: *back* taxes. **4** In arrears; overdue, as a debt. **5** In a backward direction: a *back* thrust. **6** *Phonet.* Describing those vowels produced with the tongue pulled back in the mouth, as (oo) in *food.* [OE *bæc* back]

back² (bak) *adv.* **1** At, to, or toward the rear: to move *back.* **2** In, to, or toward a former place: to go *back* home. **3** In, to, or toward a former condition: My cold has come *back.* **4** In time past; ago: years *back.* **5** In return or retort: to talk *back.* **6** In reserve or concealment: to keep something *back.* **—back and forth** First in one direction and then in the opposite. **—back of** Behind. **—to go back on** *Colloq.* **1** To refuse to keep a promise or engagement. **2** To desert or betray (a cause). [< ABACK]

back³ (bak) *n.* A brewer's tub or vat. [< Du. *bak* trough < F *bac* tub, basin]

back·ache (bak′āk′) *n.* An ache or pain in one's back.

back·bite (bak′bīt′) *v.t. & v.i.* **·bit, ·bit·ten** or *Colloq.* **·bit, ·bit·ing** To revile or traduce behind one's back; slander. See synonyms under ASPERSE. **—back′bit′er** *n.* **—back′bit′·ing** *n.*

back·blocks (bak′bloks′) *n. pl. Australian* Inland farming areas.

back·board (bak′bôrd′, -bōrd′) *n.* **1** A board forming or supporting the back of something. **2** In basketball, the vertical board behind the basket to which it is attached.

back·bone (bak′bōn′) *n.* **1** *Anat.* The spine or vertebral column. **2** Any main support or stiffening part; especially, the highest or most extensive mountain range of a region or a continent. **3** Firmness; resolution; courage. **—back′boned′** *adj.*

back·break·ing (bak′brā′king) *adj.* Physically exhausting; fatiguing.

back country Unpopulated or undeveloped areas adjoining settled areas.

back court 1 In tennis and other games, the rear part of the court. **2** In basketball, the defensive half of the court of each team.

back·cross (bak′krôs′, -kros′) *v.t. & v.i. Genetics* To cross (a hybrid offspring) with one of its parents. **—n.** The offspring of a hybrid and either of the parents.

back·door (bak′dôr′, -dōr′) *adj.* **1** Relating or belonging to the back door of a house. **2** Underhand; indirect; secret.

back·drop (bak′drop′) *n.* The curtain hung at the rear of a stage, often painted to represent a scene. Also **back cloth.**

backed (bakt) *adj.* **1** Provided with or having a back, background, or backing: often used in composition: low-*backed.* **2** In weaving, having an extra weft, warp, or another ply of cloth woven or knitted on the back.

back·er (bak′ər) *n.* **1** One who or that which backs or furnishes a back to; especially, one who supports with money; a patron. **2** One who bets or gambles on a contestant. See synonyms under ADHERENT.

back·field (bak′fēld′) *n.* **1** In American football, the players behind the forward linemen, consisting of the fullback, right and left halfbacks, and quarterback. **2** The area in which these players are regularly stationed.

back·fill (bak′fil′) *n.* Soil and other material used to refill an excavation. **—v.t.** To refill (an excavation).

back·fire (bak′fīr′) *n.* **1** A fire built to check an advancing forest or prairie fire by creating a barren area in its path. **2** Premature explosion in the cylinder of an internal-combustion engine. **3** An explosion in the back part of a gun. **—v.i. ·fired, ·fir·ing 1** To set or use a backfire. **2** To explode in a backfire. **3** To have consequences contrary to those desired: The plan to raise revenue by increasing the sales tax *backfired* when sales dropped off.

back formation *Ling.* **1** The creation, by analogy, of one word from another in cases where the original word would seem to be the derivative, as in the derivation of *emote* from *emotion.* **2** A word so formed.

back·gam·mon (bak′gam′ən, bak′gam′ən) *n.* **1** A game played by two persons, on a special board, the moves of the pieces being determined by dice throws: formerly called *tables.* **2** A victory in this game before the defeated player advances all his men beyond the first six points, resulting in a tripled score for the victor. **—v.t.** To win a backgammon from. [ME *back gamen* back game; because sometimes the pieces must go back to the start]

back·ground (bak′ground′) *n.* **1** That part in a picture which is behind the principal objects represented or which forms a setting. **2** Ground in the rear or distance. **3** A subordinate position; obscurity; retirement. **4** The aggregate of one's experiences, training, cultural environment, etc. **5** Music or sound effects employed in accompaniment to a dialog, recital, etc. **6** The events leading up to or causing a situation. **7** Information explaining a situation, person, etc.

back·hand (bak′hand′) *adj.* Backhanded. **—n. 1** Handwriting that slopes toward the left. **2** The hand turned backward in making a stroke, as with a racket. **3** A stroke made with the hand turned backward, as in tennis. **—adv.** With a backhand stroke.

back·hand·ed (bak′han′did) *adj.* **1** Delivered or made with the back of the hand, or with back of the hand turned forward, as a stroke in tennis. **2** Equivocal; insincere; ironical: a

backhanded compliment. **3** Sloping to the left, as handwriting. **4** Turned or twisted in a direction opposite to the normal, as a cable. **—back′hand′ed·ly** *adv.* **—back′hand′ed·ness** *n.*

back·house (bak′hous′) *n.* A building in the rear; a privy.

back·ing (bak′ing) *n.* **1** Support or assistance given to a person, cause, etc. **2** Supporters or promoters collectively. **3** Motion backward; the act of moving backward. **4** The back of anything, especially anything added at the back for extra support or strength. **5** The act of supporting or strengthening at or with the back. **6** *Law* Endorsement by a magistrate of a warrant.

back·lash (bak′lash′) *n.* **1** *Mech.* **a** The reaction or tendency to jar or recoil, as machinery subjected to sudden strain. **b** The amount of loose play in a part subject to such tendency or reaction. **2** In angling, a snarl or tangle of the line on a reel, as caused by a faulty cast. **3** A sudden, violent recoil or reaction, as of public opinion.

back·log (bak′lôg′, -log′) *n. U.S.* **1** A large log placed at the back of an open fireplace to maintain and concentrate the heat. **2** Any reserve, as of funds, business orders, etc.

back·most (bak′mōst) *adj.* Farthest to the rear; hindmost.

back·pack (bak′pak′) *n.* A pack or knapsack carried on the back, as by campers. **—v.t. & v.i.** To carry (equipment) in a backpack. **—back′pack′er** *n.*

back·rest (bak′rest′) *n.* A support for or at the back.

back·rope (bak′rōp′) *n. Naut.* A lateral stay from the martingale of a vessel to the bows.

back seat 1 A seat in the rear, as of a vehicle, theater, hall, etc. **2** Status of little or no importance: to take a *back seat.*

back·set (bak′set′) *n.* **1** A setback; relapse. **2** An eddy; backwater, as of a stream.

back·side (bak′sīd′) *n.* The posterior part of a person or an animal; rump.

back·sight (bak′sīt′) *n.* **1** In surveying, a sight laid on a known point in order to determine the position or elevation of an instrument. **2** A sight laid on a previously taken instrument station from a newly located point.

back·slide (bak′slīd′) *v.i.* **·slid, ·slid** or **slid·den, ·slid·ing** To return to wrong or vicious ways or opinions after reformation or conversion; relapse; apostatize. **—back′slid′er** *n.*

back–spin (bak′spin′) *n.* Reverse rotation of a round object that is moving forward, causing it to rebound.

back·stage (bak′stāj′) *adv.* In or toward the portion of a theater behind the stage proper or acting area, including the wings, dressing rooms, etc. **—n.** The back portion of the stage. **—adj.** (bak′stāj′) Placed backstage, so as to be hidden.

back·stairs (bak′stârz′) *adj.* Indirect; underhanded. Also **back′stair′.**

back·stay (bak′stā′) *n.* **1** *Naut.* A stayrope supporting a mast of a vessel on the aft side. **2** A support for various mechanical purposes. **3** The leather band at the back and sides of a shoe above the heel and below the body of the counter.

back·stitch (bak′stich′) *n.* A stitch made by carrying the thread back half the length of the preceding stitch. **—v.t. & v.i.** To sew with backstitches.

back·stop (bak′stop′) *n.* A fence or screen to stop the ball from going too far in certain games, as baseball, tennis, etc.

back·strap (bak′strap′) *n.* The harness band extending from crupper to hames or saddle. See illustration under HARNESS.

back·stretch (bak′strech′) *n.* That part of a race course farthest from the spectators: opposite of *homestretch.*

back·stroke (bak′strōk′) *n.* **1** A blow or stroke in return; a backhanded stroke. **2** In swimming, a stroke executed while on one's back. **—v. ·stroked, ·strok·ing** *v.t.* To strike, as a ball, with a backstroke. **—v.i.** To swim with a backstroke.

back·swept (bak′swept′) *adj. Aeron.* Sweptback.

back·sword (bak′sôrd′, -sōrd′) *n.* **1** A sword with one sharp edge; a broadsword. **2** A stick with a basket hilt, used in fencing practice or in single–stick play. **3** One who uses a backsword. **—back′sword′man, back′swords′·man** *n.*

back talk Impudent retort; insolent answering back.

back·track (bak'trak') v.i. U.S. **1** To retrace one's steps. **2** To withdraw from a position, undertaking, etc.

back·up (bak'up') n. **1** A support or backing. **2** An accumulation, as of water or waste, caused by a stoppage. **3** A substitute held in readiness for contingent use: often used attributively: a *backup* plan; a *backup* quarterback. Also **back'–up'**.

back·ward (bak'wərd) adj. **1** Turned to the back or rear; reversed. **2** Retiring; bashful. **3** Slow in growth or development; retarded. **4** Late; slow; behindhand. **5** Done the reverse way. — adv. **1** In the direction of the back; to the rear. **2** Into time past; toward earlier times. **3** With the back foremost. **4** In reverse order. **5** From better to worse. Also **back'wards** adv. — **back'ward·ly** adv. — **back'ward·ness** n.

back·wash (bak'wosh', -wôsh') n. **1** The water moved backward, as by a boat, oars, etc. **2** The backward current of air set up by aircraft propellers. **3** Any condition resulting from some previous act, remark, etc.

back·wa·ter (bak'wô'tər, -wot'ər) n. **1** Water set, thrown, or held back, as by a dam, a current, etc.; also, the body of water held back. **2** Any place or condition regarded as stagnant, backward, etc.

back·woods (bak'wŏŏdz') n. pl. U.S. Wild, heavily wooded, or sparsely settled districts. — adj. In, from, or like the backwoods: also **back'wood'**. — **back'woods'man** (-mən) n.

ba·con (bā'kən) n. **1** The salted and dried or smoked flesh of the hog, especially the back and sides. **2** U.S. Colloq. Money, profit, or gain from any undertaking: to bring home the *bacon*. [<OF <OHG *bacho, bakho* ham, side of bacon]

Ba·con (bā'kən), **Francis**, 1561–1626, first Baron Verulam, Viscount St. Albans, English philosopher, essayist, and statesman. — **Nathaniel**, 1647–76, American colonial leader of a rebellion (1676) demanding governmental reforms. — **Roger**, 1214?–92?, English scientist and philosopher.

Ba·co·ni·an (bā·kō'nē·ən) adj. Of or pertaining to Francis Bacon, his philosophy, or his literary style. — n. One who believes in the philosophy of Francis Bacon or in the Baconian theory.

bac·te·re·mi·a (bak'tə·rē'mē·ə) n. Pathol. The presence of bacteria in the blood.

bac·te·ri·a (bak·tir'ē·ə) n. Plural of BACTERIUM.

bacterio– combining form Of or pertaining to bacteria: *bacterioscopy*. [Gk. *baktērion*, dim. of *baktron* rod, staff]

bac·te·ri·ol·o·gy (bak·tir'ē·ol'ə·jē) n. The branch of biology and medicine that deals with bacteria. — **bac·te·ri·o·log·i·cal** (bak·tir'ē·ə·loj'i·kəl), **bac·te·ri·o·log'i·cal·ly** adv. — **bac·te'ri·ol'o·gist** n.

bac·te·ri·um (bak·tir'ē·əm) n. pl. **·te·ri·a** (-tir'ē·ə) One of numerous widely distributed unicellular micro–organisms of the class *Schizomycetes*; autotrophic, heterotrophic, parasitic or saprophytic, they exhibit both plant and animal characteristics, and in their three varieties of *bacillus, coccus,* and *spirillum* range from the harmless and beneficial to the intensely virulent and lethal.

[<NL <Gk. *baktērion*, dim. of *baktron* staff, stick] — **bac·te'ri·al** adj. — **bac·te'ri·al·ly** adv.

bac·ter·ize (bak'tər·īz) v.t. **·ized**, **iz·ing** To change by the action of bacteria. — **bac'ter·i·za'tion** n.

bac·ter·oid (bak'tə·roid) adj. Resembling the forms of bacteria. Also **bac'ter·oi'dal**, **bac·te·ri·oid** (bak·tir'ē·oid). — n. A bacterium found in tubercles on the roots of leguminous plants.

bad¹ (bad) adj. **worse, worst 1** Not good in any manner or degree; not up to standard; unsatisfactory; inferior; poor: a *bad* meal; They played a *bad* game and lost. **2** Disagreeable; unpleasant: *bad* weather; *bad* manners. **3** Inadequate; deficient: *bad* wiring. **4** Lacking skill or proficiency: a *bad* musician. **5** Rotten; decaying: *bad* apples. **6** Immoral; corrupt; wicked. **7** Mischievous; naughty; ill–behaved: a *bad* child. **8** Incorrect; erroneous: *bad* grammar. **9** Injurious; harmful: a *bad* habit. **10** Severe: a *bad* sprain. **11** Sick; in poor health. **12** Injured or diseased; not sound: a *bad* knee, a *bad* heart. **13** Sorry; concerned: to feel *bad* about it. **14** Inexpedient; wrong; improper; inauspicious: He spoke at a *bad* time and regretted it later. **15** Invalid; illegal: a *bad* check. **16** In finance, outstanding and not collectable: a *bad* debt. —**in bad** Colloq. **1** In difficulty. **2** In disfavor. —**not bad** Rather good: also **not half bad, not so bad.** — n. **1** That which is bad. **2** Those who are bad, taken collectively. **3** A bad state or condition; bad luck; wickedness. —**to go to the bad** Colloq. To degenerate; become bad. — adv. Colloq. Badly. [ME *bad, baddle*. ? <OE *bæddel* effeminate man] — **bad'ness** n.

Synonyms (adj.): abominable, baleful, baneful, base, corrupt, corrupting, decayed, decaying, deceitful, deceptive, defective, deleterious, depraved, detrimental, dishonest, evil, false, foul, fraudulent, hurtful, ill, immoral, imperfect, incompetent, inferior, injurious, mean, mischievous, naughty, noxious, pernicious, poor, putrid, rascally, rotten, sad, saddening, scurvy, serious, severe, shabby, sinful, sorrowful, sorry, unfair, unfortunate, unhappy, unlucky, unprincipled, untrue, untrustworthy, unwelcome, unwholesome, unworthy, vile, villainous, wicked, worthless, wretched. See HARD, IMMORAL, PERNICIOUS. **Antonyms**: see synonyms for GOOD.

bad² (bad) Obsolete past tense of BID.

bad blood Hostility; long–standing enmity; strife.

badge (baj) n. **1** A token, mark, decoration, or insignia of office, rank or membership. **2** Any distinguishing mark. **3** A ribbon worn on the field uniform to indicate award of a decoration, or a device to indicate branch, organization, rank, rating, or professional attainment. — v.t. **badged, badg·ing** To decorate or provide with a badge. [ME *bage, bagge*]

badg·er (baj'ər) n. **1** A small, burrowing, nocturnal, carnivorous mammal, with a broad body, short legs, and long–clawed toes. There are several species,

BADGER
(Body length about 2 feet, 4 inches; tail, 6 inches)

including the **American badger** (*Taxidea americana*), the **European badger** (*Meles taxus*), and the balisaur and the ratel of Asia. **2** In Australia, the bandicoot, the rock wallaby, or the wombat. **3** The fur of a badger, or a brush made of its hair. — v.t. To worry or persecute persistently; bait; nag. [? <BADGE, with ref. to mark on head]

bad·i·nage (bad'ə·näzh', bad'ə·nij) n. Playful raillery; banter. — v.t. **·naged, ·nag·ing** To subject to or tease with badinage. See synonyms under BANTER. [<F <*badiner* jest < *badin* silly, jesting <Provençal *bader* <LL *badare* gape]

Bad·lands (bad'landz') An arid plateau in South Dakota, Nebraska, and North Dakota, eroded into peaks, pinnacles, and valleys. Also **Bad Lands**.

bad·ly (bad'lē) adv. **1** Improperly; imperfectly; incorrectly. **2** Unpleasantly. **3** Harmfully. **4** Colloq. Very much; greatly: I need to see you *badly*.

bad·min·ton (bad'min·tən) n. **1** A game played by batting a shuttlecock back and forth over a high narrow net with a light racket. **2** A drink made with claret, sugar, and soda water. [from *Badminton* in England, the estate of the Duke of Beaufort]

bad–mouth (bad'mouth') v.t. U.S. Slang To voice damaging criticism of; speak ill of.

bad–tem·pered (bad'tem'pərd) adj. Having a bad temper; cross; irritable.

baff (baf) Scot. v.t. & v.i. **1** To beat or strike. **2** In golf, to strike the ground under the ball with the sole of a wooden club so as to send the ball too high in the air. — n. **1** A stroke; blow. **2** In golf, a baffed stroke.

Baffin Bay An arm of the North Atlantic between Greenland and the Northwest Territories, Canada.

Baffin Island The largest and most easterly island in the Arctic Archipelago, Northwest Territories, Canada; 197,754 square miles. Also **Baffin Land**.

baf·fle (baf'əl) v. **baf·fled, baf·fling** v.t. **1** To thwart or frustrate; defeat; perplex: Police detectives were completely *baffled* by the absence of a motive. **2** Naut. To beat back or hinder: The ship was *baffled* by the storm. — v.i. **3** To struggle to no avail: The gull *baffles* with the wind. — n. **1** A baffleplate. **2** A partition with a small central hole set in front of a radio loudspeaker to prevent excessive flow of air in either direction. **3** Any movable surface, as a board or blanket, used to control and direct sound effect in filming motion pictures. [Origin uncertain] — **baf'fle·ment** n. — **baf'fler** n. — **baf'fling** adj. — **baf'fling·ly** adv.

Synonyms (verb): balk, circumvent, defeat, foil, frustrate, outgeneral, outmaneuver, outwit, thwart. All the words of this list imply *defeat* by something less than direct resistance. A plan, a scheme, or an opponent may be *baffled* by any artifice sufficient to prevent success. An attempt is *foiled* which is made to miss its mark by some craft or skill of an opponent. An attempt is *frustrated* which is made vain by any means, with or without design; as, the attempt at surprise was *frustrated* by the accidental discharge of a gun. An undertaking, movement, etc., is *balked* which is effectually stopped by some obstacle. To *thwart* is to *defeat* by some force or action coming across the path. To *circumvent* is to gain an advantage by passing around; "to get round" a person or a scheme. Compare CONQUER, HINDER. **Antonyms**: abet, advance, aid, assist, encourage, help, promote, prosper.

baf·fle·plate (baf'əl·plāt) n. **1** A partition, as in a furnace, to change the direction of the gases of combustion. **2** A grating placed in a pipe or channel to control eddies and secure a uniform flow of the liquid passing through it. **3** Electronics A metal plate serving to reduce the cross–section of electromagnetic waves passing through a guide.

baf·fy (baf'ē) n. pl. **·fies** A wooden golf club with a short shaft and deeply pitched face, for lofting the ball. [<BAFF]

bag (bag) n. **1** A sack or pouch. **2** A sac or similar structure in various animals, as the udder of a cow. **3** The amount a bag will hold.

COCCUS FORMS OF BACTERIA
a. Staphylococcus.
b. Diplococcus.
c. Sarcina.
d. Streptococcus.

BACILLUS FORMS OF BACTERIA
e. Bacillus typhosus.
f. Bacillus sporagenes.
g. Bacillus subtilis.
h. Bacillus proteus.

SPIRILLUM FORMS OF BACTERIA
i. Spirillum undulam.
j. Species of spirochaete.
k. Thiospirillum.
l. Vibrio cholerae.

add,āce,câre,pälm; end,ēven; it,īce; odd,ōpen,ôrder; tŏŏk,pōōl; up,bûrn; ə = a in *above*, e in *sicken*, i in *clarity*, o in *melon*, u in *focus*; yōō = u in *fuse*; oi,oil; ou,pout; ch,check; g,go; ng,ring; th,thin; ᵺ,this; zh,vision. Foreign sounds à,œ,ü,kh,ṅ; and ♦: see page xx. < from; + plus; ? possibly.

4 The amount of game caught or killed. **5** The bulged part of any object, as of a sail. **6** *pl. Colloq.* Clothes, especially ill-fitting ones. **7** *pl. Brit. Colloq.* Men's slacks. **8** A purse. **9** A suitcase. **10** *Slang* One's personal interest or habit. **11** *Slang* A situation, matter, or problem. —**in the bag** *Slang* Virtually certain. —**to be left holding the bag** *U.S. Colloq.* To be left to assume full responsibility. —*v.* **bagged, bag·ging** *v.t.* **1** To put into a bag or bags. **2** To cause to fill out or bulge like a bag. **3** To capture or kill, as game. —*v.i.* **4** To bulge or swell like a bag. **5** To hang loosely. [?<ON *baggi* pack, bundle]

ba·gasse (bə·gas′) *n.* **1** The dry refuse of sugarcane after the juice has been expressed. **2** Similar refuse from other sources, as beets and olives: also called *megass, megasse.* Also **ba·gass′.** [<F <Sp. *bagazo* refuse of grapes, olives, etc., after pressing]

bag·a·telle (bag′ə·tel′) *n.* **1** A trifle; something of minor importance. **2** A game similar to billiards. **3** Pinball. **4** A short musical composition, especially for the piano. [<F < Ital. *bagatella,* dim. of *baga* sack]

ba·gel (bā′gəl) *n.* A doughnut-shaped roll of unsalted yeast simmered in water and baked. [<Yiddish <*beigen* bend, twist]

bag·gage (bag′ij) *n.* **1** The trunks, packages, etc., of a traveler. **2** An army's movable equipment. **3** A lively, pert, or impudent young woman. **4** *Archaic* A prostitute. [<OF *bagage* <*bague* bundle <Med. L *baga* sack]

bag·gie (bäg′ē, beg′ē) *n. Scot.* The stomach.

bag·ging (bag′ing) *n.* A coarse material for making bags.

bag·gy (bag′ē) *adj.* **bag·gi·er, bag·gi·est** Like a bag; loose; bulging or ill-fitting; puffy: a *baggy* dress. —**bag′gi·ly** *adv.* —**bag′gi·ness** *n.*

Bagh·dad (bag′dad, bäg·däd′) A city on the Tigris, capital of Iraq. Also **Bag′dad.**

Bagh·dad·i (bag·dad′ē, bäg·dä·dē) *n.* A native or inhabitant of Baghdad.

bag·man (bag′mən) *n. pl.* ·**men** (-mən) *Brit.* A traveling salesman.

bagn·io (ban′yō, bän′-) *n.* **1** A brothel. **2** A bathhouse; a bath. **3** In the Orient, a prison. [<Ital. *bagno* <L *balneum* <Gk. *balaneion* bath]

bag·pipe (bag′pīp′) *n.* Often *pl.* A reed musical instrument in which the several drone pipes and the melody pipe with its finger stops are supplied with air from a windbag filled by a pipe to the player's mouth: now played chiefly in Scotland and Ireland. —**bag′. pip′er** *n.*

BAGPIPE

ba·guette (ba·get′) *n.* **1** *Archit.* A small, bead-shaped molding. **2** A gem or crystal cut in long, narrow, rectangular form. **3** This form. Also **ba·guet′.** [<F <Ital. *bacchetta* dim. of *bacchio* <L *baculum* staff, stick]

bah (bä, ba) *interj.* An exclamation expressing contempt, scorn, or dismissal.

Ba·ha·i (bə·hä′ē) *n. pl.* **Ba·ha·is** A teacher or follower of Bahaism.

Ba·ha·ism (bə·hä′iz·əm) *n.* One of the two sectarian creeds of Babism, named after the elder brother of Mirza Yahya, Mirza Husayn Ali, who, as *Bahaullah,* proclaimed himself first successor to the Bab in 1863. —**Ba·ha′ist** *n. & adj.*

Ba·ha·ma Islands (bə·hä′mə, -hā′-) An island group in the western North Atlantic between Florida and Hispaniola, comprising a British colony; 4,375 square miles; capital, Nassau. Also **Ba·ha′mas.**

Ba·ha·sa Indonesia (bä·hä′sə) The official language of Indonesia, based on Malay.

Bah·rein Islands (bä·rān′) An archipelago in the Persian Gulf near the coast of Saudi Arabia, comprising a sheikdom under British protection; 213 square miles; capital, Manameh. Also **Bah·rain′, Bah·rayn′.**

bail¹ (bāl) *n.* A scoop or bucket for dipping out fluids, as from a boat. —*v.t. & v.i.* **1** To dip (water) as from a boat, with or as with a bail. **2** To clear (a boat) of water by dipping out. —**to bail out** To jump from an airplane or other aircraft, equipped with parachute,

in order to land; to parachute. ◆ *Homophone: bale.* [<OF *baille* <LL *bacula,* dim. of *baca, bacca* shallow trough, tub]

bail² (bāl) *n.* **1** A partition between the stalls of a stable. **2** A frame to confine a cow's head while milking. **3** In cricket, one of the crosspieces of the wicket. **4** A crossbar. **5** A bailey. **6** *pl. Obs.* Palisades. ◆ *Homophone: bale.* —**to bail up** *Austral. Slang* **1** To hold up and rob. **2** To corner or accost someone. [<OF *baile* barrier, ? < *bailler* enclose, shut]

bail³ (bāl) *Law n.* **1** One who becomes surety for the debt or default of another, especially of a person under arrest. **2** The security or guaranty given or agreed upon. **3** Release, or the privilege of release, on bail. See synonyms under SECURITY. —*v.t.* **1** To release (an arrested person) on bail for appearance at a stipulated time: often with *out.* **2** To obtain the release of (an arrested person) on bail: usually with *out.* **3** To deliver, as goods, to another's disposition or care without transference of ownership. —**to go (or stand) bail for** To provide bail for. ◆ *Homophone: bale.* [<OF, power, custody <*baillier* guard, control <L *bajulare* carry, manage]

bail⁴ (bāl) *n.* **1** The semicircular handle of a pail, kettle, etc. **2** An arch-shaped support, as for holding up the cloth of a canopy. —*v.t.* To provide with a bail or handle. ◆ *Homophone: bale.* [<ON *beygla* hook, ring]

bail·ee (bā′lē′) *n. Law* One to whom property is bailed.

bail·er¹ (bā′lər) *n.* One who bails.

bail·er² (bā′lər) *n.* In cricket, a ball that strikes the bails.

bai·ley (bā′lē) *n. pl.* **bai·leys 1** The outer court of a castle, or any court of a fortress. **2** A court of justice or a prison. Also **bai′lie.**

bai·liff (bā′lif) *n.* **1** An officer of court having custody of prisoners under arraignment. **2** A sheriff's deputy for serving processes and warrants of arrest. **3** A custodian of property and its management for the owner; steward; overseer. **4** *Brit.* A subordinate magistrate with jurisdiction limited to a certain district or to certain functions, as to keeping the peace in the hundreds. **5** The first civil officer in each of the Channel Islands. [<OF *baillif* <L *bajalus* porter, manager]

bai·li·wick (bā′lə·wik) *n.* **1** The office, jurisdiction, or district of a bailiff. **2** One's own special place or province. [<BAILI(E) + OE *wic* village]

bail·ment (bāl′mənt) *n. Law* The act of bailing an accused person, goods, etc.

bail·or (bā′lər, bā′lôr′) *n. Law* One who delivers goods, etc., in bailment.

bails·man (bālz′mən) *n. pl.* ·**men** (-mən) One who provides bail for another.

Bai·ly's beads (bā′lēz) *Astron.* A series of luminous points appearing along the advancing edge of the moon's disk just before totality in a solar eclipse. [after Francis *Baily,* 1774-1844, English astronomer]

bain-ma·rie (baṅ·mȧ·rē′) *n. pl.* **bains-ma·rie** (baṅ-) *French* A water bath, especially as used in the preparation of drugs and in cookery.

Bai·ram (bī·räm′) *n.* Either of two Moslem festivals, one of which, the **Lesser Bairam,** is in the beginning of the tenth month, at the end of Ramadan, and lasts from one to three days, while the other, the **Greater Bairam,** of four days, is seventy days later. [<Turkish]

bait¹ (bāt) *n.* **1** Food or other enticement placed as a lure in a trap, on a hook, etc. **2** Any allurement or enticement. **3** A halt on a journey for food or refreshment. —*v.t.* **1** To put food or some other lure on or in: to *bait* a trap. **2** To torment, as by setting dogs upon, for sport: to *bait* a bear. **3** To harass; heckle. **4** To lure; entice. **5** *Obs.* To feed (a horse, etc.) while resting. —*v.i.* **6** *Obs.* To stop for rest and refreshment. ◆ *Homophone: bate.* [<ON *beita* cause to bite] —**bait′er**

bait² (bāt) *n. Dial.* **1** A quantity; an amount. **2** Enough. ◆ *Homophone: bate.*

bait³ (bāt) See BATE.³

baith (bāth) *adj., pron., & conj. Scot.* Both.

baize (bāz) *n.* **1** A plain, loosely woven cotton or woolen fabric, usually dyed green and napped to imitate felt: used for table covers, etc. **2** An article made of this fabric. [<OF

baies, fem. pl. of *bai* chestnut-brown <L *badius*]

Ba·ja Ca·li·for·nia (bä′hä kä′lē·fôr′nyä) The Spanish name for LOWER CALIFORNIA.

bake (bāk) *v.* **baked, bak·ing** *v.t.* **1** To cook by dry and continuous heat, as food in an oven. **2** To harden or vitrify by heat, as bricks or pottery. **3** *Obs.* To cake; harden. —*v.i.* **4** To bake bread, pastry, meat, or other food. **5** To become baked or hardened by heat, as soil. —*n.* **1** A baking or the amount baked. **2** *U.S.* A social gathering at which certain foods are baked and served. **3** *Scot.* A cracker. [OE *bacan*]

bake·house (bāk′hous′) *n.* A bakery.

bak·er (bā′kər) *n.* **1** One who bakes and sells bread, cake, etc. **2** A portable oven.

Ba·ker (bā′kər), **Ernest Albert,** born 1869, English librarian and author. —**George Pierce,** 1866-1935, U.S. educator and editor. —**Newton Diehl,** 1871-1937, U.S. lawyer; secretary of war 1916-21. —**Ray Stannard,** 1870-1946, U.S. author: pseudonym *David Grayson.* —**Sir Samuel White,** 1821-93, English explorer in Africa.

Baker, Mount A peak in the Cascade Range, northern Washington; 10,750 feet.

Baker Island A United States possession (1936) in the Pacific Ocean near the equator, used as a refueling point; one square mile.

bakers' dozen Thirteen: from a former custom of giving an excess to make sure of avoiding the heavy penalties exacted for short weight or measure.

bak·er·y (bā′kər·ē, bāk′rē) *n. pl.* ·**er·ies 1** A place for baking bread, cake, etc. **2** A shop where bread, cake, pastry, etc., are sold at retail: also **bake′shop′.**

bak·ing (bā′king) *n.* **1** The act of baking. **2** The quantity baked.

baking powder A finely powdered mixture of baking soda and an acid salt, giving off carbon dioxide when moist: it is used as a substitute for yeast in baking.

baking soda Sodium bicarbonate.

bak·sheesh (bak′shēsh) *n.* In India, Turkey, Egypt, and other countries, a gratuity or tip. —*v.t. & v.i.* To give a tip (to). Also spelled *backsheesh, backshish.* [<Persian *bakhshish* < *bakhshīdan* give]

Bal·a·kla·va (bal′ə·klä′və) A Crimean port on the Black Sea, near which the Charge of the Light Brigade took place (1854).

bal·a·lai·ka (bal′ə·lī′kə) *n.* A Russian musical instrument having a triangular body, a guitar neck, and three strings. [<Russian]

BALALAIKA

bal·ance (bal′əns) *n.* **1** An instrument for weighing, often a bar pivoted on a central point according to the weight placed in or hung from a matched scale or pan at either end; scales: often used in the plural, either scale being called a *balance,* and the two a *pair of balances.* **2** The imaginary scales of destiny by which deeds and principles are weighed: a symbol of justice: Thou hast been weighed in the *balance* and found wanting. **3** The power to decide fate, value, etc., as by a balance. **4** A state of being in equilibrium; equipoise; equality. **5** Mental or emotional stability; sanity. **6** Harmonious proportion, as in the design or arrangement of parts in a work of art. **7** Something used to produce an equilibrium; counteracting influence; counterpoise. **8** The act of balancing or weighing. **9** Equality between the credit and debit totals of an account. **10** A difference between such totals; the excess on either side. **11** *U.S. Colloq.* Whatever is left over; remainder; surplus. **12** A balance wheel. **13** An instrument for measuring electricity or its effects by opposing some other force, as gravity. **14** A movement in dancing. See synonyms under REMAINDER. —**in the balance** Being judged; not yet settled. —**to strike a balance** To find or take an intermediate position; compromise. —*v.* ·**anced, ·anc·ing** *v.t.* **1** To bring into or keep in equilibrium; poise. **2** To weigh in a balance. **3** To compare or weigh in the mind, as alternative courses of action; estimate the importance or consequence of. **4** To offset or counteract. **5** To keep or be in proportion to. **6** To be equal to. **7** To compute the difference between the debit and credit sides of (an account). **8** To reconcile, as by making certain entries, the debit and credit sides of (an account). **9** To adjust (an account) by paying what is owed. —*v.i.* **10** To be or come into equilibrium. **11** To be equal: The accounts *balance.* **12** To hesitate or waver; tilt: to *balance* on the edge of a chasm. **13** To move or lean back and forth as from one foot to another. [< F < L *bilanx, -ancis* having two plates < *bis* two + *lanx, lancis* dish, plate] —**bal′ance·a·ble** *adj.*

bal·anc·er (bal′ən·sər) *n.* **1** One who or that which balances. **2** A tightrope dancer; an acrobat. **3** *Entomol.* One of the paired halteres on each side of the thorax of certain dipterous insects. **4** An apparatus used to increase the precision of a radio direction finder.

ba·lan·dran (bə·lan′drən) *n.* A wide wrap worn in the Middle Ages. Also **ba·lan·dra·na** (bə·lan′drə·nə). [< OF < Med. L *balandrana*]

bal·a·ta (bal′ə·tə) *n.* **1** The juice of the bullytree, used industrially as an elastic gum. **2** The tree. [< Sp. < Tupian]

ba·laus·tine (bə·lôs′tin) *n.* The pomegranate, or its dried astringent flowers, bark, or rind. [< L *balaustium* pomegranate flower < Gk. *balaustion*]

bal·brig·gan (bal·brig′ən) *n.* **1** A fine, unbleached, knitted cotton hosiery fabric first made at Balbriggan, Eire. **2** A lightweight cotton fabric made in imitation of this. **3** *pl.* Clothes, especially underwear and hose, made of balbriggan. —*adj.* Made of balbriggan.

Bal·brig·gan (bal·brig′ən) A town on the Irish Sea 20 miles north of Dublin.

bal·bu·ti·es (bal·byōō′shi·ēz) *n.* A speech defect characterized by stuttering; stammering. [< NL < L *balbutire* stammer]

bal·co·ny (bal′kə·nē) *n. pl.* **·nies** **1** A balustraded platform projecting from a wall of a building, usually before a window. **2** A projecting gallery inside a theater or other public building. [< Ital. *balcone* < *balco* a beam < OHG *balcho*] —**bal′co·nied** *adj.*

BALCONY WITH BALUSTRADE

bald (bôld) *adj.* **1** Without hair on the head. **2** Without natural covering or growth, as a mountain. **3** Unadorned; without embellishments. **4** Without disguise. **5** *Zool.* Having white feathers or fur on the head: the *bald* eagle. [< Welsh *bâl* white] —**bald′ly** *adv.* —**bald′ness** *n.*

bal·da·chin (bal′də·kin, bôl′-) *n.* **1** A heavy, rich fabric, formerly made of silk and gold: also *baudekin.* **2** A canopy of such fabric, as one carried in religious processions. **3** *Archit.* A canopy of stone or metal, as over an altar or throne. Also **bal′da·quin.** [< F *baldaquin* < Ital. *baldacchino* < *Baldacco* Baghdad, where the cloth was first made]

bald eagle A species of dark brown eagle (*Heliaeetus leucocephalus*), the adults having white head and tail feathers, formerly found throughout North America but in danger of extinction. Also called *American eagle.*

Bal·der (bôl′dər) In Norse mythology, god of sunlight, spring, and joy; son of Odin and Frigga. He was killed by the treachery of Loki. Also **Bal′dr.**

bal·der·dash (bôl′dər·dash) *n.* A meaningless flow of words; nonsense. [Origin uncertain]

bald·face (bôld′fās′) *n.* **1** The widgeon. **2** A horse having a white face.

bald-faced (bôld′fāst′) *adj.* **1** Having a white face or white markings on the face: said of animals. **2** Brash; undisguised: *bald-faced* lie.

bald·head (bôld′hed′) *n.* **1** One whose head is bald. **2** A breed of pigeons. **3** The widgeon. **4** The bald eagle.

bald-head·ed (bôld′hed′id) *adj.* Having a bald head. —*adv. U.S. Colloq.* Roughly, precipitately: to go at something *bald-headed.*

bald·ing (bôl′ding) *adj. U.S. Colloq.* Beginning to grow bald.

bald·pate (bôld′pāt′) *n.* A bald-headed person. **2** The widgeon. —**bald′-pat′ed** *adj.*

bal·dric (bôl′drik) *n.* A belt worn over one shoulder and across the breast, to support a sword, bugle, etc.: also spelled *bawdric.* Also **bal′drick.** [? < OF *baudrei*]

Bald·y (bôl′dē) **1** Old Baldy. **2** A peak in northern New Mexico; 12,623 feet.

bale¹ (bāl) *n.* A large package of bulky goods corded or otherwise prepared for transportation. —*v.t.* **baled, bal·ing** To make into a bale or bales. ◆ Homophone: *bail.* [< OF *bale* round package, ? < OHG *balla* ball]

bale² (bāl) *n. Archaic* **1** That which causes ruin or sorrow; evil. **2** Pain; woe. ◆ Homophone: *bail.* [OE *bealu* evil, wickedness]

bale³ (bāl) *n.* A balefire. ◆ Homophone: *bail.* [OE *bæl* fire, funeral pile]

Bâle (bäl) French name for BASEL.

Bal·e·ar·ic Islands (bal′ē·ar′ik, bə·lir′ik) A Spanish province in the western Mediterranean, comprising a group of four islands (Mallorca, Menorca, Iviza, and Formentera) and 11 islets; 1,936 square miles; capital, Palma, on Mallorca. *Spanish* **Is·las Ba·le·a·res** (ēz′läz vä′lā·ä′rās).

ba·leen (bə·lēn′) *n.* Whalebone. [< F *baleine* < L *balæna* < Gk. *phalaina* whale]

baleen knife A curved double-handled knife for splitting whalebone.

bale·fire (bāl′fir′) *n.* **1** A signal fire; beacon. **2** A funeral pyre. **3** Any great outdoor fire. [OE *bælfyr* < *bæl* bale³ + *fyr* fire]

bale·ful (bāl′fəl) *adj.* **1** Hurtful; malignant. **2** *Archaic* Sorrowful; miserable. See synonyms under BAD. —**bale′ful·ly** *adv.* —**bale′ful·ness** *n.*

bale hook A box hook.

bal·er (bā′lər) *n.* **1** One who or that which bales. **2** A baling machine.

Ba·li (bä′lē) One of the Lesser Sunda Islands, east of Java; 2,095 square miles; capital, Singaradja.

Ba·li·nese (bä′lə·nēz′, -nēs′) *adj.* Of or pertaining to Bali, its people, or their language. —*n. pl.* **Ba·li·nese 1** A native or inhabitant of Bali. **2** The Indonesian language of Bali.

Bal·iol (bāl′yəl), **John de,** 1248–1315, king of Scotland. —**Edward,** died 1363, son of John; king of Scotland. Also spelled *Balliol.*

bal·i·saur (bal′ə·sôr′) *n.* A long-tailed badger (*Arctonyx collaris*) of India and Siam. [< Hind. *bālusūr* < *bālu* sand + *sūr* hog]

Ba·lize (bə·lēz′) See BELIZE.

balk (bôk) *v.t.* **1** To render unsuccessful; thwart; frustrate. **2** *Obs.* To heap up in ridges or balks; also, to make a balk in (land). —*v.i.* **3** To stop short and refuse to proceed or take action. —*n.* **1** That which balks or hinders; an obstacle; hindrance. **2** An error; miss; blunder. **3** A feint or false motion, as a movement of the pitcher in baseball as if to pitch the ball, or the failure of a jumper to leap after taking his run. **4** A ridge left unplowed between furrows or between plowed strips of land. **5** A squared beam or timber. **6** The space between the balk line and the cushion of a billiard table. **7** One of the stringers or joist-shaped spars placed from boat to boat, upon which the chess or flooring of a pontoon bridge is placed. Also spelled *baulk.* See synonyms under ERROR. [OE *balca* bank, ridge]

Bal·kan (bôl′kən) *adj.* **1** Of or pertaining to the Balkan Peninsula, to the people of this region, their customs, etc. **2** Of or pertaining to the Balkan Mountains.

Balkan frame *Med.* A frame supported on four posts, with pulleys and slats for holding up the legs in the treatment of fractures. [First used in the *Balkan* States]

bal·kan·ize (bôl′kən·īz) *v.t.* **·ized, ·iz·ing** To separate (a country) into small, dissenting political units or states, as the Balkans after World War I. Also **Bal′kan·ize.** —**bal′kan·i·za′tion** *n.*

Balkan Mountains A mountain range in Bulgaria, extending 350 miles westward from the Black Sea to the Yugoslav border; highest point, 7,793 feet.

Balkan Peninsula A peninsula of SE Europe lying south of the lower Danube and bounded by the Black, Aegean, Mediterranean, Ionian, and Adriatic Seas.

Balkan States The countries occupying the Balkan Peninsula: Albania, Bulgaria, Greece, Rumania, Yugoslavia, and the western part of Turkey. Also **the Balkans.**

Bal·kis (bal′kis) The Arabic name, used in the Koran, for the QUEEN OF SHEBA.

balk line (bôk) **1** In billiards, a line partitioning off a space in the corner, along the sides, or around the entire edge of the table. **2** In sports, especially track events, a line, progress beyond which counts as a trial.

balk·y (bô′kē) *adj.* **balk·i·er, balk·i·est** Disposed to stop suddenly or refuse to go: also spelled *baulky.* See synonyms under RESTIVE.

ball¹ (bôl) *n.* **1** A spherical or nearly spherical body. **2** Such a body, of any size and made of various substances, used in a number of games. **3** Any of several such games, especially baseball. **4** The mode of throwing or pitching a ball: a foul *ball,* a high or swift *ball.* **5** In baseball, a delivery by the pitcher in which the ball fails to pass over the home plate between the batsman's shoulder and knees and is not struck at by him: distinguished from *strike.* **6** *Mil.* **a** Any spherical or conoid projectile, larger than a small shot. **b** Such projectiles collectively: to load with *ball.* **7** A roundish protuberance or part of something, especially of the human body or of some organ. **8** A planet or star, especially the earth. —**to be on the ball** *Slang* To be competent or efficient. —**to have something on the ball** *Slang* To have ability. — **to play ball 1** To begin or resume playing a ball game or some other activity. **2** *Colloq.* To cooperate. —*v.t. & v.i.* To form, gather, or wind into a ball: to *ball* worsted. —**to ball up** *Slang* To embarrass; confuse or become confused. ◆ Homophone: *bawl.* [< ON *bøllr*]

ball² (bôl) *n.* A formal social assembly for dancing. ◆ Homophone: *bawl.* [< F *bal* < dance < *baler* < LL *ballare* dance]

Ball (bôl), **John,** died 1381, English priest; a leader of Wat Tyler's peasants' revolt.

bal·lad (bal′əd) *n.* **1** A narrative poem or song of popular origin in short stanzas, often with a refrain: originally handed down orally, often with changes and additions. **2** A sentimental song of several stanzas, in which the melody is usually repeated for each stanza. [< OF *ballade* dancing song]

bal·lade (bə·läd′, ba-) *n.* **1** A verse form consisting of three stanzas of eight or ten lines each and an envoy of four or five lines: the last line of each stanza and of the envoy is the same. **2** A musical composition, usually of romantic or dramatic nature, usually for piano or orchestra. [< OF *balade* dancing song]

bal·lad·eer (bal′ə·dir′) *n.* A ballad singer.

bal·lad·mon·ger (bal′əd·mung′gər, -mong′-) *n.* **1** A seller of popular ballads. **2** A poetaster.

bal·la·drom·ic (bal′ə·drom′ik) *adj.* Pursuing a course heading for the target: said of rockets and guided missiles. [< Gk. *ballein* hurl (a missile) + *dromos* course]

bal·lad·ry (bal′əd·rē) *n.* **1** Ballad poetry. **2** The art of making or singing ballads.

ballad stanza A four-line stanza used in ballads, generally riming the second and fourth lines.

ball-and-sock·et joint (bôl′ən·sok′it) *Mech.* A joint composed of a sphere working in a bearing permitting a degree of free turning in any direction.

bal·last (bal′əst) *n.* **1** Any heavy substance, as sand, stone, etc., laid in the hold of a vessel or in the car of a balloon to steady it. **2** Gravel or broken stone laid down as a stabilizer for a railroad bed. **3** That which gives stability to character, morality, etc. —*v.t.* **1** To provide or fill with ballast. **2** To steady with or as if with ballast; stabilize. **3** *Obs.* To weigh down. [< ODan. *barlast* < *bar* bare, mere + *last* load]

ball bearing *Mech.* **1** A bearing in which the shaft at its points of support rests upon or is surrounded by small metal balls that turn freely as the shaft revolves: used to reduce friction. **2** Any of the metal balls in such a bearing.

ball cartridge *Mil.* Live ammunition as distinguished from blank ammunition.

ball cock *Mech.* A stopcock for regulating the supply of water, in which the valve is opened or shut by the rising or falling of a hollow floating ball.

BALL COCK

bal·le·ri·na (bal'ə-rē'nə) *n.* A female ballet dancer. [<Ital., fem. of *ballerino* dancer]

bal·let (bal'ā, ba-lā') *n.* 1 An elaborate kind of dramatic group dance using conventionalized movements, often for narrative effects. 2 This style of dancing. 3 Dancers of ballet, expecially a company of such dancers. 4 A danced interlude, as in an opera. 5 A musical composition written as an accompaniment to a ballet performance. [<F, dim. of *bal* a dance. See BALL².]

bal·let·o·mane (ba-let'ə-mān) *n.* A ballet enthusiast. [<F <*ballet* + -(o)*mane* <Gk. *mania* enthusiasm.]

ball·flow·er (bôl'flou'ər) *n. Archit.* A ball-like ornament resembling a ball placed in a flower of which the petals form a globe around it.

bal·li·bun·tl (bal'i·bun'təl) *n.* 1 A lightweight, glossy straw, woven of buntal. 2 A hat made of this straw. [<*Baliuag* in the Philippine Islands + BUNTAL.]

bal·lis·ta (bə-lis'tə) *n. pl.* **·tae** (-tē) An engine used in ancient and medieval warfare for

ROMAN BALLISTA

hurling missiles. [<L <Gk. *ballein* throw]

bal·lis·tic (bə-lis'tik) *adj.* Pertaining to projectiles or to ballistics.

bal·lis·tics (bə-lis'tiks) *n.* The science that deals with the motion of projectiles, either while they are still in the bore (**interior ballistics**) or after they leave the muzzle (**exterior ballistics**). — **bal·lis·ti·cian** (bal'ə-stish'ən) *n.*

ballistic table A table showing the character and values of the factors affecting the flight of a projectile, as range, angle of fire, muzzle velocity, time of flight, etc.

ballistic wave The compression of air immediately in front of a projectile in flight, regarded as a wave formation.

bal·lis·tite (bal'is·tīt) *n.* A nearly smokeless gunpowder invented by Alfred Nobel in 1888.

bal·lo·net (bal'ə·net') *n.* 1 A small balloon. 2 An airtight bag set in the interior of a spherical or nonrigid dirigible balloon to maintain pressure on the outer envelope. [<F *ballonnet*, dim. of *ballon* balloon]

bal·loon (bə-lōōn') *n.* 1 A large, airtight bag, inflated with gas lighter than air, designed to rise and float in the atmosphere: larger kinds have a car or basket attached, for carrying passengers, instruments, etc. Compare DIRIGIBLE, BLIMP. 2 A small inflatable rubber bag, used as a toy. 3 *Chem.* A spherical glass vessel. 4 A balloon-shaped outline connected with the mouth of a person, containing the words he is represented as speaking, as in comic strips. — **captive balloon** A balloon restrained from free flight by means of a cable that holds it to the ground. — **kite balloon** An elongated form of captive balloon, fitted with a tail appendage to keep it headed into the wind. — **observation balloon** A captive balloon used as an observation post. — **sounding balloon** A balloon sent up unmanned for obtaining meteorological data recorded on instruments which return to earth after the bursting of the balloon. Compare RADIOSONDE. — *v.i.* 1 To increase quickly in scope or magnitude; expand: The rumor *ballooned* into a scandal. 2 To swell out like a balloon, as a sail. 3 To travel or ascend in a balloon. — *v.t.* 4 To inflate or swell with air: A gust

of wind *ballooned* the sail. [<Ital. *ballone* large ball < *balla* ball, sphere <Gmc.] — **bal·loon'ist** *n.*

balloon cloth A closely woven cotton fabric vulcanized with thin sheets of rubber so as to be airtight: used for balloons and dirigibles.

balloon foresail *Naut.* A light fóresail set between the foretopmasthead and the jib-boom end, used mostly by yachts in light winds. Also **balloon jib.**

balloon sail A spinnaker or a balloon foresail.

balloon tire A pneumatic tire filled with air at low pressure for reducing the shock of bumps.

bal·lot (bal'ət) *n.* 1 A written or printed slip or ticket used in voting. 2 A little ball used in voting: the original sense. 3 The act or system of voting secretly by ballots or by voting machines. 4 The whole number of votes cast in an election. — **Australian ballot** A ballot bearing the names of all the candidates of all parties, so arranged as to insure absolute secrecy and liberty in polling votes. — *v.* **bal·lot·ed, bal·lot·ing** *v.i.* 1 To cast a ballot; vote or decide by ballot. 2 To draw lots or determine by lot: to *ballot* for position. — *v.t.* 3 To vote for or decide on by means of a ballot: to *ballot* a question. [<Ital. *ballotta*, dim. of *balla* ball. See BALLOON.]

bal·lotte·ment (bə-lot'mənt) *n. Med.* Impulse given to a body loosely suspended in a sac or cavity by which it rises on impact and returns again; sometimes applied in the diagnosis of pregnancy, floating kidney, etc. [<F <*ballotter* toss <*ballotte* small ball]

ball–peen (bôl'pēn') *n.* A hemispherical peen on a hammerhead, used especially for riveting. See illustration under HAMMER.

ball·play·er (bôl'plā'ər) *n. U.S.* A baseball player.

ball point pen A fountain pen having for a point a ball bearing that rolls against an ink cartridge and deposits a line on the writing surface.

ball·room (bôl'rōōm', -rŏŏm') *n.* A large room for dancing, especially one with a polished floor. [<BALL²]

ballroom dancing A kind of social dancing in which two people dance as partners.

ball turret *Aeron.* A ball-shaped projection on the bottom part of certain bombers, power-driven and containing machine-guns which can swing in any direction.

bal·ly·hoo (bal'ē·hōō) *n. Colloq.* 1 Noisy patter: the *ballyhoo* of a side-show announcer. 2 Any immoderate, unrestrained advertising. 3 Conspicuous noisiness of speech, manner, or habit. — *v.t.* & *v.i.* **·hooed, ·hoo·ing** To advocate or promote by means of ballyhoo. [Origin unknown]

balm (bäm) *n.* 1 An aromatic, resinous exudation from various trees or shrubs, used as medicine; balsam. 2 Any oily, fragrant, resinous substance. 3 Any tree or shrub yielding such a substance; especially, any tree of the genus *Commiphora*. 4 Any of various aromatic plants of the genus *Melissa*, especially *M. officinalis*. 5 Any pleasing fragrance. 6 Anything that soothes or heals. [<OF *basme* <L *balsamum* <Gk. *balsamon* ? <Semitic. Doublet of BALSAM.]

bal·ma·caan (bal'mə·kän') *n.* A loose overcoat with raglan sleeves, made of rough woolen cloth. [from *Balmacaan*, estate in Scotland]

balm of Gilead 1 Any of several Oriental trees of the myrrh family (genus *Commiphora*). 2 The fragrant balsam obtained from them. 3 The balsam fir, or the balm obtained from it. 4 A European shade tree (*Populus candicans*).

balm·y (bä'mē) *adj.* **balm·i·er, balm·i·est** 1 Having the qualities of balm; aromatic. 2 Healing; soothing; mild. 3 *Brit. Slang* Slightly crazy; overly foolish. — **balm'i·ly** *adv.* — **balm'i·ness** *n.*

bal·ne·al (bal'nē·əl) *adj.* Of or pertaining to baths and bathing. [<L *balneum* bath]

bal·ne·ol·o·gy (bal'nē·ol'ə·jē) *n.* The science of treating disease by baths and the waters of mineral springs. [<L *balneum* bath + -LOGY]

ba·lo·ney (bə·lō'nē) *n.* 1 *Slang* Stuff and nonsense; bunkum. 2 *Colloq.* Bologna sausage. Also spelled *boloney, bolony.* [def. 1 <BOLOGNA SAUSAGE]

bal·sa (bôl'sə, bäl'-) *n.* 1 A tree (*Ochroma pyramidale*) of tropical America and the West Indies. 2 The very light wood from this tree: called *corkwood.* 3 A raft originally made of light logs fastened together by a platform. 4 A catamaran. [<Sp. *balza*]

bal·sam (bôl'səm) *n.* 1 Any of a group of fragrant oleoresins obtained chiefly from the exudations of various trees. 2 Any such tree. 3 Any fragrant ointment; balm. 4 An aromatic resin containing cinnamic and benzoic acid, or the tree that yields it. 5 A flowering plant of the genus *Impatiens*, especially the common garden annual *I. balsamina*. 6 Any soothing or healing agent or circumstance. 7 The balsam fir. — *v.t.* To anoint with balsam; salve. [<L *balsamum* <Gk. *balsamon* balsam tree, ? <Semitic. Doublet of BALM.] — **bal·sa·ma·ceous** (bôl'sə·mā'shəs) *adj.*

balsam fir A tree (*Abies balsamea*) of the pine family, growing in the northern United States and Canada and yielding the Canada balsam: also called *balm of Gilead.*

bal·sam·ic (bôl·sam'ik, bal-) *adj.* 1 Of, like, or containing balsam. 2 Soothing; balmy.

bal·sam·if·er·ous (bôl'sə·mif'ər·əs, bal'-) *adj.* Yielding balsam or balm.

Balt (bôlt) *n.* A native or inhabitant of the Baltic States.

Bal·tha·sar (bal·thā'zər, -thaz'ər) 1 One of the three Magi. Also **Bal·tha'zar.** 2 The alias of Portia in Shakespeare's *Merchant of Venice.*

Bal·tic (bôl'tik) *adj.* Of or pertaining to the Baltic Sea or the Baltic States. — *n.* A branch of the Balto–Slavic languages, including Lithuanian, Lettish (or Latvian), and Old Prussian (extinct).

Baltic Sea An inlet of the Atlantic enclosed by Sweden, Denmark, East Germany, West Germany, Poland, the U.S.S.R., and Finland; 163,000 square miles.

BALTIC SEA REGION

Baltic States A collective name for Lithuania, Latvia, and Estonia, formed in 1918 as independent republics from Russian provinces and governments; annexed in 1940 by the U.S.S.R.

Bal·ti·more (bôl'tə·môr, -mōr) A port in northern Maryland at the upper end of Chesapeake Bay.

Baltimore oriole An American oriole (*Icterus galbula*): so named because the orange and black of the male were the colors of the coat of arms of Lord Baltimore.

Bal·to–Sla·vic (bôl'tō·slä'vik, -slav'ik) *n.* A subfamily of Indo–European languages, consisting of Baltic and Slavic branches.

Ba·lu·chi (bə·lōō'chē) *n.* The Indo–Iranian language of Baluchistan.

Ba·lu·chi·stan (bə·lōō'chə·stän', bə·lōō'chə·stan) A mountainous region of west Pakistan; 134,139 square miles: divided into Baluchistan proper, a province of Pakistan; 52,900 square miles; capital, Quetta; four princely states; and a small area on the SW coast belonging to Oman.

bal·us·ter (bal'əs·tər) *n.* 1 One of a set of small pillars that support a hand rail and form with the hand rail a balustrade. 2 One of the small columns forming a chair back. [<F *balustre* <Ital. *balaustro* baluster <*balaustra* pomegranate flower; so called from the resemblance in form]

bal·us·trade (bal'ə·strād') *n.* A hand rail supported by balusters. See illustration under BALCONY.

Bal·zac (bal'zak, bôl'-; *Fr.* bál·zàk'), **Honoré de,** 1799–1850, French novelist and dramatist.

bam (bam) *Slang v.t.* To cheat; bamboozle. —*n.* A cheat, imposition, or deception.

Ba·ma·ko (bä·mä·kō') A city in west Africa, capital of Mali.

bam·boo (bam·bōō') *n.* **1** A tall, treelike or shrubby grass of tropical and semi-tropical regions (genus *Bambusa* or related genera). **2** The tough, hollow, jointed stem of this plant, widely used for building, furniture, utensils, etc. [<Malay *bambu*]

bam·boo·zle (bam·bōō'zəl) *v.* **·zled, ·zling** *v.t.* **1** To impose upon; mislead; cheat. **2** To perplex. —*v.i.* **3** To practice trickery or deception. [Origin unknown] —**bam·boo'zle·ment** *n.* —**bam·boo'zler** *n.*

ban[1] (ban) *v.t.* **1** To forbid; to proscribe or prohibit. **2** To place under an ecclesiastical ban; excommunicate; anathematize; interdict. **3** *Archaic* To curse; execrate. —*n.* **1** An official proclamation or edict, especially one of prohibition. **2** *pl.* An announcement of intention to marry: often spelled *banns*. **3** Informal disapproval or prohibition, as by public opinion. **4** An ecclesiastical edict of excommunication or interdiction. **5** A sentence of outlawry or banishment. **6** The summoning of vassals to arms by a feudal lord; also, the forces so collected. **7** *Archaic* A curse or denunciation. [*v.* <OHG *bannan* curse, prohibit and Med. L *bannum* proclamation; *n.* <*v.* and OF *ban* <Med. L *bannum* <Gmc.]

ban[2] (ban) *v.t. Obs.* To summon; call forth; call for. [OE *bannan* proclaim]

ban[3] (ban) *n.* A fine muslin made in the East Indies, from the fiber of the banana leafstalk. [<BANANA]

ban[4] (ban) *n. Archaic* **1** The title of the ruler of the southern marches of Hungary. **2** The governor of Croatia and Slavonia. [<Serbo-Croatian *bân* lord, ruler]

ban[5] (bän) *n. pl.* **ba·ni** (bä'nē) A Rumanian copper coin, worth 1/100 of a leu.

ba·nal (bā'nəl, bə·nal', ban'əl) *adj.* Meaningless from overuse; commonplace; trivial. [<F <OF *ban* feudal summons (to service performed communally for a lord); hence ordinary, common] —**ba·nal·i·ty** (bə·nal'ə·tē) *n.* —**ba'nal·ly** *adv.*

ba·nan·a (bə·nan'ə) *n.* **1** A large, herbaceous plant (*Musa paradisiaca sapientium*) growing 10 to 20 feet high, cultivated in tropical climates for its edible pulpy fruit which grows in long pendent clusters. **2** The fruit of this plant. [<Sp. <native African name]

banana oil **1** Isoamyl acetate, $C_7H_{14}O_2$, a sweet-smelling, colorless, liquid ester widely used as a solvent and in artificial fruit flavors, cosmetics, etc.: also called *pear oil*. **2** *U.S. Slang* Fulsome flattery; cajolery.

Ba·na·ras (bə·nä'rəs) A sacred city of the Hindus, on the Ganges River in SE Uttar Pradesh, India: formerly *Benares*.

ba·nau·sic (bə·nô'sik) *adj. Rare* Suitable for a mechanic. [<Gk. *banausikos* mechanical < *banausos* artisan, mechanic]

Ban·bur·y (ban'ber'ē, bam'bər·ē) A municipal borough in northern Oxfordshire, England, famous for its cakes.

ban·ca (bäng'kä) *n.* In the Philippines, a form of dug-out canoe. [<Sp. <Tagalog *bangca*]

band[1] (band) *n.* **1** A flat flexible strip of any material used for binding. **2** Any strip of fabric used to finish, strengthen, or trim an article of dress. **3** *pl.* A pair of linen strips hanging from the front of the neck, worn with certain clerical or academical garments: also called **Geneva bands. 4** Any broad stripe of contrasting color, material, or surface. **5** *Physics* **a** Any of the broad stripes found in typical molecular spectra: seen as distinct lines upon high magnification. **b** A group of states whose energies are so closely spaced as to be unresolvable and which therefore provide a continuous range of energies throughout an interval. **6** *Electronics* A range of sound frequencies or wavelengths within two stated limits: the standard broadcast *band.* **7** *Mech.* A flexible driving belt, communicating motion between wheels by friction. **8** A circular strip or loop of metal; a ring: a golden *band* on one's finger. —*v.t.* **1** To unite or tie with a band; encircle. **2** To mark with a band, as birds; to mark with a stripe. [<F *bande* <OF *bende*, ult. <Gmc. Akin to BIND.]

band[2] (band) *n.* **1** A company of persons associated, organized, or bound together. **2** A company of persons organized to play musical instruments, especially wind and percussion instruments. **3** A group of certain instruments in an orchestra: the string *band.* **4** A drove of animals, nomadic peoples, etc., wandering together. —**to beat the band** *U.S. Colloq.* Inordinately; surpassingly: He shouted *to beat the band.* —*v.t.* To join or unite, as associates in a league or company: often with *together.* —*v.i.* To confederate. [<F *bande.* Akin to BIND.]

band[3] (band) *n.* That which binds, ties, or unites; a bond. [<ON. Akin to BIND.]

band·age (ban'dij) *n.* **1** A strip, usually of soft cloth, used in dressing wounds, etc. **2** Any band. —*v.t.* **·aged, ·ag·ing** To bind or cover with a bandage. [<F <*bande* band]

Band-Aid (band'ād') *n.* A gauze patch attached to an adhesive strip, used to cover minor wounds: a trade name. [<BAND³ + AID']

ban·da·lore (ban'də·lôr, -lōr) *n.* A toy worked by means of a spring which returns it to the hand on a cord when thrown. [Origin unknown]

ban·dan·na (ban·dan'ə) *n.* A large, bright-colored handkerchief with spots or figures. Also **ban·dan'a.** [<Hind. *bāndhnū* mode of dyeing < *bāndh* tie]

band·box (band'boks') *n.* A light round or oval box, for carrying hats, etc.: originally used for collars (formerly called *bands*).

ban·deau (ban·dō') *n. pl.* **·deaux** (-dōz') **1** A narrow band, especially one worn about the hair; fillet. **2** A brassière. [<F <OF *bandel*, dim of *bande* band]

ban·de·role (ban'də·rōl) *n.* **1** A small flag, pennant, or streamer, as at the end of a lance, etc., often bearing an inscription. **2** In painting and sculpture, a ribbon or scroll bearing an inscription. **3** A banner over a tomb or carried at a funeral. Also **ban'de·rol:** also **ban·nerole.** [<F <Ital. *banderuola*, dim. of *bandiera* banner]

ban·di·coot (ban'di·kōōt) *n.* **1** A large rat (*Mus* or *Nesokia bandicota*) of India and Ceylon, often over a foot in length. **2** A small insectivorous marsupial (genus *Parameles*) of Australia, Tasmania, etc. [<Telugu *pandi-kokku* pig-rat]

ban·dit (ban'dit) *n. pl.* **ban·dits** or **ban·dit·ti** (ban-dit'ē) A highwayman; brigand. See synonyms under ROBBER. [<Ital. *bandito*, pp. of *bandire* proscribe, outlaw] —**ban'dit·ry** *n.*

band·mas·ter (band'mas'tər, -mäs'tər) *n.* The conductor of a musical band.

ban·dog (ban'dôg', -dog') *n.* **1** A large, fierce dog, commonly kept chained as a watchdog. **2** A bloodhound or a mastiff. [<BAND³ + DOG]

ban·do·leer (ban'də·lir') *n.* **1** A broad band, usually of canvas webbing, with loops for holding cartridges, worn over the shoulder. **2** An ammunition box attached to this band. Also **ban'do·lier'.** [<F *bandoulière* <Ital. *bandoliera* shoulder belt, ult. < *banda* band]

ban·dore (ban·dôr', -dōr') *n.* An ancient lute-like musical instrument. [<Sp. *bandurria* <L *pandura* <Gk. *pandoura* lute]

band saw *Mech.* A saw consisting of a toothed endless belt on wheels.

band shell A concave, hemispherical bandstand for concerts.

bands·man (bandz'mən) *n. pl.* **·men** (-mən) A member of a musical band.

band·stand (band'stand') *n.* An outdoor platform for a band of musicians, often roofed. Also **band stand.**

band·wag·on (band'wag'ən) *n.* A high, decorated wagon to carry a band in a parade. —**to climb on the bandwagon** To avow adherence publicly to a political principle or candidate evidently destined to win; adopt prevalent opinions and attitudes.

ban·dy (ban'dē) *v.t.* **ban·died, ban·dy·ing 1** To give and take; exchange, as blows, quips, or words: often with *about.* **2** To pass along; circulate: to *bandy* stories. **3** To pass, throw, or knock back and forth, as a ball. —*adj.* Crooked outward at the knees; curved; bowed. —*n. pl.* **ban·dies 1** A game resembling hockey; also, a crooked stick used in this game. **2** An ancient form of tennis. [Origin uncertain]

ban·dy-leg·ged (ban'dē·leg'id, -legd') *adj.* Having crooked legs; bowlegged.

bane (bān) *n.* **1** Anything destructive or ruinous; ruin. **2** A deadly poison: now used only in composition: *henbane.* **3** *Obs.* Death. [OE *bana* murderer, destruction]

bane·ber·ry (bān'ber'ē, -bər·ē) *n. pl.* **·ries 1** The poisonous berry of any species of *Actaea.* **2** The plant bearing this berry.

bane·ful (bān'fəl) *adj.* Noxious; poisonous; injurious; deadly; ruinous. See synonyms under BAD, PERNICIOUS. —**bane'ful·ly** *adv.* —**bane'ful·ness** *n.*

Banff (bamf) **1** A mountainous county of NE Scotland; 630 square miles; county seat, Banff. Also **Banff·shire** (bamf'shir). **2** A resort town in **Banff National Park,** a scenic park in SW Alberta, Canada; 2,564 square miles.

bang[1] (bang) *n.* **1** A sudden or noisy blow, thump, whack, or explosion. **2** *Colloq.* A sudden spring; dash. **3** *U.S. Slang* Thrill; excitement: to get a *bang* out of flying. [<*v.*] —*adv.* **1** With a violent blow or loud and sudden noise. **2** All at once; abruptly. —*v.t.* **1** To beat or strike resoundingly. **2** To shut noisily, as a door. **3** To give a thrashing to; drub. —*v.i.* **4** To make a heavy, loud sound. **5** To strike noisily: The car *banged* into the wall. [<ON *banga* hammer, beat]

bang[2] (bang) *n.* Front hair cut straight across: usually in the plural. —*v.t.* To cut straight across, as the front hair. [<BANG¹, *adv.*; from the hair being cut off abruptly]

bang·kok (bang'kok) *n.* **1** Smooth, light-weight, dull straw woven of buntal fibers. **2** An article made of this straw. [from *Bangkok*]

Bang·kok (bang'kok) A port on the Chao Phraya, capital of Thailand. *Siamese* **Krung Thep** (krŏong tep').

Ban·gla Desh (bäng'glä desh') A republic in southern Asia; 54,501 square miles; capital, Dacca.

ban·gle (bang'gəl) *n.* A decorative bracelet or anklet. [<Hind. *bangrī* glass bracelet]

bang·tail (bang'tāl') *n.* **1** A horse's tail cut horizontally across. **2** *Slang* A horse, especially a race horse. [<BANG² + TAIL] —**bang'-tailed'** *adj.*

bang-up (bang'up') *adj. Slang* Excellent.

ban·ian (ban'yən) *n.* **1** A Hindu merchant or trader belonging to a caste refusing to eat meat. **2** A loose shirt, jacket, or gown. **3** Banyan. [<Pg. <Arabic *banyān*, ult. <Skt. *vanij* merchant]

ban·ish (ban'ish) *v.t.* **1** To compel to leave a country by political decree; exile. **2** To expel, as from any customary or desired place; drive away; dismiss, as a thought from one's mind. [<OF *baniss-*, stem of *banir* <LL *banire* banish < *bannum* proclamation <Gmc.] —**ban'ish·er** *n.* —**ban'ish·ment** *n.*

Synonyms: ban, discharge, dislodge, dismiss, eject, evict, exile, expatriate, expel, ostracize, oust. From a country, a person may be *banished, exiled,* or *expatriated; banished* from any country where he may happen to be, but *expatriated* or *exiled* only from his own. One may *expatriate* or *exile* himself; he is *banished* by others. *Banish* is a word of wide import; one may *banish* disturbing thoughts; care may *banish* sleep. To *expel* is to drive out with violence, and often with disgrace. See EXTERMINATE.

ban·is·ter (ban'is·tər) *n.* **1** A baluster. **2** *pl.*

A balustrade on a staircase. Also *bannister*. [Alter. of BALUSTER]

ban·jo (ban′jō) *n. pl.* **·jos** A long-necked, stringed musical instrument having a hoop-shaped body covered on top with stretched skin and played by plucking the strings with the fingers or a plectrum. [Alter. of Sp. *bandurria*. See BANDORE.] — **ban′jo·ist** *n*.

BANJO

ban·jo·rine (ban′jə-rēn′) *n.* A musical instrument similar to the banjo, but tuned a fourth higher.

bank[1] (bangk) *n.* **1** Any moundlike formation or mass; ridge. **2** A steep acclivity; rising ground. **3** The slope of land at the edge of a watercourse or of any cut or channel: often in the plural. **4** A raised portion of the bed of a river, lake, or ocean: the Newfoundland *banks*; also, a shallow; sandbar; shoal. **5** The cushion of a billiard table. **6** *Aeron.* The sidewise inclination of an airplane in making a turn. **7** The ground at the top of the shaft of a mine. — *v.t.* **1** To enclose, cover, or protect by a bank, dike, or border; embank. **2** To heap up into a bank or mound. **3** To give an upward lateral slope to, as the curve of a road. **4** To incline (an airplane) laterally. **5** In billiards and pool, to cause (a ball) to rebound at an angle from a cushion; also, to pocket (a ball) in this manner. — *v.i.* **6** To form or lie in banks. **7** To incline an airplane laterally. — **to bank** (or **bank up**) **a fire** To cover a fire with ashes or earth so as to keep it alive but burning low. [ME *banke*, ult. <Gmc. Akin to BENCH.]

Synonyms (noun): beach, border, bound, brim, brink, coast, edge, marge, margin, rim, shore, strand. *Bank* is a general term for the land along the edge of a watercourse. A *beach* is a strip or expanse of incoherent wave-worn sand, which is often pebbly or full of boulders. *Strand* is a more poetic term for a wave-washed shore, especially as a place for landing or embarking; as, the keel grates on the *strand*. The whole line of a country or continent that borders the sea is a *coast*. *Shore* is any land, whether cliff, or sand, or marsh, bordering water. We do not speak of the *coast* of a river, nor of the *banks* of the ocean, though there may be *banks* by or under the sea. *Edge* is the line where land and water meet; as, the water's *edge*. *Brink* is the place from which one may fall; as, the *brink* of a precipice, the *brink* of ruin.

bank[2] (bangk) *n.* **1** An institution for lending, borrowing, exchanging, issuing, or caring for money. **2** An office or building used for banking purposes. **3** The funds of a gaming establishment or the fund held by the dealer or banker in some gambling games. **4** In some games, reserve pieces from which the players are permitted to draw, as in dominoes. **5** A store or reserve supply of anything needed for future use or emergency: a blood *bank*. **6** Any place of storage. **7** *Obs.* A money-changer's table. — *v.t.* **1** To deposit in a bank. **2** To back financially or furnish funds for, as a business enterprise. — *v.i.* **3** To do business as or with a bank or banker. **4** In gambling, to keep the bank at a gambling table. **5** To have faith in; rely or count: with *on*. [<F *banque* <Ital. *banca* money-changer's table, ult. <Gmc.]

bank[3] (bangk) *n.* **1** A set of like articles grouped together in a line. **2** A rowers' bench in a galley; a thwart. **3** A horizontal rank of keys in a piano or organ. **4** In journalism, lines under a headline; deck. **5** *Printing* **a** The heavy sloping table on which type galleys or dead type are held. **b** A pressman's table for holding sheets. **c** The track along which the carriage of a printing press moves. — *v.t.* To bring together in a bank, as transformers. [<OF *banc* <LL *bancus* bench, ult. <Gmc. Akin to BENCH.]

bank·a·ble (bangk′ə-bəl) *adj.* Capable of being banked; receivable by or acceptable to a bank.

bank account 1 An account with a bank. **2** A sum of money deposited in a bank to the credit and subject to the withdrawal of a depositor.

bank·book (bangk′book′) *n.* A book in which a depositor's accounts are entered: held by the depositor and serving as a receipt for deposits: also called *passbook*.

bank·er[1] (bangk′ər) *n.* **1** A person or company that owns or manages a bank. **2** One who acts as dealer and keeps the bank, as in certain gambling games.

bank·er[2] (bangk′ər) *n.* A vessel or person engaged in cod-fishing on the Newfoundland banks.

bank·er[3] (bangk′ər) *n.* A stonemason's or sculptor's workbench.

bank holiday 1 *Brit.* Any of six holidays on which banks are legally closed, usually a general holiday. **2** Sunday or a legal holiday upon which banks are officially closed.

bank·ing (bangk′ing) *n.* The business of a bank or banker.

bank·note (bangk′nōt′) *n.* A promissory note, issued by a bank, payable on demand, and serving as currency.

bank·pa·per (bangk′pā′pər) *n.* **1** Banknotes. **2** Negotiable, discountable commercial papers, as securities, bank drafts, bills of exchange, etc.

bank·rupt (bangk′rupt) *n.* **1** A person unable to pay his debts or without credit or resources. **2** *Law* One who is unable to make payment of a just debt when due and demanded of him: a bankrupt is judicially declared insolvent and his property is administered for and divided among his creditors, under a bankruptcy law. — *adj.* **1** Unable to pay one's debts; insolvent. **2** Subject to the conditions of bankruptcy law. **3** Lacking in some quality. — *v.t.* To make bankrupt. [<F *banqueroute* <Ital. *banca rotta* bankruptcy <*banca* bench + *rotta* broken <L *ruptus*, pp. of *rumpere* break]

bank·rupt·cy (bangk′rupt·sē, -rəp·sē) *n. pl.* **·cies 1** The state of being insolvent; failure or inability to pay just debts. **2** Any complete ruin or failure.

bankrupt worm A threadworm (genus *Trichostrongylus*) which causes gastroenteritis in livestock: so called from the financial damage caused by this parasite.

ban·ner (ban′ər) *n.* **1** A cloth bearing a device, suspended from a pole by a crossbar. **2** Any flag or standard. **3** *Bot.* The large upper petal of a papilionaceous blossom. **4** In journalism, a headline extending across the full width of a newspaper page. — *v.t.* To furnish with a banner. — *adj.* Leading; foremost; outstanding. [<OF *banere* <LL *bandum* banner, ult. <Gmc.]

ban·ner·et[1] (ban′ə-ret′) *n.* A small banner. Also **ban′ner·ette′**.

ban·ner·et[2] (ban′ər·it, -et) *n.* **1** One of a grade of knights, next below a baron, entitled to lead vassals under his own banner. **2** The title of such a knight. Also **knight banneret**.

ban·nis·ter (ban′is·tər) See BANISTER.

ban·nock (ban′ək) *n. Scot. & Brit. Dial.* A thin cake of meal baked on a griddle. [OE *bannuc* part, piece, bit]

Ban·nock·burn (ban′ək·bûrn′) A village in NE Stirlingshire, Scotland; site of a battle, 1314, in which Robert Bruce defeated the English.

banns (banz) See BAN[1] (*n.* def. 2).

ban·quet (bang′kwit) *n.* **1** An elaborate or sumptuous feast. **2** A formal or ceremonial dinner, often followed by speeches. — *v.t. & v.i.* To entertain at a banquet; feast sumptuously or formally. [<F, dim. of *banc* table] — **ban′quet·er** *n*.

ban·quette (bang·ket′) *n.* **1** *Mil.* A raised earthen platform or bank behind an earthwork, upon which soldiers stand to deliver their fire. See illustration under BASTION. **2** An upholstered bench, as along a wall in a restaurant. **3** Any bank, ledge, etc., as a shelf on a sideboard. **4** A sidewalk. [<F, dim. of *banc* bench]

bans (banz) See BAN[1] (*n.* def. 2).

ban·shee (ban′shē, ban·shē′) *n.* In Gaelic folklore, a supernatural being whose wailing outside a house was supposed to foretell a death in the family. [<Irish *bean sídhe* <*bean* woman + *sídhe* fairy]

ban·tam (ban′təm) *n.* **1** A breed of domestic fowl characterized by small size and pugnacity. Also **Ban′tam. 2** Hence, a pugnacious person of small size. — *adj.* Like a bantam; small; combative. [from *Bantam*, Java]

ban·tam·weight (ban′təm·wāt′) *n.* A boxer or wrestler who weighs 118 pounds or less.

ban·ter (ban′tər) *n.* Good-humored ridicule; raillery; repartee. — *v.t.* To tease or ridicule good-naturedly. — *v.i.* To exchange good-natured repartee. [Origin unknown] — **ban′ter·er** *n.* — **ban′ter·ing·ly** *adv.*

Synonyms (noun): badinage, chaff, derision, irony, jeering, mockery, raillery, ridicule, sarcasm, satire. *Banter* is the touching upon some unimportant fault or weakness of another in a way half to pique and half to please; *badinage* is delicate, refined *banter. Raillery* has more sharpness, but is usually good-humored and well-meant. *Irony*, the saying one thing that the reverse may be understood, may be either mild or bitter. *Ridicule* makes a person or thing the subject of contemptuous merriment; *derision* seeks to make the object derided seem utterly despicable—to laugh it to scorn. *Jeering* is loud, rude *ridicule*, as of a hostile crowd or mob. *Mockery* may include mimicry and personal violence, as well as scornful speech. A *satire* is a formal composition; a *sarcasm* may be an impromptu sentence. The *satire* shows up follies to keep people from them; the *sarcasm* hits them because they are foolish, without inquiring whether it will do good or harm. See MOCK, RIDICULE.

bant·ling (bant′ling) *n.* **1** A young child; infant. **2** A bastard. [<G *bänkling* bastard]

Ban·tu (ban′tōō) *n. pl.* **Ban·tu** or **Ban·tus** (-tōōz) **1** A member of any of numerous Negroid tribes of central and southern Africa, including the Kaffirs, Zulus, Bechuanas, Damaras, Swahili, etc. **2** A family of agglutinative languages spoken by these tribes, including Xhosa, Zulu, Bechuana, Swahili, Kikuyu, and at least 80 other languages, and excluding Hottentot, Bushman, and the various Pygmy dialects.

ban·yan (ban′yən) *n.* An East Indian fig-bearing tree (*Ficus benghalensis*) which sends down from its branches roots that develop into new trunks, thus producing a thick and shady grove: also spelled *banian.* [<BANIAN, from the use of the ground under the tree as a market place]

BANYAN TREE
(From 80 to 100 feet high)

ban·zai (bän′zī′) *interj.* A Japanese greeting, battle cry, or cheer, meaning: (May you live) ten thousand years!

ba·o·bab (bā′ō·bab, bä′ō-) *n.* An African tree (*Adansonia digitata*) with a thick trunk, bearing edible, gourdlike fruit; the monkey-bread tree. [<native African name]

bap·tism (bap′tiz·əm) *n.* **1** The act of baptizing or of being baptized; specifically, a sacrament in which water is used to initiate the recipient into a Christian church, to symbolize purification, to acknowledge consecration to Christ, etc. **2** Any initiatory or purifying experience. **3** A religious ablution signifying a purification or consecration, as that by which proselytes were Judaized. **4** In Christian Science, purification by Spirit; submergence in Spirit. [<OF *baptesme* <LL *baptismus* <Gk. *baptismos* immersion] — **bap·tis·mal** (bap·tiz′məl) *adj.* — **bap·tis′mal·ly** *adv.*

baptismal name A name given to a person when he is baptized.

Bap·tist (bap′tist) *n.* **1** A member of various Protestant denominations holding that baptism should be given only to professed adult believers, and, generally, that baptism should be by immersion rather than by sprinkling. **2** One who baptizes. — **the Baptist** John the Baptist.

bap·tis·ter·y (bap′tis·tər·ē, -tis·trē) *n. pl.* **·ter·ies 1** A font or tank for baptism. **2** A part of a church or other building set apart for baptism. Also **bap′tis·try** (-trē).

bap·tize (bap·tīz′, bap′tīz) *v.t.* **·tized, ·tiz·ing 1** To immerse in water or pour water on in the Christian sacrament of baptism, symbolizing dedication to Christ, purification, and admission into a specific church. **2** To

christen or name at the sacrament of baptism.
3 To cleanse; sanctify. **4** To consecrate or
dedicate to special uses by some ceremony
resembling baptism. Also *Brit.* **bap·tise′.**
[< F *baptiser* < LL *baptizare* < Gk. *baptizein*
immerse, wash] — **bap·tiz′er** *n.*

bar¹ (bär) *n.* **1** A piece of solid material, evenly
shaped and long in proportion to its width
and thickness: often used as a unit of quantity,
a fastening, a barrier, etc. **2** Any barrier or
obstruction. **3** A bank, as of sand, at the
entrance to a river or harbor. **4** The enclosed
place in court occupied by counsel; also, the
place where a prisoner stands to plead; hence,
the court or any place of justice, or anything
considered as analogous; a judgment seat.
5 Lawyers collectively; the legal profession.
6 A room or a counter where liquors or refreshments are dispensed. **7** A stripe; a band,
as of color or light. **8** *Music* **a** The vertical
line that divides a staff into measures. **b** A
double bar. **c** The unit of music between two
bars; measure. **9** A horizontal timber or other

BARS IN MUSIC *(def. 8)*
a. Single. *b.* Double.

piece connecting two parts of a framework.
10 The solid metal mouthpiece of a horse's
bridle; also, the space in front of a horse's
upper molar teeth in which the bit is placed;
also, that portion of a horse's foot that bends
toward the frog. **11** In needlepoint, a transverse thread or group of threads passed from
one side or corner of an opening to another:
usually twisted or buttonholed and sometimes
finished with knots. **12** *Law* The preventing
or stopping of an action by showing that the
plaintiff has no right of action. **13** *Her.* An
ordinary formed by two parallel lines drawn
horizontally across a shield, covering one
fifth of the field. See synonyms under BAR-
RIER, IMPEDIMENT, LOCK. — **the Bars** The
Confederate flag. — *v.t.* **barred, bar·ring**
1 To fasten, lock, or secure with or as with
a bar. **2** To confine or shut out with or as
with bars. **3** To obstruct or hinder: to *bar*
the way. **4** To exclude or except. **5** To mark
with bars. See synonyms under HINDER, OB-
STRUCT. — *prep.* Barring; excepting: *bar* none.
[< OF *barre* < LL *barra* bar]

bar² (bär) *n.* The cgs international unit of
pressure, equal to 1,000,000 dynes a square
centimeter or a pressure of 29.531 inches of
mercury at 32° F. and in latitude 45°: sometimes incorrectly called *barye.* [< Gk. *baros*
weight]

Ba·rab·bas (bə·rab′əs) A thief released in place
of Jesus at the demand of the multitude. *Matt.*
xxvii 16–21.

barb¹ (bärb) *n.* **1** A backward-projecting point
on a sharp weapon, as on an arrow, fish hook,
or spear, intended to prevent easy extraction.
2 Any similar sharp point: the *barbs* on a
barbed-wire fence. **3** *Bot.* A beard, as in
certain grains and grasses; awn. **4** *Ornithol.*
One of the lateral processes of a bird's feather.
See illustration under FEATHER. **5** A band or
scarf worn about the neck and covering the
breast: the *barb* of a nun. **6** *pl.* Paps or
folds of the mucous membrane under the
tongue of cattle and horses. **7** *pl.* The disease
characterized by their inflammation. **8** *Obs.*
A beard. — *v.t.* To provide with a barb or
barbs: to *barb* an arrow. [< F *barbe* < L *barba*
beard]

barb² (bärb) *n.* **1** A horse of the breed introduced by the Moors from Barbary into
Spain: noted for speed and endurance. **2** A
blackish or dun pigeon with a short stout
beak. [< F *barbe* < *Barbarie,* ult. < Arabic
Barbar native of N. Africa]

Bar·ba·dos (bär·bā′dōz) An island in the West
Indies east of the Windward Islands, comprising a British colony; 166 square miles;
capital, Bridgetown. — **Bar·ba′di·an** *adj. & n.*

bar·bal (bär′bəl) *adj.* Of or pertaining to the
beard. [< L *barba* beard]

bar·bar·i·an (bär·bâr′ē·ən) *n.* **1** One whose
state of culture is between savagery and civi-

lization; a member of an uncivilized tribe or
race. **2** Any rude, brutal, or uncultured
person. **3** One destitute of, or not caring
for, culture. **4** According to ancient Greek
and Latin usage, a foreigner or outlander.
— *adj.* **1** Uncivilized; cruel; barbarous. **2**
Foreign; alien. See synonyms under BARBA-
ROUS. — **bar·bar′i·an·ism** *n.*

bar·bar·ic (bär·bar′ik) *adj.* **1** Of or characteristic of barbarians. **2** Wild; uncivilized;
crude. See synonyms under BARBAROUS. [<
OF *barbarique* < L *barbaricus* < *barbarus* barbarian. See BARBAROUS.]

bar·ba·rism (bär′bə·riz′əm) *n.* **1** The stage
between savagery and civilization. **2** Absence
of culture; rudeness in manners, speech, living standards, etc. **3** The usage of words or
forms not approved or standard in a language;
also, an instance of this. See synonyms under
LANGUAGE. **4** A barbarous act.

bar·bar·i·ty (bär·bar′ə·tē) *n. pl.* **·ties 1** Brutal
or barbarous conduct. **2** A barbarous deed.
3 A barbarism of language.

bar·ba·rize (bär′bə·rīz) *v.* **·rized, ·riz·ing** *v.t.*
To make barbarous; corrupt, as language,
from classical standards. — *v.i.* To become
barbarous.

bar·ba·rous (bär′bər·əs) *adj.* **1** Pertaining to
or like a barbarian. **2** Uncultivated; lacking
the refinements of advanced civilization; rude.
3 Cruel; brutal; savage. **4** Marked by barba-
risms in speech; unpolished. **5** Rude or harsh
in sound. **6** In Greek and Roman usage, of
or pertaining to foreigners. [< L *barbarus*
foreign, barbarian < Gk. *barbaros* non-
Hellenic, foreign, rude] — **bar′ba·rous·ly** *adv.*
— **bar′ba·rous·ness** *n.*

  Synonyms: atrocious, barbarian, barbaric,
brutal, cruel, inhuman, merciless, rude, savage, uncivilized, uncouth, untamed. *Barbarous*
refers to the worst side of *barbarian* life, and
to acts of cruelty. We may, however, say
barbarous nations, *barbarous* tribes, without
implying anything more than want of civilization and culture. *Antonyms:* civilized, courtly,
cultured, delicate, elegant, graceful, humane,
nice, polite, refined, tender, urbane.

Bar·ba·ry (bär′bər·ē) The Moslem countries
of northern Africa west of Egypt, including
the former Barbary States.

Barbary ape An easily trained, tailless ape
(*Macaca sylvana*) of North Africa and southern Spain: also called *magot.*

Barbary Coast 1 The coastal region of Barbary. **2** A waterfront region of San Francisco
before the earthquake of 1906, infamous for
its saloons, gambling houses, and brothels.

Barbary States Formerly, Tripolitania, Algeria, Tunisia, and, generally, Morocco; centers of piracy until occupation by the European powers in the 19th century.

bar·bate (bär′bāt) *adj.* **1** Bearded. **2** *Bot.*
Tufted with long hairs. [< L *barbatus* bearded
< *barba* beard]

bar·be·cue (bär′bə·kyoo) *n.* **1** An outdoor feast
at which the whole animal carcass is roasted
over an open fire and served. **2** Any meat
roasted on a spit over an open fire. — *v.t.*
·cued, ·cu·ing 1 To roast whole. **2** To roast
(usually beef or pork) in large pieces or whole
over an open fire or in a trench, often using
a highly seasoned sauce. **3** To cook (meat)
with a highly seasoned sauce. [< Sp. *barbacoa*
< Taino *barbacoa* framework of sticks]

barbed (bärbd) *adj.* **1** Having a barb or barbs.
2 Pointed, piercing, or wounding: a *barbed*
remark.

barbed wire Fence wire having barbs at
intervals.

bar·ber (bär′bər) *n.* One who cuts the hair,
shaves the beard, etc., as a business. — *v.t.*
To cut or dress the hair of; shave or trim the
beard of. ◆ Collateral adjective: *tonsorial.*
[< OF *barbeor,* ult. < L *barba* beard]

Bar·ber (bär′bər), **Samuel,** born 1910, U.S.
composer.

bar·ber·ry (bär′ber·ē, -bər·ē) *n.* **1** A shrub
(genus *Berberis*) bearing yellow flowers and
bright-red oblong berries. **2** Its fruit. [<
Med. L *berberis, barbaris*]

bar·ber·shop (bär′bər·shop′) *n.* The place of
business of a barber. — *adj. U.S.* Like, pertaining to, or characterized by close harmony,
especially of male voices in sentimental songs.

bar·bi·tu·rate (bär·bich′ər·it, bär′bə·tōōr′it,
-tyōōr′it) *n.* Any of various derivatives of barbituric acid which act as depressants on the central
nervous system and are often used as sedatives,
hypnotics, and anticonvulsants.

Bar·bi·zon school (bär′bə·zon, *Fr.* bár·bē·zôn′)
A group of French landscape painters of the
19th century, including Corot, Daubigny, Millet,
and Théodore Rousseau. [from *Barbizon,* a village in NE France where they worked]

Bar·bu·da (bär·bōō′də) An island dependency of
Antigua.

bar·bule (bär′byool) *n.* **1** A small barb or beard.
2 A process fringing the barb of a feather. [< L
barbula, dim. of *barba* beard]

bar car *U.S.* A railroad passenger car fitted out
for serving drinks and short orders.

bar·ca·role (bär′kə·rōl) *n.* **1** A Venetian gondolier's song. **2** A melody in imitation of such a
song. Also **bar′ca·rolle.** [< F *barcarolle* < Ital.
barcaruola boatman's song < *barca* boat]

Bar·ce·lo·na (bär′sə·lō′nə, *Sp.* bär′thä·lō′nä) **1** A
port of NE Spain. **2** A province in Catalonia,
Spain; 2,975 square miles; capital, Barcelona. **3**
A city of NE Venezuela.

Poetic A poet. [< Celtic] — **bard′ic** *adj.*

bard² (bärd) *n.* Any piece of armor worn by
horses. — *v.t.* To arm with bards. Also **barde.**
[< F *barde,* ult. < Arabic *al-barda′ah* the pack-
saddle]

Bard of Avon William Shakespeare, born in
Stratford-on-Avon.

bare¹ (bâr) *adj.* **1** Devoid of covering or dress; naked. **2** Destitute of or poorly provided with what
is used or necessary; unfurnished. **3** Unarmed;
unsheathed. **4** Not more than just suffices; mere.
5 Threadbare. **6** Exposed to view; made manifest
or apparent; undisguised. **7** Lacking in embellishment or in interest or attraction; plain; meager: *bare* description. **8** Bareheaded; also, barefoot. See synonyms under BLANK. — *v.t.* **bared,**
bar·ing To make or lay bare; reveal; expose.
Homophone: *bear.* [OE *bær*]

bare² (bâr) Obsolete past tense of BEAR.

bare·back (bâr′bak′) *adj.* Riding a horse without
a saddle. — *adv.* Without a saddle. —
bare′·backed′ *adj.*

bare·faced (bâr′fāst′) *adj.* **1** Having the face
bare. **2** Unconcealed; open. **3** Impudent; audacious. — **bare·fac·ed·ly** (bâr′fā′sid·lē, -fāst′lē) *adv.*
— **bare′·fac·ed·ness** *n.*

bare·fit (bâr′fit) *adj. Scot.* Barefoot.

bare·foot (bâr′foot′) *adj. & adv.* With the feet
bare. Also **bare′·foot′ed** *adj.*

bare·hand·ed (bâr′han′did) *adj.* With the hands
uncovered. — *adv.* **1** In the act of committing a
crime. **2** With the hands uncovered.

bare·head·ed (bâr′hed′id) *adj. & adv.* With head
bare.

bare·leg·ged (bâr′leg′id, -legd′) *adj. & adv.* With
the legs bare.

bare·ly (bâr′lē) *adv.* **1** Only just; scarcely. **2** Na-
kedly. **3** Openly; boldly; plainly. See synonyms
under BUT.

Bar·ents Sea (bar′ənts, bä′rənts) An arm of the
Arctic Ocean north of Norway and European
U.S.S.R.

bare·sark (bâr′särk) *n.* A berserk. — *adv.* Without armor. [Alter. of BERSERK]

bar·fly (bär′flī′) *n. pl.* **·flies** *Slang* A habitual fre-
quenter of barrooms.

bar·gain (bär′gən) *n.* **1** A mutual agreement between persons, especially one to buy or sell
goods. **2** That which is agreed upon or the terms
of the agreement. **3** The agreement as it affects
one of the parties to it: He made a bad *bargain.* **4**
An article bought or offered at a price favorable
to the buyer. See synonyms under CONTRACT. —
into the bargain In addition to what was agreed;
thrown in for good measure; besides. — **to strike**
a bargain To come to an agreement. — *v.i.* **1** To
discuss or haggle over terms for selling or buying. **2** To make a bargain; reach an agreement.
— *v.t.* **3** To barter, as goods for others of equal
value. — **to bargain for** To expect; count on: This
is more than I *bargained for.* [< OF *bargaine;* ult.
origin uncertain]

barge (bärj) *n.* **1** A flat-bottomed freight boat or
lighter for harbors and inland waters, or other
large boat, as for pleasure excursions. **2** A large

and elegantly furnished boat, for pleasure or for state occasions. **3** *Nav.* A boat for the use of a flag officer. **4** *Obs.* In New England, a long, open vehicle, sometimes boat-shaped, for passengers. **5** A house-boat. —*v.* **barged, barg·ing** *v.t.* **1** To transport by barge. —*v.i.* **2** To move clumsily and slowly. **3** *Colloq.* To collide with: with *into.* **4** *Colloq.* To intrude; enter rudely: with *in* or *into.* [< OF < LL *barga.* Akin to BARK³.]

barge·board (bärj′- bôrd′, -bōrd′) *n.* A board, often ornate, attached along the barge couples and following the outline of a gable end.

BARGEBOARD
a.a. Barge course.
b.b. Bargeboards.
c.c. Rafters.
d.d. Barge couples.

barge couple One of a pair of outside rafters (**barge couples**) that support the projecting end of a gable roof.

barge course 1 The part of a gable roof projecting beyond the bargeboards or end wall. **2** A course of bricks laid edgewise to form the coping of a wall.

barge·man (bärj′mən) *n. pl.* **·men** (-mən) One who has charge of or is employed on a barge; a boatman or oarsman. Also *Brit.* **bar·gee** (bär·jē′).

bar·ghest (bär′gest) *n.* A goblin, often dog-shaped, whose appearance is supposed to forebode death or misfortune. [Cf. G *berggeist* gnome]

bar·i·a·trics (bare̅·a̅t′riks) *n.* The branch of medicine concerned with the treatment of the overweight. [< Gk. *baros* weight + -IATRICS]

bar·ic¹ (bar′ik) *adj.* Of or pertaining to weight, especially of air; barometric. [< Gk. *barys* heavy]

bar·ic² (bar′ik) *adj.* Of, pertaining to, derived from, or containing barium.

bar·ite (bâr′īt) *n.* A heavy, vitreous, usually white, orthorhombic barium sulfate, BaSO₄: also called *heavy spar.*

bar·i·tone (bar′ə·tōn) *n.* **1** A male voice of a register higher than bass and lower than tenor. **2** One having such a voice. **3** A brass wind instrument, used chiefly in military bands, having a similar range. —*adj.* **1** Of, like, or pertaining to a baritone. **2** Having the range of a baritone. Also spelled **barytone.** [< Ital. *baritono* < Gk. *barytonos* deep-sounding < *barys* deep + *tonos* tone]

bar·i·um (bâr′ē·əm) *n.* An element (symbol Ba, atomic number 56) of the alkaline-earth group, resembling calcium chemically and forming salts of which the water-soluble ones and the carbonate are poisonous. See PERIODIC TABLE. [< NL < Gk. *barys* heavy]

barium yellow A pale, sulfur-yellow pigment with a greenish tone, made from barium chromate.

bark¹ (bärk) *n.* **1** The short, abrupt, explosive sound characteristically made by a dog. **2** Any sound like this. —*v.i.* **1** To utter a bark, as a dog, or to make a sound like a bark. **2** *Colloq.* To cough. **3** To speak loudly and sharply. **4** *U.S. Slang* To announce the attractions of a show at its entrance. —*v.t.* **5** To say roughly and curtly: He *barked* an order. —**to bark up the wrong tree** *Colloq.* To be mistaken as to one's object or the means of attaining it. [OE *beorcan*]

bark² (bärk) *n.* **1** The tissue covering the stems, branches, and roots of a tree or shrub, extending from the cambium layer to the outer surface. **2** This tissue removed from a particular species for its special medicinal or other properties. —*v.t.* **1** To remove the bark from; scrape; girdle. **2** To rub off or abrade the skin of. **3** To cover with or as with bark. **4** To tan or treat with an infusion of bark [< Scand.]

bark³ (bärk) *n.* **1** A three-masted vessel square-rigged except for the mizzenmast, which is fore-and-aft rigged. **2** *Poetic* Any vessel or boat. Also spelled **barque.** [< F *barque* < LL *barca* bark]

BARK

bark beetle One of several small burrowing beetles (family *Scolytidae*) which breed between the bark and wood of trees, thus destroying the trees. See illustration under INSECT (injurious).

bar·keep·er (bär′kē̅·pər) *n.* **1** One who owns or manages a bar where alcoholic liquors are served. **2** A bartender. Also **bar′keep′.**

bar·ken·tine (bär′kən·tēn) *n.* A three-masted vessel square-rigged on the foremast and fore-and-aft rigged on the other two masts: also spelled **barquentine.**

bark·er¹ (bär′kər) *n.* **1** One who or that which barks or clamors. **2** A person stationed at the door of a shop or entrance to a show to attract patrons by loud, animated patter.

bark·er² (bär′kər) *n.* One who or that which removes bark from trees or works with bark.

bark·less (bärk′lis) *adj.* Unable to bark, as certain breeds of dogs.

bar·ley¹ (bär′lē) *n.* **1** A hardy, bearded cereal grass (*Hordeum vulgare*) of temperate regions, with long leaves, stout awns, and triple spikelets at the joints which distinguish it from wheat. **2** The grain borne by this grass. [OE *baerlīc*]

bar·ley² (bär′lē) *interj. Scot.* Truce!: a cry in children's games: also spelled *barly.*

bar·ley·corn (bär′lē·kôrn) *n.* **1** A grain of barley. **2** A unit of measure, originally the breadth of a barley grain, equal to one third of an inch. **3** A planed groove between moldings. —**John Barleycorn** A humorous personification of malt liquor, or of intoxicating liquors in general.

barley sugar A clear, brittle confection made by boiling sugar with a barley extract.

barley water A drink made by boiling barley in water, for invalids, etc.

barm (bärm) *n.* The froth or foam rising on fermented malt liquors. [OE *beorma* yeast]

bar·maid (bär′mād′) *n.* A woman bartender.

Bar·me·cide (bär′mə·sīd) Any member of a former wealthy and princely family of Baghdad; specifically, in the *Arabian Nights*, the member of this family who served an imaginary feast to a beggar, setting only empty dishes before him.

Barmecide feast Any imaginary, illusory, or disappointing hospitality or generosity.

bar miz·vah (bär mits′və) In Judaism, a boy commencing his thirteenth year, the age of religious duty and responsibility; also, the ceremony celebrating this: also spelled *bar mitzvah* or *mitzwah.*

barm·y (bär′mē) *adj.* **barm·i·er, barm·i·est 1** Full of barm; frothy. **2** *Brit. Slang* Silly; flighty. Also *Scot.* **barm′ie.**

barn¹ (bärn) *n.* A building for storing hay, stabling livestock, etc. [OE *bern*]

barn² (bärn) *n. Physics* A unit of area used in measuring the cross-section of atomic nuclei: equal to 10⁻²⁴ square centimeter: so called in allusion to the phrase "He can't hit the side of a barn door."

bar·na·cle¹ (bär′nə·kəl) *n.* **1** A marine shellfish (order *Cirripedia*) that attaches itself to rocks, ship bottoms, etc.; especially, the **rock barnacle** (*Balanus balanoides*) and the **goose barnacle** (*Lepas fascicularis*), the latter so called because the barnacle goose was once supposed to hatch from it. **2** A European wild goose of northern seas (*Branta leucopsis*): also **barnacle goose. 3** Something or someone that clings tenaciously; a persistent follower; a hanger-on. [ME *bernacle*; origin uncertain] —**bar′na·cled** *adj.*

bar·na·cle² (bär′nə·kəl) *n. Usually pl.* An instrument for pinching the nose of an unruly horse. [< OF *bernacle,* dim. of *bernac* a bit]

barn dance 1 A dance held in a barn, especially with square dances, rural music, etc. **2** A country dance resembling the schottische.

barn owl A North American owl (*Tyto alba pratincola*) with brownish upper parts and white underparts flecked with black: often found in barns, where it preys on mice.

BARN OWL

barn·storm (bärn′storm′) *v.i.* **1** To tour rural districts, giving plays, making political speeches, etc. **2** To tour rural districts, giving exhibitions of stunt flying, short airplane excursions,

etc. —**barn′storm′er** *n.* —**barn′storm′ing** *n.* [< BARN + STORM, *v.*]

barn swallow The common swallow of North America and Europe: it frequently nests in the eaves of barns and other buildings.

Bar·num (bär′nəm), **P(hineas) T(aylor)**, 1810–91, U.S. showman and circus proprietor.

barn·yard (bärn′yärd′) *n.* An enclosed space adjoining a barn.

baro– *combining form* Weight; atmospheric pressure; barometric. [< Gk. *baros* weight]

bar·o·dy·nam·ics (bar′ō·dī·nam′iks) *n.* The dynamics of heavy structures, as dams, bridges, etc., especially in relation to pressure and gravitation. —**bar′o·dy·nam′ic** *adj.*

bar·o·gram (bar′ə·gram) *n.* The record of a barograph.

bar·o·graph (bar′ə·graf, -gräf) *n.* An automatically recording barometer. —**bar′o·graph′ic** *adj.*

ba·rom·e·ter (bə·rom′ə·tər) *n.* **1** An instrument for measuring atmospheric pressure: used for forecasting the weather, measuring elevations, etc. **2** Anything that indicates changes. —**bar·o·met·ric** (bar′ə·met′rik) or **·ri·cal** *adj.* —**bar′o·met′ri·cal·ly** *adv.* —**ba·rom′e·try** *n.*

bar·on (bar′ən) *n.* **1** A member of the lowest order of hereditary nobility in several European countries; also, the dignity or rank itself. The title was used at first in England to designate one who held land by military or other honorable service. **2** *U.S.* One who has great power in a commercial field: a *coal* baron. **3** In the Middle Ages, a feudal tenant of the king; a noble. ◆ Homophone: *barren.* [< OF < LL *baro, -onis* man < Gmc.]

bar·on·age (bar′ən·ij) *n.* **1** Barons collectively. **2** The dignity or rank of a baron.

bar·on·ess (bar′ən·is) *n.* **1** The wife or widow of a baron. **2** A woman holding a barony in her own right.

bar·on·et (bar′ən·it, -net) *n.* **1** An inheritable English title, below that of baron. **2** The bearer of the title, who is not a member of the nobility: A baronet is designated by "Sir" before the name and "Baronet" or the abbreviation "Bart." after.

bar·on·et·age (bar′ən·it·ij, -ə·net′-) *n.* **1** Baronets collectively. **2** The dignity or rank of a baronet.

bar·on·et·cy (bar′ən·it·sē, -ə·net′-) *n. pl.* **·cies 1** The title or rank of a baronet. **2** The patent giving such rank.

ba·rong (bä·rông′, -rong′) *n.* In the Philippines, a cutlas cleaverlike weapon used by the Moros.

ba·ro·ni·al (bə·rō′nē·əl) *adj.* Pertaining to or befitting a baron, a barony, or the order of barons.

bar·o·ny (bar′ə·nē) *n. pl.* **·nies** The rank, dignity, or domain of a baron.

ba·roque (bə·rōk′) *adj.* **1** Irregularly shaped: said of pearls. **2** Of, like, or characteristic of a style of art, architecture, and decoration characterized by extravagant and fantastic forms, curved rather than straight lines in ornament, and exaggerated and theatrical effects, as those developed in the 16th and 17th centuries in Europe. —*n.* **1** The baroque style. **2** An object, ornament, or design in this style. [< F < Pg. *barroco* rough or imperfect pearl]

BAROQUE (*def.* 2)
Venice: Church of Santa
Maria della Salute,
1631–56

bar·o·scope (bar′ə·skōp) *n.* **1** An instrument for approximately indicating atmospheric pressure; a weatherglass. **2** A device indicating the loss in weight of objects in air. —**bar′o·scop′ic** (-skop′ik) or **·i·cal** *adj.*

bar·o·switch (bar′ə·swich) *n. Meteorol.* That component of a radiosonde apparatus which indicates pressure values during the ascent and, in a definite order, actuates the temperature, humidity, and other recording components.

ba·rouche (bə·rōōsh′) *n.* A four-wheeled, low-bodied pleasure-vehicle with folding top, two inside seats facing each other, and an upper outside seat for the driver. [<G *barutsche* <Ital. *baroccio* <L *bis* twice + *rota* wheel]

Ba·roz·zi (bä·rôt′tsē), **Giacomo**, 1507–73, Italian architect: also known as *Giacomo da Vignola*. Also *Barocchio*.

barque (bärk), **bar·quen·tine** (bär′kən·tēn) See BARK[3], BARKENTINE.

bar·rack[1] (bar′ək) *n.* **1** *Usually pl.* A structure or group of structures for the lodgment of soldiers. **2** *Usually pl.* A temporary or rough shelter for a gang of laborers, etc. **3** A light adjustable roof for sheltering hay, etc. — *v.t* & *v.i.* To house in barracks. [<F *baraque* <Ital. *baracca* soldiers' tent]

bar·rack[2] (bar′ək) *v.t. & v.i. Austral.* To shout for or against (a group, team, etc.): often with *for* or *against*. [<dial. E]

barracks bag A soldier's cloth bag with a draw cord, for holding clothing and equipment. Also **barrack bag.**

bar·ra·coon (bar′ə·kōōn′) *n.* A barrack or enclosure for the confinement of slaves or convicts. [<Sp. *barracon*, aug. of *barraca* barrack]

bar·ra·cu·da (bar′ə·kōō′də) *n.* *pl.* **·da** or **·das** A voracious pike–like fish (genus *Sphyraena*) of tropical seas. The **great barracuda** (*S. barracuda*), found off the Florida coast, is often 8 feet long. [<Sp.]

bar·rage[1] (bär′ij) *n.* **1** The act of barring. **2** An artificial bar placed in a watercourse, to increase its depth for irrigating, etc. [<F <*barre* bar]

bar·rage[2] (bə·räzh′) *n.* **1** *Mil.* Concentrated fire on a part of an enemy's lines to prevent the advance of reinforcements. **2** *Mil.* A curtain of fire to close off part of the front from enemy assault, isolate part of his position, or, by movable curtain, to protect advance of troops. **3** Any overwhelming attack, as of words or blows. — **balloon barrage** A curtain of captive balloons raised above a defense area to entangle enemy aircraft and prevent penetration of the area. — **box barrage** A curtain of artillery fire falling around an area and preventing the escape or reinforcement of troops. [<F (*tir de*) *barrage* barrage (fire)]

bar·ra·mun·da (bar′ə·mun′də) *n.* *pl.* **·da** or **·das** A large, edible, dipnoan mudfish (*Neoceratodus forsteri*) of Australia: also called *ceratodus*. Also **bar·ra·mun′di** (-dē) [<native Australian name]

bar·ran·ca (bə·rang′kə) *n. SW U.S.* A deep ravine or gorge. [<Sp.]

bar·ra·tor (bar′ə·tər) *n.* One guilty of barratry. Also **bar′ra·ter.**

bar·ra·try (bar′ə·trē) *n.* *pl.* **·tries** **1** Any wilful and unlawful act committed by the master or mariners of a ship, whereby the owners sustain injury. **2** In Scots law, the acceptance of a bribe by a judge. **3** The buying or selling of ecclesiastical positions. **4** *Law* The offense of exciting lawsuits; the stirring up of quarrels, spreading false rumors, etc. Also spelled *barretry*. [<OF *baraterie* misuse of office <*barat* fraud] — **bar′ra·trous** *adj.*

barred (bärd) *adj.* **1** Fastened with bars. **2** Obstructed by bars. **3** Made of bars. **4** Ornamented with bars; striped. **5** Prohibited; not allowed.

bar·rel (bar′əl) *n.* **1** A large, round, wooden vessel, made with staves and hoops, having a flat base and top and slightly bulging sides. **2** As much as a barrel will hold: a varying measure of quantity. The standard U.S. barrel for fruits, vegetables, and other dry commodities contains 7,056 cubic inches. A barrel of petroleum contains 42 U.S. gallons. **3** Something resembling or having the form of a barrel. **4** *Ornithol.* The quill of a feather. **5** *Naut.* The rotating drum of a windlass, capstan, etc., around which the rope winds. **6** The cylindrical box containing the mainspring of a watch, around which the chain is wound. **7** In firearms, the tube through which the projectile is discharged. **8** The piston chamber of a pump. — *v.* **bar′reled** or **bar′relled, bar′rel·ing** or **bar′rel·ling** *v.t.* To put or pack in a barrel. — *v.i. U.S. Slang* To move at high speed. [<OF *baril*; ult. origin unknown]

barrel catch The mechanism which locks the barrel and cylinder of a revolver in firing position.

barrel chair An upholstered chair having a high, rounded back shaped like the vertical half of a barrel.

bar·rel·house (bar′əl·hous′) *n.* **1** A cheap drinking house. **2** An early style of jazz, originally played in barrelhouses.

barrel organ A hand organ.

barrel roll *Aeron.* A complete rotation of an airplane around its longitudinal axis.

MODERN BARREL CHAIR

bar·ren (bar′ən) *adj.* **1** Incapable of producing, or not producing, offspring; sterile. **2** Not producing fruit; unfruitful. **3** Unprofitable, as an enterprise. **4** Lacking in interest or attractiveness; dull. **5** Not producing; lacking: *barren of creative effort.* See synonyms under BLANK, MEAGER. — *n.* **1** A tract of barren land. **2** *Usually pl.* A tract of level land, having a sandy soil without trees and producing only scrubby growth. ◆ Homophone *baron.* [<OF *baraigne*] — **bar′ren·ly** *adv.* — **bar′ren·ness** *n.*

Barren Grounds An arctic prairie region of northern Canada, extending west from Hudson Bay. Also **Barren Lands.**

bar·ret (bar′it) *n.* **1** A biretta. **2** A flat cap formerly worn by soldiers. [<F *barrette* <LL *birettum* cap <*birrus* red cloak]

bar·re·try (bar′ə·trē) See BARRATRY.

bar·rette (bə·ret′) *n.* **1** A small bar or comb with a clasp used for keeping a woman's hair in place. **2** In fencing, the guard of a foil. [<F, dim. of *barre* bar]

bar·ri·cade (bar′ə·kād′, bar′ə·kād) *n.* **1** A barrier hastily built for obstruction or for defense. **2** Any obstruction or barrier closing a passage, as a street, a waterway, etc. See synonyms under BARRIER, RAMPART. — *v.t.* **·cad·ed, ·cad·ing** To enclose, obstruct, or defend with a barricade or barricades. See synonyms under OBSTRUCT. [<F <Sp. *barricada* barrier <*barrica* barrel; the first barricades having been barrels filled with earth, stones, etc.] — **bar′ri·cad′er** *n.*

Bar·rie (bar′ē), **Sir James Matthew,** 1860–1937, Scottish novelist and playwright.

bar·ri·er (bar′ē·ər) *n.* **1** Any line of boundary and separation, natural or artificial, placed or serving as a limitation or obstruction. **2** Something that bars, keeps out, obstructs progress, or prevents encroachment: a *barrier* to ambition; a language *barrier.* **3** A palisade or stockade to defend the entrance to a fortified place. **4** A fortress on a frontier commanding a main passage into a country; a customs gate. **5** A fence or railing to shut out trespassers or strangers. **6** The narrow blank space which separates the frames of a motion–picture film or divides the sound track from the picture track. **7** *pl.* The palisades enclosing the ground for a tournament; the lists. **8** *Geog. Sometimes cap.* The part of the ice cap of Antarctica extending over the ocean beyond the land. [<OF *barriere* <*barre* bar]

Synonyms: bar, barricade, breastwork, bulwark, hindrance, obstacle, obstruction, parapet, prohibition, rampart, restraint, restriction. A *bar* is something that is or may be firmly fixed, ordinarily with intent to prevent entrance or egress; as, the *bars* of a prison cell. A *barrier* obstructs, but is not necessarily impassable. *Barricade* denotes some hastily piled obstruction, commonly an improvised street fortification. A *parapet* is a low or breast–high wall, as about the edge of a roof; in military use, such a wall for the protection of troops; a *rampart* is the embankment surrounding a fort, on which the *parapet* is raised; the word *rampart* is often used as including the *parapet.* *Bulwark* is a general word for any defensive wall, but in present technical use it signifies the raised side of a ship above the upper deck, topped by the rail. Compare BOUNDARY, IMPEDIMENT, RAMPART. *Antonyms:* admittance, entrance, opening, passage, road, thoroughfare, transit.

barrier cream See COSMETIC (*n.* def. 3).

barrier reef A long, narrow ridge of rock or coral parallel to the coast and close to or above the surface of the sea.

Barrier Reef See GREAT BARRIER REEF.

bar·ring (bär′ing) *prep.* Excepting; apart from.

bar·ri·o (bär′rē·ō) *n.* *pl.* **·os** **1** In Spanish–speaking countries, a district or ward of a town or city. **2** *U.S.* A section of a city or town populated largely by Spanish–speaking people. [<Sp.]

bar·ris·ter (bar′is·tər) *n.* In English law, an advocate who argues cases in the courts, as distinguished from a *solicitor,* who prepares them. In the United States an attorney combines the two functions. [<BAR[1]]

bar·room (bär′rōōm′, -rōōm′) *n.* A room where alcoholic liquors are served across a counter.

bar·row[1] (bar′ō) *n.* **1** A frame, tray, or box, with or without a wheel or wheels, having handles or shafts by which it is pushed, pulled, or carried. **2** The load carried on or capacity of a barrow. **3** A wheelbarrow. **4** A pushcart. [OE *bearwe*]

bar·row[2] (bar′ō) *n.* **1** A burial mound; cairn. **2** A hill. [OE *beorg* hill, burial mound]

bar·row[3] (bar′ō) *n.* A castrated pig. [OE *bearg* pig]

Bar·row (bar′ō), **Point** A cape of the northernmost part of Alaska in the Arctic Ocean.

bar·tend·er (bär′ten′dər) *n.* One who serves liquors over a bar.

bar·ter (bär′tər) *v.i.* To trade by exchange of goods or services without use of money. — *v.t.* To trade (goods or services) for something of equal value. — *n.* The exchanging of commodities or a commodity given in exchange. See synonyms under BUSINESS. [<OF *barater* exchange] — **bar′ter·er** *n.*

Bar·thol·di (bär·thol′dē, *Fr.* bȧr·tôl·dē′), **Frédéric Auguste,** 1834–1904, French sculptor of the Statue of Liberty.

bar·ti·zan (bär′tə·zən, bär′tə·zan′) *n.* A turret, with loopholes, jutting out from a wall. [Alter. of *bratticing* <BRATTICE] — **bar·ti·zaned** (bär′tə·zənd, bär′tə·zand′) *adj.*

BARTIZAN ON A TOWER

Bart·lett (bärt′lit) *n.* A variety of large, juicy pear developed in England about 1770 and introduced into America by Enoch Bartlett of Dorchester, Massachusetts. Also **Bartlett pear.**

Bart·lett (bärt′lit), **John,** 1820–1905, U.S. publisher; compiled *Familiar Quotations,* 1855. — **Josiah,** 1729–1795, American physician and Revolutionary leader. — **Robert Abram,** 1875–1946, Canadian Arctic explorer.

Bar·tok (bär′tôk), **Béla** (bā′lä), 1881–1945, Hungarian composer.

Bar·to·lom·me·o (bär′tō·lōm·mâ′ō), **Fra,** 1475–1517, Florentine painter: also known as *Baccio della Porta.*

Bar·ton (bär′tən), **Clara,** 1821–1912, founder of the American Red Cross.

bar·ye (bar′ē) *n.* In the cgs system, a unit expressing a pressure of one dyne a square centimeter. [<Gk. *barys* heavy]

Ba·rye (bȧ·rē′), **Antoine Louis,** 1795–1875, French sculptor.

bar·y·on (bar′ē·on) *n. Physics* Any strongly interacting particle whose spin is half an odd integer; a nucleon or hyperon. [<Gk. *barys* heavy + -ON]

bar·y·sphere (bar′i·sfir) *n. Geol.* The centrosphere. [<Gk. *barys* heavy + SPHERE]

bar·y·ta (bə·rī′tə) *n.* Barium oxide. [<Gk. *barytēs* weight <*barys* heavy]

ba·ry·tes (bə·rī′tēz) *n.* Barite.

bar·y·tone[1] (bar′ə·tōn) *n.* In Greek grammar, a word having the last syllable unaccented. [<Gk. *barytonos* unaccented]

bar·y·tone[2] (bar′ə·tōn) See BARITONE.

ba·sal (bā′səl) *adj.* **1** Pertaining to, of, or at the base. **2** Basic; fundamental. **3** *Physiol.* Designating a standard of reference or comparison: *basal* metabolism. **4** *Surg.* Serving to prepare for deeper levels of unconsciousness: *basal* anesthesia preliminary to surgical anesthesia. — **ba′sal·ly** *adv.*

basal metabolism *Physiol.* The minimum energy, measured in calories, required by the body at rest in maintaining essential vital activities.

ba·salt (bə·sôlt′, bas′ôlt) *n.* **1** A fine-grained, igneous, volcanic rock of high density and dark color, composed chiefly of plagioclase and pyroxene, usually exhibiting a columnar structure. **2** A black, unglazed pottery resembling basalt, developed by Josiah Wedgwood: also **ba·salt′ware′.** [<L *basaltes* dark marble] — **ba·sal′tic** *adj.*

bas·cule (bas′kyōol) *n.* A mechanical apparatus

BASCULE BRIDGE
Tower Bridge, London

of which each end counterbalances the other: used in a kind of drawbridge (**bascule bridge**) operated by a counterpoise. [<F, see-saw]

base[1] (bās) *n.* **1** The lowest or supporting part of anything; bottom; foundation. **2** *Ling.* The form of a word used in making derivatives, as by adding prefixes or suffixes; root or stem. **3** A determining ingredient; a common element with which other more distinctive elements unite to form a product; essential or preponderant element or part of anything. **4** *Chem.* **a** A compound which is capable of so uniting with an acid as to neutralize its acid properties and form a salt, as sodium hydroxide, NaOH. **b** A compound that yields hydroxyl ions in solution. **c** Any molecule or radical that takes up protons. **5** A basis of military or naval operations or of supplies. **6** In baseball, any one of the four points of the diamond; also, in certain other games, or in a race, the goal or starting point. **7** Any point, part, line, number, or quantity from which a reckoning, inference, or conclusion proceeds, or on which any other dimension depends; any principle or datum; a basis: the *base* of an argument, the *base* of a triangle. **8** A very accurately measured line on the earth's surface, from whose known length other lines in a survey are determined. **9** A number on which a mathematical system or calculation depends: In the Arabic notation, 10 is the *base* of the decimal system. **10** *Geom.* **a** That side of a rectilineal figure or that face of a solid on which the figure is conceived to be erected. **b** A side or face which has some special mark or character, or to which other parts are referred. **11** *Biol.* The end opposite to the apex; the point of attachment. **12** *Archit.* The lowest member of a structure, as the basement of a building, the plinth (when present) and base moldings of a column, or the lowest course of a wall; a pedestal. **13** The celluloid component of a motion-picture film. **14** *Her.* The lower part of the shield. — **off base 1** In baseball, not on the base one should be on. **2** *Colloq.* Utterly wrong about something. — *v.t.* **based, bas·ing 1** To place or ground on a logical basis, as an argument, decision, or theory: with *on* or *upon.* **2** To make or form a base for. — *adj.* **1** Serving as a base: a *base* line. **2** Situated at or near the base: a *base* angle. ◆ Homophone: *bass*[2]. [<F <L *basis* <Gk. *basis* step, pedestal <*bainein* go]

base[2] (bās) *adj.* **1** Low in sentiment, morals, or rank. **2** Low in value. **3** Alloyed, debased, or counterfeit, as money; not silver or gold: *base* metals. **4** *Music* Bass. **5** In English law, held by villeinage: opposed to *free*: said of a tenure of an estate. **6** *Obs.* Of humble or ignoble birth; also, illegitimate. **7** Menial; servile. **8** Not classical: said of languages. ◆ Homophone: *bass*[2]. [<OF *bas* <LL *bassus* low] — **base′ly** *adv.* — **base′ness** *n.*

Synonyms: abject, beggarly, cheap, contemptible, cringing, degraded, degrading, des-

picable, groveling, ignoble, infamous, low, low-minded, mean, mean-spirited, menial, miserable, obsequious, paltry, poor, poor-spirited, scurvy, servile, shabby, slavish, sneaking, sordid, squalid, subservient, vile, worthless, wretched. *Antonyms:* arrogant, conceited, dignified, eminent, esteemed, exalted, haughty, honorable, illustrious, independent, insolent, lofty, noble, pompous, princely, proud, self-assertive, self-conceited, self-reliant, self-respectful, supercilious, superior, supreme, vain, worthy.

base·ball (bās′bôl) *n.* **1** A game played with a wooden bat and a hard ball by two teams, properly of nine players each, one team being at bat and the other in the field, alternately, for a minimum of nine innings: the game is played on a field having four bases marking the course each player must take in scoring a run. **2** The ball used in this game.

base·board (bās′bôrd′, -bōrd′) *n.* **1** A board skirting the interior wall of a room, next to the floor. **2** A board forming the base of anything.

base-born (bās′bôrn′) *adj.* **1** Born out of wedlock. **2** Of low birth; plebeian. **3** Mean.

base-burn·er (bās′bûr′nər) *n.* A coal stove or furnace in which the fuel is fed from above into a central fuel chamber.

base command *Mil.* An area organized for the unified administration of all military operations carried on by the base or bases functioning within it.

base hit In baseball, a hit by which the batter reaches base without help of an opposing player's error or without forcing out a runner previously on base.

Ba·sel (bä′zəl) A city on the Rhine in northern Switzerland: ancient *Basilia*: also *Basle*: French *Bâle.*

base·less (bās′lis) *adj.* Without foundation in fact; unfounded; groundless. See synonyms under VAIN.

base level The lowest level of erosion possible to a watercourse in any geographical area.

base·man (bās′mən) *n. pl.* **·men** (-mən) A baseball player stationed at first, second, or third base.

base·ment (bās′mənt) *n.* **1** The lowest floor of a building, usually underground and just beneath the principal story. **2** The substructure or the basal portion of any building or other structure or member.

base metal 1 Any metal which oxidizes easily when exposed to or heated in air, as iron, lead, or tin: opposed to *noble* metal. **2** *Chem.* A metal whose hydroxide is soluble in water.

ba·sen·ji (bə·sen′jē) *n.* A small, barkless dog, similar in build to a fox terrier, with a smooth, reddish coat and white-tipped tail and feet. [<Afrikaans, bush thing]

BASENJI

base of operations *Mil.* A region or area from which a military force begins an offensive action and to which it falls back in case of withdrawal.

base runner In baseball, a member of the team at bat who has reached base.

bas·es[1] (bā′siz) Plural of BASE.

ba·ses[2] (bā′sēz) Plural of BASIS.

bash (bash) *v.t.* To strike heavily; smash in. — *n.* A smashing blow. [? Akin to Dan. *baske* thwack]

bash·ful (bash′fəl) *adj.* **1** Shrinking from notice; shy; timid; diffident. **2** Characterized by or indicating sensitiveness and timid modesty. [<*bash,* var. of ABASH + -FUL] — **bash′ful·ly** *adv.* — **bash′ful·ness** *n.*

bash·lyk (bash′lik) *n.* A fitted cloth hood covering the head and ears. Also **bash′lik.** [<Russian]

ba·sic (bā′sik) *adj.* **1** Pertaining to, forming, or like a base or basis. **2** Essential; fundamental. **3** *Chem.* **a** Above normal in base-producing constituents: a *basic* salt. **b** Yielding hydroxyl ions when dissolved in an ionizing solvent. **c** Showing an alkaline reaction. **4** *Geol.* Containing comparatively little silica: said of igneous rocks, as basalt. **5** *Metall.* Designating the basic process of making steel. — *n.* In the U.S. Army, an enlisted man who

has completed or is pursuing the minimum course of military training.

ba·si·cal·ly (bā′sik·lē) *adv.* Essentially; fundamentally.

ba·sic·i·ty (bā·sis′ə·tē) *n. Chem.* **1** The state or condition of being a base. **2** The ability of an acid to unite with one or more equivalents of a base, depending upon the number of replaceable hydrogen atoms contained in a molecule of the acid.

basic oxide A metallic oxide which is capable of interacting with an acid to form a salt, as calcium oxide or lime, CaO.

basic process A method of steelmaking which uses a furnace lined with a basic refractory material, as dolomite or magnesite: it yields a **basic slag** rich in lime and phosphorus.

ba·si·fy (bā′sə·fī) *v.t.* **·fied, ·fy·ing** To change into a base by chemical means. — **ba′si·fi·ca′tion** *n.* — **ba′si·fi′er** *n.*

bas·il (baz′əl) *n.* **1** Any of certain aromatic plants of the mint family (genus *Ocimum*), especially the European *sweet basil* (*O. basilicum*). **2** The American mountain mint (genus *Pycnanthemum*) or **wild basil.** [<OF *basile* <L *basilicum* <Gk. *basilikon* (*phyton*) royal (plant), basil <*basileus* king]

bas·i·lar (bas′ə·lər) *adj.* Pertaining to or situated at the base; basal. Also **bas·i·lar·y** (bas′ə·ler′ē).

basilar membrane *Anat.* The membrane separating the two vestibules of the cochlea of the ear and acting as a receptor of the sound vibrations transmitted by the auditory nerve.

ba·sil·ic (bə·sil′ik) *adj.* **1** Pertaining to a basilica. **2** Royal. **3** *Anat.* Pertaining to the largest vein of the arm. Also **ba·sil′i·cal.** [<Gk. *basilikos* kingly]

ba·sil·i·ca (bə·sil′i·kə) *n.* **1** Originally, in ancient Athens, a portico used as a court of justice. **2** In ancient Rome, a rectangular building divided into nave and aisles: used as a hall of justice and adopted as the type of the earliest buildings for Christian worship. **3** A church shaped like a Roman basilica. **4** In the Roman Catholic Church, a church accorded certain liturgical privileges. [<L <Gk. *basilikē,* fem. of *basilikos* royal] — **ba·sil′i·can** *adj.*

bas·i·lisk (bas′ə·lisk) *n.* **1** A fabled reptile of the African desert whose breath and look were fatal. **2** A tropical American lizard (genus *Basiliscus,* family *Iguanidae*) having an erectile crest and a dilatable pouch on the head. [<L *basiliscus* <Gk. *basiliskos,* dim. of *basileus* king]

THE HOODED BASILISK

ba·sin (bā′sən) *n.* **1** A round, wide, shallow vessel, often with sloping sides, used especially for holding liquids. **2** The amount that a basin will hold. **3** A sink or wash bowl. **4** A depression in the earth's surface, as a valley, or the region drained by a river. **5** A depressed region in the floor of the ocean. **6** A comparatively circular and shallow area or arm of the sea: the Minas *Basin.* [<OF *bacin* <LL *bachinus* <*bacca* bowl] — **ba′sined** *adj.* — **ba′sin·like′** *adj.*

ba·si·net (bas′ə·nit, -net) *n.* A small, close-fitting helmet. [<OF *bacinet,* dim. of *bacin* basin]

ba·si·on (bā′sē·ən) *n. Anat.* The point where the anterior border of the foramen magnum of the skull cuts the median plane. [<Gk. *basis* base]

ba·sip·e·tal (bā·sip′ə·təl) *adj. Bot.* Growing in the direction of the base.

ba·sis (bā′sis) *n. pl.* **ba·ses** (bā′sēz) **1** That on which anything rests; support; foundation. **2** Fundamental principle. **3** The chief component or ingredient of a thing. [<L <Gk., base, pedestal]

bask (bask, bäsk) *v.i.* **1** To lie in and enjoy a pleasant warmth, as of the sun or a fire. **2** To enjoy or expose oneself to a benign influence, pleasant situation, etc.: to *bask* in the favor of a king. — *v.t.* **3** To expose to warmth. [<ON *badhask* bathe oneself]

Bas·ker·ville (bas′kər·vil), **John,** 1706–75.

English printer and type founder; designer of the type face known by his name.

bas·ket (bas'kit, bäs'-) n. **1** A container made of interwoven twigs, splints, rushes, strips, etc. **2** Something resembling a basket, as the structure under a balloon for carrying passengers or ballast. **3** The amount a basket will hold; a basketful. **4** An openwork guard over the hilt of a sword: also **basket hilt. 5** In basketball, either of the goals, consisting of a metal ring with a cord net suspended from it; also, the point or points made by throwing the ball through the basket. **6** *Mil.* The platform supporting the two operators of a tank turret, which rotates with the turret. [ME; origin unknown] — **bas'ket·like'** *adj.*

bas·ket·ball (bas'kit·bôl', bäs'-) n. **1** An indoor game played by two teams of five men each, in which the object is to throw the ball through the elevated goal (basket) at the opponent's end of a zoned, oblong court. On each team the players consist of a center, two forwards, and two guards. **2** The round, inflated leather ball used in this game.

basket dance *Anthropol.* A ceremonial dance centering the action on a basket held in the left hand of a woman dancer, who strews grain or meal from it as a symbol of vegetation fertility: danced in many culture areas of the Old and New World.

bas·ket·fish (bas'kit·fish', bäs'-) n. A starfish (genus *Gorgonocephalus*) having many branched or interlacing arms: common off the New England coast.

Basket Maker One of a class of prehistoric cave-dwelling people of SW North America, of a culture more ancient than the cliff-dwellers or Pueblos, characterized by their basket-making and lack of pottery.

basket meeting *U.S.* A social gathering to which people bring their suppers in a basket.

bas·ket·ry (bas'kit·rē, bäs'-) n. **1** Baskets collectively; basketwork. **2** The art or craft of making baskets.

bas·ket·weave (bas'kit·wēv', bäs'-) n. A weave with two or more warp and filling threads woven side by side to resemble a plaited basket.

bas·ket·work (bas'kit·wûrk', bäs'-) n. A fabric or texture of woven or plaited osiers or twigs, or an imitation of it in some other substance; wickerwork.

basking shark A shark (*Cetorhinus maximus*) of the North Atlantic, attaining a length of over 30 feet and valued for its liver oil: named from its habit of basking on the surface of the water.

Basle (bäl) See BASEL.

ba·so·phile (bā'sə·fīl, -fil) n. *Biol.* A tissue or cell having a special affinity for basic staining dyes: also spelled *basiphile.* [<BASIC (dye) + -PHILE] — **ba·so·phil·ic** (bā'sə·fil'ik), **ba·soph·i·lous** (bā·sof'ə·ləs) *adj.*

ba·so·phil·i·a (bā'sə·fil'ē·ə) n. *Pathol.* A condition in which an excessive number of basophiles are present in the blood.

basque (bask) n. A woman's closely fitting bodice, separate from the dress skirt: originally from the Basque costume.

Basque (bask) n. **1** One of a people living in the western Pyrenees in Spain and France, of unknown racial origin but having such distinctive racial traits that they are believed to be unrelated to any other racial stock. **2** The agglutinative language of the Basque people, unrelated to any other language: possibly a survival of the lost ancient Iberian. — *adj.* Of or pertaining to the Basques or to their language, or to the Basque Provinces.

Basque Provinces Three provinces in northern Spain on the Bay of Biscay; combined area, 2,803 square miles. *Spanish* **Vas·con·ga·das** (väs'kōng·gä'thäs).

Bas·ra (bus'rə) A port of SE Iraq on the Shatt-el-Arab: also *Bassora, Bussora, Busra.* Also **Bas'rah.**

bas–re·lief (bä'ri·lēf', bas'-) n. Sculpture or a piece of sculpture in which the figures project only slightly from the background: also called *basso-rilievo.* See RELIEF. [<F <Ital. *basso* low + *rilievo* relief]

bass¹ (bas) n. **1** One of various spiny-finned, marine and fresh-water food fishes, especially the European sea bass (*Dicentrarchus labrax*), the American striped bass (*Roccus lineatus*), and the black basses (genus *Micropterus*). **2** The European perch (*Perca fluviatilis*). **3** The cabrilla (def. 2). [OE *bærs*]

bass² (bās) n. *Music* **1** The lowest-pitched male singing voice. **2** A deep, low sound, as of this voice or of certain low-pitched instruments. **3** The notes in the lowest register of the piano, pipe organ, etc. **4** The lowest part in vocal or instrumental music. **5** One who sings or an instrument that plays such a part, especially a bass viol. **6** Such parts collectively. — *adj.* **1** Low in pitch; having a low musical range. **2** Pertaining to, for, or able to play bass. ◆ Homophone: *base.* [<OF *bas* low; infl. in spelling by Ital. *basso*]

bass³ (bas) n. **1** The basswood. **2** Bast. [Alter. of BAST]

bass clef (bās) *Music* **1** The sign on a staff showing that the notes are below middle C. **2** The notes so shown.

bass drum (bās) The largest of the drums, beaten on both heads and having a deep sound: also called *double drum.*

bas·set¹ (bas'it) n. A hound characterized by a long, low body, long head and nose, and short, heavy, crooked forelegs: used in hunting. Also **bas'set·hound'.** [<OF *basset,* fem. dim. of *bas* low]

bas·set² (bas'it) *Geol.* n. An outcropping. — *v.i.* **·set·ed, ·set·ing** To crop out; appear at the surface, as coal. [Origin uncertain]

Basse-terre (bäs·târ') A town on St. Kitts, capital of the St. Christopher, Nevis and Anguilla presidency of the Leeward Islands.

Basse-Terre (bäs·târ') **1** A port on the SW coast of Basse-Terre island, capital of the French overseas department of Guadeloupe. **2** One of the twin islands comprising Guadeloupe department: also *Guadeloupe.*

bas·set–horn (bas'it·hôrn') n. A tenor clarinet having a compass of three and a half octaves. It has four more low keys than the ordinary clarinet. [<Ital. *corno di bassetto* < *bassetto,* dim. of *basso* low + *corno* horn]

bass horn (bās) A tuba.

bas·si·net (bas'ə·net') n. **1** A basket, usually with a hood over one end, used as a baby's cradle. **2** A small basket for holding the clothing of an infant. **3** A kind of perambulator. [<F, dim. of *bassin* basin]

bas·so (bas'ō, *Ital.* bäs'sō) n. *pl.* **bas·sos** (bas'ōz), *Ital.* **bas·si** (bäs'sē) **1** A bass singer. **2** The bass part. [<Ital., low]

bas·soon (ba·soōn', bə-) n. *Music* **1** A large, double-reed woodwind instrument with a long, curved mouthpiece. **2** An organ stop like a bassoon in its low tone. [<F *basson,* aug. of *bas* low]

basso pro·fun·do (prə·fun'dō, *Ital.* prō·foōn'dō) **1** A singer who sings the deepest bass. **2** The lowest bass voice.

bass viol (bās) *Music* **1** The double-bass. **2** The viola da gamba.

bass·wood (bas'wood') n. The linden.

bast (bast) n. *Bot.* **1** The fibrous inner bark of trees or a cordage made from it: also called *bass.* **2** A vegetable tissue found especially in the inner bark of dicotyledons, composed of tough, spindle-shaped, thick-walled fibers or cells. **3** Phloem. [OE *bæst*]

bas·tard (bas'tərd) n. **1** An illegitimate child. **2** Any hybrid plant, tree, or animal. **3** Any spurious, irregular, inferior, or counterfeit thing. **4** A refuse sugar from previously boiled sirup. — *adj.* **1** Born out of wedlock. **2** False; spurious. **3** Resembling but not typical of the genuine thing: *bastard* mahogany. **4** Unusual in size, shape, or proportion; abnormal; irregular: *bastard* type. [<OF *bastard* < *fils de bast* packsaddle child; with ref. to the use of the saddle as a bed]

bas·tard·ize (bas'tər·dīz) v. **·ized, ·iz·ing** *v.t.* **1** To prove to be, or stigmatize as, a bastard. **2** To make degenerate; debase. — *v.i.* **3** To become debased. — **bas'tard·i·za'tion** n.

bas·tard·ly (bas'tərd·lē) *adj.* **1** Bastardlike; of illegitimate birth. **2** Debased; counterfeit.

bastard wing *Ornithol.* An alula.

bas·tard·y (bas'tər·dē) n. **1** The begetting of a bastard. **2** The state of being a bastard;

illegitimacy.

baste¹ (bāst) *v.t.* **bast·ed, bast·ing** To sew loosely together, as with long, temporary stitches. [<OF *bastir* <OHG *bestan* sew with bast]

baste² (bāst) *v.t.* **bast·ed, bast·ing** To moisten (meat or fish) with drippings, butter, etc., while cooking. [<OF *basser* soak, moisten]

baste³ (bāst) *v.t. Colloq.* **1** To cudgel; thrash. **2** To attack verbally; abuse. [prob. <Scand., cf. ON *beysta* beat]

Bas·tia (bäs'tyä) A port on the NE coast of Corsica; chief city and former capital of the island.

bas·tille (bas·tēl') n. **1** A prison; especially, one used as a government prison or operated tyrannically. **2** In ancient warfare, a small fortress. Also **bas·tile'.** [<OF, building]

Bas·tille (bas·tēl', *Fr.* bàs·tē'y') A fortress in Paris, built in 1369 and stormed and destroyed in the French Revolution on July 14, 1789.

Bastille Day The national holiday of republican France, July 14, commemorating the fall and destruction of the Bastille.

bas·ti·na·do (bas'tə·nā'dō) n. *pl.* **·does 1** A beating with a stick, usually on the soles of the feet: an Oriental punishment. **2** A stick or cudgel. — *v.t.* **·doed, ·do·ing** To beat with a stick, usually on the soles of the feet. See synonyms under BEAT. Also **bas'ti·nade'.** [<Sp. *bastonado* < *bastón* cudgel]

bast·ing (bās'ting) n. **1** The act of sewing loosely together. **2** *pl.* Long, loose, temporary stitches. **3** The thread used for this purpose. [<BASTE¹]

bas·tion (bas'chən, -tē·ən) n. **1** In fortifications, a projecting work having two faces and two flanks so constructed that the adjacent curtain may be defended from it. **2** Any fortified or strongly defended place or position. [<F <Ital. *bastione* < *bastire* build] — **bas'tioned** *adj.*

Bas·togne (bas·tōn', *Fr.* bàs·tôn'y') A town in SE Belgium; besieged and nearly destroyed during the German counter-offensive of World War II in December, 1944. *Flemish* **Bas·te·na·ken** (bäs'tə·nä'kən).

BASTION a. Boulevard. *b.* Ramps. *c.* Flank. *d.* Banquette. *e.* Salient. *f.* Face of rampart. *g.* Berm. *h.* Moat. *i.* Glacis. *j.* Scarp. *k.* Embrasure in parapet. The curtains extending from its flanks (*c*) are on both sides of the bastion.

bat¹ (bat) n. **1** Any heavy cudgel or club. **2** Batting. **3** In baseball, cricket, and other games: **a** A stick or club for striking the ball, usually having one end wider or heavier than the other. **b** A turn at bat or the right to such a turn. **c** A racket, as in tennis. **d** The act of batting. **e** The batsman, as in cricket. **4** A fragment or lump of clay. **5** *Colloq.* A blow, as with a stick. **6** *Colloq.* Speed; rate of motion. **7** *Slang* A drunken carousal; a spree. — **at bat** In the act or position of batting. — **to go to bat for** *Colloq.* To defend or advocate the cause of. — *v.* **bat·ted, bat·ting** *v.i.* **1** In baseball, cricket, and other games: **a** To use a bat. **b** To take a turn at bat. **2** *Slang* To go hurriedly. — *v.t.* **3** To strike with or as with a bat. — **to bat around** *Slang* **1** To move or travel about. **2** To discuss, as a proposal or idea. **3** In baseball, to have the whole team bat in one inning. [OE *batt* cudgel]

bat² (bat) n. Any of numerous nocturnal flying mammals (order *Chiroptera*), having greatly elongated fore limbs and digits that support a thin wing membrane extending to the hind limbs and sometimes to the tail. — **blind as a bat** Altogether blind. — **to have bats in the belfry** *Slang* To be crazy. [ME *bakke,* ? <Scand.] — **bat'like'** *adj.*

bat³ (bat) *v.t. Colloq.* To wink; flutter. — **not bat an eye** *Colloq.* Not show surprise or other reaction. [Var. of BATE³]

bat⁴ (bät) See BAHT.

batch¹ (bach) n. **1** The dough for one baking, or the quantity of bread, etc., baked. **2** The grain for one grinding; grist. **3** Any set of things made, done, dispatched, etc., at one time. **4** The amount of material, quantity of articles, etc., required for one operation. [ME *bacche.* Akin to BAKE.]

batch² (bach) *n. Slang* A bachelor.

bate¹ (bāt) *v.* **bat·ed, bat·ing** *v.t.* **1** To lessen the force or intensity of; moderate: to *bate* one's breath. **2** To deduct; take away. **3** *Obs.* To depress; decrease. —*v.i.* **4** To diminish; become reduced. ◆ Homophone: *bait.* [Var. of ABATE]

bate² (bāt) *n.* A solution of chemicals or manure containing natural or synthetic enzymes: used to soften skins or hides. —*v.t.* **1** To soak, as hides. **2** To separate and soften, as jute. ◆ Homophone: *bait.* [? <ON *beita* cause to bite. Akin to BAIT and BITE.]

bate³ (bāt) *v.i.* **bat·ed, bat·ing** In falconry, to beat or flap the wings, as an impatient hawk: also spelled *bait.* ◆ Homophone: *bait.* [<F *battre* beat <L *battuere* strike, beat]

ba·teau (ba·tō′) *n. pl.* **·teaux** (-tōz′) **1** A light, flat-bottomed boat. **2** A pontoon for a floating bridge. [<F <OF *batel,* ult. <Gmc.]

bateau bridge A pontoon bridge.

bat·fowl (bat′foul′) *v.i.* To catch birds at night by dazzling them with a light and netting or striking them down. — **bat′fowl′er** *n.* [<BAT¹ + FOWL]

bath¹ (bath, bäth) *n. pl.* **baths** (bathz, bäthz; baths, bäths) **1** The act of washing or immersing something, especially the body, in water or other liquid. ◆ Collateral adjective: *balneal.* **2** The liquid substance or element used for this. **3** The container for such a liquid; a bathtub. **4** A bathroom. **5** A set of rooms or a building for bathing: often in the plural. **6** An establishment or resort where bathing is part of a medical treatment: often in the plural. **7** *Chem.* An apparatus for applying steady heat or heat of a given degree. **8** *Phot.* Any solution, or the vessel containing it, in which photographic plates, etc., are immersed for treatment. **9** *Metall.* The molten material in a reverberatory furnace. **10** The condition of being soaked or covered with a liquid. —*v.t.* To place or wash in a bath; immerse. [OE *bæth*]

bath² (bath) *n.* An ancient Hebrew liquid measure, one tenth of a homer: equivalent to about 8 1/2 gallons. [<Hebrew]

Bath (bath, bäth) A city in NE Somersetshire, England, famous since Roman times for its hot springs.

Bath brick A fine calcareous and siliceous material, usually pressed into brick shape, used for polishing and cleansing metal objects: originally found near Bath, England.

bathe (bāth) *v.* **bathed, bath·ing** *v.t.* **1** To place in liquid; immerse. **2** To wash; wet. **3** To apply liquid to for comfort or healing; lave. **4** To cover or suffuse as with liquid: The hill was *bathed* in rosy light. —*v.i.* **5** To wash oneself; take a bath. **6** To go into or remain in water so as to swim or cool off. **7** To be covered or suffused as if with liquid. —*n. Brit.* The act of bathing, as in the sea. [OE *bathian*] — **bathe′a·ble** *adj.* — **bath′er** *n.*

ba·thet·ic (ba·thet′ik) *adj.* Pertaining to, exhibiting, or of the nature of bathos. [<BATHOS]

bath·house (bath′hous′, bäth′-) *n.* **1** A building with conveniences for taking baths. **2** A small structure at a bathing resort used as a dressing-room.

bath·ing suit (bāth′ing) A garment, sometimes consisting of two pieces, worn for swimming.

batho- *combining form* Depth: *bathometer.* [<Gk. *bathos* depth]

bath·o·lith (bath′ə-lith) *n. Geol.* A large irregular mass of intrusive igneous rock which has melted or forced its way into surrounding strata. Also **bath′o·lite** (-līt). — **bath′o·lith′ic,** **bath′o·lit′ic** (-lit′ik) *adj.*

ba·thoph·i·lous (ba·thof′ə-ləs) *adj.* Of or pertaining to organisms adapted to life at great depths in the ocean. [<BATHO- + -PHILOUS]

bath·o·pho·bi·a (bath′ə-fō′bē·ə) *n. Psychiatry* Morbid fear of depths. Compare ACROPHOBIA. — **bath′o·pho′bic** (-fō′bik, -fob′ik) *adj.*

ba·thos (bā′thos) *n.* **1** A descent from the lofty to the commonplace in discourse; anticlimax. **2** Insincere pathos; sentimentality. [<Gk. *bathos* depth <*bathys* deep]

bath·robe (bath′rōb′, bäth′-) *n.* A long, loose garment for wear before and after bathing.

bath·room (bath′rōōm′, -rŏŏm′, bäth′-) *n.* **1** A room in which to bathe. **2** A toilet (def. 4).

bath salts A perfumed mixture of crystal salts used to soften bath water.

Bath·she·ba (bath·shē′bə, bath′shi·bə) Wife of Uriah and later of David; mother of Solomon. II *Sam.* xi–xii.

bath·tub (bath′tub′, bäth′-) *n.* **1** A vessel in which to bathe. **2** Such a vessel installed as a permanent fixture in a bathroom.

bathy- *combining form* Deep: of the sea or ocean depths: *bathymeter; bathysphere.* [<Gk. *bathys* deep]

ba·tik (ba·tēk′, bat′ik) *n.* **1** A process for coloring fabrics, originating in the East Indies, in which parts of a fabric are covered with melted wax so that only the uncovered portions will take the dye, the wax then being dissolved in boiling water. The process is often repeated to obtain multicolored designs. **2** The fabric so colored. Also **battik.** [<Malay]

bat·ing (bā′ting) *prep. Archaic* Making deduction for.

ba·tiste (ba·tēst′) *n.* **1** A sheer fabric made of cotton, silk, or spun rayon. The cotton batiste is sometimes mercerized. **2** A fine woolen fabric lighter than challis. **3** Originally, a fine linen cloth. [<F; after Jean Baptiste, 13th c. French linen weaver]

ba·ton (ba·ton′, bat′n; *Fr.* bȧ·tôn′) *n.* **1** A short official staff or truncheon borne as a weapon or as an emblem of authority or privilege: a marshal's *baton.* **2** *Music* A slender stick or rod used for beating time. **3** *Her.* A bend borne sinisterwise across the shield as a mark of bastardy: also **baton sinister,** erroneously *bar sinister.* [<F *bâton* <OF *baston* <LL *bastum* stick]

Bat·on Rouge (bat′n rōōzh′) A port on the Mississippi River, capital of Louisiana.

ba·tra·chi·an (bə·trā′kē·ən) *adj.* **1** Of or pertaining to the *Batrachia,* especially to the frogs and toads; amphibian. **2** Froglike. —*n.* One of the *Batrachia.*

bat·ra·chite (bat′rə-kīt) *n.* **1** A stone that is froglike in color. **2** A fossil batrachian.

bat·ra·choid (bat′rə-koid) *adj.* Froglike.

bats·man (bats′mən) *n. pl.* **·men** (-mən) In baseball or cricket, the batter.

bat·tai·lous (bat′i-ləs) *adj. Obs.* Bellicose. [<OF *bataillos* <*bataille* battle]

bat·ta·lia (bə·tāl′yə, -tāl′-) *n. Obs.* **1** An army. **2** Order of battle.

bat·tal·ion (bə·tal′yən) *n.* **1** *Mil.* **a** A unit, normally part of a regiment, consisting of a headquarters and two or more companies, batteries, or comparable units. **b** A body of troops. **2** *Usually pl.* A large group or number. [<F *battaillon* <Ital. *battaglione* <*battaglia* battle]

bat·tels (bat′lz) *n. pl. Brit.* At Oxford University, a student's account with his college for provisions, etc. [Origin uncertain]

bat·ten¹ (bat′n) *v.i.* **1** To grow fat or thrive. **2** To prosper; live well, especially at another's expense. —*v.t.* **3** To make fat, as cattle. [<ON *batna* grow better, improve]

bat·ten² (bat′n) *n.* **1** A narrow strip of wood; a cleat, as across parallel boards in a door. **2** In the theater: **a** A cleat placed on a muslin flat or piece of scenery to stiffen it. **b** A round metal bar to which spotlights or floodlights are attached. **3** *Naut.* **a** A thin strip of wood placed in a sail to keep it flat. **b** A similar strip used to fasten down a tarpaulin covering on a hatchway. —*v.t.* **1** To make, furnish, or strengthen with battens. **2** To fasten with battens. — **tō batten down the hatches** *Naut.* To put tarpaulins over a hatchway and secure them by strips of wood. [Var. of BATON] — **bat′ten·er** *n.*

bat·ter¹ (bat′ər) *n.* **1** A heavy blow; also, repeated blows, or the condition resulting from them. **2** In ceramics, a mallet for beating a lump of plastic clay. **3** *Printing* **a** The breakage or marring of type or a plate. **b** The type thus broken. **c** The resulting defect in print. [<v.] —*v.t.* **1** To strike with repeated, violent blows. **2** To damage or injure with or as with such blows. —*v.i.* **3** To pound or beat with blow after blow; hammer. See synonyms under BEAT. [<F *battre* <L *battuere* beat]

bat·ter² (bat′ər) *n.* In baseball and cricket, the player whose turn it is to bat.

bat·ter³ (bat′ər) *n.* A thick liquid mixture of eggs, flour, and milk, beaten up for use in cookery. [<OF *bature* beating <*battre* beat]

bat·ter⁴ (bat′ər) *n.* An inward and upward slope of a wall, giving greater resistance to thrust or firmer base. —*v.t. & v.i.* To slope back from the base, as a wall. [Origin uncertain]

bat·ter·ing-ram (bat′ər·ing·ram′) *n.* A long, stout beam, with heavy head, used in ancient warfare for forcing gates and making breaches in walls, either carried by the assailants, or suspended in a frame.

BATTERING-RAM

Bat·ter·sea (bat′ər-sē) A metropolitan borough of London, on the south side of the Thames.

bat·ter·y (bat′ər·ē) *n. pl.* **·ter·ies** **1** *Mil.* **a** An earthwork or parapet for protecting one or more guns. **b** Two or more pieces of artillery constituting a tactical unit. **c** A unit of an artillery regiment equivalent to an infantry company, or their guns and other equipment. **2** *Nav.* The armament of a war vessel, or a special part of it. **3** *Electr.* **a** An arrangement of two or more primary cells, dynamos, etc., for the purpose of building up a strong electric current: a *battery* of Leyden jars. **b** Any of several types of such cells used to heat the filaments of a vacuum tube, provide current, or supply voltage: an A, B, or C *battery.* **4** *Law* The illegal beating or touching of another person. **5** In baseball, the pitcher and catcher together. **6** *Music* The percussion instruments of an orchestra, collectively. **7** *Optics* The group of prisms in a spectroscope. **8** Any unit, apparatus, or grouping in which a series or set of parts or components are assembled to serve a common end: a *battery* of tests. **9** The act of battering or beating. **10** The instrument for such an act. — **dry battery** *Electr.* A battery composed of cells whose contents are solid or nearly so; a dry pile. — **in battery** *Mil.* In firing position, after recovery from recoil: said of a heavy gun. [<F *batterie* <*battre* beat]

bat·ting (bat′ing) *n.* **1** Wadded cotton or wool prepared in sheets or rolls: used for interlinings, stuffing mattresses, comforters, etc.: also **bat, batt.** **2** The act of one who bats.

bat·tle (bat′l) *n.* **1** A combat between hostile armies or fleets; a military or naval engagement. **2** Armed combat. **3** Any fighting, conflict, or struggle: to do *battle* for a cause. **4** *Obs.* A battalion. —*v.* **bat·tled, bat·tling** *v.i.* To contend in or as in battle; struggle; strive. —*v.t.* To fight. See synonyms under CONTEND, DISPUTE. [<OF *bataille* <LL *battalia* gladiators' exercises <*battuere* beat] — **bat′tler** *n.*

Synonyms (noun): action, affair, bout, combat, conflict, contest, encounter, engagement, fight, skirmish, strife. *Conflict* is a general word which describes opponents, whether individuals or hosts, as dashed together. One continuous *conflict* between entire armies is a *battle.* Another *battle* may be fought upon the same field after a considerable interval; or a new *battle* may follow immediately, the armies meeting upon a new field. An *action* is brief and partial; a *battle* may last for days. *Engagement* is a somewhat formal expression for *battle.* A protracted war, including many *battles,* may be a stubborn *contest. Combat,* originally a hostile *encounter* between individuals, is now used also for extensive *engagements.* A *skirmish* is between small detachments or scattered troops. An *encounter* may be either purposed or accidental, between individuals or armed forces. *Fight* is a word of less dignity than *battle;* we should not ordinarily speak of Waterloo as a *fight,* unless where the word is used in the sense of fighting; as, I was in the thick of the *fight. Antonyms:* armistice, concord, peace, truce.

bat·tle·dore (bat′l-dôr, -dōr) *n.* **1** A flat paddle or bat, either of wood, webbed, or covered with parchment, used to drive a shuttlecock. **2** The game in which a shuttlecock is so batted: also **battledore and shuttlecock.** —*v.t. & v.i.* **·dored, ·dor·ing** To drive or fly back and forth. [? <Provençal *batedor* an implement for beating]

bat·tle·field (bat′l·fēld′) *n.* The ground on

which a battle is fought. Also **bat′tle·ground′**.

bat·tle·ment (bat′l-mənt) *n.* A parapet indented along its upper line. —**bat·tle·ment′ed** (bat′l-men·tid) *adj.* [<OF *ba(s)tillier* fortify]

bat·tle·plane (bat′l-plān′) *n.* Formerly any airplane for combat use.

BATTLEMENT

A. Outer view: — *a, a.* Merlons; *b, b.* Embrasures. *B.* Cross–section: — showing use of corbel, *c,* for machicolation, *d.*

battle royal 1 A fight involving numerous combatants. **2** A protracted, rigorous battle.

bat·tle-scarred (bat′l-skärd′) *adj.* **1** Having scars, marks, etc., received in combat. **2** Having received the effects of a long and varied experience; experienced.

bat·tle·ship (bat′l-ship′) *n. Nav.* A vessel having a large displacement and radius of action, maximum armament and powerful batteries.

bat·tol·o·gy (bə-tol′ə-jē) *n.* Unnecessary repetition in speaking or writing. [<Gk. *battologia* stammering] —**bat·to·log·i·cal** (bat′ə-loj′i-kəl) *adj.* —**bat·tol′o·gist** *n.*

bat·tue (ba·tōō′, -tyōō′) *n.* **1** The driving of game from cover within reach of sportsmen previously posted. **2** A hunt so conducted. **3** Any wanton slaughter. [<F, fem. pp. of *battre* beat]

bat·ty (bat′ē) *adj.* **·ti·er, ·ti·est 1** Of, pertaining to, or like a bat. **2** *U.S. Slang* Crazy; foolish; odd.

bau·ble (bô′bəl) *n.* **1** A worthless, showy trinket; gew-gaw; toy. **2** *Archaic* The wand of a jester. Also spelled **bawble.** See synonyms under GAUD. [<OF *baubel* toy, ? <L *bellus* pretty]

baud (bôd) *n.* A unit of speed in telegraphy, based on the time interval required to transmit a given signal, usually the dot. [after J. M. E. *Baudot,* 1845–1903, French inventor]

Bau·haus (bou′hous′) An institute of art study, design, and research, established by Walter Gropius in Weimar, Germany, in 1919: known for its experiments in associating technology and art.

Bau·mé (bō·mā′) *n.* **1** A hydrometer for the measurement of the densities of liquids. **2** The scale used on this instrument. [after Antoine *Baumé,* 1728–1804, French pharmacist]

bau·son (bô′sən) *n. Archaic* A badger. [<OF *bausant* spotted]

Bau·tis·ta (bou·tēs′tä) Spanish form of BAPTIST.

baux·ite (bôk′sīt, bō′zīt) *n.* A whitish to reddish brown material composed of hydrated aluminum oxides along with various siliceous, ferric, and other impurities and forming the principal commercial source of aluminum. [from Les *Baux,* town in southern France]

Ba·var·i·a (bə-vâr′ē-ə) A southeastern state of the Federal Republic of Germany; 27,119 square miles; capital, Munich; formerly a duchy, kingdom, and republic: German *Bayern.*

Ba·var·i·an (bə-vâr′ē-ən) *adj.* Of or pertaining to Bavaria, its people, or their dialect. —*n.* **1** A native or inhabitant of Bavaria. **2** The High German dialect spoken in Bavaria.

bawd (bôd) *n.* The keeper of a brothel; a procuress. [ME *bawde;* origin uncertain]

bawd·ry (bôd′rē) *n.* **1** Indecent language or behavior. **2** The occupation of a bawd.

bawd·y (bô′dē) *adj.* **bawd·i·er, bawd·i·est** Of or like a bawd; obscene; indecent. —**bawd′i·ly** *adv.* —**bawd′i·ness** *n.*

bawd·y-house (bô′dē-hous′) *n.* A brothel.

bawl (bôl) *n.* A loud shout or outcry. —*v.t.* **1** To proclaim or call out noisily; bellow. **2** *U.S. Slang* To berate: with *out.* **3** To cry for sale. —*v.i.* **4** To weep or sob noisily. See synonyms under CALL. ◆ Homophone: *ball.* [<ON *baula* low, as a cow] —**bawl′er** *n.*

bay[1] (bā) *n.* **1** A body of water partly enclosed by land; an arm of the sea. **2** A recess of low land between hills. **3** Land partly surrounded by woods. ◆ Homophone: *bey.* [<F *baie* <LL *baia*]

bay[2] (bā) *n.* **1** A space in a barn for storing hay or fodder. **2** *Engin.* A principal compartment or division, as the space between two piers or pontoons of a bridge. **3** *Archit.* **a** A division of a window between adjacent mullions. **b** Part of a vault between transverse ribs or of a ceiling between panel beams. **c** A vertical division of an arcade, as the space between two adjacent pillars. **4** The head of a canal lock. **5** *Naut.* The forward part of a ship between decks on each side: commonly used as a hospital. **6** *Aeron.* **a** A compartment in the body of an aircraft: a bomb *bay.* **b** A portion of the fuselage between adjoining struts, bulkheads, or frame positions. ◆ Homophone: *bey.* [<F *baie* <bayer gape, ult. <LL *badare*]

bay[3] (bā) *adj.* Reddish-brown: said especially of horses. —*n.* **1** A horse (or other animal) of this color. **2** This color. ◆ Homophone: *bey.* [<F *bai* <L *badius*]

bay[4] (bā) *n.* **1** A deep bark or cry, as of dogs in hunting. **2** The situation of or as of a hunted creature compelled to turn on its pursuers. **3** The condition of being kept at a standstill or in check by an opponent, quarry, etc. —**at bay 1** Cornered; with no escape. **2** Held off: He kept his attackers *at bay.* —**to bring to bay** To force into a position from which there is no escape; corner and force to fight. —*v.i.* **1** To utter a deep-throated, prolonged bark, as a hound. —*v.t.* **2** To utter as with this bark: to *bay* defiance. **3** To pursue or beset with barking of this kind so as to bring to bay. ◆ Homophone: *bey.* [Var. of *abay* <OF *abai* a barking; ult. origin uncertain; in sense "at bay" appar. <OF *tenir a bay* hold in suspense <LL *badare* gape]

bay[5] (bā) *n.* **1** Laurel (def. 1): also called *baytree.* **2** A laurel wreath, bestowed as a garland of honor, especially on a poet. **3** *pl.* Fame; poetic renown. **4** The bayberry. **5** Any of several plants resembling the laurels. **6** *U.S. Dial.* Low marshy ground abounding in bay and other shrubs: also **bay-gall** (bā′gôl′). ◆ Homophone: *bey.* [<F *baie* <L *baca* berry]

ba·ya·mo (bä-yä′mō) *n. Meteorol.* A violent wind blowing on the south coast of Cuba. [from *Bayamo,* town in eastern Cuba]

bay·ard (bā′ərd) *n.* **1** A bay horse. **2** Any horse. —*adj.* Bay in color. [<OF] *a humorous use.*

bay·ber·ry (bā′ber′ē, -bər-ē) *n. pl.* **·ber·ries 1** One of various trees, as the wax myrtle or laurel, or its fruit. **2** A tropical American tree (*Pimenta racemosa*) whose leaves are used in making bay rum. [<BAY[5] + BERRY]

bay·cu·ru root (bī-kōō′rōō′) The root of a tropical American plant (*Limonium brasiliense*) which yields a powerful astringent known as **bay·cu·rine** (bī-kōō′rēn, -rin). [<Tupian]

bay lynx The common wildcat of North America.

bay·o·net (bā′ə-nit, -net) *n.* A daggerlike weapon attachable to the muzzle of a musket

BAYONETS

A. One type of sword bayonet.
B. 18th–19th century bayonet.
C. Sword bayonet.
D. Type of United States Army bayonet.
a. Blade. *b.* Guard. *c.* Bayonet spring. *d.* Scabbard catch. *e.* Tang. *f.* Pommel. *g.* Bayonet catch. *h.* Undercut groove.

or rifle, for close fighting. —*v.t.* **·net·ed, ·net·ing** To stab or pierce with a bayonet. [<F *bayonette,* from *Bayonne,* France, where first made]

bay·ou (bī′ōō) *n.* **1** A marshy inlet or outlet of a lake or bay. **2** A branch of a stream flowing through a delta. [<Choctaw *bayuk* small stream]

bay rum An aromatic liquid used in medicines and cosmetics, originally obtained by distilling rum with the leaves of the bayberry, now consisting mainly of alcohol, water, and essential oils.

bay·tree (bā′trē) *n.* **1** Bay[5] (def. 1). **2** The magnolia of eastern North America.

bay window 1 A window structure projecting from the wall of a building and forming an extension. **2** *Slang* A protruding abdomen.

bay·wood (bā′wōōd′) *n.* A coarse mahogany from Honduras or the region around the Gulf of Campeche.

ba·zaar (bə-zär′) *n.* **1** An Oriental market place or range of shops. **2** A shop or store for the sale of miscellaneous wares. **3** A sale of miscellaneous articles, as for charity. Also **ba·zar′.** [<Persian *bāzār* market]

ba·zoo·ka (bə-zōō′kə) *n. Mil.* A long, tubular missile weapon which fires an explosive rocket, and is used for short-range action against tanks and fortifications. [from fancied resemblance to the *bazooka,* a comical musical instrument invented and named by Bob Burns, U.S. comedian]

BB A standard, commercial size of lead shot, 0.18 in. in diameter.

B battery *Electr.* The battery which supplies direct-current voltage to the plate and grid of a vacuum tube.

bdel·li·um (del′ē-əm) *n.* **1** A variety of gum resin resembling myrrh, yielded by various trees (genus *Commiphora*) of India and Africa; also, any of such trees. **2** A substance mentioned in the Old Testament, variously interpreted as crystal, carbuncle, pearl, or amber. [<L <Gk. *bdellion* a plant, and its fragrant gum]

Be *Chem.* Beryllium (symbol Be).

be (bē, *unstressed* bi) *v.i.* **been, be·ing** Present indicative: *sing.* **am, are** (*Archaic* **art**), **is,** *pl.* **are;** past indicative: *sing.* **was, were** (*Archaic* **wast** or **wert**), **was,** *pl.* **were;** present subjunctive: **be;** past subjunctive: *sing.* **were, were** (*Archaic* **wert**), **were,** *pl.* **were 1** As a substantive the verb **be** is used to mean: **a** To have existence, truth, or actuality: God *is;* There *are* bears in the zoo. **b** To take place; happen: The party *is* next week. **c** To stay or continue: She *was* here for one week. **d** To belong; befall: often with *to* or *unto:* Joy *be* unto you. **2** As a copulative verb *be* forms a link between the subject and predicate nominative or qualifying word or phrase in declarative, interrogative, and imperative sentences; it also forms infinitive and participial phrases: Money *is* nothing to me; The book *is* too expensive; He *is* sick; the pleasure of *being* here. **3** As an auxiliary verb *be* is used: **a** With the present participle of other verbs to express continuous or progressive action: I *am* working. **b** With the past participle of transitive verbs to form the passive voice: He *was* injured. **c** With the past participle of intransitive verbs to form the perfect tense: Christ *is* come; I *am* finished. **d** With the infinitive or present participle to express purpose, duty, possibility, futurity, etc.: We *are* to start on Monday; We *are* leaving Monday. The verb is defective, and its conjugation is made up of fragments of three independent verbs, furnishing **be, am** (**are, is**), **was** (**were**), respectively. ◆ For usage as to the cases of personal pronouns following impersonal forms of the verb *to be,* see note under ME. [OE *bēon*]

be- *prefix* Used to form transitive verbs from nouns, adjectives, and verbs. [OE *be-, bi-,* var. of *bī* near, by]

Be- may appear as a prefix in hyphemes or solidemes, with the following meanings: **1** (from verbs) Around; all over; throughout; as in:

beclasp	befreckle	beshackle
beclog	begirdle	beshadow
beclothe	bejumble	beshroud
becompass	bekiss	beslobber
becrimson	belick	besmother
becrust	bemingle	besmudge
bedabble	bemix	bespeckle
bedarken	berake	besprinkle
bediaper	bescour	betattered
bedimple	bescreen	bewrap
befinger	bescribble	bewreath

2 (from verbs) Completely; thoroughly; as in:

beclamor	beflatter	bescourge
becrowd	befluster	beshiver
becudgel	begall	besmear
becurse	beknotted	besoothe
bedamn	bemaddening	bethank
bedeafened	bemuddle	bethump
bedrabble	bemuzzle	betrample
bedrench	besanctify	beweary
bedrug	bescorch	bewidow

3 (from verbs) Off; away from: *behead, bereave.*

4 (from intransitive verbs) About; at; on; over; against; for; as in:

bechatter	behowl	beshout
becrawl	bejuggle	besmile
bedrivel	beleap	beswarm
begaze	bemurmur	bethunder
begroan	beshame	beweep

5 (from adjectives and nouns) To make; cause to be; as in:

beclown	bedumb	begrim
becoward	bedunce	beknight
becripple	bedwarf	bemonster
bedirty	befoul	besmooth
bedoctor	beglad	bespouse

6 (from nouns) To provide with; affect by; cover with; as in:

beblister	beflea	beslime
beblood	beflower	beslipper
becap	befringe	besmoke
becarpet	beglitter	besmut
bechalk	begloom	besnow
becharm	begulf	bethorn
becloak	bejewel	bewelcome
becrime	beliquor	bewhisker
bedinner	bemist	beworm

7 (from nouns) To call; name; as in:

bebrother	belady	berascal
becoward	bemadam	bescoundrel
behypocrite	bemonster	bevillain

8 (from nouns) To furnish with, excessively or conspicuously (almost always in participial form); as in:

be–altared	begarlanded	beruffled
bebelted	begartered	besainted
bebuttoned	behusbanded	beslaved
becapped	bejeweled	bespangled
becarpeted	belaced	bespectacled
bechained	bemedaled	bestarred
becupided	bemitered	besteepled
becurtained	bemottoed	bestrapped
becushioned	bepilgrimed	besworded
bedaughtered	berailroaded	betaxed
bedotted	beribboned	betinseled
befathered	beringed	be–uncled
befeathered	beringleted	be–uniformed
beflowered	berobed	bewinged
befrilled	berouged	bewrathed

beach (bēch) *n.* **1** The sloping shore of a body of water; strand. **2** Loose pebbles on the shore; shingle. See synonyms under BANK, MARGIN. — *v.t.* & *v.i.* To drive or haul up (a boat or ship) on a beach; strand. ◆ Homophone: *beech.* [Origin unknown]

beach·comb·er (bēch'kō'mər) *n.* **1** A vagrant living on what he can find or beg around the wharves and beaches of ports, especially such a person in the South Sea islands. **2** A long wave rolling upon the beach.

beach flea A small amphipod crustacean (family *Talitridae*) that hops like a flea: found on sea beaches.

beach–grass (bēch'gras', -gräs') *n.* A tough, coarse grass (*Ammophila arenaria*) found on lake and ocean beaches: also called *marram.*

beach·head (bēch'hed') *n. Mil.* **1** A position on a hostile shore established by an advance invasion force to make possible the landing of troops and supplies. **2** A fortified place on a beach.

beach–la–mar (bēch'lə–mär') See BÊCHE–DE–MER.

beach·y (bē'chē) *adj.* Shingly; pebbly.

Beachy Head A chalk promontory in southern Sussex, England; 565 feet high.

bea·con (bē'kən) *n.* **1** Any prominent object, as a pole, tower, flag, or the like, set on a shore, shoal, buoy, reef, or in a similar position, as a guide or warning to mariners or others. **2** Something that serves as a conspicuous warning or a guide. **3** A lighthouse. **4** *Aeron.* Any of various marker, signal light, or radio devices used to establish and plot flight courses. See RADIO BEACON. — *v.t.*

1 To furnish with a beacon. **2** To light up (darkness, etc.). **3** To guide by a light or beacon. — *v.i.* **4** To shine or serve as a beacon. [OE *bēacen* sign, signal. Related to BECKON.]

Bea·cons·field (bē'kənz·fēld) See DISRAELI.

bead (bēd) *n.* **1** Any small, usually round piece of glass, wood, stone, etc., perforated and intended to be strung with others like it on a thread or attached to a fabric for decoration. **2** *pl.* A string of beads; especially, a rosary. **3** A bubble or bubbles on the surface of a liquid; froth. **4** A liquid drop, as of sweat. **5** A small spherical knob used as the front sight of a gun. **6** *Chem.* A small mass of borax or other flux, placed on a platinum wire to receive a substance for blowpipe testing **7** *Metall.* The spherical piece of refined metal resulting from cupellation. **8** *Archit.* **a** A molding composed of a row of half-oval ornaments resembling a string of beads. **b** A small convex molding. **9** That part of a pneumatic tire which grips the rim of a wheel. — **to draw a bead on** To take careful aim at. — **to tell (count,** or **say) one's beads** To recite prayers with a rosary. — *v.t.* To decorate with , or as with beads or beading. — *v.i.* To collect in beads or drops. [OE *gebed* prayer]

bead·house (bēd'hous') *n.* An almshouse or hospital in which the inmates were required to pray for the founders: also spelled *bede-house.*

bead·ing (bē'ding) *n.* **1** *Archit.* **a** A bead. **b** Beads collectively. **2** A narrow openwork lace through which a ribbon may be run. **3** Beadwork.

bea·dle (bēd'l) *n.* **1** A minor parish officer in the Church of England whose duties include keeping order during services. **2** *Brit.* An official who leads university processions. **3** A court messenger. **4** The apparitor of a guild. [OF *bedel* messenger]

bea·dle·dom (bēd'l-dəm) *n.* **1** Beadles collectively, or their characteristics. **2** A show of petty and stupid officialism.

bead·roll (bēd'rōl') *n.* **1** Originally, a list or catalog. **2** In the Roman Catholic Church, a list of persons to be prayed for.

bead–ru·by (bēd'rōō'bē) *n. pl.* **·bies** A small perennial herb (*Maianthemum canadense*) of northern North America with small crimson berries and four–lobed terminal flowers: akin to the Solomonseal.

beads·man (bēdz'mən) *n. pl.* **·men** (-mən) **1** *Brit.* The resident of an almshouse. **2** *Scot.* A privileged or licensed beggar receiving public alms. **3** One who prays for another, especially when hired to do so: also spelled *bedeman.* Also **bead'man.** — **beads'wom'an** *n. fem.*

bead·work (bēd'wûrk') *n.* **1** Decorative work made with or of beads. **2** *Archit.* Beading.

bead·y (bē'dē) *adj.* **bead·i·er, bead·i·est** **1** Beadlike. **2** Full of or covered with beads. **3** Foamy.

bea·gle (bē'gəl) *n.* A small, short-coated hound with short legs and drooping ears. [ME *begle*; origin uncertain]

BEAGLE
(About 15 inches high at the shoulder)

beak[1] (bēk) *n.* **1** The horny projecting mouth parts of birds; the bill or neb. **2** A beaklike part or organ, as the horny jaws of cephalopods and turtles, the elongated snout of various fishes, etc. **3** *Slang* The nose of a person. **4** *Naut.* That part of ancient warships fastened to the bow and used for piercing or ramming an enemy vessel. **5** *Archit.* A downward-projecting molding on the extreme edge of the lower member of a cornice to prevent the drip from working back under it. **6** Something projecting and pointed like a beak, as the spout of a pitcher. **7** That part of a retort or still which conducts the vapor to the worm or condenser. [<F *bec* <LL *beccus*, ult. <Celtic] — **beaked** (bēkt, bē'kid) *adj.* — **beak'less** *adj.* — **beak'like** *adj.*

beak[2] (bēk) *n. Brit. Slang* **1** A policeman. **2** A magistrate. **3** At Eton, a master.

beak·er (bē'kər) *n.* **1** A large, wide–mouthed cup or goblet. **2** A cylindrical, flat–bottomed

vessel of quartz, porcelain, aluminum, or thin annealed glass, having a flaring top: used in chemical analysis, etc. **3** The contents or capacity of a beaker. [<ON *bikarr*; spelling infl. by BEAK]

be–all (bē'ôl') *n.* All that is to be; the whole of something.

beam (bēm) *n.* **1** A long, horizontal piece of wood, stone, or metal, forming part of the frame of a building or other structure. **2** The bar of a balance. **3** *Naut.* **a** One of the heavy pieces of timber or iron set transversely across a vessel to support the decks and stay the sides. **b** The greatest width of a vessel. **4** The widest part of anything. **5** A horizontal cylindrical bar, in a loom, upon which warp or woven goods are wound. **6** The pole of a carriage. **7** *Mech.* A horizontal bar that transmits power to the crankshaft through the connecting rod. **8** *Optics* A ray of light, or a group of nearly parallel rays. **9** *Aeron.* A continuous radio signal from a flying field to guide incoming pilots: also **radio beam.** **10** The main stem of a deer's antler. **11** The area of maximum sound clarity in front of a microphone. **12** The horizontal piece in a plow to which the share and the handles are attached. **13** A trough containing lights in the ceiling of a stage. — **off the beam 1** *Aeron.* Not following the radio beam. **2** *Slang* On the wrong track; wrong. — **on the beam 1** *Naut.* In a direction at right angles with the keel; abeam. **2** *Aeron.* Following the radio beam. **3** *Slang* In the right direction; just right; correct. — *v.t.* **1** To send out in or as in beams or rays. **2** In radio, to aim or transmit (a signal) in a specific direction: to *beam* a program to France. **3** *Aeron.* To guide (an airplane) to a destination by means of radio beams. — *v.i.* **4** To emit light. **5** To smile or grin radiantly. [OE, tree] — **beamed** *adj.* — **beam'less** *adj.* — **beam'like** *adj.*

beam compass A drawing compass in which the points are arranged to slide on a rod, instead of fixed on dividers.

beam–ends (bēm'endz') *n. pl. Naut.* The ends of a ship's beams. — **on beam–ends 1** *Naut.* Canted over so far as to be in danger of overturning. **2** In an embarrassing or hopeless predicament.

beam·ing (bē'ming) *adj.* Radiant; bright; cheerful. See synonyms under BRIGHT. — **beam'ing·ly** *adv.*

beam·ish (bē'mish) *adj.* Radiant; beaming with light. [<BEAM + -ISH; coined by Lewis Carroll in *Jabberwocky*]

beam·y (bē'mē) *adj.* **beam·i·er, beam·i·est** **1** Sending out beams of light; radiant. **2** Like a beam; massive. **3** *Naut.* Having much breadth of beam: said of vessels. **4** Antlered, as a stag.

bean (bēn) *n.* **1** The oval edible seed of any of various leguminous plants, especially of genus *Phaseolus.* **2** A plant that bears beans. **3** One of several beanlike seeds or plants. **4** *Slang* The head. — *v.t. U.S. Slang* To hit on the head, especially with a thrown object, as a baseball. [OE]

bean·bag (bēn'bag') *n.* A small cloth bag filled with beans, used as a toy.

bean ball In baseball, a pitch aimed at the head of the batter.

bean–pole (bēn'pōl') *n.* **1** A tall pole for a bean plant to climb on. **2** *Slang* A tall, thin person.

bean·stalk (bēn'stôk') *n.* The principal stem of a bean plant.

bear[1] (bâr) *v.* **bore** (*Archaic* **bare**), **borne** or **born, bear·ing** *v.t.* **1** To support; hold up. **2** To carry; convey. **3** To show visibly; carry: to *bear* a seal or a scar. **4** To conduct or guide. **5** To spread; disseminate: to *bear* tales. **6** To hold in the mind; maintain or entertain: to *bear* a grudge. **7** To suffer or endure; undergo. **8** To accept or acknowledge; assume, as responsibility or expense. **9** To produce; give birth to. **10** To conduct or comport (oneself). **11** To manage or carry (oneself or a part of oneself). **12** To press against or thrust back: The wind *bore* the ship backward. **13** To render; give: to *bear* witness. **14** To be able to withstand; allow: His story will not *bear* investigation. **15** To have or stand (in comparison or relation): with *to:* What relation does this *bear* to the other? **16** To possess as a right or power: to *bear* title. — *v.i.* **17** To carry burdens; convey. **18** To rest heavily; lean; press: His duties *bear* heavily upon him. **19** To endure patiently; suffer: often with *with*: *Bear* with me. **20** To produce fruit or young. **21** To move, point, or lie in a certain direction; take an aim or course: Later, we *bore* west. **22** To be relevant; have reference: with *on* or *upon*: The argument *bears* on the subject. See synonyms under ABIDE, CARRY, ENDURE, LEAN, PRODUCE, SUPPORT. **— to bear company** To accompany. **— to bear down** To force down; overpower or overcome. **— to bear down upon 1** *Naut.* To approach from the weather side: said of a vessel; hence, to approach. **2** To press hard; put pressure on. **— to bear in mind** To keep in recollection; remember. **— to bear out** To support; confirm; justify. **— to bear up** To keep up strength or spirits. **— to bear upon** To be trained upon, as cannon, so as to bring within the line of fire. [<OE *beran* carry, wear, bear, suffer]

bear² (bâr) *n.* **1** A large plantigrade carnivorous or omnivorous mammal (family *Ursidae*) with massive thick-furred body and short tail. ◆ Collateral adjective: *ursine.* **2** One of various other animals like or likened to a bear: the ant-*bear.* **3** The caterpillar of the tiger moth. **4** One of two constellations, the Great Bear or the Little Bear. **5** An ill-mannered or morose person. **6** A speculator who seeks to depress prices or who sells in the belief that there is likely to be a decline in prices. **7** *Mech.* A portable device for punching iron plates. **8** *Naut.* A weighted block of wood faced with sandstone and used for scouring the decks of a ship. **— Great Bear** A large northern constellation (*Ursa Major*). See CONSTELLATION. **— Little Bear** A northern constellation (*Ursa Minor*) including the polestar. See CONSTELLATION, POINTERS. **— the Bear** Russia. **—** *v.t.* To endeavor to depress the price of (stocks, etc.) by selling or offering to sell. ◆ Homophone: *bare.* [<OE *bera*]

bear·a·ble (bâr′ə-bəl) *adj.* Capable of being borne; endurable. **— bear′a·ble·ness** *n.* **— bear′a·bly** *adv.*

bear·ber·ry (bâr′ber′ē, -bər·ē) *n.* **1** A trailing, thick-leaved evergreen plant (*Arctostaphylos uva-ursi*) of the heath family, having small red berries and astringent leaves. **2** The deciduous holly (*Ilex decidua*): also called *possumhaw.*

beard (bird) *n.* **1** The hair on a man's face, especially on the chin, usually excluding the mustache. **2** *Zool.* **a** The long hair on the chin of some animals, as the goat. **b** The feathers near the mouth of certain birds, as the turkey; the vibrissae. **3** Any similar growth or appendage. **4** *Bot.* A tuft of hair-like processes; an awn, as of grass. **5** The barb of an arrow, or of any hook. **6** *Ornithol.* The vane or barbs of a feather. **7** *U.S. Slang* In radio broadcasting, an error in performance, usually a misreading of a part. **8** *Printing* That part of a type which divides the face from the shoulder. **—** *v.t.* **1** To take by the beard; pull the beard of. **2** To defy courageously. **3** To furnish with a beard. [OE] **— beard′ed** *adj.* **— beard′less** *adj.* **— beard′like′** *adj.*

Beards·ley (birdz′lē), **Aubrey Vincent,** 1872–1898, English artist and illustrator.

bear·er (bâr′ər) *n.* **1** One who or that which bears, carries, or has in possession. **2** A person to whom a note, check, or draft is made payable without naming him; hence, as no endorsement is required, the person who presents such instrument for collection. **3** A tree or vine producing fruit. **4** A carrier or porter. **5** A pallbearer.

bear·gar·den (bâr′gär′dən) *n.* **1** A place where bears are exhibited or kept, especially for bear-baiting. **2** Any place or scene of tumult or strife.

bear·grass (bâr′gras′, -gräs) *n.* **1** Any of various species of *Yucca.* **2** The camas (*Camassia scilloides*) of Oregon. **3** A yucca-like plant (*Dasylirion texanum*) of the lily family of the SW United States.

bear·ing (bâr′ing) *n.* **1** Deportment; manner of conducting or carrying oneself. **2** The act, capacity, or period of producing. **3** That which is produced; crops; yield. **4** The act

or capacity of enduring; endurance. **5** *Archit.* The part of an arch or beam that rests upon a support. **6** *Mech.* A part that rests on something, or on which something rests, or in which a pin, journal, etc., turns. **7** *Her.* A device or charge on a field. **8** The point of a compass in which an object is seen. **9** Often *pl.* The situation of an object relative to that of another, or of other points or places. **10** Reference or relation; connection: What *bearing* does his evidence have on the problem? See synonyms under AIR, BEHAVIOR, DIRECTION.

bear·ish (bâr′ish) *adj.* **1** Like a bear; rough; surly. **2** Tending to depress the price of stocks by offering to sell. **— bear′ish·ly** *adv.* **— bear′ish·ness** *n.*

bear-lead·er (bâr′lē′dər) *n.* **1** One who leads about a trained bear. **2** Hence, a young man's private tutor or traveling companion.

bear market In finance, a market in which prices decline.

bé·ar·naise sauce (bā·ȧr·nāz′) A variation of hollandaise sauce made with chopped parsley and vinegar.

bear·skin (bâr′skin′) *n.* **1** The skin of a bear or a coat or robe made of it. **2** A tall, black fur headdress worn as a part of some military uniforms. **3** A coarse, shaggy woolen cloth.

beast (bēst) *n.* **1** Any animal except man. **2** Any large quadruped. **3** Animal characteristics or animal nature. **4** A cruel, rude, or filthy person. See synonyms under ANIMAL. [<OF *beste* <LL *besta* <L *bestia* beast] **— beast′like′** *adj.*

beast·ie (bēs′tē) *n.* Scot. A little beast: a term of endearment.

beast·ly (bēst′lē) *adj.* **1** Resembling a beast; brutish; vile; degraded. **2** *Colloq.* Disagreeable or unpleasant; nasty; abominable. See synonyms under BRUTISH. **—** *adv. Brit. Slang* Very. **— beast′li·ness** *n.*

beast of burden An animal used for carrying loads.

beat (bēt) *v.* **beat, beat·en** (*Colloq.* **beat**), **beat·ing** *v.t.* **1** To strike repeatedly; pound. **2** To punish by repeated blows; thrash; whip. **3** To dash or strike against, as wind or waves. **4** To make, as one's way, by repeated blows: to *beat* a path to the door. **5** To forge or shape by or as by hammering. **6** To make flat by tramping or treading, as a path. **7** To subdue or defeat; master. **8** To flap; flutter, as wings. **9** *Music* To mark or measure with or as with a baton: to *beat* time. **10** To hunt over; search: to *beat* the country-side. **11** To sound (a signal) as on a drum. **12** To stir; turn (ingredients) over and over so as to make lighter or frothier. **13** *Colloq.* To baffle; perplex: It *beats* me. **14** *Slang* To defraud; swindle. **—** *v.i.* **15** To strike repeated blows. **16** To strike or smite as with blows: The sound *beats* on our ears. **17** To throb; pulsate. **18** To give forth sound, as when tapped or struck. **19** To sound a signal, as on a drum. **20** *Physics* To alternate in intensity so as to pulsate. **21** To be adaptable to beating: The yolk *beats* well. **22** To hunt through underbrush, etc., as for game. **23** To win a victory or contest. **24** *Naut.* To work against contrary winds or currents by tacking. **— to beat about** To search by one means and then another. **— to beat about the bush** To approach a subject in a round-about way. **— to beat a retreat** To give a signal for retreat, as by beat of drums; hence, to turn back; flee. **— to beat down** To force or persuade (a seller) to accept a lower price. **— to beat it** *Slang* To depart hastily. **— to beat the air** To make futile exertions. **— to beat up** *Colloq.* To thrash thoroughly. **—** *n.* **1** A stroke or blow, especially one producing sound or serving as a signal. **2** A pulsation or throb, as of the pulse. **3** *Physics* **a** A regularly recurring pulsation or throb heard when two tones not quite in unison are sounded together: caused by the interference of sound waves. **b** A similar property belonging to light waves and other waves. **4** *Naut.* A tack. **5** *Music* **a** The unit of measure for indicating rhythm. **b** The gesture or symbol for this. **6** The stroke or tick of a watch or clock. **7** A round, line, or district regularly traversed,

as by a sentry or a policeman. **8** A division of a county. **9** In newspaper slang, a scoop. **10** *U.S. Slang* A deadbeat (def. 1). **11** *Colloq.* A member of the Beat Generation. **—** *adj.* **1** *U.S. Colloq.* Fatigued; worn out. **2** Pertaining to the Beat Generation. [OE *bēatan*]

Synonyms (verb): bastinado, batter, belabor, bruise, castigate, chastise, conquer, cudgel, cuff, defeat, flog, overcome, pommel, pound, scourge, smite, strike, surpass, thrash, vanquish, whip, worst. *Strike* is the word for a single blow; to *beat* is to *strike* repeatedly. Others of the words above describe the manner of *beating*, as *bastinado*, to *beat* on the soles of the feet; *belabor*, to inflict an exhaustive *beating*; *cudgel*, to *beat* with a stick; *thrash* (originally identical with "thresh"), to *beat* with repeated blows, as wheat was *beaten* out with the old hand flail; to *pound* is to *beat* with a heavy, and *pommel* with a blunt, instrument. To *batter* and to *bruise* refer to the results of *beating*; that is *battered* which is broken or defaced by repeated blows; that is *bruised* which has suffered even one severe blow. To *beat* a combatant is to disable or dishearten him for further fighting. Hence *beat* becomes the synonym for every word which implies getting the advantage of another. Compare CONQUER, SUBDUE. Antonyms: fail, fall, surrender.

beat·en (bēt′n) *adj.* **1** Shaped by beating; having undergone blows. **2** Worn by use or travel: the *beaten* path. **3** Conquered or subdued; baffled.

beat·er (bē′tər) *n.* **1** One who or that which beats. **2** An implement or device for beating. **3** In hunting, one who arouses game and drives it from cover.

Beat Generation A group of post-World War II artists, writers, and musicians who seek spiritual fulfilment through sensual experience, disclaiming social responsibility or a hostile and thoroughly materialistic society.

be·a·tif·ic (bē′ə·tif′ik) *adj.* Making blessed or blissful. **— be·a·tif′i·cal·ly** *adv.*

be·at·i·fi·ca·tion (bē·at′ə·fi·kā′shən) *n.* **1** The act of blessing, or the state of being blessed or beatified. **2** In the Roman Catholic Church, an act of the Pope declaring a deceased person beatified (*beatus*) and worthy of a certain degree of public honor: usually the last step toward canonization.

be·at·i·fy (bē·at′ə·fī) *v.t.* **·fied, ·fy·ing 1** To make supremely happy. **2** In the Roman Catholic Church, to declare as blessed and worthy of public honor by an act of the Pope. **3** To exalt above others. [<F *béatifier* <LL *beatificare* bless <*beatus* happy + *facere* make]

beat·ing (bē′ting) *n.* **1** The action of one who or that which beats, or the process involved. **2** Punishment by blows; flogging. **3** Pulsation; throbbing, as of the heart. **4** A defeat.

be·at·i·tude (bē·at′ə·tōōd, -tyōōd) *n.* **1** Supreme blessedness or felicity. **2** A blessing. **— the Beatitudes** Eight declarations of special blessedness pronounced by Jesus in the Sermon on the Mount. *Matt.* v 3–11. [<F *béatitude* <L *beatitudo* blessedness <*beatus* happy]

beat·nik (bēt′nik) *n.* A member of the Beat Generation.

beat-note (bēt′nōt′) *n.* An audible radio frequency caused by the interaction of two frequencies of different value.

Be·a·trice (bē′ə·tris, *Ital.* bā′ä·trē′chä) A feminine personal name. Also **Be·a·trix** (bē′ə·triks; *Dan., Du., Ger., Sw.* bā·ä′triks), *Fr.* **Bé·a·trice** or **Bé·a·trix** (bā·à·trēs′), *Pg., Sp.* **Be·a·triz** (*Pg.* bā′ä·trēsh′, *Sp.* -trēth′). [<L, she who makes happy]
— Beatrice The heroine of Shakespeare's *Much Ado About Nothing.*
— Beatrice The idealized and symbolic heroine of Dante's *Divine Comedy*: identified with **Beatrice Por·ti·na·ri** (pôr′tē·nä′rē), 1266–90, Florentine lady.

Beat·ty (bē′tē), **Lord David,** 1871–1936, first Earl of Brooksby and the North Sea; British admiral of the fleet in World War I. **— James,** 1735–1803, Scottish poet.

beau (bō) *n. pl.* **beaus** or **beaux** (bōz) **1** A dandy; fop. **2** An escort. **3** A lover; swain. ◆ Homophone: *bow³.* [<F <L *bellus* fine, pretty] **— beau′ish** *adj.*

Beau Brum·mell (brum'əl) A dandy or fop. [after George ("*Beau*") *Brummell*, 1778–1840, English dandy]

Beau·fort (bō'fərt), **Henry,** 1370?–1447, English cardinal.

beaut (byōōt) *n. U.S. Slang* Something beautiful: often used ironically: *a beaut* of a black eye.

beau·te·ous (byōō'tē·əs) *adj.* Beautiful. See synonyms under BEAUTIFUL. **— beau'te·ous·ly** *adv.* **— beau'te·ous·ness** *n.*

beau·ti·cian (byōō·tish'ən) *n.* One who works in a beauty parlor, or a person trained in hairdressing, manicuring, massaging, etc.

beau·ti·ful (byōō'tə·fəl) *adj.* Possessing beauty; conforming to esthetic standards, or arousing esthetic pleasure. **— n. 1** Beauty in the abstract. **2** That which is beautiful. **— beau'ti·ful·ly** *adv.* **— beau'ti·ful·ness** *n.*

Synonyms (adj.): attractive, beauteous, bewitching, bonny, charming, comely, delightful, elegant, exquisite, fair, fine, graceful, handsome, lovely, picturesque, pretty. *Beautiful* implies softness of outline and delicacy of mold; it is opposed to all that is hard and rugged. *Pretty* expresses in a far less degree that which is pleasing to a refined taste. That is *handsome* which is superficially pleasing, and also well and harmoniously proportioned. *Handsome* is a term far inferior to *beautiful*; we may even say a *handsome* villain. *Fair* denotes what is bright, smooth, clear, and without blemish; as, a *fair* face. In a specific sense, *fair* has the sense of blond, as opposed to dark or brunette. One who possesses pleasing qualities may be *attractive* without beauty. *Comely* denotes an aspect that is smooth, genial, and wholesome, with fulness of contour and pleasing symmetry, while falling short of the *beautiful*. That is *picturesque* which would make a picture. See FINE, GRACEFUL, LOVELY. *Antonyms:* awkward, clumsy, deformed, disgusting, frightful, ghastly, grim, grisly, grotesque, hideous, horrid, odious, repulsive, shocking, ugly, unattractive, uncouth, ungainly, unlovely, unpleasant.

beau·ti·fy (byōō'tə·fī) *v.t. & v.i.* **·fied, ·fy·ing** To make or grow beautiful; embellish; adorn. See synonyms under ADORN, GARNISH. **— beau'·ti·fi·ca'tion** *n.* **— beau'ti·fied** *adj.* **— beau'ti·fi'er** *n.*

beau·ty (byōō'tē) *n. pl.* **·ties 1** Any of those qualities of objects, sounds, emotional or intellectual concepts, behavior, etc., that gratify or arouse admiration to a high degree, especially by the perfection of form resulting from the harmonious combination of diverse elements in unity. **2** A person or thing that is beautiful, especially a woman. **3** A special grace or charm. [<OF *beaute*, ult. <L *bellus* handsome, fine, pretty]

beauty parlor *U.S.* An establishment for the hairdressing, manicuring, cosmetic treatment, etc., of women. Also **beauty salon, beauty shop.**

beauty spot 1 A small black patch put on the face to enhance the brilliance of the complexion. **2** A mole or other natural mark resembling this. **3** Any place regarded as especially beautiful.

Beau·voir (bō·vwär'), **Simone de,** born 1908, French novelist.

beaux (bōz) Plural of BEAU.

Beaux (bō), **Cecilia,** 1863–1942, U.S. painter.

beaux-arts (bō·zär') *n. pl. French* The fine arts, as music, painting, sculpture, etc.

beaux yeux (bō zyœ') *French* Beautiful eyes; hence, a pretty face.

bea·ver¹ (bē'vər) *n.* **1** An amphibious rodent (family *Castoridae*), with a scaly, flat, oval tail and webbed hind feet, noted for skill in damming shallow streams: valued for its fur. **2** The fur of the beaver. **3** A high silk hat, originally made of this fur. **4** A heavy twill-woven woolen cloth with a napped finish, used for outer garments. [OE *beofor*]

BEAVER
(2 1/2 to 4 feet long, including tail)

bea·ver² (bē'vər) *n.* **1** A movable piece of medieval armor covering the lower part of the face, especially when worn with a vizor; later, both chinpiece and vizor. **2** *Slang* A beard. [<OF *bavière* child's bib <*bave* saliva]

bea·ver·board (bē'vər·bôrd', -bōrd') *n.* A light, stiff building material made of compressed or laminated wood pulp: used chiefly for walls and partitions.

Bea·ver·brook (bē'vər·brŏŏk), **Baron,** 1879–1964, William Maxwell Aitken, English publisher and statesman, born in Canada.

beaver cutting A place where the trees have been gnawed and leveled by beavers.

beaver dam A dam built by beavers.

beaver lodge A beaver den.

beaver pond A pond made by a beaver dam.

Beaver State Nickname of Oregon.

be·bee·rine (bi·bē'rēn, -rin) *n.* An amorphous alkaloid, $C_{18}H_{19}NO_3$, contained in the bark of the greenheart tree: used in medicine as a tonic and febrifuge. [<BEBEERU + -INE]

be·bop (bē'bop') *n.* A variety of jazz characterized by deliberate departures from key and extreme improvisation in rhythmic pattern, and sung with meaningless sounds. Also **be'bop'.**

be·calm (bi·käm') *v.t.* **1** To make quiet or calm; still. **2** To cause to be motionless for lack of wind, as a ship: used in the passive: The ship was *becalmed* off Africa.

be·came (bi·kām') Past tense of BECOME.

be·cause (bi·kôz') *conj.* For the reason that; on account of the fact that; since. [ME *bi cause* by cause]

Synonyms: as, for, since. *Because* is the most direct and complete word for giving the reason of a thing. *Since*, originally denoting succession in time, signifies a succession in a chain of reasoning, a natural inference or result. *As* indicates something like, coordinate, parallel. *Since* is weaker than *because*; *as* is weaker than *since*: either may introduce the reason before the main statement; thus, *since* or *as* you are going, I will accompany you. Often the weaker word is the more courteous, implying less constraint. *Antonyms:* although, however, nevertheless, notwithstanding, yet.

because of On account of; by reason of: He was unable to attend *because of* illness.

bé·cha·mel sauce (bā·shà·mel') A white sauce made of cream, butter, flour, etc., and flavored with onion and seasonings. [after Louis de *Béchamel*, steward to Louis XIV, who invented it]

be·chance (bi·chans', -chäns') *v.t. & v.i.* **be·chanced, be·chanc·ing** To befall; happen by chance.

bêche-de-mer (bâsh'də·mâr') *n.* **1** The trepang. **2** A lingua franca of largely English vocabulary, used between Europeans and the natives of the SW Pacific: originally developed through commerce with trepang fishermen: also called *beach-la-mar*. [<F, sea spade]

Bech·u·a·na (bech'ŏŏ·ä'nə, bek·yōō-) *n. pl.* **·a·na** or **·a·nas 1** One of an important Bantu tribe inhabiting the region between the Orange and Zambesi Rivers, SW Africa. **2** The Bantu language of this tribe.

Bech·u·a·na·land (bech'ŏŏ·ä'nə·land, bek·yōō-) A former British territory in southern Africa. See BOTSWANA.

beck¹ (bek) *n.* A nod or other gesture of summons. **— at one's beck and call** Subject to one's slightest wish. **— v.t. & v.i. 1** To beckon. **2** *Scot.* To recognize (a person) by a nod; bow or curtsy. [Var. of BECKON]

beck² (bek) *n.* A small brook, or the valley in which it runs. [<ON *bekkr* stream, brook]

beck·et (bek'it) *n.* **1** *Naut.* A device for holding a ship's spars, ropes, etc., in position, as a cleat, a strap, loop, or rope, or a small grommet. **2** *Slang* A trouser pocket. [Origin unknown]

Beck·et (bek'it), **Thomas à, Saint,** 1117–70, English archbishop of Canterbury, murdered for his opposition to Henry II.

beck·on (bek'ən) *v.t. & v.i.* **1** To signal, direct, or summon by sign or gesture. **2** To entice or lure. **— n.** A summoning gesture; beck. [OE *biecnan, beacnian* make signs <*bēacen* a sign. Related to BEACON.]

be·cloud (bē·kloud') *v.t.* **1** To obscure by a cloud or clouds; darken. **2** To confuse, as an issue.

be·come (bi·kum') *v.* **be·came, be·come, be·com·**ing *v.i.* **1** To undergo development; grow to be: The chick *becomes* the chicken. **2** To come to be: The land *became* dry. **— v.t. 3** To suit or befit: Your words do not *become* you. **4** To be suitable to; show to advantage: Your dress *becomes* you. **— to become of** To be the fate of: I don't know what *became of* him. [OE *becuman* happen, come about]

be·com·ing (bi·kum'ing) *adj.* **1** Appropriate; suitable. **2** Pleasing; adorning. **— be·com'·ing·ly** *adv.* **— be·com'ing·ness** *n.*

Synonyms: befitting, beseeming, comely, congruous, decent, decorous, fit, fitting, graceful, meet, neat, proper, seemly, suitable, worthy. That is *becoming* in dress which suits the complexion, figure, and other qualities of the wearer, so as to produce a pleasing effect. That is *decent* which does not offend modesty or propriety. That is *suitable* which is adapted to the age, station, situation, and other circumstances of the wearer. In conduct much the same rules apply. The dignity and gravity of a patriarch would not be *becoming* to a child; at a funeral lively, cheery sociability would not be *decorous*, while noisy hilarity would not be *decent*. *Meet* now expresses chiefly a moral fitness; as, *meet* for heaven. Compare APPROPRIATE. *Antonyms:* awkward, ill-becoming, ill-fitting, improper, indecent, indecorous, unbecoming, unfit, unseemly, unsuitable.

Becquerel rays Rays emitted by radioactive substances. [after Antoine Henri *Becquerel*, who discovered them]

bed (bed) *n.* **1** An article of furniture to rest or sleep in or on: either the stuffed tick or mattress, on which the body rests, the mattress and bedclothes, the bedstead, or all combined; a couch. **2** Any place or thing used for a couch or for sleeping in or on. **3** Something likened to or serving as a bed, foundation, or support: the *bed* of a lake, a rocky *bed*. **4** The marriage bed; marriage. **5** Conjugal cohabitation, or the right to it. **6** A heavy horizontal mass of matter or a collection of closely massed objects, especially used as a foundation or support. **7** Anything resembling or used for a bed. **8** A part or surface that serves as a foundation. **9** The part of a printing press which supports the form, or a part from which work is fed to a machine. **10** A layer of mortar in which stones or bricks are to be laid. **11** A horizontal course of a stone wall. **12** The lower side of a slate, tile, or brick. **13** A plot of ground prepared for planting some particular thing, or the plants, etc., growing in such a plot. **14** A roadbed or a foundation for rails. **15** *Geol.* Any layer in a mass of stratified rock; a seam; a deposit, as of ore, parallel to the stratification. **16** A wagon body. **— v. bed·ded, bed·ding** *v.t.* **1** To furnish with a bed. **2** To put to bed. **3** To make a bed for; provide with litter: often with *down*: to *bed* cattle down. **4** To set out or plant in a bed of earth. **5** To have sexual intercourse with. **6** To lay flat or arrange in layers: to *bed* oysters. **7** To place firmly; embed. **— v.i. 8** To go to bed. **9** To form a closely packed layer; stratify. [OE] **— bed'der** *n.*

be·daub (bi·dôb') *v.t.* **1** To smear with something oily or sticky; soil. **2** To abuse; vilify. **3** To load with vulgar ornament or flattery.

be·daz·zle (bi·daz'əl) *v.t.* **·zled, ·zling 1** To blind by excess of light. **2** To bewilder; confuse.

bed·bug (bed'bug') *n.* A bloodsucking hemipterous insect (*Cimex lectularius*) of reddish-brown color, infesting houses and especially beds. See illustration under INSECTS (injurious).

bed·cham·ber (bed'chām'bər) *n.* A sleeping apartment; a bedroom.

bed·clothes (bed'klōz', -klōthz') *n. pl.* Covering for a bed, as sheets, blankets, quilts, etc.

bed·ding (bed'ing) *n.* **1** The furnishings for a bedstead. **2** Straw or other litter for animals to sleep on. **3** A putting to bed. **4** That which forms a bed or foundation. **5** *Geol.* Stratification of rocks.

be·deck (bi·dek') *v.t.* To deck; adorn; ornament. See synonyms under ADORN.

bede·man (bēd'mən) *n.* A beadsman.

be·dev·il (bi·dev'əl) *v.t.* **·iled** or **·illed, ·il·ing** or **·il·ling 1** To torment; worry. **2** To harass with diabolical treatment or abuse. **3** To spoil; corrupt, as by witchcraft. **4** To possess with or as with a devil; bewitch. **5** To make or transform into a devil. **—be·dev′il·ment** *n.*

be·dew (bi-dōō′, -dyōō′) *v.t.* To moisten with or as with dew.

bed·fel·low (bed′fel′ō) *n.* One who shares a bed with another.

be·dight (bi-dīt′) *v.t.* **be·dight, be·dight·ing** *Archaic* To furnish with dress or ornament; adorn; apparel; bedeck.

be·dim (bi-dim′) *v.t.* **be·dimmed, be·dim·ming** To make dim; obscure.

be·diz·en (bi-diz′ən, -dī′zən) *v.t.* To dress or adorn with tawdry splendor. **—be·diz′en·ment** *n.*

bed·lam (bed′ləm) *n.* **1** An excited crowd. **2** An incoherent uproar. **3** A lunatic asylum; a madhouse. [<BEDLAM]

Bed·lam (bed′ləm) The hospital of St. Mary of Bethlehem in London, used for the insane. [Alter. of BETHLEHEM] **—Bed′lam·ite** (-īt) *n.*

bed·lam·ite (bed′ləm·īt) *n.* A lunatic.

bed linen Sheets, pillow cases, etc., for beds.

Bed·ling·ton terrier (bed′ling·tən) A muscular terrier used in hunting badgers, foxes, etc. See under TERRIER.

Bed·loe′s Island (bed′lōz) A former name for LIBERTY ISLAND.

bed·mold·ing (bed′-mōl′ding) *n. Archit.* A molding, or one of a series of moldings, under the corona in a cornice.

BEDLINGTON TERRIER
(About 16 inches high at the shoulder)

Bed·ou·in (bed′ōō·in, -ēn) *n.* **1** One of the nomadic Arabs of Syria, Arabia, etc. **2** Such nomads collectively. **3** Any nomad or vagabond. **—adj.** **1** Of or pertaining to the Bedouins. **2** Roving; nomadic. Also spelled *Beduin.* [<F <Arabic *badāwîn* desert dweller < *badw* desert]

bed·pan (bed′pan′) *n.* **1** An earthenware or porcelain vessel to be used in bed by a sick person for urination or defecation. **2** A warming pan.

bed·plate (bed′plāt′) *n. Mech.* A plate or frame to which the lighter parts of a machine are bolted.

bed·post (bed′pōst′) *n.* One of the posts supporting a bedstead.

be·drag·gle (bi-drag′əl) *v.t. & v.i.* **-gled, -gling** To make or become wet or soiled, as by dragging through mire.

bed·rid·den (bed′rid′ən) *adj.* Confined to bed, by sickness or weakness. Also **bed′rid′.** [OE *bedrida* <*bed* bed + *rida* rider]

bed·rock (bed′rok′) *n. Geol.* The solid rock underlying the looser materials of the earth's surface. **—down to bedrock 1** Down to the lowest limit: Prices dropped *down to bedrock.* **2** Down to fundamentals; down to the truth of the matter.

bed·roll (bed′rōl′) *n.* **1** Bedding compactly rolled to facilitate carrying. **2** The cover for a roll of bedding.

bed·room (bed′rōōm′, -rŏŏm′) *n.* A sleeping room.

bed·side (bed′sīd′) *n.* Place by a bed; the side of the bed. **—adj.** Pertaining to or suitable for the bedside: a *bedside* manner.

bed·sore (bed′sôr′, -sōr′) *n.* An ulcer on the body, caused by lying long in one position.

bed·spread (bed′spred′) *n.* A quilt or counterpane.

bed·spring (bed′spring′) *n.* The framework of springs supporting the mattress of a bed.

bed·staff (bed′staf′, -stäf′) *n. pl.* **-staves** (-stāvz′) **1** A stick or staff used in some way about a bed, as to smooth a featherbed or to spread the coverlets. **2** A bar at the side to keep the bedclothes in place.

bed·stead (bed′sted′) *n.* A framework for supporting a mattress, bedding, etc.

bed·time (bed′tīm′) *n.* The time for retiring to bed. **—adj.** Of or for this time: *bedtime* stories.

bed·ward (bed′wərd) *adv.* **1** Toward bed. **2** Toward bedtime. Also **bed′wards.**

bed-wet·ting (bed′wet′ing) *n.* Nocturnal enuresis.

bee[1] (bē) *n.* **1** Any of a large number of hymenopterous insects of the family *Apoidea,* solitary or social in habit, with smooth or hairy bodies, variously colored, and feeding largely upon nectar and pollen. **2** The common hive or honey bee (*Apis mellifera*). **3** A social gathering of neighbors for work or competitive activity: a quilting *bee.* **—to have a bee in one's bonnet** To be excessively concerned about or obsessed with one idea. [OE *beo*]

bee[2] (bē) *n. Naut.* A strip of timber or iron bolted to each side of the bowsprit of a vessel, through which to reeve the foretopmast stays. Also **bee block.** [OE *bēag* ring]

bee·bread (bē′bred′) *n.* A mixture of pollen and certain proteins as stored by bees for food.

beech (bēch) *n.* **1** Any of a family of trees of temperate regions with smooth, ash–gray bark, and bearing an edible nut; especially, the widely cultivated European beech (*Fagus sylvatica*) and the American beech (*F. grandifolia*). **2** One of various trees similar to the beech: the blue *beech* (*Carpinus caroliniana*). **3** The wood of this tree. ◆ Homophone: **beach.** [OE *bēce*] **—beech′en** *adj.*

beech·nut (bēch′nut′) *n.* The edible nut of the beech.

bee–eat·er (bē′ē′tər) *n.* Any of certain bright-plumaged European birds (family *Meropidae*) of insectivorous habits.

beef (bēf) *n. pl.* **beeves** (bēvz) or **beefs** *for def.* **2; beefs** *for def.* **4 1** The flesh of a slaughtered adult bovine animal. **2** Any adult bovine animal, as an ox, cow, steer, bull, etc., fattened for the butcher. **3** *Colloq.* Muscular power; brawn. **4** *U.S. Slang* A complaint. **—bully beef** Canned or pickled beef. **—dried beef** Beef preserved by salting and drying, usually in smoke. **—v.i.** *U.S. Slang* To complain or grouse. [<OF *boef* < L *bos, bovis* ox]

Beefeater One of the Yeomen of the Guard who attend the British sovereign on state occasions, or one of the similarly uniformed warders of the Tower of London.

beefed–up (bēft′up′) *adj. Colloq.* Strengthened or reinforced to increase load capacity: said of an aircraft.

beef·ing (bē′fing) *n.* **1** A kind of apple, so named because of its deep–red, beeflike color. **2** *U.S. Slang* Complaining.

bee–fly (bē′flī′) *n. pl.* **-flies** A hairy fly (family *Bombyliidae*) somewhat resembling a bee: the larvae destroy the young of wasps and other insects. For illustration see INSECTS (beneficial).

beef·steak (bēf′stāk′) *n.* A slice of beef suitable for broiling or frying.

beef·y (bē′fē) *adj.* **beef·i·er, beef·i·est 1** Like an ox; fat; dull. **2** *Colloq.* Brawny; muscular. **—beef′i·ness** *n.*

bee gum 1 A hollow gum tree in which bees nest. **2** A beehive, especially one made from a hollow gum tree.

bee·hive (bē′hīv′) *n.* **1** A hive for a colony of honey bees. **2** Any place filled with busy workers. **3** A woman's hair style in which the hair is coiled in a conical mound.

bee·keep·er (bē′kē′pər) *n.* One who keeps bees; an apiarist.

bee·line (bē′līn′) *n.* The shortest course from one place to another, as of a bee to its hive.

Be·el·ze·bub (bē·el′zə·bub) **1** The prince of the demons or of false gods; the devil. **2** In Milton's *Paradise Lost,* a chief of the lost angels ranking next to Satan. **3** A Semitic god, worshiped as the lord of flies: the original sense.

been (bin, *Brit.* bēn) Past participle of BE.

beep (bēp) *n.* A short, usually high-pitched mechanical or electronic sound used as a signal or warning. **—v.i.** **1** To make such a sound. **—v.t.** **2** To sound (a horn): taxi drivers *beeping* their horns. **3** To transmit (a message) by a beep or beeps. [Imit.]

beer (bir) *n.* **1** An alcoholic fermented liquor made from malt and hops. **2** A slightly fermented beverage made from the roots, etc., of various plants, as sassafras, ginger, spruce, etc. ◆ Homophone: **bier.** [OE *bēor*]

beer·y (bir′ē) *adj.* **1** Of, pertaining to, or like beer. **2** Stained or tainted with beer. **3** Addicted to or affected by beer: a *beery* voice. **4** Maudlin.

beest·ings (bēs′tingz) *n.* The first milk from a cow after calving; the colostrum: also spelled *biestings.* [OE *bȳsting* < *beost*]

bees·wax (bēz′waks′) *n.* A white or yellowish plastic substance, secreted by honey bees, from which they make the cells of their comb: widely used in medicine and the arts. **—v.t.** To smear with beeswax; wax.

bees·wing (bēz′wing′) *n.* **1** A filmy crust of scales of tartar on the surface of some old wines, as port. **2** The wine so crusted.

beet[1] (bēt) *n.* **1** The fleshy succulent root of a biennial herb of the goosefoot family (genus *Beta*); especially, the common or red beet (*B. vulgaris*), used as a vegetable, and the sugar beet (*B. saccharifera*), used in making sugar. **2** The plant. ◆ Homophone: **beat.** [OE *bēte* < L *beta*]

beet[2] (bēt) *v.t. Brit. Dial.* **1** To kindle or replenish, as a fire; hence, to rouse; stir. **2** *Obs.* To mend or amend; correct. Also **beete.** ◆ Homophone: **beat.** [OE *bētan* make better, amend]

Bee·tho·ven (bā′tō·vən), **Ludwig van,** 1770–1827, German composer.

bee·tle[1] (bēt′l) *n.* **1** Any coleopterous insect having biting mouth parts and hard, horny elytra that serve as a cover for the membranous posterior wings when at rest. For illustrations see under INSECT. **2** Loosely, any insect resembling a beetle. **3** A short-sighted or intellectually blind person; a blockhead. **—adj.** Shaggy; overhanging: a *beetle* brow: also **bee′tling.** **—v.i.** **·tled, ·tling** To jut out; overhang. [OE *bitula* <*bītan* bite]

bee·tle[2] (bēt′l) *n.* **1** A heavy wooden hammer or mallet; a maul. **2** A pestle or mallet for pounding clothes, or for various other purposes, as mashing potatoes. **3** A beetling machine. **—v.t.** **·tled, ·tling** To beat or stamp with or as with a beetle, mallet, beetling machine, etc. [OE *bíetel* mallet <*bēatan* beat]

bee·tle–browed (bēt′l·broud′) *adj.* Having prominent, overhanging eyebrows.

be·fall (bi-fôl′) *v.* **be·fell, be·fall·en, be·fall·ing** *v.i.* **1** To come about; happen; occur. **2** *Obs.* To fall as one's right or share; belong; be fitting. **—v.t.** **3** To happen to. [OE *bef(e)allan* fall]

be·fit (bi-fit′) *v.t.* **be·fit·ted, be·fit·ting** To be suited to; be appropriate for.

be·fit·ting (bi-fit′ing) *adj.* Becoming; adequate; suitable. See synonyms under APPROPRIATE, BECOMING. **—be·fit′ting·ly** *adv.*

be·fog (bi-fôg′, fog′) *v.t.* **be·fogged, be·fog·ging 1** To envelop in or as in fog. **2** To confuse; obscure.

be·fool (bi-fōōl′) *v.t.* **1** To make a dupe or fool of; hoodwink; delude. **2** To call or treat as a fool.

be·fore (bi-fôr′, -fōr′) *adv.* **1** In front; ahead. **2** Preceding in time; previously. **3** Earlier; sooner. **—prep.** **1** In front of; ahead of. **2** Face to face with; in the presence of: The prisoner stood *before* the court. **3** Prior to, in time; earlier or sooner than. **4** In advance of, as in rank, development, or attainment. **5** Demanding the attention of: The bill is *before* the senate. **6** In the cognizance or power of: *Before* God, I swear it. **7** Driven in front of; moved by: The ship sailed *before* the wind. **—conj.** **1** Previous to the time when; sooner than. **2** In preference to; rather than: They will die *before* yielding. [OE *beforan* in front of]

be·fore·hand (bi-fôr′hand′, -fōr′-) *adv. & adj.* In anticipation or advance; ahead of time.

be·fore·time (bi-fôr′tīm′, -fōr′-) *adv.* In former time; formerly.

be·foul (bi-foul′) *v.t.* To make foul or dirty; sully.

be·friend (bi-frend′) *v.t.* **1** To be a friend to; stand by; help in time of need. **2** To become a friend to; make friends with. See synonyms under AID, HELP.

be·fud·dle (bi-fud′l) *v.t.* **·dled, ·dling** To confuse, as with liquor or glib arguments.

---

add,āce,câre,pälm; end,ēven; it,īce; odd,ōpen,ôrder; tŏŏk,pōōl; up,bûrn; ə = a in *above,* e in *sicken,* i in *clarity,* o in *melon,* u in *focus* ; yōō = u in *fuse,* oi,oil; ou,pout; ch,check; g,go; ng,ring; th,thin; ŧħ,this; zh,vision. Foreign sounds à,œ,ü,kh,ṅ; and ◆ : see page xx. <from; + plus; ? possibly.

beg¹ (beg) *v.* **begged, beg·ging** *v.t.* **1** To ask for or solicit in charity. **2** To entreat of; beseech. —*v.i.* **3** To ask alms or charity. **4** To entreat humbly. —**to beg off** To free or attempt to free oneself (from a duty, engagement, obligation, etc.) by persuasion, excuse, or pleading. —**to beg the question** To take for granted the matter in dispute. —**to go begging 1** To fail of acceptance, adoption, or use: The office *went begging.* **2** To live the life of a beggar. [? <AF *begger* beg <OF *begard* mendicant friar. See BEGHARD.]

beg² (beg) *n.* A bey.

be·gan (bi·gan′) Past tense of BEGIN.

be·get (bi·get′) *v.t.* **be·got** (*Archaic* **be·gat**), **be·got·ten** or **be·got, be·get·ting 1** To procreate; be the father of. **2** To cause to be; occasion. [OE *begitan*] —**be·get′ter** *n.*

beg·gar (beg′ər) *n.* **1** One who asks alms, especially one who makes his living by begging. **2** A person in poor or impoverished circumstances; a pauper. **3** A fellow; rogue: used contemptuously or humorously: a sulky *beggar*; smart little *beggar.* —*v.t.* **1** To reduce to want; impoverish. **2** To outdo; exhaust the resources of: It *beggars* analysis. [<OF *begard* mendicant friar] —**beg′gar·dom, beg′gar·hood** *n.* —**beg′gar·er** *n.*

beg·gar·ly (beg′ər·lē) *adj.* **1** Miserably poor; like or characteristic of a beggar. **2** Mean; sordid; contemptible. —**beg′gar·li·ness** *n.*

beg·gar's-lice (beg′ərz·līs′) *n.* Any of various plants bearing prickly fruit which adheres readily to clothes, as bedstraws and stickseeds.

beg·gar·ticks (beg′ər·tiks′) *n.* **1** The bur marigold or its seed vessels. **2** Beggar's-lice. Also **beg′gar's-ticks′.**

beg·gar·weed (beg′ər·wēd′) *n.* **1** Any of several species of plants used for forage and a cover crop in the southern United States, especially the Florida beggarweed or clover (*Desmodium tortuosum*). **2** A low annual plant (*Spergula arvensis*), now cultivated in some regions for forage and fertilizing: also called *corn spurry.*

beg·gar·y (beg′ər·ē) *n.* **1** The state or condition of being a beggar; extreme indigence or deficiency, penury. **2** Beggars as a class. **3** The act or habit of begging. See synonyms under POVERTY.

be·gin (bi·gin′) *v.* **be·gan, be·gun, be·gin·ning** *v.t.* **1** To commence or enter upon. **2** To give origin to; start. —*v.i.* **3** To start. **4** To come into being; arise. **5** To have the essentials or the ability: used with a negative: She doesn't *begin* to sing as well as her sister. [OE *beginnan*]
Synonyms: commence, inaugurate, initiate, undertake. See INSTITUTE.

be·gin·ner (bi·gin′ər) *n.* **1** A founder; originator. **2** One beginning to learn a trade or skill, study a new subject, etc.; a novice; tyro.

be·gin·ning (bi·gin′ing) *n.* **1** The starting point in space, time or action; origin. **2** The first stage or part. **3** The source or first cause of anything.
Synonyms: commencement, foundation, fountain, inauguration, inception, initiation, opening, origin, outset, rise, source, spring, start. The Latin *commencement* is more formal than the Anglo-Saxon *beginning*, as the verb *commence* is more formal than *begin. Commencement* is for the most part restricted to some form of action, while *beginning* has no restriction, but may be applied to whatever may be conceived of as having a first part, point, degree, etc. An *origin* is the point from which something starts or sets out, often involving causal connections; as the *origin* of a nation, government, or a family. A *source* is that which furnishes a first and continuous supply; as, the *source* of a river. A *rise* is thought of as in an action; we say that a lake is the *source* of a certain river, or that the river takes its *rise* from the lake. Compare CAUSE. *Antonyms:* see synonyms for END.

be·gird (bi·gûrd′) *v.t.* To gird; encircle; encompass. [OE *begyrdan*]

beg·ohm (beg′ōm′) *n.* One billion ohms, or one thousand megohms: a unit of electrical resistance. [<*beg-* billion (on analogy with *meg-* million) + OHM]

be·gone (bi·gôn′, -gon′) *interj.* Depart! Go away!

be·gon·ia (bi·gōn′yə) *n.* A plant of a large and widely distributed semitropical genus (*Be-*

gonia) with brilliantly colored leaves and showy irregular flowers. [after Michel *Begon*, 1638–1710, French colonial administrator]

be·got (bi·got′) Past tense and past participle of BEGET.

be·got·ten (bi·got′n) A past participle of BEGET.

be·grime (bi·grīm′) *v.t.* **be·grimed, be·grim·ing** To soil; make dirty with grime.

be·grudge (bi·gruj′) *v.t.* **be·grudged, be·grudg·ing 1** To envy one the possession or enjoyment of (something). **2** To give or grant reluctantly. —**be·grudg′ing·ly** *adv.*

be·guile (bi·gīl′) *v.t.* **be·guiled, be·guil·ing 1** To deceive; mislead by guile. **2** To cheat; defraud: with *of* or *out of.* **3** To while away pleasantly, as time. **4** To charm; divert. See synonyms under DECEIVE, ENTERTAIN. —**be·guile′ment** *n.* —**be·guil′er** *n.*

Be·guine (beg′ēn, *Fr.* bā·gēn′) *n.* One of a lay Catholic sisterhood, originating in the Netherlands (12th century), devoted to a religious life, but not bound by irrevocable vows.

be·gum (bē′gəm) *n.* A Moslem princess, or woman of rank in India. [<Hind. *begam* <Turkish *bigim* princess]

be·gun (bi·gun′) Past participle of BEGIN.

be·half (bi·haf′, -häf′) *n.* The interest or defense of (anyone): preceded by *in, on,* or *upon.* [OE *be healfe* by the side (of)]

be·have (bi·hāv′) *v.* **be·haved, be·hav·ing** *v.i.* **1** To comport oneself properly: Will you *behave?* **2** To conduct oneself or itself: The car *behaves* well. **3** To react to stimuli or environment. —*v.t.* **4** To conduct (oneself) properly or suitably. [ME *be-* thoroughly + *have* hold oneself, act]

be·hav·ior (bi·hāv′yər) *n.* **1** Manner of one's conduct; demeanor; deportment. **2** Manner or action of a machine, a chemical, substance, organ, organism, etc. **3** *Psychol.* The form of nervous, muscular, and emotional response of an individual to internal or external stimuli. Also *Brit.* **be·hav′iour.**
Synonyms: action, bearing, breeding, carriage, conduct, demeanor, deportment, manner, manners. *Behavior* is our *action* in the presence of others; *conduct* is a more general term, usually having ethical reference. *Demeanor* is the bodily expression, not only of feelings, but of moral states; as, a devout *demeanor. Breeding*, unless with some adverse limitation, denotes that *manner* and *conduct* which result from good birth and training. *Deportment* is *behavior* as related to a set of rules; as, the pupil's *deportment* was faultless. A person's *manner* may be that of a moment, or toward a single person: his *manners* are his habitual *behavior* toward or before others, especially in matters of etiquette and politeness; as, good *manners* are always pleasing. Compare AIR.

be·hav·ior·ism (bi·hāv′yər·iz′əm) *n. Psychol.* The theory that human behavior and activities are the result of individual reaction to definite objective stimuli or situations, and not of subjective factors. —**be·hav′ior·ist** *n.* —**be·hav′ior·is′tic** *adj.*

be·head (bi·hed′) *v.t.* To take the head from; decapitate. —**be·head′al** *n.*

be·held (bi·held′) Past tense and past participle of BEHOLD.

be·he·moth (bi·hē′məth, bē′ə-) *n.* In the Bible, a colossal beast, probably a hippopotamus. [<Hebrew *behēmōth*, pl. of *behēmāh* beast, ? <Egyptian *p-ehe-mah* water-ox]

be·hest (bi·hest′) *n.* An authoritative request; command. [OE *behæs* promise, vow]

be·hind (bi·hīnd′) *adv.* **1** In, toward, or at the rear; backward: looking *behind.* **2** In a previous place, condition, etc.: They left their regrets *behind.* **3** In time gone by: The days of youth are *behind.* **4** In reserve; to be made known: There is no evidence *behind.* **5** In arrears; not according to schedule: to fall *behind* in one's work. **6** Retarded in time, as a train or clock. —*prep.* **1** At the back or farther side of: The house is *behind* those trees. **2** To or toward the rear: Look *behind* you as you come. **3** Following after: The infantry came *behind* the cavalry. **4** Remaining after: He left a fortune *behind* him. **5** Later than: He stayed *behind* the others that day. **6** Sustaining; supporting: He has wealth *behind* him. **7** Inferior to, as in position, accomplishments, etc.; not so well advanced as: He is *behind* the others in his lessons. **8** Not yet revealed or

made known about: something strange *behind* that remark. —**to put behind one** To refuse to accept or consider. —*n. Colloq.* The buttocks. [OE *behindan*]

be·hind·hand (bi·hīnd′hand′) *adv. & adj.* **1** Behind time; late. **2** In arrears. **3** In a backward state; not sufficiently advanced.

behind the times Old-fashioned; antiquated; out-of-date.

be·hold (bi·hōld′) *v.t.* **be·held, be·hold·ing** To look at or upon; observe. —*interj.* Look! See! See synonyms under LOOK. [OE *beh(e)aldan* hold] —**be·hold′er** *n.*

be·hold·en (bi·hōl′dən) *adj.* Indebted.

be·hoof (bi·hoof′) *n.* That which benefits; advantage; use. [OE *behōf* advantage]

be·hoove (bi·hoov′) *v.* **be·hooved, be·hoov·ing** *v.t.* To be becoming to; be needful or right for: used impersonally: It *behooves* me to leave. —*v.i. Archaic* To be needful, essential or fit: used impersonally. Also **be·hove** (bi·hōv′). [OE *behōfian*] —**be·hoove′ful** *adj.*

beige (bāzh) *n.* **1** The color of natural, undyed, unbleached wool. **2** A soft fabric of undyed, unbleached wool. —*adj.* Of the color of natural wool. [<F]

be·ing (bē′ing) Present participle of BE. —*n.* **1** Any person or thing that exists or is conceived of as existing. **2** Existence, especially, conscious existence. **3** Essential nature of anything: His whole *being* is musical.

Bei·rut (bā′root, bā·root′) A port on the Mediterranean and the capital of Lebanon: ancient *Berytus:* also *Beyrouth.*

bel (bel) *n. Physics* A unit representing the ratio of the values of two amounts of power on a logarithmic scale to the base 10. [after A. G. *Bell*]

Bel (bāl) In Babylonian mythology, the god of heaven and earth.

be·la·bor (bi·lā′bər) *v.t.* **1** To beat; thrash soundly. **2** To assail verbally. **3** *Obs.* To toil over; work at. See synonyms under BEAT. Also *Brit.* **be·la′bour.**

be·lat·ed (bi·lā′tid) *adj.* Delayed past the usual or proper time. —**be·lat′ed·ly** *adv.* —**be·lat′·ed·ness** *n.*

be·lay (bi·lā′) *v.* **be·layed, be·lay·ing** *v.t.* **1** *Naut.* To make fast (a rope) by winding on a cleat or pin. **2** In mountain-climbing, to hitch (a rope) over a rock, piton, or other support. —*v.i.* **3** *Colloq.* To stop or hold; cease: *Belay* there. —*n.* A rock or other support, about which a rope may be hitched in order to provide security for a mountain climber; also, the state of being thus secured: He was in *belay.* [OE *belecgan*]

bel can·to (bel kän′tō) The traditional Italian method of singing, characterized by ease of production and purity of tone. [<Ital., beautiful song]

belch (belch) *v.t. & v.i.* **1** To eject, throw out, or to come forth forcibly or violently; vomit. **2** To eject (gas) noisily from the stomach through the mouth; eructate. —*n.* An eructation. [OE *bealcian*] —**belch′er** *n.*

bel·dam (bel′dəm) *n.* A forbidding or malicious old woman; a hag. Also **bel·dame** (bel′·dəm, -dām′). [ME, grandmother <*bel* grand (<OF *bel* fine) + *dam* mother <OF *dame* lady]

be·lea·guer (bi·lē′gər) *v.t.* **1** To surround or shut in with an armed force. **2** To harass or annoy. See synonyms under ATTACK *verb.* [<Du. *belegeren* <*be-* about + *leger* camp] —**be·lea′guered** *adj.*

bel·em·nite (bel′əm·nīt) *n.* **1** *Paleontol.* The pointed cylindrical fossil shell of an extinct cephalopod related to the cuttlefish. **2** A thunderstone. [<NL *belemnites* <Gk. *belemnon* dart]

Be·len Pass (be·len′) A mountain defile in southern Turkey, identified with the Syrian Gates of antiquity: also *Bailan Pass, Beilan Pass.*

bel-es·prit (bel·es·prē′) *n.* *pl.* **beaux-es·prits** (bō·zes·prē′) *French* A person of culture or wit.

Bel·fast (bel′fast, -fäst) The capital of Northern Ireland; a county borough and port at the head of **Belfast Lough** (lôkh), an inlet between County Antrim and County Down.

bel·fry (bel′frē) *n.* *pl.* **·fries 1** A tower in which a bell is hung. **2** The part containing the bell. [<OF *berfrei* tower, ult. <Gmc.] —**bel′fried** *adj.*

Bel·gae (bel′jē) *n. pl.* An ancient people, occupying, in Caesar's time, the region that is now Belgium and northern France.

Bel·gian (bel′jən, -jē·ən) *adj.* Of or pertaining to Belgium. — *n.* A native or citizen of Belgium.

Belgian Congo See ZAIRE REPUBLIC.

Belgian marble Rance.

Bel·gic (bel′jik) *adj.* Of or pertaining to the ancient Belgae, to Belgium, or to the Netherlands.

Bel·gium (bel′jəm, -jē·əm) A constitutional monarchy of NW Europe; 11,779 square miles; capital, Brussels. *Flemish* **Bel·gi·ë** (bel′·gē·ə); *French* **Bel·gique** (bel·zhēk′).

Bel·grade A port on the Danube, the capital of both Yugoslavia and Serbia; *Serbo-Croatian* **Belgrade**.

Be·li·al (bē′lē·əl, bēl′yəl) **1** The ancient Hebrew personification of lawlessness; the devil. **2** Any fiend: used by Milton in *Paradise Lost* as the name of one of the fallen angels.

be·lie (bi·lī′) *v.t.* **be·lied**, **be·ly·ing** **1** To misrepresent; disguise: His clothes *belie* his station. **2** To prove false; contradict: Her actions *belied* her words. **3** To disappoint; fail to fulfil: to *belie* hopes. **4** To traduce; slander. [OE *belēogan*] — **be·li′er** *n.*

be·lief (bi·lēf′) *n.* **1** Probable knowledge. **2** Mental conviction; acceptance of something as true or actual. **3** Confidence; trust in another's veracity. **4** That which is believed; creed. **5** Religious faith.
Synonyms: admission, assent, assurance, avowal, confidence, conviction, credence, credit, creed, opinion, reliance, trust. See DOCTRINE, FAITH, FANCY, IDEA. *Antonyms*: denial, disavowal, disbelief, dissent, distrust, doubt, misgiving, rejection, unbelief.

be·lieve (bi·lēv′) *v.* **be·lieved**, **be·liev·ing** *v.t.* **1** To accept as true or real. **2** To accept the word of (someone); credit with veracity. **3** To think; assume: with a clause as object: I *believe* that I will be there tomorrow. — *v.i.* **4** To accept the truth, existence, worth, etc., of something: with *in*: I *believe* in freedom. **5** To trust someone; have confidence: with *in*: The country *believes* in you. **6** To have religious faith. See synonyms under TRUST. [ME *beleven* < *be-* completely + *leven* <OE *gelēfen* believe] — **be·liev′a·ble** *adj.* — **be·liev′er** *n.* — **be·liev′ing** *adj.* — **be·liev′ing·ly** *adv.*

be·like (bi·līk′) *adv. Obs.* Perhaps; probably.

be·lit·tle (bi·lit′l) *v.t.* **·tled**, **·tling** To cause to seem small or less; disparage; minimize. See synonyms under DISPARAGE.

Be·lize (bə·lēz′) **1** The capital of British Honduras. *Spanish* **Be·li·ce** (bā·lē′sā). **2** Former name for BRITISH HONDURAS.

bell[1] (bel) *n.* **1** A hollow metallic instrument, usually cup-shaped, which gives forth a ringing sound when it is struck. **2** Anything in the shape of or suggesting a bell. **3** The lower termination of a tubular musical instrument. **4** A bell-shaped flower or corolla, the catkin

LIBERTY BELL

of the hop, the body of a helmet, etc. **5** *Naut.* **a** A stroke on a bell to mark the time on shipboard. **b** *pl.* With a numeral prefixed, the time so marked, in half-hours, from one to eight, in each period of four hours beginning at midnight, 8 bells marking the commencement of each period. — **Liberty Bell** The first bell rung to announce the signing of the Declaration of Independence, July 4, 1776, in Philadelphia. — *v.t.* **1** To put a bell on. **2** To shape like a bell. — *v.i.* **3** To take the shape of a bell. **4** To blossom; be in bell, as hops. — **to bell the cat** To plan or perform a bold or rash act: from Aesop's fable about the mice who resolved in self-protection to hang a bell on the cat's neck. ◆ Homophone: *belle*. [OE *belle*]

bell[2] (bel) *v.i.* To cry, as a buck or stag at rutting time. — *n.* The cry of a deer, bittern, etc.; also, a bellow. ◆ Homophone: *belle*. [OE *bellan* bellow]

Bell (bel), **Alexander Graham**, 1847–1922, U.S. physicist and inventor of the telephone, born in Scotland. — **Sir Charles**, 1774–1842, Scottish anatomist and surgeon.

bel·la·don·na (bel′ə·don′ə) *n.* **1** A perennial herb (*Atropa belladonna*) with purple-red flowers and shining black berries; deadly nightshade: the leaves and roots yield a number of poisonous alkaloids, as atropine, used in medicine. **2** The belladonna lily. [<Ital. *bella donna* beautiful lady]

belladonna lily An ornamental South African plant (*Amaryllis belladonna*), with large, showy, funnel-shaped flowers of pale rose color penciled with red.

bell·boy (bel′boi′) *n.* A porter, man or boy, in a hotel. Also **bell·hop** (bel′hop′).

belle (bel) *n.* A beautiful and attractive woman; a reigning social beauty. ◆ Homophone: *bell*. [<F, fem. of *beau* beautiful]

bel·leek (bə·lēk′) *n.* A thin, delicate pottery resembling porcelain, having an iridescent or pearly glaze: made originally at Belleek. Also **belleek ware**.

Bel·leek A town of NW County Fermanagh, Northern Ireland.

Belle Isle An island (20 square miles) at the entrance to the **Strait of Belle Isle**, the northern entrance to the Gulf of Saint Lawrence, lying between Labrador and Newfoundland.

Bel·ler·o·phon (bə·ler′ə·fon) In Greek mythology, a hero who slew the Chimera with the aid of the winged horse, Pegasus, and later perished in an attempt to scale heaven.

BELLEROPHON AND PEGASUS
After a sculpture in the Spada Palace, Rome.

belles-let·tres (bel′let′rə) *n. pl.* Works of literary art, esthetic rather than informational or didactic; poetry, drama, fiction, etc.; the humanities. See synonyms under HUMANITY, LITERATURE. [<F, fine letters] — **bel·let·rist** (bel′let′rist) *n.* — **bel·le·tris·tic** (bel′le·tris′tik) *adj.*

bell·flow·er (bel′flou′ər) *n.* The campanula.

bel·li·cose (bel′ə·kōs) *adj.* Pugnacious; warlike. [<L *bellicosus* warlike < *bellum* war] — **bel′li·cose′ly** *adv.* — **bel′li·cos′i·ty** (-kos′ə·tē) *n.*

bel·lig·er·ent (bə·lij′ər·ənt) *adj.* **1** Warlike; bellicose. **2** Engaged in or pertaining to warfare. — *n.* A power or person engaged in legitimate warfare. [Earlier *belligerant* <F *belligérant* <L *belligerans, -antis*, ppr. of *belligerare* wage war] — **bel·lig′er·en·cy, bel·lig′er·ence** *n.* — **bel·lig′er·ent·ly** *adv.*

bell·ing (bel′ing) *n. Dial.* A charivari.

Bel·li·ni (bel·lē′nē) Name of three Venetian painters, **Jacopo**, 1400?–70?, and his two sons, **Gentile**, 1429?–1507, and **Giovanni**, 1430?–1516. — **Vincenzo**, 1801–35, Italian composer.

bell jar A glass vessel having the shape of a bell, used to cover articles that may be injured by dust or air currents. Also **bell glass**.

bell·man (bel′mən) *n. pl.* **·men** (-mən) A town crier.

bell metal An alloy of copper and tin, used for the manufacture of bells.

bell-mouthed (bel′mouthd′, -moutht′) *adj.* Having a bell-shaped mouth, as a flask.

bel·low (bel′ō) *v.i.* **1** To utter a loud, hollow sound; roar, as a bull. **2** To roar; shout: to *bellow* with anger. — *v.t.* **3** To utter with a loud, roaring voice. — *n.* A loud, hollow cry or roar. [ME *belwen*, ? <OE *bylgan*] — **bel′low·er** *n.*

bel·lows (bel′ōz, *earlier* bel′əs) *n.* **1** An instrument with an air chamber and flexible sides, for drawing in air and expelling it under strong pressure through a nozzle or tube.

BELLOWS
a. Kitchen. *b.* For insect powders. *c.* Blacksmith's.

2 The expansible portion of a camera. **3** *Colloq.* The lungs. [OE *belg, belig* bag; a later plural from the same source as BELLY]

bell·weth·er (bel′weth′ər) *n.* **1** The wether that wears a bell and leads a flock of sheep. **2** One who leads a group, especially a thoughtless group, in any cause.

bell·wort (bel′wûrt′) *n.* **1** A plant of the lily family (genus *Uvularia*) having terminal, solitary, drooping flowers of a yellowish color with bell-shaped perianth. **2** Any plant of the bellflower family (*Campanulaceae*).

bel·ly (bel′ē) *n. pl.* **bel·lies 1** *Anat.* **a** The anterior part of a vertebrate body, extending from the sternum to the pelvis and containing the organs below the diaphragm. **b** The under part of a quadruped or lower animal. **c** The abdomen. **d** The protuberance of a bulging muscle. **2** The stomach and its associated organs. **3** Appetite. **4** Anything resembling a belly; as, the *belly* of a flask, the *belly* of a wind-filled sail. **5** The sounding box of certain stringed instruments, as the violin, viola, etc. **6** *Obs.* The womb. — *v.t. & v.i.* **bel·lied**, **bel·ly·ing** To swell out or fill, as a sail. [OE *belg, belig* bag]

bel·ly·ache (bel′ē·āk′) *n.* Intestinal colic; pain in the bowels. — *v.i.* **·ached**, **·ach·ing** *Slang* To complain sullenly.

bel·ly·band (bel′ē·band′) *n.* A transverse strap passing beneath a draft animal, to fasten the saddle, harness, etc., or hold the shafts; a girth. See illustration under HARNESS.

bel·ly·but·ton (bel′ē·but′n) *n. Colloq.* The navel.

bel·ly·ful (bel′ē·fool′) *n.* **1** Fullness resulting from much eating. **2** *Colloq.* An excessive fullness or surfeit of anything.

be·long (bi·lông′, -long′) *v.i.* **1** To be in the possession of someone: with *to*. **2** To be a part of or an appurtenance to something: with *to*: The screw *belongs* to this fan. **3** To have a proper place; be suitable: That lamp *belongs* in this room. **4** To have relation or be a member: with *to*: He *belongs* to the club. [ME *belongen* < *be-* completely + *longen*, OE *langian* go along with]

be·long·ing (bi·lông′ing, -long′-) *n.* **1** That which or one who belongs to a person or thing. **2** *pl.* Possessions; effects, as clothes, furniture, etc.

Be·lo·rus·sia The former name of the Republic of Belorus.

be·love (bi·luv′) *v.t.* **be·loved**, **be·lov·ing** To love: now only in the passive. [ME *biloven* < *be-* completely + *loven* love]

be·lov·ed (bi·luv′id, -luvd′) *adj.* Greatly loved; dear to the heart. — *n.* One greatly loved.

be·low (bi·lō′) *adv.* **1** In or to a lower place. **2** To a place under the floor or deck: Get *below*! **3** Farther down on a page or farther on in a list, book, etc. **4** On the earth, as distinguished from heaven. **5** In or to hell or Hades. **6** Lower in rank or authority: His case will be tried in the court *below*. — *prep.* **1** Farther down than: His apartment is *below* theirs. **2** Lower down in direction or course: the town *below* this one on the river. **3** Inferior to in degree, rank, value, etc.: The yield was *below* average. **4** Unworthy of. [<BE- + LOW[1]]

Bel·shaz·zar (bel·shaz′ər) The last Babylonian king, defeated and slain by Cyrus. He gave a banquet, **Belshazzar's Feast**, at which handwriting, foretelling the downfall of Babylonia, appeared on a wall. *Dan.* v.

belt (belt) *n.* **1** A band worn around the waist.

2 *Mech.* **a** A flexible band of leather or other material passing over two or more wheels and serving to transmit power in machinery from one part to another. **b** A moving assembly line in a factory, intended to convey parts from one operation or worker to another. **3** Any broad, encircling band, region, etc. **4** *Ecol.* A characteristic zone or stretch of country favoring the development of a certain type of animal or plant life; a zone; strip; as, a forest *belt*, a corn *belt*. **5** A strait. **6** *Mil.* **a** A girdle of armor plates protecting a warship along the water line. **b** A strip of webbing designed to hold a weapon or to contain cartridges. **7** *Colloq.* A blow, as with the fist. — **below the belt 1** In boxing, under the waistband. **2** Hence, unfairly; in violation of accepted codes. — **to tighten one's belt** To practice thrift; retrench; consume less food. — *v.t.* **1** To gird with or as with a belt. **2** To fasten with a belt: to *belt* on a sword. **3** To mark with belts or bands. **4** *Colloq.* To strike with force. [OE *belt* < L *balteus* girdle]

belt·ed (bel'tid) *adj.* **1** Wearing a belt; distinguished by a belt. **2** Having a mark like a belt: the *belted* kingfisher.

Bel·ter (bel'tər) *adj.* Pertaining to or naming a type of furniture, usually of rosewood, carved in elaborate floral designs. [after John H. *Belter*, mid-19th c. New York cabinetmaker]

belt·ing (bel'ting) *n.* Belts collectively, or the material for belts.

belt line A transportation route encircling a city or district.

be·lu·ga (bə·lōō'gə) *n.* *pl.* **·ga** or **·gas 1** A dolphin (*Delphinapterus leucas*) of arctic and sub-arctic seas; adults are of a white color and from 10 to 12 feet long: also called *white whale.* **2** The great white sturgeon (*Acipenser huso*), found in the Caspian Sea and the Black Sea; its roe is **Beluga caviar.** [< Russian *byelukha* < *byelo* white]

bel·ve·dere (bel'və·dir') *n.* An elevated point of vantage affording an extensive view; especially, an upper story of an Italian building, open on one or more sides so as to command a view. — **the Belvedere** A part of the Vatican containing many famous works of art. [< Ital., beautiful view < **bel·ve·dered'** *adj.*

be·ma (bē'mə) *n.* *pl.* **be·ma·ta** (bē'mə·tə) The enclosure about the altar; sanctuary; chancel, especially in the Eastern churches. [< Gk. *bema* a step, a platform < *bainein* go, walk]

be·mean (bi·mēn') *v.t.* To lower or abase (oneself).

be·mire (bi·mīr') *v.t.* **be·mired, be·mir·ing 1** To soil with or as with mud or mire. **2** To fix or stall in mud.

be·moan (bi·mōn') *v.t.* **1** To express sympathy or pity for. **2** To lament, as a loss. — *v.i.* **3** To mourn or lament. See synonyms under MOURN. [OE *bemænan*] — **be·moan'a·ble** *adj.*

be·muse (bi·myōōz') *v.t.* **·mused, ·mus·ing** To muddle or stupefy, as with drink.

be·mused (bi·myōōzd') *adj.* **1** Stupefied; dazed. **2** Engrossed.

ben (ben) *n.* *Brit. Dial.* The inner room of a house. — *adv.* & *adj.* Within; in; inner. — **to be far ben with** To be intimate with. [OE *binnan* < *be-* by + *innan* within]

be·name (bi·nām') *v.t.* **be·named, be·named** or **be·nempt** or **be·nempted, be·nam·ing** *Obs.* To name. [OE *benemnan*]

bench (bench) *n.* **1** A long, wooden seat, with or without a back. **2** A stout table for mechanical work. **3** The judges' seat in court; the judge or the judges collectively; the judiciary; also, the court. **4** A row of stalls on platforms or benches for the exhibition of animals, as dogs. **5** *Geog.* A terrace formed in rocks; also, elevated ground along the bank of a lake or river. — *v.t.* **1** To furnish with benches. **2** To seat on a bench. **3** To exhibit, as dogs at a dog show. **4** In sports, to remove (a player) from a game by sending him to a bench on the sidelines. [OE *benc.* Akin to BANK[1], BANK[3].]

bench·er (ben'chər) *n.* *Brit.* **1** A senior member of the English bar; a governor of one of the Inns of Court. **2** One of the populace; a loafer, as about taverns.

bench hook A clamp, usually of wood, for holding work upon a carpenter's bench.

bench·leg·ged (bench'leg'id, -legd') *adj.* Having the legs wide apart: said of a dog or a horse.

bench·mark (bench'märk') *n.* **1** A permanent reference mark fixed in the ground for use in surveys, tidal observations, etc. **2** A reference point serving as a standard for comparing or judging other things.

bench·root (bench'rōōt', -rŏŏt') *n.* *Bot.* A misshapen condition of roots caused by tenacious seed coats.

bench show An exhibition of animals, especially dogs, in stalls on benches, indoors.

bench warrant A warrant issued by the judge presiding at a session, directing that an offender be brought into court.

bend[1] (bend) *v.* **bent** (*Archaic* **bend·ed**), **bend·ing** *v.t.* **1** To cause to take the form of a curve; crook; bow. **2** To direct or turn, as one's course, in a certain direction; deflect. **3** To subdue; cause to yield, as to one's will. **4** To apply closely; concentrate, as the mind. **5** *Naut.* To tie; make fast, as a rope; place in position, as a sail. **6** *Archaic* To strain; make tense: with *up.* — *v.i.* **7** To assume the form of a bow. **8** To take a certain direction. **9** To bow in submission or respect; yield; conform. **10** To apply one's energies: with *to.* — *n.* **1** A curve or crook. **2** An act of bending or bowing. **3** A loop or knot by which a rope is fastened to any object. **4** A wale or rib. **5** *Scot.* A deep draft. [OE *bendan*]

Synonyms (verb): bias, crook, curve, deflect, deviate, diverge, incline, influence, mold, persuade, stoop, submit, turn, twine, twist, warp, yield. In some cases a thing is spoken of as *bent* where the parts make an angle; but oftener to *bend* is understood to be to draw to or through a curve; as, to *bend* a bow. To *submit* or *yield* is to *bend* or surrender to another's wishes. To *incline* or *influence* is to *bend* another's wishes toward our own; to *persuade* is to draw them quite over. To *warp* is to *bend* slightly through the whole fiber, as a board in the sun. To *crook* is to *bend, turn,* or *twist* irregularly. *Deflect, deviate,* and *diverge* are said of any turning away from a direct line; *deviate* commonly of a slight and gradual movement, *diverge* of a more sharp and decided one. To *bias* is to influence feeling, opinion, or action in the direction of some prevailing (often unconscious) tendency; personal enmity against the accused will *bias* a witness or a juror so as to distort his view of the facts or motives involved in the case. *Mold* is a stronger word than *bend*; we may *bend* by a superior force that which resists the constraint; as, *bend* a bow; we *mold* something plastic entirely and permanently to some desired form. See TWIST.

bend[2] (bend) *n.* **1** *Her.* A band drawn diagonally across the shield from dexter chief to

BENDS
a. A bend. *b.* A bend cottised. *c.* A bend sinister.

sinister base. **2** In the leather trade, a butt cut in two. [OE *bend* strap; infl. in meaning by OF *bende* strip, band]

bend·er (ben'dər) *n.* **1** A person or thing that bends. **2** *Slang* A drinking spree. **3** *Brit. Slang* A sixpence.

bends (bendz) *n. pl.* Decompression disease.

bend sinister *Her.* A bend drawn diagonally from sinister chief to dexter base: a mark of bastardy. Compare BATON SINISTER.

ben·dy (ben'dē) *n.* *Anglo-Indian* Okra.

be·neath (bi·nēth') *adv.* **1** At a lower point; in a lower position. **2** On the underside of; underneath. — *prep.* **1** In a lower place or position than: a rock *beneath* the waves. **2** Pressed or crushed by: The ground gave *beneath* his foot. **3** Subdued or dominated by: *beneath* the yoke of the conqueror. **4** Influenced or controlled by: helpless *beneath* the ban. **5** Inferior to; unworthy of: His assignment was *beneath* his ability. **6** Unsuited to the dignity of; lower in rank than: She

married *beneath* her station. [OE *beneathan*]

Synonyms (prep): below, under, underneath. *Under* strictly implies that another object is directly upon or over in a vertical line. *Below* signifies that one object is lower than another, so as to be looked down upon from it, or hidden from view by it; as, *below* (not *under* nor *beneath*) the horizon. *Under* has also the sense of being subject to or subjected to; as, *under* tutors and governors, *under* examination. Antonyms: see synonyms for ABOVE.

ben·e·cep·tor (ben'ə·sep'tər) *n.* *Physiol.* An element of the nervous system, as a receptor or sense organ, specialized in the transmission of pleasurable stimuli: opposed to *nociceptor.* [< NL < L *bene* well + *-ceptor,* as in RECEPTOR]

ben·e·di·ci·te (ben'ə·dis'ə·tē) *n.* A blessing; grace or thanksgiving, especially at table. — *interj.* Bless you! [< LL, bless ye, imperative of *benedicere* bless, commend]

ben·e·dict (ben'ə·dikt) *n.* A newly married man. Also **ben'e·dick.** [< BENEDICK]

ben·e·dic·tine (ben'ə·dik'tēn) *n.* A brandy liqueur formerly made at the Benedictine monastery at Fécamp, France.

Ben·e·dic·tine (ben'ə·dik'tin, -tēn) *adj.* Pertaining to St. Benedict or his order. — *n.* One of the order of monks established by St. Benedict at Subiaco, in Italy, about 530: sometimes called "Black Monks" from the color of their robes.

ben·e·dic·tion (ben'ə·dik'shən) *n.* **1** The act of blessing, as at the close of worship. **2** The invocation of divine favor upon a person. **3** Any of various formal ecclesiastical ceremonies of blessing; a dedication or consecration. **4** Divine grace or favor; the state of blessedness. **5** The giving of thanks before or after meals; grace. [< L *benedictio, -onis* < *benedicere* bless] — **ben'e·dic'tive, ben·e·dic·to·ry** (ben'ə·dik'tər·ē) *adj.*

Ben·e·dic·tus (ben'ə·dik'təs) *n.* **1** Either of two canticles, *Luke* i 68–71, and *Matt.* xxi 9, each named from the first word, *benedictus,* "blessed," of its Latin version. **2** A musical setting of either canticle mentioned above.

ben·e·fac·tion (ben'ə·fak'shən) *n.* **1** A kindly or generous act; a gift or boon; beneficence. **2** The act of bestowing charity or conferring a benefit. See synonyms under GIFT. [< L *benefactio, -onis* < *benefacere* do well]

ben·e·fac·tor (ben'ə·fak'tər, ben'ə·fak'-) *n.* A friendly helper; a patron. — **ben'e·fac'tress** *n. fem.*

be·nef·ic (bə·nef'ik) *adj.* Beneficent; kindly. [< L *beneficus* beneficent]

ben·e·fice (ben'ə·fis) *n.* **1** An ecclesiastical living or preferment; a church office endowed with funds or property. **2** The revenue so devoted: generally limited to parsonages, rectories, vicarages, and donatives. **3** A feudal fee or life interest in a landed estate, subject to the will of the donor. — *v.t.* **·ficed, ·fic·ing** To invest with a benefice. [< OF < L *beneficium* favor]

be·nef·i·cence (bə·nef'ə·səns) *n.* **1** The quality of being beneficent; active goodness. **2** A beneficent act or gift. See synonyms under BENEVOLENCE. [< F *bénéficence* < L *beneficentia* < *beneficus* generous]

be·nef·i·cent (bə·nef'ə·sənt) *adj.* **1** Bringing about or doing good. **2** Characterized by charity and kindness. See synonyms under CHARITABLE. — **be·nef'i·cent·ly** *adv.*

ben·e·fi·cial (ben'ə·fish'əl) *adj.* **1** Benefiting or tending to benefit; conferring benefits; advantageous; helpful. **2** *Law* Entitled to receive the income of an estate without its title, custody, or control; as, a *beneficial* interest in land. [< F *bénéficial* < LL *beneficialis* < *beneficium* favor] — **ben·e·fi'cial·ly** *adv.* — **ben'e·fi'cial·ness** *n.*

ben·e·fi·ci·ar·y (ben'ə·fish'ē·er'ē, -fish'ər·ē) *adj.* **1** Pertaining to benefits or benevolence. **2** Of the nature of a charity or donation. **3** Held by feudal tenure or privilege. — *n. pl.* **·ar·ies 1** One who receives or uses a charitable provision or privilege. **2** The holder of a benefice or church living. **3** *Law* One who is lawfully entitled to the profits and proceeds of an estate or property, the title to which is vested in another, as in a trustee. **4** The person to whom the amount of an insurance policy or annuity is payable. [< L *beneficiarius* < *beneficium* favor]

ben·e·fit (ben'ə·fit) *n.* **1** Profit; advantage; promotion of welfare or prosperity; helpful result. **2** A benefaction or deed of kindness; favor bestowed; privilege. **3** A special theatrical or musical performance, at which the performers usually serve gratuitously, and the proceeds of which are bestowed on some particular person or on some charity. **4** Pecuniary aid extended by a benefit society. See synonyms under FAVOR, PROFIT, UTILITY. —*v.* **·fit·ed, ·fit·ing** *v.t.* To be helpful or useful to. —*v.i.* To profit; gain advantage. See synonyms under SERVE. [< AF *benfet*, OF *bienfait* < L *benefactum* good deed < *benefacere* do well]

Ben·e·lux (ben′ə·luks) *n.* The customs union of Belgium, the Netherlands, and Luxembourg. [< BE(LGIUM) + NE(THERLANDS) + LUX(EMBOURG)]

be·nempt (bi·nempt′), **be·nempt·ed** (bi·nemp′tid) Past participles of BENAME.

Be·nét (bi·nā′), **Stephen Vincent**, 1898–1943, U.S. poet. —**William Rose**, 1886–1950, brother of preceding, U. S. poet and critic.

be·nev·o·lence (bə·nev′ə·ləns) *n.* **1** Desire for the well-being or comfort of others; love for mankind; charitableness. **2** Any act of kindness or well-doing; charity; humanity. **3** An enforced loan sometimes exacted by English sovereigns.

Synonyms: almsgiving, beneficence, benignity, bounty, charity, generosity, humanity, kindheartedness, kindliness, kindness, liberality, munificence, philanthropy, sympathy. Originally *beneficence* was the doing well, *benevolence* the wishing or willing well to others; but *benevolence* has come to include *beneficence* and to displace it. *Charity* is now almost universally applied to some form of *almsgiving* and is much more limited in meaning than *benevolence*. *Benignity* suggests some occult power of blessing, such as was formerly ascribed to the stars; we may say a good man has the air of *benignity*. *Kindness* and *tenderness* are personal; *benevolence* and *charity* are general. *Humanity* is *kindness* and *tenderness* toward man or beast. We speak of the *bounty* of a generous host, the *liberality* or *munificence* of the founder of a college, or of the *liberality* of a person toward holders of conflicting beliefs. *Philanthropy* applies to wide schemes for human welfare, often, but not always, involving large expenditures in *charity* or *benevolence*. Compare MERCY. *Antonyms:* barbarity, brutality, churlishness, greediness, harshness, illiberality, inhumanity, malevolence, malignity, niggardliness, selfishness, self-seeking, stinginess, unkindness.

be·nev·o·lent (bə·nev′ə·lənt) *adj.* **1** Characterized by benevolence. **2** Kindly, charitable; beneficent. See synonyms under CHARITABLE, GOOD, HUMANE. [< OF *benivolent* < L *benevolens, -entis* < *bene* well + *volens*, ppr. of *velle* wish] — **be·nev′o·lent·ly** *adv.*

Ben·gal (ben·gôl′, beng-) A former province of NE British India, divided (1947) into: **(1) East Bengal**, formerly a province of Pakistan; since 1972, the country of Bangla Desh; 54,501 square miles; capital, Dacca; **(2) West Bengal**, a constituent state of the republic of India; 29,476 square miles; capital, Calcutta. —**Ben·ga·lese** (ben′gə·lēz′, -lēs′, beng′-) *adj. & n.*

Bengal, Bay of A broad arm of the Indian Ocean, between India and the Andaman Sea.

Ben·ga·li (ben·gô′lē, beng-) *adj.* Of or pertaining to Bengal. —*n.* **1** A native of Bengal. **2** The modern vernacular Indic language of Bengal.

ben·ga·line (beng′gə·lēn, beng′gə·lēn′) *n.* A silk, wool, or rayon fabric of fine weave with widthwise cords. [< BENGAL]

Ben–Gur·i·on (ben·gŏŏr′ē·ən), **David**, 1886–1973, Russian-born Israeli statesman; prime minister of Israel 1948–53 and 1955–63.

be·night·ed (bi·nī′tid) *adj.* **1** Involved in darkness or gloom, whether intellectual or moral; ignorant; unenlightened. **2** Overtaken by night. — **be·night′ed·ness** *n.*

be·nign (bi·nīn′) *adj.* **1** Gracious; generous; kindly. **2** Soft; genial; propitious; mild. **3** *Pathol.* Of a mild type: opposed to *malignant:* a *benign* tumor or disease. See synonyms under BLAND, CHARITABLE, PROPITIOUS. [< OF *benigne* < L *benignus* kindly] — **be·nign′ly** *adv.*

be·nig·nant (bi·nig′nənt) *adj.* **1** Condescending; gentle; gracious. **2** Helpful; salutary. See synonyms under AMIABLE, CHARITABLE, HUMANE, MERCIFUL. [< BENIGN, on analogy with MALIGNANT] — **be·nig′nant·ly** *adv.*

be·nig·ni·ty (bi·nig′nə·tē) *n. pl.* **·ties** **1** Kindliness; beneficence: also **be·nig·nan·cy** (bi·nig′nən·sē). **2** A gracious action or influence. See synonyms under BENEVOLENCE, MERCY.

Be·nin (be·nēn′) **1** An independent republic in western Africa; 44,290 square miles; capital, Porto–Novo: formerly *Dahomey*. **2** A river in southern Nigeria, flowing west 60 miles into the **Bight of Benin**, an Atlantic bay of the Gulf of Guinea on the coast of west central Africa. **3** A province in southern Nigeria; 8,627 square miles; capital, Benin City.

ben·i·son (ben′ə·zən, -sən) *n.* A benediction; blessing. [< OF *beneison* < LL *benedictio, -onis* benediction]

benjamin bush The spicebush; feverbush.

Ben Lo·mond (ben lō′mənd) **1** A mountain in NW Stirlingshire, Scotland; 3,192 ft. **2** The highest mountain range in Tasmania; highest peak, Legge Tor, 5,160 ft.

ben·ne (ben′ē) *n.* An East Indian plant, the sesame, widely cultivated for its seeds which yield **benne oil:** also spelled *bene.* [< Malay *bijen* seed]

ben·net (ben′it) *n.* **1** The avens; especially, either of two American species (*Geum canadense* and *G. strictum*). **2** Herb-bennet. [< OF (*herbe*) *beneite* blessed (herb) < L *benedicta*]

Ben Ne·vis (nē′vis, nev′is) A mountain in SW Invernessshire, Scotland; highest peak in Great Britain; 4,406 feet.

Ben·ning·ton (ben′ing·tən) A town in Vermont; near site of battle, 1777, in which American colonial forces defeated the British.

bent[1] (bent) Past tense and past participle of BEND. —*adj.* **1** Deflected from a straight line; crooked. **2** Made fast to a spar or other object: said of a sail, etc. **3** Fixed in a course; set; as, on pleasure *bent.* — *n.* **1** The state of being inclined or the direction in which inclined; also, inclination; penchant; tendency; bias; disposition. **2** The degree of tension; limit of endurance or capacity. **3** *Engin.* A section of a framed building; a portion of a framework or scaffolding of a building, designed to carry both vertical and transverse loads. **4** A cast of the eye. **5** *Obs.* Concentrated force; impetus. See synonyms under INCLINATION.

bent[2] *n.* **1** One of various stiff wiry grasses (genus *Agrostis*): also **bent grass. 2** The stiff flower stalk of various grasses. **3** *Brit.* The stalk or seeding spike of either of the two common species of plantain (*Plantago major* and *P. lanceolata*). **4** Land unenclosed and covered only with grass or sedge, as opposed to wood, a heath, moor, or other waste land. [OE *beonet*]

ben·thos (ben′thos) *n. Ecol.* The whole assemblage of plants or animals living on the sea bottom: distinguished from *plankton.* [< Gk., the deep, depth of the sea] — **ben·thic** (ben′thik), **ben·thon·ic** (ben·thon′ik) *adj.*

ben·tho·scope (ben′thə·skōp) *n.* An undersea research apparatus resembling a bathysphere, but designed and built to withstand pressures at a depth of 10,000 feet: intended for the study of submarine life. [< Gk. *benthos* depth + -SCOPE]

Ben·ton·ville (ben′tən·vil) A town in central North Carolina; site of one of the final major engagements in the Civil War.

bent wood Designating a style of furniture constructed of wood sections curved and bent to desired shapes.

Be·nu·e (bā′nŏŏ·ā) A river in Nigeria; flowing about 800 miles to the Niger river: also *Binue.*

be·numb (bi·num′) *v.t.* **1** To make numb; deaden. **2** To render insensible; stupefy. [OE *benumen*, pp. of *beniman* deprive. See NUMB.] — **be·numbed** (bi·numd′) *adj.* — **be·numb′ment** *n.*

ben·zal·de·hyde (ben·zal′də·hīd) *n. Chem.* A colorless, highly refractive liquid, C_7H_6O, having the characteristic odor of essence of almonds. It is used largely in the dye and perfume industries. [< BENZ(OIN) + ALDEHYDE]

ben·zene (ben′zēn, ben·zēn′) *n. Chem.* A colorless, volatile, inflammable, liquid hydrocarbon, C_6H_6, obtained chiefly from coal tar by fractional distillation. It is useful as a solvent, as an illuminant in gas–manufacture, and is important as the starting point in the formation of the compounds of the benzene series. [< BENZOIN]

benzene ring *Chem.* The graphic formula of the aromatic hydrocarbon benzene. The hexagon formula shows six carbon atoms, each associated with a hydrogen atom one or more of which may be replaced to form any of a large class of benzene derivatives. Also **benzene nucleus.**

BENZENE RING

ben·zi·dine (ben′zə·dēn, -din) *n. Chem.* A crystalline hydrocarbon, $C_{12}H_{12}N_2$, synthesized from benzene derivatives: used in the preparation of dyes and as a test for blood. Also **ben′zi·din** (-din). [< BENZOIN]

ben·zine (ben′zēn, ben·zēn′) *n.* A colorless inflammable liquid derived from crude petroleum by fractional distillation and consisting of various hydrocarbons. It is used as a solvent for fats, resins, etc., to cleanse clothing, and as a motor fuel: also called *petroleum spirit.* Sometimes confused with *benzene.* Also **ben′zin** (-zin), **ben·zo·line** (ben′zə·lēn).

ben·zo·ate (ben′zō·it, -āt) *n. Chem.* A salt of benzoic acid.

benzoate of soda Sodium benzoate.

ben·zo·ic (ben·zō′ik) *adj.* **1** Pertaining to or derived from benzoin. **2** Pertaining to benzoic acid.

benzoic acid *Chem.* An aromatic compound, $C_7H_6O_2$, contained in resins, as benzoin, and in coal-tar oil, etc., and obtained also by synthesis: used as a food preservative and in medicine.

ben·zo·in (ben′zō·in, -zoin) *n.* **1** A gum resin from various East Indian plants (genus *Styrax*), used in medicine and as a perfume: also called *benjamin.* **2** *Chem.* A crystalline chemical compound, $C_{14}H_{12}O_2$, obtained variously, as from benzaldehyde by the action of an alcoholic solution of potassium cyanide: also called *flowers of benzoin.* **3** Any plant of a small genus (*Lindera*) of North American and Asian shrubs or trees of the laurel family, including the spicebush. [< F *benjoin* < Pg. *beijoin* or Ital. *benzoi* < Arabic *lubān jāwī* incense of Java]

ben·zol (ben′zōl, -zol) *n.* A grade of crude benzene. Also **ben′zole** (-zōl).

ben·zo·phe·none (ben′zō·fē′nōn) *n. Chem.* A crystalline compound, $C_{13}H_{10}O$, a ketone obtained variously, as from calcium benzoate by dry distillation. [< BENZENE + PHENOL + -ONE]

ben·zo·yl (ben′zō·il) *n. Chem.* The univalent organic radical, C_6H_5CO, derived from benzoic acid.

benzoyl peroxide *Chem.* A white, crystalline derivative of benzoic acid, $C_{12}H_{10}C_2O_4$, used in bleaching oils, waxes, flour, etc.

ben·zyl (ben′zil) *n. Chem.* The univalent radical, $C_6H_5CH_2$, derived from toluene.

Be·o·grad (be·ô′gräd) The Serbo–Croatian name for BELGRADE.

Be·o·wulf (bā′ə·wŏŏlf) A warrior prince in an eighth century Anglo–Saxon epic poem, *Beowulf*, who kills the monsters Grendel and Grendel's mother and dies in old age of a wound received in battle with a dragon.

be·queath (bi·kwēth′, -kwēth′) *v.t.* **1** *Law* To give, as personal property, by will; make a bequest of: compare DEVISE. **2** To hand down to posterity; transmit. **3** *Obs.* To devote. [OE *becwethan*]

be·quest (bi·kwest′) *n.* The act of bequeathing or that which is bequeathed. See synonyms under GIFT. [ME *biqueste*]

be·rate (bi·rāt′) *v.t.* **be·rat·ed, be·rat·ing** To chide severely; scold.

Ber·ber (bûr′bər) *n*. **1** A member of a group of Moslem tribes inhabiting northern Africa, especially the Kabyles of Algeria. **2** The Hamitic language of the Berbers, comprising the dialects spoken in Algeria, Tunisia, Morocco, and the Sahara, as Kabyle, Tuareg, etc. —*adj*. Of or pertaining to the Berbers or their language.

Ber·ber (bûr′bər) A town on the eastern bank of the Nile in northern Sudan.

Ber·ber·a (bûr′bər·ə) A port on the Gulf of Aden, former winter capital of British Somaliland.

ber·ber·i·da·ceous (bûr′bər·i·dā′shəs) *adj*. Pertaining or belonging to the barberry family of herbs and shrubs, as the May apple.

ber·ber·ine (bûr′bər·ēn, -in) *n*. A yellow crystalline bitter alkaloid, $C_{20}H_{19}O_5N$, contained in the bark of the barberry and some other plants: it is used in medicine as a tonic. Also **ber′ber·in** (-in). [< LL *berberis* barberry]

ber·ceuse (bâr·sœz′) *n*. *pl*. **·ceuses** (-sœz′) *Music* A cradle song. [< F]

Berch·tes·ga·den (berkh′tes·gä′dən) A resort village in Upper Bavaria; noted as the private retreat of Adolf Hitler.

be·reave (bi·rēv′) *v.t*. **be·reaved** or **be·reft** (bi·reft′), **be·reav·ing 1** To deprive, as of hope or happiness. **2** To leave desolate or saddened through loss: with *of*: He was *bereaved* of his father. Commonly in past participle: *bereaved* or *bereft* of a relative, but *bereft* of love or other immaterial object. **3** *Obs*. To despoil; rob. [OE *bereafian*]

be·reave·ment (bi·rēv′mənt) *n*. The act of bereaving, or the state of being bereaved; an afflictive loss, as by death. See synonyms under MISFORTUNE.

be·reft (bi·reft′) Alternative past tense and past participle of BEREAVE. —*adj*. Deprived: *bereft* of all hope.

Ber·e·ni·ce (ber′ə·nī′sē) An ancient name for BENGASI.

be·ret (bə·rā′, ber′ā) *n*. A soft, flat cap, usually of wool, originating in the Basque regions of France and Spain. [< F, ult. < LL *birettum* cap]

Ber·e·zi·na (ber′ə·zē′nə) A river in Belorussian S.S.R. flowing south 350 miles to the Dnieper; crossed by Napoleon (1812) at the battle of Borisov.

berg (bûrg) *n*. **1** An iceberg. **2** In South Africa, a mountain.

Berg (berkh), **Alban,** 1885–1935, Austrian composer.

Ber·ga·ma (ber′gə·mä) A town of western Turkey north of Smyrna, on the site of ancient Pergamum.

Ber·ga·mo (ber′gä·mō) A city in Lombardy, northern Italy.

ber·ga·mot[1] (bûr′gə·mot) *n*. **1** A tree (*Citrus bergamia*) of the rue family, the bergamot orange. **2** Its fruit, furnishing an oil used as a perfume. **3** Any of several plants of the mint family, as the horsemint in the United States, and *Mentha aquatica* and *Mentha citrata* (also called **bergamot-mint**) in England. **4** Snuff scented with bergamot. [? from *Bergamo*, Italy]

Ber·gen (bûr′gən, *Norw*. ber′gən) A port in SW Norway.

Bergh (bûrg), **Henry,** 1820–88, U.S. philanthropist; founded Society for Prevention of Cruelty to Animals, 1866.

berg·schrund (bûrg′shrund, *Ger*. berkh′shrŏont) *n*. A crevasse or series of crevasses at the head of a glacier, near the base of the cliff against which the snow field lies. [< G]

Berg·son (berg′sən), **Henri Louis,** 1859–1941, French philosopher. —**Berg·so·ni·an** (berg·sō′nē·ən) *adj*. & *n*.

Berg·son·ism (berg′sən·iz′əm) *n*. The philosophy of Henri Bergson, who held that the world is a continuing process of creative evolution, hence, of inevitable novelty and change, rather than the result of fixed or unaltering laws of nature. Reality is the expression of the creative or vital force (*élan vital*) inherent in all organisms. Knowledge of reality comes through intuition rather than through analytical intellectual processes. Compare VITALISM.

ber·i·ber·i (ber′ē·ber′ē) *n*. *Pathol*. An oriental disease of the peripheral nerves, characterized by partial paralysis, swelling of the legs, and general dropsy: due to the absence of vitamins of the B complex in a diet consisting principally of pol-

ished rice. [< Singhalese *beri* weakness] — **ber′i·ber′ic** *adj*.

be·rime (bi·rīm′) *v.t*. **·rimed, ·rim·ing 1** To mention or celebrate in rime. **2** To compose in rime. Also spelled **berhyme.**

Ber·ing Sea (bâr′ing, bir′-) An arm of the North Pacific Ocean between Alaska and Siberia, north of the Aleutian Islands: *Russian* **Be·ring·o·vo Mo·re** (be·ring′ə·və mô′re): connected by **Bering Strait** to the Arctic Ocean. Also *Behring Sea*.

Berke·le·ian·ism (bûrk·lē′ən·iz′əm, *Brit*. bärk-) *n*. The idealistic system of philosophy propounded by George Berkeley. —**Berke·le′ian** *adj*. & *n*.

Berke·ley (bûrk′lē, *Brit*. bärk′-), **George,** 1684–1753, English prelate and philosopher born in Ireland. —**Sir William,** 1606–77, English governor of Virginia.

berke·li·um (bûrk′lē·əm) *n*. A very rare, unstable element (symbol Bk, atomic number 97) of the actinide series, first obtained by bombarding americium with alpha particles, the most stable isotope having mass number 247 and a half-life of 1400 years. See PERIODIC TABLE. [from *Berkeley*, California, location of the University of California, where first produced]

Berk·shire (bûrk′shir, -shər) *n*. One of a breed of black-haired swine from Berkshire, England, of medium size, with short legs, broad, straight backs, square hams and shoulders, and short heads.

Berk·shire (bûrk′shir, -shər; *Brit*. bärk′-) A county in southern England; 725 square miles; county seat, Reading. Shortened form **Berks** (bûrks, *Brit*. bärks).

Berk·shire Hills (bûrk′shir, -shər) A wooded region of western Massachusetts; highest peak, 3,505 feet.

ber·lin (bər·lin′, bûr′lin) *n*. **1** An automobile of limousine type but with the driver's seat entirely enclosed: also **ber·line** (bər·lin′, *Fr*. ber·lēn′). **2** A four-wheeled covered carriage with a shelter seat behind. **3** Zephyr or worsted for knitting: also **Berlin wool.** [from *Berlin*, Germany]

Ber·lin (bər·lin′, *Ger*. ber·lēn′) A city of central Prussia and the capital of Germany.

Ber·lin (bər·lin′), **Irving,** born 1888, U.S. song writer.

Ber·li·oz (ber′lē·ōz, *Fr*. bâr·lyôz′), **Hector,** 1803–69, French composer.

berm (bûrm) *n*. **1** The bank of a canal opposite the towpath. **2** A horizontal ledge part way up a slope; bench. **3** A ledge dug near the top of a trench to support beams and prevent caving in of the sides. **4** A narrow, level ledge at the outside foot of a parapet, to retain material which might otherwise fall from the slope into the moat. **5** The outside or downhill side of a ditch or trench. For illustration see BASTION. Also **berme.** [< F *berme*]

Ber·me·jo (ber·me′hō) A river in northern Argentina, flowing about 650 miles to the Paraguay.

Ber·mu·da (bər·myōō′də) An island group in the western North Atlantic, comprising a British colony; 22 square miles; capital, Hamilton. Also **Ber·mu′das.** —**Ber·mu·di·an** (bər·myōō′dē·ən) *adj*. & *n*.

Bermuda shorts Shorts which extend to just above the knees.

Bern (bûrn, bern) The capital of Switzerland. Also **Berne.**

Ber·na·dette (bûr′nə·det′, *Fr*. ber·nà·det′), **Saint,** 1844–79, Bernadette Soubirous, a French maiden who saw a vision of the Virgin Mary at Lourdes; canonized 1933.

Ber·na·dotte (bûr′nə·dot, *Fr*. ber·nà·dôt′) Family name of royal house of Sweden, founded by **Jean Baptiste Jules Bernadotte,** 1764–1844, French marshal, who became king of Sweden as Charles XIV John in 1818.

Ber·nard (ber·när′), **Claude,** 1812–78, French physiologist.

Ber·nar·din de Saint-Pierre (ber·när·daṅ′ də saṅ·pyär′), **Jacques Henri,** 1737–1814, French novelist and author.

Ber·nar·dine (bûr′nər·din, -dēn) *adj*. Pertaining to St. Bernard of Clairvaux, 1091–1153, or to the Cistercian order founded by him. —*n*. A Cistercian monk.

Ber·ners (bûr′nərz), **Lord,** 1883–1950, Gerald Hugh Tyrwhitt-Wilson, English composer and

painter.

Ber·nese (bər·nēz′, -nēs′) *adj*. Of or pertaining to Bern, Switzerland. —*n*. **1** A resident of Bern, Switzerland. **2** A Swiss mountain dog, characterized by a short, compact body, straight forelegs, long, soft coat, and usually with white feet and with white blaze on face and chest.

Bernese Alps The northern division of the Swiss Alps; highest peak, 14,026 feet: also *Bernese Oberland*. (See OBERLAND.)

Bern·hardt (bûrn′härt, *Fr*. ber·nàr′), **Sarah,** 1844–1923, French actress: original name Rosine Bernard.

Ber·ni·ci·a (bər·nish′ē·ə) An Anglian kingdom founded in 547; later included in Northumbria.

ber·ni·cle (bûr′ni·kəl, bär′-) *n*. The barnacle goose.

Ber·ni·na (ber·nē′nä), **Piz** (pēts) Highest peak (13,304 feet) of the **Bernina Alps,** a part of the Rhaetian Alps, Switzerland; traversed by **Bernina Pass,** elevation, 7,645 feet.

Ber·ni·ni (ber·nē′nē), **Giovanni Lorenzo,** 1598–1680, Italian sculptor and architect.

Ber·noul·li (*Fr*. ber·nōō·yē′, *Ger*. ber·nōō′lē), **Jacob** (or **Jacques**), 1654–1705, Swiss mathematician. —**Daniel,** 1700–82, nephew of the preceding, Swiss mathematician.

Bern·stein (bern′stīn), **Henry Léon,** 1876–1953, French dramatist.

ber·ret·ta (bə·ret′ə) *n*. A biretta.

ber·ry (ber′ē) *n*. *pl*. **ber·ries 1** Any small, succulent fruit: the black*berry*, straw*berry*, goose*berry*. **2** *Bot*. A simple fruit with the seeds in a juicy pulp, as the tomato, grape, and currant. ♦ Collateral adjective: *baccate*. **3** A coffee bean; also, the dry kernel of various grains. **4** Something likened to a berry, as an egg of a crustacean. **5** *Slang* A dollar. —*v.i*. **ber·ried, ber·ry·ing 1** To form or bear berries. **2** To gather berries. ♦ Homophone: *bury*. [OE *berie*] —**ber′ried** *adj*.

Ber·ry (be·rē′) A region and former province of central France. Also **Ber·ri′.**

Ber·sa·glie·re (ber′sä·lye′re) *n*. *pl*. **·ri** (-rē) *Italian* A marksman; rifleman; specifically, one of a special corps of sharpshooters in the Italian army.

ber·seem (bər·sēm′) *n*. A clover (*Trifolium alexandrinum*) grown as forage in Egypt and the United States. [< Arabic *birshīm* clover]

ber·serk (bûr′sûrk, ber·sûrk′) *n*. **1** In Norse mythology, a furious fighter, who could assume the form of wild beasts, and whom fire and iron could not harm; hence figuratively, one who fights with frenzied fury. **2** A freebooter. Also **ber′serk·er.** —*adj*. Violently or frenziedly destructive. —**to go berserk** To run wild; have a fit of destructive rage. [< ON *berserkr* bear-shirt]

berth (bûrth) *n*. **1** A bunk or bed in a vessel or sleeping-car, etc. **2** Any place in which a vessel may lie at anchor or at a dock; sea room. **3** A place or engagement on a vessel. **4** Office or employment in general. —**to give a wide berth to** To avoid; keep out of the way of. —*v.t*. & *v.i*. **1** To provide with or occupy a bed. **2** *Naut*. To provide with or come to an anchorage. ♦ Homophone: *birth*. [Origin unknown]

ber·tha (bûr′thə) *n*. A deep collar falling from the bodice neckline over the shoulders: in imitation of a short shoulder cape formerly so called. [after Charlemagne's mother]

Ber·til·lon system (bûr′tə·lon, *Fr*. ber·tē·yôn′) A system of coded physical measurements, later extended to include personal characteristics, such as the color of the eyes, scars, deformities, and the like (sometimes, also, photographs), used as a means for identification, especially as applied to criminals. [after Alphonse *Bertillon*, 1853–1914, French anthropologist]

Ber·wick (ber′ik) A county in SE Scotland; 457 square miles; county seat, Duns. Also **Ber′wick·shire** (-shir, -shər).

ber·yl (ber′əl) *n*. A vitreous, green or emerald-green, light-blue, yellow, pink, or white silicate of aluminum and beryllium crystallizing in the hexagonal system. The aquamarine and emerald varieties are used as gems. [< OF < L *beryllus* < Gk. *bēryllos* beryl] —**ber·yl·line** (ber′ə·lin, -līn) *adj*.

be·ryl·li·um (bə·ril′ē·əm) *n*. A hard, very light metallic element (symbol Be, atomic number 4), transparent to X rays and highly toxic, whether in compounds or metallic form. See PERIODIC TABLE. [< NL < L *beryllus* beryl]

Be·ry·tus (bə·rī′təs) The ancient name for BEIRUT.

Ber·ze·li·us (bər·zē′lē·əs, *Sw.* ber·sä′lē·ōōs), **Baron Jöns Jacob**, 1779–1848, Swedish chemist.

Bes (bes) In Egyptian mythology, a god presiding over art, the dance, and music, and having power to avert witchcraft.

Be·san·çon (bə·zäɴ·sôɴ′) A city in eastern France; ancient *Vesontio*.

be·seech (bi·sēch′) *v.t.* **be·sought, be·seech·ing 1** To entreat earnestly; implore. **2** To beg for earnestly; plead. See synonyms under ASK, PLEAD. [OE *besēcan*] —**be·seech′er** *n.* —**be·seech′ing** *adj.* —**be·seech′ing·ly** *adv.* —**be·seech′ing·ness** *n.*

be·seem (bi·sēm′) *v.i.* To be fitting or appropriate: used impersonally: It ill *beseems* you to speak thus. —**be·seem′ing** *adj.*

be·seen (bi·sēn′) *adj. Obs.* **1** Clad; adorned. **2** Accomplished; versed.

be·set (bi·set′) *v.t.* **be·set, be·set·ting 1** To attack on all sides; harass. **2** To hem in; encircle. **3** To set or stud with, as gems. See synonyms under ATTACK. [OE *besettan*] —**be·set′ment** *n.*

be·set·ting (bi·set′ing) *adj.* Constantly attacking or troubling.

be·show (bi·shō′) *n.* The black candlefish (*Anoplopoma fimbria*), of the Pacific coast of the U.S. [< N. Am. Ind. *bishowk*]

be·shrew (bi·shrōō′) *v.t. Obs.* To wish ill to; execrate: a mild imprecation.

be·side (bi·sīd′) *prep.* **1** At the side of; in proximity to: a path *beside* the river. **2** In comparison with: My merit is little *beside* yours. **3** Away or apart from: This discussion is *beside* the point. **4** Other than; over and above: I have no treasure *beside* this. —**beside oneself** Out of one's senses, as from anger, fear, etc. —*adv.* In addition to; besides. See synonyms under ADJACENT. [OE *sidan* by the side (of)]

be·sides (bi·sīdz′) *adv.* **1** In addition; as well: There are, *besides*, some remarkable books here. **2** Moreover; furthermore: He is rich; *besides*, he is virtuous. **3** Not included in that mentioned; otherwise; else: Loving me, her heart is stone to all the world *besides*. —*prep.* **1** In addition to; other than: *Besides* this we have much more. **2** Beyond; apart from: I care for nothing *besides* this.

be·siege (bi·sēj′) *v.t.* **be·sieged, be·sieg·ing 1** To beset or surround; lay siege to, as a castle. **2** To crowd around; block. **3** To harass or overwhelm, as with invitations or prayers. See synonyms under ATTACK. —**be·sieg′er** *n.* —**be·siege′ment** *n.*

Bes·kid Mountains (bes′kid, bes·kēd′) A mountain group of the Carpathians along the Czechoslovak-Polish border; highest point, 5,658 feet. Also **Bes′kids.**

be·smear (bi·smir′) *v.t.* To smear over; sully.

be·smirch (bi·smûrch′) *v.t.* **1** To soil; stain. **2** To sully; dishonor, as a reputation. —**be·smirch′er** *n.* —**be·smirch′ment** *n.*

be·som[1] (bē′zəm) *n.* **1** A bundle of twigs used as a broom; any agency that cleanses or abolishes. **2** The broom (*Cytisus scoparius*). [OE *besma* broom]

be·som[2] (bē′zəm, biz′əm) *n. Scot.* A drab; slattern; street woman.

be·sot (bi·sot′) *v.t.* **be·sot·ted, be·sot·ting 1** To stupefy, as with drink. **2** To make foolish or stupid. **3** To infatuate. —**be·sot′ted** *adj.*

be·sought (bi·sôt′) Past tense and past participle of BESEECH.

be·span·gle (bi·spang′gəl) *v.t.* **·gled, ·gling** To decorate with or as with spangles.

be·spat·ter (bi·spat′ər) *v.t.* **1** To cover or soil by spattering. **2** To spatter about. **3** To besmirch; sully.

be·speak (bi·spēk′) *v.t.* **be·spoke** (*Archaic* **be·spake**), **be·spoke** or **be·spo·ken, be·speak·ing 1** To ask or arrange for in advance; reserve. **2** To give evidence of; indicate: His face *bespeaks* his happy lot. **3** To foretell; foreshadow: The present *bespeaks* a sad future. **4** *Obs.* To speak to. [OE *bisprecan*]

be·spec·ta·cled (bi·spek′tə·kəld) *adj.* Wearing glasses.

be·spoke (bi·spōk′) Past tense and alternative past participle of BESPEAK. —*adj. Brit.* Ordered ahead of time; made to order, as a suit of clothing.

be·spread (bi·spred′) *v.t.* **be·spread, be·spread·ing** To cover or spread over thickly.

be·sprent (bi·sprent′) *adj. Obs.* Besprinkled; strewed. [OE, pp. of *besprengan* sprinkle]

be·sprin·kle (bi·spring′kəl) *v.t.* **·kled, ·kling** To scatter or spread over by sprinkling.

Bes·sa·ra·bi·a (bes′ə·rā′bē·ə) A region of SW European U.S.S.R.; about 18,000 square miles; formerly a Rumanian province. *Rumanian* **Ba·sa·ra·bia** (bä·sä·rä′byä). —**Bes′sa·ra′bi·an** *adj. & n.*

Bes·sel method (bes′əl) A method of determining one's position by sighting through points on a map correctly oriented to the corresponding features of the terrain. [after Friedrich *Bessel*, 1784–1846, German astronomer]

Bes·se·mer (bes′ə·mər) *n.* Steel prepared by the Bessemer process. [after Sir Henry *Bessemer*, 1813–98, British engineer]

Bessemer converter *Metall.* A large pear-shaped vessel for containing the molten iron to be converted into steel by the Bessemer process.

Bessemer process *Metall.* **1** A process for eliminating the carbon and silicon from pig iron by forcing a blast of air through the molten metal preparatory to its conversion into steel or ingot iron. **2** A similar process for eliminating sulfur from copper matte.

BESSEMER CONVERTER
a. CO_2 *e.* Steel.
b. SO_2 *f* Hot compressed air.
c. Sand bricks.
d. Flames. *g.* Molten iron.

best (best) *adj.* [*Superlative of* GOOD] **1** Excelling all others in a given quality. **2** Most advantageous, desirable, or serviceable. **3** Most; largest; as, the *best* part of an hour. —*n.* The most excellent thing, part, etc.; the highest degree or state; the utmost. —*adv.* [*Superlative of* WELL] **1** In the most excellent or suitable manner. **2** With the most favorable result. **3** To the utmost degree. —*v.t.* To defeat; overcome. [OE *betst*]

be·stain (bi·stān′) *v.t.* Mark with stains.

be·stead (bi·sted′) *v.t.* **be·stead·ed** or **be·sted, be·stead·ing** To be of service to; help.

bes·tial (bes′chəl, best′yəl) *adj.* **1** Pertaining to or like beasts or a beast; animal. **2** Having the qualities of an animal; brutish; sensual; depraved. **3** Irrational; rude; savage. See synonyms under BRUTISH. [< OF < L *bestialis* < *bestia* beast] —**bes′tial·ly** *adv.*

bes·ti·al·i·ty (bes′chē·al′ə·tē, -tē·al′-) *n.* **1** The quality or state of being bestial. **2** Character or conduct befitting beasts. **3** Human sexual relations with an animal; sodomy.

bes·tial·ize (bes′chəl·īz, best′yəl-) *v.t.* **·ized, ·iz·ing** To brutalize.

bes·ti·ar·y (bes′tē·er′ē) *n. pl.* **·ar·ies** A medieval allegory or moralizing treatise on animals.

be·stir (bi·stûr′) *v.t.* **be·stirred, be·stir·ring** To incite or rouse to activity.

best man The chief groomsman at a wedding.

be·stow (bi·stō′) *v.t.* **1** To present as a gift: with *on* or *upon.* **2** To expend; apply: He *bestowed* his life on science. **3** *Obs.* To give in marriage. **4** *Obs.* To deposit; store; also, to house; lodge. See synonyms under GIVE. [ME *bistowen* < *bi-* to, upon + *stowen* place] —**be·stow′a·ble** *adj.* —**be·stow′al** or **be·stow′ment** *n.*

be·strad·dle (bi·strad′l) *v.t.* **·dled, ·dling** To bestride; straddle.

be·strew (bi·strōō′) *v.t.* **be·strewed, be·strewed** or **be·strewn, be·strew·ing 1** To cover or strew (a surface). **2** To scatter about. **3** To lie scattered over. Also **be·strow** (bi·strō′). [OE *bestreowian*]

be·stride (bi·strīd′) *v.t.* **be·strode, be·strid·den, be·strid·ing 1** To mount; sit astride of; ride astride; straddle. **2** To stride over or across.

best-sell·er (best′sel′ər) *n.* A book or phono-

graph record currently selling in large numbers.

bet (bet) *v.* **bet** or (less commonly) **bet·ted, bet·ting** *v.t.* **1** To stake or pledge (money, etc.) in support of an opinion or on an uncertain outcome, as of a race. **2** To declare an in a bet: I'll *bet* he doesn't come. —*v.i.* **3** To place a wager. —**you bet** *U.S. Slang* Certainly. —*n.* **1** The act of betting; a wager. **2** The stake in any wager. **3** That on which the bet is placed: The black horse is the best *bet.* [Origin uncertain]

be·ta (bā′tə, bē′-) *n.* **1** The second letter of the Greek alphabet (B, β): corresponding to English *b*. As a numeral it denotes 2. **2** The second object in any order of arrangement or classification, as, in astronomy the second brightest star in a constellation, in chemistry the second of a group of isomeric compounds, in botany the second subspecies, etc. [< Gk.]

be·ta-block·er (bā′tə-blok′ər) *n.* A drug that relieves heart stress by inhibiting absorption of adrenalin by the heart and blood vessels.

Beta Cen·tau·ri (sen·tôr′ē) The star Beta in the constellation of Centaurus; one of the 20 brightest stars, 0.86 magnitude.

be·take (bi·tāk′) *v.t.* **be·took, be·tak·en, be·tak·ing 1** To resort to or have recourse: used reflexively: with *to*: She *betook* herself to prayer. **2** To go; take (oneself): with *to*: He *betook* himself to an inn.

beta particle An electron.

beta rays *Physics* A stream of electrons projected by radioactive substances. They are identical with cathode rays, possess great penetrative power, and are easily deflected by an electric or magnetic field in a direction opposite to that of the alpha rays.

beta rhythm A frequency of 13 to 30 per second in brain waves, characteristic of an alert or aroused state in the normal human adult.

be·ta·tron (bā′tə·tron) *n.* An electromagnetic apparatus for liberating electrons and accelerating them in a quarter-cycle alternating field to the required velocity for discharge against a chosen target. [< BETA (RAY) + (ELEC)TRON]

be·ta·tro·pic (bā′tə·trō′pik, -trop′ik) *adj. Physics* **1** Of or pertaining to a difference of one beta particle in the nucleus of an atom. **2** Designating either of two atoms, one of which has been formed by the ejection of a beta particle from the nucleus, with an increase of 1 in the nuclear charge. [< BETA (PARTICLE) + -TROPIC]

be·tel (bēt′l) *n.* A climbing plant (*Piper betle*) of Asia, the leaves of which are chewed by the natives of Malaya and other Asian countries. See BETELNUT. [< Pg. *betel* < Malay *vettila*]

Be·tel·geuse (bē′təl·jōōz, bet′əl·jœz) A giant red star, Alpha in the constellation of Orion. It is an irregular variable with a magnitude of 1.2. Also **Be′tel·guese, Be′tel·geux.** [< F *Bételgeuse* < Arabic *bat al-jauza*, ? shoulder of the giant]

be·tel·nut (bēt′l·nut′) *n.* The astringent seed of an East Indian palm, the **betel palm** (*Areca cathecu*), used for chewing with betel leaves.

bête noire (bāt′ nwär′, *Fr.* bet nwâr′) Anything real or imaginary that is an object of hate or dread; a bugaboo. [< F, black beast]

beth (beth) The second Hebrew letter. See ALPHABET.

beth·el (beth′əl) *n.* **1** A seamen's church or chapel, floating or on shore. **2** *Brit.* A dissenters' chapel. **3** A hallowed place. [< Hebrew *bēth-ēl* house of God]

Be·thes·da (bə·thez′də) *n.* **1** A pool in Jerusalem reputed to have healing properties. *John* v 2. **2** A meeting house; chapel.

be·think (bi·thingk′) *v.* **be·thought, be·think·ing** *v.t.* To remind (oneself); bear in mind; consider: generally used reflexively: *Bethink* yourself of what you are. —*v.i. Archaic* To meditate.

Beth·le·hem (beth′lē·əm, -lə·hem) **1** An ancient town in Judea, SW of Jerusalem; birthplace of Jesus. *Matt.* ii 1. **2** A town in Palestine on the same site. **3** A manufacturing city on the Lehigh River in eastern Pennsylvania. —**Beth′le·hem·ite** *n.*

be·thought (bi·thôt′) Past tense and past participle of BETHINK.

be·tide (bi-tīd′) *v.t.* & *v.i.* **be·tid·ed, be·tid·ing** To happen (to) or befall. See synonyms under HAPPEN. [ME *betiden*]

be·times (bi-tīmz′) *adv.* In good season or time; also, soon. Also *Obs.* **be·time′.** [ME *betymes* in time, seasonably]

bê·tise (be-tēz′) *n.* French **1** A stupid thing; an absurdity. **2** Stupidity; nonsense.

be·to·ken (bi-tō′kən) *v.t.* **1** To be a sign of; portend. **2** To give evidence of; indicate. See synonyms under AUGUR, IMPORT. [ME *bitacnien*] — **be·to′ken·er** *n.*

bé·ton (bā-tôn′) *n.* French A concrete of lime, sand, and cement.

bet·o·ny (bet′ə-nē) *n. pl.* **·nies 1** A European herb (genus *Stachys*, formerly *Betonica*) of the mint family, once used as an emetic. **2** One of various other plants, as a British species of figwort (the water *betony*), etc. [< F *bétoine* < L *betonica*, var. of *vettonica* < *Vettones*, a people of Portugal]

be·took (bi-took′) Past tense of BETAKE.

be·tray (bi-trā′) *v.t.* **1** To deliver up to an enemy; be a traitor to. **2** To prove faithless to; disappoint: to *betray* a trust. **3** To disclose, as secret information. **4** To reveal unwittingly: to *betray* ignorance. **5** To deceive; seduce and desert. **6** To indicate; show: The smoke *betrays* a fire. See synonyms under DECEIVE. [ME *bitraien* < *bi* over, to + OF *trair* < L *tradere* deliver, give up] — **be·tray′al, be·tray′ment** *n.* — **be·tray′er** *n.*

be·troth (bi-trōth′, -trôth′) *v.t.* **1** To engage to marry; affiance. **2** To contract to give in marriage. [ME *bitreuthien* < *bi-* + *treuthe* truth]

be·troth·al (bi-trō′thəl, -trôth′əl) *n.* **1** The act of betrothing, or the state of being betrothed. **2** Engagement or contract to marry. Also **be·troth′. ment.**

be·trothed (bi-trōthd′, -trôtht′) *adj.* Engaged to be married; affianced. —*n.* A person engaged to be married.

bet·ter¹ (bet′ər) *adj.* [Comparative of GOOD] **1** Superior in excellence, amount, or value; excelling or surpassing. **2** Larger; greater: the *better* half of the cake. **3** Improved in health; convalescent. —*n.* **1** That which is in any way better; also, advantage; superiority. **2** A superior, as in ability, rank, age, etc. —*v.t.* **1** To make better; improve. **2** To surpass; excel. —*v.i.* **3** To grow better. See synonyms under AMEND. —*adv.* [Comparative of WELL] **1** In a superior manner; more thoroughly or correctly; in a higher degree. **2** *Colloq.* More: We've been here *better* than a week. [OE *betera*]

bet·ter² (bet′ər) *n.* One who lays wagers. Also **bet′tor.**

bet·ter·ment (bet′ər·mənt) *n.* **1** Improvement. **2** An addition to the value of real property.

bet·u·la·ceous (bech′oo·lā′shəs) *adj.* Belonging to a family (*Betulaceae*) of trees and shrubs including the birch, the alder, and the hazel. [< L *betula* birch]

be·tween (bi·twēn′) *adv.* In intervening time, space, position, or relation; at or during intervals: Rest periods were few and far *between*. —**in between** In an intermediate position or state; undecided. —*prep.* **1** In or at some point within the space separating two places or objects: He stepped *between* the combatants. **2** Intermediate in relation to qualities, conditions, periods of time, etc.: a flavor *between* sweet and sour; Come *between* one and two. **3** Involving in or as in joint or reciprocal action or relation: They had only five dollars *between* them. **4** Connecting, as in continuous extent or motion: the plane *between* New York and Paris. **5** One or the other of: How can you choose *between* them? **6** As a result of: *Between* her job and her housework, she had little time for her children. [OE *betweonan* < *be-* by + *tweonan* < *twā* two]

Synonym (*prep.*): among. In strict usage *between* is used only of two objects; *among* of more than two; divide the money *between* the two, *among* the three. *Between* is, however, used at times of more than two objects, particularly when some reciprocal relation is denoted; as, a treaty *between* the three powers. See AMID.

between you and me Confidentially.

be·twixt (bi·twikst′) *adv.* & *prep. Archaic* or *Poetic* Between. See synonyms under AMID. [OE *betweohs* twofold < *be* by + *-tweohs* < *twā* two]

betwixt and between In an intermediate state or position; neither the one nor the other.

Beu·lah (byoo′lə) The land of Israel. *Isa.* lxii 4. —**Land of Beulah** In Bunyan's *Pilgrim's Progress*, the land of rest where pilgrims abide till death.

Bev or **bev** (bev) *n. Physics.* Billion (10⁹) electron volts.

bev·a·tron (bev′ə·tron) *n. Physics* An atom-smashing machine resembling the synchrotron in operating principle but capable of accelerating protons to an energy level in excess of one billion electron volts; a proton synchrotron: also called *cosmotron*. [< B(ILLION) E(LECTRON) V(OLTS) + (ELEC)TRON]

bev·el (bev′əl) *n.* **1** An inclination of two surfaces other than 90°, as at the edge of a timber, etc. **2** An adjustable instrument for measuring angles: also **bevel square.** —*adj.* Oblique; slanting; beveled. —*v.* **bev·eled** or **bev·elled, bev·el·ing** or **bev·el·ling** *v.t.* To cut or bring to a bevel. —*v.i.* To slant. [? < OF. Cf. F *beveau.*]

BEVEL SQUARE

bevel gear *Mech.* A gear having beveled teeth, as for transmitting rotary motion at an angle. See illustration under COGWHEEL.

bev·er·age (bev′rij, bev′ər·ij) *n.* Drink; that which is drunk. [< OF *bevrage* < *beivre* drinking < L *bibere* drink]

Bev·er·ly Hills (bev′ər·lē) A residential city in California, on the western boundary of Los Angeles.

bev·y (bev′ē) *n. pl.* **·ies 1** A small group of persons, usually of girls or women. **2** A flock of birds, especially of quail, grouse, or larks. **3** A small herd, especially of roes. See synonyms under FLOCK. [ME *bevey;* origin uncertain]

be·wail (bi·wāl′) *v.t.* & *v.i.* To mourn; lament. See synonyms under MOURN.

be·ware (bi·wâr′) *v.t.* & *v.i.* **be·wared, be·war·ing** To look out (for); be cautious or wary (of): often with *of, lest, that, not, how.* [OE *wær* cautious; orig. *be ware* be on guard, be cautious]

be·wil·der (bi·wil′dər) *v.t.* **1** To confuse utterly; perplex. **2** *Archaic* To cause to lose the way or course. See synonyms under ABASH. — **be·wil′dered** *adj.* —**be·wil′dered·ly** *adv.* — **be·wil′der·ing** *adj.* —**be·wil′der·ing·ly** *adv.*

be·wil·der·ment (bi·wil′dər·mənt) *n.* **1** A state or condition of being bewildered. **2** A confusion; entanglement. See synonyms under PERPLEXITY.

be·witch (bi·wich′) *v.t.* **1** To gain power over by charms or incantations. **2** To attract irresistibly; charm; fascinate. See synonyms under CHARM. —**be·witch′er** *n.* —**be·witch′. ment, be·witch′er·y** *n.*

be·witch·ing (bi·wich′ing) *adj.* Charming; captivating. See synonyms under BEAUTIFUL. — **be·witch′ing·ly** *adv.*

be·wray (bi·rā′) *v.t. Obs.* To disclose; betray. [ME *bewreien* < *be-* + *wreien,* OE *wrēgan* accuse]

bey (bā) *n.* **1** The governor of a minor Turkish province or district. **2** A native ruler of Tunis. **3** A Turkish title of respect. Also spelled *beg.* ♦ Homophone: *bay.* [< Turkish *beg* lord] — **bey′i·cal** *adj.*

bey·lik (bā′lik) *n.* **1** The authority of a bey. **2** The district ruled by a bey. Also **bey′lic.**

be·yond (bi·yond′) *prep.* **1** Farther or more distant than; on or to the far side of: the house *beyond* the turn of the road. **2** Extending further than: staying *beyond* his usual hour. **3** Out of the reach or scope of: Algebra is *beyond* me. **4** Surpassing; superior to; exceeding: a woman lovely *beyond* description. —*adv.* Farther on or away; at a distance. —**the (great) beyond** Whatever comes after death. [OE *begeondan* < *be-* near + *geondan* yonder]

Bey·routh (bā′root, bā·root′) See BEIRUT.

bez·ant (bez′ənt, bi·zant′) *n.* **1** The solidus (def. 1). **2** *Archit.* A flat disk used in ornamentation. Also spelled *byzant.* [< OF *besant* < L *Byzantius* Byzantine]

bez antler (bez, bāz) The second branch of a deer's antler, the one above the brow antler. Also **bez tine.** For illustration see ANTLER. [< OF *bes-* < L *bis* twice]

bez·el (bez′əl) *n.* **1** A bevel on the edge of a cutting tool. **2** That part of a cut gem which is above the girdle, including the table and surrounding facets. **3** A groove and flange made to receive a beveled edge, as of a watch crystal. **4** A flat, engraved gold seal. [? < OF. Cf. F *biseau.*]

be·zique (bə·zēk′) *n.* A game of cards based on the declaring of certain combinations upon taking a trick: also, such a combination in this game. [< F *bésigue*]

be·zoar (bē′zôr, -zōr) *n.* **1** A concretion found in the stomach and intestines of ruminants and some other animals, formerly supposed to have medicinal value. **2** *Obs.* An antidote or panacea. [< NL < Persian *pādzahr* < *pād* expelling + *zahr* poison]

Bha·ga·vad-Gi·ta (bug′ə·vəd·gē′tä) *n.* A sacred Hindu text consisting of philosophical dialog in the *Mahabharata,* expounding the duties of caste and the yoga doctrines of devotion to the Supreme Spirit. [< Skt., Song of the Blessed One (i.e., Krishna)]

bhang (bang) *n.* **1** Indian hemp. **2** The dried leaves and capsules of the Indian hemp: used for their intoxicant and narcotic properties. Also spelled *bang.* [< Hind. < Skt. *bhangā* hemp]

Bha·rat (bu′rut) The ancient name for INDIA.

Bhat·pa·ra (bät·pä′rə) A city in West Bengal, India; an ancient seat of Sanskrit learning.

bhees·tee (bēs′tē) *n.* In India, a native water carrier. Also **bhees′tie, bhis′tie.** [< Hind. *bhīstī* < Persian *bihishti,* lit., one from heaven]

Bhu·tan (boo·tän′) A semi-independent kingdom between NE India and Tibet; 18,000 square miles; capital Punaka.

Bhu·tan·ese (boo′tən·ez′, -ēs′) *n. pl.* **·ese 1** A native of Bhutan. **2** The Sino-Tibetan language of Bhutan. —*adj.* Of or pertaining to Bhutan, its people, or their language.

Bi *Chem.* Bismuth (symbol Bi).

bi- *prefix* **1** Twice; doubly; two; especially, occurring twice or having two; as in:

biangulate	bicephalic	biradiate
bicapitate	biciliate	bispiral
bicellular	bicolumnar	bistipular
bicentral	biflorate	bistipulate

2 *Chem.* **a** Having two equivalents of the substance named: *bichloride.* **b** Indicating the presence of the named component in double the ordinary proportion, or the doubling of a radical, etc., in an organic compound. Also: *bin-* before a vowel, as in *binaural; bis-* before *c, s,* as in *bissextile.* [< L *bi- < bis* twice]

bi·an·nu·al (bī·an′yoo·əl) *adj.* Occurring twice a year; semiannual. —**bi·an′nu·al·ly** *adv.*

bi·an·nu·late (bī·an′yə·lāt, -lit) *adj. Zool.* Having two rings or bands, as of color.

Bi·ar·ritz (bē′ə·rits, *Fr.* byá·rēts′) A resort town in SW France on the Bay of Biscay.

bi·as (bī′əs) *n. pl.* **bi·as·es** or **bi·as·ses 1** A line, cut, or seam running obliquely across the threads of a fabric: a dress sewn on the *bias.* **2** A mental predilection or prejudice. See synonyms under INCLINATION, PREJUDICE. **3** *Electronics* A grid bias. **4** In bowling, a lopsided shape of a ball, causing it to swerve; also, the swerving course of such a ball. —*adj.* Cut, running, set, or folded diagonally; slanting. —*adv.* Slantingly; diagonally. —*v.t.* **bi·ased** or **bi·assed, bi·as·ing** or **bi·as·sing 1** To influence or affect unduly or unfairly. **2** *Electronics* To impose a steady negative potential upon (a grid). [< F *biais* oblique]

bi·au·ric·u·lar (bī′ô·rik′yə·lər) *adj.* **1** Of or pertaining to two auricles. **2** Biauriculate. **3** Having two ears.

bi·au·ric·u·late (bī′ô·rik′yə·lit) *adj. Anat.* Having two auricles, as the heart.

bi·ax·i·al (bī·ak′sē·əl) *adj.* Having two axes, as a crystal. Also **bi·ax·al** (bī·ak′səl). —**bi·ax′i·al·ly** *adv.*

bib (bib) *v.t.* & *v.i.* **bibbed, bib·bing** *Obs.* To drink; tipple. —*n.* **1** A cloth worn under the chin by children at meals to catch drink or food that is dribbled. **2** A waistpiece attached to a woman's apron. **3** A bibcock. [< L *bibere* drink]

bib and tucker *Colloq.* Clothes.

bi·ba·sic (bī·bā′sik) *adj.* Dibasic.

bibb (bib) *n. Naut.* A cleat or bracket bolted to the hounds of a mast of a vessel to support the trestletrees. **2** A bibcock. [< BIB (*n.* def. 1)]

bib·ber (bib′ər) *n.* A tippler.

bib·cock (bib′kok′) *n.* A cock or faucet having

the nozzle bent downward.

bibe·lot (bib′lō, Fr. bēb·lō′) n. A small, decorative, or curious article of virtu or object of art. [<F]

bi·bi·va·lent (bī′bī·vā′lənt, bī·biv′ə-) adj. Chem. Pertaining to or designating an electrolyte that breaks down into two bivalent ions.

Bi·ble (bī′bəl) n. 1 The writings of the Old and New Testaments, as accepted by the Christian Church as a divine revelation: in certain churches embracing also parts of the Apocrypha. 2 A copy of this. 3 The Old Testament Scriptures in the form accepted by the Jews. 4 Any book, record, or history considered authoritative: in this sense usually not capitalized. —Douai Bible An English translation of the Latin Vulgate by members of the English College at Douai, 1582–1610; revised and altered for modern use in the Roman Catholic Church: also Douay Bible. —King James Bible A revision of the English Bible proposed by King James I in 1604, the work of 50 revisors, published in 1611; the most widely used Protestant version of the Bible in English-speaking countries: also called Authorized Version. Compare REVISED VERSION. [<OF <L biblia <Gk., pl. of biblion book]

Bib·li·cal (bib′li·kəl) adj. 1 Pertaining to, like, quoted, or derived from the Bible. 2 In harmony with the Bible. Also bib′li·cal. Bib′li·cal·ly adv.

Bib·li·cist (bib′lə·sist) n. 1 A person thoroughly versed in the Bible. 2 One who adheres to the letter of the Bible.

biblio- combining form Of or pertaining to a book or books, or to the Bible: bibliophile, bibliomancy. [<Gk. biblion book]

bib·li·o·film (bib′lē·ə·film′) n. A kind of microfilm used especially to reproduce rare or much-used books, etc.

bib·li·og·ra·phy (bib′lē·og′rə·fē) n. pl. **·phies** 1 The description and history of books including details of authorship, editions, dates, typography, etc.; also a book containing such descriptions. 2 A list of the works of an author, or of the literature bearing on a particular subject. — **bib′li·og′ra·pher**, **bib′li·o·graph′** n. —**bib·li·o·graph·ic** (bib′lē·ə·graf′ik) or **·i·cal** adj. [<BIB·LIO- + -GRAPHY]

bib·li·o·la·try (bib′lē·ol′ə·trē) n. 1 Extravagant homage paid to the letter of the Bible. 2 Excessive worship of books. [<BIBLIO- + Gk. latreia worship] —**bib′li·ol′a·ter** n. —**bib′li·ol′a·trous** adj.

bib·li·o·man·cy (bib′lē·ō·man′sē) n. Divination by means of reference to some passage taken at random from a book, usually the Bible.

bib·li·o·ma·nia (bib′lē·ō·mā′nē·ə) n. An intense passion for collecting and owning books. — **bib′li·o·ma′ni·ac** (-ak) n. & adj.

bib·li·op·e·gy (bib′lē·op′ə·jē) n. The art or practice of bookbinding. [<biblio- + Gk. pēgnynai fasten, join]

bib·li·o·phile (bib′lē·ə·fīl′, -fil′) n. One who loves books. Also **bib′li·o·phil′** (fil′), **bib·li·oph·i·list** (bib′lē·of′ə·list). —**bib′li·oph′i·lism** n. —**bib′li·oph′i·lis′tic** adj.

bib·li·o·pole (bib′lē·ə·pōl′) n. A dealer in rare books. Also **bib·li·op·o·list** (bib′lē·op′ə·list). [<L bibliopola <Gk. bibliopōlēs bookseller <biblion book + pōleein sell] —**bib′li·o·pol′ic** (-pol′ik) or **·i·cal** adj. —**bib′li·op′o·lism** n.

Bib·list (bib′list, bī′blist) n. A Biblicist.

bib·u·lous (bib′yə·ləs) adj. 1 Given to drink; fond of drinking. 2 Taking up moisture readily; absorbent. [<L bibulus drinking readily <bibere drink] —**bib′u·los′i·ty** (-los′ə·tē) n. — bib′u·lous·ly adv. —bib′u·lous·ness n.

bi·cam·er·al (bī·kam′ər·əl) adj. Consisting of two chambers, houses, or branches, as a legislature.

bi·cap·su·lar (bī·kap′sə·lər, -syə-) adj. Bot. 1 Having two capsules. 2 Having a two-celled capsule.

bi·car·bo·nate (bī·kär′bə·nit, -nāt) n. Chem. A salt of carbonic acid in which one of the hydrogen atoms is replaced by a metal: sodium bicarbonate.

bice (bis) n. 1 A blue or green pigment made from varieties of basic copper carbonate ore. **bice green** is now usually called malachite green and **blue bice**, azurite. 2 The color of any of

these pigments. [<OF bis dark-colored]

bi·cen·te·nar·y (bī·sen′tə·nerē, bī′sen·ten′ər·ē) adj. 1 Occurring once in 200 years. 2 Lasting or consisting of 200 years. —n. pl. **·nar·ies** 1 A period of 200 years. 2 A 200th anniversary. Also **bi·cen·ten·ni·al** (bī′sen·ten′ē·əl).

bi·ceph·a·lous (bī·sef′ə·ləs) adj. Biol. Having two heads.

bi·ceps (bī′seps) n. pl. **bi·ceps** Anat. 1 The large front muscle, or flexor, of the upper arm, the **biceps bra·chi·i** (brā′kē·ī). 2 The large flexor muscle at the back of the thigh, the **biceps cru·ris** (krŏŏr′is). 3 Loosely, muscular strength. [<L, two-headed <bis twofold + caput head]

Bi·chat (bē·shä′), **Marie François Xavier**, 1771–1802, French anatomist; founder of histology.

biche (bēch) n. A Mexican hairless dog. [<Nahuatl, naked]

bi·chlo·ride (bī·klôr′īd, -id, -klôr′īd, -rid) n. Chem. 1 A salt in which there are two atoms of chlorine. 2 Bichloride of mercury, or corrosive sublimate, a dangerous poison used as a disinfectant.

two heads. 2 Pertaining to the biceps. Also **bi·cip′i·tous** (-təs).

bick·er¹ (bik′ər) v.i. 1 To dispute petulantly; wrangle. 2 To flow noisily, as a brook; gurgle. 3 To flicker, as a flame; twinkle. —n. 1 A petulant or angry dispute; a petty altercation: also **bick·er·ing**. 2 A clattering, babbling noise. 3 A flicker, or a tremulous or unsteady motion. See synonyms under QUARREL. [ME bikeren; origin uncertain] —**bick′er·er** n.

bi·col·or (bī′kul′ər) adj. Having two colors.

bi·con·cave (bī·kon′kāv, -kong′-, bī′kon·kāv′) adj. Concave on both sides.

bi·con·vex (bī·kon′veks, bī′kon·veks′) adj. Convex on both sides.

bi·corn (bī′kôrn) n. 1 A two-cornered, crescent-shaped hat with upturned brim; specifically, the two-cornered hat worn by French gendarmes: also **bi·corne**. 2 A two-horned animal: compare UNICORN. —adj. Two-horned; two-pronged; having two hornlike projections: also **bi·cor·nous** (bī·kôr′nəs), **bi·cor·nu·ate** (bī·kôr′nyŏŏ·āt). [<L bicornis <bis twofold + cornus horn]

bi·cor·po·ral (bī·kôr′pər·əl) adj. Double-bodied, as certain signs of the zodiac. Also **bi·cor·po·re·al** (bī′kôr·pôr′ē·əl, -pōr′ē-).

bi·cron (bī′kron) n. The one-billionth part of a meter; micromillimeter.

bi·cul·tur·al·ism (bī·kul′chə·rə·liz′əm) n. The policy of union between two separate cultures within one nation.

bi·cus·pid (bī·kus′pid) adj. 1 Having two cusps or points. 2 Double-pointed, as a premolar tooth, the valve at the left auricular opening of the heart, or a curve or crescent: also **bi·cus′pi·dal** (-dəl), **bi·cus′pi·date** (-dāt). —n. A premolar tooth, of which there are eight in the normal human jaws, two between each cuspid and the first molar tooth. Also **bi·cus′pis**. [<L bis twofold + cuspis, -idis point]

bi·cy·cle (bī′sik·əl) n. A two-wheeled vehicle with the wheels in tandem, a saddle or saddles, a steering handle, and propelled by foot pedals or a motor. —v.i. **·cled**, **·cling** To ride a bicycle. Also **cycle**. [<L bis twofold + Gk. kyklos wheel] —**bi′cy·cler**, **bi′cy·clist** n.

bi·cy·clic (bī·sī′klik, -sik′lik) adj. 1 Pertaining to bicycles or bicycling. 2 Bot. Disposed in two cycles or whorls: also **bi·cy′cli·cal**.

bid (bid) n. 1 An offer to pay or accept a price. 2 The amount offered. 3 In card games, the number of tricks or points that a player engages to make; also, a player's turn to bid. 4 An effort to acquire, win, or attain: He made a bid for the governorship. 5 Colloq. An invitation. —v. **bade** (Archaic bad) for defs. 3, 4, 6 or **bid** for defs. 1, 2, 5, 7, **bid·den** or **bid**, **bid·ding** v.t. 1 To make an offer of (a price), as at an auction or for a contract. 2 In card games, to declare (the number of tricks one will engage to take) and specify (the trump suit or no-trump under which the hand will be played): I bid six spades. 3 To command; order. 4 To invite. 5 U.S. Colloq. To invite to join: The fraternity will bid you. 6 To utter, as a greeting or farewell: I bid you good day. —v.i. 7

To offer a price. —**to bid fair** To seem probable. —**to bid in** At an auction, to attempt to raise the price (of an object) by competing with spurious bids. —**to bid up** To increase the price by offering higher bids. [Fusion of OE biddan ask, demand and bēodan proclaim, command]

bi·dar·ka (bī·där′kə) n. A skin-covered canoe used by natives of Alaska. [<Russian baidarka, dim. of baidara canoe]

bid·da·ble (bid′ə·bəl) adj. 1 Of sufficient value to offer a bid on, as a bridge hand. 2 Inclined to do as bidden; obedient; docile.

bid·der (bid′ər) n. 1 One who makes a bid. 2 In contract bridge, the player who first names the trump suit, or no-trump, in which a hand is played; the declarer.

bid·ding (bid′ing) n. 1 A notification or command. 2 A solicitation or invitation. 3 The making of a bid or bids, as at a sale, in the game of contract bridge, etc.; bids collectively.

bide (bīd) v. **bid·ed** (Archaic bode), **bid·ing** v.t. 1 To endure; withstand: to bide a storm. 2 Archaic To tolerate; submit to. —v.i. 3 To dwell; abide; stay. —**to bide one's time** To await the most favorable opportunity. See synonyms under ABIDE. [OE bīdan wait, stay]

bi·den·tate (bī·den′tāt) adj. Having two teeth or toothlike processes. Also **bi·den′tal**.

bi·det (bi·dā′) n. A small porcelain commode with running water, used for cleansing the genital and anal areas. [<F]

bi·di·a·lect·al·ism (bī′dī·ə·lek′tə·liz′əm) n. The use of two distinct dialects of a single language.

bid·ing (bī′ding) n. 1 An awaiting; expectation. 2 Residence; habitation.

bid·ri (bid′rē) n. An alloy of copper, lead, and tin used for making **bidri ware**, an Indian ware damascened with silver or gold. Also **bid′ree**, **bid′der·y**. [from Bidar, town in India]

Bie·der·mei·er (bē′dər·mī′ər) adj. Of or pertaining to a style of German furniture of the first half of the 19th century, based on French Empire forms. [after Gottlieb Biedermeier, character invented by L. Eichrodt. 1827–92, German poet]

bien (bēn) adj. Scot. 1 Well-to-do; comfortably off, as a farmer. 2 Comfortably furnished; cosy, as a house. Also spelled **bein**. [<F bien well]

bien en·ten·du (byañ näñ·täñ·dü′) French Of course; lit., well understood.

bi·en·ni·al (bī·en′ē·əl) adj. 1 Occurring every second year. 2 Lasting or living for two years. —n. 1 Bot. A plant that produces leaves and roots the first year and flowers and fruit the second, then dies. 2 An event occurring once in two years. [<L biennis <bis twofold + annus year] — **bi·en′ni·al·ly** adv.

bien·ve·nue (byañ·və·nü′) n. French A welcome.

bier¹ (bir) n. A framework for carrrying a corpse to the grave; a coffin. ◆ Homophone: beer. [OE bœr]

bier² (bēr) n. German Beer.

Bierce (birs), **Ambrose Gwinnett**, 1842–1914?, U.S. journalist and author.

biest·ings (bēs′tingz) n. Beestings.

bi·fa·cial (bī·fā′shəl) adj. 1 Having two fronts, as an effigy on a medal. 2 Bot. Having the opposite faces unlike, as a leaf. 3 Being alike on the opposite surfaces.

bi·far·i·ous (bī·fâr′ē·əs) adj. 1 Two-ranked. 2 Bot. Disposed in two vertical rows, as leaves on a branch. [<LL bifarius double <bis twofold + fari speak] —**bi·far′i·ous·ly** adv.

biff (bif) Slang v.t. To give a blow. —n. A whack; blow. [Imit.]

bif·fin (bif′in) n. Brit. 1 A cooking apple: a Norfolk **biffin**. 2 A baked apple flattened into a cake. [Var. of BEEFING]

bi·fid (bī′fid) adj. Doubly cleft: forked. Also **bif·i·date** (bif′i·dāt), **bif′i·dat′ed**. [<L bifidus <bis twofold + findere split] —**bi·fid·i·ty** (bī·fid′ə·tē) n. —**bi′fid·ly** adv.

bi·fi·lar (bī·fī′lər) adj. Formed of, having, or supported by two threads. —n. A bifilar micrometer. [<BI- + L filum thread] —**bi·fi′lar·ly** adv.

bi·flag·el·late (bī·flaj′ə·lāt) adj. Zool. Having two flagella or whiplike processes.

bi·flex (bī′fleks) adj. Bent in two places; alternately convex and concave. [< BI- + L *flexus*, pp. of *flectere* bend]

bi·fo·cal (bī-fō′kəl) *adj. Optics* Having two foci: said of a lens ground of both near and far vision. [< BI- + L *focus* hearth, focus of a lens]

bi·fo·cals (bī-fō′kəlz, bī′fō-kəlz) *n. pl.* Eyeglasses with bifocal lenses ground for distant vision in the upper portion of the lenses and for near vision in the lower.

bi·fold (bī′fōld′) *adj.* Twofold.

bi·fo·li·ate (bī-fō′lē-it) *adj. Bot.* Having two leaves.

bi·fo·li·o·late (bī-fō′lē-ə-lāt′) *adj. Bot.* Having two leaflets.

bi·fo·rate (bī-fôr′āt, -fō′rāt) *adj.* Having two perforations. [< BI- + L *foratus*, pp. of *forare* bore]

bi·forked (bī′fôrkt′) *adj.* Bifurcate.

bi·form (bī′fôrm′) *adj.* Having or combining the characteristics of two distinct forms, as the Minotaur. Also **bi′formed′**.

bi·fur·cate (bī′fər-kāt, bī-fûr′kāt) *v.t. & v.i.* **·cat·ed, ·cat·ing** To fork; divide into two branches or stems. —*adj.* (bī′fər-kāt, bī-fûr′kit) Forked: also **bi′fur·cat′ed, bi·fur·cous** (bī-fûr′kəs). [< BI- + L *furca* fork] —**bi′fur·cate·ly** (-kit·lē) *adv.* —**bi′fur·ca′tion** *n.*

big¹ (big) *adj.* **big·ger, big·gest 1** Of great size, amount, or intensity; large; bulky. **2** Fruitful; pregnant. **3** Full to overflowing; teeming. **4** Puffed up; pompous. **5** Important: a *big* day in his life. **6** Generous; magnanimous. See synonyms under LARGE. —*adv. Colloq.* Pompously; extravagantly: to talk *big.* [ME; origin uncertain] —**big′gish** *adj.* —**big′ly** *adv.* —**big′ness** *n.*

big² (big) *v.t. & v.i. Scot.* To build. Also **bigg.**

big·a·mist (big′ə-mist) *n.* One guilty of bigamy.

big·a·mous (big′ə-məs) *adj.* **1** Guilty of or living in bigamy. **2** Involving bigamy. —**big′a·mous·ly** *adv.*

big·a·my (big′ə-mē) *n.* The criminal offense of marrying any other person while having a legal spouse living. [< OF *bigamie* < LL *bigamus* < *bis* twice + Gk. *gamos* wedding] —**bi·gam·ic** (bī-gam′ik) *adj.*

big·ar·reau (big′ə-rō, big′ə-rō′) *n.* A type of sweet, firm-fleshed, heart-shaped cherry. Also **big·a·roon** (big′ə-rōōn′). [< F < *bigarré.* pp. of *bigarrer* variegate]

big bang theory Astronomical theory that the universe began in a single, gigantic explosion of flammable gases.

Big Ben 1 A bell which strikes the hour in the Westminster clock in the tower of the Houses of Parliament, London. **2** The clock itself.

Big Dipper A group of seven stars resembling a dipper in outline in the constellation Ursa Major.

big·gin (big′in) *n.* **1** A head covering; especially, a child's cap. **2** *Brit.* The coif of a sergeant at law. **3** *Brit. Dial.* A nightcap. [< F *beguin* cap, orig. worn by the Beguines]

big·gi·ty (big′ə-tē) *adj. U.S. Dial.* Conceited; pompous; uppity.

big·head (big′hed′) *n.* **1** *Colloq.* Inflated conceit; pomposity. **2** A bulging of the skull of an animal, due to osteomalacia. **3** A contagious inflammation of the lungs and intestines of young turkeys.

big–heart·ed (big′här′tid) *adj.* Generous; charitable.

big–horn (big′hôrn′) *n. pl.* **·horns** or **·horn** The Rocky Mountain sheep (*Ovis canadensis*), remarkable for its large horns: also called *American argali.*

Bighorn Mountains A range of the Rockies in southern Montana and northern Wyoming; highest peak, 13,165 feet.

Bighorn River A river in northern Wyoming and southern Montana, flowing north 461 miles to the Yellowstone River.

bight (bīt) *n.* **1** A slightly receding bay; a small recess in a bay. **2** A bend in a river, or the like. **3** A loop or turn in a rope, as around a post, the two ends being fast. **4** A bending or angle. —*v.t.* To secure (a load, sail, etc.) as with a bight. ◆ Homophone: *bite.* [OE *byht* corner, bay < *būgan* bend]

big·no·ni·a (big·nō′nē·ə) *n.* Any of a genus (*Bignonia*) of woody climbing plants, mostly of tropical America, with clusters of large, trumpet-shaped flowers. [after A. J. *Bignon,* 1711–72, librarian to Louis XV]

big·ot (big′ət) *n.* An illiberal or intolerant adherent of a religious creed or of any party or opinion. [< F]

big·ot·ed (big′ət-id) *adj.* Stubbornly attached to a creed, party, system, or opinion. —**big′ot·ed·ly** *adv.*

big·ot·ry (big′ət-rē) *n. pl.* **·ries** Obstinate and intolerant attachment to a cause or creed. See synonyms under FANATICISM.

big shot *Slang* A person of importance.

big top *U.S. Colloq.* The main tent of a circus.

big tree The redwood of California.

big wheel *U.S. Slang* A person of importance.

big·wig (big′wig′) *n. Colloq.* A person of importance: in allusion to the big wigs formerly worn by people of consequence in England.

bi·jou (bē′zhōō, bē-zhōō′) *n. pl.* **bi·joux** (bē′-zhōōz, bē-zhōōz′) A jewel; a trinket. [< F]

bi·jou·te·rie (bē-zhōō′tər-ē) *n.* Jewelry; especially, an article of fine workmanship.

bi·ju·gate (bī′jōō·gāt, bī·jōō′git) *adj. Bot.* Two-paired, as a pinnate leaf with two pairs of leaflets. Also **bi·ju·gous** (bī′jōō·gəs).

Bi·ka·ner (bē′kə-nēr′) A city in northern Rajasthan; former capital of a princely state of the same name now included in Rajasthan.

bike¹ (bīk) *n. Colloq.* A bicycle. [Alter. of BICYCLE]

bike² (bīk) *n. Scot.* A nest or swarm of wild bees, wasps, ants, etc.; hence, a swarm; a crowd: also spelled *byke, beik.*

bi·ki·ni (bi·kē′nē) *n.* An extremely abbreviated or scanty bathing suit.

Bi·ki·ni (bi·kē′nē) An atoll in the Marshall islands; 2 square miles; site of U.S. atomic bomb tests, July 1946.

bi·la·bi·al (bī-lā′bē-əl) *adj.* **1** *Phonet.* Articulated with both lips, as certain consonants. **2** Having two lips. —*n. Phonet.* A speech sound formed with both lips, as (b), (p), (m), and (w).

bi·la·bi·ate (bī-lā′bē-āt, -it) *adj. Bot.* Two-lipped: said of a corolla.

bi·lat·er·al (bī-lat′ər-əl) *adj.* Pertaining to two sides; two-sided: a *bilateral* agreement. —**bi·lat′er·al·ly** *adv.* —**bi·lat′er·al·ness** *n.*

bil·ber·ry (bil′ber′ē, -bər-ē) *n.* **1** The European whortleberry. **2** Its blue-black fruit. [< Scand. Cf. Dan. *böllebær*]

bil·bo (bil′bō) *n. pl.* **·boes 1** A finely tempered Spanish sword made at Bilbao. **2** A fetter consisting of two sliding shackles attached to an iron bar. [from BILBAO]

bile (bīl) *n.* **1** *Physiol.* A bitter viscid fluid, yellowish in man and green in herbivores, secreted by the liver. **2** Anger; peevishness. [< L *bilis* bile. anger]

bile ducts *Physiol.* The excretory ducts of the gall bladder.

bile·stone (bīl′stōn′) *n. Pathol.* A biliary calculus; gallstone.

bilge (bilj) *n.* **1** *Naut.* The rounded part of a ship's bottom; specifically, that part extending from the keel to the point from which the sides rise vertically. **2** The bulge of a barrel. **3** Bilge water. **4** *Slang* Stupid or trivial chatter or writing. —*v.t. & v.i.* **bilged, bilg·ing 1** To break open the bottom of (a vessel). **2** To bulge or cause to bulge. [Var. of BULGE]

bilge·keel (bilj′kēl′) *n. Naut.* An outside keel set lengthwise on each side of the bilge of a vessel to lessen rolling. Also **bilge′piece′**.

bilge water Foul water that collects in the bilge of a ship.

bilg·y (bil′jē) *adj.* Resembling bilge water, as in smell.

bil·i·ar·y (bil′ē-er′ē) *adj.* Pertaining to or conveying bile.

bi·lin·e·ar (bī-lin′ē-ər) *adj.* Formed of or related to two lines.

bi·lin·gual (bī-ling′gwəl) *adj.* **1** Recorded or expressed in two languages. **2** Speaking two languages. —**bi·lin′gual·ly** *adv.* —**bi·lin′gual·ism** *n.*

bil·ious (bil′yəs) *adj.* **1** *Pathol.* Suffering from real or supposed disorder of the liver. **2** Of, pertaining to, containing, or consisting of bile. **3** Ill-natured; cross. [< F *bilieux* < L *biliosus*] —**bil′ious·ly** *adv.* —**bil′ious·ness** *n.*

bi·lit·er·al (bī-lit′ər-əl) *adj.* Composed of two letters. —**bi·lit′er·al·ism** *n.*

-bility *suffix* Forming nouns of quality from adjectives in *-ble: probability* from *probable.* [< F *-bilité* < L *-bilitas, -tatis*]

bilk (bilk) *v.t.* **1** To cheat; swindle; evade payment to. **2** To escape; dodge. **3** To balk. —*n.* **1** A swindler; deadbeat. **2** A trick; a hoax. [Origin unknown] —**bilk′er** *n.*

bill¹ (bil) *n.* **1** A statement of an account or of money due. **2** A banknote or treasury note: a ten-dollar *bill.* **3** A list of items: a *bill* of fare. **4** The draft of a proposed law. **5** *Law* A paper filed in a court calling for some specific action. **6** Some public notice or advertisement; the program of a theatrical performance. **7** *Brit.* A bill of exchange. **8** Loosely, a promissory note. **9** In Scots law, a petition to the court of sessions. **10** *Obs.* Any writing; a billet; petition. See synonyms under MONEY. —*v.t.* **1** To enter in a bill; charge. **2** To present a bill to. **3** To advertise by bills or placards. [< LL *billa*, var. of *bulla*. See BULL².]

bill² (bil) *n.* A beak, as of a bird. —*v.i.* To join bills, as doves; caress. — **to bill and coo** To caress lovingly; make love in soft murmuring tones. [OE *bile*]

bill³ (bil) *n.* **1** A hook-shaped instrument used by gardeners in pruning: also **bill′hook′**. **2** An ancient weapon with a hook-shaped blade; a halberd. **3** The point or peak of the fluke of an anchor. [OE *bill* sword, ax]

bill⁴ (bil) *n.* **1** A bellow or roar. **2** A boom, as of the bittern. [Var. of BELL²]

bill·a·ble (bil′ə-bəl) *adj.* Indictable.

bil·la·bong (bil′ə-bong) *n. Austral.* **1** A blind branch or channel leading from a river; an incomplete anabranch. **2** A pool of stagnant water or the backwaters of a stream. [< native Australian *billa* water + *bong* dead]

bill·board (bil′bôrd′, -bōrd′) *n.* A board, panel, or tablet intended for the display of posters or placards; a bulletin board.

bil·let¹ (bil′it) *n.* **1** A written missive; a note. **2** A requisition on a household to maintain a soldier. **3** The place where soldiers are so lodged. **4** *Brit.* A position; appointment. —*v.t. & v.i.* **1** To lodge (soldiers), or to be quartered or lodged, in a private house. **2** To serve with a missive. [< OF *billete*, dim. of *bille* < L *bulla* seal, document] —**bil′let·er** *n.*

bil·let² (bil′it) *n.* **1** A stick, as of firewood. **2** Any short, thick stick. **3** *Archit.* One of a series of short, cylindrical ornaments, forming part of a molding. **4** A harness strap that passes through a buckle; also, the loop or pocket for receiving such a strap after it passes through the buckle. **5** *Metall.* A bloom of iron or steel drawn into a small bar. [< OF *billete*, dim. of *bille* log]

bil·let–d'a·mour (bē·ye dà·mōōr′) *French* Love letter; billet-doux.

bil·let–doux (bil′ē-dōō′, *Fr.* bē·ye·dōō′) *n. pl.* **bil·lets–doux** (bil′ē·dōōz′, *Fr.* bē·ye·dōō′) A love letter; lover's note. [< F, lit., sweet note]

bill·fold (bil′fōld′) *n.* A folding case for paper money.

bill·head (bil′hed′) *n.* A heading on paper used for making out bills or itemized statements.

bil·liard (bil′yərd) *n. U.S. Colloq.* A carom. —*adj.* Of or pertaining to billiards: *billiard* cue, *billiard* player.

bil·liards (bil′yərdz) *n.* A game played with hard elastic or ivory balls (**billiard balls**) propelled by cues on an oblong, cloth-covered, cushion-edged table. [< F *billard* < OF *billart* cue < *bille* log] —**bil′liard·ist** *n.*

bill·ing (bil′ing) *n.* **1** The listing of performers or acts on a theater billboard, playbill, etc. **2** The relative eminence given to an actor or an act on such a listing.

Bil·lings (bil′ingz), **Josh** Pen name of Henry Wheeler Shaw, 1818–85, U.S. humorist.

bil·lings·gate (bil′ingz·gāt) *n.* Vulgar and abusive language. [from *Billingsgate* fish market, London]

bil·lion (bil′yən) *n.* **1** A thousand millions (1,000,000,000). **2** *Brit.* A million millions (1,000,000,000,000). [< F] — **bil·lionth** (bil′-yənth) *adj. & n.*

bil·lion·aire (bil′yən-âr′) *n.* One who owns property worth a billion of money.

bill of health An official certificate of the crew's health issued to a ship's master on departure from a port.

bill of lading A written acknowledgment of goods received for transportation.

bill of rights 1 A formal summary and declaration of the fundamental principles of government and of the rights of individuals. **2** *Often cap.* The first ten amendments to the U.S. Constitution. **3** *Often cap.* The declaration of rights setting forth those fundamental principles of the British constitution, the observance of which was to be imposed upon William and Mary upon their acceptance of the crown in 1689.

bill of sale An instrument by which the transfer of title to personal property is declared and established.

bil·lon (bil′ən) n. 1 An alloy of gold or silver with some baser metal, generally copper or tin. 2 A low alloy of silver with a large proportion of copper, used in making tokens and medals. [<F <OF bille log]

bil·low (bil′ō) n. 1 A great wave of the sea; a storm wave. 2 Any wave, as of sound, etc. 3 pl. The sea. — v.i. To rise or roll in billows; surge; swell. [<ON bylgja] — bil′low·y adj. — bil′low·i·ness n.

bil·ly[1] (bil′ē) n. pl. bil·lies 1 A short bludgeon; a policeman's club. 2 A slubbing machine, used in the manufacture of textiles. [<Billy, a nickname for William]

bil·ly[2] (bil′ē) n. Scot. A comrade; crony; chum; also, a young fellow. Also bil′lie.

bil·ly[3] (bil′ē) n. Austral. A can used for heating water. [<native Australian billa water]

bil·ly·cock (bil′ē·kok′) n. Brit. A low-crowned felt hat; derby. Also billycock hat.

billy goat A male goat.

Billy the Kid Sobriquet of William H. Bonney, 1859–81, notorious Western cattle thief and murderer.

bi·lo·bate (bī·lō′bāt) adj. Divided into or having two lobes. Also bi·lo′bat·ed.

bi·lo·ca·tion (bī′lō·kā′shən) n. The power of being in two places at the same time.

bi·loc·u·lar (bī·lok′yə·lər) adj. Biol. Two-celled; divided into two cells.

Bi·lox·i (bi·lok′sē) n. One of a tribe of North American Indians of Siouan stock.

Bi·lox·i (bi·lok′sē) A city in SE Mississippi, on a peninsula in **Biloxi Bay**, an arm of Mississippi Sound.

bil·sted (bil′sted) n. U.S. The sweetgum.

bim·a·nous (bim′ə·nəs, bī·mā′-) adj. Two-handed. [<NL bimanus <L bis twofold + manus hand]

bi·man·u·al (bī·man′yōō·əl) adj. Employing both hands. — bi·man′u·al·ly adv.

bi·men·sal (bī·men′səl) adj. Bimonthly.

bi·mes·tri·al (bī·mes′trē·əl) adj. Lasting two months. [<L bimestris]

bi·met·al·ism (bī·met′əl·iz′əm) n. The concurrent use of both gold and silver as the standard of currency and value. Also bi·met′al·lism. — bi·met′al·ist, bi·met′al·list n.

bi·me·tal·lic (bī′mə·tal′ik) adj. 1 Consisting of or relating to two metals. 2 Having a double metallic coin standard. 3 Of·or pertaining to bimetalism. [<F bimétallique]

Bim·i·ni Islands (bim′ə·nē) An island group in the NW Bahamas; 9 square miles; the legendary fountain of youth sought by Ponce de Leon was said to be here. Also **Bim′i·nis.**

bi·mo·lec·u·lar (bī′mə·lek′yə·lər) adj. Chem. Relating to two molecules: a bimolecular reaction.

bi·month·ly (bī·munth′lē) adj. & adv. Occurring once in two months. — n. A publication issued once in two months.

bi·mo·tored (bī·mō′tərd) adj. Having two motors, as an airplane.

bin (bin) n. 1 An enclosed place or large receptacle for holding meal, coal, etc. 2 A compartment in a wine cellar. 3 A basket used by hop pickers. — v.t. binned, bin·ning To store or deposit in a bin. [OE binn basket, crib <Celtic]

bin– Var. of BI–.

bi·nal (bī′nəl) adj. Double; twofold. [<L bini two]

bi·na·ry (bī′nə·rē) adj. 1 Pertaining to, characterized by, or made up of two; double; paired. 2 Astron. Denoting a pair of stars revolving about a common center. — n. pl. ·ries 1 A combination of two things; a couple; duality. 2 A binary star. [<L binarius <bini two, double]

binary star See under STAR.

binary system 1 A method of counting which has 2 for its base: still in use among certain primitive tribes of Australia and Africa. 2 Math. A system of numeration which can express any number by means of two digits, 0 and 1, in various combinations: applied especially in the operation of digital computers.·

bi·nate (bī′nāt) adj. Bot. Being or growing in couples or pairs. [<NL binatus paired <L bini double, two by two] — bi′nate·ly adv.

bi·na·tion (bī·nā′shən) n. In the Roman Catholic Church, celebration of two masses within the same day by the same priest. [<Med. L binatio, -onis duplication <bini double]

bin·au·ral (bin·ôr′əl) adj. 1 Hearing with both ears. 2 Designating an apparatus for communicating faint or distant sounds simultaneously to both ears: a binaural stethoscope. 3 Two-eared. 4 Stereophonic.

bind (bīnd) v. bound, bound (Archaic bound·en), bind·ing v.t. 1 To tie together; make fast by tying. 2 To encircle, as with a belt. 3 To bandage; swathe: often with up. 4 To cause to cohere; cement. 5 To strengthen or ornament at the edge, as a garment. 6 To fasten together and secure within a cover, as a book. 7 To make irrevocable; seal, as a bargain. 8 To constrain or oblige to do or not to do, as by moral or legal authority: often with over. 9 To make constipated or costive. 10 To apprentice: often with out. — v.i. 11 To tie up anything: to reap and bind. 12 To cohere; stick together. 13 To have binding force; be obligatory. 14 To become stiff or hard, as cement; jam, as gears. — to bind over Law To hold under bond for appearance at a future time. — n. 1 That which fastens, ties, or binds. 2 Music A curved line, tie, or brace. [OE bindan]

Synonyms (verb): compel, engage, fasten, fetter, fix, oblige, restrain, restrict, secure, shackle, tie. Binding is primarily by something flexible, as a cord or bandage drawn closely around an object or a group of objects, as when we bind up a wounded limb. We bind a sheaf of wheat with a cord; we tie the cord in a knot; we fasten by any means that will make things hold together, as a board by nails or a door by a lock. Bind has an extensive figurative use. One is bound by conscience or honor; he is obliged by some imperious necessity; engaged by his own promise; compelled by physical force or its moral equivalent. Antonyms: free, loose, unbind, unfasten, unloose, untie.

bind·er (bīn′dər) n. 1 One who or that which binds. 2 One who binds books. 3 Agric. A device on a reaping machine for binding grain. 4 An attachment on a sewing machine to secure an edging. 5 A surety or written pledge for payment or performance of a contract. 6 A folder in which sheets of paper may be fastened, as for a notebook. 7 In painting, a material used to cause the pigment to adhere to a surface, as solutions of gum, glue, or casein, oils and resins, and (in fresco painting) lime. 8 In construction, a beam of steel or wood serving to support the bridging joists in a floor. 9 Metall. A substance used to promote the cohesion of crushed ore particles or finely powdered metallic dust before or in the process of sintering. 10 The cord or braiding which binds the edges of a fabric.

bind·er·y (bīn′dər·ē) n. pl. ·er·ies A place where books are bound.

bind·ing (bīn′ding) adj. Causing to be bound; obligatory. — n. 1 The act of fastening or joining. 2 Anything that binds objects to each other, as the cover of a book. 3 Any thickening substance added to a mixture to cause the various ingredients to adhere; a binder. 4 A strip sewed over an edge for protection. 5 A course of masonry by which adjoining parts are secured. — bind′ing·ly adv. — bind′ing·ness n.

binding energy Physics The energy associated with the loss of mass occurring when the constituent particles of an atomic nucleus are closely bound together.

bine (bīn) n. A flexible shoot or climbing stem of a plant; specifically, a hop vine: used of other climbers, in composition: woodbine. [Var. of BIND]

bing[1] (bing) interj. A word imitating any sharp metallic sound, as of a rifle shot. — n. The sound thus produced. — v.i. To make this sound: The guns binged away. [Imit.]

bing[2] (bing) n. Scot. & Brit. Dial. A pile or heap of anything. [<ON bingr heap]

binge (binj) n. Slang A drunken carousal; spree. [? <dial. E binge soak]

bin·it (bin′it) n. Bit[4].

bin·na·cle (bin′ə·kəl) n. Naut. A stand or case for a ship's compass: placed usually before the steering wheel. [Var. of bittacle <Pg. bitacola <LL habitaculum little house]

bin·nogue (bin′ōg) n. A headdress formerly worn by peasant women in Ireland. [<Irish Gaelic beannōg]

bin·oc·u·lar (bə·nok′yə·lər, bī-) adj. 1 Pertaining to both eyes at once. 2 Having two eyes. — n. Often pl. A telescope, opera glass, etc., adapted for use by both eyes at once. Also bin·o·cle (bin′ə·kəl). — bin·oc′u·lar′i·ty (-lar′ə·tē) n. — bin·oc′u·lar·ly adv.

BINNACLE
a. Lamp.
b. Hood.
c. Quadrilateral sphere.
d. Compass chamber.
e. Magnet chamber.
f. Window to admit light to compass chamber.

bi·no·mi·al (bī·nō′mē·əl) adj. Consisting of two names or terms. — n. 1 Math. An algebraic expression having two terms. 2 In taxonomy, a name consisting of two words, one indicating the genus, the other the species of a plant or animal. [<Med. L binomius having two names] — bi·no′mi·al·ly adv.

binomial system The system which assigns to every plant and animal a Latinized scientific name consisting of two terms, the first indicating the genus and the second the species: Latrodectus mactans, the black-widow spider. Also **binomial nomenclature.**

binomial theorem Math. The theorem stating the general form of any power of an algebraic binomial.

bi·nom·i·nal (bī·nom′ə·nəl) adj. Of, having, or characterized by two names.

bi·nu·cle·ate (bī·nōō′klē·āt, -nyōō′-) adj. Having two nuclei, as a cell. Also bi·nu′cle·ar, bi·nu′cle·at·ed.

bio– combining form Life: biology, biography. [<Gk. bios life]

bi·o·as·say (bī′ō·as′ā) n. The determination of the properties and effects of a drug by testing it under controlled conditions in the bodies of standard laboratory animals.

bi·o·blast (bī′ə·blast) n. Bioplast.

bi·o·cat·a·lyst (bī′ō·kat′ə·list) n. An enzyme.

bi·o·cel·late (bī′ō·sə·lāt, bī′ō·sel′it) adj. Biol. Having two eyelike marks or ocelli. [<BI– + OCELLATE]

bi·o·chem·is·try (bī′ō·kem′is·trē) n. That branch of chemistry relating to vital processes, their mode of action, and their products. — bi′o·chem′ic, bi′o·chem′i·cal adj. — bi′o·chem′i·cal·ly adv. — bi′o·chem′ist n.

bi·o·chore (bī′ə·kôr, -kōr) n. Ecol. 1 That region of the earth having a climate favorable to life. 2 A climatic boundary for a given plant group. [<Gk. bios life + chōrē land, country] — bi′o·chor′ic adj.

bi·o·ci·dal (bī′ə·sīd′l) adj. Destructive of life, as certain poisons and antibiotics.

bi·o·coe·no·sis (bī′ō·sē·nō′sis) n. Ecol. An association of plants and animals in a given habitat and under similar environmental conditions. Also **bi·o·coe·nose** (bī′ō·sē′nōs). [<BIO– + Gk. koinōsis sharing] — bi′o·coe·not′ic (-not′ik) adj.

bi·o·de·grad·a·ble (bī′ō·di·grā′də·bəl) adj. Chem. Capable of being broken down, as a compound, by bacterial action. [<BIO– + DEGRADABLE]

bi·o·dy·nam·ics (bī′ō·dī·nam′iks) n. The branch of biology that treats of the activities of living organisms. — bi′o·dy·nam′ic or ·i·cal adj.

bi·o·e·lec·tric·i·ty (bī′ō·i·lek′tris′ə·tē) n. Those phenomena of electricity which are associated with and characteristic of living matter. — bi′o·e·lec′tri·cal adj.

bi·o·eth·ics (bī′ō·eth′iks) n. pl. (construed as

sing.) The study of the ethical implications of medical practice, especially in regard to the preservation of human life. —**bi′o·eth′i·cal** *adj.* —**bi′o·eth′i·cist** (-eth′ə·sist) *n.*

bi·o·feed·back (bī′ō·fēd′bak) *n.* Voluntary control by feedback of involuntary functions, as heart rate.

bi·o·gen (bī′ə·jən) *n. Biochem.* The hypothetical large protein molecular unit assumed to be active in the functioning of body tissues.

bi·o·gen·e·sis (bī′ō·jen′ə·sis) *n.* **1** The doctrine that life is generated from living organisms only. **2** Such generation itself: opposed to *abiogenesis.* Also **bi·og·e·ny** (bī·oj′ə·nē). —**bi·o·ge·net·ic** (bī′ō·jə·net′ik) or **·i·cal** *adj.* —**bi′o·ge·net′i·cal·ly** *adv.*

bi·o·ge·og·ra·phy (bī′ō·jē·og′rə·fē) *n.* The science of the geographical distribution of living organisms. —**bi′o·ge′o·graph′ic** (-jē′ə·graf′ik) or **·i·cal** *adj.* —**bi′o·ge′o·graph′i·cal·ly** *adv.*

bi·og·ra·pher (bī·og′rə·fər, bē-) *n.* One who writes an account of a person's life.

bi·og·ra·phy (bī·og′rə·fē, bē-) *n. pl.* **·phies** **1** A written account of a person's life. **2** That form of literature dealing with the facts and events of individual experience. **3** Biographies collectively. See synonyms under HISTORY. [< LGk. *biographia* < *bios* life + *graphein* write] —**bi·o·graph·ic** (bī′ə·graf′ik) or **·i·cal** *adj.* —**bi′o·graph′i·cal·ly** *adv.*

bi·o·log·i·cal (bī′ə·loj′i·kəl) *adj.* **1** Of or pertaining to biology, or to the science of vital functions, structures, and processes. **2** Used for or produced by biological research or practice. Also **bi′o·log′ic.** —**bi′o·log′i·cal·ly** *adv.*

biological engineering The artificial selection of different strains of a plant or animal species to improve the structure, function, or yield of an organism, esp. a plant or animal of economic importance.

bi·o·log·i·cals (bī′ə·loj′i·kəlz) *n. pl.* Drugs and medicinal preparations obtained from animal tissues and other organic sources.

bi·ol·o·gism (bī·ol′ə·jiz′əm) *n. Philos.* The doctrine that biological methods are applicable to the entire field of human experience.

bi·ol·o·gist (bī·ol′ə·jist) *n.* One having special knowledge of biology.

bi·ol·o·gy (bī·ol′ə·jē) *n.* The science of life and of the origin, structure, reproduction, growth, and development of living organisms collectively: its two main divisions are botany and zoology. [< BIO- + -LOGY]

bi·o·lu·mi·nes·cence (bī′ō·lōō′mə·nes′əns) *n.* The emission of light by living organisms, as fireflies, certain fungi, and deep-sea fishes. —**bi′o·lu′mi·nes′cent** *adj.*

bi·ol·y·sis (bī·ol′ə·sis) *n.* The dissolution of life. [< BIO- + Gk. *lysis* loosing] —**bi·o·lyt·ic** (bī′ə·lit′ik) *adj.*

bi·o·mass (bī′ō·mas′) *n.* The total amount of plant material in a given area, esp. when considered as an energy source.

bi·o·me·chan·ics (bī′ō·mə·kan′iks) *n.* The study of the mechanics of living organisms, especially under conditions of sudden, violent, or prolonged strain. —**bi′o·me·chan′i·cal** *adj.* —**bi′o·me·chan′i·chal·ly** *adv.*

bi·om·e·try (bī·om′ə·trē) *n.* **1** A measuring or calculating of the probable duration of human life. **2** Biology from a statistical point of view, especially with reference to problems of variation: also **bi·o·met·rics** (bī′ō·met′riks). [< BIO + -METRY] —**bi′o·met′ric** or **·ri·cal** *adj.* —**bi′o·met′ri·cal·ly** *adv.*

bi·on·ics (bī·on′iks) *n.* The science of relating the functioning of biological systems to the development of electronic devices. [< BIO- + (ELECTR)ONICS]

bi·o·nom·ics (bī′ə·nom′iks) *n.* The branch of biology treating of habits and adaptation; ecology. —**bi′o·nom′ic** or **·i·cal** *adj.* —**bi′o·nom′i·cal·ly** *adv.* —**bi·on·o·mist** (bī·on′ə·mist) *n.*

bi·o·phys·ics (bī′ō·fiz′iks) *n.* The study of biological function, structure, and organization in relation to and by the methods of physics. —**bi′o·phys′i·cal** *adj.*

bi·o·plasm (bī′ō·plaz′əm) *n.* Formative living matter; protoplasm.

bi·op·sy (bī′op·sē) *n. Med.* The clinical and diagnostic examination of tissue and other material excised from the living subject: opposed to *autopsy, necropsy.* [< BIO- + Gk. *opsis* sight] —**bi·op·sic** (bī·op′sik) *adj.*

bi·o·psy·chol·o·gy (bī′ō·sī·kol′ə·jē) *n.* Psychobiology.

bi·o·rhythm (bī′ō·rith′əm) *n.* Any cyclic pattern of activity in an organism. —**bi′o·rhyth′mic** *adj.* —**bi·o·rhyth·mic·i·ty** (bī′ō·rith′mis′ə·tē) *n.*

bi·o·scope (bī′ə·skōp) *n.* **1** A motion-picture projector. **2** An instrument used in bioscopy.

bi·os·co·py (bī·os′kə·pē) *n. Med.* An examination to ascertain whether life exists or has ceased. [< BIO- + -SCOPY] —**bi·o·scop·ic** (bī′ə·skop′ik) *adj.*

-biosis *combining form* Method of living: *aerobiosis, symbiosis.* [< Gk. *biōsis* < *bios* life]

bi·os·o·phy (bī·os′ə·fē) *n.* A system of character development and national and international peace education. [< Gk. *bios* life + *sophia* knowledge]

bi·o·sphere (bī′ə·sfir) *n.* That portion of the earth and its environment within which life in any of its forms is manifested.

bi·o·stat·ics (bī′ō·stat′iks) *n.* The branch of biology that treats of the potentialities of organisms or of structure as related to function: distinguished from *biodynamics.* —**bi′o·stat′ic** or **·i·cal** *adj.*

bi·o·syn·the·sis (bī′ō·sin′thə·sis) *n.* The chemical synthesis of organic materials, especially of a fibrous nature, from elementary living units or cells. —**bi·o·syn·thet·ic** (bī′ō·sin·thet′ik) *adj.*

bi·o·ta (bī·ō′tə) *n. Ecol.* The combined fauna and flora of any geographical area or geological period. [< Gk. *biotē* life, living < *bios* life]

bi·o·tech·nol·o·gy (bī′ō·tek·nol′jē) *n.* The application of industrial techniques to the exploitation of biological processes.

bi·ot·ic (bī·ot′ik) *adj.* Pertaining to life. Also **bi·ot′i·cal.**

biotic potential **1** *Biol.* The inherent capacity of an organism to survive and reproduce under given or optimum conditions. **2** A measure of the innate vitality of a species confronted by an unfavorable or hostile environment.

bi·ot·ics (bī·ot′iks) *n.* The science of the functions of living organisms.

bi·o·tin (bī′ə·tin) *n. Biochem.* A crystalline acid, $C_{10}H_{16}O_3N_2S$, forming part of the vitamin B complex: it is essential in preventing the death of animals from an excess of egg white in the diet: also called *vitamin H.*

bi·o·tite (bī′ə·tīt) *n.* A common, brown or dark-green magnesium iron mica. [after J. B. *Biot,* 1774–1862, French physicist] —**bi′o·tit′ic** (-tit′ik) *adj.*

bi·o·tope (bī′ə·tōp) *n. Ecol.* An area, usually small and of uniform environmental conditions, characterized by relatively stable biotypes. [< BIO- + Gk. *topos* region]

bi·o·tox·ic (bī′ō·tok′sik) *adj.* Of or pertaining to natural poisons produced by plants and animals.

bi·o·type (bī′ō·tīp) *n. Biol.* **1** A race or strain that breeds true or almost true. **2** A group of individuals all of which have the same genotype. —**bi′o·typ′ic** (-tip′ik) *adj.* —**bi′o·ty·pol·o·gy** (-tī·pol′ə·jē) *n.*

bi·pa·ri·e·tal (bī′pə·rī′ə·təl) *adj. Anat.* Of or pertaining to the two parietal bones.

bip·a·rous (bip′ə·rəs) *adj.* **1** *Bot.* Having two lateral axes, as certain cymes. **2** *Zool.* Bringing forth two at a birth. [< BI- + -PAROUS]

bi·par·ti·san (bī·pär′tə·zən) *adj.* Composed of, pertaining to, or advocated by representatives of two political parties. —**bi·par′ti·san·ship** *n.*

bi·par·tite (bī·pär′tīt) *adj.* **1** Consisting of two corresponding parts. **2** *Bot.* Two-parted almost to the base, as certain leaves. Also **bi·part′ed.** —**bi·par′tite·ly** *adv.* —**bi·par·ti·tion** (bī′pär·tish′ən) *n.*

bi·ped (bī′ped) *n.* An animal having two feet. —*adj.* Two-footed: also **bi·pe·dal** (bī′pə·dəl, bip′ə-). [< L *bipes, bipedis* two-footed]

bi·pet·al·ous (bī·pet′əl·əs) *adj. Bot.* Dipetalous.

bi·phen·yl (bī·fen′əl, -fē′nəl) *n. Chem.* A colorless crystalline hydrocarbon, $C_6H_5·C_6H_5$, found in coal tar: used in lacquers and as a preservative of citrus fruit. Also called *diphenyl.*

bi·pin·nate (bī·pin′āt) *adj. Bot.* Twice or doubly pinnate, as a leaf. Also **bi·pin′nat·ed.** —**bi·pin′nate·ly** *adv.*

bi·plane (bī′plān′) *n. Aeron.* A type of airplane having two parallel connected wings arranged one above the other: distinguished from *monoplane* and *triplane.*

bi·pod (bī′pod) *n.* A two-legged rest or stand, as

for a rifle or machine-gun. [< BI- + -POD]

bi·po·lar (bī·pō′lər) *adj.* **1** Relating to or possessing two poles. **2** *Biol.* **a** Describing marine organisms found in both polar regions but nowhere else. **b** Having two prolongations of cell matter: said of nerve cells. —**bi·po·lar·i·ty** (bī′pō·lar′ə·tē) *n.*

bi·pro·pel·lant (bī′prə·pel′ənt) *n.* A propellant for rockets consisting of two chemicals, each of which is fed separately into the combustion chamber.

bi·quad·rate (bī·kwod′rāt) *n. Math.* A fourth power or the square of a square.

bi·quad·rat·ic (bī′kwod·rat′ik) *Math. adj.* Containing or referring to a fourth power. —*n.* **1** A fourth power. **2** A biquadratic equation.

bi·ra·di·al (bī·rā′dē·əl) *adj. Biol.* Having the radii set bilaterally and radially, as certain sea anemones.

birch (bûrch) *n.* **1** Any of an important genus (*Betula*) of deciduous trees and shrubs of the northern hemisphere, often having outer bark easily separable in sheets. **2** A rod or twig from a birch tree, used as a whip. **3** The tough, close-grained hardwood of the birch tree. —*v.t.* To whip with a birch rod; flog. —*adj.* Composed or fashioned of birch: also **birch·en.** [OE *birce*]

bird (bûrd) *n.* **1** A warm-blooded, feathered, egg-laying vertebrate (class *Aves*), having the

BIRD
Nomenclature for anatomical parts

forelimbs modified as wings. ◆ Collateral adjective: *avian.* **2** A game bird; in England, a partridge. **3** *Obs.* The young of a fowl; a nestling. **4** *Slang* A peculiar or remarkable person. **5** *U.S. Slang* A hiss, or other call of disapproval, by an audience; usually in the phrases *to give* (one) *the bird, to get the bird.* **6** A clay pigeon; also, the shuttlecock in badminton. —**for the birds** *Slang* Worthless. —*v.t.* To trap or shoot birds. [OE *bridd*]

bird·call (bûrd′kôl′) *n.* **1** An instrument for decoying birds by imitating their notes. **2** A bird's note in calling.

bird dog A dog that is trained to locate birds and retrieve them for hunters; specifically, a setter or pointer.

bird·house (bûrd′hous′) *n.* **1** A small house or enclosure for birds; an aviary. **2** A small house, placed in trees, etc., in which birds may nest. Also **bird house.**

bird·ie (bûr′dē) *n.* **1** A small bird. **2** A whistling birdlike chirp, as on a radio transmission line, or in the body of an automobile, etc. **3** In golf, one stroke less than par in playing a hole.

bird of prey Any of various raptorial birds, as an eagle, hawk, vulture, falcon, etc.

birds·eye (bûrdz′ī′) *adj.* **1** Marked with spots resembling birds' eyes: *birdseye* cotton, *birdseye* maple. **2** Seen at a glance, and from above: a *birdseye* view; also, cursory. —*n.* **1** A plant with small, bright-colored flowers, the birdseye primrose (*Primula farinosa*). **2** The germander speedwell. **3** A textile fabric woven in a pattern of small eyelike indentations. **4** Any of various fabrics having such a pattern. Also **bird's′-eye′.**

birds·nest (bûrdz′nest′) *n.* **1** The mucus secreted in the salivary glands of certain Asian swifts, used for building nests, and highly esteemed for making soup. **2** One of various plants resembling a bird's nest, as the wild carrot. **3** *Naut.* A crow's-nest. Also **bird's′-nest′.**

bird·y (bûr′dē) *n.* Birdie.

bi·reme (bī′rēm) *n.* An ancient galley having two banks of oars. [< L *biremis* < *bis* twofold + *remus* oar]

bi·ret·ta (bi·ret′ə) *n.* A stiff, square cap with three or four upright projections on the crown, worn by clerics of the Roman Catholic and other churches: also spelled *berretta.* [<Ital. *berretta* or Sp. *birreta* <LL *birretum* cap, dim. of *birrus* cape, cloak]

BIRETTA FOR PRIESTS

birk (bûrk, birk) *n. Scot.* The birch. —**birk′en, birk′in** *adj.*

birl (bûrl) *v.t & v.i.* 1 To rotate rapidly. 2 To spin with a humming sound. —*n.* A droning noise. ◆ Homophone: *burl.* [Blend of BIRR and WHIRL]

birle (bûrl) *v.t. & v.i. Brit. Dial.* To ply with drink; carouse: also spelled *byrl.* Also **birl.** [OE *byrelian* pour out drink <*byrele* cupbearer]

birl·ing (bûr′ling) *n.* A game between two lumberjacks in which each stands on an end of a floating log and rotates it with his feet so as to dislodge his opponent. [Origin uncertain]

Bir·ming·ham 1 (bûr′ming·əm) A county borough and city of NW Warwickshire, England. 2 (bûr′ming·ham) A manufacturing city in north central Alabama.

birr (bûr) *n. Scot.* 1 Onward rush; momentum; emphatic and rapid utterance. 2 A whirring or buzzing sound. 3 *Obs.* A rushing wind. —*v.i.* To move with or make a whirring noise. ◆ Homophones: *bur, burr.* [<ON *byrr* favorable wind]

birse (bûrs, *Scot.* birs) *Scot.* 1 A bristle; collectively, bristles. 2 Short hair, as of the head or beard. —**to set up one's birse** To make one angry.

birth (bûrth) *n.* 1 The fact or act of being born; nativity. 2 A beginning; an origin. 3 The bringing forth of offspring; parturition. 4 Ancestry or descent; lineage; also, the class into which one is born. 5 Offspring; issue. See synonyms under AFFINITY, KIN. ◆ Homophone: *berth.* [<ON *byrth*] —**to give birth** To produce offspring.

birth canal *Anat.* The passage through which a child is delivered at birth, extending from the cervix uteri to the vulva.

birth control The regulation of conception by employing preventive methods or devices.

birth·day (bûrth′dā′) *n.* The day of one's birth or its anniversary: used also adjectively.

birth·mark (bûrth′märk′) *n.* A mark or stain existing on the body from birth; a nevus.

birth·place (bûrth′plās′) *n.* The place of one's birth or of origin in general.

birth rate The number of births per 1,000 inhabitants of a given district in any given period.

birth·right (bûrth′rīt′) *n.* Native right or privilege.

birth·root (bûrth′root′, -root′) *n.* Any of a genus (*Trillium*) of typically North American perennial herbs of the lily family; especially, *T. erectum,* which has astringent tuberlike rootstocks: sometimes used to hasten parturition.

birth·stone (bûrth′stōn′) *n.* A jewel identified with a particular month of the year: thought to bring good luck when worn by a person whose birthday falls in that month.

birth tree In folklore, a tree planted at the birth of a child in the belief that its welfare has some mysterious connection with the welfare of the child all his life.

birth·wort (bûrth′wûrt′) *n.* 1 Any plant of the genus *Aristolochia*; especially, *A. clematitis* of Europe, with stimulant tonic roots used as aromatic bitters. 2 Birthroot.

bis (bis) *adv.* 1 Twice: noting duplication or repetition. 2 Encore: a call for the repetition of a performance. [<L]

bis- Var. of BI-.

Bis·cay (bis′kā, -kē) One of the Basque provinces of northern Spain; 858 square miles; on the **Bay of Biscay,** a wide inlet of the Atlantic indenting the coast of western Europe from Brittany, France, to NW Spain: Spanish *Vizcaya.*

Bis·cayne Bay (bis′kān, bis·kān′) A shallow arm of the Atlantic south of Miami, Florida.

bis·cuit (bis′kit) *n.* 1 A kind of shortened bread baked in small cakes, raised with baking powder or soda. 2 *Brit.* A sweetened cracker or cookie. 3

Unglazed pottery which has been fired in the oven; bisque. [<OF *bescoit* <*bes* twice (<L *bis*) + *coit,* pp. of *cuire* cook <L *coquere*]

bis·cuit·root (bis′kit·root′, -root′) *n.* Wild parsley.

bise (bēz) *n.* 1 A cold northerly wind in Switzerland and parts of France, destructive to vegetation. 2 Misfortune; disaster.

bi·sect (bī·sekt′) *v.t.* 1 To cut into two parts; halve. 2 *Geom.* To divide into two parts of equal size. —*v.i.* 3 To fork, as a road. [<BI- + L *sectus,* pp. of *secare* cut] —**bi·sec′tion** *n.* —**bi·sec′tion·al** *adj.* —**bi·sec′tion·al·ly** *adv.*

bi·sec·tor (bī·sek′tər) *n.* 1 That which bisects. 2 *Geom.* A line or plane that bisects an angle or another line.

bi·sec·trix (bī·sek′triks) *n. pl.* **bi·sec·tri·ces** (bī′sek·trī′sēz) 1 The line bisecting the angle formed by the optic axes of a crystal. 2 A bisector.

bi·ser·rate (bī·ser′āt, -it) *adj.* 1 *Bot.* Doubly serrate, as a leaf. 2 *Entomol.* Serrate on both sides, as the antenna of an insect.

bi·sex·u·al (bī·sek′shōo·əl) *adj.* 1 *Biol.* Having the organs of both sexes. 2 *Bot.* Hermaphroditic, as a flower with both stamens and pistils. 3 Showing characters derived from both parents, as a hybrid. 4 *Psychol.* Equally attracted by both sexes. —**bi·sex′u·al·ism** *n.* —**bi·sex′u·al·ly** *adv.*

bish·op (bish′əp) *n.* 1 A spiritual overseer in the Christian church; in various churches, a clergyman of the highest order, and head of a diocese. 2 A hot drink made with mulled wine, sugar, oranges, etc. 3 A chessman, often carved to represent a miter, which may be moved diagonally any number of unoccupied squares of the same color. [OE *biscop* <LL *episcopus* bishop <Gk. *episkopos* overseer]

BISHOP (def. 3)

bish·op·ric (bish′əp·rik) *n.* The office or the diocese of a bishop.

bish·ops·cap (bish′əps·kap′) *n.* Any species of miterwort; especially, *Mitella diphylla.* Also **bish′op's-cap′.**

Bis·marck (biz′märk) The capital of North Dakota, a city on the Missouri River.

Bis·marck (biz′märk, *Ger.* bis′-), **Prince Karl Otto Eduard Leopold von,** 1815–98, German statesman; founder of the German Empire.

Bismarck Archipelago An island group in the United Nations Trust Territory of New Guinea, comprising New Britain, New Ireland, Lavongai, and the Admiralty Islands; total, 19,200 square miles.

Bismarck Mountains A range in NE New Guinea; highest peak, 14,107 feet.

Bismarck Sea The SW arm of the Pacific enclosed by the Bismarck Archipelago.

bis·muth (biz′məth) *n.* A heavy, grayish, brittle, metallic element (symbol Bi, atomic number 83) used in alloys and in medicines and cosmetics. See PERIODIC TABLE. [<G] —**bis·muth·al** (biz′məth·əl) *adj.*

bis·mu·thic (biz·myoo′thik, -muth′ik) *adj. Chem.* Containing bismuth in its highest valence.

bis·muth·ous (biz′məth·əs) *adj. Chem.* Containing bismuth in its lowest valence.

bi·son (bī′sən, -zən) *n.* A bovine ruminant, nearly related to the true ox; especially, the North American buffalo (*Bos* or *Bison bison*). *B. bonasus* is the European bison. [<L *bison* wild ox, ult. <Gmc.]

NORTH AMERICAN BISON (Up to 5 3/4 feet high at the shoulders)

bisque¹ (bisk) *n.* 1 A thick, rich soup made from meat or fish, especially shellfish. 2 A kind of ice-cream containing crushed macaroons. Also **bisk.** [<F]

bisque² (bisk) *n.* 1 In ceramics, biscuit. 2

Any of several shades of pinkish–beige. [< BISCUIT]

bisque³ (bisk) *n.* An advantage given to an opponent in various games, as lawn tennis, consisting of a point or stroke to be taken at any time. [<F]

Bis·sau (bi·sou′) A port; the capital of Guinea-Bissau, formerly Portuguese Guinea, transferred here in 1941 from Bolama.

bis·sex·tile (bi·seks′təl, -tīl) *adj.* 1 Pertaining to the extra day occurring in leap year. 2 Pertaining to a leap year. —*n.* A leap year. [<L *bisextilis* intercalary <*bis* twice + *sextilis* sixth; so called because the sixth day before March 1 was doubled in leap year in the Julian calendar]

bis·ter (bis′tər) *n.* 1 A non-permanent, yellowish-brown pigment made from beechwood soot: used chiefly as a water-color wash. 2 A dark-brown color. Also **bis′tre.** [<F *bistre* dark brown] —**bis′tered** *adj.*

bis·tort (bis′tôrt) *n.* 1 A perennial herb (*Polygonum bistorta*) of Europe and Asia, with creeping rootstocks having astringent properties: also called *snakeweed.* 2 An allied herb, the Virginia bistort (*Tovara virginiana*). [<F <L *bis* twice + *tortus,* pp. of *torquere* twist]

bis·tou·ry (bis′too·rē) *n. pl.* **·ries** *Surg.* A narrow-bladed knife for making minor incisions. [<OF *bistorie* dagger]

bis·tro (bis′trō, *Fr.* bē·strō′) *n. Colloq.* 1 A small night club or bar. 2 A restaurant or tavern where wine is served. [<F]

bi·sul·cate (bī·sul′kāt) *adj.* 1 Cleft in two; cloven-hoofed. 2 Two-grooved. Also **bi·sul′cat·ed.** [<L *bisulcus* <*bis* twofold + *sulcus* furrow]

bi·sul·fate (bī·sul′fāt) *n. Chem.* An acid sulfate containing the group HSO₄.

bi·sul·fide (bī·sul′fīd) *n.* Disulfide. Also **bi·sul′phide.**

bi·sym·met·ri·cal (bī′si·met′ri·kəl) *adj.* Bilaterally symmetrical. Also **bi′sym·met′ric.** —**bi′sym·met′ri·cal·ly** *adv.* —**bi·sym·me·try** (bī·sim′ə·trē) *n.*

bit¹ (bit) *n.* 1 A small piece, portion, or fragment; a little. 2 The smallest quantity; a whit; jot. 3 A small quantity of food; a morsel; taste; bite. 4 In Great Britain, a small coin, usually of a named value: a threepenny bit. 5 In the United States, the Spanish real or its equivalent, 12½ cents. 6 A short time. 7 *Slang* A typical or standard practice, procedure, or way of acting. —**a long bit** *U.S. Dial.* 15 cents. —**a short bit** *U.S. Dial.* 10 cents. —**two bits** *U.S. Colloq.* 25 cents. [OE *bita* <*bītan* bite]

Synonyms: dole, driblet, drop, installment, item, mite, morsel, particle, scrap.

bit² (bit) *n.* 1 A wood-boring tool adapted to be used with a stock or brace. 2 The metallic mouthpiece of a bridle. 3 Anything that controls or holds in subjection. 4 One of various objects somewhat like a boring bit or a bridle bit. 5 The part of a key that engages the bolt or tumblers of a lock. 6 The cutting blade of a plane. —*v.t.* **bit·ted, bit·ting** 1 To put a bit in the mouth of; train, as a horse, to the use of a bit. 2 To curb; restrain. 3 To make a bit on (a key). [OE *bite* a biting <*bītan* bite]

bit³ (bit) Past tense of BITE.

bit⁴ (bit) *n. Telecom.* A single unit of information; specifically, one of the coded digital signals forming part of a complete message in the operation of an electronic computing machine: also called *binit.* [<B(INARY) (DIG)IT]

BITS AND BITSTOCK
a. Brace.
b. Screwdriver bit.
c. Drill bit.
d. Ship auger bit.
e. Auger bit.
f. Expanding bit.
g. Cross-section of chuck for holding bits.

bitch (bich) *n.* 1 The female of the dog or other canine animal. 2 *Slang* Wench; hussy: an abusive epithet, often implying lewdness. —*v.i. Slang* To complain. —**to bitch up** *Slang* To botch. [OE *bicce*]

bite (bīt) *v.* **bit, bit·ten** or *Colloq.* **bit, bit·ing** *v.t.* 1 To seize, tear, or wound with the teeth.

2 To cut or tear off with or as with the teeth: usually with *off:* He *bit* off his words. **3** To cut or pierce, as with a sword. **4** To sting, as mosquitoes. **5** To cause to smart, as a cold wind. **6** To eat into; corrode, as acid. **7** To grip; take hold of. **8** To cheat; trick. —*v.i.* **9** To seize or cut into something with the teeth. **10** To sting; have the effect of biting, as mustard. **11** To take firm hold; grip. **12** To take a bait, as fish. **13** To be tricked; accept a deceptive offer. —**to bite off more than one can chew** To attempt something beyond one's capabilities. —**to bite the dust** (or **ground**) To be vanquished or slain. —*n.* **1** The act of biting, or the hurt inflicted by biting; also, a painful sensation; smart. **2** A morsel of food; mouthful. **3** The grip or hold taken by a tool or piece of mechanism. ◆ Homophone: *bight.* [OE *bītan*] —**bit′a·ble,** **bite′a·ble** *adj.* —**bit′er** *n.*

Bi·thyn·i·a (bi·thin′ē·ə) An ancient country in NW Asia Minor.

bit·ing (bī′ting) *adj.* Keen; pungent; stinging. See synonyms under BITTER. —**bit′ing·ly** *adv.* —**bit′ing·ness** *n.*

Bi·tolj (bē′tôl·y′) A town in southern Yugoslavia. Also **Bi·tol** (bē′tôl). Turkish **Mon·as·tir** (mun·əs·tēr′).

bit part A small role in a play.

bit·stock (bit′stok′) *n.* A brace for a bit. For illustration see BIT.

bitt (bit) *n. Naut.* A post or vertical timber on a ship's deck, to which cables, etc., are made fast: usually in pairs. —*v.t.* To take a turn of (a cable) around a bitt or pair of bitts. [? <ON *biti* beam]

bit·ten (bit′n) Past participle of BITE.

BITTS

bit·ter[1] (bit′ər) *adj.* **1** Having a peculiar acrid taste, as quinine. **2** Producing pain of body or mind; keen; poignant; severe. **3** Feeling or showing hate or resentment. **4** Stinging; sharp; severe: said of words. —*n.* **1** That which is bitter; bitterness. **2** *pl.* A bitter vegetable tonic, usually spirituous. **3** *Brit.* Bitter beer. —*v.t. & v.i.* To make or become bitter. [OE *biter* <*bītan* bite] —**bit′ter·ish** *adj.* —**bit′ter·ly** *adv.* —**bit′ter·ness** *n.*

Synonyms (adj.): acerb, acetous, acid, acidulated, acidulous, acrid, acrimonious, biting, caustic, cutting, harsh, irate, pungent, savage, sharp, sour, stinging, tart, vinegarish, virulent. *Acid, sour,* and *bitter* agree in being contrasted with *sweet,* but *acid* or *sour* applies to the taste of vinegar or lemon juice; *bitter* to that of quassia, quinine, or strychnine. *Acrid* is nearly allied to *bitter. Pungent* suggests the effect of pepper or snuff on the organs of taste or smell; as, a *pungent* odor. *Caustic* indicates the corroding effect of some strong chemical, as nitrate of silver. In a figurative sense we say a *sour* face, *sharp* words, *bitter* complaints, *caustic* wit, *cutting* irony, *biting* sarcasm, a *stinging* taunt, *harsh* judgment, a *tart* reply. *Harsh* carries the idea of intentional and severe unkindness, *bitter* of a severity that arises from real or supposed ill-treatment. *Tart* and *sharp* utterances may proceed merely from a wit recklessly keen; *cutting, stinging,* or *biting* speech indicates more or less of hostile intent. The *caustic* utterance is meant to burn. Compare MALICIOUS, MOROSE. *Antonyms:* dulcet, honeyed, luscious, nectared, saccharine, sweet.

bit·ter[2] (bit′ər) *n. Naut.* A turn of the cable round a mooring bitt. [<BITT]

bitter apple The colocynth.

bitter end 1 *Naut.* The extreme end of a cable or rope, attached to the bitt. **2** The last extremity, as defeat or death.

bit·tern[1] (bit′ərn) *n.* A small, speckled, pale-buff heron (*Botaurus lentiginosus*) of North America, which utters a booming note in the breeding season. —**least bittern** The American dwarf bittern (*Ixobrychus exilis*). [<OF *butor,* ? <L *butio, -onis* a hawk]

bit·tern[2] (bit′ərn) *n.* **1** In salt manufacture, the waste liquor remaining after crystallization from brine. **2** A bitter mixture of quassia.

bit·ter–root (bit′ər·rōōt′, -rōōt′) *n.* **1** An herb (*Lewisia rediviva*) with nutritious roots: State flower of Montana. **2** Any one of certain other North American plants, as the dogbane.

bit·ter·sweet (bit′ər·swēt′) *n.* **1** A coarse trailing plant, the woody nightshade, having oval bright–red berries. Its twigs and root have a taste at first bitter and afterward sweetish. **2** A shrubby or climbing plant (*Celastrus scandens*), with green flowers succeeded by orange pods that display a red aril. —*adj.* Combining bitter and sweet.

bit·ter·weed (bit′ər·wēd′) *n.* **1** A ragweed; especially, *Ambrosia artemisifolia.* **2** Any of various other plants yielding a bitter principle, as the horseweed and sneezeweed.

bi·tu·men (bi·tōō′mən, -tyōō′-, bich′ōō·mən) *n.* **1** Any native mixture of solid and semi-solid hydrocarbons, as naphtha or asphalt. **2** A brown paint made by mixing asphalt with a drying oil: used by artists. [<L] —**bi·tu·mi·noid** (bi·tōō′mə·noid, -tyōō′-) *adj.*

bi·tu·mi·nize (bi·tōō′mə·nīz, -tyōō′-) *v.t.* **·ized,** **·iz·ing** To render bituminous; treat with bitumen. —**bi·tu′mi·ni·za′tion** *n.*

bi·tu·mi·nous (bi·tōō′mə·nəs, -tyōō′-) *adj.* **1** Of, pertaining to, or containing bitumen. **2** Containing, as coal, many volatile hydrocarbons.

bi·va·lence (bī·vā′ləns, biv′ə-) *n. Chem.* The property of having a valence of two. Also **bi·va′len·cy.**

bi·va·lent (bī·vā′lənt, biv′ə-) *adj.* **1** *Chem.* **a** Having a valence of two, or twice that of a univalent. **b** Having two valences: also *divalent.* **2** *Biol.* Composed of or characterizing chromatin rods representing two chromosomes joined end to end. [<BI- + L *valens, -entis,* ppr. of *valere* have power]

bi·valve (bī′valv′) *n.* **1** *Zool.* An acephalous mollusk having a shell of two lateral valves. **2** *Bot.* A seed vessel that splits into two parts, as a pea pod. —*adj.* Having two valves, as a mollusk or seed vessel: also **bi′valved′, bi·val·vous** (bī′val′vəs), **bi·val·u·lar** (bī·val′vyə·lər).

biv·ou·ac (biv′ōō·ak, biv′wak) *n.* A temporary encampment with or without shelter. —*v.i.* **biv·ou·acked, biv·ou·ack·ing** To encamp for the night with or without tents. [<F <G *beiwacht* guard]

Bi·wa (bē·wä) Lake The largest lake in Japan, located in southern Honshu; 261 square miles. *Japanese* **Bi·wa·ko** (bē·wä·kō).

bi·zarre (bi·zär′) *adj.* Grotesque; odd; fantastic. See synonyms under ODD. [<F, ? ult.< Basque] —**bi·zarre′ly** *adv.* —**bi·zarre′ness** *n.*

Bi·zen (bē·zen) A former province of SW Honshu, Japan; famous for pottery known as **Biz·en·ware** (biz′ən·wâr′).

Bi·zer·te (bi·zûr′tə, *Fr.* bē·zert′) The northernmost city in Africa, a port in northern Tunisia; ancient *Hippo Zarytus.* Also **Bi·zer′ta.**

Bi·zet (bē·zā′), **Georges,** 1838–75, French composer: original name *Alexandre César Léopold Bizet.*

Bk *Chem.* Berkelium (symbol Bk).

blab (blab) *v.t. & v.i.* **blabbed, blab·bing 1** To tell or repeat indiscreetly. **2** To prattle. See synonyms under BABBLE. [<*n*] —*n.* **1** One who betrays confidence. **2** Idle chatter. [ME *blabbe* idle talker] —**blab′ber** *n.*

blab·ber·mouth (blab′ər·mouth′) *n.* One who talks too much and can't be trusted to keep secrets.

black (blak) *adj.* **1** Having little or no power to reflect light; of the color of jet: the opposite of *white.* **2** Belonging to a racial group characterized by dark skin; especially, Negroid. **3** Of or re′ating to members of such a group: *black* power. **4** Swarthy; somber; dark. **5** Destitute of light; gloomy; dismal; forbidding. **6** Soiled; stained. **7** Evil; malignant; wicked; deadly; slanderous; malicious; threatening: a *black*-hearted wretch. **8** Wearing black garments: *black* monks. See synonyms under DARK. —*n.* **1** The absence of or complete absorption of light; the darkest of all colors. **2** Something that is black; also, mourning apparel or drapery. **3** A stain. **4** A member of the so-called black race; a Negro. —**in the black** In the credit column of an account: converse of *in the red.* —*v.t. & v.i.* **1** To make or become black. **2** To blacken and polish. —**to black out 1** To extinguish or screen all light. **2** To lose vision or consciousness temporarily. **3** To censor; delete by scoring through. See BLACKOUT. [OE *blæc* dark] —**black′ly** *adv.* —**black′ness** *n.*

Black (blak), **Hugo La Fayette,** 1886–1971, associate justice of the United States Supreme Court 1937–1971.

black-and-blue (blak′ən·blōō′) *adj.* Discolored: said of skin that has been bruised.

Black and Tan Formerly, the auxiliary division of the Royal Irish Constabulary: so called from its uniform and accouterments.

black and white Writing or printing.

black art Necromancy; magic.

black·ball (blak′bôl′) *v.t.* **1** To use one's vote to ban from membership. **2** To exclude or ostracize: *blackballed* from the television industry. —*n.* **1** A single negative vote resulting in the rejection of an application for membership. **2** Any willful exclusion or act of ostracism. [<BLACK + BALL[1] from the use of a black ball to signify a negative vote during balloting] —**black′ball′er** *n.*

black bear The common American bear (*Euarctos americanus*).

black·ber·ry (blak′ber·ē, -bər·ē) *n. pl.* **·ber·ries 1** The black, edible fruit of certain shrubs (genus *Rubus*) of the rose family. **2** Any of the plants producing it.

blackberry lily A perennial herb (*Belamcanda chinensis*) of the iris family: so called from its ripened seed vessel, which resembles a blackberry.

black birch A species (*Betula lenta*) of birch of eastern North America with aromatic twigs and dark brown bark that becomes furrowed with age. Also called *sweet birch.*

black·bird (blak′bûrd′) *n.* **1** A common European thrush (*Turdus merula*), the male of which is black, with a yellow bill. **2** One of various black or blackish North American birds (family *Icteridae*), as the **crow blackbird** (*Quiscalus quiscula*), **marsh blackbird** (*Agelaius phoeniceus*), etc.

black·board (blak′bôrd′, -bōrd′) *n.* A blackened surface, for marking upon with chalk.

black body *Physics* **1** An ideal body that completely absorbs all radiant energy incident upon it. **2** The blackened interior of an opaque box or chamber with a very narrow slit.

black book A book or record of misdemeanors kept at some universities. —**to be in one's black book** To be in disfavor.

black buck 1 The common Indian antelope (*Antilope cervicapra*) of a prevailing blackish-brown color. **2** The sable antelope (*Hippotragus niger*) of South Africa.

Black·burn (blak′bərn) A county borough in central Lancashire, England.

Black Canyon 1 A gorge of the Colorado River, between Arizona and Nevada; site of Hoover Dam. See MEAD, LAKE. **2** A gorge of the Gunnison River in SW Colorado, a 10-mile section of which is included in **Black Canyon of the Gunnison National Monument,** established 1933.

black·cap (blak′kap′) *n.* **1** Any of several birds having a black crown, as the European warbler, chickadee, etc. **2** The black raspberry, or its fruit.

black·cock (blak′kok′) *n.* The male of the heath grouse.

black country A highly industrialized region of England in Staffordshire, Warwickshire, and Worcestershire.

black·damp (blak′damp′) *n.* Chokedamp.

black death A bubonic plague of exceptional virulence and duration prevalent in Asia and Europe in the 14th century.

black diamond 1 Mineral coal: only in plural. **2** Carbonado or bort.

black disease An acute, infectious, generally fatal hepatic disease of sheep, caused by an anaerobic bacterium (*Clostridium novyi*) transmitted by liver flukes.

black·en (blak′ən) *v.* **black·ened, black·en·ing** *v.t.* **1** To make black or dark. **2** To slander; defame. —*v.i.* **3** To become black; darken. —**black′en·er** *n.*

black eye 1 An eye with a black iris. **2** An eye having the adjacent surface discolored by a blow or bruise. **3** *Colloq.* A bad reputation. —**black′-eyed′** *adj.*

black-eyed Susan 1 One of the coneflowers (*Rudbeckia hirta*): the State flower of Maryland: also known as *yellow daisy.* **2** The bladder ketmia.

black·face (blak′fās′) *n.* An actor with exaggerated Negro make-up, especially a minstrel comedian. —*adj.* **1** Pertaining to or performed by actors so made up: a *blackface* show. 2 *Printing* Boldface.

Black·feet (blak′fēt′) *n. pl. sing.* **·foot** A confederacy of Algonquian North American Indian tribes, consisting of the Siksika or Blackfeet, the Kainah, and the Piegan, formerly inhabiting the territory between the Saskatchewan and Missouri Rivers, now on reservations in Alberta and Montana.

black·fel·low (blak′fel·ō) *n.* An Australian aborigine.

black·fel·low's button (blak′fel·ōz) *Austral.* An Australite.

black·fish (blak′fish) *n.* 1 One of various dark-colored cetaceans, as the pilot whale (genus *Globicephala*). 2 One of various fishes, as the tautog, the black sea bass, etc. 3 A food fish (*Dallia pectoralis*) of northern Alaskan and Siberian waters.

black·fly (blak′flī′) *n.* 1 Any of certain small, stocky, dark-colored, biting flies (genus *Simulium*) having aquatic larvae, especially common in forested mountainous regions; especially, *S. hirtipes* of North America. 2 The buffalo gnat.

Black·foot (blak′fŏŏt′) *n.* A member of any of the tribes of North American Indians known as Blackfeet. —*adj.* Pertaining or belonging to the Blackfeet tribes: *Blackfoot* tales.

Black Forest A mountainous wooded region in southern Germany; highest peak, 4,898 feet: German *Schwarzwald*.

Black Friar A Dominican: so named from his black cloak.

Black·fri·ars (blak′frī′ərz) An area in the SW angle of old London city, England: named for the large number of Dominican monasteries in the district.

black frost A frost severe enough to turn vegetation black.

black·guard (blag′ərd, -ärd) *n.* A low, vicious fellow; a scoundrel. —*v.t.* To revile; vilify. —*v.i.* To act like a blackguard. —*adj.* Of or like a blackguard; base; vile: also **black′guard·ly.·** [< *black guard*, orig., the scullions and low menials of a great house or army; later applied to any base person] —**black′guard·ism** *n.*

black·gum (blak′gum′) *n.* A large tree (*Nyssa sylvatica*) of the dogwood family, with an ovoid, blue-black drupe and close-grained wood hard to split; pepperidge; sour gum.

Black Hand 1 A society of anarchists in Spain, repressed in 1883. 2 A secret organization in the United States, especially of Italians, for the purpose of vengeance or blackmail. See MAFIA.

Black Hawk, 1767–1838, American Indian chief who fought against the United States in 1831–32.

black·head (blak′hed′) *n.* 1 An American scaup duck. 2 An infectious, often fatal protozoan disease of turkeys and certain wildfowl: it attacks chiefly the liver and intestines. 3 A facial blemish; comedo.

black·heart (blak′härt′) *n.* 1 A variety of early black cherry. 2 A blackening of the internal tissues of various trees and of the potato.

black·heart·ed (blak′här′tid) *adj.* Malign; wicked.

Black Hills A mountainous region in SW South Dakota and NE Wyoming; highest point, 7,242 feet; about 6,000 square miles.

black hole 1 A dark cell or dungeon. 2 A military lock-up: in allusion to the Black Hole in Fort William, at Calcutta, a room 18 feet square, into which 146 British subjects were forced on the night of June 20, 1756, of whom 123 died of asphyxia before morning. 3 A hypothetical hole in space into which stars and other celestial objects that have condensed to a certain radius collapse under the influence of gravity.

black·ing (blak′ing) *n.* 1 A preparation used to give blackness or luster, or both, to shoes, stoves, etc. 2 *Brit.* Shoe polish.

black·ish (blak′ish) *adj.* Somewhat black; darkened. —**black′ish·ly** *adv.*

black ivory 1 A pigment composed of carbonized ivory. 2 Formerly, Negroes as merchandise in the slave trade.

black lead Graphite.

black·leg (blak′leg′) *n.* 1 An acute, infectious, often fatal disease of young cattle,

caused by an anaerobic bacterium (*Clostridium chauvoei*) and characterized by fever and loss of appetite accompanied by swellings or tumors under the skin. 2 An injurious disease of cabbage and other cruciferous plants; also, a bacterial rot of potatoes. 3 A professional swindler or gambler; a cheat; sharper. 4 *Brit. Colloq.* A strikebreaker.

black letter *Printing* The Gothic or Old English letter.

𝕿𝖍𝖎𝖘 𝖑𝖎𝖓𝖊 𝖎𝖘 𝖎𝖓 𝖇𝖑𝖆𝖈𝖐 𝖑𝖊𝖙𝖙𝖊𝖗.

black·let·ter (blak′let′ər) *adj.* 1 Of or pertaining to manuscript printed or written in black letter. 2 Unfortunate or unlucky: a *black-letter* day. Also **black′-let′tered.**

black·light (blak′līt′) *n. Physics* Ultraviolet radiation capable of exciting fluorescence in properly treated materials or objects.

black·list (blak′list′) *n.* A list of persons or organizations under suspicion or censure, or refused approval for any cause. —*v.t.* To place the name of (a person) on or as on a blacklist.

black lung A form of pneumoconiosis that afflicts coal miners.

black·ly (blak′lē) *adv.* In a manner showing blackness or darkness; gloomily; threateningly.

black Magellanic cloud *Astron.* One of several dark spaces in the Milky Way, especially one near the Southern Cross.

black magic See under MAGIC.

black·mail (blak′māl′) *n.* 1 Extortion by threats of public accusation or of exposure. 2 *Scot.* A tax formerly paid to bandits to insure immunity from pillage. —*v.t.* 1 To levy blackmail upon. 2 To force (to do something) as by threats: with *into.* [< BLACK + MAIL³] —**black′mail′er** *n.*

Black Ma·ri·a (mə·rī′ə) *Colloq.* A prison van or police patrol wagon.

black mark A mark or symbol used to record failure or bad conduct.

black market A place or firm where merchandise is offered for sale contrary to legal restrictions, or in quantities or at terms contrary to such restrictions. Also **black bourse.**

black match Strands of twine impregnated with gunpowder, used to ignite fireworks, etc.

black nightshade The common nightshade.

black·out (blak′out′) *n.* 1 A defensive or precautionary measure against aerial attack, consisting of the extinguishment or screening of all lights visible from the air. 2 *Physiol.* The partial or complete loss of vision and sometimes of consciousness, experienced by airplane pilots during rapid changes in velocity. 3 In theatrics, a fade-out or cut-out, as of part of a scene, eliminating it from view. 4 An official ban on the publication of news in war time, imposed for security reasons.

black·poll (blak′pōl′) *n.* A North American wood warbler (*Dendroica striata*), the male of which has glossy black plumage on the top of the head.

Black·pool (blak′pōōl′) A county borough in west Lancashire, England; a seaside resort.

black·pot (blak′pot′) *n.* In ceramics, a type of coarse, unglazed pottery, manufactured chiefly in England.

black racer The blacksnake.

Black River A river in Northern Vietnam, flowing 500 miles SE to the Red River: Annamese *Song Bo.*

Black Rod 1 *Brit.* An officer of the royal household, who acts as messenger from the House of Lords to the House of Commons. 2 An usher in the legislatures of British colonies and dominions.

black rot Leaf spot.

Black Sea A large inland sea between Europe and Asia, connected with the Mediterranean by the Bosporus, the Sea of Marmara, and the Dardanelles; 159,000 square miles: also *Euxine Sea.* Ancient **Pon·tus Eux·i·nus** (pon′təs yōōk·sī′nəs).

black sheep 1 One, among a herd of white sheep, that is black. 2 An evil-disposed or disreputable member of an otherwise decent family or society.

Black Shirt 1 A member of the Italian Fascist party, in allusion to the black shirts worn by members. 2 A member of the Nazi Schutzstaffel.

black·smith (blak′smith′) *n.* A workman who works in or welds wrought iron. Compare WHITESMITH.

black·snake (blak′snāk′) *n.* 1 A large, agile, non-venomous snake of the eastern United States (*Coluber constrictor*) with smooth, satiny, black scales; the black racer. 2 A dangerous Australian snake (*Pseudechis porphyriacus*) with blue-black scales and a venom similar to that of the cobra. 3 A heavy pliant whip of braided leather or rawhide.

black spruce A North American evergreen tree (*Picea mariana*) with deep blue-green foliage and firmly attached cones.

black·thorn (blak′thôrn′) *n.* 1 A thorny European shrub (*Prunus spinosa*) of the rose family: the sloe. 2 A cane made from its wood. 3 An American hawthorn (*Crataegus calpodendron*).

black tie 1 A black bow tie. 2 A tuxedo and its correct accessories. 3 A phrase used on invitations to indicate semiformal dress.

black·top (blak′top′) *n.* Asphalt used for paving. —*v.t.* **-topped, -top·ping** To surface with blacktop.

black vomit 1 Yellow fever. 2 The dark bloody matter vomited in its later stages.

Black Watch A regiment of the British Army, officially known as the Royal Highlanders: so called because of their somber tartan.

black·wa·ter fever (blak′wô′tər, -wot′ər) *Pathol.* A dangerous form of malaria characterized by the excretion of black or dark red urine; malarial hematuria.

black·weed (blak′wēd′) *n.* The ragweed.

Black·well's Island (blak′welz, -wəlz) Former name for WELFARE ISLAND.

black whale The blackfish (*Globicephala melaena*): also called *pilot whale.*

black widow A medium-sized, venomous female spider (*Latrodectus mactans*) common in dark, sheltered places in the United States, having a black body with an hourglass-shaped red mark on the abdomen: so called from its color and its habit of eating its mate.

black·will (blak′wil′) *n.* The black bass.

black·wood (blak′wŏŏd′) *n.* The black mangrove of Florida and tropical America (*Rhizophora mangle*).

blad·der (blad′ər) *n.* 1 *Anat.* **a** A distensible membranous sac on the anterior part of the pelvic cavity, for the temporary retention of urine. **b** Some part or organ of analogous structure. ◆ Collateral adjective: *vesical.* 2 *Biol.* An air vessel or an air cell in some seaweeds. 3 Anything puffed out, empty, or unsubstantial. 4 A blister or pustule. [OE *blǣdre*]

blad·der·nut (blad′ər·nut′) *n.* 1 Any plant of the genus *Staphylea* of the soapberry family, with large, inflated, three-lobed pods. 2 A seed pod of one of these plants.

blad·der·worm (blad′ər·wûrm′) *n. Zool.* An encysted larval tapeworm; a scolex; hydatid.

blad·der·wort (blad′ər·wûrt′) *n.* Any aquatic herb of the genus *Utricularia*, usually having little bladders on the leaves, in which minute organisms are trapped for nutriment.

blad·der·wrack (blad′ər·rak′) *n.* Any rockweed of the genus *Fucus.* See FUCUS.

blad·der·y (blad′ər·ē) *adj.* 1 Like a bladder. 2 Covered with or having bladders or vesicles.

blade (blād) *n.* 1 The flat, cutting part of any edged tool or weapon. 2 The thin, flat part of any instrument or utensil, as of an oar, screw propeller, plow, etc. 3 *Bot.* The leaf of grasses or certain other plants, especially, a leaf of Indian corn. 4 A rakish young man; wild, reckless fellow. 5 A swordsman; also, a sword. 6 *Phonet.* The upper flat part of the tongue immediately behind the tip and directly below the alveolar ridge. 7 The expanded or broad flat part of a leaf, petal, etc.; the lamina. 8 *Anat.* The shoulder blade or scapula. [OE *blǣd* blade of a oar or sword] —**blad′ed** *adj.*

blae (blā, blē) *adj. Scot.* Blackish-blue or bluish-gray; livid; also, cloudy; bleak.

blah (blä) *n. Slang* Excessive hyperbole; fustian; buncombe. —*adj.* Uninteresting; dull: a *blah* story.

blain (blān) *n. Pathol.* A pustular tumor; a blister. [OE *blegen*]

Blake (blāk), **Robert**, 1599–1657, English admiral. —**William**, 1757–1827, English painter, poet, and mystic.

blam·a·ble (blā'mə·bəl) *adj.* Deserving blame; culpable; faulty. —**blam'a·ble·ness** *n.* — **blam'a·bly** *adv.*

blame (blām) *v.t.* **blamed, blam·ing 1** To accuse of fault or error: often with *for.* **2** To find fault with; reproach. **3** To place the responsibility for (an action or error): with *on.* —**to be to blame** To be at fault. —*n.* Faultfinding; censure; also, the fault; culpability. See synonyms under ANIMADVERSION. [< OF *blasmer* < LL *blasphemare* revile, reproach < Gk. *blasphēmeein.* Doublet of BLASPHEME.]

  Synonyms (verb): censure, chide, condemn, rebuke, reprehend, reproach, reprobate, reprove. We blame a person *for* a fault, or lay the blame *upon* him. See CONDEMN, REPROVE. Compare ARRAIGN. *Antonyms:* acquit, approve, eulogize, exculpate, exonerate, extol, laud, praise.

blamed (blāmd) *adj. U.S. Dial.* Damned: a *blamed* fool: a euphemism. —*adv.* Very; exceedingly: *blamed* hot.

blame·ful (blām'fəl) *adj.* **1** Deserving of blame. **2** Imputing blame. —**blame'ful·ly** *adv.* — **blame'ful·ness** *n.*

blame·less (blām'lis) *adj.* Innocent; guiltless. See synonyms under PERFECT. —**blame'less·ly** *adv.* —**blame'less·ness** *n.*

blame·wor·thy (blām'wûr'thē) *adj.* Deserving of blame. —**blame'wor'thi·ness** *n.*

Blanc (blängk, blangk; *Fr.* blän), **Cape** A cape of Tunisia on the northernmost tip of Africa. *French* **Cap Blanc** (kȧp blän')

Blanc (blän), **Jean Joseph Charles Louis**, 1811–82, French socialist and historian.

Blanc, Mont See MONT BLANC.

Blan·ca Peak (blang'kə) Highest peak in the Sangre de Cristo Mountains, southern Colorado; 14,363 feet.

blanc fixe (blän fēks') Fine–grained barium sulfate, used as a base in making certain pigments, and in water colors, where it retains its white color.

blanch[1] (blanch, blänch) *v.t.* **1** To remove the color from; bleach. **2** To cause to turn pale, as from fear or anger. **3** To remove the skin of, as almonds, by scalding. **4** To whiten, as meat, by scalding. **5** *Bot.* To bleach by removing from light, as celery or endives. **6** *Metall.* To whiten or brighten (metals), as with acids or by coating with tin. —*v.i.* **7** To turn or become white or pale. See synonyms under BLEACH. —*adj.* **1** In heraldry, white; argent. **2** In English law, based on a slight payment, often in silver: said of tenures. **3** In Scottish law, designating a merely nominal quit–rent, as a pair of gloves, or the tenure thus held. [< F *blanchir* < *blanc* white] —**blanch'er** *n.*

blanch[2] (blanch, blänch) *v.t.* To turn, as a deer, aside or back. [Var. of BLENCH[1]]

blanc·mange (blə·mänzh', -mänzh') *n.* A whitish, jellylike preparation of milk, eggs, sugar, cornstarch, flavoring, etc.: used for desserts, etc. [< F *blanc-manger* white food]

bland (bland) *adj.* **1** Affable in manner; gentle; suave. **2** Mild; balmy; genial. **3** Not stimulating or irritating. **4** Smooth and mild in flavor; as, a *bland* sauce. [< L *blandus* mild] —**bland'ly** *adv.* —**bland'ness** *n.*

  Synonyms: affable, balmy, benign, complaisant, courteous, genial, gentle, gracious, mild, smooth, soft, tender. *Antonyms:* acrid, biting, brusk, curt, harsh, rough, rude.

blan·dish (blan'dish) *v.t.* To wheedle; flatter; cajole. [< OF *blandiss-*, stem of *blandir* flatter < L *blandiri* < *blandus* mild, gentle] —**blan'dish·er** *n.*

blan·dish·ment (blan'dish·mənt) *n.* Soothing, caressing, or flattering speech or action; cajolery.

blank (blangk) *adj.* **1** Wholly or partly free from writing or print. **2** Lacking in ornament, variety, interest, or results. **3** Empty; void. **4** Without expression or animation: a *blank* stare. **5** Without rime: *blank* verse. **6** Disconcerted; confused. **7** Utter; downright. **8** Pale or white; colorless. **9** Having no finishing cuts, slots, grooves, teeth, or the like: unfinished: common in such phrases as *blank arcade, arch, file, key, saw, window,* etc. —*n.*

1 A paper containing no written or printed matter. **2** A written or printed paper with blank spaces. **3** A vacant space; void interval. **4** A lottery ticket which has drawn no prize; a disappointing result. **5** A partially prepared piece, as of wood or metal, ready for forming into a finished object, as a coin, key, button, etc. **6** The central white spot of a target; bull's–eye. **7** A blank verse. **8** A blank cartridge. —*v.t.* **1** To delete; invalidate: often with *out.* **2** In games, to prevent (an opponent) from scoring. **3** *Archaic* To disconcert; put out of countenance. [< F *blanc* white, ult. < Gmc.] —**blank'ly** *adv.* —**blank'ness** *n.*

  Synonyms (adj.): bare, barren, clear, empty, plain, unfilled, unlimited, unmarked, unsigned. See BLEAK, VACANT.

blank cartridge A cartridge loaded only with powder.

blank check *Colloq.* Carte blanche.

blan·ket (blang'kit) *n.* **1** A heavy woolen covering, as of a bed. **2** A robe of like material used, by Indians, as a garment, or for horses, etc., as a protection. **3** A sheet of other material, as cotton, of like appearance. **4** Anything that covers, conceals, or protects: a *blanket* of snow; a *blanket* of smoke; a *blanket* of rubber. —*adj.* **1** Designating anything which covers a wide range or large number of interrelated names, conditions, objects, items, or the like; covering every phase of a subject; all-embracing: a *blanket* ballot; *blanket* injunction. **2** Using blankets for garments: a *blanket* Indian. —*v.t.* **1** To cover with or as with a blanket. **2** To cover or apply uniformly: The new law *blankets* the nation. **3** To obscure or suppress; interfere: A strong broadcast *blankets* a weak one. **4** *Naut.* To deprive (a sailboat) of wind by passing close on the windward side. **5** To toss in a blanket as sport or punishment. [< OF *blankete,* dim. of *blanc* white; orig. a white or undyed cloth]

blank verse Verse without rime; specifically, iambic pentameter verse, the principal verse form in English epic and dramatic poetry.

blan·quette (blän·ket') *n.* A stew of veal, lamb, chicken, or any white meat served in an egg sauce, garnished with mushrooms and onions. [< F < *blanc* white]

blare (blâr) *v.t. & v.i.* **blared, blar·ing 1** To sound loudly, as a trumpet. **2** To announce loudly. —*n.* **1** A loud brazen sound. See synonyms under NOISE. **2** Brightness or glare, as of color. [Prob. imit.]

blar·ney (blär'nē) *n.* Wheedling flattery. —*v.t. & v.i.* To flatter, cajole, or wheedle. [< BLARNEY STONE]

Blar·ney (blär'nē) A village in central County Cork, Ireland.

Blarney Stone A stone in a 15th century castle in Blarney, Ireland, which, when kissed, reputedly endows one with invincible eloquence.

bla·sé (blä·zā', blä'zā) *adj.* Sated with pleasure; wearied or worn out, as by dissipation; indifferent. [< F, pp. of *blaser* satiate]

blas·pheme (blas·fēm') *v.* **-phemed, -phem·ing** —*v.t.* **1** To speak in an impious or irreverent manner of (God or sacred things). **2** To speak ill of; malign. —*v.i.* **3** To utter blasphemy. [< OF *blasfemer* < LL *blasphemare* < Gk. *blasphēmein* revile < *blasphēmos* evil-speaking. Doublet of BLAME.]

blas·phe·mous (blas'fə·məs) *adj.* Impious; irreverent; profane. See synonyms under PROFANE. —**blas'phe·mous·ly** *adv.* —**blas'phe·mous·ness** *n.*

blas·phe·my (blas'fə·mē) *n. pl.* **·mies 1** Evil or profane speaking of God or sacred things; claiming the attributes of God. **2** In the Old Testament, any attempt to lessen reverence for the name of Jehovah. **3** Any irreverent act or utterance. See synonyms under OATH.

blast (blast, bläst) *v.t.* **1** To rend in pieces by or as by explosion. **2** To cause to wither or shrivel; destroy. —*v.i.* **3** A strong or sudden wind. **2** *Metall.* The strong artificial current of air in a blast furnace. **3** The discharge of an explosive, or its effect. **4** The charge of dynamite or other explosive used in shattering rocks, as for a building foundation, tunnel, etc. **5** A loud, sudden sound, as of a trumpet. **6** A blight or blighting influence. **7** The draft of air near the muzzle of a cannon at its discharge. **8** *Slang* A party. **9** *Slang* An impor-

tant or surprising event or occasion. **10** *Slang* A drink of hard liquor. See synonyms under RUPTURE. —**in blast** In operation: said of a smelting furnace. —**at full blast** At capacity operation or maximum speed. [OE *blæst* blowing. Akin to BLOW[1].] —**blast'er** *n.*

-blast *combining form Biol.* Growth; sprout: *ameloblast.* [< Gk. *blastos* bud]

blast·ed (blas'tid, bläs'-) *adj.* **1** Blighted; withered or destroyed. **2** *Colloq.* Confounded: a euphemistic oath.

blas·te·ma (blas·tē'mə) *n. pl.* **·ma·ta** (-mə·tə) Embryonic protoplasm; the formative material of an ovum. [< Gk. *blastēma* offspring]

blast furnace *Metall.* A smelting furnace in which the fire is intensified by an air blast.

blast·ing (blas'ting, bläs'-) *n.* **1** The act of rending by charges of explosives. **2** A blighting or withering. **3** *Telecom.* The distortion resulting from the imposing on a microphone or loudspeaker of a greater volume of sound than can be properly transmitted.

blasto- *combining form Biol.* Growth, sprout: *blastoderm.* Also, before vowels, **blast-**. [< Gk. *blastos* a sprout]

blas·to·cele (blas'tə·sēl) *n. Biol.* The cavity of the blastodermic vesicle. Also **blas'to·coele.**

blas·to·cyst (blas'tə·sist) *n.* The blastula.

blas·to·derm (blas'tə·dûrm) *n. Biol.* The germinal disk. [< BLASTO- + Gk. *derma* skin] —**blas'to·der'mic** *adj.*

blas·to·disk (blas'tə·disk) *n. Biol.* A nucleated disk of protoplasm which forms on the surface of the yolk mass in certain eggs. Also **blas'·to·disc.**

blast·off (blast'ôf') *n.* The launching of a rocket or missile.

blas·to·gen·e·sis (blas'tə·jen'ə·sis) *n. Biol.* **1** Origin from the germ plasm: opposed to *pangenesis.* **2** Reproduction by budding. —**blas'·to·gen'ic** *adj.*

blas·to·mere (blas'tə·mir) *n. Biol.* One of the large number of small cells formed during the cleavage of the fertilized ovum. —**blas'to·mer'·ic** (-mer'ik) *adj.*

blas·to·pore (blas'tə·pôr, -pōr) *n. Biol.* The exterior opening of the primitive intestine. —**blas'to·por'ic** (-pôr'ik, -por'ik) *adj.*

blas·to·sphere (blas'tə·sfir) *n. Biol.* **1** The blastodermic vesicle of the mammalian egg. **2** A blastula.

blas·tu·la (blas'chŏŏ·lə) *n. pl.* **·lae** (-lē) *Biol.* The stage of the embryo just preceding the formation of the gastrula; a hollow sphere of one layer of blastomeres enclosing a blastocele or segmentation cavity. [< NL < Gk. *blastos* sprout] —**blas'tu·lar** *adj.*

blat (blat) *v.* **blat·ted, blat·ting** *v.t. Colloq.* To utter heedlessly; blurt out. —*v.i.* To bleat, as a sheep. [Var. of BLEAT]

bla·tant (blā'tənt) *adj.* **1** Loud or noisy; offensively loud or clamorous. **2** Making a bellowing or bleating noise: said of animals. **3** Tumid; pretentious; obtrusive. [Coined by Edmund Spenser. Cf. L *blatire* babble; ME *blait* bleat.] —**bla'tan·cy** *n.* —**bla'tant·ly** *adv.*

blath·er (blath'ər) *v.t. & v.i.* To talk garrulously or foolishly. —*n.* Foolish talk; nonsense. Also spelled *blether.* Also **blat·ter** (blat'ər). [< ON *blathra* talk stupidly < *blathr* nonsense]

blath·er·skite (blath'ər·skīt) *n.* **1** A blustering, noisy fellow; a hoodlum. **2** Blustering talk; balderdash. **3** The ruddy duck. [< BLETHER + SKATE[3]]

blau·bok (blou'bok) *n. pl.* **·bok** or **·boks 1** An extinct South African antelope (*Hippotragus leucophaeus*) with bluish hair. **2** A South African antelope (genus *Cephalopus*) about the size of a rabbit. [< Afrikaans]

blaw (blô) *v.t. & v.i. Scot.* To blow.

blawn (blôn) *Scot.* Blown.

blaze[1] (blāz) *v.* **blazed, blaz·ing** *v.i.* **1** To burn brightly. **2** To burn as with emotion: to *blaze* with anger. **3** To shine; be resplendent. —*v.t.* **4** *Rare* To cause to flame or shine brightly. See synonyms under BURN. —**to blaze away** To keep on firing; hence, to go on or proceed with anything. —*n.* **1** A vivid glowing flame; fire. **2** Brightness or brilliance and heat; effulgence; also, glare. **3** Excitement or ardor. See synonyms under FIRE, LIGHT. [OE *blæse* firebrand]

blaze[2] (blāz) *v.t.* **blazed, blaz·ing 1** To mark (a tree) by chipping off a piece of bark. **2** To mark out (a path) in this way. —*n.* **1** A white spot on the face of an animal, as a horse. **2** A mark chipped on a tree, to indicate a path; a path so indicated. [Akin to ON *blesi* white spot on a horse's face]

blaze³ (blāz) *v.t.* blazed, blaz·ing 1 To publish abroad or noise about. 2 *Obs.* To blare forth. [ON *blāsa* blow]

blaz·er (blā′zər) *n.* 1 A lightweight jacket of flannel or silk in vivid colors, usually worn in outdoor sports. 2 A dish with a small brazier under it for hot coals. 3 *Colloq.* That which blazes.

bla·zon (blā′zən) *n.* 1 *Her.* A coat of arms or armorial bearing, or a banner bearing such representation; a technical description or a graphic representation of armorial bearings. 2 A proclaiming or publishing abroad. 3 Ostentatious display. — *v.t.* 1 To inscribe or adorn, as with names or symbols. 2 *Her.* To describe technically or paint (coats of arms). 3 To proclaim; publish. See synonyms under PUBLISH. [<F *blason* coat of arms, shield] — **bla′zon·er** *n.* — **bla′zon·ment** *n.*

bla·zon·ry (blā′zən·rē) *n.* 1 The art of describing or depicting heraldic devices. 2 A coat of arms. 3 Decoration; show.

–ble See –ABLE.

bleach (blēch) *v.t.* 1 To deprive of color, as by exposure to the sun or chemicals; whiten. 2 To make pale: Fear *bleached* his face. — *v.i.* 3 To become colorless, pale or white. — *n.* 1 An act or the act of bleaching; also, the result of the act or degree of bleaching obtained. 2 A fluid or powder used as a bleaching agent. [OE *blǣcean*]

Synonyms (verb): blanch, whiten, whitewash. To *whiten* is to make white in general, but commonly it means to overspread with white coloring matter. *Bleach* and *blanch* both signify to *whiten* by depriving of color, the former permanently (as linen), the latter either permanently (as, to *blanch* celery) or temporarily (as, to *blanch* the cheek with fear). To *whitewash* is to *whiten* the surface of, literally with whitewash, or figuratively with false praise or by minimizing a fault. *Antonyms:* blacken, color, darken, dye, soil, stain.

bleach·er (blē′chər) *n.* 1 One who or that which bleaches. 2 *Usually pl.* An outdoor uncovered seat or stand for spectators.

bleach·ing (blē′ching) *n.* The process of whitening, as textile fibers and fabrics, by treatment with chemicals or exposure to the sun and weather.

bleaching powder A white or grayish-white powder with a slight odor of hypochlorous acid, formed by treating slaked lime with chlorine, and used for bleaching and as a disinfectant: also called *chloride of lime.*

bleak¹ (blēk) *adj.* 1 Exposed to wind and weather; bare; barren; dreary. 2 Cold, cutting, or penetrating. [<ON *bleikja* pale] — **bleak′ish** *adj.* — **bleak′ly** *adv.* — **bleak′ness** *n.*

Synonyms: blank, cheerless, chill, cold, cutting, desolate, dreary, exposed, piercing, stormy, unsheltered, waste, wild, windy. *Antonyms:* balmy, bright, cheerful, genial, homelike, mild, sheltered, sunny, warm.

bleak² (blēk) *n.* pl. **bleak** or **bleaks** A small European cyprinoid fish (genus *Alburnus*), whose scales are lined with a silvery pigment used in making artificial pearls. [<ON *bleikja*]

blear (blir) *adj.* 1 Dimmed, as by tears or rheum; dull. 2 Causing dimness of sight; also, dim; obscure; indistinct; hazy. — *v.t.* 1 To dim or inflame (the eyes). 2 To obscure, as the face with tears; blur. 3 To mislead; hoodwink. — *n.* That which renders vision indistinct; also, a blurry condition or look. [ME *blere.* Akin to LG *bleer-oged* bleareyed.] — **blear′y** *adj.* — **blear′i·ness** *n.*

blear-eyed (blir′īd′) *adj.* 1 Having inflamed or rheumy eyes. 2 Weak-sighted. Also **blear′y-eyed′.**

bleat (blēt) *n.* The cry of the sheep, goat, or calf; also, any sound resembling it. — *v.i.* 1 To cry, as a sheep or goat. 2 To speak with such a sound, as with fear or in complaint. — *v.t.* 3 To utter with the sound of a bleat. 4 To babble foolishly; prate. [OE *blǣtan*] — **bleat′er** *n.* — **bleat′ing** *adj.* — **bleat′ing·ly** *adv.*

bleb (bleb) *n.* A blister, or bladderlike body; a bulla. [ME *bleb*; imit.] — **bleb′by** *adj.*

bleed (blēd) *v.* **bled, bleed·ing** *v.t.* 1 To draw blood from; leech. 2 To exude, as sap, blood,

or other fluid. 3 To draw sap or other fluid from. 4 To empty of liquid or gaseous matter. 5 To extort money from; overcharge. 6 In bookbinding, to trim (a page) too closely, so as to cut into or mar the printed or engraved matter. — *v.i.* 7 To lose or shed blood. 8 To exude sap or other fluid. 9 To suffer wounds or die, as in battle: He *bled* for his country. 10 To feel grief, sympathy, or anguish. 11 To suffer by extortion; be overcharged. 12 To be cut into, as a printed page. 13 To run, as dyes in wet cloth. — **to bleed (someone) white** To extort money from in very large amounts. — *n.* 1 A page or plate so trimmed as to cut the printing or engraving. 2 The part of a page or plate on which printing or an illustration extends beyond the usual printing edge. [OE *blēdan*]

bleed·er (blē′dər) *n.* 1 One who or that which bleeds. 2 A person who bleeds profusely from slight wounds; a hemophiliac.

bleeding heart 1 Any of various plants having racemes of pink, drooping, heart-shaped flowers; especially, the ornamental garden herb (*Dicentra spectabilis*). 2 *Colloq.* One whose political views are unduly influenced by sympathy for alleged suffering.

BLEEDING HEART

bleek·bok (blēk′bok) *n.* An antelope, the oribi. [<Afrikaans]

blem·ish (blem′ish) *v.t.* To mar the perfection of; sully. — *n.* A disfiguring defect; also, moral reproach or stain. [<OF *blemiss-,* stem of *blemir* make livid <*blême* pale, wan] — **blem′ish·er** *n.*

Synonyms (noun): blot, blur, brand, crack, daub, defacement, defect, deformity, dent, disfigurement, disgrace, dishonor, fault, flaw, imperfection, injury, reproach, smirch, soil, speck, spot, stain, stigma, taint, tarnish. A *blemish* is superficial; a *flaw* or *taint* is in structure or substance. In the moral sense, a *blemish* comes from one's own ill-doing; a *brand* or *stigma* is inflicted by others; as, the *brand* of infamy; we speak of a *blot* or *stain* upon reputation; a *flaw* or *taint* in character. A *defect* is the want or lack of something; *fault,* primarily a failing, is something that fails of an apparent intent or disappoints a natural expectation. See INJURY.

blend (blend) *v.* **blend·ed** or **blent, blend·ing** *v.t.* 1 To mix, as paints or whiskies, so as to obtain a combined product of a desired quality, taste, color, or consistency. 2 To prepare by such process. — *v.i.* 3 To mix; intermingle. 4 To pass or shade imperceptibly into each other, as colors. 5 To harmonize; suit one another. See synonyms under MIX, UNITE. — *n.* 1 The act or result of mixing; a mixture. 2 *Ling.* A word resulting from the combining of parts of two distinct words of generally similar meaning, as *brunch* from *breakfast* and *lunch*: also called *portmanteau word, telescope word.* [Fusion of OE *blendan,* var. of *blandan* mix and ON *blanda* mingle]

blend·er (blen′dər) An automatic electrical device that mixes and blends foods, paints, cement, etc.

bleph·a·ri·tis (blef′ə·rī′tis) *n.* *Pathol.* Inflammation of the eyelids.

blepharo- *combining form Anat., Pathol.* Eyelid. Also, before vowels, **blephar-,** as in *blepharitis.* [<Gk. *blepharon* eyelid]

bless (bles) *v.t.* **blessed** or **blest, bless·ing** 1 To consecrate; make holy by religious rite. 2 To honor and exalt; glorify. 3 To sanctify or protect by making the sign of the cross over. 4 To invoke God's favor upon (a person or thing). 5 To bestow happiness or prosperity upon; make happy. 6 To endow, as with a gift: She was *blessed* with a beautiful face. 7 To guard; protect: used as an exclamation: God *bless* me; *Bless* me! See synonyms under PRAISE. [OE *blēdsian* consecrate (with blood) <*blōd* blood] — **bless′er** *n.*

bless·ed (bles′id, blest) *adj.* 1 Being in enjoyment of felicity in heaven; beatified. 2 Worthy of veneration or of blessing. 3 Joyful; healing. 4 Happy; favored. 5 Confounded, cursed,

or the like: a euphemistic, ironical, or merely intensive use: not a *blessed* cent. Also **blest** (blest). See synonyms under HAPPY, HOLY. — **bless′ed·ly** *adv.*

blessed event *Colloq.* The birth of a baby.

bless·ed·ness (bles′id·nis) *n.* The state of one who is blessed; felicity. — **single blessedness** The unmarried state.

Bless·ed Sacrament (bles′id) In the Roman Catholic Church, the consecrated elements in the mass, especially the Host.

bless·ing (bles′ing) *n.* 1 That which makes happy or prosperous; a gift of divine favor. 2 A benediction. 3 Grateful adoration; worship. 4 Cursing or scolding: a euphemism. See synonyms under FAVOR, MERCY.

blest (blest) *adj.* Blessed.

blet (blet) *v.i.* **blet·ted, blet·ting** To decay. internally, as a fleshy fruit after ripening. — *n.* Incipient decay in overripe fruit. [<F *blet* overripe]

blight (blīt) *n.* 1 Any of a number of destructive plant diseases, as mildew, rust, smut, etc. 2 Anything that withers hopes or prospects; also, the act of ruining or destroying. 3 A minute insect, usually an aphis, injurious to trees. 4 A deteriorating influence or condition affecting use, development, and value, as of real estate. — *v.t.* 1 To cause to decay; blast. 2 To ruin; frustrate. — *v.i.* 3 To suffer blight. [Origin unknown]

blimp (blimp) *n.* *Colloq.* 1 A non-rigid, lighterthan-air, dirigible balloon. 2 The soundproof cover enclosing a motion-picture camera: also called *bungalow.* [<Type *B-Limp,* a kind of British dirigible]

blind (blīnd) *adj.* 1 Without the power of seeing. 2 Lacking in perception or judgment. 3 Acting or proceeding at random. 4 Difficult to understand or trace; illegible; unintelligible. 5 Having no opening or outlet: a *blind* ditch. 6 Having but one opening; open at one end only: a *blind* alley. 7 Difficult to find or follow: a *blind* path. 8 Of or relating to blind persons as a class. 9 Dark; obscure. — **to go it blind** 1 To bet in a poker game before looking at one's hand. 2 Hence, to undertake anything without reasonable inquiry. — *n.* 1 Something that obstructs vision or shuts off light; particularly, a window shade; a screen or shutter. 2 A subterfuge; ruse. 3 One who is, or those who are, blind. 4 A place of ambush; hiding place. 5 A baggage car with no end door: also **blind baggage.** See synonyms under ARTIFICE. — *v.t.* 1 To make blind. 2 To dazzle. 3 To deprive of judgment or discernment. 4 To darken; obscure. 5 To outshine; eclipse. [OE]

blind alley 1 An alley, road, etc., open at one end only. 2 Any search, occupation, or the like, in which progress is blocked.

blind date A date with a person whom one has not previously seen or met, usually arranged by a third person.

blind·er (blīn′dər) *n.* 1 One who or that which blinds. 2 A flap on the side of a horse's bridle, to obstruct his side view: also called *blinker.* For illustration see HARNESS.

blind·fold (blīnd′fōld′) *v.t.* 1 To cover or bandage the eyes of. 2 To hoodwink; mislead. — *n.* A bandage, etc., over the eyes. — *adj.* 1 Having the eyes bandaged. 2 Having the mental vision darkened; rash. Also **blind′fold′ed** *adj.* [ME *blindfellen* <*blind* blind + *fellen* strike; infl. in spelling by FOLD]

blind gut The cecum.

blind hinge A shutter hinge constructed so that the shutter or other piece hinged thereby closes itself by its own weight when not held open. For illustration see HINGE.

blind·ing (blīn′ding) *adj.* Making blind or as if blind, physically or mentally: *blinding* tears; *blinding* passions. — **blind′ing·ly** *adv.*

blind·ly (blīnd′lē) *adv.* Without sight or without foresight; recklessly.

blind-man's-buff (blīnd′manz′buf′) *n.* A game in which one who is blindfolded must catch and identify someone.

blind poker A game of poker in which bets are made before the hands are seen.

blind side The weakest or most vulnerable side.

blind spot 1 *Anat.* A small area on the retina of the eye that is insensible to light because of the entrance of the fibers of the optic nerve. **2** A subject or a phase of thought in which one is unable to be objective or critical.

blind·worm (blīnd′wûrm′) *n.* A small, limbless, snakelike lizard with very small but perfect eyes; especially the slowworm (*Anguis fragilis*) of Europe and Africa.

blink (blingk) *v.i.* **1** To wink rapidly. **2** To look with half–closed eyes, as in sunlight; squint. **3** To twinkle; glimmer; also, to flash on and off. **4** To ignore something: He *blinked* at the law. —*v.t.* **5** To cause to wink. **6** To shut the eyes to; evade: to *blink* matters. **7** To send (a message) by blinker light. —*n.* **1** A glance or glimpse. **2** A shimmer or glimmer. **3** Light reflected from floating ice; iceblink. [<Du. *blinken*]

blink·er (blingk′ər) *n.* **1** One who or that which blinks. **2** A blinker light. **3** *pl.* Goggles. **4** A horse's blinder.

blinker light 1 A light set to blink at regular intervals, usually as a warning. **2** A light used to signal messages.

blin·tze (blin′tsə) *n.* A thin pancake folded about a filling, as of cheese. Also **blintz** (blints). [<Yiddish]

blip (blip) *n.* **1** *Telecom.* A visual display of a radar echo. **2** A short, sharp sound. —*v.i.* **blipped, blip·ping 1** To make blips. —*v.t.* **2** To delete (speech) from a videotape, as in censoring, thus creating a discontinuity: to *blip* swearwords. [Imit.]

bliss (blis) *n.* **1** Superlative happiness; heavenly joy. **2** Gladness; joy. **3** A cause of delight. See synonyms under HAPPINESS, RAPTURE. [OE *bliths* < *blithe* joyous] — **bliss′ful** *adj.* — **bliss′ful·ly** *adv.* — **bliss′ful·ness** *n.*

blis·ter (blis′tər) *n.* **1** A thin vesicle, especially one on the skin, containing watery matter, as from a scald, bruise, etc. **2** A similar vesicle on a plant, on steel, or on a painted surface. **3** Any substance used for blistering. **4** *Nav.* A bulge on the hull of a warship below the waterline to protect it from torpedoes. **5** *Aeron.* A bulge or projection from the fuselage of certain aircraft, containing guns and used for observation. —*v.t.* **1** To produce a blister or blisters upon. **2** To rebuke; lash with words. —*v.i.* **3** To become blistered. [OF *blestre* <ON *blāstr* swelling]

blis·tered (blis′tərd) *adj.* **1** Having blisters. **2** Covered with raised spots resembling blisters. **3** Having slits which reveal material of a different color or a different type of material, especially in 16th century costumes.

blis·ter·y (blis′tər·ē) *adj.* Marked by or full of blisters.

blithe (blīth) *adj.* Characterized by gladness or mirth; joyous; gay; merry; sprightly. See synonyms under CHEERFUL, HAPPY, MERRY. [OE] — **blithe′ly** *adv.*

blithe·some (blīth′səm) *adj.* Showing or imparting gladness; cheerful; merry. See synonyms under HAPPY. — **blithe′some·ly** *adv.* — **blithe′some·ness** *n.*

blitz (blits) *v.t. Colloq.* To attack with sudden and overwhelming force. —*n.* Sudden force; lightninglike destruction. —*adj.* Lightning-like. [<G, lightning]

blitz·krieg (blits′krēg) *n.* **1** Lightning war. **2** Sudden overwhelming attack with powerful force. [<G]

bliz·zard (bliz′ərd) *n. Meteorol.* **1** A high, cold wind accompanied by blinding snow. **2** A severe and heavy snowstorm of long duration. [<dial.E *blizzer* sudden blow, flash of lightning]

bloat¹ (blōt) *v.t.* **1** To cause to swell, as with fluid or gas. **2** To puff up; make proud or vain. —*v.i.* **3** To swell; become puffed up. —*n.* **1** One who is bloated; a drunkard. **2** An accumulation of gas in the rumen or intestinal tract of an animal brought on by the fermentation of green forage. —*adj.* Bloated; puffed; swollen. [ME *blout,* ? <ON *blautr* soft, soaked]

bloat² (blōt) *v.t.* To cure, as herring, by half-drying in smoke. —*adj.* Smoke-cured: a *bloat* herring. [ME *blote,* ? <ON *blautr* soft, soaked]

bloat·ed (blō′tid) *adj.* **1** Swollen with fluid or gas. **2** Turgid; edematous. **3** Puffed up; conceited.

bloat·er (blō′tər) *n.* **1** A selected smoked herring. **2** A whitefish (*Argyrosomus prognathus*) of the Great Lakes of North America.

blob (blob) *n.* **1** A soft, globular mass; a drop,

as of viscous liquid; a blotch or daub. **2** A noise like that made by a fish flopping in water. —*v.* **blobbed, blob·bing** *v.t.* **1** To smear with ink or color; blur. —*v.i.* **2** To rise in bubbles or produce bubbles. **3** To flop, as a fish in water. [Imit.]

bloc (blok) *n.* A group, as of politicians, combined to foster special interests or to obstruct legislative action: originally, a combination of members of different political parties in the French Chamber of Deputies. Compare BLOCK². [<F]

block¹ (blok) *n.* **1** A solid piece of wood, metal, or other material. **2** A wooden log or the like upon which chopping is done. **3** A temporary support; shore. **4** The stand on which slaves were sold at auction. **5** A wooden billet on which condemned persons are beheaded. **6** The form or piece on which the final shape is given to a hat body, or one on which a hat is placed to be ironed. **7** A wooden support for a wig: a barbers' *block.* **8** A continuous portion of land: a 10–acre *block.* **9** A sheave or pulley, or set of pulleys, in a frame or shell. **10** The land and buildings enclosed in a single square, or the like, bounded by streets; the distance along a street from

TYPES OF BLOCKS
a. Tackle. *d.* Triple–sheave steel.
b. Dock. *e.* Gin.
c. Link snatch. *f.* Square–cheeked.

one cross–street to another. **11** A group acting or considered as a unit: a *block* of theater seats; the Asian *block* of nations. **12** *Austral.* The public promenade of a city; also, one of the sections into which the public lands available for settlement are divided. **13** A section of a railroad controlled by signals. **14** A set, as of tickets, shares of stock, etc., handled as a unit. —*v.t.* **1** To shape into blocks. **2** To shape, mold, or stamp with a block, as a hat. **3** To secure or strengthen with blocks. — **to block out** To plan broadly without details. — **to block up** To raise on blocks. [<F *bloc,* ult. <Gmc.]

block² (blok) *n.* **1** That which hinders or obstructs, or the condition of being obstructed; an obstruction. **2** In sports, interference. **3** The blocking of a ball with a bat, as in cricket. **4** *Pathol.* An obstruction, as of a nerve or blood vessel. —*v.t.* **1** To obstruct; stop or impede the progress of. **2** To stop with or as with a block; blockade: often with *up.* **3** In sports, to hinder the movements of (an opposing player), usually by bodily contact; also, to stop (a ball), as with the body. **4** *Physiol.* To stop (a nerve) from functioning, as with an anesthetic. —*v.i.* **5** To act so as to hinder. See synonyms under HINDER. — **to block out** To obscure from view. — **to block up** To fill (an area or space) so as to prevent movement into or through. [<F *bloquer* obstruct <*bloc* block, ult. <Gmc.]

block·ade (blo·kād′) *v.t.* **·ad·ed, ·ad·ing** To close to traffic or communication by military or naval force; obstruct. —*n.* **1** The investing of a coast by a hostile naval force with intent to close it to maritime commerce. **2** A blockading force. **3** Any hindrance or obstruction to action. — **to run the blockade** To elude blockading forces. [<BLOCK²]

blockade runner 1 A vessel engaged in passing through a blockade. **2** The captain of such a vessel, or a member of the crew.

block·bust·er (blok′bus′tər) *n.* **1** An aerial bomb capable of devastating a large area. **2** *U.S.* One who engages in blockbusting.

block·er (blok′ər) *n.* **1** One who or that which blocks. **2** In football, a player who obstructs an opposing tackler.

block front In American furniture, a form of front, as in a desk or chest of drawers, characterized by three vertical panels, the center concave, the end panels convex or blocked. — **block′–front** *adj.*

block·head (blok′hed′) *n.* A stupid person.

block·house (blok′hous′) *n.* **1** A fortification, formerly of logs and heavy timbers, now of concrete or other very resistant material, having loopholes from which to fire guns. **2** *U.S.* A house made of hewn logs set square.

BLOCKHOUSE

block·ish (blok′ish) *adj.* Like a block; stupid; dull. Also **block′like′.**

Block Island An island resort off the south coast of and belonging to Rhode Island.

block letter 1 Printing type cut from wood. **2** A style of printing without serifs, resembling letters cut from wood. — **block–let·ter** (blok′·let′-ər) *adj.*

block·line (blok′līn′) *n.* A line passing over one or more blocks and pulleys.

block plane A small carpenter's plane for trimming wood across the grain.

block printing A method of printing from wooden blocks on which designs have been engraved.

block signal A signal functioning as part of a block system.

block system A system of regulating the running of trains on a railway, by automatic signals or otherwise, in which the track is divided into sections called blocks, on any one of which, ordinarily, only one train at a time is allowed.

block tin 1 Tin cast in ingots. **2** Pure tin as distinguished from tin plate.

block·y (blok′ē) *adj.* **·i·er, ·i·est 1** Unequally shaded, as if printed in blocks. **2** Short and stout; stocky.

blond (blond) *adj.* **1** Having a fair skin with light eyes and hair. **2** Flaxen or golden, as hair. —*n.* **1** A blond person: feminine **blonde** (blond). **2** A variety of silk lace. [<F, yellow-haired <Med.L *blondus,* probable. <Gmc.]

blood (blud) *n.* **1** The chemically complex and usually red fluid that circulates through the vascular system of most vertebrates. Consisting essentially of semi-solid corpuscles suspended in plasma, it delivers oxygen and nutrients to all the cells and tissues, distributes internal secretions, removes waste products, guards against infection, and helps to maintain homeostasis of the organism. ◆Collateral adjective: *hemal.* **2** Kinship by descent; race; especially, noble lineage. Compare FULL BLOOD, HALF BLOOD. **3** Vitality; temperament; mood. **4** Bloodshed; war; murder. **5** A dashing fellow; gallant. **6** One of various red liquids, as the sap of some trees. **7** A blood horse. **8** The life blood of a sacrificial victim, especially as in the atonement of Christ. See synonyms under AFFINITY, KIN. —*v.t.* **1** To draw blood from; bleed. **2** To give (a hunting dog) its first sight or smell of blood; also, to give (troops) their first experience of battle. —*adj.* **Blooded;** of superior breed: a fine *blood* mare. [OE *blōd*]

blood bank *Med.* A reserve of blood, either in liquid form classified according to blood groups, or in the form of dried plasma, for use in transfusion.

blood bath A massacre; slaughter.

blood–bol·tered (blud′bōl′tərd) *adj.* Daubed or clotted with blood.

blood count *Med.* A measure giving the number and proportion of red and white cells in a given sample of blood: used for clinical and diagnostic purposes.

blood–cur·dling (blud′kurd′ling) *adj.* Terrifying or horrifying enough to curdle or congeal the blood.

blood group *Physiol.* One of four great classes into which all human beings may be divided on the basis of specific genetic differences in the composition and properties of blood: in the classification of Landsteiner, they are designated as AB, A, B, and O. Also **blood type.**

blood–guilt (blud′gilt′) *n.* The crime of unrighteous bloodshed. — **blood′guilt′i·ness** *n.* — **blood′guilt′y** *adj.*

blood heat *Physiol.* The normal temperature of human blood, about 98.6°F. or 37°C.

blood·hound (blud′hound′) *n.* A large hound with an unusual ability to follow a scent: characterized by a powerful body, straight and large-boned forelegs, and loose skin: often used to track fugitives: also called *sleuthhound.*

blood·less (blud′lis) *adj.* 1 Having no blood; without color; pale. 2 Lifeless. 3 Cold-hearted. 4 Without bloodshed. —**blood′less·ly** *adv.* — **blood′less·ness** *n.*

blood·let·ting (blud′let′ing) *n.* Bleeding for a therapeutic purpose. —**blood′let′ter** *n.*

blood·line (blud′līn′) *n.* Strain or pedigree, as of livestock.

blood money Money paid to a hired murderer, or, as compensation, to the kin of a murdered man.

blood poisoning Introduction of virulent bacteria into the blood stream, usually from a local infection, such as a boil or wound; septicemia.

blood pressure *Physiol.* The pressure of the blood on the walls of the arteries, varying with the force of the heart action, resilience of the arteries and blood vessels, amount and viscosity of blood, etc.

blood-red (blud′red′) *adj.* Colored with or like blood. See synonyms under BLOODY.

blood relation A person of the same stock or parentage; a kinsman by birth.

blood·shed (blud′shed′) *n.* The shedding of blood; slaughter; carnage. Also **blood′shed′·ding.** —**blood′shed′der** *n.*

blood·shot (blud′shot′) *adj.* Suffused or shot with blood; red and inflamed or irritated: said of the eye.

blood·stain (blud′stān′) *n.* A spot produced by blood. —*v.t.* To stain with blood. —**blood′·stained′** *adj.*

blood·stone (blud′stōn′) *n.* A stone of green chalcedony flecked with particles of red jasper: often cut as a gem.

blood·stream (blud′strēm) *n.* The stream of blood coursing through a living body.

blood·suck·er (blud′suk′ər) *n.* 1 An animal that sucks blood, as a leech. 2 A cruel extortioner. — **blood′suck′ing** *adj.*

blood·thirst·y (blud′thûrs′tē) *adj.* Thirsting for blood; murderous; cruel. —**blood′thirst′i·ly** *adv.* —**blood′thirst′i·ness** *n.*

blood transfusion *Med.* The transfer of a quantity of the blood from one person into the vascular system of another.

blood type Blood group.

blood vessel Any tubular canal in which the blood circulates: an artery, vein, or capillary.

blood·wort (blud′wûrt′) *n.* 1 Any plant of the family *Haemodoraceae.* 2 The salad burnet (*Sanguisorba minor*). 3 The red-veined dock (genus *Rumex*). 4 Bloodroot.

blood·y (blud′ē) *adj.* **blood·i·er, blood·i·est** 1 Covered or stained with blood: also **blood′ied.** 2 Consisting of, containing, or mixed with blood. 3 Characterized by or delighting in bloodshed; saguinary. 4 Red like blood; suggesting blood. 5 *Brit. Slang* Damned; accursed: confounded: also used adverbially, meaning very, exceedingly, damnably; as, not *bloody* likely: a low vulgarism. —*v.t.* **blood·ied, blood·y·ing** To smear or stain with blood. — **blood′i·ly** *adv.* —**blood′i·ness** *n.*

Synonyms (adj.): blood-dyed, blood-red, bloodstained, crimson, gory, reeking, sanguinary. *Bloody* is commonly used in the literal, *sanguinary* in the figurative sense. We say a *sanguinary* or *bloody* battle, a *sanguinary* temper, a *bloody* weapon, a *bloody* field. *Crimson* refers to the color of blood; *gory* signifies covered or daubed with gore, or clotted blood, and always keeps the physical signification. *Reeking,* which is capable of other meanings, is often used alone to signify wet with steaming blood; as a *reeking* blade. *Antonyms:* bloodless, calm, conciliatory, gentle, harmless, peaceable, peaceful, tranquil, unwarlike.

bloom¹ (blōōm) *n.* 1 The act of florescence or the state of being in flower. 2 A growing or flourishing condition; freshness; also, flush; glow. 3 A flower; blossom; also, flowers collectively. 4 *Bot.* The powdery, waxy substance on certain fruits, as the plum or grape, and on certain leaves, as those of the cabbage. 5 A clouded appearance on a varnished surface. 6 A yellow appearance on tanned leather. 7 A fluorescence seen in lubricat-

ing oils. 8 *Phot.* A moist film on the surface of a lens, film, or glass plate. 9 A fine variety of sun-dried raisin: also **bloom raisin.** 10 An earthy mineral, usually bright-colored, and ordinarily a decomposition product. —*v.i.* 1 To bear flowers; blossom. 2 To glow with health and beauty; be at one's prime. 3 To glow with a warm color; be rosy. —*v.t.* 4 To bring into bloom; cause to flourish. 5 To invest with a warm color. 6 To cloud, as a varnished surface. [< ON *blōm* flower, blossom. Akin to BLOSSOM.]

bloom² (blōōm) *n.* 1 *Metall.* A mass of malleable iron from which the slag has been forced by hammer or roller. 2 A lump of melted glass. [OE *bloma* lump of metal]

bloom·er¹ (blōō′mər) *n.* 1 A costume of loose trousers under a short skirt; also, a woman so dressed. 2 *pl.* Loose, wide knickerbockers gathered at the knees: worn by women. 3 *pl.* Canvas guards attached to turrets of battleships and enclosing the barrels of turret guns to keep out dampness. [after Mrs. Amelia *Bloomer,* U.S. feminist reformer, 1818–94, who first proposed it]

bloom·er² (blōō′mər) *n. Slang* A bad mistake; an error. [? < Australian slang *a bloom(ing) er(ror)*]

bloom·ing (blōō′ming) *adj.* Coming into flower; hence, fresh and beautiful; prosperous. See synonyms under FRESH. —**bloom′ing·ly** *adv.* — **bloom′ing·ness** *n.*

bloom·y (blōō′mē) *adj.* 1 Abounding in blooms; flowery. 2 Covered with bloom, as a fruit.

bloop (blōōp) *n.* In sound reproduction of motion pictures, the dull thud caused by a poorly made patch of material placed over a splice in the sound track. [Imit.]

bloop·er (blōō′pər) *n.* 1 *U.S. Slang* An error or blunder. 2 In baseball: **a** A weakly hit fly ball reaching just beyond the infield. **b** A high, weakly thrown pitch. [Imit.]

blos·som (blos′əm) *n.* 1 A flower, especially one of a plant yielding edible fruit. 2 The state or period of flowering; bloom. 3 *Geol.* A weathered or decomposed outcrop of a coal bed or mineral bed. —*v.i.* 1 To come into blossom; bloom. 2 To prosper; thrive. See synonyms under FLOURISH. [OE *blostma.* Akin to BLOOM.] —**blos′som·less** *adj.* —**blos′·som·y** *adj.*

blot¹ (blot) *n.* 1 A spot or stain, as of ink. 2 Reproach; blemish; a stain on a reputation. 3 An erasure. See synonyms under BLEMISH, STAIN. —*v.* **blot·ted, blot·ting** *v.t.* 1 To spot, as with ink; stain. 2 To disgrace; sully. 3 To mark over or obliterate, as writing: often with *out.* 4 To dry with blotting paper. 5 To obscure; darken: usually with *out.* 6 To paint roughly; daub. —*v.i.* 7 To spread in a blot or blots, as ink. 8 To become blotted; acquire spots. 9 To absorb: This paper *blots* well. [ME *blotte;* origin uncertain]

blot² (blot) *n.* 1 In backgammon, an exposed man liable to be forfeited. 2 Any exposed point; a weak spot. [Origin uncertain]

blotch (bloch) *n.* 1 A spot or blot. 2 An inflamed eruption on the skin. —*v.t.* To mark or cover with blotches. [Blend of BLOT¹ and BOTCH²] —**blotch′y** *adj.*

blot·ter (blot′ər) *n.* 1 A sheet, pad, or book of blotting paper. 2 The daily record of arrests and charges in a police station. 3 Anything that blots or defiles.

blotting paper Unsized paper for absorbing excess ink.

blouse (blous, blouz) *n.* 1 A woman's loose waist or bodice of various types, extending from the neck to the waist or below, and worn tucked into the skirt or outside. 2 A loose, knee-length shirt or frock, usually belted at the waist, worn chiefly by French workmen. 3 A U.S. Army service coat. [< F; ult. origin uncertain]

bloused (bloust, blouzd) *adj.* 1 Wearing a blouse. 2 Made loose like a blouse, as a waist.

blow¹ (blō) *v.* **blew, blown, blow·ing** *v.t.* 1 To move by a current of air. 2 To overthrow or extinguish by a current of air. 3 To emit, as air or smoke, from the mouth. 4 To force air upon, as from the mouth: often with *up:*

to *blow up* a fire. 5 To empty or clear by forcing air through, as pipes. 6 To cause to sound, as a bugle or horn. 7 To sound (a signal): The bugle *blew* taps. 8 To form or shape, as by inflating: to *blow* glass. 9 To put out of breath, as a horse. 10 To shatter or destroy by or as by explosion: usually with *up, down, out, through,* etc.: to *blow out* a tire; to *blow down* a pole; to *blow* a hole *through* a wall; to *blow up* a house. 11 To melt (a fuse). 12 To lay eggs in, as flies in meat. 13 *Slang* To spend (money) lavishly; also, to treat or entertain: I'll *blow* you to a meal. 14 *Slang* To leave; go out of. 15 *Slang* To damn: a euphemism: Well, I'll be *blowed.* —*v.i.* 16 To be in motion: said of wind or air. 17 To move in a current of air; be carried by the wind. 18 To emit a current or jet of air, water, steam, etc. 19 To sound by being blown: The bugle *blew* at dawn. 20 To fail or become useless, as by melting: The fuse *blew.* 21 To explode: usually with *up, down, to,* etc.: The engine *blew up.* 22 To pant; gasp for breath. 23 *Colloq.* To talk boastfully. 24 *Slang* To leave; go. — **to blow a fuse** *Colloq.* To lose self-control; become enraged. — **to blow hot and cold** *Colloq.* To vacillate; be uncertain. — **to blow off** 1 To let off steam, as from a boiler. 2 *Slang* To speak in anger, as to relieve pent-up emotion. — **to blow out** To subside; become less intense: The storm will *blow* itself *out.* — **to blow over** To pass, as a storm; subside. — **to blow up** 1 To inflate. 2 To enlarge, as a photographic print. 3 *Colloq.* To lose self-control; become enraged. 4 To arise; become increasingly intense, as a storm. —*n.* 1 The act of blowing; a blast; gale. 2 The oviposition of a fly; a flyblow. 3 *Metall.* A single blast of the Bessemer converter, or the quantity of metal acted on at one time. 4 *Mining* The violent inrush of gas from or into a coal seam; also, the collapse of a mine roof. 5 *Slang* Boastfulness: oratorical *blow.* 6 Time to get the breath; the act of getting the breath when winded. [OE *blāwan.* Akin to BLAST.]

blow² (blō) *n.* 1 A sudden or violent stroke; thump; thwack. 2 A sudden misfortune. 3 A hostile or combative act: usually in the plural: coming to blows. — **at a** (or **one**) **blow** By a single stroke or action; all at one time. — **to come to blows** To start fighting one another. [ME *blaw*]

Synonyms: box, buffet, calamity, concussion, cuff, cut, disaster, hit, knock, lash, misfortune, rap, shock, stripe, stroke, thump. A *blow* is a sudden impact, as of a fist or a club; a *stroke* is a sweeping movement: the *stroke* of a sword, of an oar, of the arm in swimming. A *slap* is given with the open hand, a *lash* with a whip, thong, or the like; we speak also of the *cut* of a whip. A *cuff* is a somewhat sidelong *blow,* generally with the open hand: a *cuff* or *box* on the ear. In the metaphorical sense, *blow* is used for sudden, stunning, staggering *calamity* or sorrow; *stroke* for sweeping *disaster,* and also for sweeping achievement and success. We say a *stroke* of paralysis, or a *stroke* of genius. We speak of the *buffets* of adverse fortune. *Shock* is used of that which is at once sudden, violent, and prostrating; we speak of a *shock* of electricity, the *shock* of an amputation, a *shock* of surprise. Compare BEAT, MISFORTUNE.

blow³ (blō) *v.* **blew, blown, blow·ing** *v.t.* 1 To cause to bloom, as a plant. 2 To produce, as flowers. —*v.i.* 3 To bloom; blossom. —*n.* 1 The state of flowering. 2 A mass of blossoms; blossoms in general. [OE *blowan* blossom]

blow-back (blō′bak′) *n.* 1 The escape from the rear of a gun of gases formed by discharge of the projectile. 2 A defective cartridge or primer causing this escape.

blow-by (blō′bī′) *n.* 1 The exhaust fumes of a car, truck, etc. 2 A device on the car, etc., to reduce such fumes.

blow·er (blō′ər) *n.* 1 One who or that which blows. 2 A device for forcing a draft of air through a building, furnace, machinery, etc. 3 *Slang* A boaster.

blow·fish (blō′fish′) *n.* *pl.* **·fish** or **·fish·es** 1 The walleyed perch. 2 A swellfish or any like fish which can puff up its body.

blow·gun (blō'gun') n. A long tube through which a missile, as an arrow, may be blown by the breath.

blow–hard (blō'härd') Slang n. A braggart. — adj. Boastful.

blow·hole (blō'hōl') n. 1 Zool. The nasal openings in the heads of certain cetaceans. 2 Geol. A small crater formed on the surface of a lava flow for the escape of gas, etc. 3 A vent for the release of gas and bad air, as from mines. 4 Metall. A defect in a metal casting due to an air bubble caught during solidification. 5 A hole in the ice to which seals, whales, etc., come to breathe.

blow·ing (blō'ing) n. 1 The action of emitting or applying a current of air. 2 The act or sound of breathing, especially hard breathing, as of an animal. 3 Metall. An inrush of steam or gas through molten metal.

blown[1] (blōn) Past participle of BLOW[1]. — adj. 1 Winded from overexertion. 2 Spoiled, as food, by exposure, keeping, or oviposition; tainted. 3 Inflated or swollen with gas. 4 Made with a blowpipe: blown glass.

blown[2] (blōn) Past participle of BLOW[3]. — adj. In full flower or bloom.

blow·off (blō'ôf', -of') n. 1 The expelling of water, vapor, etc. 2 An apparatus for blowing off steam, water, etc., as from boilers.

blow·out (blō'out') n. 1 Electr. The explosive destruction of a fuse by an overcharge. 2 Slang A formal entertainment that becomes disorderly; also, an elaborate social function or, especially, an elaborate meal. 3 A puncture in or bursting of an automobile tire. 4 A flameout.

blow·pipe (blō'pīp') n. 1 A tube by which air or gas is blown through a flame for the purpose of fusing, heating, or melting something. 2 A blowtube (def. 3). 3 A blowgun.

blow·torch (blō'tôrch') n. An apparatus for vaporizing a combustible fluid under pressure and expelling it from a nozzle as a long, intensely hot flame: used for soldering, etc.

blow·tube (blō'tōōb', -tyōōb') n. 1 A pea-shooter. 2 A blowgun. 3 A tube used for blowing molten glass into the desired shape.

BLOWTORCH

blow–up (blō'up') n. 1 An explosion. 2 Colloq. Bankruptcy. 3 Colloq. Loss of self-control. 4 An enlargement, as of a photograph, page of print, etc. 5 A rapid increase in the intensity or spread of a fire.

blow·y (blō'ē) adj. blow·i·er, blow·i·est Windy.

blowz·y (blou'zē) adj. -i·er, -i·est 1 Slatternly or unkempt; slovenly. 2 Having a red or flushed face. Also **blows·y** (blou'zē), **blowzed** (blouzd). [<BLOWSE]

blub·ber[1] (blub'ər) v.t. 1 To disfigure, wet, or swell with weeping. 2 To utter sobbingly. — v.i. 3 Weep and sob noisily. [ME blubren] — **blub'ber·er** n. — **blub'ber·ing·ly** adv.

blub·ber[2] (blub'ər) n. 1 Zool. The layer of fat beneath the skin of a cetacean, used as a source of oil. 2 The act of blubbering. [ME bluber]

blub·ber·y (blub'ər·ē) adj. 1 Like blubber; very fat. 2 Swollen, as cheeks; protruding.

blu·cher (blōō'chər, -kər) n. 1 A half boot, or high shoe. 2 A shoe in which there is no front seam, the upper meeting above in two projecting flaps. [after BLÜCHER]

Blü·cher (blōō'chər, -kər, Ger. blü'khər), Gebhard Leberecht von, 1742-1819, German field marshal commanding Prussian army at Waterloo.

bludg·eon (bluj'ən) n. A short club, commonly loaded at one end, used as a weapon. — v.t. 1 To strike with or as with a bludgeon. 2 To coerce; bully. [Origin unknown]

blue (blōō) adj. blu·er, blu·est 1 Having the color of the clear sky. 2 Dismal; dreary; melancholy; despondent; also, depressing; discouraging: Things look blue. 3 Severe or Puritanic; strict: blue laws. 4 Faithful; genuine; sterling: He is true blue. 5 Livid, as from contusion, cold, or fear. 6 Devoted to literature; pedantic: said of women. 7 Denoting venous blood that shows through the skin. 8 Designating a flame, as of a candle, where the red glare is absent: said to be an omen of the presence of evil spirits. — n. 1

One of the chief colors of the spectrum, between green and violet; the color of the clear sky; azure. 2 The coloring matter or pigment used for imparting a blue color. 3 A blueprint. 4 One who wears blue clothing or insignia. 5 pl. See BLUES. 6 The bluish-gray winter coat of a deer. 7 A small butterfly of the family Lycaenidae. 8 A bluestocking. — out of the blue At an unexpected time and from an unsuspected source; completely unforeseen. — v.t. blued, blu·ing 1 To make blue. 2 To treat with bluing. [<OF bleu, ult. <Gmc.] — **blue'ly** adv. — **blue'ness** n.

Blue (blōō) n. 1 A soldier of the Federal Army in the American Civil War. Compare GRAY. 2 Brit. An athlete wearing the colors of his university in contests between Oxford (dark blue) and Cambridge (light blue). 3 Brit. A member of the Royal Horse Guard.

blue·bell (blōō'bel') n. 1 Any one of various plants that bear blue bell-shaped flowers. 2 The grape hyacinth. 3 The Virginia cowslip. 4 The wood hyacinth. 5 The harebell.

blue·ber·ry (blōō'ber'ē, -bər·ē) n. pl. -ries 1 A many-seeded, edible, blue or black American berry of the genus Vaccinium. 2 The plant that bears it. Compare HUCKLEBERRY.

blue·bird (blōō'bûrd') n. A small American passerine bird (genus Sialia), with a prevailing blue plumage, especially the eastern bluebird (S. sialis) common in North America, and the Mexican bluebird (S. mexicana).

blue blood 1 Blood of a supposed finer or purer kind. 2 Aristocratic lineage, character, or bearing. 3 A person of noble or aristocratic family. — **blue'-blood'ed** adj.

blue·book (blōō'bŏŏk') n. 1 A register of names of persons employed by the U.S. government. 2 A classified register, as of persons in high society. 3 Brit. A governmental publication, issued in blue covers.

blue chip 1 In poker, a blue-colored chip of high value. 2 A high-priced common-stock issue of a leading company that pays regular dividends. — **blue'-chip'** adj.

blue·coat (blōō'kōt') n. A person wearing a blue uniform, as a policeman; during the Civil War, a Union soldier. — **blue'-coat'ed** adj.

blue–col·lar (blōō'kol'ər) adj. Of, pertaining to, or designating employees engaged in physical or manual work that requires them to wear rough-textured, dark, or special clothing for protection or as a uniform. Compare WHITE-COLLAR.

blue devils 1 Great depression of spirits; despondency; morbid melancholy. 2 Delirium tremens.

blue–eyed (blōō'īd') adj. Having blue eyes.

blue·fish (blōō'fish') n. pl. ·fish or ·fish·es 1 A voracious food fish (Pomatomus saltatrix) common along the Atlantic Coast of the United States. 2 One of various other fishes of a bluish color, as the cunner.

blue·gill (blōō'gil') n. An edible American fresh-water sunfish (Lepomis pallidus) ranging from the Great Lakes to Florida and Mexico.

blue grass (blōō'gras', -gräs') n. 1 One of various grasses (genus Poa); esp., the Kentucky bluegrass (P. pratensis) with many running rootstocks. 2 Traditional country music, esp. of the southern United States.

Bluegrass Country A region of central Kentucky. Also the **Bluegrass**.

Bluegrass State Nickname of KENTUCKY.

blue–green algae (blōō'grēn') Primitive unicellular and unspecialized algae (class Cyanophyceae) in which the chlorophyll is mixed with a blue pigment: they give a scum to the surface of stagnant water.

blue grouse Any of several grouse of western North America (genus Dendrogapus), with dusky gray or blackish plumage: also called dusky grouse, sooty grouse.

blue·ing (blōō'ing) See BLUING.

blue·jack (blōō'jak') n. 1 Blue vitriol. 2 A small oak (Quercus cinerea) of the southern United States.

blue·jack·et (blōō'jak'it) n. An enlisted man in the U.S. Navy.

blue jay A small, crested corvine bird (Cyanocitta cristata) of eastern North America.

blue jeans Trousers made of blue denim or a similar fabric.

blue law A law proscribing or dictating private personal behavior in the interests of a narrow moral code; specifically, any such law com-

mon in the early American colonies; also, any law regulating the observance of Sunday as a day of rest.

blue·line (blōō'līn') n. Either of two blue lines across a hockey rink between the center of the rink and each goal.

blue moon A period of time considered as occurring when the moon is blue; hence, never. — once in a blue moon Seldom or hardly ever.

Blue Mountains 1 A wooded range in NE Oregon, highest point, 6,500 feet. 2 An extensive plateau west of Sydney, Australia; highest point, Bird's Rock, 3,871 feet.

blue movie, a pornographic motion picture.

blue–pen·cil (blōō'pen'səl) v.t. 1 To edit or revise (a manuscript) with or as with a blue pencil. 2 Colloq. To veto; disapprove; censor.

blue peter A square, blue flag with a white rectangle in the center. In the International Maritime Code it signifies the letter P. It is also raised to indicate that a ship is sailing within 24 hours. [<blue (re)peater]

blue plate 1 A dinner plate divided by ridges into sections for holding apart several kinds of food. 2 A main course, as of meat and vegetables, listed as a single item on a menu.

blue·print (blōō'print') n. 1 A ferricyanide positive photographic print from a transparent negative original. 2 A plan or drawing made by printing on sensitized paper, the drawing showing in white lines on a blue ground. 3 Any detailed plan. — v.t. To make a blueprint of.

blue ribbon 1 The badge of the Order of the Garter. 2 A badge indicating the first competitive prize; a prize; an honor. — **blue'-rib'bon·er**, **blue'-rib'bon·ist** n.

blue–rib·bon (blōō'rib'ən) adj. 1 Having high skill or intelligence. 2 Having special qualifications: a blue–ribbon jury.

Blue Ridge The SE portion of the Appalachian Mountains extending from Virginia into northern Georgia. Also **Blue Ridge Mountains**.

blues (blōōz) n. pl. 1 Downcast or depressed feeling; melancholy. 2 A type of popular song written in minor keys, and characterized by slow jazz rhythms and melancholy words. [Short for BLUE DEVILS]

blue–sky laws (blōō'skī') Laws enacted to prevent the sale of worthless stocks and bonds by corporations, etc., to the public.

blue–stock·ing (blōō'stok'ing) adj. Pertaining to or characteristic of a learned woman, or one affecting literary tastes. — n. A learned or literary woman.

blue·stone (blōō'stōn') n. 1 Blue vitriol. 2 A bluish sandstone, used for paving and building. 3 Any stone of a blue-gray color.

blue streak Colloq. 1 Speed as swift as lightning. 2 Light caused by swift motion. 3 Rapid and incessant language: to talk a blue streak.

blu·et (blōō'it) n. 1 One of various plants having blue flowers. 2 A delicate meadow flower of the madder family (Houstonia caerulea). 3 In England, a garden flower of the composite family. [<F bleuet, dim. of bleu blue]

blue vitriol A deep blue, crystalline copper sulfate, $CuSO_4 \cdot 5H_2O$, used in electric batteries, calico-printing, etc.: also called bluestone.

blue·weed (blōō'wēd') n. A rough, bristly herb, viper's-bugloss (Echium vulgare) of the borage family, with showy blue flowers, naturalized in the United States from Europe.

blue·wood (blōō'wŏŏd') n. A shrub or small tree (Condalia obovata) of the buckthorn family, of the SW United States.

bluff[1] (bluf) v.t. 1 To fool or deceive by putting on a bold front. 2 To frighten with empty threats. 3 In poker, to attempt to deceive (an opponent) by betting heavily on a poor hand. — v.i. 4 To pretend to knowledge, ability, strength, etc., which one does not have. — to bluff one's way To obtain (an object) by bluffing. — n. 1 Bold speech or manner intended to overawe, impress, or deceive. 2 Pretense; deceit. 3 A pretender. [? <Du. bluffen deceive, mislead] — **bluff'er** n.

bluff[2] (bluf) n. A bold, steep headland; a steep bank. — adj. 1 Blunt, frank, and hearty; rude or abrupt, but kindly. 2 Presenting an upright, broad, flattened front: said of a ship's bows or a water frontage. [? <Du. blaf flat, as in blaf aensicht broad flatface] — **bluff'ly** adv. — **bluff'ness** n.

Synonyms (adj.): abrupt, blunt, blustering, bold, brusk, coarse, discourteous, frank, impolite, inconsiderate, open, plain–spoken, rough, rude, uncivil, unmannerly. *Bluff* is a word of good meaning, as are *frank* and *open*. The *bluff* man talks and laughs loudly and freely, with no thought of annoying or giving pain to others. The *blunt* man often says things which he is perfectly aware are disagreeable, either from a defiant indifference to others' feelings, or from the pleasure of tormenting; *blunt*, in this use, is allied in meaning with *impolite, inconsiderate, rough, rude, uncivil,* and *unmannerly.* Compare BLUNT, CANDID. *Antonyms:* bland, courteous, genial, polished, polite, refined, reserved, urbane.

blu·ing (blōō′ing) *n.* **1** The giving of a blue tint to; also, the tint so given. **2** The blue coloring matter used in laundry work to counteract the yellow tinge of linen. Also **blue′ing.**

blu·ish (blōō′ish) *adj.* Somewhat blue. Also **blue′ish.** —**blu′ish·ness** *n.*

blun·der (blun′dər) *n.* A stupid mistake. See synonyms under ERROR. —*v.i.* **1** To proceed carelessly or awkwardly; stumble; bungle. **2** To make a stupid and awkward mistake; err egregiously. —*v.t.* **3** To confuse (two things); jumble. [ME *blondren* mix up, confuse. Akin to BLIND and BLEND.] —**blun′der·er** *n.* —**blun′der·ing·ly** *adv.*

blun·der·buss (blun′dər·bus) *n.* **1** An old-fashioned, short gun with large bore and flaring mouth. **2** A noisy blusterer. [Blend of BLUNDER and Du. *donderbus* thunder box]

BLUNDERBUSS *(def. 1)*

blung·er (blun′jər) *n.* **1** A wooden implement shaped like a spatula, but much larger, used in mixing clay with water in the manufacture of ceramics. **2** A pug mill. See under PUG[1].

blunt (blunt) *adj.* **1** Having a thick end or edge; not sharp or piercing. **2** Abrupt in manner; plain–spoken; unceremonious; brusk. **3** Slow of wit; dull. —*v.t. & v.i.* **1** To make or become blunt or dull. **2** To make or become less keen or poignant. [ME *blunt*; origin unknown] —**blunt′ly** *adv.* —**blunt′ness** *n.*

Synonyms (adj.): dull, edgeless, obtuse, pointless, round, smooth, thick. See BLUFF. *Antonyms:* acute, keen, pointed, sharp.

blur (blûr) *n.* **1** A smeared or indistinct marking or figure. **2** A blemish; also, a moral stain. See synonyms under BLEMISH. —*v.* **blurred, blur·ring** *v.t.* **1** To stain; blemish. **2** To make obscure or indistinct in outline. **3** To impair the perceptiveness of; render insensitive. —*v.i.* **4** To become obscure. **5** To smear; make blurs. —**blur′ry** *adj.*

blurb (blûrb) *n.* A publisher's statement concerning an author or a book, containing a description of its chief characteristics, frequently excessively commendatory. [Coined by Gelett Burgess]

blurt (blûrt) *v.t.* To utter abruptly; burst out with as if on impulse. See synonyms under BABBLE. —*n.* An ejaculatory utterance; abrupt exclamation. [? Blend of BLOW and SPURT]

blush (blush) *v.i.* **1** To redden, especially in the face; flush. **2** To become red or rosy, as flowers. **3** To feel shame or regret: usually with *at* or *for.* —*v.t.* **4** To make red. **5** To exhibit or make known by blushing: She *blushed* her pride. —*n.* **1** A reddening of the face from modesty, shame, or confusion. **2** A red or rosy tint; flush. **3** A glance; glimpse; view: obsolete except in the phrase *at* or *on first blush.* —*adj.* Colored like one blushing: a *blush* rose. [OE *blyscan* redden] —**blush′ful** *adj.* —**blush′ing** *adj.*

blush·er (blush′ər) *n.* **1** One who blushes. **2** A cosmetic to give the skin a rosy color.

blus·ter (blus′tər) *n.* **1** Boisterous talk or swagger. **2** A fitful and noisy blowing of the wind; blast. See synonyms under TUMULT. —*v.i.* **1** To blow gustily and with violence and noise, as the wind. **2** To utter loud, empty threats; swagger noisily. —*v.t.* **3** To utter noisily and boisterously. **4** To force or bully by blustering. [Cf. ON *blästr* blast, blowing] —**blus′ter·er** *n.*

blus·ter·ing (blus′tər·ing) *adj.* **1** Windy; disagreeable. **2** Noisy; swaggering. See synonyms under BLUFF, NOISY. —**blus′ter·ing·ly** *adv.*

blus·ter·y (blus′tər·ē) *adj.* Stormy; rough; violent; given to bluster. Also **blus′ter·ous, blus′·trous.**

B'nai B'rith (bə·nā′ brith′) A Jewish fraternal organization. [<Hebrew, sons of the covenant]

bo·a (bō′ə) *n. pl.* **bo·as** **1** Any of several non-venomous serpents (family *Boidae*) having vestigial hind legs in the form of stout spurs, including the anaconda and the python. **2** A tropical American snake (*Constrictor constrictor*), distinguished from a python and notable for the crushing power of its coils: also **boa constrictor.** **3** A long feather or fur neckpiece for women. [<L]

Bo·a·di·ce·a (bō′ə·də·sē′ə), died A.D. 62, British queen, suffered defeat by Romans and poisoned herself.

bo·an·thro·py (bō·an′thrə·pē) *n.* A form of dementia in which a man believes himself an ox. [<NL <Gk. *boanthrōpos* <*bous* bull, ox + *anthrōpos* man]

boar (bôr, bōr) *n. pl.* **boars** or **boar** **1** A male hog. **2** The native hog, or **wild boar**, of the Old World. **3** A medieval military engine. ◆ Homophone: bore. [OE *bār*] —**boar′ish** *n.*

board (bôrd, bōrd) *n.* **1** A flat piece of wood whose length is much greater than its width. **2** A table, spread for serving food; the food served. **3** Meals regularly furnished for pay. **4** An organized official body: a *board* of directors; also, a table at which the sessions of a council are held. **5** *pl.* The stage of a theater. **6** Pasteboard; a pasteboard bookcover. **7** A thin slab of wood, cardboard, or the like for a specific purpose: a *chessboard.* **8** *Naut.* **a** The deck or side of a vessel: *on board.* **b** The course followed by a vessel while tacking. **9** A wooden rack in the box office of a theater containing tickets: sometimes arranged according to the seating plan. **10** A bulletin board for notices of rehearsals. **11** *Telecom.* The control panel connected with all the microphones on a radio broadcast, and operated by the engineer in the control room. **12** The wooden enclosure of a hockey rink. —**binder's board** Board used by bookbinders; a single-ply pasteboard made from a base stock of kiln- or plate-dried mixed papers and ranging in thickness from .03 to .30 of an inch. —**on board** On or in a vessel; also, on or in a conveyance: He jumped *on board* the train. —**to go by the board 1** To go over the ship's side: said of a mast broken off short. **2** To go to utter wreck or ruin. —**to tread the boards** To appear as an actor. —*v.t.* **1** To cover or enclose with boards. **2** To furnish with meals or meals and lodging for pay. **3** To place (someone) where meals are provided, as in a boarding school. **4** *Naut.* To come alongside or go on board of (a ship), usually for hostile purposes. **5** To enter, as a ship or train. **6** *Obs.* To approach; accost. —*v.i.* **7** To take meals or meals and lodging. **8** *Naut.* To tack. [OE *bord*]

board·er (bôr′dər, bōr′-) *n.* **1** A person who receives regular meals, or meals and lodging at a fixed place, for pay. **2** One detailed to board an enemy's ship.

board·ing (bôr′ding, bōr′-) *n.* **1** Boards collectively; a structure of boards. **2** The obtaining of food, or food and lodging, regularly for pay. **3** The act of going on board a ship, a train, etc. **4** The operation of softening leather and developing the grain by rubbing the surfaces together. **5** The shaping of hosiery on heated metal boards.

boarding school A school in which pupils are boarded: opposed to *day school.*

board of trade 1 An association of merchants, bankers, etc., to promote business interests. **2** In England, a special committee of the privy council on commerce.

board school In England, an undenom-inational elementary school having a parliamentary grant andaged by a school board.

board·walk (bôrd′wôk′, bōrd′-) *n.* A promenade along a beach.

boar·ish (bôr′ish, bōr′ish) *adj.* **1** Pertaining to or characteristic of a boar. **2** Swinish; rough; brutal. —**boar′ish·ly** *adv.* —**boar′ish·ness** *n.*

boast[1] (bōst) *v.i.* **1** To vaunt or extol the deeds or abilities of oneself or of another; brag. —*v.t.* **2** To vaunt or extol (deeds or abilities); brag about. **3** To be proud to possess; take pride in: The school *boasts* a new laboratory. See synonyms under FLAUNT. —*n.* **1** A boastful speech. **2** A source of pride. [ME *bosten*; origin unknown]

boast[2] (bōst) *v.t.* **1** In masonry, to pare, as stone, with a broad chisel. **2** In sculpture, to block out, as a statue, before finishing in detail. [Origin uncertain]

boast·er (bōs′tər) *n.* **1** One who exults. **2** A boasting chisel.

boast·ful (bōst′fəl) *adj.* Characterized by or addicted to boasting. —**boast′ful·ly** *adv.* —**boast′ful·ness** *n.*

boast·ing[1] (bōs′ting) *adj.* Exulting; bragging; ostentatious. —**boast′ing·ly** *adv.*

boast·ing[2] (bōs′ting) *n.* The dressing of stone with a boaster.

boat (bōt) *n.* **1** A small, open watercraft propelled by oars, sails, or an engine. **2** *Colloq.* Any watercraft of any size, ranging from a rowboat to an ocean liner. **3** Any article, as a dish, resembling a boat. —**to be in the same boat** To be equally involved; to run the same risks; in the same situation. —*v.i.* **1** To travel by boat. **2** To go boating for pleasure. —*v.t.* **3** To transport or place in a boat: to *boat* oars. [OE *bāt*]

boat·a·ble (bō′tə·bəl) *adj.* **1** Navigable by boats. **2** Transportable by boat.

boat·age (bō′tij) *n.* **1** Carriage by boat, or the charge for such carriage. **2** The carrying capacity of a ship's boats.

boat·house (bōt′hous′) *n.* A building along the water used for storing boats.

boat·ing (bō′ting) *n.* **1** Boats collectively. **2** use of transportation by boats, etc.; rowing; cruising; sailing.

boat·load (bōt′lōd′) *n.* **1** The full amount that a boat can hold. **2** The load carried by a boat.

boat·man (bōt′mən) *n. pl.* **·men** **1** One who manages, rows, or works on a boat. **2** An aquatic insect (family *Corixidae*) of which one pair of legs is long and oarlike: also **boat bug.** **3** An aquatic insect (family *Notonectidae*) that swims on its back. —**boat′man·ship** *n.*

boat·swain (bō′sən, *rarely* bōt′swān′) *n.* **1** A subordinate officer of a vessel, who has general charge of the rigging, anchors, etc., and whose business it is to pipe the crew to duty with his whistle, which is his badge. **2** On a fighting ship, a warrant officer, trained in seamanship. Also spelled *bosun.*

boatswain's chair A short board slung by rope, used as a seat by a seaman working aloft, and also by painters on the outside of houses.

boat·tail (bōt′tāl′) *n.* A tapering, streamlined rear end of a shell or bomb, providing greater range and accuracy.

Bo·az (bō′az) A Bethlehemite who married Ruth. *Ruth* iii 10.

bob[1] (bob) *n.* **1** In fishing, a cork or float on a line; a set or gang of fish hooks; a grapple. **2** A large, ball-shaped bait for eels, catfish, etc., made by stringing angleworms, rags, etc. **3** A grub or worm used for bait. **4** A small, pendent object, as on a pendulum. **5** A jerky bow or curtsy; any short, jerky movement. **6** A style of haircut for women or children cut short to fall about the ears. **7** The docked tail of a horse. **8** *sing. & pl. Brit. Colloq.* A shilling. **9** *Scot.* A bunch; cluster; nosegay. **10** A short, stout sleigh–runner; also, a bobsled. **11**

BOATSWAIN'S CHAIR

The refrain of a song. —*v.* **bobbed, bob·bing** *v.t.* **1** To move up and down: to *bob* the head. **2** To effect by moving up and down: to *bob* a curtsy. **3** To cut short, as hair. —*v.i.* **4** To move up and down with an irregular motion. **5** To curtsy. **6** To fish (for eels) with a bob. — **to bob up** To appear or emerge suddenly. [ME *bobbe* a hanging cluster; origin uncertain] — **bob′ber** *n.*

bob² (bob) *v.t.* **bobbed, bob·bing** To strike lightly and quickly; tap. —*n. Obs.* A rap or blow; a shake or jog. [ME *bobben*; origin unknown]

bob³ (bob) *v.t. Obs.* **1** To mock. **2** To delude; cheat. —*n.* A trick; also, a jeer or taunt; jibe. [OF *bober*]

bobbed (bobd) *adj.* **1** Cut short, as the hair of a child or of a woman. **2** Docked, as a horse's tail.

bob·bin (bob′in) *n.* **1** A slender spool to hold weft or thread in spinning, weaving, or in machine sewing. **2** A small piece of wood attached to the end of a latchstring. **3** A small pin or spool used in making bobbin lace to steady the threads. **4** A cord or braid used in haberdashery. [< F *bobine*]

bob·bi·net (bob′ə·net′) *n.* An open reticulated fabric; a machine-made lace.

bobbin lace A hand-made lace in which several bobbins are used to form a pattern, as on a pillow. Also *pillow lace.*

bob·ble (bob′əl) *n.* **1** *Brit. Colloq.* A slight swell or sea. **2** *U.S. Slang* A fumble or miss. —*v.t.* **·bled, ·bling** *U.S. Slang* To mishandle; drop: He *bobbled* the ball. [Freq. of BOB¹]

bob·by (bob′ē) *n. pl.* **·bies** *Brit. Colloq.* A policeman. [after Sir Robert (Bobby) Peel]

bobby pin A metal hairpin so shaped as to clasp and hold the hair tightly: used with bobbed hair. Also **bobbie pin.**

bobby socks *Colloq.* Ankle-length socks worn by girls.

bob·cat (bob′kat′) *n.* The American lynx.

bob·o·link (bob′ə·lingk) *n.* An American thrushlike singing bird (*Dolichonyx oryzivorus*), the male having in spring black plumage with white or buff markings: also called *ricebird.* [Imit.; from its call]

bob·sled (bob′sled′) *n.* **1** Either of two short sleds or pairs of runners connected tandem by a top plank. **2** The entire vehicle so formed. Also *bob.* —*v.i.* To go coasting on a bobsled. Also **bob′sleigh′** (-slā′).

bob·tail (bob′tāl′) *n.* **1** A short tail or a tail cut short. **2** An animal with such a tail. **3** The rabble; common herd. **4** Dishonorable discharge from military service. —*adj.* Having the tail docked; inadequate; incomplete. —*v.t.* To cut the tail of; dock. —**bob′tailed′** *adj.*

bob·white (bob′hwīt′) *n.* The North American quail (*Colinus virginianus*); also, its cry. [Imit.; from its call]

Boc·cac·ci·o (bō·kä′chē·o, *Ital.* bôk·kät′chô), **Giovanni**, 1313–75, Italian writer and poet, author of the *Decameron.*

boc·cie (boch′ē) *n.* An Italian variety of lawn bowling, played on a small court. Also **boc·ci** (boch′ē, *Ital.* bôt′chē), **boc·cia** (boch′ə, *Ital.* bôt′chä) [< *Ital. bocce* bowls, pl. of *boccia* ball]

bock beer (bok) An extra strong beer brewed in the winter and served in early spring. Also **bock.** [< G *bockbier* < *Eimbockbier,* from *Einbeck,* town in Hanover]

bode¹ (bōd) Archaic past tense and past participle of BIDE.

bode² (bōd) *v.* **bod·ed, bod·ing** *v.t.* **1** To be a token of; presage, as good, evil, etc. **2** *Obs.* To predict; foretell. —*v.i.* **3** To presage good or ill. See synonyms under AUGUR. [OE *bodian* announce] —**bode′ment** *n.*

bo·de·ga (bō·dē′gə, *Sp.* bō·tha′gä) *n.* A wine shop or warehouse. [< Sp.]

bo·dhi·satt·va (bō′di·sat′wə) *n.* In Buddhism, a candidate for Buddhaship; one who, by his virtues and meditations, is held to be a future Buddha or savior of the world. [< Skt. < *bodhi* knowledge + *sattva* essence]

bod·ice (bod′is) *n.* **1** The waist of a woman's dress. **2** A woman's ornamental laced waist. **3** *Obs.* A corset laced in front. [Var. of *bodies,* pl. of BODY]

bod·ied (bod′ēd) *adj.* Having a body: usually with an adjective forming a compound word: *full-bodied.*

bod·i·less (bod′i·lis) *adj.* Having no body; without material form; incorporeal.

bod·i·ly (bod′ə·le) *adj.* **1** Pertaining to the body. **2** Corporeal; material. See synonyms under PHYSICAL. —*adv.* **1** In the body; in person. **2** All together; in one mass; wholly; completely.

bod·ing (bō′ding) *adj.* Portending evil; ominous. —*n.* An omen; presage, especially of evil. —**bod′ing·ly** *adv.*

bod·kin (bod′kin) *n.* **1** An instrument for drawing tape through a hem. **2** A pointed instrument for piercing holes in cloth, etc. **3** A pin for fastening the hair. **4** A pointed instrument for picking type from a form. **5** *Obs.* A stiletto. [ME *boydekin* dagger; origin unknown]

bod·le (bod′l) *n. Scot.* **1** An old Scotch copper coin worth about one third of a cent; the smallest coin. **2** A trifle. Also spelled *boddle.* [? after *Bothwell,* a Scotch mintmaster]

Bod·lei·an (bod·lē′ən, bod′lē·ən) *adj.* Of or pertaining to the library of the University of Oxford, England, restored in the seventeenth century by Sir Thomas Bodley, 1544–1613. Also **Bod·ley′an.**

bod·y (bod′ē) *n. pl.* **bod·ies** **1** The entire physical part of a man or other animal, living or dead. **2** A corpse, cadaver, or carcass. **3** The trunk, or main part, of an animal or person, distinguished from the limbs and head. **4** A person; an individual: *somebody.* **5** The principal part or mass of anything. **6** The main part of a legal document as distinguished from the recitals and other introductory parts. **7** The box of a vehicle. **8** A mass of matter: the celestial *bodies.* **9** *Geom.* A solid. **10** A collection of persons, things, facts, or the like, as one whole. **11** Opacity, density, or consistency; substance: a wine with *body.* **12** That part of a garment that covers the body; waist. **13** Matter, as opposed to spirit. **14** *Printing* The size or depth of type, as distinguished from its face or style. **15** *Naut.* The hull of a ship; also, a section of it when seen from different points: the fore *body.* **16** *Aeron.* The supporting frame of an airplane, where the planes are fixed, and on which are the mechanical apparatus, seats, etc.; fuselage. —*v.t.* **bod·ied, bod·y·ing** **1** To furnish with or as with a body. **2** To exhibit in bodily form; represent. [OE *bodig*]

Synonyms (noun): ashes, carcass, clay, corpse, dust, form, frame, remains, system, trunk. *Body* denotes the entire physical structure, considered as a whole, of man or animal; *form* looks upon it as a thing of shape and outline, perhaps of beauty; *frame* regards it as supported by its bony framework; *system* views it as an assemblage of many related and harmonious organs. *Body, form, frame,* and *system* may be either dead or living; *clay* and *dust* are ordinarily used only of the dead. *Corpse* is the plain technical word for a dead body still retaining its unity; *remains* may be used after any lapse of time. *Carcass* applies only to the *body* of an animal, or of a human being regarded with contempt and loathing. Compare COMPANY, MASS. *Antonyms:* intellect, intelligence, mind, soul, spirit.

bod·y·guard (bod′ē·gärd′) *n.* A guard of the person, as of a king; also, a retinue.

body politic The state or nation as an organized political body; the people, taken collectively.

bod·y-snatch·er (bod′ē-snach′ər) *n.* One who illegally and surreptitiously removes bodies from the grave; a grave-robber; resurrectionist. —**bod′y-snatch′ing** *n.*

Boer (bōr, bôr, boor) *n.* A Dutch colonist, or person of Dutch descent in South Africa. [< Du., farmer]

bog (bog, bôg) *n.* Wet and spongy ground; marsh; morass. —*v.t. & v.i.* **bogged, bog·ging** To sink or stick in a bog: often with *down.* [< Irish, soft] —**bog′gish** *adj.* —**bog′gish·ness** *n.*

bo·gan (bō′gən) *n. Canadian* A backwater or tributary.

bog asphodel Any species of *Narthecium* of the lily family; especially, the American *N. americanum* and *N. californicum,* and the Old World Lancashire asphodel (*N. ossifragum*).

bo·gey¹ (bō′ge) *n. pl.* **bo·geys** In golf: **1** An estimated standard score. **2** One stroke over par on a hole. Also **bo′gie.** [after Col. *Bogey,* an imaginary partner who plays a faultless game]

bo·gey² (bō′ge) *n.* Bogy¹.

bog·gle (bog′əl) *v.* **bog·gled, bog·gling** *v.i.* **1** To hesitate, as from doubt or scruples; shrink back. **2** To start with fright, as a horse. **3** To equivocate; dissemble. **4** To work in a clumsy manner; fumble. —*v.t.* **1** To make a botch of; bungle. —*n.* **1** The act of shying, as of a horse. **2** A scruple; objection; difficulty. **3** *Colloq.* A bungle. [< BOGLE] —**bog′gler** *n.*

bog·gy (bog′ē, bôg′ē) *adj.* **bog·gi·er, bog·gi·est** Swampy; miry. —**bog′gi·ness** *n.*

bo·gie¹ (bō′ge) *n.* **1** A railway truck mounted on one axle and two wheels or two axles and four wheels. **2** One of the small rollers or wheels that distribute the weight of a tractor or tank along the track. Also **bo′gy.** [< dial. E. (Northern), a kind of truck or cart]

bo·gie² (bō′ge) See BOGY¹.

bog iron An impure ferruginous deposit formed in swampy or marshy ground by the oxidizing action of bacteria and algae.

bo·gle (bō′gal) *n.* A hobgoblin or bogy; bugbear. Also **bog·gle** (bog′əl). [? Akin to BUG²]

bog oak Wood of the trunks of oaks, sunk and preserved in the peat bogs.

bog orchid **1** The addermouth. **2** A European orchid (*Malaxis paludosa*) having small green flowers. Also **bog orchis.**

bog ore An iron hydroxide ore, as limonite, from marshy places.

Bo·go·tá (bō′gə·tä′) **1** The capital of Colombia. **2** A river in central Colombia, flowing 120 miles SW to the Magdalena: also *Funza.*

bog·trot·ter (bog′trot′ər, bôg′-) *n.* **1** One who trots over or lives among bogs. **2** Humorously, an Irish peasant.

bo·gus (bō′gəs) *n. U.S.* **1** An apparatus used in making counterfeit coins. **2** Counterfeit money. **3** Any counterfeit article. —*adj.* Counterfeit; spurious; fake. [Origin unknown]

bog·wood (bog′wood′, bôg′-) *n.* Wood of trees buried and preserved in peat bogs; bog oak.

bo·gy¹ (bō′ge) *n. pl.* **bo·gies** A goblin; bugbear. Also **bo′gie, bo′gey.** [? Akin to BUG²] —**bo′gey·ism** *n.*

bo·gy² (bō′ge) See BOGIE¹.

bo·hea (bō·hē′) *n.* A black tea: once applied to the choicest picking, then to black tea, now to the poorest grade. [from the *Wu-i* Hills (pronounced bōō′ē) of China]

Bo·he·mi·a (bō·hē′mē·ə) A historic province of western Czechoslovakia; with Moravia and Silesia comprising one of the two constituent states (Slovakia is the other) of Czechoslovakia; 20,102 square miles; capital Prague; formerly a kingdom: German *Böhmen,* Czech *Cechy.*

Bo·he·mi·an (bō·hē′mē·ən) *adj.* **1** Relating to Bohemia. **2** Leading the life of a Bohemian; unconventional. —*n.* **1** An inhabitant of Bohemia. **2** A gipsy. **3** A person, usually of artistic or literary tastes, who lives in a more or less unconventional manner: also **bo·he′mi·an.** **4** A former name for the Czech dialect of Czechoslovakian. —**Bo·he′mi·an·ism** *n.*

Bohr (bōr), **Niels**, 1885–1962, Danish physicist.

Bohr theory *Physics* The theory that the spectrum lines of an atom are indicators of the energy changes produced in it by the jumps of electrons from one orbit to another.

bo·hunk (bō′hungk) *n. U.S. Slang* A foreign-born laborer, especially one of central European extraction: also called *hunky:* a prejudicial term. [< BO(HEMIAN) + HUNG(ARIAN)]

boil¹ (boil) *v.i.* **1** To be agitated, as a liquid, by gaseous bubbles rising to the surface; also said of the container in reference to the contents: The kettle *boils.* **2** To reach the boiling point. **3** To undergo the action of a boiling liquid, as meat. **4** To be agitated; to seethe: The water *boiled* with sharks. **5** To be stirred or agitated, as by violent emotion. —*v.t.* **6** To bring to the boiling point. **7** To cook or cleanse by boiling: to *boil* rice; to *boil* shirts. **8** To separate by means of evaporation caused by boiling: to *boil* sugar. —**to boil away** To evaporate in boiling. —**to boil down** **1** To reduce in bulk by boiling. **2** To condense; edit. —**to boil over** **1** To overflow (the container) while boiling. **2** To become enraged. —*n.* **1** The act or state of boiling. **2** An immersion in boiling water. [< OF *boillir* < L *bullire* boil]

boil² (boil) *n. Pathol.* A purulent and painful nodule of bacterial origin lodged beneath the skin; a furuncle. [OE *byl, byle*]

boil·er (boi'lər) *n.* **1** A utensil in which food or liquid is boiled. **2** A closed vessel, usually cylindrical, used in generating steam, as for motive power. **3** A receptacle for hot–water storage; a hot–water tank. **4** One who boils.

boil·er·plate (boi'lər·plāt') *n.* **1** Iron plate for making boilers. **2** *U.S.* Material in stereotype or mat form sent out to newspapers; filler.

boiler scale Layers of calcium sulfate and other mineral wastes deposited by the action of water on the inner surfaces of boilers.

boil·ing (boi'ling) *n.* **1** The state or process of ebullition. **2** A thing boiled or to be boiled.

boiling point The temperature at which the vapor pressure in a liquid equals the external pressure; at normal atmospheric pressure the boiling point of water is 212° F.

Boi·se (boi'zē, -sē) The capital of Idaho, in the SW part of the State.

boise·rie (bwäz'rē) *n.* Woodwork; specifically, carved wall paneling characteristic of 17th and 18th century French interiors. [<F]

bois·ter·ous (bois'tər·əs) *adj.* **1** Vociferous and rude; tempestuous; unrestrained. **2** *Obs.* Rough; coarse; big; rank. See synonyms under NOISY, TURBULENT. [ME *boistous*; origin unknown] — **bois'ter·ous·ly** *adv.* — **bois'ter·ous·ness** *n.*

bo·la (bō'lə) *n.* A missile weapon, consisting of balls fastened to cords and used in South America in hunting cattle and large game. Also **bo·las** (bō'ləs). [<Sp., a ball]

BOLA

bo·lar (bō'lər) *adj.* Pertaining to or consisting of bole; clayey. Also **bol·ar·y** (bō'lər·ē).

bold (bōld) *adj.* **1** Possessing, showing, or requiring courage; audacious; fearless; spirited. **2** Presuming; forward; brazen. **3** Regardless of conventions; striking; vigorous; as language. **4** Clear; prominent; in high relief: *bold* sculpture, *bold* outlines. **5** Abrupt; steep, as a cliff. **6** Having a swift, strong current: a *bold* stream. See synonyms under BLUFF, BRAVE, IMMODEST, IMPUDENT. — **to make bold** To take the liberty; venture. [OE *bald*] — **bold'ly** *adv.* — **bold'ness** *n.*

bold·face (bōld'fās') *n.* **1** An impudent person. **2** *Printing* A type in which the lines have been thickened to give a very black impression, often used for emphasis: also called *blackface.* — **bold'–faced'** *adj.*

bole¹ (bōl) *n.* The trunk of a tree. ♦ Homophone: *bowl.* [<ON *bolr*]

bole² (bōl) *n.* A fine, compact, soft clay. ♦ Homophone: *bowl.* [<LL *bolus* <Gk. *bōlos* clod of earth]

bole³ (bōl) *n. Scot. & Irish* A small rectangular recess in the wall of a room, or an unglazed aperture in a wall; a locker. ♦ Homophone: *bowl.*

bo·lec·tion (bō·lek'shən) *n. Archit.* A molding following the outside edge of a panel and projecting beyond the face of the frame in which the panel is held: also called *bilection.* [Origin unknown]

bo·le·ro (bō·lâr'ō) *n. pl.* **·ros 1** A short jacket open at the front, worn over a blouse or the like. **2** A Spanish dance, usually accompanied by castanets; also, the music for it. [<Sp.]

bo·le·tus (bō·lē'təs) *n.* One of a genus (*Boletus*) of fleshy, quick–rotting fungi of the family *Polyporaceae*, widely distributed in the United States. [<L *boletus* <Gk. *bōlitēs* mushroom]

Bol·eyn (bŏŏl'in), **Anne**, 1507–36, second wife of Henry VIII of England; beheaded. Also spelled *Bullen.*

bo·lide (bō'līd, -lid) *n.* A brilliant shooting star; a meteor, especially one that explodes. [<F <L *bolis, -idis* meteor <Gk. *bōlis* missile <*ballein* hurl]

bo·liv·i·a (bə·liv'ē·ə) *n.* A soft woolen or worsted pile fabric, with finish resembling velvet or plush. [from *Bolivia*]

Bo·liv·i·a (bə·liv'ē·ə) A republic of South America; 412,777 square miles; constitutional and judiciary capital, Sucre; de facto capital and chief city, La Paz. — **Bo·liv'i·an** *adj.* & *n.*

boll (bōl) *n.* **1** *Bot.* A round pod or seed capsule, as of flax or cotton. **2** A knob. — *v.i.* To form pods. [Var. of BOWL¹]

bol·lard (bol'ərd) *n.* **1** *Naut.* A vertical post, as on a wharf, to which to attach a hawser. **2** *Aeron.* A similar post located on the hull or float of a seaplane for mooring purposes. [? <BOLE¹ + -ARD]

bol·lix (bol'iks) *v.t.* **·lixed, ·lix·ing** *Slang* To bungle; botch; make a mess of: usually with *up.* [Alter. of earlier *ballocks* testicles, dim. pl. of BALL]

boll weevil A grayish curculio (*Anthonomus grandis*) that infests and destroys cotton bolls. For illustration see under INSECTS (injurious).

boll·worm (bōl'wûrm') *n.* **1** The very destructive larva of a pale–brown moth (*Platyedra gossypiella*) that feeds on cotton bolls. **2** The corn–ear worm.

bo·lo (bō'lō) *n. pl.* **·los** (-lōz) A heavy, single–edged, cutlaslike weapon used by natives of the Philippine Islands. [<Sp. <Visayan]

Bo·lo·gna (bō·lō'nyä) A city of north central Italy. — **Bo·lo·gnese** (bō'lə·nēz', -nēs') *adj.* & *n.*

bo·lo·graph (bō'lə·graf, -gräf) *Physics* A continuous automatic record of the temperature indications of the bolometer. Compare BOLOMETER. [<Gk. *bolē* ray of light + -GRAPH] — **bo'lo·graph'ic** *adj.* — **bo'lo·graph'i·cal·ly** *adv.* — **bo·log·ra·phy** (bō·log'rə·fē) *n.*

bo·lom·e·ter (bō·lom'ə·tər) *n. Physics* An instrument for the measurement of minute differences of radiant energy by changes in the electric resistance of a blackened conductor exposed to it. [<Gk. *bolē* ray of light + -METER] — **bo·lo·met·ric** (bō'lə·met'rik) *adj.*

bo·lo·ney (bə·lō'nē) See BALONEY. Also **bo·lo'ny.**

Bol·she·vik (bōl'shə·vik, bol'-) *n. pl.* **Bol·she·viks** or **Bol·she·vi·ki** (bōl'shə·vē'kē, bol'-) **1** A member of the radical and dominant branch of the Russian Social Democratic Party: since 1918, called the *Communist Party.* Compare MENSHEVIK. **2** Loosely, any radical or any communist. Also **bol'she·vik.** [<Russian *bolshe* greater; referring to the majority group in the party]

Bol·she·vism (bōl'shə·viz'əm, bol'-) *n.* **1** The Marxian doctrines and policies of the Bolsheviki. **2** A government based on these policies. Also **bol'she·vism.** — **Bol'she·vist** *n.* — **Bol'she·vis'tic** *adj.*

bol·son (bōl'sən) *n. SW U.S.* A low, enclosed basin of ground surrounded by hills. [<Sp. *bolsón,* aug. of *bolso* purse]

bol·ster (bōl'stər) *n.* **1** A long, narrow pillow as wide as a bed. **2** A pad used as a support or for protection. **3** Anything shaped like or used as a bolster. **4** *Archit.* **a** The lateral part of the volute of an Ionic capital. **b** A crosspiece of an arch centering, running from rib to rib and bearing the voussoirs. **5** *Mech.* A steel block which supports the die in a punching machine. — *v.t.* **1** To support with a pillow. **2** To prop up, as something ready to fall: with *up.* **3** To furnish with padding. [OE] — **bol'ster·er** *n.*

bolt¹ (bōlt) *n.* **1** A sliding bar or piece for fastening a door, etc. **2** A pin or rod used for holding anything in its place. **3** An arrow. **4** A long cylindrical shot for a cannon, or the like. **5** Anything coming suddenly; as, a *thunderbolt.* **6** A refusal to support a party, candidate, or policy. **7** A sudden start, departure, or spring. **8** A roll of cloth containing a certain number of yards, usually 30 or 40; also, a roll of wallpaper. **9** *Obs.* A shackle. See synonyms under LOCK. — **a bolt from the blue** A sudden and wholly unexpected event. — **to shoot one's bolt** To do one's utmost; perform at the top of one's ability. — *v.i.* **1** To move, go, or spring suddenly: usually with *out* or *from: He bolted* from the room. **2** To start suddenly; break from control and run away. **3** *U.S.* To break away, as from a political party; refuse to support party policy. — *v.t.* **4** To fasten with or as with bolts. **5** *U.S.* To break away from, as a political party. **6** To chew and swallow hurriedly; gulp; as, food. **7** To arrange or roll into bolts, as cloth. **8** To blurt out; say impulsively or hastily. — *adv.* Like an arrow; swiftly; straight. [OE *bolt* an arrow for a crossbow, the bolt of a door]

bolt² (bōlt) *n.* A rotating cylindrical or prismoidal frame, covered with silk or the like with very regular meshes, for sifting flour. — *v.t.* **1** To sift; pass through a sieve. **2** To examine as by sifting. [<OF *bulter, buleter* sift <*burete,* dim. of *bure* coarse cloth]

bolt·er¹ (bōl'tər) *n.* **1** One who or that which bolts. **2** A horse given to shying or running away. **3** A person who refuses to support a political nomination.

bolt·er² (bōl'tər) *n.* A sifter for meal or flour.

bolt·head (bōlt'hed') *n.* **1** *Chem.* A spherical glass vessel with a long, narrow neck: also called *matrass, receiver.* **2** The head of a bolt.

bolt upright In an erect position.

bo·lus (bō'ləs) *n. pl.* **bo·lus·es 1** A large pill. **2** Any dose hard to swallow. **3** Any rounded mass. [<L <Gk. *bōlos* clod of earth, lump]

Bo·ma (bō'mə) A port at the mouth of the Congo.

bomb (bom) *n.* **1** *Mil.* A hollow projectile containing explosive, incendiary, or chemical material to be discharged by concussion or by a time fuze. **2** Any similar receptacle, of any shape, containing an explosive: a dynamite *bomb.* **3** *Geol.* A roughly shaped spherical or ellipsoidal mass of lava hurled from a volcano during an explosive eruption. **4** An unexpected occurrence. **5** *U.S. Slang* A complete failure; flop; dud; disaster. **6** *Football* A long forward pass. See also GRENADE, MINE, SHELL. — **aerial bomb** Any bomb dropped from an airplane. — **atomic bomb** A bomb of formidable destructive power, utilizing the energy released by the continuing fission of atomic nuclei, especially those of radioactive elements, as uranium: also called **A–bomb, atom bomb.** — **chemical bomb** A bomb which discharges noxious chemicals, fumes, and the like. — **demolition bomb** A high–explosive bomb used to destroy buildings and installations. — **depth bomb** A drum–shaped bomb which explodes under water at a desired depth: used against underwater mines and submarines: also called *ashcan; depth charge.* — **fragmentation bomb** A shrapnel–like bomb for use against ground troops and personnel. — **hung bomb** A bomb that fails to be released from an aircraft. — **incendiary bomb** A bomb filled with any of various inflammable materials as gasoline, oil, powdered magnesium, etc. — **robot bomb** A high–explosive bomb equipped with a jet–propulsion engine or rocket mechanism permitting it to travel under its own power after being launched on the target: also called *guided missile, pilotless plane.* Also **buzz bomb, flying bomb, rocket bomb.** — *v.t.* **1** To attack or destroy with or as with bombs. — *v.i.* **2** *U.S. Slang* To fail utterly. [<F *bombe* <Ital. *bomba* <L *bombus* loud sound <Gk. *bombos* hollow noise]

AERIAL BOMB
a. Metal vanes.
b. Steel walls.
c. Bursting charge.
d. Booster charge.
e. Fuze.
f. Steel base.

bom·bard (bom·bärd') *v.t.* **1** To attack with bombs or shells. **2** To attack or press as with bombs: to *bombard* with questions. **3** To expose (substances) to the effect of radiation or to the impact of high–energy atomic particles. — *n.* (bom'bärd) **1** The earliest form of cannon. **2** A leather liquor jug; blackjack. [<MF *bombarder* < *bombarde* a cannon]—**bom·bard'er** *n.* — **bom·bard'ment** *n.*

BOMBARD (*n. def. 1*)

bom·bar·dier (bom'bər·dir') *n.* **1** *Mil.* **a** The member of the crew of a bomber who operates the bombsight and releases bombs. **b** An artilleryman in charge of mortars, etc. **2** A ground beetle *(Brachinus tscherniki)* which, on irritation, ejects an acrid liquid. [<F]

bom·bar·don (bom'bər·dən, bom·bär'dən) *n.* **1** A wind instrument of the bassoon type, used as a bass for an oboe or hautboy; a bass saxhorn. **2** A pedal reed stop on the organ with 16-foot tone. [<Ital. *bombardone*]

bom·bast (bom'bast) *n.* **1** Grandiloquent language; rant. **2** *Obs.* Stuffing; filling. [<OF *bombace* cotton padding <LL *bombax, -acis,* earlier *bambax* cotton <LGk.*bambax* (infl. by Gk. *bambyx* silk) <Gk. *pambax*<Persian *pambak* cotton]

bom·bas·tic (bom·bas'tik) *adj.* Inflated; grandiloquent. Also **bom·bas'ti·cal. —bom·bas'·ti·cal·ly** *adv.*

Bom·bay (bom·bā') **1** A constituent state of western India; 115,570 square miles; formerly a presidency of British India. **2** Its capital, a port on the Arabian Sea.

Bombay hemp Sunn.

bom·ba·zine (bom'bə·zēn', bom'bə·zēn) *n.* A fine twilled fabric usually with silk or artificial silk warp and worsted filling. Also **bom'ba·sine'.** [<F *bombasin* <LL *bombasinum* < *bombax* cotton. See BOMBAST.]

bomb bay A compartment in military aircraft in which bombs are carried and from which they are dropped.

bombe (bônb) *n.* A confection in the form of a ball; especially, a mold containing different kinds of ice-cream. [<F, bomb; so called from its shape]

bombed (bombd) *adj. U.S. Slang* Drunk.

bomb·er (bom'ər) *n.* **1** A soldier who throws bombs. **2** An airplane employed in bombing. **—dive bomber** A fast, bomb-carrying airplane which, with motors running, dives toward its target and drops its bombs at close range. **—medium bomber** An airplane equipped to carry a moderately heavy bomb load over a moderate distance.

bom·bo (bom'bō) *n. Austral. Slang* Cheap wine.

bom·bo·ra (bom·bôr'ə) *n. Austral.* A dangerous area of broken water, as near the base of a cliff with submerged rocks.Also **bom·boor'a** (-bŏŏr'ə). [<native Australian]

bomb·proof (bom'prōōf') *adj.* So constructed as to resist injury from bombs. **—n.** A structure or chamber for refuge from bombs.

bomb·shell (bom'shel') *n.* A bomb (def. 1).

bomb·sight (bom'sīt') *n. Mil.* An instrument for aiming aerial bombs.

bomb-throw·er (bom'thrō'ər) *n. Mil.* **1** A gun of the howitzer type used in firing heavy shells. **2** A catapult-like military engine for throwing bombs.

bom·byx (bom'biks) *n.* A silkworm (genus *Bombyx*). [<L <Gk. *bombyx* silkworm] **—bom·bic** (bom'bik) *adj.*

Bon (bōn) A Japanese festival celebrated in July, honoring the ancestral household spirits: sometimes called *Feast of Lanterns.*

Bo·na De·a (bō'nə dē'ə) In Roman mythology, the goddess of fertility and chastity: often identified with *Maia:* also called *Fauna.* [<L, the good goddess]

bo·na-fide (bō'nə·fīd', -fī'dē) *adj.* **1** Acting or carried out in good faith: *bona–fide* transactions. **2** Legitimate: *bona–fide* owners. [<L *bona fide* in good faith] **—bonne a·mie** (bôn á·mē') sweetheart. *fem.*

bo·nan·za (bə·nan'zə) *n.* **1** A rich mine, vein, or find of ore. **2** Any profitable operation. [<Sp., success <L *bonus* good]

Bo·na·parte (bō'nə·pärt) Name of a prominent Corsican French family: **Napoleon,** 1769–1821, French military leader and conqueror 1795–1815, emperor of the French 1804–15, as *Napoleon I;* his brothers, **Joseph,** 1768–1844, king of Naples 1806, of Spain 1808; **Louis,** 1778–1846, king of Holland 1806; **Lucien,** 1775–1840, Prince de Canino; his son **François Charles Joseph,** 1811–32, *Napoleon II,* although he never ascended the throne: often called ''l'Aiglon'' (the Eaglet); his nephew **Louis Napoleon,** 1808–73, emperor of France 1852–71, as *Napoleon III,* deposed 1871. Also spelled **Buo·na·par·te** (bwō'nä·pär'tā).

Bo·na·part·ist (bō'nə·pär'tist) *adj.* Of or pertaining to the Imperial cause in France. **—n.** An adherent of Napoleon Bonaparte or the Imperial cause. **—Bo'na·part'ism** *n.*

Bon·a·ven·tu·ra (bon'ə·ven·tōōr'ə,-tyōōr'ə), **Saint,** 1221–74, Giovanni di Fidanza, Italian Franciscan monk and theologian. Also **Bon·a·ven·ture** (bon'ə·ven'chər).

bon–bon (bon'bon', Fr. bôn·bôn') *n.* A sugared candy. [<F <*bon* good]

bon·bon·nière (bôn·bô·nyâr') *n. French* A decorated box, dish, or small metal box for confections.

bond (bond) *n.* **1** That which binds; a band; tie. **2** *pl.* Fetters; captivity. **3** An obligation or constraint. **4** *Law* An obligation in writing under seal. **5** An interest–bearing debt certificate. **6** In insurance, a policy covering losses suffered through the acts of an employee. **7** The condition of being bonded. See BONDED (def. 2). **8** Bail; a surety. **9** In building, timbers or stones which help to bind together. **10** *Chem.* A unit of combining power between the atoms of a molecule, associated with the energy of electrons. **11** The attachment of an adhesive material at the interface of two surfaces. **12** Bond paper. **—bottled in bond** *U.S.* A straight, 100–proof whiskey at least 4 years old, bottled under government supervision before payment of taxes. **—debenture bond 1** A bond acknowledging loan indebtedness and securing repayment out of some designated fund or income. **2** A certificate issued by customs officials stating that an importer is entitled to a drawback on goods imported and afterward exported. **3** A bond for the payment of money stipulating that government securities or the stock of a corporate company shall be held as security. **—indemnity bond** A release signed by a shipper, relieving a railroad of responsibility. **—v.t. 1** To put a certified debt upon; mortgage. **2** To furnish bond for; be surety for (someone). **3** To place, as goods or an employee, under bond (*n.* def. 6); guarantee. **4** In masonry, to place, as bricks, in interlocking patterns, so as to strengthen a wall, etc. **—v.i. 5** To interlock or cohere, as bricks. **—adj.** Subject to servitude; enslaved. [Var. of BAND[1]]

bond·age (bon'dij) *n.* **1** Compulsory servitude; slavery; imprisonment. **2** Captivity; subjection. **3** In old English law, villenage. *Synonyms:* captivity, enthralment, serfdom, servitude, slavery, subjection, subjugation, thraldom. See FETTER.

bond·ed (bon'did) *adj.* **1** Hypothecated for payment of bonds; mortgaged. **2** Held in bond for payment of duties. **3** Secured by bonds, as a debt. **4** Held close together, as by a strong adhesive or by chemical action.

bond·er (bon'dər) *n.* **1** One who bonds, puts goods into bond, or owns goods in bond. **2** A stone or a brick extending through a wall and binding it together: also **bond'stone'.**

bond·hold·er (bond'hōl'dər) *n.* One owning or holding bonds. **—bond'hold'ing** *adj. & n.*

bond·maid (bond'mād') *n.* A female slave.

bond·man (bond'mən) *n. pl.* **·men** (-mən) **1** A male slave or serf. **2** A villein. Also **bonds'man.—bond'wom'an, bonds'wom'an** *n. fem.*

bond paper A stiff, strong, uncalendered paper of superior fiber: used in printing bonds and banknotes, for business letters, etc.

bond·ser·vant (bond'sûr'vənt) *n.* One in servitude without wages; slave. Also **bond'slave'.**

bonds·man (bondz'mən) *n. pl.* **·men** (-mən) **1** One bound as security for another. **2** A bondman.

bone (bōn) *n.* **1** *Anat.* **a** A hard, dense, porous structure composed of calcium salts (mainly of phosphate) and organic materials, forming the skeleton of vertebrate animals. **b** A separate piece of the skeleton of a vertebrate animal. ◆Collateral adjective: *osteal.* **2** *pl.* The skeleton as a whole; mortal remains. **3** One of various objects made of bone or similar material; specifically, one of a pair of dice; also, one of a pair of clappers, as used by minstrels; also, whalebone in a waist or corset. **4** *pl. U.S.* The end man on the right in a minstrel show (who plays the bones). **5** A ground of contention. **6** *pl. Slang* Dice. **—to feel in (one's) bones** To be sure of; have an intuition of. **—to have a bone to pick** To have grounds for complaint or dispute. **—to make no bones about** To have no scruples about; find no difficulty with. **—to point (or sing) a bone at** *Austral.*To invoke death or disaster upon (someone) by an aboriginal ritual. **—v. boned, bon·ing.** *v.t.* **1** To remove the bones from. **2** To stiffen with whalebone. **3** To

fertilize with bonedust. **—v.i. 4** *Slang* To study intensely: often with *up*: to *bone up* for an exam. **5** *Austral.* To bring misfortune to; jinx. [OE *bān*]

bone ash A white, friable substance, the ash of bones, composed mainly of calcium phosphate: used in cupellation, china–making, and other arts. Also **bone earth.**

bone china Porcelain in which bone ash is used.

bone conduction The transmission of sounds to the inner ear by means of the bones of the skull rather than through the auditory canal.

bone·head (bōn'hed') *n. Colloq.* A slow–witted, stupid person.

bone house An elevated, covered platform on which certain American Indians stored the bones of their dead to await burial.

bone meal Pulverized bone, used as fertilizer.

bone oil A viscid oily substance obtained from bones by dry distillation: used in disinfectants and insecticides.

bon·er (bō'nər) *n. Slang* An error; faux pas.

bone·set (bōn'set') *n.* A bitter tonic and diaphoretic herb of the genus *Eupatorium:* also called *thoroughwort.*

bone·yard (bōn'yärd') *n.* **1** A place where the bones of horses and cattle are collected. **2** The reserve pieces in a game of dominoes. **3** *Slang* A cemetery.

bon·fire (bon'fīr') *n.* **1** Formerly, a large fire for the burning of bones, as a funeral pile, etc. **2** A large fire in the open air for amusement, burning trash, a beacon, etc. [<BONE + FIRE]

bon·go (bong'gō) *n. pl.* **·gos** A large, reddish, white–striped, forest antelope of the genus *Taurotragus* of equatorial Africa, related to the eland, and having heavy, lyrate horns in both sexes. [<native African name]

bon·go drums (bong'gō) A pair of drums, attached together and played with the hands, originally from Africa. Also **bon'gos.**

bon·ho·mie (bon'ə·mē', Fr. bô·nô·mē') *n.* Genial nature or manner; good fellowship. Also **bon'hom·mie'.** [<F]

bon·i·face (bon'ə·fās) *n.* An innkeeper; hotel landlord. [after *Boniface,* innkeeper in Farquhar's *Beaux' Stratagem*]

Bon·i·face (bon'ə·fās) Name of nine popes; especially **Boniface VIII,** 1228–1303, real name Benedict Cajetan, pope 1294–1303; emphasized the temporal supremacy of the papacy. **—Boniface, Saint,** 680–755, English monk, apostle to Germany.

bo·ni·to (bə·nē'tō) *n. pl.* **·tos** or **·toes 1** One of various large, mackerel–like marine fishes of the Atlantic and Pacific (genus *Sarda*), as the California bonito (*S. lineolata*). **2** The skipjack. [<Sp.]

BONITO
(Up to 30 inches long)

bon mot (bôn mō') *pl.* **bons mots** (bōn mōz', Fr. mō') A clever saying; terse witticism. [<F]

Bon·nard (bô·nár'), **Pierre,** 1867–1947, French painter.

bon·net (bon'it) *n.* **1** A covering, or an article of apparel, for the head. **2** An outdoor headdress for women. **3** A brimless cap for men and boys, worn especially in Scotland. **4** An American Indian headdress of feathers. **5** The velvet cap lining a crown or coronet. **6** A gambler's or auctioneer's decoy. **7** The yellow waterlily. **8** One of various constructions or devices having a form or use analogous to that of a bonnet. **9** A cover or plate which can be removed to inspect a valve or other part of machinery in a chamber. **10** Any metal hood, canopy, projection, or cowl. **11** *Naut.* A supplementary sail laced to the foot of a jib of a vessel in light winds. **12** *Brit.* The hood of an automobile. **—v.t.** To cover with or as with a bonnet. [<OF *(chapel de), bonet* (cap of) *bonet* (a fabric) < Med. L *bonetus*]

bon·ny (bon'ē) *adj.* **bon·ni·er, bon·ni·est 1** Having homelike beauty; sweet and fair. **2** Blithe; merry; cheery. **3** *Scot.* Fine; spacious. **4** *Brit. Dial.* Healthy; robust; plump. Also **bon'nie.** See synonyms under BEAUTIFUL. [< F *bon* good] **—bon'ni·ly** *adv.* **—bon'ni·ness** *n.*

bon·ny-clab·ber (bon'ē·klab'ər) *n.* Milk curdled by natural souring. [<Irish *bainne clabair* <*bainne* milk + *clabair* clabber < *claba* thick]

bon·sai (bon'sī, bōn'-) *n. pl.* **·sai** **1** A dwarfed tree or shrub trained, as by pruning, into a pleasing design. **2** The art of creating such trees or shrubs. [<Japanese]

bon·te·bok (bon'tə·bok) *n. pl.* **·bok** or **·boks** A nearly extinct South African antelope of the genus *Damaliscus,* the pied antelope. [< Afrikaans <*bont* pied + *bok* buck, deer]

bon·ton (bôn·tôn') *n.* **1** The fashionable world. **2** Good style or breeding. [<F, good tone]

bo·nus (bō'nəs) *n. pl.* **bo·nus·es** **1** An allowance in addition to what is usual, current, or stipulated: a *bonus* on stocks. **2** Compensation, as for the obtaining of a loan. **3** A grant, as of money, insurance, etc., made by a government to citizens who have rendered military service. **4** A payment out of surplus, made by a life–insurance company to its policy holders. See synonyms under SUBSIDY. [<L, good]

bon vi·vant (bôn vē·vän') *pl.* **bons vi·vants** (bôn vē·vän') **1** A high liver; an epicure. **2** A boon companion. [<F]

bon vo·yage (bôn vwá·yàzh') *French* A pleasant voyage or trip.

bon·y (bō'nē) *adj.* **bon·i·er, bon·i·est** **1** Of, like, pertaining to, or consisting of bone or bones. **2** Having prominent bones; thin; gaunt. —**bon'i·ness** *n.*

bonze (bonz) *n.* A Buddhist monk. [<F <Pg. *bonzo*<Japanese <Chinese *fan seng* religious person]

bon·zer (bon'zər) *n. Austral. Slang* Something unusually good;a stroke of good luck.

boo (boo) *n. & interj.* A vocal sound made to indicate contempt or to frighten. —*v.* **booed,** **boo·ing** *v.i.* To utter *boos.* —*v.t.* To shout *boo* at, either to startle or to express contempt for.

boob (boob) *n. U.S. Slang* A gullible person; simpleton; booby.

boobs (boobz) *n. pl. Slang* The female breasts.

boob tube *Slang* **1** Television. **2** A television set.

boo·by (boo'bē) *n. pl.* **boo·bies** **1** A dull fellow; dunce. **2** In some games, the person who makes the poorest score. **3** A gannet or swimming bird of warm seas related to the pelican, especially *Sula piscator* of the coasts of the tropical and subtropical Americas: named from its apparent stupidity. [<Sp. *bobo* fool <L *balbus* stupid, dull]

booby hatch **1** *Naut.* A small hatch giving access inside a vessel without removing the main hatches. **2** *Slang* An insane asylum.

booby prize A mock award, given in good–natured derision, for the worst score or performance in a contest, game, etc.

booby trap A concealed mechanism designed to operate and cause damage when inadvertently disturbed; specifically, a mine actuated by movements of the enemy.

boo·dle (boo'dl) *n.* **1** *U.S. Slang* Money. **2** A bribery fund; corruption money. **3** Public plunder. **4** Caboodle. **5** Counterfeit money. —*v.i.* **·dled, ·dling** To receive money corruptly. [Cf. Du. *boedel* property] —**boo'dler** *n.*

boo·dling (boo'dling) *n.* The use of bribery in politics.

boog·er (boog'ər) *n.* **1** A hobgoblin. **2** *U.S. Slang* A person who is subject to contemptuous derision; also, one held in pitying affection: also *bugger.* [Origin unknown]

boog·ie–woog·ie (boog'ē·woog'ē) *n.* **1** A style of jazz piano–playing characterized by a rhythmic, ostinato bass with melodic inventions rhapsodizing in the treble. **2** A piece of music in this style. —*adj.* Of, in, or pertaining to this style. [Origin uncertain]

boo·hoo (boo·hoo') *v.i.* **·hooed, ·hoo·ing** To weep loudly. —*n. pl.* **·hoos** Noisy sobbing. [Imit.]

book (book) *n.* **1** A number of sheets of paper bound or stitched together; especially, a printed and bound volume. **2** A literary composition or treatise of some length. **3** Any one of the writings of which the Bible is made up. **4** A subdivision of a literary composition or treatise. **5** A list of horses entered in a race, with the odds laid for and against them. **6** A booklike pack of gold leaf. **7** The words of a play or opera; a libretto: The music of the new opera is good, but the *book* is poor. **8** In whist and similar games, six tricks taken by one side; in other games, all the cards of one set. **9** A business record or register, as a ledger, etc.: often in the plural: The *books* show a steady loss. **10** A volume prepared for written entries. **11** Anything considered as a record or a setting forth of truth: the *book* of nature. **12** A bundle of tobacco leaves cut in half longitudinally and without the stems. —**by the book** According to rule; unoriginal; also, literal. —**like a book** Thoroughly: He knows the town *like a book.* —**the book** The telephone directory. —**the Book** The Bible. —**by the book** According to the correct form; in the usual manner. —**to throw the book at** *Slang* **1** To sentence a lawbreaker to the maximum penalties for all charges against him. **2** To punish or reprimand severely. —*v.t.* **1** To enter or list in a book. **2** To arrange for beforehand, as accommodations or seats. **3** To engage, as actors or a play, for performance. **4** To make a record of charges against (someone) on a police blotter. [<OE *bōc*]

book·bind·er (book'bīn'dər) *n.* One whose trade is the binding of books.

book·bind·er·y (book'bīn'dər·ē) *n. pl.* **·er·ies** A place where books are bound.

book·bind·ing (book'bīn'ding) *n.* The art or trade of binding books.

book·case (book'kās') *n.* A case containing shelves for holding books.

book–end (book'end') *n.* A support or prop used to hold upright a row of books.

book·ie (book'ē) *n. Slang* In gambling, a bookmaker.

book·ing (book'ing) *n.* **1** The act or process of registering in a book, rarely of forming into a book. **2** The buying of a passage ticket. **3** The engaging of actors for dramatic productions; also, any part thus contracted for. **4** A contracting to present a play at a theater; the contract or play itself.

book·ish (book'ish) *adj.* **1** Fond of books; book–learned. **2** Pedantic; unpractical. —**book'ish·ly** *adv.* —**book'ish·ness** *n.*

book jacket A removable cover to protect the binding of a book, usually designed to aid in displaying and advertising it.

book·keep·er (book'kē'pər) *n.* One who keeps accounts; an accountant.

book·keep·ing (book'kē'ping) *n.* The art, method, or practice of recording business transactions systematically.

book·land (book'land') *n.* A freehold as held by deed charter.

book–learn·ing (book'lûr'ning) *n.* **1** The knowledge of, or obtained from, books. **2** Mere literary culture or attainment as opposed to practical experience.

book·let (book'lit) *n.* A small book, often paperbound.

book·lore (book'lôr', -lōr') *n.* Book–learning.

book·mak·er (book'mā'kər) *n.* **1** One who compiles, prints, or binds books. **2** A professional betting man, especially as connected with the turf.

book·mark (book'märk') *n.* Any object, as a ribbon, to be placed between or in the leaves of a book to mark a place for ready reference.

book·mo·bile (book'mə·bēl') *n.* A motor truck equipped with shelves for the transport, display, and loan of books forming part of a traveling library. [<BOOK + (AUTO)MOBILE]

book·plate (book'plāt') *n.* **1** An engraved label, often artistic in design, placed on or in a book to indicate ownership or proper place in a library. **2** An electrotype or stereotype of a page of a book.

book·rack (book'rak') *n.* **1** A frame to hold an open book: also **book'rest'.** **2** A framework to hold books, as on a table.

book·sell·er (book'sel'ər) *n.* One who sells books.

book·shop (book'shop') *n.* A shop where books are sold; bookstore.

book·stack (book'stak') *n.* A tall rack containing shelves for books in a library.

book·stall (book'stôl') *n.* A stall or stand where books are sold.

book·stand (book'stand') *n.* **1** A rack for books. **2** A bookstall.

book·store (book'stôr', -stōr') *n.* A store for the sale of books.

book·work (book'wûrk') *n.* Work involving reading or writing in books.

book·worm (book'wûrm') *n.* **1** A person exclusively devoted to books and study. **2** Any of various insects destructive to books, especially one of the order *Corrodentia.*

boom[1] (boom) *n.* **1** *Naut.* A spar holding the foot of a fore–and–aft sail, or that attached to a yard or to another boom to extend it. **2** A chain of logs to intercept or retard the advance of a vessel, to confine timbers, sawlogs, etc. **3** A pole set up to mark a navigable channel. **4** A long mobile beam projecting from the foot of a derrick to carry a load raised from its outer end. —**to lower the boom** *Slang* To act decisively to correct abuses; crack down. —*v.t.* **1** To extend (a sail) by means of a boom: with *out.* **2** To shove off or away, as a vessel from a wharf: with *off.* **3** To equip (a river, lake, etc.) with a barrier to stop floating logs. [<Du. *boom* tree, beam. Akin to BEAM.]

BOOM *(def. 4)*

boom[2] (boom) *v.i.* **1** To emit a deep, resonant sound, as cannon or drums. **2** To hum loudly, as bees. **3** To rush swiftly or in tumult. **4** To grow rapidly; flourish. —*v.t.* **5** To utter or sound in a deep resonant tone: to *boom* the hour. **6** To extol; praise or advertise vigorously. **7** To cause to flourish: Prosperous times *boomed* my business. **8** To rush, as logs, down a river. —*n.* **1** A deep, reverberating sound, as of a supersonic aircraft, waves, etc. **2** Any sudden or rapid growth or popularity. [Imit. Cf. G *bummen* hum, Gk. *bombos* hollow noise.]

boom·e·rang (boo'mə·rang) *n.* **1** A curved, wooden missile weapon originated in Australia, one form of which will return to the thrower. **2** Any proceeding that recoils upon the originator. —*v.i.* To react harmfully on the doer or user. [<native Australian name]

boom town A town that has sprung up quickly, or one that has suddenly increased in population, as from a discovery of gold or oil.

BOOMERANGS

boon[1] (boon) *n.* **1** A good thing bestowed; favor; blessing. **2** *Obs.* A petition. See synonyms under FAVOR. [<ON *bon* petition]

boon[2] (boon) *adj.* **1** Possessing convivial qualities; genial; jovial. **2** Benign; bounteous. [<F *bon* <L *bonus* good]

boon·docks (boon'doks') *n. pl. U.S. Slang* An uncivilized, out–of–the–way, or backwards area: used with *the.* [<Tagalog *bundok* mountain]

boon·dog·gle (boon'dôg'əl, -dog'əl) *v.i.* **·dog·gled, ·dog·gling** *U.S. Colloq.* To work, especially for the government, on wasteful or unnecessary projects. —*n.* A wasteful or worthless project. [Origin uncertain] —**boon'dog'gler** *n.* —**boon'dog'gling** *n.*

Boone (boon), **Daniel,** 1735?–1820, American frontiersman in Kentucky and Missouri.

boor (boor) *n.* **1** A coarse rustic. **2** An ill–bred fellow. **3** A peasant, especially a Dutch peasant. [<Du. *boer* farmer, rustic]

boor·ish (boor'ish) *adj.* Rude; clownish. See synonyms under AWKWARD, RUSTIC. —**boor'ish·ly** *adv.* —**boor'ish** *n.*

boost (boost) *v.t. U.S.* **1** To raise by or as by pushing from beneath or behind. **2** *Slang* To speak in praise of; help by speaking well of. **3** *Colloq.* To increase: to *boost* prices. —*n.* **1** A lift; help. **2** *Colloq.* An increase. [Origin uncertain]

boost·er (boos'tər) *n.* **1** Any device for increasing the power or thrust of an engine, mechanism, etc. **2** *U.S. Colloq.* One who gives enthusiastic support to a person, organization, community, or cause. **3** The first stage of a multistage rocket, the source of thrust during takeoff. **4** A booster shot. **5** *Slang* A professional shoplifter.

booster shot Another injection, as of a vaccine, to reinforce immunity, administered at an interval after the initial dose.

boot[1] (boot) *n.* **1** A leather covering for the foot and leg. **2** A high shoe. **3** *Brit.* A compartment in an automobile, coach, etc., for carrying baggage. **4** A medieval instrument of torture, compressing the foot and leg. **5** A ring-shaped appliance put on the leg of a horse to prevent interference. **6** A leather flap fastened to the dashboard of an open carriage, to be drawn up as a shield from rain or mud. **7** A carbine bucket fitted to a military saddle. **8** A box encasing the lower pulley in a grain elevator. **9** The part of a reed pipe containing the reed, as of an organ. **10** *Ornithol.* A tarsal envelope of a bird, as in thrushes. **11** *Bot.* The lowest leaf-bearing segment of a stalk of wheat. **12** *Colloq.* In the U.S. Navy, a new recruit, or one but recently arrived from a training station. **—big in one's boots** Proud. **—the boot is on the other foot** The case is reversed. **—to get the boot on the wrong foot** —To make a mistake in attribution, interpretation, etc. **—to die with one's boots on 1** To die by violence; die fighting. **2** To die working, *i.e.*, without ever resting. **—to get the boot** *Slang* To be discharged. **—v.t. 1** To put boots on. **2** To torture with the boot. **3** To kick; also, in football, to punt. **4** *Slang* To dismiss; fire; eject: often with *out*. [<OF *bote*]

boot[2] (boot) *v.i. Obs.* To be of avail. **—v.t. Obs.** To benefit. **—n. 1** Something over and above given in barter. **2** Advantage; resource; help. **—to boot** In addition; over and above. [OE *bōt* profit]

boot·black (boot'blak') *n.* One who cleans and blacks boots.

boot camp The primary training station for enlisted naval personnel; so called because of the leggings or *boots* worn by the recruits.

boot·ed (boo'tid) *adj.* **1** Wearing boots. **2** *Ornithol.* Not divided into scutella except at the extreme lower portion; covered with feathers, as the tarsi of some birds.

boo·tee (boo·tē', boo'tē) *n.* **1** A woman's or child's short, light boot; a half-boot. **2** A knitted woolen boot for a baby.

Bo·ö·tes (bō·ō'tēz) A northern constellation, whose brightest star is Arcturus. See CONSTELLATION.

booth (booth, booth) *n.* **1** A stall at a fair, market, polls, etc. **2** A temporary shelter. [ME *bothe*, ult. <Scand.]

boot·leg (boot'leg') *v.t. & v.i.* **·legged, ·leg·ging** To make, sell, or carry for sale (liquor, etc.) illegally; smuggle. **—adj.** Unlawful: *bootleg* whisky. **—n. 1** The part of a boot above the instep. **2** Liquor, or other merchandise, that is unlawfully carried, produced, sold, or offered for sale. Compare BLACK MARKET. [With ref. to the smuggling of liquor in bootlegs] **—boot'leg'ger** *n.*

boot·leg·ging (boot'leg'ing) *n.* The act of producing, carrying, selling, or offering for sale liquor or other merchandise in violation of the law.

boot·less (boot'lis) *adj.* Profitless; useless; unavailing. **—boot'less·ly** *adv.* **—boot'less·ness** *n.*

boot·lick (boot'lik') *v.t. & v.i.* To flatter servilely; to toady. **—boot'lick'er** *n.* **—boot'· lick'ing** *n. & adj.*

boots (boots) *n. Brit.* A hotel bootblack.

boo·ty (boo'tē) *n. pl.* **·ties 1** The spoil of war; plunder. **2** Gain. See synonyms under PLUNDER. [<F *butin* <MLG]

booze (booz) *n.* **1** Strong drink; liquor. **2** A drunken spree; carouse. [<v.] **—v.i. boozed, booz·ing** To drink to excess; tipple. Also **boose, bouse.** [<MDu. *busen* drink, tipple] **—boozed** *adj.* **—booz'er** *n.*

booz·y (boo'zē) *adj.* Somewhat intoxicated; tipsy. Also **boos'y.** **—booz'i·ly** *adv.* **—booz'i·ness** *n.*

bop[1] (bop) *v.t.* **bopped, bop·ping** *Slang* To hit or strike. [Imit.]

bop[2] (bop) See BE-BOP.

bo·peep (bō·pēp') *n.* The game of peek-a-boo.

bo·ra (bo'rə) *n. Meteorol.* A blustering dry wind from the Julian Alps, blowing over the Adriatic in winter. See BOREAS. [<Ital.]

bo·rate (bôr'āt, bō'rāt) *n. Chem.* A salt of boric acid. **—bo'rat·ed** *adj.*

bo·rax (bôr'aks, bō'raks) *n.* A white crystalline compound, $Na_2B_4O_7 \cdot 10H_2O$, with a sweetish, alkaline taste, found native as tincal, and used as an antiseptic, in preserving food, in medicine, and as a flux, also of value in glass-manufacture and certain smelting operations. [<OF *boras* <Med. L *borax* <Arabic *bōraq* <Persian *būrah*]

bo·ra·zon (bôr'ə·zon, bō'rə-) *n. Chem.* A crystalline compound of boron and nitrogen, BN, produced under extremely high temperature and pressure: it equals the diamond in hardness but has a much higher melting point [<BOR(ON) + AZO- + -*n*]

Bor·deaux (bôr·dō') A port of SW France on the Garonne.

Bor·deaux (bôr·dō') *n.* A white or red wine produced in the vicinity of Bordeaux, France. Red Bordeaux is often called *claret.*

bor·del (bôr'dəl) *n. Archaic* A brothel. [<OF *bordel*, dim. of *borde* cottage, hut, ult. <Gmc.]

Bor·de·laise (bôr·də·lâz') *n.* A sauce made of meat stock, white wine, and flavored with onions, carrots, thyme, and garlic. [from *Bordeaux*, France]

bor·del·lo (bôr·del'ō) *n.* A house of prostitution; a brothel. [<Ital. <Med. L *bordellus,* dim. of *borda* cottage]

bor·der (bôr'dər) *n.* **1** A margin or edge; outer portion or limit; brink; verge. **2** The frontier line or district of a country or state; hence, a boundary or frontier, especially the western frontier of the United States. **3** A surrounding or enclosing strip of ground in a garden, commonly planted with flowers; also, a decorative edge or margin: a *border* of lace on a cap. **4** A shallow drop curtain hanging at the top of a stage set, to conceal lights, mask the gridiron, etc. See synonyms under BANK, BOUNDARY, MARGIN. **—the Border** or **Borders** The boundary and nearby land between England and Scotland. **—adj. 1** Of or pertaining to a territorial border. **2** Living on or characteristic of a frontier: *border* costumes. **3** Situated on a frontier: a *border* town. **—v.t. 1** To put a border or edging on. **2** To lie next to; form a boundary to. **—v.i. 3** To resemble; have the appearance: with *on* or *upon*: That *borders* on piracy. **4** To touch or abut: with *on* or *upon*. [<OF *bordure* < *bord* edge, ult. <Gmc.] **—bor'der·er** *n.* **—bor'der·ing** *adj.*

bor·dered (bôr'dərd) *adj.* Having a border distinctively marked in structure, coloring, etc.

bor·der·land (bôr'dər·land') *n.* **1** Land on or near the border of two adjoining countries. **2** Debatable or indeterminate ground: the *borderland* of history.

bor·der·line (bôr'dər·līn') *n.* A line of demarcation. Also **border line.** **—adj.** Difficult to classify, such as might conceivably fall into one or another category.

bor·dure (bôr'jər) *n. Her.* A border around a shield. See SUBORDINARY. [<F]

bore[1] (bôr, bōr) *v.* **bored, bor·ing** *v.t.* **1** To make a hole in or through, as with a drill. **2** To make (a tunnel, hole, well, etc.) by or as by drilling. **3** To advance or force (one's way). **4** To weary by monotony, iteration, etc.; tire. **—v.i. 5** To make a hole, etc., by or as by drilling. **6** To admit of being drilled: This wood *bores* easily. **7** To force one's way; advance by persistent motion. **—n. 1** A hole made by or as if by boring. **2** The interior diameter of a firearm or cylinder. **3** Caliber. **4** A tiresome person or thing; an annoyance. See synonyms under HOLE. ◆ Homophone: *boar.* [v., OE *borian* < *bor* auger; *n.* < *v.* + ON *bora* hole]

bore[2] (bôr, bōr) *n.* A high crested wave caused by the rush of flood tide up a river, as in the Amazon or the Bay of Fundy. Compare EAGER[2]. ◆ Homophone: *boar.* [<ON *bāra* billow]

bore[3] (bôr, bōr) Past tense of BEAR.

bo·re·al (bôr'ē·əl, bō'rē-) *adj.* Pertaining to the north or the north wind. [<LL *borealis* <BOREAS]

Bo·re·al (bôr'ē·əl, bō'rē-) *adj.* **1** Pertaining to or designating a climatic period of the Mesolithic Baltic culture, centering around 6,000 B.C. **2** Describing a subdivision of the Holarctic region, including the great belt of coniferous forests extending from New England to Alaska.

Bo·re·as (bôr'ē·əs, bō'rē-) *n.* In Greek mythology, the north wind. [<Gk.]

bore·dom (bôr'dəm, bōr'-) *n.* **1** The condition of being bored; ennui. **2** *Rare* The habit of being a bore. **3** *Rare* Bores as a class.

bor·er (bôr'ər, bō'rər) *n.* **1** One who or that which bores. **2** A beetle, moth, or worm that burrows in plants, wood, etc.; especially, the **metallic wood borer** (family *Buprestidae*), the **palm borer** (family *Bostrichidae*), the **maple borer** (family *Cerambycidae*). For illustration see INSECTS (injurious). **3** The shipworm.

Bor·ghe·se (bôr·gā'zā) A noble family in the Republic of Siena and later at Rome, flourishing in the 16th and 17th centuries.

Bor·gia (bôr'jä) Aristocratic Spanish family, a branch of which emigrated to Italy.
—Alfonso, 1378–1458; became Pope Calixtus III, 1455–58.
—Cesare, 1478–1507, Duc de Valentinois, Italian cardinal, soldier, and adventurer.
—Francisco de, 1510–72, Spanish Jesuit, third general of the order; canonized 1671.
—Lucrezia, 1480–1519, sister of Cesare, and wife of Alfonso, Duke of Esté; heroine of opera by Donizetti.
—Rodrigo Lanzol y, 1431–1503; became Pope Alexander VI, 1492–1503.

bo·ric (bôr'ik, bō'rik) *adj. Chem.* Of, pertaining to, or derived from boron: also called *boracic.*

boric acid *Chem.* A white crystalline compound, H_3BO_3, obtained in volcanic lagoons of Tuscany, Italy, and by treating borax with sulfuric acid: used as a preservative, and mild antiseptic. Also **bo·rac'ic acid.**

bo·ride (bôr'īd, bō'rīd) *n.* A combination of boron with another element or radical.

bor·ing (bôr'ing, bō'ring) *n.* **1** The act or process of making a hole with or as with a boring tool. **2** A hole so made; a bore hole. **3** *pl.* Material removed by boring.

born (bôrn) *adj.* **1** Brought forth or into being, as offspring. **2** Natural; ingrained: a *born* musician. [OE *boren*, pp. of *beran* bear]

borne (bôrn, bōrn) Past participle of BEAR.

Bor·ne·o (bôr'nē·ō, bôr'-) The third largest island in the world, between Sumatra and Celebes; 286,969 square miles: divided into (1) *Sabah*; (2) *Sarawak*; (3) *Brunei*; and (4) Borneo, a part of the Republic of Indonesia; 208,285 square miles; chief town, Banjermasin: formerly *Dutch Borneo. Indonesian* **Ka·li·man·tan** (kä'lē·män'tän).

Born·holm (bôrn'hōlm) A Danish island in the Baltic Sea; 228 square miles; chief port, Rönne.

born·ite (bôr'nīt) *n.* A metallic, reddish-brown, copper-iron sulfide showing purple tarnish: also called *horseflesh ore, peacock copper.* [after Ignaz von *Born,* 1742–91, Austrian metallurgist]

Bo·ro·bu·dur (bō'rō·boo·door') Site of a huge, ruined Buddhist temple in central Java. Also **Bo'ro·boe·doer'.**

bo·ron (bôr'on, bō'ron) *n.* A non-metallic element (symbol B) obtained as an odorless and very infusible powder, **amorphous boron,** from its oxide and in octahedral or prismatic diamondlike crystals, **crystalline** or **adamantine boron,** from amorphous boron heated with aluminum. See ELEMENT. [<BOR(AX) + (CARB)ON]

boron carbide *Chem.* A compound of carbon and boron, B_4C, an extremely hard material, often used in cutting tools.

bo·ro·sil·i·cate (bôr'ə·sil'ə·kit, -kāt, bō'rə-) *n. Chem.* A salt in which both boric and silicic acids are united with a base.

bor·ough (bûr'ō) *n.* **1** An incorporated village or town; a subdivision of a city, having a limited self-government; specifically, one of the five administrative divisions of New York, N.Y. **2** *Brit.* A municipal corporation, not a city, endowed by royal charter with certain privileges, a **municipal borough;** a town, whether corporate or not, entitled to representation in Parliament, a **parliamentary borough. 3** *Obs.* Any town. ◆ Homophone: *burrow.* [OE *burg, burh* fort, town, ult. <Gmc. Related to BOURG, BURG.]

bor·row (bôr'ō, bor'ō) *v.t.* **1** To take or obtain (something) on a promise to return it or its equivalent. **2** To adopt for one's own use, as words or ideas. **3** *Math.* In subtraction, to add ten to any figure of the minuend, at the same time withdrawing one from the next figure of the process. — *v.i.* **4** To borrow something. — *n.* **1** A place, as a bank of earth, where material is removed to be used as filling elsewhere. **2** *Obs.* A pledge; surety; the act of borrowing. [OE *borgian* give a pledge, borrow < *borg* pledge] — **bor′row·er** *n.*

borscht (bôrsht) *n.* A Russian beet soup, often served with sour cream and eaten hot or cold. Also **borsch** (bôrsh). [<Russian]

bort (bôrt) *n.* An impure diamond, used only for cutting and polishing: often called *carbonado*. Also **bortz** (bôrts). [? <OF *bort* bastard] — **bort′y** *adj.*

Bo·rus·sian (bō-rush′ən) *n.* The Old Prussian language. See under PRUSSIAN.

bor·zoi (bôr′zoi) *n.* A breed of Russian hounds, generally resembling the greyhound, but with a long, silky coat, usually white: also called *Russian wolfhound.* [<Russian, swift]

bos·cage (bos′kij) *n.* A mass of shrubbery; a thicket; clump. Also **bos′kage.** [<OF, ult. <Gmc. Akin to BUSH.]

Bosch (bos), **Hieronymus**, 1450?–1516, Dutch painter. Also **Jerom Bos.**
— **Bosch** (bôsh), **Karl**, 1874–1940, German chemist.

bosch·bok (bosh′bok) *n.* A bushbuck. Also **bosh′bok.** [<Du. *bosch* wood + *bok* buck]

bosch·vark (bosh′värk) *n.* A wild hog of South Africa (*Potamochoerus choeropotamus*); the bush pig. [<Du. *bosch* wood + *vark* pig]

bosh[1] (bosh) *n.* *Colloq.* Empty words; nonsense. [<Turkish, empty, worthless]

bosh[2] (bosh) *n.* *Metall.* **1** That part of one of the sloping sides of a blast furnace extending from the belly to the hearth. **2** A trough for cooling ingots, etc. [Cf. G *böschung* slope]

bosk (bosk) *n.* A thicket of bushes; a small wood. [ME, var. of *busk* bush] — **bosk′y** *adj.* — **bosk′i·ness** *n.*

bos·ket (bos′kit) *n.* A cluster of trees in a garden; a thicket. Also **bos′quet.** [<F *bosquet* <Ital. *boschetto,* dim. of *bosco* wood, ult. <Gmc.]

bos·om (bŏŏz′əm, bŏŏ′zəm) *n.* **1** The breast of a human being, especially that of a woman. **2** The breast with the arms, considered as an enclosure in embracing. **3** That portion of a garment covering the breast, as a shirt front, or the receptacle which it forms. **4** The breast as the seat of affection. **5** Any deep or enclosed place or supporting surface, suggesting, in purpose or function, the human breast: the *bosom* of the earth. — *adj.* **1** Close, as if held to the bosom; confidential; intimate; cherished: a *bosom* friend. **2** Cherished in secret: a *bosom* sin. — *v.t.* **1** To have or cherish in the bosom; embrace. **2** To hide in the bosom; conceal. [OE *bōsm*]

Bos·po·rus (bos′pə·rəs) A strait between the Black Sea and the Sea of Marmara, separating European from Asian Turkey; 17 miles long. Also **Bos·pho·rus** (bos′fə·rəs).

boss[1] (bôs, bos) *n.* **1** *U.S. Colloq.* A superintendent or employer of workmen; manager; foreman. **2** Any employer or any director of the work of others. **3** *U.S.* An organizer or dictator of a political party. See synonyms under MASTER. — *adj.* Being at the head of a working force; superintending; also, expert; master: *boss* shoemaker. — *v.t.* & *v.i.* **1** To have control (of) or supervision (over). **2** To domineer. [<Du. *baas* master]

boss[2] (bôs, bos) *n.* **1** A circular prominence; a knob; stud. **2** *Archit.* An ornament, sometimes a pendant, at the intersection of the ribs of a groined arch, or in any similar position. **3** *Mech.* An enlargement of a shaft to couple with a wheel or another shaft. **4** *Geol.* A domelike mass of igneous rock. — *v.t.* **1** To work with bosses. **2** To ornament with bosses. [<OF *boce* bump, knob]

BOSS (def. 2)

boss[3] (bos, bôs) *n.* **1** A calf or a cow. **2** A word used to call a calf or a cow. Also **boss′y.** [Cf. L *bos* cow]

bos·set (bôs′it, bos′-) *n.* A small protuberance, boss, or knob. [<F *bossette,* dim. of *bosse*

boss rule Domination of voters by political leaders.

boss·y[1] (bôs′ē, bos′ē) *adj. Colloq.* **boss·i·er, boss·i·est** Like a boss; domineering.

boss·y[2] (bôs′ē, bos′ē) *adj.* Decorated with or as with bosses.

bos·ton (bôs′tən, bos′-) *n.* **1** A game of cards, somewhat resembling whist; also, a bid to make five tricks, the lowest in the game. **2** A form of the waltz. [from *Boston,* Mass.]

Bos·ton (bôs′tən, bos′-) **1** A New England port on Boston Bay; capital of Massachusetts. **2** A municipal borough and port in eastern Lincolnshire, England. — **Bos·to·ni·an** (bôs·tō′nē·ən, bos-) *n.* & *adj.*

Boston Bay The inner portion of Massachusetts Bay.

Boston Harbor The northern arm of Boston Bay.

Boston Massacre A riot in Boston, Mass., March 5, 1770, during which several colonials were killed and others wounded by British troops.

Boston Mountains The ruggedest section of the Ozarks, in Oklahoma and Arkansas.

Boston rocker An American 19th century rocking chair having an up-curved wooden seat and a high back with spindles held at the top by a wide rail.

Boston Tea Party An uprising in Boston, Mass., in 1773, against the British customs officials, during which colonists, disguised as Indians, boarded British ships in the harbor and dumped chests of tea overboard.

bo·sun (bō′sən) *n.* Boatswain.

Bos·well (boz′wel, -wəl), **James,** 1740–95, Scottish lawyer and writer; biographer of Samuel Johnson.

bot (bot) *n.* The larva of a botfly. Also spelled *bott.* [Origin unknown]

bo·ta (bō′tə) *n.* A Portuguese wine cask or butt, holding about 128 gallons. [<Pg.]

bo·tan·i·cal (bə·tan′i·kəl) *adj.* **1** Of or pertaining to botany. **2** Connected with the study or cultivation of plants. Also **bo·tan′ic.** [<F *botanique* <Gk. *botanikos* <*botanē* plant, pasture <*boskein* feed, graze] — **bo·tan′i·cal·ly** *adv.*

bot·a·nist (bot′ə·nist) *n.* A student of or one versed in botany.

bot·a·nize (bot′ə·nīz) *v.* **·nized, ·niz·ing** *v.i.* **1** To study botanical specimens. **2** To gather plants for study. — *v.t.* **3** To explore in search of botanical specimens. — **bot′a·niz′er** *n.*

bot·a·ny (bot′ə·nē) *n. pl.* **·nies** **1** That division of biology which treats of plants with reference to their structure, functions, classification, etc. **2** The total plant life of a country, region, zone, etc.: the *botany* of Oceania. **3** The characteristics of a group of plants treated collectively: the *botany* of orchids.

botch[1] (boch) *v.t.* **1** To patch or mend clumsily. **2** To bungle; do or say ineptly. — *n.* A bungled piece of work; a bad job; an ill-finished patch. [ME *bocchen;* origin unknown] — **botch′er** *n.* — **botch′er·y** *n.*

botch[2] (boch) *n. Brit. Dial.* A superficial swelling or ulcer; a boil. [<OF *boche,* var. of *boce* knob, lump]

botch·y (boch′ē) *adj.* Imperfect; botched; poorly done. — **botch′i·ly** *adv.*

bot·fly (bot′flī′) *n.* A fly of the family *Gasterophilidae* or *Oestridae,* the larvae of which are parasitic in vertebrates, especially the **horse botfly** (*Gasterophilus intestinalis*). For illustration see under INSECTS (injurious).

both (bōth) *adj.* The two inclusively or together: *Both* girls laughed. — *pron.* The two; the one and the other; the pair: *Both* of the girls were there. — *adv.* & *conj.* Equally; alike; as well: with *and:* The bill passed *both* the House and the Senate. [<ON *badhir*]

Synonyms: twain, two. As an adjective or pronoun *both* emphasizes the idea of *two* and should not be connected with or refer to more than two objects. But as a conjunction *both* has a more extended meaning than it has as an adjective or a pronoun; thus, it is permissible to say, "He lost all his livestock—*both* horses, cows and sheep." When so used it emphasizes the extent or comprehensiveness of the assertion. *Twain* is a nearly obsolete form

of *two. The two,* or *the twain,* is practically equivalent to *both; both,* however, expresses a closer unity. Compare EVERY.

both·er (both′ər) *v.t.* **1** To pester; give trouble to. **2** To confuse; fluster. — *v.i.* **3** To trouble or concern oneself. — *n.* A source of annoyance; petty perplexity; vexation. [? dial. E (Irish) var. of POTHER]

both·er·a·tion (both′ə·rā′shən) *n. Colloq.* Annoyance; vexation.

both·er·some (both′ər·səm) *adj.* Causing bother or perplexity.

bot·o·né (bot′ə·nā) *adj. Her.* Having an ornament of three leaf–shaped or button–shaped projections. Also **bot′o·née, bot·o·ny** (bot′ə·nē). [<OF *botonné,* pp. of *botonner* bud, button]

bot·ry·oi·dal (bot′rē·oid′l) *adj.* Like a cluster of grapes. Also **bot′ry·oid.** [<Gk. *botryoeidēs* <*botrys* cluster of grapes + *eidos* form, shape] — **bot′ry·oi′dal·ly** *adv.*

bots (bots) *n.* A disease of horses, sheep, etc., caused by the botfly.

Bot·swa·na (bot·swä′nä) An independent member of the Commonwealth of Nations in southern Africa; 222,000 sq. mi.; capital, Gaberones; formerly *Bechuanaland Protectorate.*

bott (bot) *n.* A bot.

Bot·ti·cel·li (bot′ə·chel′ē, *Ital.* bōt′tē·chel′lē), **Alessandro,** 1447?–1515, Florentine painter: real name *Filipepi.*

bot·tle (bot′l) *n.* **1** A vessel for holding, carrying, and pouring liquids, having a neck and a narrow mouth that can be stopped. **2** As much as a bottle will hold: also **bot′tle·ful. 3** In the U.S., a unit of capacity for wines or spirits, equal to approximately 26 fluid ounces. **4** The act or habit of drinking intoxicants. — **to hit the bottle** To drink to excess. — *v.t.* **·tled, ·tling 1** To put into a bottle or bottles. **2** To restrain; shut in, as if in a bottle: often with *up* or *in.* [<OF *bouteille, botel* <LL *buticula* flask, dim. of *butis* vat, vessel] — **bot′tler** *n.*

bottled in bond See under BOND.

bottle glass Green glass.

bottle green A dark, dull green, like the color of bottle glass.

bottle imp 1 A Cartesian devil. **2** An imp or spirit shut up in a bottle. See ALADDIN.

bot·tle·neck (bot′l·nek′) *n.* **1** A narrow or congested way. **2** Any condition that retards progress.

bot·tle·stone (bot′l·stōn′) *n.* A mineral, sometimes used as a gemstone, having the characteristics of ordinary bottle glass; chrysolite; moldavite.

bot·tom (bot′əm) *n.* **1** The lowest part of anything; undersurface; base; support. **2** The ground beneath a body of water. **3** The real meaning; base; root; the foundation or basis of any state of affairs; idea; plan: to knock the *bottom* out of an argument. **4** Lowland along a river: often in plural. **5** *Naut.* The part of a vessel below the water line; hence, a vessel. **6** The part of the body on which one sits; the posterior; buttocks. **7** Residuum or dregs. **8** Endurance; stamina; grit. **9** All of a shoe below the upper. — *adj.* Lowest; fundamental; basal. — *v.t.* **1** To provide with a bottom. **2** To base or found: with *on* or *upon.* **3** To fathom; comprehend. — *v.i.* **4** To be founded; rest. **5** To touch or rest upon the bottom. [OE *botm*]

bottom dollar *U.S.* One's last and only dollar.

bottom land Lowland along a river.

bot·tom·less (bot′əm·lis) *adj.* **1** Having no bottom. **2** Unfathomable. **3** Baseless; visionary.

bottom line 1 *Colloq.* The line of a business accounting statement showing net profit or loss: with *the.* **2** *U.S. Slang* The condition or status of any enterprise after assets and liabilities have been calculated: with *the.*

bot·tom·ry (bot′əm·rē) *n.* A maritime contract whereby the owner or master of a vessel borrows money, pledging the vessel as security.

bot·u·lin (boch′ŏŏ·lin) *n.* A highly active nerve poison formed by an anerobic bacterium (*Clostridium botulines*) and sometimes present in spoiled or imperfectly prepared food; it has the property of resisting the action of gastrointestinal secretions.

bot·u·lism (boch′ŏŏ·liz′əm) *n.* Poisoning caused by eating spoiled food or food improperly prepared or canned, caused by botulin and characterized by acute gastrointestinal and nervous disorders. [<L *botulus* sausage; so called because the bacteria were first isolated from spoiled sausage]

bou·chée (bōō·shā′) *n. French* A small cake, tart shell, or puff, filled with cream, marmalade or forcemeat, and sometimes glazed.

bou·clé (bōō·klā′) *n.* A wool, rayon, cotton, silk, linen, or combination fabric woven or knitted with a looped or knotted surface. [< F, pp. of *boucler* buckle, curl]

bou·doir (bōō·dwär, bōō·dwär′) *n.* A lady's private sitting–room. [<F, lit., pouting room <*bouder* pout, sulk] —**bou·doir·esque** (bōō·dwär·esk′) *adj.*

bouf·fant (bōō·fänt′) *adj.* Puffed–out; flaring: a *bouffant* skirt. —*n.* A woman's hairstyle in which the hair hangs straight from the top of the head and puffs out over the ears and neck to frame the face. [<F, ppr. of *bouffer* swell]

bouffe (bōōf) *n.* Opera bouffe. [<F (*opéra*) *bouffe* comic (opera) <Ital. *buffa* joke, jest]

bou·gain·vil·le·a (bōō′gən·vil′ē·ə) *n.* Any of a genus (*Bougainvillea*) of small climbing shrubs: widely cultivated as hothouse plants. [after L. A. de *Bougainville*]

bough (bou) *n.* 1 A limb of a tree. 2 *Obs.* The gallows. ◆ Homophones: *bow*[1] and *bow*[2]. [OE *bog* shoulder, bough. Akin to BOW[1].]

bought (bôt) Past tense and past participle of BUY.

bou·gie (bōō′jē, -zhē) *n.* 1 *Med.* **a** A smooth, slender, flexible instrument to be introduced into a canal of the body, for removing obstructions, etc. **b** A suppository. 2 A wax candle. [from *Bougie*, a town in Algeria, where the candles were made]

bouil·la·baisse (bōōl′yə·bās′, *Fr.* bōō·yà·bes′) *n.* A chowder made of several varieties of fish and crustaceans, flavored with wine and saffron. [<F <Provençal *bouiabaisso* <*boui* boil + *abaisso* settle, go down]

bouil·lon (bool′yon, -yən; *Fr.* bōō·yôn′) *n.* 1 Clear soup from beef, chicken, or other meats. 2 A special preparation used as a culture medium for bacteria. [<F<*bouillir* boil]

Bou·lan·ger (bōō·län·zhā′), **Georges Ernest**, 1837–91, French general.
—**Nadia**, 1887–1979, French musician; professor of harmony and counterpoint.

boul·der (bōl′dər) *n.* A large stone moved by natural agencies from its original bed. Also **bowl′der**. [ME *bulderston* <Scand. Cf. Sw. *bullersten* rumbling stone (in a stream).]

Boul·der (bōl′dər) A university city in northern Colorado.

Boulder Dam The former name of HOOVER DAM.

bou·le[1] (bōō′lē) *n. Greek* 1 An ancient Greek legislative council. 2 The modern Greek legislative assembly, especially the lower house. Also spelled *bule*.

boule[2] (bōōl) *n.* A small mass of fused alumina, usually pear–shaped, and tinted to resemble the natural ruby, sapphire, etc. [<F, ball]

boul·e·vard (bool′ə·värd, bōō′lə-) *n.* 1 A broad city avenue, often planted with trees. 2 The decorative plot of trees, turf, or shrubbery along such an avenue. 3 Originally, a rampart; hence, a street laid out on the site of former ramparts. [<F <G *bollwerk* fortification. Akin to BULWARK.]

boul·e·ver·se·ment (bool′vers·män′) *n. French* An overthrow; confusion; convulsion.

Bou·logne (bōō·lōn′, *Fr.* bōō·lôn′y′) A port of northern France on the English Channel. Also **Boulogne–sur–Mer** (-sür·mâr′).

bounce (bouns) *v.* **bounced, bounc·ing** *v.t.* 1 To cause to bound or rebound. 2 To cause to move noisily; bang; thump. 3 *U.S. Slang* To eject forcibly. 4 *U.S. Slang* To discharge from employment. —*v.i.* 5 To bound or rebound. 6 To move suddenly and violently; jump or spring. 7 To move hurriedly: with *out of* or *into*. 8 *Informal* To be returned because of insufficient funds: said of a check. —*n.* 1 A sudden, or violent spring or leap; a bounding or elastic motion; rebound. 2 *Colloq.* Enthusiasm; vivacity; spirit; verve. 3 *Slang* Dismissal; discharge; expulsion. 4 A heavy blow; a bang. 5 *Brit. Colloq.* An audacious lie; a bouncer; boastful exaggeration; bluster; swagger. [ME *bunsen* <MLG. Cf. Du. *bonzen*.]

bounc·er (boun′sər) *n.* 1 A large or strong

person or thing. 2 One who or that which bounces. 3 *U.S. Colloq.* A strong man employed in a theater, saloon, etc., to throw out objectionable customers. 4 An audacious lie; also, a braggart.

bounc·ing (boun′sing) *adj.* 1 Strong and active. 2 Large; strapping; buxom. 3 Exaggerated; boastful.

bound[1] (bound) *v.i.* 1 To strike and spring back from a surface, as a ball. 2 To leap; move by a series of leaps. —*v.t.* 3 To cause to rebound. —*n.* 1 A light elastic leap or spring; also, a rebound. 2 The distance passed over in a leap or bound. See synonyms under LEAP. [<F *bondir* leap]

bound[2] (bound) *v.t.* 1 To set limits to; restrict. 2 To form the boundary of. 3 To describe or name the boundaries of. —*v.i.* 4 To adjoin. See synonyms under CIRCUMSCRIBE, LIMIT. [<*n.*] —*n.* 1 That which circumscribes or limits; boundary. 2 *pl.* The district included within a boundary or limits. See synonyms under BANK, BOUNDARY. [< OF *bonne, bonde* <LL *bodina* limit. Related to BOURN[1].]

bound[3] (bound) Past tense and past participle of BIND.—*adj.* 1 Made fast; tied; confined in bonds. 2 Constrained or compelled. 3 Having a cover or binding. 4 Apprenticed. 5 *Colloq.* Determined; resolved. 6 Constipated.

bound[4] (bound) *adj.* Having one's course directed; on the way; destined: with *for* or *to*. [<ON *buinn* <*bua* prepare]

bound·a·ry (boun′də·rē, -drē) *n. pl.* **·ries** 1 A limiting or dividing line or mark. 2 Any object serving to indicate a limit or confine.

Synonyms: barrier, border, bound, bourn, bourne, confines, edge, enclosure, frontier, landmark, limit, line, marches, marge, margin, term, termination, verge. The *boundary* was originally the *landmark*, that which marked off one piece of territory from another. The *bound* is the *limit*, marked or unmarked. Now, however, the difference between the two words has come to be simply one of usage. As regards territory, we speak of the *boundaries* of a nation or of an estate; the *bounds* of a college, a ball ground, etc. A *barrier* is something that bars ingress or egress. A *barrier* may be a *boundary*, as was the Great Wall of China for many centuries. *Bourn*, or *bourne*, is a poetical expression for *bound* or *boundary*. A *border* is a strip, as of land, along the *boundary*. *Edge* is a sharp terminal line, as where river or ocean meets the land. *Limit* is now used almost wholly in the figurative sense; the *limit* of discussion, of time, of jurisdiction. *Line* is a military term: within the *lines*, or through the *lines*, of an army. Compare BARRIER, END, MARGIN.

bound·en (boun′dən) *adj.* 1 Obligatory; necessary, as a duty. 2 *Obs.* Under obligations; obliged. [Var. of BOUND[3]]

bound·er (boun′dər) *n.* 1 One who fixes or marks bounds. 2 *Colloq.* One whose manners, etc., are offensive; a cad.

bound·less (bound′lis) *adj.* Having no limit; vast; measureless; infinite. See synonyms under INFINITE. —**bound′less·ly** *adv.* —**bound′less·ness** *n.*

bound–out (bound′out′) *adj.* Indentured; apprenticed.

boun·te·ous (boun′tē·əs) *adj.* 1 Giving freely and largely; generous; beneficent. 2 Marked by liberality or bounty; plentiful. —**boun′te·ous·ly** *adv.* —**boun′te·ous·ness** *n.*

boun·ti·ful (boun′tə·fəl) *adj.* 1 Bounteous; generous. 2 Abundant; displaying abundance. See synonyms under AMPLE, GENEROUS. —**boun′ti·ful·ly** *adv.* —**boun′ti·ful·ness** *n.*

boun·ty (boun′tē) *n. pl.* **·ties** 1 Liberality in giving or bestowing; munificence. 2 Gifts or favors generously bestowed. 3 A grant or allowance from a government, as for fisheries, manufactures, exports, enlistment, etc. 4 A reward paid by a government to encourage the killing of predatory animals (formerly also of Indians). See synonyms under BENEVOLENCE, GIFT, SUBSIDY. [<OF *bonté* <L *bonitas, -tatis* goodness]

boun·ty–jump·er (boun′tē·jum′pər) *n.* One who, having enlisted for the bounty, deserts as soon as possible, as in the Civil War.

bou·quet (bō·kā′, bōō·kā′ *for def.* 1; bōō·kā′ *for def.* 2) *n.* 1 A bunch of flowers; a nosegay. 2 Delicate odor; particularly, the distinctive aroma of

a wine. [<F <OF *boschet*, dim. of *bosc* wood, ult. <Gmc.]

bou·quet gar·ni (bōō·ke′ gàr·nē′) *French* A bundle of herbs and vegetables used for seasoning.

Bour·bon (bōōr′bən) 1 A dynasty which reigned over France, 1589–1792, 1815–48. 2 A member of the deposed royal house of France, or of the Spanish or Neapolitan branches of the same family. 3 One who is stubbornly conservative in politics; one opposed to progressive movement. —**Bour′bon·ism** *n.* —**Bour′bon·ist** *n.*

Bour·bon whisky (bûr′bən) Whisky distilled from corn and barley, originally in Bourbon County, Ky. Also **bour′bon**.

bour·don[1] (bōōr′dən) *n.* 1 An organ stop, commonly of 16-foot tone. 2 The drone of a bagpipe. 3 A humming, monotonous, or continuous sound. —*v.i.* To drone a melody. [<Med. L *burdo* drone]

bour·don[2] (bōōr′dən) *n. Obs.* A pilgrim's staff. [<F]

bourg (boorg) *n.* A fortified medieval town; a Continental market town. [<F <LL *burgus,* ult. <Gmc. Related to BOROUGH.]

bour·geois[1] (bōōr′zhwä, bōōr·zhwä′) *adj.* Of or pertaining to the commercial or middle class, as distinguished from the nobility or from the working class: used by some writers as signifying uncultivated; ill-bred; common. —*n. pl.* **·geois**[1] A citizen; a member of the commercial or middle class; a townsman; tradesman. 2 A 14th century coin. 3 In radical circles, anyone who owns property. [<F <OF *burgeis.* Doublet of BURGESS.]

bour·geois[2] (bər·jois′) *n.* A size of type: about 9-point. [? after a French printer]

bour·geoi·sie (bōōr′zhwä·zē′) *n.* 1 The middle class of society, especially in France: used collectively. 2 That class of society having private property. used especially by radical socialists. [<F <*bourgeois* middle class]

Bour·gogne (bōōr·gôn′y′) The French name for BURGUNDY.

Bour·gui·gnonne (bōōr·gē·nyôn′) *adj.* Prepared in a red wine sauce garnished with mushrooms and small onions. [<F, Burgundian]

bourn[1] (bôrn, bōrn, bōōrn) *n.* 1 That which limits; bound; goal; end: the *bourn* of man's life. 2 *Obs.* Realm; region; domain. Also **bourne**. See synonyms under BOUNDARY. [<F *borne* <OF *bodne* <LL *bodina* limit. Related to BOUND[2].]

bourn[2] (bôrn, bōrn, bōōrn) *n.* A brook or rivulet: used also in combination: *Eastbourne*. Compare BURN[2]. Also **bourne**. [Var. of BURN[2]]

bourre·let (bōōr·lā′) *n.* A ridgelike band between the ogive and body of a shell, fitting closely to the bore of the gun and centering the projectile. [<F]

bourse (bōōrs) *n.* An exchange or money market: applied to Continental stock exchanges, and especially to the Paris stock exchange. [<F, purse <LL *bursa* bag]

bou·stro·phe·don (bōō′strə·fēd′n, bou′-) *n.* The early Greek method of writing, alternately from right to left and from left to right, as in inscriptions. [<Gk. *boustrophēdon* turning like oxen (in plowing) <*bous* ox + *strephein* turn] —**bou·stroph·e·don·ic** (bōō′strof′ə·don′ik, bou-), **bou·stroph·ic** (bōō·strof′ik, bou-) *adj.*

bous·y (bōō′zē, bou′-) *adj.* Boozy.

bout (bout) *n.* 1 A single turn, as in mowing a field. 2 A set-to or contest, as at boxing, etc. 3 A fit of drunkenness, reveling, or illness. 4 A bend or turn, as of a rope; bight. See synonyms under BATTLE. [Var. of ME *bought* bending, turn. Cf. LG *bucht* bend, turn.]

bou·tique (bōō·tēk′) *n. French* A small retail store in which dress accessories are sold.

bou·ton·nière (bōō′tə·nyâr′) *n.* A buttonhole bouquet, or a single flower worn in the buttonhole. [<F]

bou·zou·ki (bə·zōō′kē) *n.* A mandolinlike stringed instrument having a very long neck. [<New Gk. *mpouzouki*]

bo·vid (bō′vid) *n. Zool.* One of the *Bovidae*.

Bo·vi·dae (bō′vi·dē) *n. pl.* A family of ruminants, generally embracing those having paired hollow horns ensheathing horn cores, as antelopes, cattle, sheep, goats, etc.: distinguished from the deer family especially by non-deciduous, unbranched horns. [<L *bos, bovis* ox]

bo·vine (bō′vīn, -vin) *adj.* 1 Of or pertaining to the *Bovidae* or the genus *Bos.* 2 Oxlike; slow; patient; dull. —*n.* A bovine animal, as an ox, cow, etc. [< LL *bovinus* < L *bos* ox]

bow[1] (bou) *n.* 1 The forward part of a vessel; also, the front part of an airship. 2 The forward oarsman of a boat. ◆Homophone: *bough.* [< Dan. *bov* bow of a ship. Akin to BOUGH.]

bow[2] (bou) *v.* **bowed, bow·ing** *v.t.* 1 To bend (the head, knee, etc.), as in reverence, courtesy, or assent. 2 To express with bows: to *bow* agreement. 3 To escort with bows: He *bowed* us into the room. 4 To cause to yield; coerce: He *bowed* her to his will. 5 To weigh down; cause to stoop: Fatigue *bowed* his head. —*v.i.* 6 To bend the head, knee, etc., as in reverence, courtesy, or assent. 7 To express homage, greeting, agreement, etc., by bowing. 8 To bend or incline downward: The waves *bowed* over and broke. 9 To submit; yield. —**to bow out** To withdraw; resign. —*n.* An inclination of the body or head forward and downward, as in salutation or worship. ◆Homophone: *bough.* [OE *bugan* bow, bend, flee] —**bow'er** *n.*

bow[3] (bō) *n.* 1 A bend or curve, or something bent or curved. 2 A rainbow. 3 A weapon made from a strip of elastic wood or other pliable material, bent by a cord and projecting an arrow by its recoil when suddenly released; also, an archer. 4 *Music* A rod having parallel hairs strained between raised ends, used with a violin or other stringed instrument by drawing across the strings; also, the movement or mode of moving this. 5 A knot with a loop or loops, as of ribbon, etc. 6 Any one of various bow-shaped objects. 7 A U-shaped wooden piece passing upward through a yoke and retained by pins; oxbow. 8 *Geom.* A polygonal or curved projection from a straight line or wall on the ground plane. 9 Either of the rims of a pair of spectacles or one of the curved supports passing over the ears. —*adj.* Bent; curved; bowed. —*v.t.* & *v.i.* **bow·ed, bow·ing** 1 To bend into the shape of a bow. 2 *Music* To play (a stringed instrument) with a bow. ◆Homophone: *beau.* [OE *boga*] —**bow'er** *n.*

bow arm (bō) In playing a violin, the right arm; in archery, the left.

bow compass (bō) *Geom.* A pair of very small compasses, properly having, instead of a joint, a curved metal strip between the legs, for drawing small circles or arcs of small radius.

bowd·ler·ize (boud'lər·īz) *v.t.* **·ized, ·iz·ing** To expurgate or edit prudishly. [after Dr. Thomas *Bowdler's* "family" edition of Shakespeare (1818)] —**bowd'ler·i·za'tion** *n.* —**bowd'ler·ism** *n.*

bow·el (bou'əl, boul) *n.* 1 An intestine. 2 *pl.* The intestines or entrails collectively. 3 *pl.* The inner part of anything: the *bowels* of the earth. 4 *pl.* The intestinal regions, formerly considered as the seat of the tender emotions; hence, pity; compassion; heart. —*v.t.* **·eled** or **·elled, ·el·ing** or **·el·ling** To remove the bowels from; disembowel. [< OF *boel* < L *botellus,* dim. of *botulus* sausage]

bow·er[1] (bou'ər) *n.* 1 A shady recess; a retired dwelling; a rustic cottage. 2 A private apartment; boudoir. 3 An arbor. —*v.t.* To enclose in or as in a bower; embower. [OE *bur* chamber] —**bow'er·y** *adj.*

bow·er[2] (bou'ər) *n.* Either of the two highest cards (the knave of trumps or **right bower** and the knave of the same color or **left bower**) in the game of euchre, unless the joker is used, which is then usually called the **best bower.** [< G *bauer* peasant, knave in a deck of cards]

bow·er[3] (bou'ər) *n. Naut.* A large anchor carried on the bow of a vessel. Also **bower anchor.**

bow·er·y (bou'ər·ē) *n. pl.* **·er·ies** A farm or plantation: so called by the Dutch settlers of New York. [< Du. *bouwerij* farm < *bouwer, boer* farmer]

Bow·er·y (bou'ər·ē), **the** A street and section in New York City occupying the site of Governor Stuyvesant's farm or bowery: noted for its saloons, shabby hotels, and cheap shops.

bow·knot (bō'not') *n.* An ornamental slipknot made by doubling ribbon, cord, fabric, etc., into one or more loops, usually tied so as to leave ends free to draw the loops easily through the knot. See illustration under KNOT.

bowl[1] (bōl) *n.* 1 A concave domestic vessel, nearly hemispherical and larger than a cup. 2 The amount it will hold. 3 A drinking-vessel for wine, etc. 4 A large goblet. 5 Anything shaped like a bowl, as a stadium. ◆Homophone: *bole.* [OE *bolla*]

bowl[2] (bōl) *v.t.* 1 To strike or hit with or as with a bowl; knock down. 2 To roll (a ball). 3 To carry or transport on or as on wheels. 4 In cricket, to put out (the batsman): with *out.* —*v.i.* 5 To play at bowls. 6 To throw or roll a bowl or round object. 7 In cricket, to deliver the ball to the batsman. 8 To move smoothly and swiftly: usually with *along:* The ship *bowled* along. —**to bowl over** To cause to be confused or helpless; knock down or out. —*n.* 1 A large wooden ball for playing bowls or tenpins. 2 A turn or inning at a game of bowls. 3 A roller in a knitting machine. ◆Homophone: *bole.* [< F *boule* ball < L *bulla* bubble]

bow·leg (bō'leg') *n.* A leg bent in an outward curve. —**bow'leg'ged** *adj.*

bowl·er (bō'lər) *n.* 1 One who plays bowls. 2 The player who delivers the ball. 3 *Brit.* A low-crowned, stiff felt hat; a derby hat.

bow·line (bō'lin, -līn') *n.* 1 *Naut.* A rope to keep the weather edge of a vessel's square sail forward when sailing close-hauled. 2 A knot. —**on a bowline** Close-hauled to the wind; said of a vessel.

bowl·ing (bō'ling) *n.* 1 A game played on a narrow lane along which a ball is rolled in an attempt to knock down ten pins at the far end of the lane. 2 Any of various similar games. 3 The playing of any of these games.

BOWLINE KNOTS
a. Bowline knot.
b. Running bowline.

bowling alley 1 A long, narrow, planked space for playing at tenpins. 2 A building containing one or more such alleys. 3 Any enclosure for playing bowls.

bowling ball A hard, heavy ball used in the game of bowling, usually having three finger holes for gripping.

bowling green A smooth lawn for playing at bowls.

bowls (bōlz) *n. pl. (construed as sing.)* Any of various bowling games, especially one (also called **lawn bowling**) played outdoors with weighted balls rolled at a stationary ball.

bow·man[1] (bō'mən) *n. pl.* **·men** (-mən) An archer.

bow·man[2] (bou'mən) *n. pl.* **·men** (-mən) The oarsman nearest the bow.

bow pen (bō) *Geom.* A pair of jointless compasses carrying a pen or pencil: used for drawing very small circles.

bow·pin (bō'pin') *n.* A bow-key.

bow·shot (bō'shot') *n.* The distance which an arrow may be sent from the bow.

bow·sprit (bou'sprit', bō'-) *n. Naut.* A spar projecting forward from the bow of a vessel.

bow·string (bō'string') *n.* 1 The string of a bow. 2 A string for strangling criminals. 3 Execution by strangling. —*v.t.* To execute by strangling; garrote.

bow·tie (bō'tī') *n.* A necktie worn in a bowknot.

bow window (bō) A projecting window built up from the ground level, properly one of curved ground plan. Compare BAY WINDOW.

bow-wow (bou'wou') *n.* 1 The bark of a dog, or an imitation of it. 2 A dog: a child's word. 3 *pl. Colloq.* Ruin; damnation: going to the *bow-wows.* —*v.i.* To bark.

bow·yer (bō'yər) *n.* A maker or seller of bows.

box[1] (boks) *n.* 1 A receptacle or case of wood or other material, usually having a lid. 2 Any of various objects or receptacles resembling a box. 3 *Mech.* An axle bearing, casing, or other enclosed cavity. 4 The raised seat of a coach, the body of a wagon, etc. 5 A building, structure, or compartment with some resemblance or analogy to a box, as a compartment in a theater, restaurant, etc. 6 The quantity contained in a box or that a box will hold. 7 Either of the rectangular

spaces on a baseball field in which the batsman or pitcher stands. 8 A gift or present packed in a box. 9 A box stall for a horse or bovine animal. 10 A flag house, sentry house, or similar small building for a watchman or the like. 11 A small house in the country; a shooting-box. 12 The place in a courtroom where the jury, a prisoner, or witnesses are railed in. 13 A cavity made in the trunk of a tree to collect its sap, as in extracting turpentine, etc. 14 A difficulty or predicament. —*v.t.* 1 To put into or enclose in a box: often with *up.* 2 To furnish with a bushing or box. 3 To boxhaul. 4 To fit into a mortise, as a tenon. —**to box the compass** 1 To recite in order the 32 points of the compass. 2 To make a complete revolution; adopt successively all possible opinions on a question. [OE < Med. L *buxis,* blend of L *buxus* boxwood and *pyxis* box (both < Gk. *pyxos* boxwood). Doublet of PYX.] —**box'er** *n.*

box[2] (boks) *v.t.* 1 To cuff or buffet, especially about the ears and side of the head. 2 To fight (another) in a boxing match. —*v.i.* 3 To fight in a boxing match. 4 To be a prize fighter. —*n.* A slap or cuff with the hand on the ear or the cheek. See synonyms under BLOW [ME; origin uncertain]

box[3] (boks) *n.* A small evergreen tree or shrub (genus *Buxus*) of the Old World, cultivated as a border or hedge; especially, any variety of *B. sempervirens.* [OE < L *buxus* < Gk. *pyxos* boxwood]

box·ber·ry (boks'ber'ē, -bər·ē) *n. pl.* **·ber·ries** 1 The checkerberry or wintergreen. 2 The partridgeberry.

box calf Tanned calfskin with square markings on the grain produced by lengthwise and cross-wise rolling.

box·car (boks'kär') *n.* A railway car shaped like a rectangular box, for carrying freight.

box coat 1 A coachman's heavy overcoat. 2 A greatcoat, especially one worn by travelers on the tops of coaches. 3 A loosely fitting overcoat, snug only at the shoulders.

box elder A North American tree of the maple family (*Acer negundo*) having leaves with 3 or 5 compound leaflets.

box·er[1] (bok'sər) *n.* A pugilist.

box·er[2] (bok'sər) *n.* A breed of medium-sized dog, related to the bulldog, characterized by a short, sturdy body, smooth coat, fawn or brindle in color, and a black mask. [Alter. of G *-beisser* in *Bullenbeisser* bulldog]

box·haul (boks'hôl') *v.t. Naut.* To veer (a square-rigged vessel) round instead of tacking: done when tacking is impracticable.

box hook A sickle-shaped hook with a wooden handle, usually T-shaped, used for gripping and moving heavy boxes or bales of merchandise, waste, etc.: also called *bale hook.*

box·ing[1] (bok'sing) *n.* The act or practice of sparring, as with gloves; pugilism.

box·ing[2] (bok'sing) *n.* 1 The act of enclosing in a box. 2 Material from which to make boxes. 3 A casing or niche, as for window shutters.

Boxing Day The first weekday after Christmas, a British legal holiday on which presents (Christmas boxes) are given to employees, letter-carriers, etc.

boxing glove A glove with padded back, for boxing.

boxing match A prize fight or sparring contest.

box iron A smoothing and pressing iron containing a receptacle for a heater: distinguished from *sad-iron.*

box kite A kite having two rectangular, box-shaped, covered frames fitted together.

box office The ticket office of a theater, etc.

box-of·fice (boks'ôf'is, -of'is) *adj.* Of such a character as to attract large audiences, and, therefore, destined to make large profits.

box pleat Material folded twice and in opposite directions, the edges turned under and meeting. Also **box plait.**

BOX KITE

box spring A mattress foundation consisting of an upholstered wood or metal frame set with an arrangement of coil springs to provide resiliency.

box stall A large, boxed-in stall for horses or cattle, in which they do not have to be tied.

box·wood (boks′wŏŏd′) n. 1 The hard, close-grained, durable wood of the box evergreen shrub (genus *Buxus*). 2 The shrub.

boy (boi) n. 1 A male child; lad; youth; son. 2 pl. Comrades; fellows. 3 A male servant, especially a personal servant: often used of Orientals or Africans. [ME *boi;* origin unknown]

bo·yar (bō′yär′, boi′ər) n. 1 A member of a class of the old Russian aristocracy, abolished in the time of Peter the Great. 2 In Rumania, one of a privileged class. Also **bo·yard** (bō-yärd′, boi′ərd). [< Russian *boyarin* noble]

boy·cott (boi′kot) v.t. 1 To combine together in refusing to deal or associate with, so as to punish or coerce. 2 To refuse to use or buy. —n. The act, pressure, or an instance of boycotting. [after Capt. C. *Boycott,* 1832–1897, landlord's agent in Ireland, who was first victim, 1880]

boy friend *Colloq.* 1 A girl's or woman's sweetheart, favorite male companion, etc. 2 A male friend. Also **boy·friend** (boi′frend′).

boy·hood (boi′hŏŏd) n. 1 The state or period of being a boy. 2 Boys collectively.

boy·ish (boi′ish) adj. Of, pertaining to, or like boys or boyhood. See synonyms under YOUTHFUL. —**boy′ish·ly** adv. —**boy′ish·ness** n.

boy·sen·ber·ry (boi′zən-ber′ē) n. pl. ·ries 1 A hybrid plant obtained by crossing the blackberry, raspberry, and loganberry. 2 Its edible fruit, resembling the raspberry in taste. [after Rudolph *Boysen,* 20th c. U.S. horticulturist, the originator]

Bra·ban·çonne (brá-bän-sôn′) The national anthem of the Belgians since 1830. [< F < *Brabant,* province in Belgium]

Bra·bant (brə-bant′, brä′bənt) A former duchy, now divided into North Brabant, Netherlands, and Brabant province in Belgium; 1,268 square miles; capital, Brussels.

brab·ble (brab′əl) v.i. ·bled, ·bling To quarrel noisily about trifles. [? < Du. *brabbelen* jabber] —**brab′ble·ment** n.

brac·cate (brak′āt) adj. *Ornithol.* Having the feet feathered down to the claws, as certain birds. [< L *bracatus* wearing breeches < *bracae* breeches]

BRACCATE
CLAWS

brace (brās) v. **braced,** **brac·ing** v.t. 1 To make firm or steady; strengthen by or as by equipping with braces. 2 To make ready to withstand pressure, impact, assault, etc. 3 To tie or fasten firmly, as with straps. 4 To stimulate; enliven. 5 *Naut.* To turn (the yards) by means of the braces. 6 *Slang* To ask a loan or favor from. —v.i. 7 To strain against pressure. —**to brace up** *Colloq.* To rouse one's courage or resolution. —n. 1 A support, as of wood or metal, to hold something firmly in place. 2 A cranklike handle, as for a bit. 3 A clasp or clamp used for connecting, fastening, etc. 4 A doubly curved line (‿), used in writing and printing to connect words, lines, or staves of music. 5 A pair; couple; two: a *brace* of ducks, etc. 6 The state of being braced; tension. 7 *Naut.* A rope fastened to a yardarm and reaching the deck, to swing the yard for the wind and to hold it in place. 8 pl. *Brit.* Suspenders. [< OF *bracier* embrace < *brace, brache* two arms < L *brachia,* pl. of *brachium* arm]

brace·let (brās′lit) n. 1 An ornamental band encircling the wrist or arm. 2 *Colloq.* A handcuff. [< OF, dim. of *bracel* < L *brachiale* bracelet < *brachium* arm]

brac·er (brā′sər) n. 1 That which braces or steadies; a band; support. 2 A protective covering for the forearm in archery. 3 A tonic; stimulant. 4 A stimulating drink.

brach (brach, brak) n. *Archaic* A hound bitch. Also **brach·et** (brach′it). [< OF *brachet* hunting dog < OHG]

bra·chi·al (brā′kē·əl, brak′ē-) adj. 1 Of or pertaining to the arm, especially the upper arm. 2 *Zool.* Of, pertaining to, or designating the armlike appendages or brachia of various invertebrates. 3 Armlike. [< L *brachialis < brachium* arm]

bra·chi·ate (brā′kē·it, -āt, brak′ē-) adj. *Bot.* Having branches in pairs, each pair forming a right line with each other, and standing at right angles to the stem, or widely diverging. —v.i. (-āt) **·at·ed, ·at·ing** *Zool.* To move by a swinging motion of the arms, as from branch to branch of trees: said especially of certain arboreal apes not fully adapted to the erect posture and bipedal locomotion. [< L *brachiatus* having arms < *brachium* arm] —**bra′chi·a′tion** n.

brachio- *combining form* Arm; of the arm: *brachiotomy.* Also, before vowels, **brachi-.** [< Gk. *brachīōn* arm]

bra·chi·ot·o·my (brā′kē·ot′ə·mē, brak′ē-) n. *Surg.* The cutting off or removal of an arm.

bra·chi·o·pod (brā′kē·ə·pod′, brak′ē-) n. *Zool.* One of a phylum or class (*Brachiopoda*) of nearly extinct molluscoid marine animals having a bivalve shell and a pair of brachial appendages rising from the sides of the mouth; a lamp shell. —**bra·chi·op·o·dous** (brā′kē·op′ə·dəs, brak′ē-) adj.

bra·chis·to·chrone (brə·kis′tə·krōn) n. *Physics* The line of motion along which a particle acted upon by a constraining force will move from one given point to another in the shortest time: also spelled *brachystochrone.* [< Gk. *brachistos* shortest + *chronos* time]

bra·chi·um (brā′kē·əm, brak′ē-) n. pl. **bra·chi·a** (brā′kē·ə, brak′ē-) 1 The upper arm, or its homolog in any animal. 2 Any armlike process or appendage. [< L]

brachy- *combining form* Short: *brachycranic.* [< Gk. *brachys* short]

brach·y·dac·tyl·ic (brak′i·dak·til′ik) adj. Having abnormally short fingers or toes. [< Gk. *brachydaktylos < brachys* short + *daktylos* finger] —**brach′y·dac′tyl·ism** (-dak′təl·iz′əm) n.

brach·y·dro·mic (brak′i·drom′ik) adj. Taking a deflected or slanting path with reference to the target; heading short: said of guided missiles. [< Gk. *brachydromos < brachys* short + *dromos* course]

bra·chyl·o·gy (brə·kil′ə·jē) n. Brevity and conciseness of speech; an abridged form of expression; especially, omission of a word necessary for correct grammatical expression. [< Gk. *brachylogia < brachys* short + *-logia* speech]

brach·y·u·ran (brak′i·yŏŏr′an) adj. *Zool.* Of or relating to a suborder (*Brachyura*) of decapods, comprising the crabs. Also **brach′y·u′rous** (-yŏŏr′əs). —n. A short-tailed crustacean. [< NL *brachyura < Gk. brachys* short + *oura* tail]

brac·ing[1] (brā′sing) adj. Imparting tone or vigor; invigorating; tonic.

brac·ing[2] (brā′sing) n. 1 The act of bracing, or the state of being braced. 2 A system of braces, as in bridge-building.

brack·en (brak′ən) n. 1 A brake or other large fern. 2 Brakes collectively. [ME *braken* < Scand. Cf. Sw. *bräken* fern.]

brack·et (brak′it) n. 1 A piece projecting from a wall to support a shelf or other weight. 2 A projecting gas fixture or lamp holder, etc. 3 A brace used to strengthen an angle. 4 *Printing* One of two marks [ ], used to enclose any part of the text. 5 A vinculum. 6 A number of persons considered as a group because of some common characteristics: the high-income *bracket.* —v.t. 1 To provide or support with a bracket or brackets. 2 To enclose within brackets. 3 To group or categorize together. 4 *Mil.* To fire both over and short of (a target). [< Sp. *bragueta,* dim. of *braga* < L *bracae,* pl., breeches]

brack·et·ing (brak′it·ing) n. 1 Wooden skeleton pieces to which the lath and plaster forming the surface of a cornice are fastened, and which give shape to the latter. 2 The act of furnishing with brackets. 3 A series of brackets.

brack·ish (brak′ish) adj. 1 Somewhat saline, as a mixture of salt water and fresh; briny. 2 Distasteful. [< Du. *brak* salty] —**brack′ish·ness** n.

bract (brakt) n. *Bot.* A modified leaf in a flower cluster or subtending a flower. [< L *bractea* thin metal plate] —**brac·te·al** (brak′tē·əl) adj.

brac·te·ate (brak′tē·it, -āt) adj. *Bot.* Having bracts.

brac·te·o·late (brak′tē·ə·lāt′) adj. *Bot.* Having bracteoles.

brac·te·ole (brak′tē·ōl) n. *Bot.* A diminutive bract. Also **bract·let** (brakt′lit).

BRACT
Surrounding a composite flower.

brad (brad) n. A small and slender nail, often having, in place of head, a projection on one side. [< ON *broddr* spike]

brad·awl (brad′ôl′) n. A short, non-tapering awl, with a cutting edge on the end.

Brad·dock (brad′ək), **Edward,** 1695?–1755, English general in French and Indian War.

brady- *combining form* Slow: *bradycardia.* [< Gk. *bradys* slow]

brad·y·car·di·a (brad′i·kär′dē·ə) n. *Pathol.* Slowness of the heartbeat, indicated by a pulse rate of 60 or less. [< NL < BRADY- + Gk. *kardia* heart] —**brad′y·car′dic** adj.

brae (brā) n. *Scot.* A bank; hillside; slope. ◆ Homophone: *bray.*

brag (brag) v. **bragged, brag·ging** v.i. To vaunt oneself or one's deeds or abilities. —v.t. To declare or assert boastfully; boast of. —n. 1 The act of bragging; boastfulness; boastful language. 2 The thing bragged of; boast. 3 A person who brags. 4 A game of cards resembling poker. —adj. 1 To be bragged about: a *brag* crop. 2 *Obs.* Boastful; also, spirited; valiant. [Origin uncertain] —**brag′ger** n.

brag·ga·do·ci·o (brag′ə·dō′shē·ō) n. pl. ·ci·os 1 Pretentious boasting. 2 One who talks boastfully; a swaggerer. [after *Braggadochio,* a boastful character in Spenser's *Faerie Queene*]

brag·gart (brag′ərt) n. A vain boaster. —adj. Overboastful. —**brag′gart·ism** n.

brag·get (brag′it) n. An ancient drink of ale and honey fermented with yeast; later, mulled ale sweetened and spiced. [< Welsh *bragawd*]

Brah·ma[1] (brä′mə) n. 1 In Hindu religion, the absolute primordial essence; the supreme soul of the universe, self-existent, absolute, and eternal, from which all things emanate and to which all return. 2 God, conceived of as comprising the Hindu trinity Brahma, Vishnu, and Siva; also, specifically, the personification of the first of the trinity, as supreme creator. [< Skt. *Brahmā*]

Brah·ma[2] (brä′mə, brä′-) n. A large variety of the domestic hen of an Asian breed. [from *Brahmaputra*]

Brah·man (brä′mən) n. pl. ·mans 1 A member of the first of the four Hindu castes of India; the sacerdotal class: also spelled *Brahmin.* 2 A species of cattle originally imported from India and bred in the southern United States. [< Skt. *brāhmana < brahman* praise, worship] —**Brah·man·i** (brä′mən·ē) n. fem. —**Brah·man·ic** (brä·man′ik) or **·i·cal** adj.

Brah·man·ism (brä′mən·iz′əm) n. The religious and social system of the Brahmans: also spelled *Brahminism.* —**Brah′man·ist** n.

Brah·man·y (brä′mən·ē) adj. Held sacred according to Brahmanic rites, or consecrated to the use of Brahmans: said especially of certain animals and trees: *Brahmany* bull, fig tree, etc. Also **Brah′min·y.**

Brahmany bull The white male zebu.

Brah·ma·pu·tra (brä′mə·pōō′trə) A river of southern Asia, flowing 1,800 miles across Tibet, SW China, Assam, and East Pakistan to the Bay of Bengal.

Brah·min (brä′min) n. 1 Brahman (def. 1). 2 An aristocrat; a highly cultured person; specifically, an ultra-intellectual New Englander.

Bra·min·ism (brä′min·iz′əm) n. 1 Brahmanism. 2 The attitude, mannerisms, etc., of Brahmins.

Brahms (brämz, *Ger.* bräms), **Johannes,** 1833–97, German composer.

braid[1] (brād) v.t. 1 To weave together or intertwine several strands of; plait. 2 To bind or ornament (the hair) with ribbons, etc. 3 To form by braiding: to *braid* a mat. 4 To ornament (garments) with braid. —n. 1 A narrow, flat tape or strip for binding or ornamenting fabrics. 2 Anything braided or plaited: a *braid* of hair. 3 A string or band used in arranging the hair. [OE *bregdan* brandish, weave, braid] —**braid′er** n.

braid[2] (brād) adj. *Scot.* Broad.

braid·ing (brā′ding) n. 1 Braids collectively. 2 Embroidery done with braid.

brail (brāl) n. 1 *Naut.* One of the ropes for gathering up the foot and leeches of a fore-and-aft sail for furling. 2 A leather fastening for a hawk's wing. —v.t. 1 *Naut.* To haul in (a sail) by means of brails: usually with *up.* 2 To fasten with a brail, as a hawk's wing. [< OF *braiel* < L *bracale* a belt for breeches < *bracae* breeches]

Bră·i·la (brə·ē′lä) A city on the Danube in eastern Rumania.

Braille (brāl) *n.* A system of printing or writing for the blind in which the characters consist of raised dots to be read by the fingers; also,

A B C D E F G H I J

K L M N O P Q R S T

U V W X Y Z and for of the

; ; : . ! ( ) ? " Apostrophe

Hyphen   Dash   Numeral   Letter   Capital   Accent

BRAILLE ALPHABET

the characters themselves. See POINT SYSTEM (def. 2). [after Louis *Braille*, 1809–52, French educator, who invented it]

brain (brān) *n.* 1 *Anat.* The enlarged and greatly modified portion of the central nervous system contained within the cranium of vertebrates: its functions are shared between the two cerebral hemispheres, the cerebellum, and the medulla oblongata, which are of great development in higher mammals and in man. 2 Mind; intellect: often in the plural. 3 *Zool.* The principal regulating ganglion of invertebrates. See synonyms under MIND. —**to have on the brain** To be obsessed by. —*v.t.* To dash out the brains of. [OE *brœgen*]

brain-child (brān'chīld') *n.* An idea, project, or other product of the mind considered as belonging to its creator.

brain drain emigration of highly educated persons to areas with more opportunity, e.g., from England, India to U.S. -**brain drain** v. - **brain-drainer** *n.* one who emigrates.

brain fever Inflammation of the meninges.

brain-less (brān'lis) *adj.* 1 Without a brain. 2 Destitute of intelligence; senseless. —**brain'less-ly** *adv.* —**brain'less-ness** *n.*

brain-pan (brān'pan') *n.* The bony case enclosing the brain; cranium; skull.

brain-stem (brān'stem') *n.* All the brain except the cerebellum and the cerebral cortex; that is, the segmental apparatus.

brain storm 1 Cerebral disturbance of a sudden and violent character. 2 *Colloq.* Any momentary confusion of mind. 3 *Colloq.* A burst of inspiration.

brain trust Any group of experts or, derisively, of pretended experts: used in 1933 to designate the group of educators in political science and economy who advised President Franklin D. Roosevelt.

brain-wash (brān'wosh', -wôsh') *v.t.* To alter the convictions, beliefs, etc., of by means of brainwashing.

brain-wash-ing (brān'wosh'ing, -wôsh'ing) *n.* 1 Indoctrination. 2 The systematic alteration of personal convictions, beliefs, habits, and attitudes to follow politically acceptable lines.

brain wave 1 *Physiol.* A rhythmical fluctuation of electrical potential between different parts of the brain. 2 *Colloq.* A sudden inspiration.

brain-work (brān'wûrk') *n.* Work involving primarily the use of the mind, rather than manual or mechanical skills. —**brain'work'er** *n.*

brain-y (brā'nē) *adj.* **brain-i-er**, **brain-i-est** Possessed of brains; mentally able; smart. —**brain'i-ly** *adv.* —**brain'i-ness** *n.*

braise (brāz) *v.t.* **braised**, **brais-ing** To cook (meat) by searing till brown and then simmering in a covered pan. [< F *braiser* < *braise* charcoal]

brais-er (brā'zər) *n.* A covered kettle or pan used in braising.

brake¹ (brāk) *n.* 1 A device for retarding or arresting the motion of a vehicle, a wheel, etc. 2 A harrow. 3 An instrument for separating the fiber of flax, hemp, etc., by bruising. 4 A lever for working a pump or other machine. 5 A baker's kneading machine. 6 A framework to hold a

horse's foot while it is being shod. 7 A machine for extracting juice from fruits and vegetables. 8 An old instrument of torture. —*v.* **braked**, **brak-ing** *v.t.* 1 To apply a brake to; reduce the speed of. 2 To bruise and crush, as flax. 3 To pulverize (clods) with a harrow. 4 To knead (dough). —*v.i.* 5 To operate a brake or brakes. ◆ Homophone: *break*. [MDu. *braeke* brake for flax; infl. in meaning by F *brac*, var. of *bras* arm, and by BREAK]

brake² (brāk) *n.* Break (def. 7).

brake³ (brāk) *n.* 1 A variety of fern; bracken. 2 A canebrake. ◆ Homophone: *break*. [ME < *braken* BRACKEN]

brake⁴ (brāk) *n.* A thicket. ◆ Homophone: *break*. [Cf. MLG *brake* stumps, broken branches]

brake⁵ (brāk) Archaic past tense of BREAK.

brake-age (brā'kij) *n.* The action or controlling power of a brake.

brake band A flexible band or strap which encircles a brake drum and grips it when tightened.

brake drum A metal drum attached to the axle or transmission shaft of a vehicle and connecting with the brake mechanism.

brake-man (brāk'mən) *n. pl.* **-men** (-mən) One who tends a brake or brakes on a railroad car or in a mine. Also **brakes'man.**

brake shoe A brake lining.

bra-ky (brā'kē) *adj.* Overgrown with bracken or brushwood.

Bra-man-te (brä-män'tā), **Donato d'Agnolo,** 1444–1514, Italian architect and painter.

bram-ble (bram'bəl) *n.* 1 The European blackberry, or any other species of the genus *Rubus*. 2 Any prickly plant or shrub. [OE *brœmble*. Akin to BROOM.] —**bram'bly** *adj.*

bram-bling (bram'bling) *n.* The European mountain finch (*Fringilla montifringilla*).

bran (bran) *n.* 1 The coarse, outer coat of cereals, as separated from the flour by sifting or bolting. 2 Grain by-products as used for cattle feed. [< OF *bran*, *bren*]

Bran (bran) 1 A mythical king of Britain. 2 In Celtic mythology, a god of the underworld. 3 In Icelandic saga, the faithful hound of Frithiof.

branch (branch, bränch) *n.* 1 A secondary stem of a tree, shrub, or the like; a limb: distinguished from *twig*; an offshoot. 2 A separate part; side issue; division; department. 3 *Geog.* A tributary stream; in the southern United States, any stream of water smaller than a river. 4 Anything having an analogy to a branch, as one of the subdivisions of a deer's antler, a part of a family, a subhead of a general subject, etc. 5 A local division of a highway, railroad, etc., connecting with a main line. 6 *Archit.* One of the ribs in the Gothic style of vaulting. 7 A division used in classifying the subdivisions of linguistic families and stocks, including more than a group and less than a stock. 8 A subordinate local office, store, etc. 9 *Physics* a In a band spectrum, a section of the component lines proceeding in both directions from a common zero line. b Any of the subdivisions due to varying transformations of a radioactive series. —*v.t.* 1 To divide into branches. 2 To embroider with a pattern of flowers or foliage. —*v.i.* 3 To put forth branches; divide into branches. 4 To spring off from the main part; come out from the trunk, etc. —**to branch off** 1 To separate into branches; fork, as a road. 2 To diverge; go off on a tangent. —**to branch out** To extend or expand, as one's business or interests. —*adj.* Diverging from or tributary to a trunk, stock, or main part. [< F *branche* < LL *branca* paw]

bran-chi-a (brang'kē-ə) *n. pl.* **-chi-ae** (-kē-ē) 1 *Zool.* A gill. 2 *pl.* Gills or gill-like appendages; respiratory organs of fish, modified for breathing the air contained in water. [< L < Gk. *branchia*, pl., gills] —**bran'chi-al** *adj.*

branchial cleft Gill slit.

bran-chi-ate (brang'kē-it, -āt) *adj.* Having gills.

branchio- combining form Gills: branchiopod. Also, before vowels, **branchi-.** [< Gk. *branchia*, pl., gills of fishes]

bran-chi-o-pod (brang'kē-ə-pod') *n.* One of a group (*Branchiopoda*) of aquatic crustaceans having a typically elongated body and many pairs of leaflike thoracic appendages having a respiratory function. [< BRANCHIO- + Gk. *pous*,

podos foot]

Bran-cusi (bron'kōōsh), **Constantin,** 1876–1957, Rumanian sculptor.

brand (brand) *v.t.* 1 To mark with or as with a hot iron. 2 To stigmatize; mark as infamous. [< *n.*] —*n.* 1 A burning stick; firebrand. 2 A mark burned with a hot iron. 3 A name or trademark used to identify a product or group of products of a particular manufacturer. 4 A herd of cattle marked with a certain brand. 5 Quality; kind. 6 A branding iron. 7 *Archaic* A sword. 8 *Bot.* A pustular appearance of plants, caused by a parasitic fungus. See synonyms under BLEMISH, BURN. [OE, torch, sword. Akin to BURN¹.] —**brand'er** *n.*

bran-den-burg (bran'dən-bûrg) *n.* 1 One of a series of ornamental loops worn on an outer garment in the place of buttons; a frog. 2 A facing of embroidery on a military coat: usually in parallel bars. [from *Brandenburg*]

brand-er¹ (bran'dər) *n.* 1 One who or that which brands. 2 *Dial.* A support of a grain stack. [<BRAND]

brand-er² (bran'dər) *n.* 1 *Scot.* A gridiron. 2 *Dial.* A stand for a kettle; trivet. [ME *brandire* < *branden* burn + *ire* iron]

bran-died (bran'dēd) *adj.* Mixed, flavored with, or preserved in brandy: *brandied* cherries.

branding iron An iron for burning in a brand. Also **brand iron.**

BRANDING IRON AND CATTLE BRANDS

bran-dish (bran'dish) *v.t.* To wave, shake, or flourish triumphantly, menacingly, or defiantly. See synonyms under SHAKE. —*n.* A flourish, as with a weapon. [<OF *brandiss-*, stem of *brandir* < *brand* sword] —**brand'ish-er** *n.*

brand-new (brand'nōō', -nyōō') *adj.* Quite new; fresh and bright: also *bran-new.*

bran-dy (bran'dē) *n. pl.* **bran-dies** An alcoholic liquor distilled from wine and also from the fermented juice of fruits other than the grape. —*v.t.* **bran-died**, **bran-dy-ing** 1 To mix, flavor, strengthen, or preserve with brandy. 2 To serve or refresh with brandy. [<Du. *brandewijn* brandy, lit., distilled wine]

branle (bränl) *n.* A form of dance in vogue in France in the 16th and 17th centuries, still performed by French Canadians. [<F < *branler* shake]

brash¹ (brash) *adj.* Brittle: said of wood or timber. [Cf. dial. E (Northern) *brassish* brittle]

brash² (brash) *adj.* 1 Quick-tempered; irascible; hasty; rash. 2 Saucy; pert. 3 Active; quick. [Cf. G *barsch* harsh and Sw. *barsk* impetuous] —**brash'ly** *adv.* —**brash'ness** *n.*

brash³ (brash) *n.* 1 A transient attack of sickness, especially one arising from a disordered stomach. 2 A rash or eruption. 3 An attack; bout; brush. 4 *Brit. Dial.* A shower of rain. [? Blend of BREAK and CRASH, DASH, SPLASH, etc.] —**brash'i-ness** *n.* —**brash'y** *adj.*

brash⁴ (brash) *n.* 1 A heap of rubbish. 2 Any brittle wood. [Prob. <F *brèche* rubble]

bra-sier (brā'zhər) *n.* Brazier.

Bra-sí-li-a (brə-zē'lē-ə) The capital of Brazil, in a Federal District in the central part.

brass (bras, bräs) *n.* 1 An alloy essentially of copper and zinc, harder than copper, ductile, and capable of being hammered into thin leaves. 2 Formerly, any alloy of copper, especially one with tin. 3 An ornament or utensil of brass, as a candlestick, doorknob, etc.: chiefly in the plural. 4 The brass wind instruments of an orchestra collectively. 5 *Colloq.* Impudence; effrontery. 6 *Slang* Money. 7 A bearing box or bush, properly of a copper alloy. 8 A monumental tablet of brass. 9 *Colloq.* High-ranking military officers collectively. [OE *brœs*]

bras-sage (bras'ij, bräs'-) *n.* The mintage fee for coining. Compare SEIGNIORAGE. [<F < *brasser* stir (fused metal)]

bras-sard (bras'ärd, brə-särd') *n.* 1 A cloth

band worn on the left arm by military police, umpires at maneuvers, and others, bearing insignia which denote the special duties of the wearer. **2** A piece of armor for the arm. Also **bras·sart** (bras'ərt). [<F <*bras* arm]

brass band A band of musicians using mostly brass instruments.

bras·sière (brə·zir') *n.* A woman's undergarment shaped to support the breasts. [<F, shoulder strap <*bras* arm]

brass tacks *Colloq.* Concrete facts; details.

brass winds *Music* The wind instruments of a band or orchestra that are made of metal: distinguished from *woodwinds*; specifically, the trumpet, horn, trombone, and tuba.

brass·y (bras'ē, bräs'ē) *adj.* **brass·i·er, brass·i·est 1** Covered with, made of, or like brass. **2** Impudent; shameless. **3** Debased; degenerate. — *n. pl.* **brass·ies** A wooden golf club with a brass plate on the sole: also **brass'ie.** — **brass'i·ly** *adv.* — **brass'i·ness** *n.*

brat¹ (brat) *n.* A child: now only contemptuously. [? <BRAT² (def. 1)]

brat² (brat) *n. Scot.* **1** An apron; bib; rag or clout. **2** The scum on boiled milk, porridge, etc. [OE *bratt,* ult. <Celtic]

brat·tice (brat'is) *n.* **1** A plank partition; especially, inside planking in a mine. **2** In old fortifications, a temporary parapet or breastwork. — *v.t.* **brat·ticed, brat·tic·ing** To furnish with a brattice. [<OF *bretesche,* ult. <Gmc.]

brat·tle (brat'l) *v.i.* **·tled, ·tling 1** To make a rattling or clattering noise. **2** To run with clatter; scamper noisily. — *n.* A rattling or clattering noise. [Imit.]

brat·wurst (brät'wûrst, -vûrst, brat'-) *n.* A small German sausage made mainly of pork or of pork and veal and various seasonings. [<G <*brat* fried + *wurst* sausage]

Braun (broun), **Karl Ferdinand,** 1850–1918, German physicist and inventor in wireless telegraphy.

bra·va·do (brə·vä'dō) *n. pl.* **·dos** or **·does** Arrogant defiance or menace; affectation of reckless bravery. [<Sp. *bravada* <*bravo* brave]

brave (brāv) *adj.* **brav·er, brav·est 1** Having or showing courage; intrepid; courageous. **2** Having elegance; showy; splendid. **3** *Obs.* Excellent. — *v.* **braved, brav·ing** *v.t.* **1** To meet or face with courage and fortitude. **2** To defy; challenge. **3** *Obs.* To make splendid. — *v.i.* **4** *Obs.* To boast. — *n.* **1** A man of courage; a soldier. **2** A North American Indian warrior. **3** A bully; bravo. **4** *Obs.* A boast or defiance. [<F <Ital. *bravo,* ? <L *barbarus* wild, fierce] — **brave'ly** *adv.* — **brave'ness** *n.*

Synonyms (adj.): adventurous, bold, chivalric, chivalrous, courageous, daring, dauntless, doughty, fearless, gallant, heroic, intrepid, undaunted, undismayed, valiant, venturesome. The *adventurous* man goes in quest of danger; the *bold* man stands out and faces danger or censure audaciously; the *brave* man combines confidence with firm resolution in presence of danger; the *chivalrous* man puts himself in peril for others' protection. The *daring* step out to defy danger; the *dauntless* will not flinch before anything that may come to them; the *doughty* will give and take limitless hard knocks; the *venturesome* may be simply heedless, reckless, or ignorant. The *fearless* and *intrepid* possess unshaken nerves in any place of danger. *Courageous* is more than *brave,* adding a moral element; the *courageous* man steadily encounters perils to which he may be keenly sensitive, at the call of duty; the *gallant* are *brave* in a dashing, showy, and splendid way; the *valiant* not only dare great dangers, but achieve great results; the *heroic* are nobly *daring* and *dauntless,* truly *chivalrous,* sublimely *courageous.* Compare CALM. *Antonyms:* afraid, cowardly, craven, cringing, faint-hearted, fearful, frightened, pusillanimous, shrinking, timid, timorous.

brav·er·y (brā'vər·ē) *n. pl.* **·er·ies 1** The quality or state of being brave; valor; gallantry; heroism. **2** Elegance of attire; show; splendor; beauty. **3** *Obs.* Ostentation; bravado. See synonyms under COURAGE.

bra·vis·si·mo (brä·vis'sē·mō) *interj. Italian* Excellent! splendid!

bra·vo¹ (brä'vō) *interj.* Good! well done! — *n. pl.* **·vos** A shout of "bravo!" [<Ital.

BRAVE.]

bra·vo² (brä'vō, brā'-) *n. pl.* **·voes** or **·vos** A daring villain; hired assassin; bandit. [<Ital. See BRAVE.]

bra·vu·ra (brə·vyŏŏr'ə, *Ital.* brä·vōō'rä) *n.* **1** *Music* A passage in a composition that requires dashing and brilliant execution; also, a brilliant style of execution. **2** Any pretentious attempt or display; dashing or daring style. [<Ital., dash, daring <*bravo* BRAVE]

braw (brô, brä) *adj. Scot.* Brave or bravely dressed; splendid; handsome; fine. — **braw'ly,** *Obs.* **braw'lie** *adv.*

brawl¹ (brôl) *n.* **1** A noisy quarrel or wrangle; a row. **2** A roaring stream. See synonyms under ALTERCATION, QUARREL. — *v.i.* **1** To quarrel noisily; fight. **2** To move noisily, as water. [ME *braulen,* ? <LG; cf. Du. *brallen*] — **brawl'er** *n.* — **brawl'ing·ly** *adv.*

brawl² (brôl) *n.* A dance in which one or two dancers lead the others; also, the music for it. [<F *branle* <*branler* shake, sway]

brawn (brôn) *n.* **1** Flesh; firm muscle; strength. **2** The flesh of the boar, especially when boiled, pickled, and pressed. **3** The arm, calf of the leg, or buttock. [OF *braon* slice of flesh, ult. <Gmc.]

brawn·y (brô'nē) *adj.* **brawn·i·er, brawn·i·est** Having or characterized by firm muscle; strong. — **brawn'i·ness** *n.*

braws (brôz, bräz) *n. pl. Scot.* Finery; best clothes.

brax·y (brak'sē) *n.* **1** A carbuncular fever of sheep, caused by a bacterium (*Clostridium septicum*). **2** A sheep affected with this disease. — *adj.* Affected with braxy. [Cf. OE *bræc* sickness, rheum]

bray¹ (brā) *v.t.* **1** To utter in a loud, harsh manner. — *v.i.* **2** To give forth a loud, harsh cry, as an ass. **3** To sound harshly, as a trumpet. — *n.* Any loud, harsh sound, as the cry of an ass. ♦ Homophone: *brae.* [<OF *braire* cry out] — **bray'er** *n.*

bray² (brā) *v.t.* To bruise, pound, or mix, as in a mortar. ♦ Homophone: *brae.* [<OF *breier,* ult. <Gmc.]

bray·er (brā'ər) *n.* A roller mounted for use by hand, to spread ink evenly over a printing surface. [See BRAY²]

bra·ye·ra (brə·yär'ə) *n.* Cusso. [after A. *Brayer,* 1775?–1848, French physician]

bra·za (brä'thä, -sä) *n.* A Spanish measure of length equivalent to 5.48 feet; in Argentina, 5.68 feet. [<Sp.]

braze¹ (brāz) *v.t.* **brazed, braz·ing 1** To make of brass. **2** To make hard like brass. **3** To ornament with or as with brass. **4** *Poetic* To color as with brass. [OE *brasian* <*bræs* brass]

braze² (brāz) *v.t.* **brazed, braz·ing** *Metall.* To join the surfaces of similar or dissimilar metals by partial fusion with a layer of a soldering alloy applied under very high temperature. [<F *braser* solder <OF, burn, ult. <Gmc; infl. in meaning by BRAZE¹] — **braz'er** *n.*

bra·zen (brā'zən) *adj.* **1** Made of, colored like, or resembling brass. **2** Sounding like brass. **3** Impudent; shameless. See synonyms under IMMODEST, IMPUDENT. — *v.t.* **1** To face or treat with effrontery or impudence: with *out.* **2** To make bold or reckless. — **bra'zen·ly** *adv.* — **bra'zen·ness** *n.*

bra·zier¹ (brā'zhər) *n.* A worker in brass: also spelled *brasier.* [ME *brasiere*]

bra·zier² (brā'zhər) *n.* An open pan for holding live coals: also spelled *brasier.* [<F *braiser* <*braise* hot coals]

bra·zil (brə·zil') *n.* **1** The red wood of a Brazilian tree (*Caesalpinia echinata*), or of several related species: used as a dyestuff. **2** A dyewood from several nearly allied genera. **3** The dye obtained from the wood. **4** The Oriental sapanwood (*C. sappan*). Also **bra·zil'wood'.** [<Sp. *brasil,* or Ital. *brasile,* an Oriental dyewood]

Bra·zil (brə·zil') A republic in South America; 3,287,842 square miles; capital, Brasilia: officially **The United States of Brazil.** *Portuguese* **Es·ta·dos U·ni·dos do Bra·sil** (esh·tä'thōōz ōō·nē'thōōz thōō brä·zil'). — **Bra·zil'ian** *adj. & n.*

Brazil nut One of the triangular edible seeds of a South American tree (*Bertholletia excelsa*).

brazing solder A brass alloy of high tensile strength used to make brazing joints.

brazing tongs Clamping irons used in brazing.

Braz·za·ville (braz'ə·vil, *Fr.* brá·zá·vēl') A city on the Congo, capital of the Congo Republic.

breach (brēch) *n.* **1** The act of breaking; infraction; infringement. **2** Violation of duty, right, or legal obligation. **3** A gap or break, as in a wall, dike, etc. **4** A rupture of amicable relations; dissension; quarrel. **5** The breaking of waves or surf; a surge. **6** The leaping of a whale from the water. **7** *Obs.* An injury; wound. — *v.t.* To make a breach in; break through. ♦ Homophone: *breech.* [<OE *bryce* breaking; infl. in form by F *brèche* fragment, piece. Akin to BREAK.]

Synonyms (noun): chasm, chink, cleft, crack, cranny, crevice, fissure, flaw, hole, opening, rent, rupture. Compare BREAK, GAP, HOLE, QUARREL, RUPTURE. *Antonyms:* adhesion, connection, contact, contiguity, union, unity.

breach·y (brē'chē) *adj.* **1** Apt to break out of an enclosure: said of livestock. **2** Full of breaches.

bread (bred) *n.* **1** An article of food made with flour or meal: commonly raised with yeast, kneaded, and baked. **2** Food in general: also, the necessaries of life. **3** Beebread. **4** *Slang* Money. — **light bread** Bread made with wheat flour and leavened with yeast. — *v.t.* To dress with bread crumbs before cooking. [OE, bit, crumb] — **bread'ed** *adj.*

bread and butter 1 Bread spread with butter. **2** *Colloq.* Subsistence; maintenance; livelihood.

bread·fruit (bred'frōōt') *n.* **1** The fruit of a moraceous tree of the South Sea Islands (*Artocarpus altilis*), which, when roasted, resembles bread. **2** The tree.

bread·line (bred'lin') *n.* A line of persons waiting for charitable donations of bread or other food.

BREADFRUIT (Fruit: ÷ 8 inches in diameter)

bread mold A mold developed on bread by a black fungus (*Rhizopus nigricans*).

bread·nut (bred'nut') *n.* The edible fruit of a West Indian tree (*Brosimum alicastrum*) of the mulberry family.

bread riot A people's riot caused by extreme hunger.

bread·root (bred'rōōt', -root') *n.* **1** A leguminous plant (*Psoralea esculenta*) of the plains of the United States. **2** Its starchy, edible root.

bread·stuff (bred'stuf') *n.* **1** Material for bread; grain, meal, or flour. **2** *pl.* Such materials collectively. **3** Bread.

breadth (bredth, bretth) *n.* **1** Measure or distance from side to side; as distinguished from length and thickness; width. **2** Catholicity; liberality. **3** That which has breadth; especially, a piece of a fabric of the full width. **4** The impression, in art, of largeness and comprehensiveness. [OE *braedu* <*brad* broad; *-th* added on analogy with *length*]

breadth·wise (bredth'wiz', bretth'-) *adv.* In the direction of the breadth. Also **breadth'ways'** (-wāz').

bread·win·ner (bred'win'ər) *n.* One who supports himself and others by his earnings; a producer.

break (brāk) *v.* **broke** (*Archaic* **brake**), **bro·ken** (*Archaic* **broke**), **break·ing** *v.t.* **1** To separate into pieces or make a fracture in; divide into fragments; shatter. **2** To part; sever, as a rope or bonds. **3** To disable or render useless by shattering or crushing. **4** To puncture or pierce the surface of (the skin). **5** To part the surface of, as ground or water. **6** To violate: to *break* a contract or a law. **7** To diminish the force of; moderate by interrupting: to *break* a fall. **8** To dispel or interrupt, as darkness or silence. **9** To destroy the order, continuity, or completeness of: to *break* step. **10** To interrupt the course of, as a journey; disconnect, as an electrical circuit. **11** To terminate forcibly; overwhelm: to *break* a strike. **12** To open forcibly (an entrance or way), as into or through a barrier. **13** To escape from: to *break* jail. **14** To surpass; excel, as a record. **15** To subdue or destroy the spirit or health of, as with toil or discipline. **16** To demote; reduce in rank or status. **17** To make bankrupt or short of money. **18** To discontinue (a habit): usually with *off*. **19** To cause (someone) to discontinue a habit: to *break* a child of biting his nails. **20** To tell; announce, as news. **21** *Law* **a** To enter (a shop or house) illegally. **b** To invalidate (a will) by court action. —*v.i.* **22** To become divided into fragments or pieces. **23** To dissolve and disperse; come apart: The clouds *broke*. **24** To become unusable or inoperative: The pencil *broke*. **25** To be grief-stricken, as the heart. **26** To burst away; free oneself: He *broke* free from the crowd. **27** To appear above the surface, as a periscope or arm. **28** To come into being or evidence, as the day. **29** To become bankrupt or short of funds. **30** To change or alter in direction, course, etc.: The horse *broke* from the track. **31** In baseball, to curve near the plate: said of the ball. **32** To crack, as a boy's voice. **33** *Music* To change from one quality of tone to another. —**to break bread** To take or share a meal. —**to break down 1** To become inoperative. **2** To have a physical or nervous collapse. **3** To give way to grief or strong feelings. **4** To overcome, as opposition. **5** To analyze. —**to break in** To cause to obey. —**to break into** (or **in**) **1** To interrupt or intervene. **2** To enter by force. —**to break in on** (or **upon**) To interrupt. —**to break off 1** To stop or cease, as from doing something. **2** To sever (relations); discontinue. **3** To become separate or detached. —**to break out 1** To start; have inception, as a fire or plague. **2** To have an eruption or rash, as the skin. **3** To make an escape, as from prison. —**to break out into** (or **forth in, into,** etc.) To begin to do or perform: The birds *broke* into song. —**to break up 1** To disperse; scatter: The meeting *broke up*. **2** To dismantle; take apart. **3** To put an end to; stop. **4** To distress: The loss *broke up* the old man. **5** To sever or discontinue relations: They decided to *break up*. —**to break with** To sever relations. —*n.* **1** An opening or breach; tear; fracture. **2** A starting or opening out: The *break* of day. **3** That which causes an opening, breach, or interruption. **4** *Electr.* **a** An apparatus for interrupting the flow or reversing the direction of an electric current. **b** The interruption of the current. **5** *Printing* A place where one paragraph ends and another begins. **6** In prosody, a caesura. **7** A high, four-wheeled carriage or wagonette: also brake. **8** A breach of continuity; interruption; especially, an interruption of physical continuity. **9** In writing, address, verse, etc., an interruption in the text or thought, as by an omission, or a space left to be filled out, or by a digression or aposiopesis. **10** A rupture of friendship; a falling out. **11** A sudden decline in prices. **12** *Music* The point where the chest tone changes to the head tone in singing; hence, sometimes, the point where one register or quality of voice changes to another, as alto to soprano; a similar point in the tones of a musical instrument. **13** In pool, the first play; the shot that scatters the balls. **14** In bowling, the act of playing a frame without making a strike or a spare. **15** In baseball or cricket, a deflection of the ball from a straight course when thrown. **16** In billiards, pool, and croquet, an uninterrupted series of successful shots. **17** *Colloq.* An unfortunate remark or ill-considered reaction: He made a bad *break*. **18** *Colloq.* An opportunity; a piece of luck, good or bad. **19** An agitation on the surface of water caused by the rising of a fish. **20** A dash or run; especially, an attempt to escape. **21** A sudden change in the gait of a horse. ◆ Homophone: *brake*. [OE *brecan*. Akin to BREACH.] *Synonyms* (verb): bankrupt, burst, cashier, crack, crush, demolish, destroy, fracture, rend, rive, rupture, sever, shatter, shiver, smash, split, sunder, transgress. To *break* is to divide sharply, with severance of particles, as by a blow or strain. To *burst* is ordinarily to *break* by pressure from within, as a bombshell. To *crush* is to *break* by pressure from without, as an egg shell. To *crack* is to *break* without complete severance of parts. *Fracture* has a

somewhat similar sense. A *shattered* object is *broken* suddenly and in numerous directions, as a vase is *shattered* by a blow. A *shivered* glass is *broken* into numerous minute, needle-like fragments. To *smash* is to *break* thoroughly to pieces with a crashing sound by some sudden act of violence. To *split* is to part, as wood in the way of the grain, or of other natural cleavage. To *rupture* is to cause to part less violently and completely than by explosion. To *demolish* is to beat down, as a mound, building, fortress, etc.; to *destroy* is to put by any process beyond restoration physically, mentally, or morally. Compare REND, RUPTURE. *Antonyms:* attach, bind, fasten, join, mend, repair, secure, unite, weld.

break·a·ble (brā′kə-bəl) *adj.* Capable of being broken. See synonyms under FRAGILE. —**break′a·ble·ness** *n.*

break·age (brā′kij) *n.* **1** A breaking, or the state of being broken. **2** Articles broken. **3** Compensation for damage or loss due to articles broken in shipment or use.

break·a·way (brāk′ə·wā′) *n.* **1** A motion-picture set or prop so designed as to break apart quickly. **2** In pugilism, a separation of the antagonists. **3** The start of the contestants in a race.

break·bone (brāk′bōn′) *n. Pathol.* Dengue. Also **breakbone fever.**

break·down (brāk′doun′) *n.* **1** The act of breaking down; a collapse, as of a machine, one's health, etc. **2** A shuffling, stamping dance. **3** *Chem.* Decomposition or analysis of compounds. **4** The arrangement of large groups, as of facts, figures, operations, and processes, into categories permitting more efficient interpretation or management. Also **break′-down′.**

break·er (brā′kər) *n.* **1** One who or that which breaks. **2** A wave of the sea that breaks on a beach, etc. **3** A structure in which large masses of anthracite coal are broken up, sorted in various sizes, and cleaned for the market. **4** A strip of rubberized fabric attached to a pneumatic tire before the tread is put on, serving to distribute the pressure of the tire in contact with the ground. **5** *Naut.* A small barrel or cask containing drinking water for those in a lifeboat.

break·fast (brek′fəst) *n.* **1** The first meal of the day. **2** That with which a fast is broken; a meal. —*v.t.* To give a breakfast to; furnish with a breakfast. —*v.i.* To eat breakfast. —**break′fast·er** *n.*

break·front (brāk′frunt′) *n.* A cabinet, bookcase, or the like, having a central section which extends forward from those at either side.

break·in (brāk′in′) *n.* The act of breaking into a place, as to commit burglary.

breaking and entering *Law* Burglary; housebreaking.

break·neck (brāk′nek′) *adj.* Likely to break the neck; dangerous to life and limb: at *breakneck* speed.

break·o·ver (brāk′ō′vər) *n.* The front of a forest fire that jumps across a natural barrier or control line set to confine its range of devastation: also called *slopover*.

break·through (brāk′throō′) *n.* **1** A decisive or dramatic advance, especially in research, knowledge, understanding, etc. **2** *Mil.* An attack that penetrates an enemy's defensive system into the rear area.

break·up (brāk′up′) *n.* **1** The act of breaking up. **2** *Canadian* The time when the ice breaks up in the northern streams; spring.

break·wa·ter (brāk′wô′tər, -wot′ər) *n.* A mole or wall for protecting a harbor or beach from the force of waves.

breast (brest) *n.* **1** *Anat.* The front of the chest from the neck to the abdomen. **2** One of the mammary glands; a teat. **3** That part of a garment that covers the breast. **4** The seat of the affections, etc.; the mind or heart. **5** Anything likened to the human or animal breast. **6** The front of a plow moldboard. **7** The working face of a mine, from which material is being, or may be, removed. —**to make a clean breast of** To make a complete confession of. —*v.t.* **1** To encounter or oppose with the breast. **2** To meet or oppose boldly; advance against: to *breast* one's problems. [OE *brēost*]

breast·bone (brest′bōn′) *n. Anat.* A bone in the front part of the chest, with which some of the ribs are joined; the sternum.

breast-feed (brest′fēd′) *v.t. & v.i.* **-fed, -feeding** To suckle.

breast·pin (brest′pin′) *n.* A pin worn at the breast to close a garment; brooch; scarfpin.

breast·plate (brest′plāt′) *n.* **1** A piece of defensive plate armor for the breast; also, a metalworker's protective plate. **2** A strap crossing a horse's breast. **3** A square piece of linen cloth, embroidered with gold, adorned with twelve precious stones symbolizing the twelve tribes of Israel, worn by the Jewish high priest. **4** The plastron of a turtle.

BREASTPLATE

breast pocket A pocket in a garment situated over the breast, as the inside pocket of a jacket.

breast pump A suction instrument for drawing milk from the breast.

breast-stroke (brest′strōk′) *n.* In swimming, a stroke made while lying face down, the arms being simultaneously thrust forward from the breast under or on the surface, then brought laterally back to the sides, the legs at the same time being moved in a frog kick. —**breast′-strok′er** *n.*

breast·work (brest′wûrk′) *n.* A low, temporary, defensive work, usually breast-high; a parapet. See synonyms under BARRIER, RAMPART.

breath (breth) *n.* **1** Air inhaled or exhaled in respiration. **2** A single act of respiration: He drew a long *breath*. **3** Power to breathe, or to breathe freely; life. **4** The time of a single respiration; an instant. **5** Something resembling breath; a gentle movement of air; an exhalation. **6** Some slight thing, as a word or a rumor. **7** *Phonet.* An exhalation of air without vibration of the vocal cords, as in the production of (p) and (f). **8** The moisture condensed on cold objects or in cold air caused by the act of breathing. **9** Anything caused by breathing, as an utterance. **10** Time to breathe; delay; intermission; respite. —**in the same breath** At the same moment; without a pause or break. —**to take one's breath away** To overawe; produce sudden emotion. —**under one's breath** In a whisper. [OE *brǣth* vapor, odor]

breath·a·lys·er (breth′ə·lī′zər) *n.* A balloonlike device that measures the alcoholic content of blood by analyzing expelled breath, used especially to test motorists for intoxication. [< BREATH + (AN)ALYSER, Brit. spelling of *analyzer*; the device was originated in Britain]

breathe (brēth) *v.* **breathed** (brēthd), **breathing** *v.t.* **1** To inhale and exhale, as air; respire. **2** To emit by breathing. **3** To utter; whisper. **4** To express; manifest. **5** *Phonet.* To utter with the breath only, without vibration of the vocal cords. **6** To exhaust; put out of breath. **7** To inject or infuse by or as by breathing: to *breathe* new life into a project. —*v.i.* **8** To inhale and exhale air; respire. **9** To be alive; exist. **10** To exhale, as fragrance. **11** To pause for breath. **12** To move gently, as breezes. **13** To allow air to penetrate: said of a fabric or garment. [ME *brethen* < *breth* breath]—**breath′a·ble** *adj.*

breath·er (brē′thər) *n.* **1** One who or that which breathes. **2** *Colloq.* That which exercises or exhausts the breath, as a run. **3** *Colloq.* A brief rest period: to take a *breather* during a workout.

breath·ing (brē′thing) *adj.* Respiring; living. See synonyms under ALIVE. —*n.* **1** The act of respiration; a breath. **2** Time to take breath. **3** Exercise that quickens the breath. **4** *Gram.* An aspiration; aspirate. In Greek the **rough breathing** (‘) over an initial vowel indicates the sound equivalent to our letter *h*; the **smooth breathing** (’), its absence.

breath·less (breth′lis) *adj.* **1** Out of breath. **2** Intense or eager, as if holding the breath. **3** Without breath; dead. —**breath′less·ly** *adv.* —**breath′less·ness** *n.*

breath·tak·ing (breth′tā′king) *adj.* Astounding; overawing.

breath·y (breth′ē) *adj.* Characterized by audible breathing; aspirate.

breech (brēch) *n.* **1** The posterior and lower part of the body; the buttocks. **2** The rear end of a gun, cannon, etc. —*v.t.* (brēch, brich) **1** To clothe with breeches. **2** To provide with a breech, as a gun. **3** To fasten by a breeching, as a ship's cannon. **4** *Obs.* To flog on the breech. ◆ Homophone: *breach.* [OE *brec*, pl., breeches]

breech·block (brēch′blok′) *n.* The movable piece which closes the breech of a breech-loading firearm, but is withdrawn to insert the cartridge, and replaced before firing.

breech·cloth (brēch′klôth′, -kloth′) *n.* A loincloth. Also **breech′clout′** (-klout′).

breech·es (brich′iz) *n. pl.* **1** A garment for men, covering the waist, hips, and thighs. **2** Trousers. [OE *brec* breeches]

breeches buoy *Naut.* A life-saving apparatus, consisting of canvas breeches, attachable at the waist to a ring-shaped lifebuoy, to be slung and run upon a rope stretched from the shore to a wrecked vessel.

BREECHES BUOY

A. Mast of vessel.
B. Traveling block.
C. Hawser running from mast to shore.
D. Tailblock.
E. Whip, or endless line, by which buoy is hauled to and from shore.
F Breeches buoy

breech·ing (brich′ing, brē′ching) *n.* **1** A holdback strap passing behind a horse's haunches. For illustration see HARNESS. **2** The parts composing the breech of a gun. **3** A heavy rope used for securing a ship's cannon. **4** A flogging.

breech·load·er (brēch′lō′dər) *n.* A firearm the load of which is inserted at the breech. —**breech′load′ing** *adj.*

breed (brēd) *v.* **bred, breed·ing** *v.t.* **1** To produce (offspring); give birth to; hatch. **2** To cause; favor the development of: Familiarity *breeds* contempt. **3** To cause to give birth; develop new strains in: He *breeds* horses. **4** To bring up; train, as to a profession. —*v.i.* **5** To produce young; procreate. **6** To originate or be caused: Militarism *breeds* in armies. See synonyms under PRODUCE. —*n.* **1** The progeny of one stock; a race or strain of animals deliberately cultivated by man. **2** A sort or kind. **3** The character or degree of perfection possessed by a wine. [OE *brēdan* < *brod* brood. Related to BROOD.]

breed·er (brē′dər) *n.* **1** One who or that which breeds or produces; author; source. **2** One who manages the breeding of animals. **3** An animal suitable, or intended primarily for, reproductive purposes.

breeder reactor *Physics* An apparatus for the generation of atomic energy in which the fuel is converted into more fissionable material than is consumed. Compare REACTOR (def. 4).

breed·ing (brē′ding) *n.* **1** The generating, bearing, or training of young. **2** Nurture or its effect on character and behavior. **3** Manners, especially good manners. See synonyms under BEHAVIOR, EDUCATION, NURTURE.

breeze¹ (brēz) *n.* **1** A moderate current of air; a gentle wind. See BEAUFORT SCALE. **2** *Brit. Colloq.* A flutter of excitement; agitation; disturbance. **3** A vague rumor; whisper. See synonyms under WIND. **4** *Slang* Ease; facility: The horse won in a *breeze.* —*v.i.* **breezed, breez·ing 1** To blow moderately; begin to blow: It's *breezing* up. **2** *Slang* To go or proceed quickly and blithely. —**to breeze in** *Slang* To enter in an airy, vivacious manner. —**to breeze up 1** To spring up, as a wind; also, to grow stronger.

[< Sp. and Pg. *brisa, briza* northeast wind]

breeze² (brēz) *n.* A gadfly or a botfly. [OE *breosa* gadfly]

breeze³ (brēz) *n. Brit.* Refuse cinders, small coke, or fine coal used in burning bricks in a kiln. [? < F *braise* hot embers]

breeze·way (brēz′wā′) *n.* A roofed, open passageway from house to garage or between two buildings.

breez·ing (brē′zing) *n.* The blurring of a motion picture on the screen caused by distorted focus, uneven shrinkage of film, or unevenly placed track perforations.

breez·y (brē′zē) *adj.* **breez·i·er, breez·i·est 1** Like a breeze; airy; windy. **2** Brisk or animated. **3** Somewhat pert; brash. —**breez′i·ly** *adv.* —**breez′i·ness** *n.*

breg·ma (breg′mə) *n. pl.* **·ma·ta** (-mə·tə) *n. Anat.* That point on the vault of the skull where the coronal and sagittal sutures meet. [< Gk. *bregma* front of the head]—**breg·mate** (breg′māt), **breg·mat·ic** (breg·mat′ik) *adj.*

bre·hon (brē′hən) *n.* An ancient Irish lawgiver and judge, who made the law and decided controversies. The **brehon laws** prevailed in Ireland through the 16th century. [< Irish *breitheamh* < OIrish *brithem* judge]

Bren·nan (bren′ən), **William J(oseph),** born 1906, U.S. jurist; associate justice of the Supreme Court 1956.

Bre·tagne (brə·tàn′y′) French name for BRITTANY.

breth·ren (breth′rən) *n. pl.* **1** Brothers. **2** Members of a brotherhood. [ME, pl.]

breve (brēv) *n.* **1** A mark (˘) placed over a vowel to indicate that it has a short sound, as the *a* in *hat* compare MACRON); or, in prosody, placed over a syllable to show that it is not stressed. **2** A royal or papal commission or mandate; brief. **3** A judicial writ or brief. **4** *Music* A note equivalent to two whole notes, or the sign for it. [< Ital. < L *brevis* short]

bre·vet (brə·vet′, *esp. Brit.* brev′it) *n. Mil.* **1** A commission advancing an officer in honorary rank without advance in pay or in command. **2** A commission or promotion awarded for achievement, usually on the field of battle. —*v.t.* **bre·vet·ted** or **bre·vet·ed, bre·vet·ting** or **bre·vet·ing** To raise in rank by brevet. —*adj.* Held or conferred by brevet; holding rank by brevet; brevetted. [< OF *brevet*, dim. of *bref* letter, document]

bre·vet·cy (brə·vet′sē) *n. pl.* **·cies** Brevet rank.

brevi- *combining form* Short: *brevipennate.* [< L *brevis* short]

bre·vi·ar·y (brē′vē·er′ē, brev′ē-) *n. pl.* **·ar·ies** *Eccl.* A book of daily offices and prayers for the canonical hours. [< L *breviarium* abridgment < *brevis* short]

bre·vier (brə·vir′) *n. Printing* A size of type, about 8-point. [? < G, breviary; with ref. to its use in breviaries]

brev·i·lin·e·al (brev′i·lin′ē·əl) *adj.* Denoting a type of body built along broad, short lines: opposed to *longilineal.* [< BREVI- + L *linea* line]

brev·i·pen·nate (brev′i·pen′āt) *adj. Ornithol.* Short-winged, as the ostrich, cassowary, etc. —*n.* A brevipennate bird, as the auk, guillemot, etc. [< BREVI- + L *penna* wing]

brev·i·ros·trate (brev′i·ros′trāt) *adj. Ornithol.* Having a short bill or beak. Also **brev′i·ros′tral.** [< BREVI- + L *n. rostrum* beak]

brev·i·ty (brev′ə·tē) *n. pl.* **·ties 1** Shortness of duration; brief time. **2** Condensation of language; conciseness. [< L *brevitas, —tatis* < *brevis* short]

brew (brōō) *v.t.* **1** To make, as beer or ale, by steeping, boiling, and fermentation of malt, hops, etc. **2** To make (any beverage) as by boiling or mixing. **3** To concoct; devise, as mischief. —*v.i.* **4** To make ale, beer, or the like. —**to be brewing** To be imminent; gather, as a storm, trouble, etc. —*n.* That which is brewed; the product of brewing. [OE *brēowan.* Related to BROTH.]—**brew′er** *n.*

brew·age (brōō′ij) *n.* **1** The process of brewing. **2** A drink prepared by brewing or mixing. **3** A concocted plot.

brew·er·y (brōō′ər·ē) *n. pl.* **·er·ies** An establishment for brewing.

brew·ing (brōō′ing) *n.* **1** Brewage. **2** The amount of liquor brewed at one time. **3** A mixture; concoction. **4** A gathering of storm clouds.

brew·is (brōō′is) *n.* **1** Bread or oatmeal soaked in pot liquor, hot milk, or the like. **2** Thickened broth. **3** In New England, porridge made of brown bread, milk, and butter. [ME *browes* < OF *brouet,* dim. of *breu, bro* broth; infl. by BREW]

Brewster chair An early New England type of chair with heavy turned posts and spindles arranged in tiers in the back and below the seat in front: named for William Brewster.

Brezh·nev (bryezh·nyôf′), **Leonid Ilyich,** 1906–82, Soviet statesman; first secretary of the Communist party 1964–82.

bri·ar (brī′ər), **bri·ar·root** (-rōōt′, -rōōt′), **bri·ar·wood** (-wood′) See BRIER, etc.

bri·ard (brē·ärd′) *n.* A breed of French work dog with a large head, pointed muzzle, heavily boned legs, and long, stiff coat. [< F, a native of Brie, France]

bribe (brīb) *n.* **1** Any gift or emolument used corruptly to influence public or official action. **2** Anything that seduces or allures; an allurement. See synonyms under GIFT. —*v.* **bribed, brib·ing** *v.t.* **1** To offer or give a bribe to. **2** To gain or influence by means of bribery. —*v.i.* **3** To give bribes. [< OF, piece of bread given a beggar]—**brib′a·ble** *adj.* —**brib′er** *n.*

brib·er·y (brī′bər·ē) *n. pl.* **·er·ies** The giving, offering, or accepting of a bribe.

bric-à-brac (brik′ə·brak) *n.* Objects of curiosity or decoration; rarities; antiques; knickknacks. [< F]

brick (brik) *n.* **1** A molded block of clay, sun-baked or kiln-burned in various shapes and sizes, but usually about 8 1/2 x 4 x 2 1/2 inches: used for building, paving, etc. **2** Bricks collectively; also, any object shaped like a brick. **3** *Colloq.* An admirable or first-rate fellow. —*v.t.* **1** To build or line with bricks. **2** To cover or wall in with bricks: with *up* or *in.* [< OF *brique* fragment, bit, ult. < Gmc. Cf. OE *bryce* fragment.]

brick·bat (brik′bat′) *n.* A piece of a brick, especially when used as a missile.

brick·kiln (brik′kil′, -kiln′) *n.* A structure in which bricks are burnt.

brick·lay·er (brik′lā′ər) *n.* One who builds with bricks. —**brick′lay′ing** *n.*

brick·le (brik′əl) *adj.* **1** *Dial.* Changeable; fickle; *brickle* weather. **2** *Brit. Dial.* Brittle.

brick red Any of several shades of dull, yellowish- or brownish-red, like the color of the common red clay brick. —**brick-red** (brik′red′) *adj.*

brick·work (brik′wûrk′) *n.* Any construction of bricks laid in courses.

brick·yard (brik′yärd′) *n.* A place where bricks are made.

bri·cole (bri·kōl′, brik′əl) *n.* **1** A harness worn by men for dragging field guns over ground where horses cannot be used. **2** A side stroke against the wall of a tennis court. **3** A cushion shot in billiards. **4** A medieval military engine for throwing stones or darts. [< F]

bri·dal (brīd′l) *adj.* Pertaining to a bride or a wedding; nuptial. —*n.* A marriage festival; wedding. See synonyms under MATRIMONIAL. ◆ Homophone: *bridle.* [OE *brȳldeala* wedding feast]

bri·dal·wreath (brīd′l·rēth′) *n.* A spring-flowering shrub (*Spiraea prunifolia*) of the rose family, with umbels of white flowers and ovate-oblong leaves.

bride¹ (brīd) *n.* A newly married woman, or a woman about to be married. [OE *brȳd*]

bride² (brīd) *n.* **1** A loop, tie, etc., made in lace or needlework; also, a bonnet string. **2** *Obs.* A bridle. [< F, bridle, string]

bride·groom (brīd′grōōm′, -grŏŏm′) *n.* A man newly married or about to be married. [OE *brȳdguma* < *brȳ* bride + *guma* man; infl. in ME by *grome* bride, groom]

brides·maid (brīdz′mād′) *n.* A young, usually unmarried woman who attends a bride at her wedding.

brides·man (brīdz′mən) *n. pl.* **·men** (-mən) A groomsman.

bride·well (brīd′wel, -wəl) *n.* A house of correction; a lock-up. [from St. *Bride's* well, in London, near which a prison was located]

bridge¹ (brij) *n.* **1** A structure erected to afford passage for pedestrians, vehicles, railroad trains, etc., across a waterway, a railroad, a ravine, etc.; a raised support. **2** *Naut.* An observation platform or partial deck built across and above a ship's deck for the use of the officers, the pilot, etc. **3** Something likened to a bridge. **4** The arched or central portion of the nose. **5** The part of a pair of spectacles or eyeglasses crossing over or resting upon this portion of the nose. **6** A block for raising the strings of a musical instrument, as a violin or guitar. **7** *Anat.* The pons Varolii. **8** A low, vertical, crosswise division wall, as in a boiler setting or a metallurgic furnace. **9** A mounting for holding false teeth, attached to adjoining teeth on each side. **10** *Electr.* A device used in measuring electrical resistance. **11** In billiards or pool, the hand or a notched support for a billiard cue, used when a player is about to strike a ball. **12** In the theater, a platform immediately inside the teaser, for suspending lights and providing space for electricians, etc. **— to burn one's bridges** To cut off all possibility of retreat. **— suspension bridge** Any bridge in which the roadway is hung from cables strong-

SUSPENSION BRIDGE
Brooklyn Bridge spanning East River, New York

ly anchored over towers and without support from below. See also under BASCULE, CANTILEVER, DRAWBRIDGE, PONTOON. **— v.t.** **bridged, bridg·ing** **1** To construct a bridge or bridges over. **2** To make a passage over or across by a bridge; get over. [OE *brycg*]

bridge² (brij) *n.* A card game similar to whist, except that the dealer, or his partner (the dummy), has the right to name the trump. Odd tricks vary in value according to the suit declared. Partners first scoring 30 win the game. Also BRIDGE WHIST. **— auction bridge** A variety of the game of bridge, in which, instead of the dealer or his partner having the declaration, it goes to the player who undertakes to score the highest number of points. **— contract bridge** A variation of bridge in which the declarer, if successful, scores toward game only the tricks named in the bid; the awards are high, and failure is heavily penalized. **— duplicate bridge** The game of bridge, auction bridge, or contract bridge in which a series of hands is played over again, each side holding the cards previously held by its opponent. [Origin uncertain]

bridge·board (brij'bôrd', -bōrd') *n.* A notched board to which stair treads and risers are fastened.

bridge·head (brij'hed') *n.* **1** *Mil.* A position on or near the bank of a river or defile that is established by advance troops of an attacking force to protect and cover the crossing of the main body of troops over the river or defile. **2** Loosely, a beachhead.

bridge·work (brij'wûrk') *n.* **1** *Dent.* A partial denture, variously attached to the natural teeth. **2** The construction of bridges.

bridg·ing (brij'ing) *n.* Wooden struts or braces between joists or other beams to keep them apart and to stiffen the structure.

bri·dle (brīd'l) *n.* **1** The head harness of a horse, including bit and reins. **2** Anything that restrains, limits, or guides movement, action, or development; a check; also, a curb. **3** The clevis of a plow. **4** *Anat.* A ligament or frenum attaching two parts or surfaces of an organism to each other. **5** A former instrument of torture, used for scolds. **6** *Aeron.* In the handling of airships and dirigibles, a sling of cordage or wire with ends fixed at two different points, to the bight of which a single line may be attached, movable or fixed, thus distributing the pull of the single line to two points or more in the case of a multiple bridle. **7** A span of mooring cables. **— v. bri·dled, bri·dling** *v.t.* **1** To put a bridle

on. **2** To check or control with or as with a bridle. **— v.i.** **3** To raise the head and draw in the chin through resentment, pride, etc. See synonyms under REPRESS, RESTRAIN, SUBDUE. ◆ Homophone: *bridal.* [OE *brīdel*] **— bri'dler** *n.*

bridle hand The left hand, in which the reins are usually held.

bri·dle·path (brīd'l·path', -päth') *n.* A path intended only for saddle horses or pack-animals.

bri·dle·wise (brīd'l·wīz') *adj.* Answering the pressure of the bridle rein on the neck, instead of on the bit: said of a horse.

bri·doon (bri·dōōn') *n.* A snaffle and rein of a military bridle used in connection with, or acting independently of, the curb bit and its rein. [< F *bridon* snaffle, bit < *bride* bridle, check]

Brie (brē) *n.* A soft, white, creamy cheese, mold- or bacteria-ripened. [from *Brie-Comte-Robert,* town in central France, where first made]

brief (brēf) *adj.* **1** Short in time or space; quickly passing. **2** Of few words; concise; also, curt or abrupt in speech. **3** Curtailed in extent; limited. See synonyms under TERSE, TRANSIENT. **— n.** **1** Any short or abridged statement; a summary. **2** *Law* A concise statement in writing of the law and authorities relied upon in trying a cause; also, a memorandum of all the material facts of a client's case prepared for the instruction of counsel. **3** In the Roman Catholic Church, a letter from the Pope; less formal than a bull. **4** Briefing. **— in brief** Briefly; in short. **— to hold a brief for** To be on the side of; champion; aid. **— v.t.** **1** To epitomize; make a summary of. **2** To instruct or advise in advance: He *briefed* his salesmen on the coming campaign. **3** *Brit.* To inform by a legal brief. **4** *Brit.* To retain as counsel. **— adv. Obs.** Shortly; briefly. [< OF *bref* < L *brevis* short] **— brief'ly** *adv.* **— brief'ness** *n.*

brief·case (brēf'kās') *n.* A leather portfolio for carrying briefs, commercial papers, manuscripts, etc.

brief·ing (brē'fing) *n.* Final instructions given to aircraft pilots and crew members before a flight or raid.

brief·less (brēf'lis) *adj.* Having no briefs or clients.

brig¹ (brig) *n.* *Naut.* A two-masted ship, square-rigged on both masts. [Short for BRIGANTINE]

brig² (brig) *n.* *Scot.* A bridge.

brig³ (brig) *n.* A place of confinement on shipboard. [Origin unknown]

bri·gade (bri·gād') *n.* **1** *Mil.* A tactical unit intermediate between a regiment

BRIG

and a division, commanded by a brigadier general. **2** Any considerable body of persons more or less organized: a fire *brigade.* **— v.t.** **bri·gad·ed, bri·gad·ing** **1** To form into a brigade. **2** To classify or combine. [< MF < Ital. *brigata* company, crew < *brigare* brawl, fight]

brig·a·dier (brig'ə·dir') *n.* **1** See under GENERAL. **2** In some European armies, a cavalry subaltern whose rank corresponds with that of an infantry corporal.

brig·and (brig'ənd) *n.* A robber; a bandit; especially, one of a band of outlaws and plunderers. See synonyms under ROBBER. [< F < Ital. *brigante* fighter < *brigare* brawl, fight] **— brig'and·age** (-ij) *n.* **— brig'and·ish** *adj.* **— brig'and·ism** *n.*

brig·an·dine (brig'ən·dēn, -dīn) *n.* A medieval coat of mail made of metal plates, scales, or rings, sewn upon linen, leather, or the like. [< MF, armor for fighter < *brigand.* See BRIGAND.]

brig·an·tine (brig'ən·tēn, -tīn) *n.* *Naut.* A two-masted vessel, square-rigged on the foremast, and fore-and-aft rigged on the mainmast; also called *hermaphrodite brig, jackass brig.* [< MF *brigandin* a fighting vessel < Ital.

brigantino < *brigare* fight]

bri·er (brī'ər) *n.* **1** A prickly bush or shrub, especially of the rose family, as the sweet-brier. **2** A pipe of brier-root. **3** A thorn or prickle; also, the white or tree heath. Also spelled *briar.* [OE *brēr*] **— bri'er·y** *adj.*

bri·er-root (brī'ər·rŏŏt', -rŏŏt') *n.* The root of the white or tree heath of southern Europe *(Erica arborea),* used in making tobacco pipes. Also spelled *briar-root.*

bri·er·wood (brī'ər·wŏŏd') *n.* **1** The wood of the brier-root. **2** A pipe made from it. Also spelled *briarwood.*

bright (brīt) *adj.* **1** Emitting or reflecting much light; shining; sparkling. **2** Possessing or showing quick intelligence or sparkling wit; quick-witted. **3** Full of or marked by gladness, prosperity, or hope; cheery; auspicious. **4** Illustrious; glorious. **5** Of brilliant color; clear and transparent. **6** Resplendent with excellence or beauty. **7** Watchful; alert. **— adv.** Brightly: The moon shines *bright.* **— n.** *Poetic* Brilliancy; splendor; brightness. [OE *beorht, briht*] **— bright'ly** *adv.*

Synonyms (*adj.*): beaming, brilliant, burnished, cheerful, cheering, cheery, effulgent, flashing, gleaming, glorious, glowing, luminous, lustrous, radiant, refulgent, resplendent, shining, sparkling, splendid, sunny, sunshiny. See CHEERFUL, CLEVER, FRESH, HAPPY, INTELLIGENT, VIVID. Compare LIGHT. Antonyms: See synonyms under DARK.

bright·en (brīt'n) *v.t. & v.i.* To make or become bright or brighter. **2** To make or become cheerful: The outlook is *brightening.* **— bright'en·er** *n.*

bright·ness (brīt'nis) *n.* **1** The state, quality, or condition of being bright, in any sense. **2** The luminous intensity of any surface in a given direction, per unit of projected area of the surface as viewed in that direction. **3** That attribute of a color which identifies it as equivalent to some member of the achromatic color series, ranging from black or very dim, to white or very bright. Compare LIGHTNESS, HUE, SATURATION. See COLOR.

bright·work (brīt'wûrk') *n.* Those parts of a machine, building, etc., in which the metal is made bright, as by planing, turning, or polishing.

bril·liance (bril'yəns) *n.* **1** The quality of being brilliant; brightness; radiance; luster. **2** The presence of many rich overtones and high frequencies in a sound record made under suitable conditions. **3** A high degree of insight or understanding; skill and finish of execution in artistic performance, creative work, etc. **4** In colorimetry, lightness. Also **bril'lian·cy.**

bril·liant (bril'yənt) *adj.* **1** Sparkling or glowing with luster or light; very bright. **2** Showy; accomplished; illustrious; splendid: a *brilliant* mind, *brilliant* record. **— n.** **1** A diamond of the finest cut, or one possessing a single large face surrounded by a bezel of 33 facets and, below the girdle, a pavilion of 25 facets. For illustration see DIAMOND. **2** *Printing* A small type, about 3 1/2-point. [< MF *brillant,* ppr. of *briller* sparkle, ? < L *beryllus* beryl] **— bril'liant·ly** *adv.* **— bril'liant·ness** *n.*

bril·lian·tine (bril'yən·tēn') *n.* **1** A smooth, fine, wiry fabric in plain or twill weave, having a cotton warp and worsted or mohair filling. **2** A mixture of oil and perfume, used to impart a gloss to the hair.

brim (brim) *n.* **1** The rim of a cup. **2** The margin of a river. **3** A projecting rim, as of a hat. See synonyms under BANK, MARGIN. **— v.t. & v.i.** **brimmed, brim·ming** To fill or be filled to the brim. **— to brim over** To fill to the brim and overflow. [OE *brim* seashore]

brim·ful (brim'fŏŏl', brim'fŏŏl') *adj.* Full to the brim; brimming.

brim·mer (brim'ər) *n.* A vessel full to the brim; a brimming cup.

brim·stone (brim'stōn') *n.* **1** Sulfur in its solid state or in some form derived from the solid state. **2** A spitfire; scold. [OE *brynstān* < *bryn-* burning (< *brinnen* burn) + *stān* stone] **— brim'ston'y** *adj.*

brin (brin) *n.* One of the radiating sticks of a fan.

brind·ed (brin′did) *adj.* Irregularly streaked; brindled. [Akin to BRAND]

brin·dle (brin′dəl) *adj.* Brindled. —*n.* A brindled color, or a brindled animal.

brin·dled (brin′dəld) *adj.* Tawny or grayish with irregular streaks or spots; also, barred; streaked. [Var. of BRINDED]

brine (brīn) *n.* 1 Water saturated or strongly impregnated with salt, as the water of the sea, that of salt wells and springs. 2 Saline water in which meats are preserved. 3 The water of the sea; ocean. 4 Tears. 5 A solution of sodium or calcium chloride used as a refrigerant in the making of ice. —*v.t.* **brined, brin·ing** To treat with brine; steep in brine. [OE *brȳne*] —**brin′ish** *adj.*

brine pit A salt spring, or a well the water of which yields salt on evaporation.

bring (bring) *v.t.* **brought, bring·ing** 1 To convey or cause (a person or thing) to come with oneself to or toward a′ place: *Bring* your friend to the party. 2 To cause to come about; involve as a consequence: War *brings* destruction. 3 To introduce into the mind; cause to appear: He *brought* her face into his thoughts. 4 To cause (a person) to adopt or admit, as a persuasion, course of action, etc.: He *brought* her to his point of view. 5 To sell for: The house *brought* a good price. 6 *Law* a To prefer, as a charge. b To institute: to *bring* suit. c To set forth, as evidence or an argument. —**to bring about** 1 To accomplish; cause to happen. 2 *Naut.* To reverse; turn, as a ship. —**to bring around** (or **round**) 1 To cause to adopt or admit, as an opinion or persuasion. 2 To revive; restore to consciousness. —**to bring down** 1 To cause to fall. 2 To fell by wounding or killing. —**to bring down the house** To evoke wild applause or acclaim. —**to bring forth** 1 To give birth. 2 To produce (foliage). —**to bring forward** 1 To adduce, as an argument. 2 In bookkeeping, to carry, as a sum, from one page or column to another. —**to bring home** To prove conclusively, so as to be understood. —**to bring home the bacon** *Colloq.* 1 To provide support or livelihood. 2 To gain a desired end or object. —**to bring in** 1 To import. 2 To render or submit (a verdict). 3 To yield or produce, as profits. —**to bring off** To do successfully. —**to bring on** 1 To cause; lead to. 2 To produce; cause to appear: *Bring on* the dancing girls! —**to bring out** 1 To reveal; cause to be evident, as the truth. 2 To publish or produce, as a book or play. 3 To introduce, as a young girl to society. —**to bring to** 1 To revive; restore to consciousness. 2 *Naut.* To cause (a ship) to come up into the wind and lie to. —**to bring to bear** To cause to have reference, application, or influence. —**to bring up** 1 To rear; educate. 2 To suggest or call attention to, as a subject. 3 To cough or vomit up. [OE *bringan*] —**bring′er** *n.*

brink (bringk) *n.* 1 The verge of a steep place, or of a dangerous condition, action, event, or time. 2 The margin of any water; bank; shore. See synonyms under BANK, MARGIN. [ME *brenk* <Scand.]

brink·man·ship (bringk′mən·ship) *n.* A willingness to expose oneself to major risk to achieve some end; especially, a national policy embodying such a position. [<BRINK + -manship, on analogy with *showmanship*, etc.]

brin·y (brī′nē) *adj.* **brin·i·er, brin·i·est** Of the nature of brine; salty. —*n. Colloq.* The ocean: a dip in the *briny*. —**brin′i·ness** *n.*

bri·o (brē′ō) *n. Music* Spirit; vivacity: usually in the phrase *con brio*. [<Ital.]

bri·oche (brē′ōsh, -osh, *Fr.* brē·ôsh′) *n.* A soft, sweet roll made of butter, eggs, flour, and yeast. [<F]

bri·o·lette (brē′ə·let′) *n.* A gemstone cut with triangular or long facets, generally pear- or drop-shaped. For illustration see DIAMOND. [<F <*brillant* diamond]

bri·quet (bri·ket′) *n.* A block of compressed coal dust, used as fuel. Also **bri·quette′**. [<F *briquette*, dim. of *brique* brick]

bri·sance (brē·zäns′) *n.* The shattering effect of a high-explosive shell or of any blasting substance, usually measured in terms of detonating velocity. [<F *brisant*, ppr. of *briser* crush]

Bri·se·is (brī·sē′is) In the *Iliad*, Achilles' concubine, whose seizure by Agamemnon led to a quarrel between the two men.

brisk (brisk) *adj.* 1 Moving, acting, or taking place rapidly; quick. 2 Energetic; vivacious;

spirited; lively. 3 Sharp or stimulating, as cold air. 4 Sparkling; effervescent: said of liquors. See synonyms under ACTIVE, ALERT, ALIVE, NIMBLE. —*v.t.* & *v.i.* To make or become lively; animate: with *up*. [Cf. F *brusque* abrupt, sudden] —**brisk′ly** *adv.* —**brisk′ness** *n.*

bris·ket (bris′kit) *n.* The breast of a quadruped, especially of one whose flesh is used as food. [OF *bruschet*, ult. <Gmc.]

bris·ling (bris′ling) *n.* The sprat. [<Scand.]

bris·tle (bris′əl) *n.* 1 A coarse, stiff hair, as of swine. 2 *Bot.* A slender, stiff hair; morphologically, a trichome. —*v.* **bris·tled, bris·tling** *v.i.* 1 To erect the bristles, as an animal when aroused: often with *up*. 2 To show anger, irritation, etc., as by stiffening the body: often with *up*. 3 To be thickly set as with bristles: The plain *bristled* with bayonets. —*v.t.* 4 To erect as or like bristles: often with *up*: A cock *bristles* up his crest. 5 To cover or line as with bristles. 6 To agitate; ruffle violently: The storm *bristled* the lake. [ME *bristel*, OE *byrst*] —**bris′tly** *adj.*

bris·tle·tail (bris′əl·tāl′) *n.* The silverfish.

Bristol board A fine quality of calendered cardboard. [from *Bristol*]

brit (brit) *n. pl.* **brit** A young herring, once thought to be a species. [Origin unknown]

Brit·ain (brit′n) Great Britain. Abbr. *Brit.*; *Br.*

bri·tan·ni·a (bri·tan′ē·ə, -tan′yə) *n. Metall.* A silver-white alloy of tin, copper, and antimony: used for cheap tableware. Also **Britannia metal.** [from *Britannia*]

Bri·tan·ni·a (bri·tan′ē·ə, -tan′yə) 1 The Roman name for Britain. 2 Great Britain, Ireland, and the Dominions. 3 A female figure representing Great Britain or the British Empire.

Bri·tan·nic (bri·tan′ik) *adj.* Of or pertaining to Great Britain; British. [<L *Britannicus*]

Brit·i·cism (brit′ə·siz′əm) *n.* A word, expression, or usage characteristic of Great Britain or the British. Also **Britishism, Britticism.**

Brit·ish (brit′ish) *adj.* 1 Pertaining to Great Britain, the United Kingdom, or the British Empire. 2 Of or pertaining to the ancient Britons, the original Celtic people of Britain. —*n.* 1 *pl.* The people of Great Britain or of the British Empire. 2 The language of the ancient Britons; Brythonic. [OE *Brettisc* <*Bret* a Briton]

British Columbia The westernmost province of Canada; 366,255 square miles; capital, Victoria. Abbr. *B.C.*

British thermal unit *Physics* The quantity of heat required to raise the temperature of one pound of water one degree Fahrenheit: at a starting temperature of 60° F. it is equal to 1054.6 joules. Abbr. *B.T.U.*

Brit·on (brit′n) *n.* 1 One of any of the tribes inhabiting ancient Britain before the Anglo-Saxon invasion, probably belonging to the Brythonic branch of the Celts. 2 A native or citizen of Great Britain; an Englishman. [< OF *Breton* <L *Britto, -onis* <Celtic]

Brit·ta·ny (brit′ə·nē) A region and former province of western France, occupying the peninsula between the English Channel and the Bay of Biscay: French *Bretagne*, Breton *Breiz*.

Brit·ten (brit′n), (**Edward**) **Benjamin**, 1913–1976, English composer.

brit·tle (brit′l) *adj.* Liable to break or snap; frangible;fragile. [ME *britel*. Akin to OE *bryttian* divide.] —**brit′tle·ness** *n.*

britz·ska (brits′kə) *n.* A light, four-wheeled carriage with calash top. Also **brits′ka, britz′ka.** [<Polish *bryczka*, dim. of *bryka* freight wagon]

Brno (bûr′nô) The second largest city in Czechoslovakia; former capital of Moravia.

BRITZSKA

broach¹ (brōch) *v.t.* 1 To introduce or mention for the first time, as a subject. 2 To open for the first time, as a cask of wine. 3 To draw off; let out: to *broach* wine. 4 To dress or enlarge with a broach. [<*n.*] —*n.* A pointed, tapering tool for boring or reaming; a reamer; also a spit. [<OF *broche*<Med. L *brocca* spike, spit, ult. <Celtic]

broach² (brōch) *v.t.* & *v.i.* To veer. —**to broach to** *Naut.* To fall off with the wind, especially broadside to the wind and waves, and thus risk capsizing. [? <BROACH¹, *v.*]

broach·er (brō′chər) *n.* One who or that which broaches.

broad (brôd) *adj.* 1 Extended in lateral measurement; of unusual width; wide; expanded; vast. 2 Of wide range, sympathy, etc. 3 Widely diffused; comprehensive: a *broad* education. 4 Catholic; liberal; tolerant: *broad* views. 5 Strongly dialectal; also, rude and vigorous, as speech. 6 Strongly defined; plain; clear: a *broad* hint. 7 Loose; indelicate; bold. 8 Denoting the chief features of a thing; not detailed: a *broad* outline. 9 *Phonet.* Formed with the oral passage wide open and the tongue low and flat, as the *a* in *calm*; open. See synonyms under LARGE. —*n.* 1 The broad part of anything. 2 A former English gold coin; a broadpiece. 3 A type of incandescent flood lamp used on motion-picture sets; a broadside. 4 The broadening out of a river over flat land; a fenny lake. 5 *Slang* A woman or girl. —*adv.* Completely; fully. [OE *brād*] —**broad′ly** *adv.*

broad arrow 1 A broad-headed arrow. 2 A mark shaped like a barbed arrow placed on British government property, as convicts' uniforms, ordnance stores, etc.

broad-ax (brôd′aks′) *n.* An ax with broad edge and short handle. Also **broad′-axe′.**

broad·bean (brôd′bēn′) *n.* The large, usually flat, orbicular or angular, seed of a strong, erect annual vine (*Vicia faba*) of the Old World.

broad·bill (brôd′bil′) *n.* 1 The scaup duck. 2 The shoveler duck. 3 The European spoonbill. 4 The swordfish.

BROADBILL (def 3)

broad-brim (brôd′brim′) *n.* A hat with a broad brim.

broad·cast (brôd′kast′, -käst′) *v.* ·**cast** or ·**casted, ·cast·ing** *v.t.* 1 To send or transmit (music, newscasts, etc.) by radio or television. 2 To scatter or cast, as seed, over a wide area; sow. 3 To disseminate; make public, as gossip. —*v.i.* 4 To speak, sing, etc., for broadcasting purposes. —*adj.* 1 Transmitted by radio. 2 Cast or scattered abroad, as seeds. —*n.* 1 *Telecom.* a The process of transmitting a program by radio. b A radio program. c The time period of a broadcast. 2 A casting or scattering of seed, etc., over the ground. —*adv.* By scattering abroad, or so as to scatter abroad or disseminate.

broad·cast·er (brôd′kas′tər, -käs′-) *n.* 1 One who owns or operates a broadcasting station. 2 One who makes broadcasts.

broad·cloth (brôd′klôth′, -kloth′) *n.* 1 A fine quality of woven wool, napped and calendered, in plain or twill weave: used for suits, skirts, etc. 2 A closely woven fabric of silk, cotton, etc., in plain weave with a light crosswise rib: used for shirts, dresses, etc.

broad·en (brôd′n) *v.t.* & *v.i.* To make or become broad or broader.

broad-gage (brôd′gāj′) *adj.* 1 Having a gage wider than the standard gage of 56½ inches, as a railway. 2 Broad-minde Also **broad′-gauge′, broad′-gaged′, broad′-gauged′.**

broad hatchet A hatchet with a broad blade. For illustration see HATCHET.

broad·horn (brôd′hôrn′) *n.* 1 A large flatboat, used formerly on the Mississippi and Ohio Rivers. 2 A Rocky Mountain sheep. 3 One of a herd of Texas longhorn cattle.

broad·ish (brô′dish) *adj.* Somewhat broad.

broad jump A jump for distance; a long jump.

broad-leaf (brôd′lēf′) *n.* 1 A tree (*Terminalia catappa*) of the myrobalan family, of Jamaica, with almondlike fruit. 2 Any variety of tobacco plant suitable for cigarmaking, having especially broad leaves.

broad-minded (brôd′mīn′did) *adj.* Liberal in beliefs and opinions; tolerant; free from bigotry and prejudice. —**broad′-mind′ed·ly** *adv.* —**broad′-mind′ed·ness** *n.*

broad-piece (brôd′pēs′) *n.* An English gold coin of James II.

broad·side (brôd'sīd') n. 1 All the guns on one side of a man–of–war, or their simultaneous discharge. 2 Any sweeping attack; hence, a volley of abuse or denunciation. 3 *Naut.* A vessel's side above the water line. 4 A large sheet of paper, printed on one side: also **broad'sheet'**. 5 The broad, unbroken surface of anything. 6 The side of an animal between the ham and the shoulder, used as meat; specifically, a side of bacon. 7 A flood lamp: see BROAD (n. def. 3). —*adv.* With the broadside turned, presented, or exposed.

broad·sword (brôd'sôrd', -sōrd') n. A sword with a broad cutting blade and obtuse point.

broad·tail (brôd'tāl') n. 1 A family of fat-tailed sheep. 2 The pelt of very young fat-tailed lambs, whose soft, lustrous fur lacks the tight curl characteristic of older lambs and sheep.

Broad·way (brôd'wā) 1 A street running north and south through New York City, famous for its brightly lighted entertainment district. 2 The New York entertainment industry. —*adj.* Situated on, characteristic of, or like Broadway in New York.

Broca's area *Anat.* A convolution located on the left frontal lobe of the brain: its function is the coordination of the sensory and motor processes involved in speech. [after Paul *Broca*]

bro·cade (brō·kād') n. A rich fabric of satin or twill background interwoven with raised flower or figure design in silken or gold or silver threads. —*v.t.* **·cad·ed, ·cad·ing** To weave (a cloth) with a raised design or figure. [< Sp. *brocado* < Med. L *broccata,* fem. pp. of *broccare* embroider] —**bro·cad'ed** *adj.*

broc·a·tel (brok'ə·tel') n. A brocaded fabric of silk, wool, cotton, or the like, with a more highly raised pattern than in brocade. Also **broc'a·telle'**. [< F *brocatelle* < Ital. *broccatello,* dim. of *broccato* brocade]

broc·co·li (brok'ə·lē) n. A hardy variety of cauliflower which does not head, of which the green sprouts and tender stalks are eaten. [< Ital., pl. of *broccolo* cabbage sprout]

broch (brokh) n. A type of corbelled stone tower of the Bronze Age found in Scotland. [< ON *borg* castle]

bro·ché (brō·shā') *adj.* Woven with a raised design; embossed; brocaded; stitched, as a book. [< F *broché,* pp. of *brocher* stitch, brocade]

bro·chette (brō·shet') n. A small spit used in roasting; a skewer. [< OF, dim. of *broche* skewer, spit]

bro·chure (brō·shoor') n. A pamphlet; anything written or published in pamphlet form. [< F < *brocher* stitch]

brock (brok) n. 1 A badger. 2 *Brit. Dial.* A foul, dirty fellow. [OE *broc*]

brock·et (brok'it) n. 1 A stag in its second year with its first horns as simple spikes. 2 A small deer of tropical America (genus *Mazama*). [< F *brocart* < *broche* tine of antlers]

bro·gan (brō'gən) n. A coarse, heavy shoe kept on the foot by side flaps laced or buckled over a short tongue. [< Irish *brōgan,* dim. of *brōg* shoe]

brög·ger·ite (bræg'ər·īt) n. A variety of uranite from which helium has been obtained. [after W. C. *Brögger,* 1851–1940, Norwegian mineralogist]

brogue[1] (brōg) n. A dialectal pronunciation of English, especially that of the Irish people. [< Irish *barrōg* defect of speech]

brogue[2] (brōg) n. 1 A heavy oxford with low heels, decorated with stitchings, pinkings, and perforations. 2 A rude shoe of untanned hide with the hair outside, tied with thongs: worn formerly in Ireland and the Scottish Highlands. [< Irish *brōg* brogue (def. 2)]

brogue[3] (brōg) n. *Scot.* A fraud; cheating trick.

broi·der (broi'dər) v.t. *Obs.* To embroider. [< MF *broder* stitch; infl. by ME *broid,* var. of *braid*] —**broi'der·y** n.

broil[1] (broil) v.t. 1 To cook, as meat, by subjecting to direct heat. 2 To expose to great heat; scorch. —v.i. 3 To be exposed to great heat; cook. 4 To become impatient; burn with anger. —n. 1 Something broiled. 2 A broiling heat. [< OF *bruiller*]

broil[2] (broil) n. A turmoil; noisy quarrel; brawl. See synonyms under ALTERCATION, QUARREL. —v.i. To engage in a broil; brawl; quarrel. [< F *brouiller* confuse]

broil·er (broi'lər) n. 1 A device for broiling, as a gridiron. 2 A chicken suitable for broiling. 3 *Colloq.* A very hot day.

broil·ing (broi'ling) *adj.* Extremely hot; torrid. —**broil'ing·ly** *adv.*

bro·kage (brō'kij) n. Brokerage. [< AF *brocage*]

broke[1] (brōk) v.i. **broked, brok·ing** To act as a broker.

broke[2] (brōk) Past tense and archaic past participle of BREAK. —*adj.* 1 Ruined; bankrupt. 2 *Colloq.* Without any money. —**go for broke** *Slang* To risk everything on an uncertain course of action.

bro·ken (brō'kən) Past participle of BREAK. —*adj.* 1 Separated forcibly into parts; fractured; shattered; ruptured. 2 Crushed in feeling or spirit; humbled; contrite. 3 Reduced to subjection; trained. 4 Made infirm; weakened. 5 Violated, transgressed, or disobeyed. 6 Reduced or shattered in estate or fortune; ruined; bankrupt. 7 Incomplete or interrupted, as sleep, utterance, etc. 8 Disordered or disarranged, as troops. 9 Rough, rugged, or irregular: *broken* ground; also, plowed or dug up, as land. 10 Faultily spoken: *broken* English. —**bro'ken·ly** *adv.* —**bro'ken·ness** n.

bro·ken-down (brō'kən·doun') *adj.* 1 Broken in health or strength; ruined; wrecked. 2 Having the parts or a part broken; powerless: a *broken-down* engine.

bro·ken-heart·ed (brō'kən·här'tid) *adj.* Overwhelmed or crushed in spirit, as by sorrow or grief.

bro·ken-wind·ed (brō'kən·win'did) *adj.* 1 Habitually short of breath. 2 Affected with the heaves, as a horse.

bro·ker (brō'kər) n. One who buys and sells for another on commission or who arranges for the negotiation of contracts of various types; especially, a stockbroker. [< AF *brocour* < OF *brochier* tap, broach (a wine cask)]

bro·ker·age (brō'kər·ij) n. The business or commission of a broker.

brom- Var. of BROMO-.

bro·ma (brō'mə) n. 1 The dry powder of cacao seeds after the oil has been expressed. 2 A beverage prepared therefrom. 3 *Med.* Solid food. [< Gk. *brōma* food]

bro·ma·tol·o·gy (brō'mə·tol'ə·jē) n. The study of food and diet. [< Gk. *brōma, -atos* + -LOGY]

bro·mat·o·ther·a·py (brō·mat'ə·ther'ə·pē) n. *Med.* The treatment of disease by means of food. Also **bro'ma·ther'a·py** (brō'mə-). [< Gk. *brōma, -atos* + THERAPY]

bromic (brō'mik) *adj. Chem.* Of, pertaining to, or containing bromine, especially in its higher valence.

bro·mide[1] (brō'mīd, -mid) n. 1 *Chem.* A compound of bromine with an element or an organic radical; a salt of hydrobromic acid: potassium *bromide,* KBr. 2 A photograph printed on paper, etc., that has been subjected to the effects of bromide of silver. Also **bro'mid** (-mid). [< BROM(INE) + -IDE]

bro·mide[2] (brō'mīd, -mid) n. *Colloq.* 1 One who utters platitudes; a commonplace bore. 2 A platitude; a dull remark. [< BROMIDE[1]; with ref. to the sedative effect of some bromides] —**bro·mid·ic** (brō·mid'ik) *adj.*

bro·mi·nate (brō'mə·nāt) v.t. **·nat·ed, ·nat·ing** To bromate.

bro·mine (brō'mēn, -min) n. A heavy, reddish-brown non-metallic liquid element (symbol Br, atomic number 35) belonging to the halogen group and having a toxic, suffocating vapor. See PERIODIC TABLE. Also **bro'min** (-min). [< F *brome* (< Gk. *brōmos* stench) + -INE]

bro·mism (brō'miz·əm) n. *Pathol.* Chronic poisoning by bromides.

bro·mize (brō'mīz) v.t. **·mized, ·miz·ing** *Chem.* To combine, impregnate, or treat with bromine or a bromide.

bromo- *combining form* Used to indicate the presence of bromine as a principal element in chemical compounds. Also, before vowels, **brom-**. [< BROMINE]

bron·chi (brong'kī) *Anat.* Plural of BRONCHUS.

bron·chi·a (brong'kē·ə) n. pl. *Anat.* The bronchial tubes. [< LL < Gk. *bronchia* bronchial tubes]

bron·chi·al (brong'kē·əl) *adj. Anat.* Of or pertaining to the chief air passages of the lungs.

bronchial tubes *Anat.* The subdivisions of the trachea conveying air into the lungs.

bron·chi·tis (brong·kī'tis) n. *Pathol.* Inflammation of the bronchial tubes, or, loosely, of the bronchi or trachea. [< BRONCH(O)- + -ITIS] —**bron·chit·ic** (brong·kit'ik) *adj.*

broncho- *combining form* Windpipe: *broncho-scope.* Also, before vowels, **bronch-.** [< Gk. *bronchos*]

bron·cho·cele (brong'kə·sēl) n. Goiter. [< Gk. *bronchokēlē* tumor in the throat < *bronchos* windpipe + *kēlē* tumor]

bron·cho·pneu·mon·ia (brong'kō·nōō·mōn'yə, -nyōō-) n. *Pathol.* Bronchitis complicated with inflammation of the surrounding substance of the lungs; catarrhal pneumonia.

bron·cho·scope (brong'kə·skōp) n. *Med.* An instrument for inspecting or treating the interior of the bronchi. —**bron·chos·co·py** (brong·kos'kə·pē) n.

bron·chot·o·my (brong·kot'ə·mē) n. *Surg.* The operation of making an incision into the windpipe; tracheotomy. [< BRONCHO- + -TOMY]

bron·chus (brong'kəs) n. pl. **·chi** (-kī) *Anat.* One of the two forked branches of the trachea. [< Gk. *bronchos* windpipe]

bron·co (brong'kō) n. pl. **·cos** A small, wild, or partly broken horse of the western United States. —*adj.* 1 Consisting of, or like broncos. 2 Wild; unruly. Also **bron'cho.** [< Sp. *bronco* rough]

bron·co·bust·er (brong'kō·bus'tər) n. *U.S. Colloq.* One who breaks a bronco to the saddle. Also **bron'cho·bust'er.**

Bron·të (bron'tē) Name of three English novelists, sisters: **Anne,** 1820–49; **Charlotte,** 1816–1855; **Emily Jane,** 1818–48. Pseudonyms, respectively, *Acton, Currer,* and *Ellis Bell.*

bron·tides (bron'tīdz) n. pl. *Meteorol.* Brief, thunderlike noises accompanying the activity of faint earthquakes in seismic regions. [< Gk. *brontē* thunder + -*eidēs* like, similar to]

bron·to·sau·rus (bron'tə·sôr'əs) n. *Paleontol.* A huge, herbivorous dinosaur (order *Sauropoda*) of the Jurassic period, found fossil in western North America. [Gk. *brontē* thunder + *sauros* lizard]

BRONTOSAURUS
(Up to 70 feet in length, 20 tons in weight)

Bronx (brongks), **the** A mainland borough of New York City.

Bronx cheer *U.S. Slang* A voiced and forced expulsion of the breath through nearly-closed lips to express contempt or derision.

bronze (bronz) n. 1 *Metall.* **a** A reddish-brown alloy essentially of copper and tin, used in making bells and statues. **b** A similar alloy of copper and some other metal, as aluminum or manganese. 2 A pigment of the color of bronze. 3 A statue or bust cast in bronze. —*v.* **bronzed, bronz·ing** *v.t.* To harden or color like bronze; make brown. —*v.i.* To become brown or tan. [< MF < Ital. *bronzo, bronzino,* ? < L (*aes*) *Brundisinum* (alloy) of Brundisium] —**bronz'y** *adj.*

Bronze Age *Archeol.* A period of time following the Stone Age and preceding the Iron Age during which weapons and other implements were made of bronze.

Bronze Star A U.S. military decoration in the form of a bronze star having a much smaller raised star in the center: awarded for heroic or meritorious achievement not involving participation in an aerial flight.

brooch (brōch, brōōch) n. An ornamental pin

for wearing on the breast. [Var. of BROACH¹, *n.*]

brood (brood) *n.* **1** All the young birds of a single hatching; also, offspring; progeny. **2** Species; kind; race. See synonyms under FLOCK. —*v.t.* **1** To sit upon or incubate (eggs). **2** To protect (young) by covering with the wings. —*v.i.* **3** To sit on eggs; incubate. **4** To meditate or ponder moodily and deeply: usually with *on* or *upon.* —*adj.* Kept for breeding purposes: a *brood* mare [OE *brod.* Related to BREED.]

brood·er (broo′dər) *n.* **1** A covered and warmed receptacle, usually with an outside run, for protecting chicks reared without a hen. **2** One who broods over things in thought.

brood mare A mare used for breeding.

brood·y (broo′dē) *adj.* **brood·i·er, brood·i·est** **1** Inclined to brood, or sit on eggs, as a hen. **2** Prolific; capable of breeding. **3** Meditative; moody.

brook¹ (brook) *n.* A small, natural stream, smaller than a river or creek; a rivulet. See synonyms under STREAM. [OE *brōc*]

brook² (brook) *v.t.* To put up with; endure; tolerate: usually with the negative: I cannot *brook* such conduct. See synonyms under ENDURE. [OE *brūcan* use, enjoy]

brook·let (brook′lit) *n.* A little brook.

(brook′lin) A borough of New York City on the western end of Long Island.

brook trout **1** The speckled trout *(Salvelinus fontinalis)* of eastern North America. **2** The European brown trout *(Salmo trutta).*

broom (broom, broom) *n.* **1** A brush attached to a long handle for sweeping: made chiefly of broomcorn. **2** Any of various shrubs (genus *Cytisus*) of the pea family, especially the **Scotch broom** *(C. scoparius),* with yellow flowers and stiff green branches. —*v.t.* To remove with a broom; sweep. [OE *brōm* broom. Akin to BRAMBLE.] —**broom′y** *adj.*

broom·corn (broom′kôrn′, broom′-) *n.* A canelike grass (genus *Sorghum*) of which brooms are made.

broom·stick (broom′stik′, broom′-) *n.* The handle of a broom.

brose (brōz) *n. Scot.* Porridge hastily made by pouring boiling water, or sometimes milk, beef broth, or the like, on meal, and stirring them together. —**bro′sy** *adj.*

broth (brôth, broth) *n.* **1** A fluid food made by boiling flesh, vegetables, etc., in water; a thin or strained soup. **2** *Irish Colloq.* A manly boy or young man of good character. —**a broth of a boy** A fine fellow. [OE. Related to BREW.]

broth·el (broth′əl, broth′-, brôth′əl, brôth′-) *n.* A house of prostitution. [ME, a worthless person, OE *brothen,* pp. of *breothan* ruin, decay; infl. by BORDEL]

broth·er (bruth′ər) *n. pl.* **broth·ers** or *Archaic* **breth·ren** **1** A male person having the same parent as another or others. Sons of the same two parents are **full** or **whole brothers;** those having only one parent in common are *half-brothers.* **2** A person of the same descent, profession, trade, company, etc., with another or others; one having the same racial heritage; a kinsman. **3** A fellow human being. **4** One closely united with another or others by religious, political, or family bond. **5** One of a male religious order; a monk. **6** *U.S. Colloq.* A black man; a fellow black. —*v.t.* To treat or address as a brother. [OE *brōthor*]

broth·er·hood (bruth′ər·hood) *n.* **1** Fraternal relationship; the state of being brothers. **2** A society, fraternity, guild, etc. **3** A body of persons of the same occupation, profession, etc.

broth·er-in-law (bruth′ər-in-lô′) *n. pl.* **broth·ers-in-law** A brother of a husband or wife, a sister's husband, or, loosely, a wife's sister's husband.

broth·er·ly (bruth′ər·lē) *adj.* Pertaining to or like a brother; fraternal; affectionate. See synonyms under FRIENDLY. —*adv.* Like a brother; kindly. —**broth′er·li·ness** *n.*

brought (brôt) Past tense and past participle of BRING.

brou·ha·ha (broo′hä·hä) *n.* Hubbub; uproar; hurly-burly. [< F]

brow (brou) *n.* **1** The front upper part of the head; the forehead. **2** The eyebrow. **3** The countenance in general. **4** The upper edge of a cliff or the like. [OE *brū*]

brow·band (brou′band′) *n.* **1** A band about the brow. **2** A band, as of a bridle, passing across a horse's forehead. For illustration see HARNESS.

brow·beat (brou′bēt′) *v.t.* **·beat, ·beat·en, ·beat·ing** To intimidate by a stern, overbearing manner; bully. See synonyms under FRIGHTEN.

brown (broun) *n.* **1** A dark color, shading toward red, yellow, or black, as the color of faded leaves. **2** A pigment or dye used to produce it; a thing or part that is brown. —*adj.* Of the dusky or tanned color known as brown. —**to do up brown** *Slang* To do thoroughly and perfectly. —*v.t. & v.i.* To make or become brown; tan, as by sunbathing. [OE *brun*] —**brown′ish** *adj.* —**brown′ness** *n.*

brown bagging **1** The practice of carrying in a small paper bag one's own liquor into a restaurant, where its sale is prohibited. **2** The practice of taking one's lunch to work in a brown paper bag.

brown bread **1** Bread made of unbolted wheat flour; Graham bread. **2** Bread made of rye flour and corn meal.

Brown·i·an movement (brou′nē·ən) *Physics* The rapid oscillatory movement of small particles when suspended in liquids. Also **Brownian motion.** [after Robert *Brown,* 1773–1858, English botanist, who discovered it]

brown·ie (brou′nē) *n.* **1** A homely, good-natured sprite, supposed to haunt farmhouses and do useful work at night. **2** A small, flat chocolate cake with nuts, usually square.

Brown·ing (brou′ning), **Elizabeth Barrett,** 1806–61, English poet; wife of Robert. —**Robert,** 1812–89, English poet.

brown lung Byssinosis.

brown-out (broun′out′) *n.* **1** A partial diminishing of lights as a defensive measure against aerial attacks. **2** Any diminution of electric power.

brown rice Unpolished rice grains, with the bran layers and most of the grains intact.

Brown Shirt **1** A member of the Sturmabteilung. **2** A Nazi.

brown·stone (broun′stōn′) *n.* A brownish-red sandstone used for building. —*adj.* **1** Made of brownstone. **2** Pertaining to the well-to-do class: the *brownstone* vote.

brownstone front A house having a front of brownstone.

brown study Deep meditation; absent-mindedness.

brown sugar Sugar that is unrefined or partly refined.

Brown Swiss A type of hardy dairy cattle originating in Switzerland.

browse (brouz) *v.* **browsed, brows·ing** *v.t.* **1** To crop; nibble at (leaves, grasses, etc.). **2** To graze on. —*v.i.* **1** To feed on grasses, leaves, etc. **4** To dip into books, etc., for casual reading. [< *n.,* or < MF *brouster* browse] —*n.* **1** Growing shoots or twigs used as fodder. **2** The act or process of browsing. [< MF *broust* bud, sprout] —**brows·er** *n.*

bru·cel·lo·sis (broo′sə·lō′sis) *n.* Undulant fever. [after Sir David *Bruce*]

bru·cine (broo′sēn, -sin) *n. Chem.* A bitter poisonous crystalline alkaloid, $C_{23}H_{26}O_4N_2 \cdot 4H_2O$, found, with strychnine, in the seed and bark of the nux vomica, and in other species of the same genus *(Strychnos).* Also **bru′cin** (-sin). [after J. *Bruce,* 1730–94, Scottish explorer in Africa]

Brue·ghel (broi′gəl) Family of Flemish painters, especially, **Peter,** 1520?–69, known as *the Elder,* and his sons, **Peter,** 1564?–1638?, known as *the Younger,* and **Jan,** 1568–1625. Also spelled *Breughel, Bruegel.*

Bruges (broozh, broo′jiz) A city of NW Belgium, capital of West Flanders province. *Flemish* **Brug·ge** (brœkh′ə)

bru·in (broo′in) *n.* A bear; especially, a brown bear. [< Du., brown]

bruise (brooz) *v.* **bruised, bruis·ing** *v.t.* **1** To injure, as by a blow, without breaking the surface of the skin; contuse. **2** To dent or mar the surface of. **3** To hurt or offend slightly, as feelings. **4** To crush; pound small, as with a mortar and pestle. —*v.i.* To become discolored as the result of a blow. —*n.* A surface injury caused by violent contact, usually with discoloration of the skin but without laceration or fracture; contusion. [Fusion of OE *brȳsan* crush and OF *bruisier* break, shatter]

bruis·er (broo′zər) *n.* **1** One who bruises. **2** A professional pugilist. **3** A pugnacious ruffian; a bully.

bruit (broot) *v.t.* To noise abroad; talk about:

used mainly in the passive. See synonyms under PUBLISH. [< *n.*]—*n.* **1** *Obs.* A rumor noised abroad. **2** A din; clamor. **3** *Med.* A sound, generally abnormal, heard in auscultation. ◆ Homophone: **brute.** [< F *bruit* noise < *bruire* roar, make a noise, ? < L *rugire* roar, bellow] —**bruit′er** *n.*

bru·mal (broo′məl) *adj.* Wintry. [< L *brumalis* wintry]

brum·by (brum′bē) *Austral.* A wild horse.

brume (broom) *n.* Fog; mist. [< F < L *bruma* winter] —**bru·mous** (broo′məs) *adj.*

brum·ma·gem (brum′ə·jəm) *adj.* Cheap and showy; spurious, bogus. —*n.* An imitation; a sham; especially, cheap, imitation jewelry. [Alter. of *Birmingham,* England, where cheap jewelry was made]

brunch (brunch) *n.* A late morning meal combining breakfast and lunch. [Blend of BREAKFAST and LUNCH]

Bru·nei (broo·nī′) A sultanate under British protection in NW Borneo; 2,226 square miles; capital, Brunei.

Bru·nel·les·chi (broo′nel·les′kē), **Filippo,** 1377–1446, Italian architect and sculptor. Also **Bru′nel·les′co** (-les′kō).

bru·net (broo·net′) *n.* A man or boy of dark complexion, eyes, and hair. —*adj.* Brunette.

bru·nette (broo·net′) *adj.* Dark-hued; having dark complexion, hair, and eyes. —*n.* A woman or girl of dark complexion, eyes, and hair. [< F, fem. dim. of *brun* brown]

Brun·hild (broon′hild, *Ger.* broon′hilt) In the *Nibelungenlied,* a queen of Iceland, married to Gunther, for whom she is won by Siegfried: discovering the deceit of her conquest, she persuades Hagen to avenge her by murdering Siegfried. Compare BRÜNNEHILDE, BRYNHILD.

Brünn (brün) The German name for BRNO.

Brünne·hil·de (brün·hil′də) In Wagner's *Ring of the Nibelung,* a Valkyrie who incurs the anger of Wotan for assisting Siegmund and is put in a trance in a flame-encircled fastness, but is eventually released by Siegfried. Compare BRUNHILD, BRYNHILD.

Bruns·wick (brunz′wik) **1** A port in SE Georgia. **2** A former duchy and state of north central Germany; also, its former capital, a city in Lower Saxony: German *Braunschweig.*

brunt (brunt) *n.* **1** The main force, shock, strain, or stress of a blow, an attack, etc.; the hardest part. **2** *Obs.* A blow; assault; collision. [? < ON *bruna* advance quickly, as a fire]

brush¹ (brush) *n.* **1** An implement having bristles, hair, feathers, wire, or other flexible fibrous material, fixed in a handle or a back, and used for sweeping, scrubbing, painting, cleansing, smoothing, etc. **2** The act of brushing. **3** A light, grazing touch. **4** A skirmish; a short, brisk fight. **5** Brushwork. **6** Any object resembling a brush, as the bushy tail or bushy part of the tail of various animals, especially the fox. **7** *Elect.* **a** A strip of metal, bundle of wire, or bunch of slit metal plates, bearing on the commutator cylinder of a dynamo, for carrying off the current or for an external current through a motor. **b** A brush discharge. **8** A brushlike appearance in certain phenomena of polarized light. —*v.t.* **1** To use a brush on; sweep, polish, smooth, paint, etc., with or as with a brush. **2** To remove with or as with a brush. **3** To touch lightly in passing; touch upon briefly. —*v.i.* **4** To move lightly and quickly, often with a touch: to *brush* past someone. —**to brush aside** To deny consideration to. —**to brush up 1** To refresh one's knowledge of. **2** To renovate; refurbish. —**to brush up against** To come into slight contact with. [< OF *brosse* butcherbroom, brush, ? < Gmc.]

brush² (brush) *n.* **1** A growth of small trees and shrubs; hence, wooded country sparsely settled; backwoods. **2** Lopped-off bushes or branches of trees; brushwood. [< OF *broche,* ? < Gmc.]

brush discharge *Electr.* A discharge of low luminosity which issues in brushlike form from the terminals of an electric circuit. Compare CORONA (def. 6).

brushed wool A knit or woven woolen fabric on which a nap has been raised by a process using circular brushes.

brush fire **1** A fire in the brush. **2** A fire built of brushwood.

brush hook A hook for cutting brush.

brush–off (brush′ôf′, -of′) *n.* *U.S. Colloq.* An abrupt refusal or dismissal.

brush–tail possum (brush′tāl′) A marsupial (*Trichosurus vulpecula fuliginosis*) of Tasmania, about two feet high and largest of the Australian possums.

brush turkey A jungle fowl of Australia or New Guinea; especially, the Australian *Alectura lathami,* about the size of a turkey but having a bright-yellow wattle.

brush wheel A wheel with bristles, buff leather, etc., on its periphery: used to rotate a similar wheel, or for cleaning, polishing, etc.

brush·wood (brush′wŏŏd′) *n.* **1** A low thicket; underwood. **2** Cut bushes, or branches.

brush·work (brush′wûrk′) *n.* A painter's characteristic style or way of applying paint with a brush.

brush·y (brush′ē) *adj.* **brush·i·er, brush·i·est** **1** Covered with brushwood. **2** Resembling a brush; shaggy; rough; bushy.

Bru·si·lov (brŏŏ·sē′lôf), **Alexei Alexeivich,** 1853–1926, Russian general in World War I.

brusk (brusk, *esp. Brit.* brŏŏsk) *adj.* Rude or curt; abrupt; blunt; rough. See synonyms under BLUFF. Also **brusque.** [<MF *brusque* <Ital. *brusco* rough, rude] — **brusk′ly** *adv.* — **brusk′ness** *n.*

brus·que·rie (brus′kə·rē, *Fr.* brüs·kə·rē′) *n.* Bluntness; bruskness; a brusk act or speech.

Brus·sels (brus′əlz) The capital of Belgium and of the province of Brabant. *French* **Brux·elles** (brü·sel′, brük·sel′); *Flemish* **Brus·sel** (brœs′əl).

Brussels carpet A machine-made worsted carpet of linen or cotton and linen web.

Brussels griffon A toy dog of European origin, having a flat face and shaggy, reddish-brown hair. See BELGIAN GRIFFON, BRABANÇON GRIFFON.

Brussels lace Net lace, made by machine, with designs separately made and appliquéd upon it.

Brussels sprouts **1** A cultivated variety of wild cabbage (*Brassica oleracea gemmifera*), with blistered leaves and stems covered with heads like little cabbages. **2** The small edible heads or sprouts of this plant.

BRUSSELS LACE

brut (brüt) *adj.* Dry: said of wines. [<F, lit., rough, raw <L *brutus* rough, rude]

Brut (brŏŏt) Legendary king of Britain; great-grandson of Aeneas and founder of the British race. See LAYAMON. Also **Brute, Bru′tus.**

bru·tal (brŏŏt′l) *adj.* **1** Characteristic of or like a brute; cruel; savage. **2** Unfeeling; rude; coarse. See synonyms under BARBAROUS, BRUTISH. [<L *brutus* stupid] — **bru′tal·ly** *adv.*

bru·tal·i·ty (brŏŏ·tal′ə·tē) *n. pl.* **·ties** **1** The state or quality of being brutal; cruelty. **2** A brutal or cruel act.

bru·tal·ize (brŏŏt′l·īz) *v.t. & v.i.* **·ized, ·iz·ing** To make or become brutal. — **bru′tal·i·za′·tion** *n.*

brute (brŏŏt) *n.* **1** Any animal other than man, as a horse, dog, etc. **2** A brutal person. See synonyms under ANIMAL. — *adj.* **1** Wanting the rational faculty; merely animal. **2** Unintelligent; also, sensual; brutal. **3** Merely material; inanimate. ◆ Homophone: *bruit.* [<F *brut* <L *brutus* stupid]

bru·ti·fy (brŏŏt′ə·fī) *v.t. & v.i.* **·fied, ·fy·ing** To brutalize.

brut·ish (brŏŏt′ish) *adj.* **1** Pertaining to, characteristic of, or resembling brutes. **2** Stupid; irrational; sensual; gross. — **brut′ish·ly** *adv.* — **brut′ish·ness, brut′ism** *n.*

Synonyms: animal, base, beastly, bestial, brutal, brute, carnal, coarse, ignorant, imbruted, insensible, lascivious, sensual, sottish, stolid, stupid, swinish, unintellectual, unspiritual, vile. A *brutish* man simply follows his *animal* instincts, without special inclination to do harm; the *brutal* have always a spirit of malice and cruelty. *Brute* or *animal* simply indicates what a brute or an animal might possess; *animal* leans more to the side of sensuality, *brute* to that of force, as appears in the familiar phrase "*brute* force." Hunger is an *animal* appetite; a *brute* impulse may prompt one to strike a blow in anger. *Bestial* implies an intensified and degrading animalism. *Beastly* refers largely to the outward and visible consequences of excess; as, *beastly* drunkenness. Compare ANIMAL. *Antonyms:* elevated, enlightened, exalted, grand, great, humane, intellectual, intelligent, noble, refined, spiritual.

Bru·tus (brŏŏ′təs), **Marcus Junius,** 85–42 B.C., Roman republican leader, one of Caesar's assassins.

brux·ism (bruk′siz·əm) *n.* A grinding or gnashing of the teeth in sleep or for other than chewing purposes: injurious to dental health. [<Gk. *bruchē* gnashing (of teeth) <*bruchein* gnash]

Bryn·hild (brün′hilt) In the *Volsunga Saga* and in William Morris's *Sigurd the Volsung,* a Valkyrie who is thrown into an enchanted sleep by Odin, from which she is awakened by Sigurd. Compare BRUNHILD, BRÜNNEHILDE.

bry·o·chore (brī′ə·kôr, -kōr) *n. Ecol.* The tundra region characteristic of Siberia and arctic North America. [<Gk. *bryon* moss + *chorē* country, region]

bry·ol·o·gy (brī·ol′ə·jē) *n.* The department of botany that treats of mosses. [<Gk. *bryon* moss + -LOGY] — **bry·o·log·i·cal** (brī′ə·loj′i·kəl) *adj.* — **bry·ol′o·gist** *n.*

bry·o·nin (brī′ə·nin) *n. Chem.* An amorphous bitter glucoside, $C_{48}H_{66}O_{18}$, contained in the root of bryony: used in medicine.

bry·o·ny (brī′ə·nē) *n.* A common English herb (genus *Bryonia*) of the gourd family, with white or yellowish flowers and black or red berries. [<Gk. *bryōnē*]

bry·o·phyte (brī′ə·fīt) *n. Bot.* Any moss or liverwort of the phylum *Bryophyta.* [Gk. *bryon* moss + -PHYTE] — **bry′o·phyt′ic** (-fit′ik) *adj.*

bry·o·zo·an (brī′ə·zō′ən) *n. Zool.* One of a phylum or class (*Bryozoa*) of small aquatic animals which generate by budding, usually found in permanent colonies: of delicately branched or mosslike formation, or else of flat, crustlike growth. [<Gk. *bryon* moss + *zōon* organism]

Bryth·on (brith′ən) *n.* A Briton; specifically, a Welshman or a Celt of the Brythonic group. [<Welsh]

Bry·thon·ic (bri·thon′ik) *adj.* Of or pertaining to the Brythons or to their languages. — *n.* That branch of the Celtic languages which includes Welsh, Breton, and the extinct Cornish; Cymric: distinguished from *Goidelic.*

bub (bub) *n. Colloq.* A small boy; youngster; young man: used in direct address. [Alter. of BROTHER]

bu·bal (byŏŏ′bəl) *n.* A large antelope (genus *Alcelaphus*), especially the North African bubal hartebeest (*A. boselaphus*). Also **bu·bale** (byŏŏ′bəl), **bu·ba·lis** (byŏŏ′bə·lis). [<L *bubalus* <Gk. *boubalos* African antelope. Related to BUFFALO.]

bu·ba·line (byŏŏ′bə·līn, -lin) *adj.* **1** Resembling the bubal. **2** Of, pertaining to, or like a buffalo.

bub·ble (bub′əl) *n.* **1** A vesicle of cohesive liquid, filled with air or other gas. **2** A globule of air or other gas in any confined space, as in a liquid or solid substance. **3** Anything unsubstantial; a delusion; cheat; fraud. **4** The process or sound of bubbling. [<v.] — *v.* **·bled, ·bling** *v.t.* **1** To form bubbles in, as a liquid. **2** To emit or utter by or as by bubbling: He *bubbled* the good news. **3** *Archaic* To cheat; swindle. — *v.i.* **4** To form bubbles; rise in bubbles. **5** To move or flow with a gurgling sound. **6** To express emotion, joy, etc., with a gurgling sound: He *bubbled* with glee. [ME *buble*; prob. imit.] — **bub′bly** *adj.*

bubble and squeak *Brit.* Cabbage and meat fried together. Also **bub′ble-and-squeak′** *n.*

bub·bler (bub′lər) *n.* A drinking fountain fitted with a vertical nozzle from which water flows in a small stream.

bubble sextant *Aeron.* A sextant in which an artificial horizon is represented by the position of a bubble in an instrument similar to a carpenter's level.

bu·bo (byŏŏ′bō) *n. pl.* **bu·boes** *Pathol.* An inflammatory swelling of a lymph gland in the groin, especially one due to venereal infection. [<LL <Gk. *boubōn* groin] — **bu·bon·ic** (byŏŏ·bon′ik) *adj.*

bubonic plague *Pathol.* A malignant, contagious, epidemic disease, characterized by fever, vomiting, diarrhea, and buboes: it is caused by a bacterium of the genus *Pasteurella* transmitted to man by fleas which have been infected by rats.

bu·bon·o·cele (byŏŏ·bon′ə·sēl) *n. Pathol.* Inguinal hernia. [<Gk. *boubōnokēlē* < *boubōn* groin + *kēlē* abscess]

buc·cal (buk′əl) *adj. Anat.* **1** Of or pertaining to the cheek: the *buccal* artery. **2** Pertaining to the mouth; oral. [<L *bucca* cheek]

buc·ca·neer (buk′ə·nir′) *n.* **1** A pirate or freebooter. **2** One of the piratical rovers of the 17th and 18th centuries who preyed upon the Spaniards, along the Spanish coasts of America. See synonyms under ROBBER. [<F *boucanier,* orig. one of the hunters of wild oxen in Haiti, who later turned to piracy <Tupian *boucan* a frame for the smoking and curing of meat]

buc·ci·na·tor (buk′sə·nā′tər) *n. Anat.* A muscle of the middle cheek, used in blowing. [<L, trumpeter < *buccina* trumpet]

Bu·cen·taur (byŏŏ·sen′tôr) *n.* **1** The state barge of Venice, used by the Doge on Ascension Day. **2** A mythical monster, half bull and half man. [<Ital. *bucentoro,* ? <Med. Gk. *boukentauros* bucentaur < Gk. *bous* bull + *kentauros* centaur; with ref. to the vessel's figurehead]

BUCENTAUR

Bu·chan·an (byŏŏ·kan′ən), **James,** 1791–1868, president of the United States 1857–61.

Bu·cha·rest (bŏŏ′kə·rest, byŏŏ′-) The capital of Rumania. *Rumanian* **Bu·cu·resti** (bŏŏ·kŏŏ·resht′)

Buch·en·wald (bŏŏk′ən·wôld, *Ger.* bŏŏkh′ən·vält) Site of a notorious Nazi concentration and extermination camp near Weimar, Germany.

buck¹ (buk) *n.* **1** The male of certain animals, as of antelopes, deer, goats, rabbits, and rats. **2** A dashing fellow; a young blood. **3** An adult male Negro or Indian. — *v.i.* **1** To leap upward suddenly and come down with the legs stiff, as a horse or pack-animal, in an attempt to dislodge rider or burden. **2** *U.S. Colloq.* To resist stubbornly; object. **3** *U.S. Colloq.* To move with jerks and jolts: said of vehicles. **4** To provide resistance against which a rivet may be driven or some other pounding or pushing work done. — *v.t.* **5** To throw (a rider) by bucking. **6** *U.S. Colloq.* To butt with the head. **7** *U.S. Colloq.* To resist stubbornly; oppose. **8** To provide resistance for pounding or pushing (a rivet, etc.). **9** In football, to charge into (the opponent's line) with the ball. — **to buck up** *Colloq.* To encourage or become encouraged. [Fusion of OE *buc* he-goat and *bucca* male deer]

buck² (buk) *n.* **1** A sawhorse. **2** A padded frame in the shape of a sawhorse, used by gymnasts. [<Du. *zaagbok* sawbuck]

buck³ (buk) *n.* **1** A buckskin, formerly taken as a standard of value by North American Indians. **2** *U.S. Slang* A dollar.

buck⁴ (buk) *n. Brit.* Suds or lye, for washing clothes; also, the clothes washed. [<v.] — *v.t. Dial.* To wash or bleach in lye. [ME *bouken.* Akin to LG *büken* steep in lye]

buck⁵ (buk) *n.* **1** In card games, an object placed before a player as a reminder of his turn to deal. **2** In poker, a marker occasionally put into a jackpot, indicating that he who receives the buck must order another jackpot when it is his deal. — **to pass the buck** *U.S. Colloq.* To shift responsibility, blame, etc., from oneself to someone else. [Origin uncertain]

buck·a·roo (buk′ə·rŏŏ, buk′ə·rŏŏ′) *n.* A cowboy. Also **buck·ay·ro** (buk·ā′rō). [Alter. of Sp. *vaquero* cowboy]

buck·ber·ry (buk′ber′ē, -bər·ē) n. 1 A small, wild, black huckleberry (*Gaylussacia ursina*) native in SE United States. 2 The deerberry (*Vaccineum stamineum*) common in eastern North America.

buck·board (buk′bôrd′, -bōrd′) n. A light, four–wheeled, horse–drawn vehicle having a long flexible board in place of body and springs. Also **buck′wag′on**. [<BUCK, v. (def. 3) + BOARD]

BUCKBOARD

buck·er (buk′ər) n. 1 One who or that which bucks. 2 *U.S. Slang* One who bolts from a political party.

buck·et (buk′it) n. 1 A deep cylindrical vessel, with a bail, for dipping or carrying liquids; a pail. 2 As much as a bucket will hold: also **buck′et·ful′**. 3 A compartment on a water wheel, or the like. 4 A piston, as in a lifting pump, with a valve opening upward. —v.t. & v.i. 1 To draw or carry in a bucket. 2 *Colloq.* To ride (a horse) hard. 3 To move along rapidly. —**to kick the bucket** *Slang* To die. [? <OF *buket* kind of tub; infl. by OE *bucc* pitcher]

bucket seat A single, low, often adjustable seat with a rounded back: used in racing and sports cars, airplanes, etc.

buck·et·shop (buk′it·shop′) n. An office for gambling in fractional lots of stocks, grain, etc., with no delivery of securities or commodities sold or purchased.

buck·eye (buk′ī′) n. 1 The horse chestnut of the United States. 2 The glossy brown seed or nut of this tree. [<BUCK¹ + EYE]

Buck·eye (buk′ī′) n. A native or inhabitant of Ohio.

Buckeye State Nickname of OHIO.

buck fever *U.S. Colloq.* The state of excitement felt by an inexperienced hunter when first sighting game.

buck·horn (buk′hôrn′) n. The horn of a buck deer: often used to make knife handles, buttons, etc.

buck·hound (buk′hound′) n. 1 A large hound formerly used for hunting bucks. 2 The Scottish deerhound: also called **staghound**.

buck·ish (buk′ish) adj. Dapper; foppish.

buck·le¹ (buk′əl) n. 1 A metal frame with movable tongue for fastening together two loose ends, as of straps, etc. 2 An ornament for shoes, etc., devised like a buckle. —v.t. 1 To fasten or attach with or as with a buckle. 2 To apply (oneself) assiduously. —v.i. 3 To apply oneself vigorously: often with *down to* or *to*. 4 To fight; grapple. [<F *boucle* cheek-strap, boss of a shield <L *buccula*, dim. of *bucca* cheek]

buck·le² (buk′əl) v.t. & v.i. **·led, ·ling** To bend under pressure; warp, curl, or crumple. —n. A bend; in mechanics, a permanent distortion or bend. [<F *boucler* bulge]

buck·ler (buk′lər) n. 1 A shield; especially, a small round shield. 2 One who defends or protects; one who shields. 3 A protective covering on various animals. —v.t. To shield, as with a buckler; defend; protect. [OF *boucler* having a boss]

Buck·ley's chance (buk′lēz) *Austral. Slang* No chance at all, or very little chance, of success.

buck·o (buk′ō) n. pl. **·oes** 1 A bully; blusterer.

buck private *U.S. Colloq.* An enlisted man of the lowest rank in the U.S. Army.

buck·ra (buk′rə) adj. White, or belonging to a white man; like or characteristic of white people: a term used among the Negroes of Africa, the West Indies, and the southern United States: a *buckra* house, *buckra* manners. —n. A white man. [<Efik *mbākara*]

buck·ram (buk′rəm) n. 1 A coarse, glue–sized cotton fabric, for stiffening garments, and for bookbinding. 2 Stiffness of manner. 3 *Originally*, a fine linen or cotton fabric. —adj. Of or like buckram; stiff; precise. —v.t. To stiffen with or as with buckram. [Cf. OF *boquerant*]

buck·skin (buk′skin′) n. 1 The skin of a buck: also **buck skin**. 2 A soft, strong, grayish–yellow leather, formerly made from deerskins, now chiefly from sheepskins. 3 pl. Breeches or a suit made of such skin. 4 A person clad in such skin; especially, one of the American soldiers in the Revolution. 5 A horse of a

buckskin color. 6 A cream–colored woolen cloth of close weave: also **buckskin cloth**.

buck·thorn (buk′thôrn′) n. A shrub or small tree of the genus *Rhamnus*, having alternate pinnately veined leaves and axillary flowers. —**southern buckthorn** A tree (*Bumelia lycioides*) of the southern United States. [<BUCK¹ + THORN]

buck·tooth (buk′tōōth′) n. pl. **·teeth** A projecting tooth. [<BUCK¹ + TOOTH]

buck·toothed (buk′tōōtht′, -tōōthd′) adj. Having projecting teeth.

buck·wheat (buk′hwēt′) n. A plant of the genus *Fagopyrum*, yielding triangular seeds used as fodder and for flour. 2 Its seeds. 3 The flour. [OE *bōc* beech + WHEAT, from resemblance of seeds to beech seeds]

buck·y diaphragm (buk′ē) In roentgenography, an apparatus for preventing secondary X–rays from affecting the plate, thus ensuring a clearer picture. [after Gustav *Bucky*, 1880–1963, German–American roentgenologist]

bu·col·ic (byōō·kol′ik) adj. Pertaining to or like shepherds or herdsmen; pastoral; rustic: also **bu·col′i·cal**. —n. 1 A pastoral poem. 2 A rustic; farmer: humorous usage. See synonyms under RUSTIC. [<L *bucolicus* <Gk. *boukolikos* < *boukolos* herdsman < *bous* ox] —**bu·col′i·cal·ly** adv.

bud¹ (bud) n. 1 *Bot.* a An undeveloped stem, branch, or shoot of a plant, with rudimentary leaves or unexpanded flowers. b The act or stage of budding. 2 *Zool.* A budlike projection, as in polyps, etc., developing into a new individual; also, a budlike part. 3 Any immature person or thing. —**to nip in the bud** To stop in the initial stage. —v.t. **bud·ded, bud·ding** v.t. 1 To put forth as buds. 2 To graft by inserting a bud of (a tree or plant) into the stock of another type of tree or plant. 3 To cause to bud. —v.i. 4 To put forth buds. 5 To begin to grow or develop. [ME *budde*; origin uncertain] —**bud′der** n.

bud² (bud) n. *U.S. Colloq.* A term of direct address to a man or boy. Also **buddy**. [Alter. of BROTHER]

Bu·da·pest (bōō′də·pest) The capital of Hungary, on the Danube.

Bud·dha (bōōd′ə, bōō′də) n. Literally, the Enlightened; an incarnation of selflessness, virtue, and wisdom; specifically, Gautama Siddhartha, 563?–483? B.C., the founder of Buddhism, regarded by his followers as the last of a series of deified religious teachers of central and eastern Asia. [<Skt.]

Bud·dhism (bōōd′iz·əm, bōō′diz-) n. A mystical and ascetic religious faith of eastern Asia, founded in northern India by Buddha in the sixth century B.C., teaching that Nirvana, which is the conquest of self and subsequent freedom from sorrow and mortality, is reached by the Eightfold Path of right belief, right resolution, right speech, right action, right living, right effort, right thinking, and peace of mind through meditation. —**Bud′dhist** adj. & n. —**Bud·dhis′tic** or **·ti·cal** adj.

bud·ding (bud′ing) n. 1 *Zool.* A mode of asexual reproduction, as in various polyps, ascidians, etc., in which a small part of the substance of the parent is protruded as a bud or gemma and develops into a new organism; gemmation. 2 *Bot.* A similar mode of reproduction occurring in some cryptogams.

bud·dle (bud′l) n. *Mining* 1 An inclined shallow trough, used for separating ores by shaking or raking in running water. 2 One of various circular and conical machines, stationary or rotary, working on the same principle. [Origin unknown]

bud·dy (bud′ē) n. pl. **·dies** *Colloq.* 1 Brother. 2 Pal; chum; companion. 3 Little boy: used in direct address. [See BUD²]

budge¹ (buj) v.t. & v.i. **budged, budg·ing** To move or stir slightly: usually with the negative. —n. A slight movement. [<F *bouger* stir, move]

budge² (buj) n. 1 Lambskin with the wool side out: formerly used for edgings on the gowns of scholastics, etc. 2 A leather bag made with the wool side out. —adj. 1 Trimmed with budge, or wearing budge. 2 Hence, pompous; imposing; formal. [Origin uncertain]

budg·et (buj′it) n. 1 A statement of probable revenue and expenditure and of financial proposals for the ensuing year as presented to or passed upon by a legislative body. 2

A summary of probable income for a given period, as of a family or an individual, with approximate allowances for certain expenditures over that period. 3 A collection or store, as of news, anecdotes, etc. 4 A small sack or its contents; hence, a loose bundle. —v.t. 1 To determine in advance the expenditure of (time, money, etc.) over a period of time. 2 To put on or into a budget: He *budgeted* his trip. [<F *bougette*, dim. of *bouge* <L *bulga* leather bag] —**budg·et·ar·y** (buj′ə·ter′ē) adj. —**budg′et·er** n.

Bue·nos Ai·res (bwā′nəs ī′riz, bō′nəs âr′ēz) 1 A province in eastern Argentina; 116,322 square miles; capital, La Plata. 2 The largest city of Latin America, a federal district and port on the La Plata, capital of Argentina; 77 square miles: a native of the city is known as a *Porteño*.

buff¹ (buf) n. 1 A thick, soft, flexible leather, undyed and unglazed, made from the skins of buffalo, elk, oxen, etc: also **buff leather**. 2 Its color, a light yellow. 3 A coat made of buff leather. 4 *Colloq.* The bare skin; the nude: in the *buff*. 5 A stick or wheel covered with leather, velvet, etc., and used with emery and other powders in polishing: also **buff′er**. —adj. Made of, or of the color of, buff leather; brownish–yellow. —v.t. 1 To clean or polish with or as with a buff. 2 In leather-making, to shave, as cowskin, on the grain side until very thin, producing an imitation of calf leather. 3 To make buff in color. [<F *buffle* buffalo]

buff² (buf) n. A blow; buffet: only in *blind-man's-buff*. —v.t. 1 To deaden the shock of. 2 To strike; buffet. —v.i. 3 To act as a buffer. [<OF *buffe* blow]

buff³ (buf) n. 1 Originally, a voluntary, unofficial auxiliary of a fire department. 2 One who rushes to attend fires. 3 An enthusiast in any special field, who attends all possible events: a theater *buff*. [? Special use of BUFF¹]

buf·fa·lo (buf′ə·lō) n. pl. **·loes** or **·los** 1 A large Old World ox, now extensively domesticated, one of which, the African Cape buffalo (*Syncerus caffer*), has horns that broaden at the base. ♦ Collateral adjective: *bubaline*. 2 The Indian water buffalo. 3 The North American bison. 4 A buffalo robe. 5 A buffalo fish. 6 *Naut.* One of the bulwarks on each side of the stem of the forecastle deck in the extreme bow. —v.t. *U.S. Slang* To overawe; hoodwink. [<Ital. <L *bufalus*, var. of *bubalus* <Gk. *boubalos* buffalo. Related to BUBAL.]

AFRICAN OR CAPE BUFFALO

Buf·fa·lo (buf′ə·lō) A city in western New York at the eastern end of Lake Erie.

buf·fa·lo·ber·ry (buf′ə·lō·ber′ē) n. The edible crimson berry of either of two American shrubs, the thorny silverleaf (*Shepherdia argentea*) or the russet buffaloberry (*S. canadensis*).

buf·fa·lo·grass (buf′ə·lō·gras′, -gräs′) n. 1 A low, creeping grass (*Buchloë dactyloides*) covering large prairies east of the Rocky Mountains, highly esteemed for winter forage. 2 The curly mesquite (*Hilaria belangeri*) of the SW United States and Central America.

buffalo robe The skin of the North American bison, dressed with the hair on for use as a lap robe.

buff·er¹ (buf′ər) n. One who or that which buffs. [<BUFF¹, v.]

buff·er² (buf′ər) n. A device for lessening the shock of concussion. [<BUFF², v.]

buffer state A small country situated between two larger rival powers regarded as less likely to open hostilities with each other because they have no common boundary.

buf·fet¹ (bōō·fā′, *Brit.* buf′it) n. 1 A sideboard; also, a cupboard for china, glassware, etc. 2 A counter or bar for serving lunch or refreshments; also, a public lunchroom. [<F]

buf·fet² (buf′it) v.t. 1 To strike or cuff, as with the hand. 2 To strike repeatedly; knock about. **3** To force (a way) by pushing or striking, as through a crowd. —*v.i.* **4** To fight; struggle. **5** To force a way. —*n.* A blow; cuff; assault. [<OF *buffet*, dim. of *buffe* blow, slap] —**buf′fet·er** *n.*

buf·fet car (boo·fā′) A parlor car or sleeping car on a train equipped with a small kitchen.

buf·fet supper (boo·fā′) A light meal at which the guests serve themselves. Also **buffet lunch.**

buff·ing wheel (buf′ing) Buff¹ (def. 5).

buf·fle·head (buf′əl·hed′) *n.* A North American duck (*Charitonetta albeola*) having the feathers of the head elongated, and with plumage black above and white below: also called *butterball.* [<F *buffle* buffalo + HEAD]

buf·fo (boo′fō, *Ital.* boof′fō) *n.* *pl.* **·fi** (-fē) A comic actor in opera; comic singer: usually a bass. [<Ital., foolish, comic]

buf·foon (bu·foon′) *n.* A clown; one given to jokes, coarse pranks, etc. [<F *buffon* <Ital. *buffone* clown <*buffa* jest] —**buf·foon′er·y** *n.* —**buf·foon′ish** *adj.*

buff·skin (buf′skin′) *n.* Buff¹ (def. 1).

buff·y (buf′ē) *adj.* **1** Of a buff color. **2** Characterized by or resembling buff. **3** Designating or pertaining to a buffy coat.

bug¹ (bug) *n.* **1** Any of an order (*Hemiptera*) or suborder (*Heteroptera*) of terrestrial or aquatic insects with piercing, sucking mouth parts, wingless or with two pairs of wings, the anterior pair typically horny with an apical membranous part, as the stinkbug, squashbug, bedbug. For illustrations see under INSECT. **2** Loosely, any insect or small arthropod. **3** Often *pl.* *U.S. Colloq.* Any small but troublesome defect in the design, structure, or operation of an instrument, motor, machine, or the like. **4** *Slang* An enthusiast; a monomaniac. **5** *Colloq.* A pathogenic microorganism. **6** *Colloq.* A miniature electronic microphone, used in wiretapping, etc. —*v.* **bugged, bug·ging** *v.i.* **1** To stare; stick out: said of eyes. —*v.t.* **2** *Colloq.* To fix an electronic eavesdropping device in (a room, etc.) or to a (wire, etc.). **3** *U.S. Slang* To annoy or anger; also, to bewilder or puzzle. —**to bug off** *U.S. Slang* Go away! Get lost! —**to bug out** *U.S. Slang* To quit, especially hastily or ignominiously. [Origin unknown]

bug² (bug) *n.* *Obs.* A specter; bugbear. [ME *bugge* scarecrow. Cf. Welsh *bwg* ghost.]

bug·a·boo (bug′ə·boo) *n.* *pl.* **·boos** A bugbear. [<BUG² + BOO]

bug·bear (bug′bâr′) *n.* An imaginary object of terror; a specter: also called *bugaboo.* [< BUG² + BEAR²]

bug·eye (bug′ī′) *n.* *Naut.* A centerboard sailing vessel of shallow draft, fore-and-aft rigged on two raked masts: used in dredging oysters in Chesapeake Bay.

bug–eyed (bug′īd′) *adj.* *Slang* With the eyes bulging out, as from astonishment.

bug·ger (bug′ər) *n.* **1** One guilty of sodomy. **2** A contemptible person. **3** *U.S. Slang* A chap; person; child: used in mild or humorous disparagement. [<OF *bougre* <Med. L *Bulgarus* a Bulgarian; with ref. to a Bulgarian sect of heretics (11th c.) to whom sodomy was imputed]

bug·ger·y (bug′ər·ē) *n.* Sodomy.

bug·gy¹ (bug′ē) *n.* *pl.* **·gies** **1** A light, four-wheeled, horse–drawn vehicle with a hood. **2** The caboose of a freight train. [Origin uncertain]

bug·gy² (bug′ē) *adj.* **·gi·er, ·gi·est** **1** Infested with bugs. **2** *Slang* Crazy. —**bug′gi·ness** *n.*

bug·house (bug′hous′) *U.S. Slang* *n.* An asylum for the insane. —*adj.* Crazy; insane.

Bu·gin·vil·lae·a (boo′gən·vil′ē·ə) *n.* Bougainvillea.

BUGLE

bu·gle¹ (byoo′gəl) *n.* **1** A brass wind instrument resembling a horn or trumpet, with or without keys or valves. **2** A huntsman's horn. —*v.t. & v.i.* **bu·gled, bu·gling** **1** To summon with or as with a bugle. **2** To sound a bugle. [<OF <L *buculus,* dim. of *bos* ox; because first made from the horns of oxen] —**bu′gler** *n.*

bu·gle² (byoo′gəl) *n.* A tube–shaped glass bead, commonly black, used for ornamenting gar-

ments. —*adj.* Of, resembling, or adorned with bugles. [Origin uncertain] —**bu′gled** *adj.*

bu·gle³ (byoo′gəl) *n.* A British plant of the mint family (genus *Ajuga*), especially the **carpet bugle** (*A. reptans*). [<F <LL *bugula*]

bug·light (bug′līt′) *n.* **1** A small lighthouse. **2** A small flashlight.

buhl (bool) *n.* Metal or tortoise shell inlaid in furniture; also, cabinetwork so decorated. Also **buhl′work′.** [after A. C. *Boulle,* 1642–1732, French cabinetmaker]

build (bild) *v.* **built** (*Archaic* **build·ed**), **build·ing** *v.t.* **1** To construct, erect, or make by assembling separate parts or materials. **2** To establish and increase: to *build* a business. **3** To found; make a basis for: We *build* our hopes on peace. **4** In cards, to form sequences or combinations of cards, as by suit or number. —*v.i.* **5** To be in the business of building. **6** To base or form an idea, theory, etc.: with *on* or *upon.* —**to build up 1** To renew; strengthen, as health or physique. **2** To fill, as an area, with houses. See synonyms under CONSTRUCT. —*n.* **1** The manner or style in which anything is built; form; figure. **2** A cumulative increase in power and effectiveness, as of a dramatic performance as the climax is approached. [OE *byldan* <*bold* house]

build·er (bil′dər) *n.* **1** One who or that which builds. **2** One who follows the occupation of building, or who controls or directs the actual work of building. **3** An abrasive or other substance added to soap to increase its cleansing effect.

build·ing (bil′ding) *n.* **1** An edifice for any use; that which is built, as a dwelling house, barn, etc. **2** The occupation, business, or art of constructing. **3** The act or process of erecting or establishing. See synonyms under HOUSE.

build–up (bild′up′) *n.* **1** A gradual accumulation or increase, as of buildings. **2** *Mil.* The accumulation of troops or materiel in a given area. **3** In forestry, the steady acceleration of a fire under conditions favoring its spread and in spite of attempts at effective control. **4** *Colloq.* An enhancement of reputation, as by praise or favorable publicity.

built–in (bilt′in′) *adj.* Made part of or permanently attached to the structure, as of a house or room.

bulb (bulb) *n.* **1** *Bot.* **a** A leaf bud comprised of a cluster of thickened, scalelike leaves, growing usually underground and sending forth roots from the lower face, as the onion or lily. **b** Any of several underground stems resembling bulbs, as the corm of a crocus or a dahlia tuber. **2** Any protuberance resembling a plant bulb, as the bulb at the root of a hair (see illustration under HAIR), the enlarged end of a thermometer tube, etc. **3** *Electr.* An evacuated glass container holding the filament of an incandescent electric light. **4** A vacuum tube. **5** *Anat.* The medulla oblongata. [<L *bulbus* <Gk. *bolbos* bulbous root] —**bul·ba·ceous** (bul·bā′·shəs) *adj.* —**bul′bous** *adj.*

bul·bar (bul′bər) *adj.* Of or pertaining to a bulb, especially the bulb of the medulla oblongata: *bulbar* paralysis.

bul·bif·er·ous (bul·bif′ər·əs) *adj.* Producing bulbs. [<NL *bulbifer* <L *bulbus* bulb + *ferre* bear]

bulb·i·form (bul′bə·fôrm) *adj.* Having the form of a bulb.

bul·bil (bul′bil) *n.* **1** A small bulb. **2** *Bot.* An aerial, deciduous, fleshy leaf bud, capable of developing into a new individual, as in the tiger lily: also **bul′bel** (-bel). [<NL *bulbillus,* dim. of *bulbus* bulb]

bul·bul (bool′bool) *n.* **1** Any of various thrushlike birds (family *Pycnonotidae*) of the tropics of the Old World, with short legs, rounded wings, and typically dull coloration. **2** The Persian nightingale (genus *Luscinia*). [<Persian <Arabic]

Bul·gar (bul′gär, bool′-) *n.* **1** A Bulgarian. **2** The Bulgarian language.

Bul·gar·i·a (bul·gâr′ē·ə, bool-) A state in SE Europe; 142,471 square miles; capital, Sofia: officially **People's Republic of Bulgaria.** *Bulgarian* **Bl·ga·ri·ya** (bul·gä′rē·yä).

Bul·gar·i·an (bul·gâr′ē·ən, bool-) *adj.* Of or per-

taining to Bulgaria, the Bulgarians, or to their language. —*n.* **1** A native or citizen of Bulgaria. **2** One of an ancient people considered to be of Mongolian stock, who, in the 7th century, migrated from the region west of the Ural Mountains and north of the Caspian Sea, and settled Bulgaria. **3** The language of the Bulgarians, belonging to the South Slavic group of the Balto-Slavic languages.

bulge (bulj) *v.t. & v.i.* **bulged, bulg·ing** To make or be protuberant; swell out. [<*n.*] —*n.* **1** The most convex part, as of a cask. **2** A protuberant part; swelling. **3** *U.S. Colloq.* Advantage; especially, a slight but telling advantage. —**to get the bulge on** *U.S. Colloq.* To gain the advantage over. [<OF *boulge*] —**bulg′y** *adj.* —**bulg′i·ness** *n.*

bulg·er (bul′jər) *n.* **1** In golf, a driver or a brassy having a convex face: also **bulger driver.** **2** A stick used in hockey, having a flat-faced, heavy head with a convex back.

bu·lim·i·a (byoo·lim′ē·ə) *n.* *Pathol.* Insatiable appetite, or the disease of which this is a characteristic. [<Gk. *boulimia* great hunger <*bou-* ox-like, great + *limos* hunger] —**bu·lim′ic** *adj.*

bulk¹ (bulk) *n.* **1** The substance or body of anything material considered with reference to its magnitude, as of a ship, a man, an elephant, etc. **2** A large body; mass; volume; size. **3** Greater or principal part; main body; majority. **4** *Naut.* The whole space in a ship's hold for stowing goods; also, the whole cargo. See synonyms under MAGNITUDE, MASS. —**in bulk** Loose; in mass; not in boxes, bales, sacks, or packages. —*v.i.* **1** To have an appearance of largeness or weight; be of importance: The weather *bulks* large in our plans. **2** *Obs.* To swell; expand: with *up.* —*v.t.* **3** To cause to expand or grow large: with *out.* [Cf. ON *būlki* heap, cargo, and Dan. *bulk* lump]

bulk² (bulk) *n.* A projecting part of a building; a framework in front of a shop; stall. [? <ON *bōlkr* beam]

bulk·age (bul′kij) *n.* *Physiol.* The non-assimilable accessory of food elements, such as vegetable fiber, that stimulates intestinal activity.

bulk·head (bulk′hed′) *n.* **1** *Naut.* One of various partitions in a vessel, to separate it into rooms or to divide the hold into watertight compartments. **2** A partition of stone or wood to keep back earth, gas, etc., as in a mine. **3** A horizontal or sloping door outside a house, giving entrance to the cellar. **4** A framework or casing to cover a staircase or elevator shaft. —**bulk′head′ed** *adj.*

bulk·y (bul′kē) *adj.* **bulk·i·er, bulk·i·est** Huge; large; massive; unwieldy. —**bulk′i·ly** *adv.* —**bulk′i·ness** *n.*

bull¹ (bool) *n.* **1** The male of domestic cattle or of some other animals, as of the elephant, moose, giraffe, whale, seal, etc. ◆Collateral adjective: *taurine.* **2** A dealer who seeks or expects higher prices, and buys stocks or bonds accordingly. **3** One possessing characteristics suggestive of a bull. **4** *U.S. Slang* A policeman or detective, usually in plain clothes. —*v.t.* **1** To attempt to raise the price of or in. **2** To push or force (a way). —*v.i.* **3** To go up in price: said of stocks, etc. **4** *Slang* To go or push ahead: to *bull* through a crowd. —*adj.* **1** Large; bull-like; male. **2** Going up or advancing: a *bull* market. [ME *bule;* cf. OE *bulluc* bullock]

bull² (bool) *n.* **1** An official and authoritative document issued by the Pope, usually an edict, decree, or other proclamation, sealed with a bulla. **2** Bulla (def. 1). [<L *bulla* edict, seal]

bull³ (bool) *n.* A ridiculous blunder in speech. [? <F *boule* lie, deceit <L *bulla* bubble]

bull⁴ (bool) *n.* *Slang* Nonsense; bluff.

Bull (bool) The constellation and astrological sign Taurus. See CONSTELLATION.

bul·la (bool′ə, bul′ə) *n.* *pl.* **bul·lae** (bool′·ē, bul′ē) **1** A seal of lead, used by the Pope, or of gold or other metal used by the Greek and early German emperors and sovereigns. **2** *Pathol.* A small blister or large vesicle filled with watery serum; a bleb. [<L, seal]

bul·lar·i·um (bool·âr′ē·əm) *n.* A collection of papal bulls. [<Med. L]

bul·late (bŏŏl′āt, -it, bul′-) *adj.* **1** *Biol.* Having blisterlike prominences, as a leaf or surface. **2** *Anat.* Swollen; inflated. [<L *bullatus* <*bulla* bubble]
bull-bait·ing (bŏŏl′bā′ting) *n.* The setting of dogs upon bulls: a former English sport.
bull-bat (bŏŏl′bat′) *n.* The nighthawk (genus *Chordeiles*): named from the noise it makes while flying.
bull·dog (bŏŏl′dôg′, -dog′) *n.*
1 A medium-sized, short-haired, powerful dog, originally bred in England for use in bull-baiting: also called *English bulldog.* **2** A pistol; especially, a short-barreled revolver of large caliber: also, formerly, a cannon. —*adj.* Resembling a bulldog; courageous; tenacious. —*v.t.* U.S. *Colloq.* To throw (a steer) by gripping its horns and twisting its neck.

BULLDOG
(About 16 inches high at the shoulders)

bulldog edition The early edition of a morning newspaper, often appearing the evening before, for distribution out of town.
bull-doze (bŏŏl′dōz′) *v.* **-dozed, -doz·ing** *v.t.* **1** *U.S. Slang* To intimidate; bully. **2** To clear, dig, scrape, etc., with a bulldozer. —*v.i.* **3** To operate a bulldozer. [? <BULL, *adj.* + DOSE, with ref. to the violent or excessive treatment given to the victim.]
bull-doz·er (bŏŏl′dō′zər) *n.* **1** A powerful, tractor-driven machine equipped with a heavy steel blade: used for clearing wooded areas and moving soil in road construction. **2** A power-driven machine for stamping heads on wires and small rods. **3** *U.S. Slang* One who bulldozes.
bull dust *Austral.* **1** Dry silt. **2** *Slang* Nonsense; foolish chatter; bluff.
bul-let (bŏŏl′it) *n.* **1** A small projectile for a firearm. **2** Any small ball. [<F *boulette,* dim. of *boule* ball]
bul-le-tin (bŏŏl′ə-tən) *n.* **1** A brief official summary. **2** A brief news statement, issued in printed form, as in a newspaper, or by word of mouth, as transmitted by radio. **3** A periodical publication, as of the proceedings of a society. —*v.t.* To make public by bulletin. [<F <Ital. *bulletino,* double dim. of *bulla* <L, edict] —**bul′le-tin-ist** *n.*
bul-let-proof (bŏŏl′it-prŏŏf′) *adj.* Not penetrable by bullets.
bull-fight (bŏŏl′fīt′) *n.* A combat in an arena between men and a bull or bulls, popular among the Spanish, Portuguese, and Spanish Americans. —**bull′fight′ing** *n.* —**bull′fight′er** *n.*
bull-finch (bŏŏl′finch′) *n.* **1** A European singing bird (genus *Pyrrhula*) having a short, stout bill and red breast. **2** Any of certain American grosbeaks. [<BULL, *adj.* + FINCH]
bull-finch[2] (bŏŏl′finch′) *n. Brit.* A strong high hedge. [Prob. alter. of BULL FENCE]
bull-frog (bŏŏl′frog′, -frôg′) *n.* A large North American frog (*Rana catesbiana*) with a deep bass croak.
bull-head (bŏŏl′hed′) *n.* **1** One of various fishes (genus *Ameiurus*) with a broad head, as the horned pout (*A. nebulosus*). **2** The sculpin. **3** A plover (family *Charadriidae*). **4** The goldeneye duck (*Glaucionetta clangula*). **5** An obstinate, stupid person.
bull-head-ed (bŏŏl′hed′id) *adj.* Stupid and obstinate.
bull-horn (bŏŏl′hôrn′) *n.* An electrical, hand-held voice amplifier resembling a megaphone.
bul-lion[1] (bŏŏl′yən) *n.* Gold or silver uncoined or in mass, as in bars, plates, or the like. See synonyms under MONEY. [<AF *bullion,* OF *bouillon* boiling, melting <*bouillir* boil; ? infl. by OF *billon* base metal]
bul-lion[2] (bŏŏl′yən) *n.* A heavy, twisted, cord fringe, especially that of which the cords are covered with fine gold or silver wire. [<OF *bouillon* <L *bulla* bubble]
bull-ish[1] (bŏŏl′ish) *adj.* **1** Of or characteristic of a bull. **2** Characterized by or suggesting a trend toward higher prices, as in the stock market; also, hopeful of such a trend. **3** Confidently optimistic. —**bull′ish-ly** *adv.* —**bull′ish-ness** *n.*
bull-ish[2] (bŏŏl′ish) *adj.* Having the character of a bull or blunder.
bull-neck (bŏŏl′nek′) *n.* **1** A short, thick neck

like that of a bull. **2** The canvasback. **3** The American scaup duck.
bul-lock (bŏŏl′ək) *n.* **1** A gelded bull; a steer or an ox. **2** Formerly, a bull calf. [OE *bulluc*]
bull-pen (bŏŏl′pen′) *n. U.S.* **1** An enclosure for one or more bulls; also, an enclosure for a bullfight. **2** *Colloq.* A corral for temporary detention of prisoners; hence, a jail. **3** *Colloq.* The living quarters in a lumber camp. **4** A place of practice for baseball pitchers who may be needed in an emergency.
bull-pout (bŏŏl′pout′) *n.* A catfish; bullhead.
bull-ring (bŏŏl′ring′) *n.* A circular enclosure for bullfights.
bull-roar-er (bŏŏl′rôr′ər, -rōr′-) *n.* **1** A toy consisting of a small slat of wood fastened to a thong or string, to be whirled in the air to produce a roaring sound. **2** A larger device of this kind used by Australian aborigines in their religious rites.
bull's-eye (bŏŏlz′ī′) *n.* **1** The center of a target, or a shot that hits it. **2** A circular window or mirror. **3** A thick disk or lens of glass, or a lantern fitted with one. **4** *Naut.* A small wooden block perforated for ropes. **5** A thick, rounded lump of candy, usually flavored with peppermint. **6** An old-fashioned, thick, open-faced watch. **7** A depression or wave in mirror glass which causes a distortion of the image. **8** *Meteorol.* **a** A small area of clear sky marking the center of a cyclone storm; the eye of the storm. **b** A small detached cloud indicating the top of a developing bull's-eye squall.
bull snake A gopher snake.
bull-strong (bŏŏl′strông′, -strong′) *adj.* Strong enough to hold a bull: said of fences.
bull terrier See under TERRIER.
bull-tongue (bŏŏl′tung′) *n.* In cotton farming, a heavy plow with a nearly vertical moldboard.
bull-weed (bŏŏl′wēd′) *n.* Knapweed.
bull-whip (bŏŏl′hwip′) *n.* A long, tough whip used by teamsters. —*v.t.* **-whipped, -whip-ping** To strike or beat with a bullwhip.
bul-ly[1] (bŏŏl′ē) *adj.* **bul-li-er, bul-li-est** **1** *Colloq.* Excellent, admirable. **2** Quarrelsome; blustering. **3** Jolly; dashing; gallant. —*n. pl.* **bul-lies** **1** A quarrelsome, swaggering, cowardly fellow; one who terrorizes or threatens those weaker than himself. **2** *Archaic* A hired ruffian. **3** *Obs.* A pimp. **4** *Obs.* Sweetheart; darling: a term formerly applied to both sexes. —*interj.* Well done! —*v.* **bul-lied, bul-ly-ing** *v.t.* To coerce by threats; intimidate. —*v.i.* To be quarrelsome and blustering. [Cf. Du. *boel* friend, lover]
bul-ly[2] (bŏŏl′ē) *n.* Canned or pickled beef. Also **bul′ly-beef′.** [Prob. <F *bouilli,* pp. of *bouillir* boil]
bul-ly-boy (bŏŏl′ē-boi′) *n.* A jovial fellow.
bul-ly-rag (bŏŏl′ē-rag′) *v.t.* **-ragged, -rag-ging** To bully; intimidate. [? <BULLY, *v.* + RAG[1]]
bul-ly-tree (bŏŏl′ē-trē′) *n.* One of several tropical American trees yielding balata gum, especially *Manilkara bidentata.* Also **bul′let-wood′.**
bul-rush (bŏŏl′rush′) *n.* **1** A tall, rushlike plant growing in damp ground or water, as the tall sedge (*Scirpus lacustris*), the common American rush (*Juncus effusus*), and the common English cat-tail (*Typha latifolia*). **2** Papyrus. *Exodus* ii 3. [<BULL[1], *adj.* + RUSH[2]]
bul-wark (bŏŏl′wərk) *n.* **1** A defensive wall or rampart; fortification. **2** Any safeguard or defense. **3** *Naut.* The raised side of a ship, above the upper deck: usually in the plural. See synonyms under BARRIER, DEFENSE, RAMPART. —*v.t.* To surround and fortify with, or as with, a bulwark. [<MHG *bolwerc.* Akin to BOULEVARD.]

bum[1] (bum) *n.* **1** *U.S. Colloq.* A worthless or dissolute loafer; tramp. **2** A spree; debauch. —**on the bum** **1** Out of order; broken. **2** Living as a vagrant. —*adj.* Bad; inferior. —*v.* **bum-med, bum-ming** *v.i.* **1** To live by sponging from others. **2** To live idly and in dissipation. —*v.t.* **3** To get by begging: to *bum* a ride. [Short for *bummer,* alter. of G *bummler* loafer, dawdler] —**bum′mer** *n.*
bum[2] (bum) *v.i.* **bummed, bum-ming** *Brit. Dial.* To hum, as a top. [Var. of BOOM[2]]
bum[3] (bum) *n. Brit. Slang* The buttocks. [ME *bom;* origin uncertain]
bum-bai-liff (bum′bā′lif) *n. Brit.* A sheriff's deputy or county-court bailiff whose duties

are to levy and attach. Also **bum′bail′ey** (-bā′-lē). [<BUM[3] + BAILIFF; because he follows closely behind a person]
bum-ble (bum′bəl) *v.t. & v.i.* **-bled, -bling** To bungle; confuse, especially in an officious manner. [Imit.] —**bum′bling** *adj. & n.*
bum-ble-bee (bum′bəl-bē′) *n.* Any of certain large, hairy, social bees (family *Bombidae*). [<dial. E *bumble,* freq. of BUM[2] + BEE[1]]
bum-ble-foot (bum′bəl-fŏŏt′) *n.* A suppurative swelling of the foot in domestic fowls, arising from a bacterial infection of a cut or bruise.
bum-boat (bum′bōt′) *n.* A boat employed in peddling provisions and small wares among vessels in port or offshore. [<LG *bumboot* broad-beamed boat]
bum-kin (bum′kin) *n. Naut.* A projecting boom on a vessel, placed at each side of the bow to haul the foretack to, or on the quarter, for the standing part of the mainbrace, or over the stern to extend the mizzen sail: also *bumpkin.* [<Du. *boomkin,* dim. of *boom* tree, beam]
bum-ming (bum′ing) *n.* **1** Carousing. **2** Living like a bum.
bum-ming[2] (bum′ing) *adj. Scot.* Humming.
bump (bump) *v.t.* **1** To come into contact with; knock into. **2** To cause to knock into or against. **3** *U.S. Colloq.* To displace, as from a position or seat. —*v.i.* **4** To come into contact; knock together. **5** To move or proceed with jerks and jolts. —**to bump off** *Slang* To kill, especially with a gun. —*n.* **1** A violent impact or collision; a heavy blow. **2** A protuberance like that caused by a blow. **3** The act of bumping. **4** One of the protuberances of the human head said to denote a certain faculty. **5** *Aeron.* A gust of wind striking the surface of an aircraft with the effect of a sharp blow. [Imit.]
bump-er[1] (bum′pər) *n.* **1** Something that either bumps or causes a bump. **2** A buffer, as on a railroad car. **3** A guard on the front or rear of an automobile to attenuate the shock of collision.
bump-er[2] (bum′pər) *n.* A cup or glass filled to the brim. —*adj.* Unusually full or large: a *bumper* crop. —*v.t.* **1** To fill to the brim. **2** To drink toasts to. —*v.i.* **3** To drink from bumpers. [? Alter. of F *bombarde* large cup, infl. in form by BUMP]
bump-i-ness (bum′pē-nis) *n.* **1** The state or condition of being bumpy. **2** *Aeron.* A condition of irregular atmospheric density, as from rising or falling air currents, which results in sudden jolts to aircraft.
bump-kin (bump′kin) *n.* **1** An awkward rustic; a clown; a lout. **2** A bumkin. [? <Du. *boomkin* little tree, block. Cf. BLOCKHEAD.]
bumps (bumps) *n. pl.* In motion pictures, a series of low-frequency sounds caused by irregularities in the sound track.
bump-tious (bump′shəs) *adj.* Aggressively and offensively self-conceited. —**bump′tious-ly** *adv.* —**bump′tious-ness** *n.*
bump-y (bum′pē) *adj.* **bump-i-er, bump-i-est** Having bumps or bumpiness; jolty. —**bump′i-ly** *adv.* —**bump′i-ness** *n.*
bum's rush *Slang* Forced expulsion or ejection, as of an undesirable person.
bun[1] (bun) *n.* **1** A small bread roll, sometimes sweetened or glazed with sugar, containing currants, citron, etc. **2** *Brit.* A small sweet cake. **3** A roll of hair shaped like a bun and worn at the nape of the neck. [ME *bunne;* origin uncertain]
bun[2] (bun) *n. Brit. Dial.* A rabbit's tail; hence, a rabbit or squirrel. [Cf. Irish *bun* stump]
bu-na (bŏŏ′nə, byŏŏ′-) *n. Chem.* A synthetic rubber made by the polymerization of butadiene with certain other substances, as styrene. Also **Bu′na.** [<BU(TADIENE) + NA(TRIUM)]
bunch (bunch) *n.* **1** A compact collection, usually of objects of the same kind; also, a group; cluster. **2** A hunch; hump; protuberance. —*v.t. & v.i.* **1** To make into or form bunches or groups. **2** To gather, as in pleats or folds. [ME *bonche,* *bunche;* origin unknown]
bunch-ber-ry (bunch′ber′ē, -bər-ē) *n. pl.* **-ries** The dwarf cornel (*Cornus canadensis*) with bright red, closely clustered berries.
Bunche (bunch), **Ralph Johnson,** 1904-1971, U.S. educator and United Nations statesman.
bunch-flow-er (bunch′flou′ər) *n.* A plant (*Melanthium virginicum*) of the lily family of the United States, having linear leaves and a

pyramidal panicle of greenish flowers.

bunch grass Any of various grasses growing in clumps or tufts.

bun·co (bung'kō) n. U.S. Colloq. A swindling game in which confederates join to rob a stranger. — v.t. To swindle or bilk. Also spelled bunko. [Prob. <Sp. banco, a card game]

bun·combe (bung'kəm) n. 1 Bombastic speechmaking or any specious utterance for political effect. 2 Humbug. Also spelled bunkum. [from Buncombe County, N.C., whose Congressman (1819–21) often insisted on making empty, unimportant speeches "for Buncombe"]

bun·co-steer·er (bung'kō-stir'ər) n. U.S. Slang A swindler.

bund¹ (bund) n. 1 An embankment or dike. 2 A thoroughfare along a waterfront. — the Bund, an esplanade in Shanghai, China. [<Hind. band]

bund² (bo͝ond, bund; Ger. bo͝ont) n. A confederation; league; a society. [<G]

Bund (bo͝ont) n. pl. Bün·de (bün'də) 1 A confederation of German states established in 1867. 2 The German-American Bund, a former pro-Nazi organization in the United States.

bun·der (bun'dər) n. Anglo-Indian In the Orient, a landing place: the Apollo bunder at Bombay. [<Hind. bandar]

bun·dle (bun'dəl) n. 1 A number of things or a quantity of anything bound together. 2 Anything folded or wrapped and tied up; a package. 3 A group; collection. 4 Bot. A cluster of one or more elementary tissues lying across other tissues: also called vascular bundle. ◆ Collateral adjective: fascicular. — v. ·dled, ·dling v.t. 1 To tie, roll or otherwise secure in a bundle. 2 To send away or place in summarily or in haste: with away, off, out, or into. — v.i. 3 To leave or proceed hastily or in a bustling manner: They bundled down the stairs. 4 To practice bundling. [<MDu. bondel, dim. of bond group. Akin to BIND.] — bun'dler n.

bun·dling (bun'dling) n. An old courting custom, prevalent in New England, in which sweethearts lay or slept together in bed without undressing.

bung (bung) n. 1 A stopper for the large hole through which a cask is filled. 2 Bunghole. 3 A large sac between the small intestine and the colon of beef viscera. — v.t. 1 To close with or as with a bung: often with up or down. 2 Slang To damage; maul: usually with up. [<MDu. bonghe]

bun·ga·low (bung'gə-lō) n. 1 In India, a one-storied house with wide verandas. 2 A small house or cottage, usually with one or one and a half stories. 3 The blimp of a motion-picture camera. [<Hind. banglā Bengalese <Banga Bengal]

bun·gee (bung·gē') n. Aeron. An apparatus, operated by the pilot of an aircraft, which restricts or controls the action of certain movable parts, as a bomb-bay door. [Origin uncertain]

bung·hole (bung'hōl') n. A hole in a keg or barrel from which liquid is tapped. [<MDu. bonghe a stopper, plug + HOLE]

bun·gle (bung'gəl) v.t. & v.i. ·gled, ·gling To work, make, or do (something) clumsily; botch. — n. An awkward, clumsy, and imperfect job or performance; botch. — bun'gler n. — bun'gle·some (-səm) adj. — bun'gling adj. — bun'gling·ly adv. [Cf. Sw. bangla work ineffectually]

Bu·nin (bo͞o'nyin), Ivan Alexeyevich, 1870–1953, Russian novelist and poet.

bun·ion (bun'yən) n. Pathol. A painful swelling of the foot, usually at the outer side of the base of the great toe: at first an enlarged bursa, eventually producing a distortion of the bony structure. [Akin to OF bugne swelling]

bunk¹ (bungk) n. 1 A small compartment, shelf, box, or recess, etc., used as a sleeping place, as in a vessel, lodging house, sleeping car, etc. 2 A piece of timber across a lumberman's sled; also, the sled so arranged. — v.i. 1 To sleep in a bunk. 2 To share a bed. [Cf. MDu. banc bench, shelf and BANK³ (def. 2)]

bunk² (bungk) n. Slang Inflated or empty speech; balderdash. [Short for BUNCOMBE]

bun·ker (bung'kər) n. 1 A large bin, as for coal on a ship. 2 A box or chest that serves also for a seat. 3 In golf, a sandy hollow or a mound of earth serving as an obstacle on a course. 4 Mil. a A steel and concrete fortification, usually underground. b A bulwark of earth erected to protect a gun emplacement. — v.i. To fill the coal bunkers of a ship. — v.t. In golf, to drive (a ball) into a bunker. [Cf. OSw. bunke hold of a ship and BANK³ (def. 2)]

Bun·ker Hill (bung'kər) A hill in Charlestown, Massachusetts, near which (on Breed's Hill) occurred the first organized engagement of the Revolutionary War, June 17, 1775.

bunk·house (bungk'hous') n. A structure used as sleeping quarters.

bunk·mate (bungk'māt') n. One who shares a bunk. Also bunk·ie (bung'kē), bunk'y.

bun·ko (bung'kō), bun·kum (bung'kəm) See BUNCO, BUNCOMBE.

bunn (bun) n. Bun ¹.

bun·ny (bun'ē) n. pl. ·nies A rabbit or squirrel: a pet name. [<BUN²]

bun·ny-hug (bun'ē·hug') n. U.S. A dance in ragtime rhythm, popular in about 1910.

Bun·sen (bun'sən, Ger. bo͝on'zən), Robert William Eberhard, 1811–99, German chemist and inventor.

Bun·sen burner (bun'sən) A type of gas burner in which a mixture of gas and air is burned at the top of a short metal tube, producing a very hot flame. [after R. W. E. Bunsen]

BUNSEN BURNER
a. Complete combustion.
b. Incomplete combustion.
c. Non-burning mixture.
d. Air. e. Gas.

bunt¹ (bunt) v.t. & v.i. 1 To strike or push as with horns; butt. 2 In baseball, to bat (the ball) lightly to the infield, without swinging the bat. — n. 1 A push or shove; a butt. 2 In baseball, a short hit to the infield, made by allowing a pitched ball to bounce off a loosely held bat. [Nasalized var. of BUTT¹]

bunt² (bunt) n. Naut. The middle or bellying portion of a square sail. 2 The middle, sagging part of a fishnet. 3 Naut. The middle part of a yard. — v.t. Naut. To haul up the middle part of (a square sail) in furling. — v.i. To swell out; belly. [Origin unknown]

bunt³ (bunt) n. 1 A parasitic fungus (Tilletia foetens), a species of smut, which destroys the grains of wheat by converting the interior into a fetid black powder. 2 The disease caused by it: also called stinking smut. [Origin unknown]

bunt·ing¹ (bun'ting) n. 1 A light woolen stuff used for flags. 2 A light cotton fabric resembling cheesecloth. 3 Flags, banners, etc., collectively. [? ME bonten sift]

bunt·ing² (bun'ting) n. One of various birds related to the finches and sparrows: the indigo and snow buntings. [ME bountyng; origin unknown]

bunt·line (bunt'lin, -līn) n. Naut. A rope used in hauling a square sail of a vessel up to the yard for furling.

Bun·yan (bun'yən), John, 1628–88, English preacher and author of Pilgrim's Progress. — Paul See PAUL BUNYAN.

Bun·yip (bun'yip) n. In Australian folklore, a bellowing water monster who lives at the bottom of lakes and water holes, into which he draws his human victims.

Buo·na·par·te (bwô'nä·pär'tā) See BONAPARTE.

Buo·nar·ro·ti (bwô'när·rô'tē) See MICHELANGELO.

buoy (boi, bo͞o'ē) n. 1 Naut. A float moored on a dangerous rock or shoal or at the edge of a channel, as a guide to navigators. Many are named according to shape or function: can buoy (cylindrical); nun buoy (conical); spar buoy (a spar anchored at one end); bell buoy, whistling buoy (buoys devised to sound with the motion of the waves: used to mark dangerous shoals or harbor entrances, respectively). 2 Any device or object for keeping a person in the water afloat: also called

TYPES OF BUOYS
a. Nun buoy. b. Can buoy. c. Spar buoy. d. Bell buoy. e. Whistling buoy. f. Gas-lighted buoy.

lifebuoy. Compare BREECHES BUOY. — v.t. 1 To keep from sinking in a liquid; keep afloat. 2 To sustain the courage or heart of; encourage: usually with up. 3 Naut. To mark, as a channel, with buoys. [<MDu. boeie]

buoy·age (boi'ij, bo͞o'ē·ij) n. 1 Buoys collectively. 2 A system of buoys.

buoy·an·cy (boi'ən·sē, bo͞o'yən·sē) n. 1 The property of keeping afloat. 2 Power or tendency of a liquid or gas to keep an object afloat. 3 Resultant upward pressure of fluid on an immersed or floating body. 4 Elasticity of spirits; cheerfulness. Also buoy'·ance.

buoy·ant (boi'ənt, bo͞o'yənt) adj. 1 Having buoyancy. 2 Vivacious; cheerful; hopeful. See synonyms under CHEERFUL, HAPPY, SANGUINE. [Prob. <Sp. boyante <boyar float] — buoy'ant·ly adv.

bu·pres·tid (byo͞o·pres'tid) n. Any of a family (Buprestidae) of brilliantly colored beetles with the first and second vertical segments confluent and membranous-lobed tarsi, and whose larvae are destructive woodborers. [<L buprestis <Gk. bouprēstis <bous ox + prēthein swell]

bur¹ (bûr) 1 Bot. A rough or prickly flower head, or the like, as of the chestnut and burdock. 2 The burdock or other plant that bears burs. 3 A protuberance; lump; specifically, a knot or excrescence on a tree. 4 An impediment or unwelcome adherent. — v.t. burred, bur·ring To remove burs from, as wool. Also spelled burr. ◆ Homophones: birr, burr. [<Scand. Cf. Dan. borre bur.]

bur² (bûr) See BURR¹.

bu·ran (bo͞o·rän') n. Meteorol. A violent windstorm of Siberia and the Russian steppes: a hot duststorm in summer and a blizzard in winter. Also bu·ra (bo͞o·rä'). [<Russian]

bur·ble (bûr'bəl) v.i. ·bled, ·bling 1 To bubble; gurgle. 2 To talk excitedly and confusedly. [ME; imit.]

bur·bling (bûr'bling) n. Aeron. A turbulence in the airflow around an airplane, especially such as to increase the drag.

bur·bot (bûr'bət) n. pl. ·bots or ·bot A freshwater fish (Lota lota) of the northern hemisphere, with barbels on the nose and chin: also called ling. [<F bourbotte, ult. <L barbata bearded; infl. in form by TURBOT]

burd (bûrd) n. Brit. Dial. A maiden. Also burd·ie (bûr'dē). [ME burde; origin uncertain]

bur·den¹ (bûr'dən) n. 1 Something heavy that is borne or carried; responsibility; a load. 2 Naut. a The carrying capacity of a vessel. b The weight of the cargo. 3 The employment of carrying loads: beasts of burden. — v.t. To load or overload; oppress, as with care: burdened with responsibilities. See synonyms under LOAD. Also spelled burthen. [OE byrthen load]

bur·den² (bûr'dən) n. 1 Something often repeated or dwelt upon; the prevailing idea or tone: The burden of the speech was a desire for war. 2 A refrain repeated at the end of every stanza of a song. 3 The drone of a bagpipe. Also spelled burthen. [<F bourdon bass <LL burdo drone]

bur·den·some (bûr'dən·səm) adj. Hard or heavy to bear; oppressive. See synonyms under HEAVY, TROUBLESOME. — bur'den·some·ly adv. — bur'den·some·ness n.

bur·dock (bûr'dok) n. A coarse, biennial weed (Arctium lappa) of the composite family, with a globular bur and large roundish leaves. [<BUR + DOCK⁴]

bu·reau (byo͝or'ō) n. pl. bu·reaus or bu·reaux

(byŏŏr'ōz) 1 A chest of drawers for clothing, etc., commonly provided with a mirror. 2 A public department. 3 An organized staff of literary workers, etc.; also, the place where the work is done. 4 A writing desk; escritoire. [<F, cloth–covered desk <OF *burel* coarse woolen cloth]

bu·reau·ra·cy (byŏŏ·rok'rə·sē) *n.* *pl.* ·**cies** 1 Government by bureaus, especially by rigid and arbitrary routine. 2 Government officials collectively.

bu·reau·crat (byŏŏr'ə·krat) *n.* 1 A member of a bureaucracy. 2 An official who governs by rigid routine. — **bu'reau·crat'ic** ·or ·**i·cal** *adj.* — **bu'reau·crat'i·cal·ly** *adv.*

bu·rette (byŏŏ·ret') *n.* 1 *Chem.* A finely graduated glass tube from which a small quantity of a solution can be drawn off at a time. 2 A decorated cruet; an altar cruet. Also **bu·ret'.** [<F, dim. of *buire* vase <OF *buise* drink]

burg (bûrg) *n.* 1 *Colloq.* A town; city. 2 *Archaic* A fortified place. [OE *burg.* Related to BOROUGH.]

bur·gage (bûr'gij) *n.* 1 In feudal law, a tenure by which houses and lands in an ancient borough were held of the lord at a certain yearly rent; land so held. 2 A form of tenure by which property in royal burgs is held of the king for the nominal service of watching and warding. [<OF <Med. L *burgagium* < *burgus* town <Gmc.]

bur·gee (bûr'jē) *n.* *Naut.* A triangular or swallow–tailed pennant flown on vessels for identification. [Origin unknown]

bur·geon (bûr'jən) *v.t.* & *v.i.* To put forth (buds or shoots); sprout. [<*n.*] — *n.* 1 A bud; sprout. 2 A boss for protecting the binding of a book. Also spelled *bourgeon.* [<OF *burjon*]

Burg·er (bûr'gər), **Warren Earl,** born 1907, U.S. jurist; chief justice of the Supreme Court 1969–.

bur·gess (bûr'jis) *n.* 1 A freeman, citizen, or officer of a borough or burg. 2 In colonial times, a member of the lower house of the legislature, the **House of Burgesses,** of Maryland or Virginia: now called *delegate.* 3 *Brit.* Formerly, a member of Parliament for a borough or university. [<OF *burgeis* < *bourg* town <Gmc. Doublet of BOURGEOIS[1].] — **bur'·gess-ship** *n.*

burgh (bûrg, *Scot.* bûr'ō, -ə) *n.* 1 In Scots law, a corporate body erected by charter of the sovereign, consisting of the inhabitants of the district designated in the charter; a borough. 2 *Archaic* A castle or fortification. [Var. of BOROUGH] — **burgh·al** (bûr'gəl) *adj.*

burgh·er (bûr'gər) *n.* 1 A citizen or a burgh. 2 An early Dutch inhabitant or citizen of New York. [<Du. *burger* < *burg* town. Akin to BURGESS.]

bur·glar (bûr'glər) *n.* One who commits a burglary. See synonyms under ROBBER. [<Med. L *burglator* <OF *bourg* dwelling (<Gmc.) + *laire* robbery (<L *latro* robber)]

burglar alarm A device, usually electric, by which an alarm is given, by bell, gong, flashing light, etc., upon forcible intrusion of a building, safe, etc.

bur·glar·i·ous (bər·glâr'ē·əs) *adj.* Relating to or of the nature of a burglary. — **bur·glar'i·ous·ly** *adv.*

bur·glar·ize (bûr'glə·rīz) *v.t.* ·**ized,** ·**iz·ing** 1 To commit burglary upon. 2 To enter or steal by burglary.

bur·gla·ry (bûr'glər·ē) *n.* *pl.* ·**ries** The breaking and entering of a building (primarily of a dwelling, by night), with felonious intent.

bur·gle (bûr'gəl) *v.t.* & *v.i.* ·**gled** ·**gling** *Colloq.* To commit burglary; burglarize. [Back formation <BURGLAR]

bur·go·mas·ter (bûr'gə·mas'tər, -mäs'-) *n.* 1 A Dutch, Flemish, German, or Austrian municipal magistrate; a mayor. 2 A large arctic gull (*Larus hyperboreus*). [<Du. *burgemeester*]

bur·go·net (bûr'gə·net) *n.* *Archaic* A light, open helmet. [<OF *bourguignotte* Burgundian <*Bourgogne* Burgundy, where first used]

bur·goo (bûr'gōō) *n.* *pl.* ·**goos** 1 A kind of oatmeal porridge or mush formerly served at sea. 2 *U.S. Dial.* A thick, highly seasoned soup or stew of meat; also, the meals at which this is served, especially picnics and barbecues. Also **bur'gout** (-gōō). [Cf. Turkish *burghul* porridge]

bur·grave (bûr'grāv) *n.* The governor or lord of a fortified town or a military fortress. [<G *burg* walled town + *graf* count]

Bur·gun·dy (bûr'gən·dē) A region of east central France; formerly a kingdom, duchy, and province: French *Bourgogne.* — **Bur·gun·di·an** (bər·gun'dē·ən) *adj.* & *n.*

Bur·gun·dy (bûr'gən·dē) *n.* *pl.* ·**dies** A kind of red or white wine originally made in Burgundy.

bur·i·al (ber'ē·əl) *n.* The burying of a dead body; sepulture. [OE *byrgels* tomb]

bur·i·er (ber'ē·ər) *n.* One who or that which buries.

bu·rin (byŏŏr'in) *n.*
1 An engraver's tool; graver. 2 The style or manner of execution of an engraver.

BURINS
a. For engraving on wood.
b. For carving copper or stone.
c. For carving steel.
d. For use by mechanics.

burke (bûrk) *v.t.* **burked, burk·ing** 1 To murder by suffocating, so as to leave no marks. 2 To get rid of by quietly suppressing; dispose of. [after William *Burke,* 1792–1829, Irish murderer who sold his victims' bodies for dissection]

burl (bûrl) *n.* 1 A knot or lump in wool or cloth. 2 A large, wartlike excrescence, usually a flattened hemisphere, formed on the trunks of trees. 3 A veneer made from it. — *v.t.* To dress (cloth) by removing burls, loose thread, etc. ◆ Homophone: *birl.* [<OF *bourle* tuft of wool <L *burra* shaggy hair] — **burled** *adj.* — **burl'er** *n.*

bur·lap (bûr'lap) *n.* A coarse fabric resembling canvas, made of jute, flax, hemp, or cotton: used for wrapping, bagging, etc. [Origin uncertain]

bur·lesque (bər·lesk') *n.* 1 Ludicrous imitation or representation; broad caricature; travesty. 2 A product of such imitation, as a literary or dramatic work intended to produce laughter by its caricature or satire. 3 *U.S.* A theatrical entertainment marked by low comedy, strip–tease, etc. See synonyms under CARICATURE. — *v.* ·**lesqued,** ·**les·quing** *v.t.* To represent by grotesque parody or ridicule. — *v.i.* To use burlesque. — *adj.* Marked by ludicrous incongruity or broad caricature. [<F <Ital. *burlesco* <*burla* joke] — **bur·les'quer** *n.*

bur·ley (bûr'lē) *n.* A fine, light tobacco used chiefly in plug form for chewing, and grown principally in Kentucky. Also **Bur'ley.** [? after *Burley,* name of a grower]

Bur·ling·ton (bûr'ling·tən) The largest city in Vermont, on Lake Champlain.

bur·ly[1] (bûr'lē) *adj.* **bur·li·er, bur·li·est** Large of body; bulky; stout; lusty. See synonyms under CORPULENT. [ME *borlich*; origin unknown] — **bur'li·ly** *adv.* — **bur'li·ness** *n.*

bur·ly[2] (bûr'lē) *adj.* Having burls or knots, as a tree.

Bur·ma The former name of Myanmar, a country in SE Asia bordered by India and Bangladesh on the western side and China, Laos, and Thailand on the east. Capital, Rangoon (Yangon). Formerly the Union of Burma (1948-1989). The name was changed to reflect the non-Burmese population of the country.

bur marigold An herb of the composite family (genus *Bidens*) having barbed awns: also called *beggar-ticks.*

Burma Road The road from northern Burma to Yunnan province, China: completed 1938, vital as a supply route during World War II.

Bur·mese *n.* 1 *usu. pl.* The ethnic Burmans from Myanmar (Burma) or their language. The other ethnic groups of Myanmur are the Karens, Shans, Kachins, Chins, and Chinese. 2 A native or inhabitant of Burma, written in the Pali alphabet. - *adj.* •**mese.**

burn[1] (bûrn) *v.* **burned** or **burnt, burn·ing** 1 To destroy or consume by fire. 2 To set afire; ignite. 3 To injure or kill by fire; execute by fire. 4 To injure or damage by friction, heat, steam, etc.; scald; wither. 5 To produce by fire, as a hole in a suit. 6 To brand; also, to cauterize. 7 To finish or harden by intense heat; fire. 8 To use; employ, so as to give off light, heat, etc. 9 To cause a feeling of heat in: The pepper *burned* his tongue. 10 To sunburn. 11 *Chem.* To cause to undergo combustion. 12 *Slang* To electrocute. 13 *Slang* To cheat. — *v.i.* 14 To be on fire; blaze. 15 To be destroyed or scorched by fire; undergo change by fire. 16 To give off light, heat, etc.; shine. 17 To die by fire. 18 To appear or feel hot: He *burns* with fever. 19 To be eager, excited, or inflamed. 20 *Chem.* To oxidize; undergo combustion. 21 *Slang* To be electrocuted. — **to burn down** To be razed by fire. — **to burn one's fingers** To suffer from taking part in. — **to burn out** 1 To become extinguished through lack of fuel. 2 To destroy or wear out by heat, friction, etc. 3 To burn up the house, store, or property of. 4 To drive out by heat. — **to burn the candle at both ends** To exhaust one's strength by overwork or dissipation. — **to burn up** 1 To consume by fire. 2 *Slang* To make or become irritated or enraged. — *n.* 1 An effect or injury from burning; a burnt place. 2 A brand. 3 The process of burning. 4 *Usually pl.* A defective area in window glass caused by overheating in the annealing furnace. 5 A place where vegetation has been burned away, in a forest, on the prairie, etc. [Fusion of OE *beornan* be on fire and OE *bærnan* set afire]

Synonyms (verb): blaze, brand, cauterize, char, consume, cremate, flame, flash, ignite, incinerate, kindle, scorch, singe. To *burn* is to effect either partial change or complete combustion: to *burn* wood in the fire; to *burn* one's hand on a hot stove; the sun *burns* the face. One *brands* with a hot iron, but *cauterizes* with some corrosive substance, as silver nitrate. *Cremate* is now used specifically for *consuming* a dead body by intense heat. To *kindle* is to *ignite,* the scientific word for the same thing. To *scorch* and to *singe* are superficial, and to *char* usually so. Both *kindle* and *burn* have extensive figurative use. Compare LIGHT. *Antonyms:* cool, extinguish, smother, stifle, subdue.

burn[2] (bûrn) *n. Scot.* A brook or rivulet: also spelled *bourn, bourne.*

burn·er (bûr'nər) *n.* 1 One who or that which burns. 2 The light–giving or flame–giving part of a lamp, etc.

bur·net (bûr'nit) *n.* Any of several perennial herbs (genus *Sanguisorba*) of the rose family, with alternate, pinnate leaves and small flowers in a dense head or spike. [Var. of BRUNETTE]

bur·nie (bûr'nē) *n. Scot.* A little burn; brooklet.

burn·ing (bûr'ning) *adj.* Consuming or being consumed by fire; intense; vehement; exciting. See synonyms under ARDENT, EAGER, HOT. — *n.* 1 A state or sensation of inflammation. 2 A destruction or putting to death by fire. 3 The baking, as of brick or pottery. See synonyms under FIRE.

burn·ing·bush (bûr'ning·bŏŏsh') *n.* 1 The wahoo. 2 The strawberry bush.

burning glass A convex lens for concentrating the sun's rays upon an object so as to heat or ignite it.

bur·nish (bûr'nish) *v.t.* & *v.i.* To polish by friction; make or become brilliant or shining. — *n.* Polish; luster; brightness. [OF *burniss-,* stem of *burnir* polish] — **bur'nish·ment** *n.*

bur·nish·er (bûr'nish·ər) *n.* 1 One who burnishes. 2 A tool with a smooth, rounded head used for giving a lustrous surface to metal, porcelain, etc. 3 A tool used to soften the hard lines of an engraving.

bur·noose (bər·nōōs', bûr'nōōs) *n.* A cloak with hood, worn by Arabs and Moors. Also **bur·nous', bur·nus'.** [<F *burnous* <Arabic *burnus*]

BURNOOSE

burn·out (bûrn'out') *n.* 1 *Agric.* A severe parching of the soil in areas subjected to prolonged or excessive solar heat. 2 The point at which one of the parts of a rocket or guided missile drops off the main assembly after having completed its work.

Burns (bûrnz), **Robert,** 1759–1796, Scottish poet.

burn·sides (bûrn'sīdz) *n.* *pl.* Side whiskers and mustache worn with closely shaven chin. [after Ambrose E. *Burnside,* 1824–81, U.S. major general]

burnt (bûrnt) A past tense and past participle of BURN. — *adj.* 1 Affected or consumed by fire; charred. **2** Diseased, as grain.

burnt cork A paste of powdered charred cork mixed with water: formerly used by actors to simulate Negro coloring.

burnt ocher A permanent, brick-red pigment made by heating ocher in a furnace.

burnt offering An animal, food, etc., burnt upon an altar as a sacrifice or offering to a god.

burnt orange A shade of light orange, with a brownish cast.

burnt sienna Raw sienna, calcined or roasted, noted for its dark brown color: used as an artist's pigment.

burnt umber A reddish-brown pigment made by calcining raw umber.

burp (bûrp) *n. Colloq.* A belch. —*v.t. & v.i.* To belch or cause to belch. [Imit.]

burr¹ (bûr) **1** A roughness or rough edge, especially one left on metal in casting or cutting. **2** A tool or device that raises a burr. **3** A dentist's drill with rough knothead: also **burr drill. 4** A millstone made of burstone: also spelled *buhr*. **5** The lobe of the ear. **6** A metal ring on the staff of a lance or handle of a battle-ax to keep the hand from slipping. **7** A halo around the moon or a star. **8** A blank punched out of a sheet of metal. **9** A washer to be slipped upon the end of a rivet before swaging, as in riveting leather. **10** A partly vitrified brick. **11** A hard lump of ore imbedded in a vein of softer material. **12** Bur¹. —*v.t.* **1** To form a rough edge on. **2** To remove a rough edge from. —*v.i.* **3** To operate a dentist's drill. Also spelled *bur.* ◆ Homophone: *birr.* [Var. of BUR¹]

burr² (bûr) *n.* **1** A rough guttural sound of *r* caused by the vibration of the uvula against the back part of the tongue: common in the north of England, but not to be confused with the Scottish trill. **2** Any rough, dialectal pronunciation: the Scottish *burr.* **3** A whirring sound; a buzz. —*v.t.* **1** To pronounce with a rough or guttural articulation. —*v.i.* **2** To speak with a burr. **3** To whir. Also spelled *bur.* ◆ Homophone: *birr.* [Imit.]

Burr (bûr), **Aaron,** 1756–1836, American lawyer and statesman; vice president of the United States 1801–05.

bur reed An herb (genus *Sparganium*), with ribbon-shaped leaves and spherical burlike fruit.

bur·ro (bûr′ō, bŏŏr′ō) *n. pl.* **·ros** A small donkey, used as a pack animal. [< Sp.]

bur·row (bûr′ō) *n.* **1** A hole made in and under the ground, as by a rabbit, etc., for habitation. **2** A mound or barrow. —*v.t.* **1** To make by burrowing. **2** To perforate with or as with burrows. —*v.i.* **3** To live or hide in or as in a burrow. **4** To make a burrow or hole. **5** To dig into, under, or through something; bore. ◆ Homophone: *borough.* [ME *borow.* Related to BOROUGH.] — **bur′row·er** *n.*

burr·stone (bûr′stōn′) *n.* A cellular, compact siliceous rock used for making millstones: also spelled *buhrstone, burstone.*

bur·ry (bûr′ē) *adj.* Having or resembling burs; rough; prickly.

bur·sa (bûr′sə) *n. pl.* **·sae** (-sē) **1** *Anat.* A pouch or saclike cavity; especially, one containing a viscid fluid and located at points of friction in the bodies of vertebrates. **2** *Pathol.* A cyst or abnormal sac. [< Med. L, sack, pouch]

bur·sal (bûr′səl) *adj.* **1** Of or pertaining to a bursa. **2** Of or pertaining to the public revenue.

bur·sar (bûr′sər, -sär) *n.* A treasurer, as of a college. [< Med. L *bursarius* treasurer] — **bur·sar·i·al** (bər-sâr′ē-əl) *adj.*

bur·sa·ry (bûr′sər-ē) *n. pl.* **·ries** **1** The treasury of a public institution or a religious order. **2** *Scot.* A grant for the maintenance of beneficiary students.

burse (bûrs) *n.* **1** A purse. **2** *Eccl.* A lined case used to carry the folded corporal to and from the altar. **3** A scholarship. [< F *bourse* < LL *bursa* wallet < Gk. *byrsa* hide]

bur·seed (bûr′sēd′) *n.* An Old World stickseed (*Lappula echinata*), naturalized in Canada and the northern United States.

bur·si·form (bûr′sə·fôrm) *adj.* Pouch-shaped; saclike.

bur·si·tis (bər·sī′tis) *n. Pathol.* Inflammation of a bursa.

burst (bûrst) *v.* **burst, burst·ing** *v.i.* **1** To break open or come apart suddenly and violently; explode, as from internal force. **2** To be full to the point of breaking open; bulge. **3** To issue forth or enter suddenly or violently. **4** To appear, begin; become audible or evident, etc.: A sound *burst* upon their ears. **5** To give sudden expression to passion, grief, etc.: to *burst* into tears; also, to be filled with violent emotion: He was *bursting* with rage. —*v.t.* **6** To cause to break open suddenly or violently; force open; puncture. **7** To fill or cause to swell to the point of breaking open. —*n.* **1** A sudden or violent explosion, rending, or disruption. **2** *Mil.* **a** The explosion of a bomb or shell on impact or in the air. **b** The number of bullets fired by one pressure on the trigger of an automatic weapon: a short *burst.* **3** A sudden effort; spurt; rush. **4** A sudden opening to view; prospect. [OE *berstan*]

burst·er (bûr′stər) *n.* **1** One who bursts. **2** *Mil.* An explosive which breaks open and scatters the contents of chemical shells, bombs, or mines.

bur·stone (bûr′stōn′) See BURRSTONE.

bur·then (bûr′thən) See BURDEN.

bur·ton (bûr′tən) *n. Naut.* A light hoisting tackle, usually one kept hooked to the pendant at the topmasthead of a vessel. [Origin uncertain]

Bur·ton (bûr′tən), **Harold Hitz,** born 1888, U.S. jurist; associate justice of the Supreme Court 1945–59. — **Sir Richard Francis,** 1821–1890, English traveler and writer. — **Robert,** 1577–1640, English scholar, author, and clergyman.

bury¹ (ber′ē) *v.t.* **bur·ied, bur·y·ing** **1** To put (a dead body) in a grave, tomb, or the sea; perform burial rites for; inter. **2** To cover, as for concealment. **3** To end; put out of mind: to *bury* a friendship or a difference. **4** To occupy deeply; engross: He *buried* himself in study. ◆ Homophone: *berry.* [OE *byrgan*]

Synonyms: conceal, cover, entomb, hide, inter, overwhelm. Anything which is effectually *covered* and *hidden* under any mass or accumulation is *buried.* Money is *buried* in the ground; a body is *buried* in the sea; a paper is *buried* under other documents. Whatever is *buried* is *hidden* or *concealed;* but there are many ways of *hiding* or *concealing* a thing without *burying* it. So a person may be *covered* with wraps, and not *buried* under them. *Bury* may be used of any object, *entomb* and *inter* only of a dead body. Compare HIDE, IMMERSE. *Antonyms:* disclose, disinter, exhume, expose, raise, restore, reveal, show, uncover.

bur·y² (ber′ē) *n. Obs.* A borough; castle; manor: often in composition: *Salisbury.* ◆ Homophone: *berry.* [Var. of BOROUGH]

Bur·y (ber′ē) A county borough in SE Lancashire, England.

bur·y·ing-ground (ber′ē·ing·ground′) *n.* A cemetery.

bus (bus) *n. pl.* **bus·es** or **bus·ses** **1** A large motor vehicle that carries passengers; an omnibus. **2** *Colloq.* An automobile. —*v.* **bused** or **bussed, bus·ing** or **bus·sing** *v.t.* **1** To transport by bus. —*v.i.* **2** To go by bus. **3** *Colloq.* To do the work of a bus boy. [Short form of OMNIBUS]

bus·by (buz′bē) *n. pl.* **·bies** A tall fur cap worn as part of the full-dress uniform of British hussars, artillerymen, and engineers. [Origin uncertain]

bush¹ (bŏŏsh) *n.* **1** A low, treelike or thickly branching shrub. **2** A scrubby growth, or land covered by scrub; a forest with undergrowth. **3** A bough: used as a sign for a tavern; hence, a tavern. **4** A fox's brush. **5** A bushy growth, as of hair. — **the bush 1** Country covered with thick woods and dense undergrowth. **2** A rural, arid, scrub-covered region, especially of Australia. —*v.i.* **1**

BUSBY

To grow or branch as or like a bush. **2** To be or become bushy. —*v.t.* **3** To protect (plants) with bushes or bushwood set round about; support with bushes. —*adj. U.S. Slang* Bush-league; small-time. [< ON *buskr*]

bush² (bŏŏsh) *v.t.* To line with a bushing, as an axle bearing, a pivot hole, etc. —*n.* A bushing. [< MDu. *busse* box]

bush baby Any of several species (genera *Galago* and *Euoticus*) of small, agile, gregarious nocturnal primates of African forests, having fluffy fir, long tails, and large eyes. Also **bush-baby.** Also called *galago.*

bushed (bŏŏsht) *adj. Colloq.* **1** Exhausted; worn out. **2** *Austral.* Lost; confused.

bush·el¹ (bŏŏsh′əl) *n.* **1** A measure of capacity; four pecks, 35.238 liters, or 2150.42 cubic inches. **2** A vessel holding that amount. [< OF *boissel,* dim. of *boiste* box]

bush·el² (bŏŏsh′əl) *v.t. & v.i.* To mend or alter, as men's clothes. [Cf. G *bosseln* do small jobs] — **bush′el·er, bush′el·ler** *n.* — **bush′el·man** (-mən) *n.*

bush·ing (bŏŏsh′ing) *n.* **1** A metallic lining for a hole, as in the hub of a wheel, designed to insulate or to prevent abrasion between parts. **2** A tube for insertion in a pump barrel or a pulley bore to reduce the diameter. **3** *Electr.* A lining inserted in a socket to protect an electric current.

bush jacket A hip-length jacket of strong material with a belt and four pockets.

bush·land (bŏŏsh′land′) *n. Canadian* Unsettled northern forest land.

bush league *U.S. Slang* **1** In baseball, a minor league. **2** Anything minor or second-rate. — **bush′-league′** *adj.*

bush·lea·guer (bŏŏsh′lē′gər) *n. U.S. Slang* **1** A player in a bush league. **2** Any person working or acting in a petty way.

bush·man (bŏŏsh′mən) *n. pl.* **·men** (-mən) *Austral.* A dweller or farmer in the bush.

Bush·man (bŏŏsh′mən) *n. pl.* **·men** (-mən) **1** One of a nomadic people of South Africa, considered to be related to the Pygmies. **2** The language of the Bushmen comprising many dialects, characterized by clicks, and forming a subfamily of the Khoisan family of African languages. [< Du. *boschjesman*]

bush·mas·ter (bŏŏsh′mas′tər, -mäs′-) *n.* A large and venomous pit viper (*Lachesis mutus*) of Central America and tropical South America, sometimes 12 feet long.

bush·rang·er (bŏŏsh′rān′jər) *n.* **1** One who lives as a wanderer in the bush. **2** *Austral.* A robber or brigand; originally, an outlaw living in the bush.

bush·whack (bŏŏsh′hwak′) *v.i.* **1** To cut bushes or underbrush with a bushwhacker. **2** To ride or range in the bush; fight in the bush, as a guerrilla. [< Du. *boschwachter* forest-keeper; infl. by WHACK]

bush·whack·er (bŏŏsh′hwak′ər) *n.* **1** One who ranges or fights in the bush. **2** A Confederate guerrilla. **3** A stout scythe for cutting bushes; also, one who uses it. **4** A backwoodsman. **5** *Austral.* A dweller or worker in the bush.

bush·whack·ing (bŏŏsh′hwak′ing) *n.* **1** Pulling a boat against the current by grabbing bushes. **2** Using underhand methods in politics. **3** Marauding; guerrilla fighting.

bush·y (bŏŏsh′ē) *adj.* **bush·i·er, bush·i·est** **1** Covered with or full of bushes. **2** Like a bush; shaggy. — **bush′i·ly** *adv.* — **bush′i·ness** *n.*

bus·ied (biz′ēd) Past tense and past participle of BUSY.

bus·i·ly (biz′ə·lē) *adv.* In a busy manner; industriously.

busi·ness (biz′nis) *n.* **1** A pursuit or occupation; trade; profession; calling. **2** Commercial affairs. **3** A matter or affair. **4** Interest; concern; duty. **5** A commercial enterprise or establishment. **6** Those details other than and exclusive of dialog, by which actors portray their parts and interpret a play. **7** (biz′ē·nis) *Obs.* The state of being busy: now *busyness.* — **to mean business** To be serious. [OE *bysignis*] — **busi·ness·like** *adj.*

Synonyms: art, avocation, barter, calling, commerce, concern, craft, duty, employment, handicraft, industry, job, labor, occupation, profession, trade, trading, traffic, vocation, work. A *business* is what one follows regularly and for profit; an *occupation* is what he is engaged in, either continuously or temporarily, for any purpose, whether of profit, or of amusement, learning, philanthropy, etc. *Pursuit* is an *occupation* which one follows with ardor. A *profession* implies scholarship; as, the learned *professions*. A *vocation* or a *calling* is that to which one feels himself called, as by special fitness or sense of duty, often now also used to characterize an occupation or profession; an *avocation* is a secondary interest, including hobbies and other activities whether for pleasure or profit, that interrupt one's *vocation* or *business* or that may parallel and eventually become a vocation. A *job* is a piece of *business* viewed and paid for as a single undertaking; colloquially, any regular *employment* is often termed a *job*. *Trade* and *commerce* may be used as equivalents, but *trade* may have a more limited application; as, the *trade* of a village, the *commerce* of a nation; in the special sense, a *trade* is an *occupation* involving manual training and skilled labor. *Barter* is the direct exchange of commodities without use of money. *Work* is any application of energy to secure a result, or the result thus secured; we may speak of the *work* of an artist, or a janitor. A single branch of productive *work* is called an *industry*; as, the steel *industry*. *Labor* is ordinarily used, in this connection, for unskilled *work*; *employment* for work done in the service of another. *Art* in the industrial sense is a system of rules and methods for accomplishing some practical result; as, the *art* of printing; collectively, the *arts*. A *craft* is some occupation requiring technical skill or manual dexterity, or the persons, collectively, engaged in its exercise; as, the weaver's *craft*. Compare ACTION, DUTY, TRAFFIC, TRANSACTION, WORK. *Antonyms*: idleness, inaction, inactivity, indolence, leisure, unemployment, vacation.

busi·ness·man (biz′nis·man′) *n. pl.* **·men** (-men′) One engaged in commercial or industrial activity. **—busi′ness·wom′an** *n. fem.*

bus·ing (bus′ing) *n.* 1 Transporting by bus. 2 The transportation of pupils by bus to schools other than in their own neighborhoods, in order to have racial balance in those schools.

busk[1] (busk) *n.* 1 A thin, elastic strip of wood, whalebone, or steel, placed in a corset or the like. 2 A corset. [< F *busc* ? < LL *boscum* bush, wood]

busk[2] (busk) *v.t. Scot.* or *Obs.* 1 To dress. 2 To prepare. [< ON *buask* get ready] **—busk′er** *n.*

busk·er (busk′ər) *n. Brit.* An itinerant musician or entertainer.

bus·kin (bus′kin) *n.* 1 A high shoe or half-boot reaching half-way to the knee, and strapped or laced to the ankle. 2 A laced half-boot, worn by Athenian tragic actors. 3 Tragedy. Compare SOCK[1]. [Origin uncertain]

BUSKIN

bus·kined (bus′kind) *adj.* 1 Having the feet laced in buskins, as on the stage. 2 Of or pertaining to the tragic drama. 3 Tragic, lofty, dignified.

bus·kit (bus′kit) *adj. Scot.* 1 Clothed. 2 Prepared; made ready.

bus·man (bus′mən) *n. pl.* **·men** (-mən) One who operates a bus.

Bus·ra (bus′rə) Basra. Also **Bus′rah.**

buss[1] (bus) *Colloq. n.* A kiss; smack. **—v.t. & v.i.** To kiss heartily. [Imit. Cf. dial. G *bussen*, Sw. *puss*, Sp. *buz* (? < L *basiare*]

buss[2] (boos, boos) *n. Scot.* A bush.

buss·es (bus′iz) A plural of BUS.

bust[1] (bust) *n.* 1 The human chest or breast. 2 A piece of statuary representing the human head, shoulders, and breast. [< F *buste* < Ital. *busto* trunk of the body]

bust[2] (bust) *Slang v.t.* 1 To burst. 2 To tame; train; as a horse. 3 To make bankrupt or short of funds. 4 To reduce in rank; demote. 5 To hit; strike. **—v.i.** 6 To burst. 7 To become bankrupt or short of funds. **—n.** 1 A bankruptcy. 2 Any failure; flop; dud. 3 A spree of any kind. 4 An arrest. [Alter. of BURST]

bus·tard (bus′tərd) *n.* Any member of a family (*Otididae*) of large Old World game birds related to the plovers and cranes, especially the **great bustard** (*Otis tarda*), the largest European land

bird. [< OF *bistarde, oustarde* < L *avis tarda*, lit., slow bird]

bust·er (bus′tər) *n.* 1 *Slang* Something great, large, or remarkable; a person of exceptional ability. 2 *Slang* A spree; a bust. 3 *U.S. Colloq.* Little boy: used in direct address. **—southerly buster** *Austral.* 1 A powerful southerly wind. 2 A mixed alcoholic drink.

bus·tic (bus′tik) *n.* A tree (*Dipholis salicifolia*) of southern Florida, with a very hard, strong, close-grained wood. [Origin unknown]

bus·tle[1] (bus′əl) *n.* Excited activity; noisy stir; fuss. See synonyms under TUMULT. **—v.t. & v.i. ·tled, ·tling** To hurry noisily; make a stir or fuss [? Related to BUSK[2]]

bus·tle[2] (bus′əl) *n.* 1 A frame or pad, formerly worn by women on the back below the waist to distend the skirts. 2 Fullness, as of gathered material, a bow, etc., worn over the back of a skirt below the waist. [? < BUSTLE[1]]

bus·tling (bus′ling) *adj.* Active; agitated. See synonyms under ACTIVE, ALERT, BUSY. **—bus′tling·ly** *adv.*

bus·y (biz′ē) *adj.* **bus·i·er, bus·i·est** 1 Intensely active; constantly or habitually occupied. 2 Temporarily engaged; not at leisure. 3 Officiously active; prying; meddling. 4 Pertaining to or filled with business. 5 Engaged: said of a telephone line or number. **—v.t. bus·ied, bus·y·ing** To make or be busy; occupy (oneself). See synonyms under OCCUPY. [OE *bysig* active]

Synonyms(adj.): active, assiduous, bustling, diligent, employed, engaged, industrious, occupied. *Busy* applies to an activity which may be temporary, *industrious* to a habit of life. *Diligent* indicates also a disposition, which is ordinarily habitual, and suggests more of heartiness and volition than *industrious*. We say one is a *diligent*, rather than an *industrious* reader. The *assiduous* worker gives patient and unremitting devotion to a task until it is done, or until nothing more can be done. Compare ACTIVE, INDUSTRIOUS, INDUSTRY. *Antonyms*: dilatory, dull, idle, inactive, indolent, lazy, listless, negligent, remiss, slack, slothful.

bus·y·bod·y (biz′ē·bod′ē) *n. pl.* **·bodies** One who officiously meddles with the affairs of others.

bus·y·ness (biz′ē·nis) *n.* The state of being busy: distinguished from *business*.

busy signal In a dial telephone, the sharp, recurrent buzzing tone indicating that the number called is already connected on another line. Compare DIAL TONE.

bus·y·work (biz′ē·wûrk′) *n.* Unnecessary work that is done only to keep one busy.

but[1] (but, *unstressed* bət) *conj.* 1 On the other hand; yet: I thought him honest, *but* he was lying. 2 Unless; if not: It never rains *but* it pours. 3 Excepting: Nothing would satisfy him *but* I come along. 4 Other than; otherwise than: I cannot choose *but* hear. 5 That: We don't doubt *but* matters will improve. 6 That . . . not: He is not so strong *but* a little exercise will do him good. 7 Who . . . not; which . . . not: Few sought his advice *but* were enlightened by it. **—prep.** With the exception of; save: owning nothing *but* his clothes. **—adv.** 1 Only; just: If I had *but* thought. 2 Merely; not otherwise than: She is *but* a child. **—all but** Almost: He is *all but* well. **—but for** Were it not for; without: *But for* me, how would you have succeeded? **—but what** 1 But that; but those which: There are no events *but what* have meaning. 2 *Colloq.* But that: I don't know *but what* I will. **—n.** A verbal objection; exception; condition: without any ifs or *buts.* [OE *buten* < *be* by + *ūtan* outside]

Synonyms (conj.): and, barely, besides, except, further, however, just, merely, moreover, nevertheless, notwithstanding, only, provided, save, still, that, though, unless, yet. *But* ranges from the faintest contrast to absolute negation; as, I am willing to go, *but* (on the other hand) content to stay; he is not an honest man, *but* (on the contrary) a villain. *Except* and *excepting* are slightly more emphatic than *but*. Such expressions as "words are *but* breath" (nothing *but*) may be referred to the restrictive use by ellipsis. *But* never becomes a full synonym for *and*; *and* adds something like, *but* adds something different; "brave *and* tender" implies that tenderness is natural to the brave; "brave *but* tender" implies that bravery and tenderness are rarely combined. The

omission or insertion of *but* often reverses the meaning. "I have no fear *that* he will do it" and "I have no fear *but that* he will do it" have contrary senses, the former indicating the feeling of certainty *that he will not do it*, and the latter feeling of certainty *that he will do it*. Where ambiguity or haziness results from the use of *but that*, it can ordinarily be avoided by recasting the sentence. Compare NOTWITHSTANDING.

but[2] (but) *n. Brit.* Any of various kinds of flatfish, especially the halibut and flounder: also spelled *butt*. [? < Gmc. Cf. Du. *bot* flounder, Sw. *butta* turbot.]

but[3] (but) *v.t. & v.i.* **but·ted, but·ting** To abut.

but[4] (but) *n. Scot.* The kitchen or outer room of a two-roomed house. **—to be but and ben with** To live in close intimacy with.

but[5] (but) See BUTT[4].

bu·tane (byōō′tān, byōō·tān′) *n. Chem.* A colorless, inflammable, gaseous compound, C_4H_{10}, of the aliphatic hydrocarbon series, contained in petroleum and formed synthetically by the action of zinc on ethyl iodide. [< L *butyrum* butter]

butch (booch) *adj. Slang* Masculine, as in appearance or manner: said of one who adopts a masculine role, especially a female homosexual. **—n.** 1 A closely cropped haircut for boys or men. 2 *Slang* A butch woman, especially a lesbian. [Prob. < *Butch*, a boy's nickname, often applied to young toughs]

butch·er (booch′ər) *n.* 1 One who slaughters animals or deals in meats for food. 2 A bloody or cruel murderer. 3 A vendor of candy, cigarettes, newspapers, etc., on trains. 4 In journalism, a copyreader. **—v.t.** 1 To slaughter or dress (animals) for market. 2 To kill (people or game) barbarously or brutally. 3 *Slang* To ruin by bungling treatment; botch. See synonyms under KILL. [< OF *bouchier* man who slaughters bucks < *boc* buck, he-goat] **—butch′er·er** *n.*

butch·er·bird (booch′ər·bûrd′) *n.* A shrike: named from its habit of impaling its prey upon thorns.

butch·er·y (booch′ər·ē) *n. pl.* **·er·ies** 1 Wanton or wholesale slaughter. 2 A slaughterhouse. 3 Butcher's trade. 4 The result of butchering. See synonyms under MASSACRE.

bu·te·o (byōō′tē·ō) *n.* Any of the numerous large, thickset hawks of the genus *Buteo*, having broad wings and rounded tails. Also called *buzzard*.

but·ler (but′lər) *n.* 1 A man servant in charge of the dining-room, wine, plate, etc. 2 Formerly, an official in charge of a royal wine cellar. [< OF *bouteillier* cupbearer < Med. L *buticularius* < *buticula* bottle] **—but′ler·ship** *n.*

Butler (but′lər), **Benjamin Franklin**, 1818–1893, U.S. general. **—Joseph**, 1692–1752, English theologian. **—Nicholas Murray**, 1862–1947, U.S. educator, president of Columbia University, New York, 1902–45. **—Pierce**, 1866–1939, U.S. jurist, associate justice of the Supreme Court 1923–39. **—Samuel**, 1612–1680, English satirical poet. **—Samuel**, 1835–1902, English novelist. **—Smedley Darlington**, 1881–1940, U.S. general.

butler's pantry A room between the kitchen and the dining-room, arranged for storage, serving, etc.

but·ler·y (but′lər·ē) *n. pl.* **·ler·ies** The butler's pantry.

butt[1] (but) *v.t.* 1 To strike with or as with the head or horns; ram. 2 To touch or bump against. 3 To cause to abut. 4 To abut on. 5 To join two things at the end; attach (one thing) to another, as a beam to a wall. **—v.i.** 6 To make a butting motion; move by butting. 7 To project; jut out. 8 To make a butt joint. 9 To be or lie adjacent; abut. **—n.** 1 A stroke, thrust, or push with or as with the head. 2 A thrust in fencing. **—to butt in** *Colloq.* To interrupt; interfere. [< OF *abouter* strike, ult. < Gmc.]

butt[2] (but) *n.* 1 A target, as for a rifle range. 2 *Often pl.* The range itself. 3 The shelter for the score-keeper on a rifle range. 4 The retaining wall placed behind a target to stop the bullets: also *target butt*. 5 A target for ridicule or criticism. 6 A limit; bound. [< OF *but* end, goal, ult. < Gmc.]

butt[3] (but) *n.* 1 The larger or thicker end of anything, as of a log. 2 That end or edge of a piece of timber where it comes squarely against another piece, or the joint thus formed. 3 A hinge.

4 The thick part of a tanned hide of leather. **5** The large end of the loin in beef. **6** *U.S. Colloq.* The buttocks. **7** The unused end of a cigar or cigarette. [Akin to Dan. *but* blunt, Du. *bot* short, stumpy]

butt[4] (but) *n.* **1** A large cask. **2** A measure of wine, 126 U.S. gallons. Also **but.** [< OF *boute*]

butte (byōōt) *n. Geog.* A conspicuous hill or natural turret, especially one with steep sides and a flattened top: also **bute.** [< F]

but·ter[1] (but′ər) *n.* **1** The fatty constituent of milk, separated by churning into a soft, whitish-yellow solid; also, this substance prepared and processed for cooking and table use. **2** A substance having the consistency or other qualities of butter, as the chlorides of some metals, a fruit preserve of a semisolid consistency: apple *butter,* and certain easily fused vegetable oils: peanut *butter.* —**to look as if butter would not melt in one's mouth** To look innocent. —*v.t.* **1** To put butter on. **2** *Colloq.* To flatter: usually with *up.* —**to know which side one's bread is buttered on** To be aware of the true sources of one's fortune or security and to behave accordingly. [OE *butere,* ult. < Gk. *boutyron* < *bous* cow + *tyros* cheese]

butt·er[2] (but′ər) *n.* A person or animal that butts.

but·ter-and-eggs (but′ər-ən-egz′) *n.* Any of various plants having two shades of yellow in the flower, as the toadflax in the United States, and a species of narcissus in England.

but·ter·ball (but′ər-bôl′) *n.* **1** The bufflehead. **2** *Colloq.* A very fat person.

butter bean 1 Wax bean **2** *Southern U.S.* Lima bean.

but·ter·bough (but′ər-bou′) *n.* The inkwood.

but·ter·burr (but′ər-bûr′) *n.* An Old World herb (genus *Petasites*), with round or roundish leaves often a foot wide. Also **but′ter-bur′.**

but·ter·cup (but′ər-kup′) *n.* **1** One of various species of crowfoot (genus *Ranunculus*), as *R. acris* and *R. bulbosus,* with yellow, cup-shaped flowers. **2** The flower. Also **but′ter-flow′er.**

but·ter·fat (but′ər-fat′) *n.* The fatty substance obtained from the milk of mammals, consisting of the glycerides of various fatty acids.

but·ter·fin·gers (but′ər-fing′gərz) *n.* An inept or clumsy person; one who drops things easily. —**but′ter-fin′gered** *adj.*

but·ter·fish (but′ər-fish′) *n. pl.* **·fish** or **·fish·es** One of various marine food fishes of the North Atlantic with an oily skin, as the dollarfish: also called *pumpkinseed.*

but·ter·fly (but′ər-flī′) *n. pl.* **·flies 1** A diurnal lepidopterous insect (division *Rhopalocera*) with large, often brightly colored wings, club-shaped antennae, and slender body. Compare MOTH. **2** A gay idler or trifler. [OE *buttorflēoge*]

butterfly bush Buddleia.

butterfly fish *n.* **1** One of various tropical marine fishes (family *Chaetodontidae*) having brightly colored bodies. **2** A brilliantly colored Chinese fish (*Macropodus viridiauratus*).

butterfly stroke In swimming, a stroke made while lying face down, the arms being brought forward laterally above the water: performed in conjunction with a fishtail kick.

butterfly table A small drop-leaf table, the leaves supported by brackets that resemble a butterfly's wings.

butter knife A small, blunt-edged knife for cutting or spreading butter.

but·ter·milk (but′ər-milk′) *n.* The sour liquid left after the butterfat has been separated from milk or cream.

but·ter·nut (but′ər-nut′) *n.* **1** The oily, edible nut of the North American white walnut (*Juglans cinerea*). **2** The tree, or its cathartic inner bark. **3** An oily, nutlike seed of a tall tree (*Caryocar nuciferum*), native to British Guiana, having a hard, brown, tubercled shell: also called *souari nut.* **4** The dye obtained from the bark and roots of the butternut tree. **5** A Confederate soldier; also, a Southern sympathizer in the Civil War. **6** Cloth or a garment dyed with butternut.

but·ter·scotch (but′ər-skoch′) *n.* **1** Hard, sticky candy made with brown sugar, butter, and flavoring. **2** A flavoring extract consisting of similar ingredients. —*adj.* Made of or flavored with butterscotch.

but·ter·weed (but′ər-wēd′) *n.* **1** The horseweed. **2** A groundsel (*Senecio lobatus*) of the southern United States. **3** The Indian mallow.

but·ter·wort (but′ər-wûrt′) *n.* Any of several small stemless herbs (genus *Pinguicula*), with broad fleshy leaves that secrete a greasy substance in which insects are captured.

but·ter·y[1] (but′ər-ē) *adj.* **1** Containing, like, or smeared with butter. **2** Grossly flattering; adulating.

but·ter·y[2] (but′ər-ē, but′rē) *n. pl.* **·ter·ies 1** A pantry; a wine cellar. **2** In English universities, a place in each college from which the students are supplied with provisions. [< OF *boterie* < LL *botaria* < *butta* bottle]

butt hinge A hinge composed of two plates or leaves which are screwed to the abutting surfaces of the door and the jamb. For illustration see under HINGE.

but·ting (but′ing) *n.* An abuttal.

butt joint A joint made by placing the component parts end to end and holding them in place either by welding or by side plates riveted thereto.

but·tock (but′ək) *n.* **1** *Naut.* The hinder part of a ship's hull. **2** *Anat.* **a** Either of the two fleshy prominences which form the rump. **b** *pl.* The rump. ◆ Collateral adjective: *gluteal.* [Dim. of BUTT[3]]

but·ton (but′n) *n.* **1** A knob or disk, as of bone or metal, which, when forced through a narrow opening, or buttonhole, fastens one part of a garment to another. **2** Anything resembling a button, as an emblem of membership, usually worn in the lapel, a political emblem on a celluloid disk, etc. **3** A pivoted fastener for a door, window, etc. **4** A knob or protuberance, as for operating an electric bell, at the end of a foil, etc. **5** *pl. Brit. Colloq.* A boy in attendance; a page: so called from the buttons on his uniform. **6** *Metall.* A small globular or disklike mass of metal found in a crucible after fusion. **7** *Bot.* **a** A bud or other like protuberance on a plant. **b** The small round flower head of some composite plants. **c** A small seed vessel. **d** The head of an immature mushroom. **8** *Zool.* **a** The bud that forms at the initial stage of a stag's horns. **b** The small round knob at the end of the rattles of a rattlesnake. **9** *U.S.* A guessing game. **10** *Slang* The point of the jaw. **11** *pl. Slang* Wits: Some of his *buttons* are missing. —*v.t.* **1** To fasten with or as with a button or buttons. **2** To provide with buttons. —*v.i.* **3** To admit of being buttoned. **4** To bud or form heads, as a cauliflower. [< OF *boton* button, bud] —**but′ton·er** *n.* —**but′ton-like′** *adj.*

but·ton·bush (but′n-boosh′) *n.* A North American shrub (*Cephalanthus occidentalis*): so called from its spherical white flower heads.

but·ton·hole (but′n-hōl′) *n.* A slit to receive and hold a button. —*v.t.* **·holed, ·hol·ing 1** To work buttonholes in. **2** To sew with a buttonhole stitch. **3** To detain by conversation; importune. —**but′ton-hol′er** *n.*

buttonhole stitch A perpendicular stitch fastened with a loop at the top, worked in a row or series for making a firm edge as, in buttonholes: also called *close stitch.*

BUTTONHOLE STITCH

but·ton·hook (but′n-hook′) *n.* A hook for buttoning gloves or shoes.

but·ton·mold (but′n-mōld′) *n.* A disk of wood or other material which is made into a button by covering with fabric, leather, etc.

button snakeroot 1 Any of several plants (genus *Liatris*): so called from the small round flower heads. **2** A stout-stemmed plant (*Eryngium aquaticum*), with linear leaves and globose heads of flowers.

but·ton·weed (but′n-wēd′) *n.* **1** The knapweed. **2** The Indian mallow.

but·ton·wood (but′n-wood′) *n.* **1** The sycamore or plane tree of the United States: also

but′ton·ball′. 2 A tree or shrub of tropical America and Africa (*Conocarpus erecta*) with heavy, close-grained wood and an astringent bark: also **but′ton-tree′.**

but·ton·y (but′ən-ē) *adj.* Of the nature of, like, or covered with buttons.

butt plate A plate, usually corrugated to prevent slipping on the shoulder, attached to the end of a gunstock.

but·tress (but′ris) *n.* **1** *Archit.* A structure built against a wall to strengthen it. **2** Any support or prop: *buttresses* to faith. **3** Any formation suggesting a buttress. **4** A projecting rock or hillside. **5** A horny growth on a horse's hoof. See synonyms under PROP. — **flying buttress** *Archit.* A rampant arch extending from a wall or pier to a supporting abutment, usually receiving the thrust of another arch on the other side of the wall, which it supports by its upper end. —*v.t.* **1** *Archit.* To support with a buttress. **2** To prop up; sustain; fortify: *buttressed* by her religious convictions. [< OF *bouterez,* nominative sing. of *bouteret* < *bouter* push, thrust]

butt shaft An arrow with a blunt head.

butt-weld (but′weld′) *n.* A weld made between two abutting ends or edges without overlapping.

bu·tyl (byōō′til) *n. Chem.* A univalent hydrocarbon radical, C_4H_9, from butane. [< BUT-(YRIC) + -YL]

butyl alcohol *Chem.* Any of three isomeric alcohols derived from butane, and having the formula C_4H_9OH: also *butanol.*

bux·om (buk′səm) *adj.* **1** Characterized by health and vigor; plump; comely: said of women. **2** Having a large bosom. [OE *buhsum* pliant. Akin to OE *bugan* bend, bow.] —**bux′om·ly** *adv.* —**bux′om·ness** *n.*

buy (bī) *v.* **bought, buy·ing** *v.t.* **1** To obtain for a price; purchase. **2** To be a price for. **3** To obtain by an exchange or sacrifice: to *buy* wisdom with experience. **4** To bribe; corrupt. **5** *Slang* To believe or accept, as an excuse. —*v.i.* **6** To make purchases; be a purchaser. —**to buy in 1** To buy from the owner, as at an auction when bids are too low. **2** To buy stock or an interest, as in a company. **3** *Slang* To pay money as a price for joining. —**to buy off** To obtain a promise of nonintervention by bribing. —**to buy out** To purchase the stock, interests, etc., of, as in a business. —*n. Colloq.* **1** Anything bought or about to be bought. **2** A bargain. [OE *bycgan*] —**buy′a·ble** *adj.* —**buy′er** *n.*

buzz[1] (buz) *v.i.* **1** To make a humming, vibrating sound, as a bee or hummingbird. **2** To talk, discuss, or gossip excitedly: The town *buzzed* with the news. **3** To move from place to place; bustle about. —*v.t.* **4** To utter or express in a buzzing manner; gossip. **5** To cause to buzz, as wings. **6** *Colloq.* To fly an airplane low over: He *buzzed* the ship. **7** *Colloq.* To call on the telephone. —*n.* **1** A low murmur, as of bees, talk, or distant sounds. **2** Rumor; gossip. **3** *Colloq.* A telephone call. [Imit.]

buzz[2] (buz) *v.t. Brit.* To drain to the last drop. [Origin unknown]

buzzard (buz′ərd) *n.* **1** One of several large, slow-flying hawks, as the **red-tailed buzzard** (*Buteo borealis*), an American species. **2** An American vulture; the turkey buzzard. [< OF *busart,* prob. < L *buteo* hawk]

buz·zard[2] (buz′ərd) *n. Brit. Dial.* A noisy insect, as a cockchafer, dor beetle, etc. [< BUZZ[1] + -ARD]

buzz·er (buz′ər) *n.* **1** One who or that which buzzes. **2** An electric signal making a buzzing sound, as on a telephone switchboard.

buzz saw A circular saw: so called from the sound it emits.

buzz·wig (buz′wig′) *n.* **1** A large, thick wig. **2** A person who wears such a wig. **3** A person of importance.

by (bī) *prep.* **1** Next to; near: the house *by* the road. **2** Along the course of: the railroad tracks *by* the river. **3** Past or beyond: The train flashed *by* us. **4** In the course of; during: birds flying *by* night. **5** Not later than: Be here *by* four tomorrow. **6** For the period of; according to: They work *by* the day. **7** As a result of the effort, means, or action of:

a play written *by* Shakespeare; a house struck *by* lightning. **8** With the perception of: a loss felt *by* all. **9** By means of: leading a child *by* the hand. **10** In consequence of: a case won *by* default. **11** As a means of conveyance; via: Mail your letters *by* air. **12** To the extent or amount of: insects *by* the thousands. **13** On the basis of: a road four miles long *by* actual measurement. **14** Considered according to: advancing step *by* step; reading word *by* word. **15** With reference to: to do well *by* one's friends. **16** Multiplied by: a room ten *by* twelve. **17** In the name of: swearing *by* all that is sacred. —*adv.* **1** In the presence or vicinity; at hand; near; as, to keep one's sword *by*. **2** Up to and beyond something; past: the train roared *by*. **3** Apart; aside, as discarded or saved for future use: to lay something *by*. **4** At or into a person's house, store, etc.: to stop *by*. —*adj. & n.* Bye. [OE *bī* near, about]

Synonyms (prep.): through, with. *By* refers to the agent; *through*, to the means, cause, or condition; *with*, to the instrument. *By* commonly refers to persons; *with*, to things; *through* may refer to either. The road having become impassable *through* long disuse, a way was opened *by* pioneers *with* axes. *By*, however, may be applied to any object which is viewed as partaking of action and agency; as, the metal was corroded *by* the acid; skill is gained *by* practice. "His friends were displeased *by* the selection of another chairman" means that the action displeased them; "His friends were displeased *with* the selection," etc., means that the man selected was not their choice. *Through* implies a more distant connection than *by* or *with*, and more intervening elements. Material objects are perceived *by* the mind *through* the senses. *By* is in frequent use after call, judge, know, measure, perceive, see, seem, take, understand, etc., to indicate the determining object; as, to call *by* name; I judge *by* his dress that he is poor; I saw *by* his glance that he was a rogue. *Accompanied* and *attended* take *by* of persons, *with* (commonly) of things; we say, *surrounded by*.

by- *combining form* **1** Secondary; inferior; incidental: *by-product*. **2** Near; close: *bystander*. **3** Aside; out of the way: *byway*.

by all means Certainly; on every account.

by and by 1 At some time in the future; soon; before long. **2** *Obs.* At once; immediately.

by-and-by (bī'ən-bī') *n.* Future time; hereafter.

by and large 1 Generally speaking; on the whole. **2** *Naut.* Alternatively well up to and off from the wind: This boat sails well *by and large*.

by-bid-der (bī'bid'ər) *n.* A person who runs up prices at an auction for the seller or owner. —**by'-bid'ding** *n.*

by-blow (bī'blō') *n.* **1** A side or chance blow; one that falls short of its aim. **2** An illegitimate child.

bye (bī) *n.* **1** Something of minor or secondary importance; a side issue. **2** In cricket, a run made on a ball missed by the batsman and which has passed by the wicket-keeper. **3** The position of a person who is assigned no opponent and auto-

matically advances to the next round, as in the preliminary pairings of a tennis tournament. **4** In golf, any hole or holes remaining unplayed when the match ends. —*adj.* Not principal or main; secondary. Also *by*. [Var. of BY]

bye-bye (bī'bī') *interj.* A child's word for good-bye. Also **bye**.

by-e-lec-tion (bī'i-lek'shən) *n. Brit.* A parliamentary election between general elections, held to fill a vacancy.

bye-low (bī'lō') *adv. & interj.* Hush!: a child's word, used in lullabies.

by-gone (bī'gôn', -gon') *adj.* Gone by; former; past; out-of-date. —*n.* Something past; that which has gone by: usually in the plural.

byke (bīk) See BIKE[2].

by-lane (bī'lān') *n.* **1** A byway. **2** A side passage in a mine.

by-law (bī'lô') *n.* **1** A rule or law adopted by an association, a corporation, or the like, which is subordinate to a constitution or charter. **2** *Obs.* An accessory law. [ME *bilawe* < *by*, *bi* village (< ON *bȳr*) + *lawe* law; infl. by BY]

by-line (bī'līn') *n.* The line at the head of an article in a newspaper, etc., giving the name of the writer.

by-name (bī'nām') *n.* **1** A secondary name; surname; sobriquet. **2** A nickname; epithet.

by-pass (bī'pas', -päs') *n.* **1** Any road, path, or route connecting two points in a course other than that normally used; a detour. **2** A device to lead a flow of gas or liquid around a pipe, fixed connection, or obstacle. **3** An electric switch. —*v.t.* **1** To go around (an obstacle). **2** To provide with a by-pass.

by-past (bī'past', -päst') *adj.* Bygone.

by-path (bī'path', -päth') *n.* A side, secluded, or secondary path.

by-play (bī'plā') *n.* **1** Action on the stage conducted through asides or dumb show as an accompaniment to the main action. **2** Any diversion from the main action.

by-prod-uct (bī'prod'əkt) *n.* Any material or product contingent upon or incidental to a manufacturing process: Bagasse is a *by-product* in the making of cane sugar.

byre (bīr) *n.* A cow stable. [OE, stall, shed]

byrl (bûrl, birl) See BIRLE.

Byrnes (bûrnz), **James Francis**, 1879–1972, U.S. statesman; secretary of state 1945–47.

byr-nie (bûr'nē) *n. Archaic* A coat of mail. [Var. of ME *brynie*]

by-road (bī'rōd') *n.* **1** A back road or crossroad; a private way. **2** Secret means.

By-ron (bī'rən), **Lord**, 1788–1824, George Gordon Noel Byron, sixth baron, English poet.

By-ron-ic (bī-ron'ik) *adj.* Of or pertaining to Lord Byron or his writings. **2** Like or characteristic of Byron or his style: proud, romantic, passionate, etc. Also **By-ro-ni-an** (bī-rō'nē-ən), **By-ron'i-cal.**

bys-si-no-sis (bis'ə-nō'sis) *n.* A pulmonary disease caused by the inhalation of cotton dust in mills. [< Latin *byssinum* linen + -OSIS]

bys-sus (bis'əs) *n. pl.* **bys-sus-es** or **bys-si** (bis'ī) **1** Formerly, any costly white stuff of cotton, silk, or linen. **2** *Zool.* A bunch of silky thread secreted

by the foot of certain stationary bivalve mollusks, as mussels, and serving as a means of attachment to an anchorage. **3** *Bot.* A filamentous fungus of the obsolete group *Byssi.* [< L < Gk. *byssos* fine linen]

by-stand-er (bī'stan'dər) *n.* One who stands by; a looker-on. See synonyms under SPECTATOR.

by-street (bī'strēt') *n.* A side street; a byway.

by-talk (bī'tôk') *n.* Incidental talk; small talk.

byte (bīt) *n.* A group of eight bits in a computer memory that form a character, a symbol, or a keyboard function. [< B(INAR)Y (DIGI)T E(IGHT)]

by the bye Incidentally; by the way. Also **by the by.**

by the way Incidentally; by the bye.

By-tom (bī'tôm) Polish name for BEUTHEN.

by-wa-ter (bī'wô'tər, -wot'ər) *n.* A diamond that is slightly yellowish or off color. [< BY, *adv.* (def. 3) + WATER (def. 5)]

By-wa-ter (bī'wô-tər), **Ingram**, 1840–1914, English classical scholar.

by-way (bī'wā') *n.* A branch or side road.

by-word (bī'wûrd') *n.* **1** A phrase, person, institution, etc., that has become an object of derision or mockery. **2** A nickname. **3** A trite saying; proverbial phrase. See synonyms under ADAGE. [OE *biword* proverb]

by-work (bī'wûrk') *n.* Work for odd hours during leisure time.

byz-ant (biz'ənt) See BEZANT.

Byz-an-tine (biz'ən-tēn, -tīn, bi-zan'tin) *adj.* **1** Of or pertaining to Byzantium. **2** Pertaining to a style of architecture developed in the Byzantine Empire during the fourth century, characterized by the round arch springing from four columns or piers, and in which the dome rests on

BYZANTINE ARCHITECTURE
Santa Sophia, Constantinople, A.D. 538.

pendentives, with centralized plans, colorful mosaics, and rich decoration. For illustration see under CAPITAL. —*n.* A native or inhabitant of Byzantium. Also **By-zan-ti-an** (bi-zan'-shē-ən, -shən). [< L *Byzantinus* < *Byzantium*]

Byzantine Empire The eastern part of the later Roman Empire (395–1453): Arabic *Rum:* also *Byzantium, Eastern Empire, Eastern Roman Empire.*

Byzantine rite Religious ceremonies as performed by the Greek Orthodox Church.

Bzu-ra (bzŏŏ'rä) A river in central Poland, flowing 85 miles NE to the Vistula.

C

c, C (sē) *n. pl.* **c's** or **cs, C's Cs, cees** (sēz) **1** The third letter of the English alphabet: from Phoenician *gimel*, through Hebrew *gimel*, Greek *gamma*, Roman C or G. **2** The sound of the letter *c*. See ALPHABET. —*symbol* **1** In Roman notation, the numeral 100. See under NUMERAL. **2** *Chem.* Carbon (symbol C). **3** *Music* **a** The tonic note of the natural musical scale, *do*. **b** The pitch of this tone or the written note representing it. **c** The scale built upon C. **d** Common or 4–4 time.

Ca *Chem.* Calcium (symbol Ca).

cab[1] (kab) *n.* **1** A one-horse public carriage. **2** A taxicab. **3** The covered part of a locomotive or motortruck. [Short form of CABRIOLET]

cab[2] (kab) *n.* A Hebrew measure equivalent to

about two quarts: also spelled *kab*.

ca-bal (kə-bal') *n.* **1** A number of persons secretly united for some private purpose. **2** Intrigue; conspiracy. —*v.i.* **ca-balled, ca-bal-ling** To form a cabal; plot. [< MF *cabale* < Med. L *cabbala* < Hebrew *qabbālāh* tradition]

Synonyms (noun): combination, conclave, confederacy, conspiracy, crew, faction, gang, junto. See CONSPIRACY.

cab-a-la (kab'ə-lə, kə-bä'lə) *n.* **1** The mystic theosophy of the Hebrews. **2** Any secret, occult, or mystic system. Often spelled *cabbala, kabala, kabbala.* [< Hebrew *qabbālāh* tradition < *qābal* receive] —**ca-bal'ic** *adj.* —**cab-a-lism** (kab'ə-liz'əm) *n.*

cab-a-list (kab'ə-list) *n.* **1** A student of the cabala. **2** A mystic; occultist.

cab-a-lis-tic (kab'ə-lis'tik) *adj.* **1** Pertaining to the cabala. **2** Having a mystic sense; mysterious. Also **cab'a-lis'ti-cal.** See synonyms under MYSTERIOUS. —**cab'a-lis'ti-cal-ly** *adv.*

ca-bal-la-da (kä'bəl-yä'də) *SW U.S.* A herd of horses or mules.

cab-al-le-ro (kab'əl-yâr'ō) *n. pl.* **-ros 1** A Spanish gentleman; cavalier: used with as broad a signification as the English word *gentleman.* **2** *SW U.S.* **a** A lady's escort. **b** A horseman.

cab-al-line (kab'ə-līn, -lin) *adj.* Of, pertaining to,

or suited to horses: *caballine* aloes. [< L *caballinus* < *caballus* horse]

caballine fountain The fountain Hippocrene; hence, a fountain of inspiration. Also **caballine spring.**

Ca·ba·na·tuan (kä·bä'nə·twän') A town in central Luzon; site of a Japanese prisoner of war camp in World War II.

ca·bane (kə·ban') *n. Aeron.* **1** A framework to support the wings of an airplane at the fuselage. **2** The system of trusses supporting the overhang of a wing. [< F, Cabin]

cab·a·ret (kab'ə·rā') *n.* **1** A restaurant or café which provides singing, dancing, etc., as entertainment for its patrons. **2** Entertainment of this type. **3** A tavern or wine shop. **4** A tea or coffee set, including tray and dishes. [< F]

cab·as (kab'ə, kə·bä') *n.* **1** A rush basket. **2** A woman's workbag or basket. [< F]

cab·as·set (kab'ə·set) *n.* An open helmet with a rounded top and narrow brim. [< F, dim. of *cabas* basket]

cab·bage[1] (kab'ij) *n.* **1** The close-leaved head formed by certain brassicaceous plants. **2** The plant (*Brassica oleracea*) producing it. **3** The large terminal leaf bud of the cabbage palm used as a vegetable. — *v.i.* **·baged, ·bag·ing** To form a head, as cabbage; to grow into a head. [< OF *caboche* < L *caput* head]

cab·bage[2] (kab'ij) *v.t. & v.i.* **·baged, ·bag·ing** To pilfer; take dishonestly; purloin: said originally of a tailor who appropriated a part of his customers' cloth. — *n.* Cloth appropriated by a tailor in cutting out garments; hence, anything purloined. [Origin uncertain]

cabbage bug The harlequin bug.

cabbage butterfly Any of several butterflies (genus *Pieris*) whose larvae feed on plants of the mustard family; especially *P. rapae*, the green larvae of which destroy cabbage. For illustration see under INSECT (injurious).

cabbage green The soft, grayish blue-green color of cabbage leaves.

cabbage palm 1 A palm with a terminal leaf bud used as a vegetable, as the cabbage palm (*Sabal palmetto*) of Florida. **2** The feather palm (*Ptychosperma elegans*) of Australia. **3** The fan palm.

cab·ba·la (kab'ə·lə, kə·bä'lə), etc. See CABALA.

cab·by (kab'ē) *n. pl.* **·bies** *Colloq.* A cabman.

ca·ber (kā'bər) *n. Scot.* A mastlike pole, generally the stem of a tree, used in the Highland athletic game **tossing the caber:** also spelled *kabar, kebar.*

cab·in (kab'in) *n.* **1** A small, rude house; hut. **2** A compartment in a vessel for officers or passengers. **3** *Aeron.* The enclosed space in an airplane for passengers, pilot, etc.; the cockpit. see synonyms under HOUSE, HUT. — *v.t. & v.i.* To shut up or dwell in or as in a cabin; crib; hamper. [< F *cabane* < LL *capanna* cabin]

cabin boy A boy who waits on the officers and passengers of a vessel.

cabin class A class of accommodations for steamship passengers, higher than tourist class, lower than first class.

cab·i·net (kab'ə·nit) *n.* **1** The body of official advisers of a king, president, or chief of state. **2** A council, or the chamber in which it meets. **3** A room for works of art, etc.; also, the articles collected. **4** A piece of furniture fitted with shelves and drawers. **5** *Obs.* A little cabin. **6** A small private room; a study or closet. — *adj.* **1** Pertaining to or suitable for a cabinet in any sense. **2** Secret; confidential. [< F < Ital. *gabinetto* closet, chest of drawers; in def. 4, dim. of CABIN]

cab·i·net·mak·er (kab'ə·nit·mā'kər) *n.* One who does fine woodworking, as for cabinets, furniture, etc.

cab·i·net·work (kab'ə·nit·wûrk') *n.* The work of a cabinetmaker; expert woodwork.

ca·ble (kā'bəl) *n.* **1** *Naut.* **a** A heavy rope or chain, as for mooring vessels, etc. **b** A cable's length. **2** *Electr.* An insulated electrical conductor or group of conductors, protected by a waterproof coat, as for a submarine telegraph. **3** A cablegram. — *v.t.* **ca·bled, ca·bling 1** To fasten, as by a cable; tie fast. **2** To equip with cable or cables. **3** To send, as a message, by submarine telegraph. — *v.i.* **4** To communicate by submarine telegraph. [Akin to F *câble*, Sp. *cable* < LL

capulum, caplum rope < *capere* take, grasp]

cable car A car or cage, pulled by an overhead or underground cable.

ca·ble·gram (kā'bəl·gram) *n.* A telegraphic dispatch sent by cable.

ca·ble·laid (kā'bəl·lād') *adj.* Made up of three three-stranded ropes twisted together left-handed: a ropemaking term.

cable railroad A railroad in which the cars are attached to an endless moving cable by means of an adjustable grip usually passing through a slot in the roadway.

ca·blet (kā'blit) *n.* A cable rope less than 10 inches in circumference: a hawser. [Dim. of CABLE]

cable TV or **cable television** A system for transmitting television programs by coaxial cable to individual subscribers. Abbr. CATV

cab·man (kab'mən) *n. pl.* **·men** (-mən) The driver of a cab.

ca·bob (kə·bob') See KABAB.

ca·boched (kə·bosht') *adj. Her.* Full-faced: said of the head of a stag, bull, or other beast. Also **ca·boshed'.** [< OF *caboché*, pp. of *cabocher* cut off the head < L *caput* head]

cab·o·chon (kab'ə·shon, *Fr.* kà·bô·shôn') *adj.* Cut convex and highly polished but not faceted. — *n.* Any gem so cut. — **en cabochon** Cut and polished but not faceted: said of gems. [< F, aug. of *caboche* head]

ca·boo·dle (kə·bōōd'l) *n. Colloq.* Aggregate or collection; lot; usually with an intensive, as **the whole caboodle, the whole kit and caboodle.** [Prob. intens. form of BOODLE]

ca·boose (kə·bōōs') *n.* **1** *U.S.* A car on a freight train or work train equipped with stove and bunks for the use of the train crew or work crew. **2** *Brit.* The cook's galley on a ship. Also spelled *camboose.* [< MDu. *cabuse* cook's galley]

Cab·ot (kab'ət), **John,** 1451?–98, Venetian navigator in English service; discovered American continent (Labrador) 1497. — **Sebastian,** 1474–1557, English navigator: son of preceding.

cab·o·tage (kab'ə·tij) *n.* **1** Coastwise navigation; coast pilotage; coasting trade. **2** Air transport passengers and goods within the same national territory. [< F]

ca·bres·ta (kä·bres'tä), **ca·bres·to** (-tō) See CABESTRO.

ca·bril·la (kə·bril'ə, *Sp.* kä·brē'yä) *n.* **1** One of various serranoid food fishes; specifically, one of the groupers (genus *Epinephelus*) common on the West Indian and Florida coasts. **2** A fish of the genus *Paralabrax*, as the California rock bass (*P. clathratus*). ob <Sp.]

cab·ri·ole (kab'rē·ōl) *n.* A curved, tapering leg, often with a decorative foot: characteristic of Chippendale and Queen Anne furniture. [< MF. See CABRIOLET.]

cab·ri·o·let (kab'rē·ə·lā', -let') *n.* **1** A one-horse covered carriage with two seats; a cab. **2** An automobile of the coupé type, having a collapsible top. [< F, dim. of MF *cabriole* leap < Ital. *capriola* < L *capreolus* wild goat]

cab·stand (kab'stand') *n.* A specified place where cabs are stationed for hire.

ca' can·ny (kä kan'ē, kô) **1** *Brit.* A deliberate slowing down of production on the part of workers. **2** *Scot.* Go warily.

ca·ca·o (kə·kā'ō, -kä'ō) *n. pl.* **·ca·os 1** The large, nutritive seeds of a small evergreen tropical American tree (*Theobroma cacao*): also called *chocolate nuts.* **2** The sweet-scented, yellowish oil of this tree, widely used in medicine and cosmetics, and in making cocoa and chocolate. **3** The tree producing these nuts or seeds: also called *chocolate tree.* [< Sp. < Nahuatl *cacauatl* cacao]

cacao butter A hard, yellowish, fatty substance obtained from cacao beans, consisting chiefly of glycerides of stearic, palmitic, and lauric acid; used for soap, cosmetics, etc.: also called *cocoa butter.*

cac·cia·to·re (käch'ə·tôr'ē, -tō'rē) *adj.* Stewed in tomatoes and wine: chicken *cacciatore.* [< Italian]

cach·a·lot (kash'ə·lot, -lō) *n.* The sperm whale. [< F, prob. < dial. F *cachalut* toothed]

cache (kash) *v.t.* **cached, cach·ing** To conceal or store, as in the earth; hide in a secret place. — *n.* A place for hiding or storing provisions, equipment, etc.; also, the things stored or hidden.

[< F < *cacher* hide]

ca·chec·tic (kə·kek'tik) *adj.* Of, pertaining to, or affected with cachexia. Also **ca·chec·ti·cal.** [< MF *cachectique* < L *cachecticus* < Gk. *kachektikos*]

cache·pot (kash'pot, *Fr.* käsh·pō') *n.* A jardinière or an ornamental pot or a casing concealing an ordinary flowerpot. [< F]

ca·chet (ka·shā', kash'ā) *n.* **1** A seal. **2** A distinctive mark; stamp of individuality. **3** A hollow wafer used for enclosing nauseous medicine. **4** A stamped or printed mark, picture, etc., put on mail as a slogan, commemoration mark, etc. See LETTRE DE CACHET. [< F < *cacher* hide]

ca·chex·i·a (kə·kek'sē·ə) *n. Pathol.* Malnutrition and general bad health, characterized by a waxy or sallow complexion, as in cancer, tuberculosis, etc. Also **ca·chex·y** (kə·kek'sē). [< LL *cachexia* < Gk. *kachexia* poor condition or state < *kakos* bad + *-hexia* < *echein* hold oneself, be]

cach·in·nate (kak'ə·nāt) *v.i.* **·nat·ed, ·nat·ing** To laugh immoderately or noisily. [< L *cachinnatus*, pp. of *cachinnare* laugh loudly] — **cach·in·na'tion** *n.*

cach·o·long (kash'ə·long) *n.* An opaque white, yellowish, or reddish variety of opal. [< Kalmuck *kaschschilon* beautiful stone]

ca·chou (kə·shōō', ka-) *n.* **1** An aromatic pill or pastille, used to perfume the breath. **2** Catechu. [< F < Malay *kāchū* catechu]

ca·chu·cha (kä·chōō'chä) *n. Spanish* An Andalusian dance or dance tune in 3–4 time, resembling the bolero.

ca·cique (kə·sēk') *n.* **1** A prince or chief among the Indians of the West Indies, Mexico, Peru, etc. **2** An oriole of the warmer parts of America. Also spelled *cazique.* [< Sp. < native Haitian word for "chief"]

cack·le (kak'əl) *v.* **·led, ·ling** *v.i.* **1** To make a shrill cry, as a hen that has laid an egg. **2** To laugh or talk with a sound resembling this cry. — *v.t.* **3** To utter in a cackling manner. — *n.* **1** The shrill, broken cry made by a hen after laying an egg; the gabbling of a goose. **2** Idle talk; chattering or chuckling. See synonyms under BABBLE. [Imit.] — **cack'ler** *n.*

caco- *combining form* Bad; diseased; vile: *cacography.* [< Gk. *kakos* bad, evil]

cac·o·de·mon (kak'ə·dē'mən) *n.* **1** A devil, or evil spirit. **2** One supposedly possessed by an evil spirit. Also **cac'o·dae'mon.** [< Gk. *kakodaimōn* evil genius]

cac·o·e·thes (kak'ō·ē'thēz) *n.* **1** A bad propensity or habit; a mania. **2** *Pathol.* A malignant ulcer. [< L < Gk. *kakoēthēs* < *kakos* bad + *ēthos* habit, disposition]

cacoethes lo·quen·di (lō·kwen'dī) *Latin* A passion for talking.

cac·o·gen·ics (kak'ə·jen'iks) *n.* The scientific study of race degeneration; also, race degeneration, as from inbreeding or inferior mating. [< CACO- + (EU)GENICS] — **cac'o·gen'ic** *adj.*

ca·cog·ra·phy (kə·kog'rə·fē) *n.* Bad handwriting or spelling. — **ca·cog'ra·pher** *n.* — **cac·o·graph·ic** (kak'ə·graf'ik) or **·i·cal** *adj.*

ca·col·o·gy (kə·kol'ə·jē) *n.* Mischoice or misuse of words; bad pronunciation or speech. [< Gk. *kakologia* bad style, abuse]

cac·o·mis·tle (kak'ə·mis'əl) *n.* A long-tailed, raccoonlike carnivore (genus *Bassariscus*); especially, *B. astutus* of Mexico and adjacent parts of the United States. Also **cac'o·mis'cle, cac'o·mix'l** (-mis'əl, -mik'səl), **cac'o·mix'le.** [< Sp. < Nahuatl *tlacomiztli*]

ca·coph·o·nous (kə·kof'ə·nəs) *adj.* **1** Having a harsh, discordant, disagreeable sound: opposed to *euphonious.* **2** *Music* Discordant; dissonant: opposed to *harmonious.* Also **ca·coph·on·ic** (kak'ə·fon'ik) or **·i·cal** — **ca·coph'o·nous·ly, cac'o·phon'i·cal·ly** *adv.*

ca·coph·o·ny (kə·kof'ə·nē) *n.* **1** Discord; a disagreeable sound. **2** The use of harsh combinations of sounds, words, etc., in speech. **3** *Music* Dissonance; also, the frequent use of dissonance. [< F *cacophonie* < Gk. *kakophōnia* < *kakos* bad + *phōneein* sound]

cac·ta·ceous (kak·tā'shəs) *adj. Bot.* Of or belonging to the cactus family (*Cactaceae*).

cac·tus (kak'təs) *n. pl.* **·tus·es** or **·ti** (-tī) Any one

---

of various polypetalous, green, fleshy, mostly leafless and spiny plants of the family *Cactaceae*, native in arid regions of America, often having showy flowers. [< L < Gk. *kaktos* a prickly plant]

ca·cu·men (kə·kyōō'mən) *n.* The apex or top. [< L]

ca·cu·mi·nal (kə·kyōō'mə·nəl) *adj.* 1 Pertaining to the top, as of a plant. 2 *Phonet.* Describing those consonants pronounced with the tip of the tongue turned up and back toward the hard palate, as *t* and *d* in the Indic and Dravidian languages; cerebral; retroflex. —*n. Phonet.* A consonant so formed.

cad (kad) *n.* 1 A vulgar, ill-bred, obtrusive person; one not behaving as a gentleman. 2 *Obs.* In England, one who caters to the sports of public-school boys or university students; at Oxford, a townsman. 3 *Obs.* The conductor of an omnibus. [Short form of CADET] —**cad'dish** *adj.* —**cad'dish·ly** *adv.* —**cad'dish·ness** *n.*

ca·das·ter (kə·das'tər) *n.* A register, survey, or map of the extent, ownership, value, etc., of the lands of a country, as a basis of taxation. Also **ca·das'tre.** [< F *cadastre* < LL *capitastrum* tax register < *caput* head] —**ca·das'tral** *adj.* —**cad·as·tra·tion** (kad'əs·trā'shən) *n.*

ca·dav·er (kə·dav'ər, -dā'vər) *n.* A dead body; especially, that of a human being intended for dissection; a corpse. [< L]

ca·dav·er·ine (kə·dav'ər·in, -ēn) *n. Biochem.* A thick, colorless, liquid ptomaine, $C_5H_{14}N_2$, of noxious odor, formed by putrefying animal tissue.

ca·dav·er·ous (kə·dav'ər·əs) *adj.* Like a corpse; pale; ghastly; gaunt. Also **ca·dav'er·ic.** —**ca·dav'er·ous·ly** *adv.* —**ca·dav'er·ous·ness** *n.*

cad·die (kad'ē) *n.* A messenger or errand boy, especially one paid to carry clubs for golf players. —*v.i.* **·died, ·dy·ing** To act as a caddie. Also spelled **caddy.** [< CADET]

cad·dis (kad'is) *n.* 1 A coarse, sergelike fabric. 2 A narrow, tapelike worsted fabric for bindings, etc. 3 Worsted yarn; crewel. Also **cad'dice.** [< MF *cadis*, a woolen fabric]

cad·dis fly (kad'is) Any of certain four-winged insects (order *Trichoptera*): their aquatic larvae, known as **caddis worms,** construct, inhabit, and carry cylindrical, silklined cases covered with sand, gravel, etc. [Origin uncertain]

cad·dy (kad'ē) *n. pl.* **·dies** 1 A receptacle for tea. 2 A small box or case. [< Malay *kati,* a measure of weight, equal to 1 1/4 lbs.]

cade¹ (kād) *adj.* 1 Brought up by hand: a *cade colt.* 2 Coddled. [Origin unknown]

cade² (kād) *n.* A large, bushy shrub *(Juniperus oxycedrus)* of Mediterranean regions: its wood yields a brown, thick liquid having a tarry odor, known as **cade oil,** used in soaps and medicinally. [< F]

ca·delle (kə·del') *n.* A small, black beetle *(Tenebrioides mauritanicus)* which in both larval and adult stages feeds upon stored grain. [< F]

ca·dence (kād'ns) *n.* 1 Rhythmic or measured flow or movement, as in poetry, music, oratory. 2 *Mil.* Uniform pace and time in marching expressed in so many steps to the minute; measure; beat. 3 Modulation, as of the voice or of elemental sounds; also, a fall of the voice, as at a period. 4 Intonation or inflection of the speaking voice as distinctive of a language or locality. 5 *Music* A succession of chords naturally closing a musical phrase or period: the **perfect, complete,** or **whole cadence,** proper at the end of a movement; the **imperfect** or **half cadence,** often a reversal of the dominant perfect. **b** A cadenza. See synonyms under TUNE. [< F < Ital. *cadenza* < LL *cadentia* a falling < *cadere* fall. Doublet of CHANCE, CADENZA.] —**ca'denced** *adj.*

ca·den·cy (kād'n·sē) *n. pl.* **·cies** 1 Cadence; rhythm. 2 *Her.* The relative position of the younger members of the same family or branches of the same house.

ca·dent (kād'nt) *adj.* 1 Having cadence or rhythm. 2 *Obs.* Falling.

ca·den·za (kə·den'zə, *Ital.* kä·dent'sä) *n. Music* An embellishment or flourish, prepared or improvised for a solo voice or an instrument, before the close of a movement or between divisions of a movement, especially in the first movement of a concerto. [< Ital. Doublet of CADENCE, CHANCE.]

ca·det (kə·det') *n.* 1 A student at a military or naval school. 2 A student in training at the United States Military or Coast Guard Academy for commissioning as an officer: at the United States Air Force Academy the official designation is **Air Force cadet.** 3 A younger son or brother in a noble family. 4 *Archaic.* A gentleman who entered the army without a commission so as to gain military experience and thus earn a commission. 5 *Colloq.* A pander or pimp; whoremonger. [< F, ult. < dim. of L *caput* head, chief]

ca·dette (kà·det') *n. fem.* 1 *French* A younger daughter or sister in a noble family. 2 In New Zealand, a young woman who has passed a competitive test and been appointed to the civil service.

cad·mi·um (kad'mē·əm) *n.* A soft, bluish-white, toxic metallic element (symbol Cd, atomic number 48) occurring in zinc ores and used in the manufacture of fusible alloys, in electroplating, and in controlling fission in nuclear reactors. See PERIODIC TABLE. [< NL < L *cadmia* zinc ore < Gk. *kadmeia(gē)*]

cadmium sulfide A pigment, CdS, varying in hue from lemon to orange: also **cadmium yellow** or **cadmium orange.**

cad·re (kad'rē, *Fr.* kä'dr') *n.* 1 The officers and men necessary to establish and train a military unit. 2 Trained personnel essential in the conduct and management of an organization, enterprise, etc. 3 A nucleus; skeleton; framework. [F, frame of a picture < Ital. *quadro* < L *quadrum* square]

ca·du·ce·us (kə·dōō'sē·əs, -dyōō'-) *n. pl.* **·ce·i** (-sē·ī) 1 The wand or staff of Mercury, the messenger of the gods. 2 A similar wand used in the armed services as the emblem of the medical corps or department; also often used as the symbol of the medical profession. [< L < Gk. (Doric) *karykion* herald's staff] —**ca·du'ce·an** *adj.*

CADUCEUS

ca·du·ci·ty (kə·dōō'sə·tē, -dyōō'-) *n.* 1 The state or quality of being caducous. 2 Old age; senility.

ca·du·cous (kə·dōō'kəs, -dyōō'-) *adj.* 1 *Biol.* Dropping or falling off, especially at an early stage of development, as the sepals of a poppy or the gills of salamanders, etc. 2 Having a tendency to fall or perish; perishable. [< L *caducus* falling < *cadere* fall]

cae- For words not found here, see under CE-.

cae·cil·i·an (si·sil'ē·ən) *n.* One of a family *(Caecilidae)* of tropical, burrowing, legless amphibians, resembling worms or small snakes. [< L *caecilia,* a kind of lizard]

cae·cum (sē'kəm), etc. See CECUM, etc.

cae·o·ma (sē·ō'mə) *n. Bot.* An aecium of a fungus (genus *Caeoma*) of the *Uredinales.* [< NL < Gk. *kaiein* burn; with ref. to its color]

caer·i·mo·ni·a·ri·us (ser'i·mō'nē·ā'rē·əs) *n. pl.* **·ri·i** (-rē·ī) A director of ceremonies in solemn offices, as in Roman Catholic cathedral services. [< L *caerimonia* ceremony]

caes·al·pin·i·a·ceous (sez'al·pin'ē·ā'shəs, ses'-) *adj. Bot.* Belonging to a genus *(Caesalpinia)* of tropical trees, shrubs, or herbs of the bean family. [< after A. *Caesalpinus,* 1519–1603, Italian botanist]

Cae·sar (sē'zər) 1 A masculine personal name: also spelled *Cesar.* 2 The title of any one of the Roman emperors from Augustus to Hadrian. 3 Any powerful emperor or despot.

—**Caesar, Gaius Julius,** 100–44 B. C., Roman general, statesman, and historian.

Caesarean operation *Surg.* The delivery of a child by section of the abdominal walls and the womb of the mother when ordinary delivery is apparently impossible: reported to have been performed at the birth of Julius Caesar: also spelled *Cesarean.* Also **Caesarean section.**

Cae·sar·ism (sē'zər·iz'əm) *n.* Government like that of the Caesars; imperialism; military despotism. —**Cae'sar·ist** *n.*

cae·si·um (sē'zē·əm) See CESIUM.

caes·tus (ses'təs) See CESTUS.

cae·su·ra (si·zhoor'ə, -zyoor'ə) *n. pl.* **·su·ras** or

·su·rae (-zhoor'ē, -zyoor'ē) 1 In prosody, a break or pause in the middle of a foot, usually near the middle of a verse. 2 A break or interruption. 3 *Music* A rest or pause indicating a rhythmic division point in an air or melody; also, the stressed note preceding. Also spelled *cesura.* [< L, cutting, caesura < *caedere* cut] —**cae·su'ral** *adj.*

ca·fé (kə·fā', ka-) *n.* 1 A coffee house; restaurant. 2 A barroom. 3 Coffee. [< F]

café society The set customarily frequenting cafés or night clubs, especially in New York City.

caf·e·te·ri·a (kaf'ə·tir'ē·ə) *n.* A restaurant where the patrons wait upon themselves. [< Am. Sp., coffee store]

caf·fe·ic (ka·fē'ik) *adj.* Of, pertaining to, or derived from coffee. [< F *caféique* < *café* coffee]

caf·feine (kaf'ēn, *in technical usage* kaf'ē·in) *n. Chem.* A crystallizable, slightly bitter alkaloid, $C_8H_{10}N_4O_2 \cdot H_2O$, found in the leaves and berries of coffee, and chemically identical with theine: used as a stimulant and diuretic. [< F *caféine* < *café* coffee]

caf·fe·tan·nic (kaf'ē·tan'ik) *adj. Chem.* Of, pertaining to, or derived from caffeine and tannin together. Also **caf'fe·o·tan'nic** (kaf'ē·ō·tan'ik). [< CAFFE(INE) + TANNIC]

caf·tan (kaf'tən, käf·tän') *n.* An undercoat having long sleeves and a sash, worn in Mediterranean countries: also spelled *kaftan.* [< F *cafetan* < Turkish *qaftān*]

cage (kāj) *n.* 1 A structure, with openwork of wire or bars, as for confining birds or beasts. 2 A room or place enclosed by a grating, for confining prisoners. 3 Any lockup, prison, or place of confinement, or anything that confines or imprisons. 4 Any cagelike structure, framework, or grating, as a timber framework lining a shaft. 5 A platform, elevator car, or the like, protected by gratings. 6 A wire mask worn by the catcher in baseball. 7 The iron or steel skeleton frame of a high building. 8 A table from which quick-firing guns are discharged. 9 An enclosure in a gymnasium for interior baseball practice. —*v.t.* **caged, cag·ing** To shut up in or as in a cage; confine; imprison. [< OF < L *cavea* < *cavus* empty, hollow]

cage·ling (kāj'ling) *n.* A caged bird.

ca·gey (kā'jē) *adj.* **ca·gi·er, ca·gi·est** *Colloq.* Shrewd; wary of being duped. Also **ca'gy.** —**ca'gi·ly** *adv.* —**ca'gi·ness** *n.*

ca·hier (kä·yā') *n.* 1 A memorial, report of proceedings, or the like. 2 A quarter of a quire of writing paper. 3 A few leaves, as of printed matter, loosely stitched together; a number of a book issued in parts. [< F < OF *quaier* < L *quaterni* four < *quattuor* four]

ca·hoots (kə·hōōts') *n. pl. U.S. Slang* Partnership; close cooperation; collusion: to be in *cahoots.* [? < F *cahute* cabin]

Cai·a·phas (kā'ə·fəs, kī'-) A Jewish high priest: presided at the council which condemned Jesus. *Matt.* xxvi 57–68.

cai·man (kā'mən) *n. pl.* **·mans** A tropical American crocodilian (genus *Caiman*) closely related to the alligator, as the **spectacled caiman** *(C. sclerops),* having prominent ridges above the upper eyelid. Also spelled *cayman.* [< Sp., probably < a Carib word]

Cain (kān) 1 The eldest son of Adam, who slew his brother Abel. *Gen.* iv 1–10. 2 Hence, a fratricide or murderer. —**to raise Cain** *Slang* To raise a rumpus; make a noisy disturbance.

ca·in·ca root (kə·ing'kə) The root of the tropical American snowberry: the bark of this root yields a glycoside used as a purgative. Also **ca·hin·ca root** (kə·hing'kə).

Cain·ite (kā'nīt) *n.* A member of a heretical sect of the second century which professed reverence for Cain, Esau, and other wicked Old Testament characters. —**Cain'ism** *n.* —**Cain·it·ic** (kā·nit'ik) *adj.*

Cai·no·zo·ic (kī'nə·zō'ik) See CENOZOIC.

ca·ique (kä·ēk') *n.* 1 A long, narrow, pointed skiff with from two to ten oars, used on the Bosporus. 2 A small Levantine sailing vessel. [< F < Ital. *caicco* < Turkish *qāyiq*]

cairn (kârn) *n.* A mound or heap of stones for a memorial or a marker. [< Scottish Gaelic *carn* heap of stones] —**cairned** *adj.*

cairn·gorm (kârn'gôrm) *n.* A smoky, yellow to brown variety of quartz; smoky quartz. [from *Cairngorm* Mountains]

Cai·ro (kī′rō) **1** The capital of Egypt and the largest city of Africa, on the east bank of the Nile at the head of its delta: an inhabitant of the city known as a **Cai·rene** (kī·rēn′). **2** (kâr′ō) A city in Illinois at the confluence of the Mississippi and Ohio Rivers.

cais·son (kā′sən, -son) *n.* **1** An amfjmunition chest or wagon. **2** A two-wheeled vehicle carrying such a chest to serve a gun in firing position with its immediate needs in ammunition. **3** A large watertight chamber within which work is done under water, as on a bridge pier. **4** A watertight box, or other apparatus, to be placed beneath a sunken vessel and inflated in order to raise it. **5** A gate for closing the entrance to a drydock. [< F, aug. of *caisse* box, chest]

CAISSON
A. Airlocks.   *B.* Shafts for entrance of men and materials.   *C.* Work chamber. *D.* Water level.   *E.* River bottom.   *F.* Bedrock.

caisson disease Decompression sickness.
cai·tiff (kā′tif) *n.* A base wretch. —*adj.* Vile; basely wicked. [< AF *caitif* weak, wretched < L *captivus.* Doublet of CAPTIVE.]
Cai·us (kā′əs, kī′) See GAIUS.
Ca·jal (kä·häl′) See RAMÓN Y CAJAL.
caj·e·put (kaj′ə·pət) *n.* **1** The California laurel (*Umbellularia californica*). **2** The cajuput. [< Malay *kāyupūtih* < *kāyu* tree + *pūtih* white]
ca·jole (kə·jōl′) *v.* **ca·joled, ca·jol·ing** *v.t.* To persuade or coax with flattery or delusive promises. —*v.i.* To wheedle; to practice cajolery. See synonyms under ALLURE. [< F *cajoler*] — **ca·jole′ment** *n.* — **ca·jol′er** *n.* —**ca·jol′ing·ly** *adv.*
ca·jol·er·y (kə·jō′lər·ē) *n. pl.* **·er·ies** The act of cajoling; the art or practice of wheedling by flattery.
ca·jon (kä·hōn′) *n. pl.* **ca·jo·nes** (kä·hō′nās) *SW U.S.* A canyon or narrow gorge with steep sides. [< Sp.]
Ca·jun (kā′jən) *n.* A reputed descendant of the Acadian French in Louisiana. [Alter. of ACADIAN]
caj·u·put (kaj′ə·pət) *n.* **1** A small tree (*Melaleuca leucadendron*) of the myrtle family, native in the Moluccas. **2** A greenish-yellow, odorous oil distilled from the fresh leaves and twigs of this tree: used chiefly in the treatment of skin diseases. Also **caj′a·put.** Sometimes spelled *cajeput, kajeput.* [See CAJEPUT]
cake (kāk) *n.* **1** A baked mixture of flour, eggs, milk, etc.: distinguished from bread or pudding. **2** A small or thin mass of dough, etc., baked or fried: *pancake.* **3** A hardened mass of any material: a *cake* of soap, etc. **4** *Pathol.* A morbid hardening or coagulation in the body. —**to take the cake** *Colloq.* To take the prize; be the best of or at something. —*v.t.* & *v.i.* **caked, cak·ing** To form into a hardened mass. [< ON *kaka*]
cakes and ale A carefree way of life; soft, easy living.
cake urchin A sea urchin (family *Clypeastridae*) having a disklike body with a raised central surface and a mass of velvety spines.
cake·walk (kāk′wôk) *n.* **1** Originally, a promenade or march of American Negro origin in which a cake is awarded as prize for the most original steps. **2** A dance based on this or the music for such a dance. —*v.i.* To do a cakewalk; strut. —**cake′walk′er** *n.*
cal·a·bar (kal′ə·bär) *n.* **1** The pelt of the gray Siberian squirrel. **2** The squirrel. Also **cal′a·ber** (-bər). [< F *Calabre* Calabria]
Calabar bean The highly poisonous seed of an African twining climber (*Physostigma venenosum*) of the bean family, the source of physostigmine: also called, from its use as a native test for crime or witchcraft, *ordeal bean.*
cal·a·ba·zil·la (kal′ə·bə·sēl′yə) *n.* A squash (*Cucurbita foetidissima*), the macerated root of

which is used as a remedy for hemorrhoids and the pulp of its green fruit as soap. [< Sp., dim. of *calabaza* gourd]
ca·la·di·um (kə·lā′dē·əm) *n.* One of a genus (*Caladium*) of tuberous tropical American herbs of the arum family with large, variegated sagittate leaves. [< NL < Malay *kēlādy*]
Cal·ais (kal′ā, ka·lā′, kal′is; *Fr.* kà·le′) A French port on the English Channel, facing Dover.
cal·a·man·co (kal′ə·mang′kō) *n.* **1** A glossy, woolen, Flemish fabric, or a garment made from it. **2** A glazed linen stuff. Also spelled *calimanco.* [< Sp.]
cal·a·man·der (kal′ə·man′dər) *n.* The wood of various trees of the ebony family, especially the rare *Diospyros quaesita* of Ceylon, finely veined, hard, and valued for cabinetwork. [Alter. of *Coromandel* (Coast)]
cal·a·mar·y (kal′ə·mâr′ē, -mər·ē) *n. pl.* **·mar·ies** A squid. [< L *calamarius* < *calamus* pen < Gk. *kalamos* reed]
cal·am·bak (kal·am·bak′) *n.* A wood used in fine inlay work; also called *aloes wood.*
cal·a·mif·er·ous (kal′ə·mif′ər·əs) *adj.* Bearing reeds [< CALAMUS + L *ferre* bear]
ca·lam·i·form (kə·lam′ə·fôrm) *adj.* Shaped like a reed.
cal·a·mine (kal′ə·mīn, -min) *n.* **1** Hemimorphite. **2** Smithsonite. **3** A native zinc carbonate, a pink powder much used in the form of a zinc and ferric oxide as a lotion or ointment for the treatment of skin ailments. —*v.t.* **·mined, ·min·ing** To apply calamine to. [< F < LL *calamina* < L *cadmia.* See CADMIUM.]
cal·a·mint (kal′ə·mint) *n.* A menthaceous plant (genus *Satureia*) of the north temperate zone, especially *S. calamintha.* Also **calamint balm.** [< MF *calament* < Med. L *calamentum* < L *calaminthe* < Gk. *kalaminthē*]
cal·a·mite (kal′ə·mīt) *n.* A fossil plant (genus *Calamites,* division *Pteridophyta*) of the later Paleozoic era, resembling the modern horsetails in general appearance but growing to a height of 100 feet and more. [< NL *calamites* < L *calamus* reed]
ca·lam·i·tous (kə·lam′ə·təs) *adj.* Disastrous; causing or resulting in a calamity. —**ca·lam′i·tous·ly** *adv.*
ca·lam·i·ty (kə·lam′ə·tē) *n. pl.* **·ties** **1** A misfortune or disaster. **2** A state or time of affliction, adversity, or disaster. See synonyms under ACCIDENT, ADVERSITY, BLOW, CATASTROPHE, MISFORTUNE. [< F *calamité* < L *calamitas*]
cal·a·mus (kal′ə·məs) *n. pl.* **·mi** (-mī) **1** The sweetflag. **2** The quill of a feather. [< L < Gk. *kalamos* reed]
Cal·a·mus (kal′ə·məs) *n.* A genus of oriental climbing palms; the climbing rattans. [See CALAMUS]
ca·lan·do (kä·län′dō) *adj.* & *adv. Music* Diminishing in strength of tone and in rapidity. [< Ital.]
cal·a·ver·ite (kal′ə·vâr′īt) *n.* A telluride of gold and silver, usually granular in structure, with a silvery-white metallic luster: an important ore of gold. [from *Calaveras* County, Calif.]
cal·ca·ne·um (kal·kā′nē·əm) *n. pl.* **·ne·a** (-nē·ə) *Anat.* The heel bone. See illustration under FOOT. Also **cal·ca′ne·us.** [< L *calx* heel]
cal·car[1] (kal′kär) *n.* **1** A calcining oven. **2** An annealing oven. [< L *calcaria* limekiln]
cal·car[2] (kal′kär) *n. pl.* **cal·car·i·a** (kal·kâr′ē·ə) *Biol.* A spur, or spurlike projection, as at the base of a petal or on the leg or wing of a bird. [< L, spur < *calx* heel]
cal·ca·rate (kal′kə·rāt, -rit) *adj. Biol.* Having a calcar, or spur; spurred. Also **cal′ca·rat′ed.**
cal·car·e·ous (kal·kâr′ē·əs) *adj.* **1** Composed of, containing, or of the nature of limestone or calcium carbonate. **2** Containing calcium. [< L *calcarius* of lime < *calx* lime]
cal·ca·rif·er·ous (kal′kə·rif′ər·əs) *adj. Biol.* Bearing spurs.
cal·ce·ate (kal′sē·āt, -it) *adj.* Wearing shoes; shod: said of certain religious orders. [< L *calceatus,* pp. of *calceare* shoe]
cal·ced·o·ny (kal·sed′ə·nē) See CHALCEDONY.
cal·ce·o·lar·i·a (kal·sē·ə·lâr′ē·ə) *n.* A member of a large genus (*Calceolaria*) of herbs and shrubs of the figwort family, with opposite leaves and small axillary or racemose flowers having the

lowest petal the longest: also called *slipperwort.* [< L *calceolus,* dim. of *calceus* shoe]
cal·ce·o·late (kal′sē·ə·lāt) *adj. Bot.* Slipper-shaped. —**cal′ce·o·late′ly** *adv.*
calci- *combining form* Lime: *calciferous.* [< L *calx, calcis* lime]
cal·cic (kal′sik) *adj.* Of, pertaining to, or containing calcium or lime. [< L *calx* lime]
cal·ci·co·sis (kal′si·kō′sis) *n. Pathol.* A disease of the lungs occurring among workers in limestone dust. [< L *calx* lime + -OSIS]
cal·cif·er·ol (kal·sif′ər·ōl, -ol) *n. Biochem.* The anti-rachitic vitamin D[2], a white, crystalline, fat-soluble, accessory food factor, C[28]H[44]O, formed by the ultraviolet irradiation of ergosterol: found in fish oils, milk, eggs, etc. [< CALCIFER(OUS) + (ERGOSTER)OL]
cal·cif·er·ous (kal·sif′ər·əs) *adj.* Yielding or containing calcium carbonate, as rocks. Also **cal·cif·ic** (kal·sif′ik).
cal·ci·fi·ca·tion (kal′sə·fi·kā′shən) *n.* **1** Conversion into chalk, or into stony or bony substance, by the deposition of lime salts, as in petrifaction and ossification. **2** Such a lime formation. **3** *Pathol.* A petrifactive retrogression observed in tissue which has degenerated. **4** The accumulation by a surface soil of sufficient calcium to bring soil colloids close to saturation, as in Chernozem soils.
cal·ci·form[1] (kal′sə·fôrm) *adj.* **1** *Obs.* Having the form of lime or chalk. **2** Pebble-shaped.
cal·ci·form[2] (kal′sə·fôrm) *adj.* Having a projection like a heel. [< L *calx* heel + -FORM]
cal·ci·fy (kal′sə·fī) *v.t.* & *v.i.* **·fied, ·fy·ing** To make or become stony by the deposit of lime salts.
cal·ci·mine (kal′sə·mīn, -min) *n.* A white or tinted wash consisting of whiting, or zinc white, with glue and water, for ceilings, walls, etc. —*v.t.* **·mined, ·min·ing** To apply calcimine to. Also spelled *kalsomine.* [< L *calx* lime]
cal·ci·na·to·ry (kal·sin′ə·tôr′ē, -tō′rē) *adj.* For calcining. —*n. pl.* **·ries** An apparatus for calcining, as a calcining furnace. [< LL *calcinatorium* < *calcinare* calcine]
cal·cine (kal′sin, -sin) *v.* **·cined, ·cin·ing** *v.t.* **1** To expel volatile matter (as carbon dioxide or water) from (a substance) by heat, for the purpose of rendering it friable: to *calcine* limestone. **2** To reduce to a calx, as copper ore, by subjecting to heat; roast. —*v.i.* **3** To become changed by the action of dry heat into a friable powder. Also **cal′cin·ize.** [< F *calciner* < Med. L *calcinare* < *calx* lime] —**cal′cined** *adj.* —**cal·ci·na·tion** (kal′sə·nā′shən) *n.*
cal·cite (kal′sīt) *n.* A widely diffused calcium carbonate, CaCO[3], usually colorless or whitish in hexagonal crystals: massive varieties include chalk, limestone, and marble. See ICELAND SPAR. —**cal·cit·ic** (kal·sit′ik) *adj.*
cal·ci·um (kal′sē·əm) *n.* An abundant, silvery-white metallic element (symbol Ca, atomic number 20) belonging to the alkaline-earth group and forming an essential constituent of living organisms. See PERIODIC TABLE. [< L *calx* lime]
calcium carbide *Chem.* A compound, CaC[2], made from quicklime and carbon in an electric furnace: treated with water it yields acetylene. Also **calcium acetylide.**
calcium carbonate *Chem.* A fine white amorphous powder, CaCO[3]: used in toothpowders and dental cements.
calcium chloride *Chem.* A white, very deliquescent, hygroscopic salt, CaCl[2]: used as a drying agent, preservative, refrigerant, and to prevent dust.
calcium cyanamide *Chem.* A compound, CaCN[2], produced in the electric furnace from the nitrogen of the air; an artificial fertilizer.
calcium fluoride *Chem.* A white powder, CaF[2], which becomes luminous on the application of heat: used for etching glass and in the manufacture of enamels.
calcium hydroxide *Chem.* Slaked lime, Ca(OH)[2]; also used in solution; limewater.
calcium light A powerful light produced by the incandescence of lime in an oxyhydrogen flame; the Drummond light: limelight.
calcium phosphate *Chem.* Any of a class of earthy phosphates formed in various animal tis-

sues and otherwise; especially, tribasic calcium phosphate or bone ash, $Ca_3(PO_4)_2$, used as an antacid, polishing agent, etc.

calcium sulfate *Chem.* A white compound, $CaSO_4$, occurring in nature as anhydrite and as gypsum.

calc·sin·ter (kalk'sin'tər) *n.* A loose deposit of massive calcite in caverns or river beds; travertine. [< G *kalksinter* < *kalk* chalk (< L *calx* lime) + *sinter* slag]

calc·spar (kalk'spär') *n.* Crystallized carbonate of lime. [< CALC(AREOUS) + SPAR³]

calc·tuff (kalk'tuf') *n.* *Geol.* A porous deposit of carbonate of lime found in calcareous springs. Also **calc·tu·fa** (kalk'tōō'fə, -tyōō'-). [< CALC-(AREOUS) + TUFA]

cal·cu·la·ble (kal'kyə·lə·bəl) *adj.* Capable of being calculated, estimated, or forecast; reliable. —**cal'cu·la·bly** *adv.*

cal·cu·late (kal'kyə·lāt) *v.* **·lat·ed, ·lat·ing** *v.t.* **1** To determine by computation; arrive at by arithmetical means. **2** To predict or ascertain beforehand, as by computation: to *calculate* an eclipse. **3** To adapt or fit, as to a purpose or function: used chiefly in the passive: a truck *calculated* to carry a two-ton load. **4** To estimate or determine after deliberation; reckon: He *calculated* his chances. —*v.i.* **5** To perform a mathematical process; compute. **6** *U.S. Dial. & Colloq.* To suppose or believe; think. —**to calculate on** *Colloq.* To depend or rely on. [< LL *calculatus*, pp. of *calculare* reckon < *calculus* pebble < *calx* lime; with ref. to the use of pebbles in counting]

Synonyms: account, compute, consider, count, deem, enumerate, estimate, number, rate, reckon. *Number* is the generic term. To *count* is to *number* one by one. To *calculate* is to use more complicated processes, as multiplication, division, etc. *Compute* allows more of the element of probability, which is still more strongly expressed by *estimate*; as, to *estimate* the cost of a proposed building. To *enumerate* is to mention item by item; as to *enumerate* one's grievances. To *rate* is to *estimate* by comparison, as if the object were one of a series. We *count* upon a desired future; we do not *count* upon the undesired. As applied to the present we *reckon* or *count* a thing precious or worthless. Compare ESTEEM.

cal·cu·lat·ing (kal'kyə·lā'ting) *adj.* **1** Inclined to reckon or estimate, especially for one's own chances or interests; planning; scheming: a *calculating* politician. **2** Designed for computation: a *calculating* machine.

cal·cu·la·tion (kal'kyə·lā'shən) *n.* **1** The act or art of computing. **2** A computation; reckoning. **3** An estimate of probability; a forecast or deduction; the result of calculating. **4** Shrewd caution; prudence.

cal·cu·la·tive (kal'kyə·lā'tiv) *adj.* Of or pertaining to calculation; given to calculation.

cal·cu·la·tor (kal'kyə·lā'tər) *n.* **1** One who calculates. **2** A calculating machine or set of tables.

cal·cu·lous (kal'kyə·ləs) *adj.* **1** Stony; gritty. **2** Pertaining to, like, or affected with calculus. [< L *calculosus* gritty, pebbly]

cal·cu·lus (kal'kyə·ləs) *n. pl.* **·li** (-lī) or **·lus·es** **1** *Pathol.* A stonelike concretion, as in the bladder. **2** *Math.* A method of calculating by the use of a highly specialized system of algebraic symbols. —**differential calculus** That branch of analysis which investigates the infinitesimal changes of constantly varying quantities when the relations between the quantities are given. —**integral calculus** That branch of analysis which, from the relations among the infinitesimal changes or variations of quantities, deduces relations among the quantities themselves, as in finding the area enclosed by a given curve. [< L, a pebble (used in counting)]

Cal·cut·ta (kal·kut'ə) A port on the Hooghly; the largest city in India, and the capital of West Bengal.

cal·de·ra (kal·dē'rə, *Sp.* käl·dā'rä) *n.* **1** *Geol.* A large, roughly circular depression, in many cases with a partially broken-down rim, formed by the explosive disruption of a volcanic cone, or by the collapse of a crater floor. **2** A large caldron. [< Sp.]

cal·dron (kôl'drən) *n.* A large kettle or boiler: also spelled *cauldron*. [< AF *caudron* < L *caldaria* kettle < *calidus* hot]

cal·e·fa·cient (kal'ə·fā'shənt) *adj.* Causing heat or warmth. —*n.* *Med.* Something that produces heat or warmth, as a mustard plaster. [< L *calefaciens, -entis,* ppr. of *calefacere* < *calere* be warm + *facere* make, cause] —**cal'e·fac'tion** (-fak'shən) *n.* —**cal'e·fac'tive** *adj.*

cal·e·fac·to·ry (kal'ə·fak'tər·ē) *adj.* Adapted or used for heating or warming; communicating warmth. —*n.* An artificially warmed room in a monastery.

cal·en·dar (kal'ən·dər) *n.* **1** A systematic arrangement of subdivisions of time, as years, months, days, weeks, etc. **2** An almanac. **3** A schedule or list of things or events classified or chronologically arranged: a *calendar* of causes for trial in court. **4** *Obs.* A guide; example; model. —*v.t.* To register in a calendar or list; place in the calendar of saints; digest and index, as documents. ◆ Homophone: *calender.* [< L *calendarium* account book < *calendae* calends]

—**Chinese calendar** An ancient calendar, no longer in official use, with days and years reckoned in cycles of sixty. Each year consists of twelve lunar months, with adjustment to the solar year by periodic intercalation.

—**ecclesiastical calendar** A lunisolar calendar reckoning the year from the first Sunday in Advent: used for regulating the dates of church feasts.

—**Gregorian calendar** The calendar now in general use in most parts of the world; first prescribed in 1582 by Pope Gregory XIII to correct the Julian year to the solar year; adopted in England Sept. 3/14, 1752, the first being the *Old Style* (*O.S.*) date and the last being the *New Style* (*N.S.*). (Thus, although George Washington's birthday is commemorated on February 22, he was born on February 11, 1732, by the Old Style calendar.)

—**Hebrew calendar** The present-day calendar of the Jews, based on a lunar month, and adjusted to the solar year by intercalating the month Veadar between Adar and Nisan 7 times in a 19-year cycle. The months, having alternately 30 and 29 days, are Tishri, Heshwan, Kislew, Tebet, Shebat, Adar, Nisan, Iyyar, Siwan, Tammuz, Ab, and Elul; Heshwan and Kislew, however, may add or lose a day respectively as needed. The year now begins on Tishri 1, though anciently it began in Nisan. The Hebrew calendar reckons the creation at 3760 years 3 months B.C., as compared with Archbishop Ussher's 4004 B.C.

—**Julian calendar** The calendar prescribed by Julius Caesar, which, though using the bissextile year, was in error one day in 128 years. The months, after some changes by Augustus, had the length now in use in Europe and America.

—**Mohammedan calendar** A lunar calendar of 12 months dating from A.D. 622 (July 15), the year of the Hegira. There is no seasonal intercalation, the seasons retrogressing in a period of 32 1/2 years. The names of the months, alternately 29 and 30 days, are Muharram (30 days), Saphar, Rabia 1, Rabia 2, Jomada 1, Jomada 2, Rajab, Shaaban, Ramadan, Shawwal, Dulkaada, and Dulheggia.

—**Republican** or **Revolutionary calendar** The calendar instituted on Oct. 5, 1793, by the first French Republic, and abolished Dec. 31, 1805. Its scheme divided the year into 12 months of 30 days each, with five (in leap years, six) supplementary days (*sansculottides*) at the end of the last month. The first year (Year I) began Sept. 22, 1792. The months were: Vendémiaire, Brumaire, Frimaire, Nivose, Pluviose, Ventose, Germinal, Floréal, Prairial, Messidor, Thermidor (or Fervidor), and Fructidor.

—**Roman calendar** A lunar calendar, attributed to Numa. The day of the new moon was the *calends,* and the day of the full moon the *ides* (the 13th or 15th of the month). Days were reckoned backward from these dates and from the *nones,* ninth day before the ides by inclusive reckoning.

cal·en·der¹ (kal'ən·dər) *n.* A machine for giving a gloss to cloth, paper, etc., by pressing between rollers. —*v.t.* To press in a calender. ◆ Homophone: *calendar.* [< F *calendre* < L *cylindrus* < Gk. *kylindros* roller] —**cal'en·dered** *adj.* —**cal'en·der·er** *n.*

cal·en·der² (kal'ən·dər) *n.* A mendicant dervish

of Persia or Turkey. ◆ Homophone: *calendar.* [< Persian *qalandar*]

cal·ends (kal'əndz) *n. pl.* The first day of the Roman month: also spelled *kalends.* —**at** (or **on**) **the Greek calends** At a date that will never come, the Greeks having had no calends. [< L *calendae* calends]

ca·len·du·la (kə·len'jōō·lə) *n.* **1** Any of a small genus (*Calendula*) of annual or perennial herbs of the composite family, the pot marigolds, having alternate entire leaves, and heads of yellow or orange flowers. **2** The dried florets of this plant, containing a bitter principle used to promote the healing of wounds. [< NL, dim. of *calendae* calends; because it blooms almost every month]

cal·en·ture (kal'ən·chŏŏr) *n.* *Pathol.* **1** A tropical remittent fever caused by extreme heat and accompanied by delirium and hallucinations. **2** Sunstroke. [< F < Sp. *calentura* fever < L *calere* be warm]

ca·les·cence (kə·les'əns) *n.* The condition of growing warm; increasing warmth. [< L *calescens, -entis,* ppr. of *calescere,* inceptive of *calere* be warm] —**ca·les'cent** *adj.*

calf¹ (kaf, käf) *n. pl.* **calves** (kavz, kävz) **1** The young of the cow or various other bovine animals. ◆ Collateral adjective: *vituline.* **2** The young of various large mammals, as the elephant, whale, hippopotamus, etc. **3** The skin of the calf, or leather made from it: also *calfskin.* **4** *Colloq.* A raw, gawky, witless young person; a blockhead; dolt. **5** A floating fragment of ice near an iceberg. —**the golden calf 1** The molten image made by Aaron and worshiped by the Israelites. *Ex.* xxxii. **2** Riches, as unduly prized; mammon. [OE *cealf*]

calf² (kaf, käf) *n. pl.* **calves** (kavz, kävz) The muscular hinder part of the human leg below the knee. ◆ Collateral adjective: *sural.* [< ON *kálfi*]

calf's–foot jelly (kafs'fŏŏt', käfs'-) A gelatinous deposit sometimes found between the bones of calves' feet and processed by boiling: also spelled *calvesfoot jelly.*

calf·skin (kaf'skin', käf'-) *n.* **1** The skin or hide of a calf. **2** A kind of fine leather made from the skin of a calf. Also *calf.*

Cal·ga·ry (kal'gər·ē) A city in southern Alberta, Canada.

cal·i·ber (kal'ə·bər) *n.* **1** The internal diameter of a tube. **2** *Mil.* **a** The internal diameter of the barrel of a gun, cannon, etc., expressed in decimals of an inch for small arms, millimeters for rifles, centimeters for cannon. **b** The diameter of a bullet, shell, etc. **c** The ratio of the length of a gun's bore to its diameter: a unit of length. **3** Degree of individual capacity or intellectual power; personal ability, quality, or worth. Also **cal'i·bre.** [< F *calibre,* ? < Arabic *qālib* mold, form]

cal·i·brate (kal'ə·brāt) *v.t.* **·brat·ed, ·brat·ing 1** To graduate the tube of (a measuring instrument) into appropriate units. **2** To determine the reading of (such an instrument). **3** To ascertain the caliber of. [Cf. F *calibrer*] —**cal'i·bra'tion** *n.* —**cal'i·bra'tor** *n.*

ca·li·che (kä·lē'chä) *n.* **1** The native, impure sodium nitrate of Chile, $NaNO_3$; Chile saltpeter. **2** A calcareous sediment typical of soils in warm, semiarid, or desert regions. [< Am. Sp.]

cal·i·cle (kal'i·kəl) *n.* *Zool.* A small, cup-shaped part or organ, as a polyp cell in corals or a hydrotheca in hydrozoans; a calycle. [< L *caliculus,* dim. of *calix* cup]

cal·i·co (kal'i·kō) *n. pl.* **·coes** or **·cos 1** Any cheap cotton cloth printed in bright colors. **2** *Brit.* White cotton cloth. —*adj.* **1** Made of calico: a *calico* dress. **2** Resembling printed calico; dappled or streaked; variegated: a *calico* cat. [from *Calicut*]

cal·i·co·bush (kal'i·kō·bŏŏsh') *n.* The mountain laurel. Also **cal'i·co·tree'.**

ca·lic·u·la (kə·lik'yə·lə) See CALYCLE.

ca·lif (kā'lif, kal'if), **cal·i·fate** (kal'ə·fāt, -fit), etc. See CALIPH, etc.

Cal·i·for·nia (kal'ə·fôrn'yə, -fôr'nē·ə) A Pacific State of the United States; 156,803 square miles; capital, Sacramento; entered the Union Sept. 9, 1850: nickname *Golden State.* Abbr. CA

cal·i·for·nite (kal'ə·fôr'nīt) *n.* A compact variety of vesuvianite, resembling jade, found in California.

cal·i·for·ni·um (kal'ə·fôr'nē·əm) *n.* A synthetic

radioactive element (symbol Cf, atomic number 98), having isotopic mass numbers from 242 to 253 and half-lives ranging from 3.7 minutes to approximately 800 years. See PERIODIC TABLE. [< from the University of *California*, where first produced]

ca·lig·i·nous (kə·lij′ə·nəs) *adj.* Obscure; dark; dim. [< L *caliginosus* misty, dark < *caligo* fog, darkness] —**ca·lig′i·nous·ly** *adv.* —**ca·lig′i·nous·ness, ca·lig·i·nos′i·ty** (-nos′ə·tē) *n.*

cal·i·pash (kal′ə·pash, kal·ə·pash′) *n.* The part of a turtle next to the upper shell, a greenish gelatinous substance esteemed as a table delicacy: also spelled *callipash*. [? Alter. of Sp. *carapacho* carapace]

cal·i·pee (kal′ə·pē, kal·ə·pē′) *n.* The part of a turtle next the lower shell, a yellowish gelatinous edible substance: also spelled *callipee*. [Cf. CALIPASH.]

cal·i·per (kal′ə·pər) *n.* 1 An instrument like a pair of compasses, usually with curved legs, for measuring diameters: usually in the plural: also **caliper compass. 2** A caliper rule. —*v.t.* & *v.i.* To measure by using calipers. Also spelled *calliper*. [Var. of CALIBER]

TYPES OF CALIPERS
A. Graduating.   *B.* Inside.
C. Square or beam.   *D.* Outside adjusting.

ca·liph (kā′lif, kal′if) *n.* The spiritual and civil head of a Moslem state: title taken by the sultans of Turkey, abolished in 1924: also spelled *calif, kalif, khalif*. [< F *caliphe*. < Arabic *khalīfah* successor (to Mohammed)] —**cal·i·phate** (kal′ə·fāt, -fit) *n.*

cal·i·sa·ya (kal′ə·sā′ə) *n.* Cinchona; specifically, the species rich in quinine, *Cinchona calisaya*: also called *yellowbark*. [< Sp. < Quechua]

cal·is·then·ics (kal′is·then′iks) *n. pl.* 1 Light gymnastics to promote grace and health: construed as plural. 2 The science of such exercises: construed as singular. Also spelled *callisthenics*. [< Gk. *kalli-* < *kalos* beautiful + *sthenos* strength] —**cal·is·then′ic** *adj.*

ca·lix (kā′liks kal′iks) *n. pl.* **cal·i·ces** (kāl′ə·sēz) 1 A cup; hence, any cup-shaped organ or part. 2 *Eccl.* A chalice. Compare CALYX. [< L, cup]

calk[1] (kôk) *v.t. Naut.* To make tight, as a boat's seams, by plugging with soft material, as oakum or hemp fiber. 2 To hammer or fasten together, as the edges of the plates of a boiler. 3 To plug up the crevices of, as a window frame. Also spelled *caulk*. [< OF *cauquer* < L *calcare* tread] —**calk′ing** *n.*

calk[2] (kôk) *n.* 1 A spur on a horse's shoe to prevent slipping. 2 A plate with sharp points worn on the sole of a person's boot or shoe to prevent slipping. Also **calk′er, calk′in.** —*v.t.* 1 To furnish with calks. 2 To wound with a calk. [Prob. < L *calx* heel]

call (kôl) *v.t.* 1 To appeal to by word of mouth. 2 To utter or read aloud. 3 To summon in any way; convoke, as Congress; convene; invoke solemnly: to *call* God to witness. 4 To designate or characterize in any way; name; style; suppose; assume to be so much. 5 To read aloud from a list of names: *Call* the roll. 6 To arouse, as from sleep. 7 To designate for a special work: to *call* to the ministry. 8 To lure (birds or animals) by imitating their cry with a whistle, call, or other imitative means. 9 To insist upon payment of, as by written notice. 10 To communicate by telephone. 11 To fix the time for; bring to action: to *call* a case to court. 12 *Colloq.* In the game of pool, to designate (a shot), before making the play. 13 In baseball, to stop or suspend (a game) because of rain, darkness, etc. —*v.i.* 14 To lift up

the voice in address, command, or entreaty; send out a cry of summons; appeal; sound a signal. 15 To communicate by telephone: I will *call* tomorrow. 16 To make a brief visit, stop or stay: followed by *at, on,* or *upon*: The steamer *calls* at Southampton. 17 In poker, to demand a show of hands, upon staking an amount equal to the bet of each previous player. 18 In whist and other card games, to make a demand or give a signal, as for trumps or for a particular card. 19 To ask for a showdown on anything. —**to call back 1** To summon back; recall; revoke; retract. 2 To call in return, as by telephone. —**to call one's bluff** To take a challenge; ask for a showdown. —**to call down 1** To pray heaven to send or cause to descend: to *call down* the wrath of the gods. 2 To rebuke; reprimand. —**to call off 1** To count; announce. 2 To cancel. —**to call out 1** To shout. 2 To bring an actor or actress out before the curtains by applause. 3 To summon workers to go out on strike. —**to call up 1** To bring before the memory or mind's eye. 2 To bring up for action or discussion, as a legislative measure. 3 To demand payment of, as amounts due on shares. 4 To notify to appear before some tribunal, as a court; cite. 5 To notify to appear for induction into the armed forces; also, to summon (troops) for active service. 6 To summon to stand up and speak. 7 To communicate with by telephone. —*n.* 1 A shout or cry to attract attention or response. 2 A lifting up of the voice in speech or other utterance; specifically, a thing called or indicated. 3 A summons or invitation; also, a roll call, a bugle call, or telephone call. 4 A requirement; claim; right; obligation: the *call* of duty. 5 A brief visit. 6 An assessment or demand; specifically, a contract requiring, in consideration of money paid, the delivery of some article named, as stocks, at a certain price. Compare PUT *n.* (def. 2). 7 A request by a government or corporation that holders of its redeemable bonds present them for payment. 8 An assessment on the members of a corporation or joint-stock company for the payment of subscription instalments, or for cash to meet losses. 9 A blast on a hunting horn to encourage the hounds. 10 The characteristic cry of an animal or a bird. 11 *Law* A visible natural object or an established point mentioned in the descriptive part of a deed for tracing a line of vision or boundary: a *call* of the deed. 12 An inward urge to a certain line of work; a vocation. 13 *Colloq.* Right or occasion for: You've no *call* to do that. 14 In poker, a demand for a show of hands: made only after equaling preceding bets. 15 A notice of rehearsals, instructions to actors, etc., posted on the callboard. —**at (or on) call** Payable on demand, or without previous notice, as a loan or deposit. —**to have the call** To have the advantage; also, to be the leader in popular favor. —**within call** Readily accessible or within hearing; also, subject to call. ♦ Homophone: *caul*. [< ON *kalla*]

Synonyms (verb): bawl, bellow, clamor, cry, ejaculate, exclaim, roar, scream, shout, shriek, vociferate, yell. To *call* is to send out the voice in order to attract another's attention, either by word or by inarticulate utterance. Animals *call* their mates, or their young; a man *calls* his dog, his horse, etc. The sense is extended to include summons by bell or other audible signal. To *shout* is to *call* or *exclaim* with the fullest volume of sustained voice; to *scream* or *shriek* is to utter a shriller cry. We *shout* words; in *screaming, shrieking,* or *yelling* there is often no attempt at articulation. To *bawl* is to utter senseless, noisy cries, like a child in pain or anger. *Bellow* and *roar* are applied to the utterances of animals, and only figuratively to those of persons. To *clamor* is to utter with noisy iteration; it applies also to the confused cries of a multitude. To *vociferate* is commonly applied to loud, excited speech. One may *exclaim,* or *ejaculate* with no thought of others' presence; when he *calls,* it is to attract another's attention. See CONVOKE, EXCLAIM. *Antonyms,* harken, hush, list, listen.

cal·la (kal′ə) *n.* 1 A South African plant (*Zantedeschia aethiopica*) of the arum family, with a large, milk-white spathe that resembles a flower: also called *lily-of-the-Nile*. 2 A marsh plant of North America and Europe (*Calla palustris*) bearing red berries in dense clusters. Also **calla lily.** [< L *calla,* a plant name]

call·er[1] (kô′lər) *n.* 1 One who or that which calls. 2 One making a brief, formal visit. 3 A head waiter. 4 In square dancing, one who calls the successive steps of a set.

call girl *Colloq.* A prostitute who goes to assignations in response to telephone calls.

calli- For words not found here, see under CALI-

cal·li·graph (kal′ə·graf, -gräf) *n.* A specimen of beautiful or ornamental penmanship.

cal·lig·ra·phy (kə·lig′rə·fē) *n.* 1 Beautiful penmanship. 2 Handwriting in general. [< Gk. *kalligraphia* < *kalos* beautiful + *graphein* write] —**cal·lig′ra·pher, cal·lig′ra·phist** *n.* —**cal·li·graph·ic** (kal′ə·graf′ik) *adj.* —**cal′li·graph′i·cal·ly** *adv.*

call·ing (kô′ling) *n.* 1 A speaking, crying, or shouting to command attention. 2 A convocation or summoning. 3 A solemn appointment or summons. 4 Habitual occupation; profession; vocation; business. 5 Social condition or status; rank.

cal·li·o·pe (kə·lī′ə·pē, kal′ē·ōp) *n.* A musical instrument consisting of a series of steam whistles played by means of a keyboard; a steam organ. [after *Calliope*]

cal·li·op·sis (kal′ē·op′sis) See COREOPSIS.

cal·li·per (kal′ə·pər) See CALIPER.

cal·li·pyg·i·an (kal′ə·pij′ē·ən) *adj.* Having beautiful buttocks. Also **cal′li·py′gous** (-pī′gəs). [< Gk. *kallipygos* < *kalos* beautiful + *pygē* buttocks]

cal·lis·then·ics (kal′is·then′iks) See CALISTHENICS.

cal·li·type (kal′ə·tīp) *v.t.* **·typed, ·typ·ing** To make a copy of (reading matter) on printing plates by photoengraving typewritten sheets. [< *calli-* beautiful (< Gk. *kalos*) + -TYPE] —**cal′li·typ′y** *n.*

call letters The code letters identifying a radio or television transmitting station.

call number A classifying number employed by libraries to indicate the subject and author of a book and its place on the shelves.

cal·lose (kal′ōs) *n. Biochem.* A hard, thick, insoluble carbohydrate assumed to develop in the cell walls of certain plants. [< L *callosus* hard-skinned]

cal·los·i·ty (kə·los′ə·tē) *n. pl.* **·ties 1** *Physiol.* A thickened, hardened portion of the skin, produced by or as by pressure or friction. 2 *Biol.* A hard or thickened part, as on the legs of horses, on or in a plant, etc.; a callus. 3 Hardness; insensibility.

cal·lous (kal′əs) *adj.* 1 Thickened and hardened, as the skin by friction or pressure. 2 Hardened in feeling; insensible; unfeeling. See synonyms under HARD. ♦ Homophone: *callus*. [< L *callosus* < *callus* hard skin] —**cal·loused** (kal′əst) *adj.* —**cal′lous·ly** *adv.* —**cal′lous·ness** *n.*

cal·low (kal′ō) *adj.* 1 Unfledged; not yet feathered, as a bird. 2 Inexperienced; youthful. 3 Of or pertaining to an unfledged bird or a youth. [OE *calu* bare, bald]

cal·lus (kal′əs) *n. pl.* **·lus·es 1** A callosity or thickening. 2 *Physiol.* The new bony tissue between and around the fractured ends of a broken bone in the process of reuniting. 3 *Bot.* The parenchymatous tissue which forms over a cut on a stem and protects the exposed wood. —*v.i.* To form a callosity or callus. ♦ Homophone: *callous*. [< L, hard skin]

calm (käm) *adj.* Free from disturbance or agitation; without motion; in repose; also, unmoved by passion or emotion; serene. —*n.* 1 Stillness; serenity. 2 Lack of wind or motion. See synonyms under REST. —*v.t.* To bring into repose; still; soothe. —*v.i.* To become quiet or placid. See synonyms under ALLAY, SETTLE. [< MF *calme* < Ital. *calma* < LL *cauma* heat of the day < Gk. *kauma* heat; with ref. to the rest or siesta at midday]

— **calm'ly** *adv.* — **calm'ness** *n.*

Synonyms (adj.): collected, composed, cool, dispassionate, imperturbable, peaceful, placid, quiet, sedate, self-controlled, self-possessed, serene, smooth, still, tranquil, undisturbed, unruffled. That is *calm* which is free from disturbance or agitation; in the physical sense, free from violent motion or action; in the mental or spiritual sense, free from excited or disturbing emotion or passion. We speak of a *calm* sea, a *placid* lake, a *serene* sky, a *still* night, a *quiet* home. We speak, also, of *still* waters, *smooth* sailing, which are different modes of expressing freedom from manifest agitation. *Cool,* in this connection, always suggests the recognition of some form of danger or risk. One may be *calm* by assured superiority to danger, by ignorance of its existence or of its magnitude, or by indifference to the result, or by the apathy of hopelessness, as we speak of the *calmness* of despair; one is *cool* who, while intensely alive to danger or need, has all his faculties concentrated on the means of meeting or overcoming it; a *calm* boxer would probably be an easy victim, while a *cool* boxer would be a dangerous antagonist. *Cool* is stronger than *composed* or *collected.* One is *composed* who has subdued excited feeling; he is *collected* when he has every thought, feeling, or perception awake and at command. *Tranquil* refers to a present state, *placid* to a prevailing tendency. We speak of a *tranquil* mind, a *placid* disposition. The *serene* spirit dwells as if in the clear upper air, above all storm or agitation. See PACIFIC, SOBER. *Antonyms:* agitated, boisterous, disturbed, excited, fierce, frantic, frenzied, furious, heated, passionate, raging, roused, ruffled, stormy, turbulent, violent, wild, wrathful.

cal·ma·tive (kal′mə·tiv, kä′mə-) *adj.* Having a soothing effect; sedative. — *n.* A sedative; tranquilizer.

cal·o·mel (kal′ə-mel, -məl) *n. Med.* Mercurous chloride, HgCl, a heavy, white, tasteless compound: used as a purgative. [< F < Gk. *kalos* beautiful + *melas* black]

cal·o·mon·din (kal′ə-mon′din) *n.* A hardy orange (*Citrus mitis*) with a small, acid, orange-red fruit.

cal·o·res·cence (kal′ə-res′əns) *n. Physics* The generation of visible light from invisible heat radiation, as by directing a stream of infrared rays upon a thin platinum plate. [< L *calor* heat + -ESCENCE]

ca·lor·ic (kə-lôr′ik, -lor′-) *adj.* Of or pertaining to heat. — *n.* 1 Heat. 2 Formerly, a supposed principle of heat. [< F *calorique* < L *calor* heat]

cal·o·ric·i·ty (kal′ə-ris′ə·tē) *n.* The power of developing heat, possessed by animals.

cal·o·rie (kal′ə-rē) *n.* 1 One of two recognized units of heat used especially to express the heat- or energy-producing content of foods. The **great, greater, large,** or **kilogram calorie** is the amount of heat required to raise the temperature of one kilogram of water 1° C. The **lesser, small,** or **gram calorie** is the amount of heat required to raise one gram of water 1° C. 2 *Physiol.* The large calorie, used as a measure of the energy value of foods or the heat output of organisms. Also **cal′o·ry.** [< F *calorie* < L *calor* heat]

cal·o·rif·ic (kal′ə-rif′ik) *adj.* 1 Able to produce heat; heating. 2 Carrying or conducting heat; thermal. Also **cal′o·rif′i·cal.** [< F *calorifique* < L *calorificus*]

cal·o·rif·i·ca·tion (kə-lôr′ə·fi·kā′shən, -lor′-) *n.* The production of heat.

calorific power The heat resulting from complete combustion of a gram of fuel. Also **calorific value.**

cal·o·rif·ics (kal′ə-rif′iks) *n.* 1 The science of heating. 2 The branch of physics that treats of heat.

cal·o·rim·e·ter (kal′ə-rim′ə·tər) *n.* Any apparatus for measuring the quantity of heat generated by friction, combustion, or chemical change. — **bomb calorimeter** A calorimeter in the form of a steel-walled container in which measured quantities of fuel or other substances may be burned to determine their calorific value. [< L *calor* heat + -METER] — **ca·lo·ri·met·ric** (kə-lôr′ə·met′rik, -lor′-) or **-met′ri·cal** *adj.* — **cal′o·rim′e·try** *n.*

cal·trop (kal′trəp) *n.* 1 *Mil.* A small iron instrument shaped like a ball from which four sharp-pointed curved spikes project and are so mounted that one is always upright: formerly used to impede cavalry or infantry. 2 One of various plants with spiny heads or fruit that entangle the feet, as the **hairy caltrop** (*Kalestroemia hirsutissima*), the puncturevine, the star thistle, and the water chestnut. Also **cal′trap** (-trəp). [OE *coltetraeppe* < L *calx* heel + LL *trappa* trap]

cal·u·met (kal′yə-met, kal′yə-met′) *n.* A tobacco pipe with a long, ornamented reed stem, and, usually, a red clay bowl: used by American Indians in religious and magic ceremonies, to ratify war and peace treaties, etc.: often called *peace pipe.* [< F, pipe stem < L *calamellus,* dim. of *calamus* reed]

CALUMET

ca·lum·ni·ate (kə·lum′nē·āt) *v.t.* & *v.i.* ·at·ed, ·at·ing To accuse falsely; defame; slander. See synonyms under ASPERSE, REVILE. [< L *calumniatus,* pp. of *calumniari* slander < *calumnia* slander] — **ca·lum′ni·a′tion** *n.* — **ca·lum′ni·a′tor** *n.* — **ca·lum·ni·a·to·ry** (kə·lum′·nē·ə·tôr′ē, -tō′rē) *adj.*

ca·lum·ni·ous (kə·lum′nē·əs) *adj.* Slanderous; defamatory. — **ca·lum′ni·ous·ly** *adv.*

cal·um·ny (kal′əm·nē) *n. pl.* ·nies A false, malicious, and injurious accusation or report; defamation; slander. See synonyms under SCANDAL. [< MF *calomnie* < L *calumnia* slander. Doublet of CHALLENGE.]

cal·u·tron (kal′yə·tron) *n.* An electromagnetic device for the separation of isotopes, especially in the study and production of atomic energy. [< CAL(IFORNIA) U(NIVERSITY) (CY-CLO)TRON]

cal·va·ry (kal′vər·ē) *n. pl.* ·ries A sculptured representation of the Crucifixion, usually erected in the open air.

calves (kavz, kävz) Plural of CALF.

Cal·vin (kal′vin), **John,** 1509–64, French Protestant reformer.

Cal·vin·ism (kal′vin·iz′əm) *n.* 1 *Theol.* **a** The system or doctrines of John Calvin, emphasizing the depravity and helplessness of man, the sovereignty of God, and predestination, and characterized by an austere moral code. **b** Any later system based upon the teachings of Calvin. 2 Belief in or support for such a system. — **Cal′vin·ist** *n.*

Cal·vin·is·tic (kal′vin·is′tik) *adj.* 1 Pertaining to Calvinism or Calvinists. 2 Austere: strict; severe. — **Cal′vin·is′ti·cal** *adj.* — **Cal′vin·is′ti·cal·ly** *adv.*

cal·vi·ti·es (kal·vish′i·ēz) *n.* Baldness, especially on the top or back of the head. [< L *calvus* bald]

calx (kalks) *n. pl.* **calx·es** or **cal·ces** (kal′sēz) 1 The residue from the calcination of minerals. 2 Lime or chalk. [< L]

cal·y·cine (kal′ə·sin, -sīn) *adj.* 1 Of or pertaining to a calyx. 2 Of the nature of, situated on, or like a calyx. Also **ca·lyc·i·nal** (kə·lis′ə·nəl). [< L *calyx.* See CALYX.]

cal·y·cle (kal′i·kəl) *n. Bot.* An accessory calyx outside of the true calyx: also called *calicula.* [< L *caliculus,* dim. of *calyx*]

ca·lyc·u·lar (kə·lik′yə·lər) *adj.* Having calycles. Also **ca·lyc′u·late** (-lāt, -lit).

ca·lyc·u·lus (kə·lik′yə·ləs) See CALYCLE.

ca·lyp·so¹ (kə·lip′sō) *n.* Any orchid of the genus *Cytherea,* having only one species (*C. bulbosa*), growing in boggy regions of northern Europe and North America. [after *Calypso*]

ca·lyp·so² (kə·lip′sō) *n.* A type of song, originally improvised and sung by natives of Trinidad, dealing with topical, sexual, or humorous themes and achieving its effect by only approximate rime, flexible syllabic emphasis, and colloquial language. [Origin uncertain]

ca·lyp·tra (kə·lip′trə) *n.* 1 A hood or lid. 2 *Bot.* **a** In mosses, the hood or covering of the capsule. **b** In flowering plants, any similar hood-shaped organ. Also **ca·lyp′ter** (-tər). [< NL < Gk. *kalyptra* veil < *kalyptein* cover]

ca·lyp·trate (kə·lip′trāt) *adj.* Covered with, having, or like a calyptra.

ca·lyx (kā′liks, kal′iks) *n. pl.* **ca·lyx·es** or **cal·y·ces** (kā′lə·sēz, kal′ə-) 1 The outermost series of leaflike parts of a flower, individually called sepals: usually green and more or less leaf-shaped, but frequently colored and petaloid. Compare COROLLA. 2 *Zool.* A cup-shaped part or organ. Compare CALIX. [< L < Gk. *kalyx* husk, pod]

cam (kam) *n. Mech.* A rotating piece of irregular shape, as on a wheel in a machine: used to change the direction of the motion of another part moving against it, as rotary into reciprocating or variable motion. [< Du. *cam* tooth, cog of a wheel]

ca·ma·ra·de·rie (kä′mə·rä′dər·ē) *n.* Comradeship; loyalty; fellowship. Also **com′rade·ry.** [< F]

cam·a·ril·la (kam′ə·ril′ə, *Sp.* kä·mä·rē′lyä) *n.* 1 A group of unofficial advisers, as of a king; a clique of persons exercising political powers secretly and unofficially; a cabal. 2 A little chamber; especially, the audience chamber of a king. [< Sp., dim. of *camara* chamber]

cam·as (kam′əs) *n.* 1 Any of several North American bulbous herbs of the lily family (genus *Camassia*); especially, *C. quamash,* having an edible bulb. 2 The death camas. Sometimes spelled *cammas, quamash.* Also **cam′ass.** [< Chinook jargon]

Cam·bay (kam·bā′) A town of northern Bombay state, India; capital of the former princely state of Cambay, on the **Gulf of Cambay,** an inlet of the Arabian Sea between Bombay and Kathiawar peninsula.

cam·ber (kam′bər) *v.t.* To cut or bend to a slight upward convex form. — *v.i.* To have or assume a slight upward convex curve, as a ship's, deck. — *n.* A slight upward bend or convexity, as of a timber or an airfoil; a slight central rise. [< MF *cambrer* arch < L *camerare* < *camera* curved roof, vault]

cam·bist (kam′bist) *n.* 1 A manual giving the moneys, weights, and measures of different countries, and their equivalents. 2 One versed in exchange values. [< F *cambiste* < Ital. *cambista* b < LL *cambiare* exchange]

cam·bi·um (kam′bē·əm) *n. Bot.* A zone of cells which generate new phloem and xylem in the stems and roots of many vascular plants. For illustration see EXOGEN. [< LL, exchange] — **cam·bi·al** (kam′bē·əl) *adj.*

Cam·bo·di·a (kam·bō′dē·ə) See KHMER REPUBLIC.

Cam·bo·di·an (kam·bō′dē·ən) *adj.* Pertaining to Khmer Republic (Cambodia), its people, or their language. — *n.* A native or inhabitant of Khmer Republic.

cam·bric (kām′brik) *n.* 1 A fine white linen fabric or a similar fabric of cotton. 2 A coarse cotton fabric used for linings. [< Flemish *Kameryk* Cambrai]

cambric tea *n.* A drink made of sweetened hot water and milk, sometimes flavored with a little tea.

cam·el (kam′əl) *n.* 1 A large Asian or African ruminant (genus *Camelus*) with a humped back, capable of subsisting for extended periods of time without water: used as a beast of burden. There are two species, the **Arabian camel** or **dromedary,** having one hump, and the **Bactrian camel** (*C. bactrianus*), having two. 2 A buoyant, watertight contrivance for lifting wrecks, etc. [OE < L *camelus* < Gk. *kamēlos* < Semitic] — **cam′el·ish** *adj.*

CAMELS
A. Arabian. B. Bactrian.
(7–9 feet tall)

cam·el·eer (kam′əl·ir′) *n.* A camel driver or a soldier mounted on a camel.

ca·mel·ia (kə·mēl′yə, mel′ē·ə) *n.* A tropical Asian tree or shrub (*Camellia* or *Thea japonica*) with glossy leaves and white, pink, red, or variegated flowers: also called *Japan rose.* [after George Joseph Kamel, 1661–1706, Jesuit traveler]

cam·el's-hair (kam′əlz·hâr′) *n.* A heavy, warm, tan cloth made of camel's hair, sometimes mixed with wool or other fibers. — *adj.* Made of, like, or the color of camel's-hair. Also **cam′el·hair′.**

Cam·em·bert (kam′əm·bâr, *Fr.* kȧ·män·bâr′) *n.* A rich, creamy, soft cheese. [from *Camembert,* town in NW France]

cam·e·o (kam′ē·ō) *n.* 1 A striated stone (as onyx

or agate) or shell, carved in relief so as to show the design on differently colored layers. 2 The art of so carving. Compare INTAGLIO. 3 A brief appearance by an actor or actress in a film or play. —*adj.* Miniature; on a small scale. [< Ital. *cammeo;* ult. origin unknown]

cameo glass *n.* Glass fused in layers of different colors and cut in relief like a cameo: also called **onyx glass.**

cam·er·a (kam′ər·ə, kam′rə) *n. pl.* **·er·as** for defs. 1 and 2, **·er·ae** for defs. 3, 4, 5, 6. 1 A lightproof chamber or box in which the image of an exterior object is projected upon a sensitized plate or film through a shuttered opening usually equipped with a lens or lenses. 2 An enclosed unit containing the special light-sensitive vacuum tube which converts optical images into electrical impulses for television transmission. 3 A chamber, as of the heart. 4 In Italy, a legislative chamber; also, the financial department of the papal curia. 5 *Law* A judge's chamber or private room. 6 A camera obscura. —**in camera** *Law* Not in public court; privately; secretly. [< L, vaulted room < Gk. *kamara.* Doublet of CHAMBER.]

camera gun A camera mounted on a machine-gun frame in an airplane, and used in gunnery practice to record each shot.

cam·er·al (kam′ər·əl) *adj.* Pertaining to a camera, chamber, public office, or treasury.

cam·er·al·is·tics (kam′ər·əl·is′tiks) *n.* The science of state finances. —**cam′er·al·ist** *n.* —**cam′er·al·is′tic** *adj.*

camera lu·ci·da (lo͞o′si·də) A device by which the image of a body seems to be projected on a sheet of paper or other surface, so that it may be traced.

CAMERA LUCIDA
a. Eyepiece.
b. Mirror.
c. Glass slide.
d. Image here.

cam·er·a·man (kam′ər·ə·man′, kam′rə-) *n. pl.* **·men** (-men′) The operator of a camera, especially a motion-picture camera.

camera ob·scu·ra (ob·skyo͞or′ə) A darkened box in which the real image of an object, received through a small aperture, is projected upon a plane surface, for viewing, tracing, or photographing.

cam·er·lin·go (kam′ər·ling′gō) *n.* In the Roman Catholic Church, the cardinal who administers the finances and secular interests of the Pope. Also **cam′er·len′go** (-leng′gō). [< Ital. *camerlingo* chamberlain < L *camera* chamber]

Cam·e·roun (kam′ə·ro͞on, kam′ro͞on) An independent republic in western Africa, including the southern part of the former British Cameroons; 184,252 square miles; capital, Yaoundé; formerly French Cameroons, a United Nations Trust Territory.

cam·i·sole (kam′ə·sōl) *n.* 1 Formerly, a woman's wrapper. 2 A woman's fancy underwaist or corset cover. 3 A straitjacket having long sleeves that can be tied behind the patient's back. 4 Formerly, a man's jacket or jersey with sleeves. [< F < Sp. *camisola,* dim. of *camisa* shirt]

cam·let (kam′lit) *n.* 1 A stiff, closely woven fabric of camel's-hair, or an imitation of it. 2 A garment made from this fabric. [< MF *camelot* < OF *chamelot,* ? < Arabic *khamlat* nap, pile on cloth]

cam·o·mile (kam′ə·mīl) *n.* 1 A strongly scented bitter herb of the genus *Anthemis;* especially, the European perennial (*A. nobilis*) whose bitter, aromatic flowers and leaves are used in medicine. 2 Any plant of a genus (*Matricaria*) of widely distributed herbs of the composite family. Also spelled **chamomile.** —**wild** (or **stinking**) **camomile** Mayweed. [< F *camomille* < L *chamomilla* < Gk. *chamaimēlon* < *chamai* on the ground + *mēlon* apple]

cam·ou·flage (kam′ə·fläzh) *n.* 1 *Mil.* Disguise by masking, as artillery, with an arbor of leaves built around a gun; also, artificial scenery, etc., painted on canvas to conceal military installations and movements. 2 *Nav.*

Disguise by painting, as ships, as protection from attack by submarines, etc. 3 Any disguise or pretense. —*v.t. & v.i.* **·flaged, ·flag·ing** To hide or obscure, as with disguises. [< F *camoufler* disguise] —**cam′ou·flag′er** *n.*

camp¹ (kamp) *n.* 1 A group of tents or other shelters, as for soldiers or hunters, or the place so occupied; also, a single tent, cabin, etc. 2 An army encamped; hence, military life or the field of battle. 3 A chapter or lodge of various fraternal organizations. 4 A new community or town hastily gathered around the mines: so called because the people originally lived in tents. 5 A group of buildings for temporary (usually summer) habitation, built on a lake, or seashore, or in the mountains. 6 A stage of a journey. 7 A place where open-air religious or political meetings are held. 8 A body of persons who support or defend a policy, theory, or doctrine: Avarice dominates the *camp* of the profiteers. 9 A mass of facts or arguments arrayed in support or defense of a policy, theory, or doctrine. —*v.t.* 1 To shelter or station, as troops, in a camp. —*v.i.* 2 To form an encampment. 3 To live temporarily in a camp. 4 To hold stubbornly to a position: Strikers *camped* in front of the factory. —**to camp down** To settle down. —**to camp on the trail of** To follow closely; dog. —**to camp out** To sleep in a tent; live in the open. [< MF < Ital. *campo* field < L *campus* level plain]

camp² (kamp) *n.* 1 A comical style or quality typically perceived in banal, flamboyant, or patently artificial gestures, appearances, literary works, etc., that intentionally or unwittingly seem to parody themselves. 2 A person, thing, aspect, etc., marked by this style or quality. —*adj.* Of or characterized by camp, or by a ready appreciation of camp: the *camp* sensibility; in the *camp* tradition of Hollywood's gangster films. —*v.i. Slang* 1 To behave, dress, etc., in a theatrical or bizarre way to get attention. —*v.t.* 2 To invest with a camp quality: to *camp* the play up with weird effects. [? < dial. E *camp* or *kemp* bold, impetuous fellow]

cam·paign (kam·pān′) *n.* 1 A series of connected military actions or maneuvers conducted for a particular objective, in a particular area, etc. 2 A series of connected political, commercial, or other activities designed to bring about a result: a welfare *campaign.* —*v.i.* To serve, operate in, or conduct a campaign. [< F *campagne* open country, field < Med. L *compania* < L *campus*]

cam·paign·er (kam·pā′nər) *n.* 1 One who campaigns. 2 A person of long experience in campaigns; a veteran.

cam·pa·ne·ro (käm′pä·nā′rō) *n.* The bellbird of South America. [< Sp., bellman < LL *campana* bell]

cam·pan·i·form (kam·pan′ə·fôrm) *adj.* Bell-shaped; campanulate. [< LL *campana* bell + -FORM]

cam·pa·nol·o·gy (kam′pə·nol′ə·jē) *n.* The science and art of casting and ringing bells. [< LL *campana* bell + -LOGY] —**cam′pa·nol′o·gist** *n.*

cam·pan·u·la (kam·pan′yə·lə) *n.* 1 A member of a very large genus of plants (*Campanula*), the bellflowers, as the bluebell of Scotland, Canterbury bell, etc. 2 *Zool.* A bell-shaped structure. [< NL, dim. of LL *campana* bell]

campanula blue The bluish-mauve color of various campanulas or bellflowers.

cam·pan·u·la·ceous (kam·pan′yə·lā′shəs) *adj. Bot.* Belonging to the bellflower family (*Campanulaceae*) of herbs, shrubs, and trees.

cam·pan·u·late (kam·pan′yə·lit, -lāt) *adj.* Bell-shaped, as a corolla.

camp·er (kamp′ər) *n.* 1 One who camps out or lives in a camp. 2 A member of a camp, as a summer camp for children. 3 A vehicle affording shelter and usually sleeping accommodations for travelers and campers: also **camper wagon.**

cam·pes·tral (kam·pes′trəl) *adj.* Growing in or pertaining to the fields or open country. [< L *campestris* < *campus* field]

camp·fire (kamp′fīr′) *n.* 1 A fire in an outdoor camp, for cooking, warmth, etc. 2 A fire in a camp used as the center of social evening

gatherings. 3 A meeting or social gathering; especially, a reunion. Also **camp fire.**

campfire girl A girl between 12 and 20 years of age, belonging to the **Camp Fire Girls of America,** an organization incorporated in 1914 for promoting the health and welfare of young women by encouraging outdoor life, etc.

camp follower 1 A civilian who follows an army about, usually a merchant or prostitute. 2 One who supports a movement, etc., without formally belonging to it; hanger-on.

camp·ground (kamp′ground′) *n.* An area used for a camp or a camp meeting.

cam·phene (kam′fēn, kam·fēn′) *n. Chem.* One of a series, $C_{10}H_{16}$, of solid hydrocarbons similar to camphor, isomeric with oil of turpentine: used as a camphor substitute. [< CAMPHOR]

cam·pho·gen (kam′fə·jen) *n. Chem.* Cymene.

cam·phol (kam′fōl, -fol) *n. Chem.* Borneol.

cam·phor (kam′fər) *n.* A white, volatile, translucent crystalline compound, $C_{10}H_{16}O$, with a penetrating, fragrant odor and pungent taste, distilled from the wood and bark of the camphor tree and also obtained by organic synthesis: used in medicine as a sedative, as an antispasmodic, in liniments, etc., and in the chemical and plastics industries. [< F *camphre* < Arabic *kāfūr* < Malay *kāpūr*] —**cam·phor·ic** (kam·fôr′ik, -for′-) *adj.*

cam·phor·ate (kam′fə·rāt) *v.t.* **·at·ed, ·at·ing** To treat or saturate with camphor.

camphor ball A moth ball.

camphor ice A mixture of camphor, white wax, spermaceti, and castor oil: used for chapped skin, etc.

camphor tree 1 A large evergreen tree of eastern Asia (*Cinnamomum camphora*) yielding the camphor of commerce. 2 A tree of Borneo, Sumatra, and Malaya (*Dryobalanops aromatica*) yielding borneol.

camp·ing (kamp′ing) *n.* The act or practice of living outdoors, as in tents or without any shelter, especially for recreation.

cam·pi·on (kam′pē·ən) *n.* One of various herbs of the pink family, as the **rose campion.** [Origin uncertain]

camp meeting A prolonged series of religious meetings held in a grove or field, usually in a tent.

cam·po¹ (kam′pō, käm′-) *n. pl.* **·pi** (-pē) In Italy, an open space in a town. [< Ital.]

cam·po² (kam′pō, käm′-) *n. pl.* **·pos** In South American countries, an open, level plain, with scattered shrubbery and trees. [< Sp.]

camp stool A light, folding stool or seat.

cam·pus (kam′pəs) *n.* 1 *U.S.* The grounds of a school or college or the court enclosed by the buildings. 2 In ancient Rome, an open field where military drills, games, etc., were held. [< L, field]

cam·py·lot·ro·pal (kam′pi·lot′rə·pəl) *adj. Bot.* Bent on itself so as to bring the true apex or micropyle down to the base or hilum: said of an ovule. Also **cam′py·lot′ro·pous** (-pəs). [< NL < Gk. *kampylos* bent + *tropos* direction < *trepein* turn]

cam shaft The shaft to which a cam is attached.

cam·wood (kam′wo͝od′) *n.* The red wood of a tree (*Baphia nitida*) of western Africa, used in dyeing. [? < native African name]

can¹ (kan, *unstressed* kən) *v. Present: sing.* **can, can** (*Archaic* canst), **can,** *pl.* **can;** *past:* **could** A defective verb now used only in the present and past tenses as an auxiliary followed by the infinitive without *to,* or elliptically with the infinitive unexpressed, in the following senses: 1 To be able to. 2 To know how to. 3 To have the right to. 4 *Colloq.* To be permitted to; may. [OE *cunnan* know, be able]

◆ **can, may** In informal speech and writing, *can* is now acceptable in the sense of *may,* to express permission, especially in questions or negative statements: *Can* I leave now? You *cannot.* At the formal level, the distinction between *can* and *may* is still observed: *can,* to express ability to perform, either mentally or physically; *may,* to denote permission.

can² (kan) *n.* 1 A vessel for holding or carrying liquids. 2 A vessel of tin-plated iron or other metal, in which fruit, meat, tobacco, or the like is sealed, often hermetically: called **tin**

in Great Britain. **3** A drinking mug or cup; a tankard. **4** A radio headphone. **5** *Slang* Jail; prison. **6** *Slang* Toilet; bathroom. **7** *Slang* Buttocks; backside. —**in the can** Ready for distribution or exhibition: said of a motion picture.— *v.t.* **canned, can·ning 1** To put up or preserve in cans, glass jars, or the like. **2** *Slang* To dismiss; discharge; also, to expel from school. **3** To preserve for reproduction, as on a phonograph record: *canned* music. **4** *Slang* To suppress; jail; imprison. [OE *canne* cup] —**can'ner** *n.*

Ca·naan (kā'nən) The Israelite name of the part of Palestine between the Jordan and the Mediterranean; the Promised Land.

Can·a·da (kan'ə·də) A self-governing member of the Commonwealth of Nations, comprising ten provinces and two territories in North America; 3,851,809 square miles; capital, Ottawa: also *British North America.*

Canada balsam A yellowish turpentine derived from the balsam fir.

Canada bluegrass Wiregrass.

Canada jay A non-migratory, sooty-gray bird of the crow family (*Perisoreus canadensis*), native in Canada and the NE United States: also called *venison bird.*

Canada lily An American lily (*Lilium canadense*) with drooping orange or yellow flowers, sometimes spotted with brown: also called *meadow lily.*

Ca·na·di·an (kə·nā'dē·ən) *adj.* Of or pertaining to Canada or its inhabitants, their industries, products, etc.— *n.* A native of Canada or a legally constituted citizen of Canada.

Ca·na·di·an·ism (kə·nā'dē·ən·iz'əm) *n.* **1** A trait, custom, or tradition characteristic of the people of Canada or some of them. **2** A word, phrase, or usage especially characteristic of Canadian English or French. **3** Devotion to Canada, its institutions, etc.

ca·nal (kə·nal') *n.* **1** An artificial inland waterway connecting two navigable bodies of water. **2** An artificial channel for irrigating tracts of land. **3** Any channel, groove, passage, or duct: the auditory *canal.* **4** *Zool.* A groove, as for the siphon in the shells of gastropods, or a pore, as in sponges, etc. **5** *Astron.* One of the peculiar markings visible on the face of the planet Mars. —**central canal** The ventricle of the spinal cord. — *v.t.* **ca·nalled** or **ca·naled, ca·nal·ling** or **ca·nal·ing** To build a canal or canals across or through; canalize. [< MF < L *canalis* groove. Doublet of CHANNEL.]

ca·nal·age (kə·nal'ij) *n.* **1** The construction of canals. **2** Canals collectively. **3** A charge for transportation through a canal.

canal boat A long barge, principally used on canals and drawn either by electric power or by horses or mules on a towpath.

Ca·nal du Nord (kȧ·nȧl' dü nôr') See SAINT-QUENTIN CANAL.

ca·nal·er (kə·nal'ər) *n.* **1** One who works on a canal boat. **2** A canal boat. Also **ca·nal'. ler.**

can·a·lic·u·late (kan'ə·lik'yə·lit, -lāt) *adj.* Channeled or grooved. Also **can'a·lic'u·lar** (-lər), **can'a·lic'u·lat·ed.**

can·a·lic·u·lus (kan'ə·lik'yə·ləs) *n. pl.* **·li** (-lī) *Anat.* A small tube or canal, as in a bone. [< L *canaliculus,* dim. of *canalis* pipe, groove]

ca·nal·ize (kə·nal'īz, kan'əl·īz) *v.t.* **·ized, ·iz·ing 1** To convert into a canal, as a stream or chain of lakes. **2** To furnish with a canal, or a system of canals, or waterways. **3** To furnish with an outlet. —**ca·nal·i·za·tion** (kə·nal'ə·zā'shən, kan'ə·lə-) *n.*

canal rays *Physics* A stream of positively charged ions emitted from the anode of a vacuum tube and emerging through openings in the cathode: also called *positive rays.*

Ca·nan·ga oil (kə·nang'gə) A volatile oil used in perfume, obtained from the ylang-ylang.

ca·nar·y (kə·nâr'ē) *n. pl.* **·nar·ies 1** A small finch (*Serinus canarius*) originally native in the Canary Islands, having generally yellow plumage: popular as a cage bird for its song. **2** A bright yellow color: also **canary yellow. 3** A sweet, white wine from the Canary Islands. **4** An old French dance in rapid time. — *v.i.* To dance the canary.[< F *canarie* < Sp. *canario* < L *Canaria* (*Insula*) Dog (Island) < *canis* dog; so called from a breed of dogs found there]

ca·nar·y·grass (kə·nâr'ē·gras', -gräs') *n.* A grass (*Phalaris canariensis*) native in the Ca-

nary Islands and cultivated for its seeds, which are used as food for cage birds.

Canary Islands An island group off the NW coast of Africa, comprising two Spanish provinces; 2,894 square miles. Also **Canaries.** *Spanish* **Is·las Ca·na·rias** (ēz'lȧs kä·nä'ryȧs).

ca·nas·ta (kə·nas'tə) *n.* A card game based on the principles of rummy, for two to six players, using a double deck of cards.[< Sp., basket]

ca·nas·ter (kə·nas'tər) *n.* A coarse-grained tobacco formerly packed in rush baskets. [< Sp. *canastro* < Gk. *kanastron* rush basket]

Ca·nav·er·al (kə·nav'ər·əl), **Cape** See KENNEDY, CAPE.

Can·ber·ra (kan'bər·ə) The capital of the Commonwealth of Australia, in Australian Capital Territory: formerly *Yass–Canberra.*

can but Have no other course than to. See CANNOT BUT.

can·can (kan'kan', *Fr.* kän·kän')*n.* A Parisian dance, introduced about 1830, in which the figures of the quadrille are diversified by high kicking and other wild or suggestive movements. [< F, gossip] —**can'can'ing** *adj.*

can·cel (kan'səl) *v.t.* **can·celed** or**·celled, can·cel·ing** or **·cel·ling 1** To mark out or off, as by drawing or stamping lines across written matter to signify that it is to be omitted; blot or strike out; obliterate. **2** To remove, as by cutting out; suppress, as pages of a book. **3** To render null and void; annul, revoke, or set aside. **4** To make up for; compensate; neutralize; countervail. **5** To mark or ink (a postage stamp) to show that it has been used. **6** *Math.* To eliminate (a common factor, as a figure or quantity) from the numerator and denominator of a fraction, or from both sides of an equation. — *n.* In printing and bookbinding, the striking or cutting out, omission, or suppression of a leaf, leaves, or any part of any printed matter or work; also, any printed matter thus suppressed, or the matter substituted for that stricken out. [< MF *canceller* < L *cancellare* cross out < *cancelli,* dim. pl. of *cancer* lattice]

Synonyms (verb): abolish, abrogate, annul, discharge, efface, erase, expunge, nullify, obliterate, quash, remove, repeal, rescind, revoke, vacate. *Cancel, efface, erase, expunge,* and *obliterate* have as their first meaning the removal of written characters or other forms of record. To *cancel* is, literally, to make a lattice by cross lines, exactly our English *cross out*; to *efface* is to rub off, smooth away the face of, as of an inscription; to *expunge* is to punch out with some sharp instrument, so as to show that the words are no longer part of the writing; to *obliterate* is to cover over or remove, as a letter, as was done by reversing the Roman stylus, and rubbing out with the rounded end what had been written with the point on the waxen tablet. What has been *canceled, erased, expunged,* may perhaps still be traced; what is *obliterated* is gone forever, as if it had never been. The figurative use of the words keeps close to the primary sense. Compare ABOLISH, ANNUL. *Antonyms:* approve, confirm, enact, enforce, establish, maintain, perpetuate, record, reenact, sustain, uphold.

can·cel·a·ble (kan'səl·ə·bəl) *adj.* That can be canceled. Also **can'cel·la·ble.**

can·cel·er (kan'səl·ər) *n.* **1** A person or thing that cancels. **2** A device for canceling. Also **can'cel·ler.**

can·cel·late (kan'sə·lāt) *adj.* **1** *Anat.* Latticelike in structure; also, having reticulations, as certain bones, or parts of bones. **2** Chambered; cell–like. Also **can'cel·lat·ed, can'cel·lous** (-ləs).

can·cel·la·tion (kan'sə·lā'shən) *n.* **1** That which is canceled. **2** The mark which cancels. **3** A network formed by small interlacing bars; a reticulation.

can·cel·li (kan·sel'ī) *n. pl.* **1** Bars of latticework, as in a latticed window or in the screen separating the choir from the nave of a church. **2** Bars in the railing of a court. **3** Reticulations; especially, the latticework of bony spicules that forms the spongy or interior portion of a bone.

can·cer (kan'sər) *n.* **1** *Pathol.* A malignant neoplasm or tumor, characterized by a morbid proliferation of epithelial cells in various parts of the body, spreading into adjacent tissue, with consequent progressive degeneration

which often ends fatally: also called *carcinoma, sarcoma.* **2** Any inveterate and spreading evil. —**colloid cancer** A variety of cancer which chiefly attacks the alimentary canal, uterus, or peritoneum. — *v.t.* To eat or penetrate like a cancer. [< L, crab]

can·cer·ate (kan'sə·rāt) *v.i.* **·at·ed, ·at·ing** *Pathol.* To become cancerous; develop into a cancer. —**can'cer·a'tion** *n.*

can·cer·ous (kan'sər·əs) *adj.* **1** *Pathol.* Pertaining to, of the nature of, or affected with a cancer. **2** Virulent; incurable.

cancer-root (kan'sər·rōōt', -rŏŏt') *n.* Beechdrops: so called from its supposed value in the external treatment of cancerous ulcer.

can·croid (kang'kroid) *adj.* **1** Like a crab. **2** Resembling a cancer. — *n. Pathol.* An epithelioma of the skin.

can·del·a (kan·del'ə) *n. Physics* A unit of luminous intensity equal to that of 1/60 square centimeter of a black body operating at the temperature of solidification of platinum: also called *candle, standard candle.* Abbr. **cd**

can·de·la·brum (kan'də·lä'brəm, -lä'-) *n. pl.* **·bra** or **·brums** A large, branched candlestick. Also **can'de·la'bra** *pl.* **·bras.** [< L < *candela* candle]

can·dent (kan'dənt) *adj.* Glowing with heat; incandescent. [< L *candens, -entis,* ppr. of *candere* glow]

can·des·cence (kan·des'əns) *n.* Incandescence. —**can·des'cent** *adj.*

Can·di·a (kan'dē·ə) **1** The largest city in Crete, a port on the **Gulf of Candia,** a bay of the Aegean in northern Crete: Greek *Hérakleion.* **2** A former name for CRETE.

can·did (kan'did) *adj.* **1** Sincere; ingenuous; frank. **2** Impartial; fair. **3** *Obs.* White; also, pure. [< MF *candide* pure, honest < L *candidus < candere* gleam, shine] —**can'did·ly** *adv.* —**can'did·ness** *n.*

Synonyms: aboveboard, artless, fair, frank, guileless, honest, impartial, ingenuous, innocent, naive, open, simple, sincere, straightforward, transparent, truthful, unbiased, unprejudiced, unreserved, unsophisticated. A *candid* statement is meant to be true to the real facts and just to all parties; a *fair* statement is really so. *Fair* is applied to the conduct but *candid* is not; as, *fair* treatment, a *fair* field and no favor. One who is *frank* has a fearless and unconstrained truthfulness. *Honest* and *ingenuous* unite in expressing total lack of deceit. On the other hand, *artless, guileless, naive, simple,* and *unsophisticated* express the goodness which comes from want of the knowledge or thought of evil. *Sincere* applies to the feelings as being all that one's words would imply. See HONEST. *Antonyms:* adroit, artful, crafty, cunning, deceitful, designing, diplomatic, foxy, insincere, intriguing, knowing, maneuvering, sharp, shrewd, sly, subtle, tricky, wily.

can·di·date (kan'də·dāt, -dit) *n.* A nominee or aspirant for any position or honor. [< L *candidatus* wearing white < *candidus* white; because office–seekers in Rome wore white togas] —**can·di·da·cy** (kan'də·də·sē), **can'di·date'ship, can·di·da·ture** (kan'də·də·chər, -dā'. chər) *n.*

can·died (kan'dēd) *adj.* **1** Converted into candy; preserved in sugar. **2** Coated with something resembling sugar; frosted. **3** Flattering; honeyed; sugared.

can·dle (kan'dəl) *n.* **1** A cylinder of tallow, wax, or other solid fat, containing a wick, to give light when burning. **2** Anything like a candle in shape or purpose. **3** *Mil.* A cylindrical container which, when ignited, emits a cloud of smoke or gas. **4** *Physics* A candela. —**to hold a candle to** To compare with favorably: used in the negative. — *v.t.* **·dled, ·dling 1** To test (eggs) by holding between the eye and a light, translucency indicating soundness. **2** To test (bottled wines) for clarity. [OE *candel* < L *candela < candere* shine, gleam] —**can'dler** *n.*

can·dle·ber·ry (kan'dəl·ber'ē) *n. pl.* **·ries 1** The wax myrtle or bayberry. **2** Its fruit. **3** An East Indian and Polynesian tree (*Aleurites moluccana*); the candlenut.

candleberry cactus The ocotillo.

can·dle·fish (kan'dəl·fish') *n.* An edible, oily smeltlike marine fish (*Thaleichthys pacificus*) of the northern Pacific, which, when dried, may be burned as a candle.

can·dle-foot (kan'dəl·fŏŏt') *n.* Foot–candle.

Can·dle·mas (kan'dəl·məs) n. The feast of the Purification, or of the Presentation of Christ in the temple, held on Feb. 2; also, the day itself. Also **Candlemas Day.** [OE *candelmæsse* < *candel* candle + *mæsse* mass]

can·dle·mold (kan'dəl·mōld') n. A tin mold with multiple tubular compartments in which to insert wicks and pour melted tallow or wax for making candles.

can·dle·nut (kan'dəl·nut') n. 1 The candleberry (def. 3). 2 The fruit of this tree, burned as candles by the natives of Polynesia.

CANDLEMOLD

can·dle·pin (kan'dəl·pin') n. A slender, nearly cylindrical pin used in a bowling game called **candlepins.**

can·dle·pow·er (kan'dəl·pou'ər) n. The illuminating power of a standard candle: used as a measure of other illuminants.

can·dle·stick (kan'dəl·stik') n. A support for a candle or candles. [OE *candelsticca* < *candel* candle + *sticca* stick]

can·dle·wick (kan'dəl·wik') n. The wick of a candle, or the soft, twisted fibers from which wicks are made; candlewicking. [OE *candelweoca* < *candel* candle + *weoca* wick]

can·dle·wick·ing (kan'dəl·wik'ing) n. 1 Thick, soft, cotton thread used to make wicks for candles. 2 Tuftings of such threads worked into a fabric, usually in the form of a design, to give a napped surface.

can·dle·wood (kan'dəl·wŏŏd') n. 1 Any of several trees or shrubs, as the ocotillo (*Fouquiera splendens*). 2 Any resinous wood finely split so as to give light when burned on the hearth.

can·dor (kan'dər) n. 1 Freedom from mental reservation or prejudice. 2 Openness; frankness; impartiality. 3 *Obs.* Brightness; fairness. Also *Brit.* **can'dour.** See synonyms under VERACITY. [<L, sincerity, purity < *candere* gleam, shine]

can·dy (kan'dē) n. pl. **·dies** 1 Sugar or molasses crystallized by evaporation; also, a confection of sugar or molasses crystals. 2 Any of numerous confections in various colors, flavors, and forms, and consisting chiefly of cane or beet or other sugar to which has been added chocolate, milk products, fruits, fruit extracts, nuts, or the like; also, such confections collectively: usually called *sweets* in Great Britain. — v. **·died, ·dy·ing** v.t. 1 To cause to form into crystals of sugar. 2 To preserve by boiling or. coating with sugar, as orange peels. 3 To render pleasant; sweeten. 4 To overlay with any crystalline substance, as ice or sugar. — v.i. 5 To become crystallized into or covered with sugar. [Short for *sugar candy* < F (*sucre*) *candi* < Arabic *qandī* made of sugar < *qand* sugar, ult. < Skt.]

can·dy·tuft (kan'dē·tuft') n. A plant of the mustard family (genus *Iberis*) with white, pink, or purple flowers.

cane (kān) n. 1 A walking stick. 2 A stem of cane grass. 3 The stem of a raspberry or allied plant. 4 Any rod, especially one used for flogging. — v.t. **caned, can·ing** 1 To strike or beat with a cane. 2 To bottom or back with cane, as a chair. [<OF <L *cana* <Gk. *kanna* reed <Semitic] —**can'er** n.

Ca·ne·a (kä·nē'ä) The capital of Crete, a port on the **Gulf of Canea,** a bay of the Aegean in western Crete: ancient *Cydonia:* Greek *Khania.*

cane·brake (kān'brāk') n. Land overgrown with canes.

cane grass Any of various plants with slender, flexible stems, usually jointed, as the rattan or sugarcane.

ca·nel·la (kə·nel'ə) n. The pale, orange–yellow, aromatic inner bark of a tropical American tree (*Canella winterana*): used as a tonic and condiment. Also **canella bark.** [<Med. L, dim. of *canna* reed]

ca·nes·cence (kə·nes'əns) n. A whitish color; hoariness.

ca·nes·cent (kə·nes'ənt) adj. Becoming, or tending to become, white or hoary. [<L *canescens, -entis,* ppr. of *canescere,* inceptive of *canere* be white]

cane sugar Sucrose obtained from the sugarcane.

cangue (kang) n. A heavy wooden collar or yoke, formerly worn around the neck by convicts in China as a punishment. [<F <Pg. *cango*]

ca·nine (kā'nīn) adj. 1 Of, pertaining to, or like a dog. 2 *Zool.* Of or pertaining to the dog family (*Canidae*). 3 Of or pertaining to a canine tooth. — n. 1 A dog or other canine animal. 2 A canine tooth. [<L *caninus* <*canis* dog]

canine tooth *Anat.* A tooth growing directly behind the intermaxillary suture in the upper jaw, or the opposite one of the lower jaw; an eyetooth of the upper jaw, or stomach tooth of the lower jaw.

can·ions (kan'yənz) n. pl. Sausagelike rolls worn in the 16th and 17th centuries as ornaments around the bottoms of breeches' legs. [<Sp. *cañon,* aug. of *caña* tube,]

Ca·nis (kā'nis) n. *Zool.* The genus including the dog (wild and domestic), the wolf, the fox, and the jackal. [<L, dog]

can·is·ter (kan'is·tər) n. 1 A metal case, as for tea, coffee, or spices. 2 Shot or bullets packed in a metallic cylinder, to be fired from a cannon; case shot; shrapnel. [<L *canistrum* basket <Gk. *kanastron* <*kanna* reed]

can·ker (kang'kər) n. 1 *Pathol.* Any ulcer with a tendency to gangrene; a group of small ulcers in the mouth. 2 A disease of fruit trees. 3 Any secret or spreading evil. 4 A disease affecting the feet of horses, characterized by the discharge of an evil–smelling exudate. 5 An inflammation of the external ear in cats and dogs. 6 The cankerworm. 7 *Obs.* The dog rose; also **canker blossom.** — v.t. 1 To infect with canker. 2 To eat away or into like a canker; corrode; corrupt. — v.t. 3 To fester with or be attacked by a canker. [<AF *cancre* <L *cancer* crab, ulcer]

can·kered (kang'kərd) adj. 1 Affected by or as by canker. 2 Corrupted; malignant; venomous.

can·ker·ous (kang'kər·əs) adj. 1 Of the nature of a canker; gangrenous. 2 Causing canker. 3 Corroding; corrupting.

canker rash Scarlet fever.

can·ker·root (kang'kər·rōōt', -rŏŏt') n. One of several plants with astringent roots, as the marsh rosemary.

can·ker·worm (kang'kər·wûrm') n. Any of several insect larvae which destroy fruit and shade trees; especially, the measuring worms of the family **Geometridae.**

can·na (kan'ə) n. Any of a genus (*Canna*) of erect, mostly tropical American plants with red or yellow irregular flowers. [<L <Gk. *kanna* reed] — **can·na·ceous** (kə·nā'shəs) adj.

can·na·bin (kan'ə·bin) n. A white, poisonous crystalline resin in Indian hemp, of which it is believed to be the active narcotic principle.

can·nab·in·ol (kə·nab'ə·nōl, -nol) n. *Chem.* The principal resinous ingredient of *Cannabis sativa,* $C_{21}H_{30}O_2$, a thick, reddish–yellow oil, subject to deterioration on exposure to air.

Can·na·bis (kan'ə·bis) n. 1 A genus of plants of the mulberry family having only one known species, Indian hemp, from the flowering tops of which are derived the resinous alkaloids noted for their narcotic properties. 2 Hashish. [<L <Gk. *kannabis* hemp]

canned (kand) adj. 1 Preserved in a can or jar. 2 *Slang* Recorded: *canned* music.

can·nel (kan'əl) n. A bituminous coal, rich in gas, with low heating power: also called *kennel.* Also **cannel coal.** [Alter. of *candle coal*]

can·ne·lure (kan'ə·lŏŏr) n. A groove or a fluting, especially around the rim of a bullet or the head of a rimless cartridge case. [<F] — **can'ne·lured** adj.

can·ner·y (kan'ər·ē) n. pl. **·ner·ies** A factory or other establishment where foods are canned.

Cannes (kan, kanz; *Fr.* kän) A port and resort city on the Riviera, SE France.

can·ni·bal (kan'ə·bəl) n. 1 A human being who eats human flesh. 2 An animal that devours members of its own species. — adj. Of or like cannibals or their feasts. [<Sp. *Canibales,* var. of *Caribes* Caribs] — **can'ni·bal·ism** n. — **can·ni·bal·ic** (kan'ə·bal'ik), **can'ni·bal·is'tic** adj. — **can'ni·bal·is'ti·cal·ly** adv.

can·ni·kin (kan'ə·kin) n. 1 A small can or drinking cup. 2 A small wooden pail. Also spelled *canikin.* [Dim. of CAN²]

can·ning (kan'ing) n. The act, process, or business of preserving fruits, vegetables, meats, etc., in hermetically sealed tin cans, glass jars, etc.

can·non (kan'ən) n. pl. **·nons** or **·non** 1 *Mil.* a A large tubular weapon for discharging a heavy projectile; especially, one mounted on a carriage, movable or fixed. b A big artillery gun. c Artillery collectively. 2 The great bone between the fetlock and knee or hock of the horse and allied animals: also **cannon bone.** 3 A carom. 4 *Mech.* A loose metallic sleeve on a shaft. 5 A smooth round bit for a horse: also **cannon bit.** 6 The ear of a bell; one of the parts by which it is hung. — v.t. 1 To attack with cannon shot. 2 In billiards, to cause to carom. 3 To cause to rebound from one object to another. — v.i. 4 To fire cannon repeatedly. 5 In billiards, to make a carom. 6 To rebound from one object to another. ◆ Homophone: *canon.* [<OF *canon* <Ital. *cannone,* aug. of *canna* tube, pipe]

can·non·ade (kan'ən·ād') v. **·ad·ed, ·ad·ing** v.t. To attack with cannon shot. — v.i. To fire cannon repeatedly. — n. A continued attack with or discharge of cannon.

cannon ball Any missile to be shot from a cannon; originally, a spherical solid shot.

can·non·eer (kan'ən·ir') n. 1 An artilleryman belonging to a gun squad. 2 A soldier who serves as gunner. Also **can'non·ier'.**

cannon fodder Soldiers, as considered expendable in wartime.

can·non·ry (kan'ən·rē) n. Artillery; also, its discharge.

cannon shot 1 A shot or projectile for a cannon; a cannon ball. 2 The distance which the shot of a cannon may achieve.

can·not (ka'not) v.i. Am, is, or are not able to.

cannot but Have no alternative except to: objected to by some as a double negative, but long established in formal literary usage.

can·nu·la (kan'yə·lə) n. *Med.* A tube to be inserted by means of a trocar into a cavity, through which pus, etc., may escape or medicine be introduced: also spelled *canula.* [<L, dim. of *canna* reed, tube] — **can'nu·lar** adj.

can·nu·late (kan'yə·lāt) v.t. **·lat·ed, ·lat·ing** To make hollow or tubular. — adj. (kan'yə·lit, -lāt) Tubular. Also spelled *canulate.*

cannulated needle *Surg.* A ligating needle having a bore through which the wire or thread may pass.

can·ny (kan'ē) adj. **can·ni·er, can·ni·est** 1 Careful in determining or acting; prudent; knowing; thrifty; shrewd. 2 Skilful; clever. 3 Lucky; safe. 4 Quiet; sly; dry: said of humor as characteristically Scottish. 5 Comfortable; cozy; snug. Also spelled *cannie.* [<CAN (def. 3)] — **can'ni·ly** adv. — **can'ni·ness** n.

ca·noe (kə·nōō') n. 1 A small, long, narrow boat, pointed at both ends, made from a hollowed log, bark, light wood, or animal skins, and propelled by paddles: used by primitive peoples. 2 A modern adaptation of this, made of canvas, light wood, or aluminum. Compare illustration under CATAMARAN. — v.t. 1 To convey by canoe. — v.i. 2 To paddle, sail, or travel in a canoe. 3 To operate a canoe. [<Sp. <Taino *canoa* boat] — **ca·noe'ing** n. — **ca·noe'ist** n.

CANOES
A. Dugout. B. Birch bark. C. Modern.

ca·noe·wood (kə·nōō'wŏŏd') n. Tulipwood.

can·on¹ (kan'ən) n. 1 A rule or law; standard; criterion. 2 The books of the Bible that are recognized by the Church as inspired. 3 The list of an author's works which are accepted as genuine: the Shakespearian *canon.* 4 *Eccl.* An official list or catalog, as of the saints recognized by a church, or of the members of a cathedral chapter. 5 *Eccl.* A rule of faith or discipline, especially one enacted by a church council and (in the Roman Catholic Church) ratified by the Pope. 6 *Often cap.* The portion of the mass between the Sanctus and the Lord's Prayer. 7 *Printing* A size of

---

add,āce,câre,pälm; end,ēven; it,īce; odd,ōpen,ôrder; tŏŏk,pool; up,bûrn; ə = a in *above,* e in *sicken,* i in *clarity,* o in *melon,* u in *focus;* yōō = u in *fuse;* oi,oil; ou,pout; ch,check; g,go; ng,ring; th,thin; ŧħ,this; zh,vision. Foreign sounds á,œ,ü,kh,ñ; and ◆ : see page xx. <from; + plus; ? possibly.

type nearly four times as large as pica; 48-point type. See PICA. **8** *Music* A composition having voices or parts wherein each voice or part in turn takes up the same melody (called the subject), and all combine to make harmony: the strictest form of musical imitation. **9** One of the metal loops at the top of a bell, by which it is hung. See synonyms under LAW, RULE. ◆ Homophone: *cannon.* [OE <L <Gk. *kanōn* rule, straight rod]

can·on² (kan'ən) *n.* A member of the chapter of a cathedral or collegiate church. ◆ Homophone: *cannon.* [OE *canonic* <LL *canonicus* cleric <L *canon* rule. See CANON¹.]

ca·non·i·cal (kə·non'i·kəl) *adj.* **1** Belonging to or characteristic of the canon of Scripture. **2** Regular; lawful; accepted or approved. Also **ca·non'ic.** [<Med. L *canonicalis* <L *canonicus* <L *canon.* See CANON¹.] — **ca·non'i·cal·ly** *adv.*

canonical age The age required by canon law for ordination or for the performance of any particular act.

canonical hours 1 *Eccl.* The seven stated daily periods, fixed by canon, for prayer and devotion. They are named respectively matins (including nocturns and lauds), prime, tierce, sext, nones, vespers, and compline. **2** *Brit.* The hours (from 8 a.m. to 3 p.m.) during which marriage may be legally performed in parish churches.

ca·non·i·cals (kə·non'i·kəlz) *n. pl.* The habits or robes prescribed by canon to be worn by the clergy when they officiate.

ca·non·i·cate (kə·non'i·kāt, -kit) *n.* The office of a canon.

can·on·ic·i·ty (kan'ən·is'ə·tē) *n.* **1** The quality of being canonical. **2** Conformity to the canon; orthodoxy.

can·on·ist (kan'ən·ist) *n.* One skilled in canon law. — **can'on·is'tic** or **·ti·cal** *adj.*

can·on·i·za·tion (kan'ən·ə·zā'shən, -ī·zā'-) *n.* **1** The formal enrolling of a deceased and beatified person in the Roman Catholic canon, or calendar of saints. **2** The act of canonizing or regarding as a saint; the state of being canonized.

can·on·ize (kan'ən·īz) *v.t.* **·ized, ·iz·ing 1** To place (a deceased person) in the canon, or catalog of saints; declare to be or regard as a saint. **2** To recognize as part of the canon of Scripture. **3** To sanction as being conformable to the canons of the Church. **4** To give or ascribe glory to; glorify.

canon law The body of ecclesiastical law by which a church is governed.

can·on·ry (kan'ən·rē) *n. pl.* **·ries 1** The office or dignity of a canon; the benefice of a canon. **2** Canons collectively. Also **can'on·ship.**

can·o·py (kan'ə·pē) *n. pl.* **·pies 1** A covering suspended over a throne, bed, shrine, or the like, or held over a person in a procession. **2** Any covering overhead, as the arch of the sky. **3** An ornamental feature covering a niche, or an altar or tomb, or placed over a statue. **4** *Aeron.* **a** The main lifting surface of a parachute, whose unfolding reduces the velocity of descent. **b** The semicircular sliding panel enclosing the cockpit cowling of an airplane. — *v.t.* **·pied, ·py·ing** To cover with or as with a canopy. [<F *canapé* sofa <L *canopeum* mosquito net <Gk. *kōnōpeion* bed with mosquito net <*kōnōps* mosquito]

ca·no·rous (kə·nôr'əs, -nō'rəs) *adj.* Having a singing quality; tuneful; melodious; musical. [<L *canorus* <*canor* song <*canere* sing] — **ca·no'rous·ly** *adv.*

can·so (kan·sō') *n. pl.* **·sos** A lyric poem in Provençal troubadour literature, characterized by great formal elaboration and generally concerning themes of mundane gallantry (*canso d'amor*): also spelled *canzo.* [<Provençal <L *cantio* <*canere* sing]

cant¹ (kant) *n.* **1** An inclination or tipping; a slope or set to one side. **2** A motion that produces a slant or an overturn. **3** A salient angle, as of a bolthead. **4** A slant surface, as one produced by cutting off a corner or edge. — *v.t.* **1** To set slantingly; tip up; tilt. **2** To give a bevel to. **3** To throw out or off; also, to jerk; toss. — *v.i.* **4** To tilt; slant. — *adj.* **1** Oblique; slanting. **2** Having canted sides or corners. [Prob. <OF <Med. L *cantus* corner, side]

cant² (kant) *n.* **1** Hypocritical or ostentatious religious talk. **2** Any technical or professional

jargon: legal *cant.* **3** The secret language of thieves, gipsies, beggars, etc.; argot. **4** Any jargon employed for secrecy. **5** Hackneyed phraseology assumed as a fashion or for effect. **6** Whining speech, especially of beggars. See synonyms under HYPOCRISY, SLANG. — *v.i.* **1** To say with affected religiousness or in a hypocritical way. — *v.i.* **2** To chant; whine, as a beggar. **3** To talk with hypocritical or exaggerated unction, especially about religion. — *adj.* Like cant; insincere; hypocritical. [< AF, singing <L *cantus* song <*canere* sing] — **cant'er** *n.*

can't (kant, känt) Cannot: a contraction.

can·ta·bi·le (kän·tä'bē·lā) *Music adj.* Melodious; flowing. — *n.* Music characterized by flowing melody. [<Ital.]

can·ta·loupe (kan'tə·lōp) *n.* A variety of muskmelon (*Cucumis melo cantalupensis*). Also **can'ta·loup.** [<F from *Cantalupo*, Italian castle where first grown in Europe]

can·tank·er·ous (kan·tang'kər·əs) *adj.* Quarrelsome; ill-natured; perverse. [ME *contak* strife] — **can·tank'er·ous·ly** *adv.* — **can·tank'·er·ous·ness** *n.*

can·tar (kan'tär) *n.* A unit of weight in Moslem countries, commonly between 100 and 130 pounds: also spelled *kantar.* [<Sp. *cantaro* <Arabic *qintar* hundredweight, ult. <L *centenarius* hundredfold]

can·ta·ta (kan·tä'tə) *n. Music* A choral composition in the style of an oratorio or drama, sung but not acted. [<Ital.]

Can·ta·te (kan·tä'tē) The 98th Psalm (97th in the Douai version), used as an alternative canticle in the Book of Common Prayer at Evening Prayer: so called from the first words in Latin, *Cantate Domino* (Sing unto the Lord).

Cantate Sunday The fourth Sunday after Easter, the introit for which is the first verse of the Cantate.

can·teen (kan·tēn') *n.* **1** A small, metal flask for water, coffee, etc. **2** A refreshment and liquor shop; formerly, a shop at a military camp where soldiers might buy provisions. See POST EXCHANGE. **3** An entertainment center or club operated by civilians for enlisted personnel of Army, Navy, Air Force, Marine, and other military units. [<F *cantine* <Ital. *cantina* cellar]

can·ter (kan'tər) *n.* A moderate, easy gallop. — *v.t. & v.i.* To ride or go at an easy gallop. [Short for *Canterbury gallop*; with ref. to the pace of pilgrims riding to Canterbury] — **can'ter·er** *n.*

Canterbury bell One of various cultivated bellflowers, especially *Campanula medium.*

Canterbury gallop A canter: the original term. Also **Canterbury pace, rack,** or **trot.**

Canterbury Tales An uncompleted work (1387–1400) by Chaucer, consisting of a series of tales, largely in verse, told by a group of pilgrims to each other on their way to Canterbury.

can·thar·i·des (kan·thar'ə·dēz) *n.* The dried powder obtained by crushing the Spanish fly or blister beetle: used externally as a rubefacient and vesicant and internally as a diuretic and aphrodisiac. [See CANTHARIS]

can·thar·i·din (kan·thar'ə·din) *n. Chem.* The bitter crystalline anhydride principle, $C_{10}H_{12}O_4$, contained in cantharides: a powerful blistering agent. Also **can·thar'i·dine** (-din, -dēn).

can·tha·ris (kan'thə·ris) *n. pl.* **can·thar·i·des** (kan·thar'ə·dēz) The Spanish fly. [<L <Gk. *kantharis*]

cant–hook (kant'·hŏŏk') *n.* A lever equipped with a hook for handling logs.

can·thus (kan'thəs) *n. pl.* **·thi** (-thī) *Anat.* The angle at the outer or inner junction of the eyelids. [<L <Gk. *kanthos*]

can·ti·cle (kan'ti·kəl) *n.* A non-metrical hymn, as one with words taken directly from the Bible text, to be chanted, as in certain church services. [<L *canticulum*, dim. of *canticum* song]

Can·ti·cles (kan'ti·kəlz) The Song of Solomon.

can·ti·lev·er (kan'tə·lev'ər) *n.* **1** *Engin.* One of two long structural members, as a truss, beam, or slab, lying across a support, with the two projecting arms in balance, as in a **cantilever bridge.** **2** *Archit.* A heavy bracket supporting

CANTILEVER BRIDGE

a balcony, or the like. **3** *Aeron.* A form of airfoil without external bracing. — *v.t. & v.i.* To project (a building member) outward and in balance beyond the base. Sometimes spelled *cantalever.* Also **can'ti·liv'er** (-liv'ər). [Origin uncertain]

can·til·late (kan'tə·lāt) *v.t. & v.i.* **·lat·ed, ·lat·ing** To recite by intoning or chanting: said especially of the manner of rendering the service in Jewish or other rituals. [<L *cantillatus,* pp. of *cantillare* sing low, hum <*cantare* sing] — **can'til·la'tion** *n.*

can·tle (kan'təl) *n.* **1** A piece cut or broken off; a segment; corner. **2** The hind bow of a saddle. [<AF *cantel* <LL *cantellus,* dim. of *cantus* corner]

can·to (kan'tō) *n. pl.* **·tos 1** A division of an extended poem. **2** *Archaic* The part of a musical score to which the melody is assigned; the air. [<Ital. <L *cantus* song]

can·ton (kan'tən, -ton, kan·ton') *n.* **1** A district of the Swiss confederation. **2** A subdivision of an arrondissement in France. **3** The rectangular part of a flag next the staff. **4** *Her.* The diminutive of the quarter, occupying one third of the chief, usually on the dexter side of the shield. **5** An assemblage of village communities. — *v.t.* **1** To divide into cantons. **2** To sever; separate. **3** To assign to quarters, as military troops. [<OF <Ital. *cantone,* aug. of *canto* corner <L *cantus*] — **can·ton·al** (kan'tən·əl) *adj.*

Can·ton 1 (kan·ton') A port on the Canton River, the capital of Kwangtung province, southern China: Chinese *Kwangchow.* **2** (kan'tən) A city in NE Ohio.

can·toned (kan'tənd) *adj.* **1** *Her.* Placed in the midst of four bearings or groups of bearings on a shield, as a cross, or having a single canton, as a shield. **2** *Mil.* Assigned to quarters, as soldiers.

Can·ton·ese (kan'tən·ēz', -ēs') *n. pl.* **·ese 1** A native of Canton, China. **2** The Chinese language spoken in Kwangtung province and other parts of southern China.

can·ton flannel (kan'tən) A heavy cotton fabric having a long nap, usually on one side only: used for undergarments, infants' nightwear, etc. [from *Canton,* China]

Can·ton Island (kan'tən) The largest and northernmost of the Phoenix Islands, comprising a condominium (1939) of the United States and Great Britain; 3 1/2 square miles.

can·ton·ment (kan·ton'mənt, -tōn'-, kan'tən·mənt; *Brit.* kan·tōon'mənt) *n.* **1** A group of wooden buildings for housing troops; a military station. **2** The act of cantoning troops. [<F *cantonnement* <*cantonner* quarter]

can·tor (kan'tər, -tôr) *n.* **1** A precentor; a chief singer. **2** A liturgical singer in a synagog. [<L]

can·tus (kan'təs) *n. pl.* **can·tus 1** A style of church song. **2** The principal voice of a polyphonic work. [<L, song, singing]

cantus fir·mus (fûr'məs) **1** The plain song or chant. **2** *Music* The fixed, simple melody to which other parts are added to make a polyphonic work.

can·vas (kan'vəs) *n.* **1** A heavy, strong cloth of various grades, used for sails, tents, etc. **2** A piece of such cloth; a sail. **3** A strong, closely woven cloth stretched on a frame and prepared for the reception of colors, as in paintings. **4** A painting. **5** A square-meshed fabric of linen, silk, or the like, on which embroidery or tapestry is worked with a needle. **6** A tent; especially, a circus tent. — **under canvas 1** With sails set. **2** In tents. ◆ Homophone: *canvass.* [<AF *canevas* <L

CANT–HOOK

cannabis hemp]

can·vas·back (kan′vəs·bak′) *n.* A North American sea duck (*Nyroca valisineria*) with a grayish white back, highly esteemed for its flesh.

can·vass (kan′vəs) *n.* **1** The going about to solicit orders, interest, or votes. **2** A political campaign. **3** A survey taken to ascertain sentiment. **4** A detailed examination; especially, a sifting of votes in an election; a recount. — *v.t.* **1** To go about an area to solicit, as votes. **2** To scrutinize; examine; sift. — *v.i.* **3** To go about seeking votes, orders or the like: to *canvass* for votes. See synonyms under EXAMINE. ◆ Homophone: *canvas*. [<CANVAS; with ref. to the earlier use of canvas for sifting] — **can′vass·er** *n.*

can·y (kā′nē) *adj.* Full of canes; made of cane.

can·yon (kan′yon) *n.* A deep gorge or ravine, with steep or precipitous sides: also spelled *cañon.* See synonyms under VALLEY. [<Sp. *cañón*]

can·zo·ne (kän·tsō′nā) *n. pl.* **·ni** (-nē) **1** A Provençal or Italian ballad or song. **2** The music for such a song. [<Ital. <L *cantio* song]

can·zo·net (kan′zə·net′) *n.* A short song; light air. [<Ital. *canzonetta,* dim of *canzone* song]

caout·chouc (kōō′chŏŏk, kou·chōōk′) *n.* Rubber; especially, crude rubber. [<F <Tupian *caú–uchú*]

cap¹ (kap) *n.* **1** A covering to be worn on the head; specifically, a brimless head covering, often with a shade or vizor in front. **2** A head covering for a woman or an infant made of lace or some soft fabric. **3** Any headgear of unique design to distinguish some order, office, dignity, or characteristic of the wearer. **4** Anything resembling or used as a cap: a bottle *cap.* **5** The primer of a cartridge or shell case. **6** *Bot.* The pileus of a mushroom. **7** The top of an oil well. **8** Any of various large sizes of writing paper. See FOOLSCAP, LEGAL CAP. **9** *Archit.* The upper member of a column or pilaster; a capital. — **test cap** A protective covering for the exposed end of a cable, excluding dirt, moisture, etc. — **to set one's cap for** To try to win as a suitor or husband. — *v.t.* **capped, cap·ping 1** To put a cap on, as the head. **2** To fit the top or summit of with a cover: Bees *cap* their cells. **3** To serve as a cap to; lie on top of; crown: The cloud *capped* the mountain. **4** To add the final touch to; complete. **5** To excel; top. — **to cap the climax** To surpass the climax; exceed the limit. [OE *cæppe* <LL *cappa* hooded cloak, cap, prob. <*caput* head]

cap² (kap) *n. Colloq.* A capital letter.

ca·pa·bil·i·ty (kā′pə·bil′ə·tē) *n. pl.* **·ties 1** The state or quality of being capable; capacity; ability. **2** Susceptibility to some particular form of use, treatment, or development. **3** *Usually pl.* A feature or condition that may be improved or developed. See synonyms under ABILITY.

ca·pa·ble (kā′pə·bəl) *adj.* **1** Having adequate ability or capacity to do or to receive; efficient; able; qualified; competent. **2** *Obs.* Comprehensive. **3** Adaptable; susceptible: with *of.* See synonyms under CLEVER, COMPETENT. [<F <LL *capabilis* <L *capere* take, receive] — **ca′pa·ble·ness** *n.* — **ca′pa·bly** *adv.*

ca·pa·cious (kə·pā′shəs) *adj.* Able to contain or receive much; spacious; roomy. See synonyms under LARGE. [<L *capax, -acis* able to hold, roomy <*capere* take] — **ca·pa′cious·ly** *adv.* — **ca·pa′cious·ness** *n.*

ca·pac·i·tance (kə·pas′ə·təns) *n. Electr.* **1** In a conductor or system of conductors, the ratio of electrical charge to a resulting potential. **2** That property of a body expressed by the amount of electricity required to give it a potential greater than its surroundings. [<CAPACI(TY) + (REAC)TANCE]

ca·pac·i·tate (kə·pas′ə·tāt) *v.t.* **·tat·ed, ·tat·ing 1** To render capable. **2** To qualify according to law.

ca·pac·i·tive (kə·pas′ə·tiv) *adj. Electr.* Of or relating to capacitance.

ca·pac·i·tor (kə·pas′ə·tər) *n.* A device for accumulating and holding a charge of electricity, consisting of two conductors separated by a dielectric and having equal, opposite charges.

ca·pac·i·ty (kə·pas′ə·tē) *n. pl.* **·ties 1** Ability to receive or contain; cubic extent; carrying power or space. **2** Adequate mental power to receive, understand, etc.; also, ability; talent; capability. **3** Specific position, character, or office. **4** Legal qualification. **5** *Electr.* **a** Capacitance. **b** The output of an electric generator. See synonyms under ABILITY, POWER. [<F *capacité* <L *capacitas, -tatis* <*capax.* See CAPACIOUS.]

cap and bells A cap ornamented with little bells, worn by a fool or court jester.

cap and gown The apparel worn at some academic ceremonies, consisting of a flat cap (*mortarboard*) and a long, dark gown: often used figuratively for the academic life.

ca·par·i·son (kə·par′ə·sən) *n.* **1** Decorative trappings for a horse. **2** Showy or sumptuous apparel. — *v.t.* To put ornamental trappings on; clothe richly. [<OF *caparasson* <Sp. *caparazón* <LL *cappa* cape]

Synonyms (noun): accouterments, harness, housings, trappings. *Harness* was formerly used of the armor of a knight as well as of a horse; it is now used almost exclusively of the equipment of a horse when attached to a vehicle. We speak of the *accouterments* of a soldier. *Caparison* and *trappings* denote the ornamental outfit of a horse, or, in a humorous sense, showy human apparel. Compare ARMS, DRESS.

cape¹ (kāp) *n.* A point of land extending into the sea or a lake. — **the Cape 1** The Cape of Good Hope. **2** *U.S.* Cape Cod. [<F *cap* < L *caput* head]

cape² (kāp) *n.* A circular, sleeveless upper garment; a short cloak. [<F <LL *cappa*] — **caped** (kāpt) *adj.*

cap·e·lin (kap′ə·lin) *n. pl.* **·lin** or **·lins** A small, edible fish (*Mallotus villosus*) of the smelt family, with many–rayed pectoral fins, found in northern seas: much used as cod bait: also spelled *caplin.* [<F *caplan, capelan*]

ca·per¹ (kā′pər) *n.* **1** A leaping or frisking; a skip or jump; prank; antic. **2** Any wild or fantastic action activity. — **to cut a caper** (or **capers**) To caper; frolic. — *v.i.* To leap playfully; frisk. See synonyms under FROLIC. [Short for CAPRIOLE] — **ca′per·er** *n.*

ca·per² (kā′pər) *n.* **1** The flower bud of a low shrub of Mediterranean countries, used as a condiment. **2** The shrub (*Capparis spinosa*) producing it. [<L *capparis* <Gk.*kapparis*]

cap·er·cail·lie (kap′ər·kāl′yē) *n.* A large, black European grouse (*Tetrao urogallus*). Also **cap′er·cail′zie** (-yē, -zē). [<Scottish Gaelic *capullcoille* horse of the wood]

cape·skin (kāp′skin′) *n.* A kind of leather made from lamb or sheep skins, originally from the Cape of Good Hope: used especially for gloves.

Ca·pet (kā′pit, kap′it) See HUGH CAPET.

Cape Town A port on Table Bay, capital of Cape of Good Hope Province, Republic of South Africa. Also **Cape′town′.**

Cape Verde Islands A Portuguese overseas province west of Cape Verde, comprising two groups of islands; 1,557 square miles; capital, Praia, on São Tiago. *Portuguese* **I·lhas do Ca·bo Ver·de** (ē′lyəz hthōō kä′vōō vär′di).

ca·pi·as (kā′pē·əs, kap′ē·əs) *n. pl.* **·as·es** *Law* A judicial writ issued to an officer, commanding him to take and hold in custody the person named therein subject to the order of the court; a writ of arrest. [<L, you may take]

cap·il·la·ceous (kap′ə·lā′shəs) *adj.*Hairlike; capillary. [<L *capillaceus* <*capillus* hair]

cap·il·lar·i·ty (kap′ə·lar′ə·tē) *n.* **1** The state or quality of being capillary. **2** *Physics* The interaction between the molecules of a liquid and those of a solid: a form of surface tension. When the adhesive force is stronger the liquid will tend to rise above mean level at the points of contact with the solid, as water in clean glass; when cohesion dominates, the liquid will tend to fall below this level, as mercury. [<F *capillarité*]

cap·il·lar·y (kap′ə·ler′ē) *adj.* **1** Of, pertaining to, or like hair; fine; slender. **2** Having a hairlike bore, as a tube or vessel; also, pertaining to such a tube. — *n. pl.* **·lar·ies 1** *Anat.* A minute vessel, as those connecting the arteries and veins. **2** Any tube with a fine bore. [<L *capillaris* <*capillus* hair]

cap·il·li·ti·um (kap′ə·lish′ē·əm) *n. pl.* **·li·ti·a**

(-lish′ē·ə) *Bot.* The sterile, branching or anastomosing, threadlike tubes or filaments mixed with the spores in a sporangium, or fruit body, as in myxomycetes. [<L<*capillus* hair]

cap·i·tal¹ (kap′ə·təl) *adj.* **1** Standing at the head or beginning; chief; principal. **2** Excellent; admirable. **3** Of or pertaining to the death penalty; punishable with death. **4** Of or pertaining to funds or capital. See synonyms under EXCELLENT, GOOD. — *n.* **1** The chief city or town of a country, state, province, etc., usually the seat of government. **2** A capital letter. **3** Wealth employed in or available for producing more wealth. **4** Property used in the business of a firm or corporation at a valuation on which profits and dividends are calculated. **5** The aggregate of the products of industry directly available for the support of human existence or for promoting additional production. **6** Possessors of wealth, as a class. **7** Any resource or circumstance that can be utilized for an ambitious objective. ◆ Homophone: *capitol.* [<F <L *capitalis* <*caput* head]

cap·i·tal² (kap′ə·təl) *n. Archit.* The upper member of a column or pillar. ◆ Homophone: *capitol.* [<L *capitellum,* double dim. of *caput* head]

CAPITALS
A. Doric.
  a. Abacus. *b.* Echinus.
  c. Channeled shaft.
B. Egyptian.
C. Ionic.
D. Corinthian.
E. Byzantine.
F. Romanesque.

capital account A statement of the amount and value of a business at a given time, consisting of two columns representing assets and liabilities balanced by profit and loss, indicating a surplus or a deficit.

capital expenditure Expenditure for permanent additions or improvements to property, as opposed to money spent for repairs.

cap·i·tal·ism (kap′ə·təl·iz′əm) *n.* **1** An economic system in which the means of production and distribution are for the most part privately owned and operated for private profit. **2** The possession and concentration of private capital and its resulting power and influence.

cap·i·tal·ist (kap′ə·təl·ist) *n.* **1** One who shares in or adheres to capitalism. **2** An owner of capital; especially, one who has large means employed in productive enterprise. **3** Loosely, any person of apparent wealth. — **cap′i·tal·is′tic** *adj.* — **cap′i·tal·is′ti·cal·ly** *adv.*

cap·i·tal·i·za·tion (kap′ə·təl·ə·zā′shən, -ī·zā′-) *n.* **1** The act or process of capitalizing. **2** The value of the entire property of a business, usually represented by the stock or shares issued as permanent liabilities of the business.

cap·i·tal·ize (kap′ə·təl·īz) *v.t.* **·ized, ·iz·ing 1** To begin with capital letters, or write or print in capital letters. **2** To convert into capital or cash. **3** To convert (a periodical payment) into a sum in hand; compute the value of in a single payment or capital sum. **4** To invest for profit; provide capital. **5** To organize on a basis of capital. **6** To profit by: with *on*: He *capitalized* on his enemy's errors.

capital letter In writing and printing, the form of the alphabetic letter used at the beginning of a sentence, with proper names, etc.: in printing called *cap* or *upper case letter* as distinguished from *lower case letter.* Compare CASE² (def. 3). — **small capital** A letter used in printing having the same form as but of smaller size than the CAPITAL of the same font: also called *small cap.* In this dictionary cross–references are in SMALL CAPITALS.

cap·i·tal·ly (kap′ə·təl·ē) *adv.* **1** Firstly; chiefly. **2** Excellently. **3** So as to deserve death.

capital punishment The death penalty for a crime.

capital ship A warship of large size (including aircraft carriers) carrying guns of over 8–inch caliber; battleship or battle cruiser.

cap·i·tate (kap'ə·tāt) adj. 1 Bot. Head–shaped; headed: a capitate flower. 2 Zool. Enlarged terminally, or knobbed at the end, as tentacles. [<L capitatus having a head < caput head]

cap·i·ta·tion (kap'ə·tā'shən) n. 1 An individual assessment or tax; a poll tax. 2 Any count or fee per capita. [<LL capitatio, -onis poll tax <L caput head]

cap·i·tol (kap'ə·təl) n. The building in which a State legislature convenes; a statehouse. ◆ Homophone: capital.

Cap·i·tol (kap'ə·təl) 1 The official building of the U.S. Congress in Washington. 2 The temple of Jupiter Maximus in ancient Rome, or the Capitoline Hill on which it stood. [< L Capitolium the Capitoline <caput head]

ca·pit·u·lar (kə·pich'oo·lər) adj. 1 Of or belonging to a cathedral chapter; capitulary. 2 Bot. Of, pertaining to, or growing in a capitulum. — n. 1 Any of the collections of laws issued by Charlemagne and his successors. 2 A member of a cathedral chapter. [< L capitularis <capitulum chapter, dim. f caput head]

ca·pit·u·lar·y (kə·pich'oo·ler'ē) adj. Relating to an ecclesiastical hapter. — n. pl. ·lar·ies A capitular.

ca·pit·u·late (kə·pich'oo·lāt) v. ·lat·ed, ·lat·ing v.t. To surrender, as a fort or army, to an enemy on stipulated conditions. — v.i. To surrender on stipulated terms; make terms. — adj. (kə·pich'oo·lit, -lāt) Bot. Headed; having a capitulum. [< L capitulatus, pp. of capitulare draw up in chapters, arrange terms] — ca·pit'u·la'tor n. — ca·pit·u·la·to·ry (kə·pich'oo·lə·tôr'ē, tō'rē) adj.

ca·pit·u·la·tion (kə·pich'oo·lā'shən) n. 1 A conditional surrender, or the instrument embodying it; a charter or treaty. 2 A statement, summary, or enumeration.

ca·pit·u·lum (kə·pich'oo·ləm) n. pl. ·la (-lə) 1 Bot. In phanerogams, a close, head–shaped cluster of sessile flowers, as in the button daisy. See illustration under INFLORESCENCE. 2 Anat. A small rounded body, as at the head of a rib. 3 Zool. The headlike part of ticks and mites. 4 Entomol. The enlarged tip of the antenna or mouth of certain insects. [< L, dim. of caput head]

ca·po das·tro (kä'pō däs'trō) A clamp or nut attached to the finger board of a guitar to raise uniformly the pitch of the strings. Also **capo tas·to** (täs'tō). [<Ital. capo di tastro cap for the keys]

ca·pon (kā'pon, -pən) n. A rooster gelded to improve the flesh for eating. [OE capun <L capo, -onis]

cap·o·ral[1] (kap'ə·ral') n. A form of cut tobacco. [<F (tabac du) caporal corporal's tobacco]

cap·pa·ri·da·ceous (kap'ə·ri·dā'shəs) adj. Bot. Belonging to a family (Capparidaceae) of herbs and shrubs, the caper family. [< L capparis caper]

cap pistol A toy pistol with a hammer for firing caps.

cap·re·o·late (kap'rē·ə·lāt, kə·prē'-) adj. Bot. Like or bearing a tendril. [<L capreolus tendril]

Ca·pri (kä'prē, kə·prē') A resort island at the SE entrance of the Bay of Naples; 4 square miles: a native of the island is known as a Capristano.

Ca·pri blue A vivid turquoise blue: so called from the tones of the Blue Grotto of Capri.

cap·ric (kap'rik) adj. Of, pertaining to, derived from, or like a goat. [<L caper, capri goat]

capric acid Chem. A colorless crystalline compound, $C_{10}H_{20}O_2$ of goatlike odor, found in butter, coconut oil, etc.: used in perfumery.

ca·pric·ci·o (kə·prē'chē·ō, Ital. kä·prēt'chō) n. pl. ·ci·os or Ital. **ca·pric·ci** (kä·prēt'chē) 1 Music A composition of lively and spirited mood and fancifully irregular in form. 2 A prank. [< Ital. <capro goat <L caper]

ca·pric·ci·o·so (kə·prē'chē·ō'sō, Ital. kä'prēt·chō'sō) adj. Music Fanciful; lively; irregular; fantastic. [< Ital.]

ca·price (kə·prēs') n. 1 A sudden unreasonable change of mood or opinion; a whim. 2 Any sudden, arbitrary act or fanciful idea. 3 The mood or state of mind that causes sudden changes or fancies. 4 A capriccio. See synonyms under FANCY, WHIM. [<F <Ital. capriccio. See CAPRICCIO.]

ca·pri·cious (kə·prish'əs, kə·prē'shəs) adj. Characterized by or resulting from caprice; fickle; whimsical; inconstant; unpredictable; also, fanciful. See synonyms under IRRESOLUTE. [<F capricieux] — **ca·pri'cious·ly** adv. — **ca·pri'cious·ness** n.

cap·ri·fi·ca·tion (kap'rə·fi·kā'shən) n. 1 The process and effect of exposing the cultivated fig, at the time when the flowers are within the growing fruit, to the attack of a chalcid insect that infests the wild fig, so as to hasten the ripening and improve the quality of the fruit. 2 Artificial fertilization of the fig or date by this method. [<L caprificatio, -onis <caprificare ripen figs <caprificus wild fig]

cap·ri·fo·li·a·ceous (kap'ri·fō'lē·ā'shəs) adj. Bot. Belonging to the honeysuckle family (Caprifoliaceae) of herbs, woody shrubs, and vines. [<Med. L caprifolium honeysuckle < caper goat + folium leaf]

cap·ri·form (kap'rə·fôrm) adj. Having the form or appearance of a goat. [<L caper, capri goat +-FORM]

cap·ri·ole (kap'rē·ōl) n. An upward leap made by a trained horse while standing. — v.i. ·oled, ·ol·ing To perform a capriole; leap upward. [<F <Ital. capriola, dim. of capra she–goat <L capra]

ca·pro·ic (kə·prō'ik) adj. Of or pertaining to a goat.

caproic acid Chem. A colorless, inflammable fatty acid, $C_6H_{12}O_2$, derived from butter and other sources: used in organic synthesis.

cap·sa·i·cin (kap·sā'ə·sin) n. Chem. A white crystalline compound, $C_{18}H_{27}O_3N$, extracted from cayenne pepper: used in medicine as a rubefacient. [<NL capsicum]

cap screw A screw bolt with a long thread and, generally, a square head: used to secure cylinder covers, etc.

cap·si·cum (kap'si·kəm) n. 1 An herb or shrub of the nightshade family (genus Capsicum), including the common red and other peppers producing many–seeded pods prepared as condiments or gastric stimulants. 2 The fruit of these plants. [<L capsa box (from the shape of the fruit)]

cap·size (kap·sīz', kap'sīz) v.t. & v.i. ·sized, ·siz·ing To upset or overturn. [? <Sp. capuzar sink a ship by the head <cabo head]

cap·stan (kap'stən)
n. Naut. A drumlike apparatus for hoisting anchors or other weights by exerting traction upon a cable. [<F cabestan <L capistrum halter < capere hold]

capstan bar A lever used in turning a capstan.

CAPSTAN
a. Drumhead. b. Bar-hole. c. Capstan bar. d. Barrel. e. Pawls. f. Pawl-rim.

cap·stone (kap'stōn) n. Copestone.

cap·su·late (kap'sə·lāt, -syoō-) adj. 1 Enclosed in a capsule. 2 Having or formed into a capsule or capsules. Also **cap'su·lat'ed**. [<NL capsulatus <L capsula, dim. of capsa box] — **cap'su·la'tion** n.

cap·sule (kap'səl, -syoōl) n. 1 Bot. a A dry dehiscent seed vessel made up of more than one carpel, as of a pink or a lily. b The spore case of a moss or other cryptogam. 2 Med. A small gelatinous case for containing a dose of a drug. 3 Biol. A capsulelike organ, membrane, or structure: the suprarenal capsule. 4 The cargo or passenger container of a space rocket. 5 A metallic shell, cap, or seal, as of a cartridge or percussion cap. — v.t. 1 To furnish with or enclose in or as in a capsule. 2 To summarize. — adj. Small and compact; condensed; brief. [<F <L capsula, dim. of capsa box] — **cap·su·lar** (kap'sə·lər, -syoō-) adj.

CAPSULES
A. Iris. B. Carnation. C. Poppy.

cap·tain (kap'tən, -tin) n. 1 One at the head of or in command of others; a chief; leader; commander. 2 The master or commander of a vessel, regardless of rank. 3 In the U.S. Army, Air Force, or Marine Corps, a commissioned officer ranking next above a first lieutenant and next below a major. 4 In the U.S. Navy and Coast Guard, a commissioned officer ranking next above a commander and next below a rear admiral: equal in rank to a colonel in the Army, Air Force, or Marine Corps. See table under GRADE. See synonyms under CHIEF, MASTER. — v.t. To be captain over; act as captain to; command; manage; lead. [<OF capitaine <LL capitaneus <L caput head. Doublet of CHIEFTAIN.] — **cap'tain·cy, cap'tain·ship** n.

cap·tion (kap'shən) n. 1 The title or introductory part of a legal document, showing time, place, circumstances, authority, etc., or a notary's affidavit, endorsed or affixed. 2 A heading of a chapter, section, document, etc. 3 The title of an illustration. 4 The subtitle in a motion picture. 5 Obs. Any seizure or capture. — v.t. To provide a caption for. [<L captio, -onis seizure, deception, sophism < capere take; in senses 1–4 infl. in meaning by L caput head]

cap·tious (kap'shəs) adj. 1 Apt to find fault; hypercritical. 2 Perplexing; sophistical. [<L captiosus fallacious < captio sophism < capere take] — **cap'tious·ly** adv. — **cap'tious·ness** n.
Synonyms: carping, caviling, censorious, critical, cross, cynical, faultfinding, hypercritical. Antonyms: appreciative, approving, commendatory, eulogistic, flattering, laudatory.

cap·ti·vate (kap'tə·vāt) v.t. ·vat·ed, ·vat·ing 1 To charm; win; fascinate. 2 Obs. To capture; subdue. See synonyms under ALLURE, CHARM. [<LL captivatus, pp. of captivare capture <captivus CAPTIVE] — **cap'ti·va'tion** n. — **cap'ti·va'tor** n.

cap·tive (kap'tiv) n. 1 One captured and held in confinement or restraint; a prisoner. 2 One who is held captive in will and feeling. — adj. 1 Taken prisoner, as in war; held in confinement or bondage. 2 Charmed or subdued in will or feeling. [<F captif <L captivus < capere take. Doublet of CAITIFF.]

captive balloon See under BALLOON.

cap·tiv·i·ty (kap·tiv'ə·tē) n. The state of being held captive; thraldom. See synonyms under BONDAGE.

cap·tor (kap'tər) n. One who takes or holds captive.

cap·ture (kap'chər) v.t. ·tured, ·tur·ing 1 To take captive; seize and hold or carry off, as in war. 2 To take possession of; catch; gain; win. See synonyms under ARREST, CATCH. — n. 1 A capturing, or being captured. 2 The person or thing captured. [<MF <L captura < capere take]

cap·u·chin (kap'yoō·chin, -shin) n. 1 A woman's hooded cloak, or hood. 2 A long–tailed South American ceboid monkey (genus Cebus) whose head is covered with a cowl–like growth of hair. [<Ital. cappuccino < cappuccio]

ca·put (kā'pət, kap'ət) n. pl. ca·pi·ta (kap'ə·tə) 1 The head; also, any rounded extremity of an organ; top. 2 Law The person; a citizen; one holding civil rights; the status of a citizen before the law. 3 The former governing council of Cambridge University in England. [<L, head]

cap·y·ba·ra (kap'i·bä'rə) n. A South American rodent (Hydrochoerus capybara) about 4 feet long, with coarse, dark brown fur, webbed feet, and a stumpy tail: it frequents the borders of lakes and rivers. [<Sp. capibara <Tupian kapigwara]

car (kär) n. 1 A vehicle for use on tracks. 2 Any wheeled vehicle, as an automobile. 3 Poetic A chariot. 4 The contents of a car; carload. 5 The cage of an elevator. 6 The basket of a balloon or the like. 7 A floating box for live fish. [<AF carre <LL carra, var. of carrus wagon, ult. <Celtic]

car·a·cal (kar'ə·kal) n. 1 The Persian lynx (Felis or Lynx caracal) of SW Asia and the greater part of Africa, somewhat larger than a fox, reddish–brown with black–tipped ears. 2 Its pelt or fur. [<F <Turkish qarah qulaq < qarah black + qulaq ear]

ca·ra·ca·ra (kä′rə·kä′rə) *n.* A large, vulturelike hawk of South America: **Audubon's caracara** (*Polyborus cheriway*) sometimes reaches as far north as the southern borders of the United States. [<Sp. *caracará* <Tupian]

Ca·ra·cas (kə·rä′kəs, -rak′əs; *Sp.* kä·rä′käs) The largest city and capital of Venezuela.

car·ack (kar′ək) *n.* A large Portuguese or Spanish merchant vessel, frequently armed, in use from the 15th to the 17th century: also spelled *carrack.* [<OF *carraque* <Med. L *carraca,* ? <Arabic *qaraqīr,* pl. of *qorqūr* merchant ship]

car·a·cole (kar′ə·kōl) *n.* A sudden half turn to the right or left made by a horseman in riding; curvet. — *v.* **·coled, ·col·ing** *v.t. Rare* To cause to curvet or half-wheel: He was fond of *caracoling* his horse. — *v.i.* To make or cause one's horse to make caracoles; prance; wheel in line of files, as cavalry. Also **car′a·col** (-kol). [<F <Ital. *caracollo*]

ca·rafe (kə·raf′, -räf′) *n.* A glass water bottle; decanter. [<F, ? <Arabic *gharafa* draw water]

car·a·mel (kar′ə·məl, -mel, kär′məl) *n.* **1** A confection, variously colored and flavored, composed of sugar, butter, and other ingredients. **2** Burnt sugar; the brown or black, soluble material obtained by heating sugar or molasses, or from starch by converting it into glucose: used to color soups, liquids, gravies, and the like. **3** A reddish tan, the color of burnt sugar. [<F, alter. of OF *calemele* <Med. L *calamellus,* alter. of *canna mellis* sugarcane, under the infl. of L *calamus* reed]

car·a·mel·ize (kar′ə·məl·īz′, kär′məl-) *v.t.* **·ized, ·iz·ing** To heat (sugar) slowly until melted and brown. — **car′a·mel·i·za′tion** *n.*

ca·ran·goid (kə·rang′goid) *adj.* Belonging to a family (*Carangidae*) of fishes having a rudimentary dorsal fin, and usually two anal spines forming a detached portion, as in cavallies, pompanos, etc. — *n.* Any member of this family. [<NL *caranx, -angis* <Sp. *carangue* flatfish]

car·a·pace (kar′ə·pās) *n.* **1** *Zool.* The hard bony or chitinous outer case on the back of various animals, as of a turtle or a lobster. **2** Any protective, umbrellalike covering. Also **car′a·pax** (-paks). [<F <Sp. *carapacho*] — **car′a·pa′cic** (-pā′sik) *adj.*

car·at (kar′ət) *n.* **1** A unit of weight for gems: one metric carat is 200 milligrams, or 3.086 grains. **2** Loosely, a karat. ◆ Homophone: *carrot.* [<F <Ital. *carato* <Arabic *qīrāt* weight of 4 grains <Gk. *keration* seed, small weight]

car·a·van (kar′ə·van) *n.* **1** An Oriental armed company of traders, pilgrims, etc. **2** A traveling company or menagerie. **3** A van; a house on wheels. **4** A company of people traveling together with wagons, pack horses, etc. **5** A train of wagons or pack horses, or of motor vehicles. [<F *caravane* <Persian *kārwān* caravan]

car·a·van·sa·ry (kar′ə·van′sə·rē) *n. pl.* **·ries** **1** A large square building enclosing a court for the shelter of caravans in Oriental countries. **2** A hostelry or inn. Also **car′a·van′se·rai** (-rī, -rā), **car′a·van′se·ry.** [<F *caravan-sérai* <Persian *kārwānsarāi* <*kārwān* caravan + *sarāi* inn]

car·a·vel (kar′ə·vel) *n.* A fleet vessel of Spain and Portugal in the 15th century: sometimes

CARAVELS
A. The *Santa Maria* of Columbus.
B. A caravel, showing the set of the sails.

spelled *carvel.* Also **car′a·velle.** [<MF *caravelle* <Sp. *carabela,* dim. of *caraba* boat <L *carabus* <Gk. *korabus*]

car·a·way (kar′ə·wā) *n.* A European biennial herb (*Carum carvi*) of the parsley family: its fruits, called **caraway seeds,** are small, spicy, aromatic seeds used for flavoring food. [<Sp. *alcarahueya* <Arabic *al* the + *karwīyā* caraway <Gk. *karon*]

car·ba·mate (kär′bə·māt, kär·bam′āt) *n. Chem.* A salt or ester of carbamic acid containing the univalent NH₂COO radical.

car·bam·ic (kär·bam′ik) *adj. Chem.* Of, pertaining to, or derived from the amide of carbonic acid and the amide radical NH₂.

carbamic acid *Chem.* A theoretical compound, NH_2COOH, known only by its salts and esters.

car·bam·ide (kär·bam′īd, -id, kär′bə·mīd) *n. Chem.* Urea or one of its isomers. Also **car·bam′id** (-id). [<CARB- + AMIDE]

car·ba·zole (kär′bə·zōl) *n. Chem.* A white crystalline compound, $C_{12}H_9N$, derived from coal tar: used in dyes and as a stabilizer in making explosives. [<CARB- + AZOLE]

car·bide (kär′bīd, -bid) *n. Chem.* A compound of carbon with a more positive element: calcium *carbide,* CaC_2.

car·bine (kär′bīn, -bēn) *n. Mil.* A light, short-barreled rifle originally devised for mounted troops. A magazine-fed, gas-operated carbine weighing about five pounds was adopted in the United States in World War II for certain ranks previously armed with pistols. Also spelled *carabin, carabine.* [<F *carabine*]

car·bi·neer (kär′bə·nir′) *n.* A soldier armed with a carbine: also spelled *carabineer, carabinier.*

car·bi·nol (kär′bə·nōl, -nol) *n. Chem.* Methanol. [<G; name given to wood alcohol by Adolf Kolbe, German chemist, 1818–84]

carbo- *combining form* Carbon: *carbohydrate.* Also, before vowels, **carb-**. [<L *carbo* coal]

car·bo·hy·drate (kär′bō·hī′drāt) *n. Biochem.* Any one of a group of compounds containing carbon combined with hydrogen and oxygen in the form of an aldose or a ketose, essential in the metabolism of plants and animals. The carbohydrates include sugars, starches, and cellulose.

car·bo·late (kär′bə·lāt) *n. Chem.* An ester of carbolic acid.

car·bo·lat·ed (kär′bə·lā′tid) *adj.* Carbolized.

car·bol·ic (kär·bol′ik) *adj. Chem.* **1** Of, pertaining to, or derived from carbon and oil. **2** Of or pertaining to coal-tar oil. [<CARB- + L *oleum* oil]

carbolic acid Phenol (def. 2).

car·bo·lize (kär′bə·līz) *v.t.* **·lized, ·liz·ing** *Chem.* To treat or impregnate with carbolic acid.

car·bon (kär′bən) *n.* **1** A nonmetallic element (symbol C, atomic number 6) found free as diamond, graphite, and amorphous carbon, and having the property of forming stable rings and long chains which are the basis of millions of organic compounds. See PERIODIC TABLE. **2** *Electr.* A rod of carbon, used as an electrode in an arc light. **3** A piece of carbon paper. **4** A carbon copy. —*adj.* **1** Of, pertaining to, or like carbon. **2** Treated with carbon: *carbon* paper. [<F *carbone* <L *carbo,* *-onis* coal]

carbon 13 *Physics* A heavy carbon isotope of mass 13, used as a tracer element in the study of physiological processes.

carbon 14 *Physics* Radiocarbon.

car·bo·na·ceous (kär′bə·nā′shəs) *adj.* Of, pertaining to, or yielding carbon.

car·bo·na·do¹ (kär′bə·nā′dō) *n. pl.* **·does** or **·dos** A bird, fish, or piece of meat scored and broiled. —*v.t.* **·doed, ·do·ing** *Obs.* **1** To hack or slash. **2** To score and broil. [<Sp. *carbonada* <*carbón* coal <L *carbo*]

car·bo·na·do² (kär′bə·nā′dō) *n. pl.* **·does** Bort. [<Pg., carbonated]

car·bon·ate (kär′bə·nāt) *Chem. v.t.* **·at·ed, ·at·ing** **1** To charge with carbonic acid. **2** To carbonize. —*n.* (kär′bə·nāt, -nit) A salt or ester of carbonic acid.

carbon bisulfide Carbon disulfide.

carbon black A deep, smooth, permanent black pigment made of pure carbon: also called *lampblack, ivory black.*

carbon copy 1 A copy of a typewritten letter, etc., made by means of carbon paper. **2** An exact replica; duplicate.

carbon cycle 1 *Physics* A 6-stage thermonuclear process taking place in the interior of stars, by which hydrogen is transformed into helium through the catalytic action of carbon and nitrogen. Compare PROTON-PROTON REACTION. **2** *Biol.* The biological elaboration and destruction in the biosphere of carbon compounds derived from atmospheric carbon dioxide by photosynthesis.

carbon dioxide A heavy, colorless, non-flammable gas, CO_2, formed by the oxidation of carbon, by the interaction of carbonates and acids, and in the respiration of plants and animals. It is irrespirable, extinguishes fire, and is moderately soluble in water.

carbon disulfide *Chem.* A colorless, limpid, volatile, and highly inflammable liquid, CS_2, with a disagreeable odor: used as a solvent for oils, resins, etc., and for the extermination of vermin.

car·bon·ic (kär·bon′ik) *adj.* Of, pertaining to, or obtained from carbon.

carbonic acid *Chem.* A weak, unstable dibasic acid, H_2CO_3, existing only in solution and readily dissociating into water and carbon dioxide.

car·bon·ic-ac·id gas (kär·bon′ik·as′id) Carbon dioxide.

car·bon·if·er·ous (kär′bə·nif′ər·əs) *adj.* Of, pertaining to, containing, or yielding carbon or coal.

car·bon·i·za·tion (kär′bən·ə·zā′shən, -ī·zā′-) *n.* The conversion of organic matter, as wood, into coal or charcoal.

car·bon·ize (kär′bən·īz) *v.t.* **·ized, ·iz·ing 1** To reduce to carbon; char. **2** To coat with carbon, as paper. **3** To charge with carbon.

carbonized cloth Cloth charred in a vacuum: used for high electrical resistance.

car·bon·iz·er (kär′bən·ī′zər) *n.* Carburetor (def. 1).

carbon monoxide *Chem.* A colorless, odorless gas, CO, formed by the incomplete oxidation of carbon. It burns with a blue flame to form carbon dioxide, and is highly poisonous when inhaled, since it combines with the hemoglobin of the blood to the exclusion of oxygen.

carbon paper Tissue paper so prepared with carbon or other material that it will reproduce on paper underneath a copy of anything impressed upon it, as by pencil or typewriter. Also **carbon tissue.**

carbon process A photographic printing process employing a tissue or film of gelatin colored with a permanent and insoluble pigment. Also **carbon printing.**

carbon tetrachloride *Chem.* A colorless, nonflammable liquid, CCl_4, produced by the action of chlorine on carbon disulfide: used as a solvent, local anesthetic, fire extinguisher, cleaning fluid.

car·bon·yl (kär′bən·il) *n. Chem.* **1** A bivalent organic radical, CO, known only in combination. **2** A compound of a metal and carbon monoxide: nickel *carbonyl.* —**car′bon·yl′ic** *adj.*

carbonyl chloride *Chem.* Phosgene.

Car·bo·run·dum (kär′bə·run′dəm) *n.* An abrasive of silicon carbide: a trade name.

car·box·yl (kär·bok′sil) *n. Chem.* A univalent acid radical, COOH, characteristic of nearly all organic acids. [<CARB(ON) + OX(YGEN) + -YL] —**car·box·yl′ic** (kär′bok·sil′ik) *adj.*

car·box·y·lase (kär·bok′sə·lās) *n. Biochem.* An enzyme found in yeast which splits carbon dioxide from the carboxyl group of amino acids. [<CARBOXYL + -ASE]

car·bun·cle (kär′bung·kəl) *n.* **1** *Pathol.* An inflammation of the subcutaneous tissue, resembling a boil but larger and more painful. **2** A red garnet cut without facets and concave below, to show the color. **3** Any deep red gem. [<AF <L *carbunculus,* dim. of *carbo* coal] —**car·bun·cu·lar** (kär·bung′kyə·lər) *adj.*

car·bu·ret (kär′bə·rāt, -byə·ret) *v.t.* **·ret·ed** or **·ret·ted, ·ret·ing** or **·ret·ting** To carburize; combine chemically with carbon. [<NL *carburetum* carbide] —**car·bu·re·tion** (kär′bə·rā′shən, -byə·resh′ən) *n.*

car·bu·re·tor (kär′bə·rā′tər, -byə·ret′ər) *n.* **1** An apparatus used to charge air or gas with volatilized hydrocarbons to give it illuminating power:

also called *carbonizer.* **2** A device for carrying a current of air through or over a liquid fuel, so that the air may take up the vapor to form the explosive mixture, as in internal-combustion engines. **3** A hydrocarbon so used. Also **car·bu·ret·tor** (kär′bya·ret′·ar), **car′bu·ret′ter.**

car·bu·rize (kär′bya·rīz, -bya-) *v.t.* **·rized, ·riz·ing 1** To combine or impregnate with carbon, as gas to increase its illuminating power. **2** *Metall.* To impregnate the surface layer of (low-carbon steel) with carbon: a stage in casehardening. Also *Brit.* **car′bu·rise.** [< F *carbure* carbide + -IZE] —**car′bu·ri·za′tion** *n.* —**car′bu·riz′er** *n.*

car·byl·a·mine (kär′bil·a·mēn′, -am′in) *n. Chem.* An organic compound containing the radical -NC.

car·cass (kär′kas) *n.* **1** The dead body of an animal. **2** The human body: a contemptuous or humorous use. **3** Something from which the vital principle, importance, or value has departed; lifeless or worthless remains. **4** A framework or skeleton, as of a construction. Also **car′case.** See synonyms under BODY. [< AF *carcas* < Med. L *carcasium* infl. in form by MF *carcasse* a corpse < Ital. *carcassa*]

car·cel (kär′sal) *n.* The light of a Carcel lamp burning 42 grams of colza oil an hour with a flame 40 millimeters high: a photometric standard, equal to 9.6 international candles. [after B. G. *Carcel,* 1750–1812, French inventor]

Car·cha·ri·as (kär·kā′rē·as) *n.* The typical genus of a family of sharks *(Carcharinidae).* [< NL < Gk. *karcharias* a saw-toothed shark]

car·cin·o·gen (kär′sin′a·jen) *n.* A cancer-producing substance. —**car·cin·o·gen·ic** (kär′sən·a·jen′ik) *adj.*

car·ci·no·ma (kär′sa·nō′ma) *n. pl.* **·mas** or **·ma·ta** (-ma·ta) A cancer; a malignant tumor that arises from epithelial cells and spreads by metastasis. [< L < Gk. *karkinoma* < *karkinos* cancer] —**car′ci·nom′a·tous** (-nom′a·tas, -nō′ma-) *adj.*

card[1] (kärd) *n.* **1** A piece of cardboard bearing, or intended to bear, written or printed words, symbols, etc.: used for social and business purposes. **2** A piece of cardboard imprinted with symbols, for use in certain games of chance and skill: in such use specifically called a **playing card. 3** *pl.* Any or all games played with playing cards. **4** A small advertisement or published statement printed on a card. **5** A chart giving a table of information, etc. **6** A program or a menu; hence, an authorized announcement of a coming event. **7** *Naut.* The dial of a compass. **8** *Colloq.* A person manifesting some peculiarity: He is a queer *card.* **9** Cardboard. —**on the cards 1** Listed on the program; scheduled to occur. **2** Possible; likely to happen. —**to put one's cards on the table** To reveal one's intentions or resources with complete frankness. —*v.t.* **1** To fasten or write upon a card or cards. **2** To provide with a card. [< F *carte* < Ital. *carta* card, sheet of paper < L *charta* paper < Gk. *chartēs.* Doublet of CHART.]

card[2] (kärd) *n.* **1** A wire-toothed brush for combining and cleansing wool and other fiber. **2** A similar instrument for currying cattle and horses. —*v.t.* To comb, dress, or cleanse with a card. [< MF *carde* < Ital. *carda* < Med. L < *cardus* < L *carduus* thistle] —**card′er** *n.*

car·da·mom (kär′da·mam) *n.* **1** The fruit of an East Indian or Chinese plant of the ginger family *(Elettaria cardamomum)* having aromatic seeds, used as a condiment. **2** One of the plants yielding this fruit. Also **car′da·mon** (-man), **car′da·mum.** [< L *cardamomum* < Gk. *kardamōmon* < *kardamon* cress + *amōmon* spice]

card·board (kärd′bôrd′, -bōrd′) *n.* A thin, stiff pasteboard used for making cards, boxes, etc. —*adj.* **1** Made of cardboard. **2** Flimsy; insubstantial.

card catalog A catalog made out on cards, especially for library books.

car·di·a (kär′dē·a) *n. Anat.* The upper orifice of the stomach, where the esophagus discharges. [< Gk. *kardia* heart]

car·di·ac (kär′dē·ak) *Med. adj.* **1** Pertaining to, situated near, or affecting the heart or the cardia. **2** Of, pertaining to, or designating the upper esophageal orifice of the stomach. Also **car·di·a·cal** (kär·dī′a·kal). —*n.* **1** One suffering from a heart disease. **2** A cardiac remedy or stimulant; a cordial.

cardiac neurosis *Psychiatry* Abnormal heart action due primarily to nervous disorder or emotional disturbance, without pathological change.

car·di·al·gi·a (kär′dē·al′jē·a) *n. Pathol.* A burning sensation of the stomach, caused by indigestion; gastric neuralgia; heartburn: once thought to be an affliction of the heart. Also **car′di·al′gy.** [< NL < Gk. *kardialgia* < *kardia* heart + *algos* pain] —**car′di·al′gic** *adj.*

car·di·nal (kär′da·nal) *adj.* **1** Of prime importance; chief; fundamental; principal. **2** Of a deep scarlet color. **3** Of or relating to a cardinal or cardinals. —*n.* **1** One of the ecclesiastical body of the Roman Catholic Church known as the sacred college, an electoral college by which the Pope is elected and which constitutes his chief advisory council; a prince and senator of the Church. **2** A cardinal bird. **3** A short, hooded cloak worn by women in the 18th century. **4** A deep scarlet, the color of a cardinal's cassock. **5** A dyestuff, derived from magenta, for dyeing cardinal-red. **6** A cardinal number. [< F < L *cardinalis* important < *cardo* hinge] —**car′di·nal·ly** *adv.*

car·di·nal·ate (kär′da·nal·āt′) *n.* The rank, dignity, or term of office of a cardinal. Also **car′di·nal·ship′.**

cardinal bird A North American bright-red, crested finch (genus *Richmondena*); especially, the common redbird of the eastern United States. Also **cardinal grosbeak.**

cardinal flower A perennial North American herb *(Lobelia cardinalis)* having large red flowers: also called *red lobelia.*

car·di·nal·i·ty (kär′da·nal′a·tē) *n. Math.* The property of being expressible by a cardinal number, as any finite or restricted series of numbers.

cardinal point Any one of the four principal points of the compass.

cardinal virtues Virtues of the first importance or rank, as the "natural virtues" of ancient philosophy: justice, prudence, temperance, and fortitude; with the "theological virtues," faith, hope, and charity, these form the seven cardinal virtues of medieval and modern writers.

card·ing (kär′ding) *n.* **1** The preparing of wool, flax, or cotton fibers before drawing or spinning. **2** Material as it comes from the carding machine.

cardio- *combining form* Heart: cardiogram. Also, before vowels, *cardi-.* [< Gk. *kardia* heart]

car·di·o·gram (kär′dē·a·gram′) *n.* The graphic record of heart movements produced by the cardiograph.

car·di·o·graph (kär′dē·a·graf′, -gräf′) *n.* An instrument for tracing and recording the force of the movements of the heart. —**car·di·o·graph′ic** *adj.* —**car·di·og·ra·phy** (kär′dē·og′ra·fē) *n.*

car·di·oid (kär′dē·oid) *Math.* A heart-shaped curve generated by a point in the circumference of a circle which rolls on another fixed circle of the same size.

car·di·ol·o·gy (kär′dē·ol′a·jē) *n.* The science of the heart and its physiology and pathology.

car·di·o·pul·mo·nar·y (kär′dē·ō·pōōl′ma·ner′ē) *adj.* Pertaining to or affecting the heart and lungs: cardiopulmonary resuscitation. Also **cardiorespiratory.**

cardiopulmonary resuscitation (kär′dē·ō·pōōl′ma·ner·ē, -pul′-) A first-aid method of restoring the heartbeat and breathing by alternately compressing the chest and applying mouth-to-mouth insufflation. Also *CPR.*

car·di·ot·o·my (kär′dē·ot′a·mē) *n. Surg.* Incision of the heart or of the cardiac end of the esophagus.

car·di·o·vas·cu·lar (kär′dē·ō·vas′kya·lar) *adj.* Pertaining to or affecting the heart and the blood vessels: cardiovascular disease.

car·di·tis (kär·dī′tis) *n. Pathol.* Inflammation of the muscular substance of the heart.

car·doon (kär·dōōn′) *n.* A perennial plant of the Mediterranean region *(Cynara cardunculus),* allied to the artichoke and eaten as a vegetable. [< MF *cardon* < Ital. *cardone,* aug. of *cardo* thistle < L *carduus* thistle]

card·sharp (kärd′shärp′) *n.* One who cheats at cards, especially as a profession. Also **card′sharp′er.** —**card′sharp′ing** *n.*

car·du·a·ceous (kär′jōō·ā′shas) *adj. Bot.* Of or belonging to the thistle group (formerly the *Carduaceae*) of the composite family, having heavy-headed radiate flowers. [< NL < L *carduus* thistle]

care (kâr) *v.i.* **cared, car·ing 1** To have or show

regard, interest or concern as respecting some person, thing, or event. **2** To be wishful or inclined: Do you *care* to read this book? **3** To mind or be concerned; harbor an objection: used chiefly in negative or conditional expressions: I don't *care* if it rains. —**to care for 1** To protect or provide for; guard; watch over. **2** To be interested in or concerned for some person or thing; also, to feel affection for; hold in high regard or esteem. —*n.* **1** A state of oppressive anxiety or concern; solicitude. **2** Responsible charge or oversight. **3** Watchful regard or attention; heed. **4** Any object of solicitude or guardianship. **5** Affliction; distress. [OE *carian*] —**car′er** *n.*

Synonyms (noun): anxiety, attention, caution, charge, circumspection, concern, direction, forethought, heed, management, oversight, perplexity, precaution, prudence, solicitude, trouble, vigilance, wariness, watchfulness, worry. *Care* inclines to the positive, *caution* to the negative; *care* is shown in doing, *caution* largely in not doing. *Precaution* is allied with *care, prudence* with *caution;* a man rides a dangerous horse with *care;* caution may keep him from mounting the horse; *precaution* looks to the saddle girths, bit, and bridle, and all that may make the rider secure. *Circumspection* is watchful observation and calculation, but without the timidity implied in *caution. Concern* denotes a serious interest, milder than *anxiety;* as, *concern* for the safety of a ship at sea. *Heed* implies *attention* without disquiet; it is now largely displaced by *attention* and *care. Solicitude* involves especially the element of personal concern for another not expressed in *anxiety,* and of hopefulness not implied in *care. Watchfulness* recognizes the possibility of danger, *wariness* the probability. A man who is not influenced by *caution* to keep out of danger may display great *wariness* in the midst of it. *Care* has also the sense of responsibility, with possible control, as expressed in *charge, management, oversight;* as, these children are under my *care;* send the money to me in *care* of the firm. Compare ALARM, ANXIETY, OVERSIGHT, PRUDENCE. Antonyms: carelessness, disregard, heedlessness, inattention, indifference, neglect, negligence, omission, oversight, recklessness, remissness, slight.

CARE (kâr) A non-profit organization begun after World War II to send food and clothing parcels overseas to the needy. [< C(OOPERATIVE FOR) A(MERICAN) R(EMITTANCES) E(VERYWHERE)]

ca·reen (ka·rēn′) *v.t.* **1** To cause to turn over to one side; heel over, as for repairing or cleaning the bottom of: to *careen* a ship. **2** To clean, repair, or calk (a careened ship.) —*v.i.* **3** To heel over, as a vessel in the wind. **4** To clean, repair, or calk a ship when turned on one side. **5** To lurch or twist from side to side: The car *careened* down the slope. —*n.* **1** The act of inclining a ship to one side. **2** The cleaning or repairing of a ship that is turned over. **3** A careening. [< F *cariner, caréner* < *carène* keel of a ship < L *carina*] —**ca·reen′er** *n.*

ca·reen·age (ka·rē′nij) *n.* **1** The charge for careening. **2** A place where a ship is careened for repairs.

ca·reer (ka·rir′) *n.* **1** A free and swift course; a swift run or charge. **2** A complete course or progress extending through the life or a portion of it, especially when abounding in remarkable actions or incidents: His was a remarkable *career.* **3** A course of business, activity, or enterprise; especially, a course of professional life or employment. **4** A short, rapid gallop or encounter, as in a tournament; a charge; an assault. **5** *Obs.* Originally, a racecourse. —*v.i.* To move with a swift, free, and headlong motion. [< F *carrière* racecourse < LL *carraria (via)* road for carriages < *carrus* wagon] —**ca·reer′er** *n.*

Synonyms (noun): achievement, charge, course, flight, passage, race, rush. Compare BUSINESS.

care·free (kâr′frē) *adj.* Free of troubles; without responsibilities; light-hearted.

care·ful (kâr′fal) *adj.* **1** Exercising, marked by, or done with care. **2** Attentive and prudent; circumspect. See synonyms under PRECISE, THOUGHTFUL. —**care′ful·ly** *adv.* —**care′ful·ness** *n.*

care·less (kâr′lis) *adj.* **1** Neglectful; indifferent; heedless. **2** Free from solicitude or anxiety; lighthearted. **3** Negligent; unconcerned. **4** Not studied or constrained; easy: a *careless* attitude. See synonyms under CURSORY, IMPROVIDENT, IMPRUDENT, INATTENTIVE, SECURE. —**care′less·ly** *adv.* —**care′less·ness** *n.*

ca·ress (kə·res′) *n.* A gentle, affectionate movement; an expression of affection or attachment by touching, as by patting, embracing, or stroking. —*v.t.* To touch or handle lovingly; fondle; embrace; pet. [< F *caresse* < Ital. *carezza* < L *carus* dear] —**ca·ress′er** *n.* —**ca·ress′ing** *adj.* —**ca·ress′ive** *adj.*

Synonyms (verb): coddle, embrace, flatter, fondle, kiss, pamper, pet. To *caress* is less than to *embrace. Fondling* is always by touch; *caressing* may be also by words, or other tender and pleasing attentions. See PAMPER.

car·et (kar′ət) *n.* A sign (^) placed below a line to denote an omission. [< L, it is missing]

care·tak·er (kâr′tā′kər) *n.* **1** One who takes care of a place, thing, or person. **2** One employed to watch over property or keep it in order, as a house in the absence of its owner, or the property of an insolvent, to see that nothing is removed.

care-worn (kâr′wôrn′) *adj.* Harassed with troubles or worries.

car·fare (kär′fâr′) *n.* The charge for a ride on a bus, streetcar, etc.

car·go (kär′gō) *n. pl.* **·goes** or **·gos** **1** Goods and merchandise taken on board a vessel; lading. **2** Load. [< Sp. < LL *carricum* load < *carricare* load < *carrus* wagon]

cargo vessel 1 A vessel of the merchant marine, carrying goods or merchandise exclusive of passengers or animals. **2** A naval vessel for transporting goods.

Car·ib·be·an (kar′ə·bē′ən, kə·rib′ē·ən) *n.* A Carib Indian. —*adj.* **1** Of or pertaining to the Caribbean Sea. **2** Of the Carib Indians, their language, culture, etc.

car·i·be (kar′ə·bē, *Sp.* kä·rē′bā) *n.* A carnivorous, fresh-water characin fish of tropical South America (genus *Serrasalmo*), with massive jaws and sharp trenchant teeth. They are attracted by blood, and, in schools, will attack man or the larger animals: also called *piranha, piraya.* [< Sp., cannibal]

car·i·bou (kar′ə·bōō) *n.* The North American reindeer. The **woodland caribou** (*Rangifer caribou*) is found from Maine to Lake Superior and northward, and the smaller and lighter colored (sometimes white) **Barren Grounds caribou** (*R. arcticus*) in the treeless arctic regions. [< Canadian F Algonquian *khalibu* pawer, scratcher]

CARIBOU
(About 4 feet high at the shoulder)

car·i·ca·ture (kar′i·kə·chŏŏr, -chər) *n.* **1** A picture or description deliberately making use of ridiculous exaggeration or distortion; burlesque. **2** The act or art of caricaturing. **3** A poor, inept, or badly distorted likeness or imitation. —*v.t.* **·tured, ·tur·ing** To represent so as to make ridiculous; travesty; burlesque. [< F < Ital. *caricatura*, lit., an overloading < *caricare* load, exaggerate] —**car′i·ca·tur′al** *adj.* —**car′i·ca·tur′ist** *n.*

Synonyms (noun): burlesque, exaggeration,

extravaganza, imitation, mimicry, parody, take-off, travesty.

car·ies (kâr′ēz, -i·ēz) *n. Pathol.* Ulceration and decay of a bone or of a tooth. [< L]

car·il·lon (kar′ə·lon, kə·ril′yən) *n.* **1** A set of bells so hung and arranged as to be capable of being played upon, either by hand or by machinery, as a musical instrument. **2** A small instrument provided with bells, played upon by means of a pianoforte keyboard. **3** An air arranged for a chime of bells, or any rapid ringing of changes on a chime. —*v.i.* **·lonned, ·lon·ning** To play a carillon. [< F < Med. L *quadrilio, -onis* set of four bells]

car·il·lon·neur (kar′ə·lə·nûr′) *n.* One who plays a carillon. [< F]

ca·ri·na (kə·rī′nə) *n. pl.* **·nae** (-nē) *Biol.* In certain plants and animals, a keel or keel-shaped formation. [< L, keel] —**ca·ri′nal** *adj.*

car·i·nate (kar′ə·nāt) *adj. Biol.* Having a carina; keeled; keel-shaped: said especially of birds having a breastbone. Compare RATITE. Also **car′i·nat′ed.** [< L *carinatus*, pp. of *carinare* supply with a keel]

Ca·rin·thi·a (kə·rin′thē·ə) A province of southern Austria; formerly a duchy; 3,681 square miles; capital, Klagenfurt: German *Kärnten.* —**Ca·rin′thi·an** *adj. & n.*

car·i·ole (kar′ē·ōl) *n.* A small carriage: also spelled *carriole.* [< F < Ital. *carriuola*, dim. of *carra* cart, wagon]

car·i·op·sis (kar′ē·op′sis) See CARYOPSIS.

car·i·ous (kâr′ē·əs) *adj.* Affected with caries; decayed. Also **car·ied** (kâr′ēd). See synonyms under ROTTEN. —**car′i·os′i·ty** (-os′ə·tē), **car′i·ous·ness** *n.*

carl (kärl) *n. Archaic* **1** A rustic. **2** *Scot.* A boor; churl. **3** A feudal serf. Also **carle.** [< ON *karl* man, freeman. Akin to CHURL.]

carl hemp *Bot.* The seed-bearing or female hemp plant: so named because formerly supposed to be the male. Also **carl.**

car·line[1] (kär′lin) *adj.* Of or pertaining to a genus (*Carlina*) of thistles. —*n.* A plant of the genus *Carlina.* [? after *Charlemagne*, whose soldiers were supposedly cured of a plague with it]

car·load (kär′lōd′) *n.* A minimum load carried by a railroad freight car at a lesser rate (**car·load rate**) than for a smaller shipment: a unit of measure of varying tonnage.

carload lot A freight shipment meeting the official minimum weight for a carload amount.

Car·ma·gnole (kär′mən·yōl′, *Fr.* kår·må·nyôl′) *n.* **1** A wild dance and song of the French revolutionists of 1789. **2** The coat and general costume worn by them. **3** A soldier of the French Revolution. [< F, from *Carmagnola*, a town in Piedmont occupied by the revolutionists]

car·man (kär′mən) *n. pl.* **·men** (-mən) **1** One who drives a car. **2** One who drives a cart.

car·mel·ite (kär′məl·īt) *n.* **1** A fine, usually beige or gray, woolen stuff. **2** A variety of pear. [< CARMELITE]

car·min·a·tive (kär·min′ə·tiv, kär′mə·nā′tiv) *Med. adj.* Tending to relieve flatulence; warming. —*n.* A remedy for flatulence. [< L *carminatus*, pp. of *carminare* cleanse]

car·mine (kär′min, -mīn) *n.* **1** A rich purplish-red color. **2** An impermanent lake pigment prepared from cochineal; rouge. [< F *carmin* < Med. L *carminus*, contraction of *carmesinus* < OSp. *carmesin.* Doublet of CRIMSON.] —**car·min·ic** (kär·min′ik) *adj.*

car·nage (kär′nij) *n.* **1** Extensive and bloody slaughter; massacre. **2** *Obs.* The bodies of the slain. See synonyms under MASSACRE. [< MF < Ital. *carnaggio* < LL *carnaticum* < L *caro, carnis* flesh, meat]

car·nal (kär′nəl) *adj.* **1** Pertaining to the fleshly nature or to bodily appetites. **2** Sensual; sexual. **3** Pertaining to the flesh or to the body; not spiritual; hence, worldly. See synonyms under BRUTISH. [< LL *carnalis* fleshly < *caro, carnis* flesh] —**car′nal·ist** *n.* —**car·nal·i·ty** (kär·nal′ə·tē) *n.* —**car′nal·ly** *adv.*

car·nal·lite (kär′nəl·īt) *n.* A massive, milk-white, hydrous chloride of magnesium and potassium: an important source of potassium. [after R. von *Carnall*, 1804–74, German mineralogist]

Car·nar·von (kär·när′vən) See CAERNARVON.

car·nas·si·al (kär·nas′ē·əl) *adj.* Adapted for tearing flesh; sectorial: specifically said of the last upper premolar and the first lower molar in carnivores. —*n.* A carnassial tooth. [< F *carnassier* carnivorous < Provençal *carnacier* < *carnaza* flesh < L *caro, carnis* flesh]

car·na·tion (kär·nā′shən) *n.* **1** The perennial, herbaceous, fragrant flower of any of the many cultivated varieties of the pink family (genus *Dianthus*), especially the clove pink or scarlet carnation (*D. caryophyllus*): State flower of Ohio. **2** A light pink, bright rose, or scarlet color. **3** *Obs.* In painting, the flesh tints in the human face and figure. [< F, flesh pink < L *carnatio, -onis* fleshiness < *caro, carnis* flesh]

car·nau·ba (kär·nou′bə) *n.* **1** The Brazilian wax palm (*Copernicia cerifera*). **2** The greenish or yellow wax from its leaves, used as a polish and for making phonograph records. [< Pg. < Tupian]

car·nel·ian (kär·nēl′yən) *n.* A clear red chalcedony, often cut as a gem: also spelled *cornelian.* [Earlier *cornelian* < MF *corneline* < Med. L *corneolus, cornelius* chalcedony]

car·ni·fy (kär′nə·fī) *v.t. & v.i.* **·fied, ·fy·ing** **1** To change to a fleshlike consistency. **2** To form into flesh; grow fleshy. [< L *carnificare* < *caro, carnis* flesh + *facere* make] —**car′ni·fi·ca′tion** *n.*

car·ni·val (kär′nə·vəl) *n.* **1** A period of festival and gaiety immediately preceding Lent, observed in Roman Catholic countries and in some cities in the United States, especially by the Latin peoples. It commonly lasts from three days to a week, Shrove Tuesday being the conclusion, and is marked by street revelry, masking, pageants, and the like. **2** Any gay festival, wild revel, or masquerade. **3** Riotous sport and confusion. **4** A traveling amusement show, with merry-go-round, ferris wheel, side shows, etc. [< Ital. *carnivale* < Med. L *carnelevarium* < L *caro, carnis* flesh + *levare* remove]

Car·niv·o·ra (kär·niv′ə·rə) *n. pl.* An order of flesh-eating mammals.

car·ni·vore (kär′nə·vôr, -vōr) *n.* **1** One of the *Carnivora.* **2** An insectivorous plant.

car·niv·o·rous (kär·niv′ə·rəs) *adj.* **1** Eating or living on flesh. **2** Of or pertaining to the *Carnivora.* [< L *carnivorus* < *caro, carnis* flesh + *vorare* eat, devour] —**car·niv′o·rous·ly** *adv.* —**car·niv′o·rous·ness** *n.*

car·nos·i·ty (kär·nos′ə·tē) *n. pl.* **·ties** *Pathol.* An abnormal fleshy growth or excrescence upon any bodily organ. [< OF *carnosité* < Med. L *carnositas, -tatis* < *carnosus* fleshy]

Car·not cycle (kär·nō′) *Physics.* A thermodynamic cycle consisting of four reversible changes in the operation of an ideal heat engine working at maximum efficiency. [after N. L. S. *Carnot*, 1796–1832, French physicist]

car·no·tite (kär′nə·tīt) *n.* A yellow, earthy vanadate containing potassium, uranium, and slight traces of radium, found in western Colorado: one of the sources of uranium [after M. A. *Carnot*, Inspector General of Mines in France]

car·ob (kar′əb) *n.* **1** An evergreen tree of the Mediterranean region (*Ceratonia siliqua*). **2** Its long, sickle-shaped, fleshy pods, used for fodder: sometimes called *St. John's bread:* also **carob bean.** [< F *caroube* < Arabic *kharrûbah* bean pods]

car·ol (kar′əl) *v.* **·oled** or **·olled, ·ol·ing** or **·ol·ing** *v.t.* **1** To utter in song, as a bird; sing. **2** To celebrate or praise in song. —*v.i.* **1** To sing in a cheerful or joyous strain; warble. **2** To sing. —*n.* **1** A song of joy or praise; especially, a Christmas song. **2** The warbling of birds. **3** *Obs.* A dance performed in a circle; also, the song accompanying it. See synonyms under SING. [< OF *carole*, prob. < L *choraules* a flutist < Gk. *choraulēs* < *choros* a dance + *aulein* play the flute < *aulos* a flute] —**car′ol·er, car′ol·ler** *n.*

Carolina parrot An extinct American parakeet (*Conuropsis carolinensis*), native to the Carolinas.

Carolina pink The pinkroot.

Carolina potato The common sweet potato.

Car·o·li·nas (kar′ə·lī′nəz), **the** **1** North and South Carolina. **2** The Caroline Islands.

Caroline Islands An island group east of the Philippines, comprising part of the United Nations Trust Territory of the Pacific Islands; 510 square miles; Japanese mandate, 1919–1944; formerly **New Philippines:** administered as the **Western Carolinas,** capitals, Palau and Yap; and the **Eastern Carolinas,** capitals, Ponape and Truk: also *the Carolinas.* Also **the Car′o·lines.**

car·o·lus (kar′ə·ləs) *n. pl.* **·lus·es** or **·li** (-lī) An ancient English gold coin of the value of about twenty shillings. [<Med. L, *Charles*]

car·om (kar′əm) *v.t.* To cause to make a glancing movement: He *caromed* one ball off the other. — *v.i.* To make a glancing movement: The car *caromed* off the wall. — *n.* **1** In billiards, the impact of one ball against two others in succession, or the stroke producing it. **2** In other games, the glancing of one object from another: in England, this word has been altered to *cannon.* Also spelled *car·rom.* [<F *carambole*]

car·o·tene (kar′ə·tēn) *n. Biochem.* A deep-yellow or red crystalline hydrocarbon, $C_{40}H_{56}$, which acts as a plant pigment: it occurs also in various animal tissues, and is changed in the body to vitamin A. Also **car′o·tin** (-tin): sometimes spelled *carrotin.* [<L *carota* carrot]

ca·rot·e·noid (kə·rot′ə·noid) *n. Biochem.* One of a large variety of nitrogen-free, light-yellow to deep-red lipochrome pigments found in plant and animal tissues. Also **ca·rot′i·noid.**

ca·rot·id (kə·rot′id) *adj. Anat.* Of, pertaining to, or near one of the two major arteries on each side of the neck. Also **ca·rot′i·dal.** [<Gk. *karōtides,* pl. <*karoein* stupefy; so called from the belief that pressure on them would cause unconsciousness]

ca·rotte (ka·rot′) *n.* A roll of tobacco; especially, the perique tobacco of Louisiana. [<F, carrot]

ca·rou·sal (kə·rou′zəl) *n.* A jovial feast or banquet; boisterous or drunken revelry. See synonyms under FROLIC.

ca·rouse (kə·rouz′) *v.i.* **ca·roused, ca·rous·ing** To drink deeply, freely, and jovially; engage in a carousal. — *n.* **1** A carousal. **2** *Obs.* The draining of a full bumper of liquor. See synonyms under FROLIC. [<G *gar aus (trinken)* (drink) all out] — **ca·rous′er** *n.*

car·ou·sel (kar′ə·sel′, -zel′) *n.* **1** A merry-go-round. **2** A tournament, tilting match, or military pageant. Also spelled *carrousel.* [<F *carrousel* <Ital. *carosello* tournament]

carp¹ (kärp) *v.i.* To find fault unreasonably; complain; cavil. [<ON *karpa* boast] — **carp′·er** *n.*

carp² (kärp) *n. pl.* **carp** or **carps 1** A freshwater food fish (*Cyprinus carpio*), originally of China but now widely distributed in Europe and America. **2** Any of various other cyprinoid fishes, as dace, minnows, and goldfish. [<OF *carpe* <LL *carpa*]

-carp *combining form* Fruit; fruit (or seed) vessel: *pericarp.* [Gk. *karpos* fruit]

car·pal (kär′pəl) *adj. Anat.* Of, pertaining to, or near the wrist. — *n.* A carpal bone. [<NL *carpalis* <L *carpus* wrist <Gk. *karpos*]

car·pa·le (kär·pā′lē) *n. pl.* **·li·a** (-lē·ə) *Anat.* A bone of the carpus or wrist; especially, one articulating with the metacarpal bones. [<NL, neut. of *carpalis* CARPAL]

car·pel (kär′pəl) *n. Bot.* A simple pistil or seed vessel. See illustration under FRUIT. Also **car·pel·lum** (kär·pel′əm). [<NL *carpellum* <Gk. *karpos* fruit] — **car·pel·lar·y** (kär′pə·ler′ē) *adj.*

car·pel·late (kär′pə·lāt) *adj. Bot.* Possessing, or like, carpels.

car·pen·ter (kär′pən·tər) *n.* An artificer who builds with timber or wood, as in the construction of houses, ships, and other wooden structures. — *v.t.* To make by carpentry. — *v.i.* To work with wood. [<AF *carpentier* <LL *carpentarius* carpenter, wagon-maker <L *carpentum* two-wheeled carriage] — **car′pen·ter·ing** *n.* — **car′pen·try** *n.*

carpenter bee A large, hairy, solitary bee (genus *Xylocopa*) that bores tunnels in wood for its nest, as *X. violacea* of Europe or *X. virginica* of the United States.

carpenter moth A large, light-brown moth (*Prionoxystus robiniae*), with two blue horizontal bars on its wings, whose larvae, called **carpenter worms,** bore beneath the bark of

certain trees.

car·pet (kär′pit) *n.* **1** A heavy ornamental floor covering; also, the fabric used for it. **2** Any smooth surface upon which one may walk. — **on the carpet** *Colloq.* Subjected to reproof or reprimand. — *v.t.* To cover with or as with a carpet. [<OF *carpite* <LL *carpita* thick woolen covering < *carpere* pluck]

car·pet·bag (kär′pit·bag′) *n.* A handbag for travelers; especially, one made of carpeting.

car·pet·bag·ger (kär′pit·bag′ər) *n.* A person traveling with all his possessions in a carpetbag: said originally of unscrupulous itinerant bankers of the West; later, of political or profit-seeking adventurers who infested the South after the Civil War. Compare SCALAWAG. — **car′pet·bag′ger·y, car′pet·bag′gism** *n.*

carpet beetle A beetle (*Attagenus piceus*) whose reddish-brown larvae are destructive of carpets, woolen fabrics, and animal products. Also called *buffalo bug.* See illustration under INSECTS (injurious). Also **carpet bug.**

car·pet·ing (kär′pit·ing) *n.* **1** Material or fabric used for carpets; carpets collectively. **2** The act of covering with, or as with, a carpet.

carpet knight One knighted for other than military achievements; a stay-at-home soldier: used contemptuously.

carpet weed A procumbent North American herbaceous annual (*Mollugo verticillata*), the leaves of which, clustered in whorls, form mats on the ground.

car·phol·o·gy (kär·fol′ə·jē) *n. Pathol.* A delirious, automatic picking at the bedclothes in forms of low fever. [<Gk. *karphologia* < *karphos* straw + *legein* pick, collect]

-carpic *combining form* See -CARPOUS.

carp·ing (kär′ping) *adj.* Censorious; fault-finding. — **carp′ing·ly** *adv.*

carpo- *combining form* Fruit: *carpology.* [<Gk. *karpos* fruit]

car·pog·e·nous (kär·poj′ə·nəs) *adj. Bot.* Fruit-producing: said of the cell or groups of cells from which the spores are formed in certain algae. [<CARPO- + -GENOUS]

car·po·go·ni·um (kär′pə·gō′nē·əm) *n. pl.* **·ni·a** (-nē·ə) *Bot.* The female organ of certain algae; especially, in the red algae, the carpogenous cell or cells of the procarp which, after fertilization, develop a sporocarp. [<CARPO- + -GONIUM] — **car′po·go′ni·al** *adj.*

car·pol·o·gy (kär·pol′ə·jē) *n.* That department of botany which treats of fruits in general. [<CARPO- + -LOGY] — **car·po·log·i·cal** (kär′pə·loj′i·kəl) *adj.* — **car·pol′o·gist** *n.*

car·poph·a·gous (kär·pof′ə·gəs) *adj.* Frugivorous; fruit-eating. [<CARPO- + -PHAGOUS]

car·po·phore (kär′pə·fôr, -fōr) *n. Bot.* **1** In flowering plants, a portion of the receptacle prolonged between the carpels, as in the geraniums and many umbelliferous plants. **2** In fungi, any fruit-bearing structure or organ.

car·port (kär′pôrt, -pōrt) *n.* A roof projecting from the side of a building, used as a shelter for motor vehicles.

-carpous *combining form* Having a certain kind or number of fruits: *acrocarpous.* Also **-carpic.** [<Gk. *karpos* fruit]

car·pus (kär′pəs) *n. pl.* **·pi** (-pī) **1** *Anat.* The wrist. **2** *Zool.* A part analogous to or like a wrist. [<NL <Gk. *karpos* wrist]

car·ra·geen (kar′ə·gēn) *n.* A small, purplish, edible marine alga (*Chondrus crispus*), the Irish moss of commerce: used in medicine as a demulcent. Often spelled *carageen, caragheen, carrigeen.* Also **car′ra·gheen.** [from *Carragheen,* near Waterford, Ireland]

car·riage (kar′ij) *n.* **1** A wheeled vehicle for carrying persons. **2** That which carries something, as in a machine. **3** Transportation; the charge for, or cost of, carrying. **4** Deportment; bearing. **5** The carrying of a besieged place. **6** The act of carrying. **7** Execution; management; control. **8** *Obs.* That which is carried. **9** *Obs.* Import; meaning. Compare BEHAVIOR. See synonyms under AIR, MANNER. [<AF *cariage* < *carier* CARRY]

carriage dog A Dalmatian.

carriage trade The wealthy patrons of a restaurant, theater, etc.: so called because of the former association of wealth with private carriages.

car·ried (kar′ēd) Past tense and past participle of CARRY.

car·ri·er (kar′ē·ər) *n.* **1** One who or that which carries; hence, a person or company

that undertakes to carry persons or goods for hire, as a railroad company, etc.; also, one who carries or delivers messages, letters, etc. **2** A carrier pigeon. **3** A conduit. **4** *Chem.* A material used as an intermediary or vehicle, as a catalytic agent acting to transfer an element between compounds. **5** *Mech.* A device or attachment that conveys, drives, moves, or supports something. **6** A ship for carrying aircraft. **7** *Bacteriol.* One who is immune to a disease but transmits it to others by carrying the bacteria in his body. **8** A carrier wave. — **common carrier** A person or company that undertakes to carry persons or goods for pay when called to do so, whether by land, air, or water, and that is liable for all loss or damage during transportation except such losses as arise from natural causes.

carrier pigeon A homing pigeon.

carrier wave *Telecom.* The current, wave frequency, or voltage transmitted in various forms of electrical communication; especially, in radio, the wave which is subjected to amplitude or frequency modulation.

car·ri·ole (kar′ē·ōl) See CARIOLE.

car·ri·on (kar′ē·ən) *n.* Dead and putrefying flesh; a carcass. — *adj.* **1** Feeding on carrion. **2** Like or pertaining to carrion; putrefying. [<AF *caroigne,* ult. <L *caro, carnis* flesh]

carrion crow 1 The common crow (*Corvus corone*) of Europe. **2** The black vulture (*Coragyps atratus*) of the southern United States, Mexico, and Central America.

car·ro·nade (kar′ə·nād′) *n.* Formerly, a short, chambered ordnance piece of large caliber and short range. [from the *Carron* ironworks, Scotland]

carron oil (kar′ən) A mixture of limewater and linseed oil: used for treating burns. [from the *Carron* ironworks, Scotland]

car·rot¹ (kar′ət) *n.* **1** The long, reddish-yellow, edible root of an umbelliferous plant (*Daucus carota*). **2** The plant itself. ◆ Homophone: *carat.* [<F *carotte* <L *carota* <Gk. *karōton*]

car·rot² (kar′ət) *v.t.* To brush (furs) with a mercury and nitric acid solution, in order to prepare the fibers for the operations of matting and felting: so called from the yellowish color of the furs when dried. ◆ Homophone: *carat.* [<CARROT¹] — **car′rot·ing** *n.*

car·ro·tin (kar′ə·tin) See CAROTENE.

car·rot·y (kar′ət·ē) *adj.* **1** Like a carrot. **2** Having red hair.

car·rou·sel (kar′ə·sel′, -zel′) See CAROUSEL.

car·ry (kar′ē) *v.* **·ried, ·ry·ing** *v.t.* **1** To bear from one place to another; transport; convey. **2** To have or bear upon or about one's person or in one's mind. **3** To serve as a means of conveyance or transportation: The wind *carries* sounds. **4** To lead; urge; move; influence: Love for art *carried* him abroad. **5** To win; capture. **6** To bear up; sustain; hold in position: The ship *carries* sail well. **7** To conduct (oneself) or demean (oneself); behave. **8** To transfer, as a number or figure, to another column, or, as in bookkeeping, from one account book to another. **9** To have or keep on hand: We *carry* a full stock. **10** To win, as an election; win the support of. **11** To be pregnant with. **12** To bear, as crops, or sustain, as cattle. **13** To give support to, as evidence; corroborate; confirm. **14** To extend; continue: He *carries* this farce too far. **15** In golf, to cover or pass, as a distance or object, in one stroke. **16** In hunting, to follow or trail by scent. **17** *U.S. Dial.* To conduct; escort. — *v.i.* **18** To act as bearer or carrier: fetch and *carry.* **19** To have or exert impelling or propelling power: The rifle *carries* nearly a mile. **20** To hold the head and neck habitually in a given manner: The horse *carries* well. **21** In falconry, to fly off with the game. — **to carry all before one** To meet with unimpeded and uniform success. — **to carry arms 1** To belong to the army. **2** To bear weapons. **3** To hold a weapon in a prescribed position against the shoulder. — **to carry away 1** To move the feelings greatly; enchant, as with passion or rapture. **2** To break off, as from a ship; lose by breaking off in a collision or gale. — **to carry forward 1** To progress or proceed with. **2** In bookkeeping, to transfer, as an item, to the next column or page. — **to carry off 1** To cause to die. **2** To win, as a prize or honor. **3** To face consequences boldly; brazen out. **4** To abduct. **— to carry on 1** To keep up; keep going; continue. **2** To behave in a free, frolicsome manner. **3** To perpetuate; continue, as a tradition. **— to carry out** To accomplish; bring to completion. **— to carry over 1** In bookkeeping, to repeat, as an item, on another page or in another column. **2** To influence to join the opposed party. **— to carry through 1** To carry to completion or success. **2** To sustain or support to the end. **—** *n.* *pl.* **·ries 1** A portage, as between navigable streams; also, the act of carrying, as a canoe, luggage, etc. **2** The range of a gun or a projectile; also, the distance covered by a projectile, as a golf ball. **3** *Mil.*' The position of carry arms, or carry swords, etc. [<AF *carier* <LL *carricare* L *carrus* cart. Doublet of CHARGE.]

Synonyms (verb): bear, bring, convey, lift, move, remove, sustain, take, transmit, transport. A person may *bear* a load when either in motion or at rest; he *carries* it only when in motion. The stooping Atlas *bears* the world on his shoulders; swiftly moving Time *carries* the hourglass and scythe; a person may be said either to *bear* or to *carry* a scar, since it is upon him whether in motion or at rest. If an object is to be *moved* from the place we occupy, we say *carry*; if to the place we occupy, we say *bring*. A messenger *carries* a letter to a correspondent, and *brings* an answer. *Take* is often used in this sense in place of *carry*; as, *take* that letter to the office. *Carry* often signifies to *transport* by personal strength, without reference to the direction; as, that is more than he can *carry*; yet even so, it would not be admissible to say *carry* it to me, or *carry* it here; in such case we must say *bring*. To *lift* is simply to raise an object from its support, if only for an instant, with no reference to holding or moving; one may be able to *lift* what he cannot *carry*. The figurative uses of *carry* are very numerous; as, to *carry* an election, *carry* the country, *carry* (in the sense of *capture*) a fort, *carry* an audience, *carry* a stock of goods, etc. Compare CONVEY, KEEP, SUPPORT. *Antonym:* drop.

car·ry-all (kar'ē-ôl') *n.* **1** A one-horse, four-wheeled covered vehicle. **2** A closed automobile having two seats arranged lengthwise and facing each other. [Alter. of CARIOLE]

carrying charge In instalment buying, the interest charged on the unpaid balance.

car·ry-o·ver (kar'ē-ō'vər) *n.* **1** The item or entry in bookkeeping repeated from the bottom of one page to the top of the next. **2** The remainder of a crop, supply of stock, etc., to be disposed of along with the next crop or lot.

Car·son City (kär'sən) The capital of Nevada.

cart (kärt) *n.* **1** A heavy two-wheeled vehicle, for carrying loads. **2** A light two-wheeled pleasure vehicle with springs. **3** Loosely, any two- or four-wheeled vehicle. **—** *v.t.* To convey or carry in or as in a cart. **—** *v.i.* To drive or use a cart. [OE *cræt*] **—cart'er** *n.*

cart·age (kär'tij) *n.* The act of or price charged for carting.

carte[1] (kärt) *n.* **1** A card or paper. **2** *Scot.* A playing card. **3** A bill of fare. [<F, card]

carte[2] (kärt) See QUARTE.

car·tel (kär·tel', kär'təl) *n.* **1** A written official agreement between governments, especially when at war, as for the exchange of prisoners. **2** A written challenge to single combat. **3** An international combination of independent enterprises in the same branch of production, aiming at a monopolistic control of the market by means of weakening or eliminating competition. Compare MONOPOLY, SYNDICATE, TRUST. **4** An agreement among states to maintain mutually beneficial customs rates or otherwise act as a unit for a common purpose. See ANSCHLUSS. [<F <Ital. *cartello,* dim. of *carta* paper]

Cartesian coordinate system *Geom.* **1** A plane system for indicating the curve of an equation graphically by means of two axes, graduated in both directions from the origin: when intersecting at right angles, the coordinates are called *rectangular,* when intersecting at any angle other than 90°, the coordinates are called *oblique.* **2** A three-dimensional system for indicating the shape of a solid by means of three planes inter-

secting at right angles to each other at a point called the origin: from the three points of reference required, any point in space with coordinates *x, y,* and *z* can be located. See illustration under OCTANT. Also called *rectangular coordinate system.*

Cartesian devil A hollow figure partly filled with air, and immersed in water in a glass jar, the jar being provided with an elastic cover, by pressure upon which the immersed figure is made to sink, rising again when the pressure is removed: sometimes called *bottle imp.* Also **Cartesian diver, Cartesian imp.**

car·ti·lage (kär'tə-lij) *n* *Biol.* **1** A tough, elastic supporting tissue in animals, composed of cells embedded in an opalescent matrix, either homogeneous or fibrous; gristle. **2** A structure or part consisting of cartilage. [<MF <L *cartilago* gristle]

car·ti·lag·i·nous (kär'tə-laj'ə-nəs) *adj.* **1** Of or like cartilage; gristly. **2** Having a gristly skeleton, as sharks.

cart·load (kärt'lōd') *n.* **1** As much as a cart will hold. **2** The contents of a cart.

car·to·gram (kär'tə-gram) *n.* A map giving statistical information by means of comparative diagrams. [<F *cartogramme*]

car·tog·ra·phy (kär·tog'rə-fē) *n.* The science, technology, or art of drawing or compiling, maps or charts. [<*carto-* map (<L *charta*) + -GRAPHY] **—car·to·graph** (kär'tə-graf, -gräf) *n.* **—car·tog'ra·pher** *n.* **—car'to·graph'ic** or **·i·cal** *adj.*

car·ton (kär'tən) *n.* **1** A pasteboard box. **2** Pasteboard. **3** A white disk within the bull's-eye of a target or a shot striking it. [<F. See CARTOON.]

car·toon (kär-tōōn') *n.* **1** A drawing or caricature as in a newspaper or periodical; especially, one intended to affect public opinion as to some matter or person. **2** A sketch for a fresco or mosaic. **3** A comic strip. **4** A motion-picture film, called an **animated cartoon,** made by photographing a series of carefully prepared black-and-white or colored drawings, each representing a further stage in the action of the film, which is usually synchronized for sound effects and music. See synonyms under PICTURE. **—** *v.t.* To make a caricature or cartoon of; satirize pictorially. **—** *v.i.* To make cartoons. [<F *carton* <Ital. *cartone* pasteboard, aug. of *carta* card <L *charta* paper] **—car·toon'ist** *n.*

car·toph·i·ly (kär-tof'ə-lē) *n. U.S.* The collecting of illustrative cards, as those enclosed in packages of retail goods: a humorous term. [<*carto-* card (<F *carte*) + Gk. *philia* <*phileein* love] **—car·toph'i·list** *n.*

car·touche (kär-tōōsh') *n.* **1** An oblong or oval figure containing the name of a king, queen, or deity, as on ancient Egyptian monuments and papyri. **2** *Archit.* An ornamental tablet or scroll with inscription or emblem; a scroll-shaped bracket, etc. **3** A cartridge box; a cartridge box; an ammunition bag. **4** The case containing the inflammable materials in some fireworks. **5** *Astron.* A curve exhibiting the varying visibility of an object, such as of a canal on Mars. Also **car·touch'.** [<F <Ital. *cartoccio,* aug. of *carta* card <L *charta* paper]

car·tridge (kär'trij) *n.* **1** An explosive charge

CARTRIDGE

A. Shotgun shell.
　a. Powder. *b., b.* Wads. *c.* Shot.
B. Section of center-fire metallic rifle or pistol cartridge case.
　a. Primer-cup. *b.* Percussion composition.
　c. Anvil. *d.* Vent. *e.* Base of case.

for a pistol, rifle, machine gun, or other small arm, consisting of primer, gunpowder, cardboard or metal case, and projectile or projectiles. **2** *Phot.* A roll of protected sensitized films. — **blank cartridge** A cartridge containing powder but no projectile. [Alter. of CARTOUCHE]

cartridge belt A belt having loops or pockets for cartridges or cartridge clips.

cartridge clip Clip[1] (def. 6).

car·tu·lar·y (kär'chōō·ler'ē) *n.* *pl.* **·lar·ies 1** A collection or a register of charters, etc., as of a monastery. **2** An officer in charge of such records. Also spelled *chartulary.* [<LL *cartularium*]

cart·wheel (kärt'hwēl') *n.* **1** *U.S. Colloq.* A silver dollar. **2** *Aeron.* A flight maneuver which causes an airplane to rotate about its long axis while describing an inverted U in the air: a variation of the half-roll. **3** A lateral handspring.

ca·ru·ca (ka·rōō'kə) *n.* **1** A plow. **2** A plow team of four oxen or horses yoked abreast. [<Med. L *carruca* a plow]

car·un·cle (kar'ung·kəl, kə·rung'-) *n.* **1** *Zool.* A fleshy excrescence, as a cock's comb. **2** *Bot.* A protuberant growth of the seed coat at or near the hilum. Also **ca·run·cu·la** (kə·rung'kyə·lə). [<MF <L *caruncula,* dim. of *caro, carnis* flesh] **—ca·run·cu·lar** (kə·rung'kyə·lər) or **·late** (-lit, -lāt) or **·lous** (-ləs) *adj.*

car·va·crol (kär'və·krōl, -krol) *n.* *Chem.* A colorless, oily, aromatic liquid, $C_{10}H_{14}O$, obtained from origan, camphor, thyme, and other plants of the mint family: used in perfumery and in medicine as an antiseptic. [<F *carvi* caraway + L *acer, acris* biting + -OL]

carve (kärv) *v.* **carved, carv·ing** *v.t.* **1** To cut figures or designs upon. **2** To make by cutting or chiseling. **3** To cut up, as cooked meat; divide. **—** *v.i.* **4** To make carved work or figures. **5** To cut up cooked meat served at table. See synonyms under CUT. **—** *n.* A cut or stroke in carving. [OE *ceorfan*] **—carv'er** *n.*

carv·ing (kär'ving) *n.* **1** The act of one who carves. **2** That which is carved; sculpture.

car·y·at·id (kar'ē·at'id) *n.* *pl.* **·ids** or **·i·des** (-ə·dēz) *Archit.* A supporting column in the form of a sculptured female figure. [<L *Caryatis, -ides* <Gk. *Karyiatis* a priestess of Artemis at Karyai, town of Laconia, Greece] **—car·y·at'i·dal** (kar'ē·at'ə·dəl), **car·y·at·i·de·an** (kar'ē·at'ə·dē'ən), **car·y·a·tid·ic** (kar'ē·ə·tid'ik) *adj.*

caryo- See KARYO-.

car·y·o·ki·ne·sis (kar'ē·ō·ki·nē'sis) See KARYOKINESIS.

car·y·o·phyl·la·ceous (kar'ē·ō·fi·lā'shəs) *adj.* *Bot.* **1** Pertaining or belonging to a family (*Caryophyllaceae*) of herbs, the pink family, characterized by stems enlarged at the nodes, opposite entire leaves, and perfect or rarely dioecious flowers: also called *silenaceous.* **2** Having a tubular calyx with five long-clawed petals. [<NL <Gk. *karyophyllon* <*karyon* nut + *phyllon* leaf]

car·y·op·sis (kar'ē·op'sis) *n.* *pl.* **·op·ses** (-op'sēz) or **·op·si·des** (-op'sə·dēz) *Bot.* A seedlike fruit, as the grains of wheat and rye: also spelled *cariopsis.* [<Gk. *karyon* nut + *opsis* appearance]

car·y·o·tin (kar'ē·ō'tin) See KARYOTIN.

Ca·sa·ba (kə·sä'bə) *n.* A winter variety of muskmelon with sweet white flesh and yellow rind: also spelled *Cassaba.* Also **Casaba melon.** [from *Kasaba,* a town in western Turkey]

cas·cade (kas·kād') *n.* **1** A fall of water over steeply slanting rocks, or one of a series of such falls. **2** Anything resembling a waterfall, as the lace trimming of a dress. **3** *Chem.* A connection in series of two or more electrolytic cells or tanks so arranged as to produce a flow of the electrolyte from higher to lower levels. **4** *Physics* A successive operation, as cooling a gas by utilizing the effect of a previously expanded gas. **—** *v.i.* **cad·ed, ·cad·ing** To fall in the form of a waterfall; form cascades. [<F <Ital. *cascata* <*cascare* fall <L *cadere*]

cascade amplification *Electronics* An amplifying system in which two or more vacuum tube units are connected to form a number of stages, each stage deriving its input from the output of the one preceding.

cas·cade control *Electr.* A method of turning street lights on and off in sections, each section being controlled by the energizing and de-energizing of preceding sections.

cas·car·a buckthorn (kas-kãr′ə) A buckthorn (*Rhamnus purshiana*) of the NW United States: its bark yields **cascara sa·gra·da** (sə-grä′də), used as a laxative: also called *bearwood.* Also **cas·car′a.** [<Sp. *cáscara* bark]

cas·ca·ril·la (kas′kə-ril′ə) *n.* **1** The aromatic bark of a West Indian shrub (*Croton eluteria*) of the spurge family, sometimes used as a tonic. **2** The shrub. Also **cascarilla bark.** [<Sp., dim. of *cáscara* bark]

case¹ (kās) *n.* **1** The state of things in a given instance; a special condition of affairs; juncture: *What shall be done in this case?*; also, the actual circumstance; the fact or facts: *Such is not the case.* **2** An event; contingency: *in case of fire.* **3** A particular instance or example: *a case of pneumonia; a case of fraud.* **4** *Law* A cause of action; a suit; an action. **5** *State;* physical condition or situation; plight. **6** *Gram.* **a** The syntactical relationship of a noun, pronoun, or adjective to other words in a sentence, as indicated, generally, in inflected languages, by declensional endings or, in non-inflected languages, by prepositions and word order. **b** The form of a word indicating this relationship. **c** These relationships or forms as a group. Evidence would indicate that primitive Indo-European had eight cases — nominative, genitive, dative, accusative, ablative, instrumental, locative, and vocative. See SUBJECTIVE, POSSESSIVE, and OBJECTIVE for the cases surviving in Modern English. **7** *Colloq.* A peculiar or exceptional person. See synonyms under EVENT, PRECEDENT, SAMPLE. **— in any case** No matter what; regardless. **— in case** In the event that; if. [<F *cas* <L *casus* event <*cadere* fall; the grammatical cases (def. 6) were thought of as "falling" from the nominative]

case² (kās) *n.* **1** A box, sheath, bag, or other covering in which something is or may be kept. **2** A box and the quantity or number contained in it; a set. **3** *Printing* A tray, with compartments for holding type. Cases are commonly made in pairs, called **upper** or **cap case,** for capital letters, and **lower case,** for small letters, respectively. **4** The frame or casing for a door, window, etc., or a hollow box beside a casing, as for sash weights. **5** *Archit.* An outer facing of a building, as of stone over brick. **6** The cavity in the upper anterior part of the head of a sperm whale containing the spermaceti. **7** In bookbinding, a binding or cover made separately. **8** *Her.* The skin of an animal. **9** *Obs.* The clothes of a person; also, the exterior, in any sense. **10** *Obs.* A brace or pair, as of pistols. — *v.t.*

ca·se·ase (kā′sē-ās) *n. Biochem.* A tryptic enzyme of bacterial origin which dissolves casein and hastens ripening in cheese. [< CASE(IN) + -ASE]

ca·se·ate (kā′sē-āt) *v.i.* **·at·ed, ·at·ing** To become cheesy; undergo caseation. [<L *caseatus* mixed with cheese <*caseus* cheese]

ca·se·a·tion (kā′sē-ā′shən) *n.* **1** Conversion into cheese or curd; coagulation. **2** *Pathol.* Caseous degeneration, as of the tissues.

ca·se·fy (kā′sə-fī) *v.t. & v.i.* **·fied, ·fy·ing** To make or become like cheese. [<L *caseus* cheese]

case·hard·en (kās′här′dən) *v.t.* **1** *Metall.* To harden by carburizing the surface of (iron), followed by quenching. **2** To make callous or insensible to influences, especially good influences.

case history The record of an individual, as made and filed by hospitals, social agencies, insurance companies, etc., giving the salient facts on health, family, financial condition, economic and social status.

ca·se·in (kā′sē-in, -sēn) *n. Biochem.* A phosphoprotein found especially in milk, constituting the principal ingredient in cheese: a white friable substance of acid character, used in preparing cotton cloth for calico printing, as an adhesive in certain varieties of cement, and as an important ingredient in plastics and synthetic resins. [<L *caseus* cheese] — **ca·se·ic** (kā′sē-ik) *adj.*

ca·se·in·o·gen (kā′sē-in′ə-jen, kā-sē′nə-) *n.* The casein-bearing protein of milk. [< CASEIN +

-GEN]

case law Law based upon or settled by decided cases; decisions handed down by judges and having the effect of law: distinguished from *statute law.*

case·mate (kās′māt) *n.* **1** A vaulted chamber in a fortification. **2** A bombproof shelter from which guns fire through openings, or an armored bulkhead on shipboard, with openings for guns. [<F <Ital. *casamatta,* ? <Gk. *chasmata,* pl. of *chasma* opening] — **case′·mat′ed** *adj.*

case·ment (kās′mənt) *n.* **1** The sash of a window when arranged to open on hinges at the side, or a window arranged with such sashes. **2** A case; covering; incasement. [<OF *encassement*] — **case′ment·ed** *adj.*

ca·se·ose (kā′sē-ōs) *n. Biochem.* An intermediary product in the hydration of caseins, either artificial or in the digestive process: one of the proteoses. [<L *caseus* cheese]

ca·se·ous (kā′sē-əs) *adj.* Of, pertaining to, or like cheese; cheesy.

case shot An assortment of small shot, as shrapnel or canister, enclosed in a metal case.

case·work (kās′wûrk′) *n.* The investigation and guidance by a social worker of the cases of maladjusted individuals and families. — **case′work′er** *n.*

cash¹ (kash) *n.* **1** Current money in hand or readily available. **2** Money paid down; immediate payment: *five percent discount for cash.* See synonyms under MONEY. — *v.t.* To convert into ready money, as a check; give or receive money for. **— to cash in** **1** In gambling, to turn in one's chips and receive cash. **2** *U.S. Slang* To die. **— to cash in on** To turn to advantage; make a profit from. [<F *casse* cash box, cash <Ital. *cassa* <L *capsa* box] — **cash′a·ble** *adj.*

cash² (kash) *n. pl.* **cash** Any of various little coins used as small change in parts of the East Indies and China; especially, a Chinese coin made of copper and lead, with a square hole in the middle. [<Pg. *caixa* <Tamil *kāsu* small coin]

cash basis A system of bookkeeping that includes only cash receipts as income and only cash payments as expense: opposed to *accrual basis.*

cash·ew (kash′ōō, kə-shōō′) *n.* **1** A tropical American tree (genus *Anacardium*) now naturalized in Africa and Asia. **2** Its small, kidney-shaped, edible fruit, the **cashew nut.** [<F *acajou* <Tupian *acajoba*]

cash·ier¹ (ka-shir′) *n.* **1** A custodian of money; especially, one who has charge of the receipts, disbursements, cash on hand, etc., of a banking or mercantile house. **2** A paymaster. [<F *caissier* < *caisse.* See CASH¹.]

cash·ier² (ka-shir′) *v.t.* **1** To dismiss in disgrace, as a military officer. **2** To discard. See synonyms under BREAK. [<Du. *casseren* <F *casser* <LL *cassare* annul and L *quassare* destroy]

cashier's check A check drawn by a bank's cashier upon its own funds.

cash·mere (kash′mir) *n.* **1** A fine wool obtained from Cashmere goats. **2** A soft fabric made from this or similar wool. **3** A dress, shawl, etc., made of cashmere. [from *Kashmir,* India]

cash on delivery Immediate cash payment to the bearer on delivery of goods: abbr. *C.O.D.*

ca·shoo (kə-shōō′) See CATECHU.

cash register An automatic mechanical device with keyboard, for recording, adding, and displaying the amount of cash placed in its money drawer.

cas·i·mere, cas·i·mire (kas′ə-mir) See CASSIMERE.

cas·ing (kā′sing) *n.* **1** That with which a thing or place is incased or lined, as a wall of firebrick on the door of a kiln. **2** The framework around a door or window. **3** The outer covering or shoe of an automobile tire. **4** *pl.* The intestines of cattle, hogs, etc., cleaned and salted for use as sausage containers. [<CASE²]

ca·si·no (kə-sē′nō) *n.* **1** A room or building for public amusement, dancing, gambling, etc. **2** In Italy, a summerhouse, or the like; also, a house built in imitation of the Italian casino. **3** A game of cards for from two to four players: also spelled *cassino.* [<Ital., dim. of *casa* house]

cask (kask, käsk) *n.* **1** A barrel-shaped wooden

vessel or receptacle, made of staves, hoops, and flat heads. A cask for liquor or liquids may be larger or smaller than a barrel, and is usually of heavier material. **2** The quantity a cask will hold. **3** *Obs.* A casket. ◆ Homophone: *casque.* [<Sp. *casco* skull, potsherd, cask, ? ult. <L *quassare* break. Related to *casque.*]

cas·ket (kas′kit, käs′-) *n.* **1** A small box or chest, as for jewels or other valuables. **2** A coffin. — *v.t.* To enclose in or as in a casket. [<F *cassette* <*casse* chest; form infl. by CASK]

casque (kask) *n.* **1** Any piece of armor to cover the head. **2** A helmet. **3** A helmet-like protuberance, as the bony crest of a cassowary or the horny process of a hornbill. ◆ Homophone: *cask.* [<F, ult. <L *quassare.* Related to CASK.] — **casqued** (kaskt) *adj.*

cas·quette (kas-ket′) *n.* A woman's brimless hat. [<F, dim. of *casque* helmet]

CASQUE
Surmounted by a crest.

Cass (kas), **Lewis,** 1782–1866, U.S. statesman.

cas·sa·reep (kas′ə-rēp) *n.* A condiment made from the juice of the cassava plant. [<F *cassiry* <Tupian *cachiri*]

cas·sa·tion (ka-sā′shən) *n.* **1** The act of making null or abrogating, as a judgment or decree. **2** *Music* A composition in several movements, similar to a suite. [<F <LL *cassatio, -onis* <*cassare* annul <L *cassus* empty]

cas·sa·va (kə-sä′və) *n.* **1** One of several tropical American shrubs or herbs (genus *Manihot*), cultivated for their edible roots; especially, the sweet cassava (*M. dulcis*) and the bitter cassava (*M. exculens*); manioc. **2** A starch made from the roots of these plants, valued as the source of tapioca. Also spelled *casava.* [<F *cassave* <Taino *casavi*]

casse (kas) *n.* A darkening in the color of wines due to the chemical action of excess iron or copper. [<F, a breaking]

Cas·se·grain·i·an (kas′ə-grā′nē-ən) *adj. Astron.* Describing a type of reflecting telescope which employs a hyperbolic mirror inside the prime focus to form an image which passes through an aperture in the primary mirror at the bottom of the tube. [after N. *Cassegrain,* 17th c. French physician, who invented it in 1672]

Cas·sel (kas′əl, *Ger.* käs′əl) See KASSEL.

cas·se·role (kas′ə-rōl) *n.* **1** A saucepan. **2** A baking dish of earthenware, glass, etc., in which food may be baked and served: food so served is said to be **en casserole. 3** A dish with a handle used by chemists. [<F]

cas·sette (kə-set′, ka-) *n.* **1** *Photog.* A light-proof magazine for holding a sensitized plate or film in a camera or X-ray device. **2** *Electronics* A cartridge containing magnetic tape for the storage of audio or video material, as for use in a tape recorder or television receiver. [<F, lit., small box]

cas·sia (kash′ə) *n.* **1** A coarse variety of cinnamon, especially that obtained from the bark of *Cinnamomum cassia:* also **cassia bark. 2** The tree yielding it. **3** Any of a large genus (*Cassia*) of shrubs or herbs of the senna family. **4** A medicinal product of a plant of the genus *Cassia;* especially, the laxative pulp obtained from the pods of *C. fístula* of the East Indies. Compare SENNA. [<L <Gk. *kasia* <Hebrew *qetsi'ah* < *qātsa'* strip off bark]

cas·si·mere (kas′ə-mir) *n.* A woolen cloth for men's wear: also called *kerseymere:* also spelled *casimere, casimire.* [<F *casimir* cashmere]

cas·si·no (kə-sē′no) See CASINO (def. 3).

cas·si·o·ber·ry (kas′ē-ō-ber′ē) *n. pl.* **·ries 1** The shining black edible drupe of a North American shrub (*Viburnum obovatum*). **2** The yaupon or its fruit. [<N. Am. Ind.]

cas·sis (kä-sēs′) *n.* **1** The black currant of Europe. **2** A cordial made from black currants. [<F]

cas·sit·e·rite (kə-sit′ə-rīt) *n.* A tetragonal, brown to black tin dioxide, SnO_2: the most important ore of tin. [<Gk. *kassiteros* tin]

cas·sock (kas′ək) *n.* **1** A close-fitting garment, reaching to the feet, worn by the Roman Catholic and many of the Protestant clergy. **2** A short garment or loose jacket worn under the Geneva gown by Presbyterian ministers. **3** A clergyman or the clerical office. **4** *Obs.* Any long coat or gown; especially, a military cloak. [<MF *casaque* <Ital. *casacca* greatcoat] — **cas·socked** (kas′ŏkt) *adj.*

cas·so·war·y (kas′ə·wer′ē) *n.* *pl.* **·war·ies** A large, three–toed, ratite bird of Australia and New Guinea (genus *Casuarius*), related to the emu. [<Malay *kasuārī*]

cast (kast, käst) *v.* **cast, cast·ing** *v.t.* **1** To throw with force; drive by force, as from the hand or from an engine; fling; hurl. **2** To place as if by throwing; put with violence or force, as by the sea or wind: The waves *cast* us on the beach. **3** To throw up, as with a shovel: to *cast* a mound of earth. **4** To throw down; defeat; especially with the feet upward: He *cast* his enemy to the ground. **5** To deposit; give: He *cast* his vote. **6** To draw by chance; throw, as dice. **7** To cause to fall upon or over; throw in a particular direction; emit: *cast* a shadow. **8** To throw out or forth; get rid of. **9** To let down; put out; let drop: to *cast* anchor. **10** To abandon or shed, as in the process of growth; molt. **11** To give birth to, especially prematurely; drop: The mare *cast* her foal. **12** *Metall.* To shape in a mold; make a cast of; found. **13** To stereotype or electroplate. **14** To assign roles, as in a play; to assign to a part. **15** To add; total, as a column of figures. **16** To calculate mathematically: He *cast* his horoscope. **17** *Law* To defeat in a suit. **18** To winnow, as grain, by throwing in the air. **19** To reject; discard; disqualify: to *cast* horses for bad temper. **20** In falconry, to place upon the perch. **21** *Naut.* To turn, as a ship, to another course. — *v.i.* **22** To revolve something in the mind; scheme; consider: to *cast* about for a solution. **23** To anticipate; forecast; conjecture. **24** *Metall.* To take shape in a mold, as metal. **25** To add up a column of figures; make a computation: with *up.* **26** To throw a fish line. **27** *Naut.* To turn from the wind; fall off, as in getting under way; to tack; put about. **28** To warp, as timber. **29** In hunting, to make a detour or run, as a dog, in search of a lost scent or trail. **30** To swarm, as bees. **— to cast about 1** To consider ways and means; scheme. **2** To warp; tack. **— to cast away 1** To discard; reject. **— to cast down 1** To overthrow; destroy. **2** To cause to feel dejection; discourage; depress. **— to cast off 1** To reject or discard. **2** To let go, as a ship from a dock. — *n.* **1** The act of throwing or casting: a *cast* of a fly in angling. **2** A throw of dice; also, the number or total thrown. **3** The distance to which a thing may be thrown: a stone's *cast.* **4** Anything that is thrown out or off, as an insect's skin, the dung of an earthworm, the undigested matter ejected from the stomach of an owl or hawk. **5** In angling, a leader, sometimes including the flies. **6** An object founded or run in or as in a mold, as of metal, plaster, wax, etc. **7** *Pathol.* A morbid substance molded as in one of the urinary tubules: a renal *cast.* **8** A stereotype or electrotype plate. **9** A reverse copy, in plaster of Paris or similar material, of a mold: usually distinguished from a *casting,* which is of iron or other metal or alloy. **10** The material run into molds at one operation. **11** An impression as of a harder in a softer body: a *cast* of a man's face. **12** An impressed form of the inner surface of an animal or plant, either of the bony outline or particularly of the organs of an animal: distinguished from *mold.* **13** A characteristic formation or inclination; also, stamp; type; kind; sort. **14** Shade; dash; tinge: white, with a bluish *cast.* **15** A twist or perversion; warp; squint. **16** The distribution of parts to performers in a play; also, the performers collectively. **17** In hunting, a detour in search of the scent. **18** A stroke or turn: a *cast* of one's skill. **19** A pair of hawks or other birds. **20** A course or change in a course. **21** A forecast or conjecture. **22** A contrivance; scheme. **23** A look; turning of a glance in a certain direction. ◆ Homophone: *caste.* [<ON *kasta* throw]

caste (kast, käst) *n.* **1** One of the hereditary classes into which Hindu society is divided in India. **2** The principle or practice of such division or the position it confers. **3** The division of society on artificial grounds; a social class. **4** Reputation; standing. See synonyms under CLASS. **— to lose caste** To lose one's former or rightful position in a community; lose standing. ◆ Homophone: *cast.* [<Pg. *casta* unmixed breed <L *castus* pure]

cas·tel·lan (kas′tə·lən) *n.* The keeper or commander of a castle; a chatelain. [<AF *castelain* <L *castellanus* <*castellum* castle]

cas·tel·lat·ed (kas′tə·lā′tid) *adj.* **1** Having battlements; built like a castle; fortified. **2** Having a castle or castles. [<Med. L *castellatus,* pp. of *castellare* to build a castle <L *castellum* castle] — **cas′tel·la′tion** *n.*

cas·tel·ry (kas′əl·rē, käs′-) *n.* *pl.* **·ries 1** The government, tenure, or jurisdiction of a castle. **2** The territory subject to the lord of the castle. Also spelled *castlery.*

cast·er (kas′tər, käs′-) *n.* **1** One who or that which casts. **2** A cruet for condiments. **3** A swiveling roller fastened under an article of furniture, or a similar mounting for wheels, etc. **4** An axle offset on a motor vehicle.

cas·ti·gate (kas′tə·gāt) *v.t.* **·gat·ed, ·gat·ing** To punish with or as with the rod; chastise. See synonyms under BEAT, CHASTEN. [<L *castigatus,* pp. of *castigare* chasten, ult. <*castus* pure] — **cas′ti·ga′tion** *n.* — **cas′ti·ga′tor** *n.* — **cas·ti·ga·to·ry** (kas′ti·gə·tôr′ē, -tō′rē) *adj.*

Cas·tile soap (kas′tēl, käs·tēl′) A hard, white, odorless soap made with olive oil.

cast iron *Metall.* Commercial iron produced in a blast furnace and containing a large proportion of carbon. It may be hard and brittle or soft and strong.

cast–i·ron (kast′ī′ərn, käst′-) *adj.* **1** Made of cast iron. **2** Like cast iron; rigid; unyielding.

cas·tle (kas′əl, käs′-) *n.* **1** A strong fortress. **2** Any massive or imposing building; hence, any place of defense and security. **3** A castle-shaped chessman; a rook. **4** A close helmet; casque. **5** A wooden tower on the back of an elephant. See synonyms under FORTIFICATION. — *v.* **tled, ·tling** *v.t.* **1** To place in or as in a castle; fortify. **2** In chess, to move the king two squares to the right or left, at the same time bringing the castle (rook) from that side of the board toward which the king is moved to the square over which the king has passed. — *v.i.* **3** In chess, to move the castle and king in this manner. [Fusion of OE *castel* village and AF *castel* castle, both <L *castellum,* dim. of *castrum* camp, fort]

cas·tled (kas′əld, käs′-) *adj.* **1** Having or furnished with a castle or castles. **2** Castellated; fortified.

castle in the air A fanciful, impractical scheme: also called **castle in Spain.**

cas·tle·ry (kas′əl·rē, käs′-) See CASTELRY.

cast–off (kast′ôf′, -of′, käst′-) *adj.* Thrown or laid aside; discarded: *cast–off* garments. — *n.* **1** *Printing* A computation of the space required by any matter to be printed. **2** A person or thing no longer wanted or used.

cas·tor[1] (kas′tər, käs′-) *n.* **1** A beaver, or its fur. **2** A hat of beaver or other fur; also, a silk hat. **3** An oily odorous secretion of beavers: used in medicine and perfumery: also **cas·to·re·um** (kas·tôr′ē·əm, -tō′rē·əm). [<L <Gk. *kastōr* beaver]

cas·tor[2] (kas′tər, käs′-) See CASTER (defs. 2 and 3).

castor bean 1 The seed of the castor–oil plant. **2** The plant.

castor oil A viscous fixed oil, colorless or pale yellow, extracted from the seeds of the castor–oil plant: used as a cathartic and lubricant.

cas·tor–oil plant (kas′tər·oil′, käs′-) A herbaceous plant (*Ricinus communis*) of the spurge family, native in India but widely naturalized in warm climates, yielding the castor bean: also called *palma–Christi.*

cas·tra·me·ta·tion (kas′trə·mə·tā′shən) *n.* The art or act of, or plan for, laying out a camp, especially an army camp. [<F *castramétation* <L *castrum* camp + *metari* measure, lay out]

cas·trate (kas′trāt) *v.t.* **·trat·ed, ·trat·ing 1** To remove the testicles from; emasculate; geld. **2** To remove the ovaries from; spay. **3** To expurgate, as a book; mutilate. [<L *castratus,* pp. of *castrare* castrate] — **cas·tra′tion** *n.*

Cas·tries (kås·trē′, käs′trēs) The capital of St. Lucia, Windward Islands: also *Port Castries.*

cast steel *Metall.* Steel cast in molds to provide special machine parts or other articles.

cas·u·al (kazh′ōō·əl) *adj.* **1** Occurring by chance; accidental; unusual. **2** Occurring at irregular intervals; occasional. **3** *Brit.* Of or pertaining to laborers, vagrants, or paupers who receive temporary aid or shelter. **4** Nonchalant; careless. **5** Unmethodical; haphazard. **6** Of, pertaining to, or caused by accident; a *casual* patient. **7** Informal: *casual* clothes. **8** *Obs.* Precarious. See synonyms under INCIDENTAL — *n.* **1** A casual laborer, patient, or pauper. **2** A chance visitor. **3** *Mil.* A soldier subject to individual regulation because of his physical separation from an organization or lack of assignment or attachment to one. [<F *casuel* <L *casualis* <*casus* accident <*cadere* fall] — **cas′u·al·ly** *adv.* — **cas′u·al·ness** *n.*

cas·u·al·ism (kazh′ōō·əl·iz′əm) *n.* The doctrine that chance prevails in all things. — **cas′u·al·ist** *n.*

cas·u·al·ty (kazh′ōō·əl·tē) *n.* *pl.* **·ties 1** A fatal or serious accident. **2** A chance occurrence. **3** *Mil.* **a** A soldier missing in action or removed from active duty by death, wounds, or capture. **b** *pl.* Losses arising from death, wounds, illness, capture, or desertion. See synonyms under ACCIDENT, HAZARD.

casual water Water which has temporarily accumulated on a golf course, but is not treated as a hazard except where it lodges in a bunker.

cas·u·ist (kazh′ōō·ist) *n.* A theologian, philosopher, etc., who studies or resolves ethical problems or cases of conscience involving a seeming conflict of right and wrong: often used derogatorily. [<F *casuiste* <L *casus* event, case]

cas·u·is·tic (kazh′ōō·is′tik) *adj.* **1** Pertaining to a casuist or casuistry. **2** Sophistical; equivocal. Also **cas′u·is′ti·cal.** — **cas′u·is′ti·cal·ly** *adv.*

cas·u·ist·ry (kazh′ōō·is·trē) *n.* *pl.* **·ries 1** The science or doctrine of resolving doubtful cases of conscience or questions of right and wrong according to the injunctions of sacred books or of individual authority or social conventions: often used derogatorily. **2** Sophistical or equivocal reasoning.

cat (kat) *n.* **1** A domesticated carnivorous mammal (*Felis domestica*) with retractile claws: it kills mice and rats and is of worldwide distribution in various breeds. ◆ Collateral adjective: *feline.* **2** Any animal of the cat family (*Felidae*), as a lion, tiger, lynx, ocelot, etc. **3** *Naut.* A purchase for hoisting an anchor. **4** A whip with nine lashes; a cat-o′-nine-tails. **5** A catboat. **6** A double-pointed piece of wood used in the game of tipcat; also, the game. **7** A game of ball, called from the number of batters *one old* (or *o*′) cat, *two old cat,* etc. **8** *Colloq.* A spiteful woman given to gossip and scandal. **9** *Colloq.* A prostitute. **10** *U.S. Colloq.* A Caterpillar tractor. **11** *U.S. Slang* A musician in a jazz band. **— to let the cat out of the bag** To divulge a secret. **— see which way the cat jumps** See how things turn out. — *v.t.* **cat·ted, cat·ting** To hoist or raise to and fasten at the cathead, as an anchor. **2** To flog with a cat-o′-nine-tails. [OE *cat, catte*]

cata– *prefix* **1** Down; against; upon: *cataclysm.* **2** Back; over: *cataphonic.* **3** With a pejorative or intensive sense: *cataphyllon.* Also, before vowels, **cat–;** before *h, cath–.* [<Gk. *kata–* <*kata* down, against, back]

ca·tab·a·sis (kə·tab′ə·sis) *n.* *pl.* **·ses** (-sēz) **1** A going downward; descent: opposed to *anabasis.* **2** *Pathol.* The decreasing of a disease. [<Gk. *katabasis* <*kata–* down + *bainein* go] — **cat·a·bat·ic** (kat′ə·bat′ik) *adj.*

ca·tab·o·lism (kə·tab′ə·liz′əm) *n.* *Biol.* The series of changes by which living matter or protoplasm breaks down into less complex and more stable substances within a cell or organism; destructive metabolism: opposed to *anabolism.* Also spelled *katabolism.* [<Gk. *katabolē* destruction <*kata-* down + *ballein* throw] — **cat·a·bol·ic** (kat'ə·bol'ik) *adj.* — **cat'a·bol'i·cal·ly** *adv.*

ca·tab·o·lite (kə·tab'ə·līt) *n.* Any product resulting from catabolism.

cat·a·caus·tic (kat'ə·kôs'tik) *adj. Optics* Denoting a caustic curve formed by reflected rays of light: opposed to *diacaustic.* — *n.* A catacaustic curve. [<CATA- + CAUSTIC (def. 3)]

cat·a·chre·sis (kat'ə·krē'sis) *n.* 1 The misuse of a word; application of a meaning to a word not its own, as *asset* used in the sense of *advantage;* also, a mixed or strained metaphor. 2 The use of a wrong form of a word, through a misunderstanding of its etymology. [<L <Gk. *katachrēsis* <*kata-* against + *chraesthai* use] — **cat·a·chres·tic** (kat'ə·kres'tik) or **·ti·cal** *adj.* — **cat'a·chres'ti·cal·ly** *adv.*

cat·a·clysm (kat'ə·kliz'əm) *n.* 1 An overwhelming flood. 2 *Geol.* Any violent and extensive subversion of the ordinary phenomena of nature on the earth's surface. 3 Any sudden overwhelming change or political or social upheaval. See synonyms under CATASTROPHE. [<Gk. *kataklysmos* flood <*kata-* down + *klyzein* wash] — **cat·a·clys·mal** (kat'ə·kliz'məl), **cat'a·clys'mic**, **cat'a·clys·mat'ic** (-kliz·mat'ik) *adj.*

cat·a·comb (kat'ə·kōm) *n. Usually pl.* A long underground gallery with excavations in its sides for tombs or in which human bones are stacked or piled. [<F *catacombe* <LL *catacumbas*]

cat·a·falque (kat'ə·falk) *n.* 1 A temporary raised structure or staging that supports the coffin, usually draped, of a deceased personage lying in state. 2 The drapery on or the hangings over it. 3 A stately funeral car. [<F <Ital. *catafalco*]

cat·a·log (kat'ə·lôg, -log) *n.* 1 A list or enumeration of names, persons or things, usually in alphabetical order, sometimes with accompanying description. 2 A publication listing wares for sale by a commercial establishment: a mail-order *catalog.* See synonyms under RECORD. — *v.* **·loged**, **·log·ing** *v.t.* To make an alphabetical list of; insert in a catalog. — *v.i.* To work upon or make such a list. [<F <LL *catalogus* <Gk. *katalogos* list <*kata-* down + *legein* select, choose] — **cat'·a·log'er**, **cat'a·log'ist** *n.*

ca·tal·pa (kə·tal'pə) *n.* A tree (genus *Catalpa*) of the bignonia family of China, Japan, and North America, having large, ovate leaves, large, fragrant bell-shaped flowers, and long slender pods. [<N. Am. Ind.]

ca·tal·y·sis (kə·tal'ə·sis) *n. pl.* **·ses** (-sēz) *Chem.* An alteration in the speed of a chemical reaction effected by the presence of an agent or substance that itself remains stable. [<Gk. *katalysis* dissolution <*kata-* wholly, completely + *lyein* loosen] — **cat·a·lyt·ic** (kat'ə·lit'ik) *adj. & n.*

cat·a·lyst (kat'ə·list) *n. Chem.* Any substance or agent that causes catalysis. A **positive catalyst** accelerates the speed of the reaction; a **negative catalyst** retards it.

cat·a·lyze (kat'ə·līz) *v.t.* **·lyzed**, **·lyz·ing** To submit to or decompose by catalysis. — **cat'a·lyz'er** *n.*

cat·a·ma·ran (kat'ə·mə·ran') *n. Naut.* 1 A long, narrow raft of logs, often with an outrigger. 2 A life raft of two pointed metal cylinders connected by a platform. 3 A boat having twin hulls. [<Tamil *katta-maram* tied wood]

CATAMARAN
Twin-hulled
Tahitian
war canoe.

cat·a·me·ni·a (kat'ə·mē'nē·ə) *n. pl. Physiol.* The menses. [<Gk. *katamēnia,* neut. pl. of *katamēnios* monthly <*kata-* by + *mēn* month] — **cat·a·me'ni·al** *adj.*

cat·a·mite (kat'ə·mīt) *n.* A boy used in pederasty. [<L *Catamitus,* alter. of Gk. *Ganymēdēs,* the cupbearer of Zeus]

cat·am·ne·sis (kat'əm·nē'sis) *n. Med.* The history of a patient subsequent to his illness and recovery: distinguished from *anamnesis.*

[<NL <Gk. *kata-* down + *-mnēsis* recollection <*mimnēskein* remember] — **cat'am·nes'·tic** (-nes'tik) *adj.*

cat·a·moun·tain (kat'ə·moun'tən) *n.* 1 A catamount. 2 One of various wildcats, as a leopard or panther. [Short form of *cat of the mountain*]

cat·a·phon·ic (kat'ə·fon'ik) *adj. Physics* Relating to or produced by the reflection of sound. [CATA- + Gk. *phōnē* sound]

cat·a·phon·ics (kat'ə·fon'iks) *n. Physics* The study of the reflection of sound.

cat·a·pho·re·sis (kat'ə·fə·rē'sis) *n.* 1 The movement of medicinal substances in or through living tissue under the influence of an electric field. 2 Electrophoresis. [<NL <Gk. *kata-* down + *phorēsis* carrying <*pherein* bear, carry] — **cat·a·pho·ret·ic** (-ret'ik) *adj.*

cat·a·phyll (kat'ə·fil) *n. Bot.* A rudimentary or scalelike leaf which forms the covering of a bud. [<Gk. *kata-* + Gk. *phyllon* leaf]

cat·a·pla·si·a (kat'ə·plā'zhē·ə, -zē·ə) *n. Pathol.* A reversion of cells or tissues to a more primitive or embryonic form. Also **ca·tap·la·sis** (kə·tap'lə·sis). [<NL <Gk. *kata-* back + *-plasia* a molding <*plassein* form, mold]

cat·a·plasm (kat'ə·plaz'əm) *n.* A soothing poultice, often medicated. [<Gk. *kataplasma*]

cat·a·plex·y (kat'ə·plek'sē) *n. Psychiatry* A temporary paroxysmic rigidity of the muscles often caused by sudden emotional shock. [<Gk. *kataplēxis* amazement <*kataplēssein* astound <*kata-* down + *plēssein* strike] — **cat·a·plec·tic** (-plek'tik) *adj.*

cat·a·pult (kat'ə·pult) *n.* 1 An engine of sisting of an elastic band attached to the prongs of a forked stick: used by boys for throwing missiles. 3 *Aeron.* A device for launching an airplane at flight speed, as from the deck of a ship not having a flight deck. — *v.t.* To hurl from or as from a catapult. — *v.i.* To hurtle through the air as if from a catapult. [<L *catapulta* <Gk. *katapeltēs* <*kata-* down + *pallein* brandish, hurl]

cat·a·ract (kat'ə·rakt) *n.* 1 A waterfall of great size. 2 *Pathol.* Opacity of the crystalline lens of the eye. 3 A heavy downpour or flood of water; a deluge. [<F *cataracte* <L *cataracta* <Gk. *kataraktēs* <*kata-* down + *arassein* fall headlong]

ca·tarrh (kə·tär') *n. Pathol.* Excessive secretion from an inflamed mucous membrane, especially of the air passages of the throat and head. [<F *catarrhe* <L *catarrhus* <Gk. *katarrhoos* <*kata-* down + *rheein* flow] — **ca·tarrh'al** *adj.* — **ca·tarrh'ous** *adj.*

ca·tas·tro·phe (kə·tas'trə·fē) *n.* 1 Any final event; a fatal conclusion; great and sudden misfortune. 2 In a drama, the conclusion or unraveling of the plot; the dénouement. 3 A sudden, violent change, especially of the earth's surface; cataclysm. [<Gk. *katastrophē* <*kata-* over, down + *strephein* turn] — **cat·a·stroph·ic** (kat'ə·strof'ik) *adj.*

Synonyms: calamity, cataclysm, dénouement, disaster, mischance, misfortune, mishap, sequel. A *cataclysm* or *catastrophe* is some great convulsion or momentous event that may or may not be a cause of misery to man. In *calamity,* or *disaster,* the thought of human suffering is always present. It has been held by many geologists that numerous *catastrophes* or *cataclysms* antedated the existence of man. In literature the final event of a drama is the *catastrophe,* or *dénouement. Misfortune* ordinarily suggests less of suddenness and violence than *calamity* or *disaster,* and is especially applied to that which is lingering or enduring in its effects. Pestilence is a *calamity;* a defeat in battle, a shipwreck, a failure in business are *disasters;* sickness, loss of property are *misfortunes;* failure to meet a friend is a *mischance;* the breaking of a teacup is a *mishap.* Compare ACCIDENT, MISFORTUNE. *Antonyms:* benefit, blessing, boon, comfort, favor, help, pleasure, privilege, prosperity, success.

cat·a·to·ni·a (kat'ə·tō'nē·ə) *n. Psychiatry* A complex of symptoms typical of schizophrenia, characterized by stupor, muscular rigidity, and occasional mental agitation. [<NL <*kata-* down + *tonos* tension, tone <*teinein* stretch] — **cat·a·ton·ic** (-ton'ik) *adj.*

cat·bird (kat'bûrd') *n.* A small slate-colored North American songbird (*Dumetella carolinensis*), related to the mockingbird: named from its catlike cry.

cat·boat (kat'bōt') *n. Naut.* A small one-masted sailboat, usually equipped with a centerboard and having its mast stepped well forward and carrying a single fore-and-aft sail with boom and gaff.

cat·bri·er (kat'brī'ər) *n.* Any of certain woody vines of the genus *Smilax,* especially the greenbrier.

cat·call (kat'kôl') *n.* A shrill, discordant call or whistle, in token of impatience or derision. — *v.t.* To deride or express disapproval of with catcalls. — *v.i.* To utter catcalls.

catch (kach) *v.* **caught, catch·ing** *v.t.* 1 To take, seize, or come upon, as something departing or fleeing; take captive; capture. 2 To entrap; ensnare. 3 To captivate, gain, or hold. 4 To apprehend or perceive clearly. 5 To surprise; detect, as in a misdeed. 6 To contract; incur, as a disease. 7 To arrive at or take, as a train or boat, just before its departure. 8 To arrest the motion of; entangle. 9 To grasp and retain. 10 To perceive, as something fleeting, with momentary distinction: to *catch* sight of. 11 To reach, as a person, with a blow: She *caught* him a box on the ear. — *v.i.* 12 To make a movement of grasping or seizing: He *caught* at the idea. 13 In baseball, to act as catcher. 14 To become entangled or fastened. 15 To be communicated or communicable, as a disease or enthusiasm. 16 To take fire; kindle; ignite. 17 *Naut.* To catch the wind: an elliptical expression. — **to catch it** *Colloq.* To receive a reprimand, scolding, drubbing, or the like. — **to catch (one) napping** To take off guard; outwit. — **to catch on** *Colloq.* 1 To understand. 2 To become popular or fashionable. — **to catch out** 1 In baseball, to put a batter out by catching the ball. 2 To discover (someone) in error. — **to catch up** 1 To overtake. 2 To regain by or as if by overtaking: to *catch up* on one's lessons. — **to catch up with** (or **up to**) To overtake. — *n.* 1 The act of catching; the act of grasping or seizing; specifically, the act of catching a batted or thrown ball before it reaches the ground, as in baseball, cricket, etc.; also a catcher. 2 A hold or grip, as in wrestling. 3 That which catches or fastens; a fastening. 4 That which is or may be caught or gained, such as a person or thing worth obtaining, as in marriage. 5 The amount of fish or the like caught at one time or in a given period. 6 The state in which or the extent to which a crop germinates. 7 An artful trick or question. 8 An impediment; a break, as in the voice or breathing. 9 *Music* A round; also, a scrap of song. — *adj.* Attracting or meant to attract notice; catchy; a *catch* phrase. [<AF *cachier* <LL *captiare,* freq. of *capere* take, hold. Doublet of CHASE.]

Synonyms (verb): apprehend, capture, clasp, clutch, comprehend, discover, ensnare, entrap, grasp, grip, gripe, overtake, secure, seize, snatch, take. To *catch* is to come up with or take possession of something departing, fugitive, or illusive. We *catch* a runaway horse, a flying ball, a mouse in a trap. To "catch at" is to attempt to *catch,* often unsuccessfully. We *clutch* with a swift, tenacious movement of the fingers; we *grasp* with a firm closure of the whole hand; we *grip* or *gripe* with the strongest muscular closure of the whole hand possible to exert. We *clasp* in the arms. We *snatch* with a quick, sudden, and usually a surprising motion. In the figurative sense, *catch* is used of any act that brings a person or thing into our power or possession; as, to *catch* a criminal in the act; to *catch* an idea, in the sense of *apprehend* or *comprehend.* Compare ARREST, GRASP. *Antonyms:* lose, miss, release, restore.

catch basin A filter at the entrance to a drain or sewer to stop matter which might clog the pipes.

catch·er (kach'ər) *n.* 1 One who or that which catches. 2 In baseball, the player stationed behind home plate to catch balls that pass the batter.

catch·fly (kach'flī) *n.* Any one of several weeds (genus *Silene*) of the pink family, the stem and calyx of which exude a viscid fluid which holds small insects alighting on it.

catch·ing (kach'ing) *adj.* 1 Infectious. 2 Captivating.

catch·ment (kach'mənt) *n.* 1 Drainage. 2 The collection of water over a natural drainage area.

3 The water so collected.

catchment basin *Geog.* The area drained by a river or river system. Also **catchment area.**

catch·word (kach′wûrd′) *n.* **1** A word or phrase to catch the popular fancy or attention, especially, a word or phrase used as a slogan in a political campaign. **2** In the theater, a cue. **3** A word so placed as to catch the attention. **4** An isolated word at the bottom of a page in old books, inserted to connect the text with the beginning of the next page. **5** A word at the head of a page or column, as of a dictionary, encyclopedia, etc.

catch·y (kach′ē) *adj.* **·i·er, ·i·est 1** Attractive; taking. **2** Entangling; deceptive, puzzling. **3** Broken; fitful.

cat·e·che·sis (kat′ə·kē′sis) *n. pl.* **·ses** (-sēz) **1** Oral instruction in the elements of Christianity, as given to a catechumen; catechizing. **2** A catechetic discourse or writing. [< Gk. *katēchēsis* instruction]

cat·e·chet·ic (kat′ə·ket′ik) *adj.* **1** Of or pertaining to oral instruction: consisting of question and answer. **2** Of or pertaining to instruction in the elementary doctrines of Christianity. Also **cat′e·chet′i·cal.**

cat·e·chin (kat′ə·chin, -kin) *n. Chem.* An amorphous yellow powder, $C_{15}H_{14}O_6·4H_2O$, contained in catechu: used in dyeing.

cat·e·chism (kat′ə·kiz′əm) *n.* **1** A short treatise giving in catechetic form an outline of the fundamental principles of a religious creed. **2** Any brief manual of instruction by questions and answers; an examination of candidates by interrogatories. **3** Catechetic instruction, especially in religious doctrine. [< Med. L *catechismus* < Gk. *katēchizein* instruct]

cat·e·chist (kat′ə·kist) *n.* One who teaches by question and answer; especially, an instructor of catechumens or new converts. Also **cat′e·chiz′er, cat′e·chis′er. —cat′e·chis′tic** or **·ti·cal** *adj.*

cat·e·chize (kat′ə·kīz) *v.t.* **·chized, ·chiz·ing 1** To interrogate seriously as to conduct or belief. **2** To question in a searching manner, especially with a view to judgment or reproof. **3** To give systematic oral instruction to; instruct in elementary truths of religion; teach by means of a catechism. **4** To teach the catechism to, as in preparation for confirmation. Also **cat′e·chise.** [< L *catechizare* instruct < Gk. *katēchizein*] **—cat′e·chi·za′tion** *n.*

cat·e·chol (kat′ə·chōl, -kōl) *n. Chem.* Pyrocatechol. [< CATECHU]

cat·e·chol·a·mine (kat′ə·chōl′ə·mēn, -kōl′-) *n.* Any of various amines chemically related to pyrocatechol and having a hormonal effect on the sympathetic nervous system, including epinephrine, norepinephrine, and dopamine.

cat·e·chu (kat′ə·chōō) *n.* A resinous astringent and tanning extract prepared from the wood of various Asian and East Indian plants, especially *Acacia catechu.* Also called *cashoo, cutch.* [< NL < Malay *kachu*] **—cat′e·chu′ic** *adj.*

cat·e·chu·men (kat′ə·kyōō′mən) *n.* **1** One who is under instruction in the elements of Christianity; especially, a new or a young convert in the ancient church; a beginner. **2** One undergoing initiation in any science, art, set of opinions, etc. [< L *catechumenus* < Gk. *katēchoumenos*, ppr. passive of *katēcheein* instruct] **—cat′e·chu′me·nal, cat·e·chu·men·i·cal** (kat′ə·kyōō·men′i·kəl) *adj.*

cat·e·gor·e·mat·ic (kat′ə·gôr′ə·mat′ik, -gor′-) *adj. Logic* Capable of being used alone as the complete subject or predicate of a proposition: opposed to *syncategorematic.* [< Gk. *katēgorēma* logical predicate]

cat·e·gor·i·cal (kat′ə·gôr′i·kəl, -gor′-) *adj.* **1** Without qualification; absolute; unequivocal. **2** Of or pertaining to a category; in the form of a category. **—cat′e·gor′i·cal·ly** *adv.* **—cat′e·gor′i·cal·ness** *n.*

categorical imperative *Philos.* The principle established by Immanuel Kant, which states, "Act in such a way that the maxim of your will can simultaneously apply as the basis for a universal law."

cat·e·go·rize (kat′ə·gə·rīz′) *v.t.* **·rized, ·riz·ing 1** To put into categories. **2** To treat categorically.

cat·e·go·ry (kat′ə·gôr′ē, -gō′rē) *n. pl.* **·ries 1** Any comprehensive class or description of things. **2** A

class, condition, or predicament. **3** One of the several forms of conception or knowledge that together embrace everything predicable or existent. [< L *categoria* < Gk. *katēgoria* < *katēgoreein* allege, predicate < *kata-* against + *agora* public assembly]

cat·e·lec·trot·o·nus (kat′ə·lek·trot′ō·nəs) *Physiol.* A state of increased tension produced in a nerve fiber or muscle at the negative pole of an electric current passing through it. [< CAT(HODE) + ELECTROTONUS]

ca·te·na (kə·tē′nə) *n. pl.* **·nae** (-nē) A chain or closely connected series, usually with reference to succession in time; specifically, a series of excerpts from the works of the fathers of the Church to clear up some point, as of Scriptural exegesis. [< L, chain]

cat·e·nar·y (kat′ə·ner′ē, kə·tē′nə·rē) *n. pl.* **·ies** *Math.* The curve formed by a perfectly flexible, inextensible, infinitely slender cord suspended from two points not in the same vertical line; especially, the common catenary, represented by a chain freely suspended from two fixed points. — *adj.* Relating to or like a catenary or a chain: also **cat·e·nar·i·an** (kat′ə·nâr′ē·ən). [< L *catenarius* < *catena* chain]

cat·e·nate (kat′ə·nāt) *v.t.* **·nat·ed, ·nat·ing** To connect like the links of a chain; form into a chain; link together. **—cat′e·na′tion** *n.*

cat·e·noid (kat′ə·noid) *n. Math.* The surface formed by the rotation of a catenary about its axis.

ca·ten·u·late (kə·ten′yə·lāt, -lit) *adj.* Consisting of little links; made up of parts united end to end in a chainlike series. [< L *catenula*, dim. of *catena* chain]

ca·ter (kā′tər) *v.t.* **1** To furnish food or entertainment. **2** To provide for the gratification of any need or taste. See synonyms under PROVIDE. [< AF *acater* buy < LL *acceptare* < *ad-* toward + *captare* grasp, seize] **—ca′ter·er** *n.*

cat·er-cor·nered (kat′ər-kôr′nərd) *adj.* Placed cornerwise or diagonally; diagonal: also *catty-cornered, kitty-cornered.* Also **cat′er-cor′ner.** [< *cater* diagonally < F *quatre* four < L *quattuor* + CORNERED]

cat·er·pil·lar (kat′ər·pil′ər) *n.* **1** The larva of a butterfly or moth (order *Lepidoptera*), or of certain other insects, as the sawfly. **2** Something resembling a caterpillar or its system of locomotion, as a car fitted with supplementary wheels or a device on the principle of the endless chain. [< AF *catepelose* hairy cat < L *catta* cat + *pilosus* < *pilum* hair]

Cat·er·pil·lar (kat′ər·pil′ər) *n.* A tractor whose driving wheels gear with self-laid, wide metal belts whereby its weight is distributed over a large area, permitting the tractor to move over soft or rough terrain: a trade name.

caterpillar hunter Any of a genus (*Calosoma*) of carabid beetles which prey on caterpillars, especially *C. scrutator,* having dark green elytra. For illustration see INSECTS (beneficial).

cat·er·waul (kat′ər·wôl) *v.i.* **1** To utter the discordant cry peculiar to cats at rutting time. **2** To make any discordant screeching. **3** To argue or dispute noisily. —*n.* The cry of cats at rutting time; also, any similar cry. [ME *caterwawen* < *cater* cat (cf. G *kater* tomcat) + *wawen* wail, howl] **—cat′er·waul′ing** *n.*

cat·fish (kat′fish′) *n. pl.* **·fish** or **·fish·es 1** One of numerous silurid fishes, usually carnivorous and of fresh-water habitat, having sensitive barbels around the mouth to enable them to find their prey in muddy waters. **2** Any of many other teleost fishes, as the bullhead.

cat·gut (kat′gut′) *n.* **1** A very tough cord, made from the intestines of certain animals, as sheep, and used for stringing musical instruments, making surgical ligatures, etc. **2** A violin or fiddle; hence, stringed instruments generally: a humorous use. **3** A leguminous perennial (*Tephrosia virginiana*), native in the eastern half of the United States.

cath- Var. of CATA-.

ca·thar·sis (kə·thär′sis) *n.* **1** *Med.* Purgation or cleansing of any passage of the body, especially of the alimentary canal. **2** A word used by Aristotle to express the effect of tragic drama in purifying and relieving the emotions. **3** *Psychoanal.* Abreaction. Also spelled *katharsis.* [< Gk. *ka-*

tharsis cleansing < *katharos* pure]

ca·thar·tic (kə·thär′tik) *adj.* Purgative; purifying: also **ca·thar′ti·cal.** —*n.* A purgative medicine. [< Gk. *kathartikos* < *katharos* pure] **—ca·thar′ti·cal·ly** *adv.*

ca·the·dra (kə·thē′drə, kath′ə-) *n.* **1** A bishop's seat or throne in the cathedral or chief church of his diocese; hence, the see or dignity of a bishop. **2** A professor's chair. **—ex cathedra** *Latin* **1** Literally, from the seat: applied to a pronouncement on faith or morals by the Pope as head of the Roman Catholic Church. **2** With authority: also used attributively, meaning "officially spoken": an *ex cathedra* pronouncement. [< L < Gk. *kathedra* < *kata* down + *hedra* seat. Doublet of CHAIR.]

ca·the·dral (kə·thē′drəl) *n.* **1** The church containing the cathedra or official chair of the bishop; the mother church of a diocese. **2** Any large or important church. —*adj.* **1** Pertaining to or containing a bishop's chair or see. **2** Of or pertaining to any chair of authority; authoritative; dogmatic. **3** Of, pertaining to, belonging to, or resembling a cathedral: a *cathedral* choir.

catherine wheel 1 A rotating firework; a pinwheel, especially a large, showy one. **2** *Her.* The figure of a wheel with the tire armed with hooks, to represent the legendary instrument of St. Catherine's martyrdom.

cath·e·ter (kath′ə·tər) *n. Med.* A slender, tubular, surgical instrument for introduction into canals or passages. [< L < Gk. *kathetēr* < *kata-* down + *hienai* send, let go]

cath·e·ter·ize (kath′ə·tər·īz′) *v.t.* **·ized, ·iz·ing** To introduce a catheter into.

ca·thex·is (kə·thek′sis) *n. Psychoanal.* **1** Concentration of psychic energy upon the self, another person, a phantasy, idea, or object. **2** The investment or charging of an idea or emotion with significance. [< Gk. *kathexis* holding < *kata-* thoroughly + *echein* hold, have; trans. of G *besetzung*]

cath·ode (kath′ōd) *n. Electr.* The electrode through which negative ions leave a non-metallic conductor and toward which positive ions flow from the anode. It is negative for a battery, electrolytic bath, or a vacuum tube, but positive for a voltaic cell: also spelled *kathode.* [< Gk. *kathodos* a way down < *kata-* down + *hodos* road, way] **—ca·thod·ic** (kə·thod′ik) or **·i·cal** *adj.*

CATHODE-RAY TUBE
a. Cathode.
b. Anode.
c. Vacuum.

cathode rays *Physics* A stream of electrons that pass from a cathode to the opposite wall of a vacuum discharge tube when it is excited by a current of electricity, or by a series of spark discharges.

cathode-ray tube *Electronics* A special type of electron tube in which a beam of electrons is focused by an electric or magnetic field and deflected so as to impinge upon a sensitized screen, forming an image, as on a television receiver.

cath·o·lic (kath′ə·lik, kath′lik) *adj.* **1** Broadminded, as in belief, tastes, or views; liberal; comprehensive; large. **2** Universal in reach; general. [< L *catholicus* < Gk. *katholikos* universal < *kata-* thoroughly + *holos* whole] **—ca·thol·i·cal·ly** (kə·thol′ik·lē) *adv.* **—cath·o·lic·i·ty** (kath′ə·lis′ə·tē) *n.*

Cath·o·lic (kath′ə·lik, kath′lik) *adj.* **1** Universal; of, pertaining to, belonging or addressed to all Christians: a *Catholic* epistle; the *Catholic* faith. **2** Describing the ancient, undivided Christian Church; in accordance with the decrees of the seven ecumenical councils; not heretical or schismatic: the *Catholic* fathers; a *Catholic* creed. **3** Designating the western or Latin Church as opposed to the eastern or Greek Church after their final separation in 1472; not Orthodox. **4** Describing those churches which, after the Reformation and in modern times, claim to have the apostolic doctrine, discipline, orders, and sacraments of the ancient undivided church, and including the Anglican, Eastern

Orthodox, Old Catholic, and Roman Churches. —*n.* **1** A member of the Catholic Church, in any of the above senses. **2** Specifically, a Roman Catholic. —**Cath·o·lic·i·ty** (kath'ə·lis'ə·tē) *n.*

Catholic Church The Roman Catholic Church.

Ca·thol·i·cism (kə·thol'ə·siz'əm) *n.* **1** The doctrine, system, and practice of the Church universal. **2** The system, doctrine, and practice of the Roman Catholic Church.

ca·thol·i·cize (kə·thol'ə·sīz) *v.t. & v.i.* **·cized, ·ciz·ing** To make or become catholic or Catholic.

ca·thol·i·con (kə·thol'ə·kən) *n.* A supposed universal remedy; a panacea. [<LL <Gk. *katholikos* universal]

cath·o·lyte (kath'ə·līt) *n. Chem.* The liquid formed near the cathode during electrolysis. [<CATHO(DE)+ (ELECTRO)LYTE]

cat·i·on (kat'ī'ən) *n. Chem.* **1** A positively charged particle which in electrolysis moves toward the cathode or is deposited there. **2** A positive ion, molecule, or radical. Also spelled *kation.* [<Gk. *kation*, ppr. neut. of *katienai* <*kata*- down + *ienai* go]

cat·kin (kat'kin) *n. Bot.* A deciduous scaly spike of flowers, as in the willow; an ament. [<MDu. *katteken*, dim. of *katte* cat]

cat·like (kat'līk') *adj.* **1** Like a cat; feline. **2** Noiseless; stealthy.

cat·ling (kat'ling) *n.* **1** Catgut. **2** *pl.* Stringed instruments. **3** A kitten.

cat·nap (kat'nap') *n.* A short doze, usually taken sitting up.

cat·nip (kat'nip) *n.* An aromatic herb (*Nepeta cataria*) of the mint family, of which cats are fond. Also **cat'mint'.**

cat–o'–moun·tain (kat'ə·moun'tən) See CATAMOUNT.

cat–o'–nine–tails (kat'ə·nīn'tālz) *n.* A whip with nine lashes.

ca·top·trics (kə·top'triks) *n.* That branch of optics which treats of the reflection of light and the formation of images by mirrors. [< Gk. *katoptrikos* <*katoptron* mirror]—**ca·top'·tric** or **·tri·cal** *adj.*

cat owl The great horned owl.

cat rig The rig of a catboat, consisting of one mast far forward and one sail with a long boom and a gaff. —**cat'–rigged'** *adj.*

cat's cradle A game played with a loop of string stretched over the fingers and transferred from one player's hands to another's, so as to produce intricate geometrical arrangements.

cat's–eye (kats'ī') *n.* A gemstone, usually chrysoberyl or quartz, which shows a line of light across the dome when cut en cabochon.

cat's–paw (kats'pô') *n.* **1** A person used as a tool or dupe. **2** A light wind which barely ruffles the water. **3** *Naut.* A twisting hitch in the bight of a rope. Also **cats'paw'.**

cat·sup (kat'səp, kech'əp) See KETCHUP.

Catt (kat), **Carrie Chapman,** 1859–1947, *née* Lane, U.S. suffragist.

cat–tail (kat'tāl') *n.* **1** A perennial aquatic plant (genus *Typha*), with long leaves, flowers in cylindrical terminal spikes, and downy fruit: used in making mats, chair seats, etc. **2** *Brit.* Timothy grass. **3** A catkin or ament. **4** A cirrus cloud.

cat·ta·lo (kat'ə·lō) See CATALO.

Cat·ta·ro (kät'tä·rō) The Italian name for KOTOR.

catted chimney A chimney built of sticks and clay.

CAT–TAIL

Cat·te·gat (kat'ə·gat) See KATTEGAT.

cat·tle (kat'l) *n.* **1** Domesticated bovine animals. **2** Formerly, all livestock, as horses, sheep, goats, etc. **3** Human beings: a contemptuous term. **4** *Obs.* Vermin, birds, etc. [<AF *catel* <LL *captale* <L *capitale* capital, wealth. Doublet of CHATTEL.]

cat·tle·ya (kat'lē·ə) *n.* Any of a genus (*Cattleya*) of tropical American orchids, widely cultivated in many horticultural varieties and esteemed for their showy, variously colored flowers. [<NL, after William *Cattley*, English botanist]

cat·ty¹ (kat'ē) *n. pl.* **·ties** An Oriental and Asiatic weight varying in different countries but equivalent to about 1⅓ pounds avoirdupois: also called *chang.* Also **cat'tie.** [<Malay *kātī*]

cat·ty² (kat'ē) *adj.* **·ti·er, ·ti·est 1** Pertaining to cats. **2** *Colloq.* Malicious; spiteful; backbiting. —**cat'ti·ly** *adv.* —**cat'ti·ness** *n.*

cat·ty–cor·nered (kat'ē·kôr'nərd) See CATER-CORNERED.

cat·walk (kat'wôk) *n.* **1** Any narrow walking space, as at the side of a bridge, in an aircraft, near the ceiling of the stage in a theater, etc.

cat–whisk·er (kat'hwis'kər) *n. Electronics* A fine, sharp–pointed wire used to make contact with a sensitive point on the surface of a crystal detector.

Cau·ca·sian (kô·kā'zhən, -shən, -kash'ən) *n.* **1** A member of the white–skinned division of the human race: so called from a skull found in the Caucasus, which was taken as establishing the type. **2** A member of the native peoples of the Caucasus region. **3** A family of languages spoken in the Caucasus region, including Georgian and Circassian: unrelated to the Indo–European, Semitic, Hamitic, Uralic, or Altaic families. —*adj.* **1** Belonging to the region of the Caucasus mountains, its inhabitants, or their languages. **2** Caucasoid. Also **Cau·cas·ic** (kô·kas'ik).

Cau·ca·soid (kô'kə·soid) *adj. Anthropol.* Of or pertaining to the so-called white race, characterized by a skin color ranging from very white to dark brown: variable in stature, body build, eye color, head hair, and cephalic index, with moderate to profuse body hair and generally narrow to medium–broad, high–bridged nose. —*n.* A member of this ethnic group; a Caucasian.

cau·cus (kô'kəs) *n.* **1** A private or preliminary meeting of members of a political party to select candidates or plan a campaign; a primary. **2** *Brit.* A political committee or other body in charge of shaping political policies, or of a local canvass or election. —*v.i.* **cau·cused** or **·cussed, ·cus·ing** or **·cus·sing** To meet in or hold a caucus. [from the *Caucus* Club, Boston, Mass., prob. <Algonquian *caucawasu* advisor]

cau·da (kô'də) *n. pl.* **·dae** (-dē) A tail, or tail–like appendage. [<L, tail]

cau·dad (kô'dad) *adv. Zool.* Toward the tail: opposed to *cephalad.*

cau·dal (kôd'l) *adj. Zool.* **1** Of, pertaining to, or near the tail or posterior part of the body. **2** Having the nature or form of a tail. —**cau'dal·ly** *adv.*

Cau·da·ta (kô·dā'tə) *n. pl.* An order of amphibians with naked skin, limbs, and a tail, including salamanders and newts: formerly called *Urodela.*

cau·date (kô'dāt) *adj. Zool.* Having a tail or tail–like appendage or extremity. Also **cau'·dat·ed.** [<L *caudatus* <*cauda* tail]

cau·dex (kô'deks) *n. pl.* **·di·ces** (-də·sēz) or **·dex·es** *Bot.* **1** The woody axis or trunk of a tree. **2** The woody base of a perennial plant. [<L, var. of *codex* trunk of a tree]

caught (kôt) Past tense and past participle of CATCH.

caul (kôl) *n. Anat.* **1** That part of the amniotic sac which sometimes envelops the head of a newly born child. **2** The great omentum. ◆ Homophone: *call.* [<OF *cale* cap]

caul·dron (kôl'drən) See CALDRON.

cau·les·cent (kô·les'ənt) *adj. Bot.* Having a clearly defined stem. [<L *caulis* stem + -ESCENT]

cau·li·cle (kô'li·kəl) *n. Bot.* A little stem; specifically, the rudimentary stem in the embryo of a seed. [<L *cauliculus,* dim. of *caulis* CAULIS]

cau·li·flo·rous (kô'lə·flôr'əs, -flō'rəs) *adj. Bot.* Characterized by a growth of flowers; borne on the main stem, as flowers and fruits. [<L *caulis* stem + *florus* flowering]

cau·li·flow·er (kô'lə·flou'ər, kol'i-) *n.* **1** The fleshy, edible head formed by the young flowers of a variety of cabbage (*Brassica oleracea botrytis*). **2** The plant bearing this. [<NL *cauliflora* flowering cabbage; infl. in form by FLOWER]

cau·li·form (kô'lə·fôrm) *adj. Bot.* Shaped like a stem.

cau·line (kô'lin, -līn) *adj. Bot.* Of, pertaining to, or growing on a stem. [<NL *caulinus* <L *caulis* CAULIS]

cau·lis (kô'lis) *n. pl.* **·les** (-lēz) *Bot.* The stem of a plant. [<L <Gk. *kaulos* stem of a plant]

caulk (kôk) See CALK¹.

cau·lome (kô'lōm) *n. Bot.* The axial portion

or stem of a plant as distinguished from phyllome, trichome, and root. [<Gk. *kaulos* stalk + -OME] —**cau·lom·ic** (kô·lom'ik) *adj.*

caus·al (kô'zəl) *adj.* Pertaining to, constituting, involving, or expressing a cause. —*n.* A word expressive of cause or reason. [<L *causalis* of a cause <*causa* cause] —**caus'al·ly** *adv.*

cau·sal·gi·a (kô·zal'jē·ə) *n. Pathol.* A burning pain, such as often follows injuries of the nerves; neuralgia with severe local pain. [<NL <Gk. *kausos* heat <*kaiein* burn + -*algia* pain <*algein* hurt]

cau·sal·i·ty (kô·zal'ə·tē) *n. pl.* **·ties 1** The relation of cause and effect. **2** Causal action or agency. See synonyms under CAUSE.

cau·sa·tion (kô·zā'shən) *n.* **1** The act, process, or agency of causing. **2** The relation of cause and effect. **3** The active force of the principle of causality. **4** Causative power or agency. See synonyms under CAUSE. [<L *causatio, -onis* <*causari* bring about <*causa* cause]

caus·a·tive (kô'zə·tiv) *adj.* **1** Effective as a cause. **2** *Gram.* Expressing cause or agency; indicating that the subject causes the action: *en*- in *enfeeble* is a *causative* prefix; *lay* (cause to lie) is a *causative* verb. —*n. Gram.* A form that expresses or suggests causation. [<F *causatif* <L *causativus* <*causa* cause] —**caus'a·tive·ly** *adv.* —**caus'a·tive·ness** *n.*

cause (kôz) *n.* **1** The power or efficient agent producing any thing or event. **2** Any occasion or condition upon the occurrence of which an event takes place. **3** Any rational ground for choice or action; reason. **4** A great enterprise, movement, principle, or aim. **5** *Law* An action or suit; also, a ground of action. **6** *Obs.* Behalf; interest. **7** *Philos.* The object or end for which anything is done or made; purpose; aim. —*v.t.* **caused, caus·ing** To be the cause of; produce; effect; induce; compel. [<F <L *causa* cause, legal case] —**caus'a·ble** *adj.* —**cause'less** *adj.* —**caus'er** *n.*

Synonyms (noun): actor, agent, antecedent, author, causality, causation, condition, creator, designer, former, fountain, motive, occasion, origin, originator, power, precedent, reason, source, spring. The efficient *cause,* that which makes anything to be or be done, is the common meaning of the word, as in the saying "There is no effect without a *cause."* Every man instinctively recognizes himself acting through will as the *cause* of his own actions. The *Creator* is the Great First *Cause* of all things. A *condition* is something that necessarily precedes a result, but does not produce it. An *antecedent* simply precedes a result, with or without any agency in producing it; as, Monday is the invariable *antecedent* of Tuesday, but not the *cause* of it. The direct antonym of *cause* is *effect,* while that of *antecedent* is *consequent.* An *occasion* is some event which brings a *cause* into action at a particular moment; gravitation and heat are the *causes* of an avalanche; the steep incline of the mountain side is a necessary *condition. Causality* is the doctrine or principle of causes, *causation* the action or working of causes. *Motive* is an impulse of an intelligent being which incites to action, and, if unchecked, is a *cause* of action. Compare DESIGN, REASON. *Antonyms:* consequence, creation, development, effect, end, event, fruit, issue, outcome, outgrowth, product, result.

cause·way (kôz'wā') *n.* **1** A raised road or way, as over marshy ground. **2** A sidewalk above the street level. **3** A highway. —*v.t.* **1** To make a causeway for or through, as a marshy tract. **2** To pave, as a road. [<AF *caucie* <LL *calciata,* pp. of *calciare* tread, stamp down <L *calx, calcis* heel + WAY]

caus·tic (kôs'tik) *adj.* **1** Capable of corroding or eating away tissues; burning; corrosive. **2** Causing to smart; stinging; biting; sarcastic and severe. **3** *Optics* **a** Designating a surface to which all rays emitted from one point and reflected or refracted from a curved surface are tangents: so called because along such a surface the heating effect is at the maximum. **b** Designating a curve formed by such a surface. —*n.* **1** A caustic substance. **2** *Optics* A caustic curve or surface. Also **caus'ti·cal.** See synonyms under BITTER. [<L *causticus* <Gk. *kaustikos* <*kausos* burning <*kaiein* burn] —**caus'ti·cal·ly** *adv.*

caus·tic·i·ty (kôs·tis'ə·tē) *n.* **1** The quality or state of being caustic. **2** Severity of language. See synonyms under ACRIMONY.

caustic potash Potassium hydroxide.

caustic soda Sodium hydroxide.

cau·ter·ant (kô′tər·ənt) *adj.* Of or pertaining to cautery or a caustic. —*n.* A cauterizing substance.

cau·ter·ize (kô′tər·īz) *v.t.* **·ized, ·iz·ing** **1** To sear with a caustic drug or a heated iron. **2** To make callous or insensible. Also *Brit.* **cau′ter·ise.** See synonyms under BURN. [< LL *cauterizare* < L *cauterium.* See CAUTERY.] —**cau′ter·i·za′tion, cau′ter·ism** *n.*

cau·ter·y (kô′tər·ē) *n. pl.* **·ter·ies** **1** *Med.* The application of a caustic, especially for the purpose of destroying tissue. **2** A cauterizing agent or a searing iron. [< L *cauterium* branding iron < Gk. *kautērion* < *kaiein* burn]

cau·tion (kô′shən) *n.* **1** Care to avoid injury or misfortune; prudence; wariness. **2** An admonition or warning. **3** *Colloq.* A person or thing that alarms, astonishes, or provokes great admiration. —*v.t.* To advise to be prudent; warn. See synonyms under ADMONISH. [< OF < L *cautio, -onis* < *cavere* beware, take heed]

cau·tion·ar·y (kô′shən·er′ē) *adj.* Constituting or conveying a warning; admonitory.

cau·tious (kô′shəs) *adj.* Exercising or manifesting caution; wary; prudent. —**cau′tious·ly** *adv.* —**cau′tious·ness** *n.*

cav·al·cade (kav′əl·kād′, kav′əl·kād) *n.* A company of riders; a parade. See synonyms under PROCESSION. [< MF < Ital. *cavalcata* < *cavalcare* ride on horseback < LL *caballicare* < L *caballus* horse, nag]

cav·a·lier (kav′ə·lir′) *n.* **1** A horseman; knight. **2** A lover; escort; gallant. —*adj.* **1** Free and easy; offhand. **2** Haughty; supercilious. —*v.t.* To escort or play the gallant to, as a lady. —*v.i.* To behave in a cavalier fashion; show arrogance. Also *Obs.* **cav·a·le·ro** (kav′ə·lā′rō), **cav′a·lie′ro** (-lyā′rō). [< MF < Ital. *cavaliere* < LL *caballarius* < *caballus* horse, nag. Doublet of CHEVALIER.]

cav·a·lier·ly (kav′ə·lir′lē) *adj.* Like or characteristic of a cavalier; gallant; also, haughty. —*adv.* After the manner of a cavalier; disdainfully; haughtily.

ca·val·ly (kə·val′ē) *n. pl.* **·lies** **1** A carangoid fish (genus *Caranx*); especially, a food fish (*C. hippos*) of the Atlantic. **2** The cero. Also **ca·val·la** (kə·val′ə). [< Sp. *caballa* horse mackerel < L *caballus* horse]

cav·al·ry (kav′əl·rē) *n. pl.* **·ries** **1** Mobile ground troops, organized in mounted, mechanized, or motorized units. **2** One of the principal arms or branches of the U.S. Army and of other armies. **3** Organized, mounted combat troops. **4** Riders, horsemen, etc., collectively. [< MF *cavallerie* < Ital. *cavalleria* < LL *caballarius* horseman < *caballus* horse. Doublet of CHIVALRY.] —**cav′al·ry·man** (-mən) *n.*

ca·van (kä·vän′) *n.* A measure used in the Philippines: approximately equal to 75 liters or 2 1/2 bushels. [< Sp. *cabán*]

cav·a·ti·na (kav′ə·tē′nə, *Ital.* kä′vä·tē′nä) *n. Music* A short and simple kind of aria; especially, a song without a second part. [< Ital.]

cave (kāv) *n.* **1** A natural cavity beneath the earth's surface or in a mountain; a cavern; den. ◆ Collateral adjective: *spelean.* **2** In English politics, a member of a party which seceded from the Liberals in 1866: so called from the application by John Bright of the expression **Cave of Adullam** (I *Sam.* xxii 1, 2) in referring to this party; hence, a seceder or a seceding group. See synonyms under HOLE. —*v.* **caved, cav·ing** *v.t.* **1** To hollow out. **2** To cause to fall down or in, or to become hollow by a partial falling away. **3** To place in or as in a cave. —*v.i.* **4** To fall in or down; give way, as ground when undermined. —**to cave in** **1** To fall in or down, as when undermined; cause to fall in, as by undermining. **2** *Colloq.* To yield utterly; give in, as to argument, hardship, or strain. [< OF < L *cava* < *cavus* hollow]

ca·ve·at (kā′vē·at) *n.* **1** *Law* A formal notification to a court or officer not to take a certain step till the notifier is heard. **2** A description of an invention that is not fully perfected, formerly filed in the U.S. Patent Office, which entitled the person filing it to

three months' notice before the issuing of a patent for a like invention to another. **3** A caution. [< L, let him beware]

ca·ve·a·tor (kā′vē·ā′tər) *n.* One who enters a caveat.

cave·fish (kāv′fish′) *n. pl.* **·fish** or **·fish·es** Blindfish.

cave-in (kāv′in′) *n.* A collapse or falling in, as of a mine or tunnel; also, the site of such a collapse.

cav·ern (kav′ərn) *n.* A large cave; a den; cavity. —*v.t.* **1** To make like a cavern; hollow out. **2** To enclose, shut up, or place in or as in a cavern. [< F *caverne* < L *caverna* < *cavus* hollow]

cav·er·nic·o·lous (kav′ər·nik′ə·ləs) *adj.* Living in caves: *cavernicolous* fish. [< L *caverna* cavern + *colere* dwell + -OUS]

cav·ern·ous (kav′ər·nəs) *adj.* **1** Consisting of or containing caverns; like a cavern; hollow. **2** Hollow-sounding. **3** Pertaining to rocks having cavities or various sizes and shapes. —**cav′ern·ous·ly** *adv.*

cav·es·son (kav′ə·sən) *n.* A headstall furnished with a noseband having rings attached for a rein or cord by which a trainer on foot directs a horse in circles about him. [< F *caveçon* < Ital. *cavezzone,* aug. of *cavezza* halter]

ca·vet·to (kə·vet′ō, *Ital.* kä·vet′tō) *n. pl.* **·ti** (-tē) or **·tos** *Archit.* A molding having a concave profile of not more than 90° curvature, terminating in a vertical fillet, with a projection usually about equal to its altitude. [< Ital., dim. of *cavo* hollow < L *cavus*]

cav·i·ar (kav′ē·är, kä′vē-) *n.* A relish consisting of the roe of sturgeon or other fish, either in the natural state and salted, or pressed and salted, especially as prepared in Russia: considered a delicacy. —**caviar to the general** Something too esoteric to appeal to the popular taste. Also **cav′i·are.** [< F < Turkish *khavyar*]

cav·i·corn (kav′ə·kôrn) *adj. Zool.* Having hollow horns. —*n.* Any one of the hollow-horned ruminants. [< L *cavus* hollow + *cornu* horn]

cav·il (kav′əl) *v.* **cav·iled** or **·illed, cav·il·ing** or **·il·ling** *v.t.* To find fault with. —*v.i.* To pick flaws or raise trivial objections; argue or object captiously: with *at* or *about.* —*n.* A captious objection; caviling. [< MF *caviller* < L *cavillari* < *cavilla* a jeering, a scoffing] —**cav′il·er, cav′il·ler** *n.* —**cav′il·ing, cav′il·ling** *adj.* —**cav′il·ing·ly, cav′il·ling·ly** *adv.*

cav·i·ta·tion (kav′ə·tā′shən) *n. Physics* The formation of vapor cavities in the water flowing around the blades of a propeller, due to excessive speed of rotation, and resulting in structural damage or a loss of efficiency. [< CAVITY]

cav·i·ty (kav′ə·tē) *n. pl.* **·ties** **1** A hollow or sunken space; hole. **2** A natural hollow in the body. **3** A hollow place in a tooth, especially one caused by decay. [< MF *cavité* < LL *cavitas, -tatis* a hollow < *cavus* hollow, empty]

ca·vort (kə·vôrt′) *v.i.* **1** To act up; cut up. **2** To prance and show off, as a horse; curvet. **3** To run and prance without control. [Origin unknown]

ca·vy (kā′vē) *n. pl.* **·vies** A small South American burrowing rodent with the tail absent or rudimentary, as the guinea pig (*Cavia cobaya*), the **restless cavy** (*C. porcellus*), the **southern cavy** (*C. australis*), common on the Patagonian coast, and the harelike **Patagonian cavy** (*Dolichotis patagonica*). —**giant cavy** The capybara. [< NL *Cavia* < Cariban]

caw (kô) *v.i.* To cry or call: said of crows, rooks, etc.; cry like a crow. —*n.* The cry of a crow, raven, rook, etc. [Imit.]

caw[2] (kô) See CA′.

cay (kā, kē) *n.* A coastal reef or sandy islet, as in the Gulf of Mexico. See KEY[2]. [< Sp. *cayo* shoal]

Cay·enne (kī·en′, kā-) The capital of French Guiana.

cayenne pepper A pungent red powder made from the fruit of various capsicums; red pepper. Also **cay·enne′.**

Cayes (kā) See LES CAYES.

cay·man (kā′mən) *n. pl.* **·mans** See CAIMAN.

Cay·mans (kā′mənz, kī·mänz′) A West Indies is-

land group, comprising a dependency of Jamaica; 92 square miles. Also **Cayman Islands.**

cay·ote (kī′ōt) See COYOTE.

ca·zique (kə·zēk′) See CACIQUE.

C-bi·as (sē′bī′əs) See GRID BIAS.

Cd *Chem.* Cadmium (symbol Cd)

Ce *Chem.* Cerium (symbol Ce).

Ce·a (sē′ə) See CEOS.

Ceará rubber The coagulated latex of a tropical American tree (*Manihot glaziovi*).

cease (sēs) *v.* **ceased, ceas·ing** *v.t.* To leave off or discontinue, as one's own actions. —*v.i.* To come to an end; stop; desist. —*n.* End; stopping: obsolete except after *without.* [< F *cesser* < L *cessare* stop < *cedere* withdraw, yield] —**cease′less** *adj.* —**cease′less·ly** *adv.* —**cease′less·ness** *n.*

Synonyms (verb): abstain, conclude, desist, discontinue, end, finish, intermit, pause, quit, refrain, stop, terminate. Strains of music may gradually or suddenly *cease.* A man *quits* work on the instant; he may *discontinue* a practice gradually; he *quits* suddenly and completely; he *stops* short in what he may or may not resume; he *pauses* in what he will probably resume. What *intermits* or is *intermitted* returns again, as a fever that *intermits.* Compare ABANDON, DIE, END, REST. Antonyms: begin, commence, inaugurate, initiate, institute, originate, start.

ceb·a·dil·la (seb′ə·dil′ə) See SABADILLA.

ce·boid (sē′boid) *adj. Zool.* Pertaining to or describing any member of a superfamily or group (*Ceboidea*) of monkeys believed to have evolved from the prosimians isolated in South America, and including the marmosets, capuchins, tamarins, sapajous, and spider monkeys. —*n.* A member of this superfamily or group: also **ce·bid** (sē′bid, seb′id). [< NL < Gk. *kēbos,* a long-tailed monkey]

ce·cro·pi·a moth (si·krō′pē·ə) A large, strikingly marked moth (*Samia cecropia*) common in the eastern United States. [< NL *Cecropia,* genus of an American mulberry tree, named after *Cecrops*]

ce·cum sē′kəm) *n. pl.* **ce·ca** (sē′kə) *Anat.* A blind pouch, or cavity, open at one end, especially that situated between the large and small intestines; the blind gut. Also spelled caecum. [< L < *caecus* blind] —**ce′cal** *adj.*

ce·dar (sē′dər) *n.* **1** A large tree of the pine family (genus *Cedrus*) having evergreen leaves and fragrant wood. There are several varieties, as the **cedar of Lebanon** (*C. libani*), **deodar cedar** (*C. deodara*), etc. **2** The American red cedar. **3** The arbor vitae. **4** Spanish cedar (*Cedrela odorata*), a deciduous tree of the mahogany family, whose wood is used for cigar boxes. **5** The wood of these and related trees. —*adj.* Pertaining to or made of cedar. [< OF *cedre* < L *cedrus* < Gk. *kedros*]

ce·dar·bird (sē′dər·bûrd′) *n.* The common American waxwing. Also **cedar waxwing.**

cedar brown A warm, light brown, the color of cedar wood.

cedar chest A storage chest for woolens, made of cedar wood, for protection from moths.

ce·darn (sē′dərn) *adj.* **1** Of, pertaining to, or made of cedar. **2** Lined or bordered with cedars. Also **ce′dared.**

ce·dar·wood (sē′dər·wŏŏd′) *n.* The wood from any species of cedar.

cedarwood oil A colorless to pale- or greenish-yellow essential oil obtained by the distillation of cedarwood: used in medicine and in perfumes and insecticides.

cede (sēd) *v.t.* **ced·ed, ced·ing** **1** To yield or give up. **2** To surrender title to; transfer: said especially of territory. See synonyms under ABANDON, GIVE. ◆ Homophone: seed. [< MF *céder* < L *cedere* withdraw, yield]

ce·dil·la (si·dil′ə) *n.* A mark put under the letter *c* (ç) in some French words to indicate that it is to be sounded as *s.* [< Sp., dim. of *zeda,* the letter *z* < Gk. *zēta;* orig., a small *z* placed next to a *c* to indicate its sound]

ced·u·la (sej′oō·lə, *Sp.* thā′thoō·lä) *n.* **1** An obligation of the government in certain Spanish-

American countries. 2 In the Philippines, a personal registration tax certificate; also, the tax itself. [< Sp. *cédula* note, bill]

cee (sē) *n.* The letter *c.*

ce·i·ba (sā'i·bä, sī'bə) *n.* A West Indian and Mexican tree *(Ceiba pentandra),* yielding kapok. [< Sp. < Arawakan]

ceil (sēl) *v.t.* 1 To furnish with a ceiling; line the roof of. 2 To sheathe internally; line, as an apartment. ◆ Homophone: *seal.* [< F *ciel* roof, canopy < L *caelum* heaven, sky]

ceil·ing (sē'ling) *n.* 1 The overhead covering of a room. 2 Internal sheathing, as of a vessel. 3 The act of one who ceils. 4 *Aeron.* a The maximum height to which a given aircraft can be driven. b The upward limit of visibility for flying; the distance, expressed in hundreds of feet, between the ground and the base of an overcast or broken cloud formation. 5 The top limit of anything; specifically, the highest price that can be charged for a given thing. —**absolute ceiling** *Aeron.* The greatest altitude above sea level at which an airplane can sustain horizontal flight under standard air conditions. —**service ceiling** *Aeron.* The maximum height beyond which an airplane under normal conditions may not climb faster than 100 feet a minute.

ceil·om·e·ter (sē·lom'ə·tər) *n. Meteorol.* A photoelectric device used with a mercury-vapor lamp to determine the ceiling height of clouds under all weather conditions.

cel·an·dine (sel'ən·dīn) *n.* 1 A European perennial *(Chelidonium majus)* of the poppy family, with yellow flowers. 2 The pilewort. [< OF *celidoine* < L *chelidonia* < Gk. *chelidonion* < *chelidōn* a swallow]

ce·la·tion (sə·lā'shən) *n. Med.* The concealing of pregnancy, or of the birth of a child. [< L *celatio, -onis* < *celare* conceal]

-cele[1] *combining form* Tumor or hernia: *gastrocele.* [< Gk. *kēlē* tumor]

-cele[2] *combining form* Cavity; hollow space: *blastocele.* Also spelled *-coele.* [< Gk. *koilos* hollow]

cel·e·brant (sel'ə·brənt) *n.* 1 One who celebrates. 2 The officiating priest at a mass.

cel·e·brate (sel'ə·brāt) *v.* **·brat·ed, ·brat·ing** *v.t.* 1 To observe, as a festival or occasion, with demonstrations of respect or rejoicing. 2 To make known or famous; extol, as in song or poem: to *celebrate* a hero. 3 To perform a ceremony publicly and as ordained, as with solemn rites. —*v.i.* 4 To observe or commemorate a day or event. 5 To observe the Eucharist. [< L *celebratus,* pp. of *celebrare* celebrate, honor < *celeber* famous] —**cel'e·brat'er** or **·bra'tor** *n.*

Synonyms (verb): commemorate, keep, observe, solemnize. To *celebrate* any event or occasion is to make some demonstration of respect or rejoicing because of or in memory of it, or to perform such public rites or ceremonies as it properly demands. We *celebrate* the birth, *commemorate* the death of one beloved or honored. We *celebrate* a national anniversary with music, song, firing of guns and ringing of bells; we *commemorate* by any solemn and thoughtful service, or by a monument or other enduring memorial. We *keep* the Sabbath, *solemnize* a marriage, *observe* an anniversary; we *celebrate* or *observe* the Lord's Supper in which believers *commemorate* the sufferings and death of Christ. See KEEP, PRAISE. *Antonyms:* contemn, despise, dishonor, disregard, forget, ignore, neglect, overlook, profane, violate.

cel·e·brat·ed (sel'ə·brā'tid) *adj.* 1 Famous; renowned. 2 Performed or observed with customary rites.

Synonyms: distinguished, eminent, exalted, famed, famous, glorious, illustrious, noted, renowned. See ILLUSTRIOUS. *Antonyms:* degraded, disgraced mean, obscure, unknown.

cel·e·bra·tion (sel'ə·brā'shən) *n.* 1 The act of celebrating. 2 Things done in commemoration of any event.

ce·leb·ri·ty (sə·leb'rə·tē) *n. pl.* **·ties** 1 The state or quality of being celebrated; fame. 2 A famous or much publicized person. See synonyms under FAME.

ce·ler·i·ty (sə·ler'ə·tē) *n.* Quickness of motion; speed; rapidity. [< F *célérité* < L *celeritas, -tatis* < *celer* swift]

cel·er·y (sel'ər·ē, sel'rē) *n.* A biennial herb *(Ap-*

ium graveolens), whose blanched stems are used as a vegetable or salad. [< F *céleri* < Ital. *sellari,* pl. of *sellaro* < L *selinon* parsley < Gk.]

ce·les·ta (sə·les'tə) *n.* A musical instrument, with keyboard of five octaves and hammers that strike steel plates. [< F *célesta*]

ce·les·tial (sə·les'chəl) *adj.* 1 Of or pertaining to the sky or heavens. 2 Heavenly; divine. —*n.* A heavenly being. [< OF < L *caelestis* heavenly < *caelum* sky, heaven] —**ce·les'tial·ly** *adv.*

celestial equator *Astron.* The great circle in which the plane of the earth's equator cuts the celestial sphere: also called *equinoctial circle* or *line.*

celestial globe A globe whose surface depicts the geography of the heavens, fixed stars, constellations, etc.; a spherical representation of the heavens.

celestial navigation. Celonavigation.

celestial pole Either of the two points where the earth's axis of rotation pierces the celestial sphere.

celestial sphere The spherical surface on which the heavenly bodies seem to lie: conceived by astronomers as of infinite diameter and enclosing the universe.

cel·es·tite (sel'is·tīt) *n.* A vitreous, white, often bluish orthorhombic strontium sulfate, $SrSO_4$. Also **cel'es·tine** (-tin, -tīn). [< L *caelestis* heavenly; from its blue color]

ce·li·ac (sē'lē·ak) *adj.* Of or pertaining to the abdomen: also spelled *coeliac.* [< L *coeliacus* < Gk. *koiliakos* < *koilia* belly, abdomen < *koilos* hollow]

cel·i·ba·cy (sel'ə·bə·sē) *n.* The state of being unmarried; specifically, abstinence from marriage in accordance with religious vows. [< L *caelebs* unmarried]

cel·i·bate (sel'ə·bit, -bāt) *adj.* 1 Unmarried. 2 Vowed to remain single. —*n.* An unmarried person.

cell (sel) *n.* 1 A small, close room, especially one for a prisoner. 2 *Entomol.* a A small space or cavity bounded by the veins or nerves on the surface of an insect's wing. b A single compartment of a honeycomb. 3 *Biol.* a One of the cases or cuplike cavities containing an individual zoospore. b A small, often microscopic mass of protoplasm, variously differentiated in composition, structure, and function, usually containing a central nucleus and enclosed within a semipermeable wall (plant) or membrane (animal). It is the

TYPICAL CELL

a. Vacuole.	*g.*	Plasma membrane.
b. Centriole.	*h.*	Chondriosome.
c. Centrosphere.	*i.*	Nucleolus.
d. Metaplasm.	*j.*	Nuclear sap.
e. Golgi body.	*k.*	Chromatin.
f. Cell wall.	*l.*	Karyosome.

fundamental unit of all organisms and the physicochemical basis both of individual development and of organic evolution from the simplest protozoa to the most complex forms of plant and animal life. 4 *Bot.* a The cavity of an anther, containing pollen. b The seed-bearing cavity of an ovary or pericarp. 5 *Electr.* The unit of a battery, consisting of electrodes in contact with an electrolyte and in which an electric potential is developed by means of chemical action: a voltaic *cell.* 6 *Crystall.* The fundamental structural element of a crystalline lattice: also called *unit cell.* 7 *Aeron.* a The full assembly of parts on either side of the fuselage of a biplane. b The gas compartment of a balloon or dirigible. 8 A body of persons forming a single unit in an organization of similar groups. 9 A small monastery or nunnery dependent on a larger one. 10 The room occupied by a monk or a nun. ◆ Homophone: *sell.* [< OF *celle* < L *cella*]

cel·la (sel'ə) *n. pl.* **cel·lae** (sel'ē) The enclosed interior of a temple. [< L, small room]

cel·lar (sel'ər) *n.* 1 An underground room usually under a building: used for storage. 2 A room for storing wines; hence, the wines. —*v.t.* To put or keep in or as in a cellar. [< OF *celier* < L *cellarium* pantry < *cella* cell, small room]

cell-block (sel'blok') *n.* In prisons, a group of cells considered as and divided off into a unit.

cell fusion *Biol.* The artificial creation of a cell containing replicating genetic elements from disparate sources.

cel·lo (chel'ō) *n. pl.* **·los** A violoncello. Also **'cel'lo.** Short for VIOLONCELLO. —**cel'list** *n.*

cel·loi·din (sə·loi'din) *n.* A substance composed of pyroxylin, used for embedding microscopic specimens so that they may be cut in thin sections. [< CELL(ULOSE) + -OID + -IN]

cel·lo·phane (sel'ə·fān) *n.* A specially treated regenerated cellulose which has been processed in thin, transparent, and impermeable strips or sheets, variously colored. [< CELL(ULOSE) + -PHANE]

cel·lu·lar (sel'yə·lər) *adj.* 1 Of, pertaining to, or like a cell or cells. 2 Consisting of or containing cells. [< NL *cellularis* < L *cellula.* See CELLULE.]

cel·lule (sel'yōōl) *n.* 1 *Biol.* A small cell, as on a leaf or the wings of an insect. 2 *Aeron.* A boxlike rectangular area in a biplane or triplane formed by the planes or the struts between. [< L *cellula,* dim. of *cella* cell, small room]

cel·lu·li·tis (sel'yə·lī'tis) *n. Pathol.* Inflammation of the cellular tissue.

cel·lu·lose (sel'yə·lōs) *n. Biochem.* An amorphous white carbohydrate, $(C_6H_{10}O_5)x$, isomeric with starch, insoluble in all ordinary solvents, and forming the fundamental material of the structure of plants. —*adj.* Containing cells. [< L *cellula.* See CELLULE.]

cellulose acetate *Chem.* 1 An acetic acid ester of cellulose: when coagulated or solidified it is used in making artificial leather and synthetic textile yarns and fabrics. 2 Acetate rayon.

cellulose nitrate *Chem.* A nitric acid ester of cellulose, its properties depending upon the nitrogen content: used in the manufacture of explosives and lacquers: also called *nitrocellulose.*

cel·o·nav·i·ga·tion (sel'ō·nav'ə·gā'shən) *n.* That part of navigation in which position is determined by observation of celestial bodies; nautical astronomy: also called *astronavigation.* [< L *caelum* sky + NAVIGATION]

Cel·si·us scale (sel'sē·əs) A temperature scale in which the freezing point of water is 0° and the boiling point 100°: term now preferred to *centigrade scale.* [after Anders *Celsius,* 1701–44, Swedish astronomer]

ce·ment (si·ment') *n.* 1 Any substance, as a preparation of glue, red lead, or lime, the hardening of which causes objects between which it is applied to adhere firmly. 2 Any compound or substance applied in the form of a mortar and used for producing a hard and stony, smooth, waterproof surface, coating, filling, or lining, as for a floor or cistern. Ordinary cement is made by heating limestone and clay, or a natural rock containing both materials in right proportions. When it will harden under water, it is called **hydraulic cement.** 3 That which serves to bind together persons or interests; bond of union. 4 *Metall.* a A finely divided metal obtained by precipitation: *cement* silver. b The substance in which iron is packed in the process of cementation. 5 Auriferous gravel held together by a clayey or silicic bond; also, the binding substance. 6 The glassy base of an igneous rock. 7 Cementum. —**Portland cement** A hydraulic cement made by calcining limestone with clayey matter, such as chalk a..d river mud. —*v.t.* 1 To unite or join wi.. ..i as with cement. 2 To cover or coat with cement, as a cistern. —*v.i.* 3 To become united by means of cement; cohere. [< OF *ciment* < L *caementum* rough stone, stone chip < *caedere* cut] —**ce·ment'er** *n.*

ce·men·ta·tion (sē'mən·tā'shən, sem'ən-) *n.* 1 The act of cementing; result of cementing. 2 *Metall.* a A process of making steel by heating wrought iron in charcoal until it is carburized, or in making soft malleable iron by heating cast iron in a bed of red hematite until it is partly decarburized. b The method of precipitating a metal from its solution, as the precipitation of metallic copper from a copper sulfate solution by means of metallic iron.

ce·ment·ite (si·men′tīt) *n. Metall.* Iron combined with carbon as it exists in steel before hardening; carbide of iron, Fe₃C.

ce·ment·um (si·men′təm) *n. Anat.* The layer of bony tissue developed over the roots of the teeth about the fifth month after birth: also called *cement.* [< L]

cem·e·ter·y (sem′ə·ter·ē) *n. pl.* **·ter·ies** A place for the burial of the dead; formerly, a church-yard or a catacomb; now, usually, a large parklike enclosure, laid out and kept for purposes of interment. [< L *cemeterium* < Gk. *koimētērion* < *koimaein* put to sleep]

ce·nes·the·sia (sē′nis·thē′zhə, -zhē-ə, sen′is-) *n. Psychol.* The diffuse internal awareness of bodily existence, caused by the interaction of numerous unlocalized sensations whose aggregate expression may be of any degree of pain or pleasure. Also **ce′nes·the·sis.** Sometimes spelled *coenesthesia, coenesthesis.* [< CEN(O)- + Gk. *aisthēsis* feeling] — **ce′nes·thet′ic** (-thet′ik) *adj.*

ceno– *combining form* Common: *cenobite.* Also spelled *coeno–.* Also, before vowels, **cen–.** [< Gk. *koinos* common]

cen·o·bite (sen′ə·bīt, sē′nə-) *n.* A monk; a member of a religious community (convent or monastery), as distinguished from a religious recluse, or *anchorite:* also spelled *coenobite.* [< LL *coenobita* < *coenobion* CENOBIUM] — **cen′o·bit′ic** (-bit′ik) or **·i·cal** *adj.* — **cen·o·bit·ism** (sen′ə·bit·iz′əm, sē′nə-) *n.*

ce·no·bi·um (si·nō′bē·əm) *n. pl.* **·bi·a** (-bē·ə) The abode of a society that has all things in common; especially, a monastery or other such religious community. Also **cen·o·by** (sen′ə·bē, sē′nə-). [< LL *coenobium* < Gk. *koinobion* < *koinos* common + *bios* life]

cen·o·gen·e·sis (sen′ə·jen′ə·sis, sē′nə-) *n. Biol.* A form of development in which the characters of an individual organism are not typical of the group to which it belongs: opposed to *palingenesis.* Also spelled *coenogenesis, kenogenesis.* [< CENO- + Gk. *genesis* origin] — **cen·o·ge·net·ic** (sen′ə·jə·net′ik, sē′nə-) *adj.*

ce·nog·o·nal (si·nog′ə·nəl) *adj.* **1** Having one or more angles in common. **2** *Mineral.* Pertaining to or describing different crystals some of whose angles have identical values. [< Gk. *koinos* common + *gōnia* angle]

cen·o·taph (sen′ə·taf, -täf) *n.* **1** An empty tomb. **2** A monument erected to the dead but not containing the remains. [< MF *cénotaphe* < L *cenotaphium* < Gk. *kenotaphion* < *kenos* empty + *taphos* tomb] — **cen′o·taph′ic** *adj.*

cense (sens) *v.t.* **censed, cens·ing** **1** To perfume with incense. **2** To offer burning incense to. [< INCENSE²]

cen·ser (sen′sər) *n.* A vessel for burning incense, especially in religious ceremonies; thurible. ◆ Homophone: *censor.* [< OF *censier,* short for *encensier* < Med. L *incensarius* < *incensum* incense]

cen·sor (sen′sər) *n.* **1** An official examiner of manuscripts and plays empowered to prohibit their publication or performance if offensive to the government or subversive of good morals. **2** An official who examines despatches, letters, etc., and, if necessary, prohibits forwarding or publication, especially in time of war. **3** Anyone who censures or arraigns; a critic. **4** In ancient Rome, one of two magistrates who kept the public register of citizens and of their property, and were entrusted with the supervision of public manners and morals. **5** *Psychoanal.* The subconscious mental force that disguises painful or unwanted memories and complexes or prevents them from rising to conscious recognition. — *v.t* To act as censor of; delete. ◆ Homophone: *censer.* [< L < *censere* judge] — **cen·so·ri·al** (sen·sôr′ē·əl, -sō′rē-) *adj.*

cen·so·ri·ous (sen·sôr′ē·əs, -sō′rē-) *adj.* **1** Given to censure; judging severely; faultfinding. **2** Containing or involving censure, as remarks. See synonyms under CAPTIOUS. — **cen·so′ri·ous·ly** *adv.* — **cen·so′ri·ous·ness** *n.*

cen·sor·ship (sen′sər·ship) *n.* **1** The office

term, power, system, or act of a censor or critic. **2** *Psychoanal.* The aggregate of selective agencies, both unconscious and deliberate, which are responsible for the suppression of unpleasant memories and thoughts, for the inhibition of impulses and behavior deemed improper, and for the exercise of discipline over the tendencies of the primitive ego or id.

cen·sur·a·ble (sen′shər·ə·bəl) *adj.* Deserving censure; culpable; blameworthy. — **cen′sur·a·ble·ness** *n.* — **cen′sur·a·bly** *adv.*

cen·sure (sen′shər) *n.* **1** Disapproval; condemnation or blame; adverse criticism. **2** Reprimand or discipline by ecclesiastical or political authority. **3** Critical recension of a literary work; revision. **4** *Obs.* A formal judgment or judicial sentence; opinion. — *v.t.* **·sured, ·sur·ing** **1** To express disapproval of; condemn; blame. **2** To punish by a public reprimand, with or without some other penalty. **3** *Obs.* To pass judgment upon. [< F < L *censura* < *censere* judge] — **cen′sur·er** *n.*

cen·sus (sen′səs) *n. pl.* **cen·sus·es** **1** An official numbering of the people of a country or district, embracing statistics of nativity, age, sex, employment, possessions, etc.; also, the printed record of it. **2** In ancient Rome, a similar enumeration of the people, but with special reference to their property, in order to determine taxation. [< L < *censere* assess] — **cen·su·al** (sen′shoo·əl) *adj.*

cent (sent) *n.* **1** The hundredth part of a dollar. In the United States it is legal tender for all sums not exceeding twenty-five cents. **2** Centum or cento; hundred: used only in *per cent,* etc. **3** The hundredth part of a standard unit in other money systems, as of the florin of the Netherlands. Equivalent forms are the centavo, centesimo, and centime. **4** *Music* A unit of pitch equal to one one-hundredth of the interval between any two successive semi-tones of the equally tempered scale: An octave contains 1200 *cents.* ◆ Homophone: *scent.* [< F < L *centum* hundred]

cen·tal (sen′təl) *adj.* **1** Of or pertaining to a hundred. **2** Counting by the hundred. — *n. Rare* A hundredweight. [< L *centum* hundred]

cen·tare (sen′târ, *Fr.* sän·târ′) *n.* A measure of land area, equal to one square meter: also spelled *centiare.* See METRIC SYSTEM. [< F *centi–* hundredth (< L *centum* hundred) + *are* ARE²]

cen·taur (sen′tôr) **1** In Greek mythology, one of a race of monsters, having the head, arms, and torso of a man united to the body and legs of a horse. **2** An expert horseman. [< L *Centaurus* < Gk. *Kentauros*]

Cen·tau·rus (sen·tôr′əs) A constellation of the southern sky which contains **Alpha Centauri,** the third brightest star known. See CONSTELLATION. Also **Cen′taur.**

cen·tau·ry (sen′tô·rē) *n. pl.* **·ries** **1** One of certain small, mostly annual herbs (genera *Centaurium* and *Sabatia*) of the gentian family, with opposite leaves and clusters of rose, purple, or pink flowers, especially the Old World *C. umbellatum,* reputed to have medicinal properties. **2** A milkwort (*Polygala polygama*). [< L *centaureum* < Gk. *kentaureion*]

cen·ta·vo (sen·tä′vō) *n. pl.* **·vos** (-vōz, *Sp.* -vōs) **1** A small nickel or copper coin of the Philippines, Mexico, and other countries of Latin America, usually equal to the hundredth part of a peso. **2** A similar coin of Portugal and Brazil, equal to the hundredth part of an escudo. [< Sp.]

cen·te·nar·i·an (sen′tə·nâr′ē·ən) *n.* One who has reached the age of one hundred years. — *adj.* Of or pertaining to a hundred years, or to a hundredth anniversary.

CENTAUR

cen·te·nar·y (sen′tə·ner′ē, sen·ten′ə·rē) *adj.* **1** Of or pertaining to a hundred or a century. **2** Completing a century. —*n. pl.* **·nar·ies** **1** A hundredth anniversary. **2** A period of a hundred years. [< L *centenarius* < *centum* hundred]

cen·ten·ni·al (sen·ten′ē·əl) *adj.* **1** Of or pertaining to a hundredth anniversary. **2** A hundred years old or more. —*n.* **1** A hundredth anniversary; also, its celebration. **2** A period of a hundred years; centennium. [< L *centum* hundred + *annus* a year] —**cen·ten′ni·al·ly** *adv.*

cen·ten·ni·um (sen·ten′ē·əm) *n.* A century.

cen·ter (sen′tər) *n.* **1** *Geom.* **a** The point within a circle or sphere equally distant from any point on the circumference or surface. **b** The point within a regular polygon equidistant from the vertices. **2** The middle: the *center* of the town. **3** The point, object, or place about which things cluster or to which they converge. **4** A fixed point or line about which a thing or things revolve; point of attraction or convergence; focal point: the *center* of interest. **5** The point of divergence, emanation, or radiation; nucleus; origin. **6** The earth considered as the center of the universe; the center of the earth. **7** The part of a target nearest the bull's-eye, or a shot striking this part. **8** The middle part of an army in order of battle, occupying the front between the wings. **9** *Mech.* **a** One of two conical points, as in a lathe, between which an object is held and rotated on an axial line. The one at the end from which the object is rotated is the **live center,** the other the **dead center. b** The depression in a piece of revolving work, as a shaft, into which the conical point enters to support it. **10** The person who takes the middle position of the forward line in many athletic games, as football, basketball, etc. **11** Any place considered the hub of a specific activity: a manufacturing *center.* —*v.t.* **1** To place in the center. **2** To supply with a center. **3** To draw or converge in one place; concentrate. **4** In football, to pass the ball from the line to a backfield player. **5** To determine the center of; shape a lens so as to have it thickest in the center. —*v.i.* **6** To be in or at the center; have a focal point: The riots *centered* in the industrial section of the city. **7** To gather or converge, as toward a center: The crowds *centered* in the square. —*adj.* Central; middle. Also spelled *centre.* [< L *centrum* < Gk. *kentron* point (i.e., around which a circle is described)]

Synonyms (noun): middle, midst. We speak of the *center* of a circle, the *middle* of a room or the street. The *center* is equally distant from every point of the circumference of a circle, or from the opposite boundaries on each axis of a parallelogram, etc.; *middle* is more general and less definite. The *center* is a point; the *middle* may be a line or a space. We say *at the center; in the middle. Midst* commonly implies a group or multitude of surrounding objects. Compare synonyms for AMID. *Antonyms:* bound, boundary, circumference, perimeter, rim.

cen·ter·bit (sen′tər·bit′) *n.* A bit with a cutting edge that revolves about a central point.

cen·ter·ing (sen′tər·ing) *n.* **1** The act or operation of bringing an object within the focus of a microscope, telescope, etc. **2** A temporary support of an arch or other part of a building. Also **cen′tring.**

center of mass *Physics* **1** That point in a body at which all its mass can be concentrated without altering the effect of gravitation upon it. **2** The point in which a body near the earth's surface, acted upon by gravity or other parallel forces, is balanced in all positions: commonly known as **center of gravity.**

cen·ter·piece (sen′tər·pēs′) *n.* An ornament in the center of a table, ceiling, etc., or between other ornaments: also spelled *centrepiece.*

cen·tes·i·mal (sen·tes′ə·məl) *adj.* **1** Hundredth; of or divided into hundredths. **2** Pertaining to progression by hundreds. [< L *centesimus* hundredth] —**cen·tes′i·mal·ly** *adv.*

cen·tes·i·mo (sen·tes′ə·mō; *Ital.* chen·tes′ē·mō, *Sp.* sen·tes′ē·mō) **1** *pl.* **·mi** (-mē) An Italian coin, equal to the hundredth part of a lira. **2** *pl.* **·mos**

(-mōz, *Sp.* -mōs) A small Uruguayan coin, equal to the hundredth part of a peso.

centi- *combining form* **1** Hundred: *centipede.* **2** In the metric system, hundredth: *centiliter.* [< L *centum* hundred]

cen·ti·are (sen'tē-âr) See CENTARE.

cen·ti·grade (sen'tə-grād) *adj.* Graduated to a scale of a hundred. On the **centigrade scale** (now called the *Celsius scale*) the freezing point of water at normal atmospheric pressure is 0° and its boiling point 100°. The distance between those two points in the Fahrenheit and Réaumur is 180° and 80° respectively. See TEMPERATURE. [< F < L *centum* hundred + *gradus* step, degree]

cen·ti·gram (sen'tə-gram) *n.* The hundredth part of a gram. See METRIC SYSTEM. Also **cen'ti·gramme.** [< F *centigramme*]

cen·ti·le (sen'til, -til) See PERCENTILE.

cen·ti·li·ter (sen'tə-lē'tər) *n.* The hundredth part of a liter. See METRIC SYSTEM. Also **cen'ti·li'tre** [< F *centilitre*]

cen·time (sän'tēm, *Fr.* sän·tēm') *n.* In France, Belgium, and Switzerland, a hundredth of a franc; also, a coin of this value. [< F < OF *centisme* < L *centesimus* hundredth]

cen·ti·me·ter (sen'tə-mē'tər) *n.* The hundredth part of a meter. See METRIC SYSTEM. Also **cen'ti·me'tre.** [< F *centimètre*]

cen·ti·me·ter-gram-sec·ond (sen'tə-mē'tər-gram'sek'ənd) See CGS.

cen·ti·mo (sen'tə-mō) *n. pl.* **·mos** The hundredth part of a Spanish peseta.

cen·ti·pede (sen'tə-pēd) *n.* Any of a class (Chilopoda) of carnivorous, predatory arthropods having elongate, segmented bodies bearing a pair of legs on each segment, the front pair being modified into poison claws. Also called *chilopod.* [< F < L *centipeda* < *centum* hundred + *pes, pedis* foot]

cen·ti·poise (sen'tə-poiz) *n.* The hundredth part of a poise. [< CENTI- + POISE²]

cen·ti·stere (sen'tə-stir) *n.* A hundredth of a stere. See METRIC SYSTEM. [< F *centistère*]

cent·ner (sent'nər) *n.* **1** The hundredweight of various European countries, or 110.23 pounds, equal to 50 kilograms. **2** *Metall.* A hundred pounds. **3** In assaying, one dram. —**metric centner** Quintal. [< G *centner, zentner* hundredweight < L *centenarius* of a hundred]

cen·to (sen'tō) *n. pl.* **·tos** **1** A writing composed of selections from various authors or from different works of the same author. **2** *Obs.* Patchwork. [< L, patchwork cloak]

cen·tral (sen'tral) *adj.* **1** Of or pertaining to, equidistant or acting from, the center. **2** Being a dominant or controlling factor, element, etc.; chief. **3** Constituting the principal point; a *central* event in history. **4** *Phonet.* Formed with a tongue position intermediate between front and back: said of vowels. —*n.* **1** *Colloq.* A telephone exchange; also, the operator in charge of it. **2** In Latin America, a sugar mill grinding for a number of plantations. [< L *centralis* < *centrum* center] —**cen'tral·ly** *adv.* —**cen'tral·ness** *n.*

Central African Republic An independent republic of the French Community; 238,244 square miles; capital, Bangui; formerly *Ubangi-Shari,* a French overseas territory.

Central America A narrow, winding strip of land between North America proper and

the South American continent, generally understood to include Guatemala, British Honduras, Honduras, El Salvador, Nicaragua, Costa Rica, and Panama.

central angle See under ANGLE.

Central Asia See SOVIET CENTRAL ASIA.

central heating A system of heating a building by piping hot steam, water, or air from a

central source to heat distributors located in separate rooms, apartments, etc.

cen·tral·ism (sen'trəl·iz'əm) *n.* Concentration of control in a central authority, especially of government control. —**cen'tral·ist** *n. & adj.* —**cen'tral·is'tic** *adj.*

cen·tral·i·ty (sen·tral'ə·tē) *n.* **1** The state of being central. **2** Tendency toward or situation at a center.

cen·tral·ize (sen'trəl·īz) *v.* **·ized, ·iz·ing** *v.t.* **1** To make central; bring to a center; concentrate. **2** To concentrate (power or control) in one authority. —*v.i.* **3** To come to a center; concentrate. —**cen'tral·i·za'tion** *n.* —**cen'tral·iz'er** *n.*

Central Kar·roo (kə·rōō') See GREAT KARROO.

Central Powers The countries opposed to the Allied Nations in World War I: Germany, Austria-Hungary, Bulgaria, and Turkey.

Central Provinces and Berar The former name for MADHYA PRADESH.

central spindle *Biol.* The fibrous portions of protoplasm lying between the asters in a karyokinetic division of a cell, and about which the chromosomes are grouped.

central staging See ARENA THEATER.

Central Standard Time See STANDARD TIME. Abbr. *C.S.T.*

cen·tre (sen'tər) *n., v.t. & v.i.* **·tred, ·tring** Center.

Cen·tre (sen'tər) See CENTER.

centri- *combining form* Center: equivalent of CENTRO-: used in words of Latin origin, as in *centrifugal.* [< L *centrum* center]

cen·tric (sen'trik) *adj.* **1** Central; centrally situated. **2** Belonging to or described around a center. **3** *Physiol.* Related to or connected with a nerve center. Also **cen'tri·cal.** —**cen·tri·cal·i·ty** (sen'tri·kal'ə·tē), **cen·tric·i·ty** (sen·tris'ə·tē) *n.* —**cen'tri·cal·ly** *adv.*

cen·trif·u·gal (sen·trif'yə·gəl, -ə·gəl) *adj.* **1** Directed or tending away from a center; radiating; opposed to *centripetal.* **2** Employing centrifugal force: a *centrifugal* pump. **3** *Bot.* **a** Developing from the center or apex outward, or toward the base; determinate. **b** Turned from the center toward the side of a fruit, as a radicle. **4** *Physiol.* Leading away from the central nervous system; efferent. —*n.* **1** The drum-like rotary part of a centrifuge or other centrifugal machine. **2** *pl.* Sugars from which the molasses has been removed by a centrifugal machine: also **centrifugal sugar.** [< NL *centrifugus* < L *centrum* center + *fugere* flee] —**cen·trif'u·gal·ly** *adv.*

centrifugal force *Physics* The inertial reaction of a body against a force constraining it to move in a curved path.

cen·tri·fuge (sen'trə·fyōōj) *n.* A rotary machine, with accessory containers, tubes, etc., for the separation by controlled centrifugal force of substances having different densities. —*v.t.* **·fuged, ·fug·ing** To subject to the action of a centrifuge. —**cen·trif·u·ga·tion** (sen·trif'yə·gā'shən, -ə·gā'-) *n.*

cen·tri·ole (sen'trē·ōl) *n.* *Biol.* A minute structure, frequently double, enclosed within the centrosome which forms the center of the aster in cell division, and with which it makes up the central body. For illustration see under CELL. [< CENTRI- + -OLE²]

cen·trip·e·tal (sen·trip'ə·təl) *adj.* **1** Directed, tending, or drawing toward a center: *centripetal* force. **2** Acting by drawing toward a center: a *centripetal* pump. **3** *Bot.* **a** Developing from without toward the center or in the direction of the apex. **b** Turned toward the axis of the fruit, as a radicle. **4** *Physiol.* Conducting toward the central nervous system; afferent. [< NL *centripetus* < *centrum* center + *petere* seek]

centripetal force *Physics* A force attracting a body toward a center around which it revolves.

cen·trist (sen'trist) *n.* One who takes the middle position in politics, especially in France.

centro- *combining form* Center: used in words of Greek origin, as in *centrosphere.* Also, before vowels, **centr-.** [< Gk. *kentron* center]

cen·tro·bar·ic (sen'trə·bar'ik) *adj.* *Physics* Relating to the center of gravity of a body. [< CENTRO- + Gk. *baros* weight]

cen·troid (sen'troid) *n.* **1** *Physics* Center of mass. **2** *Mech.* The point at which the area of a body may be concentrated without altering the moment of any line in its plane, as the center of a square or the intersections of the median lines of a triangle.

cen·tro·some (sen'trə·sōm) *n.* *Biol.* The small area of protoplasm at the center of each aster in cell division: it contains the centrioles. [< CENTRO- + Gk. *sōma* body] —**cen'tro·som'ic** (-som'ik) *adj.*

cen·tro·sphere (sen'trə·sfir') *n.* **1** *Geol.* The central portion of the terrestrial globe. Compare HYDROSPHERE, LITHOSPHERE. **2** *Biol.* In living cells, the sphere from which the astral rays diverge, and which surrounds the centrosome, if any. For illustration see under CELL.

cen·trum (sen'trəm) *n. pl.* **·trums** or **·tra** (-trə) **1** A center or central mass. **2** *Zool.* The body of a vertebra. [< L]

cen·tum (ken'təm) *n.* One of the two main divisions of the Indo-European languages; namely, the western division, including the Hellenic, Italic, Celtic, and Germanic languages and dialects, in which the proto-Indo-European palatalized velar stop (k) is retained as a velar, as in the Latin word *centum* "hundred." Compare SATEM. See INDO-EUROPEAN.

cen·tu·ple (sen'tə·pəl, sen·tōō'pəl, -tyōō'-) *v.t.* **·pled, ·pling** To increase a hundredfold. —*adj.* Increased a hundredfold. [< F < L *centuplus* hundredfold]

cen·tu·pli·cate (sen·tōō'plə·kāt, -tyōō'-) *v.t.* **·cat·ed, ·cat·ing** To multiply by a hundred; centuple. —*adj. & n.* (-kit) Hundredfold. [< LL *centuplicatus,* pp. of *centuplicare* increase a hundredfold < *centuplex* hundredfold]

cen·tu·ri·al (sen·tōōr'ē·əl, -tyōōr'-) *adj.* **1** Of or pertaining to a century of the Roman army or people. **2** Of or pertaining to a hundred years.

cen·tu·ried (sen'chə·rēd) *adj.* **1** Continued or maintained for one or more than one century. **2** Having endured for hundreds of years.

cen·tu·ri·on (sen·tōōr'ē·ən, -tyōōr'-) *n.* A captain of a century in the ancient Roman army. [< L *centurio, -onis*]

cen·tu·ry (sen'chə·rē) *n. pl.* **·ries** **1** One hundred consecutive years, reckoning from a specific date. **2** A period of 100 years in any system of chronology, especially in reckoning from the first year of the Christian era: the twentieth *century,* A.D. 1901–2000. **3** A body of Roman foot soldiers (at one time 100 men); one sixtieth of a legion; also, one of the 193 divisions into which the Roman people were divided according to their incomes. **4** A hundred; hundred things of the same kind collectively. [< L *centuria* < *centum* hundred]

century plant An agave (*Agave americana*) which flowers once in twenty or thirty years and then dies. Also called *American aloe.*

ce·pha·e·line (si·fā'ə·lēn, -lin) *n.* *Chem.* A white, crystalline alkaloid, $C_{28}H_{18}O_4N_2$, from ipecac: regarded as more powerful than emetine. [< NL *cephaelis,* genus name of ipecac]

ceph·a·lad (sef'ə·lad) *adv.* *Zool.* Toward the head of an animal body: opposed to *caudad.* [< Gk. *kephalē* head]

ceph·a·lal·gia (sef'ə·lal'jē·ə) *n.* A headache. [< Gk. *kephalē* head + *algos* pain]

ce·phal·ic (sə·fal'ik) *adj.* **1** Of, pertaining to, on, in, or near the head. **2** Performing the functions of a head. **3** Relatively nearer the head or the end of the body where the head is situated: the *cephalic* end of the sternum. [< Gk. *kephalē* head]

-cephalic *combining form* Head; skull: *brachycephalic.* [< Gk. *kephalē* head]

ceph·a·lin (sef'ə·lin) *n.* *Biochem.* A yellowish amorphous phospholipid obtained from the brain substance or spinal cord of mammals, which acts as a blood coagulant: also spelled *kephalin.*

ceph·a·li·za·tion (sef'ə·lə·zā'shən, -li·zā'-) *n.* *Zool.* Concentration or localization of functions, powers, or parts in or toward the head: the *cephalization* of the vertebrate nervous system.

cephalo- *combining form* Head: *cephalometer.* Also, before vowels, **cephal-.** [< Gk. *kephalē* head]

ceph·a·lo·cau·dal (sef'ə·lō·kô'dəl) *adj.* *Anat.* Of

or pertaining to the head or tail, or to the long axis of the body. Also **ceph′a·lo·cer′cal** (-sûr′kəl). [< CEPHALO- + L *cauda* tail]

ceph·a·lo·chor·date (sef′ə·lō·kôr′dāt) *adj. Zool.* Having the notochord continued into the head: said especially of the lancelets. Also **ceph′a·lo·chor′dal.** —*n.* An animal having such a notochord.

ceph·a·lom·e·ter (sef′ə·lom′ə·tər) *n.* An instrument for measuring the head or skull, as for ascertaining the size of a fetal head (in parturition); craniometer. [< CEPHALO- + Gk. *metron* measure] —**ceph′a·lom′e·try** *n.*

ceph·a·lo·pod (sef′ə·lə·pod′) *n.* Any of a class (Cephalopoda) of predaceous marine mollusks, including squids, octopuses, cuttlefish, and nautiluses, having a clearly defined head and eyes and tentacles surrounding the mouth. —*adj.* Of or pertaining to the class Cephalopoda. — **ceph·a·lop·o·dan** (sef′ə·lop′ə·dən) *adj. & n.* **ceph·a·lop·o·dous** (sef′ə·lop′ə·dəs) *adj.*

ceph·a·lo·tho·rax (sef′ə·lō·thôr′aks, -thō′raks) *n. Zool.* The anterior portion of certain arthropods, as crustaceans and arachnids, consisting of the united head and thorax. —**ceph′a·lo·tho·rac′ic** (-thə·ras′ik) *adj.*

ceph·a·lous (sef′ə·ləs) *adj.* Having a head.

-cephalous *combining form* Headed: *hydrocephalous.* [< Gk. *kephalē* head]

Ceph·e·id variable (sef′ē·id) *Astron.* Any of a class of variable stars characterized by a uniform, relatively short-term cycle of brightness associated with corresponding internal changes: so called from the star Delta in the constellation of Cepheus.

ce·ra·ceous (si·rā′shəs) *adj.* Of the nature of or like wax; waxy. [< L *cera* wax]

ce·ram·al (sə·ram′əl) *n. Metall.* A combination of metals, as iron and cobalt, with ceramic materials such as boron or titanium carbide, developed to provide alloys resistant to very high temperatures, as on the blades of turbine airplane engines. [< CERAM(IC) AL(LOY)]

ce·ram·ic (sə·ram′ik) *adj.* Pertaining to pottery and to articles made of clay that have been fired and baked. Also spelled *keramic.* [< Gk. *keramikos* < *keramos* potters' clay]

ce·ram·ics (sə·ram′iks) *n.* 1 The art of molding, modeling, and baking in clay: construed as singular. 2 Objects made of fired and baked clay: construed as plural. —**cer·a·mist** (ser′ə·mist) *n.*

ce·rar·gy·rite (sə·rär′jə·rīt) *n.* An isometric, brown, easily sectile silver chloride, AgCl; horn silver. [< Gk. *keras* horn + *argyros* silver]

ce·ras·tes (sə·ras′tēz) *n.* A horned viper of North Africa and the Near East (*Cerastes cornutus*). [< L < Gk. *kerastēs* < *keras* horn]

ce·rate (sir′āt) *n.* A medicated ointment of oil or lard mixed with resin, wax, etc. Cerates are intermediate in consistency between ointments and plasters. [< L *ceratus,* pp. of *cerare* smear with wax < *cera* wax]

ce·rat·ed (sir′ā·tid) *adj.* Covered with wax.

cerato- *combining form* Horn; of or like horn: *ceratodus.* Also, before vowels, **cerat-.** [< Gk. *keras, -atos* horn]

ce·rat·o·dus (sə·rat′ə·dəs, ser′ə·tō′dəs) *n.* The barramunda. [< NL < Gk. *keras* horn + *odous* tooth]

cer·a·toid (ser′ə·toid) *adj.* 1 Horny; horn-shaped. 2 Of or pertaining to a superfamily (*Ceratoidea*) of mostly small deep-sea fishes having luminescent organs.

Cer·ber·us (sûr′bər·əs) In Greek and Roman mythology, the three-headed dog guarding the portals of Hades. —**Cer·be·re·an** (sər·bir′ē·ən) *adj.*

cer·car·i·a (sər·kâr′ē·ə) *n. pl.* **·car·i·ae** (-kâr′i·ē) *Zool.* A larval, parasitic form of a trematode worm, originating as a bud from a birth stage and having a tail that is lost in the adult. [< NL < Gk. *kerkos* tail] —**cer·car′i·al** *adj.* —**cer·car′i·an** *adj. & n.*

cer·co·pi·the·coid (sûr′kō·pi·the′koid) *adj. Zool.*

Relating to or describing any of a superfamily or group (*Cercopithecoidea*) of Old World monkeys evolved from prosimian stock by adaptive radiation and including macaques, mandrills, baboons, langurs, and Barbary apes. —*n.* A member of this group. [< NL < L *cercopithecus* < Gk. *kerkopithēkos* < *kerkos* tail + *pithēkos* ape]

cer·cus (sûr′kəs) *n. pl.* **·ci** (-sī) *Entomol.* One of a pair of anal appendages found in many insects, as in the cockroach. [< NL < Gk. *kerkos* tail]

cere[1] (sir) *v.t.* **cered, cer·ing** 1 *Obs.* To cover with or as with wax; to wax. 2 To wrap in cerecloth; wrap (a dead body). ◆ Homophones: *sear, sere.* [< F *cirer* < L *cerare* smear with wax < *cera* wax]

cere[2] (sir) *n. Ornithol.* A waxlike, fleshy area about the bill, in parrots and birds of prey, containing the nostrils. ◆ Homophones: *sear, sere.* [< F *cire* < L *cera* wax]

ce·re·al (sir′ē·əl) *n.* 1 An edible starchy grain yielded by certain plants of the grass family, as rice, wheat, rye, oats, etc. 2 Any of the plants yielding such grains. 3 A breakfast food made from a cereal grain. —*adj.* Pertaining to edible grain. ◆ Homophone: *serial.* [< L *cerealis* of grain < *Ceres,* goddess of grain]

cer·e·bel·lum (ser′ə·bel′əm) *n. pl.* **·bel·lums** or **·bel·la** (-bel′ə) The massive, dorsally located organ of the central nervous system forming that part of the brain below and behind the cerebrum. It consists of a central lobe and two lateral lobes and acts as the coordination center of voluntary movements, posture, and equilibrium. [< L, dim. of *cerebrum* brain] — **cer′e·bel′lar** *adj.*

cer·e·bral (ser′ə·brəl, sə·rē′-) *adj.* 1 Of or pertaining to the cerebrum or the brain. 2 Appealing to the intellect; requiring mental activity; intellectual. 3 *Phonet.* Cacuminal. —*n. Phonet.* A cerebral consonant, as *t* and *ḍ* in the Indic languages. [< F *cérébral* < L *cerebrum* brain]

cer·e·brate (ser′ə·brāt) *v.* **·brat·ed, ·brat·ing** *v.t.* 1 To perform by brain action. —*v.i.* 2 To have or manifest brain action. 3 To think. [< L *cerebrum* brain]

cer·e·bra·tion (ser′ə·brā′shən) *n.* 1 The functional activity of the cerebrum. 2 The act of thinking; thought.

cer·e·brin (ser′ə·brin) *n.* A cerebroside found in brain substance and isolated as a yellowish-white powder, $C_{17}H_{33}NO_3$.

cer·e·bri·tis (ser′ə·brī′tis) *n. Pathol.* Inflammation of the cerebrum.

cerebro- *combining form* Brain; pertaining to the brain: *cerebrospinal.* Also, before vowels, **cerebr-.** [< L *cerebrum* brain]

cer·e·bro·side (ser′ə·brō·sīd′) *n. Biochem.* A nitrogenous fatty substance found in brain and nerve tissue, containing galactose and forming a series of complex fatty acids, as phrenosin: also called *galactolipin.* [< CEREBR(O)- + -OSE + -IDE]

cer·e·bro·spi·nal (ser′ə·brō·spī′nəl) *adj.* Of or pertaining to the brain and spinal cord.

cer·e·brum (ser′ə·brəm) *n. pl.* **·bra** (-brə) or **·brums** The enlarged upper and anterior part of the brain in vertebrates, consisting of two lateral hemispheres. [< L] —**cer·e·bric** (ser′ə·brik, sə·rē′-) *adj.*

cere·cloth (sir′klôth′, -kloth′) *n.* A cloth coated or saturated with wax or some gummy substance, used as a waterproof covering, a medicinal application, or a winding sheet. [orig. *cered cloth* < CERE[1]]

cere·ment (sir′mənt) *n.* A cerecloth; a garment or wrapping for the dead; usually in the plural. [< F *cirement* a waxing < *cirer* CERE[1]]

cer·e·mo·ni·al (ser′ə·mō′nē·əl) *adj.* Of or pertaining to ceremony; ritual; formal. —*n.* 1 A system of rules of ceremony; ritual; also, social etiquette. 2 A ceremony. See synonyms under FORM. — **cer′e·mo′ni·al·ism** *n.* —**cer′e·mo′ni·al·ist** *n.* —**cer′e·mo′ni·al·ly** *adv.*

cer·e·mo·ni·ous (ser′ə·mō′nē·əs) *adj.* 1 Observant of or conducted with ceremony; formal. 2 Conventional; studiously polite. 3 Ceremonial. —**cer′e·mo′ni·ous·ly** *adv.* —**cer′e·mo′ni·ous·ness** *n.*

cer·e·mo·ny (ser′ə·mō′nē) *n. pl.* **·nies** 1 A formal or symbolical act or observance, or a series of them, as on religious and state occasions. 2 The doing of some formal act in the manner prescribed by authority or usage: the *ceremonies* at an ordination, inauguration, or coronation. 3 Mere outward form. 4 Observance of etiquette or conventional forms in social matters; formal civility; adherence to the prescribed forms of amenity. —**to stand on ceremony** 1 To observe conventions. 2 To be formal, stiff, or uncordial. See synonyms under FORM, SACRAMENT. [< OF *cerymonie* < L *caerimonia* awe, veneration]

cer·e·sin (ser′ə·sin) *n.* Ozocerite. [< L *cera* wax]

ce·re·us (sir′ē·əs) *n.* Any of a genus of cactuses (*Cereus*) having large lateral tubular flowers, often nocturnal, whence several have the name of *night-blooming cereus.* [< L *cereus* waxy < *cera* wax]

ce·ri·a (sir′ē·ə) *n. Chem.* An infusible compound, CeO_2, used in the manufacture of incandescent mantles; cerium dioxide.

ce·rif·er·ous (sə·rif′ər·əs) *adj.* Yielding or producing wax. [< L *cera* wax + *ferre* bear]

cer·iph (ser′if) See SERIF.

ce·rise (sə·rēz′, -rēs′) *adj.* Of a vivid red. —*n.* A vivid red color. [< F, cherry]

ce·rite (sir′īt) *n.* A resinous, brown, orthorhombic hydrous cerium silicate. [< CERIUM]

ce·ri·um (sir′ē·əm) *n.* A silvery-white, ductile, highly reactive and electropositive metallic element (symbol Ce, atomic number 58), being the most abundant of the lanthanide series. See PERIODIC TABLE. [after the asteroid *Ceres*]

cerium metals A subgroup of the lanthanide series of elements, including lanthanum, cerium, praseodymium, neodymium, illinium, samarium, europium, and gadolinium.

cer·met (sûr′met) *n.* An alloy of a heat-resistant compound and a metal, used for strength and to withstand high temperatures. [< CER(AMIC) + MET(AL)]

cer·nu·ous (sûr′nyōō·əs) *adj. Bot.* Drooping or nodding, as a flower. [< L *cernuus* stooping]

ce·ro (sir′ō) *n. pl.* **·ros** A scombroid fish (*Scomberomorus regalis,* or *S. cavalla*) closely related to, but larger than, the Spanish mackerel. The **common cero** (*S. regalis*) weighs as much as 20 pounds, and the **spotted** or **king cero** (*S. cavalla*) up to 100 pounds. See PINTADO. [< Sp. *sierra* < L *serra* saw]

cero- *combining form* Wax: *cerotype.* Also, before vowels, **cer-.** [< L *cera* or Gk. *kēros* wax]

ce·rog·ra·phy (si·rog′rə·fē) *n.* 1 The art of engraving or writing on wax. 2 Painting by the encaustic method. 3 The wax process of printing. [< Gk. *kērographia* < *kēros* wax + *graphein* write] —**ce·ro·graph** (sir′ə·graf, -gräf) *n.* — **ce′ro·graph′ic** *adj.* —**ce·rog′ra·phist** *n.*

ce·roon (sə·rōōn′) See SEROON.

ce·ro·plas·tic (sir′ə·plas′tik) *adj.* 1 Pertaining to or of the nature of wax modeling. 2 Modeled in wax. [< Gk. *kēroplastikos* < *kēros* wax + *plassein* mold]

ce·rot·ic (si·rot′ik) *adj.* Of, pertaining to, or derived from beeswax, as **cerotic acid,** $C_{26}H_{53}COOH.$ [< Gk. *kērōtos* waxed < *kēros* wax]

ce·ro·type (sir′ə·tīp′, ser′-) *n.* 1 A process of engraving in which a metal plate is coated with wax, which is cut away according to some design, and a cast made therefrom in plaster. 2 A printing plate so produced.

cer·tain (sûr′tən) *adj.* 1 Established as fact or truth so as to be absolutely known, accepted as true, and depended upon; beyond doubt or question; demonstrable; true. 2 Absolutely confident as to truth or reality; sure; convinced. 3 Definitely settled so as not to be variable or fluctuating; fixed; determined; stated. 4 That may be absolutely predicted; sure to come; inevitable: Death is *certain.* 5 Sure in its workings or results; reliable; effectual. 6 Determinate, but not particularized or named; definite, but assumed to be determinable: a *certain* man. See synonyms under AUTHENTIC, CONSCIOUS, INCONTESTABLE, SECURE, SURE. [< OF < L *certus* < *cernere* determine]

cer·tain·ly (sûr′tən·lē) *adv.* With certainty; surely.

cer·tain·ty (sûr′tən·tē) *n. pl.* **·ties** 1 The quality

CERBERUS

or fact of being certain. **2** A known truth. **3** Precision; accuracy.

Synonyms: assurance, certitude, confidence, conviction, demonstration, evidence, infallibility, positiveness, proof, surety. See DEMONSTRATION. Compare ASSURANCE. *Antonyms*: conjecture, doubt, dubiousness, hesitation, indecision, misgiving, precariousness, uncertainty.

cer·tif·i·cate (sər·tif′ə·kit) *n.* **1** A written declaration or testimonial. **2** A writing signed and legally authenticated. **3** A writing or statement certifying that the one named therein has satisfactorily completed a certain educational course. —**gold** (or **silver**) **certificates** Certificates issued by the U.S. government, and used as currency, on the basis of gold (or silver) bullion of equal amounts deposited with the government for their redemption. —*v.t.* (-kāt) **·cat·ed, ·cat·ing** To furnish with or attest by a certificate. [< Med. L *certificatus*, pp. of *certificare*. See CERTIFY.] —**cer·tif·i·ca·to·ry** (sər·tif′ə·kə·tôr′ē, -tō′rē) *adj.*

certificate of deposit A statement issued by a bank certifying that a person has a specified sum on deposit.

cer·ti·fi·ca·tion (sûr′tə·fi·kā′shən) *n.* **1** The act of certifying; the guaranteeing of the truth or validity of; attestation. **2** A certified statement; a certificate.

certified check A check marked or stamped, as by a bank official, to certify that it is genuine and that it represents an account having sufficient funds for the bank to guarantee its payment.

cer·ti·fy (sûr′tə·fī) *v.* **·fied, ·fy·ing** *v.t.* **1** To give certain knowledge of; attest. **2** To assert as a matter of fact; assure. **3** To give a certificate of, as insanity. —*v.i.* **4** To make attestation as to truth or excellence. [< F *certifier* < Med.L *certificare* attest < L *certus* certain + *facere* make] —**cer·ti·fi·a·ble** *adj.*

cer·ti·o·ra·ri (sûr′shē·ə·râr′ē, -râr′ī) *n. Law* A writ from a superior to an inferior court, directing a certified record of its proceedings in a designated case to be sent up for review. [< LL, to be certified]

cer·ti·tude (sûr′tə·tōōd, -tyōōd) *n.* **1** Perfect assurance; confidence. **2** Assured fact or reality; sureness and precision. See synonyms under CERTAINTY. [< Med.L *certitudo* < L *certus*. See CERTAIN.]

ce·ru·le·an (sə·rōō′lē·ən) *adj. & n.* Sky blue. [< L *caeruleus* dark blue]

ce·ru·men (sə·rōō′mən) *n.* Earwax. [< NL < L *cera* wax] —**ce·ru′mi·nous** *adj.*

ce·ruse (sir′ōōs, sə·rōōs′) *n.* **1** White lead. **2** A cosmetic made from it. [< F *céruse* < L *cerussa*]

ce·rus·site (sir′ə·sīt) *n.* An orthorhombic, white to grayish-black lead carbonate, PbCO₃. Also **ce′ru·site.**

cer·vi·cal (sûr′vi·kəl) *adj. Anat.* Of, pertaining to, or situated in or near the neck or cervix: *cervical vertebrae.* [< L *cervix, -icis* neck]

cervico- *combining form* Neck: *cervicofacial.* Also, before vowels, **cervic-.** [< L *cervix, -icis* neck]

cer·vi·co·fa·cial (sûr′vi·kō·fā′shəl) *adj. Anat.* Pertaining to the neck and the face.

cer·vine (sûr′vīn, -vin) *adj.* **1** Of or pertaining to deer. **2** Designating the subfamily (*Cervinae*) of deer representing the typical deer. [< L *cervinus* < *cervus* deer]

cer·vix (sûr′viks) *n. pl.* **cer·vix·es** or **cer·vi·ces** (sər·vī′sēz, sûr′və·sēz) **1** The neck. **2** The cervix uteri. **3** A necklike part. [< L]

cer·vix u·ter·i (sûr′viks yōō′tər·ī) *Anat.* The constricted neck of the uterus which distends during parturition.

cer·void (sûr′void) *adj.* Resembling a deer. [< L *cervus* deer + -OID].

ce·si·ous (sē′zē·əs) *adj.* Pale greenish-blue: also spelled *caesious.* [< L *caesius* bluish-gray]

ce·si·um (sē′zē·əm) *n.* A steel-gray, ductile, metallic element (symbol Cs, atomic number 55) that is the most electropositive of the alkali metals. See PERIODIC TABLE. [< L *caesius* bluish-gray]

ces·pi·tose (ses′pə·tōs) *adj. Bot.* Growing in tufts or clumps, as a plant; matted; turfy: also spelled *caespitose.* [< L *caespes, caespitis* turf] —**ces′pi·tose·ly** *adv.*

ces·pi·tous (ses′pə·təs) *adj.* Cespitose.

ces·sa·tion (se·sā′shən) *n.* A ceasing; stop; pause. See synonyms under END, REST. [< L *ces-*

satio, -onis < *cessare* stop]

ces·sion (sesh′ən) *n.* **1** The act of ceding; surrender. **2** An assignment of property or rights to another or others. **3** The ceding of territory by a nation or state; also, the territory ceded. ◆ Homophone: session. [< L *cessio, -onis* surrender < *cessus* pp. of *cedere* yield]

ces·sion·ar·y (sesh′ən·er′ē) *adj.* Giving up; surrendering. —*n.* An assignee or grantee.

cess·pool (ses′pōōl) *n.* **1** A covered well or pit for the drainage from sinks, etc. **2** Any repository of filth. Also spelled *sesspool.* Also **cess′pit.** [Origin uncertain]

.ces·tus¹ (ses′təs) *n. pl.* **ces·tus** An ancient Roman device of thongs, often weighted, wound about the hands by boxers: also spelled *caestus.* [< L *caestus* < *caedere* kill]

ces·tus² (ses′təs) *n. pl.* **·ti** (-tī) **1** A belt or girdle. **2** In classical mythology, the girdle of Aphrodite, which could awaken love in whoever beheld it. [< L < Gk. *kestos*]

CESTUS

ce·su·ra (si·zhŏŏr′ə, -zyŏŏr′ə) See CAESURA.

Ce·ta·cea (si·tā′shə) *n. pl.* An order of aquatic mammals, especially those of a fishlike form with teeth conic or absent: the whales, dolphins, and porpoises. [< L *cetus* < Gk. *kētos* whale] —**ce·ta′cean** *adj. & n.* —**ce·ta′ceous** *adj.*

ce·tane (sē′tān) *n. Chem.* A saturated hydrocarbon of the methane series, C₁₆H₃₄: used as fuel for diesel engines. [< L *cetus* whale]

cetane number *Chem.* A measure of the performance characteristics of diesel engine fuels. It is the percentage of cetane (value = 100) in a mixture of cetane and *alpha*-methylnaphthalene (value = 0) which gives the same ignition performance as the fuel being tested. Compare OCTANE NUMBER.

ce·tol·o·gy (si·tol′ə·jē) *n.* The branch of zoology dealing with whales. [< Gk. *kētos* + -LOGY] —**ce·to·log·i·cal** (sē′tə·loj′i·kəl) *adj.* —**ce·tol′o·gist** *n.*

Cette (set) See SÈTE.

Ceylon moss A red seaweed of the East Indies (*Gracilaria lichenoides*), a principal source of agar-agar.

Cf *Chem.* Californium (symbol Cf).

cgs The centimeter-gram-second system of measurement in which the unit of length is the centimeter, the unit of mass the gram, and the unit of time one second. Thus, the cgs unit of force is the dyne, of work the erg, etc. Also **c.g.s., C.G.S.**

chab·a·zite (kab′ə·zīt) *n.* A rhombohedral, white or flesh-colored hydrous silicate of calcium and aluminum. Also **chab′a·site** (-sīt). [< F *chabazie*, alter. of Gk. *chalazios*, a precious stone < *chalaza* hail]

cha·blis (shà·blē′) *n.* A dry, white, Burgundy wine made in the region of **Chablis**, a town in north central France.

cha·bouk (chä′bŏŏk) *n.* A horsewhip; specifically, a long whip used in the Orient for corporal punishment. Also **cha′buk.** [< Persian *chābuk* horsewhip]

chace (chās) See CHASE¹ *n.*

chac·ma (chak′mə) *n.* A large, black and gray South African baboon (*Papio porcarius*). [< Hottentot]

cha·conne (shà·kôn′) *n.* A slow dance of the 18th century; also, the music for it. [< F < Sp. *chacona*]

Chad (chad) An independent republic of the French Community in north central Africa; 501,000 square miles; capital, Fort-Lamy; formerly a French overseas territory.

chae·ta (kē′tə) *n. pl.* **·tae** (-tē) *Zool.* A bristle or seta. [< NL < Gk. *chaitē* hair]

chaeto- *combining form* Hair: *chaetopod.* Also, before vowels, **chaet-.** [< Gk. *chaitē* hair, bristle]

chae·to·don (kē′tə·don) *n.* One of a family (*Chaetodontidae*) of fishes having the dorsal fins stiff and spiny, including certain angelfishes of West Indies and Florida waters. [< NL < Gk. *chaitē* bristle + *odous, odontos* tooth]

chae·tog·nath (kē′tog·nath) *n. Zool.* Any of a phylum (*Chaetognatha*) of small, active, widely distributed marine animals having characteristic

bristles around the mouth and elongate, arrow-shaped, almost transparent bodies adapted for swift motion through the water. [< NL < Gk. *chaitē* hair + *gnathos* jaw.]

chae·to·pod (kē′tə·pod) *n. Zool.* Any of a class (*Chaetopoda*) of annelid worms having conspicuous segments provided with locomotor organs and setae, including clamworms and earthworms. [< NL < Gk. *chaitē* + *pous, podos* foot]

chafe (chāf) *v.* **chafed, chaf·ing** *v.t.* **1** To abrade or make sore by rubbing; gall. **2** To make warm by rubbing. **3** To fret; irritate; annoy. —*v.i.* **4** To be irritated; fret; fume. —*n.* **1** Soreness or wear from friction; friction. **2** Irritation or vexation; restlessness. [< OF *chaufer* warm < L *calefacere* < *calere* be warm + *facere* make] —**chaf′er** *n.*

chaf·er (chā′fər) *n.* The cockchafer or other scarabaeid beetle. Also **chaf·fer** (chaf′ər). [OE *ceafor*]

chaff¹ (chaf, chäf) *n.* **1** The external envelopes or husks of grain. **2** Straw or hay cut fine. **3** Refuse; trifles collectively. See synonyms under WASTE. [OE *ceaf*]

chaff² (chaf, chäf) *v.t.* To poke fun at; ridicule. —*n.* Good-natured raillery; banter. See synonyms under BANTER, RIDICULE, MOCK. [Origin uncertain] —**chaff′er** *n.*

chaf·finch (chaf′inch) *n.* A European song finch (*Fringilla caelebs*), popular as a cage bird. [< CHAFF¹ + FINCH]

chaff·y (chaf′ē, chäf′ē) *adj.* **1** Of, pertaining to, or like chaff. **2** *Bot.* Paleaceous. **3** Light as chaff; unsubstantial; empty.

chaf·ing dish (chā′fing) A vessel with a heating apparatus beneath it, to cook or keep hot its contents at the table.

Cha·gas disease (chä′gäs) *Pathol.* A form of trypanosomiasis prevalent in South and Central America, communicated by the bite of the assassin bug. [after C. *Chagas*, 1879–1934, Brazilian physician]

cha·grin (shə·grin′) *n.* Distress or vexation caused by disappointment, failure, or wounded pride; mortification. —*v.t.* To humiliate; mortify: used in the passive. [< F. See SHAGREEN.]

Synonyms (noun): confusion, disappointment, discomposure, dismay, humiliation, mortification, shame, vexation. *Chagrin* unites *disappointment* with some degree of *humiliation.* A rainy day may bring *disappointment*; needless failure in some enterprise brings *chagrin. Shame* involves the consciousness of fault, guilt, or impropriety; *chagrin* of failure of judgment, or harm to reputation. A consciousness that one has displayed his own ignorance will cause him *mortification*; if there was a design to deceive, the exposure will cover him with *shame.* Compare ABASH.

Antonyms: delight, exultation, glory, rejoicing, triumph.

chain (chān) *n.* **1** A series of connected rings or links, serving to bind, drag, hold, or ornament. **2** Shackles; bonds; enthralment: usually in the plural. **3** Any connected series; a succession. **4** A range of mountains. **5** A measuring line or tape of 100 links; the **engineer's** (or **Ramden's**) **chain** is 100 feet long; the **surveyor's** (or **Gunter's**) **chain** is 66 feet long. **6** The warp threads of a fabric; also, the pattern chain of a loom. **7** *pl. Naut.* The flat iron bars on the side of a ship that receive the strain of the shrouds; a chain plate or channel plate. **8** *Chem.* A series of atoms of the same or different kinds, linked together and acting as a unit. See CLOSED CHAIN, OPEN CHAIN, SIDE CHAIN. **9** A series of associated stores, banks, etc. —*v.t.* **1** To fasten, as with a chain; also, to bring into or hold in subjection; enthrall. **2** In surveying, to measure with a chain. [< OF *chaeine* < L *catena*] —**chain′less** *adj.*

chain gang A gang of convicts chained together while doing hard labor.

chain letter 1 A letter written to a group of people and sent from one to another in rotation, each recipient adding to it before forwarding it to the next. **2** A letter, duplicates of which are sent by one person to two or more others, each of whom forwards it to two or more others.

chain lightning 1 Forked or zigzag lightning. **2** *U.S. Slang* Cheap whisky.

chain·man (chān′mən) *n. pl.* **·men** (-mən) In surveying, a man who carries one end of the measuring chain. Also **chain′bear′er**.

chain pump A pump that raises water by means of buckets or disks on an endless chain passing under water and up over a wheel.

chain reaction *Physics* **1** A series of reactions each of which develops from the energy released by the previous reaction within the system. **2** The spontaneous explosive fission of atomic nuclei through the repeated capture of free neutrons, as in an atomic bomb or in the controlled generation of atomic energy.

chain shot Cannon balls or half-balls chained together: formerly used in warfare.

CHAIN
a. Chain shot.
b. Chain stitch.

chain–smok·er (chān′smō′kər) *n.* One who smokes cigars or cigarettes in unending succession.

chain stitch 1 In sewing, a loop stitch. **2** A chainlike stitch used in crocheting, embroidery, etc. Also **chain′work′**.

chain store A retail store selling the same type of goods, food, etc., as a number of other like stores, all of which are under the same management or ownership.

chain·wale (chān′wāl, chā′nəl) See CHANNEL².

chair (châr) *n.* **1** A movable or stationary seat, usually with four legs and a back and for one person. **2** A seat of office, as of a professor or moderator. **3** An office or officer; a chairman. **4** An iron block for holding railroad tracks in place. **5** The seat with long projecting arms on which the glass-blower rolls his blowpipe; also, the set of men working with him. **6** *Obs.* A sedan. — *v.t.* **1** To put into a chair; install in office. **2** To preside over (a meeting). **3** In England, to carry in a chair in public; bear in triumph in a chair.

chair·man (châr′mən) *n. pl.* **·men** (-mən) **1** One who presides over an assembly, committee, etc. **2** *Obs.* One of the carriers of a sedan chair. — *v.t.* To take the chair at (a meeting); preside over.

chair·per·son *n.* individual who supervises at a committee or formal meeting.

chair rail A wooden molding running around the walls of a room to protect them against damage from the backs of chairs.

chair-ta·ble (châr′tā′bəl) See TABLE-CHAIR.

chair·wom·an (châr′wŏom′ən) *n. pl.* **·wom·en** (-wim′ən) A woman who presides over an assembly, committee, etc.

chaise (shāz) *n.* **1** A two-wheeled, one-horse vehicle for two persons, having a calash top, and the body usually hung on long leather straps. **2** A light, four-wheeled carriage, usually open. *Chay,* or *shay,* was formerly a common colloquial variant, from the notion that *chaise* was a plural form. [<F, var. of *chair* chair]

chaise-longue (shāz′lông′, *Fr.* shez lông′) *n.* A couchlike chair having a backrest at one end and the seat prolonged to support the sitter's outstretched legs. [<F, lit., long chair]

cha·la·za (kə·lā′zə) *n. pl.* **·zas** or **·zae** (-zē) **1** *Biol.* One of the two spirally twisted albuminous threads that are attached to each end of the lining membrane of an egg and keep the yolk in position with the germinating spot uppermost. See illustration under EGG. **2** *Bot.* The part of an ovule where the coats are united to each other and to the nucellus. [<NL <Gk., hailstone, small lump]

chal·ced·o·ny (kal·sed′ə·nē, kal′sə·dō′nē) *n. pl.* **·nies** A waxy, translucent, crypto-crystalline variety of quartz: also spelled *calcedony.* [from *Chalcedon*]

chal·ced·o·nyx (kal·sed′ə·niks, kal′sə·don′iks) *n.* A variety of agate in which white and gray layers alternate. [<CHALCED(ONY) + ONYX]

chal·cid (kal′sid) *n.* A tiny hymenopterous fly (family *Chalcididae*) whose larvae are parasitic on the larvae of other insects. Also **chalcid fly.** [<NL <Gk. *chalkos* copper; with ref. to its color]

chalco- *combining form* Copper; brass: *chal-*

cography. [<Gk. *chalkos* copper]

chal·co·cite (kal′kə·sīt) *n.* An orthorhombic, metallic, blackish-gray copper sulfide, Cu₂S: also called *copper glance.*

chal·cog·ra·phy (kal·kog′rə·fē) *n.* The art of engraving on plates of copper or steel; line engraving. [<CHALCO- + -GRAPHY] —**chal·co·graph** (kal′kə·graf, -gräf) *n.* —**chal·cog′ra·pher** *n.* —**chal′co·graph′ic** *adj.* —**chal·cog′ra·phist** *n.*

chal·co·py·rite (kal′kə·pī′rīt, -pir′īt) *n.* A tetragonal, metallic, brass-yellow copper-iron sulfide, CuFeS₂; copper pyrites.

chal·dron (chôl′drən) *n.* A weight or measure for coal and coke: in England 32 to 36 bushels; in the United States 36 bushels or 1.268 cubic meters. [Var. of CALDRON]

cha·let (sha·lā′, shal′ā) *n.* **1** A small building made of planks or of squared timbers, having a gently sloping and projecting roof, built by herdsmen in the Alpine regions of central Europe, especially in Switzerland. **2** A Swiss cottage with a projecting roof. **3** Any house built in this style. [<F]

CHALET

chal·ice (chal′is) *n.* **1** A consecrated cup used in the celebration or administration of the Lord's Supper. **2** Any drinking cup, goblet, or bowl. **3** *Bot.* A cup-shaped flower. [<OF <L *calix, calicis* cup]

chal·iced (chal′ist) *adj. Bot.* Having a cup-shaped flower.

chal·i·co·there (kal′i·kō·thir′) *n. Paleontol.* One of a family (*Chalicotheridae*) of extinct ungulates resembling both the horse and rhinoceros and having legs ending in three-clawed hoofs. [<NL <Gk. *chalix* gravel + *thēr* wild beast]

chalk (chôk) *n.* **1** A soft, grayish-white or yellowish compact limestone, largely composed of the shells of foraminifers. **2** A piece of chalk or chalklike material, either natural or artificial and frequently colored, used for marking or drawing. **3** A score in a game, because often recorded with chalk. **4** A debit, formerly often marked with chalk upon the wall or door, as of an ale house. — *v.t.* **1** To put chalk on or in; also, to mark with chalk; to bleach. **2** To record, as charges or debits; score. **3** To put an official mark on. — **to chalk up 1** To raise the price of. **2** To score. **3** To give credit. — *adj.* Made with chalk. [OE *cealc* <L *calx* limestone] —**chalk′i·ness** *n.* —**chalk′y** *adj.*

chalk·board (chôk′bôrd′, -bōrd′) *n.* A flat surface of hard material for marking upon with chalk, used for classroom instruction.

chal·ki·tis (kal·kī′tis) *n. Pathol.* An inflammation of the eyes caused by rubbing the eyes with hands that have been working on or with brass. [<NL <Gk. *chalkos* brass]

chalk·stone (chôk′stōn′) *n.* **1** *Pathol.* A gouty concretion in the joints. **2** A piece of chalk.

chal·lenge (chal′ənj) *v.* **·lenged, ·leng·ing** *v.t.* **1** To dare to a contest or trial of superiority. **2** To invite to personal combat: to *challenge* to a duel. **3** To invite or defy, as scrutiny or proof: to *challenge* criticism. **4** To claim as due, as attention or respect. **5** To call in question; dispute; object to, as a choice of jurors. **6** *Mil.* To stop and demand a countersign of, as a sentry does. — *v.i.* **7** To utter or make a challenge. **8** In hunting, to open and cry, as hounds on picking up the scent. — *n.* **1** A call or defiance to personal contest; a dare or summons to fight, especially to a duel. **2** A formal objection or exception to a person or thing. **3** *Mil.* A sentry's call, requiring one to halt and give the countersign. **4** *Telecom.* An electromagnetic signal requesting identification, as in radar communication. [<OF *chalenger* <LL *calumniare* accuse falsely < *calumnia* slander. Doublet of CALUMNY.] —**chal′leng·a·ble** *adj.* —**chal′leng·er** *n.*

chal·lis (shal′ē) *n.* A light dress fabric, usually printed. Also **chal′lie.** [Origin uncertain]

chal·u·meau (shal yə·mō′, *Fr.* shà·lü·mō′) *n.* **1** The lowest register of the clarinet. **2** An

old, single-reed wind instrument from which the clarinet developed. [<F <OF *chalemel* <L *calamellus,* dim. of *calamus* reed]

cha·lutz (khä·lŏots′) See HALUTZ.

cha·lyb·e·ate (kə·lib′ē·āt, -it) *adj.* **1** Impregnated with compounds of iron: said of mineral waters. **2** Resembling iron in taste or action. — *n.* A medicine or water containing iron in solution. [<NL *chalybeatus* <L *chalybeius.* See CHALYBEAN.]

chal·y·bite (kal′ə·bīt) *n.* Siderite.

cham·ber (chām′bər) *n.* **1** A room in a dwelling house; especially, a bedroom. **2** *pl.* A suite of rooms or offices for the use of one person; specifically, a lawyer's or judge's office or apartment. **3** Lodgings. **4** A hall where an assembly or council meets; also, the assembly itself: the *chamber* of commerce. **5** The popular branch of a legislature. **6** An enclosed space at the breech of a gun containing the explosive charge; also, one of the cavities in the cartridge cylinder of a revolver. **7** A room in which a monarch or other great personage gives audience. **8** *Anat.* A space enclosing the aqueous humor of the eye, separated by the iris into an anterior and a posterior chamber. **9** A chamber pot. **10** A lock on a canal. — **cloud chamber** *Physics* An enclosed receptacle containing air or gas saturated with water vapor whose sudden cooling indicates the presence of ions as condensation nuclei of water droplets. The movements of these nuclei are revealed by the cloud tracks marked out by the droplets. Also **expansion chamber, fog chamber.** — **lower chamber** The lower house of a bicameral legislature. — **upper chamber** The upper house of a bicameral legislature. — *v.t.* **1** To make chambers in, as a gun. **2** To fit into a chamber; also, to fit compactly, as shot in a cartridge. [<F *chambre* <L *camera* vaulted room <Gk. *kamara.* Doublet of CAMERA.] — **cham′bered** *adj.*

cham·ber·lain (chām′bər·lin) *n.* **1** A high European court official. **2** A steward or treasurer of a corporation or municipality. **3** *Obs.* The chamber attendant of a monarch or lord. [<OF *chamberlenc* <OHG *chamarlinc* < *chamara* room <L *camera.* See CHAMBER.] — **cham′ber·lain·ship′** *n.*

cham·ber·maid (chām′bər·mād′) *n.* A woman whose work is taking care of the bedrooms in a hotel.

chamber music Music written for a small number of instruments (less than ten), suitable for performance in a small room or hall.

chamber of commerce An association of merchants and businessmen for the protection and regulation of commerce.

cham·bray (sham′brā) *n.* A strong cotton fabric woven with colored warp and white filling that gives a changeable colored surface. [from *Cambrai,* France]

cha·me·le·on (kə·mē′lē·ən, -mēl′yən) *n.* **1** A tropical tree lizard (genus *Chamaeleon*) with a long protrusible tongue, prehensile limbs and tail, and the power of changing its color. **2** A person of changeable character or habits like a chameleon. [<L *chamaeleon* <Gk. *chamaileon* < *chamai* on the ground + *leon* lion] — **cha·me·le·on·ic** (kə·mē′lē·on′ik) *adj.*

cham·ois (sham′ē, *Fr.* shà·mwä′) *n. pl.* **·ois 1** A mountain antelope of Europe, the Caucasus, and western Asia (*Rupicapra rupicapra*). **2** A soft leather originally prepared from the skin of the chamois, now from sheep, goats, deer, etc.: also spelled *shammy, shamois.* Also **cham′my. 3** The color of this leather, a yellowish-beige. — *v.t.* **1** To dress (leather or skin) like chamois. **2** To clean or dry with a chamois skin, as an automobile. [<F]

CHAMOIS
(About 2 1/2 feet at the shoulder)

---

add,āce,câre,pälm; end,ēven; it,īce; odd,ōpen,ôrder; tŏŏk,pool; up,bûrn; ə = a in *above,* e in *sicken,* i in *clarity,* o in *melon,* u in *focus* ; yōō = u in *fuse,* oi,oil; ou,pout; ch,check; g,go; ng,ring; th,thin; th,this; zh,vision. Foreign sounds à,œ,ü,kh,n̄; and ◆: see page xx. <from; + plus; ? possibly.

cham·o·mile (kam′ə·mīl) See CAMOMILE.

champ[1] (champ) *v.t.* **1** To crush and chew noisily; munch. **2** To bite upon restlessly. **3** *Scot.* To mash, as potatoes; trample underfoot. — *v.i.* **4** To make a biting or chewing movement with the jaws. — *n.* The action of chewing or biting. [Prob. imit.]

champ[2] (champ) *n. Slang* Champion.

cham·pa·col (cham′pə·kōl, -kol) *n. Chem.* A white, crystalline, camphorlike substance, $C_{15}H_{26}O$, extracted from the wood of the champak tree. [<CHAMPAK + -OL[1]]

cham·pagne (sham·pān′) *n.* **1** A sparkling white wine made from grapes grown in the area of the former province of Champagne. **2** A still, white wine from this region. **3** Any light, effervescent wine made in imitation of French champagne. **4** The color of champagne, a pale, tawny or greenish yellow.

cham·paign (sham·pān′) *n.* **1** Flat and open ground; clear, level country; a plain. **2** Figuratively, field of observation; expanse. **3** *Obs.* An area of unenclosed or common land. **4** *Archaic* The field of military operation. — *adj.* Of or pertaining to level ground or open country. [<OF *champaigne* <Med. L *campania.* See CAMPAIGN.]

cham·pak (cham′pak, chum′puk) *n.* An Indian tree (*Michelia champaca*) of the magnolia family, bearing golden-yellow fragrant flowers, and whose wood yields champacol. Also **cham′pac.** [<Skt. *campaka*]

cham·per·ty (cham′pər·tē) *n. pl.* **·ties** *Law* A bargain made by one not a party to the suit to bear expenses of litigation in consideration of a share of the matter sued for. [<F *champart* <OF <L *campi pars* share of the field] — **cham′per·tous** *adj.*

cham·pi·on (cham′pē·ən) *n.* **1** Originally, one who fights in behalf of another; one who defends a person, principle, etc. **2** The victor in an open contest. **3** Something of highest excellence; anything which has been given first prize. — *adj.* Acknowledged superior to all competitors; holding the first prize, or having first excellence. — *v.t.* To defend; advocate; stand up for the rights of. [<OF <LL *campio, -onis* fighter <L *campus* field] — **cham′pi·on·ess** *n. fem.*

cham·pi·on·ship (cham′pē·ən·ship′) *n.* **1** The state of being a champion; supremacy. **2** The position or honor of a champion. **3** The act of championing; advocacy; defense.

champ·le·vé (shamp′lə·vā′) *n.* **1** An enamelware produced by cutting depressions in a metal plate, leaving a ridge between them which forms the outline of a design, the hollows then being filled with enamel powder or paste and fired. **2** The process of making this ware, or an article so made. [<F, pp. of *champlever* engrave < *champ* surface + *lever* raise]

chance (chans, chäns) *n.* **1** The unknown or the undefined cause of events not subject to calculation; luck; fortune. **2** An unknown agency, assumed to account for unusual or unexplained events. **3** The operation of this agency: often personified or, in antiquity, deified. **4** A fortuitous event; an accident. **5** A favorable conjuncture of circumstances; opportunity. **6** Undetermined probability in general; contingency. See synonyms under ACCIDENT, HAZARD, PROBABILITY. — *v.* **chanced,** **chanc·ing** *v.i.* **1** To occur accidentally; happen. — *v.t.* **2** To take the chance of; hazard: I'll *chance* it. **3** *Archaic* To befall; happen to. — **to chance upon** To find unexpectedly or undesignedly; come upon; stumble over. — *adj.* Occurring by chance; casual; accidental. [<OF *cheance* <LL *cadentia.* Doublet of CADENCE, CADENZA.]

chance·ful (chans′fəl, chäns′-) *adj.* **1** Full of chance or chances; eventful. **2** *Obs.* Dependent on chance.

chan·cel (chan′səl, chän′-) *n.* The space in a church reserved for the officiating clergy and the choir, often separated from the rest of the building by a screen or railing. [<OF <LL *cancellus* < *cancelli,* pl., lattice, railing; because it is so enclosed]

chan·cel·ler·y (chan′sə·lər·ē, chän′-, lər·ē, chäns′-) *n. pl.* **·ries** **1** The office or dignity of a chancellor. **2** The building or room in which a chancellor has his office. **3** A court and its officials. **4** The office of an embassy or legation. Also **chan·cel·ry** (chan′.səl·rē, chän′-).

chan·cel·lor (chan′sə·lər, chän′-, chans′lər, chäns′-) *n.* **1** A high officer of state or of a university. **2** A judicial officer sitting in a court of chancery or equity. **3** In Germany, formerly, the president of the Federal Council. **4** In France, formerly, the keeper of the great seal and president of the Councils. **5** A chief secretary, as of an embassy. **6** A keeper of the great seal under the Eastern Empire, the Holy Roman Empire, etc. Also **chan′cel·or.** — **lord high chancellor** In Great Britain, the highest judicial officer of the crown. Also **lord chancellor.** [<OF *chancelier* <LL *cancellarius* one who stands at the bar in a court < *cancelli.* See CHANCEL.] — **chan′cel·lor·ship′** *n.*

chancellor of the Exchequer The minister of finance in the British cabinet.

chance–med·ley (chans′med′lē, chäns′-) *n.* **1** *Law* Unpremeditated wounding or killing in self-defense in a casual affray; homicide upon sudden encounter. **2** A haphazard combination or mixture; any inadvertent act. [<OF *chance medlée* mixed case or event < *chance* CHANCE + *medlée,* pp. of *medler* mix]

chan·cer·y (chan′sər·ē, chän′-) *n. pl.* **·cer·ies** **1** In the United States, a court of equity, as distinguished from a common-law court. **2** *Brit.* Previously to 1873, the court presided over by the Lord High Chancellor of England, the highest court next to the House of Lords; since the Judicature Act of 1873, one of the five divisions of the High Court of Justice. **3** A court of records; archives. **4** A chancellery. **5** The business and legal offices of a Roman Catholic diocese or archdiocese. **6** A wrestling hold. — **in chancery 1** Pending in a court of chancery; also, under the supervision of the Lord Chancellor. **2** In a hopeless predicament. **3** In boxing, said of the head caught and held under the arm of an opponent. [<OF *chancellerie* < *chancelier.* See CHANCELLOR.]

chan·ci·fy (chan′sə·fī, chän′-) *v.* **·fied,** **·fy·ing** *v.t.* **1** To make fully random, as by the thorough mixing of an array of lottery tickets. — *v.i.* **2** To become fully random. **3** In the theory of games, to provide for the equiprobability of any in a series of results or events by deliberately altering the number, range, or effect of chance factors. [<CHANCE + -FY]

chan·cre (shang′kər) *n. Pathol.* A primary syphilitic lesion resembling a sore with a hard base. [<F <L *cancer* crab, ulcer] — **chan·crous** (shang′krəs) *adj.*

chan·croid (shang′kroid) *n. Pathol.* A venereal sore resembling chancre, but not infecting the system; soft chancre.

chan·de·lier (shan′də·lir′) *n.* A branched support for lights, as a gas or electric fixture, suspended from a ceiling. [<F <Med. L *candelarius* <L *candela* candle]

chan·delle (shan·del′) *n. Aeron.* An abrupt climbing turn of an airplane, utilizing momentum to gain altitude while the direction of flight is changed. [<F]

chan·dler (chan′dlər, chän′-) *n.* **1** A trader; dealer: ship *chandler.* **2** In England, a retailer of common groceries, provisions, and the like; a petty shopkeeper. **3** One who makes or sells candles: tallow *chandler.* [<F *chandelier* chandler, candlestick. See CHANDELIER.]

change (chānj) *v.* **changed,** **chang·ing** *v.t.* **1** To make different; alter; transmute. **2** To exchange; interchange: to *change* places. **3** To give or cause another to give the equivalent of, as money, in smaller units or foreign currency. **4** To put other garments, coverings, etc., on: to *change* the bed. — *v.i.* **5** To become different; vary. **6** To enter upon a new phase: the moon has *changed.* **7** To make a change or exchange. **8** To transfer from one train to another. **9** To put on other garments. — **to change color** To blush or turn pale. — **to change front 1** In a military sense, to face a different way; alter the direction of a line of attack. **2** To adopt a new line of argument. **3** To alter one's attitude or principles. — **to change hands** To pass from one possessor to another. — *n.* **1** The act or fact of changing; alteration; substitution or something used in substitution. **2** A place for general transaction of business; an exchange. **3** The money returned to a purchaser who has given a bill or coin of greater value than his purchase. **4** Money of smaller denomination

given in exchange for larger; small coins collectively. **5** A passage from one phase to another: the *change* of the moon. **6** *Music* **a** A modulation or variation of key. **b** Any order, other than that of the diatonic scale, in which a peal of bells is struck: usually in the plural. **7** *Obs.* Want of constancy; caprice. **8** Religious conversion. — **to ring the changes 1** To operate a chime of bells so as to produce a variety of tuneful combinations. **2** To repeat something with every possible variation of language and illustration. [<OF *changer* <LL *cambiare* exchange] — **chang′er** *n.*

Synonyms (verb): alter, commute, convert, exchange, metamorphose, modify, qualify, shift, substitute, transfigure, transform, transmute, turn, vary, veer. To *change* is to make a thing other than it has been; to *exchange,* to put or take something else in its place; to *alter* is ordinarily to *change* partially. To *exchange* is often to transfer ownership; as, to *exchange* city for country property. *Change* is often used in the sense of *exchange;* as, to *change* horses. To *transmute* is to *change* the qualities while the substance remains the same; as, to *transmute* baser metals into gold. To *transform* is to *change* form or appearance, with or without deeper and more essential change. *Transfigure* is, as in its Scriptural use, to *change* in an exalted and glorious spiritual way. To *metamorphose* is to make some remarkable change, as of a caterpillar into a butterfly, or of the crystalline structure of rocks, hence called "metamorphic rocks." To *vary* is to *change* from time to time, often capriciously. To *commute* is to put something easier, lighter, milder, etc., in place of that which is *commuted;* as, to *commute* daily fares on a railway to a monthly payment. To *convert* is primarily to *turn* about, and signifies to *change* in form, character, use, etc.; iron is *converted* into steel, joy into grief, etc. *Turn* is a popular word for *change* in any sense short of the meaning of *exchange,* being often equivalent to *alter, convert, transform, transmute,* etc. We *modify* a statement by some limitation, *qualify* it by some addition. See CONVEY. *Antonyms:* abide, bide, continue, endure, hold, keep, persist, remain, retain, stay.

Synonyms (noun): alteration, conversion, diversity, innovation, mutation, novelty, regeneration, renewal, renewing, revolution, transformation, transition, transmutation, variation, variety, vicissitude. *Mutation* is a more formal word for *change,* often suggesting repeated or continual *change;* as, the *mutations* of fortune. *Revolution* is specifically and most commonly a *change* of government. *Variation* is a partial *change* in form, qualities, position, or action; as, the *variation* of the magnetic needle or of the pulse. *Vicissitude* is sharp, sudden, or violent *change;* as, the *vicissitudes* of politics. *Transition* is change by passing from one place or state to another, especially in a natural, regular, or orderly way; as, the *transition* from spring to summer. An *innovation* is a *change* that breaks in upon an established order or custom. See MOTION. *Antonyms:* constancy, continuance, firmness, fixedness, fixity, identity, invariability, permanence, persistence, steadiness, unchangeableness, uniformity.

change·a·ble (chān′jə·bəl) *adj.* **1** Capable of being changed; alterable. **2** Likely to change or vary; inconstant. **3** Reflecting light so as to appear of different color from different points of view. See synonyms under FICKLE, MOBILE. — **change·a·bil·i·ty** (chān′jə·bil′ə·tē), **change′a·ble·ness** *n.* — **change′a·bly** *adv.*

change·ful (chānj′fəl) *adj.* Full of or given to change; variable. See synonyms under FICKLE. — **change′ful·ly** *adv.* — **change′ful·ness** *n.*

change·less (chānj′lis) *adj.* **1** Without change; monotonous. **2** Constant; enduring; unchanging. — **change′less·ly** *adv.* — **change′less·ness** *n.*

change·ling (chānj′ling) *n.* **1** An ill-favored or stupid child believed to have been substituted, especially by supernatural or demonic agency, for a normal or beautiful child. **2** A fickle person: used also adjectively. **3** *Obs.* A silly or weak-minded person; simpleton; imbecile.

change of life The menopause.

change–ring·ing (chānj′ring′ing) *n.* The art or science of producing every possible variation in the ringing of a set of bells, starting from the time the bells leave the position of rounds to the time they return to it.

chan·nel[1] (chan'əl) n. 1 The bed of a stream. 2 A wide strait: the English *Channel.* 3 Any groove or passage. 4 *Naut.* The deep part of a river, harbor, strait, or estuary, where the current or tide is strongest; especially, a navigable passage between the shoal parts. 5 That through which anything flows or passes: a news *channel.* 6 *Telecom.* a A path for the transmission of telegraph, telephone, and radio communications. b A wave band of specified frequency over which radio and television messages or programs are transmitted. 7 A flanged iron beam having a bracket-shaped section: also **channel bar.** 8 In motion pictures, a complete assemblage of all the necessary recording equipment. —*v.t.* **chan·neled** or **·nelled, chan·nel·ing** or **·nel·ling** 1 To cut or wear channels in. 2 To convey through or as through a channel. [< OF *chanel* < L *canalis* groove. Doublet of CANAL.]

chan·nel[2] (chan'əl) n. *Naut.* A flat piece of wood or iron attached to the side of a vessel, to spread the shrouds and keep them clear of the bulwarks: originally called *chainwale.* [Alter. of *chainwale* < CHAIN (def. 7) + WALE (def. 2)]

chan·son (shän'sən, *Fr.* shän·sôn') n. A song. [< F < L *cantio, -onis* song < *canere* sing.]

chan·son de geste (shän·sôn' də zhest') An Old French epic tale in verse, generally written in assonant verse of ten syllables a line, arranged in irregular stanzas, and dealing with ancient French history and legend. The most celebrated one is the *Chanson de Roland.* [< F, song of noble deeds]

chant (chant, chänt) n. 1 A melody adapted to words without strict rhythm, or containing both recitative and rhythm: the most ancient and simple form of choral music. 2 A psalm or canticle so recited. 3 A song; melody. 4 Any measured monotonous singing or reciting of words. 5 A singing intonation in speech; twang. [< *v.t.*] —*v.t.* 1 To sing to a chant; intone, as in public worship. 2 To celebrate in song: to *chant* the praises of. 3 To say repetitiously and monotonously; harp upon. —*v.i.* 4 To sing chants. 5 To make melody; sing. 6 To talk monotonously and continuously. Also spelled *chaunt.* [< OF *chanter* < L *cantare*, freq. of *canere* sing]

chant·age (chan'tij, chän'-; *Fr.* shän·täzh') n. The extortion of money by threats of exposure; blackmailing. [< F]

chant·er (chan'tər, chän'-) n. 1 A singer; especially, a singer in a chantry; a chorister; precentor. 2 The fingerpipe of a bagpipe: distinguished from *drone.* 3 The hedge sparrow. Also **chan'tor.**

chan·te·relle[1] (shän·trel') n. *Music* The highest string of certain stringed instruments, as a violin. [< F]

chan·te·relle[2] (shan'tə·rel', chan'-) n. An edible yellow mushroom (*Cantharellus cibrius*), with a short stem. [< F < NL *cantharellus,* dim. of *cantharus* drinking cup < Gk. *kantharos*]

chant·ey (shan'tē, chan'-) n. *pl.* **·eys** A rhythmical working song of sailors: also spelled *shanty.* [Alter. of F *chantez,* imperative of *chanter* sing]

Chantilly lace A fine variety of lace formerly produced in Chantilly, France.

chant ro·yal (shän rwä·yàl') A lyric poem, related to the ballade, consisting of five 11-line stanzas with an 8-line envoy, the stanzas and the envoy having the last line identical. [< F]

chan·try (chan'trē, chän'-) n. *pl.* **·tries** 1 A chapel in or attached to a church or monastery, endowed for maintaining daily masses for the soul of the founder or of others nominated by him (the chapel usually containing the tomb of the founder). 2 Formerly, the endowment itself. 3 A chapel for subsidiary church services. [< OF *chanterie* < *chanter.* See CHANT.]

cha·os (kā'os) n. 1 A condition of utter disorder and confusion, as the unformed primal state of the universe. 2 Any thing or condition of which the elements or parts are in utter disorder and confusion. 3 *Obs.* Any vast gulf or chasm; an unfathomable abyss. [< L < Gk., abyss < *chainein*

gape, yawn]

cha·ot·ic (kā·ot'ik) adj. 1 Of, pertaining to, or like chaos. 2 Unformed; completely disordered. Also **cha·ot'i·cal.** —**cha·ot'i·cal·ly** adv.

chap[1] (chap) n. 1 *Colloq.* A fellow; lad. 2 *Obs.* A chapman; a dealer; buyer. [Short for CHAPMAN]

chap[2] (chap) v. **chapped** or **chapt, chap·ping** *v.t.* 1 To cause to split, crack, or become rough. 2 *Scot.* To strike with a hammer; pound on. —*v.i.* 3 To split, crack, or redden. 4 *Scot.* To beat or knock, as on a door; to strike, as a clock. —**to chap out** *Scot.* To summon by a tap, as on the window. —*n.* 1 A crack or roughened place in the skin. 2 *Scot.* A rap on the door; a knock of any sort. [ME *chappen.* Related to CHIP, CHOP.]

chap[3] (chap, chop) n. 1 A jaw. 2 *pl.* The mouth and cheeks. 3 The jaw of a vise. Also spelled *chop.* [Cf. ME *chaf(jaw]

chapeau bras (brä) A soft, three-cornered dress hat that can be folded and carried under the arm: worn commonly in the 18th century and still with court and diplomatic dress. [< F < *chapeau* hat + *bras* arm]

chap·el (chap'əl) n. 1 A place of worship other than a large and regular church. 2 A compartment or recess of a church, where independent services may be held. 3 Any place of worship not connected with the state or established church. 4 In England, any dissenting church. 5 A building or large room in a university, college, or school, for religious services; also, the services. 6 An official choir or orchestra, as of a court or nobleman's establishment. 7 The body of journeymen printers in a given office usually organized under a chairman, known in Great Britain as the *father of the chapel.* 8 *Archaic* A printing house. [< OF *chapele* < Med. L *capella,* dim. of *cappa* cloak; orig., a sanctuary where the cloak of St. Martin was kept as a relic]

chap·el·mas·ter (chap'əl·mas'tər, -mäs'-) See KAPELLMEISTER.

chap·er·on (shap'ə·rōn) n. 1 A woman who acts as attendant or protector of a young unmarried woman in public. 2 An older person who attends a social function to maintain its decorum and propriety. —*v.t.* To attend (a young unmarried woman) in mixed company; act as chaperon to. Also **chap'er·one.** [< F, hood < *chape* cape; because she protects her charges from harm] —**chap·er·on·age** (shap'ə·rō'nij) n.

chap·fall·en (chap'fô'lən, chop'-) adj. 1 Having the chap or jaw drooping. 2 Dejected; crestfallen. Also spelled *chop-fallen.*

chap·i·ter (chap'i·tər) n. *Archit.* The capital of a pillar. See CAPITAL[2]. [< F *chapitre.* See CHAPTER.]

chap·lain (chap'lin) n. 1 A clergyman with special functions, such as conducting religious services in a legislative assembly, in a regiment, or on board a ship. 2 A clergyman attached to a chapel for permanent or occasional duty. [< OF *chapelain* < Med. L *cappellanus* < *cappella* CHAPEL] —**chap'lain·cy, chap'lain·ship** n.

chap·let (chap'lit) n. 1 A wreath or garland for the head. 2 A necklace. 3 A rosary, or, more strictly, the third part of a rosary, or fifty-five beads. 4 A string of beads, or anything resembling it, as an astragal molding, or a rope of frog or toad spawn. [< OF *chapelet,* double dim. of *chape* hood < LL *cappa* hooded cape]

chaps (shaps, chaps) n. *pl. U.S.* Leather overalls without a seat, worn over trousers by cowboys to protect the legs: also called *chaparejos.* [Short for CHAPAREJOS]

chap·ter (chap'tər) n. 1 A division of a book or treatise, usually marked by a number and heading. 2 The body of clergy connected with a cathedral or other collegiate church; also, a council of such body, or their place of assembly. 3 *Eccl.* The meeting of any order. 4 In certain church services, a short Scriptural passage read immediately after the psalms. 5 A branch of a club, brotherhood, or other association, especially of a college fraternity or sorority. —**cathedral chapter** The personnel of canons attached to a cathedral. —**conventual chapter** The assembly of the clergy of one house or of an entire order for the purpose of regulating domestic affairs. —*v.t.* To divide into chapters, as a book. [< F *chapitre* < OF *chapitle* < L *capitulum,* dim. of *caput* head, capital, chapter]

chapter house A house of assembly for a chapter or a fraternity; especially, such a structure connected with a cathedral.

char[1] (chär) n. *Brit.* A chore; an odd job; also, work done by the day. —*v.i.* **charred, char·ring** To perform arduous work, as cleaning and scrubbing; serve as a charwoman. Also spelled *chare.* [OE *cerr* turn of work]

char[2] (chär) v. **charred, char·ring** *v.t.* 1 To burn or scorch the surface of, as timber. 2 To convert into charcoal by incomplete combustion. —*v.i.* 3 To become charred. See synonyms under BURN. —*n.* Charcoal. [? < CHARCOAL]

char[3] (chär) n. *pl.* **chars** or **char** Any fish (genus *Salvelinus*) characterized by small scales and having red spots, as the brook trout: also spelled *charr.* [< Scottish Gaelic *ceara* blood-red]

char·a·cin (kar'ə·sin) n. *Zool.* Any of a large and diversified family of fishes (*Characinidae*) native to South America and Africa, including the voracious caribe and many popular aquarium species. [< NL *Characinidae* < Gk. *charax* a sea fish < *charassein* sharpen, whet]

char·ac·ter (kar'ik·tər) n. 1 The combination of qualities distinguishing any person or class of persons; any distinctive mark or trait, or such marks or traits collectively, belonging to any person, class, or race; the individuality which is the product of nature, habits, and environment. 2 High qualities; moral force. 3 Reputation. 4 A representation; assumed part; role. 5 One assuming a certain role. 6 Position; status. 7 The person holding or represented as holding a certain position or rank. 8 A figure engraved, written, or printed; mark; sign; letter. 9 A style of handwriting or printing. 10 A form of secret writing; a cipher. 11 Fidelity and vigor in artistic representation of characteristic features. 12 An individual considered as possessing a combination of distinctive features; a personage; also, popularly, a humorous or eccentric person. 13 A representation or characterization, as of one's qualities or abilities; especially, a written testimonial given by an employer to an employee to aid in obtaining employment. 14 That by which a thing is especially known or distinguished; a quality; property: Ductility is a *character* of gold. 15 *Genetics* Any structural or functional trait in an organism regarded as the expression of a gene or genes. [< F *caractère* < L *character* < Gk. *charaktēr* stamp, mark < *charassein* carve, sharpen, engrave]

char·ac·ter·is·tic (kar'ik·tə·ris'tik) adj. 1 Distinguishing or contributing to distinguish; marking; characterizing; showing the character, traits, and disposition of; typical. 2 Constituting or pertaining to the character. See synonyms under PARTICULAR. —*n.* 1 A distinctive feature; peculiarity. 2 The integral part of a logarithm; index. —**char·ac·ter·is'·ti·cal** adj. —**char·ac·ter·is'ti·cal·ly** adv.

Synonyms (noun): attribute, character, distinction, feature, indication, mark, peculiarity, property, quality, sign, singularity, trace, trait. Compare ATTRIBUTE, CHARACTER, MARK.

char·ac·ter·ize (kar'ik·tə·rīz) *v.t.* **·ized, iz·ing** 1 To describe by qualities or peculiarities; designate. 2 To be a mark or peculiarity of; distinguish. 3 To supply character to. —**char'ac·ter·i·za'tion** n. —**char'ac·ter·iz'er** n.

char·ac·ter·o·log·i·cal (kar'ik·tər·ə·loj'ə·kəl) adj. Pertaining to the study of character or personality: *characterological* features. —**charac·ter·ol'o·gy** n.

char·ac·ter·y (kar'ik·tər·ē, -trē) n. *pl.* **·ter·ies** A system of characters or signs; mode; representation.

char·ac·to·nym (ka·rak'tə·nim) n. A word or name indicating the principal charateristic, occupation, or other distinguishing mark of a person; an epithet. [< CHARACTER + Gk. *onoma* name]

cha·rade (shə·rād') n. A guessing game in which each syllable of a word, and finally the whole word, is acted in pantomime or represented in

tableau. [<F <Provençal *charrado* chatter
<*charra* chatter, prattle]

char·bon (shär'bən) *n. Pathol.* Anthrax. [<F
<L *carbo, -onis* coal]

char·coal (chär'kōl') *n.* **1** A black, porous, odorless carbonaceous substance, burning with little
or no flame, obtained by the imperfect combustion of organic matter, as of wood: it is used as a
fuel, an adsorbent, a filter, etc. **2** A drawing pencil or crayon made of charcoal dust. **3** A drawing
made in charcoal. —*v.t.* **1** To write, draw, mark,
or blacken with or as with charcoal. **2** To subject
to or suffocate with charcoal fumes. [ME *char-
cole*; origin unknown]

chard (chärd) *n.* **1** The blanched leaves, leafstalks, or midribs of certain plants, as of the
artichoke: used as a vegetable. **2** A variety
of white beet (*Beta vulgaris cicla*) cultivated
for its large leaves and leafstalks, which are
used for salad and as a vegetable: also called
Swiss chard, leaf beet. [<F *carde* <L *carduus*
thistle]

charge (chärj) *v.* **charged, charg·ing** *v.t.* **1** To
lay or impose a load upon; to burden. **2** To
put something into or upon; fill. **3** To exhort
or instruct solemnly or authoritatively: to
charge a jury. **4** *Electr.* To replenish, as a
storage battery. **5** To accuse: with *with:* They
charged him with reckless driving. **6** To make
an onset against or attack upon, as a fort.
7 To emblazon, as with heraldic emblems.
8 To set or state, as a price. **9** To set down
or record, as a debt to be paid or accounted
for. **10** To load, as a weapon. —*v.i.* **11** To
demand or fix a price: Do you *charge* for
your services? **12** To debit. **13** To make an
onset: *Charge!* **14** To crouch or lie down, as
hunting dogs. —**to charge off** To regard or
write off as a loss. —**to be in charge of** **1** To
have the responsibility or control of. **2** To be
under the supervision or control of. See synonyms under ARRAIGN, ATTACK, ATTRIBUTE,
LOAD. —*n.* **1** The quantity of gunpowder,
fuel, etc., put or to be put into a firearm, a
furnace, etc. **2** The quantity of static electricity present in a saturated storage battery.
3 *Physics* The energy, measured in electrostatic units, present in an atomic particle, as
the proton, electron, meson, etc. **4** Care and
custody of that which is under one's care.
5 A price. **6** An entry of indebtedness. **7** A
tax; expense; cost. **8** An address of instruction or admonition: the *charge* to a jury.
9 An accusation. **10** An impetuous attack or
onslaught; also, the signal for it. **11** *Her.* A
figure or device; a bearing. **12** *Obs.* A burden;
load. See synonyms under CARE, CAREER,
LOAD, OVERSIGHT, PRICE. [<OF *chargier* <LL
carricare carry <*carrus* cart. Doublet of
CARRY.]

charge·a·ble (chär'jə·bəl) *adj.* **1** Capable of
being or rightfully to be charged, as an obligation, expense, accusation, etc. **2** Liable to be
charged or rendered subject to some duty,
expense, etc.; responsible or indictable.
3 *Obs.* Burdensome; also, important.

charge account An account against which
the purchase of merchandise in a store is
charged.

char·gé d'af·faires (shär·zhā' də·fâr', *Fr.* shàr·
zhā' dà·fâr') *pl.* **char·gés d'af·faires** (shär·zhāz'
də·fâr', *Fr.* shàr·zhā' dà·fâr') **1** A person who
temporarily assumes the command of a diplomatic mission in the absence of the regularly
appointed chief: in full *chargé d'affaires ad
interim.* **2** A diplomatic representative of the
fourth rank accredited by one foreign minister to another, and not to the chief of state.
Compare MINISTER RESIDENT, DIPLOMATIC
AGENT.

char·gé des af·faires (shär·zhā' dä·zà·fâr') A
person who has custody of the archives or
other property of a mission in a country with
which formal diplomatic relations are not
maintained. He has no diplomatic status or
immunity, and his relations with the foreign
government are purely informal.

charg·er (chär'jər) *n.* **1** One who or that
which charges; especially, a war horse. **2** An
apparatus for charging electric storage batteries. **3** A large shallow dish for meat.

char·i·ly (châr'ə·lē) *adv.* In a chary manner;
warily.

char·i·ness (châr'ē·nis) *n.* **1** The quality of
being chary. **2** Integrity; scrupulousness.

char·i·ot (char'ē·ət)
n. **1** An ancient
two–wheeled vehicle
used in war and in
racing. **2** An ornate
four–wheeled car-
riage. —*v.t. & v.i.*
To convey, ride, or
drive in or as in a
chariot. [<OF, aug.
of *char* car <L
carrus cart, wagon]

char·i·o·teer (char'-
ē·ə·tir') *n.* One who
drives a chariot.
—*v.t.* To act as
driver of (a vehicle)
or for (a person).

ETRUSCAN WAR
CHARIOT OF BRONZE

cha·ris·ma (kə·riz'mə) *n.* **1** *Theol.* A gift or
power bestowed by the Holy Spirit for use in
the propagation of the truth or the edification
of the church and its adherents. **2** The aggregate of those special gifts of mind and
character which are the source of the personal
power of exceptional individuals and upon
which they depend for their capacity to secure
the allegiance of, and exercise decisive authority over, large masses of people. Also **char·ism**
(kar'iz·əm). [<Gk., grace, favor] —**char·is-
mat·ic** (kar'iz·mat'ik) *adj.*

char·i·ta·ble (char'ə·tə·bəl) *adj.* **1** Of, pertaining to, or characterized by charity.
2 Generous in gifts to the poor; liberal. **3**
Characterized by love and good will; tolerant;
benevolent; kindly; lenient. —**char'i·ta·ble·
ness** *n.* —**char'i·ta·bly** *adv.*

Synonyms: beneficent, benevolent, benign,
benignant, compassionate, considerate, forgiving, indulgent, kind, lenient, liberal, loving,
merciful, mild, patient, placable. *Antonyms:*
implacable, relentless, revengeful, unforgiving.

char·i·ty (char'ə·tē) *n. pl.* **·ties** **1** Liberality
to the poor. **2** Almsgiving; alms. **3** An institution for the help of the needy. **4** Readiness
to overlook faults; tolerance; leniency. **5**
Spiritual benevolence; Christian love. **6** *Law*
A gift of real or personal property for the
public benefit. See synonyms under BENEV-
OLENCE, LOVE. [<OF *charité* <L *caritas,
-tatis* love <*carus* dear]

cha·riv·a·ri (shə·riv'ə·rē', shiv'ə·rē', shä·rē·
vä'rē) *n.* A noisy and discordant burlesque
serenade, as to a newly married couple or an
unpopular personage, performed with tin
pans, horns, kettles, etc.: also spelled *shivaree.*
[<F]

chark (chärk) See CHAR[2]. [Back formation
from CHARCOAL]

char·kha (chûr'kə, chär'-) *n.* The spinning
wheel of India. Also **char·ka.** [<Hind.
carkhā]

char·la·tan (shär'lə·tən) *n.* A pretender to
knowledge or skill, especially to medical
knowledge; quack. —**char'la·tan·ic** (-tan'ik)
adj. —**char'la·tan·ry, char'la·tan·ism** *n.* [<F
<Ital. *ciarlatano* babbler <*ciarlare* babble
<*ciarla* chat, idle talk]

Char·le·magne (shär'lə·mān), 742–814, king of
the Franks 768–814; emperor of the West,
800–814: known as *Charles the Great.*

Charles (chärlz, *Fr.* shàrl) A masculine per-
sonal name. See CARLO, CARLOS, KARL. [<F
<L *Carolus* <Gmc., a freeman]
—**Charles I,** 1600–49, Charles Stuart, king of
England 1625–49; beheaded.
—**Charles I of Anjou,** 1226–85, king of
Sicily 1265–82; of Naples 1266–85.
—**Charles II,** 1630–85, king of England
1660–85.
—**Charles V,** 1337–80, king of France 1364–
80: known as *Charles the Wise.*
—**Charles V,** 1500–58, emperor of Germany
1519–56, and, as **Charles I,** king of Spain
1516–56; abdicated.
—**Charles VII,** 1403–61, king of France
1422–61.
—**Charles IX,** 1550–74, king of France
1560–74.
—**Charles X,** 1757–1836, king of France
1824–30.
—**Charles XII,** 1682–1718, king of Sweden
1697–1718.
—**Charles Edward Stuart** See STUART,
CHARLES EDWARD.
—**Charles Mar·tel** (mär·tel'), 688–741, Frank-
ish ruler; grandfather of Charlemagne: called
"The Hammer."

—**Charles the Great** See CHARLEMAGNE.

Charles's law (chärl'ziz) *Physics* The statement that the volume of a gas kept at constant pressure varies directly with the absolute temperature: exact only for perfect gases:
also called *Gay–Lussac law.* [after J. A. C.
Charles]

Charles's Wain See under WAIN.

Charles·ton (chärlz'tən) **1** A port in SE South
Carolina. **2** The capital of West Virginia.

char·lock (chär'lək) *n.* Wild mustard (*Brassica
arvensis*): often a troublesome weed. [OE
cerlic]

char·lotte (shär'lət) *n.* A dessert made of
fruits, whipped cream, custard, etc., in a mold
of cake, bread, or crumbs. [<F, from the
fem. name]

charlotte russe (rōōs) A dessert made of
whipped cream or custard in a mold of sponge
cake. [<F, Russian charlotte]

Char·lotte·town (shär'lət·toun) A port, capital
of Prince Edward Island province, Canada.

charm (chärm) *v.t.* **1** To attract irresistibly;
bewitch; enchant. **2** To influence as by magic
power; soothe; assuage. **3** To influence the
senses or mind of by some quality or attraction, as beauty; delight. **4** To protect as by
a spell: a *charmed* life. —*v.i.* **5** To be pleasing
or fascinating. **6** To act as a charm; work as
a spell. **7** To use spells or incantations. [<*n.*]
—*n.* **1** The power of alluring or delighting;
fascination. **2** That which charms; beauty;
appeal. **3** A magical spell. **4** A small ornament worn on a watchguard, bracelet, etc., for
decoration, to avert evil, or to insure good
fortune. **5** Originally, the chanting of a verse
supposed to possess magical power; an incantation. See synonyms under TALISMAN. [<F
charme <L *carmen* song, incantation]
—**charm'er** *n.*

Synonyms (verb): bewitch, captivate, delight,
enchant, enrapture, entice, entrance, fascinate.
See RAVISH. *Antonyms:* annoy, disenchant,
disgust, distress, disturb, irritate, repel.

char·meuse (shär·mœz') *n.* A soft, light fabric
with satin weave, having a dull back and
semilustrous surface. [<F]

charm·ing (chär'ming) *adj.* **1** Having power
to charm. **2** Enchanting; fascinating; bewitching. —**charm'ing·ly** *adv.* —**charm'ing·ness** *n.*

Synonyms: bewitching, captivating, delightful, enchanting, enrapturing, entrancing, fascinating, winning. That is *charming* or *bewitching* which is adapted to win others as if
by a magic spell. *Enchanting, enrapturing,
entrancing* represent the influence as not only
supernatural, but irresistible and *delightful.*
That which is *fascinating* may win without
delighting, as a serpent its prey; we can speak
of horrible *fascination. Charming* applies only
to what is external to oneself; *delightful* may
apply to personal experiences or emotions as
well; we speak of a *charming* manner, a *charming* dress, but of *delightful* anticipations. Compare AMIABLE, BEAUTIFUL, LOVELY.

char·nel (chär'nəl) *n.* A burying place; cemetery; mortuary; also, a sepulcher. —*adj.*
Fitted or used for the reception of dead
bodies. [<OF <LL *carnalis* fleshly <*caro,
carnis* flesh]

charnel house A room or vault, sometimes in
a church, for or filled with dead bodies or
with bones.

char·poy (chär'poi') *n.* The typical bedstead
or cot of India, usually having a bamboo
frame interlaced with twine. Also **char·pai**
(chär'pī'). [<Hind. *chārpāī* <*chār* four +
pāī foot]

charr (chär) See CHAR[3].

char·ry (chär'ē) *adj.* **·ri·er, ·ri·est** Pertaining to
or like charcoal.

chart (chärt) *n.* **1** A map on which selected
features or characteristics are clearly indicated; especially, one for the use of navigators,
aviators, and meteorologists. **2** A sheet showing facts graphically or in tabular form. **3** An
outline or diagram having some geographical
or physical application. **4** A graph showing
changes and variation of temperature, population, circulation of publications, death rate,
etc. —*v.t.* To map out; lay out on a chart.
[<OF *charte* <L *charta* <Gk. *chartē* leaf of
paper. Doublet of CARD.]

char·ta (kär'tə) *n. pl.* **·tae** (-tē) A sheet of
paper impregnated with medicines, applied
externally. [<L *charta* paper]

char·ter (chär'tər) *n.* **1** An act of incorporation

of a municipality, company, institution, or the like. **2** A writing permitting the establishment of a branch or chapter of a society. **3** A document granting special rights or privileges. **4** A lease, as of a vessel, or the contract by which it is leased: also **char′ter·par′ty**. **5** Written evidence of agreement or contract, as a deed. —*v.t.* **1** To hire by charter. **2** To hire by contract, as a train or car. **3** To establish by charter; give a charter to, as a bank, railroad, colony, etc. [<OF *chartre* <L *chartula,* dim. of *charta* paper] —**char′ter·er** *n.*

char·ter·age (chär′tər·ij) *n.* The act or business of chartering vessels; shipbrokerage; also, a shipbroker's fee.

charter colony In American history, a colony established under a royal charter, which freed it from direct parliamentary control, as Massachusetts.

charter member An original member of a corporation, or of an order or society.

Charter of the United Nations The charter adopted by the United Nations Conference on International Organization at San Francisco, April–June, 1945, making the United Nations a permanent organization, and establishing the General Assembly, the Security Council, the Economic and Social Council, the Trusteeship Council, the International Court of Justice, and the Secretariat as its component parts. See UNITED NATIONS, INTERNATIONAL COURT OF JUSTICE under COURT.

chart·less (chärt′lis) *adj.* **1** Not laid down in a chart. **2** Without a chart. **3** Unguided.

char·treuse (shär·trœz′) *n.* **1** A yellow, pale green, or white liqueur made by the Carthusian monks. **2** (*also* shär·trooz′) A pale yellowish-green color. —*adj.* Of this color. [from CHARTREUSE]

char·tu·lar·y (kär′choo·ler′ē) See CARTULARY.

char·wom·an (chär′woom′ən) *n. pl.* **·wom·en** A woman employed to do cleaning, scrubbing, etc., as in office buildings. [<CHAR¹ + WOMAN]

char·y (châr′ē) *adj.* **char·i·er, char·i·est 1** Cautious; wary. **2** Careful; prudent; sparing; hence, stingy. [OE *cearig* sorrowful, sad < *cearu* care]

chase¹ (chās) *v.* **chased, chas·ing** *v.t.* **1** To pursue with intent to catch, capture, or molest. **2** To drive away; dispel: often with *away, out* or *off.* **3** To hunt, as deer. **4** To drive by pursuing: He *chased* the hens into the coop. —*v.i.* **5** To follow in pursuit. **6** *Colloq.* To rush; go hurriedly. —*n.* **1** Earnest pursuit; also, that which is pursued; the prey or quarry. **2** The practice of hunting. **3** *Archaic* The right to hunt on a certain tract. **4** Hunters collectively; the hunt. **5** *Brit.* A private game preserve. **6** In court tennis, a scoring stroke, as when the ball bounces a second time in certain parts of the court. Also spelled **chace.** [<OF *chacier* <LL *captiare,* freq. of *capere* take, hold. Doublet of CATCH.] —**chas′ing** *n.*

chase² (chās) *n.* **1** *Printing* A strong rectangular metal frame into which pages of type are fastened for printing. **2** The part of a cannon between the trunnions and the swell of the muzzle. **3** A groove or slot: the *chase* of a water wheel. **4** A longitudinal groove for a tenon or tongue; a form of rabbet. **5** The circular trough of a cider mill, where the apples are crushed by the runner. —*v.t.* **chased, chas·ing** To ornament by indenting; also, to form by embossing, indenting, etc.: to *chase* silverware. [<F *châsse, chas* <OF *chasse* <L *capsa* box] —**chas′er** *n.*

CHASE²
(*n. def. 1*)

chas·er (chā′sər) *n.* **1** One who chases or pursues; a hunter. **2** A steeplechaser. **3** A pursuing or following airplane or vessel. **4** A gun at the bow or stern of such a vessel for use in pursuit of or by another vessel: a bow *chaser* and a stern *chaser.* **5** *U.S. Colloq.* A drink of water or of some mild beverage taken after or with whisky, rum, etc. **6** A small quantity of alcoholic liquor taken at the end of a meal; a chasse.

chasm (kaz′əm) *n.* **1** A yawning hollow; deep gorge. **2** An abrupt interruption of continuity; a gap or void. See synonyms under

BREACH, HOLE. [<Gk. *chasma* < *chainein* gape, open wide] —**chas·mal** (kaz′məl) *adj.*

chasse¹ (shàs) *n.* A small glass of alcoholic liquor served at the end of a meal. Also French **chasse-ca·fé** (-kȧ·fā′). [Short for *chasse-café* < *chasser* chase + *café* (the taste of) coffee]

chasse² (shäs) *n.* A casket for the relics of a saint. [<F *chasse* <L *capsa* box]

chas·seur (sha·sûr′) *n.* **1** A light-armed soldier of cavalry or infantry. **2** A semimilitary household servitor among the European nobility. **3** A huntsman. **4** A hotel servant. [<F, hunter < *chasser* <OF *chacier* CHASE¹]

chas·sis (shas′ē, chas′ē) *n. pl.* **chas·sis** (shas′ēz, chas′-) **1** The frame and springs of a motor vehicle; also, all other mechanical parts of the car, including the wheels and motor. **2** *Aeron.* The landing gear of an aircraft; the wheels, floats, or other structures which support the main weight of an airplane. **3** In radio: **a** The metal framework to which the tubes and other components of a receiver, amplifier, etc., are attached. **b** The assembled framework and components. **4** In coast artillery, a movable railway for running the top carriage of a gun into and out of firing position. [<F *châssis* < *chas.* See CHASE².]

chaste (chāst) *adj.* **1** Free from sexual impurity; virtuous. **2** Pure in thought. **3** Pure in style; free from literary or artistic extravagances. **4** *Obs.* Unmarried; single. See synonyms under MODEST, PURE. [<OF *chaste* <L *castus* pure] —**chaste′ly** *adv.* —**chaste′ness** *n.*

chast·en (chā′sən) *v.t.* **1** To discipline by punishment or affliction; chastise. **2** To moderate; soften; temper. **3** To refine; purify. —**chast′en·er** *n.* —**chast′en·ing** *n.*

Synonyms: afflict, castigate, chastise, correct, discipline, humble, punish, purify, refine, soften, subdue, try. *Castigate* and *chastise* refer strictly to corporal punishment, although both are somewhat archaic. *Punish* is distinctly retributive in sense; *chasten,* wholly corrective and merciful in intent and result. See REPRESS, REPROVE. [<OF *chastier* <L *castigare* correct. See CASTIGATE.]

chas·tise (chas·tīz′) *v.t.* **·tised, ·tis·ing 1** To punish, especially with the rod; whip. **2** To refine or subdue; chasten. See synonyms under BEAT, CHASTEN. [ME *chastisen*] —**chas·tis′a·ble** *adj.* —**chas·tise·ment** (chas′tiz·mənt, chas·tīz′-) *n.* —**chas·tis′er** *n.*

chas·ti·ty (chas′tə·tē) *n.* **1** The state or quality of being chaste; purity. **2** Virginity or celibacy. See synonyms under VIRTUE. [<OF *chasteté* <L *castitas, -tatis* purity < *castus* pure]

chastity belt A fettered girdle worn by women in the Middle Ages to prohibit sexual intercourse during the absence of their husbands.

chas·u·ble (chaz′yə·bəl, chas′-) *n.* The outer vestment worn by a priest in celebrating the mass or Eucharist: a sleeveless mantle falling low in front and behind, and having a cross on the back. [<F *casubla,* var. of *casula* cloak <L, dim. of *casa* house]

chat¹ (chat) *v.i.* **chat·ted, chat·ting** To converse in an easy or gossipy manner; talk familiarly. —*n.* **1** Easy and familiar speech; informal conversation. **2** Any of several singing birds: so called from their notes. See synonyms under CONVERSATION. [Short for CHATTER]

chat² (chat) *n. Bot.* The inflorescence, catkin, or seed of various plants, as the ament of the pine, the samara of the maple, etc. [<F, cat; so called from its appearance]

Cha·tal·ja (chä′täl·jä′) See ÇATALCA.

cha·teau (sha·tō′, *Fr.* shä·tō′) *n. pl.* **·teaux** (-tōz′, *Fr.* -tō′) **1** A French castle or manor house. **2** A house on a country estate, particularly a large house resembling a French manor. Also French **châ·teau′.** [<F <OF *chastel* <L *castellum* CASTLE]

château wine Any wine made, named for, and usually bottled on, the estate of a château in France where the grapes are grown, particularly those near Bordeaux.

chat·e·lain (shat′ə·lān) See CASTELLAN.

chat·e·laine (shat′ə·lān) *n.* **1** A chain, hanging from a woman's belt to hold small articles; also, a clasp to hold a watch or purse. **2** The mistress of a chateau or castle. [<F *châtelaine,* fem. of *châtelain* CASTELLAN]

cha·toy·ant (shə·toi′ənt, *Fr.* shà·twà·yäṅ) *adj.* **1** Possessing a changeable luster, like that of a cat's eye in the dark. **2** Exhibiting a narrow band of light, as certain gemstones when cut and polished. —*n.* A stone having such a luster; cat's-eye. [<F, ppr. of *chatoyer* change, as a cat's eye] —**cha·toy′an·cy** *n.*

chat·tel (chat′l) *n. Law* **1** An article of personal property; a movable. **2** Any interest or right in land less than a freehold; a leasehold estate in lands for a determinate period: called a **chattel real.** As distinguished from freeholds, chattels real are regarded as personal property; but, as being interests in real property, they are so designated to distinguish them from other chattels, which are called **chattels personal. 3** *Archaic* A bondman; serf. See synonyms under PROPERTY. [<OF *chatel* <L *capitale* property < *caput* head. Doublet of CATTLE.]

chattel mortgage A conditional transfer of rights in movable property as security for a debt or obligation, insuring the debtor reversion of ownership upon payment of the obligation.

chat·ter (chat′ər) *v.i.* **1** To click together rapidly, as the teeth in shivering. **2** To talk rapidly and trivially; blather. **3** To make rapid and indistinct sounds, as a monkey or squirrel. **4** To clatter or vibrate while operating improperly, as a power tool. —*v.t.* **5** To utter in a trivial or chattering manner. See synonyms under BABBLE. —*n.* **1** Idle prattle. **2** Jabbering, as of a monkey. **3** A rattling of the teeth. **4** The jar or vibration of a chattering tool. [Imit.]

chat·ter·box (chat′ər·boks′) *n.* A voluble talker.

chat·ter·er (chat′ər·ər) *n.* **1** One who or that which chatters. **2** A passerine bird, as a waxwing, especially the Bohemian waxwing.

chatter marks 1 *Mech.* Irregular, very fine tool markings caused by vibration of a tool. **2** *Geol.* Transverse crescent-shaped marks in a continuous series, sometimes occurring in deeply gouged glacial striae as the result of vibration.

chat·ty (chat′ē) *adj.* **·ti·er, ·ti·est** Given to chat; loquacious. —**chat′ti·ly** *adv.* —**chat′ti·ness** *n.*

chauf·fer (chô′fər, shô′-) *n.* A small chemical furnace. Also **chau′fer.** [Var. of CHAFER]

chauf·feur (shō′fər, shō·fûr′) *n.* One who drives or operates an automobile; especially, one whose work is to drive an automobile for someone else. [<F, stoker < *chauffer* warm]

chaul·moo·gra (chôl·moo′grə) *n.* An East Indian and Malayan tree (*Taraktogenos kurzii,* family *Flacourtiaceae*), from whose seeds is extracted the yellowish chaulmoogra oil, used in the treatment of leprosy and other skin diseases. Also **chaul·mu′gra.** [<Bengali *cāulmugrā*]

chaus·sure (shō·sür′) *n.* Foot covering. [<F < L *calceare* shoe < *calceus.* See CHAUSSES.]

chau·tau·qua (shə·tô′kwə) *n. U.S.* Any educational association, especially one of a number holding sessions in a circuit of communities. [from *Chautauqua*]

chau·vin·ist (shō′vən·ist) *n.* **1** Anyone absurdly jealous of his country's honor or puffed up with an exaggerated sense of national glory; an extravagant glorifier of his country. **2** One who is belligerently attached to his own race, group, etc.: white *chauvinist.* [after Nicolas *Chauvin,* an extremely devoted soldier and overzealous supporter of Napoleon Bonaparte] —**chau′vin·ism** *n.* —**chau′vin·is′tic** *adj.* —**chau′vin·is′ti·cal·ly** *adv.*

cheap (chēp) *adj.* **1** Bearing or bringing a low price in the market; that may be bought at low price; inexpensive. **2** Obtainable at a low rate. **3** Depreciated: said of money. **4** Being of little value; hence, poor; of inferior quality. **5** Not esteemed. **6** Low: a *cheap* person. **7** Embarrassed; sheepish. See synonyms under BASE, COMMON. —*n. Obs.* **1** A market; still used in combination in some place names: *Cheap*side and East*cheap* in London. **2** A bargain. —*adv.* In a cheap manner [Earlier *good cheap* a bargain <OE *ceap* business, trade] —**cheap′ly** *adv.* —**cheap′ness** *n.*

cheap·en (chē′pən) *v.t.* **1** To make cheap or cheaper. **2** *Obs.* To chaffer or bargain for. **3** To bring into contempt, belittle, or disparage. —*v.i.* **4** To become cheap. —**cheap′en·er** *n* .

cheat (chēt) *v.t.* **1** To deceive or defraud. **2** To impose upon; delude; trick. **3** To elude or escape; foil: to *cheat* the hangman. —*v.i.* **4** To practice fraud or act dishonestly. —**to cheat on** *Slang* To be sexually unfaithful to. — *n.* **1** An act of cheating; fraud; imposture. **2** *Law* The obtaining of property by imposture: indictable at common law when the act injures the public welfare. **3** A systematic cheater; swindler. **4** Any of several types of brome-grass: so called because they resemble the the grain among which they grow. See CHESS². **5** An article or object of fictitious value; a sham. See synonyms under ARTIFICE, FRAUD, HYPOCRITE. [ME *chete,* short for *achete* es-cheat] —**cheat′ing** *adj.* —**cheat′ing·ly** *adv.*

cheat·er (chē′tər) *n.* **1** One who cheats; swindler; defrauder. **2** *pl. U.S. Slang* Spectacles; eyeglasses.

che·bec (chi·bek′) *n.* The least flycatcher. [Imit.]

che·cha·ko (chē·chä′kō) See CHEECHAKO.

check (chek) *n.* **1** A sudden stopping or arrest; rebuff; reverse; delay. **2** Any person or thing that controls or restrains. **3** A check-rein. **4** A written order for money, drawn upon a bank or banker: also *Brit. cheque.* **5** A numbered tag, etc., used in duplicate to identify the owner of article. **6** Any examination, test, or comparison for verification; also, a mark for verification or identification. **7** A square in a checkered surface; also, any checkered pattern or fabric having a check-ered pattern. **8** In chess, an attack upon or menace to the king. **9** In mining, a slight fault. **10** A chip used in games. **11** A crack, as in timber, caused by uneven season-ing, or, in steel, caused by uneven tempering. **12** A notch or rabbet in a piece of wood or stone into which another piece fits. **13** A curb on administrative power, as a constitu-tional right: the *checks* and balances of re-publican government. **14** A bill in a restaurant. **15** *Obs.* Rebuke; reproof. See synonyms under ANIMADVERSION, REPROOF. —*v.t.* **1** To stop or restrain forcibly or sud-denly. **2** To curb; hold in restraint, as with a checkrein. **3** To ascertain correctness of, as by comparison; investigate. **4** To mark with a check or checks. **5** To mark with a pat-tern of criss-crosses, as cloth. **6** To cause to crack; to make checks or chinks in. **7** To re-buke; rebuff; repulse: They *checked* the at-tack. **8** In chess, to put an opponent's king in check. **9** To deposit temporarily for safe-keeping: to *check* one's luggage. **10** *Agric.* To plant so as to form checkrows. —*v.i.* **11** pause or make a stop. **12** To crack, as paint. **13** To agree item for item: My figures *check* with yours. **14** In chess, to give check to a king. **15** *U.S.* To draw on a checking account. **16** In hunting, to pause, as hounds, to locate a lost scent. **17** In fal-conry, to forsake proper quarry for baser game: with *at.* —**to check in** *U.S.* To regis-ter as a guest at a hotel. —**to check out** *U.S.* **1** To pay one's bill and leave, as from a ho-tel; also, to depart; die. **2** To investigate or confirm. **3** To be true or as expected, upon investigation. **4** To count and charge for (merchandise). **5** test the performance of. —**to check up 1** To test; examine: often with *on.* **2** To put a checkrein on. —*interj.* **1** An exclamation proclaiming that the op-ponent's king is in check. **2** Correct; that is right. —*adj.* **1** Checkered. **2** Serving to verify or confirm: a *check* test. [<OF *eschek* defeat, check <Arabic *shāh* king <Persian; orig. from chess, indicating the king was in danger]

check·book (chek′book′) *n.* A book of bank checks in blank, usually with marginal stubs for date, amount, and name of payee.

checked (chekt) *adj.* **1** Marked with squares: *checked* gingham. **2** Made of a fabric marked or woven in squares: a *checked* suit. **3** Restrained; stopped; kept in check.

check·er (chek′ər) *n.* **1** A piece in the game of checkers, usually a small disk. **2** One of the squares in a checkered surface. **3** *pl.* A game for two persons played with 24 pieces upon a checkerboard; draughts. **4** One who checks; especially, one who inspects, counts,

or supervises the disposal of merchandise, as in a market. **5** The cultivated service tree. **6** The wild European service tree (*S. torminalis*): also called **checkertree. 7** The fruit of either tree. —*v.t.* **1** To mark with squares or crossed lines. **2** To mark with vicissitudes; diversify. Also *Brit. chequer.* [<OF *eschequier* chessboard <Med. L *scaccarium* < *scacci* chess <Arabic *shāq.* See CHECK.]

check·er·ber·ry (chek′ər·ber′ē) *n. pl.* **·ries 1** The wintergreen. **2** Its red berry. **3** Loose-ly, the partridgeberry.

check·er·board (chek′ər·bôrd′, -bōrd′) *n.* A board divided into 64 squares, used in playing checkers or chess.

check·ered (chek′ərd) *adj.* **1** Divided into squares of different colors; checked, as with black and white. **2** Showing any alternating spaces of color or of light and darkness. **3** Marked by vicissitudes; alternating, as between good and evil fortune.

checking account A bank account against which a depositor may draw checks.

check list 1 A list by which something may be confirmed or verified; specifically, a roll or list of voters used at the polls on election days for checking off the names of those who vote. **2** A list of plants, animals, minerals, fossils, etc., usually limited to one natural division, for students and collectors, to check when recognized or acquired.

check·mate (chek′māt′) *v.t.* **·mat·ed, ·mat·ing 1** In chess, to put (an opponent's king) in check from·which no escape is possible, thus winning the game: commonly shortened to *mate.* **2** Hence, to defeat by a skilful maneuver. See synonyms under CONQUER. —*n.* **1** The act or position of checkmating. **2** Complete defeat. [<OF *eschec mat* <Arabic *al-shāh māt* the king is dead <Persian]

check·off (chek′ôf′, -of′) *n.* The collection of trade-union dues by deduction at source from the pay of each employee, the em-ployer's accounting office serving as collect-ing agent. Also **check′-off′.**

check·out (chek′out′) *n.* **1** The series of ac-tions by which the condition or performance of someone or something is tested. **2** The operation or act of examining and charging for purchases, as in a market.

check·rein (chek′rān′) *n.* **1** A rein from the bit of the bridle to the saddle of a harness to keep a horse's head up. **2** The branch rein connect-ing a driving rein of one horse to the bit of his mate in a double team. Also **check′line′.**

check·room (chek′room′, -room′) *n.* A room in a railway station, restaurant, theater, etc., where small packages, coats, hats, luggage, etc., may be left temporarily.

check·row (chek′rō′) *n.* One of the standing rows, as of trees, in a farm or orchard that partition it into squares. —*v.t.* To plant in this fashion.

checks and balances Complementary or bal-anced powers among the branches of a govern-ment, as among the legislative, executive, and judiciary branches.

check-up (chek′up′) *n.* A thorough examina-tion or testing of a living organism, the operation of a mechanism or machine, the progress of work or the finished work of a person or group, etc., to ascertain health, accuracy, value, etc.

check valve *Mech.* A one-way valve, as in a boiler, which closes automatically to prevent return of fluid passing through it. See illustra-tion under HYDRAULIC RAM.

ched·dite (ched′īt, shed′-) *n.* An explosive used in blasting, consisting essentially of nitrated naphthalene containing a chlorate or perchlorate mixed with an oily substance, as castor oil. [from *Chedde,* France]

cheek (chēk) *n.* **1** Either side of the face below the eye and above the mouth. ✦ Col-lateral adjective: *buccal.* **2** A side or part analogous to the side of a face: the *cheek* of a vise. **3** *Naut.* One of two corresponding projections on either side of a mast, support-ing the trestletrees. **4** *Colloq.* Assurance; impudence. —*v.t. Brit. Colloq.* To confront or address impudently. [OE *cēce, cēace*]

cheek by jowl **1** With cheek close to cheek. **2** Closely juxtaposed. **3** Confidential; inti-mate. Also *Scot.* **cheek for chow.**

cheek·y (chē′kē) *adj.* **cheek·i·er, cheek·i·est** Impudent; brazen. —**cheek′i·ly** *adv.* —**cheek′-i·ness** *n.*

chee·la (chē′lä) See CHELA¹.

cheep (chēp) *v.t. & v.i.* To utter in a faint, shrill tone; chirp; peep. —*n.* A weak chirp or squeak, as of a young bird. [Imit.] —**cheep·er** *n.*

cheer (chir) *n.* **1** A shout of applause or en-couragement. **2** State of mind: Be of good *cheer.* **3** Cheerfulness. **4** Something that promotes cheerfulness. **5** Provisions for a feast. **6** *Obs.* Expression of countenance; look. See synonyms under APPLAUSE, ENTER-TAINMENT, HAPPINESS. —*v.t.* **1** To make cheerful; fill with joy; comfort: often with *up.* **2** To applaud or salute with cheers. **3** To urge with words or cries; encourage; incite: often with *on.* **4** To act on like cheer; invigorate: The cup that *cheers.* —*v.i.* **5** To be or become cheerful, happy or glad: with *up.* **6** To utter cheers. **7** *Obs.* To be affected; feel; fare. See synonyms under ENCOURAGE, ENTERTAIN, REJOICE. [<OF *chiere, chere* face; countenance <LL *cara*] —**cheer′er** *n.* —**cheer′ing** *adj.*

cheer·ful (chir′fəl) *adj.* **1** In good spirits; joyous; lively. **2** Willing. —**cheer′ful·ly** *adv.* —**cheer′ful·ness** *n.* Synonyms: blithe, bright, buoyant, cheering, cheery, gay, genial, happy, jocund, joyous, lively, merry, mirthful, smiling, sprightly, sunny. See BRIGHT, COMFORTABLE, GOOD, HAPPY.

cheer·less (chir′lis) *adj.* Destitute of cheer; gloomy. See synonyms under BLEAK. —**cheer′-less·ly** *adv.* —**cheer′less·ness** *n.*

cheer·y (chir′ē) *adj.* **cheer·i·er, cheer·i·est 1** Abounding in cheerfulness. **2** Fitted to cheer; cheering. See synonyms under BRIGHT, CHEERFUL, COMFORTABLE, HAPPY. —**cheer′i·ly** *adv.* —**cheer′i·ness** *n.*

cheese¹ (chēz) *n.* **1** The pressed curd of milk, variously prepared and flavored; also, a cake or mass of this substance. **2** Any of various substances ground and compacted like cheese, as headcheese. [OE *cēse* <L *caseus* cheese]

cheese·cake (chēz′kāk′) *n.* **1** A cake contain-ing sweetened curds, eggs, milk, etc.: also **cheese cake. 2** *Slang* The display of a girl's legs, as in photographs.

cheese·cloth (chēz′klôth′, -kloth′) *n.* A thin cotton fabric, originally used for wrapping a cheese after pressing.

cheese mite A minute acarid infesting cheese, flour, and meal.

cheese-par·ing (chēz′pâr′ing) *adj.* Miserly; parsimonious. —*n.* **1** A paring of cheese. **2** Something of no value. **3** Any mean or stingy practice or disposition.

chees·y (chē′zē) *adj.* **·i·er, ·i·est 1** Made of or similar to cheese. **2** *Slang* Of inferior grade; second-rate.

chee·tah (chē′tə) *n.* An animal (*Acinonyx juba-tus*) of the cat family, resembling the leopard, native to SW Asia and northern Africa: often tamed and trained to hunt antelope. Also spelled *chetah.* [<Hind. *chītā* leopard]

chef (shef) *n.* **1** A head cook. **2** Any cook. **3** A chief or director. [<F]

cheg·oe (cheg′ō) See CHIGOE.

cheilo-, etc. See CHILO-, etc.

cheiro-, etc. See CHIRO-, etc.

Chei·ron (kī′ron) See CHIRON.

che·la¹ (chä′lä) *n. Anglo-Indian* A disciple or novice; especially, the disciple of a holy man. Also spelled *cheela.* [<Hind. *chelā* disciple <Skt. *cheṭaka* servant, slave]

che·la² (kē′lə) *n. pl. ·lae* (-lē) *Zool* A terminal pincerlike claw in crustaceans and arachnids, as in lobsters and scorpions. [<NL <Gk. *chēlē* claw]

che·late (kē′lāt) *adj. Zool.* Having a chela or pincerlike claw; cheliform. —*n. Chem.* A compound which has been subjected to chelation.

che·la·tion (kē·lā′shən) *n. Chem.* The inactiva-tion of metallic ions in a solution by an or-ganic reagent with whose molecules they are strongly bound in a ring structure giving maxi-mum stability for specified uses. [<Gk. *chēlē* claw]

che·li·form (kē′lə·fôrm, kel′ə-) *adj. Zool.* Hav-ing the form of a chela of a lobster; pincerlike.

che·loid (kē′loid) See KELOID.

Che·lo·ni·a (ki·lō′nē·ə) *n.* An order of reptiles with external skeletons and toothless jaws, including tortoises and turtles. [<NL <Gk. *chelōnē* tortoise] —**che·lo′ni·an** *adj. & n.*

chem·i·cal (kem′i·kəl) *adj.* **1** Of or pertaining

to chemistry or its phenomena, laws, operations, or results: *chemical* analysis. **2** Obtained by or used in chemistry. Also *Obs.* **chem′ic.** — *n.* A substance obtained by or used in a chemical process. — **chem′i·cal·ly** *adv.*

chemical agent 1 Any of numerous chemical compounds used to effect a given purpose. **2** *Mil.* A poison gas, incendiary substance, or screening smoke.

chemical bond The force, usually exerted by shared electrons, which holds atoms together in a molecule.

chemical engineering That branch of engineering which studies, develops, and supervises the applications of chemistry to industrial processes.

chemical warfare The technique of using chemical agents, such as burning or poisonous gases, incendiary materials, etc., in defensive or offensive warfare.

chem·i·cide (kem′ə·sīd) *n.* Any of various preparations intended to kill pests or vermin by chemical action.

chem·i·cul·ti·va·tion (kem′i·kul′tə·vā′shən) *n.* The treatment of crops with special chemicals in order to destroy injurious weeds and insect pests.

chem·i·lu·mi·nes·cence (kem′i·lōō′mə·nes′əns) *n.* The emission of light from a substance undergoing a chemical reaction. — **chem′i·lu′mi·nes′cent** *adj.*

che·mise (shə·mēz′) *n.* **1** A woman's undergarment. **2** A muslin surgical dressing used mainly in rectal or bladder operations. **3** A dress style. [< F *LL camisia* shirt]

chem·i·sette (shem′i·zet′) *n.* An ornamental neckpiece or dickey usually made of muslin or lace, worn by women to fill in the open neck of a dress. [< F, dim. of *chemise* CHEMISE]

chem·ism (kem′iz·əm) *n.* Chemical affinity or attraction; chemical properties or activities collectively.

chem·i·sorb (kem′i·sôrb, -zôrb) *v.t.* To adsorb or take up by chemical means. — *v.i.* To be adsorbed in this manner, especially in the presence of a catalyst. — **chem′i·sorp′tion** *n.*

chem·ist (kem′ist) *n.* **1** One versed in chemistry. **2** *Brit.* A druggist. **3** *Obs.* An alchemist. [< ALCHEMIST]

chem·is·try (kem′is·trē) *n.* **1** That science which treats of the structure, composition, and properties of substances and of the transformations which they undergo. **2** Chemical composition or processes.

chemo– *combining form* Chemical; of or with chemicals or chemical reactions: *chemotherapy.* Also, before vowels, **chem–**; **chemi–**, as in *chemicide.* [< CHEMICAL]

chem·o·cep·tor (kem′ō·sep′tər) *n.* **1** *Physiol.* An organ or nerve element of the body specialized to receive and transmit chemical stimuli, as those of smell and taste. **2** *Biol.* Those receptors within a cell which are supposed to have the power of fixing chemicals. Also **chem′o·re·cep′tor.** [< CHEMO- + (RE)CEPTOR]

chem·o·sphere (kem′ə·sfir′) A region of the atmosphere ranging from 26 to 70 miles above the earth and marked by predominant photochemical activity.

chem·o·sur·ger·y (kem′ō·sûr′jər·ē) *n.* A medical technique which utilizes chemistry, surgery, and microscopic analysis, especially in the treatment of skin cancers.

chem·o·syn·the·sis (kem′ō·sin′thə·sis) *n.* The formation of organic compounds from inorganic constituents by the energy derived from chemical changes. — **chem·o·syn·thet·ic** (kem′ō·sin·thet′ik) *adj.*

chem·o·tax·is (kem′ō·tak′sis) *n.* *Biol.* The property which certain motile living cells possess of approaching (**positive chemotaxis**) or moving away from (**negative chemotaxis**) chemical substances: also called *chemotropism.* [< CHEMO- + Gk. *taxis* order < *tattein* arrange] — **chem′o·tac′tic** (-tak′tik) *adj.* — **chem′·o·tac′ti·cal·ly** *adv.*

chem·o·ther·a·peu·tant (kem′ō·ther′ə·pyōō′tant) *n.* Any substance used in the prevention, treatment, and cure of diseases by chemotherapy.

chem·o·ther·a·py (kem′ō·ther′ə·pē) *n. Med.* The treatment of diseases by the chemical disinfection of affected organs and tissues, especially through the use of synthetic drugs

---

whose action is specific against certain pathogenic micro–organisms but non–toxic to the patient. Also **chem′o·ther′a·peu′tics.** — **chem′o·ther′a·peu′tic** *adj.* — **chem′o·ther′a·peu′tic** *adj.* — **chem′o·ther′a·pist** *n.*

che·mot·ro·pism (ki·mot′rə·piz′əm) *n.* **1** *Biol.* The response of a plant or animal organism to a chemical reaction, as by unequal growth or directed movements. **2** Chemotaxis. [< CHEMO- + TROPISM] — **chem·o·trop·ic** (kem′ō·trop′ik) *adj.*

chem·ur·gy (kem′ər·jē) *n.* The chemical exploitation of organic raw materials, especially agricultural products, in the industrial development of new products. [< CHEM(O)- + -URGY] — **chem·ur·gic** (kem·ûr′jik) *adj.* — **chem·ur′gi·cal** *adj.*

Cheng·tu (chung′dōō′) The capital of Szechwan province, southern China.

che·nille (shə·nēl′) *n.* **1** A soft, fluffy cord or yarn of silk, rayon, cotton, wool, etc., having a fuzzy pile on all sides: used for embroidery, fringes, tassels, etc. **2** Any fabric made with such yarns, used for rugs, etc. [< F, caterpillar < L *canicula,* dim. of *canis* dog; from its fuzzy appearance]

of the goosefoot family, including American wormseed (*Chenopodium anthelminticum*), used as a remedy for intestinal worms. [< NL *chenopodium* < Gk. *chēn, chēnos* goose + *pous, podos*foot] — **che·no·po·di·a·ceous** (kē′nə·pō′dē·ā′shəs, ken′ə-) *adj.*

cher·ish (cher′ish) *v.t.* **1** To care for kindly; hold dear; treat with tenderness; foster. **2** To entertain fondly, as a hope or an idea; hold closely to. [< F *chériss-,* stem of *chérir* hold dear < *cher* dear < L *carus*] — **cher′ish·er** *n.*

Synonyms: cheer, comfort, encourage, entertain, foster, harbor, nourish, nurse, nurture, protect, shelter, treasure, value. To *cherish* is both to hold dear and to treat as dear. To *nurse* is to tend the helpless or feeble. To *nourish* is strictly to sustain and build up by food; to *nurture* includes mental and spiritual training with love and tenderness; to *foster* is simply to maintain and care for.

CHESSBOARD
As at the beginning of a game.

B—Bishop	Kt (or N)—Knight	Q—Queen
K—King	P—Pawn	R—Rook

In chess notation the ranks (horizontal rows of squares) are numbered 1–8 reading away from each player, and each file (vertical row) is named for the piece standing at its head. The symbol for each piece is opposite the square it occupies at the beginning of the game, excepting the pawns, which are indicated at each end of the pawn rows. Bishops, knights, and rooks are named for the king or queen, according to their positions at the start. Pawns are named for the pieces they stand in front of.

cher·no·zem (cher′nə·zem) *n.* A soil typical of temperate subhumid grasslands, consisting of a very dark to black surface layer rich in organic materials overlying a layer of accumulated lime. [< Russian *chernozemu* black soil]

Cherokee rose A Chinese rose (*Rosa laevigata*) of trailing habit and having large, solitary white flowers, naturalized in the southern United States and the West Indies: the State flower of Georgia.

---

che·root (shə·rōōt′) *n.* A cigar cut square at both ends, generally of Manila or East Indian make: also spelled *sheroot.* [< F *cheroute* < Tamil *shuruttu* roll, cigar]

cher·ry (cher′ē) *n. pl.* **·ries 1** Any of various trees (genus *Prunus*) of the rose family, related to the plum and the peach and bearing small, round, or heart–shaped drupes enclosing a smooth pit; especially, the sweet cherry (*P. avium*), the sour cherry (*P. cerasus*), and the wild black cherry (*P. serotina*). **2** The wood or fruit of a cherry tree. **3** A bright–red color resembling that of certain cherries: also **cherry red.** — *adj.* **1** Like a cherry; red. **2** Made of cherry wood. [ME *chery,* back formation from AF *cherise* (mistaken for a plural) < L *cerasus* cherry tree < Gk. *kerasos*]

cher·ry·bird (cher′ē·bûrd′) *n.* The waxwing.

cherry bomb A red, round, highly explosive firecracker.

cherry bounce Brandy and sugar, in which cherries have been steeped.

cherry picker Any of several types of crane with a large bucket at the end of an articulated arm and mounted on a truck.

cherry stone 1 The pit of a cherry. **2** A small quahaug.

cher·so·nese (kûr′sə·nēz, -nēs) *n.* A peninsula. [< L *chersonesus* < Gk. *chersonēsos* < *chersos* dry + *nēsos* island]

chert (chûrt) *n.* A dull–colored, impure cryptocrystalline quartz or chalcedony: also called *hornstone.* [Origin uncertain]

cher·ub (cher′əb) *n. pl.* **cher·ubs** *for defs.* **1** *and* **2, cher·u·bim** (cher′ə·bim, -yə·bim) *for defs.* **3** *and* **4. 1** In art, the representation of a beautiful winged child, or the winged head of a child, the accepted type of the angelic cherub. **2** Hence, a beautiful child or infant. **3** One of an order of angelic beings ranking second to the seraphim in the celestial hierarchy. **4** In Scripture, an angelic being, especially as represented on the ark of the covenant, typifying the presence and power of the Deity. See *Ps.* xviii 10; *Ezek.* x; *Heb.* ix 5. [< LL < Hebrew *kerūbh,* an angelic being] — **che·ru·bic** (chə·rōō′bik) or **·bi·cal** *adj.* — **che·ru′bi·cal·ly** *adv.*

cher·vil (chûr′vəl) *n.* **1** Either of two European garden herbs (*Anthriscus cerefolium* or *Chaerophyllum bulbosum*) of the parsley family, the young leaves of which are used for soups, salads, etc. **2** Any one of several other plants of the same family: the great or sweet chervil (*Myrrhis odorata*). [OE *cerfille* < L *caerefolium* < Gk. *chairephyllon*]

Cheshire cat In Lewis Carroll's *Alice's Adventures in Wonderland,* a grinning cat that disappeared by gradually fading away until only its grin remained.

chess¹ (ches) *n.* A game of skill played by two persons on a checkered board (a **chess′board**) divided into 64 squares, with 16 pieces on each side. The aim of each player, proceeding by alternate moves, is to checkmate his opponent's king. [< OF *eschès,* pl. of *eschec.* See CHECK]

chess² (ches) *n.* **1** Any of several kinds of brome grass, especially *Bromus secalinus,* a pernicious weed in grain fields in America and Europe: also called *cheat.* **2** The darnel. [Origin uncertain]

chess³ (ches) *n.* The deck planks of a pontoon bridge. [Origin uncertain]

chest (chest) *n.* **1** A box of wood, metal, or other material, usually large, and having a hinged lid: used for valuables, tools, personal possessions, etc. **2** A receptacle for gases, liquids, etc.: a steam *chest.* **3** The part of the body enclosed by the ribs; the thorax. ◆ Collateral adjective: *pectoral.* **4** A case for packing certain commodities: a *chest* for indigo. **5** The quantity ordinarily carried in certain chests: a *chest* of tea. **6** A public treasury or fund; coffer; also, the funds contained there: the community *chest.* —**to get off one's chest** *Colloq.* To experience the relief of expressing openly (an emotion, opinion, etc.) that one has previously been at pains to withhold. [OE *cest* < L *cista* < Gk. *kistē* basket, box]

ches·ter·field (ches′tər·fēld) *n.* **1** A single-breasted topcoat of knee length, generally with concealed buttons and a velvet collar. **2**

A type of overstuffed sofa. [after an Earl of *Chesterfield* of the 19th c.]

chest·nut (ches'nut', -nət) *n.* 1 An edible nut, growing in a prickly bur. 2 Any of various trees (genus *Castanea*) of the beech family that bear this nut. 3 One of certain other trees: the horse *chestnut*. 4 A reddish-brown color; also, a horse of such a color. 5 *Colloq.* A worn-out joke; hence, anything trite. 6 A small, horny, wartlike callosity on the inner surface of the leg, as of a horse. —*adj.* 1 Reddish-brown. 2 Made of the wood of the chestnut tree. Also **ches'nut'.** [ME *chesten,* var. of *chesteine* < OF *chastaine* < L *castanea* < Gk. *kastanea* + NUT]

chest of drawers A piece of furniture consisting of a frame containing a set of drawers for storing linens, wearing apparel, etc.

chest on chest A chest of drawers in two sections, one placed upon the other which is usually wider and has feet.

chest register The lower or chest tones of the human voice.

che·tah (chē'tə) See CHEETAH.

cheth (kheth) See HETH.

che·vaux-de-frise (shə·val'də·frēz') *n. pl.* **che·vaux-de-frise** (shə·vō'-) 1 A portable obstacle of barbed wire supported on a sawhorse construction. 2 Formerly, an obstacle or obstruction of projecting spikes, used to hinder the progress of cavalry. [< F, lit., horse of Friesland; because first used by the Frisians]

che·va·let (shə·və·lā') *n.* The bridge of a stringed instrument. [< F, dim. of *cheval* horse]

che·val glass (shə·val') A full-length mirror mounted on horizontal pivots in a frame.

chev·a·lier (shev'ə·lir') *n.* 1 A knight or cavalier; especially, a French knight or nobleman. 2 *Obs.* A gallant gentleman; chivalrous man. 3 A member of the French Legion of Honor or other order of knighthood. 4 A cadet of the old French nobility who went into the army. 5 *Her.* An armed knight mounted. [< F < LL *caballarius.* Doublet of CAVALIER.]

che·vals (shə·valz') *n. pl.* Riding breeches.

chev·i·ot (shev'ē·ət) *n.* A type of rough woolen cloth of twill weave, used for suits, overcoats, etc., originally made from the wool of the Cheviot sheep.

chev·on (shev'ən) *n.* Goat flesh used as food. [< F *chèv(re)* goat, she-goat + *(mout)on* sheep]

chev·ron (shev'rən) *n.* 1 A V-shaped insigne, made of cloth and worn on the sleeve to indicate rank, rating, wounds, or length of service: used in the U.S. Army, the police force, etc. In the U.S. service, the rank of corporal is indicated by two chevrons, sergeant by three. 2 Any V-shaped mark or zigzag pattern, especially as used in Romanesque architecture: also **chevron molding.** 3 *Her.* An honorable ordinary. [< OF < Med. L *capro, -onis* rafter < L *caper* goat]

CHEVRONS
Sergeant—Army
a. United States.
b. Great Britain.
c. France.

chev·ro·tain (shev'rə·tān, -tin) *n.* A small, deerlike, hornless ruminant (family *Tragulidae*) of Africa and Asia; the mouse deer. [< F < OF *chevrot,* dim. of *chèvre* she-goat < L *capra,* fem. of *caper* goat]

chew (chōō) *v.t.* 1 To cut or grind with the teeth. 2 To meditate upon; consider carefully. —*v.i.* 3 To perform the act of cutting or grinding with the teeth: with *on* or *upon.* 4 To meditate: with *on* or *upon.* 5 *Colloq.* To use chewing tobacco continually. —**chew out** *Slang* To scold or reprimand severely. —**chew the fat** or **rag** *Slang* To chat; gossip —*n.* The act of chewing, or that which is chewed; a quid; cud: a *chew* of tobacco. [OE *cēowan*] —**chew'er** *n.*

chewing gum See under GUM.

che·wink (chi·wingk') *n.* One of several finches or buntings; especially, the towhee of the eastern United states. [Imit.]

chew·y (chōō'ē) *adj.* **chew·i·er, chew·i·est** Relatively soft and requiring chewing: Caramels are *chewy.* [< CHEW + -Y]

Chey·enne (shī·en') The capital of Wyoming.

chi (kī) The twenty-second letter in the Greek alphabet (see ALPHABET), transliterated into Latin, English, and German by *ch.*

chi·a (chē'ə) *n. SW U.S.* A Californian and Mexican herb (*Salvia columbariae*) of the mint family, whose seeds yield a beverage and an oil, **chia oil.** [< Sp. Nahuatl]

Chia·mus·su (jyä'mōō'sōō') See KIAMUSZE.

Chi·an (kī'ə) *adj.* Of, pertaining to, or produced in Chios: *Chian* wine. —*n.* A native of Chios.

Chiang Kai-shek (chäng' kī'shek', chang'; *Chinese* jyäng'), 1887–1975, Chinese generalissimo and statesman; head of the Nationalist government of the Republic of China: real name *Chiang Chung-cheng.*

chian·ti (kyän'tē) A red or white table wine from the Monti Chianti region; also, any similar wine.

chi·a·ro·scu·ro (kē·är'ə·skyŏŏr'ō) *n. pl.* **·ros** 1 The distribution and treatment of lights and shades in a picture. 2 A kind of painting or drawing using only light and shade to achieve its effects of depth, design, etc. 3 The characteristic use or mastery of light and shade by an artist. Also called *clair-obscure.* Also **chi·a·ro·scu·ro** (kē·är'ə·ō·skyŏŏr'ō). [< Ital. < *chiaro* clear (< L *clarus*) + *oscuro* dim, obscure < L *obscurus*]—**chi·a·ro·scu'rist** *n.*

chi·asm (kī'az·əm) *n.* 1 *Anat.* An intersecting or X-like commissure which unites the optic nerves at the base of the brain. 2 *Genetics* The point of intersection of two chromosomes. Also **chi·as·ma** (kī·az'mə). [< NL *chiasma* < Gk. < *chiazein* mark with a chi] —**chi·as'mal, chi·as'mic** *adj.*

chi·as·ma·ty·py (kī·az'mə·tī'pē) *n. Genetics* The intertwining of two homologous chromosomes during side-by-side conjugation of the chromosome threads in meiosis, resulting in blending and possible crossing over at points of contact. [< Gk. *chiasma* crossing + *typos* impression]—**chi·as'ma·type'** *adj. & n.*

chi·as·mus (kī·az'məs) *n.* In rhetoric, a contrast by parallelism in reverse order, as in Pope's "they fall successive, and successive rise." [< Gk. *chiasmos* < *chiazein* mark crosswise]

chi·as·to·lite (kī·as'tə·līt) *n. Mineral.* An andalusite in which the crystals in transverse section appear crossed or checkered: also called *macle.* [< Gk. *chiastos* crossed]

chic (shēk, shik) *adj.* Smart; stylish; elegant. —*n.* Originality, elegance, and taste, as in dress; smartness. [< F]

chi·ca·lo·te (chē'kä·lō'tā) *n.* A prickly poppy (*Argemone platyceras*) of the SW United States. [< Sp. < Nahuatl *chicalotl*]

chi·cane (shi·kān') *v.* **·caned, ·can·ing** *v.t.* 1 To overreach by trickery. 2 To quibble about. —*v.i.* 3 To resort to quibbles, shifts, or tricks. —*n.* 1 Mean, petty trickery, with pretense of fairness. 2 A bridge or whist hand containing no trumps. [< F *chicaner*]

chi·can·er·y (shi·kā'nər·ē) *n. pl.* **·er·ies** 1 The use of mean or paltry artifices, subterfuges, or shifts; especially, legal trickery or underhandedness. 2 A trick or dodge.

chick (chik) *n.* 1 A young chicken. 2 A child. 3 *Slang* A young woman. [Short for CHICKEN]

chick·a·dee (chik'ə·dē) *n.* An American titmouse (genus *Penthestes*) without a crest and with the top of the head and the throat black or dark-colored; especially, the black-capped chickadee (*P. atricapillus*) of eastern North America. [Imit. of its cry]

CHICKADEE

chick·a·ree (chik'ə·rē) *n.* The American red squirrel (*Sciurus hudsonicus*), smallest of the tree-climbing diurnal squirrels. [Imit. of its cry]

chick·en (chik'ən) *n.* 1 The young of the common domestic fowl. 2 Loosely, a fowl of any age; also, its flesh used as food. 3 *Colloq.* A child; an inexperienced person. —*adj.* 1 Containing, made from, or flavored with chicken. 2 *Slang* Cowardly. —**to chicken out** *Slang* To refrain from doing something because of fear or cowardice. [< OE *cycen*]

chicken hawk One of various hawks that prey on poultry; especially, the eastern goshawk (*Astur atricapillus*), Cooper's hawk, and the red-tailed hawk of the eastern United States.

chick·en-heart·ed (chik'ən-här'tid) *adj.* Fainthearted or cowardly.

chick·en-liv·ered (chik'ən-liv'ərd) *adj.* Cowardly or timorous.

chicken louse One of a species of wingless insects (order *Mallophaga,* the bird lice) that live on chickens, where they feed on feathers and the epidermis. For illustration see INSECTS (injurious).

chicken pox *Pathol.* A contagious disease, principally of children, caused by a virus and characterized by eruptions, a slight fever, and a typically brief course; varicella.

chick·pea (chik'pē) *n.* 1 A plant (*Cicer arietinum*) of Mediterranean regions and central Asia. 2 Its edible seed, enclosed in short, hairy pods: widely used as a food in Asia and Latin America; Egyptian pea. [Alter. of ME *chich-pease* < F *pois chiche* < *pois* pease + *chiche* < L *cicer,* a small pea]

chick·weed (chik'wēd') *n.* A spreading, white-flowered, Old World starwort (*Stellaria media*), used for feeding caged birds.

chi·cle (chik'əl) *n.* 1 The milky juice of the sapodilla: used as the basic principle of chewing gum. 2 A gum prepared from it. Also **chicle gum.** [< Sp. < Nahuatl *chictli*]

chi·co (chik'kō) *n. pl.* **·cos** The western American greasewood (*Sarcobatus vermiculatus*). [< Sp. *chicalote*]

chic·o·ry (chik'ə·rē) *n. pl.* **·ries** 1 A perennial herb of the composite family (*Cichorium intybus*) with pink, white, or azure flowers: naturalized in the United States. 2 Its dried, roasted, and ground roots, used for mixing with coffee or as a coffee substitute. Also spelled *chiccory.* [< F *cichorée* < L *cicorium* < Gk. *kichora*]

chide (chīd) *v.t. & v.i.* **chid·ed** or **chid** (chid), **chid·ed** or **chid** or **chid·den** (chid'n), **chid·ing** To scold; utter words of reproof or reprimand. See synonyms under BLAME, REPROVE. [OE *cīdan*] —**chid'er** *n.*

chief (chēf) *n.* 1 A ruler, leader, head, principal actor or agent, or principal part of anything, as of a tribe, party, army, fleet, police force, government bureau, or establishment of any kind. 2 An official superior to another or others in office or authority; one having authority. 3 One who or that which is specially eminent, esteemed, efficient, or active. 4 *Her.* The upper part of a shield. See illustration under ESCUTCHEON. —*adj.* 1 Highest in rank or authority. 2 Principal, most important, or most eminent, in any respect. 3 Most distinguished, influential, valuable, or active. 4 Main; foremost; leading; greatest. See synonyms under FIRST, PARAMOUNT, PREDOMINANT. —**in chief** 1 At the head; in or having the highest place or authority: used in titles: commander *in chief.* 2 Chiefly. [< OF *chef, chief* < L *caput* head]

Synonyms (noun): captain, chieftain, commander, head, leader, master, principal, ruler, sachem. A *chief* is either the *ruler* of a tribe or the *head* of some department of established government; as, the *chief* of police. The word is colloquially applied to one holding some analogous position in literary or mercantile life, etc. *Chieftain* is now mainly employed in poetic and literary use; it has special historic application to the *head* of a Scottish clan. A *leader* is one who is voluntarily followed because of ability to overcome and control, or as the choice of a party. A *master* is one who can enforce obedience. The highest officer of any considerable military force is called the *commander;* of all the forces of a nation, the *commander in chief.* See MASTER. *Antonyms:* adherent, attendant, follower, minion, retainer, satellite, subaltern, subordinate, vassal.

chief justice The presiding judge of a court composed of several justices.

chief·ly (chēf'lē) *adv.* 1 Most of all or above all; preeminently; especially; particularly. 2 Generally; usually.

chief magistrate The highest administrative official of civil affairs in a community; also, loosely, the president of the United States.

Chief of Staff 1 The senior officer or head of a staff. 2 *U.S.* The principal staff officer in assistance to a command officer in higher

military echelons. Compare EXECUTIVE OFFICER. **3** The ranking officer in the U.S. Army or in the U.S. Air Force, immediately under the secretary of his department.
chief·tain (chēf′tən) n. **1** The head of a Highland clan. **2** Any chief; leader. See synonyms under CHIEF. [<OF *chevetain* <LL *capitaneus* <L *caput* head. Doublet of CAPTAIN.] —**chief′tain·cy, chief′tain·ship** n.
chiel (chēl) n. *Scot.* A lad; a fellow; a child. Also **chield** (chēld).
Chieng·mai (chyeng′mī′) See CHIANGMAI.
chiff·chaff (chif′chaf′, -chäf′) n. A small, brownish-white, Old World warbler (*Phylloscopus rufus*), known for its peculiar cry. [Imit.]
chif·fon (shi·fon′) n. **1** A sheer silk or rayon fabric. **2** *Obs.* Any decorative object worn by women, as a ribbon or sash. [<F, dim. of *chiffe* rag]
chif·fo·nier (shif′ə·nir′) n. **1** An ornamental cabinet. **2** A high chest of drawers. Also **chif′fon·nier′**. [<F *chiffonnier* <CHIFFON]
chif·fo·robe (shif′ə·rōb) n. An article of furniture having a wardrobe compartment alongside a chest of drawers. [<CHIFFO(NIER) + (WARD)ROBE]
chig·e·tai (chig′ə·tī) See DZIGGETAI.
chig·ger (chig′ər) n. **1** Any of certain mites of the southern United States whose larvae burrow under the skin: also spelled *jigger*. **2** The chigoe. [Alter. of CHIGOE]
chi·gnon (shēn′yon, *Fr.* shē·nyôn′) n. A knot or roll of hair worn at the back of the head by women. [<F]
chig·oe (chig′ō) n. **1** A flea (*Tunga penetrans*) of the West Indies and South America. The female burrows under the skin, especially of the feet, causing sores: also called *chigger* or *jigger*. **2** The chigger. Also spelled *chegoe*. [<F *chique* <Cariban]
chil·blain (chil′blān) n. *Pathol.* An inflammation of the hands or feet, caused by exposure to cold; erythema. [<CHILL+ BLAIN] —**chil′blained** adj.
child (chīld) n. pl. **chil·dren 1** An offspring of either sex of human parents; a son or daughter. **2** A young person of either sex at any age less than maturity, but most commonly one between infancy and youth. **3** A descendant in any degree: the *Children* of Israel. **4** A childish person; one immature in judgment or discretion. **5** A person or thing considered as an offspring or product: Poems are the *children* of fancy. **6** A follower or disciple. **7** *Law* A legitimate son or daughter. In some States, as in Louisiana, the term includes all descendants in the direct line. —**with child** Pregnant; enceinte. [OE *cild*] —**child′less** adj.
child·bear·ing (chīld′bâr′ing) n. Producing or giving birth to children.
child·bed (chīld′bed′) n. The state of a woman who is in labor or confined to bed as the result of it.
child·birth (chīld′bûrth′) n. Parturition. Also **child′bear′ing.**
child·hood (chīld′hood′) n. The state or time of being a child. —**second childhood** A time or state in which the physical and mental powers are enfeebled or impaired by old age; dotage.
child·ing (chīl′ding) adj. **1** Child-bearing; pregnant; hence, fruitful; productive. **2** *Bot.* Having young blossoms clustered around an older blossom.
child·ish (chīl′dish) adj. **1** Of, pertaining to, or characteristic of a child. **2** Puerile; petty; mentally or physically weak. —**child′ish·ly** adv. —**child′ish·ness** n.
   Synonyms: babyish, childlike, foolish, imbecile, infantile, paltry, petty, puerile, silly, trifling, trivial. *Childlike* refers to the lovable qualities, *childish* to the less desirable traits of childhood. See YOUTHFUL. *Antonyms:* bold, manly, masculine, mature, resolute, strong, vigorous, virile.
child labor 1 Work done by children. **2** The employment of minors under 14 or 16 in industry.
child·like (chīld′līk′) adj. **1** Like a child. **2** Artless; confiding. **3** Docile; submissive. Also **child′ly**. See synonyms under CHILDISH, YOUTHFUL. —**child′like′ness** n.
child·ness (chīld′nis) n. Childish nature, hu-

mor, character, or manners.
chil·dren (chil′drən) Plural of CHILD.
Children of Israel The descendants of Jacob; Israelites; the Jews.
child's play Any easy or simple activity.
chil·e (chil′ē) n. The acrid red pod or fruit of certain peppers, especially *Capsicum frutescens*, the source of red or cayenne pepper: also spelled *chilli, chilly*. Also **chill′i.** [<Sp. <Nahuatl *chilli*]
Chil·e (chil′ē, *Sp.* chē′lä) A republic on the SW coast of South America; 286,396 square miles; capital, Santiago. —**Chil′e·an** adj. & n.
chil·e con car·ne (chil′ē kon kär′nē) A Mexican dish of red peppers minced and mixed with meat, beans, spices, etc. [<Sp., chile with meat]
Chile saltpeter See under SALTPETER.
chile sauce A spiced condiment sauce made with tomatoes, red peppers, etc.
chil·i·ad (kil′ē·ad) n. **1** A thousand. **2** A period of a thousand years; a millennium. [<L *chilias* <Gk. *chilias, -ados* <*chilioi* thousand]
chil·i·asm (kil′ē·az′əm) n. The doctrine that Christ will reign upon earth a thousand years; the millennium. [<Gk. *chiliasmos* <*chilias*. See CHILIAD.] —**chil′i·ast** n. —**chil′i·as′tic** adj.
chill (chil) n. **1** A sensation of cold, as that which precedes a fever, often with shivering or shaking. **2** A disagreeable feeling of coldness. **3** A check to ardor, joy, or the like. **4** *Metall.* A metal mold so constructed as to cool suddenly the surface of iron cast therein: also called *coquille*. —*v.t.* **1** To reduce to a low temperature. **2** To make chilly; seize with a chill. **3** To discourage; dispirit; check, as ardor. **4** To harden (metal) by sudden cooling. —*v.i.* **5** To become cold. **6** To be stricken with a chill. **7** To harden by sudden cooling, as metal. —*adj.* **1** Moderately, unpleasantly, or injuriously cold; chilly. **2** Somewhat affected by cold; feeling cold. **3** Cold in manner or disposition; distant; formal. **4** Dispiriting; discouraging. See synonyms under BLEAK. [OE *ciele, cyle*] —**chill′ing·ly** adv. —**chill′ness** n.
chill·er (chil′ər) n. **1** One who or that which chills. **2** *Metall.* One who sprays hot molds with water in steelworking. **3** *Slang* A horror story or moving picture.
chil·li (chil′ē) See CHILE.
chill·y[1] (chil′ē) adj. **chill·i·er, chill·i·est 1** Producing or feeling cold. **2** Disheartening; depressing. **3** Not genial or cordial; unfriendly. —**chil′i·ly** adv. —**chill′i·ness** n.
chill·y[2] (chil′ē) See CHILE.
chilo- *combining form* Lip: *Chilopoda*. Also, before vowels, **chil-**. [<Gk. *cheilos* lip]
chi·lo·pod (kī′lə·pod) n. Centipede. —**chi·lop·o·dan** (kī·lop′ə·dən) adj. & n.
chi·lo·pod·ol·o·gy (kī′lə·pə·dol′ə·gē) n. The branch of zoology concerned with centipedes. —**chi·lo·pod·ol′o·gist** n.
chime[1] (chīm) v. **chimed, chim·ing** *v.t.* **1** To cause to ring musically; play tunefully with or upon, as by striking. **2** To announce, as the hour, by the sound of bells. **3** To summon, welcome, or send by chiming. **4** To recite in unison or cadence. —*v.i.* **5** To ring out in harmony or unison, as bells. **6** To extract melodious sound, as by striking a bell or set of bells. **7** To harmonize; agree: with *with*: Her remarks *chimed* with his intentions. **8** To recite or intone in cadence. —**to chime in 1** To be in accord with; agree. **2** To take part in or interrupt, as a conversation. —*n.* **1** A set of bells tuned to a scale. **2** The mechanism for ringing the changes on bells; also, the music from such bells. **3** Accord; harmony. [ME *chimbe, chime,* alter. of OE *cimbal* <L *cymbalum* cymbal] —**chim′er** n.
chime[2] (chīm) n. **1** The edge or brim of a cask, barrel, or tub: also **chine. 2** A channel in a vessel's deck. —*v.t.* To make a chime in (a stave, etc.). Also **chimb** (chīm). [OE *cimb-* edge, as in *cimbing* a joint]
chi·me·ra (kə·mir′ə, kī-) n. **1** An absurd creation of the imagination; a groundless or impracticable conception or fancy; any horrible fancy. **2** *Bot.* A novel or unusual plant growth caused by the grafting of tissue from two or more plants; a graft hybrid of mixed characteristics. **3** *Biol.* An organism incorporating cells of more than one genotype. Also **chi·mae′ra.** [See CHIMERA]
chi·mere (chi·mir′, shi-) n. **1** The sleeveless upper robe of a bishop. **2** *Obs.* A loose upper robe.

Also **chim·ar** (chim′ər, shim′-), **chim′er.** [<OF *chamarre*]
chi·mer·i·cal (kə·mer′i·kəl, kī-) adj. **1** Like a chimera; imaginary; fanciful. **2** Impracticable; visionary. See synonyms under FANCIFUL. IMAGINARY, ROMANTIC. Also **chi·mer′ic.** —**chi·mer′i·cal·ly** adv.
chim·ney (chim′nē) n. **1** A flue for the smoke or gases from a fire. **2** A structure containing it, or something resembling such a structure. **3** A tube for enclosing a flame, as of a lamp. **4** *Obs.* A fireplace, hearth, or forge. **5** *Geol.* A formation of rock shaped like a chimney; specifically, a cleft in a steep mountain cliff or rock wall, wide enough to admit a climber's body and which can be ascended by pressure against the opposite sides. **b** A long spur of ore extending downward through the main vein; a pipe. [<OF *cheminée* <LL *caminata* <L *caminus* furnace, oven <Gk. *kaminos*]
chimney pot A pipe on the top of a chimney, to improve the draft.
chimney swallow 1 The chimney swift. **2** The European swallow.
chim·ney·sweep (chim′nē·swēp′) n. One who cleans chimneys, especially by the old method of ascending the flue. Also **chim′ney·sweep′er.**
chimney swift An American swift that nests in chimneys. See under SWIFT.
chim·pan·zee (chim′pan·zē′, chim·pan′zē) n. A West African arboreal anthropoid ape (*Pan troglodytes*), about 5 feet in height, with very large ears, dark-brown hair, smaller, less erect, and more intelligent than the gorilla. [<native West African name]

CHIMPANZEE
(About 4 1/2 feet standing erect)

chin (chin) n. **1** *Anat.* The central and anterior part of the lower jaw. ◆Collateral adjectives: *genial*[1], *mental*[2]. **2** *Entomol.* The second sclerite of the labium of an insect. **3** *Zool.* A small ciliated muscular process below the mouth, as in certain rotifers (genus *Pedalion*). —*v.* **chinned, chin·ning** *v.t.* To lift (oneself) by the hands until the chin is level with the hands. —*v.i. U.S. Colloq.* To talk idly. [OE *cin*]
chi·na (chī′nə) n. Porcelain or porcelain ware, originally from China. Also **chi′na·ware′.** —*adj.* Relating to or made of porcelain.
Chi·na (chī′nə) A country of eastern Asia, the most populous and second largest in the world; 3,800,000 square miles; divided (1949) into the **People's Republic of China;** capital, Peking; and the **Republic of China;** temporary capital, Taipei, on Taiwan. Abbr. *Chin., Ch.*
china bark 1 Cinchona bark. **2** Quillai.
chi·na·ber·ry (chī′nə·ber′ē) n. pl. **·ries** The baccate fruit of the chinaberry tree (def. 2).
chinaberry tree 1 The azedarach. **2** Either of two trees (*Sapindus saponaria* and *S. marginatus*) of the soapberry family: found in Mexico and the SW United States, where each is known as the **China tree.**
china closet A closet, cupboard, or cabinet, often with glass front and sides, for household china.
chin·ca·pin (ching′kə·pin) See CHINKAPIN.
chinch (chinch) n. **1** A small, brown and black hemipterous insect (*Blissus leucopterus*) destructive to grain: also **chinch bug. 2** The bedbug. [<Sp. *chinche* <L *cimex* bug]
chin·chil·la (chin·chil′ə) n. **1** A small rodent (*Chinchilla laniger*) native to the Andes, about the size of a squirrel, having a soft pearl-gray fur. **2** The valuable fur of this rodent. **3** A heavy, woolen, twilled fabric used for coating, having a napped surface that is rolled into little tufts or nubs: originally woven to resemble chinchilla

chine[1] (chīn) *n.* **1** The spine, backbone, or back. **2** A piece of meat from the back. **3** A ridge. —*v.t.* **chined, chin·ing 1** To cut through the backbone of; cut into chines. **2** To cut up. [< OF *eschine* backbone < Gmc.]

chine[2] (chīn) See CHIME[2].

chine[3] (chīn) *n. Geog.* A deep or narrow ravine or fissure. [OE *cinu*]

Chi·nese (chī·nēz′, -nēs′) *adj.* Of or pertaining to the Chinese Republic or China, its people, or their languages. —*n. pl.* **·nese 1** A native or naturalized inhabitant of China. **2** The standard language of China, based on the language spoken in Peking; Mandarin. **3** A subfamily of the Sino-Tibetan family of languages, including the many languages and dialects spoken in China, as those of Peking, Canton, Amoy, Foochow, etc. **4** Any of these languages or dialects, some of which are mutually unintelligible.

chink[1] (chingk) A small, narrow cleft; crevice. —*v.t.* **1** To make cracks or fissures in. **2** To fill the cracks of, as a wall; plug up. —*v.i.* **3** To open in clefts or cracks; crack. [ME *chynke*] —**chink′y** *adj.*

chink[2] (chingk) *n.* **1** A short, sharp, metallic sound. **2** *Slang* Coin; ready money; cash. —*v.t. & v.i.* To make or cause to make a short, sharp, clinking sound by striking together, as coins. [Imit.]

chintz (chints) *n.* A cotton fabric printed in various colors and usually glazed. Also **chints.** [< Hind. *chint* < Skt. *chitra* variegated]

chintz·y (chints′ē) *adj.* **chintz·i·er, chintz·i·est 1** Decorated with chintz. **2** *Colloq.* Cheap; sleazy. **3** *Slang* Stingy.

chi·no (chē′nō) *n.* **1** A strong, mercerized cotton fabric with a twilled weave. **2** *pl.* Trousers or slacks made of this material. [< Sp., toasted; with ref. to the original tan color]

chi·nook (chi·nook′, -nook′) *n. Meteorol.* **1** A warm wind off the Oregon and Washington coasts; first named because it came from the direction of Chinook territory. **2** A warm, dry wind that descends the eastern slopes of the Rocky Mountains in the NW United States and western Canada. **3** Any warm wind occurring during the cold season in the western United States: often called *snow-eater*.

chip[1] (chip) *n.* **1** A small piece cut or broken off. **2** A small disk or counter used in games, as in poker. **3** One of the dried droppings of animals available as fuel: usually in the plural: buffalo *chips.* **4** Anything insipid, vain, or worthless. **5** An overdone piece of meat, etc. **6** A small, crisp morsel: potato *chips.* **7** A crack produced by chipping. **8** A very small piece of silicon on which integrated circuits can be printed. —**a chip off the old block** *Colloq.* A child that resembles either of its parents. —*v.* **chipped, chip·ping** *v.t.* **1** To break or scale off a part of, as a piece of china. **2** To chop or cut, as with an ax or chisel. **3** To hew or shape by cutting off pieces. **4** *Obs.* To pare, as a crust of bread. —*v.i.* **5** To scale off in small pieces. **6** In golf, to hit a chip shot. —**to chip in 1** *Colloq.* To contribute, as help or money. **2** In poker, to put chips in as one's ante or bet. [ME *chippe.* Related to CHAP, CHOP.] —**chip′per** *n.*

chip[2] (chip) *v.i.* To cheep. —*n.* A squeak or weak chirp, as of a bird or mouse. [Imit.]

chip[3] (chip) *n.* In wrestling, a leg movement to trip one's opponent. [Cf. ON *kippa* a pull, sudden motion]

chip·munk (chip′mungk) *n.* Any of various striped North American rodents of the squirrel family of terrestrial or burrowing habits; especially, the common *Tamias striatus* of the eastern United States and Canada, and the genus *Eutamias* of the West, having many subspecies: also called *ground squirrel, striped squirrel.* Also **chip·muck** (chip′muk), **chipping squirrel.** [< N. Am. Ind.]

CHIPMUNK
(About 6 1/2 inches long; tail, 4 1/2 inches)

chipped (chipt) *adj.* Smoked and sliced thin, as beef.

chip·per (chip′ər) *v.i.* **1** To chirp, as a bird; twitter; babble, as a brook. **2** To talk quickly, in a heated way; be rude. —*adj.* **1** Brisk; hearty; cheerful. **2** Neat; spruce; smart. [< CHIP[2]]

Chip·pe·wa (chip′ə·wä, -wä, -wə) *n. pl.* **·wa** or **·was** Ojibwa. Also **Chip·pe·way** (chip′ə·wā).

chip·py (chip′ē) *n. pl.* **·pies 1** The chipping sparrow. **2** A squirrel or chipmunk. **3** *Slang* **a** A promiscuous girl or woman. **b** A prostitute.

chip shot In golf, a short, lofted shot made in approaching the green.

chi·ral·i·ty (kī·ral′ə·tē) *n. Chem., Physics.* The property by which a form is distinguishable from its mirror image; handedness. [< Gk. *cheir* hand] —**chi·ral** (kī′rəl) *adj.*

chir·i·men (chir′i·men) *n.* A Japanese silk crêpe fabric. [< Japanese]

chirk (chûrk) *v.i.* **1** *Scot.* To make a screeching or gritting noise; creak; shriek. **2** *Colloq.* To be or become cheerful: with *up.* [OE *cearcian* creak]

chirm (chûrm) *n.* Twittering; warbling, as of many birds or insects. —*v.i.* To make a twittering sound. [OE *cirm* < *cirman* cry out]

chiro- *combining form* Hand; of or with the hand: *chirograph.* Also, before vowels, **chir-**: also spelled **cheiro-.** [< Gk. *cheir, cheiros* hand]

chi·rog·no·my (kī·rog′nə·mē) *n.* The study of the hand as a means of interpreting character and personality. [< CHIRO- + -GNOMY]

chi·rog·nos·tic (kī′rog·nos′tik) *adj.* Having the ability to distinguish between the right and left sides of the body. [< CHIRO- + Gk. *gignōskein* know]

chi·ro·graph (kī′rə·graf, -gräf) *n. Law* A legal paper, as an acknowledgment of a debt written in the handwriting of the borrower.

chi·rog·ra·phy (kī·rog′rə·fē) *n.* The art, style, or character of handwriting. —**chi·rog′ra·pher** *n.* —**chi·ro·graph·ic** (kī′rə·graf′ik) or **·i·cal** *adj.*

chi·ro·man·cy (kī′rə·man′sē) *n.* Palmistry. —**chi′ro·man·cer, chi′ro·mant** *n.*

chi·ron·ja (chē·rōn′hä) *n.* A citrus fruit produced by crossing the grapefruit with the orange. [< Am. Sp. *china* orange + *toronja* grapefruit]

chi·ro·plas·ty (kī′rə·plas′tē) *n.* Plastic surgery of the hand.

chi·rop·o·dy (kə·rop′ə·dē, kī-) *n.* The treatment of ailments of the foot, as bunions, corns, etc. See PODIATRY. [< CHIRO- + Gk. *pous, podos* foot] —**chi·rop′o·dist** *n.*

chi·ro·prac·tic (kī′rə·prak′tik) *n.* A method of therapy based on the theory that disease is mainly due to a malfunction of the nerves which may be corrected by manipulation of bodily structures, especially the spinal column. [< CHIRO- + Gk. *praktikos* effective < *prattein* do, act] —**chi·ro·prac·tor** (kī′rə·prak′tər) *n.*

chi·rop·ter (kī·rop′tər) *n.* A bat; any member of the order Chiroptera. [< CHIRO- + Gk. *pteron* wing] —**chi·rop′ter·an** *adj. & n.*

chirp (chûrp) *v.i.* **1** To give a short, acute cry, as a sparrow, locust, or cricket; to cheep, as a young bird. **2** To make a similar sound, as in urging a horse. **3** To talk in a quick and cheerful manner. —*v.t.* **4** To utter with a quick, sharp sound. —*n.* A short, sharp sound, as made by some birds and insects. [ME *chirpen*, var. of *chirken* CHIRK.] —**chirp′er, n.** —**chirp′ing·ly** *adv.*

chirr (chûr) *v.i.* To make a sharp trilling sound, as that of the grasshopper, cicada, and some birds: chirp. —*n.* The trilling sound made by crickets, locusts, cicadas, etc. Also **chirre.** [Imit.]

chir·rup (chir′əp) *v.i.* **1** To chirp continuously or repeatedly, as a bird. **2** To chirp with the lips, as in urging or calling a horse. —*v.t.* **3** To utter with chirps. —*n.* A chirp; a cheery sound. [< CHIRP] —**chir′rup·y** *adj.*

chis·el (chiz′əl) *n.* A cutting tool with a beveled edge, used for cutting, engraving, or mortising metal, stone, or wood. —*v.* **chis·eled** or **·elled, chis·el·ing** or **·el·ling** *v.t.* **1** To cut, engrave, or carve, as with a chisel. **2** *Colloq.* To cheat; swindle. **3** *Colloq.* To obtain by dishonest or unfair methods. —*v.i.* **4** To use a chisel. **5** *Colloq.* To use dishonest or unfair methods. [< AF, ult. < L *caedere* cut] —**chis′el·er** or **chis′el·ler** *n.*

chis·eled (chiz′əld) *adj.* Distinctly outlined; finely molded with, or as with, a chisel; clearcut.

Also **chis′elled.**

chit-chat (chit′chat′) *n.* **1** Informal or familiar talk. **2** Gossip.

chi·tin (kī′tin) *n. Biochem.* A colorless, horny, amorphous polysaccharide, intermediate between proteins and carbohydrates, forming the principal constituent of the hard covering of insects and crustaceans. [< F *chitine* < Gk. *chitōn* tunic] —**chi′ti·nous** *adj.*

chit·ter·ling (chit′ər·ling) *n.* **1** *pl.* The small intestine of pigs or calves, especially as prepared as food: also **chit′ling. 2** *pl.* Shreds: torn to *chitterlings.* **3** *Archaic* A short frill having wrinkled folds. [< G *kutteln* entrails]

chiv (chiv) See SHIV.

chiv·al·rous (shiv′əl·rəs) *adj.* **1** Having the qualities of the ideal knight: gallant, courteous, generous, brave, etc. **2** Pertaining to the feudal system of chivalry. See synonyms under BRAVE. —**chiv′al·rous·ly** *adv.* —**chiv′al·rous·ness** *n.*

chiv·al·ry (shiv′əl·rē) *n.* **1** The feudal system of knighthood; knight-errantry; also, the spirit and customs of medieval knight-errantry. **2** Disinterested courtesy; bravery; magnanimity. **3** A body of knights, warriors, or gallant gentlemen. **4** *Obs.* Mounted and armed fighting men. [< OF *chevalerie* < LL *caballarius* cavalier. Doublet of CAVALRY.] —**chiv·al·ric** (shiv′əl·rik, shi·val′rik) *adj.*

chiv·a·ree (shiv′ə·rē′) See CHARIVARI.

chive (chīv) *n.* A perennial herb (*Allium schoenoprasum*) allied to the leek and onion: used as a flavoring in cooking. Also **chive garlic.** [< AF < L *cepa* onion]

chiv·y (chiv′ē) *v.t. & v.i.* To chevy. Also **chiv′vy.**

chlam·y·date (klam′ə·dāt) *adj. Zool.* Having a mantle, as certain mollusks. [< L *chlamydatus* cloaked < Gk. *chlamys, -ydos* cloak]

chla·myd·e·ous (klə·mid′ē·əs) *adj. Bot.* Pertaining to the floral envelope of a plant. [< Gk. *chlamys, -ydos* cloak]

chlam·y·do·spore (klam′i·dō·spôr′, -spōr′) *n.* **1** *Bot.* A non-sexual accessory spore in certain fungi, possessing a very thick membrane. **2** *Zool.* A spore with protective envelope, as formed by fission from an encysted protozoan. [< Gk. *chlamys, -ydos* cloak + -SPORE]

chlor·a·cet·o·phe·none (klôr′ə·set′ə·fi·nōn′, klôr′-) *n. Chem.* A colorless, crystalline compound, C_8H_7ClO, with an odor of apple blossoms: it is used as a lacrimator and harassing agent in chemical warfare. Symbol, CN. [< CHLOR- + ACETO- + PHEN(YL) + -ONE]

chlor·ac·ne (klôr·ak′nē, klôr-) *n.* A severe skin disorder resembling acne and caused by exposure to chlorinated organic compounds, especially dioxin.

chlo·ral (klôr′əl, klō′rəl) *n. Chem.* **1** A colorless, oily, liquid compound, CCl_3CHO, with a penetrating odor, obtained variously, as by the action of chlorine on alcohol. **2** A white crystalline pungent compound, $CCl_3CHO·H_2O$, used medicinally as a hypnotic, etc., which in large doses acts as a poison, paralyzing the heart: also **chloral hydrate.** [< CHLOR(INE) + AL(COHOL)]

chlo·ra·mine-T (klôr′ə·mēn·tē′, klō′rə-) *n. Chem.* A white crystalline compound, $C_7H_7SO_2NClNa$, used as a surgical antiseptic and decontaminating agent for mustard gas. [< CHLOR- + -AMINE]

chlor·am·phen·i·col (klôr′am·fen′i·kōl, -kol, klō′ram-) *n. Chem.* A crystalline nitrogenous compound, $C_{11}H_{12}Cl_2O_5N_2$, obtained from a soil bacillus (*Streptomyces venezuelae*) and also made synthetically: used as an antibiotic in the treatment of certain viral, bacterial, and rickettsial diseases. [< CHLOR- + AM(IDE) + PHE(NOL) + NI(TROGEN) + (GLY)COL]

chlo·ran·thy (klə·ran′thē) *n. Bot.* The transformation into leaflike organs of the parts of a flower. [< CHLOR- + Gk. *anthos* flower]

chlo·rate (klôr′āt, klō′rāt) *n. Chem.* A salt of chloric acid containing the univalent ClO_3 radical.

chlor·dane (klôr′dān, klō′r-) *n.* An oily, chlorinated hydrocarbon, $C_{10}H_6Cl_8$, used as an insecticide and very toxic to humans, being absorbable through the skin. Also **chlor·dan.**

chlo·ren·chy·ma (klə·reng′kə·mə) *n. Bot.* Stem tissue of a plant containing chlorophyll. [< CHLOR(OPHYLL) + (PAR)ENCHYMA]

chlo·ric (klôr′ik, klō′rik) *adj. Chem.* Of, pertaining to, or combined with chlorine: said specifically of chlorine compounds containing relatively more oxygen than the chlorous compounds.

chloric acid *Chem.* A monobasic, pungent acid, HClO₃, like nitric acid in oxidizing properties, but much less stable.

chlo·ride (klôr′īd, -id, klō′rīd, -rid) *n. Chem.* A compound of chlorine with a more positive element or radical, as hydrogen *chloride* (muriatic acid) or sodium *chloride* (common salt). — **chlo·rid·ic** (klə·rid′ik) *adj.*

chloride of lime *Chem.* A disinfecting and bleaching agent made by the action of chlorine gas on slaked lime; bleaching powder.

chlo·rin·ate (klôr′ə·nāt, klō′rə-) *v.t.* **·at·ed, ·at·ing** *Chem.* To treat, impregnate, or cause to combine with chlorine, as in whitening fabrics or separating gold from ore. —*n.* A soluble bleaching compound made by subjecting potassium or sodium hydroxide to the action of chlorine. — **chlo′rin·a′tion** *n.* —**chlo′rin·a′tor** *n.*

chlo·rine (klôr′ēn, -in, klō′rēn, -rin) *n.* A greenish-yellow, poisonous, readily liquefiable gaseous element (symbol Cl, atomic number 17), a very chemically active member of the halogens and an essential constituent of living organisms. See PERIODIC TABLE. [< Gk. *chlōros* green]

chlo·rin·i·ty (klə·rin′ə·tē) *n.* A measure of the total amount of chlorine per kilogram of sea water: it bears a constant relation to salinity according to the formula S = 0.03 × 1.805 × C.

chlo·rite (klôr′īt, klō′rīt) *n.* 1 Any one of several green hydrous silicates, closely related to the micas. 2 One of the salts of chlorous acid. [< Gk. *chlōritis* greenstone]

chloro- *combining form* 1 Light-green: *chlorophyll.* 2 Chlorine: *chlorohydrin.* Also, before vowels, *chlor-.* [< Gk. *chlōros* green]

chlo·ro·a·ce·tic acid (klôr′ō·ə·sē′tik, -ə·set′ik, klō′rō-) *Chem.* A colorless, corrosive compound, CH₂ClCOOH, derived from acetic acid in the form of deliquescent crystals: used chiefly in the synthesis of dyestuffs and in medicine as a caustic.

chlo·ro·form (klôr′ə·fôrm, klō′rə-) *n. Chem.* A colorless, volatile, sweetish liquid compound, CHCl₃, used as an anesthetic and anodyne and as a solvent of wax, resin, plastics, etc. —*v.t.* 1 To administer chloroform to. 2 To anesthetize or kill with chloroform. [< CHLORO- + FORM(YL)]

chlo·ro·hy·drin (klôr′ə·hī′drin, klō′rə-) *n. Chem.* Any of a group of organic compounds containing the hydroxyl radical and chlorine.

chlor·o·meth·ane (klôr′ə·meth′ān, klō′r-) *n.* Methyl chloride.

chlo·ro·phane (klôr′ə·fān, klō′rə-) *n.* A variety of fluorite emitting a green phosphorescence when heated. [< CHLORO- + Gk. *phainein* appear]

chlo·ro·phyll (klôr′ə·fil, klō′rə-) *n. Biochem.* The green nitrogenous coloring matter contained in the chloroplasts of plants and essential to their growth by photosynthesis of carbohydrates. It occurs in two forms: the bluish-green **chlorophyll-A,** C₅₅H₇₂O₅N₄Mg, the most abundant form; and the yellowish-green **chlorophyll-B,** C₅₅H₇₀O₆N₄Mg: some derivatives are used as dyes, in cosmetics, and in medicine as vulneraries. Also **chlo′ro·phyl.** [< CHLORO- + Gk. *phyllon* leaf] —**chlo·ro·phyl·la·ceous** (klôr′ə·fi·lā′shəs, klō′rə-), **chlo·ro·phyl′lose** (-fil′ōs), **chlo·ro·phyl′lous** (-fil′əs) *adj.*

chlo·ro·plast (klôr′ə·plast, klō′rə-) *n. Bot.* One of the flattened bodies or plastids containing chlorophyll found in the cell cytoplasm of plants. Also **chlo′ro·plas′tid.** [< CHLORO- + PLAST(ID)]

chlo·ro·prene (klôr′ə·prēn, klō′rə-) *n. Chem.* A colorless liquid, C₄H₅Cl, synthesized from acetylene and chlorine: in its polymerized forms it yields a number of compounds essential in the making of synthetic rubber. [< CHLORO- + (ISO)PRENE]

chlo·ro·sis (klə·rō′sis) *n.* 1 *Pathol.* An anemic disease affecting young women, characterized by a greenish pallor, hysteria, etc.; greensickness. 2 *Bot.* The blanching or etiolation of plants, usually caused by lack of iron and other mineral salts. [< NL < Gk. *chlōros* green] —**chlo·rot′ic**

(klə·rot′ik) *adj.*

chlor·pic·rin (klôr·pik′rin, klôr-) *n. Chem.* A colorless, oily liquid, CCl₃NO₂, obtained by distilling chloride of lime with picric acid; nitrochloroform: its nauseous vapor is called *vomiting gas.* Symbol, PS. Also **chlo′ro·pic′rin.**

chlor·pro·ma·zine (klôr·prō′mə·zēn, -zin, klôr-) *n. Med.* A synthetic ataractic drug used in the control of severe excitement in psychiatric cases, particularly of the manic-depressive type. [A composite word from dimethyl amino*propyl* *chloro*phenothi*azine* hydrochloride]

chlor·sul·fon·ic acid (klôr′sul·fon′ik, klôr-) *Chem.* A colorless, fuming liquid. HClSO₃, used as a smoke-producer in chemical warfare. Symbol, FS.

chlor·tet·ra·cy·cline (klôr′tet·rə·sī′klin, klôr-) *n. Chem.* An organic compound chemically related to tetracycline, obtained from the soil bacillus *Streptomyces aureofaciens:* used as an antibiotic, chiefly in the form known as Aureomycin.

cho·an·o·cyte (kō·an′ə·sīt) *n.* Collar cell. [< Gk. *choanē* funnel + -CYTE]

chock (chok) *n.* 1 A block or wedge, so placed as to prevent or limit motion. 2 *Naut.* A heavy piece of metal or wood fastened to a deck, or the like, and having jaws through which a rope or cable may pass. —*v.t.* To fit or wedge in tightly, as a boat, barrel, or wheel. —*adv.* 1 Completely: He stood *chock* still. 2 All the way: *chock* to the edge. [< AF *choque* log]

CHOCK

chock-full (chok′fŏŏl′) *adj.* 1 Completely full; full to crowding or choking. 2 Deeply moved with emotion. Also *choke-full.* [ME *chokke-fulle*]

chock·stone (chok′stōn′) *n. Geol.* A block or mass of loose rock wedged in a mountain chimney.

choc·o·late (chôk′lit, chôk′ə·lit, chok′-) *n.* 1 Cacao nuts roasted and ground without removing the fat, usually sweetened and flavored. 2 A beverage or confection made from this preparation. 3 Dark-brown color. —*adj.* Flavored, made with, or colored like chocolate. [< Sp. < Nahuatl *chocólatl*]

choice (chois) *n.* 1 The act, fact, power, or privilege of choosing; selection. 2 One who or that which is chosen or to be chosen; preference. 3 A number or a variety from which to choose; also, an alternative. 4 The power to prefer or select. 5 The right or privilege to choose; option. 6 The best part. See synonyms, under ALTERNATIVE. —*adj.* **choic·er, choic·est** 1 Meriting, preference; select; elegant; excellent; also, precious. 2 Dainty; fastidious. 3 *Dial.* Careful of; fond of. [< OF *choisir* choose] —**choice′ly** *adv.* *Synonyms (adj.):* cherished, chosen, costly, dainty, elegant, excellent, exquisite, nice, picked, precious, rare, select. See EXCELLENT. *Antonyms:* cheap, common, inferior, mean, ordinary, poor, valueless, worthless.

choir (kwīr) *n.* 1 A body of trained singers or that part of a church occupied by them; chancel. 2 Originally, any band or organized company, especially of dancers or singers. 3 One of the nine orders in the angelic hierarchy. —*v.i.* To sing, as in a choir. —*v.t.* To sing or utter in chorus. Also spelled *quire.* ♦Homophone: *quire.* [< OF *cuer* < L *chorus;* infl. in form by F *choeur.* Doublet of CHORUS.]

choke (chōk) *v.* **choked, chok·ing** *v.t.* 1 To stop the breathing of by obstructing or constricting the windpipe; strangle. 2 To keep back; suppress. 3 To fill completely. 4 To obstruct or close up by filling. 5 To retard the progress, growth, or action of. 6 To make a chokebore. 7 To lessen the air intake of the carburetor in order to enrich the fuel mixture of (a gasoline engine). —*v.i.* 8 To become suffocated or stifled. 9 To become clogged, fouled, or obstructed. —*n.* 1 The act of choking. 2 The narrowest part of a chokebored gun. 3 A device to control the supply of oxygen to a gasoline engine. 4 A choke coil. [OE *acēocian*]

choke·ber·ry (chōk′ber′ē, -bər·ē) *n. pl.* **·ries** A North American shrub (genus *Aronia*) of the rose family. 2 The small, red or purple astringent

fruit of this shrub.

choke·bore (chōk′bôr′, -bōr) *n.* 1 The bore of a shotgun narrowed at the muzzle. 2 A gun so bored.

choke·cher·ry (chōk′cher′ē) *n. pl.* **·ries** A North American wild cherry *(Prunus virginiana).*

choke coil *Electr.* A low-resistance coil of sufficient inductance to limit or suppress any fluctuating current without impeding the flow of a steady current.

choke·damp (chōk′damp′) *n.* A nonexplosive, asphyxiating atmosphere deficient in oxygen, found in mines, wells, etc. Also called *black-damp.*

chok·er (chō′kər) 1 One who or that which chokes. 2 *Colloq.* A wide white tie or neck cloth worn high around the throat. 3 A person who wears such a tie; especially, a minister. 4 A small fur neckpiece, closely fitting the neck. 5 A closely fitting necklace.

chok·y (chō′kē) *adj.* **chok·i·er, chok·i·est** 1 Suffocating; causing suffocation; stifling. 2 Somewhat choked: a *choky* voice. Also **chok′ey.**

chol·a·gog (kol′ə·gôg, -gog) *n. Med.* A purgative causing evacuations of bile. [< Gk. *cholagogos* < *cholē* bile + *agein* lead] —**chol·a·gog·ic** (kol′ə·goj′ik) *adj. & n.*

cho·lan·gi·ot·o·my (kə·lan′jē·ot′ə·mē) *n. Surg.* The opening of a bile duct through the substance of the liver, to remove gallstones. [< CHOLE- + ANGIO- -TOMY]

chol·an·gi·tis (kol′an·jī′tis) *n. Pathol.* Inflammation of the biliary ducts. Also **chol′an·gei′tis.** [< CHOL- + ANGIO- + -ITIS]

chole- *combining form* Bile; gall: *cholesterol.* Also, before vowels, **chol-:** also **cholo-.** [< Gk. *cholē* bile]

chol·e·cyst (kol′ə·sist) *n. Anat.* The gall bladder. [< NL *cholecystis* < Gk. *cholē* gall + *kystis* bladder]

cho·led·o·cho·plas·ty (kə·led′ə·kō·plas′tē) *n.* Plastic surgery on the bile duct. [< NL *choledochus* bile duct (< Gk. *cholē* bile + *dechesthai* contain) + -PLASTY] —**cho·led′o·cho·plas′tic** *adj.*

cho·le·mi·a (kə·lē′mē·ə) *n. Pathol.* The presence of bile in the blood; jaundice. Also **cho·lae′·mi·a.** [< CHOLE- + -EMIA]

chol·er (kol′ər) *n.* 1 Anger or hastiness of temper: formerly believed to be caused by disturbance of the liver or gall bladder. 2 *Obs.* Bile; also, biliousness. See synonyms under ANGER. [< OF *colère* < L *cholera* CHOLERA]

chol·er·a (kol′ər·ə) *n. Pathol.* An acute, infectious, chiefly epidemic disease, occurring in many forms and characterized principally by serious intestinal disorders: it is caused by a bacterium *(Vibrio comma)* and in its more malignant forms, as Asiatic cholera, is usually fatal. [< L < Gk., cholera morbus (in Hippocrates)]

cholera in·fan·tum (in·fan′təm) *Pathol.* A warm-weather, non-contagious, often fatal diarrhea of children, possibly caused by the bacterium *Vibrio proteus.* [< L, cholera of infants]

cholera mor·bus (môr′bəs) *Pathol.* Acute gastroenteritis, a warm-weather complaint. Also **cholera nos·tras** (nos′tras). [< L, cholera disease]

chol·er·ic (kol′ər·ik, kə·ler′ik) *adj.* 1 Of a bilious temperament; in a bilious condition. 2 Easily provoked; irascible. 3 Of the nature of anger. See synonyms under HOT.

cho·les·ter·ol (kə·les′tə·rōl) *n. Biochem.* A fatty monatomic crystalline alcohol. C₂₇H₄₅OH, derived principally from bile and present in most gallstones: it is found also in the blood, brain and nerve tissue, kidneys, liver, etc. Also **cho·les′ter·in.** [< CHOLE- + Gk. *stereos* solid + -OL²]

cho·lic acid (kō′lik, kol′ik) *Biochem.* A white, bitter crystalline acid; C₂₄H₄₀O₅, found in bile acids and in animal excrements.

cho·line (kō′lēn, kol′ēn, -in) *n.* An alkaline compound, C₅H₁₅NO₂, forming a part of the vitamin B complex and used in the biosynthesis of acetylcholine.

chol·la (chōl′yä) *n.* A variety of the prickly-pear cactus *(Cylindropuntia)* having spiny cylindrical stems: it is a frequent pest on stock ranges in the SW United States. [< Sp.]

chon·dri·fy (kon′drə·fī) *v.t. & v.i.* **·fied, ·fy·ing** To convert into or become cartilage. —**chon′dri·fi·ca′tion** *n.*

chon·dri·o·some (kon′drē·ə·sōm) *n.* *Biol.* A small granular body found, alone or in clusters, in the cytoplasm of a cell and subject to rapid changes both in shape and position: also called *mitochondria.* See illustration under CELL. [< Gk. *chondrion,* dim. of *chondros* cartilage + *sōma* body]

chon·drite (kon′drīt) *n.* A stony meteorite containing chondrules. —**chon·drit·ic** (kon·drit′ik) *adj.*

chondro- *combining form* 1 Cartilage: chondrotomy. 2 Grain: *chondr*ule. Also, before vowels, **chondr-.** [< Gk. *chondros* cartilage]

chon·droid (kon′droid) *adj.* Resembling cartilage.

chon·dro·ma (kon·drō′mə) *n.* *pl.* **·mas** or **·ma·ta** (-mə·tə) *Pathol.* A cartilaginous tumor.

chon·drot·o·my (kon·drot′ə·mē) *n.* *Surg.* The cutting of cartilages. [< CHONDRO- + -TOMY]

chon·drule (kon′drool) *n.* Any of the small, rounded beads of various mineral composition found embedded in chondrites.

choose (chōōz) *v.* **chose, cho·sen, choos·ing** *v.t.* 1 To select as most desirable; take by preference; elect. 2 To desire or have a preference for. 3 To please or think proper (to do something): with infinitive as object. —*v.i.* 4 To make selection or decision. 5 To have an alternate. —**cannot choose but** Has no alternative choice. —**to pick and choose** To select with great deliberation. [OE *cēosan*] —**choos′er** *n.*

Synonyms: cull, elect, pick, prefer, select. *Prefer* indicates a state of desire and approval; *choose,* an act of will. Prudence or generosity may lead one to *choose* what he does not *prefer. Select* implies a careful consideration of the reasons for preference and choice. Among objects so nearly alike that we have no reason to *prefer* any one to another, we may simply *choose* the nearest, but we could not be said to *select* it. Aside from theology, *elect* is popularly confined to the political sense; as, a free people *elect* their own rulers. *Cull* means to collect, as well as to *select.* In a garden we *cull* the choicest flowers. To *pick* is to *choose* for special fitness; as, a guard of *picked* men; *chosen,* in this sense, is somewhat archaic. *Antonyms:* decline, disclaim, dismiss, leave, refuse, reject.

choos·y (chōō′zē) *adj.* **choos·i·er, choos·i·est** *Colloq.* Disposed to be particular or fussy in one's choices.

chop[1] (chop) *v.* **chopped, chop·ping** *v.t.* 1 To cut or make by strokes of a sharp tool; hew. 2 To cut up in small pieces; mince. 3 To utter jerkily; cut short. 4 To make a cutting, downward stroke at (the ball), as in tennis. —*v.i.* 5 To make cutting strokes, as with an ax. 6 To interrupt abruptly, as in conversation: with *in:* to *chop in* with a remark. 7 To go, come, or move with sudden or violent motion. —*n.* 1 A cut of meat, chopped off, usually containing a rib. 2 A cleft or fissure; a crack, especially in the lip. 3 The act of chopping. 4 A tool for chopping. 5 A sudden bite or snap. 6 A sudden motion of waves; also, a choppy sea. 7 In boxing, a short, sharp, downward punch. 8 In tennis or cricket, a sharp, cutting, downward stroke. [ME *choppen.* Related to CHAP, CHIP.]

chop[2] (chop) *v.t.* 1 *Obs.* To barter; exchange. —*v.i.* 2 To veer suddenly; shift, as the wind; vacillate. 3 *Obs.* To bargain; barter. [ME *choppen.* Related to CHEAP.]

chop[3] (chop) *n.* 1 A jaw. 2 *pl.* The jaws and the parts about the mouth. 3 *pl.* The entrance or mouth of a harbor, channel, valley, etc.; especially, the entrance of the English Channel from the Atlantic. —*v.t.* 1 To seize with the jaws; snap. 2 To utter quickly and sharply. Also spelled *chap.* [Var. of CHAP[3]]

cho·pine (chō·pēn′, chop′in) *n.* A high clog worn under a shoe. Also **chop·in** (chop′in). [< Sp. *chapin* < *chapu* metal plate]

CHOPINE

chop·per (chop′ər) *n.* 1 One who or that which chops. 2 *Telecom.* A device, usually one that rotates, used to interrupt a continuous-wave radio signal in a transmitter or receiver. 3 *pl. Slang* Teeth. 4 *Slang* A helicopter.

chop·py[1] (chop′ē) *adj.* **·pi·er, ·pi·est** Full of cracks, chops, or fissures.

chop·py[2] (chop′ē) *adj.* 1 Full of short, rough waves. 2 Variable; shifting, as wind.

chop shop A place where stolen cars are disassembled so that their parts can be sold.

chop·sticks (chop′stiks′) *n. pl.* Slender rods of ivory or wood, used in pairs, in China, Japan, etc., to convey food to the mouth. [< Pidgin English *chop* quick + STICK; trans. of Chinese name]

chop-su·ey (chop′sōō′ē) *n.* A Chinese-American dish consisting of fried or stewed meat or chicken, bean sprouts, onions, celery, mushrooms, etc., cooked in their own juices and served with rice. [< Chinese *tsa-sui,* lit., mixed pieces]

cho·ral[1] (kə·ral′) *n.* A hymn characterized by a simple melody and firm rhythm, and often sung in unison. Also **cho·rale′.** [< G *choral*]

cho·ral[2] (kôr′əl, kō′rəl) *adj.* 1 Pertaining to a chorus or choir. 2 Written for or sung by a chorus. [< Med. L *choralis* < L *chorus* CHORUS] —**cho′ral·ly** *adv.*

chord[1] (kôrd) *n.* *Music* A combination of three or more tones sounded together according to the laws of harmony. The most important chords are the **common chord,** consisting of a fundamental tone with its major or minor third and its perfect fifth, and the **chord of the seventh,** called the dominant seventh. —*v.i.* To be in harmony or accord. ◆ Homophone: *cord.* [Earlier *cord,* short for ACCORD; form infl. by CHORD[2]]

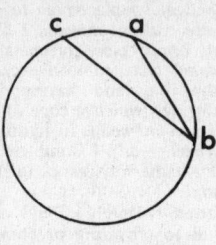

CHORD
cb and *ab* are chords.

chord[2] (kôrd) *n.* 1 A string or cord of a musical instrument; hence, emotional response or reaction. 2 *Geom.* A straight line connecting the extremities of an arc; a secant; the portion of a straight line contained by its intersections with a curve. 3 *Eng.* One of the principal members of a bridge truss, horizontal or inclined. 4 *Anat.* A tendon, a connective ligament. 5 *Aeron.* The length of an airplane. ◆ Homophone: *cord.* [< L *chorda* < Gk. *chordē* string of a musical instrument. Doublet of CORD.] —**chord′al** *adj.*

chore (chôr, chōr) *n.* 1 A small job. 2 *pl.* The routine duties of a household or farm. 3 An unpleasant or hard task. [Var. of CHAR[1]] **-chore** *combining form Bot.* Denoting a plant that is distributed in a specified manner: *anemochore.* [< Gk. *chorein* spread]

cho·re·a (kô·rē′ə, kō-) *n.* *Pathol.* A nervous disease characterized by involuntary muscular twitching; St. Vitus's dance. [< NL < Gk. *choreia* dance] —**cho·re′al** *adj.*

cho·re·o·graph (kôr′ē·ə·graf, kō′rē-) *v.t.* To provide the choreography for.

cho·re·og·ra·phy (kôr′ē·og′rə·fē, kō′rē-) *n.* 1 The art of devising ballets and incidental dances. 2 The written representation of figures and steps of dancing. 3 The art of dancing; ballet. Also **cho·reg·ra·phy** (kə·reg′rə·fē). [< Gk. *choreia* dance + -GRAPHY] —**cho′re·og′ra·pher** *n.* —**cho′re·o·graph′ic** *adj.*

cho·ri·amb (kôr′ē·amb, kō′rē-) *n.* In prosody, a metrical foot of four syllables, the second and third short and the others long (- ˘ ˘ -). Also **cho·ri·am·bus** (kôr′ē·am′bəs, kō′rē-). [< L *choriambus* < Gk. *choriambos* < *choreios* trochee + *iambos* iambus] —**cho′ri·am′bic** *adj. & n.*

cho·ri·on (kôr′ē·on, kō′rē-) *n.* 1 *Anat.* The external protective and nutritive membrane that invests the fetus of the higher vertebrates and attaches it to the uterus. 2 *Entomol.* The outer case of an insect egg. [< Gk. *chorion*]

cho·ri·pet·al·ous (kôr′ē·pet′əl·əs, kō′rē-) *adj. Bot.* Having free, unconnected petals; polypetalous. [< Gk. *chōris* apart + *petalon* leaf]

chor·is·ter (kôr′is·tər, kor′-) *n.* 1 A member of a choir; specifically, a male singer in a church choir. 2 A leader of a choir or of congregational singing; a precentor. 3 Any singer, as a bird.

cho·rog·ra·phy (kô·rog′rə·fē, kō-) *n. pl.* **·phies** 1 The delineation or mapping of regions. 2 A map or chart of any particular region. [<

Gk. *chōros* region + -GRAPHY] —**cho·rog′ra·pher** *n.* —**cho·ro·graph·ic** (kôr′ə·graf′ik, kō′rə) or **·i·cal** *adj.* —**cho′ro·graph′i·cal·ly** *adv.*

cho·roid (kôr′oid, kō′roid) *adj. Anat.* Resembling the chorion: said of highly vascular membranes. —*n.* The choroid coat, the middle or vascular tunic of the eyeball. See illustration under EYE. Also **cho·ri·oid** (kôr′ē·oid, kō′rē-).

cho·rol·o·gy (kô·rol′ə·jē, kō-) *n. Ecol.* The study of the migrations of plants and animals, especially in relation to areas of distribution. [< Gk. *chōros* region + -LOGY]

cho·ro·script (kôr′ə·skript, kō′rə-) *n.* A system of choreographic notation devised for the correct teaching and permanent recording of the steps and figures of a dance: also called *dance script.* [< Gk. *choros* dance + SCRIPT]

chor·tle (chôr′təl) *v.i.* **·tled ·tling** To chuckle or make a loud noise expressive of joy. —*n.* A chuckle; joyful vocal sound. [Blend of CHUCKLE and SNORT; coined by Lewis Carroll in *Through the Looking-Glass*]

cho·rus (kôr′əs, kō′rəs) *n.* 1 A musical composition, usually in parts, for performance by a large group of singers. 2 A body of singers, or singers and dancers, who perform together in concerts, opera, ballet, musical comedy, etc. 3 Any group of individuals singing or speaking something together simultaneously; also, that which is thus uttered. 4 The part of a work written for or performed by a chorus; the burden or refrain of a song, which others join a soloist in singing. 5 In ancient Greece, a ceremonial dance, accompanied by the singing of odes, and performed in honor of Dionysus. 6 In Greek drama, a body of actors who through song, dance, and dialog commented upon and sometimes took part in the main action of a play; also, the parts of a play so performed. 7 In later drama, especially the Elizabethan, a single actor who recites the prolog and epilog and comments upon the plot. —*v.t. & v.i.* **cho·rused** or **·russed, cho·rus·ing** or **·rus·sing** To sing or speak in concert. [< L < Gk. *choros* dance. Doublet of CHOIR.]

chose[1] (chōz) Past tense of CHOOSE.

chose[2] (shōz) *n. Law* Anything that is personal property. [< F, thing < L *causa* matter, cause]

cho·sen (chō′zən) Past participle of CHOOSE.— *adj.* 1 Made an object of choice; selected. 2 Worthy of special preference; select; choice. 3 *Theol.* Elect.

chough (chuf) *n.* A bird of the crow family, especially the red–legged or Cornish chough *(Pyrrhocorax pyrrhocorax)* with black plumage and red beak and feet. ◆ Homophone: *chuff.* [ME *choghe.*]

chow[1] (chou) *n.* 1 A medium–sized, heavy–coated, muscular dog native to China, having a thick coat of brown or black, a massive head, and characteristically blue–black tongue: also *chow–chow.* 2 *Slang* Food. [Short for CHOW–CHOW]

CHOW
(20 inches high at its shoulder)

chow[2] (chou) *n.* A Chinese subordinate district or its chief city: used frequently in combination in place names: *Foochow.*

chow–chow (chou′chou′) *n.* 1 A relish consisting of a mixture of chopped–up vegetables pickled in mustard. 2 A chow dog. —*adj.* Miscellaneous; mingled. [< Pidgin English]

chow·der (chou′dər) *n.* 1 A dish, usually of clams or fish stewed with vegetables, often in milk. 2 A picnic, usually on the seashore, where chowder is served. [< F *chaudière* kettle < L *caldaria.* See CALDRON.]

chow–mein (chou′mān′) *n.* A Chinese–American dish consisting of a stew of shredded chicken or meat, onions, mushrooms, celery, bean sprouts, etc., served with fried noodles. [< Chinese *ch'ao* fry + *mien* flour]

chre·ma·tis·tic (krē′mə·tis′tik) *adj.* Of or pertaining to the accumulation of wealth; money –making. [< Gk. *chrēmatistikos* < *chrēmatizein* deal with, transact < *chrēma* money]

chre·ma·tis·tics (krē′mə·tis′tiks) *n.* The branch

of economics that treats of the accumulation of wealth; also, political economy as a whole.

chres·ard (kres'ərd) *n. Ecol.* The available water of the soil: opposed to *echard.* [<Gk. *chrēsthai* use + *ardeia* irrigation]

chres·tom·a·thy (kres·tom'ə·thē) *n. pl.* **·thies** A collection of choice extracts; especially, one compiled for instruction in a language. [<Gk. *chrēstos* useful + *manthanein* learn]

chrism (kriz'əm) *n.* **1** An unguent of oil and balm used for anointing at baptism, confirmation, unction, etc., in the Greek Orthodox and Roman Catholic Churches. **2** Loosely, any unguent. Also spelled **chrisom.** [OE *crisma* < LL *chrisma* <Gk. <*chriein* anoint. Doublet of CREAM.] **—chris·mal** (kriz'məl) *adj.*

chris·ma·to·ry (kriz'mə·tôr'ē, -tō'rē) *n. pl.* **·ries** A vessel or container for chrism. [<Med. L *chrismatorium* <*chrisma* chrism]

chris·om (kriz'əm) *n.* **1** A baptismal or christening robe. **2** Chrism. [Var. of CHRISM]

chrisom child 1 An innocent baby; a newborn child. **2** A child who dies within a month after baptism: formerly buried in its baptismal robe.

Christ (krist) *n.* **1** The Anointed; the Messiah; the deliverer of Israel whose coming was foretold by the Hebrew prophets. **2** Specifically, a title of Jesus of Nazareth, regarded as fulfilling this prophecy: at first used as a title *(Jesus the Christ)* but later a proper name *(Jesus Christ).* **3** In Christian Science, the divine manifestation of God, which comes to the flesh to destroy incarnate error. [OE *Crist* < L *Christus* <Gk. *Christos* (<*chriein* anoint); trans. of Hebrew *māshiach* anointed] **—Christ'li·ness** *n.* **—Christ'ly** *adj.*

christ-cross (kris'krôs', -kros') *n.* **1** The mark of the cross (+), formerly placed before the alphabet in hornbooks, before and after treatises, inscriptions, etc. **2** *Brit. Dial.* A mark or cross made by a person who cannot sign his name. **3** *Obs.* The alphabet; christ-cross-row. See CRISS-CROSS. [<*Christ's cross*]

chris·ten (kris'ən) *v.t.* **1** To name in baptism: He was *christened* John. **2** To administer the rite of Christian baptism to. **3** To give a name to in baptism, or in some ceremony considered as analogous; dedicate; hence, in general, to name: The ship was *christened.* **4** To use for the first time. [OE *cristnian* < *cristen* CHRISTIAN]

chris·ten·ing (kris'ən·ing) *n.* **1** Any Christian baptismal ceremony. **2** Specifically, the baptizing and naming of an infant.

Chris·tian (kris'chən) *adj.* **1** Professing or following the religion of Christ. **2** Relating to or derived from Christ or his doctrine. **3** Manifesting the spirit of Christ or of his teachings. **4** Characteristic of Christianity or Christendom. **5** *Colloq.* Human; civilized; decent. **—n. 1** One who believes in or professes belief in Jesus as the Christ; a member of the Christian church. **2** A disciple of Jesus of Nazareth; one whose profession and life conform to the example and teaching of Jesus. **3** *Colloq.* Any human being as distinguished from a brute: That dog knows as much as a *Christian.* **4** *Colloq.* A civilized, decent, or respectable person. **5** *U.S.* A Campbellite; a member of the Disciples of Christ. [OE *cristen* < LL *christianus* <*Christus* CHRIST] **—Chris'tian·ly** *adv.*

Chris·ti·an·i·ty (kris'chē·an'ə·tē) *n.* **1** The Christian religion. **2** Christians collectively. **3** The state of being a Christian.

Christians See DISCIPLES OF CHRIST.

Christian Science A religious system embodying metaphysical healing, founded in 1866 by Mary Baker Eddy and based on her exposition of the Scriptures: officially called the **Church of Christ, Scientist.**

Chris·tian·sted (kris'chən·sted) The capital of St. Croix in the Virgin Islands; former capital of the Danish West Indies.

Christ·like (krist'līk') *adj.* **1** Resembling Christ or like that of Christ. **2** Having the spirit of Christ. **—Christ'like·ness** *n.*

Christ·mas (kris'məs) *n.* **1** The 25th of December, held as the anniversary of the birth of Jesus Christ: widely observed as a holy day or a holiday. Also **Christmas Day. 2** A church festival observed annually at this date in memory of the birth of Jesus Christ; the Feast of the Nativity;

especially, the anniversary day, the 25th of December. The season of Christmas extends from Christmas Eve (Dec. 24) to Epiphany (Jan. 6), and is known as **Christmastide.** [<CHRIST + MASS²]

Christmas Island 1 An island SW of Java, comprising part of the British crown colony of Singapore; 60 square miles. **2** The largest atoll in the Line Islands district of the Gilbert and Ellice Islands Colony; 220 square miles.

Chris·tol·o·gy (kris·tol'ə·jē) *n.* The branch of theology that treats of the person and attributes of Christ. **2** Loosely, any theory or doctrine concerning Christ. [<CHRIST + -LOGY] **—Chris·to·log·i·cal** (kris'tə·loj'i·kəl) *adj.*

chrom- Var. of CHROMO-.

chro·ma (krō'mə) *n.* Color intensity; the degree of hue and saturation in a color other than white, black, or gray. [<Gk. *chrōma* color]

chro·maf·fin (krō·maf'in) *adj. Biol.* Having the property of staining when treated with dichromate.

chro·mate (krō'māt) *n. Chem.* A salt of chromic acid.

chro·mat·ic (krō·mat'ik) *adj.* **1** Pertaining to color or colors. **2** *Music* Using or proceeding by semitones. Also **chro·mat'i·cal.**

chromatic aberration See under ABERRATION.

chro·ma·tic·i·ty (krō'mə·tis'ə·tē) *n. Physics* That quality of a color which is defined by its dominant or complementary wavelength taken together with its purity.

chro·mat·ics (krō·mat'iks) *n.* The science of colors.

chromatic scale *Music* The diatonic scale proceeding by semitones.

chro·ma·tid (krō'mə·tid) *n. Biol.* One of the four members of a tetrad formed by the longitudinal splitting of a chromosome during meiosis.

chro·ma·tin (krō'mə·tin) *n. Biol.* The deeply staining filamentous material in the protoplasm of the cell nucleus: during mitosis chromatin develops into chromosomes: also called *chromoplasm.* See illustration under CELL. [<Gk. *chrōma, -atos* color]

chro·ma·tism (krō'mə·tiz'əm) *n.* **1** *Optics* Chromatic aberration. **2** *Bot.* The assumption by normally green plant organs, as leaves, of a color approximating that of the petals. Also **chro·mism** (krō'miz·əm).

chromato- *combining form* Color; coloring or pigmentation: *chromatoscope.* Also, before vowels, **chromat-.** [<Gk. *chrōma, -atos* color]

chro·mat·o·gram (krō·mat'ə·gram) *n. Chem.* The complete array of distinctively colored bands produced by chromatography.

chro·ma·tog·ra·phy (krō'mə·tog'rə·fē) *n. Chem.* A method for the separation and analysis of small quantities of substances by passing a solution through a column of finely divided powder which selectively adsorbs the constituents in one or more sharply defined, often colored bands. [<CHROMATO- + -GRAPHY] **—chro·mat·o·graph·ic** (krō·mat'ə·graf'ik) *adj.*

chro·ma·tol·o·gy (krō'mə·tol'ə·jē) *n. pl.* **·gies 1** The science of color. **2** A treatise on colors. [<CHROMATO- + -LOGY]

chro·ma·tol·y·sis (krō'mə·tol'ə·sis) *n. Biol.* The solution and disappearance of chromatin from a neuron or other cell. [<CHROMATO- + -LYSIS]

chro·ma·to·phore (krō'mə·tə·fôr', -fōr') *n.* **1** *Zool.* One of the pigment-bearing sacs with contractile walls by which changes of color are effected in various animals, as in chameleons; a pigment cell. **2** *Bot.* A pigment-bearing plastid found in diatoms and other plants. **—chro·ma·to·phor·ic** (krō'mə·tə·fôr'ik, -for'-), **chro·ma·toph·o·rous** (krō'mə·tof'ə·rəs) *adj.*

chrome (krōm) *n.* **1** Chrome yellow. **2** Chromium. **—v.t. chromed, chrom·ing** To subject to the action of a solution of potassium dichromate. [<F <Gk. *chrōma* color]

-chrome *combining form* **1** Color; colored: *polychrome.* **2** *Chem.* Chromium: *ferrochrome.* [Gk. *chrōma* color]

chrome alum *Chem.* Any double sulfate of chromium with potassium, sodium, or ammo-

nium: *chrome alum ammonium,* $Cr(NH_4)$-$(SO_4)_2·12H_2O$, a dark, violet-red compound used as a mordant in dyeing.

chrome green 1 A green pigment derived from chromic oxide, Cr_2O_3. **2** The color of this, a dull, dark green.

chrome red A pigment made from basic lead chromate.

chrome steel *Metall.* A very hard steel alloyed with chromium: when the chrome is 12 percent or more, the resulting alloy is known as *stainless steel.* Also **chromium steel.**

chrome yellow 1 *Chem.* A yellow pigment consisting of natural lead chromate, $PbCrO_4$. **2** Any of several shades of yellow ranging from lemon to deep orange.

chro·mic (krō'mik) *adj.* **1** *Chem.* Of, from, or pertaining to chromium. **2** Pertaining to compounds in which chromium is present in its higher valency.

chromic acid *Chem.* A hypothetical acid, H_2CrO_4, known only in solution and forming chromates.

chromic oxide *Chem.* A green compound, Cr_2O_3; chromium sesquioxide: used as a pigment.

chro·mi·nance (krō'mə·nəns) *n. Physics* The colorimetric difference between a given color and a reference color of equal brightness and specified chromaticity.

chro·mite (krō'mīt) *n.* Chromic iron ore, $FeCr_2O_4$, a valuable source of chromium.

chro·mi·um (krō'mē·əm) *n.* A grayish-white, very hard metallic element (symbol Cr): used in making alloys, pigments, as a mordant, etc. See ELEMENT. [<Gk. *chrōma* color; so called from its many brightly colored, poisonous compounds]

chromium trioxide *Chem.* A red crystalline substance, CrO_3; chromic anhydride: a powerful oxidizing agent.

chro·mo (krō'mō) *n. pl.* **·mos** A picture printed in colors; a chromolithograph. [Short for CHROMOLITHOGRAPH]

chromo- *combining form* **1** Color; in or with color: *chromophotography.* **2** *Chem.* Chromium: *chromotype.* Also, before vowels, *chrom-.* [Gk. *chrōma* color]

chro·mo·gen (krō'mə·jen) *n.* **1** *Chem.* **a** Any organic coloring matter or substance capable of yielding a dye. **b** Any dye derived from naphthalene which develops a brown color on wool by oxidation. **2** *Biol.* Any substance in an animal or plant which under certain conditions becomes colored or deepens its hue. **—chro·mo·gen'ic** *adj.*

chro·mo·li·thog·ra·phy (krō'mō·li·thog'rə·fē) *n.* The process of reproducing a colored original from a set of stones by lithography.

chro·mo·mere (krō'mə·mir) *n. Biol.* One of the granules of chromatin forming the chromosome.

chro·mo·phore (krō'mə·fôr, -fōr) *n. Chem.* A group of atoms so arranged as to produce the colors of dyestuffs when combined under proper conditions with hydrocarbon radicals. **—chro·mo·phor·ic** (krō'mə·fôr'ik, -for'-), **chro·moph·o·rous** (krō·mof'ə·rəs) *adj.*

chro·mo·plasm (krō'mə·plaz'əm) *n.* Chromatin.

chro·mo·plast (krō'mə·plast) *n. Bot.* A colored protoplasmic granule of a color other than green.

chro·mo·some (krō'mə·sōm) *n. Biol.* One of the deeply staining, rod- or loop-shaped bodies into which the chromatin of the cell nucleus divides during mitosis, generally of a fixed number for any given species: regarded as a carrier of the genes or units of heredity. See HAPLOID, POLYPLOID. **— accessory chromosome** A chromosome of which the shape, size, and purpose differ from those of other chromosomes of the same cell. [<CHROMO- + -SOME²]

chro·mo·sphere (krō'mə·sfir') *n. Astron.* An envelope of incandescent red gas surrounding the sun beyond the photosphere: it is composed chiefly of hydrogen and helium. **— chro·mo·spher·ic** (krō'mə·sfer'ik) *adj.*

chro·mo·type (krō'mə·tīp') *n.* **1** A photographic process in which some salt of chromium is the sensitive agent. 2 A chromolithograph. 3 A photograph in colors. Also **chro′ma·type′**.

chro·mous (krō′məs) *adj. Chem.* Of or pertaining to chromium in its lower valence.

chro·nax·y (krō′nak·sē) *n. Physiol.* The time that a current of twice the rheobase requires to excite a muscle, nerve fiber, etc. Also **chro′nax·ie, chro·nax·i·a** (krō·nak′sē·ə). [<CHRON(O)- + Gk. *axia* value]

chron·ic (kron′ik) *adj.* 1 Continuing for a long period. 2 Inveterate; habitual: a *chronic* complainer. 3 Prolonged; lingering: said of a disease: opposed to *acute*. Also **chron′i·cal**. [<F *chronique* <L *chronicus* <Gk. *chronikos* of time <*chronos* time] — **chron′i·cal·ly** *adv.*

chron·i·cle (kron′i·kəl) *n.* A register of events in the order of time; a historical record chronologically arranged. See synonyms under HISTORY, RECORDS. — *v.t.* **·cled, ·cling** To record. [<AF *cronicle* <L *chronica*, neut. pl. of *chronicus*. See CHRONIC.] — **chron′i·cler** *n.*

chrono- *combining form* Time: *chronograph*. Also, before vowels, **chron-**. [<Gk. *chronos* time]

chron·o·gram (kron′ə·gram) *n.* 1 A record of a chronograph. 2 A writing or an inscription recording a date in numeral letters.

chron·o·graph (kron′ə·graf, -gräf) *n.* An instrument for recording graphically the moment or duration of an event, measuring intervals of time, etc.

chron·o·log·i·cal (kron′ə·loj′i·kəl) *adj.* 1 Occurring or recorded in temporal sequence, as a series of events. 2 Pertaining to or occupied with the science of time. Also **chron′o·log′ic. — chron′o·log′i·cal·ly** *adv.*

chro·nol·o·gy (krə·nol′ə·jē) *n. pl.* **·gies** 1 The science that treats of the measurement of time, or the order of events. 2 Any particular chronological system. 3 Any tabulated arrangement of events of historical or scientific import, in the order of the time of their occurrence. [<CHRONO- + -LOGY] — **chro·nol′o·ger, chro·nol′o·gist** *n.*

chro·nom·e·ter (krə·nom′ə·tər) *n.* A portable timekeeping instrument of high precision and accuracy for use in navigation and scientific work. [<CHRONO- + -METER] — **chron·o·met·ric** (kron′ə·met′rik) or **·ri·cal** *adj.* — **chron′o·met′ri·cal·ly** *adv.*

chro·nom·e·try (krə·nom′ə·trē) *n.* 1 The measurement of time. 2 The science or method of measuring time.

chron·o·scope (kron′ə·skōp) *n.* A chronograph or the like for measuring a minute interval of time. — **chron·o·scop·ic** (kron′ə·skop′ik) *adj.*

-chroous *combining form* Having (a certain) color: *isochroous*. [<Gk. *chrōs, chroos* color]

chrys- Var. of CHRYSO-.

chrys·a·lis (kris′ə·lis) *n. pl.* **chrys·a·lis·es** or **chry·sal·i·des** (kri·sal′ə·dēz) *Entomol.* 1 The pupa of an insect, especially of a butterfly; the capsule-enclosed stage between caterpillar and butterfly during which the individual develops and from which the winged adult emerges. See illustration under PUPA. 2 Anything in an undeveloped or transitory stage. [<L <Gk. *chrysallis* golden sheath of a butterfly <*chrysos* gold]

chrys·an·i·line (kris·an′ə·lin, -līn) *n. Chem.* A coal-tar dyestuff, $C_{19}H_{15}N_3$, obtained from rosaniline, that gives a golden-yellow color.

chrys·an·the·mum (kri·san′thə·məm) *n.* 1 Any of a genus of perennials (*Chrysanthemum*) of the composite family, some cultivated varieties of which have large heads of showy flowers of various colors. 2 The flower. [<L <Gk. *chrysanthemon* marigold, lit., golden flower]

chrys·a·ro·bin (kris′ə·rō′bin) *n. Chem.* An orange-yellow compound, $C_{15}H_{12}O_3$, which forms the essential principle of Goa powder. Also **chrys·a·ro·bi·num** (kris′ə·rō′bi·nəm). [<CHRYS- + Tupian *araroba* bark]

chrys·el·e·phan·tine (kris′el·ə·fan′tin) *adj.* Made or covered with gold and ivory, as certain ancient Greek statues. [<Gk. *chryselephantinos* of gold and ivory <*chrysos* gold + *elephas* ivory]

chrys·ene (kris·ēn′) *n. Chem.* A reddish-violet, fluorescent crystalline compound, $C_{18}H_{12}$, contained in coal tar and other substances.

chryso- *combining form* Gold; of a golden color: *chrysolite*. Also, before vowels, *chrys-*.

[<Gk. *chrysos* gold]

chrys·o·ber·yl (kris′ə·ber′əl) *n.* A vitreous, yellowish or greenish, transparent to translucent beryllium aluminate; used as a gem. [<L *chrysoberyllus* <Gk. *chrysoberyllos* < *chrysos* gold + *beryllos* beryl]

chrys·o·lite (kris′ə·līt) *n.* A vitreous, orthorhombic, olive-green, transparent to translucent magnesium iron silicate, $(Mg,Fe)_2SiO_4$; used as a gem: also called *olivine*. [<OF *crisolite* <Med. L *crisolitus* <L *chrysolithus* <Gk. *chrysolithos* < *chrysos* gold] — **chrys·o·lit·ic** (kris′ə·lit′ik) *adj.*

chrys·o·prase (kris′ə·prāz) *n.* A semiprecious, apple-green variety of chalcedony, colored by nickel oxide: used as a gem. [<OF *crisopace* <L *chrysoprasus* <Gk. *chrysoprasos* < *chrysos* gold + *prason* leek]

chrys·o·tile (kris′ə·til) *n.* A fibrous, silky variety of serpentine. [<CHRYSO- + Gk. *tilos* hair, fiber]

chtho·ni·an (thō′nē·ən) *adj.* 1 Of, pertaining to, or being in the nether world; underground; subterranean. 2 Specifically, pertaining to the Greek underworld gods as distinguished from those of Olympus. Also **chthon·ic** (thon′ik). [<Gk. *chthōn* the earth]

chub (chub) *n. pl.* **chubs** or **chub** 1 A European carplike fish of the cyprinoid order (genus *Leuciscus*). 2 One of various other fishes, as the fallfish, tautog, etc. [ME *chubbe*; origin unknown]

chu·bas·co (choo·bäs′kō) *n. Meteorol.* A violent thunder squall along the west coast of Central America. [<Sp.]

chub·by (chub′ē) *adj.* **·bi·er, ·bi·est** Plump; rounded. [<CHUB] — **chub′bi·ness** *n.*

chuck¹ (chuk) *n.* 1 A chick; hen. 2 A short clucking sound; a cluck. 3 An endearing sound or word. — *v.i.* To cluck, as a fowl does, or as in calling fowls. [Imit.]

chuck² (chuk) *v.t.* 1 To pat or tap affectionately or playfully, as under the chin. 2 To throw or pitch: to *chuck* a baseball. 3 *Colloq.* To throw away; discard. 4 *Colloq.* To throw out forcibly; eject: with *out*. 5 *Brit. Slang* To quit: He *chucked* his job. — *n.* 1 A playful pat, throw, or toss. 2 *Brit.* A game of pitch-and-toss, played with coins or pebbles: also called **chuck′-far′thing.** [Cf. F *choquer* shake, jolt]

chuck³ (chuk) *n.* 1 *Mech.* A clamp, chock, or wedge to hold a tool, as a drill. See illustration under BIT. 2 The part of a beef extending from the neck to the shoulder blade. 3 *Colloq.* **a** Food. **b** A meal. **c** Mealtime. — *v.t.* To place or fix in or by means of a chuck; do with a chuck. [Var. of CHOCK]

chuck·le¹ (chuk′əl) *v.i.* **·led, ·ling** 1 To laugh quietly, especially to oneself. 2 To cluck, as a hen. — *n.* A low, suppressed, or broken laugh. [Freq. of CHUCK¹] — **chuck′ler** *n.*

chuck·le² (chuk′əl) *adj.* Thick or clumsy. [? < CHUCK³ (def. 1)]

chuck wagon *U.S.* A food wagon that carries provisions and cooking equipment around to cowboys, harvest hands, etc.

chuck·wal·la (chuk′wol′ə) *n.* A large, herbivorous lizard (*Sauromalus ater*) of the deserts of the SW United States. Also **chuck·a·wal·la** (chuk′ə·wol′ə). [< N. Am. Ind.]

chuck-will's-wid·ow (chuk′wilz′wid′ō) *n.* A large goatsucker (*Caprimulgus carolinensis*) of the southern United States: so called from its note.

chu·fa (choo′fə) *n.* 1 A sedge (*Cyperus esculentus*) whose tuberous roots are eaten in southern Europe. 2 One of the tubers. [< Sp.]

chuff (chuf) *n. Brit. Dial.* 1 A rustic. 2 A boor. 3 A coarse, churlish fellow. 4 A miser. — *adj.* Gruff; crusty: also **chuf′fy.** ♦ Homophone: *chough*. [Origin unknown]

chuf·fy (chuf′ē) *adj.* Chubby; plump. Also **chuf′fie. — chuf′fi·ly** *adv.* — **chuf′fi·ness** *n.*

chug (chug) *n.* An explosive sound, as of the exhaust of an engine. — *v.i.* **chugged, chug·ging** To work or go with a series of small explosions: The old car *chugged* along. [Imit.]

chuk·ker (chuk′ər) *n.* In polo, one of the periods during which the ball is continuously in play; a chukker lasts 7½ minutes. Also **chuk′kar.** [< Hind. *chakkar* <Skt. *chakra* wheel]

chum¹ (chum) *n.* 1 Originally, a roommate. 2 An intimate companion. — *v.i.* **chummed, chum·ming** To share the same room with

someone; hence, to be very intimate. See synonyms under ASSOCIATE [? Short for CHAMBER FELLOW]

chum² (chum) *n.* Pieces of oily fish, used as fish bait, or pressed for oil. — *v.i.* To fish with chum. [Origin uncertain]

chum·my (chum′ē) *adj.* **·mi·er, ·mi·est** *Colloq.* Friendly; intimate. — **chum′mi·ly** *adv.*

chump¹ (chump) *n.* 1 A chunk of wood. 2 The thick end, as of a loin of mutton. 3 The head: a humorous use. 4 *Colloq.* A stupid or unskilful person. — **off his chump** *Brit. Slang* Out of his senses; silly. [? Var. of CHUNK]

chump² (chump) *v.t.* To chew; munch. [< CHAMP¹]

chunk (chungk) *n.* 1 A short, stout thing, person, or animal; especially, a short, thick piece of wood. 2 A lump or large piece of anything. — *v.t.* 1 To throw clods of earth, stones, etc., at. 2 To throw, as clods of earth, stones, etc. 3 To put (chunks of wood) on a fire. [Var. of CHUNK]

chunk·er (chung′kər) *n.* A coal boat on a canal.

chunk·y (chung′kē) *adj.* **chunk·i·er, chunk·i·est** 1 Short and thick-set; stocky. 2 In a chunk or chunks.

Chur (koor) A town in eastern Switzerland, capital of Grisons canton. *French* **Coire** (kwär).

church (chûrch) *n.* 1 A building for Christian worship. 2 Regular religious services; public worship. 3 A local congregation of Christians. 4 *Usually cap.* A distinct body of Christians having a common faith and discipline; a denomination: the Episcopal *Church.* 5 All Christian believers collectively. 6 Ecclesiastical organization and authority, as distinguished from secular authority: the separation of *church* and state. 7 The clerical profession; holy orders. 8 Any religious body or society. — *v.t.* 1 To call to account before the congregation; to reprimand or punish publicly according to church discipline. 2 To conduct a religious service for (a person, especially a woman after childbirth). [OE *circe*, ult. <Gk. *kyriakon (doma)* the Lord's (house) < *kyrios* Lord]

church-go·er (chûrch′gō′ər) *n.* One who goes regularly to church. — **church′-go′ing** *adj. & n.*

church·ing (chûr′ching) *n.* 1 A woman's appearance in church, to return thanks after confinement; also, the service for this occasion. 2 The process of subjecting to church discipline.

church·ly (chûrch′lē) *adj.* 1 Of, pertaining to, or suitable to a church. 2 Devoted to church polity and ritual. 3 Not secular. — **church′li·ness** *n.*

church·man (chûrch′mən) *n. pl.* **·men** (-mən) 1 A devoted supporter or member of a church, especially of an established church. 2 *Obs.* A clergyman; ecclesiastic. — **church′man·ly** *adj.* — **church′man·ship** *n.* — **church′wom′an** *n. fem.*

Church of Christ, Scientist See CHRISTIAN SCIENCE.

Church of England The church established and endowed by law as the national church of England; also called *Anglican Church.*

Church of God Any of various small religious groups in the United States, for the most part unrelated.

Church of God, Adventist See under ADVENTIST.

Church Slavonic See under SLAVONIC.

church text *Printing* Old English type.

church·war·den (chûrch′wôr′dən) *n.* 1 In the Church of England, an elected lay officer who assists in the administration of a parish, and acts as its legal representative. 2 In the Protestant Episcopal Church, one of two elected lay officers of a vestry who, with the other vestrymen, administer the property and temporal affairs of the parish, and represent the congregation on certain occasions. 3 A long-stemmed clay pipe. Also **church warden.**

church·yard (chûrch′yärd′) *n.* The yard or graveyard of a church; a cemetery.

churl (chûrl) *n.* 1 A low-bred, surly fellow. 2 A miserly or niggardly person. 3 A peasant. 4 In England of Saxon times, a freeman of low degree. [OE *ceorl.* Akin to CARL.]

churl·ish (chûr′lish) *adj.* 1 Of or like a churl;

rude; boorish. 2 Hard to work or manage; intractable. See synonyms under HAUGHTY, MOROSE. —**churl′ish·ly** *adv.* —**churl′ish·ness** *n.*

churn (chûrn) *n.* 1 A vessel in which milk or cream is agitated to separate the oily globules and gather them as butter. 2 Any vessel or receptacle similar in shape to a milk churn. —*v.t.* 1 To stir or agitate (cream or milk), as in a churn, to make butter. 2 To make by agitation, as butter. 3 To agitate violently: The oars *churned* the water. —*v.i.* 4 To stir or agitate cream or milk in making butter. 5 To produce or be in violent agitation; seethe. [OE *cyrin*] —**churn′er** *n.*

churn·ing (chûr′ning) *n.* 1 The process of churning. 2 The butter churned at one time. 3 *Med.* A splashing sound from the chest sometimes heard in pleural effusion and resembling the sound made by a churn.

churr (chûr) *n.* The whirring sound made by certain birds, as the partridge or nightjar, or insects, as the cockchafer. —*v.t.* To utter with a churr. —*v.i.* To utter a low trill or similar vibrant sound, as a partridge. [Imit.]

chute (shoōt) *n.* 1 A narrow, rocky rapid in a river. 2 A sluice through a dam for logs. 3 A passageway for fish through a dam. 4 An inclined trough or slide for grain, ore, coal, mail, baggage, etc. 5 A narrow pen for branding or shipping cattle. 6 A precipitous slide in an amusement park. 7 A toboggan slide. 8 *Colloq.* A parachute. —*v.t.* & *v.i.* **chut·ed, chut·ing** To descend or cause to descend (on) a chute. ◆ Homophone: *shoot.* [< F, fall]

chut·ney (chut′nē) *n.* A piquant relish of fruit, spices, etc. Also **chut′nee.** [< Hind. *chatni*]

chyle (kıl) *n. Physiol.* The milky emulsion of lymph and fat taken up from the intestines during digestion and passed from the thoracic duct into the veins, where it mixes with the blood. [< F < L *chylus* < Gk. *chylos* juice < *cheein* pour] —**chy·la·ceous** (kı·lā′shəs), **chy·lous** (kı′ləs) *adj.*

chyme (kım) *n. Physiol.* The partly digested food in liquid form as it passes from the stomach into the small intestines. [< L *chymus* < Gk. *chymos* juice < *cheein* pour] —**chy·mous** (kı′məs) *adj.*

chy·mif·er·ous (kı·mif′ər·əs) *adj.* Conveying or containing chyme. [< CHYME + -(I)FEROUS]

chy·mo·sin (kı′mə·sin) *n.* Rennin. [< CHYME + (PEP)SIN]

cib·ol (sib′əl) *n.* 1 The Welsh onion (*Allium fistulosum*) having hollow stems and a very small bulb: also spelled *sybo.* 2 The shallot. Also **cib′oule.** [< L *ciboule* < LL *cepulla* bed of onions < L *cepa* onion]

ci·bo·ri·um (si·bôr′ē·əm, -bō′rē-) *n., pl.* **·bo·ri·a** (-bôr′ē·ə, -bō′rē·ə) 1 An arched canopy over an altar; especially, a baldachin supported on four pillars. 2 A receptacle for the wafers of the Eucharist. [< Med. L < Gk. *kibōrion* cup]

ci·ca·da (si·kā′də, -kä′-) *n., pl.* **·das** or **·dae** (-dē) A large homopterous insect (family *Cicadidae*), the male being equipped at the base of the abdomen with vibrating membranes and sound chambers that produce a loud, shrill sound. The larvae develop underground. Often called *locust.* [< L]

CICADA

cicada killer A digger wasp (*Sphecius speciosus*) that preys upon the cicada. For illustration see under INSECTS (beneficial).

ci·ca·la (si·kä′lə) *n.* A cicada. [< Ital.]

cic·a·tric·le (sik′ə·trik′əl), *n.* 1 *Biol.* The germinating point in the yolk of an egg or in the embryo of a seed; the tread of an egg: also **cic·a·tri·cule** (sik′ə·tri·kyoōl′). 2 *Bot.* A small scar, as that left by the stem of a detached leaf. [< L *cicatricula,* dim. of *cicatrix* scar]

cic·a·trix (sik′ə·triks) *n., pl.* **cic·a·tri·ces** (sik′ə·trı′sēz) 1 *Med.* A scar or seam consisting of new tissue formed in the healing of wounded or ulcerous parts and remaining after their cure: also **cic·a·trice** (sik′ə·tris). 2 *Biol.* A scar or scar-like marking, as that left on the interior of a bivalve shell by the attachment of the adductors, or that left by the fall of a leaf or other organ. [< L]

cic·a·tri·cial (sik′ə·trish′əl), **ci·cat·ri·cose** (si·kat′ri·kōs) *adj.*

cic·a·trize (sik′ə·trız) *v.t.* & *v.i.* **·trized, ·triz·ing** To heal or become healed by the formation of a scar. —**cic·a·tri·za′tion** *n.*

cic·e·ly (sis′ə′lē) *n. pl.* **·lies** A fragrant perennial herb (*Myrrhis odorata*) of the parsley family. —**fool's-cicely** Fool's-parsley. [< L *seseli*s < Gk.; infl. in form by *Cecily,* a feminine name]

cic·e·ro (sis′ə·rō) *n. Printing* A unit of typographical measurement in Europe, similar to the pica but slightly larger: from the type size used in an edition of Cicero printed in 1458.

cich·lid (sik′lid) *n.* One of a family (*Cichlidae*) of spiny-finned, fresh-water fishes with a compressed oblong body, interrupted lateral line, and single nostril. [< NL *Cichlidae* < Gk. *kichlē,* a sea fish]

ci·cho·ri·a·ceous (si·kôr′ē·ā′shəs) *adj. Bot.* Of or pertaining to the chicory family (*Cichoriaceae*) of herbs and shrubs, yielding a milky juice which, in some species, has narcotic properties. [< NL *Cichoriaceae* < L *cichorium* chicory < Gk. *kichōrion*]

ci·cis·be·o (si·sis′bē·ō, *Ital.* chē′chēz·bā′ō) *n. pl.* **·bei** (-bi·ē, *Ital.* -bā′ē) The acknowledged gallant of a married woman. [< Ital.]

-cidal *combining form* Killing; able to kill: *homicidal.* [< L *caedere* kill]

-cide *combining form* 1 Killer or destroyer of: *regicide.* 2 Murder or killing of: *parricide.* [def. 1 < L *-cida* killer < *caedere* kill; def. 2 < L *-cidium* slaughter < *caedere*]

ci·der (sı′dər) *n.* The expressed juice of apples used to make vinegar, and as a beverage before fermentation (**sweet cider**) or after fermentation (**hard cider**). [< OF *sidre* < LL *sicera* strong drink < Hebrew *shēkār*]

ci·gar (si·gär′) *n.* A small roll of tobacco leaves prepared and shaped for smoking. [< Sp. *cigarro*]

cig·a·rette (sig′ə·ret′, sig′ə·ret) *n.* 1 A small roll of finely cut tobacco in thin paper or, rarely, in tobacco leaf. 2 A similar roll with medicinal filling. Also **cig′a·ret′.** [< F, dim. of *cigare* cigar]

cigar fish A carangoid food fish (*Decapterus punctatus*) found in the West Indies and along the Atlantic Coast of the United States: also called *round robin.*

cil·i·a (sil′ē·ə) Plural of CILIUM.

cil·i·ar·y (sil′ē·er′ē) *adj.* 1 Of, pertaining to, or like cilia. 2 *Anat.* **a** Pertaining to or situated near the eyelashes. **b** Pertaining to the set of muscle fibers which are attached to ligaments supporting the lens of the eye. [< L *cilium* eyelid]

cil·i·ate (sil′ē·it, -āt) *adj. Biol.* Having cilia or motile hairlike processes: *ciliate* leaves. Also **cil′i·at′ed.** —*n. Zool.* One of a class (*Ciliata*) of infusorians possessing cilia in both young and adult stages.

cil·ice (sil′is) *n.* 1 A coarse cloth, originally made of goats' hair. 2 A hair shirt of this; a hair shirt, formerly worn by monks and others in doing penance. [< F < L *cilicium* < Gk. *Kilikia* Cilicia, where the cloth was woven] —**ci·li·cious** (si·lish′əs) *adj.*

cil·i·o·late (sil′ē·ə·lit, -lāt) *adj.* Fringed with small cilia.

cil·i·um (sil′ē·əm) *n. pl.* **cil·i·a** (sil′ē·ə) 1 *Biol.* A vibratile, microscopic, hairlike process on the surface of a cell, organ, plant, etc. 2 An eyelash. [< L, eyelid]

ci·mex (sı′meks) *n. pl.* **eim·i·ces** (sim′ə·sēz) An insect of the genus *Cimex;* a bedbug. [< L, bug]

cim·i·tar or **cim·i·ter** (sim′ə·tər) See SCIMITAR.

cinch¹ (sinch) *n. U.S.* 1 A saddle girth, as of horsehair. 2 *Colloq.* A tight grip. 3 *Slang* A sure thing; a certainty. 4 *Slang* An easy thing to do. —*v.t.* 1 To fasten a saddle girth around. 2 *Slang* To get a tight hold upon; make sure of. —*v.i.* 3 To tighten a saddle girth: often with *up.* [< Sp. *cincha* girth < L *cingula* girdle < *cingere* bind]

cinch² (sinch) *n.* A game of cards in which the five of trumps is the most important card. [Prob. < Sp. *cinco* five]

cin·cho·na (sin·kō′nə) *n.* 1 Any of various Peruvian trees and shrubs (genus *Cinchona*) of the madder family, now widely cultivated in India and Java as a source of quinine and related alkaloids. 2 The bark of any of these trees. [after the Countess of *Cinchón,* 1576–1639, wife of the

viceroy of Peru] —**cin·chon·ic** (sin·kon′ik) *adj.*

cin·chon·i·dine (sin·kon′ə·dēn, -din) *n. Chem.* A crystalline, bitter alkaloid, $C_{19}H_{22}N_2O$, derived from cinchona, isomeric with cinchonine, but less powerful: used medicinally.

cin·cho·nine (sin′kə·nēn, -nin) *n. Chem.* A crystalline alkaloid, $C_{19}H_{22}N_2O$, derived from cinchona, similar to cinchonidine, of which it is an isomer.

cin·cho·nism (sin′kə·niz′əm) *n. Pathol.* An abnormal condition caused by overdoses of cinchona, characterized by buzzing in the head, giddiness, deafness, and temporary loss of sight.

cin·cho·nize (sin′kə·nız) *v.t.* **·nized, ·niz·ing** To bring under the influence of cinchona or quinine. —**cin′cho·ni·za′tion** *n.*

cinc·ture (singk′chər) *n.* 1 Something bound about the waist; a belt or girdle. 2 Any covering about the loins: The savages wore a *cincture* of leaves. 3 Anything that encircles or encloses; also, the act of cincturing. —*v.t.* **·tured, ·tur·ing** To surround with or as with a cincture; gird. [< L *cinctura* < *cingere* gird]

cin·der (sin′dər) *n.* 1 Any partly burned combustible substance, before it has been reduced to ashes, especially when combustion has entirely ceased. 2 A thoroughly charred bit of wood, coal, or the like; an ember. 3 *pl.* Ashes. 4 A scale of iron oxide thrown off in forging; also, light slag. 5 *pl. Geol.* Fragments of scoriaceous lava explosively ejected from a volcano during an eruption; scoria. —*v.t.* To burn or reduce to a cinder. [OE *sinder;* infl. in form by L *cinis, cineris* ash] —**cin′der·ry** *adj.*

cin·e·ma (sin′ə·mə) *n.* 1 A motion-picture theater. 2 A motion picture or motion pictures collectively. 3 The art or business of making or exhibiting motion pictures. [Short for CINEMATOGRAPH]

cin·e·mat·ic (sin′ə·mat′ik) *adj.* Of, pertaining to, or suitable for motion-picture presentation. —**cin′e·mat′i·cal·ly** *adv.*

cin·e·mat·o·graph (sin′ə·mat′ə·graf, -gräf) *n.* A camera for producing motion pictures, so constructed that a large number of separate exposures or frames are made in very rapid succession: also called *kinetograph.* —*v.t.* & *v.i.* To take photographs of (something) with a motion-picture camera: also **cin·e·ma·tize** (sin′ə·mə·tız′). [< Gk. *kinēma, -atos* movement + -GRAPH]

cin·e·ma·tog·ra·phy (sin′ə·mə·tog′rə·fē) *n.* The art and process of making motion pictures.

cin·e·ma·tome (sin′ə·mə·tōm′) *n.* An apparatus by means of which very thin sections of rock or other solid material may be sliced and then photographed on motion-picture film.

ci·ne·ma ve·ri·té (sin′ə·mə ver·ə·tā′) A kind of motion-picture technique that emphasizes realism and spontaneity. [< French *cinéma-vérité* truth cinema]

cin·e·o·graph (sin′ē·ə·graf, -gräf) *n.* A motion picture; kineograph. [< Gk. *kineein* move + -GRAPH]

cin·e·ol (sin′ē·ōl, -ol) *n.* Eucalyptol. Also **cin′e·ole** (-ōl) [Transposition of NL *ole(um) cin(ae)* oil of wormwood]

cin·e·rar·i·a (sin′ə·râr′ē·ə) *n.* A cultivated, ornamental plant (*Senecio cruentus*) of the composite family, originally from the Canary Islands, having heart-shaped leaves and showy white, red, or purple flowers. [< NL < L, fem. of *cinerarius* ashy < *cinis, cineris* ash]

cin·e·rar·i·um (sin′ə·râr′ē·əm) *n. pl.* **·rar·i·a** (-râr′ē·ə) A niche in a tomb or other place for an urn containing the ashes of a cremated body. [< L] —**cin·er·ar·y** (sin′ə·rer′ē) *adj.*

cin·er·a·tor (sin′ə·rā′tər) *n.* Incinerator.

cin·e·ri·tious (sin′ə·rish′əs) *adj.* Of the nature of ashes; ashen: said of ash-colored brain- or nerve-substance. Also **ci·ne·re·ous** (si·nir′ē·əs). [< L *cineritius* ashen]

cin·gu·lum (sing′gyə·ləm) *n. pl.* **·la** (-lə) *Zool.* A band, zone, or girdle, as of the carapace of an armadillo, of a tooth near the gum, the clitellum of an earthworm, or a raised spiral line on certain univalves. [< L < *cingere* gird] —**cin·gu·late** (sing′gyə·lit, -lāt) or **cin′·gu·lat′ed** *adj.*

cin·na·bar (sin′ə·bär) *n.* **1** A crystallized red mercuric sulfide, HgS, the chief ore of mercury. **2** A mixture formed by subliming mercury and sulfur, known as **artificial cinnabar:** used as a pigment, called *vermilion.* [< L *cinnabaris* < Gk. *kinnabari,* ult. < Persian *zinifrah*]

cinnabar lacquer Chinese carved lacquer.

cin·nam·ic (si·nam′ik, sin′ə·mik) *adj.* Of, pertaining to, or derived from cinnamon. Also **cin·na·mon·ic** (sin′ə·mon′ik).

cinnamic acid *Chem.* A colorless, crystalline, volatile compound, $C_9H_8O_2$, contained in cinnamon and various balsams, and made synthetically.

cin·na·mon (sin′ə·mən) *n.* **1** The aromatic inner bark of any of several tropical trees of the laurel family, used as a spice. **2** Any tree that yields cinnamon; especially, *Cinnamomum zeylanicum,* cultivated in Ceylon, Java, etc. **3** *Cassia.* **4** A shade of light reddish-brown. [< L *cinnamomum* < Gk. *kinnamōmon* < Hebrew *qinnāmōn*]

cinnamon bear A cinnamon-colored variety of the American black bear.

cinnamon stone A cinnamon-colored garnet; essonite.

cin·na·myl (sin′ə·mil) *n. Chem.* The univalent radical, C_9H_9, an important constituent of many compounds used in making soap, perfumes, drugs, etc. [< CINNAM(ON) + -YL]

cin·quain (sing·kān′) *n.* A stanza of five lines. [< F]

cinque·foil (singk′foil) *n.* **1** *Archit.* A five-cusped ornament or window; a five-leaved rosette. **2** *Bot.* Any one of several species of a genus (*Potentilla*) of plants of the rose family, with five-lobed leaves. [< F < L *quinque* five + *folium* leaf]

CINQUEFOIL

ci·on (sī′ən) *n. Bot.* A piece cut from a plant or tree; a twig or shoot used for grafting. See SCION. [Var. of SCION]

-cion Var. of -TION.

ci·pher (sī′fər) *n.* **1** The character 0, the symbol of the absence of quantity, in numerical notation; zero. **2** A person or thing of no value or importance. **3** A cryptogram made by rearranging the individual characters of a plain text or by substituting others in their place. **4** The method of making such a cryptogram; also, the key for deciphering it. **5** A monogram; a character consisting of two or more interwoven or interlaced letters. **6** Any numerical character; a number. Also spelled *cypher.* —*v.t.* **1** To calculate arithmetically. **2** To write in characters of hidden meaning; encipher. **3** To add a cipher to. —*v.i.* **4** To work out arithmetical examples. [< OF *cyfre* < Arabic *ṣifr.* Doublet of ZERO.]

cip·o·lin (sip′ə·lin) *n.* An Italian marble having layers of alternating white and green. [< F < Ital. *cipollino,* dim. of *cipolla* onion; with ref. to its layered structure]

cir·ca·di·an (sər·kā′dē·ən) *adj. Biol.* Pertaining to or designating those vital processes in plants and animals that tend to recur in cycles of approximately 24 hours. [< L *circa* around + *dies* day]

cir·ci·nate (sûr′sə·nāt) *adj.* **1** Ringed; ring-shaped. **2** *Bot.* Rolled inward from the apex into a coil. [< L *circinatus,* pp. of *circinare* make round < *circinus* circle] —**cir′ci·nate′ly** *adv.*

cir·cle (sûr′kəl) *n.* **1** A plane figure bounded by a curved line everywhere equally distant from the center; also, the circumference of such a figure. **2** A circular object or arrangement of objects, or whatever is included within it; an enclosure; ring; halo: a *circle* around the moon. **3** Loosely, a round or spherical body. **4** An association of persons having the same interests or pursuits; a set; class; coterie. **5** A series ending at the starting point; a repeated succession; hence, a completed series or system: the *circle* of the months. **6** A circular path or course; circuit. **7** An indirect statement; circumlocution. **8** *Logic* A form of argument in which the conclusion is virtually assumed to prove the

premise and vice versa: also called *argument in a circle.* **9** In some European countries, an administrative governmental district. **10** An astronomical or other instrument whose important parts are graduated circles. **11** A circus ring. **12** A tier of seats or gallery in a theater: the dress *circle.* **13** A crown; diadem. **14** *Astron.* The orbit of a heavenly body; formerly, the supposed sphere of a planet or other body. **15** The domain of a special influence. —*v.* **·cled, ·cling** *v.t.* **1** To enclose with or as with a circle; encompass; surround. **2** To move around, as in a circle: The dog *circles* the field. —*v.i.* **3** To move in a circle; revolve. [< L *circulus,* dim. of *circus* ring] —**cir′cler** *n.*

cir·clet (sûr′klit) *n.* A small ring or ring-shaped object, especially as used as a personal ornament. [< F *cerclet,* dim. of *cercle* ring; infl. in form by CIRCLE]

cir·cuit (sûr′kit) *n.* **1** A passing or traveling round; a revolution. **2** A journey from place to place, as by a judge or clergyman, in the discharge of duties. **3** A district or route within certain limits or boundaries; especially, a division assigned to a peripatetic judge for the holding of courts at stated intervals. **4** The persons undertaking these peripatetic journeys, as the judges. **5** In the Methodist Church, and in the Evangelical Association, a district in charge of an itinerant minister. **6** Distance around; compass; circumference. **7** *Electr.* **a** The entire course traversed by an electric current. When it is complete, so that the current will flow, it is a **made** or **closed circuit;** when interrupted, so that the current stops, it is a **broken** or **open circuit.** **b** The complete assembly of generators, conductors, vacuum tubes, switches, etc., by which an electric current is transmitted. **8** A circuit court. See under COURT. **9** A radio transmission and reception system. —**to ride the circuit** To travel an assigned route in the capacity of minister, lawyer, judge, etc. —*v.t. & v.i.* To go or move in a circuit. [< F < L *circuitus* < *circumire* < *circum-* around + *ire* go]

circuit binding A style of bookbinding in which the sides of a book are made to overlap the edge of the pages to protect them from injury.

circuit breaker *Electr.* A switch or relay for breaking a circuit under specified or abnormal conditions of current flow.

circuit judge A judge of a circuit court.

cir·cu·i·tous (sər·kyōō′ə·təs) *adj.* Of the nature of a circuit; indirect; round-about. —**cir·cu′i·tous·ly** *adv.* —**cir·cu′i·tous·ness** *n.*

circuit rider A minister who preaches at churches on a circuit or district route.

cir·cuit·ry (sûr′kit·rē) *n.* The design and arrangement of circuits in any device, instrument, or system carrying an electric current: radio *circuitry.*

cir·cu·i·ty (sər·kyōō′ə·tē) *n. pl.* **·ties** **1** Movement in a circuit; circular form or movement. **2** Indirectness; round-about procedure or speech.

cir·cu·lar (sûr′kyə·lər) *adj.* **1** Forming, or bounded by, a circle; round. **2** Moving or occurring in a circle or round. **3** Ending at the point of beginning. **4** Constantly repeated in the same or similar order: *circular* motion. **5** Intended for public circulation. **6** Circuitous; devious; indirect. —*n.* A communication for general circulation; a circular letter or announcement, such as a printed advertisement. See synonyms under ROUND. [< L *circularis* < *circulus* circle] —**cir·cu·lar·i·ty** (sûr′kyə·lar′ə·tē), **cir′cu·lar·ness** *n.* —**cir′cu·lar·ly** *adv.*

cir·cu·lar·ize (sûr′kyə·lə·rīz′) *v.t.* **·ized, ·iz·ing** **1** To make circular. **2** To ply with circulars. —**cir′cu·lar·i·za′tion** *n.* —**cir′cu·lar·iz′er** *n.*

circular measure A system of measurement for circles:

60 seconds of an arc (60″)	= 1 minute of an arc (1′)
60 minutes of an arc	= 1 degree (1°)
90 degrees	= 1 quadrant
4 quadrants (360°)	= 1 circle

circular mil A unit of measurement for the cross-sectional area of wires, equal to the area of a circle having a diameter of 1 mil.

circular sailing *Naut.* Sailing by the arc of a great circle: also called *great-circle sailing.*

circular saw A disk-shaped saw having a

toothed edge, rotated at high speed by a motor.

circular triangle *Geom.* A triangle whose sides are formed by the arcs of a circle.

cir·cu·late (sûr′kyə·lāt) *v.* **·lat·ed, ·lat·ing** *v.t.* **1** To spread about; disseminate, as news. —*v.i.* **2** To move by a circuitous course back to the starting point, as the blood through the body. **3** To spread abroad, or become diffused. **4** *Colloq.* To travel about. **5** To repeat indefinitely a number or set of numbers in a decimal quantity. See synonyms under SPREAD. [< L *circulatus,* pp. of *circulari* form a circle < *circulus* CIRCLE] —**cir′cu·la·tor** *n.*

circulating decimal A decimal number in which one or more digits are repeated indefinitely, as 0.444 . . . , 0.16353535 . . . , 0.824-37437 . . . : also called *recurring decimal, repeating decimal.*

circulating medium Currency used in exchange.

cir·cu·la·tion (sûr′kyə·lā′shən) *n.* **1** The act of circulating or state of being circulated. **2** Motion around or through something back to the starting point: the *circulation* of the blood. **3** Transmission; diffusion; dissemination. **4** The extent or amount of distribution; number of copies issued, as of a paper or periodical, etc. **5** A current medium of exchange, as coin, etc. [< L *circulatio, -onis* < *circulari.* See CIRCULATE.] —**cir′cu·la·tive** *adj.* —**cir·cu·la·to·ry** (sûr′kyə·lə·tôr′ē, -tō′rē) *adj.*

circum- *prefix* **1** About; around; on all sides; surrounding:

circumagitate	circummigration

2 Revolving around:

circumlunar	circumsolar

[< L *circum-* around, about < *circus* circle]

cir·cum·am·bi·ent (sûr′kəm·am′bē·ənt) *adj.* Extending or going around; encompassing. —**cir′cum·am′bi·ence, cir′cum·am′bi·en·cy** *n.*

cir·cum·am·bu·late (sûr′kəm·am′byə·lāt) *v.t. & v.i.* **·lat·ed, ·lat·ing** To walk around. [< L *circumambulatus,* pp. of *circumambulare* < *circum-* around + *ambulare* walk] —**cir′cum·am′bu·la′tion** *n.* —**cir′cum·am′bu·la′tor** *n.*

cir·cum·ben·di·bus (sûr′kəm·ben′di·bəs) *n.* A round-about course or method; circumlocution: a humorous usage. [Coined from L *circum* + BEND + L *-ibus*]

cir·cum·cise (sûr′kəm·sīz) *v.t.* **·cised, ·cis·ing** **1** To cut off the prepuce or, in females, the inner labia of, especially as a religious rite. **2** In the Bible, to purify from sin; to cleanse spiritually. [< OF *circonciser* < L *circumcisus,* pp. of *circumcidere* < *circum-* around + *caedere* cut] —**cir′cum·cis′er** *n.*

cir·cum·fer·ence (sər·kum′fər·əns) *n.* **1** The boundary line of a circle. **2** Distance around; circuit; compass. [< L *circumferentia* < *circum-* around + *ferre* bear] —**cir·cum·fer·en·tial** (sər·kum′fər·en′shəl) *adj.* —**cir·cum′fer·en′tial·ly** *adv.*

cir·cum·flex (sûr′kəm·fleks) *n.* A mark (‸) used over a letter to indicate the combination of a rising with a falling tone or to mark a long vowel, contraction, etc., or used as a diacritical mark in phonetics. In the pronunciations in this dictionary, the circumflex is used over *a* to indicate the vowel sound in *care* (kâr), over *o* for the vowel in *fall* (fôl), and over *u* for the vowel in *earn* (ûrn). —*adj.* **1** Pronounced or marked with the circumflex accent. **2** Bent in a curvilinear manner, as certain vessels and nerves. —*v.t.* **1** To utter with a circumflex intonation or accent; mark with a circumflex. **2** To wind around; bend about. [< L *circumflexus,* pp. of *circumflectere* < *circum-* around + *flectere* bend] —**cir·cum·flex·ion** (sûr′kəm·flek′shən) *n.*

cir·cum·flu·ent (sər·kum′flōō·ənt) *adj.* **1** Flowing around; surrounding. **2** Surrounded by, or as by, water. Also **cir·cum′flu·ous.** [< L *circumfluens, -entis,* ppr. of *circumfluere* < *circum-* around + *fluere* flow]

cir·cum·fuse (sûr′kəm·fyōōz′) *v.t.* **·fused, ·fus·ing** **1** To pour, scatter, or spread about. **2** To surround, as with a liquid. [< L *circumfusus,* pp. of *circumfundere* < *circum-* around + *fundere* pour] —**cir·cum·fu·sion** (sûr′kəm·fyōō′zhən) *n.*

cir·cum·gy·rate (sûr′kəm·jī′rāt) *v.t. & v.i.* **·rat·ed, ·rat·ing** To turn or roll about. [< CIRCUM- + L *gyratus,* pp. of *gyrare* spin [<

cir·cum·gy·ra·tion (sûr'kəm·jī·rā'shən) n. The act of turning around; rotation; motion in a circular course. — **cir·cum·gy·ra·to·ry** (sûr'kəm·jī'rə·tôr'ē, -tō'rē) adj.

cir·cum·ja·cent (sûr'kəm·jā'sənt) adj. Bordering on all sides; surrounding. [<L circumjacens, -entis, ppr. of circumjacere <circum- around + jacere lie] — **cir'cum·ja'cence, cir'cum·ja'cen·cy** n.

cir·cum·lo·cu·tion (sûr'kəm·lō·kyōō'shən) n. Indirect or round-about expression; the use of superfluous words. [<L circumlocutio, -onis < circum- around + locutio speaking <loqui speak] — **cir·cum·loc·u·tory** (sûr'kəm·lok'yə·tôr'ē, -tō'rē) adj.

Synonyms (noun): diffuseness, periphrasis, pleonasm, prolixity, redundance, redundancy, surplusage, tautology, tediousness, verbiage, verbosity, wordiness. Circumlocution is the more common, periphrasis the more technical word. Diffuseness is a scattering both of words and thought; redundance or redundancy is an overflow. Prolixity goes into endless petty details, without selection or perspective. Pleonasm may be an emphatic, tautology is a useless repetition of a word or words. "I saw it with my eyes" is a pleonasm; "all the members agreed unanimously" is tautology. Verbiage is the use of mere words without thought. Verbosity and wordiness denote an excess of words in proportion to the thought. Antonyms: brevity, compactness, conciseness, condensation, directness, succinctness, terseness.

cir·cum·mure (sûr'kəm·myōōr') v.t. **·mured, ·mur·ing** To wall around. [<CIRCUM- + LL murare build a wall <L murus wall]

cir·cum·nav·i·gate (sûr'kəm·nav'ə·gāt) v.t. **·gat·ed, ·gat·ing** To sail around. [<L circumnavigatus, pp. of circumnavigare <circum- around + navigare sail] — **cir·cum·nav·i·ga·ble** (sûr'kəm·nav'ə·gə·bəl) adj. — **cir'cum·nav'i·ga'tion** n. — **cir'cum·nav'i·ga'tor** n.

cir·cum·nu·ta·tion (sûr'kəm·nyōō·tā'shən) n. Bot. A nodding or turning successively in all directions, as observed in the tips of young and growing plant organs, such as tendrils, stems, or roots. [<CIRCUM- + L nutatio, -onis a nodding <nutare nod]

cir·cum·po·lar (sûr'kəm·pō'lər) adj. Near or surrounding one of the terrestrial or celestial poles: applied specifically to stars revolving about the pole without setting.

cir·cum·pose (sûr'kəm·pōz') v.t. **·posed, ·pos·ing** To place around. — **cir·cum·po·si·tion** (sûr'kəm·pə·zish'ən) n.

cir·cum·ro·tate (sûr'kəm·rō'tāt) v.i. **·tat·ed, ·tat·ing** To turn in the manner of a wheel; revolve. — **cir·cum·ro·ta·to·ry** (sûr'kəm·rō'tə·tôr'ē, -tō'rē), **cir'cum·ro'ta·ry** (-rō'tə·rē) adj. — **cir'cum·ro·ta'tion** n.

cir·cum·scis·sile (sûr'kəm·sis'il) adj. Bot. Dehiscent, as a capsule, in a transverse circular line, so that the top separates like a lid, as in the common purslane. [<L circumscissus, pp. of circumscindere <circum- around + scindere cut]

cir·cum·scribe (sûr'kəm·skrīb') v.t. **·scribed, scrib·ing 1** To draw a line or figure around; encircle. **2** To mark out the limits of; define. **3** To confine within bounds; restrict. **4** Geom. **a** To surround with or as with a figure that touches at every possible point: to circumscribe a triangle with a circle. **b** To cause to surround a figure thus: to circumscribe a circle about a triangle. [<L circumscribere <circum- around + scribere write] — **cir'cum·scrib'a·ble** adj. — **cir'cum·scrib'er** n.

Synonyms: bound, confine, define, delineate, describe, designate, enclose, fence, limit, restrict. See RESTRAIN. Antonyms: dilate, distend, enlarge, expand, open.

cir·cum·scrip·tion (sûr'kəm·skrip'shən) n. **1** The act of circumscribing. **2** The state of being limited or bounded; limitation; restriction. **3** The line marking the external boundary of an object; surrounding margin or edge; periphery. **4** The space or district circumscribed. **5** Obs. Definition; description. **6** Obs. Something written around, as an inscription surrounding a coin. [<L circumscriptio, -onis < circumscribere. See CIRCUMSCRIBE.] — **cir'cum·scrip'tive** adj.

cir·cum·so·lar (sûr'kəm·sō'lər) adj. Near, re-

volving about, or surrounding, the sun.

cir·cum·spect (sûr'kəm·spekt) adj. Attentive to everything; watchful in all directions, as against danger or error; cautious; wary. See synonyms under THOUGHTFUL. [<L circumspectus, pp. of circumspicere <circum- around + specere look] — **cir'cum·spect'ly** adv. — **cir'cum·spect'ness** n.

cir·cum·spec·tion (sûr'kəm·spek'shən) n. Cautious and careful observation with a view to wise conduct. See synonyms under CARE, PRUDENCE.

cir·cum·stance (sûr'kəm·stans) n. **1** Something existing or occurring incidentally to some other fact or event; a related or concomitant act or thing; an accessory detail. **2** An event, happening, or fact, especially if incidental or subordinate: a circumstance in English history. **3** pl. The surrounding facts, means, influences, etc., especially as related to one's support and way of living. **4** Environment: He is the victim of circumstance; also, environment with reference to state or condition resulting from adventitious surroundings. **5** That which is unessential or of no account; detail; circumstantiality. **6** Archaic Formal show or display; ceremony; pomp. — **under no circumstances** Never; under no conditions. — **under the circumstances** Since such is the case; things being as they are or were. — v.t. **·stanced, ·stanc·ing 1** To place in or under limiting circumstances or conditions: chiefly in past participle. **2** Obs. To set forth circumstantially; relate with details. [<OF <L circumstantia <circumstare <circum- around + stare stand]

Synonyms (noun): accompaniment, concomitant, detail, event, fact, feature, incident, item, occurrence, particular, point, position, situation. A circumstance is something existing or occurring in connection with or relation to some other fact or event, modifying or throwing light upon the principal matter without affecting its essential character; an accompaniment is something that unites with the principal matter, but is not necessary to it; as, the piano accompaniment to a song; a concomitant goes with a thing in natural connection, but in a subordinate capacity, or perhaps in contrast. A circumstance is not strictly, nor usually, an occasion, condition, effect, or result. Nor is the circumstance properly an incident. All the circumstances make up the situation. Compare ACCIDENT, CAUSE, EVENT.

cir·cum·stan·tial (sûr'kəm·stan'shəl) adj. **1** Consisting of details; minute; particular. **2** Pertaining to or dependent on circumstances; indirect; presumptive. **3** Having to do with one's circumstances: circumstantial prosperity. **4** Incidental or casual; not essential. **5** Archaic Full of circumstance or display; ceremonial. See synonyms under MINUTE, PARTICULAR.

cir·cum·stan·ti·al·i·ty (sûr'kəm·stan'shē·al'ə·tē) n. pl. **·ties 1** The quality or characteristic of being particular, detailed, or minute. **2** A particular matter; a detail.

cir·cum·stan·ti·ate (sûr'kəm·stan'shē·āt) v.t. **·at·ed, ·at·ing** To set forth or establish by circumstances or in detail.

cir·cum·val·late (sûr'kəm·val'āt) v.t. **·lat·ed, ·lat·ing** To surround with a rampart or a trench. — adj. Enclosed by or as by a wall or rampart: circumvallate papillae. [<L circumvallatus, pp. of circumvallare <circum- around + vallare fortify <vallum rampart]

cir·cum·vent (sûr'kəm·vent') v.t. **1** To get around; get the better of, as by craft, artifice, or fraud; outwit. **2** To surround or entrap, as an enemy, by craft or strategem. **3** To pass around: to circumvent a town. **4** To forestall (an occurrence or happening). See synonyms under BAFFLE, DECEIVE. [<L circumventus, pp. of circumvenire <circum- around + venire come] — **cir'cum·ven'tive** adj. — **cir'cum·ven'tion** n.

cir·cum·ven·tor (sûr'kəm·ven'tər) n. **1** One who circumvents. **2** A surveying instrument having at the top a compass box, used for laying out horizontal angles. Also **cir'cum·vent'er**.

cir·cum·vo·lu·tion (sûr'kəm·və·lōō'shən) n. **1** The act of winding. **2** A single fold or

turn of something wound. **3** A turning round an axis or center; rotation; revolution. **4** Convolution; sinuosity. [<L circumvolutus, pp. of circumvolvere <circum- around + volvere turn, spin]

cir·cum·volve (sûr'kəm·volv') v.t. & v.i. **·volved, ·volv·ing** To revolve.

cir·cus (sûr'kəs) n. **1** A traveling show in which feats of horsemanship, tumbling, and strength, as well as clowns, wild animals, etc., are exhibited; also, a performance of such a show. **2** The circular, tented enclosure in which such a show is commonly held. **3** The troupe of performers in such a show. **4** In ancient Rome, a large oval or oblong enclosure with tiers of seats around it, used for races, games, etc. **5** Brit. A circle formed by bow-shaped rows of houses. **6** Colloq. Any person or thing regarded as uproariously entertaining. [<L, a ring, racecourse <Gk. kirkos. Doublet of CIRQUE.]

cirque (sûrk) n. **1** A circular enclosure; circus. **2** Geol. A circular valley with precipitous walls, usually formed by the action of glaciers. **3** A circlet; ring: a poetical usage. [<F <L circus. Doublet of CIRCUS.]

cir·rate (sir'āt) adj. Having curls or cirri. [<L cirratus <cirrus curl]

cir·rho·sis (si·rō'sis) n. Pathol. An abnormal formation of connective tissue, with wasting of the proper tissue of the liver or other organ. [<NL <Gk. kirrhos tawny; with ref. to the color of the cirrhotic liver] — **cir·rhot·ic** (si·rot'ik) adj.

cir·ri·ped (sir'ə·ped) n. One of an order (Cirripedia) of crustaceans which become attached or parasitic in the adult stage, as the barnacles. — adj. Of or pertaining to this order.

cirro- combining form Cirrus: cirrostratus. Also **cirri-**. [<L cirrus curl]

cir·ro·cu·mu·lus (sir'ō·kyōō'myə·ləs) n. Meteorol. A mass of fleecy, globular cloudlets in contact with one another, with an average height of 5 miles; mackerel sky. — **cir'ro·cu'mu·lar** or **cir'ro·cu'mu·lous** or **cir·ro·cu·mu·la·tive** (sir'ō·kyōō'myə·lā'tiv, -lə·tiv) adj.

cir·ro·stra·tus (sir'ō·strā'təs) n. Meteorol. A fine, whitish veil of cloud with an average height of 6 miles. — **cir'ro·stra'tive** adj.

cir·rous (sir'əs) adj. **1** Having or like cirri. **2** Of or pertaining to a cirrus cloud. Also **cir·rose** (sir'ōs).

cir·rus (sir'əs) n. pl. **cir·ri** (sir'ī) **1** Meteorol. A type of white, wispy cloud, usually consisting of ice crystals and having an average height of 7 miles, seen in tufts or feathery-shaped bands across the sky. **2** Bot. A tendril. **3** Zool. A threadlike appendage serving as an organ of touch. [<L, ringlet]

cir·soid (sûr'soid) adj. Resembling a varix; varicose. [<Gk. kirsos a dilated vein]

cir·sot·o·my (sər·sot'ə·mē) n. Surg. The incision of varicose veins. [<Gk. kirsos dilated vein + -TOMY]

cis- prefix **1** On this side of: opposed to TRANS- or ULTRA-: cisatlantic. **2** Since; following: opposed to PRE-: cis-Elizabethan. [<L cis on this side]

cis·al·pine (sis·al'pīn, -pin) adj. On the Roman side of the Alps. [<L cisalpinus < cis on this side + Alpes the Alps]

cis·at·lan·tic (sis'ət·lan'tik) adj. On this side of the Atlantic: opposed to transatlantic.

cis·co (sis'kō) n. pl. **·coes** or **·cos** A whitefish (genus Leucichthys) of North America; especially, the lake herring (L. artedi) of Lakes Michigan and Ontario. [? <N. Am. Ind.]

cis·lu·nar (sis·lōō'nər) adj. On this side of the moon.

cis·soid (sis'oid)
Math. n. A curve GAP intersecting a circle at the two extremities of a diameter and having a cusp the apex of which is at the point on the circumference where the perpendicular bisector of the diameter falls; the curve traces the locus of a point

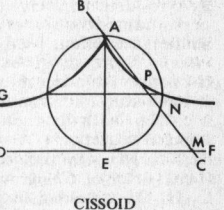

CISSOID

moving so that a straight line *BC* drawn through the apex of the cusp at *A* through the curve at any point *P* intersects the tangent *DEF* (with *E* on the circumference diametrically opposite to *A*) at point *M,* so that *AP* = *NM.* —*adj.* Contained within two curves that intersect each other, as an angle: opposed to *sistroid:* The angle interior to both curves is a *cissoid* angle; the exterior and opposite a *sistroid.* [<Gk. *kissoeidēs* like ivy <*kissos* ivy + *eidos* form]

cist[1] (sist) *n.* A casket; box. [<L *cista* CHEST]

cist[2] (sist, kist) *n.* A small sepulchral chamber, or chest, made of flat stones; a kistvaen. [< Welsh, chest <L *cista* chest]

cis·ta·ceous (sis·tā′shəs) *adj. Bot.* Designating the rockrose family (*Cistaceae*) of shrubby or herbaceous plants, with regular, perfect, often showy flowers. [<NL *Cistaceae* <Gk. *kistos* rockrose]

cis·tern (sis′tərn) *n.* 1 A reservoir, usually of masonry, wood, or metal, for storing water or other liquids; also, any natural reservoir. 2 Any analogous receptacle in which fluid is stored. 3 *Anat.* A large lymph space; a sac. [<OF *cisterne* <L *cisterna* < *cista* chest]

cis·tus (sis′təs) *n.* A plant of a genus (*Cistus*) of European evergreen shrubs of the rockrose family: gum ladanum is produced by several species. [<Gk. *kistos* rockrose]

cist·vaen (kist′vīn) See KISTVAEN.

cit·a·del (sit′ə·dəl, -del) *n.* 1 A fortress commanding a city. 2 Any strong fortress. 3 The heavily plated central casemate containing the guns in a war vessel. See synonyms under FORTIFICATION. [<F *citadelle* <Ital. *cittadella,* dim. of *città* city]

ci·ta·tion (sī·tā′shən) *n.* 1 The act of citing, or a passage quoted. 2 A public commendation for exceptional military conduct or achievement. 3 *Law* A judicial summons. 4 Recounting; enumeration. [<F <L *citatio, -onis* < *citare* CITE] —**ci·ta·to·ry** (sī′tə·tôr′ē, -tō′rē) *adj.*

cite (sīt) *v.t.* **cit·ed, cit·ing** 1 To quote or refer to as an authority, illustration, or exemplification for proof or support. 2 To refer to specifically, as in a military report. 3 *Law* To summon to appear, as before a tribunal. See synonyms under ALLEGE, ARRAIGN, QUOTE. ◆ Homophones: *sight, site.* [<F *citer* <L *citare,* freq. of *cire* call] —**cit′a·ble, cite′a·ble** *adj.*

cith·a·ra (sith′ə·rə) *n.* 1 An ancient Greek stringed instrument with a wooden case, the strings extending to the base from a crosspiece connecting the straight hollow arms: the instrument of professional musicians. 2 Loosely, any of the stringed instruments of ancient Greece. Also spelled *kithara.* [<L <Gk. *kithara.* Doublet of GUITAR and ZITHER.]

CITHARA

cith·er (sith′ər) *n.* 1 A zither. 2 A cithern. 3 A cithara.

cith·ern (sith′ərn) *n.* A medieval lute or guitar having wire strings plucked with a plectrum: the original of the zither: also spelled *cittern, zittern.* [Blend of CITHER and GITTERN]

cit·i·fied (sit′i·fīd) *adj.* Having the ways and means of city life; following city fashions: also spelled *cityfied.*

cit·i·zen (sit′ə·zən) *n.* 1 A native or naturalized person owing allegiance to, and entitled to protection from, a government: opposed to *alien.* 2 A resident of a city or town. 3 A private person; one who is not a public officer nor a soldier; a civilian. [<AF *citezein,* var. of OF *citeain* < *cité* CITY] —**cit′i·zen·ess** *n. fem.*

cit·i·zen·ry (sit′ə·zən·rē) *n.* Citizens collectively.

cit·i·zen·ship (sit′ə·zən·ship′) *n.* The status of a citizen, with its rights and duties; state of being a citizen.

citra- *prefix* On this side; cis-. [<L]

cit·ral (sit′rəl) *n. Chem.* An oily liquid aldehyde, $C_{10}H_{16}O$, contained in geranium, lemon, and other oils: used as a flavoring extract and in perfumery; geranial. [<CITR(US) + AL(DEHYDE)]

cit·rate (sit′rāt, -rit, sī′trāt) *n. Chem.* A salt of citric acid.

cit·re·ous (sit′rē·əs) *adj.* Having the yellow color of a citron or lemon; citrine. [<L *citreus* <*citrus* citron tree]

cit·ric (sit′rik) *adj.* Derived from lemons, oranges, or similar fruits.

citric acid *Chem.* A white, crystalline, sharply sour compound, $C_6H_8O_7$, contained in various fruits, and obtained from lemons, limes, and sour oranges, etc., and also made synthetically.

cit·ri·cul·ture (sit′ri·kul′chər) *n.* The cultivation of oranges, lemons, grapefruit, and other citrus fruits. —**cit′ri·cul′tur·ist** *n.*

cit·rin (sit′rin) *n. Biochem.* A constituent of vitamin P, consisting of a mixture of glycosides and occurring in citrus fruits.

cit·rine (sit′rin) *adj.* 1 Having the yellow color of a citron or lemon. 2 Pertaining to the citron, lemon, and allied trees. —*n.* 1 Citron color. 2 A light-yellow, vitreous variety of quartz so fused as to resemble topaz. [<F *citrin*]

cit·ron (sit′rən) *n.* 1 A fruit like a lemon, but larger and less acid. 2 The tree (*Citrus medica*) producing this fruit. 3 A watermelon (*Citrullus vulgaris citroides*), with a small, hard-fleshed fruit. 4 The rind of either of these fruits, preserved and used in confections. [<F <Ital. *citrone* <L *citrus* citrus tree]

cit·ron·el·la (sit′rə·nel′ə) *n.* A grass (*Cymbopogon nardus*) cultivated in Ceylon, yielding **citronella oil,** which is used in perfumery, in cooking for flavoring, and as protection against mosquitos. Also **citronella grass.** [< NL <CITRON; so called from its odor]

cit·ron·el·lal (sit′rə·nel′al) *n. Chem.* An unsaturated aldehyde, $C_9H_{17}CHO$, found in citronella oil and other essential oils: used in making soaps and perfumes.

citron wood 1 The wood of the sandarac tree, used in cabinetwork. 2 The wood of the citron tree.

cit·rus (sit′rəs) *adj.* Of or pertaining to a genus (*Citrus*) of trees or shrubs of the rue family, cultivated for their fruits. Also **cit′rous.** [<L, citron tree]

citrus fruits Fruits of the genus *Citrus:* the orange, lemon, lime, citron, grapefruit, etc.

cit·y (sit′ē) *n. pl.* **cit·ies** 1 A place inhabited by a large, permanent, organized community. 2 In the United States and Canada, a municipality of the first class, governed by a mayor and aldermen and created by charter. 3 Any one of the ancient Greek city-states. 4 The people of a city, collectively. 5 In ancient times, a citadel or central walled section used by the dwellers in a district as a market, a place of worship or festivity, and a refuge in time of invasion. —**The City** That part of London which is governed by the Lord Mayor and corporation; also, the financial center of this district. [<F *cité* <L *civitas* < *civis* citizen]

city editor On a newspaper, the editor having charge of the city news and the reportorial staff.

city father One who directs the public affairs of a city; a mayor, councilman, etc.

city hall 1 An administrative building of a city in which the chief government offices are situated. 2 The city government presently in office. 3 Bureaucratic procedures or officials characterized as obstinately unresponsive: Go fight *city hall.*

city manager An administrator not publicly elected but appointed by a city council to act as manager of the city.

City of God Heaven.

City of Seven Hills Rome.

city planning Public control of the physical development of a city, as by regulation of the size and use of buildings and streets, location of parks and public facilities, etc.

cit·y·scape (sit′ē·skāp′) *n.* A view of a city, as in a painting.

cit·y·state (sit′ē·stāt′) *n.* A state consisting of an independent city, having sovereignty over contiguous territories, as in ancient Greece.

Ciudad Vic·to·ria (vēk·tō′ryä) The capital of Tamaulipas state, Mexico.

civ·et (siv′it) *n.* 1 A substance of musklike odor, secreted by certain glands of the civet cat: used as a perfume. 2 A foxlike carnivore of Africa (genus *Viverra*), dark grey in color and banded and spotted with black, that secretes this substance: also **civet cat.** 3 The fur of this animal. See ZIBET. [< MF *civette* < Arabic *zabād*]

civ·ic (siv′ik) *adj.* Of or pertaining to a city, a citizen, or citizenship; civil. [< L *civicus* <*civis* citizen]

civ·ics (siv′iks) *n.* The science of government.

civ·il (siv′əl) *adj.* 1 Observing the social proprieties; decently polite; not rude. 2 Of or pertaining to civil or everyday life: distinguished from *ecclesiastical, naval, military.* 3 Pertaining to citizens or to the state, or to relations between the citizen and the state or between citizens, as regulated by law; belonging to private legal rights; established by law: distinguished from *criminal, political,* or *natural:* civil rights. 4 Occurring within the state or between citizens; intestine: *civil war.* 5 In accordance with the requirements of civilization; civilized. 6 Of or pertaining to civil law. See CIVIL LAW. See synonyms under POLITE. [< F < L *civilis* < *civis* citizen] —**civ′il·ly** *adv.*

civil death The total deprivation of civil rights and standing, as by life imprisonment, etc.

civil defense A program of action by civilians for the protection of the population and the maintenance of essential services in the event of overt enemy action, as nuclear bombardment.

civil disobedience Passive resistance.

civil engineer A professional engineer trained to design and build roads, bridges, tunnels, harbors, canals, docks, irrigation systems, and other public works.

ci·vil·ian (sə·vil′yən) *n.* 1 One who follows the pursuits of civil life, as distinguished from military, naval, or clerical. 2 *Obs.* One learned in the Roman or civil law. —*adj.* Of or pertaining to a civilian or civil life. [< OF *civilien* < L *civilis.* See CIVIL.]

ci·vil·i·ty (sə·vil′ə·tē) *n. pl.* **·ties** 1 The quality of being civil; courtesy; cold or formal politeness. 2 A civil act or speech. 3 *pl.* The amenities of social life. See synonyms under FAVOR.

civ·i·li·za·tion (siv′ə·lə·zā′shən, -lī·zā′-) *n.* 1 The state of human society regarded as having reached a high level of intellectual, social, and cultural development. 2 The countries and peoples considered to have reached this stage. 3 A stage in the cultural development of any specific people, country, or geographical region: Greek *civilization;* a primitive *civilization.* See CULTURE.

civ·i·lize (siv′ə·līz) *v.t.* **·lized, ·liz·ing** To bring into a state of civilization; educate from savagery; refine. Also *Brit.* **civ′i·lise.** —**civ′i·lized** *adj.* —**civ′i·liz′er** *n.*

civil liberty Freedom of the individual citizen from government control or restraint of, or interference with, his property, opinions, or affairs, except as the public good may require.

civil list 1 That part of the revenue annually appropriated in the United States for the salaries and expenses of civil officers and the government. 2 The body of such officers. 3 In Great Britain and elsewhere, the amount voted by the legislature for the personal and household expenses of the sovereign.

civil marriage A marriage solemnized as a civil contract, as distinguished from an ecclesiastical marriage considered as a sacrament.

civil rights Private, non-political privileges; specifically, exemption from involuntary servitude, as established by the 13th and 14th amendments to the U.S. Constitution and by certain acts of Congress.

civil servant One employed in the civil service.

civil service 1 The branches of governmental service that are neither military, naval, legislative, or judicial. 2 The body of persons employed in these branches.

civil war War between parties of the same government, between states within a nation, between fellow citizens, etc.

civ·ism (siv′iz·əm) *n.* Devotion to the public weal; good citizenship.

Cl *Chem.* Chlorine (symbol Cl).

clab·ber[1] (klab′ər) *n.* Milk curdled by souring. —*v.t. & v.i.* To curdle, as milk. [Short for BON-NYCLABBER]

clab·ber[2] (klab′ər) *n.* Mire; mud. [< Irish *clabar*]

clack (klak) *v.t.* 1 To strike together so as to make a cracking sound; clap; rattle. 2 To utter heedlessly; babble. —*v.i.* 3 To make a rattling, clapping, or cracking sound. 4 To talk hastily or continually; chatter. 5 To cluck or cackle, as a hen. —*n.* 1 A sharp, short, clapping sound, or something producing it. 2 Continual and confused talk; chatter. 3 *Slang* The tongue: Hold your *clack;* hence, a gossip. [Imit.] —**clack′er** *n.*

clack valve *Mech.* A valve hinged at one edge, permitting flow of fluid in one direction only.

See illustration under HYDRAULIC.

clad (klad) Past tense of CLOTHE. —*adj.* Clothed.

cla·dis·tics (klə·dis'tiks) *n.* A branch of biology dealing with the evolutionary interrelationships of organisms. [<Gk. *klados* sprout + (STAT)ISTICS]

clad·o·phyll (klad'ə·fil) *n.* *Bot.* A leaflike branch stemming from the axil of a leaf. Also **clad·ode** (klad'ōd). [<Gk. *klados* branch + *phyllos* leaf]

claim (klām) *v.t.* 1 To demand on the ground or right; affirm to be one's due; assert ownership or title to. 2 To hold to be true against implied denial or doubt. 3 To require or deserve: The problem *claims* our attention. —*v.i.* 4 To derive a right; make a claim, especially by descent: He *claims* from royal lineage. See synonyms under ALLEGE, ASSERT, ASSUME, DEMAND. —*n.* 1 The demand for something as due or on the ground of right; the assertion of a right; a right or title. 2 An assertion, as of a fact. 3 A tract of government land, petitioned for, marked out, and claimed by a settler. 4 A piece of public land staked out by a miner to be worked by him. See synonyms under RIGHT. —**Court of Claims** See under COURT. [<OF *clamer* call, claim <L *clamare* declare] —**claim'a·ble** *adj.* —**claim'er** *n.*

claim·ant (klā'mənt) *n.* One who makes a legal claim or asserts a right, title, etc.

claim-jum·per (klām'jum'pər) *n.* One who seizes another's claim.

clair de lune (klâr' də lün') 1 In ceramics, a faint, grayish-blue glaze applied to certain varieties of Chinese porcelain. 2 The color of this glaze. [<F, moonlight] —**clair-de-lune'** *adj.*

clair·voy·ance (klâr·voi'əns) *n.* 1 The ability to see things not visible to the normal human eye; second sight. 2 Intuitive sagacity or perception; mind-reading. [<F] —**clair·voy'ant** *adj. & n.*

clam (klam) *n.* 1 Any of various bivalve mollusks; especially, the edible quahog of North Atlantic American coasts, and the **long** or **soft clam** (*Mya arenaria*) of the southern Atlantic coasts. 2 *U.S. Colloq.* An uncommunicative person. —**giant clam** A huge bivalve mollusk (*Tridacna gigas*) of the Indian and Pacific Oceans: the shell may exceed 3 feet in length and weigh more than 500 pounds. —*v.i.* **clammed, clam·ming** to hunt for or dig clams. —**to clam up** *U.S. Slang* To maintain silence, as a criminal under interrogation. [Short for *clamshell* <*clam* a clamp, OE *clamm* + SHELL]

GIANT CLAM

cla·mant (klā'mənt) *adj.* 1 Calling for help or remedy; crying; insistent. 2 Clamorous; resounding: a poetic usage. [<L *clamans, -antis,* ppr. of *clamare* cry out]

clam·a·to·ri·al (klam'ə·tôr'ē·əl, -tō'rē) *adj.* *Ornithol.* Relating to a suborder (*Clamatores*) of raucous-voiced passerine birds, as the kingbirds. [<NL *Clamatores* <L *clamare* cry out]

clam·bake (klam'bāk') *n.* 1 A picnic where roasted clams are the principal dish: especially common at the seashore in New England, where the clams, often with other articles of food, are usually cooked on hot stones, sometimes in a hole covered with seaweed. 2 The meal served at such a picnic. 3 *U.S. Slang* A radio broadcast that breaks down because of bad handling and mistakes; any poor broadcast. 4 *U.S. Slang* An informal gathering of jazz musicians to improvise music for their own enjoyment.

clam·ber (klam'bər) *v.t. & v.i.* To climb up, down, or along by using hands and feet; also, to climb by attaching tendrils, as certain vines. [Akin to CLIMB] —**clam'ber·er** *n.*

clam·my (klam'ē) *adj.* **·mi·er, ·mi·est** 1 Damp and cold. 2 Soft and sticky. [<CLAM² *adj.*] —**clam'mi·ly** *adv.* —**clam'mi·ness** *n.*

clam·or (klam'ər) *n.* 1 Any loud, repeated outcry, din, or noise; vociferation; noisy confusion of voices. 2 A continuous, vehement objecting or demanding; public outcry. See synonyms under NOISE. —*v.t.* 1 To utter with loud outcry. 2 To move or drive by clamor. —*v.i.* 3 To make loud outcries, demands, or complaints; vociferate. Also *Brit.* **clam'our.** [<OF <L <*clamare* cry out] —**clam'or·er** *n.*

clam·or·ous (klam'ər·əs) *adj.* Making or made with clamor; noisy. See synonyms under NOISY.

clamp¹ (klamp) *n.* A device for compressing, holding in position, or binding together two or more parts. —*v.t.* To join or bind with or as with a clamp. [<M Du. *klampe*]

clamp² (klamp) *v.i.* To walk heavily; tramp. —*n.* A heavy tread; tramp. [Imit.]

clamp·er (klamp'ər) *n.* An attachment for fastening to shoes to prevent the wearer from slipping on ice; a creeper.

clam·shell (klam'shel') *n.* 1 The shell or half-shell of a clam. 2 A dredging box or bucket shaped and hinged like the shell of a clam.

clam·worm (klam'wûrm') *n.* Nereis.

clan (klan) *n.* 1 A united group of relatives, or families, having a common ancestor, one hereditary chieftain, and the same surname, especially in the Scottish Highlands. 2 In certain primitive societies, a body of kindred related in only one line, the members of which do not intermarry, having its own council, property, religion, etc.; an exogamous subdivision of a tribe: also called *sib.* 3 A clique, or set of persons; a fraternity; club. See synonyms under CLASS. [<Scottish Gaelic *clann*]

clan·des·tine (klan·des'tin) *adj.* Kept secret for a purpose; concealed; surreptitious; furtive; underhand. See synonyms under SECRET. [<L *clandestinus* <*clam* in secret] —**clan·des'tine·ly** *adv.* —**clan·des'tine·ness** *n.*

clang (klang) *v.t.* 1 To cause to send forth a loud, ringing metallic sound. —*v.i.* 2 To send forth such a sound: The bells *clanged.* 3 To strike together with such a sound: The shields *clanged* together. —*n.* 1 A ringing sound, as of metal struck. 2 In acoustics, a tone with its overtones; acoustic clang; timbre. 3 The ringing call of cranes or geese. [Prob. imit. Cf. L *clangere.*]

clan·gor (klang'gər, klang'ər) *n.* Repeated clanging; a clanging or noisy ringing; clamor. —*v.i.* To ring noisily; clang. Also *Brit.* **clan'gour.** [<L <*clangere* clang] —**clan'gor·ous** *adj.* —**clan'gor·ous·ly** *adv.*

clank (klangk) *n.* An abrupt, short, harsh, metallic sound. —*v.t. & v.i.* To emit, or cause to emit, a clank. [Blend of CLANG and CLINK]

clan·nish (klan'ish) *adj.* 1 Like a clan; disposed to cling together. 2 Bound by family tradition, class, or clan prejudice, etc.; narrow. —**clan'nish·ly** *adv.* —**clan'nish·ness** *n.*

clan·ship (klan'ship) *n.* Union under a chief.

clans·man (klanz'mən) *n.* *pl.* **·men** (-mən) A member of a clan or of the same clan.

clap¹ (klap) *v.* **clapped** or **clapt, clap·ping** *v.t.* 1 To strike together with a sharp, explosive sound. 2 To applaud by clapping the hands. 3 To strike suddenly, as in greeting. 4 To place quickly or suddenly. 5 To make or build hastily: often with *together* or *up.* 6 To flap, as wings. 7 *Obs.* To shut, as a door or window. —*v.i.* 8 To come together with a sharp, explosive sound, as flat surfaces. 9 To applaud by striking the hands together. 10 *Archaic* To close with a clapping sound. —**to clap eyes on** To see. —*n.* 1 A sharp sudden noise, as of two hard flat objects coming together. 2 The act of striking sharply together flatwise: a *clap* of the hands. 3 A sudden, but slight blow with the flat of the hand; a slap. 4 *Obs.* A sudden stroke or event. [OE *clæppan*]

clap² (klap) *n.* Gonorrhea: usually with *the*: a vulgarism. [<OF *clapoir* a venereal sore]

clap·board (klab'ərd, klap'bôrd', -bōrd') *n.* 1 A lapping weatherboard, usually with one edge thicker than the other. 2 A rived roofing board larger than a shingle. —*v.t.* To cover with clapboards. [Partial trans. of MDu. *klapholt* barrel stave]

clap·per (klap'ər) *n.* 1 One who or that which claps, as the tongue of a bell, or either of a pair of sticks, bones, or the like, held between the fingers and struck together, as an accompaniment to music. 2 *Slang* The tongue; also, the mouth.

clar·a·bel·la (klar'ə·bel'ə) *n.* An organ stop with open wooden pipes, giving a soft, sweet tone. [<L *clarus* clear + *bellus* pretty]

clar·ain (klâr·ān') *n.* *Geol.* A type of bituminous coal having a finely banded structure of translucent materials which impart a bright, silky luster. [<L *clarus* clear + (FUS)AIN]

Clare (klâr) Diminutive of CLARA or CLARISSA. —**Clare of Assisi, Saint** Italian founder of the Order of Poor Clares in 1212, under the rule given to her by Saint Francis.

clar·en·don (klar'ən·dən) *n.* *Printing* A style of type having a somewhat heavy and condensed face. [from the *Clarendon* Press, Oxford, England]

clar·et (klar'ət) *n.* 1 Any red table wine; especially, one from the region around Bordeaux. 2 A loose color term for various shades ranging from ruby to a deep purplish-red. [<OF (*vin*)*claret* clear (wine) <*cler* <L *clarus* bright]

Clar·i·bel (klar'ə·bel) A feminine personal name. [<L, brightly fair]

Clar·ice (klar'is, klə·rēs') See CLARISSA.

clar·i·fy (klar'ə·fī) *v.* **·fied, ·fy·ing** *v.t.* 1 To make clear or understandable. 2 To free from impurities, as wines or fats. —*v.i.* 3 To become clear or transparent. 4 To become understandable or clear: The situation *clarified.* See synonyms under PURIFY. [<OF *clarifier* <LL *clarificare* <*clarus* clear + *facere* make] —**clar'i·fi·ca'tion** *n.* —**clar'i·fi'er** *n.*

clar·i·net (klar'ə·net') *n.* 1 A cylindrical woodwind instrument with bell mouth, having a single reed mouthpiece, finger holes, and keys. Clarinets are made in various keys and sizes: those in B♭ and A are used in both orchestras and jazz bands; those in C and E♭ are used in jazz bands only. 2 An organ stop having a sound similar to that of a clarinet. Also **clar·i·o·net** (klar'ē·ə·net'). —**bass clarinet** A large clarinet pitched an octave lower than the common B♭ clarinet. [<F *clarinette,* dim. of *clarine* bell] —**clar'i·net'ist** or **clar'i·net'ist** *n.*

clar·i·on (klar'ē·ən) *n.* 1 A small trumpet. 2 The sound of a trumpet, or any sound resembling it. —*v.t. & v.i.* To proclaim with or as with a clarion; blow a clarion. —*adj.* Shrill; clear. [<OF *claron, clairon* <L *clarus* clear]

clar·i·ty (klar'ə·tē) *n.* Clearness as of sight, language, understanding, etc.

cla·ro (klä'rō) *adj.* Light in color and mild: said of cigars. [<Sp.]

clar·y (klâr'ē) *n. pl.* **clar·ies** Any of several species of sage; especially, the common clary (*Salvia sclarea*), native in Italy, Syria, etc.; and the wild English or vervain clary (*S. verbenaca*). [<F *sclarée* <Med. L *sclarea*]

clash (klash) *v.t.* 1 To strike or dash together or against with a confused, harsh, metallic sound. —*v.i.* 2 To collide with loud and confused noise; to collide. 3 To conflict; be in opposition. —*n.* A confused, resounding, metallic noise, as of striking or colliding; collision; conflict; opposition. See synonyms under COLLISION. [Imit. Cf. CLAP, DASH.]

clasp (klasp, kläsp) *n.* 1 A fastening by which things are bound together. 2 A firm grasp or embrace. 3 A small bar affixed to the ribbon of a military decoration: a **battle clasp** designates the campaign in which the wearer has taken part, a **service clasp** the country in which he has served. See synonyms under LOCK. —*v.t.* 1 To take hold of with an encircling grasp; embrace. 2 To fasten with or as with a clasp. 3 To grasp firmly in or with the hand. See synonyms under CATCH, EMBRACE, GRASP. [ME *claspe*; origin unknown]

clasp·er (klas'pər, kläs'-) *n.* 1 One who or

that which clasps. **2** *Zool.* **a** One of the paired organs accessory to copulation in various animals, as the external genital organs in male insects, etc. **b** One of the grooved cartilaginous appendages to the ventral fins of sharks, rays, etc.

class (klas, kläs) *n.* **1** A number or body of persons with common characteristics: the educated *class.* **2** Social rank; caste. **3** A group of students under one teacher, or pursuing a study together; a group of students in a school or college having the same standing and graduating together. **4** *Biol.* A group of plants or animals standing below a phylum and above an order. **5** A number of objects, facts, or events having common accidental or essential properties; a set; kind. **6** A grading according to quality, value, or rank: first-*class* mail; to travel second-*class.* **7** *Slang* Superiority; elegance. — **the classes** The wealthier, more educated, or higher social classes. — *v.t.* To arrange or group according to characteristics or properties; assign to a class; classify. — *v.i. Rare* To be placed or ranked, as in a class. [<F *classe* <L *classis* group, class] **Synonyms** (*noun*): association, caste, circle, clan, clique, club, company, coterie, grade, order, rank, set. A *caste* is hereditary; a *class* may be independent of lineage or descent; membership in a *caste* is normally for life, and hereditary; membership in a *class* may be very transient; a religious and ceremonial sacredness attaches to the *caste,* but not to the *class. Grade* implies some regular scale of valuation; as, the coarser and finer *grades* of wool. A *coterie* is a small company of persons of similar tastes. A *clique* is always fractional, implying some greater gathering of which it is a part; the *association* breaks up into *cliques.* A *set,* while exclusive, is more intensive than a *clique,* and chiefly of persons who are united by common social station, etc. *Circle* is similar in meaning to *set,* but of wider application; we speak of scientific as well as of social *circles.*

class·con·scious·ness (klas′kon′shəs·nis, kläs′-) *n.* Awareness among a social group of its own nature, interests, and unity. — **class′·con′·scious** *adj.*

clas·sic (klas′ik) *adj.* **1** Belonging to the first class or rank in literature or art. **2** Pertaining to standard and authoritative principles and forms in art, literature, music, etc. **3** Connected with or made famous by the ancient Greek or Latin authors. Compare RO-MANTIC. **4** Balanced; formal; finished; regular; simple; austere: a term variously interpreted, and often opposed to *romantic.* **5** Having literary or historical traditions: *classic* lands. See synonyms under PURE. — *n.* **1** A work of literature or art, generally recognized as excellent; especially, one of Greek or Roman workmanship or authorship. **2** *Rare* One who is familiar with classical literature. **3** Any author whose work is generally accepted as being a standard of excellence. — **the classics** Greek and Roman literature and authors. [<L *classicus* of the first rank <*classis* order, class]

clas·si·cal (klas′i·kəl) *adj.* **1** Of, pertaining to, or characteristic of ancient Greek and Roman art and literature. **2** Learned in, or based on Greek and Latin: a *classical* education. **3** Formal; finished; polished; modeled after Greek and Roman forms: often opposed to *romantic.* **4** Being of or modeled after the best in art, music, or literature. **5** *Music* **a** Following strict and established form, as a fugue or sonata. **b** Composed by the great masters. **6** *Physics* Pertaining to or describing those physical theories based upon or derived from Newtonian mechanics, especially as distinguished from relativity theory and quantum mechanics. — **clas′si·cal·ly** *adv.*

clas·si·cism (klas′ə·siz′əm) *n.* **1** Classic principles and style. **2** Any idiom found in the classics. **3** Adherence to or imitation of the classic style in literature or art. **4** Classical scholarship.

clas·si·cist (klas′ə·sist) *n.* **1** One versed in the classics. **2** An adherent or imitator of classic style.

clas·si·fi·ca·tion (klas′ə·fə·kā′shən) *n.* **1** The act, process, or result of classifying. **2** Taxonomy. **3** Systematics. **4** The systematic arrangement of books, documents, archives, and other printed material in accordance with

categories, as of subject, author, time, etc. **clas·si·fi·ca·to·ry** (klas′ə·fə·kā′tər·ē, klə·sif′ə·kə·tôr′ē, -tō′rē) *adj.* Of or pertaining to classification; taxonomical.

clas·si·fy (klas′ə·fī) *v.t.* **·fied, ·fy·ing** **1** To arrange or put in a class or classes on the basis of resemblance or differences. **2** To declare or designate as of aid to an enemy and restrict as to circulation or use, as a document, weapon, or item of information. [<L *classis* class + -FY] — **clas′si·fi′a·ble** *adj.*

clas·sis (klas′is) *n. pl.* **clas·ses** (klas′ēz) **1** A court in the Dutch and German Reformed churches, composed of ministers and ruling elders. **2** The district it represents. [<L]

class·mate (klas′māt′, kläs′-) *n.* A member of the same class in school or college.

class·room (klas′rōōm′, -rŏŏm′, kläs′-) *n.* **1** A room allotted to a certain class in a school. **2** A room in a school or college in which recitations and lectures are held.

class struggle The conflict between classes in society; particularly, the economic struggle for power between employers, as a general class or group, and employees.

class·y (klas′ē) *adj. Slang* **class·i·er, class·i·est** Grand; elegant.

clas·tic (klas′tik) *adj.* **1** *Biol.* Breaking, separating, or dividing into parts: a *clastic* cell. **2** Something that may be taken apart and reassembled: a *clastic* anatomical model. **3** *Geol.* Composed of fragments, especially of preexisting rocks: distinguished from *crystalline.* [<Gk. *klastos* broken]

clath·rate (klath′rāt) *n. Chem.* Any of a class of organic compounds whose molecules are so interlocked through hydrogen bonds as to form 3-dimensional lattices exhibiting trigonal symmetry. — *adj.* **1** Designating such a compound. **2** Having a latticelike appearance. [<L *clathri* lattice]

clat·ter (klat′ər) *v.i.* **1** To make a rattling noise or racket; give out short, sharp noises rapidly or repeatedly. **2** To advance, go, or proceed with a rattling noise. **3** To chatter; tattle. — *v.t.* **4** To cause to make a rattling noise. — *n.* **1** A rattling noise. **2** Noisy talk; chatter. See synonyms under NOISE. [OE *clatrung* a clattering noise] — **clat′ter·er** *n.*

clause (klôz) *n.* **1** *Gram.* A group of words containing a subject and predicate, but forming a subordinate part of a compound or complex sentence: distinguished from *phrase.* **2** A distinct part of a composition, as a paragraph or article. **3** A separate statement or proviso in a legal or state document. — **principal clause** *Gram.* The clause which contains the main predication of a sentence. — **relative clause** *Gram.* A subordinate clause introduced by a relative pronoun. — **subordinate** (or **dependent**) **clause** *Gram.* A clause which has the effect of a noun, adjective, or adverb in the structure of a sentence. [<OF <Med. L *clausa* <L *clausus,* pp. of *claudere* close]

claus·tral (klôs′trəl) *adj.* Cloistral.

claus·tro·pho·bi·a (klôs′trə·fō′bē·ə) *n. Psychiatry* Morbid fear of enclosed or confined places. [<L *claustrum* a closed place + -PHOBIA] — **claus′tro·pho′bic** *adj.*

clau·su·ra (klô′zhōō·rə) *n.* In the Roman Catholic Church, the rule which separates part of a monastery or convent from outsiders. [<L, a barrier <*claudere* close]

cla·vate (klā′vāt) *adj. Biol.* Denoting an organ or part having a thickened or bulbous end; club-shaped. Also **cla′vat·ed.** [<L *clavatus,* pp. of *clavare* stud with nails; infl. in meaning by L *clava* club] — **cla′vate·ly** *adv.*

clav·e·cin (klav′ə·sin) *n.* A harpsichord. [<F] — **clav′e·cin·ist** *n.*

clav·i·chord (klav′ə·kôrd) *n.* A keyboard musical instrument whose tones are produced by the blow of brass pins on horizontal strings: a forerunner of the piano. [<Med. L *clavichordium* <L *clavis* key + *chorda* string]

clav·i·cle (klav′ə·kəl) *n. Anat.* The bone connecting the shoulder blade and breastbone; collar bone. [<L *clavicula,* dim. of *clavis* key] — **cla·vic·u·lar** (klə·vik′yə·lər) *adj.*

clav·i·corn (klav′ə·kôrn) *adj. Entomol.* Of, pertaining to, or belonging to a superfamily of beetles (*Staphylinoidea,* formerly *Clavicornia*) having club-shaped antennae. [<NL *Clavicornia* <L *clava* club + *cornu* horn] — **clav·i·cor·nate** (klav′ə·kôr′nāt) *adj.*

clav·i·er (klav′ē·ər, klə·vir′ *for defs. 1 and 3;*

klə·vir′ *for def. 2*) *n.* **1** A keyboard. **2** Any keyboard stringed instrument, as a clavichord, etc.; especially, a piano. **3** A dummy keyboard: used for the perfection of technique. [<F, keyboard <L *clavis* key]

clav·i·form (klav′ə·fôrm) *adj.* Club-shaped; clavate. [<L *clava* club + -FORM]

claw (klô) *n.* **1** *Zool.* **a** A sharp, usually curved, horny nail on the toe of a bird, mammal, or reptile. **b** A limb terminating in a claw or pincers, as in certain insects and crustaceans. **2** Anything sharp and hooked. **3** A stroke, clutch, or scratch from or as with claws. — *v.t. & v.i.* To tear, scratch, dig, pull, etc., as with claws. [OE *clawu*]

claw hammer **1** A hammer with one end of its head forked and curved like a claw for drawing nails. See illustration under HAMMER. **2** *Colloq.* A swallowtail coat or dress coat: from its shape.

claw hatchet A hatchet having the head forked at one end. See illustration under HATCHET.

clax·on (klak′sən) See KLAXON.

clay (klā) *n.* **1** A common earth of various colors and fine texture, compact and brittle when dry, but plastic and tenacious when wet. It is a hydrous aluminum silicate, generally mixed with powdered feldspar, quartz, sand, iron oxides, and various other minerals. **2** Earth in general. **3** Earth as a symbol of the human body; also, the body itself. See synonyms under BODY. — *v.t.* To cover, mix, or treat with clay. [OE *clæg*] — **clay′ish** *adj.*

clay pigeon In trapshooting, a saucer-shaped disk of some brittle material, as baked clay, projected from a trap as a flying target.

clay stone **1** One of the concretionary nodules found in alluvial clay. **2** A dull-colored igneous rock containing feldspar and clay in a compact mass.

clay·to·ni·a (klā·tō′nē·ə) *n.* One of a genus (*Claytonia*) of low herbs of the purslane family: also called *springbeauty.* [after John Clayton, 1693–1773, botanist, of Virginia]

-cle *suffix* of *nouns* Small; minute: *particle; corpuscle.* [<F <L -*culus,* dim. suffix]

clean (klēn) *adj.* **1** Free from dirt, soil, impurity, or defilement; unblemished; pure. **2** Ginned: *clean* cotton. **3** Free from bungling; dexterous; complete: He's a *clean* shot. **4** Well-proportioned; symmetrical. **5** Ceremonially pure; conforming to the ceremonial law. **6** Completely cleared or rid of something. **7** Having no imperfection; perfect; whole. **8** Clear: a *clean* title to land. **9** In baseball, without error. — *v.t.* **1** To purify or cleanse; to free from dirt or impurities. **2** To draw and prepare (fowl, game, etc.) for cooking. — *v.i.* **3** To undergo or perform the act of cleaning. — **to clean out** **1** To clear of trash or rubbish. **2** To force out; overcome: to *clean* the gangsters *out* of town. **3** To empty (a place) of contents or occupants: The crowd *cleaned out* the store. **4** *Colloq.* To leave without money: The depression *cleaned* him *out.* — **to clean up** **1** To remove dirt; put in order: Today we *clean up.* **2** *Colloq.* To win a large amount or make large profits. **3** *Colloq.* To defeat: to *clean up* the enemy. **4** To remove undesirable persons or scandalous activities from: to *clean up* politics. — *adv.* In a clean manner; unqualifiedly, wholly. [OE *clæne* clear, pure] — **clean′a·ble** *adj.* — **clean′ness** *n.*

clean–cut (klēn′kut′) *adj.* **1** Cut with smooth edge or surface; made with skill and neatness. **2** Sharply defined. **3** Clear. **4** Neat in appearance; trim: a *clean–cut* young man.

clean·er (klē′nər) *n.* **1** One who or that which cleans. **2** Any substance or mechanical device which removes dirt.

clean·ly (klen′lē) *adj.* **1** Habitually and carefully clean; neat; tidy; clean. **2** Cleansing. — *adv.* (klēn′lē) In a clean manner. — **clean·li·ness** (klen′lē·nis) *n.*

cleanse (klenz) *v.t.* **cleansed, cleans·ing** To free from dirt or defilement; clean; purge. [OE *clænsian* <*clæne* clean] — **cleans′er** *n.* **Synonyms:** brush, clean, disinfect, dust, mop, purify, rinse, scour, scrub, sponge, sweep, wash, wipe. *Cleanse* implies a worse condition to start from, and more to do, than *clean;* as, Hercules *cleansed* the Augean stables. *Cleanse* and *purify* are used extensively in a moral sense; *wash* in that sense is archaic. See AMEND, PURIFY. **Antonyms:** befoul, besmear, besmirch, bespatter, contaminate, corrupt, debase, defile, deprave, pollute, soil, spoil, stain, sully, taint, vitiate.

clear (klir) *adj.* **1** Free from anything that dims or darkens; light. **2** Unclouded; distinct; intelligible. **3** Able to see, discern, or discriminate: a *clear* mind. **4** Free from obstruction or hindrance. **5** Free from encumbrance, responsibility, or guilt. **6** Free from adulteration, defect, or blemish. **7** Without deduction; net. **8** Undisturbed; serene. **9** Plain; evident. **10** Free from uncertainty. **11** Without trees or underbrush, as land. **12** Without knots or imperfections, as lumber or shingles. — *v.t.* **1** To make clear; brighten. **2** To free from foreign matter, impurities, blemishes, or muddiness. **3** To remove, as obstructions, in making clear: to *clear* dishes from the table. **4** To disentangle: to *clear* a rope. **5** To free from imputations or accusations of guilt; acquit. **6** To free from doubt or ambiguity; make plain. **7** To free from debt by payment. **8** To pass or get by or over without touching: to *clear* a fence. **9** To obtain or give clearance, as for a ship or cargo. **10** To net or gain over and above expenses. **11** To pass through a clearing-house, as a check. — *v.i.* **12** To become free from fog, cloud, or obscurity; grow bright; become fair. **13** To pass away, as mist or fog. **14** To settle accounts by exchange of bills and checks, as in a clearing-house. — **to clear for action** To prepare for battle by clearing the decks. — **to clear in** (or **inward**) *Naut.* To discharge cargo. — **to clear out 1** To leave port, as a ship. **2** To empty. **3** *Colloq.* To leave; depart. — **to clear the air** To dispel emotional tensions or disagreements. — **to clear the land** *Naut.* To get beyond danger of land and shoals into sea room. — **to clear up 1** To grow fair, as the weather. **2** To free from confusion or mystery. **3** To free from obligation. — *adv.* Wholly; completely; quite; clearly; plainly. — *n.* **1** Unbroken or unobstructed distance or space; clearance. **2** Inside measurements, from boundary to boundary. — **in the clear 1** In plain language: not written in code or cipher: said of military messages. **2** Innocent; not liable. **3** Free from limitations or obstructions. [<OF *cler* <L *clarus* clear, bright] — **clear′a·ble** *adj.*

Synonyms (*adj.*): apparent, diaphanous, distinct, evident, explicit, intelligible, limpid, lucid, manifest, obvious, pellucid, perspicuous, plain, straightforward, translucent, transparent, unadorned, unambiguous, unequivocal, unmistakable. A substance is said to be *clear* that offers no impediment to vision, is not dim, dark, or obscure; *transparent*, when objects are readily seen through it; we speak of a stream as *clear* when we think of the water itself, as *transparent* with reference to the ease with which we see the pebbles at the bottom. *Clear* is said of that which comes to the senses without dimness, dulness, obstruction, or obscurity; hence, the word is used for that which is free from any kind of obstruction; as, a *clear* field. *Lucid* and *pellucid* refer to a shining clearness, as of crystal. *Translucent* is less than *transparent*; a *translucent* body allows light to pass through, but may not permit forms and colors to be distinguished. *Limpid* refers to a liquid clearness, or that which suggests it; as, *limpid* streams. That which is *distinct* is well-defined, as in outline. That is *plain* which is level to the thought, so that one goes straight on without difficulty or hindrance; as, *plain* language; a *plain* statement. *Perspicuous* is often equivalent to *plain*, but *plain* never wholly loses the meaning of *unadorned*, so that we can say the style is *perspicuous* even if highly ornate, when we could not call it at once ornate and *plain*. Compare APPARENT, BLANK, EVIDENT, FINE, FREE, INNOCENT, MANIFEST, PLAIN, PURE, SURE, VIVID. *Antonyms*: ambiguous, cloudy, dim, dubious, foggy, indistinct, mysterious, obscure, opaque, turbid, unintelligible, vague.

clear·ance (klir′əns) *n.* **1** The act or process of clearing. **2** A certificate permitting a vessel to sail; also, the obtaining or granting of such permission. **3** The space by which a moving vehicle, machine, or part clears something. **4** The passage of checks, bank drafts,

etc., through the clearing-house.

clear-cut (klir′kut′) *adj.* **1** Distinctly and sharply outlined. **2** Concise; plainly put.

clear-eyed (klir′id′) *adj.* **1** Having bright, clear eyes; keen-sighted. **2** Acute; wise.

clear-head·ed (klir′hed′id) *adj.* Not mentally confused or befogged; clear in understanding; sensible. — **clear′-head′ed·ness** *n.*

clear·ing (klir′ing) *n.* **1** A making or becoming clear. **2** That which is clear or cleared; a tract of land cleared of trees, underbrush, etc. **3** The settlement of balances between banks arising from the interchange of checks, drafts, etc., carried on at a clearing-house. **4** *pl.* The total of checks, drafts, etc., presented daily at a clearing-house.

clear·ness (klir′nis) *n.* **1** The state or quality of being clear; distinctness to sight or understanding. **2** Transparence. **3** In rhetoric, that property of style by means of which thought is so presented as to be immediately understood, depending on precision and simplicity of diction and sentence structure.

clear-sight·ed (klir′si′tid) *adj.* Of keen vision; having accurate perception and good judgment; discerning. — **clear′-sight′ed·ly** *adv.*

clear-starch (klir′stärch′) *v.t.* To stiffen with clear or pure starch. — **clear′starch′er** *n.*

clear-sto·ry (klir′stôr′ē, -stō′rē) See CLERESTORY.

clear text Plain text.

clear·way (klir′wā′) *n. Aeron.* An unobstructed area beyond the stopway of an airport to permit safe landing of an aircraft that fails to attain a proper altitude.

clear·weed (klir′wēd′) *n.* Richweed.

clear·wing (klir′wing′) *n.* A moth of the families *Aegeriidae* or *Sphingidae*, having nearly transparent wings.

cleat (klēt) *n.* **1** A strip of wood or iron fastened across a surface, or nailed against a wall, to strengthen, support, or prevent slipping. **2** *Naut.* **a** A piece of metal or wood with arms, usually fastened in place by a bolt, on which to belay a rope. **b** A wedgelike piece of wood fastened to a spar to keep rigging from slipping up or down. **3** A piece of metal or leather fastened to the underside of a shoe to prevent slipping: used by athletes. **4** A spurlike attachment used to grip a pole or tree in climbing. — *v.t.* **1** To furnish or strengthen with a cleat or cleats. **2** *Naut.* To fasten (rope, etc.) to or with a cleat. [ME *clete*. Akin to CLOT.]

TYPES OF CLEATS
a. Pole. *b.* Surface. *c.* Deck.

cleav·age (klē′vij) *n.* **1** A cleaving or being cleft; a split; cleft; division or the manner in which a thing divides. **2** *Mineral.* A tendency in certain rocks or crystals to divide or split in certain directions. **3** *Biol.* The process of division of a fertilized ovum by which the original single cell becomes a mass of smaller cells.

cleave¹ (klēv) *v.* **cleft** or **cleaved** or **clove** (*Archaic* **clave**), **cleft** or **cleaved** or **clo·ven** (*Archaic* **clove**), **cleav·ing** *v.t.* **1** To sunder, as with an ax or wedge; split, especially along structural lines or with the grain. **2** To make or achieve by cutting. **3** To pass through; penetrate. — *v.i.* **4** To split or divide by natural lines of cleavage. **5** To pass; make one's way: with *through*. [OE *clēofan*]

cleave² (klēv) *v.i.* **cleaved** (*Archaic* **clave**), **cleaved**, **cleav·ing 1** To stick fast; adhere. **2** To be faithful: with *to*. [OE *cleofian, clifian*]

cleav·er (klē′vər) *n.* **1** One who or that which cleaves. **2** A butcher's chopper.

cleav·ers (klē′vərz) *n. pl.* A species of bedstraw (*Galium aparine*), so called because of the hooked prickles on stem and fruit: also called *catchweed*.

cle·don·ism (klē′də·niz′əm) *n.* Avoidance of the use of words considered ominous or unlucky; the practice of using euphemisms. [<Gk. *klēdōn* omen]

clef (klef) *n.* In musical notation, a symbol

CLEFS
Showing position of Middle C on each:
1. Treble or G clef. *2.* Bass or F clef.
3., 4., 5., C clefs (Soprano, Alto, Tenor).

placed upon the staff to determine the pitch: namely, **treble** or **G clef**, **bass** or **F clef**, and the **tenor** or **C clef** of ancient music. [<F <L *clavis* key]

cleft (kleft) *v.* A past tense and past participle of CLEAVE¹. — *adj.* **1** Divided partially or completely. **2** *Bot.* Divided about half-way down: said of leaves. — *n.* **1** An opening made by cleaving; a fissure in a rock; crevice; rift. **2** A chap or crack in the human skin. **3** The space between the two parts of a horse's foot. See synonyms under BREACH. [ME *clift*. Related to CLEAVE¹.]

cleft palate A congenital longitudinal fissure in the roof of the mouth.

cleisto- *combining form* Closed: *cleistogamous*. Also, before vowels, **cleist-**. [<Gk. *kleistos* closed < *kleiein* close]

cleis·tog·a·mous (klīs·tog′ə·məs) *adj. Bot.* Closed or non-expanding and self-fertilizing: said of certain closed flowers, as some violets: also spelled *clistogamous*. Also **cleis·to·gam·ic** (klīs′tə·gam′ik). [<CLEISTO- + -GAMOUS]

cleis·tog·a·my (klīs·tog′ə·mē) *n. Bot.* Self-fertilization; self-pollination.

clem·a·tis (klem′ə·tis) *n.* **1** A plant of a large genus (*Clematis*) of perennial shrubs or vines of the crowfoot family. **2** Any vine of a related genus (*Atragene*). [<Gk. *klēmatis*, dim. of *klēma* vine]

clem·en·cy (klem′ən·sē) *n. pl.* **·cies 1** Mildness of temper, especially toward offenders; leniency; mercy. **2** Mildness of climate, weather, etc. See synonyms under MERCY. [<L *clementia* < *clemens* mild]

clem·ent (klem′ənt) *adj.* **1** Lenient; merciful. **2** Mild or pleasant: said of weather. See synonyms under HUMANE. [<L *clemens, -entis* mild, merciful] — **clem′ent·ly** *adv.*

clench (klench) *v.t.* **1** To grasp or grip firmly; clamp: to *clench* something in a vise. **2** To close tightly or lock, as the fist or teeth. **3** To clinch, as a nail. **4** *Naut.* To fasten by making a clinch. — *n.* A clenching; clinch. [OE *clenc(e)an* in *beclencan* hold fast]

cle·o·me (klē·ō′mē) *n.* Any of a large genus (*Cleome*) of woody or herbaceous plants of the caper family, with solitary or racemose, often showy, white, yellow, or purple flowers: also called *spiderflower*. [<LL, a plant]

clep·sy·dra (klep′sə·drə) *n. pl.* **-dras** or **-drae** (-drē) An ancient instrument for measuring time by the regulated flow of water; a water clock. [<L <Gk. *klepsydra* < *kleptein* steal + *hydōr* water]

clep·to·ma·ni·a (klep′tə·mā′nē·ə) See KLEPTOMANIA.

clere·sto·ry (klir′stôr′ē, -stō′rē) *n. Archit.* **1** The highest story of the nave and choir of a church, with windows opening above the aisle roofs, etc. **2** A similar story or elevated part in the roofs of other structures. Also **clere′sto′rey**: sometimes spelled *clearstory*. [<earlier *clere* clear + STORY]

cler·gy (klûr′jē) *n. pl.* **·gies 1** The group of people ordained for service in a Christian church: distinguished from *laity*. **2** *Brit.* The ministers of the Established Church. — **regular clergy** The body of ecclesiastics of the Roman Catholic Church bound by monastic rules: distinguished from **secular clergy**, those not bound by such rules. [<OF *clergie* < *clerc*, cleric <LL *clericus*]

cler·gy·man (klûr′jē·mən) *n. pl.* **·men** (-mən) One of the clergy; an ordained minister.

cler·ic (kler′ik) *adj.* Clerical. — *n.* **1** A member of the clergy. **2** A member of a clerical party. [<LL *clericus*]

cler·i·cal (kler′i·kəl) *adj.* **1** Of, belonging to,

or characterizing the clergy. **2** Of or pertaining to a clerk or penmanship; composed of clerks: a *clerical* staff. — *n.* **1** A cleric. **2** One of a party seeking to preserve or extend the authority of the church in social or political matters. — **cler′i·cal·ly** *adv.*

cler·i·cal·ism (kler′i·kəl·iz′əm) *n.* The principle or policy of clerical control over education, marriage laws, etc. — **cler′i·cal·ist** *adj. & n.*

cler·id (kler′id) *n.* Any of a family (*Cleridae*) of small, slender, soft-bodied, variously colored coleopterous insects. [<NL *Cleridae* <Gk. *klēros*, a type of beetle]

cler·i·hew (kler′ə·hyōō) *n.* A satiric or comic poem in two couplets concerning some well-known personage whose name furnishes one of the rimes. [after Edmund *Clerihew* Bentley, 1875-1956, English writer, the originator]

cler·i·sy (kler′ə·sē) *n.* The literate, or well-educated class. [<Med. L *clericia*]

clerk (klûrk, *Brit.* klärk) *n.* **1** An officer or employee of a court, legislative body, corporation, society, commercial establishment, or the like, charged with the care of its records, correspondence, and accounts; a secretary. **2** A salesman or saleswoman in a store. **3** A hotel employee who assigns guests to their rooms. **4** In the Anglican Church, one who leads in the responses. **5** *Obs.* A clergyman or cleric; anciently, any person who could read or write. — *v.i.* To work or act as clerk. [OE *clerc* <LL *clericus* <Gk. *klērikos* < *klēros* lot, portion] — **clerk′li·ness** *n.* — **clerk′ly** *adj. & adv.* — **clerk′ship** *n.*

cleve·ite (klēv′īt) *n.* A radioactive variety of uraninite that is rich in uranium oxide and contains yttrium earths and helium. [after Per *Cleve*, 1840-1905, Swedish chemist]

clev·er (klev′ər) *adj.* **1** Ready and adroit with hand or brain; dexterous; capable; quick-witted; talented. **2** *U.S. Dial.* Good-natured; obliging. **3** *U.S. Dial.* Finely built; well-trained, as a horse. **4** *Dial.* Honest. **5** *Obs.* Handy; convenient; agreeable. [Cf. ME *cliver* adroit] — **clev′er·ly** *adv.* — **clev′er·ness** *n.*
Synonyms: able, adroit, apt, bright, capable, dexterous, expert, gifted, happy, ingenious, intellectual, intelligent, keen, knowing, quick, quick-witted, sharp, skilful, smart, talented. *Clever,* as used in England, implies an aptitude for study or learning, and for excellent while not preeminent mental achievement. The early New England usage as implying simple and weak good nature has largely affected the use of the word throughout the United States. *Smart,* indicating dashing ability, is now coming to have a suggestion of unscrupulousness, similar to that of the word *sharp.* The discriminating use of such words as *able, gifted, talented,* etc., is preferable to an excessive use of the word *clever.* Compare ABILITY, ACUMEN, BRIGHT, INTELLIGENT, KNOWING. *Antonyms:* awkward, bungling, clumsy, dull, foolish, idiotic, ignorant, senseless, slow, stupid, thick-headed, witless.

clev·is (klev′is) *n.* A U-shaped or stirrup-shaped piece of iron for attaching the draft chain to the end of a plow beam, wagon tongue, whiffletree, etc. [Akin to CLEAVE¹]

clew (klōō) *n.* **1** A thread that guides through a maze. **2** Something that leads to the solution of a mystery: in this sense now spelled *clue.* **3** *Naut.* A lower corner of a square sail or the lower aft corner of a fore-and-aft sail; also, a loop at the corner. **4** *pl.* The small cords by which the two ends of a hammock are slung. **5** A ball of yarn, thread, or the like. — *v.t.* **1** To move or fasten by or as by a clew or clew line. **2** To coil into a ball; roll up into a bunch. [OE *cleowan*]

HAMMOCK CLEWS

clew line *Naut.* A rope by which the clew of a sail is run up to the yards.

cli·ché (klē·shā′) *n.* **1** A fixed or stereotyped expression which has lost its significance through frequent repetition. **2** *Printing* **a** An electrotype or stereotype plate. **b** A printing block made by the half-tone or similar process. — *adj.* Being a cliché; hackneyed. [<F,

pp. of *clicher* stereotype]

click (klik) *n.* **1** A short, sharp, or dull metallic sound, as that made by the latch of a door. **2** A detent or stop; a pawl. **3** *Phonet.* An articulation occurring in the Hottentot and Bushman languages, produced by the sudden withdrawal of the tip or side of the tongue from the teeth or palate. **4** The trip, in wrestling, in which an opponent's foot is knocked from under him. — *v.t.* **1** To cause to make a click or clicks. — *v.i.* **2** To produce a click or succession of clicks. **3** *Slang* To succeed: The show *clicked.* **4** *Slang* To suit exactly; agree. [Imit.] — **click′er** *n.*

click beetle An elaterid; a snapping beetle. For illustration see INSECT (injurious).

cli·ent (klī′ənt) *n.* **1** One in whose interest a lawyer acts. **2** Hence, one who engages the services of any professional adviser. **3** Loosely, a customer or patron. **4** A dependent or follower, as of an ancient Roman patrician. [<L *cliens, -entis,* var. of *cluens,* ppr. of *cluere* hear, listen] — **cli′en·cy** *n.* — **cli·en·tal** (klī·en′təl, klī′ən·təl) *adj.*

cli·en·tele (klī′ən·tel′) *n.* A body of clients, dependents, customers, or adherents; a following. Also **cli·ent·age** (klī′ən·tij). [<F]

cliff (klif) *n.* A high steep face of rock, as on the seashore; a precipice. [OE *clif*]

cliff-hang·er (klif′hang′ər) *n.* **1** A situation marked by suspense or uncertainty of outcome. **2** A serialized drama marked by suspense at the end of each episode. Also **cliff′-hang′er.** — **cliff′hang′ing** *adj. & n.*

cliff swallow A North American swallow (*Petrochelidon albifrons*) which builds mud nests under the eaves of buildings or against cliffs.

cliff·y (klif′ē) *adj.* Abounding in or resembling cliffs; craggy.

cli·mac·ter·ic (klī·mak′tər·ik, klī′mak·ter′ik) *n.* **1** A critical year or period, or one of marked change, as in human life. **2** The menopause. — **grand climacteric** One's sixty-third year. — *adj.* **1** Of or pertaining to a climax; climactic. **2** Pertaining to or designating a critical year or period; marking, or marked by, a crisis. Also **cli·mac·ter·i·cal** (klī′mak·ter′i·kəl). [<L *climactericus* <Gk. *klimakterikos* < *klimaktēr* rung of a ladder]

cli·ma·gram (klī′mə·gram) *n. Meteorol.* Any graphic diagram representing one or more climatic elements of a region.

cli·mate (klī′mit) *n.* **1** The temperature, humidity, precipitation, winds, radiation, and other meteorological conditions characteristic of a locality or region over an extended period of time. **2** A region characterized by a certain average temperature, rainfall, dryness, etc. **3** Any region. **4** A prevailing or dominant trend in social affairs: *climate* of opinion. [<OF *climat* <LL *clima* <Gk. *klima, -atos* region, zone <*klinein* slope] — **cli·mat·ic** (klī·mat′ik) or **·i·cal** *adj.*

climato- *combining form* Climate; pertaining to climate or climatic conditions: *climatology.* Also, before vowels, **climat-.** [<Gk. *klima, -atos* region]

cli·ma·tol·o·gy (klī′mə·tol′ə·jē) *n.* The science of climate. — **cli·ma·to·log·ic** (klī′mə·tə·loj′ik) or **·i·cal** *adj.* — **cli′ma·tol′o·gist** *n.*

cli·ma·to·ther·a·py (klī′mə·tō·ther′ə·pē) *n.* The treatment of diseases by subjecting patients to appropriate climate.

cli·max (klī′maks) *n.* **1** A progressive increase in force throughout a rhetorical or musical passage, culminating at the close. **2** *Ecol.* A relatively stable community of plants and animals dominant in a given locality. **3** Loosely, the culmination; acme. — *v.t. & v.i.* To reach or bring to a climax; culminate. [<L <Gk. *klimax* ladder] — **cli·mac·tic** (klī·mak′tik) or **·ti·cal** *adj.*

climb (klīm) *v.* **climbed** (*Archaic* **clomb**), **climb·ing** *v.t.* **1** To ascend or descend, especially by means of the hands and feet; go up or down by holding or getting a foothold; mount. — *v.i.* **2** To mount, rise, or go up, especially by using the hands and feet. **3** To rise by effort, as in position or dignity. **4** To incline or slope upward. **5** To rise during growth, as certain vines, by entwining a support or clinging by means of tendrils. — *n.* **1** The act or process of climbing. ◆ Collateral adjective: *scansorial.* **2** A place that can be ascended only by climbing. ◆ Homophone: *clime.* [OE *climban*] — **climb′a·ble** *adj.*

climb·er (klī′mər) *n.* **1** One who or that which climbs. **2** *Bot.* A plant that supports its growth by its tendrils, rootlets, or the like. **3** *Colloq.* A social climber.

climbing fish See ANABAS.

cli·nan·dri·um (kli·nan′drē·əm) *n. pl.* **·dri·a** (-drē·ə) *Bot.* A depression in the summit of the column in certain orchids, in which the anther is lodged. [<NL <Gk. *klinē* bed + *anēr, andros* man]

cli·nan·thi·um (kli·nan′thē·əm) *n. pl.* **·thi·a** (-thē·ə) *Bot.* The receptacle in the heads of composite plants. [<NL <Gk. *klinē* bed + *anthos* flower]

clinch (klinch) *v.t.* **1** To secure firmly, as a nail or staple, by bending down the protruding point. **2** To fasten together by this means. **3** To grapple with. **4** To confirm, as a bargain or agreement. **5** *Naut.* To fasten by making a clinch. — *v.i.* **6** To take a strong, close hold; grapple, as combatants, with one another. **7** *Slang* To embrace or hug. — *n.* **1** A clinching, or that which clinches; especially, a clinched nail or bolt; a clamp. **2** A decisive or conclusive argument. **3** *Naut.* A rope knot made by a half-hitch and seizings: called an **inside** or an **outside clinch.** **4** A grip or struggle at close quarters, as in boxing. **5** *Slang* A close embrace. Also called *clench.* [Var. of CLENCH]

clinch·er (klin′chər) *n.* **1** One who or that which clinches. **2** A person or device that clinches nails; a clencher. **3** A nail made for clinching. **4** *Colloq.* The final unanswerable proof in or as in an argument.

cline (klīn) *n. Ecol.* A graded series of changes in a biotype, induced by corresponding gradual alterations in the environmental factors operating within a large area. [<Gk. *klinein* slope, bend]

cling (kling) *v.i.* **clung, cling·ing** **1** To hold on to something firmly, as by grasping, embracing, or winding round. **2** To remain in contact; resist separation: with *together.* **3** To stick to or continue tenaciously, as in the memory; be loyal. **4** To adhere closely; stick. [OE *clingan*] — **cling′er** *n.* — **cling′y** *adj.*

cling·fish (kling′fish′) *n. pl.* **·fish** or **·fish·es** Any of a group of small marine fishes (family *Gobiesocidae*) having a large central suction disk by which they cling to rocks, shells, etc.

clin·ic (klin′ik) *n.* **1** The teaching of medicine and surgery by treatment of or operation upon the patients in the presence of a class in a hospital or dispensary. **2** A class receiving such instruction. **3** An infirmary or dispensary connected with a hospital or medical college, for the treatment of nonresident patients. [<F *clinique* <L *clinicus* <Gk. *klinikos* < *klinē* bed < *klinein* recline]

clin·i·cal (klin′i·kəl) *adj.* **1** Of or pertaining to a sickbed or a clinic. **2** Pertaining to the practical, experimental method of medical education by the observation and treatment of patients in clinics. **3** Administered to one on a deathbed or sickbed: *clinical* baptism.

cli·ni·cian (kli·nish′ən) *n.* An active practitioner of medicine: distinguished from a teacher or from one who is consulted only at his office.

clink¹ (klingk) *v.t.* **1** To cause to make a short, slight, ringing sound. **2** *Scot. & Brit. Dial.* To clinch; rivet. — *v.i.* **3** To make a short, slight, ringing sound. **4** To rime or jingle. — *n.* **1** A tinkle, as of glass or small metallic bodies in collision. **2** *Scot.* Money; chink. **3** The shrill note of certain birds, as the whinchat. **4** A rime or jingle. [Imit. Cf. MDu. *klinken.*]

clink·er (kling′kər) *n.* **1** A thing that clinks, especially the earthy residue left by coal in burning. **2** A large, irregular porous fragment of lava. **3** A brick impregnated with niter and burned very hard. **4** A vitrified or over-burned brick; a mass of fused bricks. **5** A clincher. **6** *U.S. Slang* **a** A bad verbal mistake in a radio or television broadcast.

CLINKER-BUILT
In shipbuilding:
A. Clinker-built.
B. Carvel-built.

b A wrong note in a musical performance. **c** A failure; flop. —*v.t.* & *v.i.* To form or cause to form a clinker; become clogged with clinker. [<Du. *klinckaerd,* kind of brick]

clink·er·built (kling′kər-bilt′) *adj.* Built with overlapping and riveted planks or plates, as a ship: also *clincher-built.*

clink·stone (klingk′stōn′) *n.* A compact, grayish rock that clinks like metal when struck; phonolite.

clino– *combining form* Bend; slope; incline: *clinometer.* [<Gk. *klinein* bend]

cli·nom·e·ter (klī·nom′ə-tər, kli-) *n.* An instrument for determining angular inclination, as of guns, slopes, etc.: also *anglemeter.* [<CLINO- + -METER]

cli·no·met·ric (klī′nə·met′rik) *adj.* **1** Pertaining to or measured by the clinometer. **2** Pertaining to oblique crystalline forms or to their measurement. Also **cli′no·met′ri·cal.**

clin·quant (kling′kənt) *adj.* Glittering with or as with gold or silver; tinseled. —*n.* Imitation gold leaf; tinsel. [<F, ppr. of *clinquer* ring, glitter]

clin·to·ni·a (klin·tō′nē·ə) *n.* A plant of a small genus (*Clintonia*) of perennial herbs of the lily family, having broadly lanceolate, radical leaves, and a naked scape, bearing usually an umbel of flowers succeeded by berries. [after De Witt *Clinton*]

cli·o·met·rics (klī′ō·met′riks) *n.pl.* (construed as *sing.*) The systematic application of statistical methods to the study of history, as in the collection and analysis of quantitative data. [< CLIO + METRICS] —**cli′o·met′ric** *adj.* —**cli·o·me·tri·cian** (klī′ō·mə·trish′ən) *n.*

clip[1] (klip) *n.* **1** Any appliance that clasps, grips, or holds fast. **2** *Med.* An appliance for stopping the bleeding of arteries, etc. **3** A flange on a horseshoe, projecting upward above the calk. **4** A spring clasp for holding letters, papers, etc.: also **paper clip.** **5** A pinching device for stopping the flow of a fluid in a flexible tube. **6** A metal container holding cartridges for a rapid–fire gun, as an automatic rifle: also **cartridge clip.** —*v.t.* **clipped, clip·ping 1** *Archaic* To clasp; embrace. **2** To encircle; hold tightly. [OE *clyppan* clasp]

clip[2] (klip) *v.t.* **clipped, clip·ping 1** To cut or trim with shears or scissors, as hair or fleece. **2** To snip a part from, as a coin. **3** To cut short; curtail: to *clip* the ends of words. **4** *Colloq.* To strike with a sharp blow. **5** In football, to hurl oneself illegally across the backs of the legs of (an opponent who is not carrying the ball.) **6** *Slang* To cheat or defraud. —*v.i.* **7** To cut or trim. **8** *Colloq.* To run or move swiftly. —**to clip the wings of** To check the aspirations or ambitions of. —*n.* **1** The act of clipping, or that which is clipped off. **2** The wool yielded at one shearing or season. **3** *Colloq.* A blow with the hand or fist; a swinging or glancing hit. **4** *Colloq.* A quick pace: going at a good *clip.* **5** *pl.* Shears; snuffers. **6** *Colloq.* An effort or attempt. [<ON *klippa*]

clip·board (klip′bôrd′, bōrd′) *n.* A small board for writing and having a spring clip for holding paper in place.

clipped form A shortened form of a polysyllabic word, as *bus* for *omnibus, gym* for *gymnasium,* or *exam* for *examination.* Also **clipped word.**

clip·per (klip′ər) *n.* **1** One who or that which clips. **2** One who clips coins. **3** An instrument for clipping hair. **4** *pl.* Shears; especially, pruning shears or sheep shears. **5** *Naut.* A certain type of sailing vessel built for speed, with tall, aft–raked masts: also **clipper ship. 6** *Colloq.* One who or that which moves swiftly, as a swift horse, a sled, or smart person.

clique (klēk, klik) *n.* An exclusive or clannish set; coterie. —*v.i.* **cliqued, cli·quing** To unite in a clique; act clannishly. See synonyms under CLASS. [<F <*cliquer* click, clap]

cli·quish (klē′kish, klik′ish) *adj.* Inclined to form cliques; exclusive. Also **cli′quey, cli′quy.**

cli·sere (klī′sir) *n. Ecol.* A series of climax formations or zones which follow each other in a particular region as a consequence of a distinct change of climate. [< CLI(MATE) + SERE[2]]

clis·tase (klis′tās) *n. Ecol.* The state or condition of vegetation in a given layer of fossil plant deposits, indicating a climatic change. [< CLI(MAX), def. 2 +STASE]

clis·tog·a·mous (klis·tog′ə·məs) See CLEISTOGAMOUS.

cli·tel·lum (kli·tel′əm) *n.* The swollen, glandular portion of the skin in some earthworms. [< NL < L *clitellae* packsaddle]

cli·to·ris (klī′tə·ris, klit′ə-) *n. Anat.* An erectile organ of the female of most vertebrates, at the anterior part of the vulva: the homolog of the penis. [NL < Gk. *kleitoris* < *kleiein* close, confine]

cli·vers (klī′vərz) See CLEAVERS.

clo·a·ca (klo-ā′kə) *n. pl.* **·cae** (-sē) **1** *Zool.* The common cavity into which the various ducts of the body open in certain fishes, reptiles, insects, etc. **2** A sewer; sink; privy; a general receptacle for or repository of filth. [< L, a drain] —**clo·a′cal** *adj.*

cloak (klōk) *n.* **1** A loose outer garment. **2** Something that covers or hides; a pretext; disguise; mask. See synonyms under PRETENSE. —*v.t.* To cover with a cloak; disguise; conceal. See synonyms under HIDE, MASK, PALLIATE. [< OF *cloque, cloke* < Med. L *cloca* bell, cape; so called from its bell-like shape. Doublet of CLOCK.]

cloche (klōsh, *Fr.* klôsh) *n.* **1** A woman's close-fitting, bell-shaped hat. **2** A portable translucent cover for the protection and forcing of young plants. [< F, bell]

clock[1] (klok) *n.* **1** An instrument for measuring and indicating time by mechanical movements; a timepiece. **2** Any clocklike, mechanical, registering device for recording distance, output, etc. —**what o'clock, six o'clock,** etc. See O'CLOCK. —*v.t.* To determine the rate of speed of an automobile or of any racing event by means of a stopwatch. [< MDu. *clocke* < OF *cloque, cloche* bell < Med. L *cloca.* Doublet of CLOAK.]

clock[2] (klok) *n.* An embroidered ornament on the side of a stocking or sock at the ankle. —*v.t.* To ornament with clocks. [Origin uncertain]

clock·mak·er (klok′mā′kər) *n.* One who makes or repairs clocks.

clock·wise (klok′wīz′) *adj.* & *adv.* Moving in the direction traveled by the hands of a clock.

clock·work (klok′wûrk′) *n.* The machinery of a clock, or any similar mechanism. —**like clock-work** With regularity and precision.

clod (klod) *n.* **1** A lump of earth, clay, etc.; hence, the soil. **2** Anything earthy; as the body of man compared with his soul. **3** The cut of beef on the back part of the foreshoulder above the shank. **4** A dull, stupid fellow, —*v.t.* **clod·ded, clod·ding 1** To throw clods or stones at. —*v.i.* **2** To turn into clods; clot; coagulate. [Var. of CLOT] —**clod′dish** *adj.* —**clod′dish·ness** *n.* —**clod′dy** *adj.*

clod·hop·per (klod′hop′ər) *n.* **1** A plowman; rustic; lout. **2** *pl.* Large, heavy shoes, such as those worn by plowmen, farm workers, etc.

clog (klog) *n.* **1** Anything that impedes motion, as a block attached to an animal or a vehicle. **2** An encumbrance; a hindrance. **3** A wooden-soled shoe. **4** A clog dance. See synonyms under IMPEDIMENT, LOAD. —*v.* **clogged, clog·ging** —*v.t.* **1** To choke up or obstruct. **2** To place impediments in the way of; hinder. **3** To fasten a clog to; hamper the movements of by a clog; hobble. —*v.i.* **4** To become choked up. **5** To be retarded or hindered. **6** To adhere in a mass; coagulate. **7** To perform a clog dance. See synonyms under HINDER, OBSTRUCT. [ME *clogge* block of wood]

clog almanac An early form of calendar made by cutting notches on the edges of a square block of wood, brass, or horn, and engraving devices upon it: also called *runic staff.*

clog dance A dance performed with clogs or other shoes, the clatter of which emphasizes the rhythm of the music.

cloi·son·né (kloi′zə·nā′) *n.* **1** A method of producing designs in enamel by laying out the pattern with strips of flat wire and filling the interstices with enamel paste, which is then fused in place. **2** The ware so produced. —*adj.* Of, pertaining to, or made by this method. [< F <*cloison* a partition]

clois·ter (klois′tər) *n.* **1** A covered walk, generally following the walls of buildings enclosing a quadrangle, as in a monastery or college. **2** A building devoted to the secluded life; a monastery; convent. **3** Monastic life. —*v.t.* **1** To seclude; confine, as in a cloister. **2** To provide with cloisters. [OF *cloistre* < L *claustrum* enclosed place] —**clois′ter·er** *n.* —**clois′tral** *adj.*

Synonyms (noun): abbey, convent, friary, hermitage, monastery, nunnery, priory. *Cloister, abbey, convent,* and *priory* are for either sex; a *friary* is always for men, a *nunnery* for women, a *monastery* commonly for men. A *priory* (governed by a prior or prioress) is inferior to an *abbey* (governed by an abbot or abbess). The word *monastery* lays stress upon the loneliness; *convent* emphasizes the association of its inmates. A *hermitage* was originally for a single recluse, but the word came to be applied to collections of hermits' cells.

clone (klōn) *n.* **1** A group of organisms derived from a single individual by asexual means. **2** An exact genetic replica of an organism. **3** A duplicate. Also **clon** (klōn, klon). —*v.t.* **cloned, clon·ing 1** To produce in the form of a clone. **2** To produce a clone. [< Gk. *klōn* sprout, twig] —**clon′al** *adj.*

clo·nus (klō′nəs) *n. Pathol.* A form of muscular convulsion, characterized by violent contraction and relaxation. [< Gk. *klonos* motion] —**clon·ic** (klon′ik) *adj.* —**clo·nic·i·ty** (klə·nis′ə·tē) *n.*

close (klōs) *adj.* **clos·er, clos·est 1** Enclosed or partly enclosed; shut in or about; confined; encompassed by limits, walls, or bounds; hence, kept in confinement: a *close* prisoner. **2** Closed so as to confine, restrict, or keep out something; fast shut: a *close* box. **3** Near or near together, in space, time, etc.: The two houses were *close* to each other. **4** Divided by small intervals: a *close* sequence of events. **5** Marked by nearness in space, order, or arrangement: marching in *close* order. **6** Dense; compact: a *close* fabric. **7** Affectionately associated; trusty; intimate: a *close* friend. **8** Exactly or literally executed; near in thought or performance to some aim, purpose, or standard: a *close* copy. That shot was *close.* **9** Narrowly confined or attentive to some object; watchful; strict; searching: a *close* search. **10** Nearly even or equal, without much difference in favor of either side: a *close* election. **11** Concealing one's thoughts and feelings; secretive; reticent. **12** Not liberal; stingy. **13** Ill-ventilated; heavy; stifling; dense: *close* weather. **14** *Colloq.* Difficult to obtain; tight: said of money or the money market. **15** Shut or restricted by law; not open or free: a *close* season for fishing; a *close* corporation. **16** Fitting tightly or snugly: a *close* cap. **17** Near to the surface: a *close* shave. **18** *Phonet.* Describing those vowels pronounced with a part of the tongue relatively close to the palate, as the (ē) in *seat;* high: opposed to *open.* See synonyms under ADJACENT, AVARICIOUS, FIRM, IMMEDIATE, IMPENETRABLE, TACITURN. —*v.* (klōz) **closed, clos·ing** *v.t.* **1** To shut, as a door. **2** To fill or obstruct, as an opening or passage. **3** To bring the parts of together, as a knife or book. **4** To bring into contact; join, as parts of an electric circuit. **5** To bring to an end; terminate. **6** To shut in; enclose. —*v.i.* **7** To become shut or closed. **8** To come to an end. **9** To grapple; come to close quarters. **10** To join; coalesce; unite. **11** To come to an agreement. **12** To be worth at the end of a business day: Stocks *closed* at an average three points higher. —**to close down 1** To come upon; enfold: Night *closed down.* **2** To suppress: The law *closed down* on gambling. **3** To discontinue a business or venture. —**to close in** To advance and surround. —**to close out** *U.S.* To sell all of, as goods, usually at a reduced price. —**to close up** To make all final arrangements: to *close up* one's affairs. —*n.* (klōz) **1** The end; conclusion. **2** A grapple. **3** A junction; meeting. **4** (klōs) Any place shut in or enclosed, as by a fence; specifically, the precinct of a cathedral or abbey. **5** (klōs) *Law* Land adjoining a house. **6** (klōs) An interest in the soil entitling the holders to damages in event of trespass. —**to break close** To trespass. —*adv.* (klōs) Closely. [< OF *clos,* pp. of *clore* close < L *claudere* close] —**close·ly** (klōs′lē) *adv.* —**close·ness** (klōs′nis) *n.* —**clos·er** (klō′zər) *n.*

close-bod·ied (klōs'bod'ēd) *adj.* **1** Fitting closely, as the body of a coat. **2** Close-grained.

close call (klōs) *U.S.* A narrow escape.

closed chain (klōzd) *Chem.* Atoms of a molecule arranged in a cyclical form and represented by the symbol of a ring, as in benzene and aromatic compounds.

closed shop An establishment in which all the employees are union members.

close-fist·ed (klōs'fis'tid) *adj.* Stingy; miserly. — **close'fist'ed·ness** *n.*

close-hauled (klōs'hôld') *adj. & adv. Naut.* With the sails set for sailing as close to the wind as possible.

close-mouthed (klōs'mouthd', -moutht') *adj.* Not given to imparting formation; taciturn; uncommunicative.

close-or·der drill (klōs'ôr'dər) *Mil.* A systematic exercise in information marching and in the formal handling of arms.

close quarters 1 In fighting, an encounter at close range or hand-to-hand. **2** A small, confined space or lodgment.

clos·et (kloz'it) *n.* **1** A small chamber, side room, or recess for storage of clothes, linen, etc., or for privacy. **2** The private chamber of a ruler, used as a council chamber, or as a chapel for devotion. **3** A watercloset; privy. —*v.t.* **clos·et·ed, clos·et·ing** To shut up or conceal in or as in a closet, especially for privacy: usually used with a reflexive pronoun. —*adj.* **1** Private; confidential. **2** Based on theory rather than practice: *closet strategy.* [<OF, dim. of *clos.* See CLOSE.]

closet drama A play or dramatic poem written solely, or chiefly, for reading rather than performance.

close-up (klōs'up') *n.* **1** In motion pictures and television, a picture of a character or a scene taken with the camera at close range. **2** A close look or view.

clos·trid·i·um (klos·trid'ē·əm) *n. pl.* **·trid·i·a** (-trid'ē·ə) *n. Bacteriol.* Any of a genus (*Clostridium*) of rod-shaped, spore-bearing, anaerobic bacteria, including pathogenic forms causing botulism, gas gangrene, and tetanus. [<NL <Gk. *klōstēr* spindle]

clo·sure (klō'zhər) *n.* **1** A proceeding to stop debate in a deliberative body in order to secure a prompt vote: also *cloture.* Compare PREVIOUS QUESTION. **2** A closing or shutting up: the *closure* of a shop. **3** *Obs.* That which closes or encloses; enclosure. —*v.t.* **clo·sured, clo·sur·ing** To apply closure to (a debate, etc.). [<OF <L *clausura* a closing < *claudere* close]

clot (klot) *n.* **1** A coagulated mass. —*v.t. & v.i.* **clot·ted, clot·ting** To form into clots; coagulate; mat, fill, or cover with clots. [OE *clott* lump, mass] — **clot'ty, clot'ted** *adj.*

cloth (klôth, kloth) *n. pl.* **cloths** (klôthz, klothz, klôths, kloths) **1** A woven fabric of wool, cotton, rayon, etc.; a piece of such fabric. **2** A piece of cloth for a special use, as a tablecloth. **3** *Naut.* A sail, or a breadth of the canvas that goes to make up a sail. **4** *Obs.* Raiment; clothes. — **the cloth** Clerical attire; hence, the clerical office; the clergy. [OE *clath*]

clothe (klōth) *v.t.* **clothed** or **clad, cloth·ing 1** To cover or provide with clothes; dress. **2** To cover as if with clothing; invest. [OE *clathian*]

clothes (klōz, klōthz) *n. pl.* **1** The articles of raiment worn by human beings; garments collectively; raiment; clothing. **2** Covering for a bed; bedclothes. See synonyms under DRESS. [OE *clathas*, pl. of *clath* cloth]

clothes·horse (klōz'hôrs', klōthz'-) *n.* **1** A frame on which to hang or dry clothes. **2** *Slang* A person regarded as excessively concerned with dress or as having little ability except for dressing well.

clothes moth Any of various moths, especially of the family *Tineidae,* whose larvae are destructive of wool, fur, and other animal products. For illustration see under INSECT (injurious).

clothes·press (klōz'pres', klōthz'-) *n.* A closet or chest for clothes; wardrobe.

clothes·tree (klōz'trē', klōthz'-) *n.* A stand

having arms or hooks on which to hang hats, coats, etc.

cloth·ier (klōth'yər) *n.* One who makes or sells cloths or clothing.

cloth-yard (klôth'yärd', kloth'-) *n.* A rod used for measuring cloth, formerly 27 inches, now equal in length to the standard yard of 36 inches.

cloth-yard shaft An early English arrow for the longbow, a cloth-yard in length.

clo·ture (klō'chər) See CLOSURE (def. 1).

cloud (kloud) *n.* **1** *Meteorol.* A mass of visible vapor or an aggregation of watery or icy particles, floating in the atmosphere at various heights and exhibiting a large variety of shapes, which partly aid in the determination of weather conditions. In the International Code, clouds have been classified, according to height and typical formation, into four families and ten genera. See table below. **2** Something that darkens, obscures, dims, confuses, or threatens. **3** A dimmed appearance; a spot. **4** *Law* A defect; blemish: a *cloud* on a title. **5** A great multitude; a cloudlike mass: a *cloud* of arrows. — **in the clouds 1** Imaginary; fanciful. **2** Impractical. —*v.t.* **1** To cover with or as with clouds; dim; obscure. **2** To render gloomy or troubled. **3** To cover with obloquy or disgrace. **4** To variegate, as marble. —*v.i.* **5** To be overcast with or as with clouds. [OE *clūd* rocky mass, hill] — **cloud'less** *adj.* — **cloud'less·ly** *adv.*

CLOUD TABLE—INTERNATIONAL CODE

Families: A: high clouds, from 20,000 feet up; B: middle clouds, 6,500–20,000 feet; C: low clouds, near surface to 6,500 feet; D: vertical displacement clouds, 1,600–20,000 feet.

Type	Symbol	Family	Av. ht. miles
Altocumulus	Ac	B	2 1/2
Altostratus	As	B	3 1/2
Cirrocumulus	Cc	A	5
Cirrostratus	Cs	A	6
Cirrus	Ci	A	7
Cumulonimbus	Cb	D	4
Cumulus	Cu	D	2
Nimbostratus	Ns	C	1/4
Stratocumulus	Sc	C	1
Stratus	St	C	1/4

cloud·ber·ry (kloud'ber'ē) *n. pl.* **·ries** An arctic or alpine species of raspberry (*Rubus chamaemorus*) producing an amber-colored fruit.

cloud·burst (kloud'bûrst') *n.* A sudden flood of rain, as if a whole cloud had been discharged at once.

cloud·let (kloud'lit) *n.* A little cloud.

cloud·y (kloud'ē) *adj.* **cloud·i·er, cloud·i·est 1** Overspread with clouds. **2** Of or like a cloud or clouds. **3** Obscure; vague; confused. **4** Gloomy; sullen. **5** Not limpid or clear. **6** Marked with cloudlike spots. — **cloud'i·ly** *adv.* — **cloud'i·ness** *n.*

clour (kloor) *v.t. Scot.* To knock; thump; dent. —*n.* A blow, bump, or bash on the head.

clout (klout) *n.* **1** A piece of cloth or leather; patch; rag. **2** *Often pl.* A swaddling cloth. **3** The center of a target. **4** An iron plate. **5** A short, stout nail for boot or shoe soles; a flat-headed nail for fastening iron plates: also called *clout nail.* **6** *Colloq.* A heavy blow or cuff with the hand. **7** In baseball, a long hit to the outfield. **8** *U.S. Slang* Influence or power; especially, political weight; pull. —*v.t.* **1** *Colloq.* To hit or strike, as with the hand; cuff. **2** To patch or bandage crudely. **3** To protect with an iron plate. **4** To stud with iron nails. [OE *clut*]

clove¹ (klōv) *n.* A dried flower bud of a tropical evergreen tree (*Syzygium aromaticum*), the **clovetree** of the myrtle family: used as a spice. [<OF *clou (de girofle)* nail (of clove) <L *clavus* nail; so called from its shape]

clove² (klōv) A past tense and archaic past participle of CLEAVE¹.

clove³ (klōv) *n. Bot.* One of the small bulbs formed in the axis of the scale of a mother bulb, as in garlic. [OE *clufu*]

clove-hitch (klōv'hich') *n. Naut.* A knot consisting of two half-hitches, with the ends of the rope going in opposite directions: used for fastening a rope around a spar. See illustration under HITCH.

clo·ven (klō'vən) *adj.* Parted; split. See CLEAVE¹.

clove pink Any of several varieties of *Dianthus caryophyllus* having a sweet clovelike odor. Also **clove gilliflower.**

clo·ver (klō'vər) *n.* **1** Any of several species of plants (genus *Trifolium*) of the legume family, having dense flower heads and the leaves divided into three leaflets; especially, the common **red clover** (*T. pratense*) used for forage and adopted as the State flower of Vermont. **2** Any of certain other plants of the legume family, as melilot. — **in clover 1** Originally, in good pasture, as cattle in a clover field. **2** Prosperous; having an abundance. [OE *clæfre* trefoil]

clo·ver·leaf (klō'vər·lēf') *n.* **1** An open automobile of early style, seating three or four persons, with entrance only through doors in front of forward seats. **2** A highway intersection designed so as to route traffic without interference, by means of a system of curving ramps from one level to another, in the form of a four-leaf clover. **3** *Aeron.* A testing maneuver in which an airplane flies in a course or pattern like a double figure-8 or a highway cloverleaf.

clown (kloun) *n.* **1** A professional buffoon in a play or circus, who entertains by antics, jokes, tricks, etc.; a zany; a jester. **2** A coarse or vulgar fellow; boor. **3** A countryman. —*v.i.* To behave like a clown. [Earlier *cloune* <MLG. Cf. Du. *kloen,* dial. Frisian *klönne*] — **clown'er·y** *n.*

clown·ish (klou'nish) *adj.* Of or like a clown; rude; ill-bred. See synonyms under AWKWARD.

clown·ism (klou'niz·əm) *n.* Clownish gait and behavior, especially in certain psychiatric disorders.

cloy (kloi) *v.t.* To satiate, as with sweetness; surfeit. See synonyms under SATISFY. [Var. of earlier *accloy* <OF *encloyer* nail up, block, overload <LL *inclavare* nail <*clavus* a nail] — **cloy'ing·ly** *adv.* — **cloy'ing·ness** *n.*

club¹ (klub) *n.* **1** A stout stick or staff; cudgel; truncheon. **2** A staff with curved head of metal or wood used in golf, hockey, etc. **3** a A three-lobed spot on a playing card. **b** A card so marked. **c** *pl.* The suit so marked. **4** *Naut.* A small spar by means of which a good set is given to a gaff topsail or a staysail; also, a similar spar on a staysail or jib to which the sheet is made fast. **5** *Entomol.* A clavate organ or part. — **Indian clubs** Bottle-shaped wooden clubs used in gymnastics. —*v.* **clubbed, club·bing** *v.t.* **1** To beat, as with a stick or club. **2** *Archaic* To gather into a clublike mass, as hair. —*v.i.* **3** *Archaic* To gather in a mass. — **to club a rifle** or **musket** or **gun** To turn a firearm so that the stock is uppermost and may be used as a club. [<ON *klubba.* Akin to CLUMP.]

club² (klub) *n.* **1** An organization of persons for social intercourse or other common object. **2** A house or room reserved for the meetings of such an organization. —*v.* **clubbed, club·bing** *v.t.* To contribute for a common purpose; make common stock of: to *club* resources. —*v.i.* To combine with a common object; form a club: often with *together.* —*adj.* Of, pertaining to, or belonging to a club; *club* grounds. [Special meaning of CLUB¹]

club·foot (klub'foot') *n. pl.* **·feet 1** Congenital distortion of the foot; talipes. **2** A foot so affected. —**club'foot'ed** *adj.*

club·grass (klub'gras', -gräs') *n.* The cat-tail.

club·hand (klub'hand') *n.* **1** A deformity of the hand, analogous to clubfoot; talipomanus. **2** A hand so deformed.

club·haul (klub'hôl') *v.t. Naut.* To put (a vessel) about when in danger of drifting on a lee shore, by letting go the lee anchor, hauling to windward by the hawser, when the vessel's head has come into the wind, and cutting the hawser when the sails are trimmed on the new tack.

club·house (klub'hous') *n.* The building occupied by a club.

club·moss (klub'môs', -mos') *n.* A widely distributed evergreen herb (genus *Lycopodium*).

club sandwich A sandwich containing three or more layers of bread filled with meat, lettuce, tomatoes, mayonnaise, etc.

club steak A small beefsteak cut from the loin.

club topsail *Naut.* A sail, as a gaff topsail, extended on the foot by a club.

cluck (kluk) *v.t.* **1** To call by clucking, as chickens. **2** To utter with a like sound: to *cluck* disapproval. —*v.i.* **3** To make the noise of a hen calling her chicks or brooding. **4** To make a sound of suction in the side of the mouth, as in urging a horse; make any sound similar to a cluck. —*n.* **1** A sound like that made by a brooding hen to call her chicks. **2** A hen. **3** *Slang* A person resembling a hen in stupidity. [Imit.]

clue (klōō) *n.* A guiding fact or idea which leads to the solution of a problem or mystery. See CLEW [Var. of CLEW]

clump (klump) *n.* **1** A thick cluster; tuft; lump. **2** A dull sound, as of heavy tramping. **3** An irregular, clumsy, thick piece or mass. **4** *Bacteriol.* A mass of bacteria in a state of rest, as by the agency of agglutinins. —*v.t.* **1** To place or plant in a cluster or group. **2** To put an extra sole on (a shoe). **3** *Bacteriol.* To cluster together, as bacteria. —*v.i.* **4** To walk clumsily and noisily. **5** To form clumps. [< LG. Cf. Du. *klomp.* Akin to CLUB.] —**clump′y, clump′ish** *adj.*

clum·sy (klum′zē) *adj.* **·si·er, ·si·est** **1** Lacking dexterity, ease, or grace; awkward. **2** Rudely constructed; ill-contrived, so as to be unwieldy; ungainly. See synonyms under AWKWARD. [ME *clumsed,* pp. of *clumsen* be numb (with cold) < Scand. Cf. dial. Sw. *klumsen* benumbed.] —**clum′si·ly** *adv.* —**clum′si·ness** *n.*

clung (klung) Past tense and past participle of CLING.

clu·pe·id (klōō′pē·id) *n.* **1** Any one of a family of teleost fishes (*Clupeidae*) having compressed bodies, including the herrings, shads, etc. —*adj.* Pertaining to the *Clupeidae.* [< NL *Clupeidae* < L *clupea,* a kind of small fish]

clu·pe·oid (klōō′pē·oid) *adj.* Herringlike. —*n.* A fish of the herring family.

clus·ter (klus′tər) *n.* **1** A group or bunch, as of grapes. **2** A group of bombs dropped simultaneously. **3** An assembly; congregation. **4** In pyrotechnic illumination, a group of stars burning at the same time. —*v.t.* **1** To bring forth in or collect into clusters. **2** To provide with clusters. —*v.i.* **3** To grow in clusters, as grapes. **4** To gather in a cluster or clusters. [OE *clyster*] —**clus′tered** *adj.* —**clus′ter·y** *adj.*

cluster redpepper Bonnet pepper.

clutch[1] (kluch) *v.t.* **1** To seize eagerly; snatch, as with hands or talons. **2** To grasp and hold firmly. —*v.i.* **3** To attempt to seize, snatch, or reach: with *at:* to *clutch at* shadows. —*n.* **1** A tight, powerful grasp. **2** *pl.* Cruel, powerful claws or hands; hence, rapacious or cruel power: to fall into the *clutches* of an enemy. **3** A talon, paw, claw, or hand. **4** *Mech.* Any of variously constructed and operated devices for coupling two working parts; also, any appliance suitable for seizing and holding. See synonyms under CATCH. [ME *clucchen,* var. of *clicche,* OE *clyccan* grasp]

CLUTCH
a. Fixed member.
b. Slidable and splined member.
c. Collar.
d. Fork.
e. Lever.
The fork is controlled by the lever which slides *b* into connection with *a.*

clutch[2] (kluch) *n.* A sitting of eggs; a brood of chickens. —*v.t.* To hatch [< ON *klekja* hatch]

clut·ter (klut′ər) *n.* **1** A disordered state or collection; litter. **2** A clattering, confused noise; chattering. —*v.t.* **1** To litter, heap, or pile in a confused manner: often with *up.* —*v.i.* **2** To be littered or strewn with objects in a disorderly manner. **3** To run or move with bustle or confusion; clatter. **4** To speak hurriedly and inexactly. [Var. of earlier *clotter,* freq. of CLOT]

clyp·e·ate (klip′ē·āt) *adj.* **1** Shield-shaped: also **clyp·e·i·form** (klip′ē·ə·fôrm′). **2** Having a clypeus. Also **clyp′e·at·ed.**

clyp·e·us (klip′ē·əs) *n. pl.* **clyp·e·i** (klip′ē·ī) **1** *Entomol.* A shieldlike plate on the front part of the head of an insect. **2** *Bot.* A band encircling the perithecium of certain fungi. [< L, shield]

clys·ter (klis′tər) *n. Med.* An intestinal injection;

enema. [< F *clystère* < Gk. *klystēr* < *klyzein* wash out, rinse]

Cm *Chem.* Curium (symbol Cm).

Cnut (knōōt) See CANUTE.

Co *Chem.* Cobalt (symbol Co).

co-[1] *prefix* With; together; joint or jointly: used with verbs, nouns, adjectives, and adverbs. See the foot of the page for a list of self-explanatory words containing the prefix *co-.* [< L *co-,* var. of *com-* before *gn, h,* and vowels < *cum* with]

co-[2] *prefix* **1** *Math.* Of the complement: *cosine.* **2** *Astron.* Complement of: *codeclination.* [< L *complementum* complement]

co·a·cer·vate (kō′ə·sûr′vāt, kō·as′ər-) *n. Chem.* The material precipitated in coacervation. [< L *coacervatus,* pp. of *coacervare* pile up < *co-* together + *acervus* heap]

co·ac·er·va·tion (kō·as′ər·vā′shən) *n. Chem.* The precipitation of minute liquid droplets from a mixture of two hydrophilic colloids having opposite electric charges.

coach (kōch) *n.* **1** A large four-wheeled closed carriage. **2** A two-door, two-seated, closed automobile. **3** A stagecoach. **4** A passenger bus. **5** A railway passenger car, usually providing the lowest-priced accommodations on a train. **6** A private tutor. **7** A trainer and director in athletics. **7** In baseball, a member of the team at bat stationed near first or third base to advise the base runners. —*v.t.* **1** To tutor or train; prepare by training or drilling. **2** To place or carry in a coach. **3** In baseball, to direct base runners in their movements, as from first or third base. —*v.i.* **4** To study with or be trained by a coach or trainer. **5** To act as coach or trainer. **6** To ride or drive in a coach. [< MF *coche* < Magyar *kocsi* of Kocs, a Hungarian village where first used]

coach-and-four (kōch′ən·fôr′, -fōr′) *n.* A coach drawn by four horses.

co·act (kō·akt′) *v.i.* To act or work together. —**co·ac′tion** *n.* —**co·ac′tive** *adj.*

co·act (kō·akt′) *v.t.* To force; compel; coerce. [< L *coactus,* pp. of *cogere* compel < *co-* together + *agere* do, drive]

co·ac·tion (kō·ak′shən) *n.* The exertion of force in compulsion or restraint.

co·ac·tive (kō·ak′tiv) *adj.* Having power to compel or constrain; compulsory.

co·ad·ju·tant (kō·aj′ə·tənt) *adj.* Cooperating. —*n.* An assistant; colleague. [< CO- + L *adjutans, -antis,* ppr. of *adjutare* help]

co·ad·ju·tor (kō·aj′ə·tər, kō′ə·jōō′tər) *n.* An associate in action; a co-worker or colleague, especially one appointed to assist in official duties, as the assistant of a bishop. See synonyms under ACCESSORY, ASSOCIATE, AUXILIARY. —**co·ad′ju·tress, co·ad′ju·trix** *n. fem.*

co·ad·u·nate (kō·aj′ə·nāt) *v.t.* To join together. *adj.* (kō·aj′ə·nit, -nāt) *Biol.* Closely joined, especially during the growth of an organ or part. [< L *coadunatus,* pp. of *coadunare* unite < *co-* together + *ad* to + *unus* one] —**co·ad′u·na′tion** *n.* —**co·ad′u·na′tive** *adj.*

co·ae·val (kō·ē′vəl) See COEVAL.

co·ag·u·lant (kō·ag′yə·lənt) *n.* A coagulation agent, as rennet. [< L *coagulans, -antis,* ppr. of *coagulare* curdle]

co·ag·u·late (kō·ag′yə·lāt) *v.t. & v.i.* **·lat·ed, ·lat·ing** To change from a liquid state into a clot or jelly, as blood. [< L *coagulatus,* pp. of *coagulare* curdle] —**co·ag′u·la·bil′i·ty** *n.* —**co·ag′u·la·ble** (kō·ag′yə·bəl) *adj.* —**co·ag′u·la′tion** *n.* —**co·ag′u·la′tive** *adj.* —**co·ag′u·la′tor** *n.*

co·ag·u·lum (kō·ag′yə·ləm) *n. pl.* **·la** (-lə) Any coagulated mass, as a gel, curd, or clot. [< L, that which binds together]

coak (kōk) See COKE[1].

coal (kōl) *n.* **1** A black, brittle, compact, amorphous substance of variable physical and chemical composition, produced by the carbonization of prehistoric vegetation: found in beds or veins in the earth and used as fuel; the principal varieties are bituminous coal, anthracite, and lignite. **2** A piece of coal as broken for use; such pieces

collectively: in Great Britain commonly used in the plural. **3** A fragment of burned wood; charcoal. **4** An ember. —**to haul, rake,** etc., **over the coals** To criticize; reprimand. —*v.t.* **1** To supply with coal. **2** To reduce to coal, as wood, by burning. —*v.i.* **3** To take in coal. ♦ Homophone: **cole.** [OE *col*]

coal bank A vein of coal at the surface.

coal bed A receptacle or place for coals, as in a forge. See illustration under FORGE.

coal·er (kōl′ər) *n.* One who or that which supplies or transports coal; a collier.

co·a·lesce (kō′ə·les′) *v.i.* **·lesced, ·lesc·ing** To grow or come together into one; fuse; blend. See synonyms under UNITE. [< L *coalescere* unite < *co-* together + *alescere,* inceptive of *alere* grow up] —**co′a·les′cence** *n.* —**co′a·les′cent** *adj.*

coal·fish (kōl′fish′) *n. pl.* **·fish** or **·fish·es** **1** A dark-colored food fish (*Pollachius virens*) of the cod family; the common pollack of the Atlantic. **2** The sablefish.

coal gas **1** The poisonous gas produced by the combustion of coal. **2** A gas used for illuminating and heating: produced by the distillation of bituminous coal and consisting chiefly of methane, carbon monoxide, and hydrogen.

coal·hole (kōl′hōl′) *n.* **1** A place for storing coal. **2** A covered hole in a sidewalk, through which coal is chuted to a bin or cellar.

coal·ing (kōl′ing) *n.* **1** The burning of wood into charcoal; also, the place where this is done. **2** Loading with coal.

co·a·li·tion (kō′ə·lish′ən) *n.* **1** An alliance of persons, parties, or states. **2** Coalescence. See synonyms under ALLIANCE, UNION. [< L *coalitio, -onis* < *coalescere.* See COALESCE.] —**co′a·li′tion·ist** *n.*

coal oil Kerosene.

coal·pit (kōl′pit′) *n.* **1** A pit from which coal is obtained. **2** A pit for making charcoal.

coal·sack (kōl′sak′) *n.* **1** A sack for coal. **2** *Astron.* One of several dark spaces in the Milky Way, especially **the Coalsack,** a large space near the Large and Small Magellanic clouds in the constellation of the Southern Cross.

coal scuttle A bucketlike container with a lip and a handle, used for containing and carrying coal.

coal tar The black viscid pitch distilled from bituminous coal, and yielding a large variety of organic compounds used in the making of dyestuffs, explosives, flavoring extracts, drugs, plastics, etc. —**coal′-tar′** *adj.*

coam·ing (kō′ming) *n. Naut.* **1** A raised curb about a hatchway, well, or skylight, to keep water from entering: also spelled *combing.* **2** One of the pieces in such a curb. [Origin unknown]

co·arc·tate (kō·ärk′tāt) *adj.* **1** *Bot.* Crowded together, as a panicle of flowers; compressed. **2** *Entomol.* Constricted at the base, as the abdomen of an insect. [< L *coarctatus,* pp. of *coarctare,* var. of *coartare* confine, constrain < *co-* together + *artus* crowded]

co·arc·ta·tion (kō′ärk·tā′shən) *n.* Stricture or contraction, as of a cavity or orifice.

coarse (kôrs, kōrs) *adj.* **1** Composed of large or rough parts or particles; not fine or delicate. **2** Inferior in quality; common. **3** Low; vulgar; indelicate. See synonyms under BLUFF, BRUTISH, COMMON, IMMODEST, LARGE, ROUGH, RUSTIC, VULGAR. ♦ Homophone: *course.* [Adjectival use of COURSE in sense "customary sequence" (as in *of course*); hence, usual, ordinary] —**coarse′ly** *adv.* —**coarse′ness** *n.*

coars·en (kôr′sən, kōr′-) *v.t. & v.i.* To make or

add,āce,câre,pälm; end,ēven; it,īce; odd,ōpen,ôrder; tŏŏk,pōōl; up,bûrn; ə = a in *above,* e in *sicken,* i in *clarity,* o in *melon,* u in *focus;* yōō = u in *fuse,* oi,oil; ou,pout; ch,check; g,go; ng,ring; th,thin; ŧħ,this; zh,vision. Foreign sounds á,œ,ü,kh,ń; and ♦: see page xx. < *from;* + *plus;* ? *possibly.*

become coarse.

coast (kōst) *n.* **1** The land next to the sea; the seashore. **2** *Obs.* A region; boundary: used chiefly in the plural. **3** A slope suitable for sliding, as on a sled; also, a slide down it. **—the Coast** *U.S.* That part of the United States bordering on the Pacific Ocean. **—the coast is clear** There is no danger or difficulty now. —*v.t.* **1** To sail or travel along, as a coast or border. —*v.i.* **2** To sail or travel along a coast or littoral, keeping in sight of land; to travel from port to port along a coast. **3** To slide or ride down a slope by force of gravity alone, as on a sled or bicycle. **4** To continue moving on momentum after the source of power has been stopped. **5** To move or behave aimlessly. [< OF *coste* < L *costa* rib, flank]

coast·al (kōs′təl) *adj.* **1** Of or pertaining to the coast. **2** Bordering or skirting a coastline.

coast·er (kōs′tər) *n.* **1** One who or that which coasts, as a person or vessel engaged in the coasting trade. **2** A sled or toboggan. **3** Formerly, a tray used in passing a decanter around a dining table. **4** A small disk of glass or other material on which to set a drinking glass to protect the surface underneath from moisture or heat.

coast guard 1 Naval or military coast police. **2** A member of this police. **—United States Coast Guard** A police or military force stationed along the coasts to enforce customs, immigration, and navigation laws and maintain an ice patrol. It operates in wartime within the U.S. Navy and at other times under the Department of the Treasury.

coast·ing (kōs′ting) *n.* **1** The act of sliding down a snow-covered hill or track on a sled. **2** The act of going down grade by force of gravity, as on a bicycle or in a car. **3** Trade up and down the same coast from port to port: also **coasting trade.**

coat (kōt) *n.* **1** A sleeved outer garment opening down the front, of varying length: worn as part of an outfit or as an out-of-door covering over one's usual clothing. **2** Any outer covering, as the fur of an animal, a layer of ice or paint, etc. **3** A coat of arms. **4** *Dial.* A skirt; petticoat. **5** *Obs.* The distinctive vesture of an order of men; cloth. —*v.t.* To cover with or as with a coat, as of paint. [< OF *cote* < Med. L *cota* garment] **—coat′·less** *adj.*

coat·ed (kō′tid) *adj.* **1** Having a covering, layer, or coat. **2** In papermaking, having a calendered surface of mineral matter, as sizing or china clay.

coat·ee (kō·tē′) *n.* A short coat.

co·a·ti (kō·ä′tē) *n. pl.* **·tis** A carnivorous, raccoonlike mammal (genus *Nasua*) of tropical America, with mobile snout, plantigrade feet, elongated body, and a long, ringed tail. Also **co·a′ti·mon′di, co·a′ti·mun′di** (-mun′dē). [< Tupian]

coat·ing (kō′ting) *n.* **1** A covering layer; coat. **2** Cloth for coats.

coat of arms The armorial bearings of a person or family.

coat·tail (kōt′tāl′) *n.* **1** The loose hinder part of a coat below the waist. **2** *Usually pl.* The pendent, tapering, rear part of a man's dress coat.

coax (kōks) *v.t.* **1** To persuade or seek to persuade by gentleness and tact; wheedle. **2** To obtain by coaxing or cajolery. —*v.i.* **3** To use persuasion or cajolery. See synonyms under ALLURE, PERSUADE. —*n.* One who coaxes. **—coax′er** *n.* **—coax′ing·ly** *adv.* [< Earlier *cokes* a fool, dupe; origin unknown]

co·ax·i·al (kō·ak′sē·əl) *adj.* Having a common axis or coincident axes: also **co·ax′al** (kō-ak′səl).

coaxial cable A conducting wire for the transmission of radio or television signals or of multiple telegraph or telephone messages; held in the center of a metal tube by a series of closely-spaced disks, every element of the assembly being well insulated.

cob (kob) *n.* **1** A roundish mass, heap, or lump, as a piece of coal or stone. **2** The woody spike of an ear of corn around which the kernels grow; a corncob. **3** A strong, thick-set, short-legged horse. **4** The male of the swan. **5** *Brit. Dial.* A leading man; a leader. [ME *cobbe*; origin uncertain]

co·balt (kō′bôlt) *n.* A hard, brittle, magnetic metallic element (symbol Co, atomic number 27) usually found in iron and nickel ores, used in alloys, and biologically essential for the activity of several enzymes. See PERIODIC TABLE. [< G *kobalt*, var. of *kobold* goblin; so called by

early miners who thought it a worthless, injurious ore]

cobalt bloom Erythrite.

cobalt blue 1 A permanent deep-blue pigment resembling ultramarine, made from the oxides of cobalt and aluminum. **2** An intense, pure blue.

co·bal·tic (kō·bôl′tik) *adj. Chem.* Designating a compound containing cobalt in its higher valence.

co·bal·tite (kō·bôl′tīt, kō′bôl·tīt) *n.* A metallic, silver-white, brittle cobalt sulfarsenide, CoAsS. Also **co·bal·tine** (kō′bôl·tēn, -tin).

co·bal·tous (kō·bôl′təs) *adj. Chem.* Designating a compound containing cobalt in its lower valence.

cob·ble[1] (kob′əl) *n.* **1** A cobblestone. **2** A lump of coal as big as a cobblestone. —*v.t.* To pave with cobblestones. [Akin to COB[1]]

cob·ble[2] (kob′əl) *v.* **·bled, ·bling** *v.t.* **1** To make, patch, or repair, as boots or shoes. **2** To put together roughly. —*v.i.* **3** To work as a shoemaker. [Origin uncertain]

cob·bler[1] (kob′lər) *n.* **1** A shoemaker. **2** A clumsy workman. [< COBBLE[2]]

cob·bler[2] (kob′lər) *n.* **1** An iced drink made of wine, sugar, fruit juices, etc. **2** A deep-dish fruit pie with no bottom crust. [Origin unknown]

cob·ble·stone (kob′əl·stōn′) *n.* A rounded stone formerly much used for paving. [See COBBLE[1]]

cob coal A large round piece of coal; also, coal in such pieces or lumps.

co·bel·lig·er·ent (kō′bə·lij′ər·ənt) *n.* A country fighting on the same side with another, or others, against a common enemy: distinguished from an *ally* in international usage in that it is not bound by an alliance.

cob·nut (kob′nut′) *n.* **1** A large nut from a cultivated variety of hazel tree (*Corylus avellana grandis*). **2** The tree producing it. **3** A children's game played with such nuts. [? < COB[1] (def. 1) + NUT]

co·bra[1] (kō′brə) *n.* Any of a genus (*Naja*) of very venomous snakes of Asia and Africa that when excited can dilate their necks into a broad hood; especially, the **spectacled cobra** (*N. naja*) of India, and the **king cobra** (*Ophiophagus hannah*), the largest known of all venomous snakes. [< Pg. < L *colubra* snake]

co·bra[2] (kob′rə) See COPRA.

co·bra-de-ca·pel·lo (kō′brə·dē·kə·pel′ō) *n. pl.* **co·bras-de-ca·pel·lo** The spectacled cobra. [< Pg., snake with a hood]

Co·burg (kō′bûrg, Ger. kō′bŏŏrkh) A city in Upper Franconia, central Germany: also *Koburg.*

cob·web (kob′web′) *n.* **1** The network of fine thread spun by a spider; also, a single thread of this. **2** A snare, or anything fine-spun or flimsy. —*v.t.* **cob·webbed, cob·web·bing** To cover with or as with cobwebs. [ME *coppeweb* < *coppe* spider + WEB] **—cob′web′ber·y** *n.*

cob·work (kob′wûrk′) *n.* A structure of logs laid crosswise, with ends secured by dovetailing.

co·ca (kō′kə) *n.* **1** The dried leaves of a South American shrub (genus *Erythroxylon*), yielding cocaine and other alkaloids and sometimes chewed for their stimulant properties. **2** Either of the two species of this shrub which yield these alkaloids. [< Sp. < Quechua]

co·caine (kō·kān′, kō′kān; *in technical usage* kō′kə·ēn) *n.* A white, bitter, crystalline alkaloid, $C_{17}H_{21}NO_4$, contained in coca leaves: used in medicine as a local anesthetic and as a narcotic. Also **co·cain′.** [< COCA]

co·car·box·yl·ase (kō′kär·bok′səl·ās) *n.* A coenzyme necessary in the production and activity of carboxylase.

co·car·cin·o·gen (kō′kär′sin′ə·jən) *n.* Any non-carcinogenic agent that enhances the action of a carcinogen.

coc·cid (kok′sid) *n. Entomol.* Any member of a superfamily (*Coccoidae*) of hemipterous insects,

including mealybugs and scale insects. [< NL *Coccoidae* < Gk. *kokkos* berry]

coc·cid·i·oi·dal granuloma (kok·sid′ē·oid′l) A disease caused by a fungus (genus *Coccidioides*) superficially resembling tuberculosis, which affects the lymph nodes of some animals and of man. [< NL *Coccidioides* < Gk. *kokkos* a berry + *eidos* form]

coc·cid·i·o·sis (kok·sid′ē·ō′sis) *n.* One of a group of specific infectious diseases caused by protozoan parasites (order *Coccidia*) which attack the epithelial tissue of animals, birds, and, rarely, man. [< NL *Coccidia* (< Gk. *kokkos* a berry) + -OSIS]

coc·cif·er·ous (kok·sif′ər·əs) *adj. Bot.* Bearing or producing berries. [< Gk. *kokkos* berry + -(I)FEROUS]

coc·coid (kok′oid) *adj. Bacteriol.* Like a coccus: applied to certain forms of bacteria which tend to be round in form.

coc·co·lith (kok′ə·lith) *n. Geol.* A minute oval or rounded body often abundant in deep-sea mud. [< Gk. *kokkos* berry + -LITH]

coc·cu·lus in·di·cus (kok′yə·ləs in′də·kəs) The fishberry.

coc·cus (kok′əs) *n. pl.* **coc·ci** (kok′sī) **1** *Bot.* **a** One of the dry, one-seeded portions into which a schizocarp splits. **b** A spore mother cell in which the spores are contained for a time after their maturity. **2** *Bacteriol.* One of the principal forms of bacteria, characterized by an ovoid or spherical shape: often used in combination: *streptococcus.* See illustration under BACTERIUM. **3** *Entomol.* One of a genus (*Coccus*) of scale insects. [< NL < Gk. *kokkos* berry]

coc·cyx (kok′siks) *n. pl.* **coc·cy·ges** (kok·sī′jēz) *Anat.* The caudal end of the spine. [< L < Gk. *kokkyx* cuckoo; from a fancied resemblance to a cuckoo's bill] **—coc·cyg·e·al** (kok·sij′ē·əl) *adj.*

coch·i·neal (koch′ə·nēl′, koch′ə·nēl) *n.* A coloring matter yielding a brilliant scarlet dye, consisting of the dried bodies of the female *Dactylopius coccus*, a scale insect of tropical America and of Java. [< F *cochenille* < Sp. *cochinilla* < L *coccineus* scarlet < *coccus* a berry, grain of kermes < Gk. *kokkos*]

coch·le·a (kok′lē·ə) *n. pl.* **·le·ae** (-li·ē) *Anat.* A winding cavity in the internal ear, containing the essential organs of hearing. See illustration under EAR. [< L *cochlea* snail] **—coch′le·ar** *adj.*

coch·le·ate (kok′lē·āt) *adj.* Spirally twisted like a snail shell. Also **coch′le·at′ed.**

cock[1] (kok) *n.* **1** A full-grown male of the domestic fowl. **2** Any male bird. **3** A leader; champion. **4** A weathercock. **5** A faucet, often with the nozzle bent downward. **6** In a firearm, the hammer; also, the position at which the hammer rests when raised. **7** A significant jaunty tip or upward turn; a bending or pricking up, as of a hat brim, the ears, eyes, etc. —*v.t.* **1** To raise the cock or hammer of (a firearm) preparatory to firing. **2** To turn up or to one side alertly, jauntily, or inquiringly, as the head, eye, ears, etc. —*v.i.* **3** To raise the hammer of a firearm. **4** To stick up; be prominent. —*adj.* Male: a *cock* lobster. [OE *cocc*]

cock·ade (kok·ād′) *n.* A rosette, knot of ribbon, or the like, worn on the hat. [< MF *coquarde* < *coq* cock] **—cock·ad′ed** *adj.*

cock-and-bull (kok′ən·bŏŏl′) *adj.* Highly improbable; incredible: a *cock-and-bull* story.

cock·a·tiel (kok′ə·tēl′) *n.* An Australian cockatoo of the genus *Leptolophus*, especially *L. hollandicus.* Also **cock′a·teel′.** [< Du. *kaketielje*]

cock·a·too (kok′ə·tōō′, kok′ə·tōō) *n. pl.* **·toos** Any of various, bright-colored, crested parrots of the East Indies or Australia, especially one of the genus *Kakatoë.* [< Du. *kaketoe* < Malay *kākātūa*; infl. in form by COCK]

COCKATOO
(About 12 inches tall)

cock·a·trice (kok′ə·tris) *n.* **1** A fabulous serpent, said to be hatched from a cock's egg, deadly to those who felt its breath or met its glance. Compare BASILISK. **2** In the Bible, an unidentified species of deadly serpent. [< OF *cocatris*, infl. by *coq* cock, < Med. L *calcatrix* (< L *calcare* tread, walk), used to translate Gk. *ichneumōn* ICHNEUMON]

cock·boat (kok′bōt′) *n.* A small rowboat: also called *cock.* [< COCK[3] + BOAT]

cock·chaf·er (kok′chā′fər) *n.* Any of a widely distributed family (*Melolonthidae*) of scara-

---

*[center column — cobra illustration caption]*

COBRA
a. Indian or spectacled cobra.
b. Back of head, showing markings or "spectacles."
(Up to 6 feet in length)

baeoid beetles, especially *Melolontha melolontha*, a large, European variety destructive to vegetation. [<COCK¹ (def. 3) + CHAFER]

cock·crow (kok′krō′) *n.* The early morning. Also **cock′crow′ing.**

cocked hat (kokt) **1** A hat with the brim turned up, especially one turned up in three places; a three-cornered hat. **2** A game of bowls played with three pins. —**to knock into a cocked hat** To demolish; ruin.

cock·er (kok′ər) *n.* **1** A cocker spaniel. See under SPANIEL. **2** A cockfighter.

cock·er·el (kok′ər·əl) *n.* A young cock. [Dim. of COCK¹]

cock-eyed (kok′īd′) *adj.* **1** Cross-eyed. **2** *Slang* Off center; askew. **3** Absurd; crazy. **4** Drunk; intoxicated.

cock·fight (kok′fīt′) *n.* A battle between cocks, especially between gamecocks. Also **cock′match′.** —**cock′fight′er** *n.* —**cock′fight′ing** *adj.* & *n.*

cock·horse (kok′hôrs′) *n.* A child's rocking-horse, hobbyhorse, or the like.

cock·i·ness (kok′ē·nis) *n.* Jauntiness; also, conceit.

cock·ing (kok′ing) *n.* **1** Cockfighting. **2** The shooting of woodcocks.

cock·ish (kok′ish) *adj.* **1** Cocklike; cocky. **2** Strutting; self-assertive. —**cock′ish·ly** *adv.* — **cock′ish·ness** *n.*

cock·le¹ (kok′əl) *n.* **1** An edible European bivalve mollusk *(Cardium edule).* **2** The cockleshell. **3** A confection made with sugar and flour. **4** The fire chamber or dome of a hot-air furnace. **5** A shallow boat. — **cockles of one's heart** The depths or bottom of one's heart, or feelings. — *v.t.* & *v.i.* **cock·led, cock·ling** To wrinkle; pucker. [<F *coquille* <L *conchylium* shell <Gk. *conchylion,* dim. of *conchylē* shell, mussel]

cock·le² (kok′əl) *n.* A grass that grows among grain; the darnel. [OE *coccel*]

cock·le·bur (kok′əl·bûr′) *n.* **1** A low-branching, rank weed (genus *Xanthium*) of the composite family, with hard ovoid or oblong two-celled burs about an inch long. **2** *Brit.* The burdock.

cock·le·shell (kok′əl·shel′) *n.* **1** The shell of a cockle; especially, one valve of a scallop's shell worn in a pilgrim's hat. **2** A scallop shell. **3** A frail, light boat.

cock·loft (kok′lôft′, -loft′) *n.* A loft or attic under a roof. [Origin uncertain]

cock·ney (kok′nē) *n.* **1** One born in the East End of London, traditionally within the sound of the bells of St. Mary-le-Bow Church, in Cheapside, and speaking a characteristic dialect. **2** One having the traits or dialect of such a person; especially, an uneducated yet pretentious city person. **4** The characteristic dialect or accent of East End Londoners. **5** *Obs.* A petted child; an effeminate youth. *adj.* Of or like cockneys or their speech. [ME *cokeney,* lit., cock's egg < *coken* cock's + OE *æg* egg; later, a pampered child, a scold or effeminate person, a city man] —**cock′ney·ish** *adj.* —**cock′ney·ism** *n.*

cock of the plains A large grouse *(Centrocercus urophasianus)*: also called *sage cock, prairie cock.*

cock·pit (kok′pit′) *n.* **1** A pit or ring for cockfighting; hence, any place where many battles have taken place. **2** An apartment for the wounded in a warship. **3** *Naut.* In small yachts, a space lower than the rest of the deck. **4** *Aeron.* In some airplanes, an enclosed space for the pilot and co-pilot or a passenger. **5** *Obs.* The pit of a theater.

cock·roach (kok′rōch′) *n.* Any of a large group of swift-running, chiefly nocturnal insects (families *Blattidae* and *Phyllodromidae*) of world-wide distribution, having flat, oval, variously colored bodies, biting mouth parts, and a typically offensive odor, including such household pests as the Croton bug, the dark-brown Oriental cockroach *(Blatta orientalis)* and the large, winged American cockroach *(Periplaneta americana)*. For illustration see INSECTS (injurious). [<Sp. *cucaracha*]

cocks·comb (koks′kōm′) *n.* **1** A plant (genus *Celosia*) with red flowers, suggesting the comb of a cock. **2** A coxcomb (def. 1). **3** A

scarlet ridge on a jester's cap; also, the cap. Also spelled *coxcomb.*

cocks·head (koks′hed′) *n.* An annual shrubby herb *(Onobrychis caputgalli)* of the Mediterranean region, with purple flowers and small, crested, spine-bearing pods.

cock·spur (kok′spûr′) *n.* **1** A spur on the leg of a cock. **2** A kind of hawthorn *(Crataegus crusgalli)* with long thorns: also **cockspur thorn.**

cock·sure (kok′shoor′) *adj.* **1** Absolutely sure. **2** Self-confident; presumptuously sure. **3** *Obs.* Perfectly safe. —**cock′sure′ness** *n.*

cock·swain (kok′sən, -swān′) See COXSWAIN.

cock·tail¹ (kok′tāl′) *n.* **1** A short, mixed, alcoholic drink, variously flavored and prepared. **2** An appetizer, as chilled, diced fruits, fruit juices, or sea food seasoned with a highly spiced sauce. [? Alter. of F *coquetel,* a mixed drink popular in the 18th c.]

cock·tail² (kok′tāl′) *n.* **1** A horse with a docked tail. **2** An underbred horse. **3** A person of low breeding. [<COCK¹ (def. 1) + TAIL; with ref. to the appearance of a horse's docked tail]

cock-up (kok′up′) *n.* **1** A turned-up or cocked part or point of anything. **2** A cocked hat.

co·co (kō′kō) *n.* *pl.* ·**cos** A widely distributed tropical palm tree *(Cocos nucifera)* that produces coconuts. Also **coco palm, coconut palm.** — *adj.* Made of coco fiber. [<Pg., grinning face; with ref. to the eyes of a coconut]

co·coa (kō′kō) *n.* **1** A powder made from the roasted, husked seed kernels of the cacao; chocolate. **2** A beverage made from it. **3** The light reddish-brown color of cocoa powder. [Alter. of CACAO]

cocoa butter Cacao butter.

co·co·grass (kō′kō·gras′, -gräs′) *n.* The nutgrass.

co·con·scious·ness (kō·kon′shəs·nis) *n.* *Psychol.* A latent or accompanying consciousness, on the fringe of awareness. — **co·con′scious** *adj.* — **co·con′scious·ly** *adv.*

co·co·nut (kō′kə·nut′, -nət) *n.* The fruit of the coco palm, a white-meated seed enclosed in a hard shell, and containing a milky liquid.

co·coon (kə·koon′) *n.* **1** The envelope spun by the larvae of certain insects, as silkworms, in which they are enclosed in the pupal or chrysalis state. **2** Any analogous structure, as the egg-bearing case of spiders, earthworms, etc. **3** *Mil.* The weatherproof covering of cellophane or quick-drying synthetic resin in which military or other heavy equipment may be sealed during transport or when not in use. — *v.t.* To envelop or place in a cocoon. [<F *cocon* < *coque* shell]

coc·tion (kok′shən) *n.* The act or process of boiling. [<L *coctio, -onis* <*coquere* cook]

co·cur·ric·u·lum (kō′kə·rik′yə·ləm) *n.* The extra-curricular activities of students in the modern secondary school, such as athletics, student councils, clubs, fraternities, etc.

cod¹ (kod) *n.* **1** An important gadoid food fish *(Gadus callarias)* of the North Atlantic, found especially from Newfoundland to Norway. **2** Any other gadoid fish. [Origin unknown]

cod² (kod) *n.* **1** A pod or husk. **2** A bag or envelope. **3** *Scot.* A pillow or cushion. [OE *codd* bag]

co·da (kō′də) *n.* An independent musical passage, introduced at the conclusion of a movement, forming a more decided and usually somewhat elaborate termination; the finale of a sonata movement or of a fugue. [<Ital. <L *cauda* tail]

cod·der (kod′ər) *n.* A person or vessel occupied in codfishing.

cod·dle (kod′l) *v.t.* ·**dled, ·dling** **1** To seethe or simmer in water; cook gently. **2** To treat as a baby or an invalid; pamper. See synonyms under CARESS, PAMPER. [? Akin to CAUDLE] —**cod′dler** *n.*

code (kōd) *n.* **1** A systematized body of law. **2** A system of signals, characters, or symbols with arbitrary, conventionalized meanings, used in communication: Language is a form of code. **3** A set of prearranged symbols, usually letters, used for purposes of secrecy or brevity in transmitting messages: the mean-

ings of the symbols are given in a code book. Compare CIPHER. **4** A system of rules and regulations for the purpose of ensuring adequate standards of practice and uniformity in workmanship. See synonyms under LAW, LEGISLATION. — **civil code** A code regulating the civil relations of citizens. — **criminal** or **penal code** A code defining crimes and prescribing the method and degree of punishment. — **telegraphic code** A code convenient for use in telegraphing; specifically, the Morse or the International code, consisting of dots and dashes. — *v.t.* **cod·ed, cod·ing** **1** To systematize as laws; make a digest of. **2** To put into the symbols of a code. [<F <L *codex* writing tablet]

co·dec·li·na·tion (kō′dek·lə·nā′shən) *n.* *Astron.* The complement of the angle of declination: also called *polar distance.* [<CO-² + DECLINATION]

co·deine (kō′dēn, kō′di·ēn) *n.* *Chem.* A white crystalline alkaloid, $C_{18}H_{21}NO_3$, derived from morphine and widely used in medicine as a mild narcotic. Also **co·de·in** (kō′dē·in, kō′dēn), **co·de·ia** (kō·dē′ə). [<Gk. *kōdeia* head of a poppy]

co·dex (kō′deks) *n.* *pl.* **co·di·ces** (kō′də·sēz, kod′ə-) **1** A medieval manuscript in leaf form: distinguished from *scroll.* **2** A collection of canons or of formulas. **3** A code of laws. [<L, writing tablet]

cod·i·cil (kod′ə·səl) *n.* A supplement to a will. [<L *codicillus,* dim. of *codex* writing tablet]

cod·i·fy (kod′ə·fī, kō′də-) *v.t.* ·**fied, ·fy·ing** To systematize, as laws. —**cod′i·fi·ca′tion** *n.*

cod·ling¹ (kod′ling) *n.* **1** A young cod. **2** A gadoid fish (genus *Phycis*) with filamentous ventral fins of two or three rays; a hake. [Dim. of COD¹]

cod·ling² (kod′ling) *n.* **1** One of a group of varieties of cooking apple, elongated and tapering. **2** Formerly, any hard apple for stewing. Also **cod·lin** (kod′lin). [ME *querdling;* origin uncertain]

codling moth A moth *(Carpocapsa pomonella)* whose larvae, the apple worms, feed on the interior of apples, pears, quinces, and several other fruits. For illustration see under INSECT (injurious). Also **codlin moth.**

cod-liv·er oil (kod′liv′ər) Oil from the livers of cod, especially rich in vitamins A and D: used in cases of malnutrition.

cod·piece (kod′pēs′) *n.* An ornamented bag or flap attached to the front of the tight breeches worn by men of the 15th and 16th centuries. [ME *cod* scrotum + PIECE]

co·dress (kō′dres) *n.* A radiotelegraph message in which the address is given in the same code system as the body of the message. Compare PLAINDRESS. [<CO(DE) + (AD)DRESS]

co·ed·u·ca·tion (kō′ej·ōō·kā′shən) *n.* The education of both sexes together in the same classes or institution. — **co′·ed·u·ca′tion·al** *adj.*

co·ee-bird (kō′ē·bûrd′) *n.* The koel.

co·ef·fi·cient (kō′ə·fish′ənt) *n.* **1** A cooperating agent. **2** *Math.* A number or letter put before an algebraic expression and multiplying it. **3** *Physics* A number indicating the degree of magnitude, or the kind and amount of change under given conditions. — *adj.* Jointly efficient; acting together to a common end. — **co′ef·fi′cien·cy** *n.*

coefficient of friction *Physics* A number expressing the ratio between the force required to move one surface along another and the force, normal to the surfaces, pressing them together.

coe·la·canth (sē′lə·kanth) *n.* *Zool.* A large-bodied, hollow-spined crossopterygian fish, one species of which *(Latimeria chalumnae)* still survives. [<COEL(O)- + Gk. *akantha* spine]

COELACANTH
(From 4 to 5 1/2 feet in length)

-coele See -CELE².

coe·len·ter·ate (si·len′tə·rāt) *n.* Any of a phylum of invertebrate animals *(Coelenterata)* having an enteric cavity occupying the entire interior of the body and functioning as a vascular as well as a digestive system: the phylum includes sea anemones, corals, jellyfish, and hydras. — *adj.* Belonging or pertaining to the *Coelenterata.* [<COEL(O)- + Gk. *enteron* intestine] — **coe·len·ter·ic** (sē'len·ter'ik) *adj.*

coe·len·ter·on (si·len'tə·ron) *n.*   *pl.* **·ter·a** (-tər·ə) *Zool.* The primitive intestinal cavity of coelenterates; the archenteron.

coe·li·ac (sē'lē·ak) See CELIAC.

coelo- *combining form* Cavity; cavity of the body, or of an organ. Also, before vowels, **coel-.** [<Gk. *koilos* hollow]

coe·lom (sē'ləm) *n. Zool.* The body cavity of a metazoan; the space between the viscera and the body wall. Also **coe·lome** (sē'lōm). [<Gk. *koilōma* cavity < *koilos* hollow]

coe·lo·stat (sē'lə·stat) *n. Astron.* An instrument consisting of a mirror driven by clockwork and mounted in such a way as to keep the same celestial image reflected continuously to the eyepiece or camera attachment of a fixed telescope. [<L *caelum* heavens +*status* a standing < *stare* stand]

coe·nes·the·sia (sē'nis·thē'zhə, -zhē·ə, sen'is-) See CENESTHESIA.

coeno- See CENO-.

coe·no·cyte (sē'nə·sīt, sen'ə-) *n. Bot.* An aggregation of protoplasmic units enclosed within a common wall: exemplified in the lower algae and fungi.

coe·nure (sē'nyŏŏr) *n.* The many-headed bladderworm or larval stage of a dog tapeworm (*Taenia coenurus*), attacking the brain of sheep and producing gid or staggers. Also **coe·nu·rus** (si·nyŏŏr'əs). [<COEN(O)- + Gk. *oura* tail]

co·en·zyme (kō·en'zīm, -zim) *n. Biochem.* Any substance present in a fermenting mixture that increases the activity of the enzyme.

co·e·qual (kō·ē'kwəl) *adj.* Of the same value, age, size, or importance; equal and conjoined. — *n.* The equal of another or others. — **co·e·qual·i·ty** (kō'i·kwol'ə·tē) *n.* — **co·e'qual·ly** *adv.*

co·erce (kō·ûrs') *v.* **co·erced, co·erc·ing** *v.t.* **1** To constrain by force, law, authority, or fear; compel. **2** To bring into subjection or under control by superior force; repress. **3** To bring about by coercion: to *coerce* obedience. — *v.i.* **4** To use coercive measures, as in government. See synonyms under COMPEL. [<L *coercere* < *co-* together + *arcere* shut up, restrain] — **co·er'ci·ble** *adj.*

co·er·cion (kō·ûr'shən) *n.* **1** Forcible constraint or restraint, moral or physical; compulsion. **2** Government by force. — **co·er·cion·ar·y** (kō·ûr'shən·er'ē) *adj.* — **co·er'cion·ist** *n.*

co·er·cive (kō·ûr'siv) *adj.* Serving or tending to coerce. — **co·er'cive·ly** *adv.* — **co·er'cive·ness** *n.*

co·e·ta·ne·ous (kō'i·tā'nē·əs) *adj.* Originating at the same time; of equal age; contemporary. [<LL *coetaneus* < *co-* together + *aetas* age] — **co'e·ta·ne·ous·ly** *adv.* — **co'e·ta·ne·ous·ness** *n.*

co·e·val (kō·ē'vəl) *adj.* Of or belonging to the same age: usually implying remote time or long duration. — *n.* One of the same age; a contemporary. Also spelled *coaeval.* [<LL *coaevus* < *co-* together + *aevus* age] — **co·e'val·ly** *adv.*

co·ex·ist·ence (kō'ig·zis'təns) *n.* **1** The state of coexisting. **2** The simultaneous existence of two (or more) societies, nations, etc., which differ in ideology but which agree, often tacitly, to non-interference in each other's political affairs.

cof·fee (kôf'ē, kof'ē) *n.* **1** The seeds or beans enclosed in the dark berrylike fruit of a tropical evergreen shrub (genus *Coffea*), native in Asia and Africa and widely grown in Brazil. **2** A beverage made from the roasted and ground beans of this plant. **3** The shrub or tree itself. **4** The brown color of coffee, especially of coffee when containing milk or cream. — **black coffee** Coffee taken without milk or cream. [<Ital. *caffè* <Turkish *qahveh* <Arabic *qahwah*]

coffee break A recess from work for the purpose of taking coffee or other refreshments.

coffee pot A covered vessel in which coffee is prepared or served.

coffee shop A public restaurant or room in a hotel or a restaurant where coffee and food are served. Also **coffee room.**

coffee table Any low table, generally placed in front of a sofa, for serving refreshments.

coffee tree 1 The cascara buckthorn. **2** The Kentucky coffee tree.

coffee weed Chicory.

cof·fer (kôf'ər, kof'-) *n.* **1** A chest or box; strongbox; safe. **2** *pl.* A treasury; financial resources. **3** A decorative, sunk panel in a dome or vault. **4** A canal-lock chamber; a caisson. — *v.t.* **1** To place in a coffer. **2** To adorn with coffers, or form in coffers, as a ceiling. [<F *coffre* <L *cophinus.* See COFFIN.]

cof·fer·dam (kôf'ər·dam', kof'-) *n.* **1** A temporary enclosing dam built in the water and pumped dry, to protect workmen. **2** A watertight structure attached to a ship's side when repairs are made below the water line.

cof·fin (kôf'in, kof'-) *n.* **1** The case in which a corpse is buried. **2** The part of a horse's hoof below the coronet. — *v.t.* To put into or as into a coffin. [<OF *cofin* <L *cophinus* <Gk. *kophinos* basket]

coffin bone The bone of a horse's foot that is enclosed within the hoof.

cof·fle (kof'əl) *n.* A gang of animals or slaves, chained together for marching or sale. — *v.t.* **·fled, ·fling** To form into a coffle. [<Arabic *qāfilah* caravan]

cog¹ (kog) *n.* **1** *Mech.* A tooth or one of a series of teeth projecting from the surface of a wheel or gear to impart or receive motion. **2** A tenon on a joist or beam to fit a mortise on another. **3** A person regarded as making a minor or insignificant contribution to the working of a large organization or process. [<Scand. Cf. Sw. *kugge* cog.]

cog² (kog) *v.* **cogged, cog·ging** *v.t.* **1** To load or mishandle, as dice, in order to cheat. **2** *Obs.* To mislead or deceive. — *v.i.* **3** To cheat, as with loaded dice. — *n.* A trick; imposition; a lie. [Origin unknown]

cog³ (kog, kōg) *n.* **1** A small rowboat or fishing vessel; cockboat. **2** Formerly, a broadly built transport or other vessel: also spelled *cogue.* [<OF *cogue*]

co·gent (kō'jənt) *adj.* Compelling belief, assent, or action; forcible; convincing. See synonyms under POWERFUL. [<L *cogens, -entis,* ppr. of *cogere* compel. See COACT.]

cog·ging (kog'ing) *n. Metall.* The operation of reducing a metal ingot to a billet by application of a forging press or hammer.

cog·i·tate (koj'ə·tāt) *v.* **·tat·ed, ·tat·ing** *v.t.* To think over; ponder; meditate. — *v.t.* To think about or upon; devise. See synonyms under MUSE. [<L *cogitatus,* pp. of *cogitare* think < *co-* together + *agitare* consider] — **cog·i·ta·ble** (koj'ə·tə·bəl) *adj.* — **cog'i·ta'tor** *n.*

cog·i·ta·tion (koj'ə·tā'shən) *n.* Consideration; reflection; thought. [<OF *cogitaciun* <L *cogitatio, -onis* < *cogitare.* See COGITATE.]

cog·i·ta·tive (koj'ə·tā'tiv) *adj.* Capable of cogitation; reflective; contemplative. — **cog'i·ta'tive·ly** *adv.* — **cog'i·ta'tive·ness** *n.*

co·gnac (kōn'yak, kon'-) *n.* **1** Brandy distilled from wine produced in the Cognac region of western France. **2** Any brandy.

cog·nate (kog'nāt) *adj.* **1** Allied by blood; kindred; especially, related through females only. **2** Allied by derivation from the same source; belonging to the same stock or root: English *cold* and Latin *gelidus* are *cognate* words. **3** Allied in radical characteristics; having the same nature or quality. — *n.* One who or that which is closely related to other persons or things. [<L *cognatus* < *co-* together + (g)*natus,* pp. of (g)*nasci* be born]

cog·na·tion (kog·nā'shən) *n.* Relationship by blood or derivation.

cog·ni·tion (kog·nish'ən) *n.* **1** The act, power, or faculty of apprehending, knowing, or perceiving. **2** Knowledge; a conception, perception, or notion. [<L *cognitio, -onis* knowledge < *cognoscere* know < *co-* together + (g)*noscere* know] — **cog·ni'tion·al** *adj.* — **cog.**

ni·tive (kog'nə·tiv) *adj.*

cog·ni·za·ble (kog'nə·zə·bəl, kon'ə-) *adj.* Capable of being known or of being judicially tried or examined. — **cog'ni·za·bly** *adv.*

cog·ni·zance (kog'nə·zəns, kon'ə-) *n.* **1** Apprehension or perception; knowledge; recognition; also, the range or sphere of what can be known by observation. **2** *Law* Knowledge on which a judge acts without requiring proof; judicial notice, as of statutes or public events. **3** Jurisdiction. **4** *Law* Acknowledgment of a fine of land and tenements; a confession. [<OF *conoisance* < *conistre* know <L *cognoscere.* See COGNITION.]

cog·ni·zant (kog'nə·zənt, kon'ə-) *adj.* Having knowledge; aware: with *of.* See synonyms under CONSCIOUS.

cog·nize (kog·nīz') *v.t.* **·nized, ·niz·ing** To know, perceive, or recognize. See synonyms under KNOW. Also *Brit.* **cog·nise.** [<L *cognoscere* know. See COGNITION.]

co·gno·scen·te (kō'nyō·shen'tā) *n.*   *pl.* **·ti** (-tē) A connoisseur: also spelled *conoscente.* [<Ital.]

cog·nos·ci·ble (kog·nos'ə·bəl) *adj.* Capable of being known, recognized, or ascertained; knowable. [<L *cognoscere.* See COGNITION.] — **cog·nos'ci·bil'i·ty** *n.*

cog·no·vit (kog·nō'vit) *n. Law* A written acknowledgment, by a defendant, that the plaintiff's demand is just. [<L *cognovit* (*actionem*) he has acknowledged (the action)]

co·gon (kə·gōn') *n.* A tall, rank grass (*Imperata cylindrica*) of the Philippines: used for fodder and in thatching. [<Sp. *cogón* < Tagalog]

cog rail *n.* A cogged center rail with a cogwheel that permits a locomotive to make steep ascents. Also **cog'-rail'way.**

cogue (kog, kōg) See COG³.

cog·way (kog'wā') *n.* A rack railway.

cog·wheel (kog'-hwēl') *n.* A wheel with cogs; a gearwheel.

co·hab·it (kō·hab'it) *v.i.* **1** To live together, usually illegally, as husband and wife. **2** *Obs.* To inhabit together the same place or country. [<LL *cohabitare* < *co-* together + *habitare* live] — **co·hab'i·tant, co·hab'it·er** *n.* — **co·hab'i·ta'tion** *n.*

COGWHEELS
A. Spur-gears.
B. Spur and crown gears.
C. Bevel-gears.
D. Square gears.
E. Annular gears.
F. Elliptical gears.

Co·han (kō·han'), **George M(ichael),** 1878–1942, U.S. playwright and actor.

Co·hee (kō'hē) *n. U.S.* Formerly, a settler in western Virginia and western Pennsylvania. [? <dial. E (Scottish) *quo' he* quoth he; with ref. to a characteristic phrase in their speech]

Co·hen (kō'ən), **Morris,** 1880–1947, U.S. philosopher and logician of science, born in Russia.

co·here (kō·hir') *v.i.* **co·hered, co·her·ing** **1** To stick or hold firmly together. **2** To be logically consistent or connected. **3** To be coherent, as the parts of an address. **4** *Obs.* To agree. See synonyms under UNITE. [<L *cohaerere* < *co-* together + *haerere* stick]

co·her·ence (kō·hir'əns) *n.* **1** A sticking to or a sticking together; union; conjunction. See COHESION (def. 2). **2** Logical consistency; agreement: also **co·her'en·cy.** **3** *Physics* That relation of coincidence between two sets of waves, as light or sound waves, which will produce interference phenomena. [<MF *cohérence* <L *cohaerentia* <*cohaerere* COHERE]

co·her·ent (kō·hir'ənt) *adj.* **1** Cleaving or sticking together. **2** Logically consistent.

co·her·er (kō·hir'ər) *n.* A device formerly employed to detect radio waves, in which loosely touching metallic particles in a glass tube are made to cohere closely under the action of the wave, thus momentarily completing a local electric signaling circuit.

co·he·sion (kō·hē′zhən) *n.* **1** The act or state of cohering; union; consistency. **2** *Physics* That force by which molecules of the same kind or of the same body are held together so that the substance or body resists separation: distinguished from *adhesion*. **3** *Bot.* The joining of one part with another. [<F *cohésion* <L *cohaerere* COHERE]

co·he·sive (kō·hē′siv) *adj.* Belonging to, having, or exerting the property of cohesion; causing to cleave. — **co·he′sive·ly** *adv.* — **co·he′sive·ness** *n.*

co·ho·bate (kō′hō·bāt) *v.t.* **·bat·ed**, **·bat·ing** To redistil by restoring the distillate to the retort, to mingle again with the matter there. [<Med. L *cohobatus*, pp. of *cohobare*, ? <Arabic *ka′aba* repeat]

co·hog (kō′hôg, -hog) See QUAHAUG.

co·honk (kə·hôngk′, -hongk′) *n.* **1** The Canada goose. **2** *Obs.* The season, beginning in October, when this wild goose makes its appearance. [Imit. of its call]

co·hort (kō′hôrt) *n.* **1** The tenth of an ancient Roman military legion, 400 to 600 men. **2** A band of soldiers. **3** Any group of associates. **4** A companion or follower. [<L *cohors, cohortis.* Doublet of COURT.]

co·hosh (kō′hosh, kō·hosh′) *n.* **1** Either of two North American herbs, sometimes used medicinally; especially, the **blue cohosh** (*Caulophyllum thalictroides*), often called *squawroot*, and the black snakeroot or **black cohosh** (*Cimicifuga racemosa*). **2** The baneberry. [<N. Am. Ind.]

co·hune (kō·hoon′) *n.* A feather-leaved palm (*Orbignya cohune*) of Central and South America, from which a fatty oil is obtained. Also **cohune palm.** [<native Honduran name]

coif (koif) *n.* **1** Any close-fitting cap, hood, or headdress; especially, a close-fitting hood or skull cap for either sex, tied under the chin. **2** In England, an inner skull cap of lawn, formerly worn by sergeants at law; hence, the office or rank of a sergeant at law. **3** A soldier's thick skull cap of steel or leather, worn under the helmet. — *v.t.* To put a coif on; invest with or as with a coif. [<OF *coife* <LL *cofia* <Gmc.]

coif·fure (kwä·fyŏŏr′, *Fr.* kwà·für′) *n.* **1** An arrangement or dressing of the hair. **2** A headdress. [<F <OF *coife* COIF.]

coign (koin) *n.* A projecting angle or stone; a corner. Also **coigne.** [Var. of QUOIN]

coign of vantage An advantageous position.

coil (koil) *n.* **1** A ring or spiral formed by winding. **2** An involvement; a perplexity. **3** A spiral pipe, or a series of pipes, forming a continuous conduit which reverses two or more times. **4** An induction coil. — **Ruhmkorff coil** An induction coil with circuit breaker for use with direct and constant current. [<*v.*] — *v.t.* **1** To wind spirally or in rings; wind round and round. **2** To enwrap with coils, as a lasso or the folds of a boa constrictor. — *v.i.* **3** To form rings or coils. **4** To move in spirals, as a hawk. [<OF *coillir* <L *colligere.* See COLLECT.] — **coil′er** *n.*

coin (koin) *n.* **1** A piece of metal stamped by government authority, for use as money. **2** Metal currency, collectively. **3** Kind or means of recompense. **4** A corner; quoin. See synonyms under MONEY. — *v.t.* **1** To stamp or mint (coins) from metal. **2** To make into coins, as metal. **3** To originate or invent, as a word or phrase. **4** *Colloq.* To make or gain rapidly: to *coin* money. — *v.i.* **5** *Brit. Colloq.* To counterfeit money. [<F, wedge, die <L *cuneus* wedge] — **coin′a·ble** *adj.*

coin·age (koi′nij) *n.* **1** The making of coins, or the coins made; the system of coins of a country. **2** The cost or charge for coining money. **3** The act of fabricating, or the thing fabricated. **4** *Ling.* An artificially created word, as *blurb.*

co·in·cide (kō′in·sīd′) *v.i.* **·cid·ed**, **·cid·ing** **1** To correspond because of identity in parts, elements, space occupied, or position. **2** To agree exactly; be of one opinion, idea, or

interest. **3** To occur at the same time; endure an equal span of time. See synonyms under AGREE, ASSENT. [<MF *coincider* <Med. L *coincidere* <L *co-* together + *incidere* <*in-* upon + *cadere* fall]

co·in·ci·dence (kō·in′sə·dəns) *n.* **1** The fact or condition of coinciding; correspondence. **2** A remarkable occurrence of events, ideas, etc., at the same time or in the same way, apparently by mere accident. **3** *Geom.* Exact correspondence in space or in time. See synonyms under ANALOGY.

co·in·ci·dent (kō·in′sə·dənt) *adj.* **1** Agreeing or coinciding as in position, extent, time, etc.; concurring. **2** Exactly corresponding; identical. — **co·in′ci·dent·ly** *adv.*

co·in·ci·den·tal (kō·in′sə·den′təl) *adj.* Characterized by or involving coincidence. — **co·in′ci·den′tal·ly** *adv.*

co·in·sur·ance (kō′in·shŏŏr′əns) *n.* Joint insurance with another; specifically, a form of insurance in which the person who insures his property for less than its entire value is understood to be his own insurer for the difference which exists between the true value of the property and the amount of the insurance.

co·in·sure (kō′in·shŏŏr′) *v.t.* & *v.i.* **·sured**, **·sur·ing** **1** To insure with another or others. **2** To insure according to the specific terms of coinsurance.

coir (koir) *n.* Coconut-husk fiber, used in making cables, ropes, matting, etc.: also called *kyar.* [<Malay *kàyar* rope]

co·i·tion (kō·ish′ən) *n.* Sexual intercourse; copulation. Also **co·i·tus** (kō′i·təs). [<L *coitio, -onis: co-* together + *ire* go]

coke¹ (kōk) *n.* A solid, carbonaceous fuel obtained by distilling the volatile constituents from coal by heating in ovens or retorts. — *v.t.* & *v.i.* **coked, cok·ing** To change or be changed into coke. Also spelled *coak.* [? ME *colke*; origin uncertain]

coke² (kōk) *n. Slang* Cocaine.

coke³ (kōk) *n. Colloq.* A carbonated soft drink. [<*Coke*, short for *Coca-Cola*, a trade name]

col (kol) *n.* **1** *Geog.* A depression between two mountains; a gap in a ridge, serving as a pass from one valley to another; also called *saddle.* **2** *Meteorol.* A necklike area of low pressure between two anticyclones. [<F <L *collum* neck]

col-¹ Assimilated var. of COM-.

col-² Var. of COLO-.

co·la (kō′lə) *n.* **1** A small African tree (*Cola acuminata*), naturalized in the West Indies: also **co′la·nut′ tree.** **2** The seed of this tree or the extract of it, yielding caffeine and other substances, said to have tonic and antiseptic qualities: used in the manufacture of beverages: also **co′la·nut′.** Also spelled *kola.* [NL <native African name]

col·an·der (kul′ən·dər, kol′-) *n.* A perforated vessel for straining liquids, etc.: also spelled *cullender.* [Cf. Sp. *colador* <L *colare* strain]

co·lat·i·tude (kō·lat′ə·tōōd, -tyōōd) *n.* In navigation, the complement of the latitude; distance in degrees from the nearest pole. [<CO-² + LATITUDE]

col·can·non (kəl·kan′ən, kôl′kan·ən) *n.* An Irish dish of potatoes and greens cooked together. [< Irish *càl ceannain* white-headed cabbage]

col·chi·cine (kol′chə·sēn, kol′kə-) *n.* A pale-yellow, bitter, poisonous alkaloid, $C_{22}H_{25}O_6N$, obtained from the roots of the colchicum: used in medicine.

col·chi·cum (kol′chə·kəm, kol′kə-) *n.* **1** A plant of a genus (*Colchicum*) of Old World bulbous plants of the lily family. **2** The corm or the seed of *C. autumnale*, the autumn crocus or meadow saffron, which yields colchicine. **3** A medical preparation made from this. [<L <Gk. *kolchikon* <*Kolchis* Colchis, home of the legendary sorceress Medea]

col·co·thar (kol′kə·thər) *n.* A dark-red ferric oxide formed by heating ferrous sulfate: used as a polish and as the pigment Indian red. [<Med. L <Arabic *qolqotār*]

cold (kōld) *adj.* **1** Of a relatively low temperature as compared with a normal or standard temperature, or with the normal temperature of the hu-

man body. **2** Having no perceptible heat; gelid; frigid. **3** Dead. **4** Having the sensation due to too rapid loss of heat from the body. **5** Feeling no warmth or not sufficient warmth; chilled; chilly. **6** Having little or no liveliness, ardor, or enthusiasm; displaying no feeling or passion; unmoved; stolid; indifferent. **7** Lacking signs of life; unconscious: to be knocked *cold.* **8** Chilling or depressing to the spirits; awakening no enthusiasm; not cordial; disappointing; frigid; discouraging. **9** Weak to the taste; wanting sharpness or pungency. **10** Lacking odor or freshness: a *cold* trail. **11** Distant from the object sought; wide of the mark: said of a seeker in a game, or a guesser. **12** Bluish in tone or effect; not suggestive of warmth. —*n.* **1** A low temperature. **2** Lack of heat, or the sensation caused by it. **3** A catarrhal affection of the respiratory tract, often following exposure to cold, dampness, or draft. **4** Temperature below the freezing point. **5** The sensation characterized by lack of enthusiasm, or by fear or dejection. [OE *cald*] — **cold′ly** *adv.* —**cold′ness** *n.*

cold-blood·ed (kōld′blud′id) *adj.* **1** Lacking body heat; frigid; sensitive to cold. **2** *Zool.* Having a variable temperature dependent on the temperature of the surrounding medium, as a fish or reptile; ectothermic. **3** Unfeeling; heartless; deliberately cruel. —**cold′-blood′ed·ly** *adv.*

cold chisel A chisel of tempered steel for cutting cold metal.

cold cream A cleansing and soothing ointment for the skin.

cold deck A deck of cards prearranged to the advantage of a certain player.

cold-drawn (kōld′drôn′) *adj.* Stretched or drawn while cold: *cold-drawn* steel wire.

cold feet *Colloq.* Loss of courage; timidity. —**to get cold feet** *Colloq.* To lose courage.

cold·frame (kōld′frām′) *n.* A wooden frame set into the ground and having a glass top: used to protect plants against cold.

cold front *Meteorol.* The irregular, forward edge of a cold air mass advancing beneath and against a warmer mass.

cold-ham·mer (kōld′ham′ər) *v.t.* To hammer when cold, as metals.

cold light Light which is not produced by incandescence or combustion, as phosphorescent light.

cold pack 1 *Med.* A wrapping of cold, wet blankets or sheets about a patient as a means of therapy. **2** A canning process in which raw food is packed in cans or jars, which are then heated for sealing and cooking.

cold rubber A synthetic rubber, chemically related to buna, which has been polymerized at low temperatures of 41° F. or less to impart better wearing qualities and greater resistance to abrasion.

cold shoulder *Colloq.* A deliberate slight or show of indifference.

cold snap A sudden, short interval of very cold weather.

cold sore An eruption about the mouth or nostrils, often accompanying a cold or fever: a form of herpes.

cold storage The storage of perishable food, furs, etc. in a refrigerated chamber.

cold turkey *U.S. Slang* **1** The abrupt and total deprivation of a substance, as a narcotic drug or cigarettes, from one addicted to its use. **2** Blunt, candid talk, often unwelcome to the listener.

cold war Intense rivalry between nations in diplomacy, economic strategy, and military preparedness, falling just short of armed conflict.

cold wave *Meteorol.* An unusual drop in temperature; a spell of very cold weather, usually traveling along a specified course.

cole (kōl) *n.* A plant of the same genus as the cabbage, especially rape (*Brassica napus*). Also **cole·wort** (kōl′wûrt′). ◆ Homophone: *coal.* [OE *cawl* <L *caulis* cabbage]

co·lec·to·my (kə·lek′tə·mē) *n. Surg.* The excision of all or part of the colon.

cole·man·ite (kōl′mən·īt) *n.* A colorless, transparent, hydrous calcium borate, $Ca_2B_6O_{11} \cdot 5H_2O$, occurring massive or in monoclinic crystals: used in the manufacture of borax. [after W.T. *Coleman*, 1824–93, of California]

Co·le·op·ter·a (kō̌/lē·op′tər·ə, kole-) n. pl. A large, cosmopolitan order of insects, including the beetles and weevils, having horny front wings that fit as cases over the hind wings. [< NL < Gk. *koleos* sheath + *pteron* wing] —**co′le·op′ter, co′le·op′ter·an** n. —**co′le·op′ter·ous, co′le·op′ter·al** adj.

co·le·op·tile (kō̌/lē·op′til, kole-) n. Bot. The first leaf appearing above the ground in grass seedlings. [< NL < Gk. *koleos* sheath + *ptilon* feather]

co·le·o·rhi·za (kō̌/lē·ə·rī′zə, kole-) n. pl. **·zae** (-zē) Bot. The root sheath in certain plants, through which the radicle bursts in germination. [< NL < Gk. *koleos* sheath + *rhiza* root]

cole·seed (kōl′sēd′) n. Colza.

cole·slaw (kōl′slô′) n. A salad made of finely shredded, raw cabbage. [< Du. *kool sla* cabbage salad]

co·le·us (kō̌/lē·əs) n. A plant of a large genus (*Coleus*) of tropical African and East Indian herbs or shrubs of the mint family, cultivated for their showy foliage. [< NL < Gk. *koleos* sheath]

cole·wort (kōl′wûrt′) n. A plant of the cabbage genus; rape or kale.

col·ic (kol′ik) n. Acute spasmodic pain in the bowels. —adj. 1 Pertaining to, near, or affecting the bowels. 2 Pertaining to or like colic. [< F *colique* < L *colicus* sick with colic < Gk. *kōlikos* < *kolon* colon] —**col′ick·y** adj.

colic root 1 The intensely bitter tonic and stomachic root of a North American herb (*Aletris farinosa*) of the lily family. 2 The root of the wild yam or of the blazing star.

colic weed One of several plants, as dutchman's-breeches, the squirrel corn, or the pale corydalis (*Corydalis sempervirens*).

col·in (kol′in) n. An American quail (genus *Colinus*), especially the bobwhite. [< Am. Sp. *colín* < Nahuatl]

—**coline** See -COLOUS.

col·i·se·um (kol′ə·sē′əm) n. A large stadium or amphitheater.

co·li·tis (kə·lī′tis) n. Pathol. Inflammation of the colon: also called *colonitis*. [< COL(O)- + -ITIS]

col·lab·o·rate (kə·lab′ə·rāt) v.i. **·rat·ed, ·rat·ing 1** To labor or cooperate with another, especially in literary or scientific pursuits. 2 To cooperate willingly and traitorously with the enemy; be a collaborationist. [< LL *collaboratus*, pp. of *collaborare* < L *com-* with + *laborare* work] —**col·lab′o·ra′tion** n. —**col·lab′o·ra′tive** adj. —**col·lab′o·ra′tor** n.

col·lab·o·ra·tion·ist (kə·lab′ə·rā′shən·ist) n. A citizen of a country invaded or occupied by foreign troops who cooperates with the enemy.

col·lage (kə·läzh′) n. 1 A composition of flat objects, as newspaper, cloth, cardboard, etc., pasted together on a surface and often combined with related lines and color for artistic effect. 2 The clarifying or fining of a wine by means of an albuminous substance. [< F, pasting < *colle* glue < L *colla* < Gk. *kolla*]

col·la·gen (kol′ə·jen) n. Biochem. A protein forming the chief constituent of the connective tissues of the body, as cartilage, skin, bone, hair, etc. [< Gk. *kolla* glue + -GEN]

col·lapse (kə·laps′) v. **lapsed, laps·ing** v.i. 1 To give way; cave in. 2 To fail utterly; come to ruin. 3 To assume a more compact form by the folding in of parts, as of camp chairs. 4 To lose health or strength completely, as from exhaustion or disease; become suddenly and completely prostrated. 5 To lose courage or boldness; sink suddenly from notice. —v.t. 6 To cause to collapse. —n. 1 A falling or sinking together. 2 Extreme prostration. 3 Utter failure; ruin. [< L *collapsus*, pp. of *collabi* < *com-* together + *labi* fall]

col·lar (kol′ər) n. 1 An article worn about the neck, as a band or circlet of some fabric, worn as an article of dress; the neckpiece of a garment. 2 A band of leather or metal for the neck of an animal. 3 Biol. **a** A ring or band on or about anything, as in certain plants and insects. **b** A growth of fur or ring of color about the neck of an animal. 4 Mech. Any of various cylindrical or ring-shaped devices used to limit or control the action of machine parts, secure stability, etc. —v.t. 1 To grasp by or provide with a collar. 2 To take possession of; capture. [< AF *coler* < L *collare* < *collum* neck]

collar bone The clavicle.

collar cell Zool. A flagellate cell having the base of the flagellum surrounded by a collar-like expansion, as in certain infusorians and sponges: also called *choanocyte*.

col·lard (kol′ərd) n. A variety of cabbage that does not gather its edible leaves into a head. [Alter. of *colewort*. See COLE.]

col·late (kə·lāt′, kol′āt) v.t. **·lat·ed, ·lat·ing 1** To compare critically, as writings or facts. 2 In bookbinding, to examine (the gathered sheets to be bound) in order to verify and correct their arrangement. 3 In bibliography, to examine (the pages of a book) to see that none are missing or out of order. 4 To appoint or admit (a cleric) to a benefice. See synonyms under COMPARE. [< L *collatus*, pp. to *conferre* < *com-* together + *ferre* bear, carry]

col·lat·er·al (kə·lat′ər·əl) adj. 1 Subordinately connected; attendant or secondary; incidental. 2 Corroborative; confirmatory. 3 Being or lying alongside; parallel; bordering. 4 Descended from the same ancestor in a different line: distinguished from *lineal*. 5 Pertaining to property, as stocks or bonds, deposited as security additional to one's personal obligation: a *collateral* note. See synonyms under INCIDENTAL. —n. 1 Collateral security, which in case of default, is subject to immediate forfeiture, without recourse to legal proceedings. See COLLATERAL SECURITY. 2 A kinsman or kinswoman descended from the same ancestor in a different line. 3 An accompanying or subordinate fact, condition, or part. 4 Anat. A part connected with or derived from a main branch: the *collaterals* of a nerve fiber. See synonyms under SECURITY. [< Med. L *collateralis* < *com-* together + *lateralis* lateral < *latus, -eris* side] —**col·lat′er·al·ly** adv.

collateral security Property, money, etc., hypothecated as security additional to one's personal obligation.

col·la·tion (kə·lā′shən) n. 1 A collating; comparison. 2 The collection and critical comparison of writings or the published result of such a comparison. 3 In bookbinding, the examination of the collected sheets of a book before binding, to detect errors in arrangement. 4 A lunch or light repast: originally confined to the light evening refection of monks; also, the light supper permitted in seasons of fast, such as Lent. 5 The presentation of a clergyman to a church living. 6 In civil law, the return to an estate of property advanced to an heir, with a view to a common distribution of the whole. [< OF *collacion* < L *collatio, -onis* < *conferre*. See COLLATE.]

col·la·tive (kə·lā′tiv) adj. 1 Collating. 2 Bestowed, bestowable, or held by collation: said especially of a church living of which the bishop is patron.

col·la·tor (kə·lā′tər) n. An extensible, compartmentalized device used in offices to facilitate gathering the pages of duplicated material in proper order.

col·league (kol′ēg) n. A fellow member of an official body; an associate in office. See synonyms under ACCESSORY, ASSOCIATE. [< F *collègue* < L *collega* < *com-* together + *legere* choose] —**col′league·ship** n.

col·lect¹ (kə·lekt′) v.t. 1 To gather or come together; assemble. 2 To bring together as for a hobby, as stamps or books. 3 To gather or obtain payments of money. 4 To regain control of; bring or call back: to *collect* one's wits. —v.i. 5 To assemble or congregate, as people; accumulate, as sand. 6 To gather payments or donations. See synonyms under AMASS, CONVOKE. —adj. To be paid for on delivery: a telegram sent *collect*. [< F *collecter* < L *colligere* < *com-* together + *legere* choose] —**col·lect′a·ble** or **·i·ble** adj.

col·lect² (kol′ekt) n. A formal, condensed prayer used in several western liturgies, usually containing a single petition and varying with the season or occasion. [< F *collecte* < L *collecta* a gathering together < *colligere*. See COLLECT¹.]

col·lect·ed (kə·lek′tid) adj. 1 Assembled; gathered. 2 Composed; self-possessed. See synonyms under CALM, SOBER. —**col·lect′ed·ly** adv. —**col·lect′ed·ness** n.

col·lec·tion (kə·lek′shən) n. 1 A collecting; a group of collected objects or individuals. 2

An aggregation; accumulation. 3 A sum of money solicited and contributed, as for church expenses, missions, charity, or the like. 4 The act of receiving or enforcing payment, or the amount of such payment. 5 The act of collecting one's thoughts, feelings, etc., or the resultant state; composure. See synonyms under AGGREGATE, ASSEMBLY, COMPANY. [< L *collectio, -onis* < *colligere* COLLECT]

col·lec·tive (kə·lek′tiv) adj. 1 Relating to, consisting of, or denoting an aggregate or group: opposed to *individual*. 2 Having the power or quality of bringing together. 3 Gram. Denoting in the singular number a collection or aggregate of individuals: The word "army" is a *collective* noun. —n. 1 Gram. A singular noun naming a collection or group. It takes either a singular or a plural verb, according as it refers to the objects composing it as one aggregate (**collective singular**) or as separate individuals (**collective plural**): The audience *was* large; The audience *were* divided in opinion. 2 A collection or gathering. 3 Any collective enterprise. —**col·lec′tive·ly** adv.

collective fruit Bot. A fruit which is the product of a number of distinct flowers growing in a compact mass, as a mulberry or a pineapple: also called *multiple fruit*.

col·lec·tiv·ism (kə·lek′tiv·iz′əm) n. The doctrine that the people as a whole should own or control the material and means of production, or the spirit which determines production by the masses rather than by individuals. Compare SOCIALISM. —**col·lec′tiv·ist** adj. & n. —**col·lec′tiv·is′tic** adj.

col·lec·tiv·i·ty (kol′ek·tiv′ə·tē) n. 1 The whole taken together; the quality or state of being collective. 2 The people as a body. 3 Collectivism.

col·lec·tiv·ize (kə·lek′tiv·īz) v.t. **·ized, ·iz·ing** To organize (an agricultural settlement, industry, economy, etc.) on a collectivist basis, so that management and labor function cooperatively, the material and means of production being owned communally. —**col·lec′tiv·i·za′tion** n.

col·lec·tor (kə·lek′tər) n. 1 One who or that which collects. 2 One who receives taxes, duties, etc., or collects debts. —**col·lec′tor·ship** n.

col·lege (kol′ij) n. 1 An incorporated school for instruction in the liberal arts or professional studies; a school of higher learning that grants degrees at the completion of courses of study; one of the educational institutions of a university; especially one that offers a general, four-year course toward the bachelor's degree: distinguished from graduate and professional schools. 2 A building, or collection of buildings, owned and used by a college. 3 A body of associates or colleagues. 4 A course of lectures or studies. 5 Brit. Slang A prison. 6 Any assemblage or gathering: a *college* of bees. [< OF *collège* < L *collegium* body of associates < *collega* COLLEAGUE¹]

col·le·gian (kə·lē′jən, -jē·ən) n. A member or attendant of a college; a college student.

col·le·giate (kə·lē′jit, -jē·it) adj. Pertaining to, like or conducted like, or connected with a college or colleges. —n. A collegian. —**col·le′giate·ly** adv.

collegiate church 1 An association of churches having pastors in common: the *Collegiate* Dutch Church. 2 A Roman Catholic or an Anglican church, not a cathedral, which has a chapter of canons. 3 A Scottish church served by two or more joint incumbents.

col·len·chy·ma (kə·leng′kə·mə) n. Bot. A form of thick-walled, elastic plant tissue, composed of elongated cells strongly thickened at the angles with colloidal material. [< NL < Gk. *kolla* glue + *enchyma* infusion]

col·let (kol′it) n. 1 Mech. A collar, clutch, or clamping-piece, as for a rod. 2 The ring or rim in which a gem is set. 3 The circular flange which supports the inner terminal of the balance spring in a watch. 4 Culet. —v.t. **·let·ed, ·let·ing** To place in or furnish with a collet. [< F, dim. of *col* neck < L *collum*]

col·lide (kə·līd′) v.i. **·lid·ed, ·lid·ing 1** To come together with violent impact; crash. 2 To come into conflict; clash. [< L *collidere* < *com-* together + *laedere* strike]

col·lie (kol′ē) n. A breed of large shepherd dogs which originated in Scotland, characterized by a long, narrow head and tapering nose and an abundant long-haired coat. [Prob. <Scottish Gaelic *cuilean* puppy]

col·li·er (kol'yər) *n.* **1** A coal-miner. **2** A vessel employed in carrying coal; also, one of the crew. **3** Formerly, a dealer in coal. [ME *colier* <OE *col* coal + -IER]

col·li·gate (kol'ə·gāt) *v.t.* ·**gat·ed**, ·**gat·ing** **1** To tie, group, or fasten together. **2** *Logic* To bind together (facts) by means of some suitable conception or explanation: Certain material phenomena are *colligated* by the law of gravity. [<L *colligatus*, pp. of *colligare* <*com-* together + *ligare* bind] — **col'li·ga'tion** *n.* — **col'li·ga'tive** *adj.*

col·li·mate (kol'ə·māt) *v.t.* ·**mat·ed**, ·**mat·ing** **1** To bring into line. **2** To adjust the line of sight of, as of a telescope or other optical instrument. **3** To make parallel, as refracted rays of light or a gunsight with the axis of the gun's barrel. [<L *collimatus*, alter. of *collineatus*, pp. of *collineare* <*com-* together + *lineare* align] — **col'li·ma'tion** *n.*

col·li·ma·tor (kol'ə·mā'tər) *n. Optics* A device used to obtain parallel rays of light, as a fixed telescope or the convex lens and slit used in a spectroscope.

col·lin·e·ar (kə·lin'ē·ər) *adj.* Being in the same straight line: said of three or more points.

col·lin·si·a (kə·lin'sē·ə, -zē·ə) *n.* **1** An annual or biennial plant (genus *Collinsia*) of the figwort family with whorled leaves. **2** Any of the variously colored flowers of this plant. [after Z. *Collins*, 1764–1831, U.S. botanist]

col·li·sion (kə·lizh'ən) *n.* **1** The act of colliding. **2** Violent contact; clashing; antagonism. [<LL *collisio*, *-onis* <*collidere* COLLIDE] *Synonyms:* clash, clashing, concussion, conflict, contact, encounter, impact, meeting, opposition, shock. *Collision* is the result of motion or action and is sudden and momentary; *contact* may be a condition of rest and be continuous and permanent. *Impact* is the blow given by the striking body. *Concussion* is often by transmitted force rather than by direct *impact*; an explosion of dynamite shatters neighboring windows by *concussion*. *Shock* is the result of *collision*. *Opposition* is used chiefly of persons, less frequently of opinions or interests; *conflict* is used indifferently of all. See ENCOUNTER. *Antonyms:* agreement, amity, coincidence, concert, concord, concurrence, conformity, harmony, unison, unity.

col·lo·cate (kol'ō·kāt) *v.t.* ·**cat·ed**, ·**cat·ing** To put in certain order; arrange together. [<L *collocatus*, pp. of *collocare* <*com-* together + *locare* place] — **col'lo·ca'tion** *n.*

col·lo·di·on (kə·lō'dē·ən) *n.* A solution of guncotton or pyroxylin in ether and alcohol, deposited as a film on the evaporation of the ether, and used as a coating for wounds and for photographic plates. Also **col·lo·di·um** (kə·lō'dē·əm). [<Gk. *kollōdēs* gluelike]

col·loid (kol'oid) *n.* **1** Any gluelike or jellylike substance, as gelatin, starch, raw egg white, etc., which diffuses not at all or very slowly through vegetable and animal membranes, and whose components do not separate as in a true solution or simple mixture: distinguished from *crystalloid*. **2** *Chem.* A state of matter in which very finely divided particles of one substance (the *disperse phase*) are suspended in another (the *dispersion medium*) in such manner and degree that the electrical and surface properties acquire special importance. **3** *Med.* A translucent, gelatinous substance resulting from certain forms of tissue degeneration. —*adj.* Of or pertaining to a colloid or the colloid state: also **col·loi·dal** (kə·loid'l). [<Gk. *kollōdēs* gluelike] — **col·loi·dal·i·ty** (kol'oi·dal'ə·tē) *n.*

colloid system *Chem.* Any aggregate of substances exhibiting the properties of a colloid, as sols, gels, emulsions, etc. Eight of these systems are known, occurring in solid, liquid, and gaseous forms, each identified in terms of the relationship existing between the disperse phase and the dispersion medium. See table below.

COLLOID SYSTEMS

Components	Term	Example
Solid in solid	solid sol	alloys, paper
Solid in liquid	suspension	paints
Solid in gas	smoke	iodine vapor
Liquid in solid	gel	celluloid, glue, gelatin
Liquid in liquid	emulsion	milk, blood
Liquid in gas	fog	clouds, steam
Gas in solid	solid foam	pumice, rubber
Gas in liquid	foam	lather, froth
Gas in gas		(No example known)

col·lop (kol'əp) *n.* **1** A slice or morsel of meat for stewing. **2** A small portion or piece of anything. [Cf. Sw. *kalops* slices of stewed beef]

col·lo·qui·al (kə·lō'kwē·əl) *adj.* **1** Characteristic of or suitable to the informal language of ordinary conversation or familiar writing, but inappropriate for use on the formal level. Colloquial language is widely used by the educated in informal discourse and is not to be confused with substandard speech. **2** Conversational. Abbr. *colloq.* — **col·lo'qui·al·ly** *adv.* — **col·lo'qui·al·ness** *n.*

col·lo·qui·al·ism (kə·lō'kwē·əl·iz'əm) *n.* **1** An expression or form of speech of the type used in informal conversation. **2** Informal, conversational style.

col·lo·quy (kol'ə·kwē) *n. pl.* ·**quies** **1** An informal conference; conversation. **2** A literary work written in conversational or dialog form. [<L *colloquium* conversation <*com-* together + *loqui* speak] — **col'lo·quist** *n.*

col·lo·type (kol'ə·tīp) *n.* **1** A photomechanical printing process in which the negative is printed on a plate covered with a light-sensitive gelatin coat which is then rendered selectively ink-repellent by treatment with glycerin and salt water. **2** A print or plate made by this process. —*v.t.* ·**typed**, ·**typ·ing** To make a collotype of. [<Gk. *kolla* glue + -TYPE] — **col·lo·typ·ic** (kol'ə·tip'ik) *adj.* — **col·lo·typ·y** (kol'ə·tī'pē) *n.*

col·lude (kə·lōōd') *v.i.* ·**lud·ed**, ·**lud·ing** To cooperate secretly; conspire; connive. [<L *colludere* <*com-* together + *ludere* play, trick] — **col·lud'er** *n.*

col·lu·sion (kə·lōō'zhən) *n.* Cooperation in fraud. [<L *collusio*, *-onis* <*colludere* COLLUDE]

col·lu·sive (kə·lōō'siv) *adj.* Fraudulently concerted or devised. — **col·lu'sive·ly** *adv.* — **col·lu'sive·ness** *n.*

col·lyr·i·um (kə·lir'ē·əm) *n.* A medicated eyewash or eye salve. [<L <Gk. *kollyrion* poultice, dim. of *kollyra* bread]

Col·mar (kōl'mär, *Fr.* kôl·mär') A city of eastern France, capital of Haut-Rhin department. German **Kol·mar** (kōl'mär).

colo- *combining form* Colon: *colotomy.* Also, before vowels, *col-.* [<Gk. *kolon* colon]

Co·lô·a·ne (kōō·lô'ə·nə) See under MACAO.

col·o·cynth (kol'ə·sinth) *n.* **1** A Mediterranean vine (*Citrullus colocynthis*) of the gourd family. **2** Its small gourdlike fruit from which is obtained a cathartic drug: also called *bitter apple*, *coloquintida*. [<L *colocynthis* <Gk. *kolokynthē* gourd]

co·logne (kə·lōn') *n.* A toilet water consisting of alcohol scented with aromatic oils: often called *eau de Cologne.* Also **Cologne water.** [from *Cologne*]

Co·lom·bi·a (kə·lum'bē·ə, *Sp.* kō·lôm'byä) A republic in NW South America; 439,828 square miles; capital, Bogotá. —**Co·lom'bi·an** *adj.* & *n.*

Co·lom·bo (kə·lum'bō) The capital of Sri Lanka; a port on the west coast.

co·lon¹ (kō'lən) *n. pl.* **co·lons** for def. **1**, cola (kō'lə) for def. **2 1** A punctuation mark (:) indicating a pause greater than a semicolon, but less than a period: used as a sign of apposition or equality to connect one clause with another that explains it, as in introducing an enumeration or catalog; also used after a word introducing a speech, quotation, etc., in expressing clock time, in citations, and in mathematical proportions. **2** In ancient prosody, a member or section of a rhythmical period. [<Gk. *kōlon* member, limb, clause]

co·lon² (kō'lən) *n. pl.* **co·lons** or **co·la** (kō'lə) *Anat.* The portion of the large intestine between the cecum and the rectum. [<Gk. *kolon*] — **co·lon·ic** (kə·lon'ik) *adj.*

co·lo·nel (kûr'nəl) *n.* A commissioned officer of the sixth rank in the U.S. Army, U.S. Air Force, or U.S. Marine Corps, ranking next above a lieutenant colonel and next below a

brigadier general. —**lieutenant colonel** A commissioned officer of the fifth rank in the U.S. Army, U.S. Air Force, or U.S. Marine Corps, ranking next above a major and next below a colonel. ◆ Homophone: *kernel.* [Earlier *coronel* <F *coronnel* <Ital. *colonnello* <*colonna* column of soldiers] — **colo'nel·cy, colo'nel·ship** *n.*

co·lo·ni·al (kə·lō'nē·əl) *adj.* **1** Of, pertaining to, produced in or living in, like, or forming a colony or colonies, especially one of the thirteen British Colonies that became the United States. **2** Characteristic of colonial times; antique. —*n.* A citizen or inhabitant of a colony. — **co·lo'ni·al·ly** *adv.*

co·lo·ni·al·ism (kə·lō'nē·əl·iz'əm) *n.* The policy of a nation seeking to acquire, extend, or retain overseas dependencies; imperialism.

col·o·nist (kol'ə·nist) *n.* **1** A member or inhabitant of a colony. **2** A settler or founder of a colony.

col·o·ni·tis (kol'ə·nī'tis) See COLITIS.

col·o·ni·za·tion·ist (kol'ə·nə·zā'shən·ist, -nī·zā'-) *n.* An advocate of colonization; specifically, one of the American anti-slavery reformers who favored colonizing emancipated Negroes in Liberia.

col·o·nize (kol'ə·nīz) *v.* ·**nized**, ·**niz·ing** *v.t.* **1** To settle a colony or colonies in. **2** To establish or place as colonists. —*v.i.* **3** To establish or unite in a colony or colonies. **4** To settle in colonies. Also *Brit.* **col'o·nise.** — **col'o·ni·za'tion** *n.* — **col'o·niz'er** *n.*

col·on·nade (kol'ə·nād') *n. Archit.* A range of columns connected by an entablature. [<F <*colonne* column] — **col·on·nad'ed** *adj.*

col·o·ny (kol'ə·nē) *n. pl.* ·**nies 1** A body of emigrants or their descendants in a remote region under the control of a parent country. In Great Britain the term *colony* designates a region that has a responsible government, whether or not it has an elective legislature. **2** Any aggregation of individuals in a common group, as of alien residents in a country, or of bees, beavers, etc. **3** The territory occupied by early settlers or their descendants. **4** *Biol.* A group of organisms of the same species, usually from the same parent cell, functioning in close association and with varying degrees of independence, as certain bacteria, protozoans, and algae. **5** *Ecol.* **a** Two or more species of plants developing in a locality as a result of invasion. **b** A group of plants isolated from others of the same species, but growing in the same locality. [<L *colonia* <*colonus* farmer]

col·o·phon (kol'ə·fon, -fən) *n.* An inscription or device, often ornamental, as the publisher's distinctive emblem, at the beginning or end of books. [<LL <Gk. *kolophōn* summit]

col·o·pho·ny (kol'ə·fō'nē, kə·lof'ə·nē) *n.* Rosin. [<L *colophonia (resina)* (rosin) from Colophon]

col·o·quin·ti·da (kol'ə·kwin'ti·də) See COLOCYNTH.

col·or (kul'ər) *n.* **1** A visual attribute of bodies or substances distinct from their spatial characteristics and depending upon the spectral composition of the wavelengths of radiant energy capable of stimulating the retina and its associated neural mechanisms. **Achromatic colors** include black and white and the entire series of intermediate grays, varying only in *lightness* and *brightness.* **Chromatic colors** may also vary in *hue,* as red, green, blue, and purple; and in *saturation.* **2** A paint, dyestuff, or pigment, as used in industry and the arts. **3** An appearance; semblance; pretense; disguise. **4** *pl.* An ensign or flag of a nation, also of a military or naval unit, as a regiment, warship, etc. **5** *pl.* In the U.S. Navy, the salute made to the national flag when it is hoisted in the morning and lowered in the evening. **6** The hue of the human skin; complexion: equal rights regardless of race, creed, or *color.* **7** In art, coloring. **8** *Music* Timbre; clang; also, the tone, or characteristic effect, of a composition, as produced by specific harmonic, rhythmic, or melodic means. **9** *Law* An apparent or prima-facie right, authority, etc. **10** A small particle or trace of gold in auriferous sand

add,āce,câre,pälm; end,ēven; it,īce; odd,ōpen,ôrder; tōōk,pōōl; up,bûrn; ə = a in *above,* e in *sicken,* i in *clarity,* o in *melon,* u in *focus* ; yōō = u in *fuse,* oi,oil; ou,pout; ch,check; g,go; ng,ring; th,thin; th,this; zh,vision. Foreign sounds à,œ,ü,kh,ṅ; and ◆: see page xx. <from; + plus; ? possibly.

colorado

or gravel. **11** Liveliness or animation, vividness, especially in literary work. —**complementary color 1** Either of a pair of spectrum colors which when combined give a white or nearly white light. **2** One of two pigments whose mixture produces a third color, as blue and yellow blended to produce green. —**primary colors 1** The principal colors in which white light is separated by a prism; the colors of the rainbow. **2** The colors red, yellow, green, and blue, by mixing which any desired color or hue may be obtained; to these white and black may be added. —*v.t.* **1** To apply or give color, as by painting, staining, or dyeing. **2** To misrepresent by distortion or exaggeration. **3** To modify in nature or character. —*v.i.* **4** To take on or change color, as ripening fruit. **5** To blush or flush. Also *Brit.* **col'our** [< OF *colour* < L *color*] —**col'or·a·ble** *adj.* —**col'or·a·bly** *adv.* —**col'or·er** *n.*

col·o·ra·do (kol'ə·rä′dō) *adj.* **1** Denoting medium strength and color: said of cigars. **2** Red; reddish: used in geographic names. [< Sp., colored, red]

Col·o·ra·do (kol'ə·rä′dō, -rä′dō) A western State of the United States; 103,967 square miles; capital, Denver; entered the Union Aug. 1, 1876: nicknamed *Centennial State*: abbr. CO

col·o·ra·tion (kul'ə·rā′shən) *n.* Particular marking or arrangement of colors, as in an animal or plant; coloring.

col·o·ra·tu·ra (kul'ər·ə·tŏŏr′ə,-tyŏŏr′ə) *n.* The effect of giving color to vocal music, by means of grace notes, runs, trills, or other florid decoration. **2** The runs, etc., themselves. —*adj.* Characterized by or suitable for coloratura. Also **col·or·a·ture** (kul'ər·ə·choor). [< Ital. *coloratura* ration]

col·or·blind (kul'ər·blīnd′) *adj.* Totally or partially unable to discriminate between hues as distinguished from light or shade.

color corrector An electronic device used in the preparation of precision color negatives in photoengraving.

col·ored (kul'ərd) *adj.* **1** Having color. **2** Of a dark-skinned race; wholly or partially of African descent; loosely, of any other than the white race. Compare COLOURED. **3** Pertaining to, characteristic of, like, for, or composed of Negroes: a *colored* school. **4** Embellished or exaggerated; prejudiced; specious.

col·or·fast (kul'ər·fast′, -fäst′) *adj.* Retaining color of dye or paint substantially unfaded when fabric or surface is subjected to the action of water, cleaning fluid, or a reasonable amount of light; resistant to fading: *colorfast* fabrics; a *colorfast* paint job.

color filter A layer of substance, in solid, liquid, or gaseous form, which will absorb a certain wavelength of light: used in photography to change the relative intensities of impinging light waves. Also called **color screen.**

col·or·ful (kul'ər·fəl) *adj.* **1** Full of colors, especially contrasting colors; bright: a *colorful* scene. **2** In literature, vivid; animated: a *colorful* plot. —**col'or·ful·ly** *adv.* —**col'or·ful·ness** *n.*

color guard In the U.S. Army, Navy, and Air Force, the flagbearers and guards who conduct the colors in a ceremony.

col·or·if·ic (kul'ə·rif′ik) *adj.* Pertaining to the production or imparting of color. [< F *colorifique*]

col·or·im·e·ter (kul'ər·im′ə·tər) *n.* An apparatus for determining the hue, purity, and brightness of a color, especially as compared with a specified standard: used in chemical analysis and in medicine. [< COLOR + -(I)METER] —**col·or·i·met·ric** (kul'ər·ə·met′rik) or **·ri·cal** *adj.* —**col'or·i·met'ri·cal·ly** *adv.*

col·or·im·e·try (kul'ər·im′ə·trē) *n.* The measurement and analysis of color by comparison with a standard or in terms of physical and spectral characteristics.

color index 1 *Astron.* The difference between the photographic and visual magnitude of a star. **2** *Med.* A number expressing the amount of hemoglobin in the red blood cells. **3** *Mineral.* A number indicating the percentage of light to dark and heavy minerals in igneous rock: also called **color ratio.**

col·or·ing (kul'ər·ing) *n.* **1** The imparting of color, or that which imparts color. **2** The general color of anything; coloration; style of applying colors. **3** Peculiar style or air. **4** Appearance; especially,

---

false appearance.

col·or·ize (kul'ər·īz) *v.t.* **·ized, ·iz·ing** To add color to originally black-and-white movies by means of computer-enhanced techniques. —**col'or·i·za'tion** *n.*

col·or·less (kul'ər·lis) *adj.* **1** Without color. **2** Dull; uninteresting. See synonyms under PALE.

color line A social distinction drawn between the white and other races.

color scheme An arrangement of colors according to a planned design, as in a room.

color temperature *Physics* The temperature of a black body when its color exactly matches that of a given source of radiation.

color wheel A wheel designed to exhibit the proportion of primary colors in any shade of color.

co·los·sal (kə·los′əl) *adj.* Enormous; huge; tremendous. See synonyms under IMMENSE. —

co·los·sus (kə·los′əs) *n. pl.* **co·los·si** (kə·los′ī) or **co·los·sus·es 1** A gigantic statue. **2** Any strikingly huge or great person or object. [< L < Gk. *kolossos* gigantic statue]

co·los·to·my (kə·los′tə·mē) *n. pl.* **·mies** *Surg.* The formation of an artificial opening into the colon. [< COLO- + -STOMY]

co·los·trum (kə·los′trəm) *n.* The first milk of a mammal after parturition; beestings. [< L]

—**colous** *combining form* Dwelling in or inhabiting: *arenicolous.* [< L *colere* dwell, inhabit]

col·pi·tis (kol·pī′tis) *n.* Inflammation of the vagina; vaginitis. [< Gk. *kolpos* womb + -ITIS]

col·por·teur (kol'pôr′tər) *n.* **1** A peddler, especially one who hawks books, almanacs, etc., in country districts. **2** A traveling agent of a religious society, who sells or gives away Bibles, tracts, etc. [< F < *colporter* peddle < *col* neck + *porter* carry]

colt (kōlt) *n.* **1** A young horse, ass, etc.; specifically, a young male horse. **2** A frisky person. [OE] —**colt'ish** *adj.*

col·ter (kōl'tər) *n.* A blade or disk on the beam of a plow, to cut the sod: also spelled *coulter.* [OE *culter* < L *culter* knife]

colts·foot (kōlts'fŏŏt′) *n. pl.* **·foots** A low, perennial, Old World herb of the composite family (*Tussilago farfara*), bearing yellow flowers: formerly used in medicine.

col·u·brine (kol'yə·brīn, -brin) *adj.* **1** Of, pertaining to, or like a snake. **2** Of or pertaining to a widely distributed family of snakes (*Colubridae*); especially to the subfamily *Colubrinae*, which includes the typically nonvenomous snakes, as the garter snake, blacksnake, etc. [< L *colubrinus* < *coluber* snake]

co·lu·go (kə·lŏŏ′gō) *n. pl.* **·gos** The flying lemur.

col·um·bar·i·um (kol'əm·bâr′ē·əm) *n. pl.* **·bar·i·a** (-bâr′ē·ə) **1** A dovecot; also, a pigeonhole in a dovecot: also **col·um·bar·y** (kol'əm·ber′ē). **2** In ancient Rome, a sepulcher with niches for cinerary urns. [< L < *columba* dove]

COLUMBARIUM

Co·lum·bi·a (kə·lum′bē·ə) The capital of South Carolina.

col·um·bine (kol'əm·bīn) *n.* A herbaceous plant (genus *Aquilegia*) of the crowfoot family with variously colored flowers of five petals; especially the **Colorado columbine** (*A. coerulea*), State flower of Colorado. —*adj.* Dovelike. [< F < Med. L *columbinus* dovelike < *columba* dove; from the resemblance of its flowers to a flock of doves]

COLUMBINE

co·lum·bite (kə·lum′bīt) *n.* A black, brittle mineral, containing variable proportions of niobium and tantalum, associated with iron and manganese.

co·lum·bi·um (kə·lum′bē·əm) *n.* Former name for the element niobium. [< NL < *Columbia*, the United States]

Co·lum·bus (kə·lum′bəs) The capital of Ohio.

Co·lum·bus (kə·lum′bəs), **Christopher,** 1446–1506, Italian navigator; discovered America for Spain, Oct. 12, 1492. Spanish *Cristóbal Colón.*

---

comate

col·u·mel·la (kol'yə·mel′ə) *n. pl.* **·mel·lae** (-mel′·ē) *Biol.* A little rod, pillar, or central axis, as the central rod of the cochlea, the axial pillar of a spiral shell, etc. Also **col·u·mel** (kol'yə·mel). [< L, dim. of *columna* column]

col·umn (kol'əm) *n.*
1 *Archit.* A vertical shaft or pillar, usually having a base and a capital, and primarily for the support of superincumbent weight. **2** Any object or structure resembling a column in form position, or use: th spinal *column*; a *column* of vapor. **3** *Printing* A vertical series of lines, separated from adjoining columns by a rule or a blank space. **4** *Mil.* A unit of troops in single file, or formed several lines abreast. **5** *Naut.* A fleet of ships in single file. **6** A department of a newspaper in which a special writer presents a daily article of contemporary comment. See synonyms under PROCESSION. [< L *columna*] —**col·umned** (kol'əmd) *adj.*

co·lum·nar (kə·lum′nər) *adj.* **1** Of, pertaining to, or having the form of a column or columns; like the shaft of a column. **2** *Geol.* Describing the six-sided structural formation characteristic of basaltic rock.

ROMAN
COLUMN WITH
ENTABLATURE (*a.–c.*)
a. Cornice.
b. Frieze.
c. Architrave.
d. Capital (in Corinthian style)
e. Astragal.
f. Shaft.
g. Base.
From the Pantheon, Rome

col·um·nist (kol'əm·nist, -əm·ist) *n.* A journalist who writes or conducts a special column on a daily newspaper.

co·lure (kə·lyŏŏr′, kō′lyŏŏr) *n.* *Astron.* One of the two great circles of the celestial sphere at right angles to each other, intersecting at the poles and passing through the equinoxes and the solstices respectively. [< L *colurus* < Gk. *kolouros* < *kolos* docked + *oura* tail; because their lower parts are cut off by the horizon]

co·ly (kō′lē) *n. pl.* **co·lies** The long-tailed African mousebird, one of a genus (*Colius*) having four toes and a strong, slightly curved beak. [< NL *colius* < Gk. *kolios*, a green woodpecker]

co·ly·one (kō′lē·ōn) *n.* *Biochem.* A secretion which has the property of inhibiting the action of some organ, tissue, or part of the body: distinguished from *hormone*: also called *chalone.* [< Gk. *kōlyōn*, ppr. of *kōlyein* hinder]

col·za (kol′zə) *n.* The summer rape or coleseed whose seeds produce rape oil. [< F < Du. *koolzaad* < *kool* cabbage + *zaad* a seed]

colza oil Rape oil.

com– *prefix* With; together: *combine, compare.* Also: *co–* before *gn, h,* and vowels; *col–* before *l,* as in *collide*; *con–* before *c, d, f, g, j, n, q, s, t, v,* as in *concur, confluence, connect, conspire*; *cor–* before *r,* as in *correspond.* [< L *com– < cum* with]

co·ma[1] (kō′mə) *n. pl.* **co·mas 1** A state of unconsciousness with slow, heavy breathing: sometimes called by the names of the conditions or diseases that cause them: **diabetic coma** (occurring in diabetes), **uremic coma** (from excess of urea), etc. **2** Stupor; lethargy. [< NL < Gk. *kōma* deep sleep]

co·ma[2] (kō′mə) *n. pl.* **co·mae** (kō′mē) **1** *Astron.* The nebulosity around the nucleus of a comet. **2** *Bot.* A tuft of silky hairs, as at the end of certain seeds. **3** *Optics* The hazy border surrounding an object viewed through an imperfect lens. [< L, hair < Gk. *komē*] —**co′mal** *adj.*

co·mate (kō′māt) *adj.* **1** *Bot.* Having a coma. **2** *Entomol.* Hairy, as the heads of certain insects.

co·mate² (kō·māt′, kō′māt′) *n.* A mate; companion.

co·ma·tose (kō′mə·tōs, kom′ə-) *adj.* 1 Relating to or affected with coma. 2 Lethargic; torpid; abnormally sleepy. Also **co·ma·tous** (kō′mə·təs, kom′ə-). — **co′ma·tose′ly** *adv.*

co·mat·u·la (kō·mat′yə·lə) *n. Zool.* One of a genus (*Comatula*) of free-swimming crinoids, with plumelike arms: also called *feather star.* Also **co·mat′u·lid.** [<NL <L *comatulus,* dim. of *comatus* having hair < *coma* hair]

COMATULA
(Mostly microscopic:
some up to 2/3 of an
inch)

comb¹ (kōm) *n.* 1 A thin piece of horn, metal, ivory, or the like, with teeth, for cleansing, dressing, or fastening the hair. 2 Something resembling such a comb in appearance or use, as a currycomb or a card for dressing wool or flax. 3 The fleshy crest on the head of a fowl. 4 The crest of a hill or wave. 5 Honeycomb. 6 That part of a gunstock in which the cheek rests. 7 The ridge of a roof. — *v.t.* 1 To dress, disentangle, or smoothe out with or as with a comb, as hair; clear or cleanse with a comb. 2 To card, as wool or flax. 3 In painting, to grain with a comb. 4 To search carefully and exhaustively. — *v.i.* 5 To crest and break: said of waves. [OE *camb*]

comb² (kōm, kōm) See COOMB.

com·bat (kom′bat, kum′-) *n.* A battle or fight; struggle; contest; duel. — **close combat** Hand-to-hand fighting. — **single combat** A fight between two persons; a duel. — *v.* (kəm·bat′) **·bat·ed** or **·bat·ted, ·bat·ing** or **·bat·ting** *v.t.* 1 To fight or contend with; oppose in battle. 2 To resist. — *v.i.* 3 To do battle; struggle: with *with* or *against.* See synonyms under ATTACK, BATTLE, CONTEND, DISPUTE, OPPOSE. [<F <*combattre* <L *com-* with + *batuere* fight, beat] — **com·bat·a·ble** (kom·bat′ə·bəl, kom′bat·ə·bəl, kum′-) *adj.* — **com·bat·er** (kom′bat·ər, kum′-, kəm·bat′ər) *n.*

com·bat·ant (kəm·bat′ənt, kom′bə·tənt, kum′-) *n.* One engaged in or prepared for combat or hostilities. — *adj.* Fighting; battling; ready or disposed to combat. [<OF *combatant,* ppr. of *combattre* COMBAT]

com·bat·ive (kəm·bat′iv, kom′bə·tiv, kum′-) *adj.* Inclined or eager to fight; pugnacious. — **com·bat′ive·ly** *adv.* — **com·bat′ive·ness** *n.*

com·bi·na·tion (kom′bə·nā′shən) *n.* 1 A joining together; union; alliance. 2 A compound or group. 3 *pl.* Underwear made in one piece. 4 The series of numbers or letters forming the key symbol to a keyless lock or **combination lock;** also, the mechanism operated by such a sequence. 5 *Math.* A group of several things or symbols in which the order of arrangement is immaterial. 6 *Chem.* The union of elements in certain fixed proportions, or the compound thus resulting. 7 An alliance of politicians, or merchants, etc., to protect or further a common interest, activity, or advantage. 8 An alliance of corporations; a combine or monopoly. 9 A railroad car divided into a baggage and a passenger section. See synonyms under CABAL, UNION. [<MF <LL *combinatio, -onis* a joining by twos < *combinare.* See COMBINE.]

com·bi·na·tive (kom′bə·nā′tiv, kəm·bī′nə·) *adj.* 1 Relating to or effecting combination; tending to combine. 2 Designating those branches of algebra which depend on the theory of combinations. Also **com·bi·na·to·ri·al** (kəm·bī′nə·tôr′ē·əl, -tō′rē-).

com·bine (kəm·bīn′) *v.t.* & *v.i.* **·bined, ·bin·ing** 1 To bring or come into a close union; blend; compound; unite. 2 To unite by affinity. 3 To enter into chemical combination: Oxygen and hydrogen *combine* to form water. See synonyms under MIX, UNITE. — *n.* (kom′bīn) 1 *Colloq.* An association of persons to raise prices or obstruct the course of trade, or to gain or keep political control, often by unfair or dishonest means; a trust; ring; cabal. 2 A farm machine which combines the processes of heading, threshing, and cleaning

grain while harvesting it in the field. [<LL *combinare* <*com-* together + *bini* two by two] — **com·bin′a·ble** *adj.* — **com·bin′er** *n.*

combining form The stem of a word, usually of Greek or Latin origin (*tele-* and *-phone* in *telephone*), or in an English word unchanged (*over* in *overeat*), used in combination with other forms to create compounds.

comb jelly A ctenophore.

com·bust (kəm·bust′) *adj.* In astrology, obscured by proximity to the sun, as a planet or star. [<OF <L *combustus,* pp. of *comburere* burn up]

com·bus·ti·ble (kəm·bus′tə·bəl) *adj.* 1 Susceptible of combustion; inflammable. 2 Excitable; fiery. — *n.* Any substance that will readily burn, as pitch or coal. — **com·bus′ti·ble·ness, com·bus′ti·bil′i·ty** *n.*

com·bus·tion (kəm·bus′chən) *n.* 1 The action or operation of burning; the state of being on fire. 2 *Chem.* The combination of a substance with oxygen, accompanied by the generation of heat and sometimes light. 3 *Physiol.* Oxidation, as of fuel, or of food in the body. 4 Disturbance; tumult. See synonyms under FIRE. [<LL *combustio, -onis* < *comburere* burn up] — **com·bus′tive** *adj.*

com·bus·tor (kəm·bus′tər) *n.* The chamber of a jet-propulsion engine in which combustion occurs.

comb·y (kō′mē) *adj.* Resembling a comb or honeycomb.

come (kum) *v.* **came, come, com·ing** *v.i.* 1 To move to or toward a position or place from a point further away: opposed to *go.* 2 To move to or toward the speaker: *Come* here. 3 In the imperative, to move mentally where the speaker wills: almost an interjectional sense: *Come,* let us make a visit. 4 To arrive as the result of motion or progress: They *came* to land. 5 To attain to an end or completion: Thy kingdom *come.* 6 To arrive at some state or condition; develop. 7 To advance or move into view; become perceptible: Her color *comes* and goes. 8 To draw near in time; be present; arrive: When Christmas *comes.* 9 To arrive in due course or in orderly progression. 10 To proceed or emanate as from a source. 11 To exist as an effect or result: This *comes* of trifling. 12 To happen or befall: *Come* what may, I'll do it. 13 To get or prove to be; become: The sign *came* true. 14 To reach or extend: with *to.* 15 To be offered, obtainable, or produced: The car *comes* in many colors. 16 To be favorably inclined; yield. — *v.t.* 17 *Slang* To play the part of; act; also, to perpetrate: He *comes* a joke on us. 18 *Naut.* To loosen: with *up:* to *come up* the standing rigging. 19 *Brit. Dial.* To fit or suit; become. — **to come about** 1 To take place; happen. 2 *Naut.* To turn in order to proceed on the opposite tack. — **to come by** 1 To pass near. 2 To get, acquire, or obtain. — **to come in** 1 To give birth to a calf. 2 To join a group in some special activity. — **to come it over** *Colloq.* To outwit or humble (someone). — **to come out** 1 To speak frankly; declare one's views. 2 To pass through a contest or competition: to *come out* first. 3 To make one's début in society. — **to come through** 1 To produce (the expected thing); achieve; win. 2 To experience. — **to come to** 1 To recover consciousness; revive; be resuscitated; also, return to, as one's senses. 2 *Naut.* **a** To anchor. **b** To bring a ship close to the wind. 3 To turn sharply to the left: said of a team of oxen or horses. 4 To amount to: The bill came *to* five dollars. [OE *cuman*]

come–back (kum′bak′) *n.* 1 *Colloq.* Recovery of health or supremacy, after illness, failure, or deposition. 2 *Slang* A smart retort. 3 *Slang* Grounds for complaint; recourse: The customer has no *come-back.*

co·me·di·an (kə·mē′dē·ən) *n.* 1 A comic actor; one who plays comic parts or in comedies. 2 An entertainer who tells jokes, sings comic songs, etc. 3 One who writes comedies. 4 One who is or tries to be amusing. — **co·me·di·enne** (kə·mē′dē·en′) *n. fem.*

com·e·do (kom′ə·dō) *n. pl.* **com·e·dos** or **com·e·do·nes** (kom′ə·dō′nēz) A condition of the sebaceous glands, in which the secretion is retained in the follicle; a blackhead. [<L,

glutton < *comedere* eat up < *com-* + *edere* eat]

come–down (kum′doun′) *n.* A descent to a lower condition or position; downfall.

com·e·dy (kom′ə·dē) *n. pl.* **·dies** 1 A drama or other literary work with a happy ending. 2 A play or other work of literature, motion pictures, television, radio, etc., characterized by a humorous treatment of characters, situation, etc., and having a happy ending; an entertaining drama: distinguished from the problematic, tragic, or serious. 2 The art of writing, producing, or acting in such plays, motion pictures, etc. 3 Comedies collectively, especially as a branch of the drama. 4 Any comic or ludicrous incident or series of incidents. [<MF *comédie* <L *comoedia* <Gk. *kōmōdia* < *kōmos* revel + *aeidein* sing]

come·ly (kum′lē) *adj.* **·li·er, ·li·est** 1 Pleasing in person; handsome; graceful. 2 *Obs.* Suitable; becoming; decorous. See synonyms under BEAUTIFUL, BECOMING. [OE *cymlic*]

come–on (kum′on′, -ôn′) *n. Slang* 1 Someone or something that lures or inveigles. 2 A beckoning look or gesture.

com·er (kum′ər) *n.* 1 One who comes or arrives. 2 *Colloq.* A person, animal, or thing capable of further growth or development; someone or something showing great promise. — **all comers** All applicants, contestants, etc.: to maintain a position against *all comers.*

co·mes·ti·ble (kə·mes′tə·bəl) *adj.* Edible; pertaining to food. — *n.* An eatable: usually in the plural. [<F <LL *comestibilis* < *comedere.* See COMEDO.]

com·et (kom′it) *n. Astron.* A celestial body drawn within the sun's gravitational field and occasionally close enough to the earth or bright enough to be observed by the naked eye. It consists of a nucleus of more or less condensed material, accompanied by a tenuous coma which always points in a direction away from the sun. A number of periodic comets are now known: among them are **Biela's comet,** with a period of 7 years; **Encke's comet,** period 3 years; **Halley's comet,** period 76 years. [OE *cometa* <L <Gk. *komētēs* long-haired < *komē* hair] — **com·et·ar·y** (kom′ə·ter′ē), **co·met·ic** (kə·met′ik) *adj.*

com·et–seek·er (kom′it·sē′kər) *n. Astron.* A small telescope usually with an aperture of 3 to 5 inches, of short focal length, mounted to search for comets. Also **com′et–find′er.**

come–up·pance (kum·up′əns) *n. Colloq.* Deserved punishment; retribution.

com·fit (kum′fit, kom′-) *n.* A sweetmeat; confection. Also **com·fi·ture** (kum′fi·chŏŏr, kom′-). [<F *confit* <L *confectus.* Related to CONFECT.]

com·fort (kum′fərt) *n.* 1 Freedom or relief from pain, annoyance, or want; also, anything that contributes to such relief. 2 Relief from sorrow or distress; consolation; also, one who or that which comforts or consoles. 3 A thick, quilted bedcover; a comforter. [< *v.*] — *v.t.* 1 To give cheer or encouragement to; encourage; console; solace. 2 *Law* To countenance; abet. See synonyms under CHERISH, CONSOLE. [<OF *conforter* <LL *confortare* strengthen < *com-* with + *fortis* strong]

Synonyms (*noun*): abundance, amusement, cheer, contentment, ease, enjoyment, happiness, opulence, pleasure, plenty, satisfaction, sufficiency. *Comfort* may be used of simple freedom from pain, annoyance, or privation, with no implication of any previous trouble, sorrow, or want. Thus, we may say one has lived in *comfort* all his life. In this sense, *comfort* is more solid than *amusement,* more quiet and stable than *pleasure,* less positive and vivid than *happiness. Comfort* is also any relief of suffering, want, or sorrow, which makes the distress easier to be borne. See HAPPINESS, SATISFACTION. Antonyms: dearth, dreariness, gloom, misery, need, poverty, suffering, want, wretchedness.

com·fort·a·ble (kum′fər·tə·bəl, kumf′tə·bəl) *adj.* 1 Having or imparting comfort. 2 Out of pain; free from suffering. 3 *Colloq.* Moderate; enough: a *comfortable* income. 4 *Obs.* Comforting. — *n.* A wadded bedquilt or comforter. — **com′fort·a·ble·ness** *n.* — **com′fort·a·bly** *adv.*

Synonyms (adj.): agreeable, cheerful, cheery, commodious, contented, convenient, genial, pleasant, satisfactory, satisfied, snug. A person is *comfortable* in mind when *contented* and measurably *satisfied*. A little additional brightness makes him *cheerful*. He is *comfortable* in body when free from pain; quiet, at ease, at rest. He is *comfortable* in circumstances, or in *comfortable* circumstances, when things about him are generally *agreeable* and *satisfactory*, usually with the suggestion of sufficient means to secure that result. *Antonyms*: cheerless, disagreeable, discontented, dissatisfied, distressed, dreary, forlorn, miserable, suffering, uncomfortable, wretched.

com·fort·er (kum'fər·tər) *n.* 1 One who comforts; a consoler. 2 A thick, quilted bedcover. 3 A long woolen scarf. See JOB'S COMFORTER.

Com·fort·er (kum'fər·tər) The Holy Spirit.

comfort station A public rest-room.

com·frey (kum'frē) *n. pl.* **·freys** 1 A rough, hairy herb (genus *Symphytum*) of the borage family. 2 Its root, containing tannin: used in medicine. [<OF *confirie*]

com·ic (kom'ik) *adj.* 1 Pertaining to, like, or connected with comedy. 2 Provoking or meant to provoke mirth; funny; ludicrous. 3 Acting in or composing comedy. See synonyms under HUMOROUS. — *n.* 1 A comical person or thing; especially, a comic actor. 2 A book or motion picture made up of comic strips. 3 *pl. Colloq.* The comic strips of a newspaper. 4 The comic side of art, life, etc. [<L *comicus* <Gk. *kōmikos* < *kōmos* revelry]

com·i·cal (kom'i·kəl) *adj.* 1 Causing amusement; ludicrous; diverting. 2 *Obs.* Of or pertaining to comedy. See synonyms under HUMOROUS, ODD, RIDICULOUS. — **com'i·cal·ly** *adv.* — **com·i·cal·i·ty** (kom'ə·kal'ə·tē), **com'i·cal·ness** *n.*

comic book A magazine of comic strips, usually containing one or more complete stories.

comic strip A strip of cartoons printed in newspapers, magazines, etc., and picturing a serial sequence of comic, dramatic, or historical incidents.

com·ing (kum'ing) *adj.* 1 Approaching, especially in time: the *coming* year. 2 On the way to fame or note: He is the *coming* man. 3 Growing; increasing: a *coming* appetite. — *n.* The act of approaching; arrival; advent.

com·ing-out (kum'ing·out') *n. Colloq.* Entrance into society; debut.

com·i·ty (kom'ə·tē) *n.* 1 Kindly consideration for others; friendliness; good will; courtesy. 2 The recognition which one jurisdiction accords within its territory to the laws of another. See synonyms under FRIENDSHIP. [<L *comitas, -tatis* courtesy < *comis* kind]

com·ma (kom'ə) *n.* 1 A punctuation mark (,) indicating separation in ideas or construction within a sentence. 2 A clause, or short group of words, cut off by itself. 3 Any pause or separation. [<L <Gk. *komma* short phrase < *koptein* cut]

comma bacillus *Bacteriol.* A comma-shaped bacillus (*Vibrio comma* or *cholerae*), the causative agent of Asiatic cholera. See illustration under BACTERIUM.

com·mand (kə·mand', -mänd') *v.t.* 1 To order, require or enjoin with authority. 2 To control or direct authoritatively; rule; have at one's disposal or use. 3 To overlook, as from a height; guard. 4 To exact as being due or proper. — *v.i.* 5 To be in authority; rule. 6 To overlook something from a superior position. See synonyms under DICTATE, GOVERN, INFLUENCE. — *n.* 1 The right to command; the authority exercised by an individual over others through his rank or ability; also, the act of commanding. 2 An order; commandment. 3 The troops or district under the command of one person. 4 Dominating power; hence, range of view; control; mastery. 5 In the U.S. Air Force, a unit, usually a wing or more, directed by an officer; also, its base of operations. 6 The distance between the bore of a gun and the adjacent ground. [<OF *comander* <LL *commandare* < com- thoroughly + *mandare* order, charge. Related to COMMEND.]

com·man·dant (kom'ən·dant', -dänt') *n.* A commanding officer, as of a service school, military district, etc.

com·man·deer (kom'ən·dir') *v.t.* 1 To force into military service. 2 To take possession of or requisition by force for public use, especially under military necessity; sequester; confiscate. 3 To take over by force or by threat of force. [<Afrikaans *kommandeeren* command]

com·mand·er (kə·man'dər, -män'-) *n.* 1 One in command; a military leader. 2 In the U.S. Army, the commanding officer of a post or unit. 3 In the U.S. Navy, an officer ranking next above a lieutenant commander and next below a captain: equivalent in rank to a lieutenant colonel in the U.S. Army. — **lieutenant commander** In the U.S. Navy, an officer ranking next above a lieutenant and next below a commander: equivalent in rank to a major in the U.S. Army.

commander in chief 1 An officer commanding all the armed forces in a certain theater of war. 2 Formerly, the officer commanding the armed forces of an American Colony: often the governor.

com·mand·er·y (kə·man'dər·ē, -män'-) *n. pl.* **·der·ies** 1 *U.S.* A lodge of various orders, as of the Knights Templar, etc.; also, a division of a military officers' veterans' organization. 2 The rank of commander in an order of knighthood. 3 A district or estate under the authority of a commander; especially, a district or estate in charge of a member of a medieval order of knights; also, the house or priory of such an order: a *commandery* of the Knights of Malta.

com·mand·ing (kə·man'ding, -män'-) *adj.* 1 Fitted to command; impressive; authoritative; dignified. 2 Having a wide, overlooking view or advantageous position. See synonyms under IMPERIOUS, POWERFUL, PREDOMINANT.

com·mand·ment (kə·mand'mənt, -mänd'-) *n.* An authoritative mandate; edict; order; law; especially, a command of God, and specifically one of the divisions of the decalog or moral law. See synonyms under LAW. — **the Ten Commandments** The ten precepts given by God to Moses on Mount Sinai as recorded in *Exodus* xx 1–17; the decalog.

command module *Aerospace* A part of a space vehicle that houses the crew and navigational systems and is equipped for reentry.

com·man·do (kə·man'dō, -män'-) *n. pl.* **·dos** or **·does** 1 A special fighting force trained for quick, destructive raids into enemy territory. 2 A member of such a unit. 3 In South Africa, a militia force; also, a raid. [<Afrikaans <Pg., a group commanded < *commandar* command <LL *commandare*. See COMMAND.]

command performance A theatrical or musical performance presented at royal request.

com·meas·ure (kə·mezh'ər) *v.t.* To be coextensive with or equal to. — **com·meas'ur·a·ble** *adj.*

com·mem·o·rate (kə·mem'ə·rāt) *v.t.* **·rat·ed**, **·rat·ing** To celebrate or signalize the memory of; keep in remembrance. Also **com·mem'o·rize.** See synonyms under CELEBRATE. [<L *commemoratus*, pp. of *commemorare* recall < com- together + *memorare* remember]

com·mem·o·ra·tion (kə·mem'ə·rā'shən) *n.* The act of commemorating, or that which commemorates; a commemorative observance, celebration, recital, or action of any kind; a memorial. — **com·mem'o·ra'tion·al** *adj.*

com·mence (kə·mens') *v.t. & v.i.* **·menced**, **·menc·ing** To give origin to; begin; initiate; have or make a beginning; originate; start. See synonyms under INSTITUTE. [<OF *comencer* <LL com- together + *initiare* begin < *in-* in + *ire* go] — **com·menc'er** *n.*

com·mence·ment (kə·mens'mənt) *n.* 1 A beginning; origin. 2 A celebration of the completion of a school or college course, when degrees are conferred; also, the day so observed. See synonyms under BEGINNING.

com·mend (kə·mend') *v.t.* 1 To express a favorable opinion of; approve; praise. 2 To recommend; accredit. 3 To present the regards of. 4 To commit with confidence; entrust. 5 To place under the protection of a feudal lord. 6 To bestow *in commendam*. See synonyms under PRAISE. [<L *commendare* < com- thoroughly + *mandare* order, charge. Related to COMMAND.] — **com·mend'a·ble** *adj.*

com·men·dam (kə·men'dam) *n.* 1 The right to enjoy the revenues of a religious house or institution in the absence of a superior or during a vacancy (**in commendam**): abolished in England by act of Parliament in 1836. See COMMENDATOR. 2 The benefice so held. [<Med. L *(dare in) commendam* (give in) trust < *commendare*. See COMMEND.]

com·men·da·tion (kom'ən·dā'shən) *n.* 1 The act of commending; approbation. 2 Something that commends. 3 *Obs.* A message of good will; a greeting. See synonyms under EULOGY. [<L *commendatio, -onis* < *commendare*. See COMMEND.]

com·men·da·tor (kom'ən·dā'tər) *n.* One who held a benefice *in commendam.*

com·men·da·to·ry (kə·men'də·tôr'ē, -tō'rē) *adj.* 1 Expressing commendation; serving to commend. 2 Holding a benefice as a commendator.

com·men·sal (kə·men'səl) *adj.* 1 Eating at the same table. 2 *Biol.* Associated or living with another in close but non-parasitic relationship, as a sea anemone attached to the shell of a hermit crab. — *n.* 1 A table companion. 2 A commensal organism. [<Med. L *commensalis* < com- together + *mensa* table]

com·men·su·ra·ble (kə·men'shər·ə·bəl, -sər·ə-) *adj.* 1 Measurable by a common unit. 2 Proportionate. [<LL *commensurabilis* < com- together + *mensurabilis* measurable] — **com·men'su·ra·bil'i·ty**, **com·men'su·ra·ble·ness** *n.*

com·men·su·rate (kə·men'shə·rit, -sə·rit) *adj.* 1 Commensurable. 2 In proper proportion; proportionate. 3 Sufficient for the purpose or occasion. 4 Adequate; of equal extent. See synonyms under ADEQUATE. [<LL *commensuratus*, pp. of *commensurare* < com- together + *mensurare* measure] — **com·men'su·rate·ly** *adv.* — **com·men'su·rate·ness** *n.*

com·men·su·ra·tion (kə·men'shə·rā'shən, -sə·rā'-) *n.* 1 The act of proportioning, or the state of being proportioned. 2 Measurement by comparison.

com·ment (kom'ent) *v.i.* To make expository or critical notes or remarks; make reflections or observations. — *v.t.* To make comments or remarks upon; explain or annotate. [<n.] — *n.* 1 A note in explanation or criticism. 2 A remark made in observation or criticism. 3 Talk; conversation; gossip. See synonyms under ANIMADVERSION, REMARK. [<OF <L *commentum* invention < *comminisci* contrive] — **com'ment·er** *n.*

com·men·tar·y (kom'ən·ter'ē) *n. pl.* **·tar·ies** 1 A treatise in annotation or explanation, as of the Scriptures; a series or body of comments; exposition. 2 Anything explanatory or illustrative; systematic exposition. 3 A historical narrative or chronological record of events; journal of official acts: the Royal *Commentaries* of Peru. See synonyms under DEFINITION. [<L *commentarius* notebook < *commentari*, freq. of *comminisci* contrive, devise] — **com·men·tar·i·al** (kom'ən·târ'ē·əl) *adj.*

com·men·ta·tor (kom'ən·tā'tər) *n.* 1 A writer of commentaries; an annotator; expounder. 2 One who discusses current events, especially over the radio at regular periods. 3 An actor who serves as a link between audience and players by appropriate commentaries on the action of the play. [<L, author, contriver < *commentari*. See COMMENTARY.]

com·merce (kom'ərs) *n.* 1 Exchange of goods, products, or property, as between states or nations; extended trade. 2 Familiar or social intercourse. 3 A card game in which the hands are varied by exchanging cards. 4 Sexual intercourse. See synonyms under BUSINESS, INTERCOURSE. — **Department of Commerce** An executive department of the U.S. government established in 1913 (from 1903 to 1913 part of the Department of Commerce and Labor), headed by the Secretary of Commerce, which fosters, promotes, and develops foreign and domestic commerce, the mining, manufacturing, shipping, and fishing industries, and transportation facilities. — *v.i.* (kə·mûrs') **·merced**, **·merc·ing** To have intercourse; associate; commune. [<F <L *commercium* < com- together + *merx, mercis* wares] — **com·merc'er** *n.*

com·mer·cial (kə·mûr'shəl) *adj.* 1 Of or belonging to trade or commerce; mercantile. 2 Made or put up for the market: *commercial* sulfur. 3 Having financial gain as an object: a *commercial* novel. — *n.* In radio and television, an advertisement. — **com·mer′cial·ly** *adv.*

com·mer·cial·ism (kə·mûr′shəl·iz′əm) *n.* The spirit, methods, or principles of trade; the domination of life by such practices or aims. — **com·mer′cial·ist** *n.* — **com·mer′cial·is′tic** *adj.*

com·mer·cial·ize (kə·mûr′shəl·īz) *v.t.* **·ized, ·iz·ing** To make a matter of trade; put on a commercial basis. — **com·mer′cial·i·za′tion** *n.*

commercial paper Mercantile paper.

commercial traveler A traveling salesman.

com·merge (kə·mûrj′) *v.t. & v.i.* **·merged, ·merg·ing** To merge together; commingle.

com·mi·na·tion (kom′ə·nā′shən) *n.* A denunciation or threatening. [<L *comminatio, -onis* <*comminari* <*com-* thoroughly + *minari* threaten]

com·min·a·to·ry (kə·min′ə·tôr′ē, -tō′rē, kom′·in·ə-) *adj.* Threatening punishment or vengeance.

com·min·gle (kə·ming′gəl) *v.t. & v.i.* **·gled, ·gling** To mix together; mingle. See synonyms under MIX.

com·mi·nute (kom′ə·nōōt, -nyōōt) *v.t.* **·nut·ed, ·nut·ing** To reduce to minute particles; pulverize; triturate. [<L *comminutus,* pp. of *comminuere* <*com-* thoroughly + *minuere* lessen]

com·mi·nu·tion (kom′ə·nōō′shən, -nyōō′-) *n.* **1** Trituration; pulverization; diminution by a gradual wearing or reduction, as by slicing, rasping, etc. **2** *Surg.* A fracture in which the bones are badly crushed or splintered.

com·mis·er·a·ble (kə·miz′ər·ə·bəl) *adj.* Worthy of commiseration; pitiable.

com·mis·er·ate (kə·miz′ə·rāt) *v.* **·at·ed, ·at·ing** *v.t.* To feel or manifest pity for; sympathize. — *v.i.* To condole: with *with.* [<L *commiseratus,* pp. of *commiserari* <*com-* with + *miserari* feel pity] — **com·mis′er·a′tive** *adj.*

com·mis·er·a·tion (kə·miz′ə·rā′shən) *n.* **1** The act of commiserating. **2** A feeling or expression of sympathy, pity, sorrow, or regret; compassion. See synonyms under PITY.

com·mis·sar·y (kom′ə·ser′ē) *n.* *pl.* **·sar·ies 1** A commissioner. **2** An army officer in charge of subsistence, etc. **3** A church officer appointed by a bishop to exercise spiritual jurisdiction or hold an ecclesiastical court in distant parts of a diocese. **4** A store selling food and general provisions, as at a lumber camp. **5** An administrative division or territory, especially one in Colombia. **6** A wagon carrying food and provisions. — *adj.* Pertaining to, of, housing, or from a commissary. [<Med. L *commissarius.* See COMMISSAR.]

com·mis·sion (kə·mish′ən) *n.* **1** The act of committing, doing, or perpetrating; positive doing: contrasted with *omission.* **2** The act of entrusting; the matter entrusted; a trust; charge. **3** A certificate which confers a particular authority; specifically, a document issued by the president of the United States conferring rank and authority as an officer in the armed forces. **4** The rank or authority so conferred. **5** A body of persons acting under public authority. **6** The transaction of business for another under his authority; agency; also, an item of business so transacted. **7** The compensation of an agent. **—to put in (or into) commission 1** To put in direct command of a designated officer, as a ship of war, for active service. **2** *Brit.* To entrust temporarily to a commission, as the great seal or the functions of a high office. **—to put out of commission 1** To render unfit for use; to best or defeat thoroughly. **2** To retire the officers and crew of a naval vessel from active service, either permanently or temporarily. — *v.t.* **1** To give rank or authority to, as an officer. **2** To put into active service, as a ship of war. **3** To appoint; empower; delegate. [<OF <L *commissio, -onis* <*committere* COMMIT] — **com·mis′sion·al, com·mis·sion·ar·y** (kə·mish′ən·er′ē) *adj.*

com·mis·sion·er (kə·mish′ən·ər) *n.* **1** A person who holds a commission to perform certain acts. **2** A member of a commission. **3** A public official appointed as head of an executive department, usually on a state or municipal level. — **com·mis′sion·er·ship′** *n.*

commission plan A form of municipal government in which legislative, executive, and administrative powers are in a small elected commission or council, each municipal department being in charge of one commissioner: often called *Galveston plan.*

com·mis·sure (kom′ə·shōōr) *n.* **1** The point of union of two bodies, parts, or organs, as at the angle of the lips, etc. **2** A junction; seam; closure. **3** *Anat.* A tract or band of nerve fibers uniting corresponding right and left parts of the brain and spinal column. **4** *Bot.* The face or edge by which two carpels adhere. [<F <L *commissura* a joining <*committere* COMMIT] — **com·mis·su·ral** (kə·mish′yə·rəl, kom′·ə·sōōr′əl) *adj.*

com·mit (kə·mit′) *v.t.* **·mit·ted, ·mit·ting 1** To do; perpetrate. **2** To place in a trust or custody; consign; entrust; especially, to consign to an institution or prison. **3** To consign to any person, place, or use. **4** To devote; pledge; hence, to involve, compromise, or bind (oneself). **5** To consign for future reference, preservation, or disposal: to *commit* a speech to memory or to writing; *Commit* these bones to the earth. **6** To refer, as to a committee for consideration or report: a parliamentary term. [<L *committere* join, entrust <*com-* together + *mittere* send]

Synonyms: assign, confide, consign, entrust, relegate, trust. *Commit* is to give in charge, put into care or keeping; to *confide* or *entrust* is to *commit* especially to one's fidelity, *confide* being used chiefly of mental or spiritual, *entrust* also of material things; we *assign* a duty, *confide* a secret, *entrust* a treasure; we *commit* thoughts to writing; *commit* a paper to the flames. *Consign* is a formal word in mercantile use; as, to *consign* goods to an agent. See LEARN, TRUST. *Antonyms:* get, obtain, receive, secure, take.

com·mit·ment (kə·mit′mənt) *n.* **1** The act or process of entrusting or consigning for safekeeping. **2** An act of engagement or pledging. **3** The act of doing; perpetration. **4** *Law* A warrant (*mittimus*) for imprisonment; also, the state of being committed or act of committing to prison. **5** The act of referring a bill to a legislative body. **6** Liability incurred through buying or selling stocks, bonds, etc., or by agreeing to buy or sell. Also **com·mit′tal.**

com·mit·tee (kə·mit′ē) *n.* **1** A person or persons appointed by a larger number to act upon some matter. **2** One or more members of a legislative body appointed to investigate and report on a matter under discussion. **3** *Law* A person or persons appointed by a court to care for the person or property of another.

committee of the whole A committee consisting of all the members, as of a legislative body, sitting in deliberation on a given matter, but without legislative action, presided over by some member not the regular presiding officer.

com·mix·ture (kə·miks′chər) *n.* **1** A mixture. **2** The act or process of mixing. **3** The state of being mingled.

com·mode (kə·mōd′) *n.* **1** A low chest of drawers; a cabinet. **2** A covered washstand. **3** A low chair or cabinet enclosing a chamber pot; a nightchair. **4** A woman's high headdress, worn about 1700. [<F]

COMMODE *(def.* 4)

com·mo·di·ous (kə·mō′dē·əs) *adj* Well adapted to serve the purpose for supplying needs; especially, affording ample accommodation; convenient; spacious. See synonyms under COMFORTABLE, CONVENIENT, LARGE. [<Med. L *commodiosus* <L *commodus* convenient] — **com·mo′di·ous·ly** *adv.* — **com·mo′di·ous·ness** *n.*

com·mod·i·ty (kə·mod′ə·tē) *n.* *pl.* **·ties 1** A movable article of trade or convenience; an element of economic wealth. **2** Something bought and sold. **3** *Obs.* Convenience; suitability; conveniency; profit. [<MF *commodité* <L *commoditas, -tatis* convenience]

commodity money The currency of a suggested financial system, the unit of which, the **commodity dollar,** has a gold value determined at regular intervals by an index number based on the market prices of certain commodities.

com·mo·dore (kom′ə·dôr, -dōr) *n.* **1** In the U.S. Navy, an officer next above a captain and next below a rear admiral: a rank no longer in use since World War II. **2** In the British Navy, the commander of a squadron or division of a fleet, often having the temporary rank and pay of a rear admiral. **3** A title given to the senior captain of a naval squadron or of a fleet of merchantmen; also to the presiding officer of a yacht club. [Earlier *commandore*? <Du. *kommandeur*]

com·mon (kom′ən) *adj.* **1** Often occurring, met, or seen; frequent or usual; not distinguished or separated from the ordinary; customary; regular: a *common* occurrence. **2** Pertaining to, connected with, or participated in by two or more persons or things; joint. **3** Belonging to the public: the *common* schools. **4** The most prevalent or familiar: the *common* crow. **5** Commonplace; not excellent or distinguished in tone or quality; banal; coarse; vulgar; low. **6** *Gram.* **a** Of either gender. **b** Applicable to any individual of a class. See COMMON NOUN under NOUN. **7** Secular; profane; polluted. **8** In prosody, either long or short; doubtful in quantity. **9** Public or general; widespread: *common* knowledge. **10** *Anat.* Formed by or having similar relations with two or more organs: the *common* carotid artery. **11** *Math.* Referring to a number or quantity belonging equally to two or more quantities: a *common* denominator. — *n.* **1** Land generally, or a tract of land, considered as the property of the public, in which all persons enjoy equal rights; also, land owned by a town; land open to the use of all. **2** *Law* A profit or right of one person in the land of another: used in some specific phrases: **common of estovers** (wood necessary for the house or farm), **common of pasture, common of piscary** (fishing), **common of turbary** (cutting turf). **3** *Eccl. Sometimes cap.* The office composed of psalms, antiphons, lessons, etc., which can be used for any of certain classes of feasts: the *common* of virgins. [<OF *comun* <L *communis* common]

Synonyms (adj.): cheap, coarse, commonplace, customary, familiar, frequent, general, habitual, low, mean, normal, ordinary, popular, public, threadbare, trite, universal, usual, vile, vulgar. See FREQUENT, GENERAL, HABITUAL, MUTUAL, NORMAL, TRITE, USUAL. *Antonyms:* exceptional, infrequent, odd, peculiar, rare, singular, unusual.

com·mon·al·ty (kom′ən·əl·tē) *n.* *pl.* **·ties 1** The common people; the lower classes as opposed to persons of title or rank; the commons. **2** A body corporate; corporation: the mayor, *commonalty,* and citizens of London.

common carrier An individual or company which, for a fee, provides public transport.

com·mon·er (kom′ən·ər) *n.* **1** One of the commonalty; any subject not a peer. **2** In certain English universities, a student not dependent on the university foundation. **3** One who has a joint right in common ground. **4** Formerly, a member of the House of Commons.

com·mon–law marriage (kom′ən·lô′) A marriage, or an agreement of marriage, substantiated by writings or conduct, instead of by church or civil ceremony.

common measure 1 In prosody, a four-line stanza in which iambic lines of four stresses and three stresses alternate, usually rhyming the first with the third and the second with the fourth lines: also called *hymnal stanza.* **2** *Music* Common time.

com·mon·place (kom′ən·plās′) *adj.* Not remarkable or interesting; ordinary; trite. See synonyms under COMMON, GENERAL, TRITE. — *n.* **1** A trite remark; familiar truth; platitude; truism. **2** A note jotted down for reference; a memorandum. **3** Formerly, a book containing a methodical collection of notes, passages, etc.: also called **commonplace book 4** Commonplace quality; ordinariness. [Trans. of L *locus communis* <Gk. *koinos topos* a general theme or argument]

com·mons (kom'ənz) *n. pl.* **1** The common people; commonalty. **2** A company eating at a common table, as in a college; the provisions so furnished; hence, allowance of food; rations; fare. **3** The dining hall in a college.

common sense 1 Practical understanding; capacity to see and take things in their right light; sound judgment. **2** Ordinary mental capacity. —**com'mon-sense'** *adj.*

com·mon·wealth (kom'ən-welth') *n.* **1** The people of a state; the state. **2** A state in which the people rule; a republic; the official title of four States of the United States: the *Commonwealth* of Kentucky, of Massachusetts, of Pennsylvania, and of Virginia; also, the official title of Puerto Rico. **3** A body of persons united by some common interest and viewed as equals in authority. See synonyms under PEOPLE.

Commonwealth of England The republic established in England after the execution of Charles I in 1649 and continued till 1653, when Cromwell assumed the protectorate.

com·mo·tion (kə-mō'shən) *n.* **1** A violent agitation; excitement. **2** Popular tumult; social disorder; riot. See synonyms under TUMULT. [<L *commotio, -onis* <*commovere* <*com-* thoroughly + *movere* move]

com·mu·nal·ism (kom'yə-nal-iz'əm, kə-myoo'nəl-) *n.* **1** In France, the theory that each commune should be self-governing and the state a mere federation of communes; hence, local self-government. **2** Communal ownership of goods and property. —**com'mu·nal·ist** *n.* —**com'mu·nal·is'tic** *adj.*

com·mune[1] (kə-myoon') *v.i.* **·muned, ·mun·ing** **1** To converse or confer intimately. **2** To partake of the Eucharist. —*n.* (kom'yoon) Intimate intercourse; communion. [<OF *comuner* share <*comun* COMMON]

com·mune[2] (kom'yoon) *n.* **1** A political division of France, governed by a mayor and a council; the people and the government of such a district; also, a similar division elsewhere, as in Italy and Spain. **2** A self-governing community; also, the people of such a community. **3** The commonalty. [<F <L *communis* common]

com·mu·ni·ca·ble (kə-myoo'nə-kə-bəl) *adj.* **1** Capable of being communicated or imparted. **2** *Obs.* Ready to communicate; communicative. —**com·mu'ni·ca·bil'i·ty, com·mu'ni·ca·ble·ness** *n.* —**com·mu'ni·ca·bly** *adv.*

com·mu·ni·cant (kə-myoo'nə-kənt) *n.* **1** One who communicates or imparts, as information. **2** One who partakes or has a right to partake of the Lord's Supper. —*adj.* Communicating. [<L *communicans, -antis,* ppr. of *communicare.* See COMMUNICATE.]

com·mu·ni·cate (kə-myoo'nə-kāt) *v.* **·cat·ed, ·cat·ing** *v.t.* **1** To make another or others partakers of; impart; transmit, as news, a disease, or an idea. **2** To administer the communion to. —*v.i.* **3** To make or hold communication. **4** To be connected, as rooms. **5** To partake of communion. See synonyms under ANNOUNCE, GIVE, INFORM, PUBLISH. [<L *communicatus,* pp. of *communicare* share <*communis* common] —**com·mu'ni·ca'tor** *n.*

com·mu·ni·ca·tion (kə-myoo'nə-kā'shən) *n.* **1** The act of communicating; intercourse; exchange of ideas, conveyance of information, etc.; correspondence. **2** That which is communicated; a letter or message. **3** Means of communicating, as a highway or passage; also, a telephone, telegraph, or radio system, etc. **4** Eucharistic communion. See synonyms under CONVERSATION, INTERCOURSE.

communication theory Information theory.

com·mu·ni·ca·tive (kə-myoo'nə-kā'tiv, -kə-tiv) *adj.* **1** Ready to communicate; frank; talkative. **2** Of or pertaining to communication.

com·mun·ion (kə-myoon'yən) *n.* **1** The act of communing or sharing. **2** Sympathetic intercourse; fellowship. **3** The religious fellowship existing between man and God, between Christians, between a Christian and the church, or between autonomous churches. **4** A body or denomination of Christians having a common faith and discipline. **5** *Usually cap.* The Eucharist, or the act of celebrating

or partaking of it: often called *Holy Communion.* **6** An antiphon said or chanted after the distribution of the Sacrament. See synonyms under CONVERSATION, INTERCOURSE, SACRAMENT, SECT. [<OF<L *communio, -onis* <*communis* common]

com·mun·ion·ist (kə-myoon'yən-ist) *n.* **1** One who has a theory as to the conditions on which a person should be admitted to church communion. **2** A member of a communion. **3** A communicant.

com·mu·ni·qué (kə-myoo'nə-kā') *n.* An official message, announcement, etc. [<F]

com·mu·nism (kom'yə-niz'əm) *n.* **1** A social system in which there is community of goods. **2** A theory of social change conceived by Karl Marx, directed to the ideal of a classless society. As developed by Lenin and others, it advocates seizure of power by a conspiratorial political party, maintenance of power during an interim period by stern suppression of internal opposition, centralized public ownership of almost all productive property and the sharing of the products of labor, and mmitment to the ultimate goal of a worldwide communist state. **3** Any social theory that calls for the abolition of private property and control by the community over economic affairs. **4** *Often cap.* **a** The system in force in any state based on this theory. **b** The doctrines and practices of the Communist party of any state; specifically, of the Communist party of the U.S.S.R. —**com'mu·nist** *n.*

com·mu·nis·tic (kom'yə-nis'tik) *adj.* **1** Pertaining to or like communism. **2** Tending to, favoring, or in accordance with communism. **3** Shared in common. **4** Occupying the same nest in common, as in certain birds. Also **com'mu·nis'ti·cal.** —**com'mu·nis'ti·cal·ly** *adv.*

com·mu·ni·ty (kə-myoo'nə-tē) *n. pl.* **·ties 1** The people who reside in one locality and are subject to the same laws, have the same interests, etc. **2** A body politic. **3** The public; society at large. **4** A group of plants or animals living in a common dwelling under common conditions; also, the region in which they live. **5** A sharing or participation. **6** Identity or likeness: *community* of interest. **7** Common ownership, possession, or enjoyment of property. See synonyms under ASSOCIATION, PEOPLE. [<L *communitas, -tatis* fellowship <*communis* common]

community antenna television A television reception service in which a signal received at a master antenna is distributed to subscribers by cable. Abbr. *CATV*

community chest A general fund for charity and public welfare to which individual contributions are made, and which is drawn upon by different organizations.

community church *U.S.* A non-denominational or interdenominational church for the use of a whole community.

com·mu·nize (kom'yə-niz) *v.t.* **·nized, ·niz·ing 1** To make common; make public property. **2** To make or cause to become communistic.

com·mu·tate (kom'yə-tāt) *v.t.* **·tat·ed, ·tat·ing** *Electr.* To alter or reverse the direction of (a current).

com·mu·ta·tion (kom'yə-tā'shən) *n.* **1** A substitution of one kind of payment or service for another; also, the payment or service substituted. **2** *Law* A reduction or change of penalty. **3** *Electr.* The action of a commutator. **4** Daily or periodic travel on a commutation ticket. [<L *commutatio, -onis* <*commutare* change, alter <*com-* thoroughly + *mutare* change]

com·mu·ta·tive (kə-myoo'tə-tiv, kom'yə-tā'tiv) *adj.* Of or characterized by commutation.

com·mu·ta·tor (kom'yə-tā'tər) *n. Electr.* **1** Any contrivance for reversing the direction of the current in an electric circuit. **2** An assembly of individually insulated segments connected with the armature of a dynamo or generator and serving to collect and transmit the induced current.

com·mute (kə-myoot') *v.* **·mut·ed, ·mut·ing** *v.t.* **1** To exchange reciprocally for something else. **2** To exchange for something less severe: to *commute* a sentence, debt, or payment. **3** To pay in gross at a reduced rate, as an annuity or railroad fare, instead of in successive payments. **4** *Electr.* To commutate. —*v.i.* **5** *Archaic* To serve as or be a substitute. **6** To pay a railroad fare, etc., in gross

at a reduced rate. **7** To use a commutation ticket; specifically, to make daily or regular trips to and from work. See synonyms under CHANGE. —*n.* *U.S. Colloq.* A commuter's trip, or its duration or distance: a two-hour *commute.* [<L *commutare.* See COMMUTATION.] —**com·mut'a·ble** *adj.* —**com·mut'a·ble·ness, com·mut·a·bil'i·ty** *n.*

com·mut·er (kə-myoo'tər) *n.* One whose home and place of work are in different communities and who regularly travels between them, as a suburbanite who works in the city.

com·mu·tu·al (kə-myoo'choo·əl) *adj.* Reciprocal; mutual.

co·mose (kō'mōs) *adj. Bot.* Having hairs; hairy; tufted; comate. Also **co·mous** (kō'məs). [<L *comosus* <*coma* hair]

com·pact[1] (kəm·pakt', kom'pakt) *adj.* **1** Closely and firmly united; pressed together; solid; dense; also, fine-grained. **2** Condensed; brief; terse. **3** Packed into a small space. **4** Compound; made up: with *of.* See synonyms under FIRM, HARD, STRONG, TERSE. —*v.t.* (kəm·pakt') To pack or press closely; compress; unite closely; condense. —*n.* (kom'pakt) A small, hinged box for face powder and sometimes rouge, carried in a woman's purse. [<L *compactus,* pp. of *compangere* <*com-* together + *pangere* fasten]

com·pact[2] (kom'pakt) *n.* A covenant, agreement, or contract. See synonyms under ALLIANCE, CONTRACT. [<L *compactum* <*compacisci* <*com-* together + *pacisci* agree]

compact disc A small digital disc on which sound has been recorded, to be replayed on an electronic device utilizing a beam of laser light that reads and reproduces the original sound with a very high level of quality.

com·pan·ion[1] (kəm·pan'yən) *n.* **1** One who or that which accompanies; a comrade; associate. **2** A person, usually a woman, employed for company and assistance not of a menial nature. **3** A mate; one of a pair. See synonyms under ACCESSORY, ASSOCIATE. —*v.t.* To be a companion to; accompany; associate with. [<OF *compagnon* <LL *companio, -onis* <L *com-* together + *panis* bread]

com·pan·ion[2] (kəm·pan'yən) *n. Naut.* A companionway; also, the wooden hood over a companionway. [<Du. *kampanje* quarter-deck]

com·pan·ion·ate (kəm·pan'yən·it) *adj.* Of or pertaining to companionship or association; hence, agreed upon; shared.

companionate marriage A proposed form of marriage in which a couple agree not to have children until they are sure they wish to stay married, and which permits divorce by mutual consent.

com·pan·ion·ship (kəm·pan'yən·ship) *n.* The state of being a companion; fellowship; association. See synonyms under ACQUAINTANCE, ASSOCIATION.

com·pa·ny (kum'pə·nē) *n. pl.* **·nies 1** The society or presence of another or others; fellowship; association. **2** One or more guests or visitors; persons met for social purposes; society. **3** An assemblage or corporation. **4** A partner or partners not named. **5** A number of persons forming a corporation, guild, or partnership, or associated for some common purpose. **6** The person or persons with whom one has companionship: keeping bad *company.* **7** *Mil.* A body of men commanded by a captain, larger than a platoon and smaller than a battalion: the basic military unit, equivalent to a battery or troop. **8** *Naut.* The whole crew of a ship: a ship's *company.* **9** The entire body of actors and actresses in a play or a theater; cast; a troupe. **10** *Obs.* Friendship —**to keep company (with)** To be sweethearts (with); court. —**to part company (with)** To end friendship or association (with). —*v.t. & v.i.* **·nied, ·ny·ing** *Archaic* To keep or be in company (with); accompany; associate (with). [OF *compagnie* <*compagnon* COMPANION]

Synonyms (noun): assemblage, assembly, body, collection, conclave, concourse, conference, congregation, convention, convocation, crowd, gathering, group, host, meeting, multitude, throng. *Company* is used to include any association of those united permanently or temporarily, for business, pleasure, festivity, travel, etc., or by sorrow, misfortune, or wrong; *company* implies more unity of feeling and purpose than *crowd*, and is a less formal and more familiar word than *assemblage* or *assembly*. An *assemblage* may be of persons or of objects; an *assembly* is usually of persons. *Collection*, *crowd*, *gathering*, *group*, and *multitude* have the unorganized and promiscuous character of the *assemblage*; the other terms come under the general idea of *assembly*. *Body* is used of a number of persons so organized and unified that they can be thought of as one whole. *Congregation* is now almost exclusively religious. *Gathering* refers to a coming together, commonly of numbers from far and near; as, the *gathering* of the Scottish clans. See ASSEMBLY, ASSOCIATION, CLASS, FLOCK. *Antonyms:* dispersion, loneliness, privacy, retirement, seclusion, solitude.

company union A union of workers formed within an industrial establishment, having no affiliation with any other recognized trade union, and usually considered to be dominated by the employer of its members.

com·pa·ra·ble (kom′pər·ə·bəl) *adj.* 1 Capable of comparison. 2 Worthy of comparison.

com·par·a·tive (kəm·par′ə·tiv) *adj.* 1 Pertaining to, resulting from or using comparison. 2 Estimated by comparison; relative. 3 Almost but not quite. 4 *Gram.* Expressing a degree of an adjective or adverb higher than the positive and lower than the superlative. —*n.* *Gram.* The comparative degree, or a word or form by which it is expressed: "Better" is the *comparative* of "good." *Abbr.* *comp.* [< L *comparativus* < *comparare* COMPARE] —**com·par′a·tive·ly** *adv.*

com·pare (kəm·pâr′) *v.* **·pared, ·par·ing** *v.t.* 1 To represent or speak of as similar, analogous, or equal: with *to*. 2 To examine so as to perceive similarity or dissimilarity; state the resemblance or difference of: with *with*. 3 *Gram.* To state the degrees of comparison of (an adjective or adverb). —*v.i.* 4 To be worthy of comparison: with *with*. 5 To vie or compete. —*n.* *Archaic* or *Poetic* Comparison: usually in the phrase *beyond compare*. [< F *comparer* < L *comparare* < *com-* together + *par* equal]
   Synonyms (*verb*): assimilate, collate, liken, parallel. See CONTRAST. To compare one thing *to* another is to liken or suggest as being similar; to compare one thing *with* another is to make a detailed analysis of points of similarity or difference.

com·par·i·son (kəm·par′ə·sən) *n.* 1 A comparing; an estimate or statement of relative likeness or unlikeness. 2 *Gram.* That inflection of adjectives or adverbs which indicates differences of degree. There are three **degrees of comparison**, the positive, comparative, and superlative, the last two being regularly expressed by adding -*er* or -*est* to the positive (except in words of three syllables or more), or by using *more* or *most*, *less* or *least*, before it. 3 That which in its relation to something else serves as an illustration or example; a parallel: an act without *comparison*. 4 Any rhetorical figure that sets forth the points of similarity or contrast between one person or thing and another, such as a simile or metaphor. See synonyms under ANALOGY, SIMILE. [< OF *comparaison* < L *comparatio*, *-onis* < *comparare* COMPARE]

com·part (kəm·pärt′) *v.t.* To divide into compartments; partition. [< OF *compartir* < L *compartiri* < *com-* together + *pars*, *partis* part]

com·part·ment (kəm·pärt′mənt) *n.* 1 One of the parts into which an enclosed space is subdivided by lines or partitions. 2 Any separate section or chamber: watertight *compartments*. 3 In railway passenger cars, a small, private division with sleeping accommodations. [< F *compartiment* < Ital. *compartimento* < L *compartiri*. See COMPART.]

com·part·men·tal·ize (kom′pärt·men′təl·īz) *v.t.* **·ized, ·iz·ing** To divide into compartments.

com·pass (kum′pəs, kom′-) *n.* 1 Extent within limits; area; reach; scope. 2 A boundary, circumference, or circuit. 3 The range of a voice or instrument. 4 An instrument for determining directions by the pointing to magnetic north of a magnetic needle free to turn in a horizontal plane, and carrying a marked card, as in the **mariner's compass**. 5 A radio compass. Compare illustrations under BINNACLE, CLINOME-

TER. 6 *Obs.* A circular course or journey; round; circuit. 7 Compasses. —*v.t.* 1 To go around; make a circuit of. 2 To surround; encompass. 3 To grasp mentally; comprehend. 4 To plot or scheme. 5 To attain or accomplish; achieve. 6 *Obs.* To cause to curve; bend into circular form. [< OF *compas*, ult. < L *com-* together + *passus* step] —**com′pass·a·ble** *adj.*

compass card The circular card or dial resting on the pivot of a mariner's compass, on which the 32 points and 360 degrees of the circle are marked. Also **compass dial**.

com·pass·es (kum′pəs·iz, kom′-) *n. pl.* An instrument having two branches or legs, usually pointed, and hinged at the top by a pivoted joint, used for taking or marking measurements, describing circles, etc. Also **pair of compasses**.

compass heading *Aeron.* A specified flight course which the pilot follows by compass indications.

com·pas·sion (kəm·pash′ən) *n.* Pity for suffering, with desire to help or to spare; commiseration; sympathy. See synonyms under MERCY, PITY. [< MF < LL *compassio*, *-onis* < L *com-* together + *pati* feel, suffer]

com·pas·sion·ate (kəm·pash′ən·it) *adj.* 1 Feeling compassion or pity; merciful; sympathetic. 2 *Obs.* Pitiable; piteous. See synonyms under CHARITABLE, HUMANE, MERCIFUL. —*v.t.* (kəm·pash′ən·āt) **·at·ed, ·at·ing** To have compassion for; to pity. —**com·pas′sion·ate·ly** *adv.* —**com·pas′sion·ate·ness** *n.*

compass plant 1 A tall, rough, bristly herb (*Silphium laciniatum*) of North American prairies, belonging to the composite family and having large leaves lying in a vertical position with their edges turned north and south. 2 The prickly lettuce (*Lactuca serriola*).

com·pat·i·ble (kəm·pat′ə·bəl) *adj.* 1 Capable of existing together; congruous; congenial. 2 Describing a television set adapted to produce images in color or in black and white. [< F < Med. L *compatibilis* < L *com-* together + *pati* suffer] —**com·pat·i·bil′i·ty**, **com·pat′·i·ble·ness** *n.* —**com·pat′i·bly** *adv.*

com·pa·tri·ot (kəm·pā′trē·ət, -pat′rē·ət) *n.* 1 A fellow countryman. 2 *Colloq.* A colleague. —*adj.* Having the same country. [< F *compatriote* < LL *compatriota* < L *com-* together + *patria* native land] —**com·pa′tri·ot·ism** *n.*

com·pel (kəm·pel′) *v.t.* **·pelled, ·pel·ling** 1 To drive or urge irresistibly; constrain. 2 To force to yield; subdue. 3 To obtain by force; exact. 4 *Obs.* To seize; overpower; extort. 5 To drive together; gather in a company; herd; drive. [< L *compellere* < *com-* together + *pellere* drive] —**com·pel′la·ble** *adj.* —**com·pel′la·bly** *adv.* —**com·pel′ler** *n.*
   Synonyms: coerce, constrain, drive, force, make, necessitate, oblige. See ACTUATE, BIND, MAKE. Compare DRIVE, INFLUENCE. *Antonyms:* see synonyms under HINDER.

com·pel·la·tion (kom′pə·lā′shən) *n.* 1 Form of address; appellation. 2 The act of addressing or accosting; an address. [< L *compellatio*, *-onis* < *compellare* accost]

com·pen·di·ous (kəm·pen′dē·əs) *adj.* Briefly stated; succinct; concise; containing the substance in narrow compass. See synonyms under TERSE. [< L *compendiosus* brief < *compendium* COMPENDIUM] —**com·pen′di·ous·ly** *adv.* —**com·pen′di·ous·ness** *n.*

com·pen·di·um (kəm·pen′dē·əm) *n. pl.* **·di·ums** or **·di·a** (-dē·ə) An abridgment; abstract; a brief, comprehensive summary. See synonyms under ABBREVIATION, ABRIDGMENT. [< L < *compendere* < *com-* together + *pendere* weigh]

com·pen·sate (kom′pən·sāt) *v.* **·sat·ed, ·sat·ing** *v.t.* 1 To make suitable amends to or for; requite; remunerate. 2 To counterbalance or make up for; offset. 3 To stabilize the purchasing power of (a monetary unit) by varying gold content to counteract price fluctuations. 4 *Mech.* To provide with a counterbalancing or neutralizing device, as for a variation. —*v.i.* 5 To make returns or amends; serve as an equivalent or substitute. See synonyms under PAY, REQUITE. [< L *compensatus*, pp. of *compensare* < *com-* together + *pensare*, freq. of *pendere* weigh] —**com·pen·sa·tive**

(kəm·pen′sə·tiv), **com·pen·sa·to·ry** (kəm·pen′sə·tôr′ē, -tō′rē) *adj.*

com·pen·sa·tion (kom′pən·sā′shən) *n.* 1 The act of compensating, or that which compensates; payment; amends. 2 *Mech.* A means of counteracting variations, as of temperature; neutralizing opposing forces, as of magnetic attraction; or maintaining equilibrium. 3 *Psychol.* A form of behavior whereby an individual disguises or conceals an unpleasant sensation, feeling, or trait by giving prominence to one having desirable results. 4 *Biol.* The correction, by biological processes or medical means, of serious defects in the structure and functions of an organism or a human body. —**workmen's compensation** 1 Damages recoverable from an employer by an employee in case of accident. 2 Government insurance against illness, accident, or unemployment. —**com′pen·sa′tion·al** *adj.*

com·pen·sa·tor (kom′pən·sā′tər) *n.* 1 One who or that which compensates. 2 A device for neutralizing the influence of local attraction upon a compass needle. 3 An automatic apparatus for equalizing the pressure of gas in retorts or mains.

com·pete (kəm·pēt′) *v.i.* **·pet·ed, ·pet·ing** To contend with another or others for a prize; engage in a contest or competition; vie. See synonyms under CONTEND. [< L *competere* strive < *com-* together + *petere* seek]

com·pe·tence (kom′pə·təns) *n.* 1 The state of being competent; ability. 2 Sufficient means for comfortable living; a moderate income. 3 *Law* Qualification or admissibility; legal capacity, authority, or jurisdiction: the *competence* of a tribunal. Also **com′pe·ten·cy.** See synonyms under ABILITY.

com·pe·tent (kom′pə·tənt) *adj.* 1 Having sufficient ability or authority. 2 Possessing the requisite natural or legal qualifications; qualified. 3 Sufficient; adequate. [< MF *competent* < L *competens*, *-entis*, ppr. of *competere* be fit, be proper < *com-* together + *petere* go, seek] —**com′pe·tent·ly** *adv.* —**com′pe·tent·ness** *n.*
   Synonyms: able, adapted, adequate, capable, fit, qualified. One is *competent* who has all the natural powers, physical or mental, to meet the demands of a situation or work; the word is widely used of ability to meet all requirements, natural, legal, or other; as, a *competent* knowledge of a subject; a court of *competent* jurisdiction. *Qualified* refers to acquired abilities; a *qualified* teacher may be no longer *competent*, by reason of ill health. *Able* and *capable* suggest general ability and reserved power, *able* being the higher word of the two. An *able* man will do something well in any position. A *capable* man will come up to any ordinary demand. Compare ADEQUATE, GOOD. *Antonyms:* disqualified, inadequate, incompetent, unequal, unfit, unqualified.

com·pe·ti·tion (kom′pə·tish′ən) *n.* 1 Contention of two or more for the same object or for superiority; rivalry. 2 The independent endeavor of two or more persons to obtain the business patronage of a third by offering more advantageous terms; also, the conditions which this endeavor produces.
   Synonyms: contest, emulation, opposition, rivalry. *Competition* is the striving for something that is sought by another at the same time. *Emulation* regards the abstract, *competition* the concrete; *rivalry* is the same in essential meaning with *competition*, but differs in the nature of the objects contested for. We speak of *competition* in business, *emulation* in scholarship, *rivalry* in love, politics, etc. *Competition* may be friendly, *rivalry* is commonly hostile. Compare AMBITION, EMULATION. *Antonyms:* agreement, association, alliance, combination, confederacy, harmony, monopoly, union. In business and commercial use, the chief antonym of *competition* is *monopoly*, which by bringing all engaged in an industry under a single control forbids them to compete. [< L *competitio*, *-onis* < *competere* COMPETE]

com·pet·i·tive (kəm·pet′ə·tiv) *adj.* Pertaining to or characterized by competition. —**com·pet′·i·tive·ly** *adv.* —**com·pet′i·tive·ness** *n.*

com·pet·i·tor (kəm·pet′ə·tər) *n.* 1 One who or that which competes; especially, one striving for the same thing as another, in business, athletics, etc. **2** *Obs.* An associate; confederate. See synonyms under ENEMY. **—com·pet′i·tor·ship** *n.* **—com·pet·i·to·ry** (kəm·pet′ə·tôr′ē, -tō′rē) *adj.*

com·pi·la·tion (kom′pə·lā′shən) *n.* **1** The act or process of collecting materials for making a book, statistical table, etc. **2** That which is compiled, as a book made up of material gathered from other books: *compilations* of verse. [< F < L *compilatio, -onis* < *compilare.* See COMPILE.]

com·pile (kəm·pīl′) *v.t.* **·piled, ·pil·ing 1** To compose (a literary work, etc.) from other works. **2** To gather (materials borrowed or transcribed) into a volume or into orderly form. [< L *compilare* < *com-* thoroughly + *pilare* strip, plunder; prob. infl. in meaning by PILE] **—com·pi·la·to·ry** (kəm·pī′lə·tôr′ē, -tō′rē) *adj.* **—com·pil′er** *n.*

com·pla·cen·cy (kəm·plā′sən·sē) *n. pl.* **·cies 1** Satisfaction; self-approval. **2** Equanimity. Also **com·pla′cence.** See synonyms under SATISFACTION.

com·plain (kəm·plān′) *v.i.* **1** To express a sense of ill-treatment or of pain, grief, etc.; murmur; find fault; present a grievance. **2** To make a formal accusation; present a charge or complaint. [< F *complaindre* < LL *complangere* < *com-* thoroughly + *plangere* beat (the beast in grief)] — *Synonyms:* croak, deplore, growl, grumble, grunt, murmur, remonstrate, repine. To *complain* is to give utterance to dissatisfaction or objection, express a sense of wrong or ill-treatment. One *complains* of a real or assumed grievance; he may *murmur* through mere peevishness or ill temper; he *repines,* with vain distress, at the inevitable. *Complaining* is by speech or writing; *murmuring* is commonly said of half-repressed utterance; *repining* of the mental act alone. One may *complain* of an offense to the offender or to others; he *remonstrates* with the offender only. *Complain* has a legal meaning, which the other words have not, signifying to make a formal accusation, present a specific charge; the same is true of the noun *complaint. Antonyms:* applaud, approve, commend, eulogize, laud, praise.

com·plain·ant (kəm·plā′nənt) *n.* One who complains; especially, one who enters a formal complaint before a magistrate or other authority; a plaintiff or petitioner. [< F *complaignant* a plaintiff, orig. ppr. of *complaindre* COMPLAIN]

com·plaint (kəm·plānt′) *n.* **1** A statement of wrong, grievance, or injury. **2** *Law* The first paper setting forth the plaintiff's cause of action. **3** The act of complaining. **4** A grievance. **5** A physical ailment; disease. See synonyms under DISEASE, ILLNESS. [< F *complainte* < *complaindre* COMPLAIN]

com·plai·sant (kəm·plā′zənt, kom′plə·zant) *adj.* Showing a desire or endeavor to please; yielding; compliant. See synonyms under BLAND, FRIENDLY, POLITE. [< F, ppr. of *complaire* please < L *complacere.* Doublet of COMPLACENT.] — **com·plai′sance** *n.* **—com·plai′sant·ly** *adv.* **—com·plai′sant·ness** *n.*

com·pla·nate (kom′plə·nāt) *adj.* **1** Leveled; flattened. **2** *Bot.* Lying in the same plane, as certain leaves. [< L *complanatus,* pp. of *complanare* < *com-* together + *planare* make level] — **com′pla·na′tion** *n.*

com·ple·ment (kom′plə·mənt) *n.* **1** That which fills up or completes; that which must be added to complete a symmetrical whole. **2** Full number: The vessel has her *complement* of men. **3** An addition or appendage; an accessory. **4** *Geom.* The amount by which an angle falls short of 90 degrees. **5** *Gram.* A word or phrase used after a verb of incomplete predication to complete the meaning of the sentence. A **subjective complement** describes or identifies the subject, as the noun *president* in *He is president* or in *He was elected president* or as the adjective *happy* in *She is happy* or in *She was made happy.* An **objective complement** describes or identifies the direct object, as the noun *president* in *They elected him president* or the adjective *happy* in *It made her happy.* **6** *Music* A musical interval which, with the interval already given, will complete an octave. **7** *Immunology* A complex system of unstable, heat-sensitive proteins normally present in human and other serums where it reacts with specific antibodies to destroy related antigens.

Also called *alexin.* **—v.t.** To add or form a complement to; supplement; make complete; supply a lack in. ◆ Homophone: *compliment.* [< L *complementum* < *complere* COMPLETE] **—com·ple·men·tal** (kom′plə·men′təl) *adj.* **—com′ple·ment′er** *n.*

com·ple·men·ta·ry (kom′plə·men′tər·ē, -trē) *adj.* **1** Serving as a complement; helping to constitute a whole or to supply a lack; completing complemental. **2** Mutually providing each other's needs. **3** *Geom.* Furnishing the complement of another: see COMPLEMENTARY ANGLE under ANGLE.

complementary cell *Bot.* One of the cellular components of the lenticel in plants.

com·plete (kəm·plēt′) *adj.* **1** Having all needed or normal parts, elements, or details; lacking nothing; entire; perfect; full. **2** Thoroughly wrought; finished. See synonyms under AMPLE, IMPLICIT, RADICAL, RIPE. **—v.t. ·plet·ed, ·plet·ing** To make complete; accomplish; finish; fulfil. See synonyms under ACCOMPLISH, EFFECT, END. [< L *completus,* pp. of *complere* < *com-* thoroughly + *plere* fill] **—com·plete′ly** *adv.* **—com·plete′ness** *n.* **—com·ple′tive** *adj.*

com·ple·tion (kəm·plē′shən) *n.* **1** The act of completing, or the state of being completed. **2** Accomplishment; fulfilment. See synonyms under END.

com·plex (kəm·pleks′, kom′pleks) *adj.* **1** Consisting of various parts or elements; composite. **2** Complicated; involved; intricate. **—n.** (kom′pleks) **1** Something composite or complicated; a complication; collection. **2** *Psychoanal.* A group or cluster of interrelated and usually repressed ideas with strong emotional content which compels the individual to adopt abnormal patterns of thought and behavior. [< L *complexus,* pp. of *complectere* < *com-* together + *plectere* twist] **—com·plex′ly** *adv.* **—com·plex′ness** *n.*

Synonyms (adj.): abstruse, complicated, composite, compound, confused, conglomerate, entangled, heterogeneous, intricate, involved, manifold, mingled, mixed, multiform, tangled. That is *complex* which is made up of a number of connected parts. That is *compound* in which the parts are not merely connected, but combined into a single substance. In a *composite* object the different parts have less of unity than in that which is *complex* or *compound,* and maintain their distinct individuality. In a *heterogeneous* body, mass, or collection, unlike parts or particles are intermingled, often without apparent order or plan. *Conglomerate* (literally, globed together) is said of a *confused* mingling of masses or lumps of various substances. Things are *involved* which are rolled together so as not to be easily separated, either in thought or in fact; threads which are *tangled* or *entangled* hold and draw upon one another in a confusing and obstructive way; a knot is *intricate* when the strands are difficult to follow. An *abstruse* statement or conception is remote from the usual course of thought. *Antonyms:* clear, direct, homogeneous, obvious, plain, simple, uncombined, uncompounded, uniform, unraveled.

com·plex·ion (kəm·plek′shən) *n.* **1** The color and appearance of the skin, especially of the face. **2** General aspect; character; quality; hence, temperament; cast of mind or thought. **3** *Archaic* The combination of certain assumed qualities in a definite proportion supposed to control the nature of plants, bodies, etc.; also, the habit ascribed to such combination. [< F < L *complexio, -onis* the constitution of a body < *complectere.* See COMPLEX.] **—com·plex′ion·al** *adj.* **—com·plex′ioned** *adj.*

com·plex·i·ty (kəm·plek′sə·tē) *n. pl.* **·ties 1** The state of being complex. **2** Something complex.

com·plex·us (kəm·plek′səs) *n.* **1** A complicated system; complex. **2** *Anat.* A large muscle of the back, which passes from the spine to the head. [< L < *complectere.* See COMPLEX.]

com·pli·ance (kəm·plī′əns) *n.* **1** The act of complying, yielding, or acting in accord. **2** Complaisance. Also **com·pli′an·cy.**

com·pli·ant (kəm·plī′ənt) *adj.* Complying; yielding. See synonyms under DOCILE, OBSEQUIOUS, SUPPLE. [< COMPLY] **—com·pli′ant·ly** *adv.*

com·pli·cate (kom′plə·kāt) *v.* **·cat·ed, ·cat·ing** *v.t.* **1** To make complex, difficult, or perplexing. **2** To twist or wind around; intertwine. **—v.i. 3** To become complex or difficult. See synonyms under INVOLVE, PERPLEX. **—adj.** (kom′plə·kit) **1** Complicated; complex. **2** *Bot.* Folded lengthwise upon itself; conduplicate. **3** *Zool.* Folded longitudinally, as the wings of certain insects. [< L *complicatus,* pp. of *complicare* < *com-* together + *plicare* fold] **—com′pli·ca′tive** *adj.*

com·pli·ca·tion (kom′plə·kā′shən) *n.* **1** The act of complicating, or the state of being complicated; complexity. **2** Anything that complicates, as a disease coexisting with another disease.

com·plic·i·ty (kəm·plis′ə·tē) *n. pl.* **·ties 1** The act or state of being an accomplice. **2** Complexity.

com·pli·ment (kom′plə·mənt) *n.* **1** An expression of admiration, praise, congratulation, etc. **2** A formal greeting or remembrance: usually in the plural. **3** *Archaic* A gratuity; gift; favor. **—v.t.** (kom′plə·ment) **1** To pay a compliment to. **2** To show regard for, as by a gift or other favor. ◆ Homophone: *complement.* [< MF < Ital. *complimento* < Sp. *cumplimiento,* lit., completion of courtesy < L *complementum.* See COMPLEMENT.] **—com·pli·men·ta·ry** (kom′plə·men′tər·ē, -trē) *adj.* **—com′pli·men′ta·ri·ly** *adv.*

com·plin (kom′plin) *n.* The last of the canonical hours; also, the last service of common prayer for the day, generally just after vespers, held at this hour. Also **com·pline** (kom′plin, -plīn), **com′plines, com′plins.** [< OF *complie* < L *completa (hora)* finished (hour) < *complere* COMPLETE]

com·ply (kəm·plī′) *v.i.* **·plied, ·ply·ing 1** To act in conformity; consent; obey: with *with.* **2** *Obs.* To be complaisant or courteous; observe civilities. See synonyms under AGREE, OBEY. [< Ital. *complire* < Sp. *cumplir* complete an act of courtesy < L *complere.* See COMPLETE.]

com·po·nent (kəm·pō′nənt) *n.* **1** A constituent part. **2** *Chem.* One of the ingredients of a mixture, in which it may exist in varying proportions and without loss of its own chemical properties, as salt in water: distinguished from *constituent.* **3** *Physics* **a** The smallest number of independently variable factors needed to establish equilibrium in a given system. Compare PHASE RULE. **b** One of two or more forces which, acting in fixed directions, are the equivalent of a given force. **—adj.** Forming a part or ingredient. [< L *componens, -entis,* ppr. of *componere.* See COMPOSE.]

com·port·ment (kəm·pôrt′mənt, -pōrt′-) *n.* Behavior; deportment.

com·pose (kəm·pōz′) *v.* **·posed, ·pos·ing** *v.t.* **1** To be the constituent elements or parts of; constitute; form. **2** *Obs.* To make up of elements or parts; construct. **3** To tranquilize; calm. **4** To reconcile, arrange, or settle, as differences. **5** To create artistically, as a literary or musical work. **6** To arrange (type) in lines; set. **—v.i. 7** To engage in composition, as of a literary or musical work. **8** To set type. See synonyms under ALLAY, CONSTRUCT, MAKE, SETTLE. [< F *composer* < *com-* together + *poser.* See POSE[1].]

com·pos·er (kəm·pō′zər) *n.* **1** One who composes. **2** A writer of music.

com·pos·ing-stick (kəm·pō′zing·stik′) *n. Printing* A tray or receptacle, usually of metal, capable of adjustment so as to vary the length of a line as required, which the compositor holds in his hand, and in which he arranges in words and lines the type that he takes from the cases.

com·pos·ite (kəm·poz′it) *adj.* **1** Made up of separate parts or elements; combined or compounded. **2** *Bot.* Pertaining or belonging to a very large, cosmopolitan family (Compositae) of plants characterized by involucrate flower heads superficially resembling single flowers but typically composed of a central mass of disk florets surrounded by a fringe of ray florets. **—n. 1** That which is composed or made up of parts; a compound. **2** *Bot.* A composite plant or flower, as a sunflower, daisy, etc. [< L *compositus,* pp. of *componere* < *com-* together + *ponere* put. Doublet of COMPOST.] **—com·pos′ite·ly** *adv.* **—com·pos′ite·ness** *n.*

composite photograph A photograph formed by combining several photographs, either on the same plate, or on the same print from various negatives. Also **composite portrait.**

com·po·si·tion (kom'pə·zish'ən) *n.* **1** The act of composing, or the state or manner of being composed; specifically, the act, process, or art of inventing and producing a literary, musical, or artistic work or any part thereof. **2** The general structural arrangement or style of a work of art or a literary or musical production. **3** A literary, artistic, or musical production. **4** A compound or combination. **5** Typesetting. **6** An agreement or settlement; compromise. **7** The state or manner of being put together; also, that which is put together, or the components of which anything is made. **8** *Chem.* The structure of a compound as regards its different elements and the proportions in which they enter into the formation of the compound. See synonyms under PRODUCTION. [<F <L *compositio, -onis* <*componere.* See COMPOSITE.]

composition face The face or plane by which the parts of a twin crystal are united. Also **composition plane.**

composition of forces *Physics* The joining of two or more forces, exerted in the same or different directions, into one equivalent force, called the *resultant.*

com·pos·i·tive (kəm·poz'ə·tiv) *adj.* Having the power of compounding; synthetic.

com·pos·i·tor (kəm·poz'ə·tər) *n.* **1** A typesetter. **2** One who composes or sets in order.

com·post (kom'pōst) *n.* **1** A fertilizing mixture of decomposed vegetable matter. **2** A composition for plastering. **3** A mixture; compound. —*v.t.* To make into or cover with compost. [<OF <L *compositum,* var. of *compositum* <*componere.* Doublet of COMPOSITE.]

com·po·sure (kəm·pō'zhər) *n.* **1** Tranquillity, as of manner or appearance; calmness; serenity. **2** Composition. See synonyms under APATHY, PATIENCE.

com·pote (kom'pōt, *Fr.* kôṅ·pôt') *n.* **1** Fruit stewed or preserved in sirup. **2** A dish for holding fruits, etc. [<F <OF *composte.* See COMPOST.]

com·pound (kom'pound) *n.* **1** A combination of two or more elements, ingredients, or parts. **2** A compound engine. **3** A compound word. **4** *Chem.* A definite substance resulting from the combination of specific elements or radicals in fixed proportions: distinguished from *mixture.* —*v.* (kom·pound', kəm-) *v.t.* **1** To make by the combination of various elements or ingredients. **2** To mix elements or parts to form a compound substance; combine: to *compound* drugs. **3** To compromise; settle for less than the sum due: to *compound* a debt. **4** To cover up or condone (a crime) for a consideration: to *compound* a felony. **5** To compute, as interest, by geometric progression. **6** *Electr.* To place duplex windings on the field magnets of (a dynamo), one serving as a shunt and the other being in series with the main circuit, making the machine self-regulating. **7** *Obs.* To compose; form. —*v.i.* **8** To come to terms; take a compromise settlement. —*adj.* (kom'pound, kom·pound') Composed of, or produced by the union of, two or more elements, ingredients, or parts; composite. See synonyms under COMPLEX. [<OF *compondre* <L *componere.* See COMPOSITE.] —**com·pound'a·ble** *adj.* —**com·pound'er** *n.*

compound interest Interest computed not only on the original principal but also on interest earned in succeeding periods.

compound leaf *Bot.* A leaf having several distinct blades on a common leafstalk. See illustrations under LEAF.

compound engine A steam engine in which the exhaust steam from one or more cylinders enters and does work in one or more other cylinders.

compound flower *Bot.* The anthodium or head of the flower of a composite plant.

compound word A word composed of two or more words united either with a hyphen (hypheme) or without (solideme), and usually distinguished from a phrase by a reduction of stress on one of the elements and a shortening of the pause between the words, as *green' house'* and *a green' house'.*

com·pre·hend (kom'pri·hend') *v.t.* **1** To grasp mentally; understand fully. **2** To include, take in, or comprise. —*v.i.* **3** To understand. See synonyms under APPREHEND, CATCH, EMBRACE, KNOW, PERCEIVE. [<L *comprehendere* <*com-* together + *prehendere* seize] —**com'pre·hend'i·ble** *adj.*

com·pre·hen·si·ble (kom'pri·hen'sə·bəl) *adj.* **1** Capable of being comprehended or grasped by the mind; understandable; conceivable. **2** Capable of being comprised or included. —**com'·pre·hen'si·bil'i·ty, com'pre·hen'si·ble·ness** *n.*

com·pre·hen·sion (kom'pri·hen'shən) *n.* **1** The mental grasping of ideas, facts, etc., or the power of doing so; understanding. **2** The act or state of including, containing, or taking in; inclusion; comprehensiveness. **3** *Logic* The complete conception of a term, involving all the elements of its meaning and its correlations. See synonyms under KNOWLEDGE. [<L *comprehensio, -onis* <*comprehendere* COMPREHEND]

com·pre·hen·sive (kom'pri·hen'siv) *adj.* **1** Large in scope or content; including much; broad. **2** Having the power of fully understanding or comprehending. —**com'pre·hen'sive·ly** *adv.* —**com'pre·hen'sive·ness** *n.*

com·press (kəm·pres') *v.t.* To press together or into smaller space; condense; compact; concentrate. —*n.* (kom'pres) **1** A device for compressing. **2** *Med.* A soft pad for making local pressure on affected parts of the body. **3** An apparatus for compressing bales of cotton, etc. [<OF *compresser* <LL *compressare,* freq. of *comprimere* <*com-* together + *premere* press] —**com·press'i·bil'i·ty, com·press'i·ble·ness** *n.* —**com·press'i·ble** *adj.*

com·pres·sion (kəm·presh'ən) *n.* **1** The act of compressing or the state of being compressed. **2** The process by which a confined gas is reduced in volume through the application of pressure, as in the cylinder of an internal-combustion engine. Also **com·pres·sure**(kəm·presh'ər). [<L *compressio, -onis* <*comprimere* COMPRESS]

com·pres·sor (kəm·pres'ər) *n.* **1** One who or that which compresses. **2** *Anat.* A muscle that compresses a part of the body: the *compressor narium* of the nostrils. **3** *Surg.* An instrument for compressing a part of the body. **4** *Mech.* A power-driven machine for compressing a gas in order to utilize its expansion, as for refrigeration.

com·prise (kəm·priz') *v.t.* **·prised, ·pris·ing** To include and contain; consist of; embrace. [<F *compris,* pp. of *comprendre* <L *comprehendere* COMPREHEND] —**com·pri'sal** *n.*

com·pro·mise (kom'prə·mīz) *n.* **1** An adjustment for settlement by arbitration and mutual concession, usually involving a partial surrender of purposes or principles. **2** *Law* An adjustment of a controversy by mutual consent in order to prevent or settle a lawsuit. **3** Anything that is the result of concessions; a medium between two conflicting courses; also, the habit or spirit of concession. **4** An imperiling or surrender, as of character or reputation. —*v.* **·mised, ·mis·ing** *v.t.* **1** To adjust by concessions. **2** To expose, as to suspicion, danger, or disrepute. **3** *Obs.* To bind or pledge mutually. —*v.i.* **4** To make a settlement by concessions. [<F *compromis* <L *compromissum* a mutual agreement to accept arbitration <*com-* together + *promittere* promise] —**com'pro·mis'er** *n.*

comp·trol·ler (kən·trō'lər) *n.* A controller: the spelling sometimes employed to designate a city, State, or Federal officer in control of funds. [<Var. of CONTROLLER; infl. by COMPT]

com·pul·sion (kəm·pul'shən) *n.* **1** The act of compelling; coercion. **2** The state of being compelled. **3** *Psychol.* **a** The performance of an act contrary to the conscious will of the subject. **b** An act so performed. See synonyms under NECESSITY. [<MF <L *compulsio. -onis* <*compellere* COMPEL]

com·pul·sive (kəm·pul'siv) *adj.* **1** Compelling or tending to compel; compulsory. **2** *Psychol.* Pertaining to or describing acts or behavior independent of volition. —**com·pul'·sive·ly** *adv.* —**com·pul'sive·ness** *n.*

com·pul·so·ry (kəm·pul'sər·ē) *adj.* **1** Employing compulsion; compelling; coercive. **2** Required by law or other rule; enforced: *compulsory* education. See synonyms under NECESSARY. —**com·pul'so·ri·ly** *adv.* —**com·pul'so·ri·ness** *n.*

com·punc·tion (kəm·pungk'shən) *n.* **1** Self-reproach for wrong-doing; a sense of guilt; remorseful feeling. **2** A feeling of slight regret. See synonyms under REPENTANCE. [<LL *compunctio, -onis* <*com-* greatly + *pungere* prick, sting] —**com·punc'tious** *adj.* —**com·punc'tious·ly** *adv.*

com·pur·ga·tion (kom'pər·gā'shən) *n.* The ancient practice of clearing an accused person by the oaths of several others, usually twelve, who swore to their belief in his innocence. [<LL *compurgatio, -onis* <*com-* thoroughly + *purgare* cleanse]

com·pu·ta·tion (kom'pyə·tā'shən) *n.* **1** The act of computing; calculation. **2** A computed amount or number.

com·pute (kəm·pyōōt') *v.t.* **·put·ed, ·put·ing** To estimate numerically; calculate; reckon. —*n.* Computation. [<L *computare* <*com-* together + *putare* reckon. Doublet of COUNT[1].] —**com·put'a·bil'i·ty** *n.* —**com·put'a·ble** *adj.* —**com·put'ist** *n.*

com·put·er (kəm·pyōō'tər) *n.* **1** One who or that which computes. **2** A power-driven machine equipped with keyboards, electronic circuits, storage compartments, and recording devices for the high-speed performance of mathematical operations.

com·rade (kom'rad, -rid) *n.* **1** A friend or intimate companion. **2** A partner, associate, or fellow member, as of a political party: used as a form of address, as in the Communist party. See synonyms under ASSOCIATE. [<MF *camarade* <Sp. *camarada* roommate <L *camera* room] —**com'rade·ship** *n.*

COMSAT (kom'sat') *adj. trademark/service mark* The services and apparatus utilized in satellite and microwave telecommunications, which are produced by COMSAT Corporation. [COM(MUNICATIONS) + SAT(ELLITE)]

con[1] (kon) *v.t.* **conned, con·ning** To study; peruse carefully; learn. [Var. of CAN[1].] —**con'·ner** *n.*

con[2] (kon) *v.t.* **conned, con·ning** *Naut.* To direct the steering of (a vessel). Also **conn.** [Earlier *cond* <F *conduire* <L *conducere* CONDUCT]

con[3] (kon) *Slang adj.* Shortened form of *confidence:* used in phrases: *con* man; *con* game. —*v.t.* **conned, con·ning** To defraud; dupe; swindle. —*n.* A confidence man.

con[4] (kon) *n.* The contrary; the opposite side; the opponent, etc. —*adv.* Against. See PRO. [<L *contra* against]

con[5] (kon) *n. Slang* A convict.

con- Assimilated var. of COM-.

co·na·tion (kō·nā'shən) *n. Psychol.* The element of conscious striving and activity contained in every desire, impulse, aversion, etc. [<L *conatio, -onis* an attempt <*conari* try]

con·cat·e·nate (kon·kat'ə·nāt) *v.t.* **·nat·ed, ·nat·ing** To join or link together; connect in a series. —*adj.* Joined together; connected in a series. [<L *concatenatus,* pp. of *concatenare* <*com-* together + *catena* chain]

con·cave (kon·kāv', kon'kāv, kong'-) *adj.* **1** Hollow and rounded, as the interior of a sphere or circle; incurved: opposed to *convex.* **2** Hollow. —*n.* (kon'kāv, kong'-) A concave surface; vault. [<MF <L *concavus* <*com-* thoroughly + *cavus* hollow] —**con·cave'ly** *adv.* —**con·cave'ness** *n.*

con·ca·vo-con·cave (kon·kā'vō·kon·kāv') *adj. Optics* Concave on both sides; doubly concave. See illustration under LENS.

con·ca·vo-con·vex (kon·kā'vō·kon·veks') *adj.* **1** Concave on one side and convex on the other. **2** *Optics* Describing a lens in which the curvature of the concave side is greater than that of the convex; distinguished from *convexo-concave.* See illustration under LENS.

con·ceal (kən·sēl') *v.t.* To hide; secrete; keep from sight, discovery, or knowledge. See synonyms under BURY, HIDE, MASK, PALLIATE. [<OF *conceler* <L *concelare* <*com-* thoroughly + *ce-*

lare hide] —**con·ceal'a·ble** *adj.*

con·cede (kən·sēd′) *v.* **·ced·ed, ·ced·ing** *v.t.* **1** To grant or yield, as a right or privilege. **2** To acknowledge as true, correct, or proper; admit. — *v.i.* **3** To make a concession. See synonyms under ACKNOWLEDGE, ALLOW, CONFESS. [< L *concedere* < *com-* thoroughly + *cedere* yield, go away]

con·ceit (kən·sēt′) *n.* **1** Overweening self-esteem. **2 a** A fanciful idea; a quaint or humorous fancy; clever thought or expression. **b** An extended, flowery, strained metaphor. **3** Imagination. **4** A fancy or ingenious article or design. **5** Apprehension; understanding. **6** A conception or thought. See synonyms under EGOTISM, FANCY, IDEA, PRIDE. —**out of conceit with** Displeased with. — *v.t.* **1** *Obs.* To imagine or suppose; think. **2** *Dial.* To take a fancy to; regard favorably. **3** *Obs.* To form a conception or idea; conceive. [< CONCEIVE]

con·ceive (kən·sēv′) *v.* **·ceived, ·ceiv·ing** *v.t.* **1** To procreate; beget or become pregnant with, as young. **2** To form an idea in the mind; think of, fancy. **3** To construct in the mind; formulate, as plans. **4** To believe or suppose; form an opinion. **5** To become possessed with: to *conceive* a hatred. **6** *Obs.* To understand. — *v.i.* **7** To form a mental image; think: with *of.* **8** To become pregnant. See synonyms under APPREHEND. [< OF *conceveir* < L *concipere* < *com-* thoroughly + *capere* take] —**con·ceiv'a·ble** *adj.* —**con·ceiv'·a·bil'i·ty, con·ceiv'a·ble·ness** *n.* —**con·ceiv'a·bly** *adv.* —**con·ceiv'er** *n.*

con·cen·ter (kən·sen′tər) *v.t.* To direct or bring to a common point or center; focus. — *v.i.* To come together at a common center; combine. Also **con·cen'tre.** [< F *concentrer* < L *com-* together + *centrum* center]

con·cen·trate (kon′sən·trāt) *v.* **·trat·ed, ·trat·ing** *v.t.* **1** To draw to a common center; concenter; focus. **2** To intensify in strength or to purify by the removal of certain constituents; condense. — *v.i.* **3** To converge toward a center; become compacted or intensified. —*n.* **1** A product of concentration. **2** *Usually pl. Metall.* The product of concentration processes whereby a mass of high metal content has been obtained from the ore or other raw materials. —*adj.* Concentrated. [< CONCENTER + -ATE¹] —**con·cen·tra·tive** (kon′sən·trā′tiv, kən·sen′trə·tiv) *adj.* —**con'·cen·tra·tive·ly** *adv.* —**con'cen·tra·tive·ness** *n.* —**con'cen·tra'tor** *n.*

con·cen·tra·tion (kon′sən·trā′shən) *n.* **1** The act of concentrating: said especially of focusing the attention upon a single object, problem, task, etc. **2** That which is concentrated. **3** A medicine strengthened by evaporation of inactive ingredients. **4** *Chem.* The amount of a substance per unit volume: in a solution it is the amount of substance dissolved by a given quantity of the solvent.

concentration camp 1 A place of detention for prisoners of war, political prisoners, aliens, etc. **2** *Mil.* A place where troops are marshalled for redistribution.

con·cen·tric (kən·sen′trik) *adj.* Having a common center, as circles: opposed to *eccentric.* Also **con·cen'tri·cal.** —**con·cen'tri·cal·ly** *adv.* —**con·cen·tric'i·ty** (kon′sen·tris′ə·tē) *n.*

CONCENTRIC TREE RINGS

Con·cep·ción (kōn′sep·syōn′) A city in south central Chile.

con·cept (kon′sept) *n.* **1** An abstract notion or idea. **2** Any notion combining elements into the idea of one object. **3** A thought or opinion. See synonyms under IDEA. [< L *conceptus* a conceiving < *concipere* CONCEIVE]

con·cep·ta·cle (kən·sep′tə·kəl) *n. Bot.* A special cavity developed on the surface of many algae and fungi, for holding or enclosing reproductive organs. [< L *conceptaculum* a receptacle < *concipere.* See CONCEIVE.]

con·cep·tion (kən·sep′shən) *n.* **1** The act of conceiving or the state of being conceived. **2** The act, faculty, or power of conceiving or forming ideas or notions. **3** *Biol.* The impregnation of an ovum; act of becoming pregnant; also, an embryo; fetus. **4** A commencement; beginning; inception. **5**

Anything that is conceived; a plan or invention of the mind; a product of the inventive or constructive faculty. See synonyms under FANCY, IDEA, IMAGE, THOUGHT. —**con·cep'·tion·al** *adj.*

con·cep·tu·al·ism (kən·sep′chōō·əl·iz′əm) *n.* The doctrine that general ideas, or universals, exist in the mind only, and that the mind is capable of forming abstract ideas independently of concrete existences: a theory devised as intermediate between the extremes of nominalism and realism. —**con·cep'tu·al·ist** *n.* —**con·cep'tu·al·is'tic** *adj.*

con·cern (kən·sûrn′) *v.t.* **1** To relate or belong to; be of interest or importance to. **2** To occupy, engage, or interest. **3** To affect with solicitude; trouble: usually in the passive. — *v.i.* **4** *Obs.* To be of importance. —*n.* **1** That which concerns one; something affecting one's interest or welfare; affair; business. **2** Solicitude; interest. **3** Relation; reference. **4** A business establishment. **5** *Colloq.* Any object or contrivance. See synonyms under ANXIETY, BUSINESS, CARE. [< MF *concerner* < Med. L *concernere* regard < *com-* thoroughly + *cernere* see, discern]

con·cern·ment (kən·sûrn′mənt) *n.* **1** The fact or condition of concerning; relation; bearing; importance. **2** Anxiety; solicitude. **3** Connection; participation. **4** Anything that relates to one; affair; concern; business.

con·cert (kon′sûrt) *n.* **1** A musical performance by a number of voices or instruments, or both; also, the combination of voices or instruments to produce harmony. **2** Harmony; agreement; accordance; unity. —*adj.* Of or for concerts. —*v.* (kən·sûrt′) *v.t.* **1** To arrange or contrive by mutual agreement. **2** To plan; contrive. — *v.i.* **3** To act or plan together. [< MF < Ital. *concerto* < *concertare* agree, be in accord]

con·cer·ti·na (kon′sər·tē′nə) *n.* **1** A small musical instrument of the accordion type, with bellows and a keyboard at either end. **2** *Mil.* A portable, distensible barbed-wire entanglement, used to hinder the movements of enemy motorized equipment. [< Ital. < *concerto.* See CONCERT.]

con·cert·mas·ter (kon′sərt·mas′tər, -mäs′-) *n.* The leader of the first violin section of an orchestra, who acts as assistant to the conductor. Also **con·cert·meis·ter** (kon′sərt·mīs′tər, *Ger.* kôn′tsert′mīs′tər).

con·cer·to (kən·cher′tō) *n. pl.* **·tos,** *Ital.* **·ti** (-tē) *Music* A composition (usually of three movements) for performance by a solo instrument or instruments accompanied by an orchestra. [< Ital. See CONCERT.]

concerto gros·so (grō′sō) An early form of concerto for a small group of solo instruments and a full orchestra. [< Ital., lit., big concerto]

con·ces·sion (kən·sesh′ən) *n.* **1** The act of conceding, or that which is conceded. **2** A subsidiary business, conducted by lease or by purchase of privilege, in office buildings, railroad stations, etc.: a coatroom *concession.* **3** A strip of land, as one adjoining a port, canal, etc., conceded to an alien government for its economic use, and in which self-government and extraterritorial rights are exercised. See synonyms under FAVOR. [< MF < L *concessio, -onis* < *concedere* CONCEDE]

con·ces·sive (kən·ses′iv) *adj.* **1** Like or tending to concession. **2** *Gram.* Involving concession: said of the conjunctions *though, although,* etc., and of the subordinate adverbial clauses introduced by them.

conch (kongk, konch) *n. pl.* **conchs** (kongks) or **conch·es** (kon′chiz) **1** Any of various large marine gastropod mollusks (family Strombidae) having heavy, colorful, spiral shells. **2** The shell of such a mollusk, used to make cameos and other objects and as a crude trumpet. **3** In Roman mythology, such a shell blown as a horn by the Tritons. **4** *Archit.* A semidome, or the plain concave surface of a dome or vault. **5** *U.S. Dial.* One of a group of people native to the Florida Keys or the Bahamas. [< L *concha* < Gk. *konchē* shell]

CONCH SHELL

con·cha (kong′kə) *n. pl.* **con·chae** (kong′kē) **1** *Anat.* A structure of shell-like appearance, as the

external ear, or one of the turbinate bones. **2** *Archit.* A conch (def. 3). [< L See CONCH.]

con·chif·er·ous (kong·kif′ər·əs) *adj.* **1** Having or producing a shell; testaceous. **2** Of or pertaining to a former division of mollusks (*Conchifera*). [< L *concha* shell + -FEROUS]

con·choid (kong′koid) *n. Math.* A curve traced by the locus of a point at the end of a straight line segment of fixed length rotating about the polar axis in such a way that the length of a perpendicular from the curve to a fixed straight line (its asymptote) is in constant proportion to the length of the segment, and so that the segment of the line intercepted by the curve and its asymptote is of constant length.

CONCHOID

con·choi·dal (kong·koid′l) *adj.* Having shell-shaped depressions and elevations. Also **con'·choid.**

con·chol·o·gy (kong·kol′ə·jē) *n.* The study of shells and mollusks. [< L *concha* shell + -LOGY] —**con·cho·log·i·cal** (kong′kə·loj′i·kəl) *adj.* —**con'cho·log'i·cal·ly** *adv.* —**con·chol'o·gist** *n.*

con·cho·scope (kong′kə·skōp) *n. Med.* A speculum used in examining the anterior and middle parts of the nasal passages. [< Gk. *konchē* shell + -SCOPE]

con·ci·erge (kon′sē·ûrzh′, *Fr.* kôn·syàrzh′) *n.* **1** A doorkeeper or porter. **2** A janitor. [< F]

con·cil·i·ate (kən·sil′ē·āt) *v.t.* **·at·ed, ·at·ing 1** To overcome the enmity or hostility of; obtain the friendship of; placate; mollify: to *conciliate* an enemy. **2** To secure or attract by reconciling measures; gain; win. [< L *conciliatus,* pp. of *conciliare* < *concilium* council] —**con·cil·i·a·ble** (kən·sil′ē·ə·bəl) *adj.* —**con·cil'i·a'tor** *n.*

con·cil·i·a·tion (kən·sil′ē·ā′shən) *n.* **1** The act of bringing into agreement. **2** The settlement or attempt to settle a labor dispute by the proposal of measures acceptable to the disputants. See ARBITRATION, MEDIATION.

con·cin·ni·ty (kən·sin′ə·tē) *n. pl.* **·ties** Fitness; harmony; elegance, as of rhetorical style. [< L *concinnitas, -tatis* < *concinnus* well adjusted]

con·cise (kən·sīs′) *adj.* Expressing much in brief form; compact; terse. See synonyms under TERSE. [< L *concisus,* pp. of *concidere* < *con-* thoroughly + *caedere* cut] —**con·cise'ly** *adv.* —**con·cise'ness** *n.*

con·ci·sion (kən·sizh′ən) *n.* **1** A cutting off or asunder; schism. **2** The quality or character of being concise. **3** *Obs.* Circumcision. [< L *concisio, -onis* < *concidere.* See CONCISE.]

con·cla·mant (kən·klā′mənt) *adj.* Calling out together, as in lamentation. [< L *conclamans, -antis,* ppr. of *conclamare* < *con-* together + *clamare* cry out]

con·clave (kon′klāv, kong′-) *n.* **1** A secret council or meeting. **2** In the Roman Catholic Church, the apartments in the Vatican in which the college of cardinals meets to choose a pope, and which is kept locked until the election is over; also, the assembly or meeting of the cardinals. See synonyms under ASSEMBLY, CABAL, COMPANY. [< F < L, a place which can be locked up < *com-* together + *clavis* key]

con·clav·ist (kon′klā·vist, kong′-) *n.* An ecclesiastic attendant upon a cardinal at an electoral conclave.

con·clude (kən·klōōd′) *v.* **·clud·ed, ·clud·ing** *v.t.* **1** To come to a decision about; decide or determine. **2** To infer or deduce as a result or effect. **3** To arrange or settle finally. **4** To terminate; bring to an end. **5** *Obs.* To shut in; enclose. — *v.i.* **6** To come to an end. **7** To infer or deduce a conclusion. See synonyms under CEASE, EFFECT, END. [< L *concludere* < *com-* thoroughly + *claudere* close, shut off] —**con·clud'er** *n.*

con·clu·sion (kən·klōō′zhən) *n.* **1** The act of concluding; termination; end. **2** A conviction reached in consequence of investigation, reasoning, inference, etc. **3** A practical determination; decision. **4** The closing part, as of a discourse. **5** *Logic* A proposition the truth of which is inferred from a premise or premises; especially, the third proposition of an Aristotelian syllogism. **6** *Law* An estoppel; a bar; also, the ending of a pleading or deed.

See synonyms under DEMONSTRATION, END, INFERENCE, THOUGHT. [<F <L *conclusio, -onis* < *concludere* CONCLUDE]

con·clu·sive (kən·kloo′siv) *adj.* **1** Decisive; putting an end to doubt. **2** Leading to a conclusion; final. —**con·clu′s** *adv.* —**con·clu′· sive·ness** *n.*

con·coct (kon·kokt′, kən-) *v.t.* **1** To make by mixing ingredients, as a drink or soup. **2** To contrive; devise. [<L *concoctus*, pp. of *concoquere* <*com-* together + *coquere* cook, boil] —**con·coct′er, con·coc′tor** *n.* —**con·coc′· tive** *adj.*

con·col·or·ous (kon·kul′ər·əs) *adj.* Uniform in color; of one color. Also *Brit.* **con·col′our·ous.** [<L *concolor* <*com-* together + *color* color]

con·com·i·tant (kon·kom′ə·tənt, kən-) *adj.* Existing or occurring together; attendant. See synonyms under INCIDENTAL. —*n.* An attendant circumstance. See synonyms under APPENDAGE, CIRCUMSTANCE. [<L *concomitans, -antis,* ppr. of *concomitari* <*com-* with + *comitari* accompany <*comes* companion] — **con·com′i·tance, con·com′i·tan·cy** *n.* —**con· com′i·tant·ly** *adv.*

con·cord (kon′kôrd, kong′-) **1** Unity of feeling or interest; agreement; accord. **2** *Music* Consonance. **3** *Gram.* Agreement of words, as in gender, number, case, or person. See synonyms under HARMONY. [<F *concorde* <L *concordia* <*concors* agreeing <*com-* together + *cor, cordis* heart]

Con·cord (kong′kərd, kon′kôrd) **1** A town in NE Massachusetts; scene of a Revolutionary War battle, April 19, 1775. **2** The capital of New Hampshire.

con·cor·dance (kon·kôr′dəns, kən-) *n.* **1** An alphabetical index of words or topics in a book in their exact context; especially, such an index of the Bible. **2** Concord; agreement.

con·cor·dat (kon·kôr′dat) *n.* **1** In papal history, an agreement between the papal see and a secular power for the settlement and regulation of ecclesiastical affairs. **2** Any public act of agreement. [<Med. L *concordatum* thing agreed upon <*concordare.* See CONCORDANT.]

con·cor·po·rate (kon·kôr′pə·rāt) *v.t. & v.i.* **·rat· ed, ·rat·ing** *Obs.* To unite in one body or substance. [<L *concorporatus,* pp. of *concorporare* <*com-* together + *corpus* body]

con·course (kon′kôrs, -kôrs, kong′-)*n.* **1** An assembling or moving together; confluence. **2** An assembly; throng. **3** A large place, open or enclosed, for the passage of crowds; specifically, a boulevard or a long passageway in a railroad station, subway, etc. See synonyms under ASSEMBLY, COMPANY, THRONG. [<F *concours* <L *concursus* <*concurrere.* See CONCUR.]

con·cres·cence (kon·kres′əns) *n.* **1** *Anat.* A growing together of separate parts, as the roots of adjoining teeth. **2** *Biol.* A fusing together of the cells of an embryo during gastrulation. **3** Increase by addition of parts or particles; growth. [<L *concrescentia* < *concrescere.* See CONCRETE.]

con·crete (kon′krēt, kon·krēt′) *adj.* **1** Joined in or constituting a mass. **2** Embodied in actual existence: opposed to *abstract.* **3** Applied or relating to a particular case; individual; particular. **4** Made of concrete. —*n.* **1** A hardened mass; especially, one of sand and gravel or broken stone united by hydraulic cement. **2** A specific object or the conception of it. **3** Any mass of particles united and solidified. —*v.* (kon·krēt′ for defs. *1, 2, 4;* kon′· krēt, kon·krēt′ for def. *3*) **·cret·ed,·cret·ing** *v. t.* **1** To bring or unite together in one mass or body; cause to coalesce. **2** To bring into concrete or specific form; concretize. **3** To treat or cover with concrete. —*v.i.* **4** To coalesce; solidify. [<L *concretus,* pp. of *concrescere* <*com-* together + *crescere* grow] —**con·crete′ly** *adv.* —**con·crete′ness** *n.*

con·cre·tor (kon′krə·tər, kon·krē′tər) *n.* An apparatus for evaporating sugarcane juice and bringing it to a solid mass.

con·cu·bine (kong′kyə·bin, kon′-) *n.* **1** A woman who cohabits with a man without a marriage bond. **2** In certain polygamous societies, a secondary wife. **3** *Obs.* A paramour. [<F <L *concubina,* fem. of *concubinus* <

concumbere <*com-* with + *cumbere* lie] — **con·cu·bi·nal** (kon·kyoo′bə·nəl), **con·cu′bi· nar′y** (-ner′ē) *adj.*

con·cu·bi·tant (kon·kyoo′bə·tənt) *n. Anthropol.* One whose status at birth carries with it marriage ability with another according to a degree of consanguinity. [<L *concubit-,* stem of *concumbere* lie together + *-ANT*]

con·cu·pis·cence (kon·kyoo′pə·səns) *n.* **1** Undue or illicit sexual desire; lust. **2** Any inordinate appetite or desire. See synonyms under DESIRE.

con·cur (kən·kûr′) *v.i.* **·curred, ·cur·ring 1** To agree, as in opinion or action; cooperate or combine. **2** To happen at the same time; coincide. **3** To converge to a point, as lines. See synonyms under AGREE, ASSENT. [<L *concurrere* <*com-* together + *currere* run]

con·cur·rence (kən·kûr′əns) *n.* **1** Combination or cooperation. **2** Agreement; approval. **3** A simultaneous occurrence; coincidence. **4** *Geom.* The point where three or more lines meet. **5** Competition; rivalry. **6** *Law* A power jointly held or a claim jointly shared. Also **con·cur′ren·cy.** See synonyms under HARMONY.

con·cur·rent (kən·kûr′ənt) *adj.* **1** Occurring or acting together; meeting in the same point. **2** United in action or application; coordinate; concomitant: *concurrent* remedies or jurisdiction. —*n.* **1** A person or thing that concurs. **2** One proceeding toward the same end or purpose. **3** A rival; competitor. See synonyms under INCIDENTAL. [<L *concurrens, -entis,* pp. of *concurrere.* See CONCUR.] —**con· cur′rent·ly** *adv.*

con·cuss (kən·kus′) *v.t.* **1** To affect or injure (the brain) by concussion. **2** *Scot.* To force or intimidate into action. **3** To agitate; shake. [<L *concussus,* pp. of *concutere* < *com-* together + *quatere* strike, beat]

con·cus·sion (kən·kush′ən) *n.* **1** A violent shaking; shock; jar. **2** *Pathol.* A violent shock to some organ by a fall or sudden blow; also, the condition resulting from it. See synonyms under BLOW, COLLISION. [<L *concussio, -onis* <*concutere.* See CONCUSS.] —**con·cus′sion·al** *adj.* — **con·cus·sive** (kən·kus′iv) *adj.*

con·demn (kən·dem′) *v.t.* **1** To express opinion against; hold or prove to be wrong; censure. **2** To pronounce judicial sentence against. **3** To forbid the use of, commonly by official order, as something unfit. **4** *U.S. Law* To appropriate for public use by judicial decree; declare forfeited. **5** To pronounce hopeless; give up as incurable. **6** To close up, or to withdraw from public use, as a door, gate, or road. **7** *Obs.* To convict. [<L *condemnare* <*com-* thoroughly + *damnare* condemn] —**con·dem·na·ble** (kən·dem′nə·bəl) *adj.*— **con·dem·na·to·ry** (kən·dem′nə·tôr′ē, -tō′rē) *adj.* Synonyms: blame, censure, convict, denounce, doom, reprobate, reprove, sentence. To *condemn* is to pass judicial sentence or render judgment or decision against. *Condemn* is more final than *blame* or *censure;* a *condemned* criminal has had his trial. A person is *convicted* when his guilt is made clearly manifest; in legal usage one is said to be *convicted* only by the verdict of a jury. To *denounce* is to make public or official declaration against, especially in a violent and threatening manner. Compare ARRAIGN, BLAME, REPROVE. Antonyms: absolve, acquit, applaud, approve, exonerate, justify, pardon.

con·den·sate (kən·den′sāt) *adj.* Condensed. —*n.* **1** A product of condensation. **2** *Physics* The liquid obtained by condensing the vapor in which it is suspended. [<L *condensatus,* pp. of *condensare.* See CONDENSE.]

con·den·sa·tion (kon′den·sā′shən) *n.* **1** The act of making dense or denser, or the state of being condensed. **2** Any product of condensing. **3** *Physics* The reduction of a vapor or gas to a liquid or a solid, or of a liquid to a solid or semisolid. **4** *Chem.* The rearrangement of atoms to form a molecule of greater weight, density, or complexity. **5** *Psychol.* A fusion of events, thoughts, elements of speech, individuals, pictures, etc., as in dreams. Compare CONDENSE. See synonyms under ABBREVIATION. —**con·**

dens′a·tive *adj.*

con·dense (kən·dens′) *v.* **·densed, ·dens·ing** *v.t.* **1** To compress or make dense; consolidate. **2** To abridge or make concise; epitomize, as an essay. **3** To change from the gaseous or vaporous to the liquid or solid state, as by cooling or compression. —*v.i.* **4** To become condensed. See synonyms under ABBREVIATE, REDUCE. [<L *condensare* <*condensus* thick <*com-* together + *densus* crowded, close] —**con·dens′a·bil′i·ty** *n.* — **con·dens′a·ble** or **con·dens′i·ble** *adj.*

con·dens·er (kən·den′sər) *n.* **1** One who or that which condenses. **2** Any device for reducing a vapor to liquid by removing from the vapor its heat of evaporation, as in a steam-power plant. **3** *Electr.* An arrangement of insulated conductors and dielectrics for the accumulation of an electric charge: used to block the flow of a direct current and to modify the capacity of an electric circuit. **4** *Optics* A combination of lenses for the effective condensation of light rays.

con·de·scend (kon′di·send′) *v.i.* **1** To stoop from a position of rank or dignity; come down to equal terms with an inferior. **2** To behave as if conscious of this stooping; patronize. **3** To lower or degrade oneself. **4** *Rare* To be gracious or affable. [<F *condescendre* <LL *condescendere* <*com-* together + *descendere* stoop. See DESCEND.]

con·dign (kən·dīn′) *adj.* **1** Well-deserved; merited; deserved: said of punishment. **2** *Obs.* Deserving. [<F *condigne* <L *condignus* <*com-* thoroughly + *dignus* worthy] —**con·dign′ly** *adv.*

con·di·ment (kon′də·mənt) *n.* A sauce, relish, spice, etc. [<L *condimentum*]

con·di·tion (kən·dish′ən) *n.* **1** The state or mode in which a person or thing exists. **2** State of health; especially, a favorable or sound state of health. **3** A modifying circumstance. **4** An event, fact, or the like that is necessary to the occurrence of some other, though not its cause; a prerequisite. **5** Something required as prerequisite to a promise or to its fulfilment. **6** A grade or rank; especially, high social position. **7** *Gram.* That clause of a conditional sentence usually introduced by *if, unless,* etc. **8** A conditional proposition upon which another proposition depends as consequent. **9** *U.S.* **a** A requirement that a student who has not done satisfactory work in a college or university course do additional work to avoid failing the course. **b** A grade, often indicated by E, signifying this requirement. —*v.t.* **1** To place a stipulation or stipulations upon; prescribe. **2** To be the stipulation of or prerequisite to. **3** To specify as a stipulation or requirement. **4** To render fit. **5** *Psychol.* To train to a behavior pattern or conditioned response. **6** *U.S.* To subject (a student) to a condition. —*v.i.* **7** To stipulate. [<L *condicio, -onis* agreement <*condicere* <*com-* together + *dicere* say] —**con·di′tion·er** *n.*

con·di·tion·al (kən·dish′ən·əl) *adj.* **1** Expressing or imposing conditions: not absolute. **2** *Gram.* Expressing or implying a condition; a *conditional* clause. —*n. Gram.* A word, tense, clause, or mood expressive of a condition. —**con·di· tion·al·i·ty** (kən·dish′ən·al′ə·tē) *n.* —**con·di′· tion·al·ly** *adv.*

con·di·tioned (kən·dish′ənd) *adj.* **1** Limited by or subjected to conditions or stipulations. **2** Circumstanced; placed. **3** *Psychol.* **a** Trained to give an identical response to a given stimulus. **b** Responsive to related stimuli. **4** Accustomed (to). **5** So treated or trained as to be in good condition for some task or contest.

con·dole (kən·dōl′) *v.* **·doled, ·dol·ing** *v.i.* To grieve or express sympathy with one in affliction: with *with.* —*v.t. Rare* To grieve over with another; bewail. [<LL *condolere* <*com-* together + *dolere* grieve] —**con·do·la·to·ry** (kən· dō′lə·tôr′ē, -tō′rē) *adj.* —**con·dol′er** *n.*

con·do·lence (kən·dō′ləns) *n.* **1** Expression of sympathy with a person in pain, sorrow, or misfortune. **2** *Obs.* Lamentation. Also **con·dole′· ment.**

con·dom (kon′dəm, kun′-) *n.* A membranous penile sheath of rubber or similar material, having an anti-venereal or contraceptive function: also spelled *cundum.* [? Alter. of *Conton,* an 18th c. English physician said to have invented it.]

con·do·min·i·um (kon'də·min'ē·əm) *n.* **1** Joint government; joint sovereignty, as over property. **2** *Law* A territory jointly governed by several states under international law. **3** *U.S.* An apartment house in which the units are owned separately by individuals and not by a corporation or cooperative; also, an apartment in such a building. [< NL < L *com-* together + *dominium* rule]

con·done (kən·dōn') *v.t.* **·doned, ·don·ing** To treat (an offense) as overlooked or forgiven; forgive, See synonyms under PARDON. [< L *condonare* < *com-* thoroughly + *donare* give] **—con·do·na·tion** (kon'dō·nā'shən), **con·done'·ment** *n.* **—con·don'er** *n.*

con·dor (kon'dər) *n.* **1** A vulture of the high Andes (*Vultur gryphus*), characterized by a fleshy comb and a white downy neck ruff: it is one of the largest birds with the power of flight. **2** The California vulture (*Gymnogyps californianus*). [< Sp. < Quechua *cuntur*]

Con·dor·cet (kôn·dôr·se'), **Marquis de,** 1743–94, Marie Jean Caritat, French mathematician and philosopher.

CONDOR
(Wing spread
8 1/2 to 10 1/2
feet)

con·dot·tie·re (kon'dōt·tyä'rä) *n. pl.* **·ri** (-rē) **1** A hireling military chief of the14th and 15th centuries. **2** A freelance; adventurer. [< Ital. < *condotto* a mercenary < L *conductus* hired. See CONDUCT.]

con·duce (kən·dōōs' -dyōōs') *v.i.* **·duced, ·duc·ing** To help or tend toward a result; contribute. [< L *conducere* bring together. See CONDUCT.] **— con·duc'er** *n.* **—con·du'ci·ble** *adj.* **— con·du·ci·bil'i·ty, con·du'ci·ble·ness** *n.* **—con·du'ci·bly** *adv.*

con·du·cive (kən·dōō'siv, -dyōō'-) *adj.* Contributing; leading; helping: with *to.* Also **con·du·cent** (kən·dōō'sənt, -dyōō'-). **—con·du'cive·ly** *adv.* **—con·du'cive·ness** *n.*

con·duct (kən·dukt') *v.t.* **1** To accompany and show the way; guide; escort. **2** To manage or control. **3** To direct and lead the performance of. **4** To serve as a medium of transmission for; convey; transmit, as electricity. **5** To act or behave: reflexive *—v.i.* **6** To serve as a conductor. **7** To direct or lead. *—n.* (kon'dukt) **1** One's course of action; behavior. **2** The act of managing; direction; control; skilful management. **3** The action of leading; escort; convoy. [< L *conductus*, pp. of *conducere* < *com-* together + *ducere* lead] **— con·duct'i·bil'i·ty** *n.* **—con·duct'i·ble** *adj.*

con·duc·tance (kən·duk'təns) *n. Electr.* A measure of the ability of a circuit or circuit element to carry current that is effective in producing power, equal to the ratio of the resistance to the square of the magnitude of the impedance: expressed in mhos. Symbol *g, G*

con·duc·tion (kən·duk'shən) *n.* **1** *Physics* The transmission of heat, sound, or electricity through matter without bulk motion of the matter: distinguished from *convection.* **2** *Physiol.* The transference of a stimulus along the nerve fibers from the point of irritation to the nerve center. **3** Transmission or conveyance in general.

con·duc·ti·tious (kon'duk·tish'əs) *adj.* Employed for wages; kept for hire.

con·duc·tiv·i·ty (kon'duk·tiv'ə·tē) *n.* **1** *Physics* The capacity of a substance or body to transmit light, heat, or electricity. **2** *Electr.* The conductance between opposite parallel faces of a given material of unit length and cross-section. **3** *Physiol.* The property of nerve fibers by which they conduct stimuli.

con·duc·tor (kən·duk'tər) *n.* **1** One who or that which leads or shows the way; an escort; guide. **2** An officer of a railroad who has charge of a train or car and collects tickets and fares. **3** Any manager or director of a movement or operation; especially, the director of an orchestra or chorus. **4** Any conducting medium, material, or device; a conduit. **5** Any body or medium having sensible conductivity for electricity or heat. **6** A lightning rod. **—con·duc'tor·ship** *n.* **—con·duc'tress** *n. fem.*

con·duit (kon'dit, -dōō·it) *n.* **1** A means for con-

ducting something, as a tube or pipe for a fluid; an aqueduct. **2** A passage or subway for electric wires, underground cables, gas and water pipes, or the like. **3** A fountain or a reservoir. [< F < conduire < L conducere. See CONDUCT.]

con·du·pli·cate (kon·dōō'plə·kit, -dyōō'-) *adj.* *Bot.* Doubled together: said of leaves and cotyledons.

con·dyle (kon'dil) *n. Anat.* **1** An enlarged, rounded prominence on the end of a bone, usually associated with a joint. **2** Any process by which an appendage is articulated in a depression or cavity, as the head to the base of the mandible. [< F < L *condylus* knuckle < Gk. *kondylos*] **—con·dy·lar** (kon'də·lər) *adj.*

con·dy·lo·ma (kon'də·lō'mə) *n. pl.* **·ma·ta** (-mə·tə) *Pathol.* An indolent wartlike growth, sometimes syphilitic, usually near the anus and external genitals of either sex. **—con·dy·lom·a·tous** (kon'də·lom'ə·təs, -lō'mə·təs) *adj.*

cone (kōn) *n.* **1** A solid figure that tapers uniformly from a circular base to a point. **2** *Geom.* A solid whose surface is generated by the turning of a straight line on a fixed point, called the *vertex,* and intersecting a closed plane curve at all points on the circumference. **3** *Bot.* A dry multiple fruit, as of the pine, composed of scales arranged symmetrically around an axis and enclosing seeds. **4** *Mech.* Any of several conical instruments or parts as either of the two taper drums in the head stock of a spinning mule. **5** *Physiol.* One of the specialized, photosensitive cells in the retina of the eye concerned with the perception of color and with daylight vision. **6** A cone-shaped pastry shell used to hold a ball of ice-cream. *—v.t. & v.i.* **coned, con·ing** To shape or be shaped conically. [< L *conus* < Gk. *kōnos*]

CONES
a. Stone pine.
b. California big tree.
c. Eastern hemlock.
d. Red spruce.

cone-flow·er (kōn'flou'ər) *n.* **1** Any of several hardy annual and perennial plants of the composite family, having a broadly conical disk of dark-brown chaff and flowers. **2** A rudbeckia.

con·el·rad (kon'əl·rad) *n. Aeron.* A technique for deliberately scrambling radio signals from separate stations so as to prevent enemy aircraft from using the signals of any one station as a navigation aid or for information: used in civil defense. [< *con(trol of) el(ectromagnetic) rad(iation)*]

cone-nose (kōn'nōz') *n.* **1** A large hemipterous insect (genus *Triatoma*): the bloodsucking *cone-nose* (*T. sanguisuga*) of the United States. **2** An assassin bug.

co·ne·pa·te (kō'nä·pä'tä) *n.* A white-backed, tropical American skunk (genus *Conepatus*); specifically, the hog-nosed skunk (*C. mesoleucus*) of South and Central America. Also **co·ne·pa·tl** (kō'nä·pät'l). [< Nahuatl *conepatl* < *conetl* small + *epatl* fox]

con·fab·u·late (kən·fab'yə·lāt) *v.i.* **·lat·ed, ·lat·ing** **1** To chat; gossip; converse. **2** *Psychol.* To compensate for loss or impairment of memory by fabrication or invention of details. Also **con·fab** (kon'fab). [< L *confabulatus,* pp. of *confabulari* < *com-* together + *fabulari* chat < *fabula* story] **— con·fab·u·la'·tion, con'fab** *n.* **— con·fab·u·la·to·ry** (kən·fab'yə·lə·tôr'ē, -tō'rē) *adj.*

con·fect (kən·fekt') *v.t.* **1** To make into a confection; preserve; prepare. **2** To construct or put together. *—n.* (kon'fekt) *Obs.* A confection. [< L *confectus,* pp. of *conficere* < *com-* together + *facere* make. Related to COMFIT.]

con·fec·tion (kən·fek'shən) *n.* **1** Any mixing or compounding; also, the article produced by either process. **2** An article of confectionery; a sweetmeat. **3** Any medicated conserve or sweetmeat; an electuary; also, any compound of drugs or spices. **4** An attractive, stylish article of dress for women. *— v.t.* To make up into a confection. [< F < L *con-*

fectio, -onis < *conficere.* See CONFECT.]

con·fec·tion·ar·y (kən·fek'shən·er'ē) *adj.* Of, pertaining to, or like confections or confectionery. *—n. pl.* **·ar·ies 1** A confectioner. **2** A sweetmeat. **3** *Obs.* A room or shop where confections are prepared; a confectionery.

con·fed·er·a·cy (kən·fed'ər·ə·sē) *n. pl.* **·cies 1** A number of states or persons in league with each other; league; confederation: the *Confederacy* of the Southern States. **2** *Law* An unlawful combination; conspiracy. See synonyms under ALLIANCE, ASSOCIATION, CABAL. **— Southern Confederacy** The Confederate States of America: also **the Confederacy.** [< AF *confederacie* < L *confoederatio* < *confoederare.* See CONFEDERATE.]

con·fed·er·ate (kən·fed'ər·it) *n.* One who is united with another or others in a league or plot; an associate; accomplice. See synonyms under ACCESSORY, AUXILIARY. *—adj.* Associated in a confederacy; united or allied by treaty. *— v.t. & v.i.* (kən·fed'ə·rāt) **·at·ed, ·at·ing** To form together or join with in a league, confederacy, or conspiracy. [< LL *confoederatus,* pp. of *confoederare* join in a league < *com-* together + *foedus* league]

Con·fed·er·ate (kən·fed'ər·it) *adj.* Pertaining to the **Confederate States of America,** a league of eleven southern States of the American Union that seceded from the United States in 1860–61. They were South Carolina, Mississippi, Florida, Alabama, Georgia, Louisiana, Texas, Virginia, Arkansas, Tennessee, and North Carolina. *— n.* An adherent, soldier, or sailor of the Confederate States of America.

con·fer (kən·fûr') *v.* **·ferred, ·fer·ring** *v.t.* **1** To grant as a gift or benefit; bestow. **2** *Obs.* To collate; compare. *— v.i.* **3** To hold conference; consult. See synonyms under CONSULT, DELIBERATE, GIVE. [< L *conferre* < *com-* together + *ferre* bring, carry] **— con·fer'ment** *n.* **— con·fer'ra·ble** *adj.* **— con·fer'rer** *n.*

con·fer·ence (kon'fər·əns, -frəns) *n.* **1** A formal meeting for counsel or discussion; an official council, as of two branches of a legislature. **2** Conversation; discourse. **3** *U.S.* One of several orders of assemblies of preachers and laymen of the Methodist Episcopal Church: the Annual *Conference*; the General *Conference*; the District *Conference.* **4** A local organization representing the Congregational churches of a district. **5** The act of bestowing; conferment. **6** A league or association, as of athletic teams. See synonyms under ASSEMBLY, COMPANY, CONVERSATION. [< MF *conférence* < Med. L *conferentia* < L *conferre.* See CONFER.] **— con·fer·en·tial** (kon'fə·ren'shəl) *adj.*

con·fer·va (kən·fûr'və) *n. pl.* **·vae** (-vē) or **·vas** *Bot.* Any member of a genus (*Tribonema*) of greenish, threadlike, fresh-water algae [< L] **— con·fer'val, con·fer'void, con·fer'vous** *adj.*

con·fer·vite (kən·fûr'vīt) *n. Bot.* A fossil plant allied to the aquatic confervae and found chiefly in the formations of the Cretaceous period.

con·fess (kən·fes') *v.t.* **1** To acknowledge or admit, as a fault, guilt, or debt. **2** To acknowledge belief or faith in. **3** *Eccl.* **a** To admit or make known (one's sins), especially to a priest, to obtain absolution. **b** To hear the confession of: said of a priest. **4** To concede or admit to be true. **5** *Poetic* To demonstrate or make manifest. *—v.i.* **6** To make acknowledgment of, as a fault, crime, or error. **7** To make confession to a priest. [< F *confesser* < L *confessus,* pp. of *confiteri* < *com-* thoroughly + *fateri* own, declare] *Synonyms:* accept, acknowledge, admit, allow, avow, certify, concede, disclose, endorse, grant, own, recognize. We *accept* another's statement; *admit* any point made against us; *acknowledge* what we have said or done, good or bad; *avow* our individual beliefs or feelings; *certify* to facts within our knowledge; *confess* our own faults; *endorse* a friend's note or statement; *grant* a request; *own* our faults or obligations; *recognize* lawful authority; *concede* a claim, demand, etc. The chief present use of *confess* is in the sense of making known to others one's own error or wrong-doing; as, to *confess* a crime. *Acknowledge* may be used as a milder word in this sense, but is more freely used of matters not involving error or fault: I *acknowledge* my signature, the receipt of a letter, a check, etc. *Own* commonly indicates a somewhat reluctant acknowledgment. *Admit* and *concede* have a similar suggestion of reluctance or of possible objection. See ACKNOWLEDGE, AVOW.

con·fes·sion (kən-fesh′ən) *n.* 1 The act of confessing; the avowal or acknowledgment of an action, especially of one that is inculpatory or sinful; admission: a *confession* of crime. 2 An acknowledgment of belief (in another); recognition of a relation (to another): *confession* of Christ. 3 *Law* A voluntary declaration or acknowledgment by a party against whom some misdeed or default is alleged in respect of such allegation. 4 A formulary of faith: also called **confession of faith.** 5 A formulary of public worship embodying a general admission of common sinfulness, used in the Roman Catholic, Anglican, and other liturgies. 6 The contrite acknowledgment to a priest of any sins committed: a part of the sacrament of penance and a condition of absolution: called in full **sacramental** or **auricular confession.** 7 An organization, as a church or communion, using a confession of faith. 8 The tomb of a martyred Christian; also, an altar over such a tomb or the basilica in which the altar stood; an altar–tomb confessionary. See synonyms under APOLOGY.

con·fes·sion·al (kən-fesh′ən-əl) *adj.* Pertaining to a confession. — *n.* 1 A cabinet in a church where a priest hears confessions. 2 The act, performance, or practice of confession before a priest.

con·fes·sor (kən-fes′ər) *n.* 1 A priest who hears confessions; a spiritual adviser, as of a sovereign. 2 One who confesses or admits anything, as a crime. 3 One who confesses his faith in Christianity, especially in the face of persecution. Also **con·fess′er.** — **con·fes′- sor·ship** *n.*

con·fet·ti (kən-fet′ē) *n. pl.* 1 Small pieces of brightly colored paper thrown about at carnivals, weddings, etc. 2 Bonbons. [<Ital., pl. of *confetto* confection]

con·fi·dant (kon′fə-dant′, kon′fə-dant) *n.* A person to whom secrets are entrusted. [<F *confident* <Ital. *confidente* <L *confidens.* See CONFIDE.] — **con′fi·dante′** *n. fem.*

con·fide (kən-fīd′) *v.* **·fid·ed, ·fid·ing** *v.t.* 1 To reveal in trust or confidence. 2 To put into one's trust or keeping. — *v.i.* 3 To have faith or trust: often with *in.* See synonyms under COMMIT, TRUST. [<L *confidere* <*com-* thoroughly + *fidere* trust] — **con·fid′er** *n.*

con·fi·dence (kon′fə-dəns) *n.* 1 Trust in or reliance upon something or someone; belief in a person or thing. 2 Assurance; presumption. 3 Self–reliance; hence, courage or boldness. 4 Private conversation or communication; a secret. 5 *Obs.* That in which one confides. See synonyms under ASSURANCE, BELIEF, CERTAINTY, FAITH.

con·fi·dent (kon′fə-dənt) *adj.* 1 Having confidence; assured; self-reliant. 2 *Obs.* Forward; impudent. See synonyms under SANGUINE, SECURE, SURE. — *n.* A confidant. [<L *confidens, -entis,* ppr. of *confidere.* See CONFIDE.] — **con′fi·dent·ly** *adv.*

con·fi·den·tial (kon′fə-den′shəl) *adj.* 1 Having secret or private relations; trusted; intimate: a *confidential* clerk. 2 Imparted in confidence; secret: *confidential* information. 3 Disposed to confide in another. 4 *U.S.* Denoting defense information classified next above "for official use only": the next lowest classification. Compare TOP-SECRET, SECRET (*adj.* def. 5). — **con·fi·den·ti·al·i·ty** (kon′fə-den′shē·al′ə·tē), **con′fi·den′tial·ness** *n.*

con·fig·u·rate (kən-fig′yə-rāt) *v.* **·rat·ed, ·rat·ing** *v.t.* To give shape or fashion to. — *v.i.* To be congruous. [<LL *configuratus,* pp. of *configurare.* See CONFIGURE.]

con·fig·u·ra·tion (kən-fig′yə-rā′shən) *n.* 1 Structural arrangement; conformation; contour. 2 *Psychol.* In the Gestalt theory, a static or dynamic aggregate of sensations, feelings, reflexes, and ideas so organized as to function as a unit in individual behavior. 3 *Physics* The spatial arrangement of atoms in a molecule or of nucleons and electrons in an atom. — **con·fig′u·ra′tion·ism** *n.*

con·fine (kən-fīn′) *v.* **·fined, ·fin·ing** *v.t.* 1 To shut within an enclosure; imprison. 2 To re-

strain or oblige to stay within doors. 3 To hold or keep within limits; restrict: to *confine* remarks. — *v.i.* 4 *Obs.* To border; abut. See synonyms under CIRCUMSCRIBE, LIMIT, RESTRAIN. — *n.* 1 *Usually pl.* A boundary; limit; border; frontier. 2 *Obs.* A prison. 3 *Obs.* Region, territory, or district. See synonyms under BOUNDARY, MARGIN. [<F *confiner* <Ital. *confinare* <L *confinis* bordering <*com-* together + *finis* border] — **con·fin′a·ble** *adj.*

con·fined (kən-fīnd′) *adj.* 1 Limited; restricted. 2 In childbed.

con·fine·ment (kən-fīn′mənt) *n.* 1 The state of being confined; restriction; imprisonment. 2 Accouchement; the state of being in childbed.

con·firm (kən-fûrm′) *v.t.* 1 To assure by added proof; corroborate; verify; make certain. 2 To add firmness to; strengthen. 3 *Law* To ratify; sanction. 4 To establish in office. 5 To receive into the church by confirmation. [<OF *confermer* <L *confirmare* strengthen <*com-* thoroughly + *firmus* strong] — **con·firm′a·ble, con·firm′a·tive, con·firm·a·to·ry** (kən-fûr′mə-tôr′ē, -tō′rē) *adj.* — **con·firm′er** *n.*

Synonyms: assure, corroborate, establish, fix, prove, ratify, sanction, settle, strengthen, substantiate, sustain, uphold. *Confirm* means to add firmness or give stability to. Both *confirm* and *corroborate* presuppose something already existing to which the confirmation or corroboration is added. Testimony is *corroborated* by concurrent testimony or by circumstances; *confirmed* by *established* facts. That which is thoroughly *proved* is said to be *established;* so is that which is official and has adequate power behind it; as, the *established* government. The continents are *fixed.* A treaty is *ratified;* an appointment *confirmed.* An act is *sanctioned* by any person or authority that passes upon it approvingly. A statement is *substantiated;* a report *confirmed;* a controversy *settled;* the decision of a lower court *sustained* by a higher. Just government should be *upheld.* See RATIFY.

con·fir·ma·tion (kon′fər-mā′shən) *n.* 1 The act of confirming. 2 That which confirms; proof. 3 *Eccl.* A sacramental rite administered to baptized persons, confirming or strengthening their faith, and admitting them to all the privileges of the church. 4 *Law* An instrument that supplies some defect or omission in a former conveyance. See synonyms under PROOF.

con·fis·cate (kon′fis·kāt) *v.t.* **·cat·ed, ·cat·ing** 1 To appropriate as forfeited to the public use or treasury, usually as a penalty. 2 To appropriate by or as by authority. — *adj.* Appropriated or forfeited. [<L *confiscatus,* pp. of *confiscare* <*com-* together + *fiscus* chest, treasury] — **con·fis·ca·ble** (kən-fis′kə- bəl), **con′fis·cat′a·ble** *adj.* — **con′fis·ca′tion** *n.*

con·fla·grant (kən-flā′grənt) *adj.* Burning fiercely. [<L *conflagrans, -antis,* ppr. of *conflagrare* <*com-* thoroughly + *flagrare* burn]

con·fla·gra·tion (kon′flə-grā′shən) *n.* A great or disastrous fire; destruction by burning. [<L *conflagratio, -onis* <*conflagrare.* See CONFLAGRANT.]

con·flate (kən-flāt′) *v.t.* **·flat·ed, ·flat·ing** 1 To combine from variant readings into a composite reading. 2 To blow together; bring together from diverse sources. — *adj.* 1 Composed of a variety of elements. 2 Blown together. [<L *conflatus,* pp. of *conflare* <*com-* together + *flare* blow] — **con·fla′tion** *n.*

con·flict (kon′flikt) *n.* 1 A struggle to resist or overcome; contest of opposing forces or powers; strife; battle. 2 A state or condition of opposition; antagonism; discord: the *conflict* of testimony. 3 Active antagonism; clash; collision. 4 *Psychoanal.* Painful tension set up by a clash between opposed and contradictory impulses in an individual; specifically, the antagonism existing between primitive desires and instincts and moral, religious, or ethical ideals. — *v.i.* (kən-flikt′) 1 To come into collision; be in mutual opposition; clash. 2 To engage in battle; struggle. [<L *conflictus,* pp. of *configere* <*com-* together + *fligere* strike] — **con·flic′tion** *n.* — **con·flic′- tive** *adj.*

con·flu·ence (kon′floo·əns) *n.* 1 *Geog.* A junction of streams; the place where streams

flow together. 2 A gathering and mingling. 3 A flocking together; concourse. Also **con·- flux** (kon′fluks).

con·flu·ent (kon′floo·ənt) *adj.* Flowing together so as to form one; blended into one. — *n.* *Geog.* A stream that unites with another; a branch of a river. [<L *confluens, -entis,* ppr. of *confluere* <*com-* together + *fluere* flow]

con·form (kən-fôrm′) *v.t.* 1 To make like or similar in form or character: with *to.* — *v.i.* 2 To act in accord; correspond; comply. 3 To be or become a conformist. [<F *conformer* <L *conformare* <*com-* together + *formare* shape] — **con·form′a·bil′i·ty, con·form′a·ble- ness** *n.* — **con·form′a·ble** *adj.* — **con·form′a- bly** *adv.* — **con·form′er** *n.*

con·for·ma·tion (kon′fôr·mā′shən) *n.* 1 The manner of formation of a body; general structure, form, or outline; arrangement of parts. 2 The act of conforming, or the state of being conformed.

con·for·ma·tor (kon′fôr·mā′tər) *n.* An instrument which makes a graphic record of the size and shape of an object, as the head or bust.

con·form·ist (kən-fôr′mist) *n.* 1 One who conforms or complies. 2 In English history, one who adheres to the usages of the Established Church: opposed to *dissenter, nonconformist.*

con·form·i·ty (kən-fôr′mə·tē) *n. pl.* **·ties** 1 Correspondence in form, manner, or use; agreement; harmony; congruity. 2 The act or habit of conforming oneself; acquiescence. 3 In English history, adherence to the Church of England. See synonyms under HARMONY.

con·found (kon-found′, kən-) *v.t.* 1 To strike with confusion or amazement; perplex; overwhelm; abash. 2 To confuse with something else; mix. 3 To confuse or mingle (elements, things, or ideas) indistinguishably. 4 (kon′- found′) To imprecate ill upon: used as a mild oath. 5 *Obs.* To waste. 6 *Archaic* To defeat; overthrow; ruin, as an army or nation. See synonyms under ABASH, PERPLEX, REFUTE. [<OF *confondre* <L *confundere.* See CONFUSE.] — **con·found′er** *n.*

con·front (kən-frunt′) *v.t.* 1 To stand face to face with; face defiantly. 2 To put or face to face: with *with:* to *confront* the accused with the witnesses against him. 3 To compare. See synonyms under OPPOSE. [<F *confronter* <L *com-* together + *frons, frontis* face, forehead]

con·fron·ta·tion (kon′frən·tā′shən) *n.* 1 The act of confronting, or the state of being confronted. 2 A direct challenge to the power of an opposing group or state, as by affirmation of policy, acts of protest, or acts or threats of violence. 3 A crisis or conflict between opposing political groups or states: events leading to a *confrontation* with China.

con·fuse (kən-fyooz′) *v.t.* **·fused, ·fus·ing** 1 To perplex or perturb; confound; bewilder. 2 To throw into disorder; mix indiscriminately; derange: to *confuse* the colors of a picture. 3 To mix in such a way as to make distinction difficult or impossible: He *confused* the dates of the events. 4 *Obs.* To undo; ruin. See synonyms under ABASH, DISPLACE, EMBARRASS, MIX, PERPLEX. [<L *confusus,* pp. of *confundere* <*com-* together + *fundere* pour. Related to CONFOUND.] — **con·fus·ed·ly** (kən- fyoo′zid·lē) *adv.* — **con·fus′ed·ness** *n.* — **con- fus′ing·ly** *adv.*

con·fu·sion (kən-fyoo′zhən) *n.* 1 The act of confusing, or the state of being confused; perplexity; distraction. 2 Embarrassment; shame; intellectual discomfiture. 3 *Obs.* Destruction; ruin; overthrow. See synonyms under CHAGRIN, DISORDER, PERPLEXITY, TUMULT. — **con·fu′sion·al** *adj.*

con·fute (kən-fyoot′) *v.t.* **·fut·ed, ·fut·ing** 1 To prove to be false or invalid; refute successfully. 2 To prove (a person) to be in the wrong. 3 To confound. See synonyms under REFUTE. [<L *confutare* check, restrain] — **con- fut′er** *n.*

con·ga (kong′gə) *n.* 1 A ballroom dance of Latin-American origin in which the dancers form a winding line. 2 The music for this dance, in fast 4/4 time, with a strongly accented fourth beat. [<Am. Sp.]

con·geal (kən-jēl′) *v.t.* 1 To convert from a fluid to a solid condition, as by freezing or curdling. **2** To clot or coagulate, as blood. — *v.i.* **3** To become hard, stiff, or viscid. [<MF *congeler* <L *congelare* < *com-* together + *gelare* freeze < *gelum* frost] — **con·geal'a·ble** *adj.* — **con·geal'er** *n.* — **con·geal'ment** *n.*

con·ge·la·tion (kon'jə·lā'shən) *n.* **1** A congealing. **2** A congealed state; clot; concretion. [<L *congelatio, -onis* < *congelare.* See CONGEAL.]

con·gen·ial (kən·jēn'yəl) *adj.* **1** Having similar character or tastes; sympathetic. **2** Suited to one's disposition; agreeable. See synonyms under DELIGHTFUL. [<CON- + GENIAL] — **con·ge·ni·al·i·ty** (kən·jē'nē·al'ə·tē) *n.* — **con·gen'ial·ly** *adv.*

con·gen·i·tal (kən·jen'ə·təl) *adj.* **1** Born with a person; existing at or from birth. **2** Acquired by an individual organism in the course of uterine development subsequent to action by the genes but prior to delivery from the womb: distinguished from *hereditary.* See synonyms under INHERENT. [<L *congenitus* <*com-* together + *genitus,* pp. of *gignere* bear, produce] — **con·gen'i·tal·ly** *adv.*

con·ger (kong'gər) *n.* A marine eel *(Conger conger)* from 4 to 10 feet long, used as a food fish. Also **conger eel.** [<OF *congre* <L *conger* <Gk. *gongros*]

con·ge·ries (kon'jə·rēz, kon·jir'ēz) *n.* *pl.* **·ge·ries** A collection or aggregation of things; an assemblage of bodies; mass; heap. [<L <*congerere.* See CONGEST.]

con·gest (kən·jest') *v.t.* **1** To collect or crowd together; overcrowd. **2** *Pathol.* To surcharge an organ or member with blood. **3** *Obs.* To collect; accumulate. — *v.i.* **4** To become congested. [<L *congestum,* pp. of *congerere* <*com-* together + *gerere* bear, carry] — **con·ges'tive** *adj.*

con·ges·tion (kən·jes'chən) *n.* **1** *Pathol.* An excessive accumulation, as of blood in the blood vessels. **2** An overcrowded condition.

con·glom·er·ate (kən·glom'ər·it) *adj.* **1** Massed or clustered. **2** *Geol.* Consisting of loosely cemented heterogeneous material: *conglomerate* clay. See synonyms under COMPLEX, HETEROGENEOUS. — *n.* **1** A heterogeneous collection. **2** A large corporation formed by merging a number of separate companies, often in unrelated fields. **3** *Geol.* A rock composed of pebbles or fragments of rock loosely cemented together. — *v.t. & v.i.* (kən·glom'ə·rāt) **·at·ed, ·at·ing** To gather into a cohering mass. [<L *conglomeratus,* pp. of *conglomerare* <*com-* together + *glomus, glomeris* ball] — **con·glom·er·at·ic** (kən·glom'ə·rat'ik) or **con·glom'er·it'ic** (-ə·rit'ik) *adj.*

con·glu·ti·nant (kən·gloo'tə·nənt) *adj.* **1** Causing to stick together. **2** *Med.* Healing by adhesion, as the edges of a wound. — *n. Med.* An application for wounds.

con·glu·ti·nate (kən·gloo'tə·nāt) *v.t. & v.i.* **·nat·ed, ·nat·ing** **1** To glue or stick together; adhere. **2** *Med.* To reunite by adhesion, as wounds or fractures. — *adj.* **1** Glued together; united by adhesion. **2** *Bot.* United as if glued together, but not organically. [<L *conglutinatus,* pp. of *conglutinare* <*com-* together + *glutinare* stick <*gluten* glue] — **con·glu'ti·na'tion** *n.* — **con·glu'ti·na'tive** *adj.*

con·glu·ti·nous (kən·gloo'tə·nəs) *adj.* Causing adhesion; gluelike. — **con·glu'ti·nous·ly** *adv.*

con·go (kong'gō) *n.* **1** The congo snake. **2** The mud eel.

Congo Republic An independent republic of the French Community in western equatorial Africa; 139,000 square miles; capital, Brazzaville; formerly *Middle Congo,* a French overseas territory. — **Con'go·lese'** *adj. & n.*

congo snake A tailed aquatic salamander *(Amphiuma means)* of the SE United States, of elongate eel-like form with rudimentary limbs. Also **congo eel.**

con·gou (kong'goo) *n.* A grade of black tea from China, the third picking. Also **con·go** (kong'gō), **con'gu.** [<Chinese *kung-fu(ch'a)* labor (tea); tea on which labor has been spent]

con·grat·u·late (kən·grach'oo·lāt) *v.t.* **·lat·ed, ·lat·ing** **1** To express sympathetic pleasure in the joy, success, or good fortune of (another); felicitate. **2** *Obs.* To salute approvingly; welcome; hail. [<L *congratulatus,* pp. of *congratulari* <*com-* together + *gratulari* rejoice] — **con·grat'u·lant** *adj.* — **con·grat'u·la'tor** *n.* — **con·grat·u·la·to·ry** (kən·grach'oo·lə·tôr'ē, -tō'rē) *adj.*

con·grat·u·la·tion (kən·grach'oo·lā'shən) *n.* **1** The act of congratulating. **2** *pl.* Expressions of pleasure and good wishes on another's fortune or success; congratulatory speech or writing.

con·gre·gant (kong'grə·gənt) *n.* A member of a congregation; one who joins with others anywhere.

con·gre·gate (kong'grə·gāt) *v.t. & v.i.* **·gat·ed, ·gat·ing** To bring or come together into a crowd; assemble. — *adj.* (kong'grə·git) **1** Relating to a congregation. **2** Gathered together; collected. [<L *congregatus,* pp. of *congregare* <*com-* together + *gregare* crowd, collect <*grex, gregis* flock] — **con'gre·ga'tive** *adj.* — **con'gre·ga'tive·ly** *adv.* — **con'gre·ga'tive·ness** *n.* — **con'gre·ga'tor** *n.*

con·gre·ga·tion (kong'grə·gā'shən) *n.* **1** The act of congregating; the collecting into one mass, body, or assembly; aggregation. **2** An assemblage of people or of things. **3** A group of people met together for worship; also, the body of persons who worship in a local church; a parish. **4** In the Old Testament, the whole body of Israel. **5** *Eccl.* A religious community or order bound by a common rule. **6** Any of several committees of cardinals who administer the departments of the papal government and assist the Pope. **7** In colonial New England, a town or settlement, considered as a religious community. See synonyms under ASSEMBLY, COMPANY. — **con'gre·ga'tion·al** *adj.*

con·gre·ga·tion·al·ism (kong'grə·gā'shən·əl·iz'əm) *n.* A form of church polity in which each local congregation is autonomous in all ecclesiastical matters.

con·gress (kong'gris) *n.* **1** An assembly or conference; a gathering. **2** A coming together; intercourse. **3** Sexual union. — *v.i.* (kən·gres') To assemble; meet together. [<L *congressus* a coming together <*congredi* <*com-* together + *gredi* go, move] — **con·gres·sive** (kən·gres'iv) *adj.*

con·gres·sion·al (kən·gresh'ən·əl) *adj.* Pertaining to a congress, especially, *cap.,* the United States Congress.

con·gru·ence (kong'groo·əns) *n.* Harmony, conformity; agreement. Also **con'gru·en·cy.**

con·gru·ent (kong'groo·ənt) *adj.* **1** Having mutual agreement or conformity; correspondent; appropriate. **2** *Math.* Describing two geometric figures which may be exactly superposed on each other, or two numbers which will give the same remainders when divided by a given quantity called the *modulus.* [<L *congruens, -entis,* ppr. of *congruere* agree] — **con'gru·ent·ly** *adv.*

congruent forms In crystallography, two forms which may be derived from each other by the rotation of the crystal.

con·gru·i·ty (kən·groo'ə·tē) *n.* *pl.* **·ties** **1** Agreement; harmoniousness; appropriateness. **2** An example or case of harmoniousness. **3** Geometrical agreement.

con·gru·ous (kong'groo·əs) *adj.* **1** Harmoniously related or combined. **2** Appropriate; consistent. **3** *Math.* Having congruence. [<L *congruus* <*congruere* agree] — **con'gru·ous·ly** *adv.* — **con'gru·ous·ness** *n.*

con·ic (kon'ik) *adj.* Cone-shaped. **2** Relating to or formed by or upon a cone. Also **con'i·cal.** — *n.* A conic section. [<Gk. *kōnikos* <*kōnos* cone] — **con'i·cal·ly** *adv.*

conic projection A type of map in which the terrain is plotted on a cone, the projection then being flattened out to a plane surface.

conic section *Math.* A curve formed by the intersection of a plane with a right circular cone: an ellipse, parabola, or hyperbola, according to the inclination of the cutting plane to the axis.

conic sections That branch of mathematics which treats of the ellipse, parabola, and hyperbola. Also **con'ics.**

co·nid·i·if·er·ous (kō·nid'ē·if'ər·əs) *adj. Bot.* Bearing conidia. Also **co·nid'i·oph'o·rous** (-of'ər·əs). [<CONIDIUM + -FEROUS]

CONIC SECTIONS
a. Circle. *c.* Hyperbola.
b. Parabola. *d.* Ellipse.
e. Right line.

co·nid·i·o·phore (kō·nid'ē·ə·fôr', -fōr') *n. Bot.* A branch of the hypha in the mycelium of fungi which bears the conidia.

co·nid·i·um (kō·nid'ē·əm) *n.* *pl.* **co·nid·i·a** (kō·nid'ē·ə) *Bot.* A non-sexually produced propagative cell or spore borne upon special branches of the thallus in many species of fungi. Also **co·nid'i·o·spore** (kō·nid'ē·ə·spôr', -spōr'). [<NL <Gk. *konis* dust] — **co·nid'i·al** *adj.*

con·i·fer (kon'ə·fər, kō'nə-) *n.* Any of an order of evergreen shrubs and trees *(Coniferales)* belonging to the Gymnosperm subdivision of plants, characterized by needle-shaped leaves, strobili or cones, and a resinous wood: includes the pines, spruces, firs, and junipers. [<L <*conus* cone + *ferre* bear]

co·nif·er·in (kō·nif'ər·in) *n. Chem.* A crystalline compound, $C_{16}H_{22}O_8 \cdot 2H_2O$, found in the sap of coniferous trees: used in the preparation of vanillin.

co·nif·er·ous (kō·nif'ər·əs) *adj.* **1** Cone-bearing. **2** Containing or composed of conifers: *coniferous* forests.

co·ni·ine (kō'ni·ēn, -nē·in) *n. Chem.* A yellowish, oily, volatile alkaloid, $C_8H_{17}N$, contained in poison hemlock *(Conium maculatum)*: a narcotic, sometimes used locally to relieve pain. Also **co·nin** (kō'nin), **co·nine** (kō'nēn). [<CONIUM]

co·ni·ros·tral (kō'ni·ros'trəl) *adj. Ornithol.* Having a conical beak. [<L *conus* cone + *rostrum* beak]

co·ni·um (kō'nē·əm) *n.* Any of a genus *(Conium)* of tall, highly poisonous, biennial herbs of the parsley family; especially, *C. maculatum,* the poison hemlock. [<L <Gk. *kōneion* hemlock]

con·jec·ture (kən·jek'chər) *v.t.* **·tured, ·tur·ing** To conclude or suppose from incomplete evidence; guess; infer. — *v.i.* To make a conjecture. See synonyms under GUESS, SUPPOSE. — *n.* **1** An indecisive opinion; a guess; surmise. **2** The act of conjecturing. **3** *Obs.* Divination; prediction. See synonyms under GUESS, HYPOTHESIS. [<L *conjectura* <*jicere* <*com-* together + *jacere* throw] — **con·jec'tur·a·ble** *adj.* — **con·jec'tur·a·bly** *adv.* — **con·jec'tur·er** *n.*

con·join (kən·join') *v.t. & v.i.* To join together; associate; connect; unite. See synonyms under UNITE. [<F *conjoindre* <L *conjungere* <*com-* together + *jungere* join]

con·joint (kən·joint') *adj.* **1** Associated; conjoined. **2** Joint. [<F, pp. of *conjoindre.* See CONJOIN.] — **con·joint'ly** *adv.*

con·ju·gal (kon'joo·gəl) *adj.* Pertaining to marriage; connubial; matrimonial. [<F <L *conjugalis* <*conjunx, conjugis* spouse <*conjungere* join in marriage] — **con·ju·gal·i·ty** (kon'joo·gal'ə·tē) *n.* — **con'ju·gal·ly** *adv.*

con·ju·gate (kon'joo·gāt) *v.* **·gat·ed, ·gat·ing** *v.t.* **1** *Gram.* To give the inflections of: said of verbs. **2** *Rare* To unite or join together; couple, especially in marriage. — *v.i.* **3** *Biol.* To unite in conjugation. **4** *Rare* To unite in sexual intercourse. — *adj.* (kon'joo·git, -gāt) **1** Joined in pairs; coupled; paired. **2** *Math.* Reciprocally related; interchangeable. **3** *Chem.* Containing two or more radicals acting as one. **4** *Bot.* Composed of two leaflets: said of a pinnate leaf. **5** Kindred in origin and, usually, meaning: said of words; paronymous. Also **con'ju·gat'ed.** — *n.* (kon'joo·git, -gāt) **1** A word closely related to, and usually of kindred meaning with, another or others. **2** A member of a conjugate pair. Also **con'ju·gant.** [<L *conjugatus,* pp. of *conjugare* <*com-* together + *jugare* <*jugum* yoke]

con·ju·ga·tion (kon'joo·gā'shən) *n.* **1** Conjunction; union. **2** *Gram.* The inflection of a verb, or the expression of such inflection; also, a class of verbs similarly inflected, or the mode of inflection. **3** *Biol.* The temporary fusion of two similar protozoans during which exchange of nuclear material takes place.

con·junct (kən·jungkt', kon'jungkt) *adj.* Joined together; conjoined. [<L *conjunctus,* pp. of *conjungere.* See CONJOIN.] — **con·junct'ly** *adv.*

con·junc·tion (kən·jungk'shən) *n.* **1** The state of being joined together, or the things so joined; combination; league. **2** *Astron.* The position of an inferior planet when it is on a direct line with the earth and the sun, or of a superior planet when the sun is on the direct line between it and the earth. **3** Simultaneous occurrence of events. **4** *Gram.* A word used to connect words, phrases, clauses, or sentences: one of the eight traditional parts of speech. See synonyms under ASSOCIATION, UNION. — **coordinate conjunction** A conjunction, as *and, but, or,* which joins words or groups of words of equal rank. — **subordinate conjunction** A conjunction, as *as, because, if, that, though,* which joins clauses of minor rank to principal clauses. — **con·junc′tion·al** *adj.* — **con·junc′tion·al·ly** *adv.*

con·junc·ti·va (kon′jungk·tī′və) *n.* pl. **·vas** or **·vae** (-vē) *Anat.* The mucous membrane lining the eyelids and covering the anterior part of the eyeball. See illustration under EYE. [<NL (*membrana*) *conjunctiva* connective (membrane)]

con·junc·tive (kən·jungk′tiv) *adj.* **1** Joining; connective: *conjunctive* tissue. **2** Joined together. **3** *Gram.* **a** Serving to unite words, clauses, etc.; used as a conjunction: a *conjunctive* adverb. **b** Serving to unite both meaning and construction, as the conjunction *and.* — *n. Gram.* A conjunctive word. [<L *conjunctivus* < *conjungere.* See CONJOIN.] — **con·junc′tive·ly** *adv.*

con·junc·ti·vi·tis (kən·jungk′tə·vī′tis) *n. Pathol.* Inflammation of the conjunctiva; ophthalmia.

con·junc·ture (kən·jungk′chər) *n.* **1** A combination of circumstances; juncture; also, a crisis. **2** The act of joining; union.

con·ju·ra·tion (kon′jŏŏ·rā′shən) *n.* **1** An enchantment; incantation; spell. **2** Magic or a magical expression used in an appeal for supernatural aid. **3** A solemn invocation; adjuration.

con·jure (kən·jŏŏr′ *for v. defs. 1 and 6*; kon′jər, kun′- *for v. defs. 2–5*) *v.* **·jured,** **·jur·ing** *v.t.* **1** To call on or appeal to solemnly; adjure. **2** To summon, bring, or drive away by incantation or spell, as a devil or spirit. **3** To accomplish or effect by or as by magic. — *v.i.* **4** To practice magic or legerdemain. **5** To summon a devil or spirit by incantation. **6** *Obs.* To conspire. — *adj.* (kon′jər, kun′-) *U.S. Dial.* Given to practicing magic or curing by magic: a *conjure* man. [<OF *conjurer* <L *conjurare* <*com-* together + *jurare* swear]

con·nate (kon′āt) *adj.* **1** Born in and with one; innate; congenital. **2** Born or existing together or with another; cognate. **3** *Biol.* Congenitally or firmly united, as the parts of an organism. [<L *connatus,* pp. of *connasci,* var. of *cognasci.* See COGNATE.] — **con′nate·ly** *adv.* — **con′nate·ness** *n.*

con·nat·u·ral (kə·nach′ər·əl) *adj.* **1** Innate; congenital; inborn. **2** Allied; cognate. Also spelled *connatural.* [<Med. L *connaturalis* < *com-* together + *naturalis* NATURAL] — **con·nat′u·ral·ly** *adv.*

con·naught (kon′ôt) A cotton cloth used as a foundation for embroidery. [from *Connaught,* var. of *Connacht*]

con·nect (kə·nekt′) *v.t.* **1** To join together as by links or fastenings; unite or combine. **2** To bring into correlation; associate. **3** To think of as being similar or related; associate mentally. **4** To close or complete, as an electric circuit or telephone connection. — *v.i.* **5** To unite or join; be in close relation; be associated. **6** To meet as scheduled, as buses or trains, for transference of passengers. **7** *U.S. Colloq.* In some sports, to hit the ball or mark. [<L *connectere,* var. of *conectere* <*com-* together + *nectere* bind]

Con·nect·i·cut (kə·net′ə·kət) A State of the NE United States: 5,009 square miles; capital, Hartford; entered the Union Jan. 9, 1788, one of the original thirteen States; nickname, *Nutmeg State.* Abbr. CT

connecting rod *Mech.* A rod or bar in an engine, joining two or more moving parts.

con·nec·tion (kə·nek′shən) *n.* **1** The act or means of connecting or the state of being connected; union; combination. **2 a** Family relationship, especially by marriage. **b** A distant relative. **3** A company; denomination; a body of persons connected, or with whom one is connected, by relationship, belief, dealings, etc. **4** A direct transfer from one route to another, as in railway service. **5** Logical coherence or consistency, as the parts of an address. **6** That which connects or serves as a

bond of union: There is no *connection* between the two. **7** A mechanism or apparatus which serves to form a union of parts; specifically, a connecting rod or a connecting passageway in a series of flues. Also *Brit.* **con·nex′ion.** See synonyms under ASSOCIATION, KINSMAN.

con·nec·tive (kə·nek′tiv) *adj.* Capable of connecting, or serving to connect; causing or involving connection. — *n.* **1** That which connects. **2** *Gram.* A connecting word or particle, as a conjunction. **3** *Bot.* The portion of the filament of a stamen that unites the lobes of an anther. — **con·nec′tive·ly** *adv.*

connective tissue *Anat.* The fibrous tissue that pervades the whole body and serves to unite and support the various parts, as cartilage, bone, or tendon.

con·ning–tow·er (kon′ing·tou′ər) *n.* **1** The armored pilothouse on the deck of a warship. **2** In submarines, an observation tower serving also as an entrance.

con·ni·vance (kə·nī′vəns) *n.* **1** The act or fact of conniving. **2** Silent or indirect assent, especially to wrongdoing. **3** *Law* A guilty assent to or knowledge of a wrongful or criminal act during its occurrence. Also **con·ni′van·cy.**

con·nive (kə·nīv′) *v.i.* **·nived,** **·niv·ing** **1** To encourage or assent to a wrong by silence or feigned ignorance: with *at.* **2** To be in collusion: with *with.* [<L *connivere,* var. of *conivere* wink, shut the eyes] — **con·niv′er** *n.*

con·ni·vent (kə·nī′vənt) *adj. Biol.* Converging, as stamens or wings. [<L *connivens, -entis,* pp. of *connivere.* See CONNIVE.]

con·nois·seur (kon′ə·sûr′) *n.* A competent critical judge of anything, especially in matters of art and taste. [<F]

con·no·ta·tion (kon′ə·tā′shən) *n.* **1** The suggestive emotional content or significance of a word, additional to its explicit literal meaning; implication. **2** The act of connoting or connotating, and the quality or qualities connoted. [<Med. L *connotatio, -onis* < *connotare.* See CONNOTE.]

con·note (kə·nōt′) *v.t.* **·not·ed,** **·not·ing** To indicate or imply along with the literal meaning; mention by implication. Also **con·no·tate** (kon′ə·tāt). [<Med. L *connotare* <*com-* together + *notare* mark]

con·nu·bi·al (kə·noo′be·əl, -nyoo′-) *adj.* Pertaining to matrimony; relating to husband or wife; matrimonial; conjugal; nuptial. [<L *connubialis* <*connubium* <*com-* together + *nubere* marry] — **con·nu·bi·al·i·ty** (kə·noo′bē·al′ə·tē, -nyoo′-) *n.* — **con·nu′bi·al·ly** *adv.*

cono– *combining form* Cone; conical. Also, before vowels, **con–.** [<Gk. *kōnos* cone]

co·no·dont (kō′nə·dont, kon′ə-) *n. Paleontol.* A small toothlike fossil, found in Paleozoic rocks. [<CON(O)- + Gk. *odous, odontos* tooth]

co·noid (kō′noid) *adj.* Cone–shaped; conical. — *n.* Something having the form of a cone. [< Gk. *kōnoeides* conical] — **co·noi·dal** (kō·noid′l), **co·noi′dic** *adj.*

con·quer (kong′kər) *v.t.* **1** To overcome or subdue by force, as in war; vanquish. **2** To acquire or gain control of by or as by force of arms. **3** To overcome by mental or moral force; surmount. — *v.i.* **4** To be victorious. [<OF *conquerre* <L *conquirere* <*com-* thoroughly + *quaerere* seek] — **con′quer·a·ble** *adj.*

Synonyms: beat, checkmate, crush, defeat, discomfit, down, humble, master, overcome, overmaster, overmatch, overpower, overthrow, reduce, rout, subdue, subject, subjugate, surmount, triumph, vanquish, win, worst. A country is *conquered* when its armies are totally defeated and its territory is occupied by the enemy; it may be *subjected* to indemnity or to various disabilities; it is *subjugated* when it is held helplessly under military control; it is *subdued* when all resistance has died out. Any army is *defeated* when forcibly driven back; it is *routed* when it is converted into a mob of fugitives. Compare BAFFLE, BEAT, GAIN, HINDER, SUBDUE. *Antonyms:* capitulate, cede, fail, fall, fly, forfeit, lose, resign, retreat, submit, succumb, surrender, yield.

con·quest (kon′kwest, kong′-) *n.* **1** The act of conquering. **2** The thing conquered; that which is captured and taken forcibly, as terri-

tory, a person, or the favor of a person. See synonyms under VICTORY. — **the Conquest** The Norman Conquest. [<OF, pp. of *conquerre.* See CONQUER.]

con·quis·ta·dor (kon·kwis′tə·dôr, Sp. kōng·kēs′·tä·thôr′) *n.* pl. **·dors,** Sp. **·do·res** (-thō′rās) A conqueror; specifically, any of the Spanish conquerors of Mexico and Peru in the 16th century. [<Sp. <*conquistar* conquer]

con·san·guin·e·ous (kon′sang·gwin′e·əs) *adj.* **1** Descended from the same parent or ancestor; akin. **2** Of or pertaining to consanguinity. Also **con·san·guine** (kon·sang′gwin), **con′san·guin′e·al.** [<L *consanguineus* <*com-* together + *sanguis* blood] — **con′san·guin′e·ous·ly** *adv.*

con·san·guin·i·ty (kon′sang·gwin′ə·tē) *n.* **1** The relationship that proceeds from a common ancestry; blood relationship. **2** Any near affinity or relationship. See synonyms under AFFINITY, KIN.

con·science (kon′shəns) *n.* **1** Moral consciousness in general; the activity or faculty by which distinctions are made between right and wrong in one's own conduct and character; the act or power of moral discrimination; ethical judgment or sensibility. **2** Conformity in conduct to one's conceptions of right and wrong. **3** *Obs.* Consciousness. — **in (all) conscience 1** In truth; in reason and honesty. **2** Certainly; assuredly. [<F <L *conscientia* <*com-* together + *scire* know] — **con′science·less** *adj.*

con·sci·en·tious (kon′shē·en′shəs) *adj.* Governed or dictated by conscience; scrupulous. — **con′sci·en′tious·ly** *adv.* — **con′sci·en′·tious·ness** *n.*

conscientious objector One who, on grounds of religious or moral convictions, objects to warfare and refuses to perform military service.

con·scion·a·ble (kon′shən·ə·bəl) *adj.* Conformable to conscience or right. — **con′scion·a·bly** *adv.*

con·scious (kon′shəs) *adj.* **1** Immediately aware of; mentally recognizing, to some degree and extent, one's own inner feeling and thought, or their objective reference. **2** Unjustifiably embarrassed by the sense of one's own individuality; self-conscious. **3** Mentally alert; well aware of some object, impression, or truth. **4** Present in the mind; recognized as belonging to oneself: *conscious* superiority. **5** Cognizant of guilt or fault. **6** Deliberate: a *conscious* lie. **7** Pertaining to consciousness. **8** Having the faculty and psychical attributes of consciousness. **9** *Obs.* Possessing knowledge in common with another; mutually informed. — *n. Psychoanal.* That part of mental life of which an individual is aware.[<L *conscius* <*com-* together + *scire* know]

Synonyms (adj.): aware, cognizant, sensible. One is *aware* of that which exists without him; he is *conscious* of the inner workings of his own mind. *Sensible* may be used in the exact sense of *conscious,* or it may partake of both the senses mentioned above. One may be *sensible* of his own or another's error; he is *conscious* only of his own. A person may feel *assured* or *sure* of something false or non-existent; what he is *aware* of, still more what he is *conscious* of, must be fact. *Sensible* has often a reference to the emotions, where *conscious* might apply only to the intellect; to say a culprit is *sensible* of his degradation is more forcible than to say he is *conscious* of it. *Antonyms:* dead, deaf, ignorant, insensible, unaware, unconscious.

con·scious·ness (kon′shəs·nis) *n.* **1** The state of being conscious; sensation; knowledge. **2** The power of self-knowledge; internal perception. **3** The aggregate of the conscious states in an individual or a group of persons. **4** The awareness of some particular object, state, agency, or influence; an intuition. **5** Any form of intellectual activity or its product in direct and convincing knowledge, whether of external or internal objects. See synonyms under FEELING, MIND.

con·script (kon′skript) *adj.* **1** Registered; enrolled. **2** Compulsorily enlisted, as a soldier or an armed force. — *n.* One who is compulsorily enrolled for military service; a draftee. — *v.t.* (kən·skript′) To force into military service; draft. [< L *conscriptus*, pp. of *conscribere* enrol < *com-* together + *scribere* write]

con·scrip·tion (kən·skrip′shən) *n.* A compulsory enrolment of men for military service; draft.

con·se·crate (kŏn′sə·krāt) *v.t.* ·crat·ed, ·crat·ing 1 To set apart as sacred; dedicate to sacred uses with appointed ceremonies; to *consecrate* a church, a bishop, or the elements of the Eucharist. 2 To dedicate solemnly, as from emotions of gratitude or convictions of duty; devote: He *consecrated* his life to the cause. 3 To apotheosize; canonize. 4 To make reverend or venerable; hallow: *consecrated* by time. — *adj.* Hallowed; consecrated. [< L *consecratus*, pp. of *consecrare* < *com-* thoroughly + *sacer* holy] — **con′se·cra′tor** *n.* — **con·se·cra·to·ry** (kŏn′sə·krə·tôr′ē, -tō′rē) *adj.*

con·se·cra·tion (kŏn′sə·krā′shən) *n.* 1 The act or ceremony of separating from a common to a sacred use; the state of being consecrated. 2 Canonization, as of a saint; apotheosis, as of a god.

con·sec·u·tive (kən·sek′yə·tiv) *adj.* 1 Following in uninterrupted succession; successive. 2 Characterized by logical sequence. 3 Following as a consequence or result; consequent. 4 *Gram.* Denoting result or consequence. [< L *consecutus*, pp. of *consequi.* See CONSEQUENT.] — **con·sec′u·tive·ly** *adv.* — **con·sec′·u·tive·ness** *n.*

con·sen·su·al (kən·sen′shŏŏ·əl) *adj.* 1 *Law* Existing merely by virtue of acquiescence. 2 *Physiol.* **a** Excited by sympathetic or reflex action. **b** Denoting instinctive and reflex actions and movements which are stimulated by conscious sensations. — **con·sen′su·al·ly** *adv.*

con·sen·sus (kən·sen′səs) *n.* A collective opinion; general agreement. [< L < *consentire* < *com-* together + *sentire* feel, think]

con·sent (kən·sent′) *v.i.* 1 To yield or accede, as to a proposal or request, when one has the right, power, or wish not to do so. 2 To give assent, as to a contract; agree. 3 *Obs.* To agree together; accord. See synonyms under AGREE, ASSENT. — *n.* 1 A voluntary yielding of the will, judgment, or inclination to what is proposed or desired by another; acquiescence; compliance. 2 Harmony in opinion or sentiment; agreement; concord. 3 *Law* A rational and voluntary concurrence in an act or contract. 4 *Obs.* Harmonious correspondence or operation. See synonyms under HARMONY, PERMISSION. [< OF < L *consentire.* See CONSENSUS.] — **con·sent′er** *n.*

con·sent·i·ble (kən·sen′tə·bəl) *adj.* Capable of being established or fixed by consent of those interested.

con·sen·tience (kən·sen′shəns) *n.* 1 The state or quality of being in agreement or accord. 2 *Psychol.* The sensuous analog, in automatic or reflex action, of consciousness in conscious action. — **con·sen′tient** *adj.*

con·se·quence (kŏn′sə·kwens, -kwəns) *n.* 1 That which naturally follows from a preceding action or condition; the effect of a cause; result. 2 The conclusion of a syllogism; inference; deduction. 3 The relation between an antecedent and a consequent; causal or logical consecution; sequence. 4 Distinction; note: said of persons: a man of *consequence*; also, significance; moment: said of things: an event of no *consequence.* 5 Self-importance; consequentiality: used of persons.

con·se·quent (kŏn′sə·kwent, -kwənt) *adj.* 1 Following as a natural result or as a logical conclusion. 2 Characterized by correctness of reasoning; logical. — *n.* 1 The conclusion of an inference or syllogism; consequence. 2 That which follows something else, as in time, order, or relation, without causal connection: opposed to *antecedent.* 3 *Math.* **a** The second term of a ratio. **b** In a series of four proportionals, the second and fourth terms. 4 Having a course or direction depending on or resulting from the original slope of the surface. See synonyms under CONSEQUENCE. [< L *consequens, -entis*, ppr. of *consequi* < *com-* together + *sequi* follow]

con·se·quent·ly (kŏn′sə·kwent′lē, -kwənt·lē) *adv.* As a result; therefore. See synonyms under THEREFORE.

con·ser·va·tion (kŏn′sər·vā′shən) *n.* 1 The act of keeping or protecting from loss or injury: the *conservation* of health, or of social order. 2 The preservation of natural resources for

economical use; specifically, the preservation of forests, fisheries, harbors, etc. [< L *conservatio, -onis* < *conservare.* See CONSERVE.]

conservation of energy *Physics* The principle that in any closed material system the total amount of energy remains constant, though it may assume different forms successively.

conservation of mass *Physics* The principle that the total mass of any material system remains constant through all changes taking place within the system.

con·ser·va·tive (kən·sûr′və·tiv) *adj.* 1 Adhering to and tending to preserve the existing order of things; opposed to change or progress. 2 Conserving; preservative. 3 Moderate; cautious; within a safe margin: a *conservative* estimate or statement. 4 *N.A.* A conservative person. — **con·ser′va·tive·ly** *adv.* — **con·ser′·va·tive·ness** *n.*

Conservative Judaism Judaism as practiced especially in the U.S. by those who hold that both the Scriptures and the oral laws are divinely authoritative but that traditional rituals may be selectively observed or modified to accord with contemporary cultural conditions. Compare ORTHODOX JUDAISM, REFORM JUDAISM.

con·ser·va·tor (kŏn′sər·vā′tər, kən·sûr′və·tər) *n.* A protector; guardian; keeper.

con·ser·va·to·ry (kən·sûr′və·tôr′ē, -tō′rē) *n.* *pl.* ·ries 1 A small greenhouse or glass-enclosed room in which plants are grown and displayed. 2 A school of art, especially of music. 3 *Obs.* A place for the preservation or protection of anything: also **con·ser·va·toire** (kən·sûr′və·twär′) — *adj.* Adapted to preserve.

con·serve (kən·sûrv′) *v.t.* ·served, ·serv·ing 1 To keep from loss, decay, or depletion; supervise and protect. 2 To preserve with sugar. — *n.* (kŏn′sûrv, kən·sûrv′) 1 A kind of jam made of several fruits stewed together in sugar, often with nuts, raisins, etc. 2 A medicated confection of fresh vegetable substances and sugar. See synonyms under PRESERVE. [< F *conserver* < L *conservare* < *com-* thoroughly + *servare* keep, save] — **con·serv′a·ble** *adj.* — **con·serv′er** *n.*

con·sid·er (kən·sid′ər) *v.t.* 1 To think about or deliberate upon; examine mentally. 2 To look upon or regard as; think to be. 3 To hold as an opinion: with a clause as object. 4 To make allowance for; keep in mind. 5 To take into account; have a regard for: to *consider* the feelings of others. 6 *Archaic* To observe closely. 7 *Obs.* To fee; remunerate. — *v.i.* 8 To think closely; cogitate. [< F *considérer* < L *considerare*, ? < *com-* thoroughly + *sidus, sideris* star; with ref. to astrology]

con·sid·er·ate (kən·sid′ər·it) *adj.* 1 Exhibiting or given to consideration. 2 Thoughtful; kind; prudent. See synonyms under CHARITABLE, THOUGHTFUL. — **con·sid′er·ate·ly** *adv.*

con·sid·er·a·tion (kən·sid′ə·rā′shən) *n.* 1 The act of considering. 2 Thoughtful and kindly feeling or treatment. 3 A circumstance to be taken into account. 4 Something given in return for a service; remuneration. 5 Importance; consequence; standing. 6 *Law* The thing given or done, or to be given, done, or abstained from, by one party to a contract, in exchange for the act or promise of the other. Also *Obs.* **con·sid′er·ance.** See synonyms under FRIENDSHIP, PRUDENCE, REASON, REFLECTION, THOUGHT. [< F *considération* < L *consideratio, -onis* < *considerare.* See CONSIDER.]

con·sid·ered (kən·sid′ərd) *adj.* Premeditated; deliberated.

con·sid·er·ing (kən·sid′ər·ing) *prep.* In view of; taking into account the fact of: *Considering* his deafness, he takes a large part in the conversation. — *adv. Colloq.* Taking all the facts into account: He came out quite well, *considering.* — *conj.* In view of: *Considering* how I feel, you're lucky to see me at all.

con·sign (kən·sīn′) *v.t.* 1 To entrust or commit to the care of another. 2 To make over or relegate: They *consigned* his memory to oblivion. 3 To forward or deliver, as merchandise, for sale or disposal. 4 To set apart or devote, as for a specific purpose or use. 5 *Obs.* To impress, as with a seal; sign. — *v.i.* 6 *Obs.* To yield oneself; consent. See synonyms under COMMIT. [< F *consigner* < L *consignare* < *com-* with + *signum* a seal] — **con·sign′a·ble** *adj.* — **con·sign·or** (kən·sī′nər, kŏn′sī·nôr′), **con·sign′er** *n.*

con·sig·na·to·ry (kən·sig′nə·tôr′ē, -tō′rē) *n.* *pl.* ·ries One who signs jointly with another or others.

con·sign·ment (kən·sīn′mənt) *n.* 1 The sending of property to a person for keeping, sale, or shipment. 2 The property consigned. 3 A written instrument by which something is consigned. 4 A method of wholesale or jobber selling whereby the retailer pays for goods only after he has sold them: usually in the phrase **on consignment.**

con·sist (kən·sist′) *v.i.* 1 To be made up or constituted: with *of.* 2 To have as substance, quality, or nature: with *in*: Her beauty *consists* in her virtue. 3 To be compatible; harmonize; exist in agreement: with *with*: His story *consists* with the evidence. [< L *consistere* < *com-* together + *sistere* stand]

con·sis·ten·cy (kən·sis′tən·sē) *n.* *pl.* ·cies 1 Compatibility or harmony between things, acts, or statements; logical connection; agreement; also, agreement with what has been previously done, expressed, or agreed on. 2 The condition of holding together; firmness, nearness, or density. 3 Degree of firmness, thickness, or density. Also **con·sis′tence.** See synonyms under HARMONY.

con·sis·tent (kən·sis′tənt) *adj.* 1 Characterized by consistency; agreeing with itself; not self-contradictory. 2 Congruous; compatible. 3 Firmly united; solid. [< L *consistens, -entis* < *consistere.* See CONSIST.] — **con·sis′tent·ly** *adv.*

con·sis·to·ry (kən·sis′tər·ē) *n.* *pl.* ·ries 1 *Eccl.* **a** The highest council of the Roman Catholic Church, composed of all the cardinals, and usually presided over by the Pope. **b** In many Reformed Churches, a local governing body consisting of the ministers and elders of a congregation. **c** A court of the Lutheran state churches, appointed by the government to oversee ecclesiastical affairs. **d** A diocesan court of the Church of England, presided over by the chancelor or commissary of the diocese. 2 The place where an ecclesiastical court is held; a council house or hall of justice. 3 A council of dignitaries, as of Freemasons of the 32nd degree. [< LL *consistorium*] — **con·sis·to·ri·al** (kŏn′sis·tôr′ē·əl, -tō′rē-), **con·sis·to′ri·an** *adj.*

con·so·ci·ate (kən·sō′shē·āt) *v.t.* & *v.i.* ·at·ed, ·at·ing To bring or come into association; unite: said especially of pastors and organizations of Congregational churches. — *adj.* (kən·sō′shē·it, -āt) Associated with; united. — *n.* (kən·sō′shē·it) An associate; partner. [< L *consociatus*, pp. of *consociare* < *com-* together + *socius* ally, friend]

con·so·cies (kən·sō′shēz) *n. Ecol.* A plant or animal community marked by the dominance of one species belonging to the life forms typical of the given environment. [< NL < L *com-* together + *socius* ally]

con·so·la·tion (kŏn′sə·lā′shən) *n.* 1 The act of consoling, or the state of being consoled; solace. 2 A comforting thought, person, or fact. [< F < L *consolatio, -onis* < *consolari.* See CONSOLE.]

con·sole¹ (kən·sōl′) *v.t.* ·soled, ·sol·ing To comfort (a person) in grief or sorrow; solace; cheer. [< F *consoler* < L *consolari* < *com-* together + *solari* solace] — **con·sol′a·ble** *adj.*

Synonyms: comfort, condole, encourage, sympathize. One *condoles* with another by the expression of kindly sympathy in his trouble; he *consoles* him by considerations adapted to soothe and sustain the spirit; he *encourages* him by the hope of some relief or deliverance; he *comforts* him by whatever act or word tends to bring mind or body to a state of rest and cheer. We *sympathize* with others, not only in sorrow, but in joy. Compare ALLEVIATE, PITY. *Antonyms:* annoy, distress, disturb, grieve, hurt, sadden, trouble, wound.

CONSOLE *(def. 1)*

con·sole² (kŏn′sōl) *n.* 1 A bracket of any kind, especially one used to support cornices or ornamental fixtures; a corbel. 2 A console table. 3 The portion of an organ containing the manuals and stops. 4 A cabinet for a radio, phonograph, or television set, designed to rest on the floor. [< F, a bracket; ult. origin uncertain]

con·sol·i·date (kən·sol′ə·dāt) v. **·dat·ed**, **·dat·ing** v.t. **1** To make solid, firm, or coherent; strengthen. **2** Mil. To secure and strengthen, as a newly captured position. **3** To combine in one body or system; form a union of. — v.i. **4** To become united, solid, or firm. See synonyms under UNITE. [<L consolidatus, pp. of consolidare < com- together + solidus solid]

con·so·lute temperature (kon′sə·lōot) Critical solution temperature.

con·som·mé (kon′sə·mā′, Fr. kôṅ·sô·mā′) n. A clear soup made of meat and sometimes vegetables boiled in water. [<F, pp. of consommer <L consummare. See CONSUMMATE.]

con·so·nance (kon′sə·nəns) n. **1** Agreement; accord; harmony. **2** Physics The induced vibration of one sonorous body acting in sympathy with another, as of one piano string with another; resonance. **3** Music A combination of tones regarded as pleasing and not requiring resolution. Also **con′so·nan·cy**. See synonyms under HARMONY.

con·so·nant (kon′sə·nənt) adj. **1** Being in agreement or harmony; consistent. **2** Consonantal. **3** Music Having the quality of consonance. Also **con′so·nous**. — n. **1** Phonet. A sound produced by a contact or constriction of the speech organs which results in complete or partial blockage of the breath stream. Distinguished from vowels, which are characterized primarily by the shape of the resonance cavity, consonants are described by their place of articulation (bilabial, alveolar, etc.), vibration or non-vibration of the vocal cords (voiced or voiceless), presence or absence of nasality, and manner of formation (stop, fricative, etc.). **2** A letter representing such a sound. [<MF <L consonans, -antis, ppr. of consonare < com- together + sonare sound] — **con′so·nant·ly** adv. — **con′so·nant·ness** n.

con·sort (kon′sôrt) n. **1** A companion or associate. **2** A husband or wife; mate. **3** An accompanying vessel. **4** Companionship; company. — v.t. (kən·sôrt′) **1** To join; associate. **2** Obs. To accompany; escort. — v.i. **3** To keep company; associate. **4** To be in agreement; harmonize. [<F <L consors, consortis < com- together + sors share, lot]

con·sor·ti·um (kən·sôr′shē·əm) n. pl. **·ti·a** (-shē·ə) **1** Law The right of a husband to the society and conjugal affection of his wife. **2** Law Coalition; union, as of incorporated companies. **3** Bot. The close association of certain algae and lichens. [<L, fellowship]

con·spec·tus (kən·spek′təs) n. pl. **·tus·es** **1** A general view of a subject. **2** A digest or summary. See synonyms under ABRIDGMENT. [<L <conspicere. See CONSPICUOUS.]

con·sperse (kən·spûrs′) adj. **1** Sprinkled. **2** Ornithol. Irregularly dotted, as certain birds' eggs. [<L conspersus, pp. of conspergere sprinkle com- + spargere scatter]

con·spic·u·ous (kən·spik′yōo·əs) adj. **1** Clearly visible; prominent and distinct; obvious. **2** Readily attracting attention; unusual; striking. See synonyms under EMINENT, EVIDENT, MANIFEST. [<L conspicuus < conspicere < com- together + specere look at]

con·spir·a·cy (kən·spir′ə·sē) n. pl. **·cies** **1** An agreement between two or more persons to do an evil act in concert; a plot; secret combination of men for an evil purpose. **2** Law A combination of two or more persons to commit any act punishable by law. **3** Any striking concurrence of persons, classes, or agencies. — **con·spir·a·tor** (kən·spir′ə·tər) n.

Synonyms: cabal, combination, conclave, crew, faction, gang. A conspiracy is a combination of persons for an evil purpose, or the act of so combining. A faction is more extensive than a conspiracy, less formal in organization, less definite in plan. Faction and its adjective, factious, have always an unfavorable sense. Cabal commonly denotes a conspiracy of leaders. A gang is a company of workmen all doing the same work under one leader; the word is used figuratively only of combinations which it is meant to stigmatize as rude and mercenary; crew is used in a closely similar sense. A conclave is secret, but of larger numbers, ordinarily, than a cabal, and may have honorable use; as, the conclave

of cardinals. See CABAL.

con·spire (kən·spīr′) v. **·spired**, **·spir·ing** v.t. **1** To plot; scheme for. — v.i. **2** To form a plot, especially secretly, for evil or unlawful purposes. **3** To concur in action or endeavor, as circumstances. [<F conspirer <L conspirare < com- together + spirare breathe]

con·sta·ble (kon′stə·bəl, kun′-) n. **1** An officer of the peace; a policeman. **2** A high military officer in medieval monarchies. **3** The keeper or governor of a castle. — **Lord High Constable of England** A former military and judicial officer of high rank. [<OF conestable <LL comes stabuli count of the stable, chief groom] — **con′sta·ble·ship′** n.

con·stab·u·lar·y (kon·stab′yə·ler′ē) adj. Pertaining to or consisting of constables. Also **con·stab′u·lar** (-lər). — n. pl. **·lar·ies 1** Constables collectively. **2** A military police force.

con·stant (kon′stənt) adj. **1** Steady in purpose; resolute; persevering; faithful. **2** Steady in movement. **3** Long-continuing, or continually recurring. **4** Invariable. **5** Obs. Firm; positive; consistent. — n. **1** That which is permanent or invariable. **2** Math. A quantity which retains a fixed value throughout a given discussion. **3** In the sciences, any characteristic of a substance, event, or phenomenon, numerically determined, that remains always the same under specified conditions, as gravitation, the velocity of light, the melting or freezing point, etc. See synonyms under CONTINUAL, PERPETUAL. [<L constans, -antis, ppr. of constare < com- thoroughly + stare stand] — **con′stant·ly** adv.

con·stant·an (kon′stən·tan) n. A ductile, non-corrosive alloy of nickel and copper with high thermal and electrical resistance: used in rheostats and thermocouples. [Arbitrary coinage <CONSTANT]

con·stel·late (kon′stə·lāt) v.t. & v.i. **·lat·ed**, **·lat·ing** To group in constellations. — adj. Adorned or studded with constellations. [<LL constellatus studded with stars < com- together + stella star]

con·stel·la·tion (kon′stə·lā′shən) n. **1** Astron. An apparent group or cluster of stars, fortuitously associated on mythological or pictorial grounds. See table above. **2** An assemblage of brilliant things or persons. **3** In astrology, the aspect of the planets at the time of one's birth; hence, disposition or character as influenced by one's horoscope. **4** Psychol. A group of associated emotions, ideas, tendencies, etc., centering around a dominant element. — **con·stel·la·to·ry** (kən·stel′ə·tôr′ē, -tō′rē) adj.

con·ster·na·tion (kon′stər·nā′shən) n. **1** Complete confusion; bafflement. **2** Sudden overwhelming fear; terror with confusion; dismay.

con·sti·pa·tion (kon′stə·pā′shən) n. A morbid inactivity of the bowels; difficult evacuation.

con·stit·u·en·cy (kən·stich′ōo·ən·sē) n. pl. **·cies 1** A body of constituents. **2** The district from which a representative is elected to a legislative body.

con·stit·u·ent (kən·stich′ōo·ənt) adj. **1** Serving to form or compose as a necessary part; constituting: Chlorine and sodium are the constituent elements of salt. **2** Entitled to vote for a public officer or representative. **3** Having the power to frame or modify a constitution. — n. **1** One represented politically or in business; a voter; client. **2** A necessary part of a chemical compound: distinguished from component. See synonyms under PART. [<L constituens, -entis, ppr. of constituere. See CONSTITUTE.]

con·sti·tute (kon′stə·tōot, -tyōot) v.t. **·tut·ed**, **·tut·ing 1** To form or be the substance of; compose; make up. **2** To impart a given character to. **3** To make or form, as of materials or elements; construct. **4** To establish or found, as a school. **5** To set up or enact, as a law. **6** To depute or appoint, as to an office or function. **7** To give legal or official form to, as a court or assembly. **8** Obs. To place or put in position. See synonyms under MAKE. [<L constitutus, pp. of constituere < com- together + statuere place, station] — **con′sti·**

TABLE OF CONSTELLATIONS

Explanation: GROUP N includes all constellations within 45 degrees of the north pole. GROUP E includes all constellations within 45 degrees of each side of the equator. GROUP S includes all constellations within 45 degrees of the south pole.

NAME	Group	On the Meridian at 9 P.M.	NAME	Group	On the Meridian at 9 P.M.	NAME	Group	On the Meridian at 9 P.M.
Andromeda	E	Nov.	Delphinus	E	Sept.	Pegasus	E	Oct.
Antlia	E	April	Dorado	S	Jan.	Perseus	N	Dec.
Apus	S	July	Draco	N	June	Phœnix	S	Nov.
Aquarius	E	Oct.	Equuleus	E	Sept.	Pictor	S	Jan.
Aquila	E	Aug.	Eridanus	E	Dec.	Pisces	E	Nov.
Ara	S	July	Fornax	E	Dec.	Piscis Austrinus	E	Oct.
Aries	E	Dec.	Gemini	E	Feb.	Puppis	E	Feb.
Auriga	E	Feb.	Grus	S	Oct.	Pyxis	E	March
Boötes	E	June	Hercules	E	July	Reticulum	S	Jan.
Cælum	E	Jan.	Horologium	S	Dec.	Sagitta	E	Aug.
Camelopardalis	N	March	Hydra	E	April	Sagittarius	E	Aug.
Cancer	E	March	Hydrus	S	Dec.	Scorpius	E	July
Canes Venatici	E	May	Indus	S	Oct.	Sculptor	E	Nov.
Canis Major	E	Feb.	Lacerta	N	Oct.	Scutum	E	Aug.
Canis Minor	E	March	Leo	E	April	Serpens	E	July
Capricornus	E	Sept.	Leo Minor	E	April	Sextans	E	April
Carina	S	March	Lepus	E	Jan.	Taurus	E	Jan.
Cassiopeia	N	Nov.	Libra	E	June	Telescopium	S	Aug.
Centaurus	E	May	Lupus	E	June	Triangulum	E	Dec.
Cepheus	N	Nov.	Lynx	N	Feb.	Triangulum Australe	S	July
Cetus	E	Dec.	Lyra	E	Aug.	Tucana	S	Oct.
Chameleon	S	April	Mensa	S	Jan.	Ursa Major	N	April
Columba	E	Feb.	Microscopium	S	Sept.	Ursa Minor	N	....
Coma Berenices	E	May	Monoceros	E	March	Vela	E	March
Corona Australis	E	Aug.	Musca	S	May	Virgo	E	June
Corona Borealis	E	July	Norma	S	July	Volans	S	March
Corvus	E	May	Octans	S	....	Vulpecula	E	Sept.
Crater	E	April	Ophiuchus	E	July			
Crux	S	May	Orion	E	Jan.			
Cygnus	E	Sept.	Pavo	S	Aug.			

The four constellations Carina, Puppis, Pyxis, and Vela were formerly considered as a single one, called Argo Navis.

tut'er n. — con'sti·tu'tive adj. — con'sti·tu'·tive·ly adv. — con'sti·tu'tive·ness n.

con·sti·tu·tion (kon'stə·tōō'shən, -tyōō'-) n. 1 The act of constituting. 2 A system of related parts; composition; specifically, bodily frame or temperament. 3 The fundamental laws and practices that normally govern the operation of a state or association; especially, the Constitution of the United States of America, which was framed and adopted by a convention called for that purpose (1787), subsequently ratified by each State separately, and went into operation Mar. 4, 1789. 4 Archaic An imperial ordinance or rescript.

con·sti·tu·tion·al (kon'stə·tōō'shən·əl, -tyōō'-) adj. 1 Pertaining to, inherent in, or affecting the constitution of a person or of a state; consistent with the constitution of a state; lawful. 2 Acting under and controlled by a constitution: a constitutional monarchy. 3 Loyal to the constitution. 4 Framing or amending a constitution. See synonyms under RADICAL. — n. A walk taken for one's health.

con·sti·tu·tion·al·ism (kon'stə·tōō'shən·əl·iz'·əm, -tyōō-) n. 1 The theory or principle of constitutional government. 2 Adherence to this theory. 3 A constitutional form of government.

con·strain (kən·strān') v.t. 1 To compel by physical or moral means; oblige. 2 To confine, as by bonds. 3 To restrain; compel to inaction. 4 Obs. To violate; force. See synonyms under COMPEL, MAKE, RESTRAIN. [<OF constreindre <L constringere <com- together + stringere bind tight. Doublet of CONSTRINGE.] — con·strain'a·ble adj. — con·strain'·er n.

con·straint (kən·strānt') n. 1 The act of constraining, or the state of being constrained; compulsion. 2 Repression or embarrassment. 3 Anything that constrains. See synonyms under MODESTY, RESERVE. [<OF constreinte <constreindre. See CONSTRAIN.]

con·strict (kən·strikt') v.t. To compress or draw together at some point; bind; cramp. [<L constrictus, pp. of constringere. See CONSTRAIN.] — con·stric'tive adj.

con·stringe (kən·strinj') v.t. ·stringed, ·string·ing To cause contraction in; shrink; compress. [<L constringere. Doublet of CONSTRAIN.]

con·strin·gent (kən·strin'jənt) adj. 1 Tending to constrict. 2 Causing constriction. [<L constringens, -entis, ppr. of constringere. See CONSTRAIN.] — con·strin'gen·cy n.

con·struct (kən·strukt') v.t. 1 To put together and set up; build; arrange. 2 To devise. — n. (kon'strukt) 1 Anything systematically constructed or composed. 2 Psychol. A complex of mental images and impressions, deliberately synthesized in a form to aid the imagination in further speculation. [<L constructus, pp. of construere. See CONSTRUE.] — con·struct'er, con·struc'tor n.

con·struc·tion (kən·struk'shən) n. 1 The act of constructing; also, that which is constructed. 2 Style of building or composing. 3 The act of construing, or the interpretation thereby arrived at. 4 Gram. a The putting together of forms syntactically, as in sentences, or morphologically, as in words; also, an example of this. b The syntactical relationship of words, clauses, and sentences to each other. — con·struc'tion·al adj.

con·struc·tion·ist (kən·struk'shən·ist) n. 1 One who construes laws, etc., or one who advocates a particular construction. 2 One who interprets literally a law or body of writings, especially the U.S. Constitution or the Bible.

con·strue (kən·strōō') v. ·strued, ·stru·ing v.t. 1 To analyze the grammatical structure of (a clause or sentence) so as to determine the use, interrelations, and function of each word; parse. 2 To translate orally. 3 To deduce by inference; interpret. 4 Gram. To combine (words, etc.) according to syntax: The noun aerodynamics is construed as a singular. — v.i. 5 To determine grammatical structure. 6 To infer; deduce. 7 To admit of grammatical analysis. — n. 1 A construction or act of construing. 2 A translation according to a given construction. [<L construere <com- together + struere build up] — con·stru'a·ble adj. — con·stru'er n.

con·sub·stan·tial (kon'səb·stan'shəl) adj. Having the same substance: The Son is consubstantial with the Father. See TRINITY.

con·sub·stan·ti·ate (kon'səb·stan'shē·āt) v. ·at·ed, ·at·ing v.t. 1 To unite in one common substance. 2 To regard as being so united. — v.i. 3 To become one in substance. 4 To believe in the doctrine of consubstantiation. [<Med. L consubstantiatus, pp. of consubstantiare <com- together + substantia SUBSTANCE]

con·sub·stan·ti·a·tion (kon'səb·stan'shē·ā'shən) n. Theol. The theory of the substantial presence of Christ in the consecrated eucharistic elements, together with the unchanged substance of bread and wine.

con·sue·tude (kon'swi·tōōd, -tyōōd) n. Custom; association. [<OF <L consuetudo CUSTOM] — con·sue·tu·di·nar·y (kon'swi·tōō'də·ner'ē, -tyōō'-), con'sue·tu'di·nal adj.

con·sul (kon'səl) n. 1 An officer appointed to reside in a foreign port or city, chiefly as the representative of his country's commercial interests. 2 Either of two chief magistrates ruling conjointly in the Roman republic. 3 Any of the three chief magistrates of the French republic, 1799–1804. [<L] — con·su·lar (kon'sə·lər) adj.

con·su·late (kon'sə·lit) n. 1 The office or term of office of a consul: also con'sul·ship. 2 Government by consuls. 3 The official place of business of a consul. [<L consulatus <consul consul]

consul general A consular officer of the highest rank stationed in an important foreign commercial city, who supervises the other consuls in his district.

con·sult (kən·sult') v.t. 1 To ask advice or information of. 2 To have regard to, as interest or duty; consider. 3 Obs. To contrive or devise. — v.i. 4 To ask advice. 5 To compare views; take counsel: with with. [<L consultare, freq. of consulere seek advice]

con·sult·ant (kən·sul'tənt) n. 1 A person referred to for expert or professional advice. 2 One who consults.

con·sul·ta·tion (kon'səl·tā'shən) n. 1 The act of consulting. 2 A meeting, as of physicians, for conference.

con·sume (kən·sōōm') v. ·sumed, ·sum·ing v.t. 1 To destroy, as by burning. 2 To eat or drink up. 3 To expend wastefully; squander; use up, as money or time. 4 To hold the interest of; engross. — v.i. 5 To be wasted or destroyed. See synonyms under ABSORB, BURN. [<L consumere <com- thoroughly + sumere take up, use] — con·sum'a·ble adj.

con·sum·er (kən·sōō'mər) n. 1 One who or that which consumes. 2 One who uses up an article of exchangeable value; one of the buying public.

con·sum·er·ism (kən·sōō'mər·iz'əm) n. The policy or program of protecting the interests of the consumer. [<CONSUMER + -ISM, on analogy with capitalism, etc.]

consumers' goods Econ. Products for satisfying people's needs rather than for producing other goods or services; goods sold for use: opposed to producers' goods.

con·sum·mate (kon'sə·māt) v.t. ·mat·ed, ·mat·ing 1 To bring to completion or perfection; achieve. 2 To fulfil, as a marriage by cohabitation. See synonyms under ACCOMPLISH, EFFECT. — adj. (kən·sum'it) Of the highest degree; perfect; complete. [<L consummatus, pp. of consummare <com- together + summa sum, total] — con·sum'mate·ly adv. — con'·sum·ma'tion n. — con'sum·ma·tive, con·sum·ma·to·ry (kon·sum'ə·tôr'ē, -tō'rē) adj. — con'·sum·ma'tor n.

con·sump·ti·ble (kən·sump'tə·bəl) adj. Consumable, as by use. — n. Anything that can be consumed or used.

con·sump·tion (kən·sump'shən) n. 1 The act or process of consuming; gradual destruction, as by burning, etc. 2 Pathol. A wasting disease; specifically, pulmonary tuberculosis. 3 Econ. The use and consequent destruction of goods in the satisfying of people's needs. [<L consumptio, -onis <consumere. See CONSUME.]

con·sump·tive (kən·sump'tiv) adj. 1 Tending to, causing, or designed for consumption. 2 Connected with or affected by pulmonary tuberculosis. — n. A person affected with pulmonary tuberculosis. — con·sump'tive·ly adv. — con·sump'tive·ness n.

con·ta·bes·cence (kon'tə·bes'əns) n. Bot. A condition in which the stamens and pollen are abortive: often in hybridized plants. [<L con-

tabescens, -entis, ppr. of contabescere <com- thoroughly + tabes a wasting away, dwindling] — con'ta·bes'cent adj.

con·tact (kon'takt) n. 1 The coming together, meeting, or touching of two bodies. 2 Electr. The touching or joining of points or surfaces of conductors, permitting the passage or flow cf a current. 3 Immediate proximity or association. 4 Helpful vocational or social acquaintance. See synonyms under COLLISION. — v.t. 1 To bring or place in contact; touch. 2 Colloq. To get or be in touch with (a person); communicate with: I will contact you tomorrow. — v.i. 3 To be or come in contact; touch: with with. [<L contactus, pp. of contingere <com- together + tangere touch]

contact lens A thin corrective lens of hard or soft plastic that fits against the eyeball.

con·tac·tor (kon'tak·tər) n. Electr. A device for repeatedly opening and closing an electric circuit other than by hand.

con·ta·gion (kən·tā'jən) n. 1 The communication of disease by contact, direct or indirect, or, figuratively, of mental states by suggestion or association. 2 Pestilential influence; pestilence; plague. 3 The medium of transmission of disease; contagium. [<F <L contagio, -onis <contingere. See CONTACT.]

con·ta·gious (kən·tā'jəs) adj. 1 Transmissible by contact, as a disease, or by sympathy, as emotions. 2 Catching; spreading. 3 Transmitting disease; pestilential. — con·ta'gious·ly adv. — con·ta'gious·ness n.

con·tain (kən·tān') v.t. 1 To hold or enclose. 2 To include or comprise. 3 To be capable of containing; be able to hold. 4 To keep within bounds; restrain, as oneself or one's feelings. 5 Math. To be exactly divisible. 6 Mil. To hold, as an enemy, to a position or area, as by actual or feigned attacks. See synonyms under EMBRACE. [<OF contenir <L continere <com- together + tenere hold]

con·tain·ment (kən·tān'mənt) n. 1 Mil. The engagement of the enemy so that he is unable to extricate forces for use elsewhere. 2 In international politics, the forestalling or offsetting, by political and economic policy, of territorial or ideological extension by an inimical power.

con·tam·i·nate (kən·tam'ə·nāt) v.t. ·nat·ed, ·nat·ing To make impure by contact or admixture; taint; defile; pollute. — adj. Obs. Contaminated. [<L contaminatus, pp. of contaminare <contamen, contagmen <com- together + tag-, root of tangere touch] — con·tam'i·nant n. — con·tam'i·na'tive adj. — con·tam'i·na'tor n.

con·tem·plate (kon'təm·plāt) v. ·plat·ed, ·plat·ing v.t. 1 To look at attentively; gaze at. 2 To consider thoughtfully; ponder. 3 To intend or plan. 4 To treat of as contingent or possible: Secession was not contemplated in the Constitution. — v.i. 5 To meditate; muse. [<L contemplatus, pp. of contemplari <com- together + templum temple; with ref. to the art of divination] — con·tem·pla·ble (kən·tem'plə·bəl) adj. — con'tem·pla'tor n.

con·tem·pla·tion (kon'təm·plā'shən) n. 1 The act of keeping the eye or the mind fixed upon some object or subject. 2 Continued thought or abstraction in general; musing: contemplation of the heavens; absorbed in contemplation. 3 Expectation or intention of doing, or deliberation on something to be done, as of taking a journey. 4 Holy meditation; a life of prayer and meditation as practiced by certain Roman Catholic orders. See synonyms under REFLECTION, THOUGHT.

con·tem·pla·tive (kon'təm·plā'tiv, kən·tem'·plə-) adj. Of or given to contemplation; meditative. — con'tem·pla'tive·ly adv. — con'·tem·pla'tive·ness n.

con·tem·po·ra·ne·ous (kon·tem'pə·rā'nē·əs) adj. Living or occurring at the same time: also spelled cotemporaneous. [<L contemporaneus <com- together + tempus, temporis time] Synonym: contemporary. Contemporaneous is used chiefly of facts and events, contemporary of persons: contemporary writers; contemporaneous writings.

con·tem·po·rar·y (kən·tem'pə·rer'ē) adj. 1 Contemporaneous; living or existing at the same time. 2 Having the same age; coeval. — n. pl. ·rar·ies A person or thing that is contemporary. Also spelled cotemporary. See synonym under CONTEMPORANEOUS.

con·tem·po·rize (kən·tem′pə·rīz) v.t. & v.i. ·rized, ·riz·ing To make or be equal in respect of time; synchronize.

con·tempt (kən·tempt′) n. 1 The act of despising; disdain; scorn. 2 Law Wilful disregard of authority, as of a court. 3 The state of being despised; disgrace; shame. 4 An action implying contempt. See synonyms under SCORN. [<L contemptus <contemnere despise, disdain. See CONTEMN.]

con·tempt·i·ble (kən·temp′tə·bəl) adj. 1 Deserving of contempt; despicable; vile. 2 Obs. Contemptuous. See synonyms under BASE, LITTLE, PITIFUL. — **con·tempt′i·bil′i·ty,** con·tempt′i·ble·ness n. — **con·tempt′i·bly** adv.

con·temp·tu·ous (kən·temp′chōō·əs) adj. Disdainful. See synonyms under HAUGHTY.

con·tend (kən·tend′) v.t. 1 To maintain or assert in argument: with an objective clause. — v.i. 2 To debate earnestly; dispute. 3 To strive in competition or rivalry; vie: to contend for a prize. 4 To struggle or fight in opposition or combat. [<L contendere <com- together + tendere strive, strain] — con·tend′er n.
Synonyms: antagonize, argue, battle, combat, compete, contest, cope, dispute, fight, grapple, oppose, strive, vie, wrangle. See ARGUE, OPPOSE. *Antonyms:* see synonyms for AGREE, ALLOW.

con·tent¹ (kon′tent) n. 1 Usually pl. All that a thing contains. 2 The constituent elements of a conception, or meaning and relations involved; hence, significance or basic meaning. 3 Holding capacity; size. 4 Included area or space; extent. 5 The quantity of a specified part: the silver content of a ton of ore. — **latent content** Psychoanal. The underlying thoughts or repressed desires that motivate a dream. — **manifest content** Psychoanal. The incidents of a dream that are remembered and related by the dreamer. [<L contentum, pp. neut. of continere. See CONTAIN.]

con·tent² (kən·tent′) n. 1 Rest of mind; satisfaction; freedom from worry. 2 The means of contentment. — adj. Satisfied; not inclined to complain or desire something more or different than what one has. — v.t. To fulfil the hopes or expectations of; satisfy. See synonyms under INDULGE, SATISFY. [<L contentus, pp. of continere. See CONTAIN.]

con·ten·tion (kən·ten′shən) n. 1 The act of contending; strife; conflict; struggle; dispute. 2 An object or point in debate or controversy. 3 A statement in support of an argument; also, the argument itself. See synonyms under ALTERCATION, FEUD, QUARREL. [<F <L contentio, -onis <contendere. See CONTEND.]

con·ter·mi·nous (kən·tûr′mə·nəs) adj. Having a common boundary line; coextensive: also **coterminous**. Also **con·ter′mi·nal**. See synonyms under ADJACENT. [<L conterminus <com- together + terminus limit] — **con·ter′mi·nous·ly** adv.

con·test (kon′test) n. 1 A struggle; competition; conflict. 2 Verbal conflict; controversy. See synonyms under BATTLE, COMPETITION, FEUD, QUARREL. [< v.] — v.t. (kən·test′) 1 To fight about; contend for; strive to take, keep, or control. 2 To strive to win, as a battle. 3 To argue about, especially in opposition; challenge; litigate: to contest an election. — v.i. 4 To contend, struggle, or vie: with with or against. [<F contester <L contestari bring legal action against <com- together + testari bear witness <testis witness] — **con·test′a·ble** adj. — **con·tes·ta·tion** (kon′tes·tā′shən) n. — **con·test′er** n.

con·test·ant (kən·tes′tənt) n. 1 One who enters a contest; a competitor. 2 A defeated political candidate who challenges election returns. [<F <L contestans, -antis, ppr. of contestari. See CONTEST.]

con·text (kon′tekst) n. The portions of a discourse, treatise, etc., that immediately precede and follow and are connected with a passage quoted or considered. [<L contextus, pp. of contexere <com- together + texere weave]

con·ti·gu·i·ty (kon′tə·gyōō′ə·tē) n. 1 Nearness; proximity. 2 Uninterrupted connection; continuity. 3 An unbroken or continuous mass or series.

con·tig·u·ous (kən·tig′yōō·əs) adj. Touching or joining at the edge or boundary; adjacent. See synonyms under ADJACENT, IMMEDIATE. [<L contiguus <contingere. See CONTACT.] — **con·tig′u·ous·ly** adv. — **con·tig′u·ous·ness** n.

con·ti·nence (kon′tə·nəns) n. Self-restraint; moderation; especially, self-restraint in sexual passion; chastity. Also **con′ti·nen·cy.** See synonyms under ABSTINENCE.

con·ti·nent (kon′tə·nənt) n. 1 One of the great bodies of land on the globe, generally regarded as six in number: Africa, Asia, Australia, Europe, North America, and South America: Antarctica is sometimes regarded as the seventh continent. 2 Obs. That which contains; a boundary: also, that which is contained. — **the Continent** Europe, exclusive of the British Isles. — adj. 1 Self-restrained; abstinent; chaste. 2 Obs. Restraining; limiting. [<OF <L continens, -entis, ppr. of continere. See CONTAIN.] — **con·ti·nen·tal** (kon′tə·nen′təl) adj. — **con′ti·nent·ly** adv.

continental drift Geol. The theory that the continental land masses are subject to slow movement through the action of underlying magmatic material.

continental shelf Geog. The submerged border of a continent, of varying width and degree of slope, which separates the land mass from the ocean depths.

con·tin·gen·cy (kən·tin′jən·sē) n. pl. ·cies 1 Possibility of occurrence. 2 A fortuitous event; accident; casualty. 3 Something that is incidental. Also **con·tin′gence.** See synonyms under ACCIDENT, EVENT, HAZARD.

con·tin·gent (kən·tin′jənt) adj. 1 Likely to occur. 2 Fortuitous; possible. 3 Law Dependent upon an uncertain future event. — n. 1 A contingency. 2 A proportionate share; representation: the American contingent at the conference. 3 Mil. A quota of troops. See synonyms under INCIDENTAL. [<L contingens, -entis, ppr. of contingere. See CONTACT.] — **con·tin′gent·ly** adv.

con·tin·u·al (kən·tin′yōō·əl) adj. 1 Renewed in regular succession; often repeated. 2 Continuous (in time); uninterrupted. ● While *continual* is limited to continuity in time, and *continuous* refers to either space or time, usage now tends further to limit *continual* to the sense of "continuing after interruptions," in which sense it is not interchangeable with *continuous.* — **con·tin′u·al·ly** adv.
Synonyms: ceaseless, constant, continuous, incessant, invariable, perpetual, regular, unbroken, unceasing, uninterrupted, unremitting, unvarying. *Continuous* describes that which is absolutely without pause or break; *continual,* that which often intermits, but as regularly begins again. A similar distinction is made between *incessant* and *ceaseless,* but *ceaseless* may have the further meaning of unending, perpetual. *Constant* is sometimes used in the sense of *continual;* but its chief reference is to steadiness, as of purpose, sentiment, or movement; as, *constant* devotion; *constant* advance. See PERPETUAL.

con·tin·u·ance (kən·tin′yōō·əns) n. 1 The state of continuing; duration. 2 Uninterrupted succession; survival. 3 Law Postponement. 4 A continuation or sequel, as of a novel.

con·tin·u·ant (kən·tin′yōō·ənt) n. Phonet. A consonant whose sound may be prolonged on a single breath without a change in quality, as the fricatives (f) and (s): opposed to *stop.* [<L continuans, -antis, ppr. of continuare. See CONTINUE.]

con·tin·u·ate (kən·tin′yōō·āt) adj. 1 Closely joined together. 2 Unbroken; uninterrupted. [<L continuatus, pp. of continuare. See CONTINUE.]

con·tin·u·a·tion (kən·tin′yōō·ā′shən) n. 1 The act or state of continuing. 2 Something added which protracts, extends, or carries on; a sequel: the *continuation* of a novel. — **con·tin′u·a′tor** n.

con·tin·u·a·tive (kən·tin′yōō·ā′tiv) adj. Denoting or causing continuance or duration. — n. 1 That which causes continuation. 2 Gram. A conjunction which prolongs a sentence by introducing a subordinate clause at the end.

con·tin·ue (kən·tin′yōō) v. ·tin·ued, ·tin·u·ing v.t. 1 To extend or prolong in space or time. 2 To persist in or carry forward. 3 To cause to last or remain, as in a position or office.

4 To take up again, as a course of action or a narrative, after an interruption. 5 Law To postpone, as a judicial proceeding; grant a continuance of. — v.i. 6 To be durable; last; endure. 7 To keep on or persist. 8 To remain, as in a place or position; abide. 9 To resume after an interruption. See synonyms under ABIDE, LIVE, PERSEVERE, PERSIST, PROTRACT, STAND. [<L continuare <continuus <continere. See CONTAIN.] — **con·tin′u·a·ble** adj. — **con·tin′u·er** n.

continued proportion Math. A series of three or more quantities in which the ratio is the same between each two adjacent terms; as, 2, 4, 8, 16, where 2 : 4 ∷ 4 : 8 ∷ 8 : 16.

con·ti·nu·i·ty (kon′tə·nōō′ə·tē, -nyōō′-) n. 1 The state or quality of being continuous. 2 That which has or gives an orderly sequence, as a scenario for motion pictures or a radio script. 3 The close coordination of all details necessary to ensure smooth performance of a dramatic production, radio or television broadcast, etc.

con·tin·u·ous (kən·tin′yōō·əs) adj. 1 Connected, extended, or prolonged without a break; unbroken; uninterrupted. 2 Repeating, as a performance, without intermission: said of motion–picture showings, etc. See synonyms under CONTINUAL, GRADUAL, PERPETUAL. [<L continuus <continere. See CONTAIN.] — **con·tin′u·ous·ly** adv. — **con·tin′u·ous·ness** n.

con·tin·u·um (kən·tin′yōō·əm) n. pl. ·tin·u·a (-tin′yōō·ə) 1 A total that is continuous and uninterrupted. 2 That which has perfect continuity: the *continuum* of space. 3 A basic, common character underlying a series or aggregation of indefinite variations. 4 Math. A set of numbers or points such that between any two of them a third may be interpolated. [<L, neut. of continuus CONTINUOUS]

con·tort (kən·tôrt′) v.t. To twist violently; wrench out of shape or place. See synonyms under TWIST. [<L contortus, pp. of contorquere <com- together + torquere twist]

con·tour (kon′tŏŏr) n. The line bounding a figure or body; outline. — v.t. 1 To make or draw in outline or contour; make contour lines on or determine the contour lines of. 2 To carry, as a road, around the contour of a ridge or hill. [<F <Ital. contorno <contornare <LL com- together + tornare round off, make round]

contour feathers The outer feathers that determine the outline of a bird; pennae.

contour line 1 The line, or one of the lines, constituting the boundary of a plane. 2 In maps, the line connecting points on the earth which are at the same elevation above sea level.

contour map A map constructed to show the comparative elevation of topographic features by a series of contour lines, each separated from the next by a definite difference in height, called a **contour interval.**

CONTOUR MAP WITH INTERVALS

contour plowing Agric. A method of cultivation in which the furrows follow the contours of uneven land in such a way as to minimize the destructive action of wind and erosion.

contra- prefix Against; opposite; contrary: contradict. [< L <contra against]

con·tra (kon′trə) n. A rebel soldier in Central America, especially one in revolt during the 1980s against the Sandinistas in Nicaragua. [<Spanish, short for contra-revolucionario a counterrevolutionary]

con·tra·band (kon′trə·band) adj. Prohibited or excluded, as by military law; forbidden. — n. 1 Contraband goods or trade. 2 Any fugitive slave who took refuge within the Union lines during the Civil War. 3 Contraband of war. [< Sp. contrabanda a smuggling <Ital. contrabando <contra against + bando <LL bannum law, proclamation]

contraband of war Anything furnished by a neutral to a belligerent that is by the laws of war subject to seizure. Arms and military supplies are classed as **absolute contraband**; grain, horses, etc., as **occasional contraband**; goods consigned to a neutral country which may be transferred to a belligerent or to a belligerent country which may be used by the army or navy are **conditional contraband**.

con·tra·bass (kon′trə·bās) n. A double bass. —adj. Having its pitch an octave lower than another instrument of the same class; of deep range: a *contrabass* horn. [< Ital. *contrabasso*]

con·tra·bas·soon (kon′trə·bə·sōōn′) n. The double-bassoon.

con·tra·cep·tion (kon′trə·sep′shən) n. The prevention of conception or fecundation. [< CONTRA- +(CON)CEPTION]

con·tra·cep·tive (kon′trə·sep′tiv) adj. 1 Serving or acting to prevent conception or impregnation. 2 Pertaining to contraception. —n. Any device or substance that inhibits conception.

con·tract (kən·trakt′ *for v. defs.* 1, 2, 4–8; kon′trakt, kən·trakt′ *for v. def.* 3) v.t. 1 To reduce in size; abridge in compass or duration; shrink; narrow. 2 To wrinkle; draw together, as the brow. 3 To arrange or settle by agreement; enter upon with reciprocal obligations. 4 To acquire or become affected with, as a disease or habit. 5 *Gram.* To shorten, as a word, by omitting or combining medial letters or sounds. 6 To betroth. —v.i. 7 To shrink; become reduced in size. 8 To make a contract. —n. (kon′trakt) 1 *Law* A formal agreement, or the writing containing it. 2 A betrothal or marriage. 3 The department of law dealing with contracts. 4 Contract bridge: see under BRIDGE². —**yellow dog contract** A contract whereby an employee agrees not to join a union. [< L *contractus*, pp. of *contrahere* < *com-* together + *trahere* pull, draw]
  Synonyms (noun): agreement, arrangement, bargain, cartel, compact, convenant, engagement, promise, stipulation. An *agreement* or a *contract* may be oral or written, but a consideration or compensation is essential to a *contract*. A *covenant*, in law, is a written *contract* under seal. *Convenant* is frequent in religious usage, as *contract* is in law and business. *Compact* is essentially the same as *contract*, but is applied to international *agreements*, treaties, etc. A *bargain* is a mutual *agreement* for an exchange of values, without the formality of a *contract*. A *stipulation* is a single item in an *agreement* or *contract*.

contractile tissue *Physiol.* Body tissue composed of smooth or striated muscle cells whose contraction aids in the production of movement.

con·trac·tion (kən·trak′shən) n. 1 The act of contracting or the state of being contracted. 2 That which is contracted, as a word by the omission of one or more medial letters or sounds. See synonyms under ABBREVIATION.

con·trac·tor (kon′trak·tər, kən·trak′tər *for defs.* 1 *and* 2; kən·trak′tər *for def.* 3) n. 1 One of the parties to a contract. 2 One who executes plans under contract; especially, one who agrees to supply labor or materials, or both, on a large scale. 3 *Anat.* A muscle that serves to contract.

con·trac·ture (kən·trak′chər) n. 1 *Med.* A permanent contraction and rigidity of muscles. 2 *Archit.* The narrowing of the higher part of a column.

con·tra·dict (kon′trə·dikt′) v.t. & v.i. 1 To maintain the opposite of (a statement); refute or gainsay; deny. 2 To be inconsistent with or opposed to. See synonyms under OPPOSE. [< L *contradictus*, pp. of *contradicere* < *contra-* against + *dicere* say, speak] —**con′tra·dict′a·ble** adj. —**con′tra·dict′er** or **con′tra·dic′tor** n. —**con′tra·dic′tion** n. —**con′tra·dic′tive** adj. —**con′tra·dic′tive·ness** n.

con·tra·dic·to·ry (kon′trə·dik′tər·ē) adj. 1 Involving or of the nature of a contradiction; inconsistent; contrary. 2 Given or inclined to contradiction. See synonyms under ALIEN, CONTRARY, INCONGRUOUS, INIMICAL. —n. pl. **·ries** *Logic* A proposition by means of which another proposition is absolutely denied.

con·tra·dis·tinct (kon′trə·dis·tingkt′) adj. Distinguished by contrary qualities or by contrast. —**con′tra·dis·tinct′ly** adv.

con·tra·dis·tinc·tion (kon′trə·dis·tingk′shən) n. Distinction by contrast or by contrasting qualities: a large corporation in *contradistinction* to a small business. —**con′tra·dis·tinc′tive** adj. —

con′tra·dis·tinc′tive·ly adv.

con·trail (kon′trāl) n. *Aeron.* The vapor trail which sometimes streams out in the wake of an airplane flying at high altitudes, caused by the condensation of moisture from exhaust gases of the engine. [< *con(densation) trail*]

con·tra·in·di·cate (kon′trə·in′də·kāt) v.t. *Med.* To indicate the danger or undesirability of (a given drug or method of treatment). —**con′. tra·in′di·cant** adj. & n. —**con′tra·in′di·ca′tion** n.

con·tral·to (kən·tral′tō) n. pl. **·tos** or **·ti** (-tē) 1 The lowest female voice, intermediate between soprano and tenor: also called *alto*. 2 *Music* A part written for such a voice. 3 A singer with such a voice. [< Ital.]

con·tra·po·si·tion (kon′trə·pə·zish′ən) n. 1 *Logic* Conversion by negation, or by changing the quality of the judgment while the quantity remains unchanged; transposition. 2 A placing opposite.

con·trap·tion (kən·trap′shən) n. *Colloq.* A contrivance or gadget. [? < CONTRIVE] —**con·trap′tious** adj.

con·tra·pun·tal (kon′trə·pun′təl) adj. *Music* 1 Of or pertaining to counterpoint. 2 Characterized by the use of counterpoint; con-structed according to the principles of counterpoint. [< Ital. *contrapunto* counterpoint] —**con′tra·pun′tal·ly** adv. —**con′tra·pun′tal·ist, con′tra·pun′tist** n.

con·tra·ri·e·ty (kon′trə·rī′ə·tē) n. pl. **·ties** 1 The quality or state of being contrary. 2 A quality or a proposition contrary to another; an inconsistency; a contrary.

con·trar·i·ous (kən·trâr′ē·əs) adj. 1 Showing refractory opposition. 2 Harmful; vexatious: said of things. —**con·trar′i·ous·ly** adv. —**con·trar′i·ous·ness** n.

con·trar·i·wise (kon′trer·ē·wīz′; *for def.* 3, *also* kən·trâr′ē·wīz′) adv. 1 On the contrary; on the other hand. 2 In the reverse order; conversely. 3 Captiously; perversely.

con·trar·y (kon′trer·ē; *for adj. def.* 4, *also* kən·trâr′ē) adj. 1 Opposed in situation, direction, aim, purpose, or operation; antagonistic. 2 Adverse: *contrary* winds. 3 Opposite; opposing. 4 Characterized or swayed by perversity; inclined to opposition or contradiction; captious. —n. pl. **·trar·ies** 1 One of two opposing things. 2 The opposite. 3 *Logic* A statement whose truth is undetermined by the falsity of another, but which cannot be true if the latter is true: "The man is a perjurer" is the *contrary* of "The man is honest." —**by contraries** By way of opposition to anticipated procedure. —**on the contrary** Contrariwise; on the other hand. —**to the contrary** To the opposite effect. —adv. In a contrary manner; contrariwise. [< AF *contrarie* < L *contrarius* < *contra* against] —**con′trar·i·ly** adv. —**con′trar·i·ness** n.
  Synonyms (adj.): antagonistic, conflicting, contradictory, contrasted, different, discordant, dissimilar, incompatible, incongruous, inconsistent, opposed, opposite, unlike. Things are *contradictory* which mutually exclude each other, so that both cannot exist in the same object at the same time, as life and death. Things are *contrary* when the highest degree of both cannot exist in the same object at the same time, but where a middle term is possible, partaking of the qualities of both, as wisdom and folly, or heat and cold. See ALIEN, INCONGRUOUS, INIMICAL, PERVERSE.

con·trast (kən·trast′) v.t. 1 To place or set in opposition so as to show dissimilarities. 2 To set off; afford a contrast to. —v.i. 3 To manifest dissimilarities when placed or set in opposition. —n. (kon′trast) 1 The unlikeness between two or more things or persons, as revealed by comparison. 2 A person or thing that shows unlikeness to another. [< OF *contraster* < Ital. *contrastare* < LL < L *contra-* against + *stare* stand] —**con·trast′a·ble** adj.
  Synonyms (verb): compare, differentiate, discriminate, oppose. To *compare* is to place together in order to show likeness or unlikeness; to *contrast* is to set in opposition in order to show unlikeness. We *contrast* objects that have been already *compared*. We must *compare* them, at least momentarily, even to know that they are different. We *contrast* them when we observe their unlikeness in a general way; we *differentiate* them when we note the difference exactly and point by point.

con·tra·ter·rene (kon′trə·te·rēn′) adj. 1 Opposed to or destructive of the earth. 2 *Physics* Pertaining to or having the characteristics of antimatter. —n. Antiworld.

con·tra·val·la·tion (kon′trə·və·lā′shən) n. A chain of fortifications raised by besiegers round an invested place, to protect themselves from sallies of the garrison. [< F *contrevallation* < LL *contra-* against + *vallatio, -onis* rampart < *vallum* wall]

con·tra·vene (kon′trə·vēn′) v.t. **·vened, ·ven·ing** 1 To transgress; violate or infringe upon, as a law. 2 To deny or run counter to; oppose or be inconsistent with in principle. See synonyms under OPPOSE. [< F *contrevenir* < LL *contravenire* < L *contra-* against + *venire* come]

contre- *prefix* Counter; against; in opposition to. [<F < L *contra*. See CONTRA-.]

con·trec·ta·tion (kon′trek·tā′shən) n. The impulse to caress or fondle a person of the opposite sex. [<L *contrectatio, -onis* < *contrectare* < *com-* thoroughly + *tractare* touch, fondle]

con·tre·danse (kôn′trə·däns′) n. 1 A country dance. 2 One of the figures composing a quadrille. Also **con·tre·dance** (kon′trə·dans′, -däns′): also spelled *contradance, contradanse*. [<F, alter. of COUNTRY DANCE]

con·trib·ute (kən·trib′yōōt) v. **·ut·ed, ·ut·ing** v.t. 1 To give or furnish in common with others; give for a common purpose. 2 To submit, sell, or furnish, as an article or story, to a magazine or other publication. —v.i. 3 To share in effecting a result: These causes *contributed* to the king's downfall. 4 To make or give a contribution. [<L *contributus*, pp. of *contribuere* < *com-* together + *tribuere* grant, allot] —**con·trib′ut·a·ble** adj. —**con·trib′u·tive** adj. —**con·trib′u·tive·ly** adv. —**con·trib′u·tive·ness** n. —**con·trib′u·tor** n.

con·tri·bu·tion (kon′trə·byōō′shən) n. 1 The act of contributing, or that which is contributed. 2 A piece of writing furnished to a magazine, etc. 3 An impost; tax; levy.

con·trib·u·to·ry (kən·trib′yə·tôr′ē, -tō′rē) adj. 1 Contributing. 2 *Law* Casually sharing in some act. 3 Liable to an impost. —n. pl. **·ries** One who or that which contributes.

con·trite (kən·trīt′, kon′trīt) adj. 1 Broken in spirit because of a sense of sin; penitent; sorry. 2 Resulting from contrition. [<OF *contrit* <L *contritus*, pp. of *conterere* < *com-* together + *terere* rub] —**con·trite′ly** adv.

con·tri·tion (kən·trish′ən) n. 1 Deep and sincere sorrow for wrongdoing. 2 *Theol.* A feeling of repentance for sin, with an intention to amend, arising from love of God and consideration of His goodness (**perfect contrition**), or from inferior motives, as fear of punishment (**imperfect contrition**). Compare ATTRITION (def. 3). Also **con·trite′ness**. See synonyms under PENITENCE, REPENTANCE.

con·trive (kən·trīv′) v. **·trived, ·triv·ing** v.t. 1 To scheme or plan; devise. 2 To plot or conspire. 3 To make ingeniously; improvise; invent: He *contrived* an extra sail. 4 To manage or carry through, as by some device or scheme. —v.i. 5 To form designs; plot. [<OF *controver* find, invent, ? <L *com-* together + *turbare* stir up, disclose, find] —**con·triv′a·ble** adj. —**con·triv′. er** n.

con·trol (kən·trōl′) v.t. **·trolled, ·trol·ling** 1 To exercise a directing, restraining, or governing influence over. 2 To regulate or verify, as an experiment, by comparison with a parallel experiment or other relevant standard. 3 To check, as an account, by means of a duplicate register; verify or rectify. —n. 1 The act of controlling; restraining or directing influence; regulation; check; government. 2 One who or that which controls. 3 *Mech.* Any of variously designed and operated devices for the control of airplanes, motorcars, ships, machines, and the like. 4 *Meteorol.* An element, as atmospheric pressure, physical features, altitude, etc., serving as a determinant of climate. 5 A standard of comparison against which to check the results of an experiment, especially in the biological and medical sciences. 6 In spiritualism, a spirit presumed to act upon and through a medium in seances. [<MF *contrôler*, earlier *contreroller* keep a check list <Med. L *contrarotulus* a check list <L *contra-* against + *rotulus* list]

control chart *Stat.* A chart on which the numerical values of a series of observations are plotted in the order of their occurrence and checked to determine the extent of variation from designated standards of quality, quantity, performance, etc.

control day   Any of various days whose weather is popularly believed to control the weather of a group of following days, as St. Swithin's Day.

control experiment   An experiment designed to check the data in a series of related experiments by altering one of a group of specified factors and comparing the results with a view to exposing differences that might have causal significance.

con·tro·ver·sy (kon′trə·vûr′sē) *n.*   *pl.* **·sies** **1** Debate or disputation; discussion as to schemes or opinions. **2** A quarrel or dispute. See synonyms under ALTERCATION, FEUD, QUARREL. [<L *controversia* < *controversus* < *contra-* against + *versus*, pp. of *vertere* turn]

con·tro·vert (kon′trə·vûrt, kon′trə·vûrt′) *v.t.* To endeavor to disprove; oppose in debate. See synonyms under DISPUTE. [<L *controversus*, on analogy with *convert, revert*, etc. See CONTROVERSY.] **— con′tro·vert′er** *n.* **— con′tro·vert′i·ble** *adj.* **— con′tro·vert′i·bly** *adv.*

con·tu·ma·cy (kon′tŏŏ·mə·sē, -tyŏŏ-) *n.*   *pl.* **·cies** Contemptuous disregard of the requirements of rightful authority; insolent and stubborn perverseness; incorrigible obstinacy. Also **con·tu·mac·i·ty** (kon′tŏŏ·mas′ə·tē, -tyŏŏ-). [<L *contumacia* < *contumax* stubborn] **— con·tu·ma·cious** (kon′tŏŏ·mā′shəs, -tyŏŏ-) *adj.*

con·tu·me·ly (kon′tŏŏ·mə·lē, -tyŏŏ-, -mē′lē; kon·tŏŏ′mə·lē, -tyŏŏ′-) *n.*   *pl.* **·lies** **1** Insulting rudeness in speech or manner; scornful insolence. **2** An act or statement exhibiting haughtiness and contempt. See synonyms under SCORN. [<OF *contumelie* <L *contumelia* reproach] **— con·tu·me·li·ous** (kon′tŏŏ·mē′lē·əs, -tyŏŏ-) *adj.* **— con·tu·me·li·ous·ly** *adv.*

con·tuse (kən·tŏŏz′, -tyŏŏz′) *v.t.* **·tused, ·tus·ing** To bruise by a blow. [<L *contusus*, pp. of *contundere* < *com-* together + *tundere* beat]

con·tu·sion (kən·tŏŏ′zhən, -tyŏŏ′-) *n.* **1** The act of bruising, or the state of being bruised. **2** A bruise.

co·nun·drum (kə·nun′drəm) *n.* **1** A riddle, often depending on a pun. **2** Any perplexing question or thing. [Origin unknown]

con·ur·ba·tion (kon′ûr·bā′shən) *n.* A complex of towns, villages, and small cities closely associated with the needs and activities of a central metropolis. [<CON- + *urbs* city]

con·va·lesce (kon′və·les′) *v.i.* **·lesced ·lesc·ing** To recover from a sickness. [<L *convalescere* < *com-* thoroughly + *valescere*, inceptive of *valere* be strong]

con·va·les·cence (kon′və·les′əns) *n.* **1** Gradual recovery from illness. **2** The period of such recovery. Also **con′va·les′cen·cy.**

con·vec·tion (kən·vek′shən) *n.* **1** The act of conveying. **2** *Physics* The diffusion of heat through a liquid or gas by motion of its parts: distinguished from *conduction*. **3** *Meteorol.* A thermal process whereby atmospheric circulation is maintained through the upward or downward transfer of air masses of different temperature. [<L *convectus*, pp. of *convehere* < *com-* together + *vehere* carry] **— con·vec′tion·al** *adj.* **— con·vec′tor** *n.*

con·vene (kən·vēn′) *v.* **·vened, ·ven·ing** *v.t.* **1** To cause to come together or assemble; convoke. **2** To summon to appear, as by judicial authority. **— v.i.** **3** To come together; assemble. See synonyms under CONVOKE. [<L *convenire* < *com-* together + *venire* come] **— con·ven′er** *n.*

con·ven·ience (kən·vēn′yəns) *n.* **1** The state, time, or quality of being convenient; suitableness; fitness. **2** Freedom from difficulty or discomfort; ease. **3** That which is convenient; that which gives ease or comfort; anything handy or labor-saving. **4** A convenient occasion. Also **con·ven′ien·cy.** See synonyms under OPPORTUNITY.

con·ven·ient (kən·vēn′yənt) *adj.* **1** Conducive to comfort or ease; serviceable; suitable; commodious; favorable; timely. **2** Near at hand; handy. **3** *Obs.* Of a fit character or quality. [<L *conveniens, -entis*, ppr. of *convenire*. See CONVENE.] **— con·ven′ient·ly** *adv.*

Synonyms: adapted, commodious, favorable,

fit, fitted, handy, helpful, opportune, proper, seasonable, suitable, suited, useful. See COMFORTABLE, EXPEDIENT, GOOD. *Antonyms:* awkward, clumsy, inconvenient, superfluous, unhandy, unmanageable, unseasonable, useless.

con·vent (kon′vent, -vənt) *n.* **1** A religious community or association; a body of monks or nuns, especially the latter. **2** The building or buildings occupied by such a body. See synonyms under CLOISTER. [<L *conventus* meeting, assembly < *convenire*. See CONVENE.]

con·ven·tion (kən·ven′shən) *n.* **1** A formal or stated meeting of delegates or representatives, especially for legislative, political, religious, or professional purposes. **2** The act of coming together. **3** General consent, or something established by it; precedent; custom; specifically, a rule, principle, form, or technique in conduct or art; a conventionality. **4** A formal agreement or compact between two or more states relating usually to one specific subject: often used interchangeably with *treaty*. **5** *Law* An agreement or mutual engagement between persons. See synonyms under ASSEMBLY, COMPANY.

con·ven·tion·al (kən·ven′shən·əl) *adj.* **1** Established by convention or custom; agreed; stipulated; customary; formal. **2** Or or pertaining to a convention of delegates. **3** Represented according to artistic convention or rule, rather than to nature or fact. **— con·ven′tion·al·ism** *n.* **— con·ven′tion·al·ist** *n.* **— con·ven′tion·al·ly** *adv.*

con·ven·tion·al·i·ty (kən·ven′shən·al′ə·tē) *n.*   *pl.* **·ties** **1** Adherence to established forms, customs, or usages; conformity to the accepted and traditional. **2** The state or quality of being in accord with convention. **3** A conventional act or utterance. **— the conventionalities** The accepted procedures and customs of social intercourse; the proprieties.

con·verge (kən·vûrj′) *v.* **·verged, ·verg·ing** *v.t.* **1** To cause to tend toward one point. **— v.i.** **2** To move toward one point; come together by gradual approach. **3** To tend toward the same conclusion or result. [<LL *convergere* < *com-* together + *vergere* bend]

con·ver·gence (kən·vûr′jəns) *n.* **1** The act or process of converging. **2** State or quality of being convergent. **3** Degree or point of convergence. **4** *Meteorol.* The net horizontal inflow of air into a given layer of the atmosphere. **5** *Math.* The gradual approach of a series of values to a fixed limit as new values are added. **6** *Physiol.* The focusing of both eyes upon a near point. **7** *Biol.* The tendency of organisms of different types to develop similar functional and structural forms in response to the same environmental conditions. Also **con·ver′gen·cy** for defs. 1–3. **— con·ver′gent** *adj.*

con·ver·sant (kon′vər·sənt, kən·vûr′sənt) *adj.* **1** Familiar, as a result of study, application, etc.: with *with* or, rarely, *in*: *Conversant with* the principles of a subject. **2** *Rare* Intimately acquainted, as with a person. [<OF, ppr. of *converser* <L *conversari*. See CONVERSE.]

con·ver·sa·tion (kon′vər·sā′shən) *n.* **1** The speaking together of two or more persons; informal exchange of ideas, information, etc.; colloquy. **2** Intimate association or intercourse. **3** *pl.* Diplomatic intercourse; specifically, an informal international conference on matters to be treated more officially later. **4** *Obs.* Deportment. **5** *Obs.* The act or condition of being or living anywhere, as in intimacy. **— criminal conversation** *Law* Unlawful sexual intercourse with a married person; adultery. [<OF <L *conversatio, -onis* < *conversari*. See CONVERSE[1].] **— con′ver·sa′tion·al** *adj.* **— con′ver·sa′tion·al·ly** *adv.*

Synonyms: chat, colloquy, communication, communion, confabulation, conference, converse, dialog, discourse, intercourse, parley, talk. *Conversation* is, etymologically, an interchange of ideas with some other person or persons. *Talk* may be wholly one-sided. There may be *intercourse* without *conversation*, as by looks, signs, etc.; *communion* is of hearts, with or without words; *communication* is often by writing, and may be uninvited and unreciprocated. *Talk* may denote the mere utterance of words with little thought; thus,

we say idle *talk*, empty *talk*, rather than idle or empty *conversation*. *Discourse* is applied chiefly to public addresses. A *conference* is more formal than a *conversation*. A *dialog* may be real and informal, but the word denotes ordinarily an artificial or imaginary *conversation*, strictly of two persons, but sometimes of more. A *colloquy* is indefinite as to number, and generally somewhat informal. See INTERCOURSE. Compare BEHAVIOR.

conversation piece A type of genre painting popular in the 18th century, showing a group of people, usually of the upper classes, engaged in conversation; hence, any article of furniture, decoration, etc., that arouses comment, discussion, etc.

con·verse[1] (kən·vûrs′) *v.i.* **·versed, ·vers·ing** **1** To speak together informally and alternately; engage in familiar conversation or colloquy. **2** *Obs.* To associate; have intercourse; commune. **— n.** (kon′vûrs) **1** Conversation; interchange of thoughts. **2** Close intercourse; communion; fellowship. [<OF *converser* <L *conversari*, freq. of *convertere* < *com-* together + *vertere* turn] **— con·vers′a·ble** *adj.* **— con·vers′a·bly** *adv.* **— con·vers′er** *n.*

con·verse[2] (kən·vûrs′, kon′vûrs) *adj.* Turned about so that two parts are interchanged; transposed; reversed. **— n.** (kon′vûrs) **1** That which exists in a converse relation; opposite. **2** *Logic* A proposition that is the result of conversion. See CONVERSION BY LIMITATION. [<L *conversus*, pp. of *convertere* < *com-* thoroughly + *vertere* turn] **— con·verse·ly** (kən·vûrs′lē, kon′vûrs·lē) *adv.*

con·ver·sion (kən·vûr′zhən, -shən) *n.* **1** The act of converting, or the state of being converted, in any sense. **2** The act of turning or of being turned to religious belief. **3** *Law* **a** Wrongful appropriation to one's own use of the goods of another. **b** The exchange of real to personal property or the reverse, which is considered to have taken place where no actual exchange has been effected, as in settling the affairs of an estate. **4** *Logic* A form of immediate inference in which the subject and predicate or antecedent and consequent terms of a judgment change places in such a way that the converse or transposed form is a legitimate inference from the original judgment. **5** *Math.* The formation of a new proportion from four proportional terms by substituting for the second the difference between the first and second and for the fourth the difference between the third and fourth. **6** *Psychoanal.* The process by which a psychic conflict finds expression in motor or sensory disturbances associated with and partially satisfying the repressed emotion or desire: also **conversion hysteria;** see REPRESSION. See synonyms under CHANGE. **— con·ver′sion·al, con·ver·sion·ar·y** (kan·vûr′zhən·er′ē, -shən-) *adj.*

con·vert (kən·vûrt′) *v.t.* **1** To change into another state, form, or substance; transform. **2** To apply or adapt to a new or different purpose or use. **3** To change from one belief, doctrine, creed, opinion, or course of action to another. **4** To turn from a sinful to a righteous life. **5** To exchange for an equivalent value, as goods for money. **6** To exchange for value of another form, as preferred for common stock. **7** *Chem.* To change chemically. **8** *Logic* To transpose the subject and predicate of (a proposition) by conversion. **9** *Law* To assume possession of illegally. **— v.i.** **10** To become changed in character. **11** In football, to score the extra point after touchdown, as by kicking a field goal. **— n.** (kon′vûrt) A person who has been converted, as from a sinful to a pious life, or from one opinion, creed, etc., to another. [<OF *convertir* <L *convertere*. See CONVERSE[2].]

Synonyms (noun): disciple, neophyte, proselyte. The name *disciple* is given to the follower of a certain faith, without reference to any previous belief or allegiance; a *convert* is a person who has come to one faith from a different belief or unbelief. A *proselyte* is one who has been led to accept a religious system, whether with or without true faith; a *convert* is always understood to be a believer. A *neophyte* is a new *convert*, not yet fully indoctrinated, or not admitted to full privileges. The antonyms *apostate, pervert,* and *renegade* are condemnatory names applied to the *convert* by those whose faith he forsakes.

con·vert·er (kən·vûr′tər) *n.* **1** One who or that which converts. **2** A vessel in which materials are changed from one condition into another. **3** A Bessemer converter. **4** *Electr.* An apparatus for converting direct into alternating current and vice versa. **5** One who converts raw textiles into finished products. Also **con·ver′tor.**

con·vert·i·ble (kən·vûr′tə·bəl) *adj.* Capable of being converted. — *n.* **1** A convertible thing. **2** An automobile with a retractable top.

con·vert·i·plane (kən·vûr′tə·plān′) *n.* An aircraft combining the advantages of a helicopter with the ability to attain high speed in normal flight: also called *planicopter.* [< *converti(ble)* (*air*)*plane*]

con·vex (kon·veks′, kon′veks) *adj.* Curving outward like a segment of a globe or of a circle viewed from outside; bulging out: opposed to *concave.* Compare illustration under LENS. — *n.* (kon′veks) A convex surface or body; convexity. [< L *convexus* vaulted, curved < *convehere* < *com-* together + *vehere* bring, carry] — **con·vex′ed·ly, con·vex′ly** *adv.*

con·vex·o·con·cave (kon·vek′sō·kon·kāv′) *adj.* **1** Convex on one side and concave on the other. **2** *Optics* Describing a lens of which the convex surface has a greater curvature than the opposite concave surface: distinguished from *concavo-convex.* See illustration under LENS.

con·vey (kən·vā′) *v.t.* **1** To carry from one place to another; transport. **2** To serve as a medium or path for; transmit. **3** To make known or impart; communicate. **4** To transfer ownership of, as real estate. **5** *Obs.* To accompany; guide. [< AF *conveier* travel with < L *com-* together + *via* road, way. Doublet of CONVOY, *v.*] — **con·vey′a·ble** *adj.* — **con·vey′er, con·vey′or** *n.*

Synonyms: carry, change, give, move, remove, sell, shift, transfer, transmit, transport. *Convey, transmit,* and *transport* all imply delivery at a destination; *carry* does not necessarily imply delivery, and often does not admit of it. A man *carries* an appearance, *conveys* an impression, the appearance remaining his own, the impression being given to another; I will *transmit* the letter; *transport* the goods. *Transfer* may or may not imply delivery to another person; as, items may be *transferred* from one account to another or a word *transferred* to the following line. In law, real estate, which cannot be moved, is *conveyed* by simply *transferring* title and possession. *Transport* usually refers to material objects; *transfer, transmit,* and *convey* may refer to immaterial objects; we *transfer* possession, *transmit* intelligence; we *convey* ideas, but do not *transport* them. In the case of *convey* the figurative sense now predominates. Compare CARRY, LEAD. *Antonyms:* hold, keep, possess, preserve, retain.

con·vey·ance (kən·vā′əns) *n.* **1** The act of conveying. **2** That by which anything is conveyed. **3** A vehicle. **4** *Law* A document transferring title to property. **5** *Obs.* A device; artifice.

con·vict (kən·vikt′) *v.t.* **1** To prove guilty; find guilty after a judicial trial. **2** To awaken to a sense of sin. See synonyms under CONDEMN. — *adj. Obs.* Proved guilty. — *n.* (kon′vikt) One found guilty of or undergoing punishment for crime; a criminal. [< L *convictus,* pp. of *convincere.* See CONVINCE.]

con·vic·tion (kən·vik′shən) *n.* **1** The act of convicting. **2** The fact or state of being convicted. **3** The state or condition of being convinced or fully awakened to awareness: under *conviction* of sin. **4** A doctrine or proposition which one firmly believes. **5** Fixed belief: He spoke with *conviction.* See synonyms under FAITH. — **con·vic′tion·al** *adj.*

con·vince (kən·vins′) *v.t.* **·vinced, ·vinc·ing** **1** To satisfy by evidence; persuade by argument. **2** *Obs.* To convict. [< L *convincere* < *com-* thoroughly + *vincere* overcome, conquer] — **con·vince′ment** *n.* — **con·vinc′er** *n.*

con·viv·i·al (kən·viv′ē·əl) *adj.* Pertaining to a feast, especially a drinking feast; festive;

jovial. [< L *convivialis* < *convivium* a feast, banquet < *convivere* < *com-* together + *vivere* live] — **con·viv′i·al·ist** *n.* — **con·viv·i·al·i·ty** (kən·viv′ē·al′ə·tē) *n.* — **con·viv′i·al·ly** *adv.*

con·vo·ca·tion (kon′vō·kā′shən) *n.* **1** The act of summoning together an assembly. **2** The assembly thus summoned. See synonyms under ASSEMBLY, COMPANY. [< L *convocatio, -onis* < *convocare.* See CONVOKE.] — **con′vo·ca′tion·al** *adj.* — **con·vo·ca·tive** (kən·vok′ə·tiv) *adj.* — **con′vo·ca′tor** *n.*

con·voke (kən·vok′) *v.t.* **·voked, ·vok·ing** To call together; summon. [< F *convoquer* < L *convocare* < *com-* together + *vocare* call, summon] — **con·vok′er** *n.*

Synonyms: assemble, call, collect, convene, gather, muster, summon. A convention is *called* by some officer or officers, as by its president, its executive committee, or some eminent leaders; the delegates are *assembled* or *convened* in a certain place, at a certain hour. *Convoke* implies an organized body and a superior authority; *assemble* and *convene* express more independent action; Parliament is *convoked*; Congress *assembles.* Troops are *mustered*; witnesses and jurymen are *summoned.* *Antonyms:* adjourn, disband, discharge, dismiss, disperse, dissolve, prorogue, scatter, separate.

con·vo·lute (kon′və·loot) *adj.* **1** Rolled one part on another or inward from one side. **2** *Bot.* Coiled longitudinally, as the petals of the wallflower. Also **con′vo·lut·ed, con′vo·lu·tive** [< L *convolutus,* pp. of *convolvere.* See CONVOLVE.] — **con′vo·lute′ly** *adv.*

con·volve (kən·volv′) *v.* **·volved, ·volv·ing** *v.t.* To roll together; wind around something; twist; turn. — *v.i.* To turn or wind upon itself. [< L *convolvere* < *com-* together + *volvere* spin, twist]

con·vol·vu·la·ceous (kən·vol′vyə·lā′shəs) *adj. Bot.* Designating a family (*Convolvulaceae*) of gamopetalous, chiefly climbing herbs, shrubs, or trees with alternate leaves and showy flowers; the morning-glory family.

con·vol·vu·lar (kən·vol′vyə·lər) *adj.* **1** Winding in upon itself. **2** Twisted; wound together.

con·vol·vu·lus (kən·vol′vyə·ləs) *n.* Any of a genus (*Convolvulus*) of twining herbs with large, showy, trumpet-shaped flowers. [< L, bindweed]

con·voy (kon′voi) *n.* **1** A protecting force accompanying property in course of transportation, as a ship at sea or a military party by land. **2** The property so accompanied, as a ship or fleet at sea or a baggage train onland. **3** The act of convoying; the state of being convoyed, or the agency used in transportation or conveyance. [< MF *convoi* < *convoyer*] — *v.t.* (kən·voi′, kon′-) To escort and protect; guide; act as convoy to. < L *com-* together + *via* road. Doublet of CONVEY.]

con·vulse (kən·vuls′) *v.t.* **·vulsed, ·vuls·ing** **1** To affect with violent movements; agitate violently. **2** To cause to laugh violently. [< L *convulsus,* pp. of *convellere* < *com-* together + *vellere* pull]

con·vul·sion (kən·vul′shən) *n.* **1** A violent and abnormal muscular contraction of the body; spasm; fit. **2** Any violent commotion or disturbance. — **con·vul·sion·ar·y** (kən·vul′·shən·er′ē) *adj. & n.*

co·ny (ko′ne, kun′ē) *n. pl.* **co·nies** **1** A rabbit, especially the European rabbit. **2** Rabbit fur. **3** In the Bible, the hyrax or daman. **4** The pika. **5** *Archaic* A dupe; one who is cheated. Also **coney.** [< OF *cony* < L *cuniculus* rabbit]

coo (koo) *v.* **cooed, coo·ing** *v.t.* **1** To utter with the soft murmuring sound of a dove or pigeon. — *v.i.* **2** To utter the coo of a dove, or a similar sound. **3** To make love in low, murmuring tones: to bill and coo. — *n.* A murmuring note, as of a dove. [Imit.] — **coo′er** *n.* — **coo′ing·ly** *adv.*

cook (kook) *v.t.* **1** To prepare for consumption by the action of heat, as by roasting or boiling. **2** *Colloq.* To tamper with surreptitiously; garble; falsify. — *v.i.* **3** To do the work of a cook; act as a cook. **4** To undergo cooking. —**to cook (someone's) goose** To kill or ruin one; frustrate one's schemes or plans. —**to cook up** *Colloq.* To concoct or invent, as a plot. [< *n.*] — *n.* One who prepares food for eating. [OE *coc* < L *coquus*] — **cook′er** *n.*

cook·book (kook′book′) *n.* A book containing recipes and instructions for cooking.

cook·er·y (kook′ər·ē) *n. pl.* **·er·ies** **1** The art or practice of cooking. **2** A place for cooking.

cook·out (kook′out′) *n. U.S. Colloq.* A picnic at which the meal is cooked out-of-doors.

cook·y (kook′ē) *n. pl.* **cook·ies** **1** A small, sweet cake. **2** *Slang.* A person; also, a young woman or girl; sweetheart. Also **cook·ey, cook·ie.** [< Du. *koekje,* dim. of *koek* cake]

cool (kool) *adj.* **1** Moderate in temperature; not warm; some what cold. **2** Serving to produce or giving the effect of coolness. **3** Self-controlled; self-possessed. **4** Indifferent; chilling; slighting. **5** Audacious; impudent. **6** *Colloq.* Actual; absolute; not exaggerated: a *cool* million dollars. **7** *Art* Suggesting a sense of coolness: said of the colors blue, green, and violet. **8** *Slang* Very good; well done. See synonyms under CALM, FRESH. — *v.t.* **1** To lower the temperature of; make cooler or less hot. **2** To render less excited or excitable; allay, as passion; calm; moderate. — *v.i.* **3** To become cool or less hot. **4** To lose the heat of excitement or passion; become less ardent, angry, zealous, or affectionate. —**to cool it** *Slang* To calm down; take it easy. —**to cool one's heels** To wait long and wearily in attendance. — *n.* **1** A moderate temperature approaching cold: the *cool* of the day. **2** That which is cool. **3** *Slang* Calm detachment; composure. —**to blow one's cool** *Slang* To get excited; become emotional. [OE *col*] —**cool′ish** *adj.* —**cool′ly** *adv.* —**cool·ness** *n.*

cool·ant (kool′ənt) *n.* Any substance of low freezing point used as a cooling medium, as for an internal combustion engine.

cool·er (kool′ər) *n.* **1** That which cools, as a vessel to cool liquids. **2** A refreshing beverage. **3** *Slang* A jail.

coo·lie (kool′ē) *n.* **1** In the Orient, an unskilled laborer or menial. **2** Any such person doing heavy work, especially for low wages. Also **coo′ly.** [Prob. < *Kuli,* an aboriginal Gujarat tribe; infl. by Tamil *kuli* hire, wages]

coon·tie (koon′tē) *n.* A tropical American plant (genus *Zamia*) of the cycad family, whose stems and roots yield a starch. [< N. Am. Ind.]

coop (koop, koop) *n.* **1** An enclosure for small animals, as fowls or rabbits. **2** *Slang* A jail; prison. —**to fly the coop** *Slang* To decamp; quit. — *v.t.* To put into a coop; confine. [ME *cupe* < MLG. Cf. MDu. *kupe* cask]

co-op (ko′op, ko·op′) *n. Colloq.* A cooperative enterprise, as a store or market.

coop·er (koo′pər, koop′ər) *n.* One whose business it is to make casks, barrels, etc. — *v.t. & v.i.* To make or mend (casks, barrels, etc.) [ME *couper* < LG. Cf. MDu. *kuper* < *kupe* a cask]

co·op·er·ate (ko·op′ə·rāt) *v.i.* **·at·ed, ·at·ing** **1** To operate together for a common object: with *with.* **2** To practice economic cooperation. See synonyms under AID, HELP. [< L *cooperatus,* pp. of *cooperari* < *co-* together + *operari* < *opus* work]

co·op·er·a·tion (ko·op′ə·rā′shən) *n.* **1** Joint action; profit-sharing. **2** A union of laborers or small capitalists for the purpose of advantageously manufacturing, buying, or selling goods, or of pursuing other modes of mutual benefit. — **co·op′er·a′tion·ist** *n.*

co·op·er·a·tive (ko·op′rə·tiv, -ə·rā′tiv) *n.* **1** An organization carrying on any of various economic activities for the mutual benefit of its members. A **consumers' cooperative,** buying and selling at market prices, distributes the savings over cost of operation to its members in proportion to their patronage. A **producers' cooperative** conducts marketing operations for the pooled output of primary producers, usually farmers. **2** An apartment house owned by an organization of tenants, with each tenant's share determined by the value of his own apartment; also, an apartment in such building. — *adj.* **1** Pertaining to or organized for economic cooperation: a *cooperative* store. **2** Working together for a common purpose. — **co·op′er·a·tive·ly** *adv.*

coop·er·y (koo′pər·ē, koop′ər·ē) *n. pl.* **·ies** **1** The trade or workshop of a cooper; cooperage. **2** A cooper's wares, collectively.

co·opt (ko·opt′) *v.t.* **1** To choose by joint action; specifically, to elect to fill a vacant membership, as of a committee, board, etc. **2** To make ineffectual as an instrument for radical change by incorporating within the established order. Also **co·op′tate.** [< L *cooptare* < *co-* together + *optare* choose] —**co·op·ta·tive** (kō-op′tə-tiv) *adj.* — **co·op′tion, co′op·ta′tion** *n.*

co·or·di·nal (kō-ôr′də-nəl) *adj.* **1** *Biol.* Belonging to the same order, as in botany or zoology. **2** Having or defined by (a certain number of) coordinates.

co·or·di·nate (kō-ôr′də-nit, -nāt) *adj.* **1** Of the same order or rank; existing together in similar relation. **2** *Math.* Of or pertaining to coordinates. **3** Having separate colleges for men and women: a *coordinate* university. —*n.* **1** One who or that which is of the same order, rank, power, etc. **2** *Math.* Any of a set of magnitudes by means of which the position of a point, line, or angle is determined with reference to fixed elements. —*v.* (kō-ôr′də-nāt) **·nat·ed, ·nat·ing** *v.t.* **1** To put in the same rank, class, or order. **2** To harmonize or adjust; bring into harmonious relation or action. —*v.i.* **3** To be of the same order or rank. **4** To act in harmonious or reciprocal relation; come into adjustment. [< Med. L *coordinatus*, pp. of *coordinare* arrange < *co-* together + *ordinare* set in order < *ordo, -inis* rank] — **co·or′di·nate·ly** *adv.* — **co·or′di·nate·ness** *n.* — **co·or′di·na·tive** *adj.* —**co·or′di·na′tor** *n.*

co·or·di·na·tion (kō-ôr′də-nā′shən) *n.* **1** The act of coordinating. **2** The state of being coordinate. **3** The harmonious, integrated action of the various parts and processes of a machine, organization, organism, etc.

coost (kōōst) *Scot.* Past tense of CAST.

coot (kōōt) *n.* **1** An aquatic bird of the genus *Fulica,* resembling the rails. **2** A sea duck, especially any of the North American scoters. **3** *Slang* A common or stupid fellow. [ME *cote* < LG. Cf. Du. *koet.*]

coot·er (kōō′tər) *n.* **1** The Carolina box turtle (*Terrapene carolina*). **2** A turtle or tortoise of Florida (*Pseudemys floridana*). [Origin uncertain]

cop[1] (kop) *n.* **1** The top, as of a hill or the head of a thing. **2** The conical roll of thread formed on the spindle of a spinning machine; also, the tube on which this thread or yarn is wound. [OE *copp* summit]

cop[2] (kop) *Slang v.t.* **copped, cop·ping 1** To take; steal; appropriate. **2** To win: to *cop* a prize. **3** To catch or seize. —**to cop out** *U.S. Slang* To back down or turn away, as from one's responsibilities or ideals; renege. —*n.* A policeman: short for *copper*[2]. [? Var. of *cap* catch, take < OF *caper* < L *capere*]

co·pai·ba (kō-pā′bə, -pī′-) *n.* A viscous, aromatic South American balsam from some species of *Copaifera,* used in affections of the mucous membrane and in varnishes. Also **co·pai′va** (-və). [< Sp. < Tupian *cupauba*]

co·pal (kō′pəl) *n.* A hard, transparent resin exuded by various tropical trees, used for varnishes. [< Sp. < Nahuatl *copalli* incense]

co·palm (kō′päm) *n.* **1** The sweetgum tree. **2** The balsam obtained from it. [Origin uncertain]

co·part·ner (kō-pärt′nər) *n.* One who shares with another; specifically, an equal partner in a business. —**co·part′ner·ship** *n.*

cope[1] (kōp) *v.* **coped, cop·ing** *v.i.* **1** To contend or strive on equal terms; oppose successfully: often with *with.* **2** *Archaic* To meet or encounter: with *with.* **3** *Brit. Colloq.* To deal with a situation successfully. —*v.t.* **4** *Obs.* To deal with; meet in combat. **5** *Obs.* To requite. See synonyms under CONTEND. [< OF *couper* strike < *coup, colp* a blow < L *colaphus*]

cope[2] (kōp) *n.* **1** Anything that arches overhead: the *cope* of heaven. **2** A coping, as of a roof or over a window. **3** A semicircular mantle worn by priests or bishops on solemn or ceremonial occasions; also, a coronation, state, processional, or choral vestment often worn by laymen. —*v.t.* **coped, cop·ing 1** To dress in a cope or cloak. **2** To furnish with or form a coping, as a wall; bend or arch. **3** To form (a joint in a molding) without mitering, as in a sash frame. [< Med. L *cāpa* cape, cope, var. of LL *cappa.* See CAP.]

co·peck (kō′pek) *n.* See KOPECK.

Co·pen·ha·gen (kō′pən-hā′gən, -hä′-) A port on the east coast of Zealand Island, largest city and capital of Denmark: Danish *Köbenhavn.*

copenhagen blue A dusty, light blue.

co·pe·pod (kō′pə·pod) *n.* One of an order (*Copepoda*) of small, free-swimming, fresh-water and marine crustaceans. —*adj.* **1** Of, pertaining to, or belonging to this order. **2** Oar-footed, as a crustacean. Also **co·pep′o·dan** (kō·pep′ə·dən). [< NL < Gk. *kōpē* oar + *pous, podos* foot] — **co·pep′o·dous** *adj.*

cope·stone (kōp′stōn′) *n.* **1** The top stone of a wall. **2** One of the stones of a coping. **3** The final or crowning stroke; culmination.

cop·i·er (kop′ē·ər) *n.* **1** A copyist. **2** One who imitates closely the style of another.

co·pi·lot (kō′pī′lət) *n.* The assistant or relief pilot of an aircraft.

cop·ing (kō′ping) *n.* The top course of a wall, usually sloping to shed water.

coping saw A narrow-bladed saw set in a recessed frame and used for cutting small curved pieces from sections of wood.

cop·i·o·pi·a (kop′ē·ō′pē·ə) *n.* Eyestrain; asthenopia. [< Gk. *kopos* suffering + -OPIA]

co·pi·ous (kō′pē·əs) *adj.* **1** Possessing or showing abundance. **2** Ample; plenteous: large in quantity: *copious* notes. See synonyms under AMPLE. [< L *copiosus* < *copia* abundance] —**co′pi·ous·ly** *adv.* —**co′pi·ous·ness** *n.*

co·pla·nar (kō-plā′nər) *adj. Math.* In the same plane: said of figures.

co·pol·y·mer (ko-pol′ə·mər) *n. Chem.* A compound formed by the polymerization of two or more unlike substances and having properties different from those of either component taken singly.

co·pol·y·mer·i·za·tion (kō-pol′ə·mər·ə·zā′shən) *n. Chem.* A process similar to polymerization, but involving the union of two or more distinct molecular species, each of which is capable of being polymerized alone, and yielding a copolymer.

co·pol·y·mer·ize (kō-pol′ə·mə·rīz′) *v.t. & v.i.* **·ized, ·iz·ing** To subject to or undergo copolymerization.

cop-out (kop′out′) *n. U.S. Slang* **1** A way of avoiding responsibility; especially, an easy or cowardly resolution of a problem; evasion. **2** One who cops out. [< criminal slang *cop out, cop a plea* to plead guilty]

copped (kopt) *adj.* Conical; pointed.

cop·per[1] (kop′ər) *n.* **1** A reddish, ductile, metallic element (symbol Cu, atomic number 29) occurring native and in combination, and a very good conductor of heat and electricity. See PERIODIC TABLE. **2** An article made of this metal; specifically, a vessel in which clothes are boiled. **3** A coin made of copper. **4** Any of several shades of rich, lustrous, reddish-brown, similar to the color of polished copper. —*v.t.* **1** To cover or coat with copper. **2** *Slang* To bet against. [OE *coper* < LL *cuprum* < L (*aes*) *cyprium* Cyprian (metal) < Gk. *kyprios* < *Kypros* Cyprus] — **cop′per·y** *adj.*

cop·per[2] (kop′ər) *n. Slang* A policeman; detective; cop. [< COP[2]]

cop·per·as (kop′ər·əs) *n.* A green, crystalline, astringent ferrous sulfate, $FeSO_4 \cdot 7H_2O$, used in dyeing, inkmaking, photography, etc.: also called *green vitriol.* [< MF *couperose* < Med. L *cuperosa, cuprosa* < (*aqua*) *cuprosa* copper (water) < LL *cuprum.* See COPPER.]

copper barilla A native copper mixed with sandstone, found in Bolivia.

copper glance Chalcocite.

cop·per·head (kop′ər·hed′) *n.* A venomous North American crotaline snake (*Agkistrodon mokasen*) having reddish-brown markings on a buff-colored body: one of the pit vipers.

COPPERHEAD
(2 feet in length; rarely up to 3 feet)

cop·per·smith (kop′ər·smith′) *n.* **1** One who makes utensils of copper. **2** The crimson-breasted barbet (*Xantholaena haematocephala*), common in India, Ceylon, Burma, and the Philippines.

copper sulfate Blue vitriol.

cop·pice (kop′is) *n. & v.* Copse.

cop·ple-crown (kop′əl·kroun′) *n.* **1** A bird's

crest. **2** A hen with a crest or topknot. [< dim. of COP[1] + CROWN] —**cop′ple-crowned′** *adj.*

cop·re·mi·a (kop·rē′mē·ə) *n. Pathol.* A poisoning of the blood from retained fecal matter in cases of obstruction of the bowels. Also **cop·rae′mi·a.** [< COPR(O)- + Gk. *haima* blood]—**cop·re′mic** *adj.*

copro- *combining form* Dung; feces; filth: *coprolite.* Also, before vowels, **copr-.** [< Gk. *kopros* dung]

cop·ro·la·li·a (kop′rō·lā′lē·ə) *n. Psychiatry* Abnormal indecency of speech, regarded as a sign of mental disorder. [< COPRO- + Gk. *lalein* speak]

cop·ro·lite (kop′rə·līt) *n.* The petrified dung of extinct vertebrates, in some localities forming, in part, a phosphatic rock which is mined for a fertilizer. —**cop′ro·lit′ic** (-lit′ik) *adj.*

cop·rol·o·gy (kop·rol′ə·jē) *n.* **1** A collection of filth. **2** Indecency or filth in art or literature; also, the study of this. [< COPRO- + -LOGY]

cop·roph·a·gous (kop·rof′ə·gəs) *adj.* Feeding upon dung, as scarabaeid beetles. [< NL *coprophagos* < *kopros* dung + *phagein* eat]

cop·ro·phil·i·a (kop′rə·fil′ē·ə) *n. Psychiatry* Gratification derived from the contemplation or handling of filth. [< COPRO- + Gk. *philia* love] — **cop′ro·phil′ic** *adj.*

cop·roph·i·lous (kop·rof′ə·ləs) *adj.* **1** Growing readily on dung, as certain fungi. **2** Coprophagous. [< COPRO- + -PHILOUS]

cop·ro·phyte (kop′rə·fīt) *n.* A saprophyte found in dungheaps.

copse (kops) *n.* **1** A low-growing thicket. **2** Wood gathered from a copse; undergrowth. Also **copse′wood′.** —*v.t.* **copsed, cops·ing 1** To clip or turn down, as brushwood. **2** To plant or keep in growth, as underwood. —*v.i.* **3** To form a copse; grow up as a copse. [Earlier COPPICE < OF *copeiz* < *coper* cut]

Coptic Church The principal Christian sect of Egypt, which became a separate body in 451, adhering to the Monophysitic doctrine after this was rejected by the Council of Chalcedon. See MONOPHYSITE.

cop·u·la (kop′yə·lə) *n. pl.* **·las** or **·lae** (-lē) *Gram.* A verb that merely connects the subject and the predicate of a sentence without asserting action, particularly the verbs *be, appear, become, feel, look, seem, smell, sound,* and *taste;* a link verb. [< L *copula,* a link, band] —**cop′u·lar** *adj.*

cop·u·late (kop′yə·lāt) *v.i.* **·lat·ed, ·lat·ing** To unite in sexual intercourse. [< L *copulatus,* pp. of *copulare* fasten, link < *copula* a link] — **cop′u·la·tive** *adj. & n.* —**cop′u·la·tive·ly** *adv.* — **cop·u·la·to·ry** (kop′yə·lə·tôr′ē, -tō′rē) *adj.*

cop·u·la·tion (kop′yə·lā′shən) *n.* **1** The act of coupling; also, the state of being coupled together. **2** Sexual intercourse.

cop·y (kop′ē) *n. pl.* **cop·ies 1** A reproduction or imitation; duplicate. **2** A single printed pamphlet, book, etc., of an edition or issue. **3** A pattern given for imitation. **4** Manuscript or other matter to be reproduced in type. **5** In journalism, someone or something that is newsworthy: He is good *copy.* —**certified copy** A copy attested by an officer having charge of the original. —*v.* **cop·ied, cop·y·ing** *v.t.* **1** To make a copy of; transcribe; reproduce; make in imitation, as in writing or painting. **2** To follow as a model; imitate, as in actions or opinions. —*v.i.* **3** To make a copy or reproduction. **4** To admit of being copied: That page *copies* well. **5** To do in imitation. [< F *copie* < Med. L *copia* transcript < L, supply, abundance]

cop·y·book (kop′ē·book′) *n.* A book containing copies to be imitated in penmanship; writing book.

cop·y·boy (kop′ē·boi′) *n.* An errand boy in a newspaper office who delivers copy to the editor, composing room, etc.

cop·y·cat (kop′ē·kat′) *n. Colloq.* An imitator: a child's term of derision.

cop·y·desk (kop′ē·desk′) *n.* A desk in a newspaper office where copy is edited and prepared for the typesetters.

cop·y·graph (kop′ē·graf, -gräf) *n.* A hectograph.

copying ink An ink containing sugar, glycerin, or some similarly acting substance, for use in any writing or printing to be reproduced in the copying press.

copying paper An unsized paper used in the copying press.

copying press A press for duplicating writing or printing done with copying ink.

cop·y·ist (kop′ē·ist) *n.* **1** One whose business it is to copy. **2** An imitator.

cop·y·read·er (kop′ē·rē′dər) *n.* A person in an editorial office, or by assignment elsewhere, who edits work intended for publication.

cop·y·right (kop′ē·rīt) *n.* The exclusive statutory right of authors, composers, playwrights, artists, publishers, or distributors to publish and dispose of their works for a limited time; in the United States, for 28 years, with privilege of one renewal for an additional 28 years. The common–law property rights in unpublished works continue in effect until publication with or without copyright. —*v.t.* To secure copyright for, as a book or work of art. — **cop′y·right′a·ble** *adj.* — **cop′y·right′er** *n.*

cop·y·writ·er (kop′ē·rī′tər) *n.* One who writes copy for advertisements, including radio and television commercials.

coque·li·co (kōk′li·kō) *n.* **1** The English wild poppy (*Papaver rhoeas*). **2** The reddish-orange color of this flower. [<F]

co·quet (kō·ket′) *v.* **co·quet·ted, co·quet·ting** *v.i.* **1** To flirt; play the coquette; trifle in love: said of women. **2** To act in a trifling, undecided manner; dally. —*v.t.* **3** *Obs.* To flirt with. [<F *coqueter* < *coquet,* dim. of *coq* a cock; with ref. to its strutting]

co·quil·lage (kō·kē·yàzh′) *n.* A design made of or imitating shells, prevalent in the decorative arts of the rococo period. [<F *coquille* shell]

co·quil·la nut (kō·kēl′yə, -kē′yə) The hard-shelled, oval nut of the Brazilian palm *Attalea funifera.* [<Sp. *coquillo,* dim. of *coco* coconut]

co·quille (kō·kēl′) *n.* **1** Any of various dishes, usually of sea food, baked in a shell. **2** Chill (*n.* def. 4). [<F, shell]

co·qui·na (kō·kē′nə) *n.* A soft, highly porous, limestone rock composed of fragments of marine shells: used as building material. [<Sp.]

co·qui·to (kō·kē′tō) *n. pl.* **·tos 1** A tall, massive feather palm of Chile (*Jubaea spectabilis*), bearing a dense crown of foliage. **2** Its small, edible nut. [<Sp., dim. of *coco* coconut]

cor– Assimilated var. of COM–.

cor·a·ci·i·form (kôr′ə·sī′ə·fôrm) *adj.* Designating an order of non-passerine birds (*Coraciiformes*), including the rollers, kingfishers, hornbills, etc. [<NL <Gk. *korax, korakis* raven + -FORM]

cor·a·cle (kôr′ə·kəl, kor′-) *n.* A small fishing boat of hide or oilcloth on a wicker frame. [< Welsh *corwgl* < *corwg* boat]

FRENCH CORACLE

cor·a·coid (kôr′ə·koid, kor′-) *adj.* **1** *Zool.* Designating the posterior inferior process of the shoulder girdle, a separate bone in many animals, as birds, reptiles, and monotremes, that unites with the scapula to form the glenoid cavity. **2** Shaped like a raven's beak. —*n.* **1** The coracoid process. **2** The chief bone of the shoulder girdle of a teleost fish. [<Gk. *korakoeidēs* < *korax, korakis* raven + *eidos* form]

cor·al (kôr′əl, kor′-) *n.* **1** The calcareous skeleton secreted in or by the tissues of various, usually compound marine coelenterates and deposited in various forms and colors. **2** These skeletons collectively. **3** An animal of this type. **4** A yellowish-red color. **5** An object, as a toy or a jewel, made of coral. **6** Lobster or crab roe: so called from its appearance when cooked. —*adj.* **1** Consisting of or like coral. **2** Colored like coral. [<OF <L *coralium* <Gk. *korallion*]

cor·al·ber·ry (kôr′əl·ber′ē, kor′-) *n. pl.* **·ries** A bushy American shrub (*Symphoricarpos orbiculatus*) with dark berries somewhat resembling currants.

coralli– combining form Coral: *coralliferous.* Also, before vowels, **corall–.** [<Gk. *korallion* coral]

cor·al·lif·er·ous (kôr′ə·lif′ər·əs, kor′-) *adj.* Producing or containing coral. [<CORALLI- + -FEROUS]

cor·al·line (kôr′ə·lin, -līn, kor′-) *adj.* **1** Of, pertaining to, resembling, or like coral. **2** Pinkish–red. — *n.* **1** A calcareous, coral-like seaweed. **2** A coral or coral–like animal.

cor·al·lite (kôr′ə·līt, kor′-) *n.* **1** An individual skeleton of coral polyp; a cup coral. **2** Fossil coral. — **cor′al·lit′ic** (-lit′ik) *adj.*

cor·al·loid (kôr′ə·loid, kor′-) *adj.* Coral-shaped; especially, branching like coral: also **cor′al·loi′dal.** — *n.* A polyzoan.

co·ral·lum (kə·ral′əm) *n. pl.* **co·ral·la** (kə·ral′ə) Coral, either as a compound mass or as the skeleton of a polyp. [<LL, var. of *coralium* CORAL]

coral reef A reef, often of great extent, formed by the gradual deposit of innumerable coral skeletons, found chiefly in tropical waters.

cor·al·root (kôr′əl·root′, -root′, kor′-) *n.* Any one of a small genus (*Corallorhiza*) of brown-ish, leafless orchids with much-branched coral-like rootstocks.

coral snake Any of a genus (*Micrurus*) of venomous snakes of tropical America and the southern United States, noted for their brilliant red, black, and yellow rings; especially, *M. lemniscus* of South America and the harlequin snake (*M. fulvius*) of Mexico and the southern United States.

cor·ban (kôr′bən, kôr·bän′) *n.* An offering to God, as in fulfillment of a vow. *Mark* vii 11. [<Hebrew *qorbān*]

cor·bel[1] (kôr′bəl, -bel) *n. Archit.* **a** A projection from the face of a wall to support an overhanging weight; corbeling. **b** A short timber placed lengthwise upon a wall, etc., under a girder to increase its bearing. —*v.t.* **cor·beled** or **·belled, cor·bel·ing** or **·bel·ling 1** To support by corbels. **2** To make in the form of corbels. [<OF <LL *corvellum,* dim. of *corvus* crow; from its shape]

cor·bel[2] (kôr′bəl, -bel) *n. Archit.* A piece serving as a cushion for a capital, as in a Corinthian column, that rests on the astragal. [<OF <L *corbis* basket]

cor·bel·ing (kôr′bəl·ing) *n. Archit.* An arrangement of stones or bricks in building a wall, in which successive courses project beyond those below them. Also **cor′bel·ling.**

cord (kôrd) *n.* **1** A string of several strands. **2** A measure for wood; in the United States a pile 4 x 4 x 8 feet, equal to 128 cubic feet, or 3.62 cubic meters. **3** A wale or rib in a fabric giving a raised effect. **4** A corded fabric. **5** *Pl. U.S.* Corduroy trousers. **6** *Anat.* A cordlike structure: the spinal *cord.* **7** *Often pl.* Any feeling that draws or restrains. **6** The rope used by a hangman. — *v.t.* **1** To bind or secure with cord; furnish with cords. **2** To pile (firewood) by the cord. ◆ Homophone: *chord.* [<F *corde* <L *chorda* <Gk. *chordē* string of a musical instrument. Doublet of CHORD.] — **cord′er** *n.*

cord·age (kôr′dij) *n.* **1** Ropes and cords collectively; especially, ropes in the rigging of a ship. **2** The amount in cords, as of wood, on a given area of land.

cor·date (kôr′dāt) *adj.* Heart-shaped, as a leaf. [<L *cordatus* < *cor* heart] — **cor′date·ly** *adv.*

cord·ed (kôr′did) *adj.* **1** Bound or fastened with cord or rope. **2** Striped or ribbed as if with cords: a *corded* fabric. **3** Piled in cord measure: *corded* firewood. **4** With the hair twisted or felted into strings or curls: said of dogs. **5** *Obs.* Made of cord or rope.

cor·de·lier (kôr′də·lir′) *n.* An early type of ropemaking machine. [<F]

cor·dial (kôr′jəl) *adj.* **1** Proceeding from the heart; exhibiting or expressing kindliness; imparting vigor or joy; cheering. See synonyms under AMICABLE. — *n.* **1** That which invigorates or exhilarates. **2** A sweet, aromatic alcoholic spirit; a liqueur. [<Med. L *cordialis* <L *cor, cordis* heart] — **cor·dial·i·ty** (kôr·jal′ə·tē, -jē·al′-, -dē·al′-), **cor′dial·ness** *n.* — **cor′dial·ly** *adv.*

cor·di·e·rite (kôr′dē·ə·rīt′) *n. Mineral.* A bluish silicate of magnesium, aluminum, and iron, crystallizing in the orthorhombic system: used as a gemstone: also called *iolite.* [after P. *Cordier,* 1777–1861, French geologist]

cor·di·form (kôr′də·fôrm) *adj.* Heart-shaped; cordate. [<L *cor, cordis* heart + -FORM]

cor·dil·le·ra (kôr′dil·yâr′ə, kôr·dil′ər·ə) *n. Geog.* The entire system of mountain ranges that

borders a continent or occurs in the same general region. [<Sp. <OSp. *cordilla,* dim. of *cuerda* rope <L *chorda.* See CORD.] — **cor′dil·le′ran** *adj.*

cord·ite (kôr′dīt) *n.* A variety of smokeless powder consisting of cellulose nitrate or gun-cotton, nitroglycerin, and a mineral jelly, used chiefly as a propellant. [<CORD; with ref. to its appearance]

cor·don (kôr′dən) *n.* **1** An extended line, as of men, ships, forts, etc. **2** An ornamental lace, cord, or ribbon worn to secure something in place, as a badge of identification, or for adornment. **3** *Archit.* **a** A stringcourse. **b** A coping projecting from a scarp wall. [<F < *corde* cord]

cor·do·van (kôr′də·vən) *n.* **1** Cordwain. **2** Fine horsehide leather.

cor·du·roy (kôr′də·roi, kôr′də·roi′) *n.* **1** A thick, corded or ribbed, durable fabric, usually of cotton. **2** *pl.* Trousers made of corduroy. **3** A corduroy road, or the materials used in construction. —*adj.* **1** Made of corduroy, as trousers. **2** Formed from logs laid transversely; a *corduroy* road. —*v.t.* To make into a corduroy road. [<F *corde du roi* fabric of the king]

corduroy road A road, as over miry ground, constructed with small logs laid together transversely.

cord·wood (kôrd′wood′) *n.* Firewood sold by the cord.

cord·y (kôr′dē) *adj.* **1** In glassmaking, having stringlike imperfections due to impurities. **2** Full of cords; cordlike; having cordlike fibers or parts.

core (kôr, kōr) *n.* **1** The central or innermost part of a thing. **2** The heart, as of an apple or pear, containing the seeds. **3** The most important part of anything; the pith of a subject. **4** A solid form placed in a mold, about which metal is poured, so as to be cast hollow. **5** *Electr.* **a** The insulated conducting wires of an electric cable. **b** The iron mass or bundle of iron rods, etc., around which the wire is coiled in an electromagnet or armature. **6** *Engin.* In submarine and geological investigations, a cylindrical mass of test material brought to the surface by a special hollow drill. **7** In fingerprint identification, the inner terminus or focal point which constitutes the approximate center of a pattern and is essential to its correct interpretation. **8** *Anthropol.* A type of Paleolithic stone implement consisting of a central mass of a rock, shaped for use in one of several standard forms, chiefly hand-axes. — *v.t.* **cored, coring** To remove the core of. ◆ Homophone: *corps.* [Origin uncertain] — **core′less** *adj.*

co·re·la·tion (kō′ri·lā′shən) *n.* **1** Joint or mutual relation. **2** Correlation.

co·re·lig·ion·ist (kō′ri·lij′ən·ist) *n.* An adherent of the same religion, church, or sect as another.

co·re·mi·um (kə·rē′mē·əm) *n. pl.* **·mi·a** (-mē·ə) *Bot.* A special form of non-sexual fruit body in the fungi in which spore-bearing hyphae are arranged in parallel order, side by side, to form an erect fascicle. [<Gk. *korēma* broom]

co·re·op·sis (kôr′ē·op′sis, kō′rē-) *n.* A plant of a large genus (*Coreopsis*) of mainly North American herbs of the composite family, with heads of showy yellow or rose-colored flowers: also called *calliopsis.* [<NL <Gk. *koris* bug + *opsis* appearance; with ref. to the shape of the seed]

cor·e·plas·ty (kôr′ə·plas′tē, kor′-) *n. Surg.* Any plastic operation upon the iris. [<Gk. *korē* pupil of the eye + -PLASTY] — **cor′e·plas′tic** *adj.*

cor·er (kôr′ər, kō′rər) *n.* A utensil for removing the cores of apples and other fruit.

co·re·spon·dent (kō′ri·spon′dənt) *n. Law* A joint defendant; especially, in a suit for divorce, one charged with having committed adultery with the husband or wife from whom divorce is being sought. — **co′re·spon′den·cy** *n.*

co·ri·an·der (kôr′ē·an′dər, kō′rē-) *n.* A plant of the parsley family (genus *Coriandrum*), bearing aromatic seeds used for seasoning and in medicine as a carminative. [<F *coriandre* <L *coriandrum* <Gk. *koriannon*]

co·ri·um (kôr′ē·əm, kō′rē-) *n. pl.* **·ri·a** (-ə) **1** *Anat.* The sentient and vascular portion of the skin beneath the epidermis. **2** *Entomol.* In certain insects (order *Heteroptera*), the elongated middle section or harder portion of the forewing. [<L. skin, hide]

cork[1] (kôrk) *n.* **1** A tough, elastic, light, and porous outer bark of an evergreen tree (*Quercus suber*), the cork oak, indigenous to southern Europe: it improves in quality with the age of the tree, and has many uses in industry and the arts. **2** A piece of this bark used as a bottle stopper. **3** Any stopper of other material: a rubber *cork*. **4** *Bot.* A protective tissue that forms in the stems beneath the epidermis of dicotyledons and replaces it. —*v.t.* **1** To stop with a cork, as a bottle. **2** To restrain or confine; check. **3** *U.S.* To blacken with burnt cork. —**to cork up** *U.S. Colloq.* To silence suddenly. [<OSp. *alcorque* a cork slipper <Arabic, ? <L *quercus* oak]

cork[2] (kôrk) See CALK: erroneous usage.

cork·age (kôr′kij) *n.* A charge for serving wine at a hotel, especially when the wine is the property of the guest.

cork belt A belt or jacket made of pieces of cork enclosed in canvas, to support a person in the water; a life belt. Also **cork jacket.**

cork·board (kôrk′bôrd′, -bōrd′) *n.* A building material formed from compressed and bonded granulated cork.

cork cambium *Bot.* The phellogen, or inner active layers of bark-producing tissue. Also **cork meristem.**

corked (kôrkt) *adj.* **1** Stopped with cork, as a bottle. **2** Having acquired the taste of cork: *corked* wine. **3** *Slang* Very drunk.

cork·er (kôr′kər) *n.* **1** One who or that which corks. **2** *Slang* An argument that puts a stop to discussion; anything that stops competition.

cork oak An oak tree (*Quercus suber*) of southern Europe and North Africa, whose thick bark yields cork.

cork·screw (kôrk′skrōō′) *n.* **1** A spiral instrument for drawing corks from bottles. **2** A ringlet; curl. —*v.t. & v.i.* **1** To move or cause to move like a corkscrew; to twist. **2** *Aeron.* To fly in a spiral course in order to avoid enemy anti-aircraft fire. —*adj.* Shaped like a corkscrew; twisted; spiral.

cork·wood (kôrk′wōōd′) *n.* **1** The light, porous wood of several West Indian trees: specifically, of the custard-apple family (genus *Annona*), or of the balsa family, especially *Ochroma pyramidale*. **2** In the SE United States, a small tree (*Leitneria floridana*) with deciduous glossy leaves and a drupaceous fruit.

cork·y (kôr′kē) *adj.* **·i·er, ·i·est 1** Like cork; especially, shrunken; dried up. **2** Having the flavor or odor of cork: said especially of wines. **3** Of cork. —**cork′i·ness** *n.*

corm (kôrm) *n. Bot.* A bulblike, solid, fleshy enlargement, usually of the underground stem in plants. [<Gk. *kormos* tree-trunk]

cor·mo·rant (kôr′mər·ənt) *n.* **1** A large, web-footed, voracious aquatic bird (genus *Phalacrocorax*) of wide distribution and gregarious habits, having a strongly hooked bill and large throat gular pouch. **2** Hence, a glutton or avaricious person. —*adj.* Like a cormorant; greedy; rapacious. [<F *cormoran* <L *corvus marinus* sea crow]

CORMORANT

corn[1] (kôrn) *n.* **1** The edible seeds of cereal plants: in England, wheat, barley, rye, and oats collectively; in America, maize, or Indian corn. **2** The plants that produce corn when growing in the field; the stalks and ears, or the stalks, ears, and seeds, after harvesting. **3** *Slang* Anything regarded as trite, banal, sentimental, etc., especially popular music. **4** *Colloq.* Whisky distilled from corn. —*v.t.* **1** To preserve in salt or in brine: to *corn* beef. **2** *U.S.* To feed with corn. **3** *Scot.* To feed with oats. **4** To granulate. [OE]

corn[2] (kôrn) *n.* **1** A horny thickening of the cuticle, common on the feet. **2** A morbid condition of the forehoofs of horses caused by injuries to the tissue of the sole, producing inflammation of the horn. [<OF <L *cornu.*

Akin to HORN.]

cor·na·ceous (kôr·nā′shəs) *adj.* Designating a family (*Cornaceae*) of polypetalous shrubs or trees; the dogwood or cornel family.

corn borer The larva of certain insects which feeds on the ears and stalks of corn, especially the European corn borer (*Pyrausta nubilalis*).

corn·bread (kôrn′bred′) *n.* Bread made from the meal of maize or Indian corn. Also **corn bread.**

corn·cob (kôrn′kob′) *n.* The spike of maize round which the kernels grow. Also **corn cob.**

corn·cock·le (kôrn′kok′əl) *n.* A tall purple-flowered weed of the pink family, especially *Agrostemma githago*: also called *corn rose.*

corn crake A European crake (*Crex crex*) frequenting cornfields: also called *dakerhen.*

corn·crib (kôrn′krib′) *n.* A building for storage of corn, usually raised on posts, with walls made of slats for ventilation.

corn·dodg·er (kôrn′doj′ər) *n.* A cake of cornmeal baked or fried hard.

cor·ne·a (kôr′nē·ə) *n. Anat.* The transparent anterior part of the outer coat of the eyeball, continuous with the sclera. See illustration under EYE. Also **cornea lens.** [<Med. L *cornea* horny <L *cornu* horn] —**cor′ne·al** *adj.*

corn·ear worm (kôrn′ir′) The bollworm.

corned (kôrnd) *adj.* **1** Preserved in coarse salt or in brine: *corned* beef. **2** *U.S. Slang* Drunk.

cor·nel (kôr′nəl) *n.* Any of a genus (*Cornus*) of shrubs and small trees with hard, compact wood, as the dogwood: also called *cornus*. [<G *kornel*(*baum*) <Med. L *cornolius* <MF *cornoille*, ult. <L *cornus* cornel tree] —**cor·nel·ian** (kôr·nēl′yən) *adj.*

cor·ne·ous (kôr′nē·əs) *adj.* Consisting of horn; of a hornlike texture; horny. [<L *corneus* horny]

cor·ner (kôr′nər) *n.* **1** The point formed by the intersection of two or more lines or surfaces, or the edge formed by the intersection of two surfaces; an angle. **2** The space or surface comprised between two converging walls or lines near their meeting. **3** A retired spot; nook: the chimney *corner*. **4** A position of embarrassment or difficulty, or one from which extrication is difficult. **5** A condition of a financial market when a commodity or security has been largely bought up with a view to forcing a higher price: a *corner* in cotton or stocks. **6** A part or spot, especially a remote or obscure part, of a particular place; also, any of the four directions: the four *corners* of the earth. **7** A tool used in decorating the corners of books: sometimes called **corner-piece. 8** A metallic or other guard for the corner of a book, box, or other article. —**to trim one's corners** To take risks. —*v.t.* **1** To force or drive into a corner. **2** To place in a corner. **3** *U.S.* To place in a position of difficulty or embarrassment: to *corner* a witness. **4** To furnish with corners. **5** To acquire control of, as a commodity or stock, so as to demand a high price. —*v.i.* **6** *U.S.* To come together in a corner; be situated on a corner. **7** *Colloq.* To go round a corner, as in racing: The car *corners* beautifully. **8** To form a corner in a commodity or stock. —*adj.* **1** Located at a corner. **2** Designed for a corner. [<OF *cornier* <L *cornu* horn, point]

corner chair A small armchair having the back curved or placed at an angle around two sides of the seat, one leg supporting the front corner of the seat: also called *roundabout chair.*

cor·nered (kôr′nərd) *adj.* **1** Having corners. **2** Forced into a position of embarrassment or difficulty.

cor·ner·stone (kôr′nər·stōn′) *n.* **1** A stone uniting two walls at the corner of a building. **2** Such a stone, often inscribed and made into a repository, laid into the foundation of an edifice. **3** Something fundamental or of primary importance.

cor·ner·wise (kôr′nər·wīz′) *adv.* With the corner in front; diagonally.

cor·net[1] (kôr·net′ *for def.* 1; kôr′nit *for defs.* 2 *and* 3) **1** A small wind instrument of the trumpet class, in which the notes are determined by valves or pistons that open communication into auxiliary bands of tubing, thus varying the length of the vibrating air

column. **2** A cone-shaped paper wrapper. **3** A portion of a woman's headdress, of varying shape, from the 14th to the 17th century; also, the headdress itself; also, the tall white headdress of the Sisters of Charity. [<OF, dim. of corn <L *cornu* a horn] —**cor·net′tist** or **cor·net′ist** *n.*

CORNET
(def. 3)

cor·net[2] (kôr′nit) *n.* **1** Formerly, the lowest commissioned cavalry officer in the British army, or a pennant carried by him. **2** A flag or standard; specifically, a signaling flag. [<F, dim. of *corne* <L *cornu* horn]

cor·net·cy (kôr′nit·sē) *n. pl.* **·cies** The rank or commission of a cornet.

corn-fed (kôrn′fed′) *adj. U.S.* **1** Nourished on corn. **2** *Slang* Strong and healthy, as if fed on an ample diet of corn, but rustic and unsophisticated.

corn·field (kôrn′fēld′) *n.* An area in which corn is grown: also **corn field.** —*adj.* **1** Of, from, or growing in a cornfield. **2** Rustic: *cornfield* philosophy.

corn·flow·er (kôrn′flou′ər) *n.* Any flower growing in grainfields; especially, the blue-bottle or bachelor's-button.

corn·husk (kôrn′husk′) *n.* A corn shuck.

corn·husk·ing (kôrn′hus′king) *n. U.S.* **1** The husking of corn. **2** A social gathering for the purpose of husking corn, usually followed by refreshments, dancing, etc.; a husking bee.

cor·nice (kôr′nis) *n.* **1** *Archit.* **a** The horizontal molded projection at the top of a building or of a component part of a building, usually under the eaves. **b** The uppermost member of an entablature. See illustration under ENTABLATURE. **2** An ornamental molding around the walls of a room close to the ceiling; also, a light wooden molding around the walls of a room, gallery, etc., at a convenient height for the support of pictures by hooks. **3** A frame, upholstered or of molding, fastened to a wall or window frame so as to cover the rods and hooks used for hanging curtains, etc. **4** A mass of snow projecting from a mountain ridge. —*v.t.* **·niced, ·nic·ing** To provide or adorn with a cornice. [<Ital. <L *coronis* <Gk. *korōnis* wreath, garland] —**cor′niced** *adj.*

CORNICE

cor·nic·u·late (kôr·nik′yə·lāt, -lit) *adj.* Having horns or hornlike processes. [<L *corniculatus* < *corniculum*, dim. of *cornu* horn]

corn lily **1** Either of two species of convolvulus, the greater or lesser bindweed. **2** Any bulbous plant of the genus *Ixia* of South Africa.

corn mayweed **1** The scentless wild camomile (*Matricaria inodora*): naturalized in parts of the United States. **2** The field camomile (*Anthemis arvensis*) of the eastern United States.

corn·meal (kôrn′mēl′) *n.* **1** Meal made from corn; Indian meal. **2** *Scot.* Oatmeal. Also **corn meal.**

corn pit A section of a produce exchange devoted to business in corn.

corn pith The pith of Indian corn, used in the manufacture of paper, etc.

corn pone Bread made of cornmeal, water, and salt, usually without milk and eggs.

corn-pop·per (kôrn′pop′ər) *n.* A wire box or cylinder used for popping corn over a fire.

corn poppy A weed (*Papaver rhoeas*) growing in grain fields: also called *corn rose.*

corn salad Lamb lettuce (*Valerianella olitoria*), a European plant whose leaves are used for salad.

corn shock A conical bundle of stalks of Indian corn, often tied together at the top.

corn shuck The shuck or husk of an ear of maize: also *cornhusk.*

corn smut A widespread disease of corn, due to infection by the smut fungus, *Ustilago zeae*, and characterized by spore-containing

---

add, āce, câre, pälm; end, ēven; it, īce; odd, ōpen, ôrder; tŏŏk, pōōl; up, bûrn; ə = a in *above*, e in *sicken*, i in *clarity*, o in *melon*, u in *focus*; yōō = u in *fuse*; oi, oil; ou, pout; ch, check; g, go; ng, ring; th, thin; ŧh, this; zh, vision. Foreign sounds á, œ, ü, kh, ṅ; and ◆: see page xx. < from; + plus; ? possibly.

tumor masses attached to the ears and other aerial parts of the plant.

corn snow In skiing, fallen snow which has melted slightly and refrozen, forming a coarse, granular surface which enables the skis to slide more easily.

corn spurry Beggarweed.

corn·stalk (kôrn'stôk') *n.* A stalk of Indian corn. Also **corn stalk.**

corn·starch (kôrn'stärch') *n.* 1 Starch made from corn. 2 A purified starchy meal used in making puddings.

corn sugar Glucose obtained from corn.

cor·nu (kôr'nyoō) *n. pl.* **·nu·a** (-nyoō-ə) A horn, or anything shaped like a horn: applied to various anatomical structures: the superior and inferior *cornua* of the larynx. [<L, horn]

cor·nu·co·pi·a (kôr'nə·kō'pē·ə) *n.* 1 The horn of plenty, represented as overflowing with fruits and symbolizing peace and prosperity. See AMALTHEA. 2 A paper or cardboard horn for holding candies. 3 A superabundance. [<LL *cornucopia* <L *cornu copiae* horn of plenty] — **cor'nu·co'pi·an** *adj.*

cor·nus (kôr'nəs) See CORNEL.

cor·nute (kôr·noōt', -nyoōt') *adj.* 1 Having horns or a hornlike process or appendage. 2 Shaped like a horn. Also **cor·nut'ed.** [<L *cornutus* <*cornu* horn]

corn whisky Whisky distilled from corn.

corn·worm (kôrn'wûrm') *n.* The bollworm.

corn·y (kôr'nē) *adj.* **corn·i·er, corn·i·est** 1 Of, abounding in, or producing corn. 2 *Slang* Trite, banal, sentimental, or unsophisticated.

co·rol·la (kə·rol'ə) *n. Bot.* The second series or inner circle of flower leaves, usually colored, forming the inner floral envelope or inner perianth, and serving mainly to attract insects; the petals of a flower collectively. Also **cor·ol** (kor'əl). [<L, dim. of *corona* crown] — **cor·ol·late** (kôr'ə·lāt, kor'-), **cor'ol·lat'ed** *adj.*

cor·ol·lar·y (kôr'ə·ler'ē, kor'-; *Brit.* kə·rol'ər·ē) *n. pl.* **·lar·ies** 1 A proposition following so obviously from another that it requires little or no demonstration. 2 An inference; deduction. — *adj.* Like a corollary; deduced; resultant. [<L *corollarium* gift, orig. money paid for a garland < *corolla* garland]

co·ro·na (kə·rō'nə) *n. pl.* **·nas** or **·nae** (-nē) 1 A garland or wreath given by the ancient Greeks and Romans as a reward for distinguished achievements. 2 *Archit.* The projecting brow of a cornice. 3 A crownlike part, structure, or process, as the crown of the head or the shell of a sea-urchin. 4 *Astron.* **a** A luminous circle around one of the heavenly bodies. **b** The luminous envelope of ionized gases surrounding the chromosphere of the sun and visible during a total eclipse. 5 Loosely, any halo. 6 *Electr.* The luminous discharge at the surface of an electrical conductor under very high voltage. 7 *Bot.* A crownlike process at the top of the tube of the corolla, as in jonquils. 8 *Geol.* A zone of minerals surrounding another mineral or at the junction of two minerals. [<L, crown]

CORONA
(def. 4b)

co·ro·nal (kə·rō'nəl, kôr'ə·nəl, kor'-) *adj.* 1 Of or pertaining to a corona or halo, or to the crown of the head. 2 *Anat.* Having the direction of the coronal suture: a *coronal* plane.

coronal suture *Anat.* The suture between the frontal and the two parietal bones of the skull.

cor·o·nar·y (kôr'ə·ner'ē, kor'-) *adj.* 1 Pertaining to a crown or wreath. 2 *Anat.* Encircling, crowning: the *coronary* ligament of the liver; the two *coronary* arteries rising from the aorta. See illustration under HEART. — *n.* Coronary thrombosis. [<L *coronarius* < *corona* crown]

coronary thrombosis *Pathol.* The formation of a thrombus, or blood clot, in one of the coronary arteries, resulting in interruption of blood supply from the heart.

cor·o·na·tion (kôr'ə·nā'shən, kor'-) *n.* 1 The act or ceremony of crowning a monarch. 2 Accomplishment; fulfillment. [<OF *coronacion* <L *coronatus,* pp. of *coronare* crown]

cor·o·ner (kôr'ə·nər, kor'-) *n.* A public officer who inquires into the cause of deaths not clearly due to natural causes. [<AF *coruner* officer of the crown < *corune* crown <L *corona*] — **cor'o·ner·ship'** *n.*

than sovereign. 2 Any chaplet or wreath for the head; especially, a semicircular band worn by women above the brow as a headdress. 3 The upper margin of a horse's hoof. [<OF *coronete,* dim. of *corone* crown <L *corona*]

co·ro·ni·form (kə·rō'nə·fôrm) *adj.* Having the form of a crown. [<L *corona* crown + -FORM]

cor·po·ra (kôr'pər·ə) Plural of CORPUS.

cor·po·ral[1] (kôr'pər·əl) *adj.* 1 Belonging or relating to the body as opposed to the mind: *corporal* punishment. 2 Personal: *corporal* possession. 3 *Obs.* Having substance; corporeal; not spiritual. See synonyms under PHYSICAL. — *n.* The linen cloth on which the elements are placed during the celebration of the Eucharist: also **cor·po·ra·le** (kôr'pə·rā'lē) or **corporal cloth.** [<L *corporalis* < *corpus* body] — **cor·po·ral·i·ty** (kôr'pə·ral'ə·tē) *n.* — **cor'po·ral·ly** *adv.*

cor·po·ral[2] (kôr'pər·əl) *n.* 1 In the U.S. Army and Marine Corps, an enlisted man ranking next above a private first class and next below a sergeant. 2 In the British Navy; an assistant to the master at arms. 3 *U.S.* The fallfish (*Semotilus corporalis*). — **lance corporal** A private acting as corporal. [<MF *coporal,* var. of *caporal* <Ital. *caporale* < *capo* head <L *caput*]

corporal's guard *Mil.* The squad of men detailed for guard or other duty under a corporal; hence, any small number of persons, especially of attendants or adherents.

cor·po·rate (kôr'pər·it) *adj.* 1 Associated by legal enactment for the transaction of business; incorporated: a body politic and *corporate.* 2 Belonging to a corporation: *corporate* property. 3 Combined as a whole; considered as one; collective. 4 Having a visible body or form; corporeal; not spiritual. [<L *corporatus,* pp. of *corporare* assume a body < *corpus* body] — **cor'po·rate·ly** *adv.*

cor·po·ra·tion (kôr'pə·rā'shən) *n.* 1 An artificial person created by law, consisting of one or more natural persons united in one body under such grants as secure a succession of members without changing the identity of the body, and empowered to act in a certain capacity or to transact business of some designated form or nature like a natural person. 2 *Colloq.* A protuberant abdomen; paunch.

cor·po·ra·tive (kôr'pə·rā'tiv, -pər·ə·tiv') *adj.* 1 Of or pertaining to a corporation. 2 In political systems, regimenting the operation of the whole social and economic life through one or more corporate bodies selected from employers and employees of principal corporations and controlled by the government.

cor·po·ra·tor (kôr'pə·rā'tər) *n.* A member of a corporation; especially, an original incorporator.

cor·po·re·al (kôr·pôr'ē·əl, -pō'rē·əl) *adj.* 1 Having a body; of a material nature; physical: distinguished from *immaterial, mental,* or *spiritual.* 2 *Law* Perceivable by the bodily senses; substantial and permanent; opposed to *incorporeal: corporeal* hereditaments. See synonyms under PHYSICAL. [<L *corporeus* < *corpus* body] — **cor·po·re·al·i·ty** (kôr·pôr'ē·al'ə·tē, -pō'rē-), **cor·po're·al·ness, cor·po·re·i·ty** (kôr'pə·rē'ə·tē) *n.* — **cor·po're·al·ly** *adv.*

cor·po·sant (kôr'pə·zant) *n.* A luminous discharge of atmospheric electricity from sharp points near the earth's surface, as from steeples, treetops, the masts of ships, etc.; also called *St. Elmo's fire.* [<Pg. *corpo santo* <L *corpus sanctus* holy body]

corps (kôr) *n. pl.* **corps** (kôrz, kōrz) 1 *Mil.* **a** A tactical unit, intermediate between a division and an army, and consisting of two or more divisions. **b** A special department or subdivision: the Quartermaster *Corps.* 2 A number of persons acting together. ◆ Homophone: *core.* [<F, var. of OF *cors.* See CORPSE.]

corpse (kôrps) *n.* A dead body, usually of a human being. See synonyms under BODY. [ME *corps,* var. of *cors* <OF <L *corpus* body]

cor·pu·lent (kôr'pyə·lənt) *adj.* Having a great excess of fat; very fleshy. [<F <L *corpulentus* fleshy < *corpus* body] — **cor'pu·lence, cor'pu·len·cy, cor'pu·lent·ness** *n.*

Synonyms: adipose, burly, fat, fleshy, gross, obese, plethoric, portly, pursy, stout. *Antonyms:* bony, emaciated, gaunt, lean, poor, skinny, slight, spare, thin.

cor·pus (kôr'pəs) *n. pl.* **·po·ra** (-pər·ə) 1 A body of a man or animal. 2 The main body or substance of anything. 3 *Law* **a** A material object; especially, a corporeal property. **b** The elements or facts of a case considered collectively. 4 *Anat.* The main part or mass of an organ. [<L]

corpus cal·lo·sum (kə·lō'səm) *Anat.* A large band of commissural fibers connecting the two halves of the cerebral hemispheres. [< NL, hard body]

cor·pus·cle (kôr'pəs·əl, -pus·əl) *n.* 1 A minute particle of matter; molecule; atom; electron. 2 *Biol.* **a** Any protoplasmic granule of distinct shape or characteristic function. **b** One of the particles forming part of the blood of vertebrates, either a **red corpuscle** containing hemoglobin for oxygen transport, or a **white corpuscle,** known as a leukocyte. Also **cor·pus·cule** (kôr·pus'kyool). [<L *corpusculum,* dim. of *corpus* body] — **cor·pus·cu·lar** (kôr·pus'kyə·lər) *adj.*

corpus lu·te·um (loō'tē·əm) *pl.* **cor·po·ra lu·te·a** (-tē·ə) *Anat.* A yellow body formed by a Graafian follicle in the ovary, and appearing during menstruation and pregnancy: it secretes progesterone. [<L, yellow body]

corpus stri·a·tum (strī·ā'təm) *pl.* **cor·po·ra stri·a·ta** (-tə) *Anat.* One of two masses of ganglionic cells situated in front of the thalamus and at the base of either hemisphere of the brain. [<L, striped body]

cor·rade (kə·rād') *v.t.* **·rad·ed, ·rad·ing** *Geol.* To disintegrate, as rocks, either by solution or by solution combined with mechanical wear: said of rivers. [<L *corradere* < *com-* together + *radere* scrape, rub]

cor·ra·di·ate (kə·rā'dē·āt) *v.i.* **·at·ed, ·at·ing** To converge to a focus, as rays of light. [<COR- + RADIATE]

cor·ral (kə·ral') *n.* 1 An enclosed space or pen for livestock. 2 A space enclosed by wagons for protection against attack. — *v.t.* **·ralled, ·ral·ling** 1 To drive into and enclose in a corral; pen up. 2 To arrange in the form of a corral: to *corral* wagons. 3 *U.S. Colloq.* To seize or capture; secure. [<Sp., a yard, an enclosed space]

cor·ra·sion (kə·rā'zhən) *n. Geol.* The process of erosion by corrading; specifically, the vertical or lateral cutting performed by a river. Compare EROSION. [<L *corrasus,* pp. of *corradere.* See CORRADE.]

cor·rect (kə·rekt') *v.t.* 1 To rectify or remove error from; make right. 2 To point out the errors of; set right. 3 To rebuke or chastise. 4 To remedy or counteract, as a malfunction. 5 To make conformable to a standard: to *correct* a lens. See synonyms under AMEND, CHASTEN, RECLAIM. — *adj.* 1 Free from fault or mistake. 2 True, right, or proper; accurate; exact. [<L *correctus,* pp. of *corrigere* < *com-* together + *regere* make straight] — **cor·rect'a·ble** or **·i·ble** *adj.* — **cor·rec'tive** *adj. & n.* — **cor·rec'tive·ly** *adv.* — **cor·rect'ly** *adv.* — **cor·rect'ness** *n.* — **cor·rec'tor** *n.*

Synonyms (adj.): accurate, decorous, exact, faultless, perfect, precise, proper, right, true. See EXACT, PERFECT, PRECISE, RIGHT. *Antonyms:* erroneous, false, faulty, inaccurate, incorrect, wrong.

cor·rec·tion (kə·rek'shən) *n.* 1 The act of correcting or setting right; rectification; emendation. 2 That which is offered as an improvement. 3 The act or process of disciplining or chastening. 4 The act or process of neutralizing an undesired quality or condition. — **cor·rec'tion·al** *adj.*

cor·reg·i·dor (kə·reg'ə·dôr, *Sp.* kôr·rā'hē·thôr') *n.* 1 The chief magistrate of a Spanish-American town. 2 A similar magistrate whose jurisdiction extends over part of a province. [<Sp. <*corregir* <L *corrigere.* See CORRECT.]

cor·re·late (kôr'ə·lāt, kor'-) *v.* **·lat·ed, ·lat·ing** *v.t.* 1 To place or put in reciprocal relation; establish a mutual relation between. 2 To show the mutual relation between. — *v.i.* 3 To have a correlation; be mutually or reciprocally related. — *adj.* Having mutual or reciprocal relations. — *n.* A correlative. [< COR- + RELATE]

cor·re·la·tion (kôr'ə·lā'shən, kor'-) *n.* 1 Mutual or reciprocal relation. 2 The act of bringing under relations of union or interaction. 3 *Physiol.* The combination of nervous impulses in sensory centers resulting in adaptive reactions. 4 *Math.* A statement of the kind and degree of relationship between two or more variables. Also spelled *corelation.* — **cor're·la'tion·al** *adj.*

cor·rel·a·tive (kə·rel'ə·tiv) *adj.* 1 Having correlation; especially, mutually involving or implying one another: *correlative* structures. 2 Mutually related to grammatical or logical significance; referring to each other: *either* and *or* are *correlative* conjunctions. —*n.* 1 One of two or more persons or things united by reason of some natural relation or correspondence. 2 Either of two correlative terms. — **cor·rel'a·tive·ly** *adv.* — **cor·rel'a·tive·ness, cor·rel'a·tiv'i·ty** *n.*

cor·rep·tion (kə·rep'shən) *n.* In classical prosody, the treating of a metrically long syllable as short. Compare PROTRACTION. [<L *correptio, -onis* < *corripere* < *com-* thoroughly + *rapere* seize]

cor·re·spond (kôr'ə·spond', kor'-) *v.i.* 1 To agree or be conformable in respect to fitness; be proportional. 2 To be similar or analogous in character or in function. 3 To communicate by letters. [<Med. L *correspondere* < *com-* together + *respondere* answer] — **cor·re·spon·sive** (kôr'ə·spon'siv, kor'-) *adj.*

cor·re·spon·dence (kôr'ə·spon'dəns, kor'-) *n.* 1 The act, condition, or state of corresponding. 2 Mutual adaptation; congruity; agreement. 3 Communication by letters; also, the letters themselves. Also **cor're·spon'den·cy.** See synonyms under INTERCOURSE.

correspondence principle *Physics* The relation assumed to exist between the observed radiation characteristics of an electron orbit and those calculated by classical mechanics.

cor·re·spon·dent (kôr'ə·spon'dənt, kor'-) *n.* 1 One who communicates by means of letters; specifically, a newspaper or magazine employee who dispatches news and special reports from a seat of war or other place of public interest. 2 A person, partnership, firm, or corporation that carries on business transactions with another at a distance through letters or telegrams. 3 Anything that corresponds; a correlative. —*adj.* 1 Having correspondence; correlated in nature; adapted: with *to.* 2 *Obs.* Obedient.

cor·re·spond·ing (kôr'ə·spon'ding, kor'-) *adj.* 1 Correspondent; being similar and similarly placed: with *to.* 2 Carrying on a correspondence: with *with.* See synonyms under SYNONYMOUS. — **cor·re·spond'ing·ly** *adv.*

cor·ri·dor (kôr'ə·dər, -dôr, kor'-) *n.* 1 A gallery or passage in a building, usually having various rooms opening upon it. 2 A strip of land across a foreign country by which a landlocked nation has access to the sea. 3 A strip of territory including two or more major cities, typically heavily traveled and as a region densely populated: the Northeast *Corridor* of the United States. [<F <Ital. *corridore* < *correre* run <L *currere*]

cor·ri·gen·dum (kôr'ə·jen'dəm, kor'-) *n. pl.* **·da** (-də) 1 Something to be corrected: said of a printer's error. 2 *pl.* A list of corrected errors, as in a printed book. [<L, gerundive of *corrigere.* See CORRECT.]

cor·ri·gi·ble (kôr'ə·jə·bəl, kor'-) *adj.* Capable of being corrected or reformed. [<F <L *corrigere.* See CORRECT.] — **cor'ri·gi·bil'i·ty, cor'ri·gi·ble·ness** *n.* — **cor'ri·gi·bly** *adv.*

cor·rob·o·rant (kə·rob'ər·ənt) *adj.* Having the power to impart strength; invigorating. —*n.* Something that imparts strength or corroborates. [<L *corroborans, -antis,* ppr. of *corroborare.* See CORROBORATE.]

cor·rob·o·rate (kə·rob'ə·rāt) *v.t.* **·rat·ed, ·rat·ing** To strengthen, as conviction; confirm. See synonyms under CONFIRM, RATIFY. [<L *corroboratus,* pp. of *corroborare* < *com-* together + *robur* strength] — **cor·rob'o·ra'ter, cor·rob'o·ra'tor** *n.* — **cor·rob'o·ra'tion** *n.* — **cor·rob·o·ra·tive** (kə·rob'ə·rā'tiv, -rob'ər·ə·tiv), **cor·rob·o·ra·to·ry** (kə·rob'ər·ə·tôr'ē, -tō'rē) *adj.*

cor·rode (kə·rōd') *v.* **·rod·ed, ·rod·ing** *v.t.* 1 To eat away gradually; rust; ruin or destroy little by little. —*v.i.* To be eaten or worn away. [<L *corrodere* < *com-* thoroughly + *rodere* gnaw] — **cor·ro'dent** *adj. & n.* — **cor·ro·di·ble** (kə·rō'sə·bəl) *adj.*

cor·ro·sion (kə·rō'zhən) *n.* 1 An eating or wearing away; gradual decay. 2 The destruc-

tive breaking down of metals into their oxides or metallic salts. 3 The product of corrosive action. [<OF <LL *corrosio, -onis* < *corrodere.* See CORRODE.]

cor·ro·sive (kə·rō'siv) *adj.* Having the power of corroding: often used figuratively. —*n.* That which corrodes; a corroding agent. — **cor·ro'sive·ly** *adv.* — **cor·ro'sive·ness** *n.*

corrosive sublimate *Chem.* Mercuric chloride, a white, crystalline, poisonous compound, $HgCl_2$, formed by subliming a mixture of salt and mercuric sulfate: a strong disinfectant.

cor·ru·gant (kôr'ə·gant, -yə-, kor'-) *adj.* Having the power of corrugating. —*n.* A styptic or astringent. [<L *corrugans, -antis,* ppr. of *corrugare.* See CORRUGATE.]

cor·ru·gate (kôr'ə·gat, -yə-, kor'-) *v.t. & v.i.* **·gat·ed, ·gat·ing** To contract into alternate ridges and furrows; wrinkle. —*adj.* Contracted into ridges or folds; wrinkled: also **cor'ru·gat·ed.** [<L *corrugatus,* pp. of *corrugare* < *com-* together + *ruga* a wrinkle] — **cor'ru·ga'tion** *n.*

cor·rupt (kə·rupt') *adj.* 1 In a state of decomposition; tainted; putrid. 2 Of a perverted character; depraved. 3 Dishonest; given to bribery. See synonyms under BAD, IMMORAL, ROTTEN. —*v.t.* 1 To cause to become putrescent or putrid; spoil. 2 To render impure; taint; contaminate. 3 To destroy the fidelity or integrity of; bribe: to *corrupt* a voter. 4 To destroy morally; pervert; ruin. 5 To debase or lower the quality or purity of by changes or errors: to *corrupt* a manuscript. 6 *Archaic* To waste; consume; corrode. —*v.i.* 7 To become rotten or corrupt; degenerate. [<OF <L *corruptus,* pp. of *corrumpere* < *com-* thoroughly + *rumpere* break] — **cor·rupt'er, cor·rup'tor** *n.* — **cor·rupt'i·bil'i·ty, cor·rupt'i·ble·ness** *n.* — **cor·rupt'i·ble** *adj.* — **cor·rupt'i·bly** *adv.* — **cor·rupt'ly** *adv.* — **cor·rupt'ness** *n.*

Synonyms (verb): contaminate, debase, defile, deprave, deteriorate, pollute, putrefy, spoil, vitiate. See DECAY, DEFILE, PERVERT, POLLUTE, PUTREFY.

cor·rup·tion (kə·rup'shən) *n.* 1 The act of corrupting, or the state of being corrupted. 2 A corrupting influence, as bribery. 3 A linguistic or orthographic change in a text, word, etc., to an incorrect form; also, an example of such a change: *Porpentine* is a *corruption* of *porcupine.*

cor·rup·tion·ist (kə·rup'shən·ist) *n.* 1 A bribe-giver or bribe-taker. 2 One who defends corruption. 3 One who is guilty of corrupt practices while holding public office.

cor·sac (kôr'sak) *n.* A small, yellowish Asiatic fox *(Vulpes corsac):* also called *dog fox.* [<Turkic]

cor·sage (kôr·säzh') *n.* 1 The bodice or waist of a woman's dress. 2 A small bouquet of fresh flowers for a woman to wear, as at the waist or bodice. [<OF <*cors* body <L *corpus*]

cor·sair (kôr'sâr) *n.* 1 A pirate; also, his vessel. 2 Specifically, a privateer, formerly authorized by the Turkish and Saracen governments to harry the coasts of Christian countries: Barbary *corsairs.* [<F *corsaire* < Med. L *cursarius* < *cursus* inroad < L, a running < *currere* run. Doublet of HUSSAR.]

corse·let (kôrs'lit *for defs. 1, 2;* kôrs'sə·let' *for def. 3)* 1 The complete armor of a soldier; also a breastplate. 2 *Zool.* The thorax of an arthropod. 3 A light corset, usually without stays, worn by women. Also **cors'let.** [<MF, double dim. of *cors* body. See CORPSE.]

cor·set (kôr'sit) *n.* 1 A close-fitting undergarment, usually tightened with laces and reinforced by stays, worn to give support or a desired shape to the body. 2 A medieval garment fitting closely to the body. —*v.t.* To enclose or dress in a corset. [<OF, dim. of *cors* body. See CORPSE.]

cor·tex (kôr'teks) *n. pl.* **·ti·ces** (-tə·sēz) 1 *Bot.* The outer portion of the stem, thalli, or root in plants; specifically, the bark of trees or the rind of fruits. 2 *Zool.* In animals, the outer or investing layer of various organs. 3 *Anat.* **a** The external layer of gray matter of the cerebrum and cerebellum. **b** The external portion of the adrenal glands, enclosing the medullae and indispensable to proper glandular functioning. [<L, bark]

cor·ti·cal (kôr'ti·kəl) *adj.* 1 Of, pertaining to, or consisting of a cortex, bark, or rind; hence, ex-

ternal. 2 *Physiol.* Designating a process, function, or condition caused by or associated with the cerebral cortex: *cortical* sensibility. [<NL *corticalis* < L *cortex* bark] — **cor'ti·cal·ly** *adv.*

cor·ti·cate (kôr'ti·kit, -kāt) *adj.* Sheathed in bark or in a cortex. Also **cor'ti·cat·ed.** [<L *corticatus* < *cortex* bark]

cor·ti·cose (kôr'ti·kōs) *adj.* Like or of the nature of bark. Also **cor'ti·cous** (-kəs). [<L *corticosus* with a thick bark <*cortex* bark]

cor·ti·cos·ter·one (kôr'ti·kos'tə·rōn) *n. Biochem.* One of a group of steroids, $C_{21}H_{30}O_4$, occurring in, and closely associated with the proper functioning of, the adrenal cortex. [<*cortico-* (<L *cortex, -icis*) + STER(OID) + (HORM)ONE]

cor·ti·co·tro·pin (kôr'ti·kō·trō'pin) *n.* A hormonal preparation having adrenocorticotropic activity, obtained from the anterior lobe of the pituitary gland of hogs and other domestic animals. [<*cortico-* (<L *cortex, -icis*) +TROP(IC) + -IN] — **cor'ti·co·tro'pic** *adj.*

cor·tin (kôr'tin) *n. Biochem.* A substance containing various hormones of the adrenal cortex: used in the treatment of certain disorders, as Addison's disease. [<CORT(EX) + -IN]

cor·ti·sone (kôr'tə·sōn, -zōn) *n.* A powerful hormone extracted from the outer part (cortex) of the adrenal gland and also made synthetically: in therapeutic doses it has a palliative effect upon some forms of rheumatoid arthritis and rheumatic fever. Formerly called *compound E.* [Short for CORTICOSTERONE]

co·run·dum (kə·run'dəm) *n.* A very hard native alumina, Al_2O_3, used in abrasives and represented in colored varieties by gemstones, as rubies, sapphires, etc. [<Tamil *kurundam* <Skt. *kuruvinda* ruby]

cor·us·cate (kôr'ə·skāt, kor'-) *v.i.* **·cat·ed, ·cat·ing** To give out sparkles of light. [<L *coruscatus.* pp. of *coruscare* glitter] — **cor'us·ca'tion** *n.*

cor·vette (kôr·vet') *n.* 1 A small, swift ship armed with depth charges and guns, and used chiefly as an anti-submarine escort vessel. 2 Formerly, a warship equipped with sails and a single tier of guns, and ranking next below a frigate. Also **cor·vet** (kôr·vet', kôr'vet). [<F <Pg. *corveta* <L *corbita (navis)* cargo (ship) <*corbis* basket]

cor·vi·na (kôr·vi'nə) *n.* 1 A sciaenid food fish *(Micropogon undulatus)* found in Atlantic waters from Cape Cod to Texas. 2 A croaker *(Cynoscion parvipinnis)* of southern California, highly esteemed as a food fish. [<Sp.]

cor·vine (kôr'vin, -vin) *adj.* Of or pertaining to a crow; crowlike. [<L *corvinus* <*corvus* crow]

cor·ymb (kôr'imb, -im, kor'-) *n. Bot.* A flat-topped or convex open flower cluster of indeterminate inflorescence. [<L *corymbus* <Gk. *korymbos* flower cluster] — **co·rym·bose** (kə·rim'bōs), **co·rym·bous** (kə·rim'bəs) *adj.* — **co·rym'bose·ly** *adv.*

cor·y·phe·us (kôr'ə·fē'əs, kor'-) *n. pl.* **·phe·i** (-fē'i) 1 In ancient Greek drama, the leader of the chorus. 2 Any leader, as of a chorus, sect, etc. Also **cor'y·phae'us.** [<L <Gk. *koryphaios* leader of the chorus <*koryphē* head, top <*korys* helmet]

co·ry·za (kə·ri'zə) *n.* 1 *Pathol.* Inflammation of the mucous membrane of the nose and connecting sinuses; nasal catarrh; cold in the head. 2 A contagious bacterial disease of the upper air passages of poultry, characterized by morbid secretions in the mouth, throat, and nasal cavities. [<L <Gk. *koryza* catarrh]

cos (kôs, kos) *n.* A kind of lettuce with a cylindrical head of erect, oblong leaves. [from island of *Kos,* where first grown]

co·se·cant (kō·sē'kənt) *n. Trig.* The secant of the complement of an angle or an arc. [<CO-[2] + SECANT]

COSECANT

co·seis·mal (kō·siz'məl, -sis'-) *adj.* 1 Experiencing an earthquake shock simultaneously at all points: a *coseismal* line or zone. **2** Indicating the progress of an earthquake by a series of connected lines. Also **co·seis′·mic, —n.** A line on a map, usually forming a rough oval, and connecting the points at which simultaneous earthquake shocks are felt: often called *isoseismal.* [< CO-[1] + SEISMAL]

cosh·er[1] (kosh′ər) *v.t.* To pamper; treat fondly; coddle; pet. [? < dial. E (Northern) *cosh* snug, comfortable]

cos·in·age (kuz′ən·ij) *n.* Collateral relationship or kindred by blood; consanguinity: also spelled *cousinage.* [< OF *cousinage*]

co·sine (kō′sīn) *n.* *Trig.* The sine of the complement of a given angle or arc. [< CO[2]- + SINE]

COSINE
Of the angle ACB, the ratio of EC to BC is the cosine; or, CD being unity, the line BN is the cosine.

cos·me·col·o·gy (koz′mə·kol′ə·jē) *n.* The investigation and study of the effects of cosmic phenomena on life. [< COSM(IC) + ECO-LOGY]

cos·met·ic (koz·met′ik) *adj.* Pertaining to or used for beautifying, cleansing, or protecting, especially the skin, hair, nails, or other part of the human body, or of certain animals on exhibition. Also **cos·met′i·cal. —n. 1** Any preparation intended to be applied to any part of the human body for cleansing, beautifying, promoting attractiveness, or altering its appearance, including bath salts, face and hand creams, etc., but excluding soaps other than shampoos and shaving soaps. **2** Any cologne or perfume. **3** A vanishing cream used as a protective barrier for the skin to prevent or correct skin irritations acquired in certain paint and chemical industries: also called *barrier cream.* [< Gk. *kosmetikos* < *kosmos* order, ornament]

cos·me·ti·cian (koz′mə·tish′ən) *n.* One who manufactures, sells, or applies cosmetics.

cos·me·tol·o·gy (koz′mə·tol′ə·jē) *n.* The study or art of cosmetics and their application. [< Gk. *kosmetikos* cosmetic + -OLOGY] **—cos′me·tol′o·gist** *n.*

cos·mic (koz′mik) *adj.* **1** Pertaining to the universe at large as a harmonious system. **2** Harmonious; orderly: opposed to *chaotic.* **3** Belonging to the material universe, especially that portion outside the solar system: *cosmic changes.* **4** Of a magnitude or extent in space or time suggesting those of the universe; of vast extent or duration. **5** Relating to cosmism. Also **cos′mi·cal.** [< Gk. *kosmikos* < *kosmos* the universe] **—cos′mi·cal·ly** *adv.*

cosmic rays *Physics* Radiation of intense penetrating power and high frequency, impinging upon the earth from outer space and subdivided into high-energy *primary rays,* consisting almost entirely of positively charged particles, and *secondary rays,* formed from many types of atomic particles, positive and negative in charge.

cos·mism (koz′miz·əm) *n.* A doctrine of cosmic evolution. **—cos′mist** *n.*

cos·mi·um (koz′mē·əm) *n.* The hypothetical radioactive element of atomic number 137. [< NL < Gk. *kosmos* universe]

cosmo- *combining form* The universe: *cosmogony.* Also, before vowels, **cosm-.** [< Gk. *kosmos* the universe]

cos·mog·o·ny (koz·mog′ə·nē) *n. pl.* **·nies** A theory of creation, as of the world or of the universe. [< COSMO- + -GONY] **—cos·mo·gon·ic** (koz′mə·gon′ik) or **·i·cal, cos·mog′o·nal** *adj.* **— cos·mog′o·nist** *n.*

cos·mog·ra·phy (koz·mog′rə·fē) *n.* The science that describes the universe, including astronomy, geology, and geography. [< COSMO- + -GRAPHY] **—cos·mog′ra·pher, cos·mog′ra·phist** *n.* **—cos·mo·graph·ic** (koz′mə·graf′ik) or **·i·cal** *adj.*

cos·mol·o·gy (koz·mol′ə·jē) *n. pl.* **·gies** The general science or philosophy of the universe. [< COSMO- + -LOGY] **—cos·mo·log·ic** (koz′mə·loj′ik) or **·i·cal** *adj.* **—cos·mol′o·gist** *n.*

cos·mon (koz′mon) *n. Physics* The hypothetical particle from which the known universe developed, carrying a positive nucleonic charge in opposition to the negative charge attributed to the

anticosmon. [< Gk. *kosmos* the universe]

cos·mo·naut (koz′mə·nôt) *n.* A traveler in outer space.

cos·mo·plas·tic (koz′mə·plas′tik) *adj.* Pertaining to the formation of the universe; cosmogonic.

cos·mop·o·lis (koz·mop′ə·lis) *n.* A city with a cosmopolitan population, where many cultures meet. [< COSMO- + Gk. *polis* city]

cos·mo·pol·i·tan (koz′mə·pol′ə·tən) *adj.* **1** Common to all the world; not local or limited. **2** At home in all parts of the world. **3** *Biol.* Widely distributed, as a plant or animal. *—n.* A citizen of the world. **—cos′mo·pol′i·tan·ism, cos′mo·pol′i·tism** *n.*

cos·mop·o·lite (koz·mop′ə·līt) *n.* **1** One at home everywhere; a person of world-wide experience and travel. **2** One free from local prejudice or affection. **3** *Biol.* A plant or animal widely distributed over the world. *—adj.* World-wide in extent or existence; cosmopolitan. [< Gk. *kosmopolitēs* < *kosmos* world + *politēs* citizen < *polis* city] **—cos·mo·pol·it·i·cal** (koz′mō·pə·lit′i·kəl), **cos·mo·pol·i·tic** (koz′mō·pol′ə·tik) *adj.*

cos·mo·ra·ma (koz′mə·rä′mə, -ram′ə) *n.* An exhibition of scenes from different parts of the world. [< COSMO- + Gk. *horama* sight] **—cos′mo·ram′ic** *adj.*

cos·mos (koz′məs, -mos) *n.* **1** The world or universe considered as a system, perfect in order and arrangement: opposed to *chaos.* **2** Any harmonious and complete system evolved out of complex details. **3** Order; harmony. **4** *Bot.* Any member of a small genus *(Cosmos)* of the composite family of plants, related to the dahlia. [< Gk. *kosmos* order]

coss (kôs) *n.* In India, a unit of land measure, varying from one to three miles. [< Hind. *kos* < Skt. *krośa*]

cos·set (kos′it) *v.t.* To fondle; pet. [< *n.*] *—n.* **1** A pet lamb. **2** Any pet. [? OE *cot-sǣta* a dweller in a cottage]

cost (kôst, kost) *v.* **cost** (*for def. 3, also* **cost·ed**), **cost·ing** *v.i.* **1** To be priced at; require as the price of possession, use, or accomplishment. **2** To cause sacrifice, loss, or suffering: It *cost* him his fortune. *—v.t.* To estimate the cost of production of. *—n.* **1** The price paid for anything; outlay; expense; charge. **2** Loss; suffering; detriment. **3** *pl. Law* **a** The charges fixed by law or allowed by the court in a lawsuit; specifically, the charges payable to an attorney for the opposite side by an unsuccessful litigant. **b** *U.S.* The charges payable by a client to his attorney. See synonyms under EXPENSE, PRICE. [< OF *coster* < L *constare* < *com-* together + *stare* stand]

cos·ta (kos′tə) *n. pl.* **·tae** (-tē) **1** A rib or a riblike structure, part, or marking. **2** *Entomol.* A longitudinal vein along the anterior part of an insect's wing. [< L, rib] **—cos′tal** *adj.*

co·star (kō′stär′) *n.* An actor or actress given equal prominence with another or other players in a motion picture, play, etc. *—v.i. & v.t.* (kō′stär′) **co-starred, co-star·ring** To be or cause to be a co-star.

Cos·ta Ri·ca (kos′tə rē′kə, kôs′tə) A republic of Central America; 19,650 square miles; capital, San José. **—Cos′ta Ri′can** *adj. & n.*

cos·tive (kos′tiv, kôs′-) *adj.* **1** Constipated. **2** Producing constipation. [< OF *costevé* < L *constipatus.* See CONSTIPATE.] **—cos′tive·ly** *adv.* **—cos′tive·ness** *n.*

cost·ly (kôst′lē, kost′-) *adj.* **·li·er, ·li·est 1** Of great cost; expensive. **2** Splendid; gorgeous. **3** *Obs.* Free-handed; lavish. See synonyms under CHOICE. **—cost′li·ness** *n.*

cost·mar·y (kôst′mâr′ē, kôst′-) *n.* A fragrant southern European herb *(Chrysanthemum majus)*: used in salads. [< L *costum* an Eastern plant + *Maria* Mary]

costo- *combining form* Rib: used in anatomical, surgical, and zoological terms. Also, before vowels, **cost-.** [< L *costa* rib]

cost of living The average cost, as to an individual or family, of the necessities of life: food, clothing, shelter, etc.

cos·tot·o·my (kos·tot′ə·mē, kôs′-) *n. Surg.* The operation of cutting or dividing a rib. [< COSTO- + -TOMY]

cost-plus (kôst′plus′, kost′-) *n.* The cost of production plus a percentage of that cost for profit: a term often used in contracts.

cos·tume (kos′tōōm, -tyōōm) *n.* **1** Dress or ap-

parel, including all the garments worn at one time; external dress, especially that of a woman; hence, dress in general. **2** The dress belonging to a given country, time, class, calling, or the like. **3** Fancy dress: a *costume* ball. **4** Local color in art or literature; congruity and accuracy in the depicting of a given place or period in respect to details of dress, action, accessories, etc. *—v.t.* (kos·tōōm′, -tyōōm′) **·tumed, ·tum·ing** To furnish with costumes. See synonyms under DRESS. [< F < Ital. *costuma* fashion, guise < L *consuetudo* custom. Doublet of CUSTOM.]

cos·tum·er (kos·tōō′mər, -tyōō′-) *n.* **1** One who makes or furnishes costumes for stage wear or fancy dress. **2** A rack for clothing. Also **cos·tum·ier** (kos·tōōm′yər, -tyōōm′-; *Fr.* kôs·tü·myā′).

cot[1] (kot) *n.* **1** A cottage. **2** A finger stall. See synonyms under HOUSE, HUT. [OE]

cot[2] (kot) *n.* A light, portable bedstead. [< Hind. *khāt* < Skt. *khatvā*]

co·tan·gent (kō·tan′jənt) *n. Trig.* The tangent of the complement of an angle. [< CO-[2] + TAN-GENT]

co·tan·gen·tial (kō′tan·jen′shəl) *adj.* **1** Of or pertaining to a cotangent. **2** With the same tangent.

COTANGENT
Of the angle ACB, the ratio of DE to DC is the cotangent; or, DC being unity, the line DE is the cotangent.

cote[1] (kōt) *n.* **1** A small place of shelter for sheep, birds, or chickens, used chiefly in compounds: *dovecote.* **2** *Dial.* A little house; hut. [OE]

central France; 3,391 square miles; capital, Dijon.

co·tem·po·ra·ne·ous (kō·tem′pə·rā′nē·əs), **co·tem·po·rar·y** (kō·tem′pə·rer′ē), etc. See CON-TEMPORANEOUS, etc.

co·te·rie (kō′tə·rē) *n.* A set of persons who meet habitually; a clique. See synonyms under CLASS. [< F, earlier, an organization of tenants holding land from the same lord < *cotier* cotter < *cote* hut]

co·ter·mi·nous (kō·tûr′mə·nəs) See CONTER-MINOUS.

co·thur·nus (kō·thûr′nəs) *n. pl.* **·ni** (-nī) A buskin, or high laced shoe, worn by actors in ancient Greek or Roman tragedies: regarded as a symbol of tragedy. Also **co·thurn** (kō′-thûrn, kō·thûrn′). [< L < Gk. *kothornos*] **— co·thur′nal** *adj.*

co·ti·dal (kō·tīd′l) *adj.* Indicating simultaneity in tides.

cotidal lines Lines on a chart, atlas, or sphere indicating the places at which high tide occurs simultaneously.

co·til·lion (kō·til′yən, kə-) *n.* **1** A square dance; quadrille. **2** The music for such a dance. **3** A series of round dances; the german. Also **co·til·lon** (kō·til′yən, kə-; *Fr.* kô·tē·yôn′). [< F *cotillon* petticoat, dim of *cotte* coat]

cot·tage (kot′ij) *n.* **1** A humble dwelling. **2** A small house in the suburbs or the country. **3** *U.S.* A temporary vacation residence at a resort. See synonyms under HOUSE, HUT. [< COT[1]]

cottage cheese A soft, white cheese made of strained milk curds, usually seasoned with salt: also called *pot cheese.*

cottage pudding Cake without icing, served with a sweet sauce, whipped cream, etc.

cot·ton (kot′n) *n.* **1** The soft, fibrous, white or yellowish material, of high cellulose content, appendant to the seeds of the cotton plant. It is graded chiefly in accordance with the length of the fibers (long-staple and short-staple) and is widely used as a textile, in industry, chemistry, medicine, and the arts. **2** The cotton plant itself; also, cotton plants collectively. **3** Cotton cloth or thread. *—adj.* Woven or composed of cotton cloth or thread. *—v.t.* To wrap up in cotton; hence, to pet or coddle. **— to cotton to** *Colloq.* To become friendly with; take a liking to. **— to cotton up to** *Colloq.* To attempt to please or placate by friendly overtures or flattery. [< F *coton*

‹OSp. ‹Arabic *quṭun*]

cotton flannel Soft, warm cotton fabric, napped on one or both sides.

cotton gin A machine used to separate the seeds from the fiber of cotton. See GIN[3].

cot·ton·grass (kot′n·gras′, -gräs′) *n.* One of various rushlike plants (genus *Eriophorum*) of the sedge family, growing in swampy places and bearing cottony spikes.

cot·ton–leaf worm (kot′n·lēf′) The larva of a lepidopterous insect (*Alabama argillacea*), injurious to the cotton plant. Also **cotton worm**.

cotton linters See LINTERS.

cot·ton·mouth (kot′n·mouth′) *n.* A venomous pit viper (*Agkistrodon piscivorus*) living along lakes and streams or in swamps of the southern United States; the water moccasin.

cotton plant Any of various tropical shrubs or woody herbs (genus *Gossypium*) of the mallow family, widely cultivated for the cotton they produce; especially, in the United States, upland cotton (*G. hirsutum*) and Sea Island cotton (*G. barbadense*).

cot·ton·seed (kot′n·sēd′) *n.* The seed of the cotton plant. Also **cotton seed.**

cottonseed meal Cottonseed ground after the oil has been expressed: used in feeding cattle and as a fertilizer.

cottonseed oil A pale–yellow, viscid oil pressed from cottonseeds: used in cooking, paints, and as a lubricant.

cotton stainer Any of a genus (*Dysdercus*) of bugs that punctures the developing seeds of the cotton boll and stains them with its indelible yellow or red juices.

cot·ton·tail (kot′n·tāl′) *n.* The common American gray rabbit (genus *Sylvilagus*).

cotton tree 1 The cottonwood. **2** An East Indian tree (*Gossypium arboreum*) which produces the silk cotton used in cushions, etc.

cot·ton·weed (kot′n·wēd′) *n.* 1 A perennial herb (*Diotis candidissima*) of the composite family, grown in rock gardens. **2** The cudweed. **3** The everlasting. Also **cot′ton·rose′.**

cot·ton·wood (kot′n·wood′) *n.* 1 Any of several American species of poplar trees whose seeds discharge a cottony substance, especially *Populus deltoides*. **2** Its wood.

cot·ton·y (kot′ən·ē) *adj.* 1 Made or consisting of cotton. **2** Like cotton; fluffy; soft.

cot·y·le·don (kot′ə·lēd′n) *n.* 1 *Bot.* A seed leaf, or one of a pair or whorl of the first leaves from a sprouting seed. **2** A genus (*Cotyledon*) of succulent, ornamental herbs native to the Old World. **3** *Anat.* A subdivision of the uterine surface of the placenta. [‹L, navelwort ‹Gk. *kotylēdōn* socket ‹ *kotyle* a hollow, cavity] — **cot′y·le′do·nous, cot′y·le′do·nal** *adj.*

cot·y·loid (kot′ə·loid) *adj.* 1 Cup–shaped. **2** *Anat.* Of or pertaining to a cotyloid cavity: the *cotyloid* ligament. Also **cot′y·loi′dal.** [‹Gk. *kotyloeidēs* cup–shaped, hollow]

cotyloid cavity *Anat.* The acetabulum of the hip bone.

couch (kouch) *n.* 1 A structure on which to rest or sleep, as a bed or other support. **2** A long seat or lounge. **3** Any place for repose, as the lair of a wild animal, etc. [‹v.] — *v.t.* 1 To lay or cause to recline, as on a bed or cot. **2** To place upon a surface; deposit. **3** To embroider, as gold thread, laid flat on a surface. **4** To lower or depress, as a spear for attack: to *couch* a lance. **5** To phrase; put into words; also, to imply subtly: He *couched* a threat in his words. **6** *Surg.* To remove, as a cataract, by pushing down the opaque lens of the eye with a needle, until it lies below the line of vision. **7** In brewing, to spread out, as steeped barley, to germinate. — *v.i.* **8** To lie down; recline. **9** To lie in ambush; hide. **10** To lie in a heap or pile, as leaves. [‹F *coucher* put to bed ‹OF *culcher* ‹L *collocare* set, place. See COLLOCATE.] — **couch′er** *n.*

couch·grass (kouch′gras′, -gräs′) *n.* A perennial grass (*Agropyron repens*), multiplying injuriously in cultivated grounds by its long rootstocks: also called *cutch*, *quackgrass*, *quatchgrass*, *quickgrass*.

couch·ing (kou′ching) *n.* 1 *Surg.* The operation of removing a cataract. **2** Embroidery

made by securing laid gold threads with minute stitches.

cou·gar (kōō′gər) *n.* The puma. [‹F ‹Tupian]

cough (kôf, kof) *v.i.* 1 To expel air from the lungs in a noisy or spasmodic manner. — *v.t.* **2** To expel by a cough. **3** To utter or express by coughing. — **to cough down** To silence a speaker by continued coughing. — **to cough up** 1 To expel (phlegm, etc.) by a cough or coughs. **2** *Slang* To surrender; hand over, as money. — *n.* 1 A sudden, harsh expulsion of breath. **2** A disease productive of coughing. [ME *coghen, coughen.* Related to OE *cohhetan* cough.] — **cough′er** *n.*

cough–drop (kôf′drop′, kof′-) *n.* A small, medicated lozenge to ease a sore throat and relieve coughing.

could (kood) Past tense of CAN[1]. [ME *coude*, OE *cuthe* knew how; *l* inserted on analogy with *should* and *would*]

cou·lee (kōō′lē) *n.* 1 *Geol.* A sheet of solidified lava. **2** *U.S. Colloq.* A deep, usually dry gulch, distinguished by its inclined sides from a canyon. **3** A steep, trenchlike valley, as in the path of former glaciers. Also **cou·lée** (kōō·lā′). [‹F ‹ *couler* flow]

cou·lisse (kōō·lēs′) *n.* 1 A grooved timber, as one in which the wings of a stage setting slide. **2** A side scene in a theater or one of the spaces between the side scenes. [‹F, groove ‹ *couler* slide]

cou·loir (kōō·lwär′) *n.* 1 A deep gorge or gully, especially in rock, ice, or snow. **2** A dredging machine that employs iron buckets on an endless chain. [‹F ‹ *couler* flow]

cou·lomb (kōō·lom′) *n.* The practical unit of quantity in measuring electricity: the amount conveyed by one ampere in one second, equal to 6.3×10^{18} electrons. — **absolute coulomb** One tenth of an abcoulomb. — **international coulomb** The quantity of electricity passing any section of a circuit in one second when the current is one international ampere. [after C. A. de *Coulomb*, 1736–1806, French physicist]

cou·lom·e·ter (kōō·lom′ə·tər) *n.* An electrolytic cell for measuring the quantity of electricity by the chemical action produced: also called *voltameter.* Also **coulomb meter.**

cou·ma·rin (kōō′mə·rin) *n. Chem.* A fragrant crystalline compound, $C_9H_6O_2$, contained in Tonka beans, sweet clover, and other plants, and also made synthetically: used as a flavor extract and in perfumery: also spelled *cumarin.* [‹F *coumarine* ‹ *coumarou* Tonka bean]

cou·ma·rou (kōō′mə·rōō) *n.* The Tonka bean or its seed. [‹Tupian]

coun·cil (koun′səl) *n.* 1 An assembly of persons convened for consultation or deliberation: a *council* of physicians. **2** A body of men elected or appointed to assist in the administration of government, as of a city, or to legislate and advise, as in a territory or colony. **3** The deliberation or consultation that takes place in a council chamber: summoned from *council.* **4** A gathering of Roman Catholic ecclesiastical dignitaries and scholars, for the purpose of discussing and regulating matters of church doctrine and discipline: distinguished as **diocesan** (led by the bishop), **provincial** (led by the archbishop), **national** (led by the primate or patriarch), **general** (led by the Pope or papal legate), and **ecumenical** (world–wide) **councils. 5** The Sanhedrin. — **common council** A municipal, legislative body; also, a coordinate branch of such a body, called a **city council.** — **general council 1** A council made up of delegates representative of the whole of a certain territory or organization, as the British Parliament. **2** The deliberative body of a Scottish university. **3** The administrative board of Oxford University, properly known as the **Hebdomadal Council.** ◆ Homophone: *counsel.* [‹OF *cuncile* ‹L *concilium* ‹*com-* together + *calare* call]

coun·cil·or (koun′səl·ər, -slər) *n.* A member of a council. Also **coun′cil·lor.** — **coun′cil·or·ship′** *n.*

coun·sel (koun′səl) *n.* 1 Mutual consultation or deliberation. **2** Opinion; advice. **3** Deliberate purpose. **4** Good judgment; prudence. **5** A lawyer or lawyers engaged in a cause in court; an advocate. — **to keep one's own**

counsel To be reticent about one's opinions or affairs. — *v.* **·seled** or **·selled, ·sel·ing** or **·sel·ling** *v.t.* 1 To advise; give advice to. **2** To advise in favor of; recommend. — *v.i.* **3** To take counsel; deliberate. ◆ Homophone: *council.* [‹OF *cunseil* ‹L *consilium* ‹ *consulere* deliberate]

Synonyms (noun): admonition, advice, caution, dissuasion, hortation, persuasion, recommendation, suggestion, warning. *Advice* is an opinion suggesting or urging some course of action, on the ground of real or assumed superior knowledge. *Counsel* implies mutual conference. *Advice* may be unsought and even unwelcome; *counsel* is supposed to be desired. Yet the two words so far approach each other that one is said to seek *advice* from a lawyer, while a lawyer who is engaged to give *advice* or to act as an advocate in a legal proceeding is called the *counsel* of the person so employing him.

coun·sel·or (koun′səl·ər, -slər) *n.* 1 One who gives counsel; an adviser. **2** An attorney at law; advocate. Also **coun′sel·lor.**

count[1] (kount) *v.t.* 1 To list or call off the units of (a group or collection) one by one to ascertain the total; number; enumerate: to *count* a flock. **2** To list numerals in a progressive sequence up to: to *count* ten. **3** To believe or consider to be; judge; think. **4** To determine by computation; reckon. **5** To take note of; include in a reckoning. **6** *Obs.* To place to the account of; ascribe. — *v.i.* **7** To list numbers in sequence. **8** To rely: with *on* or *upon.* **9** To be of (much, little, no) value: His testimony *counts* for naught. **10** *Mus.* To keep time by counting or beating. — **to count in 1** To include: Count me *in.* **2** To elect by fraud. — **to count out 1** In boxing, to reach a count of ten over (a downed boxer), thus declaring him defeated. **2** To prevent a fraudulently elected candidate from taking office; also, to ignore, as certain votes. **3** To exclude or excuse: Count me *out* on the picnic. — **to count the cost** To determine the risk beforehand. — *n.* 1 The act of counting; number. **2** Attention; heed; estimation. **3** An accounting, as of a stewardship or for an action. **4** *Law* A separate charge, as in an indictment. **5** In boxing, the counting from one to ten seconds, during which time the contestant who is down must get up or lose the fight. [‹OF *conter* ‹L *computare.* Doublet of COMPUTE.] — **count′a·ble** *adj.*

count[2] (kount) *n.* In some European countries, a nobleman having a rank corresponding to that of an earl in England. [‹AF *counte* ‹L *comes* an associate]

count–down (kount′doun′) *n.* A specified interval of time measured in a descending order of units, usually seconds, to zero, at which an intended action is to occur.

coun·te·nance (koun′tə·nəns) *n.* 1 The face or features. **2** Expression; appearance. **3** An encouraging aspect; hence, approval; support. See synonyms under FAVOR. — **out of countenance** Disconcerted; without ease or composure; abashed. — *v.t.* **·nanced, ·nanc·ing** To approve; encourage; abet. See synonyms under ABET, ENCOURAGE. [‹OF *contenance* ‹L *continentia* behavior ‹ *continere.* See CONTINENT.] — **coun′te·nanc·er** *n.*

count·er[1] (koun′tər) *n.* One who or that which counts, especially a machine for counting.

coun·ter[2] (koun′tər) *n.* 1 An opposite or that which is opposite; especially, a parry; counterblow; also, the act of delivering such a blow. **2** A piece of material encircling the heel of a shoe to stiffen and support the outer leather. **3** *Naut.* The portion of a ship between the water line and the knuckle of the stern. **4** A horse's breast. — *v.t.* 1 To return, as a blow, by another blow. **2** To oppose; contradict; controvert. **3** To put a new counter on, as a shoe. — *v.i.* **4** In boxing, to give a blow while receiving or parrying one. **5** In chess, to make a countermove. — *adj.* **1** Opposing; opposite; contrary. **2** Duplicate: a *counter* list. — *adv.* Contrary; in an opposite manner or direction: *counter* to etiquette. [‹F *contre* against ‹L *contra*]

coun·ter[3] (koun′tər) *n.* 1 A piece of wood, ivory, etc., used in counting. **2** An imitation coin of inferior metal; counterfeit. **3** A table, board, etc., on which to count money or expose goods for sale. [<AF *counteour* <Med. L *computatorium* <L *computare* compute]

counter- *combining form* **1** Opposing; contrary; acting in opposition or response to the action of the main element (sometimes with the idea of outdoing or checking that action); as in:

counteraddress	counterinfluence
counteraffirmation	counterlegislation

coun·ter·act (koun'tər·akt') *v.t.* To act contrary or in opposition to; check; frustrate; hinder.

coun·ter·at·tack (koun'tər·ə·tak') *n.* An attack designed to counteract a previous hostile advance. — *v.t.* & *v.i.* (*usually* koun'tər·ə·tak') To attack in order to frustrate or offset an enemy's previous attack.

coun·ter·bal·ance (koun'tər·bal'əns) *v.t.* **·anced**, **·anc·ing** To oppose with an equal force; offset. — *n.* (koun'tər·bal'əns) **1** Any power equally opposing another. **2** A weight that balances another; counterpoise.

coun·ter·bar·rage (koun'tər·bə·räzh') *n.* An artillery barrage answering or opposing an enemy barrage.

coun·ter·blast (koun'tər·blast', -bläst') *n.* **1** An opposing blast. **2** An answering argument; a denunciation.

coun·ter·change (koun'tər·chanj') *v.t.* & *v.i.* **·changed**, **·chang·ing 1** To exchange; interchange. **2** To diversify.

coun·ter·charge (koun'tər·chärj') *n.* An opposing charge or accusation. — *v.t.* & *v.i.* (koun'tər·chärj') **·charged**, **·charg·ing** To make rebuttal, as an opposing charge or accusation.

coun·ter·check (koun'tər·chek') *n.* **1** Something which checks or opposes a course of action. **2** Something which checks or thwarts another check. — *v.t.* (*usually* koun'tər·chek') To check or thwart by counteraction.

coun·ter·clock·wise (koun'tər·klok'wīz') *adj.* & *adv.* Contrary to the direction taken by the hands of a clock around the dial; from right to left.

coun·ter·cul·ture (koun'tər·kul'chər) *n.* The special culture made up of those, chiefly of the younger generation, who reject the standards and values of established society.

coun·ter·cur·rent (koun'tər·kûr'ənt) *n.* An opposing current; a current opposed to another.

coun·ter·draw (koun'tər·drô') *v.t.* **·drew**, **·drawn**, **·draw·ing** To trace in transparent material.

coun·ter·es·pi·o·nage (koun'tər·es'pē·ə·näzh') *n.* Operations and measures intended to disrupt or counteract the effects of enemy spying.

coun·ter·feit (koun'tər·fit) *v.t.* **1** To make a copy of; imitate; hence, to feign; dissemble. **2** To make a spurious semblance of, as money or stamps, with the intent to deceive and defraud. — *v.i.* **3** To practice deception; feign. **4** To make counterfeits. [<*adj.*] See synonyms under IMITATE, PRETEND. — *adj.* Resembling or made to resemble some genuine thing, with intent to defraud; imitated; spurious. — *n.* **1** Something, as a coin, made fraudulently to resemble the genuine. **2** Any imitation, as a portrait or copy. **3** An impostor. [<OF *contrefet*, pp. of *contrefaire* <L *contra-* against + *facere* make] — **coun'ter·feit'er** *n.*

coun·ter·foil (koun'tər·foil') *n.* A coupon containing a memorandum, as of a check or draft, to be retained by the drawer; stub.

coun·ter·in·sur·gen·cy (koun'tər·in·sûr'jən·sē) *n.* Measures, usually of a military nature, designed to combat guerrilla warfare or to suppress revolutionary activities.

coun·ter·ir·ri·tant (koun'tər·ir'ə·tənt) *n. Med.* An agent employed to excite irritation in one place so as to counteract irritation or inflammation existing elsewhere.

coun·ter·mand (koun'tər·mand', -mänd', koun'· tər·mänd) *v.t.* **1** To recall or revoke, as an order. **2** To contradict; oppose. — *n.* (koun'· tər·mand, -mänd) An order contrary to or revoking one previously issued. [<OF *contremander* <L *contra-* against + *mandare* order]

coun·ter·march (koun'tər·märch', koun'tər· märch) *v.t.* & *v.i.* To march back. — *n.* (koun'· tər·märch') **1** A return march. **2** *Mil.* A reversal of front. **3** Any reversal of conduct or method.

coun·ter·mark (koun'tər·märk') *n.* An added mark. — *v.t.* (*usually* koun'tər·märk') To put

an added mark on.

coun·ter·mine (koun'tər·mīn') *v.t.* & *v.i.* **·mined**, **·min·ing 1** To mine counter to (an enemy); hence, to baffle or obstruct by secret means. **2** To sow (an area) with mines in order to detonate enemy mines. — *n.* (koun'· tər·mīn') **1** A mine or system of galleries run out to meet and destroy similar works of an enemy. **2** Hence, any stratagem to foil the designs of an opponent. **3** An underwater mine intended to detonate enemy mines.

coun·ter·move (koun'tər·mōōv') *v.t.* **·moved**, **·mov·ing** To move in a contrary direction. — *n.* (koun'tər·mōōv') A move in the opposite direction.

coun·ter·mure (koun'tər·myŏŏr) *n.* A wall raised before (and sometimes behind) a fortification wall to strengthen it. — *v.t.* (koun'tər· myŏŏr') **·mured**, **·mur·ing** To strengthen with a countermure. [<MF *contremur* <*contre* against + *mur* wall]

coun·ter·of·fen·sive (koun'tər·ə·fen'siv, koun'· tər·ə·fen'siv) *n.* A large-scale military action designed to stop the offensive of the enemy and to seize the initiative.

coun·ter·pane (koun'tər·pān') *n.* A coverlet or quilt for a bed. [Alter. of COUNTERPOINT[2], after F *pan* quilt <L *pannus* rag, cloth]

coun·ter·part (koun'tər·pärt') *n.* **1** A person precisely like another. **2** Anything closely resembling something else. **3** Something corresponding reversely, as the impression to the seal, or the right hand to the left; a complement; supplement; opposite. See synonyms under DUPLICATE.

coun·ter·point (koun'tər·point') *n.* **1** *Music* **a** The art of adding to a melody a part or parts that shall be related to but independent of it, according to the fixed rules of harmony. **b** The part or parts so arranged. **2** A point or position opposed to another. [<MF *contrepoint* <Med. L *(cantus) contrapunctus* (a melody) with contrasting notes <L *contra* against + *punctus* point, note]

coun·ter·poise (koun'tər·poiz') *v.t.* **·poised**, **·pois·ing 1** To bring to a poise by opposing with an equal weight; counterbalance. **2** To offset or frustrate. — *n.* (koun'tər·poiz) **1** A counterbalancing weight. **2** A counterbalancing force, power, or influence. **3** A state of equilibrium. [<OF *contrepeser* <L *contra* against + *pensare* weigh]

coun·ter·pro·duc·tive (koun'tər·prə·duk'tiv) *adj.* Producing an effect opposite from that intended; harmful to a purpose: The slurs on his opponent proved *counterproductive.*

coun·ter·re·con·nais·sance (koun'tər·ri·kon'ə· səns, -säns) The act of screening military operations from observation by the enemy.

coun·ter·ref·or·ma·tion (koun'tər·ref'ər·mā'· shən) *n.* A reformation aimed at counteracting and opposing a previous one.

coun·ter·sign (koun'tər·sīn', koun'tər·sīn') *v.t.* To sign alongside of or in addition to (the signature of another); authenticate by an additional signature. — *n.* (koun'tər·sīn') **1** A secret word or phrase to be given, as to a sentry; a watchword; password. **2** A countersignature.

coun·ter·ten·or (koun'tər·ten'ər) *n.* **1** A vocal part for a male voice higher than the tenor and lower than the treble. **2** A male voice of this kind. **3** A singer with such a voice.

coun·ter·vail (koun'tər·vāl', koun'tər·vāl) *v.t.* To oppose with equal power; counteract; offset. [<AF *countervaloir* <L *contra valere* avail against]

counter word A word widely used as a general term, without regard to its exact meaning, as *definitely, heavenly.*

coun·ter·work (koun'tər·wûrk') *v.t.* & *v.i.* To work or act in opposition to (a person or thing). — *n.* (koun'tər·wûrk') The act or effect of counterworking; a work in opposition; antagonism.

count·ess (koun'tis) *n.* **1** The wife or widow of a count, or, in Great Britain, of an earl. **2** A woman whose rank is equal to that of a count or earl. [<OF *contesse*, fem. of *conte*. See COUNT[2].]

count·less (kount'lis) *adj.* That cannot be counted; innumerable. See synonyms under INFINITE.

coun·tri·fied (kun'tri·fīd) *adj.* Rural or rustic, as the manners of or attributed to country people, etc.

coun·try (kun'trē) *n. pl.* **·tries 1** A land under a particular sovereignty or government, inhabited by a certain people, or within definite geographical limits. **2** A particular nation, or the institutions peculiar to it; the land of one's nativity or allegiance. **3** A tract of land of indefinite extent; a region. **4** A rural region, or farming district, as opposed to the city: with *the*: a summer in the *country.* **5** The general public; the inhabitants of any region, collectively: with *the*: The whole *country* hated him. **6** *Law* A jury. Originally, a jury was summoned from the hundred in which the facts at issue were supposed to have occurred and the question was then said to be tried by the *country.* Litigants were said to put themselves **upon the country. 7** In cricket, that part of the field which is remote from the wicket. See synonyms under LAND. — *adj.* **1** Of or pertaining to, for, from, occurring in, or situated in the rural parts, as distinct from the city; rural; rustic. **2** Wanting in refinement or culture; rude; boorish; unpolished: *country* manners. **3** *Dial.* Relating to one's own country; national. [<OF *contrée* <LL *contrata* <L *contra* on the opposite side]

coun·try-and-west·ern (kun'trē·and·west'ərn) *n.* A stylized form of popular music, based on the folk music of the rural southern and western U.S. Abbr. *c-and-w* or *C-and-W.*

country club A club in the outskirts of a town or city, with a clubhouse, grounds, and facilities for outdoor sports.

country cousin A relative from the country, to whom city life is new or confusing.

country dance 1 A kind of quadrille in which the partners are ranged in opposite lines. **2** The music for this. See CONTREDANSE.

coun·try·folk (kun'trē·fōk') *n. pl.* **1** People who live in the country, especially in a certain district. **2** Compatriots; fellow countrymen.

country gentleman A landed proprietor who lives on his estate.

coun·try·man (kun'trē·mən) *n. pl.* **·men** (-mən) **1** One living in the country; a rustic. **2** An inhabitant of a particular country; one of the same country with another.

coun·try·seat (kun'trē·sēt') *n.* A dwelling or mansion in the country.

coun·try·side (kun'trē·sīd') *n.* A section of country, or its inhabitants.

count·ship (kount'ship) *n.* The dignity or position of a count.

coun·ty (koun'tē) *n. pl.* **·ties 1** A civil division of a state or kingdom, created for political, judicial, and administrative purposes. In the United States, it is the division next below a State with the exception of Louisiana, where it is called a *parish.* In England a county is sometimes called a *shire.* In some of the British Colonies a county is a division for administrative purposes. **2** The inhabitants of a county: Your *county* is noted for its intelligence. **3** *Obs.* The domain of an earl or count. **4** *Obs.* An earl or count. [<AF *counté* <L *comitatus* <*comes* count, companion]

county seat The seat of government of a county.

coup (kōō) *n. pl.* **coups** (kōōz, *Fr.* kōō) **1** A sudden, telling blow; a master stroke; stratagem. **2** Among North American Indians, the first wound or cut inflicted by hand on an enemy. **3** A coup d'état. — *v.t.* (koup) *Scot.* To turn upside down; upset. Also *cowp.* [<F, ult. <L *colaphus* a blow with the fist <Gk. *kolaphos*]

coup·le (kup'əl) *n.* **1** Two of a kind; a pair. **2** Two persons of opposite sex, wedded or otherwise paired; partners in a dance. **3** A coupler; bond; leash. **4** *Mech.* A pair of equal forces acting in opposite and parallel lines, thus tending to turn a body around without moving it from its place. **5** *Electr.* Two dissimilar metals joined to form a voltaic element in a battery; a voltaic couple. — *v.* **coup·led, coup·ling** *v.t.* **1** To join, as one thing to another; link; unite in pairs. **2** To join in wedlock; marry. **3** *Electr.* To connect (two electric currents or circuits) magnetically or directly. — *v.i.* **4** To copulate. **5** To form a pair or pairs. [<OF *cople* <L *copula* a band, a bond]

coup·ler (kup'lər) *n.* **1** One who or that which couples. **2** A mechanical device by which objects are connected. **3** *Telecom.* A device for transferring signals from one circuit to another, or through a condenser or transformer. —**automatic coupler** A contrivance for coupling railroad cars by means of interlocking jaws.

coup·let (kup′lit) *n.* **1** Two similar things taken or considered together. **2** Two lines of verse in immediate sequence, especially of the same length and riming together. [<F, dim. of *couple* a pair]

coup·ling (kup′ling) *n.* **1** The act of joining together; specifically, the act of joining in marriage or copulation. **2** A coupler, or that which couples: a car or carriage *coupling*. **3** The length between the tops of the shoulder blades and the tops of the hip joints in a dog. **4** The part of the body joining the hindquarters of a quadruped to the front part, as in a dog or a horse. See illustrations under DOG, HORSE. **5** *Mech.* A friction or jaw clutch to connect moving parts or break the connection. **6** *Electr.* A connection between two circuits permitting transfer of power from one to the other.

cou·pon (kōō′pon, kyōō′-) *n.* **1** One of a number of dated certificates attached, as to a bond, representing interest accrued and payable at stated periods. **2** A section or detachable portion of a ticket or form, serving as a certificate that the holder is entitled to something, as transportation for a certain number of miles, etc. [<F <*couper* cut]

cour·age (kûr′ij) *n.* **1** That quality of mind which meets danger or opposition with intrepidity, calmness, and firmness; the quality of being fearless; bravery. **2** *Obs.* Heart; desire; disposition; condition. [<OF *corage* <L *cor* heart]
   Synonyms: boldness, bravery, daring, fearlessness, fortitude, gallantry, hardihood, intrepidity, mettle, pluck, resolution, spirit, valor. See FORTITUDE, PROWESS. Compare BRAVE. *Antonyms*: cowardice, fear, fright, timidity, timorousness.

cou·ra·geous (kə-rā′jəs) *adj.* Possessing or characterized by courage; brave; daring: a *courageous* man; *courageous* words. —**cou·ra′geous·ly** *adv.* —**cou·ra′geous·ness** *n.*

cou·ri·er (kōō′rē-ər, kûr′-) *n.* **1** A messenger. **2** A traveling attendant. See synonyms under HERALD. [<MF <Ital. *corriere* <*corre* run <L *currere*]

cour·lan (kōōr′lən) *n.* A rail-like, tropical or subtropical American bird (genus *Aramus*) with stiff tail feathers: also called *limpkin*. [<F <native name]

course (kôrs, kōrs) *n.* **1** The act of moving onward; career. **2** The way passed over, or the direction taken. **3** A series of connected motions, acts, or events; customary sequence. **4** Line of conduct; manner of procedure; behavior. **5** The portion of a meal served at one time. **6** A row or layer. **7** *pl.* The menses. **8** *Naut.* **a** A sail bent to the lower yard of any square-rigged mast. **b** A point of the compass. **9** A charge or bout in a tournament. **10** A continuous horizontal range, as of stones in a wall. **11** *Mining* **a** An influx of water from one direction. **b** The direction of a lode or adit. **c** A corridor; passageway; the direction in which a mine is being worked. **12** *Music* A series of strings of uniform tone; also, a bell's chime. **13** A definite period of instruction and study in a certain subject: a *course* in French. **14** A series of studies undertaken to earn a degree: a college *course*. **15** In golf, links. **16** Racecourse. See synonyms under CAREER, DIRECTION, WAY. —**of course** As one might expect; naturally. —*v.* **coursed, cours·ing** *v.t.* **1** To hunt or pursue with hounds, as hares; chase. **2** To chase after; pursue. **3** To cause to run; urge to speed: to *course* horses. **4** To run through or over; traverse swiftly. —*v.i.* **5** To move swiftly; race. **6** To take a direction; follow a course. **7** To pursue game with hounds. **8** *Obs.* To engage in a hunt or joust.
   ◆ Homophone: *coarse*. [<OF *cours* <L *cursus* a running <*currere* run]

cours·er (kôr′sər, kōr′-) *n.* **1** A fleet and spirited horse. **2** One given to the chase. **3** A swift-footed plover (genus *Cursorius*) of arid regions in Asia, Africa, and occasion-

ally Europe, as *C. cursor*. **4** The pratincole.

cours·ing (kôr′sing, kōr′-) *n.* The sport of chasing the hare or similar game with greyhounds, who follow by sight instead of by scent.

court (kôrt, kōrt) *n.* **1** A yard or space surrounded wholly by buildings or walls; a courtyard. **2** A building or group of buildings in a courtyard. **3** An imposing residence. **4** A space enclosed on three sides; a short street; a blind alley. **5** The actual residence of a sovereign, especially as the central seat of government and princely state; a palace. **6** The royal council, family, and retinue of a sovereign. **7** A sovereign and his retinue, considered as a body: the French *court*. **8** A formal assembly or reception held by a sovereign. **9** A place where justice is judicially administered. **10** A tribunal possessing civil, military, or ecclesiastical jurisdiction and duly constituted to administer justice. **11** A level space laid out for playing tennis, basketball, squash, or similar games; also, a subdivision of the ground so marked. **12** *Brit.* An official meeting of a corporation. **13** A local branch of certain fraternal orders; a lodge. **14** Flattery or homage paid to another to win favor. **15** Attention bestowed upon a woman to win her affection or love; wooing; courtship. —**Court of St. James's** The court of the monarch of Great Britain: so called from St. James's Palace. —*v.t.* **1** To make love to; woo. **2** To try to get in the good graces of; seek the favor of. **3** To solicit; attempt to gain: to *court* applause. **4** To lure; invite; entice into. —*v.i.* **5** To make love; act the courtier. —*adj.* Of or pertaining to a court: *court* customs. [<OF *cort* <L *cohors, cohortis* yard, troop of soldiers. Doublet of COHORT.]

—**Appeals, Circuit Court of** The highest U.S. court of appellate jurisdiction below the Supreme Court.

—**Appeals, Court of** A high court of justice to which cases from lower courts are taken for rehearing.

—**Arbitration, Permanent Court of** A tribunal established at The Hague in 1899 for the arbitration of disputes between nations, submission being voluntary: also called *Hague Tribunal*.

—**circuit court 1** A Federal court of the United States superior to a district court: abolished, 1911. **2** A State court presided over by a circuit judge.

—**Claims, Court of** A court at Washington, D.C., having jurisdiction over questions relating to claims against the government.

—**Common Pleas, Court of 1** A common-law court of record, having original jurisdiction over civil and criminal matters. **2** Formerly, an English court with exclusive jurisdiction in various classes of civil cases.

—**district court** A U.S. court serving a Federal judicial district; also, a State court serving a State judicial district.

—**ecclesiastical court** In the United States, one of the courts established by the various churches for legislation and discipline, holding jurisdiction only within their own respective organizations; in England, a court instituted by the sovereign, having jurisdiction over matters pertaining to the established church.

—**inquiry, court of** A tribunal for investigating matters pertaining to the military or naval service, with no power of trial or adjudication.

—**International Justice, Permanent Court of** An international tribunal established under the Covenant of the League of Nations (1921), empowered to interpret treaties and to give advisory opinions. Its functions, in general, were taken over (1945) by the International Court of Justice. Also called *World Court*.

—**Justice, International Court of** The principal judicial organ of the United Nations, functioning under a statute based on the Statute of the Permanent Court of International Justice as incorporated in the UN charter. All members of the UN are parties *ipso facto*; others join on recommendation of the Security Council.

—**juvenile court** A special court that deals with delinquents, neglected children, etc.,

under a fixed age.

—**King's (or Queen's) Bench, Court of** In England, the supreme court of common–law jurisdiction, consisting of a chief justice and four puisne or associate justices: now one of the divisions of the high courts of justice. Also *King's (or Queen's) Bench*.

—**municipal court** A local, city court having limited jurisdiction.

—**probate court** A court having jurisdiction of the proof of wills, of guardianships, and of the settlement of estates.

—**record, court of** A court keeping a record of its proceedings and having a clerk or prothonotary, a seal, and the power to fine and imprison.

—**superior court** In some States of the United States, a court between the inferior courts and those of last resort; in England, one of the principal courts at Westminster: King's Bench, Common Pleas, Exchequer.

—**Supreme Court** In the United States and in various States, a court of appellate jurisdiction and, in most cases, of last resort.

court-bar·on (kôrt′bar′ən, kôrt′-) *n.* Formerly, a court held by the steward of a manor for settling controversies between tenants, punishing misdemeanors, etc.

cour·te·ous (kûr′tē-əs) *adj.* Showing courtesy; polite; affable. See synonyms under BLAND, POLITE. [<OF *curteis*] —**cour′te·ous·ly** *adv.* —**cour′te·ous·ness** *n.*

cour·te·san (kôr′tə·zən, kōr′-, kûr′-) *n.* A prostitute or woman of loose morals. Also **cour′te·zan**. [<F *courtisan* <Ital. *cortigiano* courtier <*corte* court]

cour·te·sy (kûr′tə·sē) *n.* *pl.* **·sies 1** Polite behavior; habitual politeness; courtliness. **2** A courteous favor or act. **3** A curtsy. [<OF *curteisie*]

courtesy title A title of address of no legal validity, given by social custom to the children of peers.

court·house (kôrt′hous′, kōrt′-) *n.* **1** A public building occupied by the judicial courts. **2** *U.S. Dial.* A county seat.

court·i·er (kôr′tē-ər, -tyər, kōr′-) *n.* **1** A member of the court circle. **2** One who seeks favor by flattery and complaisance. [<OF *cortoyer* be at court]

court·ly (kôrt′lē, kōrt′-) *adj.* **·li·er, ·li·est 1** Pertaining to or befitting a court. **2** Elegant in manners. —*adv.* In a polite, stately, and refined manner. See synonyms under POLITE. —**court′li·ness** *n.*

court martial *pl.* **courts martial 1** A military court convened to try persons subject to military law. **2** A trial by such a court.

court·room (kôrt′rōōm′, -rōōm′, kōrt′-) *n.* A room in which judicial proceedings are held.

court·ship (kôrt′ship, kōrt′-) *n.* **1** The act or period of courting or wooing. **2** *Obs.* Courtly behavior.

court·yard (kôrt′yärd′, kōrt′-) *n.* An enclosed yard adjoining a building or surrounded by buildings to which it gives access; a court.

cous·in (kuz′ən) *n.* **1** One collaterally related by descent from a common ancestor, but not a brother or sister. Children of brothers and sisters are *first cousins*; children of first cousins are *second cousins* to each other. A *first cousin once removed* is the child of one's first·cousin; a *first cousin twice removed* is the grandchild of one's first cousin, etc. A *second cousin once removed* is the child of one's second cousin, etc. **2** A noble of the king's council, or a fellow sovereign: a style of address used by a king. **3** One of a kindred race: our English *cousins*. **4** *Obs.* Any collateral relative more distant than a brother or sister. —*v.t.* To claim as a cousin or relative. [<OF *cosin* <L *consobrinus* child of a maternal aunt] —**cous′in·ly** *adj. & adv.*

cou·tu·rier (kōō-tü-ryā′) *n. masc.* A dressmaker. [<F <*couture* sewing] —**cou·tu·rière** (kōō-tü-ryâr′) *n. fem.*

co·va·lence (kō′vā′ləns) *n.* *Chem.* **1** A bond formed by the mutual sharing of electrons between the atoms of a compound. **2** The number of pairs of electrons which can be shared between the atoms of different elements. —**co′va′lent** *adj.*

cove (kōv) *n.* **1** A small bay or baylike recess. **2** A recess in a mountain. **3** A strip of grassland on the prairies, leading into a wood. **4** *Archit.* A concavity; the concave curved portion interposed in some ceilings between the flat ceiling proper and the wall. —*v.t.* & *v.i.* **coved, cov·ing** To arch over. [OE *cofa* chamber, cave]

co·vel·line (kō·vel′ĭn) *n.* A massive, submetallic, indigo-blue copper sulfide, CuS, crystallizing in the hexagonal system. Also **co·vel·lite** (kō·vel′īt). [after N. *Covelli*, 1790–1829, Italian chemist]

cov·e·nant (kuv′ə·nənt) *n.* **1** An agreement entered into by two or more persons or parties; a compact. **2** God's promise of blessing to be fulfilled on the performance of a condition, as of obedience. **3** The solemn pledge by which members of a church bind themselves to maintain its faith, ordinances, etc. **4** *Law* A written agreement between parties under seal; a modifying agreement contained within a contract or deed; also, a form of action to recover damages for breach of contract. — **National Covenant** An agreement extensively signed by all classes of Presbyterians in Scotland, in 1638, to resist by force the introduction of episcopacy by Charles I. — **Solemn League and Covenant** An agreement between the English and the Scottish Parliaments, undertaken in 1643, to support Protestantism. —*v.t.* & *v.i.* To promise by or in covenant. [<OF <*covenir* agree <L *convenire* meet together, agree]

cov·er (kuv′ər) *v.t.* **1** To place something over or upon so as to protect or conceal. **2** To provide with a cover or covering; clothe; enwrap. **3** To hide or keep from view; conceal, as actions, facts, or crimes: often with *up.* **4** To provide shelter or protection for, as from evil or danger. **5** To occupy the surface of; overlay; serve as a cover or covering for. **6** To allow for or have provision for; treat of; include. **7** To be sufficient to pay, defray, or offset, as a debt, expense, or loss. **8** To incubate or sit on, as eggs. **9** To copulate with (a female): said of animals. **10** To travel over; traverse. **11** To aim directly at, as with a firearm. **12** *Mil.* **a** To have under command or protection. **b** To provide protective fire for (another person, unit, etc.). **c** To march in a position behind or in front of (another man). **13** In journalism, to report the details of, as an event or meeting. **14** In sports, to hinder the activity of (an opponent); also, to protect an area or position, as one temporarily left or vacated by another player: *The shortstop* covered *second base.* **15** To provide the equivalent of; equal, as the wager of an opponent. **16** In card games, to play a higher card than (the one previously played). **17** *Archaic* To pardon; put out of remembrance: in Biblical use. **18** *Rare* To don, or replace, as a hat, cap, or the like. —*v.i.* **19** To spread over so as to overlay or conceal something. **20** To put on a hat, cap, or the like. **21** In card games, to play a higher card than the one led. —*n.* **1** That which is spread or fitted over or which encloses anything. **2** A veil or disguise; pretext. **3** A shelter or defense; protection. **4** A thicket or underbrush, etc., sheltering game. **5** A setting of a cloth and articles for eating a meal for one person. **6** An envelope that has been marked at such time or place as to be of interest to philatelists. **7** A cover charge. — **to break cover** To come out from a hiding place. — **under cover** Secret; concealed; secretly. [<OF *covrir* <L *cooperire* <*co-* thoroughly + *operire* hide] —**cov′er·er** *n.* —**cov′er·ing** *n.*

cov·er·age (kuv′ər·ĭj) *n.* **1** The protection against risks extended by an insurance policy. **2** The amount of gold held in a national treasury as a basis for the issuance of paper currency. **3** In journalism, the extent to which a news story is covered.

cov·er·all (kuv′ər·ôl) *n.* One-piece overalls with sleeves, worn to protect the clothing. Also **cov′er·alls.**

cover charge A fixed charge added to the charge for food and drink at cabarets, hotels, etc., for the entertainment or service provided.

cover crop *Agric.* A crop sown to protect the ground through the winter and to enrich it when plowed under in the spring.

English Augustinian monk; translated the Bible into English.

COVERED WAGON

covered wagon A large, canvas-covered wagon; especially, one used by the American pioneers: also called *prairie schooner, Conestoga wagon.*

cov·er·ing (kuv′ər·ing) *n.* Anything that serves to cover, protect, conceal, etc.

cov·er·let (kuv′ər·lit) *n.* The outer covering of a bed; a quilt. Also **cov′er·lid.**

co·versed sine (kō′vûrst′) *Trig.* The versed sine of the complement of an angle or arc.

cov·ert (kuv′ərt) *adj.* **1** Concealed; secret. **2** Sheltered. **3** *Law* Under protection or authority, as a married woman. See synonyms under SECRET. —*n.* **1** Something that shelters, defends, or conceals. **2** A shady place or thicket. **3** *pl. Ornithol.* Feathers overlying the bases of the quills of a bird's wings and tail. See illustration under BIRD, FOWL. See synonyms under REFUGE. [<OF, pp. of *covrir* COVER] —**cov′ert·ly** *adv.*

cov·er-up (kuv′ər·up′) *n.* **1** An act or effort designed to prevent the facts or truth, as of an embarrassing or illegal activity, from becoming known. **2** A means of covering up or concealing something.

cov·et (kuv′it) *v.t.* & *v.i.* To have an inordinate desire for, especially for something belonging to another. [<OF *cuveiter* <L *cupiditas* eager desire <*cupere* desire] —**cov′et·a·ble** *adj.* —**cov′et·er** *n.*

cov·et·ous (kuv′ə·təs) *adj.* Inordinately desirous (of something); avaricious; greedy. See synonyms under AVARICIOUS. —**cov′et·ous·ly** *adv.* —**cov′et·ous·ness** *n.*

cov·ey (kuv′ē) *n. pl.* **·eys** **1** A flock of quails or partridges. **2** A company; set; bevy. See synonyms under FLOCK. [<OF *covée*, pp. of *cover* brood <L *cubare* lie down]

cov·ing (kō′ving) *n. Archit.* The projection of the upper stories over the lower. [<COVE¹]

cow (kou) *n. pl.* **cows** (*Archaic* **kine**) **1** The female of domestic cattle and of some other animals, as the elephant. **2** *Austral. Slang* An unpleasant person or event: also *fair cow.* [OE *cū*]

cow·ard (kou′ərd) *n.* One lacking in courage; a craven; poltroon. —*adj.* Of or pertaining to a coward or cowardice; cowardly. [<OF *couard* <*coue* tail <L *cauda*; with ref. to a dog with its tail between its legs] —**cow′ard·ly** *adj.* & *adv.* —**cow′ard·li·ness** *n.*

cow·ard·ice (kou′ər·dis) *n.* Unworthy timidity; lack of courage; state of being easily frightened; pusillanimity.

cow·bane (kou′bān′) *n.* **1** The water hemlock. **2** An erect swamp plant (*Oxypolis rigidior*) of the eastern U.S., poisonous to cattle.

cow·bell (kou′bel′) *n.* **1** A wedge-shaped bell, usually of harsh and penetrating sound, hung by a strap around the neck of a cow. **2** The bladder campion.

cow·ber·ry (kou′ber′ē, -bər·ē) *n. pl.* **·ries** Any of a species (*Vaccinium vitis-idaea*) of trailing evergreen shrubs of the heath family, bearing acid red berries: also called *foxberry.*

cow·bind (kou′bīnd′) *n.* The white-berried bryony.

cow·bird (kou′bûrd′) *n.* An American blackbird (*Molothrus ater*), often found with cattle. Also **cow blackbird.**

cow·boy (kou′boi′) *n.* In the western United States, a man, usually working on horseback, who herds and tends cattle on a ranch: also *cowhand.*

cow bunting A cowbird.

cow camp The headquarters of the cowboys engaged in a roundup; also, any place where cowboys have gathered for working a herd.

cow·catch·er (kou′kach′ər) *n.* An iron frame on the front of a locomotive to throw obstructions from the track; pilot.

cow·er (kou′ər) *v.i.* **1** To crouch tremblingly. **2** To tremble; quail. [ME *couren*, prob. <Scand.]

cow·fish (kou′fish′) *n. pl.* **·fish** or **·fish·es** **1** One of various cetaceans, as a grampus, dolphin, etc. **2** A trunkfish. **3** A sirenian.

cow·hage (kou′ij) *n.* **1** The stinging hairs on the pods of a tropical climbing plant of the bean family (genus *Stizolobium* or *Mucuna*).

2 The pods themselves. **3** The plant. Also *cowage.* [Alter. of Hind. *kawāch*, short for *kawānch*]

cow·hand (kou′hand′) *n.* A cowboy.

cow·herb (kou′ûrb′, -hûrb′) *n.* A smooth-leaved Old World annual (*Saponaria vaccaria*): also *cow soapwort.*

cow·herd (kou′hûrd′) *n.* One who herds cattle.

cow·hide (kou′hīd′) *n.* **1** The skin of a cow, either before or after tanning. **2** A heavy, flexible whip made of braided leather and tapering from stock to lash. —*v.t.* **·hid·ed, ·hid·ing** To whip with or as with a cowhide.

cow killer A large antlike wasp (*Dasymutilla occidentalis*) found in the SW United States.

cowl¹ (koul) *n.* **1** A monk's hood; also, any hooded garment. **2** A hood-shaped top for a chimney. **3** *Aeron.* A cowling. **4** That part of the body of an automobile to which the windshield, instrument board, and the rear end of the hood are attached. **5** *Scot.* A nightcap. —*v.t.* **1** To cloak with a cowl; make like or into a monk. **2** To cover with or as with a cowl. [OE *cugle, cuhle* <*cucullus* hood]

cow·lick (kou′lik′) *n.* A tuft of hair turned up over the forehead as if licked by a cow.

co-work·er (kō′wûr′kər) *n.* **1** One engaged in the same work as another. **2** One who cooperates in an organization.

cow·pars·nip (kou′pärs′nip) *n.* Any of a genus (*Heracleum*) of tall, stout, perennial herbs of the parsley family. Also **cow parsnip.**

cow·pea (kou′pē′) *n.* **1** A twining herb of the bean family (*Vigna sinensis*), cultivated in the southern United States. **2** The edible pea of this herb.

cow·pi·lot (kou′pī′lət) *n.* The pintano: so called from its supposed habit of accompanying the cowfish.

cow pony A small horse or pony used in herding cattle.

cow·pox (kou′poks′) *n.* An acute contagious disease of cows, forming pustules containing a virus which is the source of vaccine for smallpox.

cow·ry (kou′rē) *n. pl.* **·ries** A shell with a high gloss, a small variety of which is used as money in Africa and southern Asia. Also **cow′rie.** [<Hind. *kaurī*]

cow shark A large shark (*Hexanchus griseus*) with six gill openings on each side, inhabiting European and West Indian waters.

cow·shed (kou′shed′) *n.* A shelter for cows.

cow·skin (kou′skin′) *n.* The hide of a cow.

cow·slip (kou′slip′) *n.* **1** An English wild-flower (*Primula veris*) of the primrose family. **2** The marsh marigold of the United States. [OE *cūslyppe* <*cū* cow + *slyppe* dung; because it commonly grows in pastures]

cow soapwort Cowherb.

cow·tree (kou′trē′) *n.* **1** One of several trees yielding a milky juice which can be used as a food, especially the South American tree *Brosimum utile* of the mulberry family. **2** The bullytree. **3** Any of various other trees, as *Tabernaemontana utilis,* of the dogbane family, and certain members of the fig family.

cox·a (kok′sə) *n. pl.* **cox·ae** (kok′sē) **1** *Entomol.* The first joint or body joint of the leg in arthropods. **2** *Anat.* The hip or hip joint. [<L, hip] —**cox′al** *adj.*

cox·al·gi·a (kok·sal′jē·ə) *n. Pathol.* Pain in the hip. Also **cox′al·gy.** [<NL <L *coxa* hip + Gk. *algos* pain] —**cox·al′gic** *adj.*

cox·comb (koks′kōm′) *n.* **1** A pretentious and conceited fop: also spelled *cockscomb.* **2** Cockscomb (def. 1). **3** A piece of red cloth notched like a cock's comb, formerly worn in a jester's cap; also, the cap itself. **4** *Obs.* The top of the head, or the head itself. [Var. of *cockscomb*] —**cox·comb·i·cal, cox·com·i·cal** (koks·kom′i·kəl, -kō′mi-) *adj.* —**cox·comb′i·cal·ly** *adv.*

cox·comb·ry (koks′kōm′rē) *n.* **1** Coxcombs collectively. **2** Foppishness.

cox·swain (kok′sən, kok′swān′) *n.* One who steers or has charge of a small boat or a racing shell: often spelled *cockswain.* [<COCK³ + SWAIN]

coy¹ (koi) *adj.* **1** Shrinking from notice, diffident; shy: said chiefly of women. **2** Simulating diffidence; coquettish. **3** *Obs.* Disdainful. [<F *coi* <OF *quei* <L *quietus.* Doublet of QUIET.] —**coy′ish** *adj.* —**coy′ly** *adv.* —**coy′·ness** *n.*

coy·o·te (kī·ō′tē, kī′ōt) *n.* The prairie wolf (*Canis latrans*) of the western United States. Also spelled *cayote.* [<Am. Sp. <Nahuatl]

co·yo·til·lo (kō′yō·tēl′yō, kī′ō-) *n. pl.* **·los** A small shrub (*Karwinskia humboldtiana*) of the buckthorn family, producing poisonous fruit, native in northern Mexico and the SW United States. [<Am. Sp., dim. of *coyote* COYOTE]

coy·pu (koi′pōō) *n. pl.* **·pus** or **·pu** A South American aquatic, beaverlike rodent (*Myocastor coypus*), about 2 feet long, with webbed hind feet and round tail: it yields the fur known as nutria. Also **coy′pou.** [<Am. Sp. <native name]

coz·en (kuz′ən) *v.t.* & *v.i.* To cheat in a petty way. [<F *cousiner* deceive by claiming kinship <*cousin* COUSIN] —**coz·en·age** (kuz′ən·ij) *n.* — **coz′en·er** *n.*

co·zy (kō′zē) *adj.* **co·zi·er, co·zi·est** 1 Snugly and easily comfortable; contented. 2 Sociable. —*n.* A padded cap or cover for a teapot to prevent the heat from escaping after the tea is infused: also called *tea cozy.* Also spelled *cosy, cosey.* Also **co′zey.** [<dial. E (Scottish) *cosie,* prob. <Scand. Cf. Norw. *kose* comfortable.] —**co′zi·ly** *adv.* — **co′zi·ness** *n.*

CPR Cardiopulmonary resuscitation.

Cr *Chem.* Chromium (symbol Cr).

crab¹ (krab) *n.* 1 Any of various species of tenfooted crustaceans of the suborder *Brachyura* in the order *Decapoda,* characterized by a small abdomen folded under the body, a flattened carapace, and short antennae. They can walk in any direction without turning, but usually move sideways. 2 The hermit crab. 3 The horseshoe crab. 4 A crab louse, *Phthirus pubis.* 5 *Aeron.* The lateral slant in an airplane needed to maintain a flight line in a cross-wind. 6 A form of windlass. 7 *pl.* The lowest throw of a pair of dice. —**to catch a crab.** In rowing, to sink an oar blade too deeply; also, to miss the water entirely or skim the surface in making a stroke, and thus fall backward. —*v.* **crabbed, crab·bing** *v.i.* 1 To take or fish for crabs. 2 *U.S. Colloq.* To back out: to *crab* out of an agreement. 3 *Naut.* To drift sideways, as a ship. —*v.t.* 4 *Aeron.* To head (an airplane) across a contrary wind so as to compensate for drift. [OE *crabba.* Akin to CRAB³.]

crab² (krab) *n.* 1 A crab apple. 2 A crab-apple tree. 3 An ill-tempered, surly, or querulous person. —*v.* **crabbed, crab·bing** *v.t.* 1 *Colloq.* To disparage; belittle; complain about. 2 *Colloq.* To ruin or spoil: He *crabbed* the entire act. 3 *Obs.* To make surly or sour; irritate. 4 *Brit. Dial.* To cudgel or beat, as with a crabstick. —*v.i.* 5 To be ill-tempered. [? <Scand. Cf. dial. Sw. *scrabba* wild apple.]

crab³ (krab) *v.i.* **crabbed, crab·bing** To seize each other fiercely, as hawks when fighting; claw. [<MDu. *crabben* scratch. Akin to CRAB¹.]

crab angle The angle between the direction of movement of an airplane, rocket or guided missile and the direction in which the nose points, resembling the sideways motion of a crab.

crab apple A kind of small, sour apple: also called *crab.*

crab-ap·ple tree (krab′ap′əl) A tree (genus *Malus*) bearing crab apples: also called *crab, crab tree.*

crab·bed (krab′id) *adj.* 1 Sour-tempered. 2 Harsh; sour. 3 Hard to understand; abstruse. 4 Irregular in form; cramped. See synonyms under MOROSE. [<CRAB¹, *n.* (def. 1)] —**crab′bed·ly** *adv.*

crab·by (krab′ē) *adj.* **·bi·er, ·bi·est** 1 Crossgrained; ill-tempered. 2 Like or pertaining to a crab.

crab·grass (krab′gras′, -gräs′) *n.* A low-growing or procumbent grass (genus *Digitaria*) with freely rooting stems, especially *D. sanguinalis;* a lawn pest.

crab·stick (krab′stik′) *n.* 1 A cudgel made of crab-tree wood; hence, any cudgel. 2 An ill-tempered person.

crab tree 1 A tree having a bitter bark, as the dogbane, that is used medicinally. 2 The crab-apple tree.

crack (krak) *v.t.* 1 To produce fissures or seams in; break open partially or completely. 2 To cause to give forth a short, sharp sound: to *crack* a whip. 3 To break with such a sound. 4 *Slang* To open in order to drink: to *crack* a bottle. 5 *Colloq.* To break into, as a safe or building, in or-

der to rob. 6 To solve, as a puzzle, crime, or code. 7 *Slang* To tell (a joke). 8 To break or crush mentally, as with sorrow or torture: He *cracked* the man's spirit. 9 To cause (the voice) to become cracked or hoarse. 10 *Colloq.* To strike sharply or with a sharp sound: He *cracked* him on the jaw. 11 To reduce by distillation, as petroleum. 12 *Obs.* To make a boast. —*v.i.* 13 To split or break, especially with suddenness. 14 To make a sharp snapping sound, as a whip or pistol; break with such a sound. 15 Of the voice, to become hoarse or change tone. 16 To become impaired or broken, as the spirit or will. 17 *Slang* To fall back or forward; fail: said of racehorses. 18 *Archaic* To talk boastfully. —**cracked up to be** *Colloq.* Reputed or believed to be. —**to crack a book** *U.S. Slang* To open, as a textbook, and read or study. —**to crack a smile** *Slang* To smile. —**to crack down** *Colloq.* To take severe repressive measures: with *on* or *upon* —**to crack hardy** *Austral. Slang* To put on a bold front in the face of trouble. —**to crack on 1** *Naut.* To crowd on sail. 2 To travel at high speed. —**to crack up** *Colloq.* 1 To smash or destroy, as an airplane or automobile; also, to be in an automobile or airplane accident. 2 To have a breakdown, nervous or physical. —**to crack wise** *U.S. Slang* To wisecrack. —*n.* 1 An incomplete separation into two or more parts with or without a noticeable space between; a fissure; cleft; chink. 2 The narrow space between two boards, especially in a floor. 3 A sudden sharp or loud sound; report, as of a pistol or rifle. 4 A blow that resounds: He hit him a *crack.* 5 A mental or physical defect or imperfection; flaw. 6 *Colloq.* One of high skill or excellence in a certain line; the best: All the *cracks* were entered for that race. 7 A peculiar sound or tone of the voice, as when changing at puberty or weakened by age. 8 *Colloq.* A witty or sarcastic remark; a pun. 9 *Slang* A burglar; also, a burglary. 10 A moment; an exact instant; the duration of a crack: the *crack* of dawn. 11 *Scot.* A familiar chat. —*adj. Colloq.* Of superior excellence; first-class. [OE *cracian*]

crack·brain (krak′brān′) *n.* A weak-minded person. —*adj.* Weak-minded; crazy; odd: also **crack′-brained′.**

cracked (krakt) *adj.* 1 Having a crack or cracks; rent; split or broken into small pieces: *cracked* corn or ice. 2 Damaged or blemished. 3 *Colloq.* Crazy; mentally unsound.

crack·er (krak′ər) *n.* 1 A person or thing that cracks. 2 A firecracker. 3 A device consisting of two strips of paper with fulminating powder between them which explodes by friction when the strips are pulled apart, sometimes ornamented and combined with a motto, bonbon, paper cap, etc. 4 The snapper of a whip. 5 A thin brittle biscuit: an oyster *cracker.* 6 An impoverished white inhabitant of parts of the SE United States: a contemptuous term.

crack·er-bar·rel (krak′ər·bar′əl) *adj.* Denoting or characteristic of the informal, rambling discussions of those habitually gathered in a country store: *cracker-barrel* philosophy.

crack·ing (krak′ing) *n. Chem.* A process by which the molecular structure of petroleum or other complex hydrocarbons is changed under pressure by heat or distillation so that fractions of high boiling point are broken down to those of low boiling point: important in the production of high-octane gasoline.

crack·le (krak′əl) *v.* **·led, ·ling** *v.i.* 1 To crack or snap repeatedly with light, sharp noises. —*v.t.* 2 To crush or crumple, as paper with such sounds. 3 To cover, as china, with a delicate network of cracks. —*n.* 1 A succession of light, cracking sounds; crepitation. 2 The appearance or condition produced in china, porcelain, glass, and the like, by the cracking of the glaze in all directions so as to form a fine network of cracks: also **crack′le·ware′.** [Freq. of CRACK, *v.*] —**crack′ly** *adj.*

crack·ling (krak′ling) *n.* 1 The action or process of giving out small sharp sounds in rapid succession. 2 The crisp browned skin of roasted pork. 3 *pl.* The crisp refuse of fat, as of the hog, after the removal of the lard or tallow. 4 *Brit.* A cake of beef scraps used as dogs' food.

crack of doom 1 The signal announcing the dawn of Judgment Day. 2 Doomsday; the end of

the world.

crack·pot (krak′pot′) *n. Slang* A weak-minded or eccentric person; a harmless fanatic; crank. —*adj.* Eccentric; foolish; insane.

crack shot *Colloq.* An excellent marksman.

crack-up (krak′up′) *n.* 1 *Aeron.* The partial or total destruction of an aircraft due to circumstances beyond the pilot's control. 2 Any sudden, unforseen breakdown.

cra·dle (krād′l) *n.* 1 A rocking or swinging bed for an infant. 2 A place of birth; origin. 3 A scythe with fingers that catch the grain when cut. 4 An arch of thin wood or wire, to keep bedclothes from pressing on a tender part of the body; also a light case in which an injured limb can be swung. 5 *Engin.* **a** A frame, usually of heavy timber, for sustaining some heavy object or structure, as a ship on a marine railway or in drydock. **b** A scaffolding suspended by ropes. 6 A support for the frame or keel or an airship or dirigible under construction. 7 *Mining* A box on rockers, for washing auriferous dirt; a rocker; cradle-rocker. 8 *Brit.* A cage swung on gimbals in which miners ascend and descend a shaft. 9 A coarse ribbing on a vaulted surface that is to be plastered. 10 A currycomb-shaped tool for making mezzotint grounds on a metal plate; a rocker. 11 A life car or basket running on a line, to bring persons from a wreck to the shore. 12 *Mil.* The frame in a gun carriage in which the gun moves during a recoil. 13 The double-pronged, electrically connected holder for the operating unit of a handset telephone. —*v.* **·dled, ·dling** *v.t.* 1 To put into or rock in or as in a cradle; soothe. 2 To nurse in infancy; nurture. 3 To cut or reap, as grain, with a cradle. 4 To draw onto or transport in a cradle, as a ship. 5 *Mining* To wash, as goldbearing gravel, in a cradle. —*v.i.* 6 To lie or rest in or as in a cradle. 7 To cut or reap. —**to rob the cradle** *Colloq.* To marry or take as a sweetheart one much younger than oneself. [OE *cradol*]

cra·dle-snatch·er (krād′l·snach′ər) *n. Slang* One who consorts with or marries a much younger person.

cra·dle-song (krād′l·sông′, -song′) *n.* A lullaby.

craft (kraft, kräft) *n.* 1 Cunning or skill, especially as used with ignoble motives; guile; artifice. 2 Skill or ingenuity in any calling, especially in a manual employment. 3 Occupation or employment; a trade. 4 The membership of a particular trade or organized society; a guild. 5 A vessel; ship; airplane: also used collectively. See synonyms under ARTIFICE, BUSINESS, DECEPTION. [OE *cræft* skill, art, strength, courage]

-craft *combining form* Skill; trade; art of: *woodcraft.* [<CRAFT]

crafts·man (krafts′mən, kräfts′-) *n. pl.* **·men** (-mən) 1 A member of a craft. 2 A skilled mechanic. —**crafts′man·ship** *n.*

craft union A labor union in which membership is limited to workers in a single trade. Compare INDUSTRIAL UNION.

craft·y (kraf′tē, kräf′-) *adj.* **craft·i·er, craft·i·est** Skilful in deceiving; cunning. See synonyms under ASTUTE, INSIDIOUS, POLITIC. —**craft′i·ly** *adv.*

crag (krag) *n.* A rough, steep, or broken rock rising or jutting out prominently. [ME *cragg* <Celtic. Cf. Irish *creag,* Welsh *craig.*]

crag·ged (krag′id) *adj.* Having numerous crags. Also **crag′gy.** —**crag′ged·ness, crag′gi·ness** *n.*

crake (krāk) *n.* A small, short-billed bird of the rail family, with a harsh cry; especially, the corn crake and the spotted crake. [<ON *kraka* crow]

cram (kram) *v.* **crammed, cram·ming** *v.t.* 1 To press tightly; pack together; crowd. 2 To feed to satiety. 3 To force, as a mass of knowledge or facts, into the mind, as in hurried preparation for an examination. —*v.i.* 4 To eat greedily; stuff oneself with food. 5 To force knowledge into the mind by hurried study. —*n.* 1 The act or process of cramming. 2 One who crams. 3 Hastily acquired knowledge gained by cramming. [OE *crammian* stuff]

cram·bo (kram′bō) *n.* **1** A word-riming game. **2** A word that rimes with another. [Alter. of L *crambe* cabbage (<Gk. *krambē*) in phrase *crambe repetita* an unpleasant repetition; lit., cabbage served over]

cram·mer (kram′ər) *n.* **1** One who prepares himself or others for examination by cramming. **2** A mechanical device for cramming poultry. **3** *Brit. Slang* A lie.

cramp[1] (kramp) *n.* **1** A frame with one or more screws, in which pieces may be clamped or forced together, as in joinery; a clamp. **2** An adjustable device of wood or metal upon which vamps are stretched in shoe manufacturing. **3** A bench hook. **4** A narrow place in which it is necessary to deflect sharply the wheels of a vehicle in order to turn. **5** A cramp iron (def. 1).—*v.t.* **1** To restrain or confine the action of, as with a cramp; hamper; hinder. **2** To make fast; hold tightly, as with a cramp iron. **3** To shape over a cramp, as the upper of a boot. **4** To deflect, as the wheel of a vehicle, to one side in making a turn; also, to jam (a wheel) by turning too short. —**to cramp one's style** *Slang* To hamper one's customary skill or self-confidence.—*adj.* **1** Narrowed; straitened. **2** Contracted and irregular in form or action; cramped, as handwriting. [<MDu. *krampe* hook. Related to CRAMP[2].]

cramp[2] (kramp) *n.* **1** An involuntary, sudden, painful muscular contraction, occuring most frequently in the legs and often attacking swimmers; a tonic spasm, caused usually by strain or sudden chill. **2** A paralytic affection of local muscles caused by continued overexertion: writer's *cramp*. **3** Partial paralysis of the hindquarters, sometimes observed in animals during pregnancy. **4** *pl.* Acute abdominal pains. —*v.t.* **1** To affect with cramps. [<OF *crampe* <LG. Related to CRAMP[1].]

cramp·fish (kramp′fish′) *n. pl.* **·fish** or **·fish·es** The electric ray.

cramp iron **1** An iron with bent ends, serving to bind two pieces together more firmly, as in stonework: also called *cramp*. **2** A strip of metal on the side of a vehicle to prevent damage from scraping when the wheel is cramped.

cram·pon (kram′-pən) *n.* **1** *Bot.* An aerial root for climbing, as in the ivy. **2** A pair of hooked pieces of iron for raising heavy stones, etc. **3** An iron attached to the shoe for walking on ice or to aid in climbing. Also **cram·poon** (kram-pōōn′). [<F <*crampe* CRAMP[2]]

CRAMPON (def. 3)

cran·ber·ry (kran′ber′ē, -bər·ē) *n. pl.* **·ries** **1** The edible, scarlet, acid berry of a plant (*Vaccinium macrocarpum*) growing in marshy land. **2** The plant itself. —**small cranberry** The common Old World cranberry (*V. oxycoccus*). [<Du. *kranebere*]

cranberry tree The guelder-rose. Also **cranberry bush.**

crane (krān) *n.* **1** One of a family (*Gruidae*) of large, long-necked, long-legged, heronlike birds allied to the rails; especially, the sandhill crane (*G. americana*). **2** A heron or cormorant. **3** A hoisting machine having the added capacity of moving a load in a horizontal or lateral direction. **4** An iron arm, swinging horizontally, attached to the back or side of a fireplace: used for suspending pots or kettles over a fire. —*v.t. & v.i.* **craned, cran·ing** **1** To stretch out, as a crane stretches its neck; elongate or be elongated. **2** To halt and lean forward, as a horse hesitating at a leap; hence, to hesitate at anything. **3** To elevate or lift by or as if by a crane. [OE *cran*]

crane-fly (krān′flī) *n. pl.* **·flies** A fly with very long, slender legs resembling a large mosquito (family *Tipulidae*): in England often called *daddy-long-legs.*

cranes·bill (krānz′bil′) *n.* Geranium (def. 1). Also **crane's-bill.**

cra·ni·al index (krā′nē·əl) Cephalic index.

cra·ni·ate (krā′nē·it, -āt) *adj.* Possessing a cranium. —*n.* Any of a primary division (*Craniata*) of the phylum *Chordata*, which includes all vertebrates having a skull, as fishes, reptiles, birds, and mammals. [<NL *craniata* <Med. L *cranium* CRANIUM]

cranio- *combining form* Cranium; cranial: *craniograph*. Also, before vowels, **crani-.** [<Med. L *cranium* skull <Gk. *kranion*]

cra·ni·og·no·my (krā′nē·og′nə·mē) *n.* The doctrine that regards the form and proportions of the skull as an index of the mental qualities or temperament. [<CRANIO- + -GNOMY]

cra·ni·o·graph (krā′nē·ə·graf′, -gräf′) *n.* An instrument for making a topographical chart of the skull. —**cra·ni·og·ra·phy** (krā′nē·og′rə·fē) *n.*

cra·ni·ol·o·gy (krā′nē·ol′ə·jē) *n.* The branch of anatomy and medicine that treats of the structure and characteristics of skulls. [<CRANIO- + -LOGY] —**cra·ni·o·log·i·cal** (krā′nē·ə·loj′i·kəl) *adj.*

cra·ni·om·e·ter (krā′nē·om′ə·tər) *n.* An instrument for measuring skulls. [<CRANIO- + -METER] —**cra·ni·o·met·ric** (krā′nē·ə·met′rik) or **·ri·cal** *adj.* —**cra·ni·o·met·ri·cal·ly** *adv.* —**cra·ni·om·e·try** *n.*

cra·ni·os·co·py (krā′nē·os′kə·pē) *n.* **1** Scientific examination of the configuration of the skull. **2** Formerly, phrenology. [<CRANIO- + -SCOPY] —**cra·ni·o·scop·ic** (krā′nē·ə·skop′ik) *adj.* —**cra·ni·os′co·pist** *n.*

cra·ni·ot·o·my (krā′nē·ot′ə·mē) *n. Surg.* **1** Any operation on the cranium. **2** An operation in which the fetal skull is perforated and the cranium compressed to facilitate delivery in difficult parturition. [<CRANIO- + -TOMY]

cra·ni·um (krā′nē·əm) *n. pl.* **·ni·ums** or **·ni·a** (-nē·ə) That part of the skull enclosing the brain; brainpan. [<Med. L <Gk. *kranion* skull] —**cra′ni·al** *adj.*

crank[1] (krangk) *n.* **1** A device for transmitting motion, as by the hand, or for converting rotary into reciprocating motion, as a handle attached at right angles to a shaft. **2** *Colloq.* One who lacks mental balance; a person given to caprices, crotchets, or vagaries. **3** A fantastic turn of speech; quip; conceit; also, a twist or perversion of judgment; whim. **4** An eccentric notion or action. **5** *Colloq.* A grouchy, ill-tempered person. **6** *Obs.* A bend. —*v.t.* **1** To bend into the shape of a crank. **2** To furnish with a crank. **3** To operate or start by a crank. —*v.i.* **4** To turn a crank, as in starting an internal-combustion engine. **5** *Obs.* To bend; twist. [OE *cranc*, as in *crancstæf* a weaving comb]

crank[2] (krangk) *adj.* **1** Ill-balanced; easily capsized: said of a boat. **2** Hence, shaky. Also **cranky.** [Earlier *crank-sided* <Du. *krengd* heeled over <*krengan* push]

crank[3] (krangk) *adj.* Spirited; lively. [Origin uncertain]

crank·case (krangk′kās′) *n. Mech.* The case enclosing an engine crankshaft, as of an automobile or the like.

cran·kle (krang′kəl) *n.* A bend; crinkle. —*v.t. & v.i.* **·kled, ·kling** To bend; crinkle. [Dim. of CRANK]

crank·shaft (krangk′shaft′, -shäft′) *n. Mech.* A shaft that bears one or more cranks.

crank·y (krang′kē) *adj.* **crank·i·er, crank·i·est** **1** Full of whims; irritable; easily exasperated; peevish. **2** Crooked; bent. **3** Loose and rickety. — **crank′i·ly** *adv.* —**crank′i·ness** *n.*

cran·ny (kran′ē) *n. pl.* **·nies** A narrow opening; fissure. —*v.i.* **·nied, ·ny·ing** **1** To become full of fissures or crevices. **2** To enter by crannies, as the wind. See synonyms under BREACH. [<OF *cran, cren* notch] —**cran′nied** *adj.*

crape (krāp) *n.* **1** A sheer worsted fabric, usually black, used for funeral hangings and draperies. **2** A piece of this fabric, especially an armband or crêpe veil, or hung as a sign of mourning. —*v.t.* **craped, crap·ing** **1** To produce crimps or a crinkled surface in; frizz. **2** To drape with crape; place crape upon as a sign of mourning. [Var. of CRÊPE]

crape·fish (krāp′fish′) *n. pl.* **·fish** or **·fish·es** Codfish salted and pressed.

crape·hang·er (krāp′hang′ər) *n. Slang* A gloomy or pessimistic person: so called in allusion to the hanging of black crape at funerals.

crap·pie (krap′ē) *n. pl.* **·pies** or **·pie** An edible fresh-water fish (*Pomoxis annularis*) of the central United States. [Cf. F *crape* crabfish]

craps (kraps) *n. U.S.* A game of chance, played with two dice. Also **crap game, crap′shoot′ing.** [<F *crabs, craps* <E *crabs*, the lowest throw (two aces) in hazard]

crap-shoot·er (krap′shōō′tər) *n. U.S.* One who plays the game of craps.

crap·u·lence (krap′yōō·ləns) *n.* **1** Sickness caused by intemperance in eating or drinking; surfeit. **2** Gross intemperance, as in drinking.

crap·u·lent (krap′yōō·lənt) *adj.* **1** Grossly intemperate; drunken; gluttonous. **2** Sick from intemperance in drinking. Also **crap′u·lous.** [<LL *crapulentus* <*crapula* drunkenness <Gk. *kraipalē* drunken headache]

crap·y (krā′pē) *adj.* Crapelike; crimped; wavy, as hair.

crash (krash) *v.t.* **1** To break or dash in pieces noisily and with violence. **2** To force or drive noisily and with violence: He *crashed* his way through the jungle. **3** *U.S. Colloq.* To intrude upon or enter uninvited or without paying admission: to *crash* a party or dance. **4** To cause, as an airplane, truck, or train, to fall to the earth or strike an obstacle. —*v.i.* **5** To break or fall in pieces with a violent, broken sound. **6** To make a noise of clashing or breaking. **7** To move with such a noise: The boulder *crashed* down the hillside. **8** To fall to the earth or strike an obstacle, as an airplane or automobile. **9** To fail or collapse; come to ruin: The stock market *crashed* suddenly. —*n.* **1** A loud noise, as of thunder. **2** Destruction; bankruptcy. **3** A destructive accident caused by collision: an airplane *crash*. [Imit.]

cra·sis (krā′sis) *n.* **1** The coalescence of two vowels into one long vowel or diphthong (as the final and initial vowels of two successive words); syneresis. **2** *Med.* A characteristic mixture of constituent elements, as of the blood. **3** Constitutional temperament [<Gk. *krasis* mixture]

cras·pe·do·mor·phol·o·gy (kras′pə·dō·môr′fol′ə·jē) *n.* That branch of photography which deals with the sharpness of images, clarity of detail, and the resolving power of camera lenses. [<Gk. *kraspedon* border, margin + MORPHOLOGY]

crass (kras) *adj.* Coarse in manner or feeling; insensitive; indelicate: *crass* indifference to human suffering. [<L *crassus* thick] —**crass′ly** *adv.* —**crass′ness** *n.*

cras·sa·men·tum (kras′ə·men′təm) *n. Med.* A coagulum or clot, as the semisolid portion of blood. [<L, dregs, sediment]

cras·su·la·ceous (kras′yōō·lā′shəs) *adj. Bot.* Of or pertaining to a family (*Crassulaceae*) of polypetalous, usually succulent herbs or shrubs, including the sedums and houseleeks. [<NL *Crassulaceae* <L *crassus* thick]

-crat *combining form* A supporter or member of a social class or of a type of government: *democrat, aristocrat.* See –CRACY. [<F *-crate* <Gk. *-kratēs* <*krateein* rule, govern]

crate (krāt) *n.* **1** A large wickerwork hamper or framework of slats, for protection in transporting various articles: also, its contents. **2** A packing box. **3** *Slang* An old or decrepit vehicle or airplane. —*v.t.* **crat·ed, crat·ing** To put in a crate; send or transport in a crate. [<L *cratis* wickerwork. Doublet of GRATE.]

cra·ter (krā′tər) *n.* **1** The bowl-shaped depression forming the outlet of a volcano or of a hot spring. **2** Any large bowl or cavity. **3** In ancient Greece and Rome, a large bowl or vase in which wine was mixed with water before being served to guests. **4** The pit resulting from the explosion of a mine, bomb, or shell. [<L <Gk. *kratēr* bowl]

cra·vat (krə·vat′) *n.* A neckcloth or scarf; a necktie. [<F *cravate* <Cravate a Croatian <G *Krabate* <Croatian *Hrvat*; with ref. to the neckcloths worn by 17th c. Croatian soldiers]

crave (krāv) *v.* **craved, crav·ing** *v.t.* **1** To beg for humbly and earnestly. **2** To long for; desire greatly. **3** To be in need of; require: His body *craves* nourishment. —*v.i.* **4** To desire or long: with *for* or *after*. [OE *crafian*]

cra·ven (krā′vən) *adj.* Lacking in courage; cowardly. —*n.* A base coward. [<OF *cravant* <L *crepans*, ppr. of *crepare* break]

crav·ing (krā'ving) n. A yearning or appetite; intense longing. See synonyms under APPETITE, DESIRE, PETITION. — **crav'ing·ly** adv. — **crav'ing·ness** n.

craw·dad (krô'dad') n. Dial. A crayfish.

craw·fish (krô'fish') n. pl. **·fish** or **·fish·es** A crayfish. — v.i. U.S. Colloq. To back out or retreat, as from a position or a promise. [Var. of CRAYFISH]

crawl[1] (krôl) v.i. 1 To move by thrusting one part of the body forward upon a surface and drawing the other part after, as a worm; creep. 2 To move slowly, feebly, or cautiously: A sick person crawls about. 3 To move or make progress meanly and insinuatingly; seek influence by servility. 4 To have a sensation as of crawling things upon the body. 5 To progress or grow by extending branches, etc., as a vine or creeping plant. 6 To be filled with things that crawl, as a dead body. 7 Colloq. To back down from a declared position. — n. 1 The act of crawling; a creeping motion. 2 In swimming, a stroke made while lying face down, the arms being alternately thrust forward above the water.

crawl[2] (krôl) n. A pen or enclosure in the water for containing fish, turtles, etc. [Alter. of Du. kraal. See KRAAL.]

crawl space A shallow space beneath a floor, often to provide access to a building's ducts, electrical and plumbing fixtures, etc. Also **crawl·way** (krôl'wā')

cray·fish (krā'fish') n. pl. **·fish** or **·fish·es** 1 A spiny lobster. 2 A small, fresh-water crustacean (family Astacidae) resembling the lobster, especially the common American crayfish (Cambarus affinis). [Earlier crevice <OF <OHG krebiz; infl. in form by fish]

cray·on (krā'ən, -on) n. 1 A small cylinder of charcoal, prepared chalk, or other waxy material, as gypsum, and flour or pipe clay, especially colored, as with graphite, red ocher, etc., for drawing on paper. 2 An oily pencil, used in lithography. 3 A carbon point in an arc light. 4 A drawing made with crayons. 5 A piece of prepared chalk used for marking on blackboards. — v.t. To sketch or draw with a crayon or crayons. [<F, pencil < craie chalk <L creta] — **cray'on·ist** n.

craze (krāz) v. **crazed**, **craz·ing** v.t. 1 To cause to become insane or mentally ill. 2 To make full of minute intersecting cracks, as the glaze of pottery. 3 Obs. To impair or weaken; break down. — v.i. 4 To become insane. 5 To become full of minute cracks. — n. 1 Mental disorder. 2 A transient freak of fashion; a caprice or prejudice. 3 A flaw in the glaze of pottery. [ME crasen <Scand. Cf. Sw. krasa break.]

crazed (krāzd) adj. 1 Insane. 2 Cracked, as glaze.

cra·zy (krā'zē) adj. **cra·zi·er**, **cra·zi·est** 1 Insane; originating in or characterized by insanity. 2 Of or fit for an insane person. 3 Dilapidated; rickety. 4 Colloq. Inordinately eager; foolishly desirous. 5 Colloq. Inexplicable; odd or unconventional: a crazy driver.

crazy quilt A patchwork bed quilt made of pieces of various sizes, shapes, and colors.

cra·zy·weed (krā'zē·wēd') n. Loco or locoweed.

creak (krēk) v.t. & v.i. To make, or cause to make, a creak. — n. A sharp, squeaking sound, as from friction. [Imit.] — **creak'i·ly** adv. — **creak'i·ness** n. — **creak'y** adj.

cream (krēm) n. 1 A thick, oily, light-yellow substance composed chiefly of fatty globules that rise and gather on the surface of milk and combine into butter when churned. 2 Any substance formed in a similar manner. 3 A delicacy for the table resembling cream, or made in part from it; also, a candy containing a creamlike substance. 4 The part of something regarded as the choicest or most highly to be appreciated: the cream of fashion. 5 A soft, oily cosmetic for cleansing or protecting the skin. See COSMETIC. 6 A rich, sirupy cordial or liqueur. See CRÈME. 7 The lighter part of liquor which rises and gathers on the top. 8 The color of cream: a light-yellow color. — v.t. 1 To skim cream from. 2 To take the best part from. 3 To add cream to, as coffee. 4 To permit (milk)

to form cream. 5 To beat, as milk and sugar, to a creamy consistency. 6 To cook or prepare (food) with cream or cream sauce. — v.i. 7 To be covered with cream; froth. 8 To form cream. [<F crème <OF cresme <LL chrisma. Doublet of CHRISM.] — **cream'i·ness** n. — **cream'y** adj.

cream cheese Soft, unripened cheese made of cream or a mixture of cream and milk.

cream·cups (krēm'kups') n. An ornamental annual (Platystemon californicus) of the poppy family, with cream-colored flowers.

cream·er (krē'mər) n. 1 A cooler or other container in which milk is placed and the cream allowed to rise. 2 Any dish or machine in which cream is separated. 3 A cream pitcher.

cream·er·y (krē'mər·ē) n. pl. **·er·ies** 1 A place for collecting, keeping, or selling cream. 2 A place where butter and cheese are made, milk and cream are pasteurized, separated, bottled, etc.

cream of tartar Potassium bitartrate, $HKC_4H_4O_6$, a white crystalline compound with an aciduous taste, made by purifying argol: an ingredient of baking powder.

cream puff 1 A shell of pastry filled with whipped cream or custard. 2 Slang A sissy; weakling.

crease (krēs) n. 1 The mark of a wrinkle, fold, or the like. 2 In cricket, any of the lines limiting the position of the bowler or batsman. — v. **creased**, **creas·ing** v.t. 1 To make a crease, line, or fold in; wrinkle. 2 To stun or wound by a shot that grazes the flesh. — v.i. 3 To become wrinkled or fall into creases. [ME creaste, ? var. of creste a crest, ridge] — **creas'er** n. — **creas'y** adj.

cre·ate (krē·āt') v. **·at·ed**, **·at·ing** v.t. 1 To cause to come into existence; originate. 2 To be the cause of; occasion: The speech created much interest. 3 To produce, as a painting or poem, from thought and imagination. 4 To be the first to portray, as a character or part. 5 To invest with, as rank or office; appoint. — v.i. 6 Brit. Slang To make a fuss; complain noisily. See synonyms under MAKE, PRODUCE. [<L creatus, pp. of creare produce, create]

cre·a·tine (krē'ə·tēn, -tin) n. Biochem. A nitrogenous compound, $C_4H_9N_3O_2$, found in the muscle tissue, brain, and blood of all vertebrate animals. It has been isolated in the form of white crystals, and is also made synthetically. Also **cre'a·tin** (-tin). [<Gk. kreas, -atos flesh + -INE[2]]

cre·at·i·nine (krē·at'ə·nēn, -nin) n. Biochem. The anhydride of creatine, $C_4H_7ON_3$, occurring normally in blood and urine: isolated as white or yellowish prismatic crystals. [<CREATINE + -INE[1]]

cre·a·tion (krē·ā'shən) n. 1 The act of creating; especially, in a theological sense, the original act of God in bringing the world or universe into existence. 2 The universe. 3 An act of construction; the combining or organizing of existing materials into new form: the creation of an empire. 4 That which is created; any product of the power of scientific, artistic, or practical construction: the creations of genius. 5 The act of investing with a new rank or character or of placing in a new office: the creation of two additional judges. — **all creation** Everybody; everything in the world.

cre·a·tion·ism (krē·ā'shən·iz'əm) n. 1 The doctrine that the universe was originally brought into existence without preexistent material by the word of God, and also that new species or forms of being have been successively produced by the direct formative exercise of the Divine wisdom and power. 2 The doctrine that God creates a new soul whenever a human being begins to live: distinguished from traducianism. Also **cre·a'tion·al·ism**. — **cre·a'tion·ist** n. — **cre·a'tion·is'tic**, **cre·a'tion·al·is'tic** adj.

cre·a·tive (krē·ā'tiv) adj. 1 Having the power to create. 2 Productive; constructive. — **cre·a'tive·ly** adv. — **cre·a'tive·ness** n.

cre·a·tiv·i·ty (krē'ā·tiv'ə·tē) n. The quality of being able to produce original work or ideas in any field; creativeness.

cre·a·tor (krē·ā'tər) n. 1 One who creates or

brings into being. 2 That which produces or causes; creative instrumentality. See synonyms under CAUSE. — **the Creator** God, as the maker of the universe. — **cre·a'tor·ship** n.

crea·ture (krē'chər) 1 That which has been created; a creation; a human being. 2 A domestic animal. 3 A person or thing considered as arising from, governed by, or conditioned upon something else: creatures of habit. 4 A person dependent upon the power or influence of another; dependent; tool.

cre·dence (krēd'ns) n. 1 Confidence based upon external evidence; belief. 2 That which serves to accredit; credentials. 3 Eccl. A small table or shelf near the altar to hold the eucharistic elements before they are consecrated. 4 A sideboard or serving table of medieval and Renaissance Europe. See synonyms under BELIEF, FAITH. [<F crédence <Med. L credentia < credere believe]

cre·den·dum (kri·den'dəm) n. pl. **·da** (-də) An article of faith; that which is to be believed: distinguished from agendum. [<L, gerundive of credere believe]

cre·den·tial (kri·den'shəl) n. 1 That which certifies one's authority or claim to confidence. 2 pl. Certificate showing that a person is invested with certain authority or claim to confidence or consideration. — adj. Giving a title or claim to credit and confidence; accrediting.

cred·i·bil·i·ty (kred'ə·bil'ə·tē) n. 1 The capacity of being believed. 2 The capacity, as of a government or a public official, of maintaining the public's confidence that its report of the conduct of its affairs is worthy of belief.

credibility gap 1 A lessening or loss of credibility, as in a government or public official. 2 The extent or degree of a decline in credibility: The official statement only widened the credibility gap.

cred·i·ble (kred'ə·bəl) adj. Capable of being believed; worthy of credit, confidence, or acceptance. See synonyms under LIKELY, PROBABLE. [<L credibilis < credere believe]

cred·it (kred'it) n. 1 Belief in the truth of a statement or in the sincerity of a person; trust. 2 Reputation for trustworthiness; character; repute. 3 One who or that which adds honor or reputation: a student who is a credit to his class. 4 Influence derived from the good opinion or confidence of others: He has credit at court. 5 In bookkeeping, the entry in account of any amount paid by a debtor on account of his debt; the amount so entered; also, the right-hand side of an account, upon which are recorded values received: opposed to debit. 6 Transfer of property on promise of future payment. 7 Reputation for solvency and probity. 8 The amount to which a person, corporation, or business house may be financially trusted in a given case. 9 In an account, the balance in one's favor. 10 The time extended for the payment of a liability. 11 An amount placed by a bank at a customer's disposal against which he may draw. 12 In education, official certification that a course of study has been finished; also, a recognized unit of school or college work. 13 Usually pl. Acknowledgment of work done, as in the making of a motion picture. See synonyms under BELIEF, FAITH, FAME. — v.t. 1 To give credit for; accept as true. 2 To ascribe, as intelligence or honor, to: with with. 3 Archaic To reflect credit upon; bring into good repute. 4 In bookkeeping, to give credit for or enter as credit to. 5 In education, to give educational credits to (a student). [<F crédit <L creditum a loan < credere believe, trust] — **cred'it·a·bil'i·ty**, **cred'it·a·ble·ness** n. — **cred'it·a·ble** adj. — **cred'it·a·bly** adv.

cred·i·tor (kred'i·tər) n. 1 One to whom another is pecuniarily indebted. 2 In bookkeeping, that side of an account upon which are recorded values received or receivable.

credit standing Reputation for meeting financial obligations, paying bills, etc.

credit union A cooperative group for making loans to its members at low rates of interest.

cre·do (krē'dō, krā'-) n. pl. **·dos** 1 A creed, as

the Apostles' or the Nicene Creed. **2** A musical setting for the creed. [<L, I believe; the opening word of the creed]

cre·du·li·ty (krə·dōō′lə·tē, -dyōō′-) *n.* **1** The state or quality of being credulous. **2** A proneness to believe the improbable or the marvelous. [<L *credulitas, -tatis* < *credulus* CREDULOUS]

cred·u·lous (krej′ŏŏ·ləs) *adj.* **1** Apt or disposed to believe on slight evidence; easily deceived. **2** Arising from credulity. [<L *credulus* < *credere* believe] — **cred′u·lous·ly** *adv.* — **cred′u·lous·ness** *n.*

creed (krēd) *n.* **1** A formal summary of religious belief; an authoritative statement of doctrine; a confession of faith. **2** That which is believed; doctrine. See synonyms under BELIEF, FAITH. — **the Creed** The Apostles' Creed. [OE *creda* <L *credo* I believe. See CREDO.]

creek (krēk, krik) *n.* **1** A tidal or valley stream between a brook and a river in size: often written *crick.* **2** A small inlet, bay, or cove; a recess in the shore of the sea or of a river. **3** *Brit.* A small seaboard town. See synonyms under STREAM. — **up the creek** *U.S. Colloq.* **1** In a state of uncertainty or bewilderment. **2** Out of luck. [ME *creke, crike* <Scand. Cf. Sw. *krik* cove, inlet.]

creel (krēl) *n.* **1** An angler's willow basket for carrying fish. **2** A cage of wickerwork for catching lobsters. **3** A frame in a spinning machine. — *v.t.* To put in a creel. [<OF *creil* <L *craticula,* dim. of *cratis* wickerwork. Doublet of GRILLE.]

creep (krēp) *v.i.* **crept, creep·ing** **1** To move like a serpent; crawl. **2** To move imperceptibly, slowly, secretly, or stealthily. **3** To exhibit servility; cringe. **4** To have a sensation as of contact with creeping things. **5** To grow along a surface or support: *creeping* plants. **6** To slip out of place: A sleeve *creeps* up the arm. **7** To move slightly along the line of length: said of railroad tracks. — *n.* **1** The act of creeping. **2** *pl.* A nervous sensation as of insects creeping under the flesh; hence, uneasy apprehensiveness. **3** *Metall.* A phenomenon associated with metals subjected to critical temperature and stresses, and characterized by a slow slipping or flow of the material. **4** *Geol.* The gradual movement of rock waste and soil down a slope from which it has been loosened by weathering. [OE *crēopan*]

creeping myrtle Periwinkle.

creep·y (krē′pē) *adj.* **creep·i·er, creep·i·est** **1** Feeling as if something were creeping over the skin; shivering; especially, chilled with fright. **2** Characterized by creeping. — **creep′·i·ly** *adv.* — **creep′i·ness** *n.*

cre·mate (krē′māt, kri·māt′) *v.t.* **·mat·ed, ·mat·ing** To burn up; reduce, especially a dead body, to ashes. See synonyms under BURN. [<L *crematus,* pp. of *cremare* burn to ashes]

cre·ma·tion (kri·mā′shən) *n.* The act or practice of burning, especially of burning the dead.

cre·ma·to·ry (krē′mə·tôr′ē, -tō′rē, krem′-) *adj.* Related to or connected with cremation. — *n. pl.* **·ries** A place for cremating dead bodies. Also **cre′ma·to′ri·um** (-tôr′ē·əm, -tō′rē-).

crem·o·carp (krem′ə·kärp, krē′mə-) *n. Bot.* The fruit of any plant of the parsley family, consisting of two one-seeded carpels, separating when ripe and hanging from the summit of the slender axis. Also **cre′mo·car′pi·um** (-kär′pē·əm). [<Gk. *kremaein* hang + *karpos* fruit]

cre·nate (krē′nāt) *adj. Bot.* Scalloped or toothed with even, rounded notches, as a leaf or margin. Also **cre′nat·ed.** [<NL *crenatus* < *crena* a notch]

cren·a·ture (kren′ə·chŏŏr, krē′nə-) *n.* **1** The rounded tooth of a crenate organ. **2** The state of being crenate. Also **cre·na′tion** (kri·nā′shən).

cren·el (kren′əl) *n.* **1** An embrasure of a battlement; an indentation. **2** A crenature. — *v.t.* **cren·el·ed** or **·el·led, cren·el·ing** or **·el·ling** To crenelate. Also **cre·nelle** (kri·nel′). [<OF, dim. of *cren* notch]

cren·u·late (kren′yə·lit, -lāt) *adj.* Finely notched or crenate. Also **cren′u·lat′ed.** [<NL *crenulatus* < *crenula,* dim. of *crena* notch]

cren·u·la·tion (kren′yə·lā′shən) *n.* **1** The state of being crenulate. **2** A small crenature.

cre·o·dont (krē′ə·dont) *n. Paleontol.* One of a suborder (*Creodonta*) of primitive Tertiary carnivora, having incisors with closed roots, distinct fibula, and developed otic bulla. [<NL *Creodonta* <Gk. *kreas* flesh + *odous, odontos* tooth]

cre·o·lized language (krē′ə·līzd) An amalgamated language, such as Gullah, resulting from close and prolonged contact between two groups speaking dissimilar languages: it usually incorporates a simplified vocabulary from the dominant language with the grammatical system of the native language, and becomes the only language of the subject group. Compare PIDGIN.

cre·o·sol (krē′ə·sōl, -sol) *n. Chem.* A colorless, aromatic, oily liquid compound, $C_8H_{10}O_2$, derived from beech tar or guaiac by distillation. [<CREOS(OTE) + -OL²]

cre·o·sote (krē′ə·sōt) *n. Chem.* **1** An oily liquid consisting principally of cresol and other phenols, obtained by the destructive distillation of wood and having a smoky odor and burning taste: it is an antiseptic, but a poor germicide, and is used to preserve timber, meat, etc. **2** A similar liquid distilled from coal tar: also **coal–tar creosote.** — *v.t.* **·sot·ed, ·sot·ing** To treat or impregnate with creosote, as shingles, etc. [<Gk. *kreas* flesh + *sōtēr* preserver < *sōzein* save]

creosote bush A shrub (*Larrea tridentata*) of the bean caltrop family of Mexico and the Colorado desert, having a resinous foliage that smells like creosote.

crêpe (krāp) *n.* A thin, light fabric, made of silk, cotton, wool, or synthetic fibers, generally with a crinkled, pebbled, or puckered surface: also spelled *crape.* Also **crepe.** [<F *(tissu) crêpe* crinkled cloth <L *crispus* curled]

crêpe de Chine (də shēn′) A soft, thin silk dress fabric, with a pebbly surface.

crêpe hair Artificial hair, used in theatrical make-up for beards and moustaches.

crêpe paper A tissue paper resembling crêpe, used for decorative purposes.

crêpe rubber Rubber prepared in crinkled texture for the soles of shoes.

crêpes su·zette (krāp′ sōō·zet′) Thin egg pancakes, rolled in a hot, orange-flavored sauce: usually served aflame in cognac or curaçao.

crep·i·tate (krep′ə·tāt) *v.i.* **·tat·ed, ·tat·ing** To make a succession of quick snapping sounds; crackle; rattle. [<L *crepitatus,* pp. of *crepitare,* freq. of *crepare* creak] — **crep′i·tant** *adj.*

crept (krept) Past tense of CREEP.

cre·pus·cu·lar (kri·pus′kyə·lər) *adj.* **1** Pertaining to twilight; like twilight; obscure. **2** Appearing or flying in the morning or evening twilight, as certain birds and insects. Also **cre·pus′cu·lous.**

cre·pus·cule (kri·pus′kyōōl) *n.* Twilight. Also **cre·pus·cle** (kri·pus′əl). [<L *crepusculum* < *creper* dark, dusky]

cre·scen·do (krə·shen′dō, -sen′-) *n. pl.* **·dos** *Music* **1** A gradual increase in the force of sound: expressed by the sign ——— or the abbreviation *cres.* **2** A passage so performed. — *adj.* Slowly increasing in loudness or power. [<Ital. < *crescere* increase]

cres·cent (kres′ənt) *n.* **1** The visible part of the moon in its first quarter, having one concave edge and one convex edge; the new moon. **2** Something crescent-shaped, as the device on the Turkish standard; hence **The Crescent,** the Turkish or Mohammedan power. — *adj.* **1** Increasing: said of the moon in its first quarter. **2** Shaped like the moon in its first quarter. [<L *crescens, -entis,* ppr. of *crescere* increase] — **cres·cen·tic** (kre·sen′tik) *adj.*

cre·sol (krē′sōl, -sol) *n. Chem.* Any one of three isomeric liquid or crystalline compounds, C_7H_8O, obtained by the destructive distillation of coal, beechwood, or pinewood: used as an antiseptic. [Var. of CREOSOL]

cress (kres) *n.* One of various plants of the mustard family having a pungent taste and used in salads. [OE *cressa*] — **cress′y** *adj.*

cres·set (kres′it) *n.* An incombustible frame or vessel mounted to hold a torch, a beacon, or fuel for this. [<OF *craicet, craisset*]

Cres·si·da (kres′i·də) *n.* In medieval legend, in Chaucer's *Troilus and Criseyde,* and in Shakespeare's *Troilus and Cressida,* a Trojan girl unfaithful to her lover Troilus: also spelled *Criseyde.* Also **Cres′sid.** See PANDARUS.

Cres·sy (kres′ē) See CRÉCY.

crest (krest) *n.* **1** A comb or tuft on the head of an animal or bird. **2** The projection on the top of a helmet; a plume; tuft. **3** The ridge of a wave or of a mountain; the top of anything. **4** A heraldic device placed above the shield in a coat of arms. **5** *Archaic* Loftiness; pride; courage. **6** The ridge of the neck of a horse or a dog. **7** *Archit.* **a** The ridge of a roof. **b** Carved work or any continuous ornament on the ridge or other elevated parts of an edifice; a cresting. — *v.t.* **1** To serve as a crest for; cap. **2** To furnish with or as with a crest. **3** To reach the crest of. **4** To adorn with crestlike streaks or lines. — *v.i.* **5** To come to a crest, as a wave prior to breaking. [<OF *creste* <L *crista* tuft] — **crest′ed** *adj.*

COAT OF ARMS WITH CREST

crested auklet A small, brownish-black diving bird (*Aethia cristatella*), abundant in Alaska and the North Pacific.

crested flycatcher Any flycatcher having a conspicuous crest, especially the great crested flycatcher (*Myiarchus crinitus*) of eastern North America.

crest·fall·en (krest′fô′lən) *adj.* **1** Having the crest or head lowered. **2** Dispirited; dejected.

cres·yl (kres′əl, krē′səl) *n. Chem.* Tolyl. [< CRES(OL) + -YL]

cres·y·late (kres′ə·lāt) *n. Chem.* An ester derived from cresol.

cre·syl·ic (kri·sil′ik) *adj. Chem.* Of or derived from cresyl, cresol, or creosote.

cre·ta·ceous (kri·tā′shəs) *adj.* Consisting of or related to chalk; chalky. [<L *cretaceus* < *creta* chalk <*Creta* Cretan, of Crete (where large deposits of chalk occurred)]

cre·tin (krē′tin) *n.* A person afflicted with cretinism. [<F *crétin,* var. of *chrétien* Christian, human being, i.e., not an animal]

cre·tin·ism (krē′tən·iz′əm) *n. Pathol.* A disease associated with prenatal thyroid deficiency and subsequent thyroid inactivity, marked by physical deformities, arrested development, goiter, and various forms of mental retardation, including imbecility: also called *hypothyroidism.*

cre·tonne (kri·ton′, krē′ton) *n.* A heavy, unglazed cotton, linen, or rayon fabric printed in colored patterns: used especially for draperies, chair coverings, etc. [from *Creton,* a village in Normandy]

cre·vasse (krə·vas′) *n.* **1** A deep fissure, as in a glacier. **2** A breach in a levee. — *v.t.* **·vassed, ·vass·ing** To split with crevasses. [<F] — **cre·vassed′** *adj.*

crev·ice (krev′is) *n.* A small fissure or crack. See synonyms under BREACH. [<OF *crevace* <LL *crepatia* < *crepare* crack, creak]

crew¹ (krōō) *n.* **1** *Naut.* **a** The company of seamen belonging to one ship or boat: sometimes including officers, and legally including both master and officers unless specifically excepted. **b** The gang of a boatswain, gunner, carpenter, or other petty officer. **2** A body of men organized or detailed for a particular work, as to run a train. **3** A group of students trained to handle a racing shell, consisting of oarsmen and coxswain. **4** A company of people in general; crowd: a motley *crew* of ne'er-do-wells and loafers. **5** Any band or troop of armed men. See synonyms under CABAL. [<OF *creue* an increase < *croistre* grow <L *crescere* increase]

crew² (krōō) Past tense of CROW.

crew cut A closely cropped haircut.

crew·el (krōō′əl) *n.* A slackly twisted worsted yarn, used in fancywork. ◆ Homophone: *cruel.* [Origin uncertain]

crewel needle Any large-eyed needle, especially one used for crewel.

crew·el·work (krōō′əl·wûrk′) *n.* Embroidery with crewel.

crib (krib) *n.* **1** A rack or manger. **2** A stall for cattle. **3** A child's bedstead, with side railings. **4** A box, bin, or small building for grain, having slat or openwork sides. **5** A small raft. **6** A frame of wood or timber, used to retain a bank of earth. **7** *Colloq.* A petty theft, or the thing taken; plagiarism. **8** A translation or other unauthorized aid in study. **9** A house, cottage, lodging, etc. **10** In cribbage, the four discarded cards counted by the dealer. See CRIBBAGE. **11** A wickerwork basket. — *v.* **cribbed, crib·bing** *v.t.* **1** To enclose in or as in a crib; confine closely. **2** To line or bolster, as the walls of a pit, with timbers or planking. **3** *Colloq.* To take and pass off as one's own, as an answer or a piece of writing; copy; plagiarize. **4** *Colloq.* To steal; purloin. **5** In logging, to form (logs) into a raft, as for towing.

crib·bage (krib'ij) *n.* A game of cards for two, three, or four players, in which the score is kept on a small board with rows of holes into which pegs are inserted. [<CRIB, *n.* (def 10)]

crib·ble (krib'əl) *n.* **1** A coarse sieve. **2** Coarse flour or meal. — *v.t.* **·bled, ·bling** To separate with a coarse sieve or riddle; sift. Also **crib'le.** [<F *crible* <LL *cribellum,* dim. of L *cribrum* sieve]

crib·bled (krib'əld) *adj.* Covered with small punctures or dots, as in engraving or the decoration of wood or metal. [<F *criblé* < *crible* a sieve]

crib·ri·form (krib'rə·fôrm) *adj.* Having the form of a sieve; sievelike.

crib·work (krib'wûrk') *n.* **1** A frame of logs filled in with stones: used to support wharves or to prevent water from washing out ground. **2** A crib, or anything constructed with cribs.

crick¹ (krik) *n.* A spasmodic affection of the muscles, as of the neck; a cramp. — *v.t.* To turn or twist so as to produce a crick. [Origin uncertain]

crick² (krik) See CREEK (def. 1).

crick·et¹ (krik'it) *n.* A leaping orthopterous insect (family *Gryllidae*), with long antennae and three segments in each tarsus, the male of which makes a chirping sound by friction of the forewings. For illustration see under INSECT (injurious). [<OF *criquet* <LG]

crick·et² (krik'it) *n.* **1** An outdoor game played with bats, a ball, and wickets, between two opposing sides numbering eleven each: one of the most popular sports of England. **2** *Colloq.* Fair, gentlemanly behavior; sportsmanship. [<F *criquet* bat, stick <MDu. *cricke*] — **crick'et·er** *n.*

cri·coid (krī'koid) *Anat. adj.* Ringlike: designating a cartilage at the lowest part of the larynx. — *n.* The topmost cartilaginous ring of the trachea, whose posterior portion serves as a base for the arytenoids. [<Gk. *krikoeidēs* < *krikos* ring + *eidos* shape, form]

cri·co·thy·roid (krī'kō·thī'roid) *adj. Anat.* Of or pertaining to the cricoid and thyroid cartilages. See illustration under LARYNX.

cried (krīd) Past participle and past tense of CRY.

cri·er (krī'ər) *n.* One who publicly cries sales, lost articles, etc.

crime (krīm) *n.* **1** *Law* An act that subjects the doer to legal punishment; the commission or omission of an act specifically forbidden or enjoined by public law. **2** Any grave offense against morality or social order; wickedness; iniquity. See synonyms under ABOMINATION, OFFENSE, SIN. [<F <L *crimen* accusation, charge]

crim·i·nal (krim'ə·nəl) *adj.* **1** *Law* Relating to crime, or pertaining to the administration of penal as opposed to civil law. **2** Implying crime or heinous wickedness. **3** Guilty of crime: the *criminal* classes. — *n.* One who has committed an offense punishable by law. [<F *criminel* <L *criminalis*] — **crim·i·nal·i·ty** (krim'ə·nal'ə·tē), **crim'i·nal·ness** *n.* — **crim'i·nal·ly** *adv.*

Synonyms (adj.): abominable, culpable, felonious, flagitious, guilty, illegal, immoral, iniquitous, nefarious, sinful, unlawful, vicious, vile, wicked, wrong. Every *criminal* act is *illegal* or *unlawful,* but *illegal* or *unlawful* acts may not be always *criminal.* Offenses against public law are *criminal,* offenses against private rights are *illegal* or *unlawful.* All acts punishable by fine or imprisonment are both

are *criminal* in view of the law. It is *illegal* for a man to trespass on another's land, but it is not *criminal*; the trespasser is liable to civil suit for damages, but not to indictment, fine, or imprisonment. A *felonious* act is a *criminal* act punishable by imprisonment in the penitentiary or by death. A *flagitious* crime is one that brings public odium. *Vicious* refers to the indulgence of evil appetites, habits, or passions; *vicious* acts are not necessarily *criminal,* or even *illegal*; we speak of a *vicious* horse. That which is *iniquitous,* that is, contrary to equity, may sometimes be done under the forms of law. See IMMORAL. — *Antonyms*: innocent, just, lawful, legal, meritorious, moral, right, virtuous.

crim·i·nal·is·tics (krim'ə·nəl·is'tiks) *n.* That branch of criminology which deals especially with the scientific methods of crime detection.

crim·i·nate (krim'ə·nāt) *v.t.* **·nat·ed, ·nat·ing** To accuse of or implicate in crime; incriminate. [<L *criminatus,* pp. of *criminari* accuse of crime] — **crim'i·na'tion** *n.* — **crim'i·na'tive** *adj.* — **crim'i·na'tor** *n.*

crim·i·nol·o·gy (krim'ə·nol'ə·jē) *n.* The scientific study and investigation of crime and criminals. [<L *crimen, criminis* + -LOGY] — **crim·i·no·log·i·cal** (krim'ə·nə·loj'i·kəl) *adj.* — **crim'i·nol'o·gist** *n.*

crimp¹ (krimp) *v.t.* **1** To bend or press into ridges or folds; corrugate; flute. **2** To indent and close, as a cartridge case; crease. **3** To bend into shape, as the uppers of boots. **4** To gash the flesh of with a knife, as fish before cooking, in order to make it firmer and crisper. **5** To curl or wave: to *crimp* the hair. — *n.* **1** Anything crimped; especially, in the plural, waved or curled hair. **2** A crimping machine; crimper. **3** An offset in a piece of structural steel, used to fit one piece over another. **4** A collapse or breakdown of wood fibers, due to inherent weakness or a too rapid drying of timber. — *adj.* **1** Brittle and crisp; friable. **2** Inconsistent or contradictory. **3** Stiff, as if starched. [<MDu. *crimpen* wrinkle, draw together] — **crimp'age** *n.* — **crimp'er** *n.* — **crimp'y** *adj.*

crimp² (krimp) *n.* One who procures the impressment of sailors, soldiers, etc., by decoying or entrapping them. — *v.t.* To decoy or entrap into forced military or naval service. [Origin uncertain]

crim·son (krim'zən) *n.* A deep-red color having a tinge of blue, but lighter than purple. **1** Of a deep-red color. **2** Bloody. — *v.t. & v.i.* To make or become crimson; redden; blush. [<Sp. *cremesin,* var. of OSp. *carmesin, carmesi* <Arabic *qirmazi* < *qirmiz* kermes (insect used in making a red dye). Doublet of CARMINE.]

cringe (krinj) *v.i.* **cringed, cring·ing** **1** To bow in servility or cowardice; crouch. **2** To wince as with pain or fear. **3** To fawn. — *n.* A servile crouching. [ME *cringen, crengen;* related to OE *cringan* yield, fall] — **cring'er** *n.*

cri·nite¹ (krī'nīt) *adj.* **1** *Bot.* Having hair or bearded with long weak hairs. **2** Resembling a tuft of hair. [<L *crinitus,* pp. of *crinire* cover with hair < *crinis* hair]

cri·nite² (krī'nīt, krin'īt) *n.* An encrinite. [<Gk. *krinon* lily]

crin·kle (kring'kəl) *v.t. & v.i.* **·kled, ·kling** **1** To form or cause to form, mold, or move with bends, turns, twists, or wrinkles. **2** To wind in and out; wave; corrugate. **3** To crackle metallically. — *n.* A wrinkle; ripple; twist; sinuosity. [ME *crenklen,* freq. of OE *crincan,* var. of *cringan* yield, fall] — **crin'kly** *adj.*

crin·kle·root (kring'kəl·rōōt', -rŏōt') *n.* A toothwort (genus *Dentaria*) of the mustard family, especially *D. diphylla,* with small white or lilac flowers and a white-toothed rootstock with a pungent, aromatic taste: also called *pepperroot.*

cri·noid (krī'noid, krin'oid) *adj.* **1** Of or pertaining to the *Crinoidea.* **2** Containing crinoids: also **cri·noi·dal** (kri·noid'l). — *n.* One of the *Crinoidea.*

crin·o·line (krin'ə·lin, -lēn) *n.* **1** A highly sized, stiff fabric, used in puffed sleeves, hems, interlinings, etc.: originally made of horsehair and linen. **2** A skirt stiffened with such fabric.

3 A hoop skirt. — *adj.* Resembling crinoline, or serving an analogous purpose. [<F <L *crinis* hair + *linum* flax, thread]

cri·num (krī'nəm) *n.* Any of a genus (*Crinum*) of frequently cultivated tropical herbs of the amaryllis family, with tunicate bulbs and a solid scape bearing numerous long, narrow leaves and showy, fragrant flowers. [<NL <Gk. *krinon* lily]

cri·o·sphinx (krī'ə·sfingks') *n.* A sphinx with a ram's head. See SPHINX. [<Gk. *krios* ram + SPHINX]

crip·ple (krip'əl) *n.* **1** A maimed or lamed person or animal; one lacking the natural use of a limb or the body. **2** *U.S. Dial.* A piece of low, marshy land, partly covered by the tide and partly overgrown with trees and brush. **3** A staging used in cleaning windows. — *v.t.* **·pled, ·pling** To lame; impair or disable. [OE *crypel.* Akin to CREEP.]

crip·pler (krip'lər) *n.* **1** A crimping board or graining board for leather. **2** One who or that which cripples.

Cri·sey·de (kri·sā'də) See CRESSIDA.

cri·sis (krī'sis) *n. pl.* **cri·ses** (-sēz) **1** A turning point in the progress of an affair or of a series of events; a critical moment. **2** *Pathol.* Any sudden or decisive change in the course of a disease, favorable or unfavorable. [<L <Gk. *krisis* < *krinein* decide]

crisp (krisp) *adj.* **1** Firm and brittle; also, crumbling readily, as pastry. **2** Terse or pithy; curt. **3** Fresh; bracing. **4** Having curls or waves; crinkled; crisped. — *v.t. & v.i.* To make or become crisp. [OE <L *crispus* curled]

cris·pate (kris'pāt) *adj.* Having a crisped or curled appearance. Also **cris'pat·ed.** [<L *crispatus,* pp. of *crispare* curl < *crispus* curled]

cris·pa·tion (kris·pā'shən) *n.* **1** A slight contraction or spasmodic constriction. **2** A minute ripple of a liquid's surface, caused by vibration. Also **crisp·a·ture** (kris'pə·chŏŏr).

cris·sal (kris'əl) *adj.* **1** Of or pertaining to the crissum. **2** Having a bright-colored crissum.

criss-cross (kris'krôs', -kros) *v.t.* To cross with interlacing lines. — *v.i.* To move in crisscrosses. — *adj.* Crossing one another in different directions; said of lines or the like. — *n.* **1** The cross of one who cannot write. **2** A congeries of intersecting lines. **3** A game played by children. — *adv.* In different crossdirections; crosswise. [Alter. of CHRIST-CROSS]

cris·sum (kris'əm) *n. Ornithol.* The undertail coverts of a bird; the region or feathers about the anus. [<NL <L *crissare* move the haunches]

cris·tate (kris'tāt) *adj.* **1** Crested. **2** Carinate. Also **cris'tat·ed.** [<L *cristatus* < *crista* crest]

cri·te·ri·on (krī·tir'ē·ən) *n. pl.* **·te·ri·a** (-tir'ē·ə) or **·te·ri·ons 1** A standard by which a correct judgment can be made; a model or example. **2** A test, rule, or measure for distinguishing between the true or false, perfect or imperfect, etc. [<Gk. *kritērion* < *kritēs* a judge < *krinein* decide]

crit·ic (krit'ik) *n.* **1** One who judges anything by some standard or criterion, particularly one who so judges literary or artistic productions. **2** One who judges severely; a caviler. **3** *Obs.* A critique or review. — *adj.* Pertaining to criticism; critical. [<L *criticus* <Gk. *kritikos* < *kritēs* a judge. See CRITERION.]

crit·i·cal (krit'i·kəl) *adj.* **1** Of, pertaining to, or characteristic of a critic or criticism. **2** Disposed to judge or discriminate with care and precision. **3** Given to severe judgment; faultfinding; carping. **4** Based upon principles or methods of criticism; analytical. **5** Of doubtful result; risky; perilous. **6** Contributing to a decisive judgment: *critical* evidence. **7** *Pathol.* Pertaining to a crisis in the course of a disease. **8** *Math.* Relating to the coalescence of different values. **9** *Physics* Designating a constant value or point indicating a decisive change in a specified condition, as temperature, pressure, speed, etc. **10** Necessary for the prosecution of a war: said of any material for which there is no substitute and of which there is an insufficient supply. See synonyms under CAPTIOUS, MINUTE. — **crit'i·cal·ly** *adv.* — **crit'i·cal·ness** *n.*

critical point *Physics* The point at which the

densities and other physical properties of the liquid and gaseous states of a substance are indistinguishable from each other.

critical solution temperature *Physics* The temperature above which any substance is soluble in any proportion in its solvent: also called *consolute temperature.*

critical speed *Physics* The speed at which a rotating shaft becomes dynamically unstable, and which, if maintained, will result in serious vibration and resonance effects.

critical temperature *Physics* A temperature which is characterized by a change or transition; specifically, the temperature above which a substance can exist only in the gaseous state, no matter what pressure may be applied.

crit·i·cism (krit′ə·siz′əm) *n.* **1** The act or art of criticizing. **2** A discriminating judgment; an evaluation. **3** A severe or unfavorable judgment. **4** The principles or rules for judging anything, especially works of literature or art. **5** A review, article, etc., expressing a critical judgment. See synonyms under ANIMADVERSION.

crit·i·cize (krit′ə·siz) *v.t.* & *v.i.* **·cized, ·ciz·ing** **1** To examine and judge as a critic. **2** To judge severely; censure. Also *Brit.* **crit′i·cise.**

cri·tique (kri·tēk′) *n.* **1** A criticism; critical review. **2** The art of criticism. [<F]

crit·ter (krit′ər) *n. U.S. Dial.* **1** A domestic animal. **2** Any living creature. [Var. of CREATURE]

crizz·ling (kriz′ling) *n.* The fine cracks which appear in or on the surface of glass as a result of local chilling in the process of manufacture. [? <CRAZE, *v.* (def. 5)]

croak (krōk) *v.i.* **1** To utter a hoarse, low-pitched cry, as a frog or raven. **2** To speak in a low, hoarse voice. **3** To talk in a doleful tone; forbode evil; grumble. **4** *Slang* To die. — *v.t.* **5** To utter with a croak. **6** *Slang* To kill. — *n.* A hoarse vocal sound, as of a frog or raven. [Imit. Cf. OE *cracethan* croak.]

croak·er (krō′kər) *n.* **1** Any of various animals that croak; especially, one of a class of marine fishes, the grunts. **2** One who speaks dismally or forebodes evil; an alarmist.

cro·ce·in (krō′sē·in) *n. Chem.* One of many artificially produced yellow and bright-red dyes, generally formed of diazo and sulfonic-acid derivatives of benzene and naphthol. [<L *croceus* yellow + -IN]

cro·chet (krō·shā′) *v.t.* & *v.i.* **·cheted** (-shād′), **·chet·ing** (-shā′ing) To form or ornament (a fabric) by interlacing thread with a hooked needle. [< *n.*] — *n.* A kind of fancywork produced by crocheting: now chiefly attributive, as in *crochet hook.* [<F, dim. of *croche* a hook]

cro·cid·o·lite (krə·sid′ə·līt) *n.* **1** A fibrous, silky, blue or green hydrous silicate; blue asbestos. **2** A yellow alteration product of this silicate used as a gemstone; tiger's-eye. [<Gk. *krokis, -idos* nap of cloth + -LITE]

cro·cin (krō′sin) *n.* A vivid red powder, $C_{44}H_{66}O_{28}$, obtained from saffron and from the fruit of a Chinese gardenia (*Gardenia jasminoides*): used as a dye. [<L *crocus* saffron (<Gk. *krokos*) + -IN]

cro·cine (krō′sin, -sēn) *adj.* Of or pertaining to the crocus.

crock¹ (krok) *n.* **1** An earthenware pot or jar. **2** A fragment of earthenware. — *v.t.* To store in a crock, as butter. [OE *crocca*]

crock² (krok) *n.* **1** The black product of combustion; soot. **2** The coloring matter that rubs off from cloth; smut. — *v.t.* To stain; soil. [Origin uncertain]

crock·er·y (krok′ər·ē) *n.* Earthenware; earthen vessels collectively.

crock·et (krok′it) *n.* **1** A projecting ornament usually terminating in a curve or roll of foliage and flowers: used to decorate pastoral staffs and the angles of pinnacles, spires, gables, and cornices. **2** A terminal tine of a deer's antler. [<AF *croquet*, OF *crocket*, dim. of *croche* hook]

croc·o·dile (krok′ə·dīl) *n.* **1** A large, lizardlike, amphibious reptile (order *Crocodilia*) widely distributed in tropical regions, with long jaws, armored skin, and webbed feet; especially, the Nile crocodile (*Crocodylus niloticus*), and the American crocodile (*C. americanus*). The head is longer and narrower than that of an alligator, and the lower molars shut into marginal notches instead of pits. **2** A gavial. [Earlier *cocodrille* <OF <Med. L *cocodrillus,*

alter. of L *crocodilus* <Gk. *krokodilos* lizard, crocodile.]

CROCODILE
(Nile: to 18 feet long; American: to 14 feet)

crocodile bird A small black-headed plover (*Pluvianus aegyptius*) of northern Africa, that often perches on crocodiles and devours their insect parasites.

crocodile tears Simulated or pretended weeping; hypocritical grief: from the ancient tale that the crocodile weeps over those he devours.

croc·o·dil·i·an (krok′ə·dil′ē·ən) *adj.* **1** Of, pertaining to, or like a crocodile. **2** Of an order (*Crocodilia*) of crocodiles, alligators, and similar reptiles. — *n.* One of the *Crocodilia.* Also **croc′o·dil′e·an.**

cro·co·ite (krō′kō·īt) *n.* An adamantine to vitreous, hyacinth-red, translucent lead chromate, $PbCrO_4$, crystallizing in the monoclinic system: often called *red-lead ore.* Also **cro·co·i·site** (krō·kō′ə·sīt). [<Gk. *krokoeis* saffron-colored]

cro·cus (krō′kəs) *n. pl.* **cro·cus·es** or **cro·ci** (krō′sī) **1** Any of a genus (*Crocus*) of plants of the iris family, with long grasslike leaves and large flowers. **2** The flower of this plant. **3** A red or yellow polishing powder of iron oxide. [<L <Gk. *krokos* saffron]

croft (krôft, kroft) *n.* A small field near a house. — *v.t.* To bleach (fabrics or clothes) on the grass in the sun. [OE, a field]

croft·er (krôf′tər, krof′-) *n.* A tenant cultivating a croft.

crom·lech (krom′lek) *n.* **1** An ancient sepulchral structure consisting of a large flat stone resting on upright unhewn stones. **2** An ancient monument of standing stones arranged in a circle. [<Welsh <*crom* bent + *llech* flat stone]

cro·mor·na (krə·môr′nə) *n.* A clarinetlike reed-stop in an organ. [<F *cromorne,* alter. of G *krummhorn* crooked horn]

crone (krōn) *n.* **1** A withered old woman. **2** *Rare* A senile man. — *v.i.* **croned, cron·ing** To talk like a crone. [<Du. *kronye* an old ewe <OF *carogne* carcass]

cro·ny (krō′nē) *n. pl.* **·nies** A familiar friend. [<Gk. *chronios* contemporary; orig. university slang]

crook (krŏŏk) *n.* **1** A bend or curve; also, something bent or crooked. **2** The curved or bent part of a thing: the *crook* of a branch. **3** A genuflection. **4** A device; scheme; artifice. **5** An implement with a crook in it: a shepherd's *crook.* **6** *Scot.* A pothook. **7** *Colloq.* A criminal; swindler; cheat. **8** *Austral. Slang* Ill; out of sorts; also, angry; annoyed. — **to go crook at** *Austral. Slang* To be angry at. — *v.t.* To bend; make crooked. — *v.i.* To grow crooked. See synonyms under BEND, TWIST. [<ON *krōkr*]

crook·ed (krŏŏk′id) *adj.* **1** Not straight; having angles or curves. **2** Not straightforward in conduct. **3** Tricky; dishonest. — **to be (or go) crooked on** *Austral. Slang* To be ill-disposed toward. See synonyms under IRREGULAR. — **crook′ed·ly** *adv.* — **crook′ed·ness** *n.*

crook·neck (krŏŏk′nek′) *n.* One of several varieties of squash with a long, curved neck.

crool (krŏŏl) *v.i.* To gurgle. [Imit.]

croon (krŏŏn) *v.t.* & *v.i.* **1** To sing or hum in a low, monotonous manner; specifically, to sing (popular songs) with exaggerated sentiment or pathos. **2** *Rare* To bellow in a muffled tone. — *n.* **1** A low, mournful humming or singing; the sound made in crooning. **2** A crooning song. [<MDu. *kronen* sing softly, lament] — **croon′er** *n.*

croon song A song of exaggerated sentiment and pathos, adapted for crooning or humming.

crop (krop) *n.* **1** Cultivated plants or grains collectively. **2** The soil product of a particular

kind, place, or season. **3** The yield or seasonal product of things other than plants or grains: a *crop* of lambs or calves; the entire yield of anything. **4** The act of cutting; also, the result of cutting; specifically, a short haircut. **5** The first stomach of a bird: a large, pouch-like reservoir at the base of the distensible gullet, serving for preliminary maceration of food; a craw. **6** A growth of hair or beard, especially when short and stiff. **7** A hunting or riding whip with a leather loop for a lash. **8** A collection of things produced: a *crop* of lies. **9** An earmark. **10** The hollow behind a cow's shoulders. **11** An entire hide prepared for sole leather. — *v.* **cropped, crop·ping** *v.t.* **1** To cut or eat off the stems or ends of, as grass or vegetables. **2** To pluck or reap. **3** To cut off closely, as hair; trim, as a dog's ears or tail; formerly, to trim (the ears) of a criminal for punishment. **4** To raise a crop or crops on; cause to bear crops. — *v.i.* **5** To appear above the surface; sprout: with *up* or *out.* **6** To develop or come up unexpectedly: with *up* or *out.* **7** To bear or yield a crop or crops. [OE *cropp*]

crop-eared (krop′ird′) *adj.* **1** Having the ears cropped. **2** With the hair cut short above the ears: said of the Roundheads.

crop·per¹ (krop′ər) *n.* **1** One who raises crops on shares. **2** A tool or machine that crops. **3** A plant that produces a crop: generally with *good, bad, heavy,* etc.: Corn is a heavy *cropper* in Kansas.

crop·per² (krop′ər) *n.* A fall, as from a horse when one is thrown over the horse's head. — **to come a cropper 1** To fall headlong, as from a horse. **2** To fail disastrously in an undertaking. [? < *neck and crop* completely, thoroughly]

cro·quet (krō·kā′) *n.* **1** An outdoor game played by knocking wooden balls through a series of wire arches by means of mallets. **2** The act of croqueting. — *v.i.* **cro·queted** (krō·kād′), **cro·quet·ing** (krō·kā′ing) In croquet, to drive one's opponent's ball away from its objective by placing one's own ball in contact with it and striking the latter sharply, keeping it in position with the foot. [<AF *croquet,* var. of *crochet.* See CROCHET.]

cro·quette (krō·ket′) *n.* A ball or cake of previously cooked, minced food, fried in deep fat or baked. [<F <*croquer* crunch]

cro·sier (krō′zhər) *n.* **1** A staff surmounted by a crook or cross, borne by or before a bishop or archbishop on occasions of ceremony. **2** *Bot.* A circinate or coiled young fern frond. Also spelled *crozier.* [<OF *crocier* staff-bearer <Med. L *crociarius* < *crocia* bishop's crook]

cross (krôs, kros) *n.* **1** A sacred or mystic symbol in many ancient religions, consisting of two intersecting lines, supposed to have been originally emblematic of the union of the active and passive elements in nature. **2** That which resembles a cross: to mark a ballot with a *cross.* **3** An ancient instrument of torture in the form of a cross, on which criminals were fastened and exposed until they died from exhaustion. **4** Any suffering borne patiently for Christ's sake; a trial; tribulation. **5** A structure in the form of or surmounted by a cross, erected in some public place for devotional or memorial purposes. **6** *Biol.* **a** A mixing of varieties or breeds of plants or animals. **b** The product of any intermingling of strains; a hybrid or mongrel. **7** Anything that resembles or is intermediate between two other things: a *cross* between prose and poetry. **8** An old English coin stamped with a cross. **9** *Her.* A figure used as a bearing. **10** An ornament, in some form of the cross, worn as a distinction by knights of various orders and by persons honored for exceptional merit or bravery. **11** *Electr.* The accidental contact of two wires so that a portion of the current from one flows to the other. **12** The geometric mean of two formulas: used in index numbers. — **to take the cross** To turn crusader. — *v.t.* **1** To pass, move or extend from side to side of; traverse; span. **2** To cancel, as by marking with crossed lines: with *off* or *out.* **3** To lay or place over or across: to *cross* the legs. **4** To intersect, as streets or lines. **5** To draw a line across. **6** To meet and pass: Your letter *crossed* mine. **7** To transport across: He *crossed* his army yesterday. **8** To make the sign of the cross upon or over. **9** To obstruct or hinder; thwart. **10** To cause, as plants or animals, to inter-breed; hybridize; crossbreed. **11** *Naut.* To put (a yard) in place across a mast. — *v.i.* **12** To intersect; lie athwart. **13** To pass, move, or extend from side to side; traverse; span. **14** To meet and pass. **15** To breed together; interbreed. **— to cross one's mind** To occur to one. **— to cross one's palm 1** To pay a fortune-teller by marking crosses on his or her palm with a coin and then laying the coin in the fortune-teller's hand. **2** To pay someone money; make a bribe. **— to cross swords** To fight with swords; hence, to contest with. **— to cross up** *Colloq.* To play the traitor to; betray: He *crossed* me *up.* — *adj.* **1** Resulting from or expressive of peevishness or ill-humor; out of humor; disagreeable; peevish. **2** Transverse; crossing; intersecting. **3** Hybrid. **4** Contrary. See synonyms under CAPTIOUS, FRETFUL. — *adv.* **1** Across; cross-wise; transversely. **2** Adversely; contrarily; counter. [OE *cros* <ON *kross* <L *crux*]

cross·band (krôs'band', kros'-) *v.t.* To arrange (plywood) so that the grain in each layer is at right angles to the grain of the adjoining layers. **— cross'band'ing** *n.*

cross·bar (krôs'bär', kros'-) *n.* A transverse bar or line used in any structure. — *v.t.* To secure or mark with transverse bars. **— cross'barred'** *adj.*

cross–bed·ded (krôs'bed'id, kros'-) *adj. Geol.* Characterized by subsidiary beds or layers of rock cutting across the main stratification.

cross·bill (krôs'bil', kros'-) *n.* A finchlike bird (genus *Loxia*), the points of whose mandibles cross each other when the beak is closed.

cross·birth (krôs'bûrth', kros'-) *n. Med.* Any abnormal presentation of a fetus before delivery which requires a manual turning in the womb.

cross·bones (krôs'bōnz', kros'-) *n.* A representation of two bones crossing each other, usually surmounted by a skull, as a symbol of death.

cross·bow (krôs'bō', kros'-) *n.* A medieval missile weapon consisting of a bow fixed transversely on a grooved stock. **— cross'-bow'man** *n.*

cross·breed (krôs'brēd', kros'-) *v.t. & v.i.* **·bred, ·breed·ing** *Biol.* To produce a strain or animal by interbreeding or blending two varieties; mix together; hybridize. — *n.* A strain or animal produced by crossbreeding; a hybrid; mongrel. **— cross'bred'** *adj.*

cross–coun·try (krôs'kun'trē, kros'-) *adj.* Of or pertaining to a route across the country fields and lots, regardless of roads.

cross–cut (krôs'kut', kros'-) *v.t.* **-cut, -cut·ting** To cut crosswise or through; run across; inter-sect. — *adj.* Used or made for the purpose of cutting something across: a *cross-cut* saw. — *n.* A cut across or a shortcut.

cross–ex·am·ine (krôs'ig·zam'in, kros'-) *v.t.* **·ined, ·in·ing 1** To question anew (a witness called by the opposing party) for the purpose of testing the reliability of his previous testimony. **2** To cross-question generally. **— cross'–ex·am'i·na'tion** *n.*

cross–eye (krôs'ī', kros'-) *n.* Strabismus. **— cross'–eyed'** *adj.*

cross–fer·ti·li·za·tion (krôs'fûr'tə·lə·zā'shən, kros'-) *n.* **1** *Biol.* The fertilization of an organism by the union of sexually differentiated reproductive cells or gametes, one from the ovum and one from the sperm. **2** *Bot.* The fertilization of one plant or flower by the pollen from another.

cross–fer·ti·lize (krôs'fûr'tə·līz, kros'-) *v.t.* **·lized, ·liz·ing** To fertilize (a plant or animal) by cross-fertilization.

cross–fig·ure (krôs'fig'yər, kros'-) *n.* A style of pattern in veneer consisting of a roll or dip of the grain approximately at right angles to the long axis of the tree.

cross–fire (krôs'fīr', kros'-) *n.* **1** *Mil.* The intersection of two lines of fire; a shooting from two different points so that the lines of fire cross. **2** Any like situation: a *crossfire* of congratulations. **3** *Electr.* The interference in a telegraph or telephone circuit of impulse currents from another communication channel. — *v.i.* **·fired, ·fir·ing** To shoot from different points so that the lines of fire intersect.

cross–foot (krôs'fŏŏt', kros'-) *n.* A form of clubfoot which compels walking on the outer border of the foot, with the sole turned inward.

cross–grained (krôs'grānd', kros'-) *adj.* **1** Having the grain gnarled and hard to cut: a *cross-grained* board. **2** Hard to please or persuade; stubborn; perverse: a *cross-grained* man.

cross–hair (krôs'hâr', kros'-) *n.* One of two fine threads or strands, as of a spider's web, crossed in the center of the focal plane of an optical instrument, to define the exact point to which the readings of the circle or micrometer refer: also called *cross-wire.*

cross–hatch (krôs'hach', kros'-) *v.t.* To shade, as a picture, by crossed lines, either diagonal or rectangular. **— cross'–hatch'ing** *n.*

cross–head (krôs'hed', kros'-) *n. Mech.* **1** A beam across the top of something; specifically, a block sliding upon one guide bar, or between two or more bars, to move a piston in a straight line, axial with the cylinder. **2** The connection between the piston and the connecting rods of a reciprocating engine.

cross·ing (krôs'ing, kros'-) *n.* **1** The place where something, as a roadway or waterway, may be crossed; a ford. **2** Intersection, as of threads or roads. **3** The act of crossing.

cross·jack (krôs'jak', kros'-) *n. Naut.* The sail carried on the lower yard on the mizzen-mast of a full-rigged ship: commonly altered to *crojik.*

cross–light (krôs'līt', kros'-) *n.* A light whose rays cross other rays, lighting up what these left dark.

cros·sop·te·ryg·i·an (kro·sop'tə·rij'ē·ən) *n. Zool.* Any of a group (*Crossopterygii*) of bony fishes abundant in the Devonian period, having paddle-shaped, lobate fins: they are regarded as the direct ancestors of amphibians. [<NL *Crossopterygii* <Gk. *krossoi* fringe + *pterygia* fins of a fish, pl. dim. of *pteryx* wing]

cross–o·ver (krôs'ō'vər, kros'-) *n.* **1** A place at which one traverses a road, river, etc.; intersection; passageway. **2** The intersection of two electric lines. **3** A part of a woman's coat, dress, or wrap which crosses from one side to the other. **4** *Genetics* An interchange of parts between two homologous chromosomes in meiosis: known also as *recombination.*

cross–patch (krôs'pach', kros'-) *n.* A cranky, ill-tempered person.

cross–peen (krôs'pēn', kros'-) *n.* A chisel-like peen on a hammer head, with a blunted edge parallel to the shaft.

cross–piece (krôs'pēs', kros'-) *n.* A piece of material of any kind crossing another.

cross–pol·li·nate (krôs'pol'ə·nāt, kros'-) *v.t.* **·nat·ed, ·nat·ing** To cross-fertilize.

cross–pur·pose (krôs'pûr'pəs, kros'-) *n.* **1** A purpose which antagonizes another; a conflicting aim. **2** *pl.* A conversational game in which questions and answers having no natural connection are brought together.

cross–ques·tion (krôs'kwes'chən, kros'-) *v.t.* To question minutely or in different ways, especially to elicit facts. — *n.* A question asked in a cross-examination. **— cross'–ques'tion·ing** *n.*

cross–ref·er·ence (krôs'ref'rəns, kros'-) *n.* **1** A reference from one passage in a book or treatise to another passage in the same work. **2** In a library catalog, and in research and documentation, reference from one subject to another.

cross–road (krôs'rōd', kros'-) *n.* A road that crosses another, or that crosses from one main road to another. Also **cross'way'.**

cross–roads (krôs'rōdz', kros'-) *n.* A place where roads cross.

cross–sec·tion (krôs'sek'shən, kros'-) *n.* **1** A plane section of any object cut at right angles to the longitudinal axis. **2** Any specimen, figure, or diagram presenting a representation typical of the whole.

cross–stitch (krôs'stich', kros'-) *n.* **1** A double stitch in the form of a cross. **2** Needlework made with this stitch. — *v.t.* To make or mark with a cross-stitch.

cross–thread (krôs'thred', kros'-) *n.* In hem-stitching, one of those threads remaining in a fabric across the space from which a number of parallel threads have been drawn, and which are divided and fastened into clusters in the process of hemstitching. See illustration under HEMSTITCH.

cross–tie (krôs'tī', kros'-) *n.* A tie or sleeper connecting and supporting the parallel rails of a railroad track. **— cross'–tied'** *adj.*

cross·walk (krôs'wôk', kros'-) *n.* Any lane marked off, usually by white lines, to be used by pedestrians in crossing a street.

cross·wind (krôs'wind', kros'-) *n.* **1** A wind blowing across the take-off or flight path of an aircraft or the course of a ship. **2** Any wind at right angles to a given course or direction.

cross·wise (krôs'wīz', kros'-) *adv.* **1** Across. **2** In the form of a cross. **3** Contrarily; at cross-purposes. Also **cross'ways'.**

crot·a·lus (krot'ə·ləs, krō'tə-) *n.* *pl.* **·li** (-lī) Any snake of a genus (*Crotalus*) typical of the rattlesnake family (*Crotalidae*). [<NL <Gk. *krotalon* rattle] **— crot'a·line** (-lin, -līn) *adj.*

crotch (kroch) *n.* **1** A point of division or divergence; a separation into two parts or branches; bifurcation; fork: the *crotch* of a tree. **2** A forked support for a swinging boom when not in use. **3** The region of the human body where the legs separate from the pelvis. [Prob. <AF *croche* crook]

crotched (krocht) *adj.* **1** Having a crotch; forked. **2** Ill-tempered; cross; peevish; crotchety.

crotch·et (kroch'it) *n.* **1** A whimsical notion; a conceit; an eccentricity. **2** *Music* A quarter note. **3** A small hook. See synonyms under WHIM. [<F *crochet.* See CROCHET.]

crotch·et·y (kroch'ə·tē) *adj.* **1** Whimsical; eccentric. **2** Like a crotchet. See synonyms under FICKLE, QUEER. **— crotch'et·i·ness** *n.*

crotch–wood (kroch'wood') *n.* An elaborately patterned veneer obtained from the portion of a tree where two limbs join.

cro·ton (krōt'n) *n.* **1** Any member of a genus (*Croton*) of widely dispersed trees and shrubs of the spurge family. **2** An ornamental tropical shrub (*Codiaeum variegatum*) grown for its foliage. [<NL <Gk. *krotōn* a tick; so called from the appearance of the seeds]

cro·ton·ic acid (krō·ton'ik, -tō'nik) *Chem.* A compound, $C_4H_6O_2$, obtained from croton oil: used in organic synthesis and as a stabilizer in volatile organic solvents.

croton oil A pale-yellow or brownish-yellow viscid oil obtained from the seeds of a small East Indian tree (*Croton tiglium*): used as a purgative and rubefacient.

crouch (krouch) *v.i.* **1** To stoop or bend low with the limbs pressed to the body, as a person in fear or an animal ready to spring. **2** To cringe; abase oneself; cower. — *v.t.* **3** To bend low. — *n.* A crouching or the position taken in crouching. [<OF *crochir* be bent <*croc* a hook]

croup[1] (krōōp) *n. Pathol.* **1** A disease of the throat characterized by hoarse coughing, laryngeal spasm, and the formation of a false membrane. **2** Loosely, inflammation of the larynx. [Imit.] **— croup'ous, croup'y** *adj.*

croup[2] (krōōp) *n.* The rump; portion of a horse's back behind the saddle. Also **croupe.** [<F *croupe*]

crou·pi·er (krōō'pē·ər, *Fr.* krōō·pyā') *n.* **1** A clerk in charge of a gaming table, collecting winnings and paying losses. **2** The assistant chairman at a public dinner. [<F, lit., one who rides on the croup, an assistant]

crou·ton (krōō'ton, krōō·ton'; *Fr.* krōō·tôn') *n.* One of the small crusts or bits of bread fried in butter or oil, often served in soups, etc. [<F *croûton* <*croûte* crust]

crow (krō) *n.* **1** Any of various omnivorous, rau-cous, oscine birds of the genus *Corvus,* with glossy black plumage; specifically, *C. corone,* the European carrion crow; also, the rook, the raven, and the American species, *C. brachyrhyn-chos.* ◆Collateral adjective: *corvine.* **2** A crowbar. **3** The cry of a cock, or any like sound. **—as the crow flies** In a straight line. **— to eat crow** *Colloq.* To recant a statement; back down; to humiliate oneself. — *v.i.* **1** To utter the cry of a cock. **2** To exult; boast. **3**

To utter sounds expressive of delight, as an infant. —v.t. 4 To announce by crowing. [OE *crāwe*]

crow·bar (krō′bär′) *n.* A straight iron or steel bar, with the point flattened and sometimes set at an angle: used as a lever.

crow·ber·ry (krō′ber′ē, -bər-ē) *n. pl.* **·ries 1** The black berrylike drupe of a low shrubby evergreen (*Empetrum nigrum*) of the family *Emperaceae*: usually called **black crowberry. 2** This plant. **3** The bearberry. [Prob. trans. of G *krähenbeeri*]

crow blackbird A large crowlike bird; especially, the purple grackle.

crowd¹ (kroud) *n.* **1** A numerous collection of persons gathered closely together; multitude; throng. **2** A collection of things. **3** The populace mob. **4** *Colloq.* A particular set of people; a clique. See synonyms under AS-SEMBLY, COMPANY, MOB, THRONG. [< *v.*] —*v.t.* **1** To shove or push. **2** To fill to overflowing, as with a crowd; fill to excess. **3** To cram together; force into a confined space. **4** *Colloq.* To put moral pressure upon; press annoyingly. —*v.i.* **5** To gather in large numbers; throng together. **6** To push forward force one's way. **7** To shove or push. See synonyms under HUSTLE. JAM. —**to crowd off** *Naut.* To work a vessel off from the shore under heavy press of sail. —**to crowd out** To drive out or exclude by pushing or pressing, morally or physically; eliminate by pressure: The press of business has *crowded out* this matter. —**to crowd on sail** *Naut.* To spread a very great amount of sail in proportion to the strength of the wind. [OE *crūdan*] —**crowd′er** *n.*

crowd² (kroud) *n.* An ancient violinlike instrument, used in Ireland and Wales: also spelled *cruth, crwth.* Also **croud, crowth.** [< Welsh *crwth* violin]

crow·foot (krō′foot′) *n. pl.* **·foots** for def. 1. **·feet** for defs. 2–6. **1** Any plant of the genus *Ranunculus* (family *Ranunculaceae*); especially, the common meadow or bulb crowfoot (*R. bulbosus*) of the eastern United States. **2** *Naut.* A number of lines or small divergent cords rove through a euphroe to support an awning. **3** Caltrop (def. 1). **4** An arbitrary mark on drawings as for indicating limits of measurement. **5** *Electr.* A form of battery zinc used in a gravity cell. **6** *Aeron.* Crow's-foot.

crow·hop (krō′hop′) *n.* **1** A short hop. **2** *U.S.* The bucking of a horse with its back arched and legs stiffened.

crown (kroun) *n.* **1** A decorative circlet or covering for the head, especially as a mark of sovereign power. **2** A sovereign ruler: with *the.* **3** Sovereignty. **4** A wreath or garland for the head. **5** A reward; prize. **6** A complete or perfect state or type; acme. **7** The top or summit; crest; the *crown* of a hill. **8** The top of the head: a bald *crown.* **9** The head itself: Jack fell down and broke his *crown.* **10** The upper portion of a hat. **11** *Dent.* **a** The part of a tooth exposed beyond the gum; especially, the grinding surface of a molar. **b** An artificial substitute for a crown. **12** A clerical tonsure. **13** A coin stamped with a crown or crowned head; in England, a five-shilling piece. **14** A knot made with the strands at the end of a rope. **15** *Naut.* The outer point of junction of the two arms of an anchor. **16** *Archit.* **a** The upper projecting part of a cornice; the corona. **b** A lantern or spire formed by converging flying buttresses. **17** A halo. **18** A circlet for candles. **19** A crown lens. See under LENS. **20** The upper part of a tree, including the living branches with their foliage. **21** *Bot.* The point where stem and root unite in a seed plant. **22** *Her.* A bearing representing a crown. **23** The part of a cut gemstone above the girdle. See also CORONA. —*v.t.* **1** To place a crown or garland on the head of. **2** To enthrone; make a monarch of. **3** To surmount; be the topmost part of. **4** To form the ultimate ornament to or aspect of. **5** To endow with honor or dignity. **6** To finish or bring to completion; consummate. **7** To cause to round upward; make convex, as a road. **8** *Colloq.* To hit, as a person, on the head. **9** In checkers, to make into a king. [< AF *coroune* < L *corona*]

crown colony A colonial dependency of Great Britain in which the crown retains control of legislation: usually administered by a governor, with executive and legislative councils.

crown gold Gold 3.9166 fineness, especially as used in British coinage. Compare STERLING.

crown·im·pe·ri·al (kroun′im-pir′ē-əl) *n.* An ornamental plant (*Fritillaria imperialis*) of the lily family, from Persia, bearing a cluster of large, bell-shaped flowers beneath a crown of leaves.

crown land The real estate belonging hereditarily to the English sovereign: now nearly all surrendered for a fixed annual allowance. Also **crown′lands** (kroun′landz′) *n.*

crown-piece (kroun′pēs′) *n.* **1** A piece forming the top or crown of anything. **2** The strap in a bridle that goes over the horse's head and is buckled with the cheek straps. See illustration under HARNESS.

crown prince The heir apparent to a crown, a monarch's oldest living son.

crown princess 1 The wife of a crown prince. **2** The female heir apparent to a sovereign throne.

crown saw A ring-shaped saw with teeth at right angles to its plane, mounted on a cylinder, and operated with a rotary motion.

crown-vetch (kroun′vech′) *n.* Axseed.

crown-work (kroun′wûrk′) *n.* **1** A fortification running into the field, designed to cover some advantageous position and to protect other works. **2** *Dent.* The placing of artificial crowns upon teeth; also, the work so done.

crow·quill (krō′kwil′) *n.* **1** The quill of a crow. **2** A pen made from a crow's quill: used formerly for the finest kind of writing. **3** A fine metallic pen adapted for similar work.

crow's-foot (krōz′foot′) *n. pl.* **-feet 1** One of the wrinkles diverging from the outer corner of the eye. **2** A three-pointed embroidery stitch. **3** *Aeron.* An arrangement of short ropes diverging from a main rope: used to distribute strain in the handling of lighter-than-air craft; also *crowfoot.*

crow's-nest (krōz′nest′) *n.* **1** A small sheltered platform at a ship's masthead, used by the lookout. **2** Any similar lookout station, as one ashore.

croze (krōz) *n.* **1** The groove in the staves of a cask in which the edge of the head is set. **2** A crozer. [? < OF *croz* groove]

cru·cial (krōō′shəl) *adj.* **1** Determining absolutely the truth or falsity of a view or theory; decisive; searching. **2** Having the form of a cross. **3** Severe; excruciating. [< F < L *crux, crucis* cross, torture] —**cru′cial·ly** *adv.* —**cru·ci·al·i·ty** (krōō′shē-al′ə-tē) *n.*

cru·ci·ble (krōō′sə-bəl) *n.* **1** A pot or vessel made of a substance that will stand extreme heat, as clay, sand, graphite, platinum, etc., for melting metals or minerals. **2** The hollow place in the bottom of a furnace. **3** A trying and purifying test. [< Med. L *crucibulum* earthen pot]

crucible steel *Metall.* A high-grade steel made by reheating small batches of wrought iron with charcoal, ferromanganese, or other special steels in crucibles placed in specially designed furnaces.

cru·ci·fer (krōō′sə-fər) *n.* **1** Any plant of a large family (Cruciferae) of annual and perennial herbs characterized by pungent, watery juice and regular flowers with four petals in the form of a cross, as mustard, cress, etc. **2** One who bears a cross in a religious procession. [< LL < L *crux* cross + *ferre* bear] —**cru·cif·er·ous** (krōō·sif′ər-əs) *adj.*

cross. *Bot.* Having cruciate flowers; pertaining to or resembling the *Cruciferae.*

cru·ci·fix (krōō′sə-fiks) *n.* **1** A cross bearing an effigy of Christ crucified. **2** The cross as a Christian emblem. [< OF *crucefix* < L *cruci fixus* one hanged on a cross < *crux* cross + *figere* fasten]

cru·ci·fix·ion (krōō′sə-fik′shən) *n.* **1** The act of putting to death by nailing or binding to a cross. **2** Death upon the cross; especially, **the Crucifixion** of Christ on Mount Calvary. **3** Any pictorial representation of Christ's death.

CRUCIFIX
(*def. 1*)

cru·ci·form (krōō′sə-fôrm) *adj.* Cross-shaped; cruciate. [< L *crux* cross + -FORM]

cru·ci·fy (krōō′sə-fī) *v.t.* **·fied, ·fy·ing 1** To put to death by fastening to a cross. **2** Figuratively, to mortify; subdue, as impulses or desires: to *crucify* the lusts of the flesh. **3** To torture; torment. [< OF *crucifier,* ult. < L *cruci figere* fasten to a cross] —**cru′ci·fi′er** *n.*

crude (krōōd) *adj.* **crud·er, crud·est 1** In a state needing preparation for use; not refined; raw; uncooked. **2** Not having reached its complete or mature form; unripe; immature. **3** Lacking in completeness of form or arrangement; exhibiting roughness; incomplete. **4** Characterized by lack of knowledge or skill; imperfect; superficial: a *crude* effort. **5** Not disguised; bare: *crude* statements. **6** Lacking in tact or good taste; uncultured: a *crude* joke. —*n.* Petroleum as it comes from the well; unrefined petroleum and hydrocarbons. [< L *crudus* immature. Akin to CRUEL.]

cru·di·ty (krōō′də·tē) *n. pl.* **·ties 1** The state or quality of being crude. **2** A crude act, remark, etc.

cru·el (krōō′əl) *adj.* **1** Disposed to inflict suffering; indifferent to others' suffering; pitiless. **2** Unreasonably severe; harsh; distressing. See synonyms under BARBAROUS. HARD. IMPLACABLE. ◆ Homophone: *crewel.* [< F < L *crudelis* severe. Akin to CRUDE.] —**cru′el·ly** *adv.*

cru·el·ty (krōō′əl·tē) *n. pl.* **·ties 1** The disposition to inflict pain. **2** Indifference to the suffering of other beings; inhumanity. **3** The act of inflicting suffering. **4** An inhuman or brutal act.

cru·et (krōō′it) *n.* **1** A small glass bottle, as for vinegar. **2** *Brit.* A caster. [< AF, dim. of OF *crue* pot]

cruise (krōōz) *v.* **cruised, cruis·ing** *v.i.* **1** To sail about on the ocean with no set destination, as for pleasure or in search of plunder. **2** *Colloq.* To wander about; roam. **3** To move or proceed at a moderate speed, or at the optimum speed for sustained travel: This car *cruises* at 50 miles per hour. —*v.t.* **4** To sail over or about. **5** To proceed aimlessly through or across; wander. —*n.* **1** A voyage at sea; a sailing to and fro or from place to place. **2** A cruse. [< Du. *kruisen* < *kruis* cross < L *crux* cross]

cruise missile A guided missile that flies like an airplane at low altitudes.

cruis·er (krōō′zər) *n.* **1** A person, vehicle, or ship that cruises. **2** A fast, maneuverable warship, having long cruising radius, with medium tonnage and armament. **3** A small power vessel equipped with complete living arrangements: also called **cabin cruiser.**

crul·ler (krul′ər) *n.* A small, twisted cake of sweetened dough, fried brown in deep fat: also spelled *kruller.* [< Du. < *krullen* curl]

crumb (krum) *n.* **1** A small bit, as of crumbled bread. **2** A morsel. **3** The soft inner part of a loaf, as distinguished from the crust. —*v.t.* **1** To break into small pieces with the fingers; crumble. **2** In cooking, to dress or cover with bread crumbs. **3** *Colloq.* To brush crumbs from. Also **crum.** [OE *cruma; b* added on analogy with *dumb, lamb,* etc.]

crum·ble (krum′bəl) *v.t. & v.i.* **·bled, ·bling** To fall or cause to fall to small pieces; disintegrate; decay. —*n.* **1** A crumb. **2** Any crumbly material. [Freq. of CRUMB, *v.*] —**crum′bly** *adj.*

crumb·y (krum′ē) *adj.* **crumb·i·er, crumb·i·est 1** Having crumbs. **2** Soft, like the crumb of bread. **3** *U.S. Slang* Inferior; shoddy; lousy. Also **crum′my.**

crum·pet (krum′pit) *n.* A thin, leavened batter cake baked on a gridiron and usually toasted and buttered. [Short for *crumpet cake,* ME *crompid cake,* pp. of *crompen* curl up]

crum·ple (krum′pəl) *v.t. & v.i.* **·pled, ·pling 1** To become or cause to become wrinkled; rumple. **2** *Colloq.* To collapse. —*n.* A wrinkle, as in cloth or the earth; anything crumpled. [Freq. of obs. *crump,* var. of CRIMP] —**crum′pled** *adj.*

crunch (krunch) *v.t.* **1** To chew with a brittle, crushing sound; crush with the teeth. **2** To crush or grind noisily. —*v.i.* **3** To chew noisily. **4** To move or advance with a crushing sound. —*n.* **1** The act or sound of crunching. **2** *U.S. Slang* A critical time, as the moment of decision. [Imit.]

cru·node (krōō′nōd) *n. Math.* A point at which a curve crosses itself and therefore has two tangents. [< L *crux* cross + NODE] —**cru·no′dal** *adj.*

cru·or (krōō'ôr) *n.* Clotted blood; gore. [< L, gore]

crup·per (krup'ər) *n.* **1** The looped strap that goes under a horse's tail. **2** The rump of a horse; croup. [< F *croupière* < *croupe* CROUP²]

cru·ral (krōōr'əl) *adj.* Of or pertaining to the leg or the thigh. [< L *cruralis* < *crus* leg]

crus (krus) *n. pl.* **cru·ra** (krōōr'ə) **1** *Anat.* **a** That part of the leg between the knee and the ankle. **b** *Usually pl.* A stalk or peduncle: applied to compact masses of fibers which connect different parts of the brains. **2** Any part resembling or likened to a leg. [< L, leg]

cru·sade (krōō·sād') *n.* **1** Any of the military expeditions undertaken by European Christians from the 11th through the 13th century to recover the Holy Land from the Moslems. **2** Any expedition under papal sanction against heathens or heretics. **3** Any vigorous concerted movement or cause, especially against public evil. —*v.i.* **·sad·ed, ·sad·ing** To go on or engage in a crusade. [< Sp. *cruzada* < Med. L *cruciata* a crossing < *cruciare* mark with a cross < L *crux* a cross; infl. in form by related F *croisade*] — **cru·sad'er** *n.*

cruse (krōōz, krōōs) *n.* A small bottle, flask, or jug; cruet: also spelled *cruise.* [? < ON *krūs* jar, pot]

cru·set krōō'sit) *n.* A goldsmith's melting pot. [< F *creuset*]

crush (krush) *v.t.* **1** To press or squeeze out of shape; mash. **2** To smash or grind into fine fragments or particles. **3** To obtain or extract by pressure. **4** To press upon; crowd. **5** To rumple or press out of shape. **6** To put down; subdue; conquer. **7** *Archaic* To burden or oppress. **8** *Rare* To drink. —*v.i.* **9** To become broken or misshapen by pressure. See synonyms under BREAK, CONQUER, JAM, REPRESS, SUBDUE. —*n.* **1** A violent colliding; breaking, bruising, or deforming by violent pressure. **2** A pressing or crowding together; a crowd; jam. **3** *Colloq.* A sudden romantic attachment; infatuation. [< OF *croissir* break < Gmc.] —**crush'er** *n.*

crush hat 1 A soft felt hat that can be folded without injury. **2** A collapsible high hat; opera hat.

crust (krust) *n.* **1** A hard, thin coating, usually over something softer. **2** The outer part of bread; a bit of bread, especially if stale and hard. **3** The pastry envelope of a pie or the like. **4** An incrustation, especially from wine, on the interior of bottles. **5** A coating, as of coagulated blood or other solidified exudate of the body. **6** The cold, exterior portion or zone of the earth. **7** The part of a horse's hoof on which the shoe is nailed. **8** A crisp firm surface upon snow. **9** *Slang* Insolence; impertinence. —*v.t. & v.i.* To cover with or acquire a crust. [< L *crusta* crust] —**crust'al** *adj.*

crus·ta·cean (krus·tā'shən) *n.* One of a class of arthropods *(Crustacea)* having crustlike shells, and generally aquatic, including lobsters, crabs, barnacles, sow-bugs, etc. —*adj.* Of or pertaining to the *Crustacea.* [< NL *Crustacea* < L *crusta* crust; with ref. to the shell]

crus·ta·ceous (krus·tā'shəs) *adj.* **1** Having, or pertaining to, a crustlike shell. **2** Crustacean.

crust·er (krus'tər) *n. U.S.* One who hunts game, especially deer or moose, in deep snow when the ice crust will hold the weight of a man but not the quarry: a term of contempt. Also **crust'hunt·er.**

crust·y (krus'tē) *adj.* **crust·i·er, crust·i·est 1** Crustlike. **2** Having or hard as a crust. **3** Morosely curt in manner or speech; surly. See synonyms under MOROSE. —**crust'i·ly** *adv.* —**crust'i·ness** *n.*

crutch (kruch) *n.* **1** A staff with a crosspiece fitting under the armpit, used as a support in walking. **2** Any one of various mechanical devices involving the principle or use of such a support. **3** *Naut.* A forked support for a swinging boom when not in use. **4** The horn on a woman's saddle. **5** A rack. **6** A hooked rod used to immerse sheep while washing. **7** The crotch of a human body. —*v.t.* To prop up, as on crutches. [OE *crycc*]

crutched (krucht) *adj.* Bearing the sign of the cross: The *Crutched* Friars. [Earlier *crouched,* pp. of obs. *crouch* mark with a cross]

cruth, crwth (krōōth) See CROWD².

crux (kruks) *n. pl.* **crux·es** or **cru·ces** (krōō'sēz) **1** A pivotal, fundamental, or vital point. **2** A cross. **3** A tormenting or baffling problem; a perplexing difficulty. [< L, a cross]

cru·zei·ro (krōō·zā'rō, *Pg.* -rōō) *n.* The gold monetary unit of Brazil, equivalent to 100 centavos. [< *Pg.* < *cruz* cross < L *crux*]

cry (krī) *v.* **cried, cry·ing** *v.t.* **1** To utter loudly or shout out; exclaim. **2** To proclaim loudly and publicly; advertise loudly, as goods or services. **3** *Archaic* To beg or implore: I *cry* you mercy. **4** To affect (one) in §ome specified way by weeping: to *cry* oneself to sleep. —*v.i.* **5** To speak, call, or appeal loudly; shout; yell. **6** To utter sounds of grief and lamentation; weep; sob. **7** To weep or shed tears inaudibly. **8** To make characteristic calls: said of animals. See synonyms under CALL, ROAR. —**to cry down 1** To disparage. **2** To silence or put down by cries. —**to cry quits** To declare to be even, or that neither has the advantage. —*n. pl.* **cries 1** A loud or passionate utterance; a call; shout; yell. **2** The act of weeping. **3** An earnest appeal; entreaty. **4** Advertisement by outcry; proclamation: the hawker's *cry.* **5** General report or rumor; common saying; public opinion. **6** A pack of dogs; hence, in contempt, a company of persons; party. **7** A subject or topic made temporarily important for political purposes; watchword; party phrase. **8** A word or phrase to rally men in battle; war cry. **9** Demand; requisition: a *cry* for clean streets. **10** The characteristic call of a bird or an animal. —**a far cry** The farthest distance over which a cry can be heard; hence, a long way. —**in full cry** In full pursuit, as hunting dogs when baying in chorus. [< F *crier* < L *quiritare* call out]

cry·ba·by (krī'bā'bē) *n. pl.* **·bies** A person, especially a child, given to crying or complaining over his circumstances.

cry·ing (krī'ing) *adj.* Calling for immediate action or redress; self–proclaiming; notorious: a *crying* shame.

cryo– *combining form* Cold; frost: *cryogenic.* [< Gk. *kryos* frost]

cry·o·bi·ol·o·gy (krī'ō·bī·ol'ə·j) *n.* The study of the effects of freezing and low temperatures on living organisms.

cry·o·gen (krī'ə·jən) *n.* A freezing mixture.

cry·o·gen·ics (krī'ə·jen'iks) *n.* The branch of physics dealing with the phenomena of extreme cold.

cry·o·hy·drate (krī'ə·hī'drāt) *n.* A crystalline eutectic mixture of constant composition and melting point, as of salt with water, which forms below the freezing point of water.

cry·o·lite (krī'ə·līt) *n.* A vitreous, snow–white, translucent fluoride of sodium and aluminum, occurring in Greenland: used in the production of aluminum, soda, and glass, to which it gives a milky hue. Also spelled *kryolite, kryolith.*

cry·om·e·ter (krī·om'ə·tər) *n.* An instrument for measuring a lower temperature than the ordinary mercury thermometer will indicate, as an alcohol thermometer. [< CRYO– + -METER]

cry·oph·o·rus (krī·of'ər·əs) *n.* An instrument for showing the decrease of temperature in water through evaporation: socalled because such decrease may freeze the water. [< CRYO– +-PHOROUS]

cry·o·scope (krī'ə·skōp) *n.* An instrument used for determining the freezing point of liquids and other substances.

cry·os·co·py (krī·os'kə·pē) *n.* The study of the freezing points of solutions, especially in relation to the lowered freezing point of the solute.

cry·o·stat (krī'ə·stat) *n.* A receptacle, constructed on the principle of the Dewar flask, for containing substances studied in low–temperature research; a heat regulator for low temperatures.

cry·o·ther·a·py (krī'ə·ther'ə·pē) *n. Med.* The use of low or freezing temperatures as a therapeutic measure.

crypt (kript) *n.* **1** A secret recess or vault; especially, one used, as in the catacombs, for interment. **2** A vault under some churches, used as a chapel, cemetery, etc. **3** *Physiol.* A minute follicle or secreting cavity of the skin or mucous membrane. [< L *crypta* < Gk. *kryptē* < *kryptos* hidden. Doublet of GROTTO.]

cryp·ta·nal·y·sis (krip'tə·nal'ə·sis) *n. pl.* **·ses** (-sēz) The scientific study and conversion into plain text of cryptograms, ciphers, codes, and other forms of secret communication to which the key is not known. [< CRYPTO– + ANALYSIS]

cryp·tes·the·sia (krip'təs·thē'zhə, -zhē·ə) *n. Psychol.* Any of various modes of supernormal sensibility, as clairvoyance, telepathy, extrasensory perception, etc. [< CRYPTO– + ESTHESIA]

cryp·tic (krip'tik) *adj.* **1** Secret; occult; arcane. **2** Tending to concealment; puzzling; mysterious. Also **cryp'ti·cal.** [< LL *crypticus* < Gk. *kryptikos* < *kryptos* hidden]

crypto– *combining form* Hidden; secret: *cryptogram.* Also, before vowels, **crypt–.** [< Gk. *kryptos* hidden]

cryp·to·clas·tic (krip'tō·klas'tik) *adj. Geol.* Composed of microscopic fragmental grains, derived from preexisting rocks, as shale. [< CRYPTO– + CLASTIC]

cryp·to·cli·mate (krip'tō·klī'mit) *n.* The range of climatic conditions found within a house, building, or other enclosed structure, especially as compared with the *microclimate* of the local area and the *macroclimate* of the entire region.

cryp·to·crys·tal·line (krip'tō·kris'tə·lin, -lēn) *adj. Mineral.* Possessing a crystalline structure which cannot be resolved into distinct individuals even under the microscope: opposed to *phanerocrystalline.*

cryp·to·gam (krip'tə·gam) *n. Bot.* **1** Any of a former division of plants *(Cryptogamia)* that have no true flowers, but propagate by spores, as algae, fungi, lichens, and mosses. **2** A plant lacking true seeds: opposed to *phanerogam.* Also **cryp'to·phyte** (-fīt). [< CRYPTO– + Gk. *gamos* marriage] —**cryp'to·gam'ic** *adj.* —**cryp·tog·a·mous** (krip·tog'ə·məs) *adj.*

cryp·tog·a·my (krip·tog'ə·mē) *n. Bot.* The state or condition of being cryptogamic or having concealed fructification. [< CRYPTO– + -GAMY]

cryp·tog·e·nous (krip·toj'ə·nəs) *adj.* Of obscure origin. Also **cryp·to·ge·net·ic** (krip'tō·jə·net'ik), **cryp·to·gen·ic** (krip'tə·jen'ik). [< CRYPTO– + -GENOUS]

cryp·to·gram (krip'tə·gram) *n.* A written communication in the form of symbols chosen arbitrarily but according to a system permitting reconversion to the original plain text, as a cipher or code.

cryp·to·graph (krip'tə·graf, -gräf) *n.* **1** A cryptogram. **2** A system of cipher–writing; a cipher. —**cryp·to·ra·pher** (krip·tog'rə·fər), **cryp·tog'ra·phist** *n.* —**cryp'to·graph'ic** *adj.*

cryp·tog·ra·phy (krip·tog'rə·fē) *n.* **1** The art and process of writing in cipher. **2** Any system of writing in secret characters.

cryp·tol·o·gy (krip·tol'ə·jē) *n.* Enigmatic language; cryptography. [CRYPTO– + -LOGY]

cryp·tom·ne·sia (krip'təm·nē'zhə, -zhē·ə) *n. Psychol.* A form of memory which causes experiences to appear to the subject as new, without conscious recognition of or identification with their original source. [< CRYPTO– + Gk. *mnasthai* remember]

cryp·to·zo·ic (krip'tə·zō'ik) *adj. Zool.* Of, pertaining to, or designating animals which live in dark and hidden places.

crys·tal (kris'təl) *n.* **1** The solid form assumed by many minerals; specifically, colorless transparent quartz, or rock crystal. **2** *Physics* A homogeneous solid body, exhibiting a definite and symmetrical internal structure, with geometrically arranged cleavage planes and external faces that assume

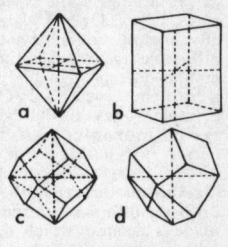

TYPES OF CRYSTALS
a. Tetragonal pyramid.
b. Tetragonal prism.
c. Dodecahedron.
d. Deltahedron.

any of a group of patterns associated with peculiarities of atomic structure. **3** Flint glass, or any fine glass, especially as made into high-grade tableware and decorative pieces. **4** A watchglass. **5** A clear, white diamond. **6** A specially shaped and ground piece of quartz or similar material, used to improve radio reception. —*adj.* Composed of or like crystal; extremely clear; limpid. [< OF *cristal* < L *crystallum* clear ice < Gk. *krystallos* < *krystainein* freeze < *kryos* frost] —**crys·tal·lic** (kris·tal′ik) *adj.*

crystal analysis *Physics* The study of the molecular, atomic, and ionic configuration in crystals, aided by X-ray methods.

crystal ball A ball of crystal or glass used in crystal-gazing.

crys·tal–gaz·ing (kris′təl·gā′zing) *n.* The act of looking into a ball of crystal and pretending to see pictures within it or to exercise divination by it; crystallomancy: also **crystal vision.**

crystal grating *Physics* A very fine diffraction grating consisting of a suitably prepared and mounted crystal: used in X-ray work.

crys·tal·lif·er·ous (kris′tə·lif′ər·əs) *adj.* Bearing or containing crystals. [< L *crystallum* clear ice, crystal + -(I)FEROUS]

crys·tal·lig·er·ous (kris′tə·lij′ər·əs) *adj.* Containing crystals. [< L *crystallum* clear ice, crystal + -(I)GEROUS]

crys·tal·line (kris′tə·lin, -lēn) *adj.* **1** Of, pertaining to, or like crystal or crystals: distinguished from *clastic.* **2** Transparent; pure; pellucid: the *crystalline* lens of the eye. —*n.* A crystallized or partly crystallized substance. [< F *cristallin* < L *crystallinus* < Gk. *krystallinos* < *krystallos.* See CRYSTAL.]

crystalline lens *Anat.* A transparent, biconvex, lentiform body situated between the iris and the vitreous body of the eye, serving to focus an image upon the retina. Also **crystalline humor.**

crys·tal·lite (kris′tə·līt) *n. Mineral.* One of certain minute, spherical, rod–shaped or hairlike bodies without the true properties of a crystal, but resulting from a crystallizing tendency, observable in thin sections of igneous rock and in slags. [< L *crystallum* clear ice, crystal + -ITE¹] —**crys·tal·lit·ic** (kris′tə·lit′ik) *adj.*

crys·tal·li·tis (kris′tə·lī′təs) *n. Pathol.* Inflammation of the crystalline lens. [< NL < Gk. *krystallos* crystal + -ITIS]

crys·tal·lize (kris′tə·līz) *v.* **·lized, ·liz·ing** *v.t.* **1** To cause to form crystals or become crystalline. **2** To bring to definite and permanent form. —*v.i.* **3** To assume the form of crystals. **4** To assume definite and permanent form. —**crys′tal·liz′a·ble** *adj.* —**crys′·tal·li·za′tion** *n.*

crystallo– *combining form* Crystal: *crystallography.* Also, before vowels, **crystall–.** [< Gk. *krystallos* crystal]

crys·tal·lo·graph·ic (kris′tə·lə·graf′ik) *adj.* Of or pertaining to crystallography. Also **crys′·tal·lo·graph′i·cal.** —**crys′tal·lo·graph′i·cal·ly** *adv.*

crystallographic axes Imaginary lines within a crystal, to which its faces can be referred.

crystallographic indices A series of numbers indicating the relative intercepts of a crystal face upon the crystal axes.

crys·tal·log·ra·phy (kris′tə·log′rə·fē) *n.* The science of crystals, including the study of their geometrical, physical, and chemical structure.

crys·tal·loid (kris′tə·loid) *adj.* Like a crystal; of or pertaining to the crystal state of matter. —*n.* **1** *Chem.* One of a class of substances, usually crystallizable, whose solutions are readily diffusible: distinguished from *colloid.* **2** *Bot.* A crystal–like protein body found in plant cells: a protein crystal. [< Gk. *krystalloeidēs* like crystal] —**crys′tal·loi′dal** *adj.*

crys·tal·lo·man·cy (kris′tə·lə·man′sē) *n.* Divination by gazing into a crystal globe. [< CRYSTALLO- + -MANCY]

crys·tal·lon (kris′tə·lon) *n.* A crystal fragment dropped into a saturated solution to provide a nucleus around which the solution may crystallize: also called *seed crystal.* [< Gk., neut. of *krystallos* of crystal]

crys·tal·lose (kris′tə·lōs) *n.* Soluble saccharin: a sweetening compound. [< CRYSTALL(O)- + -OSE]

crystal set A radio receiving set operating with a crystal detector but without vacuum tubes.

crystal system Any of the variously named

and classified fundamental patterns by which all crystals may be identified: determined on the basis of the imaginary axes drawn from each face or edge through the center of the crystal. Six major systems are generally recognized. See following table.

CRYSTAL SYSTEMS

	Name	No. of axes	Type example
I	Isometric	3	fluorite, garnet
II	Tetragonal	3	cassiterite, zircon
III	Hexagonal	4	calcite, quartz
IV	Orthorhombic	3	sulfur, topaz
V	Monoclinic	3	gypsum, augite
VI	Triclinic	3	rhodonite

crystal violet A derivative of rosaniline, used as an indicator in medicine and bacteriology.

Cs *Chem.* Cesium (symbol Cs).

cte·nid·i·um (tə·nid′ē·əm) *n. pl.* **·nid·i·a** (-nid′-ē·ə) *Zool.* **1** One of the respiratory organs of mollusks, resembling a comb. **2** One of the comblike structures situated on the toes of some birds. [< NL < Gk. *ktenidion,* dim. of *kteis* comb]

cteno– *combining form* Comb: *ctenophore.* Also, before vowels, **cten–.** [< Gk. *kteis, ktenos* comb]

cten·oid (ten′oid, tē′noid) *adj. Biol.* Having a comblike margin, as certain plants, and the scales in ctenophores. [< Gk. *ktenoeidēs* like a comb]

cten·o·phore (ten′ə·fôr, -fōr, tē′nə-) *n.* One of the *Ctenophora,* a subphylum or phylum of coelenterates which includes the marine comb jellies. [< NL *Ctenophora* < Gk. *kteis, ktenos* comb + *pherein* bear]

Cu *Chem.* Copper (symbol Cu). [L *cuprum*]

cua·ren·ta (kwä·ren′tä) *n.* A silver coin of Cuba, equal in value to forty centavos. [< Sp., forty]

cub (kub) *n.* **1** The young of the bear, fox, wolf, and certain other carnivores; a whelp. **2** A rough, awkward, uncouth, or ill-mannered youth. **3** A beginner or learner; an apprentice. —*adj.* Young; inexperienced: a *cub* reporter; *cub* pilot. [Origin uncertain] —**cub′bish** *adj.* —**cub′bish·ly** *adv.*

Cu·ba (kyōō′bə) The largest island of the West Indies, comprising a republic; 44,164 square miles; capital, Havana. —**Cu′ban** *adj. & n.*

cu·ba·ture (kyōō′bə·chŏor) *n.* **1** The process of determining the cubical contents of a solid. **2** Cubical contents. Also **cu·bage** (kyōō′bij). [< L *cubus* cube]

cub·by·hole (kub′ē·hōl′) *n.* A small, enclosed, space. [< *cubby,* dim. of dial. E *cub* shed + HOLE]

cube¹ (kyōōb) *n.* **1** *Geom.* A solid bounded by six equal squares and having all its angles right angles. **2** *Math.* The third power of a quantity; the product of three equal factors. —*v.t.* **cubed, cub·ing 1** To raise (a number or quantity) to the third power. **2** To find the cubic capacity of. **3** To form or cut into cubes or cubelike shapes; dice: to *cube* potatoes. [< MF < LL *cubus* < Gk. *kybos* cube, die²]

cu·be² (kōō′bā) *n.* A substance extracted from the roots of *Lonchocarpus nicou,* a leguminous plant native in Peru; it contains rotenone and tephrosin and is used as a fish poison. [< Sp. *quibey* < native name]

cu·beb (kyōō′beb) *n.* A berry of an East Indian shrub (*Piper cubeba*) of the pepper family: used in treating urinary and bronchial diseases and often smoked in the form of cigarettes. [< MF *cubèbe* < Med.L *cubeba* < Arabic *kabābah*]

cube root The number which, taken three times as a factor, produces a given number called its cube: 4 is the *cube root* of 64.

cu·bic (kyōō′bik) *adj.* **1** Formed like a cube. **2** Being, or equal to, a cube whose edge is a given unit: a *cubic* foot. **3** *Math.* Of the third power or degree. Also **cu′bi·cal.** [< F *cubique* < L *cubicus* < Gk. *kybikos* < *kybos* cube.] —**cu′bi·cal·ly** *adv.*

cu·bi·cle (kyōō′bi·kəl) *n.* **1** A bedroom. **2** A partially enclosed section of a dormitory. **3** Hence, any small room. [< L *cubiculum* bedroom < *cubare* lie down]

cubic measure A unit or system of units for measuring volume, or the amount of space occupied in three dimensions. The principal customary units are given in the table below. See also METRIC SYSTEM.

144 cubic inches (cu. in.)	=	1 board foot (bd. ft.)
1728 cubic inches	=	1 cubic foot (cu. ft.; ft.³)
27 cubic feet	=	1 cubic yard (cu. yd.; yd.³)
128 cubic feet	=	1 cord (cd.)

cu·bic·u·lar (kyōō·bik′yə·lər) *adj.* Of or pertaining to a bedchamber; private. Also **cu·bic′u·lar·y** (-ler′ē). [< L *cubicularis* < *cubiculum.* See CUBICLE.]

cu·bic·u·lum (kyōō·bik′yə·ləm) *n. pl.* **·la** (-lə) **1** A small bedchamber; cubicle. **2** A burial chamber with recesses in the walls for dead bodies, as in the Roman catacombs. Also *Obs.* **cu·bic′u·lo** (-lō). [< L]

cu·bi·form (kyōō′bə·fôrm) *adj.* Shaped like a cube.

cu·bism (kyōō′biz·əm) *n.* A school of modern art concerned with the analysis of form by means of abstract and geometric representation, rather than with a realistic representation of nature. —**cu′bist** *adj. & n.*

cu·bit (kyōō′bit) *n.* An ancient measure of length, originally represented by the length of the forearm: about 18 to 20 inches. [< L *cubitum* elbow]

cu·bi·tus (kyōō′bə·təs) *n. pl.* **·ti** (-tī) **1** A cubit. **2** *Entomol.* **a** The fifth longitudinal vein in an insect's wing. **b** The tibia of the anterior leg. **c** The radial or stigmal vein in the Hemiptera. **3** *Anat.* The forearm. [< L, var. of *cubitum.* See CUBIT.]

cu·boid (kyōō′boid) *n.* **1** *Anat.* The outer distal bone of the tarsus or ankle. **2** *Geom.* A rectangular parallelepiped. —*adj.* Shaped like a cube: also **cu·boi′dal.** [< Gk. *kyboeidēs* like a cube]

cub scout A member of a subdivision of the Boy Scouts, comprising boys eight to eleven years of age.

cuck·ing stool (kuk′ing) A chair in which disorderly women, scolds, and dishonest tradesmen were tied, left to public derision, and sometimes ducked. [< obs. *cuck* defecate]

cuck·old (kuk′əld) *n.* The husband of an unfaithful wife. —*v.t.* To make a cuckold of. [< OF *cucuault* < *cucu* cuckoo; with ref. to the cuckoo's habit of laying its eggs in another bird's nest.] —**cuck′old·ly, cuck′old·y** *adj.*

cuck·oo (kōōk′ōō) *n.* **1** A bird belonging to a large family (*Cuculidae*), many species of which, as the common European cuckoo (*Cuculus canorus*), deposit their eggs in the nests of other birds to be hatched and cared for. **2** Any of various birds similar to the English cuckoo, as the Australasian small owl, or the American yellow-billed cuckoo (*Coccyzus americanus*) and the black-billed cuckoo (*C. erythrophthalmus*). **3** One who repeats the saying of another or follows slavishly, as in politics; a fool; ninny. **4** A cuckoo's cry. **5** One who commits adultery. —*v.* **·ooed, ·oo·ing** *v.t.* To repeat without cessation. —*v.i.* To utter or imitate the cry of the cuckoo. —*adj.* (also kōō′kōō) *Slang* Slightly deranged mentally; crazy; silly. [< OF *cucu, coucou;* imit.]

cuckoo bud A buttercup or kingcup.

cuckoo clock A clock in which a mechanical cuckoo announces the hours.

cuckoo flower **1** A species of bittercress (*Cardamine pratensis*) with showy flowers: also called *lady-smock.* **2** Ragged robin.

cuckoo pint A tuberous herb (*Arum maculatum*) of the arum family, with long leaves and erect, purple-spotted spathes: also called *Bobbin-and-Joan, lords-and-ladies, wake robin.*

cuckoo spit **1** A frothy secretion exuded upon plants by the larvae of certain insects, as froghoppers: also called *frog spit.* **2** An insect that secretes froth; a froghopper.

cu·cu·ba·no (kōō′kə·bä′nō) *n.* The West Indian fire beetle. [< Sp.]

cu·cu·li·form (kyōō·kyōō′lə·fôrm) *adj. Ornithol.* Of or pertaining to an order of birds (*Cuculiformes*) including the cuckoos and roadrunners. [< NL *Cuculiformis* < L *cuculus* cuckoo]

cu·cul·late (kyōō′kə·lāt, kyōō·kul′āt) *adj.* **1** Hood-shaped. **2** *Bot.* Having a hoodlike part, as certain leaves. Also **cu·cul·lat·ed** (kyōō′kə·lā′tid, kyōō·kul′ā·tid). [< LL *cucullatus* < L *cucullus* hood]

cu·cul·li·form (kyōō·kul′ə·fôrm) *adj.* Having the form of a hood; cucullate. [< L *cucullus* hood + -FORM]

cu·cum·ber (kyōō′kum·bər) *n.* **1** The oblong, hard-rinded fruit of a creeping plant of the gourd family (*Cucumis sativus*), cultivated as a vegetable. **2** The plant. [< OF *cocombre* < L *cucumis, -eris*]

cucumber tree **1** A straight, tall tree (*Magno-*

lia acuminata) of the eastern United States, bearing a fruit resembling a small cucumber. 2 An East Indian tree *(Averrhoa bilimbi)* cultivated for its edible acid berries and its flowers.

cu·cu·mi·form (kyōō·kyōō′mə·fôrm) *adj.* Having the form of a cucumber. [< L *cucumis* cucumber + -FORM]

cu·cur·bit (kyōō·kûr′bit) *n.* 1 The body of an alembic, originally gourd-shaped. 2 Any similar vessel, as the cucurbitula. 3 Any plant of the gourd family. [< F *cucurbite* < L *cucurbita* gourd] —**cu·cur·bi·ta·ceous** (kyōō·kûr′bə·tā′shəs) *adj.*

cu·cur·bit·u·la (kyōō′kər·bit′yōō·lə) *n.* A cupping glass. [< L, dim. of *cucurbita* gourd, cupping glass]

cud (kud) *n.* 1 Food forced up into the mouth from the first stomach of a ruminant and chewed over again. 2 The rumen. [OE *cudu, cwida* cud]

cud·bear (kud′bâr) *n.* 1 A purplish-red dyestuff, similar to archil, made from lichens and used as a coloring for foods and drugs. 2 The lichen (genus *Lecanora*) that furnishes the dye. [Coined from his first name by Dr. *Cuthbert* Gordon, who first made it]

cud·dle (kud′l) *v.* **·dled, ·dling** *v.t.* To protect and caress fondly within a close embrace; hug. —*v.i.* To lie close; hug one another; nestle together. —*n.* An embrace; caress. [? < dial. E (Northern) *couth* snug, cozy] —**cud′dle·some** *adj.* —**cud′dly** *adj.*

cudg·el (kuj′əl) *n.* A short, thick stick used as a club. —**to take up the cudgels** To enter into a contest or controversy. —*v.t.* **·eled** or **·elled, ·el·ing** or **·el·ling** To beat with a cudgel. See synonyms under BEAT. —**to cudgel one's brains** To think hard; puzzle. [OE *cycgel*] —**cudg′el·er** or **cudg′el·ler** *n.*

cudg·el-play (kuj′əl·plā′) *n.* The art of using quarterstaves, singlesticks, or similar weapons, or a contest in which they are used.

cud·weed (kud′wēd′) *n.* Any one of various plants of the composite family (genus *Gnaphalium* or *Helichrysum*), as the everlasting. [< CUD + WEED; because given to cattle]

cue[1] (kyōō) *n.* 1 A long, tapering rod, used in billiards, pool, etc., to strike the cue ball. 2 A queue of hair. 3 A queue or line of persons. —*v.t.* **cued, cu·ing** 1 To twist, braid, or tie into a cue: to *cue* the hair. 2 In billiards, etc., to hit with a cue. [< F *queue* tail]

cue[2] (kyōō) *n.* 1 The closing words in an actor's speech, serving as a signal for his successor; hence, a catchword; hint; suggestion. 2 A part to be performed by an actor. 3 State of mind; humor. —*v.t.* **cued, cu·ing** To call a cue to (an actor); prompt. [Earlier *Q, qu,* said to have been an abbreviation of L *quando* when, written in actors' copies of plays to mark their entrances.]

cue ball A white or whitish-yellow ball struck by the cue in billiards or pool.

cue drawing One of the master drawings prepared as a basis for the succession of action drawings to be filmed as an animated cartoon.

cuff[1] (kuf) *n.* 1 A band about the wrist. 2 The lower part of a sleeve. 3 The portion of a long glove or gauntlet covering the wrist. 4 The turned-up hem on a trouser leg. 5 A handcuff. —**on the cuff** *U.S. Slang* On credit; with payment postponed. [ME *cuffe, coffe;* origin unknown]

cuff[2] (kuf) *v.t.* To strike, as with the open hand; buffet. —*v.i.* To scuffle or fight; box. —*n.* A blow, especially with the open hand. [? < Scand. Cf. Sw. *kuffa* push.]

cuff links A pair of linked buttons, etc., used to fasten shirt cuffs.

cui·rass (kwi·ras′) *n.* 1 A piece of defensive armor covering the entire upper part of the trunk, and consisting of a breastplate and backplate; also, the breastplate alone. 2 A cuirasslike covering, as the bony plates of a mailed fish, the armor of a ship, etc. —*v.t.* To cover, as with a cuirass. [< F *cuirasse*]

cui·ras·sier (kwi′rə·sir′) *n.* A mounted soldier

wearing a cuirass.

cuir·bouil·li (kwēr′bōō·yē′) *n.* Leather made extremely hard by boiling or soaking in hot water and drying, usually shaping in a mold. Also **cuir·bouil·ly′.** [< F, boiled leather]

cuish (kwish) *n.* Armor, especially plate armor, for the thigh: sometimes written *quish.* Also **cuisse** (kwis). [< OF *cuissel* < *cuisse* thigh < L *coxa* hip]

cui·sine (kwi·zēn′) *n.* 1 Style or quality of cooking. 2 The food prepared. [< F]

culch (kulch) *n.* Refuse; stuff; rubbish: also spelled *cultch.* [? < OF *culche* bed, layer]

cul-de-sac (kul′də·sak′, kōōl′-; *Fr.* kü′də·säk′) *n. pl.* **cul·de-sacs,** *Fr.* **culs·de·sac** (kü-) 1 A passage open only at one end; blind alley; trap. 2 *Anat. & Zool.* A saclike cavity or part open only at one end. 3 *Mil.* The position of a force surrounded by hostile lines. [< F, bottom of the bag]

-cule *suffix of nouns* Small; little: *animalcule.* [< F < L *-culus,* dim. suffix]

cu·let (kyōō′lit) *n. pl.* **·lets** or **·lettes** 1 The small lower terminus of a brilliant-cut gem, parallel to the table: also called *collet.* 2 One of the plates of armor for the lower part of the back: often used in the plural. [< OF, dim. of *cul* bottom < L *culus* a buttock]

cu·lex (kyōō′leks) *n.* Any of a large, cosmopolitan genus *(Culex)* of mosquitoes including the common pests of North America and Europe as well as some species that transmit viral diseases of birds, horses, and humans. —**cu·li·cine** (kyōō′lə·sēn) *adj. & n.*

cu·li·cid (kyōō·lis′id) *n.* A member of any genus (family Culicidae).

cu·li·cide (kyōō′lə·sīd) *n.* Any agent that destroys mosquitoes. —**cu′li·cid′al** *adj.*

cu·li·nar·y (kyōō′lə·ner′ē) *adj.* Of or pertaining to cooking or the kitchen. [< L *culinarius* < *culina* kitchen]

cull (kul) *v.t.* **culled, cull·ing** 1 To pick or sort out; collect apart. 2 To select and gather: to *cull* a bouquet. See synonyms under CHOOSE. —*n.* Something picked or sorted out; hence, something rejected. [< OF *cuillir* < L *colligere* collect]

cul·let (kul′it) *n.* Glass waste, variously used as a powder or in melted state. [< F *collet,* dim. of *col* neck < L *collum;* with ref. to the neck of glass left on the pipe after blowing.]

cul·lion (kul′yən) *n.* 1 A bulblike root; an orchid. 2 A poltroon. [< F *couillon* testicle] —**cul′lion·ly** *adj.*

culm[1] (kulm) *n. Bot.* The jointed, usually hollow, stem or straw of grasses. —*v.i.* To form a culm. [< L *culmus* stalk] —**cul·mif·er·ous** (kul·mif′ər·əs) *adj.*

culm[2] (kulm) *n.* 1 Anthracite refuse, or carbonaceous shale. 2 An inferior anthracite coal. [Var. of dial. *coom* soot] —**cul·mif·er·ous** (kul·mif′ər·əs) *adj.*

cul·men (kul′mən) *n.* 1 A summit or eminence. 2 *Ornithol.* The ridge or central longitudinal line of the upper mandible of bird's bill. 3 *Anat.* A small eminence on the upper surface of the cerebellum: also **culmen mon·tic·u·li** (mon·tik′yə·lī). [< L]

cul·mi·nate (kul′mə·nāt) *v.i.* **·nat·ed, ·nat·ing** 1 To attain the highest point or degree. 2 *Astron.* To reach the meridian, or the point of greatest or least altitude. 3 To come to a complete result; reach a final effect. [< LL *culminatus,* pp. of *culminare* mature < *culmen* top, highest point] —**cul′mi·nal** *adj.*

cul·mi·na·tion (kul′mə·nā′shən) *n.* 1 The highest point, condition, or degree. 2 *Astron.* The passage of a heavenly body over the meridian.

culm measures *Geol.* A rock formation belonging to the Lower Carboniferous era, alterloting marine-fossil beds with plant-fossil beds.

cu·lottes (kyōō·lots′, kōō-) *n. pl.* A woman's sportswear garment having knee-length trouser legs cut full to resemble a skirt. [< F]

cul·pa·ble (kul′pə·bəl) *adj.* Deserving of blame or censure. See synonyms under CRIMINAL. [< OF < L *culpabilis* < *culpa* fault] —**cul′pa·bil′i·ty, cul′pa·ble·ness** *n.* —**cul′pa·bly** *adv.*

cul·prit (kul′prit) *n.* 1 A guilty person; criminal. 2 In old English law, one charged with crime, but not yet convicted. [< AF *cul prit,* short for

culpable guilty (< L *culpabilis*) + *prit* ready for trial < OF *prist, prest* < L *praesto* at hand; orig., prosecutor's reply to plea of "not guilty"]

cult (kult) *n.* 1 Worship or religious devotion; especially, a form of religion. 2 A system of religious observances. 3 Extravagant devotion to a person, cause, or thing; also, the object of such devotion. [< F *culte* < L *cultus* < *colere* worship]

cultch (kulch) *n.* 1 Culch. 2 Gravel, empty shells, etc., used to form a bed to which the spawn of oysters may adhere. 3 Oyster spawn: also spelled *cutch.* [Var. of CULCH]

cul·ti·gen (kul′tə·jən) *n. Bot.* A domesticated plant species of unknown or obscure origin, distinct in its characteristics from known natural species: distinguished from *indigen.* [< CULTI(VATE) + -GEN]

cul·ti·va·ble (kul′tə·və·bəl) *adj.* Capable of cultivation. Also **cul′ti·vat′a·ble.** [< F < *cultiver* cultivate] —**cul′ti·va·bil′i·ty, cul′ti·vat′a·bil′i·ty** *n.*

cul·ti·var (kul′tə·vär) *n.* A specially cultivated horticultural or garden variety of plant, flower, etc. [< CULTI(VATED) + VAR(IETY)]

cul·ti·vate (kul′tə·vāt) *v.t.* **·vat·ed, ·vat·ing** 1 To work by stirring, fertilizing, sowing, and reaping; raise crops from. 2 To bestow labor and care upon for the purpose of aiding and improving growth. 3 To loosen the soil about (growing plants) with a cultivator, hoe, etc.: to *cultivate* potatoes twice. 4 To improve or develop by study, exercise, or training; refine; civilize. 5 To study carefully; pay special attention to; endeavor to acquire, improve, or develop by study and effort; cherish: to *cultivate* philosophy. 6 To cherish carefully the friendship or society of: to *cultivate* one's relatives. 7 To prepare a culture of bacteria. [< Med. L *cultivatus,* pp. of *cultivare* < *cultivus* tilled < L *cultus,* pp. of *cultivus* tilled < L *cultus,* pp. of *colere* care for, worship] —**cul′ti·vat′ed** *adj.*

cul·ti·va·tion (kul′tə·vā′shən) *n.* 1 The act of cultivating. 2 Improvement; development; culture. See synonyms under AGRICULTURE, EDUCATION, REFINEMENT.

cul·ti·va·tor (kul′tə·vā′tər) *n.* 1 One who cultivates. 2 *Agric.* A machine for cultivating, commonly having several shares which loosen the ground and destroy weeds.

cul·trate (kul′trāt) *adj.* 1 *Bot.* Sharp-edged and pointed, as a leaf. 2 Shaped like a pruning knife, as the beak of a bird. Also **cul′trat·ed.** [< L *cultratus* < *culter* knife]

cul·tur·al (kul′chər·əl) *adj.* 1 Of, pertaining to, or developing culture: *cultural* books. 2 Resulting from breeding or artificial cultivation, as certain varieties of fruits or plants. —**cul′tur·al·ly** *adv.*

cul·ture (kul′chər) *n.* 1 Cultivation of plants or animals, especially with a view to improvement. 2 The training, improvement, and refinement of mind, morals, or taste. 3 Tillage of the soil. 4 *Bacteriol.* **a** The development of micro-organisms, as in gelatin, beef tea, etc. **b** The organisms so developed. 5 Enlightenment or civilization: Greek *culture.* 6 *Anthropol.* The sum total of the attainments and activities of any specific period, race, or people, including their implements, handicrafts, agriculture, economics, music, art, religious beliefs, traditions, language, and story. 7 Those physical features of a terrain which are of human origin or construction, as roads, trails, canals, buildings, boundary lines; also, their symbolic representation on a map. —*v.t.* **·tured, ·tur·ing** 1 To cultivate (plants or animals). 2 *Bacteriol.* **a** To develop or grow (micro-organisms) in a gelatin or other medium. **b** To inoculate with a prepared culture. 3 *Obs.* To educate or refine. [< F < L *cultura* < *colere* care for] **cul′tur·ist** *n.*

cul·tured (kul′chərd) *adj.* 1 Possessing manifest education and refinement. 2 Cultivated. 3 Artificially propagated, as a culture of bacteria. 4 Describing a variety of pearl artificially cultivated by inserting a suitable core within the shell or mantle of a mollusk, promoting the growth of nacre around it. See synonyms under POLITE.

cul·tus (kul′təs) *n.* 1 A cult. 2 State of religious, ethical, or esthetic development. [< L. See CULT.]

cul·ver (kul′vər) *n.* A pigeon or dove. [OE *culfer*]

cul·ver·in (kul′vər·in) *n.* A long cannon used in the 16th century. [< F *coulevrin* < *couleuvre* serpent]

cul·vert (kul′vərt) *n.* An artificial, covered channel for water, as under a road. [Origin uncertain]

cum·ber (kum′bər) *v.t.* 1 To hinder by or as by a weight or burden; obstruct. 2 To weigh down; oppress; perplex. 3 *Obs.* To overwhelm; prostrate; destroy. See synonyms under LOAD. — *n. Obs.* 1 Perplexity; distress. 2 An encumbrance. [Cf. OF *encombrer* hinder]

cum·ber·some (kum′bər·səm) *adj.* 1 Moving or working heavily or with difficulty; unwieldy. 2 Vexatious; burdensome. — **cum′ber·some·ly** *adv.* — **cum′ber·some·ness** *n.*

cum·brance (kum′brəns) *n.* 1 An encumbrance. 2 A burdened condition; trouble.

cum·brous (kum′brəs) *adj.* Cumbersome. See synonyms under HEAVY. — **cum′brous·ly** *adv.*

cum·in (kum′in) *n.* 1 An annual (*Cuminum cyminum*) of the carrot family, with fennel-like leaves. 2 Its seeds, used in Eastern countries as a condiment. Also **cum′min.** [OE *cymen* < L *cuminum* < Gk. *kyminon* < Semitic]

cum·mer·bund (kum′ər·bund) *n.* A shawl or broad sash worn as a waistband; also, a girdle; a belt: sometimes spelled *kummerbund.* [< Persian *kamar–band* < *kamar* loin + *band* band]

cu·mu·late (kyoo′myə·lāt) *v.i.* ·lat·ed, ·lat·ing To collect into a heap; accumulate. — *adj.* (also kyoo′myə·lit) Massed; heaped; accumulated. [< L *cumulatus,* pp. of *cumulare* heap up < *cumulus* a heap] — **cu′mu·la′tion** *n.*

cu·mu·la·tive (kyoo′myə·lā′tiv) *adj.* 1 Gathering volume, strength, or value by addition or repetition; steadily increasing. 2 Consisting of portions gathered or collected one after another. 3 Increasing or accruing, as unpaid interest or dividends, to be paid in the future. 4 *Law* Reinforcing or proving previous evidence. — **cu′mu·la′tive·ly** *adv.*

cu·mu·li·form (kyoo′myə·lə·fôrm′) *adj. Meteorol.* Denoting clouds with dome-shaped upper surfaces and generally horizontal under surfaces, usually separated by clear spaces. [< L *cumulus* heap + -FORM¹]

cumulo- *combining form* Cumulus: *cumulonimbus.*

cu·mu·lus (kyoo′myə·ləs) *n. pl.* ·li (-lī) 1 A mass; pile; top of a heap; summit. 2 *Meteorol.* Dense clouds with dome-shaped upper surfaces and horizontal bases, seen in fair weather. See table under CLOUD. [< L] — **cu′mu·lous** *adj.*

cu·ne·al (kyoo′nē·əl) *adj.* Of or pertaining to a wedge-shaped part; cuneiform. [< Med. L *cunealis* < L *cuneus* wedge]

cu·ne·ate (kyoo′nē·it, -āt) *adj.* Wedge-shaped. Also **cu′ne·at′ed, cu·ne·at·ic** (kyoo′nē·at′ik). [< L *cuneatus,* pp. of *cuneare* make wedge-shaped < *cuneus* wedge] — **cu′ne·ate·ly** *adv.*

cuneate lobule *Anat.* A wedge-shaped portion of the median surface of the occipital lobe of the brain. Also **cu·ne·us** (kyoo′nē·əs).

cu·ne·i·form (kyoo′nē′ə·fôrm, kyoo′nē·ə·fôrm′) *adj.* 1 Of a wedge shape, as noted in the characters in some ancient Assyrian, Babylonian and Persian inscriptions. 2 *Anat.* Designating a wedge-shaped bone in the wrist, or one of three in the human foot. See illustration under FOOT. — *n.* Cuneiform writing. Also **cu·ni·form** (kyoo′nə·fôrm). [< L *cuneus* wedge + -FORM]

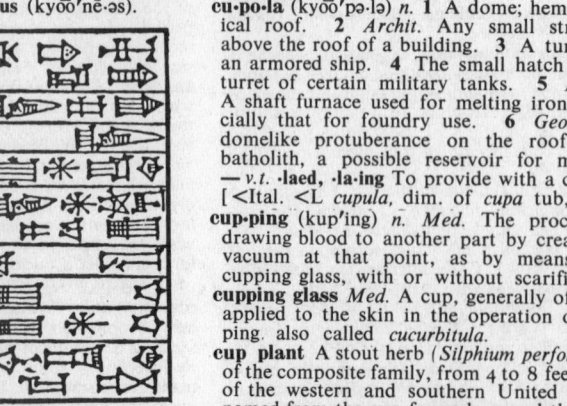

CUNEIFORM (*n.*)

Cu·ne·ne (koo·nā′nə) A river in west central Angola, SW Africa, flowing about 650 miles SW to the Atlantic: also *Kunene.*

cu·nic·u·lus (kyoo·nik′yə·ləs) *n. pl.* ·li (-lī) 1 A small underground passage or drain. 2 The track or burrow of a skin parasite. [< L, rabbit, burrow]

cun·ner (kun′ər) *n.* A small, edible fish

(*Tautogolabrus adspersus*), abundant along the North Atlantic shores of America. [Origin uncertain]

cun·ning (kun′ing) *n.* 1 Skill in deception; guile; artifice. 2 Knowledge combined with skill; dexterity. See synonyms under ARTIFICE, DECEPTION. — *adj.* 1 Crafty or shrewd; artful; guileful. 2 Attractive; bright; amusing; cute. 3 Ingenious; dexterous; made with skill: a *cunning* design. 4 *Obs.* Learned; knowing. See synonyms under ACUTE, ASTUTE, INSIDIOUS, KNOWING, POLITIC. [OE *cunnung* knowledge < *cunnan.* Related to CAN¹.] — **cun′ning·ly** *adv.* — **cun′ning·ness** *n.*

cup (kup) *n.* 1 A small open vessel of glass, porcelain, wood, waxed paper, metal, etc., used chiefly for drinking. 2 A cupful; a measure of capacity equal to 8 fluid ounces or 16 tablespoons. 3 The ornamental vessel used in administering the sacramental wine; also, the wine itself. 4 Figuratively, one's lot in life; portion. 5 Intoxicating drink, or the habit of drinking: pleasures of the *cup.* 6 A prize, usually a vase, or a cup-shaped vessel, contended for in races: the Ascot *cup.* 7 *Med.* A cupping glass or vessel for drawing blood. 8 A small hole or cuplike depression in a course; also, a hole especially made in the putting green into which the golf ball is played. 9 Any cup-shaped object: the *cup* of a flower, an oil *cup,* etc. 10 The concave part of any drinking vessel having a base and stem. 11 A beverage made of wine, generally iced, with herbs, fruits, and vegetables: claret *cup.* 12 That curvature of a board or other flat piece of lumber which runs transversely against the ‚rain. — **in one's cups** Intoxicated; also, in the act of drinking. — *v.t.* **cupped, cup·ping** 1 To bleed, as by scarification and bringing the blood to the surface under an exhausted cup. 2 To shape like or place in a cup. [OE *cuppe* < LL *cuppa* cup, var. of L *cupa* tub]

cup-bear·er (kup′bâr′ər) *n.* One who serves wine and other drinks to guests.

cup·board (kub′ərd) *n.* 1 A closet or cabinet with shelves, as for tableware. 2 Any small cabinet or closet.

cup·cake (kup′kāk′) *n.* A cake baked in cup-shaped receptacles: formerly, most of the ingredients were measured by cupfuls.

cu·pel (kyoo′pəl, kyoo·pel′) *v.t.* ·peled or ·pelled, ·pel·ing or ·pel·ling To separate from base metals by cupellation. [< *n.*] — *n.* A shallow, absorbent vessel, generally of bone ash: used in assaying gold and silver ores. [< MF *coupelle* < Med. L *cupella,* dim. of *cuppa* cup]

cu·pel·la·tion (kyoo′pə·lā′shən) *n.* The process of refining gold or silver by the use of a cupel, or in a muffle furnace. [< F]

cup·ful (kup′fool) *n. pl.* ·fuls The quantity held or measured by a cup; half a pint.

cu·pid·i·ty (kyoo·pid′ə·tē) *n.* An inordinate wish for possession, especially of wealth; avarice. [< L *cupiditas, -tatis* < *cupidus* desirous]

cu·po·la (kyoo′pə·lə) *n.* 1 A dome; hemispherical roof. 2 *Archit.* Any small structure above the roof of a building. 3 A turret on an armored ship. 4 The small hatch in the turret of certain military tanks. 5 *Metall.* A shaft furnace used for melting iron, especially that for foundry use. 6 *Geol.* The domelike protuberance on the roof of a batholith, a possible reservoir for magma. — *v.t.* ·laed, ·la·ing To provide with a cupola. [< Ital. < L *cupula,* dim. of *cupa* tub, cask]

cup·ping (kup′ing) *n. Med.* The process of drawing blood to another part by creating a vacuum at that point, as by means of a cupping glass, with or without scarification.

cupping glass *Med.* A cup, generally of glass, applied to the skin in the operation of cupping. also called *cucurbitula.*

cup plant A stout herb (*Silphium perfoliatum*) of the composite family, from 4 to 8 feet high, of the western and southern United States: named from the cup formed around the stem by the upper pair of perfoliate leaves.

cu·pram (kyoo′prəm) *n.* A fungicide formed of ammoniacal copper carbonate. [Short for CUPRAMMONIA]

cu·pram·mo·nia (kyoo′prə·mōn′yə, -mō′nē·ə) *n. Chem.* Schweitzer's reagent. [< CUPR(O)- + AMMONIA]

cu·pram·mo·ni·um process (kyoo′prə·mō′-

nē·əm) *Chem.* A process for making rayon by treating cellulose with Schweitzer's reagent.

cu·pre·ous (kyoo′prē·əs) *adj.* Of, pertaining to, containing, or like copper. [< LL *cupreus* < *cuprum* copper]

cu·pric (kyoo′prik) *adj. Chem.* Of or pertaining to copper, especially copper in its highest valence: *cupric* oxide.

cupric acetate *Chem.* Verdigris.

cupric oxide A compound, CuO, occurring in nature as the mineral tenorite and prepared by heating copper in oxygen and also by heating certain copper compounds.

cupric sulfate A white compound, $CuSO_4$, which forms blue vitriol or bluestone.

cu·prif·er·ous (kyoo·prif′ər·əs) *adj.* Yielding or containing copper. [< CUPR(O)- + -(I)FEROUS]

cu·prite (kyoo′prīt) *n.* A red, translucent cuprous oxide found in isometric crystals, and also massive, granular, or earthy: an important ore of copper.

cupro- *combining form* Copper: *cupronickel.* Also, before vowels, **cupr-.** [< L *cuprum* copper]

cu·pro·nick·el (kyoo′prō·nik′əl) *n.* Any of several alloys of copper and nickel, sometimes combined with other elements, as manganese and iron.

cu·prous (kyoo′prəs) *adj. Chem.* Of or derived from copper, especially copper in its lowest valence: *cuprous* oxide, Cu_2O.

cu·prum (kyoo′prəm) *n.* Copper. [< L]

cup-shake (kup′shāk) *n.* A division or shrinkage between the annual rings of timber: also called *ringshake.* [< CUP (def. 12) + SHAKE (def. 5)]

cu·pule (kyoo′pyool) *n.* 1 A concave or cup-shaped depression. 2 *Bot.* **a** A cup-shaped part, as the involucre of the fruit of the oak, chestnut, beech, etc. **b** The receptacle of certain fungi, mosses, and liverworts. [< LL *cupula.* See CUPOLA.]

cur (kûr) *n.* 1 A mongrel dog. 2 A mean or malicious person. [Short for earlier *kur-dogge.* Cf. dial. Sw. *kurre* dog.] — **cur′rish·ly** *adv.* — **cur′rish·ness** *n.*

cur·a·ble (kyoor′ə·bəl) *adj.* Capable of being cured. — **cur′a·bil′i·ty, cur′a·ble·ness** *n.* — **cur′a·bly** *adv.*

cu·ra·çao (kyoor′ə·sō′) *n.* A liqueur made by distilling spirits with macerated bitter orange peel. [from *Curaçao*]

cu·ra·cy (kyoor′ə·sē) *n. pl.* ·cies The position, duties, or term of office of a curate.

cu·ra·re (kyoo·rä′rē) *n.* 1 A blackish, brittle, resinous extract of certain South American trees of the genus *Strychnos,* especially *S. toxifera,* used as an arrow poison, in pharmacological research, and as an adjunct in general anesthesia. 2 The plant from which this extract is abstracted: sometimes written *woorali* or *urare.* Also **cu·ra·ra** (kyoo·rä′rə), **cu·ra′ri.** [< Sp. *curaré* < Tupian]

cu·ra·rine (kyoo·rä′rēn, -rin) *n. Chem.* A poisonous alkaloid, $C_{19}H_{26}ON_2$, obtained from curare. [< CURARE + -INE²]

cu·ra·rize (kyoor′ə·rīz, kyoo·rä′rīz) *v.t.* ·rized, ·riz·ing 1 To poison by the use of curare. 2 To administer curare to, as for paralyzing the motor nerves in vivisection. — **cu′ra·ri·za′tion** *n.*

cu·ras·sow (kyoor′ə·sō, kyoo·ras′ō) *n.* A large turkeylike South American bird (family *Cracidae*) with naked cere and tarsi: also spelled *carassow.* [from *Curaçao*]

cu·rate (kyoor′it) *n.* A clergyman assisting a parish priest, rector, or vicar. [< Med. L *curatus* < *cura* care, a cure] — **cu′rate·ship** *n.*

cur·a·tive (kyoor′ə·tiv) *adj.* 1 Possessing power or tendency to cure. 2 Relating to the cure of diseases. — *n.* A remedy. — **cur′a·tive·ly** *adv.* — **cur′a·tive·ness** *n.*

cu·ra·tor (kyoo·rā′tər) *n.* 1 A person having charge, as of a museum or library; a superintendent. 2 *Law* A guardian appointed to take charge of the property of a person not legally qualified to act for himself. 3 In some European universities, a member of a board of managers. [< L < *curare* care for < *cura* care] — **cu·ra·to·ri·al** (kyoor′ə·tôr′ē·əl, -tō′rē-) *adj.*

cu·ra·tor·ship (kyoo·rā′tər·ship) *n.* 1 A curator's office or position. 2 A body of curators collectively.

curb (kûrb) *n.* 1 A chain or strap to brace a bit against a horse's lower jaw: used to check the horse when the reins are pulled; also, a bit so arranged. 2 Anything that restrains or controls. 3 A curbstone. 4 The framework at the top of a well. **5** Originally, the street as a market for selling securities out of hours or securities not listed on the regular stock exchanges: also *curb exchange.* **6** A hard swelling on a horse's hind leg, especially back of the hock and below its point. —*v.t.* **1** To hold in subjection; control, as with reins and curb. **2** To protect with a curb. **3** To shorten and sharpen (telegraphic signals) in order to obtain more rapid transmission. Also *Brit. kerb.* See synonyms under GOVERN, REPRESS, RESTRAIN. [< F *courbe,* orig. adj., curved < L *curvus*]

curb exchange 1 An organization for the sale of securities not listed on the stock exchange, wheat exchange, etc. **2** The building in which this market operates.

curb·ing (kûr′bing) *n.* **1** Curbstones collectively. **2** Material for making a curb. **3** A curb or a part of a curb.

curb roof *Archit.* A roof having two sets of rafters, of which the upper slopes less than the lower.

curb·stone (kûrb′stōn′) *n.* A stone, or a row of stones, on the outer edge of a sidewalk: also *Brit. kerbstone.*

cur·chie (kûr′chē) *n. Scot.* A curtsy; courtesy.

cur·cu·li·o (kûr·kyōō′lē·ō) *n. pl.* **·os** One of a family (*Curculionidae*) of beetles, characterized by a prolongation of the head into a beak: many species are injurious to fruits and nuts: also called *snout beetle, weevil.* For illustration see under INSECT (injurious). [< L, weevil]

cur·cu·ma (kûr′kyōō·mə) *n.* Any of several plants (genus *Curcuma*) of the ginger family: the perennial rootstocks of *C. longa* yield turmeric, and those of *C. angustifolia* the East Indian arrowroot. [< NL < Arabic *kurkum* saffron]

cur·cu·min (kûr′kyōō·mən) *n.* **1** The yellow compound, $C_{21}H_{20}O_6$, contained in the turmeric or curcuma root, of which it is the coloring substance. **2** An artificial acid dye. Also **cur′cu·mine** (-mīn). [< CURCUMA + -IN]

curd (kûrd) *n.* The coagulated portion of milk, of which cheese is made, as distinct from the watery portion or whey. —*v.t. & v.i.* To form into or become curd; curdle. [Metathetic var. of CRUD] —**curd′i·ness** *n.* —**curd′y** adj.

cur·dle (kûrd′l) *v.t. & v.i.* **·dled, ·dling 1** To change or turn to curd; coagulate; congeal. **2** To thicken. Also *Dial.* **cruddle.** [Freq. of CURD, *v.*]

cure (kyōōr) *n.* **1** A restoration or return to a sound or healthy condition. **2** That which restores health or abolishes an evil. **3** Spiritual care; a curacy: the *cure* of souls. **4** A mode or manner of curing anything, as hams, fish, etc. —*v.* **cured, cur·ing** *v.t.* **1** To restore to a healthy or sound condition. **2** To remedy or eradicate, as a disease or bad habit. **3** To preserve, as by salting or smoking. **4** To vulcanize, as rubber. —*v.i.* **5** To bring about recovery. **6** To be preserved, as meat, by salting or drying. [< OF < L *cura* care]

cure-all (kyōōr′ôl′) *n.* That which is asserted to cure all diseases or evils; a panacea.

cure of souls The care for the spiritual needs of the faithful, which devolves upon the clergy of the Anglican and Roman Catholic Churches.

cu·ret·tage (kyōō·ret′ij, kyōōr′ə·täzh′) *n.* The use or application of the curette.

cu·rette (kyōō·ret′) *n. Med.* A small instrument, usually resembling a spoon or scoop, used for removing morbid matter by scraping from a cavity, as the ear or throat. —*v.t.* **·ret·ted, ·ret·ting** To apply a curette to. [< F < *curer* cure, restore]

cur·few (kûr′fyōō) *n.* **1** An ancient police regulation requiring fires and lights to be put out at the tolling of a bell. **2** The bell itself. **3** The hour of ringing such a bell. **4** The ringing of a bell at a certain hour in the evening, still prevailing locally, as in parts of the United States and France. **5** A police or military regulation that civilians keep off the streets after a designated hour; also, a municipal order of the same tenor applying to children only. [< AF *coeverfu,* OF *cuevrefu* < *couvrir* cover + *feu* fire]

cu·ri·a (kyōōr′ē·ə) *n. pl.* **·ae** (-ē) **1** A court of justice. **2** The collective body of officials of the papal government; also **Curia Romana. 3** The court or family residence of a medieval monarch or feudal lord. **4** A tribal division made by Rom-

ulus, or its meeting place. **5** The Roman senate house or the senate of any Italian city. [< L] —**cu·ri·al** adj.

cu·ri·al·ism (kyōō′ē·əl·iz′əm) *n.* The political principles and policy of the papal see, especially in their exclusive tendencies; ultramontanism. —**cu′ri·al·ist** *n.* —**cu′ri·al·is′tic** adj.

cu·rie (kyōōr′ē, kyōō·rē′) *n. Physics* **1** The unit of radioactivity, equal to 3.70×10^{10} disintegrations per second, of any radioactive nuclide. **2** The quantity of radon emanation in equilibrium with one gram of radium: also called **cu′rie·gram.** [after Marie *Curie*]

cur·ing (kyōōr′ing) *n.* **1** Any method of treating for preservation: said of meats, vegetables, etc. **2** A method of treating raw hides and skins so as to prevent deterioration during transport or in storage. **3** The transition of a heat-molded plastic from the liquid to the solid state without lowering the temperature.

cu·ri·o (kyōōr′ē·ō) *n. pl.* **·os** A curiosity; a rare or curious article of virtu. [Short for CURIOSITY]

cu·ri·o·log·ic (kyōōr′ē·ə·loj′ik) *adj.* Relating to pictorial hieroglyphics: also spelled *kyriologic.* Also **cu′ri·o·log′i·cal.** [< Gk. *kyriologikos* < *kyrios* literal + *logos* word] —**cu′ri·o·log′i·cal·ly** *adv.*

cu·ri·o·sa (kyōōr′ē·ō′sə) *n. pl.* Books, papers, etc., on unusual, especially pornographic, subjects. [< L, neut. pl. of *curiosus* curious, prying]

cu·ri·os·i·ty (kyōōr′ē·os′ə·tē) *n. pl.* **·ties 1** Desire for knowledge of something. **2** Inquisitive interest in the private affairs of others. **3** An interesting or strange quality. **4** Any object adapted to excite interest or inquiry. **5** *Obs.* Fastidiousness; nicety. [< L *curiositas, -tatis* < *curiosus* CURIOUS]

cu·ri·ous (kyōōr′ē·əs) *adj.* **1** Eager for information; inquisitive; prying. **2** Adapted to attract attention or excite interest; novel; odd; strange; mysterious. **3** Involving ingenuity or skill. **4** *Obs.* Fastidious; delicate; scrupulous. See synonyms under INQUISITIVE, QUEER, RARE[1]. [< OF *curios, curius* < L *curiosus* < *cura* care]

cu·ri·um (kyōōr′ē·əm) *n.* An artificially created, intensely radioactive metallic element (symbol Cm, atomic number 96) produced by bombardment of plutonium in nuclear reactors. See PERIODIC TABLE. [after Marie and Pierre *Curie*]

curl (kûrl) *v.t.* **1** To twist into ringlets or curves, as the hair. **2** To form into a curved or spiralshape. **3** *Obs.* To adorn with curls. —*v.i.* **4** To become curved; take a spiral shape. **5** To play at the game of curling. —*n.* **1** Anything coiled or spiral, as a ringlet. **2** Sinuosity. **3** A circling or wavelike marking. **4** *Bot.* A disease of plants, especially of peach trees. **5** *Physics* A vector differential operator used in studying phenomena of spin or rotation. [Metathetic var. of ME *crollid, crulled* curled < *crull* curly < MLG] —**curl′i·ness** *n.* —**curl′y** adj.

curled toe A disease of growing chicks caused by a vitamin deficiency and characterized by a twisted or flexed condition of the toes.

cur·lew (kûr′lyōō) *n.* **1** A shore bird (family *Scolopacidae*), with long bill and legs, as the European curlew (*Numenius arquatus*) and the Hudsonian curlew (*Phaeopus hudsonicus*). **2** Any bird superficially resembling the curlew. [< OF *corlieu, courlieus;* orig. imit., infl. in form by OF *courlieu* messenger]

curl·i·cue (kûr′li·kyōō) *n.* **1** Anything oddly curled or twisted, as in flourishes with a pen: *curlicues* made in skating. **2** A frolicsome trick; caper. Also **curl′y·cue.** [< CURLY + CUE[1]]

curl·ing (kûr′ling) *n.* A game in which the opposing players slide large, smooth, circular stones along the ice toward a goal or tee at either end.

curling iron An implement of metal, used when heated for curling or waving the hair. Also **curling tongs.**

cur·rant (kûr′ənt) *n.* **1** A small, round, acid berry, used for making jelly. **2** The bush (genus *Ribes*) producing it; especially, the red or white currant

(*R. sativum*) and the black currant (*R. nigrum*). **3** A small seedless raisin from the Levant. ♦ Homophone: *current.* [Back formation < *Corauntz* taken as pl. in AF (*raisins de*) *Corauntz* (raisins from) Corinth]

cur·ren·cy (kûr′ən·sē) *n. pl.* **·cies 1** The current medium of exchange; coin or bank notes. **2** The state of being current. **3** Current value or estimation; general esteem or standing: to gain *currency* without desert. See synonyms under MONEY. —**blocked currency** Currency subject to abnormal administrative restrictions, usually in the interests of controlling foreign exchange. —**flexible currency** Currency which is regulated by existing business requirements, and increased or decreased with their demands. —**managed currency** A theoretical financial arrangement intended to stabilize currency by regulation of the standard monetary unit.

cur·rent (kûr′ənt) *adj.* **1** Circulating freely. **2** Generally accepted. **3** In actual progress, or belonging to the immediate present. **4** *Math.* Differing from point to point. **5** *Rare* Moving; running; flowing. See synonyms under AUTHENTIC. —*n.* **1** A continuous onward movement, as of a stream; also, a fluid thus flowing. **2** That part of any body of water which has a more or less steady flow in a definite direction: an ocean *current.* See list of OCEAN CURRENTS below. **3** *Electr.* **a** A movement or flow of electricity passing through a conductor. **b** The rate at which it flows. **4** Any connected onward movement; course. —**alternating current** *Electr.* A current which periodically reverses its direction of flow, each complete cycle having the same value. —**direct current** *Electr.* A current flowing in one direction continuously, with negligible or zero changes in value. —**eddy current** *Electr.* A current produced in a solid conductor, such as the armature or polepiece of a dynamo or motor, which is wasted by conversion into heat: also called **Foucault current.** ♦Homophone: *currant.* [< OF *curant,* ppr. of *corre* < L *currere* run; infl. in form by L *currens, -entis,* ppr. of *currere*]

OCEAN CURRENTS

—**Agulhas current** A southern branch of the Equatorial Current, which skirts the east coast of South Africa.

—**Australia Current** A southern branch of the Equatorial Current, which flows south and east after passing along the eastern coast of Australia.

—**Brazil Current** A southern branch of the Equatorial Current, flowing southward along the coast of Brazil.

—**California Current** A broad, cold ocean current flowing southward along the Pacific coast of North America from about 50° N. to the mouth of the Gulf of California.

—**Equatorial Current** A great drift of ocean waters north and south of the Equator, set in motion by the trade winds and having a general westerly direction except when diverted by coastal features.

—**Guinea Current** An ocean current moving eastward along the upper coast of Guinea toward the Equatorial Current of the Atlantic.

—**Japan Current** A warm ocean current flowing northeastwards across the Pacific from Japan to the southern coast of Alaska: also called *Japan Stream, Kuroshiwo.* Also **Black Current.**

—**Kamchatka Current** The northern branch of the Japan Current, which flows northeast in the direction of the Aleutian Islands.

—**Labrador Current** An ocean current originating in Davis Strait and flowing southward along the coasts of Labrador and Newfoundland. Also called **Arctic Current.**

—**Peruvian Current** A cold ocean current flowing north and east along the shores of Chile and Peru. Also called **Chilean Current, Humboldt Current.**

cur·ri·cle (kûr′i·kəl) *n.* A two-wheeled, two-horse carriage with a pole. [< L *curriculum* race < *currere* run]

cur·ric·u·lum (kə·rik′yə·ləm) *n. pl.* **·lums** or **·la** (-lə) **1** A regular or particular course of study, as in a college. **2** All such courses of study, collectively. [< L, a race < *currere* run]

cur·ri·er·y (kûr′ē·ər·ē) *n. pl.* **·er·ies** The trade or occupation of a currier, or a currier's shop.

cur·rish (kûr′ish) *adj.* Like a cur; snarling; mean; nasty. **—cur′rish·ly** *adv.* **—cur′rish·ness** *n.*

cur·ry[1] (kûr′ē) *v.t.* **·ried, ·ry·ing** 1 To clean with a currycomb; groom (a horse, dog, etc.). 2 To dress (tanned hides) for use. 3 To beat or pummel. **—to curry favor** To seek favor by adulation and subserviency. [< OF *carreier, conreder* make ready, prepare]

cur·ry[2] (kûr′ē) *n. pl.* **·ries** 1 A cooked dish consisting of meats, fish, rice, etc., seasoned with curry powder or curry sauce. 2 A pungent sauce of Indian origin, made of vegetables, spices, and strong condiments: also **curry sauce.** 3 Curry powder. **—v.t.** **·ried, ·ry·ing** To flavor with curry. [< Tamil *kari* sauce]

cur·ry·comb (kûr′ē·kōm) *n.* A comb consisting of a series of upright serrated ridges, for grooming horses. **—v.t.** To comb with a currycomb.

curry powder A powdered condiment, prepared from the dried leaves of an Indian plant (*Murraya koenigi*), together with other pungent spices, turmeric, etc.: used in making curry sauce and curried dishes.

curse (kûrs) *v.* **cursed** or **curst, curs·ing** *v.t.* 1 To invoke evil or injury upon; anathematize; damn. 2 To swear at; execrate. 3 To cause evil or injury to. **—v.i.** 4 To utter imprecations; swear; blaspheme. **—n.** 1 An imprecation of evil; any profane oath. 2 Calamity invoked or threatened. 3 A source of calamity or evil; also, the evil which comes as a result of invocation or as punishment. 4 An object of execration. See synonyms under ABOMINATION, IMPRECATION, OATH. [OE *cursian* < OIrish *cursagim* blame]

curs·ed (kûr′sid, kûrst) *adj.* 1 Under a curse. 2 Deserving a curse; execrable; detestable.

cur·sor (kûr′sər) *n.* A pointer on a computer screen that shows the position where an operation is taking place.

cur·so·ri·al (kûr·sôr′ē·əl, -sōr′ē-) *adj.* 1 Fitted for running or walking, as distinguished from other modes of progression. 2 Having, or executed by means of, limbs of such a character.

cur·so·ry (kûr′sər·ē) *adj.* Rapid and superficial; hasty. Also *Obs.* **cur·so·rar·y** (kûr′sə·rer′ē). [< L *cursorius* pertaining to running < *cursor* a runner < *currere* run] **—cur′so·ri·ly** *adv.* **—cur′so·ri·ness** *n.*

Synonyms: careless, desultory, hasty, slight, superficial. *Antonyms:* careful, critical, elaborate, exhaustive, minute, painstaking, thorough.

curst (kûrst) A past tense and past participle of CURSE. **—adj.** Of a hateful disposition; vicious.

curt (kûrt) *adj.* 1 Concise and abrupt in act or expression. 2 Short and sharp in manner; brusk. [< L *curtus* shortened] **—curt′ly** *adv.* **—curt′ness** *n.*

cur·tail (kər·tāl′) *v.t.* To cut off or cut short; abbreviate; lessen; reduce. See synonyms under ABBREVIATE, RETRENCH. **—n.** The scroll-shaped end of an architectural member. [< CURTAL; infl. in form by TAIL] **—cur·tail′er** *n.* **—cur·tail′ment** *n.*

cur·tain (kûr′tən) *n.* 1 A piece of fabric, often adjustable, hung for decoration, concealment, or to shut out light, as before a wall, window, doorway, etc. 2 Something that conceals, covers or separates like a curtain. 3 Part of a rampart that connects the flanks of two bastions or towers. 4 *Archit.* That portion of a wall between two towers. 5 In the theater: **a** The drapery hanging at the front of a stage, drawn up or aside to reveal the stage. **b** The speech or situation in a play occurring immediately before the fall of the curtain. **—v.t.** 1 To supply or adorn with or as with a curtain or curtains. 2 To conceal or shut off as with a curtain; cover. [< OF *curtine* < LL *cortina*]

curtain call The prolonged applause which a performer acknowledges by appearing on the stage after the end of a play, scene, etc.

cur·tain-rais·er (kûr′tən·rā′zər) *n.* A short play or sketch presented before a longer or more important play.

cur·tate (kûr′tāt) *adj.* Shortened. [< L *curtatus,* pp. of *curtare* shorten < *curtus* shortened]

cur·te·sy (kûr′tə·sē) *n. pl.* **·sies** Courtesy.

curtesy of England In English law, the tenure by which a man holds for life the estates of his deceased wife inheritable by their children.

cur·ti·lage (kûr′tə·lij) *n.* *Law* The ground adjacent to a dwelling house, and used in connection with it. [< AF, var. of OF *cortillage* < *cortil,* dim. of *cortis, cort* COURT]

curt·sy (kûrt′sē) *n.* *pl.* **·sies** A gesture of civility or respect, consisting of a slight bending of the knees, and performed chiefly by women: sometimes spelled *courtesy.* **—v.i.** **·sied, ·sy·ing** To bend the knees and lower the body slightly, as a gesture of civility, reverence, or respect. Also **curt′sey.** [Var. of COURTESY]

cu·rule (kyoor′ool) *adj.* 1 Of or pertaining to an ancient Roman magisterial chair reserved for state dignitaries. 2 Privileged to sit in the curule chair; hence, magisterial; official. [< L *curulis* < *currus* chariot]

curule chair The official seat of Roman magistrates of the highest rank: also **curule seat.**

curule dignity The right to sit in the curule chair.

cur·va·ceous (kûr·vā′shəs) *adj.* *Colloq.* Having voluptuous curves; shapely in form: said of a woman.

cur·vate (kûr′vāt) *adj.* Evenly bent; curved. Also **cur′vat·ed.** [< L *curvatus,* pp. of *curvare* bend] **—cur·va′tion** *n.*

cur·va·ture (kûr′və·chər) *n.* 1 The act of bending, or the state of being curved; amount or rate of bending. 2 Any deviation from a normal or expected rectilinear course: a lateral *curvature* of the spine. [< L *curvatura* < *curvare* bend]

curve (kûrv) *n.* 1 A line continuously bent so that no portion of it is straight, as the arc of a circle. 2 A bending, or something bent. 3 An instrument for drawing curves: used by draftsmen. 4 *Math.* The locus of a point moving in such a way that its course can be defined by an equation. 5 *Physics* A line representing variations in force, quantity, temperature, etc. 6 In baseball, the course given to a ball by the pitcher, causing it to curve to one side or the other before crossing the plate. **—v.** **curved, curv·ing** *v.t.* 1 To cause to assume the form of a curve. **—v.i.** 2 To assume the form of a curve. 3 To move in a curve, as a projectile or ball; bend. **—adj.** Curved. [< L *curvum* < *curvus* bent]

curved (kûrvd) *adj.* Having a different direction at every point; bent. **—curv·ed·ly** (kûr′vid·lē) *adv.* **—curv′ed·ness** *n.*

cur·vet (kər·vet′, kûr′vit) *v.t.* & *v.i.* **·vet·ted** or **·vet·ed, ·vet·ting** or **·vet·ing** 1 To prance or cause to prance. 2 To frisk about. **—n.** (kûr′vit) A light, low leap of a horse, made so that at one movement all four legs are off the ground. [< Ital. *corvettare* < *corvetta,* dim. of *corva* bent < L *curvus*]

curvi- *combining form* Curved. [< L *curvus* curved]

cur·vi·fo·li·ate (kûr′və·fō′lē·it, -āt) *adj.* *Bot.* Having curved leaves.

cur·vi·lin·e·ar (kûr′və·lin′ē·ər) *adj.* Formed by curved lines. Also **cur′vi·lin′e·al.** See synonyms under ROUND.

cur·vi·ty (kûr′və·tē) *n.* The state of being curved; curvature.

cus·cus (koos′koos) *n.* Any of various arboreal phalangers (genus *Phalanger*) of Australia and New Zealand, as the **brown cuscus** (*P. orientalis*) or the **spotted cuscus** (*P. maculatus*), having long prehensile tails.

cu·sec (kyoo′sek) *n.* A cubic foot per second: a unit for measuring the rate of flow of a liquid. [< CU(BIC) + SEC(OND)]

cush·at (kush′ət, koosh′-) *n.* The European ring dove (*Columba palumbus*), having the neck partly encircled with a cream-colored mark. [OE *cūscote*]

cu·shaw (kə·shô′) *n.* A variety of the crookneck squash: also called *cashaw, China squash.* [< N. Am. Ind.]

cush·ion (koosh′ən) *n.* 1 A flexible bag or casing filled with some soft or elastic material, as feathers, air, etc. 2 Anything resembling a cushion in appearance, construction, or application; especially, any device to deaden the jar or impact of parts, as padding or inserted rubber. 3 The elastic rim of a billiard table. 4 A pincushion. 5 A pillow used in making lace. 6 The motive fluid remaining in the cylinder of a reciprocating engine after the closing of the exhaust port. 7 The fleshy part of the hind quarter of a hog, horse, etc. **—v.t.** 1 To

place, seat, or arrange on or as on a cushion; prop up. 2 To provide with a cushion. 3 To cover or hide as with a cushion. 4 To pad, as with a cushion; absorb the shock or effect of. 5 *Mech.* To compress, as exhaust steam or other motive fluid, by closing the exhaust outlet of a cylinder. **—v.i.** 6 In billiards, to cause the cue ball to strike the cushion before contact with the second object ball, either before or after striking the first. [< F *coussin,* ? var. of OF *coissin,* ult. < L *coxa* hip, thigh] **—cush′ion·y** *adj.*

cush·y (koosh′ē) *adj.* *Slang* **cush·i·er, cush·i·est** Comfortable; agreeable. [< CUSHION; orig. Brit. slang]

cusk (kusk) *n. pl.* **cusks** or **cusk** 1 An edible codlike fish (*Brosmius brosme*) of northern seas. 2 The burbot. [Origin unknown]

cusp (kusp) *n.* 1 A point or pointed end. 2 *Astron.* Either point of a crescent moon. 3 *Geom.* A point at which two branches of a curve meet and end, with a common tangent. 4 *Archit.* A projecting point between small arcs, as in medieval tracery. 5 *Anat.* **a** A prominence or point, as on the crown of a tooth. **b** The pointed fold forming a segment of the cardiac valves. 6 *Bot.* A sharp, stiff point, as of a leaf. 7 In astrology, the first entrance of a house in the determination of nativities. 8 *Geol.* An angular, projecting beach or portion of a beach, formed by the interaction of conflicting currents. [< L *cuspis, -idis* a point]

cus·pate (kus′pāt) *adj.* 1 Having a cusp or cusps. 2 Cusp-shaped. Also **cus′pat·ed, cusped** (kuspt).

cus·pid (kus′pid) *n.* A canine tooth. **—adj.** Cuspidate.

cus·pi·date (kus′pə·dāt) *adj.* 1 Having a cusp or cusps. 2 *Bot.* Ending in a cusp, as a leaf. Also **cus′pi·dat·ed, cus·pi·dal** (kus′pə·dəl).

cus·pi·da·tion (kus′pə·dā′shən) *n.* *Archit.* Decoration with cusps.

cus·pi·dor (kus′pə·dôr) *n.* A spittoon. Also **cus′pi·dore.** [< Pg., spitter < *cuspir* spit < L *conspuere* < *com-* thoroughly + *spuere* spit]

cus·pis (kus′pis) *n.* *pl.* **·pi·des** (-pə·dēz) *Latin* A cusp.

cuss (kus) *U.S. Colloq.* *v.t.* & *v.i.* To curse. **—n.** 1 A curse. 2 A worthless or disagreeable person: a humorous or contemptuous term. [Var. of CURSE]

cuss·ed (kus′id) *adj.* *U.S. Colloq.* 1 Cursed. 2 Mean; perverse. **—cuss′ed·ly** *adv.* **—cuss′ed·ness** *n.*

cus·so (kus′ō) *n.* 1 An Abyssinian tree (*Hagenia abyssinica*) of the rose family. 2 The flowers of this tree, used by natives as a vermifuge; brayera: also spelled *kousso, kusso.* [< native name]

cus·ta·lo·rum (kus′tə·lôr′əm, -lō′rəm) *n.* *Obs.* Custos rotulorum: a corruption.

cus·tard (kus′tərd) *n.* A mixture of milk, eggs, sugar, and flavoring, either boiled or baked. [Alter. of earlier *crustarde, crustade* < F *croustade,* a type of pie < L *crusta* crust]

custard apple 1 The papaw: also called **custard tree.** 2 A tropical American tree (*Annona reticulata*). 3 Its soft, edible fruit.

cus·to·di·an (kus·tō′dē·ən) *n.* A guardian; caretaker. **—cus·to′di·an·ship′** *n.*

cus·to·dy (kus′tə·dē) *n. pl.* **·dies** 1 A keeping; guardianship. 2 The state of being held in keeping or under guard; restraint of liberty; imprisonment. See synonyms under FETTER. **—to take into custody** To arrest. [< L *custodia* guard < *custos* guardian] **—cus·to·di·al** (kus·tō′dē·əl) *adj.*

cus·tom (kus′təm) *n.* 1 An ordinary or usual manner of doing or acting. 2 The habitual practice of a community or people; common usage. 3 *Law* An old and general usage that has obtained the force of law. 4 Customary frequenting, as of a hotel, or habitual purchase, as of goods, staple commodities, etc., at a particular place; business support; patronage. 5 A tariff or duty assessed by law, levied upon goods imported or exported; hence, any regular toll or tax: in the first of these senses always plural. 6 *pl.* The former ritual sacrifice of human victims in Ashanti and Dahomey, on the death of a chief or king. 7 Customary rent, tribute, or service due from a feudal tenant to his lord. **—adj.** 1 Made to order: also **cus′tom-built′, cus′tom-made.** 2 Specializing in made-to-order goods: a *custom* tailor. 5 From or for customers: *custom* ore; a *custom* smelter. [<OF *custume* <L *consuetudo* <com-thoroughly + *suescere* become used to. Doublet of COSTUME.]

Synonyms (noun): fashion, habit, manner, practice, style, use. See HABIT, TAX.

cus·tom·a·ble (kus′təm·ə·bəl) *adj.* Liable or subject to duty or customs; dutiable.

cus·tom·ar·y (kus′tə·mer′ē) *adj.* 1 Conforming to or established by custom. 2 In English law, holding, or held by custom, as a tenant or his tenancy. See synonyms under COMMON, GENERAL, HABITUAL, USUAL. — *n.* *pl.* ·ar·ies A written or printed statement of laws and customs. — **cus·tom·ar·i·ly** (kus′tə·mer′ə·lē, kus′tə·mer′ə·lē) *adv.* — **cus′tom·ar′i·ness** *n.*

cus·tom·er (kus′təm·ər) *n.* 1 One who gives his custom or trade; a purchaser. 2 *Colloq.* A person to be dealt with; a fellow: a queer *customer*; an ugly *customer.*

cus·tom·house (kus′təm·hous′) *n.* The place where entries of imports are made, vessels cleared, and duties collected; the department of customs.

customs union An association of nations that remove tariff restrictions among themselves and conduct a common tariff policy toward other nations.

cus·tos (kus′tos) *n.* *pl.* **cus·to·des** (kus·tō′dēz) 1 A custodian; keeper. 2 *Music* A direct. 3 The superior in certain religious houses. [<L, guardian]

custos mo·rum (môr′əm, mō′rəm) *Latin* Guardian of morals.

custos ro·tu·lo·rum (rō′tə·lôr′əm, -lō′rəm) A principal justice of an English county, who keeps the rolls or records of the sessions of the justices' court. [<L, keeper of the records]

cus·tu·mal (kus′chōō·məl, -tyōō-) *adj.* Belonging to the customs of a city. — *n.* A written collection of the customs of a city.

cut (kut) *v.* **cut, cut·ting** *v.t.* 1 To pierce, gash, or pass through with or as with a sharp edge. 2 To strike sharply, as with a whip. 3 To affect deeply; hurt the feelings. 4 To divide, sever, or carve into parts or segments. 5 To fell, hew, or chop down, as a tree or timber: often with *down.* 6 To mow or reap, as grain. 7 To shape, prepare, or make, as gems or carvings. 8 To hollow out, excavate. 9 To trim, shear, or pare. 10 To excise; edit out. 11 To reduce or lessen: to *cut* prices. 12 To dilute or weaken: to *cut* whisky. 13 To dissolve or break down, as fat globules: to *cut* grease. 14 To cross or intersect. 15 To castrate; geld. 16 *Colloq.* **a** To ignore socially, snub. **b** To stay away from wilfully, as work or classes. 17 To divide, as a pack of cards before dealing. 18 In racket sports, to chop (the ball) so it will spin and bound sharply and irregularly. 19 To turn the wheels of, as an automobile, so as to make the vehicle turn sharply. 20 To perform; present: to *cut* a caper. 21 To grow or acquire: to *cut* a tooth. — *v.i.* 22 To cut, cleave, or make an incision; do the work of a sharp edge. 23 To admit of being severed or cut. 24 To use an instrument for cutting. 25 To grow out through the gums: said of teeth. 26 To divide a card pack before dealing. 27 In sports, to chop the ball; also, to veer sharply while running. 28 To move or proceed by the shortest or most direct route: The boys *cut* across the field. **— to cut a figure** 1 To make a fine appearance. 2 To be of importance. 3 To make an impression: to *cut a poor figure* in scholarship. **— to cut a melon** To divide, as large profits or gains, with one's associates. **— to cut and run** Formerly, to cut the moorings of a vessel and set sail hastily; hence, to dash off without notice. **— to cut back** 1 To shorten by removing the end. 2 To curtail or cancel, as a contract, before fulfilment. 3 In sports, to run or dash erratically; change direction suddenly. **— to cut corners** To eliminate all but the most necessary items, as clothing for a trip, expenses, etc. **— to cut down** 1 To reduce the length or amount of; shorten; curtail. 2 To kill, as with a sword. **— to cut no ice** *Colloq.* To make no impression; have no significance. **— to cut in** 1 To interrupt a dancing couple in order to take the place of one partner.

2 To interrupt, as a conversation. 3 To move into (a line or queue) out of turn. **— to cut it fine** To arrange or estimate to the narrowest degree of tolerance: He *cut it fine* when he passed that car. **— to cut loose** 1 To release. 2 To speak or behave without restraint. **— to cut off** 1 To put an end to; destroy. 2 To interrupt. 3 To intercept. **— to cut out** 1 *Colloq.* To start away with haste. 2 To displace (another); supplant, as a rival. 3 To quit or renounce, as smoking. 4 To separate from the herd, as a horse or steer. 5 *Austral. Colloq.* To complete wool shearing; to complete any task. **— to cut up** 1 To slice or cut into pieces. 2 *Slang* To behave in an unruly manner. — *n.* 1 The opening, cleft, or wound made by an edged instrument; a gash; slit. 2 A cutting motion or stroke. 3 The part cut off. 4 That which cuts or hurts the feelings. 5 A cutting; excavated passage; groove; a road made through rock or a mountain for a railroad, canal, etc. 6 A direct way, as across an angle. 7 Fashion, form, style; also, number of arrangements of facets: the *cut* of a diamond. 8 An engraved block, or an impression from it. 9 A reduction, as in rates or of written matter; also, the part thus removed. 10 A refusal to recognize an acquaintance. 11 *Colloq.* An intentional failure in attendance, as at classes in college. 12 One of the bits of material used in drawing lots: to draw *cuts.* 13 The act of cutting in card playing. 14 A stroke imparting spin to a ball, in lawn tennis and cricket; also, the spin so imparted. 15 A fancy dancing step. 16 In a strip of motion-picture film, the narrow band separating one frame or exposure from the next. 17 *Chem.* **a** The quantity of resin added to each gallon of solvent. **b** A fraction of petroleum. 18 The output or seasonal yield of anything to be cut, as grain, timber, etc. 19 A group of animals, as cows or steers, separated from a herd to be driven elsewhere. 20 *U.S. Colloq.* A share. — *adj.* 1 Formed or affected by cutting; wounded; severed. 2 Dressed or finished by a tool, as stone or glass. 3 Castrated. 4 Reduced. 5 *Bot.* Incised or cleft. 6 Diluted. [ME *cutten, kytten* <Scand.]

Synonyms (verb): carve, chop, cleave, dissect, gash, hack, hew, sever, shear, slice, sunder, whittle. See RETRENCH.

cut–and–dried (kut′ən·drīd′) *adj.* 1 Prepared and arranged beforehand. 2 Lacking suspense; uninteresting; routine.

cut–and–thrust (kut′ən·thrust′) *adj.* Intended for cutting and thrusting: said of a sword.

cu·ta·ne·ous (kyōō·tā′nē·əs) *adj.* Consisting of, pertaining to, affecting, or of the nature of skin: a *cutaneous* covering; a *cutaneous* disease. [<Med. L *cutaneus* <*cutis* skin]

cut·a·way (kut′ə·wā′) *n.* A man's coat with the front corners cut slopingly away from the waist down to the back: also **cutaway coat.**

cut·back (kut′bak′) *n.* A sharp cut in the scheduled production of raw materials or manufactured goods, due to a sudden or unforeseen lessening of demand.

cutch[1] (kuch) *n.* Couchgrass.

cutch[2] (kuch) *n.* Anglo–Indian Catechu.

cute (kyōot) *adj.* 1 *U.S. Colloq.* Pretty or dainty; attractive. 2 *Dial.* Clever or sharp, especially in looking out for one's own advantage in petty ways. [Var. of ACUTE] — **cute′ly** *adv.* — **cute′ness** *n.*

cut glass See under GLASS.

cut·grass (kut′gras′, -gräs′) *n.* A swamp grass (*Leersia oryzoides*) with flat, rough-edged leaves that cut the flesh when drawn against it.

Cuth·bert (kuth′bərt), **Saint,** died 687, English monk.

cu·ti·cle (kyōō′ti·kəl) *n.* 1 The outer layer of cells that protect the true skin; epidermis; scarfskin. 2 Any superficial covering. 3 *Zool.* A thick lining membrane, as the cell integument of protozoa. 4 The crescent of toughened skin around the base of a fingernail or toenail. 5 *Bot.* A continuous hyaline film covering the surface of a plant, derived from the layers of epidermal cells. Also **cu·tic·u·la** (kyōō·tik′yə·lə). [<L *cuticula*, dim. of *cutis* skin] — **cu·tic′u·lar** *adj.*

cu·tie (kyōō′tē) *n. U.S. Slang* A pretty young woman. Also **cu′tey.** [<CUTE]

cu·ti·fy (kyōō′ti·fī) *v.i.* To form new skin. [<L *cutis* skin + -FY]

cu·tin (kyōō′tin) *n.* 1 *Bot.* A variety of fatty or waxy protective cuticle of leaves, stems, etc., of plants. 2 *Med.* A substitute for catgut or silk used in suturing wounds: it is prepared from the gut of an ox. [<L *cutis* skin + -IN]

cut–in (kut′in′) *n.* 1 The coordination of an automatic train-control system with the moving train so as to ensure application of the brakes. 2 *Printing* An insert in the text matter of a page.

cu·tin·i·za·tion (kyōō′tən·ə·zā′shən, -ī·zā′-) *n. Bot.* The modification of cell walls by the presence of cutin, making them waterproof.

cu·tin·ize (kyōō′tən·īz) *v.t.* & *v.i.* ·ized, ·iz·ing To make or become cuticular.

cu·tis (kyōō′tis) *n.* The derma or true skin; also, the corium. Also **cutis ve·ra** (vir′ə). [<L]

cut·las (kut′ləs) *n.* A short, swordlike weapon, often curved, formerly used chiefly by sailors in hand-to-hand fighting. Also **cut′lass.** [<F *coutelas,* aug. of *couteau* knife <L *culter*]

cutlas fish Scabbard fish.

CUTLASES
a. British, 10th century.
b. German, 15th century.
c. Mariner's, 17th century.

cut·ler (kut′lər) *n.* One who manufactures or deals in cutlery. [<F *coutelier* <Med. L *cultellarius* maker of knives <L *cultellus,* dim. of *culter* knife]

cut·ler·y (kut′lər·ē) *n.* 1 Cutting instruments collectively; especially, those for use at the dinner table. 2 The occupation of a cutler. [<OF *coutelerie* <*coutelier* CUTLER]

cut·let (kut′lit) *n.* 1 A thin piece of meat from the ribs or leg, for broiling or frying. 2 A flat croquette of chopped meat, fish, etc. [<F *côtelette,* double dim. of *côte* side <L *costa* rib; infl. in form by *cut*]

cut–line (kut′līn′) *n.* The title of an illustration.

cut money Money made by cutting gold and silver coins into pieces: used in the early Spanish colonies.

cut–off (kut′ôf′, -of′) *n.* 1 A short cut. 2 A mechanism that cuts off the flow of a fuel or fluid, as of steam to a boiler. 3 The point at which flow is thus cut off; the act of so doing. 4 A channel, natural or artificial, that diverts the course of a stream.

cut–out (kut′out′) *n.* 1 *Electr.* A switchlike arrangement, as for cutting a light out from a circuit. 2 A device to let the exhaust gases from an internal-combustion engine pass direct to the air without passing through the muffler. 3 The severing of the automatic train-control system from a moving train so as to prevent application of brakes.

cut–o·ver (kut′ō′vər) *adj.* Having the timber cut off: *cut-over* land.

cut–price (kut′prīs′) *adj.* Sharply reduced in price; below the usual rate.

cut·purse (kut′pûrs′) *n.* A pickpocket.

cut rate A reduced price.

cut–rate (kut′rāt′) *adj.* Sold for, or selling goods for, reduced prices: a *cut-rate* ticket; a *cut-rate* store.

cut·ter (kut′ər) *n.* 1 One who cuts, shapes, or fits anything by cutting. 2 That which cuts, as a tool or a machine. 3 *Naut.* **a** A sloop-rigged, fast-sailing vessel of narrow beam and deep draft, with bow and stern lines of the hull almost perpendicular. **b** A small, swift, armed, engined vessel, as in the revenue marine service. **c** A medium-sized boat used by a man-of-war. 4 A small sleigh usually drawn by one horse.

CUTTER (def. 4)

cut–throat (kut′thrōt′) *adj.* 1 Ruffianly;

bloodthirsty. **2** Played by three single players: said of poker and other card games. **3** Profitless: *cut-throat* stock. **4** Ruinous; merciless: *cut-throat* competition. —*n.* **1** A bloodthirsty ruffian. **2** A cut-throat card game.

cut·tie (kut′ē) *n.* An auk: also called *black guillemot.*

cut·ting (kut′ing) *adj.* **1** Adapted to cut; edged. **2** Disagreeably penetrating; sharp; chilling. **3** Tending to wound the feelings; sarcastic; bitter. See synonyms under BITTER¹, BLEAK¹. —*n.* **1** The act of severing. **2** Something obtained or made by cutting; a piece cut off or out. **3** *Bot.* A young plant shoot cut off for rooting or vegetative propagation. **4** An excavation, as for a railroad track. **5** *Chem.* In the making of soap, the separation of the final product from glycerol and aqueous products.

cut·tle (kut′l) *n.* **1** A cuttlefish. **2** Cuttlebone. [OE *cudele*]

cut·tle·bone (kut′l·bōn′) *n.* The internal calcareous plate of a cuttlefish: used as a dietary supplement for birds and, when powdered, as a polishing agent.

cut·tle·fish (kut′l·fish′) *n.* *pl.* **·fish** or **·fish·es** A carnivorous marine cephalopod (genus *Sepia*), with lateral fins, ten sucker-bearing arms, and an internal calcareous skeleton: it conceals itself by ejecting an inky fluid.

cut-up (kut′up′) *n.* *Colloq.* A person who tries to seem funny to others; a practical joker.

cut·wa·ter (kut′wô′tər, -wot′ər) *n.* **1** The forward part of the prow of a vessel. **2** The sharp edge on the up-stream side of a bridge pier.

cut·worm (kut′wûrm′) *n.* The larva of a moth (family *Noctuidae*) that cuts off young plants, usually at or near the surface of the ground. For illustration see under INSECT (injurious).

-cy *suffix* Forming nouns: **1** (*from adjectives*) Quality, state, or condition of: *secrecy, bankruptcy.* **2** (*from nouns*) Rank, order, or condition of: *chaplaincy, baronetcy.* [< F *-cie, -tie* < L *-cia, -tia* < Gk. *-kia, -keia, -tia, -teia*; or directly < L or < Gk.]

cyan- Var. of CYANO-.

cy·an·a·mide (sī·an′ə·mīd, -mid, sī′ə·nam′īd, -id) *n.* *Chem.* A white crystalline compound, CH_2N_2, formed from calcium cyanamide or by the action of cyanogen chloride on ammonia. Also **cy·an·a·mid** (sī·an′ə·mid, sī′ə·nam′id). [< CYAN- + AMIDE]

cyanamide process *Chem.* A method for the fixation of atmospheric nitrogen by passing a current of the gas over superheated calcium carbide and treating with high-pressure steam to yield ammonia.

cy·a·nate (sī′ə·nāt) *n.* *Chem.* A salt or ester of cyanic acid. [< CYAN- + -ATE³]

cy·an·ic (sī·an′ik) *adj.* **1** Of, pertaining to, or containing cyanogen. **2** Of or pertaining to blue.

cyanic acid *Chem.* A volatile liquid compound, HCNO, with a penetrating pungent odor and caustic properties, that is stable at low temperatures only. It is prepared by heating anhydrous cyanuric acid in carbonic acid gas.

cy·a·nide (sī′ə·nīd) *n.* *Chem.* A compound of cyanogen with a metallic element or radical: potassium *cyanide.* —*v.t.* **·nid·ed, ·nid·ing** *Metall.* To subject to the action of cyanide: to extract gold by *cyaniding* the ore. [< CYAN- + -IDE] —**cy·a·ni·da·tion** *n.*

cyanide process *Metall.* A process of extracting metal (chiefly gold) from ores by means of a dilute potassium-cyanide or sodium-cyanide solution which, assisted by the action of oxygen, dissolves the metal.

cy·a·nin (sī·ə·nin) *n.* *Biochem.* Any of a group of blue pigments obtained from certain flowers, as the iris, violet, and cornflower: also called *anthocyanin.* [< CYAN- + -IN]

cy·a·nine (sī′ə·nēn, -nin) *n.* *Chem.* A bluish-green, crystalline derivative, $C_{29}H_{35}N_2I$, of quinoline, used in photography as a sensitizer and indicator. [< CYAN- + -INE¹]

cy·a·nite (sī′ə·nīt) *n.* A blue, gray, or black aluminum silicate, occurring in long, bladelike, triclinic crystals, and also found columnar to fibrous in structure: often spelled *kyanite.* [< CYAN- + -ITE¹]

cyano- *combining form* **1** *Chem.* Cyanogen: *cyanogenesis.* **2** *Med.* Characterized by bluish coloring: *cyanosis.* **3** Dark-blue; blue: *cyanometer.* Also, before vowels, **cyan-**. [< Gk. *kyanos* dark-blue]

cy·an·o·gen (sī·an′ə·jən) *n.* *Chem.* **1** A colorless, intensely poisonous, liquefiable gas, C_2N_2, having an almondlike odor and burning with a purple flame. **2** The univalent radical, CN.

cy·a·no·gen·e·sis (sī′ə·nō·jen′ə·sis) *n.* *Chem.* **1** The making of hydrocyanic acid. **2** The process by which a glucoside through hydrolysis yields hydrocyanic (prussic) acid as one of its products.

cy·a·nom·e·ter (sī′ə·nom′ə·tər) *n.* *Meteorol.* An instrument for measuring the intensity of blue, as in the sky. [< CYANO- + -METER]

cy·a·nop·a·thy (sī′ə·nop′ə·thē) *n.* Cyanosis. [< CYANO- + -PATHY] —**cy·a·no·path·ic** (sī′ə·nō·path′ik) *adj.*

cy·a·noph·i·lous (sī′ə·nof′ə·ləs) *adj.* Stainable with blue dyes. [< CYANO- + -PHILOUS]

cy·a·no·pi·a (sī′ə·nō′pē·ə) *n.* *Pathol.* A diseased condition in which all things seen appear blue or bluish. Also **cy·a·nop·si·a** (sī′ə·nop′sē·ə). [< CYAN- + -OPIA]

cy·a·no·sis (sī′ə·nō′sis) *n.* *Pathol.* A disordered condition of the circulation due to inadequate airing of the blood and causing a livid bluish color of the skin. Also **cy·a·no·chroi·a** (sī′ə·nō·kroi′ə), **cy·a·no·der·ma** (-dûr′mə). [< CYAN- + -OSIS] —**cy·a·not·ic** (sī′ə·not′ik) *adj.*

cy·an·o·type (sī·an′ə·tīp′) *n.* A photographic picture, as a blueprint, made with the use of a cyanide.

cy·a·nu·ric (sī′ə·nyŏŏr′ik) *adj.* *Chem.* **1** Of or pertaining to cyanogen and urea. **2** Designating a crystalline acid, $C_3H_3O_3N_3$, obtained variously, as by the dry distillation of uric acid. [< CYAN- + URIC]

cy·ber·net·ics (sī′bər·net′iks) *n.* The science which treats of the principles underlying the common elements in the functioning of automatic machines and of the human nervous system; the theory of control and communication in machines and organisms. [< Gk. *kybernētēs* steersman + -ICS]

cy·bo·tax·is (sī′bə·tak′sis) *n.* *Physics* The arrangement of molecules in a liquid in such a manner as to suggest crystal structure, but without permanence or stability at any point. [< Gk. *kybos* cube + *taxis* arrangement] —**cy·bo·tac·tic** (-tak′tik) *adj.*

cy·cad (sī′kad) *n.* Any of a small family (*Cycadaceae*) of primitive, seed-bearing, mostly tropical plants of fernlike or palmlike appearance. [< NL *Cycas, -adis* < Gk. *kykas,* a copyist's error for *koïkas,* accusative pl. of *koïx* a palm tree] —**cy·ca·da·ceous** (sik′ə·dā′shəs) *adj.*

cyc·la·men (sik′lə·mən, -men) *n.* An Old World bulbous flowering herb (genus *Cyclamen*) of the primrose family, with white, pink, or crimson flowers: also called *sowbread.* [< NL < L *cyclaminos* < Gk. *kyklaminos, kyklamis,* ? < *kyklos* a circle; with ref. to the shape of the root]

cyc·las (sik′ləs, sī′kləs) *n.* *pl.* **cyc·la·des** (sik′lə·dēz) A close-fitting, often sleeveless tunic or surcoat worn during the Middle Ages. [< L *Gk. kyklas,* a woman's garment]

cy·cle (sī′kəl) *n.* **1** *Astron.* **a** A period of time, at the end of which certain aspects or motions of the heavenly bodies repeat themselves. **b** An orbit or circle in the heavens. **2** A round of years or of ages; a vast period; eon. **3** *Bot.* An entire turn or circle, as of a spiral leaf-structure. **4** A body of legends, poems, or romances relating to one period, person, etc.; also, a series of miracle plays: the Chester *cycle.* **5** A bicycle, tricycle, etc. **6** *Math.* A closed path in a diagram; loop. **7** A series that repeats itself. **8** *Physics* A recurring series of operations, as in gas or other internal-combustion engines, in which heat is imparted to or taken from a substance, which by expansion or contraction gives out or stores up energy and is finally returned to its original condition. **9** *Electr.* A full period of an alternating current; also, a completed series of variations in electromagnetic waves of a given frequency, as in radio transmission. —*v.i.* **cy·cled, cy·cling** **1** To pass through cycles. **2** To ride a bicycle, tricycle, or the like. [< F < LL *cyclus* < Gk. *kyklos* circle]

cycle car A light automobile with three or four

wheels, tires, and engine of similar type and size to those of a motorcycle.

cy·clic (sī′klik, sik′lik) *adj.* **1** Pertaining to or characterized by cycles; recurring in cycles. **2** *Chem.* Of, pertaining to, or characterized by a closed chain or ring formation, as benzene, naphthalene, anthracene, etc. **3** *Bot.* Having parts arranged in whorls, as a flower. Also **cy′cli·cal.**

cy·cling (sī′kling) *n.* The sport of riding the bicycle, tricycle, etc.; the art or skill of a cyclist.

cy·clist (sī′klist) *n.* One who rides a bicycle, tricycle, etc. Also **cy′cler.**

cyclo- *combining form* **1** Circular: *cyclograph.* **2** *Chem.* A saturated cyclic hydrocarbon compound: *cyclopropane.* Also, before vowels, **cycl-**. [< Gk. *kyklos* circle]

cy·clo·gen·e·sis (sī′klō·jen′ə·sis) *n.* *Meteorol.* The conditions which create a new cyclone or intensify the actions of a preexisting one. [< CYCLO(NE) + GENESIS]

cy·clo·gi·ro (sī′klō·jī′rō) *n.* *Aeron.* An aircraft equipped with airfoils designed to give support by rotating about an axis perpendicular to the longitudinal axis of the plane. Also **cy′clo·gy′ro.** [< CYCLO- + (AUTO)GIRO]

cy·clo·graph (sī′klə·graf, -gräf) *n.* **1** An instrument for drawing arcs of circles by means of two wheels of different diameters. **2** An arcograph. **3** A camera with which a panoramic view of an object may be taken.

cy·clo·hex·ane (sī′klō·hek′sān) *n.* *Chem.* A saturated hydrocarbon, C_6H_{12}, made by the hydrogenation of benzene and occurring in petroleum: it is composed of six methylene radicals arranged in cyclic form.

cy·cloid (sī′kloid) *adj.* **1** Resembling a circle or somewhat circular: specifically said of fish scales with concentric rings and smooth edges. **2** *Psychiatry* Of or pertaining to a personality type exhibiting marked alternations of mood. —*n.* *Geom.* The curve described by a point on the circumference of a circle that rolls, without slipping, along a straight line in a single plane. [< Gk. *kykloeidēs* circular] —**cy·cloi′dal** *adj.* —**cy′cloid·ism** *n.*

CYCLOID

As the circle *c* rolls along the straight line *bd*, point *a* on its circumference traces the cycloid *bad.*

cy·clom·e·ter (sī·klom′ə·tər) *n.* **1** An instrument for recording the rotations of a wheel to show speed and distance traveled; a speedometer. **2** A device for measuring circular arcs. [< CYCLO- + -METER]

cy·clom·e·try (sī·klom′ə·trē) *n.* The art of measuring circles. —**cy·clo·met·ric** (sī′klō·met′rik) *adj.*

cy·clone (sī′klōn) *n.* **1** *Meteorol.* A system of winds circulating about a center of relatively low barometric pressure, and, at the earth's surface, advancing with clockwise rotation in the southern hemisphere, counterclockwise in the northern. **2** Loosely, any violent and destructive whirling windstorm. [< Gk. *kyklōn,* ppr. of *kykloein* move in a circle < *kyklos*] —**cy·clo·nal** (sī·klō′nəl), **cy·clon·ic** (sī·klon′ik) or **·i·cal** *adj.* —**cy·clon′i·cal·ly** *adv.*

cyclone cellar An underground shelter adapted for use during cyclones and tornadoes. Also **storm cellar.**

cy·clon·o·scope (sī·klon′ə·skōp) *n.* *Meteorol.* An apparatus for detecting the approach of a cyclone or tornado. [< *cyclono-* (< CYCLONE) + -SCOPE]

cy·clo·pe·di·a (sī′klə·pē′dē·ə) *n.* **1** A work giving a summary of some branch of knowledge. **2** An encyclopedia. Also **cy′clo·pae′di·a.** [Short for ENCYCLOPEDIA]

cy·clo·pe·dic (sī′klə·pē′dik) *adj.* **1** Of or pertaining to a cyclopedia. **2** Like a cyclopedia; embracing a wide range of knowledge. Also **cy′clo·pae′dic, cy′clo·pe′di·cal, cy′clo·pae′di·cal.** —**cy′clo·pe′di·cal·ly** *adv.*

cy·clo·pe·dist (sī′klə·pē′dist) *n.* One who makes or contributes to a cyclopedia. Also **cy′clo·pae′dist.**

cy·clo·pen·tane (sī′klə·pen′tān) *n.* *Chem.* A relatively inert liquid compound, C_5H_{10}, obtained from some American and Caucasian mineral oils.

cy·clo·phon (sī′klə·fon) *n.* *Electronics* A type of

vacuum tube in which a beam of electrons serves as a switching or commutating element. [< CYCLO- + Gk. *phonē* a sound]

cy·clo·ple·gi·a (sī″klə-plē′jē-ə) *n. Pathol.* Paralysis of the ciliary muscle of the eye. — **cy′clo·ple′gic** *adj.*

cy·clo·pro·pane (sī″klə-prō′pān) *n. Chem.* A colorless, pungent, inflammable gas, C_3H_6, used as an inhalation anesthetic.

cy·clo·ram·a (sī″klə-ram′ə, -rä′mə) *n.* **1** A panorama on the interior of a cylindrical surface, appearing as in natural perspective, the spectator standing in the center. **2** A backdrop curtain, often concave, used on theater stages to give the illusion of perspective; a concave plaster structure, sometimes merely a dome, used in the same way. [< CYCLO- + Gk. *horama* a view] — **cy·clo·ram·ic** (sī″klə-ram′ik) *adj.*

cy·clo·sis (sī-klō′sis) *n. Biol.* The streaming cyclical movement of protoplasm within a cell. [< Gk. *kyklōsis* a going around]

cy·clo·spor·ine (sī″klō-spôr′ēn) *n.* A drug of fungal origin, valuable for its suppressive influence on the body's natural inclination to reject organ transplants.

cy·clo·stome (sī″klə-stōm, sik′lə-) *n.* Any of a class (*Cyclostomata*) of primitive, carnivorous, aquatic vertebrates, having round, suctorial mouths devoid of jaws, and a single nostril; the lampreys and hagfishes. —*adj.* Having a round mouth; also, pertaining to the cyclostomes: also **cy·clos·to·mate** (sī-klos′tə-māt), **cy·clo·stom·a·tous** (sī″klə-stom′ə-təs).

cy·clo·stroph·ic (sī″klə-strof′ik, -strō′fik, sik′lə-) *adj. Meteorol.* Designating the centrifugal tendency of an air mass or wind current due to the curvature of its path over the earth's surface. Compare GEOSTROPHIC. [< CYCLO- + Gk. *strophē* a turning, a twisting]

cy·clo·style (sī″klə-stīl, sik′lə-) *n.* An apparatus for manifolding manuscript. [< Gk. *kyklos* circle, wheel + STYLE (def. 7)]

cy·clo·thy·mi·a (sī″klə-thī′mē-ə) *n. Psychiatry* Manic-depressive psychosis, especially as characterized by fluctuations of mood from gaiety to depression at frequent intervals. [< CYCLO- + -THYMIA] — **cy′clo·thy′mic** *adj.*

cy·clo·tron (sī″klə-tron) *n. Physics* An apparatus which obtains high-energy deuterons by whirling a stream of electrons or ions at immense speeds in a strong magnetic field alternating in synchronism with their accelerated motion; an atom smasher. [< CYCLO- + (ELEC)TRON]

cy·e·sis (sī-ē′sis) *n.* Pregnancy. [< Gk. *kyēsis* < *kyeein* conceive, be pregnant]

cyg·net (sig′nit) *n.* A young swan. ◆ Homophone: *signet.* [< F *cygne* < L *cycnus* < Gk. *kyknos* + -ET]

cyl·in·der (sil′in-dər) *n.* **1** *Geom.* **a** A solid described by the circumference of a circle as its center moves along a straight line: the ends of the solid are parallel, equal circles. It is called a *right cylinder* when the line along which the center moves is at right angles to the plane of the circle, and *oblique cylinder* when the line is not at right angles. **b** Any curved surface generated by the motion of a straight line remaining parallel to itself and constantly intersecting a curve. **2** Any cylindrical part of a machine, especially if hollow, and proportioned so that the length exceeds the diameter. **3** *Mech.* A cylindrical member of a motor in which a piston moves and receives direct impact from the steam or other motive fluid. **4** A rotating cylindrical portion of a printing press. **5** The rotating chamber that holds the cartridges of a revolver. **6** A cylindrical stone bearing an inscription; especially, an inscribed clay tablet, found buried under the corners of edifices in Babylonia and Assyria. — *v.t.* To press or fit with a cylinder. [< L *cylindrus* < Gk. *kylindros* < *kylindein* roll]

cylinder head The detachable end cover of an internal-combustion engine, comprising a portion of the combustion chamber.

cyl·in·der-stop (sil′in-dər-stop′) *n.* The mechanism that locks each chamber in the cylinder of a revolver in alinement with the barrel. See illustration under REVOLVER.

cy·lin·dri·cal (si-lin′dri-kəl) *adj.* **1** Of or pertaining to a cylinder. **2** Having the form or shape of a cylinder. Also **cy·lin′dric.** — **cy·lin′·dri·cal·ly**

adv. — **cy·lin·dri·cal·i·ty** (si-lin′dri-kal′ə-tē) *n.*

cyl·in·droid (sil′in-droid) *n.* A solid body resembling a cylinder but having elliptical bases equal and parallel. [< Gk. *kylindroeidēs*]

cy·lix (sī′liks, sil′iks) See KYLIX.

cy·ma (sī′mə) *n. pl.* **·mae** (-mē) **1** *Archit.* A curved molding with a reversed curve as its profile: frequently placed above a cornice in Greek and Greco-Roman art. **2** *Bot.* A cyme. [< NL < Gk. *kyma* a wave]

cyma rec·ta (rek′tə) *Archit.* A cyma with the convex part nearest the wall.

cyma re·ver·sa (ri-vûr′sə) *Archit.* A cyma with the concave part nearest the wall.

cy·ma·ti·um (si-mā′shē-əm) *n. pl.* **·ti·a** (-shē-ə) *Archit.* A cyma; hence, any molding that caps a division of an entablature, separating it from the next. [< L < Gk. *kymation,* dim of *kyma* a wave]

cym·bal (sim′bəl) *n.* One of a pair of platelike metallic musical instruments played by being clashed together. ◆ Homophone: *symbol.* [OE and < OF *cymbale,* both < L *cymbalum* < Gk. *kymbalon* < *kymbē* cup, hollow of a vessel] — **cym′bal·ist, cym′bal·er** *n.*

cyme (sīm) *n. Bot.* A flat-topped flower cluster in which the central flowers bloom first. [< F < L *cyma* a wave, a sprout < Gk. *kyma*]

cy·mene (sī′mēn) *n. Chem.* One of three isomeric liquid compounds, $C_{10}H_{14}$, with lemonlike odor, contained in several volatile oils, as cumin, wild thyme, etc., and obtained by distilling camphor with phosphoric anhydride: sometimes called *camphogen.* Also **cy·mol** (sī′mōl, -mol). [< Gk. *kyminon* + -ENE]

cym·lin (sim′lin) *n.* A kind of squash: sometimes spelled *simlin.* Also **cym′bling, cym′ling.** [Var. of *simlin,* an alter. of SIMNEL]

cymo- *combining form* Wave: *cymometer.* [< Gk. *kymos* wave]

cy·mo·gene (sī′mə-jēn) *n. Chem.* A volatile, inflammable distillate of petroleum, consisting of hydrocarbons with a high butane content. [< Gk. *kyminon* cumin + -GENE]

cy·mo·graph (sī′mə-graf, -gräf) *n.* **1** An instrument for tracing in profile the outlines of architectural moldings. **2** Kymograph. — **cy′mo·graph′ic** *adj.*

cy·moid (sī′moid) *adj.* Of the form of a cyme.

cy·mo·me·ter (sī-mom′ə-tər) *n.* An instrument for the measurement of wavelengths and of small electrical capacities. [< CYMO- + -METER]

cy·mo·phane (sī′mə-fān) *n.* A variety of chrysoberyl with a changeable luster; the Oriental cat's-eye.

cy·mo·scope (sī′mə-skōp) *n.* An instrument for detecting the presence of electromagnetic waves.

cy·mose (sī′mōs, sī-mōs′) *adj. Bot.* Bearing, pertaining to, or like a cyme. Also **cy·mous** (sī′məs). — **cy′mose·ly** *adv.*

cyn·ic (sin′ik) *n.* A sneering, captious person; a misanthrope; pessimist. —*adj.* **1** Pertaining to Sirius, the Dog Star. **2** *Rare* Of or like a dog. **3** Cynical. [< Gk. *kynikos* doglike]

cyn·i·cal (sin′i-kəl) *adj.* **1** Given to distrusting evidences of virtue and disinterested motives; inclined to moral skepticism; pessimistic. **2** Currish; sneering. See synonyms under CAPTIOUS. — **cyn′i·cal·ly** *adv.*

cyn·i·cism (sin′ə-siz′əm) *n.* The state or quality of being cynical; contempt for the virtues or generous sentiments of others. Also **cyn′·i·cal·ness.**

cy·no·pho·bi·a (sī′nə-fō′bē-ə, sin′ə-) *n.* An abnormal fear of dogs. [< Gk. *kyōn, kynos* dog + -PHOBIA] — **cy′no·phobe** *n.*

cy·no·sure (sī′nə-shŏŏr, sin′ə-) *n.* An object of general interest or attention. [< MF < L *cynosura* < Gk. *kynosoura* the constellation Ursa Minor < *kyōn, kynos* dog + *oura* tail]

cy·per·a·ceous (sī′pə-rā′shəs, sip′ə-) *adj. Bot.* Designating a family (*Cyperaceae*) of glasslike or rushlike monocotyledonous herbs, the sedge family, with solid stems and closed sheaths. [< NL *Cyperaceae,* the sedge family < Gk. *kypeiros* sedge]

cy·pher (sī′fər) See CIPHER.

cy pres (sē′prā′) *Law* **1** As nearly as possible: applied in interpreting the principle whereby a gift

legal in form which cannot be administered just as the testator directed, or which is not specified in a definite manner, may be applied as nearly as possible according to the donor's intentions. [< OF *si pres* as near as]

cy·press¹ (sī′prəs) *n.* **1** An evergreen tree (family *Cupressaceae*) of southern Europe and western Asia, having durable timber; especially, *C. funebris,* having pendulous branches like a weeping willow. **2** Any of various other trees of kindred genera, as the evergreen American cypress or white cedar (genus *Chamaecyparis*), and the bald cypress (*Taxodium distichum*) of the southern United States. **3** The wood of these trees. [< OF *cypres* < LL *cypressus* < Gk. *kyparissos* cypress]

cy·press² (sī′prəs) *n. Obs.* A transparent, black lawn fabric: also spelled *cyprus.* [< OF *Cipre, Cypres* Cyprus, whence the cloth was first imported into Europe]

cypress knee A hollow, knee-shaped growth which aerates the roots of the bald cypress.

cypress vine An annual, twining plant (*Quamoclit pennata*) with leaves pinnately parted into linear, parallel lobes, and bearing narrow, funnel-shaped, scarlet, and sometimes white flowers.

cy·pri·nid (si-prī′nid, sip′rə-nid) *n.* A cyprinoid fish. —*adj.* Of, like, or pertaining to cyprinoids. [< NL *Cyprinidae,* the carp genus]

cyprino- *combining form* Carp: *cyprinodont.* Also, before vowels, **cyprin-.** [< Gk. *kyprinos* carp]

cy·prin·o·dont (si-prin′ə-dont, si-prī′nə-) *n.* Any of a family (*Cyprinidae*) of fishes with flattish, scaly heads; killifishes, guppies, minnows, etc. [< CYPRIN(O)- + Gk. *odous, odontos* tooth]

cyp·ri·noid (sip′rə-noid, si-prī′-) *adj.* Carplike. —*n.* A fish of the carp family, including barbels, breams, goldfishes, and many of the fresh-water minnows. [< Gk. *kyprinos* carp]

cyp·ri·pe·di·um (sip′rə-pē′dē-əm) *n.* Any of a genus (*Cypripedium*) of orchids, mainly terrestrial, with fibrous roots, plaited leaves, and large flowers with pouchlike lip: called *ladyslipper* and *moccasin flower.* [< NL < Gk. *Kypris* Aphrodite + *podion* a slipper, dim. of *pous, podos* a foot]

cy·prus (sī′prəs) See CYPRESS².

cyp·se·la (sip′sə-lə) *n. pl.* **·lae** (-lē) *Bot.* An achenium in plants of the sunflower family. [< NL < Gk. *kypselē* hollow vessel]

cyst¹ (sist) *n.* **1** Any membranous sac or vesicle containing liquid or semisolid material: the biliary *cyst,* the urinary *cyst.* **2** *Pathol.* Any abnormal sac or vesicle in which morbid matter may be collected and retained. **3** *Zool.* A bladderlike sac, as that with which an embryonic tapeworm surrounds itself; also, a bladderworm. **4** *Bot.* **a** A receptacle for oil in the rind of the orange and like fruits. **b** A cell or cavity containing reproductive bodies in certain cryptogams. **c** The spore case of a seaweed. [< Gk. *kystis* bladder < *kyein* contain]

cyst² (sist) *n.* A chest; cist. [Var. of CIST]

cys·tec·to·my (sis-tek′tə-mē) *n. pl.* **·mies** *Surg.* **1** An operation to remove a cyst. **2** Removal of the gall bladder. [< Gk. *kystis* bladder + *ektemnein* excise]

cys·te·ine (sis′ti-ēn, -in) *n.* An amino acid, $H_2C_3SO_2$, derived from cystine. Also **cys′te·in** (-in). [< CYSTINE]

cysti- Var. of CYSTO-.

cys·tic (sis′tik) *adj.* **1** Encysted. **2** Having cysts. **3** Of or pertaining to a cyst or to the bladder. **4** Cystlike. Also **cys′tous.**

cys·ti·cer·cus (sis′tə-sûr′kəs) *n. pl.* **·ci** (-sī) *Zool.* A hydatid cyst which develops from the larva of a tapeworm and gives rise to the head and neck (scolex) of the future tapeworm: formerly regarded as a distinct genus. [< CYSTI- + Gk. *kerkos* tail] — **cys′ti·cer′coid** *adj.*

cys·tid·i·um (sis-tid′ē-əm) *n. pl.* **·tid·i·a** (-tid′ē-ə) *Bot.* A sterile, spherical cell projecting among the basidia in fleshy fungi. [< NL < Gk. *kystis* cyst + *-idion,* dim. suffix]

cys·tine (sis′tēn, -tin) *n. Biochem.* One of the amino acids, $C_6H_{12}O_4N_2S_2$, produced by the digestion or hydrolysis of proteins in the body, and isolated from the urine in the form of white hexagonal crystals. It is an important factor in nutrition. [<CYST(O) + -INE]

cys·ti·tis (sis·tī′tis) n. Pathol. Inflammation of the bladder. [<CYST(O)- + -ITIS¹]

cys·ti·tome (sis′tə·tōm) n. Surg. An instrument used in opening the capsule of the crystalline lens.

cysto– combining form Bladder, cyst: cystoscope. Also, before vowels, **cyst–**. [<Gk. kystis bladder]

cys·to·carp (sis′tə·kärp) n. Bot. The fructification from an archicarp or procarp in fungi and red algae; a sporocarp. — **cys′to·car′pic** adj.

cys·to·cele (sis′tə·sēl) n. Pathol. A hernia or rupture involving the protrusion of the urinary bladder.

cys·toid (sis′toid) adj. Shaped like a cyst; encysted. — n. A cystoid growth.

cys·to·lith (sis′tə·lith) n. Bot. A mineral and usually somewhat crystalline concretion in the epidermal or subjacent cells of the leaf in some plants, especially of the nettle family.

cys·to·scope (sis′tə·skōp) n. Med. A catheter with a device for introducing light into the bladder to permit of ocular examination. — **cys·to·scop·ic** (sis′tə·skop′ik) adj. — **cys·tos·co·py** (sis·tos′kə·pē) n.

cys·tos·to·my (sis·tos′tə·mē) n. pl. **·mies** Surg. The making of an artificial outlet from the bladder. [<CYSTO- + Gk. stoma mouth]

cys·tot·o·my (sis·tot′ə·mē) n. pl. **·mies** Surg. A cutting into the bladder; also, the operation of puncturing an encysted tumor. [<CYSTO- + -TOMY]

cy·tase (sī′tās) n. Biochem. A digestive enzyme found in the seeds of certain plants and aiding in the formation of mannose and galactose sugars. [<CYT(O) + -ASE]

cy·tas·ter (sī·tas′tər, sī′tas′-) n. Biol. A star-like form assumed by the nucleus of a cell undergoing division; specifically, an aster

not associated with the chromosomes. [CYT(O)- + Gk. astēr star]

–cyte combining form Cell: phagocyte. [<Gk. kytos hollow vessel]

cyto– combining form Cell: cytochrome. Also, before vowels, **cyt–**. [<Gk. kytos hollow vessel < kyein contain, be pregnant with]

cy·to·chrome (sī′tə·krōm) n. Biochem. A pigment found in the respiratory cells of plants and animals, as chlorophyll, hemoglobin, and also in certain aerobic bacteria.

cy·to·di·ag·no·sis (sī′tō·dī′əg·nō′sis) n. Med. A diagnosis from the examination of cells in body fluids.

cy·to·gen·e·sis (sī′tō·jen′ə·sis) n. Biol. The formation of cells. Also **cy·to·gen·e·sis** (sis′-tō·jen′ə·sis), **cy·tog·e·ny** (sī·toj′ə·nē). — **cy·to·ge·net·ic** (sī′tō·jə·net′ik), **cy·to·gen·ic** (sī′tō·jen′ik) adj.

cy·to·ge·net·ics (sī′tō·jə·net′iks) n. The scientific investigation of the role of cells in the phenomena of heredity and evolution.

cy·to·ki·ne·sis (sī′tō·ki·nē′sis, -kī-) n. Biol. The changes which take place in the cytoplasm of the cell during mitosis, meiosis, and fertilization. [<CYTO- + Gk. kinēsis motion]

cy·tol·o·gy (sī·tol′ə·jē) n. The scientific study of the structure, organization, and function of cells. [<CYTO- + -LOGY] — **cy·to·log·ic** (sī′tə·loj′ik) or **·i·cal** adj. — **cy′to·log′i·cal·ly** adv. — **cy·tol′o·gist** n.

cy·tol·y·sis (sī·tol′ə·sis) n. Biol. The dissolution or breaking up of cells. [<CYTO- + Gk. lysis a loosing] — **cy′to·lyt′ic** (-lit′ik) adj.

cy·tom·e·ter (sī·tom′ə·tər) n. A device for measuring and counting organic cells. [<CYTO- + -METER]

cy·to·mi·cro·some (sī′tō·mī′krə·sōm) n. Biol. A cytoplasmic microsome, as differentiated from a nuclear one.

cy·to·mi·tome (sī′tō·mī′tōm, sī·tom′ə·tōm) n. Biol. The cytoplasmic threads as opposed to

those of the nuclear threadwork. [<CYTO- + Gk. mitos thread + -OME]

cy·toph·a·gy (sī·tof′ə·jē) n. Biol. The destruction of cells by other cells; phagocytosis. [<CYTO- + -PHAGY]

cy·to·phar·ynx (sī′tō·far′ingks) n. Zool. The esophageal tube of a protozoan.

cy·to·plasm (sī′tə·plaz′əm) n. Biol. All the protoplasm of a cell except that in the nucleus. — **cy′to·plas′mic** adj.

cy·to·plast (sī′tə·plast) n. Cytoplasm. — **cy′to·plas′tic** adj.

czar (zär) n. 1 An emperor or absolute monarch; especially, one of the former emperors of Russia: often spelled tsar. 2 An absolute ruler; despot. [<Russian tsare, ult. <L Caesar Caesar, a family name later used as a title of the imperial heirs]

czar·das (chär′däsh) n. A Hungarian dance consisting of a slow, melancholy section followed by a quick, fiery one. [<Hungarian csárdás]

czar·dom (zär′dəm) n. 1 The territory ruled by a czar. 2 The position or power of a czar: also spelled tsardom.

czar·e·vitch (zär′ə·vich) n. The eldest son of a czar of Russia: also written cesarevitch, tsarevitch. [<Russian tsarevich]

czar·ev·na (zä·rev′nə) n. 1 The wife of the czarevitch. 2 Formerly the title of any daughter of the czar. Also spelled tsarevna. [<Russian tsarevna]

cza·ri·na (zä·rē′nə) n. The wife of a czar of Russia. Also **cza·rit·za** (zä·rit′sə). [<Russian <G czarin]

czar·ism n. Absolutism in government; despotism; autocracy; also spelled tsarism.

Czech·o·slo·va·ki·a A former republic of east central Europe (1918-13); in 1918, the Austro-Hungarian Empire separated into Austria, Hungary, and Czechoslovakia. Czechoslovakia divided 1/1/93 into two separate republics, the Czech Republic and the Slovak Republic.

D

d, D (dē) n. pl. **d's, D's** or **Ds, ds, dees** (dēz) 1 The fourth letter of the English alphabet, from Phoenician daleth, through the Hebrew daleth, Greek delta, Roman D. 2 The sound of the letter d, usually a voiced alveolar stop. See ALPHABET. — symbol 1 In Roman notation, the numeral 500. See under NUMERAL. 2 Music a The second note in the natural scale of C; re. b The pitch of this tone, or the written note representing it. c The scale built upon D. 3 Differentiation or, in algebra, a known quantity. 4 Anything shaped like a D or a half circle, as the iron loop on a saddle to which articles are attached. 5 Pence (d., from Latin denarii) in English money. 6 Chem. Deuterium.

dab¹ (dab) n. 1 One of various flounders, especially the American **sand dab** (Limanda ferruginea) of the Atlantic and Pacific coasts. 2 Any flatfish. [Origin uncertain]

dab² (dab) Brit. Colloq. A skilful person; an adept. [Origin uncertain]

dab³ (dab) n. 1 A gentle blow; a pat. 2 A quick stroke or thrust; a peck. 3 A small lump or patch of soft substance, as butter or paint; hence, a little bit. — v.t. & v.i. **dabbed, dab·bing** 1 To strike softly; tap. 2 To peck. 3 To pat with something soft and damp. 4 To apply (paint, etc.) with light strokes. [ME dabben. Cf. G tappe footprint, MDu. dabben fumble, dabble.]

dab·ber (dab′ər) n. 1 One who or that which dabs. 2 A printers' inking ball; an engravers' pad, etc.; a dauber.

dab·bing (dab′ing) n. The process of indenting, as with a sharp hammer, the surface of a stone.

dab·ble (dab′əl) v. **·bled, ·bling** v.i. 1 To play, as with the hands, in a liquid; splash gently. 2 To engage in superficially or without serious involvement: to dabble in art. — v.t. 3 To wet slightly; bespatter, as with water or mud. [Freq. of DAB³, v.] — **dab′bler** n.

dab·chick (dab′chik) n. 1 A fledgling; hence, an immature or delicate person. 2 A small grebe of Europe (Podiceps ruficollis) or the

pied–billed grebe of North America (Podilymbus podiceps): often called helldiver. [<DAB³ + CHICK]

Dac·ca (dä′kä) The capital of Bangla Desh.

dace (dās) n. pl. **dac·es** or **dace** 1 A small cyprinoid fresh–water fish of Europe (Leuciscus leuciscus). 2 A fresh–water fish of North America (Semotilus atromaculatus). [<OF darz, dars, nominative sing. of dart, a small fish]

dachs·hund (däks′-

DACHSHUND
(From 7 to 9 inches in height at the shoulder)

hŏŏnt′, daks′hŏŏnd′, dash′-) n. A breed of dog native to Germany, of medium size, with long, compact body and short legs, short coat, usually of red or tan or black and tan. [<G <dachs badger + hund dog]

da·cite (dā′sīt) n. An igneous rock, usually volcanic, composed of plagioclase and quartz, commonly mixed with hornblende, biotite, or both. [from Dacia]

dac·ry·o·gen·ic (dak′rē·ō·jen′ik) adj. Med. Capable of producing tears. [<Gk. dakryon a tear + -GENIC]

dac·ry·on (dak′rē·on) n. pl. **·ry·a** (-rē·ə) Anat. The point near the root of the nose indicating the junction of the frontal, lacrimal, and superior maxillary bones. [<Gk. dakryon a tear]

dac·tyl (dak′təl) n. 1 In prosody, a three-syllable measure consisting of one long or accented syllable followed by two short or unaccented ones (–ᴗᴗ). 2 A finger or toe; digit. [<Gk. daktylos finger, dactyl]

dac·ty·late (dak′tə·lāt) adj. Having fingerlike organs or processes.

dac·tyl·ic (dak·til′ik) adj. Of or pertaining to dactyls. — n. A dactylic verse.

dac·tyl·i·og·ra·phy (dak·til′ē·og′rə·fē) n. The engraving of gems for rings. [<Gk. daktylios

finger ring + -GRAPHY]

dac·tyl·i·on (dak·til′ē·on) n. pl. **·tyl·i·a** (-til′ē·ə) 1 The extreme tip or end of the middle finger when the hand is fully extended: a measuring point in anthropometry. 2 The joining or webbing together of fingers; syndactylism. Also **dac·tyl′i·um** (-əm). [<NL <Gk. daktylos finger]

dactylo– combining form Finger; toe: dactylology. Also, before vowels, **dactyl–**. [<Gk. daktylos finger]

dac·tyl·o·gram (dak·til′ə·gram) n. A fingerprint.

dac·ty·log·ra·phy (dak′tə·log′rə·fē) n. The scientific study of fingerprints. [<DACTYLO- + -GRAPHY] — **dac·ty·lo·graph·ic** (dak′tə·lə·graf′ik) adj.

dac·ty·lol·o·gy (dak′tə·lol′ə·jē) n. The use of the fingers in communicating ideas, as in the deaf–and–dumb alphabet. [<DACTYLO- + -LOGY]

dac·ty·los·co·py (dak′tə·los′kə·pē) n. The examination of fingerprints as a means of identification. [<DACTYLO- + -SCOPY] — **dac·ty·lo·scop·ic** (dak′tə·lə·skop′ik) adj.

dad (dad) n. Colloq. Father: used familiarly, as by children. Also **dad′dy**.

dad·dy–long–legs (dad′ē·lông′legz′, -long′-) n. 1 A long-legged, insect–eating arachnid of the order Phalangida, resembling a spider; the harvestman. 2 Brit. The cranefly. 3 A very long–legged person.

dae·mon (dē′mən), **dae·mon·ic** (dē·mon′ik), etc. See DEMON, etc.

daf·fo·dil (daf′ə·dil) n. A plant (Narcissus pseudo–narcissus) of the amaryllis family, with solitary yellow flowers, also **daf′fa·dil′ly**, **daf′fy·down·dil′ly**, **daf′fy·down·dil′ly**. [Var. of ME affodille <Med. L affodillus <L asphodelus. Doublet of ASPHODEL.]

daf·fy (daf′ē) adj. **·fi·er, ·fi·est** Colloq. Crazy; daft. [<DAFF²]

daft (daft, däft) adj. 1 Silly; imbecile; insane. 2 Frolicsome. [OE gedæfte mild, meek] — **daft′ly** adv. — **daft′ness** n.

dag·ger (dag'ər) n. 1 A short, edged, and pointed weapon, for stabbing. 2 *Printing* A reference mark (†): the second in a series. — **double dagger** A mark of reference (‡) used in printing; a diesis: the third in a series. — v.t. 1 To pierce with a dagger; stab. 2 *Printing* To mark with a dagger. [ME *dag* pierce, stab. Cf. F *dague* dagger]

dag·gle (dag'əl) v.t. & v.i. **·gled, ·gling** To trail or draggle in the mud or wet. [Freq. of dial. *dag* dampen, bemire]

TYPES OF DAGGERS

dag·lock (dag'lok') n. A dirty or tangled lock, as of wool on a sheep: also called *taglock*. [< dial. *dag* bemire + LOCK²]

da·go·ba (dä'gə·bə) n. A dome-shaped Buddhist monument or shrine, built on a mound, and containing sacred relics. [< Singhalese *dāgaba*]

da·guerre·o·type (də·ger'ə·tīp', -ē·ə·tīp') n. 1 An early photographic process using silver-coated, light-sensitive metallic plates developed by mercury vapor. 2 A picture made by this process. [after Louis Jacques Mandé *Daguerre*, 1789–1851, French inventor, + TYPE] — **da·guerre'o·typ'er, da·guerre'o·typ'·ist** n. — **da·guerre'o·typ'y** n.

da·ha·be·ah (dä'hə·bē'ə) n. A passenger boat of the Nile, having a sharp prow and a broad stern, originally equipped with lateen sails, and now generally propelled by engines. Also **da'ha·bi'eh, da'ha·biy'eh**. [< Arabic *dhahabīyah* golden < *dhahab* gold; with ref. to the gilded royal Egyptian barges]

DAHABEAH

dahl·ia (dal'yə, däl'-, dāl'-) n. 1 A tender perennial herb (genus *Dahlia*) of the composite family, having tuberous roots and showy red, purple, yellow, or white flowers. 2 The flower or root of this herb. [after Anders *Dahl*, 18th c. Swedish botanist]

da·hoon (də·hoon') n. A small evergreen tree (*Ilex cassine*) of the holly family, found in the southern United States. [Origin uncertain]

dai·ly (dā'lē) adj. Occurring, appearing, or pertaining to every day; diurnal. — n. pl. **·lies** A daily publication. — adv. Day after day; on every day. [OE *dæglic* < *dæg* day]
  Synonym (adj.): diurnal. *Daily* is the native English and popular term, *diurnal* the Latin and scientific term. In strict usage, *daily* is the antonym of *nightly* as *diurnal* is of *nocturnal*. *Daily* is not, however, held strictly to this use; a physician makes *daily* visits if he calls at some time within each period of twenty-four hours. *Diurnal* is more exact in all its uses; a *diurnal* flower opens or blooms only in daylight; a *diurnal* bird or animal flies or ranges only by day: in contradistinction to *nocturnal* flowers, birds, etc. A *diurnal* motion exactly fills an astronomical day or the time of one rotation of a planet on its axis, while a *daily* motion is much less definite. *Antonyms*: nightly, nocturnal.

daily double In horse racing, a single bet, the winning of which depends upon choosing the winner in two specified races.

dai·mio (dī'myō) n. 1 The former class of hereditary feudal barons in Japan. 2 A member of this class. Also **dai'myo**. [< Japanese < Chinese *dai* great + *mio, myo* name] — **dai·mi·ate** (dī'mē·āt) n.

dai·mon (dī'mōn), **dai·mon·ic** (dī·mon'ik), etc. See DEMON, etc.

dain·ty (dān'tē) adj. **·ti·er, ·ti·est** 1 Refined or delicate in taste. 2 Delicious; agreeable to the taste. 3 Charming in appearance; pretty. 4 Overly nice; fastidious. [< n.] — n. pl. **·ties** Something choice, delicate, or delicious. See synonyms under CHOICE, DELICIOUS, ELEGANT, FINE, SQUEAMISH. [< OF *daintié* < L *dignitas, -tatis*. Doublet of DIGNITY.] — **dain'ti·ly** adv. — **dain'ti·ness** n.

dai·qui·ri (dī'kər·ē, dak'ər·ē) n. A cocktail made of rum, lime or lemon juice, and sugar, mixed and chilled. [from *Daiquirí*, Cuba, where the rum originally used for the drink was made]

dair·y (dâr'ē) n. pl. **dair·ies** 1 A place where milk and cream are kept and made into butter and cheese. 2 A place for the sale of milk products. 3 A dairy farm. 4 A herd of milk cattle. 5 The business of dealing in such products. [ME *deierie* < *deie* dairymaid < OE *dæge*]

dairy cattle Cows of a breed specially adapted for milk production. Also **dairy cows**.

dairy farm A farm devoted to producing dairy products.

da·is (dā'is, dās) n. 1 A raised platform in a room. 2 A seat on a dais or against a wall. [< OF *deis* < LL *discus*. Doublet of DESK. DISH. DISK.]

dai·sy (dā'zē) n. pl. **dai·sies** 1 A low European herb (*Bellis perennis*) of the composite family, having a yellow disk with white or rose-colored rays; the English daisy. 2 A common American field flower, the oxeye daisy (*Chrysanthemum leucanthemum*): also called *whiteweed*. 3 *Slang* Any very fine, excellent person or thing. [OE *dæges ēage* day's eye] — **dai'sied** adj.

Da·kar (dä·kär', də-) The capital of the Republic of Senegal; a port on Cape Verde.

da·ker·hen (dā'kər·hen') n. The corn crake.

dakh·ma (däk'mə) See TOWER OF SILENCE.

dale (dāl) n. A small valley. [OE *dæl*. Akin to DELL.]

da·leth (dä'ləth) The fourth Hebrew letter. See ALPHABET.

dalles (dalz) n. pl. In the western United States, rapids running between steep rock walls; also, steep rock walls on either side of a ravine. [< F *dalle* trough, gutter]

dal·li·ance (dal'ē·əns) n. The act of dallying; frivolous or flirtatious action.

dal·ly (dal'ē) v. **dal·lied, dal·ly·ing** v.i. 1 To make love sportively; frolic. 2 To toy with; trifle; flirt: to *dally* with death. 3 To waste time. — v.t. 4 To waste (time): with *away*.
  [< OF *dalier* converse, chat] — **dal'li·er** n.

dal·mat·ic (dal·mat'ik) n. 1 A wide-sleeved tunic, worn over the alb and cassock by the deacon at high mass. 2 A medieval state robe. [< OF *dalmatique* < L *dalmatica (vestis)* Dalmatian (robe) < *Dalmatia* Dalmatia]

dal·ton (dôl'tən) n. *Physics* The unit of atomic mass, equal to 1/12 of the mass of an atom of carbon of mass number 12, or approximately 1.6604×10^{-24} gram. [after John *Dalton*]

dal·ton·ism (dôl'tən·iz'əm) n. Colorblindness, especially to the colors red and green. [after John *Dalton*]

dam¹ (dam) n. 1 A barrier to check the flow of a stream. 2 The water held up by a dam. 3 Any barrier for preventing the passage of water, air, or gas. 4 Figuratively, any obstruction. — v.t. **dammed, dam·ming** 1 To erect a dam in; stop or obstruct by a dam. 2 To keep back; restrain: with *up* or *in*. [< MDu. *damm*]

dam² (dam) n. A female parent: said of animals. [Var. of *dame*]

dam·age (dam'ij) n. 1 Destruction or impairment of value; injury; harm. 2 pl. *Law* Money recoverable for a wrong or an injury. See synonyms under INJURY, LOSS. — v. **dam·aged, dam·ag·ing** v.t. To cause damage to; impair the usefulness or value of. — v.i. To be susceptible to damage. See synonyms under ABUSE. HURT. [< OF < *dam* loss < L *damnum*]

dam·an (dam'ən) n. A small, hyracoidean, hoofed mammal (genus *Procavia*) with rhinoceros-like molar teeth, especially *P. syriaca* of Asia Minor. [< Arabic *damān isrāīl* sheep of Israel]

dam·as·cene (dam'ə·sēn, dam'ə·sēn') v.t. **·cened, ·cen·ing** To ornament (metal, iron, steel, etc.) with wavy or variegated patterns. Also **dam·as·keen** (dam'ə·skēn, dam'ə·skēn'). — adj. Relating to damascening. — n. Work ornamented by damascening.

Da·mas·cus (də·mas'kəs) An ancient city, capital of Syria. *Arabic* **Es Sham** (ash sham'), *French* **Da·mas** (dä·mäs'). — **Dam·as·cene** (dam'ə·sēn, dam'ə·sēn') adj. & n.

dam·ask (dam'əsk) n. 1 A rich silk, linen, or wool fabric woven in elaborate patterns. 2 A fine table linen, so woven that two sets of parallel threads on the surface give the pattern different aspects from different points of view. 3 Damascus steel or Damascus work. 4 A deep pink or rose color. — adj. 1 Of, pertaining to, or from Damascus. 2 Made of damask steel or fabric. 3 Of the color of damask. — v.t. 1 To damascene. 2 To weave or ornament with rich patterns. 3 To make deep pink or rose in color. [from *Damascus*]

damask rose A large pink rose (*Rosa damascena*) of the Near East, noted for its fragrance.

dam·bo·nite (dam'bə·nīt) n. A white crystalline compound, $C_8H_{16}O_6$, contained in certain forms of caoutchouc. Also **dam·bon·i·tol** (dam·bon'ə·tōl, -tôl). [< native African *n'dambo*, the tree which produces it + -ITE¹]

dame (dām) n. 1 A woman of high social position; a lady. 2 A married or mature woman; matron. 3 *Archaic* A schoolmistress. 4 A title of address for the lady recipients of the Grand Cross (suffix, G.B.E.), or for the Dames Commanders (suffix, D.B.E.) of the Order of the British Empire, created in 1917. See under ORDER (n. def. 9). 5 A female parent or ancestress. 6 *Slang* Any woman. [< OF < L *domina* lady, fem. of *dominus* master. Doublet of DUENNA.]

dame·wort (dām'wûrt') n. A coarse herb of the mustard family (*Hesperis matronalis*), with lanceolate, toothed leaves and fragrant lilac to deep-mauve flowers: also called *dame violet, dame rocket*.

dam·i·an·a (dam'ē·an'ə, -ē·ä'nə) n. The leaves of a Mexican plant (*Turnera diffusa*), used as a nerve tonic. [< NL < Sp. < native Mexican name]

dam·mar (dam'ər) n. 1 An oleoresinous gum yielded by various evergreen trees (genus *Agathis*) of Australia, India, and Asia: used as a colorless varnish in photography, etc. 2 A similar resin from other plant sources, as *Vateria indica, Shorea wiesneri*, etc. Also **dam'ar, dam'mer**. [< Malay *damar*]

damn (dam) v.t. 1 To pronounce worthless, unfit, bad, a failure, etc.: to *damn* the opposition or a play. 2 To curse or swear at. 3 *Theol.* To condemn to eternal punishment. 4 To pronounce guilty; bring ruin upon: His words *damned* him. 5 *Obs.* To adjudge guilty; doom. — v.i. 6 To swear; curse. — **to damn with faint praise** To praise so reluctantly as to imply adverse criticism. — n. 1 A curse; an oath. 2 Anything as valueless as an oath. [< OF *damner* < L *damnare* condemn to punishment]

dam·na·ble (dam'nə·bəl) adj. Meriting or causing damnation; detestable; outrageous. [< OF < L *damnabilis* < *damnare* condemn] — **dam'na·ble·ness** n. — **dam'na·bly** adv.

dam·na·tion (dam·nā'shən) n. 1 Condemnation to future punishment or perdition. 2 The act of damning or the state of the damned. 3 Ruinous adverse criticism or public disapproval, as of a book or play. 4 Cause or occasion of eternal punishment; a mortal sin. 5 *Obs.* Condemnation. [< F < L *damnatio, -onis* < *damnare* condemn]

dam·na·to·ry (dam'nə·tôr'ē, -tō'rē) adj. Tending to convict or condemn; consigning to damnation.

damned (damd, *poetic or rhetorical* dam'nid) adj. 1 Judicially reprobated and condemned; sentenced to eternal punishment. 2 Damnable; execrably bad; detestable. — adv. *Colloq.* Very; extremely: *damned* funny; *damned* irritating.

damp (damp) n. 1 A moderate degree of moisture; dampness; fog; mist. 2 Foul air; poisonous gas, occurring especially in coal

dam·as·cene (dam'ə·sēn, dam'ə·sēn') v.t.

mines. **3** Depression of spirits, or that which produces it. —*adj.* **1** Somewhat wet; moist. **2** Dejected. —*v.t.* **1** To moisten; make damp. **2** To check or discourage (energy, ardor, etc.). **3** *Music* To check the vibrations of (a string, etc.); deaden. **4** To bank, as a fire. **5** *Physics* To reduce the amplitude of (a series of waves). [<MDu., vapor, steam] —**damp′ly** *adv.* —**damp′ness** *n.*

damp·en (dam′pən) *v.t.* **1** To make or become damp; moisten. **2** To check; depress, as ardor or spirits. —*v.i.* **3** To become damp.

damp·er (dam′pər) *n.* **1** One who or that which damps or checks. **2** A device to check the draft, as of a stove, or to stop vibration, as in a piano. **3** *Electr.* A device to check oscillation of a magnetic needle, or to control movement in an electrical mechanism. **4** *Eng.* A shock absorber.

damsel fly A slender-bodied dragonfly (order *Odonata*) with four similar elongate wings that are folded together over the back when at rest. For illustration see under INSECT (beneficial).

dam·son (dam′zən) *n.* **1** An oval purple plum of Syrian origin (*Prunus insititia*). **2** The tree producing it. Also **damson plum.** [ME *damascene* <L (*Prunum*) *Damascenum* plum from Damascus]

dam·yan·kee (dam′yang′kē, dam′-) *n.* *U.S. Colloq.* A Northerner: a contemptuous term used by Southerners since the Civil War: now chiefly jocular. Also *damned Yankee.*

dance (dans, däns) *v.* **danced, danc·ing** *v.i.* **1** To move the body and feet rhythmically, especially to music. **2** To move or skip excitedly; quiver, as from excitement or emotion. **3** To bob up and down; move about lightly and quickly. —*v.t.* **4** To perform or take part in the steps or figures of (a dance). **5** To effect or bring about by dancing: to *dance* the night away. **6** To cause to dance. **7** To dandle. See synonyms under FRISK, LEAP. —*n.* **1** A series of rhythmic concerted movements and steps timed to music. **2** A dancing party; ball. **3** A tune to dance by. **4** The intricate gyrations of swarming insects. [<OF *danser*] —**danc′er** *n.*

dance fly A small or medium-sized, slender, predacious fly (genus *Empis*, family *Empididae*) which mates in dancing swarms over the surface of land and water. For illustration see under INSECT (beneficial).

dance of death An allegory, often found in medieval art, representing Death as a skeleton leading men of all estates and conditions to the grave: also *danse macabre.*

dance·script (dans′skript′, däns′-) *n.* Choroscript.

dan·de·li·on (dan′də·lī′ən) *n.* A wide-spread plant of the composite family (*Taraxacum officinale*), having yellow flower heads and deeply toothed, edible leaves. [<F *dent de lion* lion's tooth; with ref. to the shape of the leaves]

dan·der (dan′dər) *U.S. Colloq.* Ruffled temper; anger. —**to get one's dander up** *Colloq.* To become angry. [? Var. of Scottish *dunder* ferment]

dan·di·fy (dan′də·fī) *v.t.* **·fied, ·fy·ing** To cause to resemble a dandy. —**dan′di·fi·ca′tion** *n.*

dan·druff (dan′drəf) *n.* A fine scurf forming on the scalp. Also **dan·driff** (dan′drif). [Origin unknown]

dan·dy[1] (dan′dē) *n. pl.* **·dies 1** A man excessively and ostentatiously refined in dress and affected in manner; a fop; coxcomb. **2** *Colloq.* A particularly fine specimen of its kind. **3** A dandy roll. **4** A two-wheeled hand cart used about furnaces and mills for carrying fuel, etc. **5** A yawl. —*adj.* **1** Like a dandy. **2** *U.S. Colloq.* Excellent; very fine. [Alter. of *Andy* <*Andrew*, a personal name. Cf. MERRY-ANDREW.]

dan·dy[2] (dan′dē) *n. pl.* **·dies** *Anglo-Indian* **1** A Ganges boatman. **2** A cloth hammock slung on a bamboo staff to be carried by bearers. **3** A Sivaistic ascetic who carries a small wand. Also **dan·dee, dan′di.** [<Hind. *dāndī* <*dānd* a staff, oar]

dandy roll A cylinder of wire gauze by which a web of paper pulp is given a watermark. Also **dan′dy.**

dane·wort (dān′wûrt′) *n.* The European dwarf elder (*Sambucus ebulus*): also called **Dane's-blood′, dane′weed′.**

dang (dang) *v.t.* Damn: a euphemism.

dan·ger (dān′jər) *n.* **1** Exposure to chance of evil, injury, or loss; peril; risk; also, a cause of peril or risk. **2** *Obs.* Power; control; ability to injure. [<OF, power of a lord, power to harm <L *dominium* lordship <*dominus* lord] **Synonyms:** hazard, insecurity, jeopardy, peril, risk. *Danger* is exposure to injury or evil; *peril* is exposure to imminent, threatening injury or evil. *Jeopardy* involves, like *risk*, more of the element of chance or uncertainty; a man tried upon a capital charge is said to be put in *jeopardy* of life. *Insecurity* is a feeble word, but exceedingly broad, applying to the placing of a dish, or the possibilities of a life, a fortune, or a government. Compare HAZARD. **Antonyms:** defense, immunity, protection, safeguard, safety, security, shelter.

dan·ger·ous (dān′jər·əs) *adj.* Attended with danger; hazardous; perilous; unsafe. See synonyms under FORMIDABLE, SERIOUS. —**dan′ger·ous·ly** *adv.* —**dan′ger·ous·ness** *n.*

dan·gle (dang′gəl) *v.* **·gled, ·gling** *v.i.* **1** To hang loosely; swing to-and-fro. **2** To follow or hover near someone as a suitor or hanger-on. **3** To be hanged. —*v.t.* **4** To hold so as to swing loosely to-and-fro. **5** To hang (someone). —*n.* **1** Manner or act of dangling. **2** Something which dangles. [<Scand. Cf. Dan. *dangle.*] —**dan′gler** *n.*

dan·gle·ber·ry (dang′gəl·ber′ē) See TANGLE-BERRY.

dank (dangk) *adj.* Unpleasantly damp; moist; wet. —*n.* Disagreeable humidity; wetness. [ME *danke* <Scand. Cf. Sw. *dank* marshy spot]

dap (dap) *v.i.* **dapped, dap·ping 1** To dip lightly or suddenly into water, as a bird. **2** To fish by dropping a baited hook gently on the water. **3** To bounce or skip. [Prob. var. of DAB[3]]

daph·ne (daf′nē) *n.* **1** The laurel (*Laurus nobilis*) of southern Europe. **2** Any of a genus (*Daphne*) of shrubs, some deciduous, some evergreen, with fragrant flowers. [<NL <Gk. *daphnē*]

dap·per (dap′ər) *adj.* **1** Trim; neat; natty; smartly dressed. **2** Small and active. [<MDu., strong, energetic]

dap·ple (dap′əl) *v.t.* **·pled, ·pling** To make spotted or variegated in color. —*adj.* Spotted; variegated: also **dap′pled.** —*n.* **1** A spot or dot, as on the skin of a horse. **2** An animal marked with spots. [Origin uncertain]

dare (dâr) *v.* **dared** (*Archaic* **durst**), **dar·ing** *v.t.* **1** To have the courage or boldness to undertake; venture on. **2** To challenge to attempt something as proof of courage, etc. **3** To defy; oppose and challenge. —*v.i.* **4** To have the courage or boldness to do or attempt something; venture. —**I dare say** I am reasonably certain. —*n.* **1** The act of daring; a challenge: to do something on a *dare.* **2** Daring; bravery. [OE *durran*] —**dar′er** *n.*

dare·dev·il (dâr′dev′əl) *n.* One who is recklessly bold. —*adj.* Venturesome; reckless. Indian Ocean, capital of Tanganyika.

dar·ic (dar′ik) *n.* An ancient Persian gold coin; also, a silver coin of the same design, worth one twentieth of the gold daric. [<Gk. *Dareikos* coin of Darius]

dar·ing (dâr′ing) *adj.* **1** Possessing courage; bold; brave; venturesome. **2** Audacious; presuming. See synonyms under BRAVE. —*n.* Heroic courage; bravery. See synonyms under COURAGE. —**dar′ing·ly** *adv.* —**dar′ing·ness** *n.*

dark (därk) *adj.* **1** Lacking light. **2** Of a deep shade; black; or approaching black. **3** Obscure; mysterious; not understandable. **4** Gloomy; disheartening. **5** Unenlightened. **6** Atrocious; dastardly; wicked. **7** Of brunette complexion. **8** Blind; unknowing. **9** Secretive; reticent. —*n.* **1** Lack of light. **2** A place, position, or state where there is little or no light. **3** Night. **4** Obscurity; secrecy. **5** Ignorance: especially in the phrase *in the dark.* **6** A heavy shade or shadow in a drawing or painting. —*v.t. & v.i. Obs.* To make or become dark; darken. [OE *deorc*]
Synonyms (*adj.*): black, dim, dismal, dusky, gloomy, murky, mysterious, obscure, opaque, sable, shadowy, shady, somber, swart, swarthy. Strictly, that which is *black* is absolutely destitute of color; that which is *dark* is absolutely destitute of light. In common speech, however, a coat is *black,* though not optically colorless; the night is *dark,* though the stars shine. That is *obscure, shadowy,* or *shady* from which the light is more or less cut off. *Dusky* is applied to objects which appear as if viewed in fading light; the word is often used, as are *swart* and *swarthy,* of the human skin when quite *dark,* or even verging on *black. Dim* refers to imperfection of outline, from distance, darkness, mist, etc., or from some defect of vision. *Opaque* objects are impervious to light. *Murky* is said of that which is at once *dark, obscure,* and *gloomy;* as, a *murky* den; a *murky* sky. Figuratively, *dark* is emblematic of sadness, agreeing with *somber, dismal, gloomy,* also of moral evil: as, a *dark* deed. Of intellectual matters, *dark* is now rarely used in the old sense of a *dark* saying, etc. See MYSTERIOUS, OBSCURE. **Antonyms:** bright, brilliant, clear, crystalline, dazzling, gleaming, glowing, illumined, light, lucid, luminous, radiant, shining, transparent, white. Compare synonyms for LIGHT.

dark conduction *Electr.* Conductive of residual electricity in a photosensitive substance when not illuminated.

dark current *Electr.* The current set up in a photoelectric cell when the light beam is interrupted.

dark·en (där′kən) *v.t.* **1** To make dark or darker; deprive of light. **2** To make dark in color; make black. **3** To fill with gloom; sadden. **4** To blind. **5** To obscure; confuse. —*v.i.* **6** To grow dark or darker. **7** To become sad or gloomy; grow dark or flushed, as the face with anger or hatred. **8** To become blind. —**dark′en·er** *n.*

dark-field illumination (därk′fēld′) *Optics* The lighting of the field of a microscope from the side instead of from below, so as to reveal the specimen against a dark background.

dark horse 1 An unknown or little talked-of horse that unexpectedly wins a race. **2** A little-known political candidate unexpectedly nominated.

dark lantern A lantern having a case with one transparent side, which can be covered by a shield to hide the light.

dark·ly (därk′lē) *adv.* **1** In a dark manner. **2** Obscurely; mysteriously.

dark·ness (därk′nis) *n.* **1** Total or partial absence of light; gloom. **2** Physical, mental, or moral blindness. **3** Want of clearness; obscurity; secrecy. **4** The quality of being dark in color or shade.

dark·room (därk′rōōm′, -rŏŏm′) *n. Phot.* A room equipped to exclude actinic rays, for treating plates, films, etc.

dark star See under STAR.

dar·ling (där′ling) *n.* One tenderly beloved: often a term of direct address. —*adj.* Tenderly beloved; very dear. [OE *dēorling,* dim. of *dēor* dear]

darn[1] (därn) *v.t. & v.i.* To repair (a garment or a hole or rent) by filling the gap with interlacing stitches. —*n.* A place mended by darning; also, the act of darning. [Earlier *dern,* prob. <OE *dernan* conceal <*derne* hidden]

darn[2] (därn) *v.t., adj., n., & interj. Colloq.* Damn: a euphemism.

darn·dest (därn′dist) *n. & adj. Colloq.* Damnedest: a euphemism.

dar·nel (där′nəl) *n.* A grass (*Lolium temulentum*); ryegrass; an annual weed often found in grain fields. [<dial. F *darnelle*]

darn·er (där′nər) *n.* **1** One who or that which darns. **2** A darning needle.

darning needle 1 A large-eyed needle used in darning. **2** A dragonfly: also devil's-darning-needle. **3** The Venus's-comb.

Darn·ley (därn′lē), **Lord,** 1546-67, Henry Stuart, second husband of Mary Queen of Scots; murdered.

Dar·row (dar′ō), **Clarence Seward,** 1857-1938, U.S. lawyer.

DARNEL
A. Spikelet.

dart (därt) *n.* **1** A pointed missile weapon, as a javelin; also, something like an arrow or having the effect of one. **2** A sudden and rapid motion. **3** A tapering tuck made in a garment by stitching or cutting so as to fit it to the figure. **4** An insect's sting.

— *v.t.* & *v.i.* **1** To emit swiftly or suddenly; shoot out. **2** To move swiftly and suddenly. See synonyms under THROW. [<OF <Gmc.]

dart·er (där'tər) *n.* **1** A small American perch-like fish (subfamily *Estheostomatinae*). **2** The American snakebird.

dar·tle (där'təl) *v.t.* & *v.i.* **·tled**, **·tling** To dart or shoot out repeatedly.

darts (därts) *n.* A game of skill in which small darts are thrown at a bull's-eye target.

Dar·win (där'win), **Charles Robert**, 1809–82, English naturalist; formulated the theory of evolution by natural selection. — **Erasmus**, 1731–1802, English physician and poet; grand-father of the preceding.

dash[1] (dash) *v.t.* **1** To strike with violence, especially so as to break or shatter. **2** To throw, thrust, or knock suddenly and violently: usually with *away*, *out*, *down*, etc. **3** To splash; be-spatter. **4** To do, write, etc., hastily: with *off* or *down*. **5** To frustrate; confound: to *dash* hopes. **6** To daunt or discourage. **7** To put to shame; abash. **8** To adulterate; mix: with *with*. **9** *Brit.* To damn: a euphemism. — *v.i.* **10** To strike; hit: The waves *dashed* against the shore. **11** To rush or move impetu-ously. See synonyms under THROW. — *n.* **1** A sudden advance or onset; short, spirited rush or race. **2** Impetuosity; spirit; vigor. **3** Ostentatious display, especially in the phrase *to cut a dash*. **4** A check or hindrance; dis-comfiture. **5** A slight admixture; a tinge; a small addition of some other ingredient. **6** A collision or concussion; also, its sound. **7** A horizontal line (—), as a mark of punctuation, etc. **8** The long sound in the Morse code, used in combination with dots to represent letters. **9** A dashboard. **10** The dasher of a churn. [ME *daschen* <Scand. Cf. Dan. *daske* a slap.]

dash[2] (dash) *v.t.* In West Africa, to bribe; also, offer as a bribe. — *n.* A bribe. [Earlier *dashee*, alter. of Pg. *Que das me?* What do you give me?]

dash·board (dash'bôrd', -bōrd') *n.* **1** An upright screen on the front of a vehicle to intercept mud, etc., thrown up by a horse. **2** A sprayboard at the bow of a vessel. **3** The instrument board of an automobile.

da·sheen (da·shēn') *n.* A tropical plant (*Colo-casia esculenta*) related to the taro, the root of which is a staple food of the tropics. [<F *de, Chine* of China]

dash·er (dash'ər) *n.* **1** One who or that which dashes, plunges, or cuts a dash. **2** The plunger of a churn. **3** A dashboard.

da·shi·ki (dä·shē'kē) *n. pl.* **·kis** A loose-fitting, sleeved garment of varying length, often with a print design or embroidery, worn by men and women in West Africa and elsewhere. [< Yoruba]

dash·ing (dash'ing) *adj.* **1** Spirited; bold; im-petuous. **2** Ostentatiously showy or gay. — **dash'ing·ly** *adv.*

das·tard (das'tərd) *n.* A base coward; a sneak. — *adj.* Dastardly. [? ME *dased, dast,* pp. of *dasen* daze, stupefy + -ARD]

das·tard·ly (das'tərd·lē) *adj.* Base; cowardly. — **das'tard·li·ness, das'tard·y** *n.*

das·y·ure (das'ē·oŏr) *n.* **1** An arboreal marsupial; especial-ly, a small, spotted, civetlike marsupial, as the **spotted dasy-ure** (*Dasyurus macu-latus*) of Tasmania and southern Aus-tralia. **2** The Tasmanian devil. [<Gk. *dasys* hairy + *oura* tail]

DASYURE
(Body length: 1 to 1 1/2 feet)

da·ta (dā'tə, dat'ə, dä'tə) *n. pl.* of DATUM Facts or figures from which conclusions may be drawn: often construed as a singular. [<L, neut. pl. of *datus,* pp. of *dare* give]

data bank An extensive body of information organized and stored in a computer's memory for the quick retrieval of data in response to particular queries.

data processing The operation of digital or analog computers.

da·ta·ry (dā'tə·rē) *n. pl.* **·ries** **1** A papal offi-cial, usually a bishop, having charge of grants and dispensations and the dating and registra-tion of all important documents. **2** The of-fice or employment of this official. [<Med. L *datarius* <L *dare* give, grant]

date[1] (dāt) *n.* **1** That part of a writing, in-scription, coin, etc., which tells when, or when and where, it was written, published, etc. **2** The time of some event; a point of time. **3** Duration; age. **4** *U.S. Colloq.* An engage-ment; appointment. — **down to date** Covering the current day. — **out of date** Obsolete. — **up to date** Having modern knowledge, style, etc. — *v.* **dat·ed, dat·ing** *v.t.* **1** To furnish or mark with a date. **2** To ascertain the time or era of; assign a date to. **3** *U.S. Colloq.* To make an appointment with, as a member of the opposite sex. — *v.i.* **4** To have origin in or be in existence since an era or time: usu-ally with *from*: This coin *dates* from the Renaissance. **5** To reckon time. [<F <L *data,* fem. sing. of *datus,* pp. of *dare* give; from first word of Latin formula giving a letter's date and place of writing] — **dat'er** *n.*

date[2] (dāt) *n.* **1** An oblong, sweet, fleshy fruit of the date palm, enclosing a single hard seed. **2** A lofty palm bearing this fruit (*Phoenix dactylifera* and varieties): also called **date palm.** [<OF <L *dactylus* <Gk. *daktylos* finger; with ref. to its shape]

dat·ed (dā'tid) *adj.* **1** Marked with a date. **2** Antiquated; old-fashioned.

date·less (dāt'lis) *adj.* **1** Bearing no date. **2** Without end or limit. **3** Immemorial; of permanent interest.

date line **1** The line containing the date of publication of a periodical or of any con-tribution, dispatch, etc., printed in it. **2** An imaginary line approximately congruent with 180° longitude from Greenwich, internationally agreed upon as determining those points on the earth's surface where a day is dropped on crossing it from west to east and added on crossing from east to west: also called **Interna-tional Date Line.**

da·tive (dā'tiv) *n. Gram.* **1** In inflected Indo-Eu-ropean languages, that case of a noun, pronoun, or adjective denoting the remoter, or indirect ob-ject: expressed in English by *to* or *for* with the objective or by word order, as in *I told the story to him, I told him the story.* **2** A word in this case. — *adj.* **1** *Gram.* Pertaining to or designating the dative case or a word in this case. **2** *Law* That may be disposed of at will; also, that may be re-moved; removable as opposed to perpetual: a *da-tive* officer. [<L *dativus,* trans. of Gk. *(ptōsis) dotikē* (the case of) giving <*didonai* give]

dat·o·lite (dat'ō·līt) *n.* A vitreous, translucent, brittle calcium borosilicate occurring in massive monoclinic crystals. [<Gk. *dateesthai* divide + LITE]

da·tum (dā'təm, dat'əm, dä'təm) *n. pl.* **da·ta 1** A known, assumed, or conceded fact from which an inference is made. **2** The point from which any reckoning or scale starts. [<L, neut. sing. of *datus.* See DATA.]

datum plane *Engin.* The horizontal plane from which heights and depths are measured: also **da-tum level.**

da·tu·ra (da·toŏr'a, -tyoŏr'a) *n.* One of a genus (*Datura*) of rank-smelling, poisonous plants of the nightshade fam-ily, with large funnel-shaped flowers and a prickly capsule, of which the jimsonweed is the best-known species. [<NL <Hind. *dhātūrā,* a plant]

daub (dôb) *v.t.* & *v.i.* **1** To smear or coat (something), as with plaster, grease, mud, etc. **2** To paint without skill or taste. — *n.* **1** Mud, plaster, clay, etc.; any sticky applica-tion. **2** A smear or spot. **3** A poor, coarse painting. **4** An instance or act of daubing. See synonyms under BLEM-ISH. [<OF *dauber* <L *dealbare* whitewash]

daub·er (dô'bər) *n.* **1** One who or that which daubs. **2** One who paints coarsely or cheaply. **3** A brush to put blacking on shoes; a dabber. **4** *Obs.* A flatterer. — **daub'er·y, daub'ry** *n.*

DATURA
a. Fruit.
b. Grain.

daub'ing *n.*

daub·y (dô'bē) *adj.* **1** Pertaining to or like daub; sticky. **2** Unskilfully done, as a painting; also, smeary.

daugh·ter (dô'tər) *n.* **1** A female child or descen-dant. **2** Any person or thing in a relation analo-gous to that of a female child, regarded with ref-erence to her, or its, origin. **3** *Obs.* A maiden. [OE *dohtor*] — **daugh'ter·ly** *adj.*

daughter cell *Biol.* Either of the two cells result-ing from a mitotic division of a cell.

daugh·ter-in-law (dô'tər·in·lô') *n. pl.* **daugh-ters-in-law** The wife of one's son.

daunt (dônt, dänt) *v.t.* **1** To dishearten or intimi-date; cow. **2** To pack into a barrel with a daunt. See synonyms under ABASH, FRIGHTEN. — *n.* **1** A fright. **2** A wooden disk with which to press salted fish, especially herring, into barrels. [<OF *danter, donter* <L *domitare,* freq. of *do-mare* tame]

daunt·less (dônt'lis, dänt-) *adj.* Fearless; in-trepid. See synonyms under BRAVE. — **daunt'less·ly** *adv.* — **daunt'less·ness** *n.*

dau·phin (dô'fin, *Fr.* dō·faN') *n.* The eldest son of a king of France: a title used from 1349 to 1830. [<F, a dolphin; used as a personal name and ti-tle]

dav·en·port (dav'ən·pôrt, -pōrt) *n.* **1** A large, up-holstered sofa, often one that can be used as a bed. **2** A small writing desk. [Prob. after the name of the first manufacturer]

dav·it (dav'it, dā'vit) *n. Naut.* **1** One of a pair of small cranes on a ship's side for hoisting its boats, stores, etc. **2** A curved piece of tim-ber or iron for hoist-ing the flukes of an anchor. [from *David,* proper name]

DAVIT

da·vy (dā'vē) *n. pl.* **·vies** A safety lamp.

daw[1] (dô) *n.* **1** A jackdaw. **2** A simpleton. [ME *dawe*]

daw[2] (dô) *n.* & *v.i. Scot.* Dawn.

daw·dle (dôd'l) *v.t.* & *v.i.* **·dled**, **·dling** To waste (time) in slow trifling; loiter: often with *away.* See synonyms under LINGER. [Prob. var. of DADDLE] — **daw'dler** *n.*

dawn (dôn) *v.i.* **1** To begin to grow light. **2** To begin to be understood: with *on* or *upon.* **3** To begin to expand or develop. — *n.* **1** The first ap-pearance of light in the morning; daybreak. ◆ Collateral adjective: *auroral.* **2** An awakening; beginning or unfolding. [Back formation < *dawning,* earlier *dawenyng* daybreak <Scand. Cf. Sw. *dagning.*]

day (dā) *n.* **1** The period from dawn to dark; hence, daylight or sunlight. **2** The interval rep-resented by one revolution of the earth upon its axis; twenty-four hours; also, this period as a unit in computing time. ◆ Collateral adjective: *diurnal.* See under TIME. **3** The hours appointed for labor. **4** A day's journey. **5** The period of ro-tation about its axis of any heavenly body. **6** A time or period; an age. **7** A contest or battle, or its result: The liberals won the *day.* **8** A specified epoch: in Caesar's *day.* **9** A specified date: Inde-pendence *Day.* — **day after day** Every day. — **day by day** Each day. — **day in, day out** Every day. — **(from) day to day** From one day to the next; not long-range. — **the day** *Scot.* Today: How are ye *the day?* [OE *dæg*]

day-bed (dā'bed') *n.* A lounge or couch, usually with back and sides, that can be converted into a bed at night.

day blindness Hemeralopia.

day-book (dā'boŏk') *n.* **1** In bookkeeping, the book in which transactions are recorded in the order of their occurrence. **2** A diary.

day-break (dā'brāk') *n.* Dawn; the time when the sun rises.

day camp A camp where children spend the day in supervised activities, returning home each eve-ning.

day-care center (dā'kâr') A place for the care of young children during the day, especially while their mothers are at work: also called *day nursery.*

day coach A railroad car equipped for daytime travel only, as opposed to a sleeping-car, dining-car, etc.

day·dream (dā'drēm') *n.* **1** An exercise of the fancy or imagination; a reverie. **2** A delusion of happiness. —*v.i.* To indulge the mind idly in wishful thinking. —**day'dream'er** *n.*

day flower Any species of the genus *Commelina* whose flowers last only a day.

day·fly (dā'flī') *n.* A mayfly or ephemerid insect.

day labor Labor hired and paid for by the day.

day laborer One who works for pay by the day, as at unskilled manual tasks.

day letter A lettergram sent during the day.

day·light (dā'līt') *n.* **1** The light received from the sun; the light of day. **2** The period of light during the day. **3** Insight into or understanding of something formerly puzzling. **4** Exposure to view; publicity.

day·lights (dā'līts') *n. Slang.* **1** Vital organs; life itself: The mule worked his *daylights* out. **2** Consciousness; wits: to shake the *daylights* out of one.

day·light-sav·ing time (dā'līt'sā'ving) Time in which more daylight for the working day is obtained by setting clocks one or more hours ahead of standard time, especially during the summer months.

day·lil·y (dā'lil'ē) *n. pl.* **·lil·ies** **1** Any of several lyleworts (genus *Hemerocallis*), with lanceolate leaves, and large flowers on a round thick scape, usually lasting one day. Two species, *H. fulva*, tawny red, and *H. flava*, bright yellow, are commonly cultivated. **2** A common cultivated lylewort (genus *Hosta*) of Asian origin, with large, broad, ovate or oblong leaves, and generally white flowers.

day·long (dā'lông', -long') *adj. & adv.* All day; lasting through the entire day.

day nursery A day-care center.

day school **1** A school that holds classes during the daytime: distinguished from *night school.* **2** A private school attended by pupils living outside the school: distinguished from *boarding school.*

days of grace Days (usually three) allowed for the payment of a note or bill of exchange after the date of payment expressed in the instrument itself.

day·time (dā'tīm') *n.* The time of daylight; the time between sunrise and sunset.

daze (dāz) *v.t.* **dazed, daz·ing** To stupefy or bewilder, as by a glare of light or by a physical or mental shock; stun. —*n.* The state of being dazed. [ME *dasen*. Related to ON *dasask* become weary.] —**daz·ed·ly** (dā'zid·lē) *adv.*

daz·zle (daz'əl) *v.* **·zled, ·zling** *v.t.* **1** To blind or dim the vision of by excess of light. **2** To bewilder or charm, as with brilliant display. —*v.i.* **3** To be blinded by lights or glare. **4** To excite admiration. —*n.* **1** The act of dazzling; dazzled condition. **2** Something that dazzles; brightness. [Freq. of DAZE] —**daz'zling·ly** *adv.*

de- *prefix* **1** Away; off: *deflect, decapitate.* **2** Down: *decline, descend.* **3** Completely; utterly: *derelict, denude.* **4** The undoing, reversing, or ridding of (the action or condition expressed by the main element): *decoding, decentralization, decarbonization.* [<L *de* from, away, down; also <F *dé-* <L *de-*, or <OF *des-* <L *dis-* (see DIS-)]

dea·con (dē'kən) *n.* **1** A lay church officer or subordinate minister. **2** In the Anglican, Greek, and Roman Catholic Churches, a clergyman ranking next below a priest. **3** Any cleric, as a bishop or priest, acting as chief assistant at a high mass; a gospeler. —*v.t. U.S. Colloq.* **1** To read aloud a line or two of (a hymn) at a time, as an aid to congregational singing: an office of the deacon when hymn books were scarce. **2** To arrange (garden or orchard produce) for sale with only the best showing. **3** To do dishonestly; alter; adulterate. [OE <L *diaconus* <Gk. *diakonos* servant, minister] —**dea'con·ry, dea'con·ship** *n.*

de·ac·ti·vate (dē·ak'tə·vāt) *v.t.* **·vat·ed, ·vat·ing** *Mil.* To release (a military unit, ship, etc.) from active duty; demobilize. —**de·ac'ti·va'tion** *n.*

dead (ded) *adj.* **1** Having ceased to live; lifeless. **2** In a state or condition resembling death; temporarily disabled; lacking in vitality; numb; motionless. **3** Inanimate; inorganic. **4** Complete; utter; absolute; exact: a *dead* stop, a *dead* level. **5** Unfailing; certain; sure; complete or perfect: a *dead* shot. **6** Not productively employed; also, dull or slow: *dead* capital; also, ineffective; inoperative. **7** Without break or variation; flat; unvaried; a *dead* wall. **8** Dull; uninteresting; lusterless; unburnished. **9** Without elasticity or resilience; non-resonant: a *dead* floor. **10** Extinct; obsolete: a *dead* language. **11** *Colloq.* Exhausted; worn-out. **12** Deprived of civil life, as a life-prisoner. **13** Not fresh or invigorating; lifeless; unresponsive, insensible: usually with *to.* **14** In games, not to be counted: a *dead* ball. **15** Giving no light or heat: *dead* cinders. **16** Not imparting motion; spent; also, unsupported, unrelieved, as of strains or weights. **17** Muffled, as a sound. **18** Not transmitting an electric current. **19** Bringing death; deadly. **20** Past the active point of ferment; also, tasteless, as a beverage. **21** Not required for further use, as composed type, etc. **22** Lying so near the hole that the putt is a certainty: said of a golf ball. —*n.* **1** The most lifeless or inactive period: the *dead* of night. **2** Dead persons collectively: with *the.* —*adv.* To the last degree; wholly; absolutely; exactly: *dead* right, *dead* straight. [OE *dēad*] **Synonyms** (*adj.*): deceased, defunct, departed, inanimate, lifeless. See LIFELESS. **Antonyms**: alive, animate, living.

dead air *Telecom.* A silent interval due to a failure in transmission or a breakdown in the scheduled broadcast.

dead·beat¹ (ded'bēt') *adj.* **1** Beating without recoil, as a watch escapement. **2** *Mech.* Coming to rest without oscillation. —*n.* A movement without recoil; a deadbeat escapement.

dead·beat² (ded'bēt') *n.* **1** *U.S. Colloq.* One who is notorious for not paying his bills. **2** *Slang* A sponger.

dead beat *Colloq.* Utterly exhausted: I was *dead beat.* ◆ In attributive use, **dead'-beat'**: a *dead-beat* horse.

dead center *Mech.* That position of a crank or crank motion in which the crank axle, crank pin, and connecting rod centers are all in alinement; the point where a connecting rod has no power to turn a crank. It occurs at each end of the stroke. Also *dead point.*

dead drunk So intoxicated as to be close to unconsciousness. ◆ In attributive use, **dead'-drunk'.**

dead duck *Slang* A person or thing whose career, power, influence, etc., is ruined or spent.

dead·en (ded'n) *v.t.* **1** To diminish the sensitivity, force, or intensity of. **2** To lessen or impede the velocity of; retard. **3** To render soundproof. **4** To make dull or less brilliant in color. —*v.i.* **5** To become dead. —**dead'en·er** *n.*

dead-end (ded'end') *n.* An end of a passage, street, road, etc., having no outlet; a blind alley.

dead·en·ing (ded'n·ing) *n.* **1** The act or agent by which something is deadened. **2** Any material used for dulling or shutting out sound, as in walls. **3** The act of killing trees by girdling. **4** A clearing made by girdling trees.

dead·fall (ded'fôl') *n.* **1** A trap operated by a weight that, when its support is removed, falls upon and kills or holds an animal. **2** Fallen trees and rubbish matted together.

dead·hand (ded'hand') See under MORTMAIN.

dead·head (ded'hed') *n.* **1** One who receives gratis any service or accommodation for which the general public is expected to pay. **2** A wooden buoy. **3** A sunken or partly sunken log. —*v.t. & v.i.* **1** To treat or act as a deadhead. **2** In railroading, to travel with empty cars or with no cars at all: said of locomotives.

dead heat A race in which two or more competitors finish together and there is no one winner.

dead horse *U.S. Colloq.* A debt for something already used up or worn out: so called from the old expression *to pay for a dead horse.*

dead·house (ded'hous') *n.* A morgue.

dead letter A letter which, after lying undelivered for a certain length of time, has been sent to the **dead–letter office,** the department of the general post office where unclaimed letters are examined and returned to their writers or destroyed. **2** Something, as a law, that exists in verbal form, but is not enforced or active.

dead lift **1** A lift made without help, leverage, pulleys, etc. **2** A task or effort accomplished under thankless and discouraging conditions.

dead·line (ded'līn') *n.* **1** A bounding line, as within the limits of a military prison, the crossing of which by a prisoner incurs the penalty of being fired upon by the guard. **2** The time limit before or by which one must complete news copy or other work.

dead load The fixed and permanent load of a structure, as the weight of a building or bridge.

dead·lock (ded'lok') *n.* **1** A lock worked from the outside by a key and from the inside by a handle or the like. **2** A lock in which the bolt has to be turned in each direction by a key: opposed to *springlock.* **3** A block or stoppage of business, as in a legislative or other body, caused by the refusal of opposing parties to cooperate. —*v.t. & v.i.* To cause or come to a deadlock.

dead·ly (ded'lē) *adj.* **·li·er, ·li·est** **1** Liable or certain to cause death; fatal. **2** Aiming or tending to kill; mortal; implacable. **3** Resembling death; deathly. See synonyms under NOISOME, PERNICIOUS. —*adv. Obs.* So as to cause death. —**dead'li·ly** *adv.* —**dead'li·ness** *n.*

dead·man (ded'man') *n. pl.* **·men** (-men) *Naut.* A log, concrete block, or other heavy mass, usually buried and serving as anchorage for a guy line.

deadman's handle The control mechanism or brake valve of a traction motor equipped with a safety device automatically to cut off the current or apply the brake should the operator's hand relax its pressure for any reason. Also **deadman control.**

dead·march (ded'märch') *n.* A piece of solemn music played at a funeral, especially a military one; music written for a funeral procession.

dead·net·tle (ded'net'l) *n.* Any of several herbs of the mint family (genus *Lamium*) having stingless, nettlelike leaves.

dead pan *U.S. Slang* A completely expressionless face. —**dead'-pan'** *adj. & adv.*

dead reckoning *Naut.* **1** The computation of a vessel's place at sea by log and compass without astronomical observations. **2** The position of a ship so computed.

dead set *Colloq.* Determined: with *on* or *against.*

dead shot **1** A true shot, one that exactly hits the mark. **2** A person who never misses.

dead soldier *Slang* **1** An empty bottle; especially, an empty liquor bottle: also **dead man.** **2** An old cigar or cigarette stub: also called *old soldier.* **3** A dull companion; a bore.

dead storage Storage of vehicles, equipment, etc., for an indefinite period.

dead time *Physics* An interval during which a Geiger counter or similar instrument gives no indication of radioactivity.

dead water **1** Still water. **2** The water that eddies about the stern of a moving vessel.

dead·weight (ded'wāt') *n.* **1** A burden borne without aid; an oppressive weight or load. **2** In shipping, freight charged for by weight instead of by bulk. **3** In railway transportation, weight of rolling stock as distinguished from its load.

dead·wood (ded'wŏŏd') *n. Naut.* **1** A mass of timber built up above the keel of a vessel at either end to support the cant timbers. **2** Worthless material; a profitless or burdensome person or thing. **3** Wood dead upon the tree. **4** In bowling, a fallen pin lying in front of the standing pins, and giving, if not removed, the next ball a great advantage.

deaf (def) *adj.* **1** Lacking or deficient in the sense of hearing. **2** Determined not to hear or be persuaded. [OE *dēaf*] —**deaf'ly** *adv.*

deaf·en (def'ən) *v.t.* **1** To make deaf. **2** To confuse, stupefy, or overwhelm, as with noise: The noise of the jets taking off was *deafening.* **3** To drown (a sound) by a louder sound. **4** To make soundproof.

deal¹ (dēl) *n.* A board or plank, or the wood, either fir or pine, of which it is made. [<MDu. *dele* board, plank]

deal² (dēl) *v.* **dealt** (delt), **deal·ing** *v.t.* **1** To distribute among a number of persons; mete out, as playing cards. **2** To apportion to (one person) as his or her share. **3** To deliver or inflict, as a blow. —*v.i.* **4** To conduct oneself; behave towards: with *with*: to *deal* effectively with a matter. **5** To be concerned or occupied: with *in* or *with*: I *deal* in facts. **6** To consider, discuss, or administer; take action: with *with*: The court will *deal* with him. **7** To trade; do business: with *in, with,* or *at*. **8** In card games, to act as dealer. See synonyms under APPORTION. —*n.* **1** Distribution; apportionment. **2** The act of distributing; especially, the distribution of, or right to distribute cards; a single round of play; also, the hand dealt. **3** *Colloq.* A secret bargain in politics or commerce. **4** A transaction or bargain. **5** Treatment given or received: a square *deal.* **6** An indefinite quantity, degree, or extent: a great *deal* of trouble. [OE *dælan.* Related to DOLE[1].]

deal·er (dē′lər) *n.* **1** A trader. **2** The player who distributes the cards.

deal-fish (dēl′fish′) *n.* *pl.* **·fish** or **·fish·es** A ribbonfish (*Trachypterus arcticus*) of northern seas.

deal·ing (dē′ling) *n.* **1** *Usually pl.* Any transaction with others. **2** The act of one who deals. **3** The method or manner of treatment: honest *dealing.*

de·am·i·na·tion (dē·am′ə·nā′shən) *n.* *Biochem.* The splitting off of the amino radical, NH₂, from the amino acid molecule in the body, as a stage in the formation of fatty acids from proteins. Also **de·am′i·ni·za′tion.**

dean (dēn) *n.* **1** The chief ecclesiastical officer of a cathedral or of a collegiate church. **2** *Chiefly Brit.* An ecclesiastical officer, often acting as a deputy of a bishop or archdeacon in the administration of part of a diocese: also called *rural dean.* **3** An executive officer of a college or university, having jurisdiction over a particular class or group of students, or acting as head of a faculty: *dean* of men, *dean* of the law school. **4** The senior member, in length of service, of an association or body of men: the *dean* of American composers. [< OF *deien* < LL *decanus* head of ten men < L *decem* ten]

dean·er·y (dē′nər·ē) *n.* *pl.* **·er·ies** The office, revenue, jurisdiction, or place of residence of a dean.

dean·ship (dēn′ship) *n.* The office, rank, or title of a dean.

dear[1] (dir) *adj.* **1** Beloved; precious. **2** Highly esteemed: used in letter salutations: *Dear* Sir. **3** Held at a high price, or rate; costly. **4** Characterized by high prices. **5** Intense; earnest: our *dearest* wish. **6** *Obs.* Noble; glorious. —*n.* One who is much beloved; a darling. —*adv.* Dearly. —*interj.* An exclamation of regret, surprise, etc. ◆ Homophone: *deer.* [OE *dēore*] —**dear′ness** *n.*

dear·ly (dir′lē) *adv.* **1** With much affection; fondly; tenderly. **2** At a high price or rate; at great cost. **3** Earnestly; deeply.

dearth (dûrth) *n.* **1** Scarcity; lack; famine. **2** *Obs.* Dearness; costliness. See synonyms under WANT. [ME *derthe*]

death (deth) *n.* **1** Cessation of physical life. **2** Extinction of anything; destruction. **3** Something likely to produce death; a cause or occasion of death. **4** Something considered as terrible as death. **5** The cessation, absence, or opposite of spiritual life; spiritual and eternal ruin. **6** A fatal plague. **7** A personification, type, or representation of mortality, generally a skeleton holding a scythe. **8** Slaughter; bloodshed. **9** The condition of being dead. ◆ Collateral adjectives: *lethal, mortal.* —**at death's door** Almost dead. —**to be death on** *Colloq.* **1** To dislike intensely enough to kill. **2** To have a special talent for; be very fond of. —**to death** Very much: He frightened me *to death.* —**to put to death** To kill; execute. [OE *dēath*]

death·bed (deth′bed′) *n.* The bed on which one dies; the last hours of life: also used attributively.

death bell 1 A bell announcing death; a passing bell. **2** A ringing in the ears like a tolling bell: thought by some to presage the news of a death.

death·blow (deth′blō′) *n.* A fatal blow or shock.

death camas Any of several herbaceous plants of the lily family (genus *Zygadenus*) common in the western United States and poisonous to men and animals: often confused with the edible camas.

death camp A concentration camp established for the purpose of eliminating part of the population of a country or minority group by systematic mass executions: also called *extermination camp.*

death chair The electric chair.

death·cup (deth′kup′) *n.* A common, poisonous mushroom (*Amanita phalloides*) having bright-red caps dotted with white.

death duty Inheritance taxes; a tax on property inherited.

death·ful (deth′fəl) *adj.* **1** Deadly; murderous; full of slaughter. **2** Mortal; liable to die. **3** Having the appearance of death. —**death′ful·ness** *n.*

death house That part of a prison, as a block of cells, in which prisoners condemned to death are confined.

death·less (deth′lis) *adj.* Not liable to die; undying; unending; perpetual. See synonyms under ETERNAL, IMMORTAL. —**death′less·ly** *adv.* —**death′less·ness** *n.*

death·ly (deth′lē) *adj.* **1** Having the semblance or suggestion of death: also **death′like′.** **2** Pertaining to death. **3** Deadly. See synonyms under GHASTLY. —*adv.* So as to be as one dead or dying. —**death′li·ness** *n.*

death mask A cast of the face taken just after death.

death point *Bacteriol.* The critical upper and lower temperatures beyond which microorganisms cannot live.

death rate The number of persons per thousand of population dying in a given unit of time.

death rattle The rattling sound caused by the breath passing through mucus in the throat of one dying.

death's-head (deths′hed′) *n.* A human skull or a representation of it, as a symbol of death.

death's-head moth A large, Old World sphinx moth (genus *Acherontia*), with markings like a death's-head on the upper surface of the thorax.

death-trap (deth′trap′) *n.* A building or structure where the risk of death, particularly from fire, is great.

death warrant 1 *Law* An official order for the execution of a person. **2** That which insures destruction or puts an end to hope.

death·watch (deth′woch′, -wôch′) *n.* **1** The last vigil with the dying or with the body of one dead. **2** A guard set over a condemned man before his execution. **3** A small, European, wood-boring beetle (*Xestobium rufovillosum*) that makes a ticking noise, superstitiously thought to presage death.

death whisper Sound waves of such high frequency as to be inaudible to human ears, and having the power to kill small animals, as fish in water, under certain conditions.

de·ba·cle (dā·bä′kəl, -bak′əl, di-) *n.* **1** A sudden and disastrous breakdown, overthrow, or collapse, as of a government; ruin; rout. **2** The breaking up of ice in a river, etc. **3** A violent flood carrying great masses of rock and other debris. [< F *débâcle* < *débâcler* unbar, set free]

de·bar (di·bär′) *v.t.* **·barred**, **·bar·ring** **1** To bar or shut out; exclude: usually with *from.* **2** To prohibit; hinder. See synonyms under PROHIBIT, SUSPEND. [< F *débarrer* < *dé-* away (< L *dis-*) + *barrer* bar]

de·bark (di·bärk′) *v.t.* To put ashore or unload from a ship. —*v.i.* To go ashore; disembark. Compare DISEMBARK. [< F *débarquer* < *dé-* away, from + *barque* a ship] —**de·bar·ka·tion** (dē′bär·kā′shən) *n.*

de·bar·ment (di·bär′mənt) *n.* The act of debarring; exclusion; obstruction.

de·base (di·bās′) *v.t.* **de·based**, **de·bas·ing** To lower in character, purity, or value; degrade. See synonyms under ABASE, CORRUPT, IMPAIR. [< DE- + obs. *base*, var. of ABASE] —**de·base′·ment** *n.* —**de·bas′er** *n.*

de·bate (di·bāt′) *v.* **de·bat·ed**, **de·bat·ing** *v.t.* **1** To discuss or argue about, as in a public meeting. **2** To discuss in formal argument. **3** To consider; deliberate upon in the mind, as alternatives. **4** *Obs.* To fight or contend

for or over. —*v.i.* **5** To argue; discuss. **6** To engage in formal argument. **7** To deliberate mentally; consider. See synonyms under DELIBERATE, DISPUTE. —*n.* **1** The discussing of any question; argumentation; dispute; controversy. **2** A formal argument conducted systematically to test the reasoning skill of two persons or teams taking opposing sides of a specific question (the resolution). **3** *Obs.* Combat; strife. See synonyms under ALTERCATION, REASONING. [< OF *debatre* < *de-* down (< L *de-*) + *batre* < L *batuere* strike] —**de·bat′a·ble** *adj.* —**de·bat′er** *n.*

de·bauch (di·bôch′) *v.t.* **1** To corrupt in morals; seduce; deprave. **2** *Obs.* To cause to forsake allegiance; disaffect. —*v.i.* **3** To indulge in lechery, gluttony, or drunkenness; dissipate. See synonyms under POLLUTE, VIOLATE. —*n.* **1** An act or occasion of debauchery; a carouse. **2** Excess; intemperance; lewdness. [< F *débaucher* lure from work < OF *desbaucher*]

de·bauched (di·bôcht′) *adj.* **1** Corrupted. **2** Characterized by debauchery. —**de·bauch·ed·ly** (di·bô′chid·lē) *adv.* —**de·bauch′ed·ness** *n.*

deb·au·chee (deb′ô·chē′, -shē′) *n.* One habitually profligate, drunken, or lewd; a libertine.

de·bauch·er (di·bô′chər) *n.* One who debauches; a seducer.

de·bauch·er·y (di·bô′chər·ē) *n.* *pl.* **·er·ies** **1** Licentiousness; drunkenness. **2** Seduction from virtue, purity, or fidelity. Also **de·bauch′ment.**

de·ben·ture (di·ben′chər) *n.* **1** An instrument in the nature of a bond, given as an acknowledgment of debt, and providing for repayment out of some specified fund or source of income: as, a mortgage *debenture,* one secured by a mortgage. **2** A customhouse certificate providing for a drawback. **3** A government pay order. See under BOND, STOCK. [< L *debentur* there are owing < *debere* owe]

de·bil·i·tate (di·bil′ə·tāt) *v.t.* **·tat·ed**, **·tat·ing** To make feeble or languid; weaken. [< L *debilitatus*, pp. of *debilitare* < *debilis* weak]

de·bil·i·ty (di·bil′ə·tē) *n.* *pl.* **·ties** Abnormal weakness; languor; feebleness. [< F *débilité* < L *debilitas, -tatis* < *debilis* weak]

deb·it (deb′it) *v.t.* **1** To enter on the debit side of an account. **2** To charge (a customer) for goods. —*n.* The debit side of an account; a debit or debts recorded; something owed. Compare CREDIT. [< L *debitum*, pp. of *debere* owe. Doublet of DEBT.]

deb·o·nair (deb′ə·nâr′) *adj.* Gentle or courteous; affable; complaisant; gay. Also **deb′o·naire′, deb′on·naire′.** [< F *debonnaire* < OF *de bon aire* of good mien] —**deb′o·nair′ly** *adv.* —**deb′o·nair′ness** *n.*

de·bouch (di·boosh′) *v.i.* **1** *Mil.* To come forth or issue from a defile or a wood into the open. **2** To come forth; emerge. —*v.t.* **3** To cause to emerge. —*n.* **1** An opening, especially in military works, for the passage of troops. **2** An outlet for commerce; market. Also *French* **dé·bou·ché** (dā·bōō·shā′) *n.* [< F *déboucher* < *dé-* from (< L *dis-*) + *bouche* a mouth]

de·bouch·ment (di·boosh′mənt) *n.* **1** *Geog.* The opening out of a valley, stream, etc. **2** The act of debouching. Also *French* **dé·bou·chure** (dā·boo·shür′).

dé·bride·ment (dā·brēd·män′, di·brēd′mənt) *n.* *Surg.* The excision of tissues and dead matter from the interior of wounds, to prevent septic infection. [< F *débrider* unbridle]

de·brief (dē′brēf′) *v.t.* *Mil.* To question or instruct (a pilot, agent, etc.) at the end of a mission or period of service.

de·bris (də·brē′, dā′brē; *Brit.* deb′rē) *n.* **1** Accumulated fragments; ruins; rubbish. **2** *Geol.* An aggregation of detached fragments of rocks. Also **dé·bris′.** See synonyms under WASTE. [< F *débris* < OF *débriser* < *des-* away (< L *dis-*) + *briser* break]

debt (det) *n.* **1** That which one owes. **2** An obligation. **3** The state of being indebted. **4** *Theol.* A sin; trespass. [< OF *dette* < L *debitum.* Doublet of DEBIT.]

debt·or (det′ər) *n.* **1** One who is in debt; one who is under obligation to another, as for money or goods, or for service, benefit, or help. **2** The left-hand or debit side of an account in bookkeeping. [< OF *dettor* < L

debitor < *debere* owe]

de·bunk (di·bungk′) *v.t. Colloq.* To reveal the sham, false pretensions, etc., of. [< BUNK²]

de·but (di·byōō′, dā-, dā′byōō) *n.* A first appearance, as in society or on the stage; first attempt; beginning. Also **dé·but′**. [< F *début* < *débuter* begin, lead off]

deb·u·tante (deb′yōō·tänt′, deb′yōō·tant) *n. fem.* A young girl or woman who makes a debut, especially into society. Also **dé′bu·tante′**. [< F *débutante*, fem. ppr. of *débuter* begin] —**deb′u·tant′** *n. masc.*

deca- *combining form* 1 Ten: *decapod.* 2 In the metric system, deka-. Also, before vowels, dec-.

dec·ade (dek′ād, de·kād′) *n.* 1 A period of ten years. 2 A group or set of ten. [< MF < L *decas, decadis* a group of ten < Gk. *dekas* < *deka* ten]

de·ca·dence (di·kād′ns, dek′ə·dəns) *n.* A process of deterioration; decay; a condition or period of decline, as in literature, art, morals, etc. [< F *décadence* < Med. L *decadentia* < L *decadere* < *de-* down + *cadere* fall]

de·ca·dent (di·kād′nt, dek′ə·dənt) *adj.* Falling into ruin or decay. —*n.* 1 One who has fallen from a high social position. 2 One in a state or process of mental or moral decay; a decadent person. 3 Specifically, a member of a school of French writers of the late 19th century characterized by their cultivation of subtle, refined, artificial qualities in subject and treatment.

dec·a·gon (dek′ə·gon) *n.* A plane figure with ten sides and ten angles. [< Gk. *dekagōnon* < *deka* ten + *gōnia* angle] —**de·cag·o·nal** (di·kag′ə·nəl) *adj.* —**de·cag′o·nal·ly** *adv.*

DECAGON

dec·a·gram (dek′ə·gram) See DEKAGRAM.

dec·a·he·dron (dek′ə·hē′drən) *n.* A solid bounded by ten plane faces. [< DECA- + Gk. *hedra* seat] —**dec′a·he′dral** *adj.*

dé·ca·lage (dā·kä·läzh′) *n. Aeron.* The variance in angle of incidence between two sustaining surfaces of an airplane. [< F < *décaler* shift, set at an angle]

DECAHEDRON

de·cal·ci·fi·ca·tion (dē·kal′sə·fə·kā′shən) *n.* 1 The action of decalcifying. 2 *Dent.* The removal of calcareous matter from the teeth.

de·cal·ci·fy (dē·kal′sə·fī) *v.t.* **·fied, ·fy·ing** To deprive of lime.

de·cal·co·ma·ni·a (di·kal′kə·mā′nē·ə, -mān′yə) *n.* 1 A process of transferring decorative pictures or designs from paper to glass, porcelain, etc. 2 Such a print to be transferred. 3 The decoration of glassware by gumming pictures upon it. Also **de·cal′**. [< F *décalcomanie* < *décalquer* transfer a tracing + *-manie* -MANIA]

de·ca·les·cence (dē′kə·les′əns) *n. Physics* The sudden absorption of heat by metals when the temperature passes a certain critical point, indicating internal structural changes: opposed to *recalescence.* —**de′ca·les′cent** *adj.* [< L *decalescens, -entis,* ppr. of *decalescere* < *de-* not + *calescere* grow hot]

dec·a·me·ter (dek′ə·mē′tər) *n.* 1 A dekameter. 2 Verse consisting of ten rhythmical feet. Also **dec′a·me′tre**. [< F *décamètre* < Gk. *dekametron* < *deka* ten + *metron* measure]

de·camp (di·kamp′) *v.i.* 1 To break camp or leave camp. 2 To leave suddenly or secretly; run away. See synonyms under ESCAPE. —**de·camp′ment** *n.*

dec·a·nal (dek′ə·nəl, di·kā′nəl) *adj.* Of or pertaining to a dean or deanery. [< LL *decanus.* See DEAN.] —**dec′a·nal·ly** *adv.*

de·can·drous (di·kan′drəs) *adj. Bot.* Having ten stamens. [< DEC(A)- + Gk. *anēr, andros* man]

dec·ane (dek′ān) *n. Chem.* Any of several isomeric hydrocarbons, $C_{10}H_{22}$, of the methane series, variously derived, from coal tar, etc. [< DEC(A)- + -ANE²]

de·cant (di·kant′) *v.t.* 1 To pour off gently so as not to disturb the sediment. 2 To pour from one container into another. [< F *décanter* < Med. L *decanthare* < *de-* from + *canthus* lip of a jug < Gk. *kanthos*] —**de·can·ta·tion** (dē′kan·tā′shən) *n.*

de·cant·er (di·kan′tər) *n.* An ornamental bottle for wine, etc.

de·cap·i·tate (di·kap′ə·tāt) *v.t.* **·tat·ed, ·tat·ing** To behead. [< Med. L *decapitare* < *de-* down + *caput* head] —**de·cap′i·ta′tion** *n.*

dec·a·pod (dek′ə·pod) *adj.* 1 Ten-footed or ten-armed. 2 *Zool.* Of or pertaining to the *Decapoda,* an order of crustaceans with five pairs of legs, including the crabs, lobsters, shrimps, etc. —*n.* A ten-legged crustacean; also, a ten-armed cephalopod, as a cuttlefish or squid. [< Gk. *dekapous, -podos* < *deka* ten + *pous* foot] —**de·cap·o·dal** (di·kap′ə·dəl), **de·cap′o·dous** *adj.*

DECANTER

dec·a·pod·i·form (dek′ə·pod′ə·fôrm) *adj.* Shaped like a decapod.

The removal of the enveloping membrane of an organ, especially the capsule of the kidney.

de·car·bon·ate (dī·kär′bə·nāt) *v.t.* **·at·ed, ·at·ing** To free from carbon dioxide. —**de·car′bon·a′tor** *n.*

de·car·box·y·la·tion (dē′kär·bok′sə·lā′shən) *n. Chem.* The elimination of one or more carboxyl radicals from an organic acid, with the release of carbon dioxide. [< DE- + CARBOXYL]

de·car·bu·rize (dē·kär′byə·rīz) *v.t.* **·rized, ·riz·ing** 1 To deprive wholly or in part of carbon. 2 To remove carbon from (molten steel or the cylinders of an internal-combustion engine).

dec·a·syl·la·ble (dek′ə·sil′ə·bəl) *n.* A line of verse having ten syllables. —**dec·a·syl·lab·ic** (dek′ə·si·lab′ik) *adj.*

de·cath·lon (di·kath′lon) *n.* An athletic contest consisting of ten different track and field events in which each contestant participates. [< DEC(A)- + Gk. *athlon* a contest]

dec·at·ing (dek′āt·ing) *n.* A method for the application of heat, moisture, and pressure to fabrics in order to set the nap, add luster, and control shrinkage. Also **dec·a·tiz·ing** (dek′ə·tī′zing). [< F *dicatir* sponge (a fabric) to set the gloss]

de·cay (di·kā′) *v.i.* 1 To fail slowly in health, beauty, quality, or any form of excellence. 2 To rot; decompose. —*v.t.* 3 To cause to decay. —*n.* 1 A passing into a feeble or reduced condition tending toward dissolution. 2 A gradual decline in health, size or quality; deterioration. 3 Decomposition; corruption; rottenness. 4 *Physics* The disintegration of a radioactive element. See synonyms under RUIN. [< OF *decair,* var. of *decaoir* < L *decidere* < *de-* down + *cadere* fall] —**de·cay′a·ble** *adj.* —**de·cay·ed·ness** (di·kā′id·nis) *n.*

Synonyms (verb): corrupt, decompose, molder, putrefy, rot, spoil. *Rot* is a strong and direct word. To say that a thing is *decayed* may denote only a partial result, but to say it is *decomposed* ordinarily implies that the change is complete or nearly so. *Putrefy* and the adjectives *putrid* and *putrescent,* and the nouns *putridity* and *putrescence,* are used almost exclusively of animal matter in a state of decomposition, the more general word *decay* being used of either animal or vegetable substances. *Decay* may also be extended to any process of decline or breaking down, physical, mental, social, etc. See PUTREFY.

de·cease (di·sēs′) *v.i.* **de·ceased, de·ceas·ing** To die. [< *n.*] —*n.* Departure from life; death. [< OF *déces* < L *decessus* < *decedere* < *de-* away + *cedere* go]

de·ce·dent (di·sēd′nt) *n.* A person deceased. [< L *decedens, -entis,* ppr. of *decedere.* See DECEASE.]

de·ceit (di·sēt′) *n.* The act of deceiving; deception; lying. 2 A lie or other dishonest action; trick. 3 Deceptiveness. See synonyms under DECEPTION, FRAUD, LIE. [< OF *deceite* < *deceveir* DECEIVE]

de·ceit·ful (di·sēt′fəl) *adj.* Characterized by deception; false; tricky; fraudulent. See synonyms under BAD, DECEPTIVE, INSIDIOUS, PERFIDIOUS, ROTTEN, VAIN. —**de·ceit′ful·ly** *adv.*

de·ceiv·a·ble (di·sē′və·bəl) *adj.* Capable of being deceived; liable to imposition. —**de·ceiv′a·ble·ness** *n.* —**de·ceiv′a·bly** *adv.*

de·ceive (di·sēv′) *v.* **de·ceived, de·ceiv·ing** *v.t.* 1 To mislead by or as by falsehood; impose upon; delude. 2 *Obs.* To while away (time). —*v.i.* 3 To practice deceit. [< OF *deceveir* < L *decipere* < *de-* away, down + *capere*

take] —**de·ceiv′ing·ly** *adv.*

Synonyms: beguile, betray, cheat, circumvent, defraud, delude, dupe, ensnare, entrap, mislead, outwit, overreach, trick. See MISLEAD. Compare DECEPTION.

de·ceiv·er (di·sē′vər) *n.* One who deceives. See synonyms under HYPOCRITE.

de·cel·er·ate (dē·sel′ə·rāt) *v.t. & v.i.* **·at·ed, ·at·ing** To diminish in velocity. [< DE- + L *celeratus,* pp. of *celerare* hasten < *celer* quick] —**de·cel·er·a′tor** *n.*

de·cel·er·a·tion (dē·sel′ə·rā′shən) *n.* Negative acceleration. See under ACCELERATION (def. 2).

de·cen·cy (dē′sən·sē) *n. pl.* **·cies** 1 Propriety in conduct, speech, or dress; modesty. 2 That which is decent, proper, or seemly. 3 *pl.* Things required for a proper or comfortable manner of life. [< L *decentia* < *decens.* See DECENT.]

de·cen·na·ry (di·sen′ər·ē) *adj.* Consisting of or pertaining to ten; pertaining to ten years or to a tithing: also **de·cen′a·ry.** —*n. pl.* **·ries** 1 In old English law, a tithing or group of ten freeholders and their families. 2 A period of ten years. [< L *decennis* < *decem* ten + *annus* year]

de·cen·ni·al (di·sen′ē·əl) *adj.* Continuing for or consisting of ten years; occurring every ten years. —*n.* An anniversary observed at periods of ten years. —**de·cen′ni·al·ly** *adv.*

de·cen·ni·um (di·sen′ē·əm) *n. pl.* **·cen·ni·ums** or **·cen·ni·a** (-sen′ē·ə) A period of ten years; decade. [< L *decem* ten + *annus* year]

de·cent (dē′sənt) *adj.* 1 Characterized by propriety of conduct, speech, manners, or dress; proper; decorous; respectable. 2 Free from indelicacy; modest; chaste. 3 Sufficient; passable; moderate. 4 *Obs.* Appropriate; also, symmetrical; comely. See synonyms under BECOMING, MODEST. [< L *decens, -entis,* ppr. of *decere* be fitting, be proper] —**de′cent·ly** *adv.* —**de′cent·ness** *n.*

de·cen·ter (dē·sen′tər) *v.t.* 1 To put out of center; make eccentric. 2 *Optics* To cut, as a lens for an eyeglass, so that the physical center and the optical center of the lens surfaces do not coincide. Also **de·cen′tre.**

de·cen·tral·ize (dē·sen′trəl·īz) *v.t.* **·ized, ·iz·ing** 1 To remove from a center; distribute: used especially of government or other authority. 2 *Econ.* To reorganize (a large enterprise, industry, or corporation) into smaller and more dispersed units in order to permit more efficient management and control. —**de·cen′tral·i·za′tion** *n.*

de·cep·tion (di·sep′shən) *n.* 1 The act of deceiving. 2 The state of being deceived. 3 Anything that deceives or is meant to deceive; a delusion. [< L *deceptio, -onis* < *decipere.* See DECEIVE.]

Synonyms: craft, cunning, deceit, deceitfulness, delusion, dissimulation, double-dealing, duplicity, fabrication, falsehood, finesse, fraud, guile, hypocrisy, imposition, lie, lying, prevarication, trickery, untruth. *Deceit* is especially applied to the habit, *deception* to the act; *guile* applies to the disposition out of which *deceit* and *deception* grow, and also to their actual practice. A *lie, lying,* or *falsehood* is the uttering of what one knows to be false with intent to deceive. *Untruth* is more than lack of accuracy, implying always lack of veracity; but it is a somewhat milder and more dignified word than *lie. Falsehood* and *lying* are in utterance; *deceit* and *deception* may be merely in act or implication. *Deception* may be innocent, and even unintentional, as in the case of an optical illusion; *deceit* always involves injurious intent. *Craft* and *cunning* have not necessarily any moral quality; they are common traits of animals, but stand rather low in the human scale. *Duplicity* is the habitual speaking or acting with intent to appear to mean what one does not. *Dissimulation* is rather a concealing of what is than a pretense of what is not. *Finesse* is simply an adroit and delicate management of a matter for one's own side, not necessarily involving *deceit.* Compare FRAUD, LIE. *Antonyms:* candor, frankness, guilelessness, honesty, openness, simplicity, sincerity, truth, veracity.

de·cep·tive (di·sep′tiv) *adj.* Having power or tendency to deceive. —**de·cep′tive·ly** *adv.*

Synonyms: deceitful, delusive, illusive, illusory. Persons are *deceitful:* things are *deceptive.* We speak of a *deceitful,* but not of a *deceptive* man. We speak, however, of *deceit-*

ful promises, as involving personal intent to deceive. It is more accurate to say *deceptive* than *deceitful* appearances. See BAD, COUNTERFEIT. *Antonyms:* fair, frank, genuine, honest.

de·cer·e·brate (dē·ser′ə·brāt) *v.t.* **·brat·ed**, **·brat·ing** To remove the brain from, as in certain operations and laboratory experiments. — *adj.* (-brit) Having the brain removed. [<DE- + L *cerebrum* brain] — **de·cer′e·bra′tion** *n.*

de·cer·e·brize (dē·ser′ə·brīz) *v.t.* **·brized**, **·briz·ing** To remove the cerebrum or brain from, as in vivisection.

deci- *combining form* A tenth. See METRIC SYSTEM. [<L *decimus* tenth <*decem* ten]

dec·i·are (des′ē·âr) *n.* One tenth of an are. See METRIC SYSTEM. [<F *déciare*]

dec·i·bel (des′ə·bel) *n.* *Physics* One tenth of a bel: the common unit of measure of loudness of sounds.

de·cide (di·sīd′) *v.* **·cid·ed**, **·cid·ing** *v.t.* **1** To determine; settle, as a controversy, dispute, contest, etc.; arbitrate: to *decide* who is right. **2** To cause the outcome of; settle: The charge *decided* the battle. **3** To bring (someone) to a decision. — *v.i.* **4** To give a decision. **5** To make a decision. See synonyms under SETTLE. [<MF *décider* <L *decidere* <*de-* down, away + *caedere* cut] — **de·cid′a·ble** *adj.*

de·cid·ed (di·sī′did) *adj.* **1** Free from uncertainty; unquestionable; unmistakable. **2** Determined; resolute; emphatic. See synonyms under FIRM. — **de·cid′ed·ly** *adv.* — **de·cid′ed·ness** *n.*

de·cid·u·a (di·sij′ōō·ə) *n.* *Physiol.* The thickened mucous membrane of the uterus cast off and expelled either during menstruation (*decidua menstrualis*) or at parturition (*decidua graviditatis*). [<NL (*membrana*) *decidua* (membrane) that is cast off <*deciduus.* See DECIDUOUS.] — **de·cid′u·al** *adj.*

de·cid·u·ous (di·sij′ōō·əs) *adj.* **1** *Bot.* Falling off or shed at maturity or at specific seasons, as petals, fruit, or leaves; also, characterized by such a falling off; not evergreen. **2** *Zool.* Liable to be shed at periodical times, as antlers, hair, teeth, wings of insects, etc. **3** Not enduring; evanescent; short-lived. Compare PERSISTENT. [<L *deciduus* <*decidere* <*de-* down, away + *cadere* fall] — **de·cid′u·ous·ly** *adv.* — **de·cid′u·ous·ness** *n.*

dec·i·gram (des′ə·gram) *n.* The tenth part of a gram. See METRIC SYSTEM. Also **dec′i·gramme.**

dec·i·li·ter (des′ə·lē′tər) *n.* The tenth part of a liter. See METRIC SYSTEM. Also **dec′i·li′tre.**

de·cil·lion (di·sil′yən) *n.* The numeral 1 followed by thirty-three ciphers according to American and French notation, or by sixty ciphers in English notation. [<DEC(A)- + (M)ILLION] — **de·cil′lionth** *adj.*

dec·i·mal (des′ə·məl) *adj.* **1** Pertaining to or founded on the number 10. **2** Proceeding by powers of 10 or of one tenth. — *n.* A decimal fraction or one of its digits. [<Med. L *decimalis* of tenths <*decimus* tenth <*decem* ten]

dec·i·mal·i·za·tion (des′ə·məl·i·zā′shən) *n.* The process or program of adopting the decimal system, as in currency.

decimal point A dot or period used before a decimal fraction.

decimal system A system of reckoning by tens or tenths.

dec·i·mate (des′ə·māt) *v.t.* **·mat·ed**, **·mat·ing** **1** To destroy or kill a large proportion of. **2** To select by lot and kill one out of every ten of. **3** *Obs.* To exact a tithe from; tax a tenth part of. [<L *decimatus*, pp. of *decimare* take a tenth part from <*decem* ten] — **dec′i·ma′tion** *n.* — **dec′i·ma′tor** *n.*

dec·i·me·ter (des′ə·mē′tər) *n.* The tenth part of a meter. See METRIC SYSTEM. Also **dec′i·me′tre.**

de·ci·pher (di·sī′fər) *v.t.* **1** To determine the meaning of, as hieroglyphics or illegible writing. **2** To translate from cipher into ordinary characters. **3** To determine the meaning of (anything obscure). See synonyms under INTERPRET. — **de·ci′pher·a·ble** *adj.* — **de·ci′pher·er** *n.* — **de·ci′pher·ment** *n.*

de·ci·sion (di·sizh′ən) *n.* **1** The act of deciding or making up one's mind. **2** Decisive result; settlement; judgment, as of a court. **3** The quality of being positive and firm; determination. See synonyms under DETERMINATION, WILL. [<F *décision* <L *decisio, -onis* <*decidere.* See DE-

CIDE]

de·ci·sion-making (di·sizh′ən·mā′king) *n.* **1** The process by which decisions are made, especially important decisions affecting others and made by virtue of one's office or position. **2** The power or ability to make decisions of consequence. — *adj.* Of, relating to, or requiring decision-making. — **de·ci′sion-mak′er** *n.*

de·ci·sive (di·sī′siv) *adj.* **1** Putting an end to uncertainty, debate, or question; conclusive. **2** Prompt; positive; decided. — **de·ci′sive·ly** *adv.* — **de·ci′sive·ness** *n.*

dec·i·stere (des′ə·stir) *n.* A cubic decimeter, or the tenth part of a stere. See METRIC SYSTEM.

deck (dek) *n.* **1** *Naut.* **a** A platform covering or extending horizontally across a vessel. **b** The space between two such platforms. **2** Any similar flat surface. **3** A car roof. **4** A covering or shelter. **5** A pack of cards. **6** In journalism, lines under a headline; bank. — **to hit the deck 1** *Slang* To rise from bed quickly; get up. **2** *Slang* To prepare or start to work. **3** *Slang* To drop to a prone position. — **on deck 1** Present; alive and able-bodied. **2** Next at bat in a baseball game. — *v.t.* **1** To array; dress elegantly; adorn; decorate. **2** *Naut.* To put a deck on. **3** *Obs.* To cover, clothe. See synonyms under GARNISH. [<MDu. *dek* roof, covering]

deck·le (dek′əl) *n.* **1** In papermaking by hand, a rectangular frame laid upon a wire mold to confine the paper pulp to a definite area, thus limiting the size of the sheet. **2** A raw or ragged edge of paper: also **deckle edge.** [<G *deckel*, dim. of *decke* cover]

de·claim (di·klām′) *v.i.* **1** To speak loudly and in a rhetorical manner. **2** To give a recitation. **3** To condemn or attack verbally and vehemently: with *against.* — *v.t.* **4** To utter aloud in a rhetorical manner. See synonyms under SPEAK. [<L *declamare* <*de-* completely + *clamare* shout] — **de·claim′er** *n.*

dec·la·ma·tion (dek′lə·mā′shən) *n.* **1** The act of declaiming. **2** A speech or selection recited or to be recited from memory.

de·clam·a·to·ry (di·klam′ə·tôr′ē, -tō′rē) *adj.* **1** Using, characterized by, or pertaining to declamation. **2** In a noisy, empty rhetorical style. — **de·clam′a·to′ri·ly** *adv.*

dec·la·ra·tion (dek′lə·rā′shən) *n.* **1** A formal or explicit statement; the act of declaring, or that which is declared. **2** In common-law pleading, the paper filed by the plaintiff in which he alleges the facts constituting his cause of action and demands judgment; also, a solemn declaration made by a witness under the penalties of perjury, equivalent to an oath. **3** In bridge, the naming of the trump suit and the tricks, above six, to be taken: also called *make.*

de·clar·a·tive (di·klar′ə·tiv) *adj.* Making a declaration or statement; affirmative: a *declarative* sentence. Also **de·clar·a·to·ry** (di·klar′ə·tôr′ē, -tō′rē).

de·clare (di·klâr′) *v.* **·clared**, **·clar·ing** *v.t.* **1** To assert positively; aver. **2** To announce or state formally and solemnly: to *declare* war or a dividend. **3** To manifest; make known: His actions *declare* him a saint. **4** To make full statement of, as goods liable to duty or tax. **5** In card games, to name (a suit) trumps. — *v.i.* **6** To make a declaration. **7** To proclaim a choice or decision. See synonyms under AFFIRM, ALLEGE, ANNOUNCE, ASSERT, AVOW, PUBLISH, SPEAK. [<L *declarare* <*de-* completely + *clarare* make clear <*clarus* clear] — **de·clar·ed·ly** (di·klâr′id·lē) *adv.* — **de·clar′ed·ness** *n.* — **de·clar′er** *n.*

de·clen·sion (di·klen′shən) *n.* **1** *Gram.* **a** The inflection of nouns, pronouns, and adjectives to indicate case, number, and gender. **b** A class of words similarly inflected: *Stella* and *nauta* are Latin nouns of the first *declension.* **2** Decline: deterioration. **3** The act of declining. **4** A slope; incline. [<L *declinatio, -onis* <*declinare.* See DECLINE.] — **de·clen′sion·al** *adj.*

dec·li·na·tion (dek′lə·nā′shən) *n.* **1** The act of declining; inclination; descent; slope. **2** Deterioration; decay. **3** Refusal; non-acceptance. **4** Deviation. **5** *Astron.* The angular distance of a heavenly body north or south from the celestial equator; celestial latitude. **6** The angle between the direction in which the magnetic needle points and the true meridian: often called **magnetic dec-

lination. 7** *Obs.* Grammatical declension; inflection.

de·cline (di·klīn′) *v.* **·clined**, **·clin·ing** *v.i.* **1** To refuse to accept, comply with, or do something, especially politely. **2** To lessen or fail, as in value, health, or force; wane. **3** To bend or incline downward or aside. **4** *Poetic* To fall off morally. — *v.t.* **5** To refuse to accept, comply with, or do, especially politely. **6** To cause to bend or incline downward or aside. **7** *Gram.* To give the inflected forms of (a noun, pronoun, or adjective). See synonyms under ABATE, DIE, FALL. — *n.* **1** The act or result of declining; deterioration; decay. **2** The period of such decay. **3** That stage of a disease during which the symptoms decrease in violence. **4** Any enfeebling disease, as tabes. **5** A declivity; a slope. [<OF *decliner* <L *declinare* lean down] — **de·clin′a·ble** *adj.* — **de·clin′er** *n.*

de·cliv·i·ty (di·kliv′ə·tē) *n. pl.* **·ties** A downward slope; descending surface of a hill or mountain: opposed to *acclivity.* [<L *declivitas, -tatis* <*declivis* <*de-* down + *clivus* hill, slope]

de·coc·tion (di·kok′shən) *n.* **1** The act of boiling anything, especially in water, to extract its soluble properties: distinguished from *infusion.* **2** An aqueous preparation made by boiling an animal or vegetable substance; an essence or extract.

de·code (dē·kōd′) *v.t.* **·cod·ed**, **·cod·ing** To convert (a coded message) into plain language. — **de·cod′er** *n.*

de·co·her·er (dē′kō·hir′ər) *n.* An electromagnetic device for restoring a coherer to its normal condition after the passing of an electric wave: also called *anticoherer.* See COHERER.

de·co·he·sion (dē′kō·hē′zhən) *n.* The act or state of decohering.

de·col·late (di·kol′āt) *v.t.* **·lat·ed**, **·lat·ing** To behead. [<L *decollatus*, pp. of *decollare* <*de-* down, from + *collum* neck] — **de·col′la·tor** *n.*

de·col·or (dē·kul′ər) *v.t.* To deprive of color; bleach. Also *Brit.* **de·col′our.** — **de·col′or·a′tion** *n.*

de·col·or·ant (dē·kul′ər·ənt) *adj.* Bleaching. — *n.* A bleaching substance.

de·com·mis·sion (dē′kə·mish′ən) *v.t.* To take out of active service, as a ship.

de·com·pose (dē′kəm·pōz′) *v.t. & v.i.* **·posed**, **·pos·ing** **1** To separate into constituent parts or elements. **2** To decay; putrefy. — **de′com·pos′a·ble** *adj.* — **de′com·pos′er** *n.*

de·com·pos·ite (dē′kəm·poz′it) *adj.* **1** Compounded of compounds, as a word. **2** *Bot.* Decompound, as a leaf.

de·com·po·si·tion (dē′kom·pə·zish′ən) *n.* The act, process, or result of decomposing by chemical action or by natural decay. — **double decomposition** *Chem.* The formation of two compounds by the union of the radicals formed by the decomposition of two other compounds; metathesis.

de·com·pound (dē·kom′pound′, dē′kəm·pound′) *adj. Bot.* Several times divided or compounded, as a leaf. [<DE- (def. 3) + COMPOUND]

de·com·press (dē′kəm·pres′) *v.t.* **1** To free of pressure. **2** To remove the pressure on (caisson workers, etc.), as in an airlock.

de·com·pres·sion (dē′kəm·presh′ən) *n.* The reduction or removal of pressure, especially in connection with work in caissons or under high atmospheric pressure.

decompression chamber An enclosed chamber equipped for the decompression of bodies subjected to high pressure, or for reducing normal pressure in simulation of or preparatory to high altitude flying.

de·con·tam·i·nate (dē′kən·tam′ə·nāt) *v.t.* **·nat·ed**, **·nat·ing** **1** To rid of contamination. **2** To prepare (a contaminated object or area) for normal use by destroying or neutralizing noxious chemicals or radioactivity.

de·con·trol (dē′kən·trōl′) *v.t.* **·trolled**, **·trol·ling** To remove from control, specifically, from government controls. — *n.* The removal of controls.

dé·cor (dā′kôr, dā·kôr′) *n.* **1** The plan or arrangement of furnishings and colors in an interior space, as a home or office. **2** In the theater, scenery. [<F <*décorer* decorate]

dec·o·rate (dek′ə·rāt) *v.t.* **·rat·ed**, **·rat·ing** **1** To adorn; ornament. **2** To confer a decoration or medal upon. See synonyms under ADORN, GARNISH. [<L *decoratus*, pp. of *decorare* <*decus, de-

coris grace, embellishment]

dec·o·ra·tion (dek′ə·rā′shən) *n.* **1** The act, process, or art of decorating. **2** Ornamentation; an ornament. **3** A badge or emblem conferred as a mark of honor; a medal.

dec·o·rous (dek′ər·əs, di·kôr′əs, -kō′rəs) *adj.* Proper; becoming; suitable. See synonyms under BECOMING, CORRECT, MODEST. [< L *decorus* < *decus, decoris* grace] — **dec′o·rous·ly** *adv.*

de·cor·ti·cate (di·kôr′tə·kāt) *v.t.* **·cat·ed, ·cat·ing 1** To strip off the bark or outer coat of; peel; husk; hull. **2** To strip off a portion of the cortical substance of (the brain, kidney, etc.). [< L *decorticatus,* pp. of *decorticare* < *de-* down + *cortex, corticis* bark] — **de·cor′ti·ca′tion** *n.* — **de·cor′ti·ca′tor** *n.*

de·co·rum (di·kôr′əm, -kō′rəm) *n.* *pl.* **·co·rums** or **·co·ra** (-kôr′ə, -kō′rə) **1** Propriety, as in manner, conduct, etc.; politeness. **2** An act demanded by social custom. [< L, neut. of *decorus* DECOROUS]

de·cou·page (dā′kōō·päzh′) *n.* **1** The art of using pieces cut from paper, etc., to decorate an entire surface. **2** A work produced by such means. Also **dé′cou·page′**. [< F]

de·coy (di·koi′, dē′·koi) *n.* **1** One who or that which allures or is intended to allure into danger or temptation. **2** A swindler's accomplice. **3** A lure; a bird or animal, or the likeness of one, used to lure game into a snare or net or within gunshot.

DECOY

4 An enclosed place into which game may be lured for capture. **5** *Mil.* A dummy military installation designed to distract enemy fire from a real position or installation, or to delude the foe as to the point of one's own attack. — *v.t. & v.i.* (dē′koi) To lure or be lured into danger, a snare, etc. [Earlier *coy* < Du. *kooi* a cage < L *cavea* < *cavus* hollow]

de·crease (di·krēs′) *v.t. & v.i.* **·creased, ·creas·ing** To grow, or cause to grow, less or smaller; diminish, especially by a gradual process; abate; reduce. — *n.* (usually dē′krēs) **1** The act, process, or state of decreasing. **2** The amount or degree of loss; diminution. See synonyms under ABATE, IMPAIR, RETRENCH. [< OF *decreiss-,* stem of *decreistre* < L *decrescere* < *de-* down + *crescere* grow] — **de·creas′ing·ly** *adv.*

de·cree (di·krē′) *n.* **1** A formal order determining what is to be done or not to be done in a particular matter; a law or ordinance of either a civil or an ecclesiastical ruler, council, or legislative body. **2** *Theol.* A foreordaining, eternal purpose of God. See synonyms under LAW. — *v.t.* To order, adjudge, ordain, or appoint by law or edict. — *v.i.* To issue an edict or decree. See synonyms under DICTATE. [< OF *decre, decret* < L *decretum,* neut. pp. of *decernere.* See DECERN.]

dec·re·ment (dek′rə·mənt) *n.* **1** A decreasing; waning. **2** Amount of loss by decrease or waste. **3** *Math.* A decrease in value of a variable quantity; negative increment. [< L *decrementum* < *decrescere.* See DECREASE.]

de·crep·it (di·krep′it) *adj.* Enfeebled by old age; broken down. [< L *decrepitus* < *de-* completely + *crepare* creak] — **de·crep′it·ly** *adv.*

de·crep·i·tate (di·krep′ə·tāt) *v.* **·tat·ed, ·tat·ing** *v.t.* To heat (salt, minerals, etc.) so as to cause to crepitate or crackle. — *v.i.* To crackle when heated, as salt. [< NL *decrepitatus,* pp. of *decrepitare* < *de-* completely + *crepitare,* freq. of *crepare* creak]

de·cre·tal (di·krēt′l) *n.* **1** An authoritative decree, or a letter containing such a decree; especially, a letter or rescript of the Pope determining some point in ecclesiastical law. **2** A book or compilation of decrees, orders, or laws. [< F *décrétale* < Med.L *decretale* < L *decretum.* See DECREE.]

de·cre·to·ry (dek′rə·tôr′ē, -tō′rē) *adj.* **1** Pertaining to, resulting from, or announcing a decree; judicial. **2** Definitive.

de·crim·i·nal·ize (dē·krim′ə·nəl·īz) *v.t.* **·ized, ·iz·ing** To abstain from applying criminal penalties to; regard as non-punishable. — **de·crim′i·nal·i·za′tion** *n.*

de·cru·des·cence (dē′krōō·des′əns) *n. Med.* A lessening in the intensity of the symptoms of a disease. [< DE- (def. 4) + L *crudescens, -entis,* ppr. of *crudescere* grow harsh < *crudus* harsh] — **de′cru·des′cent** *adj.*

de·cry (di·krī′) *v.t.* **·cried, ·cry·ing 1** To condemn or disparage openly; traduce. **2** To depreciate or condemn officially, as foreign or obsolete coins. See synonyms under ASPERSE, DISPARAGE. [< F *décrier* < *dé-* down (< L *de-*) + *crier* cry] — **de·cri′al** *n.* — **de·cri′er** *n.*

de·cu·ba·tion (dek′yōō·bā′shən) *n. Med.* The period of convalescence from an infectious disease, ending with the disappearance of the micro-organisms from the body. [< DE- (def. 4) + L *cubatio, -onis* a lying down < *cubare* recline]

de·cum·bence (di·kum′bəns) *n.* A decumbent or prostrate state or position. Also **de·cum′ben·cy.**

de·cum·bent (di·kum′bənt) *adj.* **1** Lying down; recumbent. **2** *Bot.* Prostrate: said of stems, shoots, etc., growing along the ground. [< L *decumbens, -entis,* ppr. of *decumbere* < *de-* down + *cumbere* lie, recline]

dec·u·ple (dek′yōō·pəl) *v.t.* **·pled, ·pling** To increase tenfold. — *adj.* Tenfold. — *n.* A number or quantity ten times as large as another or ten times repeated. [< F *décuple* < L *decuplus* < *decem* ten]

dec·u·pli·cate (dek·yōō′plə·kit) *adj.* **1** Tenfold. **2** Raised to the tenth power. — *v.t.* (-kāt) **·cat·ed, ·cat·ing** To decuple. — *n.* One of ten like things. [< DECUPLE, on analogy with *duplicate, triplicate,* etc.] — **dec·u′pli·cate·ly** *adv.* — **dec·u′pli·ca′tion** *n.*

de·cu·ri·on (di·kyōōr′ē·ən) *n.* **1** An officer who commanded ten soldiers: the lowest military officer of ancient Rome; also, a member of the Roman Senate in a colony or municipal town. **2** Any person having command over or responsibility for ten others. [< L *decurio, -onis* < *decem* ten]

de·cur·rent (di·kûr′ənt) *adj. Bot.* Extending or running downward into another structure, as leaves along a plant stem. [< L *decurrens, -entis,* ppr. of *decurrere* < *de-* down + *currere* run] — **de·cur′rent·ly** *adv.*

de·cus·sate (di·kus′āt, dek′ə·sāt) *v.i.* **·sat·ed, ·sat·ing** To intersect; cross in the form of the letter X; interlace. — *adj.* (di·kus′āt, -it) **1** Crossed; intersected. **2** *Bot.* Having each pair of leaves at right angles with the pair next below or above: also **de·cus′sat·ed.** [< L *decussatus,* pp. of *decussare* mark with an X < *decussis* the number ten, X] — **de·cus′sate·ly** *adv.*

dec·us·sa·tion (dek′ə·sā′shən) *n.* **1** The act or state of decussating; that which decussates. **2** *Anat.* A crossing over of symmetrical parts, as nerve fibers intersecting the median plane of the central nervous system to connect centers on either side.

ded·a·lous (ded′ə·ləs) *adj.* Pertaining to or like a labyrinth; involved; intricately and skilfully made. [< L *daedalus* skilfully made < Gk. *daidalos*]

ded·i·cate (ded′ə·kāt) *v.t.* **·cat·ed, ·cat·ing 1** To set apart for sacred uses; consecrate. **2** To set apart for or devote to any special use, duty, or purpose. **3** To preface with a dedication, as a work of literature. See synonyms under INSCRIBE. — *adj.* Dedicated; devoted. [< L *dedicatus,* pp. of *dedicare* < *de-* down + *dicare* proclaim] — **ded′i·ca·tive** *adj.* — **ded′i·ca′tor** *n.* — **ded′i·ca·to′ry** (-kə·tôr′ē, -tō′rē) *adj.* — **ded′i·ca·to′ri·ly** *adv.*

ded·i·ca·tion (ded′ə·kā′shən) *n.* **1** A dedicating or being dedicated. **2** An inscription in a book, etc., as to a friend or cause.

de·duce (di·dōōs′, -dyōōs′) *v.t.* **·duced, ·duc·ing 1** To derive as a conclusion; infer; conclude. **2** To trace, as derivation or origin. [< L *deducere* < *de-* down + *ducere* lead] — **de·duce′ment** *n.* — **de·duc′i·ble** *adj.*

de·duct (di·dukt′) *v.t.* To subtract; take away. [< L *deductus,* pp. of *deducere.* See DEDUCE.]

de·duc·tion (di·duk′shən) *n.* **1** The act of deducing. **2** *Logic* Reasoning from stated premises to the formally valid conclusion; reasoning from the general to the particular. **3** An inference; conclusion. **4** The act of deducting. **5** A subtraction; abatement. See synonyms under DEMONSTRATION, INFERENCE. Compare INDUCTION.

de·duc·tive (di·duk′tiv) *adj.* **1** Of or proceeding by deduction. **2** Inferential; deducible.

dee (dē) *n.* **1** The sound or the shape of the letter D. **2** A metal loop for connecting parts of harness. **3** One of a pair of D-shaped half-hollow cylinder units of a cyclotron in which the stream of entering electrons is continuously accelerated in an electromagnetic field.

deed (dēd) *n.* **1** Anything done; an act. **2** An exploit, a notable achievement. **3** Fact; truth; reality. **4** Action performed, as opposed to words. **5** *Law* A written instrument containing a grant signed and sealed by the grantor; an instrument of conveyance under seal: a *deed* for land. Any instrument in writing under seal, whether a bond, agreement, or contract of any kind, is a *deed,* but the word is more frequently used in regard to the conveyance of real estate. See synonyms under ACT, TRANSACTION, WORK. — **in deed** In fact; actually. — *v.t.* To convey or transfer by deed. [OE *dǣd*] — **deed′ful** *adj.* — **deed′less** *adj.*

deed·ed (dē′did) *adj. Law* Conveyed by a deed.

deem (dēm) *v.t. & v.i.* To judge; think; regard; believe. See synonyms under CALCULATE, ESTEEM, SUPPOSE. [OE *dēman,* judge]

de·em·pha·size (dē·em′fə·sīz) *v.t.* **·sized, ·siz·ing** To place less emphasis on. — **de·em′pha·sis** (-sis) *n.*

deem·ster (dēm′stər) *n.* **1** One who deems or dooms; a judge. **2** Either of the two highest judicial officers in the Isle of Man. [ME *demestre*] — **deem′ster·ship** *n.*

deep (dēp) *adj.* **1** Extending or situated far, or comparatively far, below the surface. **2** Extending or entering far back, in, or away from the spectator's point of view. **3** Having a depth, thickness, dimension, or quantity measured from above downward, from before backward, or from without inward. **4** Profound in nature, reach, or degree. **5** Hard to understand or fathom because abstruse, complex, or well concealed. **6** Of great and well-trained or far-reaching intellectual powers; sagacious; penetrating. **7** Of great intensity; great in degree; extreme; hence, heartfelt and earnest. **8** Artful in the concealment of plans or schemes; insidious; scheming; designing. **9** Of low, sonorous, or heavy tone; grave. **10** Of intense or dark hue. **11** Immersed; absorbed: *deep* in a book. — *n.* **1** A place or thing that has great depth; deep water; an abyss; especially, the sea or ocean. **2** Something too profound, vast, or abstruse to be easily comprehended; a mystery. **3** The most profound part; culmination: the *deep* of night. **4** *Naut.* The interval between two successive marked fathoms on a lead line or sounding line of a vessel. — *adv.* **1** Deeply. **2** Far on, in reference to time. [OE *dēop.* Akin to DIP.] — **deep′ness** *n.*

deep·en (dē′pən) *v.t. & v.i.* To make or become deep or deeper.

deep-freeze (dēp′frēz′) *n.* A refrigerator in which foods may be kept for long periods of time at temperatures approximating 0° F.

deep-fry (dēp′frī′) *v.t.* **·fried, ·fry·ing** To fry in deep fat or oil.

deep-laid (dēp′lād′) *adj.* Made with extreme care and cleverness, usually in secret: *deep-laid* plans.

deep·ly (dēp′lē) *adv.* **1** At or to a great depth. **2** To a great extent or degree; intensely; profoundly; thoroughly. **3** At a low pitch or tone. **4** With deep color. **5** Artfully; intricately.

deep reflex *Physiol.* Any reflex affecting a deep-lying muscle or other internal structure, as produced by tapping an adjacent tendon or bone.

deep-root·ed (dēp′rōō′tid, -rŏŏt′id) *adj.* **1** Having roots that reach far below the surface. **2** Firmly held: said of beliefs, prejudices, etc.

deep-sea (dēp′sē′) *adj.* Of, in, or pertaining to the depths of the sea.

deep-seat·ed (dēp′sē′tid) *adj.* So far in as to be ineradicable or almost ineradicable: said of emotions, diseases, etc.

deer (dir) *n.* *pl.* **deer 1** A ruminant (family *Cervidae*) having deciduous antlers, usually in the male only, as the moose, elk, and reindeer. Popularly, *deer* is used mainly of the smaller species. ◆ Collateral adjective: *cervine.* See FALLOW DEER, VENISON. **2** A deerlike animal. **3** Formerly, any quadruped; a wild animal. ◆ Homophone: *dear.* [OE *dēor* beast]

deer·ber·ry (dir′ber′ē) *n.* *pl.* **·ries 1** The

buckberry (def. 2). **2** The wintergreen. **3** The partridgeberry.

deer·fly (dir'flī') *n.* *pl.* **·flies** A bloodsucking fly (genus *Chrysops*), similar to a horsefly but smaller and with banded wings. For illustration see INSECT (injurious).

deer·grass (dir'gras', -gräs') *n.* **1** Meadow-beauty. **2** A forage grass (*Muhlenbergia rigens*) of Mexico and the SW United States.

deer·hound (dir'hound') *n.* A breed of sporting dog, having a long, flat head, pointed muzzle, and a shaggy, dark-gray, or brindle coat: also called *staghound.* Also **Scottish deerhound.**

DEERHOUND
(28 to 32 inches high at the shoulder)

deer·let (dir'lət) *n.* A pigmy deer.

deer·lick (dir'lik') *n.* A place, naturally or artificially salted, where deer come to lick the saline earth.

deer mouse A small, long-tailed, furry mouse (*Peromyscus maniculatus*), many varieties of which are widely distributed in North America; the white-footed mouse.

deer·skin (dir'skin') *n.* A deer's hide, or leather made from it; buckskin.

deer·stalk·er (dir'stô'kər) *n.* **1** One who hunts deer by stalking. **2** A helmet-shaped cloth cap, usually red, commonly worn by deer hunters.

deer·weed (dir'wēd') *n.* A branching, leguminous herb (*Lotus scoparius*) found in parts of Arizona and southern California: sometimes utilized for cattle food. Also **deer'vetch'.**

de·es·ca·late (dē-es'kə-lāt) *v.t.* & *v.i.* **·lat·ed, ·lat·ing** To decrease or be decreased gradually, as in scope, effect, or intensity: to *de-escalate* a war. — **de·es'ca·la'tion** *n.*

de·face (di-fās') *v.t.* **·faced, ·fac·ing 1** To mar or disfigure the face or surface of. **2** To obliterate wholly or partially, as an inscription; efface. [<obs. F *desfacier* <OF *desfacier* <*des-* down, away + *face* face <L *facies*] — **de·face·ment** (di-fās'mənt) *n.* **1** The act of defacing. **2** Anything that disfigures.

de fac·to (dē fak'tō) Actually or really existing, with or without legal sanction, as a government: distinguished from *de jure.* [<L]

de·fal·cate (di-fal'kāt) *v.i.* **·cat·ed, ·cat·ing** To commit defalcation; embezzle money. [< Med. L *defalcatus,* pp. of *defalcare* lop off <*de-* down, away + *falx, falcis* scythe] — **de·fal'ca·tor** *n.*

de·fal·ca·tion (dē'fal-kā'shən) *n.* **1** A fraudulent appropriation of money held in trust; embezzlement; also, the amount embezzled. **2** A deducting; an abatement. **3** The amount deducted.

def·a·ma·tion (def'ə-mā'shən) *n.* The act of defaming; aspersion; calumny. See synonyms under SCANDAL. [<L *diffamatio, -onis* a speaking against <*diffamare.* See DEFAME.]

de·fam·a·to·ry (di-fam'ə-tôr'ē, -tō'rē) *adj.* Slanderous.

de·fame (di-fām') *v.t.* **·famed, ·fam·ing 1** To attack the good name or reputation of; slander; libel. **2** *Obs.* To indict; accuse. See synonyms under ABUSE, ASPERSE, REVILE. [<L *diffamare* <*dis-*away, from + *fama* a report, reputation]

de·fault (di-fôlt') *n.* **1** A failure in or neglect of an obligation or duty; failure to appear or plead in a suit; failure to pay a sum due. **2** Want or deficiency; absence; lack: in *default* of evidence. **3** *Obs.* A fault; transgression. **4** The failure to appear for an athletic contest, race, etc.; failure to finish a contest. See synonyms under NEGLECT, WANT. — **in default of** Owing to lack or failure of. — **judgment by default** A judgment in a civil action rendered for failure to prosecute or defend. — *v.i.* **1** To fail or neglect to fulfil or do a duty, obligation, etc. **2** To fail to meet financial obligations. **3** *Law* To fail to appear in court; also, to lose by default. **4** In sports, to fail to compete or complete a game, etc.; also, to lose or forfeit a game, etc., by default. — *v.t.* **5** To fail to perform or pay. **6** To declare in default, especially legally. **7** In sports, to fail to compete in,

as a game; also, to forfeit by default. [<OF *defaut* <*defaillir* <*de-* down + *fallere* deceive]

de·fault·er (di-fôl'tər) *n.* **1** One who defaults; especially, one who fails to appear in court. **2** One who fails to account for trust money; a delinquent; embezzler; also, one who fails to pay debts. **3** *Brit.* A soldier who has committed an offense against military law.

de·fea·sance (di-fē'zəns) *n.* **1** A making null or void; an annulment. **2** *Law* A condition in a deed or collateral instrument by the performance of which the principal deed is rendered void. [<OF *defesance* an undoing < *defaire.* See DEFEAT.]

de·feat (di-fēt') *v.t.* **1** To overcome in any contest; vanquish. **2** To baffle; circumvent, as plans; frustrate. **3** *Law* To make void; annul. **4** *Obs.* To destroy; ruin. See synonyms under BAFFLE, BEAT, CONQUER. — *n.* **1** The act or result of defeating; an overthrow; a failure to win or succeed. **2** Prevention; frustration. **3** *Law* An annulment. **4** *Obs.* Destruction. See synonyms under LOSS, RUIN. [<OF *defeit,* pp. of *defaire* <*de-* not (<L *dis-*) + *faire* do <L *facere*]

de·feat·ism (di-fē'tiz-əm) *n.* **1** Acknowledgment or acceptance of defeat, usually on grounds of the futility of resistance. **2** The conduct, state of mind, or propaganda that makes for this. — **de·feat'ist** *n.* & *adj.*

def·e·cate (def'ə-kāt) *v.* **·cat·ed, ·cat·ing** *v.t.* **1** To clear of dregs or impurities; refine; purify. — *v.i.* **2** To become free of dregs. **3** To discharge excrement. — *adj.* Clarified; refined. [<L *defaecatus,* pp. of *defaecare* <*de-* down, away + *faex* dregs] — **def'e·ca'-tion** *n.*

def·e·ca·tor (def'ə-kā'tər) *n.* **1** One who or that which clarifies or purifies. **2** In sugar-making, an apparatus for clearing sirups, juices, etc., of impurities.

de·fect (di-fekt', dē'fekt) *n.* **1** Lack or absence of something essential; imperfection. **2** A blemish; failing; fault. See synonyms under BLEMISH, FOIBLE, WANT. — *v.i.* (di-fekt') To desert; go over to the enemy or opposition. [<L *defectus,* pp. of *deficere* fail <*de-* not + *facere* do]

de·fec·tion (di-fek'shən) *n.* **1** Abandonment of allegiance or duty; failure. **2** Apostasy; desertion.

de·fec·tive (di-fek'tiv) *adj.* **1** Incomplete or imperfect; faulty. **2** *Gram.* Lacking one or more of the declensional or conjugational forms normal for its class: Can is a *defective* verb. **3** *Psychol.* Having less than normal intelligence. — *n.* One who or that which is incomplete or imperfect; specifically, a mentally defective person. — **de·fec'tive·ly** *adv.*

de·fend (di-fend') *v.t.* **1** To shield from attack or injury; protect. **2** To justify or vindicate; support. **3** *Law* **a** To act in behalf of (an accused). **b** To contest, as a claim, charge, or suit. **4** *Obs.* To forbid. — *v.i.* **5** To make a defense. See synonyms under JUSTIFY, KEEP, PRESERVE, SHELTER. [<L *defendere* <*de-* down, away + *fendere* strike] — **de·fend'a·ble** *adj.*

de·fend·ant (di-fen'dənt) *adj.* **1** Sustaining defense. **2** *Obs.* Defensive. — *n.* **1** *Law* A person against whom an action is brought. **2** One who defends; a defender. [<F *défendant,* ppr. of *défendre* defend]

de·fend·er (di-fen'dər) *n.* One who defends or protects; a champion.

de·fen·es·tra·tion (dē-fen'ə-strā'shən) *n.* The act of throwing out of a window, or the result of or subjection to such an act: used specifically with reference to a mode of executing popular vengeance practiced in Bohemia in the later Middle Ages. [<L *de* out of, down + *fenestra* window]

de·fense (di-fens') *n.* **1** The act of defending; protection; the state of being defended. **2** Anything that defends. **3** A plea in justification; excuse; apology. **4** *Law* An opposing or denying of the truth, validity, or sufficiency of a plaintiff's complaint; also, whatever is alleged, pleaded, or offered in evidence as sufficient to defeat an action either wholly or in part. **5** The art or science of defending by force of arms; skilfulness in defending oneself, as in fencing or boxing. **6** *Obs.* A prohibitory decree. Also *defence.* — **Department of De-**

fense An executive department of the U.S. government (established in 1947), headed by the Secretary of Defense and composed of the Department of the Army, the Department of the Navy, the Department of the Air Force, and various military agencies and staffs: from 1947 to 1949 called the National Military Establishment. [<OF <L *defensus,* pp. of *defendere.* See DEFEND.]

Synonyms: apology, bulwark, exculpation, fortress, guard, justification, protection, rampart, resistance, safeguard, shelter, shield, vindication. The weak may speak or act in *defense* of the strong; none but the powerful can assure others of *protection.* A *defense* is ordinarily against actual attack; *protection* is against possible as well as actual dangers. We speak of *defense* against an assault, *protection* from the cold. *Vindication* is a triumphant *defense* of character and conduct against charges of error or wrong. Compare APOLOGY, RAMPART. *Antonyms:* abandonment, betrayal, capitulation, desertion, flight, surrender.

de·fense·less (di-fens'lis) *adj.* Having no defense or means of defense; unprotected.

de·fen·si·ble (di-fen'sə-bəl) *adj.* Capable of being defended, maintained, or justified.

de·fen·sive (di-fen'siv) *adj.* **1** Intended or suitable for defense. **2** Carried on in defense: distinguished from *offensive.* **3** Making defense. — *n.* An attitude or condition of defense: means of defense; safeguard. — **de·fen'sive·ly** *adv.*

de·fer¹ (di-fûr') *v.t.* & *v.i.* **·ferred, ·fer·ring** To delay or put off to some other time; postpone. See synonyms under PROCRASTINATE, SUSPEND. [<OF *différer* <L *differre.* Doublet of DIFFER.] — **de·fer'ra·ble** *adj.* — **de·fer'-ment** *n.*

de·fer² (di-fûr') *v.i.* **·ferred, ·fer·ring** To yield to the opinions or decisions of another: with *to.* [<MF *déférer* <L *deferre* <*de-* down + *ferre* bear, carry] — **de·fer'rer** *n.*

Synonyms: respect, revere, submit, venerate, yield. We *defer* to recognized superiors in position, ability, or attainments; we *respect* power and worth wherever found. A military officer must *defer* to the views or authority of a superior whom he may not personally *respect;* a discoverer sure of his facts may not *defer to* the incredulity of those whom on other grounds he *respects* most highly. See OBEY. *Antonyms:* defy, despise, disregard, scorn, slight.

def·er·ent (def'ər-ənt) *adj.* **1** Carrying off; bearing away; adapted to carry or convey. **2** *Anat.* Pertaining to certain ducts, as the vas deferens: opposed to *afferent.* **3** Characterized by deference; deferential. — *n.* In the Ptolemaic astronomy, the circle around the earth, as a center, on the circumference of which the center of the epicycle was supposed to move. See under EPICYCLE. [<L *deferens, -entis,* ppr. of *deferre.* See DEFER².]

def·er·en·tial (def'ə-ren'shəl) *adj.* Marked by deference; respectful; courteous. See synonyms under OBSEQUIOUS. — **def'er·en'tial·ly** *adv.*

def·er·ves·cence (def'ər-ves'əns) *n.* **1** The cessation of boiling. **2** *Med.* The fall of temperature, indicating the disappearance of fever. [<L *defervescens, -entis,* ppr. of *defervescere* cool down] — **def'er·ves'cent** *adj.*

de·fi·ance (di-fī'əns) *n.* **1** The act of defying; a challenge. **2** Bold opposition; disposition to oppose or resist; contemptuous disregard of authority or opposition.

de·fi·ant (di-fī'ənt) *adj.* Showing or characterized by defiance. [<OF ppr. of *defier.* See DEFY.] — **de·fi'ant·ly** *adv.*

de·fib·ril·late (dē-fib'rə-lāt, dē-fī'brə-) *v.t.* **·lat·ed, ·lat·ing** *Pathol.* To stop fibrillation of (the heart muscle), as by jolting with an electric current. — **de·fib'ril·la'tion, de·fib'ril·la'tor** *n.*

de·fi·bri·na·tion (dē-fī'brə-nā'shən) *n.* The removal of fibrin from the blood or lymph in order to prevent coagulation and facilitate study of the blood cells in liquid form.

de·fi·cien·cy (di-fish'ən-sē) *n.* *pl.* **·cies 1** The state of being deficient. **2** That which is deficient; lack; insufficiency; defect. Also **de·fi'cience.** See synonyms under WANT.

de·fi·cient (di·fish'ənt) *adj.* **1** Lacking an adequate or proper supply; insufficient. **2** Lacking some essential; incomplete; imperfect; defective. See synonyms under SCANTY. [<L *deficiens, -entis,* ppr. of *deficere.* See DEFECT.]

def·i·cit (def'ə·sit) *n.* A deficiency, or falling short in amount; shortage, especially of revenue. [<L, it is lacking]

de·file[1] (di·fīl') *v.t.* **·filed, ·fil·ing 1** To make foul or dirty; pollute. **2** To tarnish or sully the brightness of; corrupt the purity of. **3** To sully; profane (a name, reputation, etc.). **4** To render ceremonially unclean. **5** To corrupt the chastity of. [<OF *defouler* < *de-* down (<L *de-*) + *fouler* trample; infl. in form by ME *filen* soil, OE *fȳlan* < *fūl* foul]

Synonyms: befoul, contaminate, corrupt, infect, pollute, soil, spoil, stain, sully, taint, tarnish, vitiate. The hand may be *defiled* by a touch of pitch; swine that have been wallowing in the mud are *befouled. Contaminate* and *infect* refer to something evil that deeply pervades and permeates, as the human body or mind. *Pollute* is used chiefly of liquids; as, water *polluted* with sewage. *Tainted* meat is repulsive; *infected* meat contains germs of disease. A *soiled* garment may be cleansed by washing; a *spoiled* garment is beyond cleansing or repair. Bright metal is *tarnished* by exposure; a fair sheet is *sullied* by a dirty hand. We speak of a *vitiated* taste or style; fraud *vitiates* a title or a contract. See ABUSE, CORRUPT, POLLUTE, VIOLATE. *Antonyms:* clean, cleanse, disinfect, hallow, purify, sanctify.

de·file[2] (di·fīl', dē'fil) *v.i.* **·filed, ·fil·ing** To march in a line or by files; file off. —*n.* **1** A long narrow pass; a gorge between mountains. **2** A marching in file. [<MF *défiler* < *dé-* down (<L *de-*) + *file* FILE[1] (def. 3)]

de·fine (di·fīn') *v.t.* **·fined, ·fin·ing 1** To state the meaning of (a word or phrase). **2** To determine the limits of and specify exactly. **3** To determine and fix the boundaries of. **4** To show or bring out the form or outline of. **5** To constitute the definition of. See synonyms under INTERPRET. [<OF *definer* <L *definire* < *de-* down + *finire* finish < *finis* end] —**de·fin'a·ble** *adj.* —**de·fin'er** *n.*

def·i·nite (def'ə·nit) *adj.* **1** Having precise limits; known with exactness; determined; clear; precise. **2** *Gram.* Particularizing: The definite article in English is *the.* See synonyms under PARTICULAR, PRECISE. [<L *definitus,* pp. of *definire.* See DEFINE.] —**def'·i·nite·ly** *adv.* —**def'i·nite·ness** *n.*

def·i·ni·tion (def'ə·nish'ən) *n.* **1** A description or explanation of a word or thing, by its attributes, properties, or relations, that distinguishes it from all other things. **2** The act of stating or showing what a word means, what a thing is, or what the content of a conception is; the act of defining. **3** The state of being definite; fixed shape; definitiveness. **4** The determining of the outline or limits of anything. **5** The state of being clearly outlined or determined. **6** *Optics* The power of a lens to give a distinct image at whatever magnification. **7** In television, the clarity of detail in a transmitted image, reckoned in terms of the number of picture elements or scanning lines in each image or frame. **8** In radio, the clearness of sounds received.

Synonyms: comment, commentary, description, explanation, exposition, interpretation, rendering, translation. A *definition* is formal and exact, an *explanation* general; a *description* pictorial. A *definition* must include all that belongs to the object defined, and exclude all that does not; a *description* may include only some general features: an *explanation* may simply throw light upon some point of special difficulty. An *exposition* explains a subject in detail. *Interpretation* may translate from other languages, or give the plain meaning of difficult passages, or render the thought and emotion of worthy literature by adequate written or oral expression. *Definition, explanation, exposition,* and *interpretation* are ordinarily blended in a *commentary,* which may also include *description.* A *comment* is upon a single passage; a *commentary* may be the same, but is usually understood to be a volume of *comments.*

de·fin·i·tive (di·fin'ə·tiv) *adj.* **1** Sharply defining or limiting; determinate; explicit; positive. **2** Bringing to an end; conclusive

and unalterable. **3** *Biol.* Completely formed; fully developed. **4** Most nearly accurate, complete, etc. —*n.* A word that defines or limits. —**de·fin'i·tive·ly** *adv.* —**de·fin'i·tive·ness** *n.*

def·la·grate (def'lə·grāt) *v.t. & v.i.* **·grat·ed, ·grat·ing** To burn quickly and with dazzling light. [<L *deflagratus,* pp. of *deflagrare* < *de-* completely + *flagrare* burn] —**def·la·gra·ble** (def'lə·grə·bəl) *adj.*

def·la·gra·tion (def'lə·grā'shən) *n.* A quick and violent combustion, with or without explosion: distinguished from the instantaneous decomposition of an entire compound in a *detonation.*

def·la·gra·tor (def'lə·grā'tər) *n.* That which induces or produces very rapid combustion.

de·flate (di·flāt') *v.t. & v.i.* **·flat·ed, ·flat·ing 1** To collapse or cause to collapse by the removal of contained air or gas. **2** To take the conceit, confidence, or self-esteem out of. **3** To devaluate; lessen (currency or prices). [<L *deflatus,* pp. of *deflare* < *de-* down + *flare* blow] —**de·fla'tor** *n.*

de·fla·tion (di·flā'shən) *n.* **1** The act or condition of being deflated or reduced in volume. **2** A decrease in the amount of currency in a country. —**de·fla·tion·ar·y** (di·flā'shən·er'ē) *adj.* —**de·fla'tion·ist** *n. & adj.*

de·flect (di·flekt') *v.t. & v.i.* To turn aside; swerve or cause to swerve from a course. See synonyms under BEND. [<L *deflectere* < *de-* down + *flectere* bend] —**de·flec'tive** *adj.*

de·flec·tion (di·flek'shən) *n.* **1** A turning aside; deviation. **2** A bending of light rays; see DIFFRACTION. **3** The deviation of a galvanometer or magnetic needle from its normal position or from zero. Also *Brit.* **de·flex'ion.**

de·flex (di·fleks') *v.t.* To bend downward. [<L *deflexus,* pp. of *deflectere.* See DEFLECT.]

de·flow·er (di·flou'ər) *v.t.* **1** To despoil of flowers. **2** To deprive (a woman) of virginity; seduce. **3** To violate; rob of beauty. [<OF *desflorer, desflouer* <LL *deflorare* < *de-* down, away + *flos, floris* flower; infl. in form by flower]

de·flux·ion (di·fluk'shən) *n. Pathol.* The flowing off of fluids, as in catarrh. [<LL *defluxio, -onis* < *defluere* < *de-* down + *fluere* flow]

de·fo·li·ate (dē·fō'lē·āt) *v.* **·at·ed, ·at·ing** *v.t.* To deprive or strip of leaves. —*v.i.* To lose leaves. [<Med. L *defoliatus,* pp. of *defoliare* < *de-* down + *folium* leaf] —**de·fo'li·a'tion** *n.* —**de·fo'li·a'tor** *n.*

de·for·est (dē·fôr'ist, -for'-) *v.t.* To clear of forests or trees. —**de·for'es·ta'tion** *n.* —**de·for'est·er** *n.*

de·form (di·fôrm') *v.t.* **1** To mar or distort the form of; disfigure. **2** To spoil the beauty of; make ugly or dishonorable. **3** *Mech.* To change in form. —*v.i.* **4** To become deformed or disfigured. [<L *deformare* < *de-* away, down + *forma* figure, form] —**de·form'a·bil'i·ty** *n.* —**de·form'a·ble** *adj.* —**de·form'er** *n.*

def·or·ma·tion (def'ər·mā'shən) *n.* **1** The act of deforming; state of being deformed; misshapenness. **2** Change in form for the worse. **3** *Mech.* An alteration in the form of a body subjected to sudden or prolonged stress. **4** An altered form or shape.

de·formed (di·fôrmd') *adj.* Misshapen. —**de·form·ed·ly** (di·fôr'mid·lē) *adv.* —**de·form'ed·ness** *n.*

de·form·i·ty (di·fôr'mə·tē) *n. pl.* **·ties 1** *Pathol.* **a** A deformed or misshapen condition. **b** A deformed part; that which causes disfigurement. **2** Unsightliness; lack of symmetry. **3** Moral depravity. **4** One who or that which is deformed. See synonyms under BLEMISH. [<OF *deformité* <L *deformitas, -tatis* < *deformis* < *de-* down + *forma* form]

de·fraud (di·frôd') *v.t.* To take or withhold property, etc., from by fraud; cheat; swindle. See synonyms under DECEIVE. [<OF *defrauder* <L *defraudare* < *de-* completely + *fraus, fraudis* a cheat] —**de·fraud·a·tion** (dē'frô·dā'shən) *n.* —**de·fraud'er** *n.*

de·fray (di·frā') *v.t.* **1** To pay for; bear the expense of. **2** *Obs.* To disburse; spend. [<F *défrayer* <OF *defraier* < *de-* away (<L *de-*) + *fraier* spend < *frai* cost, charge] —**de·fray'a·ble** *adj.* —**de·fray'al, de·fray'ment** *n.* —**de·fray'er** *n.*

de·frock (dē·frok') *v.t.* To unfrock.

de·frost·er (dē·frôs'tər, -fros'-) *n.* A device

for removing the formation of ice or frost, as from an exposed surface.

deft (deft) *adj.* Neat and skilful in action; handy; apt; dexterous; clever. [OE *gedæfte* meek, gentle. Related to DAFT.] —**deft'ly** *adv.* —**deft'ness** *n.*

de·funct (di·fungkt') *adj.* Dead; deceased; extinct. —*n.* A dead person: with *the.* See synonyms under DEAD, LIFELESS. [<L *defunctus,* pp. of *defungi* < *de-* not + *fungi* perform]

de·fy (di·fī') *v.t.* **·fied, ·fy·ing 1** To resist or disregard openly or boldly. **2** To challenge: I *defy* you to cross this line. **3** To resist successfully; baffle; obstruct: to *defy* definition. **4** *Archaic* To invite to combat. See synonyms under OPPOSE. —*n. pl.* **·fies** *U.S. Slang* A challenge. [<OF *defier* <Med. L *diffidare* < *dis-* not + *fidare* be faithful < *fidus* loyal]

de·ga·me (də·gä'mə) *n.* Lemonwood. [<Sp. *dagame* < native name]

de·gas (dē·gas') *v.t.* **·gassed, ·gas·sing 1** To remove noxious and poisonous gases from (contaminated areas or affected persons). **2** To exhaust the gases from (vacuum tubes or thermionic valves).

de·gauss (di·gous') *v.t.* To make (a ship) safe against the action of magnetic mines, especially by the use of a **degaussing cable,** fitted around the hull to neutralize the magnetic field set up by the ship. [DE- + GAUSS]

de·gen·er·ate (di·jen'ə·rāt) *v.i.* **·at·ed, ·at·ing 1** To become worse or inferior. **2** *Biol.* To revert to a lower type; decline; deteriorate. —*adj.* (di·jen'ər·it) **1** Having become worse or inferior; deteriorated; degraded. **2** *Physics* Having a common value of energy but differing in other dynamical properties. —*n.* (-it) **1** A deteriorated or degraded individual, animal or human. **2** A morally degraded person. [<L *degeneratus,* pp. of *degenerare* < *de-* down, away + *generare* create] —**de·gen'er·ate·ly** *adv.* —**de·gen'er·a'tive** *adj.* —**de·gen'er·ate·ness** *n.*

de·gen·er·a·tion (di·jen'ə·rā'shən) *n.* **1** The process of degenerating; also, a degenerate condition. **2** *Biol.* Progressive deterioration of an organ, tissue, or part, especially as caused by chemical and metabolic changes in the body. **3** *Electronics* A reduction of radio signal strength by feedback.

de·glu·ti·tion (dē'glōō·tish'ən) *n. Physiol.* The act, process, or power of swallowing. [<F *déglutition* <L *deglutitio, -onis* < *de-* down + *glutire* swallow]

de·grad·a·ble (di·grā'də·bəl) *adj. Chem.* Capable of being degraded, as a compound.

deg·ra·da·tion (deg'rə·dā'shən) *n.* **1** The act of degrading. **2** The state of being reduced in rank or disgraced. **3** *Geol.* Disintegration, especially of rocks by erosion and wind. **4** The degeneration of the physiological body or an organ. —**deg'ra·da'tion·al** *adj.*

de·grade (di·grād') *v.* **·grad·ed, ·grad·ing** *v.t.* **1** To reduce in rank; remove from office, dignity, etc.; disgrace. **2** To debase or lower in character, morals, etc. **3** To bring into contempt; dishonor. **4** To reduce in quality, intensity, etc. **5** *Biol.* To reduce from a higher to a lower type. **6** *Geol.* To reduce the height of by erosion. **7** *Chem.* To break down (a compound) into less complex parts; decompose. —*v.i.* **8** To degenerate; become of a lower type. See synonyms under ABASE. [<OF *degrader* <LL *degradi* < *de-* down + *gradi* step]

de·gree (di·grē') *n.* **1** One of a succession of steps, grades, or stages. **2** Relative rank in life; attainment; station. **3** Relative extent, amount, or intensity. **4** *Gram.* One of the three forms in which an adjective or adverb is compared: the positive, comparative, and superlative *degrees.* **5** An academic rank or title conferred by an institution of learning. **6** One remove in the chain of relationship between persons in the line of descent. **7** A subdivision or unit, as in a thermometric scale. **8** The 360th part of a circle, as of longitude or latitude; the 90th part of a right angle; the unit divisions marked accordingly on various instruments. **9** *Math.* The power to which an algebraic quantity, equation, or number is raised. **10** In notation, a group of three figures in a number; a period. **11** *Music* A line or space of a staff. **12** A grade of seriousness: said of crimes: murder in the first *degree.* — **by degrees** Little by little; gradually. — **to a degree** 1 *Brit.* Extremely. 2 Somewhat. [<OF *degre* < *de-* down (<L *de-*) + *gre* <L *gradus* a step]

degree of freedom *Chem.* The particular state of a substance, compound, or body with respect to the arrangement of its parts and the number of variables, as pressure, temperature, volume, etc., required to define the system.

de·gres·sion (di·gresh′ən) *n.* 1 Decrease by steps; descent. 2 Stated decrease in tax rates on sums below a certain amount. [<LL *degressio, -onis* < *degradi*. See DEGRADE.] — **de·gres·sive** (di·gres′iv) *adj.* — **de·gres′sive·ly** *adv.*

de·gum (dē·gum′) *v.t.* **·gummed, ·gum·ming** To remove excess of gum filling from: said of silk.

de·hisce (di·his′) *v.i.* **·hisced, ·hisc·ing** *Biol.* To burst open, as the cocoon of a larva or the capsule of a plant. [<L *dehiscere* < *de-* down + *hiscere,* inceptive of *hiare* gape, yawn]

de·his·cence (di·his′əns) *n.* 1 A gape or gaping. 2 *Biol.* The opening or manner of opening, as of the cocoon of a larva or of a capsule when discharging seeds.

de·horn (dē·hôrn′) *v.t.* To remove the horns of (cattle).

de·hu·man·ize (dē·hyōō′mən·īz) *v.t.* **·ized, ·iz·ing** To divest or deprive of human qualities or attributes. — **de·hu′man·i·za′tion** *n.*

de·hu·mid·i·fi·er (dē′hyōō·mid′ə·fī′ər) *n.* An apparatus for removing moisture from the air.

de·hu·mid·i·fy (dē′hyōō·mid′ə·fī) *v.t.* **·fied, ·fy·ing** To render less humid; remove moisture from. — **de′hu·mid′i·fi·ca′tion** *n.*

de·hy·drate (dē·hī′drāt) *v.* **·drat·ed, ·drat·ing** *v.t.* 1 To deprive of water; anhydrate: to *dehydrate* alcohol. 2 To remove water from, as vegetables, so as to preserve. — *v.i.* 3 To suffer loss of water.

de·hy·dra·tion (dē′hī·drā′shən) *n.* 1 The process of removing water from a substance or body, as by heat, distillation, or chemicals. 2 The artificial drying of food products to reduce weight and preserve them for future use.

de·hy·dro·gen·ize (dē·hī′drə·jən·īz′) *v.t.* **·ized, ·iz·ing** *Chem.* To free from hydrogen; remove hydrogen from (a compound).

de·i·cide (dē′ə·sīd) *n.* 1 The killing of a god; especially, the crucifixion of Christ. 2 The slayer of a god. [<L *deus* god + -CIDE]

deic·tic (dīk′tik) *adj.* 1 *Logic* Proving by direct argument; direct: distinguished from *elenchic, refutative,* or *indirect.* 2 *Gram.* Demonstrative: a *deictic* pronoun. [<Gk. *deiktikos* able to show < *deiknynai* show, prove] — **deic′ti·cal·ly** *adv.*

de·if·ic (dē·if′ik) *adj.* 1 Making, or tending to make, divine. 2 Divine. Also **de·if′i·cal.**

de·i·form (dē′ə·fôrm) *adj.* In the form of a god; like a god. [<Med. L *deiformis* <L *deus* god + *forma* form]

de·i·fy (dē′ə·fī) *v.t.* **·fied, ·fy·ing** 1 To make a god of; rank as a deity. 2 To regard or worship as a god. [<F *déifier* <LL *deificare* <L *deus* god + *facere* make] — **de′i·fi·ca′tion** *n.* — **de′i·fi′er** *n.*

deign (dān) *v.t.* 1 To stoop so far as to grant or allow; condescend. 2 *Obs.* To deem worthy of notice or acceptance. — *v.i.* 3 To think it befitting oneself (to do something). [<OF *deignier* <L *dignari* < *dignus* worthy]

Dei·no (dī′nō) One of the Graeae.

de·in·sti·tu·tion·al·ize (dē′in·sti·tōō′shə·nə·līz, -tyōō′-) *v.t.* **·ized, ·iz·ing** 1 To remove the institutional character from. 2 *U.S. Colloq.* To remove (someone) from an institution (def. 2).

deip·nos·o·phist (dīp·nos′ə·fist) *n.* One who talks learnedly at the table. [<Gk. *deipnosophistēs* < *deipnon* dinner + *sophistēs* a wise man < *sophia* wisdom] — **deip·nos′o·phism** *n.* — **deip·nos′o·phis′tic** *adj.*

de·ip·o·tent (dē·ip′ə·tənt) *adj.* Having divine power. [<L *deus* god + *potens* powerful]

de·ism (dē′iz·əm) *n.* 1 The belief in the existence of a personal God, based solely on the testimony of reason and rejecting any supernatural revelation; natural religion. 2 The belief that God created the world and set it in motion, subject to natural laws, but takes no interest in it. 3 The belief in a first cause which is not intrinsically

perfect or complete, and therefore not a proper object for worship. [<L *deus* a god + -ISM] — **de·is′tic** or **·ti·cal** *adj.* — **de·is′ti·cal·ly** *adv.*

de·ist (dē′ist) *n.* One who subscribes to or professes deism.

de·i·ty (dē′ə·tē) *n. pl.* **·ties** 1 A god, goddess, or divine person. 2 Divine nature or status; godhead; divinity. — **the Deity** God. [<F *déité* <LL *deitas, -tatis* <L *deus* a god]

dé·jà vu (dā·zhà vü′) *Psychol.* A distortion of memory in which a new situation or experience is regarded as having happened before: a form of paramnesia. [<F, lit., already seen]

de·ject (di·jekt′) *v.t.* 1 To depress or cast down in spirit. 2 *Obs.* To throw down. — *adj.* Dejected; cast down. [<L *dejectus,* pp. of *dejicere* < *de-* down + *jacere* throw]

de·jec·ta (di·jek′tə) *n. pl.* Excrements. [<L, neut. pl. of *dejectus.* See DEJECT.]

de·ject·ed (di·jek′tid) *adj.* Having low or depressed spirits; disheartened. — **de·ject′ed·ly** *adv.*

de·jec·tion (di·jek′shən) *n.* 1 A state or condition of being dejected; depression. 2 *Med.* **a** Evacuation of the bowels. **b** Excrement.

deka- *combining form* Ten: used in the metric system, as in *dekagram, dekaliter.* Also, before vowels, **dek-.** [<Gk. *deka* ten]

dek·a·gram (dek′ə·gram) *n.* A measure of weight equal to 10 grams. See METRIC SYSTEM. Also **dek′a·gramme.**

dek·a·li·ter (dek′ə·lē′tər) *n.* A measure of capacity equal to 10 liters: also spelled *decaliter.* See METRIC SYSTEM. Also **dek′a·li′tre.**

dek·a·me·ter (dek′ə·mē′tər) *n.* A measure of length equal to 10 meters. See METRIC SYSTEM. Also **dek′a·me′tre.**

dek·are (dek′âr) *n.* In the metric system, 1,000 square meters or 10 ares: also spelled *decare.* See METRIC SYSTEM.

dek·a·stere (dek′ə·stir) *n.* A measure of volume equal to 10 steres. See METRIC SYSTEM.

de·laine (də·lān′) *n.* A light, untwilled wool, or cotton and wool, dress material. [<F *(mousseline) de laine* (muslin) of wool]

de·lam·i·nate (dē·lam′ə·nāt) *v.t.* & *v.i.* **·nat·ed, ·nat·ing** To split into thin layers.

de·lam·i·na·tion (dē·lam′ə·nā′shən) *n.* A splitting into layers: said especially of the cells of plant or animal tissue.

de·la·tor (di·lā′tər) *n.* An informer; accuser; spy.

Del·a·ware (del′ə·wâr) A Middle Atlantic State of the United States; 1,978 square miles; capital, Dover; entered the Union Dec. 7, 1787, one of the original thirteen States; nickname *Diamond State:* abbr. *Del.*

de·lay (di·lā′) *v.t.* 1 To put off to a future time; postpone; defer. 2 To cause to be late; detain. — *v.i.* 3 To linger; procrastinate. See synonyms under HINDER, PROCRASTINATE, PROTRACT, SUSPEND. — *n.* 1 A putting off; postponement; procrastination. 2 A temporary stoppage or stay; also, a loitering or lingering. See synonyms under RESPITE. [<OF *delaier*] — **de·lay′er** *n.*

de·layed-ac·tion (di·lād′ak′shən) *adj.* Designating a kind of bomb, fuze, or mine designed to explode at a set time after it has been armed or put into action.

de·le (dē′lē) *v.t.* **de·led, de·le·ing** *Printing* To take out; delete: usually an imperative represented by a sign. (℞) Compare STET. [<L, imperative of *delere* erase]

del·e·ble (del′ə·bəl) *adj.* Capable of being erased. Also **del′i·ble.**

de·lec·ta·ble (di·lek′tə·bəl) *adj.* Giving pleasure; delightful; charming. See synonyms under LOVELY. [<OF <L *delectabilis* < *delectare.* See DELIGHT.] — **de·lec′ta·ble·ness** *n.* — **de·lec′ta·bly** *adv.*

de·lec·tate (di·lek′tāt) *v.t.* **·tat·ed, ·tat·ing** To charm; delight. [<L *delectatus,* pp. of *delectare.* See DELIGHT.]

de·lec·ta·tion (dē′lek·tā′shən) *n.* 1 Delight; enjoyment. 2 Amusement; entertainment.

del·e·ga·cy (del′ə·gə·sē) *n. pl.* **·cies** 1 The action or system of delegating; authority given to act as a delegate. 2 A body of delegates. 3 The condition of being delegated.

del·e·gant (del′ə·gənt) *n.* 1 One that delegates. 2 One that assigns a debt due him to a creditor.

del·e·gate (del′ə·gāt, -git) *n.* 1 A person appointed and sent by another, with power to transact business as his representative; deputy; representative; commissioner. 2 *U.S.* A person elected or appointed to represent a Territory in the House of Representatives where he has the right to participate in debates, but not to vote. 3 A member of the House of Delegates. Compare BURGESS. 4 A person sent as a representative to a convention of any kind, to take part in the transaction of business. — **walking delegate** A member of a trade union, commissioned to visit other labor organizations and to secure the united action of employees in the advancement of common interests. — *v.t.* **(-gāt) ·gat·ed, ·gat·ing** 1 To send as a representative, with authority to act; depute. 2 To commit or entrust (powers, authority, etc.) to another as an agent or representative. 3 To assign (a debtor) to one's creditor to satisfy a claim. — *adj.* (-gāt,-git) Sent as a deputy. [<L *delegatus,* pp. of *delegare* < *de-* down + *legare* send]

Synonyms (noun): deputy, legate, proxy, representative, substitute. These words agree in designating one who acts in the place of some other or others. The *legate* is an ecclesiastical officer representing the pope. In strict usage the *deputy* or *delegate* is more limited in functions and more closely bound by instructions than a *representative.* A single officer may have a *deputy:* many persons combine to choose a *delegate* or *representative.* In the United States informal assemblies send *delegates* to nominating conventions with no legislative authority; *representatives* are legally elected to Congress and the various law-making assemblies.

del·e·ga·tion (del′ə·gā′shən) *n.* 1 The act of delegating: a *delegation* of powers or authority. 2 A person or persons appointed to act for another or others; delegates collectively.

de·lete (di·lēt′) *v.t.* **·let·ed, ·let·ing** To blot out; erase, cancel; dele. [<L *deletus,* pp. of *delere* destroy]

del·e·te·ri·ous (del′ə·tir′ē·əs) *adj.* Causing moral or physical injury; hurtful; pernicious. See synonyms under BAD, NOISOME. [<NL *deleterius* <Gk. *dēlētērios* harmful < *deleesthai* hurt] — **del′e·te′ri·ous·ly** *adv.* — **del′e·te′ri·ous·ness** *n.*

de·le·tion (di·lē′shən) *n.* The act of deleting; erasure; also, matter erased or canceled.

delft (delft) *n.* 1 A colored glazed earthenware, made first at Delft about 1310. 2 Any tableware resembling this. Also **delf** (delf), **delft′ware′.** [from DELFT]

de·lib·er·ate (di·lib′ə·rāt) *v.* **·at·ed, ·at·ing** *v.i.* 1 To think or consider carefully and at length. 2 To consider reasons or arguments for and against something so as to reach a conclusion or decision. 3 To pause to think. — *v.t.* 4 To think about or consider carefully; weigh. — *adj.* (di·lib′ər·it) 1 Acting with deliberation; carefully thought out; not hasty. 2 Done after deliberation; intentional. [<L *deliberatus,* pp. of *deliberare* < *de-* completely + *librare* weigh < *libra* a scale] — **de·lib′er·ate·ly** *adv.* — **de·lib′er·ate·ness** *n.*

Synonyms (verb): confer, consider, consult, debate, meditate, ponder, reflect, weigh. An individual *considers, meditates, ponders, reflects* by himself. *Consult* and *confer* always imply two or more persons, as does *debate,* except in rare reflexive use. *Deliberate,* which can be applied to a single individual, is also the word for a great number, while *consult* is ordinarily limited to a few; a committee *consults;* an assembly *deliberates.* Deliberating always carries the idea of slowness; a *consultation* may be hasty. We *consider* or *deliberate* with a view to action; *meditation* may be purposeless. See CONSIDER, CONSULT, MUSE.

de·lib·er·a·tion (di·lib′ə·rā′shən) *n.* 1 The act of deliberating. 2 Thoughtfulness and care in deciding or acting. 3 Forethought or intention. See synonyms under REFLECTION, THOUGHT.

de·lib·er·a·tive (di·lib′ə·rā′tiv) *adj.* 1 Pertaining to or of the nature of deliberation. 2 Characterized by or existing for deliberation. — **de·lib′er·a′tive·ly** *adv.* — **de·lib′er·a′-**

tive·ness *n.*

del·i·ca·cy (del'ə·kə·sē) *n. pl.* ·cies **1** The quality or state of being delicate; fineness; daintiness. **2** Sensitiveness of touch or perception. **3** Fragility; frailty. **4** A luxury; dainty. **5** Need of careful treatment; subtlety; nicety. **6** Refinement of feeling; fastidiousness; consideration for others. **7** *Obs.* Voluptuousness; luxuriousness.

del·i·cate (del'ə·kit) *adj.* **1** Fine and light, as in texture or color. **2** Daintily pleasing; delightful. **3** Nicely constructed or adjusted; accurate; sensitive, as an instrument. **4** Easily injured; tender; frail; fragile. **5** Requiring cautious or subtle treatment. **6** Refined and considerate. **7** Pure; chaste. **8** Fastidious; dainty. **9** Nice in discrimination; sensitive. **10** *Obs.* Voluptuous; luxurious. See synonyms under FINE, FRAGILE. —*n. Obs.* **1** A delicacy; luxury. **2** An effeminate or luxurious person. [< L *delicatus* pleasing] —del'i·cate·ly *adv.*

del·i·ca·tes·sen (del'ə·kə·tes'ən) *n. pl.* **1** Cooked or preserved foods; cooked meats, canned goods, salads, cheeses, pickles, etc.: often construed as singular. **2** A store that sells such foods. [< G, pl. of *delicatesse* dainty food]

de·li·cious (di·lish'əs) *adj.* Extremely pleasant or enjoyable; affording great pleasure, especially to the taste. [< OF < LL *deliciosus* < *delicia* a delight] —de·li'cious·ly *adv.* —de·li'cious·ness *n.*

Synonyms: dainty, delightful, exquisite, luscious, savory. That is *delicious* which affords a gratification at once vivid and delicate to the senses, especially to those of taste and smell; as, *delicious* fruit; a *delicious* odor; *luscious* has a kindred but more fulsome meaning, inclining toward a cloying excess of sweetness or richness. *Savory* is applied chiefly to cooked food made palatable by spices and condiments. *Delightful* may be applied to the higher gratifications of sense, as *delightful* music, but is chiefly used for that which is mental and spiritual. *Delicious* has a limited use in this way; as, a *delicious* bit of poetry; the word is sometimes used ironically for some pleasing absurdity; as, this is *delicious*. Compare DELIGHTFUL. *Antonyms:* acrid, bitter, nauseous, unpalatable, unsavory.

del·i·ga·tion (del'ə·gā'shən) *n.* **1** The act of binding or bandaging. **2** The application of ligatures. [< L *deligatus*, pp. of *deligare* < *de-* completely + *ligare* bind]

de·light (di·līt') *n.* **1** Great pleasure; gratification; joyful satisfaction. **2** That which affords extreme enjoyment. **3** The quality of delighting; charm. See synonyms under ENTERTAINMENT, HAPPINESS. —*v.i.* **1** To take great pleasure; rejoice: with *in* or the infinitive. **2** To give great enjoyment. —*v.t.* **3** To please or gratify highly. See synonyms under CHARM, ENTERTAIN, RAPTURE, RAVISH, REJOICE. [< OF *delit* < *deliter* < L *delectare*, freq. of *delicere* < *de-* away + *lacere* entice]

de·light·ful (di·līt'fəl) *adj.* Affording delight; extremely gratifying; charming. —de·light'·ful·ly *adv.* —de·light'ful·ness *n.*

Synonyms: acceptable, agreeable, congenial, delicious, grateful, gratifying, pleasant, pleasing, pleasurable, refreshing, satisfying, welcome. *Agreeable* refers to whatever gives a mild degree of pleasure; as, an *agreeable* perfume. *Acceptable* indicates a thing worthy of acceptance; as, an *acceptable* offer. *Grateful* is stronger than *agreeable* or *gratifying*, indicating whatever awakens a feeling akin to gratitude. A *pleasant* face and *pleasing* manners arouse *pleasurable* sensations, and make the possessor an *agreeable* companion; if possessed of intelligence, vivacity, and goodness, such a person's society will be *delightful* and *congenial*. *Satisfying* denotes anything that is received with acquiescence, as substantial food, or established truth. That is *welcome* which is received with heartiness; as, *welcome* tidings. See BEAUTIFUL, CHARMING, DELICIOUS, GRATEFUL, HAPPY, LOVELY. *Antonyms:* depressing, disappointing, distressing, hateful, horrible, melancholy, miserable, mournful, painful, saddening, woeful, wretched.

de·lim·it (di·lim'it) *v.t.* To prescribe the limits of; bound. Also de·lim'i·tate. [< F *délimiter* < L *delimitare* < *de-* completely + *limitare* bound < *limes* a boundary] —de·lim'i·ta'tion

n. —de·lim'i·ta'tive *adj.*

de·lin·e·ate (di·lin'ē·āt) *v.t.* ·at·ed, ·at·ing **1** To draw in outline; trace out. **2** To portray pictorially. **3** To describe verbally. See synonyms under CIRCUMSCRIBE. [< L *delineatus*, pp. of *delineare* < *de-* completely + *lineare* draw a line < *linea* a line] —de·lin'·e·a'tive *adj.*

de·lin·quen·cy (di·ling'kwən·sē) *n. pl.* ·cies **1** Neglect of duty; failure to do what is required. **2** A fault; offense; misdemeanor. See synonyms under OFFENSE, SIN.

de·lin·quent (di·ling'kwənt) *adj.* **1** Neglectful of or failing in duty or obligation; faulty. **2** Due and unpaid, as taxes. —*n.* One who fails to perform a duty or who commits a fault. [< L *delinquens*, *-entis*, pp. of *delinquere* < *de-* down, away + *linquere* leave] —de·lin'quent·ly *adv.*

del·i·quesce (del'ə·kwes') *v.i.* ·quesced, ·quesc·ing **1** To become liquid by absorption of moisture from the air, as certain salts. **2** To melt or pass away gradually. **3** *Bot.* **a** To become lost by repeated branching, as stems. **b** To become fluid, as a ripe agaric. [< L *deliquescere* < *de-* completely + *liquescere* melt]

del·i·ques·cent (del'ə·kwes'ənt) *adj.* **1** Liquefying in the air. **2** *Bot.* **a** Dividing; ramifying; forming many small branches, as an elm tree. **b** Becoming liquid at maturity, as certain mushrooms.

de·lir·a·tion (del'ə·rā'shən) *n.* Delirium; irrationality.

de·lir·i·ant (di·lir'ē·ənt) *n.* **1** A poison that induces delirium, as cannabis or hyoscyamine. **2** A delirious person. [< L *delirium* madness + -ANT]

de·lir·i·ous (di·lir'ē·əs) *adj.* Suffering from delirium; light-headed; raving. See synonyms under INSANE. —de·lir'i·ous·ly *adv.* —de·lir'i·ous·ness *n.*

de·lir·i·um (di·lir'ē·əm) *n.* **1** A sporadic or temporary mental disturbance associated with fever, intoxication, shock, or injury and marked by restlessness, excitement, hallucinations, and general incoherence. **2** Intense excitement; frenzy; rapture. See synonyms under INSANITY. [< L *delirare* < *de-* down, away + *lira* a furrow, track]

delirium tre·mens (trē'mənz) A violent form of delirium caused especially by excessive use of alcoholic liquors and narcotic drugs, and characterized by tremblings, acute mental distress, and delusions of the senses. [< NL, trembling delirium]

del·i·tes·cence (del'ə·tes'əns) *n.* **1** *Med.* **A** A sudden subsidence of the symptoms of a disease. **b** The latent period of an infection or a poison. **2** The state of being concealed; retirement; seclusion. Also del'i·tes'cen·cy. [< L *delitescens*, *-entis*, ppr. of *delitescere* < *de-* away + *litescere*, inceptive of *latere* lie hidden] —del'i·tes'cent *adj.*

de·liv·er (di·liv'ər) *v.t.* **1** To hand over; surrender; transfer possession of. **2** To carry and distribute. **3** To utter; give forth in words. **4** To relieve of a child in childbirth; also, to assist in the birth of (a child). **5** To free from restraint, evil, danger, etc.; set free; rescue. **6** To send forth; discharge, as a broadside. **7** To give; strike, as a blow. **8** To throw or pitch, as a ball. —*adj. Obs.* Nimble; active. [< F *délivrer* < LL *deliberare* < *de-* down, away + *liberare* set free < *liber* free] —de·liv'er·a·ble *adj.* —de·liv'er·er *n.*

Synonyms (verb): discharge, emancipate, free, liberate, ransom, redeem, rescue, save. See GIVE, RELEASE. *Antonyms:* betray, capture, confine, enslave, imprison, incarcerate.

de·liv·er·ance (di·liv'ər·əns) *n.* **1** The act of delivering or state of being delivered; rescue; release. **2** An expression of opinion; utterance. **3** *Obs.* Parturition.

de·liv·er·y (di·liv'ər·ē) *n. pl.* ·er·ies **1** The act of delivering; liberation; release; transference; surrender. **2** Parturition. **3** Mode of utterance, as in public speaking or singing. **4** Mode of projecting or discharging. **5** That which is or has been delivered: a mail *delivery.*

dell (del) *n.* A small, secluded valley; glen; dale. [< OE. Akin to DALE.]

de·lo·cal·ize (dē·lō'kəl·īz) *v.t.* ·ized, ·iz·ing To remove from place or free from local relations; enlarge the scope of; broaden. —de·lo'·cal·i·za'tion *n.*

de·louse (dē·lous') *v.t.* ·loused, ·lous·ing To remove lice or other insect vermin from.

del·phin (del'fin) *adj.* Of or pertaining to a dolphin or to a family of cetaceans (*Delphinidae*), including dolphins, porpoises, etc. —*n.* **1** *Obs.* A dolphin. **2** A neutral fat contained in the oil of certain dolphins. [< L *delphinus* < Gk. *delphis*, *delphinos* dolphin]

del·phi·nine (del'fə·nēn, -nin) *n.* A poisonous crystalline alkaloid, $C_{34}H_{47}NO_9$, found in the seeds of stavesacre: used in medicine. Also del'phi·nin (-nin). [< DELPHIN(IUM) + -INE[2]]

del·phin·i·um (del·fin'ē·əm) *n.* Any of a genus (*Delphinium*) of perennial plants of the crowfoot family, having large, spurred flowers, usually blue; the larkspur. [< NL < Gk. *delphinion* larkspur, dim. of *delphis* dolphin; so called from the shape of the nectary]

del·ta (del'tə) *n.* **1** The fourth letter in the Greek alphabet (Δ, δ): corresponding to English *d*. As a numeral it denotes 4. **2** *Geog.* An alluvial, typically triangular-shaped, silt deposit at or in the mouth of a river. **3** Anything triangular. —del·ta·ic (del·tā'ik) *adj.*

delta rays *Physics* The fringe of secondary ionization along tracks formed by the impact of primary cosmic rays upon heavy atomic nuclei.

del·toid (del'toid) *n.* **1** *Anat.* A triangular muscle of the shoulder and upper arm. **2** *Geom.* A quadrilateral formed by two unequal isosceles triangles set base to base. —*adj.* **1** Shaped like a delta; triangular. **2** Of or pertaining to the deltoid. [< Gk. *deltoeides* triangular < *delta* the letter Δ + *eidos* form]

DELTOID

de·lude (di·lood') *v.t.* ·lud·ed, ·lud·ing **1** To mislead the mind or judgment of; beguile; deceive. **2** *Obs.* To evade; elude. **3** *Obs.* To frustrate. See synonyms under DECEIVE. [< L *deludere* < *de-* down, away + *ludere* play] —de·lud'er *n.* —de·lud'ing·ly *adv.*

del·uge (del'yōoj) *v.t.* ·uged, ·ug·ing To flood with water; inundate; submerge. **2** To overwhelm; destroy. [< *n.*] —*n.* **1** A great flood; inundation. **2** Anything that comes like a flood. —the Deluge The flood in the time of Noah. *Gen.* vii. [< F *déluge* < L *diluvium* < *diluere* wash away < *dis-* away + *luere* wash]

de·lu·sion (di·loo'zhən) *n.* **1** The state of being deluded; a false belief, especially when persistent. **2** The act of deluding; deception. **3** The error thus conveyed or believed. **4** *Psychiatry* False belief about the self, often present in paranoia and dementia precox. [< L *delusio*, *-onis* < *deludere*. See DELUDE.]

Synonyms: error, fallacy, fantasm, hallucination, illusion. A *delusion* is a mistaken conviction, an *illusion* a mistaken perception or inference. An *illusion* may be wholly of the senses; a *delusion* always involves some mental error. We speak of the *illusions* of fancy or of hope, but of the *delusions* of the insane. A *hallucination* is a false image or belief which has nothing, outside of the disordered mind, to suggest it; as, the *hallucinations* of delirium tremens. Compare DECEPTION. *Antonyms:* actuality, certainty, fact, reality, truth, verity.

de·lus·ter·ing (dē·lus'tər·ing) *n.* The treatment of synthetic yarns and fabrics by special pigments or other chemicals in order to reduce their natural luster.

de luxe (di lŏoks', di luks'; *Fr.* də lüks') Elaborate and expensive; of superfine quality. [< F, of luxury]

delve (delv) *v.* delved, delv·ing *v.i.* **1** To make careful investigation for facts, knowledge, etc.: to *delve* into a crime. **2** To slope down; descend, as a road or hill. **3** *Archaic & Dial.* To engage in digging. —*v.t.* **4** *Archaic & Dial.* To turn over or dig (ground). —*n.* An excavation; pit; depression in a surface. [< OE *delfan*] —delv'er *n.*

dem·a·gog (dem'ə·gôg, -gog) *n.* **1** One who leads the populace by pandering to their prejudices and passions; an unprincipled politician. **2** Anciently, any popular leader or orator. Also dem'a·gogue. [< Gk. *dēmagōgos* < *dēmos* people

+ *agein* lead] —**dem′a·gog·ic** (-goj′ik) or **·i·cal** *adj.* —**dem′a·gog·ism** (-gog·iz·əm) or **dem′a·gogu·ism, dem′a·gogu′er·y** (-gog′ər·ē), **dem·a·go·gy** (dem′ə·gō′jē, -gôg′ē, -gog′ē) *n.*

de·mand (di·mand′, -mänd′) *v.t.* **1** To ask for boldly or peremptorily; insist upon. **2** To claim as due; ask for authoritatively. **3** To ask to know; inquire formally. **4** To have need for; require. **5** *Law* **a** To summon to court. **b** To make formal claim to (property). —*v.i.* **6** To make a demand. —*n.* **1** The act of demanding, or that which is demanded; requirement; claim; need. **2** A desire to obtain; call. **3** An actionable legal claim; also, that act of requesting payment or performance of what is due. **4** The desire to possess combined with the ability to purchase; also, the totality of such effectual desire in a given market with reference to a given commodity at a certain price. **5** An inquiry. See synonyms under TAX. —**in demand** Desired; sought after. —**on demand** On presentation; a note payable *on demand.* [< F *demander* < L *demandare* < *de-* down, away + *mandare* command; order] —**de·mand′a·ble** *adj.*

Synonyms (verb): ask, challenge, claim, exact, request, require. *Demand* is a determined and often an arrogant word; one may rightfully *demand* what is his own or his due, when it is withheld or denied; or he may wrongfully *demand* that to which he has no claim but power. *Require* is less arrogant and obtrusive than *demand,* but is exceedingly strenuous; as, the court *requires* the attendance of witnesses. *Request* is milder than *demand* or *require;* a creditor may *demand* or *require* payment; a friend *requests* a favor. We may speak of a humble *request,* but not of a humble *demand.* Compare ASK. *Antonyms:* decline, deny, refuse, reject, repudiate.

de·man·toid (di·man′toid) *n.* An emerald-green garnet. [< G *demant* diamond + -OID]

de·mar·cate (di·mär′kāt, dē′mär·kāt) *v.t.* **·cat·ed, ·cat·ing 1** To mark the bounds or limits of; delimit. **2** To distinguish; discriminate; separate. [Back formation < DEMARCATION]

de·mar·ca·tion (dē′mär·kā′shən) *n.* **1** The fixing of boundaries or limits. **2** Limitation; discrimination. **3** The limit or line fixed. Also **de′mar·ka′tion. —Line of Demarcation** The line established, chiefly in modern Brazil, by Pope Alexander VI in 1493 to prevent disputes between Spain and Portugal in regard to their discoveries in the New World. [< Sp. *demarcación* < *demarcar* < *de-* down (< L *de-*) + *marcar* mark a boundary < Gmc.]

de·ma·te·ri·al·ize (dē′mə·tir′ē·əl·īz′) *v.t. & v.i.* **·ized, ·iz·ing** To lose or cause to lose material attributes. —**de′ma·te′ri·al·i·za′tion** *n.*

deme (dēm) *n.* **1** One of the districts into which the ten tribes of Attica were divided by Cleisthenes. **2** A commune. **3** A local group of organisms whose members freely interbreed only within the group. [< Gk. *dēmos*]

de·mean[1] (di·mēn′) *v.t.* **1** To behave; conduct: always used reflexively. **2** *Obs.* To direct; control. —*n. Obs.* Behavior; conduct; bearing. [< OF *demener* < *de-* down (< L *de-*) + *mener* lead < LL *minare* threaten, drive]

de·mean[2] (di·mēn′) *v.t.* To degrade; debase in dignity or reputation. [< DE- + MEAN[2]]

de·mean·or (di·mē′nər) *n.* Behavior; bearing; deportment; mien. Also *Brit.* **de·mean′our.** See synonyms under AIR[1], BEHAVIOR, MANNER.

de·ment (di·ment′) *v.t.* To deprive of mental powers; make insane. [< L *dementare* < *de-* away + *mens, mentis* mind]

de·ment·ed (di·men′tid) *adj.* Deprived of reason; insane. —**de·ment′ed·ly** *adv.* —**de·ment′ed·ness** *n.*

de·men·tia (di·men′shə, -shē·ə) *n. Psychiatry* Unsoundness of mind resulting from organic or functional disorders, and leading to total loss or serious impairment of the faculty of coherent thought. See synonyms under INSANITY. [< L. madness]

de·mer·it (di·mer′it) *n.* **1** In schools, a mark for failure or misconduct. **2** Censurable conduct. [< Med. L *demeritum* a fault < L, pp. of *demerere* < *de-* down, away + *merere* deserve]

de·mersed (di·mûrst′) *adj. Bot.* Situated or growing under water, as leaves of aquatic plants; submersed. [< obs. *demerse* plunge down < L *demersus,* pp. of *demergere* < *de-* down + *mergere* plunge]

de·mesne (di·mān′, -mēn′) *n.* **1** In feudal law, lands held in one's own power, as distinguished from feudal lands which were held (by permission) of a superior. **2** A manor house and the adjoining lands in the immediate use and occupation of the owner of an estate. **3** The grounds appertaining to any residence, or any landed estate. **4** Any region over which sovereignty is exercised; domain. Also **de·main, de·maine** (di·mān′). [< AF *demeyne,* OF *demeine, demaine.* Doublet of DOMAIN.]

demi- *prefix* **1** Half; intermediate: *demitint, demilune.* **2** Inferior or less in size, quality, etc.; partial: *demigod.* [< F *demi* < L *dimidius* half < *dis-* from, apart + *medius* middle]

dem·i·god (dem′ē·god′) *n.* **1** An inferior or lesser deity; a hero, supposed to be the offspring of a god and a mortal. **2** A man with the attributes of a god. —**dem′i·god′dess** *n. fem.*

de·mil·i·ta·rize (dē·mil′ə·tə·rīz′) *v.t.* **·rized, ·riz·ing 1** To remove the military form of; free from militarism. **2** To transfer from military to civilian control. **3** To remove military equipment and troops from and declare neutral, as an area or zone. —**de·mil′·i·ta·ri·za′tion** *n.*

de·mise (di·mīz′) *n.* **1** Death; decease. **2** *Law* **a** Decease involving as a result the transfer of an estate. **b** A transfer or conveyance of rights or estate. **3** The immediate transfer of a sovereign's rights at his death or abdication to his successor. —*v.* **·mised, ·mis·ing** *v.t.* **1** To bestow by will; bequeath: said especially of sovereignty on the death or abdication of a king, etc. **2** *Law* To lease (an estate) for life or for a term of years. —*v.i.* **3** To pass by will or inheritance. [< OF, fem. of *demis,* pp. of *demettre* send away < L *demittere.* See DEMIT.] —**de·mis′a·ble** *adj.*

de·mis·sion (di·mish′ən) *n.* A giving up or relinquishment, as of an office; resignation. [< L *demissio, -onis* < *demittere.* See DEMIT.]

de·mit (di·mit′) *v.* **·mit·ted, ·mit·ting** *v.t.* **1** To resign (an office or dignity). **2** *Obs.* To release; dismiss. —*v.i.* **3** To resign. —*n.* A letter of dismissal or one attesting honorable resignation; a recommendation. [< L *demittere* < *de-* down, away + *mittere* send]

dem·i·tasse (dem′ē·tas′, -täs′) *n.* **1** A small cup in which after–dinner coffee is served; literally, a half cup. **2** The coffee served in such a cup. [< F]

dem·i·tint (dem′ē·tint′) *n.* **1** A half–tint; a tint intermediate between the extremes of dark and light coloring in a painting. **2** Broken tints or tertiary shades of color. **3** The portion of a work of art so tinted.

dem·i·urge (dem′ē·ûrj) *n.* **1** In Plato's philosophy, the creator of the material universe. **2** In the Gnostic systems, Jehovah as an emanation of the Supreme Being; creator of the material world: sometimes also regarded as the creator of evil. **3** One of a class of public officers or magistrates in several ancient Peloponnesian states. Also **dem′i·ur′gus** (-ûr′gəs), **dem′i·ur′gos.** [< Gk. *demiourgos* skilled or public worker < *dēmos* people + *ergein* work] —**dem′i·ur′geous** (-jəs), **dem′i·ur′gic, dem′i·ur′gi·cal** *adj.*

de·mo·bil·ize (dē·mō′bəl·īz) *v.t.* **·ized, ·iz·ing 1** To disband, as troops that have been mobilized. **2** To change, as an army, from a war to a peacetime basis. —**de·mo′bil·i·za′tion** *n.*

de·moc·ra·cy (di·mok′rə·sē) *n. pl.* **·cies 1** A theory of government which, in its purest form, holds that the state should be controlled by all the people, each sharing equally in privileges, duties, and responsibilities and each participating in person in the government, as in the city–states of ancient Greece. In practice, control is vested in elective officers as representatives who may be upheld or removed by the people. **2** A government so conducted; a state so governed; the mass of the people. **3** Political, legal, or social equality. [< F *démocratie* < Med. L *democratia*

< Gk. *dēmokratia* < *dēmos* people + *krateein* rule]

dem·o·crat (dem′ə·krat) *n.* **1** One who favors a democracy. **2** One who believes in political and social equality.

dem·o·crat·ic (dem′ə·krat′ik) *adj.* **1** Of or pertaining to democracy or a democracy; characterized by the fact, spirit, or principles of popular government. **2** Pertaining to or characteristic of any democratic party. **3** Tending to level social distinctions; practicing social equality; not snobbish. —**dem′o·crat′·i·cal·ly** *adv.*

de·mod·ed (dē·mō′did) *adj.* Out of fashion.

de·mod·u·late (dē·moj′ōō·lāt) *v.t.* **·lat·ed, ·lat·ing** *Electronics* To detect. —**de·mod′u·la′tion** *n.*

de·mog·ra·phy (di·mog′rə·fē) *n.* The study of vital and social statistics in their application to ethnology, anthropology, and public health. [< Gk. *dēmos* people + -GRAPHY]

de·mol·ish (di·mol′ish) *v.t.* **1** To tear down; raze, as a building. **2** To destroy utterly; ruin; lay waste to. [< F *démoliss-,* stem of *démolir* < L *demoliri* < *de-* down + *moliri* build < *moles* heap, mass] —**de·mol′ish·er** *n.*

Synonyms: destroy, overthrow, overturn, raze, ruin. A building, monument, or other structure is *demolished* when reduced to a shapeless mass; it is *razed* when level with the ground; it is *destroyed* when its structural unity is gone, whether or not its component parts remain. An edifice is *destroyed* by fire or earthquake; it is *demolished* by bombardment; it is *ruined* when, by violence or neglect, it has become unfit for human habitation. Compare ABOLISH, BREAK. *Antonyms:* build, construct, create, make, repair, restore.

dem·o·li·tion (dem′ə·lish′ən) *n.* The act or result of demolishing; destruction. Also **de·mol′ish·ment.** —**dem′o·li′tion·ist** *n.*

de·mon (dē′mən) *n.* **1** An evil spirit; devil. **2** A wicked or cruel person. **3** In ancient Greek religion, a supernatural intelligence; a guardian spirit; genius. **4** A person of great energy, skill, etc. —*adj.* Being or possessed of a demon. Also spelled *daemon, daimon.* [< L *daemon* evil spirit (orig., spirit, god) < Gk. *daimōn*] —**de·mon·i·an** (di·mō′nē·ən), **de·mon′ic** (di·mon′ik) *adj.*

de·mon·e·tize (dē·mon′ə·tīz) *v.t.* **·tized, ·tiz·ing 1** To deprive (currency) of standard value. **2** To withdraw from use as currency.

de·mo·ni·ac (di·mō′nē·ak) *adj.* **1** Of, like, or befitting a demon or evil spirit; devilish. **2** Influenced or produced by or as by demons; mad; violent; frenzied. Also **de·mo·ni·a·cal** (dē′mə·nī′ə·kəl) —*n.* One possessed of a demon or evil spirit; a lunatic. —**de′mo·ni′·a·cal·ly** *adv.*

de·mon·ism (dē′mən·iz′əm) *n.* Belief in the existence and power of demons. —**de′mon·ist** *n.*

de·mon·ize (dē′mən·īz) *v.t.* **·ized, ·iz·ing 1** To make a demon of. **2** To bring under demonic influence.

demono- *combining form* Demon: *demonology.* Also, before vowels, **demon-.** [< Gk. *daimōn* spirit, god]

de·mon·ol·a·try (dē′mən·ol′ə·trē) *n.* The worship of demons. [< DEMONO- + Gk. *latreia* worship] —**de′mon·ol′a·ter** *n.*

de·mon·ol·o·gy (dē′mən·ol′ə·jē) *n.* The study of or belief in demons or demonism. [< DEMONO- + -LOGY] —**de′mon·ol′o·gist** *n.*

de·mon·stra·ble (di·mon′strə·bəl, dem′ən-) *adj.* Capable of being proved. —**de·mon′stra·ble·ness, de·mon′stra·bil′i·ty** *n.* —**de·mon′stra·bly** *adv.*

dem·on·strate (dem′ən·strāt) *v.* **·strat·ed, ·strat·ing** *v.t.* **1** To explain or describe by use of experiments, examples, etc. **2** To explain the operation or use of. **3** To prove or show to be by logic; make evident. **4** To exhibit; make clear, as emotions. —*v.i.* **5** To take part in a public demonstration. **6** To make a show of military force. [< L *demonstratus,* pp. of *demonstrare* < *de-* completely + *monstrare* show, point out]

dem·on·stra·tion (dem′ən·strā′shən) *n.* **1** A pointing out; the act of making known. **2** An exhibition or expression; manifestation. **3** Proof by such evidence of facts, principles,

and arguments·as precludes denial or reasonable doubt. **4** The exhibition and description of examples in teaching an art or science. **5** A public exhibition of welcome, approval, or condemnation, as by a mass meeting or procession. **6** *Logic* A system of reasoning showing how, from given premises, such as definitions, axioms, postulates, a certain result must follow. **7** A show of military force or of aggressive movement, especially when intended as a feint, or in time of peace as a menace. **8** An exhibition and explanation of the fine points and workability of an article or commodity to be sold.
Synonyms: certainty, conclusion, consequence, deduction, evidence, induction, inference, proof. *Demonstration,* in the strict and proper sense, is the highest form of *proof* and gives the most absolute *certainty,* but cannot be applied outside of pure mathematics or other strictly deductive reasoning; there can be *proof* and *certainty,* however, in matters that do not admit of *demonstration.* A *conclusion* is the absolute and necessary result of the admission of certain premises; an *inference* is a probable *conclusion* toward which known facts, statements, or admissions point, but which they do not absolutely establish; sound premises, together with their necessary *conclusion,* constitute a *demonstration. Evidence* is that which tends to show a thing to be true. *Proof* in the strict sense is complete,·irresistible *evidence;* as, there was much *evidence* against the accused, but not amounting to *proof* of guilt. Moral *certainty* is a conviction resting on such *evidence* as puts a matter beyond reasonable doubt, while not so irresistible as *demonstration.* Compare CERTAINTY, INDUCTION, INFERENCE, PROOF.

de·mon·stra·tive (di·mon′stra·tiv) *adj.* **1** Having the power of demonstrating or pointing out; convincing and conclusive. **2** Inclined to strong expression of feeling or opinions. **3** *Gram.* Serving to indicate the person or object referred to or intended. —*n.* A demonstrative pronoun. —**de·mon′stra·tive·ly** *adv.*

dem·on·stra·tor (dem′ən·strā′tər) *n.* **1** One who demonstrates. **2** One who exhibits and explains, as in an anatomy class. **3** A salesman who demonstrates the desirability and workability of some article or product to the public. **4** The article used for demonstration, as a vacuum cleaner or automobile. Also **dem′on·strat·er.**

dem·o·pho·bi·a (dem′ə·fō′bē·ə) *n. Psychol.* Morbid fear of crowds; also called *ochlophobia.* [<Gk. *dēmos* people + -PHOBIA] —**dem′o·pho′bic** *adj.*

de·mor·al·ize (di·môr′əl·īz, -mor′-) *v.t.* ·ized, ·iz·ing **1** To corrupt or deprave. **2** To dishearten; undermine discipline among, as troops. **3** To throw into disorder. —**de·mor·al·i·za′tion** *n.* —**de·mor′al·iz′er** *n.*

de·mote (di·mōt′) *v.t.* ·mot·ed, ·mot·ing To reduce to a lower grade or rank: opposed to *promote.* [<DE- + (PRO)MOTE] —**de·mo′tion** *n.*

de·mot·ic (di·mot′ik) *adj.* **1** Of or pertaining to the people or to the population of a region, country, locality, etc.; popular. **2** Pertaining to the simplified form of the hieratic alphabet of ancient Egypt. [<Gk. *dēmotikos* <*dēmos* people]

de·mot·ics (di·mot′iks) *n.* Sociology in its most inclusive sense.

de·mul·cent (di·mul′sənt) *adj.* Soothing. —*n. Med.* A soothing application, especially one to relieve irritated mucous membranes. [<L *demulcens, -entis,* ppr. of *demulcere* <*de-* down + *mulcere* soothe]

de·mur (di·mûr′) *v.i.* murred, ·mur·ring **1** To offer objections; take exception. **2** To delay; hesitate. **3** *Law* To interpose a demurrer. —*n.* **1** A suspension of decision or action; a delay. **2** An objection. **3** *Obs.* A demurrer. [<OF *demeurer* <L *demorari* <*de-* completely + *morari* delay <*mora* a delay] —**de·mur′ra·ble** *adj.*

de·mure (di·myŏŏr′) *adj.* **1** Having a sedate or modest demeanor. **2** Affecting modesty; prim; coy. See synonyms under SERIOUS. [ME *mure* <OF *meur* <L *maturus* mature, discreet] —**de·mure′ly** *adv.* —**de·mure′ness** *n.*

de·mur·rage (di·mûr′ij) *n.* **1** The detention of a vessel or conveyance by a consigner or consignee beyond the specified time. **2** Compensation for such delay. [<OF *demourage* <*demourer* <L

demorare. See DEMUR.]

den (den) *n.* **1** A cavern occupied by animals; a lair. **2** A low haunt. **3** A room for privacy; sanctum. See synonyms under HOLE. —*v.i.* **denned, den·ning** To dwell in, or as in, a den. [OE *denn*]

de·nar·i·us (di·nâr′ē·əs) *n. pl.* ·nar·i·i (-nâr′ē·ī) **1** The most important coin of ancient Rome, made of silver and weighing, under Augustus, 1/84 of a pound; the penny of the New Testament. **2** Later, a small copper coin. **3** A gold coin, the **denarius aureus,** worth 25 silver denarii. *Denarius* was the Latin name of the English penny, the initial of which (*d.*) is preserved in monetary notation. [<L *denarius (nummus)* denary (coin); because it was worth ten asses]

ROMAN
DENARIUS

de·na·ry (den′ə·rē, dē′nə-) *adj.* Containing ten; decimal. —*n. pl.* ·ries **1** The number 10. **2** A tithing. [<L *denarius* <*deni* by tens <*decem* ten]

de·na·tion·al·ize (dē·nash′ən·əl·īz′) *v.t.* ·ized, ·iz·ing **1** To deprive of national character, status, or rights. **2** To change the nationality of. —**de·na′tion·al·i·za′tion** *n.*

de·nat·u·ral·ize (dē·nach′ər·əl·īz′) *v.t.* ·ized, ·iz·ing **1** To render unnatural. **2** To deprive of naturalization or citizenship; denationalize. —**de·nat′u·ral·i·za′tion** *n.*

de·na·ture (dē·nā′chər) *v.t.* ·tured, ·tur·ing **1** To alter the natural properties of (a substance) by adding an adulterant. **2** *Biochem.* To modify the molecular structure of (a protein or nucleic acid) by physical or chemical means. Also **de·na′tur·ize.** —**de·na′tur·ant** *n.* —**de·na′tur·a′tion** *n.*

denatured alcohol Ethyl alcohol made unfit for drinking purposes by the addition of a toxic or distasteful substance.

den·dri·form (den′drə·fôrm) *adj.* Like a tree in structure; tree-shaped.

den·drite (den′drīt) *n.* **1** *Mineral.* Any mineral crystallizing in a branching, treelike form; a rock or mineral with treelike markings. **2** *Physiol.* A filamentous, arborescent process of a nerve cell which conducts impulses toward the cell body. [<Gk. *dendritēs* of a tree]

den·drit·ic (den·drit′ik) *adj.* **1** Resembling a tree; dendriform. **2** Of or pertaining to a dendrite. Also **den·drit′i·cal.** —**den·drit′i·cal·ly** *adv.*

dendro- *combining form* Tree: *dendrochore.* Also, before vowels, **dendr-.** Also **dendri-.** [<Gk. *dendron* tree]

den·dro·chore (den′drə·kôr, -kōr) *n. Ecol.* The region of trees and forests: a major division of the biochore. —**den′dro·chor′ic** *adj.*

den·dro·chro·nol·o·gy (den′drə·krə·nol′ə·jē) *n.* The determination of the approximate dates of past events and of periods of time by a study of the growth rings on trees.

den·droid (den′droid) *adj.* Like a tree; dendritic. Also **den·droi′dal.** [<Gk. *dendroeidēs*]

den·dro·lite (den′drə·līt) *n. Bot.* A petrified or fossil shrub, plant, or part of a plant.

den·drol·o·gy (den·drol′ə·jē) *n.* That branch of botany and forestry that deals with trees. [<DENDRO- + -LOGY] —**den·drol′o·gist** *n.*

den·dron (den′dron) *n. Physiol.* A nerve dendrite. [<Gk., tree]

-dendron *combining form* Tree: *philodendron.* [<Gk. *dendron* tree]

den·gue (deng′gē, -gā) *n. Pathol.* An acute, tropical, frequently epidemic virus disease transmitted by the bite of the mosquito *Aëdes aegypti* and characterized by fever, eruptions, and severe pains in the joints: also known as *breakbone fever.* [<Sp., ult. <Swahili]

de·ni·al (di·nī′əl) *n.* **1** The act of denying; declaration that a statement made is untrue; contradiction: opposed to *affirmation.* **2** Refusal to acknowledge or admit; a disowning or disavowal; rejection. **3** Refusal to grant, indulge, or agree; non-compliance, as with something urged.

de·ni·er[1] (di·nī′ər) *n.* One who makes denial.

den·ier[2] (den′yər, də·nir′ *for def. 1,* də·nir′ *for def. 2; Fr.* də·nyā′) *n.* **1** A unit of rayon or silk yarn size, based on a standard weight of five centigrams per 450 meters of silk. **2** A silver coin, introduced by Pepin the Short in 755, which was for centuries the chief silver coin in Europe. [<F <L *denarius* DENARIUS]

den·i·grate (den′ə·grāt) *v.t.* ·grat·ed, ·grat·ing **1** To make black; blacken. **2** To slander. [<L *denigratus,* pp. of *denigrare* <*de-* completely + *nigrare* blacken <*niger* black] —**den′i·gra′tion** *n.*

den·im (den′əm) *n.* A twilled cotton used for overalls, uniforms, etc. [<F (*serge*) *de Nîmes* (serge) of Nîmes, where first made]

den·i·zen (den′ə·zən) *n.* **1** One who lives in a place; a citizen; inhabitant. **2** *Brit.* An alien who has been admitted to residence and to certain privileges of citizenship. **3** A person, animal, or thing at home in any region, although not a native. —*v.t. Brit.* **1** To admit to the rights of citizenship. **2** To populate with denizens. [<AF *deinzein* <*deinz* inside <L *de intus* from within]

Den·mark (den′märk) A kingdom in NW Europe; 16,575 square miles; capital, Copenhagen. *Danish* **Dan·mark** (dän′märk).

de·nom·i·nate (di·nom′ə·nāt) *v.t.* ·nat·ed, ·nat·ing To give a name to; call: to *denominate* him a thief. —*adj.* (-nit) Made up of units of a designated kind: opposed to *abstract.* [<L *denominatus,* pp. of *denominare* <*de-* down + *nomen* name] —**de·nom′i·na·ble** (-ə·nə·bəl) *adj.*

de·nom·i·na·tion (di·nom′ə·nā′shən) *n.* **1** The act of naming. **2** A class designation; name; epithet; appellation. **3** A body of Christians having a distinguishing name; sect. **4** A class of arithmetical units of one kind and name. **5** A unit of value: said of money: bills of all *denominations* from $1.00 to $500.00. See synonyms under NAME, SECT. —**de·nom′i·na′tion·al** *adj.* —**de·nom′i·na′tion·al·ism** *n.* —**de·nom′i·na′tion·al·ist** *n.* —**de·nom′i·na′tion·al·ly** *adv.*

de·nom·i·na·tive (di·nom′ə·nā′tiv, -nə·tiv) *adj.* **1** That gives or constitutes a name; appellative. **2** *Gram.* Derived from a noun or adjective. —*n.* **1** That which describes or denominates. **2** *Gram.* A word, especially a verb, derived from a noun or adjective, as the verb *to garden.* —**de·nom′i·na′tive·ly** *adv.*

de·nom·i·na·tor (di·nom′ə·nā′tər) *n.* **1** One who or that which names. **2** *Math.* That term of a fraction below or to the right of the line which expresses the number of equal parts into which the unit is divided; divisor. —**common denominator** Any common multiple of the denominators of a series of fractions.

de·no·ta·tion (dē′nō·tā′shən) *n.* **1** The act of denoting or distinguishing by name; a marking off; designation or separation. **2** The object or objects denoted by a word, as distinguished from the marks or qualities which it suggests: contrasted with *connotation.* **3** That which indicates; a sign. **4** That which is signified; meaning.

de·note (di·nōt′) *v.t.* ·not·ed, ·not·ing **1** To mark; point out or make known. **2** To serve as a symbol for; signify; indicate. **3** To designate; mean: said of words, symbols, etc. See synonyms under IMPORT. [<L *denotare* <*de-* down + *notare* mark] —**de·not′a·ble** *adj.*

dé·noue·ment (dā·nōō·män′) *n.* **1** The final unraveling or solution of the plot of a play, novel, or short story; issue; outcome. **2** The point in the plot where this occurs. **3** Any final issue or solution. See synonyms under CATASTROPHE. [<F <*dénouer* <*dé-* away (<L *dis-*) + *nouer* knot <L *nodare* <*nodus* a knot]

de·nounce (di·nouns′) *v.t.* ·nounced, ·nounc·ing **1** To attack or condemn openly and vehemently; inveigh against. **2** To inform against; accuse. **3** To threaten, as evil or vengeance; menace. **4** To give formal notice of, specifically, of the termination of a treaty or convention. **5** *Obs.* To announce; foretell. See synonyms under CONDEMN. [<OF *denoncer* <L *denuntiare* <*de-* down + *nuntiare* proclaim, announce] —**de·nounce′ment** *n.*

dense (dens) *adj.* **dens·er, dens·est** **1** Having its parts crowded closely together; compact in structure; thick; close. **2** Hard to penetrate; obtuse; stupid; dull. **3** *Phot.* Opaque when developed, and consequently strongly contrasted in lights and shades; intense: said of a negative. See synonyms under HARD, IMPENETRABLE. [<L *densus*] — **dense'ly** *adv.*

den·si·ty (den'sə·tē) *n.* *pl.* **·ties** **1** Compactness; the closeness of any space distribution. **2** *Physics* The mass of a substance per unit of its volume. In the metric system the unit of density is the mass of a cubic centimeter of water at 4°C. **3** *Sociol.* The number of specified units, as persons, families, or dwellings, per acre or square mile. **4** *Electr.* The quantity of current flowing through a given cross-section of a conductor: usually expressed in terms of amperes per square centimeter or square inch: also **current density. 5** *Ecol.* The relative thickness of the vegetative cover in forests, on prairies, etc., scaled in 10ths with 1 as the maximum growth. [<MF *densité* <L *densitas, -tatis* <*densus* thick]

dent (dent) *n.* A small depression made by striking or pressing; indentation. See synonyms under BLEMISH, HOLE. — *v.t.* To make a dent in. — *v.i.* To become dented. [Var. of DINT]

den·tal (den'təl) *adj.* **1** Of or pertaining to the teeth. **2** Of or pertaining to dentistry. **3** *Phonet.* Describing a consonant produced with the tip of the tongue against or near the upper front teeth, as French *t* and *d.* The English alveolars (t) and (d) are sometimes, inaccurately, called dentals. — *n.* *Phonet.* A dental consonant. [<NL *dentalis* <L *dens, dentis* a tooth]

den·tate (den'tāt) *adj.* **1** Having teeth or toothlike processes; toothed. **2** *Bot.* Having a notched edge resembling teeth, as certain leaves. [<L *dentatus* having teeth] — **den'tate·ly** *adv.*

den·ta·tion (den·tā'shən) *n.* **1** A toothed formation or condition. **2** The state or quality of being dentate.

denti– *combining form* Tooth: *dentiform.* Also, before vowels, **dent–.** [<L *dens, dentis* tooth]

den·ti·cle (den'ti·kəl) *n.* **1** A small tooth or toothlike projection. **2** *Dent.* A small, calcified mass in the pulp cavity of a tooth. **3** *Archit.* Dentil. [<L *denticulus,* dim. of *dens, dentis* tooth]

den·tic·u·late (den·tik'yə·lit, -lāt) *adj.* **1** Finely dentate or toothed. **2** *Archit.* Formed into dentils. Also **den·tic'u·lat·ed.** — **den·tic'u·late·ly** *adv.* — **den·tic'u·la'tion** *n.*

den·ti·fi·ca·tion (den'tə·fə·kā'shən) *n.* The formation of teeth. [<DENTI- + L *facere* make]

den·ti·form (den'tə·fôrm) *adj.* Tooth-shaped.

den·tine (den'tēn, -tin) *n.* The hard calcified substance forming the body of a tooth just beneath the enamel and cementum. Also **den'tin** (-tin). — **den'tin·al** *adj.*

den·ti·phone (den'tə·fōn) *n.* An instrument for hearing sounds by means of vibrations transmitted through the teeth to the auditory nerve. Also **den'ta·phone.**

den·tist (den'tist) *n.* One who practices dentistry. [<F *dentiste* <*dent* a tooth]

den·tist·ry (den'tis·trē) *n.* **1** The branch of medicine which is concerned with the diagnosis, prevention, and treatment of diseases affecting the teeth and their associated structures, including the extraction, filling, and crowning of teeth, the construction of bridges and dentures, and general oral prophylaxis. **2** The work of a dentist.

den·ti·tion (den·tish'ən) *n.* **1** The process or period of cutting teeth; teething. **2** *Biol.* The kind and number of teeth characteristic of an animal, and the manner in which they are arranged in the jaws. [<L *dentitio, -onis* teething <*dentire* cut teeth <*dens, dentis* teeth]

dento– *combining form* Dental. [<L *dens, dentis* tooth]

den·toid (den'toid) *adj.* Like a tooth. [<DENT(I)- + -OID]

den·ture (den'chər) *n.* **1** The teeth of an animal collectively. **2** A block or set of teeth. **3** *Dent.* A frame of plastic or other material adapted to fit the upper or

lower jaw and containing a partial or complete set of artificial teeth. [<F *dent* tooth]

de·nu·date (di·nōō'dāt, -nyōō'-, den'yoo·dāt) *adj.* Naked; stripped of foliage or other covering. — **den·u·date** (den'yoo·dāt, di·noo'. dāt, -nyōō'-) *v.t.* **·dat·ed, ·dat·ing** To denude; lay bare. [<L *denudatus,* pp. of *denudare.* See DENUDE.]

den·u·da·tion (den'yoo·dā'shən, dē'noo-, -nyoo-) *n.* **1** The act of denuding or state of being stripped bare. **2** *Geol.* **a** The laying bare of land, especially by erosion. **b** The slow disintegration of rock surfaces by weathering; a wearing down of hills and mountains.

de·nude (di·nōōd', -nyōōd') *v.t.* **·nud·ed, ·nud·ing** **1** To strip the covering from; make naked. **2** *Geol.* To wear away or remove overlying matter from, and so expose to view. [<L *denudare* <*de-* down, completely + *nudare* strip <*nudus* bare, naked]

de·nu·mer·a·ble (di·nōō'mər·ə·bəl, -nyōō'-) *adj.* *Math.* Capable of being put in a one-to-one correspondence with positive integers, as a set of rational numbers. — **de·nu'mer·a·bly** *adv.*

de·nun·ci·ate (di·nun'sē·āt, -shē-) *v.t. & v.i.* **·at·ed, ·at·ing** To denounce. [<L *denuntiatus,* pp. of *denuntiare.* See DENOUNCE.] — **de·nun'ci·a'tor** *n.*

de·nun·ci·a·tion (di·nun'sē·ā'shən, -shē-) *n.* **1** The act of declaring an action or person worthy of reprobation or punishment; arraignment. **2** The declaration of a threatening purpose; the proclamation of impending and deserved evil; a menace. **3** The denouncing of a treaty. **4** *Obs.* A formal announcement; proclamation. See synonyms under OATH, REPROOF. — **de·nun'ci·a'tive** *adj.* — **de·nun'ci·a'tive·ly** *adv.*

Den·ver (den'vər) The capital of Colorado.

de·ny (di·nī') *v.t.* **·nied, ·ny·ing** **1** To declare to be untrue; contradict. **2** To reject as false; declare to be unfounded or not real, as a doctrine. **3** To refuse to give; withhold. **4** To refuse (someone) a request. **5** To refuse to acknowledge; disown; repudiate. **6** To refuse access to. **7** *Obs.* To decline; refuse to accept. See synonyms under RENOUNCE. — **to deny oneself** To refuse oneself a gratification. [<OF *denier* <L *denegare* <*de-* completely + *negare* say no, refuse]

de·ob·stru·ent (dē·ob'strōō·ənt) *adj.* Having the power to remove obstructions. — *n.* A medicine for removing obstructions; an aperient. [<NL *deobstruens, -entis* <L *de-* away + *obstruens, -entis,* ppr. of *obstruere.* See OBSTRUCT.]

de·o·dar (dē'ə·där) *n.* **1** The East Indian cedar (*Cedrus deodara*), prized for its light-red wood. **2** This wood. [<Hind. <Skt. *devadāru* divine tree]

de·o·dor·ant (dē·ō'dər·ənt) *adj.* Destroying, absorbing, or disguising bad odors. — *n.* A deodorizer; specifically, any cosmetic cream, spray, or powder used to absorb or counteract body odors. [<DE- (def. 4) + L *odorans, -antis,* ppr. of *odorare* have an odor]

de·o·dor·ize (dē·ō'dər·īz) *v.t.* **·ized, ·iz·ing** To modify, destroy, or disguise the odor of.

de·on·tol·o·gy (dē'on·tol'ə·jē) *n.* The science of moral obligation or duty; ethics. [<Gk. *deon, deontos* necessary, orig. ppr. neut. of *deein* lack, need + -LOGY] — **de·on·to·log·i·cal** (dē'on'tə·loj'i·kəl) *adj.* — **de·on·tol'o·gist** *n.*

de·ox·i·dize (dē·ok'sə·dīz) *v.t.* **·dized, ·diz·ing** **1** To remove oxygen from. **2** To reduce from the state of an oxide. Also **de·ox'i·date.**

de·ox·y·gen·ate (dē·ok'sə·jə·nāt') *v.t.* **·at·ed, ·at·ing** To remove oxygen from. Also **de·ox'y·gen·ize'.** — **de·ox'y·gen·a'tion** *n.*

de·ox·y·ri·bo·nu·cle·ic acid (dē·ok'sē·rī·bō·nōō·klē'ik, -nyōō-) *Biochem.* A nucleic acid of complex molecular structure forming a principal constituent of the genes and known to play an important role in the genetic action of the chromosomes. Abbr. DNA.

de·part (di·pärt') *v.i.* **1** To go away; leave: opposed to *arrive.* **2** To deviate; differ; vary: with *from.* **3** To die. — *v.t.* **4** *Rare* To leave: to *depart* this life. See synonyms under DIE¹, ESCAPE. — *n.* *Obs.* Departure; death. [<OF *departir* <*de-* away <L *dis-*) *partir* divide <L *partire* <*pars, partis* a part]

de·part·ment (di·pärt'mənt) *n.* **1** A distinct part; a division or subdivision of an organization, business, etc. **2** A division in a secondary school, college, or university devoted to teaching courses in a certain subject: French *department, department* of sociology. **3** A subdivision of a U.S. Territory for military purposes: also **territorial department. 4** A subdivision of a governmental organization: the State *Department, Department* of Labor, etc. **5** In France, a government administrative district. [<OF <*departir.* See DEPART.]

de·par·ture (di·pär'chər) *n.* **1** The act of departing. **2** The act of deviating from a method, course of action, set of ideas, etc.; divergence. **3** The act of leaving this world; death. **4** *Naut.* **a** Distance east or west of a given meridian. **b** The position of a ship taken at the commencement of a voyage as a basis for calculations by dead reckoning.

de·pau·per·ate (dē·pô'pə·rāt) *v.t.* **·at·ed, ·at·ing** To deprive of fertility or richness; impoverish; exhaust. — *adj.* (-rit) **1** *Bot.* Diminutive or imperfectly developed, as if starved: said of plants grown in poor soil. **2** *Obs.* Impoverished. [<Med. L *depauperatus,* pp. of *depauperare* <L *de-* down + *pauperare* make poor <*pauper* poor]

de·pend (di·pend') *v.i.* **1** To trust; have full reliance: with *on* or *upon.* **2** To be conditioned or determined; be contingent: with *on* or *upon.* **3** To rely for maintenance, support, etc.: with *on* or *upon.* **4** To hang down: with *from.* **5** To be pending, undecided, or in suspension. See synonyms under LEAN¹. [<OF *dependre* <L *dependere* <*de-* down + *pendere* hang]

de·pen·dence (di·pen'dəns) *n.* **1** The act or relation of depending, or the state of being dependent on or determined by some one or something else. **2** Reliance; trust. **3** Reciprocal reliance. **4** Subordination; subjection; that which is subordinate to or contingent on something else. **5** That on which one relies. Also **de·pen'dance.**

de·pen·den·cy (di·pen'dən·sē) *n.* *pl.* **·cies 1** That which is dependent. **2** A subject or tributary state. **3** Dependence. Also **de·pen'dan·cy.**

de·pen·dent (di·pen'dənt) *adj.* **1** Depending upon something exterior; subordinate; contingent: often with *on* or *upon.* **2** Needing support or aid; needy. **3** Hanging down; pendent: often with *from.* **4** *Gram.* Subordinate. See SUBORDINATE CLAUSE under CLAUSE. See synonyms under SUBJECT. — *n.* **1** One who looks to another for support or favor; a retainer. **2** A consequence; corollary. Also **de·pen'dant.** — **de·pen'dent·ly** *adv.*

de·pict (di·pikt') *v.t.* **1** To portray or represent by drawing, sculpturing, painting, etc. **2** To describe verbally. [<L *depictus,* pp. of *depingere* <*de-* down + *pingere* paint] — **de·pic'tion** *n.*

dep·i·late (dep'ə·lāt) *v.t.* **·lat·ed, ·lat·ing** To remove hair from. [<L *depilatus,* pp. of *depilare* <*de-* away + *pilus* hair] — **dep'i·la'tion** *n.* — **dep'i·la'tor** *n.*

de·pil·a·to·ry (di·pil'ə·tôr'ē, -tō'rē) *adj.* Having the power to remove hair. — *n.* A preparation for removing hair from the human skin.

de·plete (di·plēt') *v.t.* **·plet·ed, ·plet·ing 1** To reduce or lessen, as by use, exhaustion, or waste. **2** To empty, or partially empty: to *deplete* the treasury. **3** *Med.* To lessen or remove the contents of (an overcharged organ or vessel), as by purging or bloodletting. [<L *depletus,* pp. of *deplere* <*de-* not + *plere* fill]

de·plor·a·ble (di·plôr'ə·bəl, -plō'rə-) *adj.* Lamentable; pitiable; sad. — **de·plor'a·bil'i·ty** *n.* — **de·plor'a·bly** *adv.*

de·plore (di·plôr', -plōr') *v.t.* **·plored, ·plor·ing** To feel or express deep regret or concern for; lament. See synonyms under MOURN. [<L *deplorare* <*de-* completely + *plorare* bewail]

de·ploy (di·ploi') *v.t. & v.i.* To spread out in line of battle, as troops. [<F *déployer* <OF *desployer, despleier* <LL *displicare* <*dis-* from + *plicare* fold. Doublet of DISPLAY.]

de·ploy·ment (di·ploi'mənt) *n.* *Mil.* Extension of a battle front from close order to battle formation in lines of skirmishers, foragers, etc., after development has been effected.

de·plume (dē·plōōm′) *v.t.* **·plumed, ·plum·ing** **1** To strip the plumage or feathers from. **2** To strip; despoil, as of honors or wealth. [<F *déplumer* <*dé-* away (<L *dis-*) + *plume* feather <L *pluma*]

de·po·lar·ize (dē·pō′lə·rīz) *v.t.* **·ized, ·iz·ing** **1** *Electr.* To break up or remove the polarization of, as by separating the electrodes of an electric cell. **2** To deprive of polarity.

de·pop·u·late (dē·pop′yə·lāt) *v.t.* **·lat·ed, ·lat·ing** To remove the inhabitants from, by massacre, famine, epidemics, etc. — *adj.* (-lit, -lāt) *Obs.* Depopulated. [<L *depopulatus,* pp. of *depopulari* <*de-* down + *populari* lay waste <*populus* people] —**de·pop′u·la′tor** *n.*

de·pop·u·la·tion (dē·pop′yə·lā′shən) *n.* **1** The act of depopulating, or the state of being depopulated. **2** That condition of a country in which the birth rate does not compensate for losses by the death rate.

de·port (di·pôrt′, -pōrt′) *v.t.* **1** To transport forcibly; banish. **2** To behave or conduct (oneself). [<OF *deporter* <L *deportare* <*de-* away + *portare* carry]

de·por·ta·tion (dē′pôr·tā′shən, -pōr-) *n.* **1** The act of deporting; the state of being deported; exile. **2** The sending back of an undesirable alien to the country from which he came.

de·port·ment (di·pôrt′mənt, -pōrt′-) *n.* Conduct or behavior; demeanor; bearing. See synonyms under BEHAVIOR, MANNER.

de·pose (di·pōz′) *v.* **·posed, ·pos·ing** *v.t.* **1** To deprive of official rank or office; oust, as a king. **2** To state on oath; give testimony of. **3** To take the deposition of. — *v.i.* **4** To bear witness. See synonyms under AFFIRM. [<OF *deposer* <*de-* down (<L *de-*) + *poser.* See POSE[1].] —**de·pos′a·ble** *adj.*

de·pos·it (di·poz′it) *v.t.* **1** To give in trust or for safekeeping. **2** To give as part payment or as security. **3** To put or lay on or in some place or receptacle. **4** To cause, as sediment, to form a layer or deposit. — *n.* **1** That which is or has been deposited or precipitated; especially, sediment; precipitate. **2** Money or property deposited, as in a bank for safekeeping, or as security. **3** The act of depositing, or the state of being deposited. **4** A place where anything is deposited. **5** The condition of being placed to one's order, as in a bank, in trust, or for safekeeping: on *deposit.* **6** *Geol.* An accumulated mass of iron, oil, salt, etc. **7** A layer of metal deposited by electrolytic action. [<L *depositus,* pp. of *deponere.* See DEPONE.]

de·pos·i·tar·y (di·poz′ə·ter′ē) *n.* *pl.* **·tar·ies** **1** A person entrusted with anything for safekeeping; a trustee. **2** A depository.

dep·o·si·tion (dep′ə·zish′ən, dē′pə-) *n.* **1** The act of depositing. **2** That which is deposited; especially, an accumulation or sediment. **3** The written testimony of a sworn witness; hence, allegation; evidence. **4** The act of deposing, as from office. — **the Deposition** The taking down of Christ's body from the Cross; also, in art, a representation of this. See synonyms under TESTIMONY.

de·pos·i·tor (di·poz′ə·tər) *n.* One who makes a deposit.

de·pos·i·to·ry (di·poz′ə·tôr′ē, -tō′rē) *n.* *pl.* **·ries** **1** A place where anything is deposited. **2** A person or body of persons to whom something is entrusted for safekeeping.

de·pot (dē′pō, *Mil. & Brit.* dep′ō) *n.* **1** A warehouse or storehouse. **2** *U.S.* A railroad station. **3** *Mil.* A storehouse or collecting station for personnel or materiel. [<F *dépôt* <OF *depost* <L *depositum* a pledge < *deponere.* See DEPONE.]

dep·ra·va·tion (dep′rə·vā′shən) *n.* **1** The act of depraving, or the state of being depraved or deteriorated. **2** A corrupt tendency; a depravity.

de·prave (di·prāv′) *v.t.* **·praved, ·prav·ing** **1** To render bad or worse, especially in morals; corrupt; pervert. **2** *Obs.* To vilify; slander. See synonyms under CORRUPT, POLLUTE. [<L *depravare* <*de-* completely + *pravus* corrupt, wicked] —**de·prav′er** *n.*

de·prav·i·ty (di·prav′ə·tē) *n.* *pl.* **·ties** **1** The state of being depraved; wickedness. **2** A depraved act or habit. See synonyms under SIN[1].

dep·re·cate (dep′rə·kāt) *v.t.* **·cat·ed, ·cat·ing** **1** To express disapproval of or regret for;

---

plead earnestly against. **2** To disparage or belittle; depreciate. **3** *Archaic* To desire or pray for deliverance from, as threatened evil. [<L *deprecatus,* pp. of *deprecari* <*de-* away + *precari* pray] —**dep·re·ca·ble** (dep′rə·kə·bəl) *adj.* —**dep′re·cat′ing·ly** *adv.* —**dep′re·ca′tion** *n.* —**dep′re·ca′tive** *adj.* —**dep′re·ca′tive·ly** *adv.* —**dep′re·ca′tor** *n.*

de·pre·ci·ate (di·prē′shē·āt) *v.* **·at·ed, ·at·ing** *v.t.* **1** To lessen the worth of; lower the price or rate of. **2** To disparage; belittle. — *v.i.* **3** To become less in value, etc. See synonyms under ASPERSE, DISPARAGE. [<L *depretiatus,* pp. of *depretiare* <*de-* down + *pretium* price]

de·pre·ci·a·tion (di·prē′shē·ā′shən) *n.* **1** The act of depreciating, or the state of being depreciated. **2** The wear and tear of equipment, machinery, plant, etc. **3** A diminished value; also, the amount estimated or written off to offset such loss of value.

de·pre·ci·a·to·ry (di·prē′shē·ə·tôr′ē, -tō′rē) *adj.* Tending to depreciate. Also **de·pre′ci·a′tive.**

dep·re·date (dep′rə·dāt) *v.t. & v.i.* **·dat·ed, ·dat·ing** To prey upon; pillage; plunder. [<LL *depraedatus,* pp. of *depraedari* <*de-* completely + *praeda* booty, prey] —**dep′re·da′tor** *n.* —**dep·re·da·to·ry** (dep′rə·dā′tər·ē) *adj.*

dep·re·da·tion (dep′rə·dā′shən) *n.* A plundering; robbery.

de·press (di·pres′) *v.t.* **1** To lower the spirits of; make gloomy; sadden. **2** To lessen in vigor, force, or energy; weaken; make dull. **3** To lessen the price or value of. **4** To press or push down; lower. **5** *Music* To lower the pitch of. **6** *Obs.* To subjugate; suppress. See synonyms under ABASE. [<OF *depresser* <L *depressus,* pp. of *deprimere* <*de-* down + *primere* press]

de·pres·sant (di·pres′ənt) *Med. adj.* Lessening functional activity or depressing vital force. —*n.* A drug or other substance which reduces vital functions.

de·pressed (di·prest′) *adj.* **1** Sad; dejected. **2** Lowered in position; pressed or kept down. **3** Flattened from above; sunk below the general surface, as the solid part of a plant body. **4** *Ornithol.* Broader than high, as the bill of a flycatcher.

de·pres·sion (di·presh′ən) *n.* **1** The act of depressing, or the state of being depressed; low spirits or vitality; dejection; melancholy. **2** That which is depressed; a low or hollow place. **3** A decline in business or trade; also, the period of time during which this inactivity prevails. **4** *Meteorol.* Low atmospheric pressure; also, a region of low atmospheric pressure. **5** *Astron.* The vertical angular distance of a heavenly body below the horizon: opposed to *altitude.* **6** The angular distance of an object below the horizontal plane through the point of observation: the opposite of *elevation.* **7** *Psychiatry* A lowering of vital powers; melancholy; especially, psychopathic melancholy leading to mental disorders. **8** *Music* Flatting of a tone.

de·pres·so·mo·tor (di·pres′ō·mō′tər) *adj. Physiol.* Diminishing the capacity for movement; retarding motor activity. —*n. Med.* An agent that lowers the activity of the motor centers, as a bromide.

de·pres·sor (di·pres′ər) *n.* **1** One who or that which depresses. **2** *Physiol.* A depressor nerve. **3** *Anat.* One of several muscles which depress or contract a part. **4** *Surg.* An instrument for pressing down a part.

depressor nerve *Physiol.* An afferent nerve connected with the heart, which controls blood pressure.

dep·ri·va·tion (dep′rə·vā′shən) *n.* The act of depriving, or the state of being deprived; loss; want. Also **de·priv·al** (di·prī′vəl). See synonyms under LOSS.

de·prive (di·prīv′) *v.t.* **·prived, ·priv·ing** **1** To take something away from; dispossess; divest. **2** To keep from acquiring, using, or enjoying. **3** *Obs.* To put an end to. [<OF *depriver* <L *de-* completely + *privare* strip, remove] —**de·priv′a·ble** *adj.*

de·pro·gram (dē·prō′gram) *v.t.* **-gramed** or **-grammed, -gram·ing** or **-gram·ming** To try to convince (a person) to forsake something learned well or accepted, esp. a religious belief.

dep·side (dep′sīd, -sid) *n. Chem.* One of a group of aromatic compounds formed from phenol carboxylic acids: found chiefly in lichens or made synthetically. [<Gk. *depsein* soften, tan + -IDE]

---

depth (depth) *n.* **1** The state or degree of being deep; extent or distance downward, inward, or backward. **2** A deep place. **3** The innermost part. **4** Profundity of thought or feeling; utmost extent; immensity; extremity. **5** The quality of being deep, crafty, or designing. **6** The quality of being dark in shade, or rich in color. **7** The quality of being low-pitched in tone. [ME *depthe*]

depth-sound·er (depth′soun′dər) *n.* An instrument for measuring the depth of water by sending sound waves and receiving their echoes from the bottom.

dep·u·rate (dep′yə·rāt) *v.t. & v.i.* **·rat·ed, ·rat·ing** To free or become free from morbid matter or impurities. [<Med. L *depuratus,* pp. of *depurare* <*de-* completely + *purus* pure] —**dep′u·ra′tion** *n.* —**dep′u·ra′tor** *n.*

dep·u·ra·tive (dep′yə·rā′tiv) *adj.* Purifying; purgative. —*n.* A purifying agent. Also **dep·u·rant** (dep′yə·rənt).

dep·u·ta·tion (dep′yə·tā′shən) *n.* **1** A person or persons acting for another; a delegation. **2** The act of deputing, or the state of being deputed. **3** *Brit.* A forestry license granted to a gamekeeper.

de·pute (di·pyōōt′) *v.t.* **·put·ed, ·put·ing** **1** To appoint as an agent, deputy, or delegation; send with authority. **2** To transfer, as authority, to another. [<OF *deputer* <LL *deputare* <*de-* away + *putare* think]

dep·u·ty (dep′yə·tē) *n.* *pl.* **·ties** **1** One appointed to act for another; representative agent. **2** A member of a legislative assembly in certain countries. See synonyms under DELEGATE. [<F *député,* pp. of *députer* <OF *deputer* DEPUTE]

de·rac·i·nate (di·ras′ə·nāt) *v.t.* **·nat·ed, ·nat·ing** To pull up by the roots; eradicate. [<F *déraciner* <*dé-* away (<L *dis-*) + *racine* a root <L *radix*]

de·rail (dē·rāl′) *v.t.* To cause to leave the rails, as a train. — *v.i.* To leave the rails. [<F *dérailler* <*dé-* from + *rail* a rail] —**de·rail′ment** *n.*

de·range (di·rānj′) *v.t.* **·ranged, ·rang·ing** **1** To disturb the arrangement or order of; disarrange; disorder. **2** To unbalance the reason of; craze. **3** To disturb the condition, action, or functions of. See synonyms under DISPLACE. [<F *déranger* <*dé-* away (<L *dis-*) + *ranger* RANGE, *v.*]

de·range·ment (di·rānj′mənt) *n.* **1** The act of deranging, or state of being deranged. **2** Any severe mental disorder; insanity. See synonyms under INSANITY.

der·by (dûr′bē) *n.* *pl.* **·bies** A stiff, felt hat with curved brim and round crown: in England called a *bowler.* [<DERBY]

de·reg·u·late (di·reg′yə·lāt) *v.t.* **-lat·ed, -lat·ing** To remove regulations or restrictions from.

de·re·ism (dir′ē·iz′əm) *n. Psychol.* Mental activity freed of ordinary logic, the facts of experience, or the realities of the external world: common in dreams and in certain mental disorders. [<DE- + L *res* thing + -ISM] —**de′re·is′tic** *adj.* —**de′re·is′ti·cal·ly** *adv.*

der·e·lict (der′ə·likt) *adj.* **1** Neglectful of obligation; unfaithful; remiss. **2** Deserted or abandoned. —*n.* **1** That which is deserted or abandoned. **2** Any property which is abandoned at sea, as a deserted wreck. **3** Land exposed or gained by receding of the sea. **4** One who betrays a trust. **5** A person outside the pale of respectability. [<L *derelictus,* pp. of *derelinquere* <*de-* completely + *relinquere* abandon]

der·e·lic·tion (der′ə·lik′shən) *n.* **1** Neglect or wilful omission; failure in duty. **2** Voluntary abandonment of a charge or property. **3** The state or fact of being abandoned. **4** *Law* **a** A gain of land by a permanent receding of water. **b** The land thus gained.

de·ride (di·rīd′) *v.t.* **·rid·ed, ·rid·ing** To treat with scornful mirth; ridicule. See synonyms under MOCK, RIDICULE. [<L *deridere* <*de-* completely + *ridere* laugh, mock] —**de·rid′er** *n.* —**de·rid′ing·ly** *adv.*

de·ris·i·ble (di·riz′ə·bəl) *adj.* Open to derision.

de·ri·sion (di·rizh′ən) *n.* **1** The act of deriding; ridicule; mockery; scornful laughter. **2** An object of ridicule or scorn. See synonyms under BANTER, RIDICULE, SCORN. [<L *derisio, -onis* <*deridere.* See DERIDE.]

de·ri·sive (di·rī′siv) *adj.* Expressive of or characterized by derision. Also **de·ri·so·ry** (di·rī′sər·ē).

der·i·va·tion (der′ə·vā′shən) *n.* **1** The act of deriving, or the condition of being derived. **2** The tracing of a word from its original form and meaning; also, a statement of the information thus obtained. **3** Origin; descent; extraction. **4** *Math.* **a** The process of forming a derivative. **b** The act of deriving an equation or reaching a conclusion expressed as an equation. — **de·riv·a′tion·al** *adj.*

de·riv·a·tive (di·riv′ə·tiv) *adj.* Coming or acquiring by derivation; of or pertaining to derivation or evolution; derived; not original or basic. —*n.* **1** That which is derived. **2** *Gram.* A word developed from a basic word, as by the addition of a prefix or suffix or by phonetic change: "Functional" is a *derivative* of "function." **3** *Chem.* **a** A compound formed or regarded as being formed from another, usually by partial replacement. **b** Any organic compound containing a specified radical: a benzene *derivative.* **4** *Music* A chord derived from another by inversion, or from the harmonics of an assumed root: often used in the plural. **5** *Math.* The instantaneous rate of change of a function with reference to a variable. — **de·riv′a·tive·ly** *adv.*

de·rive (di·rīv′) *v.* **·rived, ·riv·ing** *v.t.* **1** To draw or receive, as from a source, principle, or root; be descended from. **2** To deduce, as from a premise; draw, as a conclusion. **3** To trace the derivation of (a word). **4** *Chem.* To obtain (a compound) from another as by partial replacement. **5** *Obs.* To cause to come; bring: with *on, to,* or *upon.* — *v.i.* **6** To have derivation; originate. [< L *derivare* < *de-* from + *rivus* stream] —**de·riv′a·ble** *adj.* — **de·riv′er** *n.*

de·rived unit (di·rīvd′) *Physics* A unit based on or derived from any primary unit of mass, length, time, etc.

derm (dûrm) *n.* **1** *Anat.* The sensitive and vascular or true skin. **2** The skin in general: also **dermis.** Also **der·ma** (dûr′mə). [< Gk. *derma* skin]

-derm *suffix* Skin: *endoderm.* [< Gk. *derma* skin]

DERM
a. The true derm.

der·mal (dûr′məl) *adj.* Of or pertaining to the skin or epidermis, or, properly, to the corium; cutaneous: *dermal* affections. Also **der′mic.**

dermal body *Zool.* Any of the structures characterized by a glandular or sensory function which are present in the dermis and partly in the epidermis of some marine worms.

dermal layer *Zool.* A single layer of cells covering the outer surface of a sponge, through which the calcareous needle-shaped spicules project.

der·map·ter·ous (dər·map′tər·əs) *adj. Entomol.* Of or pertaining to an order (*Dermaptera*) of small, elongate, terrestrial, and mostly nocturnal insects with a pair of large, forcepslike, caudal appendages and chewing mouth parts: they are wingless or with one or two pairs of inconspicuous wings; the earwigs. [< DERM(O)- + Gk. *a-* without + *pteron* wing]

der·ma·ti·tis (dûr′mə·tī′tis) *n. Pathol.* Inflammation of the skin. [< DERMAT(O)- + -ITIS]

dermato- *combining form* Skin: *dermatology.* Also, before vowels, **dermat-.** [< Gk. *derma, dermatos* skin]

der·ma·to·bi·a·sis (dûr′mə·tō·bī′ə·sis) *n.* Infection by the larva of *Dermatobia.* [< DERMATOB(IA) + -IASIS]

der·mat·o·gen (dər·mat′ə·jən, dûr′mə·tō′jən) *n. Bot.* The outermost layer of cells in plants, forming the permanent epidermal tissue: also called *protoderm.*

der·ma·to·glyph·ics (dûr′mə·tō·glif′iks) *n.* **1** The study of the surface ridges of the skin, especially of the palm and the sole. **2** Ink impressions of such ridges taken for identification purposes. [< DERMATO- + Gk. *glyphein* carve]

der·ma·tol·o·gy (dûr′mə·tol′ə·jē) *n.* The branch of medical science that relates to the skin and its diseases. [< DERMATO- + -LOGY] —**der·ma·to·log·i·cal** (dûr′mə·tə·loj′i·kəl) *adj.*

der·ma·top·a·thy (dûr′mə·top′ə·thē) *n.* Any skin disease.

der·ma·to·phyte (dûr′mə·tō·fīt′) *n. Bot.* A plant living parasitically upon the skin, as certain fungi which produce ringworm, favus, etc. — **der′ma·to·phyt′ic** (-fit′ik) *adj.*

der·ma·to·plas·ty (dûr′mə·tō·plas′tē) *n. Surg.* The replacement of destroyed skin by flaps or skin grafts.

dermo- *combining form* Dermato-. Also, before vowels, **derm-.** [< Gk. *derma* skin]

der·moid (dûr′moid) *adj.* Like skin. —*n. Pathol.* A cystic tumor enclosing skin tissue or any skin-like substance. [< DERM(O)- + -OID]

der·mo·phy·to·sis (dûr′mō·fī·tō′sis) *n.* Athlete's foot. [< DERMO- + -PHYTE + -OSIS]

der·mo·skel·e·ton (dûr′mō·skel′ə·tən) *n. Zool.* A structure formed by the hardening of integument, as in crustaceans, insects, etc.; exoskeleton.

der·o·gate (der′ə·gāt) *v.* **·gat·ed, ·gat·ing** *v.i.* **1** To take away; detract, as from reputation, honor, or powers: with *from:* The charge cannot *derogate* from his honor. **2** To do something derogatory to one's character or position; degenerate. —*v.t.* **3** *Archaic* To take away so as to cause loss or impairment. **4** *Obs.* To disparage. —*adj.* (der′ə·git, -gāt) Derogated. [< L *derogatus,* pp. of *derogare* < *de-* away + *rogare* ask, propose a law] — **der′o·gate·ly** *adv.*

der·o·ga·tion (der′ə·gā′shən) *n.* **1** The act of derogating; detraction; disparagement. **2** The act of limiting in application, as a law, authority, etc.

de·rog·a·tive (di·rog′ə·tiv) *adj.* Tending to derogate or detract; derogatory. —**de·rog′a·tive·ly** *adv.*

de·rog·a·to·ry (di·rog′ə·tôr′ē, -tō′rē) *adj.* Lessening in good repute; detracting in estimation; disparaging. —**de·rog′a·to·ri·ly** *adv.* — **de·rog′a·to·ri·ness** *n.*

der·rick (der′ik) *n.* **1** An apparatus, as a mast with a hinged boom, or a framework, for hoisting and swinging heavy weights into place. **2** The framework over the mouth of an oil well or similar drill hole. [after *Derrick,* 17th c. London hangman]

DERRICKS
a. Hoisting derrick.
b. Oil well derrick.

der·rid (der′id) *n.* An extremely toxic, resinous alkaloid obtained from a species of derris (*Derris elliptica*): used as an arrow poison by the Malays. Also **der·ride** (der′īd).

der·rin·ger (der′in·jər) *n.* A pistol having a short barrel and a large bore. [after Henry *Derringer,* 19th c. U.S. gunsmith, who invented it]

der·ris (der′is) *n.* Any plant of a genus (*Derris*) of woody, climbing plants of the East Indies; especially, *D. tripliata* and *D. elliptica,* whose roots yield rotenone. Also **derris root.** [< NL < Gk., a covering]

der·ry (der′ē) *n. pl.* **·ries** A meaningless word used as a refrain in old songs; hence, a set of verses; a ballad. Also **der′ry-down′.**

der·vish (dûr′vish) *n.* **1** A Mohammedan mendicant friar; a fakir. **2** A member of certain fanatical tribes of Upper Egypt. [< Turkish < Persian *darvish*]

de·salt (dē·sôlt′) *v.t.* To remove the salt from, as sea water, to make potable. —**de·salt′er** *n.*

des·cant (des′kant) *n.* **1** The act of discussing; a series of remarks. **2** *Music* **a** A varied melody or song. **b** Formerly, an ornamental variation of the main subject or song. **c** A counterpoint above the plain song. **d** The composition or singing of such counterpoint or variations. **e** The upper part in part music, especially the soprano. —*v.t.* (des·kant′) **1** To discourse at length; hold forth: with *on* or *upon.* **2** To make a descant; sing. Also spelled *discant.* [< AF < Med. L *discantus* < L *dis-* away + *cantus* a song < *canere* sing]

de·scend (di·send′) *v.i.* **1** To move from a higher to a lower point; go or come down; sink. **2** To slope or incline downward, as a path. **3** To stoop; lower oneself. **4** To come down by inheritance; be inherited. **5** To be derived by heredity: with *from.* **6** To come or arrive in an overwhelming manner, as from above; attack: with *on* or *upon.* **7** To pass, as from the general to the particular. **8** *Astron.* To move southward or toward the horizon, as a star. —*v.t.* **9** To move from an upper to a lower part of; go down, as a ladder. See synonyms under FALL. [< OF *descendre* < L *descendere* < *de-* down + *scandere* climb]

de·scen·dant (di·sen′dənt) *n.* One who is descended lineally from another; offspring. —*adj.* Descendent. [< F, ppr. of *descendre.* See DESCEND.]

de·scen·dent (di·sen′dənt) *adj.* **1** Proceeding downward; descending. **2** Issuing by descent, as from an ancestor. [< L *descendens, -entis,* ppr. of *descendere.* See DESCEND.]

de·scend·er (di·sen′dər) *n.* **1** One who or that which descends. **2** *Printing* **a** The part of a letter that reaches into the bottom of the body of the type. **b** Any of such letters, as *j, g, q,* etc.

de·scend·i·ble (di·sen′də·bəl) *adj.* **1** That can be descended. **2** That can pass by descent; inheritable. Also **de·scend′a·ble.**

de·scent (di·sent′) *n.* **1** The act of descending. **2** Decline; deterioration; fall. **3** A descending way; declivity; slope. **4** Lineage; birth; extraction. **5** Descendants; issue. **6** A hostile visitation; invasion. **7** The transmission of an estate by inheritance. **8** A generation in the scale of genealogy. See synonyms under AFFINITY, KIN. [< F *descente* < *descendre.* See DESCEND.]

de·scribe (di·skrīb′) *v.t.* **·scribed, ·scrib·ing 1** To give an account of; represent, with spoken or written words. **2** To draw the figure of; delineate; outline. **3** To descry: an erroneous form. See synonyms under CIRCUMSCRIBE, RELATE. [< L *describere* < *de-* down + *scribere* write] — **de·scrib′a·ble** *adj.* —**de·scrib′er** *n.*

de·scrip·tion (di·skrip′shən) *n.* **1** The act of describing; a portrayal or explanation; a drawing or tracing. **2** A group of attributes constituting a class; sort; kind; nature. See synonyms under DEFINITION, REPORT. [< OF *description* < L *descriptio, -onis* < *describere.* See DESCRIBE.]

de·scrip·tive (di·skrip′tiv) *adj.* **1** Characterized by or containing description; serving to describe. **2** Designating a science or branch of a science concerned with the classification of material; taxonomical. **3** *Gram.* Having the function of describing: a *descriptive* adjective. See synonyms under GRAPHIC. —**de·scrip′tive·ly** *adv.* — **de·scrip′tive·ness** *n.*

descriptive geometry That application of geometry in which the representation of solids is projected upon two planes so that their metrical properties can be accurately deduced.

descriptive science Any science in which the emphasis is placed upon the classification and description of the material with which it deals: distinguished from *exact science* and *normative science.*

de·scry (di·skrī′) *v.t.* **·scried, ·scry·ing 1** To discover with the eye, as in the distance or through obscurity; discern; detect. **2** To discover or find out by observation or investigation. See synonyms under DISCERN, DISCOVER, LOOK. [< OF *descrier* < *des-* away (< L *dis-*) + *crier* cry] — **de·scri′er** *n.*

des·e·crate (des′ə·krāt) *v.t.* **·crat·ed, ·crat·ing** To divert from a sacred to a common use; profane. See synonyms under VIOLATE. [< DE- (def. 4) + L *sacratus,* pp. of *sacrare* make holy < *sacer* holy] —**des′e·crat′er** or **des′e·cra′tor** *n.*

des·e·cra·tion (des′ə·krā′shən) *n.* The act of profanation; condition of being desecrated; violation.

de·seg·re·gate (dē·seg′rə·gāt) *v.t.* **·gat·ed, ·gat·ing** To eliminate racial segregation in (schools, armed forces, public transportation, etc.).

de·seg·re·ga·tion (dē′seg·rə·gā′shən) *n.* **1** The act of ending segregation of races, as of Negroes and whites, in schools and public facilities. **2** The condition resulting from such action.

---

add,āce,câre,pälm; end,ēven; it,īce; odd,ōpen,ôrder; tŏŏk,pōōl; up,bûrn; ə = a in *above,* e in *sicken,* i in *clarity,* o in *melon,* u in *focus;* yōō = u in *fuse,* oi,oil; ou,pout; ch,check; g,go; ng,ring; th,thin; ŧh,this; zh,vision. Foreign sounds à,œ,ü,kh,ṅ; and ◆: see page xx. < from; + plus; ? possibly.

de·sen·si·tize (dē·sen′sə·tīz) v.t. **-tized, -tiz·ing** 1 To make less sensitive. 2 *Phot.* To reduce the sensitiveness to light. 3 *Physiol.* To lessen the reactive power of (an organ or tissue) to a stimulus, as an allergen, serum, etc.

des·ert[1] (dez′ərt) n. 1 A region so lacking in rainfall, moisture, and vegetation as to be uninhabitable by any considerable population. 2 Any region which is uncultivated and desolate because of deficient moisture, barren soil, or permanent frost. —*adj.* 1 Of or like a desert; barren; waste. 2 *Obs.* Deserted; forsaken. [< OF *deserte* < LL *desertum* < L, pp. neut. of *deserere* < *de-* away + *serere* join]

de·sert[2] (di·zûrt′) n. 1 The state of deserving reward or punishment; merit or demerit. 2 *Often pl.* That which is deserved or merited. 3 A meritorious or worthy act; meritoriousness. [< OF < *deservir.* See DESERVE.]

de·sert[3] (di·zûrt′) v.t. 1 To forsake or abandon, with or without right. 2 To forsake in violation of one's oath or orders, as a service, post, etc. —*v.i.* 3 To abandon one's post, duty, etc. See synonyms under ABANDON. [< F *déserter* < LL *desertare*, freq. of *deserere.* See DESERT[1].]

de·sert·er (di·zûr′tər) n. One who forsakes a service, duty, party, or friends; especially, an absconding soldier or sailor.

des·ert·i·fi·ca·tion (dez′ər·tə·fə·kā′shən) n. The process of becoming a desert.

de·ser·tion (di·zûr′shən) n. 1 The act of deserting. 2 The state of being deserted; desolation.

de·serve (di·zûrv′) v. **·served, ·serv·ing** v.t. To be entitled to or worthy of, by either merit or demerit. —*v.i.* To be worthy. [< OF *deservir* < L *deservire* < *de-* completely + *servire* serve] —**de·serv′er** n.

des·ic·cant (des′ə·kənt) adj. Producing dryness; desiccating, as a medicine or chemical agent. —n. A desiccant agent or substance.

des·ic·cate (des′ə·kāt) v. **·cat·ed, ·cat·ing** v.t. 1 To exhaust or remove the moisture from, as for preserving. 2 To dry thoroughly. —*v.i.* 3 To become dry. [< L *desiccatus*, pp. of *desiccare* < *de-* completely + *siccare* dry out < *siccus* dry] —**des′ic·ca′tion** n.

des·ic·ca·tor (des′ə·kā′tər) n. 1 One who or that which desiccates. 2 An apparatus for drying meat, vegetables, etc. 3 A tightly covered glass or porcelain vessel having a device for absorbing moisture: used to hold substances to be dried.

de·sid·er·ate (di·sid′ə·rāt) v.t. **·at·ed, ·at·ing** To feel desire or need for; feel the lack of. [< L *desideratus*, pp. of *desiderare.* See DESIRE.] —**de·sid′er·a′tion** n.

de·sid·er·a·tive (di·sid′ə·rā′tiv) adj. Having, implying, or expressing desire. —n. 1 A desideratum. 2 *Ling.* A verb derived from another verb and indicating desire to perform the action expressed in the original verb, as Latin *esurio* I wish to eat, I am hungry, from *edo* I eat.

de·sign (di·zīn′) v.t. 1 To make, draw, or prepare preliminary plans or sketches of. 2 To plan and make with art or skill, as a structure or work of art. 3 To form or make (plans, schemes, etc.) in the mind; conceive; invent. 4 To intend; purpose. 5 *Archaic* To mark out; designate. —*v.i.* 6 To make drawings or plans; be a designer. 7 To plan mentally; conceive. —n. 1 An arrangement of forms or colors, or both, intended to be wrought out for use or ornament in or on various materials; a pattern; preliminary sketch; coordination of details. 2 The art of designing; artistic invention; the artistic idea as executed; original work in the graphic or plastic arts. 3 A fixed purpose or intention; plot; scheme. 4 The adaptation of means to an end; plan; contrivance. 5 The object or reason; final purpose. [< MF *désigner* designate < L *designare.* See DESIGNATE.] —**de·sign′a·ble** adj.

Synonyms (noun): aim, device, end, intent, intention, object, plan, project, proposal, purpose, scheme. *Design* refers to the adaptation of means to an *end*, the correspondence and coordination of parts, or of separate acts, to produce a result; *intent* and *purpose* overlap all particulars, and fasten on the *end* itself. *Intention* is simply the more familiar form of the legal and philosophical *intent.* *Plan* relates to details of form, structure, and action, in themselves; *design* considers these same details all as a means to an *end.* The *plan* of a campaign may be for a series of sharp attacks, with the *design* of thus surprising and overpowering the enemy. A man comes to a fixed *intention* to kill his enemy; he forms a *plan* to en-

trap him into his power, with the *design* of then compassing his death; as the law cannot read the heart, it can only infer the *intent* from the evidences of *design.* *Intent* denotes a straining, stretching forth toward an object; *purpose* simply the placing it before oneself. *Intention* contemplates the possibility of failure; *purpose* looks to assured success, *intent* or *intention* refers especially to the state of mind of the actor, *purpose* to the result of the action. Compare AIM. END. IDEA. MODEL. PROJECT. PURPOSE. REASON.

des·ig·nate (dez′ig·nāt) v.t. **·nat·ed, ·nat·ing** 1 To indicate or make recognizable by some mark, sign, or name. 2 To name or entitle; characterize. 3 To select or appoint for a specific purpose, duty, office, etc. See synonyms under CIRCUMSCRIBE. —*adj.* (dez′ig·nit, -nāt) Designated; selected. [< L *designatus*, pp. of *designare* < *de-* completely + *signare* mark < *signum* a sign] —**des′ig·na′tive** adj. —**des′ig·na′tor** n.

des·ig·na·tion (dez′ig·nā′shən) n. 1 The act of designating. 2 A distinctive mark, name, or title. 3 Import, as of a word; character; description. See synonyms under NAME.

de·sign·er (di·zī′nər) n. 1 One who forms designs; a contriver; schemer. 2 One who invents and prepares useful, decorative, or artistic designs. See synonyms under CAUSE.

de·sign·ing (di·zī′ning) n. 1 The act or art of making designs or sketches. 2 The act of plotting or scheming. —*adj.* Artful; scheming. See synonyms under INSIDIOUS. —**de·sign′ing·ly** adv.

des·i·nence (des′i·nəns) n. 1 A termination or ending. 2 *Gram.* A formative suffix. [< MF *désinence* < L *desinentia* < *desinere* < *de-* away + *sinere* leave]

de·sip·i·ence (di·sip′ē·əns) n. Silliness; foolishness; trifling. Also **de·sip′i·en·cy.**

de·sip·i·ent (di·sip′ē·ənt) adj. Nonsensical; foolish. [< L *desipiens, -entis*, ppr. of *desipere* < *de-* away + *sapere* know, be wise]

de·sir·a·ble (di·zīr′ə·bəl) adj. Worthy or likely to be desired or wanted; worth having. See synonyms under PROFITABLE. —**de·sir′a·bil′i·ty, de·sir′a·ble·ness** n. —**de·sir′a·bly** adv.

de·sire (di·zīr′) v.t. **·sired, ·sir·ing** 1 To wish or long for; covet; crave. 2 To express a wish for; ask for; request. —n. 1 An earnest wishing for something; longing; craving; yearning. 2 A request; wish; prayer. 3 An object desired. 4 Appetite; passion; lust. [< OF *desirer* < L *desiderare,* ? < *de-* from + *sidus, sideris* star; with ref. to astrology] —**de·sir′er** n.

Synonyms (noun): appetency, appetite, aspiration, concupiscence, coveting, craving, hankering, inclination, longing, proclivity, propensity, wish. *Inclination* is the mildest of these terms; it is a quiet, or even a vague or unconscious, tendency. Even when we speak of a strong or decided *inclination* we do not express the intensity of *desire.* Desire has a wide range, from the highest objects to the lowest; *desire* is for an object near at hand, or near in thought, and viewed as attainable; a *wish* may be for what is remote or uncertain; or even for what is recognized as impossible. *Craving* is stronger than *hankering*; *hankering* may be the result of a fitful and capricious *appetite*; *craving* may be the imperious and reasonable demand of the whole nature. *Longing* is a reaching out with deep and persistent demand for that which is viewed as now distant but at some time attainable; as, the captive's *longing* for release. *Coveting* ordinarily denotes wrong *desire* for that which is another's. Compare APPETITE. FANCY, INCLINATION. *Antonyms:* see synonyms for ANTIPATHY.

de·sist (di·zist′) v.i. To cease, as from an action or proceeding; forbear; stop: often with *from.* See synonyms under CEASE, END, REST. [< L *desistere* < *de-* from + *sistere* stop, cease] —**de·sis′tance** n.

desk (desk) n. 1 A table or case specially adapted for writing or studying. 2 A stand for public reading or preaching; pulpit. [< Med. L *desca* < LL *discus.* Doublet of DAIS, DISH, DISK.]

des·moid (des′moid) adj. *Anat.* Resembling a ligament; ligamentous; also, fibrous: a *desmoid* tumor. —n. *Pathol.* A tough, very hard fibroma. [< Gk. *desmos* band + -OID]

Des Moines (də moin′, -moinz′) The capital of Iowa.

des·o·late (des′ə·lit) adj. 1 Destitute of inhabitants, dwellings, etc.; laid waste; deserted; abandoned. 2 Lonely; solitary. 3 Without friends; forlorn; sorrowful; afflicted; gloomy. See synonyms under BLEAK[1], SAD. —*v.t.* (des′ə·lāt) **·lat·ed, ·lat·ing** 1 To deprive of inhabitants. 2 To lay waste, devastate. 3 To make sorrowful, wretched, or forlorn. 4 To forsake; abandon. [< L *desolatus*, pp. of *desolare* < *de-* completely + *solus* alone] —**des′o·late·ly** adv. —**des′o·late·ness** n. —**des′o·lat′er, des·o·la′tor** n.

des·o·la·tion (des′ə·lā′shən) n. 1 The state or condition of being desolate; loneliness; dreariness; sadness; affliction; grief. 2 A desolate region; a waste. 3 The act of making desolate; devastation.

de·sorp·tion (dē·sôrp′shən) n. *Chem.* The liberation or removal of a substance, usually gaseous, from the surface of adsorbing material: opposed to *adsorption.*

de·spair (di·spâr′) v.i. To lose or abandon hope; be or become hopeless: with *of.* —*v.t. Obs.* To lose hope or faith in. —n. 1 Utter hopelessness and discouragement. 2 That which causes despair or which is despaired of. [< OF *desperer* < L *desperare* < *de-* away + *sperare* hope < *spes* hope] —**de·spair′ing** adj. —**de·spair′ing·ly** adv.

Synonyms (noun): desperation, despondency, discouragement, hopelessness. *Discouragement* is the result of so much repulse or failure as wears out courage. *Discouragements* too frequent and long continued may produce a settled *hopelessness.* *Hopelessness* is negative, and may result from simple apathy; *despondency* and *despair* are more emphatic and decided. *Despondency* is an incapacity for the present exercise of hope; *despair* is the utter abandonment of hope. *Despondency* relaxes energy and effort and is always attended with sadness or distress; *despair* may produce a stony calmness, or it may lead to *desperation.* *Desperation* is energized *despair*, vigorous in action, reckless of consequences. *Antonyms:* anticipation, assurance, cheer, confidence, courage, elation, encouragement, expectancy, expectation, hope, hopefulness, trust.

des·per·ate (des′pər·it) adj. 1 Without care for danger; reckless, as from despair. 2 Resorted to in a last extremity; instigated by or denoting despair; hazardous; frantic; furious. 3 Regarded as almost irremediable; despaired of. 4 Utterly, hopelessly bad; outrageous. 5 Hopeless of recovery; irrecoverable: said especially of a money claim. 6 *Obs.* Despairing. [< L *desperatus*, pp. of *desperare.* See DESPAIR.] —**des′per·ate·ly** adv. —**des′per·ate·ness** n.

des·per·a·tion (des′pə·rā′shən) n. 1 The state of being desperate. 2 The act of despairing. 3 The recklessness of despair; blind fury. See synonyms under DESPAIR.

des·pi·ca·ble (des′pi·kə·bəl, di·spik′ə·bəl) adj. Capable of being, or deserving to be, despised; contemptible; mean; vile. See synonyms under BASE[2], PITIFUL. [< LL *despicabilis* < *despicere.* See DESPISE.] —**des′pi·ca·bil′i·ty, des′pi·ca·ble·ness** n. —**des′pi·ca·bly** adv.

de·spise (di·spīz′) v.t. **·spised, ·spis·ing** To regard as contemptible or worthless; disdain; scorn. See synonyms under ABHOR. [< OF *despis-*, stem of *despire* < L *despicere* < *de-* down + *specere* look at] —**de·spis′a·ble** adj. —**de·spis′er** n.

de·spite (di·spīt′) n. 1 An act of defiance, malice, or injury. 2 Extreme malice; hatred; spite. 3 *Obs.* Defiance. See synonyms under SCORN n. —**in despite of** Notwithstanding, in opposition to or contradiction to: He seized my hand *in despite of* my efforts to the contrary. —*prep.* In spite of; notwithstanding: They will fight on, *despite* impediments. See synonyms under NOTWITHSTANDING. Also **de·spight′.** —*v.t.* **·spit·ed, ·spit·ing** *Obs.* 1 To despise. 2 To offend. [< OF *despit* < L *despectus* < a looking down, contempt < *despicere.* See DESPISE.]

de·spoil (di·spoil′) v.t. To strip or deprive of something by or as by force; plunder. [< OF *despoillier* < L *despoliare* < *de-* completely + *spoliare* rob < *spolium* plunder] —**de·spoil′er** n. —**de·spoil′ment** n.

de·spo·li·a·tion (di·spō'lē·ā'shən) n. The act of despoiling, or state of being despoiled or plundered. [< LL *despoliatio, -onis* < *despoliare*. See DESPOIL.]

de·spond (di·spond') v.i. To lose spirit, courage, or hope; be depressed. —n. Obs. Despondency. [< L *despondere* < *de-* away + *spondere* promise]

de·spon·dent (di·spon'dənt) adj. Dejected in spirit; disheartened. Also **de·spond'ing.** See synonyms under SAD. —**de·spon'den·cy, de·spon'dence** n. —**de·spon'dent·ly** adv.

des·pot (des'pət, -pot) n. 1 An absolute monarch; autocrat; a hard master; tyrant. 2 In Oriental countries a title, originally of a Byzantine emperor; later, of various subordinate rulers: applied also to the bishops and patriarchs of the Greek Church. See synonyms under MASTER. [< OF < Gk. *despotēs* a master]

des·pot·ic (di·spot'ik) adj. Of or like a despot or despotism; tyrannical. See synonyms under ABSOLUTE, ARBITRARY, IMPERIOUS. —**des·pot'i·cal** adj. —**des·pot'i·cal·ly** adv. —**des·pot'i·cal·ness** n.

des·pot·ism (des'pə·tiz'əm) n. 1 Absolute power; autocracy. 2 Any tyrannical control.

des·pu·mate (des'pyōō·māt, di·spyōō'māt) v. **·mat·ed, ·mat·ing** v.t. 1 To skim. 2 To throw off as scum. —v.i. 3 To throw or work off impurities in froth or scum. [< L *despumatus*, pp. of *despumare* < *de-* away + *spumare* skim < *spuma* scum] —**des'pu·ma'tion** n.

des·qua·mate (des'kwə·māt) v.i. **·mat·ed, ·mat·ing** Pathol. To peel or scale off, as the epithelial cells in certain skin ailments. [< L *desquamatus*, pp. of *desquamare* < *de-* away + *squama* a scale]

des·qua·ma·tion (des'kwə·mā'shən) n. Pathol. The scaling off of the cuticle, as in measles and scarlatina.

des·sert (di·zûrt') n. A service of something sweet, as pie, cake, pudding, fruit, etc., at the close of lunch or dinner. [< F *desservir* clear a table < *des-* away + *servir* serve]

des·ti·na·tion (des'tə·nā'shən) n. 1 A predetermined end. 2 The point to which a journey, or the course of anything, is directed; goal. 3 A destining; appointment.

des·tine (des'tin) v.t. **·tined, ·tin·ing** 1 To design for or appoint to a distinct purpose or end. 2 To determine the future of, as by destiny or fate. See synonyms under ALLOT. [< F *destiner* < L *destinare* make fast, ult. < *de-* completely + *stare* stand]

des·tined (des'tind) adj. Bound for an appointed place; assigned to go to a place designated.

des·ti·ny (des'tə·nē) n. pl. **·nies** 1 That to which any person or thing is destined; fortune; doom. 2 Inevitable necessity; divine decree; fate. See synonyms under NECESSITY. [< OF *destinée* < *destiner*. See DESTINE.]

des·ti·tute (des'tə·tōōt, -tyōōt) adj. 1 Not having or possessing; entirely lacking: with *of.* 2 Being in want; extremely poor. 3 Obs. Desolate; forsaken. [< L *destitutus*, pp. of *destituere* abandon < *de-* down + *statuere* set, place]

des·ti·tu·tion (des'tə·tōō'shən, -tyōō'-) n. The state or condition of being destitute; extreme poverty. See synonyms under POVERTY.

de·stroy (di·stroi') v.t. 1 To ruin utterly; consume; dissolve. 2 To demolish; raze; tear down. 3 To put an end to; do away with. 4 To kill. 5 To make ineffective; counteract. See synonyms under ABOLISH, ANNUL, BREAK, DEMOLISH, EXTERMINATE, SUBVERT. [< OF *destruire*, ult. < L *destruere* < *de-* down + *struere* build]

de·stroy·er (di·stroi'ər) n. 1 One who or that which destroys. 2 A speedy war vessel, smaller than a cruiser, and equipped with guns, torpedo tubes, depth bombs, and anti-aircraft batteries: widely used as an escort vessel. 3 A self-propelled anti-tank gun: also **tank destroyer.**

de·struct (di·strukt') Aerospace n. The act of destroying a defective missile or rocket after launch. —v.t. & v.i. To destroy a defective missile or rocket after launch.

de·struc·ti·ble (di·struk'tə·bəl) adj. Liable to destruction; capable of being destroyed. —**de·struc'ti·bil'i·ty** n. —**de·struc'ti·ble·ness** n.

de·struc·tion (di·struk'shən) n. 1 The act of destroying, or state of being destroyed; demolition; ruin. 2 That which destroys. See synonyms under der LOSS, RUIN. [< OF < L *destructio, -onis* < *destruere*. See DESTROY.]

de·struc·tive (di·struk'tiv) adj. 1 Tending or fitted to destroy; causing destruction. 2 Pernicious; ruinous. See synonyms under NOISOME, PERNICIOUS. —**de·struc'tive·ly** adv. —**de·struc'tive·ness** n.

destructive distillation A process in which a complex organic substance such as wood or coal is decomposed by heat in the absence of air and the volatile components are recovered by condensation.

de·struc·tor (di·struk'tər) n. A furnace or retort for burning refuse.

des·ue·tude (des'wə·tōōd, -tyōōd) n. 1 The cessation of use. 2 A condition of disuse. [< MF *désuétude* < L *desuetudo* < *desuescere* < *de-* away + *suescere* be used]

de·sul·fur·ize (dē·sul'fə·rīz) v.t. **·ized, ·iz·ing** To remove sulfur from. Also **de·sul'fur, de·sul'fur·ate, de·sul'phur·ize. —de·sul'fur·i·za'tion** n. —**de·sul'fur·iz'er** n.

de·sul·to·ry (des'əl·tôr'ē, -tō'rē) adj. 1 Passing abruptly and irregularly from one thing to another; fitful; changeable; unmethodical. 2 Starting suddenly as if by a leap; not connected with what precedes. See synonyms under CURSORY, IRREGULAR. [< L *desultorius* < *desultor* a leaper < *de-* down + *salire* leap, jump] —**des'ul·to·ri·ly** adv. —**des'ul·to·ri·ness** n.

de·tach (di·tach') v.t. 1 To unfasten and make separate; disconnect; disunite. 2 To separate and send off for a special service, duty, etc., as a regiment or a ship. See synonyms under ABSTRACT. [< F *détacher* < *dé-* away (< L *dis-*) + OF *tache* nail < Gmc.] —**de·tach'a·bil'i·ty** n. —**de·tach'a·ble** adj. —**de·tach'er** n.

de·tached (di·tacht') adj. 1 Separated from others; disconnected; disunited. 2 Mil. Designated to special duty elsewhere than with the unit to which assigned, with or without transfer of administration. 3 Pertaining to relief from assignment or attachment and assumption of another status. 4 In painting, standing alone in the foreground or distinctly separate from other objects. 5 Aloof; hence, unbiased.

detached retina Pathol. A disconnection of the inner layers of the retina from the pigment layer.

de·tach·ment (di·tach'mənt) n. 1 A detaching; separation. 2 Something detached, as a body of troops for special service. 3 Dissociation from surroundings or worldly interest; aloofness.

de·tail (di·tāl', dē'tāl) n. 1 A separately considered particular or item; minor part; accessory. 2 Mil. A small detachment assigned to some subordinate service; also, the person or persons assigned. 3 In art and architecture, a minor part essential to the completeness and finish of a work, yet secondary and accessory. See synonyms under CIRCUMSTANCE. —**in detail** Item by item; with particularity. [< v.] —v.t. (di·tāl') 1 To report or narrate minutely; enter into or give the details of. 2 Mil. (often dē'tāl) To select and send off for a special service, duty, etc. See synonyms under RELATE. [< F *détailler* cut into pieces < *dé-* completely + *tailler* cut up]

de·tain (di·tān') v.t. 1 To restrain from proceeding; stop; delay. 2 To keep back; withhold. 3 To hold in custody. See synonyms under RETAIN. [< OF *detenir* < L *detinere* < *de-* away + *tenere* hold] —**de·tain'ment** n.

de·tain·er (di·tā'nər) n. 1 One who detains, stops, or withholds. 2 Law A process for recovering possession of lands or goods wrongfully held. b A writ directing the continued holding of a prisoner in custody pending an additional action. —**forcible detainer** The seizure by violence, or keeping possession of by threats, force, or the display of arms, of lands or tenements without authority of law.

de·tect (di·tekt') v.t. 1 To discover, perceive, or find, as something obscure: to *detect* an error in spelling. 2 To expose or uncover, as a crime, fault, or a criminal. 3 Telecom. To rectify (a high-frequency carrier wave) to the desired lower frequency; to demodulate. See synonyms under DISCOVER. [< L *detectus*, pp. of *detegere* < *de-* away + *tegere* cover]

de·tec·tion (di·tek'shən) n. 1 The act of detecting; discovery. 2 Telecom. Any method of operating on a modulated signal wave so as to obtain the signal imparted to it: a process of demodulation of incoming electrical signals.

de·tec·tive (di·tek'tiv) adj. 1 Skilled in or fitted for detection; employed to detect. 2 Belonging or pertaining to detectives and their work. —n. A person, often a policeman, whose work is to investigate crimes, discover evidence, capture criminals, etc.

de·tec·tor (di·tek'tər) n. 1 One who or that which detects. 2 A device for detecting, as for showing low water in a boiler, indicating the presence of torpedoes under water, etc. 3 Electr. A device for discovering the presence of electric waves, as a coherer; also, a portable galvanometer. 4 Telecom. A demodulator or a device for obtaining the signal from a modulated carrier.

de·ten·tion (di·ten'shən) n. 1 The act of detaining. 2 The state of being detained; restraint; custody; delay. [< L *detentio, -onis* < *detinere*. See DETAIN.] —**de·ten'tive** adj.

de·ter (di·tûr') v.t. **·terred, ·ter·ring** To prevent or restrain by fear, difficulty, danger, etc., from acting or proceeding. [< L *deterrere* < *de-* away + *terrere* frighten] —**de·ter'ment** n.

de·terge (di·tûrj') v.t. **·terged, ·terg·ing** 1 To cleanse of morbid or dead matter, as a wound. 2 To wipe off; purge away. [< L *detergere* < *de-* away + *tergere* wipe]

de·ter·gent (di·tûr'jənt) adj. Having cleansing qualities; purging. —n. 1 A cleansing substance, as soap or an antiseptic. 2 Chem. Any of a class of surface-active compounds having strong cleansing effects. —**de·ter'gence, de·ter'gen·cy** n.

de·te·ri·o·rate (di·tir'ē·ə·rāt) v.t. & v.i. **·rat·ed, ·rat·ing** To make or become worse; reduce in quality, value, etc.; degenerate. See synonyms under CORRUPT, IMPAIR. [< L *deterioratus*, pp. of *deteriorare* < *deterior* worse]

de·ter·mi·na·ble (di·tûr'mi·nə·bəl) adj. 1 That may be accurately found out, settled, or decided. 2 Law Liable to be put an end to; terminable.

de·ter·mi·nant (di·tûr'mə·nənt) adj. Determinative. —n. 1 That which influences to determine. 2 Math. A set of algebraic quantities arranged in a square matrix and operated upon according to special rules for the solution of various linear systems of equations. 3 Biol. A former name introduced by Weismann for one of the hypothetical secondary units of germ plasm or hereditary substance regulating the origin and the development of cells and systems of cells.

de·ter·mi·nate (di·tûr'mə·nit) adj. 1 Definitely limited or fixed; specific; distinct. 2 Predetermined; positive. 3 Known or fixed, as a mathematical quantity. 4 Bot. Limited in extent, as an inflorescence or cyme. 5 Determined; intended; determining; decisive. —**de·ter'mi·nate·ly** adv. —**de·ter'mi·nate·ness** n.

de·ter·mi·na·tion (di·tûr'mə·nā'shən) n. 1 The act of determining; a firm resolve. 2 The quality of being earnest and decided; firmness. 3 Judicial decision; authoritative opinion or conclusion. 4 The ascertaining exactly of the character, amount, dimensions, or proportion of a thing; the result of such investigation. 5 Logic The making of a notion definite or more definite by the addition of a qualifying or limiting idea; specification; also, an attribute which determines. 6 Biol. a The classification of plants and animals. b The process whereby the cells of a developing organism become differentiated in structure and function: sex *determination.* 7 Physiol. Tendency or increased flow, as of blood, to a part. 8 The exercise of decisive force or power: *determination* of the will toward an object. 9 Obs. A limiting or putting an end to.

Synonyms: decision, resolution, resolve. *Decision* is literally a cutting off, or cutting short, of debate or questioning; *determination* is a setting of the limits within which one must act; *resolve* is a separating of the essential act from all that might cause doubt or hesitation. *Resolve* always refers to, a single act; *resolution* may have the same meaning, or it may refer to the habit of mind which

readily forms and adheres to a *resolve.*
Decision and *determination* especially mark
the beginning of action; *resolution* holds out
to the end. See AIM, PURPOSE. Compare synonyms for DESIGN. Antonyms: doubt, faltering,
fickleness, hesitancy, hesitation, indecision,
instability, irresolution, vacillation, wavering.

de·ter·mi·na·tive (di·tûr′mə·nā′tiv, -mə·nə·tiv)
adj. Tending or having power'to determine or
fix; deciding; shaping. — *n.* **1** That which
determines. **2** *Gram.* A demonstrative pronoun. **3** *Ling.* In certain languages, an
element affixed to a word which modifies or
determines its meaning, as *-sc-* in Latin
calesco I grow warm, from *caleo* I am warm.

de·ter·mine (di·tûr′min) *v.* **·mined, ·min·ing** *v.t.*
1 To settle or decide, as an argument, question, or debate. **2** To ascertain or fix, as
after thought or observation. **3** To cause to
reach a decision. **4** To regulate; fix or decide
causally: Demand *determines* supply. **5** To
give aim, purpose, or direction to. **6** To set
bounds to; limit in extent, variety, etc.
7 *Logic* To limit or define by adding differences. **8** To limit; terminate: usually in legal
usage. — *v.i.* **9** To come to a decision;
resolve. **10** To come to an end: usually in
legal usage. See synonyms under PURPOSE.
[<OF *determiner* <L *determinare* < *de-* completely + *terminare* end < *terminum* a limit]

de·ter·min·er (di·tûr′mə·nər) *n.* **1** A person
or thing that determines. **2** *Gram.* Any of
a class of words, including articles and
possessive adjectives, whose presence in a
phrase, often before a descriptive adjective,
indicates that the head word is a noun or
substantive. In *his old coat,* "his" is a
determiner.

de·ter·min·ism (di·tûr′mə·niz′əm) *n.* *Philos.*
The doctrine that man's choices, decisions,
and actions are decided by antecedent causes,
inherited or environmental, acting upon his
character: opposed to *free will.* — **de·ter′min·**
ist *adj. & n.* — **de·ter′min·is′tic** *adj.*

de·ter·rent (di·tûr′ənt) *adj.* Tending or serving
to deter. — *n.* Something that deters. — **de·**
ter′rence *n.*

de·ter·sive (di·tûr′siv) *adj.* Cleansing; detergent. — *n.* A cleansing or purging medicine
or agent.

de·test (di·test′) *v.t.* To hate; dislike with
intensity; abhor. See synonyms under ABHOR.
[<MF *détester* <L *detestari* denounce < *de-*
away + *testis* a witness] — **de·test′er** *n.* — **de·**
test′a·bil′i·ty *n.* — **de·test′a·ble** *adj.* — **de·test′a·**
ble·ness *n.* — **de·test′a·bly** *adv.*

de·throne (dē·thrōn′) *v.t.* **·throned, ·thron·ing**
To remove from the throne; depose. — **de·**
throne′ment *n.* — **de·thron′er** *n.*

det·i·nue (det′i·nyoō) *n.* *Law* An action to
recover personal property wrongfully detained; the writ used in such action; also,
the act of detaining wrongfully. [<OF *de*
tenue, pp. of *detenir.* See DETAIN.]

det·o·nate (det′ə·nāt, dē′tə-) *v.* **·nat·ed, ·nat·**
ing *v.t.* To cause to explode suddenly and
with violence. — *v.i.* To explode suddenly with
a loud report. [<L *detonatus,* pp. of *deto*
nare < *de-* down + *tonare* thunder]

det·o·na·tor (det′ə·nā′tər, dē′tə-) *n.* Any contrivance, as a primer or fuze, for detonating
the main charge of a projectile, bomb, etc.

de·tor·sion (dē·tôr′shən) *n.* The act of twisting
back or removing torsion. [<DE- + TORSION]

de·tour (dē′toor, di·toor′) *n.* A roundabout
way; any turning aside from a direct route or
course of action; specifically, a byroad substituted for part of a main road temporarily
impassable. — *v.t. & v.i.* To go or cause to
go by a roundabout way. [<F *détour* <dé
tourner <dé- away + *tourner* turn]

de·tract (di·trakt′) *v.t.* **1** To take away; withdraw. **2** *Obs.* To disparage. — *v.i.* **3** To take
away a part, especially from a reputation,
enjoyment, honor, etc. [<L *detractus,* pp. of
detrahere <de- away + *trahere* draw, pull]

det·ri·ment (det′rə·mənt) *n.* **1** Something that
impairs or injures, or causes damage or loss. **2**
Injury or loss. See synonyms under INJURY,
LOSS. [<L *detrimentum* <*deterere* <de- away +
terere rub]

det·ri·men·tal (det′rə·men′təl) *adj.* Injurious;
hurtful. See synonyms under BAD, NOISOME. —
det′ri·men′tal·ly *adv.*

de·tri·tion (di·trish′ən) *n.* The act of rubbing or
wearing off particles.

de·tri·tus (di·trī′təs) *n.* **1** *Geol.* Loose fragments
or particles separated from masses of rock by
erosion, glacial action, and other mechanical
forces. **2** Any mass of disintegrated material; debris. [<L <*deterere.* See DETRIMENT.] —
de·tri′tal *adj.*

de·trude (di·trood′) *v.t.* **·trud·ed, ·trud·ing 1** To
thrust down or out. **2** To push down forcibly.
[<L *detrudere* <de- away + *trudere* thrust] —
de·tru′sion *n.* — **de·tru′sive** *adj.*

de·trun·cate (di·trung′kāt) *v.t.* **·cat·ed, ·cat·ing**
To shorten by cutting off a part; cut off. [<L *de*
truncatus, pp. of *detruncare* <de- from + *trun*
care lop] — **de·trun·ca′tion** *n.*

de·tu·mes·cence (dē′too·mes′əns, -tyoo-) *n.*
Physiol. **1** The subsidence of any swelling in an
organ or part. **2** Subsidence of the erectile tissue
of the genitals following the orgasm. —
de′tu·mes′cent *adj.*

deuce[1] (doos, dyoos) *n.* **1** Two; especially, a card
or side of a die having two spots. **2** In tennis, a
condition of the score when it is tied at 40 or at
five games each and either side must win two
successive points for the game or two successive
games for the set. [<F *deux* <L *duo* two]

deuce[2] (doos, dyoos) *n.* The devil; plague: a mild
oath used with or without the article in exclamation, signifying disgust or surprise at an unpleasant occurrence. [Prob. <LG *de duus* the
deuce (lowest throw at dice)]

deu·ced (doo′sid, dyoo′-, doost, dyoost) *adj.*
Devilish; confounded; exceeding. —*adv.*
Deucedly.

deu·ced·ly (doo′sid·lē, dyoo′-) *adv.* Extremely;
devilishly; confoundedly.

deu·ter·a·no·pi·a (doo′tər·ə·nō′pē·ə, dyoo′-) *n.*
Pathol. An eye defect which results in an inability to see the color green. Also **deu′ter·a·nop′si·a**
(-nop′sē·ə). [<DEUTER(O)- + Gk. *an-* without +
ops eye]

deu·ter·ic (doo·tir′ik, dyoo-) *adj. Chem.* Pertaining to an acid containing deuterium.

deu·ter·ide (doo′tə·rīd, dyoo′-) *n. Chem.* Any
compound of deuterium with an element or radical.

deu·te·ri·um (doo·tir′ē·əm, dyoo-) *n.* The isotope of hydrogen having twice the mass of ordinary hydrogen. Symbol, D or ^{2}H: also called
heavy hydrogen. [<NL <Gk. *deuteros* second]

deuterium oxide Heavy water.

deutero- *combining form* Second; secondary:
deuterogamy. Also, before vowels, **deuter-.**
[<Gk. *deuteros* second]

deu·ter·o·ca·non·i·cal (doo′tər·ō·kə·non′i·kəl,
dyoo′-) *adj.* Pertaining to or constituting a second canon: applied to the books or parts of
books of the Old and New Testament whose authenticity and inspiration were at first contested
and afterward admitted by the Roman Catholic
Church; in Protestant churches, the contested
parts of the Old Testament are considered extracanonical. See APOCRYPHA.

deu·ter·on (doo′tər·on, dyoo′-) *n. Physics* The
nucleus of a deuterium atom. [<NL <Gk.,
neut. sing. of *deuteros* second]

deu·ter·op·a·thy (doo′tər·op′ə·thē, dyoo′-) *n.*
Med. A disease associated with but secondary to
another disease. [<DEUTERO- + -PATHY] —
deu·ter·o·path·ic (doo′tər·ō·path′ik, dyoo′-) *adj.*

deuto- *combining form* Deutero-.

deu·to·plasm (doo′tə·plaz′əm, dyoo′-) *n. Biol.*
The nutritive material formed within the cytoplasm of a cell; the food yolk of an ovum or egg
cell. Also **deu·ter·o·plasm** (doo′tər·ō·plaz′əm,
dyoo′-). — **deu′to·plas′mic** or **·plas′tic** *adj.*

deut·zi·a (doot′sē·ə, doit′-) *n.* Any of a genus
(*Deutzia*) of ornamental shrubs having clusters
of pink or white flowers. [<Johann van
der *Deutz,* 1743–1784, Dutch horticulturist]

de·val·u·ate (dē·val′yoo·āt) *v.t.* **·at·ed, ·at·ing 1**
To reduce or annul the value or worth of. **2** To
establish the value of (a currency) at some point
below par. Also **de·val′ue.** —**de·val′u·a′tion** *n.*

dev·as·tate (dev′ə·stāt) *v.t.* **·tat·ed, ·tat·ing** To lay
waste, as by war, fire, flood, etc.; destroy; ravage. [<L *devastatus,* pp. of *devastare* <de- completely + *vastare* lay waste < *vastus* waste] —
dev′as·tat′ing *adj.* —**dev′as·tat′ing·ly** *adv.* —
dev′as·ta′tor *n.*

dev·as·ta·tion (dev′ə·stā′shən) *n.* The act of devastating or condition of having been devastated;
waste; desolation; ravage.

de·vel·op (di·vel′əp) *v.t.* **1** To expand or
bring out the potentialities, capabilities, etc.,

of; cause to come to completeness or perfection. **2** To expand; enlarge upon, as an idea.
3 To make more extensive or productive,
as atomic power. **4** *Phot.* **a** To bring to view
by means of a developer (the latent image)
produced on a sensitized surface by means of
light. **b** To subject (a plate or film) to a
developer. **5** *Biol.* To cause to evolve to a
higher stage, as in function or structure. **6**
Music To elaborate on (a theme). **7** *Math.*
To expand (an expression) in the form of a
series. **8** *Geom.* To change the form of
(a surface) as if by bending or unbending. **9**
Obs. To disclose; reveal. —*v.i.* **10** To increase in capabilities, maturity, etc. **11** To
advance from a lower to a higher state; grow;
evolve. **12** To disclose itself; become apparent: The plot of a novel *develops.* Also
de·vel′ope. See synonyms under AMPLIFY. [<F
développer <de- away (<L *dis-*) + OF *voluper*
fold] —**de·vel′op·a·ble** *adj.*

de·vel·op·er (di·vel′əp·ər) *n.* **1** One who or that
which develops. **2** One who builds housing,
shopping centers, etc., on a speculative basis. **3**
Phot. A chemical bath or reagent used for making a latent image visible on a photographic
plate.

de·vel·op·ment (di·vel′əp·mənt) *n.* **1** Gradual
evolution or completion; also, the result of such
an evolution or completion. **2** *Biol.* The series of
changes by which an individual plant or animal
passes from a lower to a higher state of being or
from an embryonic condition to maturity. See
synonyms under EDUCATION, PROGRESS. —
de·vel·op·men·tal (di·vel′əp·men′təl) *adj.* —
de·vel′op·men·tal·ly *adv.* —**de·vel′op·men′ta·ry**
(-tər·ē) *adj.*

de·vest (di·vest′) *v.t.* **1** *Law* To take away, as a title or estate. **2** *Obs.* To remove vesture from; divest; strip. [<OF *devester, desvestir* <de- from
(<L *dis-*) + *vestir* clothe <L *vestire* <*vestis* a
garment]

de·vi·ate (dē′vē·āt) *v.* **·at·ed, ·at·ing** *v.i.* **1** To turn
aside from a straight or appointed way or
course; wander; diverge. **2** To differ, as in
thought or belief. —*v.t.* **3** To cause to turn aside.
See synonyms under BEND[1], WANDER. [<LL *de*
viatus, pp. of *deviare* <de- from + *via* a road] —
de·vi·a·tor *n.* —**de·vi·a·to·ry** (dē′vē·ə·tôr′ē,
-tō′rē) *adj.*

de·vi·a·tion (dē′vē·ā′shən) *n.* **1** The act of deviating, or its result. **2** Variation or deflection from a
straight line, from a prescribed course, or from a
customary method or standard. **3** *Stat.* The difference between one value in a series of observations and the arithmetic mean of the series.

de·vice (di·vīs′) *n.* **1** Something invented and
constructed for a special purpose; contrivance. **2**
A plan or scheme; an artifice; stratagem; plot. **3**
A fanciful design or pattern, as in embroidery or
ornamentation. **4** A motto or emblem, as on a
shield. **5** The act, state, or power of devising; inventive skill. **6** Expressed desire; inclination: now
only in the phrase *left to one's own devices.* **7** *Obs.*
Design or style of anything; cast of mind. **8** *Obs.*
A spectacle; show; masque. See synonyms under
ARTIFICE, DESIGN, PROJECT. [<OF *devis* intention, will <*diviser,* infl. by OF *devise* emblem,
design. See DEVISE.]

dev·il (dev′əl) *n.* **1** *Sometimes cap.* In Jewish
and Christian theology, the prince and ruler
of the kingdom of evil; Satan. **2** Any subordinate evil spirit; a demon. **3** In Christian
Science usage, Evil; a lie; error; neither corporeality nor mind; opposite of Truth; a
belief in sin, sickness, and death; animal
magnetism or hypnotism. **4** A wicked or
malignant person. **5** A wretched fellow: poor
devil. **6** A person of great energy, daring,
or effrontery. **7** A machine for any of various
purposes, as for cutting or tearing up rags.
8 A printer's apprentice or errand boy: also
printer's devil. 9 An expletive used profanely
or humorously: with *the.* **10** In English law,
a junior barrister who prepares a case for a
senior, receiving little or no pay. —**between
the devil and the deep blue sea** Between
equally bad alternatives; in a dilemma. —**the
devil to pay** Trouble to be expected as a con-

sequence. —**to give the devil his due** To acknowledge the ability or success of even a bad or disliked person, antagonist, etc. —*v.t.* **dev·iled** or **·illed, dev·il·ing** or **·il·ling 1** To prepare for eating by seasoning highly and sometimes broiling or frying. **2** To make fiendish. **3** To cut up, as cloth, in a devil. **4** To annoy or harass excessively; tease. [OE *dēofol* < LL *diabolus* < Gk. *diabolos* a slanderer; later, the devil < *diaballein* slander < *dia-* across + *ballein* throw]

dev·il·fish (dev′əl-fish′) *n. pl.* **·fish** or **·fish·es 1** Any of a family (*Mobulidae*) of very large top-swimming rays having a pair of fins projecting from the head with which they sweep small prey into the mouth. Also called *devil ray, manta, manta ray.* **2** The octopus.

DEVILFISH
(Often 20 feet in breadth)

devil grass Any of the several spreading, injurious grasses.

dev·il·ish (dev′əl·ish, dev′lish) *adj.* **1** Having the qualities of the devil; diabolical; malicious. **2** *Colloq.* Excessive; enormous. —*adv. Colloq.* Excessively; very. See synonyms under INFERNAL.

dev·il-may-care (dev′əl·mā·kâr′) *adj.* Careless; reckless; rollicking.

dev·il·ment (dev′əl·mənt) *n.* Mischief; impish action or tricks.

dev·il·ry (dev′əl·rē) *n. pl.* **·ries 1** Malicious mischief; deviltry. **2** Evil magic or art; demonology.

devil's advocate 1 A Roman Catholic official whose duty is to raise objections to a candidate for beatification or canonization. **2** One who argues perversely or for a bad cause.

dev·il's-darn·ing-nee·dle (dev′əlz-där′ning-nēd′l) *n.* **1** A dragonfly. **2** The Venus's-comb. Also **dev′il-darn′ing-nee′dle.**

dev·il's-food cake (dev′əlz-fōōd′) A rich, reddish-brown chocolate cake.

dev·il·wood (dev′əl-wōōd′) *n.* The American olive (*Osmanthus americanus*), a small tree of the southern Atlantic states, with a fine-grained, hard wood.

de·vi·ous (dē′vē·əs) *adj.* **1** Winding or leading away from a straight course; rambling. **2** Straying from the way of duty. See synonyms under IRREGULAR. [< L *devius* < *de-* from + *via* way]

de·vis·a·ble (di·vī′zə·bəl) *adj.* **1** *Law* That can be devised, or given by will. **2** That can be contrived or invented.

de·vi·sal (di·vī′zəl) *n.* The act of contriving or of bequeathing; a devising.

de·vise (di·vīz′) *v.* **·vised, ·vis·ing** *v.t.* **1** To form in the mind; invent; contrive; plan. **2** *Law* To transmit (real estate) by will. **3** *Obs.* To separate; distribute. **4** *Obs.* To imagine; guess. —*v.i.* **5** To form a plan. —*n. Law* **1** A gift of lands by will. **2** The act of bequeathing lands. **3** A will, or a clause in a will conveying real estate. [< OF *deviser* divide, distinguish, contrive < L *dividere* < *dis-* apart + *videre* see] —**de·vis′er** *n.*

de·vi·tal·ize (dē·vī′tal·īz) *v.t.* **·ized, ·iz·ing 1** To deprive of vital power or of the power to sustain life. **2** To destroy the vitality of; make weak. —**de·vi′tal·i·za′tion** *n.*

de·vit·ri·fi·ca·tion (dē·vit′rə·fi·kā′shən) *n.* The conversion of glassy to crystalline or lithoidal texture by slow crystallization after solidification.

de·vit·ri·fy (dē·vit′rə·fī) *v.t.* **·fied, ·fy·ing 1** To remove the glassy quality of. **2** To render opaque and hard like porcelain by long-continued great heat: said of glass. [< DE- from + VITRIFY]

de·vo·cal·ize (dē·vō′kəl·īz) *v.t.* **·ized, ·iz·ing** *Phonet.* To deprive of voice or of vocal quality.

de·voiced (dē·voist′) *adj. Phonet.* Unvoiced.

de·void (di·void′) *adj.* Not possessing; destitute: with *of.* [ME *devoided,* pp. of obs. *devoid* empty out < OF *devoidier* < *de-* down (< L *de-*) + *voidier* VOID]

dev·o·lu·tion (dev′ə·lōō′shən) *n.* **1** The act of delivering to another; a passing to a successor. **2** *Biol.* a Degeneration: opposed to *evolution.* b Involution. c Catabolism. **3** The delegation or sur-

render of the powers of a central government to local authorities. [< Med. L *devolutio, -onis* < *devolvere.* See DEVOLVE.]

de·volve (di·volv′) *v.* **·volved, ·volv·ing** *v.t.* **1** To cause to pass to a successor or substitute. **2** *Archaic* To roll down. —*v.i.* **3** To pass from a possessor to a successor or substitute: with *to, on,* or *upon.* [< L *devolvere* < *de-* down + *volvere* roll] —**de·volve′ment** *n.*

de·vote (di·vōt′) *v.t.* **·vot·ed, ·vot·ing 1** To give or apply (attention, time, or oneself) completely to some activity, purpose, etc. **2** To set apart; dedicate; consecrate. **3** *Obs.* To doom. [< L *devotus,* pp. of *devovere* < *de-* away + *vovere* vow] —**de·vote′ment** *n.*

de·vot·ed (di·vō′tid) *adj.* **1** Feeling or showing devotion; ardent; zealous; devout. **2** Set apart, as by a vow; consecrated. **3** *Obs.* Doomed. See synonyms under ADDICTED, FAITHFUL, HOLY. —**de·vot′ed·ly** *adv.* —**de·vot′ed·ness** *n.*

dev·o·tee (dev′ə·tē′) *n.* One zealously devoted, especially to religious observances; a votary; zealot. —**dev′o·tee′ism** *n.*

de·vo·tion (di·vō′shən) *n.* **1** The state of being devoted, as to religious faith or duty; zeal. **2** Strong attachment or affection expressing itself in earnest service. **3** *Usually pl.* An act of worship; prayer. **4** The act of devoting. See synonyms under ALLEGIANCE, ATTACHMENT, ENTHUSIASM, FIDELITY, FRIENDSHIP, LOVE, PRAYER, RELIGION. —**de·vo′tion·al** *adj.* —**de·vo′tion·al·ism** *n.* —**de·vo′tion·al·ly** *adv.*

de·vour (di·vour′) *v.t.* **1** To eat up greedily and voraciously. **2** To destroy; waste: The disease *devoured* him. **3** To take in greedily with the senses: He *devoured* the book. **4** To engross the attention of. **5** To engulf; absorb. [< OF *devorer* < L *devorare* < *de-* down + *vorare* gulp, swallow]. —**de·vour′er** *n.* —**de·vour′ing** *adj.* —**de·vour′ing·ly** *adv.* —**de·vour′ing·ness** *n.*

de·vout (di·vout′) *adj.* **1** Earnestly religious; pious; reverent. **2** Warmly devoted; heart-felt; sincere. **3** Containing or expressing devotion, especially religious devotion. [< OF *devot* < L *devotus.* See DEVOTE.] —**de·vout′ly** *adv.* —**de·vout′ness** *n.*

dew (dōō, dyōō) *n.* **1** Moisture condensed from the atmosphere in small drops upon the cool surfaces of plants and other bodies. **2** Anything moist, gentle, or refreshing as dew or suggesting the freshness of dewy morning: the *dew* of sleep, the *dew* of youth. **3** Moisture generally, especially that which appears in minute drops, as perspiration, tears, etc. —*v.t.* To wet with or as with dew; bedew. ♦ Homophone: **due.** [OE *dēaw*] —**dew′less** *adj.*

dew·ber·ry (dōō′ber′ē, -bər·ē, dyōō′-) *n. pl.* **·ries 1** The fruit of the low blackberry (genus *Rubus*). **2** The plant bearing it.

dew·claw (dōō′klô, dyōō′-) *n.* **1** A rudimentary toe in some dogs. **2** The false rudimentary hoof above the true hoof of hogs, deer, etc. —**dew′clawed′** *adj.*

dew·drop (dōō′drop′, dyōō′-) *n.* A drop of dew.

dew·lap (dōō′lap′, dyōō′-) *n.* **1** The pendulous skin under the throat of cattle. **2** Something likened to a dewlap, as the wattles of a turkey, or the flaccid skin sometimes seen under the chin of an aged person. [ME *dewlappe* < *dew,* origin uncertain + *lappe,* OE *læppe* lobe, fold] —**dew′lapped′** *adj.*

dew point *Meteorol.* **1** The temperature at which dew forms or condensation occurs. **2** The temperature at which a given mass of air will have a relative humidity of 100.

dew·y (dōō′ē, dyōō′ē) *adj.* **dew·i·er, dew·i·est 1** Moist, as with dew. **2** Of, like, or yielding dew. **3** Appearing as if covered with dewdrops. —**dew′i·ness** *n.*

dex·ter (dek′stər) *adj.* **1** Right-hand; right. **2** *Her.* On the wearer's right, the spectator's left. **3** Auspicious; favorable; propitious. [< L, right]

dex·ter·i·ty (dek·ster′ə·tē) *n.* **1** Readiness and skill in using the hands; expertness. **2** Mental quickness, adroitness, or skill. [< L *dexteritas, -tatis* skill, aptness < *dexter* on the right]

Synonyms: adroitness, aptitude, cleverness, expertness, readiness, skill. *Adroitness* and *dexterity*

might each be rendered "right-handedness"; but *adroitness* carries more of the idea of eluding, parrying, or checking some hostile movement, or taking advantage of another in controversy; *dexterity* conveys the idea of doing, accomplishing something readily and well, without reference to any action of others. We speak of *adroitness* in fencing, boxing, or debate; of *dexterity* in horsemanship, in the use of tools, weapons, etc. *Aptitude* is a natural *readiness,* which by practice may be developed into *dexterity. Skill* is more exact to line, rule, and method than *dexterity. Dexterity* can not be communicated; *skill* to a very great extent can be imparted. Compare ABILITY, ADDRESS, INGENUITY, POWER.

dex·ter·ous (dek′strəs, -stər·əs) *adj.* **1** Possessing dexterity; skilful or adroit; artful. **2** Done with dexterity. Also **dex·trous** (dek′strəs). See synonyms under CLEVER, GOOD, HAPPY. —**dex′ter·ous·ly, dex′trous·ly** *adv.* —**dex′ter·ous·ness, dex′trous·ness** *n.*

dex·trad (dek′strad) *adv. Anat.* On or toward the right hand or side. [< L *dexter* right + *ad* to]

dex·tral (dek′strəl) *adj.* **1** Of, pertaining to, or situated on the right side; right-hand or right-handed. **2** Propitious; favorable: said of omens. —**dex′tral·ly** *adv.* —**dex·tral·i·ty** (dek·stral′ə·tē) *n.*

dex·tran (dek′stran) *n. Biochem.* A white, gumlike substance produced by bacterial action in milk, molasses, beet juice, etc.: used as a substitute for blood plasma in the treatment of severe burns and shock. [< DEXTR(O)- + -AN(E)]

dex·trin (dek′strin) *n. Biochem.* An amorphous, colorless, water-soluble, dextrorotatory carbohydrate formed by the action of acids, heat, or diastase on starch: used as a substitute for gum arabic. Also **dex·trine** (dek′strin, -strēn). [< DEXTR(O)- + IN]

dextro- *combining form* Turned or turning to the right: used especially in chemistry and physics, as in *dextrorotatory.* Also, before vowels, **dextr-.** [< L *dexter* right]

dex·tro·ro·ta·tion (dek′strə·rō·tā′shən) *n. Optics* Clockwise rotation of the plane of polarization of light.

dex·tro·ro·ta·to·ry (dek′strə·rō′tə·tôr′ē, -tō′rē) *adj. Chem.* Causing the plane of polarization of light to rotate to the right or clockwise: said of certain crystals and compounds: opposed to *levorotatory.* Also **dex·tro·gy·rate** (dek′strə·jī′rāt), **dex·tro·ro·ta·ry** (dek′strə·rō′tər·ē).

dex·trorse (dek′strôrs, dek·strôrs′) *adj. Bot.* Rising spirally toward the right: opposed to *sinistrorse;* said of the morning-glory. Also **dex·tror′sal.** [< L *dextrorsum, dextrovorsum* < *dexter* right + *vertere* turn] —**dex′trorse·ly** *adv.*

dex·trose (dek′strōs) *n. Biochem.* The dextrorotatory form of glucose. Also called **dex·tro·glu·cose** (dek′strə·glōō′kōs) [< DEXTR(O)- + (GLUC)OSE]

dhak (däk, dôk) *n.* A tree of India and Burma (*Butea monosperma*) having trifoliolate leaves and bright orange-red flowers. [< Hind.]

dhar·ma (där′mə, dûr′-) *n.* **1** In Hinduism and Buddhism, right behavior; conformity to law; hence, truth and righteousness. **2** In Buddhism, the law which, together with Buddha and Sangha, forms the three Ratnas or treasures of Buddhism. [< Skt., law]

di- *prefix* **1** Twice; double: *digraph.* **2** *Chem.* Containing two atoms, molecules, radicals, etc.: *dichloride.* Also, before *s, dis-,* as in *dissyllable.* [Gk. *di-* < *dis* twice]

dia- *prefix* Through; across; between: *diagonal.* Also, before vowels, **di-.** [< Gk. *dia-* through]

di·a·base (dī′ə·bās) *n. Geol.* A granular igneous rock, composed essentially of plagioclase, and characterized by the feldspar having crystallized before the augite: sometimes called *dolerite.* [< Gk. *diabasis* a crossing over < *dia-* across + *bainein* go] —**di′a·ba′sic** *adj.*

di·a·be·tes (dī′ə·bē′tis, -tēz) *n. Pathol.* A disease associated with inadequate production of insulin by the pancreas and ordinarily characterized by excessive urinary secretion containing an abnormal quantity of sugar. In the form distinguished as **diabetes mel·li·tus**

(mə·lī'təs), there is also emaciation with excessive hunger and thirst. [<NL <Gk. *diabētēs* a passer through < *dia-* through + *bainein* go]

di·a·bet·ic (dī'ə·bet'ik, -bē'tik) *adj. Med.* Of, pertaining to, or affected by diabetes. Also **di'a·bet'i·cal.** — *n.* One who has diabetes.

di·a·ble·rie (dē·ä'blə·rē, *Fr.* dyȧ·blȧ·rē') *n.* 1 Demonology. 2 Fantastic and perverse behavior; deviltry; impishness. 3 Sorcery. Also **di·a'ble·ry.** [<F <*diable* devil]

di·a·bol·ic (dī'ə·bol'ik) *adj.* Of, pertaining to, or like the devil; satanic; fiendish; infernal. Also **di'a·bol'i·cal.** [<Gk. *diabolikos* < *diabolos.* See DEVIL.] — **di'a·bol'i·cal·ly** *adv.* — **di'a·bol'i·cal·ness** *n.*

di·ab·o·lism (dī·ab'ə·liz'əm) *n.* 1 Conduct befitting or inspired by the devil; devilishness. 2 Possession by the devil or devils. 3 In occultism, the conjuration or raising of evil spirits; sorcery. 4 A system of belief or doctrine in which devils are worshiped. 5 A devilish nature or disposition. — **di·ab'o·list** *n.*

di·a·caus·tic (dī'ə·kôs'tik) *adj. Optics* Denoting a caustic curve formed by refracted rays: opposed to *catacaustic.* — *n.* 1 A diacaustic curve. 2 Formerly, a burning glass for cauterization. [<DIA- + CAUSTIC (def. 3)]

di·a·cet·yl·mor·phine (dī·as'ə·təl·môr'fēn) *n.* Heroin.

di·a·chron·ic (dī'ə·kron'ik) *adj.* 1 Existing through time. 2 *Ling.* Pertaining to the study of the historical development of a language in any of its aspects. See SYNCHRONIC.

di·ach·y·lon (dī·ak'ə·lon) *n. Med.* 1 A plaster formed by combining lead oxide, olive oil, and water; lead or litharge plaster. 2 A mixture of mucilaginous vegetable juices, gums, etc., formerly used in making plasters and salves. Also **diachylon plaster, di·ach'·y·lum** (-ə·ləm). [<Med. L *diachylum* <L *diachylon* <Gk. *dia chylōn* made of juices; orig. referring to an ointment made of vegetable juices]

di·ac·id (dī·as'id) *adj. Chem.* 1 Capable of combining with two molecules of a monoacid or with one of a diacid: said of bases and alcohols. 2 Having two hydrogen atoms replaceable by radicals or atoms: said of acids. — *n.* An acid containing two hydrogen atoms.

di·ac·o·nate (dī·ak'ə·nit, -nāt) *n.* 1 The office, rank, or tenure of a deacon. 2 Deacons collectively. [<LL *diaconatus*]

di·a·crit·ic (dī'ə·krit'ik) *n.* 1 A mark, point, or sign attached to a letter to indicate its exact phonetic value, or to distinguish it from another letter: also **diacritical mark.** For a complete listing of the diacritics used in this book, see page xx. 2 A differential diagnosis. — *adj.* Of or pertaining to a diacritic. [<Gk. *diakritikos* distinguishing < *diakrinein* < *dia-* between + *krinein* distinguish]

di·a·crit·i·cal (dī'ə·krit'i·kəl) *adj.* 1 Marking a difference; distinguishing; distinctive. 2 Indicating certain variations of sounds or of form. 3 *Electr.* Denoting a current sufficient to magnetize a solenoid core to half-saturation. — **di'a·crit'i·cal·ly** *adv.*

di·ac·tin·ic (dī'ak·tin'ik) *adj.* Capable of transmitting actinic or chemical rays: said of a body or substance. — **di·ac'tin·ism** *n.*

di·a·del·phous (dī'ə·del'fəs) *adj. Bot.* Having the stamens combined by their filaments so as to form two sets or bundles. Also **di·a·del'phi·an.** [<Gk. *di-* two + *adelphos* brother]

di·a·dem (dī'ə·dem) *n.* 1 A symbol of royalty worn upon the head; a crown. 2 Regal power; sovereignty. — *v.t.* To decorate with or as with a diadem; crown. [<OF *diademe* <L *diadema* <Gk. *diadēma* < *dia-* across + *deein* bind]

DIADEL-PHOUS STAMENS Common in papilionaceous flowers in this arrangement.

di·aer·e·sis (dī·er'ə·sis), **di·ae·ret·ic** (dī'ə·ret'ik) See DIERESIS.

di·a·ge·ot·ro·pism (dī'ə·jē·ot'rə·piz'əm) *n. Bot.* Transverse or oblique geotropism: an arrangement of plant organs at right angles to the direction of gravitation. [<DIA- + GEOTROPISM] — **di·a·ge·o·trop·ic** (dī'ə·jē'ə·trop'ik, -trō'pik) *adj.*

di·ag·nose (dī'əg·nōs', -nōz') *v.* **·nosed, ·nos·ing** *v.t.* To examine or distinguish by diagnosis. — *v.i.* To make a diagnosis of a person, disease, etc.

di·ag·no·sis (dī'əg·nō'sis) *n.* 1 *Med.* **a** The art or act of discriminating between diseases and of distinguishing them by their characteristic symptoms. **b** A summary of symptoms and the conclusion arrived at. 2 *Biol.* Scientific discrimination between similar or related things or conditions for the purpose of accurate classification. [<Gk. *diagnōsis* < *diagignōskein* < *dia-* between + *gignōskein* know] — **di·ag·nos·tic** (dī'əg·nos'tik) *adj.* — **di·ag·nos'ti·cal·ly** *adv.*

di·ag·nos·ti·cian (dī'əg·nos·tish'ən) *n.* One who is versed in diagnosis.

di·ag·nos·tics (dī'əg·nos'tiks) *n.* The science or recognized principles of diagnosis.

di·ag·o·nal (dī·ag'ə·nəl) *adj.* 1 Crossing obliquely; oblique. 2 Marked by oblique lines or the like. 3 *Geom.* **a** Joining two non-adjacent or reentering angles of a figure: a *diagonal* line. **b** Joining, as a plane, two non-adjacent edges of a solid. — *n.* 1 *Geom.* A straight line or plane passing from one angle, as of a square, to any other angle not adjacent. 2 A fabric woven with diagonal ridges or lines: also **diagonal cloth.** 3 Anything running diagonally. [<L *diagonalis* < *diagonios* < *dia-* across + *gonia* angle] — **di·ag'o·nal·ly** *adv.*

di·a·gram (dī'ə·gram) *n.* 1 A line drawing, mechanical plan, or outline, as distinguished from a perspective drawing. 2 A rough projection, map, chart, etc. 3 A figure drawn to aid in demonstrating a geometrical proposition or to illustrate geometrical relations. 4 An outline figure intended to represent any object or area, or to show the relation between parts or places, or to illustrate the value or relations of quantities, forces, etc. 5 A graph. — *v.t.* **·gramed** or **·grammed, ·gram·ing** or **·gram·ming** 1 To represent by diagram. 2 To illustrate by a diagram. [<Gk. *diagramma* < *dia-* across + *graphein* write] — **di·a·gram·mat·ic** (dī'ə·grə·mat'ik) or **·i·cal** *adj.* — **di'a·gram·mat'i·cal·ly** *adv.*

diagram factor *Mech.* In the cylinder of a steam engine, the ratio between the actual average pressure and the ideal pressure as shown on an indicator diagram.

di·a·graph (dī'ə·graf, -gräf) *n.* A protractor and scale combined for drawing diagrams. [<DIA- + -GRAPH]

di·a·he·li·ot·ro·pism (dī'ə·hē'lē·ot'rə·piz'əm) *n. Bot.* A turning of plant organs so as to assume a position transverse to the light; transverse heliotropism. — **di·a·he·li·o·trop·ic** (dī'ə·hē'lē·ə·trop'ik, -trō'pik) *adj.*

di·al (dī'əl, dīl) *n.* 1 Any graduated circular plate or face, as of a watch, clock, gage, mariner's compass, or radio receiving set. 2 A plate bearing letters and numbers, used to make connections in an automatic telephone system. 3 A device for indicating time by means of the shadow of a gnomon or style thrown upon a graduated plate; a sundial. 4 A compass; especially, a miner's compass for underground surveying. 5 *Obs.* Any timepiece. — *v.t.* & *v.i.* **di·aled** or **di·alled, di·al·ing** or **di·al·ling** 1 To measure or survey with a dial. 2 To turn or adjust a dial; indicate on a dial. 3 To call by means of a telephone. 4 To adjust a radio or television set to (a station, program, etc.). [<Med. L *dialis* daily <L *dies* day] — **di'al·er, di'al·ler** *n.* — **di'al·ist, di'al·list** *n.*

di·a·lect (dī'ə·lekt) *n.* 1 A variety of speech distinguished from the standard or literary language by variations of idiom, vocabulary, phonology, and morphology peculiar to a particular geographical location: the Southern *dialect* of American English. 2 A manner of speech adopted by the members of a class, trade, or profession; jargon; cant: the *dialect* of the cultured. 3 An imperfect use of the standard language by those to whom another language is native. 4 A language developed from a root language, retaining recognizable elements of the parent but having distinctive vocabulary, pronunciation, forms, and idiom; a linguistic branch: The Romance languages are *dialects* of Latin. See synonyms under LANGUAGE. [<MF *dialecte* <L *dialectus* <Gk. *dialektos* discourse, way of speaking < *dialegesthai* < *dia-* across +

legesthai speak]

di·a·lec·tal (dī'ə·lek'təl) *adj.* Of or characterized by a dialect. Abbr. *dial.*

di·a·lec·tic (dī'ə·lek'tik) *adj.* 1 Formerly, dialectal. 2 Pertaining to dialectics; logical; argumentative. Also **di'a·lec'ti·cal.** — *n.* 1 *Usually pl.* The art or practice of examining logically, as by a method of question and answer. 2 A specific mode of argument. [<OF *dialectique* <L *dialectica* <Gk. *dialektika* (*technē*) (art) of discourse < *dialektos.* See DIALECT.]

dialectical materialism A socio-economic theory introduced by Karl Marx and Friedrich Engels, according to which history and the forms of society are interpreted as the result of conflicts between social classes arising from their relations to the means of production.

di·a·lec·ti·cism (dī'ə·lek'tə·siz'əm) *n.* 1 The character or nature distinguishing a dialect. 2 A dialectal word or peculiarity. 3 The practice of dialectics.

di·al·ing (dī'əl·ing) *n.* 1 The act of using a dial. 2 The measurement of time by sundials; the art of making sundials. 3 Underground surveying with a dial, especially in mines. Also **di'al·ling.**

di·al·lage (dī'ə·lij) *n.* A brown, gray, or green, thin-foliated variety of pyroxene, crystallizing in the monoclinic system. [<F <Gk. *diallagē* an interchange < *dia-* across + *allassein* change]

di·al·o·gism (dī·al'ə·jiz'əm) *n.* 1 A dialogue or discussion; especially, a discourse with oneself. 2 *Logic* An inference with a single premise and disjunctive conclusion.

di·al·o·gist (dī·al'ə·jist) *n.* One who writes or takes part in a dialogue. — **di·a·lo·gis·tic** (dī'ə·lō·jis'tik) or **·ti·cal** *adj.*

di·a·logue (dī'ə·lôg, -log) *n.* 1 A conversation in which two or more take part. 2 A literary work in which two or more characters are represented as conversing. 3 An exchange of opinions or ideas; free interchange of different points of view; discussion: to propose a *dialogue* among the Christian churches. See synonyms under CONVERSATION. — *v.* **·logued, ·logu·ing** *v.t.* To express in dialogue form. — *v.i.* To carry on a dialogue. Also **di'a·log.** [<F <*dialogus* <Gk. *dialogos* < *dialegesthai.* Related to DIALECT.]

dial tone The low, steady, humming tone indicating to the user of a dial telephone that a call may be put through, or that a connection has been broken. Compare BUSY SIGNAL.

di·al·y·sis (dī·al'ə·sis) *n.* *pl.* **·ses** (-sēz) 1 *Bot.* Separation of parts previously or normally joined together. 2 *Chem.* The separating of solutions of mixed substances of unequal diffusibility by means of moist membranes or septa; specifically, the separation of a colloid from a substance in true solution. See OSMOSIS. [<Gk. *dialysis* < *dialyein* < *dia-* completely + *lyein* loosen] — **di·a·lyt·ic** (dī'ə·lit'ik) *adj.*

di·a·lyze (dī'ə·līz) *v.t.* **·lyzed, ·lyz·ing** *Chem.* To subject to or prepare by dialysis; separate by dialysis.

di·a·lyz·er (dī'ə·lī'zər) *n. Chem.* An apparatus used for dialysis, especially a membranous septum stretched over a gutta-percha ring.

di·a·mag·net·ic (dī'ə·mag·net'ik) *adj. Physics* 1 Pertaining to or designating the property of substances tending to lie at right angles to the poles of a magnet. 2 Having a negative magnetic susceptibility, or a permeability less than that of a vacuum, as bismuth or copper. — *n.* A substance that possesses such properties. — **di'a·mag'net·ism** *n.* — **di'a·mag·net'i·cal·ly** *adv.*

di·am·e·ter (dī·am'ə·tər) *n.* 1 A straight line passing through the center of a figure or body and terminated at the boundaries thereof. 2 The length of such a line. 3 The thickness of an object as measured by such a line. [<OF *diametre* <L *diametrus* <Gk. *diametros* < *dia-* through + *metron* measure]

di·a·met·ri·cal (dī'ə·met'ri·kəl) *adj.* 1 Of or pertaining to a diameter; coinciding with a diameter: also **di·am·e·tral** (dī·am'ə·trəl). 2 Of or pertaining to the ends of a diameter; directly opposite, and as far removed as possible: also **di'a·met'ric.**

di·a·met·ri·cal·ly (dī'ə·met'rik·lē) *adv.* 1 In the manner of a diameter. 2 Irreconcilably: *diametrically* opposed.

di·am·ine (dī·am'ēn, -in, dī'ə·mēn, -min) *n.*

Chem. Any of a group of compounds containing two amino radicals; a double amine. Also **di·am·in** (dī-am'in, dī'ə-min).

dia·mond (dī'mənd, dī'ə-) *n.* **1** A mineral of great hardness and refractive power, consisting of carbon crystallized in the isometric system under great pressure and temperature. When pure it is a valuable gem with a beautiful display of prismatic colors, especially when cut. See list below. **2** A natural crystal face of this stone, used in cutting glass, etc. **3** *Geom.* A figure bounded by four equal straight lines, and having two of the angles

FORMS OF CUT
DIAMONDS
a.b.c. Brilliant cut.
d. Marquise cut.
e. Pitt or regent cut.
f. Kohinor cut.
g. Double rose (side view) cut.
h. Rose cut.
i. Briolette cut.

acute and two obtuse; a rhomb or lozenge. **4** *Printing* A size of type next above brilliant; 4- or 4 1/2-point. **5** A lozenge-shaped spot on a playing card, or a card or (in the plural) suit so marked. **6** The square enclosed by the lines between the bases on a baseball field. — *v.t.* To adorn with or as with diamonds. [<OF *diamant* <LL *daimas, -antis,* alter. of L *adamas.* Doublet of ADAMANT.] — **dia'mond·ed** *adj.*

dia·mond–back (dī'mənd·bak', dī'ə-) *n.* **1** An edible turtle (*Malaclemys centrata*) inhabiting salt marshes of the southern United States, having diamond-shaped markings on the shell: also **diamond–back terrapin. 2** A large rattlesnake (*Crotalus adamanteus*) of the SE United States, having diamond-shaped markings on the back: also **dia'mond–rat'tler.**

di·an·drous (dī·an'drəs) *adj. Bot.* Having two stamens. [<NL *diandrus* <Gk. *di-* two + *anēr, andros* man, male]

di·a·no·et·ic (dī'ə·nō·et'ik) *adj. Logic* Of or pertaining to a rational or discursive faculty or its products or acts; intellectual; discursive. — *n.* Logic as treating of reasoning. [<Gk. *dianoētikos* of thinking < *dia-* through + *noeein* think < *nous* mind]

di·an·thus (dī·an'thəs) *n.* Any plant of an extensive genus (*Dianthus*) of ornamental herbs of the pink family, as the carnation and the sweet william. [<NL <Gk. *Dios* of Zeus + *anthos* flower]

di·a·pa·son (dī'ə·pā'zən, -sən) *n.* **1** The basal melodic tone of a pipe organ; also, the stop producing it. In the **open diapason** the pipes are of metal and open at the top; in the **stopped diapason** the pipes are of wood and closed at the top. **2** A tuning fork, or the standard pitch given by a tuning fork. **3** In old Greek music, an octave. **4** *Archaic* Comprehensive or fundamental harmony; universal concord. [<L <Gk. *dia pasōn* (*chordōn*) through all (the notes)]

di·a·pe·de·sis (dī'ə·pə·dē'sis) *n. Pathol.* The passing of leucocytes through intact blood vessels into the adjoining tissue: noted especially during inflammation. [<NL <Gk. *diapēdēsis* <*dia-* through + *pedaein* leap, throb] — **di'a·pe·det'ic** (-det'ik) *adj.*

di·a·per (dī'ə·pər) *n.* **1** In the Middle Ages, a fine figured silken or linen cloth. **2** In art and architecture, a form of surface decoration, consisting of a system of reticulations, each of which contains a flower pattern, geometric design, etc., either carved or painted. **3** A soft, absorbent, bleached cotton fabric, of plain or birdseye weave: used for toweling, babies' breech-cloths, etc. **4** A baby's breechcloth; waist-cloth. — *v.t.* **1** To decorate with a repeated figure or similar figures. **2** To put a diaper on. [<OF *diapre,* earlier *diaspre* <Med. Gk.

A DIAPER
PATTERN (def. 2)

diaspros <*dia-* completely + *aspros* white]

di·a·pha·ne·i·ty (dī'ə·fə·nē'ə·tē) *n.* Translucency.

di·a·pha·nom·e·ter (dī'ə·fə·nom'ə·tər) *n.* An instrument for observing and measuring the transparency of materials, as fluids, paper, milk, etc., by means of transmitted light. [<Gk. *diaphanēs* transparent + -METER]

di·aph·a·no·scope (dī·af'ə·nə·skōp') *n. Med.* A device for illuminating cavities of the body to facilitate medical examination and treatment. [<Gk. *diaphanēs* transparent + -SCOPE]

di·aph·a·nous (dī·af'ə·nəs) *adj.* Showing light through its substance; transparent; translucent. See synonyms under CLEAR. [<Med. L *diaphanus* <Gk. *diaphanēs* < *dia-* through + *phainein* show] — **di·aph'a·nous·ly** *adv.*

di·aph·o·ny (dī·af'ə·nē) *n. pl.* **·nies 1** *Music* The parallel movement of voices at definite intervals from one another. **2** Anciently, dissonance: opposed to *symphony.* [<LL *diaphonia* dissonance <Gk. *diaphōnia* < *dia-* across + *phoneein* sound < *phonē* a sound] — **di·a·phon·ic** (dī'ə·fon'ik) *adj.* — **di·a·phon'ics** *n.*

di·a·pho·re·sis (dī'ə·fə·rē'sis) *n. Med.* Copious perspiration. [<LL <Gk. *diaphorēsis* < *diaphorein* perspire < *dia-* across, through + *phorein* carry]

di·a·pho·ret·ic (dī'ə·fə·ret'ik) *adj. Med.* Producing perspiration. — *n.* Any drug or agent that causes or increases perspiration. Also **di'a·pho·ret'i·cal.**

di·a·phragm (dī'ə·fram) *n.* **1** *Anat.* An important muscle used in respiration, situated between the thoracic and abdominal cavities; the midriff. **2** Any dividing membrane or partition. **3** Any device supposed to resemble a diaphragm in shape, appearance, or elasticity, as the thin vibrating disk of a telephone or phonograph, or the flexible rubber sheet of a vacuum brake. **4** The porous cup of a voltaic cell. **5** *Optics* A perforated disk whose aperture may be reduced in order to cut off marginal rays in a camera or telescope. — *v.t.* To act upon or furnish with a diaphragm. [<L *diaphragma* <Gk. < *dia-* across + *phragma* a fence] — **di·a·phrag·mat·ic** (dī'ə·frag·mat'ik) *adj.* — **di'a·phrag·mat'i·cal·ly** *adv.*

di·aph·y·sis (dī·af'ə·sis) *n. pl.* **·ses** (-sēz) *Anat.* **1** The shaft of a long bone or the part that ossifies from the center. **2** Any prominent part of a bony process, or a ligament, of the knee joint. [<NL <Gk., a growing through < *dia-* through + *phvein* grow, produce]

di·a·poph·y·sis (dī'ə·pof'ə·sis) *n. pl.* **·ses** (-sēz) *Anat.* The superior or articular part of the transverse process of a vertebra. [<DI(A) + APOPHYSIS] — **di·ap·o·phys·i·al** (dī'ap·ə·fiz'ē·əl) *adj.*

di·ar·chy (dī'är·kē) *n. pl.* **·chies** A form of government in which two persons are jointly invested with supreme power, as William and Mary in England: also spelled *dyarchy.* [<DI-² + -ARCHY]

di·ar·rhe·a (dī'ə·rē'ə) *n. Pathol.* Morbidly frequent and fluid evacuation of the bowels. Also **di'ar·rhoe'a.** [<L *diarrhoea* <Gk. *diarrhoia* < *dia-* through + *rheein* flow] — **di·ar·rhe'al** or **·rhoe'al, di·ar·rhe'ic** or **·rhoe'ic, di·ar·rhet'ic** or **·rhoet'ic** (-ret'ik) *adj.*

di·ar·thro·sis (dī'är·thrō'sis) *n. pl.* **·ses** (-sēz) *Anat.* A freely movable joint in which the ends of the bones are surrounded by a capsule and covered by cartilage. [<NL <Gk. *diarthrosis* < *dia-* completely + *arthrosis* an articulation < *arthron* a joint] — **di'ar·thro'di·al** (-dē·əl) *adj.*

di·a·ry (dī'ə·rē) *n. pl.* **·ries 1** A record of daily events; especially, a personal record of one's activities, experiences, or observations; a journal. **2** A book for keeping such record. [<LL *diarium* <L *dies* a day]

di·a·spore (dī'ə·spôr, -spōr) *n.* A variously colored, translucent to subtranslucent aluminum hydroxide, AlO.OH. [<Gk. *diaspora* a dispersion (see DIASPORA); so called from its rapid decrepitation and dispersion when heated]

di·a·stal·sis (dī'ə·stal'sis) *n. pl.* **·ses** (-sēz) *Physiol.* A downward-thrusting contraction wave forming part of the peristaltic action

of the digestive tube. [<NL <Gk. *dia-* through + *stellein* place, send] — **di·a·stal'tic** *adj.*

di·a·stase (dī'ə·stās) *n. Biochem.* A white, amorphous enzyme that converts starch and glycogen into dextrin and sugar (chiefly maltose): found in germinating grain and in various parts of plants and in animal fluids, as saliva, pancreatic juice, etc.; an amylase. [<F <Gk. *diastasis* a separation < *dia-* apart + *histanai* set, cause to stand] — **di·a·sta'sic, di·a·stat'ic** (-stat'ik) *adj.*

di·as·ter (dī·as'tər) *n. Biol.* **1** That stage of cell division in which the chromosomes have separated to form two groups of starlike radiations at the poles. **2** One of the groups of radiations so formed. [<DI-² + Gk. *aster* star]

di·as·to·le (dī·as't·lē) *n.* **1** *Physiol.* The regular expansion or dilatation of the heart and of the arteries: opposed to *systole.* **2** *Zool.* A corresponding motion in protozoans and in parts of other animal organisms. **3** In Greek and Latin prosody, the lengthening of a syllable naturally short. Compare SYSTOLE. [<LL <Gk. *diastolē* a separation, lengthening < *dia-* apart + *stellein* send, put] — **di·as·tol·ic** (dī'ə·stol'ik) *adj.*

di·as·tro·phism (dī·as'trə·fiz'əm) *n. Geol.* **1** The process of deformation of the earth's crust, producing continents and ocean beds, plateaus, mountains, valleys, folds, and faults. **2** Any deformation so caused. [<Gk. *diastrophē* <*dia-* across + *strephein* turn] — **di·a·stroph·ic** (dī'ə·strof'ik) *adj.*

di·a·ther·man·cy (dī'ə·thûr'mən·sē) *n. Physics* The property of being transparent to infrared rays, or of transmitting them. Also **di'a·ther'mance, di'a·ther'ma·cy** (-mə·sē). [<F *diathermansie* <Gk. *dia-* through + *thermansis* a heating] — **di·a·ther·ma·nous** (dī'ə·thûr'mə·nəs) *adj.*

di·a·ther·my (dī'ə·thûr'mē) *n. Med.* Application of heat to the deeper tissues of the body by means of high-frequency electric currents; thermopenetration. Also **di·a·ther·mi·a** (dī'ə·thûr'mē·ə). [<NL *diathermia* <Gk. *dia-* through + *thermē* heat]

di·ath·e·sis (dī·ath'ə·sis) *n.* **1** *Med.* A predisposition to certain forms of disease: a gouty *diathesis.* **2** Any mental or physical predisposition. [<NL <Gk. *diathēsis* an arrangement, disposition < *dia-* apart + *tithenai* place] — **di·a·thet·ic** (dī'ə·thet'ik) *adj.*

di·a·tom (dī'ə·təm, -tom) *n.* A marine and fresh-water plankton, unicellular or colonial, belonging to the family *Chlorophyceae* of microscopic green algae, characterized by bivalve walls containing silica. [<NL *diatoma* <Gk. *dia-* through + *temnein* cut] — **di·a·to·ma·ceous** (dī'ə·tə·mā'shəs) *adj.*

diatomaceous earth The siliceous skeletons of diatoms, dried and used in the manufacture of dynamite, pottery, abrasives, glaze, etc.; kieselguhr. Also **di·at·o·mite** (dī·at'ə·mīt).

di·a·tom·ic (dī'ə·tom'ik) *adj. Chem.* **1** Containing only two atoms: a *diatomic* molecule. **2** Containing two replaceable univalent atoms. **3** Bivalent.

di·a·ton·ic (dī'ə·ton'ik) *adj. Music* Designating the regular tones of a major or minor key (or scale), in distinction from chromatic or occasional tones; having eight tones to an octave. [<MF *diatonique* <LL *diatonicus* <Gk. *diatonikos* < *dia-* through + *teinein* stretch] — **di'a·ton'i·cal·ly** *adv.*

di·a·tribe (dī'ə·trīb) *n.* An abusive discourse; denunciation; invective. [<F <L *diatriba* <Gk. *diatribē* a wearing away of time < *dia-* through + *tribein* rub]

di·at·ro·pism (dī·at'rə·piz'əm) *n. Bot.* The propensity of some plant organs to arrange themselves transversely to the line of action of an external stimulus. [<DIA- + TROPISM] — **di·a·trop·ic** (dī'ə·trop'ik) *adj.*

di·a·zine (dī'ə·zēn, -zin, dī·az'in) *n. Chem.* One of three isomeric cyclic hydrocarbon compounds, the ring of which contains two nitrogen and four carbon atoms. Also **di·a·zin** (dī'ə·zin, dī·az'in). [<DIAZ(O)- + -IN]

di·az·o (dī·az'ō, dī·ā'zō) *adj. Chem.* Pertaining to or designating any of a group of very reactive compounds in which two nitrogen atoms are united to a hydrocarbon radical:

used in dyestuff manufacture. In compounds, **diazo–** or, before vowels, **diaz–,** as in **diazomethane, diazine.** [<DI-² + AZO(TE)]

di·a·zole (dī′ə·zōl, dī·az′ōl) *n. Chem.* Any member of a class of heterocyclic hydrocarbon compounds, the ring of which contains two nitrogen and three carbon atoms. [<DIAZ(O)- + -OLE¹]

di·az·o·meth·ane (dī·az′ō·meth′ān, dī·ā′zō-) *n. Chem.* An odorless, poisonous, yellow gas, CH_2N_2, used in organic syntheses.

di·a·zo·ni·um (dī′ə·zō′nē·əm) *n. Chem.* A basic organic radical which forms aromatic nitrogen compounds. [<DIAZ(O)- + (AMM)ONIUM]

diazonium salt *Chem.* Any of a group of salts formed by the action of nitrous acid at low temperature upon a salt of a primary aromatic amine.

di·az·o·re·ac·tion (dī·az′ō·rē·ak′shən, dī·ā′zō-) *n. Med.* A reaction, especially in typhoid fever, in which the urine becomes deep red in color when treated with certain reagents.

di·az·o·tize (dī·az′ə·tīz) *v.t.* **·tized, ·tiz·ing** *Chem.* To bring about chemical reactions or changes that form a diazo compound or derivative. — **di·az′o·ti·za′tion** *n.*

di·ba·sic (dī·bā′sik) *adj. Chem.* **1** Containing two atoms of hydrogen replaceable by a base or basic radical, as sulfuric acid. **2** Of or derived from such an acid: said of salts.

di·bran·chi·ate (dī·brang′kē·it, -āt) *n.* Any of an order (*Dibranchiata*) of cephalopods including the squids and octopuses, with 8 or 10 sucker-bearing arms surrounding the mouth, 2 internal gills, and a sac and siphon for emitting an inky liquid. — *adj.* Of or pertaining to the *Dibranchiata.* [<NL *dibranchiata* <Gk. *di-* two + *branchia* gills]

di·bro·mide (dī·brō′mīd, -mid) *n. Chem.* A compound containing two atoms of bromine.

di·bro·mo·gal·lic acid (dī′brō·mə·gal′ik) Gallobromal.

di·car·box·yl·ic acid (dī·kär′bok·sil′ik) *Chem.* An organic compound having two carboxyl radicals.

dice (dīs) *n. pl.* of **die** **1** Small cubes of bone, ivory, or composition, having the sides marked with spots from one to six. **2** A game played with such cubes. — **poker dice** Dice marked with card faces from nine to ace inclusive. — *v.* **diced, dic·ing** *v.t.* **1** To cut into small cubes. **2** To decorate with a dice-like pattern. **3** To gamble away or win with dice. — *v.i.* **4** To play at dice. [See DIE²]

di·ceph·a·lous (dī·sef′ə·ləs) *adj.* Having two heads.

di·cer·ous (dis′ər·əs) *adj.* Having two horns or antennae. [<Gk. *dikeros* <*di-* two + *keras* horn]

di·cha·si·um (dī·kā′zhē·əm, -zē·əm) *n. pl.* **·si·a** (-zhē·ə, -zē·ə) *Bot.* A cymose inflorescence in which two lateral branches grow from the primary axis below the flower, each branch repeating the division; a two-parted cyme. [<NL <Gk. *dichasis* a division <*dicha* in two] — **di·cha′si·al** *adj.*

di·chlor·a·mine (dī·klôr′ə·mēn) *n. Chem.* A yellowish-white, crystalline compound, $C_7H_7SO_2NCl_2$, used as an antiseptic in treating wound infection. [<DI-² + CHLOR- + -AMINE]

di·chlor·eth·yl sulfide (dī′klôr-eth′əl) See MUSTARD GAS.

di·chlo·ride (dī·klôr′īd, -id, -klō′rīd, -rid) *n. Chem.* A compound having two atoms of chlorine combined with an element or radical; a bichloride. Also **di·chlo·rid** (dī·klôr′id, -klō′rid).

di·chlor·o·di·phen·yl·tri·chlor·o·eth·ane (dī·klôr′ō-dī·fen′yl·trī·klôr′ō·eth′ān) *n.* DDT.

dicho– *combining form* In two; in pairs: *dichotomy.* Also, before vowels, **dich–.** [<Gk. <*dicha* in two <*dis* twice]

di·chog·a·my (dī·kog′ə·mē) *n. Bot.* A condition, brought about by the maturity at different times of the anthers and stigmas, for promoting intercrossing between hermaphrodite flowers: distinguished from *homogamy.* [<DICHO- + -GAMY] — **di·chog′a·mous** *adj.*

di·chot·o·mize (dī·kot′ə·mīz) *v.* **·mized, ·miz·ing** *v.t.* **1** To cut or part into two sections; subdivide or separate and classify into pairs. **2** *Astron.* To exhibit as a half disk, as the moon. — *v.i.* To be or become separated into two parts. — **di·chot′o·mi·za′tion** *n.*

di·chot·o·mous (dī·kot′ə·məs) *adj.* **1** Pertaining to or involving dichotomy. **2** Dividing into two parts or branches. Also **di·cho·tom·ic**

(dī′kə·tom′ik). — **di·chot′o·mous·ly, di·cho·tom′i·cal·ly** *adv.*

di·chot·o·my (dī·kot′ə·mē) *n. pl.* **·mies 1** The state of being divided in two; division into two parts or into two branches; division by pairs. **2** *Logic* The division of a class into two mutually exclusive subclasses, one positive and the other negative, as minerals into gold and not-gold. **3** *Astron.* The aspect of the moon, Mercury, or Venus, at first and last quarter, when half the apparent disk is illuminated. **4** *Bot.* **a** A forking in pairs, as the stem of a plant; successive bifurcation. **b** A system of branching in which each successive axis forks or bifurcates into two equally developed branches. [<Gk. *dichotomia* <*dicho-* in two + *temnein* cut]

di·chro·ic (dī·krō′ik) *adj.* **1** Of, pertaining to, or exhibiting dichroism. **2** Dichromatic. Also **di·chro·it·ic** (dī′krō·it′ik).

di·chro·ism (dī′krō·iz′əm) *n.* **1** *Physics* The property of showing different colors when viewed in different directions, exhibited by doubly refracting crystals. **2** *Chem.* The property of being differently colored in different degrees of concentration: shown by some solutions. [<Gk. *dichroos* two-colored <*di-* two + *chrōs* color]

di·chro·ite (dī′krō·īt) *n.* The mineral iolite. [<Gk. *dichroos* two-colored + -ITE¹]

di·chro·mate (dī·krō′māt) *n. Chem.* A compound containing two chromium atoms: potassium *dichromate.*

di·chro·mat·ic (dī′krō·mat′ik) *adj.* **1** Having either of two colors. **2** *Zool.* Having two color phases: said of certain birds and insects, etc., that, apart from changes due to age or sex, exhibit a coloration differing from the normal. **3** *Pathol.* Affected with blue–, green–, or red-blindness; able to see only two of the three primary colors.

di·chro·ma·tism (dī·krō′mə·tiz′əm) *n.* The state of being dichromatic, especially with reference to colorblindness. Also **di·chro′mism.**

di·chro·mic (dī·krō′mik) *adj.* **1** Containing two atoms of chromium, or their equivalents. **2** Dichromatic.

dichromic acid *Chem.* A dibasic acid, $H_2Cr_2O_7$, known only through its salts, the dichromates or bichromates.

di·chro·scope (dī′krə·skōp) *n.* An instrument for examining or exhibiting dichroism, as of crystals. Also **di·chro·o·scope** (dī·krō′ə·skōp). [<Gk. *dichroos* two-colored + -SCOPE] — **di·chro·scop·ic** (dī′krə·skop′ik) *adj.*

dick·cis·sel (dik·sis′əl) *n.* A bunting (*Spiza americana*) of the Mississippi region, distinguished by its black throat and lively call. Also **dick·sis′sel.** [Imit.]

dick·er (dik′ər) *n. U.S.* **1** A petty trade; a bargain. **2** A political deal. — *v.t. & v.i.* **1** To trade by haggling or bartering, especially on a small scale. **2** In politics, to bargain; work toward a deal. [ME *dyker,* OE (unrecorded) *dicor* a lot of ten, esp. skins or hides, ult. <L *decuria* a group of ten]

dick·ey (dik′ē) *n.* **1** A detachable article of clothing, as a false shirt front, or sweater front; also, a bib; pinafore. **2** A driver's outside seat on a carriage; also, one behind the body, for servants. **3** A donkey. **4** *Colloq.* Any small bird. Also **dick′y.** [<*Dicky,* double dim. of RICHARD]

di·cli·nous (dī′kli·nəs, dī·klī′-) *adj. Bot.* Having stamens in one flower and pistils in another; unisexual. [<DI-² + Gk. *klinē* bed]

di·cot·y·le·don (dī′kot·ə·lēd′n, dī·kot′-) *n. Bot.* **1** A plant having two cotyledons or seed leaves. **2** A member of the class *Dicotyledones.*

di·cot·y·le·do·nous (dī′kot·ə·lē′də·nəs, dī·kot′-) *adj. Bot.* Belonging or pertaining to the largest, most important subclass (*Dicotyledones*) of angiosperms or flowering plants, characterized by having seeds with two cotyledons. It embraces the majority of deciduous trees and of herbs and shrubs.

di·crot·ic (dī·krot′ik) *adj. Physiol.* Having an abnormal heartbeat, with a double pulse beat to each systole of the heart. Also **di·cro·tal** (dī·krō′təl),**di·cro·tous** (dī′krə·təs). [<Gk. *dikrotos* <*di-* two + *krotos* beat] — **di·cro·tism** (dī′krə·tiz′əm) *n.*

dic·tate (dik′tāt, dik·tāt′) *v.* **·tat·ed, ·tat·ing** *v.t.* **1** To utter or read aloud (something) to be recorded by another, as by writing. **2** To give, impose, or prescribe authoritatively, as

commands, terms, rules, etc. — *v.i.* **3** To utter aloud something to be recorded by another. **4** To give orders. — *n.* (dik′tāt) **1** An authoritative suggestion or prompting; a rule, precept, or maxim. **2** A positive order. [<L *dictatus,* pp. of *dictare,* freq. of *dicere* say, speak]

Synonyms (*verb*): command, decree, direct, enjoin, order, prescribe, require. See SPEAK. **Antonyms:** accept, follow, obey, submit, yield.

dic·ta·tion (dik·tā′shən) *n.* **1** The act of dictating. **2** The matter or material dictated. **3** Arbitrary control. — **dic·ta′tion·al** *adj.*

dic·ta·tor (dik′tā·tər, dik·tā′tər) *n.* **1** One invested with absolute power, especially in a state in time of emergency. **2** One who dictates or prescribes. **3** In ancient Rome, a chief magistrate with supreme authority, appointed by the Senate in cases of emergency for a term of about six months. — **dic·ta·tor·ship′** *n.* — **dic·ta′tress** *n. fem.*

dic·tion (dik′shən) *n.* **1** The use, choice, and arrangement of words and modes of expression. **2** The manner of speaking or of any vocal expression; enunciation. [<L *dictio, -onis* speech <*dicere* say, speak]

Synonyms: expression, language, phrase, phraseology, style, verbiage, vocabulary, wording, words. An author's *diction* is strictly his choice and use of words, with no special reference to thought; *expression* regards the words simply as the vehicle of the thought. *Phrase* and *phraseology* apply to words or combinations of words which are somewhat technical; as, in legal *phraseology;* in military *phrase. Diction* is general; *wording* is limited; we speak of the *diction* of an author or of a work, the *wording* of a proposition, of a resolution, etc. *Verbiage* is wordiness. *Style* includes *diction, expression,* rhetorical figures such as metaphor and simile, the effect of an author's prevailing tone of thought, of his personal traits—in short, all that makes up the clothing of thought in words. Compare LANGUAGE.

dic·tion·ar·y (dik′shən·er′ē) *n. pl.* **·ar·ies 1** A book containing the words of a language, or of a department of knowledge, arranged alphabetically, usually with their syllabication, pronunciation, definition, and etymology; lexicon; wordbook. **2** A similar work having definitions or equivalents in another language: a German-English *dictionary.* [<Med. L *dictionarium* a collection of words and phrases <*dictio.* See DICTION.]

dic·tum (dik′təm) *n. pl.* **dic·ta** (-tə) **1** An authoritative, dogmatic, or positive utterance; a pronouncement. **2** *Law* An opinion by a judge on a point not essential to the decision on the main question in the case on trial. **3** A popular saying; a maxim. See synonyms under ADAGE. [<L <*dicere* say]

dic·ty·nid (dik′tə·nid) *n.* One of a family (*Dictynidae*) of spiders that build their webs of a curled thread and in irregular forms. [<NL <Gk. *diktyon* a net]

did (did) Past tense of DO¹.

di·dac·tic (dī·dak′tik, di-) *adj.* **1** Pertaining to or of the nature of teaching; intended to instruct; expository. **2** Morally instructive; preceptive. **3** Overly inclined to teach; pedantic. Also **di·dac′ti·cal.** [<Gk. *didaktikos* apt to teach <*didaskein* teach] — **di·dac′ti·cal·ly** *adv.* — **di·dac′ti·cism** *n.*

di·dac·tics (dī·dak′tiks, di-) *n.* The science or art of instruction or education.

didg·er·i·du (dij′ər·ē·doo′) *n. Austral.* An aboriginal musical instrument, a foot to eight feet long, that amplifies a nasal whine. [<native Australian]

di·drach·ma (dī·drak′mə) *n. pl.* **·mas** or **mae** (-mē) **1** A double drachma in ancient Greece. **2** The earliest Roman silver coin. [<Gk. <*di-* two + *drachma* a drachma]

di·dym·i·um (dī·dim′ē·əm, di-) *n.* A mixture of the elements neodymium and praseodymium of the lanthanide series, found in cerite and formerly regarded as one of the elements. [<NL <Gk. *didymos* double]

did·y·mous (did′ə·məs) *adj.* **1** *Bot.* Twin; formed in pairs; growing double, as umbelliferous fruits. **2** Double, as markings. [<Gk. *didymos* double]

die¹ (dī) *v.i.* **died, dy·ing 1** To suffer death; pass from life; expire. **2** To suffer the pains of death: The coward *dies* a thousand deaths. **3** To lose energy or power; pass: with *away: down,* or *out.* **4** To cease to exist; fade away, The smile *died* on his lips. **5** To become extinct: with *out* or *off.* **6** To become indifferent or insensible: with *to:* to *die* to the world. **7** To desire exceedingly, as if to death: He's *dying* to meet her. **8** To stop functioning, as an engine. **9** To faint or swoon. **10** *Theol.* To suffer spiritual death. **—to die game** To die fighting. ◆ Homophone: *dye.* [< ON *deyja*]

Synonyms: cease, decease, decline, depart, expire, perish, wither. *Die* is applied to anything which has the appearance of life; an echo, a strain of music, a tempest, a topic, an issue, *dies. Expire* is a softer word for *die;* it is used figuratively of things that *cease* to exist by reaching a natural limit; as, a lease *expires;* the time has *expired.* To *perish* is oftenest used of death by privation or exposure; sometimes, of death by violence. Knowledge and fame, art and empires, may be said to *perish;* the word denotes destruction and decay. *Antonyms:* begin, exist, flourish, grow, live, survive.

die[2] (dī) *n. pl.* **dice** *for defs.* **1** *and* **2 dies** *for defs.* **3** *to* **6. 1** A small cube used in games. See DICE. **2** A cast, as in playing dice; stake; hazard. **3** *Mech.* **a** A hard metal pattern for stamping or cutting out some object; specifically, one of a pair between which a metal blank is forced or forged into a special shape, as a spoon. **b** One of a pair of such patterns, one cameo and the other intaglio, between which a sheet of metal is embossed. **c** A block or counter having an orifice through which a punch passes. Also **die plate. 4** A tool for cutting screw threads on a nut, bolt, etc. **5** The cubical part of a pedestal. **6** Any small cubical block or body. **—the die is cast** The choice is made that commits one to an irrevocable course of action —*v.t.* To cut or stamp with or as with a die. ◆ Homophone: *dye.* [< OF *de* < L *datum* something given]

die·back (dī'bak') *n.* Arrested or retarded development in the twigs of certain woody plants, due to parasites or to being winter-killed: also called *twig blight.*

die-hard (dī'härd') *n.* **1** One who fights to the last. **2** One who obstinately refuses to abandon or modify his views; especially, a political conservative who obstinately opposes a winning liberal measure.

di·el·drin (dī-el'drin) *n.* A toxic chlorinated hydrocarbon, $C_{12}H_8Cl_6O$, stereoisomeric with endrin and likewise used as a pesticide.

di·e·lec·tric (dī'ə-lek'trik) *Electr. adj.* **1** Non-conducting. **2** Capable of sustaining an electric field, as by induction. Also **di'e·lec'tri·cal.** —*n.* A dielectric substance, medium or material. — **di'e·lec'tri·cal·ly** *adv.*

di·en·ceph·a·lon (dī'en·sef'ə·lon) *n. Anat.* That part of the brain forming the posterior part of the prosencephalon, from which are developed the pineal body, the pituitary, and other structures of the third ventricle; the interbrain or middle brain: also called *thalamencephalon.* [< NL < Gk. *di(a)-* between + *enkephalos* brain]

-diene *suffix Chem.* Denoting an open-chain unsaturated hydrocarbon compound having two double bonds: *butadiene.* [< DI-[2] + -ENE]

di·er·e·sis (dī·er'ə·sis) *n. pl.* **·ses** (-sēz) **1** Two dots (¨) placed over the second of two adjacent vowels that are to be pronounced separately. **2** The separation of syllables or vowels by dots. **3** In the pronunciations in this book, a diacritic used over *a* to indicate the vowel sound in *palm* (päm). See also **ü,** Foreign Sounds page xx. **4** The coincidence of the end of a metrical foot with the end of a word in a verse. Also spelled *diaeresis.* Compare SYNERESIS. [< LL *diaeresis* < Gk. *diairesis* a division < *diairein* < *dia-* apart + *haireein* seize] —**di·e·ret·ic** (dī'ə·ret'ik) *adj.*

die·sel engine (dē'zəl) An internal-combustion engine, in which crude oil, used as fuel, is ignited by the heat resulting from the high compression of air drawn into the cylinder. Also **Diesel engine.** [after Rudolf *Diesel,* 1858–1913, German inventor]

di·e·sis (dī'ə·sis) *n.* **1** *Music* The difference in tone between a major and a minor semi-

tone, represented by the ratio of vibrations 125:128; also, an interval smaller than a half-step. **2** In Greek music, one of several intervals varying from a semitone to a quartertone. **3** *Printing* The double dagger (‡): a reference mark for the third in a series. [< L < Gk. < *diienai* < *dia-* through + *hienai* send]

Diest (dēst) A town in north central Belgium.

die·stock (dī'stok') *n.*
Mech. A double-handled holder for a die used to cut threads on screws, bolts, etc.

DIESTOCK

di·et[1] (dī'ət) *n.* **1** A regulated course of eating and drinking; a specially prescribed regimen. **2** The daily fare; victuals. **3** *Obs.* Allowance of food; ration. See synonyms under FOOD. —*v.t.* **1** To regulate or restrict the food and drink of. —*v.i.* **2** To take food and drink according to a regimen; eat discriminatingly. **3** To take food; eat. [< OF *diete* < L *diaeta* < Gk. *diaita* a way of living] —**di'et·er** *n.*

di·et[2] (dī'ət) *n.* **1** A legislative assembly. **2** *Scot.* A single session, as of a court; a day appointed for a session. [< Med. L *dieta* < L *dies* a day]

di·e·tar·y (dī'ə·ter'ē) *n. pl.* **·tar·ies 1** A system or regimen of dieting. **2** A standard or regulated allowance of food. —*adj.* Pertaining or relating to diet: also **di·e·tet·ic** (dī'ə·tet'ik), **di·e·tet'i·cal.** —**di'e·tet'i·cal·ly** *adv.*

di·e·tet·ics (dī'ə·tet'iks) *n.* The branch of hygiene that treats of diet and dieting and the feeding of individuals or of great numbers.

di·eth·y·lene glycol (dī·eth'ə·lēn) *Chem.* An organic compound, $O(CH_2CH_2OH)_2$, used as an anti-freeze mixture and as an agent in many chemical processes for the production of solvents, plastics, explosives, etc.

di·eth·yl·stil·bes·trol (dī·eth'əl·stil·bes'trōl) *n. Biochem.* A synthetic compound, $C_{18}H_{20}O_2$, having estrogenic and carcinogenic properties.

di·e·ti·tian (dī'ə·tish'ən) *n.* One skilled in the principles of dietetics and in their practical application in health and disease. Also **di·e·tet·ist** (dī'ə·tet'ist), **di·e·ti·cian.**

diet kitchen 1 An institution, usually connected with a dispensary or hospital, that provides food for the invalid poor. **2** A kitchen where special diets are prepared and from which they are served under the supervision of a dietitian who gives student nurses dietetic training.

dif- Assimilated var. of DIS-.

dif·fer (dif'ər) *v.i.* **1** To be unlike in quality, degree, form, etc.; often with *from.* **2** To disagree; dissent: often with *with.* **3** To quarrel: sometimes with *over* or *about.* [< OF *differer* < L *differre* < *dis-* apart + *ferre* carry. Doublet of DEFER[1].]

dif·fer·ence (dif'ər·əns, dif'rəns) *n.* **1** The state or quality of being other or unlike, or that in which two things are unlike; dissimilarity; variation. **2** A mark or peculiarity which distinguishes. **3** A disagreement in sentiment or opinion; controversy; quarrel. **4** A separate treatment; discrimination. **5** *Math.* The result obtained by subtracting one number from another. **6** *Logic* The specific difference; differentia. **7** In commerce, a margin that has become payable. **8** *Her.* A device in blazons to distinguish persons bearing the same arms. —*v.t.* **·enced, ·enc·ing 1** To make or mark as different; distinguish; discriminate. **2** *Her.* To add a mark of difference to.

Synonyms (noun): contrariety, contrast, disagreement, discrepancy, discrimination, disparity, dissimilarity, dissimilitude, distinction, divergence, diversity, inconsistency, inequality, unlikeness, variation. A *difference* is in the things compared; a *discrimination* is in our judgment of them; a *distinction* is in our definition or description or mental image of them. Careful *discrimination* of real *differences* results in clear *distinctions. Disparity* is stronger than *inequality,* implying that one thing falls far below another; as, the *disparity* of our achievements when compared with our ideals. *Dissimilarity* is between things sharply contrasted; there may be a *difference* between

those almost alike. There is a *discrepancy* in accounts that fail to balance. *Diversity* involves more than two objects; *variation* is a *difference* in the condition or action of the same object at different times. *Antonyms:* agreement, consonance, harmony, identity, likeness, resemblance, sameness, similarity, uniformity, unity.

dif·fer·ent (dif'ər·ənt, dif'rənt) *adj.* **1** Not the same; distinct; other: A *different* clerk is there now. **2** Marked by a difference; completely or partly unlike; dissimilar. **3** Unusual. See synonyms under CONTRARY. [< F *différent* < L *differens, -entis,* ppr. of *differre.* See DIFFER.] —**dif'fer·ent·ly** *adv.* —**dif'fer·ent·ness** *n.* ◆ **different from, than, to** In American usage, *from* is established as the idiomatic preposition to follow *different;* when, however, a clause follows the connective, *than* is gaining increasing acceptance: a result *different than* (= *from that which* or *from what*) had been expected. This last is established British usage, which also accepts *to* on a par with *from:* She is *different* to *her* sister.

dif·fer·en·ti·a·ble (dif'ə·ren'shē·ə·bəl) *adj.* **1** That can be differentiated. **2** *Math.* Belonging to or having a differential coefficient.

dif·fer·en·tial (dif'ə·ren'shəl) *adj.* **1** Relating to, making, or marked by a difference. **2** Distinctive; discriminative. **3** *Math.* Pertaining to or involving differentials or differentiation. **4** *Mech.* Characterized by a construction in which a movement is obtained by the difference in two motions in the same direction, See DIFFERENTIAL GEAR. —*n.* **1** *Math.* **a** An infinitesimal increment of a quantity: indicated by the symbol Δ. **b** The derivative of a function multiplied by the increment of the independent variable. **2** A differential rate. **3** *Mech.* A differential gear. **4** *Electr.* One of two resistance coils the current of which flows in a direction opposite to that of the other. —**dif'fer·en'tial·ly** *adv.*

differential coefficient *Math.* The ratio of the infinitesimal increase of a function to that of a variable on which the function depends; a derivative. Also **differential quotient.**

differential equation *Math.* An equation in which derivatives or differentials of an unknown function appear.

differential gear or **gearing** *Mech.* A coupling consisting of an epicyclic train used to connect shafts, as in the driving axle of an automobile, so that a rigid union is effected when moving in a straight line, but permitting of independent motion when describing a curve.

DIFFERENTIAL GEAR
a. Drive shaft. *b.* Driveshaft gear. *c.* Axles.
d. Ring gear. *e.* Epicyclic train of gears.

differential windlass See under WINDLASS.

dif·fer·en·ti·ate (dif'ə·ren'shē·āt) *v.* **·at·ed, ·at·ing** *v.t.* **1** To constitute a difference between; mark off. **2** To perceive and indicate the differences of or between. **3** *Biol.* To cause to be unlike; develop differences in. **4** *Math.* To derive the differential of (a function). —*v.i.* **5** To discriminate; perceive a difference. **6** To become specialized; acquire a distinct character. See synonyms under CONTRAST.

dif·fer·en·ti·a·tion (dif'ə·ren'shē·ā'shən) *n.* **1** The process of making or becoming different. **2** *Biol.* **a** Progressive change from the general to the special, as in all organs and tissues in course of development. **b** The setting apart of special organs for special work: distinguished from ordinary cellular growth in that the cells produced by division are dissimilar to the parent cells. **3** *Logic* Distinction on grounds of difference; discrimination. **4** *Math.* The finding of a differential.

dif·fi·cult (dif'ə·kult, -kəlt) *adj.* **1** Hard to do or be done; arduous; troublesome to understand; perplexing. **2** Hard to persuade, overcome, or satisfy; intractable; exacting. [Back formation < DIFFICULTY] —**dif'fi·cult·ly** *adv.*

Synonyms: arduous, exhausting, hard, laborious, onerous, severe, toilsome, trying. *Arduous* applies to that which involves great and sustained exertion; great learning can only be won by *arduous* toil. Anything is *hard* that involves tax and strain whether of the physical or mental powers. *Difficult* is not used of that which merely taxes physical force; a dead lift is called *hard* rather than *difficult*; that is *difficult* which involves skill, sagacity, or address, with or without a considerable expenditure of physical force; a geometrical problem may be *difficult* to solve, a mountain *difficult* to ascend. *Hard* may be active or passive; a thing may be *hard* to do or *hard* to bear. *Arduous* is always active. That which is *laborious* or *toilsome* requires the steady application of labor or toil till accomplished; *toilsome* is the stronger word. That which is *onerous* is mentally burdensome or oppressive. See ARDUOUS, HARD, OBSCURE, SQUEAMISH, TROUBLESOME. *Antonyms:* easy, facile, light, pleasant, slight, trifling, trivial.

dif·fi·cul·ty (dif'ə·kul'tē, -kəl-) *n. pl.* **·ties** 1 The state or quality of being difficult or of presenting or constituting an obstacle to achievement or mastery. 2 An obstacle; hindrance; something difficult to effect or to understand. 3 Reluctance; objection. 4 A quarrel. 5 *Usually pl.* Financial embarrassment; a strait; trouble: generally in the plural. See synonyms under IMPEDIMENT. [< L *difficultas, -tatis* < *difficilis* < *dis-* away, not + *facilis* easy < *facere* do, make]

dif·fi·dent (dif'ə·dənt) *adj.* 1 Affected or possessed with self-distrust; timid; shy; modest. 2 *Obs.* Distrustful of others; doubtful. [< L *diffidens, -entis,* ppr. of *diffidere* < *dis-* away + *fidere* trust < *fides* faith]

dif·fract (di·frakt') *v.t.* 1 To separate into parts. 2 To subject to diffraction. [< L *diffractus,* pp. of *diffringere* < *dis-* away + *frangere* break] —**dif·frac'tive** *adj.* —**dif·frac'tive·ly** *adv.* —**dif·frac'tive·ness** *n.*

dif·frac·tion (di·frak'shən) *n. Physics* 1 A deviation of rays of light from a straight course when partially cut off by any obstacle or passing near the edges of an opening, or through a minute hole, generally accompanied by prismatic colors due to interference. Diffraction is a phenomenon accompanying all forms of wave motion, its effect being more marked as the wavelength increases. It is best shown by **diffraction gratings**, plates of glass or polished metal ruled closely with parallel lines, by means of which **diffraction spectra** are obtained. 2 A similar deviation of sound waves in passing the angle or edge of a large body.

dif·fuse (di·fyōōz') *v.t. & v.i.* **·fused, ·fus·ing** 1 To pour or send out so as to spread in all directions; spread abroad; circulate; permeate. 2 To subject to or spread by diffusion. See synonyms under SPREAD. —*adj.* (di·fyōōs') 1 Characterized by redundancy; prolix; verbose. 2 Widely spread out; extended. [< L *diffusus,* pp. of *diffundere* < *dis-* away, from + *fundere* pour] —**dif·fuse·ly** (di·fyōōs'lē) *adv.*

dif·fu·sion (di·fyōō'zhən) *n.* 1 The act or process of diffusing, or the state of being diffused; a scattering; dissemination; dispersion; circulation. 2 Prolixity; diffuseness of verbal expression. 3 The scattering and criss-crossing of light rays, producing general illumination rather than direct radiation. 4 *Physics* The intermingling by thermal agitation of the atoms or molecules of two substances initially unmixed but in contact. 5 *Anthropol.* The transmission of culture traits from one area, group, or people to another.

dig (dig) *v.* **dug** (*Archaic* **digged**), **dig·ging** *v.t.* 1 To break up, turn up, or remove (earth, etc.), as with a spade, claws, or the hands. 2 To make or form by or as by digging. 3 To take out or obtain by digging: to *dig* clams. 4 To thrust or force into or against, as a tool, heel, or elbow. 5 To discover or bring out by careful effort or study: often with *up* or *out:* to *dig* up evidence of political corruption. 6 *U.S. Slang* To understand. —*v.i.* 7 To break or turn up earth, etc. 8 To force or make a way by or as by digging. 9 *U.S. Colloq.* To work hard and steadily; plod. — **to dig in** 1 To dig trenches. 2 To entrench (oneself). 3 *Colloq.* To begin to work intensively. —*n. Colloq.* 1 A thrust; poke. 2 A sarcastic remark; jibe; slur. 3 An archeological excavation. 4 *U.S.* A hard-working student. [< OF *diguer* < Gmc. Akin to DIKE.]

di·gam·ma (dī·gam'ə) *n.* The original, but early disused, sixth letter in the Greek alphabet [F], equivalent in sound to *W*, but in form to *F*. [< Gk. < *di-* two + *gamma* the letter G] —**di·gam·mat·ed** (dī·gam'ā·tid) *adj.*

di·gas·tric (dī·gas'trik) *adj. Anat.* 1 Having fleshy ends and a central tendon, as one of the muscles that depress the lower jaw. 2 Having two bellies. [< DI-² + Gk. *gastēr* belly]

di·gen·e·sis (dī·jen'ə·sis) *n. Biol.* Reproduction by two methods, a sexual followed by an asexual; alternation of generations. [< DI-² + GENESIS] —**di·ge·net·ic** (dī'jə·net'ik) *adj.*

di·gest (di·jest', dī-) *v.t.* 1 To convert (food) into chyme in the stomach and intestines; prepare for assimilation. 2 To take in or assimilate mentally. 3 To arrange in systematic form, usually by condensing; summarize and classify. 4 To tolerate patiently; endure. 5 *Chem.* a To expose to heat or moisture so as to become softened or decomposed. b To treat, as wood, etc., with chemical agents under pressure so as to obtain a desired result. 6 *Obs.* To distribute; disperse. —*v.i.* 7 To be assimilated, as food. 8 To assimilate food. 9 To be subjected to heat, moisture, chemical agents, or pressure. —*n.* (dī'jest) 1 A systematic arrangement, as of writings; classified and abridged summary, as of news; compilation. 2 *Law* A compilation of statutes systematically arranged under proper heads and titles; a brief synopsis of the adjudications of courts as recorded in the original reports. See synonyms under ABRIDGMENT. [< L *digestus,* pp. of *digerere* < *dis-* away + *gerere* carry]

di·ges·tant (di·jes'tənt, dī-) *n.* Any drug which assists digestion. —*adj.* Digestive.

di·gest·er (dī·jes'tər, di-) *n.* 1 One who makes a digest, analysis, or summary. 2 A digestant. 3 A strong, closed vessel in which substances may be exposed to the action of water or other liquids at temperatures above their boiling points, to soften or decompose them or to extract some ingredient.

di·ges·tion (di·jes'chən, dī-) *n.* 1 *Physiol.* a The process of dissolving and chemically changing food in the stomach, so that it can be assimilated by the blood and furnish nutriment to the body. b The power to digest; the digestive functions. 2 Mental reception and assimilation. 3 Exposure of a substance to heat and moisture preparatory to a chemical or other operation; solution. 4 Any absorption and assimilation, as of carbon dioxide, or of insects and other animal matter, by plants.

di·ges·tive (di·jes'tiv, dī-) *adj.* Pertaining or conducing to digestion. —*n.* A medicine to aid digestion.

digger wasp A wasp (family *Sphecidae*) which digs a hole in the ground for its nest, especially the common American genera, *Sphex* or *Ammophila,* and *Bembidula.* For illustration see INSECT (beneficial).

dig·it (dij'it) *n.* 1 A finger or toe. 2 Any one of the ten Arabic numeral symbols, 0 to 9: so named from counting upon the fingers. 3 *Astron.* The twelfth part of the diameter of the sun or moon. 4 An old English measure of length, equal to about three fourths of an inch. [< L *digitus* finger]

dig·i·tal (dij'ə·təl) *adj.* 1 Of, pertaining to, or like the fingers or digits. 2 Digitate. 3 Showing information, such as numerals, by means of electronics: *digital* watches. —*n.* A key of the piano or organ. —**dig'i·tal·ly** *adv.*

digital computer An electronic computing machine which receives problems and processes the answers in numerical form, especially one using the binary system. Compare *analog computer.*

dig·i·tal·in (dij'ə·tal'in, -tā'lin) *n.* 1 A crystalline, poisonous glucoside, C₃₆H₅₆O₁₄, contained in the leaves of the foxglove, of which it is the active principle. 2 Any of several different extracts of foxglove.

dig·i·tal·is (dij'ə·tal'is, -tā'lis) *n.* 1 Any of a genus (*Digitalis*) of tall, Old World herbs of the figwort family, including *D. purpurea,* the foxglove, often cultivated: sometimes called *fairy gloves.* 2 The dried leaves of foxglove, containing several glucosides, some of which are used as a heart tonic. [< NL < L, finger-shaped < *digitus* finger]

dig·i·tal·ism (dij'ə·təl·iz'əm) *n. Pathol.* The effect on the body resulting from the excessive administration of digitalis.

dig·i·tate (dij'ə·tāt) *adj.* 1 *Bot.* Having parts, as leaflets, arranged like the fingers of a hand. 2 *Zool.* Having fingerlike processes. [< L *digitatus* < *digitus* finger] —**dig'i·tat·ed** *adj.* —**dig'i·tate·ly** *adv.*

digiti- *combining form* Finger; toe: digitiform. [< L *digitus* finger, toe]

dig·i·ti·grade (dij'ə·tə·grād') *adj. Zool.* Walking on the toes, without resting on the whole sole of the foot, as dogs, cats: opposed to *plantigrade.*

dig·i·tox·in (dij'ə·tok'sin) *n.* A powerful form of digitalin. [< DIGI(TALIS) + TOXIN]

dig·ni·fied (dig'nə·fīd) *adj.* 1 Characterized by or invested with dignity; stately. 2 Invested with dignities; promoted in rank; honored. See synonyms under GRAND. —**dig'ni·fied·ly** *adv.*

dig·ni·fy (dig'nə·fī) *v.t.* **·fied, ·fy·ing** 1 To impart or add dignity to; honor; ennoble. 2 To give a high-sounding name to. [< OF *dignefier* < Med. L *dignificare* < *dignus* worthy + *facere* make]

dig·ni·tar·y (dig'nə·ter'ē) *n. pl.* **·tar·ies** One having high official position; especially, a churchman of rank above a canon or priest.

dig·ni·ty (dig'nə·tē) *n. pl.* **·ties** 1 Grave or stately bearing; stateliness. 2 High rank; title, office, or position; distinction, especially in the church. 3 A dignitary; persons of high rank collectively. 4 The state or quality of being excellent, worthy, or honorable. 5 Grade of elevation; rank. [< OF *digneté* < L *dignitas, -tatis* < *dignus* worthy]

di·graph (dī'graf, -gräf) *n.* Consisting of two letters which represent only one sound. —*n.* A union of two characters representing a single sound, as *oa* in *boat, sh* in *she.* Compare LIGATURE, DIPHTHONG.

di·gress (di·gres', dī-) *v.i.* To turn aside from the main subject in speaking or writing; ramble; wander. See synonyms under WANDER. [< L *digressus,* pp. of *digredi* < *di-* away, apart + *gradi* go, step]

di·gres·sion (di·gresh'ən, dī-) *n.* 1 The act of digressing. 2 That which digresses; any part of a discourse or writing that deviates from the main subject. 3 Deviation; divergence. —**di·gres'sion·al** *adj.*

di·he·dral (dī·hē'drəl) *adj.* 1 Two-sided; formed by or having two plane faces. 2 *Aeron.* Having two or more plane faces: said of an airplane. [< DI-² + Gk. *hedra* base]

di·hy·dro·mor·phi·none hydrochloride (dī·hī'drō·môr'fə·nōn) A white, crystalline derivative of morphine, C₁₇H₁₉O₃N·HCl, a narcotic and analgesic of great potency: sometimes used as a substitute for morphine.

dik-dik (dik'dik') *n.* A small NE African antelope (genera *Madoqua* and *Rhynchotragus*) about a foot tall. [< native name]

dike (dīk) *n.* 1 An embankment to protect low land from inundation. 2 A bank formed by the excavation of a ditch; a causeway. 3 A low wall of stone or turf for dividing or enclosing land. 4 *Mining* A fissure which has been filled with solid material other than the ore through which it cuts. 5 *Geol.* A mass of igneous rock filling a fissure in other rocks, into which it has been intruded. —*v.t.* **diked, dik·ing** 1 To surround or furnish with a dike. 2 To drain by ditching. Also spelled *dyke.* [OE *dic.* Related to DITCH.] —**dik'ing, dik'er** *n.*

DIK-DIK

di·lac·er·ate (di·las'ə·rāt, dī-) *v.t.* **·at·ed, ·at·ing** To tear asunder; rip to pieces. [< L *dilaceratus,* pp. of *dilacerare* < *dis-* apart + *lacerare* tear, rip]

di·lap·i·date (di·lap'ə·dāt) *v.t. & v.i.* **·dat·ed, ·dat·ing** To fall or cause to fall into partial ruin or decay. [< L *dilapidatus,* pp. of *dilapidare* < *dis-* away + *lapidare* throw stones < *lapis, idis* stone] —**di·lap'i·dat·ed** *adj.* —**di·lap'i·da'tion** *n.*

di·la·tant (di·lā'tənt, di-) *adj.* Having the property of increasing in volume when changed in shape; dilating. —*n.* A dilating substance or instrument. —**di·la'tan·cy** *n.*

di·la·ta·tion (dī'lə·tā'shən, dil'ə-) *n.* 1 The act or process of dilating. 2 The state of being dilated. 3 That which is dilated. 4 *Pathol.* An excessive enlargement of an organ, orifice, or part. 5 *Med.*

A restoration to normal functioning of a small passageway, as in the throat or rectum.

di·late (dī·lāt′, di-) v. **·lat·ed, ·lat·ing** v.t. **1** To make wider, larger or expanded; cause to swell or spread. —v.i. **2** To expand, become larger or wider. **3** To speak or write diffusely; enlarge; expatiate: with *on* or *upon*. See synonyms under AMPLIFY. [< L *dilatare* spread out < *dis-* apart + *latus* wide] —**di·lat′a·ble** adj. —**di·lat′a·ble·ness, di·lat′a·bil′i·ty** n. —**di·lat′a·bly** adv.

dil·a·tom·e·ter (dil′ə·tom′ə·tər) n. An apparatus for measuring the expansion of substances, whether due to mechanical or chemical action. [< DILATE + -(O)METER] —**dil′a·tom′e·try** n.

di·la·tor (dī·lā′tər, di-) n. **1** One who or that which dilates. **2** *Med.* An instrument for opening or expanding a wound, aperture, or cavity. Also **di·la·ta·tor** (dī′lə·tā′tər, dil′ə-), **di·lat′er.**

dil·a·to·ry (dil′ə·tôr′ē, -tō′rē) adj. **1** Given to or characterized by delay; tardy; slow. **2** Tending to cause delay. See synonyms under SLOW, TEDIOUS. —**dil′a·to′ri·ly** adv. —**dil′a·to′ri·ness** n.

di·lem·ma (di·lem′ə) n. **1** A necessary choice between equally undesirable alternatives, a perplexing predicament. **2** *Logic* A syllogistic argument which presents an antagonist with two (or more) alternatives, but is equally conclusive against him, whichever alternative he chooses. —**the horns of a dilemma** The equally undesirable alternatives between which a choice must be made. [< LL < GK. *dilēmma* < *di-* two + *lēmma* a premise] —**dil·em·mat·ic** (dil′ə·mat′ik) adj.

dil·et·tan·te (dil′ə·tan′tē, dil′ə·tänt′) n. pl. **·ti** or **·tes 1** A person who interests himself in a subject merely for amusement or superficially. **2** A person who loves the arts. —adj. Pertaining to or like a dilettante. [< Ital., ppr. of *dilettare* delight < L *delectare*] —**dil′et·tan′tish, dil′et·tan′oo·te·ish** adj.

dil·et·tan·te·ism (dil′ə·tan′tē·iz′əm, dil′ə·tän′tiz·əm) n. The attitude or characteristics of a dilettante; a superficial approach or interest. Also **dil′et·tan′tism.**

dil·i·gence (dil′ə·jəns, *for def. 3 also Fr.* dē·lē·zhäns′) n. **1** Assiduous application; industry. **2** Proper heed or attention; meticulous care. **3** A Continental, four-wheeled, public stage-coach, divided into three compartments and having a driver's seat on top: used especially in 18th-century France: also **dil·ly** (dil′ē). See synonyms under INDUSTRY.

DILIGENCE

dil·i·gent (dil′ə·jənt) adj. **1** Possessed of or showing diligence; industrious. **2** Done or pursued diligently; painstaking: *diligent* search. See synonyms under ACTIVE, BUSY, INDUSTRIOUS. [< OF < L *diligens, -entis* attentive; orig. ppr. of *diligere* choose] —**dil′i·gent·ly** adv.

dill (dil) n. **1** An Old World annual of the parsley family (genus *Anethum*) with long-stalked umbels of yellow flowers and aromatic, pungent, medicinal seeds: referred to as *anise* in the Bible. **2** The seeds or leaves of this plant. [OE *dile*]

dill pickle A cucumber pickled in vinegar and flavored with dill.

dil·ly (dil′ē) n. **1** The daffodil. **2** *Colloq.* A good one; lulu. [Short for DAFFODIL]

dil·ly-dal·ly (dil′ē-dal′ē) v.i. **·dal·lied, ·dal·ly·ing** To waste time, especially in indecision or vacillation; loiter or trifle. [Varied reduplication of DALLY]

dil·u·ent (dil′yŏŏ·ənt) adj. **1** Serving to dilute, weaken, or thin by admixture; diluting. **2** Having the property of dissolving, solvent. —n. That which dilutes. [< L *diluens, -entis,* ppr. of *diluere.* See DILUTE.]

di·lute (di·lŏŏt′, dī-) v.t. **·lut·ed, ·lut·ing 1** To make weaker or more fluid by admixture. **2** To weaken; to reduce the intensity, strength,

or purity of (a color, drug, etc.) by admixture. —adj. (also dī′lŏŏt, -lyŏŏt) Weak; diluted. [< L *dilutus,* pp. of *diluere* < *dis-* away + *luere* wash]

di·lu·tion (di·lŏŏ′shən, dī·lyŏŏ′shən) n. **1** The act of diluting or weakening by admixture. **2** The state of being diluted. **3** Something diluted.

di·lu·vi·al (di·lŏŏ′vē·əl) adj. **1** Of or pertaining to a flood, especially the Noachian deluge. **2** *Geol.* Produced by a deluge or by floods; consisting of or related to diluvium. Also **di·lu′vi·an.**

di·lu·vi·um (di·lŏŏ′vē·əm) n. *Geol.* Coarse rock material transported and deposited by glaciers; glacial drift. [< NL < L, a flood < *diluere* wash away. See DILUTE.]

dim (dim) adj. **dim·mer, dim·mest 1** Obscure from faintness of light or from lack of visual or mental perception; indistinct; shadowy; misty; also, faint, as a sound. **2** Not seeing or perceiving clearly; purblind; obtuse. **3** Lacking luster; tarnished. See synonyms under DARK, FAINT, OBSCURE. —v.t. & v.i. dimmed, **dim·ming** To render or grow dim; fade. [OE *dim(m)*] —**dim′ly** adv. —**dim′ness** n.

dime (dīm) n. A silver coin, one tenth of a dollar. [< OF *disme* < L *decima* a tenth part < *decem*]

di·men·hy·drin·ate (dī′mən·hī′drə·nāt) n. *Chem.* A white, crystalline, odorless compound, $C_{17}H_{22}NO$, resembling the antihistamines in action.

di·men·sion (di·men′shən) n. **1** Any measurable extent or magnitude, as length, breadth, or thickness. **2** Importance; extent; bulk. **3** pl. Material parts, as of the human body; proportions. **4** *Math.* A factor used to characterize a term: $a^2 b^3 c^4$ is a term of nine *dimensions,* counting all the exponents. See synonyms under MAGNITUDE. [< MF < L *dimensio, -onis* < *dis-* apart + *metiri* measure]

di·mer (dī′mər) n. *Chem.* A compound formed by the polymerization of two molecules of the same substance. [< DI-2 + Gk. *meros* part]

di·mer·cap·rol (dī′mər·kap′rol) n. *Chem.* A colorless liquid compound, $C_3H_8OS_2$, containing two sulfhydryl radicals: used in medicine for the treatment of poisoning by arsenic, gold, and mercury. Also called *BAL.* [< DI-2 + MERCAP(TAN) + PR(OPANE) + -OL1]

dim·er·ous (dim′ər·əs) adj. **1** Composed of two members or parts. **2** *Bot.* Composed of two members in each circle or whorl: frequently written *2-merous.* **3** *Entomol.* Having two-jointed tarsi. —**dim′er·ism** n.

dim·e·ter (dim′ə·tər) n. In prosody, a verse of two metrical feet. [< DI-2 + -METER]

di·meth·yl (dī·meth′əl) n. *Chem.* An alkyl radical, $(CH_3)_2$, generally occurring in combination with other compounds: used in the making of drugs, dyestuffs, solvents, etc.

di·met·ric (dī·met′rik) adj. Tetragonal.

di·mid·i·ate (di·mid′ē·āt) adj. *Bot.* Divided in half; lop-sided: said of parts appearing to lack half of a member, or with halves functionally or structurally different. —v.t. **·at·ed, ·at·ing** To cut in half. [< L *dimidiatus,* pp. of *dimidiare* halve < *dimidium* a half < *dis-* apart + *medius* middle] —**di·mid′i·a′tion** n.

di·min·ish (di·min′ish) v.t. **1** To make smaller or less; lessen; decrease. **2** *Music* To lessen (an interval) by a half-step. —v.i. **3** To grow or become smaller or less; dwindle; decrease. See synonyms under ABATE, IMPAIR, RETRENCH. [Fusion of ME *diminuen* lessen (< OF *diminuer* < L *diminuere* < *de-* down + *minuere* lessen < *minus* less) and ME *menusen* < OF *menusier* MINISH] —**di·min′ish·a·ble** adj.

di·min·ish·ing return (di·min′ish·ing) *Econ.* The theory that an added increment of capital or labor, exceeding a fixed amount, causes a proportionately lower increase in production.

di·min·u·en·do (di·min′yŏŏ·en′dō) *Music* adj. & adv. Gradually lessening in volume of sound: expressed by *dim., dimin.,* or the sign $\diagdown$. —n. pl. **·dos** Diminution, as in force; a diminuendo passage in music. Also called *decrescendo.* [< Ital., ppr. of *diminuire* lessen < L *diminuere.* See DIMINISH.]

dim·i·nu·tion (dim′ə·nŏŏ′shən, -nyŏŏ′-) n. **1** The act of diminishing, or the condition of

being diminished: reduction. **2** *Music* The repetition of a theme in notes of one half or one quarter the time value of those first used: opposite of *augmentation.* [< AF *diminuciun* < L *diminutio, deminutio, -onis* < *diminuere.* See DIMINISH.]

di·min·u·tive (di·min′yə·tiv) adj. **1** Of relatively small size; small; little. **2** Diminishing or tending to diminish. **3** Expressing diminished size: said of certain suffixes. —n. **1** A word formed from another to express diminished size, or familiarity, affection, etc.: Johnny is a *diminutive* of John, Tom of Thomas, etc. Abbr. **dim. 2** Anything very small; a very small variety or form of anything. See synonyms under LITTLE, MINUTE.

dim·is·so·ry (dim′ə·sôr′ē, -sō′rē, də·mis′ər·ē) adj. **1** Sending away; dismissing to another jurisdiction: said of episcopal letters. **2** Granting leave to go away. [< LL *dimissorius* < L *dimittere* DISMISS]

dim·i·ty (dim′ə·tē) n. pl. **·ties** A sheer cotton fabric woven with stripes, cords, or checks: used for dresses, curtains, etc. [< Ital. *dimito* < Gk. *dimitos* having a double thread < *di-* two + *mitos* thread]

dim·mer (dim′ər) n. **1** Anything that dims. **2** *Electr.* An adjustable rheostat used for varying the intensity of illumination in a lamp system.

di·morph (dī′môrf) n. A form exhibiting dimorphism.

di·mor·phism (dī·môr′fiz·əm) n. **1** The quality of existing in two different forms. **2** *Bot.* The existence of two distinct forms of the same organ on the same plant, or on the same species of plant. **3** *Zool.* A difference in form, color, etc., between individuals of the same species, characterizing two distinct types. **4** *Physics* Crystallization of the same substance in two forms. **5** *Ling.* The existence of a word in two different forms in the same language, as *dent* and *dint, card* and *chart;* a doublet. [< Gk. *dimorphos* < *di-* two + *morphē* form] —**di·mor′phic, di·mor′phous** adj.

dim·ple (dim′pəl) n. A slight depression on the cheek or chin, or on any smooth surface. —v.t. & v.i. **dim·pled, dim·pling** To mark with dimples; form dimples. [ME *dympull*; origin uncertain] —**dim′ply** adj.

dim·wit (dim′wit′) n. *Slang.* A stupid or simple-minded person. —**dim′wit′ted** adj.

din (din) n. A loud continuous noise or clamor; a rattling or clattering sound. See synonyms under NOISE. —v. **dinned, din·ning** v.t. **1** To assail with confusing noise. **2** To urge or press with repetition or insistence. —v.i. **3** To make a din. [OE *dyne*]

di·nar (di·när′) n. **1** A gold coin of medieval Arabia, especially one issued by the caliphs of Damascus. **2** An Iranian money of account. **3** A silver coin of Yugoslavia. [< Arabic *dīnār* < LGk. *dēnarion* < L *denarius* DENARIUS]

dine (dīn) v. **dined, din·ing** v.i. **1** To eat dinner. **2** To eat any meal. —v.t. **3** To entertain at dinner. —**to dine out** To take a meal away from home. [< F *dîner* < OF *disner* < *dis-* away + *jejunus* fast] —**din′ing** adj. & n.

din·er (dī′nər) n. **1** One who dines. **2** A railroad dining-car. **3** A restaurant built in the form of a railroad car.

di·ner·ic (dī·ner′ik) adj. *Chem.* Of or relating to the surface separating two contiguous liquids in the same container. [DI-2 + Gk. *nēros* liquid]

di·ne·ro (dē·nā′rō) n. pl. **·ros 1** A Peruvian silver coin, one tenth of a sol. **2** *U.S. Slang* Money. [Sp., penny < L *denarius* DENARIUS]

di·nette (dī·net′) n. **1** An alcove where meals are served. **2** A little dinner. [< F]

di·neu·tron (dī·nŏŏ′tron, -nyŏŏ′-) n. *Physics* A transitory atomic particle believed to consist of two neutrons produced by tritons in a nuclear reaction and acting as a unit under certain special conditions.

ding (ding) v.t. **1** To ring; sound, as a bell. **2** *Colloq.* To instill by constant iteration; din. **3** *U.S. Slang & Brit. Dial.* To beat; strike. —v.i. **4** To ring or sound. **5** *Colloq.* To speak with constant iteration. —n. The sound of a bell or a sound like it. [Imit. Cf. ON *dengja* hammer, Dan. *dænge* bang, beat]

ding·bat (ding′bat′) *n. Colloq.*
1 Any small object, especially one hurled at another object. **2** A small thing, the name of which is unknown or unrecalled. **3** *Printing* An ornament. [< dial. *ding* knock, dash + BAT[1]]

ding-dong (ding′dong′, -dông′) *n.* **1** The peal of a bell. **2** Any monotonous repetition. **3** A device in a clock for striking the quarter-hours. —*adj.* **1** Characterized by successive blows. **2** *Colloq.* Energetically and closely contested, as a race. [Imit.]

DINGBATS
(def. 3)

din·ghy (ding′gē, ding′ē) *n. pl.* **·ghies** **1** Any of various kinds of small rowing boats, as a small, clinker-built skiff, a ship's boat, etc. **2** A sleeping car for railway employees. Also **din′gey, din′ghy, din′gy.** [<Hind. *dīngī*, boat]

din·gle (ding′gəl) *n.* **1** A narrow valley; glen. **2** *U.S. Dial.* The enclosed weather porch of a house. See synonyms under VALLEY. [ME *dingel*; origin unknown]

din·go (ding′gō) *n. pl.* **din·goes** The native wild dog (*Canis dingo*) of Australia, having a foxlike face, bushy tail, and reddish-brown color. [< native name]

ding·us (ding′əs) *n. Slang* A thing or device: said of something the name of which is unknown or forgotten. [<Afrikaans <*ding* a thing]

din·gy (din′jē) *adj.* **din·gi·er, din·gi·est** Of a dusky color, as if soiled; dull; tarnished; grimy; shabby. [Origin uncertain] — **din′gi·ly** *adv.* — **din′gi·ness** *n.*

dinitro– *combining form Chem.* Having two nitro groups, NO₂, as certain isomeric compounds.

di·ni·tro·ben·zene (dī-nī′trō-ben′zēn) *n. Chem.* One of three isomeric compounds, $C_6H_4(NO_2)_2$, that crystallizes in colorless flexible needles, formed by heating benzene with a mixture of nitric and sulfuric acids.

di·ni·tro·cre·sol (dī-nī′trō-krē′sol) *n. Chem.* A poisonous, orange, coal-tar dye, $C_7H_6O_5N_2$: sometimes used as a substitute for true saffron and in insecticides and rat-killers.

di·ni·tro·phe·nol (dī-nī′trō-fē′nol) *n. Chem.* Any of six isomeric nitrogen compounds, $C_6H_4O_5N_2$: used in the manufacture of dyes.

din·ner (din′ər) *n.* **1** The principal meal of the day. **2** A banquet in honor of a notable person or event. **3** A formal feast. [< F *dîner*. See DINE.]

din·ner·ware (din′ər-wâr′) *n.* The dishes used in a household for serving food.

dino– *combining form* Terrible; huge: *dinosaur.* [< Gk. *deinos* terrible]

di·noc·er·as (dī-nos′ər-əs) *n. Paleontol.* A gigantic, extinct, herbivorous mammal of the Tertiary period (order *Amblypoda*), having three pairs of protuberances on the upper surface of the head. [< DINO- + Gk. *keras* horn]

di·no·saur (dī′nə-sôr′) *n. Paleontol.* One of a group of reptiles (orders *Saurischia* and *Ornithischia*) existing on all the continents, but extinct by the end of the Mesozoic period. They varied in size from small, two-footed, pigeonlike carnivores to gigantic, four-footed, aquatic and terrestrial forms, many of them heavily armored, both herbivorous and carnivorous habits. [< DINO- + Gk. *sauros* lizard] —**di′no·sau′ri·an** *adj. & n.*

di·no·there (dī′nə·thir) *n. Paleontol.* One of an extinct Miocene genus (*Dinotherium*) of elephantlike mammals having a pair of huge tusks extending downward from the lower jaw. [< DINO- + Gk. *thēr* wildbeast]

dint (dint) *n.* **1** A small depression made by a blow; a dent. **2** Active agency; force; efficacy: by *dint* of. —*v.t.* To make a dent or dint in; to drive in forcibly. [OE *dynt* blow]

di·oc·e·san (dī-os′ə-sən, dī′ə-sē′sən) *adj.* Of or pertaining to a diocese. —*n.* A bishop in charge of a diocese.

di·o·cese (dī′ə-sēs, -sis) *n.* The territory or the churches under a bishop's jurisdiction. [< OF *diocise* < Med. L *diocesis* < L *dioecesis* a district < Gk. *dioikēsis*, orig. management of a house < *dia-* completely + *oikeein* dwell, manage]

di·ode (dī′ōd) *n. Electronics* A vacuum tube which permits the stream of electrons to pass in one direction only, from the cathode to the an-

ode; a rectifier. [< DI(A)- + Gk. *hodos* a road, way]

di·oe·cious (dī-ē′shəs) *adj. Bot.* Having the male and female organs borne by different individuals, as a plant with stamens and pistils in separate individuals: also spelled *diecious.* Also **di·oi·cous** (dī-oi′kəs). [< DI-[2] + Gk. *oikia* house, dwelling] —**di·oe′cious·ly** *adv.* —**di·oe′cious·ness** *n.*

di·oes·trum (dī-es′trəm, -ēs′-) *n. Zool.* The period of calm in the estrus or mating cycle of animals. [< NL < Gk. *dia-* between + *oistros* passion, frenzy] —**di·oes′trous** *adj.*

di·o·nae·a (dī′ə-nē′ə) *n.* The Venus flytrap. [< NL < Gk. *Diōnē* Dione]

di·op·side (dī-op′sīd, -sid) *n.* A grayish-white or grayish-green variety of pyroxene. [< F < Gk. *di-* two + *opsis* view]

di·op·tase (dī-op′tās) *n.* A vitreous, emerald-green, transparent to translucent, hydrous copper silicate, crystallizing in the hexagonal system. [< F < Gk. *dia-* through + *optos* visible]

di·op·ter (dī-op′tər) *n. Optics* The unit for measuring the refractive power of a lens, expressed as the reciprocal of its focal length in meters: a convergent lens of 1 meter focal length has a power of +1 diopter; a divergent lens, of −1 diopter. Also **di·op′tre, di·op′try.** [< MF *dioptre* < L *dioptra* < Gk., an optical instrument]

di·op·tom·e·ter (dī′op·tom′ə·tər) *n.* An optical instrument for measuring refraction and accommodation of the eye. [< DI(A)- + OPTOMETER]

di·op·tric (dī-op′trik) *adj. Optics* **1** Aiding the vision by refraction, as a lens. **2** Of or pertaining to dioptrics. **3** Of or pertaining to a diopter, or the system of numbering optical glasses metrically. Also **di·op′tri·cal.** [< Gk. *dioptrikos* belonging to the use of the dioptra < *dioptra* diopter]

di·op·trics (dī-op′triks) *n.* The branch of optics treating of light-refraction by transparent media.

di·o·ra·ma (dī′ə·rä′mə, -ram′ə) *n.* **1** A painting, or a series of paintings, for exhibition, in which, by the use of cloth transparencies and arrangements of lights, alterations in the pictures are produced in view of the spectators. **2** A group of modeled figures, for exhibition, set in a naturalistic foreground blended into a painted background. **3** A building in which such a picture or group is exhibited. [< Gk. *dia-* through + *horama* a sight] —**di·o·ram·ic** (dī′ə·ram′ik) *adj.*

di·o·rite (dī′ə·rīt) *n.* A granular, crystallized, igneous rock composed of feldspar and hornblende. Also **di′o·ryte.** [< F < Gk. *diorizein* divide < *dia-* through + *horos* limit] —**di·o·rit·ic** (dī′ə·rit′ik) *adj.*

di·ox·ane (dī-ok′sān) *n. Chem.* A colorless liquid derivative of glycol, $C_4H_8O_2$, having a pleasant, faint odor: used as a solvent for resins, oils, waxes, and organic compounds. [< DI-[2] + OX(A)- + -ANE[2]]

di·ox·ide (dī-ok′sīd, -sid) *n. Chem.* An oxide containing two atoms of oxygen to the molecule. Also **di·ox·id** (dī-ok′sid).

di·ox·in (dī-ok′sən) *n.* An extremely toxic and mutagenic, fat-soluble compound produced inadvertently in the large-scale manufacture of polychlorinated biphenyls.

dip (dip) *v.* **dipped, dip·ping** *v.t.* **1** To put or let down into a liquid momentarily and then take out. **2** To obtain or lift up and out by scooping, bailing, etc.: to *dip* crackers from a barrel, or water from a boat. **3** To lower and then raise, as a flag in salute. **4** To baptize by immersion. **5** To plunge (animals) into a disinfectant so as to rid of insects, germs, etc. **6** To dye by immersion. **7** *Chem.* To coat (a metallic surface) by immersion in a solution of readily decomposed salt. **8** To make (candles) by repeatedly immersing wicks in wax or tallow. **9** *Obs.* To wet. **10** *U.S. Colloq.* To apply snuff to the gums and teeth. —*v.i.* **11** To plunge into and come out of water or other liquid, especially briefly and quickly. **12** To plunge one's hand or a receptacle into water, etc., or into a container, especially so as to take something out. **13** To sink or go down suddenly. **14** To incline downward; go down; decline. **15** *Geol.* To lie at an angle to the horizon, as rock strata. **16** *Aeron.* To drop rapidly and then climb. **17** To engage in or inquire into something slightly or

superficially; dabble. **18** To read here and there, as in a book or magazine; browse. —**to dip into** To take a part of (something held in reserve, saved, etc.): to *dip into* one's savings account. See synonyms under IMMERSE. —*n.* **1** The act of dipping; a plunge; bath; depression. **2** A liquid into which something is to be dipped. **3** Inclination, as of the magnetic needle. **4** A candle made by dipping a wick repeatedly into melted tallow. **5** Magnetic dip. **6** *Geol.* Position, other than horizontal, or rock strata; also, the angle between strata and the horizontal plane. **7** *Aeron.* A rapid drop of an airplane followed by a climb. **8** *Colloq.* A pickpocket. **9** A small amount of snuff taken into the mouth on a moistened brush. **10** An antiseptic solution in which sheep are dipped to kill parasites: also called *sheep dip.* [OE *dyppan.* Related to DEEP.]

di·pet·al·ous (dī-pet′əl-əs) *adj. Bot.* Having two petals: also *bipetalous.*

di·phase (dī′fāz′) *adj. Electr.* **1** Having two phases: said of a current compounded of two alternating currents, the maxima and minima of which differ from one another by 90 degrees. **2** The circuit carrying such a current or the generator producing it. Also **di·phas·ic** (dī-fā′zik).

di·phen·yl (dī-fen′əl, dī-fē′nəl) *n.* Biphenyl.

di·phen·yl·a·mine (dī-fen′əl-ə-mēn′, -am′in, -fē′nəl-) *n. Chem.* A crystalline aromatic amine, $(C_6H_5)_2NH$, obtained by heating aniline hydrochloride with aniline: used as a stabilizer and in the manufacture of dyestuffs. Also **di·phen′yl·am′in** (-am′in).

di·phen·yl·am·ine·chlor·ar·sine (dī-fen′əl-am′in-klôr′sēn, -sin, -fē′nəl-) *n.* Adamsite.

di·phen·yl·cy·an·ar·sine (dī-fen′əl-sī′ə·när′sēn, -sin, -fē′nəl-) *n. Chem.* A lung irritant compound, $(C_6H_5)_2AsCN$, with an odor of garlic and bitter almonds: used in chemical warfare.

di·phen·yl·hy·dan·toin sodium (dī-fen′əl-hī-dan′tō-in, -fē′nəl-) *Chem.* A white, odorless, slightly bitter compound, $C_{15}H_{11}N_2O_2Na$: used in the treatment of epileptic convulsions. Also called *Dilantin.*

di·pho·ni·a (dī-fō′nē-ə, -fōn′yə, di-) *n.* A speech condition in which the same voice produces two distinct tones; double voice. [< NL < Gk. *di-* two + *phonē* sound]

di·phos·gene (dī-fos′jēn) *n. Chem.* A chemical warfare agent, $C_2O_2Cl_4$, an oily liquid with a suffocating odor and a destructive effect on the lungs.

diph·the·ri·a (dif-thir′ē-ə, dip-) *n. Pathol.* An acute contagious disease, caused by the Klebs–Loeffler bacillus (*Corynebacterium diphtheriae*) and characterized by inflammation, usually of the pharynx, the formation of a false membrane on mucous surfaces, and toxemia. [< NL < F *diphthérie* < Gk. *diphthera* leather, membrane]

diph·the·rit·ic (dif′thə·rit′ik, dip-) *adj. Pathol.* **1** Pertaining to diphtheria. **2** Resembling, or having symptoms characteristic of diphtheria. Also **diph·the′ri·al, diph·the′ric.**

diph·thong (dif′thông, -thong, dip′-) *n.* **1** *Phonet.* A combination of two vowels in one syllable, whether written with two letters, as *oi* in *coil* and *ou* in *doubt,* or with a single letter, as *i* in *fine* and *a* in *bate.* **2** In popular usage, either of the ligatures æ, œ, pronounced as a single sound, but which were true diphthongs in classical Latin. See DIGRAPH, TRIGRAPH. [< F *diphthongue* < LL *diphthongus* < Gk. *diphthongos* < *di-* two + *phthongos* sound] — **diph·thon′gal** *adj.* — **diph·thong′ic** *adj.*

diph·thong·ize (dif′thông-īz, -thong-, dip′-) *v.* **·ized, ·iz·ing** *v.t.* **1** To make a diphthong of; combine with another sound in a diphthong. **2** To pronounce as a diphthong. —*v.i.* **3** To become a diphthong. — **diph′thong·i·za′tion, diph′thong·a′tion** *n.*

di·phyl·lous (dī-fil′əs) *adj. Bot.* Two-leaved. [< DI- + Gk. *phyllon* leaf]

diph·y·o·dont (dif′ē-ō-dont′) *adj. Zool.* Having two sets of teeth, one deciduous, the second permanent. [< Gk. *diphyēs* double + *odous, odontos* tooth]

diplo– *combining form* Double: *diplococcus.* Also, before vowels, **dipl–.** [< Gk. *diploos* double]

dip·lo·car·di·a (dip′lə-kär′dē-ə) *n. Anat.* A condition in which the right and left sides of the heart are distinctly separated, as by a fissure.

[<DIPLO- + Gk. *kardia* heart] — **dip′lo·car′·di·ac** (-ak) *adj.*

dip·lo·coc·cus (dip′lə-kok′əs) *n. pl.* **·coc·ci** (-kok′sī) **1** A cell or micro-organism consisting of two cells united. **2** *Bacteriol.* Any of a genus (*Diplococcus*) of parasitic bacteria, Gram-positive, usually encapsulated and occurring in pairs or chains, including *D. pneumoniae*, the infective agent of lobar pneumonia. See illustration under BACTERIA.

dip·lo·e (dip′lō-ē) *n. Anat.* The reticulate bony tissue between the two walls of the cranial bones. [<NL <Gk., a fold]

dip·loid (dip′loid) *adj.* **1** Twofold or doubled. **2** *Biol.* Having two sets of chromosomes in the somatic cells, as of all higher organisms. — *n.* **1** A cell having double the haploid number of chromosomes. **2** An isometric crystal with 24 trapezoidal planes.

di·plo·ma (di-plō′mə) *n.* **1** A writing, usually under seal, granting some privilege or authority, or bestowing some honor; especially, the official certificate of graduation in arts, medicine, law, etc., bestowed by a college or university. **2** An instrument authorizing a person to practice a profession. **3** An official document; charter. [<L <Gk. *diploma* paper folded double, a letter]

di·plo·ma·cy (di-plō′mə-sē) *n. pl.* **·cies 1** The art, science, or practice of conducting negotiations between nations. **2** Tact, shrewdness, or skill in conducting any affair. [<F *diplomatie* <*diplomate* DIPLOMAT]

dip·lo·mat (dip′lə-mat) *n.* One employed or skilled in diplomacy. [<F *diplomate* <*diplomatique* <NL *diplomaticus* <L *diploma* DIPLOMA]

dip·lo·mat·ic (dip′lə-mat′ik) *adj.* **1** Of or pertaining to diplomacy. **2** Characterized by special tact in negotiation; wary; adroit; tactful. **3** Pertaining to diplomatics. Also **dip′lo·mat′i·cal.** See synonyms under POLITIC.

diplomatic immunity Exemption of diplomatic agents or representatives, their staffs and premises, from the ordinary processes of local law.

dip·lo·mat·ics (dip′lə-mat′iks) *n.* **1** The science of deciphering ancient documents, charters, etc. **2** Diplomacy.

di·plo·ma·tist (di-plō′mə-tist) *n.* **1** A diplomat. **2** One remarkable for tact and shrewd management.

di·plo·pi·a (di-plō′pē-ə) *n. Pathol.* A derangement of the visual axes whereby two distinct impressions are received from a single object; double vision. Also **dip·lo·py** (dip′lə-pē). [<NL <Gk. *diploos* double + *ops* eye] — **di·plop·ic** (di-plop′ik) *adj.*

dip·lo·pod (dip′lə-pod) *n. Zool.* Any of a class (*Diplopoda*) of segmented terrestrial arthropods; the millipedes. [<NL *Diplopoda* <Gk. *diploos* double + *pous, podos* foot]

di·plo·sis (di-plō′sis) *n. Genetics* The union of two haploid sets of chromosomes by syngamy of the male and female gametes. [<DIPL(O)- + -OSIS]

dip·lo·some (dip′lə-sōm) *n. Biol.* A small, paired body in the cell, as a double centriole within the centrosome.

dip·lo·so·mi·a (dip′lə-sō′mē-ə, -sōm′yə) *n. Pathol.* An abnormal joining of two bodies. Also **dip·lo·so·ma·tia** (dip′lə-sō-mā′shə, -shē-ə). [<NL <Gk. *diploos* double + *sōma* body]

dip·lo·ste·mo·nous (dip′lə-stē′mə-nəs) *adj. Bot.* Having twice as many stamens as petals. [<DIPLO- + Gk. *stēmōn* thread (used for *stēma* a stamen)]

dip needle An inclinometer (def. 2), used in magnetic compasses.

dip·no·an (dip′nō-ən) *n.* Any of a group (*Dipnoi*) of fishes with regular gills, a single or double lung, and nostrils inside as well as outside the mouth; a lungfish. — *adj.* Of or pertaining to the *Dipnoi.* [<NL <Gk. *dipnoos* <*dis-* two + *pnoē* breath]

dip·o·dy (dip′ə-dē) *n. pl.* **·dies** In prosody, a dimeter. [<L *dipodia* <Gk. <*dis-* two + *pous, podos* foot]

di·pole (dī′pōl′) *n.* **1** *Physics* Any material system having two electric charges, equal in magnitude but of unlike sign, as the proton and electron of a hydrogen atom, or two equal but opposite magnetic poles. **2** *Chem.*

A molecule exhibiting polar separation of positive and negative charges.

dip·per (dip′ər) *n.* **1** A long-handled, bowl-shaped utensil, used principally for dipping water, as from a larger vessel into a smaller one. **2** Any of several American birds, so called because they are quick divers; specifically, the dabchick or pied-billed grebe, the small bufflehead duck of North America, and the water ouzel.

dip·sas (dip′səs) *n. pl.* **dip·sa·des** (dip′sə-dēz) **1** A serpent whose bite was fabled to produce extreme thirst. **2** Any of several tropical colubrine snakes (subfamily *Dipsadomorphinae*). [<L <Gk. <*dipsa* thirst]

dip·sey (dip′sē) *adj.* Deep-sea. — *n. pl.* **·sies 1** A sinker for a fishing line. **2** A line equipped with a number of hooks and sinkers used for bottom fishing. Also **dip′sie, dip′sy.** [Alter. of DEEP-SEA]

dip·so·ma·ni·a (dip′sə-mā′nē-ə) *n.* An uncontrollable craving for alcoholic drink. [<Gk. *dipsa* thirst + -MANIA]

dip·so·ma·ni·ac (dip′sə-mā′nē-ak) *adj.* Pertaining to or affected by dipsomania: a dipsomaniac diathesis: also **dip·so·ma·ni·a·cal** (dip′sə-mə-nī′ə-kəl) — *n.* A person affected with dipsomania; a confirmed drunkard.

dip·ter·al (dip′tər-əl) *adj.* **1** *Archit.* Having or resembling a double peristyle or colonnade. **2** Dipterous. [<L *dipteros* <Gk. *dipteros*. See DIPTEROUS.]

dip·ter·an (dip′tər-ən) *n.* A dipterous insect. Also **dip′ter·on** (-on).

dip·ter·ous (dip′tər-əs) *adj.* **1** *Entomol.* Of or pertaining to an order (*Diptera*) of insects having a single pair of membranous wings with a posterior pair of balancers and a sucking proboscis, including the flies, gnats, mosquitoes, etc. **2** *Bot.* Two-winged, as a seed or fruit. [<Gk. *dipteros* two-winged <*di-* twice + *pteron* wing]

dip·tych (dip′tik) *n.* **1** A double tablet; especially, two tablets of wood, metal, or ivory, hinged together and covered on the inside with wax, on which the ancient Greeks and Romans wrote with a stylus. **2** A cover for a book, resembling this. **3** A double picture or design on a pair of hinged tablets or panels. [<LL *diptycha* <Gk., pair of tablets; orig. neut. pl. of *diptychos* folded <*di-* twice + *ptyssein* fold]

DIPTYCH (*def.* 3)

dire (dīr) *adj.* **dir·er, dir·est** Extremely calamitous; dreadful; terrible. See synonyms under AWFUL. [<L *dirus* fearful] — **dire′ful** *adj.*

di·rect (di-rekt′, dī-) *v.t.* **1** To control or conduct the affairs of; manage; govern. **2** To order or instruct with authority; command: often with a clause as object. **3** *Music* To lead as a conductor. **4** To tell (someone) the way. **5** To cause to move, face, or go in a desired direction; aim: He *directed* his gaze toward her. **6** To indicate the destination of, as a letter. **7** To intend, as remarks or insults, to be heard by a person; address: Did you *direct* that remark at me? — *v.i.* **8** To give commands or guidance. **9** To lead performances, musicians, etc. See synonyms under DICTATE, GOVERN, LEAD, REGULATE. — *adj.* **1** Having or being the straightest course; straight; shortest; nearest. **2** Free from intervening agencies or conditions; immediate; exact; in the speaker's words: *direct* discourse. **3** Straightforward, as in meaning, statement or intention; unambiguous; candid; plain. **4** Of succession, lineal: opposed to *collateral*. **5** *Electr.* **a** Continuous as opposed to alternating, as a current. **b** Having the same direction as the primary: said of an induced current: opposed to *inverse*. **6** *Astron.* Designating motion on the celestial sphere from west toward east, in the direction of the sun's movement among the stars: opposed to *retrograde*. **7** *Chem.* Of or pertaining to dyes applied to fabrics without the use of mordants; substantive. See synonyms under IMMEDIATE,

RIGHT. — *adv.* By direct course: directly. — *n. Music* A mark (∨ or ∧) at the end of a line or page of music indicating the position of the first note on the next. [<L *directus*, pp. of *dirigere* <*dis-* apart + *regere* set straight]

di·rect–ac·tion (di-rekt′ak′shən, dī-) *adj. Mech.* Having no transmitting mechanism, such as gearwheels, between the part driven and the power that drives it.

di·rec·tion (di-rek′shən, dī-) *n.* **1** The position of one point in relation to another without reference to the intervening distance. **2** The trend of a line or of a course of motion, as determined by its spatial relation with some fixed standard of reference; loosely, the trend of a line or course as determined by its extremity. **3** Tendency; aim. **4** The act of directing, governing, or ordering; superintendence; administration. **5** Instruction; command; order. **6** The name and residence of a person; address. **7** *Music* A sign, phrase, or word, in a score designating the proper mood, intensity, etc., of a passage.

Synonyms: aim, bearing, course, inclination, tendency, way. The *direction* of an object is the line of motion or of vision toward it, or the line in which the object is moving, considered from one's own standpoint. *Way*, literally the road or path, comes naturally to mean the *direction* of the road or path. *Bearing* is direction with reference to another object or to the points of the compass. *Course* is the direction of a moving object; *inclination*, that toward which an object leans; *tendency*, that toward which anything stretches or reaches out; *tendency* is stronger and more active than *inclination*. See AIM, CARE, INCLINATION, ORDER, OVERSIGHT.

di·rec·tion·al (di-rek′shən-əl, dī-) *adj.* **1** Pertaining to direction in space. **2** *Telecom.* **a** Adapted for indicating from which of several directions signals are received. **b** Describing an antenna which radiates or receives radio waves more effectively in or from some directions than from others.

di·rec·tive (di-rek′tiv, dī-) *n.* **1** An order or regulation. **2** The document or the vehicle through which the order is transmitted: applied especially to governmental and military pronouncements. — *adj.* **1** That directs or points out, rules, or governs. **2** Responsive to direction.

di·rect·ly (di-rekt′lē, dī-) *adv.* **1** In a direct line or manner. **2** Without medium, agent, or go-between. **3** Immediately; as soon as possible. **4** Exactly; precisely. See synonyms under IMMEDIATELY. — *conj. Brit.* As soon as.

direct mail Mail sent directly to individuals that promotes the sale of merchandise or services or solicits contributions.

di·rect·ness (di-rekt′nis, dī-) *n.* The quality of being direct; straightness; straightforwardness.

di·rec·tor (di-rek′tər, dī-) *n.* **1** One who or that which directs; specifically, a member of a governing body, as of a club or corporation. **2** A conductor of an orchestra. **3** One who supervises a dramatic production. **4** In the Roman Catholic Church, a spiritual guide. **5** *Mil.* An apparatus that systematically computes firing data for use against moving enemy targets. Also **di·rect′er.** See synonyms under MASTER. — **di·rec′tress** *n. fem.*

di·rec·to·ry (di-rek′tər-ē, dī-) *n. pl.* **·ries 1** An alphabetical or classified list, as of the names and addresses of the inhabitants or business houses of a city. **2** A collection of rules; especially a book of directions for church worship, as the ordinal of the Roman Catholic Church, or the rules adopted by the Scottish General Assembly in 1645, still observed in the Presbyterian Church. **3** A body of directors. — *adj.* Containing directions.

di·rec·trix (di-rek′triks, dī-) *n. pl.* **·tri·ces** (-trī-sēz) or **·trix·es 1** *Mil.* In gunnery, the median line in the plane of fire. **2** *Geom.* A line which so determines the motion of another line, or of a point, that the latter shall describe some surface or curve.

dire·ful (dīr′fəl) *adj.* Most dire; dreadful; terrible. See synonyms under AWFUL, FRIGHTFUL. — **dire′ful·ly** *adv.* — **dire′ful·ness** *n.*

dirge (dûrj) *n.* **1** A song, tune, lament, or

wail expressing grief and mourning. **2** A hymn or choral service at a funeral. [<L *dirige* (imperative of *dirigere* DIRECT), the first word of the antiphon (*Psalms* v 8) of matins in the Latin burial office] — **dirge′·ful** *adj.*

dir·i·ga·tion (dir′ə·gā′shən) *n.* **1** The power of controlling or modifying involuntary bodily functions, such as the pulse, temperature, or digestion. **2** The exercise of that power. [<L *dirigere* DIRECT + -ATION]

dir·i·gi·ble (dir′ə·jə·bəl) *adj.* **1** That may be directed or controlled: a *dirigible* balloon.

A RIGID TYPE OF DIRIGIBLE

2 *Aeron.* Designating an airship, the outer envelope of which is of elongated form, provided with a propelling system, cars, rudders, and stabilizing surfaces. The form of the envelope may be **nonrigid**, by the pressure of the contained gases assisted by the car-suspension system; **rigid**, by a framework contained within the envelope; or **semirigid**, by means of attachment to an exterior girder construction containing the cars. — *n.* An airship. [<L *dirigere* DIRECT + -IBLE] — **dir′i·gi·bil′i·ty** *n.*

dir·i·ment (dir′ə·mənt) *adj.* Rendering absolutely void; nullifying. [<L *dirimens, -entis,* ppr. of *dirimere* < *dis-* apart + *emere* take]

dirk (dûrk) *n.* A dagger or poniard. — *v.t.* To stab with a dirk. [Origin unknown]

dirn·dl (dûrn′dəl) *n.* **1** A woman's dress with a full skirt gathered to a tight bodice. **2** Such a skirt without the bodice: also **dirndl skirt.** [<G *dirndl* girl]

dirt (dûrt) *n.* **1** Any foul or filthy substance; refuse; trash. **2** Loose earth; garden loam. **3** Uncleanness in action or speech; abuse or obscenity. **4** In placer mining, washed-down material or detritus containing precious metal: called **pay dirt** when it yields more than enough to compensate for working. — *adj.* Made of earth: a *dirt* road. [Metathetical var. of earlier *drit* <ON, dirt, bird droppings]

dirt·y (dûr′tē) *adj.* **dirt·i·er, dirt·i·est 1** Unclean; foul; imparting dirt; filthy. **2** Base; despicable; contemptible; also, mean or unkind. **3** Impure; not clear: said of colors. **4** Uncomfortable or disagreeable to the traveler, as weather or roads. **5** Obscene. See synonyms under FOUL. — *v.t. & v.i.* **dirt·ied, dirt·y·ing** To make or become dirty or soiled. — **dirt′i·ly** *adv.* — **dirt′i·ness** *n.*

dirty work 1 *Colloq.* Trickery; deceit; foul play. **2** A difficult job or the most difficult part of a job.

dis-¹ *prefix* **1** Apart; away from: *disembody, dislodge, dismiss, dissolve.* **2** The reverse of or the undoing of (what is expressed in the rest of the word): *disarm, disband, disconnect, disrobe, disown.* **3** Deprivation of some quality, power, rank, etc.: *disable, disbar, discolor, disenfranchise.* **4** Not: *disadvantageous, disloyal, distasteful.* **5** Completely; thoroughly (simple intensive with an already negative word): *disannul.* Also: *di-* before *b, d, l, m, n, r, s, v,* and usually before *g,* as in *digress, direct, diverge* (in Late Latin this was often changed back to the full form, as in *dismiss, disrupt*); *dif-* before *f,* as in *differ.* The living English prefix is always in the form *dis-.* [<L *dis-,* sometimes replacing OF *des-* (see DE-)]

dis-² *prefix* Var. of DI-². [<Gk. *dis* twice]

dis·a·bil·i·ty (dis′ə·bil′ə·tē) *n. pl.* **·ties 1** That which disables. **2** Lack of ability; inability. **3** Legal incapacity or inability to act.

disability clause In insurance policies, a clause waiving premiums upon certain disabilities of the policyholders.

dis·a·ble (dis·ā′bəl) *v.t.* **·a·bled, ·a·bling 1** To render incapable or unable; cripple; impair. **2** To render legally incapable, as of inheriting property, etc. — **dis·a′ble·ment** *n.*

dis·a·bled (dis·ā′bəld) *adj.* Incapacitated.

dis·a·buse (dis′ə·byōoz′) *v.t.* **·a·bused, ·a·bus·ing** To rid of a false notion or impression.

di·sac·cha·ride (dī·sak′ə·rīd, -rid) *n. Biochem.* One of a series of carbohydrates, as lactose

and maltose, constituting the chief ingredients of sugarcane and milk: on hydrolysis, they yield two monosaccharides. Also **di·sac′cha·rid** (-rid). [<DI-² + SACCHARIDE]

dis·ac·cord (dis′ə·kôrd′) *n.* The state of being inharmonious; disagreement; incongruity. — *v.t.* To disagree; refuse assent. [<OF *desacorder* < *des-* away + *acorder* ACCORD]

dis·ac·cus·tom (dis′ə·kus′təm) *v.t.* To free of a habit or of anything to which one has been habituated. — **dis′ac·cus′tomed** *adj.* — **dis′ac·cus′tomed·ness** *n.*

dis·ad·van·tage (dis′əd·van′tij, -vän′-) *n.* **1** That which hinders, prevents, or is prejudicial to success. **2** Prejudice to interest, reputation, credit, or other good; loss; drawback; injury. **3** A state of inferiority; unfavorable condition: The army was at a *disadvantage.* See synonyms under INJURY, LOSS. — *v.t.* **·taged, ·tag·ing** To injure the interest of; prejudice; hinder. [<OF *désavauntage* < *dés-* away (<L *dis-*) + *avauntage* ADVANTAGE]

dis·ad·van·taged (dis′əd·van′tjəd) *adj.* Having less than what is regarded as basic or minimal for decent living, as money, social position, etc.; underprivileged.

dis·ad·van·ta·geous (dis·ad′vən·tā′jəs) *adj.* Attended with disadvantage; detrimental; inconvenient. — **dis·ad′van·ta·geous·ly** *adv.*

dis·af·fect (dis′ə·fekt′) *v.t.* To destroy or weaken the affection or loyalty of; alienate.

dis·af·fect·ed (dis′ə·fek′tid) *adj.* Alienated in feeling or loyalty; estranged. See synonyms under INIMICAL. — **dis·af·fect′ed·ly** *adv.*

dis·af·fil·i·ate (dis′ə·fil′ē·āt) *v.t. & v.i.* **·at·ed, ·at·ing** To sever affiliation (with).

dis·af·firm (dis′ə·fûrm′) *v.t.* **1** To deny; contradict. **2** *Law* **a** To reverse; set aside, as a decision. **b** To repudiate; disclaim, as a contract. — **dis·af·firm′ance, dis·af·fir·ma′tion** (dis·af′ər·mā′shən) *n.*

dis·af·for·est (dis′ə·fôr′ist, -for′-) *v.t.* **1** In English law, to reduce from the privileges of a forest to common ground. Compare AF-FOREST. **2** To clear of forests. [<Med.L *disafforestare* < *dis-* away + *afforestare* AFFOREST]

dis·a·gree (dis′ə·grē′) *v.i.* **·a·greed, ·a·gree·ing 1** To vary in opinion; differ; dissent. **2** To quarrel. **3** To fail to agree or harmonize, as facts. **4** To be unfavorable or injurious in action or effect, as food or climate: with *with.* [<OF *desagreer* < *des-* away (<L *dis-*) + *agreer* AGREE]

dis·a·gree·a·ble (dis′ə·grē′ə·bəl) *adj.* ʽRepugnant to taste, sentiment, opinion, or the senses; not agreeable; displeasing; unpleasant.

dis·a·gree·ment (dis′ə·grē′mənt) *n.* Failure to agree; dissimilarity; variance; unsuitableness; incongruity; altercation; quarrel. See synonyms under DIFFERENCE, QUARREL.

dis·al·low (dis′ə·lou′) *v.t.* **1** To refuse to allow or permit. **2** To reject as untrue or invalid. See synonyms under PROHIBIT. [<OF *desalouer* < *des-* away (<L *dis-*) + *alouer* ALLOW]

dis·a·noint (dis′ə·noint′) *v.t.* To invalidate the consecration of.

dis·ap·pear (dis′ə·pir′) *v.i.* **1** To pass from sight or view; fade away; vanish. **2** To cease to exist. — **dis′ap·pear′ance** *n.*

disappearing carriage *Mil.* A mechanism by which coastal artillery of large caliber is raised above a protective embankment before firing and automatically lowered behind it after the discharge.

dis·ap·point (dis′ə·point′) *v.t.* **1** To fail to fulfil the expectation, hope, or desire of (a person). **2** To prevent the fulfilment of (a hope or plan); frustrate. [<OF *desappointer* < *des-* away (<L *dis-*) + *appointer* APPOINT]

dis·ap·point·ment (dis′ə·point′mənt) *n.* **1** The state, condition, or sense of being disappointed. **2** That which disappoints: failure; frustration. See synonyms under CHAGRIN, MISFORTUNE.

dis·ap·pro·ba·tion (dis·ap′rə·bā′shən) *n.* Disapproval; unfavorable judgment. — **dis·ap·pro·ba·to·ry** (dis·ap′rə·bə·tôr′ē, -tō′rē) *adj.*

dis·ap·prov·al (dis′ə·prōō′vəl) *n.* The act of disapproving; the withholding of approval; disapprobation. See synonyms under ANIMAD-VERSION.

dis·ap·prove (dis′ə·prōōv′) *v.* **·proved, ·prov·ing** *v.t.* **1** To regard with disfavor or censure; condemn. **2** To refuse assent to; decline to approve. — *v.i.* **3** To have or express an unfavorable opinion: often with *of.* — **dis′ap-**

prov′ing *adj.* — **dis′ap·prov′ing·ly** *adv.*

dis·arm (dis·ärm′) *v.t.* **1** To deprive of weapons. **2** To render harmless; make unable to do damage, attack, or defend. **3** To allay or reduce, as suspicion or antagonism. — *v.i.* **4** To lay down arms. **5** To reduce or restrict the size of armed forces. [<OF *desarmer* < *des-* away (<L *dis-*) + *armer* arm <L *armare* < *arma* arms]

dis·ar·ma·ment (dis·är′mə·mənt) *n.* **1** The act of disarming. **2** The reduction or limitation of armed forces or of certain types of weapons.

dis·arm·ing (dis·är′ming) *adj.* Removing suspicion or anger.

dis·ar·range (dis′ə·rānj′) *v.t.* **·ranged, ·rang·ing** To disturb the arrangement of. See synonyms under DISPLACE. — **dis′ar·range′ment** *n.*

dis·ar·ray (dis′ə·rā′) *n.* **1** Want of array or regular order; disorder; confusion. **2** Scantiness of dress; negligent or disordered dress. — *v.t.* **1** To impair the order of; throw into disorder, as an army. **2** To undress.

dis·ar·tic·u·late (dis′är·tik′yə·lāt) *v.* **·lat·ed, ·lat·ing** *v.t.* To separate the joints of. — *v.i.* To become separated or unjointed. — **dis′-ar·tic′u·la′tion** *n.* — **dis′ar·tic′u·la′tor** *n.*

dis·as·sem·ble (dis′ə·sem′bəl) *v.t.* **·bled, ·bling** To take apart.

dis·as·sem·bly (dis′ə·sem′blē) *n.* A state of being separated into component parts; a disassembling.

dis·as·so·ci·ate (dis′ə·sō′shē·āt) *v.t.* **·at·ed, ·at·ing** To dissociate. — **dis′as·so·ci·a′tion** *n.*

dis·as·ter (di·zas′tər, -zäs′-) *n.* **1** Crushing misfortune; a calamity; a terrible accident. **2** *Obs.* An evil portent; especially, in astrology, the inimical aspect or action of a star or planet. See synonyms under ACCIDENT, BLOW, MISFORTUNE. [<MF *désastre* < *des-* away + *astre* a star <L *astrum* <Gk. *astron*]

dis·as·trous (di·zas′trəs, -zäs′-) *adj.* **1** Occasioning or accompanied by disaster; calamitous. **2** Threatening disaster; ill-boding; gloomy; dismal; ill-starred. — **dis·as′trous·ly** *adv.* — **dis·as′trous·ness** *n.*

dis·a·vow (dis′ə·vou′) *v.t.* To refuse to acknowledge; disclaim responsibility for or approval of; disown; repudiate. See synonyms under RENOUNCE. [<OF *desavouer* < *des-* away (<L *dis-*) + *vouer* AVOW]

dis·band (dis·band′) *v.t.* To break up the organization of; remove from military service. — *v.i.* To break up; scatter; cease to be an organization. [<MF *desbander* < *des-* away (<L *dis-*) + *bander* tie < *bande* a band]

dis·bar (dis·bär′) *v.t.* **·barred, ·bar·ring** To deprive of the status of a lawyer; expel from the bar. — **dis·bar′ment** *n.*

dis·be·lief (dis′bi·lēf′) *n.* A conviction that a statement is untrue; positive unbelief. See synonyms under DOUBT.

dis·be·lieve (dis′bi·lēv′) *v.t. & v.i.* **·lieved, ·liev·ing** To refuse to believe; deem false.

dis·bos·om (dis·bōōz′əm) *v.t.* To reveal, as a secret; unbosom; confess.

dis·branch (dis·branch′, -bränch′) *v.t.* **1** To deprive of branches, as a tree; prune; trim. **2** To cut off, as a branch.

dis·bur·den (dis·bûr′dən) *v.t.* **1** To relieve (someone or something) of a burden; unload. **2** To unload or get rid of (a burden). — *v.i.* **3** To put off a load or burden; unburden.

dis·burse (dis·bûrs′) *v.t.* **·bursed, ·burs·ing** To pay out; expend. [<OF *desbourser* < *des-* away (<L *dis-*) + *bourse* a purse] — **dis·burs′a·ble** *adj.* — **dis·burs′er** *n.*

dis·burse·ment (dis·bûrs′mənt) *n.* **1** The act of disbursing. **2** That which is expended; money paid out.

dis·calced (dis·kalst′) *adj.* Having the shoes off; bare-footed: applied especially to those religious orders whose members go unshod or wear sandals. [<L *discalceatus* < *dis-* not + *calceatus* a shoe, orig. pp. of *calceare* shoe]

dis·card (dis·kärd′) *v.t.* **1** To cast aside as useless or undesirable; reject; dismiss. **2** In card games, to throw out (a card or cards) from one's hand; also, to play (a card, other than a trump, of a different suit from the suit led). — *v.i.* **3** In card games, to throw out a card or cards from one's hand. See synonyms under RENOUNCE. — (dis′kärd) *n.* **1** The act of discarding. **2** A card or cards discarded. **3** A person or thing cast off or dismissed.

dis·case (dis·kās′) *v.t.* **·cased, ·cas·ing** To

remove the case or covering of; unsheathe.

dis·cept (di·sept′) *v.i.* To dispute or debate. [<L *disceptare* <*dis*- away + *ceptare*, freq. of *capere* take] — **dis′cep·ta′tion** *n.*

dis·cern (di·zûrn′, di·sûrn′) *v.t.* **1** To perceive, as with sight or mind; recognize; apprehend. **2** To discriminate mentally; recognize as separate and different. — *v.i.* **3** To distinguish; discriminate. [<OF *discerner* <L *discernere* <*dis*- apart + *cernere* separate] *Synonyms:* descry, discriminate, distinguish, perceive, recognize. What we *discern* we see apart from all other objects; what we *discriminate* we judge apart; what we *distinguish* we mark apart, or *recognize* by some special mark or manifest difference. We *descry* (originally *espy*) what is difficult to discover. Compare DISCOVER, KNOW, LOOK.

dis·cern·i·ble (di·zûr′nə·bəl, -sûr′-) *adj.* Capable of being discerned; perceivable. See synonyms under EVIDENT. — **dis·cern′i·ble·ness** *n.* — **dis·cern′i·bly** *adv.*

dis·cern·ing (di·zûr′ning, -sûr′-) *adj.* Quick to discern; discriminating; penetrating. See synonyms under ACUTE, ASTUTE, INTELLIGENT, KNOWING, SAGACIOUS. — **dis·cern′ing·ly** *adv.*

dis·cern·ment (di·zûrn′mənt, -sûrn′-) *n.* **1** The act or process of discerning. **2** The mental power of discerning; keenness of judgment; insight. See synonyms under ACUMEN, UNDERSTANDING, WISDOM.

dis·charge (dis·chärj′) *v.* **·charged**, **·charg·ing** *v.t.* **1** To unload; remove the contents of: to *discharge* a ship. **2** To remove or send forth: to *discharge* passengers or cargo. **3** To send forth; emit (fluid). **4** To shoot or fire, as a gun, bow, shot, or arrow. **5** To dismiss from office; fire. **6** To release; set at liberty, as a prisoner, soldier, or patient. **7** To relieve of duty or obligation: to *discharge* a jury. **8** To perform or fulfil the functions and duties of (a trust, office, etc.). **9** To pay (a debt) or meet and satisfy (an obligation or duty). **10** In dyeing, to remove (color) from textiles. **11** *Obs.* To free of blame or accusation. **12** *Electr.* To free of an electrical charge. — *v.i.* **13** To get rid of a load, burden, etc. **14** To go off, as a cannon. **15** To give or send forth contents: The wound *discharges* constantly. **16** *Electr.* To lose a charge of electricity. See synonyms under ABSOLVE, ACCOMPLISH, BANISH, CANCEL, DELIVER, PAY, RELEASE. — *n.* (*also* dis′chärj) **1** The act of removing a load or charge. **2** A firing of a weapon; a release of a missile. **3** An emission; ejection; an issuing forth. **4** The rate or amount of outflow. **5** That which is discharged or released, as blood from a wound. **6** A relieving or freeing from burden or obligation. **7** The payment of a debt. **8** Fulfilment; execution: the *discharge* of one's duty. **9** Release or dismissal from service, employment, or custody. **10** Something which releases or dismisses, as a certificate separating one from military service. **11** *Electr.* **a** The equalization of difference of potential between terminals of a condenser or of a current source, when connected by a conductor, or placed in very near contact. **b** The removal of an electrostatic charge, as from a Leyden jar, a battery, etc. [<OF *descharger* <*des*- away (<L *dis*-) + *chargier* CHARGE] — **dis·charge′a·ble** *adj.* — **dis·charg′er** *n.*

dis·ci·ple (di·sī′pəl) *n.* One who accepts and follows a teacher or a doctrine; a pupil or learner. **2** One of **the disciples**, the twelve chosen companions and apostles of Jesus. See synonyms under ADHERENT, CONVERT. — *v.t.* **·pled**, **·pling** **1** To cause to become a disciple; convert. **2** *Obs.* To train; teach. [OE *discipul* <L *discipulus* <*discere* teach; infl. in form by OF *diciple*, *disciple* <L *discipulus*] — **dis·ci′ple·ship** *n.*

Disciples of Christ A religious body that originated in Pennsylvania in 1809, in connection with the labors of Thomas and Alexander Campbell, holding to Christian union on the basis of the Bible alone, rejecting creeds and party names, and practicing immersion and weekly communion: also called *Christians.*

dis·ci·pli·nal (dis′ə·plī′nəl, dis′ə·plin·əl) *adj.* Of or pertaining to discipline.

dis·ci·pli·nar·i·an (dis′ə·plə·nâr′ē·ən) *n.* One who disciplines; one strict in discipline; a

martinet. — *adj.* Disciplinary.

dis·ci·pli·nar·y (dis′ə·plə·ner′ē) *adj.* Of, relating to, or having the nature of discipline; employed in discipline.

dis·ci·pline (dis′ə·plin) *n.* **1** Systematic training or subjection to authority; especially, the training of the mental, moral, and physical powers by instruction and exercise. **2** The result of this; subjection; habit of obedience. **3** Training resulting from misfortune, troubles, etc. **4** Punishment for the sake of training; correction; chastisement. **5** A system of rules, or method of practice, as of a church. **6** The studies collectively embraced in a course of learning. **7** The self-scourging of some ascetics of the Roman Catholic Church; also, a scourge. See synonyms under EDUCATION. — *v.t.* **·plined**, **·plin·ing** **1** To train to obedience or subjection. **2** To drill; educate. **3** To punish or chastise. See synonyms under CHASTEN, TEACH. [<OF <L *disciplina* instruction <*discipulus* DISCIPLE] — **dis′ci·plin·a·ble** *adj.* — **dis′ci·plin·er** *n.*

dis·cis·sion (di·sish′ən, -sizh′-) *n.* **1** A cutting into a part. **2** *Surg.* An operation to relieve a soft cataract by lacerating the capsule of the lens. [<LL *discissio*, *-onis* <*dis*- apart + *scindere* cleave, cut]

disc jockey An announcer on a radio program that presents recorded music, usually interspersed with comments and commercials.

dis·claim (dis·klām′) *v.t.* **1** To disavow any claim to, connection with, or responsibility for; disown; reject. **2** To reject or deny the claim or authority of; deny. **3** *Law* To renounce a right or claim to. — *v.i.* **4** *Law* To renounce or repudiate a legal claim. See synonyms under RENOUNCE. [<AF *desclamer* <*des*- away (<L *dis*-) + *clamare* cry]

dis·claim·er (dis·klā′mər) *n.* **1** One who disclaims. **2** A disclaiming act, notice, or instrument.

dis·cla·ma·tion (dis′klə·mā′shən) *n.* A disavowal.

dis·close (dis·klōz′) *v.t.* **·closed**, **·clos·ing** **1** To expose to view; lay bare; uncover. **2** To make known; divulge; open. **3** *Obs.* To open. See synonyms under CONFESS, DISCOVER, INFORM, PUBLISH. [<OF *desclos-*, stem of *desclore* close] — **dis·clos′er** *n.*

dis·clo·sure (dis·klō′zhər) *n.* **1** The act or process of disclosing. **2** Anything disclosed.

dis·cob·o·lus (dis·kob′ə·ləs) *n.* A discus thrower. Also **dis·cob′o·los.** — **the Discobolus** A famous Greek statue of a discus thrower, attributed to Myron. [<L <Gk. *diskobolos* <*diskos* a discus + *ballein* throw]

dis·coid (dis′koid) *adj.* **1** *Zool.* Having the form of a disk, as certain univalve shells with the whorls coiled in one plane. **2** Pertaining to, like, or forming a disk or disks. **3** *Bot.* Disk-shaped; rayless, as the tubular central florets of a composite flower, such as the sunflower: also **dis·coi′dal.** — *n.* A disk or disklike object. [<L *discoïdes* <Gk. *diskoeidēs* <*diskos* a discus + *eidos* form]

dis·col·or (dis·kul′ər) *v.t.* To give an unnatural color to; stain. — *v.i.* To become stained, faded, or of a changed color. Also *Brit.* **dis·col′our.** [<OF *descolorer* <*des*- away (<L *dis*-) + *colorer* color <L *colorare* <*color* a color]

dis·col·or·a·tion (dis·kul′ə·rā′shən) *n.* **1** The act or process of discoloring; a discolored state or appearance; changed hue or aspect. **2** A stain or discolored spot or part. Also **dis·col′or·ment.**

dis·com·fit (dis·kum′fit) *v.t.* **1** To defeat the plans or purposes of; frustrate. **2** To rout; vanquish. See synonyms under CONQUER. — *n. Obs.* Rout. [<OF *desconfit*, pp. of *desconfire* <*des*- away (<L *dis*-) + *confire* <L *conficere*. See CONFECT.]

dis·com·fi·ture (dis·kum′fi·chər) *n.* The act of discomfiting or the state of being discomfited: defeat. See synonyms under RUIN.

dis·com·fort (dis·kum′fərt) *n.* **1** The state of being positively uncomfortable; disquietude. **2** That which causes an uncomfortable condition. See synonyms under PAIN. — *v.t.* **1** To make uneasy; trouble. **2** *Obs.* To dishearten; dismay. [<OF *desconfort* <*desconforter* <*des*- away (<L *dis*-) + *conforter* COMFORT]

dis·com·mend (dis′kə·mend′) *v.t.* **1** To express disapproval of. **2** To speak of dissuasively. **3** *Obs.* To cause to be regarded unfavorably. — **dis′com·mend′a·ble** *adj.* — **dis′com·men·da′·tion** *n.*

dis·com·mod·i·ty (dis′kə·mod′ə·tē) *n. pl.* **·ties 1** The state, fact, or quality of being inconvenient, troublesome, or injurious. **2** Something that causes annoyance, inconvenience, trouble, or loss.

dis·com·pose (dis′kəm·pōz′) *v.t.* **·posed**, **·pos·ing 1** To disturb the composure of; make uneasy; ruffle; agitate. **2** To disorder or disarrange; derange. See synonyms under ABASH.

dis·com·po·sure (dis′kəm·pō′zhər) *n.* Agitation; disorder; perturbation.

dis·co·my·cete (dis′kə·mī·sēt′) *n. pl.* **·cetes** (-sēts) *Bot.* Any of a group (*Discomycetes*) of fungi belonging to the *Ascomycetes*; a cup fungus. [<NL <Gk. *diskos* disk + *mykēs, mykētos* fungus]

dis·con·cert (dis′kən·sûrt′) *v.t.* **1** To disturb the self-possession or composure of; confuse; upset. **2** To throw into confusion; frustrate, as a plan. See synonyms under ABASH. [<MF *disconcerter* <*dis*- apart + *concerter* agree] — **dis′con·cert′ing** *adj.* — **dis′con·cert′ing·ly** *adv.* — **dis′con·cer′tion, dis′con·cert′ment** *n.*

dis·con·cert·ed (dis′kən·sûr′tid) *adj.* Confused; perturbed; discomposed. — **dis′con·cert′ed·ly** *adv.* — **dis′con·cert′ed·ness** *n.*

dis·con·form·i·ty (dis′kən·fôr′mə·tē) *n. pl.* **·ties** Lack of conformity; nonconformity.

dis·con·nect (dis′kə·nekt′) *v.t.* To undo or dissolve the connection of; disunite; separate. — **dis′con·nec′tion, Brit. dis′con·nex′ion** *n.*

dis·con·nect·ed (dis′kə·nek′tid) *adj.* **1** Not connected; disjointed. **2** Incoherent; rambling. — **dis′con·nect′ed·ly** *adv.* — **dis′con·nect′ed·ness** *n.*

dis·con·so·late (dis·kon′sə·lit) *adj.* **1** Destitute of consolation; inconsolable; sad. **2** Marked by gloominess; cheerless; saddening. See synonyms under SAD. [<Med. L *disconsolatus* <*dis*- not + *consolatus*, pp. of *consolari* CONSOLE[1]] — **dis′con′so·late·ly** *adv.* — **dis′con′so·late·ness** *n.*

dis·con·tent (dis′kən·tent′) *n.* Lack of content; dissatisfaction; uneasiness: also **dis′con·tent′ed·ness, dis′con·tent′ment.** — *v.t.* To render discontented; dissatisfy. — **dis′con·tent′ing** *adj.*

dis·con·tent·ed (dis′kən·ten′tid) *adj.* Ill at ease; dissatisfied. — **dis′con·tent′ed·ly** *adv.*

dis·con·tin·u·ance (dis′kən·tin′yoo·əns) *n.* **1** The act of discontinuing, or state of being discontinued; interruption or intermission. **2** Discontinuity. **3** *Law* The interruption of a suit, as by failure of the plaintiff to follow it up: distinguished from *dismissal.*

dis·con·tin·ue (dis′kən·tin′yoo) *v.* **·tin·ued**, **·tin·u·ing** *v.t.* **1** To break off or cease from; stop. **2** To cease using, receiving, etc.: to *discontinue* a newspaper. **3** *Law* To abandon (a suit, etc.) by discontinuance. — *v.i.* **4** To come to an end; stop. See synonyms under ABANDON, CEASE, SUSPEND. [<OF *discontinuer* <Med. L *discontinuare* <*dis*- not + L *continuare* CONTINUE] — **dis′con·tin′u·a′tion** *n.* — **dis′con·tin′u·er,** *Law* **dis′con·tin′u·or** *n.*

dis·con·ti·nu·i·ty (dis′kon·tə·noo′ə·tē, -nyoo′-) *n.* **1** Lack of continuity. **2** A gap, as in a structure or electric current.

dis·con·tin·u·ous (dis′kən·tin′yoo·əs) *adj.* Not continuous; characterized by interruptions or breaks. — **dis′con·tin′u·ous·ly** *adv.* — **dis′con·tin′u·ous·ness** *n.*

dis·cord (dis′kôrd) *n.* **1** Variance or strife; lack of agreement; contention. **2** *Music* A combination of dissonant sounds; lack of harmony. **3** A harsh or disagreeable medley of noises; dissonance. — *v.i.* To be out of accord or harmony; disagree; clash. [<OF *descord* <*descorder* disagree <L *discordare* <*discors* at variance <*dis*- away (<L *cor, cordis* heart]

dis·cor·dance (dis·kôr′dəns) *n.* **1** A discordant

state or quality. **2** A discord. Also **dis·cor′dan·cy.**

dis·cor·dant (dis·kôr′dənt) *adj.* **1** Contradictory; inconsistent. **2** Quarrelsome. **3** Not harmonious; dissonant. **4** *Geol.* Lacking in conformity, as in the direction or sequence of rock strata. See synonyms under CONTRARY, HETEROGENEOUS, INCONGRUOUS. [< OF *descordant*, ppr. of *descorder.* See DISCORD.] **—dis·cor′dant·ly** *adv.*

dis·co·thèque (dis·kə·tek′) *n.* A night club offering recorded music for dancing instead of music played by a band of live musicians. [< F, lit., record library]

dis·count (dis′kount) *n.* **1** An amount counted off or deducted from a sum owing or to be paid: ten per cent *discount* for cash. **2** The interest allowed and deducted from the face amount for advancing money on negotiable paper. **3** The act of discounting. **4** The rate of discount. **—at a discount** At less than the face value; below par; hence, not in esteem. **—true** or **arithmetical discount** That interest at a given rate and term which, added to the principal received, gives the face value of the discounted paper. —*v.t.* (dis′kount, dis·kount′) **1** To set aside or deduct, as a portion of an amount owed; make an allowance of. **2** To buy or sell (a bill or note) for face value less the amount of interest to be accumulated before maturity. **3** To disregard; take no account of. **4** To believe only part of; allow for exaggeration in. **5** To take into account beforehand; diminish by anticipation, especially so as to lessen value, effect, enjoyment, etc. —*v.i.* **6** To lend money, deducting the interest beforehand. [< MF *descompte, desconte* < OF *descompter* < Med. L *discomputare* < *dis-* away + *computare* COMPUTE] **—dis′count·a·ble** *adj.* **—dis′count·er** *n.*

dis·coun·te·nance (dis·koun′tə·nəns) *v.t.* **·nanced, ·nanc·ing** **1** To look upon with disfavor; disapprove or discourage. **2** To abash; disconcert. —*n.* *Obs.* Disapprobation; abashment. [< MF *descontenancer* < *des-* away (< L *dis-*) + *contenancer* favor < *contenance* COUNTENANCE]

dis·cour·age (dis·kûr′ij) *v.t.* **·aged, ·ag·ing** **1** To deprive of courage; dispirit; dishearten. **2** To deter or dissuade with *from.* **3** To obstruct; hinder: Malnutrition *discourages* growth. **4** To attempt to repress or prevent by disapproval. [< OF *descoragier* < *des-* away (< L *dis-*) + *corage* courage]

dis·cour·age·ment (dis·kûr′ij·mənt) *n.* **1** The act of discouraging, or the state of being discouraged. **2** That which discourages. See synonyms under DESPAIR.

dis·course (dis′kôrs, dis·kôrs′) *n.* **1** Connected communication of thought sequence; continuous expression or exchange of ideas. **2** Familiar conversation; talk. **3** Formal expression of thought, oral or written; a long treatise or dissertation; a sermon. **Direct discourse** is spoken or written language quoted in the exact words of the speaker or writer, as in *I will go,* and is contrasted with **indirect discourse,** in which his words are reported with change of person or tense, as in *he said he would go.* **4** An act, the exercise, or the power of analytical and consecutive thought; ratiocination. See synonyms under CONVERSATION, SPEECH. —*v.* (dis·kôrs′) **·coursed, ·cours·ing** *v.i.* **1** To set forth one's thoughts and conclusions concerning a subject: with *on* or *upon.* **2** To converse; confer. —*v.t.* **3** *Obs.* To discuss. [< OF *discours* < L *discursus* < *dis-* apart + *cursus* a running < *currere* run]

dis·cour·te·ous (dis·kûr′tē·əs) *adj.* Showing discourtesy; rude. See synonyms under BLUFF². **—dis·cour′te·ous·ly** *adv.* **—dis·cour′te·ous·ness** *n.*

dis·cour·te·sy (dis·kûr′tə·sē) *n.* *pl.* **·sies** Rude behavior; impoliteness.

dis·cov·er (dis·kuv′ər) *v.t.* **1** To find or gain knowledge of, especially for the first time. **2** *Archaic* To act or speak so as to expose or betray, especially unwittingly. **3** *Archaic* To remove the covering of; reveal; disclose. **4** *Obs.* To distinguish, as black from white. [< OF *descovrir* < *des-* away (< L *dis-*) + *covrir* COVER] **—dis·cov′er·a·bil′i·ty** *n.* **—dis·cov′er·a·ble** *adj.* **—dis·cov′er·er** *n.*

Synonyms: ascertain, descry, detect, discern, disclose, expose, find, invent. Of human actions or character, *detect* is used almost without exception of what is evil; *discover* may be used in

either the good or the bad sense, oftener in the good; he was *detected* in a fraud; real merit is sure to be *discovered.* In scientific language, *detect* is used of delicate indications that appear in course of careful watching; as, a slight fluttering of the pulse could be *detected.* We *discover* what has existed but has not been known to us; we *invent* combinations or arrangements not before in use. *Find* is the most general word for every means of coming to know what was not before certainly known. Compare CATCH, KNOW. *Antonyms:* see synonyms for HIDE.

dis·cov·er·y (dis·kuv′ər·ē) *n.* *pl.* **·er·ies** **1** The act of discovering; disclosure. **2** Something discovered.

dis·cre·ate (dis′krē·āt′) *v.t.* **·at·ed, ·at·ing** To undo (what has been created); destroy; annihilate. **—dis′cre·a′tion** *n.*

dis·cred·it (dis·kred′it) *v.t.* **1** To disbelieve. **2** To injure the credit or reputation of; dishonor. **3** To show to be unworthy of belief or confidence. —*n.* **1** The act of discrediting. **2** The state of being discredited or disbelieved. **3** Lack of credit; impaired reputation; dishonor. See synonyms under ABASE, DISPARAGE.

dis·cred·it·a·ble (dis·kred′it·ə·bəl) *adj.* Hurtful to credit or reputation; disreputable.

dis·creet (dis·krēt′) *adj.* **1** Wise in avoiding errors or in selecting the best means to accomplish a purpose. **2** Judicious; prudent; careful. See synonyms under POLITIC. ◆ Homophone: *discrete.* [< OF *discret* < LL *discretus* learned, orig. pp. of *discernere* discern] **—dis·creet′ly** *adv.* **—dis·creet′ness** *n.*

dis·crep·an·cy (dis·krep′ən·sē) *n.* *pl.* **·cies** A disagreement or difference; state or point of variance; inconsistency. Also **dis·crep′ance.** See synonyms under DIFFERENCE.

dis·crep·ant (dis·krep′ənt) *adj.* Inharmoniously different; opposite; inconsistent; contrary; discordant. See synonyms under INCONGRUOUS. [< OF < L *discrepans, -antis* < *dis-* away + *crepare* creak, make a noise]

dis·crete (dis·krēt′) *adj.* **1** Disconnected from others; distinct or separate. **2** Made up of distinct parts or separate units; discontinuous. **3** Denoting opposition or contrariety. **4** *Bot.* Separate; not coalescent, as leaves; distinct; segregate: opposed to *confluent.* ◆ Homophone: *discreet.* [Var. of DISCREET] **—dis·crete′ly** *adv.* **—dis·crete′ness** *n.*

dis·cre·tion (dis·kresh′ən) *n.* **1** Cautious and correct judgment; prudence; sagacity; the quality of being discreet. **2** Liberty of action; freedom in the exercise of judgment. **3** *Law* The act or the liberty of deciding according to justice and propriety, and one's idea of what is right and proper under the circumstances, without wilfulness or favor. **4** *Obs.* Distinction or separation; disjunction. See synonyms under ADDRESS, PRUDENCE, WISDOM. **—at discretion** At will; according to one's own judgment. [< OF < L *discretio, -onis* < *discretus* discrete]

dis·cre·tion·al (dis·kresh′ən·əl) *adj.* Discretionary. **—dis·cre′tion·al·ly** *adv.*

dis·cre·tion·ar·y (dis·kresh′ə·ner′ē) *adj.* **1** Exercisable at or left to discretion. **2** Uncontrolled legally except by discretion.

dis·crim·i·nate (dis·krim′ə·nāt) *v.* **·nat·ed, ·nat·ing** *v.i.* **1** To treat someone or something with partiality: with *against* or in *favor of:* to *discriminate* against a group or in favor of a relative. **2** To observe a difference; make a distinction: with *between.* —*v.t.* **3** To discern the difference in or between. **4** To make or constitute a difference in or between: The meter *discriminates* a poem from the other. See synonyms under CONTRAST, DISCERN, KNOW. —*adj.* (-nit) **1** Noting differences; discriminating. **2** Discriminated. [< L *criminatus,* pp. of *discriminare* < *discrimen, -inis* < *dis-* apart + *crimen* a judgment] **—dis·crim′i·nate·ly** *adv.* **—dis·crim′i·nate·ness** *n.*

dis·crim·i·nat·ing (dis·krim′ə·nā′ting) *adj.* **1** Having power to distinguish keenly: a *discriminating* intellect. **2** Serving to distinguish: a *discriminating* mark. **3** Establishing distinction or inequality. See synonyms under ASTUTE. **—dis·crim′i·nat′ing·ly** *adv.*

dis·crim·i·na·tion (dis·krim′ə·nā′shən) *n.* **1** The act or power of discriminating; the discernment of distinctions. **2** Differential treatment; bias: *discrimination* against minorities. **3** The state or condition of being dis-

criminated; distinction; sometimes, unjust distinction. See synonyms under DIFFERENCE.

dis·crim·i·na·tive (dis·krim′ə·nā′tiv) *adj.* **1** Discriminating. **2** Distinctive or characteristic. Also **dis·crim′i·na·to′ry** (-nə·tôr′ē, -tō′rē).

dis·cur·sive (dis·kûr′siv) *adj.* Passing from one subject to another; wandering away from the point or theme; digressive. [< L *discursus.* See DISCOURSE.] **—dis·cur′sive·ly** *adv.* **—dis·cur′sive·ness** *n.*

dis·cus (dis′kəs) *n.* *pl.* **dis·cus·es** or **dis·ci** (dis′ī) **1** A heavy circular plate thrown in athletic contests: originally, in Greek and Roman games, of stone or metal; quoit. **2** The exercise of throwing this plate. For illustration see DISCOBOLUS. **3** *Biol.* A disc. [< L < Gk. *diskos*]

dis·cuss (dis·kus′) *v.t.* **1** To treat of in conversation or in writing; talk about; argue the faults and merits of. **2** *Colloq.* To test by eating or drinking, as a meal. **3** In civil law, to exhaust proceedings against (the principal debtor) before proceeding against the surety or sureties. See synonyms under DISPUTE, EXAMINE. [< L *discussus,* pp. of *discutere* discuss, orig. < *dis-* apart + *quatere* shake]

dis·cus·sant (dis·kus′ənt) *n.* One who takes part in a discussion; an active participant in a symposium.

dis·cus·sion (dis·kush′ən) *n.* **1** The act of discussing; argumentative examination; debate. See synonyms under ALTERCATION, QUARREL, SPEECH. **2** *Obs.* The scattering or dispersion of any effusion, tumor, or swelling in the body. [< OF < LL *discussio, -onis* < *discutere.* See DISCUSS.]

dis·dain (dis·dān′) *v.t.* **1** To consider unworthy of one's regard or notice; treat with contempt or scorn. **2** To reject as beneath oneself; scorn. —*n.* A feeling of superiority and dislike; proud contempt. See synonyms under ARROGANCE, SCORN. [< OF *desdeignier* < *des-* away (< L *dis-*) + *deignier* DEIGN]

dis·dain·ful (dis·dān′fəl) *adj.* Filled with or expressing disdain; scornful. See synonyms under HAUGHTY. **—dis·dain′ful·ly** *adv.* **—dis·dain′ful·ness** *n.*

dis·ease (di·zēz′) *n.* **1** Disturbed or abnormal structure or physiological action in the living organism as a whole, or in any of its parts. **2** A morbid condition resulting from such disturbance. **3** Any disturbed or abnormal condition in organic substances, as wines, liquors, etc.; a taint. **4** *Obs.* Uneasiness; inconvenience; discomfort; discontent. —*v.t.* **·eased, ·eas·ing** **1** To cause disease in; disorder; derange. **2** *Obs.* To make uneasy; distress. [< AF, OF *desaise* < *des-* away (< L *dis-*) + *aise* EASE] **—dis·eased′** *adj.*

Synonyms (noun): affection, ailment, complaint, disorder, distemper, illness, indisposition, infirmity, malady, sickness, unhealthiness, unsoundness. *Disease* is the general term for deviation from health; in a more limited sense it denotes some definite morbid condition; *disorder* and *affection* are rather partial and limited; as, a nervous *affection;* a *disorder* of the digestive system. Although *sickness* was generally used in English speech and literature, till the close of the eighteenth century at least, for every form of physical *disorder,* there is now a tendency to restrict the words *sick* and *sickness* to nausea, and to hold *ill* and *illness* as the proper words to use in a general sense. We speak of trifling *ailments,* a slight *indisposition,* a serious or a deadly *disease;* a slight or severe *illness;* an insidious, serious, severe, or deadly *disease.* *Complaint* is a popular term, which may be applied to any degree of ill health, slight or severe. *Infirmity* denotes a chronic or lingering weakness or disability, as blindness or lameness. See ILLNESS. *Antonyms:* health, robustness, sanity, soundness, strength, sturdiness, vigor.

dis·em·bark (dis′em·bärk′) *v.t.* & *v.i.* To put or go ashore from a ship; land; unload. [< MF *desembarquer* < *des-* away (< L *dis-*) + *embarquer* EMBARK] **—dis·em′bar·ka′tion, dis′em·bark′ment** *n.*

dis·em·bod·y (dis′em·bod′ē) *v.t.* **·bod·ied, ·bod·y·ing** To free from the body; free from physical existence. **—dis′em·bod′i·ment** *n.*

dis·em·bogue (dis′em·bōg′) *v.t.* & *v.i.* **·bogued, ·bo·guing** **1** To pour out or discharge (waters) at the mouth; empty: said of rivers, streams, etc. **2** *Obs.* To sail out of a river, bay, or harbor. [<Sp. *desembocar* <*des-* out (<L *dis-*) + *embocar* put into the mouth <L *in-* into + *bucca* mouth] —**dis·em·bogue′ment** *n.*

dis·em·bos·om (dis′em·bōoz′əm) *v.t. & v.i.* To reveal (a secret); to disburden (oneself) of a secret.

dis·em·bow·el (dis′em·bou′əl, -boul′) *v.t.* **·bow·eled** or **·bow·elled, ·bow·el·ing** or **·bow·el·ling 1** To take out the bowels of; eviscerate. **2** To remove the contents of. —**dis′em·bow′el·ment** *n.*

dis·en·chant (dis′en·chant′, -chänt′) *v.t.* To free from enchantment; disillusion. [<OF *desenchanter* <*des-* away (<L *dis-*) + *enchanter* ENCHANT] —**dis′en·chant′er** *n.* —**dis′·en·chant′ment** *n.*

dis·en·cum·ber (dis′en·kum′bər) *v.t.* To free from encumbrance or burden. [<OF *desencombre, desencombrer* <*des-* away (<L *dis-*) + *encombrer* ENCUMBER] —**dis′en·cum′ber·ment, dis′en·cum′brance** *n.*

dis·en·fran·chise (dis′en·fran′chīz) *v.t.* **·chised, ·chis·ing** To disfranchise. —**dis′en·fran′chise·ment** (-chiz·mənt) *n.*

dis·en·gage (dis′en·gāj′) *v.t. & v.i.* **·gaged, ·gag·ing** To set or be free from engagement, entanglement, or occupation; become detached; withdraw. See synonyms under RELEASE.

dis·en·gage·ment (dis′en·gāj′mənt) *n.* **1** The act of disengaging, or the state of being disengaged; extrication. **2** Freedom from toil or care; leisure; ease.

dis·en·tan·gle (dis′en·tang′gəl) *v.t.* **·gled, ·gling** To free or relieve of entanglement or perplexity; unravel. —**dis′en·tan′gle·ment** *n.*

dis·en·thral (dis′en·thrôl′) *v.t.* **·thralled, ·thral·ling** To release from or as from thraldom; set free: also spelled *disinthral.* Also **dis′en·thrall′.** —**dis′en·thral′ment** or **dis′en·thrall′ment** *n.*

dis·en·ti·tle (dis′en·tīt′l) *v.t.* **·tled, ·tling** To take away the title from; deprive of a right.

di·sep·a·lous (dī·sep′ə·ləs) *adj. Bot.* Having two sepals. [<DI-² + SEPALOUS]

dis·es·tab·lish (dis′es·tab′lish) *v.t.* **1** To deprive of established character. **2** To withdraw state patronage from: to *disestablish* a church. —**dis′es·tab′lish·ment** *n.*

dis·es·teem (dis′es·tēm′) *v.t.* To feel a lack of esteem for; regard slightingly or with dislike; disapprove of. —*n.* Lack of esteem.

dis·fa·vor (dis·fā′vər) *n.* **1** Lack of favor; disapproval; dislike. **2** The state of being discountenanced, disliked, or opposed; odium. **3** An unkind act. **4** *Obs.* Ugliness; homeliness. —*v.t.* To treat or regard without favor; discountenance; oppose. Also *Brit.* **dis·fa′vour.**

dis·fig·ure (dis·fig′yər) *v.t.* **·ured, ·ur·ing** To mar or destroy the figure or beauty of; render unsightly; deform. [<OF *desfigurer* <*des-* away (<L *dis-*) + *figurer* <L *figurare* form, fashion <*figura* a shape] —**dis·fig′ur·er** *n.* —**dis·fig′ured** *adj.* —**dis·fig′ure·ment, dis·fig′u·ra′tion** *n.*

dis·for·est (dis·fôr′ist, -for′-) *v.t.* **1** To clear of forest; deforest. **2** *Law* To disafforest. —**dis·for′es·ta′tion** *n.*

dis·fran·chise (dis·fran′chīz) *v.t.* **·chised, ·chis·ing 1** To deprive of a privilege, right, or grant. **2** To dispossess of a citizen's privileges, as of the ballot. —**dis·fran′chis·er** *n.* —**dis·fran′chise·ment** (-chiz·mənt) *n.*

dis·frock (dis·frok′) *v.t.* To unfrock.

dis·gorge (dis·gôrj′) *v.t.* **·gorged, ·gorg·ing 1** To throw out, as from the throat or stomach; eject; vomit. **2** To give up unwillingly, especially something wrongfully obtained. —*v.i.* **3** To throw up; vomit. [<OF *desgorger* <*des-* from (<L *dis-*) + *gorge* throat]

dis·grace (dis·grās′) *v.t.* **·graced, ·grac·ing 1** To bring reproach or shame upon. **2** To dismiss from favor; treat with dishonor. —*n.* **1** Disfavor. **2** Infamy; ignominy. **3** That which disgraces. [<MF *disgracier* <Ital. *disgraziare* <*disgrazia* <*dis-* away (<L *dis-*) + *grazia* <L *gratia* favor] —**dis·grac′er** *n.*

dis·grace·ful (dis·grās′fəl) *adj.* Characterized by or causing disgrace; shameful. See synonyms under FLAGRANT, INFAMOUS. —**dis·grace′ful·ly** *adv.* —**dis·grace′ful·ness** *n.*

dis·grun·tle (dis·grun′təl) *v.t.* **·grun·tled, ·grun·tling** To disappoint and make discontented; cause to sulk.

dis·guise (dis·gīz′) *v.t.* **·guised, ·guis·ing 1** To change the appearance of; hide or conceal the identity of, as by a mask. **2** To obscure or cover up the actual nature or character of by false representation; dissemble; misrepresent. See synonyms under HIDE¹, MASK¹. —*n.* **1** The act of disguising, or the state of being disguised. **2** Something that disguises, alters the appearance of, or renders difficult of recognition. See synonyms under PRETENSE. [<OF *desguisier* <*des-* down (<L *de-*) + *guise* GUISE] —**dis·guis′ed·ly** (-id·lē) *adv.* —**dis·guis′er** *n.*

dis·gust (dis·gust′) *v.t.* **1** To affect with physical nausea; offend the senses of. **2** To offend the sensibilities of; affect with loathing or aversion. —*n.* Strong aversion or repugnance. See synonyms under ABOMINATION, ANTIPATHY. [<MF *desgouster* <*des-* away (<L *dis-*) + *gouster* taste <L *gustare*]

dis·gust·ed (dis·gus′tid) *adj.* Affected with loathing or disgust. —**dis·gust′ed·ly** *adv.* —**dis·gust′ed·ness** *n.*

dis·gust·ful (dis·gust′fəl) *adj.* **1** Disgusting. **2** Full of or characterized by disgust. —**dis·gust′ful·ly** *adv.* —**dis·gust′ful·ness** *n.*

dis·gust·ing (dis·gus′ting) *adj.* Serving or fitted to provoke disgust; odious; revolting. —**dis·gust′ing·ly** *adv.*

dish (dish) *n.* **1** A concave or hollow vessel for serving food at meals; anything of similar shape. **2** The amount of food served in a dish: also **dish′ful. 3** Food prepared in a special way. **4** Concavity. —*v.t.* **1** To place in a dish or dishes; serve as food: often with *up* or *out.* **2** To make concave. **3** *Slang* To ruin; cheat. —*v.i.* **4** To become concave; sink in. [<OE *disc* <L *discus.* Doublet of DAIS, DESK, DISK.]

dish·cloth (dish′klôth′, -kloth′) *n.* A cloth used in washing dishes. Also **dish′clout′** (-klout′), **dish′rag′** (-rag′).

dis·heart·en (dis·här′tən) *v.t.* To weaken the spirit or courage of; dispirit; discourage. See synonyms under ABASH. —**dis·heart′en·ing** *adj.* —**dis·heart′en·ing·ly** *adv.* —**dis·heart′en·ment** *n.*

dished (disht) *adj.* **1** Shaped like a dish; concave. **2** Of wheels, slanted inward at the bottom. **3** *Slang* Worn out; exhausted.

di·shev·el (di·shev′əl) *v.t.* **·eled** or **·elled, ·el·ing** or **·el·ling** To disorder (the hair); disarrange (the dress) [<MF *descheveler* <*des-* away (<L *dis-*) + *chevel* hair <L *capillus*] —**di·shev′el·ment** *n.*

dish-faced (dish′fāst′) *adj.* Having a round, flat face.

dis·hon·est (dis·on′ist) *adj.* **1** Lacking in honesty; untrustworthy. **2** Characterized by dishonesty; fraudulent; See synonyms under BAD¹, IMMORAL. [<OF *deshoneste* <LL *dis-* away + *honestus* honest] —**dis·hon′est·ly** *adv.*

dis·hon·es·ty (dis·on′is·tē) *n. pl.* **·ties 1** The quality of being dishonest. **2** Fraud or violation of trust; a dishonest action.

dis·hon·or (dis·on′ər) *v.t.* **1** To deprive of honor; disgrace; insult. **2** To violate the chastity of; seduce. **3** To decline or fail to pay, as a note. See synonyms under ABASE, BLEMISH, DISPARAGE, POLLUTE, STAIN. —*n.* **1** Lack of honor or of honorable character. **2** Degradation. **3** Insult; reproach; stain. **4** Refusal or failure to pay a note, etc., when due. Also *Brit.* **dis·hon′our.** See synonyms under SCORN. [<OF *deshonor* <L *dis-* away + *honor* HONOR] —**dis·hon′or·er** *n.*

dis·hon·or·a·ble (dis·on′ər·ə·bəl) *adj.* **1** Characterized by or bringing dishonor or reproach; discreditable; mean; ignoble: a *dishonorable* motive or act. **2** Lacking honor or honorableness: a *dishonorable* lawyer. **3** In a state of dishonor or disesteem; dishonored: a *dishonorable* grave. See synonyms under INFAMOUS. —**dis·hon′or·a·ble·ness** *n.* —**dis·hon′or·a·bly** *adv.*

dis·il·lu·sion (dis′i·lōo′zhən) *v.t.* To free from illusion or delusion; disenchant. Also **dis′il·lu′sion·ize.** —*n.* The act of freeing or state of being freed from illusion. Also **dis′il·lu′sion·ment.**

dis·il·lu·sive (dis′i·lōo′siv) *adj.* Tending to dispel an illusion.

dis·in·cen·tive (dis′in·sen′tiv) *n.* Something that deters, or reduces incentive.

dis·in·cli·na·tion (dis′in·klə·nā′shən) *n.* Distaste; aversion; unwillingness.

dis·in·cline (dis′in·klīn′) *v.t. & v.i.* **·clined, ·clin·ing** To make or be unwilling or averse.

dis·in·cor·po·rate (dis′in·kôr′pə·rāt) *v.t.* **·rat·ed, ·rat·ing 1** To free from incorporation; deprive of chartered rights or character, as a company. **2** To separate from a corporation.

dis·in·fect (dis′in·fekt′) *v.t.* **1** To purify from infection. **2** To free from morbid or pathogenic matter, as a wound, clothing, etc. See synonyms under CLEANSE.

dis·in·fec·tant (dis′in·fek′tənt) *adj.* Disinfecting. —*n.* A substance used to disinfect or to destroy the germs of infectious and contagious diseases, as chlorine, carbolic acid, etc.

dis·in·fec·tion (dis′in·fek′shən) *n.* The act of disinfecting; fact or state of being disinfected.

dis·in·fest (dis′in·fest′) *v.t.* To exterminate vermin from; delouse. —**dis·in′fes·ta′tion** *n.*

dis·in·fla·tion (dis′in·flā′shən) *n. Econ.* The process, usually governmental, of attempting to reduce the price level, or to hold it steady, through restrictions of credit and other monetary measures, resulting in a decline in industrial production and reduced pressure on foreign exchange reserves: distinguished from *deflation* by a lesser depressant effect in the economy.

dis·in·for·ma·tion (dis′in·fər·mā′shən) *n.* False, misleading information deliberately disseminated.

dis·in·gen·u·ous (dis′in·jen′yōo·əs) *adj.* Not sincere or ingenuous; artful; deceitful. —**dis·in·gen′u·ous·ly** *adv.* —**dis·in·gen′u·ous·ness** *n.*

dis·in·her·it (dis′in·her′it) *v.t.* To deprive of an inheritance. —**dis·in·her′i·tance** *n.*

dis·in·hume (dis′in·hyōom′) *v.t.* **·humed, ·hum·ing** To exhume; disinter.

dis·in·te·grate (dis·in′tə·grāt) *v.* **·grat·ed, ·grat·ing** *v.t.* To break or reduce into component parts or particles; destroy the wholeness of. —*v.i.* To become reduced to fragments or particles; crumble. —**dis·in′te·gra·ble** (-grə·bəl) *adj.* —**dis·in′te·gra′tor** *n.*

dis·in·te·gra·tion (dis·in′tə·grā′shən) *n.* **1** The act of disintegrating, or the state of being disintegrated; a crumbling away. **2** *Geol.* The gradual decay and wasting, as of rocks under elemental action. **3** *Physics* The disappearance of an initial quantity of any radioactive element due to its conversion into another element as a result of the changes in nuclear properties attendant on the emission of alpha or beta particles.

dis·in·ter (dis′in·tûr′) *v.t.* **·terred, ·ter·ring 1** To dig up, as from a grave; exhume. **2** To bring to light or life as if from a grave. [<MF *désenterrer* <*des-* away + *enterrer* INTER] —**dis′in·ter′ment** *n.*

dis·in·ter·est (dis·in′tər·ist, -trist) *n.* **1** Lack of interest; indifference. **2** Freedom from bias; impartiality.

dis·in·ter·est·ed (dis·in′tər·is·tid, -tris·tid, -tə·res′-) *adj.* **1** Free from self-interest or bias; unselfish; impartial. **2** Loosely, uninterested.

dis·ject (dis·jekt′) *v.t.* To split apart forcibly; separate; break asunder. [<L *disjectus,* pp. of *disjicere* <*dis-* apart + *jacere* throw]

dis·join (dis·join′) *v.t.* To keep apart; undo or prevent the joining of; separate. —*v.i.* To become divided or separated. [<OF *desjoindre* <*des-* away (<L *dis-*) + *joindre* JOIN]

dis·joint (dis·joint′) *v.t.* **1** To put out of joint; dislocate. **2** To take apart; disconnect the pieces of. **3** To destroy the coherence, connections, or sequence of; disorder. —*v.i.* **4** To break into parts; become out of joint. —*adj. Obs.* Out of joint; disconnected. [<OF *desjoint,* pp. of *desjoindre.* See DISJOIN.] —**dis·joint′ly** *adv.*

dis·joint·ed (dis·join′tid) *adj.* Dislocated; disconnected; incoherent. —**dis·joint′ed·ly** *adv.* —**dis·joint′ed·ness** *n.*

dis·junct (dis·jungkt′) *adj.* **1** *Entomol.* Having the head, thorax, and abdomen separated by constrictions. **2** Not connected; detached. Compare illustrations under INSECT. [<L *disjunctus,* pp. of *disjungere* <*dis-* away + *jungere* join]

dis·junc·tion (dis·jungk′shən) *n.* **1** Sundering; separation: also **dis·junc′ture. 2** *Biol.* The moving apart of each pair of homologous chromosomes during the anaphase of cell mitosis.

dis·junc·tive (dis·jungk′tiv) *adj.* **1** Helping or serving to disjoin. **2** *Gram.* Expressing separation or disjoining, as certain conjunctions, as *either—or, else, otherwise*, etc. —*n.* **1** That which disjoins. **2** *Gram.* A disjunctive conjunction. **3** A Hebrew character used to separate words and clauses in sentences. **4** *Logic* A disjunctive proposition. —**dis·junc′tive·ly** *adv.*

disk (disk) *n.* **1** A flat plate of any material that is circular, or approximately circular; also, any surface that is flat and circular, or apparently so: the *disk* of a planet. **2** *Biol.* Any approximately flat circular outgrowth, organ, or structure of a planet or animal: in this sense usually spelled **disc. 3** In the Roman Catholic Church, a paten or plate for the eucharistic bread. **4** A quoit or discus. See Illustration under DISCOBOLUS. **5** *Agric.* A disk harrow. **6** *Astron.* The figure of a heavenly body, irrespective of its actual form. **7** A disc (def. 1). —**winged disk** In Egyptian art, the disk or symbol of the sun, supported by two uraei and the expanded wings of a vulture: also **sun disk.** [< L *discus* < Gk. *diskos* disk, platter. Doublet of DAIS, DESK, DISH.]

disk brake A brake in which a pad of durable, heat-resistant material is pressed against a metal disk: also called *spot brake.*

disk flower Any of the small, tubular florets, usually containing both stamens and pistil, that make up the central disk of a composite flower head. Also **disk floret.**

disk harrow *Agric.* A harrow consisting of a series of rolling, saucer-shaped disks set on edge and at an angle along one or more axles.

DISK HARROW
Number and type of disks may be varied for different types of plowing.

disk wheel A wheel with a continuous, flat, convex, or concave outer surface from hub to rim, used on many automobiles.

dis·like (dis·līk′) *v.t.* **·liked, ·lik·ing** To regard with aversion or antipathy. See synonyms under ABHOR. —*n.* Distaste; repugnance; aversion. See synonyms under ANTIPATHY, HATRED. —**dis·lik′a·ble** *adj.*

dis·lo·cate (dis′lō·kāt, dis·lō′kāt) *v.t.* **·cat·ed, ·cat·ing 1** *Anat.* To put out of joint, as a bone. **2** To put out of proper place or order; displace; disarrange. [< Med. L *dislocatus,* pp. of *dislocare* < *dis-* away + L *locare* set, place < *locus* a place]

dis·lo·ca·tion (dis′lō·kā′shən) *n.* **1** *Anat.* The partial or complete displacement of one or more of the bones of a joint. **2** The act of displacing or disarranging, or the resulting condition; disarrangement; disorder. **3** *Geol.* A fault in or a shifting of rocks, generally followed by a displacement on either side. **4** *Physics* A disturbance of the normal atomic or molecular configuration in a crystal, revealed by changes in crystal properties.

dis·lodge (dis·loj′) *v.* **·lodged, ·lodg·ing** *v.t.* To remove or drive out, as from an abode, hiding place, or fortification. —*v.i.* To leave a place of abode; move. See synonyms under BANISH. [< OF *desloger, deslogier* < *dis-* away + *loger* LODGE] —**dis·lodg′ment,** *Brit.* **dis·lodge′ment** *n.*

dis·loy·al (dis·loi′əl) *adj.* False to one's allegiance or obligations; faithless. See synonyms under PERFIDIOUS. [< OF *desloial* < *des-* not (< L *dis-*) + *loial* LOYAL] —**dis·loy′al·ly** *adv.*

dis·mal (diz′məl) *adj.* **1** Producing or expressing depression or gloom of feeling; cheerless; mournful. **2** Relating to adversity or trouble; direful; horrible. **3** Calamitous; ill-omened. See synonyms under DARK, SAD. —*n.* **1** *Colloq.* Usually *pl.* Gloomy feelings; depression. **2** *U.S.* A piece of swampy land along or near the southern Atlantic coast. Also **dismal swamp.** [< L *dies mali* evil or unpropitious days] —**dis′mal·ly** *adv.* —**dis′mal·ness** *n.*

dis·man·tle (dis·man′təl) *v.t.* **·tled, ·tling 1** To strip of furniture, equipments, or defenses. **2** To take apart; reduce to pieces. **3** *Obs.* To divest of clothing. [< MF *desmanteller* < *des-* away +

manteller cover with a cloak < *mantel* a cloak]

dis·may (dis·mā′) *v.t.* To paralyze with fear; deprive of courage and the ability to act; daunt utterly. See synonyms under FRIGHTEN. —*n.* A state of overwhelming embarrassment and fright; consternation; terror. See synonyms under ALARM, CHAGRIN, FEAR, FRIGHT. [ME *dismayen,* prob. < OF. Cf. OF *dismayé* dismayed.]

dis·mem·ber (dis·mem′bər) *v.t.* **1** To cut or pull limb from limb or part from part. **2** To divide; separate into parts and distribute, as an empire. [< OF *desmembrer* < L *dis-* apart + *membrum* a limb, member] —**dis·mem′ber·ment** *n.*

dis·miss (dis·mis′) *v.t.* **1** To put out of office or service by an act of authority; discharge. **2** To cause or allow to depart; send away. **3** To put away or aside; reject; put beyond consideration. **4** *Law* To send out of court; reject without further hearing: The case was *dismissed.* See synonyms under BANISH. [< LL *dismissus* < *dis-* away + *missus,* pp. of *mittere* send] —**dis·miss′i·ble** *adj.* —**dis·mis′so·ry, dis·mis′sive** *adj.*

dis·mis·sal (dis·mis′əl) *n.* **1** Removal from office; a dismissing; discharge. **2** A notice of discharge. Also **dis·mis′sion** (-mish′ən).

dis·mount (dis·mount′) *v.i.* **1** To get off or alight from a horse, etc. —*v.t.* **2** To remove from a mounting, as a cannon or a jewel. **3** To come down; descend. **4** To take (a machine) to pieces. **5** To remove from or deprive of horses. —*n.* The act or manner of dismounting. —**dis·mount′a·ble** *adj.*

dis·o·be·di·ent (dis′ə·bē′dē·ənt) *adj.* Neglecting or refusing to obey; refractory. See synonyms under REBELLIOUS. [< OF *desobedient* < L *dis-* not + *obediens, -entis* OBEDIENT] —**dis′o·be′di·ence** *n.* —**dis′o·be′di·ent·ly** *adv.*

dis·o·bey (dis′ə·bā′) *v.t. & v.i.* To refuse or fail to obey. [< OF *desobeir* < LL *dis-* away + *obedire* OBEY] —**dis′o·bey′er** *n.*

dis·o·blige (dis′ə·blīj′) *v.t.* **1** To neglect or refuse to oblige. **2** *Colloq.* To discommode or inconvenience. **3** To slight; affront. [< OF *desobliger* < L *dis-* not + *obligare* OBLIGE] —**dis·ob′li·ga′tion** *n.*

dis·o·blig·ing (dis′ə·blī′jing) *adj.* Not disposed to oblige; unaccommodating. —**dis′o·blig′ing·ly** *adv.* —**dis′o·blig′ing·ness** *n.*

di·so·di·um (dī·sō′dē·əm) *adj. Chem.* Characterized by the presence of two sodium atoms in a molecule. —**di·so′dic** *adj.*

dis·or·der (dis·ôr′dər) *n.* **1** The state of being disarranged; disorderliness. **2** Hence, disregard or neglect of orderliness. **3** A disturbance of the peace; an infraction of law or discipline; minor uprising or tumult. **4** Derangement of the bodily or mental functions; disease. **5** *Obs.* Agitation. —*v.t.* **1** To throw out of order; disarrange. **2** To disturb the natural functions of, as body or mind; unsettle; derange. **3** *Obs.* To agitate. [< OF *desordre* < L *dis-* away from, out of + *ordo* order]

Synonyms (noun): anarchy, clutter, confusion, disturbance, irregularity. See DISEASE, ILLNESS, TUMULT. Antonyms: method, order, regularity, system.

dis·or·dered (dis·ôr′dərd) *adj.* **1** Having no order or arrangement; confused. **2** Mentally deranged.

dis·or·der·ly (dis·ôr′dər·lē) *adj. & adv.* **1** Being in or causing disorder; not orderly; without order. **2** Lawless; disreputable. See synonyms under IRREGULAR, TURBULENT. —*n. pl.* **·lies** A disorderly person; offender against public order: a term used in police courts. —**dis·or′der·li·ness** *n.*

dis·o·ri·ent (dis·ôr′ē·ənt, -ō′rē-) *v.t.* **1** To cause to lose the sense of direction. **2** *Psychol.* To cause to lose appreciation of spatial, temporal, or human relationships. [< F *désorienter* < *des-* away (< L *dis-*) + *orienter* ORIENT] —**dis·o′ri·en·ta′tion** *n.*

dis·own (dis·ōn′) *v.t.* To refuse to acknowledge or to admit responsibility for or ownership of; deny; repudiate. See synonyms under RENOUNCE.

dis·par·age (dis·par′ij) *v.t.* **·aged, ·ag·ing 1** To speak of slightingly; undervalue. **2** To bring discredit or dishonor upon. [< OF *desparagier* match unequally < *des-* down, away (< L *dis-*) + *parage* equality, rank] —**dis·par′ag·er** *n.* —**dis·par′ag·ing·ly** *adv.*

Synonyms: belittle, decry, depreciate, discredit, dishonor, lower, underestimate, underrate, un-

dervalue. To *decry* is to cry down, in some noisy, public, or conspicuous manner. A witness or a statement is *discredited;* the currency is *depreciated;* a good name is *dishonored* by unworthy conduct; we *underestimate* in our own minds; we may *underrate* or *undervalue* in statement to others. To *disparage* is to *belittle* by damaging comparison or suggestion. These words are used, with few exceptions, of things such as qualities, merits, attainments, etc. See ASPERSE. Antonyms: see synonyms for PRAISE.

dis·par·age·ment (dis·par′ij·mənt) *n.* **1** The act of depreciating, aspersing, slighting, or undervaluing; derogation. **2** A condition of low estimation or valuation; a reproach; disgrace. **3** An unjust classing or comparison with that which is of less worth; degradation.

dis·pa·rate (dis′pə·rit) *adj.* That cannot be compared; dissimilar; radically different; different in essential qualities. [< L *disparatus,* pp. of *disparare* < *dis-* apart + *parare* make ready; infl. in meaning by L *dispars, -partis* unequal] —**dis′pa·rate·ly** *adv.* —**dis′pa·rate·ness** *n.*

dis·pa·ra·tion (dis′pə·rā′shən) *n. Pathol.* An optical distortion, consisting of double images of objects within or beyond the focal point of the eyes.

dis·par·i·ty (dis·par′ə·tē) *n. pl.* **·ties** The state of being dissimilar; inequality; difference. [< MF *disparité* < L *dis-* apart + *paritas* equality]

dis·pas·sion (dis·pash′ən) *n.* Freedom from passion or emotion; lack of bias.

dis·pas·sion·ate (dis·pash′ən·it) *adj.* Free from passion; unprejudiced. See synonyms under CALM, SOBER. —**dis·pas′sion·ate·ly** *adv.* —**dis·pas′sion·ate·ness** *n.*

dis·patch (dis·pach′) *v.t.* **1** To send off, especially on official business or for special purposes. **2** To transact with promptness; finish quickly. **3** To execute; kill summarily. —*v.i.* **4** *Obs.* To make haste. See synonyms under KILL. —*n.* **1** The act of dispatching; a forwarding to some destination: usually with the implication of promptness or celerity: the *dispatch* of a messenger. **2** A message sent by special means and with haste, as by telegraph; especially, a communication on public matters sent by one official to another. **3** Quick transaction, as of business; the prompt performance and completion of work; expedition; speed. **4** The act of killing; a putting to death. **5** An organization or conveyance for the speedy transmission of money, goods, or messages: I will send it by *dispatch.* **6** *Obs.* Dismissal; deliverance; riddance. Also, in diplomatic use, spelled *despatch.* [< Ital. *dispacciare,* ? ult. < LL *dis-* away, not + *pactare* fasten, fix] —**dis·patch′ful** *adj.*

dis·patch·er (dis·pach′ər) *n.* **1** One who dispatches. **2** One who directs the movement of trains, trucks, etc., and maintains records of such movement: also spelled *despatcher.*

dis·pel (dis·pel′) *v.t.* **·pelled, ·pel·ling** To scatter in various directions; break up and drive away; disperse. [< L *dispellere* < *dis-* away + *pellere* drive]

dis·pen·sa·ble (dis·pen′sə·bəl) *adj.* **1** That can be dispensed with. **2** That can be distributed or administered to others. **3** That can be removed by or made the subject of dispensation; pardonable. —**dis·pen′sa·bil′i·ty, dis·pen′sa·ble·ness** *n.*

dis·pen·sa·ry (dis·pen′sər·ē) *n. pl.* **·ries** A place or establishment, often public, where medicines are compounded and dispensed gratis or at a nominal price.

dis·pen·sa·tion (dis′pən·sā′shən) *n.* **1** The act of dispensing; a dealing out; distribution. **2** That which is bestowed on or appointed to one from a higher power. **3** The divine arrangement and administration of the affairs of the world: the *dispensation* of Providence. **4** A specific plan: a special *dispensation* of nature. **5** Special exemption granted from the requirements of a law, rule, or obligation; specifically, in the Roman Catholic Church, exemption by express ecclesiastical authority from an obligation incurred at the free will of the individual. Compare INDULGENCE. **6** *Theol.* One of the several systems or bodies of law in which at different times God has revealed his mind and will to man, or the continued state of things resulting from the operation of one of these systems: the Mosaic *dispensation*; also, the period during which a particular revelation of God's mind and will has been directly operative on mankind: during the Christian *dispensation*. [<OF <L *dispensatio, -onis* < *dispensare*. See DISPENSE.] — **dis·pen·sa·tion·al** *adj.*

dis·pen·sa·to·ry (dis-pen′sə-tôr′ē, -tō′rē) *adj.* Of or pertaining to dispensing or dispensation: also **dis·pen′sa·tive.** — *n. pl.* **·ries** A book in which medicinal substances are described; a pharmacopoeia.

dis·pense (dis-pens′) *v.* **·pensed, ·pens·ing** *v.t.* **1** To give or deal out in portions; distribute. **2** To compound and give out (medicines). **3** To administer, as laws. **4** To relieve or excuse; absolve. — *v.i.* **5** To grant exemption or dispensation. See synonyms under APPORTION. — **to dispense with** To waive the observance of; relinquish; forgo. [OF *despenser* <L *dispensare*, freq. of *dispendere* < *dis-* away + *pendere* weigh]

di·sper·mous (dī-spûr′məs) *adj. Bot.* Two-seeded. [<DI-² + Gk. *sperma* seed]

di·sper·my (dī-spûr′mē) *n. Biol.* The fecundation of one egg with two spermatozoa. — **di·sper′mic** *adj.*

dis·per·sal (dis-pûr′səl) *n.* The act or fact of scattering or dispersing; dispersion.

dis·perse (dis-pûrs′) *v.* **·persed, ·pers·ing** *v.t.* **1** To cause to scatter and go off in various directions. **2** To dispel; dissipate: The sun *dispersed* the mists. **3** To spread abroad; diffuse. **4** To separate (light) into its component spectral colors. — *v.i.* **5** To scatter and go off in various directions; dissipate. See synonyms under SPREAD. [<MF *disperser* <L *dispersus*, pp. of *dispergere* < *dis-* away + *spargere* scatter] — **dis·pers′i·ble** *adj.*

dis·persed (dis-pûrst′) *adj.* **1** Scattered; dissipated. **2** Placed near together but in a random manner. — **dis·pers′ed·ly** (-id·lē) *adv.*

disperse phase *Chem.* In a colloid system, that constituent which is dispersed in · the medium: gold particles are the *disperse phase* of colloidal gold. See COLLOID. Also **dispersed phase**

dis·per·sion (dis-pur′zhən, -shən) *n.* **1** The act of dispersing; the state or result of being dispersed; also **dis·per′sal. 2** *Mil.* The dispersed pattern of hits made by bombs dropped under the same conditions, or by bullets or shells shot from one gun with the same firing data. **3** *Physics* **a** The separation of light rays of different colors by the action of a prism or lens. **b** The process of sorting out emissions, as of electrons, in accordance with the values or magnitudes of selected properties, physical, chemical, electrical, etc. **4** *Chem.* The condition of the components making up a colloid system: distinguished from *solution*. **5** *Stat.* The arrangement of a series of values around the median or mean of a distribution.

dis·per·soid (dis-pûr′soid) *n. Chem.* A colloid system.

dis·pir·it (dis-pir′it) *v.t.* To render cheerless or hopeless; depress; dishearten. — **dis·pir′it·ed·ly** *adv.* — **dis·pir′it·ed·ness** *n.* — **dis·pir′it·ing·ly** *adv.*

dis·pir·it·ment (dis-pir′it·mənt) *n.* **1** The act of dispiriting, or the state of being dispirited; dejection. **2** That which dispirits, as a sorrow.

dis·pit·e·ous (dis-pit′ē·əs) *adj.* Remorseless; without pity.

dis·place (dis-plās′) *v.t.* **·placed, ·plac·ing 1** To remove or shift from the proper place. **2** To take the place of; supplant. **3** To remove from a position or office; discharge. **4** *Chem.* To release from combination: Zinc *displaces* the hydrogen of an acid. **5** *Obs.* To banish. [<OF *desplacer* <*des-* away (<L *dis-*) + *placer* place]

Synonyms: confuse, derange, disarrange, disturb, jumble, mislay, misplace, remove, unsettle. Objects are *displaced* when moved out of the place they have occupied; they are *misplaced* when they are put into a place where they should not be. One may know where to find what he has *misplaced*; what

he has *mislaid* he cannot locate. *Antonyms:* adjust, array, assort, classify, dispose, group, order, place, sort.

dis·placed person (dis-plāst′) Any inhabitant forced by military action or calamity to flee his country or leave his home. *Abbr. DP*

dis·place·ment (dis-plās′mənt) *n.* **1** The act of displacing, or the state of being displaced. **2** *Astron.* An apparent change of position, as of a star. **3** *Physics* **a** The weight of water displaced by a body floating in it, this weight being equal to the weight of the body. **b** The quantity of air displaced by an airplane, balloon, etc. **4** The relation between the position of a moving object at any time and its original position. **5** Electric displacement. **6** *Geol.* A fault. **7** *Psychoanal.* Substitution of a secondary, harmless, or unimportant element for a primary and significant one, as in a dream, for purposes of concealment.

displacement law *Physics* **1** The principle that an atom deprived of one of its electrons acquires the physicochemical properties of the element preceding it in the periodic table. See ELECTROMOTIVE SERIES. **2** The statement that radioactive emission of an alpha particle lowers the atomic number of the element by 2, while emission of a beta particle raises the atomic number by 1.

dis·plant (dis-plant′, -plänt′) *v.t.* **1** To take (a plant) from the ground; uproot. **2** *Obs.* To dislodge; displace. [<OF *desplanter* <L *dis-* away + *plantare* plant] — **dis·plan·ta′tion** *n.*

dis·play (dis-plā′) *v.t.* **1** To show; make apparent to the eye or the mind. **2** To show off; exhibit ostentatiously. **3** To unfold; unfurl, as a flag or sail. **4** In printing, to give special prominence to, as by size, style, or spacing of type. See synonyms under FLAUNT. — *n.* **1** The act of spreading out, unfolding, exhibiting, or bringing to the view or to the mind. **2** Ostentatious show. **3** *Printing* A style of type calculated to attract attention. **4** The matter so displayed. See synonyms under OSTENTATION, SPECTACLE. [<OF *despleier* <LL *displicare*. Doublet of DEPLOY.]

dis·please (dis-plēz′) *v.* **·pleased, ·pleas·ing** *v.t.* To cause displeasure in or annoyance to; vex; offend. — *v.i.* To cause displeasure or annoyance. See synonyms under AFFRONT, PIQUE¹. [<OF *desplaisir, desplaire*, ult. <L *displicere* < *dis-* not + *placere* please] — **dis·pleas′ing** *adj.* — **dis·pleas′ing·ly** *adv.*

dis·pleas·ure (dis-plezh′ər) *n.* **1** The state of being displeased; dissatisfaction; vexation; indignant disapproval. **2** An annoyance; offense. See synonyms under ANGER, OFFENSE, PIQUE¹.

dis·port (dis-pôrt′, -pōrt′) *v.i.* To gambol; display oneself sportively. — *v.t.* To amuse or display (oneself). See synonyms under ENTERTAIN. — *n.* Diversion; pastime; sport. [<OF *desporter* <L *dis-* away + *portare* carry]

dis·pos·a·ble (dis-pō′zə·bəl) *adj.* Subject to disposal; free to be used as occasion may require.

dis·po·sal (dis-pō′zəl) *n.* **1** The act of disposing; arrangement; order; distribution. **2** A getting rid of, a transfer, as by gift or sale. **3** Power of control, outlay, management, or distribution.

dis·pose (dis-pōz′) *v.* **·posed, ·pos·ing** *v.t.* **1** To put in order; arrange properly by sequence or interrelation. **2** To incline or influence the mind of; give a tendency to. **3** To put or set in a particular place or location. **4** *Archaic* To prepare; make ready. — *v.i.* **5** To arrange or settle something. — **to dispose of 1** To settle; finish. **2** To throw away. **3** To get rid of by selling or giving. — *n. Obs.* **1** Disposal. **2** Order; arrangement. **3** Disposition; deportment. [<OF *disposer* <*dis-* apart (<L *dis-*) + *poser*. See POSE.] — **dis·posed′** *adj.*

dis·pos·er (dis-pō′zər) *n.* One who disposes or orders.

dis·po·si·tion (dis′pə·zish′ən) *n.* **1** The act of disposing; arrangement, as of troops. **2** Distribution; state or manner of disposal; final settlement. **3** Control; power: usually with *at*: at his *disposition*. **4** Natural tendency; temper or temperament; characteristic spirit; bent; propensity. **5** Natural tendency of animate or inanimate things. **6** *Archit.* Arrange-

ment, as of plan, perspective, etc.: distinguished from *distribution*. See synonyms under APPETITE, CHARACTER, INCLINATION, MIND, WILL¹. [<F <L *dispositio, -onis* < *dis-* away + *ponere* place]

dis·pos·sess (dis′pə·zes′) *v.t.* To deprive (someone) of possession, as of a house or land; eject; oust. [<OF *despossesser* <*des-* away (<L *dis-*) + *possesser* POSSESS] — **dis′pos·ses′·sion** (-zesh′ən) *n.* — **dis′pos·ses′sor** *n.*

dis·pos·ses·so·ry (dis′pə·zes′ər·ē) *adj.* Referring to or partaking of dispossession.

dis·praise (dis-prāz′) *v.t.* **·praised, ·prais·ing** To speak of with disapproval or censure; disparage. — *n.* The expression of unfavorable opinion; disparagement; censure. [<OF *despreisier* <*dis-* not (<L *dis-*) + *preisier* PRAISE] — **dis·prais′er** *n.* — **dis·prais′ing·ly** *adv.*

dis·pread (dis-pred′) *v.t. & v.i.* **·pread, ·pread·ing** To spread out or abroad; diffuse; expand: also spelled *disspread*.

dis·proof (dis-prōōf′) *n.* Refutation; confutation.

dis·pro·por·tion (dis′prə·pôr′shən, -pōr′-) *n.* Want of due relative proportion; lack of symmetry; also, inadequacy. — *v.t.* To make of unsuitable size or proportions. [<F] — **dis·pro·por′tion·a·ble** (dis′prə·pôr′shən·ə·bəl, -pōr′-) *adj.* Unsuitable; inadequate.

dis·pro·por·tion·ate (dis′prə·pôr′shən·it, -pōr′-) *adj.* Out of proportion with regard to size, form, or value; disproportioned. Also **dis′·pro·por′tion·al.** — **dis′pro·por·tion·ate·ly,** **dis′·pro·por′tion·al·ly** *adv.* — **dis′pro·por′tion·ate·ness** *n.*

dis·prove (dis-prōōv′) *v.t.* **·proved, ·prov·ing** To prove (a statement, claim, etc.) to be false or erroneous; refute. [<OF *desprouver* < *des-* not (<L *dis-*) + *prouver* prove] — **dis·prov′·a·ble** *adj.* — **dis·prov′al** *n.*

dis·put·a·ble (dis′pyōō′tə·bəl, dis′pyōō·tə·bəl) *adj.* That can be disputed; controvertible; doubtful. — **dis·put′a·bil′i·ty** *n.* — **dis·put′a·bly** *adv.*

dis·pu·tant (dis′pyōō·tənt, dis-pyōō′tənt) *adj.* Engaged in controversy; disputing. — *n.* One who disputes. [<L *disputans, -antis*, ppr. of *disputare.* See DISPUTE.]

dis·pu·ta·tion (dis′pyōō·tā′shən) *n.* **1** The act of disputing; controversy; discussion; argumentation. **2** A rhetorical or logical exercise; a scholastic debate. See synonyms under ALTERCATION. [<L *disputatio, -onis* < *disputare.* See DISPUTE.]

dis·pu·ta·tious (dis′pyōō·tā′shəs) *adj.* Characterized by or pertaining to dispute. — **dis′·pu·ta′tious·ly** *adv.* — **dis′pu·ta′tious·ness** *n.*

dis·pute (dis-pyōōt′) *v.* **·put·ed, ·put·ing** *v.t.* **1** To argue about; discuss. **2** To question the validity, genuineness, etc., of; controvert. **3** To strive for; contest for, as a prize. **4** To resist; oppose. — *v.i.* **5** To argue. **6** To quarrel; wrangle. — *n.* **1** A controversial discussion; a verbal contest. **2** An altercation; wrangle; quarrel. See synonyms under ALTERCATION, FEUD, QUARREL. [<OF *desputer* <L *disputare* < *dis-* away + *putare* think] — **dis·put′er** *n.*

Synonyms (verb): antagonize, argue, battle, combat, contend, contest, controvert, debate, discuss, oppose, quarrel, question, reason, wrangle.

dis·qual·i·fy (dis-kwol′ə·fī) *v.t.* **·fied, ·fy·ing 1** To render unqualified or unfit; incapacitate; disable. **2** To pronounce unqualified or ineligible; especially, in sports, to deprive (a competitor) of a prize for rule infractions; also, to debar from further competition for such infractions.

dis·qui·et (dis-kwī′ət) *n.* An unsettled or disturbed condition; lack of quiet; restlessness; uneasiness: also **dis·qui′et·ness,** **dis·qui′e·tude** (-tōōd, -tyōōd). See synonyms under ALARM, ANXIETY, FEAR. — *v.t.* To make anxious or uneasy; disturb; alarm. — *adj. Rare* Restless; uneasy; impatient. — **dis·qui′et·ly** *adv.*

dis·qui·si·tion (dis′kwi·zish′ən) *n.* A systematic treatise or discourse; dissertation. [<L *disquisitio, -onis* an investigation <*dis-* from + *quaerere* seek, ask]

dis·qui·si·tor (dis-kwiz′ə·tər) *n.* One who makes disquisitions: an investigator.

dis·rate (dis-rāt′) *v.t.* **·rat·ed, ·rat·ing** To

lower in rating or rank, as a petty officer; degrade.

dis·re·gard (dis'ri·gärd') *v.t.* **1** To pay no attention to; ignore. **2** To treat as undeserving of consideration, respect, or attention; slight. — *n.* Want of regard; neglect; slight. See synonyms under NEGLECT, SLIGHT. — **dis're·gard'er** *n.* — **dis're·gard'ful** *adj.*

dis·rel·ish (dis·rel'ish) *v.t.* To dislike; have a distaste for. — *n.* **1** A feeling of slight repugnance; distaste or dislike. **2** Lack of palatableness; the quality of being displeasing or distasteful.

dis·re·pair (dis'ri·pâr') *n.* The state of being out of repair.

dis·rep·u·ta·ble (dis·rep'yə·tə·bəl) *adj.* Being in or causing ill repute; disgraceful. See synonyms under INFAMOUS. — **dis·rep'u·ta·ble·ness** *n.* — **dis·rep'u·ta·bly** *adv.*

dis·re·pute (dis'ri·pyōōt') *n.* Lack or loss of reputation; ill repute. Also *Obs.* **dis·rep'u·ta'·tion.**

dis·re·spect (dis'ri·spekt') *n.* Lack of respect; discourtesy. — *v.t.* To treat or regard with lack of respect.

dis·re·spect·ful (dis'ri·spekt'fəl) *adj.* Wanting in respect; discourteous. — **dis're·spect'ful·ly** *adv.* — **dis're·spect'ful·ness** *n.*

dis·robe (dis·rōb') *v.t. & v.i.* **·robed, ·rob·ing** To undress. — **dis·robe'ment** *n.*

dis·root (dis·rōōt', -rŏŏt') *v.t.* **1** To tear up by the roots. **2** To tear from the foundation.

dis·rupt (dis·rupt') *v.t. & v.i.* To burst or break asunder. — *adj. Obs.* Burst asunder; rent. [< L *disruptus,* pp. of *disrumpere* < *dis-* apart + *rumpere* burst] — **dis·rupt'er, dis·rup'tor** *n.*

dis·rup·tion (dis·rup'shən) *n.* **1** The act of bursting or tearing asunder. **2** The state of being so torn. See synonyms under RUPTURE.

dis·rup·tive (dis·rup'tiv) *adj.* Producing, resulting from, or attending disruption; rending; bursting. — **dis·rup'tive·ly** *adv.*

diss (dis) *n.* The fibrous stems of a reedlike Mediterranean plant (*Ampelodesma mauritanicus*): used for making hats, paper, cordage, etc. [< Arabic *dīs*]

dis·sat·is·fac·tion (dis'sat·is·fak'shən) *n.* A dissatisfied state or feeling; discontent.

dis·sat·is·fac·to·ry (dis'sat·is·fak'tər·ē) *adj.* Giving dissatisfaction or discontent; unsatisfactory. — **dis'sat·is·fac'to·ri·ness** *n.*

dis·sat·is·fy (dis·sat'is·fī) *v.t.* **·fied, ·fy·ing** To fail to satisfy; disappoint; displease.

dis·seat (dis·sēt') *v.t.* To unseat.

dis·sect (di·sekt') *v.t.* **1** To cut apart or divide, as an animal body or a plant, in order to examine the structure; anatomize. **2** To analyze critically; examine. See synonyms under CUT. [< L *dissectus,* pp. of *dissecare* < *dis-* apart + *secare* cut]

dis·seize (dis·sēz') *v.t.* **-seized, -seiz·ing** *Law* To oust from the possession of an estate in freehold, usually unlawfully. Also **dis·seise'.** [< AF *disseisir,* OF *dessaisir* < *des-* away (< L *dis-*) + *saisir* SEIZE] — **dis·sei'zor** (-zər, -zôr), **dis·sei'sor** *n.*

dis·sei·zin (dis·sē'zin) *n. Law* The unlawful entry upon the freehold of another and wrongful ouster of him from possession. Also **dis·sei'sin, dis·sei·zure** (dis·sē'zhər). [< AF *disseisine* < *disseisir.* See DIS-SEIZE.]

1 To conceal or disguise the true nature of (intentions, feelings, etc.) so as to deceive; dissimulate. **2** To pretend not to notice; ignore. **3** *Obs.* To feign. — *v.i.* **4** To conceal one's true nature, intentions, etc.; act hypocritically. See synonyms under HIDE[1], MASK[1]. [Earlier *dissimule* < OF *dissimuler* < L *dissimulare* < *dis-* not, away + *similis* alike; infl. in form by RESEMBLE] — **dis·sem'bler** *n.* — **dis·sem'bling·ly** *adv.*

dis·sem·i·nate (di·sem'ə·nāt) *v.t.* **·nat·ed, ·nat·ing** To spread about; scatter, as seed in sowing; promulgate. See synonyms under SPREAD. [< L *disseminatus,* pp. of *disseminare* < *dis-* away + *seminare* sow < *semen* seed] — **dis·sem'i·na'tion** *n.* — **dis·sem'i·na'tive** *adj.* — **dis·sem'i·na'tor** *n.*

dis·sem·i·nule (di·sem'ə·nyōōl) *n. Bot.* A seed fruit modified for migration. [< DISSEMIN(ATE) + -ULE]

dis·sen·sion (di·sen'shən) *n.* Angry or violent difference of opinion; discord; strife. See synonyms under ALTERCATION, QUARREL.

dis·sent (di·sent') *v.i.* **1** To differ in thought or opinion; disagree; to withhold approval or

consent. **2** To refuse adherence to an established church. — *n.* **1** The act or state of dissenting; disagreement. **2** Refusal to conform to an established church; nonconformity. [< L *dissentire* < *dis-* apart + *sentire* think, feel]

dis·sent·er (di·sen'tər) *n.* **1** One who dissents or disagrees; one who declares his disapproval or disagreement. **2** *Often cap.* A Protestant who refuses assent to the doctrines, or compliance with the usages, of an established or state church, especially the Church of England: opposed to *conformist.* See synonyms under HERETIC.

dis·sen·tient (di·sen'shənt) *adj.* Dissenting; expressing disagreement. — *n.* A dissenter. [< L *dissentiens, -entis,* ppr. of *dissentire.* See DISSENT.]

dis·sent·ing (di·sen'ting) *adj.* Disagreeing; avowing or expressing disagreement or dissent. — **dis·sent'ing·ly** *adv.*

dis·sen·tious (di·sen'shəs) *adj. Rare* Contentious; quarrelsome. — **dis·sen'tious·ly** *adv.*

dis·sep·i·ment (di·sep'ə·mənt) *n.* **1** *Bot.* A partition, as one of those that divide a compound pericarp into two or more cells. **2** *Zool.* A horizontal plate between the vertical septa in corals. [< L *dissaepimentum* < *dis-* apart + *saepire* fence in < *saepes* a fence, a hedge]

dis·ser·ta·tion (dis'ər·tā'shən) *n.* An extended and argumentative treatise or discourse; disquisition; thesis. See synonyms under SPEECH.

dis·serve (dis·sûrv') *v.t.* **-served, -serv·ing** To serve or to treat badly; do an ill turn to.

dis·serv·ice (dis·sûr'vis) *n.* Ill service; an ill turn.

dis·sev·er (di·sev'ər) *v.t.* **1** To divide; separate. **2** To separate into parts. — *v.i.* **3** To separate; part. [< AF *deseverer,* OF *dessever* < L *disseparare* < *dis-* apart + *separare* SEPARATE] — **dis·sev'er·ance, dis·sev'er·ment** *n.*

dis·si·dence (dis'ə·dəns) *n.* Disagreement; dissent.

dis·si·dent (dis'ə·dənt) *adj.* Dissenting; differing. — *n.* A dissenter. [< L *dissidens, -entis,* ppr. of *dissidere* < *dis-* apart + *sedere* sit]

dis·sil·i·ent (di·sil'ē·ənt) *adj.* **1** Springing or flying open. **2** *Bot.* Bursting asunder, as.the dry pod of the jewelweed. [< L *dissiliens, -entis,* ppr. of *dissilire* < *dis-* apart + *salire* leap] — **dis·sil'i·ence** or **dis·sil'i·en·cy** *n.*

dis·sim·i·lar (di·sim'ə·lər) *adj.* Unlike, different: often with *to.* See synonyms under CONTRARY, HETEROGENEOUS. — **dis·sim'i·lar·ly** *adv.*

dis·sim·i·late (di·sim'ə·lāt) *v.t. & v.i.* **-lat·ed, -lat·ing** **1** To make or become unlike. **2** *Phonet.* To undergo or cause to undergo dissimilation. [< DIS-[1] + L *similis* alike]

dis·si·mil·i·tude (dis'si·mil'ə·tōōd, -tyōōd) *n.* Lack of resemblance; unlikeness. [< L *dissimilitudo* < *dissimilis* < *dis-* not + *similis* alike]

dis·sim·u·late (di·sim'yə·lāt) *v.t. & v.i.* **·lat·ed, ·lat·ing** To conceal (intentions, feelings, etc.) by pretense; dissemble. [< L *dissimulatus,* pp. of *dissimulare.* See DISSEMBLE.] — **dis·sim'u·la·tive** *adj.* — **dis·sim'u·la·tor** *n.*

dis·sim·u·la·tion (di·sim'yə·lā'shən) *n.* False pretense; hypocrisy. See synonyms under DECEPTION, HYPOCRISY, PRETENSE.

dis·si·pate (dis'ə·pāt) *v.* **·pat·ed, ·pat·ing** *v.t.* **1** To disperse or drive away; dispel. **2** To disintegrate; destroy or dissolve utterly. **3** To squander; spend lavishly and wastefully. — *v.i.* **4** To become dispersed; scatter. **5** To engage in excessive or dissolute pleasures. See synonyms under SQUANDER. [< L *dissipatus,* pp. of *dissipare* < *dis-* away + *supare* throw]

dis·si·pa·tion (dis'ə·pā'shən) *n.* **1** The act of dissipating or state of being dissipated. **2** Excessive indulgence, especially in vicious pleasures. **3** Distraction, as of the mind, or anything that distracts. See synonyms under EXCESS.

dis·so·cia·ble (di·sō'shə·bəl, -shē·ə-) *adj.* **1** Not well assorted or associated; incongruous; unsociable. **2** Capable of being separated or dissociated. **3** Unsociable. — **dis·so'cia·bil'i·ty, dis·so'cia·ble·ness** *n.* — **dis·so'cia·bly** *adv.*

dis·so·cial (di·sō'shəl) *adj.* Unsocial; unfriendly.

dis·so·ci·ate (di·sō'shē·āt) *v.* **·at·ed, ·at·ing** *v.t.* **1** To break the association of; disconnect; separate. **2** To regard as separate in concept or nature. **3** *Chem.* To resolve by dissocia-

tion. — *v.i.* **4** To break an association. **5** *Chem.* To undergo dissociation. [< L *dissociatus,* pp. of *dissociare* < *dis-* apart + *sociare* join together < *socius* a companion] — **dis·so'ci·a·tive** *adj.*

dis·so·ci·a·tion (di·sō'sē·ā'shən, -shē·ā'-) *n.* **1** The act of dissociating; state of separation. **2** *Chem.* **a** The resolution of a compound into simpler constituents by a change in physical state, as by heat or pressure, with recombination when the original conditions are restored. **b** Electrolytic dissolution. **3** *Psychiatry* A mental disorder in which one or several groups of ideas become split off from the main body of the personality and are not accessible to conscious control: contrasted with *association.*

dis·sol·u·ble (di·sol'yə·bəl) *adj.* **1** Separable into parts. **2** Capable of being dissolved or decomposed. [< L *dissolubilis* < *dissolvere.* See DISSOLVE.] — **dis'sol·u·bil'i·ty, dis·sol'u·ble·ness** *n.*

dis·so·lute (dis'ə·lōōt) *adj.* Abandoned; profligate. See synonyms under IMMORAL, IRREGULAR. [< L *dissolutus,* pp. of *dissolvere.* See DISSOLVE.] — **dis'so·lute·ly** *adv.* — **dis'so·lute·ness** *n.*

dis·so·lu·tion (dis'ə·lōō'shən) *n.* **1** The act or state of dissolving; disintegration. **2** *Chem.* Decomposition; separation into elements or components. **3** Liquefaction. **4** Separation; breaking up, as of an assembly or corporation, or of a partnership, in accordance with the articles of co-partnership, or by the death or incompetence of a partner, or by the decree of a court. **5** Death, the separation of soul and body.

1 To change (a substance) from a solid to a fluid condition. **2** To cause to pass into or combine with a solution; melt; liquefy. **3** To end the existence, functions, or meetings of: to *dissolve* Parliament. **4** To end or conclude (a relationship or association): to *dissolve* a partnership or a marriage. **5** *Law* To set aside; annul, as an injunction. **6** To disunite. — *v.i.* **7** To pass into or as into a liquid state; melt; become fluid. **8** To come to an end; disperse, as a meeting. **9** To fade away; vanish, as an image. **10** In motion pictures, to change gradually from one picture or scene to another, the two overlapping in the process. See synonyms under MELT. — *n.* In motion pictures and television, the slow emergence of one scene out of another, caused by the lapping of a fade-in over a fade-out; a lap-dissolve. [< L *dissolvere* < *dis-* apart + *solvere* loosen] — **dis·solv'a·ble** *adj.* — **dis·sol'vent** *adj. & n.*

dis·so·nance (dis'ə·nəns) *n.* **1** A discordant mingling of sounds; discord. **2** *Music* A combination of tones regarded as displeasing and requiring resolution. **3** Harsh disagreement; incongruity; discord. Also **dis'so·nan·cy.**

dis·so·nant (dis'ə·nənt) *adj.* **1** Harsh in sound; inharmonious. **2** Naturally hostile; incongruous. **3** *Music* Having the quality of dissonance. [< L *dissonans, -antis,* ppr. of *dissonare* < *dis-* away + *sonare* sound] — **dis'so·nant·ly** *adv.*

dis·suade (di·swād') *v.t.* **·suad·ed, ·suad·ing** **1** To change or alter the plans of (a person) by persuasion or advice: with *from.* **2** *Obs.* To advise against (a course of action). See synonyms under ADMONISH. [< L *dissuadere* < *dis-* away + *suadere* persuade] — **dis·suad'er** *n.*

dis·syl·la·ble (di·sil'ə·bəl, dis'il'ə·bəl) *n.* A word of two syllables: also spelled *disyllable.* [< F < L *disyllabus* < Gk. *disyllabos* < *dis-* twofold + *syllabos* SYLLABLE] — **dis·syl·lab'ic·a'tion** *n.*

dis·sym·me·try (dis·sim'ə·trē) *n.* Lack of symmetry. — **dis'sym·met'ric** or **·ri·cal** *adj.* — **dis'sym·met'ri·cal·ly** *adv.*

dis·taff (dis'taf, -täf) *n. pl.* **dis·taffs** or *Rare* **dis·taves** (dis'tāvz) **1** A rotating vertical staff that holds the bunch of flax or wool for use in spinning by hand. **2** Figuratively, woman, as the holder of a distaff; also, woman's work or domain. [OE *distæf* < *dis* bundle of flax + *stæf* staff]

dis·tal (dis'təl) *adj. Biol.* Relatively remote from the center of the body or the point of attachment; peripheral: opposed to *proximal.* [< DIST(ANT) + -AL[1]] — **dis'tal·ly** *adv.*

dis·tance (dis'təns) *n.* **1** Length of separation in space, or, by extension, in time. **2** The state of being distant; separation; remoteness; a remote point. **3** Reserve; haughtiness; coldness. **4** Separation in rank, relationship, or succession. **5** In art, the part of a picture that represents distant objects. **6** *Music* The interval between two notes. **7** In horse racing, an interval measured back from the winning post to a point on the course marked by a flag or post, called the **distance post**. To be allowed to run in succeeding heats of the race, a horse must reach the distance post before the winning horse reaches the finish line. — *v.t.* **·tanced, ·tanc·ing** **1** To leave behind, as in a race; outstrip; excel. **2** To separate by a space. **3** To cause to appear distant.

dis·tant (dis'tənt) *adj.* **1** Separated in space or time; far apart; not closely related in qualities or in position; far away; remote. **2** Reserved or unapproachable; formal. **3** Indistinct; faint. **4** Not obvious or plain; indirect. See synonyms under ALIEN, HAUGHTY. [<F <L *distans, -antis,* ppr. of *distare* <*dis-* apart + *stare* stand] — **dis'tant·ly** *adv.*

dis·taste (dis·tāst') *n.* **1** Aversion to food or drink; disrelish. **2** Alienation; disapproval; dislike. See synonyms under ANTIPATHY. — *v.t. Rare* **1** To dislike. **2** To displease; cause the dislike of.

dis·taste·ful (dis-tāst'fəl) *adj.* **1** Causing distaste; disagreeable. **2** Denoting distaste: a *distasteful* glance. — **dis·taste'ful·ly** *adv.* — **dis·taste'ful·ness** *n.*

dis·tem·per[1] (dis-tem'pər) *n.* **1** Any of several infectious diseases of animals, especially a catarrhal affection of puppies associated with a filtrable virus. **2** An improper or disordered temper; ill humor. **3** Political or civil disturbance; riot; disorder. [< *v.*] — *v.t.* **1** To disturb or derange the faculties or functions of; disorder. **2** To ruffle; disturb. [<Med. L *distemperare* <*dis-* away + *temperare* regulate, mix]

dis·tem·per[2] (dis-tem'pər) *n.* **1** A pigment mixed with a vehicle (as yolk of eggs or glue) soluble in water, used chiefly for mural decoration and scene painting. **2** The art or process of painting with such materials, or a painting executed in them. — *v.t.* **1** To mix, as colors, for distemper painting. **2** To color or paint with distemper. — *adj.* Of or pertaining to internal decoration done with distemper. [<OF *destemprer* <Med. L *distemperare* <*dis-* apart + *temperare* mix, mingle, soak]

dis·tend (dis-tend') *v.t. & v.i.* To expand; swell; dilate, as from or by pressure from within. [<L *distendere* <*dis-* apart + *tendere* stretch]

dis·tich (dis'tik) *n.* In prosody, a couplet; a two-line stanza considered as a unit. [<L *distichon* <Gk., neut. sing. of *distichos* <*di-* two + *stichos* row, line]

dis·ti·chous (dis'ti·kəs) *adj. Bot.* Disposed in two longitudinal rows on opposite sides of a common axis, as leaves. [<L *distichus* <Gk. *distichos.* See DISTICH.] — **dis'ti·chous·ly** *adv.*

dis·til (dis-til') *v.* **·tilled, ·til·ling** *v.t.* **1** To subject to or as to distillation, so as to purify, concentrate, or refine. **2** To extract volatile substances from by distillation: to *distil* corn. **3** To extract or produce by distillation: to *distil* whisky. **4** To give forth or send down in drops: The clouds *distil* rain. — *v.i.* **5** To undergo distillation. **6** To exude in drops; trickle; drip. Also **dis·till'.** [<L *distillare,* var. of *destillare* <*de-* down + *stillare* drop, trickle] — **dis·til'la·ble** *adj.*

dis·til·la·tion (dis'tə·lā'shən) *n.* **1** The act of distilling; separation of the more volatile parts of a substance from those less volatile by vaporizing and subsequently condensing, as by heating in a retort or still and cooling in a retort or worm. **2** The purification or rectification of a substance by this process. **3** The substance separated by distilling; a distillate. **4** The essential or abstract quality of anything.

dis·til·ler·y (dis·til'ər·ē) *n. pl.* **·ler·ies** An establishment for distilling, especially for producing alcoholic liquors by distillation.

dis·tinct (dis·tingkt') *adj.* **1** Clear to the senses or mind; plain; unmistakable. **2** Clearly standing apart, as in space or thought, from other objects; evidently not identical; observably or decidedly different. **3** Standing apart by itself; disjoined; unconnected. **4** Us-

ing or marked by clear vision and understanding; not obscure nor confused: a man of *distinct* ideas. **5** *Poetic* Adorned; variegated. See synonyms under CLEAR, EVIDENT, MANIFEST, PARTICULAR, PLAIN[1]. [<L *distinctus,* pp. of *distinguere.* See DISTINGUISH.] — **dis·tinct'ly** *adv.* — **dis·tinct'ness** *n.*

dis·tinc·tion (dis-tingk'shən) *n.* **1** A distinguishing mark or quality; a characteristic difference; also, the relation of difference between objects having distinguishing marks or qualities. **2** The act of distinguishing; discrimination. **3** Heed or regard to differences, as of rank or character. **4** A mark of honor; superiority; honorable position. See synonyms under CHARACTERISTIC, DIFFERENCE, FAME.

dis·tinc·tive (dis-tingk'tiv) *adj.* **1** Characteristic; distinguishing. See synonyms under PARTICULAR. **2** *Ling.* Relevant. — **dis·tinc'tive·ly** *adv.* — **dis·tinc'tive·ness** *n.*

dis·tin·guish (di-sting'gwish) *v.t.* **1** To mark as different; indicate or constitute the differences of or between. **2** To recognize as separate or distinct; discriminate. **3** To divide into classes or categories; classify. **4** To bring fame, celebrity, or credit upon. **5** To apperceive by one of the physical senses. — *v.i.* **6** To make or discern differences; discriminate: often with *among* or *between.* See synonyms under DISCERN, KNOW. [<F *distinguer* (<L *distinguere* separate) + *-ISH*[2]] — **dis·tin'guish·a·ble** *adj.* — **dis·tin'guish·a·bly** *adv.* — **dis·tin'guish·er** *n.*

dis·tin·guished (di-sting'gwisht) *adj.* Conspicuous; eminent. See synonyms under EMINENT, ILLUSTRIOUS.

dis·tome (dis'tōm) *n.* One of a genus (*Distoma*) of trematode, parasitic worms: also called *flukes.* [<NL<Gk. *di-* two + *stoma* mouth]

dis·tort (dis-tôrt') *v.t.* **1** To twist or bend out of shape; make crooked or misshapen. **2** To twist the meaning of; misrepresent; pervert. See synonyms under PERVERT. [<L *distortus,* pp. of *distorquere* <*dis-* apart + *torquere* twist] — **dis·tort'er** *n.* — **dis·tort'ed** *adj.* — **dis·tort'ed·ly** *adv.* — **dis·tort'ed·ness** *n.*

dis·tor·tion (dis-tôr'shən) *n.* **1** The act of distorting. **2** A deformity; perversion. **3** *Optics* An imperfect image due to a defective lens or retina. **4** *Telecom.* A change in the wave form of a signal caused by non–uniform transmission at different frequencies. **5** *Psychoanal.* The process whereby certain objectionable elements of the mental life are altered so as to make them acceptable to the conscious ego. Compare CENSORSHIP (def. 2). — **dis·tor'tion·al** *adj.*

dis·tract (dis-trakt') *v.t.* **1** To draw or divert (the mind, etc.) in a different direction. **2** To turn or draw (the mind or attention) in various directions; bewilder; confuse. **3** To make frantic; craze. See synonyms under PERPLEX. [<L *distractus,* pp. of *distrahere* <*dis-* away + *trahere* draw] — **dis·tract'i·ble** *adj.* — **dis·tract'ing, dis·trac'tive** *adj.*

dis·tract·ed (dis·trak'tid) *adj.* **1** Bewildered; harassed. **2** Mentally deranged; mad. See synonyms under INSANE. — **dis·tract'ed·ly** *adv.*

dis·trac·tion (dis·trak'shən) *n.* **1** A drawing off or diversion of the mind, as from some object or from troubles or cares. **2** Mental disturbance or confusion; perplexity. **3** Strong agitation, excitement, or distress; wild or violent grief. **4** Mental aberration; frenzy; madness. **5** Anything that distracts; a disturbing or diverting object or cause; an interruption or diversion. See synonyms under PERPLEXITY.

dis·train (dis-trān') *v.t. Law* **1** To take and detain (personal property) by distress as security for a debt, claim, etc. **2** To subject (a person) to distress. — *v.i.* **3** To impose a distress. [<OF *destreindre* <L *distringere* <*dis-* completely + *stringere* draw tight, compress] — **dis·train'a·ble** *adj.* — **dis·train'er** *or* **dis·train'or** *n.* — **dis·train'ment** *n.*

dis·traught (dis-trôt') *adj.* In a state of distraction. [Var. of earlier *distract,* pp. of DISTRACT]

dis·tress (dis·tres') *v.t.* **1** To inflict suffering upon; cause agony, anxiety, or worry to; afflict. **2** To constrain by suffering or pain. **3** *Law* To distrain. See synonyms under PERSE-

CUTE. — *n.* **1** Acute or extreme suffering or its cause; pain; trouble. **2** An afflicted, wretched, or exhausted condition; dangerous situation. **3** *Law* Distraint; goods taken by distraint. See synonyms under AGONY, GRIEF, MISFORTUNE, PAIN, POVERTY. [<OF *destresser,* OF *destrecier* <LL *districtiare* <*distringere.* See DISTRAIN.] — **dis·tress'ful** *adj.* — **dis·tress'·ful·ly** *adv.* — **dis·tress'ful·ness** *n.* — **dis·tress'·ing·ly** *adv.*

dis·trib·u·tar·y (dis-trib'yoo-ter'ē) *n. pl.* **·tar·ies** A river branch flowing away from the main branch and not returning to it: opposed to *tributary.*

dis·trib·ute (dis-trib'yoot) *v.t.* **·ut·ed, ·ut·ing** **1** To divide and deal out in shares; apportion; allot. **2** To divide and classify; categorize: to *distribute* plants into orders. **3** To scatter or spread out, as in an area or over a surface. **4** To divide and arrange into distinctive parts or functions. **5** *Logic* To use (a term) in its full extension, so as to include all members of the class which it names. **6** *Printing* To separate (type) and return the letters to the proper boxes. See synonyms under ALLOT, APPORTION, SPREAD. [<L *distributus,* pp. of *distribuere* <*dis-* away + *tribuere* give, allot] — **dis·trib'ut·a·ble** *adj.*

dis·tri·bu·tion (dis'trə·byoo'shən) *n.* **1** The act of distributing; apportionment; arrangement; disposition. **2** That which is distributed. **3** The state or manner of being distributed. **4** *Archit.* The arrangement and interdependence of interior subdivisions, etc., as distinguished from *disposition.* **5** In commerce, the total of all steps involved in the delivery of goods from producer to consumer, including such items as sales methods, transport, storage, financing, accounting, etc.

dis·trib·u·tive (dis-trib'yə-tiv) *adj.* **1** Serving or tending to distribute; pertaining to distribution. **2** Denoting individual action or consideration. **3** *Gram.* Denoting objects or groups composed of individuals acting individually: The *distributive* pronouns "each," "every," "either," and "neither" are called *distributive* adjectives when they modify nouns. **4** Expressing the act of taking singly: the Latin *distributive* numeral "bini" (two by two). **5** *Logic* Indicating or effecting the distribution of a term. — *n.* A distributive pronoun, adjective, or numeral, as *each, every,* etc. — **dis·trib'u·tive·ly** *adv.* — **dis·trib'u·tive·ness** *n.*

dis·trict (dis'trikt) *n.* **1** A portion of territory specially set off or defined, as for judicial, political, educational, or other purposes. **2** A subdivision of the United States or of one State having its own Federal or State court. **3** Any region of space; a tract. See synonyms under LAND. — *v.t.* To divide into districts. [<MF <Med. L *districtus* jurisdiction <L *distringere.* See DISTRAIN.]

District of Columbia A Federal district, capital of the United States, coextensive with the city of Washington on the Potomac River; 69 square miles: abbr. DC

dis·trust (dis-trust') *v.t.* To feel no trust for or confidence in; doubt; suspect. — *n.* Doubt; suspicion; discredit. See synonyms under DOUBT.

dis·turb (dis-tûrb') *v.t.* **1** To destroy or interfere with the repose, tranquility, or peace of. **2** To agitate the mind of; disquiet; trouble. **3** To upset the order, system, or progression of: She has *disturbed* the rhythm of my days. **4** To interrupt; break in on. **5** To cause inconvenience to. See synonyms under DISPLACE. [<OF *destorber* <L *disturbare* <*dis-* completely + *turbare* disorder] — **dis·turb'er** *n.*

dis·tur·bance (dis-tûr'bəns) *n.* **1** A change, or alteration, whether as the result of internal or external action, from a condition of order, repose, or peace to one of agitation or disorder. **2** The act of effecting this change. **3** A tumult or commotion by which the public peace is disturbed. **4** A disordered condition of the mind; mental agitation, distraction, or confusion. See synonyms under ALTERCATION, ANXIETY, DISORDER, TUMULT. [<OF *destorbance* <*destorber.* See DISTURB.]

dis·tyle (dis'til) *adj. Archit.* Having two columns; specifically, referring to a portico in antes. See ANTA. — *n.* A building so constructed. [<DI-[2] + Gk. *stylos* pillar]

dis·un·ion (dis·yōōn′yən) *n.* **1** The state of being disunited; severance; rupture. **2** A condition of disagreement; breach of concord.

dis·un·ion·ist (dis·yōōn′yən·ist) *n.* **1** An advocate of disunion. **2** In U.S. history, one who, before and during Civil War of 1861, favored the dissolution of the Union.

3 In English history, an opponent of the Act of Union with Ireland of 1801. Compare UNIONIST. — **dis·un′ion·ism** *n.*

dis·use (dis·yōōs′) *n.* The state of being excluded or retired from use; desuetude: also **dis·us′age** (-ij). — *v.t.* (dis·yōōz′) **·used**, **·us·ing** To cease to use or practice; discontinue.

dis·u·til·i·ty (dis′yōō·til′ə·tē) *n.* Injuriousness; harmfulness.

dis·val·ue (dis·val′yōō) *v.t.* **·val·ued**, **·val·u·ing** To treat as of little value; disparage.

dis·yoke (dis·yōk′) *v.t.* **·yoked**, **·yok·ing** To unyoke.

di·ta (dē′tə) *n.* A Philippine forest tree (*Alstonia scholaris*) of the dogbane family. The wood is used in making furniture, and a substitute for quinine is obtained from the bark. Also **di′taa**. [< native name]

ditch (dich) *n.* A narrow trench in the ground, as for drainage; an irrigation trench. — *v.t.* **1** To dig or lay a ditch or ditches in. **2** To run or throw into a ditch; derail. **3** *U.S. Slang* To abandon; get rid of. — *v.i.* **4** To make a ditch or ditches. [OE *dīc*. Related to DIKE.]

di·the·ism (dī′thē·iz′əm) *n.* *Theol.* The doctrine that maintains the existence of two coequal gods or powers of good and evil; Manicheism. [<DI-² + Gk. *theos* god] — **di′·the·ist** *n.* — **di′the·is′tic** *adj.*

dith·er (dith′ər) *v.i.* To tremble; shake; vibrate. — *n.* **1** A trembling; vibration; state of nervousness or anxiety. **2** *pl. Colloq.* An attack of nerves. [Var. of earlier *didder* tremble, shake; origin uncertain] — **dith′er·y** *adj.*

dith·y·ramb (dith′ə·ram, -ramb) *n.* **1** In ancient Greece, a wild, passionate choric hymn sung in honor of Dionysus. **2** A metrical composition resembling this. **3** A wild or vehement speech or writing. Also **dith′y·ram′·bus**. [<L *dithyrambus* <Gk. *dithyrambos*] — **dith′y·ram′bic** (-ram′bik) *adj.*

dit·ta·ny (dit′ə·nē) *n. pl.* **·nies** **1** A perennial American herb of the mint family (*Cunila origanoides*), with small, purplish or lilac blossoms; the stonemint. **2** Any of various plants of the mint family, as the **Cretan dittany** (*Origanum dictamnus*). **3** Fraxinella. [<OF *ditan, dictamne* <L *dictamnis* <Gk. *diktamon*, ? from *Diktē*, a mountain in Crete where it grew]

dit·to (dit′ō) *n. pl.* **·tos** The same thing repeated; the aforesaid: often written *do.*, or expressed by two inverted commas, called **ditto marks**, beneath the word intended to be duplicated. — *adv.* As before; likewise. — *v.t.* **·toed**, **·to·ing** To copy; duplicate. [<Ital. *detto, ditto* aforesaid <L *dictum*. See DICTUM.]

dit·to·gram (dit′ō·gram) *n.* One letter or more unconsciously repeated in the copying of a manuscript. Also **dit′to·graph** (-graf, -gräf). [<Gk. *dittos* double + -GRAM]

dit·ty (dit′ē) *n. pl.* **·ties** **1** A short, simple song; lay. **2** *Obs.* A refrain. [<OF *dittié, ditié* <L *dictatum* a thing said <*dictare*. See DICTATE.]

dit·ty-bag (dit′ē-bag′) *n.* A sailor's bag for needles, thread, personal belongings, etc. [Origin uncertain]

di·u·re·sis (dī′yōō·rē′sis) *n. Pathol.* Excessive excretion of urine. [<NL <Gk. *dia-* thoroughly + *ourēsis* urination]

di·u·ret·ic (dī′yōō·ret′ik) *adj.* Stimulating the secretion and flow of urine: also **di′u·ret′i·cal**. — *n.* A diuretic medicine.

di·ur·nal (dī·ûr′nəl) *adj.* **1** Happening every day; daily; also, performed in a day: a planet's *diurnal* revolution. **2** Done in or pertaining to the daytime: opposed to *nocturnal*. **3** *Med.* Increasing in violence by day, as the symptoms of a disease. **4** *Bot.* Expanding by day and closing at night, as certain flowers. **5** Lasting only one day; ephemeral. See synonyms under DAILY. — *n.* **1** *Eccl.* A service book containing the offices for prime, tierce, sext, nones, vespers, and compline. **2** A diurnal bird or insect. **3** *Obs.* A journal; diary. **4** *Obs.* A daily newspaper. [<L *diurnalis* <*diurnus* daily <*dies* day. Doublet of JOURNAL.] — **di·ur′nal·ly** *adv.*

di·va (dē′və) *n. pl.* **·vas** or **·ve** (-vā) A celebrated female operatic singer; a prima donna. [<Ital., fem. of *divo* divine <L *divus*]

di·va·gate (dī′və·gāt) *v.i.* **·gat·ed**, **·gat·ing** **1** To wander or stray aimlessly. **2** To digress. [<L *divagatus*, pp. of *divagari* <*dis-* away + *vagari* wander] — **di′va·ga′tion** *n.*

di·van (di·van′, dī′van) *n.* **1** A cushioned or pillowed place for reclining; a couch. **2** A café; smoking-room. **3** An Oriental governmental council; a council chamber. **4** A collection of poems usually written by one man: also spelled *diwan*. [<Turkish *dīvān* <Persian *dēvān*, orig. a collection of poems, a register; later, a council, a chamber, a bench]

di·var·i·cate (di·var′ə·kāt, dī-) *v.t.* & *v.i.* **·cat·ed**, **·cat·ing** To branch off or cause to branch off; diverge. — *adj.* (di·var′ə·kit, -kāt, dī-) Branching off; widely diverging. [<L *divaricatus*, pp. of *divaricare* <*dis-* apart + *varicare* straddle <*varicus* straddling] — **di·var′i·cate·ly** *adv.* — **di·var′i·ca′tor** *n.*

dive (dīv) *v.* **dived** (*U.S. Colloq.* **dove**), **dived**, **div·ing** *v.i.* **1** To plunge, usually headfirst, into water, etc. **2** To submerge, as a submarine. **3** To plunge the body, hand, or an object into something, usually so as to obtain a part: He *dived* into the candy. **4** To enter suddenly or abruptly: He *dived* into the forest. **5** To descend at a steep angle and at high speed: The hawk *dived* toward the earth. **6** To work under water as a diver. **7** To become engrossed or deeply involved: to *dive* into politics. — *v.t.* **8** To thrust or plunge (the body, hand, or an object) into something. **9** To cause (an airplane) to descend at a steep angle. — *n.* **1** A plunge headforemost into or as into water. **2** A steep downward plunge of an airplane. **3** *Colloq.* A disreputable resort; den. [Blend of OE *dūfan* dive and *dȳfan* immerse]

di·verge (di·vûrj′, dī-) *v.* **·verged**, **·verg·ing** *v.i.* **1** To extend or lie in different directions from the same point: opposed to *converge*. **2** To vary from a typical form; differ. **3** *Math.* To fail to converge toward a limit: said of an infinite series, the sum of whose terms has no limit. — *v.t.* **4** To make divergent, cause to fork. See synonyms under BEND, WANDER. [<NL *divergere* <*dis-* apart + *vergere* incline]

di·vers (dī′vərz) *adj.* **1** More than one, but not a great number; several; sundry. **2** *Archaic* Of different kinds; various. See synonyms under MANY. [<OF <L *diversus* different; orig. pp. of *divertere*. See DIVERT.]

♦ *Divers* implies severalty; *diverse*, difference. Hence we say: "The Evangelists narrate events in *divers* manners" but "The views of the two parties were quite *diverse*."

di·verse (di·vûrs′, dī-, dī′vûrs) *adj.* **1** Differing essentially; distinct. **2** *Obs.* Capable of various forms; multiform. [<L *diversus*. See DIVERS.] — **di·verse′ly** *adv.*

di·ver·si·fi·ca·tion (di·vûr′sə·fə·kā′shən, dī-) *n.* **1** Variation; variety. **2** The act of branching out into diverse lines of activity: product *diversification*.

di·ver·si·fy (di·vûr′sə·fī, dī-) *v.t.* **·fied**, **·fy·ing** To make diverse; impart variety to.

di·ver·sion (di·vûr′zhən, -shən, dī-) *n.* **1** The act of diverting. **2** *Mil.* An attack or feint intended to divert enemy troops from the point where a full-scale attack is to be made. **3** That which diverts; amusement; recreation. See synonyms under ENTERTAINMENT, SPORT.

di·ver·si·ty (di·vûr′sə·tē, dī-) *n. pl.* **·ties** **1** The state of being diverse; dissimilitude. **2** Variety: a *diversity* of interests. See synonyms under CHANGE, DIFFERENCE.

di·vert (di·vûrt′, dī-) *v.t.* **1** To turn aside; deflect, as in direction, course, interest, or purpose. **2** To draw off the attention of. **3** To amuse; entertain. See synonyms under ENTERTAIN, RELAX. [<L *divertere* <*dis-* apart + *vertere* turn] — **di·vert′er** *n.* — **di·vert′ing** *adj.* — **di·vert′ing·ly** *adv.*

di·ver·tic·u·lum (dī′vər·tik′yə·ləm) *n. pl.* **·la** (-lə) *Anat.* A blind pouch or structure which has arisen or developed from another larger one, as the cecum, the air bladder of a fish, or the lungs of a vertebrate, all of which arise from the intestinal canal. [<L *diverticulum, deverticulum* a by-path <*divertere*. See DIVERT.] — **di′ver·tic′u·lar** *adj.*

di·ver·ti·men·to (di·ver′ti·men′tō) *n. pl.* **·ti** (-tē) *Music* **1** A light and graceful instrumental composition in several movements. **2** A potpourri. [<Ital., diversion]

di·ver·tisse·ment (dē·ver·tēs·män′) *n.* **1** A brief performance, often a ballet, between the acts of a play. **2** *Music* A divertimento. **3** A diversion; amusement. [<F, diversion]

di·vest (di·vest′, dī-) *v.t.* **1** To strip, as of clothes, ornaments, or equipment. **2** To dispossess; deprive, as of office, rights, or honors. [<Med. L *divestire, disvestire* <OF *desvestir*. See DEVEST.]

di·vest·i·ture (di·ves′tə·chər, dī-) *n.* **1** The act of divesting, or the state of being divested. Also **di·vest′ment**. **2** *Law* The act of taking from one the possession of his property. Also **di·ves′ture** (-ves′chər).

di·vide (di·vīd′) *v.* **·vid·ed**, **·vid·ing** *v.t.* **1** To cut or separate into parts. **2** To distribute in shares; portion out. **3** To separate into classes; categorize. **4** To separate; keep apart. **5** To form the partition or boundary between. **6** To graduate with lines; calibrate. **7** *Math.* **a** To subject to division. **b** To be an exact divisor of. **8** To cause to disagree; cause discord among. — *v.i.* **9** To be or come apart; separate. **10** To differ in opinion; disagree. **11** *Brit. Govt.* To vote in two groups, one for and one against a measure. **12** To share. See synonyms under ALLOT, APPORTION. — *n.* **1** *Geol.* A mountain range or area of high land separating one drainage system from another; a watershed. **2** The boundary line between life and death. **3** *Colloq.* The division of profits, booty or spoils. [<L *dividere* separate] — **di·vid′a·ble** *adj.*

div·i·dend (div′ə·dend) *n.* **1** A quantity divided, or to be divided, into equal parts. **2** A sum of money to be distributed according to some fixed scheme, as profit on shares, share of surplus or assets, etc. [<L *dividendum* thing to be divided <*dividere* separate, divide]

div·i·na·tion (div′ə·nā′shən) *n.* **1** The act or art of trying to foretell the future or the unknown. **2** A forecast; augury. **3** A successful or clever guess.

di·vine (di·vīn′) *adj.* **1** Pertaining to, proceeding from, or of the nature of God or of a god; sacred. **2** Addressed or offered up to God in service or adoration; religious; holy. **3** Altogether excellent or admirable; godlike. **4** Pertaining to a deity or to divinity or theology. — *n.* One versed in divinity; a theologian; clergyman. — *v.* **·vined**, **·vin·ing** *v.t.* **1** To foretell or prophesy, supposedly with supernatural aid. **2** To surmise or conjecture intuitively; guess. **3** *Obs.* To portend; presage. — *v.i.* **4** To practice divination. See synonyms under AUGUR, GUESS, PROPHESY. [<OF *devin, divin* <L *divinus* <*divus* <*deus* a god] — **di·vine′ly** *adv.* — **di·vine′ness** *n.* — **di·vin′er** *n.*

divine right of kings Royal authority considered as God-given.

diving beetle Any aquatic, predacious beetle of the family *Dytiscidae*: the larva is called *water tiger*.

diving bell A hollow, watertight vessel, open below and supplied with air under pressure, in which divers may be lowered into and work under water.

diving board A springboard.

diving suit A waterproof garment with detachable helmet worn by divers doing underwater work, supplied with air from the surface or from portable tanks.

divining rod A forked twig, usually of witch hazel, held by the tips and believed to bend downward when carried over unrevealed sources of water, mineral deposits, etc.: so called for its assumed supernatural power. See RHABDOMANCY.

di·vin·i·ty (di·vin′ə·tē) *n. pl.* **·ties** **1** The quality or character of being divine. **2** A lesser deity. **3** Theology. **4** An attribute, virtue, or quality assumed to be divine. **5** A being who partakes of the divine nature or qualities. — **the Divinity** The Deity; God. [<OF *devinité* <L *divinitas, -tatis* godhead, deity <*divinus* DIVINE]

div·i·nize (div′ə·nīz) *v.t.* **·nized**, **·niz·ing** To make or treat as divine. — **div′i·ni·za′tion** *n.*

di·vis·i·ble (di·viz′ə·bəl) *adj.* **1** Capable of being divided. **2** *Math.* Admitting of division without a remainder. — **di·vis′i·bil′i·ty**, **di·vis′i·ble·ness** *n.* — **di·vis′i·bly** *adv.*

di·vi·sion (di·vizh′ən) *n.* **1** The act of dividing. **2** A part; section. **3** Separation; disagreement; discord. **4** That which separates, divides, or makes different. **5** *Math.* The operation of finding how often one quantity is contained in another, or the ratio of one to another: opposed to *multiplication*. **6** *Mil.* A large tactical and administrative unit. In the U.S. Army it is larger than a brigade and smaller than a corps and is under the command of a major general. **7** In the U.S. Navy, a group of three battleships, four cruisers, or two aircraft-carriers, under the command of a rear admiral; or four destroyers, commanded by a captain; also, a portion of a ship's company. **8** A voting of a legislative body, specifically by going into affirmative and negative lobbies, as in the British Parliament. **9** *Music* A series of notes sung to one syllable as a showy or brilliant passage. **10** *Zool.* A category of animals having common characters but of no established rank in taxonomy. **11** *Bot.* A category of plants analogous to a phylum in zoology. See synonyms under PART. [<OF <L *divisio, -onis* < *dividere* divide]

di·vi·sion·al (di-vizh′ən-əl) *adj.* Pertaining to dividing or to a division. Also **di·vi′sion·ar′y.**

di·vi·sive (di-vī′siv) *adj.* **1** Causing or expressing division. **2** Causing discord.

di·vi·sor (di-vī′zər) *n. Math.* That by which a number or quantity is divided. — **common divisor** A number or quantity that is contained in another number or quantity without leaving a remainder.

di·vorce (di-vôrs′, -vōrs′) *n.* **1** Legal dissolution of a marriage relation. **2** Hence, severance; separation. **3** A decree dissolving a marriage. — *v.* **·vorced, ·vorc·ing** *v.t.* **1** To free by legal process from the relationship of husband and wife. **2** To sunder; sever; separate. **3** To obtain a legal divorce from. — *v.i.* **4** To get a divorce. [<F <L *divortium* < *divertere* divert] — **di·vorce′ment** *n.* — **di·vorc′er** *n.*

di·vor·cé (di-vôr′sā′, -vôr′-, di-vôr′sā, -vôr′-) *n.* A divorced man. — **di·vor′cée′** *n. fem.* [<F, pp. of *divorcer* divorce]

di·vor·cee (di-vôr′sē′, -vôr′-) *n.* A divorced person.

div·ot (div′ət) *n.* **1** A piece of turf cut from the sod by the stroke of a golf club. **2** *Scot.* An oblong piece of turf or sod used for thatching, etc.

di·vul·gate (di-vul′gāt) *v.t.* **·gat·ed, ·gat·ing** To make known; publish. [<L *divulgatus*, pp. of *divulgare.* See DIVULGE.] — **di·vul′gat·er** *n.* — **div·ul·ga·tion** (div′əl-gā′shən) *n.*

di·vulge (di-vulj′) *v.t.* **·vulged, ·vulg·ing** **1** To tell, as a secret; disclose; reveal. **2** *Obs.* To proclaim publicly. See synonyms under INFORM[1], PUBLISH, SPREAD. [<L *divulgare* < *dis-* away + *vulgare* make public] — **di·vulge′ment** *n.* — **di·vulg′er** *n.*

di·vul·gence (di-vul′jəns) *n.* A revelation; disclosure.

di·vul·sion (di-vul′shən) *n.* **1** The act of plucking or pulling apart. **2** A rupturing or dilating. [<L *divulsio, -onis* < *dis-* apart + *vellere* pull] — **di·vul′sive** *adj.*

div·vy (div′ē) *Slang n. pl.* **·vies** A share; dividend. — *v.t.* **·vied, ·vy·ing** To divide. Also **divvy up.** [Short for DIVIDE]

Dix·ie (dik′sē) **1** Traditionally, those States which comprised the southern Confederacy during the Civil War; hence, the southern United States: also **Dixie Land. 2** A song composed by D. D. Emmett in 1859, adopted by the Confederate Army as a marching song.

Dix·ie·crat (dik′sē-krat) *n.* A member of the U.S. Democratic party who rejected the plank of civil liberties of the party platform and its candidate for the presidency, especially one from the southern States who voted for the States' Rights party candidates. [<DIXIE + (DEMO)CRAT; coined during the 1948 presidential campaign]

Dix·ie·land (dik′sē-land′) *n.* A style of jazz in two-beat or four-beat rhythm, originally played in New Orleans and other cities in the South.

dix·it (dik′sit) *n.* A statement or a declaration made upon personal authority. [<L, he has said]

diz·en (diz′ən, dī′zən) *v.t.* To deck out; bedizen. [<MDu. *disen* put flax on a distaff] — **diz′en·ment** *n.*

diz·zy (diz′ē) *adj.* **·zi·er, ·zi·est 1** Having a feeling of whirling and confusion, with a tendency to fall; giddy. **2** Causing or caused by giddiness; having vertigo. **3** *Colloq.* Thoughtless; capricious; silly; stupid. — *v.t.* **·zied, ·zy·ing** To make giddy; confuse. [OE *dysig* foolish] — **diz′zi·ly** *adv.* — **diz′zi·ness** *n.*

D-lay·er (dē′lā′ər) *n.* A region of the atmosphere lying just below the Heaviside layer and capable of reflecting very long radio waves.

D-line (dē′līn′) *n. Physics* One of the two closely associated yellow lines in the emission spectrum of sodium.

Dmi·tri (dmē′trē) Russian form of DEMETRIUS.

do[1] (dōō) *v.* Present: *sing.* **do, do** (*Archaic* **thou do·est** or **dost**), **does** (*Archaic* **do·eth** or **doth**), *pl.* **do**; *past:* **did** (*Archaic* **thou didst**); *pp.* **done**; *ppr.* **do·ing** *v.t.* **1** To perform, as an action; execute or fabricate, as a piece of work. **2** To finish; complete. **3** To deal with or take care of: to *do* chores. **4** To cause or produce; bring about: to *do* good or evil. **5** To exert; put forth: He *did* his best. **6** To work at as one's occupation. **7** To translate. **8** To present (a play, etc.): They are *doing* Hamlet tonight. **9** To play the part of: to *do* Ophelia. **10** To cover; travel: to *do* a mile in four minutes. **11** To visit; make a tour of: to *do* the Louvre. **12** To serve; be sufficient for: Five dollars will *do* me. **13** To extend; render: to *do* homage. **14** To solve; work out, as a problem. **15** To serve, as a term in prison. **16** *Colloq.* To cheat; swindle. — *v.i.* **17** To exert oneself; be active; strive: to *do* or die. **18** To conduct or behave oneself. **19** To fare; get along: I *did* badly in the race. **20** To suffice; serve the purpose. — **to do away with 1** To throw away; discard. **2** To kill; destroy. — **to do by** To act toward. — **to do for 1** To provide for; care for. **2** *Colloq.* To ruin; kill. — **to do in** *Slang* To kill. — **to do over** *Colloq.* To redecorate. — **to do to death** To execute; kill. — **to do up 1** To wrap or tie up, as a parcel. **2** To roll up or arrange, as the hair. **3** To clean; repair. **4** To tire out. — **to make do** To get along with whatever is available. — **auxiliary** As an auxiliary, *do* is used: **1** Without specific meaning in negative, interrogative, and inverted constructions: I *do* not want it; *Do* you want to leave?; Little *did* he know. **2** To add force to imperatives: *Do* hurry. **3** To express emphasis: I *do* believe you. **4** As a substitute for another verb to avoid repetition: I will not affirm, as some *do*; Did he come? Yes, he *did*. — *n.* **1** *Colloq.* A trick; cheat: It is a regular *do*. **2** Deed; duty: chiefly in the phrase *to do one's do*. **3** *Colloq.* Festivity. **4** *Obs.* Bustle; stir. [OE *dōn*]

Synonyms (verb): accomplish, achieve, actualize, commit, complete, consummate, discharge, effect, execute, finish, fulfil, perform, perpetrate, realize, transact. *Do* is the one comprehensive word which includes this whole list.

do[2] (dō) *n. Music* The first of the syllables commonly used in solmization; the keynote of any key. [<Ital.]

do·a·ble (dōō′ə-bəl) *adj.* Capable of being done.

do-all (dōō′ôl′) *n.* A general helper; factotum.

doat·y (dō′tē) *adj.* Stained by decay: *doaty* birch. Also spelled **doty.** [Var. of DOTY] — **doat′i·ness** *n.*

dob·ber[1] (dob′ər) *n.* A dabchick. [Origin uncertain]

dob·ber[2] (dob′ər) *n. U.S.Dial.* A float on a fishing line. [<Du., float, cork]

dob·bin (dob′in) *n.* A horse, especially a plodding or patient one; a workhorse. [from *Dobbin*, var. of *Robin* <*Robert*]

dob·by (dob′ē) *n. pl.* **·bies** A mechanical attachment on a loom for weaving small designs, known as **dobby weave.** [Dim. of *Dobbin*. See DOBBIN.]

Do·bell's solution (dō′belz) A solution of phenol, borax, sodium bicarbonate, and glycerin, used as a spray for throat and nasal infections. [after H. B. *Dobell*, 1828–1917, English physician]

Do·ber·man pin·scher (dō′bər-mən pin′shər) See PINSCHER.

do·bla (dō′blä) *n.* An ancient Spanish gold coin. [<Sp. <*doble* double <L *duplus*]

do·blon (də-blôn′) *n. pl.* **·blo·nes** (-blô′nās) A former Spanish and Spanish-American gold coin. See also DOUBLOON. [<Sp. *doblón*]

do·bra (dō′brə) *n.* Any of several former Portuguese gold coins. [<Pg. <*dobre* double <L *duplus*]

dob·son (dob′sən) *n.* The hellgrammite. [? from *Dobson*, a surname]

dobson fly A large, North American, megalopterous insect (*Corydalis cornutus*), the adult of the hellgrammite or dobson.

do·cent (dō′sənt) *n.* A person licensed to teach in a university, but without regular faculty rank; a tutor. [<G (*Privat*)*dozent* <L *docens, -entis*, ppr. of *docere* teach] — **do′cent·ship** *n.*

doc·ile (dos′əl, *Brit.* dō′sil) *adj.* **1** Amenable to training; easy to manage; tractable. **2** Easily worked or handled. [<MF <L *docilis* able to be taught <*docere* teach] — **doc′ile·ly** *adv.* — **do·cil·i·ty** (dō-sil′ə·tē, do-) *n.*

Synonyms: amenable, compliant, gentle, manageable, obedient, pliable, pliant, submissive, tame, teachable, tractable, yielding. One who is *docile* is easily taught; one who is *tractable* is easily led; one who is *pliant* is easily bent in any direction; *compliant* represents one as inclined or persuaded to agreement with another's will. Compare DUTY. *Antonyms:* determined, dogged, firm, inflexible, intractable, obstinate, opinionated, resolute, self-willed, stubborn, unyielding, wilful.

dock[1] (dok) *n.* **1** An artificial basin for vessels. **2** The space between two adjoining piers or wharves; also, the piers themselves; hence, a wharf. **3** The front portion of a theater beneath the stage. — *v.t.* To bring (a vessel) into a dock. — *v.i.* To come into a dock. [<MDu. *docke*]

dock[2] (dok) *n.* **1** The stump of a tail. **2** A leather case to cover a horse's tail when doubled. — *v.t.* **1** To cut off the end of (a tail, etc.); clip. **2** To take a part from (wages, etc.). **3** To clip short the tail of. **4** To take a part from the wages of. [Cf. LG *dokke* bundle]

dock[3] (dok) *n.* An enclosed space for prisoners on trial in a criminal court. [<Flemish *dok* cage]

dock[4] (dok) *n.* **1** Any of various plants of the sorrel or buckwheat family (genus *Rumex*) or the **sour dock** (*R. acetosa*), a troublesome weed. **2** Any plant resembling these. [OE *docce*]

dock·et (dok′it) *n.* **1** A condensed statement of a document, generally minuted upon the back of the same; summary; abstract. **2** *Law* An entry on the records of a court of the principal steps taken in a case; the registry of judgments of a court; also, the book in which such entries are made or such judgments registered. **3** A calendar of the cases to be called at any time of the court; a trial docket; hence, any calendar of business, as in an ecclesiastical assembly. **4** A tag or label attached to a parcel ready for delivery. — *v.t.* **1** To place, as a cause or announcement, on a calendar or program to determine order of precedence or a routine of procedure. **2** To make an abstract of (a case) and keep for record. **3** To make a minute on the back of; endorse. **4** To attach a docket, tag, or label to. [Origin uncertain]

dock·mack·ie (dok′mak·ē) *n.* A shrub (*Viburnum acerifolium*) of the United States and Canada, with slender cymes of white flowers and crimson fruit. [<N. Am. Ind.]

dock·wal·lop·er (dok′wol′əp·ər) *n. Slang* A worker on docks or wharves.

dock·yard (dok′yärd′) *n.* **1** A place for collecting and storing naval material, and for building or repairing ships. **2** *Brit.* A navy yard.

doc·tor (dok′tər) *n.* **1** A qualified practitioner of medicine or surgery in any of its branches. **2** A person who has received a diploma of the highest degree in a faculty, as of divinity, law, literature, etc. **3** *Mech.* A device in a machine, for doing some special work; specifically, an auxiliary or donkey engine. **4** A long knife for distributing and removing color on a printing roller. **5** A steel edge on a calender roll to scrape off dirt. **6** On sailing vessels, the steward or the cook. **7** *Colloq.* The cook in a logging camp or on shipboard. **8** Among primitive peoples, a medicine man, wizard, or conjurer. **9** Any of several varieties of brightly colored, artificial flies, used for fishing. **10** *Obs.* A person of great learning qualified to instruct. —*v.t. Colloq.* **1** To prescribe for or treat medicinally. **2** To repair. **3** To alter; falsify, as evidence. —*v.i. Colloq.* **4** To practice medicine. **5** To take medicine or undergo medicinal treatment. [< L, a teacher < *docere* teach] —**doc′tor·al** *adj.*

doc·tor·ate (dok′tər·it) *n.* The degree, status, or title of a doctor.

doc·tri·naire (dok′trə·nâr′) *adj.* Theoretical; visionary. —*n.* One whose views are derived from theories rather than from facts; a scholastic or impractical theorist. —**doc′tri·nair′ism** *n.*

doc·tri·nal (dok′trə·nəl, *also Brit.* dok·trī′nəl) *adj.* **1** Pertaining to or characterized by doctrine. **2** Having to do with teaching; instructive. See synonyms under DOGMATIC. —**doc′·tri·nal·ly** *adv.*

doc·trine (dok′trin) *n.* **1** That which is taught or set forth for acceptance or belief; that which is held to be true by any person, sect, or school; especially, in religion, a tenet, or body of tenets; belief; dogma. **2** *Obs.* Instruction; teaching. [< OF < L *doctrina* teaching < *docere* teach]
Synonyms: article, belief, dogma, precept, principle, teaching, tenet. *Doctrine* primarily signifies that which is taught; *principle*, the fundamental basis on which the *teaching* rests. A *doctrine* is reasoned out, and may be defended by reasoning; a *dogma* rests on authority, as of the decision of the church, etc. A *doctrine* or *dogma* is a statement of some one item of *belief*; a *creed* is a summary of *doctrines* or *dogmas*. *Dogma* has commonly the signification of a *belief* arrogantly asserted. *Tenet* is simply that which is held, and is applied to a single item of *belief*. Compare FAITH, LAW.

doc·u·dra·ma (dok′yə·drä′mə, -dra′-) *n.* A television drama or series based on fact but presented in the style of a documentary.

doc·u·ment (dok′yə·mənt) *n.* **1** An original piece of written or printed matter conveying authoritative information or evidence. **2** One of the several papers affixed to a documentary bill and testifying to or effecting the transfer of goods, as a bill of lading, certificate of insurance, etc. **3** A documentary. **4** *Obs.* A cautionary example. **5** *Obs.* Instruction. **6** *Obs.* Evidence. See synonyms under RECORD. —*v.t.* **1** To furnish with documents. **2** To prove by documentary evidence. **3** To supply with references and notes to authoritative material: to *document* a text. [< OF < L *documentum* a lesson < *docere* teach] —**doc′u·men′tal** *adj.*

doc·u·men·tal·ist (dok′yə·men′təl·ist) *n.* A specialist in the assembling, classifying, and organizing of documents; an archivist with special training in the field of documentation.

doc·u·men·ta·ry (dok′yə·men′tər·ē) *adj.* Of, pertaining to, supported by, or based upon documents: also **doc′u·men′tal.** —*n. pl.* **·ries** A motion-picture film that records or exhibits a phase of regional, social, or cultural life without fictionalization.

doc·u·men·ta·tion (dok′yə·men·tā′shən) *n.* **1** The preparation or supplying of documents, references, records, etc. **2** The documents thus furnished. **3** The act of citing sources in a literary work.

dod·der[1] (dod′ər) *v.i.* To tremble or totter, as from age. [Cf. ME *didder* tremble]

dod·der[2] (dod′ər) *n.* Any of several leafless, twining herbs of the genus *Cuscuta*, parasitic on various plants to which they adhere by suckers. [ME *doder*]

dod·dered (dod′ərd) *adj.* **1** Having lost the top or branches through age or decay: said of trees. **2** Shattered; infirm. [ME *dodden* clip]

dod·der·ing (dod′ər·ing) *adj.* Shaky; infirm; hence, senile.

dodeca- *combining form* Twelve; of or having twelve: *dodecagon.* Also, before vowels, **dodec-.** [< Gk. *dōdeka* twelve]

do·dec·a·gon (dō·dek′ə·gon) *n. Geom.* A figure, especially a plane figure, with twelve sides and twelve angles. [< Gk. *dōdekagōnon*] —**do·de·cag·o·nal** (dō′de·kag′ə·nəl) *adj.*

do·dec·a·phon·ic (dō′dek·ə·fon′ik) *adj. Music* Twelve-tone.

dodge (doj) *v.* **dodged, dodg·ing** *v.t.* **1** To avoid, as a blow, by a sudden turn or twist. **2** To evade, as a duty or issue, by cunning or trickery. —*v.i.* **3** To move quickly to one

side or change position suddenly, as to avoid a blow. **4** To practice trickery; be deceitful. —*n.* An act of dodging; evasion; hence, a trick to deceive or cheat; any trick. See synonyms under ARTIFICE. [Origin unknown]

dodg·er (doj′ər) *n.* **1** One who dodges; a tricky fellow. **2** A small handbill. **3** A cooked cake of Indian meal; corn dodger.

do·do (dō′dō) *n. pl.* **·does** or **·dos** A large, extinct bird (genus *Rapheco*) of Mauritius and Réunion, about the size of a turkey, with rudimentary, functionless wings. [< Pg. *doudo* foolish]

doe (dō) *n.* The female of the deer, antelope, hare, rabbit, or kangaroo. ◆ Homophone: **dough.** [OE *dā*]

do·er (dōō′ər) *n.* One who acts, does, or performs; an agent. See synonyms under AGENT.

does (duz) Present tense, third person singular, of DO.

doe·skin (dō′skin′) *n.* **1** The skin of a doe, especially when dressed. **2** A heavy, twilled, cotton fabric napped on one side; also, a heavy, short-napped, woolen fabric resembling doeskin.

does·n't (duz′ənt) Does not: a contraction.

doff (dof, dôf) *v.t.* **1** To take off or remove, as clothing. **2** To take off (the hat) in salutation. **3** To throw away; discard. [Contraction of DO OFF] —**doff′er** *n.*

dog (dôg, dog) *n.* **1** A domesticated carnivorous mammal (*Canis familiaris*), of world-wide distribution and many varieties, noted for its adaptability and its devotion to man. ◆ Collateral adjective: *canine.* **2** One of

DOG
Nomenclature for anatomical parts

various other species of the family *Canidae*, as the dingo, etc. **3** The male of the dog and various other animals of the *Canidae*: a dog fox. **4** In the western United States, a prairie dog. **5** *Mech.* Any small device that holds or grips; a catch, detent, or pawl. **6** The hammer of a firearm. **7** An andiron. **8** *Meteorol.* A sundog or fog dog. **9** A fellow; man-about-town: a gay *dog.* **10** A scoundrel; rascal. **11** *U.S. Slang* A hot dog. **12** *pl. Slang* Feet. — **dead dog** *Slang* A person or thing of no use or value. —**to put on the dog** *U.S. Slang* To make a pretentious display. —*adj.* Very; utterly: used in combination: *dog-tired.* —*v.t.* **dogged, dog·ging** **1** To follow persistently; hound; hunt. **2** To fasten with or as with a dog or catch. [OE *dogga*]

Dog (dôg, dog) **1** Either of two southern constellations, called *Canis Major* and *Canis Minor.* See CONSTELLATION. **2** Sirius, the Dog Star.

dog-ape (dôg′āp′, dog′-) *n.* A baboon or similar ape.

dog·bane (dôg′bān′, dog′-) *n.* Any of a genus (*Apocynum,* family *Apocynaceae*) of smooth, reddish-stemmed herbs about 3 feet high, having an acrid, milky juice; especially, the **hemp dogbane** (*A. cannabinum*), used in medicine as a cardiac tonic, and the **spreading dogbane** (*A. androsaemifolium*) of North America.

dog·ber·ry (dôg′ber·ē, dog′-) *n. pl.* **·ries 1** The European dogwood (*Cornus sanguinea*). **2** Its fruit. **3** The chokeberry. **4** The bearberry (genus *Arctostaphylos*). **5** The English dog rose.

dog-bri·er (dôg′brī′ər, dog′-) *n.* The dog rose.

dog-cart (dôg′kärt′, dog′-) *n.* **1** A one-horse vehicle, usually two-wheeled, with two seats set back to back and, originally, an enclosed space for dogs beneath the rear seat. **2** A cart hauled by one or more dogs.

doge (dōj) *n.* The elective chief magistrate, holding princely rank, in the former republics of Venice and Genoa. [< Ital. < L *dux, ducis* chief. Doublet of DUKE.] —**doge′dom, doge′·ship** *n.*

dog-ear (dôg′ir, dog′-) *n.* The corner of a page of a book, turned down to mark a place or by careless use. —*v.t.* To turn or fold down the corner of (a page). Also **dog′s-ear.** —**dog′-eared′** *adj.*

dog-fen·nel (dôg′fen′əl, dog′-) *n.* **1** Mayweed. **2** The heath aster.

dog·fight (dôg′fīt′, dog′-) *n.* **1** A fight between or as between dogs. **2** *Mil.* Combat at close quarters between aircraft or tanks.

dog·fish (dôg′fish′, dog′-) *n. pl.* **·fish** or **·fish·es** One of various small, littoral sharks, as the common spiny dogfish (*Squalus acanthias*) of North American waters, and the smooth dogfish (genus *Mustelus*).

dog·ged (dôg′id, dog′-) *adj.* Silently or sullenly persistent; stubborn; obdurate. See synonyms under MOROSE, OBSTINATE. —**dog′ged·ly** *adv.* —**dog′ged·ness** *n.*

dog·ger (dôg′ər, dog′-) *n. Naut.* A two-masted fishing vessel, broad of beam and having a fish-well in the center, used in the North Sea. [ME *doggere*; origin uncertain]

dog·ger·el (dôg′ər·əl, dog′-) *n.* Trivial, awkwardly written verse, usually comic or burlesque in effect. —*adj.* Of or composed of such verse. Also **dog′grel.** [ME; origin unknown] —**dog′ger·el·ist** *n.*

dog·ger·y (dôg′ər·ē, dog′-) *n. pl.* **·ger·ies 1** Dogs collectively. **2** Canaille; the mob; riff-raff. **3** Doglike conduct.

dog·gish (dôg′ish, dog′-) *adj.* **1** Like a dog; snappish. **2** *Colloq.* Showily fashionable; pretentious. —**dog′gish·ly** *adv.* —**dog′gish·ness** *n.*

dog·go (dôg′ō, dog′-) *adv. Slang* In a place of concealment; in hiding: to lie *doggo.*

dog·gy (dôg′ē, dog′-) *adj.* **·gi·er, ·gi·est 1** Of or pertaining to dogs; doglike: a *doggy* smell. **2** *Colloq.* Admirable; fashionable; attractive. —*n. pl.* **·gies** A dog, especially a little or pet dog. Also **dog′gie.**

doggy bag A bag containing leftover food which a restaurant customer may carry home for his dog.

dog house 1 A kennel. **2** The caboose on a freight train. —**in the dog house** *Slang* Out of favor.

do·gie (dō′gē) *n.* In the western United States, a stray or motherless calf: also spelled *dogy.* [Origin unknown]

dog in the manger One who will neither enjoy a thing himself nor permit others to.

dog-leg·ged (dôg′leg′id, -legd′, dog′-) *adj.* Having a bend like a dog's hind leg: said of stairs, etc. Also **dog′-leg.**

dog·ma (dôg′mə, dog′-) *n. pl.* **·mas** or **·ma·ta** (-mə·tə) **1** *Theol.* A doctrine or system of teachings of religious truth as maintained by the Christian church or any portion of it; hence, a statement of religious faith or duty formulated by a body possessing or claiming authority to decree or decide. **2** Doctrine asserted and adopted on authority, as distinguished from that which is the result of one's own reasoning or experience; a dictum. **3** Any settled opinion or conviction; an accepted principle, maxim, or tenet. See synonyms under DOCTRINE. [< L < Gk. *dogma, -atos* opinion, tenet < *dokeein* think]

dog·mat·ic (dôg·mat′ik, dog-) *adj.* **1** Marked by positive and authoritative assertion; stating opinions without evidence. **2** Hence, arrogant. **3** Of or pertaining to dogma. Also **dog·mat′i·cal.** —**dog·mat′i·cal·ly** *adv.* —**dog·mat′i·cal·ness** *n.*
Synonyms: arrogant, authoritative, dictatorial, doctrinal, domineering, imperious, magisterial, opinionated, overbearing, positive, self-opinionated, systematic.

dog·ma·tism (dôg′mə·tiz′əm, dog′-) *n.* **1** Positive or arrogant assertion, as of belief, without proof. **2** *Philos.* An uncritical faith in the presumptions of reason or a priori principles: opposed to *scepticism.*

do-good·er (dōō′good′ər) *n.* An idealistic philanthropist or reformer: a derisive term.

dog rose The wild brier (*Rosa canina*) of European hedges and thickets, bearing single pink flowers and fruits known as *hips*.

dog sled A sled drawn by one or more dogs. Also **dog sledge.**

dog's–let·ter (dôgz'let'ər, dogz'-) *n.* A name for the letter *r*, especially when pronounced with a trill. [Trans. of L *litera canina*, so called because it resembles a dog's growl]

dog's life *Colloq.* A wretched existence.

dog's–tail (dôgz'tāl', dogz'-) *n.* An Old World perennial grass (genus *Cynosurus*) with flat leaves and spikelets in dense clusters, especially the crested dog's–tail (*C. cristatus*), naturalized in eastern North America: also *dogtail.*

Dog's Tail The constellation Ursa Minor.

Dog Star The star Sirius (Alpha of the constellation Canis Major).

dog's–tooth violet (dôgz'tōōth', dogz'-) *n.* **1** A spring–flowering European herb of the lily family (*Erythronium dens–canis*) bearing yellow, purple, or white flowers: also called *adder's–tongue.* **2** One of various American plants, as *Erythronium albidum*, bearing pinkish flowers, and the yellow–flowered *E. americanum.* Also **dogtooth violet.**

dog tag 1 A pendant or small metal plate for the collar of a dog, usually indicating ownership. **2** *Colloq.* A soldier's identification tag, worn around the neck.

dog·tail (dôg'tāl', dog'-) See DOG'S-TAIL.

dog·tooth (dôg'tōōth', dog'-) *n.* **1** A human canine tooth or eyetooth. **2** An English architectural ornament, popular in the 13th century, generally composed of four radiating leaves, suggesting a dog's tooth. Also **dog tooth.**

dog–trot (dôg'trot', dog'-) *n.* A regular and easy trot.

dog·wood (dôg'wŏŏd', dog'-) *n.* Any of certain trees or shrubs (family *Cornaceae*); specifically, the European **red dogwood** (*Cornus sanguinea*) and the **flowering** or **Virginia dogwood** (*C. florida*) of the United States, with large decorative pinkish–white flowers.

Do·ha (dō'ha) Capital of Qatar sheikdom.

doi·ly (doi'lē) *n.* *pl.* **·lies** A small, matlike, ornamental napkin, used under dishes, as a decoration, etc.: also spelled *doyley, doyly.* [after *Doily* or *Doyley*, 17th c. English draper]

dol (dol) *n.* A unit of pain intensity, corresponding to a barely perceptible sensation from the application of heat rays to the skin, with a maximum for any given subject of about 10 dols. [<L *dolor* pain]

do·lab·ri·form (dō-lab'rə-fôrm) *adj. Bot.* Ax- or hatchet-shaped, as leaves, etc. [<L *dolabra* ax + (I)FORM]

dol·ce (dol'chā) *adj. Music* Smooth and sweet in performance. — *adv. Music* Sweetly; softly. — *n.* A soft-toned organ stop. [<Ital. <L *dulcis* sweet]

dol·drums (dol'drəmz) *n. pl.* **1** Those parts of the ocean near the equator where calms or baffling winds prevail. **2** A becalmed state. **3** A dull, depressed, or bored condition of mind; the dumps. [Cf. ME *dold*, pp. of *dollen* make dull]

dole (dōl) *n.* **1** That which is doled out; a small portion; a gratuity. **2** Specifically, a sum of money officially paid to an unemployed person for sustenance; in Great Britain, government relief for the unemployed, instituted 1911, consisting of weekly payments from a special fund contributed by workers, employers, and government: so called since 1918. **3** *Obs.* Lot; portion. — *v.t.* **doled, dol·ing** To dispense in small quantities; distribute: usually with *out.* [OE *dāl.* Related to DEAL².]

dole·ful (dōl'fəl) *adj.* Melancholy; mournful. Also **dole'some.** [<DOLE²] — **dole'ful·ly** *adv.* — **dole'ful·ness** *n.*

dol·er·ite (dol'ə-rīt) *n.* **1** A coarse, crystalline basalt, containing labradorite and augite: sometimes used interchangeably with *diabase.* **2** *U.S.* Any dark, greenish igneous rock not readily identified by visual examination. [<Gk. *doleros* deceptive < *dolos* deceit + -ITE¹; so called because not easily identified] — **dol'er·it·ic** (-rit'ik) *adj.*

dol·i·cho·ce·phal·ic (dol'i-kō-sə-fal'ik) *adj.* Having a long skull, the breadth less than one third of the length, the cephalic index being 75.9 or less: distinguished from *brachycephalic.* Also **dol'i·cho·ceph'a·lous** (-sef'ə-ləs). [<Gk. *dolichos* long + *kephalē* head] — **dol'i·ceph'al** *adj. & n.* — **dol'i·cho·ceph'a·lism, dol'i·cho·ceph'a·ly** *n.*

dol·i·cho·mor·phic (dol'i-kō-môr'fik) *adj.* Longilineal.

doll (dol) *n.* **1** A child's toy representing a person; a puppet. **2** A pretty but superficial woman. **3** A pretty child. **4** *Slang* Any girl or woman. Also *dolly.* — *v.t. & v.i. Slang* To dress up; dress elaborately: with *up.* [from *Doll*, a nickname for Dorothy.] — **doll'ish** *adj.* — **doll'ish·ly** *adv.* — **doll'ish·ness** *n.*

dol·lar (dol'ər) *n.* **1** The standard monetary unit of the United States and of various other countries which use the $ sign for their coinage, as Canada and Argentina. Specifically, a U.S. silver coin, of the legal value of 100 cents, authorized in 1792 by Congress. **2** A U.S. gold piece, coined 1849–90. **3** A U.S. legal tender note, either a greenback or a silver certificate. **4** The Spanish milled dollar (first coined 1728) or piece–of–eight, the metallic basis of the monetary system in the British American colonies, from which the American dollar was taken. **5** A loose term for the German thaler, the peso, the Haitian gourde, and other coins. [<earlier *daler* <LG <G *taler, thaler*, contraction of *Joachimstaler* money of Joachimstal, Bohemian city where first coined]
— **Hong Kong dollar, British dollar, Straits Settlements dollar** Coins issued by the British for use in parts of the Commonwealth.
— **Levant dollar** or **Maria Theresa dollar** A silver coin issued for trade purposes by Austria since 1780.
— **trade dollar** A U.S. special silver dollar, heavier than normal and of special composition, used in Oriental trade, 1873–87.

dol·lar·fish (dol'ər-fish') *n.* *pl.* **·fish** or **·fish·es** **1** A spiny-finned butterfish of oval, compressed form (genus *Poronatus*), common on the Atlantic coast of the United States. **2** The moonfish.

dollar mark or **sign** The sign ($) meaning dollar or dollars when placed before a number.

dol·ly (dol'ē) *n.* *pl.* **·lies** **1** A doll: child's word. **2** *Mining* A contrivance for stirring ore while it is being washed. **3** *Austral.* A rude ore–crushing device. **4** *Mech.* A block or other extension placed on a pile to lengthen it while being driven. **5** A tool for holding one end of a rivet while a head is formed at the other. **6** A small narrow-gage locomotive for use in switching. **7** A light hand truck, with wheels or rollers, used for moving heavy loads, as books, boxes, lumber, etc. **8** *Brit. Dial.* A wooden instrument for beating or stirring clothes while washing. **9** A low, wheeled platform on which a motion-picture or television camera is set. — *v.t.* **·lied, ·ly·ing 1** To crush or concentrate (ore) with a dolly. **2** *Brit. Dial.* To stir or wash (clothes) with a dolly. — *v.i.* **3** To move a television or motion-picture camera toward a scene or subject: with *in.* [from *Dolly*, a nickname for Dorothy]

Dolly Var·den (vär'dən) **1** A dress with a printed or figured design, worn over a petticoat of a plain color. **2** A woman's large, flower-trimmed hat. **3** A salmonoid fish (*Salvelinus malma*) of the Rocky Mountain streams, having red spots on the back and sides and resembling the eastern brook trout: also **Dolly Varden trout.** [after *Dolly Varden*, a character in Dickens' *Barnaby Rudge*]

dol·man (dol'mən) *n.* *pl.* **dol·mans 1** A long Turkish outer garment. **2** A woman's coat with dolman sleeves or capelike arm pieces. **3** The capelike uniform jacket of a hussar. [<F *doliman* <Turkish *dōlāmān* long robe]

dolman sleeve A sleeve on a coat or dress, tapering from a wide opening at the armhole to a narrow one at the wrist.

dol·o·mite (dol'ə-mīt) *n.* A brittle calcium magnesium carbonate, occurring abundantly in white to pale–pink rhombohedral crystals. Many so–called marbles are dolomites. [after D. de *Dolomieu*, 1750–1801, French geologist] — **dol'o·mit'ic** (-mit'ik) *adj.*

do·lor (dō'lər) *n. Poetic* Sorrow; anguish. Also *Brit.* **do'lour.** [<L, pain]

dol·or·im·e·try (dol'ə-rim'ə-trē) *n.* The measurement of the intensity of pain in terms of dols. [<L *dolor, -oris* pain + -METRY]

do·lo·ro·so (dō'lə-rō'sō) *adj. & adv. Music* With sorrow or a plaintive quality. [<Ital., sorrowful]

do·lor·ous (dō'lər-əs, dol'ər-) *adj.* Expressing or causing sorrow or pain; pathetic. — **do'lor·ous·ly** *adv.* — **do'lor·ous·ness** *n.*

do·lose (də-lōs', dō'lōs) *adj. Law* Characterized by criminal intent, as speech or action. [<L *dolosus* < *dolus* fraud]

dol·phin (dol'fin) *n.* **1** Any of various cetaceans (family *Delphinidae*), with beaklike snouts; specifically, the common dolphin (*Delphinus delphis*), about seven feet long, of the Mediterranean and temperate Atlantic; and the **bottle–nosed dolphin** (*Turiops truncatus*) of the American Atlantic coast: loosely called

THE COMMON DOLPHIN

porpoise. **2** Either of two fish of the genus *Coryphaena* of southern waters; especially, the edible *C. hippurus*: also called *dorado.* **3** *Naut.* **a** A spar or block of wood attached to an anchor and used for small boats to ride by. **b** A mooring post or buffer, or a series of such posts contiguous to each other. **c** A group of protective rope fenders just beneath the gunwale of a boat. — *adj.* Of or pertaining to devices having a fancied resemblance to the dolphin. [<OF *daulphin* <L *delphinus* <Gk. *delphis, -inos*]

Dol·phin (dol'fin) The constellation Delphinus. See CONSTELLATION.

dolt (dōlt) *n.* A stupid person; blockhead; dunce. [ME *dold* dulled, stupid] — **dolt'ish** *adj.* — **dolt'ish·ly** *adv.* — **dolt'ish·ness** *n.*

Dom (dom) *n.* **1** In Portugal and Brazil, a title of respect given to a gentleman: used with the given name. **2** A title given to certain Roman Catholic monks and other church dignitaries. [<Pg. <L *dominus* master]

-dom *suffix of nouns* **1** State or condition of being: *freedom.* **2** Rank of; domain of: *kingdom.* **3** The totality of those having a certain rank, state or condition: *Christendom.* [OE *-dōm* < *dōm* state]

do·main (dō-mān') *n.* **1** A territory over which dominion is exercised; commonwealth; province. **2** A department, as of knowledge; range; scope. **3** A manor. **4** Absolute proprietorship in land. **5** Dominion; empire; rule. [<MF *domaine* <OF *demeine, demaine* <L *dominicum*, neut. sing. of *dominicus* of a lord < *dominus* lord. Doublet of DEMESNE.] — **do·ma·ni·al** (dō-mā'nē-əl) *adj.*

dome (dōm) *n.* **1** *Archit.* The vaulted roof of a rotunda; a cupola. **2** Any cuplike covering, vertical extension, or dome-shaped top. **3** A majestic building; specifically, following Italian and German usage, a cathedral. **4** In the orthorhombic, monoclinic, and triclinic crystal systems, a form whose faces intersect the vertical axis and one lateral axis. When the face is parallel to the shorter axis, it is called a *brachydome*; when parallel to the longer axis, a *macrodome.* — *v.* **domed, dom·ing** *v.t.* **1** To furnish or cover with a dome. **2** To shape like a dome. — *v.i.* **3** To rise or swell upward like a dome. [<F *dôme* <Ital. *duomo* cupola <L *domus* house]

domes·day (dōōmz'dā') *n.* Doomsday.

do·mes·tic (də-mes'tik) *adj.* **1** Belonging to the house or household; concerning or relating to the home or family. **2** Given to the concerns of home; fond of or adapted to family life, duties, or employments; devoted to housekeeping. **3** Domesticated; tame. **4** Of or pertaining to one's own state or country; produced at home; not foreign; home-made. — *n.* **1** A family servant. **2** *pl.* Home-made fabrics or cloth: sometimes restricted to cotton goods. [<L *domesticus* < *domus* house] — **do-**

mes'ti·cal·ly *adv.*

do·mes·ti·cate (də·mes'tə·kāt) *v.* ·cat·ed, ·cat·ing *v.t.* **1** To train for domestic use; tame. **2** To civilize. **3** To cause to feel at ease or at home, make domestic. — *v.i.* **4** To become domestic. Also **do·mes'ti·cize.** [< Med. L *domesticatus,* pp. of *domesticare* live in a house < L *domus* house] — **do·mes'ti·ca'tion** *n.*

do·mes·tic·i·ty (dō'mes·tis'ə·tē) *n. pl.* ·ties **1** The state of being domestic; fondness of home and family. **2** A household habit or affair.

domestic science Home economics.

do·mi·cal (dō'mi·kəl, dom'i-) *adj.* Of or like a dome, or characterized by a dome or domes. — **do'mi·cal·ly** *adv.*

dom·i·cile (dom'ə·səl, -sīl) *n.* **1** A settled place of abode; home, house, or dwelling. **2** The place where a person has his legal abode. See synonyms under HOME, HOUSE. — *v.* ·ciled, ·cil·ing *v.t.* To establish in a place of abode. — *v.i.* To have one's abode; dwell: also **dom'·i·cil·i·ate.** Also **dom'i·cil.** [< F < L *domicilium* < *domus* house]

dom·i·cil·i·ar·y (dom'ə·sil'ē·er'ē) *adj.* Pertaining to a fixed or a private residence.

dom·i·nance (dom'ə·nəns) *n.* **1** Control; ascendancy. **2** *Genetics* The condition of having or exhibiting only one of a pair of contrasting genetic characteristics. Also **dom'i·nan·cy.**

dom·i·nant (dom'ə·nənt) *adj.* **1** Ruling; governing; predominant. **2** *Genetics* Designating a character transmitted by one parent of a hybrid offspring, in which it appears to the masking of the contrasted character transmitted by the other parent: opposed to *recessive.* — *n. Music* The fifth tone of a diatonic scale. [< F < L *dominans, -antis,* ppr. of *dominare* DOMINATE]

dom·i·nate (dom'ə·nāt) *v.* ·nat·ed, ·nat·ing *v.t.* **1** To exercise control over; govern. **2** To tower above; loom over: The city *dominates* the plain. — *v.i.* **3** To have control; hold sway. [< L *dominatus,* pp. of *dominare* rule, dominate < *dominus* lord] — **dom'i·na'tive** *adj.* — **dom'i·na'tor** *n.*

dom·i·na·tion (dom'ə·nā'shən) *n.* **1** Control; dominion. **2** *pl. Theol.* The fourth order in the hierarchy of heavenly beings: also called *dominions.*

dom·i·neer (dom'ə·nir') *v.t. & v.i.* **1** To rule arrogantly or insolently; tyrannize; bully. **2** To tower or loom (over or above). [< Du. *domineren* < F *dominer* < L *dominus* lord]

dom·i·neer·ing (dom'ə·nir'ing) *adj.* Overbearing. See synonyms under ARBITRARY, DOGMATIC, IMPERIOUS. — **dom'i·neer'ing·ly** *adv.*

do·min·i·cal (də·min'i·kəl) *adj.* **1** Relating to Christ as the Lord. **2** Relating to Sunday as the Lord's day. — *n.* **1** A church edifice. **2** A dominical letter. **3** One who celebrates the Christian Sunday: opposed to *Sabbatarian.* **4** *Obs.* The veil worn by women when attending divine service in the Roman Catholic Church; also, a Sunday dress. [< LL *dominicalis* of the Lord < L *dominicus* < *dominus* lord]

dominical letter One of the first seven letters of the alphabet, used in the ecclesiastical calendar to designate the Sundays in a given year, and to aid in determining the date of Easter.

do·min·ion (də·min'yən) *n.* **1** Sovereign authority; sway. **2** *Law* The right of absolute possession and use; ownership; dominium. **3** A country under a particular government. **4** Formerly, a self-governing member of the Commonwealth of Nations. **5** *pl.* Domination (def. 2). [< F < L *dominium* < *dominus* lord]

Dominion Day In Canada, the anniversary of the federation of Canada into a dominion (July 1, 1867): a legal holiday.

Dom·i·nique (dom'ə·nēk') *n.* An American breed of domestic fowls, with gray-barred plumage, yellow legs, and rose comb. Also **Dom'i·nick.** [< F, Dominica]

do·min·i·um (də·min'ē·əm) *n. Law* The absolute right of ownership and control of property, especially of land: *dominium* in fee simple. [< L < *dominus* lord]

dom·i·no¹ (dom'ə·nō) *n. pl.* ·noes or ·nos **1** A small mask for the eyes. **2** A loose robe, hood and mask worn at masquerades. **3** A person wearing this. **4** A hooded garment forming an outer ecclesiastical vestment. [< MF, a clerical garment < L *dominus* lord]

dom·i·no² (dom'ə·nō) *n. pl.* ·noes or ·nos **1** A

---

small, flat block, as of wood or plastic, divided on one side into halves, each left blank or marked with usually one to six dots. **2** *pl.* A game played with a set (usually 28) of such pieces, the object being to match the halves having the same number of dots: construed as singular. — *adj.* Describing the view or political theory that a series of events is unavoidably contingent on the occurrence of an initial event, as a row of dominoes collapses when the first is toppled: the *domino* theory of Communist aggrandizement.

don¹ (don) *n.* **1** A Spanish gentleman or nobleman. **2** An important personage. **3** *Colloq.* In English universities a head, residential fellow, or tutor of a college. [< Sp. < L *dominus* lord]

don² (don) *v.t.* **donned, don·ning** To put on, as a garment. [Contraction of *do on*]

Don (don) *n.* Seignior; sir: a title of respect or address, used with the given name in Spain and Spanish-speaking countries.

Do·na (dō'nə) *n.* The Portuguese form of DOÑA.

Do·ña (dō'nyä) *n.* Lady; madam: the feminine title corresponding to *Don.* [< Sp. < L *domina* mistress]

do·nate (dō'nāt) *v.t.* ·nat·ed, ·nat·ing To bestow as a gift, especially to a cause; present; contribute. [< L *donatus,* pp. of *donare* give < *donum* a gift] — **do'na·tor** *n.*

do·na·tion (dō·nā'shən) *n.* **1** The act of donating. **2** That which is donated; a gift; grant; offering. See synonyms under GIFT.

Don·a·tist (don'ə·tist) *n.* One of a fourth-century, schismatic sect of North Africa. [< Med. L *Donatista,* after *Donatus,* North African bishop and founder of the sect] — **Don'a·tis'tic** or ·ti·cal *adj.*

don·a·tive (don'ə·tiv, dō'nə·tiv) *adj.* Belonging by deed of gift. — *n.* A donation; gift.

done (dun) Past participle of DO¹. — *adj.* **1** Completed; finished; ended; agreed. **2** Cooked sufficiently.

do·nee (dō·nē') *n.* One who receives a gift. [< DON(OR) + -EE]

done for 1 Tired; exhausted. **2** Finished; put out of the running; ruined. **3** Dead or about to die.

don·ga (dong'gə) *n. Afrikaans* The dry bed of a stream.

don·go·la (dong'gə·lə) *n.* Sheepskin, goatskin, or calfskin tanned by the use of mineral and vegetable substances (called the **dongola** process), producing a finish resembling kid. Also **Dongola kid, Dongola leather.** [from DONGOLA, where originally made]

Do·ni·zet·ti (don'ə·zet'ē, *Ital.* dō'nē·dzet'tē), **Gaetano,** 1797–1848, Italian operatic composer.

don·jon (dun'jən, don'-) *n.* The principal tower or keep of a medieval castle. Also **don'jon-keep'.** [Archaic var. of DUNGEON]

Don Juan (don jōō'ən, *Sp.* dôn hwän') **1** A legendary Spanish nobleman and seducer of women, the hero of many poems, operas, plays, etc. **2** Any rake or seducer.

don·key (dong'kē, dung'-) *n.* **1** An ass. **2** A stupid or stubborn person. [? from DUNCAN]

DONJON
Chateau de Viviennes,
France

donkey engine A small subsidiary engine for pumping, hoisting, etc.

don·na (don'ə, *Ital.* dôn'nä) *n.* An Italian lady. [< Ital. < L *domina* lady]

Don·na (don'ə, *Ital.* dôn'nä) *n.* Lady; madam: a title of respect or address, used with the given name in Italy and Italian-speaking countries.

Donne (dun), **John,** 1573?–1631, English poet and clergyman.

don·nerd (don'ərd) *adj. Scot.* **1** Stupid; dunderheaded. **2** Dazed; stunned. Also **don'nered, don'nert** (-ərt).

don·nish (don'ish) *adj.* **1** Of, characteristic of,

---

or pertaining to the dons of an English university. **2** Formal; distant; pedantic. — **don'nish·ness** *n.*

do·nor (dō'nər) *n.* **1** A giver; donator. **2** One who gives his blood for transfusion, or tissue, skin, etc., for surgical grafting, for another. [< AF *donour,* OF *doneur* < L *donator* < *donare* give]

do-nothing (dōō'nuth'ing) *n.* An idler; procrastinator. — *adj.* Idle; indolent, procrastinating.

Don Quix·ote (don kwik'sət, ki·hō'tē; *Sp.* dôn kē·hō'tä) **1** The hero of Cervantes' romance of that name, a satire on chivalry, written in 1605 and followed by a continuation in 1615. **2** Anyone who naively undertakes to do extravagantly romantic things. Also **Don Qui·jo'te.** See QUIXOTIC.

don't (dōnt) Do not: a contraction.

doo·dad (dōō'dad) *n. Colloq.* **1** A doo-hickey. **2** A small ornament; bauble.

doo·dle¹ (dōō'd'l) *v.t.* ·dled, ·dling To play (the bagpipe). [< G *dudeln*]

doo·dle² (dōō'd'l) *v.i. Colloq.* To draw pictures, symbols, etc., abstractedly, on whatever material comes to hand, while the mind is otherwise occupied. — *n.* The drawings or symbols so made. [Cf. dial. E *doodle* be idle, trifle]

doo·dle·bug (dōō'd'l·bug') *n.* **1** Any device supposed to be able to detect the location of minerals, water, etc. **2** *Entomol.* The larva of the ant-lion. For illustration see under INSECT (beneficial). **3** Loosely, any droning insect, as the tumblebug. **4** *Colloq.* A robot plane. See under BOMB. [? < dial. E *doodle* an idler, a fool + BUG]

doo·dle·sack (dōō'd'l·sak') *n.* A bagpipe. [< G *dudelsack*]

doo·hick·ey (dōō'hik'ē) *n. Colloq.* Any contrivance or device, the name of which is not known or immediately recalled; doodad. Also, **doo'·hick'us, doo'hink'ey.**

doom (dōōm) *v.t.* **1** To pronounce judgment or sentence upon; condemn. **2** To destine to a disastrous fate. **3** To decree as a penalty. See synonyms under CONDEMN. [< *n.*] — *n.* **1** The act of dooming, or the state of being doomed. **2** Death; ruin; sad or evil destiny. **3** Judicial decision; condemnation; sentence. **4** The Last Judgment. **5** *Obs.* An enactment; decree. — **crack of doom** The signal for the Last Judgment: also **day of doom** [OE *dōm*]

doom palm A palm of northern Africa (*Hyphaene thebaica*), the fruit of which has the flavor of gingerbread: also called *gingerbread tree*: also spelled *doum palm.* [< F *doum* < Arabic *dawm*]

dooms·day (dōōmz'dā') *n.* The day of the Last Judgment, or of any final judgment: also spelled *domesday.* [OE *domesdæg* judgment day < *dōm* doom + *dæg* day]

door (dôr, dōr) *n.* **1** A hinged or sliding frame used for closing or opening an entrance or exit, as to a house. **2** Doorway. **3** Any means or avenue of exit or entrance; passageway; access. See synonyms under ENTRANCE. [Fusion of OE *duru* pair of doors and *dor* a gate]

door·bell (dôr'bel', dōr'-) *n.* A device at the entrance to a building or apartment to sound a signal within.

door check A device, usually operated by compressed air, for closing a door automatically and for preventing it from being slammed.

door·jamb (dôr'jam', dōr'-) *n.* The vertical piece at the side of a doorway supporting the lintel.

door·keep·er (dôr'kē'pər, dōr'-) *n.* A guardian or keeper of a door; a minor official of an organized meeting or assembly.

door·knob (dôr'nob', dōr'-) *n.* The handle for turning the catch to open a door.

door·man (dôr'man', -mən, dōr'-) *n. pl.* ·men (-men', -mən) An attendant at the door of a hotel, apartment house, etc., who assists persons entering and leaving the building.

door·mat (dôr'mat', dōr'-) *n.* A mat placed at an entrance for wiping off mud and moisture from the shoes.

door·nail (dôr'nāl', dōr'-) *n.* A nail or stud against which a knocker is struck. — **dead as a doornail** Quite dead.

door·plate (dôr'plāt', dōr'-) *n.* A metal plate

on a door, with the occupant's name, address, etc. Also **door plate.**

door·post (dôr'pōst', dōr'-) n. The post on either side of a doorway: also **door post.**

door·sill (dôr'sil', dōr'-) n. The sill or threshold of a door: also **door sill.**

door·step (dôr'step', dōr'-) n. A step or one of a series of steps leading to a door.

door·stop (dôr'stop', dōr'-) n. A device to keep a door open or to prevent it from slamming.

door·way (dôr'wā', dōr'-) n. The passage for entrance and exit into and out of a building, room, etc.

door·yard (dôr'yärd', dōr'-) n. A yard around, or especially in front of, a house.

dop (dop) n. A small metal cup on a long stem or holder in which a gemstone is held while being cut or polished. [<Du., lit., shell]

dope (dōp) n. 1 Slang Any potentially harmful narcotic used for inducing euphoria. 2 Slang A dope fiend. 3 A drug given to a race horse to influence its speed. 4 Slang Information as to the condition, past performance, etc., of a race horse. 5 Slang Any information; also, a calculation or forecast based on it; hence, confidential or inside information. 6 Any thick liquid or semifluid, as an article of food, a lubricant, etc.; specifically, axle grease. 7 An absorbent material for holding a thick liquid, as cotton waste, or a substance for holding nitroglycerin, as in dynamite. 8 Aeron. Any material used in treating the cloth surface of airplane members to increase strength or produce or maintain tautness. 9 Slang A stupid person. — v.t. 1 To give or administer dope to (a race horse). 2 Slang To stupefy or exhilarate as by a drug: often with up. — to dope out U.S. Slang 1 To plan, as a course of action. 2 To figure out; solve. [<Du. doop dipping sauce <doopen dip]

dope fiend Slang A habitual user of a narcotic drug.

dope ring A combination of persons trafficking illegally in narcotics.

dope sheet Slang An information sheet on horses in the day's races, giving their pedigree, past performance, etc.

do·pey (dō'pē) adj. ·pi·er, ·pi·est Slang Stupid from or as if from narcotics; dull; heavy.

Dop·pler (dop'lər), **Christian Johann,** 1803–1853, Austrian physicist and mathematician.

Doppler effect Physics The change in the frequency of a sound, light, or radio wave due to the motion of the observer or of the source toward or away from one another. Also **Doppler shift.** [after C. J. Doppler]

dor (dôr) n. 1 A black European dung beetle (genus Geotrupes), known by its droning flight. 2 The June beetle. For illustration see under INSECT (injurious). Also **dor beetle, dor bug, dorr, dorr beetle.** [OE dora bumblebee]

do·ra·do (də·rä'dō) n. A fish of the genus Coryphaena. See DOLPHIN. [<Sp., gilded <LL deauratus, pp. of deaurare <de- completely + aurum gold]

Do·ra·do (də·rä'dō) n. A southern constellation, the Swordfish. See CONSTELLATION.

Dor·cas society (dôr'kəs) A women's society, usually connected with a church, for supplying garments to the poor. [after Dorcas, a female disciple. See Acts ix 36.]

Dor·ches·ter (dôr'ches·tər, -chis-) A municipal borough, capital of Dorset, England.

do·ri·a (dō'rē·ə, dō'rē·ə) n. An East Indian cotton fabric with stripes of varying widths. [<Hind. doriyā <dor thread, stripe]

Do·ri·an (dō'rē·ən, dō'rē-) n. A member of one of the four major tribes of ancient Greece. The Dorians settled in the Peloponnesus about 1100 B.C. — adj. Doric.

Dor·ic (dôr'ik, dor'-) adj. 1 Relating to or characteristic of Doris or its inhabitants: also Dorian. 2 Archit. Constructed in accordance with the earliest and simplest of the three orders of Greek architecture: called the **Doric order.** For illustration see under ARCHITECTURE, CAPITAL. — n. 1 A dialect of ancient Greek, spoken by the Dorians in northern Greece, the Peloponnesus, Crete, Sicily, etc.: used by Pindar and many other lyric poets. 2 A rustic dialect of English.

Dor·is (dôr'is, dor'-) 1 A small mountainous

district of west central Greece, traditionally the home of the Dorians. 2 An ancient district on the coast of SW Asia Minor, consisting of Dorian settlements.

Dor·king (dôr'king) n. One of a breed of domestic fowls, characterized by five toes on each foot and a large, heavy body. [from Dorking, a town in Surrey, England]

dor·man·cy (dôr'mən·sē) n. A state of torpidity; lethargy; inactivity.

dor·mant (dôr'mənt) adj. 1 Being in a state of, or resembling, sleep; torpid. 2 Bot. Resting, as plants or parts of plants in winter. 3 Geol. Quiescent; not erupting: said of a volcano. 4 Inactive; unused. 5 Not asserted or enforced, as claims. 6 Her. In the attitude of sleep. Compare COUCHANT, RAMPANT. [< OF, ppr. of dormir <L dormire sleep]

dor·mer (dôr'mər) n. 1 Archit. **a** A vertical window in a small gable rising from a sloping roof: also **dormer window. b** The roofed projection or gable in which this window is set. **c** A sleeper or beam. 2 Archaic A sleeping room. [<OF dormeor <L dormitorium. See DORMITORY.]

dor·mi·to·ry (dôr'mə·tôr'ē, -tō'rē) n. pl. ·ries 1 A large room in which many persons sleep. 2 A building providing sleeping and living accommodations, especially at a school, college, or resort. [<L dormitorium < dormire sleep]

DORMER WINDOW

dor·mouse (dôr'mous') n. pl. ·mice One of the various small, arboreal, Old World, squirrel–like rodents (family Gliridae). [? <F dormir sleep <L dormire + MOUSE]

dor·my (dôr'mē) adj. In golf, being as many holes ahead of an opponent as there are holes still to play. Also **dor'mie.** [<dial. E dorm doze, ult. <L dormire sleep; so called because no further effort is needed]

DORMOUSE
(2 to 3 inches long)

dor·nick (dôr'nik) n. A heavy damask cloth, used for hangings, carpets, etc. Also **dor'nock** (-nək). [<Flemish Doornik Tournai, where originally made]

dor·sad (dôr'sad) adv. Anat. Toward the back. [<L dorsum back + ad toward]

dor·sal (dôr'səl) adj. 1 Zool. Of, pertaining to, on, or near the back: opposed to ventral. 2 Bot. Pertaining to the under surface, as of a leaf. 3 Phonet. Describing those consonants produced with the back of the tongue, as (k) in cool. — n. Dossal. [<Med. L dorsalis <L dorsum back] — **dor'sal·ly** adv.

dorsal fin The long, unpaired fin along the backbone of fish and other aquatic vertebrates. For illustration see FISH.

dorsi- combining form 1 On, to, or of the back: dorsiferous. 2 Dorso-. [<L dorsum back]

dor·sif·er·ous (dôr·sif'ər·əs) adj. Bot. Borne on the back, as the sori of ferns. [<DORSI- + -FEROUS]

dor·si·ven·tral (dôr·si·ven'trəl) adj. 1 Bot. Having distinct surfaces on both sides, as most leaves. 2 Dorsoventral.

dorso- combining form Dorsal; dorsal and: dorsoventral. [<L dorsum back]

dor·so·ven·tral (dôr'sō·ven'trəl) adj. Zool. Extending from the back to the ventral side. — **dor'so·ven'tral·ly** adv.

dor·sum (dôr'səm) n. pl. ·sa (-sə) Anat. 1 The back. 2 Any part of an organ corresponding to or resembling a back. See illustration under BIRD. 3 Phonet. The back of the tongue. [<L]

do·ry[1] (dôr'ē, dō'rē) n. pl. ·ries A deep, flat-bottomed rowboat with a sharp prow and flat triangular stern, adapted for rough weather: used especially by North Atlantic fishermen. [< native Honduran name]

do·ry[2] (dôr'e, dō'rē) n. pl. ·ries 1 The wall-eyed pike. 2 The john dory. [<F dorée, pp. fem. of dorer gild <LL deaurare. See DORADO.]

dor·y·line ant (dôr'ē·līn', dō'rē-) The driver ant.

dos·age (dō'sij) n. 1 The administering of medicine in prescribed quantity. 2 The total amount to be given. 3 The process of adding sugar, liqueur, etc., to wines to improve quality and flavor or to increase strength.

dose (dōs) n. 1 The quantity of medicine prescribed to be taken at one time; also, the quantity and strength of X-rays or other radiation to be taken in a certain period of time. 2 Anything disagreeable given as a prescription or infliction. 3 A determinate quantity or portion of whatever tends to benefit or reform individuals or society. — v. dosed, dos·ing v.t. 1 To give medicine to in a dose or doses. 2 To give, as medicine or drugs, in doses. 3 To perform the process of dosage upon: said of wines. — v.i. 4 To take medicines. [<MF <L dosis <Gk., orig., a giving] — **dos'er** n.

do·sim·e·ter (dō·sim'ə·tər) n. Med. An instrument for measuring the dosage of X-rays; also called quantimeter. [<Gk. dosis a dose + -METER]

do·sim·e·try (dō·sim'ə·trē) n. Med. 1 The accurate measurement of doses. 2 A method for the regular administration of alkaloids of definite strength, usually in granular form. — **do·si·met·ric** (dō'si·met'rik) adj.

dos·sal (dos'əl) n. A hanging of silk, etc., for the back of an altar, throne, etc.: also spelled **dorsal.** Also **dos'sel.** [<Med. L dossalis, var. of dorsalis of the back <L dorsum]

dos·ser (dos'ər) n. 1 A rich hanging for a hall or church. 2 A pannier. [<OF dossier < dos back <L dorsum]

dos·si·er (dos'ē·ā, dos'ē·ər; Fr. dô·syā') n. A collection of memoranda, papers, documents, etc., relating to a particular matter or person. [<F, bundle of papers]

dos·sil (dos'əl) n. 1 A plug or spigot. 2 Printing A cloth roll for wiping ink from an engraved plate. 3 A soft pledget for cleaning out a wound. [<OF dosil <LL duciculus, dim. of dux, ducis a leader]

Dos·to·ev·ski (dôs'tô·yef'skē), **Feodor Mikhailovich,** 1821–81, Russian novelist. Also **Dos'to·yev'sky.**

dot[1] (dot) n. 1 A minute, round, or nearly round mark; a speck, spot, or point. 2 In writing and printing, a small spot used as a part of a letter, in punctuation, etc. 3 Music A point, written after a note or rest, which lengthens its value by half. 4 A little lump; clot. 5 A precise moment of time: on the dot. 6 Telecom. A signal of shorter duration than the dash, with which it is combined in the transmission of messages in the Morse or any similar code. — v. dot·ted, dot·ting v.t. 1 To mark with a dot or dots. 2 To spread or scatter like dots. 3 To diversify with, or delineate by means of, dots. — v.i. 4 To make a dot or dots. — to dot one's i's and cross one's t's To be or to make one's work perfect in every detail. [OE dott head of a boil]

dot[2] (dot) n. A woman's marriage portion; dowry. [<F <L dos, dotis] — **do·tal** (dōt'l) adj.

do·tage (dō'tij) n. 1 Feebleness of mind, as a result of old age; senility. 2 Foolish and extravagant affection; also, any object of it. 3 A feeble or foolish fancy of a dotard. [<DOTE + -AGE]

do·tard (dō'tərd) n. One in his dotage. Also **do'tant.**

do·ta·tion (dō·tā'shən) n. 1 The act of making or apportioning a dowry. 2 An endowment, as of a public institution. [<OF <L dotatio, -onis <dotare endow]

dote[1] (dōt) v.i. dot·ed, dot·ing 1 To lavish extreme fondness: with on or upon. 2 To be in one's dotage. [ME doten. Cf. MDu. doten be silly.] — **dot'er** n.

dote[2] (dōt) n. A form of decay in wood fibers. [<DOTE[1]]

doth (duth) Do: obsolescent or poetic third person singular, present tense of DO.

dot–se·quen·tial (dot'si·kwen'shəl) adj. Pertaining to a system of color television in which the three primary colors are dissected, projected, transmitted, and received in sequence as a series of dots interwoven to produce the image in its original form. Compare FIELD–SEQUENTIAL, LINE–SEQUENTIAL.

dot·ted (dot′id) *adj.* **1** Marked or flecked with dots: spotted. **2** Distinguished by a dot or dots.

dot·ter·el (dot′ər·əl) *n.* **1** A migratory plover (genus *Eudromias*) of northern Europe and Asia, noted for the ease with which it can be taken. **2** A person easily deceived; dupe. Also **dot′trel** (-rəl). [< ME *dotrelle*. Related to DOTE¹.]

dot·tle (dot′l) *n.* The unconsumed tobacco left in a pipe after smoking. Also **dot′tel**. [? Dim. of DOT]

dot·ty (dot′ē) *adj.* **·ti·er, ·ti·est** **1** Consisting of or marked with dots. **2** *Colloq.* Of unsteady or feeble gait; hence, slightly demented; imbecile.

do·ty (dō′tē) *adj.* **·ti·er, ·ti·est** Decayed: said of trees, etc. Compare DOATY. [< DOTE²]

doub·le (dub′əl) *adj.* **1** Having two of a sort together; being in pairs; coupled. **2** Twice as large, much, strong, heavy, valuable, or many. **3** Twofold; hence, ambiguous, deceitful, or two-faced. **4** Doubled; folded. **5** *Bot.* Having the petals increased in number: said of flowers. **6** In musical instruments, making tones an octave lower. —*n.* **1** Something that is twice as much. **2** A fold or plait. **3** A person or thing that closely resembles another; hence, an apparition or wraith. **4** A backward turn, as of a hunted fox; a trick or stratagem. **5** A player or singer who understudies the part of a principal artist, so as to be able to supply his or her place in case of illness, etc.; an understudy. **6** *pl.* A tennis game between two pairs of players; also, two successive faults in tennis. **7** *Eccl.* A feast at which the antiphon is said both before and after the psalms. **8** In baseball, a two-base hit. **9** A domino piece bearing the same number of pips on each half. **10** In card playing, the act of doubling. See DOUBLE (*v.* def. 13). **11** A double star. —**on** (or **at**) **the double** In double-quick time: a military command. —*v.* **doub·led, doub·ling** *v.t.* **1** To make twice as great in number, size, value, force, etc.; increase by adding an equal amount. **2** To fold or bend one part of upon another; make of two thicknesses: usually with *over, up, back,* etc. **3** To do over again; repeat. **4** To be twice the quantity or number of. **5** To act or be the double of. **6** In baseball, to advance (a base runner) by hitting a double: He *doubled* him home. **7** *Naut.* To sail around: to *double* a cape. **8** *Music* To add the upper or lower octave to. —*v.i.* **9** To become double; increase by an equal amount. **10** To turn and go back on a course: often with *back.* **11** To act or perform in two capacities. **12** In baseball, to hit a double. **13** In bridge, to declare each trick in the suit last bid by an opponent to be of twice the normal value in points: done in the expectation of defeating the hand and thereby exacting an increased penalty. —**to double in brass** *U.S. Slang* To take more than one part in anything, as in addition to one's specialty: originally said of musicians. —**to double up 1** To bend over or cause to bend over, as from pain or laughter. **2** To fold or clench, as a fist. **3** To share one's quarters, bed, etc., with another. **4** In baseball, to complete a double play upon. —*adv.* **1** In twofold degree; twice. **2** In twice the quantity. **3** Deceitfully. Also **doub′ly** *adv.* [< OF *duble* < L *duplus* double]

double bar *Music* A double vertical line on a staff, indicating the end of a piece of music or of a section of it.

doub·le-bar·reled (dub′əl·bar′əld) *adj.* **1** Having two barrels, as a shotgun. **2** Doubly powerful or effective: *double-barreled* oratory. **3** Ambiguous as to meaning.

doub·le-bass (dub′əl·bās′) *n. Music* The largest and deepest toned of the stringed instruments played with a bow: also called *bass viol, contrabass, string bass.* —*adj.* Contrabass.

doub·le-bas·soon (dub′əl·bə·sōōn′) *n.* An instrument of the oboe family, an octave below the ordinary bassoon in pitch.

double bed A bed wide enough for two people: usually about 54 inches across.

doub·le-blind (dub′əl·blīnd′) *adj.* Describing a method of minimizing bias in conducting experiments with human subjects by concealing from both researchers and subjects the identity of those receiving the treatment under investigation and those acting as a control, who receive a superficially similar treatment.

double boiler A cooking utensil consisting of two pots, one fitting into the other so that food placed in the upper pot is cooked by boiling water in the lower one.

doub·le-breast·ed (dub′əl·bres′tid) *adj.* Having two rows of buttons and fastening so as to provide a double thickness of cloth across the breast: said of a coat or vest.

double chin A fat, fleshy fold under the chin.

doub·le-cross (dub′əl·krôs′, -kros′) *Slang v.t.* To betray by not acting, or by failing to act, as promised; be treacherous to; cheat. —*n.* (-krôs, -kros′) The act of or an instance of cheating or betraying an associate. —**doub′le-cross′er** *n.*

double date *Colloq.* An appointment made by two couples.

doub·le-deal·ing (dub′əl·dē′ling) *adj.* Treacherous; deceitful. —*n.* Treachery; duplicity. See synonyms under DECEPTION.

doub·le-deck·er (dub′əl·dek′ər) *n.* **1** *Naut.* A vessel with two decks above the water line. **2** A vehicle with an upper deck. **3** A bed containing two decks. **4** A sandwich made with three slices of bread and two layers of filling.

dou·ble-dig·it (dub′əl·dij′it) *adj.* Being at least 10 percent: *double-digit* inflation.

double drum A bass drum.

doub·le-du·ty (dub′əl·dōō′tē, -dyōō′-) *adj.* **1** Built to stand twice as much wear or use. **2** Serving a dual function.

dou·ble-en·ten·dre (dōō·blän·tän′dr′) *n.* A word or phrase of double meaning, the less obvious one often of doubtful propriety. [Alter. of F *double entente*]

double entry A method of bookkeeping in which every transaction is made to appear as both debtor and creditor. —**doub′le-en′try** *adj.*

doub·le-faced (dub′əl·fāst′) *adj.* **1** Having two faces. **2** Having a pattern on each side: said of a fabric. **3** Deceitful; hypocritical: a *double-faced* friend.

double feature A program of two full-length motion pictures.

doub·le-head·er (dub′əl·hed′ər) *n.* **1** A long, heavy train pulled by two engines. **2** Two games, especially of baseball, played in succession on the same day by the same two teams.

double indemnity A clause in a life insurance policy by which a payment of double the face value of the policy is made in the event of accidental death.

doub·le-joint·ed (dub′əl·join′tid) *adj. Anat.* Characterized by a form of diarthrosis in which the bones move freely backward and forward.

doub·le-mind·ed (dub′əl·mīn′did) *adj.* **1** Unsettled; wavering. **2** Deceitful.

doub·le-ness (dub′əl·nis) *n.* **1** The state or quality of being double. **2** Duplicity.

doub·le-park (dub′əl·pärk′) *v.t. & v.i.* To park (a motor vehicle) alongside another already parked along the curb. —**doub′le-park′ing** *n.*

double play In baseball, a play in which two base runners are put out.

double pneumonia Pneumonia affecting both lungs.

doub·le-quick (dub′əl·kwik′) *n.* In the U.S. Army, a rate of march of 180 steps a minute: now usually called *double-time.* —*v.t. & v.i.* To march or cause to march at this pace.

doub·le-reed (dub′əl·rēd′) *n. Music* A wind instrument with a reed consisting of two segments united at the lower end and separated at the upper end. —*adj.* **1** Having such a reed. **2** Designating a group of instruments having such a reed, as the oboe, bassoon, etc.

double standard A standard of conduct permitting greater sexual liberty to men than to women.

doub·le-take (dub′əl·tāk′) *n.* A delayed reaction, with visible evidence of surprise, to a joke or situation.

double talk 1 A manner of speech, adopted to confuse the listener, in which meaningless syllable combinations are substituted for expected words. **2** Ambiguous talk meant to deceive.

doub·le-think (dub′əl·thingk′) *n.* **1** The capacity to hold contradictory opinions in full knowledge of their contradiction. **2** Confused

thought. Also **dou′ble·think′.**

doub·le-time (dub′əl·tīm′) See DOUBLE-QUICK.

doub·le-tongue (dub′əl·tung′) *v.i.* **-tongued, -tongu·ing** To apply the tongue rapidly to the teeth and hard palate alternately, as in executing a staccato passage for the flute or cornet.

doub·le-tongued (dub′əl·tungd′) *adj.* Characterized by duplicity of speech.

doub·ling (dub′ling) *n.* **1** The act of one who or that which doubles. **2** Something doubled over or together; a fold; plait. **3** *Her.* The fur lining of a mantle or robe.

doub·loon (du·blōōn′) *n.* A former Spanish gold coin worth about $16. See DOBLA. DOBLON. [< Sp. *doblón,* aug. of *doble* double; orig. worth two pistoles]

doubt (dout) *v.t.* **1** To hesitate to accept as true; hold as uncertain; disbelieve. **2** *Obs.* To be apprehensive of; fear. —*v.i.* **3** To be in doubt; be uncertain. **4** To be mistrustful. —*n.* **1** Lack of certain knowledge; uncertainty regarding the truth or reality of something. **2** A matter or case of dubitation; indecision. **3** A question requiring settlement, an objection. **4** *Obs.* Fear; dread. [< OF *duter, douter* < L *dubitare*; spelling refashioned after L] —**doubt′a·ble** *adj.* —**doubt′er** *n.*

Synonyms (verb): distrust, mistrust, surmise, suspect. To *doubt* is to lack conviction. Incompleteness of evidence may compel one to *doubt,* or some perverse bias of mind may so incline him. *Distrust* may express simply a lack of confidence. *Mistrust* and *suspect* imply that one is almost assured of positive evil; one may *distrust* himself or others; he *suspects* others. *Mistrust* is rarely used of persons, but only of motives, intentions, etc. *Distrust* is always serious: *mistrust* is often used playfully. Compare DOUBT *n.,* QUESTION, SUPPOSE. *Antonyms:* believe, trust.

Synonyms (noun): disbelief, distrust, hesitancy, hesitation, incredulity, indecision, irresolution, misgiving, perplexity, question, scruple, suspense, suspicion, uncertainty. *Doubt* is lack of conviction; *disbelief* is conviction to the contrary; *unbelief* refers to a settled state of mind. *Perplexity* seeks a solution; *doubt* may be content to linger unresolved. Any improbable statement awakens *incredulity.* As regards practical matters, *uncertainty* applies to the unknown or undecided; *doubt* implies some negative evidence. *Suspense* regards the future, and is eager and anxious; *uncertainty* may relate to any period, and be quite indifferent. *Misgiving* is ordinarily in regard to the outcome of something already done or decided; *hesitation, indecision,* and *irresolution* have reference to something that remains to be decided or done and are due oftener to infirmity of will than to lack of knowledge. *Distrust* and *suspicion* apply especially to the motives, character, etc., of others, and are more decidedly adverse than *doubt. Scruple* relates to matters of conscience and duty. See PERPLEXITY, QUESTION. *Antonyms:* assurance, belief, certainty, confidence, conviction, decision, determination, persuasion, reliance, resolution, resolve, trust.

doubt·ful (dout′fəl) *adj.* **1** Subject to, entertaining, or admitting of doubt. **2** Uncertain; undecided; contingent. **3** Indistinct; vague; ambiguous. **4** Questionable; dubious. See synonyms under EQUIVOCAL, IRRESOLUTE, PRECARIOUS. —**doubt′ful·ly** *adv.* —**doubt′ful·ness** *n.*

doubt·less (dout′lis) *adj.* **1** Confident; fearless. **2** Indubitable; certain. —*adv.* Without doubt; unquestionably: also **doubt′less·ly.**

douche (dōōsh) *n.* **1** A jet of water or vapor sprayed on or into the body for medicinal or hygienic reasons. **2** The instrument for administering it. **3** A bath taken by making use of these facilities. —*v.t. & v.i.* **douched, douch·ing** To give or take a douche. [< F < Ital. *doccia* a water pipe, ult. < L *ducere* lead]

dough (dō) *n.* **1** A soft mass of moistened flour or meal, mixed for cooking into bread, cake, etc. **2** Any soft pasty mass. **3** *Slang* Money. ◆ Homophone: *doe.* [OE *dāh*] —**dough′y** *adj.*

dough·boy (dō′boi′) *n.* **1** A dumpling of raised dough. **2** *U.S. Colloq.* An infantry soldier: also **dough′foot′** (-fŏot′).

dough·face (dō′fās′) *n. U.S.* **1** A mask or false face. **2** In American history, a Northern politician who was accused of truckling to the slave power during the period of anti-slavery agitation.

dough·nut (dō′nut) *n.* A small cake made of dough raised by baking powder or yeast and fried in deep fat; a fried cake: usually cut with a hole in the center before frying.

Doug·las (dug′ləs) Name of a family prominent in Scottish history; especially, **Sir William the Hardy,** first Lord of Douglas, died 1298?, a follower of Wallace; his son, **Sir James the Good,** 1286–1330: known as *Black Douglas,* follower of Robert the Bruce; **James,** 1358–1388, second Earl of Douglas and Mar; **Gawin,** 1474?–1522, Scottish poet.

Douglas fir A large timber tree (*Pseudotsuga taxifolia*) of the pine family, growing on the Pacific Coast of the United States: often called *red fir, Oregon fir.* Also called **Douglas hemlock, Douglas pine, Douglas spruce.** [after David Douglas, 1798–1834, Scottish botanist]

Doug·lass (dug′ləs), **Frederick,** 1817–95, U.S.

dou·pi·on (dōō′pē·ən) *n.* **1** Silk thread of uneven weight and thickness, spun from two cocoons in close contact with each other. **2** A fabric made from such thread, as pongee, nankeen, or shantung. Also **doup·pi·on·i** (dōō′pē·on′ē, -ō′nē). Also *dupion, dupioni.* [< F *doppione,* aug. of *doppio* double < L *duplus*]

dou·ri·cou·li (dōōr′i·kōō′lē) *n.* A small, bushy-tailed, arboreal monkey (genus *Aotes*) of South America, having large eyes adapted for nocturnal vision. [< S. Am. Ind.]

dou·rine (dōō·rēn′) *n.* An infectious disease of horses and asses transmitted through sexual contact by a parasitic micro-organism (*Trypanosoma equiperdum*): also called *equine syphilis.* [< F <Arabic *darin* unclean]

douse (dous) *v.* **doused, dous·ing** *v.t.* **1** To plunge into water or other liquid; dip suddenly; duck. **2** To drench with water or other liquid. — *v.i.* **3** To become drenched or immersed. See synonyms under IMMERSE. — *n.* A ducking or drenching. Also spelled *dowse.* [Origin unknown]

douse (dous) *v.t.* **doused, dous·ing** **1** To strike; give a blow to. **2** *Naut.* To take in or haul down quickly, especially a sail. **3** *Colloq.* To take off, as clothes. **4** *Colloq.* To put out; extinguish. [Cf. MDu. *dossen* beat, strike]

DO·VAP (dō′vap) *n.* A method for determining the course and velocity of high-altitude, long-range rockets by radio waves whose return frequencies are interpreted on the principle of the Doppler effect. [Do(PPLER) V(ELOCITY) A(ND) P(OSITION)]

dove[1] (duv) *n.* **1** A pigeon; especially, the mourning dove, turtledove, etc. **2** *Eccl.* A symbol of the Holy Spirit. **3** A symbol of peace. **4** One who seeks to resolve a war primarily by means of limited military action, negotiation, or unilateral withdrawal: opposed to *hawk*[1] (def. 4). **5** Any gentle, innocent creature. [< ON *dūfa*]

dove[2] (dōv) *U.S. Colloq. & Brit. Dial.* Past tense of DIVE.

dove·cot (duv′kot) *n.* A house for tame pigeons; generally, a houselike box set on a pole or on the roof or side of a building. Also **dove′cote** (-kōt′, -kot′).

dove hawk The goshawk.

dove·kie (duv′kē) *n.* **1** The little auk (*Alle alle*), an arctic bird about 7 1/2 inches long, black above, white below. **2** The black guillemot. Also **dove′key.**

Do·ver (dō′vər) *n.* **1** A port in eastern Kent, England, on the **Strait of Dover** (French *Pas de Calais*), a strait 21 miles wide at the eastern end of the English Channel. **2** The capital of Delaware.

dove·tail (duv′tāl′) *n.* **1** A manner of joining boards, timbers, etc., by interlocking wedge-shaped tenons and spaces. **2** The joint so made. — *v.t. & v.i.* **1** To join by means of a dovetail or dovetails. **2** To fit in closely or aptly.

dov·ish (duv′ish) *adj.* Disposed to rely on conciliation to resolve a war: opposed to *hawkish.*

Dow (dou), **Gerard,** 1613–1675, Dutch painter. Also spelled *Dou.*

DOVETAIL JOINT
a. Before joining.
b. Joined.

dow·dy (dou′dē) *adj.* **·di·er, ·di·est** Ill-dressed; not neat or fashionable; in bad taste; shabby. Also **dow′dy·ish.** — *n. pl.* **·dies** **1** A slatternly woman. **2** A fruit pie baked in a deep dish. [ME *doude* a slut; origin unknown] — **dow′di·ly** *adv.* — **dow′di·ness** *n.*

dow·el (dou′əl) *n.* **1** A pin or peg, usually cylindrical, for joining together two adjacent pieces, as parts of a barrelhead: distinguished from a *tenon.* **2** A piece of wood built or driven into a wall, to which to nail finishings: also **dowel pin.** — *v.t.* **·eled** or **·elled, ·el·ing** or **·el·ling** To fasten or furnish with dowels. [< MLG *dovel* plug]

DOWELS

dow·er (dou′ər) *n.* **1** A widow's life portion (usually a third) of her husband's lands and tenements. **2** The sum of one's natural gifts; endowment. — *v.t.* **1** To provide with a dower. **2** To endow, as with a talent or quality. [OF *douaire* < LL *dotarium* < L *dos, dotis* a dowery] — **dow′er·less** *adj.*

dow·er·y (dou′ər·ē) See DOWRY.

dow·itch·er (dou′ich·ər) *n.* **1** The gray snipe (*Limnodromus griseus*) of eastern North America. **2** A related bird, the long-billed *dowitcher* (*L. griseus scolopaceus*). [< N. Am. Ind.]

dowl (doul) *n.* **1** A filament of a feather. **2** Down or a fiber of down. Also **dowle.** [Origin uncertain]

down[1] (doun) *adv.* **1** From a higher to a lower place, level, position, etc.: Come *down* from that ladder! **2** In or into a lower place, position, etc.: The cattle put their heads *down.* **3** On or to the ground: The house burned *down.* **4** To or toward the south: Come *down* to Florida this winter. **5** To or in an outlying or distant place: life *down* on the farm. **6** Below the horizon: The sun went *down.* **7** From an upright to a prone or prostrate position: to knock a man *down.* **8** From a former or earlier time or owner: This necklace came *down* to me from my ancestors. **9** To or toward the end; away from the start: Read from the beginning *down* to chapter five. **10** To a smaller bulk, greater density, heavier consistency, etc.: The mixture boiled *down* to a hard crust. **11** To or into a less active or violent state: The tumult died *down.* **12** To a diminished pitch or volume: Turn the radio *down!* **13** To a lower rate, price, demand or amount: The market has gone *down.* **14** Into or in an attitude or state of close application, intensity, earnestness, etc.: to get *down* to work; to track *down* a clue. **15** In a depressed mental or emotional state: His troubles had him *down.* **16** In or into ill health: He came *down* with a fever. **17** In or into a degraded, inferior, or helpless state; in subjection: His competitors kept him *down.* **18** Completely; entirely: used as an intensive: loaded *down* with honors. **19** In cash, as at the time of purchase: half the price *down* and the rest in instalments. **20** On or as on paper or other material for writing: Take *down* his words. **21** *Naut.* To or toward the lee side of a vessel: to put the helm *down.* —**down with** (Let us) do away with or overthrow: an exclamation of disfavor or disapproval. —*adj.* **1** Going, facing, or directed toward a lower position or place: the *down* side of the subway station. **2** In a lower place; on the ground: The wires are *down* because of the storm. **3** Gone, brought, or paid down: a *down* payment. **4** Downcast; dejected. **5** Bedridden: He is *down* with a cold. **6** In games, behind an opponent's score by (a number of) points, goals, strokes, etc.: opposed to *up.* **7** In football, not in play. —**down and out 1** In boxing, knocked out. **2** Disabled, destitute, or socially outcast. Also **down′-and-out′.** —**down on** Opposed to as from anger, ill will, or enmity. — *v.t.* **1** To knock, throw, or put *down;* subdue. **2** To swallow; gulp *down.* — *v.i.* **3** *Rare* To go, fall, or sink *down.* See synonyms under CONQUER. —*prep.* **1** In a descending direction along, upon, or in: The logs floated *down* the river. **2** From an earlier to a later period in the duration of: The story has remained the same *down* the ages. —*n.* **1** A down-

ward movement; a descent. **2** A reverse of fortune: the ups and *downs* of life. **3** In football, any of the four consecutive plays during which a team must advance the ball at least ten yards in order to maintain possession of it. [OE *dūne,* aphetic var. of *adūne < of dune* from the hill]

down[2] (doun) *n.* **1** The fine, soft plumage of birds under the feathers, especially that on the breast of water birds. **2** The first feathering of a bird. **3** The soft hairs that first appear on the human face. **4** *Bot.* Soft, short hairs; pubescence, as on plants or fruits. **5** Any feathery, fluffy substance. [< ON *dunn*]

down[3] (doun) *n.* **1** A hill having a broad, treeless, grass-grown top; also, the open space on its top. **2** *pl.* Turf-covered, undulating tracts of upland. **3** A dune. [OE *dūn.* Akin to DUNE.]

dow·na (dou′nə) *Scot.* Cannot. See DOW.

down·beat (doun′bēt′) *n. Music* **1** The first accent of each measure. **2** The downward gesture made by the conductor to indicate this accent.

down·cast (doun′kast′, -käst′) *adj.* **1** Directed downward or to the ground: a *downcast* look. **2** Low in spirits; dejected; depressed. See synonyms under SAD. —*n.* A shaft down which a ventilating air current passes.

down·er (doun′ər) *n. Slang* Any of various drugs that depress the central nervous system, as barbiturates.

down·fall (doun′fôl′) *n.* **1** A falling or flowing downward. **2** A sudden, heavy fall of rain. **3** A fall; disgrace. **4** A trap operating as by the descent of a weight; a deadfall. See synonyms under RUIN.

down·grade (doun′grād′) *n.* A descending slope, as of a hill or road. —**on the down-grade** Declining in health, reputation, status, etc. —*adj.* Downhill. —*v.t.* **·grad·ed, ·grad·ing** To reduce in status, salary, etc.

down·heart·ed (doun′här′tid) *adj.* Dejected, discouraged; low-spirited. —**down′heart′ed·ly** *adv.* —**down′heart′ed·ness** *n.*

down payment In instalment buying, the initial payment on a purchase.

down·play (doun′plā′) *v.t.* To play down.

down·pour (doun′pôr′, -pōr′) *n.* A copious and heavy fall of rain.

down·right (doun′rīt′) *adj.* **1** Straight to the point; unequivocal; plain; outspoken. **2** Directed downward. **3** Thorough; utter; absolute. —*adv.* **1** Directly downward. **2** Without doubt or qualification. **3** In the extreme; utterly. See synonyms under FLAT[1]. —**down′right·ly** *adv.* —**down′right·ness** *n.*

down·spout (doun′spout′) *n.* A pipe for draining rain water, etc., from a roof or from a gutter along a roof.

Down's syndrome (dounz) *Pathol.* Congenital mental and physical retardation due to a chromosomal anomaly, accompanied by variable signs including a flat face and pronounced epicanthic folds: also called *Mongolism.* [< J.L.H. *Down,* 1828–96, Eng. physician]

down·stage (doun′stāj′) *n.* The half of a stage, from left to right, that is nearest to the audience. —*adj.* Belonging or pertaining to the front half of a stage. —*adv.* Toward, near, or on the front half of a stage.

down·stairs (doun′stârz′) *adj.* Below the stairs; on a lower floor. —*n.* The downstairs region of a building. —*adv.* Down the stairs; toward a lower floor.

down·stream (doun′strēm′) *adj. & adv.* In the direction of the current; down the stream.

down·take (doun′tāk′) *n.* A downward air passage: the *downtake* to the blowers of a boiler.

down·time (doun′tīm′) *n.* The time during working hours when a machine, computer, section, or entire factory is not functioning.

down·town (doun′toun′) *adj.* **1** Of or in the part of a city or town geographically lower than the other parts: opposed to *uptown.* **2** Of, in, or characteristic of the chief business section of a city or town. —*adv.* To, toward, or in the geographically lower or chief business part of a town or city. —*n.* The downtown section of a town or city.

down·trod·den (doun′trod′n) *adj.* Trodden under foot; oppressed. Also **down′-trod.**

down·ward (doun′wərd) adj. 1 Descending or tending from a higher to a lower level (literally or figuratively). 2 Descending from that which is more remote. —adv. 1 From a higher to a lower position. 2 From that which is more remote, as in place or time. 3 Toward the extremities. Also **down′ward·ly, down′wards** adv.

down·y (doun′ē) adj. **down·i·er, down·i·est** 1 Of, pertaining to, like, or covered with down. 2 Soft; quiet; soothing. —**down′i·ness** n.

dow·ry (dou′rē) n. pl. **·ries** 1 The property a wife brings to her husband in marriage. 2 Archaic A reward paid for a wife. Gen. xxxiv 12. 3 Any endowment or gift. Also spelled **dowery**. [< AF dowarie, var. of OF douaire DOWER]

dowse (douz) v.i. **dowsed, dows·ing** To search for water, minerals, etc., with a dowsing-rod: also spelled **douse**. [Origin uncertain] —**dows′er** n.

dows·ing-rod (dou′zing-rod′) n. A divining-rod. paramour; a prostitute. Also **dox′ie.** [< MDu. docke a doll]

dox·y[2] (dok′sē) n. A doctrine; belief, especially a religious one. [< -doxy, as in orthodoxy, heterodoxy]

doze (dōz) v. **dozed, doz·ing** v.t. To spend or pass (time) listlessly or in a doze: to doze one's hours away. —v.i. To sleep unsoundly or lightly; nap; be drowsy. —n. A light, unsound sleep. [< Scand. Cf. Dan. döse make dull.] —**doz′er** n.

doz·en (duz′ən) n. Twelve things of a kind, collectively. —**a long dozen** Thirteen. [< OF dozeine < douze twelve < L duodecim < duo two + decim ten] —**doz′enth** adj.

do·zy (dō′zē) adj. **·zi·er, ·zi·est** Drowsy; soporific. —**do′zi·ly** adv. —**do′zi·ness** n.

drab[1] (drab) adj. 1 Dull; colorless. 2 Of the color drab. 3 Made of drab. [< n.] —n. 1 A yellow-gray color. 2 A special kind of cloth so colored. [< F drap cloth < LL drappus, ? < Gmc.] —**drab′ly** adv. —**drab′ness** n.

drab[2] (drab) n. A slattern; a slut. —v.i. **drabbed, drab·bing** To associate with drabs. [Cf. Irish drabog a slattern]

draff (draf) n. Refuse grain from breweries and distilleries; also, lees or dregs. [Prob. <ON draf]

draff·ish (draf′ish) adj. Worthless. Also **draff′y, draft′y.**

draft (draft, dräft) n. 1 A current of air. 2 The act of drinking or inhaling, as a liquid or air; also, that which is so drawn into the mouth or throat in one drink or gulp. 3 Naut. The depth to which a vessel sinks in the water. 4 The act of drawing or drawing out, or the fact of being drawn; also, that which is drawn or drawn out, or its weight or resistance; a haul; pull; drag; a load. 5 The result of a drawing, as of a net in fishing. 6 A plan; outline; sketch. See synonyms under SKETCH. 7 A writing of articles or propositions as framed or drawn up, but not adopted or enacted. 8 An order drawn by one party or person on another for the payment of money to a third. 9 An order for money drawn by one bank and payable at another to the person designated in the order; a bill of exchange. 10 A damper, door, or other device for controlling the airflow in a furnace, stove, etc. 11 A military or naval conscription; levy. 12 That which tends to reduce or exhaust by drawing away a part: a draft on one's time, strength, etc. 13 An allowance on the invoices of goods for samples drawn from the packages. 14 Metall. The bevel given to the pattern for a casting so that it may be drawn from the mold without injuring the latter; in general, a taper given to an article or part. 15 The total sectional area of the openings in a turbine wheel, or the area of the opening of a sluicegate. 16 A line or border chiseled on a stone to guide in its dressing. 17 A ravine; a gully. 18 pl. Draughts. —**on draft** Ready to be drawn, as beer, etc., from a cask or the like. —v.t. 1 To outline in writing; sketch; delineate. 2 To select and draw off, as for military service; conscript. 3 In weaving, to pull through the heddles. 4 To draw off or away. 5 To cut a draft on (a stone). —adj. 1 Suitable or used for pulling heavy loads: a draft animal. 2 Not bottled, as beer; drawn from a cask. Also (esp. for n. defs. 1, 2, 3, 5, 10, and adj. 2) **draught**. [ME draht <OE dragan draw] —**draft′er** n. —**draft′i·ness** n.

drafts·man (drafts′mən, dräfts′-) n. pl. **·men** (-mən) 1 One who draws or prepares plans, designs, deeds, conveyances, etc.: also spelled **draughtsman**. 2 A draughtsman. —**drafts′·man·ship** n.

drag (drag) v. **dragged, drag·ging** v.t. 1 To pull along by main force; haul. 2 To sweep or search the bottom of, as with a net or grapnel; dredge. 3 To catch or recover, as with a grapnel or net. 4 To draw along heavily and wearily. 5 To harrow (land). 6 To protract; continue tediously: often with on or out. 7 To introduce (an irrelevant subject or matter) into a discussion, argument, etc. —v.i. 8 To be pulled or hauled along; trail to or as to the ground. 9 To move heavily or slowly: The procession dragged along. 10 To lag behind: The tenor dragged in his part. 11 To pass slowly, as time. 12 To operate a dredge. 13 To cause a feeling of clutching or tugging: Worry dragged at him. See synonyms under DRAW. —**to drag one's feet** U.S. Colloq. To act or work with deliberate slowness. —n. 1 The act of dragging or that which drags or is dragged, as a grapple, a dredge, a dragnet; a brake or shoe for causing a carriage wheel to drag, as in going down a hill; a runnerless sled; a dragrope, as of a gun; hence, any clog or impediment. 2 A long, high, four-wheeled carriage; a four-in-hand coach. 3 A slow or difficult movement: to walk with a drag. 4 An artificial scent used in hunting, as an aniseed bag. 5 The scent or trail of a fox before it is found and started by the hounds: so called because originally the fox was hunted by the line of scent left by it on its return from a predatory expedition. 6 A draghunt. 7 Aeron. That component of the total air force acting on a body which is parallel to the relative wind: said of aircraft in flight. 8 The last of a herd of cattle; the stragglers. 9 Slang Influence resulting in special favors; pull. 10 Slang A puff of a cigarette. 11 U.S. Slang A dull, boring person or thing. 12 U.S. Slang Women's clothing worn by a man. [OE dragan; infl. in form by ON draga. Related to DRAW.]

DRAG
One type of drag; others are open-topped; usually drawn by four horses.

drag·gle (drag′əl) v. **·gled, ·gling** v.t. 1 To make soiled or wet by dragging in mud or over damp ground; muddy. —v.i. 2 To become wet or soiled; drag in the mud. 3 To follow slowly; lag. [Freq. of DRAG]

drag·gle·tail (drag′əl·tāl′) n. An untidy person.

drag·net (drag′net′) n. 1 A net to be drawn along the bottom of the water or along the ground, for taking fish or small animals. 2 Any device or plan by which a criminal can be caught.

drag·on (drag′ən) n. 1 A fabulous, serpentlike, winged monster. 2 In the Authorized Version, a word variously understood as a large reptile, a marine monster, a jackal, etc. 3 A fierce or overbearing person; especially, a duenna. 4 Bot. A plant of the arum family. 5 A short, large-bored firearm of the 17th century. 6 Zool. A small, arboreal, Asian lizard (genus Draco) capable of making long glides between trees by means of winglike expansions of the skin which are supported by the elongated and extensible hind ribs; a flying lizard. [< F < L draco, -onis <Gk. drakōn serpent]

DRAGON LIZARD

Drag·on (drag′ən) A northern constellation, Draco. See CONSTELLATION.

drag·on·et (drag′ən·it) n. 1 The yellow gurnard. 2 A small dragon. [< OF, dim. of dragon a dragon]

drag·on·fly (drag′ən·flī′) n. pl. **·flies** A pred-

atory insect (order Odonata), having a slender body, four finely veined wings, large eyes, and strong jaws: also called darning needle, devil's-darning-needle. For illustration see under INSECT (beneficial).

drag·on·head (drag′ən·hed′) n. Any of a genus (Dracocephalum) of hardy annual or perennial herbs of the mint family.

drag·on·root (drag′ən·rōōt′, -rŏŏt′-) n. The green dragon.

drag·on's–blood (drag′ənz·blud′) n. One of various reddish–brown resins used as a pigment, especially those obtained from the fruit of a Malayan rattan palm (Daemonorops draco) and from the dragon tree.

dragon tree n. A gigantic tree of the Canary Islands (Dracaena draco), yielding dragon's-blood.

dragon withe A West Indian climbing plant (genus Banisteriopsis or Heteropteris), bearing winged fruit: the roots of some species have been used as an adulterant of ipecac.

dra·goon (drə-gōōn′) n. 1 In some European armies, a cavalryman. 2 Obs. A soldier who served on horseback or on foot as occasion required. 3 Obs. Dragon (def. 5). —v.t. 1 To harass by dragoons. 2 To coerce; browbeat. [<F dragon dragon (def. 5)]

drag·rope (drag′rōp′) n. 1 A rope with chain and hook attached, used as a brake on a gun carriage. 2 A guiderope. 3 A rope dragged by a balloon over the ground to check speed and control height of ascent.

drain (drān) v.t. 1 To draw off gradually, as a fluid; cause to run off. 2 To draw water or any fluid from: to drain a swamp. 3 To empty; drink completely. 4 To filter. 5 To exhaust; use up: to drain one's vitality; to drain a region of resources. —v.i. 6 To flow off or leak away gradually. 7 To become empty. —n. 1 The act of draining. 2 Continuous strain, leak, or outflow. 3 A pipe or trench for draining; a drainpipe. 4 Surg. An appliance to facilitate the discharge of matter from a wound. 5 pl. Draff. [OE drēahnian strain out] —**drain′er** n.

drain·age (drā′nij) n. 1 The act or means of draining; a system of drains. 2 That which is drained off; waste water. 3 The area drained; drainage basin. 4 Surg. The gradual drawing off of morbid fluids from deep–seated wounds or abscesses.

drainage basin A large surface area whose waters are drained off into a principal river system.

drain·pipe (drān′pīp′) n. Pipe used for draining.

drake[1] (drāk) n. 1 A male duck. 2 A flat stone used in the game of ducks and drakes. [Cf. dial. G draak]

drake[2] (drāk) n. 1 A mayfly, used as bait in angling: also **drake′fly′**. 2 A small brass cannon of the 17th and 18th centuries. 3 Obs. A dragon, or an ancient standard bearing a dragon for its emblem. [OE draca <L draco. See DRAGON.]

DRAKE (def. 1)

Drake (drāk), **Sir Francis,** 1540–96, English admiral and circumnavigator of the globe.

Dra·kens·berg (drä′kənz·bûrg) A mountain range in South Africa; highest peak, 11,425 feet: also Quathlamba.

Drake Passage (drāk) A strait joining the South Pacific and the South Atlantic between Cape Horn and the South Shetland Islands.

dram (dram) n. 1 An apothecaries' weight equal to 60 grains, 3.88 grams, or one eighth of an ounce. 2 An avoirdupois measure equal to 27.34 grains, 1.77 grams, or one sixteenth of an ounce. 3 A drachma. 4 A drink of spirits: a dram of whisky. 5 In pharmacy, a fluid dram. 6 A small portion; a bit. —**fluid dram** A measure of capacity equal to one eighth of an ounce, 60 minims, or 3.69 cubic centimeters. Also **fluid drachm**: sometimes spelled fluidram, fluidrachm. —v.t. & v.i. **drammed, dram·ming** To use intoxicants freely; to treat to liquor. [<OF drame <L drachma. Doublet of DRACHMA.]

dra·ma (drä′mə, dram′ə) n. 1 A literary composition that tells a story, usually representing human conflict by means of dialog and action to be performed upon the stage; a play. 2 Stage representations collectively; the art or profession of writing, acting, or producing plays; the institution of the theater: often with *the.* **3** A series of actions, events, or purposes, considered collectively as possessing dramatic quality. [<LL, a play <Gk., a deed, an action <*draein* act, do]

Dram·a·mine (dram′ə·mēn) *n.* Proprietary name of a brand of dimenhydrinate.

dra·mat·ic (drə·mat′ik) *adj.* Of, connected with, or like the drama; especially, involving conflict. Compare LYRIC. Also **dra·mat′i·cal.** — **dra·mat′i·cal·ly** *adv.*

dra·mat·ics (drə·mat′iks) *n. pl.* **1** Dramatic performance, especially by amateurs: construed as plural. **2** The art of staging or acting plays: construed as singular or plural.

dram·a·tis per·so·nae (dram′ə·tis pər·sō′nē) *Latin* The characters of a play; also, a list of these.

dram·a·tist (dram′ə·tist) *n.* One who writes plays.

dram·a·ti·za·tion (dram′ə·tə·zā′shən, -tī·zā′-) *n.* **1** The act or process of dramatizing. **2** A dramatized version.

dram·a·tize (dram′ə·tīz) *v.t.* **·tized, ·tiz·ing 1** To present in dramatic form; convert for stage use. **2** To tell, represent, or interpret (events, one's personality, etc.) in a theatrical manner. Also *Brit.* **dram′a·tise.**

dram·a·turge (dram′ə·tûrj) *n.* The author of a drama, especially one who also directs and oversees the performance of it; a playwright. Also **dram′a·tur′gist.** [<F <Gk. *dramatourgos* <*drama, -atos* a play + *ergein* work]

dram·a·tur·gy (dram′ə·tûr′jē) *n.* The art of making dramas and placing them properly on the stage; dramatic composition and representation.

dram·shop (dram′shop′) *n.* A saloon; bar.

drank (drangk) Past tense of DRINK.

drape (drāp) *v.* **draped, drap·ing** *v.t.* **1** To cover or adorn in a graceful fashion, as with drapery or clothing. **2** To arrange (drapery, etc.) in graceful folds. — *v.i.* **3** To hang in folds. — *n.* **1** *Usually pl.* Drapery; curtain. **2** The way in which cloth hangs, as in clothing. [<F *draper* weave <*drap* cloth]

drap·er·y (drā′pər·ē) *n. pl.* **·er·ies 1** Loosely hanging attire or its arrangement, especially on figures in art. **2** Hangings; curtains, tapestry, etc. **3** *Brit.* The business of a draper. **4** Cloth in general.

dras·tic (dras′tik) *adj.* Acting vigorously; extreme; violently effective. — *n.* A powerful medicine; a strong purgative. [<Gk. *drastikos* effective <*draein* act, do] — **dras′ti·cal·ly** *adv.*

drat (drat) *interj.* An exclamation of anger or annoyance. — *v.t.* Confound; damn: *Drat* him! [Alter. of *God rot*] — **drat′ted** *adj.*

draw (drô) *v.* **drew, drawn, draw·ing** *v.t.* **1** To cause to move to or with the mover by means of strength, force, etc.; pull; haul. **2** To acquire or obtain, as from a receptacle: to *draw* water. **3** To cause to flow forth: to *draw* blood or tears. **4** To cause to come forth; induce: to *draw* praise, laughter, criticism, etc. **5** To take or pull off, on, or out, as gloves or a sword: She *drew* off her gloves. **6** To get or receive; earn, as a salary or interest. **7** To take out; remove, as money from a bank. **8** To deduce; extract by mental process; formulate: to *draw* a conclusion or comparison. **9** To attract; allure: Honey *draws* flies. **10** To close, as against light; shut, as curtains, a bag, etc. **11** To elicit; bring out, as truth or information. **12** To stretch out; manufacture by stretching or hammering, as wire or dies. **13** To disembowel: to *draw* a chicken. **14** To take in; inhale, as breath. **15** To drain of contents, as a pond. **16** To win (a prize) in a lottery; to obtain, as by chance. **17** *Naut.* To require (a specified depth) to float: said of vessels. **18** To depict, as a sketch or diagram; to describe pictorially or verbally; delineate. **19** To write out; draft, as a check or deed: often with *up.* **20** In card games, **a** To ask for or take an additional card or cards. **b** To force (a card or cards) to be played: to *draw* trumps. **21** In billiards, to cause (the cue ball) to recoil after contact. **22** In cricket, to deflect (the ball) by a slight turn of the bat. **23** In curling, to play (the stone) gently. **24** To leave undecided, as a game or contest. — *v.i.*

25 To exert a pulling force. **26** To come or go: to *draw* near or away. **27** To exercise or exert an attracting influence. **28** To pull out or unsheathe a weapon. **29** To shrink; tauten; become contracted, as a wound. **30** To cause redness and irritation of the skin, as a poultice or blister. **31** To obtain money, supplies, etc., from some source. **32** To produce a current of air: The fire *draws* well. **33** To end a contest without decision; tie. **34** *Naut.* To fill or swell out with wind: The sails are *drawing* now. **35** In hunting, **a** To track game by scent. **b** To approach game slowly after pointing: said of hounds. — **to draw a blank** To be unsuccessful. — **to draw a** (or **the**) **long bow** To exaggerate. — **to draw and quarter** In medieval executions: **a** To disembowel and dismember after hanging. **b** To tie each of the victim's arms and legs to a different horse and whip the horses in different directions. — **to draw back** To recoil, as from an unfavorable situation. — **to draw fire** To be a target of attack. — **to draw first blood 1** In dueling, to inflict the first wound. **2** To score first in any contest or competition. — **to draw on 1** To rely upon or make requirements of: He *drew* on his reputation. **2** To lure or entice. **3** To approach its end: The evening is *drawing* on. — **to draw out 1** To protract; prolong. **2** To cause (someone) to give information or express opinions. — **to draw the line** To fix the limit; refuse to go further. — **to draw up 1** To put in required legal form, as a will or deed. **2** To overtake: He *drew up* with the leader. **3** To form in ranks; marshal, as troops. **4** To straighten (oneself); stiffen, as in anger or resentment. — *n.* **1** An act of drawing or state of being drawn; also, that which is drawn. **2** An indecisive contest; a tie game. **3** The movable section of a drawbridge. **4** Anything that draws; specifically, an exhibition that attracts a crowd. **5** A drawn chance or ticket, as in a lottery. **6** A quantity drawn. **7** The act of drawing a revolver or knife: quick on the *draw.* **8** In various card games, cards dealt or drawn after the discard. **9** A ravine or coulee. [OE *dragan*]

Synonyms (verb): allure, attract, drag, entice, haul, incline, induce, lead, lure, pull, tow, tug. One object *draws* another when it moves it toward itself or in the direction of its own motion by the exertion of adequate force, whether slight or powerful. To *attract* is to exert a force that tends to *draw,* while it may produce no actual motion; all objects are *attracted* toward the earth, but they may be sustained from falling. To *drag* is to *draw* against strong resistance; as, to *drag* a sled over bare ground, or a carriage up a steep hill. To *pull* is to exert a *drawing* force, whether adequate or inadequate; as, the fish *pulls* on the line; a dentist *pulls* a tooth. To *tug* is to *draw,* or try to *draw,* a resisting object with a continuous straining motion. To *haul* is to *draw* somewhat slowly a heavy object; as, to *haul* a seine; to *haul* logs. One vessel *tows* another. In the figurative sense, *attract* is more nearly akin to *incline, draw* or *induce.* We are *attracted* by one's appearance, *drawn* to his side. See ACTUATE, ALLURE, INFLUENCE. *Antonyms:* alienate, estrange, push, rebuff, reject, repel, repulse. See synonyms for DRIVE.

draw·back (drô′bak′) *n.* **1** Anything that checks or hinders progress, success, prosperity, enjoyment, contentment, etc.; a disadvantage. **2** An allowance, consisting in a total or partial paying back, as of duties previously paid on imported articles on their being exported, or as of freight paid to a railway company; rebate.

draw·bar (drô′bär′) *n.* A projecting bar or heavy beam beneath the body of a locomotive, railway car, or tractor, and used as a coupling.

draw·bore (drô′bôr′, -bōr′) *n.* In carpentry, a hole passing through a tenon and the cheeks of its mortise, to enable the former to be drawn up to its shoulder by driving in a pin (called a **drawbore pin**).

draw·bridge (drô′brij′) *n.* A bridge of which the whole or a part may be raised, let down, or drawn aside.

draw·er (drô′ər) *n.* **1** One who draws. **2** One

who draws a bill of exchange, money order, etc. **3** (drôr) A sliding receptacle, as in a bureau, table, etc. **4** A draftsman. **5** *Archaic* A tapster.

draw·ers (drôrz) *n. pl.* A trouserlike undergarment.

draw·ing (drô′ing) *n.* **1** The act of one who or that which draws. **2** A picture, sketch, delineation, or design. **3** The art of representing objects by lines; delineation. **4** *pl. Brit.* The receipts of sales in a shop or other establishment. **5** A small quantity of tea for steeping. See synonyms under PICTURE, SKETCH.

draw·ing-room (drô′ing·rōōm′, -rōōm′) *n.* **1** A room for reception of company. **2** A reception held or the company assembled in such a room. **3** *Brit.* A court reception. **4** *U.S.* A small private room in a sleeping-car on a train. [Short for WITHDRAWING ROOM]

draw·knife (drô′nīf′)
n. pl. **·knives** (-nīvz′) A knife with a handle at each end, used for cutting with a drawing motion. Also **draw′-ing-knife.**

DRAWKNIFE

drawl (drôl) *v.t.* & *v.i.* To speak or pronounce slowly; to lengthen speech sounds, especially vowels. — *n.* The act of drawling; the attenuation of sounds giving an impression of slowness of speech: said of the patterns of speech in part of the southern United States. [Cf. Du. *dralen* loiter] — **drawl′er** *n.* — **drawl′ing·ly** *adv.* — **drawl′y** *adj.*

drawn (drôn) *adj.* **1** Equally contested; undecided, as a game. **2** Eviscerated: a *drawn* fowl. **3** Having all iron removed by magnets: said of brass filings. **4** Subjected to a process of elongation: hard-*drawn* wire. **5** Haggard: His face looked *drawn.*

drawn butter Butter melted and prepared as a sauce.

drawn work Ornamental openwork made by pulling out threads of fabric and embroidering or hemstitching the edges of the openings thus made. For illustration see HEMSTITCH.

draw·plate (drô′plāt′) *n.* **1** The plate on a locomotive to which the drawbar is attached. **2** *Mech.* A hard plate with holes of successively diminishing diameters for drawing out metal rods or wire.

draw·shave (drô′shāv′) *n.* A drawknife.

draw·string (drô′string′) *n.* A string, ribbon, or cord run through a casing or hem, which pulls together, contracts the size of, or closes an opening. Also **drawing string.**

draw·tube (drô′tōōb′, -tyōōb′) *n. Optics* The tube, consisting of two sliding parts, containing the lenses of a microscope.

dray (drā) *n.* **1** A strong, heavy vehicle, usually low for convenience in loading heavy articles. **2** A rude sledge. — *v.t.* To transport by means of a dray. [Cf. OE *dræge* drag-net <*dragan* draw]

dread (dred) *v.t.* & *v.i.* **1** To anticipate with great fear or anxiety. **2** *Obs.* To be in awe (of). — *adj.* **1** Causing great fear; terrible. **2** Exciting awe or reverential fear. See synonyms under AWFUL. — *n.* **1** Unconquerable fright; shrinking horror; terrifying anticipation. **2** Fear joined to deep respect; awe. See synonyms under ALARM, ANXIETY, FEAR, FRIGHT, VENERATION. [ME *dreden* <OE *andrædan* <*and* + *drædan* fear] — **dread′less** *adj.*

dread·ful (dred′fəl) *adj.* **1** Inspiring dread or awe; terrible. **2** Awful. See synonyms under AWFUL, FRIGHTFUL. — *n.* A sensational novelette, or a periodical that prints melodramatic stories: a penny *dreadful.* Compare DIME NOVEL. — **dread′ful·ly** *adv.* — **dread′ful·ness** *n.*

dread·nought (dred′nôt′) *n.* **1** One of a class of heavily armed battleships formerly used in the British navy, typified by the *Dreadnought,* of 17,900 tons and carrying an armament of 10 12-inch guns and 24 quick-firing guns. **2** Any battleship of great size carrying large-caliber guns. **3** A heavy cloth or a garment made of it. **4** One who fears nothing. Also **dread′naught′.**

dream (drēm) *n.* **1** A train of thoughts or images passing through the mind in sleep. **2** A mental condition similar to that of one sleeping; abstracted imagining; daydreaming.

3 A visionary idea, anticipation, or fancy; also, anything real having a dreamlike quality. **4** *Psychoanal.* A medium for the expression during sleep of various aspects of the ego and superego typically withdrawn from consciousness but, when recorded and analyzed, having some value in the diagnosis, interpretation, and treatment of certain maladjustments of the personality. — *v.* **dreamed** or **dreamt** (dremt), **dream·ing** *v.t.* **1** To see or imagine in a dream. **2** To imagine or envision as in a dream. **3** To while away, as in idle reverie. — *v.i.* **4** To have a dream or dreams. **5** To have a vague idea or conception of something. — **to dream up** *Colloq.* To concoct or create, especially by artistic invention or unbridled fancy. See synonyms under MUSE. [OE *drēam*; infl. in meaning by ON *draum* a dream] — **dream'ful** *adj.* — **dream'ful·ly** *adv.* — **dream'·less** *adj.* — **dream'less·ly** *adv.*

   Synonyms (noun): daydream, fancy, fantasy, hallucination, illusion, reverie, romance, trance, vision. A *dream* is strictly a train of thoughts, fantasies, and images passing through the mind during sleep; a *vision* may occur when one is awake and in clear exercise of the senses and mental powers; *vision* is often applied to something seen by the mind through supernatural agency, whether in sleep or wakefulness, conceived as more real and authoritative than a *dream*; a *trance* is an abnormal state, which is different from normal sleep or wakefulness. A *reverie* is a purposeless drifting of the mind when awake, under the influence of mental images; a *daydream* that which passes before the mind in such condition. A *fancy* is some image presented to the mind, often in the fullest exercise of its powers. *Hallucination* is the seeming perception of non-existent objects, as in insanity or delirium. In the figurative sense, we speak of *dreams* of fortune, *visions* of glory, with little difference of meaning except that the *vision* is thought of as fuller and more vivid. We speak of a *trance* of delight when the emotion almost sweeps one away from the normal exercise of the faculties. Compare DELUSION. *Antonyms:* certainty, fact, reality, realization, substance, verity.

dream·y (drē'mē) *adj.* **dream·i·er**, **dream·i·est** **1** Of, causing, pertaining to, or given to dreams. **2** Appropriate to dreams; shadowy; vague; also, soothing; soft. **3** Filled with dreams; visionary. See synonyms under IMAGINARY, ROMANTIC, VAIN. — **dream'i·ly** *adv.* — **dream'i·ness** *n.*

drear (drir) *adj. Poetic* Dreary.

drear·y (drir'ē) *adj.* **drear·i·er**, **drear·i·est** **1** Causing or manifesting sadness, loneliness, or gloom; dismal. **2** Causing or showing weariness; monotonous; lifeless; dull. **3** Sorrowful. See synonyms under BLEAK[1], SAD, TEDIOUS. [OE *drēorig* sad, bloody < *drēor* gore] — **drear'i·ly** *adv.* — **drear'i·ness** *n.* — **drear'i·some** *adj.*

dredge[1] (drej) *n.* An appliance for bringing up mud, silt, etc., from under water; a dredging machine. — *v.* **dredged**, **dredg·ing** *v.t.* **1** To clear or widen by means of a dredge. **2** To remove, catch, or gather by a dredge. — *v.i.* **3** To use a dredge. [ME *dreg.* Akin to DRAW.]

FLOATING DREDGE

dredge[2] (drej) *v.t.* **1** To sprinkle or dust with flour before cooking. **2** To sift; sprinkle. [< earlier *dragie* a sweetmeat < OF ? ult. < Gk. *tragema, -atos* a condiment]

dreg·gy (dreg'ē) *adj.* **·gi·er**, **·gi·est** Containing dregs; full of dregs; foul. — **dreg'gi·ness** *n.* — **dreg'gish** *adj.*

dregs (dregz) *n. pl.* **1** The sediment of liquids, especially of beverages. **2** Worthless residuum; the coarse part: the *dregs* of society. **3** *sing.* The remaining part; residuum. See synonyms under WASTE. [< ON *dreggjar*]

Drei·bund (drī'bŏŏnt) *n.* A triple alliance; specifically, that of Germany, Austria-Hungary, and Italy (1882–1915). [< G < *drei* three + *bund* alliance]

drench (drench) *v.t.* **1** To wet thoroughly; soak. **2** In veterinary medicine, to administer a potion to; force to swallow a draft. — *n.*

1 A liquid medicine, administered by compulsion, as to a horse. **2** A large draft or quantity of fluid. **3** A water solution for drenching. **4** The act of drenching; also, that which drenches. [OE *drencan* cause to drink] — **drench'er** *n.*

Dres·den (drez'dən, *Ger.* drās'dən) *n.* A fine china made in Dresden, Germany.

Dres·den (drez'dən, *Ger.* drās'dən) The capital of Saxony, east central Germany, on the Elbe.

dress (dres) *v.* **dressed** or **drest**, **dress·ing** *v.t.* **1** To clothe; supply with clothing. **2** To trim or decorate; adorn, as a Christmas tree or a store window. **3** To treat medicinally, as a wound or sore. **4** To comb and arrange (hair). **5** To curry (a horse). **6** To prepare (stone, timber, fabrics, etc.) for use or sale. **7** To clean (fowl, game, fish, etc.) for cooking. **8** To till, trim, or prune. **9** To put in proper alinement, as troops. **10** *Colloq.* To scold; reprove severely: usually with *down*. — *v.i.* **11** To put on or wear clothing, especially formal clothing. **12** To come into proper alinement. — **to dress ship** To display the national colors, all signal flags, and bunting, as in honor of an individual or event. — **to dress up** To put on or wear formal attire or clothing more elaborate than usually worn. — *n.* **1** Covering for the body; clothes collectively; especially, elegant or fashionable attire. **2** The art of dressing correctly. **3** A gown or frock of a woman or child. **4** Full dress as opposed to business attire, etc. **5** External appearance; guise. **6** Dressing or size, as of leather. — *adj.* **1** Of, pertaining to, or suitable for making dresses: *dress* goods. **2** To be worn on formal occasions: a *dress* suit, *dress* uniform. [< OF *dresser*, ult. < L *directus.* See DIRECT.]

   Synonyms (noun): apparel, array, attire, clothes, clothing, costume, garb, garments, habiliments, habit, raiment, robes, uniform, vestments, vesture.

dres·sage (dres'ij, *Fr.* dre·säzh') *n.* **1** In equitation, the act of guiding a mount through a set of paces or maneuvers by imperceptible movements on the part of the rider, usually for exhibition purposes. **2** The technique of training a horse to respond to such movements.

dress circle A section of seats in a theater or concert hall, usually comprising the first gallery behind and above the orchestra: so called because originally reserved for patrons in evening dress.

dress coat The coat of a man's dress suit.

dressed (drest) *adj.* **1** Prepared, as animal skins, for use; tanned, dyed, softened, etc. **2** Prepared for use, as lumber or stone. **3** Prepared for cooking, as fowl. **4** Clothed; especially, wearing formal dress.

dress·er[1] (dres'ər) *n.* **1** One who dresses something, as shop windows, leather, etc. **2** One who assists another to dress. **3** One who dresses well or in a particular way: a fancy *dresser*. **4** *Brit.* A surgical assistant assigned to dress and bandage wounds.

dress·er[2] (dres'ər) *n.* **1** A chest of drawers supporting a swinging mirror, useful in a dressing-room. **2** A cupboard for dishes. **3** *Obs.* A table on which meat is dressed. [OF *dresseur* < *dresser* dress]

dress goods Fabrics for dresses.

dress·ing (dres'ing) *n.* **1** The act of dressing. **2** That with which anything, as a wound, is dressed. **3** A seasoned sauce served with salads and vegetables; also, a stuffing for fowl or meats. **4** *pl. Archit.* Moldings around the wall openings in a brick building. **5** The mechanical preparation of ore for smelting. **6** *Colloq.* A beating or scolding. **7** The preparation for use of skins, lumber, stone, etc. **8** Fertilizer.

dressing station *Mil.* A medical field station for giving immediate aid to the wounded.

dress·ing-ta·ble (dres'ing-tā'bəl) *n.* A small table equipped with a mirror and used in making one's toilet; a vanity.

dress·mak·er (dres'mā'kər) *n.* One who makes women's dresses, etc. — *adj.* Not severely tailored, but having soft, dressy, or feminine lines: a *dressmaker* suit.

dress parade A formal military parade in dress uniform.

dress rehearsal The last rehearsal of a play before the public performance, in full costume and using all properties.

dress shield A crescent-shaped piece of fabric with waterproof lining, worn to protect clothes from underarm perspiration.

dress suit A man's suit, usually black, for formal evening wear, characterized by a low-cut vest and an open coat with long, wide lapels, cut to the hips in front, curving into a bifurcated tail, extending almost to the knee: also called *full-dress suit.*

dress·y (dres'ē) *adj.* **dress·i·er**, **dress·i·est** *Colloq.* **1** Fond of dress. **2** Showy; elegant. — **dress'i·ness** *n.*

drib (drib) *v.t.* **dribbed**, **drib·bing** *Obs.* **1** To let fall in drops. **2** To do or say (something) little by little. [Var. of DRIP]

drib·ble (drib'əl) *v.t. & v.i.* **·bled**, **·bling** **1** To fall or let fall in drops; drip. **2** To drool; drivel. **3** In basketball, to propel (the ball) by bouncing with the hands. **4** In soccer, to propel (the ball) by successive pushes or kicks with the feet. — *n.* **1** A small quantity of a liquid falling in drops or flowing in a scanty and broken stream. **2** *Scot.* Showery or drizzly weather. **3** In basketball and soccer, the act of dribbling. [Freq. of DRIB] — **drib'bler** *n.*

drib·let (drib'lit) *n.* **1** A small piece, part, or sum. **2** A drop or clot formed as if by dribbling: money paid in *driblets.* Also **drib'·blet.**

dried (drīd) Past tense and past participle of DRY.

dri·er (drī'ər) *n.* **1** One who or that which dries. **2** A substance added to paint, etc., to make it dry more quickly. **3** A mechanical device for drying: also spelled *dryer.*

drift (drift) *n.* **1** That which is driven or carried onward by a current: a *drift* of clouds across the sky. **2** A heap of any matter piled up by wind or sea. **3** A course along which or an end toward which anything moves on; tendency; meaning: the *drift* of a discourse. **4** A driving; an urgent force; hence, controlling power or influence. **5** A number of objects moving onward by one force; especially, anything floating or moving with the current of a river or stream, as logs, trees, etc.; driftwood. **6** A ford. **7** The fact or condition of being driven; the action of drifting. **8** A boring tool. **9** *Geol.* Material which has been transported by moving masses of ice or by running water created by glaciers, and deposited over portions of the earth's surface. **10** *Mining* A horizontal or nearly horizontal passage in a mine; also, the direction of a passage or gallery. **11** The direction of a current. **12** *Naut.* Leeway; the distance which a vessel is driven from her direct course by wind or sea or other causes. **13** A fishing net that drifts with the tide; a drift net. **14** *Aeron.* The angular difference between the long axis of an aircraft and the line of its flight path: also **drift angle.** **15** The movement of a herd of cattle, as before a storm. See synonyms under HEAP, INCLINATION, PURPOSE, STREAM. — *v.t.* **1** To carry along, as on a current. **2** To cause to pile up in heaps, as snow or sand. — *v.i.* **3** To float or be carried along, as by a current. **4** To wander. **5** To accumulate in heaps. [ME < OE *drīfan* drive]

drift·age (drif'tij) *n.* **1** The operation or process of drifting. **2** Anything carried by currents of wind or sea.

drift fence A fence to halt the drifting of cattle.

drift-me·ter (drift'mē'tər) *n. Aeron.* An instrument for measuring the drift of an aircraft and also for taking bearings from ground objects. Also **drift'-in'di·ca'tor** (-in'də-kā'tər).

drift·wood (drift'wŏŏd') *n.* Wood floated or drifted by water, especially that cast ashore by the sea.

drift·y (drif'tē) *adj.* Forming or full of drifts; drifting.

drill[1] (dril) *n.* **1** A boring tool for metal or other hard substance. **2** The art or action of training in military exercises; hence, thorough and regular discipline in any branch of knowledge, activity, or industry. See synonyms under PRACTICE. **3** *Zool.* A mollusk (*Urosalpinx cinereus*) which kills oysters by drilling holes in their shells. — *v.t.* **1** To pierce or bore with or as with a drill. **2** To bore (a hole). **3** To train in military exercises. **4** To instruct by methodical exercises. **5** To impart by

DRILLS

a. V–drill (metal).   *d.* Countersink (wood or metal).
b. Twist drill (metal).   *e.* Twist bit (wood).
c. Center bit (wood).   *f.* Earth borer.

methodical exercises: He *drilled* the lessons into his students. — *v.i.* **6** To use a drill. **7** To engage in military exercises. **8** To engage in methodical exercises. See synonyms under PIERCE, TEACH. [<Du. *dril, drille* <*drillen* bore]

drill[2] (dril) *Agric. n.* **1** A machine for planting seeds in rows. **2** A small furrow in which seeds are sown. **3** A row of seeds so planted. — *v.t.* To plant in rows: to *drill* a field; to *drill* seeds. — *v.i.* To sow or plant in drills. [Origin uncertain]

drill[3] (dril) *n.* Heavy, twilled linen or cotton cloth. Also **drill′ing.** [Short for *drilling* <G *drilich* cloth with three threads <L *trilix* <*tres* three + *licium* thread]

drill[4] (dril) *n.* A black–faced baboon of West Africa (genus *Papio*), similar to the mandrill. For illustration see MANDRILL. [? <native name]

drill·er (dril′ər) *n.* **1** One who or that which drills. **2** A drilling machine.

drill·ing (dril′ing) *n.* **1** Material excavated by a drill. **2** The act of one who drills; the act of using a drill.

drill·mas·ter (dril′mas′tər, -mäs′tər) *n.* A trainer in military or gymnastic exercises.

drill·press (dril′pres′) *n.* An upright drilling machine for working in metal.

drill·stock (dril′stok′) *n.* A holder for a drill. See DRILL[1] (def. 1).

drink (dringk) *v.* **drank** (*Obs.* **drunk**), **drunk** (*Obs.* **drunk·en**), **drink·ing** *v.t.* **1** To take into the mouth and swallow, as water. **2** To soak up or absorb (a liquid or moisture). **3** To take in eagerly through the senses or the mind: often with *in.* **4** To drink the health of; toast. **5** To swallow the contents of. — *v.i.* **6** To swallow a liquid. **7** To drink alcoholic liquors, especially to excess or habitually; tope. **8** To drink a toast: with *to.* — *n.* **1** Any liquid that is or may be swallowed; a beverage. **2** Alcoholic liquor. **3** The practice of drinking to excess. **4** As much as is or may be taken at one time; a draft. — **in drink** Overcome by liquor. [OE *drincan*]

Drinker respirator An iron lung. [after Philip *Drinker*, born 1894, U.S. Public Health engineer]

drip (drip) *n.* **1** A falling, or letting fall, in drops. **2** Dripping; that which drips. **3** *Archit.* A projecting molding over an opening for a window or a door. **4** Condensed moisture, as in gas pipes. **5** *U.S. Slang* A person regarded as socially inept. — *v.t.* & *v.i.* **dripped, drip·ping** To fall or let fall in drops. [OE *dryppan*]

drip·stone (drip′stōn′) *n. Archit.* A label or projecting molding over a window or door.

drive (drīv) *v.* **drove, driv·en, driv·ing** *v.t.* **1** To push or propel onward with force; urge or press forward; impel. **2** To force to act or work; urge on by or as by coercion: He *drives* his workers too hard. **3** To bring to a state or condition as if by coercion: Failure *drove* him to despair. **4** To cause to penetrate or pass through: often with *in*: to *drive* in a nail. **5** To form by penetrating or passing through: to *drive* a well. **6** To control the movements or direction of: to *drive* an automobile. **7** To transport in a vehicle. **8** To carry on or complete (trade, a bargain, etc.) with energy. **9** In sports, to strike and propel (a ball) with force. **10** *Mech.* To provide power for: The wind *drives* the generator. **11** In hunting, **a** To chase (game) from cover or into traps, nets, etc. **b** To search (an area) in such a manner. **12** *Mining* To excavate (a tunnel) horizon-

tally. — *v.i.* **13** To move forward or onward rapidly or with force: The ship *drove* before the wind. **14** To operate or travel in a vehicle: We all *drove* together into town. **15** To have an object or intention: with *at*: What are you *driving* at? **16** To aim a blow: with *at.* — **to drive home 1** To force in all the way, as a nail. **2** To make clear or evident; complete. — **to let drive at** To aim or discharge a shot, blow, missile, etc. — *n.* **1** The act of driving. **2** A road for driving; also, an approach for vehicles to a private house or other building. **3** A journey or excursion in an automobile or other vehicle. **4** Urgent pressure, as of business. **5** A hunt by driving; a drove or drift, as of cattle; a round–up; also, any objects driven, collectively. **6** A special sale at reduced price. **7** *Mil.* An advance of troops in mass against an enemy so as to break through defenses and drive back the defenders. **8** In golf, a stroke from the tee made with a wooden club; the distance traveled by the ball. **9** In certain games, as baseball, cricket, croquet, etc., the act of driving the ball, or the stroke by which the ball is driven; also, the flight of the ball. **10** *Mining* A driven tunnel. **11** *Mech.* A driving gear; a means of transmitting power, as from the motor of an automobile to the wheels. **12** *Energy*; vitality; also, aggressiveness. **13** *Logs* felled in the winter to be floated downstream in the spring. **14** The mass of logs floating down a river or stream. **15** An organized money–raising campaign: a Red Cross *drive.* See synonyms under WAY. [OE *drifan*]

Synonyms (verb): compel, impel, propel, push, repel, repulse, resist, ride, thrust. To *drive* is to move an object with some force or violence before or away from oneself; it is the direct reverse of *draw, lead,* etc. A man leads a horse by the halter, *drives* him with whip and rein. One may be *driven* to a thing or from it; hence, *drive* is a synonym equally for *compel* or for *repel* or *repulse. Repulse* is stronger and more conclusive than *repel*; one may be *repelled* by the very aspect of the person whose favor he seeks, but is not *repulsed* except by the direct refusal or ignoring of his suit. It is common to speak of *driving* in a car, *riding* upon a horse; though many good authorities use *ride* in the older and broader sense as signifying to be supported and borne along by any means of conveyance. Compare ACTUATE, BANISH, COMPEL, INFLUENCE, PUSH. *Antonyms:* see synonyms under DRAW.

drive·bolt (drīv′bōlt′) *n.* **1** A tool for driving bolts home. **2** A bolt used to drive out another bolt: also called *driftbolt.*

driv·el (driv′əl) *v.* **driv·eled** or **driv·elled, driv·el·ing** or **driv·el·ling** *v.i.* **1** To let saliva flow from the mouth; slobber. **2** To flow like saliva. **3** To talk or act in a foolish or stupid manner. — *v.t.* **4** To let flow from the mouth. **5** To say in a foolish manner. — *n.* **1** An involuntary flow of saliva from the mouth. **2** Senseless talk; twaddle. [OE *dreflian*] — **driv′el·er** or **driv′el·ler** *n.*

driven well A well made by driving a pipe into the ground until the perforated tip reaches a stratum where water is found. Compare illustration under ARTESIAN WELL. Also **drive·well** (drīv′wel′).

driv·er (drī′vər) *n.* **1** One who or that which drives; a coachman; locomotive engineer; the operator of any motor vehicle. **2** *Mech.* Any of various machine parts which communicate motion; especially, the driving wheel of a locomotive; also, in power transmission, any wheel which moves another, as distinguished from the follower; a driving wheel. See illustration under ECCENTRIC. **3** *Naut.* A four-cornered fore-and-aft sail; a spanker. **4** A wooden-headed golf club with full-length shaft, somewhat supple, for driving the greatest distances from the tee. See illustration under GOLF CLUB. **5** The overseer of a group of laborers. **6** One who works on a log drive. **7** A carriage horse.

driver ant Any of a subfamily (*Dorylinae*) of carnivorous, stinging ants of tropical Africa and South America (genera *Dorylus* and *Eciton*), which live in temporary nests and raid the countryside in huge armies: also called *legionary ant, doryline ant.*

drive shaft *Mech.* A shaft for transmitting power from an engine to the working parts of machinery, especially one connecting the transmission with the rear axle of an automobile.

drive train A mechanical system for transmitting motion from the source of power to its point of application, as the engine, transmission, drive shaft, differential gearing, axles, and driving wheels of an automobile: also called *power train.*

drive·way (drīv′wā′) *n.* **1** A private road providing access to a building or house. **2** A road.

driv·ing (drī′ving) *adj.* **1** Transmitting power: a *driving* wheel. **2** Active and energetic: a *driving* personality.

driving wheel 1 One of the large wheels of a locomotive which converts the energy of steam into motion. **2** Any wheel used to communicate motion to any part of a machine.

driz·zle (driz′əl) *v.t.* & *v.i.* **·zled, ·zling** To rain steadily in fine drops. — *n.* A light rain. [? Freq. of ME *dresen,* OE *drēosan* fall] — **driz′zly** *adj.*

droit (droit, *Fr.* drwà) *n.* **1** A legal right or claim of ownership, as distinguished from possession; also, that to which one has a legal claim. **2** Right in general; law; justice; equity. **3** *pl.* Customs duties. [<F, a right <LL *directum* <L *dirigere* set straight]

droit·u·ral (droi′chər·əl) *adj.* Relating to a right of ownership as distinguished from possession.

droll (drōl) *adj.* Facetiously or humorously odd; comical; ludicrous; funny; queer. See synonyms under HUMOROUS, JOCOSE, ODD, QUEER, RIDICULOUS. — *n.* **1** A jester; a funny fellow. **2** A farce. **3** A comical tale. — *v.i.* To jest; play the jester. [<MF *drôle* a jester] — **droll′ly** *adv.*

–drome *combining form* Racecourse; place for running: *hippodrome.* [<Gk. *dromos* a running]

drom·e·dar·y (drom′ə·der′ē) *n. pl.* **·dar·ies 1** The swift, one–humped Arabian camel (*Camelus dromedarius*) trained for riding. For illustration see CAMEL. [<OF *dromedaire* <LL *dromedarius* <L *dromas* <Gk., a running]

dro·mo·ma·ni·a (drō′mə·mā′nē·ə, màn′yə, drom′ə-) *n. Psychiatry* An abnormal desire to travel: also called *periomania.* [<Gk. *dromos* a running + -MANIA]

dro·mo·pho·bi·a (drō′mə·fō′bē·ə, -fōb′yə, drom′ə-) *n. Psychiatry* A morbid fear of crossing streets. [<Gk. *dromos* a running + -PHOBIA] — **dro′mo·pho′bic** *adj.*

–dromous *combining form* Running: *catadromous.* [<-DROME + -OUS]

drone[1] (drōn) *v.* **droned, dron·ing** *v.i.* **1** To make a dull, monotonous, humming sound; hum. **2** To speak in a slow, dull tone. — *v.t.* **3** To say in a slow, dull tone. — *n.* **1** A dull, monotonous, humming sound, as of a bee. **2** One of the single–note reed pipes of the bagpipe: distinguished from *chanter*; also, a bagpipe or similar instrument. See illustration under BAGPIPE. **3** *Music* A sustained bass commonly of one note. **4** A drawling speaker. [ME *dronen* <*drone* a male bee]

drone[2] (drōn) *n.* **1** A stingless male bee, that gathers no honey. **2** Hence, an idler. **3** *Aeron.* An unmanned airplane piloted by remote control. — *v.* **droned, dron·ing** *v.t.* To spend idly. — *v.i.* To live in idleness; be indolent. [OE *dran*] — **dron′ish** *adj.*

dron·go (drong′gō) *n.* A crowlike, insectivorous bird (*Dicrurus forficatus*) of the East Indies and Africa, with a long, forked tail and dark plumage. Also **drongo shrike.** [<Malagasy]

drool (drool) *v.t.* & *v.i.* To drivel; slaver. — *n.* **1** Spittle. **2** *Colloq.* Foolish talk; stuff and nonsense. [Contraction of DRIVEL]

droop (droop) *v.i.* **1** To sink down; hang downward. **2** To lose vigor or vitality. **3** To become dejected; lose spirit. — *v.t.* **4** To allow to hang or sink down. See synonyms under FALL. — *n.* A sinking or hanging down; specifically, the bending under its own weight of the long barrel of an artillery gun. [<ON *drūpa*] — **droop′ing** *adj.* — **droop′ing·ly** *adv.*

drop (drop) *n.* **1** A globule of liquid; also, a very small quantity of anything, as of a beverage. **2** Anything that resembles or hangs like a drop of liquid, or that is made in drops or by dropping; a pendant earring, small piece of candy, etc. **3** A fall; the distance fallen; a sudden change of level; descent. **4** Any one of various contrivances that drop or depend, or are employed in lowering, as the drop curtain of a theater; also, in the theater, a drop scene. **5** *Mech.* **a** A forging machine. **b** A press used for forging, stamping, etc. **6** A trap door; especially, the platform of a gallows. **7** *pl.* Any liquid medicine given by the drop. **8** *Naut.* The vertical depth of a course on its central line. **9** A letter-drop. **10** A fall in prices: Stocks took a *drop.* **— at the drop of a** (or **the**) **hat** At once; with little or no hesitation or provocation. **— to have the drop on** To have the advantage over; specifically, to have (a person) covered with a gun before he can draw his. **—** *v.* **dropped, drop·ping** *v.t.* **1** To let fall in drops. **2** To let fall in any way; release and let fall; lower. **3** To give birth to: said of animals. **4** To say as if casually or incidentally: to *drop* a hint. **5** To write and send (a note, etc.) hastily and informally. **6** To bring down or cause to fall, as by tackling, striking, or shooting. **7** To stop treating of or associating with: to *drop* a subject or a friend. **8** To leave at a specific place, as from a ship or vehicle. **9** To omit (a syllable, letter, or word): He *dropped* the *von* from his name. **10** To sprinkle with drops. **11** *Slang* To lose (money or the like), as in gambling. **12** *U.S.* To discharge (an employee); to dismiss (a student). **13** *Naut.* To outdistance; sail away from. **—** *v.i.* **14** To fall in drops, as a liquid. **15** To fall rapidly; come down. **16** To fall down exhausted, injured, or dead. **17** To crouch, as a hunting dog at sight of game. **18** To come to an end; cease; stop. **19** To fall into some state or condition: to *drop* into a habit. **20** To fall behind or to the rear: often with *behind* or *back.* See synonyms under FALL. **— to drop down** To move down a stream or along a coast, as a vessel. **— to drop in** To happen in, as for a call. **— to drop out** To leave; withdraw from. [OE *dropa*]

drop curtain A theater curtain lowered in front of the stage between the acts.

drop·forge (drop′fôrj′) *v.t.* **·forged, ·forg·ing** To forge (metal) between dies by a machine employing the mechanical force of a dropped weight. **— drop′forg′ing** *n.*

drop hammer A machine for forging, stamping, etc., in which a heavy weight sliding between vertical guides strikes blows at regular intervals or at the will of the operator.

drop·kick (drop′kik′) *n.* In football, a kick given the ball just as it is rebounding after being dropped. **— drop′kick′er** *n.*

drop–kick (drop′kik′) *v.t. & v.i.* To kick (a football) in the manner of a dropkick.

drop leaf A hinged section of a table that may be folded down when not in use. **— drop′-leaf** *adj.*

drop·let (drop′lit) *n.* A little drop.

drop·sy (drop′sē) *n.* **1** *Pathol.* An abnormal accumulation of serous fluid in cellular tissue as in some body cavity. **2** A disease of certain plants, due to an excess of water. [Short for HYDROPSY]

hemlock dropwort. **3** A North American marsh plant (*Oxypolis rigidior*) of the parsley family.

dro·soph·i·la (drō-sof′ə-lə, drə-) *n. pl.* **·lae** (-lē) Any of a genus (*Drosophila*) of fruit flies, especially *D. melanogaster,* used for research in genetics and heredity. See FRUIT FLY. [<NL <Gk. *drosos* dew + *phileein* love]

dross (drôs, dros) *n.* **1** *Metall.* Refuse or impurity in melted metal; slag; cinders. **2** Waste matter; refuse. See synonyms under WASTE. [OE *drôs*] **— dross′i·ness** *n.* **— dross′y** *adj.*

drought (drout) *n.* **1** Long–continued dry weather; want of rain. **2** Scarcity; dearth. **3** Thirst. Also **drouth** (drouth). [OE *drugoth.* Related to DRY.]

drove[1] (drōv) Past tense of DRIVE.

drove[2] (drōv) *n.* **1** A number of animals driven or herded for driving. **2** A moving crowd of human beings. **3** A stone mason's broad-edged chisel: also called **drove chisel.** **4** The surface of stone smoothed by a drove: also

called **drove′work′.** See synonyms under FLOCK[1]. **—** *v.t.* **·droved, drov·ing** **1** To drive (cows, etc.) for some distance; work as a drover. **2** To dress (stone) with a broad-edged chisel. [OE *drāf.* Related to DRIVE.]

drown (droun) *v.t.* **1** To kill by immersion and suffocation in water or other liquid. **2** To flood; deluge. **3** To overwhelm; overpower; extinguish. **—** *v.i.* To die by immersion and suffocation in water or other liquid. [ME *drūnen, drounen;* origin uncertain]

drowse (drouz) *v.* **drowsed, drows·ing** *v.i.* **1** To be sleepy; doze; be listless. **—** *v.t.* **2** To make sleepy. **3** To pass (time) in drowsing. **—** *n.* The state of being half asleep; a doze. [OE *drūsian* become sluggish]

drow·sy (drou′zē) *adj.* **·si·er, ·si·est** **1** Heavy with sleepiness; dull. **2** Lulling; soporific. See synonyms under SLOW. **— drow′si·ly** *adv.* **— drow′si·ness** *n.*

drub (drub) *v.t.* **drubbed, drub·bing** **1** To beat, as with a stick; cudgel; thrash. **2** To vanquish; overcome. **3** To stamp (the feet). **—** *n.* A blow; thump. [? <Arabic *darb* a beating <*daraba* beat] **— drub′ber** *n.*

drub·bing (drub′ing) *n.* **1** A thrashing; a beating. **2** Defeat.

drudge (druj) *v.i.* **drudged, drudg·ing** To toil; work hard and slavishly at menial tasks. **—** *n.* One who toils at menial tasks. [Prob. related to OE *drēogan* work, labor]

drudg·er·y (druj′ər-ē) *n. pl.* **·er·ies** Dull, wearisome, or menial work. See synonyms under TOIL, WORK.

drug (drug) *n.* **1** Any substance, other than food, intended for use in the diagnosis, cure, mitigation, treatment, or prevention of disease in man or other animals. **2** Any article or substance recognized in the U.S. pharmacopoeia. **3** Any narcotic; also, any substance or chemical agent, exclusive of food, employed for other than medical reasons to obtain a given physiological effect or to satisfy a craving. **4** A commodity that is overabundant or in excess of demand: a *drug* on the market. **—** *v.t.* **drugged, drug·ging** **1** To mix drugs with (food, drink, etc.), especially narcotic or poisonous drugs. **2** To administer drugs to. **3** To stupefy or poison with or as with drugs; overcome: *drugged* with sleep. [<MF *drogue;* ult. origin unknown]

drug·get (drug′it) *n.* **1** A coarse woolen or wool and cotton fabric for rugs, etc. **2** A rug made of such material. **3** A kind of dress fabric; woolen rep. [<MF *droguet*]

drug·gist (drug′ist) *n.* **1** One who compounds prescriptions and sells drugs; a pharmacist. **2** A dealer in drugs.

drug·store (drug′stôr′, -stōr′) *n.* A place where prescriptions are compounded, and drugs and miscellaneous merchandise are sold; a pharmacy.

dru·id (drōō′id) *n.* One of an order of priests or teachers of religion in ancient Gaul, Britain, and Ireland. [<MF *druide* <L *druidae, druides* <Celtic] **— dru′id·ess** (-is) *n. fem.*

dru·id·ism (drōō′id·iz′əm) *n.* The religious system of ancient Gaul, Britain, and Ireland, administered by the druids; also, its ceremonies, rites, and philosophy. Also **dru′id·ry** (-rē).

drum (drum) *n.* **1** A hollow cylinder of wood or metal, with skin or vellum stretched upon ringlike frames fitted over each end, kept taut with hoops and cords, and played by beating the head or the heads with drumsticks; also, the sound produced by beating this instrument. **2** The body of a banjo, tambourine, etc. **3** *Anat.* The tympanum, or middle ear. **4** A drummer. **5** Anything resembling a drum in

HOISTING DRUM

shape, as a cylindrical receptacle for oil, fruit, fish, etc. **6** The drumfish. **7** Any mechanical construction or device shaped like a drum. **8** *Obs.* A social gathering; formerly, a crowded and noisy fashionable card party at a private house. **—** *v.t.* **drummed, drum·ming** *v.t.* **1** To perform on or as on a drum. **2** To expel in disgrace: usually with *out.* **3** To summon by beating a drum. **4** To force into

the mind or upon the attention by constant repetition. **—** *v.i.* **5** To beat a drum. **6** To beat on anything continuously or rhythmically. **7** To make a loud, beating noise: said especially of the wings of certain birds, as partridge or grouse. **— to drum up** To seek or solicit: to *drum* up trade. [Prob. <MDu. *tromme*]

drum·beat (drum′bēt′) *n.* The sound of a drum; also, the action of beating a drum.

drum brake A brake in which a shoe lined with a durable, heat–resistant material is pressed outward against the inner rim of a drum.

drum·fish (drum′fish′) *n. pl.* **·fish** or **·fishes** **1** A sciaenoid fish (*Pogonias cromis*) of the North American Atlantic coast which makes a drumming sound, especially in the breeding season. **2** Any of similar fishes, as the fresh-water drum (*Aplodinotus grunniens*) of the Great Lakes and the Mississippi.

drum·head (drum′hed′) *n.* **1** The membrane stretched over the end of a drum, especially the end that is beaten. **2** *Naut.* The circular top of a capstan. See illustration under CAPSTAN. **3** *Anat.* The tympanic membrane; the eardrum. See illustration under EAR. **4** An Australian grasstree.

drum·mer (drum′ər) *n.* **1** One who or that which drums. **2** *U.S.* A traveling salesman.

Drummond light **1** The calcium light. **2** A type of heliostat. [after T. *Drummond,* 1797–1840, Scottish engineer, who invented it]

drum·stick (drum′stik′) *n.* **1** A stick for beating a drum. **2** The lower joint of the leg of a cooked fowl.

drunk (drungk) Past participle of DRINK; former past tense. **—** *adj.* **1** Inebriated; intoxicated; figuratively, saturated; satiated; glutted: *drunk* with slaughter. **2** *Obs.* Drenched. **—** *n. Colloq.* **1** A spree; fit of drunkenness. **2** A drunken person; a case of drunkenness.

drunk·ard (drungk′ərd) *n.* One who habitually drinks to intoxication; a sot.

drunk·en (drungk′ən) *adj.* **1** Given to, resulting from, or characterized by drunkenness; drunk; tipsy. **2** Saturated. **— drunk′en·ly** *adv.* **— drunk′en·ness** *n.*

drupe (drōōp) *n. Bot.* A soft, fleshy fruit enclosing a hard–shelled stone or seed, as in the peach or cherry. See illustration under FRUIT. [<NL *drupa* <L *drupa* (*oliva*) an overripe (olive) <Gk. *druppa*]

dry (drī) *adj.* **dri·er, dri·est** **1** Lacking moisture; not wet or damp; not fresh; not green, as wood; also, lacking lubrication, as bearings. **2** Thirsty. **3** Lacking interest; lifeless; dull. **4** Slyly jocose or satirical; shrewd, as wit. **5** Free from sweetness: said of wines; also, denoting any wine having 14 percent or less of alcohol. **6** Subject to or in favor of a prohibitory liquor law: a *dry* town. **7** Not giving milk: a *dry* cow. **8** Not liquid; solid: said of merchandise, etc. **9** Tearless: said of the eyes. **10** Characterized by absence of bloodshed. **11** Without butter: said of toast. **12** Wanting in cordiality; not genial. **—** *v.* **dried, dry·ing** *v.t.* **1** To make dry; rid of moisture. **2** To cure or preserve, as meat, fish, etc., by evaporation or desiccation. **—** *v.i.* **3** To become dry. **— to dry up** **1** To cease or cause to cease flowing. **2** *Colloq.* To stop talking. **—** *n. pl.* **dries** **1** A state or condition of dryness; especially, a drought. **2** *Often cap. Colloq.* A prohibitionist. [OE *drȳge*] **— dry′ly, dri′ly** *adv.* **— dry′ness** *n.*

dry·ad (drī′əd, -ad) *n.* In Greek mythology a wood nymph. [<L *dryas, -adis* <Gk. <*drys, dryos* an oak tree] **— dry·ad′ic** *adj.*

dry·clean (drī′klēn′) *v.t.* To clean (clothing, etc.) with solvents other than water, such as carbon tetrachloride, etc. Also **dry′cleanse′.** **— dry′clean′er** *n.* **— dry′clean′ing** *n.*

dry fog *Meteorol.* Haze formed from a suspension of fine dust or smoke particles in the atmosphere.

dry kiln A heated oven or chamber for drying and seasoning lumber.

dry law A law prohibiting the sale of spirituous liquors.

dry measure A unit or system of units for measuring the volume of dry commodities, as fruits, grain, etc. The principal customary U.S. units are as in the table below. See also METRIC SYSTEM.

2 pints (pt., pts.) = 1 quart (qt., qts.)
8 quarts = 1 peck (pk., pks.)
4 pecks = 1 bushel (bu.)

dry·nurse (drī'nûrs') *v.t.* **·nursed,** **·nurs·ing** **1** To nurse without suckling. **2** To coach or give hints to, as in or concerning the duties of an office. —*n.* **1** A nurse who nourishes and rears a child without suckling it. **2** One who cares for another; particularly, one who instructs his superior in the latter's duties.

Dry·o·pi·the·cus (drī'ō·pi·thē'kəs) *Paleontol. n.* Any of a genus of extinct apes of the Miocene and Pliocene epochs: closely related types are *Sivapithecus* and *Proconsul.* [NL <Gk. *drys, dryos* an oak tree + *pithēkos* a monkey, ape]

dry·point (drī'point') *n.* **1** A fine etching needle used to incise copperplate in fine lines, without the use of acid or etching ground. **2** A line or work thus engraved, or the method thus used.

dry·rot (drī'rot') *n.* **1** A fungous disease of timber, causing it to crumble into powder. **2** A disease of potato tubers and other vegetables. **3** Inward and gradual corruption, as of morals.

dry–run (drī'run') *n.* **1** *Mil.* Practice in aiming and firing weapons without using live ammunition. **2** Any rehearsal or practice exercise.

dry·salt (drī'sôlt') *v.t.* To preserve (food) by salting and removing moisture.

dry socket *Dent.* A morbid condition of a tooth socket after extraction of a tooth, resulting from the disintegration of a blood clot without the formation of pus and accompanied by a foul odor and severe pain.

dry wash **1** Laundry which has been washed and dried, but not ironed. **2** *U.S.* A gully or arroyo which contains water only after a heavy rain.

du·ad (dōō'ad, dyōō'-) *n.* A pair of units. [<Gk. *dyas, -ados* the number two]

du·al (dōō'əl, dyōō'-) *adj.* **1** Denoting or relating to two. **2** Composed of two, as of two natures; twofold; binary. —*n.* *Gram.* In some languages, as Sanskrit and Greek, the form of the noun or verb indicating its application to two persons or things: the dual number: distinguished from *singular* and *plural.* ◆ Homophone: *duel.* [<L *dualis* <*duo* two] —**du·al·i·ty** (dōō·al'ə·tē, dyōō-) *n.*

Du·a·la (dōō·ä'lä) *n.* **1** One of a Bantu people inhabiting the Cameroons, West Africa. **2** Their language.

Dual Alliance An alliance (1879) between Germany and Austria–Hungary against Russia.

du·al·ism (dōō'əl·iz'əm, dyōō'-) *n.* **1** The state of being twofold; duality. **2** A system or theory which asserts a twofoldness of nature, being, or operation; specifically, **theological dualism,** or the doctrine that there are two eternal and opposing principles, or beings, one good and the other evil; **philosophical dualism,** or the theory that the nature of the universe is twofold, *i.e.,* comprised of mind and matter, as opposed either to idealistic or materialistic monism; **psychological** or **psychophysical dualism,** the theory that the body and mind of man are two different existences but are placed by the order of nature in a most intimate system of correlations or interactions; or **ethical dualism,** the system of morals which demands and justifies one kind of conduct toward one's fellows in the same social group and another kind of conduct toward other men. **3** *Gram.* The expression of the condition of duality.

du·al·ist (dōō'əl·ist, dyōō'-) *n.* A believer in some form of dualism.

du·al·is·tic (dōō'əl·is'tik, dyōō'-) *adj.* **1** Of or pertaining to dualism. **2** Having a dual nature. —**du·al·is'ti·cal·ly** *adv.*

dub[1] (dub) *v.t.* **dubbed, dub·bing** **1** To confer knighthood upon by tapping on the shoulder with a sword. **2** To name or style; entitle. **3** To smooth or rub; dress, as timber. [OE *dubbian*]

dub[2] (dub) *v.t.* & *v.i.* **dubbed, dub·bing** **1** To push or thrust. **2** To beat (a drum). —*n.* **1** A blow. **2** A beat of a drum. [Prob. imit.]

dub[3] (dub) *Slang* *n.* A clumsy, blundering person; a poor or second-rate player in any game. —*v.t.* **dubbed, dub·bing** To bungle. [? <DUB[2]]

dub (dub) *v.t.* **dubbed, dub·bing** To re–record (a sound record) in order to change volume or frequency. —**to dub in** **1** In motion pictures, to insert (a new sound track) into a film. **2** To blend (new sounds, music, etc.) into the sound track of a film, or into a radio or television broadcast. [Short for DOUBLE]

dub·bing[1] (dub'ing) *n.* **1** Material for softening leather and making it waterproof. **2** Pieces of wood, etc., for filling up deep depressions or interstices in a wall before plastering. **3** The material of the body of a fishing fly. [<DUB[1]]

dub·bing[2] (dub'ing) *n.* The re–recording of a sound record, in whole or in part, where a change in volume levels or frequency characteristics is necessary; especially, the synchronized conversion of a motion–picture sound track from one language of the original cast into some other language. [<DUB[5]]

Dub·he (dōōb'he) The star Alpha in the constellation Ursa Major: the larger of the two stars which together make the Pointer toward the Pole Star.

du·bi·e·ty (dōō·bī'ə·tē, dyōō'-) *n.* The state of being doubtful or dubious; doubt; doubtfulness. Also **du·bi·os·i·ty** (dōō'bē·os'ə·tē, dyōō'-). [<LL *dubietas, -tatis* <*dubius* doubtful]

du·bi·ous (dōō'bē·əs, dyōō'-) *adj.* **1** Unsettled in judgment or opinion; in a state of doubt; doubtful. **2** Being a subject or matter of doubt; causing doubt. **3** Of uncertain result; not yet settled; problematic. **4** Of questionable propriety; open to objections, especially of a moral kind, or to suspicion; questionable. **5** Being the occasion of doubt; difficult of explanation; equivocal. See synonyms under EQUIVOCAL, PRECARIOUS. [<L *dubiosus* <*dubium* doubt] —**du'bi·ous·ly** *adv.* —**du'bi·ous·ness** *n.*

du·bi·ta·ble (dōō'bə·tə·bəl, dyōō'-) *adj.* Doubtful; debatable. —**du'bi·ta·bly** *adv.*

du·bi·tate (dōō'bə·tāt, dyōō'-) *v.i.* **·tat·ed, ·tat·ing** *Rare* To doubt. [<L *dubitatus,* pp. of *dubitare* doubt] —**du'bi·ta'tion** *n.*

du·bi·ta·tive (dōō'bə·tā'tiv, dyōō'-) *adj.* Tending to or expressing doubt; also, hesitating. —**du'bi·ta'tive·ly** *adv.*

Dub·lin (dub'lin) **1** The capital of Ireland, a port on the Liffey river at **Dublin Bay,** an inlet of the Irish Sea on the eastern coast of Ireland: Irish *Baile Atha Cliath.* **2** A county of Leinster province, eastern Ireland: 356 square miles; county seat, Dublin.

du·bon·net (dōō'bə·nā') *n.* A reddish purple, the color of Dubonnet.

Du·bon·net (dōō'bə·nā', *Fr.* dü·bô·ne') *n.* A fortified French red wine: a trade name.

Du·buque (də·byōōk') A city in eastern Iowa on the Mississippi.

du·cal (dōō'kəl, dyōō'-) *adj.* Of or pertaining to a duke or a duchy. [<MF <LL *ducalis* <*dux* leader] —**du'cal·ly** *adv.*

duc·at (duk'ət) *n.* **1** One of several European coins of varying value, the first struck by Roger II of Sicily. **2** A former coin of Venice and Holland. **3** *Slang* A ticket, usually for the theater or a sports event. [<MF <Ital. *ducato* <LL *ducatus,* orig. a duchy <*dux* leader]

duch·ess (duch'is) *n.* **1** The wife or widow of a duke. **2** The female sovereign of a duchy. [<OF *duchesse* <LL *ducissa* <L *dux* leader]

duch·y (duch'ē) *n.* *pl.* **duch·ies** The territory or dominion of a duke; a dukedom. [<OF *duché* <L *dux* leader]

duck[1] (duk) *n.* **1** A web–footed, short–legged, broad–billed water bird of the *Anatidae* family comprising fresh–water and wood ducks *(Anatinae),* the sea and bay ducks *(Fuligulinae),* and the mergansers *(Merginae).* ◆ Collateral adjective: *anatine.* **2** The female of this bird: distinguished from *drake.* **3** The flesh of this bird. **4** *Colloq.* A dear; darling. **5** *Slang* A person; a fellow. [OE *duce,* lit. diver]

duck[2] (duk) *v.t.* & *v.i.* **1** To plunge suddenly

AMERICAN MALLARD DUCK
(About 23 inches in length)

under water; dive. **2** To lower quickly; bob, as the head. **3** To dodge; evade (a blow or punishment). **4** To avoid (a duty, person, etc.). **5** To move quickly and abruptly: He ducked through the crowd. See synonyms under IMMERSE. —*n.* A sudden downward movement, as of the head; a bob or nod; also, a quick plunge under water. [ME *duken, douken* dive, ult. <Gmc.]

duck[3] (duk) *n.* **1** A strong tightly woven linen or cotton fabric with a plain weave, similar to canvas; sailcloth: heavier weights are used for tents, sails, and military and naval equipment; light weights for trousers, middy blouses, etc. **2** *pl.* Trousers made of this fabric. [<Du. *doek* cloth]

duck[4] (duk) *n.* *Mil.* An amphibious military vehicle of World War II, having a watertight body and equipped with a propeller and a rudder for use when traveling on water. [<DUKW, code word for this type of vehicle]

duck·bill (duk'bil') *n.* The platypus.

duck·board (duk'bôrd', -bōrd') *n.* A board or section of boarding laid over a wet floor or muddy ground to form a raised surface for walking.

ducking stool A stool on which the culprit was tied and plunged into water; a cucking stool: formerly used as a punishment in New England, especially for quarrelsome women.

duck·ling (duk'ling) *n.* A young duck.

duck·mole (duk'mōl') *n.* The platypus.

duck·pin (duk'pin') *n.* A pin 9 inches high and 3 1/2 inches in diameter at the body: used in the game of tenpins called **duckpins.**

ducks and drakes A game in which one skims or skips flat stones, shells, etc., along the surface of water. —**to make** (or **play**) **ducks and drakes** To throw away or squander: with *of* or *with.*

duck·weed (duk'wēd') *n.* **1** Any of several small, disk–shaped, aquatic plants (genus *Lemna*) common in streams and ponds in the United States. **2** A somewhat larger plant of the same family, the large duckweed *(Spirodela polyrhiza).* Also **duck'meat'.**

duct (dukt) *n.* **1** Any tube, canal, or passage by which a fluid is conveyed. **2** *Anat.* A tubular passage for fluid, especially one by which a secretion is carried away from a gland: the nasal *duct.* **3** *Electr.* A tubular channel for carrying electric power, telegraph or telephone cables. [<L *ductus* a leading <*ducere* lead]

duc·tile (duk'til) *adj.* **1** Capable of being hammered into thin layers or of being drawn out into wire, as certain metals. **2** Easily led; tractable; pliant. [<F <L *ductilis* <*ducere* lead] —**duc·til'i·ty, duc'tile·ness** *n.*

dud[1] (dud) *n.* *Colloq.* **1** A garment. **2** *pl.* Clothing; especially, old clothes. **3** *pl.* Belongings in general. [ME *dudde* a cloak; origin uncertain]

dud[2] (dud) *n.* **1** *Mil.* A shell that fails to explode. **2** *Colloq.* Any person or thing that is inadequate or fails to operate. [<Du. *dood* dead]

dude (dōōd, dyōōd) *n.* **1** *U.S.* A fop; an affected man. **2** A city person, especially one from the eastern United States who is vacationing on a ranch. [Coined 1883, ? <*duds* clothing] —**dud'ish** *adj.* —**dud'ism, dud'ish·ness** *n.*

dudg·eon[1] (duj'ən) *n.* Sullen displeasure; resentment. [Origin unknown]

dudg·eon[2] (duj'ən) *n.* **1** The root of the boxwood tree, formerly used for dagger hilts. **2** Any mottled or veined wood. **3** *Obs.* A wooden hilt of a dagger; a dudgeon dagger. [<AF *digeon;* ult. origin unknown]

due (dōō, dyōō) *adj.* **1** Owing and demandable; owed; especially, payable because of the arrival of the time set or agreed upon. **2** That should be rendered or given; justly claimable; appropriate. **3** Suitable; lawful; sufficient; regular. **4** Appointed or expected to arrive; having had time to arrive. **5** That may be charged or attributed; ascribable; owing: with *to:* The delay was *due* to rain. ◆ *Due to* as a preposition, though widely used, is still questioned by some, who would substitute for it *because of* or *on account of: Because of* (not *due to*) rain, we were delayed. —*n.* **1** That

add, āce, câre, pälm; end, ēven; it, īce; odd, ōpen, ôrder; tŏŏk, pōōl; up, bûrn; ə = a in *above,* e in *sicken,* i in *clarity,* o in *melon,* u in *focus;* yōō = u in *fuse;* oi, oil; ou, pout; ch, check; g, go; ng, ring; th, thin; ŧħ, this; zh, vision. Foreign sounds á, œ, ü, kh, ń; and ◆: see page xx. < from; + plus; ? possibly.

which is owed or rightfully required; a debt or obligation. **2** *pl.* Legal charge or fee: club **dues.** — *adv.* **1** Directly; exactly: *due* east. **2** Duly. ◆ Homophone: *dew.* [<OF *deü*, pp. of *devoir* owe <L *debere*]

du·el (dōō′əl, dyōō′-) *n.* **1** A prearranged combat between two persons, usually fought with deadly weapons in the presence of witnesses or seconds. **2** A struggle between two contending parties. — *v.t. & v.i.* **du·eled** or **·elled, du·el·ing** or **·el·ling** To fight or fight with, in a duel. ◆ Homophone: *dual.* [<F <Ital. *duello* <L *duellum,* var. of *bellum* war] — **du′el·er, du′el·ist** *n.* — **du′el·ist, du′el·list** *n.*

du·en·na (dōō·en′ə, dyōō-) *n.* An elderly woman who watches over a young woman in Spanish and Portuguese families; hence, a chaperon. [<Sp. <L *domina* lady. Doublet of DAME.]

du·et (dōō·et′, dyōō-) *n.* A musical composition for two voices or performers. [<Ital. *duetto,* dim. of *duo* a duet <L *duo* two]

duf·fel (duf′əl) *n.* **1** A woolen fabric; a heavyweight kersey. **2** Outfit; supplies; especially, camping outfit. Also **duf′fle.** [from *Duffel,* a town near Antwerp]

duffel bag A sack, usually of canvas or duck, used to carry clothing and personal possessions.

duf·fer (duf′ər) *n.* **1** *Colloq.* One who performs in an incompetent or perfunctory manner. **2** *Brit. Dial.* A peddler or hawker; especially, one who sells spurious or flashy articles. **3** *Slang* Any counterfeit or sham. **4** *Austral.* A stealer of horses or cattle. [Origin uncertain]

duf·fle coat (duf′əl) A heavy woolen outer coat, usually knee-length and hooded. Also **duf′fel coat.** [Var. of DUFFEL]

dug¹ (dug) Past tense and past participle of DIG.

dug² (dug) *n.* A teat or udder. [Cf. Dan. *dægge* suckle]

du·gong (dōō′gong) *n.* An aquatic, herbivorous mammal (genus *Dugong*) of the East Indies

DUGONG
(From 9 to 12 feet in length; 450 to 2000 pounds)

and Australia, having flippers in front, a paddlelike tail, and tusks which in the male grow to large size: also called *sea cow.* [<Malay *duyong*]

dug–out (dug′out′) *n.* **1** A canoe formed of a hollowed log. See illustration under CANOE. **2** A rude dwelling excavated in a hillside; a cave. **3** An underground shelter against bombs and shells, or for protection from tornadoes, etc. **4** A low, boxlike structure facing a baseball diamond, to shelter the players when not at bat or in the field.

dui·ker·bok (dī′kər·bok′) *n.* A small antelope (genus *Cephalophus*) widely distributed over southern and tropical Africa, with short conical horns set far back, a tufted head, and very short tail. Also **dui′ker, dui′ker·buck′.** [<Du. <*duiker* ducker, diver + *bok* buck; from its habit of plunging through thickets]

duke (dōōk, dyōōk) *n.* **1** An English temporal peer of the highest rank, yielding precedence to a prince of the blood or an archbishop, and ranking above a marquis or a bishop. **2** A Continental noble or prince of corresponding rank. **3** A reigning prince of less importance than a king ruling over a duchy or a small state. **4** Formerly, a powerful semi-independent vassal. — *v.t.* **duked, duk·ing** To play the duke. [<F *duc* <L *dux* leader]

duke·dom (dōōk′dəm, dyōōk′-) *n.* **1** A duchy. **2** The dignity or title of a duke.

dukes (dōōks, dyōōks) *n. pl. Slang* The fists. [Short for *Duke of Yorks,* orig. riming slang for forks; later fingers, hands, fists]

dul·ci·an·a (dul′sē·an′ə) *n.* An organ stop of soft and delicate tone. [<Med. L *dulciana* <L *dulcis* sweet]

du·li·a (dōō·lī′ə, dyōō-) *n. Theol.* A secondary kind of worship, as distinguished from *latria,* or supreme worship: used in the sense of *veneration* of the saints and angels. [<Gk. *douleia* service <*doulos* slave]

dull (dul) *adj.* **1** Not sharp or keen; having a blunt edge or point. **2** Not acute or intense: *dull* pain. **3** Not quick, as in thought; sluggish; listless; stupid; lacking in perception, sensibility, or responsiveness. **4** Not brisk or active. **5** Not bright or spirited; wearisome; boring; sad. **6** Lacking luster; cloudy; dim. **7** Of sounds, indistinct; heavily muffled. See synonyms under BLUNT, FLAT, HEAVY, LIFELESS, NUMB, SAD, SLOW, TEDIOUS. — *v.t. & v.i.* To make or become dull. [ME *dul.* Akin to OE *dol* foolish] — **dull′ish** *adj.* — **dull′ly** *adv.* — **dull′ness, dull′ness** *n.*

dull·ard (dul′ərd) *n.* A dull or stupid person.

Du·long and Pe·tit's law (dü·lôn′, pe·tēz′) *Physics* A statement that the specific heat of any solid element, multiplied by the atomic weight is nearly a constant (approximately, 6.4). [after P. L. *Dulong,* 1785–1838; A. T. *Petit,* 1791–1820, French physicists]

du·lo·sis (dōō·lō′sis, dyōō-) *n. Entomol.* A form of slavery practiced by certain genera of ants. [<NL <Gk. *doulōsis* enslavement] — **du·lot′·ic** (-lot′ik) *adj.*

dulse (duls) *n.* A reddish-brown seaweed (*Rhodymenia palmata*) eaten in Ireland, Scotland, and elsewhere as a vegetable. Also **dulce.** [<Irish *duileasg*]

du·ly (dōō′lē, dyōō′-) *adv.* In accordance with what is due; fitly; becomingly; regularly; in due time or manner.

Du·ma (dōō′mä) *n.* The former Russian national assembly elected indirectly by the people; created by an imperial ukase in 1905: also spelled *Douma.* [<Russian]

dumb (dum) *adj.* **1** Unable to make articulate sounds; having no power of speech: deaf and *dumb.* **2** Refraining from speaking; not using words or sounds; mute; silent. **3** Not having usual characteristics, symptoms, accompaniments, or powers; latent: *dumb* ague or chill. **4** *U.S. Colloq.* Stupid. **5** *Naut.* Having no sails: a *dumb* barge. See synonyms under TACITURN. In def. 4, infl. by cognate G *dumm* stupid] — **dumb′ly** *adv.* — **dumb′ness** *n.*

dumb ague A form of chills and fever in which the symptoms of the disease are concealed or obscure.

dumb·bell (dum′bel′) *n.* **1** A gymnastic implement consisting of a handle with a weighted ball at each end. **2** *U.S. Slang* A stupid person.

dumb·found (dum′found′) *v.t.* To strike dumb, confuse; confound. Also **dumb′found′er.** [Blend of DUMB and CONFOUND]

dumb show **1** Gestures and signs without words; pantomime. **2** In early English drama, pantomime representation of part of the action of a play.

dumb·wait·er (dum′wā′tər) *n.* A movable serving table or elevator for carrying things from one room or floor to another.

dum·dum bullet (dum′dum′) A small-arms bullet having a soft point or a jacket which has been cut across at the point so that it will mushroom on impact and tear a gaping wound. [from *Dumdum,* a town near Calcutta, India, where first made]

dum·my (dum′ē) *n. pl.* **dum·mies 1** *Colloq.* One who is dumb; a mute; hence, a stupid person; dolt. **2** A silent person, as an actor without a speaking part. **3** A figure used by a ventriloquist. **4** A comparatively noiseless steam locomotive without a blast pipe. **5** A dumbwaiter. **6** A thing made to represent something else; a model; a figure on which clothes can be displayed. **7** A figure stuffed with straw or sawdust, used in bayonet practice; also, a similar figure used by football players in tackling practice. **8** In certain card games, an exposed hand played by the opposite player; also, the player to whom that hand has been dealt. **9** A person who represents another in a transaction, but who poses as acting for himself; a straw man. **10** *Printing* A model book, usually blank, made up as a pattern. — **double dummy** Whist or bridge as played by two persons, each playing two hands, one of which is exposed. — *adj.* **1** Sham; counterfeit. **2** Silent. **3** Having no explosive charge: *dummy* ammunition. **4** Made to resemble some object, but having no real use; artificial: a *dummy* door. — *v.t.* **dum·mied, ·my·ing** To lay out (printed matter) as a guide for making up. — **to dummy up** *U.S. Slang* To become silent. [<DUMB]

du·mor·ti·er·ite (dōō·môr′tē·ə·rīt′, dyōō-) *n.* An

aluminum borosilicate mineral resembling lapis lazuli: used in the making of refractories and high-grade porcelain dielectrics and sometimes cut as a gemstone. [after E. *Dumortier,* French paleontologist]

dump¹ (dump) *v.t.* **1** To drop or throw down abruptly or heavily. **2** To empty out, as from a container. **3** To empty (a container), as by overturning. **4** To throw (goods or commodities) on a market, especially a foreign market, in quantity and at low prices. **5** To get rid of; throw away. — *v.i.* **6** To fall or drop. **7** To unload goods or commodities. **8** To unload. — *n.* **1** A dumping ground; especially, a place where city refuse is dumped. **2** That which is dumped. **3** A place where ammunition, stores, or supplies are held for rapid distribution. **4** *U.S. Slang* A poor, ill-kept dwelling or place; also, lodgings. **5** A leaden counter used by boys in various games. **6** Something short, thick, and heavy. **7** *Brit.* A large globular sweetmeat; a bull's-eye. **8** A coin more or less thick and shapeless. [ME <Scand. Cf. Norw. *dumpa* fall suddenly.] — **dump′er** *n.*

dump² (dump) *n.* **1** *pl.* A gloomy state of mind; melancholy. **2** *Obs.* A slow, melancholy dance, or the music for it. [Cf. MD *domp* mental haze]

dump·ish (dump′ish) *adj.* Depressed in spirits; sad; morose. — **dump′ish·ly** *adv.* — **dump′ish·ness** *n.*

dump·ling (dump′ling) *n.* **1** A small piece of pie crust or biscuit dough filled with fruit and baked or steamed. **2** A small mass of dough dropped into boiling soup or stew. **3** A short, stocky person or animal.

dump truck A truck for hauling gravel, coal, etc., which unloads by tilting back the cargo bin and opening the tailboard.

dump·y¹ (dump′ē) *adj.* **dump·i·er, dump·i·est** Sullen or discontented; sulky; gloomy or cast down.

dump·y² (dump′ē) *adj.* **dump·i·er, dump·i·est** Short and thick; stocky. — **dump′i·ly** *adv.* — **dump′i·ness** *n.*

dumpy level A surveyor's level consisting of a short telescope rigidly attached to the spindle connecting it with the horizontally rotating table.

dun¹ (dun) *v.t. & v.i.* **dunned, dun·ning** To press (a debtor) for payment; importune; pester. — *n.* **1** One who duns. **2** A demand for payment. [Prob. var. of DIN]

dun² (dun) *adj.* Of a grayish-brown or reddish-brown color. — *n.* **1** Dun color. **2** A dun-colored horse. **3** *Obs.* A nickname for an old horse; a jade. **4** A dun fly. — *v.t.* **dunned, dun·ning 1** To make dun-colored. **2** *U.S.* To cure (fish) by salting and packing in a dark place. [OE *dunn*]

dunce (duns) *n.* A stupid or ignorant person. [after Johannes *Duns* Scotus]

dunce cap A conical paper cap formerly placed on the head of a dull-witted pupil.

dun·der·head (dun′dər·hed′) *n.* A blockhead; dunce. Also **dun′der·pate′** (-pāt′). [<dial. E (Scottish) *dunder* rumble, boom + HEAD] — **dun′der·head′ed** *adj.*

dune (dōōn, dyōōn) *n.* A hill of loose sand heaped up by the wind: usually near a shore; a down. [<F <MDu. Akin to DOWN³.]

dun·fish (dun′fish′) *n. U.S.* Codfish cured by dunning.

dun fly An artificial fly variously imitative of the mayfly, used in angling.

dung (dung) *n.* **1** Animal excrement; feces; manure. **2** Anything foul. — *v.t.* To cover or enrich with or as with dung. [OE] — **dung′y** *adj.*

dun·ga·ree (dung′gə·rē′) *n.* **1** A coarse cotton cloth, originally from the East Indies, used for sailors' working clothes, tents, sails, etc. **2** *pl.* Working clothes made of this fabric. [<Hind. *dungrī*]

dung beetle Any of various scarabaeid beetles that breed in dung, as the tumblebug and the sacred scarab of Egypt. Also **dung chafer.**

dun·geon (dun′jən) *n.* **1** A dark underground prison. **2** A donjon. For illustration see DONJON. See synonyms under HOLE. [<OF *donjon* <Gmc.]

dung·hill (dung′hil′) *n.* **1** A heap of manure. **2** Figuratively, a vile abode or condition. — *adj.* From or of the dunghill; ignoble.

dun·ite (dun′īt) *n.* A variety of peridotite either wholly composed of olivine or with a small amount of chromite or ilmenite. [from *Dun* Mountain, New Zealand]

dunk (dungk) *v.t.* & *v.i.* To dip or sop (bread, doughnuts, etc.) into tea, coffee, soup, etc., while eating. [<G *tunken* dip] — **dunk′er** *n.*

Dun·ker (dung′kər) *n.* One of a body of German–American Baptists, practising triple immersion and opposed to military service and the taking of legal oaths: officially called *German Baptist Brethren.* Also **Dun′kard.** [<G *tunker* < *tunken* dip]

dun·lin (dun′lin) *n.* The red-backed sandpiper (*Pelidna alpina*) of the northern hemisphere.

dun·nage (dun′ij) *n.* **1** *Naut.* Mats and battens used to protect cargo on board ship. **2** A layer of planks placed under stored goods to protect them from contact with the ground. **3** Sailors' baggage. **4** Camp equipment. [Origin uncertain]

dun·nite (dun′īt) *n.* A shock-resistant explosive composed largely of ammonium picrate: used in armor-piercing projectiles: also called *explosive D.* [after Major B. W. *Dunn,* 1860–1936, U.S. inventor]

du·o (dōō′ō, dyōō′ō) *n.* *pl.* **du·os** or **du·i** (-ē) *Music* An instrumental duet. [<Ital.]

duo– *combining form* Two: *duogravure.* [<L *duo* two]

du·o·dec·i·mal (dōō′ō-des′ə-məl, dyōō′-) *adj.* Pertaining to twelve; reckoning by twelves. — *n.* **1** One of the numbers used in duodecimal arithmetic; a twelfth. **2** *pl.* A method of computing by twelves instead of by tens. [<L *duodecimus* twelfth < *duodecim* twelve]

du·o·dec·i·mo (dōō′ō-des′ə-mō, dyōō′-) *adj.* **1** Having twelve pages or leaves to one sheet of printing paper. **2** About 4 1/2 by 7 1/2 inches in size: said of a page or book. Written also *12 mo, 12°.* — *n.* *pl.* **·mos 1** The size of a page folded twelve to a sheet; also, a page or a book of this size. **2** *Music* An interval of a twelfth. [<L (*in*) *duodecimo* (in) twelfth]

du·o·dec·u·ple (dōō′ō-dek′yōō-pəl, dyōō′-) *adj.* Consisting of twelve; having twelve parts or members; twelvefold; also, taken by twelves. — *n.* A number or sum twelve times as great as another. [<L *duodecim* twelve; infl. in form by DECUPLE]

du·o·de·cu·pli·cate (dōō′ō-de·kyōō′plə-kit, dyōō′-) *adj.* **1** Twelvefold. **2** Raised to the twelfth power. — *v.t.* (-kāt) **·cat·ed, ·cat·ing** To multiply by twelve. — *n.* One of twelve like things. — **du′o·de·cu′pli·cate·ly** *adv.*

du·o·den·a·ry (dōō′ō-den′ər·ē, -dē′nər·ē, dyōō′-) *adj.* **1** Pertaining to or determined by the number twelve. **2** Denoting or belonging to a system of arithmetical numeration of which the base is twelve. [<L *duodenarius* containing twelve]

du·o·de·ni·tis (dōō′ə·də·nī′tis, dyōō′-) *n.* *Pathol.* Inflammation of the duodenum. [<DUODEN(O)- + -ITIS]

duodeno– *combining form* Of or pertaining to the duodenum. Also, before vowels, **duoden–.** [<Med. L *duodenum* the duodenum]

du·o·de·num (dōō′ə·dē′nəm, dyōō′-, dōō·od′ə-nəm) *n.* *pl.* **·na** (-nə) *Anat.* That part of the small intestine extending from the pylorus to the jejunum. [<Med. L *duodenum* (*digitorum*) of twelve (fingers) < *duodecim* twelve; with ref. to its length] — **du′o·de′nal** *adj.*

du·o·gra·vure (dōō′ō·grə·vyōōr′, -grā′vyər, dyōō′-) *n.* **1** A process in photoengraving in which two plates are used to produce a print in two shades of one color. **2** A print made by this process. Also **du·o·graph** (dōō′ə-graf, -gräf, dyōō′-).

du·o·log (dōō′ə-lôg, -log, dyōō′-) *n.* A literary composition for two speakers; dialog. Also **du′o·logue.** [<DUO- + (MONO)LOG]

du·o·mo (dwō′mō) *n.* *pl.* **·mi** (-mē) *Italian* A cathedral.

du·o·tone (dōō′ə-tōn′, dyōō′-) *n.* A duogravure; any illustration in two tones of the same color.

du·o·type (dōō′ə-tīp′, dyōō′-) *n.* A picture produced from two halftones, the plates being from one negative, but dissimilar in etching.

dupe[1] (dōōp, dyōōp) *n.* One misled through credulity; a victim of deception. — *v.t.* **duped, dup·ing** To make a dupe of; impose upon; deceive; trick. See synonyms under DECEIVE. [<OF <L *upupa* a hoopoe (a bird thought to be stupid)] — **dup′a·bil′i·ty** *n.* — **dup′a·ble** *adj.* — **dup′er** *n.*

dupe[2] (dōōp, dyōōp) *n.* In motion pictures, a negative film made from the positive, as a source for further positives. [Short for DUPLICATE]

dup·er·y (dōō′pər·ē, dyōō′-) *n.* *pl.* **·er·ies** The act or practice of duping; the condition of being deceived.

du·pi·on (dōō′pē·ən), **du·pi·on·i** (dōō′pē·on′ē, -ō′nē) See DOUPION.

du·ple (dōō′pəl, dyōō′-) *adj.* **1** Double; twofold. **2** Having two beats to a measure, as 2–2 or 2–4 time. [<L *duplus.* See DOUBLE]

du·plex (dōō′pleks, dyōō′-) *adj.* **1** Having two parts; double; twofold. **2** Having different faces, as some kinds of paper. **3** *Mech.* Working mechanically in two ways, whether in opposite directions along the same line, upon two things, by two similar parts, or by two separate operations at once. **4** *Biol.* Double, or with twice the number of parts; twinned. — *n.* A duplex house or apartment. [<L *duo* two + stem of *plicare* fold] — **du·plex′i·ty** *n.*

duplex apartment An apartment having rooms on two floors instead of on one.

duplex house A house having two one-family units.

duplex telegraphy Telegraphy adapted to the sending of two messages simultaneously over a single wire and in opposite directions.

du·pli·cate (dōō′plə·kit, dyōō′-) *adj.* **1** Made or done exactly like an original. **2** Growing in pairs; double. **3** Replayed by other players with the same cards as originally dealt: *duplicate* whist. See also DUPLICATE BRIDGE under BRIDGE[2]. — *n.* A double or counterpart; something that exactly corresponds to an original from which it is made; a copy: originally one of two, now one of any number of like objects considered in their relation to the original and not to one another. — *v.t.* (dōō′plə·kāt′, dyōō′-) **·cat·ed, ·cat·ing 1** To make an exact copy of; reproduce exactly. **2** To double; make twofold. **3** To repeat, as an action or effort; do a second time. See synonyms under IMITATE. [<L *duplicatus,* pp. of *duplicare* double < *duplex* twofold] — **du′pli·cate·ly** *adv.*

Synonyms (noun): copy, counterpart, facsimile, imitation, likeness, replica, reproduction, transcript. A *copy* is as nearly like the original as the copyist has power to make it; a *duplicate* is exactly like the original; a carbon *copy* of a typewritten document must be a *duplicate*; we may have an inaccurate *copy,* but never an inaccurate *duplicate.* A *facsimile* is like the original in appearance; a *duplicate* is the same as the original in substance and effect; a *facsimile* of the Declaration of Independence is not a *duplicate.* A *facsimile* of a key might be quite useless; a *duplicate* will open the lock. A *counterpart* exactly corresponds to another object, but perhaps without design, while a *copy* is intentional. An *imitation* is always thought of as inferior to the original; as, an *imitation* of Milton. A *replica* is a *copy* of a work of art by the maker of the original. In law, a *transcript* is an official *copy,* authenticated by the signature of the proper officer, and by the seal of the appropriate court. *Antonyms:* archetype, model, original, pattern, prototype.

du·pli·ca·tion (dōō′plə·kā′shən, dyōō′-) *n.* The act of duplicating, or the state of being duplicated; doubling. — **du′pli·ca′tive** *adj.*

du·pli·ca·tor (dōō′plə·kā′tər, dyōō′-) *n.* **1** One who makes anything in duplicate. **2** A contrivance or device for making duplicates, as written or typewritten matter or a drawing.

du·pli·ca·ture (dōō′plə·kā′chər, dyōō′-) *n.* *Biol.* A doubling or folding, as of a membrane.

du·plic·i·ty (dōō·plis′ə·tē, dyōō′-) *n.* *pl.* **·ties 1** Tricky deceitfulness; double-dealing. **2** *Obs.* The state of being two; doubleness. See synonyms under DECEPTION, FRAUD. [<OF *duplicité* <LL *duplicitas, -tatis* doubleness < *duplex* twofold] — **du·plic′i·tous** *adj.*

du·ra[1] (dōōr′ə, dyōōr′ə) *n.* **1** Duramen. **2** The dura mater.

du·ra[2] (dōōr′ə) See DURRA.

du·ra·bil·i·ty (dōōr′ə·bil′ə·tē, dyōōr′-) *n.* **1** The quality of being durable. **2** The power of long resistance to decay or change. Also **du′ra·ble·ness.** — **du′ra·bly** *adv.*

du·ra·ble (dōōr′ə·bəl, dyōōr′-) *adj.* Able to continue long in the same state; lasting. See synonyms under PERMANENT. [<OF <L *durabilis*

< *durare* endure < *durus* hard]

du·rain (dōō·rān′, dyōō-) *n.* *Geol.* Bituminous coal having bands of a dense, hard, granular structure, often flecked with thin streaks of brighter material. [<L *durus* hard + (FUS)AIN]

du·ral (dōōr′əl, dyōōr′-) *adj.* Of, pertaining to, or derived from the dura mater.

Du·ral·u·min (dōō·ral′yə·min, dyōō-) *n.* A light, strong alloy of aluminum and copper, with addition of magnesium and manganese: a trade name.

du·ra ma·ter (dōōr′ə mā′tər, dyōōr′ə) *Anat.* The tough fibrous membrane forming the outermost covering of the brain and spinal cord. [<Med. L <L *dura* hard + *mater* mother, trans. from Arabic]

du·ra·men (dōō·rā′min, dyōō-) *n.* *Bot.* The heartwood of an exogenous stem or tree trunk; the darker central portion of the wood, comprised of dead tissue, surrounded by the alburnum. See illustration under EXOGEN. [<L, a ligneous vine branch]

dur·ance (dōōr′əns, dyōōr′-) *n.* **1** Personal restraint; imprisonment. **2** *Obs.* Duration; continuance. [<OF, duration < *durer* last <L *durare*]

du·ra·tion (dōō·rā′shən, dyōō-) *n.* **1** The period of time during which anything lasts. **2** Continuance; time in general. [<LL *duratio, -onis* < *durare* endure]

dur·a·tive (dōōr′ə·tiv, dyōōr′-) *adj.* *Gram.* Designating an aspect of the verb that expresses the action as incomplete or continuing; imperfective. — *n.* The durative aspect, or a verb in this aspect.

du·ress (dōōr′is, dyōōr′-, dōō·res′, dyōō-) *n.* Constraint by force or fear; compulsion; imprisonment. Also **du·resse′.** See synonyms under *fetter.* [<OF *duresse* hardness, constraint <L *duritia* < *durus* hard]

Dur·ham (dōōr′əm) *n.* One of a breed of short-horned beef cattle. [from *Durham,* England]

du·ri·an (dōōr′ē·ən) *n.* **1** A tall forest tree (*Durio zibethinus*) cultivated throughout the Malay Peninsula. **2** The fruit of this tree, often ten inches in length with thick, spiny rind, and custard-like pulp having a fetid odor. The seeds are eaten roasted like chestnuts. Also **du′ri·on.** [<Malay < *duri* a thorn]

dur·ing (dōōr′ing, dyōōr′-) *prep.* **1** Throughout the time, existence, or action of: The noise continued *during* the night. **2** In the course of; at some period in: He interrupted *during* the speech. [Orig. ppr. of DURE]

DURIAN FRUIT AND BLOSSOM (The tree about 80 feet in height)

dur·mast (dûr′mast, -mäst) *n.* **1** The valuable dark, tough, elastic wood of the European oak (*Quercus petraea*). **2** The tree itself. [Origin uncertain]

du·ro (dōō′rō) *n.* *pl.* **·ros** The Spanish and Spanish-American silver dollar. [<Sp. (*peso*) *duro* hard (peso) <L *durus* hard]

dur·ra (dōōr′ə) *n.* A grain sorghum of southern Asia and northern Africa; Indian millet: also spelled *dhoura, doura, dura.* Also **durr** (dōōr). [<Arabic *dhura*]

du·rum (dōōr′əm, dyōōr′-) *n.* A species of wheat (*Triticum durum*) widely grown for macaroni and spaghetti products; introduced into the United States from southern Russia and the Mediterranean. [<L, neut. sing. of *durus* hard]

dusk (dusk) *n.* **1** A state between darkness and light; twilight. **2** Swarthiness; shadowiness. — *adj.* **1** Somewhat dark or obscure by reason of failing or feeble light; dim. **2** Dark in color; swarthy. — *v.t.* & *v.i.* To make, grow, or appear shadowy or dim; darken. [OE *dox*]

dusk·i·ness (dus′kē·nis) *n.* Moderate darkness.

dusk·y (dus′kē) *adj.* **dusk·i·er, dusk·i·est 1** Somewhat dark; dim; obscure; swarthy.

2 Gloomy; dejected. Also **dusk′ish.** See synonyms under DARK. — **dusk′i·ly** adv.

dusky glider The greater glider.

dusky grouse A blue grouse (*Dendrogapus obscurus*).

dust (dust) n. **1** Any substance, as earth, reduced to powder. **2** A cloud of pulverized earth; hence, figuratively, a bewildering cloud of words, arguments, etc.; confusion; controversy. **3** Gold dust. **4** A dead body; remains. **5** The earth; the grave; figuratively, downfall or humiliation. **6** *Brit.* Rubbish; anything worthless; ashes and household sweepings. See synonyms under BODY. — **to bite the dust** To fall wounded or dead. — **to make the dust fly 1** To act or go with energy and speed. **2** To create a fuss. — **to throw dust in one's eyes** To deceive; mislead. — v.t. **1** To wipe or brush dust from. **2** To sprinkle with powder, etc. **3** To soil with dust. — v.i. **4** To wipe or brush dust from furniture, etc. **5** *Slang* To hurry away: often with *off* or *out*. See synonyms under CLEANSE. [OE *dūst*] — **dust′·less** adj.

Dust Bowl A desert region in the south central United States where the eroded topsoil of fallow lands has been blown away by dust storms. Also **dust bowl.**

dust devil *Meteorol.* A small whirlwind, often of great intensity, which lifts dust, leaves, straw, and other light material to heights of two or three hundred feet in dry or desert areas.

dust·er (dus′tər) n. **1** One who or that which dusts. **2** A cloth or brush for removing dust; a receptacle for sprinkling a powder. **3** A garment or covering to protect from dust.

dust jacket A removable covering for a book, usually of paper, and often bearing printed matter.

dust·pan (dust′pan′) n. An implement, resembling a short-handled shovel, into which dust from a floor is swept.

dust·proof (dust′prōōf′) adj. Capable of excluding dust.

dust·storm (dust′stôrm′) n. A windstorm carrying clouds of dust along with it. Also **dust storm.**

dust·y (dus′tē) adj. **dust·i·er, dust·i·est 1** Covered with or as with dust. **2** Of the color of dust. **3** Powdered, like dust. — **dust′i·ly** adv. — **dust′i·ness** n.

dusty pink A very light dull red.

Dutch (duch) adj. **1** Belonging or relating to, or characteristic of the Netherlands or its people. **2** *Archaic* Belonging or relating to the Teutonic or German peoples. **3** *Slang* German: a humorous or derogatory use. — n. **1** The people of the Netherlands: with *the*. **2** *Slang* The Germans: with *the*. **3** The Low German, West Germanic language of the Netherlands. Abbr. *Du.* — **Middle Dutch** The pre-Reformation, literary language of Flanders, Brabant, and Limburg. Abbr. *MDu.* — **to beat the Dutch** *Slang* **1** To exceed in causing surprise; surpass in strangeness. **2** To overcome stubborn resistance. **3** Excessively; extremely: adverbial use. — **to get in Dutch** *Slang* To incur disapproval. — **to go Dutch** *U.S. Colloq.* To have each participant pay his own expenses. — **to talk like a Dutch uncle** To talk with severity and kindness at the same time. [< MDu. *dutsch* Germanic, Dutch]

Dutch Belted A breed of dairy cattle originating in the Netherlands and characterized by a wide white band around the middle of the body.

Dutch Borneo See BORNEO.

Dutch cheese 1 A hard, round, skim-milk cheese; also, cottage cheese. **2** The common mallow.

Dutch door A door divided horizontally in the middle, thus allowing the opening of one half or of both.

Dutch East Indies See NETHERLANDS EAST INDIES.

Dutch elm disease A fungus disease of elms which attacks the leaves, causing defoliation, decay, and death.

Dutch foil, Dutch gold, Dutch leaf See DUTCH METAL.

Dutch Guiana See SURINAM.

dutch·man (duch′mən) n. pl. **·men** (-mən)

DUTCH DOOR

1 A piece inserted in a crevice to fill it or hide bad fitting, or to take the place of a defective piece cut out or a piece broken. **2** A shim. **3** A stick placed transversely in a load of logs to serve as a brace. **4** A buried log, or the like, serving as an anchor; a deadman.

Dutch·man (duch′mən) n. pl. **·men** (-mən) **1** A native of the Netherlands. **2** A Dutch ship. **3** *Slang* A German.

dutch·man's-breech·es (duch′mənz·brich′iz) n. A low woodland herb (*Dicentra cucullaria*) of the fumitory family, with widely spreading spurs suggesting the name. Also **dutch′mans-breech′es.**

dutch·man's-pipe (duch′mənz·pīp′) n. A climbing shrub (*Aristolochia durior*) of the Mississippi Valley, which has a calyx tube shaped like the bowl of a meerschaum pipe.

Dutch metal A malleable alloy of copper, tin, and zinc, used in the form of thin leaves as a substitute for gold leaf in bookbinding, toymaking, etc.; tombac.

Dutch oven 1 A brick oven heated by fire within it and cooking by the heat retained when the embers are removed. **2** A shallow, iron, lidded baking pot, heated by surrounding or covering it with coals. **3** A tin or sheet-steel oven used in front of an open fire, cooking by reflected heat.

du·te·ous (dōō′tē·əs, dyōō′-) adj. Rendering due respect and obedience; dutiful. — **du′te·ous·ly** adv. — **du′te·ous·ness** n.

du·ti·a·ble (dōō′tē·ə·bəl, dyōō′-) adj. Subject to impost duty.

du·tied (dōō′tēd, dyōō′-) adj. *U.S.* Subjected to taxes or customs duties.

du·ti·ful (dōō′ti·fəl, dyōō′-) adj. **1** Performing the duties of one's position; submissive to superiors; obedient. **2** Expressive of respect or of a sense of duty; respectful. See synonyms under GOOD, MORAL. — **du′ti·ful·ly** adv. — **du′ti·ful·ness** n.

du·ty (dōō′tē, dyōō′-) n. pl. **·ties 1** That which one is bound, by any natural, legal, or moral obligation, to pay, do, or perform. **2** Specific obligatory service or function, as of a soldier, sailor, etc.: He is on sea *duty*. **3** The obligation to do that which is prescribed or required, especially by the moral law; moral obligation; right action. **4** An impost or customs tax, as upon goods imported, exported, or consumed. **5** *Agric.* **a** The quantity of water necessary, in artificial irrigation, to supply adequately a definite surface of land. **b** The acreage which a stated amount of water will adequately serve: called **duty of water. 6** *Mech.* **a** The efficiency of or useful work done by an engine or motor under stated conditions. **b** The efficiency of a steam engine expressed in terms of its capacity to lift a definite weight one foot high while consuming a certain quantity of coal. **7** A formal expression of respect. — **customs duty** A tax levied on imports (or exports) for purposes of revenue or, more commonly, for the protection of domestic manufacturers. [< AF *duete* < *du* DUE]

Synonyms: accountability, business, function, obligation, office, responsibility, right, righteousness. Etymologically, *duty* is that which is owed or due; *obligation*, that to or by which one is bound; *right*, that which is correct, straight, or in the direct line of truth and goodness; *responsibility*, that for which one must answer. *Duty* and *responsibility* are thought of as to some person or persons; *right* is impersonal. One's *duty* may be to others or to himself; his *obligations* and *responsibilities* are to others. *Duty* arises from the nature of things; *obligation* and *responsibility* may be created by circumstances, as by one's own promise, or by the acceptance of a trust, etc. We speak of a parent's *duty*, a debtor's *obligation*; or of a child's *duty* of obedience, and a parent's *responsibility* for the child's welfare. *Right* is that which accords with the moral system of the universe. *Righteousness* is *right* incarnated in action. In a more limited sense, *right* may be used of what one may rightly claim, and so be the converse of *duty*. It is the creditor's *right* to demand payment, and the debtor's *duty* to pay. Compare BUSINESS, TAX, VIRTUE.

du·ty-free (dōō′tē·frē′, dyōō′-) adj. & adv. Free from customs duties.

du·um·vir (dōō·um′vər, dyōō-) n. pl. **·virs** or **·vi·ri** (vi·rī) One of two ancient Roman magistrates holding an office jointly. [< L < *duo* two + *vir* man] — **du·um′vi·ral** adj.

du·um·vi·rate (dōō·um′və·rit, dyōō-) n. **1** The joint office of duumviri. **2** A combination of two men; government by a pair of associated officials.

du·ve·tyn (dōō′və·tēn, dōō′və·tēn′) n. Twillweave fabric with a napped surface, made of wool, rayon, cotton, or silk, or combinations of fibers. Also **du′ve·tine, du′ve·tyne.** [< F *duvet* down]

dux (duks) n. pl. **du·ces** (dōō′sēz, dyōō′-) or **dux·es 1** *Scot.* The head or leader of a class in a school. **2** *Music* The subject or principal melody of a fugue. [< L, leader]

dwarf (dwôrf) n. A person, animal, or plant that is unnaturally small; especially, an adult human being less than four feet tall. — v.t. **1** To prevent the natural development of; stunt. **2** To cause to appear small by comparison. — v.i. **3** To become stunted; grow smaller. — adj. Smaller than others of its kind; diminutive; stunted. [OE *dweorh*]

dwarf alder The smaller alder-leafed buckthorn (*Rhamnus alnifolia*).

dwarf chestnut The chinkapin.

dwarf cornel A woody perennial herb (genus *Cornus*) of the dogwood family, especially the bunchberry.

dwarf mallow See under MALLOW.

dwarf star See under STAR.

dwell (dwel) v.i. **dwelt** or **dwelled, dwell·ing 1** To have a fixed abode; reside. **2** To linger, as on a subject; pause; expatiate: with *on* or *upon*. **3** To remain; continue in a state or place. See synonyms under ABIDE. — n. **1** The short cessation of motion of a part of a machine to effect its allotted service. **2** *Obs.* Stoppage; delay; pause. [OE *dwellan* mislead, hinder, stay] — **dwell′er** n.

dwell·ing (dwel′ing) n. A residence; domicile; abode. See synonyms under HOME, HOUSE.

dwelling house A house built for habitation; a domicile. In law it may embrace the dwelling itself and such buildings as are used in connection with it.

dwin·dle (dwin′dəl) v.t. & v.i. **·dled, ·dling** To diminish or become less; make or become smaller; decline. [Freq. of DWINE]

dy·ad (dī′ad) adj. **1** *Chem.* Having a combining power of two; bivalent. **2** Dyadic. — n. **1** A pair of units; duad. **2** *Chem.* An atom, radical, or element that has a combining power of two. See VALENCE. **3** *Biol.* **a** One of a pair of chromosomes, especially in the prophases of the second division in the formation of gametes. See TETRAD. **b** A secondary unit made up of an aggregate of monads. [< L *dyas, dyadis* < Gk. *dyas* the number two]

dy·ad·ic (dī·ad′ik) adj. **1** Of or pertaining to a dyad. **2** Based on or relating to the number 2; binary.

Dy·ak (dī′ak) n. **1** One of the aboriginal people of Borneo, linguistically akin to the Malays, but differing from them in stature, type, and culture. **2** The Indonesian language of these people. Also spelled *Dayak*.

dye (dī) v. **dyed, dye·ing** v.t. **1** To fix a color by soaking in liquid coloring matter. **2** To stain; tinge. — v.i. **3** To take or give color: This cloth *dyes* badly. See synonyms under STAIN. — n. A fluid or coloring matter used for dyeing; also, the color or hue so produced. According to the method of application, dyes are classified as *substantive*, or *direct*, when they color by simple immersion; *adjective*, or *mordant*, when a fixing agent is used; *ingrain*, or *ice*, when deposited by chemical reaction; *vat*, when applied in an alkalisoluble state and oxidized; and *sulfur*, when used in a sodium sulfide bath followed by oxidation. ◆ Homophone: die. [OE *dēagian* < *deag* dye, color]

dye·house (dī′hous′) n. A building in which dyeing is done.

dyed-in-the-wool (dīd′in·thə·wōōl′) adj. **1** Dyed before being woven. **2** Thoroughgoing; complete.

dye·ing (dī′ing) n. The act, process, or trade of fixing colors in cloth or the like.

dy·er (dī′ər) n. One who or that which dyes; especially, a person engaged in the business of dyeing.

dy·er's-broom (dī′ərz·broom′, -broom′) *n.* A shrubby plant *(Genista tinctoria)* yielding a yellow dye which with woad becomes a permanent green; woadwaxen: also called *dyeweed.* Also **dyer's-green-weed** (dī′ərz-grēn′-wēd′).

dy·er's-weed (dī′ərz-wēd′) *n.* Any of several plants that yield dyeing matter, such as dyer's woad *(Isatis tinctoria).*

dy·ing (dī′ing) *adj.* **1** Becoming dead; near to death; expiring; closing. **2** Destined to die; mortal; perishable. **3** Relating to death; given, uttered, or manifested just before death.

dyna- *combining form* Power: *dynameter.* Also, before vowels, **dyn-.**

dy·nam·e·ter (dī·nam′ə·tər) *n. Optics* A device for measuring the magnifying power of telescopes. [< DYNA- + METER]

dy·nam·ic (dī·nam′ik) *adj.* **1** Of or pertaining to forces not in equilibrium, or to motion as the result of force: opposed to *static.* **2** Pertaining to or characterized by mechanical force. **3** Producing or involving activity or action of any kind; motive; efficient; causal. **4** Mentally or spiritually energetic, forceful, or powerful: a *dynamic* leader. **5** Of or pertaining to musical dynamics. Also **dy·nam′i·cal.** [< Gk. *dynamikos* powerful < *dynamis* power] **—dy·nam′i·cal·ly** *adv.*

dy·nam·ics (dī·nam′iks) *n. pl. (construed as singular in defs. 1,2, and 4)* **1** The branch of physics that treats of the motion of bodies and the effects of forces in producing motion, and of the laws of the motion thus produced *(kinetics)*: opposed to *statics.* **2** The science that treats of the action of forces, whether producing equilibrium or motion; in this sense including both statics and kinetics. **3** The forces producing or governing activity or movement of any kind; also, the methods of such activity: spiritual *dynamics.* **4** *Music* **a** The words, symbols, etc., used to indicate degrees of loudness: also **dynamic marks. b** The act or technique of producing varying degrees of loudness.

dy·na·mism (dī′nə·miz′əm) *n.* **1** *Philos.* One of various doctrines that endeavor to explain the phenomena of the universe, chiefly or wholly, in terms of force or energy. **2** *Psychol.* Any of various psychic forces, as repression, sublimation, etc., acting to produce certain effects upon behavior or the personality: also called *mechanism.* **—dy′na·mist** *n.* **—dy′na·mis′tic** *adj.*

dy·na·mite (dī′nə·mīt) *n.* **1** An explosive composed of nitroglycerin held in an absorbent substance. **2** *Slang* Anything wonderful or spectacular: The news was *dynamite!* —*v.t.* **·mit·ed, ·mit·ing 1** To blow up or shatter with or as with dynamite. **2** To charge with dynamite; as a mine. [< Gk. *dynamis* power]

dy·na·mo (dī′nə·mō) *n. pl.* **·mos** A machine for the conversion of mechanical energy into

DYNAMO

electrical energy through the agency of electromagnetic induction. Compare GENERATOR and ELECTRIC MOTOR. [Short for DYNAMOELECTRIC MACHINE]

dynamo- *combining form* Force; power: *dynamograph.* [< Gk. *dynamis* power]

dy·na·mo·e·lec·tric (dī′nə·mō·i·lek′trik) *adj.* Pertaining to the relation between electricity and mechanical force. Also **dy′na·mo·e·lec′tri·cal.**

dy·na·mog·e·ny (dī′nə·moj′ə·nē) *n. Physiol.* Production of increased nervous activity; the reinforcing effect of sensorial stimuli upon muscular action. [< DYNAMO- + -GENY]

dy·nam·o·graph (dī·nam′ə·graf, -gräf) *n.* A recording dynamometer; specifically, one used to register muscular power. Also **dy′no·graph.**

dy·na·mom·e·ter (dī′nə·mom′ə·tər) *n.* An instrument for measuring force exerted or power expended, as by a machine. [< DYNAMO- + -METER] **—dy·na·mo·met·ric** (dī′nə·mō·met′rik) or **·ri·cal** *adj.*

dy·na·mo·path·ic (dī′nə·mō·path′ik) *adj. Med.* Having an effect upon the character or course of bodily functions.

dy·nast (dī′nast, -nəst) *n.* A monarch; ruler. [< L *dynastes* < Gk. *dynastēs* < *dynasthai* be powerful]

dy·nas·ty (dī′nəs·tē) *n. pl.* **·ties** A succession of sovereigns in one line of family descent governing the same country; also, the length of time during which one family is in power. **—dy·nas′tic** (dī·nas′tik) or **·ti·cal** *adj.* **—dy·nas′ti·cal·ly** *adv.*

dy·na·tron (dī′nə·tron) *n. Electronics* A four-electrode vacuum tube designed to utilize the secondary emission of electrons to decrease the plate current as the plate voltage increases; used as an oscillator in radio. [< DYNA- + (ELEC)TRON]

dyne (dīn) *n. Physics* The fundamental unit of force in the cgs system that, if applied to a mass of one gram, would give it an acceleration of one centimeter per second per second. Abbr. *d., D.* [< F < Gk. *dynamis* power]

dys- *combining form* Bad; defective; difficult; hard: *dysphasia, dyspnea:* opposed to *eu-.* [< Gk. *dys-* bad, difficult]

dys·cra·si·a (dis·krā′zhē·ə, -zhə) *n. Pathol.* **1** A depraved condition of the system and especially of the blood, due to constitutional disease. **2** General bad health. [< Med. L < Gk. *dyskrasia* bad temperament < *dys-* bad + *krasia* mixture] **—dys·cra′si·al, dys·cras·ic** (dis·kraz′ik, -kras′-) *adj.*

dys·e·mi·a (dis·ē′mē·ə) *n. Pathol.* A morbid or vitiated condition of the blood, especially as due to mineral poisoning. Also **dys·ae′mi·a.** [< NL < Gk. *dys-* hard + *haima* blood]

dys·en·ter·y (dis′ən·ter′ē) *n. Pathol.* A severe inflammation of the mucous membrane of the large intestine, attended with bloody evacuations, griping pains, and some fever; bloody flux. [< OF *dysenterie* < L *dysenteria* < Gk. *< dys-* bad + *enteron* intestine] **—dys′en·ter′ic** or **·i·cal** *adj.*

dys·es·the·si·a (dis′əs·thē′zhē·ə, -zhə) *n. Pathol.* Loss of sensation, partial or complete; numbness. Also **dys′aes·the′si·a.**

dys·func·tion (dis·fungk′shən) *n.* Deterioration of the natural action of (anything); malfunction.

dys·gen·ic (dis·jen′ik) *adj.* Relating to or causing the biological impairment or deterioration of a strain or race, especially man: opposite of *eugenic.*

dys·gen·ics (dis·jen′iks) *n. pl. (construed as singular)* The science dealing with the factors operating to produce biological, and especially genetic, deterioration in the offspring of animals.

dys·ge·og·e·nous (dis′jē·oj′ə·nəs) *adj. Bot.* Growing on soils, such as granite or hard rocks generally, which do not readily yield a detritus: said of plants. [< DYS- + Gk. *gē* earth, soil + -GENOUS]

dys·ki·ne·si·a (dis′ki·nē′zhē·ə, -zhə) *n. Pathol.* Loss or impairment of the power of voluntary movement. [< Gk. *dyskinēsia* < *dys-* hard + *kinesis* movement] **—dys′ki·net′ic** *adj.*

dys·lex·i·a (dis·lek′sē·ə) *n. Pathol.* Loss of the ability to read due to a central brain lesion. [< NL < Gk. *dys-* hard + *lexis* speech, word]

dys·lo·gis·tic (dis′lō·jis′tik) *adj.* Conveying disapproval or censure: opposed to eulogistic. [< DYS- + (EU)LOGISTIC] **—dys′lo·gis′ti·cal·ly** *adv.*

dys·men·or·rhe·a (dis·men′ə·rē′ə) *n. Pathol.* Difficult or painful menstruation. Also **dys·men′or·rhoe′a.** [< NL < Gk. *dys-* hard + *mēn, mēnos* month + *rheein* flow]

dys·pep·si·a (dis·pep′shə, -sē·ə) *n.* Difficult or painful digestion, generally chronic. [< L < Gk. *< dys-* hard + *peptein* cook, digest]

dys·pha·gi·a (dis·fā′jē·ə) *n. Pathol.* Great difficulty in swallowing due to some constriction of the muscles of the throat. [< NL < Gk. *dys-* hard + *phagein* eat] **—dys·phag′ic** (-faj′ik) *adj.*

dys·pha·sia (dis·fā′zhə, -zhē·ə) *n.* Partial aphasia or incoherent speech due to a brain lesion. **—dys·pha′sic** *adj.* [< NL < Gk. *dys-* hard + *phasis* utterance]

dys·pho·ni·a (dis·fō′nē·ə) *n. Psychiatry* Difficulty in uttering articulate sounds; harsh, abnormal, or indistinct vocalization. [< NL < Gk. *dysphōnia* roughness of sound < *dys-* hard + *phōnē* sound] **—dys·phon′ic** (-fon′ik) *adj.*

dys·pho·ri·a (dis·fôr′ē·ə, -fō′rē·ə) *n. Pathol.* A chronic feeling of illness and discontent: opposite of *euphoria.* [< NL < Gk. *dysphoria* < *dys-* hard + *phoreein* suffer]

dys·phot·ic (dis·fot′ik, -fō′tik) *adj.* Dimly illumined, as the bottom of a deep canyon or the sea depths. **—***n.* Any plant or animal adapted to such surroundings. [< Gk. *dys-* hard, defective + *phōs, phōtos* light]

dysp·noe·a (disp·nē′ə) *n. Pathol.* Labored, difficult breathing. Also **dysp·ne′a.** [< NL < L *dyspnoea* < Gk. *dyspnoia* < *dys-* hard + *pneein* breathe] **—dysp·noe′al** or **·ic, dysp·ne′al** or **·ic** *adj.*

dys·tax·i·a (dis·tak′sē·ə) *n. Pathol.* Muscular tremor, resulting from disorder of the spinal cord. [< NL < Gk. *dys-* hard, defective + *taxis* arrangement]

dys·tro·phy (dis′trə·fē) *n.* Defective or perverted nutrition. Also **dys·tro·phi·a** (dis·trō′fē·ə). [< NL *dystrophia* < Gk. *dys-* hard, defective + *trophē* nourishment]

dys·tro·py (dis′trə·pē) *n. Psychiatry* Abnormal behavior, however caused. [< DYS- + Gk. *tropē* a turning, change] **—dys·trop′ic** (-trop′ik) *adj.*

dys·u·ri·a (dis·yoor′ē·ə) *n. Pathol.* Difficult, painful, or incomplete urination. [< LL < Gk. *dysouria* < *dys-* hard + *ouron* urine] **—dys·u′ric** *adj.*

Dzaoud·zi (dzoud′zē) Capital of the Comoro Islands.

Dzau·dzhi·kau (dzou·jē′kou) A city on the Terek, capital of North Ossetian Autonomous S.S.R.: formerly *Ordzhonikidze.*

Dzer·dzhinsk (dyer·zhinsk′) A city on the Oka in European Russian S.F.S.R.

E

e, E (ē) *n. pl.* **e's, E's** or **es, Es, ees** (ēz) **1** The fifth letter of the English alphabet: from Phoenician *he,* through Hebrew *he,* Greek *epsilon,* and Roman *E.* **2** Any sound of the letter *e.* See AL-

PHABET.

—*symbol* **1** *Music* **a** The third tone in the natural scale of C, *mi;* the pitch of this tone, or the note representing it. **b** The scale built upon E. **2** *Math.* The limit of the expression $(1 + 1/n)^n$, as *n* increases without limit: 2.7182818284+: the base to which Napierian logarithms are calculated: written *e.*

each (ēch) *adj.* Being one of two or more indi-

e- Reduced var. of EX-.

viduals that together form an aggregate; every. —*pron.* Every one of any number or aggregation considered individually; each one. See synonyms under EVERY. —*adv.* For or to each person, article, etc.; apiece: one dollar *each.* [OE *ælc* < *a* ever + *gelic* alike]

each other A compound reciprocal pronoun used in oblique cases: They saw *each other.* that is, Each saw the other. The possessive case is *each other's.*

ea·ger¹ (ē′gər) *adj.* 1 Impatiently anxious for something. 2 Showing insistent or intense feeling or desire. 3 *Obs.* Sour; tart; pungent. [< OF *aigre* < L *acer* sharp] —**ea′ger·ly** *adv.* —**ea′ger·ness** *n.* — *Synonyms:* animated, anxious, ardent, avid, burning, desirous, earnest, enthusiastic, fervent, glowing, hot, impatient, impetuous, importunate, intense, intent, keen, longing, vehement, yearning, zealous. One is *eager* who impatiently desires to accomplish some end; one is *earnest* with a desire that is less impatient, but more deep, resolute, and constant; one is *anxious* with a desire that foresees rather the pain of disappointment than the delight of attainment. One is *eager* for the gratification of any appetite or passion; he is *earnest* in conviction, purpose, or character. *Eager* usually refers to some specific and immediate satisfaction, *earnest,* to something permanent and enduring; the patriotic soldier is *earnest* in his devotion to his country, *eager* for a decisive battle. See ARDENT, HOT. Compare ENTHUSIASM. *Antonyms:* apathetic, calm, careless, cold, cool, dispassionate, frigid, heedless, indifferent, negligent, phlegmatic, purposeless, regardless, stolid, stony, stupid, unconcerned, uninterested, unmindful, unmoved.

ea·ger² (ē′gər, ā′-) *n.* A sudden flood of the tide in an estuary: also *eagre.* See BORE². [Prob. OE *ēa* river + *gār* storm]

ea·gle (ē′gəl) *n.* 1 Any of various species of very large diurnal predatory birds of the family Accipitridae of worldwide distribution, notable for keen sight and strong flight. ◆ Collateral adjective: *aquiline.* 2 A gold coin of the United States, value $10, weight 258 grains: withdrawn from circulation 1934. 3 A Roman military standard, bearing the image of an eagle; also adopted as a standard by France during the two empires. 4 Any article in the design of which an eagle is prominent. 5 In golf, two strokes less than par in playing a hole. [< OF *egle, aigle* < L *aquila*]

Ea·gle (ē′gəl) The constellation Aquila. See CONSTELLATION.

ea·gle-eyed (ē′gəl-īd′) *adj.* Keen-sighted like an eagle.

eagle owl A large predatory European owl (*Bubo bubo*).

eagle ray Any of a family (Myliobatidae) of rays having the eyes and spiracles at the sides of the head and usually bearing a single dorsal spine on the long, whiplike tail.

ea·glet (ē′glit) *n.* A young eagle.

ear¹ (ir) *n.* 1 The organ of hearing: in man and other mammals it consists of an *auricle*

NOMENCLATURE: FRONTAL SECTION OF HUMAN EAR

piece, handle, etc. 5 The external ear alone. 6 *pl.* Spiritual understanding. —**about one's ears** Surrounding one on all sides, as falling objects. —

and external auditory *meatus* for collecting sounds, a *tympanum,* containing the *ossicles* for transmitting them, and a *labyrinth* that includes the *cochlea* for delivering them to the end organs of the auditory nerve. ◆ Collateral adjective: *aural.* 2 The sense of hearing; especially, nice perception of musical sounds. 3 Attentive consideration; heed. 4 Anything like the external ear, as a projecting by the ears In close struggle or conflict; at variance; as in to set by the ears, to cause discord between. —up to the ears *Colloq.* Almost covered, as one sinking; almost at the end of one's resources. [OE *ēare*] —**ear′less** *adj.*

ear² (ir) *n.* The fruit-bearing part of a cereal plant; the head. —**in** (or **on**) **the ear** On the cob, as corn; unhusked, as grain. —*v.i.* To form ears, as grain. [OE *ēar*]

ear·ache (ir′āk′) *n.* Pain in the middle or internal ear; otalgia.

ear·drum (ir′drum′) *n.* The tympanum or the tympanic membrane.

eared seal Any of a family (*Otariidae*) of seals; the sea lion and the fur seals.

earl (ûrl) *n.* A member of the British nobility next above a viscount. *Earl* is the equivalent of the Norman *count,* in Norman French, and the wife of an earl is still called *countess.* [OE *eorl* nobleman]

ear·lap (ir′lap′) *n.* 1 The external ear; especially, the lobes. 2 An earflap.

earl·dom (ûrl′dəm) *n.* The dignity, prerogative, or territory of an earl.

ear·ly (ûr′lē) *adj.* **·li·er, ·li·est** 1 Being near the beginning of any stated period of time or definite course of existence; being or occurring among the first in a series; ancient. 2 Being or occurring sooner than is usual or necessary. 3 About to be or happen; soon to occur. [< *adv.*] —*adv.* 1 At or near the beginning of a period of time. 2 In good time or season. —**early on** Near the beginning. [OE *ærlīce* < *ær* sooner + -*līce* -ly] —**ear′li·ness** *n.*

ear·mark (ir′märk′) *v.t.* 1 To make a mark of identification on. 2 To mark an animal's ear. 3 To set aside for special purposes, as money. —*n.* An owner's mark on an animal's ear; any mark of identification.

ear·mind·ed (ir′mīn′did) *adj.* Having a marked preference for auditory images in the various mental processes. —**ear′·mind′ed·ness** *n.*

ear·mold (ir′mōld′) *n.* A plastic mold to be worn in the ear as a means of conducting sound from the earphone of a hearing aid.

ear·muff (ir′muf′) *n.* One of a pair of adjustable coverings for the ears, worn as a protection against cold.

earn (ûrn) *v.t.* 1 To receive, as salary or wages, for labor or exertion. 2 To merit as a result, reward, or punishment; deserve: He *earned* our condemnation. 3 To bring in (interest, etc.) as gain or profit. See synonyms under GAIN¹, GET, OBTAIN. ◆ Homophones: *erne, urn.* [OE *earnian*] —**earn′er** *n.*

ear·nest¹ (ûr′nist) *adj.* 1 Intent and direct in purpose; zealous; fervent: of persons. 2 Marked by deep feeling or conviction; heart-felt; hearty: of words or acts. 3 Requiring careful consideration; serious; important. See synonyms under EAGER, SERIOUS. —*n.* Seriousness; reality, as opposed to pretense or trifling. —**in earnest** With full and serious intent; real and intended. [OE *eorneste*] —**ear′nest·ly** *adv.* —**ear′nest·ness** *n.*

ear·nest² (ûr′nist) *n.* 1 Money paid in advance to bind a bargain. 2 An assurance of something to come; pledge. See synonyms under SECURITY. [Prob. < OF *erres* < L *arra, arrhabo* < Gk. *arrhabōn* < Hebrew *'ērābōn;* infl. by EARNEST¹]

earn·ing (ûr′ning) *n. Usually pl.* That which is earned; compensation; wages; salary.

ear·phone (ir′fōn′) *n.* 1 A headphone. 2 That part of an electronic hearing aid which transmits sound by air conduction through the earmold.

ear·plug (ir′plug′) *n.* A wax or plastic mold inserted into the ear to exclude water or noise, as in swimming or sleeping.

ear·ring (ir′ring′) *n.* A ring or hook usually with a pendant, worn at the ear.

ear·shot (ir′shot′) *n.* The distance at which sounds may be heard.

ear·split·ting (ir′split′ing) *adj.* Painfully loud or

high-pitched; deafening.

earth (ûrth) *n.* 1 The solid portion or surface of the globe; ground. 2 Soil as distinguished from rock. 3 Those who inhabit the globe; the world at large. 4 The hole of a burrowing animal. 5 *Electr.* a The ground that forms part of an electric circuit. b A fault in a telegraphic or telephonic line, caused by connection of the conductor with the ground; also such connection. 6 Any natural soft soil, as clay and ocher. 7 *Chem.* A rare earth. 8 Temporal and transient interests and pursuits as contrasted with those that are spiritual; material things; worldly matters. 9 *Obs.* A locality upon the earth; country. See synonyms under LAND. —**down to earth** Realistic; unfanciful. —**to run to earth** To hunt down and find, as a fox. —*v.t.* 1 To bank up or protect with earth, as plants, flowers, etc. 2 To chase, as a fox, into a burrow or hole. 3 *Electr.* To ground. —*v.i.* 4 To burrow or hide in the earth, as a fox. [OE *eorthe*]

Earth (ûrth) 1 The third planet in order of distance from the sun and fifth in order of size among the planets. It has an area of 196,400,000 square miles, a mass of 6.57 sextillion tons (6.57×10^{21}), a mean diameter of 7,918 miles, and a mean solar distance of 93,000,000 miles. ◆ Collateral adjectives: *telluric, terrestrial.* 2 The abode of man, considered as distinct from Heaven and Hell.

earth-born (ûrth′bôrn′) *adj.* 1 Born out of the earth; of earthly origin. 2 Of terrestrial birth, as distinguished from celestial origin. 3 Springing from earthly or temporal considerations; mean or ignoble.

earth-bound (ûrth′bound′) *adj.* 1 Having only material interests. 2 Firmly fixed in or on the earth.

earth color Any of several pigments or paints prepared from naturally occurring earth materials, as umber, ocher, chalk.

earth current 1 *Electr.* A direct current induced in the earth by grounded currents near powerhouses and thought responsible for the corrosion of the lead sheaths of cables, etc. 2 An electrical current, variable in strength, duration, and direction, which circulates within the earth's crust.

earth-en (ûr′thən) *adj.* Made of earth or baked clay; earthly.

earth-en-ware (ûr′thən-wâr′) *n.* Pottery, especially of inferior grade, as distinguished from porcelain and stoneware.

earth flax 1 Asbestos. 2 Amianthus.

earth inductor *Electr.* An induction coil which may be sharply rotated in the earth's magnetic field in order to determine the intensity of the field by the strength of the induced current as read on a galvanometer.

earth inductor compass A form of earth inductor designed to aid the pilot of an aircraft in maintaining a correct flight path with reference to the earth's magnetic field.

earth-i-ness (ûr′thē-nis) *n.* The quality of being earthy or like earth.

earth-light (ûrth′līt′) *n.* 1 Light sometimes visible at night, not directly attributable to sun, moon, or stars. 2 Earthshine.

earth-ling (ûrth′ling) *n.* A worldling or mortal.

earth-ly (ûrth′lē) *adj.* 1 Pertaining to the earth or the world of the present; material; secular; worldly; carnal. 2 *Colloq.* Possible; imaginable: of no *earthly* use. —**earth′li·ness** *n.*

earth-nut (ûrth′nut′) *n.* 1 The tuber of any one of several sedges. 2 The peanut. 3 Either of two European herbs (genus *Carum*) of the parsley family, as the caraway. 4 A truffle.

earth pea The hog peanut.

earth plate *Electr.* A ground plate.

earth-quake (ûrth′kwāk′) *n.* A vibration or sudden undulation of a portion of the earth's crust, caused by the splitting or faulting of a mass of rock or by volcanic or other disturbances. ◆ Collateral adjective: *seismic.*

earth return *Electr.* The return path through the earth of an electric circuit which is completed by it: also called *ground-return circuit.*

earth-shine (ûrth′shīn′) *n. Astron.* Sunlight reflected from the earth so as to illuminate slightly those parts of the moon not in the direct rays of the sun.

earth-star (ûrth′stär′) *n.* A fungus (genus *Geaster*) having the outer coat distinct from the inner and split into several reflexed divisions suggestive of a star.

earth·ward (ûrth'wərd) *adv.* Toward the earth: also **earth'wards.** — *adj.* Moving toward the earth.

earth·work (ûrth'wûrk') *n.* **1** *Mil.* An offensive or wholly of earth. **2** *Engin.* An operation or work, as a cutting or an embankment, requiring the removal of or filling in with earth. **3** Anything similar to a military earthwork.

earth·worm (ûrth'wûrm') *n.* **1** A burrowing terrestrial annelid (family *Lumbricidae*), useful for enriching the soil. **2** A weak and insignificant or sordid person.

earth·y (ûr'thē) *adj.* **earth·i·er, earth·i·est** **1** Of, pertaining to, or like earth or soil; made of earth. **2** Unrefined; coarse.

ear trumpet An instrument made to collect and concentrate sound. Compare HEARING AID.

ear·wax (ir'waks') *n.* A waxy substance secreted by the glands lining the passages of the external ear; cerumen.

ear·wig (ir'wig') *n.* **1** An insect (family *Forficulidae*) with horny, short (or absent) forewings and a caudal pair of forceps: erroneously believed to enter the human ear. For illustration see under INSECT (injurious). **2** Loosely, in the United States, a small centipede. **3** *Obs.* A secret informer. — *v.t.* **·wigged, ·wig·ging** To influence by secret and stealthy counsel; to insinuate against by or as by whispering in the ear. [OE *earwicga*]

ease (ēz) *n.* **1** Freedom from pain, agitation, or perplexity; comfort. **2** Freedom from or absence of apparent effort; facility. **3** Freedom from affectation or constraint. — *v.* **eased, eas·ing** *v.t.* **1** To relieve the mental or physical pain or oppression of; comfort. **2** To make less painful or oppressive: This will *ease* your pain. **3** To lessen the pressure, weight, tension, etc., of: to *ease* an axle. **4** To move, lower, or put in place gradually and with care. **5** *Colloq.* To rob: with *of*: a humorous usage: He was *eased* of his wallet. **6** *Rare* To facilitate. — *v.i.* **7** To diminish in severity, speed, etc.: often with *up* or *off*: The pain *eased.* — **to ease away** (or **off**) To move away slightly, as one ship from another. — **to ease the helm** *Naut.* To put the helm a trifle to midships so as to reduce the strain on the rudder. [< OF *aise* < LL *adjacens, -entis* neighboring. See ADJACENT.] — **ease'ful·ly** *adv.* — **ease'ful·ness** *n.*

Synonyms (noun): easiness, expertness, facility, knack, readiness. *Ease* may be either of condition or of action; *facility* is always of action; *readiness* is of action or of expected action. One lives at *ease* who has no pressing cares; one stands at *ease*, moves or speaks with *ease*, when wholly without restraint. *Facility* is always active; *readiness* may be active or passive; the speaker has *facility* of expression, *readiness* of wit. *Ease* of action may imply merely the possession of ample power; *facility* always implies practice and skill. *Readiness* in the active sense includes much of the meaning of *ease* with the added idea of promptness or alertness. *Easiness* applies to the thing done, rather than to the doer. *Expertness* applies to the more mechanical processes of body and mind; we speak of the *readiness* of an orator, but of the *expertness* of a gymnast. Compare COMFORTABLE, DEXTERITY, POWER. *Antonyms:* annoyance, awkwardness, constraint, difficulty, discomfort, disquiet, trouble, uneasiness, vexation, worry.

ea·sel (ē'zəl) *n.* A folding frame for supporting a picture, panel, etc. [< Du. *ezel* easel, orig. an ass]

ease·ment (ēz'mənt) *n.* **1** *Law* The incorporeal privilege or right of making limited use of another's adjacent property, as for access over a road or path, or for a telephone line, water pipe, or the like. **2** Relief. **3** Anything that gives ease or relief.

eas·i·ly (ē'zə·lē) *adv.* In an easy manner; readily; quietly.

eas·i·ness (ē'zi·nis) *n.* The state of being at ease, or of being easy to do or accomplish.

east (ēst) *n.* **1** The point of the compass at which the sun rises at the equinox, directly opposite *west*. See COMPASS CARD. **2** Any direction, region, or part of the horizon near that point. — **Far East** Eastern Asia, including China, Japan, and adjacent islands. — **Middle East** **1** The region generally including the countries of SW Asia lying west of Pakistan and India. **2** *Brit.* This region with the exception of Turkey and including India, Pakistan, Burma, Tibet, Libya, Ethiopia, and Somaliland. — **Near East** **1** The countries lying east of the Mediterranean, mostly in SW Asia, including Turkey, Syria, Lebanon, Israel, Jordan, Saudi Arabia, etc., and sometimes the Balkans and Egypt. **2** *Brit.* The Balkans. — **the East** **1** The part of the earth including Asia and the adjacent islands; the Orient. **2** In the United States: **a** The region eastward of the Mississippi and north of the Ohio. **b** The region east of the Allegheny Mountains and north of Maryland. — *adj.* **1** To, toward, facing, or placed in the east; eastern. **2** Coming from the east: the *east* wind. **3** Near the altar of a church as seen from the nave. — *adv.* In or toward the east; in an easterly direction. — *v.i.* To go or turn toward the east; proceed in an easterly direction. [OE]

east·bound (ēst'bound') *adj.* Going eastward. Also **east'bound.**

east by north One point north of east on the mariner's compass. See COMPASS CARD.

east by south One point south of east on the mariner's compass. See COMPASS CARD.

East·er (ēs'tər) *n.* **1** A Christian festival commemorating the resurrection of Christ. **2** The day on which this festival is celebrated, the Sunday immediately after the first full moon that occurs on or after March 21: also **Easter Day.** [OE *Eastre* goddess of spring]

east·er·ly (ēs'tər·lē) *adj.* **1** Situated, moving, or directed toward the east; eastward. **2** Coming from the east: said of winds. — *adv.* Toward the east: also **east'ern·ly.**

East·ern·er (ēs'tərn·ər) *n.* *U.S.* One who dwells in the eastern part of the United States.

Eastern Standard Time See STANDARD TIME. Abbr. *E.S.T.*

East·er·tide (ēs'tər·tīd') *n.* **1** The season of Easter; a period extending in various churches from Easter to Ascension Day, Whitsunday, or Trinity Sunday. **2** The week beginning with and immediately following Easter. [< EASTER + TIDE[1] (def. 4)]

East Flanders A province of NW Belgium; 1,147 square miles; capital, Ghent. *Flemish* **Oost–Vlaan·de·ren** (ôst'vlän'də·rən).

East India Company The name of various mercantile associations organized in the 17th and 18th centuries by Europeans to carry on trade with the East Indies: notably the British, Dutch, and French companies.

East Indies **1** The islands of the Malay Archipelago. **2** SE Asia. **3** *Archaic* India. Also **East India.** — **East Indian.**

east–north·east (ēst'nôrth'ēst') *adj., adv.,* & *n.* Midway between east and northeast. See COMPASS CARD.

Eas·ton (ēs'tən) A city on the Delaware River in eastern Pennsylvania.

east–south·east (ēst'south'ēst') *adj., adv.,* & *n.* Midway between east and southeast. See COMPASS CARD.

East St. Louis A city in SW Illinois on the Mississippi River.

east·ward (ēst'wərd) *adj.* Running, tending, or situated in an easterly direction. — *adv.* Toward the east: also **east'wards.** Also **east'ward·ly.**

eas·y (ē'zē) *adj.* **eas·i·er, eas·i·est** **1** Not involving great exertion, discomfort, or difficulty. **2** Free from discomfort or anxiety; comfortable. **3** Possessed of a sufficient competence. **4** Free from embarrassment or affectation; natural. **5** Yielding; indulgent. **6** Gentle; tractable. **7** Causing no disquiet or discomfort; not burdensome. **8** Self-indulgent. **9** Not straitened or tight, as money. **10** To be paid in small instalments: *easy* terms. **11** Not having much current: *easy* water. — **to go easy on** To be moderate in the use of; also, to be tactful about. — **to live on easy street** To be in good financial circumstances. [< OF *aisé*, pp. of *aiser, aisier* put at ease]

eas·y–go·ing (ē'zē·gō'ing) *adj.* **1** Not inclined to effort or worry; complacently unconcerned. **2** Moving at an easy pace, as a horse.

eat (ēt) *v.* **ate** (ēt) *or Brit.* **eat** (et), **eat·en, eat·ing** *v.t.* **1** To take (food) into the mouth and swallow. **2** To consume or destroy by or as by eating: often with *away* or *up*. **3** To wear into or away; corrode; rust. **4** To make (a way or hole) by or as by gnawing or chewing. — *v.i.* **5** To take in food; have a meal. **6** To bore into or corrode something: with *through* or *into*. — **to eat crow** To accept what one had been against; submit to humiliation. — **to eat humble pie** To make humble apologies. — **to eat one's words** To retract what one has said. — **to eat up** **1** To consume completely. **2** To pass over rapidly: to *eat up* the miles. [OE *etan*] — **eat'er** *n.*

eat·a·ble (ē'tə·bəl) *n.* Something edible: often in the plural. — *adj.* Fit to be eaten; edible.

eat·ing (ē'ting) *n.* **1** The act of taking food. **2** Food: Brook trout are good *eating.*

Eau Claire (ō klâr') A city in west central Wisconsin.

eaves (ēvz) *n. pl.* The projecting edge of a roof. [OE *efes* edge]

eaves·drip (ēvz'drip') *n.* An ancient law forbidding the erection of a building so close to a boundary line that the eaves would drip on the land of another.

eaves·drop (ēvz'drop') *v.i.* **·dropped, ·drop·ping** To listen, or try to listen, secretly, as to a private conversation. — *n.* **1** Water that drops from the eaves. **2** The line near the wall of a house made by such droppings. Also **eave'drop'.** [< *eavesdrop, n.*; with ref. to one who listens within the eavesdrop] — **eaves'drop'per** *n.* — **eaves'drop'ping** *n.*

ebb (eb) *v.i.* **1** To recede, as the tide. **2** To decline; fail. — *n.* **1** The reflux of tidewater to the ocean; low tide: opposed to *flood*: also **ebb tide.** **2** Decrease; condition or period of decline. See synonyms under ABATE. [OE *ebbian*]

E·bi·o·nite (ē'bē·ə·nīt') *n.* One of a party in the early church, second to fourth century, chiefly made up of Pharisees and Essenes. Compare NAZARENE. [< L *ebionita* < Hebrew *'ebyôn* poor] — **E'bi·o·nit'ic** (-nit'ik) *adj.*

eb·on (eb'ən) *adj.* **1** Of ebony. **2** Very black. — *n.* Ebony.

eb·on·ite (eb'ən·īt) *n.* Black vulcanite, or hard rubber.

eb·on·ize (eb'ən·īz) *v.t.* **·ized, ·iz·ing** To stain or polish, as wood, in imitation of ebony.

eb·on·y (eb'ən·ē) *n. pl.* **·on·ies** **1** A hard, heavy wood, usually black, used for cabinetwork, etc. It is furnished by various species of a tropical genus (*Diospyros*) of hardwood trees. **2** Any tree of this genus, especially *D. ebenum* of Ceylon and Southern India. — *adj.* Made of ebony; ebonylike. [< L *hebeninus* < Gk. *hebeninos* of ebony < *ebenos* ebony < Egyptian *hebni*]

e·brac·te·ate (ē·brak'tē·āt) *adj. Bot.* Without bracts. [< NL *ebracteatus* < L *ex-* without + *bractea* plate, bract]

e·bul·lient (i·bul'yənt) *adj.* **1** Bubbling over with enthusiasm. **2** In a boiling condition; boiling. [< L *ebulliens, -entis*, ppr. of *ebullire* < *ex-* out + *bullire* boil] — **e·bul'lient·ly** *adv.* — **e·bul'lience, e·bul'lien·cy** *n.*

eb·ul·lism (eb'ə·liz'əm) *n. Pathol.* The bubbling out or vaporizing of body fluids when their boiling point drops below the normal temperature of 98°F.: a condition associated with high-altitude space travel. [< L *ebullire* boil out]

eb·ul·li·tion (eb'ə·lish'ən) *n.* **1** The bubbling of a liquid; boiling. **2** Any sudden or violent agitation. [< L *ebullitio, -onis* < *ebullire*. See EBULLIENT.]

eb·ur·nat·ed (eb'ər·nā'tid) *adj.* Condensed and hardened like bone.

eb·ur·na·tion (eb'ər·nā'shən) *n. Pathol.* **1** Ossification of joint cartilage. **2** Condensation of a bone structure to the hardness of ivory. [< L *eburnus* ivory + -ATION]

e·bur·ne·an (ē·bûr'nē·ən) *adj.* Of or pertaining to ivory. Also **e·bur'ni·an.** [< L *eburnus* ivory]

ec- Var. of EX-[2].

e·cad (ē'kad) *n. Ecol.* A habitat plant form or modification due to non-inherited adaptation

---

add,āce,câre,pälm; end,ēven; it,īce; odd,ōpen,ôrder; tŏŏk,pool; up,bûrn; ə = a in *above*, e in *sicken*, i in *clarity*, o in *melon*, u in *focus*; yŏŏ = u in *fuse*, oi,oil; ou,pout; ch,check; g,go; ng,ring; th,thin; ŧħ,this; zh,vision. Foreign sounds á,œ,ü,kh,ṅ; and ◆: see page xx. < from; + plus; ? possibly.

to unusual environment. [<EC(OLOGY) + -AD]

E·car·di·nes (ē·kär′də·nēz) n. pl. An order of brachiopods with hornlike or calcareous shells joined only by muscles: formerly called *Inarticulata*. [<NL <L e- away + *cardo, cardinis* hinge]

Ec·bat·a·na (ek·bat′ə·nə) The capital of ancient Media, on the present site of HAMADAN, Iran.

ec·bol·ic (ek·bol′ik) adj. Med. Causing contraction of the uterus and thus inducing abortion or promoting parturition. — n. An ecbolic drug. [<Gk. *ekbolē* a casting out (<*ex-* out + *ballein* throw) + -IC]

ec·cen·tric (ek·sen′trik) adj. 1 Departing from the usual custom or practice; peculiar; erratic. 2 Not in the center. 3 Math. Not having the same center: said of circles, ellipses, spheres, etc.: opposed to *concentric*. 4 Not being a perfect circle, as an ellipse. 5 Of or pertaining to an eccentric. 6 Not holding to an identical purpose. 7 Removed or apart from a nerve center. 8 Colloq. Odd or unconventional to a degree short of mental unbalance: said of persons whose actions are considered peculiar to a marked degree. See synonyms under IRREGULAR, ODD, QUEER. — n. 1 Mech. A disk mounted out of center on a driving shaft, bound to it by a key, and surrounded by a collar or strap connected with a rod, effecting a crank motion. 2 One who or that which is eccentric. 3 Math. A circle not having the same center as another that partly coincides with it: also spelled *excentric*. [<LL *eccentricus* <Gk. *ekkentros* <*ek-* out, away + *kentron* center] — **ec·cen′tri·cal** adj. — **ec·cen′tri·cal·ly** adv.

ECCENTRIC
r. Driving shaft, eccentric to center of disk *d. k.* Key binding disk to shaft. *c.* Collar connecting with rod *r.*

ec·cen·tric·i·ty (ek′sen·tris′ə·tē) n. pl. ·ties 1 The state or quality of being eccentric; oddity. 2 An odd or capricious act. 3 The distance between the centers of two eccentric circles or objects. 4 The condition or quality of being eccentric. 5 Math. The ratio of the distance between the focus and the center of a conic to half of its transverse axis; formerly, the distance itself. Also spelled *excentricity*.

ec·chy·mosed (ek′i·mōzd) adj. Med. Discolored by reason of a contusion, as in the case of a black eye.

ec·chy·mo·sis (ek′i·mō′sis) n. pl. ·ses (-sēz) Med. A discoloration, as a black-and-blue spot, resulting from the rupture of small blood vessels by a blow or contusion. [<NL <Gk. *ekchymōsis* <*ek-* out + *chymos* humor (def. 4)] — **ec′chy·mot′ic** (-mot′ik) adj.

ec·cle·si·a (i·klē′zhē·ə, -zē·ə) n. pl. ·si·ae (-ē) 1 The popular or legislative assembly in Athens and other ancient Greek states in which every free citizen could vote. 2 A body of Christians organized for worship and religious work; a church; congregation. [<L <Gk. *ekklēsia* <*ekkaleein* <*ek-* out + *kaleein* call]

ec·cle·si·arch (i·klē′zē·ärk) n. A church ruler, especially one in high authority. [<ECCLESIA + Gk. *archos* chief]

Ec·cle·si·as·tes (i·klē′zē·as′tēz) One of the books of the Old Testament, formerly attributed to King Solomon. [<Gk. *ekklēsiastēs*, trans. of Hebrew *qōhēleth* a preacher]

ec·cle·si·as·tic (i·klē′zē·as′tik) Ecclesiastical. — n. 1 One officially set apart for the service of the church; a cleric; a churchman: used chiefly in episcopal communions. 2 In early church history, a member of the established or orthodox church, as distinguished from heretics and unbelievers. [<Gk. *ekklēsiastikos* for the assembly <*ekklēsia* assembly]

ec·cle·si·as·ti·cal (i·klē′zē·as′ti·kəl) adj. Of or pertaining to the church, especially considered as an organized and governing power: distinguished from *civil*. Abbr. Eccl. — **ec·cle′si·as′ti·cal·ly** adv.

ec·cle·si·as·ti·cism (i·klē′zē·as′tə·siz′əm) n. 1 Devotion to the principles of the church or to its privileges and forms. 2 The spirit that leads to such devotion. 3 Systematically exercised ecclesiastical authority.

Ec·cle·si·as·ti·cus (i·klē′zē·as′ti·kəs) One of the

books of the Old Testament Apocrypha, resembling in form the Proverbs of Solomon: accepted as canonical by the Roman Catholic Church: called also *The Wisdom of Jesus, the Son of Sirach*.

ec·cle·si·ol·a·try (i·klē′zē·ol′ə·trē) n. Worship of the church; extreme veneration for the authority, forms, and traditions of the church. [<Gk. *ekklēsia* church + *latreia* worship] — **ec·cle′si·ol′a·ter** n.

ec·cle·si·ol·o·gy (i·klē′zē·ol′ə·jē) n. 1 The study of the organization, government, liturgy, and ritual of the Christian church. 2 The study of church architecture and decoration. — **ec·cle′si·o·log′ic** (-zē·ə·loj′ik) or **-i·cal** adj.

ec·dem·ic (ek·dem′ik) adj. Med. Of or pertaining to diseases originating at a distance: opposed to *endemic*. [<EC- + Gk. *dēmos* people]

ec·dy·sis (ek′di·sis) n. pl. ·ses (-sēz) The act of casting off an integument, as in serpents and insects. [<NL <Gk. <*ek-* off + *dyein* dress, clothe]

e·ce·sis (i·sē′sis) n. Ecol. The adjustment of a plant to a new habitat; the establishment of a migrant organism. [<NL <Gk. *oikēsis* a dwelling]

ec·hard (ek′härd) n. Ecol. The non-available water of the soil: opposed to *chresard*. [Gk. *echthos* outside + *ardeia* irrigation]

ech·e·lon (esh′ə·lon) n. 1 A staggered troop, fleet, or airplane formation, one rank, ship, or airplane behind the other, but extending farther toward one flank than the preceding rank, ship, or airplane: often V-shaped.

ECHELON (def. 1)

2 Mil. a One of the different fractions of a command arranged from front to rear, to which a particular combat mission is assigned: assault *echelon*, support *echelon*. b One of the various subdivisions from front to rear of a military headquarters: forward *echelon*, rear *echelon*. c A military unit regarded as having a distinct function: command *echelon*, first *echelon* maintenance, etc. 3 Optics A diffraction grating made of glass plates so constructed that each overlaps the one below, forming a stairlike pattern. —*v.t.* & *v.i.* To form in echelon. [<F *échelon* <*échelle* ladder <L *scala*]

e·chid·na (i·kid′nə) n. pl. ·nae (-nē) An egg-laying monotreme of Australia, etc. (*Echidna aculeata*), having a vermiform tongue, tubular snout with nostrils near the tip, fossorial feet, and strong spines intermixed with fur; a spiny ant-eater. [<NL <Gk., adder]

ECHIDNA
(About 15 inches in body length)

ech·i·na·ce·a (ek′ə·nā′shē·ə) n. A genus of hardy perennial plants of the composite family native in the United States; the root of *E. angustifolia* has medicinal properties. [<NL <Gk. *echinos* hedgehog]

ech·i·nate (ek′ə·nāt) adj. Set or armed thickly with prickles; bristly; spiny. Also **ech′i·nat·ed**.

e·chi·ni·form (i·kī′nə·fôrm) adj. Having the form of a sea urchin.

echino- *combining form* Spiny; prickly: *echinoderm-*: also, before vowels, **echin-**. Also **echini-**. [<Gk. *echinos* hedgehog]

e·chi·no·derm (i·kī′nə·dûrm) n. Any of a phylum (Echinodermata) of coelomate, bottom-dwelling marine animals, as starfishes, sea cucumbers, etc., characterized by pentamerous radial symmetry, a skeleton of calcite plates just beneath the skin, and a water-vascular system which serves primarily for locomotion. — **e·chi′no·der′ma·tous** (-dûr′mə·təs), **e·chi′no·der′mal** adj.

e·chi·noid (i·kī′noid) n. Any of a class (Echinoidea) of echinoderms, including sea urchins, sand dollars, etc. —*adj.* Echiniform. — **ech·i·noi·de·an** (ek′i·noi′dē·ən) adj. & n.

e·chi·nus (i·kī′nəs) n. pl. ·ni (-nī) 1 Archit. The cushion of the capital of a Doric column, or the

corresponding part in some other order. For illustration see under CAPITAL. 2 A sea urchin or echinoid. 3 A hedgehog. [<L <Gk. *echinos* hedgehog, sea urchin]

ech·o (ek′ō) n. pl. ·oes 1 The sound produced by the reflection of sound waves from an opposing surface. 2 Reproduction of another's views or thoughts; a close imitation. 3 Prompt response. 4 The repetition of a musical phrase in soft tone; an echo-stop; an echo-organ. 5 A verse construction wherein one line repeats the last syllable or syllables of the line preceding. 6 Telecom. A retarded sound wave in radio reception; a signal received in addition to or later than the expected one. 7 In bridge, the play of a conventional card after a lead, to inform one's partner. —*v.t.* 1 To repeat or send back (sound) by echo: The walls *echoed* the shot. 2 To repeat the words, opinions, etc., of. 3 To repeat (words, opinions, etc.) in imitation of another. —*v.i.* 4 To give back sound; reverberate. 5 To be repeated or given back; resound. [<L <Gk. *ēchō*] — **ech′o·er** n.

ech·o·gram (ek′ō·gram) n. A pictorial representation, as of an organ or other structure within the body, of objects under water, etc., detected by means of reflected ultrasound. Also called *sonogram*.

ech·o·lo·ca·tion (ek′ō·lō·kā′shən) n. The determination of the distance and position of objects by the interpretation of sound waves transmitted to and returned from them. Compare RADAR. SONAR.

ech·o·or·gan (ek′ō·ôr′gən) n. A group of pipes or stops of a pipe organ, set apart from the main instrument, and enclosed for echo effects.

ech·o·stop (ek′ō·stop′) n. On a pipe organ, a stop with pipes enclosed so as to echo the tones produced.

é·clair (ā·klâr′, i·klâr′) n. A small oblong pastry shell filled with custard or whipped cream and usually iced with chocolate. [<F, lit., flash of lightning]

ec·lamp·si·a (ek·lamp′sē·ə) n. Pathol. A sudden convulsive seizure, without loss of consciousness, especially during pregnancy or childbirth. [<NL <Gk. *eklampsis* <*ek-* forth + *lampein* shine]

é·clat (ā·klä′, i·klä′) n. 1 Showiness of achievement; brilliancy; splendor. 2 Renown; celebrity; glory. [<F <*éclater* burst out]

ec·lec·tic (ek·lek′tik, ik-) adj. 1 Selecting or made by selection from different systems or sources. 2 Having broad views; liberal. 3 Composed of selections: an *eclectic* review. Also **ec·lec′ti·cal**. — n. One who practices selection from all systems or sources, as in philosophy or medicine. [<Gk. *eklektikos* <*ek-* out + *legein* select] — **ec·lec′ti·cal·ly** adv.

e·clipse (i·klips′) n. 1 Astron. The dimming or elimination of light reaching an observer from a heavenly body. A **lunar eclipse** is caused by the passage of the moon through the earth's shadow; a **solar eclipse** by the passage of the moon between the sun and the observer. 2 Any hiding or obscuring. See ANNULAR ECLIPSE.

ECLIPSE
S. Sun. *E.* Earth. *M.* Moon. *EO.* Earth's orbit.
MO. Moon's orbit.

When the moon passes between the sun and the earth, it causes an eclipse of the sun, this solar eclipse being total to observers within the umbra (darker shaded portions) of the moon's shadow and partial to those within the penumbra (lighter portions). When the moon passes through the earth's shadow, earth observers witness a total or partial lunar eclipse.

—*v.t.* **e·clipsed, e·clips·ing** 1 To cause an eclipse of; darken. 2 To obscure the beauty, fame, worth, etc., of; overshadow. [<OF <L *eclipsis* <Gk. *ekleipsis* <*ek-* out + *leipein* leave]

ec·lo·gite (ek′lə·jīt) n. A rock consisting of red garnet, greenish pyroxene, and emerald-green smaragdite. [<Gk. *eklogē* selection <*ek-* out + *legein* select]

ec·logue (ek′lôg, -log) n. 1 A poem containing discourses or dialogs, with shepherds as principal speakers. **2** A short pastoral poem; bucolic. Also **ec′log.** [<F *éclogue* <L *ecloga* <Gk. *eklogē.* See ECLOGITE.]

e·clo·sion (i·klō′zhən) *n.* **1** *Biol.* The process of hatching from an egg. **2** *Entomol.* The emergence of the mature insect from the pupa. [<F *éclosion* <*éclore* be hatched]

ec·o·cide (ek′ō·sīd) *n.* The disruption of an eco-system, as by the reckless introduction of an agent or process that destroys some key element in the system. —**ec′o·cid′al** *adj.*

e·col·o·gy (i·kol′ə·jē) *n.* **1** That division of biology which treats of the relations between organisms and their environment; bionomics. **2** The study of human populations and of their reciprocal relations in terms of physical en-vironment, spatial distribution, and cultural characteristics. [<Gk. *oikos* home + -LOGY] —**ec′o·log′ic** (ek′ə·loj′ik) or **·i·cal** *adj.* — **ec′·o·log′i·cal·ly** *adv.* —**e·col′o·gist** *n.*

e·con·o·met·ric (i·kon′ə·met′rik) *adj.* Pertain-ing to a system of analysis of economic affairs using a specialized statistical technique for large masses of assembled data.

e·con·o·met·rics (i·kon′ə·met′riks) *n.* The ap-plication of the principles of mathematical analysis to economic problems, specifically those pertaining to business and finance. [<ECONOMY + -METRICS] —**e·con′o·met′ric** *adj.*

ec·o·nom·ic (ek′ə·nom′ik, ē′kə-) *adj.* **1** Relat-ing to the science of economics; pertaining to money matters or wealth. **2** Economical. **3** Of practical utility: *economic botany.* **4** *Obs.* Pertaining to the management of household affairs. [<L *oeconomicus* <Gk. *oikonomia.* See ECONOMY.]

ec·o·nom·ics (ek′ə·nom′iks, ē′kə-) *n. pl. (Con-strued as singular)* The science that treats of the production and distribution of wealth.

e·con·o·mist (i·kon′ə·mist) *n.* **1** One who is proficient in economics. **2** A manager of do-mestic or pecuniary resources. **3** One who is careful and thrifty in management.

e·con·o·mize (i·kon′ə·mīz) *v.* **·mized, ·miz·ing** *v.t.* To use thriftily. —*v.i.* To be frugal or economical. Also *Brit.* **e·con′o·mise.** See syn-onyms under RETRENCH. — **e·con′o·miz′er** *n.*

e·con·o·my (i·kon′ə·mē) *n. pl.* **·mies 1** Dis-position to save or spare; carefulness in outlay; freedom from extravagance or waste; frugal-ity: *economy* of words, *economy* in dress. **2** Cheapness of operation, relative or absolute, as expressed in steam, fuel, or money. **3** The management of household matters: usually with a qualifying adjective: domestic *economy.* **4** Any practical system in which means are adjusted to ends, especially in the natural world: the *economy* of nature, the animal *economy,* the *economy* of a plant. **5** The prac-tical adjustment, organization, or administra-tion of affairs or resources, especially of in-dustrial resources of a state: political *economy.* **6** A method of divine management of human affairs or a system of laws and regulations, rites, and ceremonies; specifically, any par-ticular method of divine government: the Mo-saic *economy.* **7** The handling and presentation of doctrine in a judicious manner. See syno-nyms under FRUGALITY, LEGISLATION. [<L *oeconomia* <Gk. *oikonomia* <*oikos* house + *nemein* manage]

e·co·spe·cies (ē′kə·spē′shēz, ek′ə-) *n. Ecol.* A species of plant, natural or cultivated, highly adapted to its habitat. [<Gk. *oikos* home, habitat + SPECIES]

ec·o·sys·tem (ek′ō·sis′təm) *n. Ecol.* A commu-nity of organisms and their nonliving environ-ment. [<Gk. *oikos* habitat + SYSTEM]

e·co·tone (ē′kə·tōn, ek′ə-) *n. Ecol.* A zone where two different forms of vegetable life compete. [<Gk. *oikos* habitat + *tonos* stress]

e·co·tope (ē′kə·tōp, ek′ə-) *n. Ecol.* A special-ized habitat within a larger region. [<Gk. *oikos* habitat + *topos* place]

e·co·type (ē′kə·tīp, ek′ə-) *n. Ecol.* A biotype adapted for life in a particular kind of hab-itat. [<Gk. *oikos* habitat + TYPE]

ec·ru (ek′rōō, ā′krōō) *adj.* **1** Unbleached. **2** Having the color of unbleached linen or of hemp. —*n.* **1** The color of unbleached linen; a light–yellowish brown. **2** Goods made of unbleached linen. Also **é′cru.** [<F <OF *escru* <L *ex-* thoroughly + *crudus* raw]

ec·sta·sy (ek′stə·sē) *n. pl.* **·sies 1** The state of being beside oneself through some extravagant and overpowering emotion or mental exalta-tion: an *ecstasy* of joy. **2** An enrapturing or transporting influence; a rapture. **3** In mysti-cism, the state of trance supposed to accom-pany inspiration. **4** Religious rapture. **5** *Obs.* Madness. See synonyms under ENTHUSIASM, HAPPINESS, RAPTURE. [<OF *extasie* <LL *ec-stasis* <Gk. *ekstasis* distraction <*ek-* out + *histanai* place]

ec·stat·ic (ek·stat′ik) *adj.* Pertaining to or of the nature of ecstasy; transporting; enraptured: also **ec·stat′i·cal.** — *n.* **1** A person subject to ecstasies or trances; an enthusiast. **2** *pl.* Rapturous emotions.

ec·thy·ma (ek·thī′mə) *n. pl.* **·thym·a·ta** (-thim′-ə·tə) *Pathol.* A virus disease characterized by the formation on the skin of ulcerating pus-tules whose discharge produces vesicular lesions. [<Gk. *ekthyma* pustule <*ek-* out + *thuein* seethe]

ecto- *combining form* Without; outside; exter-nal: *ectoderm.* Also, before vowels, **ect-.** [<Gk. *ekto-* <*ektos* outside]

ec·to·blast (ek′tə·blast) *n. Biol.* The embry-onic stage of the ectoderm. — **ec′to·blas′tic** *adj.*

ec·to·derm (ek′tə·dûrm) *n. Biol.* **1** The outer layer of the integument of a multicellular or-ganism. **2** The outer germ layer of the em-bryo, from which the epithelial structures of the surface of the body and the nervous sys-tem develop by the process of gastrulation: often called *exoderm.* — **ec′to·der′mal, ec′to-der′mic** *adj.*

ec·to·en·zyme (ek′tō·en′zīm, -zim) *n. Biochem.* An enzyme which functions outside of the cell and acts directly upon the surrounding blood or tissue: opposed to *endoenzyme,* and often spelled *exoenzyme.* — **ec′to·en′zym** (-zim) *n.*

ec·to·mor·phic (ek′tə·môr′fik) *adj.* Denoting a physical and personality type associated with the body structure as developed from the ectodermal layer of the embryo, and charac-terized by predominance of the nervous sys-tem. Compare ENDOMORPHIC and MESOMOR-PHIC.

-ectomy *combining form* Removal of a part by cutting out: used in surgical terms to indicate certain kinds of operations; as, *appendectomy.* [<Gk. *ektomē* <*ek-* out + *temnein* cut]

ec·to·par·a·site (ek′tə·par′ə·sīt) *n. Biol.* A para-site that lives upon the exterior of its host, as a louse.

ec·to·phyte (ek′tə·fīt) *n.* An ectoparasite which attacks plants.

ec·to·pi·a (ek·tō′pē·ə) *n. Pathol.* Displacement of parts or organs, especially when congenital. [<NL <Gk. *ek-* out, from + *topos* place] — **ec·top′ic** (-top′ik) *adj.*

ec·to·plasm (ek′tə·plaz′əm) *n.* **1** *Biol.* The firm outer layer of the cytoplasm of a unicellular organism or of a plant cell. **2** The substance alleged to emanate from the body of a spiritu-alist medium during a trance: also called *teleplasm.* — **ec′to·plas′mic** *adj.*

ec·to·sarc (ek′tə·särk) *n. Biol.* The ectoplasm of protozoans. [<ECTO- + Gk. *sarx* flesh]

ec·tos·to·sis (ek′tos·tō′sis) *n. Pathol.* Ossifica-tion around the exterior of a cartilage. [< ECT(O)- + OST(EO)- + -OSIS]

ec·to·troph·ic (ek′tə·trof′ik, -trō′fik) *adj. Bot.* Nourished by the outside (of roots): said of certain fungi. [<ECTO- + Gk. *trophikos* < *trephein* grow, nourish]

ec·trog·e·ny (ek·troj′ə·nē) *n. Pathol.* The loss or absence, usually congenital, of an organ or part of the body. [< *ectro-* absence <Gk. *ektrōsis* an abortion) + -GENY] — **ec·tro·gen·ic** (ek′trə·jen′ik) *adj.*

ec·tro·pi·um (ek·trō′pē·əm) *n. Anat.* A turning outward, partial or complete, of a part, as an eyelid, or the lips of the neck of the womb. Also **ec·tro′pi·on.** [<NL <Gk. *ektropion* < *ektropos* <*ek-* out + *trepein* turn]

ec·type (ek′tīp) *n.* **1** An imitation or repro-duction of an original: opposed to *prototype* and distinguished from *replica.* **2** *Archit.* A figure or other work in relief. **3** A repro-duction, in a world of time and sense, of an eternal and non–sensuous idea: contrasted with *archetype.* **4** *Psychiatry* A physical or mental constitution that varies markedly from

the average. [<Gk. *ektypos* <*ek-* out + *typos* < *typtein* stamp] — **ec′ty·pal** *adj.*

Ec·ua·dor (ek′wə·dôr) A republic in NW South America; 108,478 square miles; capital, Quito. — **Ec′ua·do′re·an, Ec′ua·do′ri·an** *adj.* & *n.*

ec·u·men·i·cal (ek′yōō·men′i·kəl) *adj.* **1** Of or pertaining to the habitable world; general; universal. **2** Belonging to or accepted by the Christian church throughout the world: an *ecumenical* council. Also spelled *oecumenical.* Also **ec′u·men′ic.** [<LL *oecumenicus* <Gk. *oikoumenikos* <*oikoumenē (gē)* the inhabited (world) <*oikeein* dwell] — **ec′u·men′i·cal·ly** *adv.*

ec·u·men·ism (ek′yōō·men′iz·əm) *n.* The be-liefs, principles, or practices of those who de-sire and work for world–wide unity and co-operation among all Christian churches. Also **ec·u·men·i·cism** (ek′yōō·men′ə·kəl·iz·əm), **ec-u·men·i·cism** (ek′yōō·men′ə·siz′əm).

ec·ze·ma (ek′sə·mə, eg′zə·mə, eg·zē′mə) *n. Pathol.* An inflammatory disease of the skin attended by itching, watery discharge, and the appearance of lesions. [<Gk. *ekzema* <*ek-* out + *zeein* boil] — **ec·zem′a·tous** (-zem′ə-təs) *adj.*

-ed¹ *suffix* Used in the past tense of regular verbs: *walked, killed, played.* [OE *-ede, -ode, -ade*]

-ed² *suffix* **1** Used in the past participles of regular verbs: *clothed, washed.* **2** Forming adjectives from adjectives in *-ate,* with the same general meaning: *bipinnated.* [OE *-ed, -ad, -od*]

-ed³ *suffix* **1** Having; possessing; character-ized by: *toothed, green–eyed.* **2** Like; resem-bling: *bigoted.* [OE *-ede*]

e·dac·i·ty (i·das′ə·tē) *n.* Excess in eating; glut-tony. Also **e·da′cious·ness.**

e·daph·ic (i·daf′ik) *adj. Ecol.* Of, pertaining to, or affected by the state or condition of the soil rather than by climate; indigenous; local. [<Gk. *edaphos* ground]

ed·dy (ed′ē) *n. pl.* **·dies 1** A whirl or back-ward–circling current of water or air; a whirl-pool. **2** Figuratively, a turning aside or de-parture from the main current of thought or life. See synonyms under STREAM. — *v.t.* & *v.i.* **·died, ·dy·ing** To move, or cause to move, in or as in an eddy. [Prob. <ON *idha*]

e·del·weiss (ā′dəl·vīs) *n.* A small perennial alpine herb of the composite family *(Leontopodium alpinum),* with white woolly leaves suggesting a flower, and dense terminal cymes. [<G <*edel* noble + *weiss* white]

e·de·ma (i·dē′mə) *n. pl.* **·ma·ta** (-mə·tə) *Pathol.* A morbid accumulation of serous fluid in various organs or tissues of the body, as the pleural cavity or the retina: also spelled *oedema.* [<NL < Gk. *oidēma* a tumor < *oidein* swell] — **e·dem·a·tous** (i·dem′ə·təs), **e·dem′a-tose** (tōs) *adj.*

EDELWEISS
(Plant about 4 inches high over all)

E·den (ēd′n) **1** In the Bible, the garden that was the first home of Adam and Eve: often *Paradise.* **2** Any delightful region or abode; a paradise.

e·den·tate (ē·den′tāt, i·den′-) *adj.* **1** Toothless. **2** Of or pertaining to an order of placental mammals *(Edentata or Xenarthra),* some of which lack teeth, including sloths, ant–eaters, and armadillos. —*n.* **1** One of the *Edentata.* **2** A creature without teeth. [<L *edentatus* <*ex-* without + *dens, dentis* tooth]

e·den·tu·lous (ē·den′chōō·ləs, i·den′-) *adj.* Having no teeth. Also **e·den′tu·late** (-lit, -lāt).

e·des·tin (i·des′tin) *n. Biochem.* A crystalline protein found in the castor–oil bean, hemp seed, and other seeds. [<Gk. *edestos* edible + -IN]

edge (ej) *n.* **1** The thin, sharp cutting part of a blade. **2** Sharpness; acuteness. **3** An abrupt border or margin; verge; brink; rim: the *edge* of a cliff. **4** A bounding or dividing line: the *edge* of a plain. See synonyms under BANK¹, BOUNDARY, MARGIN. —**on edge 1** Nervous; irritable. **2** Keenly eager. — *v.*

edged, edg·ing *v.t.* **1** To put a cutting edge on; sharpen. **2** To put an edging or border on. **3** To move cautiously sidewise: to *edge* one's way through a mob. **4** To move by degrees; inch: to *edge* one's chair closer. **5** *U.S. Colloq.* To defeat by a slight margin: The home team just *edged* the visitors. — *v.i.* **6** To move sidewise. **7** To move by degrees: to *edge* away. [OE *ecg*] **—edged** *adj.* **—edge'·less** *adj.*

edge tool 1 Any sharp, cutting tool. **2** A tool for making an edging, or finishing an edge.

edge·wise (ej'wīz') *adv.* With the edge forward; on, by, with, along, or in the direction of the edge. Also **edge'ways'**.

edg·ing (ej'ing) *n.* **1** Anything serving as or attached to an edge; trimming. **2** The making, dressing, or ornamenting of edges.

edg·y (ej'ē) *adj.* **1** Brought out too sharply; edgelike, as the outlines of a sculptured figure. **2** Irritable; sharp-tempered; eager. **—edg'i·ness** *n.*

ed·i·ble (ed'ə·bəl) *adj.* Fit to eat. — *n. Usually pl.* Something suitable for food. [<LL *edibilis* < L *edere* eat] **—ed·i·bil'i·ty** *n.* **—ed'i·ble·ness** *n.*

e·dict (ē'dikt) *n.* **1** That which is uttered or proclaimed by authority as a rule of action; a public ordinance emanating from a sovereign and having the force of law. **2** Any proclamation of command or prohibition. See synonyms under LAW. [<L *edictum*, pp. neut. of *edicere* <*ex*- out + *dicere* say] **—e·dic'tal** *adj.* **—e·dic'tal·ly** *adv.*

ed·i·fice (ed'ə·fis) *n.* A large structure of impressive architecture; a building. See synonyms under HOUSE. [<F *édifice* <L *aedificium* <*aedes* building + *facere* make] **—ed·i·fi·cial** (ed'ə·fish'əl) *adj.*

ed·i·fy (ed'ə·fī) *v.t.* **fied, fy·ing** To build up or strengthen, especially in morals or religion; instruct; improve; enlighten. [<OF *edifier* <L *aedificare* <*aedes* building + *facere* make] **—ed'i·fi·ca'tion** *n.* **—ed'i·fi'er** *n.* **—ed'i·fy'ing** *adj.* **—ed'i·fy'ing·ly** *adv.*

Ed·i·son (ed'ə·sən), **Thomas Alva,** 1847–1931, U.S. inventor.

ed·it (ed'it) *v.t.* **1** To manage the preparation and publication of (a newspaper, etc.). **2** To compile, arrange and emend for publication: to *edit* memoirs or letters. **3** To correct and prepare (a manuscript, copy, etc.) for publication. [<L *editus,* pp. of *edere* <*ex*- out + *dare* give]

e·di·tion (i·dish'ən) *n.* **1** A published form of a literary work, or a copy of the form so published. **2** The total number of copies of a book, magazine, newspaper, etc., issued at one time.

ed·i·tor (ed'i·tər) *n.* **1** One who prepares manuscripts, copy, etc., for publication. **2** One having charge of a publication.

ed·i·to·ri·al (ed'i·tôr'ē·əl, -tō'rē-) *adj.* Of or pertaining to or emanating from an editor. — *n.* An article in a journal, or periodical, presumably written by the editor or by his subordinate, and published as an official argument or expression of opinion; a leading article. **—ed'i·to'ri·al·ly** *adv.*

ed·i·to·ri·al·ize (ed'i·tôr'ē·əl·īz', -tō'rē-) *v.t. & v.i.* **ized, iz·ing 1** To express opinions on (a subject) editorially. **2** To insert editorial opinions into (a news item, etc.).

editorial plural The editorial "we": the first person plural substituted for the first person singular in editorial writing.

editor in chief *pl.* **editors in chief** The chief editor of a publication; the one responsible for carrying out policies.

ed·i·tor·ship (ed'i·tər·ship') *n.* The office and duties of an editor.

Ed·na (ed'nə) A feminine personal name. [< Hebrew, rejuvenation]

E·dom·ite (ē'dəm·īt) *n.* A descendant of Esau, or an inhabitant of Edom. **—E'dom·it'ish** *adj.*

ed·u·ca·ble (ej'oo·kə·bəl) *adj.* Capable of being educated.

ed·u·cate (ej'oo·kāt) *v.t.* **·cat·ed, ·cat·ing 1** To develop or train the mind, capabilities, and character of by or as by formal schooling or instruction; teach. **2** To train for some special purpose: He was *educated* for the ministry. **3** To develop and train (taste, special ability, etc.). **4** To provide schooling for. See synonyms under TEACH. [<L *educatus,* pp. of *educare* bring up <*educere.*

See EDUCE.] **—ed'u·cat'a·ble** *adj.*

ed·u·cat·ed (ej'oo·kā'tid) *adj.* **1** Developed and informed by education; instructed; trained. **2** Having a cultivated mind, speech, manner, etc. See synonyms under INTELLIGENT.

ed·u·ca·tion (ej'oo·kā'shən) *n.* **1** The systematic development and cultivation of the natural powers, by inculcation, example, etc. **2** Instruction and training in an institution of learning. **3** The knowledge and skills resulting from such instruction and training. **4** Teaching as a system, science, or art; pedagogy. **5** The training of animals. **6** The culture of bees, bacteria, etc. **—Education, Office of** See UNITED STATES OFFICE OF EDUCATION. **—ed'u·ca'tion·al** *adj.* **—ed'u·ca'tion·al·ly** *adv.* **—ed'u·ca'tion·ar'y** *adj.*

Synonyms: breeding, cultivation, culture, development, discipline, information, instruction, knowledge, learning, nurture, reading, schooling, study, teaching, training, tuition. *Education* (L. *educere,* to lead or draw out) is the systematic *development* and *cultivation* of the mind and other natural powers. It begins in the nursery, continues through school, and also through life, whether we will or not. *Instruction,* the impartation of *knowledge* by others is but a part of education. *Teaching* is the more familiar and less formal word for *instruction. Training* refers not merely to the impartation of *knowledge,* but to the exercising of one in actions with the design to form habits. *Discipline* is systematic and rigorous *training,* with the idea of subjection to authority and perhaps of punishment. *Tuition* is the technical term for *teaching* as the business of an instructor or as in the routine of a school. We speak of the *teaching, training,* or *discipline,* rather than of the *education* or *tuition* of a dog or a horse. Compare KNOWLEDGE, LEARNING, NURTURE, REFINEMENT, WISDOM. *Antonyms:* ignorance, illiteracy. Compare synonyms for IGNORANT.

ed·u·ca·tion·al·ist (ej'oo·kā'shən·əl·ist) *n.* **1** One interested in educational forms or methods; one employed in educational pursuits; a practical educator. **2** One versed in educational theories or devoted to educational interests: also **ed'u·ca'tion·ist.**

ed·u·ca·tive (ej'oo·kā'tiv) *adj.* Instructive; developing; educating.

ed·u·ca·tor (ej'oo·kā'tər) *n.* A teacher. **—ed'u·ca·to'ry** (-tôr'ē, -tō'rē) *adj.*

e·duce (i·doos', i·dyoos') *v.t.* **e·duced, e·duc·ing 1** To call forth; draw out; evoke. **2** To develop or formulate, as from data or experimentation. [<L *educere* <*ex*- out + *ducere* lead] **—e·duc'i·ble** *adj.* **—e·duc·tive** (i·duk'tiv) *adj.* **—e·duc'tor** *n.*

e·duct (ē'dukt) *n.* **1** That which is educed; something brought out or developed from another. **2** *Chem.* A substance or body derived from another body in which it originally existed, as opposed to a *product* resulting from chemical change.

e·duc·tion (i·duk'shən) *n.* **1** The act or process of educing. **2** An educt. **3** The act of exhausting, as an engine cylinder, of steam: used in various self-explaining compounds, as **eduction pipe:** now superseded by *exhaust.*

e·dul·co·rate (i·dul'kə·rāt) *v.t.* **·rat·ed, ·rat·ing 1** To correct the acidity or acridity of; soften; sweeten. **2** *Chem.* To cleanse or free from soluble acids, salts, etc., by washing with water. [<L *edulcoratus,* pp. of *edulcorare* <*ex*- out + *dulcis* sweet] **—e·dul'co·ra'tion** *n.* **—e·dul'co·ra'tive** *adj.*

— Edward I, 1239–1307, king of England 1272–1307: known as *Edward Longshanks.*

— Edward II, 1284–1327, king of England 1307–27; defeated by Bruce at Bannockburn, 1314; murdered.

— Edward III, 1312–77, king of England 1327–77; defeated the Scots and French.

— Edward IV, 1442–83, king of England 1461–70, 1471–83; overthrew the Lancastrians.

— Edward V, 1470?–83, king of England 1483; murdered in the Tower.

— Edward VI, 1537–53, king of England 1547–53; son of Henry VIII and Jane Seymour.

— Edward VII, 1841–1910, king of England 1901–10.

— Edward VIII, 1894–1972, succeeded his father George V as king of England, Jan. 20, 1936; abdicated Dec. 10, 1936; became the

Duke of Windsor.

Ed·ward·i·an (ed·wär'dē·ən) *adj.* **1** *Law* Relating to Edward I as regards the writs founded on the statute of Gloucester, which enforced the law that a grant in fee simple by a tenant for life, or in dower, caused forfeiture of the entire estate. **2** *Archit.* Indicating the style of the time of the first three Edwards. **3** *Eccl.* Pertaining to the adoption of a new ritual and important changes in church management, under Edward VI. **4** Relating to Edward VII, his reign and especially the literature, manners, and decorative styles characterizing this period.

-ee *Suffix of nouns* **1** A person who undergoes the action or receives the benefit of the main element: *payee:* often used in legal terms and opposed to *-er, -or,* as in *grantor, grantee.* **2** A person who is described by the main element: *absentee.* [AF *-é,* suffix of pp. <L *-atus*]

eel (ēl) *n. pl.* **eels** or **eel 1** A voracious teleost fish belonging to the order *Apodes,* having an elongated snakelike body, usually without scales or pelvic fins, and of both marine and fresh-water habitat; especially the **American eel** (*Anguilla bastoniensis*) and the **European eel** (*A. anguilla*). **2** Any of certain other eel-like fishes, as the lamprey, frequently called the lamprey eel, electric eel, etc. **3** An eelworm. [OE *æl*] **—eel'y** *adj.*

AMERICAN EEL
(Average length under 3 feet, maximum 4 feet)

eel-grass (ēl'gras', -gräs') *n.* An herb (*Zostera marina*) of the pondweed family, of grasslike appearance, and growing wholly under water: used as a sound insulator, for packing, etc.

eel·pout (ēl'pout') *n. pl.* **·pouts** or **·pout** A marine fish with an eel-like body tapering backward. *Zoarces anguillaris* is the American and *Z. viviparus* the European eelpout. [OE *ælepute*]

eel·worm (ēl'wûrm') *n.* **1** A threadworm or nematode, especially *Ascaris lumbricoides,* parasitic in the human digestive tract. **2** The vinegar eel.

-eer *suffix of nouns and verbs* **1** One who is concerned with, works with, or produces: *engineer:* now often used disdainfully, as in *pamphleteer.* **2** Be concerned with: *electioneer.* [<F *-ier* <L *-arius*]

ee·rie (ē'rē, ir'ē) *adj.* **1** Inspiring fear or awe; weird. **2** Affected by fear; awed. Also **ee'ry.** [ME *eri* timid, var. of *erg* <OE *earg*] **—ee'ri·ly** *adv.* **—ee'ri·ness** *n.*

ef·fa·ble (ef'ə·bəl) *adj.* That can be uttered or explained. [<L *effabilis* <*ex*- out + *fari* speak]

ef·face (i·fās') *v.t.* **·faced, ·fac·ing 1** To rub out, as written characters; erase; cancel. **2** To obliterate or destroy, as a memory. **3** To make (oneself) inconspicuous or insignificant. See synonyms under CANCEL. [<F *effacer* <L *ex*- out + *facies* face] **—ef·face'a·ble** *adj.* **—ef·face'ment** *n.* **—ef·fac'er** *n.* **—ef·fa'cive** *adj.*

ef·fect (i·fekt') *n.* **1** A result or product of some cause or agency; a consequence. **2** Practical efficiency. **3** The substance of a statement; gist. **4** Active operation; execution. **5** Fact or reality: following *in.* **6** *pl.* Movable goods. **7** Useful work performed by a machine. **8** A mental state or attitude resulting from observation or external impression: the *effect* of a picture. See synonyms under ACT, CONSEQUENCE, END, OPERATION, PRODUCT. — *v.t.* **1** To bring about; produce as a result; cause. **2** To achieve; accomplish. [<L *effectus,* pp. of *efficere* <*ex*- out + *facere* do, make] **—ef·fect'er** *n.* **—ef·fect'i·ble** *adj.*

Synonyms (verb): accomplish, achieve, close, complete, conclude, consummate, do, end, execute, finish, fulfil, perform, produce, realize.

ef·fec·tive (i·fek'tiv) *adj.* **1** Producing, or adapted to produce, an effect; efficient. **2** Impressive; moving, as oratory. **3** In force, as a law. **4** Ready, as an army. — *n.* **1** One who is fit for duty. **2** The number of men available for active service: a war *effective* of 250,000. **3** That which effects; a cause. **4** Silver or gold currency, as distinguished from paper; coin.

See synonyms under EFFICIENT, POWERFUL. — **ef·fec′tive·ly** adv. — **ef·fec′tive·ness** n.

ef·fec·tor (i·fek′tər) n. Physiol. A specialized structure at the periphery of a motor nerve, as a muscle or gland, serving to transform efferent nerve impulses into physical action, or to innervate them. Compare RECEPTOR.

ef·fec·tu·al (i·fek′chōō·əl) adj. 1 Possessing or exercising adequate power to produce a designed effect; completely efficient; efficacious: effectual measures. 2 In force; legal, as a rule or law. See synonyms under POWERFUL. [<OF effectuel <LL effectualis <effectus. See EFFECT.] — **ef·fec′tu·al′i·ty** (-al′ə·tē) n. — **ef·fec′tu·al·ness** n.

ef·fem·i·nate (i·fem′ə·nit) adj. Having womanish traits or qualities; unmanly; voluptuous; delicate. See synonyms under FEMININE. [<L effeminatus, pp. of effeminare <ex- out + femina a woman] — **ef·fem′i·nate·ly** adv. — **ef·fem′i·nate·ness** n.

ef·fer·ent (ef′ər·ənt) adj. Physiol. Carrying or carried outward, as impulses from the central nervous system to muscles, the cells of glands, etc.; discharging: opposed to afferent. — n. 1 An efferent duct, vessel, or nerve. 2 A stream carrying off water, as from a pond. [<L efferens, -entis, ppr. of efferre <ex- out + ferre carry]

ef·fer·vesce (ef′ər·ves′) v.i. ·vesced, ·vesc·ing 1 To bubble up; give off bubbles of gas, as water charged with carbon dioxide. 2 To come away in bubbles, as a gas. 3 To show exhilaration or lively spirits. [<L effervescere <ex- out + fervescere boil, inceptive of fervere be hot]

ef·fer·ves·cence (ef′ər·ves′əns) n. 1 The escape of bubbles of gas from a liquid otherwise than by boiling, or the condition of a substance resulting therefrom. 2 A bubbling up: the effervescence of a carbonate with an acid. 3 Irrepressible excitement or emotion. Also **ef′fer·ves′cen·cy.** [<L effervescens, -entis, ppr. of effervescere. See EFFERVESCE.]

ef·fer·ves·cent (ef′ər·ves′ənt) adj. 1 Giving off bubbles of gas; coming off in bubbles, as gas from a liquid. 2 Effervescing, or having the property of effervescing. — **ef′fer·ves′ci·ble** adj. — **ef′fer·ves′cive** adj.

ef·fete (i·fēt′) adj. Worn out and incapable of further production, as an animal, a plant, or soil; exhausted; barren. [<L effetus <ex- out + fetus a breeding] — **ef·fete′ness** n.

ef·fi·ca·cious (ef′ə·kā′shəs) adj. Producing or capable of producing an intended effect; having efficacy. See synonyms under EFFICIENT, POWERFUL. [<L efficax, -cacis <efficere. See EFFECT.] — **ef′fi·ca′cious·ly** adv. — **ef′fi·ca′cious·ness** n.

ef·fi·ca·cy (ef′ə·kə·sē) n. pl. ·cies Power to produce an effect; effective energy. See synonyms under POWER, WEIGHT.

ef·fi·cien·cy (i·fish′ən·sē) n. pl. ·cies 1 The character of being efficient; effectiveness. 2 The ratio of the work done or energy expended by an organism or machine to the energy supplied in the form of food or fuel. Also **ef·fi′· cience.** See synonyms under ABILITY, POWER.

ef·fi·cient (i·fish′ənt) adj. 1 Acting or having power to act effectually; competent: an efficient leader. 2 Productive of effects; causative. — n. 1 A qualified person; specifically, in the British Army, a volunteer certified for his qualifications. 2 An efficient cause. [<L efficiens, -entis, ppr. of efficere. See EFFECT.] — **ef·fi′cient·ly** adv.

Synonyms (adj.): effective, effectual, efficacious.

ef·fi·gy (ef′ə·jē) n. pl. ·gies 1 A figure representing a person, as in sculpture or numismatics. 2 A representation of a person who has incurred odium. — **to burn** (or **hang**) **in effigy** To burn or hang publicly an image of a person who is hated. [<F effigie <L effigies <ex- out + fingere fashion] — **ef·fig·i·al** (e·fij′ē·əl) adj.

ef·fla·tion (i·flā′shən) n. That which is blown or breathed forth; an emanation. [<L efflatus <ex- out + flare blow]

ef·fleu·rage (e·flœ·räzh′) n. French A gentle rubbing with the palm of the hand; massage.

ef·flo·resce (ef′lô·res′, -lō-) v.i. ·resced, ·resc·ing 1 Bot. To blossom, bloom, or flower. 2 Chem. **a** To become powdery, wholly or in part, and lose crystalline structure through loss of water of crystallization on exposure to the air. **b** To become covered with a crust of saline particles left by evaporation, as the ground. [<L efflorescere <ex- thoroughly + florescere bloom <flos, floris a flower]

ef·flo·res·cence (ef′lô·res′əns, -lō-) n. 1 Bot. The time or act of flowering. 2 Pathol. A rash on the skin. 3 The process, act, or result of efflorescing. 4 A crystalline deposit on the surface of a mineral or on the face of a stone wall. Also **ef′flo·res′cen·cy.**

ef·flo·res·cent (ef′lô·res′ənt, -lo-) adj. 1 Bot. Blossoming out; blooming. 2 Tending or liable to effloresce. 3 Chem. **a** Forming into white threads or powder. **b** Covered with efflorescence. [<L efflorescens, -entis, ppr. of efflorescere. See EFFLORESCE.]

ef·flu·ence (ef′lōō·əns) n. A flowing out; emanation. Also **ef′flu·en·cy.**

ef·flu·ent (ef′lōō·ənt) adj. Flowing out. — n. 1 Sewage after purification treatment. 2 An outflow, as of water from a lake or stream. [<L effluens, -entis, ppr. of effluere <ex- out + fluere flow]

ef·flu·vi·um (i·flōō′vē·əm) n. pl. ·vi·a (-vē·ə) 1 An invisible emanation. 2 A noxious or ill-smelling exhalation from decaying matter: commonly in the plural: the effluvia from foul drains. 3 A theoretic imponderable agent formerly regarded as the source of the electric and magnetic forces of certain substances. [<L, a flowing out] — **ef·flu′vi·al, ef·flu′vi·ous** adj.

ef·flux (ef′luks) n. An outflow; effluence; emanation; effluvium. [<L effluxus <ex- out + fluere flow]

ef·fort (ef′ərt) n. 1 A voluntary exertion of power; strenuous endeavor; attempt. 2 A result or display of consciously directed power; an achievement. 3 Mech. Force exerted against the inertia of a body. See synonyms under ENDEAVOR, INDUSTRY. [<F <efforcer <L ex- out + fortis strong]

ef·front·er·y (i·frun′tər·ē) n. pl. ·er·ies Insolent assurance; audacity; impudence. [<F effronterie <OF esfront shameless <L effrons <ex- out + frons, frontis forehead, face]
Synonyms: assurance, audacity, boldness, brass, hardihood, impudence, insolence, shamelessness.

ef·fulge (i·fulj′) v.t. & v.i. ·fulged, ·fulg·ing To shine forth; radiate. [<L effulgere <ex- out + fulgere shine]

ef·ful·gence (i·ful′jəns) n. A shining forth brilliantly; beaming brightness; splendor. [<L effulgens, -entis, ppr. of effulgere. See EFFULGE.] — **ef·ful′gent** adj. — **ef·ful′gent·ly** adv.

ef·fuse (i·fyōōs′) adj. 1 Bot. Spreading loosely, as the panicle of the common rush, or spreading flat, as the plant body of some thallophytic epiphytes. 2 Bacteriol. Profuse, as a thin spreading film of bacteria in a culture. 3 Entomol. Composed of loosely joined parts; not compact, as an insect's body. 4 Zool. Having the lips separated by a groove, as a shell; expanded. 5 Obs. Poured out freely: profuse. — v. (i·fyōōz′) ·fused, ·fus·ing v.t. 1 To pour forth; shed. — v.i. 2 To emanate; exude. 3 Physics To flow through a porous diaphragm or aperture under pressure: said of gases. [<L effusus, pp. of effundere <ex- out + fundere pour]

ef·fu·sion (i·fyōō′zhən) n. 1 The act or process of pouring forth, or that which is poured forth. 2 An outpouring, as of fancy or sentiment: applied ironically to literary compositions. 3 Sentimental demonstration. 4 Pathol. The pouring out of the blood or other fluid, as into the cellular tissue. 5 Physics The flow of gases under pressure through openings in the container.

ef·fu·sive (i·fyōō′siv) adj. 1 Overflowing with sentiment; demonstrative; gushing. 2 Pouring forth; shedding abroad: with of. — **ef·fu′sive·ly** adv. — **ef·fu′sive·ness** n.

Ef·ik (ef′ik) n. pl. **Ef·ik** 1 One of a Negro people inhabiting Nigeria. 2 The language of these people, showing Sudanic characteristics.

eft (eft) n. 1 A newt. 2 Formerly, a small lizard. [OE efeta]

e·gal (ē′gəl) Obs. adj. Equal. — n. An equal. [<F égal]

e·gal·i·tar·i·an (i·gal′ə·târ′ē·ən) n. One who believes in or works for equal rights. — adj. Equalitarian. [<F égalitaire] — **e·gal′i·tar′i·an·ism** n.

e·gest (ē·jest′) v.t. To eject or void, as feces or perspiration; excrete. [<L egestus, pp. of egerere <ex- out + gerere carry]

e·ges·ta (ē·jes′tə) n. Excreta: opposed to ingesta. [<L, neut. pl. of egestus. See EGEST.]

e·ges·tion (ē·jes′chən) n. The expulsion or voiding of digested matter; defecation.

e·ges·tive (ē·jes′tiv) adj. Excretory: opposed to ingestive.

HEN'S EGG

ch.	Chalazae.	s.	Shell.
ym.	Yolk membrane.	sm.	Shell membrane.
yy.	Yellow food yolk.	ach.	Air chamber.
y.	Germinal vesicle.	a.	Albumin, or white of the egg.
wy.	White yolk.		

egg¹ (eg) n. 1 A reproductive body containing the germ and the food yolk of birds, insects, reptiles, or fishes, enclosed in a membranous or shell-like covering. 2 In common usage, such a body, especially that of the domestic fowl. See also illustration under EMBRYOLOGY, FROG. 3 The female reproductive cell of animals which, when fertilized, becomes a zygote; an ovum or germ cell. 4 Something like or likened to an egg. 5 Figuratively, that which contains a germ. — v.t. 1 To mix or cover with eggs. 2 U.S. To pelt with eggs. — v.i. 3 To collect birds' eggs. — **lay an egg** U.S. Slang To fail: said of a play, joke, etc. [<ON]

egg² (eg) v.t. To instigate or incite; urge: usually with on. [<ON eggja]

egg-and-an·chor (eg′ənd·ang′kər) n. Archit. An ornamental molding carved with series of alternate egg-shaped and anchor-shaped, or dart- or tongue-shaped figures. Also **egg′-and-dart′, egg′-and-tongue′.**

EGG–AND–ANCHOR MOLDING

egg-beat·er (eg′bē′tər) n. A kitchen utensil for beating an egg after it has been removed from the shell.

eg·ger (eg′ər) n. 1 Any of several European moths (genera Lasiocampa and Eriogaster). 2 The tent caterpillar. Also called **eg′ger moth.** Also spelled **eg′gar.** [Prob. <EGG, with ref. to the shape of the cocoon]

egg-nog (eg′nog′) n. A drink made of beaten eggs and milk with sugar and nutmeg and sometimes with brandy, rum, or other liquor. [<EGG + NOG² (def. 1)]

egg-plant (eg′plant′, -plänt′) n. 1 A widely cultivated herb (Solanum melongena) of the nightshade family, with large egg-shaped edible fruit. 2 The fruit, used as a vegetable. 3 A very dark blackish-purple; the color of the skin of the eggplant.

egg-shell (eg′shel′) n. 1 The hard, brittle, outer envelope of an egg. 2 A light ivory shade; the color commonly associated with that of a hen's egg. 2 A very thin and delicate porcelain: also **eggshell china, eggshell**

porcelain.

egg tray A tray to hold eggs in an incubator. See illustration under INCUBATOR.

egg white The albumen of an egg as distinguished from the yolk: also *white of egg*.

e·gis (ē'jis) See AEGIS.

eg·lan·tine (eg'lən·tīn, -tēn) *n.* Either of two roselike plants, the sweetbrier, and the dog rose. Also *Obs.* **eg·la·tere** (eg'lə·tir'). [<F *églantine* <OF *aiglent*, ult. <L *acus* needle]

e·go (ē'gō, eg'ō) *n. pl.* **·gos** **1** Self, considered as the seat of consciousness. **2** In philosophy, the entire man, body and mind. **3** *Psychol.* The self, considered as the aggregate of all conscious acts and states, whether organized or sporadic, but having a unity and continuity differentiating it from all others. **4** *Psychoanal.* The superficial conscious part of the id, developed in response to the physical and social environment. **5** In metaphysics, the permanent real being to whom all the conscious states and attributes belong. **6** *Colloq.* Self-centeredness; egotism; conceit. [<L, I]

e·go·cen·tric (ē'gō·sen'trik, eg'ō-) *adj.* **1** Self–centered; reacting to all things from a personal point of view; caring only for self or personal interests. **2** *Philos.* Proceeding from self as the center, as one's knowledge of the nature of the outside world. — **e'go·cen·tric'·i·ty** (-sen·tris'ə·tē) *n.*

e·go·ism (ē'gō·iz'əm, eg'ō-) *n.* **1** In ethics, the doctrine that the supreme end of human conduct is the perfection or happiness of the ego, or self, and that all virtue consists in the pursuit of self–interest; also, that part of the theory or practice of conduct or duty that has reference to oneself, as distinguished from *altruism*. **2** Selfishness. **3** Egotism. See synonyms under EGOTISM.

e·go·ma·ni·a (ē'gō·mā'nē·ə, -mān'yə, eg'ō-) *n.* Abnormal or excessive egotism. — **e'go·ma'· ni·ac** *n. & adj.*

e·go·tism (ē'gə·tiz'əm, eg'ə-) *n.* The habit or practice of thinking and talking much of oneself, or the spirit that leads to this practice; self-exaltation.
Synonyms: conceit, egoism, self-assertion, self–conceit, self-confidence, self-consciousness, self–esteem, vanity. *Egoism* is the giving the "I" undue supremacy in thought; *egotism* is giving the "I" undue prominence in speech and action. *Self-assertion* is the claim of what one believes to be his due; *self-conceit* is an overestimate of one's own powers or deserts. *Self-consciousness* (as here considered) is the keeping of one's thoughts upon oneself, with the constant anxious question of what others will think. *Vanity* is an overweening admiration of self, craving equal admiration from others. *Self-esteem* is more solid and better founded than *self-conceit*; but is ordinarily a weakness, and never has the worthy sense of *self-confidence*. Compare ASSURANCE, PRIDE. *Antonyms:* bashfulness, deference, diffidence, humility, modesty, self-distrust, self-forgetfulness, shyness, unobtrusiveness, unostentatiousness.

e·go·tist (ē'gə·tist, eg'ə-) *n.* One characterized by egotism. — **e'go·tis'ti·cal** *adj.* — **e'go·tis'· ti·cal·ly** *adv.*

e·gress (ē'gres) *n.* **1** A going out; passing forth, as from a building. **2** A place of exit. **3** *Astron.* The end of the apparent passage of a small body over the face of a larger one, as the end of an eclipse. Also **e·gres'sion.** [<L *egressus* <*ex-* out + *gradi* go]

e·gret (ē'grit) *n.* **1** A heron characterized, in the breeding season, by long and loose plumes drooping over the tail, and usually white plumage; especially the American egret (*Casmerodius albus*), and the snowy egret (*Egretta thula*). **2** A plume or tuft of its feathers, called an *aigrette*. [Var. of AIGRET]

SNOWY EGRET
(Length of body about 2 feet)

E·gypt (ē'jipt) A republic of NE Africa; 386,186 square miles, of which about 12,000 square miles are cultivated; capital, Cairo; divided into **Lower** Egypt, the Nile Delta, and **Upper Egypt,** the Nile Valley between a point a few miles south of Cairo and the Sudan. Officially *Arab Republic of Egypt.*

Egyptian blue A blue pigment made from a mixture of copper silicates and widely used by the early Egyptians, Cretans, and Romans: now imitated by coal-tar colors.

E·gyp·tol·o·gist (ē'jip·tol'ə·jist) *n.* A student of or one versed in Egyptology. Also **E'gyp·tol'o·ger.**

E·gyp·tol·o·gy (ē'jip·tol'ə·jē) *n.* The science or scientific investigation or study of the antiquities of Egypt. — **E·gyp·to·log·ic** (ē·jip'tə·loj'ik), or **·i·cal** *adj.*

eh (ā, e) *interj.* What: used as an interrogative.

ei·der (ī'dər) *n.* A large sea duck of northern regions (genus *Somateria*), having plumage mostly white above and black below. Also **eider duck.** [<ON *œdhr-* in *œdhar-dūn* eider down; infl. in form by Sw. *eider* eider]

eider down 1 The down of the eider used for stuffing pillows and quilts. **2** A warm, light-weight cotton or woolen fabric with a woolen nap. [<ON *œdhar-dūn*]

ei·det·ic (ī·det'ik) *adj. Psychol.* Of or pertaining to the faculty, voluntary or otherwise, of clearly visualizing objects previously seen. [<Gk. *eidētikos* pertaining to images]

eidetic imagery *Psychol.* The phenomenon of visual reproduction of previously seen objects: usually associated with pre-adolescent children.

ei·do·graph (ī'də·graf, -gräf) *n.* An instrument for copying drawings, usually on a reduced scale. [<Gk. *eidos* form + -GRAPH]

ei·do·lon (ī·dō'lən) *n. pl.* **·la** (-lə) **1** A representation; image. **2** A phantom. [<Gk. *eidōlon* image]

Eiffel Tower An iron tower in Paris, 984.25 feet high: designed for the Exposition of 1889 by A. G. Eiffel.

eight (āt) *n.* **1** The cardinal number following seven and preceding nine, or any of the symbols (8, viii, VIII) used to represent it. ◆ Collateral adjective: *octonary.* **2** Anything made up of eight units or members, as the crew of a racing shell, or a playing card with eight pips. —*adj.* Being or consisting of one more than seven; twice four. [OE *eahta*]

eight ball A black pool ball bearing a figure 8, and, in certain games, incurring a penalty on the player who pockets it. —**behind the eight ball** *U.S. Slang* In a dangerous or undesirable position.

eight·een (ā'tēn') *adj.* Consisting of eight more than ten. —*n.* **1** The sum of ten and eight. **2** The symbols (18, xviii, XVIII) representing this number. [OE *eahtatēne*]

eight·een·mo (ā'tēn'mō') See OCTODECIMO.

eight·eenth (ā'tēnth') *adj.* Eighth in order after the tenth: the ordinal of *eighteen.* —*n.* One of eighteen equal parts; the quotient of a unit divided by eighteen.

Eighteenth Amendment An amendment to the Constitution of the United States prohibiting the manufacture, sale, and transportation of intoxicating liquors for beverage purposes: ratified in 1919 and put into effect, January, 1920: repealed in 1933 by the Twenty-first Amendment.

eight·fold (āt'fōld') *adv.* So as to be eight times as many or as great; octuplicate. —*adj.* **1** Consisting of eight parts. **2** Eight times as many or as great.

eighth (ātth, āth) *adj.* **1** Next in order after the seventh. **2** Being one of eight equal parts. —*adv.* In the eighth order, place, or rank: also, in formal discourse, **eighth'ly.** —*n.* An eighth number or part.

eighth note *Music* A quaver.

eight·i·eth (ā'tē·ith) *adj.* **1** Tenth in order after the seventieth. **2** Being one of eighty equal parts. —*n.* **1** One of eighty equal parts. **2** That which follows the seventy-ninth.

eight·score (āt'skôr', -skōr') *adj. & n.* Eight times twenty.

eight·y (ā'tē) *adj.* Consisting of ten more than seventy. —*n.* **1** Eight times ten. **2** The symbols (80, lxxx, LXXX) representing this number. [OE *eahtatig*]

eight·y-nin·er (ā'tē·nī'nər) *n.* One of the Oklahoma homestead settlers of 1889.

ei·gon (ī'gon) *n. Med.* A compound of iodine with certain protein substances: used as an antiseptic.

ein·korn (īn'kôrn) *n.* A variety of wheat (*Triticum monococcum*) with narrow, slender curved spikelets usually bearing only one fertile floret; one-grained wheat: cultivated especially in central Europe. [<G; trans. of NL *monococcum,* species name <Gk. *monos* one + *kokkos* grain]

Ein·stein (īn'stīn), **Albert,** 1878–1955, mathematical physicist, developed the theory of relativity; born in Germany, active in Switzerland and the United States.

ein·stein·i·um (īn·stīn'ē·əm) *n.* A synthetic transuranium element (symbol Es, atomic number 99) originally detected in the debris of a thermonuclear explosion, the most stable isotope having a half-life of 276 days. See PERIODIC TABLE. [after Albert *Einstein*]

Ei·sen·how·er (ī'zən·hou'ər), **Dwight David,** 1890–1969, president of the United States 1953–61; supreme commander of Allied forces in invasion of Europe, World War II.

Ei·sen·stadt (ī'zən·shtät) The capital of Burgenland, Austria.

eis·tedd·fod (ā·steth'vod, es·teth'-) *n. pl.* **·fods** or **·fod·au** (-vod'ī) An annual assembly of bards, in Wales, to foster national, musical, and literary interests. Also **eis·tedd'vod.** [<Welsh, session <*eistedd* sit] — **eis'tedd·fod'ic** *adj.*

ei·ther (ē'thər, ī'-) *adj.* **1** One or the other of two: Use *either* foot on the pedal. **2** Each of two; one and the other: on *either* side. See synonyms under EVERY. —*pron.* One of two; one or the other. —*conj.* In one of two or more cases, indeterminately or indifferently: used as a disjunctive correlative introducing a first alternative, the second and any other being preceded by *or: Either* I shall go *or* he will come. —*adv.* At all; any more so: used after the denial of an alternative: He could not speak, and I could not *either.* [OE *œgther*]

ei·ther-or (ē'thər-ôr', ī'thər-) *adj.* Offering a choice between two alternatives, with other possibilities excluded.

e·jac·u·late (i·jak'yə·lāt) *v.* **·lat·ed, ·lat·ing** *v.t.* **1** To say vehemently and suddenly. **2** To throw out suddenly; eject, as fluids from the body. — *v.i.* **3** To exclaim. See synonyms under CALL, EXCLAIM. [<L *ejaculatus,* pp. of *ejaculari* <*ex-* out + *jaculari* throw] — **e·jac'u·la'tive** *adj.* — **e·jac'u·la'tor** *n.*

e·jac·u·la·tion (i·jak'yə·lā'shən) *n.* **1** The uttering of brief, sudden exclamations; an exclamation. **2** *Eccl.* A brief prayer; a short, pious utterance. **3** *Physiol.* The forceful expulsion of semen during the orgasm; an emission.

e·ject (i·jekt') *v.t.* **1** To throw or drive out by sudden force; expel. **2** To evict. See synonyms under BANISH. —*n.* (ē'jekt) *Psychol.* A perception, mental state, etc. (of another) inferred as an entity by one's own consciousness, but which is essentially inaccessible to consciousness. [<L *ejectus,* pp. of *ejicere* <*ex-* out + *jacere* throw] — **e·jec'tor** *n.*

e·jec·ta (i·jek'tə) *n. pl.* Matter or refuse that has been cast out, as by a volcano or the body. Also **e·jec·ta·men·ta** (i·jek'tə·men'tə). [<L, neut. pl. of *ejectus,* see EJECT.]

e·jec·ta·ble (i·jek'tə·bəl) *adj.* Capable of being ejected.

e·jec·tion (i·jek'shən) *n.* **1** The act of ejecting; expulsion. **2** Matter ejected. —**e·jec'tive** *adj.* — **e·jec'tive·ly** *adv.*

e·ject·ment (i·jekt'mənt) *n.* **1** A casting out; eviction. **2** *Law* An action to recover possession of real estate, with damages for wrongful withholding; also, the writ by which this action is instituted.

ejector seat A pilot's seat which can be catapulted from an aircraft, thus enabling the pilot to bail out at high speeds.

e·ji·do (ā·hē'thō) *n.* A communal farm, specifically in Mexico. [<Sp.]

eke (ēk) *v.t.* **eked, ek·ing 1** To supplement; make small additions to; piece out: usually with *out.* **2** To obtain or produce (a living) with difficulty. **3** *Obs.* To protract; lengthen; increase. —*n. Obs.* An addition, as to a bell rope; postscript; appendix. [Var. of ECHE]

e·kis·tics (i·kis'tiks) *n. pl.* (construed as sing.) The study of human settlements, including area planning and the relationship between communities. [<Gk. *oikos* habitat + -ICS] —**e·kis'tic** *adj.*

El (el) *n.* An elevated railroad. Also *L.* [Short for ELEVATED]

el- Assimilated var. of EN-[2].

e·lab·o·rate (i·lab′ə·rāt) v. **·rat·ed, ·rat·ing** v.t. **1** To create and work out with care and in detail: to *elaborate* a system. **2** To produce by labor; make. —v.i. **3** To speak or write so as to embellish a matter, subject, etc., with additional details; be more specific: with *on* or *upon.* —adj. (-ər·it) Developed in detail with care or painstaking; carefully wrought out; done with thoroughness or exactness. [< L *elaboratus,* pp. of *elaborare* < e- out + *laborare* work] —**e·lab′o·rate·ly** adv. —**e·lab′o·rate·ness** n. —**e·lab′o·ra′tion** n. — **e·lab′o·ra′tive** adj. —**e·lab′o·ra′tor** n.

e·lae·o·lite (i·lē′ə·līt) n. A coarsely crystallized or massive opaque variety of nephelite with a resinous luster: also spelled *eleolite.* [< Gk. *elaion* oil + -LITE]

el·ae·op·tene (el′ē·op′tēn) n. Chem. The liquid hydrocarbon or terpene constituent of an essential oil: distinguished from *stearoptene.* [< Gk. *elaion* oil + *ptenos* flying]

el·ai·o·plast (el′ē·ō·plast) n. Bot. One of the highly refractive oil-secreting protoplasmic granules found near the nuclei of plant cells: also spelled *eleoplast.*

E·lam·ite (ē′ləm·īt) n. **1** One of the ancient inhabitants of Elam. **2** An extinct, unrelated, agglutinative language, or group of languages, spoken in Elam: also **E·lam·it·ic** (ē′ləm·it′ik): also called *Susian.* —adj. Of or pertaining to Elam, its inhabitants or their language: also **E′lam·it′ic, E′lam·it′ish** (-ī′tish).

é·lan (ā·län′) n. Ardor; dash; vivacity. [< F < *élancer* < é- out + *lancer* dart, throw]

e·land (ē′lənd) n. A large oxlike African antelope with twisted horns (genus *Taurotragus*); especially; the common eland (*T. oryx*), of SE Africa. [< Du., elk]

élan vi·tal (vē·tàl′) French Literally, life force; vital energy; in Bergson's philosophy, the creative life impulse of all evolution.

ELAND

el·a·phine (el′ə·fin, -fīn) adj. **1** Of or pertaining to a genus (*Elaphodus*) of deer native in China. **2** Describing the antlers characteristic of this genus. [< L *elaphus* < Gk. *elaphos* a stag]

el·a·pine (el′ə·pīn, -pin) adj. Zool. Of or pertaining to a subfamily (*Elipinae*) of tropical snakes, including many of the most venomous species, as the coral snake, cobra, and harlequin snake. [< NL < Gk. *elaps,* var. of *ellops,* a kind of serpent]

e·lapse (i·laps′) v.i. **e·lapsed, e·laps·ing** To slip by; pass away: said of time. [< L *elapsus,* pp. of *elabi* < e- out, away + *labi* glide]

e·las·mo·branch (i·las′mō·brangk, i·laz′-) n. Any of a subclass (Elasmobranchii) of fishes having cartilaginous skeletons and lamellate gills, including sharks and rays. —adj. Pertaining to or belonging to the subclass Elasmobranchii. [< NL < Gk. *elasmos* metal plate + *branchia* gills]

e·las·tic (i·las′tik) adj. **1** Spontaneously returning to a former size, shape, or configuration after being altered from it; springy; accommodating. **2** Capable of quick recovery, as from misfortune or depression; buoyant. **3** Increasing or diminishing readily in response to a changing stimulus, demand, or other causative influence: an *elastic* price, one that soars or drops quickly owing to sudden variations in demand. **4** Capable of expansion and contraction, as a gas; flexible. —n. A strip, cord, or piece of india rubber or of webbing made elastic by india-rubber threads woven therein, used as a band, suspender, etc.; specifically, a garter. [< NL *elasticus* < Gk. *elastikos* driving, propulsive < *elaunein* drive] — **e·las′ti·cal·ly** adv.

e·las·tic·i·ty (i·las′tis′ə·tē, ē′las-) n. **1** Physics That property of matter by virtue of which a body tends to resist deformation, returning to its former or normal size, shape, or configuration,

after being deflected, compressed, expanded, twisted or drawn. **2** The rebounding quality of bodies; resilience; springiness: the *elasticity* of the air. **3** The tendency to recover from depression or misfortune; buoyancy.

e·las·tin (i·las′tin) n. Biochem. The protein substance, of high glycine and leucine content, which is found in tendons, cartilage, connective tissue, and bone.

e·las·to·mer (i·las′tə·mər) n. Chem. One of a class of polymerized compounds characterized by elastic, rubberlike properties, as the synthetic rubbers and various plastics. [< ELAST(IC) + -o- + Gk. *meros* part]

e·late (i·lāt′) v.t. **·lat·ed, ·lat·ing** To raise the spirits of; excite. —adj. Exalted or triumphant; exultant. [< L *elatus,* pp. for *efferre* < ex- out + *ferre* bear] —**e·lat′ed** adj. —**e·lat′ed·ly** adv. — **e·lat′ed·ness** n.

el·a·ter (el′ə·tər) n. **1** Entomol. **a** A click beetle or elaterid. **b** A spring or terminal bristlelike abdominal appendage of a springtail or podurid insect. **2** Bot. **a** In the horsetail family of plants (*Equisetaceae*), one of the four club-shaped membranous bands attached at a single point on a spore formed by the splitting of the outer coat. **b** A sterile, elastic, spirally twisted filament for the dispersion of spores, as in liverworts, puffballs, and slime molds. [< NL < Gk. *elatēr* < *elaunein* drive]

el·a·ter·id (i·lat′ər·id) adj. Of or pertaining to a family (*Elateridae*) of beetles with serrate antennae, including the click beetles or snapping beetles. —n. An elaterid beetle. [< NL < Gk. *elatēr.* See ELATER.]

el·a·ter·in (i·lat′ər·in) n. Chem. A bitter crystalline compound, $C_{20}H_{28}O_5$, contained in elaterium and having a powerful cathartic effect. [< ELATER(IUM) + -IN]

el·a·ter·ite (i·lat′ə·rīt) n. An elastic, resinous, dark-brown, subtranslucent mineral hydrocarbon, found in soft masses. [< obs. *elater* elasticity (< Gk. < *elaunein* drive) + -ITE[1]]

el·a·te·ri·um (el′ə·tir′ē·əm) n. **1** The squirting cucumber (*Ecballium elaterium*). **2** A purgative derived from its juice. **3** A greenish to gray strongly cathartic substance contained in the juice of the fruit of the squirting cucumber. [< L < Gk. *elatērion* a purgative < *elaunein* drive]

e·la·tion (i·lā′shən) n. Exalted feeling, as from pride or joy; exultation.

El·ba (el′bə) The largest island of the Tuscan Archipelago; 86 square miles; a sovereign principality under the exiled Napoleon I, 1814–15.

El·be (el′bə) A river of central Europe, flowing 691 miles NW to the North Sea near Hamburg. Czechoslovakian **La·be** (la′be).

el·bow (el′bō) n. **1** The joint at the bend of the arm; also, the joint resembling an elbow in the shoulder or hock of a quadruped. Compare illustration under HORSE. **2** Any outward bend resembling an elbow, as a short angular pipe fitting, or a projection on the side of a chair or sofa on which to rest the arm. —v.t. **1** To push or jostle with or as with the elbows. **2** To make (one's way) by such pushing. —v.i. **3** To make one's way by pushing or jostling. [OE *elboga*]

elbow grease Colloq. Steady application; hard work.

elbow room Ample room; scope for activity or occupation.

el·der[1] (el′dər) n. **1** A shrub (genus *Sambucus*) of the honeysuckle family, with white flowers and purple-black or red berries; the roots of some species contain a very poisonous alkaloid, but the flowers and berries are often used in medicine. **2** Any one of various trees or plants resembling elder: the poison *elder* (*Rhus vernix*). [OE *ellærn*]

eld·er[2] (el′dər) adj. **1** Having lived longer; earlier born. **2** Senior: alternative comparative of *old.* **3** Earlier in time. **4** Prior in rank. —n. **1** A prince or head of a tribe or family. **2** A church officer or minister. **3** An older or aged person. **4** An ancestor. [OE *eldra*] — **eld′er·ship** n.

el·der·ber·ry (el′dər·ber·ē, -bər·ē) n. pl. **·ber·ries** The drupe of the common elder.

eld·er·ly (el′dər·lē) adj. Somewhat old; approaching old age.

eld·est (el′dist) adj. First-born; oldest; superlative of OLD See ELDER[2].

E·le·at·ic (ē′lē·at′ik) adj. Pertaining to or characteristic of Elea or the school of philosophy founded there by Xenophanes and Parmenides. —n. **1** A native of Elea. **2** A disciple of the Eleatic school of philosophy, which developed the conception of the universal unity of being. [< L *Eleaticus* < *Elea* ELEA] —**El′e·at′i·cism** n.

el·e·cam·pane (el′i·kam·pān′) n. **1** A tall perennial herb of the composite family (*Inula helenium*), having large leaves, yellow flowers, and a mucilaginous root yielding a tonic. **2** A coarse candy flavored with an extract made from the root of this herb. [< Med. L *enula* elecampane + *campana* of the field]

e·lect (i·lekt′) v.t. **1** To choose for an office by vote. **2** To take by choice or selection. **3** Theol. To choose or set aside for eternal life. —v.i. **4** To make a choice. —adj. **1** Elected to office, but not yet in charge: used as the second element in compounds, as president-*elect.* **2** Theol. Chosen of God for salvation; of saintly or divine character. **3** Selected; chosen; picked out. —n. **1** Theol. A person, or body of persons, chosen of God for salvation or for special service. **2** One who is favored or preferred. [< L *electus,* pp. of *eligere* < ex- out + *legere* choose]

e·lec·tion (i·lek′shən) n. **1** The selecting of a person or persons for office, as by ballot. **2** A popular vote on any question. **3** A choice, as between alternatives; choice in general. **4** In Calvinism, the predestination of some individuals to be saved from God's wrath and punishment. See synonyms under ALTERNATIVE.

e·lec·tive (i·lek′tiv) adj. **1** Of or pertaining to a choice by vote. **2** Obtained or bestowed by election. **3** Exerting the privilege of choice. **4** Subject to choice; optional. **5** Chem. Having a tendency to attract and combine with some substances and not with others: *elective* absorption. —n. An optional study in a fixed college curriculum. — **e·lec′tive·ly** adv. —**e·lec′tive·ness** n.

e·lec·tor (i·lek′tər) n. **1** One who elects; a person qualified to vote at an election. **2** U.S. A presidential elector. **3** One of the great princes who formerly (12th to 18th century) had the right of electing the Holy Roman Emperor. —**presidential electors** The persons chosen by the several States and the District of Columbia' to elect the president and vice president of the United States. The District of Columbia has three electors; each State sends a number equal to its total of senators and representatives.

e·lec·tor·al (i·lek′tər·əl) adj. Pertaining to, of, or comprising electors.

electoral college The whole corporate body of the presidential electors chosen at one election, although they never meet as a body; also, those of a single State, which do meet: a popular, unofficial term, first used informally in 1821.

e·lec·tor·ate (i·lek′tər·it) n. **1** Those who elect; the mass of voters. **2** The rank or territory of an elector in the Holy Roman Empire.

e·lec·tor·ess (i·lek′tər·is) n. **1** A woman qualified to vote at an election. **2** The wife or widow of an elector of the Holy Roman Empire. Also **e·lec′tress** (-tris).

E·lec·tra (i·lek′trə) **1** In Greek legend, a daughter of Agamemnon and Clytemnestra who persuaded her brother Orestes to kill their mother and their mother's lover Aegisthus to avenge their father's murder. **2** One of the Pleiades. Also *Elektra.*

Electra complex Psychoanal. A compulsive, strongly repressed sexual attachment of the daughter to her father: the female analog of the *Oedipus complex.*

e·lec·tret (i·lek′trit) n. A dielectric, usually rod-shaped, which may be strongly charged with positive electricity at one pole and with negative electricity at the other: it is the electrical analog of the magnet. [< ELECTR(ICITY) + (MAGN)ET]

e·lec·tric (i·lek′trik) adj. **1** Relating to, derived from, produced, or operated by electricity. **2** Containing, producing, or carrying electricity. **3**

Spirited; magnetic; thrilling. Also **e·lec'tri·cal.** — *n.* **1** A street car, train, or other vehicle run by electricity. **2** Any substance or material, as amber or resin, which can be given an electric charge by rubbing. [< NL *electricus* < L *electrum* amber < Gk. *ēlektron*] —**e·lec'tri·cal·ly** *adv.*

electric breeze 1 A stream of ions repelled from an electrified point. **2** A brush discharge as used in therapeutics.

electric cell Any of a large variety of devices consisting of two dissimilar metals or materials immersed in an electrolyte, capable of generating an electric charge by chemical action.

ELECTRIC CELL
c. Carbon (positive pole).
z. Zinc (negative pole).

electric chair 1 A chair used for electrocuting criminals by sending a high voltage of electricity through the body of the person fastened into it. **2** Hence, the death penalty.

electric clock Any of variously designed clocks which are actuated by electricity in any way; especially, a clock operated by plugging in on an alternating current transmitting electromagnetic impulses from a master clock.

electric current A stream of electrons flowing through a conducting body; it is usually measured and expressed in terms of amperes, coulombs, and volts. See ELECTRON.

electric displacement The theoretical movement of the electricity in a dielectric as a result of changes in the electric field where the latter is located.

electric eel A cyprinoid, eel-like fish (*Electrophorus electricus*) of tropical America, which sometimes reaches a length of six feet, carrying in its tail organs capable of delivering powerful electric shocks.

electric eye A photoelectric cell.

electric field A field of force surrounding a charged object or a moving magnet.

electric fish Any fish having organs capable of imparting an electric shock.

e·lec·tri·cian (i·lek'trish'ən, ē'lek-) *n.* **1** One versed in the science of electricity. **2** An inventor, maker, or repairer of electrical apparatus.

e·lec·tric·i·ty (i·lek'tris'ə·tē, ē'lek-) *n.* **1** A fundamental property of matter, associated with atomic particles whose movements, free or controlled, lead to the development of fields of force and the generation of kinetic or potential energy. The electron is the basic unit of *negative* electricity, and the proton of *positive* electricity. Any accumulation of one kind of electricity in excess of an equivalent of the opposite kind is called a *charge* and is measured in appropriate units. A charge fixed at one point or within a circumscribed field of force, as a Leyden jar, is *static* electricity; a charge which flows through a conductor is *current* electricity. **2** The property of many substances, as amber, fur, glass, etc., mutually to attract or repel each other when subjected to friction. **3** The science which deals with the phenomena, laws, theory, and application of this property.

electric ray Any of a family (Torpedinidae) of rays with usually round bodies and short tails having an organ in each winglike fin that delivers an electric shock as a means of stunning prey or of defense against predators. Also called *crampfish, numbfish, torpedo.*

e·lec·tri·fy (i·lek'trə·fī) *v.t.* **·fied, ·fy·ing 1** To act upon, charge with, or subject to electricity. **2** To equip, as a house, for the use of electricity. **3** To adapt for operation by electric power, as a railroad. **4** To arouse; startle; thrill. — **e·lec'tri·fi'a·ble** *adj.* —**e·lec'tri·fi·ca'tion** *n.* — **e·lec'tri·fi'er** *n.*

e·lec·trine (i·lek'trin) *adj.* **1** Made of electrum. **2** Made of or related to amber. —*n.* An imaginary substance, supposed by some to be the basis of electricity. [< Gk. *ēlektrinos* < *ēlektron* amber]

e·lec·tro (i·lek'trō) *n. pl.* **·tros 1** An electrotype. **2** Electroplating. —*v.t.* **·troed, ·tro·ing** To make an electrotype of; electroplate. [Short for ELECTROTYPE]

electro- *combining form* **1** Electric; by, with, or of electricity: *electrocardiogram.* **2** Electrolytic: *electroanalysis.* Also, before vowels, sometimes **electr-.** [< Gk. *ēlektron* amber]

e·lec·tro·a·cous·tics (i·lek'trō·ə·kōō'stiks) *n.* The branch of acoustics which studies the design, operation, and efficiency of equipment used in the electrical and electronic transmission of sound, as microphones, loudspeakers, soundtrack apparatus, tape-recorders, etc. — **e·lec'tro·a·cous'tic** *adj.*

e·lec·tro·a·nal·y·sis (i·lek'trō·ə·nal'ə·sis) *n.* An analysis by and in accordance with the methods of electrolysis.

e·lec·tro·bi·ol·o·gy (i·lek'trō·bī·ol'ə·jē) *n.* The study of electrical phenomena associated with the functioning and behavior of living organisms.

e·lec·tro·bi·os·co·py (i·lek'trō·bī·os'kə·pē) *n.* The determination of the presence of absence of life in an organism by means of suitably applied electric currents. —**e·lec'tro·bi'o·scop'ic** (-bī'ə·skop'ik) *adj.*

e·lec·tro·cap·il·lar·i·ty (i·lek'trō·kap'i·lar'ə·tē) *n.* That change in the surface tension between two conducting liquids in contact which occurs when an electric current is passed between them.

e·lec·tro·car·di·o·gram (i·lek'trō·kär'dē·ə·gram') *n. Med.* A graph indicating electromotive variations in the action of the heart.

e·lec·tro·car·di·o·graph (i·lek'trō·kä'dē·ə·graf', -gräf') *n. Med.* An instrument for recording the electric current produced by the action of the heart muscle: used in the diagnosis of diseases affecting the heart. —**e·lec'tro·car·di·og·ra·phy** (i·lek'trō·kär'dē·og'rə·fē) *n.*

e·lec·tro·chem·is·try (i·lek'trō·kem'is·trē) *n.* The branch of chemistry that treats of electricity as active in effecting chemical change. — **e·lec'tro·chem'i·cal** *adj.* —**e·lec'tro·chem'i·cal·ly** *adv.* —**e·lec'tro·chem'ist** *n.*

e·lec·tro·co·ag·u·la·tion (i·lek'trō·kō·ag'yə·lā'shən) *n.* The destructive coagulation of protoplasmic material or of living tissue, healthy or morbid, by the passage through it of an electric current.

e·lec·tro·cul·ture (i·lek'trō·kul'chər) *n.* The stimulation of the growth, development, and maturing of plants by electrical means, especially by static electricity and fields of force in the atmosphere.

e·lec·tro·cute (i·lek'trə·kyōōt) *v.t.* **·cut·ed, ·cut·ing 1** To execute in the electric chair. **2** To kill by electricity. [< ELECTRO- + (EXE)CUTE] — **e·lec'tro·cu'tion** *n.*

e·lec·trode (i·lek'trōd) *n. Electr.* Either of the two conducting elements through which a current leaves or enters an electrolytic cell, vacuum tube, electric arc or furnace, or any non-metallic conductor; an anode or cathode. Compare illustration under ELECTRIC CELL. [< ELECTR(O) + -ODE[1]]

e·lec·tro·de·pos·it (i·lek'trō·di·poz'it) *v.i.* To deposit chemically, as metal from a solution, by means of an electric current. —*n.* That which is so deposited. —**e·lec'tro·dep'o·si'tion** (-dep'ə·zish'ən, -dē'pə-) *n.*

e·lec·tro·des·ic·ca·tion (i·lek'trō·des'ə·kā'shən) *n.* The destruction of animal tissues by means of controlled high-frequency electric-spark discharges: also called *fulguration.*

e·lec·tro·dy·nam·ics (i·lek'trō·dī·nam'iks) *n.* The branch of physics which deals with the forces of electrical attraction and repulsion and with the energy transformations of magnetic fields and electric currents.

e·lec·tro·dy·na·mom·e·ter (i·lek'trō·dī'na·mom'ə·tər) *n.* An instrument for measuring electrical current, voltage, or power, in which the deflecting force arises from the interaction of two wire coils carrying currents.

e·lec·tro·en·ceph·a·lo·gram (i·lek'trō·en·sef'ə·lə·gram') *n.* A record of electrical impulses and changes in the brain: important in the diagnosis of certain diseases, as epilepsy. —**e·lec'tro·en·ceph'a·lo·graph'** (-graf',-gräf') *n.*

e·lec·tro·en·dos·mo·sis (i·lek'trō·en'dos·mō'sis) *n.* The diffusion of fluids through permeable membranes or diaphragms by the application of an electrical potential.

e·lec·tro·form·ing (i·lek'trō·fôr'ming) *n.* The production of metal tubing, medals, and the like by the electrolytic deposition of metal upon a mold of the desired shape or pattern.

e·lec·tro·gas·tro·graph (i·lek'trō·gas'trə·graf, -gräf) *n. Med.* A device for indicating electrical changes caused by muscular contractions of the stomach.

e·lec·tro·graph (i·lek'trō·graf, -gräf) *n.* **1** The linear record of an electrometer. **2** An apparatus for tracing a design to be etched for use in printing wallpaper, calico, etc. **3** A roentgenogram. —**e·lec'tro·graph'ic** *adj.* —**e·lec·trog·ra·phy** (i·lek'trog'rə·fē, ē'lek-) *n.*

e·lec·tro·ki·net·ic (i·lek'trō·ki·net'ik) *adj.* Pertaining to or caused by electricity in motion.

e·lec·tro·ki·net·ics (i·lek'trō·ki·net'iks) *n.* That branch of electrical science which treats of the motion of electricity and the forces producing or regulating it: opposed to *electrostatics.*

e·lec·tro·ky·mo·graph (i·lek'trō·ki'mə·graf, -gräf) *n. Med.* An instrument for measuring the action of the heart by means of X-rays which project the heart shadow upon a fluorescent screen used in conjunction with a photocell.

e·lec·tro·lu·mi·nes·cence (i·lek'trō·lōō'mə·nes'·əns) *n.* **1** Light produced by the agency of electricity. **2** The emission of a soft, uniformly diffused light from phosphor powders embedded in the surface of a panel of glass or other insulating material which is directly subjected to the action of an alternating electric field. — **e·lec'tro·lu'mi·nes'cent** *adj.*

e·lec·trol·y·sis (i·lek'trol'ə·sis) *n.* **1** The decomposing of a chemical compound by passing an electric current through it. **2** The use of an electrified needle to destroy the roots of unwanted body hair. [< ELECTRO- + -LYSIS]

e·lec·tro·lyte (i·lek'trə·līt) *n.* **1** A substance, usually in solution, which will transmit an electric current by the formation of ions. **2** A solution which conducts an electric current between the electrodes of a cell, accompanied by the release of a gas or the deposition of a solid. [< ELECTRO- + Gk. *lytos* loosed < *luein* loosen] — **e·lec·tro·lyt·ic** (i·lek'trə·lit'ik) or **·i·cal** *adj.* — **e·lec'tro·lyt'i·cal·ly** *adv.*

e·lec·tro·mag·net (i·lek'trō·mag'nit) *n.* A core of soft iron or the like, which temporarily becomes a magnet during the passage of an electric current through a coil of wire surrounding it. — **e·lec'tro·mag·net'ic** (-mag·net'ik) or **·i·cal** *adj.* — **e·lec'tro·mag·net'i·cal·ly** *adv.*

e·lec·tro·mag·net·ism (i·lek'trō·mag'nə·tiz'əm) *n.* **1** Magnetism developed by electricity. **2** That science which treats of the relations between electricity and magnetism and the phenomena due to these relations. Also **e·lec'tro·mag·net'ics.**

e·lec·tro·met·al·lur·gy (i·lek'trō·met'ə·lûr'jē, -mə·tal'ər·jē) *n.* The art or science of electrolytically depositing metals, or of separating them from their ores or alloys by electrolysis or the electric furnace. —**e·lec'tro·met'al·lur'gi·cal** *adj.*

e·lec·trom·e·ter (i·lek'trom'ə·tər, ē'lek-) *n.* An instrument for measuring the voltage in an electric circuit by the electrostatic forces exerted between two charged bodies.

e·lec·tro·mo·tion (i·lek'trə·mō'shən) *n.* **1** The passage of an electric current in a voltaic circuit. **2** Motion produced by electricity employed as power.

e·lec·tro·mo·tive (i·lek'trə·mō'tiv) *adj.* Producing, or tending to produce an electric current; distinguished from *magnetomotive.*

n. Med. An instrument for determining the location and extent of nerve lesions by the application of an electric stimulus to muscles whose responses are converted into both sound and visual records. —**e·lec'tro·my·og'ra·phy** (-mī·og'rə·fē) *n.* **e·lec'tro·my'o·graph'i·cal** *adj.*

e·lec·tron (i·lek'tron) *n.* An electrically charged particle of the atom: it carries the unit charge of negative electricity, estimated at 4.8×10^{-10} cgs electrostatic units, and has a mass approximately one eighteen-hundredth (more exactly 1/1837) of that of the proton. Electrons are emitted in the form of beta particles and cathode rays. —**free electron** An electron not permanently bound to any atom and free to move within the limits of a given substance or material, as in a galvanic current. [< Gk. *ēlektron* amber]

e·lec·tro·neg·a·tive (i·lek'trō·neg'ə·tiv) *adj.* **1** Appearing, as an element in electrolysis, at the positive electrode. **2** Having the property of becoming negatively electrified by contact with or the chemical action of another element.

electron gun An apparatus, usually in the form of a slender tube with thermionic filaments and focusing and accelerating electrodes, used in television for directing a steady stream of electrons in a given direction.

e·lec·tron·ic (i·lek'tron'ik, ē'lek-) adj. **1** Of or pertaining to electrons. **2** Operating or produced by the movement of free electrons or other carriers of electric charge, as in an electron tube. **3** Pertaining to electronics. — **e·lec'tron'i·cal·ly** adv.

e·lec·tron·ics (i·lek'tron'iks, ē'lek-) n. pl. (Construed as singular) The study of the properties and behavior of electrons under all conditions, especially with reference to technical and industrial applications.

electron lens A distribution of an electric field surrounding the path of an electron beam such that the beam may be concentrated in a focus similar to that of an optical lens.

electron microscope A microscope which uses high-voltage streams of electrons in order to bring into visibility objects not accessible to the relatively large wavelengths of visible light used by the most powerful optical microscopes.

e·lec·tro·nog·ra·phy (i·lek'trō·nog'rə·fē) n. A method of printing without pressure between paper and the inked surface, by means of an applied electric charge which ionizes the ink particles, causing them to migrate to the oppositely charged printing surface. [< ELECTRON + -(O)GRAPHY]

electron optics A method for the control of electron beams or rays by properly adjusted magnetic or electric fields so that the flow of electrons will simulate the effect of light rays in an optical instrument.

electron shell Physics The orbital arrangement of electrons outside the nucleus of an atom.

electron tube A high vacuum tube in which a stream of electrons is emitted from a heated cathode and subjected to the controlling action of a grid which amplifies and directs the current.

electron volt A unit of energy equal to that acquired by an electron which passes through a potential difference of one volt: equal to 1.602 $\times 10^{-12}$ erg: also called equivalent volt.

e·lec·tro·op·tics (i·lek'trō·op'tiks) n. Physics The study of the modification of optical phenomena by the application of an electric field.

e·lec·trop·a·thy (i·lek'trop'ə·thē, ē'lek-) n. Med. The treatment of disease by means of electricity. — **e·lec'tro·path'ic** (-trə·path'ik) adj. — **e·lec'tro·path'i·cal·ly** adv.

e·lec·tro·plate (i·lek'trə·plāt') v.t. ·plat·ed, ·plat·ing To coat with metal by electrolysis, the object being immersed in a solution of a salt of the metal in connection with the negative pole of a battery or dynamo. — n. An electroplated article. — **e·lec'tro·plat'er** n.

e·lec·tro·pos·i·tive (i·lek'trō·poz'ə·tiv) adj. **1** Appearing at the negative electrode: said of an element in electrolysis. **2** Having the property of becoming positively electrified by contact or chemical action.

e·lec·tro·scis·sion (i·lek'trō·sizh'ən) n. Surg. The cutting or division of tissues by an electrically operated knife.

e·lec·tro·scope (i·lek'trə·skōp) n. An instrument for detecting the presence of electricity upon a conductor by the attraction or repulsion of pith balls or strips of gold leaf. See illustration. — **e·lec'tro·scop'ic** (-skop'ik) adj.

ELECTROSCOPE
Metallic pole (m), electrically charged by (e), conducts the impulse to strips (s) that acquire the charge and move apart in electrostatic repulsion.

e·lec·tro·shock (i·lek'trō·shok') n. Psychiatry A shock to the nervous system of a mental patient, produced by a carefully regulated electric current passed through the head.

e·lec·tro·stat·ics (i·lek'trō·stat'iks) n. That branch of electrical science which treats of the phenomena of electricity at rest or of frictional electricity: opposed to electrokinetics. — **e·lec'tro·stat'ic** or ·i·cal adj. — **e·lec'tro·stat'i·cal·ly** adv.

e·lec·tro·stenol·y·sis (i·lek'trō·sti·nol'ə·sis) n. The depositing of metallic particles in the

pores of a high–resistance membrane by electrolysis.

e·lec·tro·tax·is (i·lek'trō·tak'sis) n. Biol. **1** That property of protoplasm which makes it susceptible to the influence of an electric stimulus, as shown by the direction of movements. **2** Any similar property in simple organisms. Also **e·lec'trot'ro·pism** (i·lek'trot'rə·piz'əm, ē'lek-). — **e·lec'tro·tac'tic** (-tak'tik) adj.

e·lec·tro·tech·nics (i·lek'trō·tek'niks) n. The science of the methods, processes, and operations by which electricity is applied in the industrial arts. — **e·lec'tro·tech'nic** (-nik) or ·ni·cal adj.

e·lec·tro·ther·a·peu·tics (i·lek'trō·ther'ə·pyoo'·tiks) n. The treatment of disease by electricity, or the laws, etc., of such treatment. Also **e·lec'tro·ther'a·py** (-ə·pē). — **e·lec'tro·ther'a·peu'tic** (-tik) or ·ti·cal adj.

e·lec·tro·ther·a·pist (i·lek'trō·ther'ə·pist) n. A practitioner of electrotherapeutics. Also **e·lec'·tro·ther'a·peu'tist**.

e·lec·trot·o·nus (i·lek'trot'ə·nəs, ē'lek-) n. Physiol. The change in the activity of a nerve or muscle induced by a voltaic current. [< NL < ELECTRO- + Gk. tonos tension] — **e·lec·tro·ton·ic** (i·lek'trō·ton'ik) adj.

e·lec·tro·type (i·lek'trō·tīp') n. **1** A metallic copy of any surface, as a coin, made by electric deposition, especially one of a page of type for printing. **2** An impression from an electrotyped cut. **3** The process of electrotyping; electrotypy. — v.t. ·typed, ·typ·ing To make an electrotype of.

e·lec·tu·ar·y (i·lek'choo·er'ē) n. pl. ·ar·ies A medicine mixed with honey or sirup to form a paste. [< LL electuarium <Gk. ekleikton < ek out + leichein lick]

el·e·gance (el'ə·gəns) n. **1** The state or quality of being elegant or refined. **2** Anything elegant. Also **el'e·gan·cy**.

el·e·gant (el'ə·gənt) adj. **1** Marked by refinement, grace, or symmetry, as of action, form or structure; also, possessing or exhibiting refined taste. **2** Possessing a fine sense of beauty or fitness. **3** Colloq. Excellent; capital. **4** Marked by completeness and simplicity; appropriate: an elegant solution. [< F élégant

< L elegans, -antis fastidious] — **el'e·gant·ly** adv.

— Synonyms: dainty, exquisite. Elegant (Latin elegans, select) refers to the lighter, finer elements of beauty in form or motion, but is often misused as a general term of approval. Exquisite denotes the utmost perfection of the elegant in minute details; we speak of an elegant garment, and exquisite lace. Exquisite is also applied to intense keenness of any feeling; as, exquisite delight; exquisite pain. Dainty, at its best, applies to what is at once slight, delicate, and pleasing; in its extreme use, it may apply to sensibilities or feelings too delicate for the demands of practical life, overnice, squeamish. See BEAUTIFUL, CHOICE, FINE[1], POLITE. Antonyms: common, coarse, harsh, rude.

el·e·gi·ac (el'ə·jī'ək, i·lē'jē·ak) adj. **1** Pertaining to elegies. **2** Of the nature of an elegy; sad; plaintive. **3** In ancient prosody, written in distichs consisting of hexameter and pentameter. Also **el'e·gi'a·cal**. — n. **1** A poet who writes in the tone or in the meter of the elegy. **2** pl. Verse composed in the elegiac spirit or form.

el·e·gy (el'ə·jē) n. pl. ·gies **1** A funeral song. **2** A meditative poem with sorrowful theme. **3** A classical poem written in elegiac verse. [< F élégie <L elegia <Gk. elegeia <elegos a song]

el·e·ment (el'ə·mənt) n. **1** A component or essential part; especially, a simple part of anything complex; a constituent; ingredient. **2** pl. First principles or fundamental ideas; rudiments. **3** Eccl. The bread and wine of the Lord's Supper. **4** An ultimate and essential principle in the make–up of anything; essential constituent; anciently, one of the substances —earth, air, fire, and water—supposed to make up all things: still in popular use: the fury of the elements, the devouring element. **5** The natural sphere or environment: The element of fishes is water. **6** Physics One of a limited number of substances each of which is composed entirely of atoms having an invariant nuclear charge and none of which may be decomposed by ordinary chemical means, as

TABLE OF CHEMICAL ELEMENTS
(See also PERIODIC TABLE OF ELEMENTS.)

NAME	Symbol	Atomic No.	NAME	Symbol	Atomic No.	NAME	Symbol	Atomic No.
Actinium	Ac	89	Gold (aurum)	Au	79	Polonium	Po	84
Aluminum	Al	13	Hafnium	Hf	72	Potassium (kalium)	K	19
Americium	Am	95	Helium	He	2	Praseodymium	Pr	59
Antimony (stibium)	Sb	51	Holmium	Ho	67	Promethium	Pm	61
Argon	A	18	Hydrogen	H	1	Protactinium	Pa	91
Arsenic	As	33	Indium	In	49	Radium	Ra	88
Astatine	At	85	Iodine	I	53	Radon	Rn	86
Barium	Ba	56	Iridium	Ir	77	Rhenium	Re	75
Berkelium	Bk	97	Iron (ferrum)	Fe	26	Rhodium	Rh	45
Beryllium	Be	4	Krypton	Kr	36	Rubidium	Rb	37
Bismuth	Bi	83	Lanthanum	La	57	Ruthenium	Ru	44
Boron	B	5	Lawrencium	Lw	103	Samarium	Sm	62
Bromine	Br	35	Lead (plumbum)	Pb	82	Scandium	Sc	21
Cadmium	Cd	48	Lithium	Li	3	Selenium	Se	34
Calcium	Ca	20	Lutetium	Lu	71	Silicon	Si	14
Californium	Cf	98	Magnesium	Mg	12	Silver (argentum)	Ag	47
Carbon	C	6	Manganese	Mn	25	Sodium (natrium)	Na	11
Cerium	Ce	58	Mendelevium	Md	101	Strontium	Sr	38
Cesium	Cs	55	Mercury			Sulfur	S	16
Chlorine	Cl	17	(hydrargyrum)	Hg	80	Tantalum	Ta	73
Chromium	Cr	24	Molybdenum	Mo	42	Technetium	Tc	43
Cobalt	Co	27	Neodymium	Nd	60	Tellurium	Te	52
Columbium	(Cb)		Neon	Ne	10	Terbium	Tb	65
See NIOBIUM			Neoytterbium			Thallium	Tl	81
Copper (cuprum)	Cu	29	See YTTERBIUM			Thorium	Th	90
Curium	Cm	96	Neptunium	Np	93	Thulium	Tm	69
Dysprosium	Dy	66	Nickel	Ni	28	Tin (stannum)	Sn	50
Einsteinium	Es	99	Niobium	Nb	41	Titanium	Ti	22
Erbium	Er	68	Niton See RADON			Tungsten		
Europium	Eu	63	Nitrogen	N	7	See WOLFRAM		
Fermium	Fm	100	Nobelium	No	102	Uranium	U	92
Fluorine	F	9	Osmium	Os	76	Vanadium	V	23
Francium	Fr	87	Oxygen	O	8	Wolfram	W	74
Gadolinium	Gd	64	Palladium	Pd	46	Xenon	Xe	54
Gallium	Ga	31	Phosphorus	P	15	Ytterbium	Yb	70
Germanium	Ge	32	Platinum	Pt	78	Yttrium	Yt	39
Glucinum See BERYLLIUM			Plutonium	Pu	94	Zinc	Zn	30
						Zirconium	Zr	40

gold, carbon, sodium, etc.
7 One of the primary parts of an organism; also, a cell or morphological unit. **8** One of a number of parts composing a symmetrical whole. **9** *Geom.* One of the forms or data which together compose a figure, as a line, a point, a plane, a space. **10** *Math.* **a** An infinitely small portion of a magnitude; a generatrix. **b** A term in an algebraic expression. **11** One of the dissimilar substances in a voltaic cell or battery, etc. **12** A group or class of people distinguished from a larger group to which it belongs by its own peculiar beliefs, attitudes, behavior, etc.: the conservative *element* in the party; a rowdy *element* in the crowd. See synonyms under PART, PARTICLE. — **to be in one's element** To be in pleasing surroundings or be engaged in activities in which one excels. [<L *elementum* first principle]
el·e·men·tal (el'ə·men'təl) *adj.* **1** Pertaining to the fundamental or basic constituent of anything; primary; simple. **2** Having to do with rudiments or first principles. **3** Pertaining to or like one of the four elements of ancient physics, fire, air, earth, and water. **4** Pertaining to the forces, phenomena, or powers of physical nature, often as personified: *elemental* spirits. **5** Comparable to the great primal powers of nature: *elemental* storms. **6** Of or pertaining to chemical elements, or one of the chemical elements; uncompounded. — **el'·e·men'tal·ly** *adv.*
el·e·men·ta·ry (el'ə·men'tər·ē) *adj.* **1** Of, pertaining to, or being an element or elements, in any sense. **2** Treating of the first principles of anything; rudimentary: an *elementary* analysis. **3** Having the nature of an infinitesimal part of a quantity or magnitude. — **el'e·men'ta·ri·ly** *adv.* — **el'e·men'ta·ri·ness** *n.*
elementary education Public school and private education beyond kindergarten and preceding secondary school, from six to eight years in length, dealing with the fundamentals of education.
el·e·mi (el'ə·mē) *n.* Any one of several gum resins obtained from tropical trees of various genera, especially Manila elemi, from the pili tree of the Philippines: used in drugs and varnishes. [<Sp. *elemi,* ? <Arabic *al-lāmī*]
e·len·chus (i·leng'kəs) *n. pl.* **·chi** (-kī) **1** The contradictory opposite of a proposition; hence, a refuting argument; a refutation. **2** A false refutation; sophism. Also **e·lench** (i·lengk'). [<L <Gk. *elenchos* a cross-examination] — **e·len'chic** or **·chi·cal, e·lenc'·tic** or **·ti·cal** *adj.*
el·e·phant (el'ə·fənt)
n. **1** A massively built, almost hairless ungulate mammal of Asia and Africa (family *Elephantidae),* the largest of existing land animals, having a flexible proboscis or trunk, and the upper incisors developed as tusks valued as the chief source of ivory. There are two genera: the small-eared Asian elephant, *Elephas Maximus* and the African elephant, *Loxodonta africana,* with large flapping ears. **2** Something unwieldy, burdensome, or hard to dispose of. See WHITE ELEPHANT. **3** A size of paper, 23 by 38 inches. [<OF *olifant* <L *elephantus* <Gk. *elephas, -antos* ivory; ult. origin unknown]

AFRICAN ELEPHANT
(Height at the shoulder rarely above 11 feet; the Indian elephant slightly smaller; the cows, 7 to 9 feet)

elephant foot A South African twining vine (*Testudinaria elephantipes)* of the yam family, having a conical, cormlike stem covered with a barky substance which, becoming deeply cracked, forms large angular protuberances like those on the shell of a tortoise (whence the name *tortoise plant):* often cultivated in greenhouses. Also called *Hottentot bread.* Also **el'e·phant's-foot'.**
el·e·phan·ti·a·sis (el'ə·fən·tī'ə·sis) *n. Pathol.* The final chronic stage of a filariasis caused by the presence in the blood and lymph of a parasitic nematode worm (*Wuchereria bancrofti).* It is characterized by a thickening and hardening of the skin, together with an enor-

mous enlargement of the part affected, usually the lower extremities. [<L <Gk. <*elephas* elephant]
el·e·phan·tine (el'ə·fan'tēn, -tin, -tīn) *adj.* **1** Pertaining to an elephant. **2** Enormous; unwieldy.
el·e·vate (el'ə·vāt) *v.t.* **·vat·ed, ·vat·ing** **1** To raise; lift up. **2** To raise in rank, status, position, etc.; promote. **3** To raise the spirits of; cheer; inspire. **4** To raise the pitch or loudness of. **5** To raise the moral character or intellectual nature of, as a conversation. See synonyms under HEIGHTEN, PROMOTE, RAISE. [<L *elevatus,* pp. of *elevare* <*ex-* out + *levare* lighten]
el·e·vat·ed (el'ə·vā'tid) *adj.* **1** Lofty in situation; high: an *elevated* plateau. **2** Lofty in character; sublime: *elevated* sentiments. See synonyms under GRAND, HIGH. — *n. Colloq.* An overhead railroad.
el·e·va·tion (el'ə·vā'shən) *n.* **1** The act of elevation; exaltation. **2** An elevated place. **3** *Archit.* A geometrical drawing of the upright parts of a structure, as shown in blueprints and scale drawings. **4** *Eccl.* **a** The raising of the eucharistic elements: also **elevation of the Host. b** The music of voice or instrument that accompanies the elevation of the Host. **5** Height above the sea level. **6** *Astron.* The angular distance of a celestial body above the horizon. See synonyms under HEIGHT, RAMPART.
el·e·va·tor (el'ə·vā'tər) *n.* **1** One who or that which elevates. **2** A hoisting mechanism for grain. **3** A warehouse where grain is elevated and distributed. **4** A movable platform or cage in a building, for carrying freight or passengers up or down. **5** *Aeron.* An auxiliary airfoil, by the tilting or dipping of which the ascent or descent of the airplane is regulated: also called *diving rudder.* See illustration under AIRPLANE.
el·e·ven (i·lev'ən) *adj.* Consisting of one more than ten. — *n.* **1** The cardinal number preceding twelve and following ten. **2** Any of the symbols (11, xi, XI) representing this number. **3** A team or side of eleven players, as in cricket or football. [OE *endleofan*]
el·e·ven·fold (i·lev'ən·fōld') *adj.* Consisting of eleven; eleven times as great or as much; undecuplicate.
el·e·venth (i·lev'ənth) *adj.* **1** Next in order after the tenth. **2** Being one of eleven equal parts. — *n.* **1** One of eleven equal parts. **2** The quotient of a unit divided by eleven: five is one *eleventh* of fifty-five. **3** In a series, the unit or thing after the tenth.
eleventh hour The latest possible time; the last opportunity.
el·e·von (el'ə·von) *n. Aeron.* A combined aileron and elevator, used in certain types of airplanes. [<ELEV(ATOR) + (AILER)ON]
elf (elf) *n. pl.* **elves** (elvz) **1** In folklore, a dwarfish, mischievous sprite. **2** A dwarf or diminutive person: a pet name for a lively child. [OE *ælf.* Akin to OAF.]
elf-child (elf'chīld') *n.* A child believed to have been left by elves in place of one that they have stolen; a changeling.
elf·in (el'fin) *adj.* Relating or belonging to elves. — *n.* **1** An elf. **2** A sportive child.
elf·ish (el'fish) *adj.* Relating to elves; mischievous. — **elf'ish·ly** *adv.* — **elf'ish·ness** *n.*
elf-land (elf'land') *n.* The supposed home of the elves; fairyland.
elf-lock (elf'lok') *n.* A lock of hair tangled as if by elves; a straggling lock.
Elgin marbles A collection of Greek sculpture in the British Museum, formerly on the Acropolis at Athens. [after the Earl of *Elgin,* who had the collection brought to England, 1803–12]
e·lic·it (i·lis'it) *v.t.* To draw out or forth, as by some attraction or inducement; bring to light: to *elicit* truth. [<L *elicitus,* pp. of *elicere* <*ex-* out + *lacere* entice] — **e·lic'i·ta'tion** *n.* — **e·lic'i·tor** *n.*
e·lide (i·līd') *v.t.* **e·lid·ed, e·lid·ing** **1** To omit (a vowel or syllable) in writing or pronouncing a word. **2** To suppress; omit; ignore. **3** *Law* To annul. [<L *elidere* <*ex-* out + *laedere* strike] — **e·lid'i·ble** *adj.*
el·i·gi·ble (el'ə·jə·bəl) *adj.* Capable of being chosen or elected; worthy of acceptance. — *n.* One who is eligible in any sense. [<F *éligible* <L *eligere.* See ELECT.] — **el'i·gi·bil'i·ty, el'i·gi·ble·ness** *n.* — **el'i·gi·bly** *adv.*

e·lim·i·nate (i·lim'ə·nāt) *v.t.* **·nat·ed, ·nat·ing** **1** To expel; get rid of. **2** To disregard as irrelevant or incorrect; ignore. **3** *Physiol.* To void; excrete. **4** *Math.* To remove (a quantity) from a system of algebraic equations. [<L *eliminatus,* pp. of *eliminare* <*ex-* out + *limen* a threshold]
e·lim·i·na·tion (i·lim'ə·nā'shən) *n.* **1** The act of eliminating. **2** The state of being cast out or expelled. — **e·lim'i·na·tive** *adj.* — **e·lim'i·na·tor** *n.* — **e·lim'i·na·to·ry** (-tôr'ē, -tō'rē) *adj.*
e·li·sion (i·lizh'ən) *n.* **1** The eliding or striking out of a part of a word, as in "o'er" for "over." **2** A suppression of a part. [<L *elisio, -onis* <*elidere.* See ELIDE.]
e·lite (ā·lēt', i·lēt') *n.* **1** The choicest part, as of a society, army, etc.; the pick. **2** A size of typewriter type, equivalent to 10-point, with 12 characters to the inch. Also **é·lite'.** [<F *élite* <Med. L *electa* choice <L *eligere.* See ELECT.]
e·lix·ir (i·lik'sər) *n.* **1** A sweetened alcoholic medicinal preparation; a cordial; formerly a compound tincture. **2** An imaginary liquid or soluble substance by means of which alchemists once hoped to change base metals into gold. **3** An imaginary cordial supposed to be capable of sustaining life indefinitely: also *Obs.* **elixir vi·tae** (vī'tē). **4** The essential principle; concentrated essence. [<Med. L <Arabic *al-iksīr* <Gk. *xerion* medicated powder <*xeros* dry]
E·liz·a·beth (i·liz'ə·bəth) A feminine personal name. Also **E·li·za** (i·lī'zə), **E·lis·a·beth** (i·liz'ə·bəth, *Dan., Du., Ger.* ā·lē'zä·bet), *Fr.* **É·li·sa·beth** (ā·lē·zà·bet'), *Ital.* **E·li·sa·bet·ta** (ā·lē'·zä·bet'tä). [<Hebrew, God has sworn]
— **Elizabeth,** the mother of John the Baptist. *Luke* ii 5–14.
— **Elizabeth,** born 1900, Elizabeth Angela Marguerite Bowes-Lyon, wife of George VI of England, king 1937–52.
— **Elizabeth,** pseudonym of Countess Elizabeth Mary Russell. See RUSSELL.
— **Elizabeth, Saint,** 1207–31, Hungarian princess; queen of Thuringia 1221–27.
— **Elizabeth I,** 1533–1603, queen of England 1558–1603; daughter of Henry VIII and Anne Boleyn.
— **Elizabeth II,** born 1926, Elizabeth Alexandra Mary, queen of Great Britain 1952– ; daughter of George VI; married to Prince Philip.
— **Elizabeth Pe·trov·na** (pe·trôv'nə), 1709–62, empress of Russia 1741–62.
E·liz·a·be·than (i·liz'ə·bē'thən, -beth'ən) *adj.* Relating to Elizabeth I of England, or to her era. — *n.* **1** An Englishman who lived during the reign of Elizabeth. **2** An author who wrote during her reign or during the reign of James I.
elk (elk) *n. pl.* **elks** or **elk** **1** A large deer of northern Europe and Asia (genus *Alces*), with palmated antlers and the upper lip forming a proboscis for browsing upon trees. **2** The American wapiti. [ME *elke* <OE *elh*]

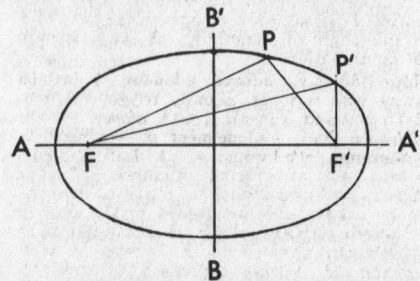
ELK

elk·hound (elk'hound') *n.* A sporting dog of Norwegian origin, of medium size, with a short, robust body and thick gray coat.
el·lipse (i·lips') *n. Geom.* **1** A plane curve such that the sum of the distances from any

ELLIPSE
A–A' Major axis. *B–B'* Minor axis.
F, F' Foci. *P,P'* Points on curve.
$FP + PF' = FP' + P'F'$

point of the curve to two fixed points, called *foci*, is a constant. **2** A conic section. [<L *ellipsis*. See ELLIPSIS.]

el·lip·sis (i·lip′sis) *n*. *pl*. **·ses** (-sēz) **1** The omission of a word or words necessary to complete a sentence or expression. **2** Marks indicating omission, such as . . . or * * *. Also *eclipsis*. [<L <Gk. *elleipsis* <*en-* in + *leipsis* a leaving <*leipein* leave]

el·lip·soid (i·lip′soid) *n*. *Geom*. A solid of which every plane section is an ellipse or a circle. —*adj*. Resembling a compressed sphere or ellipsoid: also **el·lip·soi·dal** (ē′lip·soid′l).

el·lip·tic (i·lip′tik) *adj*. **1** Of, pertaining to, or shaped like an ellipse; oblong with rounded ends. **2** Characterized by ellipsis; shortened. Also **el·lip′ti·cal**. —**el·lip′ti·cal·ly** *adv*.

el·lip·tic·i·ty (el′ip·tis′ə·tē, i·lip′-) *n*. **1** The state of being elliptic. **2** The degree of deviation of an ellipse from a circle.

El·lis Island (el′is) An island in upper New York Bay; formerly site of the chief United States immigration station.

el·lit·or·al (i·lit′ər·əl) *adj*. Of or pertaining to that part of the ocean from a depth of below 120 feet to as far as the light will penetrate.

ell·wand (el′wänd) *n*. A measuring stick one ell in length.

elm (elm) *n*. **1** A deciduous shade tree of America, Europe, and Asia (genus *Ulmus*), with a broad, spreading, or overarching top: *U. americana* is the American elm and *U. fulva* the slippery elm. **2** The wood of this tree.

elm–bark beetle (elm′bärk′) Any of various beetles (family *Scolytidae*) destructive of elm trees, especially a European species (*Scolytus multistratus*) introduced into America, which acts as the carrier of a parasitic fungus.

elm–leaf beetle (elm′lēf′) A coleopterous insect (*Galerucella xanthomelaena* or *luteola*), yellowish-green with dark lateral spots: introduced from Europe. Both larvae and adults are injurious to elm trees.

elm·y (el′mē) *adj*. Consisting of or abounding in elm trees.

el·o·cu·tion (el′ə·kyōō′shən) *n*. **1** The art of correct intonation, and inflection, in public speaking or reading. **2** Manner of utterance. [<L *elocutio, -onis* <*eloqui* <*ex-* out + *loqui* speak] —**el′o·cu′tion·ar′y** *adj*.

el·o·cu·tion·ist (el′ə·kyōō′shən·ist) *n*. One who is skilled in or teaches elocution; especially, one who gives public elocutionary readings.

E·lo·him (e·lō′him′, -lō′·him) God: Hebrew name used in the Old Testament. [<Hebrew *'Elōhīm*, pl. of *'Elōah* God]

E·lo·hist (e·lō′hist) *n*. The author of those portions of the Hexateuch that are characterized by the use of *Elohim* for God instead of *Yahweh* or *Jehovah*. Compare YAHWIST.

E·lo·his·tic (el′ō·his′tik) *adj*. **1** Of or pertaining to those portions of the Hexateuch where *Elohim* occurs in the Hebrew text and not *Yahweh* or *Jehovah*. **2** Written by the Elohist.

e·loin (i·loin′) *v.t. Law* To remove beyond the jurisdiction of; carry away, as property. Also **e·loign′**. [<OF *esloignier* carry off <LL *elongare*. See ELONGATE.] —**e·loin′er, e·loign′er** *n*. —**e·loin′ment, e·loign′ment** *n*.

e·lon·gate (i·lông′gāt, i·long′-) *v.t. & v.i.* **·gat·ed, ·gat·ing** To make or grow longer; lengthen. —*adj*. Elongated. See synonyms under PROTRACT. [<LL *elongatus*, pp. of *elongare* <*ex-* away + *longe* far off]

e·lon·ga·tion (ē′lông·gā′shən, ē′long-) *n*. **1** The act of elongating, or the state of being elongated. **2** An addition or appendage that adds to the length of something. **3** An extension or continuation.

e·lope (i·lōp′) *v.i.* **e·loped, e·lop·ing** **1** To run away with a lover, usually to get married. **2** To abscond; run off. [<AF *aloper*. Cf. OE *ahleapen* flee] —**e·lope′ment** *n*. —**e·lop′er** *n*.

el·o·quence (el′ə·kwəns) *n*. **1** Lofty, impassioned, and convincing utterance. **2** The quality of being eloquent, moving, forceful, or persuasive. See synonyms under SPEECH.

el·o·quent (el′ə·kwənt) *adj*. **1** Possessed of or manifesting eloquence. **2** Persuasive; convincing. **3** Visibly expressive of emotion. [<L *eloquens, -entis* ppr. of *eloqui*. See ELOCUTION.] —**el′o·quent·ly** *adv*.

El Pas·o (el pas′ō) A city on the Rio Grande in western Texas.

El Sal·va·dor (el sal′və·dôr, *Sp*. el säl′vä·thōr′) A republic in western Central America; 13,176 square miles; capital, San Salvador. —**Sal′va·dor′an, Sal′va·do′ri·an,** *adj*. & *n*.

else (els) *adv*. **1** In a different place, time, or way; elsewhere. **2** If the case or facts were different; otherwise; besides; instead. —*adj*. Additional; different: somebody *else*: What *else* can I do? —*conj*. If not; under other conditions. [OE *elles*]

♦ The expressions *someone else, anyone else, everyone else, somebody else*, etc., are in good usage treated as substantive phrases and have the possessive inflection upon the *else*: somebody *else's* umbrella.

else·where (els′hwâr′) *adv*. In or to another place or places; somewhere or anywhere else.

El·si·nore (el′sə·nôr, -nōr) A port on Zealand Island, Denmark; scene of Shakespeare's *Hamlet*: Danish *Helsingør*.

e·lu·ci·date (i·lōō′sə·dāt) *v.t.* **·dat·ed, ·dat·ing** To throw light upon; clear up; make plain. See synonyms under INTERPRET. [<LL *elucidatus*, pp. of *elucidare* <*ex-* out + *lucidus* clear] —**e·lu′ci·da′tive, e·lu′ci·da·to′ry** (-də·tôr′ē, -tō′rē) *adj*. —**e·lu′ci·da′tor** *n*.

e·lude (i·lōōd′) *v.t.* **e·lud·ed, e·lud·ing** **1** To avoid or escape from by dexterity or artifice. **2** To escape the notice or understanding of: Your meaning *eludes* me. See synonyms under ESCAPE. [<L *eludere* <*ex-* out + *ludere* play] —**e·lud′i·ble** *adj*.

e·lu·sion (i·lōō′zhən) *n*. The act of eluding or escaping; evasion. [<Med. L *elusio, -onis* <L *eludere*. See ELUDE.]

e·lu·sive (i·lōō′siv) *adj*. **1** Tending to slip away or escape; hard to understand; baffling. **2** Hard to grasp or keep: the *elusive* dream of wealth. Also **e·lu′so·ry** (-sər·ē). —**e·lu′sive·ly** *adv*. —**e·lu′sive·ness** *n*.

e·lute (i·lōōt′) *adj. Entomol.* Having indistinct or barely visible markings: said especially of insects. [<L *elutus*, pp. of *eluere* <*ex-* away + *luere* wash]

e·lu·tri·ate (i·lōō′trē·āt) *v.t.* **·at·ed, ·at·ing** **1** To purify by washing. **2** To separate, as finer from coarser powder, by washing and straining or decanting. [<L *elutriatus*, pp. of *elutriare* wash off] —**e·lu′tri·a′tion** *n*.

e·lu·vi·a·tion (i·lōō′vē·ā′shən) *n*. The process, mechanical or chemical, of removing the fine particles of soil from an area. [<L *eluvies* a washing away + -ATION]

e·lu·vi·um (i·lōō′vē·əm) *n. Geol.* A deposit of soil and dust particles remaining where they were formed by the decomposition of rock masses. [<NL <L *eluvies* <*eluere*. See ELUTE.] —**e·lu′vi·al** *adj*.

el·ver (el′vər) *n*. A young eel. [Var. of *eelfare* the journey of young eels upstream <EEL + FARE]

elves (elvz) Plural of ELF.

elv·et (el′vit) *n. Rare* A little elf.

elv·ish (el′vish) *adj*. Elfish; prankish. Also **elv′an**. —**elv′ish·ly** *adv*.

E·ly·sian (i·lizh′ən, -ē·ən) *adj*. **1** Belonging to, or like, Elysium. **2** Supremely blessed or happy.

E·ly·si·um (i·lizh′ē·əm, i·liz′-) **1** In Greek mythology, the abode of the blessed dead, represented as in Hades, or in the Islands of the Blest in the Western Ocean: also **Elysian Fields**. **2** A place or a condition of supreme delight; a paradise. [<L <Gk. *ēlysion (pedion)* the Elysian (field)]

el·y·tra (el′ə·trə) Plural of ELYTRON.

el·y·troid (el′ə·troid) *adj*. Sheathlike; like an elytron.

el·y·tron (el′ə·tron) *n. pl.* **·tra** *Entomol.* One of the thickened forewings of certain insects, as beetles; a wing cover: usually in the plural for the wing pair. Also **el′y·trum** (-trəm). [<Gk. *elytron* case <*eiluein* wrap up]

em (em) *n*. **1** The name of the thirteenth letter in the English alphabet, written M or m. **2** *Printing* The square of the body size of a type; especially, a pica *em*, about 1/6 of an inch, used as a standard unit of measurement: originally, the space occupied by the letter M in a font.

em-¹ *prefix* Var. of EN-¹, used before the labials *b, p,* and *m,* as in *embody, empower,* etc.

em-² Assimilated var. of EN-².

'em (əm, m) *pron. Colloq.* Them. [OE *heom* dative pl. of *he* he]

e·ma·ci·ate (i·mā′shē·āt) *v.t.* **·at·ed, ·at·ing** To make abnormally lean; cause to lose flesh. [<L *emaciatus*, pp. of *emaciare* waste away <*ex-* out + *macies* leanness] —**e·ma′ci·a′tion** *n*.

e·ma·ci·at·ed (i·mā′shē·ā′tid) *adj*. Very thin; wasted away.

em·a·nant (em′ə·nənt) *adj*. Issuing from a source; emanating. [<L *emanans, -antis*, ppr. of *emanare*. See EMANATE.]

em·a·nate (em′ə·nāt) *v.i.* **·nat·ed, ·nat·ing** **1** To come or flow forth, as from a source. **2** To take rise; originate; emerge. [<L *emanatus*, pp. of *emanare* <*ex-* out + *manare* flow]

em·a·na·tion (em′ə·nā′shən) *n*. **1** The act of issuing or flowing forth from some origin or source. **2** That which proceeds from an origin or source; efflux; effluence. **3** The pantheistic doctrine that all existing things have been created as effluxes of the Divine Essence; hence, an outcome or product of such a process. **4** *Physics* An inert gaseous product of disintegration in certain radioactive substances, as radon and thoron. —**em′a·na′tive** *adj*. —**em′a·na′tive·ly** *adv*.

e·man·ci·pate (i·man′sə·pāt) *v.t.* **·pat·ed, ·pat·ing** **1** To release from bondage or slavery, or any physical or spiritual oppression or authority; liberate; set free. **2** In Roman law, to free (a child) from its father's control. [<L *emancipatus*, pp. of *emancipare* <*ex-* out + *manus* hand + *capere* taken] —**e·man′ci·pa·to′ry** (-pə·tôr′ē, -tō′rē) *adj*. —**e·man′ci·pa·tive** *adj*. —**e·man′ci·pa·tor** *n*.

e·man·ci·pa·tion (i·man′sə·pā′shən) *n*. **1** The act of emancipating, or the state of being emancipated. **2** Liberation from bondage, disability, or dependence, or from any injurious or undue restraint or influence: *emancipation* from evil associations. **3** In Roman law, the enfranchisement of a minor by his father. See synonyms under LIBERTY.

Emancipation Proclamation A proclamation issued by President Abraham Lincoln on January 1, 1863, declaring free all Negro slaves in the seceded States: reinforced by the 13th Amendment (1865), which freed the slaves in eight other States.

e·mar·gi·nate (i·mär′jə·nit, -nāt) *adj. Bot.* Having the margin interrupted or notched; specifically, notched at the summit: said of leaves, petals, etc. Also **e·mar′gi·nat′ed**. [<L *emarginatus*, pp. of *emarginare* <*ex-* off, away + *margo, -inis* border, edge]

e·mas·cu·late (i·mas′kyə·lāt) *v.t.* **·lat·ed, ·lat·ing** **1** To deprive of procreative power; castrate; geld. **2** To deprive of strength; weaken; make effeminate. **3** To impair by cutting down or censoring, as a literary work. —*adj*. (i·mas′kyə·lit) Emasculated; weakened. [<L *emasculatus*, pp. of *emasculare* <*ex-* away + *masculus* male] —**e·mas′cu·la′tion** *n*. —**e·mas′cu·la·tive** *adj*. —**e·mas′cu·la′tor** *n*. —**e·mas′cu·la·to′ry** (-tôr′ē, -tō′rē) *adj*.

em·ball (im·bôl′) *v.t. Obs.* To ensphere.

em·balm (im·bäm′) *v.t.* **1** To preserve from decay, as a dead body, by treatment with balsams, antiseptic preparations, drugs, and chemicals. **2** To perfume. **3** To preserve from oblivion. Also spelled *imbalm*. [<F *embaumer* <*em-* in (<L *in-*) + *baume* <OF *basme* BALM]

em·balm·er (im·bä′mər) *n*. **1** One who embalms the dead. **2** Anything that preserves from decay.

em·balm·ment (im·bäm′mənt) *n*. The act of embalming.

em·bank (im·bangk′) *v.t.* To confine or protect by a bank, dike, or the like.

em·bank·ment (im·bangk′mənt) *n*. **1** A protecting or supporting bank. **2** The process of strengthening by a bank. See synonyms under RAMPART.

em·bar (im·bär′) *v.t.* **·barred, ·bar·ring** **1** To enclose within bars; fasten in. **2** To stop; check, as by a bar. —**em·bar′ment** *n*.

em·bar·ca·tion (em′bär·kā′shən) See EMBARKATION.

em·bar·go (im·bär′gō) *n. pl.* **·goes** **1** A prohibition by the sovereign power of a nation temporarily restraining vessels from leaving or entering its ports. **2** Authoritative stoppage of foreign commerce or of any special trade. **3** Any imposed impediment; a check or hindrance; specifically, in railroad operation, a notice forbidding massing of cars at specified places. —*v.t.* **·goed, ·go·ing** To lay an embargo upon. [<Sp. <*embargar* <*em-* in (<L *in-*) + *bargar* <LL *barra* a bar]

em·bark (im·bärk′) *v.t.* **1** To put or take aboard a vessel. **2** To invest (money) or involve (a person) in a venture. —*v.i.* **3** To go aboard a vessel, as for a voyage. **4** To engage in a venture. [<F *embarquer* <LL *imbarcare* <*in-* in + *barca* boat] —**em·bark′ment** *n.*

em·bar·ka·tion (em′bär·kā′shən) *n.* The act of embarking. Also spelled *embarcation.*

embarkation center A military establishment near a port for the care of troops about to embark.

em·bar·rass (im·bar′əs) *v.t.* **1** To make ill at ease, self-conscious, and uncomfortable; abash; disconcert. **2** To involve in difficulties, especially in business. **3** To hamper; encumber. **4** To render difficult; complicate. [<F *embarrasser* <*em-* in (<L *in-*) + *barre* <OF BAR] —**em·bar′rass·ing** *adj.* —**em·bar′rass·ing·ly** *adv.*

Synonyms: abash, confuse, discomfit, disconcert, faze, hamper, hinder, impede, rattle. *Embarrass* implies some influence which impedes freedom of thought, speech, or action and refers to persons and things they plan to do. One is *embarrassed* in the presence of others, and because of their presence. *Confusion* is of the intellect, *embarrassment* of the feelings. A witness may be *embarrassed* by annoying personalities, so as to become *confused* in statements. As applied to mental action, a solitary thinker may be *confused* by some difficulty in a subject, or by some mental defect. *Rattle* is a colloquialism which implies a disorganization of one's mental processes. *Faze* is an Americanism usually found in negative expressions, but sometimes carries the implications of *abash* and *rattle*; as, Nothing can *faze* him. *Hamper* is used either literally or figuratively; as, *hampered* by debt; encumbered. *Hinder* is used in the sense of obstruction; as, Adverse winds *hindered* the ship. Compare ABASH, HINDER, INVOLVE, OBSTRUCT, PERPLEX. Antonyms: assure, cheer, compose, embolden, encourage, help, relieve, sustain.

em·bar·rass·ment (im·bar′əs·mənt) *n.* **1** The state of being embarrassed. **2** That which embarrasses.

em·bas·sage (em′bə·sij) *n. Obs.* **1** The sending, business, office, or message of an ambassador or an embassy. **2** The body of ambassadors or embassy itself.

em·bas·sy (em′bə·sē) *n. pl.* **·sies** **1** An ambassador together with his suite; the person or body of persons deputed for a mission from one government to another. **2** The mission or office of an envoy of an ambassador. **3** The official residence of an ambassador and his suite. [Var. of earlier *ambassy* <OF *ambassé* <Med. L *ambactia,* ult. <Celtic]

em·bathe (em·bāth′) *v.t.* **·bathed, ·bath·ing** To bathe; drench; immerse: also spelled *imbathe.*

em·bat·tle¹ (em·bat′l) *v.t.* **·tled, ·tling** To form in line of battle; prepare or equip for battle. [<OF *embataillier* <*en-* in (<L *in-*) + *bataille* BATTLE]

em·bat·tle² (em·bat′l) *v.t.* **·tled, ·tling** To furnish with battlements. [<EM-¹ + BATTLE in obs. sense of "fortify" <OF *bastiller* build]

em·bat·tled (em·bat′ld) *adj.* **1** Drawn up in battle array; ready for battle. **2** Made the scene of a muster or battle. **3** Having battlements.

em·bay (em·bā′) *v.t.* **1** To put or force into a bay, as a ship. **2** To shut in by arms of land.

em·bay·ment (em·bā′mənt) *n.* **1** A bay or large inlet. **2** The process of forming a bay.

em·bed (im·bed′) *v.t.* **·bed·ded, ·bed·ding** **1** To place in or as in a bed. **2** To set firmly in surrounding matter. **3** To hold in the mind; keep in memory. Also spelled *imbed.* —**em·bed′ment** *n.*

em·bel·lish (im·bel′ish) *v.t.* **1** To beautify by adding ornamental features; decorate. **2** To heighten the interest of, as a story, by adding fictitious details. See synonyms under ADORN,

GARNISH. [<OF *embelliss-,* stem of *embellir* beautify <*em-* in (<L *in-*) + *bel* beautiful <L *bellus*]

em·ber (em′bər) *n.* **1** A live coal or an unextinguished brand. **2** *pl.* A dying fire. [OE *æmerge*]

Ember days *Eccl.* A three-day period of fasting and prayer observed quarterly on the Wednesday, Friday, and Saturday after the first Sunday in Lent, after Whitsunday, after September 14, and after December 13. [OE *ymbrene, ymbryne* circuit, cycle <*ymb* around + *ryne* a running]

Ember week A week including Ember days.

em·bez·zle (im·bez′əl) *v.t.* **·zled ·zling** **1** To appropriate fraudulently to one's own use. **2** *Obs.* To misappropriate secretly; make off with. See synonyms under STEAL. [<AF *embesiler* <*em-* in + *besiler* destroy] —**em·bez′zle·ment** *n.* —**em·bez′zler** *n.*

em·bit·ter (im·bit′ər) *v.t.* To render bitter, unhappy, or resentful. —**em·bit′ter·ment** *n.*

em·bla·zon (im·blā′zən) *v.t.* **1** To adorn with or as with heraldic designs; decorate. **2** To adorn magnificently; set off in resplendent colors. **3** To extol; celebrate the fame or virtues of. —**em·bla′zon·er** *n.* —**em·bla′zon·ment** *n.*

em·blem (em′bləm) *n.* **1** An object suggesting something which it does not directly represent; a figurative representation; symbol. **2** A distinctive badge; ensign. **3** An allegorical picture, usually having a motto. **4** *Obs.* An inlaid or inserted ornament. —*v.t.* *Rare* To emblematize. [<L *emblema* inlaid work <Gk. *emblēma* an insertion <*em-* in + *ballein* throw]

Synonyms: attribute, figure, sign, symbol, token, type. An *emblem* has some natural fitness to suggest that for which it stands; a *symbol* has been chosen or agreed upon to suggest something else, with or without natural fitness; a *sign* does actually suggest the thing with or without reason, and with or without intention or choice. A *symbol* may be also an *emblem.* On the other hand, the same thing may be both a *sign* and a *symbol;* a letter of the alphabet is a *sign* which indicates a sound; but letters are often used as mathematical, chemical, or astronomical *symbols.* A *token* is some object given or act done as a pledge or expression of feeling or intent; a ring, the natural *emblem* of eternity, and also its accepted *symbol,* is frequently given as a *token* of friendship or love. Compare FIGURE, IMAGE, LETTER, SIGN.

em·blem·at·ic (em′blə·mat′ik) *adj.* Of, pertaining to, or serving as an emblem; symbolic. Also **em′blem·at′i·cal.** —**em′blem·at′i·cal·ly** *adv.*

em·blem·a·tize (em·blem′ə·tīz) *v.t.* **·tized, ·tiz·ing** **1** To serve as an emblem of. **2** To represent by a symbol or emblem.

em·ble·ments (em′blə·mənts) *n. pl. Law* **1** Growing crops produced by the labor of the cultivator of the soil. **2** The right to or profits from such crops. [<OF *emblaement* <*emblaer,* sow with grain <LL *imbladare* <*in-* in + *bladum* grain]

em·blem·ize (em′blə·mīz) *v.t.* **·ized, ·iz·ing** To represent by an emblem; make into an emblem.

em·bod·i·ment (im·bod′i·mənt) *n.* **1** The act or process of embodying, the state of being embodied, or that which embodies; incarnation. **2** A concrete example: She is the *embodiment* of wit.

em·bod·y (im·bod′ē) *v.t.* **·bod·ied, ·bod·y·ing** **1** To invest with or as with a body; incarnate; make corporeal. **2** To collect into one whole; incorporate. **3** To express concretely.

em·bold·en (im·bōl′dən) *v.t.* To make bold; give courage to. See synonyms under ABET, ENCOURAGE.

em·bo·lec·to·my (em′bə·lek′tə·mē) *n. Surg.* Removal of an embolus. [<EMBOL(US) + -ECTOMY]

em·bol·ic (em·bol′ik) *adj.* **1** *Pathol.* Of, pertaining to, or caused by embolism or an embolus: *embolic* abscesses. **2** Embolismic. **3** *Biol.* Growing or pushing inward: *embolic* invagination.

em·bo·lism (em′bə·liz′əm) *n.* **1** *Pathol.* The stopping up of a vein or artery, as by a blood clot or foreign particle. **2** Intercalation, as of days, for the adjustment of the calendar. [<LL *embolismus* <Gk. *embolismos* intercalary <*embolos.* See EMBOLUS.]

em·bo·lis·mic (em′bə·liz′mik) *adj.* **1** Of or pertaining to embolism or intercalation. **2** Adjusted by intercalation; intercalated.

embolismic year The period covered by 13 lunar months or 384 days; the year in which there is an intercalation.

em·bo·lus (em′bə·ləs) *n. pl.* **·li** (-lī) **1** Anything inserted or shaped for insertion, as a wedge, sucker of a pump, plunger, or piston. **2** *Pathol.* Any solid body (as a piece of fibrin or a blood clot) that forms an obstruction in a blood vessel. [<L <Gk. *embolos* peg <*en-* in + *ballein* throw]

em·bor·der (em·bôr′dər) *v.t.* To furnish with a border.

em·bos·om (em·booz′əm, -boo′zəm) *v.t.* **1** To take to the bosom; embrace. **2** To cherish. **3** To shelter; enclose.

em·boss (im·bôs′, -bos′) *v.t.* **1** To cover or adorn (a surface) with raised figures, designs, etc. **2** To raise or represent (designs, figures, etc.) from or upon a surface. **3** To decorate sumptuously. [<OF *embocer* <*em-* in + *boce* a boss] —**em·boss′er** *n.* —**em·boss′ment** *n.*

em·bou·chure (äm·boo·shoor′, *Fr.* äⁿ·boo·shür′) *n.* **1** The mouth, as of a river or stream; point of discharge. **2** Any opening resembling a mouth: the *embouchure* of a cannon or embrasure. **3** A mouthpiece, or the place where the mouth is applied. **4** Position or adjustment of the lips, tongue, and other organs in playing a wind instrument or in vocalization. [<F <*emboucher* <*em-* in (<L *in-*) + *bouche* mouth <L *bucca* cheek]

em·bow (em·bō′) *v.t.* To bend or curve like a bow; arch. —**em·bow′ment** *n.*

em·bowed (em·bōd′) *adj.* Bent like a bow; curved outward; arched: an *embowed* window.

em·bow·el (em·bou′əl, -boul′) *v.t.* **·eled** or **·elled, ·el·ing** or **·el·ling** **1** To disembowel; figuratively, to rend. **2** To embed deeply: *emboweled* in the earth. [Def. 1 <OF *emboweler,* alter. of *esboueler* <*es-* out (<L *ex-*) + *boel* BOWEL; def. 2 <EN-¹ + BOWEL]

em·bow·er (em·bou′ər) *v.t. & v.i.* To cover, shelter, or rest in or as in a bower.

em·brace¹ (im·brās′) *v.* **·braced, ·brac·ing** *v.t.* **1** To take or infold in the arms; hug. **2** To accept willingly; adopt, as a religion or doctrine. **3** To avail oneself of: to *embrace* an offer. **4** To surround; encircle. **5** To include; contain. **6** To take in visually or mentally. **7** To have sexual intercourse with. —*v.i.* **8** To hug each other. —*n.* The act of embracing; a clasping in the arms; a hug. [<OF *embracer* <LL *in-* in + *bracchia* arm] —**em·brace′ment** *n.* —**em·brac′er** *n.*

Synonyms (*verb*): adopt, clasp, comprehend, comprise, contain, encircle, enclose, encompass, entwine, environ, espouse, grasp, hold, hug, surround. See CARESS. Antonyms: disown, exclude, refuse, reject, repel, repulse.

em·brace² (im·brās′) *v.t.* **·braced, ·brac·ing** *Law* To influence, or attempt to influence, corruptly. [Back formation from EMBRACER]

em·brac·er·y (im·brā′sər·ē) *n. Law* The act of influencing or trying to influence, corrupt, or bribe a jury, judge, etc.

em·branch·ment (em·branch′mənt, -bränch′-) *n.* A branching out or off, as of an arm of a river; a branch, ramification, or division.

em·bran·gle (em·brang′gəl) *v.t.* **·gled, ·gling** To entangle; complicate; confuse. [<EM-² + dial. *brangle* brawl] —**em·bran′gle·ment** *n.*

em·bra·sure (em·brā′zhər) *n.* **1** An opening in a wall, as for a cannon. **2** *Archit.* **a** The sloping or beveling of an opening in a wall, as of a window or door, so as to enlarge its interior profile. **b** The opening itself, or the space within it. For illustrations see BASTION, BATTLEMENT. [<F <*embraser* widen <*em-* in (<L *in-*) + *braser* bevel]

em·brit·tle (em·brit′l) *v.t.* **·tled, ·tling** To make brittle, as steel by sudden cooling.

em·brit·tle·ment (em·brit′l·mənt) *n.* A deterioration of the lining metal of steam boilers, due to the presence of excess sodium carbonate in the water.

em·bro·cate (em′brō·kāt) *v.t.* **·cat·ed, ·cat·ing** To moisten and rub, as with liniment or oil. [<Med. L *embrocatus,* pp. of *embrocha* an ointment <Gk. *embrochē*]

em·broi·der (im·broi′dər) *v.t.* **1** To ornament with designs in needlework. **2** To execute in needlework. **3** To embellish or adorn; exaggerate, as a narrative with fictitious details.

—*v.i.* **4** To make embroidery. [<EN-¹ + BROIDER] — **em·broi'der·er** *n.*

em·broil (em·broil') *v.t.* **1** To involve in dissension or strife. **2** To throw into uproar or tumult. **3** To render complicated or confused; entangle. See synonyms under INVOLVE. [<F *embrouiller* < *em-* in (<L *in-*) + *brouiller* confuse]

em·bry·ec·to·my (em'brē·ek'tə·mē) *n. Surg.* An operation for removing an embryo through an incision in the abdomen.

em·bry·o (em'brē·ō) *n. pl.* **·os** **1** The germ or rudimentary form of anything in its earliest stage; specifically, the germ of an organism before it has developed its distinctive form. **2** The germ of a viviparous animal in the first stages of its existence (in the human species the first two months). **3** *Bot.* The rudimentary plant within the seed, which makes its appearance soon after fertilization of the ovule by the pollen and then passes through a period of rest until the germination or sprouting of the seed. Also **em'bry·on** (-on). — **in embryo** In an undeveloped or incipient stage or state; not yet developed or advanced, as a project or undertaking. For illustrations see under EGG, EMBRYOLOGY, FROG. — *adj.* Pertaining to an embryo; rudimentary: also **em'bry·al.** [<Gk. *embryon* <*en-* in + *bryein* swell]

embryo– *combining form* Embryo; embryonic: *embryogenesis*. Also, before vowels, **embry–**. [<Gk. *embryon* embryo]

em·bry·o·gen·e·sis (em'brē·ō·jen'ə·sis) *n.* The development of an organism from its embryonic stage. Also **em'bry·og·e·ny** (em'brē·oj'ə·nē) — **em'bry·o·gen'ic** or **·ge·net'ic** (-jə·net'ik) *adj.*

em·bry·ol·o·gy (em'brē·ol'ə·jē) *n.* The science which deals with the origin, structure, and

A B
C D
E F

EMBRYOLOGY OF A CHICKEN

A. Before incubation, a germinal disk shown by small black spot. *B.* Three-day-old embryo, showing blood vessels radiating from heart. *C.* The fourth day. *D.* The fifth day. *E.* The seventh day. *F.* The nineteenth day, when chick absorbs remaining yolk. The chick hatches on the twenty–first day.

development of the embryo. — **em'bry·o·log'i·cal** (-ə·loj'i·kəl) *adj.* — **em'bry·o·log'i·cal·ly** *adv.* — **em'bry·ol'o·gist** *n.*

em·bry·o·nal (em'brē·ə·nəl) *adj.* Of or pertaining to an embryo or embryonic stage; embryonic.

em·bry·on·ic (em'brē·on'ik) *adj.* **1** Of, pertaining to, or like an embryo. **2** Undeveloped.

embryo sac *Bot.* The sac, formed of one cell, rarely more, within the nucleus of the ovule of flowering, seed–producing plants, containing the embryonal vesicle.

em·bry·o·scope (em'brē·ə·skōp') *n.* A device for observing embryonic development, especially in the eggs of birds. — **em·bry·os·co·py** (em'brē·os'kə·pē) *n.*

em·cee (em'sē') *Colloq. n.* Master of ceremonies. — *v.i. & v.t.* **em·ceed, em·cee·ing** To act or direct as master of ceremonies.

[<M(*aster of*) C(*eremonies*)]

e·mend (i·mend') *v.t.* **1** To make corrections or changes in the form or wording of (a literary work, etc.), especially after scholarly study. **2** To free from faults; correct. Also **e·men·date** (ē'men·dāt). [<L *emendare* <*ex-* out + *menda* a fault] — **e·mend'a·ble** *adj.*

Synonyms: amend, correct, rectify, redress, reform, remedy, revise. *Amend, emend, correct,* and *mend* all imply the *correction* of an evil. To *amend* is to *rectify* defects by positive means, generally by adding or altering, as to *amend* a law. *Emend* means negatively to remove particular faults in a literary work by alteration of letters, single words, or passages.

e·men·da·tion (ē'men·dā'shən, em'ən-) *n.* A correction or alteration. [<L *emendatio, -onis* <*emendare.* See EMEND.] — **e'men·da'tor** *n.* — **e·mend·a·to·ry** (i·men'də·tôr'ē, -tō'rē) *adj.*

em·er·ald (em'ər·əld, em'rəld) *n.* **1** A bright-green variety of beryl, which when clear and nearly flawless is one of the most highly valued gems. **2** In the Bible, an unidentified precious stone. **3** A rich and vivid green. **4** One of various green moths. **5** *Printing* A size of type intermediate between minion and nonpareil. — **Oriental emerald** A valuable transparent variety of corundum. — *adj.* **1** Pertaining to or like the emerald. **2** Of a rich green color. [<OF *emeraude, esmeraldus* <L *smaragdus.* Doublet of SMARAGD.]

emerald green A brilliant green, highly poisonous pigment made from copper and arsenic.

emerald nickel Zaratite.

e·merge (i·mûrj') *v.i.* **e·merged, e·merg·ing** **1** To rise, as from a fluid. **2** To come forth into view or existence; become noticeable or apparent. [<L *emergere* <*ex-* out + *mergere* dip]

e·mer·gence (i·mûr'jəns) *n.* **1** The process or result of emerging. **2** *Bot.* An outgrowth, as a prickle or hair growing from the tissue under the epidermis of a plant.

e·mer·gen·cy (i·mûr'jən·sē) *n. pl.* **·cies** A sudden condition or state of affairs calling for immediate action.

e·mer·gent (i·mûr'jənt) *adj.* **1** Rising or emerging, as from a fluid or from concealment. **2** Coming unexpectedly; urgent. **3** *Biol.* New and unforeseen in the evolution of plant and animal organisms. — *n.* That which emerges; the result of a natural process. [<L *emergens, -entis,* ppr. of *emergere* EMERGE]

e·mer·i·tus (i·mer'ə·təs) *adj.* Retired from active service (as on account of age), but retained in an honorary position: pastor *emeritus.* [<L, pp. of *emerere* <*ex-* out + *merere* deserve]

e·mersed (ē·mûrst') *adj. Bot.* Standing above and out of water, as the stems and leaves of aquatic plants. [<L *emersus,* pp. of *emergere* EMERGE]

e·mer·sion (ē·mûr'shən, -zhən) *n.* **1** The act or process of emerging. **2** *Astron.* The rising out of or from behind something, as the moon from the earth's shadow during an eclipse.

em·er·y (em'ər·ē, em'rē) *n.* A very hard, black or grayish–black variety of corundum mixed with magnesite and other minerals; used as an abrasive. [F *émeri* <OF *esmeril* <LL *smericulum* <Gk. *smēris* emery powder]

emery bag A small bag, often the size and shape of a strawberry, filled with emery powder: used to keep needles clean of rust.

emery board A small, flat board covered with powdered emery, used in manicuring.

emery cloth Cloth coated with powdered emery, used for fine abrading and polishing.

em·e·sis (em'ə·sis) *n. Pathol.* Vomiting. [<NL <Gk. <*emeein* vomit]

e·met·ic (i·met'ik) *adj.* Tending to produce vomiting. — *n.* A medicine used to induce vomiting. [<Gk. *emetikos* <*emeein* vomit]

–emia *combining form Med.* Blood; condition of the blood: used in names of diseases: *leukemia.* Also spelled *–aemia.* [<Gk. *haima* blood]

em·i·grant (em'ə·grənt) *adj.* Moving from one place or country for the purpose of settling in another: opposed to *immigrant.* — *n.* **1** A person who leaves one country, or section of a country, to settle in another. **2** A person from the eastern United States who went west to settle new lands. [<L *emigrans, -antis,* ppr.

of *emigrare.* See EMIGRATE.]

em·i·grate (em'ə·grāt) *v.i.* **·grat·ed, ·grat·ing** To go from one country, or section of a country, to settle in another. [<L *emigratus,* pp. of *emigrare* <*ex-* out + *migrare* move]

Synonyms: immigrate, migrate. To *migrate* is to change one's dwelling place, usually with the idea of repeated change, or of periodical return; it applies to wandering tribes of men, and to many birds and animals. *Emigrate* and *immigrate* carry the idea of a permanent change of residence to some other country or some distant region; the two words are used distinctively of human beings, and apply to the same person and the same act, according to the side from which the action is viewed. A person *emigrates from* the land he leaves, and *immigrates to* the land where he takes up his abode.

em·i·nence (em'ə·nəns) *n.* **1** A lofty place; a hill. **2** An exalted rank, condition, or degree. **3** A title of honor applied to cardinals of the Roman Catholic Church. Also **em'i·nen·cy.** See synonyms under FAME, HEIGHT. [<L *eminentia* <*e-* forth + *minere* project]

em·i·nent (em'ə·nənt) *adj.* **1** High in station, merit, or esteem; distinguished; prominent; conspicuous: an *eminent* scholar. **2** Rising above other things; high in relative position; lofty: an *eminent* tower. [<L *eminens, -entis,* ppr. of *eminere* project] — **em'i·nent·ly** *adv.*

Synonyms: conspicuous, distinguished, famed, famous, known, lofty, noted, prominent, remarkable, signal. See CELEBRATED, HIGH, ILLUSTRIOUS, PARAMOUNT. *Antonyms:* common, commonplace, inferior, low, mean, ordinary.

eminent domain *Law* The right or power of the state to take private property for public use or to control its use, usually at an adequate compensation.

e·mir (ə·mir') *n.* **1** Any independent prince or commander in the Moslem East, especially in Arabia. **2** A descendant of Mohammed through Fatima, his favorite daughter. **3** A high Turkish official. Also spelled *emeer.* [<Arabic *amir* ruler]

e·mir·ate (ə·mir'it) *n.* The jurisdiction of an emir.

em·is·sar·y (em'ə·ser'ē) *n. pl.* **·sar·ies** **1** A person sent on a mission as an agent or representative of a government, as to negotiate or gather information. **2** A secret agent; spy. **3** *Archaic* A channel, as for water: also **em·is·sa·ri·um** (em'ə·sā'rē·əm). **4** *Archaic* An excretory or connecting canal in the body. See synonyms under SPY. — *adj.* Sent forth or out. [<L *emissarius* <*emittere.* See EMIT.]

e·mis·sion (i·mish'ən) *n.* **1** The act of emitting or that which is emitted. **2** *Electronics* The ejection of electrons from the heated cathode or filament of a vacuum tube. **3** *Med.* A discharge of body fluids, especially semen. [<L *emissio, -onis* <*emittere.* See EMIT.]

emission spectrum *Physics* The spectrum of a substance indicating the type of radiation which it emits: distinguished from *absorption spectrum.*

e·mis·sive (i·mis'iv) *adj.* Sending or sent out or forth; emitting.

emissive power *Physics* The rate at which a body at a given temperature will radiate energy per unit of surface area.

em·is·siv·i·ty (em'ə·siv'ə·tē) *n. Physics* Emissive power or rate; specifically, the total emissive power of a radiating surface, expressed as a ratio to that of a black body of identical area and temperature.

e·mit (i·mit') *v.t.* **e·mit·ted, e·mit·ting** **1** To send or give out; discharge. **2** To utter (sounds, oaths, etc.). **3** To promulgate, as a law or decree. **4** To put into circulation, as paper money. [<L *emittere* <*ex-* out + *mittere* send] — **e·mit'ter** *n.*

em·men·a·gog (i·men'ə·gôg, -gog) *n.* Any medicine or substance that stimulates or renews the menstrual flow. Also **em·men'a·gogue.** [<Gk. *emmēna* the menses < *agōsos* leading < *agein* lead]

em·me·tro·pi·a (em'ə·trō'pē·ə) *n.* The normal state of the eye as regards the power of accommodation or refraction. [<NL <Gk. *emmetros* <*en-* in + *metron* measure + *ōps* eye] — **em'me·trop'ic** (-trop'ik) *adj.*

Em·my (em′ē) *n.* A gold-plated statuette awarded annually since 1949 by the Academy of Television Arts and Sciences for exceptional performances and productions on television. [Alter. of *immy*, short for *image orthicon tube.* See under ORTHICON.]

em·o·din (em′ə-din) *n. Chem.* An orange-red crystalline glucoside, $C_{15}H_{10}O_5$, obtained from rhubarb, senna, aloes, and various other related plants: used as a cathartic. [<NL *(Rheum) emodi,* a species of rhubarb (<Gk. *ēmōdos* Himalaya) + -IN]

e·mol·les·cence (em′ə-les′əns) *n.* The state or degree of softness in which a body begins to lose its shape, as in melting; incipient fusion. [<E- + L *mollescere* become soft + -ENCE]

e·mol·li·ate (i·mol′ē-āt) *v.t.* ·at·ed, ·at·ing *Obs.* To render soft; make effeminate.

e·mol·lient (i·mol′yənt, -ē-ənt) *adj.* Softening or relaxing; soothing. —*n. Med.* A softening or soothing external application. Also *molli·ent.* [<L *emolliens, -entis,* ppr. of *emollire* <*ex-* thoroughly + *mollire* soften <*mollis* soft]

e·mol·u·ment (i·mol′yə-mənt) *n.* 1 The compensation, salary, fees, perquisites, advantage, gain, or profit arising from an office or employment. 2 General advantage; gain; profit. See synonyms under PROFIT. [<L *emolimentum* <*emolere* <*ex-* out + *molere* grind]

e·mote (i·mōt′) *v.i.* **e·mot·ed, e·mot·ing** *Colloq.* To exhibit an exaggerated emotion, as in acting a melodramatic role: a humorous use. [Back formation <EMOTION]

e·mo·tion (i·mō′shən) *n.* 1 Any strong manifestation or disturbance of the conscious or the unconscious mind, typically involuntary and often leading to complex bodily changes and forms of behavior; an act or state of excited feeling: *emotions* of fear. 2 The power of feeling, with or without a corresponding trend of activities; sensibility; sentiment. 3 *Obs.* Unusual or disturbed motion. See synonyms under FEELING, SENSATION, WARMTH. [<L *emotio, -onis* <*emovere* <*ex-* out + *movere* move]

e·mo·tion·al (i·mō′shən-əl) *adj.* 1 Of, pertaining to, or expressive of emotion. 2 Having capacity for emotion. 3 Moving or suited to move the feelings or passions: an *emotional* poem. —**e·mo′tion·al·ly** *adv.*

e·mo·tion·al·ism (i·mō′shən-əl-iz′əm) *n.* 1 The expression of emotion. 2 The disposition or tendency to see and judge all things from an emotional point of view. 3 The act or habit of appealing to the emotions.

e·mo·tive (i·mō′tiv) *adj.* 1 Tending to excite emotion. 2 Expressing or characterized by or inducing emotion: *emotive* eloquence. —**e·mo′tive·ly** *adv.* —**e·mo′tive·ness, e·mo·tiv·i·ty** (ē′mō-tiv′ə-tē) *n.*

em·path·ic (em·path′ik) *adj.* Characterized by or pertaining to empathy. —**em·path′i·cal·ly** *adv.*

em·pa·thize (em′pə-thīz) *v.t. & v.i.* ·thized, ·thiz·ing To regard with or feel empathy.

em·pa·thy (em′pə-thē) *n.* 1 *Psychol.* A strong imaginative or emotional projection of one's self into a work of art; esthetic appreciation. 2 *Psychoanal.* The mental identification of the ego with the character and experiences of another person. [<Gk. *empatheia* <*en-* in + *pathos* feeling; trans. of G *Einfühlung*]

em·per·or (em′pər-ər) *n.* 1 The sovereign of an empire. 2 One of various moths, as the **emperor moth** *(Samia cecropia),* or butterflies, as the **purple emperor** *(Apatura iris),* or the **tawny emperor** *(Asterocampa clyton),* etc. [<OF *empereor* <L *imperator* commander <*imperare* order]

emperor goose A small goose of the Alaskan coasts *(Philacte canagica)* with barred plumage, a short neck, and short wings.

em·pha·sis (em′fə·sis) *n. pl.* ·ses (-sēz) 1 A stress laid upon some word or words in speaking or reading: indicated in print or writing by underscoring or underlining, by italics, or by accent marks. 2 The act of emphasizing; distinctiveness; stress of thought or importance; significance. [<L <Gk. <*en-* in + *phainein* show]

em·pha·size (em′fə·sīz) *v.t.* ·sized, ·siz·ing To make especially distinct or prominent; put stress on; give emphasis to.

em·phat·ic (im·fat′ik) *adj.* 1 Speaking or spoken with emphasis or stress. 2 Conveying or ex-

pressing emphasis; habitually forceful and decisive; striking; forcible; positive. Also **em·phat′i·cal.** [<Gk. *emphatikos,* var. of *emphantikos* <*emphainein.* See EMPHASIS.] —**em·phat′i·cal·ly** *adv.*

em·phy·se·ma (em′fə·sē′mə, -zē′mə) *n. Pathol.* A puffed condition of body tissues or organs caused by the infiltration of air; especially, a condition of the lungs marked by difficulty in breathing because of enlargement and consequent loss of elasticity of the alveoli, or air sacs. [<NL <Gk. *emphysēma* an inflation <*en-* in + *physaein* blow] —**em′phy·sem′a·tous** (-sēm′ə·təs, -zēm′ə·təs) *adj.*

em·piece·ment (em·pēs′mənt) *n.* In sewing, an insertion.

em·pire (em′pīr) *n.* 1 A state, or union of states, governed by an emperor. 2 A union of dispersed territories, dominions, colonies, states, and unrelated peoples under one sovereign rule. 3 Wide and supreme dominion. —**Holy Roman Empire** Certain portions of the old Roman Empire of the West together with the Frankish possessions of Charlemagne, who was crowned emperor by Pope Leo III at Rome in 800. In 962 the real Holy Roman-German Empire began. It became extinct in 1806, when Francis II resigned the elective imperial crown for the hereditary one of Austria. [<F <L *imperium* rule, authority]

em·pir·ic (em·pir′ik) *n.* 1 One who uses trial-and-error methods; one who believes experiment is the source of knowledge. 2 *Archaic* A quack or charlatan. —*adj.* Empirical. [<L *empiricus* <Gk. *empeirikos* <*empeiria* experience <*en-* in + *peira* a trial]

Em·pir·ic (em·pir′ik) *n.* Among the ancient Greeks, one of a school of physicians maintaining that experiment was the one requisite.

em·pir·i·cal (em·pir′i·kəl) *adj.* 1 Relating to or based on experience or observation. 2 Relying entirely or to excess upon direct, repeated, and uncritically accepted experience: opposed to metempirical. 3 Given to or skilled in experiments. 4 *Archaic* Generalizing hastily from limited facts; hence, befitting a charlatan. Also **em·pir′ic.** —**em·pir′i·cal·ly** *adv.*

em·pir·i·cism (em·pir′ə·siz′əm) *n.* 1 Empirical character, method, or practice. 2 Belief in experiment and repudiation of theory; quackery. 3 *Philos.* The doctrine that all knowledge is derived from experience through the senses. —**em·pir′i·cist** *n.*

em·place·ment (im·plās′mənt) *n.* 1 The position assigned to guns or to a battery within a fortification; also, a gun platform or the like. 2 A setting in place; location. [<F]

em·plas·tic (im·plas′tik) *adj.* Glutinous. —*n.* 1 A constipating medicine. 2 An adhesive substance. [<Gk. *emplastikos* <*em-* in + *plassein* mold, form]

em·ploy (im·ploi′) *v.t.* 1 To hire; engage the services of. 2 To provide work and livelihood for; have as employees. 3 To make use of as a means or instrument: to *employ* cunning. 4 To devote or apply: to *employ* one's energies in research. —*n.* The state of being employed; service. [<F *employer* <L *in-* in + *plicare* fold. Doublet of IMPLY.] —**em·ploy′a·ble** *adj.* —**em·ployed′** *adj.*

Synonyms (verb): engage, engross, hire, use. In general terms it may be said that to *employ* is to devote to one's purpose, to *use* is to render subservient to one's purpose; what is *used* is viewed as more absolutely an instrument than what is *employed;* a merchant *employs* a clerk; he *uses* pen and paper; hence, *use,* as applied to persons, inclines to the derogatory sense; as, The conspirators *used* him as a go-between. That which is *used* is often consumed in the *using;* as, We *used* twenty tons of coal last winter; in such cases we could not substitute *employ.* A person may be *employed* in his own work or in that of another; in the latter case the service is always understood to be for pay. In this connection *employ* is a word of more dignity than *hire;* a general is *employed* in his country's service; a mercenary adventurer is *hired* to fight; *hire* now implies that the one *hired* works directly and primarily for the pay. See OCCUPY, RETAIN.

em·ploy·ee (im·ploi′ē, em′ploi·ē′) *n.* One who works for another in return for a salary, wages, or other consideration. Also **em·ploy′e.**

em·ploy·er (im·ploi′ər) *n.* 1 One who employs. 2 A person or business firm that employs

workmen, servants, etc., for wages.

em·ploy·ment (im·ploi′mənt) *n.* 1 The act of employing, or the state of being employed. 2 The work upon which one is or may be engaged; occupation; trade. See synonyms under BUSINESS, EXERCISE, WORK.

em·po·ri·um (em·pôr′ē·əm, -pō′rē-) *n. pl.* ·ri·ums or ·ri·a (-ē·ə) 1 A store carrying general merchandise. 2 The chief mart of a wide territory. 3 A bazaar. [<L <Gk. *emporion* a market <*emporos* merchant, traveler <*en-* in + *poros* journey]

em·pow·er (em·pou′ər) *v.t.* 1 To authorize; delegate authority to. 2 To enable; permit. See synonyms under PERMIT.

em·press (em′pris) *n.* 1 A woman who rules an empire. 2 The wife or widow of an emperor. [<OF *emperesse,* fem. of *emperere,* var. of *empereor* EMPEROR]

emp·ty (emp′tē) *adj.* ·ti·er, ·ti·est 1 Having nothing within; containing nothing; void; vacant: often with reference to particular, usual, or proper contents, as food or inhabitants: an *empty* pitcher. 2 Without force, weight, value, or meaning: *empty* protestations, *empty* promises. 3 Without substance or significance; hollow; unreal; unsubstantial. 4 Destitute of intelligence, ideas, manners, etc.; senseless; inane; frivolous; contemptible: *empty* talk. 5 Being without supplies, etc.; unsupplied; unsatisfied; unfed. 6 Not carrying or drawing anything: *empty* hands. 7 Having no fruit; barren. 8 *Colloq.* Hungry. See synonyms under BLANK, FLAT[1], VACANT, VAIN. —*v.* **emp·tied, emp·ty·ing** *v.t.* 1 To make empty. 2 To transfer the contents of as if to another place or container: He *emptied* the bucket onto the fire. 3 To transfer (the contents) as if to another place or container: He *emptied* the milk into the street. 4 To remove (the contents): often with *out:* He *emptied* out the water. —*v.i.* 5 To become empty. 6 To discharge or pour out: The river *empties* into the bay. —*n. pl.* **emp·ties** A boat, barge, freight car, tank, etc., containing or transporting nothing. [OE *ǣmetig* <*ǣmetta* leisure] —**emp′ti·ly** *adv.* —**emp′ti·ness** *n.*

em·py·e·ma (em′pi·ē′mə, -pī-) *n. Pathol.* A collection or formation of pus, especially in the pleural cavity, often associated with various bacterial infections. [<NL <Gk. *empyēma* suppuration <*en-* in + *pyon* pus]

em·pyr·e·al (em·pir′ē·əl, em′pə·rē′əl, -pī-) *adj.* 1 Of or pertaining to the highest region of heaven; celestial. 2 Most highly refined; originally, formed of light or fire. —*n.* The empyrean. [<Med. L *empyreus* <Gk. *empyros* in the fire <*en-* in + *pyr* fire]

em·py·re·an (em′pə·rē′ən, -pī-) *n.* 1 The ancient supposed region of pure fire; the highest heaven. 2 Hence, the abode of God and the angels. 3 The upper sky. Also **em′py·rae′um.** —*adj.* Empyreal.

em·py·reu·ma (em′pə·rōō′mə, -pī-) *n.* The disagreeable odor produced when organic substances are decomposed by heat in a closed vessel. [<Gk. *empyreuma* covered live coal <*empyros.* See EMPYREAL.] —**em·py·reu·mat·ic** (em′pə·rōō·mat′ik) or ·i·cal *adj.*

e·mu (ē′myōō) *n.* A large ostrichlike Australian bird (genus *Dromiceius*), with neck and most of the head feathered: also spelled *emeu, emew.* [Prob. <Pg. *ema* ostrich]

EMU
(About 5 feet tall; second largest living bird)

em·u·late (em′yə·lāt) *v.t.* ·lat·ed, ·lat·ing 1 To try to equal or surpass. 2 To rival with some success. [<L *aemulatus,* pp. of *aemulari* rival <*aemulus* jealous] —**em′u·la·tive** *adj.* —**em′u·la·tive·ly** *adv.* —**em′u·la·tor** *n.*

em·u·la·tion (em′yə·lā′shən) *n.* 1 Effort or ambition to equal or excel another in any act or quality. 2 *Obs.* Selfish rivalry and strife.

Synonyms: ambition, competition, opposition, rivalry. We speak of *competition* in business, *emulation* in scholarship, *rivalry* in love, politics, etc.; *emulation* of excellence, success, achievement; *competition* for a prize. *Competition* may be friendly; *rivalry* is commonly hostile. See AM-

BITION, COMPETITION.

e·mul·gent (i·mul′jənt) *adj.* Milking out or straining. —*n.* Any preparation to aid an excretory organ or duct. [< L *emulgens, -entis,* ppr. of *emulgere* < *ex-* out + *mulgere* milk]

em·u·lous (em′yə·ləs) *adj.* **1** Eager or striving to equal or excel another; competitive. **2** *Obs.* Envious; jealous. —**em′u·lous·ly** *adv.* —**em′u·lous·ness** *n.*

e·mul·sion (i·mul′shən) *n.* **1** A liquid mixture in which a fatty or resinous substance is suspended in minute globules, as butter in milk. **2** Any milky liquid. **3** *Phot.* A substance, as a silver salt, held in suspension in collodion or gelatin, and used to coat dry plates. **4** *Physics* A colloid system, consisting of the globules or particles of one liquid finely dispersed in another. See COLLOID. [< LL *emulsio, -onis* < L *emulgere.* See EMULGENT.]

e·mul·sive (i·mul′siv) *adj.* **1** Capable of emulsifying. **2** Of the nature of an emulsion; softening. **3** Producing oil on being pressed.

e·munc·to·ry (i·mungk′tər·ē) *adj.* Serving to discharge excrementitious matter. —*n. pl.* **·ries** An organ for removing waste matter, as the kidneys, intestines, etc. [< NL *emunctorius* < L *emunctorium* a snuffer < *emungere* < *ex-* out + *mungere* blow the nose]

en (en) *n.* **1** The name of the fourteenth letter in the English alphabet, written N or n. **2** *Printing* A space half the width of an em.

en-[1] *prefix* Forming transitive verbs: **1** (from nouns) To cover or surround with; to place into or upon: *encircle.* **2** (from adjectives and nouns) To make; cause to be or to resemble: *enable, enfeeble.* **3** (from verbs) Often with simple intensive force, or used to form transitive verbs from intransitives: *enact, encompass.* Also, **em-** before *b, p,* and sometimes *m,* as in *embark.* Many words in *en-* have variant forms in *in-* because of the confusion between Old French *en-,* Latin *in-,* and native English *in-.* Compare IN-[2] and IN-[3]. [< OF < L *in-* < *in* in, into]

en-[2] *prefix* In, into; on: *endemic.* Also: *el-* before *l,* as in *ellipse; em-* before *b, m, p, ph,* as in *embolism, empathy; er-* before *r,* as in *errhine.* [< Gk. *en-* < *en* in, into]

-en[1] *suffix* Forming verbs: **1** (from adjectives) Cause to be; become: *deepen, harden.* **2** (from nouns) Cause to have; gain: *hearten, strengthen.* [OE *-nian*]

-en[2] *suffix of adjectives* Made of; resembling: *woolen, brazen.* [OE]

-en[3] *suffix* Used in the past participles of many strong verbs: *broken, beaten.* [OE]

-en[4] *suffix* Used in the plural of certain nouns: *oxen, children.* [OE *-an,* plural ending of the weak declension]

-en[5] *suffix* Small; little: *chicken, kitten.* [OE]

en·a·ble (in·ā′bəl) *v.t.* **·bled, ·bling** **1** To make able; give means or power to. **2** To make possible or more easy.

en·act (in·akt′) *v.t.* **1** To make into a law. **2** To carry out in action; perform. **3** To represent in or as in a play. —**en·act′a·ble** *adj.* —**en·ac′tor** *n.*

en·a·lid (en′ə·lid) *n. Bot.* A plant growing on the sea bottom, as eelgrass. [< Gk. *enalios* (< *en-* in + *hals, halos* the sea) + ID[1]]

en·al·la·ge (en·al′ə·jē) *n.* In rhetoric, the use of one part of speech, gender, etc., for another. [< L < Gk. *enallagē* exchange < *en-* in + *allassein* change]

en·am·el (in·am′əl) *n.* **1** A semi-opaque, vitreous material that is applied by fusion to gold, silver, copper, or other metals, or to porcelain, either as a decoration in colors or to form a surface for encaustic painting; also, as a lining for culinary and chemical vessels. **2** A work executed in such material: a fine cloisonné *enamel.* **3** One of various glossy lacquers or varnishes used for leather, paper, etc. **4** A kind of cosmetic or paint for the face, supposed to imitate exactly the natural gloss of the complexion. **5** *Anat.* The layer of hard, glossy, calcareous material forming the exposed outer covering of the teeth and protecting the dentine. —*v.t.* **·eled** or **·elled, ·el·ing** or **·el·ling 1** To cover or inlay, with enamel. **2** To surface with or as with enamel. **3** To adorn with different colors, as if with enamel. [< AF *enamyller* < *en-* on + *amayl,* OF *esmail* enamel

< Gmc.] —**en·am′el·er, en·am′el·ler** *n.* —**en·am′el·ist, en·am′el·list** *n.*

en·am·or (in·am′ər) *v.t.* To inspire with ardent love: used chiefly in the past participle, and followed by *of* or *with.* Also *Brit.* **en·am′our.** [< OF *enamourer* < *en-* in (< L *in-*) + *amour* love < L *amor*] —**en·am′ored** *adj.*

en·an·ti·o·morph (en·an′tē·ə·môrf′) *n.* Either of a pair of molecular or crystalline forms which are mirror images of each other. —**en·an′ti·o·morph′ism** *n.* —**en·an′ti·o·mor′phous** *adj.* [< Gk. *enantios* opposite + *morphē* form]

en·an·ti·op·a·thy (en·an′tē·op′ə·thē) *n.* **1** *Pathol.* A morbid condition or disease which is hostile to or preventive of another. **2** The curing of one disease by inducing another. Also **en·an·ti·o·path·i·a** (en·an′tē·ə·path′ē·ə). [< Gk. *enantios* opposite + -PATHY] —**en·an′ti·o·path′ic** (-tē·ə·path′ik) *adj.*

en·ar·thro·sis (en′är·thrō′sis) *n. Anat.* An articulation in which the rounded head of a bone is received into a corresponding cavity; a ball-and-socket joint, as the hip joint. [< NL < Gk. *enarthrōsis* < *enarthros* jointed < *en-* in + *arthron* a joint] —**en·ar·thro′di·al** (-dē·əl) *adj.*

e·nate (ē′nāt, i·nāt′) *adj.* **1** Growing out. **2** Related on the mother's side: distinguished from *agnate.* —*n.* A relative on the mother's side. [< L *enatus,* pp. of *enasci* < *ex-* out + *nasci* be born] —**e·nat′ic** (i·nat′ik) *adj.*

e·na·tion (i·nā′shən) *n. Bot.* An excessive development in plants, consisting in the formation of supplementary lobes or excrescences, usually on the upper surface of other organs, as scales on petals.

en·cage (in·kāj′) *v.t.* **·caged, ·cag·ing** To shut up in a cage: also spelled *incage.*

en·camp (in·kamp′) *v.i.* To go into camp; live in a camp. —*v.t.* To place in a camp.

en·camp·ment (in·kamp′mənt) *n.* **1** The act of pitching a camp. **2** A camp, or the persons occupying it.

en·car·nal·ize (in·kär′nəl·īz) *v.t.* **·ized, ·iz·ing 1** To invest with flesh and blood; to embody. **2** To make gross or sensual.

en·caus·tic (en·kôs′tik) *adj.* **1** Painted and having the hues fixed by heat. **2** Painted in wax and burnt in. —*n.* The art of encaustic painting. [< L *encausticus* < Gk. *enkaustikos* < *en-* in + *kaiein* burn]

encaustic painting A method of painting statues or architectural details with hot, colored wax or with cold, colored wax later fused with hot irons.

en·cave (in·kāv′) *v.t.* **·caved, ·cav·ing** To put in or as in a cave.

-ence *suffix of nouns* Forming nouns of action, quality, state or condition from adjectives in *-ent,* as in *diffidence, prominence.* Compare -ENCY. See note under -ANCE. [< F *-ence* < L *-entia,* a suffix used to form nouns from present participles; or directly < L]

en·ce·phal·ic (en′sə·fal′ik) *adj.* **1** Of or pertaining to the encephalon. **2** Situated within the cranial cavity.

en·ceph·a·li·tis (en′sef·ə·lī′tis, en·sef′-) *n. Pathol.* Inflammation of the brain; brain fever. —**en′ceph·a·lit′ic** (-lit′ik) *adj.*

encephalitis le·thar·gi·ca (li·thär′ji·kə) *Pathol.* An acute, frequently epidemic, viral encephalitis, deeply involving the central nervous system, and accompanied by widely varying symptoms, including fever, lethargy, and numerous sensory disturbances. Also called *sleeping sickness.*

en·ceph·a·li·za·tion (en·sef′ə·lə·zā′shən, -lī·zā′-) *n. Biol.* **1** The developmental processes resulting in the formation of the head. **2** The gradual association of various physiological functions, sensory and motor, with localized areas in the brain.

encephalo- *combining form* Brain: *encephalogram.* Also, before vowels, **encephal-.** [< Gk. *enkephalos* brain < *en-* in + *kephalē* head]

en·ceph·a·lo·cele (en·sef′ə·lə·sēl′) *n. Pathol.* Hernia of the brain, usually through a traumatic or congenital fissure in the skull.

en·ceph·a·lo·di·al·y·sis (en·sef′ə·lō·dī·al′ə·sis) *n. Pathol.* Softening of the brain. [< ENCEPHALO- + Gk. *dialysis* dissolution]

en·ceph·a·lo·gram (en·sef′ə·lə·gram′) *n.* An

X-ray photograph of the brain, obtained by replacing the cerebral fluid by air, oxygen, or helium. —**en·ceph′a·log′ra·phy** (-log′rə·fē) *n.*

en·ceph·a·lol·o·gy (en·sef′ə·lol′ə·jē) *n.* The study of the anatomy, physiology, and pathology of the brain. —**en·ceph′a·lol′o·gist** *n.*

en·ceph·a·lo·ma (en·sef′ə·lō′mə) *n. pl.* **·ma·ta** (-mə·tə) *Pathol.* A growth upon the brain; a brain tumor.

en·ceph·a·lo·ma·la·ci·a (en·sef′ə·lō·mə·lā′shē·ə) *n. Pathol.* Morbid softening of the brain. [< ENCEPHALO- + Gk. *malakos* soft]

en·ceph·a·lo·my·e·li·tis (en·sef′ə·lō·mī′ə·lī′tis) *n. Pathol.* One of a number of inflammatory diseases affecting the brain and the spinal cord. [< ENCEPHALO- + MYEL(O)- + -ITIS]

en·ceph·a·lon (en·sef′ə·lon) *n. pl.* **·la** (-lə) *Anat.* The brain. Also **en·ceph′a·los.** [< NL < Gk. *enkephalos*] —**en·ceph′a·lous** *adj.*

en·ceph·a·lop·a·thy (en·sef′ə·lop′ə·thē) *n. Pathol.* Any degenerative disease of the brain. —**en·ceph·a·lo·path′ic** (en·sef′ə·lə·path′ik) *adj.*

en·chain (in·chān′) *v.t.* **1** To bind with or as with a chain. **2** To hold fast or captive, as attention.

en·chant (in·chant′, -chänt′) *v.t.* **1** To put a magic spell upon; bewitch. **2** To delight; charm completely. **3** *Obs.* To mislead; delude. See synonyms under CHARM[1], RAVISH. [< F *enchanter* < L *incantare* < *in-* in + *cantare* sing] —**en·chant′ing** *adj.* —**en·chant′ing·ly** *adv.*

en·chant·ment (in·chant′mənt, -chänt′-) *n.* **1** The act of enchanting, or the state of being enchanted. **2** Illusive charm.

en·chase (en·chās′) *v.t.* **·chased, ·chas·ing 1** To incase in a setting, as a jewel in gold. **2** To enrich or decorate with engraved, chased, or inlaid work. **3** To engrave or work (figures, designs, etc.). [< F *enchâsser* < *en-* in (< L *in-*) + *châsse* case < L *capsa*]

en·chon·dro·ma (en′kon·drō′mə) *n. pl.* **·ma·ta** (-mə·tə) or **·mas** *Pathol.* A cartilaginous tumor; chondroma. [< NL < Gk. *en-* in + CHONDR(O) + -OMA] —**en·chon·drom·a·tous** (en′kon·drom′ə·təs, -drō′mə-) *adj.*

en·cho·ri·al (en·kôr′ē·əl, -kō′rē-) *adj.* Peculiar to a country; native; popular; indigenous. Also **en·chor·ic** (en·kôr′ik, -kor′-), **en·cho′ri·ous,** **en′cho·ris′tic.** [< Gk. *enchorios* native < *en-* in + *chōra* country]

en·chy·ma (eng′kə·mə) *n. Physiol.* The formative juice of tissues elaborated from chyme. [< NL < Gk. *enchyma* infusion < *en-* in + *chyma* fluid < *cheein* pour]

en·ci·na (en·sē′nə) *n.* **1** The California live oak (*Quercus agrifolia*). **2** The live or holm oak (*Q. virginiana*). [< Sp. < LL *ilicina* < L *ilex, ilicis* an oak] —**en·ci′nal** (-sī′nəl) *adj.*

en·ci·pher (en·sī′fər) *v.t.* To convert (a message, report, etc.) from plain text into cipher.

en·cir·cle (en·sûr′kəl) *v.t.* **·cled, ·cling 1** To form a circle around. **2** To go around; make a circuit of. See synonyms under EMBRACE[1], TWIST. —**en·cir′cle·ment** *n.*

en·clasp (en·klasp′, -kläsp′) *v.t.* To hold in or as in a clasp; embrace.

en·clave (en′klāv) *n.* **1** Part of a country surrounded by the territory or possessions of a foreign government, as East Prussia after World War I. **2** A substance removed from its normal place in the body and enclosed in another organ or tissue. Also **en·cla′vure** (-klä′vyər). —*v.t.* **·claved, ·clav·ing** To surround, as a region or country, with the territories of another country. [< F < *enclaver* enclose < LL *inclavare* < *in-* in + *clavis* key]

en·clit·ic (en·klit′ik) *adj.* **1** *Gram.* Attached to and dependent on a preceding word in stress and accent, as *ge* in Greek and *-que* in Latin. Such forms yield their own accent and generally change that of the word to which they are attached, usually causing a secondary accent to be laid on the final syllable of the latter. The particles *de, ge,* and *te* in Greek and *-que, -ne,* and *-ve* in Latin are examples. **2** *Anat.* Having the planes of the fetal head inclined to those of the maternal pelvis: opposed to *synclitic.* —*n.* An unaccented word attached to a preceding accented word. [< LL *encliticus* < Gk. *enklitikos* < *en-* on + *klinein* lean]

en·close (in·klōz′) *v.t.* **·closed, ·clos·ing 1** To close in; fence in. **2** To place in a cover, envelope, etc.

3 To place, as a check, in a cover, envelope, etc., with a letter or message. **4** To surround; trap. Also spelled *inclose*. See synonyms under CIRCUMSCRIBE, EMBRACE[1]. [<EN-[1] + CLOSE, after OF *enclos*, pp. of *enclore* shut in] —**en·clos′er** *n.*

en·code (en·kōd′) *v.t.* **·cod·ed, ·cod·ing** To transform a message, document, etc., from plain text into code. —**en·cod′ing** *n.*

en·co·mi·um (en·kō′mē·əm) *n. pl.* **·mi·ums** or **·mi·a** (-me·ə) A formal expression of praise; a eulogy. See synonyms under EULOGY, PRAISE. [<L <Gk. *enkōmion* a eulogy]

en·com·pass (in·kum′pəs) *v.t.* **1** To form a circle around; encircle. **2** To surround, either protectively or hostilely; shut in. **3** *Obs.* To outwit. See synonyms under EMBRACE[1]. —**en·com′pass·ment** *n.*

en·core (äng′kôr, -kōr, än′-) *v.t.* **·cored, ·cor·ing** To call for a repetition of (a performance) or by (a performer). —*n.* **1** The call for a repetition, as of some part of a performance. **2** The repetition itself. —*adv.* Again; once more. [<F]

en·coun·ter (in·koun′tər) *n.* **1** A coming together, especially when casual or unexpected. **2** A hostile meeting, contest; battle. **3** *Obs.* Manner of meeting; address. See synonyms under BATTLE, COLLISION. —*v.t.* **1** To meet accidentally; come upon. **2** To meet in conflict; face in battle. **3** To be faced with (opposition, difficulties, etc.). —*v.i.* **4** To meet accidentally or in battle. See synonyms under ATTACK. [<OF *encontrer* <LL *incontrare* <in- in + *contra* against]

en·cour·age (in·kûr′ij) *v.t.* **·aged, ·ag·ing 1** To inspire with courage, hope, or resolution. **2** To help or foster; be favorable toward. [<OF *encoragier* <en- in (<L *in-*) + *corage* COURAGE] —**en·cour′ag·er** *n.*

Synonyms: animate, arouse, cheer, countenance, embolden, excite, forward, hearten, impel, inspire, inspirit, instigate, promote, prompt, rally, reassure, stimulate. See ABET, AID, CHERISH, CONSOLE[1], HELP, PROMOTE.

en·cri·nite (en′krə·nīt) *n. Paleontol.* A fossil crinoid, especially one with cylindrical stem and developed arms. Also *crinite*. [<NL *Encrinus*, name of the genus (<Gk. *en-* in + *krinon* lily) + -ITE[1]]

en·croach (in·krōch′) *v.i.* **1** To intrude upon the possessions or rights of another by or as by stealth; trespass: with *on* or *upon*. **2** To advance or make inroads beyond the proper or usual limits, extent, etc.: The water is *encroaching* on the land. [<OF *encrochier* <en- in + *croc* a hook] —**en·croach′er** *n.*

en·croach·ment (in·krōch′mənt) *n.* **1** Entrance upon the rights or domain of another; especially, gradual intrusion. **2** That which is gained or seized by encroaching. See synonyms under AGGRESSION, ATTACK, INVASION.

en·crypt (en·kript′) *v.t.* To convert (a message) from plain text into a cryptogram. —**en·cryp·tion** (en·krip′shən) *n.*

en·cul·tu·ra·tion (in·kul′chə·rā′shən) *n. Sociol.* The processes whereby individuals are conditioned by, adjusted to, and integrated with the cultural norms prevalent in the society of which they are members. —**en·cul′tu·ra·tive** *adj.*

en·cum·ber (in·kum′bər) *v.t.* **1** To obstruct or hinder in action or movement, as with a burden; impede. **2** To obstruct or make hard to use; block: The decks were *encumbered* with fallen spars. **3** To weigh down or burden with a duty, financial obligations, mortgages, etc. Also spelled *incumber*. See synonyms under HINDER[1]. [<OF *encombrer* <LL *incombrare* < *in-* in + *combrus* an obstacle]

en·cum·brance (in·kum′brəns) *n.* **1** That which encumbers. **2** *Law* Any lien or liability attached to real property. **3** One's wife, child, or dependent. Also spelled *incumbrance*. See synonyms under IMPEDIMENT, LOAD. [<OF *encombrance* < *encombrer*. See ENCUMBER.]

-ency *suffix of nouns* A variant of -ENCE, as in *decency, urgency*, used to form words expressing quality, state or condition, the earlier form being reserved largely for nouns of action. [<L *-entia*]

en·cyc·li·cal (en·sik′li·kəl, -sī′kli-) *adj.* Intended for general circulation; circular: said of letters: also **en·cyc′lic**. —*n. Eccl.* A circular letter addressed by the pope to all the bishops, dealing with matters affecting the church in general. [<LL *encyclicus* <Gk. *enkyklios* general, common < *en-* in + *kyklos* circle]

en·cy·clo·pe·di·a (en·sī′klə·pē′dē·ə) *n.* **1** A work containing information on all subjects, or exhaustive of one subject; a cyclopedia. **2** A work of this kind by some of the intellectual leaders of the French Revolution, the French Encyclopedists. **3** The entire circle of knowledge. Also **en·cy′clo·pae′di·a.** [<NL *encyclopaedia* <Gk. *enkyklopaideia*, a misreading for *enkyklios paideia* a general education]

en·cy·clo·pe·dic (en·sī′klə·pē′dik) *adj.* Pertaining to, of the character of, or proper to an encyclopedia; comprehending a wide range of topics. Also **en·cy′clo·pae′dic, en·cy′clo·pe′di·ac** or **en·cy·clo·pe·di·a·cal** (en·sī′klə·pi·dī′ə·kəl), **en·cy′clo·pe′di·al, en·cy′clo·pe′di·an.**

en·cy·clo·pe·dist (en·sī′klə·pē′dist) *n.* **1** A writer for or compiler of an encyclopedia. **2** One whose studies embrace all sciences. Also **en·cy′clo·pae′dist.** — **French Encyclopedist** One of the writers of the *Encyclopédie ou Dictionnaire raisonné des sciences, des arts, et des métiers* (1751–65): among these were the two editors, Diderot and D'Alembert, and a number of contributors, of whom Voltaire and Rousseau are the best known.

en·cyst (en·sist′) *v.t. & v.i. Biol.* To envelop or become enclosed in a cyst, sac, etc. — **en·cyst′ed** *adj.*

en·cyst·ment (en·sist′mənt) *n. Biol.* A process by which certain protozoans, after retraction of the pseudopodia or other processes, become enclosed in a cyst, usually preparatory to reproduction, but also for protection against desiccation or putrefaction, in hibernation, etc. Also **en·cys·ta′tion.**

end (end) *n.* **1** The terminal point or part of any material object that has length. **2** The part of an object that is near either extremity. **3** The point in time at which some process ceases; hence, the conclusion of any work or operation. **4** The farthest limit of the space occupied by any extended object. **5** The purpose in view. **6** An inevitable or natural consequence. **7** The close of life. **8** A fragment; remnant. **9** A player stationed at the end of a line, as in football. **10** In archery, a unit of shooting toward a butt; in England, three arrows; in the United States, six. — **at loose ends** In an unsettled or confused state. — **in the end** At last. — **to the end that** In order that. —*v.t.* **1** To bring to a finish or termination; conclude. **2** To be the end of. **3** To cause the death of; kill. —*v.i.* **4** To come to an end. **5** To die. [OE *ende*]

Synonyms (noun): accomplishment, achievement, bound, boundary, cessation, close, completion, conclusion, consequence, consummation, design, effect, expiration, extent, extremity, finale, finis, finish, fulfilment, goal, intent, issue, limit, outcome, period, point, purpose, result, termination, terminus, tip, utmost, uttermost. The *end* is the terminal part of a material object that has length; the *extremity* is distinctively the terminal *point*, and may thus be but part of the *end* in the general sense of that word; the *extremity* is viewed as that which is most remote from some center, or some mean or standard position; the southern *end* of South America includes all Patagonia, the southern *extremity* or *point* is Cape Horn. *Tip* has nearly the same meaning as *extremity*, but is said of small or slight and tapering objects; as, the *tip* of the finger; *point* in such connections is said of that which is drawn out to exceeding fineness or sharpness; as the *point* of a needle, a fork, or a sword; *extremity* is said of something considerable; we do not speak of the *extremity* of a needle. A *goal* is an *end* sought or striven for, as in a race. For the figurative senses of *end* and its associated words, compare the synonyms for the verb END; also for AIM, CONSEQUENCE, DESIGN, EVENT, PURPOSE, REASON. *Antonyms:* see synonyms for BEGINNING.

Synonyms (verb): cease, close, complete, conclude, desist, expire, finish, quit, terminate, top. That *ends*, or is *ended*, of which there is no more, whether or not more was intended or needed; that is *closed, completed, concluded*, or *finished* which has come to an expected or appropriate end. A tumult in the audience may cause a speech to be *ended* when it is neither *closed, completed*, nor *finished*, nor, in the strict sense, *concluded*. An argument may be *closed* with nothing proved; when an argument is *concluded* all that is deemed necessary to prove the point has been stated. To *finish* is to do the last thing there is to do. To *terminate* may be to bring either to an arbitrary or to an appropriate end; as, He *terminated* his remarks abruptly; The spire *terminates* in a cross. A thing *stops* that comes to rest from motion; or the motion *stops* or *ceases* when the object comes to rest; *stop* frequently signifies to bring or come to a sudden and decided cessation of motion, progress, or action of any kind. Compare ABOLISH, CEASE, EFFECT, FINISH, TRANSACT. *Antonyms:* commence, found, inaugurate, initiate, institute, open, originate, start, undertake. Compare INSTITUTE (*verb*).

en·dam·age (en·dam′ij) *v.t.* **·aged, ·ag·ing** To cause damage to; injure.

en·da·me·ba (en′də·mē′bə) *n.* Any of a genus (*Endamoeba*) of protozoan organisms, some species of which are parasitic on man, especially *E. histolytica*, a causative agent in dysentery and liver abscess: also spelled *entamoeba*. Also **en′da·moe′ba.** [<END(O)- + AMEBA]

en·dan·ger (en·dān′jər) *v.t.* To expose to danger.

en·dar·te·ri·um (en′där·tir′ē·əm) *n. Anat.* The innermost coat of an artery. [<NL <Gk. *endo-* within + *artēria* artery]

end·brush (end′brush′) *n. Physiol.* The tufted branching fibrils forming the termination of many nerve cells.

en·dear (in·dir′) *v.t.* **1** To make dear or beloved. **2** *Obs.* To win or secure the affection of.

en·dear·ing (in·dir′ing) *adj.* **1** Making dear or beloved. **2** Manifesting affection; caressing. —**en·dear′ing·ly** *adv.*

en·dear·ment (in·dir′mənt) *n.* **1** Something, as an act, that expresses or attracts affection; an utterance of fondness; a caress. **2** The act of endearing, or the state of being endeared; hence, affection; love.

en·deav·or (in·dev′ər) *n.* An attempt or effort to do or attain something; earnest exertion for an end. —*v.t.* To make an effort to do or effect; try: usually with an infinitive as object. —*v.i.* To make an effort; strive: usually with *at, after*, or *for*. Also *Brit.* **en·deav′our.** [ME *endeveren* <EN[1] + DEVOIR. Cf. F *se mettre en devoir* make it one's duty, set about]

en·dem·ic (en·dem′ik) *adj.* **1** Peculiar to or prevailing in or among some (specified) country or people. **2** *Ecol.* Indigenous or native to a restricted area: said of plants and animals: opposed to *ecdemic*. **3** *Pathol.* Pertaining to a disease confined to or characteristic of a given locality, as distinguished from an epidemic or sporadic disease. Also **en·de·mi·al** (en·dē′mē·əl), **en·dem′i·cal.** [<Gk. *endēmos* native < *en-* in + *dēmos* people]

en·de·mic·i·ty (en′də·mis′ə·tē) *n. Ecol.* The condition of growing in only one natural area, or of being restricted in distribution to a given locality. Also **en′de·mism.**

end·er (en′dər) *n.* One who or that which brings something to an end.

En·der·bur·y Island (en′dər·ber′ē) One of the Phoenix Islands, comprising a condominium (1939) of Great Britain and the United States; 2 square miles.

En·der·by Land (en′dər·bē) A region on the coast of Antarctica south of the continent of Africa.

en·der·mic (en·dûr′mik) *adj. Med.* Acting by being absorbed in or through the skin. [<EN-[2] + Gk. *derma* skin] —**en·der′mism** *n.*

en dés·ha·bil·lé (än dā·zà·bē·yā′) *French* In dishabille.

En·di·an·dra (en′dē·an′drə) *n.* A genus of close-grained, straight-fibered hardwood trees of the laurel family native to Australia, bearing large globular fruit, especially *E. glauca*, with an aromatic teaklike wood.

end·ing (en′ding) *n.* **1** The act of bringing or coming to an end; also, an end; extremity. **2** One or more letters or syllables added to the base of a word, especially to indicate an inflection.

en·dive (en′dīv, än′dēv) *n.* **1** An herb (*Cichorium endivia*) allied to chicory. There are many varieties, divided into two groups, the **curled** or **narrow-leaved endive** (variety *crispa*) and the **broad-leaved endive** (variety *latifolia*). **2** The blanched leaves of this herb, used as a salad. [<F <L *in-*

tibus endive]

end·less (end′lis) *adj.* **1** Enduring everlastingly; eternal. **2** Having no end in space; boundless; infinite. **3** Continually recurring; incessant. **4** Forming a closed loop or circle; continuous. See synonyms under ETERNAL, IMMORTAL, PERPETUAL. —**end′less·ly** *adv.* —**end′less·ness** *n.*

endo- *combining form* Within; inside: *endocarp*. Also, before vowels, **end-**. [< Gk. < *endon* within]

en·do·blast (en′dō-blast) *n. Biol.* The hypoblast: also spelled *entoblast*. —**en′do·blas′tic** *adj.*

en·do·car·di·tis (en′dō-kär·dī′tis) *n. Pathol.* Inflammation of the endocardium. —**en′do·car·dit′ic** (-dit′ik) *adj.*

en·do·car·di·um (en′dō-kär′dē·əm) *n. Anat.* The delicate endothelial membrane lining the chambers of the heart. [< NL < Gk. *endo-* within + *kardia* heart]

en·do·carp (en′dō-kärp) *n. Bot.* The inner layer of a pericarp, as the hard inner part of a cherry stone.

en·do·cen·tric (en′dō-sen′trik) *adj. Ling.* Denoting a syntactic construction which as a unit has the same function as any one of its component parts, as the phrase *healthy boys and girls* in *healthy boys and girls eat well*: opposed to *exocentric.*

en·do·cho·ri·on (en′dō-kôr′ē·ən, -kō′rē-) *n.* **1** *Anat.* The inner chorion associated with the fetal membrane. **2** *Entomol.* The inner layer of the chorion or shell, covering an insect egg.

en·do·crine (en′dō-krin, -krīn) *adj.* **1** Producing an internal secretion. **2** Pertaining to or produced by an endocrine gland or glands. **3** Hormonal. Also **en′do·cri′nal** (-krī′nəl), **en·doc·ri·nous** (en-dok′rə-nəs), **en′do·crin′ic** (-krin′ik). —*n.* The secretion of an endocrine gland; a hormone. [< ENDO- + Gk. *krinein* separate]

endocrine gland Any of numerous ductless, hormone-secreting structures in various sites in the body which release secretions into surrounding tissue and thence into the bloodstream, either directly or through the lymphatic system.

ENDOCRINE GLANDS

Name	Location
Adrenals (2)	Anterior to the kidneys
Gonads	Sex glands collectively
Ovaries (2)	Paired sex glands of the female
Pancreas	Upper abdominal cavity
Parathyroids	In pairs, near the thyroid
Pineal	Attached to the brain, near the pituitary
Pituitary	In the floor of the skull
Testes (2)	Paired sex glands of the male
Thymus	Above the heart
Thyroid	Paired lobes, one on each side of the trachea

en·do·cri·nol·o·gy (en′dō-kri·nol′ə·jē, -krī-) *n.* That branch of medicine which treats of the anatomy, physiology, and pathology of the endocrine glands and the properties and functions of the various internal secretions. —**en′do·cri·nol′o·gist** *n.*

en·do·cyte (en′dō-sīt) *n. Biol.* A foreign substance found inside a cell.

en·do·derm (en′dō-dûrm) *n. Biol.* **1** The innermost of the germ layers of the embryo. **2** The inner layer of the integument of an organism. Also spelled *entoderm.*

en·do·der·mis (en′dō-dûr′mis) *n. Bot.* A sheath of one or more layers of modified parenchymatous cells between the cortex and the central zone of the stem or root in plants: also spelled *entoderm.* [< ENDODERM, on analogy with *epidermis*] —**en′do·der′mal, en′do·der′mic** *adj.*

en·do·don·tics (en′dō·don′tiks) *n.* The branch of dentistry which is concerned with the prevention, diagnosis, and treatment of diseases of the tooth pulp, as root canal work. Also **en′do·don′tia** (-don′shə), **en′do·don·tol′o·gy** (-don′tol′ə·jē). [< ENDO- + Gk. *odous, odontos* a tooth + -ICS] —**en′do·don′tist** *n.*

en·dog·a·my (en·dog′ə·mē) *n.* **1** *Anthropol.* The custom of marriage within the group, class, caste, or tribe; inbreeding: opposed to *exogamy.* **2** *Bot.* The fertilization of plants by pollination between two flowers on the same plant. —**en·dog′a·mous, en·do·gam·ic** (en′dō-gam′ik) *adj.*

en·do·gen (en′dō-jen) *n. Bot.* A plant that increases by the growth of new vascular and cellular tissue among that already formed; a monocotyledon: opposed to *exogen.*

ENDOGEN
A. Vertical section.
B. Cross-section.

en·dog·e·nous (en-doj′ə-nəs) *adj.* Originating or produced internally; due to internal causes. —**en·dog′e·nous·ly** *adv.*

en·dog·e·ny (en-doj′ə-nē) *n.* **1** Growth from within; specifically, endogenous cell formation. **2** Endogamy.

en·do·me·tri·um (en′dō-mē′trē·əm) *n. Anat.* The mucous membrane which lines the uterus. [< NL < Gk. *endo-* within + *mētra* womb] —**en′do·me′tri·al** *adj.*

en·dom·e·try (en-dom′ə-trē) *n.* The measurement of cavities; specifically of the interior of body organs, as the cranium. —**en·do·met·ric** (en′dō-met′rik) or **·ri·cal** *adj.*

en·do·morph (en′dō-môrf) *n. Mineral.* A mineral enclosed within another, as a crystal of tourmaline in quartz.

en·do·mor·phic (en′dō-môr′fik) *adj.* **1** *Mineral.* **a** Of or pertaining to an endomorph. **b** Occurring on the inside; produced by endomorphism. **2** Pertaining to a physical and personality type associated with the development of the endodermal layer of the embryo, and characterized by predominance of the abdominal system. Compare ECTOMORPHIC and MESOMORPHIC.

en·do·mor·phism (en′dō-môr′fiz·əm) *n. Geol.* The changes produced in igneous rocks by the action upon them of underlying and intrusive magmatic material.

en·do·par·a·site (en′dō-par′ə·sīt) *n. Biol.* A parasite that lives in the internal parts of its host, as an intestinal worm. —**en′do·par′a·sit′ic** (-sit′ik) *adj.*

en·do·path·ic (en′dō-path′ik) *adj. Pathol.* Pertaining to those diseases originating from within the organism. —**en·do·pa·thy** (en-dop′ə·thē) *n.*

en·do·phyte (en′dō-fīt) *n. Bot.* A plant living within another organism, usually as a parasite, as certain algae and fungi. Also spelled *entophyte.* —**en′do·phy′tal** *adj.* —**en′do·phyt′ic** (-fit′ik) *adj.* —**en′do·phyt′i·cal·ly** *adv.*

en·do·plasm (en′dō-plaz′əm) *n. Biol.* The inner granular portion of the cytoplasm of the cell, enclosing the nucleus. Also **en·do·sarc** (en′dō-särk). —**en·do·plas′mic** *adj.*

en·dor·phin (en-dôr′fin) *n.* Any of several peptides produced by the brain and having a morphinelike effect. [< ENDO- + (M)ORPHIN(E)]

en·dorse (in-dôrs′) *v.t.* **·dorsed, ·dors·ing** **1** To write upon the back of; especially, to write one's name on the back of (a check, draft, etc.) to assign it or to guarantee its payment; to write one's name on the back of (a check, etc.) in exchanging the document for the cash it represents. **2** To indicate receipt of (a sum) by signing one's name. **3** To give sanction to. See synonyms under ACKNOWLEDGE, AFFIRM, CONFESS, JUSTIFY, RATIFY. Also spelled *indorse.* [< OF *endosser* < Med.L *indorsare* < L *in-* on + *dorsum* back; partially refashioned after L] —**en·dors′a·ble** *adj.* —**en·dors′er, en·dor′sor** *n.*

en·do·scope (en′də·skōp) *n. Med.* An instrument for viewing the inside of a body cavity or hollow organ, especially the womb, rectum, urethra, and bladder. —**en·dos·co·py** (en·dos′kə·pē) *n.*

en·do·skel·e·ton (en′dō-skel′ə·tən) *n. Zool.* The internal supporting structure of an animal, characteristic of all vertebrates; all of the skeleton not of dermal origin: opposed to *exoskeleton.* —**en′do·skel′e·tal** *adj.*

en·dos·mo·sis (en·dos·mō′sis, -doz-) *n. Chem.* **1** Osmosis in that direction in which the fluid traverses the septum most rapidly. **2** Osmosis from an outer vessel to one within it. Also **en′dos·mose′** (-mōz′). —**en′dos·mot′ic** (-mot′ik) *adj.*

en·do·sperm (en′dō·spûrm) *n. Bot.* The albumen of a seed; nutritive substance within the embryo sac of an ovule.

en·do·spore (en′dō·spôr, -spōr) *n. Bot.* **1** A spore formed within the membrane of a cell. **2** The delicate inner layer of the wall of a spore: also **en′do·spo′ri·um. 3** An asexual spore produced by certain bacteria: opposed to *arthrospore.* —**en·dos·po·rous** (en-dos′pər·əs) *adj.*

en·dos·te·um (en·dos′tē·əm) *n., pl. ·te·a** (-tē·ə) *Anat.* The thin, vascular membrane lining the medullary cavity of a bone. [< NL < Gk. *endo-* within + *osteon* bone]

en·do·the·li·um (en′dō-thē′lē·əm) *n., pl. ·li·a* (-lē·ə) *Anat.* A membrane, composed of flat, thin cells, that lines blood vessels, lymphatic tubes, and cavities. [< NL < Gk. *endo-* within + *thēlē* nipple] —**en′do·the′li·al** *adj.* —**en′do·the′li·oid, en·doth·e·loid** (en-doth′loid) *adj.*

en·do·therm (en′dō-thûrm) *n.* An animal that maintains a uniform temperature independent of and usually higher than the ambient temperature; a warm-blooded animal.

en·do·ther·mic (en′dō-thûr′mik) *adj.* **1** *Chem.* Pertaining to, attended by, or produced from the absorption of heat; heat-absorbing: *endothermic* combination or reaction: opposed to *exothermic.* **2** *Zool.* Warm-blooded. Also **en′do·ther′mal.**

en·do·tox·in (en′dō-tok′sin) *n. Bacteriol.* A toxic product liberated by the disintegration of certain bacteria which fails to induce the formation of an antitoxin in an animal organism. —**en′do·tox′ic** *adj.*

en·do·troph·ic (en′dō-trof′ik, -trō′fik) *adj. Bot.* Relating to the condition of fungi which live in and feed upon the internal cells of plant parts, such as roots.

en·dow (in-dou′) *v.t.* **1** To bestow a permanent fund or income upon. **2** To furnish or equip, as with talents or natural gifts: usually with *with.* **3** *Obs.* To provide with a dower. Also spelled *indow.* [< OF *endouer* < *en-* in (< L *in-*) + *douer* < L *dotare* give]

en·dow·ment (in-dou′mənt) *n.* **1** Money or property given for the permanent use of an institution, person, or object. **2** Any natural gift, as talent or beauty. **3** The act of endowing. Also spelled *indowment.*

end papers In bookbinding, those papers, plain or variously colored and decorated, placed at the front and back of a book, one leaf being pasted to the binding or cover, the others acting as fly-leaves.

end·plate (end′plāt′) *n.* **1** *Electronics* One of the electrodes of a vacuum tube, carrying a negative potential to prevent the escape of electrons at the anode. **2** *Physiol.* The termination of a motor nerve, usually embedded in muscle fiber.

en·due (in-dōō′, -dyōō′) *v.t.* **·dued, ·du·ing 1** To provide or endow, as with some quality or power: with *with.* **2** To put on; don. **3** To clothe; garb. Also spelled *indue.* [Fusion of OF *enduire* introduce < L *inducere* (see INDUCE) and OF *enduire* clothe < L *induere*; infl. in meaning by ENDOW]

en·dur·ance (in-dōōr′əns, -dyōōr′-) *n.* **1** The capacity or power to endure; ability to suffer pain, distress, hardship, or any very prolonged stress without succumbing; patient fortitude. **2** The act or experience of enduring or suffering. **3** *Obs.* Hardship. See synonyms under FORTITUDE.

en·dure (in-dōōr′, -dyōōr′) *v.* **·dured, ·dur·ing** *v.t.* **1** To bear or undergo, as pain, grief, or injury, especially without yielding; withstand; suffer. **2** To tolerate; put up with. —*v.i.* **3** To last; continue to be. **4** To suffer without yielding; hold out. [< OF *endurer* < L *indurare* < *in-* in + *durare* harden < *durus* hard]

Synonyms: abide, afford, allow, bear, brook, permit, suffer, support, sustain, tolerate, undergo. *Bear* is the most general of these words; it is metaphorically to hold up or keep up a burden of care, pain, grief, annoyance, or the like, without sinking, lamenting, or repining. *Allow* and *permit* involve large concession of the will; whispering is *allowed* by the schoolteacher who does not forbid nor censure it; a state *tolerates* a religion which it would be glad to suppress. To *endure* is to *bear* with strain and resistance, but with conscious power; *endure* conveys a fuller suggestion of contest and conquest than *bear*. One may choose to *endure* the pain of a surgical operation rather than take anesthetics; he *permits* the thing to come which he must brace himself to *endure* when it comes. To *afford* is to be equal to a pecuniary demand, that is, to be able to *bear* it. *Abide* combines the senses of await and *endure*; as, I will *abide* the result. Compare ABIDE, LIVE, PERSEVERE, PERSIST, STAND, SUPPORT. *Antonyms*: break, despair, droop, fail, faint, fall, falter, sink, succumb, surrender, yield.

-ene *suffix Chem.* **1** Denoting an open-chain, unsaturated, hydrocarbon compound having one double-bond: *ethylene*. **2** Denoting an aromatic compound of the benzene series.

en·e·ma (en′ə·mə) *n. pl.* **·mas** or **e·nem·a·ta** (e·nem′ə·tə) *Med.* **1** A liquid injected into the rectum for cleansing or nutritive purposes. **2** The injection of such a liquid. **3** The apparatus for such an injection. [< Gk. *< enienai < en-* in + *hienai* send]

en·e·my (en′ə·mē) *n. pl.* **·mies** **1** One who cherishes resentment or malicious purpose toward another; an adversary; foe. **2** One of a hostile army or nation. **3** A hostile nation or military force collectively. —*adj.* **1** Of or pertaining to a hostile army or power. **2** *Obs.* Unfriendly; hostile. [< OF *enemi* < L *inimicus* < *in-* not + *amicus* friend]

Synonyms (noun): adversary, antagonist, competitor, foe, opponent, rival. An *enemy* in private life is one who is moved by hostile feeling with active disposition to injure; but in military language all who fight on the opposite side are called *enemies* or collectively "the *enemy*," where no personal animosity may be implied; *foe*, which is rather a poetical and literary word, implies intensely hostile spirit and purpose. An *antagonist* is one who opposes and is opposed actively and with intensity of effort; an *opponent*, one in whom the attitude of resistance is the more prominent; one who seeks the same object for which another is striving; *antagonists* in wrestling, *competitors* in business, *opponents* in debate may contend with no personal ill will; *rivals* in love, ambition, etc., rarely avoid inimical feeling. *Adversary* now commonly denotes one who not only opposes another in fact, but does so with hostile spirit or perhaps out of pure malignity. Compare synonyms for AMBITION. *Antonyms*: abettor, accessory, accomplice, ally, friend, helper, supporter.

en·er·ge·sis (en′ər·jē′sis) *n. Bot.* The chemical and physical changes which set free the energy produced by the respiratory processes in plant cells. [< NL < Gk. *energeein* be active]

en·er·get·ic (en′ər·jet′ik) *adj.* **1** Having or displaying energy. **2** Acting with prompt, rapid, and effective force; forceful and efficient; strenuous. Also **en′er·get′i·cal.** [< Gk. *energetikos* < *energeein* be active] —**en′er·get′i·cal·ly** *adv.*

en·er·get·ics (en′ər·jet′iks) *n. pl. (construed as singular)* **1** The science of the laws and phenomena of energy in all its forms. **2** The philosophic doctrine which attributes all natural phenomena to the action of energy.

en·er·gid (i·nûr′jid) *n. Biol.* The cytoplasm and nucleus of a cell considered as a unit. [< Gk. *energos* active + -ID¹]

en·er·gize (en′ər·jīz) *v.* **·gized, ·giz·ing** *v.t.* To give energy, force, or strength to; activate. —*v.i.* To be in operation; be active. —**en′er·giz′er** *n.*

en·er·gu·men (en′ər·gyōō′mən) *n.* One who is supposed to be possessed by evil spirits; a demoniac; hence, a fanatical enthusiast. [< LL *energumenus* < Gk. *energoumenos*, ppr. of *energeein* be active]

en·er·gy (en′ər·jē) *n. pl.* **·gies** **1** The power by which anything acts effectively to move or change other things or accomplish any result. **2** Habitual tendency to and readiness for effective action. **3** Power in active exercise; force in operation. **4** *Physics* The capacity of doing work and of overcoming inertia, as by heat, light, radiation, or mechanical and chemical forces. **Potential energy** is that due to the po-

sition of one body relative to another; **kinetic energy** is manifested by bodies in motion. The units of energy and work are mutually convertible, and energy itself is regarded as functionally related to the mass and velocity of a material system. See QUANTUM. **5** Vigor and forcefulness of style or expression. See synonyms under POWER, WARMTH. [< LL *energia* < Gk. *energeia* < *energēs* < *en-* on + *ergon* work]

energy level *Physics* Any of several discrete states which an electron may assume within an atom, transition between which is associated with the emission of quanta: also called *quantum state.*

en·er·vate (en′ər·vāt) *v.t.* **·vat·ed, ·vat·ing** To deprive of nerve, energy, or strength; weaken. —*adj.* (i·nûr′vit) Rendered feeble or effeminate; weakened. [< L *enervatus*, pp. of *enervare* weaken < *ex-* out + *nervus* a sinew] —**en′er·va′tor** *n.*

en·fee·ble (en·fē′bəl) *v.t.* **·bled, ·bling** To render feeble. See synonyms under IMPAIR. —**en·fee′ble·ment** *n.* —**en·fee′bler** *n.*

en·feoff (en·fēf′, -fef′) *v.t.* **1** *Law* To invest with a fee or fief. **2** *Obs.* To surrender, as a vassal; give over, as oneself. Also spelled *infeoff.* [< OF *enfeoffer < en-* in + *fief* FIEF]

en·fet·ter (en·fet′ər) *v.t.* To enchain.

en·fleu·rage (än′flœ·räzh′) *n.* The extraction of perfumes by exposing odorless fats to the exhalations of the more delicate flowers. [< F *< enfleurer < en-* in + *fleur* flower]

en·force (in·fôrs′, -fōrs′) *v.t.* **·forced, ·forc·ing** **1** To compel obedience to, as laws. **2** To compel (performance, obedience, etc.) by physical or moral force. **3** To make convincing; give weight to, as an argument. **4** *Obs.* To force; coerce. See synonyms under EXECUTE. [< OF *enforcier < LL infortiare < in-* in + *fortis* strong] —**en·force′a·ble** *adj.* —**en·forc′er** *n.*

en·frame (in·frām′) *v.t.* **·framed, ·fram·ing** To enclose in or as in a border or a frame. —**en·frame′ment** *n.*

en·fran·chise (en·fran′chīz) *v.t.* —**·chised, ·chis·ing** **1** To endow with a franchise, as the right to vote. **2** To set free, as from bondage. **3** *Law* In England, to convert (a copyhold estate) into a freehold, either by payment in gross or by setting a fixed annual rent charge. [< OF *enfranchiss-,* stem of *enfranchir < en-* in + *franc* free. See FRANK.]

en·gage (in·gāj′) *v.* **·gaged, ·gag·ing** *v.t.* **1** To bind by a promise, pledge, etc. **2** To promise to marry; betroth: usually in the passive. **3** To hire, as a lawyer, or his services; secure the use of, as a room. **4** To hold the interest or attention of. **5** To hold (interest or attention); occupy. **6** To occupy or take up the extent, energies, etc., of: How do you *engage* your time? **7** To win over; attract: to *engage* affections. **8** To begin a battle with: We *engaged* the enemy. **9** *Mech.* To mesh or interlock. —*v.i.* **10** To bind oneself by a promise, pledge, etc. **11** To devote or occupy oneself: to *engage* in research. **12** To begin a battle. **13** *Mech.* To mesh. See synonyms under BIND, EMPLOY, INTEREST, OCCUPY, RETAIN. [< F *engager < en-* in + *gager* pledge]

en·gaged (in·gājd′) *adj.* **1** Affianced. **2** Occupied or busy. **3** Partially sunk or built into another part of a structure, or so appearing. **4** *Mech.* Geared together; driven by gearing. **5** Involved in a contest or conflict. See synonyms under BUSY, INDUSTRIOUS.

en·gage·ment (in·gāj′mənt) *n.* **1** The act of engaging. **2** The condition of being engaged; a betrothal. **3** Something that engages or binds; an obligation; agreement; promise; contract. **4** An entering into or being in battle; a battle. **5** *Mech.* The state of being in gear. **6** *pl.* Pecuniary obligations. **7** A salaried position. See synonyms under BATTLE, CONTRACT.

en·gag·ing (in·gā′jing) *adj.* Attracting interest; winning. See synonyms under AMIABLE. —**en·gag′ing·ly** *adv.*

Eng·els (eng′əls), **Friedrich,** 1820–95, German socialist and author; associate of Karl Marx.

en·gen·der (in·jen′dər) *v.t.* **1** To cause to exist; produce. **2** *Rare* To beget. —*v.i.* **3** To come into being. See synonyms under PRODUCE, PROPAGATE. [< OF *engendrer* < L *ingenerare < in-* in + *genus, generis* race]

en·gild (en·gild′) *v.t.* To gild or brighten.

en·gine (en′jin) *n.* **1** A machine by which en-

ergy is applied to the doing of work, notably one that converts heat energy into mechanical work: a steam *engine*, gas *engine*, etc. **2** A locomotive, taken as a whole. **3** Any large mechanism or material contrivance for producing some effect, especially of destruction or disintegration: an *engine* of war. **4** Any agency or instrumentality designedly employed. [< OF *engin* < L *ingenium < in-* in + *gen-,* root of *gignere* beget]

en·gi·neer (en′jə·nir′) *n.* **1** One versed in or practicing any branch of engineering. **2** One who runs or manages an engine; engine-driver. **3** A manager; inventor; plotter. **4** A member of the division of an army which constructs forts and bridges, clears and builds roads, etc. Also *Obs.* **en′gin·er.** —*v.t.* **1** To put through or manage by contrivance: to *engineer* a scheme. **2** To plan and superintend as engineer: to *engineer* an aqueduct.

en·gi·neer·ing (en′jə·nir′ing) *n.* **1** The art of designing, building, or using engines and machines, or of designating and constructing public works or the like. The general art is now subdivided into numerous branches, dealing chiefly with the application of scientific knowledge for purposes useful to man: chemical *engineering,* civil *engineering,* electrical *engineering,* hydraulic *engineering,* mining *engineering.* **2** Painstaking management; maneuvering.

en·gi·nous (en′jə·nəs) *adj. Obs.* Tricky; crafty; deceitful. [< OF *engineus* < L *ingeniosus* INGENIOUS]

Eng·land (ing′glənd) The southern part and largest political division of Great Britain, south of Scotland and east of Wales; 50,874 square miles; capital, London: Latin *Anglia.* See COMMONWEALTH OF NATIONS, GREAT BRITAIN, UNITED KINGDOM.

Eng·lish (ing′glish) *adj.* **1** Of, pertaining to, or derived from England or its people. **2** Expressed in or belonging to the English language. —*n.* **1** The people of England collectively: with *the.* **2** The Low German, West Germanic language spoken by the people of the British Isles and most of the British Commonwealth, and of the United States, its territories, and possessions. — **Old English** or **Anglo–Saxon,** the English language from about A.D. 450 to A.D. 1150, consisting of the Kentish, West Saxon, Mercian, and Northumbrian dialects: represented by the epic poem *Beowulf* and the writings of Alfred the Great. The language in this period is synthetic in form and consists of an almost purely Germanic vocabulary. Abbr. *OE* — **Middle English,** the language of England after the Norman Conquest, from about 1150 to 1500: represented by the works of Chaucer. The characteristics of this period are the gradual loss of inflections accompanied by a stabilizing of word order, extensive borrowings from Latin, French, and the Low German languages, and the rise of the East Midland dialect as the standard. Abbr. *ME* — **Modern English,** the English language after 1500. **3** An English rendering or equivalent: "John" is the *English* of the French "Jean." **4** The English pronunciation, style, syntax, vocabulary, etc., of a particular region, time, or person: Chaucerian *English,* American *English.* **5** *Printing* A size of type between pica and great primer: about 14 points; also, a type face resembling German text: more commonly called **Old English.** **6** In billiards, a horizontal twist or spin given to the cue ball by striking it on one side; by the British called *side*: also applied in other games to the spin given to a ball. — **king's English** Spoken or written English considered as correct by official (or the king's) authority: also **queen's English.** — **plain English** A direct simple statement: This is the *plain English* of it. —*v.t.* **1** To translate into English. **2** To make English; Anglicize, as a foreign word. **3** In billiards and other games, to apply English to (a ball). [OE *Englisc* < *Engle* the Angles]

English Channel An arm of the Atlantic between England and France, connecting the North Sea with the Atlantic Ocean: French *La Manche.*

en·globe (en·glōb′) *v.t.* **·globed, ·glob·ing** **1** To ensphere. **2** To take up or assimilate within a globular body: An ameba *englobes* nutriment.

SOVEREIGNS OF ENGLAND, GREAT BRITAIN, AND THE UNITED KINGDOM

SOVEREIGNS OF ENGLAND[1]	Began to reign
ANGLO-SAXON LINE	A.D.
Egbert	800
Ethelwulf (son)	836
Ethelbald (son)	857
Ethelbert (brother)	860
Ethelred I (brother)	866
Alfred *the Great* (brother)	871
Edward *the Elder* (son)	901
Athelstan (son)	925
Edmund I (brother)	940
Edred (brother)	946
Edwy (nephew)	955
Edgar (brother)	957
Edward *the Martyr* (son)	975
Ethelred II, *the Unready* (half-brother)	979
Edmund II, *Ironside* (son)	1016
DANISH LINE	
Canute (son of Sweyn, a Viking)	1017
Harold I, *Harefoot* (son)	1036
Hardicanute (half-brother)	1039
SAXON LINE (RESTORED)	
Edward *the Confessor* (son of Ethelred II)	1041
Harold II (son of Earl Godwin)	1066
NORMAN LINE	
William I	1066
William II (son)	1087
Henry I (brother)	1100
Stephen (nephew)	1135
PLANTAGENET LINE	
Henry II (grandson of Henry I)	1154
Richard I (son)	1189
John (brother)	1199
Henry III (son)	1216
Edward I (son)	1272
Edward II (son)	1307
Edward III (son)	1327
Richard II (grandson)	1377
HOUSE OF LANCASTER	
Henry IV (grandson of Edward III)	1399
Henry V (son)	1413
Henry VI (son)	1422
HOUSE OF YORK	
Edward IV (great-great-grandson of Edward III)	1461
Edward V (son)	1483
Richard III (uncle)	1483

	Began to reign
HOUSE OF TUDOR	A.D.
Henry VII (great-great-great-grandson of Edward III)	1485
Henry VIII (son)	1509
Edward VI (son)	1547
Mary I (half-sister)	1553
Elizabeth I (half-sister)	1558

SOVEREIGNS OF GREAT BRITAIN

STUART LINE	
James I of England or VI of Scotland (son of Mary Queen of Scots, great-granddaughter of Henry VII)	1603
Charles I (son)	1625
COMMONWEALTH (during which Oliver Cromwell ruled as Lord Protector 1653-58, being succeeded by Richard Cromwell, his son, 1658-59; a year of anarchy followed)	
STUART LINE (RESTORED)	
Charles II (son of Charles I)	1660
James II (brother)	1685
HOUSE OF ORANGE	
William III (nephew) and Mary II (daughter of James II)	1688
STUART LINE	
Anne (daughter of James II)	1702
HOUSE OF HANOVER	
George I (great-grandson of James I)	1714
George II (son)	1727

SOVEREIGNS OF THE UNITED KINGDOM[2]

George III (grandson)[3]	1760
George IV (grandson)	1820
William IV (brother)	1830
Victoria (niece of William IV)	1837
SAXE-COBURG LINE	
Edward VII (son)	1901
HOUSE OF WINDSOR[4]	
George V (son)	1910
Edward VIII (son): abdicated	1936
George VI (brother)	1936
Elizabeth II (daughter)	1952

The British Sovereign has, from Norman times, been advised in the conduct of the government by a Committee of his *Privy Council,* known later as the *Cabinet.* See these words. [2]United, 1801. [3]Son of Frederick, Prince of Wales, who died 1751. [4]Created by Royal Proclamation July 17, 1917. Relationship is to previous sovereign, unless otherwise stated.

en·gorge (en·gôrj′) *v.t.* **·gorged, ·gorg·ing 1** To fill with blood, as an artery. **2** To devour or swallow greedily. [< F *engorger* < *en-* in + *gorge* throat]

en·graft (en·graft′, ·gräft′) *v.t.* **1** To graft (a cion) to another type of tree or plant for propagation. **2** To implant; set firmly. Also spelled *ingraft.* —**en·graft′ment** *n.*

en·grail (en·grāl′) *v.t.* To ornament the edge of with a series of concave notches; indent the edge of. [< OF *engresler* indent as by hailstones < *en-* in + *gresle* hail] —**en·grailed′** *adj.*

en·grain (in·grān′) *v.t.* **1** To ingrain. **2** To grain in imitation of wood.

en·gram (en′gram) *n. Psychol.* **1** A memory picture latent in consciousness. **2** The trace or impression assumed in a certain theory of mnemonics to be left in cells subjected to a constantly repeated stimulus. [< EN-[2] + -GRAM]

en·grave (in·grāv′) *v.t.* **·graved, ·grav·ing 1** To carve or etch figures, letters, etc., into (a surface). **2** To impress deeply. **3** To cut (pictures, lettering, etc.) into metal, stone, or wood, for printing. **4** To print from plates made by such a process. See synonyms under INSCRIBE. [< EN-[1] + GRAVE[3]; cf. F *engraver*]

en·gross (in·grōs′) *v.t.* **1** To occupy completely; absorb. **2** To copy legibly; make a formal transcript of. **3** To monopolize, as the supply of a marketable product. See synonyms under ABSORB, EMPLOY. [< AF *engrosser* < LL *ingrossare* write large < *in-* in + *grossus* large] —**en·gross′ing** *adj.* —**en·gross′ing·ly** *adv.*

en·gulf (in·gulf′) *v.t.* **1** To swallow up in or as in a gulf. **2** To bury or overwhelm completely.

en·hance (in·hans′, ·häns′) *v.t.* **·hanced, ·hanc·ing** To make higher or greater, as in reputation, cost,

beauty, quality, etc. See synonyms under AGGRAVATE, HEIGHTEN, INCREASE. [< AF *enhauncer,* prob. var. of OF *enhaucer* < *en-* in, on + *haucer* lift, ult. < L *altus* high]

en·har·mon·ic (en′här·mon′ik) *Music adj.* **1** Having intervals less than a half-step. **2** Pertaining to that perfectly true intonation which is violated on keyed instruments to avoid complexity: C-sharp and D-flat are not the same in the *enharmonic* scale, though they are on the pianoforte. **3** Relating to that Greek scale whose intervals were quartertones and major thirds: distinguished from the *diatonic* and *chromatic* tetrachords. —*n.* **1** An enharmonic chord or note. **2** *pl.* Music distinguished by enharmonic intervals. [< L *enharmonicus* < Gk. *enharmonikos* < *en-* in + *harmonia* HARMONY] —**en′har·mon′i·cal** *adj.* —**en′har·mon′i·cal·ly** *adv.*

e·ni·ac (ē′nē·ak) *n.* An electronically operated calculating machine designed to solve complicated mathematical problems at high speed: a trade name. [< E(LECTRONIC) N(UMERICAL) I(NTEGRATOR) A(ND) C(OMPUTER)]

e·nig·ma (i·nig′mə) *n.* **1** An obscure or ambiguous saying; a riddle. **2** Anything that puzzles or baffles. See synonyms under RIDDLE. [< L *aenigma* < Gk. *ainigma* < *ainissesthai* speak in riddles < *ainos* tale]

en·jambe·ment (in·jam′mənt, ·jamb′-; *Fr.* än·zhänb·män′) *n.* In prosody, the running over of a sentence or thought from one couplet or line to the next, without a pause at the end of the line or verse division. Also **en·jamb′ment.** [< F *enjamber* encroach < *en-* in + *jambe* leg]

en·join (in·join′) *v.t.* **1** To order authoritatively and emphatically; direct (a person or group) to a course of action, conduct, etc. **2** To impose (a

condition, course of action, etc.) on a person or group. **3** To forbid or prohibit, especially by judicial order or injunction. See synonyms under DICTATE. [< OF *enjoindre* < L *injungere* < *in-* on + *jungere* join] —**en·join′er** *n.*

en·joy (in·joi′) *v.t.* **1** To experience joy or pleasure in; receive pleasure from the possession or use of. **2** To have the use or benefit of. —**to enjoy oneself** To be happy; receive pleasure from an experience, party, etc. See synonyms under ADMIRE, REJOICE. [< OF *enjoir* < *en-* in (< L *in-*) + *joir* < L *gaudere* rejoice] —**en·joy′a·ble** *adj.* —**en·joy′a·ble·ness** *n.* —**en·joy′a·bly** *adv.* —**en·joy′er** *n.*

en·joy·ment (in·joi′mənt) *n.* **1** The act or state of enjoying; pleasure. **2** Something that gives joy or satisfaction. See synonyms under COMFORT, ENTERTAINMENT, HAPPINESS, SATISFACTION.

en·keph·a·lin (en·kef′ə·lin) *n.* A neurohormone elaborated by the pituitary and acting as an endogenous opiate.

en·kin·dle (en·kin′dəl) *v.t.* **·dled, ·dling 1** To set on fire; kindle. **2** To stir to action; excite; inflame. —**en·kin′dler** *n.*

en·lace (in·lās′) *v.t.* **·laced, ·lac·ing 1** To bind or wrap with or as with laces. **2** To intertwine; entangle. Also spelled *inlace.* [< F *enlacer* < *en-* in + *lacer* < OF *las* LACE] —**en·lace′ment** *n.*

en·large (in·lärj′) *v.* **·larged, ·larg·ing** *v.t.* **1** To make greater or larger; increase the amount or extent of; expand. **2** *Phot.* To increase the size of (a photograph) by projection printing. —*v.i.* **3** To become greater or larger; increase; widen. **4** To express oneself in greater detail or at greater length; expatiate: with *on* or *upon.* See synonyms under ADD, AMPLIFY, INCREASE. [< OF *enlarger* < *en-* in + *large* large] —**en·larg′er** *n.*

en·large·ment (in·lärj′mənt) *n.* **1** The act of making or growing larger; also, the state of being enlarged; an addition or extension. **2** Increase of range or capacity; expansion; dilatation: *enlargement* of the mind. **3** A photograph made larger than its original negative. **4** *Obs.* A setting at liberty. **5** Fullness of statement. See synonyms under ACCESSION, INCREASE.

en·light·en (in·līt′n) *v.t.* **1** To impart intellectual or spiritual knowledge to; cause to know or understand; teach. **2** *Obs.* To light up. See synonyms under TEACH. —**en·light′en·er** *n.*

en·light·en·ment (in·līt′n·mənt) *n.* **1** The act or result of enlightening, or the state of being enlightened. **2** Great moral and intellectual advancement. See synonyms under WISDOM.

En·light·en·ment (in·līt′n·mənt) *n.* A philosophical movement of the 18th century, characterized by rationalistic methods and skepticism of established dogmas.

en·list (in·list′) *v.t.* **1** To engage for service, as in the army or navy. **2** To gain the help or interest of (a person or his services). —*v.i.* **3** To enter military or naval services voluntarily. **4** To join in some venture, cause, etc. See synonyms under ENROL, RECRUIT.

en·li·ven (in·lī′vən) *v.t.* **1** To make lively, cheerful, or sprightly. **2** To make active or vigorous; stimulate. See synonyms under ENTERTAIN. —**en·li′ven·er** *n.*

en·mesh (en·mesh′) *v.t.* To ensnare or entangle in or as in a net: also spelled *inmesh.*

en·mi·ty (en′mə·tē) *n. pl.* **·ties 1** The spirit of an enemy; hostility. **2** The state of being an enemy; a hostile condition. [< OF *enemistié,* ult. < L *inimicus* hostile < *in-* not + *amicus* a friend]

Synonyms: acrimony, animosity, antagonism, bitterness, hatred, hostility, malevolence, malice, malignity, rancor, spite. *Enmity* is the state of being an enemy or the feeling and disposition characterizing an enemy (compare ENEMY). *Animosity* denotes a feeling more active and vehement, but often less enduring and determined, than *enmity.* *Hostility* is *enmity* in action; the term *hostilities* between nations denotes actual armed collision. *Bitterness* is a resentful feeling arising from a belief that one has been wronged; *acrimony* is a kindred feeling, but deeper and more persistent, and may arise from the crossing of one's wishes or plans by another, where no injustice or wrong is felt. *Antagonism* does not necessarily imply *enmity*, but ordinarily suggests a shade, at least, of hostile feeling. *Malice* is a disposition or intent to injure others, for the gratification of some evil passion; *malignity* is intense and violent *enmity, hatred,* or *malice.* Compare synonyms for ACRIMONY, ANGER, FEUD, HATRED. *Antonyms*: agreement, alliance, amity, concord, friendship, harmony, kindliness, kindness, regard, sympathy.

en·ne·ad (en′ē-ad) *n.* The number nine; any system or group containing nine objects. [< Gk. *enneas, enneados*]

en·ne·a·gon (en′ē-ə·gon) *n. Geom.* A figure, especially a plane figure, with nine sides and nine angles.

en·ne·a·he·dron (en′ē-ə·hē′drən) *n. pl.* **·drons** or **·dra** (-drə) *Geom.* A solid bounded by nine surfaces. —**en′ne·a·he′dral** *adj.*

en·ne·an·drous (en′ē·an′drəs) *adj. Bot.* Having nine stamens.

en·ne·a·style (en′ē-ə·stīl′) *adj. Archit.* Having nine columns. [< ENNEA- + Gk. *stylos* a pillar]

en·no·ble (i·nō′bəl, en-) *v.t.* **·bled, ·bling** 1 To make honorable or noble in nature, quality, etc. 2 To confer a title of nobility upon. [< F *ennoblir* < *en-* in (< L *in-*) + *noble* NOBLE] —**en·no′bler** *n.*

en·nui (än′wē, *Fr.* än·nwē′) *n.* A feeling of listless weariness resulting from satiety, boredom, inactivity, etc. —*v.t.* **en·nuied, en·nuy·ing** To oppress with tedium and lack of interest; bore. [< F *ennui* < L *in odio.* See ANNOY.]

e·nol (ē′nōl, -nol) *n. Chem.* An organic compound in which a hydroxyl group is joined with a doubly linked carbon atom. [Prob. < Gk. *en,* neut. of *heis* one + -OL[1]]

e·nol·o·gy (i·nol′ə·jē) *n.* The science or study of wines. Also *oenology, oinology.* [< Gk. *oinos* wine + -LOGY] —**e·no·log·i·cal** (ē′nə·loj′i·kəl) *adj.*

e·nor·mi·ty (i·nôr′mə·tē) *n. pl.* **·ties** 1 The state of being outrageous or extremely wicked. 2 A great or flagrant instance of wickedness or depravity; an outrageous offense; atrocity.

e·nor·mous (i·nôr′məs) *adj.* 1 Excessive or extraordinary in size, amount, or degree. 2 Wicked above measure; atrocious. See synonyms under FLAGRANT, IMMENSE, LARGE. —**e·nor′mous·ly** *adv.* —**e·nor′mous·ness** *n.*

e·no·sis (e·nō′sis) *n.* Union, especially as proposed between Cyprus and Greece. [< Gk. *énōsis* union]

e·nough (i·nuf′) *adj.* Adequate for any demand or need; sufficient. —*n.* An ample supply; a sufficiency. —*adv.* So as to be sufficient; sufficiently. —*interj.* It is enough; stop. [OE *genoh, genog*]

Synonyms (adj.): ample, sufficient. *Enough* is relative, denoting a supply equal to a given demand. A temperature of 70° Fahrenheit is *enough* for a living-room; of 212° *enough* to boil water; neither is *enough* to melt iron. *Sufficient* is an equivalent of the Saxon *enough,* with no perceptible difference of meaning, but only of usage, *enough* being the more blunt, homely, and forcible word, while *sufficient* is in many cases the more elegant or polite. *Sufficient* usually precedes its noun; *enough* preferably follows. See AMPLE.

e·nounce (i·nouns′) *v.t.* **e·nounced, e·nounc·ing** 1 To make a formal statement of; announce. 2 To give verbal expression to; utter; enunciate. [< F *énoncer* < L *enuntiare.* See ENUNCIATE.] —**e·nounce′ment** *n.*

en pas·sant (än pȧ·sän′) 1 By the way; in passing. 2 In chess, applied to the taking of a pawn that, in its first move, passes over a square commanded by a hostile pawn. [< F]

en·phy·tot·ic (en′fī·tot′ik) *adj. Bot.* Of regular occurrence in a locality: said of certain fungus diseases of plants. [< Gk. *en-* in + *phyton* plant]

en·rage (in·rāj′) *v.t.* **·raged, ·rag·ing** To throw into a rage; infuriate. See synonyms under INCENSE. [< OF *enrager* < *en-* in + *rage* RAGE]

en·rapt (in·rapt′) *adj.* Overpowered by emotion.

en·rap·ture (in·rap′chər) *v.t.* **·tured, ·tur·ing** To bring into a state of rapture; delight extravagantly. See synonyms under CHARM[1], RAVISH, REJOICE.

en·rav·ish (en·rav′ish) *v.t.* To enrapture.

en·reg·is·ter (en·rej′is·tər) *v.t.* To put on record; enrol; register. [< F *enregistrer*]

en·rich (in·rich′) *v.t.* 1 To make rich; increase the wealth of. 2 To make fertile, as soil. 3 To increase or enhance the level, quality, etc., of: to *enrich* a poem with images. 4 To increase the food value of, as bread. 5 To increase the beauty of; adorn. [< OF *enricher* < *en-* in + *riche* rich] —**en·rich′er** *n.*

en·rol (in·rōl′) *v.* **·rolled, ·rol·ling** *v.t.* 1 To write or record (a name) in a roll; register; list. 2 To enlist. 3 To place on record; record, as a document or decree. 4 To roll up; wrap. —*v.i.* 5 To place one's name on a list; register oneself. Also **en·roll′.** [< OF *enroller* < *en-* in + *rolle* ROLL]

Synonyms: enlist, enter, incorporate, initiate, list, register. Compare RECORD (noun). *Antonyms:* disband, dismiss, expel, refuse, reject.

en·rol·ment (en·rōl′mənt) *n.* 1 The act of enrolling. 2 An enrolled entry; a record. Also **en·roll′ment.**

en·root (en·rōōt′, -rŏot′) *v.t.* To cause to take root; implant deeply: used chiefly in the past participle.

en route (än rōōt′, *Fr.* än rōōt′) On the road; on the way.

ens (enz) *n. pl.* **en·ti·a** (en′shē·ə) In scholastic philosophy, the abstract conception of being, or being as absolute, without regard to any question of actual existence. [< LL, orig. ppr. formed from *esse* be]

en·san·guine (en·sang′gwin) *v.t.* **·guined, ·guin·ing** To cover or stain with or as with blood.

en·sconce (en·skons′) *v.t.* **·sconced, ·sconc·ing** 1 To fix securely or comfortably in some place; settle snugly. 2 To shelter; hide.

en·seal (en·sēl′) *v.t. Obs.* To seal up; put a seal upon. [< OF *enseeler* < *en-* in + *seel* SEAL]

en·sem·ble (än·säm′bəl, *Fr.* än·sän′bl′) *n.* 1 The parts of a thing viewed as a whole; general effect. 2 A combination of clothing and accessories that match or harmonize in color. 3 *Music* The union of soloists and chorus in a concerted number. 4 The scene in a play, usually the last, that includes the entire cast. [< F < L *insimul* < *in-* in + *simul* at the same time]

en·sep·ul·cher (en·sep′əl·kər) *v.t.* **·chered, ·cher·ing** To put into or as into a sepulchre; entomb. Also **en·sep′ul·chre.**

en·shrine (in·shrīn′) *v.t.* **·shrined, ·shrin·ing** 1 To place in or as in a shrine. 2 To cherish devoutly; hold sacred. —**en·shrine′ment** *n.*

en·shroud (en·shroud′) *v.t.* To cover as with a shroud; conceal.

en·si·form (en′sə·fôrm) *adj. Bot.* Sword-shaped, as certain leaves. [< L *ensis* sword + -FORM]

en·sign (en′sīn) *n.* 1 A distinguished flag or banner; especially, a national standard or naval flag. 2 (en′sən) In the U.S. Navy or Coast Guard, a commissioned officer of the lowest grade, ranking with a second lieutenant in the U.S. Army, Air Force, or Marine Corps. 3 In the British Army, until 1871, a commissioned officer who carried the flag of a regiment or company. 4 A badge or symbol, as of office. 5 *Obs.* A signal. [< F *enseigne* < L *insignia* < *in-* in + *signum* mark]

en·sign·cy (en′sən·sē) *n. pl.* **·cies** The function, rank, or commission of an ensign. Also **en′sign·ship.**

en·si·lage (en′sə·lij) *n.* 1 The process of preserving succulent fodder in closed pits or silos. 2 The fodder thus preserved: also called *silage.* —*v.t.* **·laged, ·lag·ing** To store in a silo for preservation: also **en·sile** (en·sīl′). [< F *ensiler* < *en-* in + *silo* SILO]

en·slave (in·slāv′) *v.t.* **·slaved, ·slav·ing** To make a slave of; dominate. —**en·slave′ment** *n.* —**en·slav′er** *n.*

en·snare (en·snâr′) *v.t.* **·snared, ·snar·ing** To catch in a snare; trick. Also spelled *insnare.* See synonyms under CATCH, DECEIVE.

en·soul (en·sōl′) *v.t.* 1 To endow with a soul. 2 To receive or put into the soul. Also spelled *insoul.*

en·sphere (en·sfir′) *v.t.* **·sphered, ·spher·ing** 1 To enclose in a sphere. 2 To give the form of a sphere to.

en·sta·tite (en′stə·tīt) *n. Mineral.* A variety of orthorhombic pyroxene low in iron oxide: a constituent of many basic igneous rocks. [< Gk. *enstatēs* adversary + -ITE[1]; so called from its refractory nature]

en·sue (en·sōō′) *v.i.* **·sued, ·su·ing** 1 To follow; occur afterward or subsequently. 2 To

follow as a consequence; result. [< OF *ensu-, stem of *ensuivre* < L *insequor* < *in-* on, in + *sequi* follow]

en·swathe (en·swäth′) *v.t.* **·swathed, ·swath·ing** To enwrap, as in swaddling clothes; swathe: also spelled *inswathe.* —**en·swathe′ment** *n.*

-ent *suffix of nouns and adjectives* 1 Having the quality, or performing the action of (the main element): *potent.* 2 One who or that which performs the action of (the main element): *superintendent.* Compare -ANT. [< F *-ent* < L *-ens, -entis,* suffix of present participial]

ent- See ENTO-.

en·tab·la·ture (en·tab′lə·chər) *n. Archit.* 1 The uppermost member of a classical order or columnar system, consisting of the architrave, frieze, and cornice. 2 A projecting frieze or cornice of several members, as on the front of an edifice 3 A platform. [< MF < Ital. *intavolatura* < *in-* in + *tavola* base, table < L *tabula*]

ENTABLATURE
A. Cornice. B. Frieze. C. Architrave. D. Capital on shaft. *a, b, c.* Fasciae.

en·ta·ble·ment (en·tā′bəl·mənt) *n. Archit.* 1 An entablature. 2 The series of platforms supporting a statue above the dado and base. [< F < *en-* in, on + *table* TABLE]

en·tail (in·tāl′) *v.t.* 1 To impose or result in (labor, concentration, etc.) as a necessary consequence. 2 *Law* To restrict the inheritance of (real property) to an unalterable succession of heirs. 3 To leave (anything) to an unalterable succession of heirs. —*n.* 1 Anything transmitted as an inalienable inheritance. 2 An estate in fee limited to a particular class of heirs, as eldest sons. 3 The act or custom of thus limiting inheritance. [< EN-[1] + TAIL[2]] —**en·tail′ment** *n.*

en·tan·gle (in·tang′gəl) *v.t.* **·gled, ·gling** 1 To catch in or as in a snare; hamper. 2 To make tangled; snarl; interlace; complicate. 3 To involve in difficulties; perplex; embarrass. See synonyms under INVOLVE, PERPLEX. —**en·tan′gled** *adj.* —**en·tan′gler** *n.*

en·ta·sis (en′tə·sis) *n.* 1 *Archit.* A slight convex curve in the vertical outlines of the shaft of a pilaster or of a column. 2 *Physiol.* Spasmodic contraction of a muscle; a tonic spasm: also **en·ta·si·a** (en·tā′zhē·ə). [< NL < Gk. *entasis* a stretching < *enteinein* < *en-* in + *teinein* stretch] —**en·tas·tic** (en·tas′tik) *adj.*

en·tel·e·chy (en·tel′ə·kē) *n. pl.* **·chies** *Philos.* 1 In Aristotle's metaphysics, completed realization, as distinguished from potentiality. 2 In the philosophy of Driesch, Bergson, etc., the non-physicochemical principle, or vital force, assumed to be responsible for life and growth. [< L *entelechia* < Gk. *entelecheia* actuality < *en telei echein* be complete]

en·tel·lus (en·tel′əs) *n.* The hanuman or East Indian bearded monkey (genus *Presbytis*). [< NL, appar. after a character in the *Aeneid*]

en·tente (än·tänt′, *Fr.* än·tänt′) *n.* An understanding. 2

ENTELLUS
(Body length 2 1/2 to 3 feet)

entente cor·diale (kôr·dyȧl′) Cordial understanding; in politics, friendliness between governments; especially, **Entente Cordiale,** the alliance between France and England, formed in 1904; enlarged to include Russia in 1907, and then called the **Triple Entente.** [< F]

en·ter (en′tər) *v.t.* 1 To come or go into. 2 To make a way into; penetrate; pierce. 3 To set or insert in: to *enter* a·wedge. 4 To become a member of; join. 5 To begin; pass within the limits of; start: to *enter* middle age. 6 To obtain admission; enrol, as in a school or competition. 7 To write or record, as in a list, book, etc. 8 To report (goods, a vessel, etc.) to the customhouse. 9 *Law* a To place on the records of a court, as evidence, a plea, or an appearance. **b** To go upon or into feloniously or as a trespasser. **c** To file for title to (public lands). — *v.i.* **10** To come or go inward; make an entrance. **11** To come onto the stage: *Enter* the queen, weeping. — **to enter into 1** To begin; start. **2** To become a party to; engage in: to *enter into* a discussion. **3** To take an interest in; join in: to *enter into* the plans for a party. **4** To form a part of; be a constituent of: Oxygen *enters into* many compound bodies. **5** To consider or discuss: to *enter into* the particulars. — **to enter on** (or **upon**) To begin; set out on: to *enter upon* a career of dissipation. [<F *entrer* <L *intrare* <*intra* within]

en·ter·al·gi·a (en′tər·ral′jē·ə) *n. Pathol.* Intestinal neuralgia.

en·ter·ec·to·my (en′tə·rek′tə·mē) *n. Surg.* Excision of a portion of an intestine.

en·ter·ic (en·ter′ik) *adj.* **1** Of or pertaining to the intestine. **2** Having an intestine. [<Gk. *enterikos* <*enteron* intestine <*entos* within]

en·ter·i·tis (en′tə·rī′tis) *n. Pathol.* Inflammation of the intestines, particularly of the small intestine.

entero- *combining form* Intestine. Also, before vowels, **enter-**. [<Gk. *enteron* intestine]

en·ter·o·gas·trone (en′tə·rō·gas′trōn) *n. Biochem.* A hormone obtained from the mucous lining of the upper intestine and having the power to inhibit the action of the gastric juices. [<ENTERO- + GASTR(O)- + (HORM)ONE]

en·ter·o·ci·ne·sia (en′tə·rō·si·nē′zhə) *n. Physiol.* Peristalsis. [<ENTERO- + Gk. *kinēsis* movement] — **en′ter·o·ci·net′ic** (-si·net′ik) *adj.*

en·ter·o·ki·nase (en′tə·rō·kī′nās, -kin′ās) *n. Biochem.* An intestinal enzyme which converts trypsinogen into trypsin.

en·ter·o·lith (en′tə·rō·lith′) *n. Pathol.* An intestinal concretion; a bezoar.

en·ter·ol·o·gy (en′tə·rol′ə·jē) *n.* The study of the intestines.

en·ter·on (en′tə·ron) *n. pl.* **·ter·a** (-tər·ə) *Anat.* The entire intestine or alimentary canal; the gut. [<NL <Gk.]

en·ter·op·to·sis (en′tə·rop·tō′sis) *n. Pathol.* Prolapse of the intestines. [<NL <Gk. *enteron* intestine + *ptosis* <*piptein* fall] — **en′ter·op′tic** *adj.*

en·ter·o·scope (en′tər·ə·skōp′) *n. Med.* An instrument equipped with an electric light for examining the intestines. — **en·ter·os·co·py** (en′tə·ros′kə·pē) *n.*

en·ter·o·sta·sis (en′tə·rō·stā′sis) *n. Pathol.* A stoppage of food in the intestinal passages; intestinal stasis.

en·ter·o·stax·is (en′tə·rō·stak′sis) *n. Pathol.* Gradual hemorrhage through the mucous membrane of the intestine. [<ENTERO- + Gk. *staxis* <*stazein* drip]

en·ter·os·to·my (en′tə·ros′tə·mē) *n. Surg.* The formation of a permanent artificial opening through the abdominal wall into the intestine.

en·ter·ot·o·my (en′tə·rot′ə·mē) *n. Surg.* Any cutting operation upon the intestines.

en·ter·o·tox·e·mi·a (en′tə·rō·tok·sē′mē·ə) *n.* Severe intestinal poisoning of sheep caused by the toxins of certain bacteria, especially *Clostridium perfringens.*

en·ter·prise (en′tər·prīz) *n.* **1** Any projected task or work; an undertaking. **2** Boldness, energy, and invention in practical affairs. [<F *enterprise* <*entreprendre* <*entre-* between (<L *inter-*) + *prendre* take <L *prehendere*]

en·ter·tain (en′tər·tān′) *v.t.* **1** To hold the attention of; amuse; divert. **2** To extend hospitality to; receive as a guest. **3** To take into consideration, as a proposal. **4** To keep or bear in mind; maintain: to *entertain* a grudge. **5** *Obs.* To keep up; maintain. — *v.i.* **6** To receive and care for guests: to *entertain* lavishly. [<F *entretenir* <*entre-* between (<L *inter-*) + *tenir* hold] — **en′ter·tain′a·ble** *adj.* — **en′ter·tain′er** *n.*

Synonyms: amuse, beguile, cheer, delight, disport, divert, enliven, gratify, interest, occupy, please, recreate.

en·ter·tain·ing (en′tər·tā′ning) *adj.* Of a character to entertain; amusing; diverting. — **en′ter·tain′ing·ly** *adv.* — **en′ter·tain′ing·ness** *n.*

en·ter·tain·ment (en′tər·tān′mənt) *n.* **1** The act of receiving and caring for guests; hospitable accommodation in the inn or dwelling of a host; the furnishing of food, lodging, and service to a guest. **2** A source or means of amusement; a diverting performance, especially a public performance, as a concert, drama, or the like. **3** Pleasure afforded by an amusing act or spectacle; amusement. **4** A social party; also, the refreshments provided for guests. **5** *Obs.* Maintenance; employment; service.

Synonyms: amusement, cheer, delight, diversion, enjoyment, frolic, fun, merriment, pastime, pleasure, recreation, sport.

en·thal·py (en·thal′pē, en′thəl·pē) *n. Physics* The quantity of heat in a substance or physical system per unit of mass; heat content. [<Gk. *enthalpein* <*en-* in + *thalpein* warm]

en·thet·ic (en·thet′ik) *adj.* **1** Introduced from without. **2** *Med.* Communicated by inoculation: said of infectious diseases. [<Gk. *enthetikos* fit for implanting <*en-* in + *tithenai* put]

en·thral (in·thrôl′) *v.t.* **·thralled, ·thral·ling 1** To keep spellbound; fascinate; charm. **2** To put or keep in thraldom; enslave. Also spelled **inthral.** Also **en·thrall′.** — **en·thral′ment, en·thrall′ment** *n.*

en·throne (in·thrōn′) *v.t.* **·throned, ·thron·ing 1** To put upon a throne. **2** To invest with sovereign or ecclesiastical power. **3** To exalt; revere. Also spelled **inthrone.** — **en·throne′ment** *n.*

en·thuse (in·thooz′) *v.t. & v.i.* **·thused, ·thus·ing** *U.S. Colloq.* To make enthusiastic; yield to or display enthusiasm. [Back formation from ENTHUSIASM]

en·thu·si·asm (in·thoo′zē·az′əm) *n.* **1** Earnest and fervent feeling; ardent zeal for a person or cause. **2** *Archaic* Exalted or ecstatic feeling; also, irrational religious ecstasy; divine fury or frenzy; possession. **3** An object of great interest to a person. [<LL *enthusiasmus* <Gk. *enthusiasmos*, ult. <*entheos, enthous* inspired <*en-* in + *theos* god]

Synonyms: ardor, devotion, eagerness, earnestness, ecstasy, excitement, extravagance, fanaticism, fervency, fervor, frenzy, inspiration, intensity, passion, rapture, transport, vehemence, warmth, zeal. The old meaning of *enthusiasm* implies a pseudo-*inspiration,* an almost frantic *extravagance* in behalf of something supposed to be an expression of the divine will. This sense remains as the controlling one in the kindred noun *enthusiast. Enthusiasm* has now chiefly the meaning of an earnest and commendable *devotion,* an intense and eager interest. *Zeal* is burning *earnestness,* always tending to vigorous action with all the *devotion* of *enthusiasm,* but often without its hopefulness. Compare WARMTH. *Antonyms:* calculation, calmness, caution, coldness, deadness, dulness, indifference, lukewarmness, policy, prudence, timidity, wariness.

en·thu·si·ast (in·thoo′zē·ast) *n.* One prone to or moved by enthusiasm; an ardent adherent; zealot.

en·thu·si·as·tic (in·thoo′zē·as′tik) *adj.* Given to enthusiasm; ardent; zealous. Also **en·thu′·si·as′ti·cal.** See synonyms under EAGER, SANGUINE. — **en·thu′si·as′ti·cal·ly** *adv.*

en·thy·meme (en′thə·mēm) *n. Logic* An argument in which one of the premises of the syllogism is not stated. [<L *enthymema* <Gk. *enthymēma* <*enthymeesthai* think <*en-* in + *thymos* mind]

en·tice (in·tīs′) *v.t.* **·ticed, ·tic·ing** To lead on or attract by arousing hope of pleasure, profit, etc.; allure. See synonyms under ALLURE, CHARM¹, DRAW, PERSUADE. [<OF *enticier* arouse <L *in-* in + *titio* a firebrand] — **en·tic′er** *n.* — **en·tic′ing** *adj.* — **en·tic′ing·ly** *adv.*

en·tire (in·tīr′) *adj.* **1** Complete in all its parts; undivided; whole. **2** Free from admixture; unalloyed; pure. **3** *Bot.* Having the margin of a leaf not serrated, as a tiger lily. **4** Consisting of only one piece. **5** Uncastrated: an *entire* horse. See synonyms under PERFECT, RADICAL. — *n.* The whole; the entirety. [<OF *entier* <L *integer.* See INTEGER.] — **en·tire′ly** *adv.* — **en·tire′ness** *n.*

en·tire·ty (in·tīr′tē) *n. pl.* **·ties 1** The state or condition of being entire; completeness. **2** That which is entire; a whole. See synonyms under AGGREGATE.

en·ti·tle (in·tīt′l) *v.t.* **·tled, ·tling 1** To give a right to demand or expect; authorize or qualify: His position *entitles* him to do it. **2** To give a name or designation to. **3** To give (a person) a title designating rank, honor, etc. Also spelled *intitle.* [<AF *entitler,* OF *entituler* <LL *intitulare* <*in-* in + *titulus* a title]

en·ti·tle·ments benefits that one may receive upon request, esp. from a government agency.

en·ti·ty (en′tə·tē) *n. pl.* **·ties 1** Anything that exists or may be supposed to exist· being. **2** A fact or conception regarded as complete in itself. [<L *entitas, -tatis* <*ens,* ppr. of *esse* be]

ento- *combining form* Within, interior: *entozoic.* Also, before vowels, **ent-.**

en·tomb (in·toom′) *v.t.* **1** To place in or as in a tomb; bury. **2** To serve as a tomb for. Also spelled *intomb.* See synonyms under BURY, HIDE. [<OF *entoumber* <*en-* in + *tombe* a tomb] — **en·tomb′er** *n.* — **en·tomb′ment** *n.*

entomo- *combining form* Insect: *entomogenous.* Also, before vowels, **entom-.** [<Gk. *entoma* insects, orig. neut. pl. of *entomos* cut up <*en-* in + *temnein* cut; with ref. to their body structure]

en·to·mog·e·nous (en′tə·moj′ə·nəs) *adj. Bot.* Growing in or upon insects, as certain fungi.

en·to·mol·o·gist (en′tə·mol′ə·jist) *n.* A student of or one versed in entomology.

en·to·mol·o·gy (en′tə·mol′ə·jē) *n.* The branch of zoology that treats of insects. — **en·to·mo·log·i·cal** (en′tə·mə·loj′i·kəl) or **·log′ic** *adj.* — **en′to·mo·log′i·cal·ly** *adv.*

en·to·moph·a·gous (en′tə·mof′ə·gəs) *adj.* Feeding on insects.

en·to·moph·i·ly (en′tə·mof′ə·lē) *n. Bot.* The condition or state of being pollinated by insects. [<ENTOMO- + Gk. *philos* loving]

en·to·mos·tra·can (en′tə·mos′trə·kan) *adj.* Designating a subclass (*Entomostraca*) of crustaceans, chiefly marine, including the branchiopods, copepods, etc. — *n.* A member of this subclass. [<ENTOM(O) + Gk. *ostrakon* shell]

en·top·ic (en·top′ik) *adj. Med.* Situated or occurring in its normal place: opposed to *ectopic.* [<Gk. *entopos* in a place <*en-* in + *topos* place]

en·top·tic (en·top′tik) *adj. Med.* **1** Of or pertaining to the interior of the eye. **2** Describing visual perception dependent on the eye itself, and not on anything external to it: *entoptic* phenomena. [<ENT- + Gk. *optikos* optic] — **en·top′ti·cal·ly** *adv.*

en·top·tics (en·top′tiks) *n.* The science of the eye with reference to its interior functions and the phenomena of visual perception.

en·tot·ic (en·tot′ik) *adj. Med.* Of or pertaining to the interior of the ear. Compare illustration under EAR. [<ENT- + Gk. *otos, otos* ear]

en·tou·rage (än′too·räzh′, *Fr.* än·too·räzh′) *n.* **1** Associates, companions, or attendants collectively, especially of a person of rank. **2** Environment. [<F *entourer* surround <*entour* around]

en·to·zo·an (en′tə·zō′ən) *n.* Any of a branch (*Entozoa*) of metazoans, chiefly parasitic worms, characterized by the possession of a gut cavity and a two-layered cell arrangement. — *adj.* Entozoic. [<ENTO- + Gk. *zōon* animal]

en·to·zo·ic (en′tə·zō′ik) *adj. Biol.* **1** Living within another animal. **2** Of, pertaining to, or caused by entozoans. Also **en′to·zo′al, en′·to·zo′i·cal.**

en·trails (en′trālz, -trəlz) *n. pl.* The internal parts, especially the intestines, of an animal. [<F *entrailles* <LL *intralia* intestines]

en·train¹ (en·trān′) *v.t. Physics* To draw along after itself: Steam *entrains* water. [<F *entraîner* <*en-* away (<L *inde*) + *trainer* drag]

en·train² (en·trān′) *v.t. & v.i.* To put or go aboard a railway train. — **en·train′ment** *n.*

en·trance¹ (en′trəns) *n.* **1** The act of entering, in any sense. **2** A passage into a house or other enclosed space. **3** The right or power of entering; entrée. **4** The entry of a vessel at a port. **5** The point or moment at which an actor first enters a scene. **6** *Obs.* Commencement; beginning. [<OF *entrer* ENTER]

Synonyms: access, accession, adit, admission,

admittance, door, doorway, entry, gate, gateway, ingress, inlet, introduction, opening, penetration, portal.

en·trance[2] (in·trans', -träns') *v.t.* **·tranced, ·tranc·ing 1** To fill with rapture or wonder; delight; charm. **2** To put into a trance. See synonyms under CHARM[1], RAVISH. — **en·trance'·ment** *n.* — **en·tranc'ing** *adj.* — **en·tranc'ing·ly** *adv.*

en·trant (en'trənt) *adj.* Entering; admitting. — *n.* **1** One who enters; a beginner. **2** One who competes in a contest.

en·trap (in·trap') *v.t.* **·trapped, ·trap·ping 1** To catch in or as in a trap. **2** To trick into danger or difficulty; deceive; ensnare. See synonyms under CATCH, DECEIVE. — **en·trap'ment** *n.*

en·treat (in·trēt') *v.t.* **1** To beg of abjectly; beseech; implore. **2** To ask for earnestly. **3** *Obs.* To act toward; treat. — *v.i.* **4** To ask earnestly. See synonyms under ASK, PLEAD, PRAY. [<OF *entraiter* <*en-* in + *traiter* TREAT] — **en·treat'ing·ly** *adv.* — **en·treat'ment** *n.*

en·treat·y (in·trē'tē) *n.* *pl.* **·treat·ies** An earnest request; supplication. See synonyms under PETITION.

en·trée (än'trā, *Fr.* än·trā') *n.* **1** The act or privilege of entering; entrance; admission. **2** The principal course at a dinner or luncheon. **3** Formerly, a subordinate dish served between the fish and meat courses or directly before the main course. [<F, orig. pp. of *entrer* ENTER]

en·trench (in·trench') *v.t.* **1** To fortify or protect with or as with a trench or trenches. **2** To establish firmly: The idea was *entrenched* in his mind. — *v.i.* **3** To encroach or trespass: with *on* or *upon*. Also spelled *intrench*.

en·trench·ment (in·trench'mənt) *n.* **1** A breastwork of earth, especially one with a ditch. **2** Any defense or protection. **3** The act of entrenching, or the state of being entrenched. **4** Encroachment. Also spelled *intrenchment*.

en·tre·pre·neur (än'trə·prə·nûr', *Fr.* än·trə·prə·nœr') *n.* **1** One who undertakes to start and conduct an enterprise or business, assuming full control and risk. **2** One who originates and manages entertainments, especially musical productions; an impresario. [<F <*entreprendre*. See ENTERPRISE.]

en·tro·pi·on (en·trō'pē·on) *n.* *Anat.* A turning inward of the edge of the eyelid or of any similar structure. [<NL <Gk. *entropē*. See ENTROPY.]

en·tro·py (en'trə·pē) *n.* **1** *Physics* An index of the degree in which the total energy of a thermodynamic system is uniformly distributed and is thus unavailable for conversion into work. **2** In information theory, a measure of the uncertainty of our knowledge. [<Gk. *entropia*, var. of *entropē* a turning <*en-* in + *trepein* turn]

en·trust (in·trust') *v.t.* **1** To give over (something) for care, safekeeping, or performance: I will *entrust* this task to you. **2** To place something in the care or trust of; trust, as with a duty, responsibility, etc. Also spelled *intrust*. See synonyms under COMMIT.

en·try (en'trē) *n.* *pl.* **·tries 1** The act of coming or going in; entrance. **2** A place of entrance; a small hallway. **3** The act of entering anything in a register, list, etc., or the item, name, or statement entered. **4** The act of reporting at a customhouse, as prescribed by law, the arrival of a ship in port and the nature of her cargo. **5** The act of assuming actual possession of lands or tenements by entering upon them. **6** A contestant listed for a race, prize competition, etc. See synonyms under ENTRANCE[1], RECORD. [<F *entrée* <*entrer*. See ENTER.]

en·try·man (en'trē·mən) *n.* *pl.* **·men** (-mən) *U.S.* One who takes action for an entry upon; that is, for legal possession of, a portion of the public land; a homesteader.

en·try·way (en'trē·wā') *n.* A way of entrance; entry.

en·twine (in·twīn') *v.t.* & *v.i.* **·twined, ·twin·ing** To twine around; twine or twist together: also spelled *intwine*. See synonyms under EMBRACE[1], TWIST.

en·twist (in·twist') *v.t.* To twist; intertwine: also spelled *intwist*.

e·nu·cle·ate (i·nōō'klē·āt, -nyōō'-) *v.t.* **·at·ed, ·at·ing 1** To shell, as a kernel. **2** *Surg.* To extract, as a tumor, eyeball, etc.; to extract from a sac without cutting. **3** To explain

clearly; disclose. **4** *Biol.* To remove the nucleus from, as a cell. — *adj.* (-it, -āt) Without a nucleus. [<L *enucleatus*, pp. of *enucleare* <*ex-* out + *nucleus* kernel] — **e·nu'·cle·a'tor** *n.*

e·nu·cle·a·tion (i·nōō'klē·ā'shən, -nyōō'-) *n.* *Surg.* The operation of extracting a tumor in its entirety.

e·nu·mer·ate (i·nōō'mə·rāt, -nyōō'-) *v.t.* **·at·ed, ·at·ing 1** To name one by one; list. **2** To count or ascertain the number of. See synonyms under CALCULATE. [<L *enumeratus*, pp. of *enumerare* <*ex-* out + *numerare* count] — **e·nu'mer·a'tive** *adj.*

e·nu·mer·a·tion (i·nōō'mə·rā'shən, -nyōō'-) *n.* **1** Detailed mention of things in succession; a catalog; a census. **2** The act of ascertaining a number by counting. See synonyms under RECORD.

e·nu·mer·a·tor (i·nōō'mə·rā'tər, -nyōō'-) *n.* One who enumerates; specifically, one of the minor officials employed in taking a census.

e·nun·ci·a·ble (i·nun'sē·ə·bəl, -shē-) *adj.* That may be enunciated, in any sense. — **e·nun'ci·a·bil'i·ty** *n.*

e·nun·ci·ate (i·nun'sē·āt, -shē-) *v.* **·at·ed, ·at·ing** *v.t.* **1** To pronounce or articulate (words), especially clearly and distinctly. **2** To state with exactness, as a theory or dogma. **3** To announce or proclaim. — *v.i.* **4** To utter or pronounce words. See synonyms under ANNOUNCE, SPEAK. [<L *enunciatus*, pp. of *enunciare* <*ex-* out + *nunciare* announce <*nuntius* a messenger] — **e·nun'ci·a'tive, e·nun'ci·a·to'ry** (-ə·tôr'ē, -tō'rē) *adj.* — **e·nun'ci·a·tive·ly** *adv.* — **e·nun'ci·a·tor** *n.*

e·nun·ci·a·tion (i·nun'sē·ā'shən, -shē-) *n.* **1** The utterance or mode of utterance of vocal sounds. **2** Definite statement.

en·u·re·sis (en'yə·rē'sis) *n.* *Pathol.* Incontinence of urine. [<NL <Gk. *enoureein* <*en-* in + *ourein* urinate]

en·vel·op (in·vel'əp) *v.t.* **·oped, ·op·ing 1** To wrap; enclose. **2** To hide from sight or understanding; obscure. **3** To surround. Also **en·vel'ope**. [<OF *enveloper* <*en-* in + *voluper* fold] — **en·vel'op·er** *n.*

en·ve·lope (en'və·lōp, än'-) *n.* **1** A case or wrapper of paper with gummed edges, for enclosing a letter or the like. **2** Any enclosing covering; a wrapper. **3** *Aeron.* The outer fabric covering of an aerostat. **4** *Biol.* The enclosing membrane of an organ. **5** *Electronics* The glass or metal casing of a vacuum tube. **6** *Geom.* A curve or surface to which another curve or surface, varying or moving according to any law, is invariably tangent. **7** *Astron.* A curved sheet of nebulous matter rising and expanding from the nucleus of a comet on the side toward the sun. Also **en'·ve·lop**. [<F *enveloppe* <*envelopper* <OF *enveloper* ENVELOP]

en·ven·om (en·ven'əm) *v.t.* **1** To impregnate with venom; poison. **2** To render vindictive; embitter. [<OF *envenimer* <*en-* in + *venim* venom]

en·vi·a·ble (en'vē·ə·bəl) *adj.* Adapted to excite envy; covetable. — **en'vi·a·bly** *adv.*

en·vi·ous (en'vē·əs) *adj.* **1** Having, showing, or cherishing envy; characterized or caused by envy; grudging: an *envious* feeling. **2** *Obs.* Jealous; emulous. **3** *Obs.* Spiteful. [<AF <OF *envieus* <L *invidiosus*. Doublet of INVIDIOUS.] — **en'vi·ous·ly** *adv.* — **en'vi·ous·ness** *n.*
Synonyms: jealous, suspicious. One is *envious* who cherishes selfish ill will toward another because of his superior success, endowments, possessions, or the like. A person is *envious* of that which is another's, and to which he himself has no right or claim; he is *jealous* of intrusion upon that which is his own, or to which he maintains a right or claim. An *envious* spirit is always bad; a *jealous* spirit may be good or bad, according to its object and tendency. A free people must be *jealous* of their liberties if they would retain them. One is *suspicious* of another from unfavorable indications or from a knowledge of wrong in his previous conduct, or even without reason. Compare DOUBT. *Antonyms:* contented, friendly, kindly, satisfied, trustful.

en·vi·ron (in·vī'rən) *v.t.* To be or extend around; encircle; surround. See synonyms under EMBRACE[1]. [<F *environner* <*environ* about]

en·vi·ron·ment (in·vī'rən·mənt, -ərn-) *n.* **1** Whatever encompasses. **2** *Biol.* The aggregate

of all external and internal conditions affecting the existence, growth, and welfare of organisms. **3** One's surroundings or external circumstances collectively. **4** The act of environing, or the state of being environed. — **en·vi'ron·men'tal** *adj.*

en·vi·rons (in·vī'rənz) *n.* *pl.* The surrounding region; outskirts; suburbs. [<F <*environ* about]

en·vis·age (in·viz'ij) *v.t.* **·aged, ·ag·ing 1** To face; look into the face of. **2** To form a mental image of; visualize. — **en·vis'age·ment** *n.*

en·vi·sion (en·vizh'ən) *v.t.* To see or foresee in the imagination: to *envision* the future.

en·voy[1] (en'voi) *n.* **1** A diplomatic agent. See PLENIPOTENTIARY. **2** A diplomat dispatched on a special mission. **3** Any one entrusted with a mission; a commissioner. [<F *envoyé*, pp. of *envoyer* send <OF *envoiier* <*en voie* on the way]

en·voy[2] (en'voi) *n.* **1** A postscript to or the closing lines of a poem: generally printed *l'envoi*. **2** *Obs.* The act of sending a message. [<OF *envoye* <*envoiier*. See ENVOY[1].]

en·vy (en'vē) *v.* **·vied, ·vy·ing** *v.t.* **1** To regard enviously. **2** To feel envy because of; begrudge. **3** To covet; desire; want. — *v.i.* **4** To feel or show envy. — *n.* *pl.* **·vies 1** Selfish and unfriendly grudging of what another enjoys; in a mild sense, the longing for a good possessed by another, without ill will toward the possessor. **2** An object of envy. **3** *Obs.* Hatred; ill will. [<F *envie* <L *invidia* <*in-* on + *videre* see, look] — **en'vi·er** *n.* — **en'vy·ing·ly** *adv.*

en·wreathe (en·rēth') *v.t.* **·wreathed, ·wreath·ing** To wrap or encircle with or as with a wreath: also spelled *inwreathe*.

en·zo·öt·ic (en'zō·ot'ik) *adj.* Endemic among animals, as a disease. [<Gk. *en-* in + *zōon* animal]

en·zyme (en'zīm, -zim) *n.* *Biochem.* A complex organic substance, usually a protein, produced by cells and having the power to initiate or accelerate specific chemical reactions in the metabolism of plants and animals; a ferment; an organic catalyst: also called *biocatalyst*. Also **en'zym** (-zim). [<L <Gk. *enzymos* leavened <*en-* in + *zymē* leaven] — **en·zy·mat·ic** (en'zī·mat'ik, -zī-) *adj.*

en·zy·mol·o·gy (en'zī·mol'ə·jē) *n.* The branch of biochemistry which treats of the structure, properties, and functions of enzymes.

en·zy·mol·y·sis (en'zī·mol'ə·sis) *n.* The chemical change induced by the action of enzymes. Also **en'zy·mo'sis** (-mō'sis).

eo- *combining form* Earliest; early part of: used in geology, paleontology, archeology, etc. [<Gk. *ēōs* dawn, daybreak]

e·o·bi·ont (ē'ō·bī'ənt) *n.* A living organism; specifically, one produced by biopoesis. [<EO- + Gk. *biōn, biontos* ppr. of *bioein* live]

E·o·cene (ē'ə·sēn) *Geol.* *adj.* Of, pertaining to, or existing in the Lower Tertiary period of the Cenozoic era, following the Paleocene and succeeded by the Oligocene. — *n.* The second epoch of the Cenozoic era, associated with a warm climate and the rise of mammals. See chart under GEOLOGY. [<EO- + Gk. *kainos* new]

e·o·cli·max (ē'ō·klī'maks) *n.* *Ecol.* The climax of the period of dominance of a given plant population. See EOSERE.

E·o·gene (ē'ə·jēn) *adj.* *Geol.* Of or pertaining to the Paleocene, Eocene, and Oligocene epochs of the Cenozoic era; Paleogene.

E·o·hip·pus (ē'ō·hip'əs) *n.* *Paleontol.* A genus of primitive, now extinct, small, four-toed horses, connected through a complete series of succeeding types with the present horse; associated with the lower Eocene of the western United States. [<EO- + Gk. *hippos* horse]

e·ol·i·pile (ē·ol'ə·pīl) *n.* **1** A reaction engine consisting of a hollow sphere upon trunnions, usually above a boiler connected with it. At right angles to its trunnions, two or more radial pipes project from the sphere, their openings so disposed that the forcible ejection of steam rotates the sphere in the opposite direction. **2** One of various devices working on the same principle, as for operating toys, etc. Also

EOLIPILE

e·ol'o·pile: often spelled *aeol-* or *-pyle*. [<L *aeolipilae* an instrument for investigating the nature of the wind <*Aeolus* god of the winds + *pila* a ball]

e·o·lith (ē'ə·lith) *n.* A stone tool of the earliest form; a celt. For illustration see CELT. [<EO- + Gk. *lithos* stone]

E·o·lith·ic (ē'ə·lith'ik) *adj. Anthropol.* Of or pertaining to a period of protohuman culture extending from the late Pliocene to the first glacial epoch of the Pleistocene and followed by the Paleolithic period: known only by the rudest implements of bone and chipped stone.

e·on (ē'on) *n.* **1** An incalculable period of time; an age; eternity. **2** *Geol.* A time interval including two or more eras. Also spelled *aeon.* [<L *aeon* <Gk. *aiōn* age]

e·o·nism (ē'ə·niz'əm) *n.* The adoption by a male of female habits, clothing, etc.; transvestitism. [after Chevalier Charles *d'Éon,* 1728–1810, French diplomat]

e·o·sere (ē'ə·sir) *n. Ecol.* The total development of a particular vegetation, such as ferns, conifers, etc., throughout a geological period that was dominated by plant population.

-eous *suffix* Of the nature of: *vitreous.* [<L *-eus*]

E·o·zo·ic (ē'ə·zō'ik) *adj. Geol.* Of or pertaining to the upper portion of the Pre–Cambrian period, immediately underlying the Paleozoic, and showing the first signs of invertebrate life. [<EO- + Gk. *zōē* life]

ep- Var. of EPI-.

e·pact (ē'pakt) *n. Astron.* **1** The excess of the solar year over 12 lunar months, generally about 11 days. **2** The number of days in the age of the moon on the first day of any particular year. [<LL *epacta* <Gk. *epaktē,* fem. sing., added <*epi-* upon + *agein* lead]

ep·arch (ep'ärk) *n.* **1** The chief administrator of a Grecian eparchy. **2** In the Greek Church, a metropolitan or bishop. — **ep·ar'chi·al** *adj.*

ep·ar·chy (ep'är·kē) *n. pl.* **·chies** **1** In ancient Greece, a district corresponding to a Roman province, under the jurisdiction of an eparch. **2** In modern Greece, a governmental subdivision of the country. **3** In the Greek Church, an ecclesiastical province or diocese. [<Gk. *eparcheia* <*eparchos* <*epi-* on + *archein* rule]

ep·au·let (ep'ə·let) *n.* **1** *Mil.* A fringed shoulder ornament of commissioned officers: no longer used in the British Army; used in the U.S. Army and Navy with full dress. **2** A shoulder ornament of women's dresses designed to give the effect of width to the shoulder line. Also **ep'au·lette.** [<F *épaulette,* dim. of *épaule* shoulder, OF *espale* <L *spatula*; from its having been used as a device to hold a shoulder belt or protect the shoulder bearing a musket. See SPATULA.]

EPAULETS
United States
a. Full dress, 1812.
b. Captain, Navy.
c. Brigadier General, Army.

e·pei·ro·gen·ic (i·pī'rō·jen'ik) *adj. Geol.* Of, pertaining to, or designating continent-making movements of the earth's crust, or the rising and sinking of vast areas: also spelled *epirogenic.* Also **e·pei'ro·ge·net'ic** (-jə·net'ik). [<Gk. *ēpeiros* mainland + -GENIC]

ep·ei·rog·e·ny (ep'ī·roj'ə·nē) *n. Geol.* The process of the formation of a continent or of the greater masses that compose a continent: also spelled *epirogeny.* See DIASTROPHISM.

ep·en·ceph·a·lon (ep'en·sef'ə·lon) *n. pl.* **·la** (-lə) *Anat.* **1** The hind brain. **2** The cerebellum. — **ep·en·ce·phal·ic** (ep'en·si·fal'ik) *adj.*

ep·en·dy·ma (ep·en'di·mə) *n. Anat.* The tissue lining the central cavities of the brain and spinal cord and derived from the original epithelium of the neural tube. [<NL <Gk. <*epi-* upon + *endyma* a garment] — **ep·en'dy·mal** *adj.*

ep·en·the·sis (ep·en'thə·sis) *n. pl.* **·ses** (-sēz) **1** The intrusion of a letter or syllable within a word, as the *d* in *thunder* (Old English *thunor*). **2** The phonetic change resulting from the transference of a semivowel to the syllable preceding, as (in the Greek) in changing *karjo* to *kairo.* [<LL <Gk. <*epi-* upon + *en-* in + *tithenai* place] — **ep·en·thet·ic** (ep'en·thet'ik) *adj.*

e·pergne (i·pûrn', ā·pârn') *n.* An ornamental centerpiece for a dinner table, often consisting of several grouped dishes for fruit, sweets, flowers, etc. [? <F *épargne* economy, thrift]

ep·ex·e·ge·sis (ep·ek'sə·jē'sis) *n.* Something added by way of further elucidation; fuller statement or explanation. [<Gk. *epexēgēsis* <*epi-* upon + *exēgēsis* explanation. See EXEGESIS.]

ep·ex·e·get·ic (ep·ek'sə·jet'ik) *adj.* Explanatory of or additional to a preceding explanation; of the nature of epexegesis. Also **ep·ex'e·get'i·cal.** — **ep·ex'e·get'i·cal·ly** *adv.*

eph- Var. of EPI-.

ep·har·mone (ep·här'mōn) *n. Ecol.* A plant form differing from the normal through influences of the environment in which it lives. [<EPHARMONY]

ep·har·mo·ny (ep·här'mə·nē) *n. Ecol.* The growth and form of plants as determined by their adaptability to environmental influences, or the harmony between the structure of a plant and the external factor. Also **ep'har·mo'sis** (-mō'sis). [<EP(H)- outside + HARMONY]

e·phe·bic (e·fē'bik) *adj.* **1** Of or pertaining to an ephebus. **2** Of or relating to the adult stages of an organism.

e·phe·bus (e·fē'bəs) *n. pl.* **·bi** (-bī) In ancient Greece, especially Attica, a free-born youth between 18 and 20 years of age, who, having passed an examination, was entered on the list of his tribe. Also **e·phe'bos.** [<L <Gk. *ephēbos* youth <*epi-* upon + *hēbē* youth]

e·phed·rine (e·fed'rin, ef'ə·drēn) *n. Chem.* An alkaloid, $C_{10}H_{15}ON$, isolated from plants of the genus *Ephedra,* and also made synthetically; used as a cardiac depressant and for asthma. Also **e·phed'rin** (i·fed'rin, ef'ə·drin). [<NL *Ephedra,* a genus of plants + -INE[2]]

e·phem·er·a (i·fem'ər·ə) *n. pl.* **·as** or **·ae** (-ē) **1** An ephemerid or mayfly. **2** Anything of very short life or duration. [<Gk. *ephēmeros* for a day <*epi-* on + *hēmera* day]

e·phem·er·al (i·fem'ər·əl) *adj.* **1** Living one day only, as certain insects. **2** Transitory. See synonyms under TRANSIENT. — *n.* Anything lasting for a very short time. — **e·phem'er·al·ly** *adv.*

e·phem·er·id (i·fem'ər·id) *n.* Any of a widespread order (*Ephemerida*) of insects with aquatic early stages and a very short-lived adult stage; of fragile build, with two or three long caudal filaments, hind wings reduced in size, and vestigial mouth parts; a mayfly, dayfly, or shadfly. [<NL *Ephemeridae* <Gk. *ephēmeros.* See EPHEMERA.]

e·phem·er·is (i·fem'ər·is) *n. pl.* **eph·em·er·i·des** (ef'ə·mer'ə·dēz) **1** A table showing the calculated positions and motions of a heavenly body, or of several such bodies, from day to day or at regular intervals. **2** A collection of such tables, or an annual publication giving such tables: an astronomical almanac. **3** Ephemera. **4** *Obs.* A diary or other diurnal record of events. [<L, a diary <Gk. *ephēmeris* <*ephēmeros.* See EPHEMERA.]

ep·i (ep'ē) *n.* **1** A short spur of a railroad, sometimes used for mounting coastal artillery. **2** (ā·pē') *Archit.* A protection for the apex of a spire or sharply pointed roof; a finial. [<F, lit., ear of grain <L *spica*]

epi- *prefix* **1** Upon; above; among; outside: *epidermis.* **2** Besides; over; in addition to: *epilog.* **3** Near; close to; beside: *epifocal.* Also: *ep-,* before vowels, as in *eponym; eph-,* before an aspirate, as in *ephemeral.* [<Gk. *epi-, ep-, eph-* <*epi* upon, on]

EPI

ep·i·blast (ep'ə·blast) *n.* **1** *Biol.* The outermost of the germ layers of the embryo; the ectoderm. **2** *Bot.* A small scalelike appendage in front of the embryo in the seed of certain grasses. — **ep'i·blas'tic** *adj.*

ep·i·bol·ic (ep'ə·bol'ik) *adj. Biol.* Of, pertaining to, or exhibiting epiboly: *epibolic invagination.*

e·pib·o·ly (e·pib'ə·lē) *n. Biol.* The inclusion of one set of segmenting cells within another by means of the more rapid division of the latter. Also **e·pib'o·lism.** [<Gk. *epibolē* <*epi-* upon + *ballein* throw]

ep·ic (ep'ik) *n.* A poem celebrating in stately, formal verse the achievements of heroes, gods, and demigods: also **heroic epic.** Homer's *Iliad* and *Odyssey,* Vergil's *Aeneid* are famous classical epics; the Hindu *Mahabharata* and *Ramayana,* and the Babylonian *Creation Epic* are among the world's greatest, as are also the medieval French *Chanson de Roland* and the 12th century Spanish *Poema del Cid.* The conscious **art epic** is typified by Milton's *Paradise Lost.* — *adj.* Of, pertaining to, or like an epic; grand; noble; heroic: also **ep'i·cal.** [<Gk. *epikos* <*epos* word] — **ep'i·cal·ly** *adv.*

ep·i·ca·lyx (ep'ə·kā'liks, -kal'iks) *n. pl.* **·ca·lyx·es** or **·ca·ly·ces** (-kā'lə·sēz, -kal'ə-) *Bot.* An external involucel or accessory calyx outside the true calyx of a flower. Compare illustration under INVOLUCEL.

ep·i·can·thic fold (ep'ə·kan'thik) *Anat.* A vertical fold of skin on the nasal side of the eyelid whose presence gives the slant-eyed effect noted chiefly in certain Mongoloid peoples. Also **ep'i·can'thus.** [<NL *epicanthus* <Gk. *epi-* upon + *kanthos* corner of the eye]

ep·i·car·di·um (ep'ə·kär'dē·əm) *n. pl.* **·di·a** (-dē·ə) *Anat.* The portion of the pericardium that is directly united with the substance of the heart. [<NL <Gk. *epi-* upon + *kardia* heart] — **ep'i·car'di·ac** (-ak), **ep'i·car'di·al** *adj.*

ep·i·carp (ep'ə·kärp) *n. Bot.* The outer layer of a pericarp. Compare illustration under FRUIT.

ep·i·ce·di·um (ep'ə·sē'dē·əm) *n. pl.* **·di·a** (-dē·ə) A dirge; funeral hymn; lament. [<L <Gk. *epikēdeion,* neut. sing. of *epikēdeios* funereal <*epi-* upon + *kēdos* care, funeral]

ep·i·cene (ep'ə·sēn) *adj.* **1** Of common gender. **2** Belonging to or partaking of the characteristics of both sexes. **3** Loosely, sexless. — *n.* **1** A noun that includes both sexes, as *bird, rat.* **2** A person who exhibits characteristics of both sexes. Also **ep'i·coene.** [<L *epicoenus* <Gk. *epikoinos* <*epi-* upon + *koinos* common] — **ep'i·cen'ism** *n.*

ep·i·cen·ter (ep'ə·sen'tər) *n. Geol.* The point or area on the earth's surface vertically above the focus or point of origin of an earthquake. Also **ep'i·cen'trum.** — **ep'i·cen'tral** *adj.*

ep·i·cot·yl (ep'ə·kot'l) *n. Bot.* That part of the young stem of a plant seedling above the cotyledons. [<EPI- + COTYL(EDON)]

e·pic·ri·sis[1] (i·pik'rə·sis) *n. pl.* **·ses** (-sēz) **1** An elaborate or detailed literary criticism. **2** *Med.* Critical discussion and analysis of a disease subsequent to its termination. [<Gk. *epikrisis* <*epi-* upon + *krinein* judge]

ep·i·cri·sis[2] (ep'ə·krī'sis) *n. pl.* **·ses** (-sēz) *Med.* A supplementary crisis in a disease. [<EPI- + CRISIS]

ep·i·crit·ic (ep'ə·krit'ik) *adj. Physiol.* Of or pertaining to nerve fibers in the skin which are responsive to very delicate variations in touch and temperature stimuli: opposed to *protopathic.* [<Gk. *epikritikos* <*epikrisis.* See EPICRISIS[1].]

ep·i·cure (ep'ə·kyōor) *n.* One given to refined indulgence in the pleasures of the table; originally, a sensualist. [after *Epicurus*] — **ep'i·cu·re'an** (-kyōo·rē'ən) *adj. & n.* — **ep'i·cu·re'an·ism** *n.* — **ep'i·cur·ism** *n.*

Ep·i·cu·rus (ep'ə·kyōor'əs), 342?–270? B.C., Greek philosopher who maintained that freedom from pain and peace of mind constitute the chief good, to be gained by self-control and the pursuit of virtue: mistakenly regarded as the philosopher of pleasure and indulgence of the senses.

ep·i·cy·cle (ep'ə·sī'kəl) *n.* **1** In the Ptolemaic

cosmogony, a small circle whose center moves on the circumference of a larger circle (the deferent) concentric with the earth, while its own circumference forms the orbit of a planet. **2** *Geom.* A circle that rolls upon the exterior or interior of the circumference of another circle. [< L *epicyclus* < Gk. *epikyklos* < *epi-* upon + *kyklos* a circle] —**ep′i·cy′clic** (-sī′klik, -sik′lik), **ep′i·cy′cli·cal** *adj.*

epicyclic train *Mech.* A train of gear wheels in which, in addition to the motions of the wheels about their respective axes, one has a fixed axis about which the other axes revolve.

EPICYCLE
c. Earth.
e. Epicycle.
d.d.d. Deferent.
p. Planet.

ep·i·cy·cloid (ep′ə·sī′kloid) *n. Math.* The curve traced by a point on the circumference of a circle which rolls without slipping upon the outside of the circumference of a fixed circle.

ep·i·dem·ic (ep′ə·dem′ik) *adj.* Affecting many in a community at once: also **ep′i·dem′i·cal.** —*n.* **1** *Med.* A disease temporarily prevalent in a community or throughout a large area. **2** Any widespread excitement, influence, etc. [< F *épidémique* < *épidémie* a plague < LL *epidemia* < Gk. *epidēmia* < *epi-* upon + *dēmos* people] —**ep′i·dem′i·cal·ly** *adv.* —**ep·i·de·mic·i·ty** (ep′ə·də·mis′ə·tē) *n.*

ep·i·der·mis (ep′ə·dûr′mis) *n.* **1** *Anat.* The outer, non-vascular covering of the skin, overlying the corium; the cuticle. **2** Any integument or tegumentary covering. **3** *Bot.* The outermost layer of cells covering the surface of a plant when there are several layers of tissue. Also **ep′i·derm.** [< NL < Gk. < *epi-* upon + *derma* skin] —**ep′i·der′mal, ep′i·der′mic** *adj.*

ep·i·di·a·scope (ep′ə·dī′ə·skōp) *n.* A device for projecting the images of opaque or transparent objects upon a screen: also called *aphengoscope.* [< EPI- + DIA- + -SCOPE]

ep·i·did·y·mec·to·my (ep′ə·did′ə·mek′tə·mē) *n. Surg.* Removal of the epididymis.

ep·i·did·y·mis (ep′ə·did′ə·mis) *n. pl.* **ep·i·di·dym·i·des** (ep′ə·di·dim′ə·dēz) *Anat.* An oblong body composed of the convoluted efferent duct of the testis, at the posterior part of that organ. [< NL < Gk. < *epi-* upon + *didymos* testicle] —**ep′i·did′y·mal** *adj.*

ep·i·fo·cal (ep′ə·fō′kəl) *adj. Geol.* Of, pertaining to, or situated near the focus of an earthquake; epicentral.

ep·i·gam·ic (ep′ə·gam′ik) *adj. Biol.* Attractive to the opposite sex, especially during the mating season: said of animal coloration.

ep·i·gas·tric (ep′ə·gas′trik) *adj. Anat.* **1** Relating to the anterior walls of the abdomen. **2** Of or pertaining to the epigastrium or the abdomen generally. Also **ep′i·gas′tri·al.**

ep·i·gas·tri·um (ep′ə·gas′trē·əm) *n. pl.* **·tri·a** (-trē·ə) *Anat.* The upper part of the abdomen, especially the region over the stomach and its walls. See illustration under ABDOMINAL. [< NL < Gk. *epigastrion*, neut. sing. of *epigastrios* < *epi-* upon + *gastēr* stomach]

ep·i·ge·al (ep′ə·jē′əl) *adj.* **1** *Bot.* Epigeous. **2** *Zool.* Keeping close to ground, as certain insects. Also **ep′i·ge′an.**

ep·i·gene (ep′ə·jēn) *adj. Geol.* **1** Produced or occurring at the surface of the earth: *epigene* disintegration, *epigene* rocks: contrasted with *hypogene.* **2** Pseudomorphous; irregular; changed from its original formation: said of crystals. [< F *épigène* < Gk. *epigenēs* < *epi-* on, upon + *gen-*, root of *gignesthai* be born]

ep·i·gen·e·sis (ep′ə·jen′ə·sis) *n.* **1** *Biol.* The theory that the structure, organization, and development of new organisms, as in embryos, is the result of the successive interactions between male and female cells subsequent to fertilization: opposed to the doctrines of *preformation* and *syngenesis.* **2** *Geol.* An alteration in the character of rocks due to external forces or agents. **3** *Med.* An accessory or secondary symptom of a disease. —**ep′i·ge·net′ic** (-jə·net′ik) *adj.*

ep·i·ge·nous (i·pij′ə·nəs) *adj. Bot.* Growing on the surface, especially the upper surface, as fungi on leaves. [< EPIGENE + -OUS]

ep·i·ge·ous (ep′ə·jē′əs) *adj. Bot.* Related or pertaining to plants or plant parts which appear above the surface of the ground, especially ap-

plied to cotyledons. [< Gk. *epigeios* < *epi-* upon + *gē* earth]

ep·i·glot·tis (ep′ə·glot′is) *n. Anat.* The leaf-shaped cartilaginous lid, at the base of the tongue, that covers the trachea, or windpipe, during the act of swallowing. [< NL < Gk. *epiglōttis* < *epi-* upon + *glōtta* tongue] —**ep′i·glot′tal** *adj.*

ep·i·gram (ep′ə·gram) *n.* **1** A pithy, caustic, or thought-provoking saying. **2** A short, pithy poem, especially one ending with a caustic point. [< L *epigramma* < Gk., an inscription < *epi-* upon + *graphein* write] —**ep′i·gram′ma·tism** *n.* —**ep′i·gram′ma·tist** *n.*

ep·i·graph (ep′ə·graf, -gräf) *n.* **1** A carved inscription on a monument, tomb, etc. **2** The superscription prefixed to a book or chapter. [< Gk. *epigraphē* < *epi-* upon + *graphein* write] —**ep′i·graph′ic** or **·i·cal** *adj.* —**ep′i·graph′i·cal·ly** *adv.*

ep·ig·y·nous (i·pij′ə·nəs) *adj. Bot.* Having floral organs adnate to and near the summit of the ovary. [< EPI- + -GYNOUS] —**e·pig′y·ny** *n.*

ep·i·lep·sy (ep′ə·lep′sē) *n. Pathol.* A chronic nervous affection characterized by sudden loss of consciousness, sometimes accompanied by paroxysmal seizures of varying intensity and duration: primarily a symptom complex associated with various neuropsychiatric disorders. See also GRAND MAL, PETIT MAL. Also **ep′i·lep′si·a.** [< OF *epilepsie* < LL *epilepsia* < Gk. *epilēpsia* < *epi-* upon + *lambanein* seize]

ep·i·lep·tic (ep′ə·lep′tik) *adj.* Pertaining to or affected with epilepsy. —*n.* One affected with epilepsy. —**ep′i·lep′ti·cal·ly** *adv.*

ep·i·log (ep′ə·lôg, -log) *n.* **1** The conclusion of a discourse. **2** A short poem or speech to the audience delivered by an actor after the conclusion of a play. **3** The close of a novel or a narrative or dramatic poem. Also **ep′i·logue.** [< F *épilogue* < L *epilogus* < Gk. *epilogos* a peroration < *epi-* upon, in addition + *legein* say] —**ep′i·log′ic** (-loj′ik) or **·i·cal** *adj.* —**ep′i·lo·gis′tic** (-lō·jis′tik) *adj.*

ep·i·mor·pha (ep′ə·môr′fə) *n. pl. Zool.* Larvae having all their segments fully formed before hatching. [< NL < Gk. *epi-* on, upon + *morphē* form]

ep·i·mor·pho·sis (ep′ə·môr·fō′sis) *n. Biol.* The proliferation of new tissue preceding the regeneration of a part, as in many invertebrate animals.

ep·i·nas·ty (ep′ə·nas′tē) *n. Bot.* Downward curvature of a plant member, induced by a more active growth on its upper side. [< EPI- + Gk. *nastos* compact] —**ep′i·nas′tic** *adj.*

ep·i·neph·rine (ep′ə·nef′rin, -rēn) *n.* A hormone, $CaH_{13}NO_3$, secreted by the adrenal medulla, which stimulates heart action and causes constriction of blood vessels, thus increasing blood pressure. Also *Brit.* **adrenaline.** [< EPI- + Gk. *nephros* kidney]

ep·i·neu·ri·um (ep′ə·nŏŏr′ē·əm, -nyŏŏr′-) *n. pl.* **·ri·a** (-ē·ə) *Anat.* The sheath of connective tissue that surrounds a nerve trunk. [< NL < Gk. *epi-* upon + *neuron* nerve, sinew] —**ep′i·neu′ri·al** *adj.*

ep·i·no·sis (ep′ə·nō′sis) *n.* **1** *Pathol.* A morbid condition subordinate to an original and primary illness. **2** *Psychoanal.* A secondary illness or disorder exploited by the patient to gain relief from the primary affliction and to obtain further sympathy. [< EPI- + Gk. *nosos* illness] —**ep′i·no′sic** *adj.*

ep·i·on·tol·o·gy (ep′ē·on·tol′ə·jē) *n.* The study of the geographic distribution of plants. [< Gk. *epiōn, -ontos,* ppr. of *epienai* < *epi-* upon + *ienai* go) + -LOGY] —**ep′i·on′to·log′i·cal** (-tə·loj′i·kəl) *adj.* —**ep′i·on·tol′o·gist** *n.*

ep·i·pet·a·lous (ep′ə·pet′ə·ləs) *adj. Bot.* Inserted or growing on a petal, as a stamen.

e·piph·a·ny (i·pif′ə·nē) *n. pl.* **·nies** A bodily manifestation, as of a deity. [< OF *epiphanie* < Gk. *epiphainein* manifest < *epi-* upon + *phainein* show]

E·piph·a·ny (i·pif′ə·nē) *n. Eccl.* A festival, observed on January 6, commemorating the manifestation of Christ to the Gentiles, represented by the Magi: also called *Twelfth Day.*

ep·i·phe·nom·e·non (ep′ə·fə·nom′ə·non) *n. pl.* **·na** (-nə) A phenomenon which is secondary to or a by-product of one or more other phenomena; one which is a mere accompaniment of some effect and exerts no causal influence on the effect.

ep·i·phyl·lous (ep′ə·fil′əs) *adj. Bot.* Situated or growing upon a leaf, especially with reference to stamens inserted on a perigonium. Also **ep′i·phyl′line** (-in, -ēn). [< EPI- + Gk. *phyllon* leaf]

e·piph·y·sis (i·pif′ə·sis) *n. pl.* **·ses** (-sēz) *Anat.* **1** The extremity of a long bone, originally separated from it by cartilage but later consolidated with it by ossification. **2** The pineal body. [< NL < Gk., an outgrowth < *epi-* upon + *phyein* grow] —**ep·i·phys·i·al** (ep′ə·fiz′ē·əl), **ep′i·phys′e·al** *adj.*

ep·i·phyte (ep′ə·fīt) *n. Bot.* **1** A plant growing nonparasitically upon another plant or on a non-living support and deriving nutrients and moisture from the air; also called *air plant, aerophyte.* **2** A plant, as a fungus, parasitic upon the exterior surface of an animal. —**ep·i·phyt′ic** (-fit′ik) or **·i·cal** *adj.*

ep·i·phy·tot·ic (ep′ə·fī·tot′ik) *adj.* Having or characterized by a wide-spreading plant disease. Compare EPIDEMIC, EPIZOOTIC.

ep·i·po·di·um (ep′ə·pō′dē·əm) *n. pl.* **·di·a** (-dē·ə) *Zool.* A lateral part of the foot in certain mollusks. [< NL < Gk. *epipodios* on the feet < *epi-* upon + *pous, podos* foot]

e·pis·co·pa·cy (i·pis′kə·pə·sē) *n. pl.* **·cies** **1** Government of a church by bishops. **2** A bishop's state or office. **3** The body of bishops collectively. [< LL *episcopatus* < *episcopus* BISHOP]

e·pis·co·pal (i·pis′kə·pəl) *adj.* **1** Of or pertaining to bishops. **2** Having a government vested in bishops; characterized by episcopacy. **3** Advocating or supporting episcopacy. [< LL *episcopalis* < *episcopus* BISHOP] —**e·pis′co·pal·ly** *adv.*

E·pis·co·pal (i·pis′kə·pəl) *adj.* Belonging or pertaining to the Protestant Episcopal Church, or to any church in the Anglican communion.

e·pis·co·pa·li·an (i·pis′kə·pā′lē·ən, -pāl′yən) *n.* An advocate of episcopacy. —*adj.* Pertaining to or favoring episcopal government.

E·pis·co·pa·li·an (i·pis′kə·pā′lē·ən, -pāl′yən) *n.* A member of the Protestant Episcopal Church. —*adj.* Episcopal. —**E·pis′co·pa′li·an·ism** *n.*

e·pis·co·pal·ism (i·pis′kə·pəl·iz′əm) *n.* That view of the constitution of the church that places the supreme power in the hands of a body of bishops, and recognizes no single supreme head, as the pope, with ordinary jurisdiction over the whole church.

e·pis·co·pate (i·pis′kə·pit, -pāt) *n.* **1** The office, dignity, or term of office of a bishop. **2** A bishopric. **3** Bishops collectively.

ep·i·sode (ep′ə·sōd) *n.* **1** An incident or story in a literary work, separable from, yet related to it. **2** A notable incident or action occurring as a break in the regular course of events. **3** An intermediate passage in a musical composition whereby the development of the subject is for a time suspended for the sake of variety and relief. **4** A portion of a Greek tragedy occurring between two choric songs. See synonyms under EVENT. [< Gk. *epeisodion* < *epeisodios* coming in besides < *epi-* upon + *eisodos* entrance < *eis-* into + *hodos* way, road] —**ep′i·sod′ic** (-sod′ik) or **·i·cal, ep′i·so′dal** or **·di·al** *adj.* —**ep′i·sod′i·cal·ly** *adv.*

ep·i·spas·tic (ep′ə·spas′tik) *adj.* Raising blisters; blistering. —*n.* A blistering medicament. [< NL *epispasticus* < Gk. *epispastikos* < *epi-* on + *spaein* draw]

ep·i·sperm (ep′ə·spûrm) *n. Bot.* The outer covering of a seed. —**ep′i·sper′mic** *adj.*

ep·i·spore (ep′ə·spôr, -spōr) *n. Bot.* The outer integument or coat of a spore.

e·pis·ta·sis (i·pis′tə·sis) *n.* **1** *Genetics* The masking of one factor in Mendelian inheritance by another not allelomorphic to it. **2** *Med.* The stoppage of a hemorrhage or other fluid discharge of the body. [< NL < Gk., a stoppage < *epi-* upon + *histanai* stand]

ep·i·stat·ic (ep′ə·stat′ik) *adj. Genetics* **1** Pertaining to the dominance of one factor over another not of the same allelomorphic factor. **2** Possessing such a factor: opposed to *hypostatic.*

ep·i·stax·is (ep′ə·stak′sis) *n. Pathol.* Nosebleed. [< NL < Gk. *epistaxis* < *epi-* upon + *stazein* drop, drip]

e·pis·te·mol·o·gy (i·pis′tə·mol′ə·jē) *n.* That department of philosophy which investigates critically the nature, grounds, limits, and criteria, or validity, of human knowledge;

theory of cognition. [<Gk. *epistēmē* knowledge + -LOGY] — **e·pis·te·mo·log·i·cal** (i·pis'tə·mə·loj'i·kəl) *adj.* — **e·pis'te·mo·log'i·cal·ly** *adv.* — **e·pis'te·mol'o·gist** *n.*

e·pis·tle (i·pis'əl) *n.* **1** A written message; communication; letter: more formal than *letter*, and especially applied to ancient epistolary writings of sacred character or of literary excellence: the Pauline *epistles*. **2** *Eccl.* *Usually cap.* A selection, usually from an apostolic epistle, read in the communion service of the Greek, Roman, and Anglican churches. [OE *epistol* <L *epistola* <Gk. *epistolē* <*epi-* on + *stellein* send]

e·pis·tler (i·pis'lər) *n.* **1** One who writes epistles. **2** *Eccl.* The reader of the Epistle at the Eucharist; the subdeacon. Also **e·pis'to·ler** (-tə·lər).

e·pis·to·lar·y (i·pis'tə·ler'ē) *adj.* Belonging or suitable to correspondence by letter; included in or maintained by letters: also **ep·is·tol·ic** (ep'is·tol'ik), **ep'is·tol'i·cal.** — *n. pl.* **·lar·ies** A book containing the epistles of a liturgy.

e·pis·tro·phe (i·pis'trə·fē) *n.* **1** In rhetoric, that form of repetition in which successive clauses or sentences end with the same word. **2** A musical refrain. **3** *Bot.* The arrangement of chlorophyll granules (as on the upper and under walls of leaf cells) when exposed to diffused light. [<EPI- + Gk. *strophe* turning about]

ep·i·taph (ep'ə·taf, -täf) *n.* **1** An inscription on a tomb or monument in honor or in memory of the dead. See EPIGRAPH. **2** A sentiment in prose or verse written as for inscription on a tomb. [<L *epitaphium* a eulogy <Gk. *epitaphios* at a tomb <*epi-* upon, at + *taphos* a tomb] — **ep'i·taph'ic** (-taf'ik), **ep'i·taph'i·al** *adj.*

ep·i·the·li·oid (ep'ə·thē'lē·oid) *adj. Biol.* Resembling epithelium or epithelial tissue.

ep·i·the·li·o·ma (ep'ə·thē'lē·ō'mə) *n. pl.* **·o·ma·ta** (-ō'mə·tə) or **·o·mas** *Pathol.* A tumor originating in or affecting epithelial tissue; specifically, cancer of the skin. — **ep·i·the·li·om·a·tous** (ep'ə·thē'lē·om'ə·təs) *adj.*

ep·i·the·li·um (ep'ə·thē'lē·əm) *n. pl.* **·li·ums** or **·li·a** (-lē·ə) *Biol.* A membranous tissue consisting of one or more layers of cells of various types and sizes, compactly joined and serving to line the canals, cavities, and ducts of the body as well as all free surfaces exposed to the air. [<NL <Gk. *epi-* upon + *thēlē* nipple]

ep·i·thet (ep'ə·thet) *n.* **1** A phrase or word used adjectively to express some characteristic attribute or quality. **2** An expressive surname or nickname, as Harry *Hotspur, Old Hickory.* Also **e·pith·e·ton** (i·pith'ə·ton). See synonyms under NAME. [<L *epitheton* <Gk. <*epitithenai* attribute <*epi-* upon + *tithenai* place] — **ep'i·thet'ic** or **·i·cal** *adj.*

e·pit·o·me (i·pit'ō·mē) *n.* **1** A typical example; embodiment: the *epitome* of arrogance. **2** An extreme example; climax or culmination. **3** A concise summary; abridgement. See synonyms under ABBREVIATION, ABRIDGMENT. [<L <Gk. *epitomē* <*epi-* upon + *temnein* cut] — **ep·i·tom·ic** (ep'ə·tom'ik) or **·i·cal** *adj.* — **e·pit'o·mist** or **e·pit'o·miz'er** or *Brit.* **e·pit'o·mis'er** *n.*

ep·i·troch·le·a (ep'ə·trok'lē·ə) *n. Anat.* The bony prominence on the inner side of the humerus at its lower end; the inner condyle.

ep·i·zeux·is (ep'ə·zōōk'sis) *n.* That form of figurative repetition in which a word is repeated without any intervening words or clauses. Example: He is brave—brave beyond measure. [<LL <Gk. <*epizeugnunai* <*epi-* upon + *zeugnunai* yoke, join]

ep·i·zo·on (ep'ə·zō'on) *n. pl.* **·zo·a** (-zō'ə) An animal parasite living on the outside of the body.

ep·i·zo·ot·ic (ep'ə·zō·ot'ik) *adj.* Common to or affecting many animals at the same time: said especially of diseases. — *n.* An epizootic disease: also **ep'i·zo'o·ty** (-zō'ə·tē).

ep·och (ep'ək, *Brit.* ē'pok) *n.* **1** A point in the onward course of history from which succeeding years are counted: Atomic energy marks an *epoch* in history. **2** An interval of time or a series of years, regarded as a whole, memorable for extraordinary events and far-reaching results; any definite period of history.

3 *Geol.* A minor subdivision of time; a time interval less than a period: the Pleistocene *epoch.* See chart under GEOLOGY. **4** *Astron.* A moment of time when a planet reaches a certain known position with reference to the sun. [<Gk. *epochē* a stoppage, point of time < *epi-* upon + *echein* have]

ep·o·nym (ep'ə·nim) *n.* **1** A personage assumed as the founder and name–giver of a race, state, or city; also, the name of that personage. **2** A name or phrase formed from the name of a person to designate a people, period, scientific theory, disease, etc. **3** A high official in ancient Assyria, whose name was given to the year during which he held office. [<Gk. *epōnymos* <*epi-* upon + *onyma* name]

e·pox·y (i·pok'sē) *n. Chem.* The radical –O–, especially as bonded to different atoms already joined in different ways to form the durable **epoxy resins** much used for varnishes and adhesives.

ep·si·lon (ep'sə·lon) *n.* The fifth letter and second vowel of the Greek alphabet (E, ε), equivalent to English short *e.* As a numeral it denotes 5. [<Gk. *epsilon* < *e e* + *psilon* simple]

eq·ua·bil·i·ty (ek'wə·bil'ə·tē, ē'kwə-) *n.* Evenness, as of temper or action. Also **eq'ua·ble·ness.**

eq·ua·ble (ek'wə·bəl, ē'kwə-) *adj.* Of uniform condition or movement; steady; even; not readily disturbed: an *equable* disposition. [<L *aequabilis* <*aequare* make equal] — **eq'ua·bly** *adv.*

e·qual (ē'kwəl) *adj.* **1** Of the same degree with another or with each other, as in magnitude or value; neither greater nor less. **2** Equable. **3** Adequate for the purpose; commensurate. **4** *Archaic* Equitable; just. **5** Having the same rank, rights, or importance. **6** Level. **7** Uniform in operation: *equal* laws. See synonyms under ADEQUATE, ALIKE. — *v.t.* **e·qualed** or **e·qualled, e·qual·ing** or **e·qual·ling** **1** To be or become equal to. **2** To do or produce something equal to. **3** To recompense in full. **4** *Obs.* To make equal; equalize. — *n.* A person or thing equal to another; a person of the same rank or condition. [<L *aequalis* <*aequus* even] — **e'qual·ly** *adv.* — **e'qual·ness** *n.*

e·qual·i·tar·i·an (i·kwol'ə·târ'ē·ən) *adj.* Of or pertaining to the doctrine that all men are equal. — *n.* A believer in this doctrine.

e·qual·i·ty (i·kwol'ə·tē) *n. pl.* **·ties** **1** The state of being equal. **2** Exact agreement; uniformity.

e·qual·i·za·tion (ē'kwəl·ə·zā'shən, -ī·zā'-) *n.* **1** The act of equalizing. **2** An equal state.

e·qual·ize (ē'kwəl·īz) *v.t.* **·ized, ·iz·ing** **1** To make equal. **2** To render uniform. Also *Brit.* **e'qual·ise.**

e·qual·iz·er (ē'kwəl·ī'zər) *n.* **1** One who or that which equalizes. **2** *Mech.* A device for equalizing pressure or strain between parts of a structure, as the springs and wheels of a locomotive. **3** *Electr.* **a** A conductor of low resistance used to join the currents of two generators and equalize their voltage. **b** Any contrivance for equalizing the pull of electromagnets. **4** *U.S. Slang* A revolver.

equal rights Equality of rights, especially between men and women.

e·quan·gu·lar (i·kwang'gyə·lər) *adj.* Equiangular.

e·qua·nim·i·ty (ē'kwə·nim'ə·tē, ek'wə-) *n.* Evenness of mind or temper; composure; calmness. [<L *aequanimitas, -tatis* <*aequus* even + *animus* mind]

e·quan·i·mous (i·kwan'ə·məs) *adj.* Even-tempered.

e·quate (i·kwāt') *v.t.* **e·quat·ed, e·quat·ing** **1** To make equal; treat or consider as equivalent. **2** *Math.* To indicate the equality of; express as an equation. **3** To reduce to an average; correct so as to reduce to a common standard. [<L *aequatus*, pp. of *aequare* make even < *aequus* even]

e·qua·tion (i·kwā'zhən, -shən) *n.* **1** The process or act of making equal; equal division; equality. **2** *Math.* A statement expressing (usually by the symbol =) the equality of two quantities. **3** *Chem.* A symbolic representation of a chemical reaction, as $Na_2CO_3 + H_2SO_4 = Na_2SO_4 + CO_2 + H_2O$. The first member includes the substances reacting; the second, the products. The sum of the quantities

of the two members must be equal. — **e·qua'tion·al** *adj.* — **e·qua'tion·al·ly** *adv.*

e·qua·tor (i·kwā'tər) *n.* **1** A great circle of the earth, a planet, etc., lying at right angles to its axis and equidistant from the poles. **2** Any similar circle, as of the sun, a planet, etc. **3** The celestial equator. [<LL *(circulus) aequator* equalizer (circle); so called because day and night are equal when the sun crosses the equator]

EQUATOR
e. Equator.
n. North pole.
s. South pole.

e·qua·to·ri·al (ē'kwə·tôr'ē·əl, -tō'rē-) *adj.* Relating to, near, or determined by an equator: *equatorial* climate. — *n. Astron.* A telescope turning on two axes at right angles to each other, the principal one being parallel to the axis of the earth.

equatorial plate *Biol.* In cell division, the group of chromosomes collected into a disk midway between the centrosomes, just prior to the anaphase: also called *nuclear plate.* See MITOSIS, also illustration under CELL.

e·ques·tri·an (i·kwes'trē·ən) *adj.* **1** Pertaining to horses or horsemanship; skilled in horsemanship. **2** Representing as on horseback. **3** Composed of or pertaining to knights. — *n.* One skilled in horsemanship. [<L *equester, -tris* <*eques* a horseman < *equus* a horse]

equi- *combining form* Equal; equally: *equidistant.* [<L *aequus* equal]

e·qui·an·gu·lar (ē'kwē·ang'gyə·lər) *adj.* Having equal angles.

e·qui·dis·tant (ē'kwə·dis'tənt) *adj.* Equally distant. — **e'qui·dis'tance** *n.*

e·qui·lat·er·al (ē'kwə·lat'ər·əl) *n.* A side of equal length with another, or a figure with equal sides. — *adj.* Having all the sides equal. — **e'qui·lat'er·al·ly** *adv.*

equilateral hyperbola *Math.* A rectangular hyperbola.

e·qui·len·in (ē'kwə·len'in) *n. Biochem.* A sex hormone obtained from the urine of pregnant mares: a derivative of estrone. [<L *equus* horse]

e·quil·i·brant (i·kwil'ə·brənt) *n. Physics* A force or system of forces which, applied to a body, counteracts another force or system and produces equilibrium. [<F *équilibrant*, ppr. of *équilibrer* balance < *équilibre* <L *aequilibrium* equilibrium]

e·qui·lib·ri·um (ē'kwə·lib'rē·əm) *n.* **1** A state of balance produced by the counteraction of two or more forces; equipoise. **2** *Physics* A condition of balance among forces acting within or upon a body or material system such that there is no change in the state of rest or motion of the system. **3** *Chem.* The state in a chemical process when the components no longer react among themselves or react in such a way as to maintain a balanced condition. **4** Equal balance of the mind between conflicting or differing motives or reasons; hence, fairness of judgment; well-balanced state. Also **e'qui·lib'ri·ty.** [<L *aequilibrium* <*aequus* equal + *libra* a balance]

EQUILIBRIUM
A. Stable. *B.* Unstable.
C. Neutral.
g. Center of gravity.

e·qui·mul·ti·ple (ē'kwə·mul'tə·pəl) *adj.* Produced by multiplying by the same number. — *n.* One of two or more products of different quantities by the same multiplier.

e·quine (ē'kwīn) *adj.* Of, pertaining to, or like a horse. — *n.* A horse, or a related animal. [<L *equinus* <*equus* horse]

e·qui·noc·tial (ē'kwə·nok'shəl) *adj.* **1** Occurring at or near the time when the sun crosses the celestial equator. **2** Of or pertaining to the equinox, or equality of day and night. **3** *Bot.* Opening and closing at regular hours: said of certain flowers, as the four-o'clock. **4** Of or pertaining to the equator or equatorial regions. — *n.* **1** *Meteorol.* A severe storm occurring usually at or near the equinox: also called, locally, *line storm.* **2** The equator. See EQUINOX. [<L *aequinoctialis* <*aequinox* EQUINOX]

equinoctial line The celestial equator.

equinoctial points The points of intersection of the equator and the ecliptic; the equinoxes.

equinoctial time Time reckoned from the moment at which the sun passes the vernal equinox.

e·qui·nox (ē'kwə-noks) *n.* One of two opposite points at which the sun crosses the celestial equator, when the days and nights are equal; also, the time of this crossing (about Mar. 21, the **vernal** or **spring equinox,** and Sept. 21, the **autumnal equinox**). [<L *aequinox* <*aequus* equal + *nox* night]

e·quip (i·kwip') *v.t.* **e·quipped, e·quip·ping 1** To furnish or fit out with whatever is needed for any purpose or undertaking. **2** To dress or attire; array. [<F *équiper* <OF *esquiper,* prob. <ON *skipa* outfit a vessel <*skip* a ship]

e·qui·par·ti·tion (ē'kwə·pär·tish'ən) *n. Physics* **1** The balanced arrangement of atoms, as in a crystal. **2** That state of the molecules in a gas where they keep the same average distance apart under the same pressure. Also **equipartition of energy.**

e·quip·ment (i·kwip'mənt) *n.* **1** The act or process of equipping. **2** The state of being equipped or furnished. **3** Whatever constitutes an outfit for some special purpose or service. **4** Personal acquirements, as of an instructor, a diplomatist, etc. **5** The rolling stock and apparatus for operating a railroad or other transportation system, as distinguished from stations, trackage, and personnel.

e·qui·poise (ē'kwə·poiz, ek'wə-) *n.* **1** Equality or equal distribution, as of weight and power; equilibrium. **2** A counterpoise.

e·qui·pol·lence (ē'kwə·pol'əns) *n.* The state or quality of being equipollent. Also **e'qui·pol'len·cy.**

e·qui·pol·lent (ē'kwə·pol'ənt) *adj.* **1** Equal in weight, power, effect, etc.; equivalent. **2** Equivalent in meaning and force. **3** Equal and parallel. —*n.* An equivalent. [<F *équipollent* <L *aequipollens, -entis* <*aequus* equal + *pollere* be strong]

e·qui·pon·der·ance (ē'kwə·pon'dər·əns) *n.* Equality of weight; equipoise. — **e'qui·pon'der·ant** *adj.*

e·qui·po·ten·tial (ē'kwə·pō·ten'shəl) *adj.* **1** Having equal power or influence. **2** *Electr.* Of equal potential at all points.

e·qui·prob·a·ble (ē'kwə·prob'ə·bəl) *adj.* Having an equal chance of occurring or being selected, as any one of a group of numbers, objects, events, etc., forming part of a random array. Compare CHANCIFY. — **e'qui·prob'a·bil'i·ty** *n.*

eq·ui·se·tum (ek'wə·sē'təm) *n. pl.* **·se·ta** (-sē'tə) Any of a widely distributed genus (*Equisetum*) of rushlike, non–seed–bearing plants; the horsetail. [<NL <L *equus* horse + *saeta* bristle]

e·qui·so·nance (ē'kwə·sō'nəns) *n. Music* The consonance which exists between octaves.

eq·ui·ta·ble (ek'wə·tə·bəl) *adj.* **1** Characterized by equity, or fairness and just dealing; impartial. **2** *Law* Of or pertaining to the principles of right and justice as administered by courts of equity, having relation to the system of rules and remedies enforced by those courts, as distinguished from courts of common law. **3** Within the cognizance of a court of equity. See synonyms under HONEST, JUST, RIGHT. [<F *équitable* <*équité* EQUITY] — **eq'ui·ta·ble·ness** *n.* — **eq'ui·ta·bly** *adv.*

eq·ui·ta·tion (ek'wə·tā'shən) *n.* **1** Horsemanship. **2** The art of riding on horseback. [<L *equitatio, -onis* <*equitare.* See EQUITANT.]

eq·ui·tes (ek'wə·tēz) *n. pl.* The equestrian order of knights in ancient Rome, consisting originally of the mounted soldiers. [<L, pl. of *eques* horseman]

eq·ui·ty (ek'wə·tē) *n. pl.* **·ties 1** Fairness or impartiality; justness. **2** Something that is fair or equitable. **3** *Law* **a** Justice administered between litigants which is based on natural reason or ethical judgment. **b** That field of jurisprudence superseding the legal remedies of statute law and common law when these are considered inadequate or inflexible for the purposes of justice to the parties concerned. **c** A right recognized by a court of equity. **4** Value in excess of mort-

gage or other liens. See synonyms under JUSTICE. [<F *équité* <L *aequitas, -tatis* < *aequus* equal]

e·quiv·a·lence (i·kwiv'ə·ləns) *n.* **1** The state of being equivalent or of having equal values. **2** *Chem.* The property of having equal valences. **3** Valence. Also **e·quiv'a·len·cy.**

e·quiv·a·lent (i·kwiv'ə·lənt) *adj.* **1** Equal in value, force, meaning, or the like. **2** Equal in area or volume. **3** *Chem.* Having the same valence or the same combining weight. See synonyms under ALIKE, IDENTICAL, SYNONYMOUS. —*n.* **1** That which is equivalent; something equal in value, power, or effect. **2** *Chem.* **a** A number or amount representing one of the relative weights in which elements unite with each other to form compounds, or replace other elements in compounds. **b** The· combining weight of an element, compound, or radical, or that weight which combines with or displaces 8 parts of oxygen or 1.008 parts of hydrogen. [<LL *aequivalens, -entis* ppr. of *aequivalere* < *aequus* equal + *valere* be worth] — **e·quiv'a·lent·ly** *adv.*

equivalent volt An electron volt.

e·quiv·o·cal (i·kwiv'ə·kəl) *adj.* **1** Having a doubtful meaning; susceptible of different interpretations. **2** Of uncertain significance, origin, character, or value; questionable. [<LL *aequivocus* ambiguous < *aequus* equal + *vox* voice] — **e·quiv'o·cal·ly** *adv.* — **e·quiv'o·cal·ness** *n.*·

Synonyms: ambiguous, doubtful, dubious, enigmatic, enigmatical, indefinite, indeterminate, indistinct, obscure, perplexing, questionable, suspicious, uncertain. *Ambiguous* is applied only to spoken or written statements; *equivocal* has other applications. A statement is *ambiguous* when it causes the mind of the reader or hearer to fluctuate between two meanings, which would fit the language equally well; it is *equivocal* when it would naturally be understood in one way, but is capable of a different interpretation; an *equivocal* expression is, as a rule, intentionally deceptive, while an *ambiguous* utterance may result merely from a lack of clear thought or of adequate expression. That which is *enigmatical* must be guessed like a riddle. That is *doubtful* which is fairly open to doubt; that is *dubious* which has become the subject of doubts so grave as scarcely to fall short of condemnation; as a *dubious* reputation. *Questionable* may be used nearly in the sense either of *dubious* or of *doubtful*; a *questionable* statement is one that must be proved before it can be accepted. A *suspicious* character gives reason to be suspected; a *suspicious* temper is inclined to suspect the others, with or without reason. Compare CLEAR, PRECARIOUS. *Antonyms:* certain, clear, distinct, evident, indisputable, indubitable, lucid, manifest, obvious, perspicuous, plain, unambiguous, unequivocal, unquestionable, unquestioned.

e·quiv·o·cate (i·kwiv'ə·kāt) *v.i.* **·cat·ed, ·cat·ing** To use ambiguous language with intent to deceive. [<LL *aequivocatus,* pp. of *aequivocare* call by the same name <*aequivocus.* See EQUIVOCAL.]

eq·ui·voke (ek'wə·vōk) *n.* **1** An ambiguous term or expression; an equivocal word or phrase. **2** An equivocation. **3** A play upon words; pun. Also **eq'ui·voque.**

E·quu·le·us (i·kwoo'lē·əs) A southern constellation, near Aquarius. See CONSTELLATION.

er– Assimilated var. of EN–².

–er¹ *suffix of nouns* **1** A person or thing that performs the action of the root verb: *checker.* **2** A person concerned with or practicing a trade or profession: *glover.* **3** One who lives in or comes from: *New Yorker.* **4** A person, thing, or action related to or characterized by: *three–decker.* ◆ Nouns of agency are generally formed in English by adding –er to a verb, as in *leader,* but some such nouns, on analogy with those from French or Latin, are formed with –or. There is no definite rule regarding the use of these suffixes. [OE *-ere, -are*]

–er² *suffix of nouns* A person or thing concerned with, or related to: *jailer.* [<AF *-er,* OF *-ier* <L *-arius, -arium*]

–er³ *suffix* More: used in the comparative degree of adjectives and adverbs: *harder, later.* [OE *-ra, -or*]

–er⁴ *suffix* Repeatedly: used in frequentative

verbs: *stutter.* [OE *-rian*]

–er⁵ *suffix* Denoting the action expressed by the root word: *waiver:* used mostly in legal terms. [<F *-er,* infinitive ending]

e·ra (ir'ə, ē'rə) *n.* **1** A historical period or reckoning of years, dating from some important event or fixed point of time; a period running from a fixed epoch established as the basis of a chronology. **2** A period of time characterized by some coextensive phenomenon or order of things, or social, intellectual, or physical conditions, etc. **3** A date or event from which time is reckoned; a time or age marked by a remarkable event; the beginning of a period; an epoch: the Christian *era.* **4** *Geol.* A division of geological history of highest rank: the Cenozoic *era.* See chart under GEOLOGY. [<LL *aera* counters; orig. pl. of *aes* brass, money]

e·ra·di·ate (i·rā'dē·āt) *v.t.* & *v.i.* **·at·ed, ·at·ing** To radiate. — **e·ra'di·a'tion** *n.*

e·rad·i·cate (i·rad'ə·kāt) *v.t.* **·cat·ed, ·cat·ing 1** To pull up by the roots; root out. **2** To destroy utterly; extirpate; erase. See synonyms under ABOLISH, EXTERMINATE. [<L *eradicatus,* pp. of *eradicare* <*e-* out + *radix, -icis* a root] — **e·rad'i·ca·ble** (-ə·kə·bəl) *adj.* — **e·rad'i·ca'tor** *n.*

e·rase (i·rās') *v.t.* **e·rased, e·ras·ing 1** To obliterate, as by scraping or rubbing out; efface. **2** *U.S. Slang* To kill. See synonyms under CANCEL. [<L *erasus,* pp. of *eradere* <*e-* out + *radere* scrape] — **e·ras'a·ble** *adj.*

e·ras·er (i·rā'sər) *n.* **1** One who or that which erases. **2** A sharp tool or a rubber for removing pencil or ink marks. **3** An oblong device of wood, felt, etc., for removing chalk marks.

e·ra·sion (i·rā'zhən) *n.* **1** The act of erasing; erasure. **2** *Surg.* The operation of scraping away diseased material; specifically, that of laying open a diseased joint and removing morbid tissue by scraping.

e·ra·sure (i·rā'shər, -zhər) *n.* **1** The act of erasing or the state of being erased. **2** Anything erased.

er·bi·um (ûr'bē·əm) *n.* A metallic element (symbol Er) of the lanthanide series, first isolated in crude form by C. G. Mosander in 1843. It is found in gadolinite and some other minerals. See ELEMENT. [<NL <(*Ytt*)*erby,* town in Sweden where first found]

ere (âr) *Archaic & Poetic prep.* Prior to; before in time. —*conj.* **1** Rather than; before. **2** Sooner than; rather than. [OE *ǣr*]

e·rect (i·rekt') *v.t.* **1** To construct, as a house; build. **2** To assemble the parts of; set up. **3** To set upright; lift up: to *erect* a flagpole. **4** To construct or establish; formulate, as a theory. **5** *Geom.* To draw upon a given base, as a geometrical figure. **6** *Optics* To cause (an inverted image) to become upright. **7** *Obs.* To raise to a higher position; exalt. See synonyms under CONSTRUCT, INSTITUTE, RAISE. —*adj.* **1** Upright in position, form, or person; vertical. **2** Directed upward. **3** Free from depression or humiliation. **4** Attentive; alert. [<L *erectus,* pp. of *erigere* <*e-* out + *regere* make straight] — **e·rect'ly** *adv.* — **e·rect'ness** *n.*

e·rec·tile (i·rek'təl, -til) *adj.* Susceptible of erection: *erectile* feathers. Also **e·rect'a·ble.** — **e'rec·til'i·ty** *n.*

e·rec·tion (i·rek'shən) *n.* **1** The act or process of building or constructing; also, the state of being erected. **2** A raising to and fixing in an upright position; a setting up. **3** A building or structure. **4** *Physiol.* **a** The raising up or stiffening of a part through the accumulation of blood in erectile tissue. **b** The state of being so raised and stiffened.

e·rec·tive (i·rek'tiv) *adj.* Tending to erect or raise.

e·rec·tor (i·rek'tər) *n.* **1** One who or that which erects. **2** *Anat.* Any of various muscles which stiffen or hold up a part of the body.

ere·long (âr'lông', -long') *adv.* Before much time has passed; soon.

er·e·ma·cau·sis (er'ə·mə·kô'sis) *n. Biochem.* The process of gradual decay by oxidation in animal or vegetable matter when in contact with air and moisture. [<NL <Gk. *erema* slightly + *kausis* a burning <*kaiein* burn]

e·re·mic (i·rē'mik) *adj. Ecol.* Designating plant communities adapted to deserts and steppes. [<Gk. *erēmos* deserted]

er·e·mite (er'ə·mīt) *n.* A hermit. [<LL *eremita* <LGk. *erēmitēs* <*erēmia* a desert <*erēmos* deserted] —er·e·mit·ic (er'ə·mit'ik) or ·i·cal, er'e·mit'ish (-mī'tish) adj.

er·e·mo·phil·i·a (er'ə·mō·fīl'ē·ə, -fēl'yə) n. Psychiatry A morbid craving for solitude. [<NL <Gk. erēmos deserted + -PHILIA]

er·e·mo·phyte (er'ə·mō·fīt') n. Ecol. Any individual of a society of desert plants. [<Gk. erēmos deserted + -PHYTE]

ere·now (âr'nou') adv. Before this time; heretofore.

e·rep·sin (i·rep'sin) n. Biochem. An enzyme or group of associated enzymes found in the intestinal and pancreatic juices of animals: it splits peptones into amino acids and ammonia. Also e·rep'tase (-tās). [<L ereptus, pp. of eripere set free + -sin, as in pepsin] —e·rep'tic adj.

er·e·thism (er'ə·thiz'əm) n. Physiol. Abnormal excitability or irritability in any part of the body. [<Gk. erethismos < erethizein irritate] —er'e·this'mic adj.

erg (ûrg) n. Physics In the cgs system, the unit of work and of energy, being the work done in moving a body one centimeter against the force of one dyne. See UNIT. Also er·gon (ûr'gon). [<Gk. ergon work]

er·gas·the·ni·a (ûr'gəs·thē'nē·ə, -thēn'yə) n. A condition of debility and exhaustion from overwork. —er'gas·then'ic (-then'ik) adj.

er·ga·tes (ûr'gə·tēz) n. Entomol. A worker ant. [<Gk. ergatēs workman]

er·go (ûr'gō) conj. & adv. Latin Hence; therefore. [<L]

ergo– combining form Work; of or related to work: ergometer. Also, before vowels, erg–. [<Gk. ergon work]

er·go·gen·ic (ûr'gō·jen'ik) adj. Tending to increase the quantity of work done under given conditions.

er·go·graph (ûr'gō·graf, -gräf) n. Physiol. An instrument for registering on a moving drum the movement of a finger or a contracting muscle in doing work: used as an index of mental excitement, fatigue, etc.

er·gom·e·ter (ûr·gom'ə·tər) n. Physiol. An apparatus, as a geared bicycle wheel, for measuring the metabolism rate or the amount of energy expended in doing work.

er·go·nom·ics (ûr'gə·nom'iks) n. The study of the relationship between man and his working environment, with special reference to anatomical, physiological, and psychological factors; human engineering. [<ERGO– + (ECO)NOMICS] —er'go·nom'ic adj.

er·go·phile (ûr'gō·fīl, -fil) n. A lover of work.

er·gos·ter·ol (ûr·gos'tə·rōl) n. Biochem. An inert sterol, $C_{28}H_{44}O$, obtained from ergot, yeast, and certain other plants: irradiation by sunlight or ultraviolet light converts it into vitamin D_2. [<ERGO(T) + STEROL]

er·got (ûr'gət) n. 1 A fungus (Claviceps purpurea) that sometimes takes the place of the grain in rye and other grasses; it yields several alkaloids which are used medicinally in parturition. 2 The disease of rye and other cereal grasses caused by this growth. 3 The dried sclerotia of rye ergot, used in medicine to contract muscle fibers, especially those of the uterus, in order to check hemorrhage. [<F <OF argot spur of a cock] —er'got·ed adj.

er·got·in·ine (ûr·got'ə·nēn, -nin) n. Chem. A crystalline alkaloid, $C_{35}H_{39}N_5O_5$, obtained from ergot: used in medicine.

er·got·ism (ûr'gə·tiz'əm) n. 1 Pathol. A morbid condition produced by excessive doses of ergot; poisoning from ergotized grain. 2 The formation of ergot in grasses.

er·i·ca·ceous (er'ə·kā'shəs) adj. Bot. Of or relating to the heath family (Ericaceae) of trees, shrubs, or herbs, natives of temperate or cold climates, including the azalea, rhododendron, wintergreen, mountain laurel, etc. [<NL Ericaceae < Erica, name of a genus <L erica heath <Gk. ereikē]

E·rid·a·nus (i·rid'ə·nəs) n. A southern constellation, containing the bright star Achernar. See CONSTELLATION. [<L, the Po river]

E·rie (ir'ē) n. pl. E·rie or E·ries One of a tribe of North American Indians of Iroquoian stock, formerly inhabiting the southern shores of Lake Erie.

e·rig·er·on (i·rij'ə·ron) n. Any plant of a large genus (Erigeron) of mainly North American weedy herbs of the composite family, usually

bearing solitary heads with numerous violet, purple, or white ray flowers. Certain species, as E. canadensis, yield oil of erigeron, used as a hemostatic drug. [<L, groundsel <Gk. ērigerōn < ēri early + gerōn old man; with ref. to a hoary growth on some species]

Er·in (âr'in, ir'in) Poetic Ireland.

er·i·na·ceous (er'ə·nā'shəs) adj. Of or like a hedgehog. [<L erinaceus hedgehog]

er·i·om·e·ter (er'ē·om'ə·tər) n. An instrument for measuring by diffraction the diameters of very small objects. [<Gk. erion wool, fibre + -METER] —er'i·om'e·try n.

e·ris·tic (e·ris'tik) adj. 1 Relating to controversy. 2 Prone to dispute: also e·ris'ti·cal. —n. 1 A person given to controversy. 2 A scholar of Euclid's Eristic or Megarian school of philosophy. [<Gk. eristikos < eris strife]

E·ri·tre·a (er'i·trē'ə) An autonomous state in eastern Africa on the Red Sea, federated with Ethiopia; formerly an Italian colony; 45,754 square miles; capital, Asmara. —Er'i·tre'an adj. & n.

Er·len·mey·er flask (ûr'lən·mī'ər) A conical glass flask with a narrow neck and very broad base, extensively used in laboratory work in chemistry, physiology, and medicine. [after Emil Erlenmeyer, 1825–1909, German chemist]

erl·king (ûrl'king') n. In Teutonic folklore, the king of the elves, malicious toward children.

er·mine (ûr'min) n. 1 A long–bodied, slender, voracious weasel (genus Mustela) of the northern hemisphere; the stoat, especially in its winter dress, which is white, with a black tail tip. 2 Its fur, used in Europe for the facings of official robes, as of judges. 3 The judicial office or its ideal purity. [<OF (h)ermine. ? <Gmc.] —er'mined adj.

ERMINE
(Body: 9 to 12 inches; tail: 3 to 3 1/2 inches)

ermine moth A moth (Yponomeuta padella), whose larvae destroy the foliage of apple and related trees.

er·myte (er'mit) n. Obs. A hermit.

erne (ûrn) n. A sea eagle (genus Haliaetus). Also ern. ♦ Homophones: earn, urn. [OE earn]

e·rode (i·rōd') v. e·rod·ed, e·rod·ing v.t. 1 To eat or wear into or away. 2 Geol. To wear down, as rocks, soil, etc., by the action of wind, water, and other agencies; also, to form, as a canyon, by such action. —v.i. 3 To become eroded. [<L erodere <e- off + rodere gnaw]

e·ro·dent (i·rōd'nt) adj. 1 Causing erosion. 2 Caustic, as certain drugs. —n. A caustic drug; that which erodes or burns away. [<L erodens, -entis, ppr. of erodere. See ERODE.]

e·rog·e·nous (i·roj'ə·nəs) adj. Producing erotic feeling; exciting sexual desire. Also er·o·gen·ic (er'ə·jen'ik). [<Gk. erōs love, + -GENOUS]

e·rose (i·rōs') adj. 1 Appearing as if gnawed. 2 Bot. Having an irregularly toothed margin, as some leaves. [<L erosus, pp. of erodere. See ERODE.]

e·ro·sion (i·rō'zhən) n. 1 Geol. The wearing away of materials, as rocks by wind and water; denudation. 2 Med. The eating away of body tissue, bone, etc.

e·ro·sive (i·rō'siv) adj. 1 Having the power or property of gnawing or wearing away. 2 Acting by erosion: an erosive acid.

e·rot·ic (i·rot'ik) adj. Of or pertaining to passionate love; amorous; amatory: also e·rot'i·cal. —n. 1 An amatory poem. 2 A theory or science of love: also e·rot'ics. 3 An erotic person. [<Gk. erōtikos < erōs love] —e·rot'i·cal·ly adv.

e·rot·i·ca (i·rot'i·kə) n. pl. Erotic pictures, books, etc. [<Gk. erōtika, neut. pl. of erōtikos EROTIC]

e·rot·i·cism (i·rot'ə·siz'əm) n. Erotic tendency or character.

er·o·tism (er'ə·tiz'əm) n. 1 Eroticism. 2 Psychoanal. Sexual life in all its phases of physical and mental development and manifestations.

e·ro·to·ma·ni·a (i·rō'tə·mā'nē·ə, i·rot'ə-) n. 1 Psychiatry A morbid propensity to love or make love; uncontrollable sexual desire. 2 Melancholia caused by love.

err (ûr) v.i. erred, err·ing 1 To make a mistake; be wrong. 2 To go astray morally; sin. 3 Obs. To wander; stray. See synonyms under WANDER. [<OF errer <L errare wander]

er·ran·cy (er'ən·sē) n. 1 The condition of erring or of containing errors. 2 Liability to err.

er·rand (er'ənd) n. 1 A trip or journey made to carry a message or do a commission. 2 The object of a going or coming; the business or commission to be done or message to be given by a messenger. [OE ærende message, news]

er·rant (er'ənt) adj. 1 Roving or wandering. 2 Erring; erratic. 3 Obs. See ARRANT. [<OF errant, ppr. of errer travel <L iter a journey; infl. by OF errant <errer wander. See ERR.] —er'rant·ly adv.

er·rant·ry (er'ənt·rē) n. The vocation, conduct, or career of a knight errant; knight–errantry.

er·ra·ta (i·rä'tə, e·rä'tə) Plural of ERRATUM.

er·rat·ic (i·rat'ik) adj. 1 Not conforming to rules or standards; irregular; eccentric. 2 Wandering; straying. 3 Geol. Transported from the original site by natural agencies: erratic rocks or gravel. Also er·rat'i·cal. See synonyms under IRREGULAR, QUEER. [<L erraticus <errare wander] —er·rat'i·cal·ly adv.

er·ra·tum (i·rä'təm, e·rä'-) n. pl. ·ra·ta (-rä'tə, -rä'tə) An error, as in writing or printing. [<L]

er·rhine (er'in, -in) adj. Med. Promotive of sneezing and nasal discharges. —n. A medicine to be snuffed; a sternutatory. [<NL errhinum <Gk. errhinon <en- in + rhis, rhinos nose]

err·ing (ûr'ing, er'ing) adj. 1 Sinning; doing wrong. 2 In error; wrong. —err'ing·ly adv.

er·ro·ne·ous (ə·rō'nē·əs, e·rō'-) adj. Marked by error; incorrect; mistaken. —er·ro'ne·ous·ly adv. —er·ro'ne·ous·ness n.

er·ror (er'ər) n. 1 The condition of erring, or going astray from the truth, especially in matters of opinion or belief; also, deviation from a right standard of judgment or conduct, as through ignorance or inadvertence; mistake. 2 Something done, said, or believed wrongly; a deviation from correctness or accuracy, or from truth. 3 Any misplay in baseball which prolongs the batsman's time at bat or permits a base runner to make one or more bases. Misplays, as a passed ball or a wild pitch, made by catcher or pitcher, are not scored as errors. 4 A violation or neglect of duty; transgression; sin. 5 Math. a The difference between the observed value of a magnitude and the true or mean value as determined by a series of measurements of the same quantity. b Any deviation from the true or mean value not due to gross blunders of observation and measurement. 6 In Christian Science, the contradiction of truth; a belief without understanding; that which seems and is not. [<OF <L errare wander]

Synonyms: balk, blunder, fallacy, falsity, fault, hallucination, mistake, omission, oversight, unsoundness. See DELUSION, FOIBLE.

er·satz (er·zäts') n. A substitute; equivalent; replacement, usually inferior to the original product or material. —adj. Substitute. [<G <ersetzen replace]

erst (ûrst) Archaic adv. 1 Formerly; long ago; once. 2 In the beginning. —adj. First. [OE ærest]

erst·while (ûrst'hwil') adj. Former. —adv. Archaic Formerly.

er·u·bes·cence (er'oo·bes'əns) n. Med. The process or condition of growing red; redness; blush. Also er'u·bes'cen·cy. [<LL erubescentia <L erubescere blush] —er'u·bes'cent adj.

e·ruct (i·rukt') v.t. & v.i. To belch. Also e·ruc'tate. [<L eructare <e- out + ructare belch]

e·ruc·ta·tion (i·ruk·tā'shən, ē'ruk-, er'ək-) n. 1 The act of belching. 2 That which is thrown off in belching. [<L eructatus, pp. of eructare. See ERUCT.] —e·ruc·ta·tive (i·ruk'tə·tiv) adj.

er·u·dite (er'yoo·dīt, er'oo-) adj. Very learned; scholarly. [<L eruditus, pp. of erudire instruct

< *e-* out + *rudis* untrained] —**er′u·dite·ly** *adv.* —**er′u·dite·ness** *n.*

er·u·di·tion (er′yŏŏ·dish′ən, -ŏŏ-) *n.* **1** Extensive knowledge of history, literature, languages, etc.; accomplished scholarship. **2** *Obs.* The act of instructing. See synonyms under KNOWLEDGE, LEARNING, WISDOM. —**er′u·di′tion·al** *adj.*

e·ru·gi·nous (i·rŏŏ′jə·nəs) *adj.* See AERUGINOUS. [< L *aeruginosus* < *aerugo, -inis* copper rust < *aes* copper]

e·rum·pent (i·rum′pənt) *adj. Bot.* Bursting forth, as if through the epidermis, as the spore clusters of certain fungi. [< L *erumpens, -entis,* ppr. of *erumpere.* See ERUPT.]

e·rupt (i·rupt′) *v.i.* **1** To cast forth smoke, lava, etc., suddenly and with violence: The volcano *erupted.* **2** To be thrown forth: Steam is *erupting* from the volcano. **3** *Dent.* To become visible in the mouth, as teeth. —*v.t.* **4** To cause to burst forth. [< L *eruptus,* pp. of *erumpere* < *e-* out + *rumpere* burst]

e·rup·tion (i·rup′shən) *n.* **1** A breaking forth with violence; bursting out. **2** That which bursts forth, as lava from a volcano. **3** A breaking out, as in a rash. **4** Any sudden outbreak, as of armed forces.

-ery *suffix of nouns* **1** A business, place of business, or place where something is done: *brewery.* **2** A place or residence for: *nunnery.* **3** A collection of goods, wares, etc.: *pottery;* or things pertaining to: *popery.* **4** The qualities, principles, or practices of: *snobbery.* **5** An art, trade, or profession: *cookery.* **6** A state, or condition of being: *slavery.* Also *-ry,* as in *jewelry.* [< OF *-erie* < *-ier* (< L *-arius*) + *-ie* < L *-ia.* See -ARY, -Y².]

e·ryn·go (i·ring′gō) *n.* **1** Any of various coarse herbs of the genus *Eryngium:* the roots are used in medicine. **2** *Obs.* The candied root of sea eryngo *(E. maritimum),* formerly deemed an aphrodisiac. Also spelled *eringo.* [? Alter. of Ital. *eringio* < L *eryngion* < Gk. *eryngion* < *eryngos*]

er·y·sip·e·las (er′ə·sip′ə·ləs, ir′ə-) *n. Pathol.* An acute inflammatory disease of the skin, due to infection by various strains of streptococcus and accompanied by fever. [< NL < Gk., ? < *erysis* a reddening + *pella* skin] —**er·y·si·pel·a·tous** (er′ə·si·pel′ə·təs, ir′ə-), **er′y·sip′e·lat′ic** (-lat′ik) *adj.* —**er′y·sip′e·lous** *adj.*

er·y·the·ma (er′ə·thē′mə) *n. Pathol.* **1** A superficial skin disease characterized by abnormal redness, but without swelling or fever. **2** Abnormal redness of the cheek in hectic fever. [< NL < Gk. *erythēma* redness < *erythros* red] —**er′y·them′a·tous** (-them′ə·təs, -thē′mə-), **er′y·the·mat′ic** (-thi·mat′ik), **er′y·the′mic** *adj.*

er·y·thre·an (er′i·thrē′ən) *adj.* Red. Also **er′y·thrae·an.** [< L *erythraeus* < Gk. *erythraios* < *erythros* red]

e·ryth·rin (i·rith′rin) *n. Chem.* A crystalline compound, $C_{20}H_{22}O_{10}$, contained in various lichens, as *Rocella tinctoria,* from which it is extracted by milk of lime. Also **e·ryth′rine.**

e·ryth·rism (i·rith′riz·əm) *n.* **1** Morbid fondness for red. **2** Abnormal or excessive redness, especially when exhibited by certain dichromatic birds, as the screech owl, which has two distinct plumage phases, one grayish and the other red. —**er·y·thris·mal** (er′ə·thriz′məl), **er′y·thris′tic** *adj.*

e·ryth·rite (i·rith′rīt) *n.* **1** A crimson and peach-red transparent, hydrous cobalt arsenate, found amorphous and also crystallized in the monoclinic system; cobalt bloom. **2** Erythritol.

erythro- *combining form* Red: *erythrocyte.* Also, before vowels, **erythr-.** [< Gk. *erythros* red]

e·ryth·ro·blast (i·rith′rō·blast) *n. Anat.* One of the colored ameboid cells from which the red corpuscles of the blood are believed to be developed: found in the red marrow of bones.

e·ryth·ro·ca·tal·y·sis (i·rith′rō·kə·tal′ə·sis) *n.* Destruction of red blood corpuscles by phagocytes.

e·ryth·ro·chlo·ro·pi·a (i·rith′rō·klôr′ə·pē′ə, -klō·rə-) *n. Pathol.* A visual defect which allows correct perception only of red and green. Also **e·ryth·ro·chlo·rop′si·a** (-klô·rop′sē·ə, -klō·rop′-).

e·ryth·ro·cyte (i·rith′rō·sīt) *n. Anat.* A red blood cell, formed in the red bone marrow and, in all mammals, lacking a nucleus: it contains hemoglobin and transports oxygen to all tissues of the body. —**e·ryth·ro·cyt′ic** (-sit′ik) *adj.*

e·ryth·ro·cy·tom·e·ter (i·rith′rō·sī·tom′ə·tər) *n.* A device for counting erythrocytes.

e·ryth·ro·cy·to·sis (i·rith′rō·sī·tō′sis) *n. Pathol.* An excessive increase in the number of red blood corpuscles in the circulatory system.

er·y·throl (er′ə·thrōl, -thrôl) *n.* A crystalline alkaloid, $C_4H_{10}O_4$, found in certain lichens: the compound **erythrol tetranitrate** is used medicinally as a substitute for amyl nitrite and nitroglycerin in heart ailments, and also in explosives as a detonator.

e·ryth·ro·me·lal·gi·a (i·rith′rō·mə·lal′jē·ə) *n. Pathol.* A nervous disease of the extremities, characterized by persistent redness on the soles of the feet or palms of the hands, with burning pain. [< ERYTHRO- + Gk. *melos* limb + -ALGIA]

er·y·troph·i·lous (er′ə·throf′ə·ləs) *adj. Biol.* Having an affinity for red coloring matter.

e·ryth·ro·pho·bi·a (i·rith′rō·fo′bē·ə) *n.* A morbid fear of the color red; specifically, fear of blushing. —**e·ryth′ro·pho′bic** *adj.*

es- *prefix* Out: used in words borrowed into English from Old French: *escape, escheat.* It was often later refashioned to *ex-* after Latin, as in *exchange,* formerly *eschange.* [< OF < L *ex-.* See EX-¹.]

-es¹ An inflectional ending used to form the plural of nouns ending in a sibilant *(glasses, fuses, fishes)* or an affricate *(witches, judges).* After such consonants it is pronounced as a separate syllable; after vowels, as in *potatoes,* it merely extends the syllable. [OE *-as*]

-es² An inflectional ending used to form the third person singular present indicative of verbs ending in a sibilant, affricate, or vowel: *goes, kisses, poaches.* [ME *-es*]

es·ca·drille (es′kə·dril′, *Fr.* es·kä·drē′y′) *n.* **1** In France, a unit of six military airplanes. **2** A squadron of naval vessels. [< F, dim. of *escadre* a squadron; infl. by Sp. *escuadrilla,* dim. of *escuadra* a squadron; both ult. < L *ex-* completely + *quadrare* make square < *quattuor* four]

es·ca·lade (es′kə·lād′) *v.t.* **·lad·ed, ·lad·ing** To attack and force a way into or over (a fort, rampart, etc.) by means of ladders. —*n.* An attack by escalading. [< F < Sp. *escalada* < *escalar* climb < L *scala* a ladder]

es·ca·late (es′kə·lāt) *v.t. & v.i.* **·lat·ed, ·lat·ing 1** To ascend or raise on an escalator. **2** To increase or be increased in a gradual manner. **3** To determine the upward trend of material and labor costs in adjusting (price contracts). [Back formation from ESCALATOR] —**es′ca·la′tion** *n.*

Es·ca·la·tor (es′kə·lā·tər) *n.* A moving stairway, built on the endless-chain principle, used in stores, railroad stations, etc.: a trade name. [< ESCAL(ADE) + (ELEV)ATOR]

es·ca·pade (es′kə·pād) *n.* **1** An act in reckless disregard of propriety; a mischievous prank. **2** An escape from restraint. **3** *Obs.* A plunging or kicking, as of a horse. [< F < Sp. *escapada* < *escapar* escape]

es·cape (ə·skāp′, e·skāp′) *v.* **es·caped, es·cap·ing** *v.t.* **1** To get away from; flee from, as guards or prison. **2** To avoid, as harm or evil. **3** To be uttered involuntarily; slip from: No cry *escaped* him. **4** To slip away from or elude (notice or recollection); fail to be understood or remembered. —*v.i.* **5** To get free from or avoid arrest, custody, danger, etc. **6** To elude notice or recollection. **7** To come forth; emerge; leak: Gas is *escaping* from the stove. **8** *Bot.* To grow wild, as a newly introduced plant. —*n.* **1** A successful flight from, or evasion of, custody, pursuit, danger, injury, or annoyance. **2** Mental relief from monotony, anxiety, etc.: literature of *escape.* **3** Issue, as of a fluid; leakage. **4** *Bot.* Any plant formerly cultivated that now grows wild in fields. **5** *Obs.* An outburst; sally. **6** *Obs.* An inadvertence; act of transgression. [< AF *escaper* < L *ex-* out + *cappa* a cloak] —**es·cap′er** *n.*

Synonyms (verb): abscond, avoid, decamp, depart, elude, evade, flee, fly, shun. To *escape* is to get away clear; to *flee* or *fly* is to attempt it, with or without success; to *avoid* success is both to *flee* and to hide, or at least to seek concealment and obscurity. To *escape* may be noble and worthy; to *abscond* is ordinarily an act of cowardice and guilt. See AVOID.

escape lung A respiratory device for underwater breathing, especially in escaping from submarines: it consists of a tightly fitting mask with a nose clamp, connected with an oxygen-filled rubber chamber and a canister of powdered charcoal or other adsorbent material.

escape mechanism *Psychol.* The process whereby the mind evades its problems, anxieties, responsibilities, etc.

ESCAPEMENT
OF A WATCH
a. Anchor.
l. Lever or fork.
ip. Impulse pallet.
lp. Locking pallet.
r. Roller.

es·cape·ment (ə·skāp′mənt, e·skāp′-) *n.* **1** *Mech.* A device used in timepieces for securing a uniform movement, consisting of an escape wheel and a detent or lock, through which periodical impulses are imparted to the balance wheel, to keep it in oscillation, and to which, in turn, motion is imparted by the return movement of the balance wheel actuated by a mainspring or a weight. **2** *Obs.* The act of escaping; an escape or a means of escape; a vent.

escape wheel A toothed wheel in an escapement: also called *scape wheel.* See illustration under PENDULUM.

es·cap·ist (ə·skā′pist, e·skā′-) *adj.* Offering or intended to offer relief from unpleasant or monotonous realities of life: *escapist* drama; *escapist* novels. —*n.* One who seeks to avoid the realities of life. —**es·cap′ism** *n.*

es·car·got (es·kär·gō′) *n. French* A snail, especially one of an edible variety.

es·carp (es·kärp′) *n.* The inner wall or side of the ditch at the foot of a rampart: distinguished from *counterscarp,* the further or outer side. See illustration under BASTION. —*v.t.* **1** To cause to slope steeply. **2** To provide with a scarp. [< F < Ital. *scarpa* a scarp]

es·carp·ment (es·kärp′mənt) *n.* **1** A precipitous artificial slope about a fortification or position. **2** A steep slope; the precipitous face of a more or less extended line of cliffs: sometimes called *scarp.*

-esce *suffix of verbs* To become or grow; begin to be or do (what is indicated by the main element): *phosphoresce.* [< L *-escere,* suffix of inceptive verbs]

-escence *suffix of nouns* Forming nouns of state or quality corresponding to adjectives in *-escent: effervescence.* [< L *-escentia*]

-escent *suffix of adjectives* Beginning to be, have, or do (what is indicated by the main element): *effervescent.* [< L *-escens, -escentis,* suffix of ppr. of inceptive verbs]

es·char (es′kär) *n. Med.* The dry crust produced by mortification or cauterization; a slough or scab. [< L *eschara* < Gk. *eschara* a hearth]

es·cha·rot·ic (es′kə·rot′ik) *adj. Med.* Able to destroy living tissue and form an eschar; caustic. —*n.* A powerful caustic.

es·cha·tol·o·gy (es′kə·tol′ə·jē) *n.* The branch of theology that treats of death, resurrection, immortality, the end of the world, final judgment, and the future state. [< Gk. *eschatos* last + -LOGY] —**es′cha·to·log′ic** (-tə·loj′ik) or **·i·cal** *adj.* —**es′cha·tol′o·gist** *n.*

es·cheat (es·chēt′) *Law v.t. & v.i.* To revert, or cause to revert, to the state or crown. —*n.* **1** The reversion of lands, in the United States to the state, in England to the crown, in default of heirs or devisees. **2** In feudal law, reversion of an estate to the lord of the fee on failure of heirs or service. **3** Forfeiture of property, real or personal, for default; confiscation. [< OF *eschete, escheoite* < *escheoir* < es- out (< L *ex-*) + *cadere* < *cadere* fall] —**es·cheat′a·ble** *adj.* —**es·cheat′age** *n.*

es·chew (es·chŏŏ′) *v.t.* To shun, as something unworthy or injurious. [< OF *eschiver,* ult. < Gmc. Akin to SHY¹.] —**es·chew′al** *n.*

Esch·scholt·zi·a (e·shōlt′sē·ə, e·sholt′-, esh·kolt′-) *n.* A genus of smooth herbs of the poppy family with dissected leaves and long-peduncled yellow flowers of western North America. The California poppy is the best known. [< NL, after J. F. von *Eschscholtz,* 1793–1831, German naturalist]

es·co·pette (es′kō·pet′) *n. SW U.S.* A short carbine. Also **es′co·pe′ta** (-pā′tə), **es′co·pet′,**

es·co·pate′ (-pāt′). [<Sp. *escopeta*; infl. in form by F *escopette* a musket]

es·cort (es·kôrt′) *v.t.* To accompany; go with, as from courtesy or to protect; conduct; convoy. See synonyms under LEAD. [<*n.*] —*n.* (es′kôrt) **1** A guard accompanying a person or property in transit, for protection, surveillance, as compulsion, or as a mark of respect. **2** Safeguard; protection. **3** A companion at a social affair. [<F *escorte* <Ital. *scorta* <*scorgere* lead <L *ex-* out + *corrigere*. See CORRECT.]

es·cri·toire (es′kri·twär′) *n.* A secretary; writing desk. [<OF *escriptoire* <L *scriptorium* place for writing <*scribere* write] —**es′cri·to′ri·al** (-tôr′ē·əl, -tō′rē·) *adj.*

es·croll (es·krōl′) *n.* **1** *Her.* A scroll. **2** *Obs.* An escrow. Also **es·crol′**. [<OF *escroele*, dim. of *escroe*. See ESCROW.]

es·crow (es′krō, es·krō′) *n.* *Law* An instrument, under seal, placed in the hands of a third person for delivery to the grantee on some condition, the instrument being of no effect until delivery. [<AF *escrowe*, OF *escroe* a scroll <Gmc.]

es·cu·lent (es′kyə·lənt) *adj.* Suitable for food; edible. —*n.* Anything suitable for food, especially a plant that is edible. [<L *esculentus* <*esca* food]

es·cutch·eon (i·skuch′ən) *n.* **1** *Her.* The surface, usually shield-shaped, upon which armorial bearings are displayed; a heraldic shield. See under FIELD. **2** Any shield-shaped surface or device. **3** *Entomol.* The scutum of the mesothorax in certain insects. **4** An ornamented plate about a keyhole, or one to which a door knocker is attached. **5** *Naut.* That part of a ship's stern on which her name is inscribed. [<AF *escuchon* <L *scutum* shield]

ESCUTCHEON
Divisions of shield:
a. Dexter chief.
b. Middle chief.
c. Sinister chief.
d. Dexter flank.
e. Fess point.
f. Sinister flank.
g. Dexter base.
h. Middle base.
i. Sinister base.
j. Honor point.
k. Nombril point.

Es·dra·e·lon (ez′drə·ē′lən) See JEZREEL, PLAIN OF.

Es·dras (ez′drəs, *Fr.* ez·dràs′) **1** Variant of EZRA. **2** The name of the first two books of the Old Testament Apocrypha.

-ese *suffix of nouns and adjectives* **1** A native or inhabitant of: *Milanese*. **2** The language or dialect of: *Chinese*. **3** Originating in; denoting the inhabitants or language of: *Tirolese*. **4** In the manner or style of: *journalese*. [<OF *-ese* <L *-ensis*]

es·ker (es′kər) *n. Geol.* A ridge of glacial gravel, deposited by a subglacial stream between banks of ice. Also **es′kar**. [<Irish *escir* ridge]

Es·ki·mo (es′kə·mō) *n. pl.* **·mos** **1** One of a Mongoloid people indigenous to the Arctic coasts of North America, Greenland, and NE Siberia. **2** The language of the Eskimos, belonging to the Eskimo-Aleut family. Also spelled *Esquimau*. [<Dan. <F *Esquimaux* <N. Am. Ind., eaters of raw flesh]

Es·ki·mo–Al·e·ut (es′kə·mō·al′ē·ōōt) *n.* A family of polysynthetic languages spoken along the shores of Greenland, the coasts of Labrador, in the Hudson Bay area, along the entire Arctic coast of North America, in western and northern Alaska, the Chukchi peninsula of NE Siberia, and the Aleutian Islands: possibly related to the Altaic languages.

e·soph·a·gos·to·my (i·sof′ə·gos′tə·mē) *n. Surg.* The forming of an artificial opening into the esophagus. [<ESOPHAGUS + -STOMY]

e·soph·a·gus (i·sof′ə·gəs) *n. pl.* **·gi** (-jī) *Zool.* The tube in vertebrate and invertebrate animals through which food passes from the mouth to the stomach: also *oesophagus*. [<NL <Gk. *oisophagos*] —**e·so·phag·e·al** (ē′sō·faj′ē·əl, i·sof′ə·jē′əl), **e·soph′a·gal** (-ə·gəl) *adj.*

es·o·ter·ic (es′ə·ter′ik) *adj.* **1** Confined to a select circle; confidential. **2** Adapted exclusively for the initiated and enlightened few; abstruse; profound: opposed to *exoteric*. [<Gk. *esōterikos* inner <*esō* inside] —**es′o·ter′i·cal·ly** *adv.*

ESP Extrasensory perception.

---

es·pa·drille (es′pə·dril′, *Fr.* es·pà·drē′y′) *n.* A canvas shoe soled with rope: used in sports and in mountain-climbing. [<F]

es·pal·ier (es·pal′yər) *n.* **1** A trellis on which small fruit trees, shrubs, etc., are trained to grow flattened out. **2** A tree or row of plants

ESPALIER
A tree espaliered against a wall.

trained on a wall or framework. —*v.t.* To train on or furnish with an espalier, as small trees. [<F <Ital. *spalliera* <*spalla* a shoulder]

es·par·to (es·pär′tō) *n.* A hardy perennial rush-like grass (genera *Lygeum* and *Stipa*) of sandy regions in northern Africa and southern Spain: used for weaving and for making a grade of paper. Also **esparto grass**. [<Sp. <L *spartum* <Gk. *sparton* a fiber rope < *spartos* esparto]

es·pe·cial (es·pesh′əl) *adj.* **1** Exceptional; noteworthy. **2** Particular or individual; special. [<OF <L *specialis* <*species* kind, type]

es·pe·cial·ly (es·pesh′əl·ē) *adv.* Preeminently; particularly.

Es·pe·ran·to (es′pə·rän′tō) *n.* An artificial language designed for universal use, invented by Ludwig Zamenhof, a Russian scholar, and published in 1887. Its vocabulary, as far as was found practicable, consists of words common to every important European language, spelled more or less phonetically. [after Dr. *Esperanto* (Dr. Hopeful), pen name of inventor] —**Es′pe·ran′tism** *n.* —**Es′pe·ran′tist** *n.*

es·pi·al (es·pī′əl) *n.* **1** The action of a spy. **2** A watching in secret; concealed observation. **3** *Obs.* A company of spies, or a spy. **4** The catching or being caught sight of.

es·pi·o·nage (es′pē·ə·nij, -näzh; *Fr.* es·pyô·näzh′) *n.* **1** The practice of spying; excessive or offensive surveillance. **2** The employment and activities of spies and secret agents in time of war. [<F *espionnage* <*espier* espy]

es·pla·nade (es′plə·nād′, -näd′) *n.* A level open space, as before a fortress or along a waterside, for promenading, driving, etc. [<F <Sp. *esplanada* <*explanar* <L *explanare* <*ex-* out + *planus* level]

es·pou·sal (es·pou′zəl) *adj.* Of or pertaining to a betrothal or marriage. —*n.* **1** The act of espousing; plighting of troths; betrothal; marriage. **2** The adoption, as of a cause or principle.

es·pouse (es·pouz′) *v.t.* **·poused, ·pous·ing** **1** To take as a spouse; marry. **2** To promise or give in marriage. **3** To make one's own; adopt, as a cause or doctrine. **4** *Obs.* To pledge; commit. See synonyms under EMBRACE. [<OF *espouser* <L *sponsare* <*sponsus*. See SPOUSE.] —**es·pous′er** *n.*

es·py (es·pī′) *v.t.* **es·pied, es·py·ing** **1** To catch sight of (something distant or hidden); see; descry. **2** *Obs.* To observe closely; explore; spy. [<OF *espier* <Gmc.]

-esque *suffix of adjectives* Like; in the manner or style of: *picturesque, arabesque*. [<F <Ital. *-esco* <Gmc.]

es·quire (es·kwīr′, es′kwīr) *n.* **1** A title of dignity, office, or courtesy ranking below that of *knight*. In the United States, the title is given specially to lawyers and justices of the peace, but occasionally to any man as a mark of respect. **2** In England, a landed proprietor; squire. **3** A gentleman who escorts a lady in public. —*v.t.* (es·kwīr′) **es·quired, es·quir·ing 1** *Rare* To squire. **2** To address or raise to the title of esquire. [<OF *esquier* <LL *scutarius* shield-bearer <*scutum* a shield]

ess (es) *n. pl.* **ess·es 1** The letter *S, s*. **2** Anything shaped like an *S*. [<L *es* letter *s*]

-ess *suffix* Female: *goddess, lioness*: used to form the feminine of many nouns. [<F *-esse* <LL *-issa* <Gk.]

es·say (e·sā′) *v.t.* **1** To try to do or accomplish; attempt. **2** To test the nature, quality, etc., of. See synonyms under ENDEAVOR. [Var. of ASSAY, *v.*] —*n.* (es′ā, es′ā) **1** (es′ā) A literary composition on some special subject, analytical, expository, critical, or reflective and personal, commonly briefer and less complete and formal than a *treatise*; latterly, any dissertation on a particular subject, a form of pure representative discourse. **2** An endeavor; attempt; effort. **3** *Obs.* An assay. **4** In philately, a rejected or unused design for a stamp. See synonyms under ENDEAVOR, PROOF. [<OF *essai*. Doublet of ASSAY, *n.*]

es·sence (es′əns) *n.* **1** The intrinsic nature of anything; that which makes a thing what it is. **2** Being or existence in the abstract. **3** A being, especially a spiritual being. **4** A solution, as of an essential oil in alcohol. **5** The active principle of a plant or medicinal substance. **6** Perfume; scent. [<F <L *essentia* <*esse* be]

es·sen·tial (ə·sen′shəl) *adj.* **1** Of or pertaining to the essence or intrinsic nature of anything; substantial; basal; characteristic. **2** Indispensable, necessary, or highly important, as to success or completeness; absolutely requisite; cardinal. **3** Constituting, containing, or derived from the essence or any distinguishing constituent, as of a plant; constitutive: *essential oils*. **4** Having real existence; real; actual: distinguished from *accidental*. **5** Having the appearance or properties of an essence. See synonyms under INHERENT, NECESSARY, RADICAL. See ESSENCE.] —*n.* **1** That which is essential or characteristic. **2** A necessary element, organ, or part. See synonyms under NECESSITY. [<LL *essentialis* <*essentia*. See ESSENCE.] —**es·sen·ti·al·i·ty** (-shē·al′ə·tē) *n.* —**es·sen′tial·ly** *adv.* —**es·sen′tial·ness** *n.*

essential amino acid Any of some eight amino acids that must be present in the human diet because they are required for protein synthesis but are not themselves synthesized in the human body.

es·soin (i·soin′) *n.* **1** In English law, an excuse for non-appearance in court, or the allegation of such excuse. **2** The person so excused. **3** *Obs.* Excuse; delay. —*v.t.* To excuse for not appearing at court. Also **es·soign′**. [<OF *essoine, essoigne* <*essoignier* <Med. L *exsoniare* <*ex-* out + *soniare* <*sonia* excuse]

-est¹ *suffix* Most: used in the superlative degree of adjectives and adverbs: *hardest, latest*. [OE *-ast, -est, -ost*]

-est² An archaic inflectional ending used in the second person singular present and past indicative, with *thou: eatest, walkest*. Also, in contracted forms, *-st*, as in *hast, didst*.

es·tab·lish (es·tab′lish) *v.t.* **1** To settle or fix firmly; make stable or permanent. **2** To set up; found, as an institution or business. **3** To set up; install (oneself or someone else) in business, a position, etc.: to *establish* oneself in an apartment. **4** To make firm; build up securely: to *establish* a reputation. **5** To put into effect permanently; ordain, as laws. **6** To gain acceptance for; prove, as a theory or argument. **7** To appoint (a church) as a national or state institution. **8** In card games, to gain command of (a suit). See synonyms under CONFIRM, INSTITUTE, MAKE, RATIFY, SET, SETTLE. [<OF *establiss-*, stem of *establir* <L *stabilire* <*stabilis* STABLE¹] —**es·tab′lish·er** *n.*

es·tab·lish·ment (es·tab′lish·mənt) *n.* **1** The act of establishing. **2** The state of being established, in any sense of the word. **3** Anything established. **4** A household; a family residence, with its grounds and equipment. **5** An organized staff of servants or employees, together with the building in which they are located. **6** A place of business, together with its equipment. **7** An organized civil, military, or naval force. **8** The act of recognizing a church as a state church. **9** A church so recognized. **10** A settlement in life; particularly, a fixed allowance or income. —**the Establishment** Those collectively who occupy positions of influence and status in a society.

es·ta·cade (es′tə·kād′, -käd′) *n. Mil.* A stockade

or dike of piles in a morass, sea, or river, to prevent any enemy's approach; also, any defensive work of stakes or piles. Also **es'ta·ca'do** (-kä'dō). [< F < Sp. *estacada* < *estaca* stake, post]

es·tate (es·tāt') *n.* **1** One's entire property; a tract of land. **2** Property left after death. **3** Condition or state; social standing; rank; dignity. **4** A class or order of persons in a state. **5** *Brit.* The lords spiritual, lords temporal, and commons. **6** *Law* The degree, nature, and amount of one's lawful interest in any property. **7** *Obs.* Pomp; display. See synonyms under PROPERTY. —**third estate** The commons, as distinguished from the clergy and the nobles, the **first** and the **second estates.** —*v.t. Obs.* To set up in or as in an estate. [< OF *estat* < L *status* STATE]

es·teem (es·tēm') *n.* **1** Favorable opinion or estimation on the basis of worth, especially that based on moral characteristics; respect; regard. **2** Character that commands respect or consideration; estimableness: a person of *esteem.* **3** *Obs.* Estimation or judgment of merit or demerit; opinion; estimation. [< *v.*] —*v.t.* **1** To value highly; regard as having worth or excellence. **2** To think to be; deem; consider: to *esteem* one fortunate. [< F *estimer* < L *aestimare* value]

Synonyms (noun): estimate, estimation, favor, regard, respect. *Esteem* for a person is a favorable opinion on the basis of worth, especially of moral worth, joined with a feeling of interest in and attraction toward the person. *Regard* for a person is the mental view or feeling that springs from a sense of his excellence, with a cordial and hearty friendliness. *Regard* is more personal and less distant than *esteem,* and adds a special kindliness; *respect* is a more distant word than *esteem. Respect* may be wholly on one side, while *regard* is commonly mutual; *respect* in the fullest sense is given to what is lofty, worthy, and honorable, or to a person of such qualities; but we may pay *respect* to station or office, regardless of the person holding it. *Estimate* has more of calculation; as, My *estimate* of the man, or of his abilities, is very high. *Estimation* involves the idea of appraisal, and is especially used of the feeling entertained by numbers of people; as, He stood high in public *estimation.* Compare ESTEEM *verb,* ATTACHMENT, FRIENDSHIP, LOVE, REGARD. *Antonyms:* abhorrence, antipathy, aversion, contempt, dislike, hatred, loathing, repugnance.

Synonyms (verb): appreciate, calculate, consider, deem, estimate, hold, prize, regard, think, value. *Esteem* and *estimate* alike imply to set a certain mental value upon, but *esteem* is less precise and mercantile than *calculate* or *estimate.* We *esteem* a jewel precious; we *estimate* it to be worth so much money. In popular usage *esteem,* as said of persons, denotes a union of respect and kindly feeling and, in the highest sense, of moral approbation; as, one whom I highly *esteem.* To *appreciate* anything is to be deeply or keenly sensible of or sensitive to its qualities or influence; as, to *appreciate* beauty or harmony; to *appreciate* one's services. To *prize* is to set a high value on for something more than merely commercial reasons. To *regard* (F *regarder* look at, observe) is to have a certain mental view favorable or unfavorable; as, I *regard* him as a friend; or, I *regard* him as a villain; *regard* has a distinctively favorable sense as applied to institutions, proprieties, duties, etc., but does not share the use of the noun *regard* as applied to persons; we *regard* the Sabbath; we *regard* a person's feelings; we have a *regard* for the person. See ADMIRE, APPRECIATE, LIKE. Compare ESTEEM *noun. Antonyms:* see synonyms for ABHOR.

es·ter (es'tər) *n. Chem.* Any of a class of organic compounds formed by the reaction of an acid with an alcohol: they include oils, natural fats, and waxes, and are important in the manufacture of explosives, plastics, rayon, etc. [Coined by Leopold Gmelin, 1788–1853, German chemist]

es·ter·ase (es'tə·rās) *n. Biochem.* A hydrolytic enzyme having the power of accelerating the breakdown of esters, as the lipases.

es·ter·i·fi·ca·tion (es·ter'ə·fə·kā'shən) *n. Chem.* The formation of an ester by the direct action of an acid on an alcohol in the presence of hydrogen ions, and accompanied by the

removal of water.

es·ter·i·fy (es·ter'ə·fī) *v.t. & v.i.* **·fied, ·fy·ing** To make or change into an ester.

es·the·sia (es·thē'zhə, -zhē·ə) *n. Physiol.* The capacity or state of feeling or sensation; sensibility: also *aesthesia, aesthesis.* Also **es·the'·sis** (-sis). [< NL < Gk. *aisthēsis* a feeling, sensation]

es·the·si·om·e·ter (es·thē'zē·om'ə·tər) *n.* An instrument for measuring the degrees of discriminative sensitiveness to touch.

es·thete (es'thēt) *n.* A votary of the beautiful; a possessor of or a pretender to fine taste and artistic culture: also spelled *aesthete.* [< Gk. *aisthetēs* one who feels]

es·thet·ic (es·thet'ik) *adj.* **1** Pertaining to beauty, taste, or the fine arts; artistic. **2** Appreciating or loving the beautiful. Also **es·thet'i·cal.** —*n.* **1** The philosophy of the beautiful; the principles underlying beauty. **2** Esthetics. Also spelled *aesthetic.* [< Gk. *aisthētikos* perceptive] —**es·thet'i·cal·ly** *adv.*

es·the·ti·cian (es'thə·tish'ən) *n.* One devoted to esthetics; an expert in matters of taste.

es·thet·i·cism (es·thet'ə·siz'əm) *n.* Devotion to beauty in its sensuous forms; also, the principles or spirit of those devoted to beauty in its sensuous forms.

es·thet·ics (es·thet'iks) *n. pl. (construed as singular)* **1** The science of beauty and taste. **2** Knowledge of the fine arts and art criticism. Also spelled *aesthetics.*

es·ti·mate (es'tə·māt) *v.* **·mat·ed, ·mat·ing** *v.t.* **1** To form an approximate opinion of (size, amount, number, etc.); calculate roughly. **2** To form an opinion about; judge, as character. —*v.i.* **3** To make or submit an estimate. See synonyms under APPRECIATE, CALCULATE, ESTEEM. —*n.* (es'tə·mit) **1** A valuation based on opinion or roughly made from imperfect or incomplete data; a calculation not professedly exact; appraisement; also, a statement, as by a builder, in regard to the cost of certain work. **2** Carefully weighed judgment; formal opinion: an *estimate* of a person's character. [< L *aestimatus,* pp. of *aestimare* value] —**es'ti·ma'tive** *adj.* —**es'ti·ma'tor** *n.* —**es'ti·ma·to·ry** (-mə·tôr'ē, -tō'rē) *adj.*

es·ti·ma·tion (es'tə·mā'shən) *n.* **1** The act of estimating. **2** The conclusion arrived at; an estimate. **3** Esteem; regard. See synonyms under ATTACHMENT, ESTEEM.

es·ti·val (es'tə·vəl, es·tī'-) *adj.* Of or pertaining to summer; appearing in summer: also spelled *aestival.* [< LL *aestivalis* < L *aestas* summer]

es·ti·vate (es'tə·vāt) *v.i.* **·vat·ed, ·vat·ing 1** To pass the summer. **2** To pass the summer in torpor: said of certain animals. Compare HIBERNATE. Also spelled *aestivate.* [< L *aestivatus,* pp. of *aestivare* < *aestas* summer] —**es'ti·va'tor** *n.*

es·ti·va·tion (es'tə·vā'shən) *n.* **1** The act of spending the summer. **2** *Zool.* The dormancy in summer of certain animals. **3** *Bot.* The disposition of the parts of a flower in the bud; prefloration. Also spelled *aestivation.*

es·toile (es·toil', -twäl') *n.* A heraldic star, having six, eight, or more points. [< OF < L *stella* star]

es·top (es·top') *v.t.* **·topped, ·top·ping 1** *Law* To prevent by estoppel. **2** *Obs.* To bar; plug. [< AF *estopper,* OF *estoper* < OF *estoupe* tow < L *stuppa*] —**es·top'page** (-ij) *n.*

es·top·pel (es·top'əl) *n.* **1** *Law* An impediment to a right of action, whereby one is forbidden to contradict or deny one's own previous statement or act. **2** Prohibition. [< OF *estoupail* < *estouper,* var. of *estoper.* See ESTOP.]

es·to·vers (es·tō'vərz) *n. pl. Law* **1** Necessaries or supplies allowed by law, as wood taken by a tenant for his own use. **2** Alimony allowed to a wife separated from her husband; also, a widow's allowance. [< OF *estover < estovoir* be necessary]

es·trange (es·trānj') *v.t.* **·tranged, ·trang·ing 1** To make (someone previously friendly or affectionate) indifferent or hostile; alienate, as affections. **2** To remove or dissociate (oneself, etc.): to *estrange* oneself from society. [< OF *estranger* < L *extraneare* < *extraneus.* See STRANGE.]

es·trange·ment (es·trānj'mənt) *n.* The act of estranging, or the condition of being estranged.

es·tray (es·trā') *n.* **1** *Law* A stray or un-

claimed domestic animal. **2** Something which has gone astray. —*v.t.* To go astray. [< OF *estraié,* pp. of *estraier.* See STRAY.]

es·treat (es·trēt') *Brit. Law n.* An exact copy of a record or writing, especially of fines and amercements on court rolls. —*v.t.* **1** To copy from the records of a court for prosecution. **2** To levy (a fine, etc.) under estreat of record; exact, as a fine. [< AF *estrete,* OF *estrait,* pp. of *estrai're* < L *extrahere.* See EXTRACT.]

es·tri·ol (es'trē·ōl, -ol) *n. Biochem.* An estrogen, $C_{18}H_{24}O_3$, found in the urine of pregnant women: also *oestriol.* [< ESTRUS + -OL[1]]

es·tro·gen (es'trə·jən) *n. Biochem.* Any of several hormones found in the ovarian fluids of the mammalian female and exercising a more or less specific and critical influence on the sexual cycle: also called *oestrin.* [< ESTRUS + -GEN] —**es'tro·gen'ic** *adj.*

es·trus (es'trəs, ēs'-) *n.* **1** *Zool.* The peak of the sexual cycle in animals, culminating in ovulation; heat or rut, especially in female mammals. **2** A violent or passionate impulse, craving, or stimulus; specifically, erotic desire. Also spelled *oestrus, oestrum.* [< L *oestrus* frenzy, passion < Gk. *oistros* a gadfly] —**es'tru·al** *adj.*

es·tu·ar·y (es'chōō·er·ē) *n. pl.* **·ar·ies** The wide mouth of a river where it is met and invaded by the sea, especially in a depression of the coast. [< L *aestuarium* < *aestus* tide] —**es'·tu·ar'i·al** (-är'ē·əl), **es'tu·ar'i·an, es·tu·a·rine** (es'chōō·ə·rin, -rīn) *adj.*

e·su·ri·ent (i·sŏor'ē·ənt) *adj.* Hungry; greedy; eager for food. [< L *esuriens, -entis,* ppr. of *esurire* be greedy < *edere* eat] —**e·su'ri·ence, e·su'ri·en·cy** *n.* —**e·su'ri·ent·ly** *adv.*

-et *suffix* Small; little: *islet:* often without appreciable force, as in *sonnet.* [< F]

e·tae·ri·o (i·tē'rē·ō) *n. pl.* **·ri·os** *Bot.* An aggregate fruit, such as the strawberry. Also **e·tae'ri·um.** [< Gk. *hetairia* society < *hetairos* companion]

é·ta·gère (ā·tá·zhâr') *n.* An ornamental stand with shelves; a what-not. [< F < *étage* stage]

et·a·lon (et'ə·lon) *n. Physics* An interferometer for studying the fine lines of a spectrum by means of multiple reflection between parallel, half-silvered plates of glass or quartz arranged at fixed distances. [< F *étalon* a standard (def. 4)]

et·a·mine (et'ə·mēn) *n.* A loosely woven, buntinglike fabric. Also **et'a·min** (-min). [< F *étamine*]

é·tape (ā·táp') *n.* **1** A public warehouse. **2** A halting place. **3** Supplies allotted to troops during a march. **4** The distance marched in one day. [< F < OF *estaple* < MDu. *stapel* a warehouse]

etch (ech) *v.t.* **1** To engrave by means of acid or other corrosive fluid, especially for making a design on a plate for printing. **2** To outline or sketch by scratching lines with a pointed instrument. [< Du. *etsen* < G *ätzen* < MHG *etzen,* causative of *ezzen* eat] —**etch'er** *n.*

etch figure *Physics* The pattern etched on a crystal or metal surface by a reagent, valuable in indicating molecular structure.

etch·ing (ech'ing) *n.* **1** A process of engraving in which lines are scratched with a needle on a plate covered with wax or other coating, and the parts exposed are subjected to the biting of an acid. **2** A figure or design formed by etching. **3** An impression from an etched plate.

e·ter·nal (i·tûr'nəl) *adj.* **1** Having neither beginning nor end of existence; infinite in duration. **2** Having no end; everlasting. **3** Continued without interruption; perpetual. **4** Independent of time or its conditions, or of the things that are perishable; unchangeable; immutable. **5** Of or pertaining to eternity. **6** Appearing interminable; perpetual; incessant: often implying weariness or disgust: George and his *eternal* jokes. —*n.* One who or that which is everlasting: usually in the plural. —**the Eternal** God. [< OF < LL *aeternalis* < *aeternus* < *aevum* an age] —**e·ter'nal·ly** *adv.* —**e·ter'nal·ness, e·ter·nal·i·ty** (i·tûr·nal'ə·tē) *n.*

Synonyms (adj.): deathless, endless, eonian, everlasting, everliving, fadeless, immortal, imperishable, interminable, never-ending, never-failing, perennial, perpetual, timeless, unceasing, undying, unending, unfading, unfailing. *Eternal* strictly signifies without beginning or end; *everlasting* applies to that which may or may not have beginning, but can never cease; *endless,* without end, in its utmost reach, is not distinguishable from *everlasting,* but is constantly used in inferior senses, especially in mechanics, as in the phrases "an *endless* screw," "an *endless* chain." *Everlasting, endless,* and *interminable* are used in a limited sense of protracted, indefinite, but not infinite duration; as, the *everlasting* hills; *endless* debates; *interminable* quarrels. *Immortal* applies to that which now has life and is forever exempt from death. *Timeless* carries the fullest idea of *eternal,* as above and beyond time, and not to be measured by it. See IMMORTAL, INFINITE, PERPETUAL.

e·ter·ni·ty (i·tûr′nə·tē) *n. pl.* **·ties** 1 Infinite duration or existence. 2 An endless or limitless time. 3 Immortality. 4 That which is eternal or immortal. [< OF *eternité* < L *aeternitas, -tatis*]

e·ter·nize (i·tûr′nīz) *v.t.* **·nized, ·niz·ing** 1 To make eternal. 2 To perpetuate the fame of; immortalize. Also *Brit.* **e·ter′nise.** —**e·ter′ni·za′tion** *n.*

e·te·sian (i·tē′zhən) *adj. Meteorol.* Annually periodic, as certain northerly Mediterranean summer winds. [< L *etesius* < Gk. *etēsios* < *etos* a year]

-eth[1] An archaic inflectional ending used in the third person singular present indicative of some verbs: *eateth, drinketh.* Also, in contracted forms, *-th,* as in *hath, doth.* [OE *-ath, -eth, -oth*]

-eth[2] *suffix* Var. of -TH[2].

eth·ane (eth′ān) *n. Chem.* A colorless, odorless, gaseous compound, C_2H_6, of the paraffin series contained in the gases given off by petroleum and in illuminating gas; an alkane or saturated hydrocarbon of the methane series. [< ETHER]

eth·a·nol (eth′ə·nōl, -nol) *n.* Alcohol (def. 1); an organic compound, C_2H_5OH, representing the second member of the homologous series of alcohols of the general formula $C_nH_{2n+1}OH$. Also called *ethyl alcohol, grain alcohol.*

eth·ene (eth′ēn) *n.* Ethylene.

e·ther (ē′thər) *n.* 1 *Chem.* **a** A colorless, mobile, volatile, aromatic liquid compound, ethyl oxide, $(C_2H_5)_2O$, made by the action of sulfuric acid on alcohol: used as an anesthetic and solvent. **b** Any of a group of organic compounds in which an oxygen atom is joined with two organic radicals. 2 A solid or semisolid, perfectly elastic medium formerly assumed to pervade all of space and to be responsible for the transmission of light, heat, gravitational effects, and all forms of energy and radiation. 3 The upper air. Also spelled *aether* (for defs. 2 and 3). [< L *aether* sky < Gk. *aithēr* < *aithein* burn, shine]

e·the·re·al (i·thir′ē·əl) *adj.* 1 Having the nature of ether or air. 2 Light; airy; fine; subtle; exquisite. 3 Existing in or belonging to the ether or upper air; aerial; heavenly. 4 Of or pertaining to ether. See synonyms under AIRY. —**e·the′re·al·i·ty, e·the′re·al·ness** *n.* —**e·the′re·al·ly** *adv.* —**e·the′re·ous** *adj.*

e·ther·i·fy (i·ther′ə·fī) *v.t.* **·fied, ·fy·ing** *Chem.* To form ether from (an alcohol). —**e·ther′i·fi·ca′tion** *n.*

e·ther·ize (ē′thə·rīz) *v.t.* **·ized, ·iz·ing** 1 To subject to the influence of ether; anesthetize. 2 To change into ether. —**e′ther·i·za′tion** *n.* **e′ther·iz′er** *n.*

eth·ic (eth′ik) *adj.* Ethical; moral. —*n.* 1 The philosophy of morals; ethics: now in revived use by some philosophical writers instead of *ethics.* 2 The standard of character set up by any race or nation. [< L *ethicus* < Gk. *ēthikos* < *ethos* character]

eth·i·cal (eth′i·kəl) *adj.* 1 Pertaining or relating to ethics. 2 Treating of morals. 3 In accordance with right principles, as defined by a given system of ethics or professional conduct. See synonyms under MORAL. —**eth′i·cal′i·ty, eth′i·cal·ness** *n.* —**eth′i·cal·ly** *adv.*

eth·ics (eth′iks) *n. pl. (construed as singular in defs.* 1 *and* 3*)* 1 The study and philosophy of human conduct, with emphasis on the determination of right and wrong: one of the normative sciences. 2 The basic principles of right action. 3 A work or treatise on morals.

E·thi·o·pi·a (ē′thē·ō′pē·ə) 1 A native empire in eastern Africa; 350,000 square miles; capital, Addis Ababa; annexed by Italy, 1936; recovered by British forces, 1941: also *Abyssinia.* 2 An ancient country south of Egypt.

E·thi·o·pi·an (ē′thē·ō′pē·ən) *adj.* 1 Of or pertaining to Ethiopia, or to the Ethiopians. 2 Of or pertaining to a group of Hamitic languages spoken in Abyssinia and regions to the south. 3 *Ecol.* Designating a zoogeographical region including Africa south of the Sahara, southern Arabia, and Madagascar. —*n.* 1 A native of modern Abyssinia. 2 A member of the Ethiopian race. 3 A blackamoor. 4 **a** The Hamitic language of Abyssinia and the regions to the south; Cushitic. **b** Ethiopic.

eth·moid (eth′moid) *n. Anat.* A bone, cubical in man, composed of thin plates and situated at the base of the skull, behind the nose. —*adj.* Of or pertaining to the ethmoid; sievelike. [< Gk. *ēthmoeidēs* < *ēthmos* sieve + *eidos* form] —**eth·moi′dal** *adj.*

eth·nic (eth′nik) *adj.* 1 Of or pertaining to race, races, or peoples. 2 Pertaining to groups or stocks of mankind as having certain physical, mental, or cultural characteristics in common, and usually but not necessarily living within a given geographic area; ethnological. 3 Belonging distinctively to a race. 4 Pertaining to peoples neither Jewish nor Christian; gentile; heathen; pagan. Also **eth′ni·cal.** —*n. Colloq.* A member of a minority ethnic group, esp., in the U.S., a nonblack minority. [< Gk. *ethnikos* < *ethnos* nation] —**eth′ni·cal·ly** *adv.*

ethno- *combining form* Race, nation; peoples: *ethnogenic, ethnozoology.* Also, before vowels, **ethn-.**

eth·no·bi·ol·o·gy (eth′nō·bī·ol′ə·jē) *n.* The study of human societies in relation to their biological environment, especially as regards plant life and food supply; human ecology.

eth·no·bot·a·ny (eth′nō·bot′ə·nē) *n.* The study of plants in relation to the needs and customs of a given ethnic group or people. —**eth′no·bo·tan′i·cal** (-bə·tan′i·kəl) *adj.* —**eth′no·bot′a·nist** *n.*

eth·no·cen·trism (eth′nō·sen′triz·əm) *n. Sociol.* The concept, formulated by W. G. Sumner, that the attitudes, beliefs, and customs of one's own group, nation, or people are of central importance and a basis for judging all other groups. —**eth′no·cen′tric** *adj.*

eth·no·gen·ic (eth′nō·jen′ik) *adj.* 1 Of or pertaining to the origin of races and ethnic groups. 2 Producing races or peoples.

eth·nog·e·ny (eth·noj′ə·nē) *n.* The department of ethnology that deals with the origin of races and ethnic groups.

eth·nog·ra·pher (eth·nog′rə·fər) *n.* One who studies or is proficient in ethnography. Also **eth′no·graph·ist.**

eth·nog·ra·phy (eth·nog′rə·fē) *n.* 1 The branch of anthropology that considers man geographically and descriptively, treating of the subdivision of races and peoples, the causes of migration, etc. 2 Formerly, ethnology.

eth·no·lin·guis·tics (eth′nō·ling·gwis′tiks) *n.* The study, through linguistic methodology, of the relation between language and ethnology.

eth·nol·o·gist (eth·nol′ə·jist) *n.* A student of or an expert in ethnology.

eth·nol·o·gy (eth·nol′ə·jē) *n.* The science of the subdivisions and families of men, their origins, characteristics, distribution, and physical and linguistic classification. —**eth·no·log·i·cal** (eth′nō·loj′i·kəl) or **eth′no·log′ic** *adj.* —**eth′no·log′i·cal·ly** *adv.*

eth·no·zo·ol·o·gy (eth′nō·zō·ol′ə·jē) *n.* The study of a regional fauna in relation to the needs, uses, and customs of a given people or ethnic community. —**eth′no·zo·o·log′i·cal** (-zō′ə·loj′i·kəl) *adj.* —**eth′no·zo·ol′o·gist** *n.*

e·thog·ra·phy (i·thog′rə·fē) *n.* A description of the moral attributes and customs of mankind. [< Gk. *ēthos* character + -GRAPHY]

e·thol·o·gy (i·thol′ə·jē) *n.* 1 The scientific study of animal behavior. 2 The science of the formation of human character. [< Gk. *ēthos* character

+ -LOGY] —**e·tho·log·ic** (ē′thə·loj′ik) or **·i·cal** *adj.*

e·thos (ē′thos) *n.* 1 The characteristic spirit, disposition, or tendency of a people or community regarded as an endowment and as expressed in their customs. 2 The genius or spirit of an institution or a system. 3 The essential characteristics, or ideal attributes, of a work, or period in art or literature, or the type to which the art or period corresponds, as opposed to what is merely emotional, incidental, and transient. Compare PATHOS. [< Gk. *ēthos* character]

eth·yl (eth′il) *n. Chem.* 1 A univalent hydrocarbon radical, C_2H_5, of the paraffin series, denoting the presence of the radical in any of numerous compounds widely used in industry, medicine, and the arts: *ethyl* acetate, *ethyl* cellulose, etc. 2 Any gasoline treated with tetraethyl lead to reduce knock. [< ETHER + -YL] —**eth·yl′ic** *adj.*

ethyl alcohol Ethanol.

eth·y·late (eth′ə·lāt) *v.t.* **·lat·ed, ·lat·ing** To treat or combine so as to cause the introduction of ethyl or its compounds. —**eth′y·la′tion** *n.* —**eth′y·lat′ed** *adj.*

eth·yl·u·re·thane (eth′əl·yŏor′ə·thān) *n. Chem.* Urethan.

e·ti·o·late (ē′tē·ə·lāt) *v.t. & v.i.* **·lat·ed, ·lat·ing** To whiten, or become white, as a plant or person kept from sunlight. [< F *étioler* < OF *estieuler* grow up in stalks, ? ult. < L *stipula* straw]

e·ti·o·la·tion (ē′tē·ə·lā′shən) *n.* A blanching or yellowing, specifically in plants deprived of light or deficient in chlorophyll.

e·ti·ol·o·gy (ē′tē·ol′ə·jē) *n.* 1 The science of efficient, as distinguished from final, causes. 2 That department of medicine that treats of the causes of disease. 3 The giving of a cause or reason for anything; also, the reason itself. Also spelled *aetiology.* [< LL *aetiologia* < Gk. *aitiologia* < *aitia* cause + *logos* word, study] —**e·ti·o·log·i·cal** (ē′tē·ə·loj′i·kəl) *adj.* —**e·ti·o·log′i·cal·ly** *adv.* —**e′ti·ol′o·gist** *n.*

et·i·quette (et′ə·ket, -kət) *n.* The usages of polite society or professional intercourse. [< F < OF *estiquette.* Doublet of TICKET.]

é·toile (ā·twäl′) *n.* A lustrous satin fabric with plain or changeable surface. [< F, star]

et se·quens (et sē′kwənz) *pl.* **et se·quen·ti·a** (-kwen′shē·ə) *Latin* And the following. Abbr. *et seq.*

-ette *suffix* 1 Little, small: *kitchenette.* 2 Resembling; like; imitating: *leatherette.* 3 Feminine: *farmerette.* [< F *-ette,* fem. of *-et,* dim. suffix]

et·tle (et′l) *Scot. v.t. & v.i.* To aim; intend. —*n.* 1 Intention; aim. 2 Opportunity.

é·tude (ā′tōōd, -tyōōd; *Fr.* ā·tüd′) *n. Music* 1 A composition designed to illustrate some phase of technique. 2 A composition meant to be played for its esthetic effect, but also exemplifying some aspect of technical virtuosity. [< F. See STUDY.]

é·tui (ā·twē′) *n. pl.* **é·tuis** A case for carrying small articles. Also **et·wee′.** [< F]

et·y·mo·log·i·cal (et′ə·mə·loj′i·kəl) *adj.* Relating to or based upon the study of etymology. Also **et′y·mo·log′ic.** —**et′y·mo·log′i·cal·ly** *adv.*

et·y·mo·log·i·con (et′ə·mə·loj′i·kon) *n. pl.* **·ca** (-kə) An etymological dictionary or a treatise on the derivation of words. [< LL < Gk. *etymologikon* of an etymologist]

et·y·mol·o·gist (et′ə·mol′ə·jist) *n.* A student of or one versed in the derivations, form changes, and meanings of words.

et·y·mol·o·gize (et′ə·mol′ə·jīz) *v.t. & v.i.* **·gized, ·giz·ing** To trace or give the derivation of (a word or words).

et·y·mol·o·gy (et′ə·mol′ə·jē) *n. pl.* **·gies** 1 The history of a word as indicated by breaking it down into basic elements, or by tracing it back to the earliest known form or root, with all its changes in form and meaning; also, a statement of this. 2 The study of the derivation of words. See FOLK ETYMOLOGY. [< F *etymologie* < L *etymologia* < Gk. < *etymon* original meaning + *logos* word, study]

et·y·mon (et′ə·mon, -mən) *n. pl.* **·mons** or **·ma** (-mə) 1 The radical or root form of a word. 2 The primitive signification of a word. [< L < Gk., original meaning; orig. neut. sing. of *etymos* true, genuine]

eu- *prefix* Good; well; easy; agreeable: *euphony, eupnea:* opposed to *dys-.* [< Gk. *eu-* < *eus* well]

Eu·bac·te·ri·a·les (yōō'bak·tir'ē·ā'lēz) *n. pl.* A large and highly diversified order of bacteria, including many of the disease–producing genera, as the cholera, typhoid, anthrax, and dysentery groups. See illustration under BAC-TERIA. [<NL *Eubacterium,* one of an order of bacteria <Gk. *eu-* good, typical + *bacterium* BACTERIUM]

eu·caine (yōō·kān', yōō'kə·in) *n. Chem.* Either of two important compounds similar in effect to cocaine, but less toxic, used for local anesthesia, known as **eucaine A** and **eucaine B.** [<EU- + (CO)CAINE]

eu·ca·lypt (yōō'kə·lipt) *n.* A tree of the genus *Eucalyptus.* —**eu'ca·lyp'tic** *adj.*

eu·ca·lyp·te·ol (yōō'kə·lip'tē·ōl, -ol) *n. Chem.* A crystalline compound, $C_{10}H_{16}·2HCl$, with a camphorlike odor, derived from eucalyptol. Also **eucalyptene hydrochloride.**

eu·ca·lyp·tol (yōō'kə·lip'tōl, -tol) *n.* A colorless camphoraceous liquid compound, $C_{10}H_{18}O$, contained in eucalyptus oil: used as an antiseptic and expectorant: also called *cineol.* [<EUCALYPT(US) + -OL²]

eu·ca·lyp·tus (yōō'kə·lip'təs) *n. pl.* **-lyp·ti** (-tī) or **-lyp·tus·es** Any of a genus (*Eucalyptus*) of large, chiefly Australian evergreen trees of the myrtle family: widely used as timber, for ornamental purposes, and in the preparation of drugs, especially the volatile, pungent, essential **oil of eucalyptus.** [<NL <Gk. *eu-* well + *kalyptos* covered <*kalyptein* cover; from the covering of the buds]

eu·cha·ris (yōō'kə·ris) *n.* Any plant of a small genus (*Eucharis*) of bulbous South American plants of the amaryllis family, with elliptic or ovate leaves and white, fragrant flowers in umbels. [<NL <Gk. *eucharis* agreeable <*eu-* good + *charis* grace]

Eu·cha·rist (yōō'kə·rist) *n.* **1** A Christian sacrament in which bread and wine are consecrated, distributed, and consumed in commemoration of the passion and death of Christ. **2** The consecrated bread and wine of this sacrament. See synonyms under SACRAMENT. [<OF *eucariste* <LL *eucharistia* <Gk. <*eu-* well + *charizesthai* give thanks] —**eu'cha·ris'tic** or **·ti·cal** *adj.*

eu·char·is·ti·al (yōō'kə·ris'chəl) *n.* A pyx (def. 1).

eu·chre (yōō'kər) *n.* **1** A card game for two to four players, played with 32 cards, one side in choosing trumps being required to take three to five tricks to win. See BOWER². **2** An instance of euchring an opponent or of being euchred. —*v.t.* **eu·chred** (-kərd), **eu·chring 1** In the game of euchre, to defeat (the trump–making side) by taking three tricks. **2** *Colloq.* To outwit or defeat. [Origin uncertain]

eu·clase (yōō'klās) *n.* A very brittle pale–green silicate of beryllium and aluminum, used rarely as a gem. [<EU- + Gk. *klasis* breaking <*klaein* break]

Eu·clid (yōō'klid) **1** An Athenian geometer who lived about 300 B.C. **2** The work on geometry written by him. **3** An elementary textbook of geometry. **4** Impersonally, the science of geometry or its principles.

Eu·clid·e·an (yōō·klid'ē·ən) *adj.* Of or pertaining to Euclid; accordant with the axioms and postulates of his geometry. Also **Eu·clid'i·an.**

eu·de·mon (yōō·dē'mən) *n.* A benevolent spirit or genius. Also **eu·dae'mon.** [<Gk. *eudaimōn* fortunate <*eu-* well + *daimōn* spirit]

eu·de·mo·ni·a (yōō'də·mō'nē·ə) *n.* A state of complete well–being, as defined by the philosophy of Aristotle; good fortune; true happiness, as arising from a rational satisfaction. Also **eu'dae·mo'ni·a, eu·de'mo·ny.** [<Gk. *eudaimonia* <*eudaimōn.* See EUDEMON.]

eu·de·mon·ic (yōō'də·mon'ik) *adj.* Of, pertaining to, or tending to produce happiness; conceived or done for the sake of happiness: *eudemonic* morals. Also **eu'de·mon'i·cal.**

eu·de·mon·ics (yōō'də·mon'iks) *n.* **1** The branch of ethics that discusses happiness. **2** Means of comfort or happiness. **3** Eudemonism.

eu·de·mon·ism (yōō·dē'mən·iz'əm) *n.* Any of several philosophical theories which maintain that man's greatest good exists in some form of mental or spiritual happiness. See HEDON-ISM. —**eu·de'mon·ist** *n.* —**eu·de'mon·is'tic** or **·ti·cal** *adj.* —**eu·de'mon·is'ti·cal·ly** *adv.*

eu·di·om·e·ter (yōō'dē·om'ə·tər) *n. Chem.* A graduated glass vessel used in the volumetric analysis of gases. [<Gk. *eudios* clear, fine

+ -METER; orig. used to measure the amount of oxygen in the air] —**eu·di·o·met·ric** (yōō'· dē·ə·met'rik) or **·ri·cal** *adj.* —**eu·di·o·met'ri·cal·ly** *adv.* —**eu'di·om'e·try** *n.*

eu·gen·ic (yōō·jen'ik) *adj.* **1** Relating to the development and improvement of human stocks. **2** Well–born. Also **eu·gen'i·cal.** [< Gk. *eugenēs* well–born (<*eu-* well + *genos* race) + -IC] —**eu·gen'i·cal·ly** *adv.*

eu·gen·ics (yōō·jen'iks) *n. pl.* (*construed as singular*) The science and art of improving human breeds by so applying the ascertained principles of genetics and inheritance as to secure a desirable combination of physical characteristics and mental traits in the offspring of suitably mated parents. [Coined by Sir Francis Galton in 1883]

eu·ge·nist (yōō'jə·nist, yōō·jen'ist) *n.* A student or advocate of eugenics. Also **eu·gen·i·cist** (yōō·jen'ə·sist).

eu·ge·nol (yōō'jə·nōl, -nol) *n. Chem.* A colorless oil, $C_{10}H_{12}O_2$, of spicy odor and burning taste contained in oil of cloves, oil of bay, and other oils: used medicinally and in the manufacture of vanillin. [<EUGEN(IA) + -OL²]

Eu·gle·na (yōō·glē'nə) *n. Zool.* A genus of microscopic fresh–water protozoans (class *Mastigophora*) having one flagellum and a red eyespot or stigma, especially *E. viridis,* noted for its green chromatophores. [<NL <Gk. *eu-* well + *glēnē* eyeball]

eu·he·mer·ism (yōō·hē'mə·riz'əm, -hem'ə-) *n.* The rationalistic system of **Euhemerus,** a Sicilian philosopher of the fourth century B.C., who explained mythology as the deification of earth–born kings and heroes, and denied the existence of divine beings. —**eu·he'mer·ist** *n.* —**eu·he'mer·is'tic** *adj.* —**eu·he'mer·is'ti·cal·ly** *adv.*

eu·he·mer·ize (yōō·hē'mə·rīz, -hem'ə-) *v.t.* **·ized, ·iz·ing** To explain (myths) by euhemerism.

eu·lo·gi·a (yōō·lō'jē·ə) *n.* **1** In the Greek Church, unconsecrated bread which is blessed and distributed to non–communicants after the Eucharist. **2** In patristic writings, the Eucharist itself. [<LL <Gk. See EULOGY.]

eu·lo·gist (yōō'lə·jist) *n.* One who speaks in high or extravagant praise; the author of a eulogy. Also **eu'lo·giz'er.**

eu·lo·gize (yōō'lə·jīz) *v.t.* **·gized, ·giz·ing** To speak or write a eulogy about; to praise highly. Also *Brit.* **eu'lo·gise.** See synonyms under PRAISE. —**eu·lo·gis·tic** (yōō'lə·jis'tik) or **·ti·cal, eu·lo·gi·ous** (yōō·lō'jē·əs) *adj.* —**eu'lo·gis'ti·cal·ly** *adv.*

eu·lo·gy (yōō'lə·jē) *n. pl.* **·gies** A spoken or written laudation of a person's life or character; praise. Also **eu'lo·gism, eu·lo·gi·um** (yōō·lō'jē·əm). [<Gk. *eulogia* praise <*eu-* well + *legein* speak] —**eu·log·ic** (yōō·loj'ik) *adj.* —**eu·log'i·cal·ly** *adv.*

Synonyms: applause, commendation, encomium, laudation, panegyric, praise. *Panegyric* is *commendation* expressed *to* an assembly, and *applause* is *commendation* expressed *by* an assembly. *Eulogy* is now used almost in the very sense of *panegyric,* a laudatory address before an audience; as Blaine's *eulogy* on Garfield; *eulogy,* however, is regarded as more discriminating than *panegyric,* which is unstinted *praise.* Compare APPLAUSE, PRAISE. *Antonyms:* abuse, calumny, denunciation, detraction, invective, obloquy, philippic, slander, vilification, vituperation.

Eu·men·i·des (yōō·men'ə·dēz) *n. pl.* The Furies. [<Gk., the kind ones]

eu·nuch (yōō'nək) *n.* An emasculated man, formerly employed as a harem attendant or an Oriental palace official. [<L *eunuchus* <Gk. *eu-nouchos* chamber attendant <*eunē* bed + *echein* keep, guard]

eu·nuch·oid (yōō'nək·oid) *adj.* Having the appearance of a eunuch.

eu·on·y·mus (yōō·on'ə·məs) *n.* Any of a widely distributed genus (*Euonymus*) of shrubs or small trees having inconspicuous flowers and many-colored fruits; especially, the wahoo: also spelled *evonymus.* [<L *euonymos* <Gk. *euōnymos* <*eu-* well + *onyma* name]

eu·pa·to·ri·um (yōō'pə·tôr'ē·əm, -tō'rē-) *n.* Any plant of the large, principally American genus (*Eupatorium*) of herbaceous or shrubby plants of the composite family, the thoroughworts, with mainly aromatic or bitter leaves and numerous corymbose heads of small flowers, as the joe-pye–weed, the boneset, the white snakeroot, and hemp agrimony. [<NL <Gk. *eupatorion* agri-

mony; named after Mithridates VI, called *Eupator* <*eu-* good + *patēr* father]

eu·pat·rid (yōō·pat'rid, yōō'pə·trid) *adj.* Of or pertaining to the eupatridae; of patrician birth. —*n.* One of the eupatridae; a patrician.

eu·pep·si·a (yōō·pep'sē·ə, -shə) *n.* Healthy digestion: opposed to *dyspepsia.* Also **eu·pep·sy** (yōō'pep·sē, yōō·pep'-). [<NL <Gk. <*eu-* good + *pepsia* digestion]

eu·pep·tic (yōō·pep'tik) *adj.* **1** Pertaining to good digestion. **2** Promoting digestion. **3** Optimistic; sanguine.

eu·phe·mism (yōō'fə·miz'əm) *n.* A mild or agreeable expression substituted for a realistic description of something disagreeable. [<Gk. *euphēmismos* <*euphēmizein* <*eu-* well + *phēmizein* <*phanai* speak] —**eu'phe·mist** *n.* —**eu'phe·mis'tic** or **·ti·cal** *adj.* —**eu'phe·mis'ti·cal·ly** *adv.*

eu·phe·mize (yōō'fə·mīz) *v.t.* & *v.i.* **·mized, ·miz·ing** To say in euphemistic form; express oneself euphemistically. —**eu'phe·miz'er** *n.*

eu·phon·ic (yōō·fon'ik) *adj.* Agreeable in sound; pertaining to euphony; euphonious. Also **eu·phon'i·cal.** —**eu·phon'i·cal·ly** *adv.* —**eu·phon'i·cal·ness** *n.*

eu·pho·ni·ous (yōō·fō'nē·əs) *adj.* Pleasant in sound, as a word; characterized by euphony. —**eu·pho'ni·ous·ly** *adv.* —**eu·pho'ni·ous·ness** *n.*

eu·pho·ni·um (yōō·fō'nē·əm) *n. Music* **1** A bass and tenor brass wind instrument, producing a mellower tone than the baritone saxhorn, and having the same range (E to B flat). **2** A musical instrument consisting of glass tubes connected by steel bars. [<NL <Gk. *euphōnos.* See EU-PHONY.]

eu·pho·nize (yōō'fə·nīz) *v.t.* **·nized, ·niz·ing** To make euphonious. —**eu'pho·nism** *n.*

eu·pho·ny (yōō'fə·nē) *n. pl.* **·nies 1** Agreeableness of sound. **2** Pleasant–sounding combination or arrangement of words. See synonyms under ME-TER. [<Gk. *euphōnia* <*euphōnos* <*eu-* good + *phōnē* sound]

eu·phor·bi·a (yōō·fôr'bē·ə) *n.* Any plant of a large and widely distributed genus (*Euphorbia*) of herbs of the spurge family, characterized by their milky juice and various medicinal properties. [<NL <L *euphorbea* <Gk. *euphorbion*; named after *Euphorbos,* a Greek physician] —**eu·phor'bi·a'ceous, eu·phor'bi·al** *adj.*

eu·pho·ri·a (yōō·fôr'ē·ə, -fō'rē-) *n.* **1** Physical comfort or well–being. **2** *Psychiatry* An exaggerated buoyancy and sense of bodily health. [<NL <Gk. *euphoria* <*eupherein* be well] —**eu·phor·ic** (yōō·fôr'ik, -for'-) *adj.*

eu·pho·ri·ant (yōō·fôr'ē·ənt, -fō'rē-) *n. Med.* A drug or other agent which induces euphoria.

eu·phot·ic (yōō·fot'ik) *adj. Ecol.* Of or pertaining to the receipt of the maximum amount of sunlight: The *euphotic* zone. [<Gk. *eu-* well + *phōs, photos* light]

eu·phra·sy (yōō'frə·sē) *n.* Eyebright. [<Med. L *euphrasia* <Gk, delight <*eu-* well + *phrēn* mind]

eu·phroe (yōō'frō, -vrō) *n. Naut.* A long wooden block having several holes through which to reeve a cord: used in adjusting an awning on shipboard, also sometimes in tightening tent ropes: also spelled *uphroe.* [<Du. *juffrouw,* orig., a maiden]

eu·phu·ism (yōō'fyōō·iz'əm) *n.* **1** An affectation of elegance in writing; a high–flown periphrastic style, such as that of John Lyly. **2** An instance of such a style. **3** Affected elegance in dress, etc. [after *Euphues,* character created by John Lyly] —**eu'phu·ist** *n.* —**eu'phu·is'tic** or **·ti·cal** *adj.* —**eu'phu·is'ti·cal·ly** *adv.*

eu·phu·ize (yōō'fyōō·iz) *v.t.* **·ized, ·iz·ing** To speak or write in an affected style.

eu·plas·tic (yōō·plas'tik) *adj. Biol.* Readily transformable into organic tissue. —*n.* Matter thus transformable. [<Gk. *euplastos* easily molded <*eu-* well + *plassein* form]

eu·ploid (yōō'ploid) *adj. Genetics.* Having a number of chromosomes that is an exact multiple of the haploid number. —*n.* A euploid cell or organism. —**eu·ploid·y** *n.*

eup·ne·a (yōōp·nē'ə) *n. Med.* Easy, natural breathing; normal respiration: opposed to *dyspnea.* Also **eup·noe'a.** [<EU- + Gk. *pnoia* breath <*pneein* breathe]

Eur·a·sia (yōō·rā'zhə, -shə) The land mass comprising the continents of Europe and Asia.

Eur·a·sian (yōō·rā'zhən, -shən) *adj.* **1** Pertaining

to both Europe and Asia. **2** Of European and Asian descent. —*n.* A half-caste of mixed European and Asian parentage. Also **Eur·a·si·at·ic** (yŏŏ·rā'zhē·at'ik, -shē-), **Eu·ro·pa·sian** (yŏŏr'ə·pā'zhən, -shən).

eu·re·ka (yŏŏ·rē'kə) *interj.* I have found (it): attributed to Archimedes on his discovery of a method of determining the ratio of weight to volume: the motto of the State of California. [< Gk. *heurēka*]

Eu·rip·i·des (yŏŏ·rip'ə·dēz), 480–406 B.C., Greek tragic dramatist.

eu·ri·pus (yŏŏ·ri'pəs) *n. pl.* **·pi** (-pī) **1** An arm of the sea where the tide rushes in strong, shifting currents. **2** A scene or occasion of violent changes. [< L < Gk. *euripos* a strait < *eu-* well + *rhipē* rush]

Eu·ro·com·mu·nism (yŏŏr'ō·kom'yə·niz·əm) *n.* A form of Communism practiced in some Western European countries that emphasizes the importance of democratic methods.

Eu·ro·dol·lar (yŏŏr'ō·dol'ər) *n. Econ.* A U.S. dollar on deposit outside the United States, especially in one of the western European countries. [< EUR(OPE) + DOLLAR]

Eu·rope (yŏŏr'əp) A continent comprising a vast western peninsula of the Eurasian land mass; about 3,800,000 square miles, or excluding European U.S.S.R. and Turkey about 1,902,600 square miles.

Eu·ro·pe·an (yŏŏr'ə·pē'ən) *adj.* Relating to or derived from Europe or its inhabitants. —*n.* A native of Europe.

European Economic Community A customs union of France, Italy, West Germany, and the Benelux nations. Also **European Common Market**.

Eu·ro·pe·an·ize (yŏŏr'ə·pē'ən·īz) *v.t.* **·ized, ·iz·ing** To make European in characteristics, views, culture, etc. —**Eu'ro·pe'an·i·za'tion** *n.*

European plan The system of hotel-keeping by which lodging and service are charged for separately from meals, these being furnished to order. Compare AMERICAN PLAN.

eu·ro·pi·um (yŏŏ·rō'pē·əm) *n.* A rare metallic element (symbol Eu, atomic number 63) of the lanthanide series. See PERIODIC TABLE. [< NL < L *Europa* Europe]

eury- *combining form* Wide; broad: *eurychoric*. [< Gk. *eurys* wide]

eu·ry·ce·phal·ic (yŏŏr'i·sə·fal'ik) *adj. Anat.* Broad-headed. Also **eu'ry·ceph'a·lous** (-sef'·ə·ləs).

eu·ry·cho·ric (yŏŏr'i·kôr'ik, -kō'rik) *adj. Ecol.* Of or pertaining to a wide distribution in varying climates, as plant species. [< EURY- + Gk. *chóros* country]

eu·ryg·na·thous (yŏŏr'ig·nā'thəs) *adj. Anat.* Having a wide upper jaw. Also **eu'ryg·na'thic**. [< EURY- + Gk. *gnathos* jaw]

eu·ry·on (yŏŏr'ē·on) *n. Anat.* The point on either side of the head above the ear having the greatest lateral projection: the distance between the two euryons is a measure of the head width. [< Gk. *eurys* broad]

eu·ryp·ter·id (yŏŏ·rip'tər·id) *n. Paleontol.* Any member of an extinct Silurian order (*Eurypterida*) of very large aquatic arthropods related to the *Arachnida* and to the king crab. —*adj.* Belonging to this order. [< NL *Eurypterida* < Gk. *eurys* broad + *pteron* wing]

eu·ry·ther·mic (yŏŏr'i·thûr'mik) *adj. Biol.* Designating plant or animal organisms capable of withstanding a wide range of temperature conditions, as bacteria. [< EURY- + Gk. *thermē* heat]

eu·ryth·mics (yŏŏ·rith'miks) *n.* A method of free-style rhythmical bodily movements in interpretation of musical compositions: devised by Émile Jaques-Dalcroze (1860–1950), Swiss composer. Also spelled *eurhythmics*.

eu·ryth·my (yŏŏ·rith'mē) *n.* Harmony and just proportion. Also spelled *eurhythmy*. [< L < Gk. *eurythmia* harmony < *eu-* well + *rhythmos* rhythm] —**eu·ryth'mic** or **·mi·cal** *adj.*

eu·sol (yŏŏ'sōl, -sol) *n.* A chlorinated antiseptic solution for wound treatment. [< E(DIN-BURGH) U(NIVERSITY) SOL(UTION)]

eu·spo·ran·gi·ate (yŏŏ'spə·ran'jē·āt) *adj. Bot.* Having sporangia developed from a group of cells, instead of from a single cell. [< EU- + SPORANGIA]

Eustachian tube *Anat.* A passage between the pharynx and the inner ear; it forms the auditory canal and serves to equalize air pressure between the inner ear, the tympanic cavity of the middle ear, and the external air.

See illustration under EAR. [after Bartolommeo *Eustachio*]

eu·tax·it·ic (yŏŏ'tak·sit'ik) Of or pertaining to ore deposits occurring in stratified form: opposed to *ataxitic*.

eu·tax·y (yŏŏ·tak'sē) *n.* Good arrangement; orderly disposition. [< Gk. *eutaxia* < *eu-* good + *taxis* arrangement < *tassein* arrange]

eu·tec·tic (yŏŏ·tek'tik) *adj. Chem.* Melting readily or at a low temperature: said of an alloy or a solution that has the lowest possible fusing point, usually below that of any of the components taken separately. —*n.* A eutectic substance, as an alloy. [< GK. *eutēktos* < *eu-* well, easily + *tēkein* fuse]

eu·tha·na·si·a (yŏŏ'thə·nā'zhē·ə, -zhə) *n.* **1** Painless, peaceful death. **2** The deliberate putting to death of a person suffering from a painful and incurable disease; mercy killing. Also called *active euthanasia*. **3** Death resulting from the cessation of heroic measures to prolong a life. Also called *passive euthanasia*. [< Gk. < *eu-* easy + *thanatos* death]

eu·then·ics (yŏŏ·then'iks) *n. pl.* (construed as singular) **1** The science of improving the human race by external influences, apart from considerations of heredity. **2** The science which aims at securing the most favorable environmental conditions for the growth of plants and animals. Compare EUGENICS. [< GK. *euthenia* well-being] —**eu'the·nist** *n.*

Eu·the·ri·a (yŏŏ·thir'ē·ə) *n.* A subclass of mammals characterized by a highly developed placenta and lengthy prenatal development of offspring: includes man and most of the mammalian types: formerly called *Monodelphia*. [< NL < Gk. *eu-* good, typical + *thērion* animal]

eu·troph·ic (yŏŏ·trof'ik, -trō'fik) *adj. Ecol.* Of a lake or other body of water, characterized by an advanced stage of eutrophication; rich in nutrients; mature. [< Gk. *eutrophos* well-nourished]

eu·troph·i·ca·tion (yŏŏ·trof'ə·kā'shən, -trō'fə-) *n. Ecol.* The process by which a body of water, as a lake, matures and ages, characterized by an environment growing progressively richer in mineral and organic nutrients, resulting in a seasonally recurring depletion in oxygen that is ultimately incompatible with animal life. [< EU-TROPHIC + -ATION]

e·vac·u·ant (i·vak'yŏŏ·ənt) *adj. Med.* Producing evacuation; cathartic, diuretic, or emetic. —*n.* Something that assists evacuation.

e·vac·u·ate (i·vak'yŏŏ·āt) *v.* **·at·ed, ·at·ing** *v.t.* **1** *Mil.* **a** To give up or abandon possession of; withdraw from, as a fortress or city. **b** To withdraw (troops, inhabitants, etc.) from a threatened area or place. **2** To make empty; vacate. **3** To remove the contents of. **4** *Physiol.* To discharge or eject, as from the bowels. —*v.i.* **5** To withdraw, as from a threatened area or place. [< L *evacuatus*, pp. of *evacuare* < *e-* out + *vacuare* make empty < *vacuus* empty] —**e·vac'u·a·tive, e·vac'u·a·to·ry** (-tôr'ē, -tō'rē) *adj.* —**e·vac'u·a·tor** *n.*

e·vac·u·a·tion (i·vak'yŏŏ·ā'shən) *n.* **1** The act of evacuating or making empty: the *evacuation* of a fort. **2** *Physiol.* That which is evacuated or ejected by excretory passages, especially by the bowels. **3** The act of making void or null, as a contract.

e·vac·u·ee (i·vak'yŏŏ·ē') *n.* One who has been removed from or has abandoned his home.

e·vade (i·vād') *v.* **e·vad·ed, e·vad·ing** *v.t.* **1** To escape or get away from by tricks or cleverness; save oneself from: to *evade* pursuers or a crisis. **2** To avoid or get out of; get around: to *evade* a question or a duty. **3** To baffle; elude: The facts *evade* explanation. —*v.i.* **4** To practice evasion. **5** *Rare* To escape; get away. See synonyms under ESCAPE. [< L *evadere* < *e-* out + *vadere* go] —**e·vad'a·ble, e·vad'i·ble** *adj.* —**e·vad'er** *n.*

e·vag·i·nate (i·vaj'ə·nāt) *v.t.* **·nat·ed, ·nat·ing** *Biol.* To turn inside out, as a tubular organ; protrude by eversion; unsheathe. [< LL *evaginatus*, pp. of *evaginare* < *e-* out + *vagina* a sheath]

e·vag·i·na'tion *n.*

e·val·u·ate (i·val'yŏŏ·āt) *v.t.* **·at·ed, ·at·ing** **1** To find or determine the amount, worth, etc., of; appraise. **2** *Math.* To determine the numerical value of. [< F *évaluer* < *e-* out (< L *ex*) + *valuer* < OF *valoir*. See VALUE.]

e·val·u·a·tion (i·val'yŏŏ·ā'shən) *n.* Accurate appraisal of value.

ev·a·nesce (ev'ə·nes') *v.t.* **·nesced, ·nesc·ing** To disappear by degrees; vanish gradually. [< L *evanescere* < *e-* out + *vanescere* vanish < *vanus* empty] —**ev'a·nes'ci·ble** *adj.*

ev·a·nes·cent (ev'ə·nes'ənt) *adj.* Passing away, or liable to pass away, gradually or imperceptibly. See synonyms under TRANSIENT. [< F *évanescent* < L *evanescens, -entis*, ppr. of *evanescere*. See EVANESCE.] —**ev'a·nes'cence** *n.* —**ev'a·nes'cent·ly** *adv.*

e·van·gel[1] (i·van'jəl) *n.* **1** The message of redemption through Jesus Christ; the Christian gospel. **2** *Usually cap.* One of the four Gospels of the New Testament. **3** Any good news or glad tidings. [< OF *evangile* < LL *evangelium* < Gk. *euangelion* good news < *eu-* good + *angellein* announce]

e·van·gel[2] (i·van'jəl) An evangelist. [< MGk. *euangelos* < *eu-* good + *angelos* messenger]

e·van·gel·i·cal (ē'van·jel'i·kəl, ev'ən-) *adj.* **1** In or agreeing with the four Gospels or the teachings of the New Testament. **2** Denoting the adherents of a school of Protestant theology stressing the divine inspiration, authority, and sufficiency of the Scriptures, the fallen state of man, salvation by faith in the redeeming work of Christ, and spiritual regeneration, and denying in whole or in part the efficacy of the sacraments and the authority of the church. **3** *U.S.* Loosely, orthodox; Trinitarian in belief. **4** Zealous or fervent: *evangelical* preaching. **5** Pertaining to the work of an evangelist; evangelistic: *evangelical* labors. —*n.* A member of an evangelical church, or of an evangelical party within a church, as of the Low Church party in Anglicanism. Also **e'van·gel'ic**. [< LL *evangelicus* < Gk. *euangelikos* < *euangelion*. See EVANGEL[1].] —**e'van·gel'i·cal·ism, e'van·gel'i·cism** *n.* —**e'van·gel'i·cal·ly** *adv.* —**e'van·gel'i·cal·ness, e·van·ge·lic'i·ty** (i·van'jə·lis'ə·tē) *n.*

e·van·gel·ism (i·van'jə·liz'əm) *n.* **1** The zealous preaching or spreading of the gospel. **2** The work of an evangelist.

e·van·gel·ist (i·van'jə·list) *n.* **1** *Usually cap.* One of the four writers of the New Testament Gospels; Matthew, Mark, Luke, or John. **2** An itinerant or missionary preacher; a revivalist. **3** In the Mormon Church, a patriarch.

e·vap·o·ra·ble (i·vap'ər·ə·bəl) *adj.* Capable of being converted into vapor. —**e·vap'o·ra·bil'i·ty** *n.*

e·vap·o·rate (i·vap'ə·rāt) *v.* **·rat·ed, ·rat·ing** *v.t.* **1** To convert into vapor, usually by application of heat; vaporize. **2** To remove moisture from by a drying or heating process; to concentrate (fruit, milk, etc.) by evaporation. —*v.i.* **3** To become vapor; pass off as vapor. **4** To yield vapor. **5** To vanish; disappear. [< LL *evaporatus*, pp. of *evaporare* < *e-* out, away + *vapor*. See VAPOR.] —**e·vap'o·ra'tive** *adj.*

e·vap·o·ra·tion (i·vap'ə·rā'shən) *n.* **1** The act or process of changing or being changed into vapor, specifically, at temperatures below the boiling point. **2** A rising of or passing off in vapor. **3** The act of drying or concentrating. **4** The result of evaporation; vapor.

e·vap·o·ra·tor (i·vap'ə·rā'tər) *n.* An apparatus for drying substances, as fruits, by evaporation.

e·vap·o·rim·e·ter (i·vap'ə·rim'ə·tər) *n.* An apparatus for testing the rate of evaporation of a liquid; an atmometer. Also **e·vap'o·rom'e·ter**.

e·va·sion (i·vā'zhən) *n.* The act, means, or result of evading; equivocation; subterfuge. [< LL *evasio, -onis* < *evadere*. See EVADE.]

e·va·sive (i·vā'siv) *adj.* Tending or seeking to evade; marked by evasion; elusive. —**e·va'sive·ly** *adv.* —**e·va'sive·ness** *n.*

eve (ēv) *n.* **1** *Poetic* Evening. **2** The evening before a church festival or saint's day: Christmas *Eve*. **3** The time immediately preceding some event. [Var. of EVEN[2]]

e·vec·tics (i·vek'tiks) *n. pl* (construed as singular)

1 The art of developing health, physical vigor, strength, and energy. **2** Hygiene. [< Gk. *euektikē* (*technē*) (skill) of good health < *eu echein* be well]

e·vec·tion (i·vek′shən) *n. Astron.* The largest inequality in the motion of the moon, due to the action of the sun, which causes periodic changes in the eccentricity of the moon's orbit. [< LL *evectio, -onis* < *evehere* < *e-* out + *vehere* carry] — **e·vec′tion·al** *adj.*

e·ven[1] (ē′vən) *adj.* **1** Free from inequalities or irregularities; level; uniform. **2** Divisible by 2 without remainder: said of numbers. **3** On the same level or line. **4** Without advantage on either side; of the same character; equal; fair; impartial. **5** Unvarying in disposition, action, or quality. **6** Whole or entire: said of money, numbers, etc.: *even* dollars. See synonyms under FLAT, HORIZONTAL, JUST, LEVEL, SMOOTH. —**of even date** *Law* Of identical date. —**on an even keel** Smoothly: from a nautical phrase applied to a ship with the same draft of water forward and aft. —**to get even** To get revenge; retaliate. —*adv.* **1** To a like degree; at the very time; so far or so much as; exactly; precisely; fully; quite: used to express emphasis, surprise, concession, or extension to what might not be expected: *even* to the end, intelligible *even* to a child. **2** As much as; yet: They would not believe the report, nor *even* the evidence. **3** Smoothly; regularly; evenly: His verses ran *even.* **4** *Obs.* Exactly. —*v.t.* & *v.i.* **1** To make or become even or level; balance: often with *up.* **2** To make or become equal; equalize. [OE *efen* level] —**e′ven·ly** *adv.* —**e′ven·ness** *n.*

e·ven[2] (ē′vən) *n. Archaic* **1** Evening. **2** The eve before a church festival, an event, etc. [OE *æfen*]

e·ven-hand·ed (ē′vən·han′did) *adj.* Treating all alike; impartial. —**e′ven-hand′ed·ly** *adv.* —**e′ven-hand′ed·ness** *n.*

eve·ning (ēv′ning) *n.* **1** The closing part of the day and beginning of the night; in a strict sense, from sunset till dark; in common speech, the latter part of the day and the earlier part of the night, until bedtime: used also adjectively: *evening* prayer. ◆ Collateral adjective: *vesperal.* **2** *U.S. Dial.* Afternoon until dark. **3** A closing or declining part of any state or period: the *evening* of life. [OE *æfnung* < *æfnian* grow to evening]

evening primrose 1 A stout, erect American biennial herb (*Oenothera biennis*), with conspicuous yellow flowers opening in the evening. **2** Any other species of this genus.

evening star A bright planet when visible in the west just after sunset: especially applied to Venus: also called *Hesperus* and *Vesper.*

e·ven-mind·ed (ē′vən·mīn′did) *adj.* Characterized by equanimity; fair; just.

e·vent (i·vent′) *n.* **1** Anything that happens or comes to pass. **2** The result or outcome of any action. **3** A contingent occurrence or state of things. **4** One incident in a series, as of games. **5** *Philos.* Anything that occurs, usually manifesting changes and lasting only a relatively short time: thus opposed to *object,* which endures. [< OF < L *eventus* < *e-* out + *venire* come] —**e·vent′less** *adj.*
Synonyms: case, chance, circumstance, consequence, contingency, end, episode, fact, fortune, incident, issue, occurrence, outcome, possibility, result, sequel. Etymologically, the *incident* is that which falls in, the *event* that which comes out; *event* is thus greater and more signal than *incident*; we speak of trifling *incidents,* great *events*; *incidents* of daily life, *events* of history. *Circumstance* agrees with *incident* in denoting a matter of relatively slight importance, but implies a more direct connection with the principal matter as indicated in the phrase "circumstantial evidence." An *occurrence* is, etymologically, that which we run against, without thought of its origin, connection, or tendency. An *episode* is connected with the main course of *events,* like an *incident* or *circumstance,* but is of more independent interest and importance. *Outcome* is the Saxon, and *event* the Latin for expressing the same original idea. *Consequence* and *result* express more of logical connection and are more comprehensive. The *end* may be simple cessation; the *event* is what has been

accomplished; the *event* of a war is victory or defeat; the *end* of the war is reached when a treaty of peace is signed. Since the future is contingent, *event* comes to have the meaning of a *contingency*; as, In the *event* of his death, the policy will at once fall due. Compare CIRCUMSTANCE, CONSEQUENCE, END.

e·vent·ful (i·vent′fəl) *adj.* Attended or characterized by important or noteworthy events; also, momentous. —**e·vent′ful·ly** *adv.* —**e·vent′ful·ness** *n.*

e·ven·tu·al (i·ven′chōō·əl) *adj.* **1** Pertaining to or being a result; consequential; ultimate. **2** Dependent upon a final contingency. —**e·ven′tu·al·ly** *adv.*

e·ven·tu·al·i·ty (i·ven′chōō·al′ə·tē) *n. pl.* **·ties 1** The character of happening contingently or as a result. **2** A consequential event or issue.

e·ven·tu·ate (i·ven′chōō·āt) *v.t.* **·at·ed, ·at·ing 1** To have a particular event or issue; result. **2** To be the event or issue; happen. —**e·ven′tu·a′tion** *n.*

ev·er (ev′ər) *adv.* **1** At any time; in any case: better than *ever.* **2** In any degree: Run as fast as *ever* you can. **3** Under all circumstances; invariably; always. [OE *æfre*]

ever and anon Now and then; at one time and at another; repeatedly.

ev·er·glade (ev′ər·glād) *n.* A tract of low swampy land covered with tall grass. —**The Everglades** A swampy subtropical region of southern Florida; 100 miles long, 50–75 miles wide.

ev·er·green (ev′ər·grēn′) *adj.* Retaining verdure throughout the year: opposite of *deciduous.* —*n.* **1** A tree or other plant which retains its foliage throughout the year, as the pine, fir, hemlock, laurel, etc. **2** A branch or twig of an evergreen plant or tree, or the plant, used for decoration: Christmas *evergreens.*

evergreen oak Any of various live oaks of the United States; especially, *Quercus nigra* of the South, and encina.

ev·er·last·ing (ev′ər·las′ting, -läs′-) *adj.* **1** Lasting forever; eternal. **2** Interminable; incessant. —*n.* **1** Past or future endless duration; eternity. **2** A plant, the flowers of which retain their form and color when dried, as the cudweed. **3** Prunella, a durable woolen material. **4** A game of cards. See synonyms under ETERNAL, IMMORTAL. —**the Everlasting** The Eternal; God. —**ev·er·last′ing·ly** *adv.* —**ev·er·last′ing·ness** *n.*

ev·er·more (ev′ər·môr′, -mōr′) *adv.* During all time; always.

e·ver·si·ble (i·vûr′sə·bəl) *adj.* Capable of being everted.

e·ver·sion (i·vûr′zhən) *n.* A turning outward or inside out. [< L *eversio, -onis* < *evertere.* See EVERT.]

e·vert (i·vûrt′) *v.t.* To turn inside out; turn outward. [< L *evertere* < *e-* out + *vertere* turn] —**e·ver·tile** (i·vûr′til) *adj.*

e·ver·tor (i·vûr′tər) *n. Anat.* A muscle which serves to rotate an organ or a part outward.

eve·ry (ev′rē, ev′ər·ē) *adj.* **1** Each individual or part, as of an aggregate whole; all taken one by one. **2** All possible; very great: Show him *every* consideration. **3** *Obs.* All: with plural noun. —*pron. Law* Every one; each. [ME < OE *æfre* ever + *ælc* each]
Synonyms (*adj.*): all, any, both, each, either. *Any* makes no selection and may not reach to the full limits of *all*; *each* and *every* make no exception or omission, and must extend to *all*; *all* sweeps in the units as part of a total. *each* and *every* proceed through the units to the total. A promise made to *all* omits none; a promise made to *any* may not reach *all*; a promise made to *every* one is so made that no individual shall fail to be aware of it; a promise made to *each* is made to the individuals personally, one by one. *Each* divides, *both* unites; if a certain sum is given to *each* of two persons, *both* (together) receive twice the amount; a man may fire *both* barrels of a gun by a single movement; if he fires *each* barrel, he discharges them separately. *Either* denotes one of two, indefinitely to the exclusion of the other; *either* is also in good, but somewhat rare, use, in the sense of *each* or *both* of two, taken separately and indifferently; as, on *either* side of the river.

eve·ry·bod·y (ev′rē·bod′ē, -bud′ē) *pron.* Every

person; everyone.
◆ **everybody, everyone** *Everybody,* like *everyone,* calls for a singular verb and singular pronouns of reference: *Everybody* here has had *his* turn.

eve·ry·day (ev′rē·dā′, -dā′) *adj.* **1** Suitable for every day; ordinary; *everyday* clothes. **2** Happening every day. **3** Having general utility; practicable. See synonyms under GENERAL, USUAL.

every once in a while Every now and then.

eve·ry·one (ev′rē·wun′, -wən) *pron.* Everybody; every person: *Everyone* likes ice-cream. See note under EVERYBODY.

every one Each individual person or thing out of the whole number, excepting none: *Every one* of the men is ill.

eve·ry·thing (ev′rē·thing′) *pron.* Each one in a collection or number of things, none being omitted; whatever exists; whatever pertains to some specified person, thing, place, condition, etc. —*n.* That which is of the highest importance or which includes all things: Health is *everything* to the worker.

eve·ry·where (ev′rē·hwâr′) *adv.* **1** At or in every place. **2** Wherever.

Eve's-cup (ēvz′kup′) *n.* An insectivorous American pitcherplant (*Sarracenia flava*) with trumpet leaves, crimson throat, and yellow flowers.

e·vict (i·vikt′) *v.t.* **1** To expel (a tenant) by legal process; dispossess; put out. **2** To recover, as property, by legal process. See synonyms under BANISH. [< L *evictus,* pp. of *evincere* < *e-* out + *vincere* conquer] —**e·vic′tion** *n.* —**e·vic′tor** *n.*

ev·i·dence (ev′ə·dəns) *n.* **1** That which makes evident or clear, whether taken singly or collectively. **2** Any ground or reason for knowledge or certitude in knowledge. **3** Proof, whether immediate or derived by inference. **4** A fact or body of facts on which a proof, belief, or judgment is based. **5** *Law* That by means of which a fact is established: distinguished from *proof,* which is the result of evidence, and *testimony,* which is evidence given orally. **6** Evidentness; clearness. See synonyms under CERTAINTY, DEMONSTRATION, PROOF, TESTIMONY. —**circumstantial evidence** Evidence consisting of circumstances which furnish reasonable ground for believing or deciding as to the existence of fact, or the guilt or innocence of an accused person. —**in evidence** Present; at hand; to be seen; conspicuous. —*v.t.* **·denced, ·denc·ing 1** To make evident; show clearly; display. **2** To support by one's testimony; attest.

ev·i·dent (ev′ə·dənt) *adj.* Plain, manifest, or clear, as to the mind or the senses; obvious. [< L *evidens, -entis,* ppr. of *evidere* < *e-* out + *videre* see] —**ev′i·dent·ly** *adv.*
Synonyms: apparent, clear, conspicuous, discernible, distinct, glaring, indubitable, manifest, obvious, open, overt, palpable, patent, perceptible, plain, tangible, transparent, unmistakable, visible.

ev·i·den·tial (ev′ə·den′shəl) *adj.* **1** Of the nature of or furnishing evidence. **2** Based or relying on evidence. —**ev′i·den′tial·ly** *adv.*

e·vil (ē′vəl) *adj.* **1** Morally bad; contrary to divine or righteous law; wrong or wicked; sinful or depraved. **2** Possessing injurious nature or qualities; unwholesome; noxious. **3** Characterized by calamity, trouble, or sorrow. **4** Of ill repute. See synonyms under BAD[1], IMMORAL, PERNICIOUS. —*n.* **1** Wicked conduct or disposition as showing depravity or as being destructive of good; sinfulness as injurious; moral depravity. **2** Something that harms or hurts; that which hinders prosperity, diminishes welfare, or prevents the enjoyment of a good; affliction. **3** King's evil. See synonyms under ABOMINATION, INJURY, SIN. —*adv.* In an evil manner. [OE *yfel*] —**e′vil·ly** *adv.* —**e′vil·ness** *n.*

Evil One Satan.

e·vince (i·vins′) *v.t.* **e·vinced, e·vinc·ing 1** To show plainly or certainly; make evident; display. **2** *Obs.* To conquer. [< L *evincere.* See EVICT.] —**e·vin′ci·ble** *adj.* —**e·vin′ci·bly** *adv.*

e·vin·cive (i·vin′siv) *adj.* Capable of proving; convincing.

ev·i·ra·tion (ev′i·rā′shən) *n.* **1** Castration. **2** *Psychiatry* A paranoid condition in which a man develops the conviction that he is a woman, especially in relation to sexual behavior and personality traits. [< L *e-* out

+ *vir* man + -ATION]

e·vis·cer·ate (i·vis′ə·rāt) *v.t.* **·at·ed, ·at·ing**
1 To disembowel. **2** To remove the essential
or vital parts of (anything). — *adj.* (i·vis′ə·
rit) *Surg.* Disemboweled: an *eviscerate* abdomen. [< L *evisceratus,* pp. of *eviscerare* < *e-*
out + *viscera* entrails]

ev·i·ta·ble (ev′ə·tə·bəl) *adj.* That may be
escaped, avoided, or shunned; avoidable. [< L
evitabilis < *evitare* < *e-.* out + *vitare* shun]

ev·o·ca·ble (ev′ə·kə·bəl) *adj.* Capable of being
evoked or called forth.

ev·o·ca·tion (ev′ə·kā′shən) *n.* **1** A calling forth
or out; summoning, as of memories, etc. **2**
Specifically, the summoning of a spirit, or of
the dead, from a grave. **3** The formula used
in such a summons. **4** In civil law, the transference of a suit from a lower to a higher
court. [< L *evocatio, -onis* < *evocare.* See
EVOKE.]

e·voc·a·tive (i·vok′ə·tiv, -vō′kə-) *adj.* Evoking;
calling forth; fitted or calculated to evoke or
call forth.

ev·o·ca·tor (ev′ə·kā′tər) *n.* One who summons
up spirits.

e·voke (i·vōk′) *v.t.* **e·voked, e·vok·ing 1** To
call or summon forth; elicit, as an emotion
or reply. **2** To summon up (spirits) by or as
by spells. [< L *evo-*
care < *e-* out + *vo-*
care call]

ev·o·lute (ev′ə·lōōt) *n.*
Math. A curve which
is the locus of the
center of curvature
of another curve, its
involute, and there-
fore tangent to all
its normals; a curve
that is the envelope
of all the normals
of another curve.
[< L *evolutus,* pp.
of *evolvere.* See
EVOLVE.]

EVOLUTE OF
AN ELLIPSE

ABC is the evolute of ellipse *ADC.* Cord *AC,* if
fastened at *A* and swung
so as to encompass *AB,*
will describe arc *CD* of
the ellipse.

ev·o·lu·tion (ev′ə·
lōō′shən) *n.* **1** The
act or process of
unfolding; develop-
ment or growth,
usually in slow stages and from simpler forms
to those which are more complex: the *evolution* of the telephone. **2** *Biol.* **a** The doctrine
that all forms of life originated by descent,
with gradual or abrupt modifications, from
preexisting forms which themselves trace backward in a continuing series to the most rudimentary organisms. **b** The series of changes
by which a given type of organism has acquired the physiological and structural characteristics differentiating it from other types;
phylogeny. **3** The old theory of preformation,
that the germ contains all the parts of the
mature organism in minute form; development from such a germ: opposed to *epigenesis.*
4 *Math.* The operation of extracting a root.
5 A move or maneuver, as of troops. **6** *Philos.*
The cosmological theory that accounts for the
universe and its contents by the combination
of separate and diffused atoms existing originally in a condition of absolute homogeneity.
7 A movement forming one of a series of complex motions; hence, any intricate or involved
form: the *evolutions* of the labyrinth. **8** Anything evolved; also, a series unfolded. — **ev′o-
lu′tion·al** *adj.* — **ev′o·lu′tion·al·ly** *adv.* — **ev′o-
lu′tion·ism** *n.* — **ev′o·lu′tion·ist** *adj.* & *n.*

ev·o·lu·tion·ar·y (ev′ə·lōō′shən·er′ē) *adj.* Pertaining or relating to evolution, in any sense.

e·volve (i·volv′) *v.* **e·volved, e·volv·ing 1** To
unfold or expand. **2** To work out; develop:
to *evolve* a plan. **3** *Biol.* To develop, as by a
differentiation of parts or functions, to a more
highly organized condition. **4** To give or throw
off (vapor, heat, etc.); emit. — *v.i.* **5** To
undergo the process of evolution. **6** To come
out; develop. [< L *evolvere* unroll < *e-* out
+ *volvere* roll] — **e·volv′a·ble** *adj.* — **e·volv′ent**
adj. & *n.* — **e·volve′ment** *n.*

e·von·y·mus (i·von′ə·məs) See EUONYMUS.

e·vul·sion (i·vul′shən) *n.* A plucking out; forcible extraction. [< L *evulsio, -onis* < *e-* out +
vellere pluck]

ewe (yōō, *Dial.* yō) *n.* A female sheep. ◆ Homophone: *yew.* [OE *eowu*]

ex¹ (eks) *prep.* **1** In finance, without the right
to have or to participate in; excluding: said
of stocks, as *ex* bonus, *ex* dividend, etc. **2** In
commerce, free out of; not subject to charge
until taken out of, as *ex* elevator, *ex* ship, *ex*
store, etc. **3** *U.S.* From, but not having graduated with a given class: *ex* '54. [< L *ex-* out]

ex² (eks) *n.* *pl.* **ex·es** The letter X, x.

ex-¹ *prefix* **1** Out; out of: *exit, exhale.* **2** Remove from; free from: *exonerate.* **3** Thoroughly: *exasperate, excruciate.* **4** Without;
not having: *excaudate.* **5** Once; formerly
(hyphenated): *ex-president.* Also: *e-* before
consonants except *c, f, p, q, s, t,* as in *edentate,
erode, evade; ef-* before *f,* as in *efferent.* [< L
ex- < *ex* from, out of]

ex-² *prefix* Out of; from; forth: *exodus.* Also,
before consonants, *ec-,* as in *eclipse.* [< Gk.
ex-, ek- < *ex* out]

ex-³ Var. of EXO-.

ex·ac·er·bate (ig·zas′ər·bāt) *v.t.* **·bat·ed, ·bat·ing**
1 To make more sharp or severe; aggravate
(feelings, a disease, pain, etc.). **2** To embitter
or irritate (someone). [< L *exacerbatus,* pp. of
exacerbare < *ex-* completely + *acerbus* bitter,
harsh]

ex·ac·er·ba·tion (ig·zas′ər·bā′shən) *n.* **1** The
act of exacerbating, or the state of being ex-
acerbated. **2** *Pathol.* Increased severity, as
in the symptoms of a disease.

ex·act (ig·zakt′) *adj.* **1** Perfectly conformed
to a standard; nicely adjusted; strictly accurate
or correct. **2** Precise: the *exact* sum. **3** Accurately or precisely conceived or expressed;
characterized by definite knowledge or principles; rigorously determined; definite: *exact*
thinking. **4** Capable of yielding results of high
precision and accuracy: an *exact* instrument.
See synonyms under CORRECT, JUST, MINUTE,
PARTICULAR, PRECISE. — *v.t.* **1** To compel the
yielding or payment of; extort. **2** To demand;
insist upon as a right. **3** To require; call for:
The task will *exact* great effort. See synonyms
under DEMAND. [< L *exactus,* pp. of *exigere*
determine < *ex-* out + *agere* drive. Related to
EXAMINE.] — **ex·act′a·ble** *adj.* — **ex·act′er, ex·
ac′tor** *n.*

ex·act·ing (ig·zak′ting) *adj.* Making unreasonable or inconsiderate demands; taxing; arduous. See synonyms under HARD, IMPERIOUS.
— **ex·act′ing·ly** *adv.* — **ex·act′ing·ness** *n.*

ex·ac·tion (ig·zak′shən) *n.* **1** The act of exacting; extortion. **2** Something exacted; a compulsory levy. See synonyms under TAX.

ex·act·ly (ig·zakt′lē) *adv.* **1** In an exact manner;
precisely. **2** Yes indeed; quite so.

ex·act·ness (ig·zakt′nis) *n.* The condition or
quality of being accurate and precise. Also
ex·act′i·tude (-tōōd, -tyōōd).

exact science A science the data of which are
susceptible to precise formulation and rigorous
mathematical analysis, especially one that permits accurate prediction of future events within
its prescribed field, as physics or astronomy:
distinguished from *descriptive science, normative science.*

ex·ag·ger·ate (ig·zaj′ə·rāt) *v.* **·at·ed, ·at·ing** *v.t.*
1 To describe or represent beyond the bounds
of truth; overstate. **2** To increase or enlarge
immoderately. — *v.i.* **3** To use exaggeration.
See synonyms under INCREASE. [< L *exaggera-
tus,* pp. of *exaggerare* < *ex-* out + *agger*
mound, heap] — **ex·ag′ger·at·ed** *adj.* — **ex·ag′·
ger·at·ed·ly** *adv.* — **ex·ag′ger·at·ing·ly** *adv.*
— **ex·ag′ger·a′tor** *n.*

ex·ag·ger·a·tion (ig·zaj′ə·rā′shən) *n.* The act
of exaggerating; overstatement; hyperbole. See
synonyms under CARICATURE.

ex·ag·ger·a·tive (ig·zaj′ə·rā′tiv) *adj.* Tending
to or marked by exaggeration. Also **ex·ag′ger·
a·to′ry** (-tôr′ē, -tō′rē). — **ex·ag′ger·a·tive·ly**
adv. — **ex·ag′ger·a·tive·ness** *n.*

ex·alt (ig·zôlt′) *v.t.* **1** To raise on high; lift up;
elevate. **2** To raise in rank, character, honor,
etc. **3** To glorify or praise; pay honor to. **4** To
fill with delight, pride, etc. **5** To increase the
force or intensity of, as colors. See synonyms
under HEIGHTEN, PROMOTE, RAISE. [< L *exaltare*
< *ex-* out + *altus* high] — **ex·alt′er** *n.*

ex·alt·ed (ig·zôl′tid) *adj.* **1** Raised up or aloft;
elevated. **2** Raised in rank, position, or dignity. **3** Dignified; sublime: *exalted* poetry.

4 Intensely joyous or abnormally elated. —
ex·alt′ed·ly *adv.* — **ex·alt′ed·ness** *n.*

ex·am (ig·zam′) *n. Colloq.* An examination.

ex·am·i·na·tion (ig·zam′ə·nā′shən) *n.* **1** The
act or process of examining or being examined;
careful scrutiny or inquiry; investigation; inspection. **2** A testing of knowledge, progress,
skill, qualifications, etc: an *examination* in
history, civil service *examination.* **3** *Law*
Inquiry by means of interrogation or testimony; the result of such inquiry; testimony
reduced to writing. See synonyms under IN-
QUIRY. [< F < L *examinatio, -onis* < *examinare.*
See EXAMINE.] — **ex·am′i·na′tion·al** *adj.*

ex·am·ine (ig·zam′in) *v.t.* **·ined, ·in·ing 1** To
inspect or scrutinize with care; investigate
critically. **2** To test by questions or exercises
as to qualifications, fitness, etc., as a pupil.
3 To question in order to elicit facts, etc.
4 To assay; analyze. [< OF *examiner* < L
examinare < *examen* a testing < *ex-* out + *ag-,*
root of *agere* drive. Related to EXACT.] — **ex·
am′in·a·ble** *adj.* — **ex·am′i·na·to′ri·al** (-tôr′ē·əl,
-tō′rē-) *adj.* — **ex·am′i·nee′** *n.* — **ex·am′in·er** *n.*
Synonyms: canvass, consider, criticize, dis-
cuss, explore, inspect, interrogate, investigate,
observe, overhaul, ponder, question, ransack,
scrutinize, search, study, test, try, view, weigh.
See CONSIDER, INQUIRE, REVIEW. Compare synonyms for DELIBERATE.

ex·am·ple (ig·zam′pəl, -zäm′-) *n.* **1** A thing or
person suitable to be used as a model. **2** An
instance of something to be avoided; an act,
especially a punishment, serving or designed
to serve as a warning. **3** A sample; specimen.
4 An instance serving to illustrate a rule. **5** A
problem to be solved. **6** That with which something may be compared; precedent; parallel.
— *v.t. Obs.* **1** To exemplify. **2** To teach by
example. [< OF, earlier *essample* < L *exemplum* something taken out < *eximere* < *ex-*
out + *emere* buy. Doublet of SAMPLE.]
Synonyms (noun): archetype, exemplar, exemplification, ideal, model, pattern, precedent,
prototype, sample, specimen, standard, type,
warning. From its original sense of *sample* or
specimen (L *exemplum*), *example* derives the
seemingly contradictory meanings, on the one
hand of a *pattern* or *model,* and on the other
hand of a *warning*—a *sample* or *specimen* of
what is to be followed, or of what is to be
shunned. An *example,* however, may be more
than a *sample* or *specimen* of any class; it may
be the very *archetype* or *prototype* to which
the whole class must conform. *Example* comes
nearer to *model* than to the necessary exactness
of the *pattern.* In its application to a person
or thing, *exemplar* can scarcely be distinguished
from *example;* but *example* is most frequently
used for an act, or course of action, for which
exemplar is not used; as, one sets a good (or
a bad) *example.* An *exemplification* is an illustrative working out in action of a principle or
law, without any reference to its being copied
or repeated; an *example* guides, an *exemplification* illustrates or explains. Compare AR-
CHETYPE, MODEL, PRECEDENT, SAMPLE.

ex·an·i·mate (ig·zan′ə·mit, -māt) *adj.* **1** Deprived of life; inanimate. **2** Having no animation; dispirited; spiritless. [< L *exanimatus,*
pp. of *exanimare* kill < *ex-* out + *animus*
breath, life]

ex·an·i·ma·tion (ig·zan′ə·mā′shən) *n.* Real or
apparent death; swooning.

ex·an·the·ma (ek′san·thē′mə) *n.* *pl.* **·them·a·ta**
(-them′ə·tə, -thē′mə·tə) *Pathol.* A breaking out
upon the skin; a rash, or a disease accompanied by rash, as smallpox or measles; specifically, usually in the plural, the eruptive fevers.
[< LL < Gk. *exanthēma* a blossoming < *ex-*
out + *anthos* a flower] — **ex·an·the·mat·ic**
(ek·san′thi·mat′ik), **ex′an·them′a·tous** (-them′-
ə·təs) *adj.*

ex·as·per·ate (ig·zas′pə·rāt) *v.t.* **·at·ed, ·at·ing**
1 To irritate exceedingly; enrage. **2** To make
worse; intensify; inflame. See synonyms under
AFFRONT, INCENSE. [< L *exasperatus,* pp. of
exasperare < *ex-* out + *asper* rough] — **ex·as′·
per·at·er** *n.* — **ex·as′per·at·ing** *adj.* — **ex·as′·
per·at·ing·ly** *adv.*

ex·ca·vate (eks′kə·vāt) *v.t.* **vat·ed, ·vat·ing**
1 To make a hole or cavity in; hollow or dig
out. **2** To form or make by hollowing, digging

out, or scooping. **3** To remove by digging or scooping out, as soil. **4** To uncover by digging, as ruins. [<L *excavatus*, pp. of *excavare* <*ex-* out + *cavus* hollow]

ex·ca·va·tion (eks'kə·vā'shən) *n.* **1** A digging out. **2** A cavity or hollow formed by excavating. See synonyms under HOLE.

EXCAVATOR
Side view of 27-ton ditch excavator
operated by one man.

ex·ca·va·tor (eks'kə·vā'tər) *n.* **1** One who or that which excavates. **2** A steam shovel or dredging machine.

ex·ceed (ik·sēd') *v.t.* **1** To go or be beyond; surpass, as in quantity, quality, measure, or value. **2** To go beyond the limit or extent of: to *exceed* one's income. — *v.i.* **3** To be superior; surpass others. [<F *excéder* <L *excedere* <*ex-* out, beyond + *cedere* go]

ex·ceed·ing·ly (ik·sē'ding·lē) *adv.* To a greater degree than usual; extremely.

ex·cel (ik·sel') *v.t. & v.i.* **·celled, ·cel·ling** To go beyond or above; outdo; surpass (another or others). See synonyms under LEAD. [<OF *exceller* <L *excellere* rise]

ex·cel·lence (ek'sə·ləns) *n.* **1** Possession of eminently good qualities; great merit, virtue, or goodness. **2** A superior trait. See synonyms under VIRTUE. Also **ex'cel·len·cy.**

ex·cel·lent (ek'sə·lənt) *adj.* **1** Having good qualities in a high degree; superior in worth or value. **2** *Obs.* Eminent; excelling. [<OF <L *excellens, -entis*, ppr. of *excellere* rise]
Synonyms: admirable, capital, choice, fine, first-class, first-rate, precious, prime, select, superior, transcendent, valuable, worthy. That which is *excellent* excels, but an object that is *valuable* or a man who is *worthy* so far excels the majority of persons or things that these words have become close synonyms for *excellent.* See CHOICE, FINE, GOOD, MORAL. *Antonyms:* bad, base, defective, deficient, good-for-nothing, imperfect, inferior, mean, poor, unworthy, useless, valueless, vile, worthless.

ex·cept (ik·sept') *v.t.* To leave or take out; exclude; omit. — *v.i.* To object; take exception: with *to.* — *prep.* With the exception of; excluding; leaving out; save; but: Tell no one *except* me. — *conj. Archaic* If not that; unless: *except* a man be born again. [<F *excepter* <L *exceptare*, freq. of *excipere* <*ex-* out + *capere* take] — **ex·cep'tor** *n.*

ex·cep·tion (ik·sep'shən) *n.* **1** That which is excluded, as from a list. **2** The act of excepting; exclusion. **3** A captious objection, complaint, or quibble. **4** *Law* A formal objection to the decision of a court during trial. — **to take exception** To take offense; object.

ex·cep·tion·al (ik·sep'shən·əl) *adj.* Unusual or uncommon; superior. See synonyms under IRREGULAR. — **ex·cep'tion·al·ly** *adv.*

ex·cerpt (ek'sûrpt) *n.* An extract from written or printed matter. — *v.t.* (ik·sûrpt') To take out, as a passage or quotation; extract. See synonyms under QUOTE. [<L *excerptus*, pp. of *excerpere* <*ex-* out + *carpere* pluck, seize] — **ex·cerp'tion** *n.* — **ex·cerp'tive** *adj.* — **ex·cerp'tor** *n.*

ex·cess (ik·ses') *n.* **1** That which passes the ordinary, reasonable, or required limit. **2** Inordinate gratification of appetite. **3** The amount by which one thing is greater than another; overplus. — *adj.* (*also* ek'ses) Being above a stipulated amount; extra. [<OF

exces <L *excessus* a departure <*excedere.* See EXCEED.]
Synonyms (noun): dissipation, exorbitance, extravagance, intemperance, lavishness, overplus, prodigality, profusion, redundance, redundancy, superabundance, superfluity, surplus, waste, wastefulness. *Excess* is more than enough of anything, and, since this in many cases indicates a lack either of judgment or of self-control, the word is used frequently in an unfavorable sense. Careless expenditure in *excess* of income is *extravagance*; we may have also *extravagance* of language, professions, etc. As *extravagance* is *excess* in outlay, *exorbitance* is *excess* in demands, especially in pecuniary demands. *Overplus* and *superabundance* denote in the main a satisfactory, and *superfluity* an undesirable, *excess*; *lavishness* and *profusion*, a generous or bountiful *excess. Surplus* has none of the unfavorable meaning that often attaches to *excess*; a *surplus* is that which remains over after all demands are met. *Redundance* or *redundancy* refers chiefly to literary style, denoting an *excess* of words or matter. *Excess* in the moral sense is expressed by *dissipation, prodigality, intemperance,* etc. *Antonyms:* dearth, defect, deficiency, destitution, economy, failure, frugality, inadequacy, insufficiency, lack, need, poverty, scantiness, shortcoming, want.

ex·ces·sive (ik·ses'iv) *adj.* Being in, tending to, marked by excess; immoderate; extreme. See synonyms under IMMODERATE, REDUNDANT. — **ex·ces'sive·ly** *adv.* — **ex·ces'sive·ness** *n.*

ex·change (iks·chānj') *n.* **1** The act of giving or receiving one thing as an equivalent for another; a trade; a bartering: an *exchange* of prisoners. **2** Interchange: an *exchange* of wit, remarks, etc. **3** The mutual giving and receiving of equivalents in money, goods, or labor. **4** The system by which titles to commodities in distant localities are transferred by means of credits, drafts, etc. **5** The rate of exchange. **6** The percentage of difference between currencies of values at two given places. **7** Bills, drafts, etc., presented to a clearing house for settlement. **8** A transition from one experience or condition to another. **9** That which is given or received by interchange, as a periodical or an advertisement exchanged for another. **10** A place where merchants or brokers effect exchanges: a stock *exchange.* See CURB¹. **11** A central telephone office. **12** *Physics* The mutual interaction between the electrons, protons, and other components of the same or different atoms. **13** *Brit.* A labor exchange. See synonyms under INTERCOURSE. — **bill of exchange** A written order or request from one person to another for the payment of money to a third, the amount to be charged to the drawer of the bill. — **par of exchange** The comparison of value in gold of the monetary units of two different countries. — **rate of exchange** The price at which a bill drawn in one country upon a drawee in another country may be sold where drawn. — *v.* **·changed, ·chang·ing** *v.t.* **1** To give or part with for something regarded as of equal value, etc.: to *exchange* francs for dollars. **2** To give and receive in turn; reciprocate. **3** To replace by or give up for something else: to *exchange* poverty for wealth. — *v.i.* **4** To be given or taken in exchange: American money *exchanges* well. **5** To make an exchange. See synonyms under CHANGE. [<AF *eschaunge* <LL *excambium* <*excambiare* <*ex-* out + *cambiare* exchange] — **ex·change'a·bil'i·ty** *n.* — **ex·change'a·ble** *adj.* — **ex·change'a·bly** *adv.*

ex·cheq·uer (iks·chek'ər, eks'chek·ər) *n.* **1** The treasury of a state. **2** *Colloq.* Finances; pecuniary resources. [<OF *eschequier.* See CHECKER.]

ex·cip·i·ent (ik·sip'ē·ənt) *n. Med.* Any inert substance used to give drug preparations a suitable form or pleasant taste. [<L *excipiens, -entis*, ppr. of *excipere.* See EXCEPT.]

ex·cise¹ (ik·sīz', ek'sīz) *n.* **1** An indirect tax on commodities manufactured, produced, sold, used, or transported within a country, including license fees for various sports, trades, or occupations. **2** *Brit.* A branch of the department of the civil service having charge of the inland revenue taxes and duties. See synonyms under TAX. — *v.t.* (ik·sīz')

·cised, ·cis·ing To levy an excise upon. [<MDu. *excijs, accijs* <OF *acceis* <L *ad-* to + *census* a tax] — **ex·cis'a·ble** *adj.*

ex·cise² (ik·sīz') *v.t.* **·cised, ·cis·ing** To cut out or off; remove; extirpate; expunge. [<L *excisus*, pp. of *excidere* <*ex-* out + *caedere* cut] — **ex·ci·sion** (ik·sizh'ən) *n.*

ex·cit·a·ble (ik·sī'tə·bəl) *adj.* **1** Easily excited; high-strung. **2** *Physiol.* Susceptible to stimuli. See synonyms under ARDENT, IMPETUOUS. — **ex·cit'a·ble·ness** *n.* — **ex·cit'a·bly** *adv.*

ex·ci·tant (ik·sī'tənt, ek'sə·tənt) *n.* A drug that excites or stimulates. — *adj.* Adapted or tending to excite or stimulate: also **ex·ci'ta·tive, ex·ci'ta·to·ry** (-tôr'ē, -tō'rē). [<L *excitans, -antis*, ppr. of *excitare.* See EXCITE.]

ex·cite (ik·sīt') *v.t.* **·cit·ed, ·cit·ing** **1** To arouse (a feeling, interest, etc.) into being or activity; evoke: to *excite* admiration or jealousy. **2** To arouse feeling in; stimulate the emotions of: to *excite* someone to hatred. **3** To cause action in; stir to activity or motion: Wine *excites* the tongue. **4** To bring about; stir up: to *excite* a riot. **5** *Physiol.* To cause increased activity in; stimulate (muscles or nerves). **6** *Electr.* To initiate or develop a magnetic field in, as a dynamo. **7** *Physics* To raise an atom or molecule to a higher energy or quantum state, as by heat, radiation, or electron bombardment. See synonyms under ACTUATE, ENCOURAGE, INFLUENCE, INTEREST, PROMOTE, STIR. [<OF *exciter* <L *excitare*, freq. of *exciere* <*ex-* out + *ciere* arouse, stir up] — **ex·cit'ed** *adj.* — **ex·cit'ed·ly** *adv.*

ex·cite·ment (ik·sīt'mənt) *n.* **1** The act of exciting; stimulation. **2** That which excites. **3** The state of being excited, agitated, or aroused; disturbance; agitation. Also *excitation.* See synonyms under ENTHUSIASM, WARMTH.

ex·cit·ing (ik·sī'ting) *adj.* Of a nature to excite; stirring; rousing. — **ex·cit'ing·ly** *adv.*

ex·ci·tor (ik·sī'tər) *n. Physiol.* An afferent nerve connected with the spinal division of the nervous system. Also **ex·cit'er.**

ex·claim (iks·klām') *v.t. & v.i.* To say or cry out abruptly; speak vehemently, as in surprise or anger. [<F *exclamer* <L *exclamare* <*ex-* out + *clamare* cry] — **ex·claim'er** *n.*
Synonyms (verb): call, ejaculate. We may *exclaim* by mere interjections, or by connected words. To *ejaculate* is to throw out brief, disconnected, but coherent utterances of joy, regret, and of appeal, petition, prayer; such devotional utterances are named "ejaculatory prayer." See CALL.

ex·cla·ma·tion (eks'klə·mā'shən) *n.* **1** Clamorous or passionate outcry. **2** An abrupt or emphatic expression; an interjection. **3** An exclamation mark.

exclamation mark A point, note, or mark (!) placed after an interjection or exclamation to indicate its character. Also **exclamation point.**

ex·clam·a·to·ry (iks·klam'ə·tôr'ē, -tō'rē) *adj.* **1** Of the nature of exclamation. **2** Given to or characterized by the use of exclamation.

ex·clave (eks'klāv) *n.* A minor part of a country disjoined from the main part and lying within an alien territory. Compare ENCLAVE. [<EX- + (EN)CLAVE]

ex·clo·sure (eks·klō'zhər) *n. Ecol.* An area set apart from its surroundings as a means of studying the characteristics of a region under controlled conditions. [<EX- + (EN)CLOSURE]

ex·clude (iks·klōōd') *v.t.* **·clud·ed, ·clud·ing** **1** To keep from entering; shut out, as from a place or group. **2** To refuse to notice, consider, or allow for; leave out: opposed to *include.* **3** To put out; eject. [<L *excludere* <*ex-* out + *claudere* close] — **ex·clud'a·ble** *adj.* — **ex·clud'er** *n.*

ex·clu·sion (iks·klōō'zhən) *n.* **1** The act of excluding. **2** The state of being excluded. **3** That which is excluded. [<L *exclusio, -onis* <*excludere.* See EXCLUDE.] — **ex·clu'sion·ism** *n.* — **ex·clu'sion·ist** *n.*

ex·clu·sive (iks·klōō'siv) *adj.* **1** Intended for or possessed by a single group or individual; not shared: *exclusive* fishing rights; *exclusive* information. **2** Restricting membership or patronage; fastidiously reluctant to accept outsiders; hence, snobbish: an *exclusive* club. **3** Singly devoted; undivided: *exclusive* attention to music. **4** Not including; not comprising: usually followed by *of: exclusive* of fees.

5 Not counting the specified terminal points: 20 to 30 *exclusive* (including 21 through 29 and excluding 20 and 30): opposed to *inclusive*. — **ex·clu'sive·ly** *adv.* — **ex·clu'sive·ness** *n.*

ex·cog·i·tate (iks·koj'ə·tāt) *v.t.* **·tat·ed, ·tat·ing** To think out carefully; invent; devise. [<L *excogitatus*, pp. of *excogitare* <*ex-* out + *cogitare* think]

ex·com·mu·ni·cate (eks'kə·myoo'nə·kāt) *v.t.* **·cat·ed, ·cat·ing 1** To punish by an ecclesiastical sentence of exclusion from the sacraments and communion of the church. **2** To expel in disgrace from any organization. — *adj.* Excommunicated. — *n.* An excommunicated person. [<LL *excommunicatus*, pp. of *excommunicare* <*ex-* out + *communicare* share <*communis* common] — **ex'com·mu'ni·ca'tor** *n.*

ex·com·mu·ni·ca·tion (eks'kə·myoo'nə·kā'shən) *n.* The act of excommunicating, or the state of having been excommunicated; a cutting off of an offender from all privileges of church membership.

ex·co·ri·ate (iks·kôr'ē·āt, -skō'rē-) *v.t.* **·at·ed, ·at·ing 1** *Physiol.* To strip off the skin or covering of; flay; abrade; gall. **2** To denounce scathingly. [<L *excoriatus*, pp. of *excoriare* <*ex-* out, off + *corium* skin] — **ex·co'ri·a'tion** *n.*

ex·cre·ment (eks'krə·mənt) *n.* Refuse matter discharged from an animal body; feces. [<L *excrementum* <*excernere*. See EXCRETE.] — **ex'cre·men'tal, ex'cre·men'ta·ry, ex'cre·men·ti'tial** (-tish'əl), **ex'cre·men·ti'tious** (-tish'əs) *adj.*

ex·cres·cence (iks·kres'əns) *n.* **1** An unnatural or disfiguring outgrowth, as a wart on the human body or a nutgall on the oak. **2** Any unnatural addition, outgrowth, or development. **3** A natural outgrowth, as hair.

ex·cres·cent (iks·kres'ənt) *adj.* **1** Of the nature of or pertaining to an excrescence; superfluous. **2** *Phonet.* Intrusive. [<L *excrescens, -entis*, ppr. of *excrescere* <*ex-* out + *crescere* grow]

ex·cre·ta (iks·krē'tə) *n. pl.* **1** *Physiol.* All useless matter eliminated from the bodily system, especially that which has entered into the constitution of the body and is removed in urine or sweat. **2** Noxious or worthless matter generated in a plant body by destructive metabolism. [<NL <L <*excernere*. See EXCRETE.] — **ex·cre'tal** *adj.*

ex·crete (iks·krēt') *v.t.* **·cret·ed, ·cret·ing** To throw off or eliminate, as waste matter, by normal discharge from an organism or any of its tissues. [<L *excretus*, pp. of *excernere* <*ex-* out + *cernere* separate]

ex·cre·tion (iks·krē'shən) *n.* **1** The act of excreting. **2** Matter excreted, particularly sweat, urine, and the juices exuded from certain plants: distinguished from *secretion*.

ex·cru·ci·ate (iks·kroo'shē·āt) *v.t.* **·at·ed, ·at·ing** To inflict extreme pain or agony upon; torture. [<L *excruciatus*, pp. of *excruciare* <*ex-* completely + *cruciare* torture <*crux, crucis* cross] — **ex·cru'ci·a'tion** *n.*

ex·cru·ci·at·ing (iks·kroo'shē·ā'ting) *adj.* Causing or inflicting intense pain; agonizing. — **ex·cru'ci·at'ing·ly** *adv.*

ex·cul·pate (eks'kəl·pāt, ik·skul'-) *v.t.* **·pat·ed, ·pat·ing** To declare free from blame; prove innocent of guilt or fault; exonerate. See synonyms under JUSTIFY. [<EX-¹ + L *culpatus*, pp. of *culpare* blame <*culpa* a fault] — **ex·culp'a·ble** *adj.*

ex·cur·rent (ik·skûr'ənt) *adj.* **1** Running or passing out. **2** *Biol.* Running through to the surface, summit, or tip, as the midrib of a leaf, or the canal of a sponge. [<L *excurrens, -entis*, ppr. of *excurrere* <*ex-* out + *currere* run]

ex·cur·sion (ik·skûr'zhən, -shən) *n.* **1** A short journey, usually for pleasure. **2** A boat or train trip at reduced rates, accommodating groups of excursionists to specified points. **3** A body of excursionists collectively. **4** A digression; deviation. **5** A running out or going forth. **6** *Physics* Half the amplitude of vibration; the movement of a vibrating or oscillating body from its mean to either of its extreme states or positions. **7** *Astron.* The apparent movement to and fro of a heavenly body, as of a satellite about its primary. See synonyms under JOURNEY. [<L *excursio, -onis* <*ex-*

currere. See EXCURRENT.]

ex·cur·sus (eks·kûr'səs) *n. pl.* **·sus·es** or **·sus 1** A supplemental dissertation added to a work. **2** A wandering off; digression. [<L, a going out <*excurrere*. See EXCURRENT.]

ex·cuse (ik·skyooz') *v.t.* **·cused, ·cus·ing 1** To pardon and overlook (a fault, offense, etc.); regard as unimportant. **2** To try to free (someone) from blame; seek to remove blame from: I *excused* myself to him. **3** To offer a reason or apology for (an error, fault, etc.); try to obtain pardon for or minimize. **4** To be or serve as a reason for; justify: His energy does not *excuse* his lateness. **5** To release from attendance, a duty, promise, etc. **6** To refrain from exacting or enforcing, as a demand or claim. See synonyms under JUSTIFY, PALLIATE, PARDON. — *n.* (ik·skyoos') **1** A plea in extenuation of an offense, neglect, or failure. **2** The act of excusing. **3** A reason for excusing. See synonyms under APOLOGY, PRETENSE. [<OF *excuser* <L *excusare* <*ex-* out, away + *causa* charge, accusation] — **ex·cus'a·ble** *adj.* — **ex·cus'a·ble·ness** *n.* — **ex·cus'a·bly** *adv.* — **ex·cus'er** *n.*

ex·e·crate (ek'sə·krāt) *v.* **·crat·ed, ·crat·ing** *v.t.* **1** To curse, or call down evil upon. **2** To detest; abhor. — *v.i.* **3** To utter curses. [<L *execratus*, pp. of *execrari* curse <*ex-* out + *sacrare* devote to a god <*sacer* holy, accursed] — **ex'e·cra'tor** *n.*

ex·ec·u·tant (ig·zek'yə·tənt) *n.* One who executes or performs; specifically, a skilled musical performer.

ex·e·cute (ek'sə·kyoot) *v.t.* **·cut·ed, ·cut·ing 1** To do or carry out fully: to *execute* an order. **2** To put in force; administer, as a law. **3** To put to death by legal sentence. **4** *Law* To make legal or valid by fulfilling all requirements of law. **5** To do or perform, as a maneuver or a musical work. **6** To produce, as according to a preconceived plan or design: to *execute* a portrait in oils. [<L *executus*, var. of *exsecutus*, pp. of *exsequi* <*ex-* out + *sequi* follow] — **ex'e·cut'a·ble** *adj.* — **ex'e·cut'er** *n.*

Synonyms: administer, do, enforce, perform.

ex·e·cu·tion (ek'sə·kyoo'shən) *n.* **1** The act of executing. **2** *Law* A judicial writ, as for the seizure of goods, etc. **3** The act of carrying into effect or enforcing any legislative or judicial act or decree. **4** The signing, as of a deed. **5** The infliction of capital punishment. **6** Style of performance; technical skill, as in music or art. **7** Effective work: said especially of warlike operations. See synonyms under ACT, OPERATION.

ex·ec·u·tive (ig·zek'yə·tiv) *adj.* **1** Having the function, power, or skill of executing or performing. **2** Having ability or aptitude for directing or controlling. **3** Connected with or pertaining to direction or control; carrying into effect; administrative, as distinguished from *judicial* and *legislative:* an *executive* department of the government. Compare JUDICIAL, LEGISLATIVE. **4** Adroit or dexterous in execution. — *n.* **1** An official personage or body charged with the administration of a government: applied in the United States to the president and to governors. **2** The executive branch of government. **3** A director of a business or other organization.

executive agreement *U.S.* An international agreement concluded by the president and not requiring Senate ratification.

Executive Mansion 1 The White House, Washington, D.C.: the official residence of the president of the United States. **2** The residence of the governor of a State.

executive officer *U.S.* The principal officer assisting a commanding officer. Compare CHIEF OF STAFF (def. 2).

executive session A session of the U.S. Senate, closed to the public and convened to consider confidential business.

ex·ec·u·tor (ig·zek'yə·tər) *n.* **1** *Law* A person nominated by the will of another to execute the will. **2** One who executes, in any sense.

ex·ec·u·to·ri·al (ig·zek'yə·tôr'ē·əl, -tō'rē-) *adj.* **1** Executive. **2** In Scots law, of or pertaining to the execution of a judicial writ.

ex·ec·u·to·ry (ig·zek'yə·tôr'ē, -tō'rē) *adj.* **1** Pertaining to execution; executive; adminis-

trative. **2** *Law* That is to be executed or put into effect; especially, becoming operative on a future contingency; an *executory* consideration, contract, or devise.

ex·ec·u·trix (ig·zek'yə·triks) *n. fem. pl.* **ex·ec·u·trix·es** or **ex·ec·u·tri·ces** (-trī'sēz) *Law* A female executor.

ex·e·dra (ek'sə·drə, ik·sē'drə) *n. pl.* **·drae** (-drē) *Archit.* **1** In classical antiquity, a range of permanent seats, or a platform with seats, by the roadside, in a court, or otherwise placed, built of masonry and often curved in plan, intended for rest and conversation. **2** A curved seat, accommodating several persons, for use in the open air. **3** An apse, niche, window recess, or the like. [<L <Gk. *exedra* <*ex-* out + *hedra* a seat]

EXEDRA

ex·e·ge·sis (ek'sə·jē'sis) *n. pl.* **·ses** (-sēz) Explanation of the language and thought of a literary work; especially, Biblical exposition or interpretation. [<Gk. *exēgēsis* <*exegeesthai* explain <*ex-* out + *hegeesthai* <*agein* lead]

ex·e·get·ic (ek'sə·jet'ik) *adj.* Pertaining to exegesis; expository; explanatory. [<Gk. *exegētikos* <*exēgēsis*. See EXEGESIS.] — **ex'e·get'i·cal·ly** *adv.*

ex·em·plar (ig·zem'plər, -plär) *n.* **1** A model, pattern, or original, to be copied or imitated. **2** The mental conception or image of something to be produced. **3** A specimen or transcript; especially, a specimen copy of a book or writing. **4** A typical example; archetype. See synonyms under EXAMPLE. [<OF *exemplaire* <L *exemplarium* <*exemplum* EXAMPLE; infl. in form by L *exemplar* typical <*exemplum*]

ex·em·pla·ry (ig·zem'plər·ē) *adj.* **1** Serving or fitted to serve as a model or example worthy of imitation; commendable: *exemplary* conduct. **2** Serving as or furnishing a warning example: *exemplary* damages; a most *exemplary* punishment. **3** Serving to exemplify; illustrative. — **ex·em'pla·ri·ly** *adv.* — **ex·em'pla·ri·ness** *n.*

ex·em·pli·fy (ig·zem'plə·fī) *v.t.* **·fied, ·fy·ing 1** To show by example; illustrate. **2** *Law* **a** To prove by an attested copy. **b** To make an authenticated transcript from, as a public record. [<Med. L *exemplificare* <*exemplum* EXAMPLE + *facere* make] — **ex·em'pli·fi·ca'tive** *adj.*

ex·empt (ig·zempt') *v.t.* **1** To free or excuse from some obligation to which others are subject; grant immunity to: to *exempt* one from military service. **2** *Obs.* To take or put away; remove. See synonyms under ABSOLVE, RELEASE. — *adj.* **1** Free, clear, or excused, as from some liability, restriction, or burden. **2** *Obs.* Remote; separated. See synonyms under FREE. — *n.* A person who is exempted, as from military service. [<L *exemptus*, pp. of *eximere* <*ex-* out + *emere* buy, take] — **ex·empt'i·ble** *adj.*

ex·emp·tion (ig·zemp'shən) *n.* **1** The act of exempting. **2** The state of being exempt; a dispensation giving freedom from duty or penalty; freedom or immunity from some liability, requirement, or evil: *exemption* from punishment. See synonyms under RIGHT.

ex·en·ter·ate (eks·en'tə·rāt) *v.t.* **·at·ed, ·at·ing** *Surg.* To eviscerate. [<L *exenteratus*, pp. of *exenterare* <*ex-* out + Gk. *enteron* intestine] — **ex·en'ter·a'tion** *n.*

ex·e·qua·tur (ek'sə·kwā'tər) *n.* In international law, the official recognition given to a consul or commercial agent by the government of the country in which he is to exercise his functions. [<L, let him perform]

ex·e·quy (ek'sə·kwē) *n. pl.* **·quies 1** *pl.* Funeral ceremonies; obsequies. **2** A funeral procession. [<OF *exequies* <L *exequiae* <*exequi, exsequi*. See EXECUTE.]

ex·er·cise (ek'sər·sīz) *v.* **·cised, ·cis·ing** *v.t.* **1** To subject to drills, systematic movements, etc., so as to train or develop (troops, muscles, the mind, etc.). **2** To make use of; employ: to *exercise* caution or a right. **3** To perform or execute, as the duties of an office. **4** To wield; exert, as influence or authority. **5** To do habitually; make a habit of: used reflexively

or in the passive: to be *exercised* in good works. **6** To occupy the mind of; especially, to make anxious; worry. —*v.i.* **7** To take exercise. **8** To undergo training. [< *n.*] —*n.* **1** A putting into use, action, or practice. **2** Activity for health, development, or training. **3** An act of speaking, reading, etc., as at a school exhibition or religious meeting: usually in the plural. **4** An act of worship; a religious service. **5** A lesson assigned to a student; also, the written or oral fulfilment of that assignment. [< OF *exercice* < L *exercitium* < *exercere* practice < *ex*- out, away + *arcere* restrain] —**ex'er·cis'a·ble** *adj.*
Synonyms (noun): act, action, activity, application, employment, exertion, occupation, operation, performance, practice, use. See ACT, PRACTICE. *Antonyms:* idleness, inaction, inactivity, relaxation, rest.

ex·er·cised (ek'sər·sīzd) *adj.* Harassed; agitated; excited.

ex·er·ci·ta·tion (ig·zûr'sə·tā'shən) *n.* **1** An exercise, as a disciplinary mental act. **2** Exercise or practice. [< OF < L *exercitatio, -onis* < *exercitare*, freq. of *exercere.* See EXERCISE.]

ex·ergue (ig·zûrg', ek'sûrg) *n.* The space beneath the principal design on the reverse of a coin or medal, with date, place of coining, etc. [< F < Gk. *ex* out + *ergon* work]

ex·ert (ig·zûrt') *v.t.* **1** To put forth or put in action, as strength, force, or faculty; bring into strong or vigorous action. **2** *Obs.* To push or thrust forth. —**to exert oneself** To put forth effort. [< L *exertus,* var. of *exsertus,* pp. of *exserere* thrust out < *ex*- out + *serere* bind] —**ex·er'tive** *adj.*

ex·er·tion (ig·zûr'shən) *n.* The act of putting some power or faculty into vigorous action; a strong effort. See synonyms under ACT, ENDEAVOR, EXERCISE, INDUSTRY, WORK.

ex·e·sion (ig·zē'zhən, -shən) *n. Pathol.* The slow superficial destruction of organic tissues, especially bone, by the action of abscesses and other agencies. [< L *exesus,* pp. of *edere* eat + -ION]

ex·e·unt (ek'sē·ənt, -ŏont) They go out: a stage direction. [< L]

ex·fo·li·ate (eks·fō'lē·āt) *v.t. & v.i.* **·at·ed, ·at·ing** **1** To remove scales or splinters (from). **2** To peel or scale off in thin flakes, as the bark of a tree. **3** *Geol.* To split off in scales or sheets, as a heated mineral or weathered rock. [< LL *exfoliatus,* pp. of *exfoliare* < *ex*- off + *folium* a leaf] —**ex·fo'li·a'tive** *adj.*

ex·ha·lant (eks·hā'lənt, ig·zā'-) *adj.* Having the property of exhaling. —*n.* Anything exhaled or which exhales; specifically, a duct used for exhaling. [< F < L *exhalans, -antis,* pp. of *exhalare* EXHALE]

ex·hale (eks·hāl', ig·zāl') *v.* **·haled, ·hal·ing** *v.i.* **1** To expel air or vapor; breathe out. **2** To pass off or rise as a vapor or effluence; evaporate. —*v.t.* **3** To breathe forth or give off, as gas, vapor, or an aroma. **4** To draw off; cause to evaporate: Heat *exhales* the earth's moisture. [< F *exhaler* < L *exhalare* < *ex*- out + *halare* breathe] —**ex·hal'a·ble** *adj.*

ex·haust (ig·zôst') *v.t.* **1** To make tired; wear out completely. **2** To drain of resources, strength, etc.; use up. **3** To draw off, as gas, steam, etc., from or as from a container. **4** To empty (a container) of contents; drain. **5** To study, treat of, or develop thoroughly and completely: to *exhaust* a subject. **6** In pharmacy, to remove the essential principles of by means of a solvent, thus leaving an inert remainder. —*v.i.* **7** To pass out as the exhaust: The steam *exhausts* from the pipe. See synonyms under ABSORB. —*n.* **1** The fluid discharged or escaping from the cylinder of a steam engine after expansion. **2** The formation of air currents by creating a partial vacuum. **3** The device used in flour mills to conduct dust particles away by means of air currents. **4** The escape of the waste gases from the cylinders of an internal-combustion engine; also, more loosely, the muffler which regulates this escape. **5** Foul air escaping from an apartment by a special register or pipe. **6** Emission. [< L *exhaustus,* pp. of *exhaurire* < *ex*- out + *haurire* draw] —**ex·haust'er** *n.* —**ex·haust'i·bil'i·ty** *n.* —**ex·haust'i·ble** *adj.*

ex·haust·ed (ig·zôs'tid) *adj.* **1** Used up; consumed; spent. **2** Emptied: an *exhausted* cask. **3** Depleted of essential ingredients: said

specifically of soil. **4** Deprived of air; having a vacuum. **5** Weakened; tired out. —**ex·haust'ed·ly** *adv.*

exhaust velocity The velocity of exhaust gases at the moment of their expulsion from an internal-combustion engine, jet engine, rocket motor, or the like.

ex·hib·it (ig·zib'it) *v.t.* **1** To present to view; display. **2** To show or reveal: to *exhibit* ill will. **3** To present for public inspection or entertainment, as a product, play, etc. **4** *Law* To present formally or officially, as evidence. **5** *Med.* To administer, as a remedy. —*v.i.* **6** To place something on display. See synonyms under FLAUNT. —*n.* **1** Any object or objects exhibited. **2** *Law* A document or object marked for use as evidence. **3** A showing or manifestation; especially, a written statement of the condition of anything. [< L *exhibitus,* pp. of *exhibere* < *ex*- out + *habere* hold, have] —**ex·hib'i·tor, ex·hib'it·er** *n.*

ex·hi·bi·tion (ek'sə·bish'ən) *n.* **1** The act of exhibiting; display. **2** Anything exhibited; a show; especially, a public showing of works of art, athletic prowess, cattle, agricultural or manufactured products, etc. **3** An examination of students before an audience. **4** A display of student work. **5** *Brit.* A bursary. See synonyms under SPECTACLE. [< OF *exhibicion* < L *exhibitio, -onis* < *exhibere.* See EXHIBIT.]

ex·hi·bi·tion·ism (ek'sə·bish'ən·iz'əm) *n.* **1** The tendency to display one's personal qualities in a manner that will attract attention. **2** *Psychiatry* The tendency, usually compulsive, to obtain sexual gratification by public exposure of one's body or genitalia. —**ex'hi·bi'tion·ist** *n.*

ex·hil·a·rate (ig·zil'ə·rāt) *v.t.* **·rat·ed, ·rat·ing** To induce a lively or enlivening feeling in; enliven; cheer; stimulate. See synonyms under REJOICE. [< L *exhilaratus,* pp. of *exhilarare* gladden < *ex*- completely + *hilarare* < *hilaris* glad] —**ex·hil'a·rat'ing** *adj.* —**ex·hil'a·rat'ing·ly** *adv.* —**ex·hil'a·ra'tor** *n.*

ex·hil·a·ra·tion (ig·zil'ə·rā'shən) *n.* The act of exhilarating, or the state of being exhilarated; animation; enlivenment; stimulation. —**ex·hil'a·ra·to'ry** (-tôr'ē, -tō'rē) *adj.*

ex·hort (ig·zôrt') *v.t.* To urge by earnest appeal or argument; advise or caution strongly. —*v.i.* To utter exhortation. [< L *exhortari* < *ex*- completely + *hortari* urge]

ex·hor·ta·tion (eg'zôr·tā'shən, ek'sər-) *n.* **1** The act or practice of exhorting; attempt to arouse or incite, as by appeal, argument, or admonition. **2** That which is spoken in exhorting; admonition; earnest advice. See synonyms under COUNSEL. [< L *exhortatio, -onis* < *exhortari.* See EXHORT.]

ex·hu·ma·tion (eks'hyōō·mā'shən) *n.* The digging up of that which has been buried; disinterring; especially, the disinterring of a human body.

ex·hume (ig·zyōōm', iks·hyōōm') *v.t.* **·humed, ·hum·ing** To dig out of the earth, as a dead body; disinter. [< F *exhumer* < Med. L *exhumare* < L *ex*- out + *humus* ground]

ex·i·gen·cy (ek'sə·jən·sē) *n. pl.* **·cies** **1** The state of being urgent or exigent; pressing need or demand. **2** A case requiring immediate attention, assistance, or remedy. **3** A critical period or condition; a pressing necessity. Also **ex'i·gence.** See synonyms under NECESSITY.

ex·i·gent (ek'sə·jənt) *adj.* **1** Demanding immediate aid or action; urgent. **2** Feeling the need; requiring; exacting. [< L *exigens, -entis,* ppr. of *exigere.* See EXACT.]

ex·ile (eg'zīl, ek'sīl) *n.* **1** Banishment from one's home or native land; expatriation. **2** One driven or wandering away from country or home; an expatriate. —**the Exile** The Babylonian captivity of the Jews. —*v.t.* **ex·iled, ex·il·ing** To expel from one's own country or home; banish; expatriate. [< F *exiler* < L *exilium,* var. of *exsilium* banishment < *ex*- out + root of *salire* to leap]

ex·ist (ig·zist') *v.i.* **1** To have actual being or reality; be. **2** To continue to live or be: Animal life cannot *exist* without oxygen. **3** To be present; occur: This species now *exists* only in Australia. See synonyms under LIVE. [< F *exister* < L *existere* < *ex*- out + *stare* stand]

ex·is·tence (ig·zis'təns) *n.* **1** Being; the state or fact of being, or of continuing to be, whether as substance, essence, personality, or consciousness: a brief or an endless *existence,* real or idle *existence.* **2** Possession or continuance of animate or vital being; life: a fight for *existence.* **3** Anything that exists or has the quality of objectivity; an entity; actuality.

ex·is·ten·tial (eg'zis·ten'shəl) *adj.* **1** Of or pertaining to existence. **2** Expressing or stating the fact of existence. —**ex'is·ten'tial·ly** *adv.*

ex·is·ten·tial·ism (eg'zis·ten'shəl·iz'əm) *n.* **1** A movement in 20th century philosophy, influenced in its development by Kierkegaard and Nietzsche and popularized in France by Sartre, emphasizing the active participation of the will, rather than the reason, in confronting the problems of a non-moral or absurd universe. Man is defined in existentialism as the sum total of his acts rather than his intentions or potentialities, and exists in order to will himself to act. **2** A cult of nihilism and pessimism popularized in France after World War II, supposedly based on the doctrines of Sartre and other existentialist writers. —**ex'is·ten'tial·ist** *adj. & n.*

ex·it (eg'zit, ek'sit) *n.* **1** A way or passage out; egress. **2** The departure of an actor from the stage. **3** Any departure, as that from the scenes of life; death. —*v.i.* **1** To go out. **2** (He or she) goes out: a stage direction. [< L *exitus* < *exire* < *ex*- out + *ire* go]

exo- *combining form* Out; outside; external: *exocarp.* Also, before vowels, **ex-.** [< Gk. *exo-, ex- < exō* outside]

ex·o·car·di·a (ek'sō·kär'dē·ə) *n. Pathol.* A displacement of the heart from its normal position. [< NL < Gk. *exo-* out + *kardia* heart]

ex·o·car·di·ac (ek'sō·kär'dē·ak) *adj.* Situated outside the heart. Also **ex'o·car'di·al.**

ex·o·carp (ek'sō·kärp) *n. Bot.* The outer wall of a fruit covering, when it is possible to distinguish more than one; epicarp. Compare ENDOCARP and illustrations under FRUIT.

ex·o·cen·tric (ek'sō·sen'trik) *adj. Ling.* Denoting a syntactic construction which as a unit functions differently from any of its component parts, as *Jim works hard* is an *exocentric* construction: opposed to *endocentric.*

ex·od·ic (ek·sod'ik) *adj.* **1** Of or pertaining to an exodus. **2** Efferent.

ex·o·don·tia (ek'sō·don'shə, -shē·ə) *n.* The branch of dentistry concerned with the extraction of teeth. [< NL < Gk. *ex-* out + *odon, odontos* a tooth] —**ex'o·dont'ist** *n.*

ex·o·dus (ek'sə·dəs) *n.* A going forth, or departure, as of a multitude, from a place or country. —**the Exodus** The departure of the Israelites from Egypt under the guidance of Moses, described in Exodus, the second book of the Old Testament. [< L < Gk. *exodos* < *ex*- out + *hodos* way]

ex·og·a·my (eks·og'ə·mē) *n.* **1** The custom of certain peoples forbidding any man to marry within his own tribe or clan. **2** Marriage outside of one's tribe, clan, or family: opposed to *endogamy.* **3** *Biol.* The union of two protozoans of different ancestry, with fusion of nuclei, as the commencement of a new cycle of growth. —**ex·og'a·mous, ex·o·gam·ic** (ek'sō·gam'ik) *adj.*

EXOGEN
A. Vertical section; *B.* Cross-section;
showing growth rings for three
successive years at *1, 2, 3.*

b. Bark.	*s.* Sapwood	*m.* Medullary
c. Cambium	(alburnum).	sheath.
layer.	*h.* Heartwood	*p.* Pith.
	(duramen).	

ex·o·gen (ek'sə·jən) *n. Bot.* A plant which increases in size by successive concentric additions or rings beneath the bark and outside the previous growth; a dicotyledon: opposed to *endogen.*

ex·og·e·nous (eks·oj'ə·nəs) *adj.* **1** Originating outside the organism. **2** Due to external causes. **3** Growing by addition at the outer surface. —**ex·og'e·nous·ly** *adv.*

ex·on·er·ate (ig·zon′ə·rāt) v.t. ·at·ed, ·at·ing 1 To free from accusation or blame; acquit; exculpate. 2 To relieve or free from a responsibility or the like. See synonyms under ABSOLVE, JUSTIFY. [< L *exoneratus*, pp. of *exonerare* < *ex-* out, away + *onus, oneris* burden] —**ex·on′er·a′tion** n. —**ex·on′er·a′tive** adj.

ex·o·path·ic (ek′sō·path′ik) adj. Pathol. Of or resulting from causes external to the organism: an *exopathic* disease.

ex·o·ra·ble (ek′sər·ə·bəl) adj. Capable of being persuaded or moved by entreaty; capable of relenting. [< L *exorabilis* < *ex-* out, away + *orare* pray] —**ex′o·ra·bil′i·ty** n.

ex·or·bi·tance (ig·zôr′bə·təns) n. Excessiveness in degree or amount; extravagance; a tendency to be exorbitant. Also **ex·or′bi·tan·cy**. See synonyms under EXCESS.

ex·or·bi·tant (ig·zôr′bə·tənt) adj. 1 Going beyond usual and proper limits, as in price or demand; excessive; extravagant. 2 Out of the realm of the law; illegal. See synonyms under IMMODERATE. [< LL *exorbitans, -antis*, ppr. of *exorbitare* go astray < *ex-* out + *orbita* a track] —**ex·or′bi·tant·ly** adv.

ex·or·cise (ek′sôr·sīz) v.t. ·cised, ·cis·ing 1 To cast out (an evil spirit) by prayers or incantations. 2 To free of an evil spirit. 3 Obs. To summon or conjure up, as a demon. Also **ex′or·cize**. [< OF *exorciser* < LL *exorcizare* < Gk. *exorkizein* < *ex-* out + *horkos* an oath]—**ex′or·cis′er** or ·**ciz′er** n.

ex·or·di·um (ig·zôr′dē·əm, ik·sôr′-) n. pl. ·**di·ums** or ·**di·a** (-dē·ə) The introductory part, as of a discourse; a prelude. [< L *exordiri* < *ex-* out + *ordiri* begin] —**ex·or′di·al** adj.

ex·o·re·ic (ek′sə·rē′ik) adj. Pertaining to or designating a region whose surface drainage reaches the oceans, as the greater part of North and South America. [< EXO- + Gk. *rheein* flow]

ex·o·skel·e·ton (ek′sō·skel′ə·tən) n. Biol. An external skeleton; any bony or horny external covering, armor, or structure of hardened integument, especially in invertebrates; dermoskeleton: opposed to *endoskeleton*.

ex·os·mo·sis (ek′sos·mō′sis, -soz-) n. Chem. 1 Osmosis in that direction in which the fluid crosses the septum most slowly. 2 Osmosis from an inner to an outer vessel; opposed to *endosmosis*. Also **ex′os·mose**. —**ex′os·mot′ic** (-mot′ik) adj. —**ex·os′mic** adj.

ex·o·sphere (ek′sō·sfir) n. The outermost region of the earth's atmosphere, beginning at a height of about 400 miles.

ex·o·spore (ek′sō·spôr, -spōr) n. Bot. 1 The outer wall of a spore. 2 An outer coat of the spores of certain fungi.

ex·os·to·sis (ek′sos·tō′sis) n. pl. ·**ses** (-sēz) Pathol. An excessive bony outgrowth or tumor formed on either the outer or the inner surface of a bone or on a cartilage. [< NL < Gk. < *ex-* out + *osteon* bone]

ex·o·ter·ic (ek′sə·ter′ik) adj. 1 Adapted or intelligible, as a doctrine, to those outside the inner circle of disciples, or to the uninitiated; suitable for popular comprehension: opposed to *esoteric*. 2 External. Also **ex′o·ter′i·cal**. [< LL *exotericus* < Gk. *exōterikos* < *exōterō*, comparative of *exō* outside] —**ex′o·ter′i·cal·ly** adv. —**ex′o·ter′i·cism** n.

ex·o·ther·mic (ek′sō·thûr′mik) adj. Chem. Designating those reactions which are accompanied by the liberation of heat: opposed to *endothermic*. Also **ex·o·ther′mal**. [< EXO- + Gk. *thermē* heat]

ex·ot·ic (ig·zot′ik) adj. Belonging by nature or origin to another part of the world; brought in from abroad; foreign; strange: an *exotic* flower. —n. Something not native, as a plant, person, word, etc. [< L *exoticus* < Gk. *exōtikos* foreign < *exō* outside] —**ex·ot′i·cal·ly** adv. —**ex·ot′i·cism** n.

ex·o·tox·in (ek′sō·tok′sin) n. Biochem. A toxin formed within and excreted by an organism which is not itself toxic: distinguished from *endotoxin*. —**ex′o·tox′ic** adj.

ex·pand (ik·spand′) v.t. 1 To increase the range, scope, volume, size, etc., of: to *expand* a business. 2 To spread out by unfolding or extending; open: The peacock *expands* his tail. 3 To write or develop in full the details or form of, as a

thought, argument, etc. —v.i. 4 To grow larger, wider, etc.; unfold; increase. See synonyms under AMPLIFY, SPREAD. [< L *expandere* < *ex-* out + *pandere* spread. Doublet of SPAWN.] —**ex·pand′er** n.

ex·panse (ik·spans′) n. That which lies spread out; a vast continuous area or stretch: the blue *expanse* of heaven. [< L *expansum* < *expandere*. See EXPAND.]

ex·pan·sion (ik·span′shən) n. 1 The act of expanding, in any sense. 2 The condition or state of being expanded. 3 The amount of increase in size, scope, or the like. 4 That which is expanded; an expanded continuation or result; an extended surface; an expanded part; an enlargement. 5 The extent or space over or through which a thing expands; hence, extent in general; unlimited space; expanse; immensity. 6 Physics Increase of volume, as of steam in an engine cylinder when cut off from connection with the supply of pressure, or of the exploding gas in an internal-combustion engine. 7 Math. Development of a mathematical function into a series; also, the full expression as developed: the *expansion* of (a + b)³ into $a^3 + 3a^2b + 3ab^2 + b^3$.

ex·pan·sive (ik·span′siv) adj. 1 Capable of enlarging or being expanded; tending to expand; causing or characterized by expansion. 2 Presenting an expanse; extending; extensive. 3 Comprehensive; broad in mind or sympathies; liberal. 4 Amiable and effusive: an *expansive* personality. —**ex·pan′sive·ly** adv. —**ex·pan′sive·ness** n.

ex·pa·ti·ate (ik·spā′shē·āt) v.i. ·at·ed, ·at·ing 1 To speak or write in a lengthy manner; elaborate: with *on* or *upon*. 2 Rare To roam at large; range widely or unrestrainedly. See synonyms under AMPLIFY. [< L *ex(s)patiatus*, pp. of *ex(s)patiari* < *ex-* out + *spatiari* walk < *spatium* space] —**ex·pa′ti·a′tion** n. —**ex·pa′ti·a′tor** n. —**ex·pa′ti·a·to·ry** (-tôr′ē, -tō′rē) adj.

ex·pa·tri·ate (eks·pā′trē·āt) v.t. ·at·ed, ·at·ing 1 To drive (a person) from his native land; exile; banish. 2 To withdraw (oneself) from one's native land. —n. (-it, -āt) One exiled. —adj. Banished; exiled. [< Med. L *expatriatus*, pp. of *expatriare* < *ex-* out + *patria* native land] —**ex·pa′tri·a′tion** n.

ex·pect (ik·spekt′) v.t. 1 To look forward to as certain or probable; anticipate in thought. 2 To look for as right, proper, or necessary; require. 3 Colloq. To presume; suppose. 4 Obs. To wait for. See synonyms under ABIDE, ANTICIPATE. [< L *ex(s)pectare* < *ex-* out + *spectare* look at]

ex·pec·tan·cy (ik·spek′tən·sē) n. pl. ·**cies** 1 The act or state of expecting; expectation. 2 An object of expectation. 3 Law The state of being expected; abeyance: an estate in *expectancy*. See synonyms under ANTICIPATION. Also **ex·pec′tance**.

ex·pec·tant (ik·spek′tənt) adj. 1 Waiting or looking forward in expectation. 2 Awaiting the birth of a child: an *expectant* mother. —n. One who is anticipating confidently. [< OF < L *ex(s)pectans, -antis*, ppr. of *ex(s)pectare*. See EXPECT.] —**ex·pec′tant·ly** adv.

ex·pec·ta·tion (ik′spek·tā′shən) n. 1 The act of looking confidently for something; expectancy. 2 Anticipation; prospect of good to come, as of wealth: often plural. 3 Something expected. 4 The present value of a probability. See synonyms under ANTICIPATION. [< L *ex(s)pectatio, -onis* < *ex(s)pectare*. See EXPECT.]

ex·pec·to·rant (ik·spek′tər·ənt) adj. Relating to or promotive of expectoration. —n. A medicine to promote expectoration. [< L *expectorans, -antis*, ppr. of *expectorare*. See EXPECTORATE.]

ex·pec·to·rate (ik·spek′tə·rāt) v.t. & v.i. ·rat·ed, ·rat·ing 1 To discharge, as phlegm, by hawking or coughing up and spitting from the mouth. 2 To spit. [< L *expectoratus*, pp. of *expectorare* < *ex-* out + *pectus, -oris* breast]

ex·pe·di·en·cy (ik·spē′dē·ən·sē) n. pl. ·**cies** 1 The quality of being proper, suitable, and advantageous under given circumstances; advantageousness; fitness. 2 That which is most practicable, all things considered. 3 In ethics, the doing of what is useful, politic, or advantageous, regardless of justice or right.

See synonyms under PROFIT, UTILITY. Also **ex·pe′di·ence**.

ex·pe·di·ent (ik·spē′dē·ənt) adj. 1 Serving to promote a desired end; suitable under the circumstances; contributing to personal advantage; advisable. 2 Pertaining to utility or advantage rather than principle. 3 Obs. Speedy; expeditious. —n. 1 That which furthers or promotes an end. 2 A device; shift. [< OF < L *expediens, -entis*, ppr. of *expedire*. See EXPEDITE.] —**ex·pe′di·ent·ly** adv.

Synonyms (adj.): advantageous, beneficial, convenient, favorable, paying, profitable, sensible, suitable, useful, wise, worthwhile. See PROFITABLE. Compare synonyms for PROFIT, UTILITY. *Antonyms*: absurd, ill-adapted, ill-considered, ill-devised, ill-judged, inexpedient, irrational, reckless, unsuitable, unwise.

ex·pe·dite (ek′spə·dīt) v.t. ·dit·ed, ·dit·ing 1 To speed up the process or progress of; facilitate. 2 To do quickly. 3 To send or issue officially; dispatch. See synonyms under PUSH. —adj. Prompt; expeditious. [< L *expeditus*, pp. of *expedire* < *ex-* out + *pes, pedis* foot]

ex·pe·di·tion (ek′spə·dish′ən) n. 1 A journey, march or voyage, generally of several or many persons, for a definite purpose: an Arctic *expedition*. 2 The body of persons engaged in such a journey, march, or voyage, together with their equipment. 3 The quality of being expeditious; speed; dispatch. See synonyms under JOURNEY.

ex·pel (ik·spel′) v.t. ·pelled, ·pel·ling 1 To drive out by force or authority; force out. 2 To dismiss, as a pupil from a school; eject. See synonyms under BANISH, EXTERMINATE. [< L *expellere* < *ex-* out + *pellere* drive, thrust] —**ex·pel′la·ble** adj.

ex·pend (ik·spend′) v.t. To pay out or spend; use up. [< L *expendere* < *ex-* out + *pendere* weigh]

ex·pend·a·ble (ik·spen′də·bəl) adj. That may be expended; capable of being, or to be, consumed, used, or sacrificed, as men and materiel in warfare.

ex·pen·di·ture (ik·spen′də·chər) n. 1 The act of expending; outlay; disbursement. 2 That which is expended; expense. See synonyms under EXPENSE, PRICE. [< Med. L *expenditus*, irreg. pp. of *expendere*. See EXPEND.]

ex·pense (ik·spens′) n. 1 The laying out or expending, as of money or other resources; expenditure. 2 Loss: at the *expense* of health. 3 Money expended; outlay. 4 Anything requiring expenditure. [< AF < LL *expensa* < *expendere*. See EXPEND.]

Synonyms: cost, expenditure, outgo, outlay. The *cost* of a thing is whatever one surrenders or gives up for it, intentionally or unintentionally, or even unconsciously; *expense* is what is laid out by calculation or intention. We say, "He won his fame at the *cost* of his life"; "I know it to my *cost*"; we speak of a joke at another's *expense*; at another's *cost* would seem to make it a more serious matter. There is a tendency to use *cost* of what we pay for a possession, *expense* of what we pay for a service; we speak of the *cost* of goods, the *expense* of manufacture. *Outlay* is used of some definite *expenditure*, as for the purchase of supplies; *outgo* of a steady drain or of incidental *expenses*. See PRICE. *Antonyms*: gain, income, proceeds, product, profit, profits, receipt, receipts, return, returns.

ex·pen·sive (ik·spen′siv) adj. Causing or involving much expense; costly. —**ex·pen′sive·ly** adv. —**ex·pen′sive·ness** n.

ex·pe·ri·ence (ik·spir′ē·əns) n. 1 Knowledge derived from one's own action, practice, perception, enjoyment, or suffering; experimental knowledge; especially, the state of such knowledge in an individual as an index of wisdom or skill: He is a lawyer of *experience*. 2 Something undergone, enjoyed, etc. 3 Spiritual exercise of mind; conversion. 4 Every form of knowledge due to one's immediate observation; also, the sum total of such knowledge in the life of an individual. 5 Length, duration, or state of occupation with or employment in a particular study, business, or work. See synonyms under ACQUAINTANCE, KNOWLEDGE. —v.t. ·enced, ·enc·ing To undergo personally; feel. See synonyms under KNOW. —**to**

experience religion To undergo a change of heart; be converted. [<OF <L *experientia* <*experiri* try out]

ex·per·i·ment (ik·sper′ə·mənt) *n.* **1** An act or operation designed to discover, test, or illustrate a truth, principle, or effect; a test, especially one intended to confirm or disprove something which is still in doubt. **2** The conducting of such operations or tests. **3** Something undergoing the test of actual experience, as opposed to that whose practicability or usefulness has been fully demonstrated: often used depreciatively: Your boasted institutions are but an *experiment.* **4** *Obs.* Experience. — *v.i.* (-ment) To make experiments; make a test or trial. [<OF <L *experimentum* <*experiri* try out] — **ex·per′i·ment′er** *n.*

ex·per·i·men·tal (ik·sper′ə·men′təl) *adj.* **1** Pertaining to, growing out of, or known by methods of controlled testing and direct observation under stated conditions: *experimental* science: opposed to *speculative.* **2** Designating or pertaining to that which is learned by experience: distinguished from *theoretical.* — **ex·per′i·men′tal·ism** *n.* — **ex·per′i·men′tal·ist** *n.* — **ex·per′i·men′tal·ly** *adv.*

ex·pert (ek′spûrt) *n.* **1** One who has special skill or knowledge; a specialist. **2** In the U.S. Army, the highest of three grades for skill in the use of small arms. **3** A soldier having this grade. Compare MARKSMAN, SHARPSHOOTER. — *adj.* (*also* ik·spûrt′) **1** Skilful as the result of practice; dexterous; marked by skill. **2** Proceeding from an expert. See synonyms under CLEVER, GOOD. [<L *expertus,* pp. of *experiri* try out] — **ex·pert′ly** *adv.* — **ex·pert′ness** *n.*

ex·pi·ate (ek′spē·āt) *v.t.* **·at·ed, ·at·ing** To atone for; make amends for. [<L *expiatus,* pp. of *expiare* <*ex-* completely + *piare* appease <*pius* pious] — **ex′pi·a·tor** *n.*

ex·pi·a·tion (ek′spē·ā′shən) *n.* **1** The active means of expiating, or of making reparation or satisfaction, as for offense or sin. **2** The removing of guilt by suffering punishment; atonement. ◆ Collateral adjective: *piacular.* See synonyms under PROPITIATION. — **ex′pi·a·to·ry** (-tôr′ē, -tō′rē) *adj.*

ex·pire (ik·spīr′) *v.* **·pired, ·pir·ing** *v.i.* **1** To exhale one's last breath; die. **2** To die out, as the embers of a fire. **3** To come to an end; terminate, as a contract or magazine subscription. **4** To breathe out air from the lungs; exhale. — *v.t.* **5** To breathe out from the lungs. **6** *Obs.* To emit (a vapor or odor). See synonyms under DIE, END. [<L *ex(s)pirare* <*ex-* out + *spirare* breathe] — **ex·pir′er** *n.*

ex·plain (ik·splān′) *v.t.* **1** To make plain or clear; make understandable. **2** To give a meaning to; interpret. **3** To give reasons for; state the cause or purpose of. — *v.i.* **4** To give an explanation. See synonyms under INTERPRET. [<L *explanare* <*ex-* out + *planare* make level <*planus* flat] — **ex·plain′a·ble** *adj.*

ex·pla·na·tion (ek′splə·nā′shən) *n.* **1** The act or means of explaining; elucidation. **2** Meaning; significance; sense. **3** The process of settling a disagreement, or reconciling a difference, by explaining the circumstances; reconciliation. See synonyms under DEFINITION. [<L *explanatio, -onis* <*explanare.* See EXPLAIN.]

ex·plan·a·to·ry (ik·splan′ə·tôr′ē, -tō′rē) *adj.* Serving or tending to explain. Also **ex·plan′a·tive.** — **ex·plan′a·to·ri·ly** *adv.*

ex·plant (iks·plant′, -plänt′) *v.t.* To place outside its habitat, as an organ of the body or bacteria in a medium, for purposes of observation and study.

ex·ple·tive (eks′plə·tiv) *n.* **1** An interjection, often profane. **2** A word or syllable employed for rhetorical or rhythmical effect. **3** Something serving to fill out. — *adj.* Added for emphasis; redundant: also **ex′ple·to·ry** (-tôr′ē, -tō′rē). [<LL *expletivus* <L *expletus,* pp. of *explere* <*ex-* completely + *plere* fill]

ex·pli·ca·ble (eks′pli·kə·bəl, *frequently* iks·plik′ə·bəl) *adj.* Capable of explanation.

ex·pli·cate (eks′plə·kāt) *v.t.* **·cat·ed, ·cat·ing** To clear from obscurity; explain. See synonyms under INTERPRET. [<L *explicatus,* pp. of *explicare* <*ex-* out + *plicare* fold] — **ex′pli·ca′tor** *n.*

ex·plic·it (ik·splis′it) *adj.* **1** Plainly expressed, or that plainly expresses. **2** Having no

disguised meaning or reservation; definite; open; unreserved. **3** *Logic* Brought out definitely in words; not merely implied: opposed to *implicit.* [<L *explicitus,* var. of *explicatus.* See EXPLICATE.] — **ex·plic′it·ly** *adv.* — **ex·plic′it·ness** *n.*

Synonym: express.

ex·plode (ik·splōd′) *v.* **·plod·ed, ·plod·ing** *v.t.* **1** To cause to expand violently or pass suddenly from a solid to a gaseous state: to *explode* gunpowder. **2** To cause to burst or blow up violently and with noise: to *explode* a bomb. **3** To disprove utterly; refute: to *explode* a theory. **4** *Phonet.* To pronounce with an explosion. **5** *Obs.* To drive from the stage, as an actor. — *v.i.* **6** To be exploded, as gunpowder. **7** To burst into pieces or fragments; blow up. **8** To make a noise as if bursting: to *explode* with laughter. [<L *explodere,* orig. drive off the stage, hiss <*ex-* out + *plaudere* clap] — **ex·plod′er** *n.*

ex·ploit (eks′ploit, ik·sploit′) *n.* A deed or act, especially one marked by heroism, daring, skill, or brilliancy. See synonyms under ACT. — *v.t.* (ik·sploit′) **1** To use for one's own advantage; take advantage of: Rulers often *exploit* the people. **2** To put to use; make use of: to *exploit* water power. [<OF *esploit* <L *explicitum,* neut. sing. of *explicitus.* See EXPLICIT.] — **ex·ploit′a·ble** *adj.*

ex·ploi·ta·tion (eks′ploi·tā′shən) *n.* **1** The act of exploiting. **2** Selfish employment for one's own use or advantage.

ex·plo·ra·tion (eks′plə·rā′shən) *n.* **1** The act of exploring; especially, geographical research in unknown regions. **2** The examination of internal organs or parts. [<L *exploratio, -onis* <*explorare.* See EXPLORE.]

ex·plor·a·to·ry (ik·splôr′ə·tôr′ē, ik·splō′rə·tō′rē) *adj.* Of, for, or relating to exploration. Also **ex·plor′a·tive.**

ex·plore (ik·splôr′, -splōr′) *v.* **·plored, ·plor·ing** *v.t.* **1** To search through or travel in or over, as new lands, for discovery. **2** To look into carefully; scrutinize. **3** *Med.* To examine: to *explore* a wound with a probe. — *v.i.* **4** To make explorations. See synonyms under EXAMINE. [<L *explorare* investigate <*ex-* out + *plorare* cry out]

ex·plo·sion (ik·splō′zhən) *n.* **1** The act of exploding; rapid combustion or other similar process, usually causing a loud report. **2** The power stroke of an internal-combustion engine. **3** *Physiol.* The sudden discharge of a neural cell or group of cells. **4** A sudden and violent outbreak as of physical forces or of human emotion. **5** *Phonet.* Plosion. [<L *explosio, -onis* <*explodere.* See EXPLODE.]

ex·plo·sive (ik·splō′siv) *adj.* **1** Pertaining to explosion. **2** Liable to explode or to cause explosion. **3** *Phonet.* Plosive. — *n.* **1** *Physics* Any substance or mixture of substances which, on impact or by ignition, reacts by a violent rearrangement of its molecules accompanied by the sudden expansion of gases and the liberation of relatively large amounts of thermal energy. **2** *Phonet.* A plosive consonant. — **ex·plo′sive·ly** *adv.* — **ex·plo′sive·ness** *n.*

ex·po·nent (ik·spō′nənt) *n.* **1** One who or that which explains, interprets, or expounds. **2** *Logic* An illustrative example of a general proposition. **3** *Math.* Any number or symbol placed as a superscript to the right of a quantity to indicate a power or the reciprocal or root of a power: thus, $3^2 = 3 \times 3$; $3^{-2} = 1/3^2$; $3^{\frac{1}{2}} = \sqrt{3}$. **4** Any person or thing that represents the character or principles of something: Franklin was the *exponent* of American principles in France. [<L *exponens, -entis,* ppr. of *exponere* indicate <*ex-* out + *ponere* place] — **ex·po·nen·tial** (ek′spō·nen′shəl) *adj.* — **ex′po·nen′tial·ly** *adv.*

ex·po·ni·ble (ik·spō′nə·bəl) *adj.* Needing explanation, as in logic, when propositions must be restated to be intelligible. — *n.* An exponible statement.

ex·port (ik·spôrt′, -spōrt′, eks′pôrt, -pōrt) *v.t.* To carry or send, as merchandise or raw materials, to other countries for sale or trade. — *n.* (eks′pôrt, -pōrt) **1** The act of exporting; exportation. **2** That which is exported; especially, merchandise sent from one country to another: usually in the plural. — *adj.* Of or pertaining to exports or exportation. [<L *exportare* <*ex-* out + *portare* carry] — **ex·port′a·ble** *adj.* — **ex·port′a·bil′i·ty** *n.* — **ex·port′er** *n.*

ex·por·ta·tion (ek′spôr·tā′shən, -spōr-) *n.* **1** The act or practice of exporting. **2** An export commodity.

ex·pose (ik·spōz′) *v.t.* **·posed, ·pos·ing 1** To lay open, as to harm, attack, ridicule, censure, etc. **2** To leave open to the action of a force or influence. **3** To present to view; show; display: The dress *exposed* her shoulders. **4** To cause to be known; make public, as a conspiracy or crime. **5** To lay open or make known the crimes, faults, etc., of (a person): to *expose* a traitor. **6** To abandon so as to cause the death of: to *expose* an unwanted child. **7** *Phot.* To admit light to (a sensitized film or plate). **8** In the Roman Catholic Church, to show for adoration or worship, as the Host. See synonyms under DISCOVER. [<MF *exposer* <*ex-* out + *poser.* See POSE¹.] — **ex·po′sal** *n.* — **ex·pos′er** *n.*

ex·po·sé (ek′spō·zā′) *n.* **1** An undesirable or embarrassing disclosure or exposure. **2** A revelation or disclosure of something to the public, as corruption, political graft, social injustice, etc. — *adj.* Given to exposing discreditable things: an *exposé* magazine. [<F, pp. of *exposer.* See EXPOSE.]

ex·po·si·tion (eks′pə·zish′ən) *n.* **1** A public exhibition of the arts, products, achievements, etc., of a specific region, country, or group, as a world's fair. **2** An explanation; commentary. **3** Rhetorical analysis. **4** The part of a dramatic composition that unfolds the plot. **5** In the Roman Catholic Church, a service in which the blessed sacrament is exposed for adoration. **6** *Music* The initial presentation or statement of the themes of a movement; especially, in a fugue, the introduction of the several parts or voices. See synonyms under DEFINITION. [<OF <L *expositio, -onis* <*exponere.* See EXPONENT.]

ex post fac·to (eks pōst fak′tō) Arising or enacted after the fact but retroacting upon it; retroactive; retrospective. [<L]

ex·pos·tu·late (ik·spos′chə·lāt) *v.i.* **·lat·ed, ·lat·ing** To reason earnestly with a person, against some action: usually with *with.* [<L *expostulatus,* pp. of *expostulare* <*ex-* out + *postulare* demand] — **ex·pos′tu·la′tor** *n.*

ex·po·sure (ik·spō′zhər) *n.* **1** The act or process of exposing, or the state of being exposed in any sense; disclosure of the hitherto hidden truth, usually discreditable, about a person or situation. **2** An open situation or position in relation to the sun, elements, or points of the compass; outlook; aspect: The house had a southern *exposure.* **3** In ancient Greece and Rome, the practice of abandoning sickly and deformed (and often female) infants. **4** *Phot.* The act of submitting a sensitized plate or film to the action of actinic rays. **5** *Geol.* The portion of a rock mass exposed to view. **6** *Law* Offensive public display of one's body.

ex·pound (ik·spound′) *v.t.* **1** To set forth in detail; state; declare, as a doctrine or theory. **2** To explain the meaning or significance of; interpret. See synonyms under INTERPRET. [<OF *espondre* <L *exponere.* See EXPONENT.] — **ex·pound′er** *n.*

ex·press (ik·spres′) *v.t.* **1** To put (thought or opinion) into spoken or written words. **2** To make apparent; reveal: His actions *express* his anger. **3** To represent in art, poetry, etc.; depict by symbols: The rose *expresses* love. **4** *Math.* To represent by a figure, symbol, letter, etc. **5** *U.S.* To send by express. **6** To press out; squeeze out, as juice or moisture. **7** To force out by or as by pressure. **8** To send or cause to be sent by express, as a package. — **to express oneself 1** To make known one's thoughts. **2** To give expression to one's imagination or emotions, especially in artistic activity. See synonyms under SPEAK. — *adj.* **1** Set forth distinctly; explicit; plain; direct. **2** Specially prepared; adapted to a specific purpose: There was *express* provision for strangers. **3** Done, traveling, or carried with speed or in haste: an *express* train. **4** Exactly resembling an original: an *express* likeness. **5** Of or pertaining to an express company. See synonyms under EXPLICIT. — *adv.* With speed; not stopping at local stations: This train runs *express.* — *n.* **1** A system of transportation for trunks, small parcels, packages, etc., by organized corporations. **2** The packages, parcels, etc., sent by this system. **3** Any means of rapid transmission. **4** A message; dispatch; special communication sent with speed. **5** A messenger bearing dispatches; a courier. **6** An express rifle. **7** An express train. [< OF *expresser* < L *ex-* out + *pressare* < *premere* press]

ex·pres·sion (ik·spresh′ən) *n.* **1** The act or mode of uttering or representing, as by language or gesture. **2** Any act or object by which some truth or idea is conveyed: the *expression* of pleasure. **3** That which is uttered; a saying; any embodiment of a thought: a common *expression* among doctors. **4** Outward aspect; especially, the ensemble of the face as indicating the feelings, etc.; look. **5** The quality of having proper expressive methods; the effective utterance of thought or feeling; expressiveness. **6** The development or revelation of character and sentiment in art, music, etc., by shadings, nuances, variations in style. **7** A pressing out. **8** *Math.* A group of characters, numbers, and symbols composing a statement. Also *Obs.* **ex·pres′sure.** See synonyms under AIR, DICTION, LANGUAGE, TERM. [< F < L *expressio, -onis* < *exprimere* < *ex-* out + *premere* press] — **ex·pres′sion·less** *adj.*

Ex·pres·sion·ism (ik·spresh′ən·iz′əm) *n.* A movement in the arts, originating in Europe at about the time of World War I, which had as its object the free expression of the inner experience of the artist rather than the realistic representation of appearances. — **ex·pres′-sion·ist** *n. & adj.* — **ex·pres′sion·is′tic** *adj.*

ex·pres·sive (ik·spres′iv) *adj.* **1** Of, pertaining to, or characterized by expression. **2** Conveying or containing expression, in any sense of the word. **3** Manifesting special significance or force. See synonyms under MOBILE. — **ex·pres′sive·ly** *adv.* — **ex·pres′sive·ness** *n.*

ex·press·ly (ik·spres′lē) *adv.* With definitely stated intent or application; exactly and unmistakably; in direct terms: The condition was *expressly* named.

ex·pro·pri·ate (eks·prō′prē·āt) *v.t.* **·at·ed, ·at·ing** **1** To take from the owner, especially for public use. **2** To deprive of ownership or property. [< LL *expropriatus*, pp. of *expropriare* < *ex-* out + *proprium* property < *proprius* one's own] — **ex·pro′pri·a′tor** *n.*

ex·pro·pri·a·tion (eks·prō′prē·ā′shən) *n.* **1** The act, process, or result of expropriating. **2** The act of taking land for public use by right of eminent domain.

ex·pul·sion (ik·spul′shən) *n.* **1** The act of expelling; forcible ejection. **2** The state of being expelled. [< L *expulsio, -onis* < *expellere.* See EXPEL.] — **ex·pul′sive** *adj.*

ex·punc·tion (ik·spungk′shən) *n.* The act of expunging; erasure. [< L *expunctio, -onis* < *expungere.* See EXPUNGE.]

ex·punge (ik·spunj′) *v.t.* **·punged, ·pung·ing** To blot or scratch out, as from a record or list; obliterate; efface. See synonyms under CANCEL. [< L *expungere* < *ex-* out + *pungere* prick] — **ex·pung′er** *n.*

ex·pur·gate (eks′pər·gāt) *v.t.* **·gat·ed, ·gat·ing** To clear, as a book, of whatever is considered objectionable, immoral, etc. [< L *expurgatus*, pp. of *expurgare* < *ex-* out + *purgare* cleanse] — **ex′pur·ga′tion** *n.* — **ex·pur·ga·to·ry** (ik·spûr′gə·tôr′ē, -tō′rē) *adj.*

ex·qui·site (eks′kwi·zit, ik·skwiz′it) *adj.* **1** Characterized by fineness and delicacy; dainty in make or quality; satisfying to the esthetic faculties; refined; delicately beautiful. **2** Having unusually refined perception or judgment; delicately sensitive and accurate; of keen esthetic discrimination; nice; fastidious: *exquisite* taste. **3** Causing or marked by intense or extreme emotion; exciting or fitted to excite extreme pleasure or pain; intense or poignant: *exquisite* rapture or pain. **4** *Obs.* Very careful; curious. **5** *Obs.* Particular; choice. See synonyms under BEAUTIFUL, CHOICE, DELICIOUS, ELEGANT, FINE. — *n.* A person very dainty in dress or manners; a fop; dandy; dude. [< L *exquisitus*, pp. of *exquirere* < *ex-* out + *quarere* seek] — **ex′qui·site·ly** *adv.* — **ex′qui·site·ness** *n.*

ex·san·guine (eks·sang′gwin) *adj.* Having no blood; anemic.

ex·scind (ek·sind′) *v.t.* To cut out; sever. [< L *exscindere* < *ex-* out + *scindere* cut]

ex·se·cant (eks′sē′kənt, -kant) *n. Trig.* A function of an angle expressible as the secant of the angle minus one. See TRIGONOMETRICAL

FUNCTIONS. [< EX(TERIOR) SECANT]

ex·sect (ek·sekt′) *v.t.* To cut out. [< L *exsectus*, pp. of *exsecare* < *ex-* out + *secare* cut] — **ex·sec′tion** *n.*

ex·sert (ek·sûrt′) *v.t.* To push out; protrude. [< L *exsertus.* See EXERT.] — **ex·ser′tile** (-til) *adj.* — **ex·ser′tion** *n.*

ex·sic·ca·tae (ek′sə·kā′tē) *n. pl.* Dried specimens of plants, especially in numbered sets for herbariums. [< L, fem. pl. of *exsiccatus.* See EXSICCATE.]

ex·sic·cate (ek′sə·kāt) *v.t. & v.i.* **·cat·ed, ·cat·ing** To dry up or out. [< L *exsiccatus*, pp. of *exsiccare* < *ex-* out + *siccus* dry] — **ex·sic′-cant** (ek·sik′ənt) *adj. & n.* — **ex′sic·ca′tion** *n.* — **ex′sic·ca′tive** *adj.* — **ex′sic·ca′tor** *n.*

ex·stro·phy (ek′strə·fē) *n. Pathol.* The turning of an inner part outward, as the bladder. [< Gk. *ex-* out + *strephein* turn]

ex·tant (ek′stənt, ik·stant′) *adj.* **1** Still existing and known; living. **2** *Obs.* Standing out; manifest; conspicuous. [< L *ex(s)tans, -antis*, ppr. of *exstare* < *ex-* out + *stare* stand]

ex·tem·po·ra·ne·ous (ik·stem′pə·rā′nē·əs) *adj.* **1** Done or made with little or no preparation; composed or uttered on the spur of the moment; unpremeditated. **2** Given to speaking without notes. [< LL *extemporaneus* < *ex-* out + *tempus, temporis* time] — **ex·tem′po·ra′ne·ous·ly** *adv.* — **ex·tem′po·ra′ne·ous·ness** *n.* — *Synonyms:* extempory, extempore, impromptu, improvised, offhand, unpremeditated.

ex·tem·po·rar·y (ik·stem′pə·rer′ē) *adj.* **1** Extemporaneous. **2** Made for the occasion; extemporized: an *extemporary* shelter. — **ex·tem′po·rar′i·ly** *adv.* — **ex·tem′po·rar′i·ness** *n.*

ex·tem·po·re (ik·stem′pər·ē) *adj.* Done on the spur of the moment; extemporaneous; unstudied; offhand. — *adv.* Without special preparation; extemporaneously. See synonyms under EXTEMPORANEOUS. [< L *ex tempore* out of the time]

ex·tend (ik·stend′) *v.t.* **1** To open or stretch to full length. **2** To cause to stretch to a specified point, in a given direction, or for a given distance; make longer. **3** To cause to last until or for a specified time; continue. **4** To widen or enlarge the range, area, scope, meaning, etc., of: to *extend* the duties of an office. **5** To hold out or put forth, as the hand. **6** To give or offer to give: to *extend* hospitality. **7** To straighten, as a leg or arm. **8** In business, to put off the date of completion or payment of, as a contract or debt, beyond that originally set. **9** *Law* **a** *Brit.* To assess; appraise. **b** To seize under a writ of extent. — *v.i.* **10** To be extended; stretch. **11** To reach, as in a specified direction: This road *extends* west. — **to extend oneself** To put forth great effort. See synonyms under ADD, AMPLIFY, INCREASE, PROTRACT, SPREAD. [< L *extendere* < *ex-* out + *tendere* stretch] — **ex·tend′i·ble** *adj.*

ex·tend·ed (ik·sten′did) *adj.* **1** Covering a great extent of time or space. **2** Pulled or stretched out. **3** Broad in proportion to height: said of type: an *extended* letter. — **ex·tend′ed·ly** *adv.*

ex·ten·si·ble (ik·sten′sə·bəl) *adj.* That may be extended. — **ex·ten′si·bil′i·ty, ex·ten′si·ble·ness** *n.*

ex·ten·sile (ik·sten′sil) *adj.* Extensible.

ex·ten·sion (ik·sten′shən) *n.* **1** The act or process of extending. **2** An annex; addition. **3** That property of matter by virtue of which it occupies space. **4** *Logic* The capacity of a general concept to cover the specific classes or individual things connoted by it; the degree of applicability belonging to a notion. **5** *Surg.* Traction of a fractured or dislocated limb in order to replace its parts. **6** *Anat.* The straightening of a limb: opposed to *flexion.* **7** The act of a creditor allowing to a debtor further time in which to pay a debt. See synonyms under ACCESSION, APPENDAGE, INCREASE. [< L *extensio, -onis* < *extendere.* See EXTEND.]

ex·ten·si·ty (ik·sten′sə·tē) *n.* **1** The quality of extension; extensiveness. **2** *Psychol.* An element of sensation yielding the spatial qualities of perception.

ex·ten·sive (ik·sten′siv) *adj.* **1** Extended widely in space, time, or scope; great; wide. **2**

Designating a method of land cultivation in which the crop depends on the area treated rather than (as in *intensive* agriculture) on the fertilization and care of a restricted area. **3** Of or pertaining to extension. See synonyms under LARGE. — **ex·ten′sive·ly** *adv.* — **ex·ten′sive·ness** *n.*

ex·ten·som·e·ter (eks′ten·som′ə·tər) *n. Mech.* A micrometer by which to measure the expansion of a body, as a bar of metal. Also **ex′ten·sim′e·ter.**

ex·ten·sor (ik·sten′sər, -sôr) *n. Anat.* A muscle that causes extension. Compare FLEXOR.

ex·tent (ik·stent′) *n.* **1** The dimension or degree to which anything is extended; compass; reach; size; range; also, the limit to which anything reaches. **2** Size within given bounds: the *extent* of his power. **3** *Law* A writ directing the appraisal of lands at their yearly value, and their delivery to a creditor for a limited time to satisfy his claim. **4** *Logic* Extension (def. 4). **5** Any continuous magnitude, as of a line, surface, or solid. See synonyms under END, MAGNITUDE. [< L *extentus*, pp. of *extendere.* See EXTEND.]

ex·ten·u·ate (ik·sten′yōō·āt) *v.t.* **·at·ed, ·at·ing** **1** To represent as less blameworthy; make excuses for. **2** To cause to seem less serious or blameworthy. **3** *Rare* To make thin or weak; attenuate. **4** *Obs.* To diminish in estimation; depreciate; detract from. [< L *extenuatus*, pp. of *extenuare* weaken < *ex-* out + *tenuis* thin] — **ex·ten′u·at′ing** *adj.* — **ex·ten′u·a′tor** *n.*

ex·ten·u·a·tion (ik·sten′yōō·ā′shən) *n.* The act of extenuating, in any sense; palliation; excuse. — **ex·ten′u·a′tive** *adj. & n.* — **ex·ten′-u·a·to·ry** (-tôr′ē, -tō′rē) *adj.*

ex·te·ri·or (ik·stir′ē·ər) *adj.* **1** External; outlying. **2** Manifest to the senses. **3** Acting from without. **4** Pertaining to foreign countries; foreign. — *n.* **1** That which is outside; external features or qualities. **2** Hence, the sum of observable qualities or traits: one's physiognomy, demeanor, general appearance, or outward conduct. [< L *exterior*, compar. of *exterus* outside] — **ex·te′ri·or·ly** *adv.*

ex·te·ri·or·i·za·tion (ik·stir′ē·ər·ə·zā′shən) *n. Psychiatry* The act or process of turning the thoughts and emotions away from the self and toward the external world: used in the treatment of schizophrenia and related mental disorders.

ex·ter·mi·nate (ik·stûr′mə·nāt) *v.t.* **·nat·ed, ·nat·ing** To destroy entirely; annihilate. Also *Obs.* **ex·ter′mine.** [< L *exterminatus*, pp. of *exterminare* < *ex-* out + *terminus* a boundary] — **ex·ter′mi·na·ble** *adj.* — **ex·ter′mi·na′tive, ex·ter′mi·na·to·ry** (-tôr′ē, -tō′rē) *adj.* — *Synonyms:* annihilate, banish, demolish, destroy, eradicate, expel, extirpate, overthrow, remove, uproot. The word *exterminate* is applied to groups or masses of men or animals; individuals are said to be *banished, expelled, destroyed,* etc. *Eradicate* is primarily applied to numbers or groups of plants; a single tree may be *uprooted*, but is not said to be *eradicated.* To *extirpate* is to *destroy* the very stock, so that the race can never be restored; we speak of *eradicating* a disease, of *extirpating* a cancer, *exterminating* wild beasts or hostile tribes; we seek to *eradicate* or *extirpate* vice. See ABOLISH. *Antonyms:* augment, beget, cherish, colonize, develop, foster, increase, plant, populate, propagate, replenish, settle.

ex·ter·mi·na·tion (ik·stur′mə·nā′shən) *n.* The act or process of exterminating; annihilation.

ex·ter·mi·na·tor (ik·stûr′mə·nā′tər) *n.* **1** Someone or something that exterminates. **2** A person whose business is destroying rodents, insects, etc. **3** A chemical preparation used to destroy rodents, insects, etc.

ex·tern (eks′tûrn) *n.* **1** *Brit.* A pupil who does not live at the school he attends; a day scholar. **2** A member of the house staff of a hospital who does not reside in the institution; opposed to *intern.* Also **ex′terne.** — *adj.* (ik·stûrn′) *Obs.* External. [< F *externe* < L *externus* outer < *ex* out]

ex·ter·nal (ik·stûr′nəl) *adj.* **1** Situated or occurring outside of the subject; being on or relating to the exterior. **2** Visible from the outside; hence, often; superficial: *external* polish. **3** Belonging to the material or phenomenal world as distinguished from the mind that perceives it; objective. **4** Relating to the surface of the body: an *external* disease. **5** Pertaining to or coming from foreign lands or people; foreign: *external* traffic. **6** Extraneous; extrinsic. — *n.* **1** An exterior or outer part. **2** *pl.* Outward symbols, as of religion. [<L *externus* outer < *ex* out] — **ex·ter'nal·ly** *adv.*

ex·ter·nal–com·bus·tion (ik·stûr'nəl·kəm·bus'· chən) *adj.* Pertaining to or designating a type of engine in which ignition of the fuel–air mixture takes place outside the engine cylinder.

ex·ter·nal·ism (ik·stûr'nəl·iz'əm) *n.* **1** *Philos.* The doctrine that only things which are the objects of sense perception have reality, or can be known to have it; phenomenalism. **2** Devotion to externals, especially in matters of religion.

ex·ter·nal·i·ty (ek'stər·nal'ə·tē) *n.* **1** Location on the outside, or as on a surface outside. **2** Regard for or devotion to externals.

ex·ter·nal·ize (ik·stûr'nəl·īz) *v.t.* **·ized, ·iz·ing** **1** To give shape to; embody. **2** To make outwardly real. — **ex·ter'nal·i·za'tion** *n.*

ex·ter·o·cep·tor (ek'stər·ō·sep'tər) *n. Physiol.* A peripheral sense organ that responds to stimulation from external agents, as in sight, hearing, touch, etc. Compare INTEROCEPTOR. [<L *exterus* external + (RE)CEPTOR] — **ex'· ter·o·cep'tive** *adj.*

ex·ter·ri·to·ri·al (eks'ter·ə·tôr'ē·əl, -tō'rē-) *adj.* Extraterritorial. — **ex'ter·ri·to'ri·al'i·ty** *n.* — **ex'ter·ri·to'ri·al·ly** *adv.*

ex·tinct (ik·stingkt') *adj.* **1** Extinguished; inactive; quenched: an *extinct* volcano. **2** Exterminated; no longer existing: an *extinct* animal or species. **3** Void; lapsed: an *extinct* title. See synonyms under LIFELESS. [<L *ex(s)tinctus,* pp. of *ex(s)tinguere* EXTINGUISH]

ex·tinc·tion (ik·stingk'shən) *n.* **1** The act of extinguishing or state of being extinguished; extinguishment. **2** A putting an end to something; a destroying; complete destruction; annihilation. **3** A quenching or slaking, as of quicklime with water. **4** *Physics* A diminution in the intensity of radiation due to absorption by or scattering in the medium; also, the stopping of incident X–rays by the outer layers of atoms in a crystal.

ex·tinc·tive (ik·stingk'tiv) *adj.* Calculated to extinguish; extinguishing.

ex·tin·guish (ik·sting'gwish) *v.t.* **1** To put out; quench, as a fire. **2** To make extinct; wipe out. **3** To obscure or throw into the shade; eclipse. **4** *Law* To cause to end and become extinct; pay off and satisfy in full. See synonyms under ANNUL, SUBVERT. [<L *ex(s)tinguere* < *ex-* completely + *stinguere* quench] — **ex·tin'guish·a·ble** *adj.* — **ex·tin'guish·er** *n.* — **ex·tin'guish·ment** *n.*

ex·tir·pate (ek'stər·pāt, ik·stûr'-) *v.t.* **·pat·ed, ·pat·ing** To root out or up; eradicate; destroy wholly. See synonyms under ABOLISH, EXTERMINATE. [<L *ex(s)tirpatus,* pp. of *ex(s)tirpare* < *ex-* out + *stirps* stem, root] — **ex·tir'pa·ble** *adj.* — **ex'tir·pa'tion** *n.* — **ex'tir·pa'tive** *adj.* — **ex'tir·pa'tor** *n.* — **ex·tir·pa·to·ry** (ik·stûr'· pə·tôr'ē, -tō'rē) *adj.*

ex·tol (ik·stōl', -stol') *v.t.* **·tolled, ·tol·ling** To praise in the highest terms; magnify. See synonyms under ADMIRE, PRAISE. Also **ex·toll'.** [<L *extollere* < *ex-* out, up + *tollere* raise] — **ex·tol'ler** *n.* — **ex·tol'ment** or **ex·toll'ment** *n.*

ex·tort (ik·stôrt') *v.t.* To obtain from a person by violence, threat, oppression, or abuse of authority; wring; wrest. See synonyms under STEAL. [<L *extortus,* pp. of *extorquere* < *ex-* out + *torquere* twist] — **ex·tort'er** *n.* — **ex·tor'tive** *adj.*

ex·tor·tion (ik·stôr'shən) *n.* **1** The act or practice of extorting. **2** That which has been extorted. **3** *Law* The offense, committed by an official, of taking money under color of his office, with the consent of the victim, either where none is due, in excess of what is due, or before it is due. — **ex·tor'tion·er** or **·ist** *n.*

ex·tor·tion·ar·y (ik·stôr'shən·er'ē) *adj.* Practicing extortion.

ex·tor·tion·ate (ik·stôr'shən·it) *adj.* Characterized by extortion; oppressive. — **ex·tor'· tion·ate·ly** *adv.*

ex·tra (eks'trə) *adj.* Being over and above what is required; additional. — *n.* **1** Something beyond what is usual or required. **2** A copy or an edition of a newspaper issued for some special purpose, or at a time different from

that of the regular edition. **3** In cricket, any run resulting from a by, leg–by, no–ball, or wide. **4** Something of a special quality. **5** An actor, not a member of the regular cast, hired for a special scene, as a mob scene, or for a small part. — *adv.* Unusually. [<L, outside, beyond]

extra– *prefix* Beyond; outside; outside the scope of: *extraordinary* beyond the ordinary; *extra–oral* outside the mouth. [<L *extra–* < *extra* < *exter* on the outside < *ex* out]

ex·tra–bold (eks'trə·bōld') *adj. Printing* Denoting a very heavy face of type.

ex·tra–ca·non·i·cal (eks'trə·kə·non'i·kəl) *adj.* Being outside the canon; non–canonical: *extra–canonical* writings.

ex·tra–con·densed (eks'trə·kən·denst') *adj. Printing* Extremely narrow in proportion to the height: said of type.

ex·tract (ik·strakt') *v.t.* **1** To draw or pull out by force: to *extract* a tooth. **2** To obtain from a substance by pressing, treatment with chemicals, etc. **3** To draw out or obtain as if by such process; derive, as instruction or pleasure. **4** To copy out; select for quotation. **5** *Math.* To calculate (the root of a number). See synonyms under QUOTE. — *n.* (eks'trakt) **1** Something extracted or drawn out. **2** A selection from a book; a passage quoted. **3** The portion of a plant or substance removed by solvents and used in drug preparations in solid, powdered, or liquid form. [<L *extractus,* pp. of *extrahere* < *ex-* out + *trahere* draw, pull] — **ex·tract'a·ble** or **ex·tract'i·ble** *adj.*

ex·trac·tion (ik·strak'shən) *n.* **1** The act of extracting. **2** That which is extracted. **3** Lineage; descent.

ex·trac·tive (ik·strak'tiv) *adj.* **1** That extracts or tends to extract. **2** Capable of extraction. — *n.* **1** Something capable of being extracted. **2** That portion of an extract which becomes insoluble.

ex·trac·tor (ik·strak'tər) *n.* **1** One who or that which extracts. **2** The device in a fire-arm or cannon which withdraws a spent round of ammunition from the chamber prior to ejection.

ex·tra·cur·ric·u·lar (eks'trə·kə·rik'yə·lər) *adj.* Of or pertaining to those activities which are not a part of the curriculum, but which form an important part of school or college life, as athletics, fraternities, campus publications, etc. Also **ex'tra–cur·ric'u·lum.**

ex·tra·dit·a·ble (eks'trə·dī'tə·bəl) *adj.* Liable to or warranting extradition.

ex·tra·dite (eks'trə·dīt) *v.t.* **·dit·ed, ·dit·ing** **1** To deliver up, as to another state or nation. **2** To obtain the extradition of. [Back formation from EXTRADITION]

ex·tra·di·tion (eks'trə·dish'ən) *n.* The surrender of an accused person by a government to the justice of another government, or of a prisoner by one authority to another. [<F <L *extraditio, -onis* < *ex-* out + *traditio* a surrender. See TRADITION.]

ex·tra·dos (eks·trā'dos) *n. Archit.* The exterior curve of an arch. For illustration see under ARCH. [<F < *extra-* EXTRA- + *dos* the back <L *dorsum*]

ex·tra·ga·lac·tic (eks'trə·gə·lak'tik) *adj. Astron.* Beyond the Galaxy.

ex·tra·ju·di·cial (eks'trə·jŏŏ·dish'əl) *adj.* Happening out of court; out of the jurisdiction of the proper court. — **ex'tra·ju·di'cial·ly** *adv.*

ex·tra·mun·dane (eks'trə·mun'dān, -mun·dān') *adj.* Existing outside of our world or beyond the limits of the material universe.

ex·tra·mu·ral (eks'trə·myŏŏr'əl) *adj.* **1** Situated without or beyond the walls, as of a fortified city. **2** Beyond the boundaries of an educational institution: *extramural* games: opposed to *intramural.*

ex·tra·ne·ous (eks·trā'nē·əs) *adj.* Not intrinsic or essential to matter under consideration; foreign. [<L *extraneus* foreign. Doublet of STRANGE.] — **ex·tra'ne·ous·ly** *adv.* — **ex·tra'ne·ous·ness** *n.*

ex·traor·di·nar·y (ik·strôr'də·ner'ē; *esp. for def. 3,* eks'trə·ôr'də·ner'ē) *adj.* **1** Being beyond or out of the common order, course, or method. **2** Exceeding the ordinary degree; not ordinary; unusual; remarkable: an *extraordinary* accident. **3** Employed for a special purpose or on an exceptional occasion; special: an envoy *extraordinary.* **4** *Optics* Designating that component of a plane-polarized ray of light which, on passing

through a doubly refracting crystal, has different speeds in different directions. [<L *extraordinarius* < *extra* beyond + *ordo, ordinis* order] — **ex·traor'di·nar'i·ly** *adv.*

Synonyms: amazing, egregious, marvelous, monstrous, peculiar, preposterous, prodigious, remarkable, signal, singular, strange, striking, uncommon, unprecedented, unusual, unwonted, wonderful. See ODD, RARE[1]. **Antonyms:** common, commonplace, frequent, natural, ordinary, unimportant, usual.

ex·trap·o·late (eks·trap'ə·lāt, eks'trə·pə·lāt') *v.t. & v.i.* **·lat·ed, ·lat·ing** **1** *Math.* To estimate those values of a magnitude or a function which lie beyond the range of known or determined values: distinguished from *interpolate.* **2** To infer (a possibility) beyond the strict evidence of a series of facts, events, observations, etc. [<EXTRA- + (INTER)POLATE]

ex·tra·sen·so·ry (eks'trə·sen'sər·ē) *adj. Psychol.* **1** Of or pertaining to phenomena outside of or beyond normal sensory perception. **2** Designating those powers of perception not yet scientifically explained in relation to any of the senses, as telepathy, clairvoyance, etc. Compare PARAPSYCHOLOGY.

ex·tra·ter·ri·to·ri·al (eks'trə·ter'ə·tôr'ē·əl, -tō'· rē-) *adj.* **1** Exempt from territorial jurisdiction; not subject to the laws of one's abode: the *extraterritorial* rights of an ambassador. **2** Of or pertaining to things beyond the national territory: *extraterritorial* possessions. — **ex'tra·ter'ri·to'ri·al·ly** *adv.*

ex·tra·ter·ri·to·ri·al·i·ty (eks'trə·ter'ə·tôr'ē·al'· ə·tē, -tō'rē-) *n.* In international law, the state or privilege of freedom from (local) territorial jurisdiction, accorded to foreign sovereigns, to diplomatic representatives, their suites, and to a certain extent their dwellings.

ex·traught (eks·trôt') *adj. Obs.* **1** Extracted. **2** Distraught. [Var. of EXTRACT]

ex·trav·a·gance (ik·strav'ə·gəns) *n.* **1** An extravagant act or group of such acts; especially, undue expenditure of money; lavishness: prodigality; excess. **2** Overly exaggerated statement or language. **3** Ridiculous action. Also **ex·trav'a·gan·cy.** See synonyms under ENTHUSIASM, EXCESS.

ex·trav·a·gant (ik·strav'ə·gənt) *adj.* **1** Exceeding ordinary limits; needlessly free or lavish in expenditure. **2** Immoderate; fantastic; unrestrained, as language or behavior. **3** Excessive; exorbitant. **4** *Obs.* Straying beyond bounds; wandering abroad. See synonyms under IMMODERATE, ROMANTIC. [<MF <Med. L *extravagans, -antis,* ppr. of *extravagari* <L *extra-* outside + *vagari* wander] — **ex·trav'a·gant·ly** *adv.* — **ex·trav'a·gant·ness** *n.*

ex·trav·a·gate (ik·strav'ə·gāt) *v.i.* **·gat·ed, ·gating** **1** To roam at will. **2** To exceed proper bounds. [<Med. L *extravagatus,* pp. of *extravagari.* See EXTRAVAGANT.]

ex·trav·a·sate (ik·strav'ə·sāt) *v.* **·sat·ed, ·sating** *v.t.* **1** *Pathol.* To cause or allow the escape of from the proper vessels, as blood or air. **2** *Geol.* To gush out, as lava. — *v.i.* **3** *Pathol.* To filter or ooze into surrounding tissues, as blood from an artery or vein following a bruise. [<EXTRA- + L *vas* a vessel + -ATE[2]]

ex·tra·vas·cu·lar (eks'trə·vas'kyə·lər) *adj. Anat.* **1** Situated outside the vascular system. **2** Having no blood vessels; non–vascular.

ex·tra·ver·sion (eks'trə·vûr'zhən, -shən), **ex·tra·vert** (eks'trə·vûrt) See EXTROVERSION, EXTROVERT.

ex·treme (ik·strēm') *adj.* **1** At or to the farthest limit; outermost; utmost. **2** Last; final. **3** In the utmost degree; far removed from the normal or average: *extreme* joy; *extreme* poverty. **4** Immoderate or radical: *extreme* opinions. — *n.* **1** The utmost or highest degree: the *extreme* of cruelty. **2** Either of two ends (of a line, series, scale, etc.): *extremes* of temperature. **3** *Math.* The first or last term of a proportion or series. **4** *Logic* **a** Either the subject or predicate of a proposition, distinguished from the copula. **b** Either of the two terms of a syllogism which, separated in the premises, are joined in the conclusion. [<OF <L *extremus,* superl. of *exterus* outside] — **ex·treme'ly** *adv.* — **ex·treme'ness** *n.*

ex·trem·i·ty (ik·strem'ə·tē) *n. pl.* **·ties** **1** The utmost or farthest point; termination, end, or edge. **2** The greatest degree. **3** Desperate distress or need. **4** *pl.* Extreme measures. **5** *Usually pl.* The end part of a limb or appendage. See synonyms under END, NECESSITY.

ex·tri·cate (eks'trə·kāt) v.t. **·cat·ed, ·cat·ing**
1 To free from hindrance, difficulties, etc.;
disentangle. **2** To cause to be given off; evolve,
as gas or moisture. See synonyms under RE-
LEASE. [<L *extricatus*, pp. of *extricare* <*ex*-
out + *tricae* troubles] — **ex·tri·ca·ble** (eks'-
tri·kə·bəl) adj. — **ex'tri·ca·bly** adv.

ex·trin·sic (ek·strin'sik) adj. **1** Being outside
of the nature of an object or case; not inherent
or included in a thing; not essential: opposed
to *intrinsic*. **2** *Anat.* Originating beyond the
limits of a body or limb: *extrinsic* muscles.
3 Irrelevant; extraneous. Also **ex·trin'si·cal.**
[<F *extrinsèque* <L *extrinsecus* outwardly
< *exter* outside + *secus* besides] — **ex·trin'·
si·cal·ly** adv. — **ex·trin'si·cal·ness** n.

ex·tro·ver·sion (eks'trō·vûr'zhən, -shən) n.
1 *Psychol.* The turning of one's interests toward the outside world or toward persons
other than oneself; the quality of finding
interest and pleasure in outside interests; opposed to *introversion*. Also **extraversion. 2**
Anat. Extroversion. [<*extro*- outwards (<EX-
TRA-) + L *versio, -onis* a turning <*vertere*
turn]

ex·tro·vert (eks'trō·vûrt) n. A person highly
adapted to living in and deriving satisfaction
from the external world: opposed to *introvert*. Also **extravert.**

ex·trude (ik·strōōd') v. **·trud·ed, ·trud·ing** v.t.
1 To force, thrust, or push out; expel. **2** To
force (a plastic, metal, or other substance)
through a shaped opening in order to give it
a desired cross–section. — v.i. **3** To protrude.
[<L *extrudere* <*ex*- out + *trudere* thrust]
ex·tru·sion (ik·strōō'zhən) n. **1** The act or
process of extruding; expulsion. **2** *Geol.* An
overflow of lava upon the earth's surface
through conduits or fissures in the rocks;
effusion.

ex·u·ber·ance (ig·zōō'bər·əns) n. **1** Abounding
variety or copiousness. **2** Superabundance:
an *exuberance* of imagination. Also **ex·u'ber·
an·cy.**

ex·u·ber·ant (ig·zōō'bər·ənt) adj. **1** Effusive;
overflowing; lavish. **2** Marked by plentiful-
ness; producing copiously. See synonyms under FERTILE, REDUNDANT. [<L *exuberans,
-antis* <*ex*- completely + *uberare* be fruitful
< *uber* rich] — **ex·u'ber·ant·ly** adv.

ex·u·date (eks'yōō·dāt) n. *Biol.* Any substance
which filters through the walls of living cellular tissue and is available for removal or
extraction, as gums and resins. [<L *ex-
(s)udatus*, pp. of *ex(s)udare*. See EXUDE.]

ex·ude (ig·zōōd', ik·sōōd') v.t. & v.i. **·ud·ed,
·ud·ing** To give off or come forth gradually;
ooze or trickle forth, as sweat. [<L *ex(s)udare*
< *ex*- out + *sudare* sweat]

ex·ult (ig·zult') v.i. To rejoice in or as in
triumph; take great delight. [<F *exulter* <L
ex(s)ultare, freq. of *exsilire* leap up < *ex*-
out + *salire* leap] — **ex·ult'ing·ly** adv.

ex·ul·ta·tion (eg'zul·tā'shən, ek'sul-) n. The
act or state of exulting; triumphant joy. Also
ex·ul'tance, ex·ul'tan·cy. [<L *ex(s)ultatio,
-onis* <*ex(s)ultare*. See EXULT.]

ex·urb (eks'ûrb') n. A residential area outside
a city beyond the suburbs, usually characterized by relative affluence. [<EX- + -*urb* (on
analogy with *suburb*) <L *urbs* city] — **ex·
urb·an** (eks·ûr'bən) adj.

ey·as (ī'əs) n. A young hawk; nestling. [ME
nyas <F *niais* <L *nidus* a nest; in ME *a nyas*
became *an eyas*]

eye[1] (ī) n. **1** The organ of vision in animals;
especially, the human eye, a nearly spherical
mass set in a cavity of the skull and consisting

Superior rectus muscle
Retina
Choroid
Sclera
Optic nerve
Inferior rectus muscle
Conjunctiva sac
Upper eyelid
Lens
Iris
Aqueous chamber
Cornea
Lower eyelid

CROSS–SECTION OF THE HUMAN EYE

of the cornea, iris, pupil, lens, with associated
muscles and optic nerve, also the eyelids, eyelashes, and eyebrows. **2** Ocular perception;
sight. **3** Capacity for seeing or discerning.
4 Attentive observation; watchful care. **5** A
particular look or expression; mien. **6** Mental
or moral vision; estimation; also, regard;
desire. **7** Anything that resembles the human
organ of sight, or its socket, in shape, place,
or office: the *eye* of a needle, the *eye* of a
potato, apple, gooseberry, dahlia, etc.
8 *Meteorol.* The calm central area of an
advancing hurricane or cyclone: also **eye of
the storm. — to keep an eye out** or **peeled** To
watch for; keep alert. — **to lay eyes on** To see.
— v.t. **eyed, ey·ing** or **eye·ing 1** To look at
carefully; scrutinize. **2** To make a hole in, like
the eye of a needle. ◆ Homophones: *aye, I.*
[OE *ēage*]

eye[2] (ī) n. A brood, as of pheasants. ◆ Homophones: *aye, I.* [ME *nye* <OF *ni* <L *nidus*
a nest: in ME *a nye* was altered to *an eye*]

eye·ball (ī'bôl') n. The globe or ball of the eye.

eye bank *Med.* A collection of healthy corneas
stored at very low temperatures, for use in transplanting on eyes which have been seriously injured by accident or disease.

eye·bar (ī'bär') n. *Engin.* A heat-treated steel bar
of high tensile strength, usually rectangular in
cross-section, with holes punched in the terminal
heads for attachment to other structural members, as suspension cables, trusses, etc.

eye·beam (ī'bēm') n. A quick look or glance of
the eye.

eye·bolt (ī'bōlt') n. *Mech.* Any of various forms
of bolt having, in place of a head, an eye or ring
to receive a rope, hook, etc.

eye·bright (ī'brīt') n. **1** A low annual herb of the
figwort family (*Euphrasia officinalis*), formerly
used in eye lotions. **2** The red or scarlet pimpernel.

eye·brow (ī'brou') n. **1** The arch over the eye. **2**
Its covering, especially the hairs. ◆ Collateral adjective: *superciliary.*

eye·cup (ī'kup') n. **1** A small cup of glass or
metal, with rim curved to fit the eye, used in applying lotions. **2** *Anat.* An embryonic structure
which develops into the retina.

eye·glass (ī'glas', ī'gläs') n. **1** pl. A pair of lenses
resembling spectacles without bows; a pincenez:
frequently called **glass'es. 2** Any lens used to assist vision; a monocle. **3** The glass nearest the eye
in a telescope or microscope. **4** An eyecup.

eye·ground (ī'ground') n. *Anat.* The fundus, or
inner side of the back of the eyeball, especially as
seen in an ophthalmoscope.

eye·hole (ī'hōl') n. **1** A round opening through
which to pass a pin, hook, rope, or the like. **2** A

hole or crevice through which one may look;
peephole. **3** The socket containing the eye.

eye·hook (ī'hook') n. A hook permanently attached to a reinforced ring at the end of a rope,
chain, etc. See illustration under HOOK.

eye·lash (ī'lash') n. One of the stiff curved hairs
growing from the edge of the eyelids. ◆ Collateral adjective: *ciliary.*

eye·less (ī'lis) adj. Lacking eyes; deprived of
sight.

eye·let (ī'lit) n. **1** A small hole or opening; a little
eye or aperture. **2** A hole made in canvas,
leather, paper, or the like, either bushed with
metal or worked around with buttonhole stitch.
3 A metal ring for protecting such a perforation:
also **eye'let-ring'. 4** *Entomol.* An ocellus. —v.t.
To make eyelets in. [<F *oeillet*, dim. of *oeil* an
eye]

eye·lid (ī'lid') n. One of the curtains of loose integument that cover the eyeballs in front. ◆ Collateral adjective: *palpebral.*

eye-o·pen·er (ī'ō'pən·ər) n. *U.S.* **1** Anything that
opens the eyes, actually or figuratively. **2** An incredible tale or piece of news. **3** *Colloq.* Something enabling one to comprehend what was before a mystery or unheeded. **4** *Colloq.* A drink of
liquor, especially one taken early in the morning.

eye·piece (ī'pēs') n. *Optics* The lens or combination of lenses nearest the eye in a telescope or microscope.

eye shadow A cosmetic preparation, tinted
blue, green, black, etc., applied to the eyelids to
enhance the eyes.

eye·shot (ī'shot') n. Reach or scope of the eye;
view; sight.

eye·sight (ī'sīt') n. **1** The power or sense of sight.
2 Extent of vision; view.

eye·sore (ī'sôr', ī'sōr') n. **1** A diseased place on or
near the eye. **2** Anything that offends the sight.

eye speculum An instrument for retracting the
eyelids and holding them apart.

eye·splice (ī'splīs') n. *Naut.* A loop formed by
bending back the end of a rope and splicing it
into the rope.

eye·spot (ī'spot') n. *Biol.* **1** One of the rudimentary visual organs of many invertebrates, consisting of a few pigment cells overlaying a nerve
filament sensitive to light. **2** The rudimentary eye
in an embryo. **3** An ocellus. **4** An eyelike marking.

eye·stalk (ī'stôk') n. *Zool.* A stalk or peduncle
that supports an eye, as in lobsters and crabs.

eye·stone (ī'stōn') n. A small smooth calcareous
disk with one side convex, used to remove foreign substances from the eye.

eye·strain (ī'strān') n. An affection caused by excessive or improper use of the eyes.

eye·string (ī'string') n. *Anat.* A muscle or tendon
that holds or moves the eye.

eye·tooth (ī'tōōth') n. pl. **eye·teeth** One of the
upper canine teeth. —**to cut one's eyeteeth** To
grow old enough to gain wisdom by experience.

eye·wash (ī'wosh', ī'wôsh') n. **1** A medicinal
wash for the eye. **2** *Slang* Nonsense; bunk.

eye·wa·ter (ī'wô'tər, ī'wot'ər) n. **1** The natural
water that forms in the eye; tears. **2** A medicated
lotion for the eyes.

eye·wit·ness (ī'wit'nis) n. One who has seen a
thing or an occurrence with his own eyes and
hence can give testimony about it.

eye worm A nematode worm (*Thelazia califor-
niensis*), whitish in color and about half an inch
long, which lives underneath the eyelids and in
the tear ducts, causing inflammation and discomfort: parasitic on dogs, sheep, cats, and man.

F

f, F (ef) pl. **f's, F's** or **fs, Fs, effs** (efs) n. **1** The
sixth letter of the English alphabet, from
Phoenician *vau*, through Hebrew *vau*, Greek *di-
gamma*, which was early dropped from the

Greek alphabet, but was restored by the Romans. **2** The sound of the letter *f*, usually a
voiceless labiodental fricative. See ALPHABET.
—symbol **1** *Music* **a** The fourth tone in the mus-

ical scale of C; the pitch of this tone, or the note
representing it. **b** The scale built upon F. **c** The
bass clef in musical notation. **2** *Chem.* Fluorine
(symbol F). **3** *Genetics* A filial generation, usu-

ally followed by a subscript numeral, as F₁, F₂, for the first, second, etc., filial generation offspring of a given mating. **4** In education, a grade meaning failure, or, sometimes, fair.

fa (fä) *n.* The fourth tone of any key in music, or of the so-called natural key. [< Ital.]

fa' (fô) *n. Scot.* **1** Lot; luck. **2** Share. **3** Fall. Also spelled **faw.**

fa·ba·ceous (fə-bā'shəs) *adj. Bot.* Designating a very large family (*Leguminosae;* formerly *Fabaceae*) of herbs, shrubs, and trees, characterized by stipulate leaves, irregular flowers, and fruits that are true pods or legumes; the bean or pea family. [< L *fabaceus* leguminous < *faba* a bean]

Fabian Society An English association of socialists, formed in 1884, including many able writers on economics, having as their object the achievement of socialism by easy stages.

fa·ble (fā'bəl) *n.* **1** A brief story or tale embodying a moral and introducing persons, animals, or inanimate things as speakers an actors. **2** A foolish or improbable story; fabrication. **3** *Archaic* The plot of an epic or dramatic poem. **4** Common talk. See synonyms under ALLEGORY, FICTION. —*v.t. & v.i.* **fa·bled, fa·bling** To invent or tell (fables or stories); fabricate; lie. [< OF < L *fabula* < *fari* say, speak] —**fa'bler** *n.*

fa·bled (fā'bəld) *adj.* **1** Recorded in fable; made famous by fable. **2** Existing only in fable; mythical.

fab·li·au (fab'lē-ō, *Fr.* fȧ·blē-ō') *n. pl.* **·aux** (-ōz, *Fr.* -ō') A short, comic or gay tale, usually in eight-syllable verse: the genre which arose in France in the 12th and 13th centuries. [< F, ult. < OF *fable.* See FABLE.]

fab·ric (fab'rik) *n.* **1** A woven, felted, or knitted material, as cloth, felt, hosiery, or lace; also, the material used in its making. **2** Something that has been fabricated, constructed, or put together; any complex construction. **3** An edifice: St. Paul's, that noble *fabric.* **4** The manner of construction; workmanship; texture: cloth of a very intricate *fabric.* **5** *Geol.* The texture or structure of igneous rock. See synonyms under FRAME. [< OF *fabrique* < L *fabrica* a workshop < *faber* a workman. Doublet of FORGE.]

fab·ri·cate (fab'rə·kāt) *v.t.* **·cat·ed, ·cat·ing** **1** To make or manufacture; build. **2** To make by combining parts; assemble. **3** To invent, as lies or reasons; concoct. See synonyms under CONSTRUCT, MAKE. [< L *fabricatus,* pp. of *fabricare* construct < *faber* a workman] —**fab'ri·ca·tor** *n.*

fab·ri·ca·tion (fab'rə·kā'shən) *n.* **1** The art of fabricating. **2** Something fabricated, as a structure or contrivance. **3** A contrived or trumped-up story; a falsehood. See synonyms under DECEPTION, FICTION, LIE.

fab·u·lous (fab'yə·ləs) *adj.* **1** Belonging to fable; fictitious; mythical. **2** Passing the limits of belief; incredible. —**fab'u·lous·ly** *adv.* —**fab'u·lous·ness** *n.*

fa·çade (fə·säd', fa-; *Fr.* fȧ·sȧd') *n.* **1** *Archit.* The front or chief face of a building. **2** The front, visible part, or most conspicuous part of an institution, often designed to convey a favorable impression of the whole. [< F < *face* a face, on analogy with Ital. *facciata,* both ult. < L *facies* a face]

face (fās) *n.* **1** The anterior portion of the head, in which the eyes, nose, and mouth are situated, comprising in man the surface between the top of the forehead and the bottom of the chin, and extending laterally from ear to ear. **2** The surface, or most important surface, of anything; a front or working surface; that side or edge presented to view, or to any particular adjustment for operating; a side or surface of a solid: the *face* of a dam, one of the *faces* of a crystal, the *face* of a playing card, the *face* of a molar tooth. **3** The façade. **4** The flat portion of a propeller blade. **5** The flat or rounded striking surface of a hammer. **6** The long outer slope of a bastion; also, that part of the line of defense ending with the curtain and the angle of the shoulder. **7** *Mining*

a The end of a drift or tunnel. **b** The sharply defined and more important joint in coal running at right angles to the plane of stratification. **8** *Printing* **a** The impression surface of a type body or of a printing plate. **b** The letter or other character cut on the type, or the size or style of the character cut on the type. **9** The dial of a clock or watch. **10** The obverse of a coin, or medal, which bears the effigy; occasionally the reverse side. **11** The inscribed side of a document, or printed side of a sheet. **12** One of the sides of any military formation, as of a square. **13** The external aspect or appearance; look; show; outward effect or impression: He put a bold *face* on the matter. **14** Personal force, influence, opinion, or will, as if expressed in the countenance: He set his *face* steadily against it. **15** Personal presence; immediate cognizance; sight: before the *face* of, to one's *face.* **16** *Colloq.* Effrontery; audacity; assurance. **17** The value as expressed on the written or printed surface: said of any commercial paper, as a note or bond. **18** In golf, the striking side of a club head; the side or slope of a hillock or bunker. — **in the face of** **1** In the presence of; confronting. **2** In opposition to; in defiance of; in spite of. — **to save face** To save one's reputation or standing; protect one's dignity in the opinion of others. — **to lose face** To lose standing or reputation. — **to make faces** To grimace. — *v.* **faced, fac·ing** *v.t.* **1** To bear or turn the face toward; front upon: The house *faces* the street. **2** To cause to turn in a given direction, as soldiers. **3** To meet face to face; confront, as with courage or boldness: to *face* great odds. **4** To realize or be aware of: to *face* facts. **5** To cover with a layer or surface of another material: to *face* brick with stucco or a garment with silk. **6** To make smooth the surface of; dress: to *face* stone. **7** To turn face upward, as a playing card. — *v.i.* **8** To be turned or placed with the face in a given direction: The house *faces* west. **9** To turn in a given direction: The soldiers *faced* right. See synonyms under OPPOSE. — **to face down** To abash or disconcert by a bold stare or audacious manner. — **to face out** To see to completion or endure, as by a persevering manner. — **to face the music** *U.S. Slang* To accept the consequences. — **to face up to** To meet with courage; confront. **2** To realize; become aware of. [< F, ult. < L *facies* a face] —**face'a·ble** *adj.*

fac·et (fas'it) *n.* **1** One of the small plane surfaces cut upon a diamond or other gem. For illustration see DIAMOND. **2** *Archit.* A flat projecting fillet between the flutes of a column. **3** *Zool.* A unit of a compound eye in insects and crustaceans; also, the surface or cornea of such an eye. **4** One side, view, or phase of a subject or of a person's mind or character. **5** *Anat.* A small flat surface on a bone. **6** *Dent.* A flat abraded spot on a tooth: also **fac'ette.** — *v.t.* **fac·et·ed** or **·et·ted, fac·et·ing** or **·et·ting** To cut or work a facet or facets upon. [< F *facette,* dim. of *face* FACE]

fa·ce·tious (fə·sē'shəs) *adj.* Indulging in, characterized by, or marked by wit or humor; jocular; jocose; waggish; witty; funny; humorous. See synonyms under HUMOROUS, JOCOSE, MERRY. [< L *facetia* wit + -OUS] —**fa·ce'tious·ly** *adv.* —**fa·ce'tious·ness** *n.*

fa·cial (fā'shəl) *adj.* Of, near, or affecting the face. — *n. Colloq.* A massage or other treatment of the face for the purpose of enhancing health and beauty of facial skin.

facial angle *Anat.* The angle subtended between the line representing the face-height and the axis of the skull from the edge of central incisors to the auricular point.

facial index A number expressing the ratio of the breadth to the length of the face.

facial mask A face pack.

facial nerve *Anat.* The seventh cranial nerve, one of a pair which actuate the muscles controlling facial expression.

fa·ci·es (fā'shi·ēz) *n.* **1** The general aspect

FACIAL ANGLE
a. Glabella.
c. Edge of central incisors.
f. Auricular point.
acf. Facial angle.

or external appearance of anything. **2** *Geol.* The aggregate of the characteristics which determine the origin, composition, and mode of formation of rock deposits. **3** *Med.* The expression of the face in a given disease. **4** A surface. [< L, face, appearance]

fac·ile (fas'il) *adj.* **1** Easy of performance. **2** Easily gained; readily mastered. **3** Easily moved or persuaded; pliant; yielding. **4** Ready or quick in performance; dexterous; skilful. [< F < L *facilis* easy to do < *facere* do] —**fac'ile·ly** *adv.* —**fac'ile·ness** *n.*

fa·cil·i·tate (fə·sil'ə·tāt) *v.t.* **·tat·ed, ·tat·ing** To make easier or more convenient. —**fa·cil'i·ta'tion** *n.*

fa·cil·i·ty (fə·sil'ə·tē) *n. pl.* **·ties** **1** Ease or readiness in doing; dexterity. **2** Readiness of compliance; pliancy. **3** Any aid or convenience: *facilities* for travel. **4** A place or office equipped to fulfill a special function: a government *facility.* [< L *facilitas, -tatis* ability < *facere* do]

fac·ing (fā'sing) *n.* **1** A covering in front serving any purpose. **2** A covering plate or layer in front, for ornament or protection against wear or corrosion, or to alter the contour. **3** The lining of a garment on parts exposed by being turned back, as the lapel of a coat or a hem, cuff, etc. **4** Any heavy, durable fabric used for this. **5** An improvement to the appearance of a food product, as by the addition of coloring matter. **6** *Mech.* A smooth, machined surface for attachment to another part. **7** *pl.* The different-colored collars and cuffs on a military uniform, often indicative of the branch of the service.

fac·sim·i·le (fak·sim'ə·lē) *n.* An exact copy or reproduction, often differing in scale but always identical or closely imitative in detail, material, etc. See synonyms under DUPLICATE. — *adj.* **1** Exactly copied or reproduced; exactly similar or corresponding: a *facsimile* autograph. **2** Producing exact copies or facsimiles. [< L *fac simile* make like]

fact (fakt) *n.* **1** Anything that is done or happens, as an act or deed. **2** Anything actually existent. **3** Any statement strictly true; truth; reality. **4** *pl. Law* The issues raised by the pleadings and evidence in an action and upon which the jury must base their verdict. **5** *Obs.* A thing done; a deed; performance. See synonyms under CIRCUMSTANCE, EVENT, PROOF. [< L *factum* < *facere* do. Doublet of FEAT.]

fac·tice (fak'tis) *n.* A fluffy, rubberlike material obtained by vulcanizing linseed oil with sulfur or sulfur chloride. [< F < L *factitius.* See FACTITIOUS.]

fac·tion (fak'shən) *n.* **1** A number of persons combined for a common purpose. **2** A party within a party; an irregular association of partisans; a cabal. **3** Violent opposition, as to a government; turbulence; dissension. See synonyms under CABAL. [< F < L *factio, -onis* < *facere* do. Doublet of FASHION.] —**fac'tion·ist,** *Obs.* **fac'tion·ar'y** *n.*

fac·tious (fak'shəs) *adj.* Given to, characterized by, or promoting faction; turbulent; partisan. See synonyms under PERVERSE. —**fac'tious·ly** *adv.* —**fac'tious·ness** *n.*

fac·ti·tious (fak·tish'əs) *adj.* **1** Artificial; conventional; affected; unnatural. **2** Proceeding from or created by art as opposed to nature. [< L *factitius* artificial < *facere* do] —**fac·ti'tious·ly** *adv.* —**fac·ti'tious·ness** *n.*
    Synonyms: affected, artificial, manufactured, pretended, sham, simulated, spurious.

fac·ti·tive (fak'tə·tiv) *adj. Gram.* Pertaining to or designating a verb which takes, in addition to an object, a characterizing complement. Examples: They elected *him president;* He called *John* a *villain.* [< NL *factitivus* < *factitare,* freq. of *facere* do] —**fac'ti·tive·ly** *adv.*

fac·tor (fak'tər) *n.* **1** *Math.* One of two or more quantities that, when multiplied together, produce a given quantity. **2** One of several elements or causes that produce a result. **3** *Brit.* A commission merchant; agent. **4** *Scot.* A bailiff or steward; also, a person legally appointed to care for forfeited property. **5** *U.S.* In some States, a garnishee. **6** A specialized commercial banker who finances manufacturers and dealers, accepting receivables as collateral. **7** The unit of heredity. See GENE. **8** *Physiol.* An element important in metabolism and nutrition, as a vitamin, enzyme, or hormone. **9** The agent controlling one of the remaining posts of the Hudson's Bay Company. See synonyms under AGENT. — *v.t.* **1** To manage as a factor. **2** *Math.* To resolve into factors; factorize. [<L, maker < *facere* make]

fac·tor·age (fak'tər·ij) *n.* **1** A factor's commission. **2** The conduct of a factor's business.

fac·to·ri·al (fak·tôr'ē·əl, -tō'rē-) *n. Math.* The product of a series of consecutive positive integers from 1 to a given number; thus, *factorial* four (written 4! or ⌊4) = 1 × 2 × 3 × 4 = 24. — *adj.* Pertaining to a factor or a factorial.

fac·tor·ship (fak'tər·ship) *n.* **1** The business of a factor or a factory. **2** A body of factors.

fac·to·ry (fak'tər·ē) *n. pl.* **·ries** **1** An establishment devoted to the manufacture of something, including the building or buildings and machinery necessary to such manufacture; a manufactory. **2** A business establishment in charge of factors or agents in a foreign country.

fac·to·tum (fak·tō'təm) *n.* An employee hired to do all kinds of work. [<Med. L *fac*, sing. imperative of *facere* do + *totum* everything]

fac·tu·al (fak'chŏŏ·əl) *adj.* Pertaining to, containing, or consisting of facts; literal and exact; genuine.

fac·u·la (fak'yə·lə) *n. pl.* **·lae** (-lē) *Astron.* A small spot on the sun brighter than the rest of the photosphere. [<L, dim. of *fax* torch]

fac·ul·ta·tive (fak'əl·tā'tiv) *adj.* **1** Producing or imparting faculty or power; enabling; qualifying. **2** Endowing with authority or power, but allowing the use of it at option or contingently. **3** Empowering but not requiring one to perform some act; providing, as a law, for optional action: distinguished from *obligative*. **4** *Biol.* Having the power to exist in and become adapted to changed conditions, as aerobic bacteria, which may become anaerobic: distinguished from *obligate*. **5** Related or pertaining to a faculty or faculties.

fac·ul·ty (fak'əl·tē) *n. pl.* **·ties** **1** Any mode of bodily or mental behavior regarded as implying a natural endowment or acquired power: the *faculty* of seeing, feeling, reasoning. **2** Any special form of skill, or unusual ability, whether natural or acquired; knack; turn; native facility. **3** One of the native complex capacities or powers into which the older psychology analyzed, and to which it ascribed, the phenomena of conscious mental life: the *faculty* of perception, memory, thought, etc. **4** The members of any one of the learned professions, collectively: the *faculty* of law or medicine. **5** The body of instructors in a university, college, or higher educational institution. **6** A department of learning or instruction at a university: the English *faculty*. **7** In the Roman Catholic Church, the right to perform certain ecclesiastical functions, bestowed by a prelate upon a subordinate; formerly, also, power or privilege in general bestowed or otherwise obtained: chiefly in the plural. **8** Ability to do or manage: executive skill and efficiency, especially in domestic matters: a housekeeper of notable *faculty*. **9** Pecuniary resources; means. See synonyms under ABILITY. [<OF *faculté* <L *facultas, -tatis* < *facilis*. See FACILE.]

fad (fad) *n.* A passing fancy or fashion; hobby. [Cf. dial. E *fad* be busy with trifles] — **fad'·dist** *n.*

fade (fād) *v.* **fad·ed**, **fad·ing** *v.i.* **1** To lose brightness or clearness; become indistinct; dim. **2** To lose freshness, vigor, youth, etc.; wither; wane. — *v.t.* **3** To cause to fade. **4** *U.S. Slang* In dice, to cover (a bet). — **to fade in** In motion pictures, to come into view gradually. — **to fade out** In motion pictures, to disappear gradually. See synonyms under DIE[1]. [<OF *fader* < *fade* pale, insipid]

fade-a·way (fād'ə·wā') *n.* In baseball, a slow, curved ball, seemingly pitched fast, that breaks inward toward the batter.

fade-in (fād'in') *n.* A gradual appearance of a motion-picture sequence on the screen, often, as by double exposure, etc., replacing a preceding sequence.

fade·less (fād'lis) *adj.* Unfading. See synonyms under ETERNAL. — **fade'less·ly** *adv.*

fade-out (fād'out') *n.* A gradual disappearance

of a motion-picture sequence on the screen.

fad·er (fā'dər) *n.* In motion pictures, a potentiometer for the control of sound volume in reproduction, or for controlling the amount of light in developing the film.

fad·ing (fā'ding) *n. Telecom.* A lessening in the strength of electromagnetic signals owing to increased distance from the transmitting station, atmospheric condition, or mechanical defect.

fa·ga·ceous (fə·gā'shəs) *adj. Bot.* Of or pertaining to a large family (*Fagaceae*) of trees and shrubs having alternate simple leaves, sterile flowers, and one-celled, one-seeded nuts; the beech family. [<NL *Fagaceae*, the beech family <L *fagus* a beech]

fag-end (fag'end') *n.* **1** The frayed end, as of a rope. **2** A remnant or last part, usually of slight utility.

fag·ot (fag'ət) *n.* **1** A bundle of sticks, twigs, or branches, as used for fuel. **2** A bundle of pieces of wrought iron or steel to be worked over. — *v.t.* **1** To make a fagot of. **2** To ornament by fagoting. Also *faggot.* [<F]

fag·ot·ing (fag'ət·ing) *n.* A mode of ornamenting textile fabrics, in which a number of threads of a material are drawn out and the cross-threads tied together in the middle; in basketry, hemstitching. Also **fag'got·ing.**

FAGOTING
Hemstitch   Drawn work

fahl·band (fäl'band', Ger. fäl'bänt') *n. Geol.* A band or stratum of rock containing metallic sulfides. [<G < *fahl* pale + *band* band]

Fahr·en·heit (far'ən·hīt, Ger. fär'ən·hīt) *adj.* **1** Designating a temperature scale in which zero is the temperature of a mixture of equal weights of snow and common salt; the freezing point of water is 32° and the boiling point 212°, all under standard atmospheric pressure. **2** Noting a thermometer graduated to this scale. Abbr. *F.* or *Fahr.* See TEMPERATURE. [after Gabriel Daniel *Fahrenheit*, 1686–1736, German physicist]

fa·ience (fī·äns', fä-; *Fr.* fà·yäns') *n.* A variety of majolica, usually highly decorated. [<F, pottery from Faenza]

fail (fāl) *v.i.* **1** To be unsuccessful; be unable. **2** To be deficient or wanting, as in ability, faithfulness, etc.; prove disappointing: He *failed* in his duty. **3** To give out: His strength *failed.* **4** To become extinct; die out. **5** To fade away; disappear: The light *failed* rapidly. **6** To weaken gradually, as in illness or death. **7** To become insolvent; go bankrupt. **8** To receive a failing grade. — *v.t.* **9** To prove to be inadequate or of no help to; abandon; forsake: My courage *fails* me. **10** To leave undone or unfulfilled; neglect: with infinitive as object: He *failed* to carry out orders. **11** In education: **a** To receive a failing grade in (a course or test). **b** To assign a failing grade to (a pupil). See synonyms under FALL, SUSPEND. — *n.* Failure: in the phrase *without fail.* [<OF *faillir* <L *fallere* to deceive]

fail·ing (fā'ling) *n.* A minor fault; foible; infirmity. See synonyms under FOIBLE. — *adj.* **1** Characterized by failure. **2** Diminishing; weakening. — **fail'ing·ly** *adv.*

fail·ure (fāl'yər) *n.* **1** The act of failing, cessation of supply, power, etc.: *failure* of sight. **2** A becoming bankrupt or proving unsuccessful in business or in any profession or trade. **3** Neglect or non-performance. **4** That which fails; anything unsuccessful. **5** One who fails conspicuously or in some specific effort. See synonyms under LOSS, MISFORTUNE, NEGLECT. [Earlier *failer* <AF, orig. var. of OF *faillir*. See FAIL.]

faint (fānt) *v.i.* **1** To lose consciousness; swoon: often with *away.* **2** *Archaic* To fail in courage or hope. **3** *Obs.* To become weak. See synonyms under FALL. [<adj.] — *adj.* **1** Lacking in purpose, courage, or energy; timid. **2** Ready to faint; weak. **3** Evincive of weakness, feebleness, or lack of purpose; slight. **4** Indistinct; feeble; dim. — *n.* A swoon; syncope: also **faint'·ing.** ◆ Homophone: *feint.* [<OF, pp. of *faindre* FEIGN] — **faint'er** *n.* — **faint'ish** *adj.* — **faint'·ish·ness** *n.* — **faint'ly** *adv.* — **faint'ness** *n.*

Synonyms (*adj.*): dim, exhausted, faded, fainthearted, faltering, fatigued, feeble, half-hearted, ill-defined, indistinct, irresolute, languid, listless, purposeless, timid, weak, wearied, worn. *Faint*, with the general sense of lacking strength or effectiveness, covers a wide range of meaning, signifying overcome by physical weakness or exhaustion, or lacking in purpose, courage, or energy, as said of persons; or lacking definiteness or distinctness of color or sound, as said of written characters, voices, or musical notes. A person may be *faint* when physically *wearied*, or when overcome by fear; he may be a *faint* adherent because naturally *feeble* or *purposeless*, or because *half-hearted* in the cause; he may be a *faltering* supporter because naturally *irresolute* or because *faint-hearted* and *timid* in view of perils that threaten, a *listless* worker, through want of mental energy and purpose. Written characters may be *faint* or *dim*, either because originally written with poor ink, or because they have become *faded* by time and exposure. Antonyms: bright, brilliant, clear, conspicuous, daring, energetic, fresh, hearty, resolute, strong, sturdy, vigorous.

faint-heart·ed (fānt'här'tid) *adj.* Timorous; cowardly. — **faint'-heart'ed·ly** *adv.* — **faint'-heart'ed·ness** *n.*

faints (fānts) *n. pl.* The dilute and impure spirit produced during the first and last stages of the distillation of whisky: also spelled *feints.*

fair[1] (fâr) *adj.* **1** Free from clouds; not obscure; sunshiny; clear. Compare def. 13. **2** Open; distinct. **3** Free from spot or blemish. **4** Showing no partiality, prejudice, or favoritism; hence, just, upright; honest. **5** Having light or clear color or hue; not dark or sallow: *fair* hair or complexion. **6** Pleasing to the eye or the mind; comely; beautiful. **7** Nearly or fully up to the average; moderately satisfactory or excellent; passably good or large: a *fair* crop. **8** Easily legible; well-formed and distinct: a *fair* print; a *fair* handwriting. **9** Apparently good and plausible, but not sincere: *fair* promises. **10** Accurately trimmed; even; regular; flowing: said of timbers, lines, or the like. **11** In games and sports, according to rule: a *fair* tackle; a *fair* walking. **12** In a favorable direction: *fair* wind. **13** *Meteorol.* Having the sky cloudless to half covered with clouds; no aspect of rain, snow, or hail; fine; bright; sunny. **14** Properly open to attack: He is *fair* game. See synonyms under BEAUTIFUL, CANDID, GOOD, HONEST, JUST[1], PURE, RIGHT. — *adv.* **1** In a spirit of justice and reason; fairly, justly; honestly: deal *fair* with me. **2** In clear view; distinctly: *fair* in sight. **3** Favorably; fortunately; happily; to bid *fair.* **4** Politely; kindly; plausibly; to speak *fair.* **5** *Obs.* Deliberately; quietly. — *v.t.* To make smooth, as timbers. — *v.i. Dial.* To become fair or clear: said of weather. — *n.* **1** A fair one; sweetheart. **2** Women: with *the*: also *the fair sex.* **3** *Obs.* Good fortune; good luck. **4** *Obs.* Beauty. — **for fair** For sure. ◆ Homophone: *fare.* [OE *fæger*] — **fair'ness** *n.*

fair[2] (fâr) *n.* **1** An exhibit and sale of fancy-work, etc., for the especial benefit of some object. **2** An occasional or periodical exhibit of agricultural products, manufactures, or other articles of value or interest: a county *fair*, an industrial *fair.* **3** A stated or regular market; a gathering of buyers and sellers. ◆ Homophone: *fare.* [<OF *feire* <L *feria* a holiday]

Fair Deal The domestic program and policies of the administration of President Truman, as set forth in his State of the Union message to the U.S. Congress, January 5, 1949.

fair-faced (fâr'fāst') *adj.* **1** Having a fair face. **2** Specious.

fair green In golf, a fairway.

fair·ground (fâr'ground') *n.* The ground or enclosure in which a fair is held.

fair-haired (fâr'hârd') *adj.* **1** Flaxen-haired. **2** Favorite.

fair·ly (fâr'lē) *adv.* **1** In a just manner; equitably; properly. **2** Moderately; tolerably: a *fairly* tall building. **3** Positively; completely: The crowd *fairly* roared. **4** Clearly; distinctly. **5** *Obs.* Handsomely; courteously. **6** *Obs.* Softly; gently.

---

fair-mind·ed (fâr′mīn′did) *adj.* Free from bias or bigotry; open to reason; honest-minded. — **fair′mind′ed·ness** *n.*

fair play 1 Fairness in playing, contending, debating, etc. **2** The ideal and practice of justice, unaffected by prejudice or partiality.

fair-spo·ken (fâr′spō′kən) *adj.* Having grace of speech; plausible.

fair-trade (fâr′trād′) *v.t.* -trad·ed, -trad·ing To set a price no less than the manufacturer's minimum price on (a branded or trademarked product). — *adj.* Of or pertaining to such a price.

fair·wa·ter (fâr′wô′tər, -wot′ər) *n.* A stream-lined covering of metal or plastic shaped to fit over the superstructures of a submarine as a protection against the mechanical and chemical action of sea water.

fair·way (fâr′wā′) *n.* **1** The proper course through a channel or harbor. **2** That part of a links or golf course, between the several tees and putting greens, on which the grass is constantly kept short: also called *fair green.*

fair-weath·er (fâr′weth′ər) *adj.* **1** Suitable for or restricted to fair weather, as a racetrack. **2** Useful or dependable only in favorable circumstances; not helpful in adversity: *fair-weather* friends.

fair·y (fâr′ē) *n.* *pl.* **fair·ies 1** An imaginary being, ordinarily of small and graceful human form, capable of working good or ill to mankind. **2** *Slang* A male homosexual. — *adj.* **1** Of or pertaining to fairies. **2** Resembling fairies. Also *Obs. faery* or *faerie.* [<OF *faerie* enchantment < *fae.* See FAY².] — **fair′y·like′** *adj.*

fairy gloves Digitalis; foxglove.

fair·y·hood (fâr′ē-hŏŏd) *n.* **1** Enchantment by fairies. **2** Fairy nature or characteristics. **3** The race of fairies.

fair·y·ism (fâr′ē-iz′əm) *n.* **1** Belief in fairies; fairy lore. **2** Resemblance to fairies or to their supposed habitations, customs, or characteristics.

fair·y·land (fâr′ē·land′) *n.* The fancied abode of the fairies.

fairy rings Circles in lawns or pastures, usually caused by the spreading of the mycelia of certain fungi, but popularly said to be made by fairies.

fairy stone 1 A fossil sea urchin or echinite. **2** A stone arrowhead. **3** A variously shaped concretion found in alluvial clays in Scotland.

fairy tale 1 A tale about fairies; an imaginative or legendary story. **2** An incredible statement.

fairy wand Blazing star (def. 1).

faith (fāth) *n.* **1** Belief without evidence. **2** Confidence in or dependence on a person, statement, or thing as trustworthy. ◆ Collateral adjective: *fiducial.* **3** Belief in God or the testimony of God as revealed in Scripture. **4** A doctrine or system of doctrines, propositions, etc., held to be true: the Christian *faith.* **5** Anything given adherence or credence: a man's political *faith.* **6** Allegiance or loyal adherence to something; faithfulness: to pledge *faith* in a venture. — **bad faith** Deceit; dishonesty. — **in faith** Indeed; truly. — **in good faith** Honestly; with honorable intentions. — **to break faith 1** To betray one's principles or beliefs. **2** To fail to keep a promise. — **to keep faith 1** To adhere to one's principles or beliefs. **2** To keep a promise. — *interj.* In truth; indeed. [<OF *feit, feid* <L *fides* < *fidere* trust]

Synonyms (noun): assent, assurance, belief, confidence, conviction, credence, credit, creed, doctrine, opinion, reliance, trust. *Belief,* as an intellectual process, is the acceptance of something as true on other grounds than personal observation and experience. We give *credence* to a report, *assent* to a proposition or to a proposal. *Belief* is stronger than *credence; credence* might be described as a prima-facie *belief; credence* is a more formal word than *belief,* and seems to imply somewhat more of volition; we speak of giving *credence* to a report, but not of giving *belief.* Goods are sold on *credit;* we give one *credit* for good intentions. *Conviction* is a *belief* established by argument or evidence; *assurance* is *belief* beyond the reach of argument; as, the Christian's *assurance* of salvation. *Faith* is a union of *belief* and *trust. Faith* is often personal; *belief* may be quite impersonal, but as soon as a *belief* is strong enough to be followed by def-

inite action, the *belief* becomes *faith.* In religion it is common to distinguish between intellectual *belief* of religious truth, as any other truth might be believed, and *belief* of the heart, or saving *faith.* Compare FIDELITY, OPINION, RELIGION, TRUST. *Antonyms:* denial, disbelief, dissent, distrust, doubt, incredulity, infidelity, misgiving, rejection, skepticism, suspicion, unbelief.

faith cure 1 The alleged cure of disease by virtue of prayer, with faith in its efficacy. **2** The procedure, prescribed acts, etc., to effect such cure.

faith·ful (fāth′fəl) *adj.* **1** True or trustworthy in the performance of duty, especially in the fulfilment of promises, obligations, vows, and the like: a *faithful* servant, *faithful* to one's agreement. **2** True in detail; accurate in correspondence, or exact in description: a *faithful* copy. **3** Truthful; worthy of belief or confidence: a *faithful* witness, a *faithful* saying. **4** Full of faith; strong or firm in faith: *faithful* convictions. — **the faithful 1** In the early church, all true believers in God. **2** The members in good standing of the Christian church, or any part of it. **3** In Islam, the followers of Mohammed. **4** The devoted members of a group or organization. — **faith′ful·ly** *adv.* — **faith′ful·ness** *n.*

Synonyms: devoted, firm, incorruptible, loyal, staunch, sure, true, trustworthy, trusty, unwavering. A person is *faithful* who will keep faith, whether with or without power to aid or serve; a person or thing is *trusty* that possesses such qualities as to justify the fullest confidence and dependence. We may speak of a *faithful* but feeble friend; we say a *trusty* agent, a *trusty* steed, a *trusty* sword. See HONEST, MORAL. *Antonyms:* capricious, faithless, false, fickle, unfaithful, untrue, untrustworthy.

faith healer One who heals by faith cures.

faith·less (fāth′lis) *adj.* **1** Untrue to promise or obligation; unfaithful; disloyal. **2** Tending or calculated to delude; deceptive and unreliable. **3** Lacking in or devoid of faith, especially in the Christian religion. See synonyms under PERFIDIOUS. — **faith′less·ly** *adv.* — **faith′less·ness** *n.*

fake¹ (fāk) *n. Colloq.* Anything or any person not genuine; a counterfeit. — *adj.* Spurious. — *v.* **faked, fak·ing** *v.t.* **1** To make up and attempt to pass off as genuine: to *fake* a pedigree. **2** To simulate; feign: to *fake* gratitude. **3** To improvise, as in music or a play. — *v.i.* **4** To practice faking. [? Var. of obs. *feague, feak* <Du. *vegen* beat, dust off]

fake² (fāk) *n. Naut.* A single coil or turn of a rope or cable. — *v.t.* **faked, fak·ing** To coil, as a rope. [Origin uncertain]

fa·kir (fə-kir′, fā′kər) *n.* **1** A Mohammedan ascetic, religious mendicant, or mendicant priest. **2** Loosely, a Hindu Yogi or mendicant devotee. Also **fa·keer** (fə-kir′). [<Arabic *faqīr* poor]

fal·cate (fal′kāt) *adj.* Sickle- or scythe-shaped: also **fal′cat·ed.** — *n.* A sickle-shaped figure. [<L *falcatus* < *falx, falcis* sickle] — **fal·ca′tion** *n.*

fal·ci·form (fal′sə-fôrm) *adj.* Curved like a sickle; falcate.

fal·con (fôl′kən, fô′-, fal′-) *n.* **1** A diurnal bird of prey (genus *Falco*) used by falconers; especially, the peregrine falcon (*F. peregrinus*), with long, pointed wings, the hobby, merlin, or gerfalcon. **2** A falconine bird, whether used in falconry or not, having the upper mandible toothed, and circular nostrils, as a kestrel, duck hawk, prairie falcon (*F. mexicanus*), or sparrow hawk. **3** A small cannon of the 15th–17th centuries, firing a shot of around six pounds. [<OF *faucon, falcun* <LL *falco, -onis* <L *falx, falcis* a sickle]

FALCON

fal·con·er (fôl′kən·ər, fô′-, fal′-) *n.* One who breeds, trains or hunts with falcons for sport.

fal·co·net (fôl′kə·net, fô′-, fal′-) *n.* **1** A little falcon. **2** A small cannon of the 16th century.

fal·con-gen·tle (fôl′kən·jen′təl, fô′-, fal′-) *n.* **1** The European goshawk. **2** A female falcon. Also **fal′con-gen′til.**

fal·co·ni·form (fal·kō′nə·fôrm) *adj. Ornithol.* Belonging to the order of birds (*Falconiformes*) which includes the vultures, hawks, falcons, and eagles.

fal·con·ry (fôl′kən·rē, fô′-, fal′-) *n.* The training or using of falcons for sport.

fal·cu·la (fal′kyə·lə) *n.* **1** A sharp, curved claw, as in birds of prey. **2** *Anat.* A sickle-shaped process of the dura mater between the lobes of the cerebellum: also called *falx cerebelli.* [<L, dim. of *falx* a sickle]

fald·stool (fôld′stōōl′) *n.* **1** A desk at which the litany is read, as in the Church of England. **2** A folding seat, stool, or chair, especially one used by a king, or by a bishop when performing pontifical acts away from his cathedral, or in the presence of a superior. **3** A camp stool. [<Med. L *faldistolium* <OHG *faldstuol* a folding stool]

Falk·land Island Dependencies (fôk′lənd) The territories in the South Atlantic administered by Great Britain along with the Falkland Islands, including South Georgia, the South Shetland, South Orkney, and South Sandwich islands, and Palmer Peninsula in Antarctica.

Falk·land Islands (fôk′lənd) A British crown colony in the South Atlantic, 4,618 square miles; capital, Stanley. *Spanish* **Is·las Mal·vi·nas** (ēs′läs mäl·vē′näs).

fall (fôl) *v.* **fell, fall·en, fall·ing** *v.i.* **1** To drop from a higher to a lower place or position because of removal of support or loss of hold or attachment. **2** To drop from an erect to a less erect or prone position: He *fell* to his knees. **3** To collapse; come down: The bridge *fell.* **4** To become less in height, number, force, volume, value, etc. **5** To descend or become less in rank, estimation, importance, etc. **6** To be wounded or slain, as in battle. **7** To be overthrown; lose power, as a government. **8** To be taken or captured: The fort *fell.* **9** To yield to temptation; sin. **10** To hit; land: The bombs *fell* short. **11** To slope downward: The road *falls* into the valley. **12** To hang down; droop. **13** To begin and continue: Night *fell.* **14** To pass into a state or condition: to *fall* asleep. **15** To experience or show dejection: His face *fell.* **16** To come or happen by chance or lot: Suspicion *fell* on him. **17** To happen; occur: Hallowe'en *falls* on Tuesday. **18** To pass by right or inheritance, as an estate. **19** To be uttered as if accidentally: An oath *fell* from his lips. **20** To be born, as a lamb. **21** To happen or come at a specific place: The accent *falls* on the last syllable. **22** To be classified or divided: with *into.* — *v.t.* **23** *U.S.* To fell or cut down, as a tree. — **to fall afoul (or foul) of 1** To collide with, as a vessel. **2** To quarrel or argue with. — **to fall away 1** To become lean or emaciated. **2** To die; decline. — **to fall away from** To renounce allegiance to. — **to fall back** To recede; retreat. — **to fall back on (or upon) 1** *Mil.* To retreat to. **2** To resort to; have recourse to. — **to fall behind 1** To drop back; lose ground. **2** To be in arrears. — **to fall down on** *U.S. Slang* To fail in. — **to fall flat** To fail to produce the intended effect or result. — **to fall for** *U.S. Colloq.* **1** To be deceived by. **2** To fall in love with. — **to fall in** *Mil.* To take proper place in a formation or group. — **to fall in with 1** To meet and accompany. **2** To agree with; conform to. — **to fall off 1** To leave or withdraw. **2** To become less: Attendance is *falling off.* **3** *Naut.* To veer to leeward from the former course. — **to fall on (or upon) 1** To attack; assail. **2** To find; discover. — **to fall out 1** To quarrel. **2** To happen; result. **3** *Mil.* To leave ranks. — **to fall through** To come to nothing; fail. — *adj.* **1** Of or pertaining to autumn; happening, or for use in, the fall of the year: *fall* weather, *fall* planting, a *fall* coat. **2** *Slang* Easily duped: a *fall* guy. — *n.* **1** The act, process, or result of falling, in any sense of the word: the *fall* of Adam, a *fall* in price, the *fall* of Rome. **2** *Usually pl.* A waterfall; cataract; cascade. **3** A flowing or discharge, as of one stream or body of water into another. **4** That which falls or is caused to fall; also, the amount of descent. **5** *Often cap.* The season coming between summer and winter; autumn. **6** A falling band or ruff for the neck; also, a veil. **7** In wrestling, the throwing of or being thrown by one's opponent, or the method of doing it. **8** That which acts by falling, as a *deadfall.* **9** In music and oratory, a cadence; a sinking of tone or decrease of volume of sound. **10** A hoisting rope, or the part of a hoisting rope or tackle to which power is applied or by which power is exerted; the rope of a tackle or purchase. **11** The birth of animals. See synonyms under RUIN. — **the fall of man** The disobedience of Adam and Eve. [OE *feallan*]

Synonyms (*verb*): decline, descend, droop, drop, fail, faint, lapse, set, sink, subside. See HAPPEN. *Antonyms*: ascend, climb, mount, rise, soar.

fal·la·ci·a (fə-lā'shē-ə, -shə) *n. Psychiatry* An illusion or hallucination: *fallacia optica*, an optical illusion. [<L. See FALLACY.]

fal·la·cious (fə-lā'shəs) *adj.* Of, pertaining to, embodying, or involving a fallacy; deceptive; misleading; delusive. — **fal·la'cious·ly** *adv.* — **fal·la'cious·ness** *n.*

fal·la·cy (fal'ə-sē) *n. pl.* **·cies 1** Anything that deceives the mind or eye; deception. **2** A flaw in reasoning; fallaciousness. **3** *Logic.* Any reasoning, exposition, argument, etc., contravening the canons of logic. See synonyms under DELUSION, ERROR. [<L *fallacia* <*fallax, fallacis* deceptive <*fallere* deceive]

fal·lal (fal·lal') *n.* **1** An ornament or trinket; gew-gaw. **2** Pretentiousness. Also **fal·lal'er·y.** [Cf. FALBALA]

fall dandelion An herb (*Leontodon autumnalis*) of the composite family having yellow flowers.

fall·en (fô'lən) *adj.* **1** Having come down by falling. **2** Overthrown; disgraced; ruined.

fall·fish (fôl'fish') *n. pl.* **·fish** or **·fish·es 1** A fresh-water cyprinoid fish (genus *Semotilus*) of eastern North America, about 18 inches long, bluish above, with silvery sides. **2** One of various other cyprinoids, as the **red fallfish** (*Notropis rubricroceus*).

fal·li·ble (fal'ə-bəl) *adj.* ¯**1** Liable to error or mistake. **2** Liable to be misled or deceived. **3** Liable to be erroneous, incorrect, or false. [<Med. L *fallibilis* <*fallere* deceive] — **fal'li·bil'i·ty, fal'li·ble·ness** *n.* — **fal'li·bly** *adv.*

fall·ing-leaf (fô'ling·lēf') *n. Aeron.* A flight maneuver in which an airplane loses altitude by a series of lateral oscillations resembling those of a falling leaf.

falling star A shooting star; a meteor. Also **falling stone.**

fall line The brink of a plateau, as indicated by waterfalls.

Fal·lo·pi·an tube (fə-lō'pē-ən) *Anat.* One of a pair of long, slender ducts in mammals, serving as a passage for the ovum from the ovary to the uterus.

fall·out (fôl'out') *n. Physics* **1** The descent of minute particles of radioactive material resulting from the explosion of an atomic or thermonuclear bomb. **2** The particles themselves. **3** Any incidental result; unplanned or unpredictable consequences. Also **fall'out'.**

fal·low[1] (fal'ō) *adj.* Left unseeded after being plowed; uncultivated. — *n.* **1** Land left unseeded after plowing; also, cleared woodland. **2** The act or system of plowing or working land and leaving it unseeded for a time. — *v.t.* & *v.i.* To make, keep, or become fallow. [OE *fealga* fallow land] — **fal'low·ness** *n.*

fal·low[2] (fal'ō) *adj.* Pale-yellow or pale-red. [OE *fealu* tawny]

fallow crop A crop alternated with the main crop to nourish the soil.

fallow deer A European deer (genus *Dama*), about 3 feet high at the shoulders and spotted white in the summer.

fall term 1 A court session beginning in the fall. **2** A school session beginning in the fall.

fall·way (fôl'wā') *n.* A hoistway through several floors, as of a warehouse.

FALLOW DEER

false (fôls) *adj.* **1** Contrary to truth or fact. **2** Deceptive; counterfeit; artificial; not real or genuine. **3** Incorrect; irregular. **4** Lying; dishonest; faithless; treacherous. **5** Supplementary; substitutive. **6** Out of tune. See synonyms under BAD, COUNTERFEIT, PERFIDIOUS. — *adv. Obs.* Falsely. [<OF *fals, faus* <L *falsus*, orig. pp. of *fallere* deceive] — **false'ly** *adv.* — **false'ness** *n.*

false foxglove Any of several widely distributed plants of the figwort family (genus *Aureolaria*) bearing bright yellow flowers.

false glottis The space between the false vocal cords. See VOCAL CORD.

false·hood (fôls'hŏŏd) *n.* **1** Lack of accord to fact or truth; untruthfulness. **2** An intentional untruth; a lie. **3** Act of lying; falsification. **4** An untrue belief or idea. See synonyms under DECEPTION, FICTION, LIE.

false pretenses Wilful misrepresentations made to cheat and defraud; swindling.

false ribs *Anat.* Ribs that do not unite directly with the sternum; in man, there are five on each side. See RIB.

false step 1 A stumble. **2** An error or blunder in behavior. See FAUX PAS.

fal·set·to (fôl·set'ō) *n. pl.* **·tos 1** The artificial tones of the voice, higher than the chest voice or natural voice. **2** A singer possessing such a voice. — *adj.* Having the quality of the falsetto; shrill; artificial. [<Ital., dim. of *falso* false]

false·work (fôls'wûrk') *n.* **1** A temporary scaffolding to facilitate the erection of a permanent structure. **2** That part of a structure designed to improve its shape or increase its efficiency, but without carrying any of the fundamental stresses, as an airplane fairing.

fal·si·fi·ca·tion (fôl'sə-fə-kā'shən) *n.* **1** The act or process of falsifying. **2** *Law* The intentional alteration of a record, an account, or any document, so as to render it untrue. Compare SURCHARGE.

fal·si·fy (fôl'sə-fī) *v.* **·fied, ·fy·ing** *v.t.* **1** To misrepresent; tell lies about. **2** To prove to be false; disprove. **3** *Law* To tamper with, as a document. **4** In prosody, to alter (an accent in a poem) from the usual form or rule. — *v.i.* **5** To tell falsehoods; lie. See synonyms under PERVERT. [<F *falsifier* <LL *falsificare* <L *falsificus* making false <*falsus* FALSE + *facere* make] — **fal'si·fi'er** *n.*

fal·si·ty (fôl'sə-tē) *n. pl.* **·ties 1** The quality of being false. **2** A false statement, thing, or appearance. See synonyms under ERROR.

falt·boat (fält'bōt') *n.* A collapsible, kayaklike boat, seating one person, propelled by a double-bladed paddle: used chiefly on rivers: also *foldboat*. [<G *faltboot* folding boat]

fal·ter (fôl'tər) *v.i.* **1** To be hesitant or uncertain; waver; give way. **2** To stumble; move unsteadily. **3** To speak haltingly; stammer. — *v.t.* **4** To utter haltingly. — *n.* A faltering hesitation; a trembling. [? <ON *faltrask* be encumbered] — **fal'ter·er** *n.* — **fal'ter·ing** *adj.* — **fal'ter·ing·ly** *adv.*

fame (fām) *n.* **1** Public or general reputation; renown. **2** *Obs.* Report; rumor. — *v.t.* **famed, fam·ing 1** To speak of widely; celebrate. **2** To make famous. [<F <L *fama* report, reputation <*fari* speak]

Synonyms (*noun*): celebrity, credit, distinction, eminence, glory, honor, laurels, notoriety, renown, reputation, repute. *Fame* is the widely disseminated report of a person's character, deeds, or ability, and is oftenest used in the favorable sense. *Reputation* and *repute* are more limited than *fame*, and may be either good or bad. *Notoriety* is evil *repute* or a dishonorable counterfeit of *fame. Eminence* and *distinction* may result from rank, station, or character. *Celebrity* is limited in range; we speak of local *celebrity*, or world-wide *fame. Fame* in its best sense may be defined as the applause of numbers; *renown*, as such applause worthily won: we speak of the conqueror's *fame*, the patriot's *renown. Glory* and *honor* are of good import; *honor* may be given for qualities or acts that should not win it, but it is always given as for something good and worthy; we speak of an evil *fame*, but not of evil *honor; glory* has a more exalted and often a sacred sense. *Antonyms*: contempt, contumely, discredit, disgrace, dishonor, disrepute, humiliation, ignominy, infamy, oblivion, obscurity, shame.

fa·mil·ial (fə-mil'yəl) *adj.* **1** Of, pertaining to, involving, or associated with the family.

2 *Genetics* Transmitted within the family, as certain hereditary diseases. [<L *familia* family]

fa·mil·iar (fə-mil'yər) *adj.* **1** Having close knowledge; well acquainted; thoroughly versed: followed by *with*. **2** Having the relation of an intimate or near friend; arising from or characterized by close acquaintance; not distant; informal. **3** Exercising undue intimacy; forward; intrusive. **4** Well known, as from habitual use or long acquaintance; common; frequent; customary. **5** Domesticated; attached: said of animals. See synonyms under COMMON, GENERAL, HABITUAL, USUAL. — *n.* **1** An intimate friend. **2** A person with whom one frequently associates. **3** A spirit supposed to attend and obey a sorcerer: also **familiar spirit. 4** A servant of a prelate of the Roman Catholic Church, or the Inquisition. [<L *familiaris* of the family <*familia* family] — **fa·mil'iar·ly** *adv.*

fa·mil·i·ar·i·ty (fə-mil'ē-ar'ə-tē, -mil'yar'-) *n. pl.* **·ties 1** The state or condition of being familiar; intimacy; intimate knowledge or acquaintance, as with a subject. **2** Conduct implying familiar intimacy. **3** *Often pl.* Offensively familiar conduct. See synonyms under ACQUAINTANCE, ASSOCIATION.

fa·mil·iar·ize (fə-mil'yə-rīz) *v.t.* **·ized, ·iz·ing 1** To make (oneself or someone) accustomed or familiar. **2** To cause to be well known or familiar. — **fa·mil'iar·i·za'tion** *n.*

fam·i·ly (fam'ə-lē, fam'lē) *n. pl.* **·lies 1** A group of persons, consisting of parents and their children. **2** The children as distinguished from the parents. **3** A group of persons forming a household, including servants, etc.; a household. **4** A succession of persons connected by blood, name, etc.; a house; line; clan; tribe; race. **5** Distinguished or ancient lineage with its traditions; descent. **6** *Biol.* A taxonomic category higher than a *genus*; for animals, family names end in *-idae*, for plants, in *-aceae*. **7** Any class or group of like or related things. **8** *Ling.* A grouping of languages, such as Indo-European, assumed, from certain shared characteristics, to be descended from a common parent: often subdivided into *subfamily, branch*, and *group*. — *adj.* Of, belonging to, or suitable for a family. [<L *familia* family <*famulus* servant]

family planning Control by means of contraceptive measures of the timing and number of births in a family.

fam·ine (fam'in) *n.* **1** A wide-spread scarcity of food; dearth. **2** A great scarcity of anything: a water *famine*. **3** Starvation. [<OF <L *fames* hunger]

fam·ish (fam'ish) *v.t.* & *v.i.* To suffer or die, or to cause to suffer or die, from lack of nourishment; starve. [Earlier *fame* <F *afamer*; refashioned after verbs in *-ish*, as *banish, finish*, etc.] — **fam'ish·ment** *n.*

fa·mous (fā'məs) *adj.* **1** Having fame or celebrity; renowned. **2** *Colloq.* Admirable, excellent. See synonyms under EMINENT, ILLUSTRIOUS. — **fa'mous·ly** *adv.* — **fa'mous·ness** *n.*

fam·u·lus (fam'yə·ləs) *n. pl.* **·li** (-lī) An assistant or servant; specifically, the assistant or amanuensis of a scholar or the familiar of a magician. [<L, servant]

fan[1] (fan) *n.* **1** An implement or device for agitating the air; specifically, a light, flat implement, often collapsible, spreading a wedge-shaped sheet from a stem or point, with a stock or handle. **2** One of various implements or machines for stirring up currents of air or doing something similar. **3** A kind of basket formerly

FANS
a. Folding. *b.* Palm leaf.
c. Collapsible.

used for winnowing grain, by tossing the grain in the air. **4** A winnowing machine. **5** A small sail or vane to keep the sails of a windmill at right angles to the wind. **6** A propeller; also, one of its blades. **7** Something that excites or stimulates. — *v.* **fanned, fan·ning** *v.t.* **1** To move or stir (air) with or as with a fan. **2** To direct air upon; cool or refresh with or as with a fan. **3** To move or stir to action; excite, as fire or rage. **4** To winnow (grain or chaff). **5** To spread like a fan. **6** In baseball, to cause (a batter) to strike out. — *v.i.* **7** To spread out like a fan. **8** In baseball, to strike out. [OE *fann* < L *vannus* winnowing fan]

fan² (fan) *n. Colloq.* **1** An enthusiastic devotee of any sport or diversion, as of baseball or of motion pictures; a fanatic. **2** An ardent admirer, usually of a public character, writer, artist, etc. [? < *the fancy* (see under FANCY)]

fa·nat·ic (fə·nat'ik) *adj.* Actuated by extravagant or intemperate zeal; inordinately and unreasonably enthusiastic: also **fa·nat'i·cal.** — *n.* One who is motivated by intemperate zeal; one who is moved by a frenzy of enthusiasm; especially, a religious zealot. [< L *fanaticus* inspired < *fanum* a temple] — **fa·nat'i·cal·ly** *adv.*

fa·nat·i·cism (fə·nat'ə·siz'əm) *n.* The spirit or conduct of a fanatic; unreasonable zeal. Also **fa·nat'i·cal·ness.**

Synonyms: bigotry, credulity, intolerance, superstition.

fa·nat·i·cize (fə·nat'ə·sīz) *v.t. & v.i.* **·cized, ·ciz·ing** To make or to become fanatical; act like a fanatic.

fan·ci·er (fan'sē·ər) *n.* **1** A breeder and seller of birds or animals. **2** One having a taste for special objects; an amateur. **3** A dreamer; visionary.

fan·ci·ful (fan'si·fəl) *adj.* **1** Proceeding from or produced by fancy; ideal; odd; curious in appearance. **2** Existing only in the fancy; unreal; visionary. **3** Whimsical. — **fan'ci·ful·ly** *adv.* — **fan'ci·ful·ness** *n.*

Synonyms: chimerical, fantastic, grotesque, imaginative, visionary. That is *fanciful* which is dictated or suggested by fancy independently of more serious considerations; the *fantastic* is the *fanciful* with the added elements of whimsicalness and extravagance. The *fanciful* swings away from the real or the ordinary lightly and pleasantly, the *fantastic* extravagantly, the *grotesque* ridiculously. A *fanciful* arrangement of objects is commonly pleasing, a *fantastic* arrangement is striking, a *grotesque* arrangement is laughable. A *fanciful* theory or suggestion may be clearly recognized as such; a *visionary* scheme is erroneously supposed to have a basis in fact. Compare synonyms for DREAM, IDEA, IDEAL, IMAGINARY, IMAGINATION, ROMANTIC. *Antonyms:* accurate, calculable, calculated, commonplace, literal, ordinary, prosaic, real, reasonable, regular, sensible, solid, sound, sure, true.

fan·ci·less (fan'si·lis) *adj.* Lacking fancy; unimaginative.

fan·cy (fan'sē) *n. pl.* **·cies** **1** The power or act of forming pleasing, graceful, whimsical, or odd mental images, or of combining them with little regard to rational processes of construction; imagination in its lower form; hence, in former usage, the re-imaging faculty of the mind; fantasy. **2** Any product of the exercise of this faculty; an imaginary notion, representation, or image; whimsical notion; vagary. **3** A baseless or visionary idea; notion; illusion. **4** An unreasoned liking or fondness, resulting from caprice; preference. **5** A pet pursuit; an object sought after to gratify the taste or a whim without regard to utility; a hobby; fad. **6** Taste exhibited in production; artistic invention; design: The edifice showed a cultivated *fancy.* **7** *Obs.* A specter; phantom. **8** *Obs.* Love. — **the fancy** The votaries collectively of any special art, sport, or amusement. — *adj.* **·ci·er, ·ci·est** **1** Adapted to please the fancy; ornamental; decorative: *fancy* embroidery. **2** Evolved from the fancy; imaginary; ideal. **3** Capricious; whimsical; fanciful. **4** In commerce, of higher grade than the average; choice; characterized by variety, excellence, or special request: *fancy* fruits. **5** Extravagant; exorbitant: *fancy* prices. **6** Selectively bred to a type, as an animal. **7** Performed with exceptional

grace and skill: the *fancy* bowing of a violinist. — *v.t.* **·cied, ·cy·ing** **1** To imagine; picture. **2** To take a fancy to; like. **3** To believe without proof or conviction; suppose. **4** To breed, as animals, for conventional points of symmetry or beauty. [Short for FANTASY]

Synonyms (noun): belief, caprice, conceit, conception, desire, humor, idea, image, imagination, inclination, liking, mood, preference.

fan·cy·work (fan'sē·wûrk') *n.* Embroidery, tatting, crocheting, lacework, etc.

fan·dan·go (fan·dang'gō) *n. pl.* **·gos** **1** A Spanish dance in triple time, usually accompanied by castanets. **2** The music for this dance. **3** A dancing party or ball. [< Sp.]

fan delta An alluvial cone.

fane (fān) *n.* A sanctuary; temple. ◆ Homophones: *fain, feign.* [< L *fanum* temple]

fa·ne·ga (fä·nā'gä) *n.* A Spanish dry measure equal to a little more than 1 1/2 bushels, but variable in Latin-American countries. Also **fan·ga** (fäng'gä). [< Sp.]

fa·ne·ga·da (fä'nä·gä'thä) *n.* A Spanish unit of area, equal to 6.92 acres or 7,449 square feet.

fan·fare (fan'fâr') *n.* A flourish, as of trumpets; a noisy parade or demonstration. [< F]

fan·fa·ron·ade (fan'fə·rə·nād') *n.* A blustering, ranting, or vainglorious speech or style; a boastful or bullying manner; rodomontade. — *v.i.* **·ad·ed, ·ad·ing** To swagger; bluster. [< F < Sp. *fanfarronada* < *fanfarrón.* See FANFARON.]

fang (fang) *n.* **1** A long pointed tooth or tusk by which an animal seizes, holds, or tears its prey, as the canine tooth of a boar or dog. **2** One of the long, curved, hollow or grooved, usually erectile teeth with which a venomous serpent injects its poison into its victim. **3**

FANGS OF THE RATTLESNAKE

A. Fang and accompanying bones: *f.* fang; *a.* external pterygoid; *b.* internal pterygoid; *c.* palatal; *d.* superior maxillary; *e.* lacrimal. *B.* Muscles related to the venom gland and fang: *f.* fang; *a.* anterior temporal muscles; *b.* internal pterygoid; *c.* venom gland; *d.* the fang, half erected; *e.* point where the venom enters the channel of the fang.

One of various pointed or incurved objects, organs, or devices, especially for clutching or holding fast, as the root of a tooth or the claw or talon of a bird. — *v.t.* **1** *Obs.* To seize or take hold of. **2** To sink fangs into. [OE *fang* catching, seizing] — **fanged** (fangd) *adj.* — **fang'less** *adj.* — **fang'like** *adj.*

fan·jet (fan'jet') *n.* A turbofan (def. 2).

fan·light (fan'līt') *n.* **1** A fan window. **2** *Brit.* A transom.

fan mail Complimentary letters to public performers, as actors, musicians, and the like.

fan·nel (fan'əl) *n.* A fanon. [< Med. L *fanula,* dim. of *fano.* See FANON.]

fan·ny (fan'ē) *n. U.S. Slang* The buttocks.

fan·on (fan'ən) *n. Eccl.* **1** A maniple or napkin used by a celebrant at mass. **2** A cape worn only by the pope, as he presides at solemn pontifical mass. Also **fan·o** (fan'ō), **fan·um** (fan'əm). [< OF *fanon* < Med. L *fano, -onis* a banner, napkin < Gmc.]

fan palm Any palm with fan-shaped leaves; especially, the talipot palm of Ceylon and the Malabar Coast, having immense leaves; the palmetto of Florida; and the California or Washington fan palm (*Washingtonia filifera*), occurring in California and Lower California.

fan·tail (fan'tāl') *n.* **1** A variety of domestic pigeon having fanlike tail feathers. **2** An Australian or Oriental flycatcher (genus *Rhipidura*) having fanlike tail feathers. **3** A fan-shaped joint or mortise. **4** Any end or tail shaped like a fan. **5** Any of certain species of fancy-bred goldfish, having double anal and dorsal fins. **6** *Naut.* The overhanging stern of some vessels.

FANTAIL PIGEON

fan-tailed (fan'tāld') *adj.* Having the tail feathers arranged like a fan or capable of expansion like a fan, as the flycatcher.

fan·ta·si·a (fan·tā'zē·ə, -zhə, fan'tə·zē'ə) *n.* **1** A fanciful, irregular, fantastic composition, not observing strict musical forms. **2** A piece of orchestral music less formal than an overture; also, a prelude to an organ fugue. [< Ital., a fancy]

fan·ta·size (fan'tə·sīz) *v.* **·sized, ·siz·ing** *v.i.* **1** To imagine or daydream about fantastic events. — *v.t.* **2** To create in fantasy, as in daydreaming. — **fan'ta·sist** *n.*

fan·tasm (fan'taz·əm) *n.* **1** An imaginary appearance; a phantom. **2** A mental image; fancy. Also spelled *phantasm.* See synonyms under DELUSION. [< Gk. *phantasma.* Doublet of PHANTOM.]

fan·tas·ma·go·ri·a (fan·taz'mə·gôr'ē·ə, -gō'rē·ə) *n.* **1** A changing, incoherent series of apparitions or fantasms. **2** An exhibition of pictures projected on a screen and made to increase or diminish in size rapidly while continually in focus. Also **fan·tas'ma·go'ry:** also spelled *phantasmagoria.* [< NL < Gk. *phantasma* an apparition + prob. *agora* assembly, crowd] — **fan·tas'ma·go'ri·al, fan·tas'ma·gor'ic** (-gôr'ik, -gor'-) or **·i·cal** *adj.*

fan·tas·mal (fan·taz'məl) *adj.* Of or like a fantasm; unreal or illusive. Also **fan·tas'mic.**

fan·tast (fan'tast) *n.* **1** One who believes in or advocates a fantastic delusion as a true doctrine. **2** A dreamer or visionary. [< Med. L *phantasta* < Gk. *phantastēs* a boaster < *phantazein* boast]

fan·tas·tic (fan·tas'tik) *adj.* **1** Of an odd appearance; grotesque. **2** Capricious; whimsical: a *fantastic* imagination. **3** Of the nature of fantasy; fanciful; illusory. See synonyms under FANCIFUL, ODD, QUEER, ROMANTIC. — *n.* One who is fantastic in conduct or appearance: also *Obs.* **fan·tas'ti·co.** Also **fan·tas'ti·cal.** [< Med. L *fantasticus* < L *phantasticus* < Gk. *phantastikos* < *phantastēs.* See FANTAST.] — **fan·tas'ti·cal·ly** *adv.* — **fan·tas'ti·cal·ness** *n.*

fan·tas·ti·cal·i·ty (fan·tas'ti·kal'ə·tē) *n.* **1** The quality of being fantastic. **2** Anything which is fantastic or grotesque.

fan·ta·sy (fan'tə·sē, -zē) *n. pl.* **·sies** **1** A fantastic notion or mental image; fancy. **2** A fantastic design, as in embroidery. **3** *Psychol.* The form of representation that brings before the mind a sequence of images serving to fulfil a need not gratified in the real world; a daydream. **4** *Music* A fantasia. **5** A capricious mood. See synonyms under DREAM, IDEA, IMAGINATION. — *v.t.* **·sied, ·sy·ing** To imagine; conceive. Also spelled *phantasy.* [< F *fantasie* < L *phantasia* < Gk., appearance < *phainein* show]

fan tracery *Archit.* Bar tracery, diverging like a fan to form a section of fan vaulting rising from a capital or corbel, as in Henry VII's chapel, Westminster.

fan vaulting *Archit.* A system of vaulting in which the ribs spread out like a fan: used in later English Gothic.

fan window *Archit.* A semicircular window containing a sash with bars radiating from the middle of its base.

fan·wort (fan'wûrt') *n.* An American aquatic plant (*Cabomba caroliniana*) which occurs in the southern United States; one of the water-lily family: also called *fishgrass.*

far (fär) *adv.* **1** At a remote or distant point or place; so as to be a long way off: *far* distant. **2** To a great distance; so as to reach to a point a long way off; so as to occupy or cover an extent of time or space: How *far* did Caesar march? **3** To a great degree; by much; very greatly: *far* wiser than their ancestors. **4** From afar; from a long distance: a *far*-traveled guest. — **by far** In a great degree; by much. — *adj.* **far·ther** or **fur·ther, far·thest** or **fur·thest**: see FARTHER. **1** Situated at a great distance in space or time; being a long way off; remote: He went into a *far* country. **2** Extending widely or at length; reaching a long way. **3** Being the more distant of two: the *far* end of the garden. **4** Advanced; progressed, as in age. [OE *feor*]

far·ad (far'əd, -ad) *n. Electr.* The unit of capacitance; the capacitance of a condenser that retains one coulomb of charge with one volt difference of potential. [after Michael *Faraday*]

far·a·day (far'ə·dā) n. Electr. The quantity of electricity required in electrolysis to liberate one unit equivalent weight of an element, equal to 96,500 coulombs per gram equivalent. [after Michael Faraday]

Far·a·day (far'ə·dā), **Michael**, 1791–1867, English chemist and physicist; discovered electromagnetic induction.

fa·rad·ic (fə·rad'ik) adj. Pertaining to or caused by induced electric currents. Also **far·a·da·ic** (far'ə·dā'ik).

far·ad·me·ter (far'əd·mē'tər, -ad-) n. An instrument, usually graded in microfarads, for measuring the strength of an induced electric current.

far·an·dine (far'ən·dīn) n. A fabric of silk mixed with hair or wool, used during the 17th century. [<F ferrandine, after Ferrand de Lyon, its inventor]

far·an·dole (far'ən·dōl, Fr. fȧ·rän·dôl') n. A rapid dance in which the participants whirl in a circle, alternately facing in and out.

far and wide Everywhere; in every place. Also **far and near.**

far·a·way (fär'ə·wā') adj. 1 Distant: a faraway town. 2 Absent-minded; abstracted.

farce (färs) n. 1 A short comedy with exaggerated effects and incidents. 2 A ridiculous proceeding; an absurd failure. — v.t. **farced, farc·ing** 1 To fill out with witticisms, jibes, etc., as a play. 2 Obs. To fill with dressing; stuff, as a fowl. [<F, orig. stuffing <farcer stuff <L farcire] — **far·cial** (fär'shəl) adj.

far·ceur (fär·sœr') n. One who writes or acts a farce; a jester; wag. Also **farc·er** (fär'sər). [<F]

far·ci·cal (fär'si·kəl) adj. Of, pertaining to, or of the nature of a farce; absurd. See synonyms under RIDICULOUS. — **far'ci·cal·ly** adv. — **far'ci·cal·ness, far'ci·cal'i·ty** n.

far·cy (fär'sē) n. A contagious disease, primarily of the horse, characterized by pustular eruptions; glanders. [Var. of obs. farcin <F <L farcimimum, a disease of horses]

far·cy-bud (fär'sē·bud') n. A swollen gland, as in glanders.

far·del (fär'dəl) n. Archaic A bundle; pack; burden. [<OF, dim. of farde <Arabic fardah a bundle]

fare (fâr) v.i. **fared, far·ing** 1 To be in a specified state; get on. 2 To turn out; happen. 3 To eat; be supplied with food. 4 Archaic To go; travel. — n. 1 Passage money. 2 A passenger carried for hire. 3 Food and drink; diet; eatables. See synonyms under FOOD. ◆ Homophone: fair. [OE faran go, travel]

fare·box (fâr'boks') n. A box into which passengers boarding a street car or bus deposit their fares.

far·er (fâr'ər) n. One who travels: most commonly in compounds, as wayfarer, etc.

fare·well (fâr'wel') n. 1 A parting salutation; a good-by; adieu. 2 The act of taking leave; parting. — inter. (fâr'wel') May you fare well; may you prosper: now used only at parting. — adj. Parting; closing; valedictory. — v.t. Poetic To take leave of. — **to a fare-you-well** U.S. Colloq. Completely; with finality: beaten to a fare-you-well: also **to a fare-thee-well.** [Earlier fare well. See FARE.]
  Synonyms (noun): adieu, congé, good-by, leave-taking, valediction, valedictory. Good-by is the homely and hearty parting salutation. Adieu, from the French, is still more ceremonious than farewell; congé, also from the French, is commonly contemptuous or supercilious, and equivalent to dismissal. Valediction is a learned word never in popular use. A valedictory is a public farewell to a company or assembly.

far-fetched (fär'fecht') adj. 1 Brought in only by laborious or strained effort. 2 Neither natural nor obvious.

far-flung (fär'flung') adj. Having great range; extending over great distances.

fa·ri·na (fə·rē'nə) n. 1 A meal or flour obtained chiefly from cereals, nuts, potatoes, or Indian corn, and used as a breakfast food. 2 Starch. 3 A mealy powder found on certain insects. [<L <far spelt]

far·i·nose (far'ə·nōs) adj. 1 Yielding farina: farinose plants. 2 Bot. Covered with or as if

---

with a white meal–like powder, as the under side of the leaves of certain primroses.

far·kle·ber·ry (fär'kəl·ber'ē) n. pl. **·ries** A shrub or small tree (Vaccinium arboreum) of the heath family, with globose black berries. [Origin uncertain]

farm (färm) n. 1 A tract of land forming a single property and devoted to agriculture, stock-raising, dairying, or some allied activity. 2 A tract of water used for the cultivation of marine life: an oyster farm. 3 Obs. a The system of farming our revenues or taxes. b A fixed annual sum paid as a rent or tax. 4 In baseball, a minor-league club used by a major-league club for training its recruits. — v.t. 1 To cultivate (land). 2 To take a lease of, as the use of a business or the collection of taxes, for a fixed rental, retaining the profits. 3 To let at a fixed rental, as lands, collection of taxes, etc.: usually with out: to farm out taxes. 4 To let out the services of (a person) for hire. 5 To agree to maintain òr care for at a fixed price, as paupers. 6 To arrange for (work) to be performed by persons or a firm not in the main organization; subcontract: with out. 7 In baseball, to place (a player) with a minor-league team for training: often with out. — v.i. 8 To practice farming; be a farmer. [<F ferme <Med. L firma a fixed payment <L firmare fix, settle <firmus firm]

farm·er (fär'mər) n. 1 One who follows the occupation of farming; an agriculturist. 2 One who collects revenues for a percentage or commission.

farmer general pl. **farmers general** A member of a privileged class in France before the revolution of 1789, who farmed or leased the public revenues. — **farm'er-gen'er·al·ship** n.

Farm·er-La·bor party (fär'mər·lā'bər) A minor U.S. political party, 1919–23: active since 1923 in Minnesota.

farm·er·y (fär'mər·ē) n. Brit. The buildings, yards, etc., of a farm.

farm·hand (färm'hand') n. One who works for wages on a farm. Also **farm laborer.**

farm·house (färm'hous') n. The homestead on a farm, commonly occupied by the farmer's family.

farm·ing (fär'ming) n. The act of one who farms; the management of or labor on a farm; agriculture. See synonyms under AGRICULTURE. — adj. Engaged in, suitable for, or used for, agriculture: a farming region, farming implements.

farm·stead (färm'sted) n. A farm and the buildings on it. Also **farm'stead·ing.**

farm·yard (färm'yärd') n. A space surrounded by farm buildings, and enclosed for confining stock, etc.

far·ne·sol (fär'nə·sōl, -sol) n. Chem. An alcohol with a delicate fragrance, $C_{15}H_{25}O$, extracted from the flowers of the acacia and from various essential oils: used in perfumery. [<NL (Acacia) farnesiana, a species of acacia + -OL]

far·o (fär'ō) n. A game of cards in which the players bet against the dealer as to the order in which certain cards will appear. [alter. of Pharaoh, ? from a picture originally on one of the cards]

far-off (fär'ôf', -of') adj. Situated at a great distance; remote.

far-point (fär'point') n. Physiol. The farthest point at which the eye, under conditions of relaxation, can see objects distinctly: greatest in normal and hypermetropic vision.

far·ra·go (fə·rā'gō, -rä'-) n. pl. **·goes** A confused mixture; medley: a farrago of nonsense. [<L, salad, mixture <far spelt] — **far·rag·i·nous** (fə·raj'ə·nəs) adj.

far-reach·ing (fär'rē'ching) adj. 1 Producing effects that extend far; having profound consequences: a far-reaching decision. 2 Reaching far either in time or in space.

far·ri·er (far'ē·ər) n. Brit. 1 One who shoes horses. 2 A veterinary surgeon. [<OF ferrier <L ferrarius <ferrum iron]

far·row[1] (far'ō) n. 1 A litter of pigs. 2 Obs. A little pig. — v.t. & v.i. To give birth to (young): said of swine. [OE fearh young pig]

far·row[2] (far'ō) adj. Not producing young during a given year, as a cow. [Cf. Flemish varvekoe cow no longer fertile]

---

far-see·ing (fär'sē'ing) adj. 1 Seeing afar. 2 Having foresight.

far-sight·ed (fär'sī'tid) adj. 1 Able to see things at a distance more clearly than things near at hand; hypermetropic. 2 Far-seeing; prescient, as a statesman. — **far'-sight'ed·ly** adv. — **far'-sight'ed·ness** n.

far·ther (fär'thər) Comparative of FAR. — adj. More distant in space; more advanced. — adv. 1 To or at a more forward or distant point in space. 2 At a more forward stage; more fully or completely. [Var. of FURTHER; infl. in form by far]
  ◆ **farther, further** Farther is used only with reference to literal, spatial distance; further is employed in figurative senses involving time, degree, or quantity: further in the future; further (=additional) damage. Because it is often hard to tell whether the meaning is spatial or figurative, further is also used where some might prefer farther. We drove no further that day.

far·thest (fär'thist) Superlative of FAR. — adj. & adv. Most distant or advanced in space. [Var. of FURTHEST; infl. by far]

far·thing (fär'thing) n. 1 One fourth of an English penny, at par value, about one half of a cent. 2 A small trifle. [OE feorthing < feortha a fourth]

far·thin·gale (fär'thing·gāl) n. A woman's hoop skirt of the 16th and 17th centuries: so called because distended by hoops of green osier, willow, or rattan. [<OF verdugale, alter. of Sp. verdugado <verdugo a rod, hoop]

Faruk (fə·rook') See FAROUK.

Fas (fäs) The Arabic name for FEZ.

fas·ces (fas'ēz) n. pl. In ancient Rome, a bundle of rods enclosing an ax, borne by lictors before consuls and other magistrates as a symbol of power. [<L]

FARTHINGALE

fas·ci·al (fash'ē·əl) adj.

fas·ci·a (fash'ē·ə) n. pl. **·ci·ae** (-i·ē) 1 Anat. Condensed connective tissue forming sheets or layers, for the investment of organs or the insertion of muscles. 2 Archit. A flat member or broad volute; a jutting brick course in any story of a building except the uppermost. See illustration under ENTABLATURE. 3 Something that binds together, as a fillet; a band. 4 A bandage. 5 A distinct band of color, as in certain plants and animals. [<L, a band] — **fas'·ci·al** adj.

fas·ci·cle (fas'i·kəl) n. 1 A small collection; bundle; cluster; group. 2 Anat. A bundle of fibers in the body; a fasciculus. 3 Bot. A cluster or bundle, as of leaves, flowers, or stalks, which proceed from a common point. 4 A number of sheets of printed work bound together. [<L fasciculus, dim. of fascia bundle]

fas·cic·u·lar (fə·sik'yə·lər) adj. Of or pertaining to a fascicle.

fas·cic·u·late (fə·sik'yə·lit) adj. Composed of or growing in bundles. Also **fas'ci·cled, fascic'u·lat'ed** — **fas·cic'u·late·ly** adv. — **fas·cic'u·la'tion** n.

fas·cic·u·lus (fə·sik'yə·ləs) n. pl. **·li** (-lī) A fascicle; especially, a bundle of nerve fibers.

fas·ci·nate (fas'ə·nāt) v. **·nat·ed, ·nat·ing** v.t. 1 To attract irresistibly, as by beauty or other qualities; captivate. 2 To hold spellbound, as by terror or awe. 3 Obs. To bewitch. — v.i. 4 To be fascinating. See synonyms under CHARM. [<L fascinatus, pp. of fascinare charm <fascinum a spell] — **fas'ci·nat'ing** adj. — **fas'ci·nat'ing·ly** adv.

fas·ci·na·tion (fas'ə·nā'shən) n. 1 The act of fascinating. 2 The state of being fascinated. 3 Enchantment; charm.

fas·cism (fash'iz·əm) n. Any authoritarian, anti-democratic, anti-communist system of government in which economic control by the state, militaristic nationalism, propaganda, and the crushing of opposition by means of secret police emphasize the supremacy of the state over the individual. [<Ital. fascismo < fascio political club <L fascis a bundle] —

---

fas′cist n. —**fa·scis′tic** adj. —**fa·scis′ti·cal·ly** adv.

Fas·cism (fash′iz·əm) n. The system of one-party government, developed by the Fascisti in Italy, which exercised a centralized autocratic control over the activities of all individuals, especially through the economic agency of state corporations.

Fas·cist (fash′ist) n. One of the Fascisti.

Fa·scis·ti (fə·shis′tē, Ital. fä-shē′stē) n. pl. of **Fa·scis′ta** The members of a totalitarian, syndicalist society in Italy, formed in 1919 under Benito Mussolini to oppose socialism and communism: in control of the government, 1922–43. [<Ital. <fascio a political club; meaning infl. by L fasces a bundle of rods. See FASCES.] —**Fas′cism,** Italian **Fa·scis·mo** (fä·shēs′mō).]

fash·ion (fash′ən) n. 1 The prevailing mode, especially in dress; the usage of polite society. 2 Manner of doing a thing; method; way. 3 The make or shape of a thing; external appearance; form. 4 Fashionable people, collectively. 5 Common practice or custom; usage. 6 A thing that is fashionable. See synonyms under AIR, CUSTOM, HABIT. —**after a fashion** In a way; not thoroughly, well, or enthusiastically: also **in a fashion.** —v.t. 1 To give shape or form to; frame; mold; make. 2 To conform; accommodate; fit. See synonyms under ADAPT, MAKE. [<AF fachon, var. of OF façon <L factio, -onis. Doublet of FACTION.]

fash·ion·a·ble (fash′ən·ə·bəl) adj. 1 Conforming to the current edicts of fashion. 2 Established and approved by the prevailing custom or polite usage. 3 Of, pertaining to, or like persons of fashion. —n. A person of fashion. —**fash′ion·a·ble·ness** n. —**fash′ion·a·bly** adv.

fashion plate 1 A picture representing the prevailing fashions in wearing apparel. 2 Colloq. One whose attire is perfect, according to the current mode.

fast¹ (fast, fäst) adj. 1 Firm in place; not easily moved. 2 Firmly secured or bound. 3 Constant; steadfast. 4 Unfadable: said of colors. 5 Resistant: acid–fast. 6 Sound or deep, as sleep. 7 Acting or moving quickly; swift. 8 Performed quickly: fast work. 9 Adapted to, or suitable for, quick movement: a fast track. 10 Requiring rapidity of action or motion: a fast schedule. 11 Indicating a time in advance of the true time: The clock is fast. 12 Given to dissipation or moral laxity: fast living. 13 Phot. Intended for short exposure, as a high–velocity shutter or a highly sensitive film. —adv. 1 Firmly; fixedly; securely. 2 Soundly: fast asleep. 3 Quickly; rapidly; swiftly. 4 In quick succession: His thoughts came fast. 5 Dissipatedly; recklessly: to live fast. 6 Archaic Near: fast by. —n. 1 Something which is firm or fixed, as shore ice. 2 A mooring line. [OE fæst]

fast² (fast, fäst) v.i. 1 To abstain from food. 2 To go without food, wholly or in part, as in observance of a religious duty. —n. 1 Abstinence from food, partial or total, or from prescribed kinds of food, particularly as a religious duty. 2 A period prescribed for religious fasting and other observances: opposed to feast. [OE fæstan]

fast·en (fas′ən, fäs′-) v.t. 1 To attach or secure to something else; connect. 2 To make fast; secure: to fasten a door. 3 To direct, as attention or the eyes, steadily. 4 To cause to cling or be attributed: to fasten blame. —v.i. 5 To take fast hold; cling: usually with on. 6 To become firm or attached. See synonyms under BIND. [OE fæstnian <fæst fixed] —**fast′en·er** n.

fas·tid·i·ous (fas·tid′ē·əs) adj. Hard to please; overnice; squeamish. See synonyms under SQUEAMISH. [<L fastidiosus <fastidium disgust] —**fas·tid′i·ous·ly** adv. —**fas·tid′i·ous·ness** n.

fas·tig·i·ate (fas·tij′ē·it, -āt) adj. 1 Tapering toward a point. 2 Zool. Forming a conical bundle. 3 Bot. Nearly parallel and pointing upward, as the branches of a Lombardy poplar. [<L fastigium top + -ATE¹]

fast·ness (fast′nis, fäst′-) n. 1 A fortress; stronghold. 2 The state of being firm or fixed; security. 3 Rapidity. 4 Dissipation. See synonyms under FORTIFICATION.

fat (fat) adj. **fat·ter, fat·test** 1 Having much or superfluous flesh; corpulent; obese. 2 Con-

taining much oil, grease, etc. 3 Broad: said of a ship's quarter, of type bodies, etc. 4 Printing Profitable, because containing a large proportion of open space, illustrations, etc.: said of type matter or copy for it: also spelled phat. 5 Stupid; sluggish; dull. 6 Prosperous; thriving; flourishing. 7 Rich in products or in profits; rewarding: fat lands, a fat office. 8 Resinous; as fat wood. 9 Well–filled: a fat larder. 10 Plump, well–nourished, and healthy, as cattle. See synonyms under CORPULENT. —n. 1 Biochem. A gray to white, greasy, easily melted compound contained in certain specialized cells of plants and animals, and forming an important food reserve as well as a source of hormones, vitamins, and other products essential in metabolism. 2 The richest or most desirable part of anything: the fat of the land. 3 Chem. Any of various compounds of carbon, oxygen, and hydrogen which are glycerol esters of certain acids, as stearic, palmitic, etc.; they include waxes, lipids, and sterols, are insoluble in water, and in the pure state are generally colorless, odorless, and tasteless. —**the fat is in the fire** The mischief is done. —v.t. & v.i. **fat·ted, fat·ting** To fatten. [OE fæt] —**fat′ly** adv. —**fat′ness** n.

fa·tal (fāt′l) adj. 1 Bringing or connected with death or ruin; destructive; deadly. 2 Portentous; ominous. 3 Fraught with or determining fate or destiny; fateful. 4 Obs. That must be; inevitable. [<L fatalis <fatum FATE]

fa·tal·ism (fā′təl·iz′əm) n. 1 Philos. The doctrine that every event is predetermined by fate and inevitable. 2 A disposition to accept every event as preordained.

fa·tal·ist (fā′təl·ist) n. A believer in fatalism. —**fa·tal·is′tic** adj. —**fa·tal·is′ti·cal·ly** adv.

fa·tal·i·ty (fā·tal′ə·tē, fə-) n. pl. **·ties** 1 A state of being fated. 2 Destiny; a decree of fate. 3 A disastrous or fatal event; death. 4 Tendency to danger or disaster. See synonyms under NECESSITY.

fa·tal·ly (fā′təl·ē) adv. 1 In a disastrous manner; ruinously; mortally. 2 According to the decrees of fate.

fat·back (fat′bak′) n. 1 The menhaden. 2 The American striped mullet. 3 Unsmoked salt pork.

fat·bird (fat′bûrd′) n. 1 The pectoral sandpiper (Pisobia melanota). 2 The guacharo.

fat·body (fat′bod′ē) n. Entomol. The tissue of oily cells closely associated with the nutritive and metabolic functions of insects.

fat–cell (fat′sel′) n. Biol. One of a class of nucleated cells filled with fatty matter. See illustration under HAIR.

fate (fāt) n. 1 Predetermined and inevitable necessity; that power which is thought to determine one's future, success or failure, etc. 2 Destiny; fortune; lot. 3 Evil destiny; doom; destruction; death. 4 Outcome; final result. See synonyms under NECESSITY. —v.t. **fat·ed, fat·ing** To predestine: obsolete except in passive. [<L fatum, orig. neut. sing. of fatus, pp. of fari speak]

fate·ful (fāt′fəl) adj. 1 Fraught with fate. 2 Fatal. 3 Controlled by fate. —**fate′ful·ly** adv. —**fate′ful·ness** n.

Fates (fāts) In Greek mythology, three goddesses who control human destiny: Clotho spins the thread of life, Lachesis decides its length, and Atropos severs it: identified with the Roman Parcae: also Destinies.

fa·ther (fä′thər) n. 1 The male human parent. 2 Any male ancestor; forefather. 3 A patriarch; an aged and reverend man or honored official. 4 a In the Roman Catholic and, sometimes, in the Anglican Church, a priest: often used as a title and capitalized when preceding a name. b A church dignitary, as a bishop or abbot. 5 Eccl. Any one of the early historical or doctrinal writers of the Christian Church. 6 An author; founder. 7 Brit. The oldest member of a class or body; doyen. 8 One who bears a paternal relationship toward another. 9 A member of the ancient Roman Senate. 10 pl. The chiefs of a city or assembly. —v.t. 1 To beget as a father. 2 To found, create, or make. 3 To acknowledge as one's offspring. 4 To act as a father to. 5 To take or accept the responsibility of. [OE fæder] —**fa′ther·like′** adj. & adv.

Fa·ther (fä′thər) n. The Deity; God; the first person in the Trinity.

father confessor A priest of the Roman

Catholic Church or of any other church to whom the members confess their faults and sins; hence, any one in whom one confides.

fa·ther·hood (fä′thər·hŏŏd) n. The state of being a father.

fa·ther–in–law (fä′thər·in·lô′) n. pl. **fa·thers–in–law** The father of one's husband or wife.

fa·ther·land (fä′thər·land′) n. The land of one's birth.

fa·ther·less (fä′thər·lis) adj. Not having a living father.

fa·ther·ly (fä′thər·lē) adj. 1 Of, pertaining to, or like a father. 2 Manifesting the affection of a father; paternal. —**fa′ther·li·ness** n.

fath·om (fath′əm) n. pl. **·oms** or **·om** A measure of length, 6 feet, or 1.829 meters: used principally in marine and mining measurements. —v.t. 1 To find the depth of; sound. 2 To get to the bottom of; understand; interpret. [OE fæthm the span of two arms outstretched] —**fath′om·a·ble** adj.

fa·thom·e·ter (fə·thom′ə·tər) n. A device for registering ocean depths by measuring the time required for the transmission and reflection of sound waves.

fath·om·less (fath′əm·lis) adj. Unfathomable.

fa·tid·ic (fə·tid′ik) adj. Able to prophesy; oracular. Also **fa·tid′i·cal.** [<L fatidicus <fatum FATE + dicere speak]

fat·i·ga·ble (fat′ə·gə·bəl) adj. Capable of causing or experiencing fatigue; tiring; wearying.

fat·i·gate (fat′ə·gāt) adj. Obs. Fatigued; exhausted. [<L fatigatus, pp. of fatigare tire]

fa·tigue (fə·tēg′) n. 1 Exhaustion of strength by toil; weariness. 2 Wearing toil. 3 Physiol. a A condition of lessened activity of an organism or any of its parts, resulting from prolonged exertion. b A diminished susceptibility to stimulation of the central nervous system, affecting primarily the junction between nerve and muscle fibers. 4 Metall. The failure of metals under prolonged or repeated stress, characterized by local deformation of structure. 5 Fatigue duty. 6 pl. Strong, durable clothes worn on fatigue duty. —v.t. & v.i. **·tigued, ·ti·guing** To weary; tire out. [<F fatiguer tire <L fatigare]

fatigue duty Common labor done by soldiers.

fat·ten (fat′n) v. **fat·tened, fat·ten·ing** v.t. 1 To make fat or plump. 2 To make (land) fertile or productive. 3 To make rich or richer. —v.i. 4 To become fat. —**fat′ten·er** n.

fat·tish (fat′ish) adj. Somewhat fat. —**fat′tish·ness** n.

fat·ty (fat′ē) adj. **fat·ti·er, fat·ti·est** Fat; unctuous. —**fat′ti·ly** adv. —**fat′ti·ness** n.

fatty acid Chem. A derivative of the paraffin series formed by oxidizing one of the monatomic alcohols. The physical characteristics of the higher complex fatty acids, as palmitic and stearic acids, give the name to the group.

fatty degeneration Pathol. A condition in which the efficient cells in an organ are enveloped in or replaced by fat.

fa·tu·i·ty (fə·tŏŏ′ə·tē, -tyŏŏ′-) n. 1 Obstinate or conceited folly. 2 Imbecility; idiocy; feeble–mindedness. [<F fatuité <L fatuitas, -tatis <fatuus foolish] —**fa·tu′i·tous** adj.

fat·u·oid (fach′ŏŏ·oid) n. A species of wild oat (Avena fatua) resembling the cultivated variety; it is frequently a troublesome weed.

fat·u·ous (fach′ŏŏ·əs) adj. 1 Stubbornly blind or foolish; idiotic. 2 Baseless; illusory, like the will-o′-the-wisp. [<L fatuus foolish] —**fat′u·ous·ly** adv. —**fat′u·ous·ness** n.

fau·cal (fô′kəl) adj. Anat. Of or pertaining to the fauces; produced in the fauces; deeply guttural. Also **fau·cial** (fô′shəl).

fau·ces (fô′sēz) n. pl. Anat. The parts bordering on the opening between the back of the mouth and the pharynx. [<L]

fau·cet (fô′sit) n. A spout fitted with a valve, for drawing liquids through a pipe. [<OF fausset, prob. <fausser break into, damage <L falsare <falsus FALSE]

TYPES OF FAUCETS
a. Sink. b. Hose.
c. Mixing.

faugh (fô) interj. An exclamation of disgust, contempt, or rejection.

Faulk·ner (fôk′nər), **William,** 1897–1962, U.S. novelist: also spelled *Falkner.*

fault (fôlt) *n.* **1** A slight offense; failure; negligence. **2** Whatever impairs excellence; an imperfection or defect in a person or thing; failure; blemish. **3** *Geol.* **a** A dislocation of a stratum or vein of ore which breaks its continuity. **b** A displacement or break in the

FAULT (*def. 3*)

continuity of rock masses, caused by disturbances of the earth's crust and resulting in a wide variety of surface features. **4** A missing or losing of the trail or scent: said of hunting dogs. **5** *Electr.* A deflection or leak in a current, due to abnormal connection of circuits or defective insulation of a conductor. **6** In tennis, rackets, etc., a failure by the server to drive the ball into the proper part of his opponent's court; also, a failure by the server to have both feet on the ground behind the service line in serving: usually called **foot fault. 7** *Obs.* Default; lack. See synonyms under BLEMISH, ERROR, OFFENSE. **— at fault 1** In the wrong. **2** Worthy of blame. **3** Off the scent. **4** Hence, at a loss; in a quandary. **— in fault** Blameworthy. **— to a fault** Exceedingly; excessively: generous *to a fault.* *—v.t.* **1** *Rare* To find fault with; blame. **2** *Geol.* To cause a fault in. *—v.i.* **3** *Archaic* To commit a fault; err. **4** *Geol.* To crack or fracture so as to produce a fault. [<OF *faute,* ult. <L *fallere* deceive] **—fault′· ful·ly** *adv.* **—fault′ful·ness** *n.*

fault–current (fôlt′kûr′ənt) *n. Electr.* A current flowing from conductor to ground or to another conductor because of faulty connections.

fault·less (fôlt′lis) *adj.* Without fault; flawless. See synonyms under CORRECT, INNOCENT, PERFECT. **—fault′less·ly** *adv.* **—fault′less·ness** *n.*

fault plane *Geol.* The fracture along which faulting occurs, commonly a curved surface.

fault·y (fôl′tē) *adj.* **fault·i·er, fault·i·est 1** Having faults or blemishes. **2** Characterized by faults of conduct. **3** *Obs.* Guilty of faults; blamable. **—fault′i·ly** *adv.* **—fault′i·ness** *n.*

fau·na (fô′nə) *n. pl.* **fau·nas** or **fau·nae** (-nē) **1** The animals living within a given area or environment or during a stated period: distinguished from *flora.* **2** A treatise upon a fauna. See synonyms under ANIMAL. [<NL, after L *Fauna,* a rural goddess] **—fau′nal** *adj.* **—fau′nal·ly** *adv.*

Fauves (fōv), **Les** (lā) A group of French painters, including Derain, Dufy, Matisse, and Vlaminck, who, about 1906, revolted from what they regarded as the limitations of Impressionism as well as from those of academic art. [<F, wild beasts] **—Fau′vism** *n.* **—Fau′vist** *n.*

fa·ve·o·late (fə·vē′ə·lāt) *adj.* Pitted; honeycombed; alveolate. Also **fa·vose** (fā′vōs, fə·vōs′). [<NL *faveolus,* dim. of *favus* a honeycomb <L + -ATE[1]]

fa·vo·ni·an (fə·vō′nē·ən) *adj.* **1** Of or pertaining to Favonius, the west wind, promoter of vegetation. **2** Auspicious.

fa·vor (fā′vər) *n.* **1** An act or course of generosity; kind and favorable feeling; privilege granted. **2** The state or condition of being favored or approved. **3** Favoritism; bias; partiality. **4** Kind permission. **5** Convenience; facility. **6** Something given as a token; a gage. **7** A letter, especially a business letter. **8** That which is favored. **—in favor of 1** On the side of. **2** To the benefit of; payable to. *—v.t.* **1** To look upon with favor or kindness; like. **2** To treat with partiality; show preference for. **3** To make easier; facilitate. **4** To be in favor of; support; help. **5** To do a favor for; oblige. **6** To use carefully; spare, as a lame foot. **7** *Colloq.* To look like; resemble. See synonyms under INDULGE. Also *Brit.* **fa′vour.** [<L *favere* favor] **—fa′vor·er** *n.*

Synonyms (noun): benefit, blessing, boon, civility, concession, condescension, countenance, gift, grace, kindness, patronage, predilection, preference, regard. A *favor* is a *benefit* or *kindness* that one is glad to receive, but cannot demand or claim, hence always indicating good will or *regard* on the part of the person by whom it is conferred. See ESTEEM, FRIENDSHIP, GIFT, MERCY. *Antonyms*: disapproval, disfavor, dislike, harm, hostility, hurt, injury, insult, repulse.

fa·vor·a·ble (fā′vər·ə·bəl) *adj.* **1** Convenient; advantageous. **2** Friendly; propitious. Also *Brit.* **fa′vour·able.** See synonyms under AMICABLE, AUSPICIOUS, CONVENIENT, EXPEDIENT, FRIENDLY, GOOD, PROPITIOUS. **—fa′vor·a·ble· ness** *n.* **—fa′vor·a·bly** *adv.*

fa·vored (fā′vərd) *adj.* **1** Having an aspect or appearance; in compounds: ill-*favored.* **2** Wearing a favor. **3** Befriended; aided; privileged. See synonyms under FORTUNATE.

fa·vor·ite (fā′vər·it) *adj.* Regarded with special favor; preferred. *—n.* **1** A person or animal that is considered to have the best chance of success in a race or other contest. **2** A person or thing particularly liked or favored. Also *Brit.* **fa′vour·ite.** [<OF *favorit* <Ital. *favorito,* pp. of *favorire* favor <L *favor*]

fa·vor·it·ism (fā′vər·ə·tiz′əm) *n.* **1** A disposition to favor unfairly or unreasonably. **2** The state or condition of being a favorite. Also *Brit.* **fa′vour·it·ism.**

fa·vus (fā′vəs) *n. Pathol.* A contagious disease as of the scalp, caused by a parasitic fungus (*Achorion schönleinii*) an.′ producing yellow flattened scabs and baldness; scaldhead. [<L, honeycomb]

fawn[1] (fôn) *v.i.* **1** To show cringing fondness, as a dog: often with *on* or *upon.* **2** To show affection or seek favor by or as by cringing. ◆ Homophone: *faun.* [OE *fahnian,* var. of *fægnian* rejoice] **—fawn′er** *n.* **—fawn′ing** *adj.* & *n.* **fawn′ing·ly** *adv.* **—fawn′ing·ness** *n.*

fawn[2] (fôn) *n.* **1** A young deer; a buck or doe in its first year. **2** The color of a fawn. *—adj.* Fawncolored. ◆ Homophone: *faun.* [<OF *faon,* ult. <L *fetus* offspring]

fay[1] (fā) *v.t.* & *v.i.* To fit or join closely; lie closely together, as two timbers. *—n.* A fitting smoothly, as of one plank to another. [OE *fegan*]

fay[2] (fā) *n.* A fairy. [<OF *fae* <L *fata* the Fates, pl. of *fatum* fate]

fay·al·ite (fā′əl·it, fī·äl′īt) *n.* A black magnetic iron silicate crystallizing in the orthorhombic system. [from *Fayal* + -ITE[1]]

Fe *Chem.* Iron (symbol Fe). [L *Ferrum*]

fe·al·ty (fē′əl·tē) *n. pl.* **·ties 1** Fidelity, as of a vassal to his lord. **2** Devoted faithfulness; loyalty. See synonyms under ALLEGIANCE, FIDELITY. [<OF *feaute, feaulte* <L *fidelitas.* Doublet of FIDELITY.]

fear (fir) *n.* **1** An emotion excited by threatening evil or impending pain, accompanied by a desire to avoid or escape it; apprehension; dread. **2** Uneasiness about a thing; solicitude accompanied with dread. **3** That which causes fear. **4** Alarming character; formidableness. **5** Reverence for constituted authority, especially when accompanied by obedience thereto: the *fear* of God. *—v.t.* **1** To be afraid of; be fearful of. **2** To look upon with awe or reverence; venerate: to *fear* God. **3** To be anxious about; be apprehensive about. *—v.i.* **4** To be afraid; feel fear. **5** To be anxious or doubtful. [OE *fær* peril, sudden attack] **—fear′er** *n.*

Synonyms (noun): affright, apprehension, awe, consternation, dismay, disquiet, dread, fright, horror, misgiving, panic, terror, timidity, trembling, tremor, trepidation. *Fear* is the generic term denoting an emotion excited by threatening evil with a desire to avoid or escape it; *fear* may be sudden or lingering, in view of present, of imminent, or of distant and only possible danger; in the latter sense *dread* is oftener used. *Horror* (etymologically a shivering or shuddering) denotes a shuddering *fear* accompanied by abhorrence, or such a shock to the feelings and sensibilities as may exist without *fear,* as when one suddenly encounters some ghastly spectacle; we

say of a desperate but fettered criminal, "I looked upon him with *horror.*" Where *horror* includes *fear,* it is *fear* mingled with abhorrence. (See ABHOR.) *Timidity* is′ a quality, habit, or condition, a readiness to be affected with *fear.* A person of great *timidity* is constantly liable to needless *alarm* and even *terror.* *Dread* is terrifying anticipation of evil, and is lingering and oppressive. *Dismay* is a helpless sinking of heart in view of some overwhelming peril or sorrow, actual or prospective. *Dismay* is more reflective, enduring, and despairing than *fright;* a horse is subject to *fright* or *terror,* but not to *dismay. Awe* is a reverential *fear.* Compare ALARM, ANXIETY, FRIGHT. *Antonyms:* see synonyms for FORTITUDE. Compare BRAVE.

fear·ful (fir′fəl) *adj.* **1** Experiencing fear; afraid; apprehensive. **2** Timid; timorous. **3** Inspiring fear; terrible. **4** Caused by fear: *fearful* tremblings. **5** Full of awe and reverential fear. **6** *Colloq.,* Very bad; appalling. See synonyms under AWFUL, FRIGHTFUL. **—fear′ful·ly** *adv.* **—fear′ful·ness** *n.*

fear·some (fir′səm) *adj.* **1** Causing fear; alarming. **2** Timid; frightened. **—fear′some·ly** *adv.* **—fear′some·ness** *n.*

fea·sance (fē′zəns) *n. Law* Performance of a duty; fulfilling a condition. [<AF *fesance* < *faire* do <L *facere*]

fea·si·ble (fē′zə·bəl) *adj.* **1** That may be done; practicable. **2** Open to being dealt with successfully. [<OF *faisable* < *faire* do <L *facere*] **—fea′si·bil′i·ty, fea′si·ble·ness** *n.* **—fea′si·bly** *adv.*

fea·sor (fē′zər) *n. Law* A doer; one who does a tort or wrong. See TORT. [<OF]

feast (fēst) *n.* **1** A sumptuous repast. **2** Anything affording great pleasure or enjoyment. **3** A day set aside for the commemoration of some person or event with rejoicing; a festival or joyous anniversary: opposed to *fast. —v.t.* **1** To give a feast for; entertain lavishly. **2** To delight; gratify: He *feasted* his eyes on her beauty. *—v.i.* **3** To partake of a feast; eat heartily. **4** To dwell delightedly, as on beauty. [<OF *feste* <L *festa,* neut. pl. of *festus* joyful] **—feast′er** *n.*

feat (fēt) *n.* **1** A notable act or performance, as one displaying skill, endurance, or daring; an achievement. **2** *Obs.* An act of any kind. See synonyms under ACT. *—adj. Obs.* **1** Dexterous; neat; ingenious. **2** Fit; befitting. [<OF *fait* <L *factum.* See FACT.]

feath·er (feth′ər) *n.* **1** One of the horny, elongated structures which form the body covering of birds and provide the flight surface for their wings. It consists of a central *shaft* composed of a hollow part near the body called the *quill* and a distal solid part, the *rachis,* along each side of which is a series of processes, the *barbs.* The barbs are provided with a fringe of smaller processes, the *barbules,* which in turn

FEATHER
a. Aftershaft.
b. Shaft.
c. Barbs.

are equipped with *barbicels,* or hooklets, the whole composing the *vane* of the feather. **2** Something resembling a feather, as in mechanisms; a tongue, wedge, or fin. **3** Kind; class or species: birds of a *feather.* **4** Frame of mind; mood; spirits. **5** In rowing, the act of feathering. **6** The wake of the periscope of a submarine. **7** An irregular flaw in a gem. **8** The hairy fringe on the backs of the legs and on the tail of some dogs. **9** *pl.* Plumage; by extension, dress or attire. **10** A fin or guide on the shaft of an arrow. **11** Anything light or trivial: A *feather* would upset him. **— a feather in one's cap** An achievement to be proud of; a thing to one's credit. **— in full feather** In full force; fully equipped. **— in high, fine,** or **good feather** In a cheerful or confident frame of mind. — *v.t.* **1** To fit with a feather, as an arrow. **2** To cover, adorn, or fringe with feathers. **3** To join by a tongue and groove. **4** In rowing, to turn (the oar blade) as it comes from the water until it is horizontal or nearly horizontal, thus offering the least resistance while reaching for a new stroke. **5** *Aeron.* To turn one edge of (the propeller blade) into the wind, thus minimizing drag. — *v.i.* **6** To grow or become covered with feathers. **7** To move, spread, or expand like feathers. **8** To feather an oar or propeller blade. — **to feather one's nest** To provide well for one's own future while acting as the agent of another. [OE *fether*]

feath·ered (feth′ərd) *adj.* **1** Provided with feathers or featherlike appendages. **2** Winged; swift.

feather grass **1** An ornamental grass (*Stipa pennata*) of southern Europe, having a feathered beard. **2** A related species (*S. comata*) of the western United States, sometimes called *needle grass.*

feath·er·less (feth′ər-lis) *adj.* Without feathers.

feather palm Any of various palms having feather-shaped or pinnate leaves.

feather star One of a genus (*Comatula*) of free-swimming crinoids with plumelike arms.

feath·er·stitch (feth′ər-stich′) *n.* A kind of decorative stitch, resembling a feather, made by taking one or more short stitches alternately on either side of a straight line. — **feath′er·stitch′ing** *n.*

feath·er·veined (feth′ər·vānd′) *adj. Bot.* Having the veins all proceeding from opposite sides of a midrib.

feath·er·weight (feth′ər·wāt′) *n.* **1** A boxer or wrestler weighing from 118 to 126 pounds. **2** The least weight allowed to a race horse in a handicap. **3** A person weighing very little; hence, anyone of little ability or importance. — *adj.* Of little weight; insignificant; unimportant.

feath·er·wood (feth′ər·wŏŏd′) *n.* A hickorylike, hardwood timber tree of Australia (*Polyosma cunninghami*).

fea·ture (fē′chər) *n.* **1** Any part of the human face. **2** *pl.* The whole face. **3** A salient point. **4** A magazine or newspaper article or story on a special subject. **5** A full-length motion picture. **6** *Archaic* Make; shape; form. See synonyms under CHARACTERISTIC, CIRCUMSTANCE. — *v.t.* **fea·tured, fea·tur·ing** **1** To make a feature of, as in a newspaper story. **2** To be a feature of. **3** To portray or outline the features of. **4** *U.S. Slang* To imagine; fancy. **5** *Colloq.* To resemble; favor. [< OF *faiture* < L *factura* < *facere* do] — **fea′ture·less** *adj.*

fea·tured (fē′chərd) *adj.* **1** Chiseled; shaped or fashioned. **2** Having or exhibiting features. **3** Given special prominence.

fea·ture-length (fē′chər·length′) *adj.* Full-length: said especially of a motion picture.

febri- *combining form* Fever: *febrifuge.* Also, before vowels, **febr-.** [< L *febris* fever]

fe·bric·i·ty (fə·bris′ə·tē) *n.* The condition of being feverish.

fe·bric·u·la (fə·brik′yə·lə) *n.* A light and passing fever. [< L, little fever]

feb·ri·fa·cient (feb′rə·fā′shənt) *n.* A substance that produces fever. — *adj.* Producing or promoting fever.

fe·brif·ic (fə·brif′ik) *adj.* **1** Causing fever. **2** Feverish. Also **fe·brif′er·ous.**

feb·ri·fuge (feb′rə·fyŏŏj) *n.* A medicine efficacious in reducing or removing fever. [< FEBRI- + L *fugere* flee] — **feb·rif·u·gal** (fə·brif′yə·gəl) *adj.*

fe·brile (fē′brəl, feb′rəl) *adj.* Pertaining to fever; caused by or indicating fever; feverish. [< F *fébrile* < L *febrilis* < *febris* fever]

Feb·ru·ar·y (feb′rŏŏ·er′ē) The second month of the year, having twenty-eight or, in leap years, twenty-nine days. See LEAP YEAR. [< F *Februarius* (*mensis*) (month) of purification < *februa,* a Roman purificatory festival, celebrated on Feb. 15]

fe·ces (fē′sēz) *n. pl.* **1** Animal excrement; ordure. **2** Any foul refuse matter or sediment. Also spelled *faeces.* [< L *faex, faecis* sediment] — **fe·cal** (fē′kəl) *adj.*

feck·less (fek′lis) *adj.* Feeble; good-for-nothing; irresponsible. — **feck′less·ly** *adv.* — **feck′·less·ness** *n.*

fec·u·la (fek′yə·lə) *n. pl.* **·lae** (-lē) **1** Starch, especially as extracted by washing farinaceous

pulp; also called **amylaceous fecula.** **2** The sediment or dregs precipitated from an infusion. [< L *faecula* crust of wine, orig. dim. of *faex* dregs]

fec·u·lence (fek′yə·ləns) *n.* **1** The condition or quality of being feculent; foulness; muddiness. **2** That which is feculent; dregs. Also **fec′u·len·cy.**

fec·u·lent (fek′yə·lənt) *adj.* Turbid or foul from impurities; fecal. [< L *faeculentus* < *faecula.* See FECULA.]

fe·cund (fē′kund, fek′und) *adj.* Fruitful; fertile; prolific. [< OF *fecond* < L *fecundus*]

fe·cun·date (fē′kən·dāt, fek′ən-) *v.t.* **·dat·ed, ·dat·ing** **1** To make fruitful or fecund. **2** To impregnate; fertilize. [< L *fecundatus,* pp. of *fecundare* fertilize < *fecundus* fruitful] — **fe′·cun·da′tion** *n.*

fe·cun·di·ty (fi·kun′də·tē) *n.* Productiveness; fruitfulness.

fed (fed) Past tense and past participle of FEED.

fed·er·a·cy (fed′ər·ə·sē) *n. pl.* **·cies** A confederacy.

fed·er·al (fed′ər·əl) *adj.* **1** *Govt.* Of or pertaining to a form of government in which certain states agree by compact to grant control of common affairs to a central authority but retain individual control over internal affairs. **2** Of or pertaining to a union or central authority so established. **3** Favoring or supporting a government formed by a union of several states. **4** Relating to, arising from, or founded upon a league or covenant. — *n.* An advocate of federalism. [< F *fédéral* < L *foedus, -eris* a compact, league] — **fed′er·al·ly** *adv.*

Fed·er·al (fed′ər·əl) *adj.* **1** Of, pertaining to, owned or used by, or representing the United States of America: a *Federal* building, the *Federal* Bureau of Investigation. **2** Supporting the Union cause in the American Civil War of 1861–65: the *Federal* forces. — *n.* One who favored or fought for the Union cause in the American Civil War.

Federal Bureau of Investigation A branch of the Department of Justice which investigates all violations of Federal laws other than those specifically assigned to other agencies: popularly the FBI.

Federal Communications Commission An agency of the U.S. government which supervises wire, radio, and television communication in the interest of maximum efficiency and public service.

Federal District A district reserved by a country for the location of the national government; in Argentina, including Buenos Aires, 74 square miles; in Brazil, including Rio de Janeiro, 154 square miles; in Mexico, including Mexico City, 573 square miles; in Venezuela, including Caracas, 745 square miles; in the United States, the District of Columbia, including Washington, 61 square miles. Spanish and Portuguese *Distrito Federal.*

fed·er·al·ism (fed′ər·əl·iz′əm) *n.* **1** The doctrine of federal union in government. **2** *Cap.* The principles of the Federal party.

fed·er·al·ist (fed′ər·əl·ist) *n.* An advocate of federalism.

Fed·er·al·ist (fed′ər·əl·ist) *n.* One who supported the federal union of the American colonies and the adoption of the Constitution of the United States; a member of the Federal party. — *The Federalist* A series of 85 essays by Alexander Hamilton, John Jay, and James Madison, explaining, and recommending for ratification, the Constitution of the United States.

Federal party A political party (1787–1830) originally under the leadership of Alexander Hamilton, which advocated the adoption of the United States Constitution and the formation of a strong national government.

Federal Power Commission An agency of the U.S. government which supervises the development and utilization of power resources on Federal property, regulates the activities of public utilities engaged in interstate commerce, and provides for a uniform system of accounts in the management of electric power enterprises.

Federal Reserve System A banking system created by the **Federal Reserve Act** (1913) and controlled by a **Federal Reserve Board** of eight members, established to provide an elastic currency and to concentrate the na-

tional banking resources in a system of twelve **Federal reserve banks,** each designed to regulate and aid the member banks in its respective **Federal reserve district.** The **Federal reserve cities** are Boston, New York, Philadelphia, Cleveland, Richmond, Atlanta, Chicago, St. Louis, Minneapolis, Kansas City, Dallas, and San Francisco.

Federal Trade Commission An agency of the U.S. government which enforces Federal laws against unfair trade practices, as price-fixing, false advertising claims, etc.

fed·er·a·tion (fed′ə·rā′shən) *n.* **1** The act of uniting under a federal government. **2** A federated body; league. **3** A national union. See synonyms under ALLIANCE, ASSOCIATION.

fe·do·ra (fə·dôr′ə, -dō′rə) *n.* A low hat, usually of soft felt, with the crown creased lengthwise. [after *Fédora,* a play by V. Sardou]

fee (fē) *n.* **1** A payment, as for professional service. **2** A charge for a special privilege, as admission to an entertainment or membership in a society or club. **3** A gratuity. **4** *Law* An estate of inheritance, either in *fee-simple,* in which the heir has unqualified ownership and power of disposition, or in *fee-tail,* in which inheritance is limited to a man and his heirs or to certain classes of heirs. **5** In feudal law, a fief. **6** Ownership; property. See synonyms under SALARY. — *v.t.* **feed, fee·ing** **1** To give a fee to; tip, as a waiter. **2** *Scot.* To hire. **3** *Obs.* To bribe. [< AF, var. of OF *fé, fief* < Med. L *feudum* FEUD²]

fee·ble (fē′bəl) *adj.* **fee·bler, fee·blest** **1** Lacking muscular power; frail; infirm. **2** Lacking strength for support or resistance; weak: a *feeble* barrier. **3** Lacking force, energy, or vigor. See synonyms under FAINT, LITTLE, MEAGER, PUSILLANIMOUS. [< OF *feble* < *fleible* weak < L *flebilis* tearful < *flere* weep. Related to FOIBLE.] — **fee′ble·ness** *n.* — **fee′blish** *adj.* — **fee′bly** *adv.*

feed (fēd) *n.* **1** Anything that is used for food; especially, food for domestic animals; fodder, such as hay and grain. **2** The amount of food given to an animal at one time. **3** The motion that carries material into a machine or work toward a tool. **4** The machinery by which motion of the work toward the tool or of the tool toward the work is produced. **5** The material supplied to a machine to be operated upon or consumed, as wool to a carding engine or water to a boiler. **6** *Colloq.* A meal. See synonyms under FOOD. [< *v.*] — *v.* **fed, feed·ing** *v.t.* **1** To give food to; supply with food. **2** To give as food. **3** To furnish with what is necessary for the continuance, growth, or operation of: to *feed* a furnace. **4** To supply (what is necessary) for operation, manufacture, etc.: to *feed* steel to a factory. **5** To enlarge; increase, as if by causing to grow: Compliments *feed* his vanity. **6** To cue an actor with (lines). **7** In sports, to hand or throw (the ball or puck) to a player who will try for a goal, etc. — *v.i.* **8** To take food; eat: said of animals. **9** To subsist; depend: usually with *on:* to *feed* on hopes. [OE *fēdan*]

feed·back (fēd′bak′) *n.* **1** *Electronics* The transfer of a portion of the energy from the output circuit of an electronic system to the input circuit; when properly controlled and in correct phase, it is positive or regenerative; reversed or improper forms anywhere in the system are negative or degenerative. **2** A similar energy transfer occurring in certain biological processes, as in the transmission of stimuli along an interconnected system of nerve fibers.

feed·er (fē′dər) *n.* **1** One who or that which feeds, as a person or appliance for supplying material to a machine. **2** A person, animal, or plant that takes in nourishment. **3** Anything that supplies the wants, or increases the importance, of something else, as a tributary stream, a branch railroad, a small vein in a mine, running into a main lode. **4** One who fattens livestock for market. **5** An animal intended for intensive feeding in preparation for slaughter, or an animal that is on such feed. **6** A plant root. **7** A large box or container for feed for animals. **8** *Electr.* A conductor or group of conductors between different generating or distributing units of a power system.

feel (fēl) v. felt, feel·ing v.t. 1 To touch; examine by touching or handling. 2 To perceive or become aware of by the senses: to *feel* the prick of a pin. 3 To be conscious of the effects of: to *feel* the weight of a storm. 4 To be conscious of mentally; experience: to *feel* joy. 5 To have the emotions stirred by; be affected by: to *feel* a slight. 6 To be convinced of intellectually; believe in: to *feel* the need for reform. —v.i. 7 To have perception as if by the sense of touch: I *feel* cold. 8 To seem; appear: The air *feels* humid to me. 9 To have the emotions or opinions stirred: I *feel* strongly about the matter. 10 To make examination with or as with the hands; grope: to *feel* around a room. —to feel like Colloq. To have a desire or inclination for: to *feel* like a swim. —to feel one's oats Colloq. To act in a high-spirited manner. —to feel out 1 To examine the possibilities of (a situation). 2 To talk to (a person) so as to determine opinions, ideas, etc. —to feel up to To feel able to do. —n. 1 The sense of touch. 2 Sensation; perception by touch. 3 Perception in general as accompanied with feeling: the *feel* of joy. 4 The quality of a thing that is perceived by the touch: Fur has a soft *feel*. [OE *fēlan*]

feel·er (fē'lər) n. 1 One who or that which feels. 2 Zool. An antenna; tentacle. 3 Bot. A tendril of a vine. 4 An indirect approach; a trial venture.

feel·ing (fē'ling) n. 1 The sense of touch or immediate contact, as aroused by stimulating receptors in the skin, muscles, or internal organs. 2 The fact or the power of perceiving the qualities of the objects arousing the sensations: the *feeling* of a glassy or metallic surface. 3 The collective state or general tone of consciousness due to more or less complex and obscure combinations of classes of sensations: a rested *feeling*, etc. 4 Any emotion as apart from the body; mental stirring; emotion; sentiment; presentiment: to express *feelings* of sympathy: The *feeling* of the meeting was hostile. 5 Sensitiveness, or the capacity to feel deeply; refined sensibility shown in tenderness or ready sympathy; by extension, sentimentality: a woman of *feeling*, to hurt one's *feelings*. 6 Psychol. The affective, emotional aspect of all mental life and its phenomena, as distinguished from the intellectual and voluntary, or active, aspects. 7 That quality by which expression is given to the emotions, and which should actuate a painter in the conception and execution of his design; sympathetic expression in art. —adj. 1 Possessed of warm sensibilities; sympathetic. 2 Marked by, or indicating deep sensibility or fervor and earnestness; hence, affecting. —feel'ing·ly adv.
Synonyms (noun): consciousness, emotion, impression, passion, pathos, sensation, sense, sensibility, sensitiveness, sentiment, tenderness. See IMPULSE. LOVE. SENSATION.

fee-sim·ple (fē'sim'pəl) n. Law An estate of inheritance free from condition.

feet (fēt) Plural of FOOT.

fee-tail (fē'tāl') n. Law An estate limited to a person and the heirs of his body, or to a particular class of them.

feign (fān) v.t. 1 To make a false show of; simulate; pretend. 2 To invent deceptively, as excuses. 3 To make up or imagine, as myths or stories. —v.t. 4 To pretend; dissimulate. See synonyms under ASSUME. PRETEND. ◆Homophones: fain, fane. [<OF *feindre* <L *fingere* shape] —feign·ed·ly (fā'nid·lē), —feign'ing·ly adv. —feign'er n.

feint (fānt) n. 1 A deceptive appearance or movement; a ruse or pretense. 2 In boxing, fencing, war, etc., an apparent or pretended blow or attack meant to divert attention from an attack to be made on another part. 3 pl. Faints. —v.i. To make a feint. —adj. Obs. Feigned; pretended. ◆ Homophone: faint. [<F *feinte* <*feindre*. See FEIGN.]

Fei·sal I (fī'səl), 1885–1933, king of Iraq 1921–1933. —Feisal II, 1935–58, king of Iraq 1939–58. Also spelled *Faisal*.

feis·ty (fīs'tē) adj. U.S. Colloq. Frisky; meddlesome; spunky.

feld·spar (feld'spär, fel'-) n. Any one of a group of crystalline rock-forming materials which consist of silicates of aluminum with potassium, sodium, or calcium: sometimes spelled *felspar*. Also feld'spath (-spath). [Partial trans. of G *feldspat* <*feld* field + *spat* spar³] —feld·spath'ic, feld·spath'ose adj.

feld·spath·oid (feld·spath'oid) n. One of a group of rock-forming minerals, as leucite, nepheline, sodalite, etc.; in general, silicates of aluminum and potassium or sodium, which act like the feldspars in the formation of igneous rocks.

fe·lic·i·tate (fə·lis'ə·tāt) v.t. ·tat·ed, ·tat·ing 1 To wish joy or happiness to; congratulate. 2 Rare To make happy. —adj. Made happy. [<L *felicitatus*, pp. of *felicitare* <*felix* happy]

fe·lic·i·tous (fə·lis'ə·təs) adj. 1 Marked by or producing felicity. 2 Happy in operation or effect; appropriate; apt. See synonyms under HAPPY. —fe·lic'i·tous·ly adv. —fe·lic'i·tous·ness n.

fe·lic·i·ty (fə·lis'ə·tē) n. pl. ·ties 1 A state of great and well-founded happiness, comfort, and content; good fortune; blissfulness. 2 Something causing happiness; a source of content or satisfaction. 3 Happy faculty or turn; tact or knack. 4 A clever, happy, or apt expression. See synonyms under HAPPINESS. [<L *felicitas*, -tatis <*felix* happy]

fe·lid (fē'lid) n. Any member of a family of carnivores (Felidae), the cat family, including the lion, tiger, leopard, puma, lynx, etc., and the domestic cat. [<NL <L *felis* a cat]

fe·line (fē'līn) adj. 1 Of or pertaining to cats or catlike animals. 2 Catlike; sly. —n. A cat; one of the cat family. [<L *felinus* <*felis* cat] —fe'line·ly adv. —fe'line·ness, fe·lin·i·ty (fə·lin'ə·tē) n.

fell¹ (fel) v.t. 1 To cause to fall; cut down. 2 In sewing, to finish with a flat seam. —n. 1 A seam made by joining edges, folding them under, and stitching flat. 2 The end of the web in weaving. 3 The timber cut down during one season. [OE *fellan*] —fell'a·ble adj.

fell² (fel) Past tense of FALL.

fell³ (fel) adj. 1 Characterized by fierceness or cruelty; inhuman; barbarous. 2 Hideous. 3 Scot. Strong; sharp; heroic: *fell* liquor. 4 Scot. Huge; immense. [<OF, cruel, orig. nominative of *felon*. See FELON.]

fell⁴ (fel) n. 1 Hair; a growth of hair. 2 A hide or pelt. [OE, hide]

fell field An area of scattered dwarf plants, chiefly cryptogams, usually in very cold zones or on mountains above the timber line.

fel·low (fel'ō) n. 1 A man; boy. 2 A person or individual; one: A *fellow* can't work day and night. 3 A companion; mate; a counterpart or one of a pair; an equal. 4 An inferior or worthless person. 5 A trustee or member of the corporation in some educational institutions. 6 A member of a society. 7 A graduate or student of a university holding a fellowship or stipend awarded for excellence in and the further pursuit of a special field of study. See FELLOWSHIP. 8 Colloq. A girl's beau. See synonyms under ASSOCIATE. —v.t. 1 To make or proclaim an equal to another. 2 To produce an equal to; match. —adj. Joined or associated; associate; having the same relation to something. ◆ Homophone: *felloe*. [OE *fēolaga* business partner <*feoh* property + *lag-*, stem of *lecgan* lay]

fel·low·ship (fel'ō·ship) n. 1 The state of being a companion or fellow; association; communion; friendly intercourse: the *fellowship* of students. 2 The condition of being sharers or partakers; community of interest, condition, or feeling; joint interest or experience: *fellowship* in prosperity or adversity. 3 A body of persons associated by reason of a community of taste, views, or interests; a company. 4 A position to which graduate members of a college may be elected, carrying with it certain privileges. 5 A foundation, as in a college or university, the income of which is bestowed upon a student, to aid him in pursuing further studies. 6 The rules for determining the shares of partners in the gains or losses of a business; partnership. See synonyms under ACQUAINTANCE, ASSOCIATION, INTERCOURSE. —v. ·shiped or ·shipped, ·ship·ing or ·ship·ping v.t. To admit to religious fellowship. —v.i. U.S. To unite with others in fellowship.

fellow traveler A person who favors the ideology or program of a political party (specifically, the Communist party) without membership in the party.

fel·on¹ (fel'ən) n. 1 One who has committed a felony. 2 Obs. A criminal or depraved person. —adj. 1 Obtained by felony. 2 Wicked; criminal; treacherous. [<OF, base, ult. <L *fellare* suck (in obscene sense)]

fel·on² (fel'ən) n. Pathol. Inflammation of the cellular tissue and periosteum, as on a finger; a whitlow. [Origin uncertain]

fe·lo·ni·ous (fə·lō'nē·əs) adj. 1 Showing criminal purpose; malicious; villainous. 2 Like or involving legal felony. See synonyms under CRIMINAL. — fe·lo'ni·ous·ly adv. — fe·lo'ni·ous·ness n.

fel·on·ry (fel'ən·rē) n. A body of felons; a convict population, as of a penal colony.

fel·o·ny (fel'ə·nē) Law n. pl. ·nies 1 In common law, an offense the punishment of which carried with it the forfeiture of lands or goods, or both. 2 One of the highest class of offenses, variously limited by common law or by statute, and punishable by imprisonment or death. Included are treason, murder, rape, robbery, arson, etc., and punishment is in a State prison.
In modern usage, and especially in American law, forfeiture of estate for crime being generally abolished, the word is used, as defined above, as distinct from *misdemeanor*, an offense of minor degree, punishable by fine or imprisonment in a county jail. Hence, *felony* is now a generic term that denotes a general class or grade of offenses, usually those of greater enormity.

felony murder A murder perpetrated during the commission of a crime of arson, rape, robbery, or burglary.

fel·site (fel'sīt) n. A cryptocrystalline mixture of quartz and feldspar: the groundmass of the quartz porphyries, and often the product of devitrification. Also fel'stone (-stōn). [<G.*fels* rock] — fel·sit·ic (fel·sit'ik) adj.

fel·spar (fel'spär) see FELDSPAR.

felt¹ (felt) Past tense and past participle of FEEL.

felt² (felt) n. 1 A fabric made by compacting wool, fur, or hair, or a mixture thereof, by mechanical or chemical action, moisture, and heat. 2 A piece of material so made; also, some article manufactured therefrom. 3 A thick fabric made of asbestos by weaving or other process. 4 In papermaking, one of two woolen or cotton blankets on which the sheet is carried and between which it is pressed on passing through the rolls of the machine. —adj. Made of felt. —v.t. 1 To make into felt. 2 To overlay with felt. —v.i. 3 To become matted together. [OE]

fe·luc·ca (fə·luk'ə, fe-) n. A small, swift Mediterranean vessel propelled by lateen sails and by oars. [<Ital. <Arabic *falūkah*]

FELUCCA

fe·male (fē'māl) adj. 1 Of or pertaining to the sex that brings forth young or produces ova. 2 Characteristic of a woman; feminine. 3 Bot. Designating a plant which has a pistil but no stamen; pistillate; capable of being fertilized and producing fruit. 4 Mech. Denoting some object having a correlative known as the male; specifically, a part having a hollow or bore into which the correlative may enter. 5 Obs. Effeminate. See synonyms under FEMININE. —n. 1 A person or animal of the female sex. ◆ The use of the word to mean a woman is a survival of an old English usage now regarded with disfavor by good speakers and writers. But *female* is correctly used as the correlative of *male*, whether the latter be expressed or not: "Statistics of population show that there is an excess of *females* in many cities." 2 A pistillate plant. [<OF *femelle* <L *femella*, dim. of *femina* woman]

fem·i·nine (fem'ə·nin) adj. 1 Belonging to or characteristic of womankind; having qualities, as modesty, delicacy, tenderness, tact, etc., normally characteristic of women. **2** Lacking in manly qualities; effeminate. **3** *Gram.* Applicable to females only or to objects classified with them. —*n.* **1** Women, or a woman. **2** *Gram.* A word belonging to the feminine gender. [< L *femininus* < *femina* a woman] —**fem′i·nine·ly** *adv.* —**fem′i·nine·ness** *n.*

Synonyms (*adj.*): effeminate, female, womanish, womanly. We apply *female* to the sex, *feminine* to the qualities, especially the finer physical or mental qualities that distinguish the *female* sex in the human family, or to the objects appropriate for or especially employed by them. A *female* voice is the voice of a woman; a *feminine* voice may belong to a man. *Womanish* denotes the undesirable, *womanly* the admirable or lovely qualities of woman. *Womanly* tears would suggest respect and sympathy, *womanish* tears a touch of contempt. The word *effeminate* is always used reproachfully, and only of men as possessing *womanish* traits such as are inconsistent with true manliness. *Antonyms:* See synonyms for MASCULINE.

feminine ending 1 The termination of an iambic verse (line of poetry) with an unaccented final syllable. **2** *Gram.* A termination or final syllable indicating feminine gender.

feminine rime Rime of the two final syllables of two or more verses in which the accent falls on the next to the last syllable, as in Keats's *Endymion,*

> A thing of beauty is a joy forever:
> Its loveliness increases; it will never . . .

fem·i·nin·i·ty (fem′ə·nin′ə·tē) *n.* **1** The quality or state of being feminine. **2** Women collectively. Also **fe·min′i·ty.**

fem·i·nism (fem′ə·niz′əm) *n.* **1** The doctrine which declares the equality of the sexes and advocates equal social, political, and economic rights for women. **2** *Med.* The existence of female characteristics in the male. — **fem′i·nist** *n.* — **fem′i·nis′tic** *adj.*

fem·o·ral (fem′ər·əl) *adj. Anat.* Pertaining to the femur or thigh: the *femoral* artery.

fe·mur (fē′mər) *n. pl.* **fe·murs** or **fem·o·ra** (fem′ər·ə) **1** *Anat.* The long bone that forms the chief support of the thigh; thigh bone; thigh. **2** *Entomol.* The third, strongest, and most prominent segment of the leg in insects, situated between the trochanter and the tibia. Compare illustration under KNEE JOINT. [< L, thigh]

fen (fen) *n.* A marsh; bog. — **The Fens** A low, flat district in Cambridgeshire, Norfolk, Huntingdonshire, and Lincolnshire, England. [OE *fenn*]

fence (fens) *n.* **1** An enclosing structure of rails, pickets, wires, or the like. **2** A defense; shield; bulwark. **3** The art of using weapons in self-defense; especially, the skilful use of the épée, rapier, or saber; hence, skill in repartee or debate. **4** *Mech.* A guard, guide, or gage. **5** A receiver of stolen goods, or the place where such goods are received. See synonyms under RAMPART. — **on the fence** Undecided or non-committal as to opposing opinions, parties, etc. — **worm fence** A zigzag fence of rails crossed at their ends: varieties of this fence are known as *panel, serpent, snake,* and *Virginia rail fence.* —*v.* **fenced, fenc·ing** *v.t.* **1** To enclose with or as with a fence. **2** To separate with or as with a fence. **3** *Archaic* To protect; shield. **4** *Obs.* To keep out; ward off. —*v.i.* **5** To engage in the art of fencing. **6** To attempt to avoid giving direct answers; parry. **7** To deal in stolen goods. See synonyms under CIRCUMSCRIBE. [Aphetic var. of DEFENSE]

fenc·er (fen′sər) *n.* **1** One who fences, as with foil or sword. **2** A horse adept at leaping fences. **3** One who builds or mends fences.

fence-rid·er (fens′rī′dər) *n.* One who rides along fences on a cattle ranch to find and repair breaks: also called a *line-rider.*

fence-sit·ter (fens′sit′ər) *n. Colloq.* A person remaining neutral, usually waiting to see which side will win.

fence-view·er (fens′vyōō′ər) *n.* In New England, a township official in charge of the inspection and erecting of fences, and the settling of line disputes.

fenc·ing (fen′sing) *n.* **1** The art of attacking and defending as with a foil or sword. **2** Skilful debate or the parrying of prying questions. **3** Material for fences; fences collectively.

fend (fend) *v.t.* **1** To ward off; parry: usually with

off. **2** *Archaic* To defend. —*v.i.* **3** To offer resistance; parry. **4** *Colloq.* To provide or get along: with *for:* to *fend for* oneself. [Aphetic var. of DEFEND]

fend·er (fen′dər) *n.* **1** One who or that which fends or wards off. **2** A metal guard before an open fire, to keep burning coals from falling onto the floor. **3** *Naut.* Any timber, rope plaiting, or other device hanging against or lying along a vessel's side as a protection from injury. **4** A plate of pressed steel over the wheels of a motor vehicle; a mudguard.

fen·es·tel·la (fen′is·tel′ə) *n. pl.* **·lae** (-ē) *Archit.* **1** A small window. **2** A niche in the wall to the side of the altar of a Roman Catholic church, containing a piscina and often the credence. [< L, dim. of *fenestra* window]

fe·nes·tra (fə·nes′trə) *n. pl.* **·trae** (-trē) **1** *Anat.* A windowlike aperture in the body: the **fenestra ovalis,** the opening between the tympanum and the vestibule of the middle ear, closed by the foot of the stapes. See illustration under EAR. **2** *Entomol.* A transparent, glassy spot, as in the wings of some insects. [< L] —**fe·nes′tral** *adj.*

fe·nes·trate (fə·nes′trit, -trāt) *adj.* **1** Having windows or windowlike openings. **2** Having transparent spots. Also **fe·nes′trat·ed.** [< L *fenestratus,* pp. of *fenestrare* furnish with windows < *fenestra* window]

Fe·ni·an (fē′nē·ən, fēn′yən) *n.* **1** A member of an Irish society called the Fenian Brotherhood, formed in New York in 1857 to seek independence for Ireland. **2** One sympathizing with the Fenian Brotherhood. **3** One of the Fianna, the warriors of Fionn MacCumal, Irish chieftain of the second and third centuries. —*adj.* Of or belonging to, composed of, or characteristic of the Fenians or the Fianna. [< Irish *Fiann,* a legendary Irish warrior; infl. by OIrish *fene* an Irishman]—*Fen′i·an·ism n.*

Fenian cycle A body of Old Irish tales dealing with the expoits of Fionn MacCumal and his warriors, called the Fianna, in the second and third centuries A.D.

fen·land (fen′land′) *n.* Low, boggy land; marsh.

fen·nec (fen′ek) *n.* A small, fawn-colored African fox (*Vulpes zenda*) having very large, pointed ears. [< Arabic *fanak*]

fen·nel (fen′əl) *n.* **1** A tall, stout European herb (*Foeniculum vulgare*) of the parsley family, with finely dissected leaves and yellow flowers: cultivated in the United States for use in sauces and for its aromatic seeds. **2** The seeds of this plant. —**giant fennel** An Old World herb (*Ferula communis*) of the parsley family, sometimes attaining a height of 15 feet. [OE *fenugl, fenol* < L *faeniculum* fennel, dim. of *faenum* hay]

fen·nel·flow·er (fen′əl·flou′ər) *n.* **1** An ornamental annual herb (genus *Nigella*) of the crowfoot family; ragged lady. **2** The nutmeg flower (*N. sativa*), the seeds of which are used as seasoning.

fen·ny (fen′ē) *adj.* Marshy; boggy. Also **fen′nish.**

fent (fent) *n. Brit.* **1** A remnant or flawed piece of fabric. **2** *Dial.* A slit or vent in a garment. [< F *fente* < *fendre* split < L *findere*]

fen·u·greek (fen′yōō·grēk′) *n.* **1** An Old World herb (*Trigonella foenum-graecum*) of the pea family, having strong-scented leaves and mucilaginous seeds. **2** The seeds, used in medicine and as curry powder. [OE *feno-graecum* < L *faenum Graecum* Greek hay]

feoff (fef, fēf) *Law v.t.* **feoffed, feoff·ing** To give or grant a fief to; enfeoff. —*n.* A fief; fee. [< AF *feoffer,* OF *fieffer* < *fief* FIEF]

feoff·ee (fef·ē′, fēf·ē′) *n. Law* One to whom a feoffment is made.

feoff·er (fef′ər, fēf′-) *n.* One who grants a feoffment. Also **feof′for.**

feoff·ment (fef′mənt, fēf′-) *n.* **1** A grant of lands in fee by deed with delivery. **2** The accompanying deed.

-fer *combining form* One who or that which bears: *conifer.* [< L < *ferre* bear]

fe·ra·cious (fə·rā′shəs) *adj.* Fruitful; fertile. [< L *ferax, feracis* < *ferre* bear] —**fe·rac·i·ty** (fə·ras′ə·tē) *n.*

fe·ral (fir′əl) *adj.* **1** Undomesticated; existing in a wild state; savage. **2** Pertaining to or characteristic of the wild state. Also **ferine.**

fer-de-lance (fâr′də·läns′) *n.* A venomous crotaline snake (*Bothrops atrox*) of tropical South America and Martinique, related to the copperhead. [< F, iron head of a lance]

Fer·di·nand (fûr′di·nand, *Du.,* Ger. fer′dē-

nänt; *Fr.* fär·dē·nän′) A masculine personal name. Also *Ital.* **Fer·di·nan·do** (fer′dē·nän′dō). [< Gmc., ? brave life]
—**Ferdinand I,** died 1065, king of Castile and Leon.
—**Ferdinand I,** 1503–64, king of Bohemia and Hungary; Holy Roman Emperor 1556–64.
—**Ferdinand II,** 1578–1637, king of Bohemia and Hungary; Holy Roman Emperor 1619–1637; grandson of preceding; involved in the Thirty Years' War.
—**Ferdinand III,** 1608–57, king of Bohemia and Hungary; Holy Roman Emperor 1637–57; son of Ferdinand II; signed Peace of Westphalia, 1648.
—**Ferdinand V,** 1452–1516, king of Castile and Aragon; established the Inquisition at Seville; expelled the Jews and Moors; promoted the expeditions of Columbus and Vespucci. Known as *Ferdinand the Catholic.*
—**Ferdinand VII,** 1784–1833, king of Spain 1808, 1814–33.

fer·e·to·ry (fer′ə-tôrē, -tō′rē) *n. pl.* **·ries** **1** A portable shrine for the relics of saints; a reliquary. **2** The place in a church where the shrine is kept; a fixed shrine. [Alter. of earlier *fertre* < OF *fiertre* < L *feretrum* < Gk. *pheretron* < *pherein* bear]

FERETORY (def. 1)

fer·i·ty (fer′ə-tē) *n.* Wildness; fierceness; cruelty. [< L *feritas, -tatis* < *ferus* wild, fierce]

fer·ma·ta (fer·mä′tä) *n. Music* A pause of indeterminate length. Also *German* **fer·ma·te** (fer·mä′tə). [< Ital.]

Fer·mat's spiral (fûr′mats) A parabolic spiral.

fer·ment (fûr′ment) *n.* **1** A substance productive of fermentation, as yeast; an enzyme. **2** Fermentation. **3** Excitement or agitation. —*v.t. & v.i.* (fər·ment′) **1** To undergo fermentation or produce fermentation in; work. **2** To stir with anger; agitate or be agitated by emotions or passions. [< F < L *fermentum* < *fervere* boil] —**fer·ment′a·ble** or **·i·ble** *adj.* —**fer·ment′a·bil′i·ty** *n.*

fer·men·ta·tion (fûr′mən·tā′shən) *n.* **1** *Chem.* The gradual decomposition of organic compounds induced by the action of living organisms, by enzymes, or by chemical agents; specifically, the conversion of glucose into ethyl alcohol through the action of zymase. **2** Commotion, agitation, or excitement.

fer·ment·a·tive (fər·men′tə·tiv) *adj.* Causing, capable of causing, or caused by fermentation; fermenting.

fer·mi (fer′mē, fûr′-) *n. Physics* A unit for the measurement of the radii of atomic particles, equal to 10^{-13} centimeter. [after E. *Fermi*]

Fer·mi (fer′mē), **Enrico,** 1901–54, Italian nuclear physicist active in the United States.

fer·mi·um (fer′mē·əm, fûr′-) *n.* A synthetic radioactive element (symbol Fm, atomic number 100) produced by neutron bombardment of plutonium and by other nuclear reactions, first identified in residue from a thermonuclear explosion. See PERIODIC TABLE. [after E. *Fermi*]

fern[1] (fûrn) *n.* Any of a widely distributed class (*Filicineae*) of flowerless, seedless pteridophytic plants, having roots and stems and feathery leaves (fronds) which carry the reproductive spores in clusters of sporangia called *sori:* related to the horsetails and clubmosses. See SORUS. [OE *fearn*] —**fern′like** *adj.*

fern[2] (fûrn) *Obs. adj.* Former. —*adv.* Formerly; in olden times. [OE *fyrn*]

FERNS

fern·er·y (fûr′nər·ē) *n. pl.* **·er·ies** A place in which ferns are grown.

fern seed The reproductive spores of the fern which were formerly supposed to render one carrying them invisible.

fern·wort (fûrn′wûrt′) *n.* Any pteridophyte or fern.

fern·y (fûr′nē) *adj.* Of, pertaining to, abounding in, or resembling ferns.

fe·ro·cious (fə·rō′shəs) *adj.* **1** Of a fierce and savage nature; rapacious. **2** Very intense: *ferocious* heat. See synonyms under FIERCE, GRIM. [< L *ferox, ferocis* < *ferus* wild beast] — **fe·ro′cious·ly** *adv.* — **fe·ro′cious·ness** *n.*

fe·roc·i·ty (fə·ros′ə·tē) *n. pl.* **·ties** The state or quality of being ferocious or savage; fierce cruelty.

-ferous *combining form* Bearing or producing: *coniferous.* [< -FER + -OUS]

fer·ral·i·um (fə·ral′ē·əm) *n.* A medicine or drug containing iron; a chalybeate. [Erroneous sing. of NL *ferralia* < L *ferralis* containing iron < *ferrum* iron]

fer·rate (fer′āt) *n. Chem.* A salt of the hypothetical ferric acid, especially **sodium ferrate,** Na_2FeO_4, a deep-red or purple, unstable solution.

fer·ret[1] (fer′it) *n.* **1** A small, red-eyed domesticated polecat of Europe (genus *Mustela*), about 14 inches long: used to hunt rodents and other vermin. **2** A black-footed weasel

FERRET

of the western United States (*M. nigripes*), which preys on prairie dogs. — *adj.* Ferret-like; red, like the eyes of a ferret. — *v.t.* **1** To drive out of hiding with a ferret. **2** To search out by careful investigation: with *out.* **3** To hunt with ferrets. — *v.i.* **4** To hunt by means of ferrets. **5** To search. [< OF *fuiret,* dim. of *fuiron* < LL *furon* robber < *fur* a thief] — **fer′ret·er** *n.* — **fer′ret·y** *adj.*

fer·ret[2] (fer′it) *n.* A narrow ribbon or tape, used for binding fabrics, etc. Also **fer′ret·ing.** [< Ital. *fioretto,* dim. of *fiore* a flower < L *flos, floris*]

fer·ret[3] (fer′it) *n.* A glassmaker's iron rod for trying the melted material. [< F, dim. of *fer* iron < L *ferrum*]

ferret badger A stout-bodied carnivore (genus *Helictis*) of SE Asia.

ferri- *combining form Chem.* Containing iron in the ferric condition: *ferricyanide.* [Var. of FERRO-]

fer·ri·age (fer′ē·ij) *n.* **1** The act of ferrying; conveyance by ferry. **2** The toll charged for ferrying.

fer·ric (fer′ik) *adj. Chem.* **1** Pertaining to iron. **2** Pertaining to or designating compounds of iron in its higher valence. [< L *ferrum* iron + -IC]

ferric acetate *Chem.* A reddish-brown powder, $FeO_5H_7C_4$, widely used as an ingredient in many chemicals as a mordant, and in certain drug preparations.

ferric oxide Hematite.

ferric sulfate *Chem.* A compound of iron, $Fe_2(SO_4)_3$, uniting with water in the form of colorless crystals: used alone or as iron alum in tanning and dyeing.

fer·ri·cy·an·ic (fer′ə·sī·an′ik) *adj. Chem.* Of or pertaining to a compound of iron in its higher valence and cyanogen: *ferricyanic* acid, $H_3Fe(CN)_2$.

fer·ri·cy·a·nide (fer′ə·sī′ə·nīd, -nid) *n. Chem.* A salt containing the trivalent negative ion radical $Fe(CN)_6$, as potassium ferricyanide, $K_3Fe(CN)_6$.

fer·rif·er·ous (fə·rif′ər·əs) *adj.* Yielding iron, as rocks.

Fer·ris wheel (fer′is) A giant, vertical, power-driven wheel that revolves on a stationary axle and bears swinging observation cars for passengers. Also **ferris wheel.** [after G. W. G. *Ferris,* 1859–96, U.S. engineer]

fer·rite (fer′it) *n.* **1** *Geol.* Indeterminable reddish decomposition products in altered igneous rocks, presumably containing iron. **2** *Chem.* Any compound, such as franklinite (zinc ferrite); considered as a derivative of the ferric hydroxide, $Fe(OH)_3$. **3** *Metall.* The pure

metallic constituent in iron and steel. [< L *ferrum* iron + -ITE[1]]

ferro- *combining form* **1** Derived from, containing, or alloyed with iron: *ferromanganese.* **2** *Chem.* Containing iron in the ferrous condition: *ferrocyanide.* [< L *ferrum* iron]

fer·ro·al·loy (fer′ō·al′oi, -ə·loi′) *n. Metall.* An alloy of iron with certain other metals used in the making of special steels, as nickel, manganese, chromium, etc.

fer·ro·type (fer′ō·tīp′) *n.* A tintype.

fer·rous (fer′əs) *adj. Chem.* Of or pertaining to bivalent iron, where its combining value is lowest: *ferrous* chloride, $FeCl_2$: also spelled *ferreous.* [< L *ferrum* iron + -OUS]

ferrous carbonate A compound, $FeCO_3$, precipitated as a white solid, uniting readily with the free oxygen of the air; also found as a mineral, which is an important iron ore.

ferrous sulfate A compound, $FeSO_4·H_2O$, which unites with free oxygen to form ferric sulfate. See COPPERAS.

ferrous sulfide A compound, FeS, formed either as a black solid precipitated by the action of an iron salt solution with an alkaline sulfide, or as a brittle solid from the union of sulfur and iron under heat: a source of hydrogen sulfide.

fer·ro·va·na·di·um (fer′ō·və·nā′dē·əm) *n.* An alloy of iron and vanadium: used in the manufacture of a special steel.

fer·ru·gi·nous (fə·rōō′jə·nəs) *adj.* **1** Of or like iron. **2** Rust-colored. [< L *ferruginus* < *ferrugo, -inis,* iron rust < *ferrum* iron]

ferruginous thrush The brown thrasher.

fer·rule (fer′əl, -ōol, -ōol) *n.* **1** A metal ring or cap, as on the end of a cane or around the handle of a tool. **2** A bushing or thimble. **3** The frame of a slate. **4** A ferule. — *v.t.* **·ruled, ·rul·ing** To furnish with a ferrule. [Earlier *verrel* < OF *virelle* < L *viriola,* dim. of *viriae* bracelets; infl. in form by L *ferrum* iron]

fer·ry (fer′ē) *n. pl.* **·ries** **1** Transportation by boat or airplane across a body of water. **2** The place of crossing a river, bay, strait, or the like by boat. **3** The legal right to run a ferry and to charge toll for transporting passengers and goods. **4** A boat for such transportation; a ferryboat. — **trail ferry** A raft connected with a cable crossing a stream and so adjusted as to utilize the force of the current for motive power. [< *v.*] — *v.* **fer·ried, fer·ry·ing** *v.t.* **1** To carry across a body of water in a boat. **2** To cross (a river, bay, etc.) in a boat. **3** To bring or take (an airplane or vehicle) to a point of delivery under its own power. — *v.i.* **4** To cross a body of water in a boat or by ferry. [OE *ferian* carry, convey]

fer·ry·boat (fer′ē·bōt′) *n.* A boat, often double-ended, used to transport passengers, vehicles, goods, etc., across a river, bay, strait, etc.

fer·ry·man (fer′ē·mən) *n. pl.* **·men** (-mən) **1** One who has charge of a ferry: also **fer′ry·mas′ter.** **2** A member of the crew of a ferry.

ferry slip A landing dock for a ferryboat.

fer·tile (fûr′təl) *adj.* **1** Producing or capable of producing abundantly; fruitful or prolific; rich; productive; inventive. **2** Reproducing or capable of reproducing. **3** *Bot.* **a** Bearing or capable of producing fruit; capable of fertilizing or of being fertilized, as perfect anthers and pistils. **b** Productive of spore-bearing organs: said of ferns, etc. **4** *Biol.* Capable of growth or development; productive: said of seeds or eggs. **5** Causing or imparting productiveness: *fertile* rains. **6** Produced abundantly; plentiful. [< OF *fertil* < L *fertilis* < *ferre* bear] — **fer′tile·ly** *adv.*

Synonyms: exuberant, fecund, fruitful, luxuriant, productive, prolific, rich, teeming.

Fertile Crescent **1** Originally, the arc-shaped area in the Near and Middle East in which agriculture was supposedly first practiced. **2** A similar region extending from the Levant to modern Iraq.

fer·til·i·ty (fər·til′ə·tē) *n.* **1** The state or quality of being fertile. **2** Procreative capacity; fruitfulness. **3** Quickness; readiness. Also **fer′tile·ness.**

fer·til·i·za·tion (fûr′təl·ə·zā′shən) *n.* **1** The act or process of fertilizing or rendering productive. **2** *Biol.* The fusion of two gametes or of the sperm or male cell with an egg, to form a new individual, the zygote. **3** *Bot.* Pollina-

tion. **4** The treatment of soils to increase their crop productivity.

fer·til·ize (fûr′təl·īz) *v.t.* **·ized, ·iz·ing** **1** To render fertile or fruitful. **2** To impregnate an egg, ovum, or seed. **3** To enrich, as soil. — **fer′til·iz′a·ble** *adj.*

fer·til·iz·er (fûr′təl·īz′ər) *n.* **1** One who or that which fertilizes. **2** A fertilizing material applied to soil, as guano, manure, etc.

fer·u·la (fer′yōō·lə, -ōo·lə) *n. pl.* **·lae** (-lē) or **·las** **1** Any of a large genus (*Ferula*) of chiefly Mediterranean herbs of the parsley family, with dissected leaves and umbels of yellow flowers. Several species supply important medicinal products, as asafetida, galbanum, and sumbul or muskroot. **2** A ferule; rod. **3** A scepter, especially that of the Byzantine emperors. [< L, giant fennel, whip, rod]

fer·u·la·ceous (fer′yōō·lā′shəs, -ōō-) *adj.* Pertaining to reeds or canes; having a stalk like a reed.

fer·ule (fer′əl, -ōol) *n.* **1** A flat stick or ruler sometimes used for punishing children. **2** Punishment; discipline. — *v.t.* **fer·uled, fer·ul·ing** To punish with a ferule. [< L *ferula* FERULA]

fer·vent (fûr′vənt) *adj.* **1** Ardent in feeling; fervid. **2** Burning, or very hot. See synonyms under ARDENT, EAGER, HOT. [< L *fervens, -entis,* pp. of *fervere* be hot] — **fer′ven·cy** *n.* — **fer′vent·ly** *adv.* — **fer′vent·ness** *n.*

fer·vid (fûr′vid) *adj.* **1** Burning with zeal or eagerness; vehement. **2** Hot; glowing; fiery. [< L *fervidus* hot, violent < *fervere* be hot] — **fer·vid′i·ty, fer′vid·ness** *n.* — **fer′vid·ly** *adv.*

fer·vor (fûr′vər) *n.* **1** Ardor, or intensity of feeling; zeal. **2** Heat; warmth. Also *Brit.* **fer′vour.** See synonyms under ENTHUSIASM, WARMTH. [< OF < L, heat, passion < *fervere* be hot]

Fes·cen·nine (fes′ə·nīn, -nin) *adj.* Relating to the ancient festivals attributed to Fescennium, a town in Etruria, and to the rude jests and licentious verses that characterized the festivals; hence, obscene; indelicate.

fes·cue (fes′kyōō) *n.* **1** Any of a genus (*Festuca*) of slender, tough grasses, valuable for pasturage. **2** A twig or straw formerly used to point out the letters to children learning to read. [< OF *festu* < L *festuca* a stalk, straw]

fess (fes) *n. Her.* A horizontal band across the middle of the shield and having a breadth equal to one third of the field. Compare illustration under ESCUTCHEON. Also **fesse.** [< OF *fesse* < L *fascia* band]

FESS

fess·wise (fes′wīz′) *adv. Her.* Horizontally. Also **fesse′wise′.**

fes·tal (fes′təl) *adj.* Pertaining to a festival, feast, or holiday; festive. [< OF < L *festum* a feast] — **fes′tal·ly** *adv.*

fes·ter (fes′tər) *v.i.* **1** To generate morbid matter; ulcerate. **2** To become embittered; rankle. **3** To decay; rot. — *v.t.* **4** To cause to fester or rankle. [< *n.*] — *n.* **1** The act of festering; rankling. **2** An ulcerous sore. [< OF *festre* < L *fistula* ulcer]

fes·ti·na len·te (fes·tī′nə len′tē) *Latin* Make haste slowly.

fes·ti·na·tion (fes′tə·nā′shən) *n.* **1** *Psychiatry* Involuntary haste in walking, as in certain nervous diseases. **2** Haste.

fes·ti·val (fes′tə·vəl) *adj.* **1** Of, pertaining to, or suitable to a feast. **2** *Obs.* Joyous; merry. — *n.* **1** A period of feasting or celebration, as an anniversary. **2** A season devoted periodically to some form of entertainment. **3** An entertainment, as a supper, bazaar, etc., to raise funds for some charitable or other purpose: a church *festival.* [< OF < Med. L *festivalis* < L *festivus* FESTIVE]

fes·tive (fes′tiv) *adj.* Pertaining or suited to a feast; gay; joyful. [< L *festivus* < *festum* feast] — **fes′tive·ly** *adv.* — **fes′tive·ness** *n.*

fes·toon (fes·tōon′) *n.* **1** A decorative garland or band hanging in a curve between two points. **2** An ornamental carving resembling a wreath or garland. — *v.t.* **1** To decorate with festoons. **2** To fashion into festoons. **3** To link

---

add, āce, câre, pälm; end, ēven; it, īce; odd, ōpen, ôrder; tōōk, pōōl; up, bûrn; ə = a in *above,* e in *sicken,* i in *clarity,* o in *melon,* u in *focus;* yōō = u in *fuse;* oi, oil; ou, pout; ch, check; g, go; ng, ring; th, thin; th, this; zh, vision. Foreign sounds à, œ, ü, kh, ṅ; and ●: see page xx. < from; + plus; ? possibly.

together by festoons. [<F *feston* <Ital. *festone* <*festa* a feast <L *festus*] — **fes·toon'y** *adj.*

fe·tal (fē'tl) *adj.* Pertaining to the fetus: also spelled *foetal.*

fetal rickets Achondroplasia.

fe·ta·tion (fē·tā'shən) *n.* Pregnancy: also spelled *foetation.*

fetch (fech) *v.t.* **1** To go after and bring back. **2** To cause to come; draw; bring, as a reply. **3** To heave (a sigh); to utter (a groan). **4** To bring as a price; sell for. **5** To execute; perform, as a leap or other movement. **6** *Colloq.* To captivate; charm. **7** *Naut.* To reach or arrive at. **8** *Colloq.* To strike or deliver, as a blow. — *v.i.* **9** To go after and bring things back. **10** In hunting, to retrieve game. **11** *Naut.* **a** To take a course. **b** To reach or get. — **to fetch and carry** To perform menial tasks; be a servant. — **to fetch up** To rear; bring up. — *n.* **1** The act of fetching. **2** The distance something is brought. **3** A stratagem. [OE *feccan,* var. of *fetian.* See FET.]

fetch (fech) *n.* The apparition of one still living; a wraith. [Origin uncertain]

fetch·er (fech'ər) *n.* One who or that which goes and brings.

fetch·ing (fech'ing) *adj. Colloq.* Calculated to attract; taking; fascinating. — **fetch'ing·ly** *adv.*

fête (fāt) *n.* A festival; holiday. — *v.t.* **fêt·ed, fêt·ing** To honor with festivities; give a feast or celebration for. [<F <OF *feste.* See FEAST.]

fet·e·ri·ta (fet'ə·rē'tə) *n.* A variety of sorghum introduced as fodder in the United States: also called *Sudan durra.* [< native Sudanese name]

fe·ti·a·les (fē'shē·ā'lēz) *n.pl.* A college of twenty priests or heralds in ancient Rome who conducted the negotiations and the ceremonies attending declarations of war and peace. [<L; ult. origin unknown]

fe·ti·cide (fē'tə·sīd) *n.* **1** *Law* The felonious killing of an unborn child. **2** The intentional production of abortion. Also spelled *foeticide.* [<L *fetus* fetus + -CIDE] — **fe·ti·ci'dal** *adj.*

fet·id (fet'id) *adj.* Emitting an offensive odor: also spelled *foetid.* See synonyms under NOISOME, ROTTEN. [<L *fetidus* <*fetere* stink] — **fet'id·ly** *adv.* — **fet'id·ness** *n.*

fe·tip·a·rous (fə·tip'ər·əs) *adj.* Bringing forth undeveloped young, as marsupials: also spelled *foetiparous.* [<L *fetus* fetus + -PAROUS]

fe·tish (fē'tish, fet'ish) *n.* **1** A natural object believed to be the dwelling of a spirit, or to represent a spirit that may be induced or compelled magically to help and safeguard the possessor, and to protect him from harm or disease: an object of worship among savages. **2** Any object of devotion or blind affection. Also **fe'tich.** [<F *fétiche* <Pg. *feitiço* a charm, orig. an adj. <L *factitius* artificial]

fe·tish·ism (fē'tish·iz'əm, fet'ish-) *n.* **1** The belief in, devotion to, or worship of fetishes, or rites used in fetish-worship. **2** The mental state which characterizes such worship; superstition. **3** *Psychiatry* Sensual or sexual pleasure derived from fixing the attention on a part of the body or on a piece of wearing apparel belonging to a person. Also **fe'tich·ism.** — **fe'tish·ist** *n.* — **fe'tish·is'tic** *adj.*

fet·lock (fet'lok') *n.* **1** The tuft of hair above a horse's hoof. **2** The projection and the joint at this place. See illustration under HORSE. [ME *fitlok, fetlak,* prob. <LG. Cf. Du. *vitlok.*]

fe·tor (fē'tər, -tôr) *n.* A stench: also spelled *foetor.* [<L]

fet·ter (fet'ər) *n.* A shackle for the ankles or a rope that binds, etc.; hence, anything that confines. — *v.t.* **1** To fasten fetters upon; shackle. **2** To prevent the activity of; restrain. [OE *feter, fetor.* Related to FOOT.]

Synonyms (noun): bondage, bonds, chains, custody, durance, duress, gyves, handcuffs, imprisonment, irons, manacles, shackles.

fetter bone The first phalanx or great pastern of a horse's foot, just below the fetlock. See illustration under HORSE.

fet·ter·bush (fet'ər·boosh') *n.* **1** An evergreen shrub (*Lyonia lucida*) of the heath family, with alternate leaves and fragrant white flowers, of the southern United States. **2** A related shrub (*Pieris floribunda*), with white, bell-shaped flowers.

fet·tle (fet'l) *v.t.* **fet·tled, fet·tling** **1** *Metall.* To line or cover with a refractory material: to *fettle* the hearth of a puddling furnace. **2** *Brit. Dial.* To put in repair or good condition.

---

3 To beat; thrash. — *n.* **1** State of repair; condition. **2** The fettling used in a furnace. — **fine fettle** Good condition; high spirits. [ME *fetlen* prepare, lit., gird up <OE *fetel* a belt]

fet·tling (fet'ling) *n. Metall.* Iron ore, cinder, or other oxidizing agents, used to cover the hearth of a puddling furnace before charging it.

fet·tuc·ci·ne (fet'ə·chē'nē) *n.pl.* (construed as *sing.* or *pl.*) Flat noodles, often prepared with butter, cheese, heavy cream, etc. Also **fet'tu·ci'ne, fet'tu·ci'ni.** [<Ital., lit., dim. of *fettucia* ribbon]

fe·tus (fē'təs) *n.* *pl.* **fe·tus·es** The young in the womb of viviparous animals in the later stages of development; specifically, in women, from the end of the second month, prior to which it is called the *embryo;* unborn offspring: also spelled *foetus.* [<L]

feu (fyōō) *n.* **1** Tenure of lands based on agricultural service, or rent in grain or money: distinguished from *ward-holding,* the military tenure of the country; also, a perpetual lease at a stipulated rent. **2** The ground so held. **3** A piece of land held in feu. — *v.t.* In Scots law, to grant (land) upon feu. [<OF, var. of *fé.* See FEE.]

feud[1] (fyōōd) *n.* **1** Vindictive strife or hostility between families or clans, commonly hereditary. **2** Any quarrel or conflict. — *v.i.* To engage in a feud; quarrel bitterly. [ME *fede* <OF <OHG *fehida* hatred, revenge] — **feud'ist** *n.*

Synonyms: animosity, bitterness, contention, contest, controversy, dispute, dissension, enmity, hostility, quarrel, strife. A *feud* is *enmity* between families, clans, or parties, with acts of *hostility* mutually retaliated and avenged; *feud* is rarely used of individuals, never of nations. While all the other words of the group may refer to that which is transient, a *feud* is long-enduring, and often hereditary. *Dissension* is used of a number of persons, of a party or other organization. *Bitterness* is in feeling only; *enmity* and *hostility* involve will and purpose to oppose or injure. Compare QUARREL.

feud[2] (fyōōd) *n.* *Law* Land granted of a superior on condition of rendering service; a fief: also spelled *feod.* [<Med. L *feudum* <Gmc.]

feu·dal (fyōō'dəl) *adj.* **1** Pertaining to the relation of lord and vassal, or to the feudal system. **2** Relating to or of the nature of a feud or fee. — **feu'dal·ly** *adv.*

feu·dal·ism (fyōō'dəl·iz'əm) *n.* The medieval European system of land tenure on condition of military aid and other services. — **feu'dal·is'tic** *adj.*

feudal system A politico-social system in force throughout Europe from the 9th to the 15th century, founded on the tenure of feuds, or fiefs, given as compensation for military services rendered by chiefs and by them sublet by allotments to their subordinates and vassals.

feu·da·ry (fyōō'dər·ē) *adj.* Relating to a feudal tenure. — *n.* *pl.* **·ries** One holding land by feudal tenure; a vassal.

Feu·illant (fœ·yän') *n.* **1** A reformed Cistercian of the order instituted by Jean de la Barrière and approved by the pope in 1586: so called from the monastery of Feuillants in Languedoc. **2** A member of a club of conservative royalists in the French Revolution of 1789: named from the convent of the Feuillants, where it met.

fe·ver (fē'vər) *n.* **1** Body temperature above the normal; pyrexia. **2** A disorder marked by high temperature, rapid pulse, increased tissue-destruction, loss of appetite, restlessness, and delirium. ◆ Collateral adjective: *febrile.* **3** Emotional excitement; great interest, enthusiasm, or urge. — *v.t.* To affect with fever. [OE *fēfer* <L *febris* <*fervere* be hot] — **fe'vered** *adj.*

fever blister A form of herpes affecting the lips. Also **fever sore.**

fe·ver·bush (fē'vər·boosh') *n.* **1** The benjamin-bush. **2** The winterberry.

fe·ver·few (fē'vər·fyōō') *n.* An erect bushy herb (*Chrysanthemum parthenium*) of the composite family, bearing white-rayed flowers, once used to make a medicinal tea. [OE *feferfuge* <LL *febrifugia* <L *febris* fever + *fugare* put to flight]

FEVERFEW

---

fe·ver·ous (fē'vər·əs) *adj.* Feverish. — **fe'ver·ous·ly** *adv.*

fever therapy Pyretotherapy.

fever tree **1** The bluegum tree (*Eucalyptus globulus*) from which eucalyptol is obtained. **2** An American tree (*Pinckneya pubens*), with a bark of tonic and febrifugal properties.

fe·ver·weed (fē'vər·wēd') *n.* Any of a genus (*Eryngium*) of herbs of the parsley family having medicinal uses.

fe·ver·wort (fē'vər·wûrt') *n.* A perennial weedy herb (*Triosteum perfoliatum*) of the honeysuckle family having brownish-purple flowers and a nauseous odor. Its root is a purgative and emetic. Also **fe'ver·root'** (-rōōt', -rōōt').

few (fyōō) *adj.* Small or limited in number; not many. — *n.* A small number; some: Give me a *few.* — **the few** The minority. — **quite a few** An appreciable number. ◆ **fewer, less** See LESS (def. 3). [OE *fēawe*]

few·ness (fyōō'nis) *n.* The state of being few; scarcity.

fey (fā) *adj.* **1** Affected by association with the fairies; enchanted, under a spell; hence, out of touch with reality. **2** Visionary; touched in the head. [<F *fé,* pp. of *féer* enchant <*fee, fae.* See FAY[2].]

fez (fez) *n.* A brimless felt cap, usually red with a black tassel, formerly worn by the Turks. [<F <Turkish *fes,* after *Fez* in Morocco, where these caps were formerly manufactured] — **fezzed** *adj.*

fi·a·cre (fē·ä'kər, *Fr.* fyȧ'kr') *n.* A small four wheeled public carriage; a French hackney coach. [<F, after Hotel St. *Fiacre,* a Parisian inn]

fi·an·cé (fē'än·sā', fē·än'sā; *Fr.* fē·äṅ·sā') *n. masc.* An affianced or betrothed person. [<F] — **fi'an·cée'** *n. fem.*

fi·as·co (fē·as'kō) *n.* *pl.* **·cos** or **·coes** A complete or humiliating failure. [<Ital., a flask; semantic development uncertain]

fi·at (fī'at, -ət) *n.* **1** A positive and authoritative command that something be done; an order or decree. **2** Authorization. [<L, let it be done]

fib (fib) *n.* A petty falsehood. — *v.i.* **fibbed, fib·bing** To tell a fib. [? Alter. of FABLE] — **fib'ber** *n.*

fi·ber (fī'bər) *n.* **1** A fine filament. **2** A slender or threadlike component of a substance, as of wood, or spun glass. **3** An individual filament, as of wool or cotton. **4** A structure composed of filaments; especially, any natural or synthetic material that may be separated into threads for spinning, weaving, etc.: the *fiber* of hemp, flax, rayon, or wool, etc. **5** *Bot.* **a** A slender, elongated, and thickened cell in the strengthening tissue of plants. **b** A filamentous wool; also, a rootlet. **6** The texture of anything. **7** Character; nature; make-up: a woman of strong *fiber.* Also **fi'bre.** [<F *fibre* <L *fibra* fiber] — **fi'bered** *adj.* — **fi'ber·less** *adj.*

fi·ber·board (fī'bər·bôrd', -bōrd') *n.* A tough, pliable, water-resistant material made of wood or other plant fibers compressed and rolled into sheets of varying thickness.

Fi·ber·glas (fī'bər·glas', -gläs') *n.* A flexible, non-flammable, moisture- and rot-proof material made of glass spun into filaments: it is widely used for textiles, insulators, mats, filters, etc.: a trade name.

fiber optics A branch of optics concerned with optical fibers and their applications.

fi·bril (fī'brəl) *n.* A minute fiber, especially a nerve or muscle filament. **2** *Bot.* A root hair. [<NL *fibrilla,* dim. of L *fibra* fiber]

fi·bril·la (fī·bril'ə) *n.* *pl.* **·lae** (-ē) *Biol.* One of the filamentous structures found in the cytoplasm of cells and thought to be essential in cell development and function. [<NL, dim. of L *fibra* a fiber]

fi·bril·la·tion (fī'brə·lā'shən, fī'brə-) *n.* **1** The formation of fibers. **2** *Physiol.* A localized twitching of certain muscle fibers. **3** *Pathol.* Rapid, irregular, uncoordinated contractions of the muscle fibers of the heart.

fi·bril·lose (fī'brə·lōs) *adj.* Composed of fibers or fibrils.

fi·brin (fī'brin) *n.* **1** *Biochem.* An insoluble protein which forms an interlacing network of fibers in clotting blood, with resulting coagulation of the plasma and separation of the serum. **2** The fibrous portion of flesh. **3** *Bot.* Gluten, or vegetable fibrin.

fi·brin·o·gen (fī-brin′ə-jən) *n. Biochem.* A complex protein of the globulin group, found in blood plasma and in other body fluids. It is associated with a ferment, thrombin, in the formation of fibrin during the process of coagulation. — **fi′brin·o·gen′ic, fi·bri·nog·e·nous** (fī′brə-noj′ə-nəs) *adj.*

fi·bri·no·ly·sin (fī′brə-nō-lī′sin) *n. Biochem.* A toxic substance having the power to liquefy human fibrin. It is formed by the action of certain pathogenic bacteria, as staphylococci.

fi·bri·no·sis (fī′brə-nō′sis) *n. Pathol.* A condition of excess fibrin in the blood.

fi·bri·nous (fī′brə-nəs) *adj.* Possessed of the properties, characteristics, or nature of fibrin.

fibro– *combining form* Related to or composed of fibrous tissue; having a fibrous structure: *fibrovascular.* Also, before vowels, **fibr–.** [< L *fibra* fiber]

fi·broid (fī′broid) *adj.* Of the nature of fiber; fibrous: as a *fibroid* tumor.

fi·bro·in (fī′brō·in) *n. Biochem.* A white, lustrous protein, forming the principal ingredient in natural silk and spider webs.

fi·bro·ma (fī·brō′mə) *n. pl.* **·ma·ta** (-mə·ta) *Pathol.* A fibrous tumor. — **fi·bro′ma·tous** *adj.*

fi·bro·sis (fī·brō′sis) *n. Pathol.* Morbid increase of fibrous tissue in the body; fibroid degeneration, as of the blood capillaries.

fi·brous (fī′brəs) *adj.* Composed of, or having the character of fibers.

fi·bro·vas·cu·lar (fī′brə-vas′kyə-lər) *adj. Bot.* Composed or consisting of woody fibers and vessels, as **fibrovascular tissue,** a tissue composed of elongated, thick-walled, and generally fusiform elements, as wood and bast.

fib·u·la (fib′yōō-lə) *n. pl.* **·lae** (-lē) **1** *Anat.* The outer of the two bones forming the lower part of the leg or hind limb; the calf bone. ◆ Collateral adjective: *peroneal.* **2** An ancient type of ornamental brooch, fastening somewhat like a safety pin. [< L, a clasp < *figere* fasten] — **fib′u·lar** *adj.*

-fic *suffix* Making, rendering, or causing: *beatific, scientific.* [< L *-ficus* < *facere* make, render]

-fication *suffix* The making, rendering, or causing to be of a certain sort of character: *beatification, glorification.* [< L *-ficatio, -onis* < *-ficare* < *facere* make]

fick·le (fik′əl) *adj.* Inconstant in feeling or purpose; changeful; capricious. [OE *ficol* crafty] — **fick′le·ness** *n.*

Synonyms: capricious, changeable, changeful, crotchety, fitful, inconstant, irresolute, mutable, shifting, unstable, unsteady, vacillating, variable, veering, wavering, whimsical. See IRRESOLUTE, MOBILE. *Antonyms:* constant, decided, determined, firm, fixed, immutable, invariable, reliable, resolute, steadfast.

fic·tile (fik′til) *adj.* **1** Made of molded earth or clay; pertaining to pottery. **2** Capable of being molded; plastic. [< L *fictilis* < *fingere* form]

fic·tion (fik′shən) *n.* **1** The act of feigning or imagining that which does not exist or is not actual. **2** That which is feigned or imagined, as opposed to that which is actual. **3** The department of literature that embraces fictitious narrative, including romances, novels, short stories, art epics, etc. See NOVEL. **4** A legal assumption, for the furtherance of justice, that a certain thing which is or may be false is true. **5** *Obs.* The act of fashioning; also, a device; fabric. **6** *Obs.* Pretense; deceit. [< F < L *fictio, -onis* a making < *fingere* form]

Synonyms: allegory, apolog, fable, fabrication, falsehood, figment, invention, legend, myth, novel, romance, story. *Fiction* is now chiefly used of a prose work in narrative form in which the characters are partly or wholly imaginary, and which is designed to portray human life, with or without a practical lesson; a *romance* portrays what is picturesque or striking, as a mere *fiction* may not do; *novel* is a general name for any continuous fictitious narrative, especially a love story. The moral of the *fable* is expressed formally; the lesson of the *fiction,* if any, is inwrought. A *fiction* is studied; a *myth* grows up without intent. A *legend* may be true, but cannot be historically verified; a *myth* has been received as true at

some time. A *fabrication* is designed to deceive; it is a less odious word than *falsehood,* but is really stronger, as a *falsehood* may be a sudden unpremeditated statement, while a *fabrication* is a series of statements carefully studied and fitted together in order to deceive; the *falsehood* is all false; the *fabrication* may mingle the true with the false. A *figment* is something imaginary which the one who utters it may or may not believe to be true; we say, "That statement is a *figment* of his imagination." The *story* may be either true or false, and covers the various senses of all the words in the group. *Apolog,* a word simply transferred from Greek into English, is the same as *fable.* Compare ALLEGORY. *Antonyms:* certainty, fact, history, literalness, reality, truth, verity.

fic·tion·al (fik′shən-əl) *adj.* Belonging to fiction; ideal. — **fic′tion·al·ly** *adv.*

fic·ti·tious (fik·tish′əs) *adj.* **1** Belonging to or of the nature of fiction. **2** Counterfeit; false; assumed. See synonyms under COUNTERFEIT, ROMANTIC. — **fic·ti′tious·ly** *adv.* — **fic·ti′tious·ness** *n.*

fic·tive (fik′tiv) *adj.* **1** Of the nature of a figment; imaginary. **2** Having to do with the creation of fiction: *fictive* ability. — **fic′tive·ly** *adv.*

Fi·cus (fī′kəs) *n.* A large genus of plants, mostly tropical trees, shrubs, and vines, belonging to the mulberry family and including the fig, banyan, and rubber plant. [< L, a fig tree]

fid·dle (fid′l) *n.* **1** A violin. **2** *Naut.* A rack or frame used at table on board ship in rough weather to keep the dishes in place. — *v.* **fid·dled, fid·dling** *v.i.* **1** To play on a fiddle. **2** To pass the time in trifling matters. **3** To toy with an object. — *v.t.* **4** To play (an air, tune, etc.) on a fiddle. **5** To trifle; fritter: to *fiddle* time away. [OE *fithele,* found in *fithelere* a fiddler. Akin to VIOL.]

fiddle block *Mech.* A pulley block with two sheaves, the larger one above the smaller.

fid·dler (fid′lər) *n.* **1** One who plays a fiddle. **2** A fiddler crab. — **to pay the fiddler** To suffer the consequences.

fiddler crab A small burrowing crab (genus *Uca*) the male of which flourishes its enlarged claw as if fiddling: found on the Atlantic coast of the United States.

FIDDLER CRAB
(Carapace about 1/2 to 1 inch in width)

fid·dle·stick (fid′l-stik′) *n.* **1** A fiddle bow. **2** A trifling or absurd thing.

fid·dle·sticks (fid′l-stiks′) *interj.* Nonsense!

fid·dle·wood (fid′l-wŏŏd′) *n.* Any one of several species of trees of the vervain family (*Citharexylum* and allied genera): used in tropical America for building.

fi·de·i·com·mis·sar·y (fī′de·ī·kom′ə-ser′ē) *n. Law* A beneficiary in a trust estate, or one for whose benefit a trust has been created. [< L *fidei commissarius*] — **fi′de·i·com′mis·sar′i·ly** *adv.* — **fi·de·i·com·mis′sion** *n.* — **fi′de·i·com·mis′sion·er** *n.*

fi·de·jus·sion (fī′də·jush′ən) *n. Law* The condition of being bound as surety for another; suretyship. [< L *fideiussio, -onis* < *fideiubere* < *fide,* ablative sing. of *fides* faith + *iubere* order] — **fi′de·jus′so·ry** (-jus′ər-ē) *adj.*

fi·del·i·ty (fī-del′ə-tē, fə-) *n. pl.* **·ties** **1** Faithfulness in the discharge of duty or of obligation. **2** Hearty allegiance to those to whom one is bound in affection or honor; loyalty; devotion: matrimonial *fidelity, fidelity* to a father or friend. **3** Strict adherence to truth or fact; reliability; veracity. **4** *Electronics* A measure of the accuracy and freedom from distortion with which a sound-reproducing system, as radio, will receive and transmit the input signals; it may be high, medium, or low. [< F *fidelité* < L *fidelitas, -tatis* < *fides* faith]

Synonyms: allegiance, constancy, devotion, faith, faithfulness, fealty, honesty, integrity, loyalty, truth, truthfulness. See ALLEGIANCE. *Antonyms:* disloyalty, infidelity, treachery, treason.

fidg·et (fij′it) *v.i.* **1** To move about restlessly. **2** To toy with something nervously. — *v.t.* **3** To make restless; worry. — *n.* **1** Nervous restlessness: often in the plural: to have the *fidgets.* **2** A restless person; one who fidgets. [< obs. *fidge* move about; ultimate origin unknown] — **fidg′et·y** *adj.* — **fidg′et·i·ness** *n.*

fi·du·cial (fī-dōō′shəl, -dyōō′-) *adj.* **1** Of the nature of or indicating faith or practical confidence. **2** Of the nature of a trust; fiduciary. **3** *Physics* Fixed as a basis of measurement or reference: the *fiducial* point of a scale. [< L *fiducialis* < *fiducia* trust] — **fi·du′cial·ly** *adv.*

fi·du·ci·ar·y (fī-dōō′shē·er′ē, -shə-rē, -dyōō′-) *adj.* **1** Pertaining to a position of trust or confidence; confidential: a *fiduciary* relation, as that of an attorney, guardian, or trustee. **2** Unwavering; trustful; undoubting. **3** Relying on the confidence of the public as for paper currency or value. **4** Held in trust. — *n. pl.* **·ar·ies** *Law* A person who holds a thing in trust; a trustee.

fie (fī) *interj.* An expression of impatience or disapproval. [< OF *fi, fy* < L *fi,* an expression of disgust]

fief (fēf) *n.* A landed estate held under feudal tenure; a fee: also spelled *feoff.* [< OF < Med. L *feudum* FEUD[2]]

field (fēld) *n.* **1** A piece of cleared land set apart and enclosed for tillage or pasture. ◆ Collateral adjective: *campestral.* **2** A plot of land set apart for a particular use: the potter's *field.* **3** A region of the countryside considered as yielding some natural product: the *coalfields* of Pennsylvania. **4** *Mil.* **a** A sphere of action or place of contest. **b** A battleground. **c** A battle: a hard-fought *field.* **5** Open or unenclosed countryside: the beast of the *field.* **6** Any wide or open expanse: the *fields* of ocean. **7** Sphere of study, investigation or practice. **8** In painting, the surface of canvas upon which the figures of a composition are set. **9** That portion of the face of a coin or medal which is not occupied by the type or principal figure. **10** The ground of each section of a flag: a blue *field* with white stars. **11** In games, the plot of ground on which the game is played; especially, in baseball, the outfield, or part outside the diamond; in baseball and cricket, the fielders collectively. For illustration see BASEBALL. **12** *Her.* The whole surface of the escutcheon upon which the charges and bearings are depicted, or of each separate coat when the shield contains quarterings or impalements. See illustration under ESCUTCHEON. **13** *Physics* **a** A portion of space at every point of which force is exerted. **b** The force exerted therein: the magnetic *field,* a *field* of force. **14** *Optics* The space or apparent surface within which objects are seen in a telescope or other optical instrument. **15** The participants in a hunt; all the competitors in a contest or race; also, the contestants exclusive of the favorites in the betting. — **to keep the field 1** To hold one's ground against all opposers. **2** To continue active operations. — *adj.* **1** Of, pertaining to, or found in the fields: *field* flowers. **2** Used in, or for use in, the fields: a *field* gun. **3** Played on a field: *field* sports. — *v.t.* In baseball, cricket, etc. **1** To catch and return (a ball in play). **2** To put (a player or team) on the field. — *v.i.* **3** In baseball, cricket, etc., to play as a fielder. [OE *feld*]

field artillery Light or heavy artillery so mounted as to be freely movable, and suitable for use with troops in the field. Hence, **Field Artillery,** a branch of the U.S. Army.

field coil An insulated coil for exciting a field magnet.

field colors 1 Small flags used for marking the position for companies and regiments, especially in peacetime field maneuvers, reviews, parades, etc. **2** Any regimental headquarters flags, used in field service.

field corn Any of several kinds of Indian corn used for feeding livestock.

field day 1 A day when army troops are taken to the field for exercise and maneuvers. **2** In the navy, a day for general cleaning up. **3** A school holiday devoted to athletic sports. **4** Any day of display, excitement, celebration, or success. **5** A day of outdoor scientific excursion.

field·er (fēl'dər) *n.* In baseball, cricket, etc., a player stationed in the field to stop, or catch, and return the balls. Compare illustration under BASEBALL.

fielder's choice In baseball, the decision by a player to attempt to retire a base runner rather than the batter, the latter being credited with a time at bat but not with a hit.

field events The jumping, vaulting, and casting contests at an athletic meet: distinguished from *track events.*

field·fare (fēld'fâr') *n.* A European thrush (*Turdus pilaris*), deep brown above, with a pearl-gray head and black tail, streaked on the breast and throat with blackish-brown. [OE *feldeware,* ? misspelling of *feldefare* (< *feld* field + *faran* go); or < *feld* field + *warian* dwell]

field glass 1 A small, portable, terrestrial telescope, monocular or binocular; a spyglass. 2 A field lens.

field hand An agricultural laborer.

field hospital A hospital established on a field of battle; also, its medical officers and attendants, with their equipment for service.

field intensity *Electr.* A measure of the direction and magnitude of the force exerted upon a unit charge at a given point.

field lark 1 The American meadowlark. 2 The English skylark. 3 Any of various larklike birds, as the pipit.

field lens *Optics* The anterior of the two lenses in the eyepiece of a telescope or microscope, whose purpose is to enlarge the field of view.

field magnet 1 The magnet of a magnetoelectric or dynamoelectric machine, which produces the *magnetic field.* 2 A small magnet, commonly of horseshoe shape, used in determining the existence of iron ore in minerals.

field marshal A general officer of high rank in the armies of several European nations.

field martin The kingbird.

field mouse A mouse inhabiting fields and meadows, as the common European vole (*Microtus agrestis*) and the small short-tailed vole of North America (*M. pennsylvanicus*): also called *meadow mouse.*

field music 1 The drummers, buglers, fifers, etc., who play for military troops on the march, sound regimental calls, etc. 2 The music produced by them.

field notes 1 A surveyor's notes detailing a survey. 2 A naturalist's notes taken in the field.

field officer An officer intermediate between a company and a general officer; a major, lieutenant colonel, or colonel.

field of honor 1 The ground where a duel is fought. 2 A battlefield.

field sparrow A small light-breasted American sparrow (*Spizella pusilla*).

field sports 1 Outdoor sports, especially hunting, shooting, and racing. 2 Athletic games played on the field, as opposed to races, hurdles, etc., on the track.

field stop An opening in an opaque screen, generally circular, for determining the size of the field of view of an optical instrument.

field strength *Electr.* The magnitude of a field, expressed as a vector quantity in volts per unit length at a given point.

field trip A trip outside the classroom for purposes of first-hand observation and study.

field winding *Electr.* The winding of the field-magnet coils of a dynamoelectric machine.

field·work (fēld'wûrk') *n.* A temporary fortification thrown up in the field.

field work Observations or performance in the field, as by scientists, surveyors, etc.

fiend (fēnd) *n.* 1 An evil spirit; a devil; demon. 2 An intensely malicious or wicked person; one having a cruel, diabolical spirit. 3 *Colloq.* One unduly devoted to some theory or occupation; one exceptionally interested in and clever or talented in a certain subject: an algebra *fiend;* a crank; monomaniac: a fresh-air *fiend.* 4 *Colloq.* One morbidly addicted to the use of a narcotic drug or some deleterious habit: a cocaine *fiend.* 5 An implacable enemy; foe. — **the Fiend** Satan; the devil. [OE *fēond* enemy, devil]

fiend·ish (fēn'dish) *adj.* Of, pertaining to, or resembling a fiend or his conduct; diabolical. — **fiend'ish·ly** *adv.* — **fiend'ish·ness** *n.*

fierce (firs) *adj.* 1 Having a violent and cruel nature or temper; savage; ferocious. 2 Violent in action; furious. 3 Vehement; passionate; extreme. 4 *Slang* Very bad; atrocious. [<OF *fers, fiers,* nominative sing. of *fier* proud <L *ferus* wild] — **fierce'ly** *adv.* — **fierce'ness** *n.*

Synonyms: ferocious, fiery, furious, impetuous, raging, savage, uncultivated, untrained, violent, wild.

fi·e·ri fa·ci·as (fī'ə·rī fā'shē·əs) *Law* A writ of execution commanding a levy on goods, etc., to satisfy a judgment; literally, that you cause to be done. [<L]

fier·y (fīr'ē, fī'ər·ē) *adj.* **fier·i·er, fier·i·est** 1 Of or pertaining to fire; having the appearance of or containing fire; glowing; glaring; burning; hot: a *fiery* furnace. 2 Of the nature of ardor, rage, or animation; passionate; impetuous; fervid; spirited: a *fiery* disposition. 3 Inflammable: a *fiery* gas in a coal mine. See synonyms under ARDENT, FIERCE, HOT, IMPETUOUS. — **fier'i·ly** *adv.* — **fier'i·ness** *n.*

fiery hunter A large, black ground beetle of the United States (*Calosoma calidum*) with small coppery spots on the wing covers. For illustration see under INSECT (beneficial).

fi·es·ta (fē·es'tə, *Sp.* fyes'tä) *n.* A feast day; holiday. [<Sp. <L *festa.* See FEAST.]

fife (fīf) *n.* A small, shrill-toned, flute-like, martial wind instrument. — *v.t.* & *v.i.* **fifed, fif·ing** To play on a fife. [<G *pfeife* pipe <OHG *pfifa* <(assumed) LL *pipa* <L *pipare* peep, chirp. Doublet of PIPE.] — **fif'er** *n.*

FIFE

fife rail *Naut.* A railing around a mast for holding belaying pins, etc.

fif·teen (fif'tēn') *adj.* Consisting of five more than ten; quindecimal. — *n.* 1 The sum of ten and five: a cardinal number. 2 Any of the symbols (15, xv, XV) representing this number. [OE *fīftēne*]

fif·teenth (fif'tēnth') *adj.* 1 Fifth in order after the tenth: the ordinal of *fifteen.* 2 Being one of fifteen equal parts: a *fifteenth* share. — *n.* 1 One of the fifteen equal parts of anything. 2 The quotient of a unit divided by fifteen.

Fifteenth Amendment An amendment to the Constitution of the United States, providing that the right of citizens to vote shall not be denied or abridged on account of "race, color, or previous condition of servitude. . . ."

fifth (fifth) *adj.* 1 Next in order after the fourth: the ordinal of *five.* 2 Being one of five equal parts: a *fifth* part. — *n.* 1 One of five equal parts of anything. 2 The quotient of a unit divided by five. 3 *Music* a The interval between any note and the fifth note above it in the diatonic scale, counting the starting point as one (see SCALE²). b A note separated by this interval from any other, considered in relation to that other; specifically, the fifth above the keynote; the dominant. 4 One fifth of a U.S. gallon used as a measure of spirituous liquors. — *adv.* In the fifth order, place, or rank: also, in formal discourse, **fifth'ly.**

Fifth Amendment An amendment to the Constitution of the United States, providing that no person "shall be compelled in any criminal case to be a witness against himself. . . ."

fifth column A group, within a city or country, of civilian sympathizers with an enemy, who act as spies, saboteurs, and propagandists: first applied to Franco agents and sympathizers in Madrid by Gen. Emilio Mola (1887–1937), who led four armed columns against that city in 1936.

fifth wheel 1 A horizontal metallic circle or segment of a circle attached to the upper side of the fore axle of a carriage or wagon to give support to the body in turning; a circle iron. 2 An additional wheel carried with a vehicle as a replacement in case of accidents. 3 A superfluous thing or person.

fif·ty (fif'tē) *adj.* Consisting of ten more than forty or five times ten. — *n. pl.* **fif·ties** 1 The sum of ten and forty; five times ten. 2 Any of the symbols (50, l, L) representing this number. [OE *fīftig*]

fif·ty–fif·ty (fif'tē·fif'tē) *adj. Colloq.* Sharing equally, as benefits: *fifty-fifty* partners in

business.

fig (fig) *n.* 1 The small, edible, pear-shaped fruit of a tree (genus *Ficus*), cultivated in warm climates. 2 The tree (*F. carica*) that bears the fruit. 3 Any tree or plant bearing a fruit somewhat like the fig, or the fruit of such a tree or plant. 4 One of several Australian trees and shrubs of the fig family, as *F. macrophylla,* used as fodder for cattle. 5 A petty matter; trifle. 6 An insulting gesture; a fico. — *v.t. Obs.* To make a fico at; insult. [<OF *fige, figue* <L *ficus* a fig]

fig–eat·er (fig'ē'tər) *n.* 1 A large velvety-green scarabaeid beetle (*Cotinis nitida*) common in the southern United States, injurious to ripe fruits. 2 The beccafico. 3 The grape-eater.

fight (fīt) *v.* **fought, fight·ing** *v.t.* 1 To struggle against in battle or physical combat. 2 To struggle against in any manner. 3 To carry on or engage in (a battle, duel, court action, etc.). 4 To make (one's way) by struggling. 5 To maneuver or handle, as troops or a gun, in battle. 6 To cause to fight, as dogs or game-cocks. — *v.i.* 7 To take part in battle or physical combat. 8 To struggle in any manner. See synonyms under CONTEND. — **to fight shy of** To avoid meeting (an opponent or an issue) squarely. — **to fight it out** To fight until a final decision is reached. — *n.* 1 Strife or struggle between adversaries; battle; conflict; combat. 2 Strife to attain an object in spite of difficulties or opposition. 3 Power or disposition to fight; pugnacity. 4 *Obs.* A temporary bulwark or screen on a ship when in action, to conceal the men. See synonyms under BATTLE. [OE *feohtan*]

fight·er (fī'tər) *n.* 1 One who fights; a combatant; warrior. 2 A pugnacious or spirited person. 3 *Mil.* A fast, highly maneuverable airplane designed to hunt out and destroy enemy planes in the air.

fight·er–bomb·er (fī'tər·bom'ər) *n. Mil.* An aircraft which combines the functions of the fighter and the bomber.

fighter command A division of the U.S. Air Force intermediate between a wing and an air force, used for interception of enemy aircraft and for support of air and ground offensive forces.

fighter plane A pursuit plane.

fight·ing (fī'ting) *adj.* 1 Qualified, equipped, trained, or ready to fight; active in war or battle. 2 Of, pertaining to, suitable for, engaged in, or used for conflict. — *n.* Strife; struggle; battle; conflict.

fighting chance A bare possibility of success, contingent on a hard struggle.

fighting fish A brightly colored Siamese aquarium fish (*Betta splendens*), the males of which are noted for their nesting habits and pugnacity.

fighting top On war vessels, a platform at the lower masthead for the fire-control lookout, or for light anti-aircraft guns.

fig·ment (fig'mənt) *n.* 1 Something imagined or feigned; a fiction. 2 *Obs.* An object molded or shaped. [<L *figmentum* anything made. < *fingere* form]

fig·u·line (fig'yŏŏ·lin, -līn) *adj.* 1 Capable of being used in the manufacture of porcelain or earthenware. 2 Made or molded as in potter's clay. — *n.* 1 Fictile ware; any object made of potter's clay, especially if decorated. 2 Potter's clay. [<L *figulinus* <*figulus* potter < *fingere* form]

fig·ur·al (fig'yər·əl) *adj.* 1 Represented by or consisting of figures or delineation. 2 *Music* Figurate.

fig·u·rant (fig'yŏŏ·rant, *Fr.* fē·gü·rän') *n.* 1 An accessory character on the stage. 2 A non-featured ballet dancer. [<F, ppr. of *figurer* figure] — **fig·u·rante** (fig'yŏŏ·rant', -ränt'; *Fr.* fē·gü·ränt') *n. fem.*

fig·ur·ate (fig'yər·it) *adj.* 1 Having a definite or characteristic figure or shape; resembling anything of definite form. 2 *Music* Florid; figured. [<L *figuratus,* pp. of *figurare* form <*figura.* See FIGURE.]

fig·ur·a·tive (fig'yər·ə·tiv) *adj.* 1 Not literal; metaphorical; symbolic. 2 Ornate; florid. 3 Of or pertaining to the representation of form or figure. 4 Representing by means of a form or figure; emblematic. — **fig'ur·a·tive·ly** *adv.* — **fig'ur·a·tive·ness** *n.*

fig·ure (fig'yər, *Brit.* fig'ər) *n.* 1 The visible form of any person or thing; fashion; shape;

outline; appearance; hence, any visible object thus recognized. **2** The representation or likeness of the form of a person or other object, as in wax or marble, in a painting or drawing, upon a fabric, or as embodied in a diagram or illustration; a cut. **3** A combination of lines, points, surfaces, or solids representing an object or illustrating a condition or relation, or simply for decoration; a diagram, drawing, or pattern. **4** *Geom.* **a** A surface enclosed by lines, as a square, triangle, etc.: called a **plane figure. b** A space enclosed by planes or surfaces, as a cube, sphere, etc.: called a **solid figure. 5** Any person, thing, or act that figures or prefigures, or is a type of some other or future thing or person. **6** Any personage or character, especially one who is active or conspicuous; one who plays a prominent part. **7** The appearance that a person or his conduct makes: to make a sorry *figure.* **8** A character representing a number: the *figure* 5; hence, amount stated in numbers; price; value: to sell goods at a high *figure.* **9** One of the regular movements or divisions of a dance, in which a certain set of steps or evolutions is completed. **10** Something conjured up by the imagination; a fancy; fantasm; imagination; idea. **11** A form of expression that deviates intentionally from the ordinary mode of speech for the sake of more powerful, pleasing, or distinctive effect; pictorial or poetic language. **12** An intentional deviation from ordinary form or construction, as in syntax, euphony, or prosody. **13** *Logic* The character of a syllogism with reference to the places occupied by the middle term in the major and minor premises. **14** *Music* **a** Any short succession of notes, either as melody or a group of chords, which produces a single, complete, and distinct impression; a musical phrase. **b** A theme or melody repeated throughout a whole movement as an accompaniment or bond of connection. **c** A numeral written in connection with the bass to show the unwritten harmony of a piece. **15** A horoscope; the diagram of the aspects of the astrological houses. — *v.* **fig·ured, fig·ur·ing** *v.t.* **1** To make an image, picture, or other representation of; depict. **2** To form an idea or mental image of; imagine. **3** To ornament or mark with a design. **4** To compute numerically; calculate. **5** To express metaphorically; symbolize. **6** *Colloq.* To think; believe; predict. **7** *Music* **a** To embellish, as by adding passing notes. **b** To mark with figures above or below the staff, indicating accompanying chords. — *v.i.* **8** To be conspicuous; appear prominently. **9** To make computations; do arithmetic. — **to figure on** (or **upon**) **1** To think over; consider. **2** To plan; expect. — **to figure out** To reckon; ascertain; solve. [< F < L *figura* < *fingere* form] — **fig'ur·er** *n.*

Synonyms (noun): appearance, aspect, attribute, comparison, delineation, diagram, drawing, emblem, form, illustration, image, likeness, metaphor, simile, similitude, shape, symbol, type.

fig·ured (fig'yərd) *adj.* **1** Adorned or marked with figures or designs: *figured* cottons. **2** Represented by figures; pictured. **3** *Music* **a** Figurate. **b** Indicated by figures, as a bass.

figure eight 1 *Aeron.* A flight maneuver which consists in tracing the figure eight above the ground, with two conspicuous points as the pivots around which to describe each loop. **2** A similar maneuver in ice skating. **3** A style of knot. See illustration under KNOT.

fig·ure·head (fig'yər·hed') *n.* **1** *Naut.* A carved or ornamental figure on the prow of a vessel. **2** A person having nominal leadership but without real power, responsibility, or authority.

figure of speech An expression, usually within a sentence, which deviates from simple, normal speech to produce a fanciful or vivid impression, as simile, metaphor, personification, etc.

FIGUREHEAD

fig·wort (fig'wûrt') *n.* **1** A plant (genus *Scrophularia*) with small, dark-colored flowers, formerly supposed to cure scrofula. **2** Any plant of the figwort family (*Scrophulariaceae*).

fil·a·ment (fil'ə·mənt) *n.* **1** A fine thread, fiber, or fibril. **2** Any threadlike structure or appendage. **3** *Bot.* The stalk or support of an anther. **4** *Electr.* The slender wire of tungsten, carbon, or other material, which, when an electric current is passed through it in a vacuum, is heated to a brilliant glow and produces light. See illustration under INCANDESCENT LAMP. **5** *Electronics* A similar wire, forming the cathode of a vacuum tube, from which electrons are emitted under the action of heat. **6** *Ornithol.* The barb of a feather. [< F < LL *filamentum* < *filare* spin < *filum* a thread]

fil·a·men·tous (fil'ə·men'təs) *adj.* Like, consisting of, or bearing filaments; threadlike. Also **fil'a·men'ta·ry.**

fi·let (fi·lā', fil'ā; *Fr.* fē·le') *n.* **1** Net lace having a square mesh. **2** Fillet (def. 2 and 3). [< F. See FILLET.]

filet de sole (də sôl') *French* · Fillet of sole.

fi·let mi·gnon (fi·lā'min·yon') A small fillet of beef cooked with a garnish of bacon. [< F]

fil·i·al (fil'ē·əl, fil'yəl) *adj.* **1** Of, pertaining to, or befitting a son or daughter; due to parents. **2** *Genetics* Pertaining to a generation following the parental. The first filial generation is designated F_1, the second F_2, etc. [< LL *filialis* < L *filius* a son]

LACE FILET

fil·a·ture (fil'ə·chər) *n.* **1** The act or process of forming threads or of reeling off raw silk from cocoons. **2** An apparatus, machine, or establishment for reeling silk, etc. [< F < L *filare* spin < *filum* a thread]

fil·bert (fil'bərt) *n.* **1** The edible nut of the European or the Oriental hazel (*Corylus avellana*); and also, sometimes, of the American hazel (*C. americana* and *C. cornuta*). **2** The bushy shrub or small tree that bears the nut. [Earlier *filbert nut* < dial. F *noix de filbert* nut of Philibert, after St. *Philibert,* near whose feast (Aug. 22) these nuts ripen]

filch (filch) *v.t.* To steal slyly and in small amounts; pilfer. See synonyms under STEAL. [Origin uncertain] — **filch'er** *n.*

file[1] (fīl) *n.* **1** Any device, as a pointed wire, to keep papers in order for reference; also, a cabinet, drawer, or the like, in which papers are filed. **2** A collection of papers or documents arranged systematically for reference. **3** Any orderly succession or line of men or things; especially a line or row of men standing or marching one behind another: distinguished from *rank*; a small detachment; corporal's guard. **4** Place or standing on a list for advancement, as in the army. **5** A roll; list. **6** A vertical row of squares running directly across a chessboard from one player to the other. — **single file** An arrangement of persons or things one behind another in a single line: also *Indian file.* — *v.* **filed, fil·ing** *v.t.* **1** To put on file in systematic order, as papers for reference. — *v.i.* **2** To march in file, as soldiers. **3** To make an application, as for a job. [Fusion of F *fil* thread and *file* a row, both ult. < L *filum* a thread] — **fil'er** *n.*

file[2] (fīl) *n.* **1** A hard steel abrading or smoothing instrument with ridged cutting surfaces. **2** Figuratively, anything used to abrade, smooth, or polish. **3** *Brit. Slang* A shrewd or artful person. — *v.t.* **filed, fil·ing 1** To cut, smooth, or sharpen with a file. **2** To remove with a file: with *away* or *off*: to *file away* rust. [OE *fīl*] — **fil'er** *n.*

file·fish (fīl'fish') *n.* ·**fish** or ·**fish·es 1** Any of certain fish (family *Balistidae*) with roughly granulated skin, especially the triggerfish. **2** Any of certain fish (family *Monacanthidae*) with prickly scales.

fil·i·ate (fil'ē·āt) *v.t.* ·**at·ed,** ·**at·ing** To affiliate. [< LL *filiatus,* pp. of *filiare* have a son < *filius* son]

fil·i·a·tion (fil'ē·ā'shən) *n.* **1** The relation of a child to a parent. **2** *Law* The judicial determination of parentage; affiliation. **3** Causal connection or relationship; descent. **4** The formation of offshoots, as of a language.

fil·i·bus·ter (fil'ə·bus'tər) *n.* **1** *U.S.* A member of a legislative body who attempts to obstruct legislation by prolonged speaking to consume time; hence, any such prolonged speech. **2** A freebooter or buccaneer; pirate. **3** An adventurer who takes part in an unlawful military expedition into a foreign country. — *v.i.* **1** *U.S.* To obstruct legislation by long speeches and constant delay. **2** To act as a freebooter or adventurer. — *v.t.* **3** *U.S.* To block passage of (legislation) by constant delay. [< Sp. *filibustero* < Du. *vrijbuiter* freebooter] — **fil'i·bus'ter·er** *n.* — **fil'i·bus'trous** *adj.*

fil·i·cide (fil'ə·sīd) *n.* **1** One who kills his child. **2** The act of killing one's child. [< L *filius* a son + -CIDE] — **fil'i·ci'dal** *adj.*

Fil·i·cin·e·ae (fil'ə·sin'i·ē) *n. pl.* A large class of pteridophyte plants; the ferns. [< NL *filicineus* < *Filicales,* an order of ferns < L *filix, filicis* a fern]

fil·i·coid (fil'ə·koid) *adj.* Resembling a fern; fernlike: a *filicoid* pattern. See illustration under FROST. [< L *filix, filicis* a fern + -OID]

fil·i·form (fil'ə·fôrm) *adj.* Threadlike; filamentous; thready. [< L *filum* thread + -FORM]

fil·i·gree (fil'ə·grē) *n.* **1** Delicate ornamental work formed of intertwisted gold or silver wire. **2** Anything fanciful and delicate, but purely ornate. — *adj.* Made of or adorned with filigree; fanciful; ornate. — *v.t.* **·greed, ·gree·ing** To adorn with filigree; work in filigree. Sometimes spelled *filagree* or *fillagree.* Also *Obs.* **fil'i·grain.** [Short for *filigreen,* var. of *filigrane* < F < Ital. *filigrana* < L *filum* thread + *granum* a grain]

fil·ing (fī'ling) *n.* **1** The act or process of using a file. **2** A particle removed by a file.

Fil·i·pi·no (fil'ə·pē'nō) *n. pl.* **·nos** A native or inhabitant of the Philippines. — *adj.* Of or pertaining to the Philippines.

fill (fil) *v.t.* **1** To make full; put as much in as possible. **2** To occupy to capacity; pack. **3** To abound in. **4** To stop up or plug: to *fill* a tooth. **5** To supply with what is necessary or ordered: to *fill* a prescription. **6** To occupy (an office or position). **7** To put someone into (an office or position): to *fill* the governorship with a good man. **8** To feed to fullness; to satisfy; glut. **9** *Engin.* To build up or make full, as an embankment or a ravine, by adding fill. **10** *Naut.* **a** To distend (a sail): said of the wind. **b** To trim (a yard) so the wind will distend the sail. — *v.i.* **11** To become full. See synonyms under SATISFY. — **to fill in 1** To fill up, as an excavation. **2** To insert (something), as into a blank space. **3** To insert something into (a blank space). **4** *Colloq.* To be a substitute. — **to fill in on** *Colloq.* To tell or bring (someone) up to date on additional details or facts. — **to fill out 1** To become fuller or more rounded. **2** To make complete, as a document. — **to fill the bill** *Colloq.* To do or be what is wanted or needed. — *n.* **1** That which fills or is sufficient to fill; a full supply. **2** An embankment, especially a section of a road or railroad bed built up by filling in with stone, gravel, etc., over low ground. **3** The stone, gravel, etc., used to make such an embankment. [OE *fyllan* fill]

filled gold (fild) A layer of gold rolled upon base metal and not merely electroplated on it.

fil·let (fil·lit, *usually for defs.* 2 *and* 3 fil'ā) *n.* **1** A narrow band or ribbon for binding the hair. **2** A strip of lean meat. **3** A flat slice of fish without the bone. **4** A thin band, strip, or engraved line. **5** *Archit.* **a** A small band or molding, usually rectangular, narrow, and flat, used to separate or ornament larger moldings or members. **b** The narrow ridge or strip between the flutes of a column or filling any similar function; a facet. **c** A strip or molding fastened to a wall or the like. **6** *Physiol.* An important nerve tract by which sensory impressions are conveyed to the higher cerebral centers. **7** *Her.* A diminutive ordinary occupying the lower fourth part of the chief. **8** The loins of a horse. **9** Fairing[1] (def. 1). — *v.t.* **1** To bind or adorn with a fillet or band. **2** (also fil'ā, fi·lā') To slice into fillets; cook as a fillet. [< F *fi·let,* dim. of *fil* a thread < L *filum*]

fill·ing (fil'ing) *n.* **1** The act of making or becoming full. **2** Something used to fill a cavity or vacant space: a *filling* of gold for a tooth. **3** In weaving, the weft or woof, which crosses the

add, āce, câre, pälm; end, ēven; it, īce; odd, ōpen, ôrder; tŏŏk, pōōl; up, bûrn; ə = a in *above*, e in *sicken*, i in *clarity*, o in *melon*, u in *focus*; yōō = u in *fuse*; oi, oil; ou, pout; ch, check; g, go; ng, ring; th, thin; th, this; zh, vision. Foreign sounds á, œ, ü, kh, ṅ; and ⬥: see page xx. < from; + plus; ? possibly.

warp. **4** A custard, jelly, or fruit-and-nut mixture placed between layers of a cake.

fil·lip (fil′əp) *n.* **1** A sudden flip of a finger from contact with the thumb; a quick snap or blow with the end of a finger. **2** Anything which serves as an incitement or gives impulse, as to an ambition. —*v.t.* **1** To strike by or as by a fillip; snap with the finger. **2** To project or impel, as by a fillip. —*v.i.* To make a fillip. [Var. of FLIP]

fil·lis·ter (fil′is·tər) *n. Mech.* **1** A plane for making grooves. **2** A rabbet on a sash bar, for receiving the edge of the glass and the putty. **3** A type of screw with a round head. [Origin unknown]

fil·ly (fil′ē) *n. pl.* **fil·lies** A young mare. [< ON *fylia* < *fōli* foal]

film (film) *n.* **1** A thin coating, layer, or membrane. **2** *Phot.* **a** A thin coating of a light-sensitive emulsion laid on a glass plate or on a flexible base, for making photographs. **b** The base itself. **3** A motion picture. **4** A delicate filament, as of a cobweb. **5** *Pathol.* A morbid growth on the cornea of the eye. —*v.t.* **1** To cover or obscure by or as by a film. **2** To photograph on a film; especially, to take motion pictures of. —*v.i.* **3** To become covered or obscured by a film. **4** To take motion pictures. [OE *filmen* membrane]

fi·lose (fī′lōs) *adj.* Having a threadlike appendage. [< L *filum* thread + -OSE[1]]

fil·ter (fil′tər) *n.* **1** Any device or porous substance, as paper, cloth, fine clay, or charcoal, used as a strainer for clearing or purifying fluids. Compare illustration under FUNNEL. **2** *Electr.* A device which permits the passage of currents of certain frequencies and limits the flow of certain others, such as a **band filter**, which passes currents neither above nor below a given range, a **high-pass filter**, which selects certain high-frequency currents and a **low-pass filter**, which permits the flow of certain low-frequency currents; also used in power transmission. **3** *Phot.* A colored screen of glass, or of other translucent material, placed in front of a camera lens to control the kind and relative intensity of light waves in an exposure. —*v.t.* **1** To pass (liquids) through a filter; strain. **2** To separate (solid matter) from liquid by a filter. —*v.i.* **3** To pass through a filter. **4** To move slowly; leak out, as news. See synonyms under PURIFY. ◆ Homophone: *philter.* [< OF *filtre* < Med. L *fēltrum.* Related to FELT[2].] —**fil′ter·a·bil′i·ty**, **fil·tra·bil′i·ty** (fil′trə·bil′ə·tē), **fil′ter·a·ble·ness** *n.* —**fil′ter·a·ble**, **fil·tra·ble** (fil′trə·bəl) *adj.*

filter bed A reservoir with a sand or gravel bottom for purifying large quantities of water.

filter feeder Any aquatic organism that feeds on small organisms which are strained out of the surrounding water as it is channeled through a specialized sieve or filtering system.

filter paper A soft porous paper suitable for filtering.

filth (filth) *n.* **1** Anything that soils, or makes foul; that which is foul or dirty. **2** Moral defilement; obscenity. [OE *fȳlth*]

fil·trate (fil′trāt) *v.t.* **·trat·ed**, **·trat·ing** To filter. —*n.* The liquid or other substance separated by filtration. [< NL *filtratus*, pp. of *filtrare* < Med. L *filtrum* a filter]

fil·tra·tion (fil·trā′shən) *n.* **1** The act or process of filtering. **2** The separation of liquids from solids. **3** The sterilization of liquids by the mechanical removal of bacteria and other impurities.

fi·lum (fī′ləm) *n. pl.* **·la** (-lə) *Anat.* A thread or threadlike structure. [< NL < L]

fim·ble (fim′bəl) *n.* The male hemp plant, which is generally harvested before the female plant. [< Du. *femel* < F (*chanvre*) *femelle* female (hemp)]

fim·bri·a (fim′brē·ə) *n. Zool.* A fringe or fringelike structure, as around the mouth of a tube or duct in certain animals. [< NL < L, a fringe]

fim·bri·ate (fim′brē·āt) *v.t.* **·at·ed**, **·at·ing** *Biol.* To furnish with a fringe or border; fringe. —*adj.* (-it) Having such a fringe or border. — **fim′bri·a′tion** *n.*

fim·bri·at·ed (fim′brē·ā′tid) *adj.* Having a fringe or fringelike processes; fimbriate.

fim·bril·late (fim·bril′it) *adj. Biol.* Having a fine fringe or border. [< NL *fimbrilla*, dim. of *fimbra* a fringe]

fin (fin) *n.* **1** A membranous extension from the body of a fish or other aquatic animal, serving to propel, balance, or steer it in the water. For illustrations see FISH, RORQUAL. **2** Any finlike or projecting part, appendage, or attachment. **3** *Naut.* A finlike appendage to a submarine boat or the like; a fin keel. **4** *Aeron.* A fixed supplementary surface of an aircraft, usually vertical: a tail *fin.* See illustration under AIRPLANE. **5** A projecting rib on a radiator or on the cylinder of an internal-combustion engine. **6** Any finlike part, as on a rocket, bomb, etc. **7** A flipper (def. 2). **8** *Mech.* The projecting ridge of a metal casting at the line of junction with the mold. —*v.* **finned**, **fin·ning** *v.t.* To cut up or trim off the fins (of a fish). —*v.i.* To beat the water with the fins, as a whale when dying. [OE *finn*]

fin·a·ble (fī′nə·bəl) *adj.* **1** Liable to or involving a fine. **2** Capable of being refined or purified. Also *fineable.*

fi·na·gle (fi·nā′gəl) *v.* **·gled**, **·gling** *Colloq. v.t.* **1** To get (something) by trickery or deceit. **2** To cheat or trick (someone). —*v.i.* **3** To use trickery or deceit; be sly. **4** In card games, to renege. [Var. of FAINAIGUE] —**fi·na′gler** *n.*

fi·nal (fī′nəl) *adj.* **1** Pertaining to, or coming at or as, the end; ultimate; last. **2** Precluding, or making unnecessary, further action or controversy; conclusive; decisive. **3** Relating to or consisting in the end or purpose aimed at: a *final cause.* —*n.* **1** Something that is terminal, last, or final; that which makes an end; a finale. **2** The last, deciding match in a tournament or series of games. **3** The last examination of a term in a school or college. [< F < L *finalis* < *finis* end]

fi·na·le (fi·nä′lē, -nal′ē; *Ital.* fē·nä′lä) *n.* **1** The last act, part, or scene; end. **2** The last movement in a musical composition. See synonyms under END. [< Ital., final]

fi·nal·ist (fī′nəl·ist) *n.* In athletics, a contestant who takes part in the final round, as of a tournament, race, etc.

fi·nal·i·ty (fī·nal′ə·tē) *n. pl.* **·ties** **1** The state or quality of being final. **2** A final, conclusive, or decisive act, determination, offer, etc. **3** *Philos.* The doctrine of final causes, that design actuates the universe; teleology. **4** The belief that there can be no progress or change.

fi·nal·ize (fī′nəl·īz) *v.t.* **·ized**, **·iz·ing** **1** To bring to a state of completion, as a transaction, sale, or agreement. **2** To put into final or complete form.

fi·nal·ly (fī′nəl·ē) *adv.* **1** At or in the end; ultimately. **2** Lastly. **3** Completely; irrecoverably.

fi·nance (fi·nans′, fī′nans) *n.* **1** The science of monetary affairs. **2** *pl.* Monetary affairs; pecuniary resources; funds; revenue; income. —*v.t.* **·nanced**, **·nanc·ing** **1** To manage the finances of. **2** To supply the money for. [< OF, payment < *finer* settle < *fin* end. See FINE[2].]

fi·nan·cial (fi·nan′shəl, fī-) *adj.* **1** Of or pertaining to finance; monetary. **2** Of or pertaining to those dealing professionally with money and credit. —**fi·nan′cial·ly** *adv.*

Synonyms: fiscal, monetary, pecuniary. These words all relate to money, receipts, or expenditures. *Monetary* relates to actual money, coin, currency; as, the *monetary* system; a *monetary* transaction is one in which money is transferred. *Pecuniary* refers to that in which money is involved, but less directly; we speak of one's *pecuniary* affairs or interests, with no special reference to the handling of cash. *Financial* applies especially to governmental revenues or expenditures, or to private transactions of considerable moment; we speak of a *pecuniary* reward, a *financial* enterprise; we give a needy person *pecuniary* (not *financial*) assistance. *Fiscal* applies to the state treasury or public finances or accounts; it is common to speak of the *fiscal* rather than the *financial* year.

finch (finch) *n.* A small, seed-eating bird (family *Fringillidae*), as a bunting, sparrow, grosbeak, bullfinch, goldfinch, greenfinch, canary, chaffinch, or weaverbird. ◆ Collateral adjective: *fringilline.* [OE *finc*]

find (find) *v.* **found**, **find·ing** *v.t.* **1** To come upon unexpectedly; discover. **2** To perceive or discover; come upon by search or examination. **3** To learn or become aware of by ex-

perience. **4** To recover (something lost). **5** To reach; arrive at; attain. **6** To give a decision upon: The judge *found* him in contempt. **7** To gain or recover the use of: He *found* his tongue. **8** To furnish; provide. —*v.i.* **9** To arrive at and express a judicial decision: to *find* for the plaintiff. See synonyms under DISCOVER. —**to find fault** To complain of some defect or deficiency. —**to find oneself** **1** To become aware of one's special ability or vocation. **2** To fare in health; feel. —**to find out** To detect or discover, as a thief. —**to find out about** To learn the truth concerning. —*n.* A finding; a thing found or discovered; especially, a valuable discovery. [OE *findan*]

find·ing (fīn′ding) *n.* **1** The act of finding; that which is found; discovery. **2** *Law* A conclusion arrived at before an official or a court. **3** Support; expense.

find·ings (fīn′dingz) *n. pl.* **1** Small tools and supplies which a workman provides for himself. **2** Sewing essentials, as thread, needles, tape, buttons, etc.; notions. **3** *Law* Conclusions as to matters of fact arrived at through testimony heard before an official or a court.

fine[1] (fīn) *adj.* **fin·er**, **fin·est** **1** Excellent in quality; admirable; superior. **2** Suggesting lightness; light or delicate; not coarse, gross, or dull; subtle; thin; keen. **3** Showy in appearance or style; pretentious; ostentatious. **4** Delicate of perception; refined; sensitive; nice. **5** Refined, as sirup. **6** Having a high or specified degree of purity, as gold or silver. **7** Distinguished or noteworthy. **8** Enjoyable; pleasant. **9** Trained to the highest point of efficiency: said of an athlete, a horse, etc. **10** Cloudless; rainless. —*adv.* **1** *Colloq.* Very nicely; finely; well; excellently. **2** In billiards, in a manner producing a fine carom, etc. —*v.t. & v.i.* **fined**, **fin·ing** To make or become purified, thin, or slender. [< OF *fin* perfected < LL *finus*, a back formation < L *finire* complete < *finis* end] —**fine′ly** *adv.*

Synonyms (adj.): beautiful, clarified, clear, comminuted, dainty, delicate, elegant, excellent, exquisite, gauzy, handsome, keen, minute, nice, polished, pure, refined, sensitive, sharp, slender, slight, small, smooth, splendid, subtile, subtle, tenuous, thin.

fine[2] (fīn) *n.* **1** A pecuniary penalty; the money so required, or anything forfeited as a penalty. **2** In English law, an amicable adjustment of a suit either actual or fictitious; a final agreement as for the possession of lands. **3** *Obs.* End; conclusion; death. —**in fine** Finally. —*v.t.* **fined**, **fin·ing** To punish by fine; exact a fine from. [< OF *fin* settlement < L *finis* end]

fine[3] (fēn) *n. French* A drink of brandy, especially one served with meals.

fi·ne[4] (fē′nā) *n. Music* A mark denoting the end; finis. [< Ital.]

fine–draw (fīn′drô′) *v.t.* **·drew**, **·drawn**, **·drawing** **1** To sew or close up, as a tear, so that the joining is imperceptible. **2** To draw out, as wire, to an extreme degree of fineness.

fine–drawn (fīn′drôn′) *adj.* Drawn out finely; hence, developed very subtly or too subtly.

fine–frame (fīn′frām′) *n.* A special frame used in making high-grade yarns of Sea Island cotton.

fine–grained (fīn′grānd′) *adj.* Having a close, fine grain, as in texture or surface: said of some leathers and woods.

fine·ness (fīn′nis) *n.* **1** The state or quality of being fine. **2** The degree of subdivision of the particles of a powder or other granular substance. **3** The purity of an alloy, especially one containing gold or silver, expressed in parts per thousand.

fin·er·y (fī′nər·ē) *n. pl.* **·er·ies** Showy or fine clothes or decoration.

fines herbes (fēn ârb) *French* A mixture of herbs used to season soups, stews, etc.

fine–spun (fīn′spun′) *adj.* **1** Drawn or spun out to an extreme degree of tenuity. **2** Subtle.

fi·nesse (fi·nes′) *n.* **1** Subtle contrivance; artifice; stratagem. **2** Dexterity; artfulness; skill. **3** In card-playing, an attempt on the part of a player to take a trick with a lower card when he holds a higher (as a queen when he holds the ace), in the hope that the opposing hand yet to play will not hold a taking card (as the king). See synonyms under ARTIFICE, DECEPTION. —*v.* **fi·nessed**, **fi·ness·ing** *v.t.* **1** To change or bring about by finesse. **2** In card games, to play as a finesse. — *v.i.* **3** To use finesse. **4** In card games, to make a finesse. [<F <*fin* FINE[1]]

fine-toothed comb (fīn'tōōtht') A comb with fine teeth very close together. — **to go over with a fine-toothed comb** To search carefully; leave no part unsearched or unexamined.

fine-top (fīn'top') *n.* Redtop.

fin-fish (fin'fish') *n.* True fish: not shellfish.

fin-foot-ed (fin'fŏŏt'id) *adj.* **1** Having webbed feet. **2** Having lobate toes.

fin-gent (fin'jənt) *adj.* Forming; making; molding. [<L *fingens, -entis*, ppr. of *fingere* form]

fin-ger (fing'gər) *n.* **1** One of the digits of the hand, usually excluding the thumb. **2** Any small projecting piece or part, like a finger, as a lever. **3** A measure of length; the length of the middle finger. **4** A measure of depth, equal to the width of the finger. **5** That part of a glove which covers a finger. — **to burn one's fingers** To suffer the consequences of meddling or interfering. — **to have a finger in the pie** To take part in some matter. — **to have at one's finger tips** To have ready and available knowledge of. — **to put one's finger on** To identify or indicate correctly. — **to put the finger on** *U.S. Slang* **1** To betray to the police. **2** To indicate (the victim) of a planned crime. — **to twist around one's (little) finger** To be able to influence or manage with ease. — *v.t.* **1** To touch or handle with the fingers; toy with. **2** To steal; purloin. **3** *Music* **a** To play (an instrument) with the fingers. **b** To mark the notes of (music) showing which fingers are to be used. **4** *U.S. Slang* **a** To betray. **b** To point out (the victim) of a planned crime. — *v.i.* **5** To touch or feel anything with the fingers. **6** *Music* **a** To use the fingers on a musical instrument in a certain manner. **b** To be arranged for playing by the fingers: said of instruments. [OE]

fin-ger-board (fing'gər-bôrd', -bōrd') *n.* **1** A guideboard bearing a pointing finger. **2** In stringed instruments, the strip of wood upon which the strings are pressed by the fingers of the player. **3** In instruments of the piano or organ class, a keyboard.

fin-ger-breadth (fing'gər-bredth') *n.* The breadth of a finger, from 3/4 inch to one inch.

finger hole **1** A hole in any object into which a finger may be fitted, as in a bowling ball. **2** One of a series of holes in various wind instruments, as a flute, oboe, etc., over which the finger is manipulated in order to change the tones. **3** One of a series of small holes in a dial telephone.

fin-ger-ing[1] (fing'gər-ing) *n.* **1** The act of touching or feeling with the fingers. **2** *Music* **a** The act or order of using the fingers in playing an instrument, as the flute or piano. **b** The notation indicating what fingers are to be used.

fin-ger-ing[2] (fing'gər-ing) *n.* A finely twisted woolen yarn of medium weight, used for knitting and crocheting. Also **fingering yarn.**

fin-ger-ling (fing'gər-ling) *n.* **1** A young fish, especially a salmon or trout, no bigger than a man's finger. **2** A being of very small size. Compare THUMBLING. **3** *Obs.* A glove finger; a finger covering; a thimble.

fin-ger-nail (fing'gər-nāl') *n.* The horny growth on the end and along the upper surface of a finger.

finger painting A technique of applying paint to wet paper with the fingers and palms to form a design or picture.

fin-ger-print (fing'gər-print') *n.* An impression of the skin pattern on the inner surface of a finger tip: especially used in the identification of criminals, in the military, naval, and police services, and in various commercial transactions. — *v.t.* To take the fingerprints of. See synonyms under MARK[1]. — **fin'ger-print'ing** *n.*

FINGERPRINT
The whorl type of print.

fin-i-al (fin'ē-əl) *n.* **1** *Archit.* An ornament at the apex of a spire, pinnacle, or the like. **2** Any terminal part pointing upward. [<L *finis* end + -IAL]

FINIAL

fin-i-cal (fin'i-kəl) *adj.* Overnice or fastidious in dress, manners, and the like. Also **fin'ick-ing, fin'ick-y, fin'i-kin.** See synonyms under SQUEAMISH. [<FINE[1]] — **fin'i-cal-ly** *adv.* — **fin'i-cal-ness** *n.*

fin-i-cal-i-ty (fin'ə-kal'ə-tē) *n.* **1** The characteristic of being finical. **2** That which is finical.

fin-ing (fī'ning) *n.* **1** The process of making fine. **2** The removal of gas bubbles from fused glass. **3** The purification and clarifying of wines. **4** Any substance used in clarifying liquids.

fin-ish (fin'ish) *v.t.* **1** To complete or bring to an end; come to the end of. **2** To perfect finally or in detail, as a portrait. **3** To use up; dispose of. **4** *Colloq.* To kill or destroy. **5** *Colloq.* To defeat; make powerless. — *v.i.* **6** To reach or come to an end; stop. **7** *Obs.* To die. — *n.* **1** The conclusion or last stage of anything. **2** The process or effect of perfecting or beautifying anything: the *finish* of a statue; cloth of a fine *finish.* **3** Perfection in speech or manner; social poise. **4** The joinery and cabinetwork necessary to complete the interior of a building. **5** That which finishes or completes. **6** A material, as oil, used in finishing. See synonyms under END. [<OF *feniss-*, stem of *fenir* end <L *finire* <*finis* an end]

Synonyms (verb): accomplish, achieve, close, complete, conclude, elaborate, end, perfect, polish, terminate.

fin-ished (fin'isht) *adj.* **1** Carried to a high degree of perfection; polished. **2** Ended; concluded. **3** Completed; done. See synonyms under PERFECT, RIPE.

fin-ish-ing (fin'ish-ing) *n.* The final operation or set of operations in any manufacturing process: the *finishing* of furs, etc.

fi-nite (fī'nīt) *adj.* **1** Having bounds, ends, or limits, as opposed to that which is infinite. **2** That may be determined, counted, or measured. **3** Subject to creature limitations, especially those that affect human life. **4** *Gram.* Limited by number and person: said of verb forms that can serve as predicates in sentences: distinguished from infinitives, participles, and gerunds that have no such limitations. **5** *Math.* **a** That may be equaled or exceeded by counting: said of numbers. **b** Limited and determinate, in theory or by observation; not infinite or infinitesimal: said of a magnitude. — *n.* Finite things collectively, or that which is finite: usually with *the.* [<L *finitus* limited; orig. pp. of *finire* end] — **fi'nite-ly** *adv.* — **fi'nite-ness** *n.*

fin-i-tes-i-mal (fin'ə-tes'ə-məl) *adj. Math.* Denoted by the ordinal of a finite number. [<FINITE + *-esimal*, as in *centesimal* <L *-esimus*, suffix of ordinal numbers]

fin-i-tude (fin'ə-tōōd, -tyōōd, fī'nə-) *n.* The mode or fact of being finite; limitation. [<L *finitus* limited]

Fin-land (fin'lənd) A republic of northern Europe, NE of the Baltic Sea; 130,091 square miles; capital, Helsinki: Finnish *Suomi.*

Finland, Gulf of An eastern arm of the Baltic Sea, between Finland and the U.S.S.R.

Finn (fin) *n.* **1** A native or inhabitant of Finland. **2** A member of a people speaking a Finnic language. [OE *Finnas* Finns]

fin-nan had-die (fin'ən had'ē) Smoked haddock. Also **fin'nan had-dock** (had'ək). [<*Findhorn haddock*, from *Findhorn*, a Scottish town where originally prepared]

finned (find) *adj.* Having fins or finlike extensions.

Finn-ic (fin'ik) *n.* A branch of the Finno-Ugric subfamily of Uralic languages, including Finnish, Estonian, and Lapp. — *adj.* Finnish.

fin-nick-ing (fin'i-king), **fin-nick-y** (fin'i-kē) See FINICAL.

Finn-ish (fin'ish) *adj.* Of or pertaining to Finland, the Finns, or their language. — *n.* The

Uralic language of the Finns.

Fin-no-U-gric (fin'ō-ōō'grik, -yōō'grik) *n.* A subfamily of the Uralic languages, embracing the Finnic (Finnish, Estonian, Lapp, etc.) and Ugric (Magyar, Ostyak, Vogul) branches. — *adj.* Pertaining to the Finns and the Ugrians, or to their languages. Also **Fin'no-U'gri-an.**

fin-ny (fin'ē) *adj.* **1** Having fins; fishlike. **2** Abounding in fish.

fi-no-chi-o (fi-nō'kē-ō) *n.* A variety of fennel (*Foeniculum vulgare dulce*) whose young sweet shoots are esteemed as a food and salad. [<Ital. *finocchio* <L *faeniculum* FENNEL]

fin ray One of the cartilaginous or bony rods supporting the membrane of a fish's fin: also called *ray.*

Fin-sen light (fin'sən) A strong actinic light obtained either from an electric lamp or by passing sunlight through an ammoniacal solution of copper sulfate: used in treating certain skin diseases. [after N. R. *Finsen*, 1860–1904, Danish physician, its originator]

fiord (fyôrd, fyōrd) *n.* A long and narrow arm of the sea, with high rocky banks: also spelled *fjord.* [<Norw. *fjord*]

fip-pence (fip'əns) *n. Brit.* Fivepence.

fip-pen-ny (fip'ə-nē, fip'nē) Short for FIVE-PENNY.

fip-ple (fip'əl) *n.* A plug with a lip, as in certain wind instruments, such as the *fipple* flute. [? <ON *flipi* lip of a horse]

fi-que (fē'kā) *n.* A succulent plant of the amaryllis family (*Furcraea macrophylla*) native in tropical America, yielding a fiber similar to jute. [<Sp.]

fir (fûr) *n.* **1** An evergreen tree of the pine family (genus *Abies*), cone-bearing and resinous, especially the balsam fir (*A. balsamea*). **2** Its wood. ◆ Homophone: *fur.* [OE *fyrh*]

Fir-bolg (fir'bul-əg) Literally, men of the leather boats: one of a legendary pre-Celtic people of Ireland, defeated and run out by the Fomorians. [<Irish *fir* men + *bolg* leather coracle]

fire (fir) *n.* **1** The evolution of heat and light by combustion. **2** The combustion thus manifested, especially the flame, or the fuel as burning. **3** A destructive burning, as of a building. **4** The discharge of firearms. **5** A spark or sparks; a light, luster, or flash. **6** Intensity of feeling or action; ardor; passion; vivacity. **7** Any raging evil; affliction; trial. **8** Fever. **9** A combustible device or substance for producing fire or for display; fireworks. **10** Lightning. **11** *Poetic* A luminous object in the sky, as a star or meteor. **12** Torture or death by or as by burning; also, any severe trial. **13** *Obs.* A North American Indian term for a family or a nation; hence, by transference, one of the United States, especially one of the first thirteen. — **colored fire** A mixture of combustibles, as sulfur with a mineral salt that yields a colored light when burning: used for signals, fireworks, etc. — **Greek fire** An incendiary composition, used by the Byzantine Greeks to fire enemy ships: said to ignite on contact with water. — **on fire** Burning; ablaze; hence, ardent; zealous. — **under fire** Exposed to gunshot or artillery fire; hence, under attack of any kind. — *v.* **fired, fir-ing** *v.t.* **1** To set on fire; cause to burn. **2** To tend the fire of; put fuel in: to *fire* a furnace. **3** To bake, as pottery, in a kiln. **4** To cure, as tobacco, by exposure to heat. **5** To cauterize. **6** To inflame the emotions or passions of; excite. **7** To discharge, as a gun or bullet. **8** *Colloq.* To impel or hurl, as with force: to *fire* questions. **9** To cause to glow or shine. **10** *U.S. Colloq.* To discharge peremptorily from employment. — *v.i.* **11** To take fire; become ignited. **12** To discharge firearms. **13** To discharge a missile. **14** To become inflamed or excited. **15** To tend a fire. **16** To become blotched or yellow: said of flax and grain. See synonyms under INCENSE[1]. — **to fire away** To begin; start. — **to fire up 1** To start a fire, as in a furnace. **2** To become enraged. [OE *fyr*]

Synonyms (noun): blaze, burning, combustion, conflagration, flame.

fire-ac-tion (fir'ak'shən) *n.* The fire of small

arms or artillery estimated as a force in attack or defense.

fire alarm **1** An alarm calling attention to a fire or its whereabouts. **2** An apparatus for giving an alarm of fire, especially a telegraphic alarm.

fire-and-brim·stone (fīr'ən·brim'stōn') *adj.* Impassioned; also, threatening hell: a *fire-and-brimstone* sermon.

fire ant A destructive, mound-building red ant (*Solenopsis geminata*) common in the SE United States: its sting is very painful and often fatal to animals.

fire·arm (fīr'ärm') *n.* Any weapon from which a missile, as a bullet, is hurled by an explosive: usually restricted to small arms.

fire·back (fīr'bak') *n.* **1** The rear wall of a furnace or fireplace. **2** One of various Asian pheasants, having the plumage of the back a bright metallic red.

fire·ball (fīr'bôl') *n.*
1 A sack of canvas filled with combustibles. **2** A meteor brighter than the planet Venus. **3** Ball-shaped lightning. **4** *Physics* The dense, mushroom-shaped or globular mass of radioactive debris and fall-out material produced by the explosion of an atomic or thermonuclear bomb.

FIREBALL (def. 4)

fire balloon **1** A balloon inflated with hot air supplied by fire from underneath, particularly a paper toy balloon carrying a lighted ball or sponge. **2** A balloon carrying inflammable explosives or fireworks, to ignite at a certain height.

fire beetle Any of various elaterid beetles (genus *Pyrophorus*) of the West Indies, especially the cucubano (*P. luminosus*), which emits a greenish light from two spots near the head and a red light from the abdomen.

fire·bird (fīr'bûrd') *n.* Any of various, small, brilliantly colored birds, as the Baltimore oriole, the vermilion flycatcher, and the scarlet tanager.

fire·blight (fīr'blīt') *n.* A serious bacterial disease of various pome fruits, caused by *Erwina amylovora* and attacking blossoms, leaves, twigs, and fruit.

fire·board (fīr'bôrd', -bōrd') *n.* A board to close a fireplace not in use; chimney board.

fire boat A steamboat provided with fire-extinguishing apparatus: used to protect shipping and wharves.

fire·box (fīr'boks') *n.* The chamber in which the fuel of a locomotive, furnace, etc., is burnt.

fire·brand (fīr'brand') *n.* **1** A burning or glowing piece of wood or other substance. **2** An incendiary; a mischief-maker.

fire·brat (fīr'brat') *n.* A small, wingless, scaly insect (*Thermobia domestica*) which inhabits warm houses and is destructive of wallpaper, clothing, and starchy materials: related to the silverfish. For illustration see under INSECT (injurious).

fire·break (fīr'brāk') *n.* A strip of plowed or cleared land made to prevent the spread of fire in woods or on a prairie.

fire·brick (fīr'brik') *n.* A brick made of fireclay, used for lining furnaces.

fire brigade A company of firemen.

fire·clay (fīr'klā') *n.* A refractory material, usually finely powdered aluminum silicate, mixed with iron oxide, lime, and other constituents to improve its fire-resistant qualities.

fire·crack·er (fīr'krak'ər) *n.* A firework made of a small paper cylinder charged with gunpowder.

fire·cure (fīr'kyŏŏr') *v.t.* **-cured, -cur·ing** To season with the heat and smoke of an open fire, as tobacco; to smoke.

fire·damp (fīr'damp') *n.* **1** A combustible gas (chiefly methane) which enters mines from coal seams. **2** The explosive mixture formed by this gas and air.

fire department That part of the public service, including buildings, fire-extinguishing apparatus, and men, devoted to the preven-

tion or extinguishment of fires.

fire·drake (fīr'drāk') *n.* A fire-breathing dragon of Germanic mythology; specifically, the dragon that killed Beowulf. Also **fire'drag'on** (-drag'ən). [OE *fÿrdraca* < *fÿr* fire + *draca* a dragon]

fire drill **1** The drilling of a fire company. **2** Drilling, as of pupils in a school, to accustom them to proper action in case of fire.

fire engine A heavy motor truck equipped with fire-fighting apparatus, especially power-driven pumps for throwing water and chemicals under high pressure.

fire escape A ladder or other device attached to the outside of a building and furnishing a means of escape from a burning building.

fire extinguisher A portable fire-fighting apparatus containing certain chemicals that are ejected by pressure through a short hose.

fire·fang (fīr'fang') *v.i.* To deteriorate by oxidation, as cheese. [<FIRE + FANG, *v.*]

fire·find·er (fīr'fīn'dər) *n.* An instrument consisting of a map with an azimuth circle, an alidade, spirit level, and other accessories: used by forest rangers to locate the position of a fire.

fire·fly (fīr'flī') *n. pl.* **·flies** Any of various phosphorescent, night-flying beetles (family *Lampyridae*); specifically, the North American genera *Photinus* and *Photuris*, whose females and phosphorescent larvae are called *glowworms*.

fire-foam (fīr'fōm') *n.* A thick foamlike substance, formed by the chemical union of aluminum sulfate and sodium bicarbonate with other materials, which smothers a fire: a trade name.

fire·guard (fīr'gärd') *n.* **1** A space in fields, grasslands, woods, and forests, cleared of all combustible matter and serving as a protection against the spread of fire. **2** A metal screen placed before an open fire as a guard against sparks.

fire-i·rons (fīr'ī'ərnz) *n.* Poker, shovel, and tongs.

fireless cooker An insulated container in which hot foods may be placed to finish cooking or to be kept warm.

fire·light (fīr'līt') *n.* The light from a fire, as a campfire.

fire line **1** A firebreak. **2** A barrier made by police against approach to a burning building.

fire·lock (fīr'lok') *n.* An old form of musket discharged by any device for producing sparks; a flintlock.

fire·man (fīr'mən) *n. pl.* **·men** (-mən) **1** One who aids in extinguishing fires; a member of a professional fire-fighting company or crew. **2** One who tends the firing on a locomotive; a stoker.

fire·pan (fīr'pan') *n.* **1** A brazier; a grate. **2** The priming receptacle of a flintlock gun.

fire·pink (fīr'pingk') *n.* A catchfly (*Silene virginica*) of the eastern United States, with crimson or scarlet flowers.

fire·place (fīr'plās') *n.* A recess or structure in or on which a fire is built; especially that part of a chimney that opens into a room.

fire·plug (fīr'plug') *n.* A hydrant for use in case of fire.

fire point A flash point.

fire·pow·er (fīr'pou'ər) *n. Mil.* **1** Capacity for delivering fire, as from the guns of a ship, battery, etc. **2** The total amount of fire delivered by a given weapon or unit.

fire·proof (fīr'prōōf') *adj.* **1** Made resistant against fire; incombustible. **2** Of a nature to protect from fire. — *v.t.* To make resistant to fire.

fire sale A sale of goods reduced in price because of slight damage by fire.

fire ship A ship filled with combustibles, fired and floated toward an enemy for the purpose of destroying ships, bridges, etc.

fire station A firehouse.

fire·stone (fīr'stōn') *n.* **1** Flint or pyrites used for striking fire. **2** A stone that will withstand the action of fire.

fire surface That part of the surface of a boiler which is exposed to the fire; the heating surface.

fire·thorn (fīr'thôrn') *n.* An evergreen, typically thorny shrub (genus *Pyracantha*) of the rose family, bearing white flowers and a scarlet or orange fruit, and cultivated as an ornamental hedge plant.

fire·tow·er (fīr'tou'ər) *n.* A watchtower, usually in a wooded area, from which a fire can be seen and reported.

fire·trap (fīr'trap') *n.* A building notoriously inflammable, or one not provided with an escape for use in case of fire.

fire·wall (fīr'wôl') *n.* **1** A fireproof wall designed to block the progress of a fire. **2** *Aeron.* A bulkhead of fire-resistant material placed between the engine compartment of an aircraft and the rest of the structure to limit the spread of fire from the engines.

fire·war·den (fīr'wôr'dən) *n.* An officer who has charge of the prevention and extinguishing of fires.

fire·weed (fīr'wēd') *n.* **1** The willow herb. **2** The jimsonweed.

fire·works (fīr'wûrks') *n.* **1** A case or cases containing combustibles and explosives, producing brilliant or colored light or scintillations in burning. **2** A pyrotechnic display.

fire·worm (fīr'wûrm') *n.* **1** A glowworm. **2** The larva of a tortricid moth (*Rhopobota naevana*), which devours the leaves of the cranberry, leaving the plant apparently burned.

fir·ing (fīr'ing) *n.* **1** The act or process of applying fire or intense heat to anything, as in stoking, burning, baking, or vitrifying, as bricks or pottery in a kiln; also, in cauterizing. **2** The discharge of firearms. **3** Fuel, as wood or coal.

firing line **1** The line of active engagement in battle. **2** The main body of troops in action within effective rifle range of the enemy. **3** The foremost position in any activity.

firing pin That part of a firearm or a fuze which, on being actuated, strikes the primer or detonator. See illustration under BOMB (aerial).

firing squad A military or naval detachment selected to show honor to a deceased person by firing over his grave, or to execute a sentence of death by shooting.

firm¹ (fûrm) *adj.* **1** Solidly compacted; unyielding; solid. **2** Fixedly settled; difficult to move; stable. **3** Strong, steadfast, or determined in character; vigorous; resolute; enduring. **4** Solid; not liquid or gaseous. **5** Not fluctuating widely, as prices. — *v.t.* & *v.i.* **1** To make or become firm, solid, or compact. **2** *Obs.* To confirm; establish. — *adv.* Solidly; resolutely; fixedly: to stand *firm* against the foe. [<L *firmus*] — **firm'ly** *adv.* — **firm'ness** *n.* Synonyms (*adj.*): close, compact, decided, determined, established, fast, fixed, hard, immovable, immutable, resolute, robust, rugged, secure, solid, stable, steadfast, steady, strong, sturdy, unchanging, unfailing, unfaltering, unshaken. See FAITHFUL, HARD, IMPLICIT, OBSTINATE.

firm² (fûrm) *n.* **1** A union of two or more persons for the purpose of conducting business; a commercial, industrial, or financial partnership; a business house. **2** The style or title under which such a house carries on business; firm name. [<Ital. *firma* a signature <L *firmare* make firm < *firmus* firm]

fir·ma·ment (fûr'mə·mənt) *n.* The expanse of the heavens; sky. [<L *firmamentum* a support < *firmare* make firm] — **fir'ma·men'tal** *adj.*

firm·er (fûr'mər) *adj.* Designating a cutting tool with a thin, narrow blade, for manual use in shaping wood. — *n.* A firmer chisel or gouge. For illustration see under GOUGE.

firm power Electric power from a generating station available for use under all conditions.

firn (firn) *n. Meteorol.* Snow, partly consolidated into ice, found in Alpine regions; névé. [<G <*firn*, adj., of last year]

first (fûrst) *adj.* **1** Preceding all others in the order of numbering: the ordinal of *one*. **2** Prior to all others in time; earliest. **3** Nearest or foremost in place from a given point. **4** Highest or foremost in character, rank, etc.; leading; chief; best. — **at (the) first blush** On first presentation; at first thought, without mature consideration. — **at first hand** Directly from the original source; without intervening assistance. — *n.* **1** That which comes or is first; the beginning. **2** *Music* The leading or upper part, voice, or instrument; also, a unison. **3** In English universities, the highest rank in examinations for honors; also, one taking the highest rank.

4 A winning position in a contest. **5** The first day of a month; the first year in a period or reign. **6** *pl.* The best grade of certain commercial products, as butter, sugar, etc. **— at first** (or **from the first**) At the beginning or origin. **—** *adv.* **1** Before all others in order, as in counting, time, place, or rank; also, in formal discourse, **first'ly.** **2** Before, or in preference to, some proposed act or anticipated event; sooner: He will never confess: he would die *first.* **3** For the first time. [OE *fyrst,* superlative of *fore* before]

Synonyms (adj.): chief, earliest, foremost, front, highest, leading, original, primary, primeval, primitive, primordial, principal, pristine, supreme. *Antonyms:* hindmost, inferior, insignificant, last, least, lowest, secondary, subordinate, subsequent, subservient, subsidiary, trifling, trivial, unimportant.

first aid Treatment given in any emergency while awaiting qualified medical or surgical attention. **— first–aid** (fûrst'ād') *adj.*

first base In baseball, the base first reached by the runner, at the right-hand angle of the infield. Compare illustration under BASEBALL. **— to get to first base** *U.S. Slang* To succeed in the first phase of an enterprise.

First Cause 1 God as uncaused, the original source and creator of all things. **2** In Aristotelian philosophy, prime mover.

first–class (fûrst'kläs', -kläs') *adj.* **1** Belonging to the first class; of the highest rank or the best quality. **2** Consisting of sealed letters or other sealed matter transmitted by the post: *first–class* mail. **3** Pertaining to, for, or using, the most luxurious accommodations on a steamer, train, plane, etc.

First Day Sunday: name used by the Society of Friends.

first–fruit (fûrst'frōōt') *n., usually pl.* **1** The first gatherings of a season's produce. *Ex.* xxiii 19. **2** The first outcome, effects, results, or rewards of anything.

first–hand (fûrst'hand') *adj.* Obtained direct from the origin or producer; without intermediary. **—** *adv.* Direct from the original source.

First Lady The wife of the President of the United States or if he has no wife, the lady chosen by him to be the hostess of the White House.

first papers Papers declaring intent to become a citizen of the United States: first step in the naturalization of a foreigner.

first–rate (fûrst'rāt') *adj.* Of the first or finest class, quality, or character. **—** *adv.* In a high degree; well; excellently. **— first'–rat'er** *n.*

first water 1 The finest quality and purest luster: said of gems, especially of diamonds and pearls. **2** The utmost excellence of anything.

fisc (fisk) *n.* The treasury of a state; any treasury. [< F < L *fiscus* a purse]

fis·cal (fis'kəl) *adj.* **1** Of or pertaining to the treasury or finances of a government. **2** Financial. **—** *n.* In Spain, Portugal, and some other countries in Europe, a public prosecutor.

fish (fish) *n. pl.* **fish** or (with reference to different species) **fish·es** **1** A vertebrate, cold-blooded craniate animal with permanent gills, belonging to the superclass *Pisces* in the phylum *Chordata;* adapted solely for aquatic life, it has a typically elongate, tapering body, usually covered with scales and provided with

FISH
(Anatomical features of a trout)
a Eye socket. *b* Brain case. *c* Dorsal fin. *d* Fin ray. *e* Adipose fin. *f* Caudal fin. *g* Anal fin. *h* Anus. *i* Ventral fin (also called abdominal, thoracic, or jugular, according to its deviation from normal position). *j* Ribs. *k* Pectoral fin.

fins for locomotion. **◆** Collateral adjective:

piscine. **2** Loosely, any animal habitually living in the water. **3** The flesh of a fish used as food. **4** *Naut.* **a** A strip used to strengthen or mend a spar, rail joint, etc., or to join parts. **b** An apparatus for weighing anchor; anchor tackle: also called **fish tackle.** **5** A person with fishlike characteristics, such as cold-bloodedness, stupidity, etc. **— to have other fish to fry** To have other business to do. **—** *adj.* Pertaining to, like, consisting of, or made from, fish: *fish* market, *fish* beam, *fish* glue; also, for fish: *fish* bowl, *fish* sauce. **—** *v.t.* **1** To catch or try to catch fish in (a body of water). **2** To catch or try to catch (fish, eels, etc.). **3** To search for by dragging, diving, etc. **4** To grope for and bring out: usually with *up* or *out.* **5** *Naut.* **a** To repair or strengthen by strips fastened lengthwise: to *fish* a spar. **b** To bring the flukes of (an anchor) to the gunwale or rail. **—** *v.i.* **6** To catch or try to catch fish. **7** To try to get something in an artful or indirect manner: usually with *for:* to *fish* for compliments. **— to fish or cut bait** To make a choice, as of joining or being left out of an enterprise. **— to fish out** To exhaust of fish. [OE *fisc*] **— fish'a·ble** *adj.*

fish ball A fried ball or cake made of chopped fish (often salt codfish) mixed with mashed potatoes. Also **fish cake.**

fish beam A beam cut with a downward bulge, like the belly of a fish.

fish·ber·ry (fish'ber'ē) *n. pl.* **·ber·ries** The berry of an East Indian vine (*Anamirta cocculus*), yielding picrotoxin. Also called *cocculus indicus.*

fish·bone (fish'bōn') *n.* **1** A bone of a fish. **2** *Mil.* A network of subterranean passages constructed by military engineers for purposes of defense, attack, and as listening posts close to enemy positions.

fish bowl (fish'bōl') *n.* A bowl, usually glass, serving as a small aquarium for fish.

fish crow A crow (*Corvus ossifragus*) of the Atlantic coast of the United States that feeds mainly on fish.

fish–cul·ture (fish'kul'chər) *n.* The artificial breeding of fishes; pisciculture. **— fish'–cul'-tur·ist** *n.*

fish·er (fish'ər) *n.* **1** One who fishes; a fisherman. **2** A weasel–like carnivore (*Martes pennanti*) of eastern North America, related to the martens. **3** The dark–brown fur of this animal. **◆** Homophone: *fissure.*

fish·er·man (fish'ər·mən) *n. pl.* **·men** (-mən) **1** One who catches fish; a fisher; an angler. **2** A fishing boat.

fish·er·y (fish'ər·ē) *n. pl.* **·er·ies** **1** The operation or business of catching fish; fishing industry. **2** A place for fishing. **3** *Law* The right to fish in a given place at a given time. **4** A fish–hatchery.

fish–hatch·er·y (fish'hach'ər·ē) *n. pl.* **·er·ies** A place designed for the artificial propagation, hatching, and nurture of fish.

fish hawk The osprey.

fish·ing (fish'ing) *n.* **1** The operation or the sport of catching or trying to catch fish. **2** A right of, a place for, fishing; a fishery. **◆** Collateral adjective: *piscatorial.*

fish·ing–frog (fish'ing·frog', -frôg') *n.* The angler (def. 1).

fish joint A splice made by fastening two rails together by fishplates bolted across the meeting ends.

fish ladder A chute or series of steps in a dam, covered with flowing water, to facilitate the upstream migrations of fish: also called *fishway.*

fish·meal (fish'mēl') *n.* **1** Ground dried fish: used in soups. **2** Ground fish waste: used as fertilizer.

fish·mon·ger (fish'mung'gər, -mong'-) *n.* A dealer in fish.

fish owl A large Asian or African owl (genera *Ketupa* and *Scotopelia*), feeding mostly on fish.

fish·plate (fish'plāt') *n.* One of the iron plates used in forming a fish joint.

fish·pole (fish'pōl') *n.* A long, flexible rod to which a line and hook are attached for catching fish.

fish story *Colloq.* An extravagant or incredible narrative.

fish tackle A tackle used to raise an anchor to the gunwale of a ship by means of an iron hook.

fish–tail (fish'tāl') *adj.* Like the tail of a fish in shape or in action. **—** *v.i. Aeron.* To swing the tail of an aircraft from side to side as a retarding action: also called *yaw.*

fishtail kick In swimming, a kick in which both legs are drawn up and then thrust simultaneously backward while held together.

fish–tracks (fish'traks') *n. pl. Physics* Visible trails made by the particles activated in a cloud chamber.

fish–well (fish'wel') *n.* A compartment, as in the hold of a fishing smack, open to the water beneath, used for storing live fish.

fish·wife (fish'wīf') *n. pl.* **·wives** (-wīvz') **1** A woman who sells fish. **2** An abusive virago.

fish·y (fish'ē) *adj.* **fish·i·er, fish·i·est** **1** Suggestive of, pertaining to, or like fish. **2** Abounding in fish. **3** *Colloq.* Of the nature of a fish story; incredible. **4** Vacant of expression; dull, as the eyes; lacking luster. **— fish'·i·ly** *adv.* **— fish'i·ness** *n.*

fis·sate (fis'āt) *adj.* Deeply cleft; fissured.

fissi– *combining form* Split; cleft: *fissiparous.* Also, before vowels, **fiss–.** [< L *fissus,* pp. of *findere* split]

fis·sile (fis'əl) *adj.* **1** Capable of being split or separated into layers. **2** Tending to split. [< L *fissilis* < *findere* split] **— fis·sil·i·ty** (fi·sil'ə·tē) *n.*

fis·sion (fish'ən) *n.* **1** The act of splitting or breaking apart. **2** *Biol.* Spontaneous division of a cell or organism into new cells or organisms, especially as a mode of reproduction; cell division. **3** *Physics* The disintegration of the nucleus of a radioactive atom initiated by bombardment with nucleons or gamma rays, leading to the formation of nuclei of more stable atoms and the release of energy. **4** In astrophysics, the breaking up of a large gaseous body into separate masses subject to mutual attraction: regarded as the possible origin of binary and double stars. [< L *fissio,* *-onis* < *fissus,* pp. of *findere* split] **— fis'sion·a·ble** *adj.*

fission fungus A bacterium; any member of the group *Schizomycetes* of the *Thallophyta* division of plants.

fis·si·pal·mate (fis'i·pal'māt) *adj.* Partially web–footed. **— fis'si·pal·ma'tion** *n.*

fis·sip·a·rous (fi·sip'ər·əs) *adj. Biol.* **1** Reproducing by fission. **2** Separating by fission. **— fis·sip'a·rous·ly** *adv.*

fis·si·ped (fis'i·ped) *adj.* Having the toes separated: also **fis·sip·e·dal** (fi·sip'ə·dəl, fis'i·ped'l), **fis·si·pe'di·al** (-pē'dē·əl). **—** *n. Zool.* Any of a suborder (*Fissipedia*) of terrestrial carnivores with separate toes, as cats, bears, etc. [< LL *fissipes, -pedis*]

fis·si·ros·tral (fis'i·ros'trəl) *adj. Ornithol.* Having a wide beak deeply cleft, as swifts, nighthawks, etc.

fis·sure (fish'ər) *n.* **1** A narrow opening, cleft, crevice, or furrow. **2** Cleavage. **3** *Anat.* **a** Any cleft or furrow of the body, as between the lobes of the liver or the bones of the skull. **b** One of the furrows on the surface of the brain. See synonyms under BREACH. **—** *v.t.* & *v.i.* **fis·sured, fis·sur·ing** To crack; split; cleave. **◆** Homophone: *fisher.* [< L *fissura* < *findere* split]

fist[1] (fist) *n.* **1** The hand closed tightly, as for striking; the clenched hand; also, grip, clutch. **2** *Colloq.* The hand. **3** *Colloq.* Handwriting. **4** *Printing* An index mark (☞). **—** *v.t.* **1** To strike with the fist. **2** *Naut.* To grasp with the fist. [OE *fӯst*] **— fist'ful** *n.*

fist[2] (fist) See FICE.

fist·ic (fis'tik) *adj.* Pertaining to the fist; pugilistic.

fist·i·cuff (fis'ti·kuf) *v.t. & v.i.* To beat or fight with the fist. **—** *n.* **1** A cuff with the fist. **2** *pl.* A pugilistic encounter.

fis·tu·la (fis'chōō·lə) *n. pl.* **·las** or **·lae** (-lē) **1** *Pathol.* Any abnormal opening or duct leading into a natural canal, hollow organ, or other part of the body. **2** A deep-seated suppurative inflammation, as in the withers of horses, ordinarily resulting from a bruise. **3** *Obs.* A reed or pipe. — **gastric fistula** An opening into the stomach through the abdominal wall, usually of traumatic origin. [<L, a pipe] — **fis′tu·lar** *adj.*

fis·tu·lous (fis′chŏŏ·ləs) *adj.* **1** Cylindrical and hollow like a reed. **2** Of or pertaining to a fistula. Also **fis′tu·late** (-lit, -lāt), **fis′tu·lat′ed.**

fist·wise (fist′wīz′) *adj. & adv.* Like a fist.

fit[1] (fit) *adj.* **fit·ter, fit·test 1** Adapted to an end, aim, or design; adequate; competent; qualified. **2** Conformed to a standard, suitable; appropriate. **3** In a state of preparation; ready. **4** In good physical condition and training: originally a sporting use. **5** Suitable to the person or occasion; convenient; becoming; proper. See synonyms under ADEQUATE, APPROPRIATE, BECOMING, COMPETENT, CONVENIENT, GOOD, RIPE. — *v.* **fit·ted** or **fit, fit·ting** *v.t.* **1** To be suitable for: Dark days *fit* dark deeds. **2** To be of the right size and shape for. **3** To make or alter to the proper size or purpose: to *fit* a suit. **4** To provide with what is suitable or necessary: to *fit* a ship for sea. **5** To prepare or make qualified or ready: His experience *fits* him for the position. **6** To put in place carefully or exactly: to *fit* an arrow to a bow. — *v.i.* **7** To be suitable or proper. **8** To be of the proper size, shape, etc.: This shoe *fits*. See synonyms under ADAPT, ACCOMMODATE, TEMPER. — *n.* **1** An adjustment or agreement in size, form, or the like; suitability; adaptation. **2** A making ready; preparation. **3** *Mech.* **a** A part upon which something fits snugly; specifically, that part of a car axle upon which the wheel is forced. **b** The closeness or completeness of contact in machine parts, usually classified as loose, free, medium, snug, and wringing. **4** That which fits, as a piece of clothing. [ME *fyt*; origin uncertain] — **fit′ly** *adv.* — **fit′ness** *n.* — **fit′ter** *n.*

fit[2] (fit) *n.* **1** A sudden onset of an organic or functional disorder, often attended by convulsions, as in epilepsy; spasm. **2** A sudden overmastering emotion or feeling; a mood: a *fit* of rage. **3** Impulsive and irregular exertion or action: a *fit* of industry. — **by fits (or by fits and starts)** Spasmodically; irregularly. [OE *fitt* struggle]

fit[3] (fit) *n.* **1** A song, story, or ballad. **2** A division of a ballad or song. [OE *fitt*]

fitch (fich) *n.* A fitchew or its fur. [<MDu. *vitsche* a polecat]

Fitch (fich), **John,** 1743–98, U.S. inventor; pioneer in steam navigation. — **(William) Clyde,** 1865–1909, U.S. playwright.

fitch·ew (fich′ōō) *n.* **1** The polecat of Europe. **2** The fur of this animal: also called *fitch.* Also **fitch′et** (-it), **fitch′ole** (-ōl). [<OF *fissel, fissau.* Cf. MDu. *fisse, vitsche.*]

fit·ful (fit′fəl) *adj.* Occurring in fits; marked by fits; spasmodic; capricious; unstable. See synonyms under FICKLE, IRREGULAR, IRRESOLUTE. — **fit′ful·ly** *adv.* — **fit′ful·ness** *n.*

fit·ting (fit′ing) *adj.* Fit or suitable for any purpose; proper; appropriate. — *n.* **1** The act of adjusting or connecting properly. **2** A fixture or a piece of apparatus. **3** Anything designed as an accessory to any system of working parts in a machine: usually in the plural. See synonyms under ADEQUATE, BELONGING, JUST. — **fit′ting·ly** *adv.* — **fit′ting·ness** *n.*

fit to kill *Colloq.* Excessively: He laughed *fit to kill.*

Fitz– *prefix* Son of: an element in surnames, as in *Fitzgerald*: formerly used in forming the surnames of illegitimate children of royalty. [<AF, var. of OF *fiz, filz* <L *filius* son]

five (fīv) *n.* **1** The cardinal number following four and preceding six, or any of the symbols (5, v, V) used to represent it. **2** Anything made up of five units or members, as a basketball team, or representing five, as a playing card having five spots, or a five-dollar bill. ◆ Collateral adjective: *quinary.* — *adj.* Being five. [OE *fīf*]

Five Civilized Nations or **Tribes** The Cherokee, Chickasaw, Choctaw, Creek, and Seminole tribes of Oklahoma.

five-fin·gers (fīv′fing′gərz) *n.* **1** Any of several plants, as cinquefoil, bird′s-foot trefoil, oxlip, Virginia creeper. **2** A starfish with five arms.

five·fold (fīv′fōld′) *adj.* Made up of five; five

times as much or as great; quintuplicate. — *adv.* In a fivefold manner or degree.

Five Nations Five confederated tribes of Iroquois Indians within the borders of the State of New York; namely, Mohawks, Oneidas, Onondagas, Cayugas, and Senecas. These five tribes, together with a sixth, the Tuscaroras, which returned from self-exile in 1712, formed the famous *Six Nations* of American history.

five-spot (fīv′spot′) *n.* A small delicate annual herb (*Nemophila maculata*) of the waterleaf family, with white purple-spotted flowers: common in California.

fix (fiks) *v.t.* **1** To make firm or secure; attach securely; fasten. **2** To set or direct (attention, gaze, etc.) steadily: He *fixed* his eyes on the door. **3** To look at steadily or piercingly: He *fixed* her with his eyes. **4** To attract and hold; get, as attention or regard. **5** To decide definitely; settle: The decision *fixed* his fate. **6** To decide or agree on; determine: We *fixed* a date for the next meeting. **7** To place firmly in the mind. **8** To lay, as blame or responsibility, on. **9** *U.S.* To repair. **10** To arrange or put in order; adjust, as clothing or the hair. **11** *U.S.* To make ready and cook (food or a meal). **12** *U.S. Colloq.* To arrange or influence the outcome, decision, etc., of (a race, game, jury, etc.) by bribery or collusion: to *fix* a race. **13** To prepare (specimens) for microscopic study. **14** *Chem.* To cause to form a non-volatile or solid compound. **15** *Phot.* To bathe (a film or plate) in chemicals which remove substances still sensitive to light, thus preventing fading. **16** To regulate or stabilize (wages, prices, etc.). — *v.i.* **17** To become firm or fixed. **18** *Colloq.* To intend or prepare: I′m *fixing* to go. — **to fix on** To decide upon; choose. — **to fix up** *Colloq.* **1** To repair. **2** To arrange or put in order. **3** To supply the needs of. — *n.* **1** *Colloq.* A position of embarrassment; dilemma. **2** *Naut.* A ship′s position as decided by reference to certain fixed points on shore or to astronomical observations; location. **3** On a chart or map, the point of intersection of two or more bearings, which serve to establish the position of an aircraft on its course. [<Med. L *fixare* fasten <L *fixus*, pp. of *figere* fasten] — **fix′a·ble** *adj.*

Synonyms (verb): See BIND, CONFIRM, SET, SETTLE. The best usage avoids such expressions as ″*Fix* the furniture in the room,″ ″*Fix* the books on the shelves,″ when the meaning is *set* or *arrange* them. We *fix* a statue on its pedestal, a stone in the wall. *Fix* in the sense of *repair* is a convenient American and British colloquialism, rooted in popular use. In the United States, to *fix* a thing is to do to or with it whatever is needed to make it answer its purpose; to *fix* a furnace is to put it in working order by whatever process.

fix·ate (fik′sāt) *v.t & v.i.* **·at·ed, ·at·ing 1** To render fixed; become fixed. **2** To fix or concentrate, as the eyes or attention, upon something. **3** To render constant or unchanged. **4** *Psychoanal.* To concentrate the libido on a particular object, blocking further development or new attachment. [<Med. L *fixatus*, pp. of *fixare.* See FIX.]

fix·a·tion (fik·sā′shən) *n.* **1** The act of fixing, or the state of being fixed; stability. **2** *Chem.* **a** A state of non-volatility in a chemical compound, or the entering into such a state. **b** The making permanent of a dye or color. **c** The conversion of free nitrogen from the air into useful compounds; any similar process applied to an oil or a gas. **3** *Psychoanal.* An excessive concentration of the libido on a particular object, as the exaggerated attachment of a child for one of its parents, manifested in periods of adult emotional stress in some types of psychosis or psychoneurosis. **4** A sustained focusing of the eyes upon a definite object. **5** *Bacteriol.* The prevention of hemolysis by the action of the complement.

fix·a·tive (fik′sə·tiv) *adj.* Serving to render permanent. — *n.* **1** That which serves to render permanent, as a mordant or varnish. **2** In art, a solution applied to pastel and crayon pictures to reduce fragility.

fixed (fikst) *adj.* **1** Of an established, unchanging, or permanent character; settled; lasting; stable. **2** Keeping nearly the same relative position. **3** Without days of grace: said of bills, notes, etc. **4** Attached; not loco-

motory: said of plants and certain organisms. **5** Equipped: all *fixed* for camp. **6** Settled; located: *fixed* in a new home. **7** *U.S. Colloq.* Bribed: a *fixed* jury. **8** *U.S. Colloq.* Provided with money, possessions, etc.: He′s well *fixed.* — **fix·ed·ly** (fik′sid·lē) *adv.* — **fix′ed·ness** *n.*

fixed charge A charge that cannot be changed or escaped; specifically, such a charge payable at fixed intervals.

fixed idea *Psychiatry* An obsessional idea, often delusional, which tends to influence a person′s whole attitude or mental life: also *idée fixe.*

fixed star *Astron.* A self-luminous celestial body far beyond the bounds of our solar system: so called because such bodies preserve the same relative positions as observed from the earth.

fix·ing (fik′sing) *n.* **1** The act of fastening, securing, repairing, solidifying, deciding, etc. See FIX. **2** *Phot.* The process of treating a developed picture so that it will not be changed by the further action of light. **3** *pl. U.S. Colloq.* Furnishings, ornaments, or trappings of any kind. **4** *pl. U.S. Colloq.* Foods prepared as accompaniments to a main dish.

fix·ture (fiks′chər) *n.* **1** Anything fixed firmly in its place; gas *fixtures.* **2** One who or that which is regarded as permanently fixed. **3** *Law* **a** Personal articles or chattels affixed to a freehold which may be removed by the tenant only without injury to the realty: also **movable fixtures. b** Anything affixed to a freehold of such a permanent nature as to be a legal part thereof: also **immovable fixtures.** [<FIXURE; infl. in form by *mixture*]

fix·ure (fik′shər) *n. Obs.* Fixed condition; firmness. [<LL *fixura* a fastening <L *figere* fasten]

fizz (fiz) *v.i.* To make a hissing noise. — *n.* **1** A hissing noise. **2** An effervescing beverage. **3** *Brit.* Champagne. Also **fiz.** [Imit.] — **fizz′y** *adj.*

fiz·zle (fiz′əl) *v.i.* **fiz·zled, fiz·zling 1** To make a hissing noise, as wet wood or gunpowder when burning. **2** *Colloq.* To fail, especially after a good start. — **to fizzle out** To become a failure. — *n.* **1** A spluttering; fizzing. **2** A person, an attempt, or an undertaking that fails or comes to nothing; an ignominious failure, as in a recitation. [Freq. of obs. *fise* break wind]

flab (flab) *n.* Flabby body tissue. [Back formation <FLABBY]

flab·ber·gast (flab′ər·gast) *v.t. Colloq.* To astound; confound, as by extraordinary news. [? Blend of FLABBY and AGHAST] — **flab′ber·gas·ta′tion** *n.*

flab·by (flab′ē) *adj.* **·bi·er, ·bi·est 1** Lacking muscle or healthy fiber; flaccid. **2** Lacking in moral or intellectual vigor; languid; feeble. [Var. of *flappy* <FLAP + -Y[1]] — **flab′bi·ly** *adv.* — **flab′bi·ness** *n.*

fla·bel·late (flə·bel′it, -āt) *adj. Zool.* Fanshaped: *flabellate* antennae.

flabelli– *combining form* Fan-shaped: *flabelliform.* [<L *flabellum* a fan, orig. dim. of *flabrum* a breeze <*flare* blow]

fla·bel·li·form (flə·bel′ə·fôrm) *adj.* Fan-shaped; flabellate.

fla·bel·lum (flə·bel′əm) *n. pl.* **·la** (-ə) **1** A fan, especially one used ceremonially in the Greek and Roman Catholic churches. **2** Any fanshaped structure. **3** *Anat.* A group of fibers radiating from the corpus striatum of the brain. [<L, fan]

flac·cid (flak′sid) *adj.* Lacking firmness or elasticity; having no resistance; flabby. [<F *flaccide* <L *flaccidus* <*flaccus* limp] — **flac′cid·ly** *adv.* — **flac·cid′i·ty, flac′cid·ness** *n.*

flag[1] (flag) *n.* **1** A piece of cloth commonly bearing a device and attached to a staff or halyard: used as a standard, symbol, or signal. See COLOR, ENSIGN, GUIDON, PENNANT, STANDARD. **2** The bushy part of the tail of a dog, as that of a setter. **3** *pl. Ornithol.* The long feathers on the leg of a hawk or other bird of prey; also, those on the second joint of a bird′s wing. **4** The tail of a deer. — **black flag** A flag with a black field surmounted by white skull and crossbones, traditionally flown by pirate ships: the Jolly Roger.— **Christian flag** A flag with a white field (peace) and a blue canton (sincerity), emblazoned with a red cross: adopted by most Protestant churches. — **papal flag** A yellow-and-white banner, in which the crossed keys of Saint Peter surmounted by the papal triple crown occupy the center of the white half. — **service flag** A flag with red border and white center on which one or more blue or gold stars are sewn, each representing a man or woman in or formerly in the armed forces. — *v.t.* **flagged, flag·ging** 1 To mark out or adorn with flags. 2 To signal with a flag. 3 To send (information) by signals. 4 To decoy, as deer, by or as by waving a flag. — **to flag down** To cause to stop, as a train, by signaling with a flag or with a waving motion. [? <FLAG[2]] — **flag'ger** *n.* — **flag'gy** *adj.*

flag[2] (flag) *n.* 1 One of various monocotyledonous plants of the genus *Iris*, having sword-shaped leaves and growing in moist places; especially, the **yellow flag** of Europe (*I. pseudacorus*) and the common **blue flag** (*I. versicolor*) of the United States, the State flower of Tennessee. 2 The leaf of a flag. — *v.t.* **flagged, flag·ging** To calk the seams of (a cask) with flags or rushes. [Cf. Du. *vlag* iris]

flag[3] (flag) *v.i.* **flagged, flag·ging** 1 To grow spiritless or languid; become tired or weak. 2 To hang down; become limp. [? < obs. *flack* flutter; infl. by OF *flaquir* droop < *flac* droopy <L *flaccus*]

flag[4] (flag) *n.* Split stone for paving; a flagstone. — *v.t.* **flagged, flag·ging** To pave with flagstones. [<ON *flaga* slab of stone. Akin to FLAKE.] — **flag'ger** *n.*

Flag Day A holiday commemorating the day, June 14, 1777, on which Congress proclaimed the Stars and Stripes the national standard of the United States.

flag·el·lant (flaj'ə·lənt, flə·jel'ənt) *n.* A zealot given to whipping or scourging himself, to secure pardon from sin: also **flag'el·la·tor**. — *adj.* Using a scourge; scourging; practicing flagellation. [<L *flagellans, -antis*, ppr. of *flagellare* scourge <*flagellum* a whip]

flag·el·late (flaj'ə·lāt) *v.t.* **·lat·ed, ·lat·ing** To whip; scourge. — *adj.* Biol. 1 Having or producing flagella or whiplike processes, or runnerlike branches. 2 Shaped like a flagellum. Also **flag'el·lat'ed** *adj.* [<L *flagellatus*, pp. of *flagellare*. See FLAGELLANT.]

flag·el·la·tion (flaj'ə·lā'shən) *n.* 1 A scourging, specifically as an incitement of abnormal sexual desire. 2 A massaging by strokes or blows. 3 Self-scourging as a means of religious discipline. 4 *Biol.* The development of flagella by certain protozoan organisms.

fla·gel·lum (flə·jel'əm) *n.* *pl.* **·la** (-ə) 1 *Biol.* A lashlike appendage, as the terminal part of an antenna in insects, or the mobile process of a protozoan. 2 A scourge. [<L, whip]

flag·eo·let (flaj'ə·let') *n.* 1 A musical instrument resembling the flute, but blown at the end instead of at the side. It usually has six finger holes and a mouthpiece with a fipple.

FLAGEOLET

2 An organ stop. [<F, dim. of OF *flageol*; ult. origin uncertain]

flag·ging[1] (flag'ing) *adj.* Growing weak; becoming languid or exhausted; failing; drooping.

flag·ging[2] (flag'ing) *n.* 1 A pavement of flagstones; flagstones collectively. 2 The act of paving with flagstones.

fla·gi·tious (flə·jish'əs) *adj.* 1 Flagrantly wicked; atrocious; heinous. 2 Guilty of extraordinary vice; extremely criminal. See synonyms under CRIMINAL, FLAGRANT. [<L *flagitiosus* <*flagitium* disgraceful act] — **fla·gi'tious·ly** *adv.* — **fla·gi'tious·ness** *n.*

flag·on (flag'ən) *n.* 1 A vessel with a handle and a spout, and often having a hinged lid, used to serve liquors at table. 2 A large wine bottle. [<OF *flacon, flascon* <Med. L *flasco, -onis* <Gmc.]

fla·gran·cy (flā'grən·sē) *n.* *pl.* **·cies** Notoriousness; heinousness. Also **fla'grance**.

fla·grant (flā'grənt) *adj.* 1 Openly scandalous; notorious; heinous. 2 *Obs.* Burning; blazing; also, raging. [<L *flagrans, -antis*, ppr. of *flagrare* blaze, burn] — **fla'grant·ly** *adv.*

Synonyms: atrocious, disgraceful, enormous, flagitious, heinous, monstrous, nefarious, outrageous, scandalous, shameful, shocking. **Antonyms**: see synonyms for EXCELLENT.

flag·ship (flag'ship') *n.* The ship in a naval formation that carries a flag officer and displays his flag. See FLAG OFFICER.

flag·smut (flag'smut') *n.* A disease of wheat, caused by the smut fungus *Ustilago tritici* affecting the leaves and culms.

Flag·staff (flag'staf, -stäf) A city in north central Arizona.

flag station A station on a railway at which a train stops only on signal. Also **flag stop**.

flag·stone (flag'stōn') *n.* 1 A broad, flat stone suitable for pavements. 2 Any fine-grained rock from which such slabs may be split. [<FLAG[4] + STONE]

flail (flāl) *n.* 1 An implement consisting of a wooden bar (the swingle) hinged or tied to a handle, for separating grain by beating. 2 A medieval weapon with spiked iron swingle. — *v.t. & v.i.* To beat with or as with a flail; use a flail; thresh. [OE *flygel*, prob. <L *flagellum* a whip]

FLAIL (def. 2)

flail joint *Pathol.* A disorder characterized by excessive mobility of a limb, usually after resection of a joint.

flair (flâr) *n.* 1 Discernment; talent; aptitude. 2 Inclination; fondness; strong liking. 3 *Colloq.* A showy or dashing style: to wear clothes with *flair*. [<OF <*flairer* smell, ult. <L *fragrare*]

flak (flak) *n.* 1 Anti-aircraft fire. 2 *U.S. Colloq.* Criticism: political *flak*. [<G *fl(ieger)* aircraft + *a(bwehr)* defense + *k(anonen)* guns]

flake[1] (flāk) *n.* 1 A small flat fragment or loosely cohering mass; a thin piece or chip of anything; scale; fleck. 2 A carnation having stripes of any single color on a white ground. 3 A gleam of light; flash. 4 *Naut.* The flat coil of a stowed cable; a fake. — *adj. Anthropol.* Denoting that form of Paleolithic stone implement shaped from the thin flakes chipped off the core of a large lump. — *v.t. & v.i.* **flaked, flak·ing** 1 To peel off in flakes. 2 To form into flakes. 3 To spot or become spotted with flakes. [ME <Scand. Akin to FLAG[4].]

flake[2] (flāk) *n.* 1 A light staging or platform for drying fish. 2 A flap on a saddle to keep the rider's knee from the horse. [<ON *flaki* hurdle]

flake[3] (flāk) *v.* **flaked, flak·ing** *Slang v.i.* 1 To retire or go to sleep, as from exhaustion: usually with *out*. — *v.t.* 2 To fatigue; exhaust: usually with *out*.

flak·ing (flā'king) *n.* 1 The operation of making flint flakes by chipping, as for gunlocks. 2 The breaking away of small bits of paint or plaster from covered surfaces.

flak·y (flā'kē) *adj.* **flak·i·er, flak·i·est** Resembling or consisting of flakes; easily separable into flakes. — **flak'i·ly** *adv.* — **flak'i·ness** *n.*

flam·boy·ant (flam·boi'ənt) *adj.* 1 Characterized by extravagance; showy; bombastic. 2 Bursting into flame; blazing. 3 Having a wavy edge, as of flame. [<F, ppr. of *flamboyer* <OF *flambeiier* <*flambe* FLAME] — **flam·boy'ance, flam·boy'an·cy** *n.* — **flam·boy'ant·ly** *adv.*

flamboyant architecture A highly florid style of French Gothic architecture.

flame (flām) *n.* 1 A stream of vapor or gas made luminous by heat; gas or vapor in combustion. 2 An appearance or color like that of a blaze; glow; brilliancy; a red-yellow color, called **flame-scarlet**.

FLAMBOYANT ARCHITECTURE

---

3 Excitement, as from rage, strife, or passionate desire. 4 An ardent affection; passionate love. 5 *Slang* A sweetheart. See synonyms under FIRE, LIGHT[1]. — *v.* **flamed, flam·ing** *v.i.* 1 To give out flame; blaze; burn. 2 To light up or burn as if on fire; flash: His face *flamed* with rage. 3 To become enraged or excited (with anger, indignation, etc.): He *flamed* with indignation. — *v.t.* 4 To subject to heat or fire. 5 *Obs.* To inflame; excite. See synonyms under BURN. [<OF *flamme, flambe* <L *flamma* a flame] — **flam'ing** *adj.* — **flam'ing·ly** *adv.*

flame arc An electric arc produced and maintained between two carbons impregnated with mineral salts.

fla·men·co (flə·meng'kō, -men'-, flä-) *n.* A style of singing and dancing practiced by the Gipsies of Andalusia; also, a song or dance in this style. [<Sp., Flemish, because the Gipsies were thought to be from Flanders]

flame-throw·er (flām'thrō'ər) *n.* *Mil.* A weapon that throws a stream of burning napalm or other gasoline mixture.

fla·min·go (flə·ming'gō) *n.* *pl.* **·gos** or **·goes** A long-necked, small-bodied wading bird (genus *Phoenicopterus*) of a pink or red color, having very long legs, webbed feet, and a bent bill. [<Pg. *flamingo* or Sp. *flamenco*, ult. <L *flamma* flame + Gmc. *-enc* -ING[3]]

FLAMINGO

flam·ma·ble (flam'ə·bəl) *adj.* Combustible; inflammable.

flam·y (flā'mē) *adj.* **flam·i·er, flam·i·est** Relating to, composed of, or resembling flame.

flan (flan, *Fr.* flän) *n.* 1 A piece of metal ready to be made into a coin by receiving the stamp or the die; a blank. 2 A tart filled with cheese, cream, or fruit; also a custard or soufflé. [<F]

flange (flanj) *n.* 1 A spreading or flaring part. 2 A projecting rim or edge, as on a car wheel, a section of pipe, length of shafting, etc. 3 A tool used to shape flanges. — *v.* **flanged, flang·ing** *v.t.* To supply with a flange. — *v.i.* To have or take the form of a flange. [Prob. <OF *flangir* bend]

flank (flangk) *n.* 1 The hinder part of an animal's side, between the ribs and the hip. See illustration under HORSE. 2 *Entomol.* The side of an insect's thorax; the pleura. 3 The side, or the lateral portion or anything, especially of a military or naval force, or of a marching column. 4 That part of a bastion between the curtain and the face, or any part of a fortification that defends another work by a fire along its face; also, the lateral part of a fortification. See illustration under BASTION. — **by the right** or **left flank** A drill command preparatory to the marching maneuver in which every marcher makes a 90-degree turn to the right or left. — *v.t.* 1 To stand or be on one or both sides of. 2 *Mil.* **a** To get around and in back of (an enemy position or unit); turn the flank of. **b** To attack or threaten the flank of. **c** To guard the flank of (a friendly position or unit). — *adj.* 1 Pertaining to the flank or side. 2 Cut from the side, or situated at the side: a *flank* steak. 3 Coming from or toward the side: a *flank* attack. [<F *flanc* <Gmc.]

flan·nel (flan'əl) *n.* 1 A loosely-woven fabric of cotton, or of cotton and wool, with soft, naplike surface. 2 Plain cloth in the first stage of manufacture. 3 *pl.* Clothing made of flannel. — *v.t.* **·neled** or **·nelled, ·nel·ing** or **·nel·ling** To wrap in or rub with flannel. [Prob. <Welsh *gwlanen* flannel <*gwlan* wool] — **flan'nel·ly** *adj.*

flap (flap) *n.* 1 A broad, limber, and loosely hanging part or attachment. 2 The act of flapping. 3 An implement for brushing away flies. 4 *Surg.* A piece of skin or flesh cut away except at its base. 5 The flapping tongue of a valve. 6 *pl.* A disease of the lips of horses. 7 *Aeron.* A movable hinged

---

section along the rear or trailing edge of a wing of an airplane, used to increase drag. **8** *Slang* An agitated or tempestuous reaction. [< *v.*] — *v.* **flapped, flap·ping** *v.t.* **1** To move by beating: to *flap* the wings. **2** To move with a flapping sound. **3** To strike with something flat and flexible. — *v.i.* **4** To beat the wings or move by beating the wings. **5** To move to and fro, as if blown by the wind. **6** *Slang* To lose one's composure. [Imit.]

flap·jack (flap'jak') *n.* A griddle cake.

flap·per (flap'ər) *n.* **1** One who or that which flaps or slaps, or calls attention. **2** A young bird unable to fly. **3** A flipper. **4** *Colloq.* A young girl, especially in the 1920's, given to exaggerated styles and to sophisticated conduct.

flare (flâr) *v.* **flared, flar·ing** *v.i.* **1** To blaze or burn with a brilliant, wavering light, as a candle in the wind. **2** To break out in sudden or violent emotion: often with *up* or *out*. **3** To open or spread outward: A ship's bows *flare.* — *v.t.* **4** To cause to flare. **5** To signal (information) with flares. — *n.* **1** A large, bright, but unsteady and flickering light; unsteady glare. **2** A widening or spreading outward, as of the sides of a funnel. Compare illustrations under FUNNEL. **3** *Phot.* Unwanted light falling on the image plane in a camera projector or printer due to reflection of light between the lens surface or the interior of the lens barrel. **4** A brilliant burst of flame or light used as a signal or guide or as illumination. **5** Any sudden display, as of temper. See synonyms under LIGHT. [? Blend of FLY[1] and BARE[1]]

flash (flash) *v.i.* **1** To break forth with light or fire suddenly and briefly: Lightning *flashed* across the sky. **2** To gleam; glisten: Their helmets *flashed* in the sun. **3** To be in view fleetingly; move very quickly: A train *flashed* by. **4** To come suddenly; be known or perceived in an instant: The memory *flashed* into my mind. **5** *Colloq.* To make a display. — *v.t.* **6** To send forth (fire, light, etc.) in brief flashes; cause to flash: His sword *flashed* fire in the sun. **7** To send or communicate with great speed: to *flash* news. **8** *Colloq.* To show or display briefly or ostentatiously: to *flash* a badge. **9** In glassmaking: **a** To cover with a thin coating of colored glass. **b** To apply (colored glass) as a coating. See synonyms under BURN[1]. — *n.* **1** A sudden and transient blaze; gleam. **2** A sudden outburst, as of wit, anger, etc. **3** A moment; instant. **4** Display; pomp; specifically, a vulgar display. **5** The coating of glass which is flashed upon other glass. **6** A mixture of capsicum, caramel, etc.: used in adulterating liquors. **7** A reservoir and sluiceway in a stream for storing water to float boats over a shoal. **8** A brief news dispatch sent right after the event, usually as a preliminary to fuller coverage. **9** *Archaic* Thieves' jargon. See synonyms under LIGHT[1]. — **a flash in the pan 1** An explosion of the powder in the pan of a flintlock that does not discharge the weapon. **2** Hence, any abortive attempt, or weak outburst. — *adj.* **1** Obtained by flashlight, as a photograph. **2** Flashy; smart; sporty. **3** *Archaic* Of, pertaining to, or used by thieves: *flash* slang. [ME *flaschen*; prob. imit.]

flash·back (flash'bak') *n.* **1** In fiction, drama, motion pictures, etc., a break in continuity made by the presentation of a scene, episode, or event occurring earlier. **2** The scene, episode, or event so presented.

flash flood A sudden, rushing flood of short duration.

flash·ing (flash'ing) *n.* **1** The act of one who flashes, in any sense. **2** A reheating of imperfectly formed glassware. **3** The twirling of a hollow globe of heated glass to spread it into a flat disk. **4** The fusing of a thin coating of colored glass on plain glass. **5** A lap joint, or a turned-up flange, usually of metal, to keep a roof watertight at an angle or where it joins a chimney, etc. **6** The act of flushing, as a stream or sewer. **7** The operation of perfecting the vacuum in a lamp bulb or vacuum tube by suddenly increasing the voltage passing through the filaments or

FLASHING
a, b. Parts of a lap joint.

cathode. — *adj.* Emitting flashes. — **flash'-ing·ly** *adv.*

flash·light (flash'līt') *n.* **1** *U.S.* A light, as in a lighthouse, shown only at regular intervals. **2** A brief and brilliant light for taking photographs. **3** A small portable electric light. Also **flash light.**

flash·o·ver (flash'ō'vər) *n. Electr.* A disruptive leakage of current through or around an insulator.

flash point The lowest temperature at which the vapors of petroleum or other combustible liquids will give a flash or slight explosion on exposure to a flame.

flash spectrum *Astron.* In a total eclipse of the sun, the instantaneous emission of bright lines in the spectrum of the chromosphere at the moment of totality.

flask (flask, fläsk) *n.* **1** A small bottle or similar vessel. **2** A small container, often of metal, for carrying liquids or liquor on the person. **3** A metal or horn vessel used by hunters to carry gunpowder. **4** A thin long-necked glass bottle covered with straw, as for oil. **5** A frame for holding a founding mold. **6** Any of variously shaped receptacles of glass or other material, used in laboratory work. **7** The commercial unit for the measurement and sale of mercury, equal to 76 pounds. **8** The iron container in which mercury is sold. [<F *flasque* <Med. L *flasca,* var. of *flasco.* See FLAGON.]

flat[1] (flat) *adj.* **flat·ter, flat·test 1** Having a surface that is a horizontal plane, or nearly so; level; without unevenness or inclination. **2** Without prominences or depressions; not curved or round or uneven: a *flat* country. **3** Lying prone upon the ground; prostrate; hence, overthrown; ruined. **4** Not qualified or softened in any way; positive; absolute: a *flat* refusal. **5** Deficient in distinctness, form, or interesting qualities; monotonous; stupid; tasteless; dull; insipid: a *flat* sermon, a *flat* market, *flat* wine. **6** *Music* Below pitch; minor or diminished: a *flat* third; having flats in the signature: a *flat* key. **7** *Phonet.* **a** Designating the vowel sound in *man,* as opposed to the sound in *calm.* **b** Of consonants, voiced; opposed to *sharp.* **8** Without gloss, as a painted surface. **9** Uniform in tint. **10** Lacking in contrast; without distinguishing light and shadow: an effect often aimed at in mural-painting. **11** Of a golf club, having the head set at a very obtuse angle to the shaft. **12** *Gram.* Having no inflectional or distinguishing ending or mark, as an adverb not ending in *-ly,* or a noun used as an adjective without the addition of a characterizing suffix, as in such expressions as to breathe *deep,* the *sister* arts, etc. **13** Not varying with changing conditions; uniform: a *flat* rate. **14** Wanting in tonal quality: said of a sound or accent. — *adv.* **1** In a level state or position; so as to be flat; flatly. **2** *Music* Below the true pitch. **3** In finance, without interest. **4** Exactly; precisely: used of amounts, distances, and the like: It weighed ten pounds *flat.* — *n.* **1** A plane surface; a level. **2** Low meadowland over which the tide flows, never completely submerged by water: used for pasturage or planting. **3** Shoal: commonly in the plural. **4** Anything that is flat; the flat side of a thing. **5** *Music* A tone a half step lower than a tone from which it is named, represented by the character ♭. **6** A strip of high, level land. **7** An oblong wooden frame covered with canvas; a unit of a box-set of stage scenery. **8** A platform car. **9** A flat-bottomed boat, used for transporting heavy cargoes; a flatboat. **10** A deflated automobile tire. **11** A shallow, earth-filled tray for earlier seed germination to advance the flowering period. — *v.* **flat·ted, flat·ting** *v.t.* **1** To make flat. **2** *Music* To lower (a tone) in playing or composing, especially by a semitone. — *v.i.* **3** To become flat. **4** *Music* To sing or play below pitch. [ON *flatr*] — **flat'ly** *adv.* — **flat'ness** *n.*

Synonyms (adj.): absolute, characterless, downright, dull, empty, even, horizontal, insipid, level, lifeless, mawkish, pointless, spiritless, stupid, tame, vapid.

flat[2] (flat) *n.* **1** A set of rooms on one floor, for the occupancy of a family; apartment. **2** A house containing such flats. [Var. of obs. *flet,* a floor OE *flet;* infl. by FLAT[1]]

flat·boat (flat'bōt') *n.* A large boat with a flat

bottom much in use on rivers for freighting merchandise: also *flat.* Also **flat'bot'tom** (-bot'əm).

flat car A railroad freight car, usually without sides or covering; a platform car. Also *flat.*

flat·fish (flat'fish') *n. pl.* **·fish** or **·fish·es** Any of an order (*Heterosomata*) of fishes having a compressed body with unsymmetrical sides and with both eyes on one side, as the flounder, halibut, sole, etc.

flat·foot (flat'fŏŏt') *n.* **1** *Pathol.* The deformed condition of a foot caused by a falling of the arch. **2** *pl.* **flat·feet** *Slang* A policeman.

flat foot A foot having a flat sole.

flat–foot·ed (flat'fŏŏt'id) *adj.* **1** Having flat feet. **2** Uncompromising; resolute; positive. — **flat'–foot'ed·ly** *adv.*

flat·i·ron (flat'ī'ərn) *n.* An iron with a smooth, polished surface for smoothing cloth by the action of heat and pressure.

flat knot A reef knot.

flat silver Silver spoons, knives, forks, etc., collectively, as distinguished from silver bowls, pitchers, goblets, etc.

flat·ten (flat'n) *v.t. & v.i.* **1** To make or become flat or flatter. **2** To make or become prostrate. — **to flatten out 1** To make or become flat or flatter. **2** *Aeron.* To change or become changed in angle of flight so as to fly horizontally, as after diving or climbing. — **flat'ten·er** *n.*

flat·ter[1] (flat'ər) *v.t.* **1** To praise unduly or insincerely. **2** To try to win over or gain the favor of by flattery. **3** To play upon the hopes or vanity of; beguile. **4** To please or gratify: She *flattered* me by saying "Yes." **5** To represent too favorably: The picture *flatters* her. — *v.i.* **6** To use flattery. See synonyms under CARESS, PRAISE, PUFF. — **to flatter oneself** To believe: I *flatter* myself that my gifts are acceptable. [<OF *flater* fawn, caress. Akin to FLAT[1].] — **flat'ter·er** *n.* — **flat'ter·ing** *adj.* — **flat'ter·ing·ly** *adv.*

flat·ter[2] (flat'ər) *n.* **1** One who or that which flattens. **2** A flat–holed drawplate through which watch springs, skirt wire, etc., are drawn. **3** A flat–faced hammer used by blacksmiths.

flat·ter·y (flat'er·ē) *n. pl.* **·ter·ies 1** The act or practice of the flatterer. **2** Undue or insincere compliment; adulation. See synonyms under PRAISE. [<OF *flaterie* <*flater* fawn, caress]

flat–top (flat'top') *n.* A U.S. naval aircraft-carrier.

FLAT–TOP — AN AIRCRAFT-CARRIER

flat·u·lence (flach'ə·ləns, -yŏŏ-) *n.* **1** The accumulation of gas in the stomach and bowels. **2** Windiness; vanity. Also **flat'u·len·cy.** [<F, ult. <L *flatus* a blowing <*flare* blow] — **flat'u·lent, flat'u·ous** *adj.* — **flat'u·lent·ly** *adv.*

fla·tus (flā'təs) *n. pl.* **·tus·es 1** A breath; puff of wind. **2** Windiness; wind or gas in the stomach or bowels. **3** The condition of being puffed out with wind; inflation. [<L <*flare* blow]

flat·ware (flat'wâr') *n.* **1** Dishes that are more or less flat, as plates and saucers, taken collectively: distinguished from *holloware.* **2** Table utensils, as knives, forks, and spoons.

flat·worm (flat'wûrm') *n.* Any flat-bodied worm, as a tapeworm, fluke, planarian, etc.

flaunt (flônt) *v.i.* **1** To make an ostentatious or gaudy display; parade impudently: to *flaunt* through the streets. **2** To wave or flutter freely. — *v.t.* **3** To show or display in an ostentatious or impudent manner. — *n.* **1** The act of flaunting. **2** A boast; vaunt. [ME

flant <Scand. Cf. Norw. *flanta* gad about.]
— **flaunt′er** *n.*
  Synonyms (verb): boast, display, exhibit, flourish, flutter, parade, vaunt, wave.

flaunt·ing (flôn′ting) *adj.* Making a parade or ostentatious display; jaunty and gay. Also **flaunt′y.** — **flaunt′ing·ly** *adv.*

flau·tist (flô′tist) *n.* One who plays the flute; a flutist.

fla·ves·cent (flə·ves′ənt) *adj.* Turning yellow; yellowish. [<L *flavescens, -entis,* ppr. of *flavescere* become yellow <*flavus* yellow]

fla·vin (flā′vin) *n.* 1 *Biochem.* One of a group of yellow pigments widely distributed in plant and animal tissues and constituting an important element of the vitamin B₂ complex, as ribo*flavin.* 2 Quercetin. [<L *flavus* yellow + -IN]

fla·vism (flā′viz·əm) *n.* The condition or state of being yellow.

fla·vo·pur·pu·rin (flā′vō·pûr′pyə·rin) *n.* *Chem.* A crystalline coal-tar dye, C₁₄H₈O₅, isomeric with purpurin and similar to alizarin except that it produces colors with a yellowish tinge. [<L *flavus* yellow + PURPURIN]

fla·vor (flā′vər) *n.* 1 The quality of a thing as affecting the sense of taste or the senses of taste and smell; odor; scent. 2 The characteristic taste of a thing, especially if pleasant. 3 Distinctive quality or characteristic: the *flavor* of speech. 4 Flavoring. — *v.t.* To give flavor or any distinguishing quality to. Also, *Brit.,* **fla′vour.** [<OF *flaor, fleur,* prob. ult. <L *flare* blow; *v* added on analogy with *savor*] — **fla′vor·y** *adj.*

fla·vor·ing (flā′vər·ing) *n.* A substance, as an essence or extract, for giving a flavor to anything.

fla·vous (flā′vəs) *adj.* Nearly pure yellow.

flaw¹ (flô) *n.* 1 An inherent defect, as in construction or constitution; especially, a defect that destroys or impairs strength, force, or legal validity; weak spot. 2 A crack; fissure: a *flaw* in a casting. See synonyms under BLEMISH, BREACH. — *v.t. & v.i.* To make flaws in; become cracked or defective. [? <ON *flaga* slab of stone] — **flaw′less** *adj.* — **flaw′less·ness** *n.* — **flaw′less·ly** *adv.*

flaw² (flô) *n.* 1 A sudden squall of wind; a transient but violent windstorm. 2 *Obs.* A tumult. [Prob. <ON *flaga* gust]

flax (flaks) *n.* 1 An annual plant (genus *Linum*) with stems about two feet high and blue flowers, having a mucilaginous seed, called *flaxseed* or *linseed,* and an inner bark which yields the flax of commerce. 2 The soft fiber obtained from the bark of the flax plant, used in the manufacture of linen. 3 Any plant resembling flax. — *v.t. & v.i.* To beat or thrash. — **to flax around** *U.S. Colloq.* To stir about busily. — **to flax out** *U.S. Colloq.* 1 To knock out; beat, as in a fight. 2 To become fatigued or exhausted. [OE *fleax*]

FLAX

flax·en (flak′sən) *adj.* 1 Of, pertaining to, or made of flax. 2 Like flax. 3 Of a light golden color.

flax·seed (flaks′sēd′, flak′-) *n.* 1 The mucilaginous seed borne by the common flax; linseed: used medicinally for soothing and softening. 2 A low European herb of the flax family, having similar seed vessels.

flax·wort (flaks′wûrt) *n.* Any plant of the flax family (*Linaceae*).

flay (flā) *v.t.* 1 To strip off the skin from, as by flogging. 2 To pillage; rob. 3 To attack with scathing criticism. [OE *flēan*] — **flay′er** *n.*

flea (flē) *n.* 1 A wingless insect (order *Siphonaptera*), parasitic upon a mammal or a bird, and having a compressed body, limbs adapted for leaping, and a head armed with piercing mandibles and a suctorial proboscis. For illustration see under INSECT (injurious). ◆ Collateral adjective: *pulicene.* 2 One of several small beetles or crustaceans that jump like fleas, as a beach flea or sand hopper. ◆ Homophone: *flee.* [OE *flēa.* Akin to FLEE.] — **a flea in one's** (or **the**) **ear** A warning; cau-

tion; sometimes, an irritating reply or rebuff.

fleam (flēm) *n.* 1 A surgeon's lancet. 2 The angle made by the cutting edge of a saw tooth with the plane of the blade. [<OF *flieme,* ult. <LL *flebotomum* <Gk. *phlebotomon.* See PHLEBOTOMY.]

flea market A market, often outdoors, for the sale of a wide assortment of old or second-hand articles, antiques, etc.

flea·wort (flē′wûrt) *n.* 1 A European plant (genus *Inula*) of the composite family: a reputed repellent of fleas. 2 A plant (*Plantago psyllium*) of the plantain family, whose seeds are used medicinally.

flèche (flesh) *n. Archit.* Any spire; more particularly, one over the intersection of the nave and transepts. [<F, lit., arrow]

fleck (flek) *n.* 1 A dot or speck; a spot; dapple. — *v.t.* To mark with spots or flecks. [Cf. ON *flekkr* spot] — **fleck′less** *adj.* — **fleck′y** *adj.*

flec·tion (flek′shən) *n.* 1 The act of bending or turning. 2 A curved or bent part. 3 A turning as of the eye; glance; cast. 4 *Anat.* Flexion. 5 *Gram.* Inflection. Also, for defs. 1–3, *Brit. flexion.* [<L *flexio, -onis* <*flectere* bend]

fled (fled) Past tense and past participle of FLEE¹.

fledge (flej) *v.* **fledged, fledg·ing** *v.t.* 1 To furnish with feathers, as an arrow. 2 To bring up (a young bird) until ready for flight. — *v.i.* 3 To grow enough feathers for flight. [<obs. *fledge* ready to fly, ME *flegge,* OE *-flycge* in *unflycge* not ready to fly]

fledg·ling (flej′ling) *n.* 1 A young bird just fledged. 2 A tyro; an inexperienced person. Also **fledge′ling.**

fledg·y (flej′ē) *adj.* **fledg·i·er, fledg·i·est** Feathery; downy; feathered.

flee¹ (flē) *v.* **fled, flee·ing** *v.i.* 1 To run away, as from danger, harm, or enemies. 2 To move away quickly; disappear. 3 To move swiftly; leave abruptly. — *v.t.* 4 To run away from; avoid or try to avoid. 5 To leave or go away from abruptly: to *flee* the country. See synonyms under ESCAPE, FLY¹. ◆ Homophone: *flea.* [OE *flēon.* Akin to FLEA.]

flee² (flē, flā) *Scot. v.t. & v.i.* To fly; let fly. — *n.* A fly: also spelled *flie.*

fleece (flēs) *n.* 1 The coat of wool covering a sheep. 2 The entire coat of wool sheared from a sheep. 3 Anything resembling a fleece in quality or appearance. 4 A textile fabric with a soft silky pile, used for linings, etc.; also, the nap. 5 Meat from the ribs of buffalo. 6 Bear fat, used as food. — *v.t.* **fleeced, fleec·ing** 1 To shear the fleece from. 2 To swindle; defraud. 3 To cover or fleck as with fleece. [OE *flēos*] — **fleece′a·ble** *adj.*

fleer (flir) *v.t.* To jeer at; deride. — *v.i.* To laugh or grin coarsely or scornfully; sneer. — *n.* 1 Derision or scorn. 2 A leer. [Prob. <Scand. Cf. Norw. *flira* laugh, grin.] — **fleer′ing** *adj.* — **fleer′ing·ly** *adv.*

fleet¹ (flēt) *v.i.* 1 To move swiftly. 2 *Naut.* To change place; shift. 3 *Archaic* To fade. 4 *Obs.* To float. — *v.t.* 5 *Rare* To cause to pass quickly; while away. 6 *Naut.* To change the position of, as a cable. — *adj.* 1 Moving, or capable of moving, swiftly; rapid; swift; nimble. 2 Passing; evanescent. 3 *Brit. Dial.* Thin; shallow. [OE *flēotan* float] — **fleet′ly** *adv.* — **fleet′ness** *n.*

fleet² (flēt) *n.* 1 A number of vessels in company or under one command; especially ships of war. 2 The entire number of vessels belonging to one government; a navy. 3 The number of vessels in one command: the Pacific *fleet.* 4 A number of vessels, aircraft, or vehicles, collectively, engaged in the same activity, or operated as a unit: a fishing *fleet,* a *fleet* of trucks. [OE *flēot* ship]

fleet·ing (flē′ting) *adj.* Passing quickly; transitory. See synonyms under TRANSIENT.

Flem·ish (flem′ish) *adj.* Of or pertaining to Flanders, its people, literature, or language. — *n.* 1 Flemings collectively: with the definite article. 2 The language of Flanders, belonging to the Low German branch of the Germanic languages. [<MDu. *Vlaemisch*]

flense (flens) *v.t.* **flensed, flens·ing** To strip the blubber or the skin from, as a whale or a seal.

Also **flench** (flench). [<Dan. *flense*] — **flens′er** *n.*

flesh (flesh) *n.* 1 The portion of an animal body that consists of the softer tissues; especially, the muscular part of the body, but the fats being often included: distinguished from the fluids, bones, and integuments. 2 Animal food or meat as distinguished from vegetable; in a restricted sense, the meat of mammals and birds as distinguished from fish. 3 The material part of man as distinguished from the spiritual; the body as opposed to the soul. 4 Mankind in general; the human race. 5 In Scriptural and theological use, human nature; specifically, the carnal nature of man as affected with evil inclinations. 6 Desire for the gratification of sensual passions. 7 *Poetic* Kind-heartedness; gentleness of nature. 8 The outer appearance or color of a person's body: a man of dark *flesh.* 9 Animal life as a whole. 10 The soft, pulpy parts of fruits and vegetables, as distinguished from skin, etc. 11 The color of the skin of a white person; flesh-colored. 12 Kin; family stock. — **in the flesh** 1 In person. 2 Alive. — **own flesh and blood** One's own family, relations, or descendants. — *v.t.* 1 To plunge, as a sword, into the flesh, especially for the first time. 2 To inure or initiate, as troops, by giving a first experience of warfare. 3 To incite, as hawks for hunting, with a first experience of killing. 4 To scrape the flesh from, as a hide. 5 To invest or pad out with flesh. 6 To make fat or fleshy. — *v.i.* 7 To become fat or fleshy. — **flesh out** To give substance or the appearance of reality to; develop fully: to *flesh out* an idea. [OE *flǣsc*]

flesh·er (flesh′ər) *n.* 1 One who strips the flesh from hides; also, an instrument used for this. 2 *Scot.* A butcher.

flesh fly A carnivorous dipterous insect (genus *Sarcophaga*) that deposits its eggs or larvae in animal matter.

flesh·i·ness (flesh′ē·nis) *n.* Plumpness; corpulence.

flesh·mon·ger (flesh′mung′gər, -mong′-) *n.* 1 A dealer in meat; butcher. 2 A procurer.

flesh wound A superficial wound not injuring the bones or vital organs.

flesh·y (flesh′ē) *adj.* **flesh·i·er, flesh·i·est** 1 Having much flesh; plump; corpulent; fat. 2 Pertaining to flesh or to carnal nature; composed of flesh. 3 Consisting of firm pulp; succulent, as a peach or an apple.

fletch (flech) *v.t.* To provide with feathers, as arrows; fledge. [Alter. of FLEDGE; infl. by *fletcher*]

Fletch·er·ism (flech′ə·riz′əm) *n.* 1 The doctrine that perfect health requires complete mastication of food. 2 The practice of this doctrine. [after Horace *Fletcher,* 1849–1919, U.S. dietician]

Fletsch·horn (flech′hôrn) A peak in southern Switzerland; 13,121 feet.

fleur-de-lis (flœr′də·lē′, -lēs′) *n. pl.* **fleurs-de-lis** (-də·lēz′) 1 The iris. 2 A heraldic device, the bearing of the former royal family of France. Also **fleur′-de-lys′.** [<F, flower of lily]

fleured (flœrd) *adj.* Decorated with fleurs-de-lis.

FLEUR-DE-LIS

fleu·ry (floo′rē) *adj. Her.* Terminating in the three leaves of, or strewed with, the fleur-de-lis; specifically, tipped with a fleur-de-lis: said of the arms of a cross. For illustration see under CROSS.

flew¹ (floo) See FLUE¹.

flew² (floo) Past tense of FLY¹.

flews (flooz) *n. pl.* The large chops or hanging parts of the upper lip of certain dogs: term used especially of hounds. See illustration under DOG. [Origin unknown] — **flewed** *adj.*

flex (fleks) *v.t. & v.i.* 1 To bend. 2 To contract, as a muscle. — *n.* 1 A bend; flexure. 2 *Brit.* A length of pliant, usually insulated, copper wire, as for an electric plug-in connection. [<L *flexus,* pp. of *flectere* bend]

flex·i·ble (flek′sə·bəl) *adj.* 1 Capable of being bent, turned, or twisted, without breaking. 2 Pliant; plastic. 3 Tractable; yielding; compliant. Also **flex·ile** (flek′sil). — **flex′i·bil′i·ty, flex′i·ble·ness** *n.* — **flex′i·bly** *adv.*

flex·ion (flek'shən) n. 1 Anat. The bending or turning of a part, as a limb, muscle, etc.: opposed to extension. 2 Brit. Flection (defs. 1–3).

flex·or (flek'sər) n. Anat. A muscle that operates to bend a joint.

flex·time (fleks'tīm') n. The system of allowing workers to arrange working hours according to their own convenience.

flex·u·ose (flek'shoo-ōs) adj. 1 Bot. Bending gently to and fro in opposite directions, as certain plants; zigzag. 2 Flexuous. [< L flexuosus < flexus bent. See FLEX.]

flex·u·ous (flek'shoo-əs) adj. 1 Winding or turning about; having bends or turns. 2 Unsteady; wavering. 3 Flexuose. [< L flexuosus < flexus; see FLEX] —flex·u·os·i·ty (flek'shoo-os'ə-tē), flex'u·ous·ness n. —flex'u·ous·ly adv.

flex·u·ral (flek'shər-əl) adj. Of or pertaining to bending or curving.

flex·ure (flek'shər) n. 1 A bending; the state of being bent or flexed. 2 A bent part; turn; curve; fold.

fli·aum (flī'ôm) n. The orange rockfish (Sebastodes pinniger) of the American Pacific coast. [Origin uncertain]

flick[1] (flik) v.t. 1 To strike with a quick, light stroke, as with a whip or finger. 2 To throw or remove with such a motion: to flick dust. 3 To cause to move, as a whip, in a quick, darting manner. —v.i. 4 To move in a quick, darting manner: His fist flicked out. 5 To flutter. [< n.] —n. 1 A quick, light stroke, as with a whip. 2 The sound of such a stroke. 3 A streak or splash. [Imit.]

flick[2] (flik) n. Slang A movie. [Short for FLICKER[1]]

flick·er[1] (flik'ər) v.i. 1 To burn or shine with an unsteady or wavering light. 2 To move quickly or jerkily, as lightning. 3 To flutter the wings. —v.t. 4 To cause to flicker. —n. 1 A waving or fluctuating light. 2 A flickering or fluttering motion. See synonyms under LIGHT[1]. 3 In motion pictures, the effect of discontinuity due to faulty projection. [OE flicorian move the wings] —flick'er·ing adj. —flick'er·ing·ly adv. —flick'er·y adj.

flick·er[2] (flik'ər) n. A woodpecker, especially the golden–winged woodpecker (Colaptes auratus) of eastern North America. [Imit.]

flick·er·tail (flik'ər-tāl') n. A medium–sized ground squirrel (Citellus richardsonii) with a buff–to–grayish coat and a bushy tail, black above and brown beneath: common in Montana and North Dakota.

flied (flīd) Past tense and past participle of FLY[1] (def. 7).

fli·er (flī'ər) n. 1 That which flies; a flying bird, airplane, or the like; a fugitive. 2 An aviator or airman. 3 A rapidly moving piece in a machine. 4 U.S. A printed handbill. 5 A single step in a straight flight of stairs; in the plural, a straight flight. 6 A bus or express train with a fast schedule. 7 Colloq. A venture, as in the stock market. Also spelled flyer.

flight (flīt) n. 1 The act, process, or power of flying; swift movement of any kind. ◆ Collateral adjective: volar. 2 The distance traveled, as by a projectile. 3 A group or flock flying through the air together. 4 The art of traveling through the air in aircraft. 5 A single trip of an airplane. 6 In the U.S. Air Force, a tactical unit of two or more aircraft. 7 A soaring and sustained effort or utterance. 8 An ascent or continuous series (of stairs or steps). 9 A light, slender arrow for shooting at long distances: also flight arrow. 10 In angling, a device for whirling the bait rapidly. 11 The act of fleeing or escaping. See synonyms under CAREER. —to put to flight To cause to flee or run; defeat decisively; rout. —v.i. Obs. To migrate or move in flights, as birds. [OE flyht] —flight'·less adj.

flight engineer Aeron. The crew member of an airplane in charge of mechanical performance during flight.

flight feather Ornithol. One of the strong, stiff feathers that are essential to the flight of a bird.

flight formation Aeron. A maneuver in which two or more aircraft fly in a definite pattern with reference to the complete unit.

flight officer U.S. In World War II, a specially created rank in the Air Force, corresponding to a warrant officer in grade.

flight path Aeron. The path traced out by the center of gravity of an aircraft with reference to the earth.

flight plan Aeron. The essential details of a proposed aircraft flight, including type of airplane, points of departure and arrival, cruising altitude, course, speed, etc.

flight–re·cord·er (flīt'ri-kôr'dər) n. Aeron. An automatic electronic device for recording temperature and pressure changes in an aircraft in flight: used primarily on test flights.

flight station Aeron. The compartment of a large airplane containing equipment for controlling mechanical performance during flight, and manned by crew members other than the pilot.

flight strip Aeron. An auxiliary landing field for aircraft.

flight·y (flī'tē) adj. flight·i·er, flight·i·est 1 Given to light–headed fancies or caprices; volatile. 2 Slightly delirious. 3 Fleeting; passing swiftly. —flight'i·ly adv. —flight'i·ness n.

flim·sy (flim'zē) adj. ·si·er, ·si·est Lacking substantial texture or structure; thin and weak; ineffective. —n. pl. flim·sies 1 A thin paper used for carbon copies. 2 A dispatch or article received on thin paper. [< FILM, by metathesis; infl. in form by clumsy, tipsy, etc.] —flim'si·ly adv. —flim'si·ness n.

flinch (flinch) v.i. 1 To shrink back, as from pain or danger; waver; wince. 2 In croquet, to allow the foot to slip from one's ball during the action of driving an opponent's ball from the field of play. —n. Any act of shrinking back, wavering, or wincing. [< OF flenchir, var. of flechier bend; ult. origin uncertain] —flinch'er n. —flinch'ing·ly adv.

flin·der (flin'dər) n. A small fragment; splinter; shred: usually in the plural. [Cf. Norw. flindra splinter]

fling (fling) v. flung, fling·ing v.t. 1 To cast or throw with violence; hurl. 2 To cast off; discard. 3 To put abruptly or violently, as if by throwing: They flung him into prison. 4 To put (oneself) into something completely or with energy: He flung himself into the battle. 5 To throw to the ground, as in wrestling; overthrow. 6 To send forth; emit, as a fragrance. —v.i. 7 To move, rush, or flounce, as with anger or contempt. 8 To make abusive remarks; speak bitterly or critically. 9 To kick and plunge: said of horses. —n. 1 The act of casting out, down, or away; a throw. 2 A sneering insinuation; aspersion. 3 A kick, flounce, leap, or the like. 4 Free range for action or indulgence; dash; swagger. 5 A lively Scotch dance. [ME flingen < Scand. Cf. ON flegja beat.] —fling'er n.

flint (flint) n. 1 A dull–colored variety of quartz resembling chalcedony but more opaque; it is very hard, and produces a spark when struck with steel. 2 A piece of such stone, shaped for some purpose, as for striking fire. 3 Anything very hard, obdurate, or cruel. —v.t. To provide with a flint. [OE]

flint·lock (flint'lok') n. 1 A gunlock in which a flint was used to ignite the powder in the pan. 2 A firearm equipped with such a gunlock.

flint paper A paper covered with powdered flint, resembling sandpaper.

flint·y (flin'tē) adj. flint·i·er, flint·i·est 1 Made of, containing, or resembling flint. 2 Hard; cruel; obdurate. See synonyms under HARD. —flint'i·ly adv. —flint'i·ness n.

flip (flip) v. flipped, flip·ping v.t. 1 To throw or put in motion with a jerk; flick. 2 To toss, as a coin or cigarette, by or as by a fillip. —v.i. 3 To move abruptly or with a jerk. 4 To make a fillip; strike lightly and quickly. —n. 1 A quick movement of the hand or finger; sudden toss; snap; fillip; flick. 2 A drink made with some liquor, as sherry, mixed with egg, sugar, and spices. —adj. Colloq. Pert; saucy; impertinent. [Imit.]

flip·pant (flip'ənt) adj. 1 Light, pert, and trifling; shallow and impertinent. 2 Obs. Fluent; free of speech. [< FLIP, v. + -ANT] —flip'pan·cy, flip'pant·ness n. —flip'pant·ly adv.

flip·per (flip'ər) n. 1 A limb used to swim with, as by seals, turtles, etc. 2 Usually pl. One of a pair of rubber shoes having a long, flat, paddlelike piece projecting beyond the toes, used by skin divers and other swimmers: also called fin. 3 Slang The hand.

flirt (flûrt) v.i. 1 To play at courtship; try to attract attention or admiration; coquet. 2 To trifle; toy: to flirt with danger. 3 To move with sudden jerky motions. —v.t. 4 To toss or throw with a jerk. 5 To move briskly or back and forth. —n. 1 A person, especially a woman, who coquets; a trifler. 2 The act of flirting; a flirting motion; fling. [Imit.] —flirt'er n. —flirt'y adj.

flir·ta·tion (flər-tā'shən) n. Insincere lovemaking. Also flirt'ing. —flir·ta'tious adj. —flir·ta'tious·ly adv. —flir·ta'tious·ness n.

flit (flit) v. flit·ted, flit·ting v.i. 1 To move or fly rapidly and lightly; dart; skim. 2 To pass away, as time. 3 Dial. To leave; depart. 4 Scot. & Brit. Dial. To move from one dwelling to another. —v.t. 5 Scot. To transfer; move. See synonyms under FLY[1]. —n. A flitting motion or action; flutter. [< ON flytja remove, move] —flit'ter n. —flit'ting n.

flitch (flich) n. 1 A side (of a hog) salted and cured; side of bacon. 2 A strip or steak cut from the side of certain fishes, smoked or adapted for smoking. 3 In carpentry, one of the parts of a compound beam. 4 A length of stripped log from whose circumference thin sheets of veneer are cut; also, the sheet so cut. —v.t. To cut into flitches. [OE flicce]

flit·ter[1] (flit'ər) n. A thin bit or bits of tin, brass, or the like, used in decorative work. [Alter. of obs. fitters pieces, fragments]

flit·ter[2] (flit'ər) v.t. & v.i. To flutter; flit. [Freq. of FLIT]

flit·ter·mouse (flit'ər·mous') n. pl. ·mice (-mīs') A bat. [Cf. G fledermaus]

float (flōt) v.i. 1 To rest on the surface of a liquid. 2 To drift on or as on the surface of a liquid; move gently. 3 To move or drift without purpose or destination. 4 To hover; stay vaguely: The image floated in his mind. —v.t. 5 To cause to rest on the surface of a liquid. 6 To put in circulation; place on sale: to float a loan. 7 To find support for, as a business venture. 8 To irrigate; flood. 9 To smooth the surface of (soft plaster). —n. 1 An object, as a ball, that floats on a liquid or buoys up something, as a cork on a bait line or a hollow ball in a cistern. 2 One of various devices or appliances, as a plasterer's spreading trowel, a shoemaker's rasp, etc. 3 A truck or wheeled platform, decorated for display in a pageant. 4 Naut. A dock or basin in which a ship is floated. For illustration see DRYDOCK. 5 Geol. Rock or rocky debris detached from the original formation. 6 Aeron. That portion of the landing gear of a seaplane which provides buoyancy when it is resting on the surface of the water. 7 In banking, time drafts and out-of-town checks in transit for collection. See TRANSIT. 8 A mechanical device for elevating performers above the stage in spectacular plays; also, the footlights. 9 The passage of a filling thread under or over several warp threads without engaging them. 10 Electr. A voltage equalizer; storage battery. 11 Biol. A hollow or inflated organ that supports an animal in water. 12 A milk shake with a ball of ice-cream floating in it. [OE flotian float] —float'a·ble, float'y adj.

Synonym (verb): swim. An object floats which is upborne in a fluid without action; a living being swims when borne up, or borne onward, in a liquid by action; one wearied with swimming may rest himself by floating; a cork floats on water; the hawk seems to float in the upper air. Antonyms: drown, sink.

float·board (flōt'bôrd', -bōrd') n. One of the paddles of a water wheel or of a paddle wheel.

float-feed (flōt'fēd') adj. Mech. Furnished with a feed controlled by a float, as the carburetor of an internal-combustion engine.

floating axle Mech. In an automobile, a live axle which floats in a housing: it supports none of the weight, its sole function being to transmit propelling power to the wheels.

floating debt The general unfunded indebtedness of a state or a corporation.

float·ing-heart (flō'ting-härt') n. An aquatic herb (genus Nymphoides), with floating heart-shaped leaves.

float·ing-island (flō'ting-ī'lənd) n. A dessert consisting of boiled custard with the beaten whites of eggs or whipped cream floating on the surface.

floating kidney *Pathol.* An abnormal condition, usually congenital, in which the kidneys are movable or unstable in position: also called *movable kidney, wandering kidney.*

floc (flok) *n.* A tiny flaky mass, as in smoke; a chemical precipitate: also spelled *flock.* [Short for FLOCCULE]

floc·cil·la·tion (flok′si·lā′shən) *n. Pathol.* A delirious picking at the bedclothes by a patient. [< NL *floccillus,* dim. of *floccus* lock of wool + ATION]

floc·cose (flok′ōs, flo·kōs′) *adj.* 1 Woolly. 2 *Bot.* Having tufts of soft hairs or wool. [< LL *floccosus* < *floccus* lock of wool]

floc·cu·late (flok′yə·lāt) *v.t. & v.i.* **·lat·ed, ·lat·ing** 1 To gather or be joined together in small lumps, as some soils. 2 To collect in flaky masses, as the particles of a finely divided precipitate. 3 To form large masses, as clouds. —*adj.* (-lit) Having a tuft of stiff hairs or a flocculus. —**floc′cu·la′tion** *n.*

floc·cule (flok′yōōl) *n.* 1 A loose tuft, like wool. 2 *Chem.* One of the flakes in a flocculent precipitate. 3 A small flocculent mass. Also **floc·cus** (flok′əs). [< NL *flocculus,* dim. of *floccus* lock of wool]

floc·cu·lent (flok′yə·lənt) *adj.* 1 Resembling wool; woolly. 2 Of, pertaining to, or like the down of a young bird. 3 Covered with a soft waxy secretion, as certain insects. 4 Coalescing in flakes, as the clumping together of microscopic particles in a liquid. —**floc′cu·lence, floc′cu·len·cy** *n.* —**floc′cu·lent·ly** *adv.*

floc·cu·lus (flok′yə·ləs) *n. pl.* **·li** (-lī) 1 A little flake; floccule. 2 A small tuft of wool or woollike hairs. 3 *Astron.* One of the gaseous cloudlike masses in the chromosphere of the sun. 4 *Anat.* One of a pair of small lateral lobes in the cerebellum of the higher vertebrates. [< NL. See FLOCCULE.]

flock[1] (flok) *n.* 1 A company or collection of animals, as sheep, goats, or birds. 2 The persons belonging to a congregation, church, parish, or diocese. 3 An unorganized company of persons; a crowd. —*v.i.* To assemble or go in flocks, crowds, etc.; congregate. [OE *flocc*]

Synonyms (noun): bevy, brood, company, covey, drove, gam, group, hatch, herd, litter, lot, pack, set, swarm. *Group* is the general word for any gathering of a small number of objects, whether of persons, animals, or inanimate things. The individuals in a *brood* or *litter* are related to each other; those in the other *groups* may not be. *Brood* is used chiefly of fowls and birds, *litter* of certain quadrupeds which bring forth many young at a birth; we speak of a *brood* of chickens, a *litter* of puppies. *Bevy* is used of birds, and figuratively of any bright and lively *group* of women or children, but rarely of men. *Flock* is applied to birds and to some of the smaller animals; *herd* is confined to the larger animals; we speak of a *bevy* of quail, a *covey* of partridges, a *flock* of blackbirds, or a *flock* of sheep, a *gam* of whales, a *herd* of cattle, horses, buffaloes, or elephants, a *pack* of wolves, a *pack* of hounds, a *swarm* of bees. A collection of animals driven or gathered for driving is called a *drove.*

flock[2] (flok) *n.* 1 Finely ground wool, felt or vegetable fiber; wool dust. 2 A tuft of wool, or the like. 3 Short refuse wool, used as stuffing and in upholstery. 4 A tufted or flakelike mass, especially if produced by precipitation: also spelled *floc.* —*v.t.* To cover or fill with flock, as a cushion. [Prob. < OF *floc* < L *floccus* lock of wool]

flock paper Wallpaper sized and covered with or figured with flock; velvet paper.

floe (flō) *n.* A tabular mass, or a collection of such masses, of floating ice. ✦ Homophone: *flow.* [< ON *flo* a layer]

flog (flog, flôg) *v.t.* **flogged, flog·ging** To beat with a whip, rod, etc.; to whip. See synonyms under BEAT. —*n.* A sound resembling the impact of a blow; also, the act of flogging. [? < L *flagellare*] —**flog′ger** *n.* —**flog′ging** *n.*

flong (flong) *n.* A sheet of specially prepared paper used for making a stereotype mold or matrix.

[Var. of FLAN]

flood (flud) *n.* 1 An unusually large flow of water; freshet; inundation; deluge. ✦Collateral adjective: *diluvial.* 2 The coming in of the tide; the tide at its height; high tide: also called *flood tide.* 3 A copious flow or stream, as of sunlight, lava, etc.; abundant or excessive supply. 4 Any great body of water; the sea; a river. 5 A stage light that throws a broad beam. —**the Flood** or **Noah's flood** See under DELUGE. —*v.t.* 1 To cover or inundate with a flood; deluge. 2 To fill or overwhelm as with a flood: They *flooded* him with advice. 3 To supply with too much: He *flooded* the engine with gasoline. —*v.i.* 4 To rise to a flood; overflow. 5 To flow in a flood; gush. [OE *flōd*] —**flood′er** *n.*

flood·gate (flud′gāt′) *n.* 1 *Engin.* A gate for regulating the flow of water, as a raceway. 2 Any free vent for an outpouring, as of wrath or tears.

flood·light (flud′līt′) *n.* Artificial illumination of great brilliancy and broad beam; specifically, a lighting unit equipped with a highpowered projector, enveloping the desired object in a broad flood of light.

flood plain An area of flat country bordering a stream and subject to flooding in periods of high water.

flood tide See FLOOD *n.* (def. 2).

floor (flôr, flōr) *n.* 1 The surface in a room or building upon which one walks. 2 The space between two adjacent levels of a building; a story. 3 Any natural area made smooth or level, corresponding in character or use to a floor; also, the surface of something built, as a bridge. 4 In any parliamentary body, the part of the hall occupied by its members; hence, the right or privilege to address the house during a given time and to the exclusion of other speakers. 5 The main business hall of an exchange. 6 *Naut.* The vertical plates between the inner and outer bottoms of a ship extending from one side (bilge) to the other. 7 The bottom limit of anything; specifically, the lowest price charged for a given thing. —*v.t.* 1 To cover or provide with a floor. 2 To throw or knock down; overthrow. 3 *Colloq.* To silence; defeat. 4 *Colloq.* To baffle; confound. [OE *flōr*] —**floor′er** *n.*

floor leader A party leader in either house of the U.S. Congress, in charge of party organization and many of the privileges of the floor.

flop (flop) *v.* **flopped, flop·ping** *v.i.* 1 To move or beat about with or as with thuds. 2 To fall loosely and heavily: to *flop* to the ground. 3 *Colloq.* To fail. —*v.t.* 4 To cause to strike, slap, or drop with or as with a thud. —*n.* 1 The sound or act of flopping. 2 *Colloq.* An utter failure, or a person who has failed. [Var. of FLAP] —**flop′per** *n.* — **flop′py** *adj.* —**flop′pi·ly** *adv.* —**flop′pi·ness** *n.*

flop·house (flop′hous′) *n.* A cheap lodging house or hotel.

floppy disc A small, flexible recording disc on which data may be stored in the memory of a digital computer.

flo·ra (flôr′ə, flō′rə) *n. pl.* **·ras** or **·rae** (-ē) 1 The aggregate of plants indigenous to a country or district: distinguished from *fauna.* 2 A work systematically describing such plants. [< NL, after L *Flora,* goddess of flowers]

flo·ral (flôr′əl, flō′rəl) *adj.* Of, like, or pertaining to flowers.

floral envelope *Bot.* The corolla and calyx of a flower.

Flor·ence (flôr′əns, flor′-) A city on the Arno in central Italy: Italian *Firenze.* Ancient **Flo·ren·ti·a** (flō·ren′shē·ə).

Florence flask 1 A round or pear-shaped bottle of thin glass in which liquids are heated. 2 A straw-covered glass flask in which olive oil or wine is imported from Italy.

flor·en·tine (flôr′ən·tēn, -tīn, flor′-) *n.* A stout and durable kind of silk dress goods.

flo·res·cence (flô·res′əns, flō-) *n. Bot.* 1 The state of being in blossom. 2 Inflorescence. For illustrations see INFLORESCENCE. [< NL *florescentia* < L *florescere,* inceptive of *florere* bloom]— **flo·res′cent** *adj.*

flo·ret (flôr′it, flō′rit) *n.* 1 A little flower. 2 *Bot.* One of the small individual flowers that make

up a cluster or head, as in sunflowers, dandelions, etc., of the composite family. 3 A silk yarn or floss. [< OF *florete,* dim. of *flor* a flower < L *flos, floris*]

flo·ri·at·ed (flôr′ē·ā′tid, flō′rē-) *adj.* Decorated with flower designs.

flo·ri·cul·ture (flôr′ə·kul′chər, flō′rə-) *n.* The cultivation of flowers or ornamental plants. See synonyms under AGRICULTURE. [< L *flos, floris* a flower +CULTURE]—**flo′ri·cul′tur·al** *adj.* — **flo′ri·cul′tur·al·ly** *adv.* —**flo′ri·cul′tur·ist** *n.*

flor·id (flôr′id, flor′-) *adj.* 1 Having a bright color; of a lively reddish hue. 2 Excessively ornate. 3 Blooming; flowery. 4 Full of ornamental musical phrases. [< L *floridus* flowery < *flos, floris* a flower]—**flo·rid·i·ty** (flə·rid′ə·te), **flor′id·ness** *n.* —**flor′id·ly** *adv.*

Flor·i·da (flôr′ə·də, flor′-) The southernmost Atlantic State of the United States; 58,560 square miles; capital, Tallahassee; entered the Union March 3, 1845: nickname, *Everglade State.* Abbr. FL —**Flo·rid′e·an** (flô·rid′ē·ən, flō-), **Flor·i·dan** (flôr′-, flor′-) *adj. & n.*

flo·rif·er·ous (flô·rif′ər·əs, flō-) *adj.* Bearing flowers. [< L *florifer* bearing flowers +-OUS]

flor·in (flôr′in, flor′·in) *n.* 1 The unit of value of the Netherlands: also called *guilder.* 2 A British silver coin, equal to one tenth of a pound, or two shillings. 3 A gold coin first issued in England in 1343. 4 A coin first issued by Florence, made of gold, and weighing about 54 grains: also **flor′ence.** 5 Any of several ancient coins of England, Tuscany, Germany, etc. [< OF < Ital. *fiorino* < *fiore* a flower; so called from the figure of a lily stamped on it]

FLORIN
(Obverse)

flo·rist (flôr′ist, flō′rist, flor′ist) *n.* A grower of or dealer in flowers.

-florous *combining form Bot.* Having (a specified number, kind, etc., of) flowers: *uniflorous.* [< L *-florus* < *flos, floris* a flower]

flos fer·ri (flos′ fer′ī) A variety of aragonite, suggesting coral. [< L, flower of iron]

floss[1] (flôs, flos) *n.* 1 Floss silk. 2 The silk of some plants, as Indian corn. 3 The stray silk on the outside of cocoons of silkworms and of spiders. 4 A flossy surface; fluff. [< OF *flosche*]

floss[2] (flôs, flos) *n. Metall.* A slag that floats on molten metal. [< G *flosz*]

floss silk A soft, downy silk fiber suitable for embroidery.

flo·ta·tion (flō·tā′shən) *n.* 1 The act or state of floating. 2 The science of bodies that float. 3 The act of floating or financing, as of an issue of bonds, etc., by bankers. 4 *Metall.* A method of separating pulverized ores by placing them in a froth of oils and chemicals in water, and applying a current of air so that the valuable ore particles float on or adhere to the surface. Also spelled *floatation.*

flo·til·la (flō·til′ə) *n.* 1 A fleet of small vessels; a small fleet. 2 In the U.S. Navy, an organized group of destroyers, composed of two or more squadrons. 3 In the U.S. Army, a seagoing unit for laying mines. [< Sp., dim. of *flota* a fleet]

flot·sam (flot′səm) *n.* 1 *Law* Goods cast or swept from a vessel into the sea and found floating. Compare JETSAM, LAGAN. 2 Any objects floating on the sea. 3 Hence, vagrants or unattached persons: the *flotsam* of society. Also spelled **flot′san** (-sən), **flot′son.** [< AF *floteson* < *floter* float < OE *flotian*]

flounce[1] (flouns) *n.* A gathered or plaited strip on a skirt. —*v.t.* **flounced, flounc·ing** To furnish with flounces. [Var. of FROUNCE]

flounce[2] (flouns) *v.i.* **flounced, flounc·ing** 1 To move or go with exaggerated tosses of the body, as in anger or petulance. 2 To plunge; founder: said of animals. —*n.* The act of flouncing; a fling. [< Scand. Cf. dial. Sw. *flunsa* plunge]

floun·der[1] (floun'dər) v.i. **1** To struggle clumsily; move awkwardly as if mired or injured. **2** To proceed, as in speech or action, in a clumsy or confused manner; muddle. —n. A stumbling or struggling motion. [? Blend of FLOUNCE[2] and FOUNDER[2]] —**floun'der·ing·ly** adv.

floun·der[2] (floun'dər) n. **1** One of certain species of flatfish, valued as a food fish; especially, the winter flounder (*Pseudopleuronectes americanus*) of the North Atlantic coast, and the California flounder (*Platichthys stellatus*). **2** Any of several flat fish other than sole. [< AF *floundre*, prob. < Scand. Cf. Sw. *flundra*.]

flour (flour) n. **1** The ground and bolted substance of wheat. **2** The finely ground particles of any specified cereal: rye *flour*. **3** Any finely powdered substance. **4** Loose, finely crystallized saltpeter, used in making gunpowder. —v.t. **1** To make into flour; pulverize, as wheat. **2** *Metall.* To break up into minute particles: to *flour* mercury in the amalgamating process. **3** To sprinkle or cover with flour. [Var. of FLOWER] —**flour'y** adj.

flour·ish (flûr'ish) v.i. **1** To grow or fare well or prosperously; thrive. **2** To be at the peak of success or development; be at the height or in the prime: Alchemy *flourished* in the Middle Ages. **3** To move with sweeping motions; be displayed or waved about: Swords *flourished* in the air. **4** To write with sweeping or ornamental strokes. **5** *Music* **a** To play a showy passage. **b** To sound a fanfare. **6** *Obs.* To blossom. —v.t. **7** To wave about or brandish; flaunt, as a weapon or flag. **8** To embellish, as with ornamental lines or figures. —n. **1** An ornamental mark or design, especially a sweeping stroke, as in writing or embroidery; anything done for display alone. **2** The act of brandishing or waving. **3** A musical passage for display; fanfare. See synonyms under OSTENTATION. [< OF *floriss-*, stem of *florir* < L *florere* bloom] —**flour'ish·ing** adj. —**flour'ish·ing·ly** adv.

Synonyms (verb): advance, blossom, flower, gain, grow, increase, prosper, thrive. See FLAUNT, GAIN[1], SUCCEED. *Antonyms:* see synonyms for FALL.

flout (flout) v.t. To show or express scorn or contempt for; scoff at. —v.i. To express one's contempt; mock; jeer. See synonyms under MOCK. —n. A gibe; scoff; mockery. [Prob. ME *flouten* play the flute, deride] —**flout'er** n. —**flout'ing·ly** adv.

flow (flō) v.i. **1** To move along in a stream, as water or other fluid. **2** To move along, as with the qualities of a liquid: The crowd *flowed* through the gates. **3** To stream forth; proceed from a source. **4** To move with continuity and pleasing rhythm, as verse or music. **5** To fall or lie in waves, as garments or hair. **6** To be full or too full; abound; overflow: The creeks are *flowing* with gold. **7** To come in or rise, as the tide: opposed to ebb. —v.t. **8** To flood; inundate. **9** *Obs.* To cause to flow. —n. **1** The act of flowing, or that which flows; also, a continuous stream or current. **2** The incoming of the tide. **3** The quantity, as of water, that passes through an orifice or by a given point in a given time. **4** A copious outpouring. **5** Any easy, gentle movement, as of speech. ◆Homophone: *floe*. [OE *flōwan*] —**flow'ing** adj. & n. —**flow'ing·ly** adv. —**flow'ing·ness** n.

flow-chart (flō'chärt') n. A diagram showing all the steps in a logical sequence, as in a computer program.

flow·er (flou'ər, flour) n. **1** *Bot.* **a** The organ, or the combination of organs of reproduction in a plant; blossom; bloom. **b** In mosses, the reproductive organs with their enveloped or associated leaves. **2** A blooming plant. **3** The brightest, finest, choicest part, period, or specimen of anything. **4** Any flowerlike ornament. **5** A flowery figure of speech. **6** *pl.* A very light powder obtained by sublimation and usually a metallic

FLOWER
a. Calyx.   e. Pollen.
b. Petal.   f. Stamen.
c. Sepal.   g. Corolla.
d. Pistil.   h. Pedicel.
             i. Bract.

oxide: *flowers* of antimony; flour (def. 3). —v.i. **1** To put forth blossoms; bloom. **2** To come to full development; be at the full: The Renaissance *flowered* in Italy. —v.t. **3** To decorate with flowers or a floral pattern. [< OF *flour*, *flor* < L *flos*, *floris* a flower] —**flow'er·er** n. —**flow'er·less** adj. —**flow'er·y** adj. —**flow'er·i·ly** adv. —**flow'er·i·ness** n.

flow·er-de-luce (flou'ər-də-lōōs', flour'-) n. pl. **flow·ers-de-luce** A flower of the iris variety. FLEUR-DE-LIS.

flow·er·et (flou'ər·it, flou'rit) n. A small flower, or a floret.

flower head *Bot.* A dense headlike cluster of sessile florets.

flowering maple A plant (*Abutilon striatum*) with maplelike leaves and orange flowers veined in dark crimson: also called *redvein maple.*

flow·er-of-an-hour (flou'ər·uv·ən·our', flour'-) n. The bladder ketmia.

flow·me·ter (flō'mē'tər) n. An apparatus designed to measure the rate of flow of a liquid or a gas through any part of a transmitting system.

flown[1] (flōn) Past participle of FLY[1].

flown[2] (flōn) adj. **1** Coated, as a glaze, with color freely blended or flowed. **2** Eased off; slack, as a sheet. [< obs. pp. of FLOW]

flow relay *Electr.* A relay circuit adjusted to operate under specified conditions of flow in a gas or liquid.

flow-sheet (flō'shēt') n. A diagram, chart, or expository outline showing the successive operations through which material progresses in a manufacturing process.

flu (flōō) n. *Colloq.* Influenza: a contraction.

flub (flub) *U.S. Colloq.* v.t. & v.i. **flubbed, flub·bing** To do or manage (something) badly; botch or bungle: to *flub* one's chance. —n. A blunder; failure. [Origin unknown]

fluc·tu·ant (fluk'chōō·ənt) adj. **1** Showing fluctuation. **2** Moving or shaped like a wave.

fluc·tu·ate (fluk'chōō·āt) v. **·at·ed, ·at·ing** v.i. **1** To change or vary often and in an irregular manner; waver; be unsteady. **2** To move with successive rise and fall; undulate. —v.t. **3** To cause to fluctuate. [< L *fluctuatus*, pp. of *fluctuare* wave < *fluctus* a wave < *fluere* flow] —**fluc'tu·a·bil'i·ty** n. —**fluc'tu·a·ble** adj.

Synonyms: hesitate, oscillate, swerve, undulate, vacillate, vary, veer, waver.

fluc·tu·a·tion (fluk'chōō·ā'shən) n. **1** Frequent irregular change; varying movement or action. **2** A rising and falling, as of prices. **3** *Biol.* A variation in an organism which is not inherited.

flue[1] (flōō) n. **1** A channel or passage for smoke, air, or gases of combustion; a chimney. **2** An organ pipe of flute or diapason quality. **3** Any of several types of fishing nets. Also spelled *flew*. [Origin uncertain]

flue[2] (flōō) n. Any fine, flocklike refuse of wool or the like; lint; down. [< Flemish *vluwe* down]

flue[3] (flōō) n. A fluke; barb, as of a harpoon, feather, or anchor. [Cf. Sw. *fly*]

flue gas The by-product of combustion in a heating system, consisting mostly of nitrogen, with varying proportions of carbon dioxide, oxygen, and, under improper conditions, carbon monoxide.

flu·ent (flōō'ənt) adj. **1** Ready in speaking or writing; voluble; copious. **2** Marked by fluency; flowing; smooth. **3** Flowing freely; mobile; changeable. [< L *fluens*, *-entis*, ppr. of *fluere* flow] —**flu'en·cy** (-sē), **flu'ent·ness** n. —**flu'ent·ly** adv.

flue pipe *Music* An organ pipe in which the tone is produced by a current of air striking an aperture or flue.

flue stop *Music* A stop controlling the flue pipes of an organ.

flu·ey (flōō'ē) adj. Containing or like flue or lint; downy; fluffy.

fluff[1] (fluf) n. **1** Nap or down. **2** Anything downy or fluffy. **3** *Colloq.* An error made in reading or speaking (lines): said of actors, etc. —v.t. **1** To shake or pound so as to cause to puff out and become fluffy. **2** *Colloq.* To make an error in reading or speaking (lines). —v.i. **3** To become fluffy. **4** *Colloq.* To make a fluff (def. 3). [? Blend of FLUE[2] + PUFF]

fluff[2] (fluf) n. A flash, as of loose powder; puff. [Imit.]

fluff·y (fluf'ē) adj. **fluff·i·er, fluff·i·est** Downy; feathery. —**fluff'i·ly** adv. —**fluff'i·ness** n.

fluffy glider A flying phalanger (*Petaurus aus-*

tralis) of Australia: also called *yellow-bellied glider.*

Flü·gel·horn (flōō'gəl·hôrn', Ger. flü'gəl·hôrn') n. A brass wind instrument similar in pitch and design to a cornet yet mellower in tone. [< G *flügel* wing + *horn* a horn; so called from its shape]

flu·id (flōō'id) adj. Capable of flowing; liquid or gaseous. —n. A substance that yields to any force tending to change its form; a liquid or gas. [< F *fluide* < L *fluidus* < *fluere* flow] —**flu·id'ic** adj. —**flu·id'i·ty, flu'id·ness** n. —**flu'id·ly** adv.

Synonyms (noun): gas, liquid. In comparison with the substance, *fluid*, a *liquid* is a body in a state in which the particles move freely among themselves, but remain in one mass, keeping the same volume, but taking always the form of the containing vessel; a *liquid* is an inelastic *fluid*; a gas is an elastic *fluid* that tends to expand to the utmost limits of the containing space. All *liquids* are *fluids*, but not all *fluids* are *liquids*; air and all the *gases* are *fluids*, but they are not *liquids* under ordinary circumstances, even if capable of being reduced to a *liquid* form by special means, as by cold and pressure. Water at the ordinary temperature is at once a *fluid* and a *liquid*. *Antonym:* solid.

fluid drive An automobile transmission in which a driving rotor, turning in oil, transmits driving force to a driven rotor by forcing it to rotate in response to the action of the oil: usually automatically operated. Also called *hydraulic transmission.*

flu·id·ex·tract (flōō'id·eks'trakt) n. A solution in alcohol of the active principle of a vegetable drug so prepared that 1 cubic centimeter has the strength of 1 gram of the dry drug.

fluke[1] (flōōk) n. **1** *Naut.* The part of an anchor that holds to the ground. **2** One of the lobes of the tail of a whale. **3** A barb on a harpoon, arrow, etc. [? < FLUKE[2]]

fluke[2] (flōōk) n. **1** A leaflike, parasitic, trematode worm infesting sheep, and also man and other animals: also called **fluke worm. 2** A flatfish or flounder. [OE *flōc*]

FLUKE[1] (def. 3)

fluke[3] (flōōk) n. **1** A lucky stroke or accident, as in billiards, etc. **2** *Colloq.* An accidental failure or disappointment, as from a capricious wind in sailing. [Origin unknown]

flume (flōōm) n. **1** A conduit, as for a millwheel. **2** A narrow passage through which a torrent passes. **3** A chute. —v.t. **flumed, flum·ing 1** To drain away or divert by means of a water chute or conduit, as in mining. **2** To move or transport, as logs, by means of a flume. See synonyms under STREAM. [< OF *flum* < L *flumen* river < *fluere* flow]

flu·mi·nous (flōō'mə·nəs) adj. Of or pertaining to rivers; watered by streams. [< L *flumen*, *-inis* a river]

flum·mer·y (flum'ər·ē) n. pl. **·mer·ies 1** A light dish made of flour or cornstarch; blanc-mange. **2** A glutinous refuse product of the manufacture of wheat starch. **3** Originally, a dish of oatmeal steeped in water and turned sour; pap. **4** Hence, anything vapid or insipid; empty compliment; flimsy show; humbug. [< Welsh *llymru*]

flum·mox (flum'əks) v.t. *Slang* To confuse; confound; perplex. [Cf. dial. E *flummocks* maul, mangle]

flung (flung) Past tense and past participle of FLING.

flunk (flungk) *U.S. Colloq.* v.t. **1** To fail in, as an examination. **2** To give a failing grade to. —v.i. **3** To fail, as in an examination. **4** To back out; give up. —**to flunk out** To leave or cause to leave a class, school, or college because of failure in studies. —n. A complete failure; a giving up. [? Blend of FLINCH and FUNK]

flunk·y (flung'kē) n. pl. **flunk·ies 1** An obsequious fellow; servile imitator; toady. **2** A servant in livery. Also **flunk'ey.** [? Alter. of *flanker* < FLANK, v.] —**flunk'y·ism** n.

flu·o·resce (flōō'ə·res') v.i. **·resced, ·resc·ing** To become fluorescent; exhibit fluorescence. [Back formation < FLUORESCENCE]

flu·o·res·cence (flōō'ə·res'əns) n. *Physics* **1** The property of certain substances to absorb radiation of a particular wavelength and to re-emit it as light of a different, usually greater, wavelength; the emitted radiation persists only as long as the stimulus is active: distinguished from *phosphorescence.* **2** The light so produced. [< FLUOR(SPAR); coined on analogy with OPALESCENCE]

flu·o·res·cent (floo′ə·res′ənt) *adj.* Having or exhibiting fluorescence.

fluorescent lamp An electric-discharge lamp, usually tubular in shape, containing a metallic vapor which becomes luminous on the passing of the current and energizes a layer of fluorescent material coating the tube.

fluorescent screen A surface of glass coated with a fluorescent material, as platinocyanide; it fluoresces on exposure to electron bombardment and is used in cathode-ray vacuum tubes.

flu·or·ic (floo·ôr′ik, -or′-) *adj.* Pertaining to, derived from, or containing fluorine or fluorite.

fluor·i·date (floor′ə·dāt, floo′ə·ri·dāt) *v.t.* **·dat·ed, ·dat·ing** To add sodium fluoride to (drinking water), especially as a means of preventing tooth decay. **—fluor′i·da′tion** *n.*

flu·o·ride (floo′ə·rīd, -rid) *n. Chem.* A binary compound of fluorine and another element. Also **flu′o·rid** (-rid).

fluor·i·dize (floor′ə·dīz, floo′ə·ri·dīz) *v.t.* **·dized, ·diz·ing** To treat (teeth) with a fluoride, especially as a preventive of tooth decay. **—fluor′i·di·za′tion** *n.*

flu·o·rim·e·ter (floo′ə·rim′ə·tər) *n. Physics* An absorbing screen used to measure the intensity of fluorescence from different sources, as X-rays, radium, etc.

flu·o·ri·na·tion (floo′ər·i·nā′shən, floor′ə-) *n.* The act or process of introducing fluorine into an organic compound.

flu·o·rine (floo′ə·rēn, -rin) *n.* A pale yellow, toxic, corrosive gaseous element (symbol F, atomic number 9), the most electronegative and reactive of all elements. See PERIODIC TABLE.

flu·o·rite (floo′ə·rīt) *n.* A cleavable, isometric, variously colored calcium fluoride, CaF₂: used as a flux in making steel and glass: also called *fluor, fluorspar.*

fluoro- *combining form* **1** *Chem.* Indicating the presence of fluorine in a compound. **2** Fluorescence: *fluoroscope*: also, before vowels, *fluor-*, as in *fluoride.*

flu·o·ro·car·bon (floo′ə·rō·kär′bən) *n. Chem.* Any of a group of very stable compounds in which hydrogen has been replaced by fluorine: used as solvents, lubricants, and insulators.

flu·or·o·chem·i·cal (floo′ə·rō·kem′ə·kəl) *n.* Any of various chemicals containing fluorine, as the fluorocarbons.

flu·or·om·e·try (floo′ə·rom′ə·trē) *n.* The measurement of the color and intensity of fluorescence.

fluor·o·scope (floor′ə·skōp, floo′ər·ə-) *n.* A device for observing, by means of some fluorescent substance, the shadows of objects enclosed in media opaque to ordinary light, but transparent to X-rays. **—fluor′o·scop′ic** (-skop′ik) *adj.*

flu·o·sil·i·cate (floo′ə·sil′ə·kāt, -kit) *n. Chem.* A salt of silicic acid.

flur·ry (flûr′ē) *v.* **·ried, ·ry·ing** *v.t.* To bewilder or confuse; agitate; fluster. **—***v.i.* To move in a flurry. [< *n.*] **—***n. pl.* **flur·ries 1** A sudden commotion; nervous agitation. **2** Flutter; hurry. **3** A light gust of wind. **4** A light snowfall or rain. **5** The spasmodic contortions of a dying whale. See synonyms under TUMULT. [Blend of FLUTTER and HURRY]

flush¹ (flush) *v.i.* **1** To become red in the face or overspread with color; redden; blush. **2** To flow and spread suddenly; rush: The blood *flushes* in his veins. **3** To be washed out or cleansed by a sudden flow of water. **—***v.t.* To cause to color, as with a rush of blood; make red or florid. **5** To encourage; excite: *flushed* with victory. **6** To wash out by a flow of water, as a sewer or an obstacle. **—***n.* **1** A heightened color; warm glow; blush. **2** Sudden elation or excitement. **3** A sudden blossoming out; growth; bloom. **4** A sudden gush or flow of water. **5** Full of life; vigorous. **2** Powerful and direct, as a blow. **—***adv.* In a direct manner; squarely; straight.

[? < FLUSH⁴: infl. in meaning by *flash, flow, bluish,* etc.] **—flush′er** *n.*

flush² (flush) *adj.* **1** Having the surfaces in the same plane; level. **2** *Printing* Set even with the left edge of the type page; having no indention. **3** *Naut.* Of or pertaining to a ship with an upper deck extending in one level from stern to stern. **4** Full; copious. **5** Well supplied with money; spending freely. **—***v.t.* To make level or straight. **—***n.* **1** A level or unbroken surface. **2** Abundance. **—***adv.* **1** With level, unbroken surface or form. **2** *Printing* Without indention; straight. [? < FLUSH¹]

flush⁴ (flush) *v.t. & v.i.* To drive or to be startled from cover; start up, as birds. **—***n.* The act of startling a bird; also a bird or birds startled from cover. [ME *flusschen*; origin uncertain]

flus·ter (flus′tər) *v.t. & v.i.* To make or become confused, agitated, or befuddled. **—***n.* Confusion of mind; flurry; intoxication. [Cf. Icel. *flaustr* hurry]

flus·trate (flus′trāt) *v.t.* **·trat·ed, ·trat·ing** To fluster; befuddle. Also **flus′ter·ate.** [< FLUSTER + -ATE¹] **—flus′ter·a′tion, flus·tra′tion** *n.*

flute (floot) *n.* **1** A tubular wind instrument of small diameter with holes along the side. **2** A flute stop in an organ; flue. **3** *Archit.* A groove, usually of semicircular section, as in a column. **4** A corrugation; crimping. **5** A tall, slender wineglass. **—***v.* **flut·ed, flut·ing.** **—***v.i.* **1** To play on a flute. **2** To produce a flutelike sound. **—***v.t.* **3** To sing or utter with flutelike tones. **4** To make flutes in, as a column. [< OF *flaüte*] **—flut′y** *adj.*

flut·ed (floo′tid) *adj.* **1** Having parallel grooves or flutes. **2** Having the tone of a flute.

flut·ing (floo′ting) *n.* **1** A flute or groove. **2** Flutes or grooves collectively. **3** The act of making a flute, as by carving a column: the reverse of *reeding.* **4** A crimp, as in the ruffle of a woman's dress.

flut·ist (floo′tist) *n.* A flute-player: also called *flautist.*

flut·ter (flut′ər) *v.i.* **1** To wave or flap rapidly and irregularly, as in the wind. **2** To flap the wings rapidly, in or as in erratic flight. **3** To move or proceed with irregular motion: to *flutter* to the ground. **4** To move about lightly and quickly; flit. **5** To be excited or nervous, as with hope, fear, or expectation. **—***v.t.* **6** To cause to flutter. **7** To excite; fluster. See synonyms under SHAKE. **—***n.* **1** The act of vibrating or quivering. **2** Agitation; confused or tumultous emotion. **3** An up-and-down motion of the feet used in various swimming strokes, especially the crawl. **4** *Aeron.* A periodic oscillation set up in any part of an airplane by mechanical disturbances and maintained by inertia, structural characteristics, etc. **5** Tremololike pulsations in the sound track of a motion picture, due to rapid fluctuations in motor speed. **6** *Pathol.* An abnormally rapid but rhythmical contraction of the atria of the heart; also **auricular flutter.** [OE *flotorian*] **—flut′ter·er** *n.* **—flut′ter·y** *adj.*

flu·vi·al (floo′vē·əl) *adj.* **1** Of, pertaining to or formed by a river. **2** Existing in a river. Also **flu·vi·at·ic** (floo′vē·at′ik), **flu·vi·a·tile** (floo′vē·ə·til). [< L *fluvialis* < *fluvius* river]

fluvio- *combining form* River: *fluviograph.* [< L *fluvius* a river]

flu·vi·o·graph (floo′vē·ə·graf′, -gräf′) *n.* A mechanical contrivance for measuring the rise and fall of a river.

flux (fluks) *n.* **1** A continuous flowing or discharge: a thermal or electrical *flux.* **2** The act or process of melting. **3** *Pathol.* A morbid discharge of fluid matter from the body. **4** *Metall.* A substance that promotes the fusing of minerals or metals, as borax. **5** Any readily fusible glass or enamel used as a base or ground in ceramic work. **6** *Physics* The rate of flow or transfer of water, heat, electricity, etc. **7** A state of constant movement: the *flux* of the tide. See synonyms under STREAM. **—bloody flux** Dysentery. **—***v.t.* **1** To make fluid; melt; fuse. **2** To treat, as metal, with a flux. **3** *Obs.* To purge. **—***v.i.* **4** *Obs.* To flow; move. [< F < L *fluxus* < *fluere* flow] **—flux·a′tion** *n.*

fly¹ (flī) *v.* **flew** or **flied** (def. 7), **flown, fly·ing** *v.i.* **1** To move through the air by using wings, as a bird. **2** To move through the air in an aircraft; travel by aircraft. **3** To move through the air with speed, as an arrow or bullet. **4** To wave or move in the air, as a flag. **5** To pass swiftly: The years *flew* by. **6** To move swiftly or with violence: The door *flew* open. **7** In baseball, to bat a fly. **8** To take flight; flee. **9** In hawking, to hunt with or as with a hawk. **—***v.t.* **10** To cause to wave or float in the air. **11** To operate (an aircraft). **12** To pass over in an aircraft: to *fly* the Atlantic. **13** To transport by aircraft. **14** To flee from. **15** In hawking, to hunt with a hawk. **—to fly at** To attack. **—to fly in the face of** To defy openly. **—to fly out** In baseball, to be retired by batting a ball which is caught by an opposing player before it touches the ground. **—***n. pl.* **flies.** **1** An object or device that moves or swings rapidly through the air, or has some relation to such motion. **2** A speed-regulating device, as of vanes upon a rotating shaft, used in music boxes, in the striking part of clocks. **3** *Printing* A long-fingered frame oscillating quickly upon a horizontal axis, taking the sheets from the tapes or cylinder of a printing press and delivering them flat upon a pile. **4** A knitting-machine latch. **5** The length of a flag measured from the staff to its farthest edge, as distinguished from the *hoist.* **6** That part of a flag farthest from the staff, or beyond the canton. **7** The revolving part of a vane that shows the direction of the wind. **8** *Mech.* **a** A flywheel, a weighted arm, or other mechanical device involving the flywheel principle. **b** The heavily weighted lever which enables a fly press to acquire momentum. **c** A fly press. **9** A strip or lap on a garment, to cover the buttons or other fasteners; hence, something used to cover or connect; a flap, as of a bootee. **10** An upper covering to a ridge-pole tent; also, the flap at the entrance of a tent. **11** The condition or movement of a ball when sent flying through the air as in baseball; also, the ball thus flying. **12** Waste cotton. **13** The act or state of flying; flight. **14** A public carriage; also, a delivery wagon. **15** In a theater, the space above the stage and behind the proscenium containing the borders, the mechanism for handling and setting the scenery, the overhead lights, etc. **—on the fly** While flying; while in the air; in haste. [OE *flēogan*]

Synonyms (verb): flee, flit, haste, hasten, run, soar, speed. See ESCAPE.

fly² (flī) *n. pl.* **flies 1** One of various small dipterous insects (family *Muscidae*), especially the common housefly (*Musca domestica*). **2** Any of various other flying insects not of the family *Muscidae*: the Spanish *fly*, or the *mayfly*. **3** A fish hook concealed by feathers, etc., to imitate some insect. **4** *pl.* **flys** A light carriage. [OE *flȳge*]

fly·a·gar·ic (flī′ə·gar′ik, -ag′ə·rik) *n.* A common species of poisonous mushroom (*Amanita muscaria*) with a brightly colored pileus. Also **fly·am·a·ni·ta** (-am′ə·nī′tə).

fly·blow (flī′blō′) *n.* The egg or young larva of a blowfly. **—***v.t. & v.t.* **·blew, ·blown, ·blow·ing 1** To taint (food) with flyblows. **2** To spoil.

fly·catch·er (flī′kach′ər) *n.* Any of a large order of perching birds (*Passeriformes*) that feed upon insects; especially, the American tyrant flycatcher (family *Tyrannidae*) and the Old World flycatcher (family *Muscicapidae*)–**least flycatcher** A small American flycatcher; the chebec (*Empidonax minimus*).

fly·frame (flī′frām′) *n.* Any of several machines used to draw and twist textile fibers preparatory to spinning, as a roving frame.

fly·ing (flī′ing) *adj.* **1** Intended or adapted for swift or easy motion, or motion through the air; moving with or as with wings. **2** Moving rapidly or continuously; hurried: a *flying* bird or trip. **3** Floating or suspended so as to float in the air: a *flying* banner. **4** Extending or being beyond the ordinary; extra: a *flying* jib. **—***n.* **1** The act of flight; flight, as of a bird or an aircraft. **2** *pl.* Loose material, as fibers, floating in the air. — **instrument flying** Navigation of an aircraft by means of instruments alone: also called **blind flying.**

flying boat A large seaplane, supported on water by its own hull rather than by floats.

flying buttress *Archit.* A rampant arch extending from a wall or pier to a supporting abutment, usually receiving the thrust of another arch on the other side of the wall.

flying fatigue Aeroneurosis.

flying field *Aeron.* A field with a graded portion for taking off and landing and an unimproved area for flying operations.

flying fish A fish (family *Exocoetidae*) of warm and temperate seas, with large pectoral fins that enable it to glide through the air for short distances.

fly·ing-fox (flī′ing·foks′) *n.* A large fruit-eating bat, especially a genus (*Pteropus*) of the warmer parts of the Old World, with foxlike snout.

flying frog A ranoid tree frog (*Rhacophorus pardalis*) of Borneo, having elongated, webbed toes which serve as supports during leaps.

flying gurnard A marine fish (family *Dactylopteridae*) having very long horizontal pectoral fins divided into a smaller upper and a longer lower or posterior portion and able to flutter for short distances in the air.

flying jib, flying-jib boom See under JIB¹.

flying lemur An insect-eating mammal (genus *Cynocephalus*) having the fore and hind limbs connected by a fold of skin, by the aid of which it makes flying leaps: native of East Indies: also called *colugo.*

fly·ing-mare (flī′ing-mâr′) *n.* In wrestling, a throw accomplished by seizing an opponent's wrist, turning around and jerking the opponent over one's shoulder.

flying phalanger Any of several arboreal marsupials (genera *Acrobates, Petaurus, Schoinobates*) of Australia and New Guinea, having folds of skin along the sides that enable them to make long, gliding leaps. Also called *glider, gliding possum, possum glider.*

flying saucer Any of various oddly shaped objects alleged to have been seen flying at high altitudes; an unidentified flying object (UFO).

flying squirrel A squirrel (genus *Glaucomys*) having on each side a fold of skin forming a parachute, by the help of which the animal can make long sailing leaps.

flying start 1 In racing, the passing of the starting post at full speed. **2** Any rapid beginning.

flying trip A quick, hurried trip.

flying wing 1 An airplane without a fuselage. **2** *Canadian* In football, a player whose position varies behind the line of scrimmage.

FLYING SQUIRREL
(Head and body about 5 inches long; tail. 4 inches)

fly·leaf (flī′lēf′) *n. pl.* **·leaves** A blank leaf at the beginning or end of a book, pamphlet, or similar printed matter.

fly·net (flī′net′) *n.* **1** A net worn by horses to keep off flies. **2** Any netting, as in a window, for excluding insects.

fly·o·ver (flī′ō′vər) *n.* A public display of military aircraft as a demonstration of strength, variety of types, and maneuverability; a military air show. Also **fly′-past′** (-past′).

fly·pa·per (flī′pā′pər) *n.* An adhesive paper, or one impregnated with poison, for catching or killing flies.

fly press A press for stamping and punching metal blanks, equipped with a hand screw and a heavily weighted cross arm.

fly·trap (flī′trap′) *n.* **1** A trap for catching flies. **2** An insectivorous plant, as the pitcher plant and the Venus flytrap.

fly·weight (flī′wāt′) *n.* A boxer weighing 112 lbs. or less: the lightest weight class.

fly·wheel (flī′hwēl′) *n.* A heavy wheel whose weight resists sudden changes of speed, thus securing uniform motion in the working parts of

an engine or machine.

Fm *Chem.* Fermium (symbol Fm).

foal (fōl) *n.* The young of an equine animal; a colt. —*v.t. & v.i.* To give birth to (a foal). [OE *fola*]

foam (fōm) *n.* **1** A collection of minute bubbles forming a frothy mass. **2** *Chem.* A colloid system of gas dispersed in liquid. **3** Frothy saliva or sweat. **4** The white crest of a breaking wave; hence, the sea. **5** Figuratively, rage or fury. —*v.i.* To gather, produce, or form foam; froth. —*v.t.* To cause to foam. [OE *fām*] —**foam′less** *adj.*

foam-flow·er (fōm′flou′ər) *n.* A hardy herbaceous perennial (*Tiarella cordifolia*) of the saxifrage family, with purple or red flowers and decorative foliage.

foam rubber Natural or synthetic rubber which has been treated with various chemicals and expanded into a cellular structure adapted for a wide range of uses as an insulating and buoyancy material and in upholstery.

foam·y (fō′mē) *adj.* **foam·i·er, foam·i·est** Covered with or full of foam; foamlike. —**foam′i·ly** *adv.* —**foam′i·ness** *n.*

fob¹ (fob) *n.* **1** A watch pocket in the waistband of trousers. **2** A chain or ribbon hanging from it; also, an ornament on a watch chain or ribbon. [Cf. dial. G *fuppe* a pocket]

fob² (fob) *v.t.* **fobbed, fob·bing** *Archaic* To cheat; trick: also spelled *fub.* —**to fob off 1** To dispose of or palm off by craft or deceit. **2** To put off; attempt to placate, as with promises. [? < FOB¹]

fo·cal (fō′kəl) *adj.* Pertaining to, at, or limited to a certain point or focus.

focal epilepsy Jacksonian epilepsy.

focal infection *Pathol.* An infection originating in and often spreading from a circumscribed region of the body.

fo·cal·ize (fō′kəl·īz) *v.t. & v.i.* **·ized, ·iz·ing 1** To adjust or come to a focus; focus. **2** *Med.* To confine or be confined to a small area, as an infection. —**fo′cal·i·za′tion** *n.*

focal length *Optics* The distance from the second principal plane of a lens or mirror to the point where rays from a distant object converge. Also **focal distance.**

fo·c′s·le (fōk′səl) *n. Naut.* Forecastle.

fo·cus (fō′kəs) *n. pl.* **·cus·es** or **·ci** (-sī) **1** *Optics* **a** The point to which a system of light rays converges after passage through a lens or other optical arrangement, or after reflection from

FOCI

A. Concavo-concave lens—showing light rays *a. a.* refracting as at *b. b.* and forming the virtual focus at *c.*
B. Convexo-convex lens—showing light rays *d. d.* converging to the principal focus at *e.*

a mirror. **b** The point from which such rays appear to diverge. **c** The place where a visual image is clearly formed, as in the eye or a camera. The point of convergence of the rays is called the **real focus;** the point where diverging rays would meet if their directions were reversed is called the **virtual focus. 2** *Physics* The meeting point of any system of rays, beams, or waves: an acoustic *focus.* **3** *Geom.* **a** One of two points, the sum or difference of whose distances to a conic section is a constant. **b** A point in some other curve, having similar properties. **4** Any central point: the *focus* of an earthquake. —*v.t. & v.i.* **fo·cused** or **fo·cussed, fo·cus·ing** or **fo·cus·sing 1** To adjust the focus of (the eye or an optical instrument). **2** To bring or come to a focus or point, as rays. [< L, hearth] —**fo′cal** *adj.*

fod·der (fod′ər) *n.* Coarse feed, for horses, cattle, etc., as the stalks and leaves of field corn. See synonyms under FOOD. —*v.t.* To supply with fodder. [OE *fōdor*]

foe (fō) *n.* **1** One actively hostile. **2** A hostile force; an enemy; adversary. **3** One who or that which opposes or injures; anything injurious or detrimental. See synonyms under ENEMY. [Fu-

sion of OE *fah* hostile and *gefa* an enemy]

foe·man (fō′mən) *n. pl.* **·men** (-mən) An active or open enemy.

foe·tal (fē′təl), **foe·ta·tion** (fē·tā′shən), **foe·tus** (fē′təs), etc. See FETAL, etc.

fog¹ (fog, fôg) *n. Agric.* **1** Dead or decaying grass. **2** Aftermath (def. 2). Also *foggage.* [ME *fogge,* prob. <Scand. Cf. Norw. *fogg* long grass on wet ground.] —**fog′gy** *adj.*

fog² (fog, fôg) *n.* **1** Condensed watery vapor suspended in the atmosphere at or near the earth's surface. **2** *Chem.* A colloid system of the liquid–in–gas type (see COLLOID SYSTEM). **3** *Meteorol.* Any hazy condition of the atmosphere, or the material causing it: a dust *fog.* **4** Bewilderment; obscurity. **5** *Phot.* A coating obscuring a developed photographic plate. —*v.* **fogged, fog·ging** *v.t.* **1** To surround with or as with fog. **2** To confuse; bewilder. **3** *Phot.* To cloud (a plate) with a fog. —*v.i.* **4** To become foggy. [Prob. back formation < *foggy,* in the sense "marshy" <FOG¹; infl. in meaning by Dan. *fog* spray]

fog·bow (fog′bō′, fôg′-) *n. Meteorol.* A white or very faintly colored arc of light seen opposite the sun in fog.

fog chamber A cloud chamber. See under CHAMBER.

fog dog A clearing spot in a fog bank, indicating the lifting of the fog: also called *sea dog.*

fog-fruit (fog′frōōt′, fôg′-) *n.* An American creeping plant (genus *Lippia*) of the vervain family bearing closely bracted heads of bluish–white flowers, especially *L. lanceolata.*

fog·gage (fog′ij, fôg′-) *n.* **1** Long grass, left standing over winter, for feeding cattle in the spring. **2** The privilege of pasturing cattle on fog; also, such pasturing.

fog·gy (fog′ē, fôg′ē) *adj.* **fog·gi·er, fog·gi·est 1** Full of or marked by the presence of fog. **2** Mentally confused; obscure; cloudy. **3** *Phot.* Fogged; indistinct. See synonyms under THICK. [<FOG¹] —**fog′gi·ly** *adv.* —**fog′gi·ness** *n.*

fog·horn (fog′hôrn′, fôg′-) *n.* **1** A horn or whistle for sounding a warning during a fog on the water: also **fog′-sig′nal, fog′-whis′tle. 2** Hence, a powerful, harsh voice.

foi·ble (foi′bəl) *n.* **1** A personal weakness; slight fault of character. **2** The portion of a sword blade or foil blade from the middle to the point: distinguished from *forte.* [<F, obs. var. of *faible* FEEBLE]

Synonyms: defect, error, failing, frailty, imperfection, infirmity, peccadillo, weakness.

foil¹ (foil) *v.t.* **1** To prevent the success of; balk; frustrate; baffle. **2** In hunting, to cross and recross (a scent or trail) so as to confuse pursuers. See synonyms under BAFFLE, HINDER¹. —*n.* **1** *Archaic* A thwarting; frustration. **2** In wrestling, an incomplete fall. **3** An animal's trail. [<OF *fouler, fuler* crush, trample down <LL *fullare* full cloth <*fullo* a fuller]

foil² (foil) *n.* **1** Metal in very thin pliable sheets or leaves. **2** A leaf of bright metal placed by jewelers beneath an inferior gem to heighten the color or luster. **3** Anything serving to adorn or set off by contrast something different or superior. **4** The reflecting amalgam on the back of a mirror. **5** *Archit.* A leaflike division in ornamentation; a lobe, as in tracery. A group of three foils is called *trefoil;* of four, *quatrefoil;* of five, *cinquefoil;* etc. **6** *Obs.* A leaf. —*v.t.* **1** To apply foil to; cover with foil. **2** To intensify or set off by contrast. **3** *Archit.* To adorn, as windows, with foils. [<OF <L *folium* leaf]

FOILS (def. 5)
Foliated tracery in Gothic window, Grace Church Chantry, New York.

foil³ (foil) *n.* **1** A blunted rapierlike implement, sometimes having a button on its end, used in fencing. **2** The art of fencing. [Origin uncertain]

foist (foist) *v.t.* **1** To put in or introduce slyly or improperly: to *foist* a candidate on a party. **2** To pass off (something spurious) as genuine. [Prob. < dial. Du. *vuisten* hold in the hand, palm]

fold¹ (fōld) *v.t.* **1** To turn back (something)

upon itself one or more times. **2** To bring down upon itself; close; collapse: to *fold* an umbrella; to *fold* wings. **3** To place together and interlock: to *fold* one's hands. **4** To wrap up; enclose. **5** To mix, as beaten egg whites or whipped cream, into other ingredients, by gently turning one part over the other with a spoon: with *in*. **6** To embrace; enfold: She *folded* him in her arms. — *v.i.* **7** To come together in folds. **8** *U.S. Slang* To fail; close: often with *up*. — *n.* **1** One part doubled over another; a plait; ply; a lap; also, the space between two folded-over parts. **2** The crease made by folding. **3** *Geol.* A smooth bend or flexure in a layer of rock; an anticline or syncline. **4** That which envelops; an embrace. [OE *fealdan*]

fold[2] (fōld) *n.* **1** A pen, as for sheep. **2** A flock of sheep. **3** Any group needing care, as the congregation of a church. **4** *Brit. Dial.* A farmstead. — *v.t.* To shut up in a fold, as sheep. [OE *fald*]

-fold *suffix* **1** Having (a specified number of) parts: a *threefold* blessing. **2** (A specified number of) times as great, or as much: to reward *tenfold*. [OE *-feald* < *fealdan* fold]

fold·er (fōl'dər) *n.* **1** One who or that which folds. **2** A timetable or other printed paper that may be readily folded or readily spread out. **3** A large envelope or binder for loose papers.

fold·ing (fōl'ding) *n.* The gathering or keeping of sheep in a fold.

fo·li·a·ceous (fō'lē·ā'shəs) *adj.* **1** Of the nature or form of a leaf. **2** Leaflike. **3** Having leaves; foliate. [< L *foliaceus* < *folium* a leaf]

fo·li·age (fō'lē·ij) *n.* **1** Any growth of leaves; leaves collectively. **2** A representation of leaves, flowers, and branches, used in architectural ornamentation. [Earlier *foillage* < F *feuillage* < *feuille* a leaf < L *folium*; refashioned after the Latin form]

foliage green Any of several shades of dark, dull green; a color like that of the leaves of trees in the summer.

fo·li·ar (fō'lē·ər) *adj.* Of, pertaining to, consisting of, or resembling leaves.

fo·li·ate (fō'lē·āt, -it) *adj.* **1** Having leaves; leafy; leaf-shaped. **2** Decorated with leaf-shaped ornaments; beaten into leaf. — *v.* ·at·ed, ·at·ing *v.t.* **1** To beat or form into a leaf or thin plate, as gold. **2** To coat or back with metal foil. **3** To number the leaves of (a book). **4** *Archit.* To adorn or ornament with foils or foliage. — *v.i.* **5** To split into leaves or. laminae. **6** To put forth leaves. [< L *foliatus* leafy < *folium* a leaf] — **fo'li·at'ed** *adj.*

fo·li·a·tion (fō'lē·ā'shən) *n.* **1** *Bot.* **a** The leafing-out of plants. **b** The disposition of leaves in a bud. **2** The act or process of making into thin sheet metal or foil, or of covering or backing with foil, as a mirror. **3** *Archit.* Decoration or enrichment with cusps, lobes, or foliated tracery; also, one of such ornaments. **4** The state of being foliaceous or foliated. **5** *Geol.* A crystalline segregation of certain minerals in a rock, in dominant planes. **6** The numbering of the leaves of a book, etc., instead of its pages. Also **fo·li·a·ture** (fō'lē·ə·chŏor').

fo·lic acid (fō'lik) *Biochem.* A nitrogen-containing acid having vitaminlike properties and often included in the vitamin-B complex. It is found abundantly in green leaves, and in mushrooms, yeast, and some animal tissues.

fo·li·o (fō'lē·ō, fōl'yō) *n. pl.* ·li·os **1** A sheet of paper folded once or of a size adapted to folding once. **2** A book, or the like, composed of sheets folded but once; hence, a book of the largest size. **3** The size of a book so made up. **4** A page of a book; sometimes, in bookkeeping, two opposite pages numbered alike. **5** *Printing* The number of a page. **6** *Law* A certain number of words (72–100), recognized as a unit for estimating the length of a document. **7** A leaf of manuscript or of a book. **8** A holder made of heavy paper for protecting sheets of manuscript, music, etc. — *adj.* Consisting of or resulting from a sheet or sheets folded once; having two leaves, hence, four pages. — *v.t.* To number the pages

or locate the folios of (a book or manuscript) consecutively. [< L, ablative sing. of *folium* a leaf]

fo·li·o·late (fō'lē·ə·lāt') *adj. Bot.* Of, pertaining to, or composed of leaflets: used in composition: *bifoliolate*, composed of two leaflets. [< L *foliolum*, dim. of *folium* a leaf + -ATE[1]]

fo·li·um (fō'lē·əm) *n. pl.* ·li·ums or ·li·a (-lē·ə) **1** *Usually pl.* A thin layer or stratum, especially of rocks. **2** *Geom.* A segment of a curve closed by its node; a loop. [< L, a leaf]

folium of Descartes *Geom.* A plane cubic curve with one loop, a node, and two branches asymptotic to the same line.

folk (fōk) *n. pl.* **folk** or **folks** **1** A people; nation; race. **2** *Usually pl.* People of a particular group or class: ·old *folks*; poor *folks*; town *folk*. **3** *pl. Colloq.* People in general: *Folks* say; *folks* disagree. **4** *pl. Colloq.* One's family and relatives. — *adj.* Originating among or characteristic of the common people of a district or country. [OE *folc*]

folk etymology **1** Modification of an unfamiliar word resulting from an incorrect analysis of the elements, causing it to assume the shape or pronunciation of better known forms, as *agnail* (in Middle English, a painful nail) became *hangnail*. **2** Nonscientific word derivation. Also called *popular etymology*.

folk·land (fōk'land') *n.* In old English law, land of the folk or people, of the community, or of the nation, held by folkright: distinguished from *bookland*, requiring written title. [OE *folcland*]

folk laws The laws of the common people; specifically, the laws of the Salian Franks.

folk·lore (fōk'lôr', -lōr') *n.* **1** The traditions, beliefs, customs, sayings, stories, etc., preserved among the common people. **2** The study of folk cultures. — **folk'lor·ist** *n.*

folk·ways (fōk'wāz') *n. pl.* The traditional habits, customs, and behavior of a given group, tribe, or nation. [Coined by W. G. Sumner]

fol·li·cle (fol'i·kəl) *n.* **1** *Anat.* A small cavity or saclike structure in certain parts of the animal body, having a protective or secretory function: a hair *follicle*. See illustration under HAIR. **2** *Bot.* **a** A dry seed vessel of one carpel. **b** A small bladder on the leaves of some mosses. [< L *folliculus*, dim. of *follis* bag]

fol·lic·u·lar (fə·lik'yə·lər) *adj.* **1** Of, pertaining to, or like a follicle. **2** Affecting the follicles, as of the pharynx.

fol·lies (fol'ēz) *n. pl.* of **folly** A theatrical performance having no plot sequence, consisting of many elaborate scenes of music and dance; revue.

fol·low (fol'ō) *v.t.* **1** To go or come after and in the same direction. **2** To succeed in time or order. **3** To seek to overtake or capture; pursue. **4** To accompany; attend. **5** To hold to the course of: to *follow* a road. **6** To conform to; act in accordance with. **7** To move or act in the cause of; be under the leadership or authority of: He *follows* Plato. **8** To work at as a profession or livelihood; employ oneself in: men who *follow* the sea. **9** To come after as a consequence or result: The effect *follows* the cause. **10** To use or take as a model; imitate: to *follow* an example. **11** To watch or observe closely; be attentive to: to *follow* sports. **12** To understand the course, sequence, or meaning of, as an explanation. **13** To strive after; try to attain or obtain: to *follow* one's star. — *v.i.* **14** To move or come after or in the direction of something preceding in time, sequence, or motion. **15** To attend; understand: Do you *follow*? **16** To come as a result or consequence. — **to follow out** **1** To follow to the end, as an argument. **2** To comply with, as orders or instructions. — **to follow suit** **1** In card games, to play a card of the suit led. **2** To follow another's example. — **to follow through** **1** To swing to the full extent of the stroke after having struck the ball, as in tennis or golf. **2** To perform fully; complete. — **to follow up** **1** To pursue closely. **2** To achieve more by acting upon what has already been achieved, as an advantage. — *n.* The act of following; specifically, a stroke in billiards that causes

the cue ball, after impact, to follow the object ball. [OE *folgian*]

Synonyms (verb): accompany, attend, chase, copy, ensue, heed, imitate, obey, observe, practice, pursue, result, succeed.

fol·low·er (fol'ō·ər) *n.* **1** One who or that which follows; an adherent, imitator, or attendant. **2** *Mech.* A part of a machine put into action by another part, as a driven pulley. **3** *Brit. Colloq.* An admirer; a beau.

fol·low·ing (fol'ō·ing) *adj.* **1** Next in order; succeeding or ensuing. **2** That is about to follow, be recounted, be mentioned, or the like. — *n.* A body of adherents, attendants, or disciples.

fol·low·up (fol'ō·up') *adj.* Pertaining to steady or repeated action or to a second or immediately following action or thing; reinforcing; supplementary. — *n.* A supplementary letter or visit to a business prospect, urging favorable action on a previous proposal.

fol·ly (fol'ē) *n. pl.* ·lies **1** The condition or state of being foolish, or deficient in understanding; foolish conduct, idea, or act. **2** The result of a ruinous undertaking or enterprise, as a costly and useless structure left unfinished; also, any extravagant structure or undertaking, considered as showing the bad judgment of the originator. **3** An object of foolish or vicious attention or pursuit. **4** Immoral conduct; sin. See synonyms under IDIOCY. [< F *folie* < *fol* fool]

Fol·som culture (fol'səm) *Anthropol.* A supposed prehistoric North American culture represented by typically Neolithic artifacts discovered near Folsom, northeastern New Mexico.

Fo·mal·haut (fō'məl·hôt) The bright star Alpha in the constellation of Piscis Austrinus; magnitude, 1.3.

fo·ment (fō·ment') *v.t.* **1** To stir up or instigate; incite, as rebellion or discord. **2** To treat with warm water or medicated lotions; apply a poultice to. See synonyms under PROMOTE. [< F *fomenter* < LL *fomentare* < *fomentum* a poultice < *fovere* warm, keep warm] — **fo·ment'er** *n.*

fo·men·ta·tion (fō'mən·tā'shən) *n.* **1** The act of fomenting, warming, or cherishing. **2** The use of any warm, moist application, as a poultice; also, the lotion applied. **3** Instigation or incitement, as to mutiny.

fo·mes (fō'mēz) *n. pl.* **fom·i·tes** (fom'i·tēz, fō'mi-) *Med.* An object or substance other than food capable of transmitting an infection, as bedding, clothes, etc. [< L, tinder]

fond[1] (fond) *adj.* **1** Disposed to love or to regard with pleasure, tenderness, or desire; enamored: followed by *of*, formerly by *on*. **2** Loving or affectionate; devotedly attached: sometimes with an implication of unwise tenderness or weak indulgence. **3** Cherished or regarded with affection; doted on. **4** *Archaic.* Foolish or simple; silly. See synonyms under FRIENDLY. [Earlier *fonned*, pp. of obs. *fon* be foolish]

fond[2] (fond, *Fr.* fôn) *n.* A groundwork or background, especially of lace. [< F < L *fundus* bottom]

fon·dant (fon'dənt, *Fr.* fôn·dän') *n.* A soft, molded confection. [< F, orig. ppr. of *fondre* melt]

fon·dle (fon'dəl) *v.* ·dled, ·dling *v.t.* **1** To handle lovingly; caress. **2** *Obs.* To pamper; coddle. — *v.i.* **3** To display fondness, as by caressing. See synonyms under CARESS. [Freq. of obs. *fond* caress] — **fon'dler** *n.*

fond·ling (fond'ling) *n.* One who or that which is fondled.

fond·ly (fond'lē) *adv.* **1** In a fond manner; tenderly; dotingly. **2** Credulously. **3** *Obs.* Foolishly.

fond·ness (fond'nis) *n.* **1** Extravagant or foolish affection. **2** Strong preferment, liking or relish. **3** *Obs.* Foolishness.

fon·due (fon·dōo', *Fr.* fôn·dü') *n.* A dish made of grated cheese, melted with eggs, butter, etc. [< F]

font[1] (font) *n.* **1** A receptacle for the water used in baptizing. **2** A receptacle for holy water. **3** A fountain; hence, origin; source. [OE < LL *fons, fontis* a fountain]

font[2] (font) *n.* A full assortment of printing type of a particular face and size: also *Brit.*

fount. [<F *fonte* < *fondre* melt]

font·al (fon'təl) *adj.* Pertaining to a font or fountain, and hence to an origin or source.

fon·ta·nel (fon'tə·nel') *n.* **1** *Anat.* A soft, pulsating, unossified area in the fetal and infantile skull. **2** *Surg.* An artificial opening for the discharge of body fluids; a seton. Also **fon'ta·nelle'.** [<F *fontanelle,* dim. of *fontaine.* See FOUNTAIN.]

food (food) *n.* **1** That which is eaten or drunk or absorbed for the growth and repair of organisms and the maintenance of life; nourishment; nutriment; aliment. **2** Nourishment taken in solid as opposed to liquid form: *food* and drink. **3** That which increases, keeps active, or sustains. [OE *fōda*]
Synonyms: aliment, diet, fare, feed, fodder, forage, nourishment, nutriment, nutrition, pabulum, provender, regimen, sustenance, viands, victuals. *Food* is, in the popular sense, whatever one eats in contradistinction to what one drinks. Thus we speak of *food* and drink, of wholesome, unwholesome, or indigestible *food;* in a more scientific sense whatever, when taken into an organism, serves to build up structure or supply waste may be termed *food;* thus we speak of liquid *food,* plant *food,* etc.; in this wider sense *food* is closely synonymous with *nutriment, nourishment,* and *sustenance. Victuals* is a plain, homely word for whatever may be eaten; we speak of choice *viands,* cold *victuals. Diet* refers to the quantity and quality of *food* habitually taken, with reference to preservation of health. *Regimen* considers *food* as taken by strict rule, in which use it is closely synonymous with *diet,* but applies more widely to the whole ordering of life. *Fare* is a general word for all table supplies, good or bad; as, sumptuous *fare;* wretched *fare. Feed, fodder,* and *provender* are used only of the food of the lower animals, *feed* denoting anything consumed, but more commonly grain, *fodder* denoting hay, corn stalks, or the like, sometimes called long *feed; provender* is dry *feed,* whether grain or hay, straw, etc. *Forage* denotes any kind of *food* suitable for horses and cattle, primarily as obtained by a military force in scouring the country, especially an enemy's country. Compare NUTRIMENT.

Food and Drug Administration A division of the U.S. Department of Health, Education, and Welfare, which enforces laws relating to the purity, standards, branding, and labeling of foods, drugs, and cosmetics.

food chain *Ecol.* The relationship of organisms considered as food sources or consumers or both, as the relationship of a flowering plant to a bee to a bird.

Foo dog (foo) A lion dog (def. 1): a western commercial term. [<Chinese *Foo,* var. of *Fo* Buddha + dog]

fool¹ (fool) *n.* **1** A person lacking in understanding, judgment, or common sense; a simpleton. **2** A person, fantastically dressed and equipped, formerly kept at court and in great households to make sport; a professional jester. **3** One who is fooled or made a fool of; butt; victim. **4** *Obs.* An idiot; imbecile. **5** *Obs.* One without spiritual wisdom; wicked person. — *v.i.* To act like a fool; be foolish or playful. — *v.t.* To make a fool of; impose upon; deceive. — **to fool around** *U.S. Colloq.* **1** To waste time on trifles. **2** To hang about idly. — **to fool away** *Colloq.* To spend foolishly; squander, as money. — **to fool with 1** To meddle with. **2** To joke with. **3** To play with. — *adj. Colloq.* **1** Stupid: that *fool* cook. **2** Foolish: a *fool* story. [<F *fou* <L *follis* a bellows; later, a windbag, a simpleton]

fool² (fool) *n.* Crushed stewed fruit with whipped cream. [Prob. <FOOL¹]

fool·har·dy (fool'här'dē) *adj.* Bold without judgment; reckless; rash. See synonyms under IMPRUDENT. — **fool'har'di·ly** *adv.* — **fool'har'·di·ness** *n.*

fool·ish (foo'lish) *adj.* **1** Showing folly; wanting in judgment. **2** Resulting from folly or stupidity. **3** *Archaic* Insignificant; small; humble. See synonyms under ABSURD, CHILDISH. — **fool'ish·ly** *adv.* — **fool'ish·ness** *n.*

fool·proof (fool'proof') *adj.* So simple as to be understood or operated by a fool; so constructed as to operate smoothly and safely no matter how ignorant the operator.

fools·cap (foolz'kap') *n.* **1** A size of writing paper about 13 by 16 inches, making when folded a page 13 by 8 inches. **2** *Brit.* A size of printing paper 13 1/2 by 17 inches: so called from the watermark of a fool's cap and bells used by old papermakers. **3** A fool's cap.

fool's cap 1 A pointed, belled cap, formerly worn by jesters. **2** A dunce's cap of this shape: formerly used as a punishment for school children.

fool's errand A profitless undertaking.

fool's gold Pyrite, a gold-colored mineral.

fool's paradise A state of deceptive happiness based on vain hopes or delusions.

foot (foot) *n. pl.* **feet 1** The terminal segment of the limb of a vertebrate animal upon which it rests in standing or moving. ◆ Collateral adjective: *pedal.* **2** Any part serving as or likened to a foot. **3** Anything corresponding in form, use, or position to the foot. **4** The part of a boot or stocking which receives the wearer's foot. **5** A part in a sewing machine, to hold the fabric down: also called **presser foot. 6** *Naut.* The lower edge of a four-sided sail. **7** The lowest part; bottom; base; foundation; also, the last row, line, or series; the inferior part or end. **8** A measure of length, equivalent to 12 inches, or 30.48 centimeters. **9** Soldiers, collectively, who march and fight on foot: distinguished from *horse* (cavalry). **10** A primary measure of poetic rhythm, corresponding to a *bar* in music. — **on foot 1** Walking; not riding. **2** Happening; going on; proceeding. — **to put one's foot down** To be decisive or determined. — **to put one's foot in it** To get into a difficulty or scrape. — **under foot 1** Under the feet; hence, in the way. **2** On the ground: wet *under foot.* — *v.i.* **1** To go afoot; walk. **2** To move the foot to music; dance. **3** *Naut.* To move or sail faster. — *v.t.* **4** To move on or through by walking or dancing; set foot on. **5** To furnish with a foot, as a stocking. **6** To add, as a column of figures, and place the sum at the bottom. **7** *Colloq.* To pay, as a bill. — **to foot it** To walk, run, or dance. — **to foot up** To amount to when counted or added. [OE *fōt*]

LONGITUDINAL SECTION OF HUMAN FOOT

a. Tibia.
b. Astragal.
c. Calcaneum.
d. Navicular.
e. Internal cuneiform bone.
f. First metatarsal.
g, h. Phalanges of great toe.
i. Inferior ligament.
j. Plantar fasciae, supporting the plantar arch.
k. Achilles' tendon.

foot·age (foot'ij) *n.* **1** Length in running feet, as of lumber, of tunneling or mining, or of film in a motion picture. **2** Payment at a rate of so much a foot for work done.

foot-and-mouth disease (foot'ən·mouth') A contagious, febrile disease of domestic animals, in which ulcers are formed about the mouth and hoofs. It is caused by a filtrable virus.

foot·ball (foot'bôl') *n.* **1** *U.S.* A game played between two teams, properly of eleven men

FOOTBALL PLAYING FIELD
A. Goal lines.   *C.* Goal posts.
B. End lines.   *D.* End zones.
The field of play is marked off in guidelines spaced 5 yards apart and so identified, as 20-yard line, etc.

each, on a field with goals at each end, points being scored by running or passing an ellipsoidal leather ball across the opponent's goal line, or kicking it between the goal posts placed on or behind the goal line. **2** The ball itself. **3** *Brit.* **a** Soccer. **b** Rugby football. **4** Any person, idea, etc., bandied or shunted back and forth.

foot·board (foot'bôrd', -bōrd') *n.* **1** Something to rest the feet upon. **2** An upright piece at the foot of a bedstead.

foot·can·dle (foot'kan'dəl) *n.* The illumination on one square foot of surface, all points of which are at a distance of one foot from one international candle. — **apparent foot-candle** See FOOT-LAMBERT.

foot·fall (foot'fôl') *n.* The sound of a footstep; a footstep.

foot·hill (foot'hil') *n.* A low hill at the base of a mountain.

foot·ing (foot'ing) *n.* **1** A place to stand or walk on; hence, position or condition; especially, secure position. **2** An established mode of mutual consideration and treatment. **3** The adding of a column or columns of figures, or the sum thus obtained. **4** A footstep; tread; especially, measured tread; dancing. **5** The act of adding a foot to anything; that which is added as a foot. **6** A strong foundation of greater lateral dimensions than the wall, embankment, or structural member which it supports.

foot ladder A ladder with flat steps to place the feet upon.

foot-lam·bert (foot'lam'bərt) *n.* A unit of brightness, equal to the brightness of a uniformly diffusing surface which emits or reflects one lumen per square foot: also called *apparent foot-candle.*

foot·lights (foot'līts') *n. pl.* **1** Lights in a row near the front of the stage, as in a theater. **2** The stage.

foot·lock·er (foot'lok'ər) *n.* A small trunk, usually used by soldiers for personal belongings and clothing.

foot·log (foot'lôg', -log') *n.* A log across a stream from bank to bank, on which a person may cross.

foot·loose (foot'loos') *adj.* Free to travel or rove around; not bound to any person or duty; unattached.

foot·man (foot'mən) *n. pl.* **·men** (-mən) **1** A male servant in livery who attends a carriage, answers the door, waits at table, etc. **2** *Obs.* A pedestrian.

foot·note (foot'nōt') *n.* A note at the foot of a page or column.

foot·path (foot'path', -päth') *n.* A path for persons on foot.

foot·pound (foot'pound') *n.* The work done in moving a pound's weight one foot against gravity: a unit of mechanical work.

foot·pound·al (foot'poun'dəl) *n.* A measure of the work done in moving through one foot against a force of one poundal.

foot·print (foot'print') *n.* An impression left by a foot. See synonyms under MARK, TRACE.

foot·rest (foot'rest') *n.* A stool, chair extension, etc., for supporting the feet.

foot·rot (foot'rot') *n.* An infectious disease of sheep, characterized by inflammation of the foot, progressive degeneration of the tissues, ill-smelling discharges, and lameness: caused by any of several micro-organisms, bacterial or of fungous origin.

foot soldier An infantryman.

foot·sore (foot'sôr', -sōr') *adj.* Having sore feet, as from walking.

foot·stalk (foot'stôk') *n. Bot.* **1** The petiole of a leaf, or the peduncle of a flower. **2** A stem or part supporting the body or an organ; a pedicel.

foot·step (foot'step') *n.* **1** The impression or mark of a foot; footprint; track. **2** The action of a foot in stepping. **3** The sound of a step; tread; footfall. See synonyms under TRACE.

foot·stone (foot'stōn') *n.* The stone at the foot of a grave.

foot·stool (foot'stool') *n.* A low stool for the feet.

foot·stove (foot'stōv') *n.* A metal container for live coals, enclosed in a box having a perforated top: used for warming the feet.

foot·ton (foot'tun') *n.* The work done in raising a long ton a distance of one foot against the force of gravity.

foot·wall (foot'wôl') *n.* **1** *Mining* The layer of rock lying just beneath a vein of ore. **2** *Geol.* That side of an inclined fault that lies below the hanging wall.

foot·way (foŏt'wā') *n.* A path or passage for pedestrians; footpath.

foot·wear (foŏt'wâr') *n.* Clothing for the feet; boots, shoes, socks, stockings.

foot·work (foŏt'wûrk') *n.* Use or control of the feet, as in boxing or tennis.

foot·worn (foŏt'wôrn', -wōrn') *adj.* **1** Weary with walking. **2** Worn by the feet, as a path.

fop (fop) *n.* A man affectedly fastidious in dress or deportment; a dandy. [Cf. Du. *foppen* cheat]

fop·pish (fop'ish) *adj.* Characteristic of a fop; dandified. —**fop'pish·ly** *adv.*

for (fôr, *unstressed* fər) *prep.* **1** To the extent of: The ground is flat *for miles.* **2** Through the duration or period of: The coupon is good *for* a week. **3** To the number or amount of: a check *for* six dollars. **4** At the price or payment of: He bought the hat *for* ten dollars. **5** On account of; as a result of: He is respected *for* his ability. **6** In honor of; by the name of: He is called Walter *for* his grandfather. **7** Appropriate to: a time *for* work. **8** In place or instead of: using a book *for* a desk. **9** In favor, support, or approval of: a vote *for* peace. **10** In the interest or behalf of: My lawyers will speak *for* me. **11** Tending toward, as with longing or desire: a passion *for* jewelry; an eye *for* bargains. **12** As affecting (in a particular way): good *for* your health. **13** Belonging, given, attributed, or assigned to: a package *for* you; the reason *for* going. **14** In proportion to: big *for* his age. **15** As the equivalent to or requital of: blow *for* blow. **16** In spite of: I believe in it *for* all your sophistry! **17** In order to reach or go toward: He left *for* his office. **18** In order to become, find, keep, or obtain: using *for* damages; looking *for* a hat. **19** At (a particular time or occasion): We agreed to meet *for* Easter. **20** In the character of; as being, seeming, or supposed to be: We took him *for* an honest man. —**for . . . to . . .** To have: The child pulled at her skirt *for* her *to* notice him. —**O** (Now, etc.) **for . . .** ! Would that I had !: O *for* a horse! —*conj.* **1** In view of the reason that; seeing that: It is no easy matter to decide, *for* its elements are complex. **2** Owing to the fact that; because: He could not leave, *for* he was expecting a visitor. See synonyms under BECAUSE. [OE]

for- *prefix* **1** Away; off (in a privative sense); past: *forget, forgo.* **2** Very; extremely: *forlorn.* [OE *for-, fær-*]

for- See also words beginning FORE-.

for·age (fôr'ij, for'-) *n.* **1** Any food suitable for horses or cattle. **2** The act of foraging or seeking food. —*v.* **for·aged**, **for·ag·ing** *v.t.* **1** To strip of provisions; search through for supplies; ravage. **2** To provide with forage. **3** To obtain or provide by or as by foraging. —*v.i.* **4** To search for food or supplies. **5** To search: usually with *out* or *for.* **6** To make a foray. See synonyms under FOOD. [< F *fourrage* < OF *feurre* < Gmc.] —**for'ag·er** *n.*

foraging ant Any of various tropical ants (family *Formicidae*) that make forays for food in large bodies; especially, the driver ant and army ant of Africa, and the tropical American legionary ant (genus *Eciton*).

fo·ra·men (fô·rā'mən) *n. pl.* **·ram·i·na** (-ram'ə·nə) *Anat.* **1** An orifice or short passage, as in a bone. **2** An opening; aperture. [< L < *forare* bore]

foramen magnum *Anat.* The large orifice by which the spinal cord passes into the skull and becomes continuous with the medulla oblongata.

for·a·min·i·fer (fôr'ə·min'ə·fər, for'-) *n.* One of a large order (*Foraminifera*) of rhizopods usually having a typically calcareous or chitinous shell perforated by many minute apertures. They are chiefly marine and virtually microscopic. [< L *foramen, -inis* a hole +-*fer* having < *ferre* bear] —**fo·ram·i·nif·er·al** (fə·ram'ə·nif'ər·əl), **fo·ram·i·nif·er·ous** *adj.*

for·ay (fôr'ā, for'ā) *v.t. & v.i.* To ravage; pillage; raid. —*n.* A marauding expedition; raid. See synonyms under INVASION. [Prob. back formation < *forayer* a raider < OF *forrier* < *forre*, var. of *feurre* FORAGE]

forb (fôrb) *n.* A weed, in the range stockman's usage; a non-grasslike herb. [Appar. < Gk. *phorbē* fodder]

for·bade, **for·bad** (fər·bad', fôr-) Past tense of FORBID.

for·bear¹ (fôr·bâr', fər-) *v.* **·bore**, **·borne**, **·bear·ing** *v.t.* **1** To refrain or abstain from; avoid (an action) voluntarily. **2** *Archaic* To put up with; endure. —*v.i.* **3** To abstain or refrain. **4** To be patient or act patiently. See synonyms under REFRAIN. [OE] —**for·bear'er** *n.*

for·bear·ance (fôr·bâr'əns, fər-) *n.* **1** The act of forbearing; patient endurance of offenses. **2** *Law* A refraining from claiming or enforcing a right. **3** A refraining from retaliation or retribution. See synonyms under MERCY, PATIENCE, RESPITE.

for·bid (fər·bid', fôr-) *v.t.* **for·bade** or **for·bad**, **for·bid·den** or **for·bid**, **for·bid·ding** **1** To command (a person) not to do, use, enter, etc. **2** To prohibit the use or doing of; interdict. **3** To make impossible. See synonyms under PROHIBIT. [OE *forbēodan*] —**for·bid'dance** *n.* —**for·bid'der** *n.*

forbidden fruit 1 In the Bible, the fruit of the tree of knowledge of good and evil, forbidden to Adam and Eve. **2** Prohibited pleasure.

force (fôrs, fōrs) *n.* **1** *Physics* Anything that changes or tends to change the state of rest or motion in a body: the fundamental cgs unit of force is the dyne. **2** The action of one body upon another; any operating energy. **3** Any moral, social, or political cause, or aggregate of causes. **4** Power or energy as lodged in an individual agent. **5** Power or energy considered as exerting constraint or compulsion; coercion. **6** The capacity to convince or move; weight; import. **7** Binding effect; efficacy. **8** An organized or aggregated body of individuals; especially, a military aggregate; an army; troop or naval unit. **9** Rhetorical vigor; energy; animation; strength. **10** A group of workers. See synonyms under ARMY, IMPULSE, OPERATION, POWER, —**coercive** or **coercitive force** *Physics* The power of resisting magnetization or demagnetization. —**the force** The police of a certain district. —*v.t.* **forced**, **forc·ing** **1** To compel to do something by or as by force; coerce; constrain. **2** To get or obtain by or as by force: to *force* an answer. **3** To bring forth or about by or as by effort: to *force* a smile. **4** To drive or move despite resistance; press: to *force* the enemy back. **5** To assault and capture, as a fortification. **6** To break open, as a door or lock. **7** To make, as a passage or way, by force. **8** To press or impose upon someone as by force: to *force* one's opinion on someone. **9** To exert to or beyond the utmost; strain, as the voice. **10** To stimulate the growth of artificially, as plants in a hothouse. **11** To rape. **12** *Obs.* To put in force, as a law. **13** In baseball: **a** To put out (a base runner) who has been compelled by another baserunner to leave one base for the next. **b** To allow (the base runner on third base) to score by walking the batter when the bases are full. **c** To allow (a run) in such a manner. **14** In card games: **a** To compel (a player) to trump a trick by leading a suit of which he has none. **b** To play so as to compel (a player) to reveal the strength of his hand. **c** To compel a player to play (a particular card). [< F < L *fortis* brave, strong] —**force'a·ble** *adj.* —**forc'er** *n.*

forced feeding Compulsory feeding of a person.

force-feed (fôrs'fēd', fōrs'-) *n.* The supply of lubricating oil under pressure to an internal-combustion engine.

force·ful (fôrs'fəl, fōrs'-) *adj.* Acting with force; strong; effective. —**force'ful·ly** *adv.* —**force'ful·ness** *n.*

force·meat (fôrs'mēt', fōrs'-) *n.* Finely chopped, seasoned meat served separately or used as stuffing. [< *force*, alter. of FARCE, *v.* + MEAT]

force-out (fôrs'out', fōrs'-) *n.* In baseball, an out made when a runner, forced from his base, fails to reach the next base before it is tagged by a fielder holding the ball.

ford (fôrd, fōrd) *n.* A place in a stream that can be crossed in a vehicle or by wading. —*v.t.* **1** To go on foot or in a vehicle across (a stream, river, etc.). **2** To drive across a river or stream at a ford, as cattle, etc. [OE *ford*] —**ford'a·ble** *adj.* —**ford'less** *adj.*

fore (fôr, fōr) *adj.* **1** Preceding in place or time; forward; antecedent; prior. **2** Situated at or toward the front in relation to something else. —*n.* **1** The foremost part; the leading place. **2** *Naut.* The foremast. —**to the fore 1** To or at the front; into prominence or conspicuous view. **2** At hand; available. **3** Alive; still active. —*prep. & conj. Archaic* or *Dial.* Before. —*adv.* **1** *Naut.* At or toward the bow of a ship. **2** Before; forward; in front. —*interj.* In golf, a warning to any person who stands in the way of a stroke or of the ball. [OE]

fore- See also words beginning FOR-.

fore-and-aft (fôr'ən·aft', fōr'-) *adj. & adv. Naut.* Lying or going in the direction of the ship's length; also, toward both bow and stern; in or at the bow and stern.

fore·arm¹ (fôr·ärm', fōr-) *v.t.* To arm beforehand.

fore·arm² (fôr'ärm', fōr'-) *n.* **1** The part of the arm between the elbow and the wrist. ◆ Collateral adjective: *cubital.* **2** A wooden grip on the barrel of a gun to guard the firer's hand against being burned.

fore·bear (fôr'bâr', fōr'-) *n.* An ancestor. [< Earlier *fore-be-er*, one who has existed formerly]

fore·bode (fôr·bōd', fōr-) *v.t. & v.i.* **·bod·ed**, **·bod·ing 1** To have a premonition of (evil or harm). **2** To portend; presage; foretell. See synonyms under AUGUR. [< FORE- + BODE²] —**fore·bode'ment** *n.* —**fore·bod'er** *n.*

fore·brain (fôr'brān', fōr'-) *n. Anat.* **1** The first embryonic cerebral vesicle, from which develop the interbrain and endbrain. **2** The prosencephalon.

fore·cast (fôr'kast', -käst', fōr'-) *v.t.* **·cast**, **·cast·ing 1** To calculate or plan beforehand. **2** To predict; foresee. **3** To foreshadow. See synonyms under ANTICIPATE, AUGUR. —*n.* **1** *Meteorol.* An antecedent calculation or determination, especially in regard to weather conditions over a short period of time on the basis of charted data. **2** Previous contrivance; also, plan. **3** Forethought; foresight. **4** A prophecy. See synonyms under ANTICIPATION, PRUDENCE.

fore·cas·tle (fōk'səl, -käs'-, fôr'-, fōk'səl) *n. Naut.* **1** The forward part of a ship. **2** In a merchant vessel, the forward part or compartment with living quarters for common sailors. Also spelled *fo'c's'le.*

fore·close (fôr·klōz', fōr'-) *v.* **·closed**, **·clos·ing** *v.t.* **1** *Law* **a** To deprive (a mortgager in default) of the right to redeem mortgaged property. **b** To take away the power to redeem (a mortgage or pledge). **2** To shut out; exclude. —*v.i.* **3** To foreclose a mortgage. [< OF *forclos*, pp. of *forclore* exclude < *for-* outside (< L *fors*) + *clore* < L *claudere* close] —**fore·clos'a·ble** *adj.* —**fore·clo'sure** (-klō'zhər) *n.*

fore·con·scious (fôr·kon'shəs, fōr-) *n.* The preconscious.

fore·course (fôr'kôrs', fōr'kōrs') *n. Naut.* In a square-rigged vessel, the foresail.

fore·court (fôr'kôrt', fōr'kōrt') *n.* In tennis, handball, etc., the zone nearest the net or wall.

fore·date (fôr·dāt', fōr-) *v.t.* **·dat·ed**, **·dat·ing** To antedate.

fore·deck (fôr'dek', fōr'-) *n. Naut.* The forward part of a deck, especially of an upper deck.

fore·fa·ther (fôr'fä'thər, fōr'-) *n.* An ancestor; especially a remote ancestor.

fore·front (fôr'frunt', fōr'-) *n.* The foremost part or position.

fore·glimpse (fôr'glimps', fōr'-) *n.* A glimpse of the future, or a glance ahead at the outset.

fore·go¹ (fôr·gō', fōr-) See FORGO.

fore·go² (fôr·gō', fōr-) *v.t. & v.i.* **fore·went**, **fore·gone**, **fore·go·ing** To go before or precede in time, place, etc. [OE *foregān*]

fore·go·ing (fôr·gō'ing, fōr-) *adj.* Occurring previously; antecedent. See synonyms under ANTECEDENT.

fore·gone (fôr·gôn', -gon', fōr'-) *adj.* Determined already; previous. —**fore'gone'ness** *n.*

fore·ground (fôr'ground', fōr'-) *n.* That part of a landscape or picture nearest the spectator.

fore·gut (fôr'gut', fōr'-) *n. Zool.* In vertebrates, the anterior part of the embryonic alimentary canal.

fore·hand (fôr'hand', fōr'-) *adj.* 1 Done prior to. 2 Front. 3 Of or pertaining to a tennis stroke made to the right of the body (when the player is right-handed): distinguished from *backhand.* — *n.* 1 The part of a horse in front of the rider. 2 Superiority; advantage. 3 A forehand tennis stroke; also, the position in playing such a stroke.

fore·head (fôr'id, -hed, for'-) *n.* 1 The upper part of the face, between the eyes and the natural line of the hair. ◆ Collateral adjective: *frontal.* 2 The front part of a thing.

for·eign (fôr'in, for'-) *adj.* 1 Belonging to, situated in, or derived from another country; not native; alien. 2 Connected with other countries; bearing a relation to other countries. 3 Of, pertaining to, or resulting from some person or thing aside from that under discussion. 4 *Biol.* Occurring in that place or body in which it is not normally or organically found. 5 Having only remote relation or no relation; not pertinent; irrelevant. 6 *Law* Not subject to the laws or jurisdiction of a country; extraterritorial. 7 *Obs.* Outside one's family circle. See synonyms under ALIEN. [<F *forain,* ult. <L *foras* out of doors]

foreign affairs International affairs in relation to the home government.

foreign bill A bill of exchange drawn in one country or state and made payable in another: also called **foreign draft.**

for·eign-born (fôr'in·bôrn', for'-) *adj.* Born in another country; not native.

for·eign·er (fôr'in·ər, for'-) *n.* A native or citizen of a foreign country. See synonyms under ALIEN.

foreign exchange 1 The transaction of monetary affairs, payment of debts, etc., between residents of different countries. 2 The value of the money of one country in terms of the money of another; also, the difference between this and par.

foreign legion A military unit of foreign volunteers serving in a national army.

Foreign Legion A volunteer infantry regiment of the French army composed chiefly, in its enlisted ranks, of non-French troops and originally serving in North Africa. Also **French Foreign Legion.**

foreign mission 1 A group of people organized and sent to spread religious teaching, medical knowledge, etc., in a foreign country. 2 A group of government representatives sent to a foreign country on diplomatic or other business.

for·eign·ness (fôr'in·nis, for'-) *n.* 1 The state or quality of being foreign. 2 Absence of connection or relation; extraneousness.

fore·judge (fôr·juj', fōr-) *v.t.* **·judged, ·judg·ing** To prejudge; pass judgment on before hearing the evidence.

fore·knowl·edge (fôr'nol'ij, for'-) *n.* Knowledge of a thing before it manifests itself or of an event before it takes place; prescience.

fore·land (fôr'land, for'-) *n.* 1 A projecting point of land; a cape. 2 Territory situated in front: opposed to *hinterland.*

fore·lay (fôr·lā', fōr-) *v.t.* **·laid, ·lay·ing** *Dial.* To plan or lay down beforehand.

fore·leg (fôr'leg', for'-) *n.* A front leg of a quadruped. Also **fore leg.**

fore·lock[1] (fôr'lok', for'-) *n.* A lock of hair growing over the forehead.

fore·lock[2] (fôr'lok', for'-) *n. Mech.* An iron pin or wedge passed through the end of a bolt or the like, to prevent its withdrawal; linchpin; key.

fore·man (fôr'mən, for'-) *n. pl.* **·men** (-mən) 1 The overseer of a body of workmen. 2 The head man; chief man; especially, the spokesman of a jury. See synonyms under MASTER. — **fore'man·ship** *n.*

fore·mast (fôr'mast', -mäst', -məst, for'-) *n. Naut.* The foremost mast of a vessel.

fore·most (fôr'mōst, -məst, for'-) *adj.* First in place, time, rank, or order; chief. See synonyms under FIRST, PARAMOUNT. — *adv.* In the first place; soonest; first. [OE *formest*]

fo·ren·sic (fə·ren'sik) *adj.* 1 Pertaining to courts of justice or to public disputation; argumentative; rhetorical. 2 Relating to or used in legal proceedings: *forensic* medicine.

Also **fo·ren'si·cal.** [<L *forensis* <*forum* market place, forum] — **fo·ren'si·cal·ly** *adv.*

fore·or·dain (fôr'ôr·dān', for'-) *v.t.* To ordain beforehand; predestinate.

fore·part (fôr'pärt', for'-) *n.* The first part in time, place, or sequence.

fore·peak (fôr'pēk', for'-) *n. Naut.* The extreme forward part of a ship's hold within the angle of the bow under the lowest deck.

fore·quar·ter (fôr'kwôr'tər, for'-) *n.* The front portion of a side of beef, etc., including the leg and adjacent parts.

fore·rank (fôr'rangk', for'-) *n.* The front or first rank.

fore·reach (fôr·rēch', for-) *v.t. Naut.* 1 To gain upon or pass, as a ship. — *v.i.* 2 To move forward suddenly and unexpectedly. 3 To gain.

fore·run (fôr·run', for-) *v.t.* **·ran, ·run, ·run·ning** 1 To be the precursor of; foreshadow; herald. 2 To run in advance of; precede. 3 To forestall.

fore·run·ner (fôr·run'ər, for-, fôr'run'ər, for'-) *n.* 1 A precursor; predecessor; ancestor. 2 One who or that which runs before; a herald; a harbinger. 3 A portent or prognostic. — **the Forerunner** John the Baptist. See synonyms under HERALD.

fore·said (fôr'sed', for'-) *adj.* Aforesaid.

fore·sail (fôr'sāl', -səl, for'-, fō'səl) *n. Naut.* 1 A square sail, bent to the foreyard; the lowest sail on the foremast of a square-rigged vessel. 2 The fore-and-aft sail on a schooner's foremast, set on a boom and gaff. 3 The forestaysail of a cutter or sloop.

fore·see (fôr·sē', for-) *v.t.* **fore·saw, fore·seen, fore·see·ing** To see beforehand; anticipate. — **fore·see'a·ble** *adj.* — **fore·seer'** *n.*

fore·shad·ow (fôr·shad'ō, for-) *v.t.* To suggest or indicate beforehand; prefigure. — *n.* The indistinct representation or indication of something to come. — **fore·shad'ow·er** *n.*

fore·short·en (fôr·shôr'tən, for-) *v.t.* In drawing, to reduce the lines or parts of (a drawing, etc.) so as to create the illusion of depth and distance while retaining the proper proportions of size and extent. — **fore·short'en·ing** *n.*

fore·show (fôr·shō', for-) *v.t.* **·showed, ·shown, ·show·ing** To show or indicate beforehand; prophesy. Also *Archaic* **fore·shew'** (-shō).

fore·side (fôr'sīd', for'-) *n.* 1 The front. 2 Land along the shore.

fore·sight (fôr'sīt', for'-) *n.* 1 The act or capacity of foreseeing; a looking forward. 2 Thoughtful care for the future. See synonyms under ANTICIPATION, PRUDENCE, WISDOM. — **fore'sight'ed** *adj.* — **fore'sight'ed·ness** *n.*

fore·skin (fôr'skin', for'-) *n.* The prepuce.

for·est (fôr'ist, for'-) *n.* 1 A large tract of land covered with a natural growth of trees and underbrush. ◆ Collateral adjective: *sylvan.* 2 In English law, wild land generally belonging to the crown and kept for the protection of game. — *adj.* Of, pertaining to, or inhabiting woods or forest. — *v.t.* To overspread or plant with trees; make a forest of. [<OF <Med. L *(silva) foresta* an unenclosed (wood) <*foris* outside]

fore·stall (fôr·stôl', for-) *v.t.* 1 To hinder, prevent, or guard against by taking preventive measures. 2 To deal with, think of, or realize beforehand; anticipate. 3 To affect (the market) in one's favor by buying up or diverting goods. 4 *Obs.* To intercept. See synonyms under PREVENT. [OE *foresteall* an ambush] — **fore·stall'er** *n.* — **fore·stall'ing** *n.*

for·est·a·tion (fôr'is·tā'shən, for'-) *n.* 1 Forest extension; the planting of, or conversion of land into, forests. 2 Practical forestry.

fore·stay (fôr'stā', for'-) *n. Naut.* A guy from the head of the foremast to the stem.

fore·stay·sail (fôr'stā'sāl', -səl, for'-) *n. Naut.* A triangular sail in front of the foremast, hoisted on the forestay: in some rigs called *foresail.*

forest cover The sum total of vegetation in a forest; more especially, herbs, shrubs, and the litter of leaves, branches, fallen trees, and decayed vegetable matter composing the **forest floor.**

for·est·ed (fôr'is·tid, for'-) *adj.* Covered with trees or woods.

for·est·er (fôr'is·tər, for'-) *n.* 1 One skilled in the science of forestry; one in charge of

a forest, its timber, or its game. 2 Any forest dweller. 3 A spotted moth (family *Agaristidae*) of the United States; especially, the velvety-black eight-spotted forester (*Alypia octomaculata*). 4 The great gray kangaroo of Australia (*Macropus giganteus*).

forest fly A small, dipterous insect (*Hippobosca equina*) widely distributed in the Old World, infesting horses, mules, camels, and related quadrupeds: also called *horse tick.*

forest reserve A tract of forest land set aside by government order for protection and cultivation.

for·est·ry (fôr'is·trē, for'-) *n.* The science of planting, developing, and managing forests.

Forest Service A branch of the Department of Agriculture which administers the National Forests, directs forest research, and promotes the conservation of forest resources.

fore·taste (fôr·tāst', for-) *v.t.* **·tast·ed, ·tast·ing** To have some experience or taste of beforehand. See synonyms under ANTICIPATE. — *n.* (fôr'tāst', for'-) A taste or brief experience beforehand. See synonyms under ANTICIPATION.

fore·tell (fôr·tel', for-) *v.t. & v.i.* **·told, ·tell·ing** To tell or declare in advance; predict; prophesy. See synonyms under AUGUR, PROPHESY. — **fore·tell'er** *n.*

fore·thought (fôr'thôt', for'-) *adj.* Devised or thought of in advance; planned. — *n.* 1 Consideration beforehand; deliberate planning. 2 Prudent care for the future. See synonyms under ANTICIPATION, CARE, PRUDENCE. — **fore·thought'ful** *adj.* — **fore·thought'ful·ly** *adv.* — **fore·thought'ful·ness** *n.*

fore·time (fôr'tīm', for'-) *n.* Time gone by; the past.

fore·to·ken (fôr·tō'kən, for-) *v.t.* To foreshow or presage; foreshadow. — *n.* (fôr'tō'kən, for'-) A token in advance.

fore·tooth (fôr'tooth', for'-) *n. pl.* **·teeth** An incisor.

fore·top (fôr'top', for'-; *for def. 3, also* fôr'təp, for'-) *n.* 1 The forelock; especially of a horse. 2 The front part of a wig. 3 *Naut.* A platform at the head of the lower section of a foremast.

for·ev·er (fôr·ev'ər, fər-) *adv.* 1 Throughout eternity; to the end of time; everlastingly. 2 Incessantly. Also *Brit.* **for ever.**

fore·warn (fôr·wôrn', for-) *v.t.* To caution beforehand; inform or instruct in advance. — **fore·warn'ing** *n.*

fore·wom·an (fôr'woom'ən, for'-) *n. pl.* **·wom·en** (-wim'in) A woman who oversees other employees.

fore·word (fôr'wûrd', for'-) *n.* An introduction; preface.

fore·yard[1] (fôr'yärd', for'-) *n. Naut.* The lowest yard on the foremast of a square-rigged vessel.

fore·yard[2] (fôr'yärd', for'-) *n.* A front yard of a house, temple, etc.

for·feit (fôr'fit) *v.t.* To incur the loss of through some fault, omission, error, or offense. [<*n.*] — *adj.* Forfeited. — *n.* 1 A thing lost by way of penalty for some default. 2 *pl.* Any game in which some piece of personal property is taken as a fine for a breach of the rules, and is redeemable by some playful penalty; also, the articles so taken. 3 Forfeiture. [<OF *forfait* a misdeed <Med. L *foris factum* <*foris* outside + *factum.* See FACT.] — **for'feit·a·ble** *adj.* — **for'feit·er** *n.*

for·fei·ture (fôr'fi·chər) *n.* 1 The act of forfeiting. 2 That which is forfeited.

for·fi·cate (fôr'fi·kit) *adj.* Deeply furcate, or forked, as the tail of a frigate bird. [<L *forfex, forficis* scissors + -ATE[1]]

for·gath·er (fôr·gath'ər) *v.i.* 1 To meet or gather together; assemble. 2 To meet or encounter, especially by chance. 3 To associate; converse socially. Also spelled *foregather.*

for·gave (fôr·gāv', fər-) Past tense of FORGIVE.

forge (fôrj, forj) *v.t. & v.i.* **forged, forg·ing** To move, go, or impel slowly forward. [? Alter. of FORCE]

forg·er·y (fôr'jər·ē, for'-) *n. pl.* **·ger·ies** 1 The act of falsely making or materially altering, with intent to defraud, any writing which, if genuine, might be of legal efficacy or the foundation of a legal liability. 2 The act of counterfeiting coin. 3 A spurious article bearing a false signature, as a painting, sculpture, or book. **4** *Obs.* The exercise of invention.

Synonym: counterfeiting.

for·get (fər·get′, fôr-) *v.* **for·got** (*Archaic* **for·gat**), **for·got·ten** or **for·got**, **for·get·ting** *v.t.* **1** To be unable to recall (something previously known) to the mind; fail or cease to remember. **2** To fail (to do something) unintentionally; neglect. **3** To fail to take through forgetfulness; leave behind accidentally. **4** To lose interest in or regard for; overlook purposely; disregard or slight: *I* will never *forget* you. **5** To leave unmentioned; fail to think of. — *v.i.* **6** To lose remembrance of something. — **to forget oneself 1** To be unselfish. **2** To lose self-control and act in an unbecoming manner. **3** To lose consciousness. **4** To be lost in thought. [OE *forgietan*] — **for·get′ter** *n.*

for·get·ful (fər·get′fəl, fôr-) *adj.* **1** Having little power to retain or recall. **2** Neglectful; inattentive; careless. **3** *Obs.* Producing forgetfulness or oblivion. — **for·get′ful·ly** *adv.* — **for·get′ful·ness** *n.*

for·get–me–not (fər·get′mē·not′) *n.* A small herb (genus *Myosotis*) of the borage family, with blue, rose, or white flowers. One species (*M. alpestris*) is the official flower of Alaska Territory.

forg·ing (fôr′jing, fôr′-) *n.* A tool or implement that has been forged.

for·give (fər·giv′, fôr-) *v.* **for·gave, for·giv·en, for·giv·ing** *v.t.* **1** To grant pardon for or remission of (something); cease to demand the penalty for. **2** To grant freedom from penalty to (someone). **3** To cease to blame or feel resentment against. **4** To remit, as a debt. — *v.i.* **5** To show forgiveness; grant pardon. See synonyms under ABSOLVE, PARDON. [OE *forgiefan*] — **for·giv′a·ble** *adj.* — **for·giv′er** *n.*

for·give·ness (fər·giv′nis, fôr-) *n.* **1** The act of forgiving; pardon. **2** A disposition to forgive. See synonyms under MERCY.

for·go (fôr·gō′) *v.t.* **for·went, for·gone, for·go·ing 1** To refrain from. **2** To give up; go without. **3** *Obs.* To overlook; neglect. Also spelled *forego.* See synonyms under ABANDON. [OE *forgān* pass over] — **for·go′er** *n.*

for·got (fər·got′, fôr-) Past tense and alternative past participle of FORGET.

for·got·ten (fər·got′n, fôr-) Past participle of FORGET.

fork (fôrk) *n.* **1** A utensil consisting of a handle and two or more tines or prongs, used for handling food at the table or in cooking. **2** A pronged agricultural or mechanical implement for tossing, turning, carrying, digging, lifting, etc.: a *pitchfork.* **3** Anything of like use or shape. **4** An offshoot: diverging branch. **5** The angular opening or place of division.

FARM FORKS
a.   Spading fork.
b.   Hay fork.
c.   Ensilage fork.
d.   Barley fork.
e.   Manure fork.

6 The point at which two roads or streams unite. **7** Each of the roads or streams: the west *fork*; also, the ground in the angle made by the junction of two streams. **8** A dilemma. **9** The barb of an arrow. — *v.t.* **1** To make fork-shaped. **2** To pierce, pitch, or dig with or as with a fork. **3** In chess, to attack (two pieces) simultaneously. — *v.i.* **1** To branch; bifurcate: The trail *forked.* — **to fork out** (or **over** or **up**) *Slang* To pay or hand over. [OE *forca* <L *furca*]

forked (fôrkt, fôr′kid) *adj.* **1** Having a fork, or shaped like a fork. **2** Diverging into two branches: *forked* lightning. — **fork′ed·ly** *adv.* — **fork′ed·ness** *n.*

forked tongue A lying or treacherous tongue.

fork·y (fôr′kē) *adj.* Like a fork; forked; bifurcate.

for·lorn (fər·lôrn′, fôr-) *adj.* **1** Left in distress without help or hope; deserted. **2** Miserable; pitiable. **3** Lonely; dreary. [Orig. pp. of obs.

---

forlese lose, abandon, OE *forleosan*] — **for·lorn′ly** *adv.* — **for·lorn′ness** *n.*

forlorn hope 1 A desperate enterprise. **2** Those who undertake a hopeless task, as the members of a storming party. [<Du. *verloren hoop* lost troop]

form (fôrm) *n.* **1** The outward or visible shape of a body as distinguished from its substance or color. **2** *Philos.* The intelligible structure of a thing, which determines its substance or species, as distinguished from its matter. **3** A body, especially of a living being. **4** A mold or frame for shaping. **5** A specific structure, condition, or appearance: carbon in the *form* of diamonds; disease in all its *forms.* **6** A specific type or species of a larger group: democracy as a *form* of government. **7** In art, music, and literature, style and manner, as opposed to content. **8** System; order; formal procedure: to convene as a matter of *form.* **9** Behavior or conduct according to custom, ceremony, or decorum; formality; manners. **10** Manner or fashion of doing something: He swam in good *form.* **11** Fitness in respect to health, spirits, training, etc.: The horse was in good *form* for the race. **12** A formula or draft; a specimen document used as a guide in drawing up others. **13** A document with spaces left for the insertion of information: an application *form.* **14** The lair of an animal, especially of a hare. **15** A cotton bud. **16** A long bench without a back. **17** *Brit.* A grade or class in a school. **18** *Printing* The body of type and cuts secured in a chase. Also *Brit.* **forme. 19** *Gram.* Any of the various shapes assumed by a word in a particular context, as *talk, talks, talked, talking.* **20** *Ling.* A linguistic form. See BOUND FORM, FREE FORM. — *v.t.* **1** To give shape to; mold; fashion. **2** To construct in the mind; devise: to *form* a plan. **3** To combine into; organize into: The men *formed* a club. **4** To develop; acquire, as a habit or liking. **5** To give a specific or exemplified shape or character to: He *formed* his ideals on those of Wilson. **6** To go to make up; be an element of: Guesswork *forms* the larger part of his theory. **7** To shape by discipline or training; mold: Education *forms* the mind. **8** *Gram.* To construct (a word) by adding or combining elements: to *form* an adverb by adding *–ly* to an adjective. — *v.i.* **9** To take shape; assume a specific form or arrangement. **10** To begin to exist. See synonyms under CONSTRUCT. [<OF *fourme* <L *forma*]

Synonyms (noun): appearance, aspect, ceremonial, ceremony, configuration, conformation, contour, fashion, figure, formality, method, mode, mold, observance, outline, rite, ritual, shape. See BODY, FIGURE, FRAME.

-form *combining form* Like; in the shape of: *ensiform.* [<L *-formis -*like *< forma* form]

for·mal[1] (fôr′məl) *adj.* **1** Made, framed, or done in accordance with regular and established forms and methods, or with proper dignity and impressiveness; orderly. **2** Of or pertaining to established forms or methods. **3** Of or pertaining to the external appearance or form as opposed to real substance: *formal* religion; perfunctory. **4** Having outward show, but lacking reality; outward; mechanical. **5** Having regard to or done in accordance with a scrupulous observance of social forms, customs, and etiquette; punctilious; ceremonious; conventional. **6** Of or pertaining to the form as opposed to the content of logical reasoning. **7** *Philos.* Of or pertaining to the characteristic composition of anything; essential instead of material.

for·mal[2] (fôr·mal′) *n.* Methylal.

for·mal·de·hyde (fôr·mal′də·hīd) *n. Chem.* A colorless pungent gas, CH_2O, obtained variously by the partial oxidation of methyl alcohol: used as an antiseptic, reagent, preservative, and disinfectant, for which it is prepared by solution in water or absorption into porous materials. It is also the basis of many important plastic materials, such as Bakelite, Formica, etc. Also **for·mal′de·hyd** (-hid). [<FORM(IC) + ALDEHYDE]

for·mal·ism (fôr′məl·iz′əm) *n.* **1** Scrupulous observance of prescribed forms, especially in religious worship, social life, art, etc. **2** An instance of such observance. **3** Gestalt or

---

configuration psychology. — **for′mal·ist** *n.* — **for′mal·is′tic** *adj.*

for·mal·i·ty (fôr·mal′ə·tē) *n. pl.* **·ties 1** The state or character of being formal, precise, stiff, or elaborately ceremonious. **2** Adherence to standards and rules; ceremony; conventionality. **3** A proper order of procedure. **4** Form without substance or meaning. See synonyms under FORM.

formal logic The branch of logic which deals only with the formal structure of propositions and with the operations by which conclusions are deduced from them; the art of deductive reasoning.

for·mal·ly (fôr′mə·lē) *adv.* **1** In accordance with forms; in a formal manner; stiffly. **2** In an authorized manner.

for·mat (fôr′mat) *n.* The form, size, type face, margins, and general style of a book or other publication, when printed and bound; especially, its shape and size as determined by the number of times the original sheet forming the leaves has been folded. [<F <L (*liber*) *formatus* a (book) made up *< formare* form]

for·ma·tion (fôr·mā′shən) *n.* **1** The act or process of forming or of making by the combination of materials; also, the taking on of specific form; development. **2** Manner in which anything is shaped or composed. **3** The disposition of military troops as in column, line, or square. **4** Anything that is formed. **5** *Geol.* **a** Earthy or mineral deposits, or rock masses, named with reference to mode of origin. **b** A series of associated rocks, having similar conditions of origin. **6** *Ecol.* A fully developed plant association in a given area.

form·a·tive (fôr′mə·tiv) *adj.* **1** Competent, serving, or aiding to form; capable of being formed or influenced; plastic. **2** Pertaining to formation. **3** *Gram.* Serving to form words. — *n. Gram.* **1** An element, as an affix, added to the root of a word to give it a new and special grammatical form. **2** A word formed by the addition of a new element to, or a modification of, the root.

form class A group of linguistic forms having certain syntactical characteristics in common, as all words functioning as the subjects of sentences in English.

form·er[1] (fôr′mər) *n.* One who or that which forms or molds; a maker; pattern.

for·mer[2] (fôr′mər) *adj.* Going before in time; previously mentioned; preceding; ancient. — **the former** The first of two mentioned persons or things: opposed to *the latter.* See synonyms under ANTECEDENT, ANTERIOR, CAUSE. [ME *formere,* a back formation *< foremost*]

for·mic (fôr′mik) *adj.* **1** Pertaining to or derived from ants. **2** Derived from formic acid. [<L *formica* ant]

for·mi·cant (fôr′mə·kənt) *adj.* **1** Antlike. **2** *Med.* Pertaining to the feeble, creeping motion of the pulse noted in certain conditions.

for·mi·car·y (fôr′mə·ker′ē) *n. pl.* **·car·ies** A nest of ants, consisting of galleries and chambers excavated in the earth and covered by a mound of debris.

for·mi·cate (fôr′mə·kāt) *v.i.* **·cat·ed, ·cat·ing** To swarm; collect in swarms, as ants. [<L *formicatus,* pp. of *formicare* crawl *< formica* an ant] itching sensation like the creeping of ants.

for·mi·ci·a·sis (fôr′mə·sī′ə·sis) *n. Pathol.* The itching, swollen condition following ant bite.

for·mi·da·ble (fôr′mi·də·bəl) *adj.* **1** Exciting fear; felt as dangerous to encounter. **2** Difficult to accomplish. [<MF <L *formidabilis* <*formidare* fear] — **for′mi·da·ble·ness** *n.* — **for′mi·da·bly** *adv.*

Synonyms: dangerous, redoubtable, redoubted, terrible, tremendous. That which is *formidable* is worthy of fear if encountered or opposed; as, a *formidable* array of troops, or of evidence. *Formidable* is a word of more dignity than *dangerous,* and suggests more calm and collected power than *terrible; formidable* is less overwhelming than *tremendous.* A loaded gun is *dangerous;* a battery of artillery is *formidable.* A *dangerous* man is likely to do mischief, and needs watching; a *formi-*

---

dable man may not be *dangerous* if not attacked; an enraged maniac is *terrible*; the force of ocean waves in a storm, the silent pressure in the ocean depths, are *tremendous*. *Antonyms:* contemptible, despicable, feeble, harmless, helpless, powerless, weak.

form·less (fôrm′lis) *adj.* Without form; shapeless. — **form′less·ly** *adv.* — **form′less·ness** *n.*

for·mu·la (fôr′myə·lə) *n.* *pl.* **·las** or **·lae** (-lē) **1** An exact method or form of words prescribed as a guide for thought, action, expression, or statement; fixed rule or set form. **2** A medical prescription. **3** *Math.* A rule or combination expressed in algebraic or symbolic form. **4** *Chem.* A symbolic representation of the nature, composition, and structure of a chemical compound. The principal types are: the **empirical formula,** giving the quantitative values of the constituents, as H_2SO_4, sulfuric acid; the **structural formula,** showing the linkages of each atom, as CH_3CH_3, ethane; and the **graphic formula,** showing the spatial relations of the constituents, as

$$H-\overset{\displaystyle H}{\underset{\displaystyle |}{C}}-\overset{\displaystyle H}{\underset{\displaystyle |}{C}}-OH, \text{ ethyl alcohol } C_2H_6O, \text{ or } CH_3CH_2OH.$$

5 A confession of religious faith, or a formal statement of doctrine. See synonyms under LAW, RULE. [<L, dim. of *forma* form]

for·mu·late (fôr′myə·lāt) *v.t.* **·lat·ed,** **·lat·ing** **1** To express in a formula, or as a formula. **2** To put or state in exact, concise, and systematic form. — **for′mu·la′tion** *n.* — **for′·mu·la′tor** *n.*

for·mu·lism (fôr′myə·liz′əm) *n.* Observance or use of, or adherence to, formulas. — **for′mu·lis′tic** *adj.*

for·myl (fôr′mil) *n.* *Chem.* The univalent radical CHO, constituting the base of formic acid. [<FORM(IC) + -YL]

for·ni·cate[1] (fôr′nə·kit) *adj.* *Archit.* Arched; vaulted. [<L *fornicatus* <*fornix, -icis* an arch]

for·ni·cate[2] (fôr′nə·kāt) *v.i.* **·cat·ed,** **·cat·ing** To commit fornication. [<L *fornicatus,* pp. of *fornicare* <*fornix, -icis* a vault, brothel] — **for′ni·ca′tor** *n.*

for·ni·ca·tion (fôr′nə·kā′shən) *n.* **1** Illicit sexual intercourse of unmarried persons. **2** In Scriptural use: **a** Adultery or harlotry, or incest. **b** Idolatry.

for·nix (fôr′niks) *n.* *pl.* **for·ni·ces** (-nə·sēz) **1** *Anat.* **a** A vaulted or reflected surface. **b** The bands of white fibers beneath the corpus callosum of the brain, connecting the two hemispheres of the cerebrum. **2** *Archit.* A vault or arch, commonly one within a building. [<L, vault]

for·sake (fər·sāk′, fôr-) *v.t.* **for·sook, for·sak·en, for·sak·ing** **1** To leave or withdraw from; renounce. **2** To abandon; desert. **3** *Obs.* To reject. See synonyms under ABANDON. [OE *forsacan*]

for·sooth (fər·sōōth′, fôr-) *adv.* In truth; certainly: chiefly ironical. [OE *forsóth*]

for·spent (fôr·spent′) *adj.* Tired out; exhausted: also spelled forespent. [Orig. pp. of *forspend* exhaust, OE *forspendan*]

for·swear (fôr·swâr′) *v.* **swore, sworn, swear·ing** *v.t.* **1** To renounce upon oath; repudiate; abjure. **2** To deny upon oath. — *v.i.* **3** To swear falsely; commit perjury. — **to for·swear oneself** To swear falsely. See synonyms under ABANDON, RENOUNCE. [OE *forswerian* swear falsely]

for·sworn (fôr·swôrn′, -swōrn′) *adj.* Perjured.

for·syth·i·a (fôr·sith′ē·ə, -sī′thē·ə, fər-) *n.* One of a genus (*Forsythia*) of slender shrubs of the olive family native to China and Japan. Two species, *F. viridissima* and *F. suspensa,* are widely cultivated as ornamental plants. [after Wm. *Forsyth,* 1737–1804, British botanist, who brought the shrub from China]

fort (fôrt, fōrt) *n.* A single enclosed military work capable of independent defense; any fortification held by a garrison; a fortification: fortress. [<F, orig. an adj. <L *fortis* strong]

fort·a·lice (fôr′tə·lis) *n.* An outwork of a fortification; a small fort. [<Med. L *fortalitia* <*fortis* strong]

forte[1] (fôrt) *n.* **1** That which one does most readily or excellently. **2** The strongest part of a sword blade: distinguished from *foible*. [<F *fort.* See FORT.]

for·te[2] (fôr′tā, -tē) *Music n.* A musical chord or passage to be performed loudly. — *adj.* & *adv.* Loud: often as a direction to the player. [<Ital., strong <L *fortis*]

forth (fôrth, fōrth) *adv.* **1** Forward in place, time, or order. **2** Outward, as from seclusion. **3** Away; out, as from a place of origin; abroad. — *prep. Archaic* Forth from; out of. [OE, forwards]

forth·com·ing (fôrth′kum′ing, fōrth′-) *adj.* Ready or about to appear. — *n.* A coming forth.

forth·right (fôrth′rīt′, fōrth′-) *adj.* Straightforward; direct. — *n. Archaic* A direct path or course. — *adv.* **1** Straightforwardly; with directness or frankness. **2** At once; straightway.

forth·with (fôrth′with′, -with′, fōrth′-) *adv.* Without delay; immediately.

for·ti·eth (fôr′tē·ith) *adj.* **1** Tenth in order after the thirtieth: the ordinal of *forty.* **2** Being one of forty equal parts. — *n.* One of forty equal parts of anything; the quotient of a unit divided by forty.

for·ti·fi·ca·tion (fôr′tə·fə·kā′shən) *n.* **1** The act, art, or science of fortifying. **2** A military defensive work; a fort. **3** A strengthening of any kind.
Synonyms: castle, citadel, fastness, fort, fortress, stronghold. *Fortification* is the general word for any artificial defensive work; a *fortress* is a *fortification* of especial size and strength, regarded as permanent, and ordinarily an independent work; a *fort* or *fortification* may be temporary; a *fortification* may be but part of a defensive system; we speak of the *fortifications* of a city. A *citadel* is a *fortification* within a city, or the fortified inner part of a city, or a *fortress* within which a garrison may be placed to overawe the citizens, or to which the defenders may retire if the outer works are captured; the medieval *castle* was the fortified residence of a king or baron. *Fort* is the common military term for a detached fortified building or enclosure of moderate size occupied or designed to be occupied by troops. The *fortifications* of a modern city usually consist of a chain of *forts.* Any defensible place, whether made so by nature or by art, is a *fastness* or *stronghold.* See RAMPART.

for·ti·fied (fôr′tə·fīd) *adj.* **1** Strengthened; said especially of wines whose alcoholic content has been increased by the addition of brandy. **2** Enriched, as bread.

for·ti·fy (fôr′tə·fī) *v.* **·fied, ·fy·ing** *v.t.* **1** To provide with defensive works; strengthen against attack. **2** To give physical or moral strength to; invigorate or encourage. **3** To confirm; corroborate. **4** To strengthen the structure of; reenforce. **5** To strengthen, as wine, by adding alcohol. **6** To enrich (food) by adding minerals, vitamins, etc. — *v.i.* **7** To raise defensive works. [<F *fortifier* <L *fortificare* <*fortis* strong + *facere* make] — **for′ti·fi′a·ble** *adj.* — **for′ti·fi′er** *n.*

for·tis (fôr′tis) *Phonet. adj.* Strongly articulated: opposed to *lenis.* — *n.* A consonant, usually a stop, pronounced with tension of the speech organs or with strong plosion. [<L, strong]

for·tis·si·mo (fôr·tis′ə·mō, *Ital.* fôr·tēs′sē·mō) *adj.* & *adv. Music* Very loud. [<Ital., superl. of *forte* strong]

for·ti·tude (fôr′tə·tōōd, -tyōōd) *n.* **1** Strength of mind to meet or endure unfalteringly pain, adversity, or peril; patient and constant courage. **2** *Obs.* Physical strength or force. [<F <L *fortitudo* <*fortis* strong]
Synonyms: courage, endurance, heroism, resolution. *Fortitude* (L. *fortis,* strong) is the strength or firmness of mind or soul to endure pain or adversity patiently and determinedly. *Fortitude* has been defined as "passive *courage,*" which is a good definition, but not complete. *Fortitude* might be termed "still *courage,*" or "enduring *courage*"; it is that quality which is able not merely to endure pain or trial, but steadily to confront dangers that cannot be actively opposed, or against which one has no adequate defense; it takes *courage* to charge a trench, *fortitude* to withstand an enemy's fire. *Resolution* is of the mind; *endurance* is partly physical; it requires *resolution* to resist

temptation, *endurance* to resist hunger and cold. Compare COURAGE, PATIENCE.

for·ti·tu·di·nous (fôr′tə·tōō′də·nəs, -tyōō′-) *adj.* Having or showing courage and endurance.

fort·night (fôrt′nīt, -nit) *n.* A period of two weeks; fourteen days. [OE *féowerténe* fourteen + *niht* nights]

fort·night·ly (fôrt′nīt′lē) *adj.* Occurring, coming, or issued every fortnight. — *adv.* Once a fortnight.

for·tress (fôr′tris) *n.* A large permanent fort; a stronghold; castle. See synonyms under DEFENSE, FORTIFICATION. — *v.t.* To furnish or strengthen with a fortress; fortify. [<OF *forteresse* <L *fortis* strong]

for·tu·i·tism (fôr·tōō′ə·tiz′əm, -tyōō′-) *n.* The doctrine that phenomena or events come to pass by chance rather than in accordance with intelligent design or natural law. — **for·tu′i·tist** *n.* & *adj.*

for·tu·i·tous (fôr·tōō′ə·təs, -tyōō′-) *adj.* **1** Occurring by chance; casual; accidental. **2** Fortunate; lucky. See synonyms under INCIDENTAL. [<L *fortuitus* <*fors* chance] — **for·tu′i·tous·ly** *adv.* — **for·tu′i·tous·ness** *n.*

for·tu·i·ty (fôr·tōō′ə·tē, -tyōō′-) *n.* *pl.* **·ties** Chance occurrence; also, chance. See synonyms under ACCIDENT, HAZARD.

for·tu·nate (fôr′chə·nit) *adj.* **1** Happening by a favorable chance; lucky. **2** Favored with good fortune. — **for′tu·nate·ly** *adv.* — **for′tu·nate·ness** *n.*
Synonyms: favored, happy, lucky, prospered, prosperous, successful. A man is *successful* in any case if he achieves or gains what he seeks; he is known as a *successful* man if he has achieved or gained worthy objects of endeavor; he is *fortunate* or *lucky* if advantages have come to him without or beyond his direct planning or achieving. *Lucky* is the more common and colloquial, *fortunate* the more elegant word; *fortunate* is more naturally applied to the graver matters, as we speak of the *fortunate,* rather than the *lucky,* issue of a great battle; *lucky* more strongly emphasizes the element of chance, as when we speak of a *lucky* hit, a *lucky* guess, or of one as "born under a *lucky* star." *Favored* is used in a religious sense, implying that one is the object of divine favor. *Happy,* in this connection, signifies possessed of the means of happiness. One is said to be *happy* or *prosperous* whether his prosperity be the result of fortune or of achievement; *prospered* rather denotes the action of a superintending Providence. See AUSPICIOUS, HAPPY. *Antonyms:* broken, crushed, fallen, ill-starred, miserable, unfortunate, unhappy, unlucky, woeful, wretched.

for·tune (fôr′chən) *n.* **1** Chance or luck as the cause of changes in human affairs: often personified. **2** That which befalls one as his lot; good or bad luck. **3** Future destiny; fate: to tell *fortunes.* **4** Good luck; success; prosperity. **5** An amount of wealth; usually great wealth. See synonyms under EVENT. — *v.* **·tuned, ·tun·ing** *v.t. Rare* To bestow wealth upon. — *v.i.* To happen; occur by chance. [<OF <L *fortuna* <*fors* chance] — **for′tune·less** *adj.*

for·tune-hunt·er (fôr′chən·hun′tər) *n.* One who seeks to obtain wealth by marriage. — **for′tune-hunt′ing** *n.*

for·tune-tell·er (fôr′chən·tel′ər) *n.* One who claims to foretell events in a person's future. — **for′tune-tell′ing** *n.* & *adj.*

for·ty (fôr′tē) *adj.* Consisting of ten more than thirty, or of four times ten. — *n.* *pl.* **·ties** **1** The sum of ten and thirty; four times ten: a cardinal number. **2** Any of the symbols (40, xl, XL) representing this number. **3** *U.S.* Forty acres, or one-sixteenth of a section of land. [OE *féowertig*]

for·ty-nin·er (fôr′tē-nī′nər) *n.* *U.S.* An adventurer or pioneer who went to California in 1849, the year of the gold rush.

forty winks *Colloq.* A short nap.

fo·rum (fôr′əm, fō′rəm) *n.* *pl.* **·rums** or **·ra** (-rə) **1** The public market place of an ancient Roman city, where popular assemblies met, and most legal and political business was transacted. **2** A tribunal; a court. **3** An assembly for free discussion of public affairs. [<L]

for·ward (fôr′wərd) *adj.* **1** At, or belonging to, the fore part, as of a ship. **2** Directed toward a position in front; onward: a *forward* course. **3** For deferred delivery: a *forward* purchase. **4** Advanced toward maturity or completion; specifically, precocious. **5** Bold; presumptuous. **6** Advanced; extreme; said of opinions or actions. — *adv.* **1** Toward the future. **2** Toward the front; ahead; onward. **3** At or in the fore part, as of a ship. **4** To a prominent position; forth; into view: to come *forward*; to bring *forward* an idea. Also *forwards*. — **forward of** In advance of. — *n.* **1** In American football, one of the players in the front line who attack in advance of the backfield and try to thwart the opponents. **2** In basketball, soccer, hockey, etc., one of those players who lead the attack and specialize in making goals. — *v.t.* **1** To help onward or ahead; promote. **2** To send; transmit; especially, to send (mail) on to a new address. **3** To prepare (a book) for finishing by covering, etc. See synonyms under ENCOURAGE, PROMOTE. [OE *foreweard*]

forward delivery Delivery at a future time.
for·ward·er (fôr′wər·dər) *n.* **1** A person, firm, or corporation whose business it is to receive goods for transportation and send them to their destination; a forwarding merchant or agent. **2** One who carries or promotes anything, as a reform.
for·ward·ly (fôr′wərd·lē) *adv.* **1** In a forward or front position. **2** In a forward manner; eagerly; boldly.
for·ward·ness (fôr′wərd·nis) *n.* **1** Presumption; overeagerness to put oneself forward; boldness; brazenness. **2** Willing readiness; eagerness. **3** State of being forward or in advance; precocity.
forward pass See under PASS.
forward quotation A price set for goods to be delivered at a future time.
for·wards (fôr′wərdz) See FORWARD *adv.*
foss (fôs, fos) *n.* An artificial ditch or moat, as in a fortification. Also **fosse.** [<F *fosse* <L *fossa* <*fodire* dig]
fos·sa (fôs′ə, fos′ə) *n.* *pl.* **fos·sae** (-ē) *Anat.* A shallow depression or cavity in the body. [<L. See FOSS.]
fos·sick (fôs′ik, fos′-) *v.i. Austral.* **1** *Mining* To search for gold in abandoned mines, waste heaps, etc.; also, to search for surface gold. **2** To rummage about for something: used with *about* or *around.* [Cf. dial. E *fussock* bustle] — **fos′sick·er** *n.*
fos·sil (fos′əl, fôs′-) *n. Paleontol.* **1** The actual remains of plants or animals, preserved in the rocks of the earth's crust; also, material evidences of early organisms, as in petrified forms, coprolites, casts, impressions, imprints, etc. **2** *Geol.* One of certain inorganic objects or substances which in extinct or mineralized forms preserve in themselves records of the natural activities or phenomena of ancient geological ages, as solidified ripple marks. **3** Buried records of human activities, even within historic times. **4** *Colloq.* A person or thing that is behind the times, antiquated, or out of date. — *adj.* **1** Dug out of the earth; petrified. **2** Of or like a fossil; outworn; antiquated. [<F *fossile* <L *fossilis* dug up <*fossa.* See FOSS.]
fos·sil·if·er·ous (fos′əl·if′ər·əs) *adj.* Containing fossils.
fos·sil·ize (fos′əl·īz) *v.* **·ized, ·iz·ing** *v.t.* **1** To change into a fossil; petrify. **2** To make antiquated or out of date. — *v.i.* **3** To become a fossil. **4** To search for or gather fossil specimens. — **fos′sil·i·za′tion** *n.*
fos·so·ri·al (fo·sôr′ē·əl, -sō′rē-) *adj.* **1** Digging; burrowing: a *fossorial* animal. **2** Adapted for or used in digging in the earth, as the legs and other organs of the moles, armadillos, etc. [<LL *fossorius* <L *fodire* dig]
fos·ter (fôs′tər, fos′-) *v.t.* **1** To rear; bring up, as a child. **2** To promote the growth of; forward; help: to *foster* genius. **3** To keep as if affectionately; cherish; nurse: to *foster* a grudge. **4** *Obs.* To provide with food. See synonyms under AID, CHERISH, HELP, PROMOTE. — *adj.* Having the relation of, in the sense of giving, sharing, or receiving nourishment, shelter, affection, and care, but unrelated by blood; as in

foster brother	foster father	foster parent
foster child	foster land	foster sister
foster daughter	foster mother	foster son

[OE *fostrian* nourish] — **fos′ter·age** *n.* — **fos′·ter·er** *n.* — **fos′tress** *n. fem.*
fos·ter·ling (fôs′tər·ling, fos′-) *n.* A foster child.
Foucault current See under CURRENT.
Fouc·quet (foo·ke′) See FOUQUET.
fou·droy·ant (foo·droi′ənt, *Fr.* foo·drwà·yän′) *adj.* **1** Sudden and overwhelming, as lightning. **2** *Pathol.* Beginning in an aggravated form, as a disease. [<F, ppr. of *foudroyer* strike with lightning <*foudre* lightning]
fought (fôt) Past tense and past participle of FIGHT.
foul (foul) *adj.* **1** Offensive or loathsome to the physical, moral, or esthetic sense; filthy. **2** Obstructing, entangling or injuring by anything that clogs or is harmful; contrary; disagreeable. **3** Impeded or encumbered by something detrimental; clogged; entangled; encumbered; a *foul* chimney, a *foul* anchor. **4** Not according to justice or rule; unfair. **5** *Printing* **a** Full of errors; inaccurate; dirty. **b** Having the characters badly mixed; said of a type case. **6** Unfavorable; unlucky: a *foul* wind. **7** *Obs.* Ugly; homely. **8** In baseball, of or pertaining to a foul ball or foul line. — *n.* **1** An act of fouling, colliding, or becoming entangled. **2** A breach of rule in various sports and games. **3** In baseball, a foul ball. — *adv.* In a foul manner. — *v.t.* **1** To make foul or dirty; befoul. **2** To clog or choke, as a drain. **3** To entangle; snarl, as a rope in a pulley. **4** *Naut.* To cover or encumber (a ship's bottom) with barnacles, seaweed, etc. **5** To collide with. **6** To dishonor; disgrace. **7** In sports, to commit a foul against. **8** In baseball, to bat (the ball) outside of the foul lines. — *v.i.* **9** To become foul or dirty. **10** To become clogged or encumbered. **11** To become entangled. **12** To collide. **13** In sports, to violate a rule. **14** In baseball: **a** To bat a foul ball. **b** To be retired by batting a foul ball which is caught before it strikes the ground: usually with *out.* — **to foul up** *Slang* To bungle; make a mess (of). ◆ Homophone: *fowl.* [OE *ful*]
  Synonyms (adj.): defiled, dirty, filthy, gross, impure, indelicate, muddy, nasty, obscene, odious, offensive, soiled, stained, sullied, unclean, vile. See BAD, NOISOME. *Antonyms:* see synonyms for PURE.
foul ball In baseball, a ball batted so that it falls outside the foul lines.
foul line 1 In baseball, a line drawn from home plate through first or third base to the limits of the field. **2** In basketball, the line from which foul shots are made. **3** In bowling, tennis, etc., any line limiting the area of play or action.
foul·ly (foul′lē) *adv.* **1** In a foul manner. **2** Undeservedly: *foully* maligned.
foul-mouthed (foul′mouthd′, -moutht′) *adj.* Using abusive, profane, or obscene language.
foul·ness (foul′nis) *n.* **1** The state or quality of being foul. **2** Foul matter.
foul play 1 Unfairness; in games and sports, a violation of rule. **2** Any unfair or treacherous conduct, often with the implication of murder.
foul shot In basketball, a free throw awarded a player who has been fouled by an opposing player, and if successful scored as one point.
foul tip In baseball, a pitched ball swung at by the batter and glancing off the bat into the catcher's hands: the batter is retired if there are two strikes against him.
fou·mart (foo′märt) *n.* The European polecat; the fitchew. Also **fou·li·mart** (foo′lē·märt). [ME *fulmard*, OE *fūl* foul + *mearth* marten]
found¹ (found) *v.t.* **1** To lay the foundation of; establish on a foundation or basis: to *found* a theory. **2** To give origin to; establish; set up: to *found* a college or a family. — **to found on 1** To form and base one's opinion. **2** To rest as on a foundation. [<OF *fonder* <L *fundare* <*fundus* base, bottom] — **found′er** *n.*
found² (found) *v.t.* **1** To cast, as iron, by melting and pouring into a mold. **2** To make by casting molten metal. [<F *fondre* <L *fundere* pour]
found³ (found) Past tense and past participle of FIND. — *adj.* Provided with food, lodging, equipment, etc. — **and found** Plus board and lodging, as part payment.

foun·da·tion (foun·dā′shən) *n.* **1** The act of founding or establishing. **2** That on which anything is founded and by which it is supported or sustained. **3** A fund for the permanent maintenance of an institution; an endowment. **4** An endowed institution. **5** A structure upon which a building or a machine is erected, usually wholly or principally of masonry; that part of a building below the surface of the ground, or the portion that constitutes a base; sometimes, a platform, on which the upper portions rest. **6** An inner, fitted lining of a garment. **7** Theatrical greasepaint applied to the face, hands, etc., before adding the final make-up details. — **foun·da′·tion·al** *adj.*
foundation garment A girdle or corset, often combined with a brassière.
foundation sire In horse breeding, the named stallion from which the genealogy of all horses of a given breed is traced.
found·er¹ (foun′dər) *n.* One who makes metal castings.
found·er² (foun′dər) *v.i.* **1** *Naut.* To fill with water and sink. **2** To collapse; cave in; fail. **3** To stumble; go lame, as a horse. **4** To have founder. — *v.t.* **5** *Naut.* To cause to sink. **6** To cause to go lame. — *n.* **1** Inflammation of the tissue in the foot of a horse, commonly due to overfeeding: also called *laminitis.* **2** Act of foundering. [<OF *fondrer* sink <*fond* bottom <L *fundus*]
founders' shares Shares of stock, often privileged to extra dividends, issued to the promoters or founders of a company as payment for organizing expenses and reward for initiative.
found·ing (foun′ding) *n.* The business of making articles of cast iron, brass, etc.
found·ling (found′ling) *n.* A deserted infant of unknown parentage. [ME *fundeling* <*funde*, pp. of *find* + -LING¹]
foun·dry (foun′drē) *n. pl.* **·dries 1** An establishment in which articles are cast from metal. **2** The act or operation of founding. Also **foun′der·y.**
foundry proof *Printing* A final proof of composed type before stereotyping or electrotyping.
fount (fount) *n.* A fountain; hence, any source. [<F *font* <L *fons, fontis* fountain]
foun·tain (foun′tən) *n.* **1** A spring or jet of water issuing from the earth; especially, the source of a stream. ◆ Collateral adjective: *fontal.* **2** The origin or source of anything. **3** A jet or spray of water forced upward artificially, to provide water for drinking, cooling the air, or display. **4** A structure designed for such a jet to rise and fall in. **5** A reservoir or supply chamber for holding oil, ink, etc., as in a lamp, printing press, or inkstand. **6** A soda fountain. See synonyms under BEGINNING, CAUSE. [<OF *fontaine* <LL *fontana,* orig. fem. singular of *fontanus* of a spring <*fons, fontis* fountain]
foun·tain·head (foun′tən·hed′) *n.* **1** The source of a stream. **2** Any primal source or originating cause.
fountain pen A pen having a reservoir for ink within the holder.
four (fôr, fōr) *adj.* Consisting of one more than three; twice two; quaternary. — *n.* **1** The cardinal number following three and preceding five, or any of the symbols (4, iv, IV) used to represent it. **2** Anything made up of four units or members; especially, a crew of four oarsmen, a team of four horses, a playing card with four pips, etc. [OE *feower*]
four·chette (foor·shet′) *n.* **1** A forked piece between glove fingers, uniting the front and back parts. **2** *Ornithol.* The furculum or wishbone of a bird. **3** The frog of a horse. **4** *Anat.* A fold of mucous membrane forming the posterior commissure of the vulva. [<F, dim. of *fourche* a fork <L *furca*]
four-cy·cle (fôr′sī′kəl, fōr′-) A cycle of operation in an engine in which air is taken into the cylinder, compressed, burned, and exhausted in four successive strokes.
four-di·men·sion·al (fôr′di·men′shən·əl, fōr′-) *adj.* **1** Having, or pertaining to, four dimensions. **2** *Math.* Relating to a system or a set of magnitudes whose elements can be completely defined only by four coordinates.

Four·drin·i·er (foor·drin′ē·ər) *adj.* Of, pertaining to, or designating a papermaking machine, the first to make a continuous web: invented by Louis Robert of France and patented by him there, but improved in England by Henry and Sealy Fourdrinier early in the 19th century. — *n.* A Fourdrinier machine.

four-eyed fish (fôr′īd′, fōr′-) The anableps.

four-flush (fôr′flush′, fōr′-) *n.* A valueless poker hand containing four cards of one suit and one of another. — *v.i.* To bet on a hand containing four cards of one suit but lacking the fifth. **2** *Slang* To bluff.

four·fold (fôr′fōld′, fōr′-) *adj.* Made up of four; quadruplicate. — *n.* That which is four times as many or as much. — *adv.* In quadrupled measure.

Four Freedoms Freedom of speech and religion and freedom from want and fear: the world-wide goals of U.S. foreign policy stated by President F. D. Roosevelt in a message to Congress, January 6, 1941.

four-hand·ed (fôr′han′did,′ fōr′-) *adj.* **1** Having four hands; quadrumanous, as monkeys. **2** Needing four hands, as certain games, a piano duet, etc.

four hundred The most exclusive social group of a place: a term originally applied to the wealthiest set in New York by Ward McAllister.

Fou·ri·er·ism (foor′ē·ə·riz′əm) *n.* The social reform system advocated by F. M. C. Fourier about 1815, proposing small, voluntary cooperative groups for economic production and maintenance, the achievement of social justice, and the fulfilment of individual desires. — **Fou′ri·er·ist, Fou′ri·er·ite′** *n.*

four-in-hand (fôr′in·hand′, fōr′-) *adj.* **1** Consisting of a four-horse team driven by one person. **2** Designating a necktie tied in a slipknot with the ends hanging vertically. — *n.* **1** A four-horse team driven by one person; also, a vehicle drawn by four horses. **2** A four-in-hand necktie.

four-leafed rose (fôr′lēft′, fōr′-) *Geom.* The polar curve of equation $r = a \sin 2\theta$: a curve of four symmetrical loops with the node at the origin.

four·pence (fôr′pəns, fōr′-) *n.* **1** The sum of four English pennies; also, a silver piece of that value. **2** A silver coin used before the Civil War, worth 6 1/4 cents; the Spanish half-real: called *fourpence halfpenny* in New England, *fippenny bit* in Pennsylvania and elsewhere.

four-post·er (fôr′pōs′tər, fōr′-) *n.* A bedstead with four tall posts at the corners. and worn around the left shoulder. [< F]

four·score (fôr′skôr′, fōr′skôr′) *adj. & n.* Four times twenty; eighty.

four·some (fôr′səm, fōr′-) *adj.* Consisting of four: said of anything in which four are needed to take part together. — *n.* **1** A game, especially of golf, in which four players take part, two on each side; also the players. **2** Any group of four.

four·square (fôr′skwâr′, fōr′-) *adj.* **1** Having four equal sides and angles; square. **2** Frank, firm; solid; also, sincere; without guile. — *n.* An object having four equal sides; a square.

four·teen (fôr′tēn′, fōr′-) *adj.* Consisting of four more than ten, or of twice seven. — *n.* **1** The sum of ten and four; twice seven. **2** Any symbol (14, xiv, XIV) representing this number. [OE *fēowertēne*]

Fourteen Points The peace aims set forth by President Woodrow Wilson in an address, January 8, 1918, ten months before the end of World War I. Also **Fourteen Peace Points.**

fourth (fôrth, fōrth) *adj.* **1** Next in order after the third. **2** Being one of four equal parts. — *n.* **1** One of four equal parts of anything; the quotient of a unit divided by four; a quarter. **2** A fourth person, thing, or group. **3** *Music* **a** The interval between any note and the fourth note above it in a diatonic scale, counting the starting point as one. **b** A note at this interval above or below any other, considered in relation to that other; specifically, the fourth above the keynote; the subdominant. **c** Two notes at this interval written or sounded together; the consonance thus produced. See INTERVAL. — **the Fourth** July 4th; Independence Day. — *adv.* In the fourth order, rank, or place: also, in formal discourse, *fourthly.* ◆ Homophone: *forth.*

fourth-class (fôrth′klas′, -kläs′, fōrth′-) *adj.* Designating mail matter consisting of merchandise, and carried at the lowest rate.

fourth dimension **1** *Math.* A hypothetical, usually spatial dimension in addition to height, width, and thickness. **2** In the theory of relativity, the temporal coordinate of space time. — **fourth′-di·men′sion·al** *adj.*

fourth estate **1** The newspapers; journalism, in general. **2** *Brit.* The reporters' gallery in the House of Commons.

Fourth of July *U.S.* Independence Day.

Fourth Republic The republic formed in France in 1945.

four-wheel (fôr′hwēl, fōr′-) *adj.* **1** Having four wheels. **2** Affecting or controlling all four wheels: *four-wheel* drive.

fo·ve·a (fō′vē·ə) *n. pl.* **·ve·ae** (-vi·ē) *Anat.* A shallow rounded depression: the central *fovea* of the retina directly in the axis of vision; a fossa. [< L, a small pit] — **fo′ve·al** *adj.*

fo·ve·ate (fō′vē·āt, -it) *adj.* Having foveae; covered with little pits.

fo·ve·o·la (fə·vē′ə·lə) *n. pl.* **·lae** (-lē) A small fovea or pit. Also **fo·ve·ole** (fō′vē·ōl), **fo′ve·o·let** (-let). [< L, dim. of *fovea* a small pit]

fo·ve·o·late (fō′vē·ə·lāt) *adj.* Having foveolae or little pits. Also **fo′ve·o·lat′ed.**

fowl (foul) *n. pl.* **fowl** or **fowls** **1** The common domestic cock, hen, or chicken. **2** The flesh of fowls, especially of the full-grown domestic hen. **3** Poultry in general. **4** Birds collectively: wild *fowl.* **5** *Obs.* Any bird. — *v.i.* To catch or hunt wild fowl. ◆ Homophone: *foul.* [OE *fugol*] — **fowl′er** *n.*

fowl cholera An infectious intestinal disease, chronic or acute, of domestic fowl caused by a pathogenic bacterium, *Pasteurella avicida.*

fox (foks) *n.* **1** A burrowing canine mammal (family *Canidae*, genus *Vulpes*) having a long, pointed muzzle and long bushy tail, commonly reddish-brown in color, noted for its cunning. The common **European red fox** *(V. vulpes)* is reddish-brown above and white beneath, with a white-tipped tail. It inhabits a burrow, and preys on poultry, rabbits, etc. The **North American red fox** *(V. fulva)* is a similar species of which the **cross fox** (having a dark cross mark on its back) and **black** or **silver fox** are color varieties. The **gray fox** *(Urocyon cinereoargenteus)* is found from Pennsylvania southward, and differs in habits from the red. ◆ Collateral adjective: *vulpine.* **2** The fur of the fox. **3** A sly, crafty person. **4** A small rope made by hand of two or more rope yarns. **5** *Obs.* A sword. — *v.t.* **1** To trick; outwit. **2** To make drunk; intoxicate. **3** To stain, as paper or timber, with a reddish color. **4** To make sour, as beer, in fermenting. **5** To repair or mend, as shoes, with new uppers. — *v.i.* **6** To become drunk. **7** To become sour. **8** To become reddish in color. [OE]

Fox (foks) *n.* One of an Algonquian tribe of North American Indians, formerly inhabiting the neighborhood of Green Bay, Wisconsin: combined with the Sacs, 1760.

fox·bane (foks′bān′) *n.* A European herb *(Aconitum lycoctonum)* of the crowfoot family; wolf's-bane.

NORTH AMERICAN RED FOX

(Average length 2 feet; tail, 13 inches; height, 13 inches)

FOWL
Nomenclature for anatomical parts.

fox·ber·ry (foks′ber′ē) *n. pl.* **·ries** The cowberry.

fox brush The tail of a fox.

fox-chase (foks′chās′) *n.* A fox hunt.

fox earth The burrow of a fox.

foxed (fokst) *adj.* **1** Discolored by decay: applied to timber. **2** Having light-brown stains or spots, as the paper of books, prints, etc. **3** Repaired or ornamented with a foxing, as the upper leather of a shoe.

fox-fire (foks′fīr′) *n.* The phosphorescent light emitted by foxed or rotten wood.

fox-fish (foks′fish′) *n. pl.* **·fish** or **·fish·es** **1** The dragonet. **2** The fox shark.

fox·glove (foks′gluv′) *n.* Any plant of a genus *(Digitalis)* of the figwort family, especially the English variety *(D. purpurea),* having flowers in long one-sided racemes; the leaves are a source of digitalis.

ENGLISH FOXGLOVE
(From 2 1/2 to 5 feet tall)

fox grape Either of two species of American grapes, called the **northern fox grape** *(Vitio labrusca)* and the **southern fox grape** *(V. rotundifolia).*

fox-hole (foks′hōl′) *n.* A shallow pit dug by a combatant as cover against enemy fire: so called from the earth burrow of a fox.

fox-hound (foks′hound′) *n.* One of a breed of large, strong, very swift dogs trained for fox-hunting.

fox-hunt (foks′hunt′) *n.* The hunting of foxes with hounds. Also **fox hunt.**

fox shark The thresher shark *(Alopias vulpes),* having a powerful tail as long as its body: also called *foxfish.*

fox-skin (foks′skin′) *n.* **1** The dressed skin of a fox. **2** A fur cap made of such skin.

fox squirrel Any of several large North American arboreal squirrels; especially *Sciurus niger.*

fox-tail (foks′tāl′) *n.* **1** The tail of a fox. **2** Any of various species of grass bearing a dense spike of flowers like a fox's tail; especially the meadows foxtail *(Alopecurus pratensis).*

fox terrier See under TERRIER.

fox-trot (foks′trot′) *n.* **1** A pace between a trot and a walk: used of horses. **2** A modern dance step of syncopated two-four time.

fox-wood (foks′wood′) *n.* Decayed or foxed wood.

fox·y (fok′sē) *adj.* **fox·i·er, fox·i·est** **1** Of or like a fox; crafty. **2** Reddish-brown in color. **3** Discolored; foxed. **4** Soured; improperly fermented, as wine. **5** Defective, as in quality. **6** Denoting a wild flavor found in wine made from some American grapes. — **fox′i·ness** *n.*

foy·er (foi′ər, -ā; *Fr.* fwȧ·yā′) *n.* **1** A public room or lobby, as in a theater or hotel. **2** An entrance room in a house. [< F < LL *focarium* hearth < *focus*]

Fr *Chem.* Francium (symbol Fr).

fra·cas (frā′kəs) *n.* A noisy fight; brawl. See synonyms under ALTERCATION, QUARREL. [< F < Ital. *fracasso* an uproar < *fracassare* shatter]

frac·tion (frak′shən) *n.* **1** A disconnected part; fragment; hence, a tiny bit. **2** *Math.* A quantity less than a unit, or one expressed as the sum of a number of aliquot parts of a unit. See list of principal kinds of fractions below. **3** *Obs.* The act of breaking. **4** A piece of land smaller than the standard unit of measurement. **5** *Chem.* One of the components separated from a substance by fractional distillation: Naphtha is a *fraction* of petroleum. — *v.t.* To set or separate into fractions. See synonyms under PART. [< OF < L *fractio, -onis* < *fractus,* pp. of *frangere* break]

— **common fraction** A fraction expressed by two numbers, a denominator, indicating the number of equal parts into which the unit is to be divided, and a numerator, indicating the number of those parts to be taken. Also called **vulgar fraction.**

— **complex fraction** A fraction in which either the numerator or the denominator is a fraction. Also called **compound fraction.**

— **continued fraction** A fraction whose denominator is another integer plus another fraction, and so on.

— **decimal fraction** A fraction whose denominator is any power of 10 and which may be expressed in decimal form, as 7/10 (0.7), 3/100 (0.03), etc.

—**improper fraction** A fraction in which the numerator exceeds the denominator.

—**partial fraction** One of a set of fractions whose algebraic sum is a given fraction.

—**proper fraction** A fraction in which the numerator is less than the denominator.

—**similar fraction** Any of a group of fractions having a common denominator or the same number of decimal places.

—**simple fraction** A fraction in which both numerator and denominator are integers.

—**unit fraction** A fraction whose numerator is unity.

frac·tion·al (frak'shən·əl) *adj.* 1 Pertaining to or constituting a fraction. 2 Broken; small. 3 *Chem.* Designating a process or method of separating a complex of substances into component parts on the basis of specific differences in selected properties, as solubility, boiling point, crystallization, etc.

fractional section A piece of land of less than 640 acres, having topographical irregularities.

fractional township A tract of land of more or less than 36 sections, having various topographical irregularities.

fractionating column *Chem.* A long vertical tube divided into segments and attached to a still for the fractional distillation of liquid mixtures: also called *dephlegmator.*

frac·tious (frak'shəs) *adj.* Disposed to rebel; restive; unruly; peevish. See synonyms under FRETFUL, PERVERSE, RESTIVE. —**frac'tious·ly** *adv.* —**frac'tious·ness** *n.*

frac·tog·ra·phy (frak·tog'rə·fē) *n.* The microscopic study of the fractures and other structural defects occurring in metals. [< L *fractus* broken + -GRAPHY] —**frac·to·graph·ic** (frak'tə·Jean graf'ik) *adj.*

frac·ture (frak'chər) *n.* 1 The act, mode, or result of breaking, or the state of being broken. 2 A break. 3 The breaking of a bone; a break in a bone. —**comminuted fracture** A fracture in which the bone is splintered or crushed. —**compound fracture** One leading to an open wound, often exposing the bone. —**impacted fracture** One in which the broken parts are driven into each other. —**simple fracture** One without any break in the skin: also **closed fracture.** 4 A rupture; crack. 5 The characteristic appearance of the freshly broken surface of a mineral, as a conchoidal *fracture.* —*v.t. & v.i.* **·tured, ·tur·ing** To break or be broken; crack. See synonyms under BREAK, RUPTURE. —**frac'tur·a·ble** *adj.* —**frac'tur·al** *adj.*

frag·ile (fraj'əl) *adj.* Easily broken; frail; delicate. [< L *fragilis* < *frangere* break. Doublet of FRAIL.] —**frag'ile·ly** *adv.* —**fra·gil·i·ty** (frə·jil'ə·tē), **frag'ile·ness** *n.*
Synonyms: breakable, brittle, delicate, frail, frangible, infirm, slight, tender, weak.

frag·ment (frag'mənt) *n.* A part broken off; a small detached portion. See synonyms under PART. [< F < L *fragmentum* fragment, remnant]

frag·men·tar·y (frag'mən·ter·ē) *adj.* Composed of fragments; broken; incomplete. Also **fragmen'tal.** —**frag'men·tar'i·ly** *adv.* —**frag'men·tar'i·ness** *n.*

frag·men·ta·tion (frag'mən·tā'shən) *n.* 1 The breaking up into fragments. 2 The scattering in all directions of the fragments of an exploding grenade, shell, or bomb. 3 *Biol.* In cell division, the breaking up of one or more chromosomes into pieces smaller than the normal.

frag·ment·ed (frag'mən·tid) *adj.* Broken into pieces or fragments.

frag·ment·ize (frag'mən·tīz) *v.t.* **·ized, ·iz·ing** To break into small pieces.

fra·grance (frā'grəns) *n.* The state or quality of being fragrant; a sweet odor. Also **fra'gran·cy.**

fra·grant (frā'grənt) *adj.* Having an agreeable or sweet smell. [< L *fragrans, -antis,* ppr. of *fragrare* smell sweet] —**fra'grant·ly** *adv.*

frail[1] (frāl) *n.* 1 A basket made of rushes: used for containing dried fruits, and as a measure. 2 The weight measure of raisins in such a basket, about 50 pounds avoirdupois. [< OF *fraiel* basket]

frail[2] (frāl) *adj.* 1 Delicately constituted; easily broken or destroyed. 2 Easily tempted; liable to be led astray. See synonyms under FRAGILE.

[< OF *fraile* < L *fragilis.* Doublet of FRAGILE.] —**frail'ly** *adv.*

frail·ty (frāl'tē) *n. pl.* **·ties** 1 The state of being frail. 2 A fault or moral weakness. Also **frail'ness.** See synonyms under FOIBLE.

frame (frām) *v.* **framed, fram·ing** *v.t.* 1 To surround with or put in a frame. 2 *Colloq.* To incriminate falsely. 3 To put together; build, as a house. 4 To put in words; utter: to *frame* a reply. 5 To draw up; put in proper form: to *frame* a law. 6 To think out; arrange; conceive, as a plan or theory. 7 To shape or adapt to a purpose; dispose: to *frame* oneself to obedience. —*v.i.* 8 *Obs.* To move; go. See synonyms under CONSTRUCT, MAKE. —*n.* 1 Something composed or constructed of parts, whether physical or mental, united and adjusted to one another in a system; a construction. 2 The general arrangement or constitution of a thing. 3 Structure or build, as of a person. 4 The supporting and formative parts of a structure, put together so as to sustain and give shape to the whole. 5 A machine characterized by a wooden framework or structure: a silk *frame.* 6 A case or border made to enclose or surround a thing. 7 A mental state or condition; mood. 8 In tenpins and bowling, a division of the game during which a player bowls at one setting of the pins. 9 The triangular frame in which the balls in a pool game are bunched ready for the break. 10 One of the complete exposures in a roll of motion-picture film. 11 In television, a single complete scanning of the field of view by the electronic or other scanning device. 12 Form; proportion. 13 The act of contriving or inventing. 14 *Colloq.* A frame-up. [OE *framian* benefit]
Synonyms (noun): fabric, form, framework, order, structure, system. See BODY, FORM, TEMPER.

frame frequency In television, the number of frames per second completed by the scanning spot.

frame house A house built on a wooden framework covered on the outside by shingles, boards, stucco, etc.

fram·er (frā'mər) *n.* One who or that which frames; a maker.

frame·work (frām'wûrk') *n.* A skeleton structure for supporting or enclosing something.

fram·ing (frā'ming) *n.* 1 A framework. 2 The act of erecting or making a frame; the act of composing or drawing up. 3 *Colloq.* The act of conspiring against.

franc (frangk) *n.* 1 A French coin, originally silver and once valued at about 19 1/2 cents: equivalent to 100 centimes: the monetary unit of France. 2 The corresponding monetary unit of Belgium, Switzerland, etc. 3 A French gold piece, first coined in 1360; also, a silver piece, first coined in 1575. [< OF *Franc(orum rex)* king of the Franks, the motto on the first of these coins]

France (frans, fräns) A republic in western Europe; 212,659 square miles; capital, Paris. Abbr. *Fr.*

fran·chise (fran'chīz) *n.* 1 A political or constitutional right reserved to or vested in the people, as the right of suffrage. 2 *Law* A special privilege emanating from the government by legislative or royal grant and vested in an individual person or in a body politic and corporate; a right to do something, as run a railroad, a bus line, etc. 3 The territory or boundary of a special privilege or immunity. 4 Authorization granted by a manufacturer to distributor or retailer to sell his products. See synonyms under RIGHT. —*v.t. Obs.* To enfranchise. [< OF < *franc, franche* free]

Fran·cis (fran'sis, -sis) A masculine personal name. Also **Fran·cis·cus** (*Dan., Du.* frän·sēs'kəs; *Ger.* frän·tsēs'kəs), *Fr.* **Fran·çois** (frän·swä'), *Ital.* **Fran·ces·co** (frän·ches'kō), *Pg., Sp.* **Fran·cis·co** (*Pg.* frän·sēs'kōō, *Sp.* frän·thēs'kō). Compare FRANCES. [< Gmc., free]

—**Francis I,** 1494–1547, king of France 1515–1547.

—**Francis II,** 1768–1835, Holy Roman Emperor 1792–1806, emperor of Austria 1804–35.

—**Francis Ferdinand,** 1863–1914, archduke of Austria; assassinated.

—**Francis Joseph,** 1830–1916, emperor of Austria 1848–1916. Also *Ger.* **Franz Josef.**

—**Francis of Assisi, Saint,** 1182–1226, Italian mendicant; founder of the Franciscan order.

—**Francis of Sales, Saint,** 1567–1622, French prelate; founded the Order of Visitation, 1610. See SALESIAN.

—**Francis Xavier, Saint** See XAVIER.

Fran·cis·can (fran·sis'kən) *n.* A member of the mendicant order (*Gray Friars* or *Minorites*) founded in 1209 by St. Francis of Assisi. The three branches of the order are *Capuchins, Conventuals,* and *Observantines.* See also POOR CLARE. —*adj.* 1 Of or pertaining to St. Francis. 2 Belonging to a religious order or institution following the rule of St. Francis.

fran·ci·um (fran'sē·əm) *n.* A short-lived radioactive metallic element (symbol Fr, atomic number 87) occurring as a decay product of actinium and having a half-life of 22 minutes. See PERIODIC TABLE. [after FRANCE]

fran·co·lin (frang'kə·lin) *n.* An Old World, now chiefly Asian, partridge (genus *Francolinus*), having richly colored plumage and a rather long tail and bill. [< F < Ital. *francolino*]

Fran·co·phile (frang'kə·fil) *n.* A non-French admirer of France or of French customs, etc. —*adj.* Kindly disposed toward France. — **Fran'co·phil'i·a** (-fil'ē·ə) *n.*

Fran·co·phobe (frang'kə·fōb) *n.* A person who fears or dislikes France or French things. —*adj.* Fearful of France. —**Fran'co·pho'bi·a** *n.*

Fran·co-Prus·sian War (frang'kō-prush'ən) See table under WAR.

franc-ti·reur (frän·tē·rœr') *n. pl.* **francs-ti·reurs** (frän·tē·rœr') A French soldier, one of the sharpshooters of a light infantry force. [< F < *franc* free + *tireur* shooter < *tirer* shoot]

fran·gi·ble (fran'jə·bəl) *adj.* Easily broken; brittle; fragile. [< OF < L *frangere* break] — **fran'gi·bil'i·ty, fran'gi·ble·ness** *n.*

fran·gi·pan·i (fran'ji·pan'ē, -pä'nē) *n.* 1 A perfume derived from or resembling that of the West Indian red jasmine (*Plumera rubra*). 2 The plant. Also **fran'gi·pane** (-pān). [after Marquis *Frangipani,* who created the perfume]

frank (frangk) *adj.* 1 Candid and open; ingenuous. 2 *Obs.* Giving freely; generous. 3 *Law* Free, in the sense of privileged, exempt, or unhindered in action. See synonyms under BLUFF, CANDID, HONEST. —*v.t.* 1 To mark, as a letter or package, so as to be sent free of charge. 2 To send, as a letter, free of charge. 3 To convey free of charge. 4 *Chiefly Brit.* To mark or stamp (mail) by machine (a *franking machine*) to indicate that postage has been paid. —*n.* 1 The right to send mail matter free. 2 The package so sent. 3 The signature that authenticates it: extended commercially to telegrams, etc. [< OF *franc* frank, free] — **frank'ly** *adv.* —**frank'ness** *n.* —**frank'er** *n.*

Frank (frangk) *n.* 1 A member of one of the Germanic tribes settled on the Rhine early in the Christian era. 2 In the Near East, any European. [< L *Francus* a Frank < Gmc., a spear (cf. OE *franca* lance); named from their weapon]

Frank·en·stein (frangk'ən·stīn) *n.* 1 The hero of Mary Wollstonecraft Shelley's *Frankenstein,* a medical student who fashions a man monster which commits numerous atrocities and finally slays its maker. 2 Any person destroyed by his own handiwork. 3 Loosely, Frankenstein's monster. 4 Any work or created thing that gets beyond the control of the inventor and causes his destruction.

frank·furt·er (frangk'fər·tər) *n.* A highly seasoned sausage of mixed meats. Compare WIENERWURST. Also **frank'fort·er, frankfurt (or frankfort) sausage.** [after *Frankfurt,* Germany] tice of the Supreme Court, 1939–1962.

frank·in·cense (frangk'in·sens) *n.* An aromatic gum or resin from various trees of East Africa, especially *Boswellia carteri:* used as an incense and in medicine as a stimulant and expectorant: also called *olibanum.* [< OF *franc* pure + *encens* incense]

Frank·ish (frang'kish) *adj.* Of or pertaining to the Franks, or, in the Near East, to Europeans in general. —*n.* The language spoken by the Franks, belonging to the western branch of the Germanic languages.

frank·lin (frangk'lin) *n.* In late medieval England, a freeholder; a non-noble landholder ranking below the gentry. [ME *frankeleyn* < Med. L

francus free]

Frank·lin (frangk′lin) **1** A temporary state, 1784–88, comprising lands of western North Carolina ceded to Congress in 1784; now part of eastern Tennessee. **2** The northernmost district of Northwest Territories, Canada; 541,753 square miles.

frank·lin·ite (frangk′lin-īt) *n.* A metallic, iron-black, slightly magnetic oxide of zinc, iron, and manganese, crystallizing in the isometric system: a valuable ore of zinc. [after *Franklin*, N. J., where it is found]

Franklin stove An open-faced cast-iron stove resembling a fireplace: invented by Benjamin Franklin.

frank·ly (frangk′lē) *adv.* Candidly; openly.

frank·pledge (frangk′plej′) *n.* **1** In old English law, a system of mutual suretyship that required all men to combine in groups of ten to stand as sureties for one another's good behavior. **2** A member of such a group. **3** One such group; a tithing.

FRANKLIN
STOVE

fran·tic (fran′tik) *adj.* Manifesting, or caused by, excessive excitement; frenzied. See synonyms under INSANE. [<OF *frenetique* <LL *phreneticus* <Gk. *phrenitikos* delirious <*phrenitis* delirium <*phrēn* mind] —**fran′ti·cal·ly, fran′tic·ly** *adv.*— **fran′tic·ness** *n.*

frap (frap) *v.t.* **frapped, frap·ping** *Naut.* To draw or bind firmly. [<OF *fraper* strike]

frap·pé (fra-pā′) *U.S. adj.* **frap·pée** *fem.* Iced; chilled. —*n.* **1** A fruit juice frozen to a mush. **2** A liqueur or other beverage poured over shaved ice. [<F, pp. of *frapper* chill]

fra·ter·nal (frə-tûr′nəl) *adj.* **1** Pertaining to or befitting a brother; brotherly. **2** Of or pertaining to a fraternal order or association. [<L *fraternus* <*frater* brother] —**fra·ter′nal·ism** *n.*— **fra·ter′nal·ly** *adv.*

fraternal society An organization for the attainment of some mutual benefit. Also **fraternal association** or **order.**

fraternal twins *Genetics* Twins that develop from separately fertilized ova and thus are as distinct in hereditary characteristics as though born at different times. They may be of the same or opposite sex: distinguished from *identical* twins.

fra·ter·ni·ty (frə-tûr′nə-tē) *n. pl.* **·ties 1** The condition or relation of brotherhood; brotherly affection. **2** An organization, for social or other purposes, of men students of American colleges, usually having Greek letter names and secret rites, and represented by chapters in many in stitutions. **3** A similar organization outside of colleges. **4** A group of men of the same profession, sporting interests, etc.: the medical *fraternity.*

frat·er·ni·za·tion (frat′ər·nə·zā′shən) *n.* The act of fraternizing; specifically, intercourse between occupying military forces and civilians, often in contravention of regulations.

frat·er·nize (frat′ər·nīz) *v.* **·nized, ·niz·ing** *v.i.* **1** To be friendly or fraternal. **2** To be friendly with the enemy or with the people of an occupied or conquered territory; especially, to have sexual relations with women of such a territory. —*v.t.* **3** To bring into fraternal association. —**frat′er·niz′er** *n.*

frat·ri·ci·dal (frat′rə·sī′dəl) *adj.* Of, pertaining to, or guilty of fratricide.

frat·ri·cide (frat′rə·sīd) *n.* **1** One who kills his brother. **2** The killing of a brother. [Def. 1 <F <L *fratricida* <*frater* brother + *caedere* kill; def. 2 <F <L *fratricidium*]

fraud (frôd) *n.* **1** Deception in order to gain by another's loss; craft; trickery; guile. **2** One who acts fraudulently; a cheat. **3** A deceptive or spurious thing. **4** *Law* Any artifice or deception practiced to cheat, deceive, or circumvent another to his injury. [<OF *fraude* <L *fraus, fraudis* deceit] —**fraud′ful** *adj.* —**fraud′ful·ly** *adv.* —**fraud′less** *adj.* **fraud′less·ly** *adv.* — **fraud′less·ness** *n.*

Synonyms: artifice, cheat, cheating, deceit, deception, dishonesty, duplicity, imposition, imposture, swindle, swindling, treachery, treason, trick. A *fraud* is an act of deliberate *deception* with the design of securing something by taking unfair advantage of another. A *deceit* or *decep-*

tion may be designed merely to gain some end of one's own, with no intent of harming another; an *imposition* is intended to take some small advantage of another, or simply to make another ridiculous. An *imposture* is designed to obtain money, credit, or position to which one is not entitled, and may be practiced by a street beggar or by the pretender to a throne. All action that is not honest is *dishonesty*, but the term *dishonesty* is generally applied in business, politics, etc., to deceitful practices which are not distinctly criminal. *Fraud* includes *deceit*, but *deceit* may not reach the gravity of *fraud*; a *cheat* is of the nature of *fraud*, but of a petty sort; a *swindle* is more serious than a *cheat*, involving larger values and more flagrant *dishonesty. Fraud* is commonly actionable at law; *cheating* and *swindling* are for the most part out of the reach of legal proceedings. Compare ARTIFICE, DECEPTION, TREACHERY. *Antonyms:* fairness, honesty, integrity, truth, uprightness.

fraud·u·lence (frô′jə·ləns) *n.* The quality to being fraudulent; unfairness. Also **fraud′u·len·cy.**

fraud·u·lent (frô′jə·lənt) *adj.* Proceeding from, characterized by, or practicing fraud. See synonyms under BAD, COUNTERFEIT. —**fraud′u·lent·ly** *adv.*

fraught (frôt) *adj.* **1** Involving; full of. **2** *Archaic* Freighted; laden. —*n. Obs.* Freight; cargo. [Orig. pp. of obs. *fraught* load, ult. <MDu. *vrachten*]

Fraunhofer's lines A series of groups of dark lines in the spectrum of the sun and other stars, each group appearing to the eye as a single transverse line: also called *F lines.*

frax·i·nel·la (frak′sə·nel′ə) *n.* A Eurasian herb *(Dictamnus albus)* of the rue family with white flowers and a powerful odor: also called *dittany* and *gas plant.* [<NL, dim. of L *fraxinus* ash tree]

fray[1] (frā) *n.* A fight; an affray. —*v.t. Obs.* To frighten. —*v.i. Obs.* To fight. [Aphetic var. of AFFRAY]

fray[2] (frā) *v.t. & v.i.* To wear, rub, or become worn, as by friction; ravel. — *n.* A fretted spot in a cloth, etc. [<F *frayer* <L *fricare* rub]

fra·zil (frə·zil′, fraz′əl, frā′zəl) *n.* Ice of a granular, spicular, or platelike shape formed in agitated or flowing water. Also **frazil ice.** [Cf. F *fraisil* cinders]

fraz·zle (fraz′əl) *Colloq. v.t. & v.i.* **·zled, ·zling 1** To fray or become frayed; fret, or tatter. **2** To tire out; weary. — *n.* Frayed ends; state of being frayed. — **beat to a frazzle** Beat into shreds and tatters; hence, overcome completely. — **worn to a frazzle** Worn to shreds; hence, tired out; utterly exhausted. [? Blend of FRAY[2] + obs. *fasel* ravel]

freak (frēk) *n.* **1** A sudden causeless change of mind; a whim. **2** A malformation; monstrosity. **3** *Slang* One given to the use of drugs, especially illegal drugs. **4** *Slang* One who is very unconventional. **5** *Slang* One who is very enthusiastic about something: an opera *freak.* —*adj.* Strange; abnormal. —**to freak out** *Slang* **1** To experience, often unpleasantly, the effects of drugs, especially psychedelic drugs. **2** To behave as though one were under the influence of a psychedelic drug. [Origin unknown] — **freak′y** *adj.*

freak·ish (frē′kish) *adj.* Inclined to freaks; eccentric; also, like a freak, capricious; prankish. — **freak′ish·ly** *adv.* — **freak′ish·ness** *n.*

freck·le (frek′əl) *n.* A small, brownish, or dark-colored spot on the skin. — *v. freck·led, freck·ling* *v.t.* To mark or cover with freckles. — *v.i.* To become marked with freckles. [ME *fracel*, var. of *frekne* <ON *freknur* freckles]

freck·led (frek′əld) *adj.* Marked with freckles. Also **freck′ly.**

free (frē) *adj.* **fre·er, fre·est 1** Not bound by restrictions, physical, governmental, or moral; exempt from arbitrary domination or distinction; independent. **2** Not enslaved or in bondage. **3** Not believing in or permitting slavery. **4** Self-determining, whether as implying the absence of control through external causes in the form of physical forces, legal commands, or moral influences, or as asserting the mysterious and inexplicable spontaneity of the self as possessed of so-called *free* will. **5** Having, conferring, or characterized by political liberty; not subject to despotic or arbitrary rule; living under a government based on the consent of the people: a

free nation. **6** Liberated, by reason of age, from the authority of parents or guardians: At 21 years a man is *free.* **7** Invested with certain franchises; enjoying certain immunities; given or allowed all privileges of: *free* of the city. **8** Exempt from or not subject to; not dominated by; clear of: followed by *from*, or rarely by *of.* **9** Characterized by disregard of conventionality, ceremony, or formality; accessible; frank; ingenuous. **10** Characterized by disregard of duty or propriety; forward; impertinent, indelicate or immodest; careless; immoderate; reckless. **11** Without impediment or restraint; moving or ranging at will; not repressed, checked, or hampered; unobstructed; unrestricted; unconstrained. **12** Without restriction; especially, without charge or cost; open; gratuitous: *free* seats. **13** Employing or giving unrestrainedly or without parsimony; liberal; profuse; generous; also, not obtained by solicitation. **14** Expending energy without stint; ready and prompt in action or movement without urging; ready; spirited. **15** Not closely bound to an original or pattern, nor limited by strict technical rules; exercising some liberty or discretion: a *free* choice, a *free* translation. **16** Not attached, bound, or fixed; capable of moving; loose: the *free* end of a rope. **17** Uncombined chemically: *free* hydrogen. **18** Available: *free* energy. **19** *Naut.* Favorable: applied to winds more than six points from being dead ahead. **20** Of or pertaining to a freeman: opposed to *base.* —*adv.* **1** Gratuitously. **2** Freely; willingly. **3** With the wind more than six points from being dead ahead. —*v.t.* **freed, free·ing 1** To make free; release from bondage, obligation, worry, etc. **2** To clear or rid of obstruction or hindrance; disentangle; disengage. See synonyms under ABSOLVE, DELIVER, RELEASE. [OE *frēo*] —**free′ly** *adv.*

Synonyms (adj.): clear, emancipated, exempt, independent, unchecked, unconfined, unfettered, unhindered, unimpeded, unobstructed, unrestrained, untrammeled. See GENEROUS. *Antonyms:* bound, clogged, dependent, enslaved, fettered, hindered, impeded, restrained, restricted, shackled, subdued, subjected, subjugated.

–free *combining form* Free of; devoid of: *carefree, duty-free.*

free agency The power or capacity of a personality to act freely without constraint of his will. See WILL.

free agent A person regarded as self-determining and thus capable of responsible choice, and whose actions are determined by his own unconstrained will.

free association 1 *Psychol.* An association of ideas unrestricted by definite control or limiting factors. **2** *Psychoanal.* A method of revealing unconscious processes by encouraging a spontaneous and unselective association of ideas.

free·board (frē′bôrd′, -bōrd′) *n.* **1** *Naut.* The side of a vessel between the water line and the main deck. **2** The distance between the underframe of an automobile and the ground.

free·boot·er (frē′bōō′tər) *n.* One who plunders; especially a pirate or buccaneer. [<MDu. *vrijbuiter* <*vrij* free + *buit* booty]

free·born (frē′bôrn′) *adj.* Not born in servitude.

free city A city having an independent government, as certain German cities, that at one time were virtually small republics.

free coinage The mintage of certain specified bullion that may be offered at the mint by any person, with or without a fixed charge.

freed·man (frēd′mən) *n. pl.* **·men** (-mən) An emancipated slave, especially an emancipated American Negro after the Civil War. — **freed′wom′an** *n. fem.*

free·dom (frē′dəm) *n.* **1** Exemption or liberation from slavery or imprisonment. **2** Exemption from political restraint or autocratic control; independence. **3** Liberty of choice or action. **4** *Philos.* The state of the will as the first cause of human actions; self-determination in rational beings. **5** Exemption; immunity: *freedom* from want; *freedom* from arrest. **6** Exemption or release from obligations, ties, etc. **7** Ease; facility. **8** Frankness or familiarity in speech or manner. **9** The right to enjoy the privileges of membership or citizenship: *freedom* of the city. **10** Unrestricted use: He had *freedom* of the library.

11 Ease of motion. See synonyms under LIBERTY. — **free′dom·less** adj. [OE *frēodōm*]

freedom of the press The right freely to publish without censorship or other government interference, usually restricted in practice by laws barring obscenity, sedition, and libel.

free electron See under ELECTRON.

free energy *Physics* That portion of the energy of a physicochemical system that is available to perform work.

free form *Ling.* A morpheme which can occur meaningfully in isolation: opposed to *bound form.*

free gold **1** Gold held by the U. S. Treasury over and above that in the gold reserve. **2** Pure gold found loose, as in placer mining.

free·hand (frē′hand′) adj. Executed with the hand without aid of measurements or drawing instruments: *freehand* drawing.

free hand Authority to act on one's own.

free-hand·ed (frē′han′did) adj. **1** Having the hands free or unrestricted. **2** Open-handed; generous. — **free′-hand′ed·ness** n.

free·hold (frē′hōld′) n. **1** An estate in lands. **2** Land held without limitations or conditions; absolute ownership of an estate. — **free′hold′er** n.

free lance **1** A medieval soldier who sold his services to any state or cause. **2** One who writes, performs, or offers services without being regularly employed. **3** One who supports a cause or causes independently and without personal allegiance.

free-lance (frē′lans′, -läns′) v.i. **-lanced, -lanc·ing** To serve or work as a free lance. — adj. Working or acting as a free lance.

free·man (frē′mən) n. pl. **-men** (-mən) **1** A man who is free; one not a slave or serf. **2** An inhabitant of a city. **3** In English law, a person admitted to the freedom of a corporate town or borough or of any other corporate body and hence having full rights and privileges. **4** In feudal law, an allodial proprietor, as distinct from a vassal. **5** In old English law, a freeholder, as distinct from a villein. **6** In colonial America, a freeholder and hence, in most colonies, an enfranchised citizen.

free·mar·tin (frē′mär′tən) n. A female calf twinned with a male calf and generally barren. [Origin uncertain]

free·ma·son (frē′mā′sən) n. In the Middle Ages, a stonemason belonging to a craft guild that had secret signs and passwords, and that admitted as honorary members persons not connected with their craft, who were designated *accepted masons.*

Free·ma·son (frē′mā′sən) n. A member of an extensive secret order or fraternity, dating from the Middle Ages, the members denoting themselves *Free and Accepted Masons.* — **Free·ma·son·ic** (frē′mə·son′ik) adj. — **Free′ma′son·ry** n.

free·ma·son·ry (frē′mā′sən·rē) n. Instinctive sympathy or community of interests.

free·ness (frē′nis) n. The state of being free.

free on board Put on board a train, ship, or other freight or baggage carrier, without charge: abbreviated *f.o.b.*

free oscillations *Electr.* Oscillations within a circuit of a frequency determined by the inductance and capacity of the circuit uninfluenced by impressed voltages. Compare FORCED OSCILLATIONS.

free path *Physics* The distance traveled by a particle, as an ion, electron, or molecule, before colliding with another.

free port **1** A port open to all trading vessels on equal terms. **2** The whole or part of a port area where no customs duties are levied on goods intended for transshipment rather than for import.

free ship **1** A ship belonging to a neutral power, and hence free from liability to seizure in time of war. **2** A ship that, while foreign built, may receive U.S. registry when owned by a citizen or citizens of the United States.

free·si·a (frē′zhē·ə, -sē·ə, -zhə) n. A South African plant (genus *Freesia*) of the iris family, having bell-shaped, various colored, fragrant flowers. [<NL, after E. M. *Fries*, 1794–1878, Swedish botanist]

free silver The free and unlimited coinage of silver, particularly at a fixed ratio to gold, as 16 to 1 (advocated by a section of the Democratic party in 1896). — **free′-sil′ver** adj.

Free-soil (frē′soil′) adj. *U.S.* Of or pertaining to the Free-soil party, organized in 1848 to oppose the extension of slavery. — **Free′-soil′er** n.

free-spo·ken (frē′spō′kən) adj. Unreserved or frank in speech. — **free′spo′ken·ly** adv. — **free′·spo′ken·ness** n.

free·stone (frē′stōn′) adj. Having a pit from which the pulp easily separates, as a plum or peach. — n. **1** Any stone, as sandstone or limestone, easily wrought for building purposes. **2** A peach easily freed from its pit.

free-style (frē′stīl′) adj. In competitive swimming, using or marked by the freedom to use whichever stroke the swimmer chooses. — n. Free-style swimming.

free-think·er (frē′thing′kər) n. An independent thinker; especially, one who forms his own religious beliefs without regard to church authority. — **free′think′ing** adj. & n.

free thought Thought or belief, especially in religious matters, based on reason alone and uninfluenced by authority or dogma.

free trade **1** Commerce between different countries free from restrictions or burdens, as tariff or customs; specifically, commerce not subjected to restrictions, discriminations, or favors of any kind designed to influence its normal course. **2** The practice, policy, or system of unrestricted trade. **3** The trade system of a country whose duties are levied only for revenue and without regard to their effect on home industries. Compare PROTECTION, PROTECTIVE TARIFF. **4** *Archaic or Obs.* Smuggling.

free verse Verse depending for its poetic effect upon irregular rhythmical pattern, either absence or irregularity of rime, and the use of cadenced speech rhythms rather than conventional verse forms; vers libre.

free water Soil water in excess of that absorbed by the soil: also called *gravity water.*

free·way (frē′wā′) n. A multiple-lane road designed for rapid transportation.

free wheel *Mech.* **1** A form of automotive transmission including a clutch which allows the driving shaft to run freely when its speed exceeds that of the engine shaft. **2** A brake device attached to the rear wheel of a bicycle which permits wheel motion without pedal action. — **free′-wheel′ing** n. & adj.

free will **1** The power of self-determination regarded as a special faculty. **2** *Philos.* The doctrine that man is entirely unrestricted in his ability to choose between good and evil: opposed to *determinism.*

free-will (frē′wil′) adj. Made, done, or given of one's own free choice; voluntary.

freeze (frēz) v. **froze, fro·zen, freez·ing** v.i. **1** To become converted from a fluid to a solid state by loss of heat; become ice. **2** To become stiff or hard with cold, as wet clothes. **3** To be very cold: It's *freezing* in here! **4** To become covered or obstructed with ice. **5** To adhere by freezing: It *froze* to the ground. **6** To be damaged or killed by freezing or frost. **7** To become motionless, as if frozen. **8** To be chilled or made motionless, as if by fear or other emotion. **9** To become formal or unyielding in manner. — v.t. **10** To change into ice; cause to become frozen. **11** To make stiff or hard by freezing the moisture of. **12** To cover or obstruct with ice. **13** To damage or kill by freezing or frost. **14** To make or hold motionless or in position. **15** To chill or make motionless, as if by fear, awe, or other emotion; frighten; discourage. **16** To fix or stabilize (prices, stocks, wages, etc.) so as to prevent change, as by government order. **17** *Med.* To anesthetize: to *freeze* a tooth. — **to freeze to** (or **onto**) **1** To keep close or cling to (a person). **2** To hold on to. — **to freeze out** *U.S. Colloq.* To exclude or drive away, as by unfriendliness or severe competition. — n. **1** The act of freezing or the state of being frozen. **2** A spell of freezing weather. **3** The stabilizing or fixing of prices, labor, etc., in order to prevent profiteering, migration of workers, etc. ◆ Homophone: *frieze.* [OE *frēosan*]

freez·er (frē′zər) n. **1** That which freezes. **2** A refrigerator within which a low temperature is maintained for the purpose of preserving or freezing foods, etc. **3** An apparatus containing ice or brine, for freezing ice-cream.

freeze-up (frēz′up′) n. The freezing over of lakes, rivers, streams, etc., in severe winter weather; also, such weather.

freezing mixture Any mixture, as of salt and ice, that can lower the temperature of surrounding bodies or substances to various levels below the freezing point.

freezing point *Physics* The temperature at which a liquid passes into the solid state under given pressure; for fresh water at sea-level pressure this temperature is 32 degrees above zero Fahrenheit, or zero degrees Celsius. Compare MELTING POINT.

free zone A section of a port or city for the receipt and storage of goods, duty-free.

freight (frāt) n. **1** *U.S. & Can.* **a** The service of transporting commodities by land, air, or water; specifically, ordinary transportation as opposed to *express.* **b** The commodities so transported. **2** *Brit.* **a** The service of transporting commodities by air or water. **b** The commodities so transported. In Great Britain, commodities transported by land are known as *goods.* **3** The price paid for the transportation of commodities. **4** *U.S. & Can.* A freight train: in Great Britain, called a *goods* train. — **dead freight** Money paid for cargo space, as on shipboard, that was not used. — v.t. **1** To load with commodities for transportation. **2** To load; burden. **3** To send or transport as or by freight. [<MDu. *vrecht*, var. of *vracht.* See FRAUGHT.]

freight·age (frā′tij) n. **1** A cargo; lading. **2** The price charged or paid for carrying goods. **3** The transportation of merchandise.

freight car A railway car for carrying freight.

freight·er (frā′tər) n. **1** One who has freight transported. **2** One who contracts to transport freight for others; especially, the charterer of a ship for carrying merchandise. **3** One engaged in transporting merchandise by fleets or trains of vehicles. **4** A freight-carrying vessel or aircraft.

freight train *U.S.* A railroad train comprised of freight cars.

frem·i·tus (frem′i·təs) n. pl. **·tus** *Pathol.* A palpable vibration, as of the wall of the chest; resonant thrill. [<L, a roar]

fre·na·tor (frē′nā·tər) n. *Anat.* Anything which checks or restrains body motion. [<L, a tamer < *frenare* curb, restrain]

french (french) v.t. To prepare (chops or rib roasts) by trimming the meat from the ends of the bones.

French (french) adj. Pertaining to, from, or characteristic of France, its people, or their language. — n. **1** The people of France collectively: with *the.* **2** The Romance language of France, belonging to the Italic subfamily of Indo-European languages. — **Old French** The French language from about 850 to 1400, directly descended from Vulgar Latin as it developed in Gaul. Old French had two especially important dialects, the *langue d'oïl,* spoken north of the Loire, and the *langue d'oc* (Provençal), spoken south of it. Modern French is derived from the former, with the central French dialect of Paris as the standard. Abbr. *OF* — **Middle French** The French language as spoken from about 1400 to 1600. Abbr. *MF* — **Modern French** The language of France after 1600. Abbr. *F* [OE *Frencisc* <*Franca* a Frank]

French and Indian War That part of the war between France and England, 1754–60, waged in America, in which the French received support from Indian allies.

French Canada **1** The province of Quebec. **2** French-Canadians collectively.

French Community A political association that includes France, Central African Republic, Chad, Congo Republic, Dahomey, Gabon Republic, Ivory Coast Republic, Malagasy Republic, Mauritania, Republic of Niger, Senegal, and Republic of the Upper Volta, together with the French overseas departments and territories.

French curve An instrument used by draftsmen and architects for drawing curves.

French doors A pair of adjoining doors, often set with glass panes, attached to opposite door jambs and opening in the middle.

French Equatorial Africa A former group of French overseas territories in west central Africa. Formerly **French Congo**. See CENTRAL AFRICAN REPUBLIC, CHAD, CONGO REPUBLIC, GABON REPUBLIC.

French-fried (french'frīd') *adj.* Cooked by frying crisp in deep fat.

French Gui·an·a (gē·an'ə) An overseas department of France on the NE coast of South America, including the inland Territory of Inini; 34,740 square miles; capital, Cayenne. *French* **Guy·ane Fran·çaise** (gē·än' frän·sez').

French heel A high, forward-slanting heel, used on women's dress shoes.

French horn A keyed, brass wind instrument with long twisted tube whose diameter increases gradually from the mouthpiece to a widely flaring bell shape: developed from the hunting horn.

FRENCH HORN

French·i·fy (fren'chə·fī) *v.t.* **·fied, ·fy·ing** To make French in form or characteristics.

French India Formerly, the overseas territories of France in India, consisting of the settlements of Chandernagore, Karikal, Mahé, Pondicherry, and Yanam, with adjoining territory; total, 193 square miles; capital, Pondicherry. *French* **É·ta·blisse·ments fran·çais dans l'Inde** (ā·tà·blēs·män' frän·sā' dän länd')

French Indochina A former name for INDO-CHINA (def. 2).

French Morocco A former French protectorate and associated state in the French Union, in NW Africa: since 1956 a part of the sultanate of Morocco.

French North Africa A former name for Algeria, French Morocco, and Tunisia.

French Polynesia A French overseas territory spread over a wide area of the South Pacific, comprising Gambier, Tubuai, Marquesas, and Society Islands, and Tuamotu Archipelago; 1,575 square miles; capital, Papeete, on Tahiti; *French* **Po·ly·né·sie Fran·çaise** (pô·lē·nä·zē' frän·sez'). Formerly called **French Oceania,** *French* **Établissements français de l'Océanie.**

French pastry A rich fancy pastry often having a filling of whipped cream, custard, or preserved fruits.

French Revolution See under REVOLUTION.

French roof A modified mansard roof.

French seam A seam sewed on both sides so that no raw edges are exposed.

French telephone A handset telephone, with the receiver and the transmitter mounted on one handle.

French toast Bread dipped in a batter of beaten eggs and milk, and fried in shallow fat.

French Union A former political association of France, its overseas departments and territories, and other associated states and territories. See also FRENCH COMMUNITY.

French West Africa A former group of French overseas territories comprised in the western bulge of Africa. See DAHOMEY, GUINEA, IVORY COAST REPUBLIC, MALI, MAURITANIA, REPUBLIC OF NIGER, REPUBLIC OF SENEGAL, REPUBLIC OF THE UPPER VOLTA.

French West Indies Islands in the Caribbean, comprising two overseas departments of France: Martinique and Guadeloupe.

fre·num (frē'nəm) *n. pl.* **·na** (-nə) *Anat.* A restraining band or fold; the *frenum* of the tongue: also spelled *fraenum*. [<L, bridle]

fren·zied (fren'zēd) *adj.* Affected with frenzy or madness; frantic.

fren·zy (fren'zē) *n. pl.* **·zies** Violent agitation; fury; madness; delirium. — *v.t.* **·zied, ·zy·ing** To throw into frenzy; make frantic. [<OF *frenesie* <LL *phrenesis* <LGk. *phrenēsis,* var. of *phrenitis* delirium <*phrēn* mind]
Synonyms (noun): fanaticism, fury, insanity, madness, mania, raving. See ENTHUSIASM, IN-

SANITY. *Antonyms:* composure, coolness, equanimity, equipoise, sanity, sobriety.

Fre·on (frē'on) *n. Chem.* Any of a group of stable, colorless, non-toxic, non-flammable organic compounds of chlorine and fluorine used as solvents, refrigerants, and propellants for aerosol insecticides: a trade name.

fre·quence (frē'kwəns) *n.* Frequency.

fre·quen·cy (frē'kwən·sē) *n. pl.* **·cies** **1** The property or state of being frequent. **2** *Physics* The number of occurrences of a periodic quantity, as waves, vibrations, oscillations, in a unit of time; usually expressed as cycles per second. **3** *Stat.* A ratio expressing the number of times a given case, value, or score occurs in a total of relevant classified data: the *frequency* of marriage in a specified population. **4** *Ecol.* The relative number of plant and animal species in a given region.

frequency band *Telecom.* A channel included between certain specified wavelengths for the efficient transmission of radio, television, and other forms of electromagnetic signals.

frequency bridge *Electr.* A device similar to the Wheatstone bridge, used in the measurement of alternating-current frequencies.

frequency condition *Physics* The state of an atom or molecule in which it may emit radiation of a given frequency.

frequency curve *Stat.* A graphic representation of the frequencies of the values of specified variables as presented in a **frequency distribution** table and arranged by order of magnitude: also called *distribution curve.* See HISTOGRAM.

frequency level *Physics* A logarithmic expression of the tone interval between a given sound frequency and a reference keynote; one octave has a frequency level of unity.

frequency meter An instrument, calibrated in cycles, kilocycles, or megacycles, for measuring the wavelength or frequency of radio signals.

frequency modulation *Telecom.* A system of radio transmission in which the carrier wave is varied by the modulation signal in frequency rather than in amplitude. This system can utilize narrower channels than does the amplitude modulation system and is exceptionally free of static and other atmospheric disturbances.

fre·quent (frē'kwənt) *adj.* **1** Occurring or appearing often. **2** Repeating or inclined to repeat often; reiterating; persistent. **3** *Obs.* Crowded; full; thronged. — *v.t.* (fri·kwent') **1** To visit often. **2** To be in or at often or habitually. [<L *frequens, -entis* crowded] — **fre·quent'er** *n.*
Synonyms (adj.): common, constant, general, numerous, recurrent, recurring, repeated, returning, usual. See COMMON, GENERAL, MANY, USUAL. *Antonyms:* few, occasional, rare, scanty, solitary, uncommon, unusual.

fre·quent·ly (frē'kwənt·lē) *adv.* Often; repeatedly; at short intervals.

fres·co (fres'kō) *n. pl.* **·coes** or **·cos** **1** The art of painting on a surface of plaster, especially while the plaster is still fresh. **2** A picture so painted. — *v.t.* **fres·coed, fres·co·ing** To paint in fresco. [<Ital., fresh] — **fres'co·er, fres'co·ist** *n.*

fresh[1] (fresh) *adj.* **1** Newly made, obtained, received, etc.: *fresh* coffee; *fresh* footprints. **2** New; recent: *fresh* news. **3** Additional; further: *fresh* supplies. **4** Not salted, pickled, smoked, etc. **5** Not spoiled, stale, musty, etc. **6** Not faded, worn, etc.: *fresh* colors; *fresh* memories. **7** Not salt: *fresh* water. **8** Pure; refreshing: *fresh* air. **9** Appearing healthy or youthful. **10** Not fatigued; active. **11** Inexperienced; unsophisticated. **12** *Meteorol.* Moderately rapid and strong; specifically designating a breeze (No. 5) or a gale (No. 8) of the Beaufort scale. **13** Having a renewed supply of milk: said of a cow that has recently calved. — *n.* **1** A freshet. **2** A pool or stream of fresh water. **3** A fresh-water stream running into tidewater; also the adjoining lands. [OE *fersc,* infl. by OF *freis,* both ult. <Gmc.] — **fresh'ly** *adv.* — **fresh'ness** *n.*
Synonyms (adj.): blooming, bright, cool, green, new, novel, recent, renewed, ruddy, undimmed, unfaded, unimpaired, unskilled, untarnished, untried, unworn, verdant, vigorous, young, youthful. See MODERN, NEW. *Antonyms:* blasé, decayed, dim, dull, exhausted, faded, jaded, moldy, musty.

fresh[2] (fresh) *adj. Slang* Forward; presump-

tuous. [<G *frech* impudent]

fresh·en (fresh'ən) *v.t.* **1** To make fresh, vigorous, or less salty. **2** *Naut.* To relieve (a hawser or rope) by changing the position of the part exposed to chafing. — *v.i.* **3** To become fresh. **4** To have a calf: said of cows. **5** To come into milk. — **fresh'en·er** *n.*

fresh·et (fresh'it) *n.* **1** A sudden flood in a stream; an inundation. **2** A fresh-water stream flowing into the sea.

fresh·man (fresh'mən) *n. pl.* **·men** (-mən) A student in the first year of the course in a college, high school, etc.

fresh-wa·ter (fresh'wô'tər, -wot'ər) *adj.* **1** Pertaining to or living in fresh water. **2** Experienced in sailing on fresh water only; hence, untrained; of no experience. **3** Inland; not situated on the coast. **4** *U.S.* Not well known; somewhat provincial: a *fresh-water* college. **5** Untrained; unskilled.

fres·nel (frā·nel') *n. Physics* A unit of wave frequency, equal to 10^{12} cycles per second. [after A. J. Fresnel]

fres·no (frez'nō) *n. pl.* **·noes** or **·nos** A wide, shallow, scooplike, metal scraper for moving earth. Also **fresno scraper.** [after *Fresno,* Cal., where first made]

Fres·no (frez'nō) A city in central California.

fret[1] (fret) *v.* **fret·ted, fret·ting** *v.t.* **1** To irritate; worry; annoy. **2** To wear or eat away, as by chafing or gnawing; corrode; fray. **3** To form or make by wearing away. **4** To make rough; agitate: to *fret* the surface of a pond. — *v.i.* **5** To be angry, troubled, or irritated; chafe. **6** To be worn or eaten away. **7** To become rough or agitated. See synonyms under PIQUE. — *n.* **1** The act of fretting. **2** An abrasion, corrosion, or wearing away. **3** An abraded, worn, or eroded spot. **4** A state of irritation, ill temper, or vexation. [OE *fretan* devour]

fret[2] (fret) *n.* A ridge on a musical instrument, as a guitar, against which the strings may be stopped. — *v.t.* **fret·ted, fret·ting** To provide with frets, as of a stringed instrument. [Cf. OF *frete* ring]

fret[3] (fret) *n.* **1** Ornamental work in relief,

TYPES OF FRET

done by carving, cutting, or embossing; in a broad sense, perforated or interlaced ornamental work in wood or stone or in painting. **2** An ornament characterized by angular interlocked or interlacing lines. **3** A headdress of wire of precious metal, often ornamented with gems: worn by women in medieval times. — *v.t.* **fret·ted, fret·ting** To ornament with fretwork; embroider with gold or silver thread. [Prob. <OF *frette* a lattice, trellis]

fret·ful (fret'fəl) *adj.* Inclined to fret; peevish; worrying; agitated. — **fret'ful·ly** *adv.* — **fret'ful·ness** *n.* — **fret·some** *adj.*
Synonyms (adj.): complaining, cross, fractious, fretting, impatient, irritable, peevish, pettish, petulant, snappish, snarling, testy, touchy, vexed, waspish, worried, worrying. See RESTIVE. *Antonyms:* forbearing, genial, gentle, kind, lovely, loving, meek, mild, patient, sweet, uncomplaining.

fret saw A saw with a long, narrow blade and fine teeth: used for fretwork, scrollwork, etc.

fret·ty (fret'ē) *adj.* **·ti·er, ·ti·est** **1** Fretful; peevish. **2** *Colloq.* Rubbed; inflamed, as a sore.

fret·work (fret'wûrk') *n.* **1** Interlaced ornamental work composed of frets. **2** Perforated architectural work. **3** Variable movement, as of light and shade.

FRET SAW

Freud (froid, *Ger.* froit), **Sigmund,** 1856–1939, Austrian neurologist; founder of modern theory of psychoanalysis.

Freu·di·an (froi'dē·ən) *adj.* Of, pertaining to, or conforming to the teachings of Sigmund Freud, especially regarding the cause and cure of neurotic and psychotic disorders, and the significance of dreams. — *n.* One who upholds the theories of Freud. — **Freu'di·an·ism** *n.*

fri·a·ble (frī'ə·bəl) *adj.* Easily crumbled or pulverized. [<F <L *friabilis* < *friare* crumble] — **fri'a·bil'i·ty, fri'a·ble·ness** *n.*

fri·ar (frī'ər) *n.* **1** A brother or member of one of the mendicant religious orders, as the Augustinians, Carmelites (*White Friars*), Dominicans (*Black Friars*), or Franciscans (*Gray Friars*). **2** *Printing* An area on a printed sheet or page containing too little ink: opposed to *monk.* [<OF *frere* <L *frater* brother]

fri·ar·bird (frī'ər·bûrd') *n.* An Australian honey-eating bird (genus *Philemon*) having a bare head: also called *four-o'clock.*

friar's balsam A soothing balsam, composed of benzoin, myrrh, aloe, balsam of Tolu, and other ingredients dissolved in alcohol.

fri·ar's–lan·tern (frī'ərz·lan'tərn) *n.* The will-o'-the-wisp.

frib·ble (frib'əl) *v.* **frib·bled, frib·bling** *v.t.* To waste; fritter away. — *v.i.* To act in a frivolous way; trifle. — *adj.* Of little importance; frivolous. — *n.* **1** Trifling action. **2** A trifler. [Cf. FRIVOLOUS] — **frib'bler** *n.* — **frib'bling** *adj.*

fric·an·deau (frik'ən·dō') *n. pl.* **·deaux** (-dōz) A cutlet of veal or other meat, roasted or braised and served with sauce. Also **fric'·an·do'.** [<F]

fric·as·see (frik'ə·sē') *n.* A dish of meat cut small, stewed, and served with gravy. — *v.t.* **·seed, ·see·ing** To make into a fricassee. [<F *fricassé*, orig. pp. of *fricasser* sauté]

fric·a·tive (frik'ə·tiv) *Phonet. adj.* Describing those consonants that are produced by the forced escape and friction of the breath through a narrow aperture, as (f), (v), (th). — *n.* A consonant so produced. Also called *spirant.* [<NL *fricativus* <L *fricare* rub]

fric·tion (frik'shən) *n.* **1** The rubbing together of two bodies. **2** Resistance to motion due to the contact of two surfaces moving relatively to each other. **3** Lack of harmony; conflict of opinions; disagreement. [<F <L *frictio, -onis* < *fricare* rub] — **fric'tion·al** *adj.* — **fric'·tion·al·ly** *adv.*

Synonyms: abrasion, attrition, chafing, fretting, grating, grinding, interference, rubbing, wearing.

friction clutch *Mech.* Any of various arrangements for transferring the motion of one system of parts to another by regulating the frictional contact between designated elements. Also **friction coupling.**

friction drive *Mech.* A drive in which motion is obtained by the frictional contact of surfaces, one being connected with the power system, the other with the transmission system.

friction fabric Fabric impregnated with rubber: used in the making of automobile tires. Also **friction stock.**

friction gear *Mech.* Any machine element that transmits power by frictional contact between surfaces, as of rotating wheels, disks, etc.

friction layer *Meteorol.* That portion of the atmosphere, from 1,500 to 3,000 feet altitude, in which air flow is strongly affected by the rotational friction of the earth.

friction loss Loss of power through friction, as in the contact surfaces of a machine, the surface tension of flowing water in pipes, etc.

friction match A match tipped with a chemical mixture that ignites by friction.

friction tape Cotton tape impregnated with an adhesive, moisture-resisting compound: used in electrical and mechanical work.

friction test A test for determining the amount of power absorbed by a specified lubricant.

Fri·day (frī'dē, -dā) The sixth day of the week. — **Good Friday** The Friday before Easter. [OE *Frigedæg* Frigg's day; trans. of LL *Veneris dies* day of Venus]

fried (frīd) Past tense and past participle of FRY.

fried cake A cruller or doughnut fried in deep fat.

friend (frend) *n.* **1** One who cherishes kind regard for another person; an intimate and trustworthy companion. **2** One who regards a thing with favor; a promoter. **3** An adherent; ally; one of the same nation or party. See synonyms under ASSOCIATE. — *v.t. Obs.* To befriend. [OE *frēond*]

friend·less (frend'lis) *adj.* Having no friends; forlorn. — **friend'less·ness** *n.*

friend·ly (frend'lē) *adj.* **·li·er, ·li·est** **1** Pertaining to or like a friend; befitting friendship; amicable. **2** Propitious; favorable. — **friend'li·ly, friend'ly** *adv.* — **friend'li·ness** *n.*

Synonyms: accessible, affable, affectionate, amicable, brotherly, companionable, complaisant, cordial, favorable, fond, genial, hearty, kind, kindly, loving, neighborly, sociable, social, tender, well-disposed.

Friendly Islands See TONGA ISLANDS.

friend·ship (frend'ship) *n.* **1** Mutual regard cherished by kindred minds. **2** The state or fact of being friends.

Synonyms: affection, amity, attachment, comity, consideration, devotion, esteem, favor, friendliness, love, regard. *Friendship* is a deep, quiet, enduring *affection*, founded upon mutual respect and *esteem. Friendship* is always mutual; one may have friendly feelings toward an enemy, but while there is hostility or coldness on one side there cannot be *friendship* between the two. *Friendliness* is a quality of friendly feeling, without the deep and settled *attachment* implied in the state of *friendship. Comity* is mutual, kindly courtesy, with care of each other's right, and *amity* a friendly feeling and relation not necessarily implying special *friendliness;* as, the *comity* of nations, or *amity* between neighboring countries. *Affection* may be purely natural; *friendship* is a growth. *Friendship* is more intellectual and less emotional than *love;* it is easier to give reasons for *friendship* than for *love; friendship* is more calm and quiet, *love* more fervent, often rising to intensest passion. Compare ACQUAINTANCE, ASSOCIATION, ATTACHMENT, LOVE. *Antonyms:* see synonyms for BATTLE, ENMITY, FEUD, HATRED.

frieze[1] (frēz) *n. Archit.* **1** The middle division of an entablature. It may be flat and plain, as in the Roman Tuscan order; conventionally ornamented, as in the Greek Doric; or highly enriched with sculpture. For illustration see ENTABLATURE. **2** Any ornamented horizontal band or strip in a wall. ◆ Homophone: *freeze.* [<F *frise* <Med. L *frisium,* ? ult. <L *Phrygium (opus)* Phrygian (work, ornament)]

frieze[2] (frēz) *n.* A coarse woolen cloth with shaggy nap, now made almost exclusively in Ireland. — *v.t.* **friezed, friez·ing** *Obs.* To produce a nap on. ◆ Homophone: *freeze.* [<MF *frise* < *friser* curl]

FRIGATE

frig·ate (frig'it) *n.* **1** A sailing war vessel, in use from 1650 to 1840, smaller than a ship of the line but larger than a corvette. **2** A modern anti-submarine warship, somewhat larger than the 600-ton corvette; used to escort merchant convoys. **3** Originally, a light and swift vessel of the Mediterranean, propelled by both oars and sails. [<F *frégate* <Ital. *fregata*]

frigate bird Either of two species of large raptorial birds (genus *Fregata*) with great powers of flight, having the upper mandible hooked and extraordinarily long wings and tail feathers: also called *man–of–war bird.*

fright (frīt) *n.* **1** Sudden and violent alarm or fear. **2** *Colloq.* Anything ugly, ridiculous, or shocking in appearance, producing aversion or alarm. — *v.t. Poetic* To frighten. [OE *fryhto*]

Synonyms (noun): affright, dismay, dread, fear, horror, panic, terror. *Affright, fright,* and *terror* are always sudden, and in actual presence of that which is terrible; *fear* may be controlled by force of will; *fright* and *terror* overwhelm the will; *terror* paralyzes; *fright* may cause wild or desperate action. *Fright* is largely a matter of the nerves; *fear* of the intellect and the imagination; *terror* of all the faculties, bodily and mental. *Panic* is a sudden *fear* or *fright,* affecting numbers at once; vast armies or crowded audiences are liable to *panic* upon slight occasion. In a like sense we speak of a financial *panic.* Compare ALARM, FEAR.

fright disease A nervous disorder of dogs, characterized by sporadic attacks of running and barking, with manifestations of great fear: also called *running fits, canine hysteria.*

fright·en (frī'tn) *v.t.* **1** To throw into a state of fear or fright; terrify; scare. **2** To drive by scaring: with *away* or *off.* — **fright'en·er** *n.* — **fright'en·ing** *adj.* — **fright'en·ing·ly** *adv.*

Synonyms: affright, alarm, appal, browbeat, cow, daunt, dismay, intimidate, scare, terrify. The sudden rush of an armed madman may *frighten;* the quiet leveling of a highwayman's pistol *intimidates.* A savage beast is *intimidated* by the keeper's whip. Employers may *intimidate* their employees from voting contrary to their will by threat of discharge. To *browbeat* or *cow* is to bring into a state of submissive fear; to *daunt* is to give pause or check to a violent, threatening, or even a brave spirit. To *scare* is to cause sudden, unnerving fear; to *terrify* is to awaken fear that is overwhelming. To *appal* (literally to make *pale*) is to overcome momentarily by some staggering or chilling fear or shocked repugnance; to *dismay* (literally to deprive of power) is to cause a sinking fear, make faint with dread or terror. Compare ALARM, FRIGHT.

fright·ened (frī'tnd) *adj.* Terrified; alarmed.

fright·ful (frīt'fəl) *adj.* Apt to induce terror; shocking. — **fright'ful·ly** *adv.* — **fright'ful·ness** *n.*

Synonyms: alarming, appalling, awful, direful, dreadful, fearful, hideous, horrible, horrid, portentous, shocking, terrible, terrific, terrifying. See AWFUL.

frig·id (frij'id) *adj.* **1** Of low temperature; cold. **2** Lacking in warmth of feeling; stiff, formal, and forbidding. **3** Lacking in sexual feeling or response: said of women. Compare IMPOTENT. [<L *frigidus* < *frigere* be cold] — **frig'id·ly** *adv.* — **frig'id·ness** *n.*

fri·gid·i·ty (fri·jid'ə·tē) *n.* **1** Coldness; formality. **2** Sexual unresponsiveness. Compare IMPOTENCE.

frill (fril) *n.* **1** An ornamental band of textile fabric, especially of lace or fine lawn, gathered in folds on one edge, the other edge being left loose; a flounce; ruffle. **2** *pl.* Affected airs and manners; fripperies, as of dress. **3** *Zool.* A ruff or frill-like part, appendage, or fold, as of elongated feathers on the neck of some birds, of long hairs on the neck of some dogs, and of membrane on the frilled lizard. **4** *Bot.* A thin membrane surrounding the stem of certain fungi near the pileus or hood, as in *Agaricus:* also called *armilla.* **5** *Phot.* A loosening and bulging of a plate or film around the edges, caused by uneven action of the emulsion; frilling. — *v.t.* **1** To make into a frill. **2** To put frills on. — *v.i.* **3** *Phot.* To wrinkle at the edges, as a gelatin film. [Origin uncertain] — **frill'er** *n.* — **frill'y** *adj.*

frilled lizard A large arboreal lizard (*Chlamydosaurus kingii*) of Australia, about three feet long, and having on each side of the neck a broad erectile membrane.

frill·ing (fril'ing) *n.* Gathered trimming in general; ruffles; frills.

fringe (frinj) *n.* **1** An ornamental border or trimming of pendent cords, loose threads, or tassels. **2** Any fringelike border, edging, or margin. **3** Any outer or bounding portion: a *fringe* of shrubs in a garden, a *fringe* of land seen in the distance. **4** *Optics* One of the alternate light and dark bands produced by the interference of light, as in diffraction. — *v.t.* **fringed, fring·ing 1** To ornament with or as with a fringe. **2** To serve as a fringe or border for. [<OF *frenge* <L *fimbria* a fringe]

fringed orchis An orchid of the hardy terrestrial group (genus *Habenaria*) with tuberous roots and flowers having a fringed lip.

fringe lily A perennial herb of the lily family (genus *Thysanotus*) having clusters of purple flowers with fringed edges, native in Western Australia, but now found in California. Also **fringed violet.**

fringe tree A small tree (*Chionanthus virginicus*) of the olive family of the eastern United States with dark-blue drupes and white flowers; the dried root bark has medicinal properties.

frin·gil·line (frin·jil'īn, -in) *adj.* **1** Finchlike. **2** Of or pertaining to a family (*Fringillidae*) of small birds of which the finches and sparrows are characteristic. [<L *fringilla*, a small bird + -INE[1]]

frip·per·y (frip'ər·ē) *n. pl.* **·per·ies 1** Mean or worthless things; trumpery; tawdry finery; gew-gaws. **2** *Obs.* Cast-off or old clothes. **3** *Obs.* Traffic in old clothes, or a place where they are sold. [<F *friperie* <OF *freperie* <*frepe* a rag]

frisk (frisk) *v.t.* **1** To move briskly or playfully. **2** *U.S. Slang* To search (someone) for concealed weapons, smuggled goods, etc., by running the hand rapidly over his clothing. **3** *U.S. Slang* To steal from in this way. — *v.i.* **4** To leap about playfully; gambol; frolic. — *n.* **1** A playful skipping about. **2** *U.S. Slang* A frisking or searching. [< obs. *frisk* lively <F *frisque*; ult. origin unknown] — **frisk'er** *n.*

Synonyms (verb): caper, dance, frolic, gambol, play, sport. See LEAP. *Antonyms:* droop, mope, muse, repose, rest.

fris·ket (fris'kit) *n. Printing* **1** A light frame to hold the printing surface between the tympan and the form of a platen press. **2** A similar frame attached to a hand press of the Washington type. [<F *frisquette*] — **frisk'i·ly** *adv.* — **frisk'i·ness** *n.*

frit (frit) *v.t.* **frit·ted, frit·ting** To decompose and partly melt: to *frit* glassmaking materials before final fusion. — *n.* **1** An imperfectly vitrified mass, formed in making glass. **2** The material from which soft fictile wares are made. **3** A partially fused composition used as a basis for glazes. Also **fritt.** [<F *fritte* <Ital. *fritta*, pp. of *friggere* fry]

frit fly A small fly (*Oscinosoma frit*), very destructive of cereal grains.

frit·il·lar·y (frit'ə·ler'ē) *n. pl.* **·lar·ies 1** One of a genus (*Fritillaria*) of arctic or north-temperate bulbous plants of the lily family in which the flowers are checkered with pale and dark purple. **2** One of various butterflies (*Argynnis, Dione,* and related genera) having wings checkered with black and light brown, whose caterpillars feed on the violet and related plants. [<NL *Fritillaria* <L *fritillus* a dice box; from its checkered markings]

frit·ter[1] (frit'ər) *v.t.* **1** To waste or disperse little by little: usually with *away.* **2** To break or tear into small pieces. [<n.] — *n.* A small piece or fragment: a shred. [Cf. OF *fraiture* <L *fractura* <*frangere* break]

frit·ter[2] (frit'ər) *n.* A small fried cake, often containing fruit or pieces of meat. [<F *friture* <L *frigere* fry]

Fri·u·li·an (frē·ōō'lē·ən) *n.* **1** One of a people of Celtic origin inhabiting the region of Friuli. **2** The Rhaeto-Romanic dialect of these people.

friv·ol (friv'əl) *v.i.* **friv·oled** or **friv·olled, friv·ol·ing** or **friv·ol·ling** *Colloq. v.i.* To behave frivolously; trifle. — *v.t.* To fritter: with *away.* [Back formation <FRIVOLOUS] — **friv'ol·er, friv'ol·ler** *n.*

fri·vol·i·ty (fri·vol'ə·tē) *n. pl.* **·ties 1** The quality or condition of being frivolous. **2** A frivolous act, thing, or practice. See synonyms under LEVITY.

friv·o·lous (friv'ə·ləs) *adj.* **1** Void of significance or reason; petty; trivial; unimportant. **2** Characterized by lack of seriousness, sense, or reverence; trifling; silly. [<L *frivolus* silly] — **friv'o·lous·ly** *adv.* — **friv'o·lous·ness** *n.*

frizz[1] (friz) *v.t. & v.i.* **frizzed, frizz·ing 1** To

form into tight, crisp curls, as the hair. **2** To make or form into small, tight tufts or knots, as the nap of cloth. — *n.* **1** That which is frizzed, as hair. **2** The condition of being frizzed. Also **friz.** [Var. of FRIEZE[2], v.] — **friz'zer, friz'er** *n.* — **frizz'i·ly** *adv.* — **frizz'i·ness** *n.*

frizz[2] (friz) *v.t. & v.i.* **frizzed, friz·zing** To fry with a sizzling noise. [<FRY + imit. suffix]

frock (frok) *n.* **1** The principal outer garment of women and girls; a dress. **2** A monk's robe, long and very loose. **3** A coarse loose outer garment worn by laborers, brewers, butchers, etc. **4** A woolen jersey worn by sailors. **5** In English military service, an undress regimental coat. **6** A frock coat. — *v.t.* **1** To furnish with or clothe in a frock. **2** To invest with ecclesiastic office. [<OF *froc*; ult. origin uncertain]

frock coat A coat for men's wear, usually double-breasted, having knee-length skirts.

froe (frō) *n.* A cleaving knife with the blade at right angles to the handle, used for riving staves, shingles, etc. Also spelled *frow.* [Appar. <FROWARD, in sense "turned away," with ref. to the blade]

STAGES IN THE DEVELOPMENT OF THE FROG
a. Eggs. *b.* Embryo. *c–h.* Development of the tadpole. *i.* Young frog. *j.* Adult frog.

frog (frog, frôg) *n.* **1** One of a genus (*Rana*) of small, tailless, amphibious, web-footed animals; especially, the North American bullfrog (*R. catesbina*), the leopard frog (*R. pipiens*), and the green edible European frog (*R. esculenta*). Frogs are distinguished from the toads in having smooth skin, webbed feet, and greater leaping and swimming powers. **2** Any of several arboreal frogs (family *Ranidae*), as the tree *frog,* flying *frog.* **3** The triangular prominence in the sole of a horse's foot. **4** A section of a railway track where one rail crosses or diverges from another. **5** A metal device used to stop the action in a power loom when the warp becomes entangled with the shuttle. **6** A small bundle of certain types of Cuban, Puerto Rican, or other imported tobaccos, having a V-shaped notch at the ends where the heaviest part of the stems has been removed. **7** An ornamental fastening on a cloak or a coat. **8** The loop of a scabbard. **9** *Slang* A Frenchman: a derogatory term. — **a frog in one's throat** A slight laryngeal hoarseness. — *v.i.* **frogged, frog·ging** To hunt frogs. [OE *frogga*] — **frog'like'** *adj.*

frog·bit (frog'bit', frôg'-) *n.* **1** A little aquatic European plant (*Hydrocharis morsus-ranae*) which floats on water and bears white flowers. **2** An American plant (*Limnobium spongia*) of the same family (*Hydrocharitaceae*), found in stagnant water. Also **frog's'-bit'.**

frog-eye (frog'ī', frôg'ī') *n.* **1** A fungus disease affecting the leaves of apple trees and caused by various species of a fungus (*Physalospora*). **2** Any similar leaf blight of fungus origin characterized by concentric whitish spots. — **frog'-eyed'** *adj.*

frog·gy (frog'ē, frôg'ē) *adj.* **·gi·er, ·gi·est** Of, pertaining to, or abounding in frogs. — **frog'gi·ness** *n.*

frog·hop·per (frog'hop'ər, frôg'-) *n.* A broad, squat leafhopping insect (family *Cercopidae*); the nymphs of many species are enclosed in a frothy mass; a spittle insect. See FROG SPIT.

frog kick In swimming, a kick in which both legs are drawn up with the heels together and the knees apart, then simultaneously thrust backward.

frog lily The yellow waterlily (*Nuphar advena*).

frog·mouth (frog'mouth', frôg'-) *n.* **1** An East Indian nocturnal bird (genus *Podargus*) with very broad, deeply cleft bill: found also in Australia and locally named *mopoke.* **2** The snapdragon.

frol·ic (frol'ik) *n.* **1** A scene of gaiety. **2** A gay or sportive outburst or act; a prank. **3** A gathering for social merriment; a party. **4** A gathering of neighbors to do or finish some kind of work; a bee: a harvesting *frolic.* [<adj.] — *v.i.* **frol·icked, frol·ick·ing** To play merrily; gambol. — *adj.* Full of or characterized by mirth or playfulness; sportive; merry. [<Du. *vrolijk* merry <MDu. *vro* glad] — **frol'ick·er** *n.* — **frol'ick·y** *adj.*

Synonyms (noun): amusement, caper, carousal, entertainment, festivity, fun, gambol, game, gaiety, lark, merrymaking, prank, spree, sport. See AMUSEMENT, ENTERTAINMENT, SPORT.

frol·ic·some (frol'ik·səm) *adj.* Full of frolic; playful. Also **frol'ick·y.** See synonyms under AIRY, MERRY. — **frol'ic·some·ly** *adv.* — **frol'ic·some·ness** *n.*

from (frum, from; *unstressed* frəm) *prep.* **1** Starting at (a particular place or time): the plane *from* Chicago; busy *from* six until nine. **2** Out of (something serving as a holder or container): She drew a pistol *from* her purse. **3** Not near to or in contact with: far *from* the madding crowd. **4** Out of the control or authority of: released *from* custody. **5** Out of the totality of: six cigarettes *from* the pack. **6** As being other or another than: He couldn't tell me *from* my brother. **7** As being in adverse relation to: *from* grave to gay. **8** Because of: having as the foundation, origin, or cause: Skill comes *from* practice. **9** With (some person, place, or thing) as the instrument, maker, or source: a note *from* your mother; silks *from* Rome. [OE *fram, from*]

frond (frond) *n. Bot.* **1** A leaflike expansion in which the functions of stem and leaf are not fully differentiated, as the so-called leaf of ferns and seaweeds. See illustration under FERN. **2** The leaf of a palm. [<L *frons, frondis* leaf]

front (frunt) *n.* **1** The fore part or side of anything: opposed to *back.* **2** The position directly before a person or thing: the steps in *front* of the church. **3** A face of a building; usually the face on the entrance side. **4** The foremost ground occupied by an army; battle zone. **5** Land facing a road, body of water, etc.; frontage. **6** *Brit.* A promenade facing a beach. **7** In the theater, the audience part of the auditorium. **8** *Archaic* The forehead; by extension, the face. **9** Bearing or attitude in facing a problem, etc.: a bold *front.* **10** Bold assurance; effrontery. **11** *Colloq.* An outward semblance of wealth or position. **12** A person chosen for his prestige to serve as an official, usually titular, of an organization; a figurehead. **13** A person, group, or business serving as a cover for underhanded activities. **14** A coalition of diverse forces working for a common political or ideological aim: a labor *front.* **15** A dickey (def. 1); also, a large cravat. **16** In hotels, the bellhop first in line: generally used as a call to the desk. **17** *Meteorol.* The boundary, diffuse or sharp, which separates masses of cold air and warm air. **18** *Phonet.* The part of the tongue immediately behind the blade and directly below the hard palate. — *adj.* **1** Of or pertaining to the front; situated in front. **2** Considered from the front: a *front* view. **3** *Phonet.* Describing those vowels produced with the front of the tongue raised toward the hard palate, as (ē) in *feed.* See synonyms under ANTERIOR, FIRST. — *v.t.* **1** To have the front opposite to or in the direction of; face. **2** To confront; meet face to face; defy. **3** To furnish with a front. **4** To serve as a front for. — *v.i.* **5** To have the front or face turned in a specific direction. [<OF <L *frons, frontis* forehead]

front·age (frunt'tij) *n.* **1** Linear extent of front: the *frontage* of a lot. **2** The fact or action of facing in a certain direction; outlook; exposure.

fron·tal[1] (frun'təl) *adj.* Pertaining to the front or to the forehead. — *n. Anat.* A bone of the anterior part of the skull, forming the skeleton of the forehead. [<NL *frontalis* <L *frons, frontis* forehead] — **fron'tal·ly** *adv.*

fron·tal² (frun′təl) *n.* **1** A front part. **2** Something to cover the front or forehead. **3** *Eccl.* A movable hanging to cover the front of an altar. **4** *Archit.* A small pediment or other front piece above a minor door or window. [<OF *frontel* <LL *frontale* < *frons, frontis* forehead, front]

fron·tier (frun·tir′) *n.* **1** The part of a nation's territory that abuts upon another country; the border; confines. **2** That portion of a country bordering on the wilderness, newly or thinly settled by pioneer settlers. **3** Any region of thought or knowledge not yet explored: a *frontier* of science. **4** *Obs.* A fort. See synonyms under BOUNDARY. — *adj.* Of, from, inhabiting, situated on, or characteristic of a frontier. [<OF *frontiere* < *front* FRONT]

fron·tiers·man (frun·tirz′mən) *n. pl.* **·men** (-mən) One who lives on the frontier or on or beyond the borders of civilization. Also **fron·tier′man.**

fron·tis·piece (frun′tis·pēs′, fron′-) *n.* **1** An illustration in the front of a book. **2** An ornamental front; a façade. [Earlier *frontispice* <F <Med. L. *frontispicium* face <L *frons, frontis* forehead + *specere* look at; infl. in form by *piece*]

front·let (frunt′lit) *n.* **1** A band worn on the forehead. **2** The forehead of a bird or animal when distinguished by color or the like. **3** A frontstall. [<OF *frontelet*, dim. of *frontel*. See FRONTAL.]

fronto– *combining form* **1** *Anat.* Pertaining to the frontal bone or frontal region of the skull. **2** *Meteorol.* Pertaining to a front. [<L *frons, frontis* forehead, front]

fron·to·gen·e·sis (frun′tō·jen′ə·sis) *n. Meteorol.* The development of a boundary between cold air and warm air masses, or the intensification of an already existing boundary.

fron·tol·y·sis (frun·tol′ə·sis) *n. Meteorol.* The disappearance or subsidence of a front: opposed to *frontogenesis.*

fron·to·ma·lar (frun′tō·mā′lər) *adj. Anat.* Pertaining to the frontal and cheek bones.

front–page (frunt′pāj′) *adj.* Of great significance or importance; meriting placement on the front page of a publication.

frost (frôst, frost) *n.* **1** Minute crystals of ice

FROST PATTERNS
a. Spongiform. *b.* Filicoid. *c.* Stellate.

formed directly from atmospheric water vapor; frozen dew; hoarfrost. **2** Freezing weather; the **degree of frost** is the number of degrees below the freezing point. **3** The formation of ice; frozen moisture within a porous substance. **4** Coldness and austerity of manner. **5** *Slang* A failure. — *v.t.* **1** To cover with frost. **2** To damage or kill by frost. **3** To apply frosting to. [OE] — **frost′less** *adj.*

frost·bite (frôst′bīt′, frost′-) *n.* The gangrenous condition of having some part of the body, as the ears or fingers, partially frozen. — *v.t.* **·bit, ·bit·ten, ·bit·ing** To injure, as a part of the body, by partial freezing. — **frost′bit·ten** *adj.*

frost·ed (frôs′tid, fros′-) *adj.* **1** Covered with frost or frosting. **2** Presenting a surface resembling frost, as an iced cake or matted electric bulb. **3** Frostbitten.

frost–flow·er (frôst′flou′ər, frost′-) *n.* A small bulbous plant of the lily family (*Milla biflora*) with scape 6–18 inches high, bearing starlike, fragrant, white, waxy flowers; native in southwestern U. S.

frost·ing (frôs′ting, fros′-) *n.* **1** A mixture of sugar, egg white or fat, and flavoring of various kinds, used to coat or cover a cake; also called *icing.* **2** The rough surface produced on metal, glass, etc., in imitation of frost. **3** Coarsely powdered glass, etc., used for decorative work.

frost itch A complaint affecting certain persons only in winter and usually in dry climates; a form of pruritis: also called *winter itch.*

frost line The depth to which frost penetrates the ground, expressed in terms of a single season, a seasonal average, or the maximum attained.

frost·weed (frôst′wēd′, frost′-) *n.* A cistaceous plant, the rockrose (*Crocanthemum canadense*). Also **frost′wort′** (-wûrt′).

frost·work (frôst′wûrk′, frost′-) *n.* **1** Hoarfrost deposited upon exposed objects in delicate tracery. **2** Any surface ornamentation in imitation of such effect.

froth (frôth, froth) *n.* **1** A mass of bubbles resulting from fermentation or agitation; a colloid system of gas dispersed in a liquid. **2** Any foamy excretion or exudation; foam. **3** Any light, unsubstantial matter; vain or senseless display of wit; idle pleasure; vanity. — *v.t.* **1** To cause to foam. **2** To cover with froth. **3** To give forth in the form of froth. — *v.i.* **4** To form or give off froth; foam. [<ON *frodha*]

froth·ing–a·gent (frô′thing·ā′jənt, froth′ing-) *n. Chem.* Any substance, as saponin or oleic acid, which will produce froth in an agitated liquid.

froth·y (frô′thē, froth′ē) *adj.* **froth·i·er, froth·i·est** **1** Consisting of, covered with, or full of froth. **2** As unsubstantial as froth; empty; pretentious; trivial. — **froth′i·ly** *adv.* — **froth′i·ness** *n.*

frounce (frouns) *v.t. & v.i.* **frounced, frounc·ing** **1** To curl. **2** *Archaic* To wrinkle; pleat. — *n. Archaic* Affectation; empty pretence. [<OF *froncier* < *fronce* a fold, ? <Gmc.]

fro·ward (frō′ərd, -wərd) *adj.* Disobedient; intractable; perverse. [<FRO + WARD] — **fro′ward·ly** *adv.* — **fro′ward·ness** *n.*

frown (froun) *v.i.* **1** To contract the brow, as in displeasure or concentration; scowl. **2** To look one's displeasure or disapproval: with *on* or *upon.* — *v.t.* **3** To make known (one's displeasure, disgust, etc.) by contracting one's brow. **4** To silence, rebuke, etc., by or as by a frown. — *n.* **1** A wrinkling of the brow, as in dislike, anger or abstraction; a scowl. **2** Hence, any manifestation of displeasure or lack of favor. [<OF *froignier*, prob. <Gmc.] — **frown′er** *n.* — **frown′ing** *adj.* — **frown′ing·ly** *adv.*

frow·zy (frou′zē) *adj.* **·zi·er, ·zi·est** Slovenly in appearance; unkempt; untidy. Also **frou′zy, frow′sy.** [? Akin to FROWSTY]

fro·zen (frō′zən) *adj.* **1** Congealed, benumbed, or killed by cold; having become, or overspread with, ice. **2** Subject to extreme cold, as a climate or region. **3** Quick-frozen, as *frozen* food. **4** *Econ.* Arbitrarily maintained at a given level: said of prices, wages, employment status, etc.

fruc·tif·er·ous (fruk·tif′ər·əs) *adj.* Fruit-bearing.

fruc·ti·fy (fruk′tə·fī) *v.* **·fied, ·fy·ing** *v.t.* To make fruitful; fertilize. — *v.i.* To bear fruit. [<F *fructifier* <L *fructificare* < *fructus* fruit + *facere* do, make] — **fruc′ti·fi·ca′tion** *n.*

fruc·tose (fruk′tōs) *n.* A very sweet, levorotatory monosaccharide, $C_6H_{12}O_6$, occurring in sugar cane and fruits: also called *fruit sugar, levulose.*

fruc·tu·ous (fruk′choo·əs) *adj.* Productive; fertile; fruitful. [<OF <L *fructuosus* < *fructus* fruit]

fru·gal (froo′gəl) *adj.* **1** Exercising economy; saving; sparing. **2** Marked by economy; meager; stinted. [<L *frugalis* < *frugi* temperate, orig. dative singular of *frux* food] — **fru′gal·ly** *adv.*

fru·gal·i·ty (froo·gal′ə·tē) *n. pl.* **·ties** **1** Strict economy; thrift. **2** Wise and sparing use: *frugality* of praise. Also **fru′gal·ness.**

Synonyms: economy, miserliness, parsimoniousness, parsimony, providence, prudence, saving, scrimping, sparing, thrift. *Economy* is a wise and careful administration of the means at one's disposal; *frugality* is a withholding of expenditure, or *sparing* of supplies or provision, to a noticeable and often to a painful degree; *parsimony* is excessive and unreasonable *saving* for the sake of *saving.* *Frugality* exalted into a virtue to be practiced for its own sake, instead of as a means to an end,

becomes the vice of *parsimony. Miserliness* is the denying oneself and others the ordinary comforts or even necessaries of life, for the sake of hoarding. *Prudence* and *providence* look far ahead, and sacrifice the present to the future, saving as much as may be necessary for that end. (See PRUDENCE.) *Thrift* seeks not merely to save, but to earn. *Economy* manages, *frugality* saves, *providence* plans, *thrift* at once earns and saves, with a view to wholesome and profitable expenditure at a fitting time. See ABSTINENCE. *Antonyms:* abundance, bounty, extravagance, liberality, luxury, opulence, riches, waste, wealth.

fru·giv·o·rous (froo·jiv′ər·əs) *adj.* Fruit-eating. [<L *frux, frugis* fruit + -VOROUS]

fruit (froot) *n.* **1** *Bot.* **a** The edible, pulpy mass covering the seeds of various plants and

FRUIT
A. Cross–section of an apple:
  a. Seeds. *b.* Pulp. *c.* Limb of calyx. *d.* Core. *e.* Carpels.
B. Cross–section of an orange.
C. Schizocarpous fruit of the maple.
D. Ripe capsule of a poppy.
E. Pyxis of henbane with outer carpel removed.
F. Legume of pea.

trees. They are classified as *fleshy*, as gourds, melons, oranges, apples, pears, berries, etc.; *drupaceous*, as cherries, peaches, plums, apricots, and others containing stones; *dry*, as nuts, capsules, achenia, follicles, legumes, etc. **b** In flowering plants, the mature seed vessel and its contents, together with such accessory or external parts of the inflorescence as seem to be integral with them. **c** In cryptogams, the spores with their enveloping or accessory organs. **2** Any vegetable product used as food, or otherwise serviceable to man, as grain, cotton, or flax; also, such products collectively: the *fruits* of the earth. **3** That which is produced, as the young of man or animals. **4** The consequence or result of any action; any outcome, effect, or result: the *fruit* of evil, the *fruits* of industry. — *v.t. & v.i.* To bear or make bear fruit. [<OF <L *fructus* < *frui* enjoy]

Synonym (noun): vegetable. In the botanical sense not only apples, pears, peaches, tomatoes, figs, etc., but all berries, nuts, grains, beans, peas, pumpkins, squashes, cucumbers, and melons, as well as pine cones, the samaras or winged seeds of the maple, ash, or elm, and many other products, are *fruits.* Popular usage, however, is narrower. The *grains* have been dropped, and the tendency is to drop *nuts* also, so that a *fruit* is now generally understood to be the fleshy and juicy product of some plant, usually tree or shrub (and nearly always containing the seed), which, when ripe, is edible without cooking, and adapted for use as a dessert as well as a salad. The quince, however, while usually cooked before eating, is classed among *fruits*, and we sometimes speak of poisonous *fruits* as the *berries* of the nightshade. A *vegetable*, in the popular sense, is any part of a herbaceous plant commonly used for culinary purposes, and may consist of the *root*, as in the beet and turnip; the *stem*, as in the asparagus, celery, and rhubarb; a *tuber*, or underground stem, as in the potato; the *foliage*, as in cabbage and spinach, or of that which is botanically the *fruit*, as in the tomato, bean, pea, and eggplant. See synonyms under HARVEST, PRODUCT.

fruit fly 1 One of various flies of the family *Trypetidae* whose larvae attack fruit, especially a member of the destructive tropical genera, *Ceratitis* and *Anastrepha*. 2 A pomace fly (*Drosophila melanogaster*) whose larvae feed on ripe or overripe fruit and whose various species have been used in fundamental researches on the mechanism of genetics and heredity.

fruit·ful (frōōt′fəl) *adj.* 1 Bearing fruit or offspring abundantly; prolific; productive. 2 Bringing results. See synonyms under FERTILE. — **fruit′ful·ly** *adv.* — **fruit′ful·ness** *n.*

fru·i·tion (frōō·ish′ən) *n.* 1 The bearing of fruit. 2 The yielding of natural or expected results; realization; fulfilment. 3 Enjoyment. [<OF <LL *fruitio, -onis* enjoyment <*frui* enjoy]

fruit·less (frōōt′lis) *adj.* 1 Yielding no fruit; barren. 2 Yielding no good results; useless; idle. See synonyms under USELESS, VAIN. — **fruit′less·ly** *adv.* — **fruit′less·ness** *n.*

fruit rot Leaf rot.

fruit sugar Fructose.

fruit tree A tree, particularly a cultivated tree, producing an edible, succulent fruit.

fruit·y (frōō′tē) *adj.* **fruit·i·er, fruit·i·est** Like fruit in taste, flavor, etc. — **fruit′i·ness** *n.*

fru·men·ta·ceous (frōō′mən·tā′shəs) *adj.* 1 Belonging to the cereals. 2 Resembling or made of cereal grain. [<LL *frumentaceus* <*frumentum* grain]

fru·men·ty (frōō′mən·tē) *n.* A seasoned dish of hulled wheat boiled in milk: also spelled *fromenty, furmenty*. [<OF *frumentée* <L *frumentum* grain]

frump (frump) *n.* A dowdily dressed, sometimes ill-tempered, woman. [? <MDu. *frompelen,* var. of *verrompelen* wrinkle]

frump·ish (frum′pish) *adj.* 1 Dowdy; old-fashioned in dress. 2 Ill-tempered; morose. Also **frump′y.**

frus·trate (frus′trāt) *v.t.* **·trat·ed, ·trat·ing** 1 To keep (someone) from doing or achieving something; baffle the efforts or hopes of. 2 To keep, as plans or schemes, from being fulfilled; thwart; bring to naught. See synonyms under BAFFLE, HINDER. — *adj.* 1 Without effect; vain; null; void. 2 Frustrated; baffled. [<L *frustratus,* pp. of *frustrari* disappoint <*frustra* in vain] — **frus′trat·er** *n.* — **frus′tra·tive** *adj.*

frus·tra·tion (frus·trā′shən) *n.* State of being frustrated or thwarted; bafflement.

frus·tule (frus′chōōl) *n.* The siliceous shell of a diatom. [<F < LL *frustulum,* dim. of *frustum* a bit, small piece]

frus·tum (frus′təm) *n. pl.* **·tums** or **·ta** (-tə) 1 *Geom.* **a** That which is left of a solid after cutting off the upper part: said of a cone or a pyramid. **b** That part of a solid included between any two planes, or, in the case of a sphere, that part between two parallel planes. 2 *Archit.* A fragment; a broken shaft of a column. [<L, fragment]

FRUSTUM
OF A PYRAMID

fru·tes·cent (frōō·tes′ənt) *adj.* 1 Somewhat shrubby. 2 Becoming a shrub. [<L *frutex* a shrub + -ESCENT] — **fru·tes′cence** *n.*

fru·ti·cose (frōō′ti·kōs) *adj.* Of, pertaining to, or having the characteristics of a true shrub. [<L *fruticosus* <*frutex, fruticis* a shrub]

fry¹ (frī) *v.t. & v.i.* **fried, fry·ing** 1 To cook or be cooked in hot fat, usually over direct heat. 2 *Obs.* To vex; worry; be agitated. — *n. pl.* **fries** 1 A dish of anything fried. 2 A social occasion, usually a picnic, at which foods are fried and eaten: a fish *fry.* 3 The viscera or testes of an animal fried and served for the table: calf's *fry* (pluck), pig's *fry* (liver), lamb's *fries* (testes). [<F *frier* <L *frigere*]

fry² (frī) *n. pl.* **fry** 1 Very young fish. 2 The young of other animals, especially when spawned or littered in large numbers. 3 Small adult fish. 4 A multitude or quantity of persons or objects of little importance. [<ON *frió* seed]

fry·er (frī′ər) *n.* 1 One who or that which fries. 2 A young chicken, suitable for frying. 3 A high-power electric lamp for use in color

photography. Also spelled *frier.*

frying pan A shallow metal pan, with a long handle, for frying food.

fuch·sia (fyōō′shə, -shē·ə) *n.* 1 A plant (genus *Fuchsia*) of the evening-primrose family, with red, pink, white, or purple drooping, four-petaled flowers. 2 A perennial herb, the California fuchsia (*Zauschneria californica*), with scarlet flowers. 3 A bright bluish-red, the typical color of the fuchsia. [after Leonhard *Fuchs,* 1501–66, German botanist]

fuch·sin (fōōk′sin) *n. Chem.* A crystalline coal-tar product, superficially green in the solid state, but deep red in solution. Obtained by treating rosaniline with hydrochloric acid, it is used as a dye and in printing. Also called *magenta.* Also **fuch′sine** (-sin, -sēn). [<FUCHSIA + -IN]

fu·coid (fyōō′koid) *adj.* 1 Resembling or belonging to seaweeds, of the family *Fucaceae* which includes the rockweeds. 2 Containing fucoids or impressions of them. Also **fu·coi′dal, fu′cous.** — *n.* 1 A large, coarse, olive-brown seaweed. 2 A plant, either living or fossil, that resembles a seaweed.

fu·cus (fyōō′kəs) *n. pl.* **·ci** (-sī) or **·cus·es** 1 Any of a genus (*Fucus*) of algae, typified by certain large olive-brown seaweeds, known as *rockweed* or *bladderwrack.* 2 *Obs.* A paint or dye. [<L]

fudge (fuj) *n.* 1 A soft confection made of butter, sugar, chocolate, etc. 2 Humbug; nonsense: commonly used as a contemptuous interjection. 3 An attachment to a rotary newspaper press, for printing late news, usually in a different color from the remainder of the publication. 4 The news so printed. — *v.t.* **fudged, fudg·ing** To make, adjust, or fit together in a clumsy or dishonest manner. [Origin uncertain]

fu·el (fyōō′əl) *n.* 1 Combustible matter, as wood or coal, used to feed a fire. 2 Whatever feeds or sustains any expenditure, outlay, passion, or excitement. — *v.t. & v.i.* **fu·eled** or **fu·elled, fu·el·ing** or **fu·el·ling** To supply with or take in fuel. [<OF *fouaille* <LL *focalia* <*focus* hearth] — **fu′el·er, fu′el·ler** *n.*

fuel cell Any of various devices for the generation of electrical energy from the chemical energy of continuously supplied fuels, chiefly hydrogen and oxygen, in contact with a suitable electrolyte.

fuel injection The providing of fuel to an engine by direct injection into the cylinders for the purpose of obtaining precise distribution of the fuel.

fuel tank A tank for holding fuel.

fu·ga·cious (fyōō·gā′shəs) *adj.* 1 Having a fugitive tendency; transitory; volatile. 2 *Bot.* Falling very early, as the petals of a poppy. [<L *fugax, fugacis* <*fugere* flee] — **fu·ga′cious·ly** *adv.* — **fu·ga′cious·ness** *n.*

fu·gac·i·ty (fyōō·gas′ə·tē) *n.* 1 The quality of being transitory; fugaciousness. 2 In thermodynamics, the tendency of a substance in a heterogeneous mixture to escape from a given phase in order to reestablish chemical equilibrium. 3 The amount of this tendency.

fu·gi·o (fyōō′jē·ō) *n.* A copper coin, issued 1787, bearing the word *fugio* beside a meridian sun; the Franklin cent: the first U.S. coinage authorized by Congress. [<L, I flee]

FUGIO

fu·gi·tive (fyōō′jə·tiv) *adj.* 1 Fleeing or having fled, as from pursuit, danger, arrest, etc.; escaping or escaped; runaway. 2 Not fixed or lasting; transient; fading or liable to fade; evanescent. 3 Treating of subjects of passing interest; occasional. See synonyms under TRANSIENT. — *n.* 1 One who or that which flees, as from pursuit, danger, bondage, restraint, or duty; a runaway or deserter. 2 An exile or refugee. [<F *fugitif* <L *fugitivus* <*fugere* flee] — **fu′gi·tive·ly** *adv.* — **fu′gi·tive·ness** *n.*

fu·gle·man (fyōō′gəl·mən) *n. pl.* **·men** (-mən) 1 A soldier who stands in front of a line or body of men and leads them in military exer-

cises; a file-leader. 2 One who leads or sets an example in anything. [<G *flügelmann* <*flügel* wing + *mann* man]

fugue (fyōōg) *n. Music* 1 A form, or sometimes a complete composition in strict polyphonic style in which a theme is introduced by one part, harmonized by contrapuntal rule, and reintroduced throughout. 2 *Psychiatry* An interval of flight from reality, during which an individual will assume a personality and perform actions in themselves rational but entirely forgotten upon the return of normal consciousness: a form of amnesia. [<F <Ital. *fuga* <L, a flight] — **fug′al** *adj.*

-ful *suffix* 1 Full of; characterized by: *joyful.* 2 Able to; tending to: *fearful.* 3 Having the character of: *manful.* 4 The quantity or number that will fill: *cupful.* [OE *-full, -ful* <*full* full] ◆ Nouns ending in *-ful* form the plural by adding *-s,* as in *cupfuls, spoonfuls.*

Ful·bright Act (fōōl′brīt) A Congressional act of 1946 that provides for a large part of the proceeds from the sale of United States war surplus property in foreign countries to be used for financing the mutual exchange of students, teachers, and other cultural workers: named for James William Fulbright, born 1905, U.S. senator.

ful·crum (fōōl′krəm) *n. pl.* **·crums** or **·cra** (-krə) 1 The support on or against which a lever rests. 2 Any prop or support. 3 *Zool.* In many ganoid fishes one of the rows of spinelike scales arranged along the forward edge of the median and paired fins: usually in the plural. [<L, bed post <*fulcire* prop up]

FULCRUM

ful·fil (fōōl·fil′) *v.t.* **ful·filled, ful·fil·ling** 1 To perform, as a duty or command. 2 To bring into effect or to consummation. 3 To finish; come to the end of. 4 To fill the requirements of; satisfy, as the conditions of a contract. Also **ful·fill′.** See synonyms under EFFECT, KEEP. [OE *fullfyllan*] — **ful·fil′ler** *n.* — **ful·fil′ment, ful·fill′ment** *n.*

ful·gent (ful′jənt) *adj.* Beaming or shining brightly; radiant; gleaming; effulgent; resplendent. [<L *fulgens, -entis,* ppr. of *fulgere* gleam] — **ful′gen·cy** *n.* — **ful′gent·ly** *adv.*

ful·gid (ful′jid) *adj.* 1 Fulgent. 2 Fiery red. [<L *fulgidus* <*fulgere* gleam]

ful·gor (ful′gər) *n. Archaic* Dazzling brightness. Also **ful′gour.** [<L <*fulgere* gleam]

ful·gu·rant (ful′gyər·ənt) *adj.* Flashing; lightninglike.

ful·gu·rate (ful′gyə·rāt) *v.i.* **·rat·ed, ·rat·ing** To flash or throw out flashes, as of lightning. [<L *fulguratus,* pp. of *fulgurare* lighten <*fulgur* lightning]

ful·gu·ra·tion (ful′gyə·rā′shən) *n.* 1 The act of flashing or lightening. 2 The sensation of stabbing pain. 3 Lightning stroke. 4 Destruction of animal tissue by electric sparks.

ful·gu·rite (ful′gyə·rīt) *n.* 1 A vertical tube with fused walls, formed in sand or rock by the passage of lightning. 2 An explosive: a type of dynamite.

ful·gu·rous (ful′gyər·əs) *adj.* Flashing, moving, or acting like lightning.

fu·lig·i·nous (fyōō·lij′ə·nəs) *adj.* 1 Like soot or smoke; also, sooty-brown. 2 Dark, as if shrouded in smoke. [<L *fuliginosus* <*fuligo, -inis* soot] — **fu·lig′i·nous·ly** *adv.*

full¹ (fōōl) *adj.* 1 Containing or having all that can or should be admitted; having no empty or vacant space; filled. 2 Abounding in something; also, engrossed or excited as with some thought: with *of.* 3 Perfectly sufficient or complete. 4 Ample in extent or volume; well-filled or rounded out; plump. 5 Having the disk wholly illuminated, as the moon. 6 Filled or satisfied with food or drink; hence, intoxicated. 7 Filled with emotion or with knowledge. 8 High, as the tide. 9 Possessing depth or volume: said of sounds. 10 Unblended; pure: said of color. 11 Having plenty of body: said of wines, etc. 12 Distended by wind, as a sail. 13 Having folds or plaits: a *full* skirt. See synonyms under AMPLE, IMPLICIT. — *n.* 1 The highest state, point, or degree. 2 The phase (of the moon) when the whole disk is illuminated. — *adv.* 1 Without abatement, diminution, qualification, etc.; fully; completely; to the utmost extent. 2 Very: to run *full* fast. — *v.t.* To make full; gather, as a sleeve. — *v.i.* To become full. [OE *ful*] — **full′ness, ful′ness** *n.* — **ful′ly** *adv.*

full² (fŏŏl) *v.t. & v.i.* To make or become thicker and more compact, by shrinking: said of cloth. [Back formation <FULLER, *n.*]

full-back (fŏŏl′bak′) *n.* In American football, one of the backfield, originally the player farthest from the line of scrimmage.

full-blood (fŏŏl′blud′) *n.* A person or animal of unmixed breed.

full blood 1 The condition of being thorough-bred: an Indian of *full blood.* 2 The relation-ship between kindred of any degree who possess to the full the degree of kinship named. — **full′-blood′** *adj.*

full-blown (fŏŏl′blōn′) *adj.* 1 Fully expanded or blossomed out. 2 Fully matured, per-fected, or attired. 3 Filled with wind.

full-dress (fŏŏl′dres′) *adj.* 1 Characterized by or requiring full dress: a *full-dress* dinner. 2 Formal and thoroughgoing: a *full-dress* debate.

full dress Costume worn at court receptions or at formal social gatherings.

full-er¹ (fŏŏl′ər) *n.* One who fulls and cleanses cloth. [OE *fullere* <L *fullo*]

full-er² (fŏŏl′ər) *n.* 1 A blacksmith's tool with a round edge, used in grooving or spreading hot iron; a form of swage. 2 A groove made by a fuller. — *v.t.* To groove or crease by the use of a fuller: to *fuller* a bayonet blade. [? <FULL¹, *v.*]

Full-er-board (fŏŏl′ər·bôrd′, -bōrd′) *n.* A card-board used as insulating material and for other protective purposes in the electrical industry: a trade name. Also called *electrical pressboard, presspahn.*

fuller's earth A soft earthy material occur-ring in nature as an impure hydrous alu-minum silicate: it is used as a filter and in removing grease from cloth and wool, and also in medicine, as a dusting powder and, with glycerin, in poultices.

ful-ler's-tea-sel (fŏŏl′ərz·tē′zəl) *n.* A stout coarse herb (*Dipsacus fullonum*) resembling a thistle, with opposite connate leaves, and ob-long heads of flowers.

full-er-y (fŏŏl′ər·ē) *n. pl.* **·er-ies** A place where cloth is fulled; a fulling mill.

full-fashioned (fŏŏl′fash′ənd) *adj.* Knitted to conform to the shape of the lower leg, the human figure, etc.: said of hosiery and sweaters.

full-fledged (fŏŏl′flejd′) *adj.* 1 Full-feathered. 2 Fully developed; having gone into full operation. 3 Of full rank.

full moon 1 The moon when it shows its whole disk illuminated. 2 The time when this occurs.

full-scale (fŏŏl′skāl′) *adj.* 1 Unreduced; scaled to actual size: a *full-scale* drawing. 2 All-out: a *full-scale* attack.

full stop A period.

full swing Unrestrained liberty or license; free course. — **in full swing** Going on vigor-ously and unrestrainedly.

full-time (fŏŏl′tīm′) *adj.* Requiring all one's working hours.

ful-mar (fŏŏl′mər) *n.* A large sea bird (*Ful-marus glacialis*) of the Arctic; also, the **giant fulmar** (*Macronectes giganteus*) of southern seas. [<ON *full mar* stinking mew]

ful-mi-nant (ful′mə·nənt) *adj.* 1 Fulminating. 2 Beginning suddenly, as a fever.

ful-mi-nate (ful′mə·nāt) *v.* **·nat-ed, ·nat-ing** *v.i.* 1 To explode or detonate violently. 2 To shout accusations, threats, etc.; denounce. 3 *Rare* To thunder and lighten. — *v.t.* 4 To cause to explode violently. 5 To shout (accusations, threats, etc.). — *n. Chem.* 1 A salt of fulminic acid, that explodes under percussion. 2 A mixture containing such a salt. [<L *fulminatus,* pp. of *fulminare* lighten <*fulmen, fulminis* lightning] — **ful′mi-na′tion** *n.* — **ful′mi-na′tor** *n.* — **ful′mi-na-to-ry** (-tôr′ē, -tō′rē) *adj.*

fulminating compound A fulminate. Also **fulminating powder.**

ful-mine (ful′min) *v.t. & v.i.* **·mined, ·min-ing** To fulminate. [<F *fulminer* <L *fulminare.* See FULMINATE.]

ful-min-ic (ful·min′ik) *adj.* Relating to or pro-ducing a detonation.

fulminic acid *Chem.* An isomer of cyanic acid, CNOH, that unites with bases to form explosive salts, called fulminates.

ful-mi-nous (ful′mə·nəs) *adj.* Of, pertaining to, or like thunder and lightning.

ful-some (fŏŏl′səm, ful′-) *adj.* 1 Offensive and distasteful because excessive: *fulsome* praise. 2 Coarse; indelicate. [<FULL, *adj.* + -SOME; infl. by FOUL] — **ful′some-ly** *adv.* — **ful′some-ness** *n.*

ful-vous (ful′vəs) *adj.* Reddish-yellow; tawny. [<L *fulvus*]

fu-mar-ic (fyŏŏ·mar′ik) *adj. Chem.* Of, per-taining to, or occurring in fumitory plants: *fumaric* acid, C₄H₄O₄.

fu-ma-role (fyŏŏ′mə·rōl) *n.* A small hole from which volcanic vapors issue. [<F *fumerolle* <LL *fumariolum,* dim. of *fumarium* chimney <*fumus* smoke]

fu-ma-to-ri-um (fyŏŏ′mə·tôr′ē·əm, -tō′rē-) *n. pl.* **·ri-ums** or **·ri-a** An airtight chamber or apparatus for an arboretum, etc., to contain gases or the like, with which to destroy insects, fungous scales, etc. [<NL <L *fumare* smoke <*fumus* smoke]

fu-ma-to-ry (fyŏŏ′mə·tôr′ē, -tō′rē) *adj.* Of or pertaining to smoking. — *n.* A fumatorium.

fum-ble (fum′bəl) *v.* **fum-bled, fum-bling** *v.i.* 1 To feel about blindly or clumsily; grope: with *for, at, with,* or *after.* 2 In sports, to fail to catch or hold the ball. — *v.t.* 3 To handle clumsily or awkwardly. 4 In sports, to fumble (the ball). — *n.* The act of fum-bling. [Prob. <Scand. Cf. Sw. *fumla* grope] — **fum′bler** *n.*

fume (fyŏŏm) *n.* 1 Reek; smoke. 2 Vapor, visible or invisible, especially as having narcotic or choking qualities. 3 Any odorous smoke or vapor. 4 Furious anger. 5 Incense; aromatic smoke. — *v.* **fumed, fum-ing** *v.i.* 1 To give off smoke, vapor, etc. 2 To pass off in a mist or vapor. 3 To express or show anger, irritation, etc. — *v.t.* 4 To expose to or treat or fill with fumes, smoke, etc. [<OF *fum* <L *fumus* smoke] — **fum′er** *n.* — **fum′-ing** *adj.*

fu-mi-gant (fyŏŏ′mə·gənt) *n.* Any substance, as hydrogen cyanide, whose vapors are ca-pable of destroying vermin, rats, insects, etc., in an enclosed space; a gaseous disinfectant or insecticide.

fu-mi-gate (fyŏŏ′mə·gāt) *v.t.* **·gat-ed, ·gat-ing** 1 To subject to smoke or fumes, as for dis-infection. 2 *Archaic* To perfume. [<L *fumigatus,* pp. of *fumigare* smoke <*fumus* smoke + *agere* drive] — **fu′mi-ga′tion** *n.* — **fu′-mi-ga′tor** *n.*

fu-mi-to-ry (fyŏŏ′mə·tôr′ē, -tō′rē) *n. pl.* **·ries** Any of a genus (*Fumaria*) of climbing herbs; especially, a low herb (*F. officinalis*) with terminal racemes of rose-colored flowers, used medicinally as an alterative and tonic. [<F *fumeterre* <Med. L *fumus terrae* smoke of the earth]

fu-mu-lus (fyŏŏ′myə·ləs) *n. Meteorol.* A deli-cate, almost invisible veil of cloud that may form at all heights from cirrus to stratus: most observable in low latitudes and on hot days. [<NL, dim. of *fumus* smoke]

fum-y (fyŏŏ′mē) *adj.* **fum-i-er, fum-i-est** Yield-ing or containing fumes; smoky; vaporous. — **fum′i-ly** *adv.* — **fum′i-ness** *n.*

fun (fun) *n.* 1 That which excites merriment; frolic; sport; amusement. 2 Drollery; jocular-ity; a joke. 3 Frolicsome doings; also, the mirth and enjoyment derived therefrom. See synonyms under ENTERTAINMENT, LAUGHTER, SPORT, WIT. — **to make fun of** To ridicule. — **for** or **in fun** Not seriously; sportively, jokingly. — *v.i.* **funned, fun-ning** *Colloq.* To indulge in fun; make sport; jest. [< obs. *fonnen* befool]

fu-nam-bu-list (fyŏŏ·nam′byə·list) *n.* A per-former on a tight or slack rope. [<L *funam-bulus* <*funis* rope + *ambulare* walk] — **fu-nam′bu-la-to-ry** (-tôr′ē, -tō′rē) *adj.* — **fu-nam′-bu-lism** *n.*

func-tion (fungk′shən) *n.* 1 The specific, natural, or proper action that belongs to an agent. 2 One's appropriate or assigned busi-ness, duty, part, or office. 3 The proper em-ployment of faculties or powers. 4 The

normal action of any organ or set of organs: the respiratory *function.* 5 A public or official ceremony or formal entertainment. 6 *Math.* A quantity whose value is dependent on the value of some other quantity. 7 *Ling.* The part played by a linguistic element in a form or construction. See synonyms under DUTY. — *v.i.* 1 To perform as expected or required; operate properly. 2 To perform the rôle of something else. 3 *Ling.* To perform a specific function. [<OF <L *functio, -onis* <*fungi* perform]

func-tion-al (fungk′shən·əl) *adj.* 1 Of or be-longing to the proper office or work of an agent or agency. 2 Designed for or suited to a particular operation or use: *functional* architecture. 3 *Med.* Affecting only the func-tions of an organ or part; not structural or organic: a *functional* disease. — **func′tion-al-ly** *adv.*

func-tion-al-ism (fungk′shən·əl·iz′əm) *n.* In art, architecture, etc., a doctrine that holds func-tion to be of prime importance, modifying such factors as form and structure so that they may contribute the utmost to the effective functioning of the finished product. — **func′-tion-al-ist** *n.*

functional shift *Ling.* The assuming of a new syntactic function by a word, without a change in form, as when an adjective serves as a noun in English.

func-tion-ar-y (funk′shən·er′ē) *n. pl.* **·ar-ies** A public official.

function word *Ling.* A word which is used to indicate the function of, or the relationship between, other words in a phrase or sentence, as a preposition or conjunction.

fund (fund) *n.* 1 A sum of money or stock of convertible wealth employed in, set aside for, or available for a business enterprise or other purpose; specifically, the quick capital or available assets of a business firm or corpora-tion. 2 *pl.* Money lent to government; a funded debt. 3 A reserve store; an ample stock: a *fund* of humor. 4 *pl.* Money in general: out of *funds.* 5 *Obs.* Bottom. See synonyms under STOCK, MONEY. — *v.t.* 1 To convert into a more or less permanent debt bearing a fixed rate of interest: to *fund* a pub-lic debt. 2 To furnish a fund for the payment of the principal or interest of (a debt). 3 To make a fund of; amass. [<L *fundus* bottom] — **fund′a-ble** *adj.*

fun-da-men-tal (fun′də·men′təl) *adj.* 1 Relat-ing to or constituting a foundation; indis-pensable; basal. 2 *Geol.* Located at the bottom; constituting the lowest stratum or formation: *fundamental* rock. 3 *Music* Radi-cal: applied to the lowest note of a chord, considered as being its foundation or root. 4 *Physics* Designating that component of a wave form or other periodic oscillation on which all harmonic frequencies are based. See synonyms under RADICAL. — *n.* 1 Anything that serves as the foundation or basis of a system of belief, as a truth, law, or principle; a primary and necessary truth; an essential. 2 *Music* The note on which a chord is formed. 3 *Physics* That frequency on which a har-monic or group of harmonics is based. — **fun′-da-men′tal-ly** *adv.*

fun-da-men-tal-ism (fun′də·men′təl·iz′əm) *n.* 1 The belief that all statements made in the Bible are literally true. 2 In the United States, a movement among Protestants holding that such belief is essential to Christian faith: opposed to *modernism.* — **fun′da-men′tal-ist** *n.*

fun-dus (fun′dəs) *n. Anat.* The rounded base, bottom, or farther end or part of any hollow organ: the *fundus* of the eye. [<L]

fu-ner-al (fyŏŏ′nər·əl) *n.* 1 The rites and cere-monies preceding and accompanying burial; obsequies. 2 A gathering or procession of persons on the occasion of a burial. — *adj.* Pertaining to, suitable for, or used at a funeral. [<OF *funeraille* <Med. L *funeralia,* neut. pl. of *funeralis* <*funus, funeris* a burial rite]

fun-gal (fung′gəl) *adj.* Fungous. — *n.* A fun-gus.

Fun-gi (fun′jī) *n. pl.* One of the subdivisions of the *Thallophyta:* non-flowering plants of wide distribution and great variety, devoid of chlorophyll, reproducing chiefly by asexual means and obtaining nourishment either as *parasites* on living organisms or as *saprophytes* on dead organic matter. They include the molds, mildews, rusts, and mushrooms, and are subdivided into bacteria or fission fungi (*Schizomycetes*), slime fungi (*Myxomycetes*), algal fungi (*Phycomycetes*), ascus fungi (*Ascomycetes*), basidium fungi (*Basidomycetes*), and the Fungi Imperfecti, not yet classified. [See FUNGUS.]

fungi- *combining form* Fungus: *fungicide*. Also, before vowels, **fung-**. [<L *fungus* a mushroom]

fun·gi·ble (fun'jə·bəl) *adj.* **1** Capable of being replaced in kind, as movables. **2** That may be measured, counted, or weighed. — *n.* **1** Anything fungible. **2** *Law* A thing of which one portion may be taken or used in the place of another portion to fulfil an obligation. [<Med. L *fungibilis* < *fungi* perform] — **fun'·gi·bil'i·ty** *n.*

fun·gi·cide (fun'jə·sīd) *n.* Anything that kills fungi or destroys their spores; especially, any chemical compound used for this purpose. — **fun'gi·ci'dal** *adj.*

fun·gous (fung'gəs) *adj.* **1** Pertaining to or of the nature of a fungus; spongy. **2** Springing up suddenly. **3** Bearing or containing fungi.

fun·gus (fung'gəs) *n.* *pl.* **fun·gus·es** or **fun·gi** (fun'jī) **1** Any of the *Fungi* group of thallophytic plants, comprising the mushrooms, puffballs, molds, smuts, etc. **2** A soft, spongy growth on an animal body. [<L, a mushroom. Akin to SPONGE.]

fu·ni·cle (fyōo'ni·kəl) *n.* *Anat.* **1** A small cord, ligature, or fiber. **2** A funiculus. [<L *funiculus*, dim. of *funis* a rope]

fu·nic·u·lar (fyōo·nik'yə·lər) *adj.* **1** Pertaining to, consisting of, or like a funicle. **2** Pertaining to a cord or funiculus. **3** Operated by a cable, cord, or rope: a *funicular* railway. — *n.* A cable railway. Also **funicular railway.**

fu·nic·u·late (fyōo·nik'yə·lit, -lāt) *adj.* **1** *Bot.* Provided with funicles. **2** *Zool.* Forming a narrow ridge.

fu·nic·u·lus (fyōo·nik'yə·ləs) *n.* *pl.* **·li** (-lī) **1** A small cord, rope, or the like. **2** *Anat.* The umbilical cord. **3** *Bot.* The cord or stalk that connects the ovule or seed with the peridium of a plant. [<L]

fun·nel (fun'əl) *n.* **1** A wide-mouthed conical vessel, terminating in a tube, for filling close-necked vessels with liquids: also called *tunnel*. **2** A smoke pipe, chimney, or flue. **3** A smokestack on a steamship. **4** Any funnel-like part or process: the *funnel* cell in a leaf. — *v.t. & v.i.* **·neled** or **·nelled, ·nel·ing** or **·nel·ling** To pass or move through or as through a funnel; focus. [Earlier *fonel*, ult. <L *infundibulum* < *infundere* pour < *in-* into + *fundere* pour]

FUNNELS

fun·ny (fun'ē) *adj.* **·ni·er, ·ni·est** **1** Affording fun; comical; ludicrous; laughable. **2** *Colloq.* Puzzling; strange; unusual. — **fun'ni·ly** *adv.* — **fun'ni·ness** *n.*
  Synonyms: amusing, comical, diverting, droll, facetious, farcical, grotesque, humorous, jocose, jocular, jolly, jovial, laughable, ludicrous, merry, mirthful, odd, queer, ridiculous, whimsical, witty. Compare AMUSE. *Antonyms:* see synonyms for SAD.

fur (fûr) *n.* **1** The soft, fine, hairy coat covering the skin of many mammals. **2** *pl.* or *collective sing.* Skins of fur-bearing animals, as ermine, sable, beaver, etc.; also, apparel made of them. **3** Any fuzzy covering, as coating on the tongue. **4** A piece of wood nailed under a bent rafter to straighten it. [< *v.*] — **to make the fur fly** To attack a person or thing vigorously; fight. — *v.t.* **furred, fur·ring** **1** To cover, line, or trim with fur. **2** To clothe with fur. **3** To cover with a coating, as of scum. **4** To apply furring to, as for lathing. ◆ Homophone: *fir*. [<OF *forrer* line with fur <Gmc.]

fur·be·low (fûr'bə·lō) *n.* **1** A plaited flounce, ruffle, or similar ornament. **2** Hence, any ornament in feminine dress. — *v.t.* To decorate elaborately or fussily. [Alter. of FALBALA]

fur·bish (fûr'bish) *v.t.* **1** To make bright by rubbing; burnish. **2** To restore to brightness or beauty; renovate: often with *up*. See synonyms under GARNISH. [<OF *forbiss-*, stem of *forbir* <OHG *furban* clean] — **fur'bish·er** *n.*

fur·cal (fûr'kəl) *adj.* Forked; branched; furcate.

fur·cate (fûr'kāt) *v.i.* **·cat·ed, ·cat·ing** To separate into diverging parts; fork. — *adj.* Forked: also **fur'cat·ed.** [<Med. L *furcatus* cloven < *furca* fork] — **fur'cate·ly** *adv.* — **fur·ca'tion** *n.*

fur·crae·a (fər·krē'ə) *n.* One of a genus (*Furcraea*) of tropical American plants of the amaryllis family; especially *F. macrophylla*, which yields a valuable fiber. See FIQUE. [<NL, after A. F. *Fourcroy*, 1755–1809, French chemist]

fur·cu·lum (fûr'kyə·ləm) *n.* *pl.* **·la** (-lə) The united clavicles of a bird; the wishbone. [< NL, incorrectly formed as dim. of *furca* fork]

fur·fur·al (fûr'fə·ral) *n.* *Chem.* A colorless liquid heterocyclic aldehyde, $C_5H_4O_2$, obtained by distillation of the pentose sugars occurring in corncobs, oat hulls, and other agricultural waste products: widely used as a solvent and reagent in the dyestuffs, plastics, and other industries. Also **fur'fur·ol** (-ôl, -ol). [<L *furfur* bran + AL(DEHYDE)]

Fu·ries (fyŏor'ēz) *n. pl.* In Greek and Roman mythology, the three goddesses who take vengeance on unpunished criminals—Alecto, Megaera, and Tisiphone: also called *Erinyes, Eumenides.*

fu·ri·o·so (fyōo'rē·ō'sō) *adj.* *Music* With fury or vehemence. [<Ital.]

fu·ri·ous (fyŏor'ē·əs) *adj.* **1** Full of fury; raging; frantic. **2** Wildly rushing; violent; tempestuous; as waves, a storm, etc. See synonyms under FIERCE. [<L *furiosus* < *furere* rage] — **fu'ri·ous·ly** *adv.* — **fu'ri·ous·ness** *n.*

furl (fûrl) *v.t.* To roll up and make secure, as a sail to a spar. — *v.i.* To become furled. — *n.* **1** The act of furling. **2** Something furled.

fur·long (fûr'lông, -long) *n.* A measure of length, one eighth of a mile, 220 yards, or 201.168 meters. [OE *furlang* < *furh* furrow + *lang* long]

fur·lough (fûr'lō) *n.* An authorized leave of absence of more than three days granted to an enlisted man in the army or navy. Compare LEAVE, PASS. — *v.t.* To grant a furlough to. [<Du. *verlof*]

fur·nace (fûr'nis) *n.* **1** A structure or apparatus containing a chamber for heating, fusing, hardening, etc., by means of a fire beneath, as for melting metal, baking pottery, evaporating water, etc. **2** A large stove in the basement or cellar of a house, equipped with conduits for heating the upper rooms. See ELECTRIC FURNACE. [<OF *fornais* <L *fornax, fornacis* < *furnus* oven]

fur·nish (fûr'nish) *v.t.* **1** To equip, or fit out, as with fittings or furniture. **2** To supply; provide. See synonyms under ACCOMMODATE, GIVE, PRODUCE, PROVIDE. [<OF *furniss-*, stem of *furnir* <OHG *frumjan* provide] — **fur'nish·er** *n.*

fur·nish·ing (fûr'nish·ing) *n.* **1** *pl.* Fixtures or fittings, as hardware for cabinetwork, etc. **2** The act of supplying with furniture.

fur·ni·ture (fûr'nə·chər) *n.* **1** That with which anything is furnished or supplied; equipment or outfit; specifically, movable household articles, such as chairs, tables, bureaus. **2** Ornamental appendages or external adjuncts that serve to complete anything. **3** *Printing* The strips and blocks of wood or metal, made in multiples of picas, which are locked between the page forms and the chase. **4** *Obs.* The action of providing for, equipping, or furnishing. [<F *fourniture* < *fournir* FURNISH]

fu·ror (fyŏor'ôr) *n.* **1** Fury. **2** Great excitement or enthusiasm. **3** An object of enthusiasm; a fad; a craze. **4** Religious frenzy. Also **fu·rore** (fyŏor'ôr, fyōo·rôr'ē, -rō'rē) *n.* [<L *furor* < *furere* rage]

fur·phy (fûr'fē) *Austral.* A rumor; canard. [after *Furphy*, a foundry owner]

furred (fûrd) *adj.* **1** Bearing fur; also, trimmed with fur. **2** Provided with furring.

fur·ri·er (fûr'ē·ər, -yər) *n.* A dealer in furs or fur goods; a dresser of furs for garments.

fur·ring (fûr'ing) *n.* **1** Fur, or fur trimmings. **2** A coating or scale, as on the inner surface

of boiler pipes; also, the process of removing it. **3** Pieces of wood attached to a surface, as for lathing. **4** The act of applying or adjusting, as pieces of wood or metal for lathing.

fur·row (fûr'ō) *n.* **1** A trench made in the earth by a plow. **2** One of the grooves in the face of a millstone. **3** Any groove or wrinkle. **4** *Obs.* A plowed field. — *v.t.* **1** To make furrows in; plow. **2** To make wrinkles in, as the brow. — *v.i.* **3** To become wrinkled. [OE *furh*] — **fur'row·er** *n.*

fur·ry (fûr'ē) *adj.* **1** Of or like fur. **2** Covered with or clad in fur. — **fur'ri·ness** *n.*

fur seal An eared seal that yields a fur of great commercial value, especially *Callorhinus alascanus*, the Alaska fur seal of the Pribilof Islands. See SEAL[2].

fur·ther (fûr'thər) Comparative of FAR. — *adj.* **1** More distant or advanced in time or degree. **2** Wider or fuller; additional. **3** More distant in space; farther. See note under FARTHER. — *adv.* **1** More remotely; farther. **2** In addition; besides; also. See synonyms under YET. — *v.t.* To help forward; promote. See synonyms under PROMOTE. [OE *furthra*] — **fur'ther·er** *n.*

fur·ther·ance (fûr'thər·əns) *n.* **1** The act of furthering; advancement. **2** That which furthers.

fur·ther·more (fûr'thər·môr', -mōr') *adv.* In addition; moreover.

fur·ther·most (fûr'thər·mōst') *adj.* Furthest or most remote.

fur·thest (fûr'thist) Superlative of FAR. — *adj.* **1** Most distant, remote, or advanced in time or degree. **2** Most distant in space. — *adv.* **1** At or to the greatest distance in time or degree. **2** Farthest.

fur·tive (fûr'tiv) *adj.* Stealthy or sly; stolen; secret; elusive. See synonyms under SECRET. [<F *furtif* <L *furtivus* stolen < *fur* a thief] — **fur'tive·ly** *adv.* — **fur'tive·ness** *n.*

fu·run·cle (fyŏor'ung·kəl) *n.* A boil or inflammatory sore caused by bacterial infection of the subcutaneous tissue. [<L *furunculus*, dim. of *fur* thief] — **fu·run·cu·lar** (fyŏo·rung'kyə·lər) *adj.* — **fu·run'cu·lous** *adj.*

fu·ry (fyŏor'ē) *n.* *pl.* **·ries** **1** A state of violent anger; ungovernable rage. **2** A storm of anger; a fit of raving passion. **3** Violent action or agitation; impetuosity; fierceness; frenzy. **4** Intense passion of any kind; inspiration; enthusiasm. **5** A person of violent temper, especially a turbulent woman; termagant. See synonyms under ANGER, FRENZY, VIOLENCE. [<L *furia* < *furere* rave]

furze (fûrz) *n.* A spiny evergreen shrub (*Ulex europaeus*) of the bean family, having many branches and yellow flowers: also called *gorse, whin*. [OE *fyrs*] — **furz'y** *adj.*

Fu·san (fōo·sän) Japanese name for PUSAN.

fus·cous (fus'kəs) *adj.* Grayish-brown or tawny; dusky. [<L *fuscus* dusky]

fuse[1] (fyōoz) *n.* **1** *Electr.* A protective device of fusible metal set in a circuit so as to be directly heated and destroyed by the passage of an excess current through it. **2** A textile cord, ribbon, or the like impregnated with combustible material for communicating fire to explosives, as in mining, blasting, and pyrotechnics; black match: distinguished from *fuze.* [<Ital. *fuso* <L *fusus* a spindle]

fuse[2] (fyōoz) *v.t. & v.i.* **fused, fus·ing** **1** To liquefy by heat; melt. **2** To join or cause to join as if by melting together. See synonyms under MELT, MIX, UNITE. [<L *fusus*, pp. of *fundere* pour]

fu·see (fyōo·zē') *n.* **1** A wooden match having a bulb of inflammable material at its end and not extinguishable by wind. **2** A flare used as a railroad signal. **3** *Mech.* A spirally grooved cone, as in a watch or a spring clock, about which is wrapped a chain or cord, which is also wound about a cylindrical barrel containing or driven by a spiral spring. Its use is to give the spring increasing leverage as its power lessens by unwinding. Also spelled *fuzee*. [<F *fusée* <Med. L *fusata* <L *fusus* spindle]

fu·se·lage (fyōo'sə·lij, -läzh, -zə-) *n.* *Aeron.* The main structural framework of an airplane which supports the power plant, cockpit, fuel container, wings, cargo, crew and passenger space, etc. See illustration under AIRPLANE. [<F, ult. <L *fusus* a spindle]

fu·sel oil (fyōo'zəl, -səl) A volatile, poisonous, oily liquid, consisting largely of amyl alcohol, and having a disagreeable odor and taste, obtained when corn, potato, or grape spirits are rectified: used as a solvent in various chemical processes. Also **fu′sel.** [<G *fusel* inferior spirits]

fu·si·ble (fyōō′zə·bəl) *adj.* Capable of being fused or melted by heat. —**fu′si·ble·ness** *n.* —**fu′si·bly** *adv.*

fusible metal Any alloy, as one containing bismuth, which melts at a comparatively low temperature. Also **fusible alloy.**

fu·si·form (fyōō′zə·fôrm) *adj.* Tapering from the middle toward each end; spindle-shaped. [<L *fusus* spindle + -FORM]

fu·si·liers (fyōō′zə·lirz′) *n. pl.* A title borne by certain British infantry regiments: from soldiers who formerly carried fusils. Also **fu′si·leers′.**

fu·sil·lade (fyōō′zə·lād′) *n.* A simultaneous discharge of firearms. —*v.t.* ·**lad·ed,** ·**lad·ing** To attack or kill by a fusillade. Also **fu′si·lade′.** [<F <*fusiller* shoot <*fusil* a musket]

fu·sion (fyōō′zhən) *n.* 1 The act of blending, or the state of being blended throughout. 2 The act of coalescing of two political parties, or the state of coalescence: also used attributively: a *fusion* ticket. 3 The act or process of changing, or the state of being in the course of change, from a solid into a liquid by the agency of heat; melting. 4 A state of fluidity due to the action of heat. 5 *Physics* A thermonuclear reaction in which the nuclei of a light element undergo transformation into those of a heavier element, with the release of great energy: the reverse of *fission.* 6 *Ling.* A coalescing of two originally distinct words because of a similarity in form and meaning, as in the development of the verb *bid* from the Old English verbs *biddan* "ask" and *bēodan* "command." See synonyms under ALLIANCE. [<L *fusus, -onis* <*fundere* pour]

fusion welding A process of joining metal parts by applying high temperatures to the contact surfaces, thus bonding them together without the use of rivets or other mechanical means.

fuss (fus) *n.* 1 Disturbance about trivial matters; trouble; ado. 2 One who worries about trifles: also **fuss′er.** See synonyms under QUARREL. —*v.i.* To make a fuss or bustle over trifles. —*v.t.* To bother or perplex with trifles. [Origin unknown]

fuss–budg·et (fus′buj′it) *n. Colloq.* A nervous, fussy person.

fuss·y (fus′ē) *adj.* **fuss·i·er, fuss·i·est** 1 Inclined to fuss; fidgety; fretful. 2 Troublesome to do or make. —**fuss′i·ly** *adv.* —**fuss′i·ness** *n.*

fus·tian (fus′chən) *n.* 1 Formerly, a kind of stout cloth made of cotton and flax; now, a coarse, twilled cotton fabric, such as corduroy or velveteen. 2 Pretentious verbiage; bombast. —*adj.* 1 Made of fustian. 2 Pompous, bombastic. [<OF *fustaine* <Med. L *(pannus) fustaneus* (<L *fustis* a cudgel), trans. of Gk. *xylinon* wooden <*xylon* wood]

fus·tic (fus′tik) *n.* 1 The wood of a tropical tree *(Chlorophora tinctoria)* used as a yellow dyestuff; yellow wood. 2 Any of several other woods used for dyeing. [<F *fustoc* <Sp. < Arabic *fustug,* prob. <Gk. *pistakē* pistachio]

fus·ti·gate (fus′tə·gāt) *v.t.* ·**gat·ed,** ·**gat·ing** To beat with a stick; cudgel: now in humorous use. [<L *fustigatus,* pp. of *fustigare* <*fustis* club + *agere* do, drive] —**fus′ti·ga′tion** *n.*

fus·tin (fus′tin) *n.* 1 The coloring matter of fustic and sumac. 2 *Chem.* A glucoside, $C_{36}H_{26}O_{14}$, from the wood of the smoke tree. [<FUST(IC) + -IN]

fust·y (fus′tē) *adj.* **fust·i·er, fust·i·est** 1 Musty; moldy; rank. 2 Old–fashioned; fogeyish. —**fust′i·ly** *adv.* —**fust′i·ness** *n.*

fu·thark (fōō′thärk) *n.* The runic alphabet. Also **fu′tharc, fu′thorc** (-thôrk), **fu′thork.** [from the first six letters, *f, u, þ (th), a* (or *o*), *r, c*]

fu·tile (fyōō′təl, -til; *Brit.* -tīl) *adj.* 1 Of no avail; done in vain; useless. 2 Frivolous; trivial: *futile* chatter. See synonyms under USELESS, VAIN. [<F <L *futilis* pouring out easily, useless] —**fu′tile·ly** *adv.* —**fu′tile·ness** *n.*

fu·til·i·tar·i·an (fyoo·til′ə·târ′ē·ən) *adj.* Convinced of the futility of human enterprise. —*n.* One so convinced.

fu·til·i·ty (fyōō·til′ə·tē) *n. pl.* ·**ties** 1 The quality of being ineffective or useless. 2 Unimportance; triviality. 3 A futile act, event, thing, etc.

fu·tur·al (fyōō′chər·əl) *adj.* Of or pertaining to the future or futures.

fu·ture (fyōō′chər) *n.* 1 The time yet to come. 2 Prospects or outlook. 3 Any security sold or bought upon agreement for future delivery: usually plural: to deal in *futures.* 4 *Gram.* **a** A verb tense denoting action that will take place at some time to come. **b** A verb in this tense. —*adj.* 1 Such as will or may be hereafter. 2 Pertaining to or expressing time to come. 3 Pertaining to the state of the soul after death: the *future* life. [<OF *futur* <L *futurus,* future participle of *esse* be]

fu·ture·less (fyōō′chər·lis) *adj.* Having or knowing no future; lacking foresight or forethought.

future perfect *Gram.* The verb tense expressing an action completed before a specified future time. Example: He *will have finished* by tomorrow.

future shock A state of stress and disorientation brought on by a quick succession of changes, esp. in new standards of behavior and values.

fu·tur·ism (fyōō′chə·riz′əm) *n.* A movement in art, music, and literature originating in Italy in 1910, and aiming at originality, intensity, and force unhampered by tradition. —**fu′·tur·ist** *n.*

fuze (fyōōz) *n.* A mechanical or electrical device that initiates the explosive charge of a shell, bomb, grenade, etc.: distinguished from *fuse* (def. 2). —**all–ways fuze** A fuze, used especially on mortar shells, which detonates the explosive charge on contact, regardless of the position of the projectile. —**non–delay fuze** A fuze which detonates on impact. [Var. of FUSE[1]]

fuzz (fuz) *n.* 1 Loose, light, or fluffy matter. 2 A mass or coating of such matter. 3 *Slang* A policeman or the police. —*v.t. & v.i.* To cover or become covered with fuzz. [Origin unknown]

fuzz·y (fuz′ē) *adj.* **fuzz·i·er, fuzz·i·est** 1 Covered with fuzz. 2 Lacking sharpness: said of motion–picture sound track on visual inspection. 3 Having distorted sound: said of recorded music, especially of high frequencies. —**fuzz′i·ly** *adv.* —**fuzz′i·ness** *n.*

-fy *suffix of verbs* 1 Make; form into: *deify.* 2 Cause to be; become: *liquefy.* [<OF *-fier* < L *-ficare* <*facere* do, make]

FUZES
A. Artillery VT (proximity) fuze:
a. Radio unit.
b. Battery.
B. Aerial bomb time fuze.

G

g, G (jē) *n. pl.* **g′s, G′s** or **gs, Gs, gees** (jēz) 1 The seventh letter of the English alphabet: from Phoenician *gimel,* through Greek *gamma,* Roman *G.* 2 A sound of the letter *g.* See ALPHABET. —*symbol* 1 *Music* **a** The fifth, or dominant, tone in the scale of C major. **b** The pitch of this tone. **c** A printed or written note representing it. **d** A scale built upon G. **e** The treble clef. 2 *Physics* The acceleration of a body due to gravity, about 32 feet per second per second: written in lower case.

G–1, G–2, G–3 See under GENERAL STAFF.

gab[1] (gab) *n. Colloq.* Idle talk; loquacity. —*v.i.* **gabbed, gab·bing** To talk much or idly; chatter. [Prob. <ON *gabba* mock]

gab[2] (gab) *n. Mech.* A hook, as on a rod conveying the motion of an eccentric. For illustration see ECCENTRIC. [Cf. Flemish *gabbe* a notch]

gab·ar·dine (gab′ər·dēn, gab′ər·dēn′) *n.* 1 A firm, twilled, worsted fabric, having a diagonal raised weave, used for coats, suits, etc. 2 A similar, softer fabric of mercerized cotton. 3 A gaberdine. [Var. of GABERDINE]

gab·ble (gab′əl) *v.* **·bled, ·bling** *v.i.* 1 To talk rapidly and incoherently; babble. 2 To utter rapid, cackling sounds, as geese. —*v.t.* 3 To utter rapidly and incoherently. —*n.* 1 Noisy and incoherent or foolish talk. 2

Cackling, as of geese. See synonyms under BABBLE. [Freq. of GAB[1]] —**gab′bler** *n.*

gab·bro (gab′rō) *n. pl.* ·**bros** *Geol.* Any of a class of igneous rocks of granular texture, consisting essentially of pyroxene, usually augite or diallage, and plagioclase. [<Ital.] —**gab′broid** *adj.*

gab·by (gab′ē) *adj. Colloq.* ·**bi·er, ·bi·est** Given to talk; loquacious.

gab·er·dine (gab′ər·dēn, gab′ər·dēn′) *n.* 1 A loose, coarse coat or frock. 2 A long, loose, coarse cloak worn by Jews in medieval times. 3 Gabardine. [<Sp. *garbardina* <MHG *wallevart* a pilgrimage]

ga·bi·on (gā′bē·ən) *n.* A bottomless wicker basket or cylinder, to be stuffed with sand or earth to form a fortification, foundation, etc. [<F <Ital. *gabbione,* aug. of *gabbia* a cage <L *cavea* cage] —**ga′bi·oned** *adj.*

ga·bi·on·ade (gā′bē·ən·ād′) *n.* A defensive work formed principally of gabions. Also **ga′bi·on·nade′.**

gable end *Archit.* The triangular wall between the eaves and the apex of the roof on the end of a building having a gable.

gable roof A ridge roof terminating in a gable at each end.

gable window A window in a gable, or one having a gable top.

gad[1] (gad) *v.i.* **gad·ded, gad·ding** To roam abroad idly; ramble; stray. —*n.* The act of gadding. [? Back formation from obs. *gadling* vagabond] —**gad′der** *n.*

gad[2] (gad) *n.* 1 A punch or metal-pointed tool for breaking up ore or rock; also, a percussion drill. 2 A goad for driving cattle; any small rod or switch. 3 A large nail, spike, or wedge. —*v.t.* **gad·ded, gad·ding** 1 To break up with a gad. 2 To use a gad or rod upon. [<ON *gaddr* goad, spike]

gad·fly (gad′flī′) *n. pl.* ·**flies** 1 A large fly (family *Tabanidae*) that torments cattle and horses. 2 A botfly or warblefly. 3 A restless, annoying busybody. [<GAD[2] + FLY]

gadg·et (gaj′it) *n.* 1 Any small mechanical device or contrivance, especially one of which the name cannot be recalled. 2 In glassmaking, a tool for grasping a piece of ware in the course of treatment. [Origin uncertain]

gadg·e·teer (gaj′ə·tir′) *n.* A habitual user or contriver of gadgets.

gadg·et·ry (gaj′ət·rē) *n.* 1 The devising of gadgets. 2 Gadgets collectively.

ga·doid (gā′doid) *adj.* Of or pertaining to a large family *(Gadidae)* of chiefly marine fishes with soft fins, somewhat elongated bodies, large mouths, and wide gill openings. The family includes the codfish, hake, and haddock. —*n.* One of the *Gadidae.* Also **ga′did.** [< NL *gadus* codfish < Gk. *gados,* a kind of fish + -OID]

gad·o·lin·ite (gad′ə·lin·īt′) *n.* A black, vitreous silicate ore which yields gadolinium and other rare-earth elements.

gad·o·lin·i·um (gad′ə·lin′ē·əm) *n.* A metallic element (symbol Gd, atomic number 64) of the lanthanide series, having six naturally occurring stable isotopes and one weakly radioactive isotope. See PERIODIC TABLE. [after John *Gadolin,* 1760–1852, Finnish chemist]

gad·wall (gad′wôl) *n. pl.* **·walls** or **·wall** A large fresh-water duck (*Chaulelasmus streperus*) of the northern hemisphere, with black and white markings and numerous fine lamellae on the bill: highly esteemed as game. [Origin unknown]

Gae·a (jē′ə) In Greek mythology, the goddess of earth, mother and wife of Uranus, and mother of the Titans, etc.: identified with the Roman *Tellus:* also called *Gaia, Ge.* Also **Gæ′a.** [< Gk. *Gaia* Earth]

Gaek·war (gīk′wär, jēk′-) *n.* Title of the native ruler of Baroda, India: also spelled *Gaikwar, Guicowar.* [< Marathi *Gāekvād,* a family name; lit., cowherd]

Gael (gāl) *n.* One of the Celtic people of Ireland, the Scottish Highlands, and the Isle of Man: also spelled *Gadhel.* [< Scottish Gaelic *Gaidheal*]

Gael·ic (gā′lik) *adj.* Belonging or relating to the Celtic Gaels, or to their languages. —*n.* 1 The languages of the Gaels; namely, Irish (*Irish Gaelic*), Manx, and, specifically, the speech of the Scottish Highlanders (*Scottish Gaelic*). 2 The Goidelic branch of the Celtic languages.

gaff[1] (gaf) *n.* 1 A sharp iron hook at the end of a pole, for landing a large fish. 2 *Naut.* A spar for extending the upper edge of a fore-and-aft sail. 3 A gamecock's steel spur. —*v.t.* 1 To strike or land with a gaff: to *gaff* a sailfish. 2 *Brit. Slang* To trick; cheat. —**to stand the gaff** *U.S. Colloq.* To endure hardship, ridicule, or pain without complaining or quitting; be game. [< OF *gaffe,* prob. < Celtic]

gaff[2] (gaf) *n.* 1 Loud, rude talk; raillery. 2 An outburst of laughter; a guffaw. [Cf. OE *gafspræc* ribald talk]

gaf·fer (gaf′ər) *n.* 1 An old man: correlative of *gammer;* an aged rustic: now contemptuous. 2 *Brit.* A foreman of laborers. 3 *U.S. Slang* The chief electrician in a motion-picture studio. [Alter. of GODFATHER]

gaff-headed (gaf′hed′id) *adj. Naut.* Having a gaff rig.

gaff rig *Naut.* A type of rig consisting of a fore-and-aft sail with the head supported by a gaff. —**gaff′-rigged′** *adj.*

gaff-top·sail (gaf′top′səl, -sāl) *n. Naut.* A light sail set above a gaff and having its foot extended thereby.

gag (gag) *n.* 1 Any appliance for completely obstructing the vocal organs or restraining speech; hence, any restraint upon free speech or discussion. 2 Something nauseating. 3 An instrument for holding open the jaws during an operation. 4 An interpolation by an actor in a play; a joke, humorous remark, story, etc.; also, a practical joke. [< *v.*] —**to pull a gag** *U.S. Slang* To perpetrate a hoax; tell an untrue story in a playful spirit. —*v.* **gagged, gag·ging** *v.t.* 1 To keep from speaking or crying out by means of a gag. 2 To keep from speaking or discussing freely, as by force or authority: to *gag* the press. 3 To cause nausea in; cause to retch. 4 *Surg.* To hold open (the mouth) with a gag. 5 *Slang* To make fun of; hoax. 6 *Slang* To introduce one's own words or speeches into (a theatrical role): often with *up.* —*v.i.* 7 To heave with nausea; retch. 8 *Slang* To make jokes or speeches of an improvised nature. [ME *gaggen;* prob. imit.]

gage[1] (gāj) *v.t.* **gaged, gag·ing** 1 To determine the dimensions, amount, force, etc., of by means of a gage. 2 To determine the contents or capacity of, as a cask. 3 To estimate; appraise or judge. 4 To cut or rub (stones or bricks) to uniform size. 5 To mix (plaster) in the right proportions so as to dry in a desired time. —*n.* 1 An instrument for measuring, indicating, or regulating the capacity, quantity, dimensions, power, amount, proportions, etc., of anything. 2 A standard of comparison: the *gage* of the boiler; and, figuratively: the *gage* of his genius. 3 A standard measurement,

dimension, quantity, or amount. 4 The distance between rails or between wheel treads, as in a railway. See the adjectives BROAD-GAGE, NARROW-GAGE, and STANDARD-GAGE. 5 The exposed length of a tile, slate, or shingle. 6 The amount of gypsum added to lime plaster to hasten its setting. 7 The composition of plaster of Paris and other substances used in making moldings, decorations, etc. 8 The diameter of the bore of a gun. 9 *Printing* A strip of metal or other material by which the exact space occupied by type of a certain kind, or the length of a page, or the width of a margin, is determined. 10 *Naut.* a The position of a vessel with regard to the wind and to another vessel. When to windward of another vessel, a ship is said to have the *weather gage;* when to leeward, the *lee gage.* b The draft of a vessel. 11 A measurement standard indicating relative fineness of hose, as determined by the number of needles used per inch. Also spelled *gauge.* [< OF *gauger* measure]

gage[2] (gāj) *v.t.* **gaged, gag·ing** *Archaic* 1 To bind or pledge as a guaranty or forfeit. 2 To wager; stake. —*n.* Something given or thrown down as security for some act, as a gauntlet in token of readiness for combat; a pledge. See synonyms under SECURITY. [< OF *gager* < *gage* a pledge < Gmc. Doublet of WAGE.]

gage[3] (gāj) *n.* One of several varieties of plum, as the *greengage.* [after Sir William *Gage,* 1777–1864, who introduced it into England]

gag·er (gāj′ər) *n.* 1 One who gages. 2 An officer of the revenue service who measures the contents of casks, etc. Also spelled *gauger.*

gag·ger (gag′ər) *n.* 1 One who gags. 2 A piece of iron used to keep a core in its place in a mold.

gag·gle (gag′əl) *v.i.* **gag·gled, gag·gling** To utter the cackle of the goose; gabble. —*n.* 1 A flock of geese. 2 A group, as of talkative women. 3 A cackle. [Imit.]

gag·man (gag′man′) *n. pl.* **·men** (-men′) A professional humorist; one employed to write humorous lines and sketches for stage, screen, radio, etc.

gag rule A rule of parliamentary procedure limiting speech or discussion; especially, a rule adopted by the U.S. Congress in 1836 tabling all matters relating to slavery.

gahn·ite (gän′īt) *n.* A zinc aluminate, subtranslucent to opaque and varying in color from green to black and brown, crystallizing in the isometric system. [after J. G. *Gahn,* 1745–1818, Swedish chemist]

gai·e·ty (gā′ə·tē) *n. pl.* **·ties** 1 The state of being gay; merriment; fun: often used in the plural. 2 Gay appearance; finery; show: *gaiety* of attire. Also spelled *gayety.* See synonyms under FROLIC, HAPPINESS, SPORT. [< F *gaieté* < *gai.* See GAY.]

gail·lar·di·a (gā·lär′dē·ə) *n.* Any plant of a genus (*Gaillardia*) of western American herbs of the composite family with alternate resinous dotted leaves and large shiny terminal heads of fragrant yellow or reddish-purple flowers. [after *Gaillard* de Charentonneau, French botanist]

gai·ly (gā′lē) *adv.* In a gay manner; joyously; merrily; showily: also spelled *gayly.*

gain[1] (gān) *v.t.* 1 To obtain by or as by effort; earn. 2 To get in competition; win. 3 To reach; arrive at. 4 To get or undergo as an increase, profit, addition, etc.: to *gain* interest or weight. 5 To get the friendship or support of; win over. —*v.i.* 6 To make progress; increase; improve. 7 To draw nearer or farther away: He *gained* on me steadily. —*n.* 1 That which is obtained as an advantage; a desired acquisition; commercial profit. 2 Amount of increase; accession. 3 The pursuit or the acquisition of riches. 4 *Electronics* The ratio of output to input in a sound-transmitting circuit. See synonyms under PROFIT. [< F *gagner* < OF *gaaignier* < Gmc.]

Synonyms (verb): achieve, acquire, attain, conquer, earn, flourish, get, learn, master, obtain, procure, realize, reap, win. See ACHIEVE, FLOURISH, GET, OBTAIN, REACH. *Antonyms:* forfeit, lose, miss, surrender.

gain[2] (gān) *n.* 1 A groove across a board or plank; a cut to receive a timber, as a girder. 2 A

beveled shoulder in a binding joist. —*v.t.* To fasten with notches or gains, or cut gains in, as floor timbers. [Origin uncertain]

gain·er (gā′nər) *n.* 1 One who gains profit or advantage for himself. 2 A fancy dive, consisting of a back somersault from a front-diving take-off.

gain·ful (gān′fəl) *adj.* Yielding profit; lucrative. —**gain′ful·ly** *adv.* —**gain′ful·ness** *n.*

gain·less (gān′lis) *adj.* Profitless. —**gain′less·ness** *n.*

gain·say (gān′sā′) *v.t.* **gain·said, gain·say·ing** 1 To deny. 2 To contradict; controvert. 3 To speak or act against; oppose. —*n. Rare* A contradiction. [OE *gegn-* against + SAY[2]] —**gain′say′er** *n.*

'gainst (genst) *prep.* Against: an abbreviated form.

gait (gāt) *n.* 1 The manner of walking or stepping; carriage of the body in going; walk. 2 The movement of a horse's feet in going, as the canter, pace, trot, run, single-foot, etc. —*v.t.* 1 To train to or cause to take a particular gait: to *gait* a horse. 2 To put in working order; set up: to *gait* a loom. ◆ Homophone: *gate.* [< ON *gata* way]

gait·ed (gā′tid) *adj.* Having a (particular) gait.

gai·ter (gā′tər) *n.* 1 A covering for the lower leg or ankle, fastened at the side and usually strapped under the foot. 2 A shoe covering the ankle and having no opening in front and usually elastic sides. 3 An overshoe with a cloth top. [< F *guêtre*]

gaiting pole A device for keeping a horse straight in the shafts of a racing sulky; a pole on which a roller is mounted which rubs against the horse when he swerves.

Ga·ius (gā′əs, gī′-) A Roman praenomen: also *Caius.*

—**Gaius** Roman jurist of the second century A.D.

gal (gal) *n. U.S. Colloq.* A girl.

ga·la (gā′lə, gal′ə, gä′lə) *n.* A festivity; show. —*adj.* Festive; appropriate for a festive occasion. [< F < Ital., holiday dress]

ga·lac·ta·gog (gə·lak′tə·gog, -gog) *adj.* Promotive of the flow of milk. —*n.* Any medicine promoting the secretion of milk. Also **ga·lac′ta·gogue, ga·lac′to·gogue.** [< GALACT(O)- + Gk. *agōgos* producing]

ga·lac·tan (gə·lak′tən) *n. Biochem.* A polymeric anhydride of galactose, found in gums, algae, lichens, agar, and in fruit pectins. [< GALACT(O)- + AN(HYDRIDE)]

ga·lac·tic (gə·lak′tik) *adj. Astron.* Pertaining to the Galaxy or Milky Way.

galactic circle *Astron.* The great circle passing centrally along the Milky Way.

galactic latitude *Astron.* The angular distance of a celestial body from the galactic plane.

galacto- *combining form* Milk; milky: *galactopoietic.* Also, before vowels, **galact-.** [< Gk. *gala, galaktos* milk]

ga·lac·to·cele (gə·lak′tə·sēl) *n. Pathol.* A tumor of the female breast caused by blockage of a milk duct.

ga·lac·to·lip·in (gə·lak′tō·lip′in) See CEREBROSIDE.

gal·ac·tom·e·ter (gal′ək·tom′ə·tər) *n.* A lactometer.

ga·lac·to·poi·et·ic (gə·lak′tō·poi·et′ik) *adj.* Promoting the secretion of milk. [< GALACTO- + Gk. *poiētikos* capable of making]

ga·lac·to·scope (gə·lak′tə·skōp) *n.* An instrument for testing milk for butterfat content.

ga·lac·tose (gə·lak′tōs) *n. Chem.* A sweet crystalline glucose, $C_6H_{12}O_6$, the dextrorotatory form of which is obtained when milk sugar is treated with dilute acids.

ga·lac·to·se·mi·a (gə·lak′tə·sē′mē·ə) *n. Pathol.* A metabolic disease in which the body is unable to tolerate milk in any form because of the lack of an enzyme which converts galactose into glucose: often fatal in newborn children. [< GALACTOSE + -EMIA]

ga·lac·to·ther·a·py (gə·lak′tō·ther′ə·pē) *n.* Treatment of disease by means of milk.

gala day A holiday; festival.

gal·a·lith (gal′ə·lith) *n.* A hard, thermoplastic casein plastic, available in colors, used to make buttons, clips, etc., and for trimming apparel and accessories. Also called *milkstone.* [< Gk. *gala* milk + *lithos* stone]

ga·lan·gal (gə·lang′gəl) *n.* The aromatic rootstocks of various East Indian herbs (genus *Alpi-*

nia) of the ginger family: also spelled *galingale*. [< OF *galingal* < Arabic *khalanjān* < Chinese *Ko-liang-kiang* mild ginger from the province Ko]

gal·an·tine (gal′ən·tēn) *n.* A cold preparation of boned, stuffed, and seasoned chicken, veal, etc., served in its own jelly. [< F]

ga·lan·ty show (gə·lan′tē) A shadow pantomime in miniature, the shadows being cast by figures cut from paper. [Prob. < Ital. *galante* gallant]

gal·a·te·a (gal′ə·tē′ə) *n.* A strong twill cotton fabric, white or striped, used in making women's and children's garments. [after the *Galatea*, a British warship]

ga·lax (gā′laks) *n.* A stemless evergreen herb (*Galax aphylla*) bearing a raceme of white flowers; its leaves are much used for funeral decoration. [< NL < Gk. *gala* milk]

gal·ax·y (gal′ək·sē) *n. pl.* **·ax·ies 1** *Astron.* Any of the very large systems of stars, nebulae, and other celestial bodies, comparable with but assumed to be independent of our own; an island universe. **2** Any brilliant group, as of persons. [< F *galaxie* < L *galaxias* the Milky Way < Gk. *gala* milk]

Gal·ax·y (gal′ək·sē) *n. Astron.* The aggregate of all celestial bodies in the universe to which the sun belongs, including the luminous band of stars known as the Milky Way.

gal·ba·num (gal′bə·nəm) *n.* A bitter and odorous gum resin obtained from certain umbelliferous herbs, especially the giant fennel: used as a stimulant, expectorant, and anti-spasmodic. [< L *galbanum* < Gk. *chalbanē* < Hebrew *helbenah*]

gale[1] (gāl) *n.* **1** A strong wind less violent than a hurricane, but stronger than a stiff breeze (7–10 on the Beaufort scale). **2** In poetic usage, a breeze; zephyr. **3** Figuratively, a noisy outburst: *gales* of merriment. [Origin uncertain]

gale[2] (gāl) *n.* A branching, sweet-smelling marsh shrub (*Myrica gala*) of the eastern United States. See SWEETGALE. [OE *gagel*]

ga·le·a (gā′lē·ə) *n. pl.* **·le·ae** (-li·ē) **1** *Entomol.* A helmetlike membrane attached to the maxillae of certain insects. **2** *Bot.* The upper sepal of the flower of monkshood. **3** *Anat.* A structure connecting the separate parts of one of the muscles of the scalp. **4** *Med.* A type of bandage for the head. [< L, helmet]

ga·le·ate (gā′lē·āt) *adj.* Covered with, wearing, or having a galea. Also **ga′le·at′ed**.

ga·le·i·form (gā′lē·ə·fôrm) *adj.* Helmet-shaped; resembling a casque or helm. [< L *galea* helmet + -*i*- + -FORM]

Ga·len (gā′lən), **Claudius**, 130?–200?, Greek physician and writer on medicine. — **Ga·len·ic** (ga·len′ik, -lē′nik) or **·i·cal** *adj.*

ga·le·na (gə·lē′nə) *n.* A metallic, lead-gray, cleavable, isometric lead sulfide, PbS: an important ore of lead; lead glance. Also **ga·le·nite** (gə·lē′nīt). [< L, lead ore]

ga·len·i·cal (gə·len′i·kəl, -lē′ni-) *n.* **1** A medicine or drug prepared in accordance with the principles of Galen. **2** A drug containing a standard proportion of naturally occurring organic substances as distinguished from chemical ingredients.

Ga·len·ism (gā′lən·iz′əm) *n.* The theory or practice of medicine followed by Galen. — **Ga′len·ist** *n.*

ga·le·o·pi·the·cus (gā′lē·ō·pi·thē′kəs) *n.* Any member of a genus (*Galeopithecus*, family *Galeopithecidae*) of insectivorous mammals, as the flying lemur. [< Gk. *galeē* weasel + *pithēkos* ape]

gal·er·o·pi·a (gal′ə·rō′pē·ə) *n.* Abnormally clear vision and perception of objects. Also **gal′er·op′si·a** (-op′sē·ə) [< Gk. *galeros* cheerful + *ōps* eye]

GALEATE SEPAL
A monkshood flower showing galeate upper sepal (*a*).

Gal·i·lee (gal′ə·lē) A region in northern Palestine.

Galilee, Sea of A fresh-water lake in northern Palestine on the Israel–Jordan border, through which the river Jordan flows: Old Testament *Sea of Chinnereth*; New Testament *Sea of Gennesaret*: also *Lake Tiberias*.

Galilee porch A porch or chapel at the west end of some abbey churches. Also **Gal′i·lee.**

Gal·i·le·o (gal′ə·lē′ō), 1564–1642, Italian astronomer and founder of the science of mechanics; condemned by the Roman Inquisition: full name *Galileo Galilei*.

gal·i·ma·ti·as (gal′ə·mā′shē·əs, -mat′ē·əs) *n.* Confused or meaningless talk; gibberish. [< F]

gal·in·gale (gal′in·gāl) *n.* **1** A tall, perennial, and rare sedge (*Cyperus longus*) of southern England, with aromatic tuberous roots. **2** Galangal. [See GALANGAL]

gal·i·ot (gal′ē·ət) *n.* **1** A small galley propelled by sails and oars. **2** A one- or two-masted Dutch or Flemish merchant vessel. Also spelled *galliot*. [< OF, dim. of *galie* < Med. L *galea* a galley]

gal·i·pe·a (gal′ə·pē′ə) *n.* A tropical American shrub (*Galipea officinalis*) of the rutaceous family which yields angostura bark. [< NL]

gal·i·pot (gal′i·pot) *n.* The white turpentine resin formed on the bark of a pine (*Pinus pinaster*) of southern Europe: when refined it is called *white, yellow,* or *Burgundy pitch*: also spelled *gallipot*. [< F]

gall[1] (gôl) *n.* **1** *Physiol.* The bitter fluid secreted by the liver; bile. **2** Bitter feeling; malignity. **3** Any bitter and trying experience. **4** *Anat.* The sac containing the bile: also **gall bladder. 5** *U.S. Slang* Cool impudence; effrontery. [OE *gealla*]

gall[2] (gôl) *n.* **1** An abrasion or excoriation, as by the friction of harness on a horse. **2** *Brit.* A blemish. **3** A locality made barren by exhaustion of the soil. **4** *U.S. Dial.* Low-lying wet land. **5** A person or thing that irritates or galls. — *v.t.* **1** To make sore or injure (the skin) by friction; chafe. **2** To vex or irritate. — *v.i.* **3** To be or become chafed or irritated. See synonyms under INCENSE. [Prob. < GALL[1]]

gall[3] (gôl) *n.* **1** An excrescence on plants, caused by insects, bacteria, or a parasitic fungus. The galls of commerce are produced by a gallfly which lays its eggs in the soft twigs of an oak (*Quercus lusitanica*) of western Asia and southern Europe. Galls contain tannin, and are used in inkmaking, dyeing, etc. **2** A similar excrescence on animals. [< F *galle* < L *galla* the gallnut]

gal·lant (gal′ənt) *adj.* **1** Possessing an intrepid spirit; brave; chivalrous. **2** Stately; imposing; noble. **3** Marked by showiness; gay: said chiefly of attire. **4** (gə·lant′, gal′ənt) Polite and attentive to women; courteous. See synonyms under BRAVE. — *n.* (gal′ənt, gə·lant′) **1** A man of gay and dashing manners; an intrepid youth. **2** A man who pays court to women; also, a man of fashion. — *v.t.* (gə·lant′) **1** To accompany (a woman); escort. **2** To court or dally with (a woman). — *v.i.* **3** To play the gallant. [< OF *galant*, ppr. of *galer* rejoice]

gal·lant·ly (gal′ənt·lē) *adv.* Bravely; politely.

gal·lant·ry (gal′ənt·trē) *n. pl.* **·ries 1** Courage; heroism; chivalrousness. **2** Polite or excessive attention to women. **3** A gallant act or polite speech. **4** The calling or manner of a gallant. **5** Gallants collectively. See synonyms under COURAGE, PROWESS.

gall–ap·ple (gôl′ap′əl) *n.* A gallnut.

gall–ber·ry (gôl′ber′ē) *n. pl.* **·ries** The inkberry.

gall bladder *Anat.* A small, pear-shaped muscular pouch situated beneath the liver in man and serving as a reservoir for bile conducted through the **gall duct.**

gal·le·on (gal′ē·ən) *n.* A sailing vessel of the 15th to 17th centuries, usually armed and having three or four decks; especially, the vessel used by Spain in trade with her Central American possessions. [< Sp. *galeón*, aug. of *galea* < Med. L. See GALLEY.]

gal·ler·y (gal′ər·ē) *n. pl.* **·ler·ies 1** A long, narrow balcony or other passage having balustrades or rails and projecting from the

inner or outer wall of a building. **2** *U.S.* In the South, a veranda. **3** A platform with seats which projects from the rear or side walls of a theater, legislative chamber, church, etc., out over the main floor; specifically, in a theater, the highest of such platforms, containing the cheapest seats. **4** The audience occupying the gallery seats; hence, the general public. **5** *Naut.* A balcony projecting from the after part of a ship's hull. **6** A long, narrow room or corridor. **7** A room or building used for the display of works of art. **8** A collection of works of art. **9** A room suggestive of a gallery, used for business purposes: a shooting *gallery*; a photographer's *gallery*. **10** *Mil. & Mining* A horizontal underground passage; a driftway. **11** An underground passage made by an animal. — *v.* **gal·ler·ied, gal·ler·y·ing** *v.t.* To furnish or adorn with a gallery or galleries. — *v.i. Mil.* To make an underground passage. [< F *galerie* < Med. L *galeria*, ? alter. of *galilaea* a Galilee porch]

gal·let (gal′it) *n.* A small piece of stone; a chip. — *v.t.* To fill the joints of (a wall) with bits of stone. [< F *galet* a pebble]

gal·ley (gal′ē) *n. pl.* **·leys 1** A long, low vessel used in ancient and medieval times, propelled by oars and sails or by oars alone. **2** A large rowboat. **3** The kitchen of a ship; also, the cookstove. **4** *Printing* **a** A long tray, for holding composed type. **b** A proof (**galley proof**) printed from such type. [< OF *galee* < Med. L *galea* < LGk. *galaia*]

galley slave 1 A slave who rowed in a galley. **2** Formerly, a convict sentenced to labor at the oar of a galley. **3** Hence, a drudge; hack.

gall–fly (gôl′flī′) *n. pl.* **·flies 1** Any of various small hymenopterous insects (family *Cynipidae*), resembling wasps in appearance, whose larvae promote the growth of galls on plants. Also called **gall wasp. 2** A gall midge.

gal·lic (gal′ik) *adj. Chem.* **1** Of, pertaining to, or derived from the element gallium. **2** Relating to or derived from gallnuts; specifically, designating a white, odorless, crystalline organic compound, **gallic acid**, $C_7H_6O_5 \cdot H_2O$, widely distributed in the vegetable kingdom and used in the making of inks, dyestuffs, paper, etc.

Gal·lic (gal′ik) *adj.* Of or pertaining to ancient Gaul or modern France. [< L *Gallicus* < *Gallus* inhabitant of Gaul]

Gal·li·can (gal′ə·kən) *adj.* Of or pertaining to Gaul or France, or especially to a former party in the Roman Catholic Church there. — *n.* A member of the Gallican party.

gal·li·fi·ca·tion (gal′ə·fi·kā′shən) *n.* The production of galls.

gal·li·gas·kins (gal′i·gas′kinz) *n. pl.* **1** Long loose hose, worn in the 16th century. **2** Loose breeches. **3** A sportsman's leather leggings. [Alter. of MF *garguesque*, var. of *greguesque* < Ital. *grechesca*, fem. of *grechesco* Greek]

gal·li·mau·fry (gal′i·mô′frē) *n. pl.* **·fries 1** A hash or hodgepodge. **2** A confused jumble or medley of any kind. [< F *gallimafrée*; ult. origin unknown]

gal·li·na·cean (gal′ə·nā′shən) *n.* A gallinaceous bird.

gal·li·na·ceous (gal′ə·nā′shəs) *adj.* Of or pertaining to an order of birds (*Galliformes*), including the common hen, turkeys, partridges, etc. [< L *gallinaceus* < *gallina* a hen]

gal·li·na·zo (gal′i·nä′zō) *n. pl.* **·zos** or **·zoes 1** A turkey buzzard. **2** A tropical carrion crow. [< Sp. *gallinaza* vulture, aug. of *gallina* a hen]

gall·ing (gô′ling) *adj.* Chafing and rendering sore; hence, irritating; harrowing: *galling* bondage. — **gall′ing·ly** *adv.*

gal·li·nip·per (gal′ə·nip′ər) *n.* A large mosquito; a cranefly. [Origin uncertain]

gal·li·nule (gal′ə·nyōōl, -nōōl) *n.* Any of several cootlike birds allied to the rails; especially, the Florida gallinule (*Gallinula chloropus*). [< NL *gallinula*, dim. of *gallina* a hen]

gal·li·pot[1] (gal′i·pot) *n.* A small earthen jar as for ointments, jam, etc., especially as used by apothecaries. [? < GALLEY + POT, because orig. imported on galleys]

gal·li·pot[2] (gal′i·pot) See GALIPOT.

gal·li·um (gal′ē·əm) *n.* A rare metallic element

(symbol Ga, atomic number 31) having a low melting point. See PERIODIC TABLE. [< NL < L *gallus* a cock, trans. of *Lecoq* de Boisbaudran, 1838–1912, its discoverer]

gal·li·vant (gal'ə·vant, gal'ə·vant') *v.i.* To go about, especially with members of the opposite sex, in search of fun and pleasure; gad: also spelled *galavant, galivant.* [? Alter. of GALLANT]

gal·li·vat (gal'ə·vat) *n.* A large boat propelled by oars and a large, triangular sail: formerly used by Malay pirates. [Ult. < Pg. *galeota* a galley]

gal·li·wasp (gal'i·wosp', -wôsp') *n.* 1 A lizard (genus *Diploglossus*) of Jamaica, greatly feared, but harmless. 2 A lizard fish. Also spelled *gallywasp.* [Appar. < GALLEY + WASP; orig. an insect which infested West Indian ships]

gall midge Any of various small, slender, hairy gnats (family *Cecidomyiiae*) whose larvae produce galls on plants, especially on those of the composite and willow families. Also **gall'fly', gall gnat.** For illustration see INSECT (injurious).

gall·nut (gôl'nut') *n.* The gall of any gall-bearing oak: a source of tannic acid. Also **gall'·ap'ple.**

gal·lo·bro·mal (gal'ō·brō'məl) *n. Chem.* An organic compound, $C_7H_4O_5Br_2$, obtained by treating bromine with gallic acid: used in medicine as a sedative and hypnotic.

gal·lon (gal'ən) *n.* 1 An English and American liquid measure of various capacities: the **Winchester** or **wine gallon**, containing 231 cubic inches or four quarts, or 3.78 liters, which is the common standard of the United States; the **imperial gallon** of Great Britain of 277.42 cubic inches, or 4.5459 liters. 2 *Brit.* A dry measure; one eighth of a bushel. [< AF *galon*, ? < Celtic]

gal·lon·age (gal'ən·ij) *n.* Quantity or capacity reckoned in gallons.

gal·loon (gə·lōōn') *n.* A narrow braid, tape, or trimming of worsted, silk, or rayon, sometimes of gold or silver thread. [< OF *galon* < *galonner* adorn with ribbons] —**gal·looned', ga·looned'** *adj.*

gal·lop (gal'əp) *n.* 1 A gait of a quadruped characterized by a regular succession of leaps, in which the foot sequence is left hind, right hind, left fore, right fore, in repeating sequence. 2 The act of riding, or a ride at a gallop. 3 Speedy and careless action. —*v.i.* 1 To ride at a gallop. 2 To go, run, or move very fast or at a gallop. —*v.t.* 3 To cause to run at a gallop. [< OF *galop* < *galoper* < Gmc. Doublet of WALLOP.] —**gal'lop·er** *n.*

gal·lo·pade (gal'ə·pād') *n.* 1 A sidewise gallop, or curveting motion. 2 A brisk dance, or the music for it.

gal·lous (gal'əs) *adj. Chem.* Designating a compound containing bivalent gallium: *gallous* bromide.

Gal·lo·way (gal'ə·wā) *n.* 1 A small horse, originally from Galloway, Scotland, now nearly or quite extinct. 2 A breed of dark cattle from Galloway, Scotland.

gal·lows (gal'ōz) *n.* *pl.* **·lows·es** or **·lows** 1 A framework consisting of two or more uprights supporting a crossbeam, used for hanging criminals. 2 *Naut.* A similar structure used to support spars on a vessel, or for other purposes: also called *gallows bitts.* [OE *galga*]

gal·lows-bird (gal'-oz·bûrd') *n.* One who either has been hanged or deserves hanging.

gal·lows-tree (gal'-oz·trē') *n.* A gallows.

A TYPE OF GALLOWS

gall·stone (gôl'stōn') *n. Pathol.* A solid substance found in the gall bladder, liver, etc.; biliary calculus.

Gal·lup poll (gal'əp) A sampling or cross-section of public opinion on given subjects, as conducted by George Horace *Gallup*, born 1901, U.S. statistician.

gall wasp A gallfly.

gal·op (gal'əp) *n.* 1 A lively dance in double measure. 2 The music for it. Also **gal·o·pade** (gal'ə·pād'). [< F, gallop]

ga·lore (gə·lôr', -lōr') *adj.* Very many; abundant: used after its noun. —*n. Obs.* Abundance. —*adv.* In abundance. [< Irish *go leór*, enough]

ga·losh (gə·losh') *n.* 1 *Usually pl.* An overshoe reaching above the ankle and worn in stormy weather. 2 *Obs.* A heavy wooden shoe; a clog or patten; hence, any boot or shoe. Also spelled *golosh.* Also **ga·loshe'.** [< F *galoche*, ult. < Gk. *kalopous* wooden shoe]

ga·lu·chat (gá·lü·shá') *n.* 1 Ornamental sharkskin leather, tanned without removal of pebbly surface. 2 A type of sharkskin fabric. [< F]

gal·van·ic (gal·van'ik) *adj.* 1 Pertaining to galvanism. 2 Resembling the movement of a limb of a dead animal subjected to an electric current; spasmodic. Also **gal·van'i·cal.** —**gal·van'i·cal·ly** *adv.*

galvanic battery A battery of primary cells.

galvanic pile A voltaic pile.

gal·va·nism (gal'və·niz'əm) *n.* 1 A flow of electricity as produced by chemical action. 2 *Med.* The therapeutic application of a continuous electric current from voltaic cells. [after Luigi *Galvani* + -ISM] —**gal'va·nist** *n.*

gal·va·nize (gal'və·nīz) *v.t.* **·nized, ·niz·ing** 1 To stimulate to muscular action by electricity. 2 To rouse to action; startle; excite. 3 To coat with metal by galvanic process; electroplate; also, to coat iron with zinc. Also *Brit.* **gal'va·nise.** —**gal'va·ni·za'tion** *n.* —**gal'va·niz'er** *n.*

galvanized iron Iron coated with zinc, primarily by the electrolytic process.

galvano- *combining form* Galvanic; galvanism: produced by a galvanic current: *galvanometer.*

gal·va·no·cau·ter·y (gal'və·nō·kô'tər·ē) *n. pl.* **·ter·ies** *Med.* The operation or result of cauterizing by electricity.

gal·va·nom·e·ter (gal'və·nom'ə·tər) *n. Electr.* An apparatus for measuring current strength or potential difference. —**gal·va·no·met·ric** (gal'və·nō·met'rik, gal·van'ō-) or **·ri·cal** *adj.*

gal·va·nom·e·try (gal'və·nom'ə·trē) *n.* The science, art, or process of measuring electric currents.

gal·va·no·plas·ty (gal'və·nō·plas'tē, gal·van'ō-) *n.* The reproduction of the forms of objects by electrodeposition; electrotypy. Also **gal'va·no·plas'tics.** —**gal'va·no·plas'tic** *adj.*

gal·va·no·scope (gal'və·nō·skōp', gal·van'ə-) *n.* An instrument for detecting an electric current and showing its direction, differing from a galvanometer in being only qualitative. —**gal·va·no·scop·ic** (gal'və·nō·skop'ik, gal·van'ō-) *adj.*

gal·va·nos·co·py (gal'və·nos'kə·pē) *n.* 1 Use of the galvanoscope. 2 *Med.* Diagnosis by galvanism.

gal·va·no·sur·ger·y (gal'və·nō·sûr'jər·ē) *n.* Use .of galvanic electricity in surgery.

gal·va·no·tax·is (gal'və·nō·tak'sis) *n.* Electrotaxis. Also **gal·va·not·ro·pism** (gal'və·not'rə·piz'əm).

gal·va·no·ther·my (gal'və·nō·thûr'mē) *n.* Production of heat by galvanism.

Gal·way (gôl'wā) A maritime county in western Ireland; 2,293 square miles; capital, Galway.

gal·yak (gal'yak) *n.* A flat fur from the skin of a prematurely born kid or lamb. [< Russian *golyak* bare]

gam¹ (gam) *n.* 1 A herd or school of whales. 2 *U.S. Dial.* An exchange of visits between whaling vessels and crews.—*v.* **gammed, gam·ming** *v.i.* 1 *U.S. Dial.* To visit back and forth while at sea. 2 To come together in a gam: said of whales.—*v.t.* 3 *U.S. Dial.* To make a visit or visits to. [? Var. of GAME¹]

gam² (gam) *n. Slang.* A leg or calf, especially of a woman. [Var. of GAMB]

Gam·bi·a (gam'bē·ə) An independent state in the Commonwealth of Nations, in western Africa; 4,000 square miles; capital, Bathurst; comprising an enclave along 300 miles of the lower course of the **Gambia River,** a river flowing 700 miles west from French Guinea to the Atlantic: *French Gambie* (gän·bē').

Gam·bier Islands (gam'bir) A part of French Oceania at the southern end of the Tuamotu group; 12 square miles; capital, Rikitea on Mangareva: also *Mangareva.*

gam·bir (gam'bir) *n.* Pale catechu, the dried extract from the leaves and twigs of an Asian woody vine (*Uncaria gambir*): used as an astringent and tonic, and in tanning, dyeing, etc. Also **gam'bi·a** (-bē·ə), **gam'bier.** [< Malay]

gam·bit (gam'bit) *n.* One of various openings in chess, in which a pawn or piece is risked to obtain an attack. [< F < OF *gambet,* a tripping up, ult. < LL *gamba* a leg]

gam·ble (gam'bəl) *v.* **gam·bled, gam·bling** *v.i.* 1 To risk or bet something of value on the outcome of an event, a game of chance, etc. 2 To take a risk to obtain a desired result: He *gambled* on finding the window open. —*v.t.* 3 To wager or bet (something of value). 4 To lose or squander by gaming: usually with *away.* —*n. Colloq.* 1 Any risky or uncertain venture. 2 A gambling venture or transaction. ◆ Homophone: *gambol.* [Cf. ME *gamenen,* OE *gamenian* sport, play] —**gam'bling** *n.*

gam·boge (gam·bōj', -bōōzh') *n.* A brownish Oriental gum resin obtained from a tropical tree (*Garcinia hanburyi*), used as a pigment and cathartic. [< NL *gambogium,* from *Cambodia,* where found]

gam·bol (gam'bəl) *v.i.* **·boled** or **·bolled, ·boling** or **·bol·ling** To skip or leap about in play; frolic. See synonyms under FRISK, LEAP. —*n.* A skipping about in sport. See synonyms under FROLIC, SPORT. ◆ Homophone: *gamble.* [Earlier *gambald* < F *gambader* < *gambade* a spring, leap < Ital. *gambata* < *gamba* leg]

gam·brel (gam'brəl) *n.* 1 The hock of an animal. 2 A stick used for hanging meat. 3 *Archit.* A roof having its slope broken by an obtuse angle: also called **gambrel roof.** [< OF *gamberel,* dim. of *gambe* leg < LL *gamba*]

Gam·bri·nus (gam·brī'nəs), 1251–94, duke of Brabant, reputed to be the inventor of beer.

GAMBREL (*def.* 3)

game (gām) *n.* 1 Any contest undertaken for recreation or prizes, played according to rules, and depending on strength, skill, or luck to win. 2 *pl.* Organized athletic contests. 3 Amusement: diversion; play. 4 Fun; sport. 5 A strategy; scheme; plan. 6 A proceeding conducted like a game: the *game* of diplomacy. 7 A set of equipment used in playing certain games, as backgammon or darts. 8 Success in a match: The *game* is ours. 9 The number of points required to win: *Game* is 100 points. 10 A definite portion of a match terminated by a victory or draw, as a *game* in bridge or tennis. 11 Manner or art of playing: He plays a poor *game.* 12 That which is hunted in a chase; prey. 13 Wild animals or birds, collectively, pursued or caught for sport or profit; also their flesh. 14 Any object of pursuit or attack: They were fair *game* for ridicule. 15 Pluck; spirit; intrepidity. 16 *Slang* A business; vocation; especially one involving risk: the advertising *game.* See synonyms under FROLIC. —*v.* **gamed, gam·ing** *v.i.* To gamble at cards, dice, etc., for money or other stakes. —*v.t.* To lose or squander by gambling: with *away.* —*adj.* 1 Of or pertaining to hunted wild animals or their flesh. 2 Plucky; spirited; intrepid. 3 Ready; willing. [OE *gamen*]

game bird Any bird commonly hunted as game, as pheasant, wild duck, or partridge.

game·cock (gām'kok') *n.* A rooster bred and trained for fighting. Also **game cock.**

game fowl 1 One of several breeds of fowl used in cockfighting. 2 Any bird hunted as game.

game laws Laws passed by Federal or State legislatures to protect wild game (animals, birds, fish) by setting the season and manner of capture and sale.

game preserve A large tract of land set apart by law as a refuge and natural breeding ground for wild game.

games·man·ship (gāmz'mən·ship) *n.* The art of winning by the use of any and all means available while seeming to honor the recognized dictates of sportsmanship. [Coined by Stephen Potter, born 1900, English writer]

game·some (gām'səm) *adj.* Playful; sportive; gay; merry. —**game'some·ly** *adv.* —**game'some·ness** *n.*

gam·e·tan·gi·um (gam'ə·tan'jē·əm) *n. pl.* **·gi·a** *Bot.* The plant cell or organ in which gametes are produced. [< GAMETE + Gk. *angeion* vessel]

gam·ete (gam'ēt, gə·mēt') *n. Biol.* Either of two mature reproductive cells, an ovum or sperm, which in uniting produce a zygote. [< NL *gameta* < Gk. *gametē* wife, or *gametēs* husband] — **ga·met·ic** (gə·met'ik) *adj.* — **ga·met'i·cal·ly** *adv.*

gameto– *combining form* Gamete: *gametophore.* [< Gk. *gametēs* husband < *gamos* marriage]

ga·me·to·cyte (gə·mē'tə·sīt) *n. Biol.* A cell which produces gametes.

gam·e·tog·e·ny (gam'ə·toj'ə·nē) *n. Biol.* The formation of gametes. Also **gam·e·to·gen·e·sis** (gam'ə·tō·jen'ə·sis). — **gam'e·to·gen'ic** *adj.*

ga·me·to·phore (gə·mē'tə·fôr, -fōr) *n. Bot.* A modified branch or filament which bears reproductive organs or gametes, as in certain liverworts.

ga·me·to·phyte (gə·mē'tə·fīt) *n. Bot.* That phase or generation of a plant which produces the sexual organs: distinguished from the non-sexual form. — **gam·e·to·phyt·ic** (gam'ə·tō·fit'ik) *adj.*

gam·ic (gam'ik) *adj.* **1** Pertaining to or produced by the congress of the sexes; sexual. **2** *Biol.* Capable of development only after fecundation: *gamic* ova. [< Gk. *gamikos* < *gamos* marriage]

gam·ing (gā'ming) *n.* The act or practice of gambling.

gam·ma (gam'ə) *n.* **1** The third letter in the Greek alphabet (Γ, γ): corresponding to *g* (as in *go*). As a numeral it denotes 3. **2** *Physics* A unit of magnetic field intensity, equal to 10^{-5} gauss. **3** A unit of weight, equal to one thousandth of a milligram. **4** *Phot.* A number expressing the degree to which a negative has been developed as compared with the range of light values in the subject photographed. [< Gk.]

gam·ma·cism (gam'ə·siz'əm) *n.* Inability to utter such letters as *g, k*; baby talk.

gam·ma·di·on (gə·mā'dē·ən) *n.* **1** A cross made of four capital gammas; a swastika; a fylfot. **2** A Greek cross formed of four capital gammas all facing outward so that the ends of the arms of the cross are open. Also **gam·ma'tion** (-shən). [< LGk. < *gamma,* the letter G]

gamma globulin A globulin present in blood plasma which contains antibodies effective against certain pathogenic micro-organisms.

gamma rays *Physics* A type of emission from radioactive substances, consisting of electromagnetic radiation of great penetrating power and of wavelengths lying beyond the region of the shortest X-rays.

gamma test *Phot.* A test using a strip of film to determine the degree of density in a photographic image in comparison with the degree of illumination of the object photographed.

gam·mon (gam'ən) *n.* In backgammon, a defeat in which the winner throws all his men before the loser throws off any. — *v.t.* To obtain a gammon over. [? ME *gamen* a game]

gam·mon² (gam'ən) *n.* **1** A cured ham. **2** The bottom part of a flitch of bacon. — *v.t.* To cure by salting and smoking. [< OF *gambon* < *gambe* a leg < LL *gamba*]

gamo– *combining form* **1** Sexually joined: *gamogenesis.* **2** Fused; united: *gamophyllous.* [< Gk. *gamos* marriage]

gam·o·gen·e·sis (gam'ə·jen'ə·sis) *n. Biol.* Sexual generation.

gam·o·ge·net·ic (gam'ə·jə·net'ik) *adj.* Of, pertaining to, or resulting from gamogenesis. — **gam'o·ge·net'i·cal·ly** *adv.*

gamp (gamp) *n.* A long piece of metal with a raised center, fitted to a sewing machine to produce a rounded tuck on fabric. [< F *guimpe.* See GUIMPE.]

gam·ut (gam'ət) *n.* **1** *Music* The diatonic scale of musical notes. **2** The whole range of anything: the *gamut* of emotions. [< Med. L *gamma ut* < *gamma,* the first note of the early musical scale + *ut* (later, *do*); the names of the notes of the scale were taken from a medieval Latin hymn: *Ut* queant laxis *Re*sonare fibris, *Mi*ra gestorum *Fa*muli tuorum, *Sol*ve polluti *La*bii reatum, *S*ancte *I*ohannes]

gam·y (gā'mē) *adj.* **gam·i·er, gam·i·est** **1** Having the flavor of game, especially game that has been kept raw until somewhat tainted, as preferred by gourmets. **2** Full of pluck; disposed to fight.

–gamy *combining form* Marriage or union for reproduction: used in anthropology, biology, and sociology: *polygamy.* [< Gk. *gamos* marriage]

gan·der (gan'dər) *n.* **1** A male goose. **2** A dunce. [OE *gandra*]

Gan·dhi (gän'dē, gan'-), **Mohandas Karamchand,** 1869–1948, Hindu nationalist leader: known as *Mahatma Gandhi.*

Gan·do (gän'dō) A former emirate including parts of Nigeria and French West Africa. Also **Gan'du** (-dōo).

gan·dou·rah (gän·dōo'rä) *n.* A sleeveless garment resembling a shirt, worn by Arabs in the Near East. Also **gan·dou'ra.** [< Arabic *ghandūrah*]

gang (gang) *n.* **1** A number of persons acting or operating together; a group; squad. **2** A group cooperating for evil purposes. **3** A set of tools or other objects of one kind operated together. **4** Gangue. See synonyms under CABAL. — *v.t.* **1** To unite into or as into a gang. **2** *Colloq.* To attack as a group. — *v.i.* **3** To come together as a gang; form a gang. — **to gang up on** *U.S. Slang* To attack or act against together: They *ganged up on* me. [OE *gang* a going < *gangan* go]

gang·ing (gang'ing) *n. Electronics* A system of coupling two or more coils or condensers of a radio receiving set so that they may be controlled by a single dial.

gang knife A set of knives used to slice fish, etc., into pieces of predetermined length.

gan·gli·at·ed (gang'glē·ā'tid) *adj.* Possessing ganglia. Also **gan'gli·ate** (-it, -āt), **gan·gli·on·at·ed** (gang'glē·ən·ā'tid).

gan·gling (gang'gling) *adj.* Awkwardly tall and loosely built. Also **gan'gly.** [Cf. dial. E *gangrel* a lanky person]

ganglio– *combining form* Ganglion. Also, before vowels, **ganglion-,** as in *ganglionitis.*

gan·gli·oid (gang'glē·oid) *adj.* Resembling a ganglion.

gan·gli·on (gang'glē·ən) *n. pl.* **·gli·ons** or **·gli·a** (glē·ə) *Physiol.* **1** A collection of nerve cells, acting as a center of nervous influence. **2** Any center of energy, activity, or strength. **3** *Pathol.* A hard globular tumor proceeding from a tendon. [< LL < Gk. *ganglion* tumor] — **gan·gli·on·ic** (gang'glē·on'ik) *adj.*

gan·gli·on·ec·to·my (gang'glē·ən·ek'tə·mē) *n. Surg.* Removal of a ganglion.

gan·gli·on·i·tis (gang'glē·ən·ī'tis) *n. Pathol.* Inflammation of a ganglion.

gang·plank (gang'plangk') *n.* A temporary bridge for passengers between a vessel and a wharf.

gang plow A set of plowshares arranged to work simultaneously.

gan·grene (gang'grēn, gang·grēn') *n. Pathol.* Mortification or death of a part of the body, caused by failure or lack of an adequate blood supply; massive necrosis of the tissue. — *v.t. & v.i.* **gan·grened, gan·gren·ing** To cause gangrene in or become affected by gangrene. [< L *gangraena* < Gk. *gangraina*] — **gan'gre·nous** (-grə·nəs) *adj.*

gang saw An arrangement of circular saws geared to one shaft and used to perform several cutting operations simultaneously.

gang·ster (gang'stər) *n.* A member of a gang of toughs, gunmen, or the like. — **gang'ster·dom** *n.*

gangue (gang) *n. Mining* The non-metalliferous or worthless minerals found in a vein of ore. [< F < G *gang* vein of ore]

gang·way (gang'wā') *n.* **1** A passageway through, into, or out of any enclosure; especially, a temporary passageway made of planks. **2** *Brit.* An aisle between rows of seats in the British House of Commons, separating members of the government or ex-ministers who are in opposition from the rank and file of their parties. **3** *Naut.* **a** Either side of the upper deck of a ship, from the mainmast to the quarter-deck. **b** An opening in a vessel's bulwarks to afford entrance

for passengers or freight; also, a gangplank. **4** *Mining* The main level in a coal mine. **5** The gradient up which logs are conveyed into a sawmill: also called *logway.* — *interj.* Get out of the way! Stand aside! [OE *gangweg*]

gan·is·ter (gan'is·tər) *n.* **1** A very siliceous claystone of the lower coal measures of England, used chiefly for flagging and refractory furnace linings. **2** A mixture of ground quartz and fire clay used in lining Bessemer converters. Also **gan'nis·ter.** [< dial. G *ganster* < MHG, a spark]

gan·net (gan'it) *n.* **1** Any of several large sea birds (family *Sulidae*) related to the pelicans. The common gannet (*Moris bassana*) of the North Atlantic coasts is of a prevailing white color with blackish feet. **2** The wood ibis of Florida. [OE *ganot*]

gan·oid (gan'oid) *adj.* **1** Pertaining to a subclass (*Ganoidei*) of teleost fishes having scales consisting of laminated bone covered with a shiny enamel surface, as sturgeons, bowfins, etc. — *n.* A ganoid fish. [< Gk. *ganos* brightness + -OID]

gant·let¹ (gônt'lit, gant'-) *n.* **1** A punishment wherein the victim runs between two rows of men who strike him with clubs or switches as he passes. **2** A series of risks or unpleasant events. **3** A narrowing of two lines of railway track almost into the space of one, as on a bridge or in a tunnel, without breaking the continuity of either track. — **to run the gantlet** To be exposed to a series of hostile attacks or unpleasant incidents. — *v.t.* To form a gantlet by running together (railway tracks). Also spelled *gauntlet.* [Earlier *gantlope,* alter. of Sw. *gatlopp* a running down a lane]

gant·let² (gônt'lit, gant'-) See GAUNTLET¹.

gan·try (gan'trē) *n. pl.* **·tries** **1** The frame of a traveling crane, or the crane and frame together. **2** A framework for supporting railway signals usually bridging the tracks. **3** A frame to hold a barrel horizontally. Also spelled *gauntry, gauntree.* [Alter. of OF *gantier, chantier* < L *canterius* beast of burden, framework < Gk. *kanthēlios* pack ass]

GANTRY (*def.* 1)

gap (gap) *n.* **1** An opening or parting in anything; aperture; breach; chasm. **2** *Geog.* A deep notch or ravine in a mountain ridge. **3** A break in continuity; an interruption; a period in chronology or a range of phenomena about which nothing is known. **4** *Aeron.* The vertical distance between two supporting planes of an airplane. See synonyms under BREACH, HOLE. — *v.t.* **gapped, gap·ping** To make a breach or opening in. [< ON *gap* gap, abyss < *gapa* gape] — **gap'less** *adj.*

gape (gāp, gap) *v.i.* **gaped, gap·ing** **1** To stare with or as with open mouth, as in awe or surprise. **2** To open the mouth wide, as in yawning. **3** To be or become open wide; present a wide opening. — *n.* **1** The act of gaping. **2** *Zool.* The expanse of the open mouth, as in birds; also, the opening between the shells of a bivalve the edges of which do not naturally shut tight together, as in soft clams. **3** A gap. — **the gapes** **1** A fit of gaping or yawning. **2** A disease of young fowls, caused by the presence of gapeworms obstructing the breathing and causing much gaping. [< ON *gapa*] — **gap'er** *n.*

gape·worm (gāp'wûrm', gap'-) *n.* A nematode worm (*Syngamus trachealis*) that causes the gapes.

gar (gär) *n. pl.* **gars** or **gar** Any of several fishes having a spearlike snout and elongate body, including the North American species (*Tylosurus marinus*); the common European species (*Belone vulgaris*), esteemed as a food fish; and the teleost marine varieties also called *billfishes, needlefishes.* [Short for GARFISH]

garb (gärb) n. **1** Style of apparel, especially as characteristic of some office, rank, etc. **2** Clothes. **3** Obs. External seeming; appearance; demeanor; manner. **4** Obs. Custom; style. See synonyms under DRESS. —v.t. To clothe; dress. [< MF garbe gracefulness, ult. < Gmc.]

gar·bage (gär′bij) n. **1** Animal or household refuse. **2** Low or vile things collectively. [Prob. < AF. Cf. OF garbe a sheaf of grain, animal fodder]

gar·ban·zo bean (gär·bän′sō) The Mexican chickpea.

gar·ble (gär′bəl) v.t. **gar·bled, gar·bling 1** To mix up or confuse; make incomprehensible: to garble a message. **2** To change or alter the meaning or emphasis of (a document, report, etc.) with intent to mislead or misrepresent. **3** Obs. To take the best part of. **4** Obs. To cull or sift. See synonyms under PERVERT. —n. **1** The act of garbling; a perversion, as of a text. **2** pl. Impurities separated from drugs, spices, etc.; refuse; trash. [< Ital. garbellare < Arabic gharbala sift < ghirbal a sieve, ult. < L cribellum, dim. of cribrum a sieve]

gar·dant (gär′dənt) adj. Her. Looking directly toward the observer, as an animal on a shield: also spelled guardant. [< F, orig. ppr. of garder watch]

gar·den (gär′dən) n. **1** A place for the cultivation of flowers, vegetables, or small plants. **2** Hence, any fertile or highly cultivated territory. **3** A piece of ground, commonly with ornamental plants or trees, used as a place of public resort: a botanical garden. —adj. **1** Grown, or capable of being grown in a garden; hence, hardy. **2** Ordinary; common. **3** Like a garden; ornamental: garden spot of the world. —v.t. To cultivate as a garden. —v.i. To till or work in a garden. [< AF gardin < Gmc.]

garden balsam An ornamental plant (Impatiens balsamina), cultivated in many varieties.

gar·den·er (gärd′nər, gär′dən·ər) n. One who tends gardens, or is skilled in gardening.

garden heliotrope A species of valerian (Valeriana officinalis) having clusters of small pink or white flowers and roots with a penetrating aroma, reputed to have curative properties. Also called allheal, valerian.

gar·de·ni·a (gär·dē′nē·ə, -dēn′yə) n. Any of a considerable genus (Gardenia) of mainly tropical shrubs or trees of the madder family, with large and fragrant yellow or white axillary flowers. The Cape jasmine (G. jasminoides) is the best known in cultivation. [< NL, after Alexander Garden, 1730–91, U.S. botanist]

gar·den·ing (gärd′ning, gär′dən·ing) n. The art of making and caring for a garden; also, the work involved. See synonyms under AGRICULTURE.

garden sorrel The common sorrel, or sour dock.

gar·fish (gär′fish′) n. pl. **·fish** or **·fish·es** A fish with a spearlike snout, as a garpike. See GAR[1]. [OE gar spear + FISH]

gar·ga·ney (gär′gə·nē) n. A teal (Anas querquedula) of Europe and Asia, having a broad white line on each side of the head and neck. [< Ital. garganello]

Gar·gan·tu·an (gär·gan′chōō·ən) adj. Huge; gigantic; prodigious.

gar·get (gär′git) n. **1** An infectious bacterial disease of cattle, sheep, and swine, characterized by inflammation of the udder, deficient or contaminated milk, distemper, and other symptoms: also called mastitis. **2** The pokeweed. [< OF gargate throat < L gurges a whirlpool]

gar·gle (gär′gəl) v. **gar·gled, gar·gling** v.t. **1** To rinse (the throat) with a liquid agitated by air from the windpipe. —v.i. **2** To use a gargle. **3** To make a sound as if gargling. —n. A liquid for gargling. [< OF gargouiller gargle < gargouille throat]

gar·goyle (gär′goil) n. A waterspout, usually carved in a grotesque human or animal figure, projecting from the gutter of a building. Also spelled gurgoyle. [< OF gargouille throat] —**gar′goyled** adj.

gar·i·bal·di (gar·ə·bôl′dē) n. A loose blouse resembling those worn by the soldiers of Garibaldi.

Gar·i·bal·di·an (gar·ə·bôl′dē·ən) adj. Of or pertaining to Giuseppe Garibaldi or his troops. —n. One of the soldiers of Giuseppe Garibaldi

Ga·ri·glia·no (gä·rē·lyä′nō) The lower reaches of the Liri.

gar·ish (gâr′ish) adj. **1** Marked by a dazzling glare. **2** Displaying a gaudy effect. **3** Extravagantly conceited. Also formerly spelled gairish. [Cf. obs. gaure stare] —**gar′ish·ly** adv. — **gar′ish·ness** n.

gar·land (gär′lənd) n. **1** A wreath of leaves, flowers, etc., as a token of victory, joy, or honor. **2** A collection of literary gems. **3** A wire framework covered with cloth or burlap strips and used in camouflage. **4** Something resembling a garland or wreath. **5** A strop used to hoist spars. —v.t. To deck with or as with a garland. [< OF garlande]

gar·lic (gär′lik) n. **1** A hardy bulbous perennial (Allium sativum) of the same genus as the onion. **2** Its pungent bulb, used in cooking. [OE gárléac < gár spear + léac leek] —**gar′lick·y** adj.

gar·ment (gär′mənt) n. An article of clothing. See synonyms under DRESS. —v.t. To clothe: usually in the past participle. [< OF garnement < garnir garnish]

gar·ner (gär′nər) v.t. To gather or store as in a garner; collect. —n. **1** A place for the storing of grain; a granary. **2** Any storage place. [< OF gernier, grenier < L granarium a granary < granum grain]

gar·net[1] (gär′nit) n. **1** Any of a group of mineral double salts (silicates) of isometric crystalline form and varied composition, used as gemstones and abrasives. **2** A variable deep red color characteristic of certain varieties of garnet, as pyrope and almandine. [< OF grenat < Med. L granatum < L, a pomegranate; so called from its color]

gar·net[2] (gär′nit) n. Naut. A form of tackle or purchase. [Origin uncertain]

gar·net·ting (gär·net′ing) n. A process of reducing wool or cotton shoddy and rags to fibers that can be re-used. [from Garnett machine, named after the inventor]

gar·ni·er·ite (gär′nē·ə·rīt′) n. An amorphous, apple-green, hydrous silicate of nickel and magnesium, forming an important ore of nickel. [after Jules Garnier, French geologist]

gar·nish (gär′nish) v.t. **1** To decorate, as with ornaments; embellish. **2** In cookery, to decorate (a dish) with flavorsome or colorful trimmings for the table. **3** Law To give warning to (someone) to answer to an action; garnishee. —n. **1** Something placed around a dish for ornamentation or a relish. **2** Anything added as an ornament; embellishment. **3** Obs. In English jails, a fee collected from a new prisoner by the jailer. [< OF garniss-, stem of garnir prepare. Akin to WARN.]

Synonyms (verb): adorn, beautify, deck, decorate, dress, embellish, furbish, ornament. See ADORN. Antonyms: blemish, deface, denude, disfigure, dismantle, spoil, strip.

gar·nish·ee (gär′nish·ē′) v.t. **·eed, ·ee·ing** Law **1** To secure by garnishment (any debt or property, in the hands of a third person, which is due or belonging to the defendant in attachment). **2** To warn (a person) by garnishment. —n. Law A person warned not to pay or deliver money or effects to a defendant, pending a judgment of a court.

gar·nish·er (gär′nish·ər) One who garnishes or garnishees.

gar·nish·ment (gär′nish·mənt) n. **1** The act of garnishing. **2** That which garnishes; embellishment; ornament. **3** Law A warning or summons; specifically, a notice not to pay or deliver money or effects to a defendant, but to appear and answer the plaintiff's suit.

gar·ni·ture (gär′ni·chər) n. Anything used to garnish; embellishment. [< F < garnir. See GARNISH.]

gar·pike (gär′pīk′) n. pl. **·pike** or **·pikes 1** A large ganoid fish of the fresh waters of eastern North America (family Lepisosteidae), having an elongated spearlike snout. **2** A garfish. [< GAR[1] + PIKE]

gar·ret (gar′it) n. A story or room directly under a sloping roof. [< OF garite a watchtower < garir watch, defend < Gmc.]

gar·ret·eer (gar′it·ir′) n. One who lives in a garret.

gar·ri·son (gar′ə·sən) n. **1** The military force defending a fort, town, etc. **2** The place where such a force is stationed. ◆ Collateral adjective: presidial. —v.t. **1** To place troops in, as a fort or town, for its defense. **2** To station (troops) in a fort, town,

etc. **3** To be the garrison of. [< OF garison < garir defend < Gmc.]

garrison cap A military cap having a round cloth top and a stiff, shiny visor, worn with the dress uniform.

gar·rote (gə·rot′, -rōt′) n. **1** A Spanish instrument for strangling, formerly used as a means of capital punishment. **2** The mode of punishment inflicted by the garrote. **3** Any similar method of strangulation, especially in order to rob. —v.t. **gar·rot·ed, gar·rot·ing 1** To execute with a garrote. **2** To throttle in order to rob. Also **ga·rote′, ga·rotte′, gar·rotte′**. [< Sp. garotte, orig. a stick, cudgel < Celtic]

gar·ru·line (gar′ōō·lin, -lin, -yōō-) adj. Of or pertaining to a subfamily of corvine birds (Garrulinae), which includes the jays. —n. Any bird of this subfamily. [< NL < L garrulus talkative]

gar·ru·lous (gar′ə·ləs, -yə-) adj. Given to continual and tedious talking; habitually loquacious. [< L garrulus talkative] —**gar′ru·lous·ly** adv. — **gar′ru·lous·ness** n.
    Synonyms: chattering, loquacious, talkative, verbose.

gar·ter (gär′tər) n. A band worn around the leg to hold a stocking in place; loosely, any stocking supporter. —v.t. To support or fasten with a garter. [< AF gartier < OF garet bend of the knee < Celtic]

Gar·ter (gär′tər) n. **1** The distinctive badge of the Order of the Garter, the highest order of knighthood in Great Britain. **2** The order itself, or membership therein.

garter snake Any of various small, harmless, viviparous, brightly striped snakes (genus Thamnophis): most common of American snakes.

garth (gärth) n. **1** The open space or courtyard enclosed by a cloister. **2** Archaic A yard; garden. [< ON gardhr a yard]

Gar·y (gâr′ē) A city in NW Indiana, on Lake Michigan.

gas (gas) n. **1** Physics That fluid form of matter which is compressible within limits, and which, owing to the relatively free movement of its molecules, diffuses readily and is capable of indefinite expansion in all directions. **2** Any gaseous or vaporous mixture other than air: illuminating gas, fuel gas, etc. **3** A single jet of flame supplied by illuminating gas. **4** Laughing gas. **5** Mining An explosive mixture of atmospheric air with firedamp. **6** Slang Empty boasting; chatter. **7** U.S. Colloq. Gasoline. **8** Chlorine or some other highly poisonous or asphyxiating substance used in warfare: also **poison gas**. **9** Flatulence. See synonyms under FLUID. —v. **gassed, gas·sing** v.t. **1** To overcome, affect, or kill by gas or gas fumes. **2** To treat or saturate with gas. **3** To supply with gas or gasoline. **4** To singe so as to free of loose fibers: to gas lace. **5** U.S. Slang To talk boastfully or nonsensically to. —v.i. **6** To give off gas. **7** U.S. Slang To talk in an idle or empty manner; boast. [Coined by J. B. van Helmont, 1577–1644, Belgian chemist]

gas alarm 1 A warning of a gas attack. **2** The device by which the warning is given.

gas analysis The qualitative and quantitative determination of gases, especially in regard to their physiological and thermodynamic properties.

gas attack A military attack using asphyxiating or poisonous gases to overcome the enemy, as by bombardment with gas shells.

gas bacillus The micro-organism producing gas gangrene in gunshot wounds, specifically Bacillus welchii.

gas-bag (gas′bag′) n. **1** An expansible container for holding gas. **2** Slang A tiresome, garrulous person.

gas balance An instrument for determining the specific gravity of gases.

gas black Carbon black, produced by carbonizing natural gas: used as a substitute for animal and vegetable carbon.

gas bleaching Bleaching by means of a gas, as by chlorine.

gas bomb A bomb or shell filled with poison gas which is released when the shell explodes. Also **gas shell**.

gas bracket A bracket bearing one or more gas burners.

gas burner A tube or tip, usually attached to a gas fixture, for regulating the flame of the gas consumed.

gas carbon A compact, amorphous carbon deposited in the retorts of gasworks, which is a good conductor of heat and electricity, and is used for battery plates and in the electric arc light. Also **gas coke.**

gas cell 1 *Aeron.* One of the individual compartments containing the gas in an airship: also **gas container. 2** An electrolytic cell composed of two gas electrodes: also **gas battery.**

gas chamber A chamber in which executions are performed by means of poisonous gas.

gas coal A bituminous coal from which illuminating gas may be made.

gas·con (gas′kən) *n.* A boaster. —*adj.* Boastful; blustering. [< F, a native of Gascony]

gas electrode An electrode capable of dissolving a gas or holding it on its surface; it is usually made of finely divided metal and in the solution behaves as a reversible electrode.

gas·e·lier (gas′ə·lir′) See GASOLIER.

gas engine An internal-combustion engine, especially one using illuminating or natural gas.

gas·e·ous (gas′ē·əs, -yəs) *adj.* **1** Having the nature or form of gas; aeriform. **2** Unsubstantial.

gas fading Fume fading.

gas filter A filter for removing solid or liquid particles from a gas.

gas fitter One who fits and puts up gas fixtures.

gas fittings The appliances connected with the introduction and use of gas in a building.

gas fixture A tube, with burners and stopcocks, connected with a gas pipe.

gas focusing *Physics* A method of focusing a stream of electrons through the action of an ionized gas.

gas furnace A furnace in which gas is used for fuel, or one for making gas.

gas gangrene *Pathol.* Gangrene with gas formation in the tissues of gunshot wounds; caused chiefly by anaerobic bacteria, as *Bacillus welchii.*

gas groove *Chem.* A groove formed by a stream of hydrogen or other gas rising continuously along the surface of an electrochemical metallic deposit while it is forming.

gash[1] (gash) *v.t.* To make a long, deep cut in. See synonyms under CUT. —*n.* A long, deep incision; a flesh wound. [Earlier *garse* < OF *garser* scratch]

gash[2] (gash) *adj. Scot.* **1** Fluent; intelligent **2** Neat; trim.

gas helmet A gas mask.

gas-hold·er (gas′hōl′dər) See GASOMETER.

gas-house (gas′hous′) *n.* A gasworks: often used figuratively to designate the rowdy district around a gashouse.

gas·i·form (gas′ə·fôrm) *adj.* Gaseous.

gas·i·fy (gas′ə·fī) *v.t. & v.i.* ·**fied,** ·**fy·ing** To make into or become gas. —**gas′i·fi′a·ble** *adj.* — **gas′i·fi·ca′tion** *n.* —**gas′i·fi′er** *n.*

gas jet 1 A burner on a gas fixture. **2** The jet of flame on a gas burner.

gas·ket (gas′kit) *n.* **1** *Mech.* A ring, disk, or plate of packing to make a joint watertight. **2** *Naut.* A rope or cord used to confine furled sails to the yard or boom. Also **gas′kin** (-kin), **gas′king** (-king). [Cf. Ital. *gaschetta* end of rope]

gas·kin (gas′kin) *n.* **1** The hinder part of a horse's leg, between the stifle and the hock. See illustration under HORSE. **2** *pl.* Galligaskins. See GASKET (def. 2). [? < GALLIGASKINS]

gas liquor A by-product obtained by subjecting soft coal to destructive distillation: the chief source of ammonia.

gas log An imitation log concealing a gas burner, used in a fireplace.

gas main A trunk gas pipe for conveying gas to the service pipes.

gas mantle A mantle surrounding the flame of a gas jet, which radiates light when heated.

gas mask A protective headpiece worn to prevent poisoning by noxious fumes or gases.

gas meter An apparatus for measuring the quantity of gas that passes through it.

gas·o·gene (gas′ə·jēn) *n.* **1** A fuel gas made from charcoal. **2** A portable contrivance for producing gas for aerating water. [< F *gazogène*]

gas·o·hol (gas′ə·hôl, -hol) *n.* A mixture of 90 percent gasoline and usu. 10 percent alcohol, used in internal-combustion engines as a petroleum-saving fuel.

gas·o·lier (gas′ə·lir′) *n.* A pendent fixture having branches ending in gas burners: also spelled **gasalier, gaselier.** [< *gaso-* (< GAS) + (CHANDE)LIER]

gas·o·line (gas′ə·lēn, gas′ə·lēn′) *n.* A colorless, volatile, inflammable hydrocarbon product of the distillation of crude petroleum, having a specific gravity of .629 to .667 and boiling at from 75° to 90° C. It is used as fuel, for carbonizing water gases, to propel machinery, and as a solvent for fats. Also **gas′o·lene.** [< GAS + -OL[2] + -INE[2]]

gas·om·e·ter (gas·om′ə·tər) *n.* **1** An apparatus for measuring gases, used in chemical manipulations. **2** An apparatus adapted to collecting, holding, or mixing gases; a gas-holder.

gas·om·e·try (gas·om′ə·trē) *n.* The measurement of gases. —**gas·o·met·ric** (gas′ə·met′rik) *adj.*

gas·op·er·at·ed (gas′op′ə·rā′tid) *adj.* Operated by the action of expanding gases: said especially of certain automatic and semi-automatic weapons. See GARAND RIFLE.

gasp (gasp, gäsp) *v.i.* **1** To take in the breath suddenly and sharply; breathe convulsively, as from fear or exhaustion. **2** To have great longing or desire: with *for* or *after.* —*v.t.* **3** To say or utter with gasps. —*n.* An act of convulsive and interrupted breathing. [< ON *geispa* yawn]

gas pipe A pipe for carrying gas, especially illuminating gas.

gas plant The herb fraxinella.

gas pot A receptacle containing lacrimatory or other poison gases and used principally in training for chemical warfare.

gastero- *combining form* Gastro-.

gas·ter·o·my·ce·tous (gas′tər·ō·mī·sē′təs) *adj.* Of or pertaining to a subgroup (*Gasteromycetes*) of fleshy fungi having spores enclosed in cavities within the fruit body, as puffballs and earthstars. [< GASTERO- + Gk. *mykēs, mykētos* fungus + -OUS]

gas thermometer A thermometer which indicates temperature changes by variations in the pressure or volume of a contained gas, usually hydrogen.

gas-tight (gas′tīt′) *adj.* Not permitting the escape of gas.

gas·tral·gi·a (gas·tral′jē·ə) *n.* **1** *Pathol.* Neuralgia in the stomach. **2** Gastric pain.

gas·trec·to·my (gas·trek′tə·mē) *n. Surg.* An operation to remove a portion of the stomach.

gas·tric (gas′trik) *adj.* Of, pertaining to, or near the stomach. Compare illustration under ABDOMINAL.

gastric fever *Pathol.* **1** A bilious remittent fever; harvest fever. **2** Acute dyspepsia.

gastric juice *Biochem.* A thin acid fluid secreted by the glands of the stomach and containing several enzymes; the chief digestive fluid, acting mainly on proteins.

gas·trin (gas′trin) *n. Biochem.* A hormone secreted by the stomach membrane and promoting digestion by activating gastric juices.

gas·tri·tis (gas·trī′tis) *n. Pathol.* Inflammation of the stomach. —**gas·trit·ic** (gas·trit′ik) *adj.*

gastro- *combining form* **1** Stomach: *gastrolith.* **2** Stomach and: *gastroenterology.* Also **gastero-.** [< Gk. *gastēr* stomach]

gas·tro·coel (gas′trə·sēl) *n. Anat.* The archenteron. [< GASTRO- + Gk. *koilia* cavity]

gas·tro·col·ic (gas′trə·kol′ik) *adj. Anat.* Of, pertaining to, or attached to the stomach and the transverse colon.

gas·tro·di·aph·a·ny (gas′trō·dī·af′ə·nē) *n. Med.* Examination of the stomach by means of a small electric light inserted through the esophagus. Also **gas·tro·di·aph·a·nos·co·py** (gas′trō·dī·af′ə·nos′kə·pē). [< GASTRO- + Gk. *diaphanēs* transparent < *dia-* through + *phainein* appear]

gas·tro·en·ter·i·tis (gas′trō·en′tə·rī′tis) *n. Pathol.* Inflammation of the lining membrane of the stomach and bowels. —**gas·tro·en·te·rit·ic** (-tə·rit′ik) *adj.*

gas·tro·en·ter·ol·o·gy (gas′trō·en′tə·rol′ə·jē) *n.* The study of the anatomy, physiology, and pathology of the stomach and intestines. —**gas·tro·en·ter·ol′o·gist** *n.*

gas·tro·en·ter·os·to·my (gas′trō·en′tə·ros′tə·mē) *n. Surg.* An operation by which a passage is formed between the stomach and the intestine.

gas·tro·ga·vage (gas′trō·gə·väzh′) *n. Med.* Artificial feeding through an opening in the abdominal wall to the stomach. Also **gas·tros·to·ga·vage** (gas′tros′tō·gə·väzh′). [< GASTRO- + F *gavage* cramming < *gaver* gorge]

gas·tro·he·pat·ic (gas′trō·hi·pat′ik) *adj. Anat.* Of or pertaining to the stomach and the liver.

gas·tro·in·tes·ti·nal (gas′trō·in·tes′tə·nəl) *adj. Anat.* Of or pertaining to the stomach and the intestines.

gas·tro·lith (gas′trō·lith) *n. Pathol.* A calculus or stony formation in the gastric region.

gas·trol·o·gy (gas·trol′ə·jē) *n.* The study of the anatomy, physiology, and pathology of the stomach.

gas·tron·o·mer (gas·tron′ə·mər) *n.* An epicure. Also **gas·tro·nome** (gas′trə·nōm), **gas·tron′o·mist.**

gas·tro·nom·ic (gas′trə·nom′ik) *adj.* Of or pertaining to gastronomy. Also **gas·tro·nom′i·cal.** —**gas·tro·nom′i·cal·ly** *adv.*

gas·tron·o·my (gas·tron′ə·mē) *n.* The art of good eating; epicurism. [< F *gastronomie* < Gk. *gastronomia* < *gastēr* stomach + *nomos* law]

Gas·troph·i·lus (gas·trof′ə·ləs) *n.* A genus of dipterous insects whose larvae are parasitic on horses, especially *G. intestinalis,* a botfly: also called *Gasterophilus.* [< NL < Gk. *gastēr* stomach + *philos* loving]

gas·tro·pod (gas′trə·pod) *n.* Any of a large and diverse class (Gastropoda) of mollusks usually having a spiral shell and moving by means of a ventral muscular organ, including snails, slugs, limpets, and conches. —*adj.* Of or pertaining to the class of gastropods. [< NL < Gk. *gastēr* stomach + *pous, podos* foot] —**gas·trop·o·dan** (gas·trop′ə·dən), **gas·trop′o·dous** *adj.*

gas·trop·to·sis (gas′trop·tō′sis) *n. Pathol.* Prolapse of the stomach. [< GASTRO- + Gk. *ptosis* a falling]

gas·tro·scope (gas′trə·skōp) *n. Med.* An electrical apparatus for illuminating and inspecting the human stomach. —**gas·tro·scop·ic** (-skop′ik) *adj.*

gas·tros·co·py (gas·tros′kə·pē) *n. Med.* An examination of the abdomen to discover disease.

gas·tro·stege (gas′trə·stēj) *n. Zool.* One of the abdominal scales of a reptile. [< GASTRO- + Gk. *stegē* a covering]

gas·trot·o·my (gas·trot′ə·mē) *n. Surg.* An opening of or cutting into the stomach or abdomen, as to remove a foreign substance.

gas·trot·ri·chan (gas·trot′rə·kən) *n.* Any of a class (Gastrotricha) of minute fresh-water animals, possibly related to the rotifers, having spindle-shaped bodies partly or entirely covered with spines, bristles, or scales. [< GASTRO- + Gk. *thrix, trichos* hair]

gas·tro·vas·cu·lar (gas′trō·vas′kyə·lər) *adj. Physiol.* **1** Serving both a circulating and a digestive function. **2** Of or pertaining to organs having such a dual function.

gas·tru·la (gas′trōō·lə) *n. pl.* ·**lae** (-lē) *Biol.* That embryonic form of metazoic animals which consists of a two-layered sac enclosing a central cavity or archenteron and having an opening or blastopore at one end. [< NL, dim. of Gk. *gastēr* stomach] —**gas′tru·lar** *adj.*

gas·tru·la·tion (gas′trōō·lā′shən) *n.* The formation of a gastrula.

gas tube *Physics* A vacuum tube in which the pressure of the contained gas or vapor is such as to affect the electrical characteristics of the tube appreciably.

gas turbine A turbine engine in which liquid or gaseous fuel is burned under pressure and the expansion gases sent through a rotor unit connected with a generator.

gas warfare Warfare in which noxious or poisonous gases are dispersed by gas bombs or other means among enemy forces.

gas weld A fusion of metals by use of high-temperature gas flames, mixtures of hydrogen or acetylene with oxygen.

---

add, āce, câre, pälm; end, ēven; it, īce; odd, ōpen, ôrder; tōōk, pōōl; up, bûrn; ə = a in *above,* e in *sicken,* i in *clarity,* o in *melon,* u in *focus;* yōō = u in *fuse,* oi, oil; ou, pout; ch, check; g, go; ng, ring; th, thin; ᵗh, this; zh, vision. Foreign sounds á, œ, ü, kh, ń; and ♦: see page xx. < from; + plus; ? possibly.

gas well A well from which natural gas flows.

gas·works (gas'wûrks') *n.* A factory where illuminating gas or heating gas is made.

gate (gāt) *n.* **1** A movable barrier, commonly swinging on hinges: often distinguished from a door by having openwork. **2** An opening or passageway, as in a barrier, fence, wall, or enclosure, often with its surrounding masonry or woodwork; a portal. **3** *Geog.* A mountain gap or natural passageway. **4** That which gives or affords access: the *gates* of hell. **5** A frame in which a saw (or set of saws) is stretched. **6** *Mech.* A valve controlling the water supply of a water wheel or the like. **7** *Metall.* **a** A pouring hole in a mold. **b** A sprue or waste piece on a casting formed in a pouring hole. **8** A thing. See illustration under HINGE. **9** The total paid admissions at a sports event; the total attendance. See synonyms under ENTRANCE. —*v.t.* **gat·ed, gat·ing** *Brit.* To keep (a college student) within the gates as a punishment. ◆ Homophone: *gait.* [OE *gatu,* plural of *geat* opening]

gate hinge *Mech.* A type of hinge formed of two detachable sections, one of which pivots on a cylindrical core projecting from the other. See illustration under HINGE.

gate·house (gāt'hous') *n.* A house beside, over, or at a gate, as a power station, a porter's lodge, or a medieval defensive structure.

gate-leg table (gāt'leg') A table with swinging legs which support drop leaves and fold against the frame when the leaves are let down.

gate money Money paid for admission to a sports event, theatrical performance, etc.

gate-post (gāt'pōst') *n.* Either of two posts between which a gate swings.

gate·way (gāt'wā') *n.* **1** An entrance that is or may be closed with a gate. **2** That which is regarded as a means of ingress or egress. **3** The guides of a saw frame. See synonyms under ENTRANCE.

gath·er (gath'ər) *v.t.* **1** To bring together in one place or group. **2** To bring together from various places, sources, etc. **3** To pick, harvest, or collect. **4** To collect or summon up, as one's energies, for an effort, trial, etc. **5** To acquire or gain in increasing amount or degree: The storm *gathered* force. **6** To come to understand, believe, or infer. **7** To clasp or enfold: to *gather* someone into one's arms. **8** To draw into folds or plaits, as by shirring. **9** To wrinkle (the brow). —*v.i.* **10** To come together. **11** To increase by accumulation. **12** To wrinkle up, as the brow. **13** To come to a head; contract, as a boil. See synonyms under AMASS, CONVOKE. —**to gather up** To pick up and collect together in one place. —*n.* A plait or fold in cloth, held by a thread passing through the folds; a drawing together. [OE *gadrian*] —**gath·er·a·ble** *adj.*

gat·ing (gā'ting) *n.* **1** A form of punishment. See GATE[1] *v.* **2** *Mech.* A gate in a lock tumbler for the passage of the stub.

gauche (gōsh) *adj.* Awkward; clumsy; boorish. [< F, left-handed]

gauche·rie (gōsh'rē) *n.* **1** An awkward or tactless action. **2** Clumsiness; tactlessness. [< F]

gaud (gôd) *n.* An article of vulgar finery. [< OF *gaudir* be merry < L *gaudere* rejoice]
  Synonyms: bauble, finery, gew-gaw, gimcrack, kickshaw, toy, trinket, trumpery.

gaud·y[1] (gô'dē) *adj.* **gaud·i·er, gaud·i·est** Obtrusively brilliant in color: garish; flashy. —**gaud'i·ly** *adv.* —**gaud'i·ness** *n.*

gaud·y[2] (gô'dē) *n.* *Brit.* A feast or festival; an entertainment; especially, an annual dinner given by a college in one of the English universities. [< L *gaudium* joy]

gauf·fer (gôf'ər) See GOFFER.

gauge (gāj) See GAGE[1].

Gau·guin (gō·gaṅ'), **Paul,** 1848–1903, French painter.

Gaul (gôl) An ancient name for the territory south and west of the Rhine, west of the Alps, and north of the Pyrenees; roughly the area of modern France: Latin *Gallia.* See also CISALPINE GAUL, TRANSALPINE GAUL, TRANSPADANE GAUL.

Gaul (gôl) *n.* **1** A native of ancient Gaul. **2** A Frenchman. [< F *Gaule* < L *Gallus*]

Gaul·ish (gô'lish) *adj.* Of ancient Gaul, its people, or their Celtic language. —*n.* The extinct continental Celtic language of Gaul.

Gaull·ism (gôl'iz'əm) *n.* The policies or philosophy of Charles de Gaulle and his followers. —

Gaull·ist *adj. & n.*

gaul·the·ri·a (gôl·thir'ē·ə) *n.* **1** Any of a large genus (*Gaultheria*) of aromatic shrubs or undershrubs with thick, shining, evergreen leaves and axillary white or rose-colored nodding flowers. The wintergreen is a well-known North American species. **2** Oil of wintergreen: also called **oil of gaultheria.** [< NL, after Dr. Jean-François *Gaultier,* 1708?–56, Canadian physician and botanist]

gaunt (gônt) *adj.* **1** Emaciated, as from lack of food; lank; lean; meager; thin. **2** Grim; desolate. [? < OF *gent* elegant, infl. in meaning by ON *gand* a tall, thin person] —**gaunt'ly** *adv.* —**gaunt'ness** *n.*
  Synonyms: emaciated, famished, hungry, lank, lean, meager, pinched, thin, wan, wasted. See MEAGER.

gaunt·let[1] (gônt'lit, gänt'-) *n.* **1** In medieval armor, a leather glove covered with metal plates. **2** A modern glove with long wrist-extension; also, the part of the glove covering the wrist.

GAUNTLET *(def. 1)*

—**to throw** (or **fling**) **down the gauntlet** To challenge to combat or contest. Also spelled *gantlet.* [< OF *gantelet,* dim. of *gant* mitten] —**gaunt'let·ed** *adj.*

gaunt·let[2] (gônt'lit, gänt'-) See GANTLET[1].

gaun·try (gôn'trē), **gaun·tree** See GANTRY.

gaur (gour) *n.* A large wild ox (*Bos gaurus*) of southeastern Asia, having a hump on the dorsal ridge and horns curving backward.[< Hind.]

gauss (gous) *n. pl.* **gauss** *Physics* The cgs unit of magnetic induction, equal to a field exerting a force of one dyne on unit magnetic pole, or 0.7958 ampere-turn per centimeter. [after K. F. *Gauss*]

gauze (gôz) *n.* **1** A light perforated fabric in which the warp threads are crossed or twisted around the filling. **2** Any thin open-woven material: wire *gauze.* **3** A mist; light fog. —*adj.* Resembling or made of gauze. [< MF *gaze,* appar. from *Gaza,* where originally made]

gave (gāv) Past tense of GIVE.

gav·el (gav'əl) *n.* A mallet used by a presiding officer to call for order or attention. [Prob. var. of KEVEL]

ga·vi·al (gā'vē·əl) *n.* The great Indian crocodile (*Gavialis gangeticus*), having long, slender jaws, the upper one knobbed at the end. [< F < Hind. *ghariyal*]

ga·votte (gə·vot') *n.* **1** A vivacious French dance, resembling the minuet. **2** Music appropriate to such a dance. Also **ga·vot'.** [< F < Provençal *gavoto* Alpine dance < *gavot* an inhabitant of the Alps]

gawk (gôk) *v.i. Colloq.* To stare or behave awkwardly and stupidly. —*n.* An awkward, stupid fellow. [Cf. dial. E *gawk* left-handed]

gawk·y (gô'kē) *adj.* **gawk·i·er, gawk·i·est** Awkward and dull; clownish; clumsy. See synonyms under AWKWARD. —*n. pl.* **gawk·ies** A gawk. —**gawk'i·ly** *adv.* —**gawk'i·ness** *n.*

gay (gā) *adj.* **1** Filled with or inspiring mirth; merry; sportive. **2** Brilliant; showy. **3** Loving pleasure; wanton. **3** *Slang* Homosexual; also, intended for homosexuals: a *gay* bar. See synonyms under AIRY, CHEERFUL, HAPPY, MERRY, VIVACIOUS, WANTON. —*n. Slang* A homosexual person. —*adv. Scot.* Fairly; considerably: sometimes spelled *gey;* also **gay'lie.** [< OF < Gmc.] —**gay'ness** *n.* —**gay'some** *adj.*

gay·al (gā'əl, gə·yäl') *n.* A semi-domesticated bovine (*Bos frontalis*) of southeastern Asia, very similar to the closely related wild and slightly larger gaur. [< Hind.]

Gay Nine·ties (nīn'tēz) The decade from 1890 to 1900.

Ga·za (gä'zə) A city in SW Palestine; since 1948 administered with the surrounding coastal district (**Gaza strip**) by Egypt, since 1957, by United Nations. *Arabic* **Ghaz·ze** (gaz'zē).

ga·za·bo (gə·zā'bō) *n. U.S. Slang* An awkward or eccentric man or boy; a queer fellow. [Cf. Sp. *gazapo* a shrewd fellow]

gaze (gāz) *v.i.* **gazed, gaz·ing** To look earnestly and steadily, as in scrutiny, admiration, or concern. —*n.* **1** A continued or intense look. **2** Something gazed at. See synonyms under LOOK.

—**at gaze** *Brit.* In a gazing attitude; in the act of looking around with fear or apprehension, as a stag on hearing hounds. [ME *gasen* < Scand. Cf. dial Sw. *gasa* stare.] —**gaz'er** *n.*

ga·ze·bo (gə·zē'bō, -zā'-) *n. pl.* **·bos** or **·boes** A structure commanding a wide view, such as a summerhouse, or projecting window or balcony; a belvedere. [? < GAZE, imitating a Latin form]

gaze·hound (gāz'hound') *n.* A hound that hunts by sight.

ga·zelle (gə·zel') *n.* A small, delicately formed antelope of northern Africa and Arabia (genus *Gazella*), with recurved horns and large, gentle eyes. [< OF < Arabic *ghazal* gazelle]

GAZELLE

ga·zette (gə·zet') *n.* **1** A newspaper, or printed account of current events. **2** *Brit.* Any official government journal announcing appointments, promotions, etc. —*v.t. Brit.* **ga·zet·ted, ga·zet·ting** To publish or announce in a gazette. [< F < Ital. *gazzetta* < dial. Ital. (Venetian) *gazeta* a coin, orig. the price of the paper]

gaz·et·teer (gaz'ə·tir') *n.* **1** A dictionary of geographical names. **2** A writer or contributor of news for a gazette.

gaz·pa·cho (gäz·pä'chō) *n. pl.* **·chos** A cold Spanish soup made with fresh tomatoes, peppers, olive oil, vinegar, garlic, and spices, to which cucumber and bread are added. [< Sp.]

Gd *Chem.* Gadolinium (symbol Gd).

Ge (zhā) *n.* A large and important South American Indian linguistic stock of eastern and central Brazil: also called *Tapuyan.*

Ge *Chem.* Germanium (symbol Ge).

ge·an·ti·cline (jē·an'tə·klīn) *n. Geol.* A vast upward flexure of the earth's crust: opposed to *geosyncline.* [< Gk. *gē* earth + ANTICLINE] —**ge·an·ti·cli'nal** *adj. & n.*

gear (gir) *n.* **1** *Mech.* **a** The moving parts or appliances that constitute a whole or set, serving to transmit motion or change its rate or direction: valve *gear,* reversing *gear.* **b** A cogwheel. **c** The engagement of toothed wheels or other parts in a mechanical assembly. **2** *Naut.* The ropes, blocks, etc., used in working a spar or sail; all the rigging of a ship. **3** Fitness for harmonious and effective action; working relationship: out of *gear.* **4** Any equipment, as dress, vestments, warlike accouterments, harness, tools, or household necessaries. **5** *Archaic* Property; possessions; goods. **6** *Archaic* Arms; armor. —*v.t.* **1** *Mech.* **a** To put into gear. **b** To equip with gears. **c** To connect by means of gears. **2** To regulate so as to match or suit something else: to *gear* production to demand. **3** To put gear on; harness; dress. —*v.i.* **4** To come into or be in gear; mesh. [< ON *gervi* equipment]

gear·box (gir'boks') *n.* The gears and gearcase comprising the variable transmission of an automobile.

gear·case (gir'kās') *n. Mech.* A metal housing for the gears of machinery.

gear·ing (gir'ing) *n. Mech.* **1** Power-transmitting gear in general. **2** Working parts collectively. **3** Ropes and tackle.

gear·shift (gir'shift') *n. Mech.* A device for engaging or disengaging the gears in a power-transmission system.

gear·wheel (gir'hwēl') *n. Mech.* A cogwheel.

geck·o (gek'ō) *n. pl.* **geck·os** or **geck·oes** Any of a family (*Geckonidae*) of small lizards having toes with adhesive disks; wall lizard. [< Malay *gēkoq,* imit. of its cry]

ged (ged) *n. Scot.* A fish, the pike. Also **gedd.**

gee[1] (jē) *n.* The letter G, g, or its sound.

gee[2] (jē) *v.t. & v.i.* **1** To turn to the right. **2** To evade; swerve. —*interj.* Turn to the right! a call in driving animals without reins: opposed to *haw[4].* Also spelled *jee.* [Origin uncertain]

Gee (jē) *interj.* A minced oath: a euphemism for Jesus.

geek (gēk) *n.* A carnival performer who publicly eats or swallows live animals as a sensational

GECKO

spectacle. [Prob. var. of GECK]

geese (gēs) Plural of GOOSE¹.

geest (gēst) *n. Geol.* 1 Material derived from rock decay in its natural place. 2 Gravel; especially, alluvium. [< Du., barren, dry soil]

Ge·ez (gē·ez′, gēz) *n.* Ethiopic.

gee·zer (gē′zər) *n. Slang* A queer old person. [Var. of *guiser* mummer < GUISE, *v.* (def. 3)]

ge·gen·schein (gā′gən·shīn) *n. Astron.* A patch of faint, hazy light sometimes observable at night on the point of the ecliptic opposite the sun: associated with the zodiacal light. Also called *counterglow.* [< G]

Ge·hen·na (gi·hen′ə) *n.* 1 In the Bible, the valley of Hinnom near Jerusalem, where offal was thrown and fires kept burning to purify the air. 2 A place of torment. 3 In the New Testament, hell; hellfire. [< LL < Gk. *geenna* < Hebrew *ge-hinnom* valley of *Hinnom*]

Gei·ger counter (gī′gər) *Physics* A sensitive instrument for counting ionizing particles in the air, as alpha particles or cosmic rays and also for detecting the amount of radioactivity in a given area. Also called *counting tube.* [after Hans *Geiger*]

gei·sha (gā′shə) *n. pl.* **·sha** or **·shas** A Japanese girl trained to furnish entertainment by singing, dancing, etc. [< Japanese]

Geiss·ler tube (gīs′lər) *Physics* A sealed and partly evacuated glass tube containing electrodes: used for the study of electric discharges through gases. [after Heinrich *Geissler,* 1814–79, German physicist]

gel (jel) *n. Chem.* A colloidal dispersion of a solid in a liquid which may range from the nearly liquid to the solid state, but is typically a semisolid and of a jellylike consistency, as gelatin, mucilage, uncooked egg white, etc. —*v.i.* **gelled, gel·ling** To change into a gel; jellify. [Short for GELATIN]

gel·a·tin (jel′ə·tin) *n.* A hard, transparent, tasteless, colloidal protein produced from bones, white connective tissue, and skin of animals. It is soluble in hot water, cooling to a jelly, but insoluble in alcohol or chloroform. Edible gelatin, used for foods, drugs, etc., is a highly refined product of yellowish tint; technical gelatin is used in photography, lithography, in the manufacture of sizing, plastics, etc. Also **gel′a·tine** (-tin, -tēn). [< F *gélatine,* orig. a soup made from fish < Ital. *gelatina* < *gelata* jelly < L. See JELLY.]

ge·lat·i·nate (ji·lat′ə·nāt) *v.t. & v.i.* **·nat·ed, ·nat·ing** To change into gelatin or a jellylike substance. —**ge·lat′i·na′tion** *n.*

ge·lat·i·nize (ji·lat′ə·nīz) *v.* **·nized, ·niz·ing** *v.t.* 1 To gelatinate. 2 To treat or coat with gelatin. —*v.i.* 3 To be changed into gelatin or jelly. —**ge·lat′i·ni·za′tion** *n.*

ge·lat·i·noid (ji·lat′ə·noid) *adj.* Like jelly or gelatin. —*n.* A gelatinlike substance.

ge·lat·i·nous (ji·lat′ə·nəs) *adj.* 1 Of the nature of gelatin; like jelly. 2 Of or pertaining to or consisting of gelatin. —**ge·lat′i·nous·ly** *adv.* —**ge·lat′i·nous·ness** *n.*

ge·la·tion (ji·lā′shən) *n.* Solidification, especially by cooling.

geld¹ (geld) *n.* In early English history, a tax or tribute. [OE]

geld² (geld) *v.t.* **geld·ed** or **gelt, geld·ing** 1 To castrate; emasculate; also, to spay. 2 To deprive of an essential part; weaken. [< ON *gelda* castrate]

geld·ing (gel′ding) *n.* A castrated animal, especially a horse.

gel·id (jel′id) *adj.* Very cold; icy; frozen. [< L *gelidus*] —**ge·lid′i·ty** *n.* —**gel′id·ly** *adv.*

gel·se·mine (jel′sə·min, -mīn) *n. Chem.* A white, crystalline, very poisonous alkaloid, $C_{22}H_{26}O_2N_2$, obtained from gelsemium: used as a depressant and mydriatic.

gel·se·mi·um (jel·sē′mē·əm) *n.* 1 The poisonous root of the yellow jasmine (*Gelsemium sempervirens*). 2 A medical preparation made from it. [< NL < Ital. *gelsomino* jasmine]

gem (jem) *n.* 1 A precious stone, especially when set as an ornament. 2 Anything rare, delicate, and perfect, as a work of literature or art. 3 A carved or engraved semiprecious stone; any

jewel. 4 *Printing* A size of type between brilliant and diamond. 5 A light cake somewhat like a muffin. —*v.t.* **gemmed, gem·ming** To adorn with or as with gems. [OE *gim* < L *gemma* jewel]

Ge·ma·ra (gə·mä′rə, -môr′ə) *n.* The second part of the Jewish Talmud, an exposition of the first part (Mishna). [< Aramaic, completion]

gem·el (jem′əl) *adj.* Paired; coupled: a *gemel* window. [< OF < L *gemellus* doubled]

gem·i·nate (jem′ə·nāt) *v.t. & v.i.* **·nat·ed, ·nat·ing** 1 To make or become double; pair. 2 *Ling.* To double a phoneme, particularly a consonant. —*adj.* (-nit) *Bot.* Occurring in pairs or couples, as leaves. [< L *geminatus,* pp. of *geminare* < *geminus* a twin] —**gem′i·na′tion** *n.*

Gem·i·ni (jem′ə·nī) 1 A constellation, the Twins. See CONSTELLATION. 2 The third sign of the zodiac.

gem·ma (jem′ə) *n. pl.* **·mae** (-ē) *Bot.* 1 A bud. 2 The budlike product of gemmation. [< L]

gem·mate (jem′āt) *adj. Bot.* Bearing buds; reproducing by buds. [< L *gemmatus,* pp. of *gemmare* bud]

gem·ma·tion (jem·ā′shən) *n. Bot.* 1 Reproduction by budlike outgrowth that becomes an independent individual. 2 The period of the expansion of buds.

gem·me·ous (jem′ē·əs) *adj.* Relating to, having the nature of, or resembling gems.

gem·mip·a·rous (jem·ip′ər·əs) *adj. Bot.* Reproducing by, or producing, buds. [< L *gemma* bud + -PAROUS] —**gem·mip′a·rous·ly** *adv.*

gem·mu·la·tion (jem′yōō·lā′shən) *n. Biol.* Reproduction by, or formation of, gemmules.

gem·mule (jem′yōōl) *n.* 1 *Bot.* A small bud or gemma. 2 *Biol.* One of the minute hypothetical granules that, according to the doctrine of pangenesis, reproduce the cells or organic units from which they are thrown off. 3 *Zool.* A small internal reproductive bud in certain fresh-water sponges. [< LL *gemmula,* dim. of *gemma* bud]

gem·my (jem′ē) *adj.* 1 Full of, set with, or containing gems. 2 Like a gem; bright; sparkling.

gem·ol·o·gy (jem·ol′ə·jē) *n.* The scientific study and investigation of gems. —**gem·o·log·i·cal** (jem′ə·loj′i·kəl) *adj.* —**gem·ol′o·gist** *n.*

gems·bok (gemz′-bok) *n. pl.* **·bok** or **·boks** A South African antelope (*Oryx gazella*) having long, sharp, nearly straight horns and a tufted tail. [< Afrikaans < G *gemse* chamois + *bock* a buck]

GEMSBOK

gem·stone (jem′stōn′) *n.* A mineral or petrified organic material of a quality suitable for cutting, polishing, and using in jewelry.

-gen *suffix of nouns* 1 *Chem.* That which produces: *oxygen.* 2 *Biol.* That which is produced: *antigen.* [< F -*gène* < Gk. -*genēs,* < *gen-,* stem of *gignesthai* be born, become]

gen·darme (zhän′därm, *Fr.* zhän·därm′) *n. pl.* **·darmes** (-därmz, *Fr.* -därm′) One of a corps of armed police, especially in France. [< F < *gens d'armes* men-at-arms]

gen·darm·e·rie (zhän′där·mə·rē, zhän·därm′ə·rē; *Fr.* zhän·därm·rē′) *n.* Gendarmes collectively. Also **gen·darm′e·ry.**

gen·der (jen′dər) *n.* 1 *Gram.* In many languages, as in the Indo-European and Semitic families, a grammatical category of nouns governing the form assumed by the words which modify or refer to them. **Natural gender** corresponds to sex or lack of sex; animate beings are either masculine or feminine, inanimate objects are neuter. This is true of English, which indicates natural gender by pronoun reference (*he, she, it,* etc.), by suffixes and prefixes (*aviator, aviatrix, emperor, empress, he-bear, she-bear,* etc.), or by completely different forms (*cow, bull,* etc.). **Grammatical gender** may have a partial correspondence to sex for animate beings, but sexless objects can be of any gender. Latin and German have three grammatical genders (masculine, feminine, and neu-

ter) often without reference to sex, as seen in Latin *nauta* sailor, which is in a feminine declension. French and Hebrew have two genders, the names of inanimate objects being either masculine or feminine. In some languages, as in the Algonquian family, gender classification is made on another basis entirely—that of animate and inanimate categories. 2 *Colloq.* Sex. 3 *Obs.* A kind; genus. —*v.t. & v.i. Obs.* To engender. [< OF *gendre* < L *genus, -eris.* Doublet of GENUS, GENRE.]

gene (jēn) *n. Biol.* The chemically complex unit which is assumed to be the carrier of specific physical characters from parents to offspring, being transmitted through the chromosomes of the gametes and subject to many influences, as mutation, translocation, crossing over, radiation, X-rays, etc.: also called *factor.* [< Gk. *genea* breed, kind]

gen·e·al·o·gist (jē′nē·al′ə·jist, jen′ē-) *n.* One versed in genealogies.

gen·e·al·o·gy (jē′nē·al′ə·jē, jen′ē-) *n. pl.* **·gies** 1 A record of descent from some ancestor; a list of ancestors and their descendants. 2 Descent in a direct line; pedigree. 3 The science that treats of pedigrees. [< Gk. *genea* race + -LOGY] —**gen·e·a·log·i·cal** (jē′nē·ə·loj′i·kəl, jen′ē-) *adj.* —**gen·e·a·log′i·cal·ly** *adv.*

gen·er·al (jen′ər·əl) *adj.* 1 Pertaining to, including, or affecting all of the whole; not local or particular: a *general* election; a *general* anesthetic. 2 Common to or current among the majority; prevalent: the *general* opinion. 3 Extended in scope, meaning, or content; not restricted in application: a *general* principle. 4 Not limited to a special class; miscellaneous: a *general* cargo. 5 Not detailed or precise: a *general* idea. 6 Usual or customary: one's *general* habit. 7 Dealing with all branches of a business or pursuit; not specialized: a *general* store; a *general* practitioner. 8 Superior in rank: attorney *general.* —*n.* 1 *Mil.* **a** In the U.S. Army, Air Force, or Marine Corps, an officer ranking next above a lieutenant general, equivalent in rank to an admiral in the Navy. **b** Any general officer, as a brigadier general, lieutenant general, etc.: a shortened form. **c** In

a	b	c	d	e

INSIGNIA OF GENERALS—UNITED STATES ARMY
a. Brigadier general.   *c.* Lieutenant general.
b. Major general.   *d.* General.
e. General of the Army.

many foreign armies, an officer of superior grade, usually ranking just below a marshal or field marshal. 2 *Eccl.* The chief of a religious order. 3 A general statement, fact, or principle. 4 *Archaic* The people or the public. —**brigadier general** An officer in the U.S. Army, Air Force, or Marine Corps ranking next above a colonel and next below a major general. —**in general** For the most part; in the main. —**lieutenant general** An officer in the U.S. Army, Air Force, or Marine Corps ranking next above a major general and next below a general. —**major general** An officer in the U.S. Army, Air Force, or Marine Corps ranking next above a brigadier general and next below a lieutenant general. [< OF < L *generalis* of a race or kind < *genus, generis* kind]

Synonyms (adj.): common, commonplace, customary, everyday, familiar, frequent, habitual, normal, ordinary, popular, prevalent, public, universal, usual.

general agent *Law* One appointed by a principal to act for him solely or particularly.

General Assembly 1 The deliberative body of the United Nations, meeting in annual or special

add,āce,câre,pälm; end,ēven; it,īce; odd,ōpen,ôrder; tōōk,pōōl; up,bûrn; ə = a in *above,* e in *sicken,* i in *clarity,* o in *melon,* u in *focus;* yōō = u in *fuse;* oi,oil; ou,pout; ch,check; g,go; ng,ring; th,thin; ŧħ,this; zh,vision. Foreign sounds á,œ,ü,kh,ṅ; and ◆: see page xx. <from; + plus; ? possibly.

sessions, in which every member nation is represented. **2** *U.S.* The legislature in some States. **3** The highest ecclesiastical governing body of certain denominations.

gen·er·al·cy (jen′ər·əl·sē) *n.* Rank, authority, or tenure of office of a general.

general delivery 1 A post-office department that delivers mail to an addressee when called for. **2** Mail so addressed.

general election An election on a set date in which every constituency chooses a representative.

gen·er·al·is·si·mo (jen′ər·əl·is′i·mō) *n. pl.* **·mos** A supreme military or military and naval commander. [< Ital.]

gen·er·al·i·ty (jen′ə·ral′ə·tē) *n. pl.* **·ties 1** The main part; chief portion; majority: the *generality* of voters. **2** Anything general or not specific; especially, a vague general statement: to deal in *generalities.* **3** The state of being general or generalized. Also **gen·er·al·ty** (jen′ər·əl·tē).

gen·er·al·i·za·tion (jen′ər·əl·ə·zā′shən, -ī·zā′-) *n.* **1** Act of generalizing. **2** A statement or proposition expressed in general terms, applying to a class or numerous members of a class, rather than covering only an individual case; opposite of *particularization.*

gen·er·al·ize (jen′ər·əl·īz′) *v.* **·lized, ·liz·ing** *v.t.* **1** To treat as having general or wide application. **2** To cause to be used or understood generally or widely; popularize. **3** To draw or frame (a general rule or principle) from particular evidence, facts, etc. **4** To draw or frame a general rule or principle from (particular evidence, facts, etc.). —*v.i.* **5** To talk in general rather than particular terms; make generalizations; be vague. **6** To draw general ideas or inferences from particulars.

gen·er·al·ly (jen′ər·əl·ē) *adv.* **1** For the most part; ordinarily; in most but not all cases. **2** Without going into particulars. **3** So as to include or apply to all; collectively or universally.

general officer Any army officer holding a rank higher than colonel.

General of the Air Force The highest ranking officer of the U.S. Air Force.

General of the Armies A special title and rank conferred upon John J. Pershing in 1919.

General of the Army An officer of the highest rank in the U.S. Army: equivalent to marshal or field marshal in other armies. For insignia see illustration under GENERAL.

general semantics A discipline for human living, formulated by Alfred Korzybski, involving a critical analysis of verbal and non-verbal symbols as these enter into behavioral responses, and a denial of the universality of Aristotelian logic: in practice using a methodology based on modern science, distinguishing carefully between levels of abstraction, between statements and the events they represent, generalizations and the particular, etc., avoiding polarized (either-or) orientations, and emphasizing unity and relationships within wholes.

gen·er·al·ship (jen′ər·əl·ship) *n.* **1** A general's office or rank. **2** A general's military skill or management. **3** Management or leadership of any sort.

general staff 1 A body of officers who direct the military policy and strategy of a national state. **2** A group of officers charged with directing a division or higher unit and operating from a headquarters under a commander in chief.

General Staff In the U.S. Army, the supreme military staff for policy and strategy, consisting of the Chief of Staff, several deputy and assistant Chiefs of Staff, including those heading sections of personnel administration (G-1), military intelligence (G-2), and operations and training (G-3), the Comptroller of the Army, the Director of the Women's Army Corps, and other officers.

gen·er·ate (jen′ə·rāt) *v.t.* **·at·ed, ·at·ing 1** To produce or cause to be; bring into being. **2** To beget as a parent; procreate. **3** *Geom.* To trace out by motion: A moving point *generates* a line, or a line a surface. See synonyms under PRODUCE, PROPAGATE. [< L *generatus,* pp. of *generare* generate]

gen·er·a·tion (jen′ə·rā′shən) *n.* **1** The process, act, or function of begetting or procreating; reproduction. **2** Production or origination by any process; creation: the *generation* of electricity. **3**

A step or degree in natural descent. **4** The period between successive steps in natural descent, usually taken at 30 years in humans. **5** All persons removed in the same degree from an ancestor. **6** A body of persons existing at the same time or period. **7** A body of persons overlapping other existing bodies, but typified by difference in mental, moral, or ethical outlook: the jazz *generation.* **8** The average lifetime of the persons in a community. **9** *Geom.* The formation of a magnitude by the motion of a point, line, or surface. **10** Race or family. **11** Progeny; offspring. —**spontaneous generation** Abiogenesis.

gen·er·a·tive (jen′ə·rā′tiv) *adj.* **1** Of or pertaining to generation. **2** Having the power to produce or originate.

gen·er·a·tor (jen′ə·rā′tər) *n.* **1** One who or that which generates, produces, or originates. **2** An apparatus in which the generation of a gas is effected. **3** A machine that transforms heat or mechanical work directly into electric energy; a dynamo.

gen·er·a·trix (jen′ə·rā′triks) *n. pl.* **gen·er·a·tri·ces** (jen′ər·ə·trī′sēz) **1** *Geom.* A line, point, or figure that generates another figure by its motion. **2** A female that generates or produces.

ge·ner·ic (ji·ner′ik) *adj.* **1** Pertaining to a genus or a class of related things: contrasted with *specific* or *varietal.* **2** Having a general application; abstract; not concrete. Also **ge·ner′i·cal.** [< L *genus, -eris* race, kind + -IC] —**ge·ner′i·cal·ly** *adv.*

gen·er·os·i·ty (jen′ə·ros′ə·tē) *n. pl.* **·ties 1** The quality of being generous; liberality. **2** A generous act. See synonyms under BENEVOLENCE.

gen·er·ous (jen′ər·əs) *adj.* **1** Giving or bestowing heartily and munificently; munificent: a *generous* contributor. **2** Having noble qualities; honorable; high-minded: a *generous* nature. **3** Abundant; bountiful: a *generous* fare. **4** *Obs.* Of good descent: said either of men or of animals. **5** Having stimulating qualities; strong: *generous* wine. [< F *généreux* < L *generosus* of noble birth < *genus.* See GENUS.] —**gen′er·ous·ly** *adv.* —**gen′er·ous·ness** *n.*

Synonyms: bountiful, chivalrous, disinterested, free, free-handed, free-hearted, liberal, magnanimous, munificent, noble, open-handed, open-hearted.

ge·ne·si·al (ji·nē′zē·əl) *adj.* Of or pertaining to reproduction or generation. Also **ge·ne·sic** (ji·nē′zik).

ge·ne·si·ol·o·gy (ji·nē′zē·ol′ə·jē) *n.* The study of the reproduction of organisms. [< GENESIS + -(o)LOGY]

gen·e·sis (jen′ə·sis) *n. pl.* **·ses** (-sēz) **1** The act or mode of originating; creation. **2** Origin; beginning. [< L < Gk. *genēsis* creation, origin]

Gen·e·sis (jen′ə·sis) The first book of the Pentateuch in the Old Testament.

-genesis *combining form* Development; genesis; evolution: *biogenesis.* [< Gk. *genēsis* origin]

gen·et[1] (jen′it, jə·net′) *n.* **1** Any of certain small carnivores (genus *Genetta*) related to the civets but having only rudimentary scent glands. **2** The fur of the genet. Also **ge·nette′.** [< F *ge·nette* < Sp. *gineta* < Arabic *jarnait* genet]

GENET
(Body 1 foot, 10 inches; tail, 1 foot, 6 inches)

gen·et[2] (jen′it) *n.* A jennet.

ge·neth·li·ac (jə·neth′lē·ak) *adj.* Relating to nativities or their calculation; showing the position of the stars at birth. Also **gen·eth·li·a·cal** (jen′əth·lī′ə·kəl). [< F *généthliaque* < LL *genethliacus* < Gk. *genethliakos* of one's birth] —**gen·eth·li·a·cal·ly** *adv.*

ge·net·ic (jə·net′ik) *adj.* **1** Of, pertaining to, dealing with, or based on genesis. **2** Of or relating to genetics. **3** *Biol.* Designating those characteristics of an organism due to inheritance or to the action of genes. Also **ge·net′i·cal.** [< GENESIS; formed on analogy with *synthetic, antithetic,* etc.] —**ge·net′i·cal·ly** *adv.*

genetic engineering The application of techniques of genetic recombination to produce desired alterations in genetic material.

ge·net·ics (jə·net′iks) *n.* **1** That branch of biol-

ogy which deals with the interaction of the genes in producing the similarities and differences between individuals related by descent. **2** The science of plant- and animal-breeding. **3** The inherited characteristics of an organism or group of organisms. —**ge·net′i·cist** *n.*

ge·net·o·troph·ic (jə·net′ō·trof′ik, -trō′fik) *adj. Biol.* Pertaining to, exhibiting, or characterized by inherited defects in body chemistry resulting in an inability to assimilate enough of the essential elements in nutrition. [< GENETIC +TROPHIC]

ge·ne·va (jə·nē′və) *n.* Gin, especially Holland gin. [< MDu. *genever* < OF *genevre* gin < L *juniperus* juniper]

Geneva bands A pair of linen strips, hanging from the front of the neck: worn with clerical or academic garments.

Geneva Convention A convention for the amelioration of the condition of the wounded and of prisoners in time of war, signed at Geneva, Switzerland, in 1864: also called *Red Cross Convention.*

Geneva gown A loose academic gown with large sleeves: used as an ecclesiastical vestment.

Geneva movement *Mech.* The movement effected by a mechanism having its driving wheel so geared as to give intermittent motion to another wheel which is toothed: used in watches, motion-picture projectors, etc.

gen·ial[1] (jēn′yəl, jē′nē·əl) *adj.* **1** Kindly in disposition; cordial and pleasant in manner. **2** Imparting warmth, comfort, or life; supporting life or growth. **3** *Rare* Exhibiting or relating to genius. See synonyms under BLAND, CHEERFUL, COMFORTABLE, FRIENDLY, GOOD. [< L *genialis* of one's tutelary deity < *genius.* See GENIUS.] —**ge′nial·ly** *adv.*

ge·ni·al[2] (jə·nī′əl) *adj. Anat.* Of, pertaining to, or near the chin. [< Gk. *geneion* chin]

ge·ni·al·i·ty (jē′nē·al′ə·tē) *n.* Kindness of disposition; warmth; friendly cheerfulness.

gen·ic (jen′ik) *adj.* Of, pertaining to, or like a gene or genes; genetic.

-genic *combining form* Related to generation or production: *biogenic.* [< -GEN + -IC]

ge·nic·u·late (jə·nik′yə·lāt, -lit) *adj. Biol.* **1** Having kneelike joints or protuberances. **2** Bent abruptly, like a knee. [< L *geniculatus* < *geniculum,* dim. of *genu* knee]

ge·ni·o·plas·ty (jə·nī′ə·plas′tē) *n.* Plastic surgery of the chin and lower cheek.

gen·i·pap (jen′ə·pap) *n.* **1** A tropical American tree (*Genipa americana*) of the madder family. **2** Its edible fruit, about the size of an orange. [< Pg. *genipapo* < native name]

gen·i·tal (jen′ə·təl) *adj.* **1** Of or pertaining to the reproductive organs, or to the process of generation. **2** *Psychoanal.* Of or relating to a stage of psychosexual development in which the genitals are the dominant source of libidinal gratification in the context of mature personal relations with others: compare ANAL, ORAL. [< L *genitalis* of generation < *genitus,* pp. of *gignere* beget]

gen·i·ta·li·a (jen′ə·tā′lē·ə, -tāl′yə) *n. pl.* The genitals. [< L, neut. plural of *genitalis.* See GENITAL.]

gen·i·tals (jen′ə·təlz) *n. pl.* The external organs of generation; sexual organs.

gen·i·ti·val (jen′ə·tī′vəl) *adj.* Pertaining to the genitive case; having a genitive form. —**gen′i·ti′val·ly** *adv.*

gen·i·tive (jen′ə·tiv) *adj.* **1** Indicating source, origin, possession, or the like. **2** *Gram.* Pertaining to a case in Latin, Greek, etc., corresponding in part to the English possessive. —*n. Gram.* **1** The genitive case. **2** A word in this case. [< L *genitivus* < *gignere* beget]

genito- *combining form* Of or related to the genitals. [< L *genitus,* pp. of *gignere* beget]

gen·i·tor (jen′ə·tər, -tôr) *n. Obs.* A progenitor; a begetter. [< L]

gen·i·to·u·ri·nar·y (jen′ə·tō·yŏŏr′ə·ner′ē) *adj. Anat.* Of or pertaining to the genital and the urinary organs.

gen·ius (jēn′yəs) *n. pl.* **gen·ius·es** *for defs.* 2–5, 7, 8; **ge·ni·i** *for defs.* 6 *and* 9. **1** Extraordinary intellectual gifts, evidenced in original creation, expression, or achievement. **2** Remarkable aptitude for some special pursuit; a distinguishing natural capacity or tendency: a *genius* for oratory. **3** A person of phenomenal and original powers for productivity in art, science, statesmanship, etc.: such a *genius* as Mozart, Shakespeare, Napoleon, Einstein, etc. **4** The dominant influence or essential animating principle of anything; the prevalent feeling or thought (of a nation or era). **5** A representative type; impersonation; embodiment. **6** In Roman antiquity, a beneficent spirit or demon supposed to accompany one through life, or either of two attendant spirits, one good, the other bad; a guardian or tutelary spirit of a person, place, or thing. **7** Hence, a person having an extraordinary influence over another. **8** The traditions, history, associations, influences, etc., of a locality or place. **9** In Mohammedan folklore, a jinni. [< L, tutelary spirit < *gen-*, stem of *gignere* beget.]

Synonyms: talent, talents. *Genius* is exalted intellectual power capable of operating independently of tuition and training, and marked by extraordinary faculty for original creation, invention, discovery, expression, etc. *Talent* is marked mental ability, and in a special sense, a particular and uncommon aptitude for some special mental work or attainment. *Genius* is higher than *talent*, more spontaneous, less dependent upon instruction, less amenable to training; *talent* is largely the capacity to learn, acquire, appropriate, adapt oneself to demand. Compare CHARACTER, INGENUITY, MIND, POWER. *Antonyms:* dulness, folly, imbecility, obtuseness, senselessness, stupidity.

ge·ni·us lo·ci (jē′nē·əs lō′sī, -kē) *Latin* **1** The spirit or guardian deity of the place. **2** The unique quality of a place as felt by an observer.

gen·o·cide (jen′ə·sīd) *n.* The systematic extermination of racial and national groups: term first used in indictment of German war criminals after World War II. [< Gk. *genos* race, tribe +-CIDE; coined by Raphael Lemkin, 1944.]

gen·om (jen′om) *n. Biol.* A full set of chromosomes with their associated genes. Also **gen′ome** (-ōm). [< GENE+-OM(E)]

gen·o·type (jen′ə·tīp) *n. Biol.* **1** The genetic constitution of an organism, expressed and latent: contrasted with *phenotype.* **2** A type representative of a group of organisms; the most typical species of a genus. [< Gk. *genos* race, kind +-TYPE]—**gen·o·typ·ic** (jen′ə·tip′·ik) or **·i·cal** *adj.*

gen·re (zhän′rə) *n.* **1** A genus, sort, or style; especially, a category of art or literature characterized by a certain form, style, subject matter, or atmosphere. **2** A class of painting or other art portraying everyday life; distinguished from the historical, romantic, etc., style. [< F < L *genus, -eris* race, kind. Doublet of GENDER, GENUS.]

gens (jenz) *n. pl.* **gen·tes** (jen′tēz) **1** *Anthropol.* In primitive society, a body of blood kindred having a common gentile name, and distinguished by a totem or crest. **2** In Roman antiquity, a clan or house composed of several families having a common ancestor; a subdivision of a tribe. [< L]

gen·teel (jen·tēl′) *adj.* **1** Well-bred or refined; elegant; polite. **2** Suitable for or pertaining to the station or needs of well-bred persons. **3** Stylish or fashionable. ◆This word is now used chiefly in a somewhat derogatory or humorous sense: *genteel* poverty. See synonyms under POLITE. [< MF *gentil.* Doublet of GENTLE.]—**gen·teel′ly** *adv.* —**gen·teel′ness** *n.*

gen·tian (jen′shən) *n.* **1** Any of a large genus (*Gentiana*) of European and American flowering herbs, as the **yellow gentian** of Europe (*G. lutea*), the **fringed gentian** of America (*G. crinita*), with blue, conspicuously fringed solitary flowers, and the **closed** or **bottle gentian** (*G. andrewsi*), with purple-blue, non-opening flowers. **2** The root of the yellow gentian, having tonic properties. [< L *gentiana*, appar. after *Gentius*, an Illyrian king]

GENTIAN
a. Bottle or closed.
b. Fringed.

gen·tian·a·ceous (jen′shən·ā′shəs) *adj. Bot.* Be-

longing to a family (*Gentianaceae*) of annual or perennial herbs, with showy, perfect, regular flowers.

gen·tian·el·la (jen′shən·el′ə) *n.* **1** A European alpine dwarf gentian (*Gentiana acaulis*) having attractive blue flowers. **2** A shade of blue. [< NL, dim. of L *gentiana* GENTIAN.]

gentian violet *Chem.* A purple dye of the rosaniline group, used medicinally as an antiseptic and bactericide: also called *methylrosaniline.*

gen·tile (jen′tīl) *adj.* **1** Of or pertaining to a nation, gens, or clan. **2** *Gram.* Denoting racial, national, or local extraction: said of a noun or adjective. **3** Heathen; pagan. —*n.* **1** *Gram.* A noun or an adjective denoting race, country, etc. **2** In Roman law, a member of a gens or clan. [< F *gentil* < LL *gentilis* foreign. Doublet of GENTLE.]

Gen·tile (jen′tīl) *n.* **1** Among the Jews, one of a non-Jewish people; one not a Jew. **2** Among Christians: **a** One who is not a Jew; a pagan. **b** A Christian, especially one formerly a pagan. **3** Among Mormons, a non-Mormon. —*adj.* **1** Pertaining to or characteristic of a non-Jewish people. **2** Belonging to or like Christians, as distinguished from Jews. **3** Of or pertaining to non-Mormons.

gen·til·i·ty (jen·til′ə·tē) *n. pl.* **·ties 1** The quality of being genteel or well-bred; refinement: now often used ironically. **2** Gentle birth; good extraction. **3** Well-born or well-bred persons collectively; gentry. [< OF *gentilite* < L *gentilitas, -tatis* < *gentilis.* See GENTLE.]

gen·tle (jen′təl) *adj.* **1** Belonging to a family distinguished by blood, birth, or station. **2** Befitting one of high birth or station. **3** *Archaic* Noble; chivalrous: a *gentle* knight. **4** Considerate; generously inclined: *gentle* reader. **5** Mild in disposition; refined in manners. **6** Tame; docile: a *gentle* horse. **7** Soft; moderate; not harsh: a *gentle* touch. **8** Not steep, sharp, or abrupt: a *gentle* slope. **9** *Meteorol.* Designating a moderate breeze, No. 3 on the Beaufort scale. —*v.t.* **gen·tled, gen·tling 1** To make easy to control; tame, as a horse. **2** To make gentle. **3** *Obs.* To raise to the rank of gentility. [< OF *gentil* < L *gentilis* of good birth < *gens, gentis* race, clan. Doublet of GENTEEL, GENTILE.]—**gen′tly** *adv.* —**gen′tle·ness** *n.*

gen·tle·man (jen′təl·mən) *n. pl.* **·men** (-mən) **1** A well-bred man with good manners. **2** Any man: in the plural the usual form of address in public assemblies: Ladies and *gentlemen.* **3** *Brit.* A man above a yeoman in social rank. —**fine gentleman** A fashionable gentleman; also a dandy; fop.

gentleman's agreement An agreement, usually diplomatic or political, and less formal than a treaty or contract, guaranteed only by the honor of the parties involved.

gen·tle·wom·an (jen′təl·woom′ən) *n. pl.* **·wom·en** (-wim′in) **1** A woman of good birth and social position: a lady. **2** A considerate, gracious, well-mannered woman. **3** Formerly, a woman in attendance on a lady of rank.

Gen·too (jen·tōō′) *n. pl.* **·toos** (-tōōz′) **1** In India, a Hindu, especially a Telugu, as distinguished from a Moslem. **2** The language of the Gentoos. [< Pg. *gentio* gentile < L *gentilis.*]

gen·tri·fi·ca·tion (jen′trə·fə·kā′shən) *n.* The rebuilding or restoration of deteriorating city residential properties for purchase or use by middle- or upper-class buyers.

gen·try (jen′trē) *n.* **1** People of good position or birth; in England, the upper class exclusive of the nobility. **2** Any specified class of people: commonly an ironical term. **3** *Obs.* Gentle birth or condition. **4** *Obs.* Urbanity; politeness. [Appar. a back formation from GENTRICE, incorrectly taken as a plural]

ge·nu (jē′nōō, -nyōō) *n. pl.* **gen·u·a** (jen′yōō·ə) *Anat.* **1** The knee. **2** A kneelike structure, as a bend of the corpus callosum. [< L]

gen·u·flect (jen′yə·flekt) *v.i.* To bend the knee, as in worship. [< Med. L *genuflectere* < *genu* knee + *flectere* bend]

gen·u·ine (jen′yōō·in) *adj.* **1** Of the original or true stock. **2** Authentic; of the authorship claimed. **3** Not spurious, adulterated, or counterfeit. **4** Not affected or hypocritical; frank; sincere; true. See synonyms under AUTHENTIC, HONEST, PURE. [< L *genuinus* innate]

—**gen′u·ine·ly** *adv.* —**gen′u·ine·ness** *n.*

ge·nus (jē′nəs) *n. pl.* **gen·e·ra** (jen′ər·ə) **1** *Biol.* A class or category of plants and animals ranking next above the species and next below the family or subfamily. The genus and species names together constitute the scientific name of an organism, the genus name (capitalized) standing first; as *Homo sapiens* for the human species. **2** *Logic* A class of things divisible into two or more subordinate classes, or species. **3** A kind; class. [< L, race, kind]

-geny *combining form* Mode of production of; generation or development of: *anthropogeny, cosmogeny.* [< F *-génie* < L *-genia* < Gk. *-geneia* < *gen-*, stem of *gignesthai* become]

geo- *combining form* Earth; ground; soil: *geocentric, geology.*

ge·ode (jē′ōd) *n. Geol.* **1** A stone having a cavity lined with crystals. **2** The cavity in such a stone. [< F *géode* < L *geodes*, a precious stone < Gk. *geōdēs* earthy]—**ge·od·ic** (jē·od′ik) *adj.*

geodesic line *Math.* The shortest line connecting two points on a given surface.

ge·od·e·sy (jē·od′ə·sē) *n. Math.* The study and measurement of extensive areas of the earth's surface, especially with reference to the determination of the magnitude and figure of the earth: distinguished from *surveying* (of limited areas). [< F *géodésie* < NL *geodaesia* < Gk. *geodaisia* < *gē* earth + *daiein* divide] —**ge·od′e·sist** *n.*

ge·o·dy·nam·ics (jē′ō·dī·nam′iks) *n.* The study of the forces that affect the structure and modifications of the earth. —**ge′o·dy·nam′ic, ge′o·dy·nam′i·cal** *adj.*

materials of the earth, their structure, characteristics, and interrelationships; structural geology. [< GEO- + Gk. *gnōsis* knowledge]

ge·o·graph·ic determinism (jē′ə·graf′ik) *Sociol.* The theory that attributes the forms and characteristics of a given society, community, or nation to the molding influence of geographic factors.

ge·og·ra·phy (jē·og′rə·fē) *n. pl.* **·phies 1** The science that describes the surface of the earth and its associated physical, biological, economic, political, and demographic characteristics, especially in terms of large areas and the complex of interrelationships obtaining among them. **2** The natural aspect, features, etc., of a place or area: the *geography* of the Arctic. [< L *geographia* < Gk. < *gē* earth + *graphein* write, describe] —**ge·og′ra·pher** *n.* —**ge′o·graph′ic** or **·i·cal** *adj.* —**ge′o·graph′·i·cal·ly** *adv.*

ge·oid (jē′oid) *n.* The earth considered as an ellipsoidal solid whose surface coincides with the mean level of the ocean. [< Gk. *geoidēs* earthlike < *gē* earth + *eidos* form]

ge·ol·o·gist (jē·ol′ə·jist) *n.* One versed in geology. Also **ge·ol′o·ger.**

ge·ol·o·gy (jē·ol′ə·jē) *n. pl.* **·gies 1** The science that treats of the origin, history, constitution, and structure of the earth, including the operation of the physical forces affecting its development and appearance and the history of living or extinct forms as recorded in the rocks. See Time Scale page 406. **2** A treatise on this subject. See HISTORICAL GEOLOGY. —**ge·o·log·ic** (jē′ə·loj′ik) or **·i·cal** *adj.* —**ge′o·log′i·cal·ly** *adv.*

ge·o·man·cy (jē′ə·man′sē) *n.* Divination by means of some aspect of the earth, particularly by the observation of points and lines on the earth. —**ge′o·man′cer** *n.* —**ge′o·man′tic** *adj.*

ge·o·med·i·cine (jē′ō·med′ə·sin) *n.* The branch of medicine that treats of the geographic factors of disease.

ge·om·e·ter (jē·om′ə·tər) *n.* One skilled in geometry. Also **ge·om·e·tri·cian** (jē·om′ə·trish′·ən, jē′ə·mə-). [< L *geometres* < Gk. *geōmetrēs* one who measures land]

ge·o·met·ric (jē′ə·met′rik) *adj.* **1** Pertaining to or according to the rules and principles of geometry. **2** Forming, consisting of, or characterized by regular lines, curves, and angles, as the markings on certain insects, or on the primitive pottery of the Mycenaean era, which is recognized by its rectilinear decorations. Also **ge′o·met′ri·cal** —**ge′o·met′ri·cal·ly** *adv.*

GEOLOGICAL TIME SCALE

Read from bottom to top.

ERAS	TIME PERIODS ROCK SYSTEMS	TIME EPOCHS ROCK SERIES	APPROX. DURATION MILLION YEARS	APPROX. PERCENT TOTAL AGE	LIFE FORMS
CENOZOIC	QUATERNARY	RECENT / PLEISTOCENE	1		Rise and dominance of Man.
CENOZOIC	UPPER TERTIARY	PLIOCENE / MIOCENE	65	2	Modern animals and plants.
CENOZOIC	LOWER TERTIARY	OLIGOCENE / EOCENE / PALEOCENE			Rapid development of modern mammals, insects, and plants.
MESOZOIC	UPPER CRETACEOUS		75		Primitive mammals; last dinosaurs; last ammonites.
MESOZOIC	LOWER CRETACEOUS				Rise of flowering plants.
MESOZOIC	JURASSIC		45	5	First birds, first mammals. Diversification of reptiles; climax of ammonites; coniferous trees.
MESOZOIC	TRIASSIC		45		Rise of dinosaurs; cycadlike plants; bony fishes.
PALEOZOIC	PERMIAN		45		Rise of reptiles. Modern insects. Last of many plant and animal groups.
PALEOZOIC	PENNSYLVANIAN (CARBONIFEROUS)		75		First reptiles. Amphibians; primitive insects; seed ferns; primitive conifers.
PALEOZOIC	MISSISSIPPIAN (CARBONIFEROUS)				Climax of shell-crushing sharks. Primitive ammonites.
PALEOZOIC	DEVONIAN		50	9	First amphibians, first land snails. Primitive land plants. Climax of brachiopods.
PALEOZOIC	SILURIAN		20		First traces of land life. Scorpions. First lungfishes. Widespread coral reefs.
PALEOZOIC	ORDOVICIAN		70		First fish. Climax of trilobites. First appearance of many marine invertebrates.
PALEOZOIC	CAMBRIAN		50		First marine invertebrates, including trilobites.
PROTEROZOIC (PRE-CAMBRIAN)			About 3,000	84	First signs of life. Algae.
ARCHEOZOIC (PRE-CAMBRIAN)					

Age of oldest dated rocks: about 3,500,000,000 years.

geometric progression *Math.* A sequence of terms of which each member except the first is greater than its predecessor by a constant ratio, as 2, 4, 8, 16, 32, 64: distinguished from *arithmetic progression.*

ge·om·e·trid (jē·om′ə·trid) *n.* Any of a family (*Geometridae*) of moths whose larvae are called measuring worms, because they walk by moving their abdominal and anal prolegs, thus forming the body into a loop, giving the impression that they are measuring the space below. [< NL *Geometridae* < L *geometres.* See GEOMETER.]

ge·om·e·try (jē·om′ə·trē) *n. pl.* **·tries** The branch of mathematics that treats of space and its relations, especially as shown in the properties and measurement of points, lines, angles, surfaces, and solids. [< OF *geometrie* < L *geometria* < Gk. *geōmetria* < *gē* earth + *metrein* measure]

ge·o·mor·phic (jē′ə·môr′fik) *adj.* **1** Resembling the earth, as in contour. **2** Of or pertaining to the earth's form or the configuration of its surface features.

ge·on·o·my (jē·on′ə·mē) *n.* The study of the earth in all its geological, physical, chemical, and mechanical aspects; earth science. —**ge·o·nom·ic** (jē′ə·nom′ik) *adj.*

ge·oph·a·gy (jē·of′ə·jē) *n.* Dirt-eating; morbid appetite for dirt, clay, etc. —**ge·oph′a·gism** (-jiz′əm) *n.* —**ge·oph′a·gist** *n.*

ge·o·phys·ics (jē′ə·fiz′iks) *n.* The science that treats of the physical forces and phenomena associated with the earth, and studies the nature of deep-lying areas by means of seismographs, the torsion balance, and various electromagnetic instruments. —**ge′o·phys′i·cal** *adj.* —**ge′o·phys′i·cist** *n.*

ge·o·phyte (jē′ə·fīt) *n. Bot.* An earth-growing plant; especially, one whose buds, mycelia, etc., are deeply buried in the substratum.

ge·o·pol·i·tics (jē′ō·pol′ə·tiks) *n.* **1** The study of geography, geology, climate, and the natural resources of the earth in relation to the development of peoples, cultures, and states. **2** A method of studying geography and power politics in terms of national security in international relations, embracing geography, natural resources, industrial development, and political strength. **3** The former German doctrine of living space as the primary element in, and strongest guaranty of, state power and world domination. See LEBENSRAUM.

ge·o·pon·ic (jē′ə·pon′ik) *adj.* Pertaining to agri-

culture; hence, rustic. [< Gk. *geōponikos* < *geōponos* a farmer < *gē* earth + *ponos* labor]

ge·o·po·ten·tial (jē′ə·pə·ten′shəl) *n. Meteorol.* The potential energy of unit mass, equal to the work required to lift it from the zero potential of sea level to its actual position: applied especially in air-mass analysis.

George (jôrj) A masculine personal name. Also *Dan., Ger., Sw.* **Ge·org** (gā′ôrg), *Fr.* **Georges** (zhôrzh) or **Geor·get** (zhôr·zhe′), *Latin* **Geor·gi·us** (jôr′jē·əs). [< Gk., husbandman]
—**George I,** 1660–1727, elector of Hanover; king of England 1714–27.
—**George I,** 1845–1913, king of Greece 1863–1913.
—**George II,** 1683–1760, king of England 1727–60.
—**George II,** 1890–1947, king of Greece 1922–23, 1935–47.
—**George III,** 1738–1820, king of England 1760–1820.
—**George IV,** 1762–1830, king of England 1820–30.
—**George V,** 1865–1936, king of England 1910–36.
—**George VI,** 1895–1952, king of England 1936–52.
—**George, Saint,** martyred 303?, patron saint of England.

geor·gette crepe (jôr·jet′) A sheer, dull fabric with a crepelike surface, originally made of silk: used for blouses, gowns, millinery, etc.: a trade name. [after Mme. *Georgette* de la Plante, French modiste]

Geor·gia (jôr′jə) **1** A southern Atlantic State of the United States; 58,876 square miles; capital, Atlanta; entered the Union Jan. 2, 1788, one of the original thirteen States: nickname, *Cracker State:* abbr. GA **2** A constituent republic of the U.S.S.R. in the southern Caucasus on the Black Sea; 29,400 square miles; capital, Tiflis: Russian *Gruziya;* Georgian *Sakartvelo:* also **Georgian Soviet Socialist Republic.**

Geor·gian (jôr′jən) *adj.* **1** Of or pertaining to the reigns or period of the four Georges in England, 1714–1830, or of George V, 1910–36. **2** Of or pertaining to the State of Georgia. **3** Of or pertaining to Georgia in the U.S.S.R., to the Georgians, or to their language. —*n.* **1** A native or inhabitant of the State of Georgia. **2** One of an ancient mountain people native to the Caucasus; also, one of their modern descendants, a native of the Georgian Republic. **3** The agglutinative South Caucasian language of the Georgians of the Soviet Union. **4** A person belonging to either of the Georgian periods in England, or having Georgian taste.

Georgia pine 1 The long-leaved southern yellow pine (*Pinus palustris*). **2** The wood of this tree.

geor·gic (jôr′jik) *adj.* Pertaining to husbandry or rural affairs: also **geor′gi·cal.** —*n.* A poem on husbandry. [< L *georgicus* < Gk. *geōrgikos* < *geōrgia* husbandry]

ge·o·stat·ic (jē′ə·stat′ik) *adj.* Of or pertaining to the pressure of the earth.

ge·o·stat·ics (jē′ə·stat′iks) *n.* The statics of rigid bodies in relation to balanced forces on or beneath the earth's surface.

ge·o·strat·e·gist (jē′ō·strat′ə·jist) *n.* A specialist in the problems, objectives, and doctrines of geostrategy.

ge·o·strat·e·gy (jē′ō·strat′ə·jē) *n.* Military strategy as related to and determined by geopolitical factors. [< GEO(POLITICS) + STRATEGY] —**ge′o·stra·te′gic** (-strə·tē′jik) *adj.*

ge·o·stroph·ic (jē′ə·strof′ik) *adj. Meteorol.* Designating a regional drift of air masses caused by the rotation of the earth. Compare CYCLOSTROPHIC. [< GEO- + Gk. *strephein* turn]

ge·o·syn·cline (jē′ə·sin′klīn) *n. Geol.* A massive downward flexure of the earth's crust: opposed to *geanticline.* —**ge′o·syn·cli′nal** *adj. & n.*

ge·o·tax·is (jē′ə·tak′sis) *n. Biol.* The arrangement of an organism or any of its parts with respect to the force of gravitation. See GEOTROPISM.

ge·o·tech·nol·o·gy (jē′ō·tek·nol′ə·jē) *n.* The application of the mineral arts and sciences to the improvement of old and development of new methods, techniques, processes, and products, as in ceramics, glassmaking, metallurgy, etc. —**ge′o·tech′no·log′i·cal** (-nə·loj′i·kəl) *adj.* —**ge′o·tech·nol′o·gist** *n.*

ge·o·tec·ton·ic (jē′ō·tek·ton′ik) *adj. Geol.* Relating to the structure of the rock masses of the earth's crust and to their shape, composition, and distribution.

ge·o·ther·mal (jē′ə·thûr′məl) *adj.* Pertaining to or of the earth's internal heat. Also **ge′o·ther′mic.**

ge·ot·ro·pism (jē·ot′rə·piz′əm) *n. Biol.* A tendency exhibited by organisms, especially the roots of growing plants, to turn toward the center of the earth: distinguished from *apogeotropism.* Compare GEOTAXIS. —**ge·o·trop·ic** (jē′ə·trop′ik) *adj.* —**ge′o·trop′i·cal·ly** *adv.*

ge·ra·ni·a·ceous (ji·rā′nē·ā′shəs) *adj. Bot.* Belonging or pertaining to a family *(Geraniaceae)* of polypetalous herbs, shrubs, and trees, the geranium family, widely scattered in temperate and subtropical regions. [< NL *Geraniaceae* < L *geranium* GERANIUM]

ge·ra·ni·al (ji·rā′nē·əl) *n.* Citral.

ge·ra·ni·ol (ji·rā′nē·ôl, -ōl) *n. Chem.* An oily colorless alcohol of the terpene group, $C_{10}H_{18}O$, a constituent of oil of roses, geranium, citronella, and other plants: used in perfumery and cosmetics.

ge·ra·ni·um (ji·rā′nē·əm) *n.* 1 Any of a widespread genus *(Geranium)* of plants typical of the family Geraniaceae. Also called *cranesbill.* 2 Pelargonium. 3 A very deep pink to vivid red color. [< L < Gk. *geranion* < *geranos* crane]

ger·bil (jûr′bil) *n.* Any of a subfamily *(Gerbillinae)* of rodents found in Asia, Africa, and SE Europe, with long hind legs, hairy tail, and narrow incisors. Also **ger·bille′.** [< F *gerbille* < NL *gerbillus,* dim. of *gerbo* a jerboa]

ge·rent (jir′ənt) *n.* A governing power; ruler; manager. [< L *gerens, -entis,* ppr. of *gerere* carry on, do]

ge·re·nuk (ge′rə·nook′) *n.* An East African antelope *(Lithocranius walleri)* with extremely long legs and a massive head. [< native name]

ger·e·ol·o·gy (jer·ē·ol′ə·jē) *n.* Gerontology. Also **ger′a·tol′o·gy** (-ə·tol′ə·jē). [< Gk. *gēras* old age + -LOGY]

ger·fal·con (jûr′fôl′kən, -fô′-) *n.* A large falcon *(Falco rusticolus)* of the Arctic regions, with feathered shanks: also spelled *gyrfalcon.* [< OF *gerfaucon* < OHG *gir* vulture + OF *faucon* a falcon]

ger·i·at·ric (jer′ē·at′rik) *adj.* Of or pertaining to geriatrics or to old people.

ger·i·a·tri·cian (jer′ē·ə·trish′ən) *n.* A specialist in the diseases of old age. Also **ger·i·at·rist** (jer′ē·at′rist).

ger·i·at·rics (jer′ē·at′riks) *n.* 1 The branch of medicine which deals with the structural changes, physiology, diseases, and hygiene of old age. 2 Gerontology. [< Gk. *gēras* old age + -IATRICS]

ger·i·o·psy·cho·sis (jer′ē·ō·sī·kō′sis) *n.* Mental disorder associated with old age; a psychosis of the senile. [< Gk. *gēras* old age + PSYCHOSIS]

germ (jûrm) *n.* 1 Any rudimentary vital element. 2 *Biol.* **a** The formative protoplasm of an egg or ovum, or of an ovule; a gamete; germ cell. **b** The earliest stage of an organism. 3 *Bot.* A growing point, as a young bud. 4 The primary source of anything; that from which a thing may be developed as from a seed. 5 A micro-organism; especially, one likely to cause disease; a microbe. 6 An embryo. —*adj.* 1 Germinative. 2 Pertaining to or arising from disease germs. [< F *germe* < L *germen* sprig]

ger·man¹ (jûr′mən) *n.* The cotillion, or a dance at which it is the chief feature. [Short for *German* cotillion]

ger·man² (jûr′mən) *adj.* Having the same parents or grandparents: used after the noun: cousins *german,* brothers *german.* [< OF *germain* < L *germanus* closely related]

Ger·man (jûr′mən) *n.* 1 A native or citizen of Germany. 2 The West Germanic language of the Germans. —**High German** The standard literary and spoken language used throughout most of Germany and in parts of Switzerland, Austria, and Alsace: also called **New High German.** Abbr. *HG* —**Low German** 1 The collective languages of the Low Countries, including Dutch,

Flemish, and Frisian, and of the northern lowlands of Germany (Plattdeutsch). 2 The division of West Germanic which includes Dutch, Flemish, Frisian, English, etc. Abbr. *LG* —**Old High German** The language of southern Germany from about 800 to 1100. Abbr. *OHG* —**Middle High German** The High German language from 1100 to 1450, as exemplified in the *Nibelungenlied.* Abbr. *MHG* —**Middle Low German** The low German language from 1100 to 1450. Abbr. *MLG*

ger·man·der (jər·man′dər) *n.* 1 A labiate herb (genus *Teucrium*) of the mint family, with pale purple flowers; especially the American germander (*T. canadense*). 2 The germander speedwell. See under SPEEDWELL. [< OF *germandree* < Med. L *germandra,* alter. of LGk. *chamandrya* < Gk. *chamaidrys* < *chamai* on the ground + *drys* an oak]

ger·mane (jər·mān′) *adj.* 1 In close relationship; relevant; appropriate; pertinent. 2 Akin; german. [See GERMAN²]

ger·man·ic (jər·man′ik) *adj. Chem.* Containing germanium in its higher valence.

Ger·man·ic (jər·man′ik) *adj.* 1 Of or pertaining to a group of early Indo-European tribes living in the region between the Rhine, Danube, and Vistula rivers: later extended to include the Germans, English, Dutch, Flemings, Danes, Scandinavians, and German-Swiss. 2 Relating to the language or customs of any of these people. —*n.* 1 A subfamily of the Indo-European family of languages, divided into the branches **East Germanic,** including Gothic (extinct); **North Germanic** or Scandinavian, including Norwegian, Swedish, Danish, Icelandic, and Faroese; and **West Germanic,** including all the High and Low German languages and dialects, among which are German, Dutch, Flemish, Frisian, English, Yiddish, Plattdeutsch, etc. 2 The prehistoric parent of these languages: called **Primitive Germanic.** Also called *Teutonic.*

ger·ma·ni·um (jər·mā′nē·əm) *n.* A brittle, grayish white crystalline element (symbol Ge, atomic number 32) with a metallic luster, important as a semiconductor in the manufacture of electronic instruments. See PERIODIC TABLE. [< NL < L *Germania* Germany]

German measles Rubella.

Germano- *combining form* German: *Germanophile.*

ger·man·ous (jûr′mən·əs) *adj. Chem.* Of or pertaining to germanium in its lower valence.

German shepherd A breed of dog having a large, muscular body, a thick, smooth coat, and unusual adaptability to work with policemen, blind persons, etc. Also called *police dog, Alsatian.*

German silver A while alloy of copper, nickel, and zinc, used in cutlery and as a base for plated ware; nickel silver.

Ger·ma·ny (jûr′mə·nē) A country of central Europe, known as the *German Empire* 1871–1918, divided in 1949 into: **a** The *Federal Republic of Germany (West Germany);* 84,634 square miles; capital, Bonn; **b** The *German Democratic Republic (East Germany);* 41,700 square miles; capital, Berlin: German *Deutschland,* French *Allemagne.*

ger·mar·i·um (jər·mâr′ē·əm) *n. Zool.* The formative part of the ovary of certain invertebrates, as the flatworm, containing the primary cell elements. [< NL < L *germen* a sprig]

germ cell *Biol.* A cell specialized for reproduction: distinguished from *somatic cell.*

ger·mi·cide (jûr′mə·sīd) *n.* That which is capable of killing germs; any agent used to destroy disease germs or other micro-organisms, as chlorine. [< GERM + -(I)CIDE] —**ger′mi·ci′dal** *adj.*

ger·mi·cul·ture (jûr′mə·kul′chər) *n.* The artificial cultivation of bacteria or disease germs for scientific research. —**ger′mi·cul′tur·ist** *n.*

ger·mi·nal (jûr′mə·nəl) *adj.* Pertaining to or constituting a germ; germinative. [< NL *germinalis* < L *germen, -inis* a sprig]

germinal disk *Biol.* 1 A disklike area of the blastoderm of eggs of amniotic vertebrates, in which the embryo proper first appears. 2 In meroblastic eggs with much yolk, the disklike protoplasmic part, which undergoes segmentation.

Also called *blastodisk.* Compare illustration under EMBRYOLOGY.

germinal vesicle 1 *Biol.* The nucleus of the animal ovum. 2 *Bot.* The oosphere within the embryo sac of the ovule of plants.

ger·mi·nate (jûr′mə·nāt) *v.* **·nat·ed, ·nat·ing** *v.i.* To begin to grow or develop; sprout. —*v.t.* To cause to sprout. [< L *germinatus,* pp. of *germinare* sprout] —**ger′mi·na·ble** (-nə·bəl) *adj.* —**ger′mi·nant** *adj.* —**ger·mi·na′tion** *n.* —**ger′mi·na′tor** *n.*

ger·mi·na·tive (jûr′mə·nā′tiv) *adj.* 1 Pertaining to or tending to produce germination; capable of germinating. 2 Capable of growing.

germ layer *Biol.* One of the three principal layers of cells from which the embryo develops, as the ectoderm, mesoderm, or endoderm.

germ plasm *Biol.* The part of the cell protoplasm which is the material basis of heredity, transferred from one generation to another. Also **germ plasma.**

germ theory 1 *Pathol.* The theory that infectious diseases, as typhoid fever, are caused by bacteria or other micro-organisms. 2 The doctrine of biogenesis.

ger·o·don·tia (jer′ə·don′shə) *n.* The branch of dentistry which specializes in the dental condition of elderly people. [< NL < Gk. *gēras* old age + *odous, odontos* tooth]

ger·o·mor·phism (jer′ə·môr′fiz·əm) *n. Pathol.* Premature senility and old age. [< Gk. *gēras* old age + *morphē* form + -ISM] —**ger′o·mor′phic** *adj.*

ge·ron·tic (ji·ron′tik) *adj.* Senile; of or pertaining to an old person or to old age. [< Gk. *gerontikos* < *gerōn, gerontos* old man]

geronto- *combining form* Old age; pertaining to old people: *gerontology.* Also, before vowels, **ger·ont-.** [< Gk. *gerōn, gerontos* old man]

ger·on·toc·ra·cy (jer′on·tok′rə·sē) *n.* Government by the old; specifically, in certain primitive African Negro cultures, the control of social life by members of the oldest age group. —**ge·ron·to·crat·ic** (ji·ron′tō·krat′ik) *adj.*

ge·ron·to·ge·ic (ji·ron′tō·jē′ik) *adj.* Of or pertaining to the Old World: opposed to *neogeic.* [< GERONTO- + Gk. *gē* earth]

ger·on·tol·o·gy (jer′on·tol′ə·jē) *n.* 1 The scientific study of the processes and phenomena of aging. 2 Geriatrics. —**ger′on·tol′o·gist** *n.*

ge·ron·to·ther·a·py (ji·ron′tō·ther′ə·pē) *n.* The therapeutic management of the disorders and processes associated with aging: distinguished from *geriatrics.*

-gerous *suffix* Bearing or producing: crystalligerous. [< L *gerere* bear + -OUS]

ger·ry·man·der (jer′i·man′dər, ger′-) *n.t.* To alter unfairly or abnormally, as the political map of a state, etc. —*n.* An unnatural and arbitrary redistricting of a state or county. [< GERRY (SALA)MANDER: from the salamander shape of one of the districts formed in Massachusetts while Elbridge Gerry was governor]

Gersh·win (gûrsh′win), **George,** 1898–1937, U.S. composer. —**Ira,** 1896-1983 U.S. lyricist; brother of George.

ger·und (jer′ənd) *n. Gram.* 1 In Latin, a verbal noun used only in the oblique cases of the singluar, as furor *scribendi,* a rage for *writing.* 2 In English, a verbal noun ending in *-ing,* functioning as a noun, but capable of taking objects and adverbial modifiers. Example: *Writing* poetry well is an art. [< LL *gerundium* < *gerere* carry on, do] —**ge·rundi·al** (jə·run′dē·əl) *adj.*

ge·run·dive (jə·run′div) *Gram. adj.* Like, pertaining to, or having the nature of the gerund. —*n.* In Latin, a verbal adjective having the gerund stem and used as future passive participle, expressing obligation, fitness, or necessity, as *regendus,* that must or should be ruled, or *amandus,* to be loved, that should be loved, etc. [< LL *gerundivus* < *gerundium* GERUND]

ges·so (jes′ō) *n.* 1 A ground of plaster, as gypsum or plaster of Paris, prepared to be painted on. 2 Gypsum or plaster of Paris prepared for use in sculpture. [< Ital. < L *gypsum* GYPSUM]

Ge·stalt (gə-shtält′) *n. pl.* **-stalt·en** (-shtält′ən) *Psychol.* An arrangement of separate elements of experience, emotion, etc., in a form, pattern, or configuration so integrated as to appear and function as a unit that is more than a simple summation of its parts. [< G, form]

Gestalt psychology A school of psychology which interprets biological and psychic processes in terms of the action and interplay of closely integrated patterns or *Gestalten*; the observed effect of a Gestalt, as well as the mechanism of its action, cannot be adequately explained through a simple analysis of its constituent parts.

Ge·sta·po (gə-stä′pō) *n.* The secret police of Nazi Germany. [< G *Ge(heime) Sta(ats)-po(lizei)* Secret State Police]

ges·tate (jes′tāt) *v.t.* **·tat·ed, ·tat·ing** To carry in the womb during gestation. [< L *gestatus*, pp. of *gestare* carry young]

ges·ta·tion (jes·tā′shən) *n.* Pregnancy; especially, the period of carrying a fetus in the womb from conception until birth. **—ges′ta·to·ry** (-tôr′ē, -tō′rē) *adj.*

ges·tic (jes′tik) *adj.* Of or pertaining to bodily motion, especially dancing. Also **ges′ti·cal.**

ges·tic·u·late (jes·tik′yə·lāt) *v.* **·lat·ed, ·lat·ing** *v.i.* To make motions with the hands or arms, as in speaking. **—v.t.** To express by gestures. [< L *gesticulatus*, pp. of *gesticulari* < *gesticulus*, dim. of *gestus* bearing, gesture] **—ges·tic′u·la′tive** *adj.* **—ges·tic′u·la′tor** *n.*

ges·ture (jes′chər) *n.* **1** An expressive motion or action, as of the hand or hands in speaking, used for emphasis or to express some idea or emotion. **2** Such motions collectively, or the art of making them. **3** Something said or done as a mere concession to manners, courtesy, etc. **4** *Obs.* Deportment; posture. **—v.** **·tured, ·tur·ing** *v.i.* To make gestures; gesticulate. **—v.t.** To express by gestures. [< Med. L *gestura* < *gerere* carry on, do] **—ges′tur·er** *n.*

  Synonym (noun): gesticulation. *Gesticulation* often conveys the idea of jerky, sudden, or undignified motions; a *gesture* is any expressive movement of the limbs or body.

get (get) *v.* **got** or *Archaic* **gat, got** or *U.S.* **got·ten, get·ting** *v.t.* **1** To come into possession of; obtain. **2** To go and bring back or obtain: to *get* one's hat. **3** To cause to come, go, move, etc.: to *get* baggage through customs. **4** To take; carry away: *Get* your things out of this house. **5** To prepare; make ready: to *get* breakfast. **6** To cause to be; bring to a state or condition: to *get* the work done. **7** To find out; ascertain by calculation, experiment, etc.: To *get* the range of a gun. **8** To obtain as a result: Divide two into six and you will *get* three. **9** To receive as a reward, punishment, evaluation, etc.: to *get* ten years in jail for robbery. **10** To obtain, receive, or earn (something desired or needed): to *get* permission. **11** To receive as a salary, gift, etc.: What did you *get* for Christmas? **12** To learn by memorizing: to *get* a lesson by heart. **13** To become sick with; contract: to *get* malaria. **14** To board; catch, as a train. **15** To beget: said chiefly of animals. **16** *U.S. Colloq.* To come to an understanding of; comprehend: I *get* the idea. **17** *Colloq.* To possess, or to have as a characteristic: with *have* or *has*: He has *got* quite a temper. See note under GOT. **18** To square accounts with: I'll *get* you yet. **19** *Colloq.* To be obliged or forced to do: with *have* or *has*: I have *got* to go home. See note under GOT. **20** *Colloq.* To strike; hit: That shot *got* him in the arm. **21** *Slang* To puzzle; baffle; also, to cause irritation or pleasure to: His impudence *gets* me. **22** *Archaic* Betake: *Get* thee behind me. **—v.i.** **23** To arrive: When does the train *get* there? **24** To come or go: *Get* in here! **25** To board; enter: to *get* on a train or into a car. **26** To become: arrive at a condition or state: to *get* drunk; to *get* stuck in the mud. **27** To acquire profits or property. **28** *Colloq.* To find time, means, or opportunity: to *get* to go. **—to get about 1** To become known. **2** To move about. **—to get across 1** To make or be convincing or clear, as to an audience. **2** To be successful, as in projecting one's personality, entertaining, etc. **—to get ahead** To succeed; prosper. **—to get along 1** To leave; go. **2** To be successful or fairly successful, as in business. **3** To be friendly; harmo-

nize. **4** To proceed. **5** To grow old or older. **—to get around 1** To become known. **2** To move about. **3** To avoid; circumvent. **4** To flatter, cajole, etc., so as to obtain the favor of. **—to get at 1** To reach; arrive at: to *get at* the truth. **2** To intend; mean: I don't see what you're *getting at.* **3** To apply oneself to: to *get at* a problem. **4** *Colloq.* To bribe; corrupt. **—to get away 1** To escape. **2** To leave; go. **3** To start. **—to get away with** *Slang* To do (something) without discovery, criticism, or punishment. **—to get back at** *Slang* To revenge oneself on. **—to get by 1** To pass: This *got by* the censor. **2** *Colloq.* To manage to survive. **—to get in 1** To arrive. **2** To interject effectively, as a remark or the last word. **—to get off 1** To descend from; dismount. **2** To leave; depart. **3** To be relieved, as of duty. **4** To be released without punishment; escape penalty. **5** To utter: to *get off* a joke. **—to get on 1** To mount, as a horse. **2** To get along. **—to get out 1** To depart. **2** To escape. **3** To become known, as a secret. **4** To publish; issue. **—to get over 1** To recover from, as illness or surprise. **2** To get across. **—to get together 1** To collect, as facts or goods. **2** To meet; assemble. **3** *Colloq.* To come to an agreement. **—to get up 1** To rise, as from sleep. **2** To prepare and arrange; devise. **3** *Colloq.* To dress up; bedeck, as with finery. **4** To acquire or work up knowledge of: to *get up* German for an examination. **5** To climb; ascend. **—n.** **1** The act of begetting, or that which is begotten; breed; progeny: the *get* of the stallion. **2** In tennis, handball, etc., the retrieval of a shot apparently beyond reach. [< ON *geta*] **—get′ta·ble** *adj.*

  Synonyms (verb): achieve, acquire, attain, earn, gain, obtain, procure, receive, secure, win. *Get* is a most comprehensive word. A person *gets* whatever he comes to possess or experience, with or without endeavor, expectation, or desire; he *gets* a bargain, a blow, a fall, a fever; he *gains* what he comes to by effort or striving; the swimmer *gains* the shore; a man *acquires* by continuous and ordinarily by slow process; as, One *acquires* a foreign language. A person is sometimes said to *gain* and often to *acquire* what has not been an object of direct endeavor; in the pursuits of trade, he incidentally *gains* some knowledge of foreign countries; he *acquires* by association with others a correct or incorrect accent; he *acquires* a bronzed complexion by exposure to a tropical sun; in such use, what he *gains* is viewed as desirable, what he *acquires* as slowly and gradually resulting. A person *earns* what he gives an equivalent of labor for, but he may not *get* it. On the other hand, he may *get* what he has not *earned;* the temptation to all dishonesty is the desire to *get* a living or a fortune without *earning* it. Compare ATTAIN, GAIN[1], LEARN, MAKE, OBTAIN, PURCHASE, REACH. *Antonyms:* see synonyms for ABANDON.

geth·sem·a·ne (geth·sem′ə·nē) *n.* A place or time of agony.

Geth·sem·a·ne (geth·sem′ə·nē) A garden outside Jerusalem at the foot of the Mount of Olives; the scene of the agony, betrayal, and arrest of Jesus. *Matt.* xxvi 36. [< Gk. *Gethsēmanē* < Aramaic *gath shemānīm* oil press]

Get·tys·burg (get′iz·bûrg) A town in southern Pennsylvania; scene of a Confederate defeat in the Civil War, July 1–3, 1863.

Gev *abbr. Physics* Giga (10⁹) electron volts.

gew·gaw (gyoo′gô) *adj.* Showy; gaudy. **—n.** A flashy, useless ornament; bauble. See synonyms under GAUD. [ME *giue-goue;* origin uncertain]

gey·ser (gī′zər) *n.* **1** A natural hot spring from which intermittent jets of steam, hot water, or mud are ejected in a fountainlike column. **2** *Brit.* A gas hot-water heater. [< Icel. *geysir* gusher, name of a hot spring < *geysa* gush]

gey·ser·ite (gī′zər·īt) *n.* A concretionary opaline quartz deposited in various forms around the orifices of geysers and hot springs, sometimes forming terraces.

ghaist (gāst) *n. Scot.* A ghost.

Gha·na (gä′nä) An independent state (1957) in the Commonwealth of Nations, comprising the former Gold Coast Colony and the protectorates of Ashanti, Northern Territories, and British Togoland in western Africa; 91,690 square miles;

capital, Accra: formerly *Gold Coast.*

ghast·ly (gast′lē, gäst′-) *adj.* **·li·er, ·li·est** **1** Having a haggard, deathlike appearance. **2** Terrifying or shocking. **—adv.** Like a specter; fearfully. [ME *gastlich,* OE *gæstan* terrify + *-lich* LY[1]] **—ghast′li·ness** *n.*

  Synonyms (adj.): cadaverous, deathlike, deathly, hideous, pale, pallid, spectral, wan. See PALE[2]. *Antonyms:* blooming, bright, buxom, comely, fresh, ruddy.

ghat (gôt) *n. Anglo-Indian* **1** A stairway on a river bank leading to a temple, or to a landing place or wharf. **2** A mountain pass or a descent from a mountain range. Also **ghaut.** [< Hind. *ghāt*]

Ghaz·ni (gäz′nē) A city in eastern Afghanistan; former capital of the first Moslem dynasty in Afghanistan.

ghee (gē) *n. Anglo-Indian* **1** Clarified butter. **2** A solid white oil obtained from a tree of northern India *(Madhuca butyracea),* used in soaps and ointments. Also **ghi.** [< Hind. *ghī* < Skt. *ghṛta*]

Gheel (khāl) A city in northern Belgium, known since the 14th century for its community treatment of the insane. Also **Geel.**

Ghent (gent) A city in NW Belgium: Flemish *Gent,* French *Gand.*

gher·kin (gûr′kin) *n.* **1** A small prickly cucumber *(Cucumis anguria),* used for pickles. **2** Any small, immature cucumber used for pickling: also spelled **gerkin.** [< Du. *agurk* cucumber < G < Slavic, ult. < LGk. *angourion*]

GHERKIN — VINE, FLOWER AND FRUIT

ghet·to (get′ō) *n. pl.* **·tos** or **·ti** (-tē) **1** A part of a city or town, especially in Italy, in which Jews were formerly required to live. **2** A section of a city, often rundown or overcrowded, inhabited chiefly by a minority group that is effectively barred from living in other communities, as because of racial prejudice or for economic or social reasons. [< Ital.]

ghost (gōst) *n.* **1** A disembodied spirit. **2** The soul or spirit. **3** A shadow or semblance; slight trace. **4** A spirit of any kind. **5** *Optics* **a** A false or secondary image, or a spot of light, as from a defect in a lens or instrument. **b** In television, a secondary image, appearing as a doubling of the image to the right, caused by reception of a reflected signal a fraction of a second later than the primary image. **6** *Obs.* The Holy Ghost. **7** *U.S. Slang* An addict to opium-smoking. **8** *Metall.* A narrow band of metal on steel ingots or forgings, harder than the adjoining parts; it becomes more evident on machining: also **ghost line.** See synonyms under SPECTER. **—to give up the ghost.** To die. **—v.t. & v.i.** **1** To haunt as a ghost. **2** *Colloq.* To write as a ghost writer. [OE *gāst* spirit] **—ghost′like′** *adj.*

ghost dance A dance performed by certain North American Indian tribes, in which both sexes take part, believed to bring the dancer into communion with the souls of dead friends.

ghost·ly (gōst′lē) *adj.* **·li·er, ·li·est** **1** Pertaining to the soul or religion; spiritual. **2** Pertaining to apparitions; spectral. **—ghost′li·ness** *n.*

ghost town A deserted town; especially, a former boom town now empty and decayed.

ghost-write (gōst′rīt′) *v.i. & v.t.* **-wrote, -written, -writing** To do literary work credited to another. **—ghost writer.**

ghoul (gool) *n.* **1** In Oriental legend, an evil spirit supposed to prey on corpses. **2** A person who robs dead bodies; a grave-robber; body-snatcher. **3** One who delights in morbid and revolting things. [< Arabic *ghūl*] **—ghoul′ish** *adj.* **—ghoul′ish·ly** *adv.* **—ghoul′ish·ness** *n.*

GI (jē′ī′) *n. Colloq.* A soldier, especially an enlisted man, in the U.S. Army —*adj.* Of, pertaining to, or issued by the U.S. Army. See GOVERNMENT ISSUE. Also **G.I.** [< *G(overnment) I(ssue)*]

gi·ant (jī'ənt) *n.* **1** In mythology, a being of human form, but of enormous size. **2** Any person or thing of great size, either physically, mentally, or figuratively. **3** Any imaginary person of gigantic size. —*adj.* Gigantic. [< OF *géant* < L *gigas, -antis* < Gk. *gigas, -antos*] —**gi'ant·ess** *n. fem.* — **gi'ant·ship** *n.*

giant cactus A large desert cactus of SW United States (*Cereus giganteus*), with an erect columnar trunk, sometimes branching, many ribs, strong spines, and flowering tops: also called *saguaro, sahuaro.*

gi·ant·ism (jī'ənt·iz'əm) *n.* **1** The quality or condition of being a giant. **2** Gigantism.

giant kelp A very large, tough and massive seaweed (*Macrocystis pyrifera*) belonging to the brown algae, found mainly in the Pacific.

giant powder A variety of dynamite.

gi·ar·di·a·sis (jē'är·dī'ə·sis) *n. Pathol.* An intestinal disorder attributed to the presence of a parasitic flagellate protozoan, *Giardia lamblia;* flagellate diarrhea. [< NL *Giardia*, a genus name + -IASIS]

gib (gib) *n. Mech.* **1** A wedge-shaped or other piece of metal that holds another in place or adjusts a bearing, etc. **2** A bearing surface, usually of brass, let into the cross-head of a steam engine to reduce friction. —*v.t.* **gibbed, gib·bing** To fasten with a gib or gibs; supply with a gib. [? < GIBBET]

gib·ber (jib'ər, gib'-) *v.i.* To talk rapidly and incoherently; jabber. —*n.* Gibberish. [Imit.]

gib·ber·el·lic acid (jib'ə·rel'ik) *Chem.* A fermentation product of gibberellin, $C_{19}H_{22}O_6$, used as a plant-growth regulator.

gib·ber·el·lin (jib'ə·rel'in) *n. Chem.* Any of a group of closely related plant hormones that regulate certain processes in all higher plants, as flowering, germination of seeds, stem elongation, etc. [after *Gibberella fujikuroi*, a pathogenic fungus from which they were first isolated]

gib·ber·ish (jib'ər·ish, gib'-) *n.* Incoherent or unintelligible gabble. See synonyms under LANGUAGE.

gib·bet (jib'it) *n.* An upright timber with a crosspiece projecting at right angles from its upper end, upon which criminals were formerly hanged; hence, any gallows. —*v.t.* **·bet·ed** or **·bet·ted, ·bet·ing** or **·bet·ting 1** To execute by hanging. **2** To hang and expose on a gibbet. **3** To hold up to public contempt. [< OF *gibet*, dim. of *gibe* a staff]

gib·bon (gib'ən) *n.* A slender, long-armed arboreal anthropoid ape of southern Asia (genus *Hylobates*). [< F; ult. origin uncertain]

Gib·bon (gib'ən), **Edward,** 1737–94, English historian.

Gib·bons (gib'ənz), **James,** 1834–1921, U.S. cardinal. —**Orlando,** 1583–1625, English composer.

gib·bos·i·ty (gi·bos'ə·tē) *n. pl.* **·ties 1** The state of being gibbous, or convex. **2** A rounded protuberance; hump.

BLACK–CAPPED GIBBON

gib·bous (gib'əs) *adj.* **1** Irregularly rounded; convex, as the moon when less than full and yet more than half full. **2** Humpbacked. **3** *Bot.* Swollen on one side, as the calyx of a lupine. Also **gib·bose** (gib'ōs, gi·bōs'). [< L *gibbosus* < *gibbus* a hump] —**gib'bous·ly** *adv.* —**gib'bous·ness** *n.*

gibe¹ (jīb) *v.t. & v.i.* **gibed, gib·ing** To mock; sneer; scoff. See synonyms under MOCK, SCOFF. —*n.* An expression of sarcasm and ridicule. See synonyms under SNEER. Also spelled *jibe.* [Cf. OF *giber* treat roughly in play] —**gib'er** *n.* — **gib'ing·ly** *adv.*

gibe² (jīb) See JIBE¹.

Gib·e·on (gib'ē·ən) A city NW of Jerusalem in ancient Palestine.

Gib·e·on·ite (gib'ē·ən·īt) *n.* **1** One of the inhabitants of Gibeon, condemned by Joshua to be "hewers of wood and drawers of water" for the Israelites. *Josh.* ix 27. **2** *Obs.* A drudge; a slave's slave.

gib·let (jib'lit) *n.* One of the edible visceral parts of a fowl, as the gizzard, heart, or liver. [< OF *gibelet* a stew made from game]

Gi·bral·tar (ji·brôl'tər) *adj.* A British crown colony, fortress, and naval base on the southern coast of Spain: called *Key of the Mediterranean* and identified with one of the *Pillars of Hercules;* 2 1/4 square miles, including the **Rock of Gibraltar** (ancient *Calpe:* also *the Rock*) 1,396 feet high, and dominating the **Strait of Gibraltar**, the passage between Spain and Africa at the western end of the Mediterranean.

Gibson girl An idealization of the American girl of the 1890's as portrayed by Charles Dana Gibson; also, the style of dress fashionable in that period. —**Gib'son-girl'** *adj.*

gid (gid) *n.* A parasitic disease chiefly affecting sheep and goats, caused by the presence in the brain or spinal cord of the cysticercus of a tapeworm (*Coenurus cerebralis*). [< GIDDY]

gid·dy (gid'ē) *adj.* **·di·er, ·di·est 1** Having a whirling or swimming sensation in the head; dizzy. **2** Tending to cause such a sensation: a *giddy* precipice. **3** Marked by foolish levity or impudence; heedless; fickle. —*v.t. & v.i.* **gid·died, gid·dy·ing** To make or become dizzy or unsteady. [OE *gydig* insane] —**gid'di·ly** *adv.* —**gid'di·ness** *n.*

Gide (zhēd), **André,** 1869–1951, French author. —**Charles,** 1847–1932, French economist.

Gid·e·on (gid'ē·ən) A masculine personal name. [< Hebrew, hewer] —**Gideon** An Israelite judge. *Judges* vi 11.

Gid·e·ons (gid'ē·ənz), **The International** A society of American businessmen founded in 1899 to advance the distribution of Bibles in hotels, hospitals, prisons, and public schools.

gier-ea·gle (jir'ē·gəl) *n.* A bird of prey, probably the Egyptian vulture (*Neophron percnopterus*). *Lev.* xi 18. [< Du. *gier* vulture +EAGLE]

gift (gift) *n.* **1** That which is given; a donation; present. **2** The act, right, or power of giving. **3** A natural endowment; aptitude; talent. **4** *Obs.* A bribe; also, an offering. —*v.t.* **1** To bestow or confer upon. **2** To endow with a talent or faculty. [OE < *gifan* give]

Synonyms (noun): benefaction, bequest, boon, bounty, bribe, donation, grant, gratuity, largess, present, tip. A *gift* is that which is voluntarily bestowed without expectation of return or compensation. *Gift* is almost always used in the good sense, *bribe* is the evil sense to signify payment for a dishonorable service under the semblance of a *gift.* A *benefaction* is a charitable *gift*, generally of large amount, and viewed as of enduring value, as an endowment for a college. A *donation* is something, perhaps of great, seldom of trivial value, given to a cause or to a person representing a cause; as, a *donation* to a charity. A *gratuity* is usually of moderate value and is always given as of favor, not of right; as, a *gratuity* to a waiter; commonly called a *tip. Largess* is archaic for a bountiful *gratuity*, usually to be distributed among many, as among the heralds at ancient tournaments. A *present* is a *gift* of friendship, or conciliation, and given as to an equal or a superior. A *boon* is something that has been desired or craved or perhaps asked, or something freely given where that meets some great desire. A *grant* is commonly considerable in amount and given by public authority; as, a *grant* of public lands for a college. See FAVOR, SUBSIDY. *Antonyms:* compensation, earnings, guerdon, penalty, remuneration, wages.

gift·ed (gif'tid) *adj.* Endowed with mental power or talent. See synonyms under CLEVER. —**gift'ed·ness** *n.*

gig¹ (gig) *n.* **1** A light, two-wheeled, one-seated vehicle drawn by one horse. **2** A machine for raising a nap on a cloth by passing it over cylinders fitted with teasels. **3** *Naut.* A ship's boat in which the oarsmen are seated on alternate thwarts; also, a speedy, light rowboat. —*v.*

gigged, gig·ging *v.i.* To ride in a gig. —*v.t.* To raise the nap on (cloth). [Origin uncertain]

gig² (gig) *n.* **1** A pronged fishspear. **2** An arrangement of four barbless fish hooks fastened back to back and drawn through a school of fish to catch them in the bodies. —*v.t. & v.i.* **gigged, gig·ging** To spear or catch (fish) with a gig. [< FISHGIG]

gig³ (gig) *Slang n.* A demerit, as in the army, school, etc. —*v.t.* **gigged, gig·ging 1** To give a demerit to. **2** To punish with a gig. [Origin unknown]

giga- *combining form* In systems of measurement, one billion (10⁹) times (the specified unit): *gigavolt.*

gi·gan·tesque (jī'gan·tesk') *adj.* Like or suited to giants.

gi·gan·tic (jī·gan'tik) *adj.* **1** Like a giant; colossal; huge. **2** Tremendous; extraordinary. Also **gi·gan·te·an** (jī'gan·tē'ən). See synonyms under IMMENSE, LARGE. [< L *gigas, -antis* GIANT + -IC]

gi·gan·tism (jī·gan'tiz·əm) *n.* **1** Abnormal size. **2** *Pathol.* Excessive growth of the body due to disturbances in the function and growth of the anterior lobe of the pituitary gland: also called *giantism.* Also **gi·gan·to·so·ma** (-tə·sō'mə).

giganto- *combining form* Gigantic; very large: *gigantocyte.* Also, before vowels, **gigant-.** [< Gk. *gigas, -antos* giant]

gi·gan·to·cyte (ji·gan'tə·sīt) *n. Physiol.* An excessively large erythrocyte.

gi·gan·tom·a·chy (jī'gan·tom'ə·kē) *n.* In classical mythology, the battle of the giants; the war of the giants against Zeus and the Olympian gods. Also **gi·gan·to·ma·chi·a** (ji·gan'tō·mä'kē·ə). [< Gk. *gigantomachia* < *gigas, -antos* giant + *machē* battle]

Gi·gan·to·pith·e·cus (ji·gan'tō·pith'ə·kəs) *n. Paleontol.* A giant hominoid primate of the early Pleistocene, represented only by several very large fossilized molar teeth discovered in Hong Kong apothecary shops between 1935 and 1939. Also **Gi·gant·an·thro·pus** (jī'gan·tan'thrə·pəs). [< NL < Gk. *gigas, -antos* giant + *pithēkos* ape]

gig·gle (gig'əl) *v.i.* **gig·gled, gig·gling** To laugh in a high-pitched, nervous manner; titter. —*n.* A convulsive laugh; titter. [Imit.] —**gig'gler** *n.* —**gig'gle·some** *adj.* —**gig'gling** *adj. & n.* —**gig'gly** *adj.*

gig·o·lo (jig'ə·lō, *Fr.* zhē·gô·lō') *n. pl.* **·los** (-lōz, *Fr.* -lō') **1** A professional male dancer in dance halls, cabarets, or the like, who attends women patrons or visitors. **2** A woman's paid escort. A man who is supported by a woman; a kept man. [< F, prob. < *gigolette* a prostitute]

gig·ot (jig'ət) *n.* **1** A leg of mutton. **2** A sleeve having the shape of a leg of mutton. [< F]

gigue (zhēg) *n. Music* A lively composition often forming the final movement of a suite. [< F. See JIG.]

Gi·la monster (hē'lə)A large, poisonous lizard (*Heloderma suspectum*) with a stout orange-and-black body, ranging from southern Utah and Nevada through Arizona and New Mexico into northern Mexico. The beaded lizard (*H. horridum*), an allied form found in Mexico, is also poisonous.

GILA MONSTER
(Up to 20 inches over all in length)

Gila woodpecker A woodpecker (*Centurus uropygialis*) of the SW United States, habitually nesting in the stem of the giant cactus.

gil·bert (gil'bərt) *n. Electr.* The cgs unit of magnetomotive force; equal to 0.7958 ampere-turn. [after William *Gilbert*, 1540–1603, English physicist]

gild¹ (gild) *v.t.* **gild·ed** or **gilt, gild·ing 1** To coat with or as with gold or gold leaf. **2** To give a pleasing or attractive appearance to; gloss over. **3** *Obs.* To redden or smear (with blood). See synonyms under ADORN. ◆ Homophone: *guild.* [OE *gyldan*] —**gild'er** *n.*

gild² (gild), **gild·hall** (gild'hôl'), **gild·ry** (gild'rē), etc. See GUILD.

gild·ed (gil′did) *adj.* **1** Thinly overlaid with or as with gold. **2** Fashionable; wealthy.

Gilded Age, the A post-Civil War period (1870–98) of waxing plutocratic accumulation and display in the United States: from *The Gilded Age* (1871), a novel by Mark Twain and Charles Dudley Warner depicting the newly emergent plutocracy with its conspicuous consumption and waste.

gild·ing (gil′ding) *n.* **1** The art of overlaying a surface thinly with gold. **2** A mixture of finely divided gold, brass, or other substance to simulate gold, and a drying liquid: used as a decorative paint. **3** A specious or superficial appearance. Also **gilt, gild.**

Gil·e·ad (gil′ē·əd) A mountainous region of ancient Palestine east of the Jordan. *Josh.* xii 2.

Gil·e·ad·ite (gil′ē·əd·īt′) *n.* An inhabitant of Gilead. *Judges* xii 4.

gill¹ (gil) *n.* **1** An organ for breathing the air dissolved in water, consisting, in aquatic vertebrates, as fishes and amphibians, of leaflike or threadlike vascular processes of mucous membrane on either side of the neck. Fishes take in water for the gills through the mouth and force it out mostly through the gill slits. **2** A gill-like part, as the wattle of a fowl. **3** *Bot.* One of the thin radial plates on the under side of the cap of a mushroom. —*v.t.* **1** To catch by the gills, as fish in a gill net. **2** To gut (fish). [ME *gile*, prob. < Scand. Cf. Sw. *gäl* gill.]

gill² (jil) *n.* A liquid measure, one fourth of a pint or 0.118 liter: also spelled *jill.* [< OF *gelle* measure for wine]

gill³ (gil) *n.* **1** A ravine; a deep narrow gully. **2** A brook; narrow mountain stream. Also *ghyll.* [< ON *gil* gorge]

gill arch *Zool.* One of the arches in gill-bearing vertebrates that carry the gills. In the higher vertebrates, the gill arches are transformed to perform other functions.

gill cleft Gill slit.

gill filament *Zool.* A threadlike vascular process of the mucous membrane of the gill.

gill fungus Any fungus of the genus *Agaricus;* an agaric.

gil·li·flow·er (jil′ē·flou′ər) *n.* **1** One of various plants of the mustard family, as the common stock, the wallflower, or the rocket. **2** A plant of the pink family, as the clove pink: the Middle English and Elizabethan sense. **3** The feathered gilliflower *(Dianthus plumarius)* and ragged robin. **4** A variety of apple. Also **gil′ly·flow′er.** [Alter. of ME *gilofre* < OF, var. of *girofle* a clove < L *caryophyllum* < Gk. *karyophyllon* a clove tree]

gill net A net, set upright in the water by means of weighted stakes, in the meshes of which fish become entangled by their gills.

gill raker *Zool.* One of a row of processes projecting from the gill arches of fishes and screening the gills from injurious substances.

gill slit Any of a bilateral series of narrow external openings in the pharynx of embryonic chordates which persists throughout life in some aquatic forms, as sharks. Also called *gill cleft, branchial cleft.*

gilt¹ (gilt) Alternative past tense and past participle of GILD. —*adj.* Gilded; yellow like gold. —*n.* **1** The material used in gilding. **2** Superficial or meretricious show. ◆ Homophone: *guilt.*

gilt² (gilt) *n.* A young female pig. ◆ Homophone: *guilt.* [< ON *gyltr*]

gilt-edge (gilt′ej′) *adj.* **1** Having the edges gilded: said of leaves of paper either for writing or as bound in a book. **2** Of the best quality or highest price; first-class: *gilt-edge securities.* Also **gilt′-edged′.**

gilt·head (gilt′hed′) *n.* **1** One of various European fishes, as the sea bream *(Pagrus auratus)* of the Mediterranean. **2** A cunner.

gim·bals (jim′bəlz, gim′-) *n. Naut.* A contrivance for allowing a suspended object, as a ship's compass, to tip freely in all directions, thus remaining level, however the ship moves: also spelled *gymbals.* [Alter. of OF *gemelle* twin < L *gemellus,* dim. of *geminus* twin, double]

gim·crack (jim′krak) *n.* A gew-gaw; bauble. See synonyms under GAUD.

GIMBALS

—*adj.* Cheap and showy. [Origin uncertain]

gim·crack·er·y (jim′krak·ər-ē) *n.* Worthless ornament or show.

gim·el (gim′əl) *n.* The third Hebrew letter. See ALPHABET.

gim·let (gim′lit) *n.* A small boring tool with a cross-head and a cutter-pointed screw tip. See illustration under AUGER. —*v.t.* To make a hole in with a gimlet. [< OF *guimbelet.* Akin to WIMBLE.]

gim·mick (gim′ik) *n. Slang* **1** A secret device for controlling the movements of a prize wheel. **2** Any tricky device or means. **3** Any contrivance, the name of which is not known or cannot be recalled. [Origin uncertain]

gimp¹ (gimp) *n.* **1** A narrow, flat, ornamental trimming, used for dresses, furniture, etc.: also **gimp′ing. 2** A coarse thread for forming edges and outlines in pillow lace. —*v.t.* To border with gimp. [Cf. OF *guimpre,* var. of *guipure,* a kind of trimming]

gimp² (gimp) *U.S. Slang n.* **1** Lameness; a limp. **2** One who limps; a cripple. —*v.i.* To limp. [Origin unknown]

gin (jin) *n.* An aromatic alcoholic liquor, distilled from various grains and flavored with juniper berries; also, such a liquor with other flavoring. [Short for GENEVA]

gin (jin) *n.* **1** A machine for separating cotton fibers from the seeds. **2** A portable hoisting machine. **3** A pump worked by a windmill. **4** A pile driver. **5** A snare or trap. **6** *Obs.* Artifice of any sort. —*v.t.* **ginned, gin·ning 1** To catch in or as in a gin or trap. **2** To remove the seeds from (cotton) in a gin. [Aphetic var. of OF *engin* ingenuity. See ENGINE.]

gin·ge·ley (jin′ji·lē) *n.* The sesame. Also **gin′ge·li, gin′gel·ly, gin′ge·ly.** [< Hind. *jingalī*]

gin·ger (jin′jər) *n.* **1** The pungent, spicy rootstock of a tropical plant *(Zingiber officinale),* either whole or pulverized: used in medicine and cookery. With the outer covering scraped off, the rootstock is called **white ginger,** and is regarded as superior to the East Indian or **black ginger,** in which the covering is not removed. **2** The plant itself. **3** A tawny, sandy, or reddish-brown color. **4** *Colloq.* Something of pungent quality; liveliness; spunk. —*v.t.* **1** To treat or spice with ginger. **2** *Colloq.* To make lively or piquant; enliven: often with *up.* [OE *gingifer* < LL *gingiber* < Gk. *zingiberis,* ult. < Skt.]

ginger ale An effervescent soft drink flavored with ginger.

ginger beer An effervescent drink made with yeast and flavored with ginger, popular in England, Canada, etc.

gin·ger·bread (jin′jər·bred′) *n.* **1** A light sweet cake flavored with ginger. **2** A ginger-flavored cooky cut into odd shapes and ornamented with colored icings. **3** Gaudy or unnecessary ornament. [Alter. of OF *gingembras* preserved ginger < LL *gingiber* GINGER]

gingerbread tree 1 The doom palm. **2** A tree of the rose family of West Africa *(Parinarium macrophylla),* bearing a farinaceous stone fruit called the gingerbread plum.

gin·ger·ly (jin′jər·lē) *adj.* Cautious, or fastidious, as an act or movement. —*adv.* **1** In a cautious, scrupulous, or fastidious manner. **2** *Obs.* Daintily. [Cf. OF *gensor, gentchur,* compar. of *gent* delicate]

gin·ger·snap (jin′jər·snap′) *n.* A small, flat, brittle cooky or biscuit flavored with ginger and molasses.

gin·ger·y (jin′jər·ē) *adj.* **1** Resembling ginger; spicy; hot-flavored. **2** Having a reddish or sandy color.

ging·ham (ging′əm) *n.* A plain-weave cotton fabric, usually in checks or stripes. [< F *guingan,* ult. < Malay *ginggang* striped]

gin·gi·val (jin·jī′vəl, jin′jə-) *adj.* **1** Of or pertaining to the gums. **2** *Phonet.* Produced with the aid of the gums; alveolar: *gingival* sounds. [< L *gingiva* gum]

gingival line *Pathol.* A line across the gums indicating chronic metal poisoning: in lead poisoning the line has a bluish tinge.

gin·gi·vi·tis (jin′jə·vī′tis) *n. Pathol.* Inflammation of the gums.

gin·gly·mus (jing′glə·məs, ging′-) *n. pl.* **·mi** (-mī) *Anat.* A joint that permits flexion and extension in a single plane, as at the elbow and knee; a hinge joint. [< NL < Gk. *ginglymos* a hinge]

gink·go (ging′kō, jing′kō) *n. pl.* **·goes** A deciduous resinous tree *(Ginkgo biloba),* native in China but cultivated in the United States for its fanlike foliage; the maidenhair tree: also spelled *jinkgo.* Also **ging′ko.** [< Japanese]

GINKGO
Branch showing leaf and nut. Regarded as the only surviving member of a family that had flourished millions of years ago, during the time of the dinosaurs.

gin rummy A variety of rummy, in which a player may meld his hand whenever his unmatched cards are worth 10 points or less.

gin·seng (jin′seng) *n.* **1** An herb (genus *Panax)* native in North America and China, having a root of aromatic and stimulant properties, in great esteem in China. **2** The root, or a preparation made from it. [< Chinese *jen shen*]

gip·sy (jip′sē) *n. pl.* **·sies** One of any wandering group of people living the gipsy life; an itinerant tinker, farrier, etc. —*v.i.* **·sied, ·sy·ing** To live or wander like a gipsy. —*adj.* Of, pertaining to, or like a gipsy or the Gipsies; unconventional; wandering; Bohemian. Also spelled *gypsy.*

Gip·sy (jip′sē) *n. pl.* **·sies 1** A member of a wandering, dark-haired, dark-skinned people originating in India and appearing in Europe in the 15th century, now known in every part of the world as itinerant metalworkers, musicians, fortune-tellers, and, formerly, horse dealers. **2** Romany, their language. Also spelled *Gypsy.* [< Earlier *gipcyan,* aphetic var. of *Egypcyan* Egyptian]

gipsy moth A European moth *(Porthetria* or *Lymantria dispar)* naturalized in eastern New England about 1869, having larvae highly destructive to foliage: the male is light-brown, the larger female nearly white. For illustration see under INSECT (injurious).

gi·raffe (jə·raf′, -räf′) *n. pl.* **·raffes** or **·raffe 1** A large spotted African ruminant *(Giraffa camelopardalis),* having a very long neck and limbs; the tallest of the quadrupeds, sometimes attaining a height of 18 feet. **2** A cagelike mine car especially adapted for inclines. [< F, ult. < Arabic *zarāfah*]

GIRAFFE

gir·an·dole (jir′ən·dōl) *n.* **1** A branching chandelier or bracket light. **2** A rotating firework. **3** A rotating water jet. **4** In fortification, a connection of several mines. **5** A pendent piece of jewelry. [< F < Ital. *girandola* < *girare* rotate < L *gyrare.* See GYRATE.]

gird¹ (gûrd) *v.t.* **gird·ed** or **girt, gird·ing 1** To surround with a belt or girdle. **2** To encircle; hem in. **3** To prepare (oneself) for action. **4** To clothe; equip; endue, etc. [OE *gyrdan*]

gird² (gûrd) *n.* **1** A sarcastic thrust; taunt; gibe; sneer. **2** *Obs.* A cutting stroke; hence, a pang. **3** *Obs.* A spurt. —*v.t. & v.i.* To attack with sarcasm; gibe; jeer. [ME *girden;* origin unknown] —**gird′er** *n.*

gird·er (gûr′dər) *n.* **1** A principal horizontal beam, or a compound structure acting as a beam, receiving a vertical load and bearing vertically upon its supports. **2** One who or that which girds or encompasses.

GIRDERS

gird·er·age (gûr′dər·ij) *n.* Girders collectively.

gir·dle (gûr′dəl) n. **1** A belt used for girding a loose garment about the waist; specifically, in ecclesiastical language, the narrow belt adorned with tassels, used to secure the alb; called also *cincture*. **2** Anything which encircles like a belt; especially, a woman's undergarment, more flexible and lighter than a corset, not coming above the waistline. **3** *Obs.* A small band or fillet encompassing a column. **4** *Mining* A thin sandstone stratum in a vein of coal. **5** *Anat.* The ringlike arrangement of bones, by which the limbs of a vertebrate animal are attached to the trunk. **6** The peripheral line of a cut gem, at which it is held in the setting. **7** An encircling cut through the bark of a branch or tree. — *v.t.* **gir·dled, gir·dling** **1** To fasten a girdle or belt around. **2** To encircle; encompass. **3** To make an encircling cut through the bark of (a branch or tree). [OE *gyrdel*]

gir·dler (gûrd′lər) n. **1** One who makes girdles. **2** One who or that which girdles or encircles. **3** *Entomol.* Any insect which cuts through the bark of twigs or branches; especially, the American twig girdler (*Oncideres cingulata*), which severs the twigs of hickory, poplar, and many other trees.

girl (gûrl) n. **1** A female infant or child, or a young unmarried woman. **2** A maid servant. **3** A sweetheart. [ME *gurle*; origin uncertain]

girl Friday A female office worker who performs various tasks. [<GIRL + (MAN) FRIDAY]

girl friend *Colloq.* **1** A boy or man's sweetheart, favorite female companion, etc. **2** A female friend.

girl·hood (gûrl′hŏŏd) n. The state or time of being a girl.

girl scout A member of an organization, **Girl Scouts of America**, formed in the United States in 1912 by Juliette Low to develop health, character, etc.

girt[1] (gûrt) v.t. **1** To gird. **2** To measure the girth of. **3** To fasten with a girth, strap, etc. — *v.i.* **4** To measure in girth. — n. Girth. [<GIRD[1]; also partly <n.]

girt[2] (gûrt) Past tense and past participle of GIRD[1]. — adj. **1** Encircled; bound or fastened with a girth or girdle. **2** *Naut.* Moored with taut cables, so as to prevent swinging by wind or tide, as a vessel. **3** *Entomol.* Braced, as a chrysalis.

girth (gûrth) n. **1** A band or strap for fastening a pack or saddle to a horse's back. **2** Anything that girds or binds; a girdle. **3** The circumference of a circular or cylindrical object; especially, the measure around the waist. **4** A circular bandage. — *v.t.* **1** To bind with a girth. **2** To encircle; girdle. **3** To find the girth of. [<ON *gjordh*]

gist (jist) n. **1** The substance or fundamental fact of a matter in law, the essential cause of legal action. **2** The substance or pith of any matter; the point or main idea. [<OF *giste* place of rest <*gesir* lie <L *jacere*]

git·a·lin (jit′ə·lin, jə·tä′lin, -tal′in) n. *Chem.* A glucoside, $C_{35}H_{59}O_{12}$, in crystalline or powdered form, from the leaves of digitalis, similar in action to digitalis. [<(DI)GITAL(IS) + -IN]

gi·ta·no (ji·tä′nō, *Sp.* hē·tä′nō) n. pl. **·nos** A Spanish gipsy. [<Sp.]

git·tern (git′ərn) n. A medieval musical instrument, like a cithern, but having gut instead of metal strings: predecessor of the guitar. [<OF *guiterne*]

give (giv) v. **gave, giv·en, giv·ing** *v.t.* **1** To transfer the possession or title of to another without compensation of any kind. **2** To transfer to the possession or control of another for a price or equal value. **3** To hand over to another for safekeeping, delivery, etc.: to *give* a letter to a postman. **4** To offer as entertainment: to *give* a play, party, etc. **5** To yield as a product or result: Two plus two *gives* four. **6** To be the cause or source of: The sun *gives* light. **7** To provide or furnish; impart: to *give* evidence; to *give* form to an idea. **8** To express in words; declare: to *give* a ruling or reply. **9** To impose or grant, as a punishment or reward: They *gave* him the death penalty. **10** To emit or show, as a movement, shout, etc. **11** To

administer, as medicine. **12** To deal; inflict, as a blow or pain. **13** To concede; yield or grant: to *give* ground; to *give* permission. **14** To devote or sacrifice, as to a cause: to *give* one's time or one's life. — *v.i.* **15** To make gifts. **16** To yield, as from pressure, melting, or thawing; collapse. **17** To be springy or resilient; bend. — **to give away** **1** To bestow as a gift. **2** To bestow (the bride) upon the bridegroom in a marriage ceremony. **3** *Colloq.* To reveal or disclose; betray. — **to give birth (to)** **1** To bear (offspring). **2** To result in. — **to give in** **1** To yield, as in a fight or argument. **2** To collapse, as under stress. — **to give off** To send forth; emit, as odors. — **to give out** **1** To send forth; emit. **2** To serve out or distribute. **3** To make known; publish. **4** To fail; become worn out or exhausted. — **to give over** **1** To hand over, as to another's care. **2** To cease; desist. — **to give rise to** To cause or result in. — **to give tongue** To bark or bay: said of hunting dogs in pursuit. — **to give up** **1** To surrender; cede; hand over. **2** To stop; cease. **3** To desist from as hopeless. **4** To lose all hope for, as a sick person. **5** To devote wholly: to *give* oneself *up* to art. — n. The quality of being yielding; elasticity; the process or act of giving way. [Fusion of OE *giefan* and ON *gefa*] — **giv′er** n.

— *Synonyms* (verb): bestow, cede, communicate, confer, deliver, furnish, grant, impart, supply. To *give* is primarily to transfer to another's possession or ownership without compensation; in its secondary sense in popular use, it is to put into another's possession by any means and on any terms whatever; a buyer may say "*Give* me the goods, and I will *give* you the money"; we speak of *giving* answers, information, etc., and often of *giving* what is not agreeable to the recipient, as blows, medicine, reproof. To *grant* is to put into one's possession in some formal way, or by authoritative act; as, Congress *grants* lands to a railroad corporation. *Confer* has a similar sense; as, to *confer* a degree or an honor; we *grant* a request or petition, but do not *confer* it. To *impart* is to *give* of that which one still, to a greater or less degree, retains; the teacher *imparts* instruction. To *bestow* is to *give* that of which the receiver stands in especial need; we *bestow* charity.

give–and–take (giv′ən·tāk′) n. **1** Fair exchange; equal compromise. **2** Repartee; a flow or exchange of ideas or wit: He is adept at such *give-and-take*.

give·a·way (giv′ə·wā′) n. **1** A betrayal to ridicule or detection, often unintentional. **2** That which betrays a secret or a person. — adj. Featuring awards of money or prizes: said of a radio or television show.

giv·en (giv′ən) adj. **1** Habitually inclined: with *to*. **2** Specified; stated; also, in law, dated. **3** Donated; presented. **4** Admitted as a fact or a premise. — n. A datum; premise.

given name The name given at birth or baptism.

give–up (giv′up′) n. The practice of splitting a stockbroker's commission with another broker at the direction of the customer.

Gi·za (gē′zə) A city in Upper Egypt on the Nile; site of the pyramids: also **El Gizeh**.

giz·zard (giz′ərd) n. **1** The second stomach of birds, in which the food is ground. **2** *Entomol.* The first stomach of insects, provided with horny plates for macerating or sifting food. **3** *Slang* The stomach. [<OF *gezier* <L *gigeria* cooked entrails of poultry]

gla·bel·la (glə·bel′ə) n. pl. **·lae** (-ē) *Anat.* The smooth prominence on the forehead just above the nose and between the eyebrows. See illustration under FACIAL ANGLE. [<NL <L, dim. of *glaber* smooth]

gla·brate (glā′brāt) adj. **1** Glabrous. **2** Becoming glabrous.

gla·bres·cent (glə·bres′ənt) adj. Shedding hair; becoming glabrous.

gla·bri·ros·tral (glā′brē·ros′trəl) adj. *Ornithol.* Having the mouth free from bristles, as some birds. [<L *glaber* smooth + ROSTRAL]

gla·brous (glā′brəs) adj. *Biol.* **1** Without hair or down. **2** Having a smooth surface. [<L *glaber* smooth]

gla·cé (gla·sā′, *Fr.* glȧ·sā′) adj. **1** Iced; frozen

or cooled. **2** Having a glossy surface resembling ice. **3** Smooth and glossy, as certain leathers. — *v.t.* **·céed, ·cé·ing** **1** To cover with icing. **2** To render smooth and glossy. [<F, pp. of *glacer* freeze <*glace* ice]

gla·cial (glā′shəl) adj. **1** Pertaining to or caused by ice masses. **2** Icy, or icily cold. **3** Of or pertaining to the glacial epoch. **4** *Chem.* Crystallizing or assuming an icelike appearance at ordinary temperature: *glacial* acetic acid. [<F <L *glacialis* <*glacies* ice] — **gla′cial·ly** adv.

glacial deposits *Geol.* Unstratified earth materials and debris transported by glaciers and left at the place of melting.

glacial epoch *Geol.* **1** Any portion of geological time characterized by the formation of ice sheets over large portions of the earth's surface. **2** One of four such epochs identified as succeeding one another during the Pleistocene: beginning with the oldest, they are the Günz, the Mindel, the Riss, and the Würm.

gla·cier (glā′shər) n. A field of ice, formed in regions of perennial frost from compacted snow, which moves slowly downward over slopes or through valleys until it either melts, as in the lowlands, or breaks off in the form of icebergs on the borders of the sea. [<F <L *glacies* ice] — **gla′ciered** adj.

glacier milk The milky water of a stream issuing from a glacier and containing suspended silt or finely divided rock particles.

glacier theory *Geol.* The theory that large elevated portions of the temperate and frigid zones were covered during the earlier geologic epochs by slowly moving glaciers that transported vast masses of drift to lower latitudes.

gla·ci·ol·o·gy (glā′sē·ol′ə·jē) n. That branch of geology which studies the forms, movements, causes, and effects of glaciers. — **gla·ci·o·log·ic** (glā′sē·ə·loj′ik) or **·i·cal** adj. — **gla′ci·ol′o·gist** n.

gla·cis (glā′sis, glas′is) n. A defensive slope in front of a fortification. See illustration under BASTION. [<F, orig. a slippery place <OF *glacier* slip]

glad (glad) adj. **glad·der, glad·dest** **1** Having a feeling of joy, pleasure, or contentment; joyful; gratified: often with *of* or *at*. **1** Having an appearance of joy or brightness; gladsome; joyous. **3** Suggestive of or exciting joy: *glad* tidings. See synonyms under HAPPY, MERRY. — *v.t.* & *v.i.* **glad·ded, glad·ding** *Obs.* To gladden. [OE *glæd* shining, glad] — **glad′ly** adv. — **glad′ness** n.

glad·den (glad′n) v.t. & v.i. To make or become glad. See synonyms under REJOICE. — **glad′den·er** n.

glade (glād) n. **1** A clearing or open space in a wood. **2** A smooth tract of uncovered ice, or an unfrozen open space in the ice of a river or lake. **3** An everglade. [Prob. akin to *glad* in obs. sense "bright," "sunny"]

glad·i·a·tor (glad′ē·ā′tər) n. **1** A man who fought with deadly weapons, as in the ancient Roman amphitheater, for popular amusement. **2** Hence, one who engages in any kind of spirited contest. [<L <*gladius* sword]

a   **b**   **c**   **d**

ROMAN GLADIATORS
a. Retiarius.   *c.* Andabata.
b. Mirmillon.   *d.* Thracian.

glad·i·o·lus (glad′ē·ō′ləs, glə·dī′ə·ləs) *n. pl.* **·lus·es** or **·li** (-lī) **1** Any of a large Old World genus (*Gladiolus*) of plants of the iris family with fleshy bulbs, sword-shaped leaves, and spikes of colored flowers. **2** Its corm or flower. Also **glad·i·o·la** (glad′ē·ō′lə, glə·dī′ə·lə), **glad′i·ole** (-ōl). [< L, dim. of *gladius* sword]

glad·some (glad′səm) *adj.* **1** Causing, feeling, or expressive of joy; joyous; pleasing. **2** Having a feeling of joy or pleasure: cheerful. See synonyms under MERRY. **—glad′some·ly** *adv.* **—glad′some·ness** *n.*

Glad·stone (glad′stōn, -stən) *n.* **1** A suitcase, generally of leather, hinged in the middle lengthwise so that it may open into halves: also called **Gladstone bag.** **2** A four-wheeled pleasure carriage having a driver's seat and two inside seats. [after W. E. *Gladstone*]

glair (glâr) *n.* **1** The white of eggs mixed with vinegar: used as a size in gilding, etc. **2** Any similar viscous matter; anything slimy or slippery. — *v.t.* To treat with glair, as a book cover before gilding. Also **glaire.** ◆Homophone: *glare.* [< F *glaire* < L *clarus* clear]

glair·e·ous (glâr′ē·əs) *adj.* Of the nature of glair; glairy.

glair·y (glâr′ē) *adj.* **1** Like glair. **2** Exhibiting glair. **—glair′i·ness** *n.*

glai·zie (glā′zē) *adj. Scot.* Glossy; sleek.

glam·or·ous (glam′ər·əs) *adj.* Radiating glamour; gorgeous. **—glam′or·ous·ly** *adv.*

glam·our (glam′ər) *n.* **1** A delusion wrought by magic spells; charm; enchantment. **2** Any artificial interest or association by which an object is made to appear delusively magnified or glorified; illusion; fascination; witchery. Also **glam′or.** [Scottish alter. of GRAMARY. Related to GRAMMAR.]

glance¹ (glans, gläns) *v.* **glanced, glanc·ing** *v.i.* **1** To strike something at an angle and bounce off. **2** To look quickly or hurriedly. **3** To glint; flash. **4** To make passing reference; allude. — *v.t.* **5** To cause to strike something at an angle and bounce off. See synonyms under LOOK. — *n.* **1** A quick or passing look; sudden or transient thought. **2** A momentary gleam. **3** An oblique movement or rebound. **4** In cricket, a stroke with the bat held slanting and thus sending the ball to one side of the wicket. [< OF *glacier* slip, ?infl. by ME *glenten* shine]

glance² (glans, gläns) *n.* A mineral, usually a sulfide, having a vitreous sheen: lead *glance.* [Short for *glance ore* < Du. *glanserts* luster ore]

gland (gland) *n.* **1** *Anat.* Any of various organs, composed of specialized epithelial tissue, intended for the secretion of materials essential to the bodily system or for the elimination of waste products: the salivary *glands,* endocrine *glands.* **2** A glandlike structure; a lymph *gland.* **3** *Aeron.* A tube so fitted to the envelope or gas bag of an airship as to allow the passing of a line through it without leakage of air or gas. **4** *Bot.* A special secreting organ in plants. **5** *Mech.* One of various parts of a mechanism that hold something in place; especially, a device for compressing the packing in a stuffing box in order to prevent leakage of a fluid under pressure. [< F *glande* < OF *glandre* < L *glandula,* dim. of *glans, glandis* acorn]

glan·ders (glan′dərz) *n.* A serious contagious disease of horses, mules, and other equines, caused by a bacillus (*Malleomyces mallei*) and characterized by nasal discharges and ulcerative lesions of the lungs and other organs: occasionally found in other animals and in man. When affecting the skin it is called *farcy.* [< OF *glandres,* pl. of *glandre* a gland] **—glan′dered, glan′der·ous** *adj.*

glan·dif·er·ous (glan·dif′ər·əs) *adj.* Acorn-bearing. [< L *glans, glandis* an acorn +-(I)FEROUS]

glan·di·form (glan′də·fôrm) *adj.* Acorn-shaped.

glan·du·lar (glan′jə·lər) *adj.* **1** Pertaining to, bearing, or of the nature of glands. **2** Affecting glands: a *glandular* infection. Also **glan′du·lous.**

glandular fever Infectious mononucleosis.

glan·dule (glan′jōōl) *n.* A small gland.

glans (glanz) *n. pl.* **glan·des** (-dēz) **1** An acorn, or an acornlike part or instrument. **2** *Anat.* The rounded extremity of the penis or clitoris. [< L, an acorn]

glare¹ (glâr) *v.* **glared, glar·ing** *v.i.* **1** To shine with great and dazzling intensity. **2** To gaze or stare fiercely. **3** To be conspicuous or ostentatious. —

v.t. **4** To express or send forth with a glare. — *n.* **1** A dazzling light. **2** An intense and piercing look or gaze, usually hostile. **3** Gaudiness; vulgar splendor. See synonyms under LIGHT¹. ◆ Homophone: *glair.* [ME *glaren* < LG]

glare² (glâr) *n.* A glassy, smooth surface. — *adj.* Having a glassy, smooth surface. ◆Homophone: *glair.* [? < GLARE¹, *n.*]

glass (glas, gläs) *n.* **1** A hard, amorphous, brittle, usually transparent substance made by fusing one or more of the oxides of silicon, boron, or phosphorus with certain basic oxides, followed by rapid cooling to prevent crystallization. ◆ Collateral adjectives: *hyaline, vitreous.* Principal types are:
—borosilicate glass A tough optical and thermal glass; Pyrex glass.
—bottle glass A soda-lime-silica glass with a greenish color caused by iron impurities.
—crown glass Hard optical sodium-silicate glass of low refraction.
—cut glass Glass ornamented by cutting or grinding on a wheel of stone, iron, or wood into grooves, leaving prismatic or crystal-like elevations between them.
—flint glass Soft optical lead-oxide glass of high refraction.
—ground glass Glass having a smooth, semi-opaque surface that diffuses light.
—lime glass Plate, window, and container glass; made of lime and soda.
—milk glass Opaque milky glass containing cryolite.
—optical glass High-quality glass specialized in refractive and dispersive powers for lenses.
—plate glass Sheets of glass poured, rolled, and polished: used for mirrors and display windows.
—safety glass Glass in two sheets enclosing a film of transparent adhesive plastic tightly pressed between them; laminated glass: often called *shatterproof glass.*
—stained glass Glass colored by the addition of pigments in the form of metallic oxides: used decoratively, as for church windows.
—window glass Ordinary blown glass, flattened from cylinder shapes.
—wire glass Glass sheets reinforced with wire netting. **2** Any fused substance resembling glass. **3** Any article made of glass, as a window pane, a goblet or tumbler, a mirror, spectacles, etc. **4** A telescope; also, a barometer. **5** A glass devised for measuring time by the passage of sand or the like through an orifice. See HOURGLASS. **6** The contents of a glass or drinking vessel: He drank a *glass* of wine. **7** Glassware collectively. — *v.t.* **1** To enclose with glass. **2** To reflect; mirror. **3** To give a glazed surface to. — *adj.* Made of, relating to, or like glass. [OE *glæs*]

glass bead Any small, solid or hollow sphere of glass.

glass·blow·ing (glas′blō′ing, gläs′-) *n.* The process of blowing viscid molten glass into any desired form. **—glass′-blow·er** *n.*

glass furnace A furnace for fusing the materials of which glass is made, or one for remelting glass frit and making it ready for working.

glass gall A porous scum of impurities formed on the surface of molten glass.

glass·house (glas′hous′, gläs′-) *n.* **1** A factory where glass is made. **2** *Brit.* A hothouse or greenhouse.

glass paper Paper coated with glue and sprinkled with powdered glass: used as an abrasive.

glass snake **1** A slender legless lizard of the southern United States (*Ophisaurus ventralis*) having a very brittle tail. **2** A similar Old World snakelike lizard (*O. apus*).

glass·ware (glas′wâr′, gläs′-) *n.* Articles made of glass.

CHAMPAGNE   CLARET   SHERRY   LIQUEUR

WATER   LONG DRINKS   OLD-FASHIONED   COCKTAIL

GLASSWARE FOR MODERN TABLE USE

glass·wool (glas′wŏŏl′, gläs′-) *n.* Fibers of spun glass of wool-like appearance: used in fireproofing fabrics, as insulator material, as a filter, and in draining wounds.

glass·work (glas′wûrk′, gläs′-) *n.* **1** The manufacture of glass articles, etc. **2** Articles made of glass. **—glass′work′er** *n.*

glass·worm (glas′wûrm′, gläs′-) *n.* The arrowworm.

glass·wort (glas′wûrt′, gläs′-) *n.* Any of several low saline seaside herbs (genus *Salicornia*) whose ashes were formerly used in glassmaking.

glass·y (glas′ē, gläs′ē) *adj.* **glass·i·er, glass·i·est** **1** Composed of or like glass; having a hard, fixed appearance. **2** Fixed, blank, and uncomprehending: a *glassy* stare. **—glass′i·ly** *adv.* **—glass′i·ness** *n.*

Glauber's salts A white crystalline sodium sulfate, used medicinally as a cathartic. Also **Glauber salt.**

glau·cine (glô′sēn, -sin) *n. Biochem.* A yellowish, bitter, crystalline alkaloid, $C_{21}H_{25}O_4N$, from the sap of the yellow-horned poppy (*Glaucium flavum*): it suspends heart action and inhibits muscular activity.

glauco– *combining form* Bluish-gray: *glauconite.* Also, before vowels, **glauc–.** [< Gk. *glaukos* bluish-gray]

glau·co·ma (glô·kō′mə) *n. Pathol.* An affection of the eye characterized by opacity of the vitreous humor and impaired vision that may, if not given early therapeutic treatment, lead to blindness. [< L < Gk. *glaukōma* < *glaukos* bluish-gray] **—glau·com·a·tous** (glô·kom′ə·təs) *adj.*

glau·co·nite (glô′kə·nīt) *n.* An amorphous, olive-green, loosely granular, massive hydrous silicate, chiefly of iron and potassium, found in greensand. [< Gk. *glaukon,* neut. of *glaukos* bluish-gray + -ITE¹]

glau·cous (glô′kəs) *adj.* **1** Having a yellowish-green color; also, sea green. **2** *Bot.* Covered with a bluish-white bloom, as grapes, blueberries, etc. [< L *glaucus* < Gk. *glaukos* bluish-gray]

glaze (glāz) *v.* **glazed, glaz·ing** *v.t.* **1** To fit, as a window, with glass panes. **2** To provide (a building, etc.) with windows. **3** To coat, as pottery, with a glasslike surface applied by fusing. **4** To cover with a glaze, as meat or biscuits. **5** To make glossy, as by polishing. **6** In painting, to cover with a thin, transparent color so as to modify the tone. — *v.i.* **7** To become glassy; take on a glaze. — *n.* **1** A smooth, shining, transparent surface; a glossy coating, or a substance used to produce it, as on pottery or tiles: distinguished from *enamel.* **2** A sheet of ice; an icy surface. **3** Stock or icing cooked to a thin paste and applied to the surface of meat, fish, vegetables, fruits, or nuts. [ME *glasen* < *glas* glass] **—glaz′er** *n.* **—glaz′i·ness** *n.* **—glaz′y** *adj.*

gla·zier (glā′zhər) *n.* **1** One who fits panes of glass. **2** One who applies glaze to pottery. **—gla′zier·y** *n.*

glaz·ing (glā′zing) *n.* **1** A glaze; material used to produce a glaze. **2** The act or art of applying glaze. **3** Window panes collectively; glasswork. **4** The act or art of setting glass.

gleam (glēm) *n.* **1** A moderate light; a passing or intermittent glimmer; flash. **2** Something likened to a flash of light: a *gleam* of wit. See synonyms under LIGHT. — *v.i.* **1** To shine or glitter with a gleam or gleams. **2** To appear clearly and briefly, as a signal fire. — *v.t.* **3** To show with a gleam or gleams: His eyes *gleamed* hatred. See synonyms under SHINE. [OE *glæm.* Akin to GLIM, GLIMMER.]

glean (glēn) *v.t. & v.i.* **1** To collect (information, facts, etc.) by patient effort. **2** To gather (the leavings) from a field after the crop has been reaped. **3** To gather the leavings from (a field, etc.). [< OF *glener* < LL *glenare* < Celtic] **—glean′er** *n.*

glean·ing (glē′ning) *n.* **1** *pl.* That which is collected by a gleaner; a remaining portion. **2** The act of a gleaner.

gle·ba (glē′bə) *n. pl.* **·bae** (-bē) *Bot.* The chambered spore-bearing tissue within the closed sac or peridium of a puffball fungus. [< NL < L, a clod]

glede (glēd) *n.* **1** The European kite (genus *Milvus*). **2** Any of several similar birds. Also **gled** (gled). [OE *glida*]

glee (glē) *n.* **1** Mirth; gaiety; merriment. **2** A

musical composition for three or more voices, without accompaniment. See synonyms under LAUGHTER. [OE *glēo*] — **glee'some** (-səm) *adj.*

glee club A musical club or group organized, formerly, to sing glees, now, any songs.

glee·ful (glē'fəl) *adj.* Feeling or exhibiting glee; mirthful. — **glee'ful·ly** *adv.* — **glee'ful·ness** *n.*

glee·man (glē'mən) *n. pl.* **-men** (-mən) *Archaic* A wandering singer or minstrel.

gleet (glēt) *Pathol. n.* **1 a** A slimy mucous discharge succeeding inflammation of the urethra. **b** A chronic discharge from any mucous membrane. **2** A chronic discharge from the nasal cavities, as in horses. — *v.i.* To emit a thin, watery liquid; ooze. [<OF *glette* mucus, pus] — **gleet'y** *adj.*

glei·za·tion (glī·zā'shən) *n. Geol.* The process by which moisture acts upon rock materials to produce a greenish or bluish waterlogged soil, often with formation of peat bogs.

glen (glen) *n.* A small, secluded valley. [<Scottish Gaelic *glenn*]

Glen·coe (glen·kō') A valley in Argyllshire, Scotland; scene of massacre of the MacDonalds by the Campbells and the English, 1692.

gle·noid (glē'noid) *adj.* **1** *Anat.* Hollowed like a shallow pit, as the articular cavities or fossae of the scapula and the temporal bone. **2** Having a shallow cavity. [<Gk. *glēnoeidēs* like a socket <*glēnē* a socket]

gli·a·din (glī'ə·din) *n. Biochem.* Any of a group of simple proteins derived from the gluten of wheat, rye, or other grains. [<F *gliadine* <Gk. *glia* glue]

glib (glib) *adj.* **glib·ber, glib·best 1** Speaking with smooth fluency without much thought: a *glib* talker. **2** More facile than sincere: a *glib* compliment. **3** Characterized by easiness or quickness, as of manner. [Cf. obs. *glibbery* <MLG *glibberich* slippery] — **glib'ly** *adv.* — **glib'ness** *n.*

glide (glīd) *v.* **glid·ed, glid·ing** *v.i.* **1** To move, slip, or flow smoothly or easily. **2** To pass unnoticed or imperceptibly, as time: often with *by.* **3** *Aeron.* To descend gradually and without the use of motor power: also, to operate or fly in a glider. **4** *Music & Phonet.* To produce a glide. — *v.t.* **5** To cause to glide. — *n.* **1** The act of gliding; a gliding motion. **2** *Music* An unbroken passage from tone to tone; a slur. **3** *Phonet.* **a** A transitional sound made in passing from the position of one speech sound to that of another, as the (w) heard between (ōō) and (a) in *bivouac.* **b** A semivowel. **4** A gliding step in waltzing; also, a waltz in which this movement is used. **5** The movement of a glider. [OE *glīdan*]

glid·er (glī'dər) *n.* **1** One who or that which glides. **2** *Aeron.* An aircraft similar in general structure to an airplane but without an engine, supported by rising currents of air. **3** A couch hung in a metal frame and arranged so as to glide back and forth. **4** *Austral.* A flying phalanger: also **gliding possum.**

GLIDER—TWO-SEATED TRAINER

glid·ing (glī'ding) *n.* The act of one who or that which glides. — *adj.* Having the action or motion of a glide.

gliding angle See under ANGLE.

gliding plane *Mineral.* A plane parallel to which a differential movement of the parts of a crystal can take place without rupture.

gliding range *Aeron.* The greatest distance that can be traveled by an aircraft from a given height under normal gliding conditions. Also **gliding distance.**

glim·mer (glim'ər) *v.i.* **1** To shine with a faint, unsteady light; flicker. **2** To appear fitfully or faintly. — *n.* **1** A faint, unsteady light; a flickering gleam. **2** A momentary apprehension; glimpse; a vague idea: a *glimmer* of the truth. See synonyms under LIGHT[1]. [ME *glimeren* shine. Akin to GLEAM.]

glimpse (glimps) *n.* **1** A momentary view or look. **2** A swift, passing appearance. **3** An inkling. **4** A sudden, passing gleam. — *v.* **glimpsed, glimps·ing** *v.t.* **1** To see for an in-

stant; catch a glimpse of. — *v.i.* **2** To look for an instant; glance. [ME *glimsen* shine faintly. Akin to GLEAM.]

glint (glint) *v.i.* **1** To gleam; glitter. **2** To move quickly; glance aside. — *v.t.* **3** To reflect; shine. — *n.* **1** A gleam; flash. **2** *Scot.* A glimpse. [ME *glinten*, var. of *glenten* shine <Scand. Cf. dial. Sw. *glänta* shine.]

gli·o·ma (glī·ō'mə) *n. pl.* **-ma·ta** *Pathol.* A tumor containing elements similar to neuroglia cells, occurring in connective tissue. [<NL <Gk. *glia* glue + *-ōma* -OMA] — **gli·o·ma·tous** (glī·ō'mə·təs, -om'ə-) *adj.*

gli·o·sa (glī·ō'sə) *n. Anat.* The gray matter which surrounds the central canal of the spinal cord. [<NL <Gk. *glia* glue]

glis·sade (gli·säd', -sād') *v.i.* **-sad·ed, -sad·ing** To slide or glide. — *n.* **1** The act of gliding down a slope, as of ice or snow. **2** A sliding step in dancing; glide. [<F <*glisser* slip]

glis·san·do (gli·sän'dō) *n. pl.* **-di** (-dē) A gliding effect, as in the playing of a run on the piano by sliding a finger rapidly over the keys. [<F *glissant*, ppr. of *glisser* slip + Ital. *-ando*, ppr. suffix]

glis·ten (glis'ən) *v.i.* To sparkle, especially with reflected light; shine; gleam. See synonyms under SHINE. — *n.* A shining, as by reflection from a wet surface. See synonyms under LIGHT[1]. [OE *glisnian* shine] — **glis'ten·ing** *adj.*

glit·ter (glit'ər) *v.i.* **1** To shine with a gleaming light; sparkle. **2** To be bright or colorful. — *n.* Sparkle; brilliancy. See synonyms under LIGHT[1]. [<ON *glitra*]

glit·ter·y (glit'ər·ē) *adj.* Having, or shining with, a glitter.

gloat (glōt) *v.i.* To look with cruel or triumphant satisfaction; think about something with exultation or avarice: usually with *over.* [Cf. ON *glotta* grin]

glob·al (glō'bəl) *adj.* **1** Spherical. **2** Pertaining to or involving the world in its entirety: *global* war. **3** *Pathol.* Entire; all-inclusive: *global* aphasia.

globe (glōb) *n.* **1** A perfectly round body; ball; sphere. **2** The earth: with the definite article. **3** A sphere on which is a map of the earth or of the heavens: also **terrestrial** or **celestial globe. 4** A hollow globular vessel or the like. **5** Any planetary or celestial body. **6** A ball, usually of gold, borne as an emblem of authority. — *v.t. & v.i.* **globed, glob·ing** To form into a globe. [<F <L *globus* ball]

globe·fish (glōb'fish') *n. pl.* **·fish** or **·fish·es** **1** A teleost fish (*Diodon hystrix*) of tropical seas, covered with long, horny spines and able, when disturbed, to inflate its body into a globular form: also called *porcupine fish.* **2** A puffer.

globe·flow·er (glōb'flou'ər) *n.* Any of a genus (*Trollius*) of ranunculaceous plants having globular, yellow flowers.

GLOBEFISH
a. Normal. *b.* Inflated.
(About 7 inches long)

globe·trot·ter (glōb'trot'ər) *n.* A habitual traveler; especially, one who travels all over the world. — **globe'-trot'ting** *n. & adj.*

glo·bin (glō'bin) *n. Biochem.* A protein constituent of red blood corpuscles. [<L *globus* a ball + -IN]

glo·bose (glō'bōs) *adj.* Spherical. Also **glo'bous** (-bəs). [<L *globosus* <*globus* a ball] — **globose'ness** *n.* — **glo·bos·i·ty** (glō·bos'ə·tē) *n.*

glob·u·lar (glob'yə·lər) *adj.* **1** Spherical. **2** Formed of globules. **3** World-wide.

glob·u·lar·in (glob'yə·lər·in) *n.* A white, bitter powder, $C_{15}H_{20}O_8$, obtained from the leaves of the globe daisy (*Globularia alypum*): a glucoside similar to caffeine in action.

glob·ule (glob'yōol) *n.* **1** A small globe or spherical particle. **2** A small pill. **3** *Med.* A corpuscle (def. 3). [<F <L *globulus*, dim. of *globus* a ball]

glob·u·li·cide (glob'yə·lə·sīd') *n.* An agent destructive of red blood corpuscles. — **glob·u·li·ci'dal** *adj.*

glob·u·lif·er·ous (glob'yə·lif'ər·əs) *adj.* **1** Having or containing globules. **2** Containing red blood corpuscles.

glob·u·lim·e·ter (glob'yə·lim'ə·tər) *n.* An instrument for determining the number of red blood corpuscles in a given amount of blood.

glob·u·lin (glob'yə·lin) *n. Biochem.* Any one of a class of simple plant and animal proteins, insoluble in water but soluble in dilute saline solutions. [<GLOBULE]

glo·chid·i·ate (glō·kid'ē·āt) *adj. Biol.* Barbed, as hairs and bristles.

glo·chid·i·um (glō·kid'ē·əm) *n. pl.* **·chid·i·a** (-kid'ē·ə) *Zool.* A larva of a mussel with a bivalve embryonic shell provided with hooked processes by which it may attach itself to a fish and there pass a brief phase of its life. [<NL, dim. of Gk. *glōchis* point of an arrow]

GLOCKENSPIEL

glock·en·spiel (glok'ən·spēl) *n.* **1** A portable musical instrument consisting of a series of metal bars tuned in chromatic range and played by striking with two wooden or composition hammers. **2** A set of bells; a carillon. [<G *glocken* bells + *spiel* play]

glom·er·ule (glom'ər·ōol) *n. Bot.* A cymose flower cluster which is condensed into a head-like form. [<F <NL *glomerulus*, dim. of *glomus*, *-eris* a mass]

glo·mer·u·lus (glə·mer'yə·ləs) *n. pl.* **·li** (-lī) **1** A glomerule. **2** *Anat.* A coil of blood vessels forming a small tuft at the expanded end of each uriniferous tubule. [<NL. See GLOMERULE.]

glon·o·in (glon'ō·in) *n.* Nitroglycerin, especially as used in medicine. Also **glon'o·ine** (-in, -ēn). [<GL(YCERIN) + O, oxygen, and NO_3, nitric anhydride + -IN]

gloom (glōōm) *n.* **1** Partial or total darkness; heavy shadow. **2** Darkness or depression of the mind or spirits. **3** A dark or gloomy place. **4** *Scot.* A sulky look; frown. [< *v.*] — *v.i.* **1** To look sullen, displeased, or dejected. **2** To be or become dark or threatening. — *v.t.* **3** To make dark, sad, or sullen. ◆ Homophone: *glume.* [ME *glom(b)en* look sad]

gloom·ing (glōō'ming) *n.* **1** Gloaming. **2** A frown; sulky fit.

gloom·y (glōō'mē) *adj.* **gloom·i·er, gloom·i·est 1** Dark; dismal; obscure. **2** Affected with gloom or melancholy; morose. **3** Productive of gloom or melancholy. See synonyms under DARK, MOROSE, SAD. — **gloom'i·ly** *adv.* — **gloom'i·ness** *n.*

glo·ri·a (glôr'ē·ə, glō'rē·ə) *n.* **1** *Eccl.* A hymn or ascription of praise to God; a doxology. **2** *Eccl. Usually cap.* **a** A movement of the mass, following the Kyrie, during which the *Gloria in excelsis* is sung. **b** In the Anglican and some other churches, a similar section in the Eucharist. **3** A musical setting for a gloria, especially the *Gloria in excelsis.* **4** A gloriole; glory. **5** An ornament for the head in imitation of a gloriole. **6** A mixture of wool and silk or similar material, used as a substitute for silk in covering umbrellas and in dressmaking. [<L, glory]

Gloria in ex·cel·sis (ek·sel'sis) **1** A Latin doxology beginning *Gloria in excelsis*; the greater doxology. **2** An English translation of this. [<LL *Gloria in excelsis (Deo)* Glory (to God) in the highest. See *Luke* ii 14.]

glo·ri·fy (glôr'ə·fī, glō'rə-) *v.t.* **·fied, ·fy·ing 1** To give a glorious or exaggerated appearance to: to *glorify* military life. **2** To give exaggerated praise to; extol. **3** To honor or make glorious by prayer or action; worship. **4** To give glory to; make exalted or blessed. See synonyms under PRAISE. [<OF *glorifier* <LL *glorificare* <L *gloria* glory + *facere* make] — **glo'ri·fi'er** *n.*

glo·ri·ous (glôr'ē·əs, glō'rē-) *adj.* ¯ **1** Full of glory; of exalted honor, dignity, or majesty. **2** Extremely delightful; splendid: a *glorious* time. **3** *Obs.* Resplendent. **4** Eager for glory or distinction; vainglorious. See synonyms under BRIGHT, ILLUSTRIOUS. [<L *gloriosus* <*gloria* glory] — **glo'ri·ous·ly** *adv.*

— **glo'ri·ous·ness** *n.*

glo·ry (glôr′ē, glō′rē) *n. pl.* **·ries** 1 Distinguished honor or praise; exalted reputation. 2 Something which occasions praise or renown; an object of praise. 3 Adoration; worshipful praise: give *glory* to God. 4 Splendor; magnificence: the *glory* of Rome. 5 The bliss of heaven: to go to *glory.* 6 A state of exaltation or extreme well-being: He was in his *glory.* 7 Radiance; brilliancy. 8 The emanation of light surrounding the head or the entire figure of a divine being; a nimbus; halo. See synonyms under FAME. — *v.i.* **glo·ried, glo·ry·ing** To rejoice proudly or triumphantly; exult; take pride: with *in.* [<OF *glorie* <L *gloria*]

gloss[1] (glôs, glos) *n.* 1 The brightness or sheen of a polished surface. 2 A deceptive or superficial show. — *v.t.* 1 To make smooth or lustrous, as by polishing or buffing. 2 To hide or attempt to hide (errors, defects, etc.) by falsehood or equivocation: with *over.* — *v.i.* 3 To become shiny. [<Scand. Cf. ON *glossi* blaze, spark.] — **gloss′er** *n.*

gloss[2] (glôs, glos) *n.* 1 An explanatory note; especially, a marginal or interlinear note. 2 A glossary. 3 A plausible explanation to cover fault or defect. — *v.t.* 1 To write marginal explanations for (a text, word, etc.); annotate. 2 To excuse or change by false explanations: to *gloss* the truth of a matter. — *v.i.* 3 To make glosses. [<OF *glose* a note <L *glossa* a difficult word (in a text) <Gk. *glōssa* a foreign word; orig., tongue] — **gloss′er** *n.*

glos·sal (glôs′əl, glos′-) *adj.* Of or pertaining to the tongue; having a tongue; lingual.

glos·sa·rist (glôs′ə·rist, glos′-) *n.* One who writes glosses; also, one who compiles a glossary. Also **glos·sa·tor** (glo·sā′tər, glô-).

glos·sa·ry (glôs′ə·rē, glos′-) *n. pl.* **·ries** 1 A lexicon of the obsolete, obscure, or foreign words of a work. 2 Any explanatory vocabulary, as of a science. [<L *glossarium* <*glossa* GLOSS[2]] — **glos·sar·i·al** (glo·sâr′ē·əl, glô-) *adj.*

glos·sec·to·my (glo·sek′tə·mē, glô-) *n. Surg.* Total or partial removal of the tongue or of a glossal lesion.

glos·si·tis (glo·sī′tis, glô-) *n. Pathol.* Inflammation of the tongue. — **glos·sit·ic** (-sit′ik) *adj.*

glosso- *combining form* The tongue; pertaining to the tongue: *glossography.* Also, before vowels, **gloss-.** [<Gk. *glōssa* tongue]

glos·sog·ra·phy (glo·sog′rə·fē, glô-) *n.* 1 A description of the tongue. 2 The making of glosses or of glossaries. — **glos·sog′ra·pher** *n.*

glos·so·la·li·a (glôs′ə·lā′lē·ə, glos-) *n.* 1 The gift of tongues. 2 (In some Pentecostal churches) A speaking in sounds that do not correspond linguistically to those of any known language.

gloss·y (glôs′ē, glos′ē) *adj.* **gloss·i·er, gloss·i·est** 1 Having a lustrous surface; polished. 2 Outwardly or speciously fair. See synonyms under SMOOTH. — **gloss′i·ly** *adv.* — **gloss′i·ness** *n.*

glost (glôst, glost) *n.* Lead glaze used in making pottery; also, glazed pottery. [Variant of GLOSS[1]]

-glot *combining form* Able to speak, or written in, a number of languages: *polyglot.* [<Gk. *glōtta,* var. of *glōssa* tongue, language]

glot·tal (glot′l) *adj.* Of, pertaining to, or articulated in the glottis.

glottal stop *Phonet.* A sound produced in the larynx by an instantaneous closure of the glottis, as at the beginning of a cough, or in one pronunciation of *bottle:* not a phoneme in English.

glot·tic (glot′ik) *adj.* 1 Of or pertaining to the tongue. 2 Of, pertaining to, or produced by the glottis; glottal. 3 *Obs.* Linguistic.

glot·tis (glot′is) *n. pl.* **·ti·des** (-ə·dēz) *Anat.* The cleft or opening between the vocal folds at the upper orifice of the larynx, the mouth of the windpipe. [<NL <Gk. *glōttis* <*glōtta* tongue]

glove (gluv) *n.* A covering for the hand, having a separate sheath for each finger. —**the gloves** Boxing gloves. — *v.t.* **gloved, glov·ing** 1 To put gloves on. 2 To cover with or as with a glove. 3 To serve as a glove for. [OE *glōf*]

glov·er (gluv′ər) *n.* A maker of or a dealer in gloves.

glow (glō) *v.i.* 1 To give off light and heat, especially without flame; be incandescent. 2 To shine as if greatly heated. 3 To show a strong, bright color; be bright or red, as with heat or anima-

tion; blush. 4 To be animated with strong emotion. 5 To be excessively hot; burn. — *n.* 1 The incandescence of a heated substance. 2 Bright color; redness; flush; ruddiness. 3 Fervid heat; strong emotion or ardor. 4 Bodily warmth, as caused by exercise, etc. See synonyms under LIGHT[1], WARMTH. [OE *glōwan*]

glow-dis·charge (glō′dis-chärj′) *n.* The initial luminous electrical discharge in a gas, as observed in neon lamps, etc.

glow·er (glou′ər) *v.i.* 1 To stare with an angry frown; scowl sullenly. 2 *Scot.* To stare. — *n.* The act of glowering; a fierce or threatening stare. Also *Scot.* **glour, glowr.** [? Freq. of obs. *glow* stare] — **glow′er·ing** *adj.* — **glow′er·ing·ly** *adv.*

glow-fly (glō′flī′) *n.* A firefly.

glow·ing (glō′ing) *adj.* Having a glow; ardent; bright; also, enthusiastic. — **glow′ing·ly** *adv.*

glow lamp An incandescent lamp, usually electrical.

glow potential The voltage marking the beginning of a glow-discharge.

glow-worm (glō′wûrm′) *n.* 1 A European beetle (genus *Lampyris*), the larva and wingless female of which display phosphorescent light. 2 The luminous larva of American fireflies.

glox·in·i·a (glok·sin′ē·ə) *n.* Any plant of a genus (*Sinningia*), with opposite leaves and large bell-shaped spotted flowers. [after B. P. *Gloxin,* 18th century German physician]

glu·ca·gon (glōo′kə·gon) *n.* A hormone secreted by the pancreas that increases the level of sugar in the blood by stimulating the breakdown of glycogen to glucose.

glu·ci·num (glōo·sī′nəm) *n.* The former name for beryllium. [<NL <Gk. *glykys* sweet; because some of its salts are sweet to taste]

glu·cose (glōo′kōs) *n. Chem.* 1 Dextrose or grape sugar; a monosaccharide carbohydrate having the formula $C_6H_{12}O_6$. It is widely distributed in plants and animals and is obtained by the hydrolysis of starch and other carbohydrates. It is fermentable but less sweet than cane sugar. 2 A thick yellowish sirup containing dextrose, maltose, and dextrin, obtained by incomplete hydrolysis of starch and used in confectionery, baking, etc. [<Gk. *glykys* sweet + -OSE[2]] —**glu·cos′ic** (-kos′ik) *adj.*

glue (glōo) *n.* 1 A viscid cement or adhesive preparation, usually a form of impure gelatin derived from boiling certain animal substances, as skin, bones, and cartilage, in water. It is a typical colloid. 2 Any of a number of sticky substances. — *v.t.* **glued, glu·ing** To stick or fasten with or as with glue. [<OF *glu* birdlime <LL *glus, glutis*] —**glue′y** *adj.*

glum (glum) *adj.* **glum·mer, glum·mest** Moody and silent; sullen. [Akin to GLOOM] —**glum′ly** *adv.* —**glum′ness** *n.*

glume (glōom) *n. Bot.* A chafflike scale on the lowest bracts of a grass spikelet. ◆ Homophone: *gloom.* [<L *gluma* husk]

glut[1] (glut) *v.* **glut·ted, glut·ting** *v.t.* 1 To fill or supply to excess; satiate; gorge. 2 To supply (the market) with an excessive quantity of an article and bring on a lowering of prices. — *v.i.* 3 To eat gluttonously; gormandize. See synonyms under PAMPER, SATISFY. — *n.* 1 An excessive supply; plethora. 2 A full supply. 3 The condition of being glutted; act of glutting. [<obs. *glut* a glutton <OF *gloutir* swallow <L *glutire*]

glut[2] (glut) *n.* A wooden wedge used in splitting logs. [Cf. dial. *clut* a cleat]

glu·te·al (glōo·tē′əl, glōo′tē·əl) *adj. Anat.* Of or pertaining to the muscles of the buttocks. [<GLUTEUS]

glu·te·lin (glōo′tə·lin) *n. Biochem.* Any of a class of simple proteins found in certain plants, as wheat. [<GLUTEN + *-lin,* an arbitrary ending]

glu·ten (glōot′n) *n.* A mixture of plant proteins found in cereal grains; a tough, sticky substance obtained by washing out the starch from wheat flour: used as an adhesive and thickener. [<L, glue] —**glu′te·nous** *adj.*

glu·te·us (glōo·tē′əs) *n. pl.* **·te·i** (-tē′ī) *Anat.* Any of three muscles in the region of the buttocks. [<NL <Gk. *gloutos* rump]

glu·ti·nous (glōo′tə·nəs) *adj.* 1 Resembling glue; sticky. 2 Pervaded with sticky matter. See synonyms under ADHESIVE. — **glu′ti·nous·ly** *adv.* — **glu′ti·nous·ness** *n.*

glut·ton[1] (glut′n) *n.* 1 One who gluts himself; an excessive eater. 2 One who has an excessive appetite for anything. [<OF *glouton* <L *gluto, -onis* a glutton]

glut·ton[2] (glut′n) *n.* A musteline carnivore; the wolverine *(Gulo luscus),* especially the Old World form. [Trans. of G *vielfrass* great eater]

glut·ton·ous (glut′ən·əs) *adj.* Voracious. — **glut′ton·ous·ly** *adv.*

glut·ton·y (glut′ən·ē) *n. pl.* **·ton·ies** The act or habit of eating to excess.

gly·cer·ic (gli·ser′ik, glis′ər-) *adj.* Of or derived from glycerol.

glyceric acid *Chem.* A colorless, sirupy compound, $C_3H_6O_4$, formed during alcoholic fermentation and by oxidizing glycerol with nitric acid.

glyc·er·ide (glis′ər·īd, -id) *n. Chem.* An ether or ester of glycerol with a fatty acid.

glyc·er·in (glis′ər·in) See GLYCEROL. Also **glyc′er·ine** (-in, -ēn).

glyc·er·ol (glis′ər·ōl, -ol) *n. Chem.* A sweet, oily, nearly colorless trihydric alcohol, $C_3H_8O_3$, formed by decomposition of natural fats with alkalis or superheated steam; also obtained from petroleum products. Also called *glycerin.* [<Gk. *glykeros* sweet + -OL[2]]

glyc·er·yl (glis′ər·il) *n. Chem.* The trivalent glycerol radical C_3H_5. [<GLYCER(IN) + -YL]

gly·cine (glī′sēn, glī·sēn′) *n. Chem.* A sweet, colorless amino acid, $C_2H_5O_2N$, obtained from various proteins. [<Gk. *glykys* sweet + -INE[2]]

gly·co·gen (glī′kə·jən) *n. Biochem.* A white, mealy, amorphous polysaccharide, $(C_6H_{10}O_5)_x$, contained in animal tissues, principally the liver: also called *animal starch.* [<Gk. *glykys* sweet + -GEN]

gly·co·gen·ase (glī′kə·jə·nās′) *n. Biochem.* An enzyme present in the liver which converts glycogen to a saccharide. [<GLYCOGEN + -ASE]

gly·co·gen·ic (glī′kə·jen′ik) *adj.* 1 Relating to the formation of glycogen. 2 Caused by glycogen.

gly·col (glī′kōl, -kol) *n. Chem.* 1 A colorless, sweetish compound, $C_2H_6O_2$, formed by decomposing certain ethylene compounds: used as a solvent, as a freezing mixture, and in the manufacture of explosives, intermediates, etc. 2 Any dihydroxyl alcohol of the glycol group having the general formula $C_nH_{2n}(OH)_2$. [<GLYC(ERIN) + -OL[1]]

gly·col·ic acid (glī·kol′ik) *Chem.* An acid, $C_2H_4O_3$, found in the juice of cane sugar and unripe grapes: also made synthetically.

glyph (glif) *n.* 1 *Archit.* A vertical groove or channel, as in a Doric frieze. Compare TRIGLYPH. 2 A picture or carving representing an idea; hieroglyph. [<Gk. *glyphē* a carving <*glyphein* carve] — **glyph′ic** *adj.*

glyp·tic (glip′tik) *adj.* 1 Pertaining to carving or engraving. 2 Exhibiting figures, as in a mineral. [<Gk. *glyptikos* <*glyphē* a carving]

glyp·to·dont (glip′tə·dont) *n.* Any of a genus *(Glyptodon)* of extinct American armadillos. [<NL *Glyptodon* <Gk. *glyptos* carved + *odous, odontos* a tooth]

GLYPTODONT
(From 12 to 14 feet long)

glyp·to·graph (glip′tə·graf, -gräf) *n.* A design cut on a gem. — **glyp·tog·ra·pher** (glip·tog′rə·fər) *n.* — **glyp′to·graph′ic** *adj.*

glyp·tog·ra·phy (glip·tog′rə·fē) *n.* 1 The art or operation of engraving on gems. 2 The study of engraved gems. [<Gk. *glyptos* carved + -GRAPHY]

gnar (när) *v.i.* **gnarred, gnar·ring** To snarl or growl. Also **gnarr.** [Imit.]

gnarl[1] (närl) *v.i.* To snarl; growl. [Freq. of GNAR]

gnarl[2] (närl) *n.* A protuberance on a tree; a tough knot. [Back formation from GNARLED]

gnarled (närld) *adj.* Exhibiting gnarls; knotty; cross-grained; distorted. Also **gnarl′y.** [Var. of KNURLED]

gnash (nash) *v.t.* 1 To grind or snap (the teeth) together, as in rage or pain. 2 To bite or chew with grinding teeth. — *v.i.* 3 To grind the teeth together. — *n.* A snap or bite of the teeth. [Var. of obs. *gnast* <Scand. Cf. ON *gnista* gnash.]

gnat (nat) *n.* **1** Any of various small dipterous flies with long, many-jointed antennae, as the buffalo gnats, punkies, and midges. **2** A mosquito. [OE *gnæt*]

gnath·ic (nath′ik) *adj.* Of or pertaining to the jaw. [<Gk. *gnathos* jaw]

gnathic index A measure of the prominence of the jaw, expressed as the ratio of the distance from nasion to basion taken as 100, to the distance from the basion to the alveolar point. Compare illustration under FACIAL ANGLE.

gnatho- *combining form* Jaw: *gnathostome.* [<Gk. *gnathos* jaw]

gna·thon·ic (na-thon′ik) *adj.* Fawning; flattering. [after *Gnatho,* a sycophant in Terence's *Eunuchus*]

gnath·o·stome (nath′ə·stōm) *n.* Any of a division (*Gnathostomata*) of vertebrates having mouths provided with jaws.

-gnathous *combining form* Jaw: *prognathous.* [<Gk. *gnathos* jaw + -OUS]

gnaw (nô) *v.t.* **gnawed, gnawed** or **gnawn, gnaw·ing 1** To bite or eat away little by little with or as with the teeth. **2** To make by gnawing: to *gnaw* a hole. **3** To bite on repeatedly: He *gnawed* his lip in rage. **4** To torment or oppress with fear, pain, etc. —*v.i.* **5** To bite, chew, or corrode persistently or continually. **6** To cause constant worry, pain, etc. [OE *gnagan*] —**gnaw′er** *n.*

gneiss (nīs) *n.* **1** A metamorphic rock consisting essentially of the same components as granite but in which there is a more or less distinctly foliated arrangement of the components, and especially of the mica. **2** Any of a number of highly metamorphic rocks containing feldspar. ◆ Homophone: *nice.* [<G] —**gneiss′ic** *adj.*

gnome[1] (nōm) *n.* **1** In folklore, one of a race of dwarfs believed to live underground as guardians of treasure, mines, etc. **2** The pigmy owl of North America. [<F <NL *gnomus*] —**gnom′ish** *adj.*

gnome[2] (nōm) *n.* A pithy proverbial saying; maxim. [<Gk. *gnōmē* thought, maxim]

gno·mic (nō′mik, nom′ik) *adj.* **1** Dealing in maxims. **2** Expressing a maxim or a universal truth. Also **gno′mi·cal.**

gno·mon (nō′mon) *n.* **1** The triangular piece whose shadow points out the time of day on a sundial, or anything, as a pillar, used for a similar purpose. **2** The index of the hour circle of a globe. **3** *Geom.* The figure that remains after a parallelogram has been removed from the corner of a similar but larger parallelogram, as *BCIGDE* or *FCAGHE.* The diagonally opposite parallelograms *ADEB, EHIF,* or *GHED, EFCB,* are called *complements* of each other or of the whole parallelogram. **4** *Math.* One of the terms of an arithmetical series by which polygonal numbers are found: also **gnomonic number.** [<Gk. *gnōmōn* an indicator <*gnō-,* stem of *gignōskein* know]

GNOMON

-gnomy *combining form* Knowledge or art of judging: *physiognomy.* [<Gk. *gnōmē* judgment]

gno·sis (nō′sis) *n.* Cognition; especially, the knowledge of spiritual mysteries; Gnosticism. [<NL <Gk. *gnōsis* knowledge <*gignōskein* know]

-gnosis *combining form* *Med.* Knowledge; recognition: *prognosis.* [<Gk. *gnōsis* knowledge]

gnos·tic (nos′tik) *adj.* Of, pertaining to, or possessing knowledge; claiming esoteric insight or wisdom. Also **gnos′ti·cal.** [<Gk. *gnōstikos* knowing <*gnōsis.* See GNOSIS.] —**gnos′ti·cal·ly** *adv.*

Gnos·tic (nos′tik) *adj.* Of or pertaining to the Gnostics or Gnosticism. —*n.* An adherent or advocate of Gnosticism.

Gnos·ti·cism (nos′tə·siz′əm) *n.* A philosophical and religious system (first to sixth century)

teaching that knowledge rather than faith was the key to salvation.

gnu (noo, nyoo) *n. pl.* **gnus** or **gnu** A South African antelope (genus *Connochaetes*) having an oxlike head with curved horns, a mane, and a long tail; a wildebeest. Also **gnoo.** ◆ Homophone: *new.* [<Kaffir *nqu*]

GNU
(From 4 to 4 1/2 feet high at the shoulder)

go (gō) *v.* **went, gone, go·ing** *v.i.* **1** To proceed or pass along; move, as at a given speed. **2** To move from a place; leave; depart. **3** To move from one place to another for or as for a purpose: She *went* to dress for dinner. **4** To pass away; disappear; end: The opportunity has *gone.* **5** To be free or freed: They let him *go.* **6** To be in motion or operation; work properly: The watch is *going* now. **7** To extend or reach: The pipe *goes* into the next room. **8** To be, continue, or appear in a specified state or condition: Should these crimes *go* unpunished? **9** To pass into a state or condition; become: to *go* insane. **10** To proceed or end in a specified manner: The election *went* badly for him. **11** To be suitable; have its usual place; fit; belong: The music *goes* with these words. **12** To be considered or ranked: a good lunch, as lunches *go.* **13** To be phrased or expressed; have proper form or order: The song *goes* like this. **14** To emit or produce a specified sound or signal: The chain *goes* clank. **15** To attend; engage oneself in an occupation: to *go* to sea; to *go·* fishing. **16** To pass: said of time. **17** To be guided or regulated; conform: to *go* with the times. **18** To be awarded, given, or applied: This *goes* toward canceling the debt. **19** To have recourse; make appeal; resort: to *go* to court. **20** To be known: What name does she *go* by? **21** To be sold or bid for: These shoes will *go* at a high price. **22** To help; tend: This *goes* to prove my argument. **23** To serve as a part; contribute: the graces that *go* to make a lady. **24** To be abolished or surrendered: The poll tax must *go.* **25** To collapse; fail: The walls *went* last in the fire. **26** To subject or put oneself: He *went* to great pains to do it. **27** To die. **28** To be about to do or act: used only in the progressive form and followed by the present infinitive: They were *going* to protest. —*v.t.* **29** To furnish; put up: to *go* bail. **30** To contribute; share: to *go* halves. **31** *Colloq.* To risk or bet; wager. **32** *Colloq.* To put up with; tolerate: I cannot *go* that music. —**to go about 1** To be occupied or busy with. **2** To set about to do (something). **3** *Naut.* To change to the other tack. —**to go around 1** To move about or circulate. **2** To be enough to furnish even shares. —**to go at 1** To attack. **2** To work at. —**to go back on 1** To forsake; be untrue to. **2** To fail to fulfil or abide by. —**to go by 1** To pass. **2** To conform to or be guided by: to *go by* the rules. —**to go for 1** To reach for; try to get: He *went for* his gun. **2** To attack. **3** *Colloq.* To be strongly attracted by. —**to go in for** *Colloq.* **1** To strive for or advocate: to *go in for* social reform. **2** To prefer; have a liking for: to *go in for* classical music. —**to go into 1** To investigate. **2** To take up, as an occupation: He *went into* business for himself. **3** To be contained in: Four *goes into* twelve three times. —**to go in with 1** To join. **2** To share expenses or risks with. —**to go off 1** To explode or be discharged, as a gun. **2** *Colloq.* To succeed; result: How did the party *go off?* —**to go on 1** To act; behave. **2** To happen: What's *going on* here? **3** *Colloq.* To talk aimlessly; chatter. **4** In the theater, to appear on stage. —**to go one better (than)** To surpass by a single degree or quality. —**to go out 1** To cease or be extinguished, as a light. **2** To advance or be drawn forth in sympathy: My heart *goes out* to him. **3** To strike: The union *went out* for higher wages. **4** To become obsolete. **5** To go to social affairs, the theater, etc. —**to go**

over 1 To turn on its side: The car *went over.* **2** To rehearse; repeat. **3** To examine closely or carefully. **4** *Colloq.* To succeed. —**to go through 1** To search thoroughly. **2** To experience; undergo. **3** To practice, as a role or part. **4** To be passed, as legislation. **5** To spend completely; use up: to *go through* a fortune. —**to go through with** To complete; undertake to finish. —**to go together 1** To be suitable; harmonize. **2** *Colloq.* To keep company, as sweethearts. —**to go under 1** To be overwhelmed or conquered. **2** To fail, as a business. —**to go up** To increase, as prices or values. —**to go with 1** To be suitable to; harmonize with. **2** *Colloq.* To keep company with. —**to go without** To do or be without. —**to let go of 1** To release one's hold of. **2** To abandon one's interest or share in. —*n.* **1** The act of going: the come and *go* of the seasons. **2** *Colloq.* The capacity for energetic action; vigor: He has plenty of *go.* **3** *Colloq.* A try; attempt: to have a *go* at something. **4** *Colloq.* A success: He made a *go* of it. **5** *Colloq.* A bargain. **6** *Colloq.* The fashion; mode: with *the.* **7** *Colloq.* A proceeding; turn of affairs. —**no go** *Colloq.* Useless; hopeless. —**on the go** *Colloq.* Busy; in constant motion. —*adj. Aerospace* Operating or proceeding as planned. [OE *gān*] —**go′er** *n.*

go·a (gō′ə) *n.* A black-tailed gazelle (*Procapra picticaudata*) of the mountains of Tibet. [<Tibetan *dgoba*]

goad (gōd) *n.* **1** A point set in the end of a stick for urging oxen or other beasts. **2** Something that spurs or incites. —*v.t.* To prick or drive with or as with a goad; incite. See synonyms under INCENSE[1], PIQUE[1], SPUR. [OE *gād*]

goads·man (gōdz′mən) *n. pl.* **·men** (-mən) A driver of oxen, cattle, etc.

goal (gōl) *n.* **1** A point toward which effort or movement is directed; the objective point or terminus that one is striving to reach; the end aimed at: the *goal* of one's ambition. **2** In any game, race, contest, or competition, a mark, line, post, pole, or the like, made or set up to indicate the limit, winning point, or safety place of the game; in football, a pair of upright posts, **goal posts,** with a crosspiece over which the players strive to kick the ball. **3** In football and similar games, the act of propelling the ball over or past the goal, so as to win a point; also, the point so won. See synonyms under AIM, END. [ME *gol*; origin uncertain]

goal·keep·er (gōl′kē′pər) *n.* In certain games, as hockey, soccer, etc., a player stationed to protect the goal. Also **goal′tend′er.**

go·an·na (gō-an′ə) *n.* Any of several large, predatory, Australian lizards (family *Varanidae*) resembling the iguana, especially the black-and-yellow tree goanna (*Varanus varius*). [Alter. of IGUANA]

Goa powder A bitter yellow powder found in cavities of the Brazilian araroba tree (*Andira araroba*): used in medicine.

goat (gōt) *n.* **1** A hollow-horned ruminant (genus *Capra*) of rocky and mountainous regions, related to the sheep and including wild and domesticated forms. ◆ Collateral adjective: *hircine.* **2** A lecherous man. **3** *Slang* A scapegoat; the butt of a joke. —**to get one's goat** *Slang* To get a strong reaction (from someone) by teasing, tormenting, etc. [OE *gāt*] —**goat′like′** *adj.*

goat antelope Any of certain ruminant mammals related to the goats and antelopes, as the chamois, Rocky Mountain goat, etc.

goat·beard (gōt′bird′) *n.* **1** A European plant, the salsify (*Tragopogon pratensis*) with long, feathery pappus, naturalized in the United States. **2** A perennial herb of the rose family (*Aruncus sylvester*) with long compound panicles of whitish flowers. Also **goats′beard′.**

goat·ee (gō·tē′) *n.* A man's beard so trimmed as to resemble the pointed beard of a goat.

goat·fish (gōt′fish′) *n. pl.* **·fish** or **·fish·es 1** A tropical marine fish of the mullet family, having a beardlike appendage below the mouth, especially the European red mullet, esteemed as a food fish. **2** The European filefish.

goats·rue (gōts′roo′) *n.* **1** A hardy perennial herb (*Galega officinalis*) of the Old World. **2** An American herb of the pea family (*Taph-*

rosia virginiana).

goat·suck·er (gōt′suk′ər) *n.* **1** Any of numerous nocturnal, insectivorous birds (family *Caprimulgidae*) with flattened heads and wide mouths, as the whippoorwill or nighthawk. **2** The frogmouth.

gob (gob) *n.* A small piece, mass, or chunk; a lump. [<OF *gobe* mouthful, lump, ? <Celtic]

gobbe (gob) *n.* A creeping annual (*Voandzeia subterranea*), resembling the common peanut: much cultivated in Africa and South America. [< native Cariban name]

gob·bet (gob′it) *n.* **1** A piece or fragment, especially a morsel of cooked meat, highly seasoned. **2** A chunk; lump. **3** *Archaic* A mouthful. [<OF *gobet,* dim. of *gobe* GOB¹]

gob·ble¹ (gob′əl) *v.* **gob·bled, gob·bling** *v.t.* **1** To swallow (food) greedily and in gulps. **2** *U.S. Slang* To seize or acquire in a grasping manner. — *v.i.* **3** To eat greedily and quickly. [<F *gover* bolt, devour] — **gob′bler** *n.*

gob·ble² (gob′əl) *n.* The sound made by the turkey cock. — *v.i.* **gob·bled, gob·bling** To utter a gobble, as turkeys. [Var. of GABBLE]

gob·let (gob′lit) *n.* **1** A drinking vessel with a stem and no handle. **2** A large, shallow bowl or drinking vessel for ceremonious or festive occasions. [<OF *gobelet,* dim. of *gobel* a drinking cup <Celtic]

gob·lin (gob′lin) *n.* A supernatural, grotesque creature regarded as malicious or mischievous. [<OF *gobelin* <Med. L *gobelinus,* ? <Gk. *kobalos* a rogue]

go·bo (gō′bō) *n. pl.* **·bos** **1** A portable sound–absorbing panel used to control sound effects in motion–picture production. **2** A device for shielding the lens of a television camera from the direct rays of light. [Origin uncertain]

gob·stick (gob′stik′) *n.* An implement for removing a hook from a fish's mouth. [<dial. E *gob* the mouth + STICK]

go·by (gō′bē) *n. pl.* **·by** or **·bies** Any of a widely distributed family (*Gobiidae*) of spiny–rayed, chiefly marine fishes having ventral fins united into a funnel–shaped suction disk, as the rock goby (*Gobius paganellus*) and the California blind goby (genus *Typhlogobius*). [<L *gobius* <Gk. *kōbios,* a small fish]

go·cart (gō′kärt′) *n.* **1** A light framework on rollers designed to support a baby learning to walk. **2** A small, light, baby carriage having the front wheels smaller than the rear. **3** A light carriage.

god (god) *n.* **1** A being regarded as possessing superhuman or supernatural qualities or powers, and made an object of worship or propitiation; a higher intelligence supposed to control the forces of good and of evil; a personification of any of the forces of nature or of some human attribute, interest, or relation; a divinity; deity. **2** Any person or thing exalted as the chief good, or made an object of supreme devotion. **3** Anything that absorbs one's attentions or aspirations: Money is his *god.* **4** The embodiment of some aspect of reality or of some being regarded as the ultimate principle of the universe: the *god* of justice. **5** An image or symbol of a deity; idol. — *v.t.* *Rare* **god·ded, god·ding** To deify; idolize. [OE]

God (god) The one Supreme Being, self–existent and eternal; the infinite creator, sustainer, and ruler of the universe: conceived of as omniscient, good, and almighty.

god·child (god′chīld′) *n.* A child for whom a person becomes sponsor at baptism.

god·daugh·ter (god′dô′tər) *n.* A female godchild.

god·dess (god′is) **1** A female divinity. **2** Figuratively, a woman surpassingly beloved, good, or beautiful. — **god′dess·hood** *n.*

go·dev·il (gō′dev′əl) *n.* **1** A dray sled for hauling rocks, logs, etc. **2** A pointed iron weight dropped into the bore of an oil well to explode the charge of dynamite. **3** A railroad handcar used by work gangs. **4** A jointed, flexible device for cleaning a pipeline of obstructions.

god·fa·ther (god′fä′thər) *n.* A man who becomes sponsor for a child at its baptism or confirmation. — *v.t.* To act as a godfather to.

god·head (god′hed′) *n.* Godhood; divinity.

God·head (god′hed′) *n.* The essential nature of God; the Deity.

god·hood (god′hŏŏd) *n.* The state or quality of being divine.

god·less (god′lis) *adj.* Ungodly; atheistical; wicked. See synonyms under PROFANE. — **god′·less·ness** *n.*

god·like (god′līk′) *adj.* Similar to God or to a god; divine; of supreme excellence or beauty. — **god′like′ness** *n.*

god·ling (god′ling) *n.* A minor divinity.

god·ly (god′lē) *adj.* **·li·er, ·li·est** Filled with reverence and love for God; pious. — **god′li·ly** *adv.* — **god′li·ness** *n.*

god·moth·er (god′muth′ər) *n.* A female sponsor at baptism. — *v.t.* To act as godmother to.

god·par·ent (god′pâr′ənt) *n.* A godfather or godmother.

god·send (god′send′) *n.* An unexpected stroke of good fortune regarded as sent by God. [Earlier *God's send* <GOD + ME *sande* message]

god·ship (god′ship) *n.* The rank or character of a god; deity.

god·son (god′sun′) *n.* A male godchild.

God·speed (god′spēd′) *n.* God speed you: a wish for a safe journey or for success.

God·ward (god′wərd) *adv.* Toward or in connection with God. Also **God′wards.**

god·wit (god′wit) *n.* A curlewlike shore bird (genus *Limosa*) with long legs and a long, tilted bill, as the American marbled godwit (*L. fedoa*). [Origin uncertain]

goe·thite (gō′thīt, gœ′tīt) *n.* An imperfect, adamantine, reddish or blackish–brown ferric hydroxide, crystallizing in the orthorhombic system: also spelled *göthite.* [after Goethe]

gof·fer (gof′ər, gôf′-) *n.* **1** A fluting or crimp. **2** A tool used in crimping lace, paper, etc. — *v.t.* **1** To form plaits or flutes in; crimp, as lace or paper. **2** To raise in relief. Also spelled *gauffer.* [< F *gaufrer* crimp cloth < *gaufre* a honeycomb]

Gog (gog) **and Ma·gog** (mā′gog) In the Bible, the nations, led by Satan, which will war against the kingdom of God. *Rev.* xx 8.

gog·gle (gog′əl) *n.* **1** A rolling of the eyes. **2** *pl.* Spectacles, often with colored lenses, and attachments to fit close to the face as protection against strong light, wind, and dust. [< *v.*] — *adj.* Prominent; staring. — *v.* **gog·gled, gog·gling** *v.i.* **1** To roll the eyes about or stare with bulging eyes. **2** To roll sidewise or stare protrusively: said of the eyes. — *v.t.* **3** To roll (the eyes). [ME *gogelen* look aside, prob. <Celtic]

gog·gle-eye (gog′əl-ī′) *n.* A staring eye. — **gog′gle-eyed′** *adj.*

gog·let (gog′lit) *n.* In the East Indies, a jar or vase of porous pottery for keeping water cool by evaporation: also called *gurglet.* [<Pg. *gorgoleta*]

go-go (gō′gō) *adj.* *Slang* **1** Of or describing discothèques, the usually unrestrained, erotic dances performed there, or the dancers, typically young women, who entertain with such dances. **2** Lively, modern, glamorous, etc. **3** In finance, characterized by rapid speculative trading to realize profit quickly. **4** Aggressively enterprising or ambitious [<F *à gogo* joyfully]

Goi·del·ic (goi·del′ik) *n.* A branch of the Celtic languages including Irish, the Gaelic of the Scottish Highlands, and Manx; Gaelic. — *adj.* Of or pertaining to the Gaels or their languages. Also spelled *Gadelic, Gaedhelic.* Also **Goi·dhel′ic.** [<OIrish *Gōidel* a Gael]

go·ing (gō′ing) *n.* **1** The act of departing or moving; leaving. **2** The condition of the ground, paths, or roads. **3** Style of walking; gait. **4** *Obs.* The manner of conducting oneself; deportment. — **goings·on** *Colloq.* Behavior; conduct; actions: used to express disapproval. — *adj.* **1** Continuing to function: a *going* concern. **2** Arising from continued operation: the *going* value of a business. **3** In existence: available: the best bargain *going.* **4** Departing; leaving. — **going on** *Colloq.* Approaching (a particular age or time).

goi·ter (goi′tər) *n.* *Pathol.* **1** A morbid enlargement of the thyroid gland, variously caused, visible as a swelling on the front part of the neck. **2** The condition itself; bronchocele. See also EXOPHTHALMIC GOITER. Also *goi′tre.* [<F, back formation from *goitreux,* ult. < L *guttur* throat] — **goi′trous** *adj.*

goi·tro·gen (goi′trə·jən) *n.* Any substance capable of initiating or promoting a goiter.

Gol·con·da (gol·kon′də) A city in Hyderabad, India, famous in the 16th century for diamond marketing.

gold (gōld) *n.* **1** A soft, heavy, malleable and ductile metallic element (symbol Au, atomic number 79) found uncombined in nature, resistant to oxidation and to most chemical reagents. See PERIODIC TABLE. **2** The metal in the form of a coin. **3** Wealth; riches. **4** Gilding, or a golden–yellow color. See synonyms under MONEY. — *adj.* Pertaining to, like, made of, containing, or producing gold, or used in mining gold. [OE]

gold basis The basis of values calculated on a gold standard.

gold·beat·er (gōld′bē′tər) *n.* One who makes gold leaf.

gold beetle 1 A leaf beetle (*Coptocycla bicolor*): so called from its metallic luster. **2** A brilliant beetle (family *Chrysomelidae*) found on the sweet potato.

gold·brick (gōld′brik′) *n.* **1** *Colloq.* A brick or bar of base metal gilded, used by swindlers, or a brick or bar of gold for which something else is substituted in delivery to the purchaser; hence, any swindle: also **gold brick. 2** *Slang* A soldier or sailor who shirks or tries to shirk work: also **gold′brick′er.** — *v.t. & v.i.* *Slang* **1** To shirk (work or duty). **2** To cheat.

gold·bug (gōld′bug′) *n.* **1** A gold beetle. **2** *U.S. Colloq.* An advocate of the gold standard.

gold certificate A U.S. Treasury note redeemable in gold at its face value, not now issued.

Gold Coast 1 A former name for GHANA. **2** A section of the African shore line on the Gulf of Guinea between the Ivory Coast and the Slave Coast. **3** *U.S.* Any residential or resort district frequented by rich people.

Gold Coast Colony A former British colony on the coast of western Africa. See GHANA.

gold·dig·ger (gōld′dig′ər) *n.* **1** One who or that which digs for gold. **2** *Colloq.* A woman who uses her personal relations with men to get money and gifts from them.

gold dust Gold in fine particles.

gold·en (gōl′dən) *adj.* **1** Made of or consisting of gold. **2** Having the color or luster of gold; bright–yellow; resplendent. **3** Resembling gold in worth or scarcity; unusually valuable or excellent; rare. **4** Characterized by a condition of great happiness and prosperity: the *golden* age. — **gold′en·ly** *adv.* — **gold′en·ness** *n.*

golden age 1 In Greek and Roman legend, a mythical period when perfect innocence, peace, and happiness reigned. **2** The most flourishing period of a nation's history. **3** In Roman literature, the period (27 B.C. to A.D. 14) of the finest classical writers; hence, in any country, the periods of literature most nearly corresponding to this: also called *Augustan age.*

golden anniversary See under ANNIVERSARY

golden aster A North American perennial (genus *Chrysopsis*) of the composite family, with yellow–rayed flowers.

golden eagle A rare eagle (*Aquila chrysaetos*) ranging throughout the Northern Hemisphere, having dark brown feathers tipped with golden brown at the nape.

gold·en·eye (gōl′dən·ī′) *n.* A large sea duck (*Glaucionetta clangula*) having the upper parts black and the lower parts white.

Golden Fleece In Greek legend, a fleece of gold that hung in a sacred grove in Colchis, guarded by a dragon: stolen by Jason with the aid of Medea. See PHRIXUS.

gold·en·glow (gōl′dən·glō′) *n.* A summer–flowering, erect herb (*Rudbeckia laciniata*) of the composite family, with showy terminal heads of yellow–rayed flowers.

golden goose In Greek legend, a goose that laid golden eggs, killed by its owner who thought to obtain all of them at once.

Golden Legend The name given by Caxton to his translation, published in 1483, of a medieval collection of the lives of the saints, composed in Latin by Jacobus de Voragine, 1230–98, archbishop of Genoa: also called *Legenda Aurea.*

golden mean A wise moderation; the avoidance of extremes.

golden number *Eccl.* A number indicating the place of a year in a Metonic cycle of 19 years, used in calculating the movable feasts.

golden pheasant A vividly colored pheasant (*Chrysolophus pictus*) of China and Tibet.

golden robin The Baltimore oriole.

gold·en·rod (gōl′dən·rod′) *n.* A widely distributed North American biennial or perennial herb (genus *Solidago*) of the composite family, with erect stalks carrying small heads of flowers, usually yellow and sometimes in clusters, blooming in summer and autumn. State flower of Alabama, Kentucky, and Nebraska.

golden rule The rule of life given in *Matt.* vii 12: "Whatsoever ye would that men should do to you, do ye even so to them."

gold·en·seal (gōl'dən·sēl') *n.* **1** An herb (*Hydrastis canadensis*) of the United States, with a yellow rootstock, a single radical leaf, a hairy stem, and a single greenish-white flower. **2** This plant's rootstock.

golden section 1 In Euclidean geometry, the division of a line segment in extreme and mean ratio. **2** In esthetics, the division of a line or of a figure in which the smaller length or area is to the larger as the larger is to the whole; also, that proportion of a plane figure in which the smaller dimension is to the larger as the larger is to the sum of the dimensions; broadly a ratio of 3:5, thought to be especially pleasing esthetically. In sculpture, this is applied to the proportion of the frontal plane of the figure. In the Petrarchan sonnet, the relationship between the octave and the sestet is very like that of the golden section, with the 14 lines divided in a ratio of 8 : 6. (The true section of 14 is 8.65 : 5.35.) In bookbinding, the proportion of an octavo binding also approximates this ratio.

GOLDEN SECTION
On line *AB*, square *ABIG* is constructed; *AG* is bisected at *C*, whereby *CD* = *CB*, and square *DEFA* is constructed. Ratio: *DA : AG :: AG : DG*.

golden wattle A plant of the genus *Acacia* (especially *A. pycnantha*) related to the mimosa and having yellow flowers: widely distributed in Australasia.

golden wedding Fiftieth wedding anniversary.

gold·en·winged warbler (gōl'dən·wingd') A North American warbler with yellow wings (*Vermivora chrysoptera*).

gold-ex·change standard (gōld'iks·chānj') A monetary system based on currency at par in another country that maintains a gold standard.

gold·eye (gōld'ī') *n.* A small fresh-water fish (*Amphiodon alosoides*) of northern and western North America: also called *Winnipeg goldeye*.

gold-filled (gōld'fīld') *adj.* Denoting an extra heavy or thick plate of gold on a base metal foundation, as in watchmaking.

gold·finch (gōld'finch') *n.* **1** A European finch (genus *Carduelis*) having a black hood and a yellow patch on the wings. **2** An American finch (*Spinus tristis*) of which the male, in the summer, has a yellow body with black tail.

gold·fin·ny (gōld'fin'ē) *n.* *pl.* **·nies** A bright-colored European wrasse (genus *Ctenolabrus*).

gold·fish (gōld'fish') *n.* *pl.* **·fish** or **·fish·es** A small carp of golden color (genus *Carassius*), originally of China, now cultivated in many varieties as an ornamental aquarium fish.

gold foil Thin sheets of gold, thicker than gold leaf. — **gold–foil** (gōld'foil') *adj.*

gold·i·locks (gōld'ə·loks') *n.* **1** A European herb (*Linosyris vulgaris*) with yellow flower heads. **2** The European buttercup. **3** A girl with golden hair.

gold lace A lace wrought with gold or gilt thread.

gold leaf A very fine leaf made from beaten gold. — **gold–leaf** (gōld'lēf') *adj.*

gold note A banknote to be paid in gold.

gold number *Chem.* A number expressing the weight in milligrams of a lyophilic colloid (gelatin) just insufficient to prevent a change from red to violet in 10 cc. of colloidal gold to which has been added 1 cc. of a 10 percent solution of sodium chloride.

gold-of-pleas·ure (gōld'əv·plezh'ər) *n.* An erect annual herb (*Camelina sativa*) with long, lanceolate leaves, small, numerous flowers, and obovoid or pear-shaped pods: naturalized from Europe; false flax.

gold point 1 That point in the rate of foreign exchange at which bullion çan be shipped in payment of accounts without entailing a loss. **2** *Physics* The melting point of gold, 1063°C., used as a reference temperature.

gold reserve 1 Gold held in reserve by the U. S. Treasury to protect and formerly to redeem U. S. promissory notes; established by Congress, 1882. **2** The quantity of gold bullion or coin owned by the central bank of a country.

gold rush A mass movement of people to an area where gold has been discovered.

gold shell A copper–zinc alloy thinly plated with gold and used for making cheap jewelry: also called *Talmi gold.*

gold·smith (gōld'smith') *n.* A worker in gold. — **gold'smith'er·y** *n.* — **gold'smith'ing** *n.*

goldsmith beetle A large European scarabaeid beetle (*Cetonia aurata*) of a brilliant golden color: also called *rose beetle.*

gold standard A monetary system based on gold of a specified weight and fineness as the unit of value.

gold·stone (gōld'stōn') *n.* Aventurine glass having numerous gold specks which give it a jeweled appearance.

gold–thread (gōld'thred') *n.* **1** A North American evergreen herb (*Coptis groenlandica*) of the crowfoot family, with long, bright-yellow, fibrous roots. **2** The roots of this plant.

golf (gôlf, golf) *n.* An outdoor game played on a large course with a small resilient ball and a set of clubs, the object being to direct the ball into a series of variously distributed holes (usually nine or eighteen) in as few strokes as possible. — *v.i.* To play golf. [Cf. dial. E (Scottish) *gowf* strike] — **golf'er** *n.*

golf club 1 One of several clubs used in playing golf. **2** An organization of golfers; also, the building and grounds used by them.

TYPES OF GOLF CLUBS

a. Driver.	*d.* No. 5 iron.
b. Brassie.	or mashie.
c. No. 2 iron	*e.* No. 6 iron.
or midiron.	*f.* No 7 iron.

g. No. 8 iron.
h. No. 9 iron
or niblick.
i. Putter.

golf links The course over which a game of golf is played. Also **golf course.**

Golgi apparatus *Biol.* A netlike structure of rod-shaped elements found in the cytoplasm of animal cells. Also **Golgi body.** See illustration under CELL.

gol·go·tha (gol'gə·thə) *n.* **1** A burial place; graveyard; charnel house. **2** Any place of torment or sacrifice. [from *Golgotha*]

Gol·go·tha (gol'gə·thə) A place near Jerusalem where Jesus was crucified. *Matt.* xxvii 33. [<LL <Gk. <Aramaic *gogoltha* skull <Hebrew *gulgōleth*]

gol·iard (gōl'yərd) *n.* One of a class of wandering student jesters of the 12th and 13th centuries who wrote and sang Latin satirical verses. [<OF, a glutton <*gole* gluttony <L *gula*] — **gol·iar·der·y** (gōl·yär'dər·ē) *n.* — **gol·iar'dic** *adj.*

gol·li·wog (gol'ē·wog) *n.* **1** A grotesque, black doll. **2** A grotesque person. Also **gol'li·wogg.** [after illustrations drawn (1895) by Florence Upton for a series of children's books]

gom·broon (gom·brōōn') *n.* A Persian pottery of a semitransparent white. Also **gom·broon'-ware.** [from a town on the Persian Gulf].

Go·mor·rah (gə·môr'ə, -mor'ə) A city on the shore of the Dead Sea, destroyed with Sodom because of the wickedness of its people. *Gen.* xiii 10. Also **Go·mor'rha.**

gom·pho·sis (gom·fō'sis) *n. Anat.* An articulation or union by the firm implantation of one part in a socket situated in another, as

the setting of teeth in the jaw or the styloid process in the temporal bone. [<NL <Gk. *gomphos* a bolt]

go·mu·ti (gō·mōō'tē) *n.* **1** The Malayan feather palm (*Arenga pinnata*): a source of palm sugar. **2** A durable, black, hairlike fiber obtained from this palm: valuable for cordage, etc., because it does not rot in water. [<Malay *gumuti*]

gon- Var. of GONO-.

-gon *combining form* Having (a certain number of) angles: *pentagon.* [<Gk. *gonia* an angle]

gon·ad (gon'ad, gō'nad) *n. Anat.* A male or female sex gland, in which the gametes develop; an ovary or testis. [<GON- + -AD¹] — **gon'a·dal, go·na·di·al** (gō·nā'dē·əl), **go·nad·ic** (gō·nad'ik) *adj.*

Gond (gond) *n.* A Dravidian of the hilly country of central India.

gon·do·la (gon'də·lə) *n.* **1** A long, narrow, flat-bottomed Venetian boat, high-peaked at the ends, and rowed with one oar by a gondolier who stands near the stern. **2** A large flat-bottomed river boat of light build. **3** A long, shallow, open freight car. **4** *Aeron.* The car hanging below or attached to a dirigible balloon for the accommodation of engines, crew, or the like. [<Ital. < *gondola* rock]

TRADITIONAL VENETIAN GONDOLA

gon·do·lier (gon'də·lir') *n.* The rower of a gondola.

gone (gôn, gon) Past participle of GO. — *adj.* **1** Passed beyond help or hope; ruined; lost: a *gone* case. **2** Marked by faintness or weakness: a *gone* sensation. **3** Ended; past; dead. **4** Depressed and hopeless. — **gone on** *Colloq.* In love with.

gon·fa·lon (gon'fə·lon) *n.* An ensign fixed to a revolving frame or a crossyard, generally with two or three streamers; a banderole. Also **gon·fa·non** (gon'fə·non). [<Ital. *gonfalone* <OHG *gundfano* war banner]

gon·fa·lon·ier (gon'fə·lə·nir') *n.* **1** A gonfalon-bearer; a chief standard-bearer, as of the Church of Rome. **2** The title of the chief magistrate of Florence, after 1293, and of other Italian medieval republics.

gong (gông, gong) *n.* **1** A metal musical instrument shaped like a shallow dish, sounded by beating. **2** A fixed signal bell of flattened curvature. [<Malay]

Gon·gor·ism (gong'gə·riz'əm) *n.* An ornate and euphuistic literary style of the type cultivated by the Spanish poet **Luis de Gongora y Argote,** 1561–1627.

go·nid·i·um (gō·nid'ē·əm) *n. pl.* **·nid·i·a** (-ə) *Bot.* **1** In algae, a naked or membranous-coated propagative cell produced asexually. **2** In mosses, a cell filled with green granules. **3** In lichens, one of the green algal cells of a thallus. [<NL, dim. of Gk. *gonos* seed] — **go·nid'i·al** *adj.*

gonio- *combining form* Angle; corner: *goniometry.* [<Gk. *gōnia* a corner]

go·ni·om·e·ter (gō'nē·om'ə·tər) *n.* **1** An instrument for measuring angles, as in crystallography, surveying, etc., either by direct contact as in the **contact goniometer,** or more accurately, by utilizing beams of light, as in the **reflecting goniometer.** **2** An electrical direction-finder for aircraft. — **go·ni·o·met·ric** (gō'nē·ə·met'rik) or **·ri·cal** *adj.*

go·ni·om·e·try (gō'nē·om'ə·trē) *n.* **1** The art of measuring angles. **2** The branch of trigonometry that treats of angles.

go·ni·on (gō'nē·on) *n. pl.* **·ni·a** (-ə) *Anat.* The tip of the angle of the lower jaw. [<NL <Gk. *gonia* an angle]

go·ni·um (gō'nē·əm) *n. pl.* **·ni·a** (-ə) *Biol.*

One of the primitive germ cells which aggregate from male or female sex cells. [<NL]
-gonium *combining form* Seed; reproductive cell: *sporogonium.* [<Gk. *gonos* seed]
gono- *combining form* Procreative; sexual: *gonophore.* Also, before vowels, **gon-**. [<Gk. *gonos* seed]
gon·o·coc·cus (gon′ə-kok′əs) *n.* *pl.* **·coc·ci** (-kok′sī) The Gram-negative, strictly parasitic bacterium (*Neisseria gonorrheae*) which causes gonorrhea. [<NL. See GONO-, COCCUS.]
gon·o·phore (gon′ə-fôr, -fōr) *n.* **1** *Bot.* A stalk bearing male and female organs; an elongation of the axis of a flower lifting the stamens and pistil high above the floral envelopes. **2** *Biol.* An accessory generative organ that conveys the generative products, as an oviduct or spermiduct.
gon·o·poi·et·ic (gon′ə-poi·et′ik) *adj.* *Biol.* Yielding or producing reproductive elements, as ova or spermatozoa.
gon·or·rhe·a (gon′ə-rē′ə) *n.* *Pathol.* A specific contagious inflammation of the mucous membrane of the genital organs, caused by the gonococcus and accompanied by a discharge of morbid matter. Also **gon′or·rhoe′a.** [<LL <Gk. *gonorrhoia* <*gonos* seed + *rheein* flow]
-gony *combining form* Generation or production of: *cosmogony.* [<L *-gonia* <Gk. <*gonos* seed, reproduction; cf. -GENY]
good (good) *adj.* **bet·ter, best 1** Satisfactory in quality or kind: *good* food; *good* soil. **2** Striking in appearance: a *good* figure. **3** Morally excellent; virtuous. **4** Worthy: in *good* standing; a *good* name; a *good* family. **5** Kind; benevolent. **6** Well-behaved: a *good* child. **7** Proper; desirable: *good* manners. **8** Pleasing; agreeable: *good* company; *good* news. **9** Beneficial; salutary: *good* for business; *good* advice. **10** Favorable; approving: a *good* opinion. **11** Skilful; proficient: *good* at arithmetic; a *good* swimmer. **12** Orthodox; conforming: a *good* Democrat. **13** Reliable; safe: a *good* investment. **14** Considerable; rather great in degree, measure, or extent: a *good* supply; a *good* while; a *good* beating. **15** Full: a *good* two miles off. **— as good as** Practically; virtually: It is *as good as* done. **— to make good 1** To compensate for; replace. **2** To carry out; accomplish. **3** To prove; substantiate. **4** To be successful. **— n. 1** That which is desirable, fit, serviceable, etc.: opposed to the *bad* or *evil.* **2** Benefit; profit; advantage: for the *good* of mankind; to get some *good* out of it. **3** That which is morally or ethically desirable: to do *good*. See synonyms under PROFIT, SERVICE. **— for good (and all)** Finally; for the last time. **— to the good** In excess of assets over liabilities: fifty dollars *to the good*. **— interj.** An exclamation of satisfaction or assent. **— adv.** *Illit. & Dial.* Well. [OE *gōd*]
— good′ness *n.*
Synonyms (*adj.*): able, adequate, admirable, advantageous, agreeable, beneficial, benevolent, capital, cheerful, cheering, companionable, competent, complete, considerable, convenient, dexterous, dutiful, excellent, expert, fair, favorable, fit, friendly, genial, genuine, godly, gracious, gratifying, holy, honorable, humane, immaculate, kind, lively, merciful, obliging, perfect, pious, pleasant, precious, profitable, proper, ready, real, religious, right, righteous, satisfactory, serious, serviceable, skilful, social, sound, staunch, sterling, suitable, thorough, true, unblemished, unfeigned, unimpeached, unsullied, untarnished, upright, useful, valid, valuable, virtuous, well-adapted, well-disposed, well-qualified, wholesome, worthy. *Good* may at some time be a synonym of almost any adjective in the language implying advantage, benefit, utility, worth, etc. *Good* almost always carries a silent connotation of the connection or purpose with reference to which it is affirmed. A horse that is sound, kind, and serviceable, whether swift, as a racer, or strong and heavy, as a dray horse, is a *good* horse; a ship that is *staunch* and seaworthy is a *good* ship; a use of money that brings in sure and ample returns is a *good* investment; a man of high and true moral character is a *good* man; one of very different character, if brave and skilful in war, is a *good* soldier. Compare AMIABLE, BENEFICIAL, CHOICE, EXCELLENT, HONEST, MORAL, RIGHT, USEFUL, VIRTUOUS, WELL². *Antonyms:* see synonyms for BAD.
good-by (good′bī′) *adj., n. & interj.* *pl.* **-bys**

(-bīz′) Farewell; adieu. Also **good-bye.** See synonyms under FAREWELL. [Contraction of GOD BE WITH YOU]
Good Conduct Medal A decoration awarded for efficiency, honor, and fidelity in the U.S. Army: a bronze medal on which is an eagle standing on a closed book.
good fellow A boon companion; any sociable person.
good-fel·low·ship (good′fel′ō-ship) *n.* Merry society; companionableness. Also **good′-fel′low·hood** (-hood).
good for 1 Able or likely to produce: That patch is *good for* ten bushels. **2** Entitling (one) to, or acceptable for: a ticket *good for* ten trips, or *good for* a year. **3** Admitting to: The pass is *good for* any performance.
Good Friday The Friday before Easter.
good-heart·ed (good′här′tid) *adj.* Kind. **— good′heart′ed·ly** *adv.* **— good′heart′ed·ness** *n.*
Good Hope, Cape of A promontory in SW Cape Province, Republic of South Africa.
good humor A cheery, kindly mood or temper.
good-hu·mored (good′hyoo′mərd, -yoo′-) *adj.* **1** Having or marked by a cheerful, kindly temper; pleasant. **2** Done or said in a pleasant, kindly way. **— good′hu′mored·ly** *adv.*
good·ish (good′ish) *adj.* **1** Somewhat good; not bad; rather good. **2** Of appreciable extent; considerable.
good-look·ing (good′look′ing) *adj.* Attractive; handsome.
good·ly (good′lē) *adj.* **·li·er, ·li·est 1** Having a pleasing appearance or superior qualities; comely; attractive. **2** Large; sizable. **— good′·li·ness** *n.*
good-na·tured (good′nā′chərd) *adj.* Having a pleasant disposition; not easily provoked. See synonyms under AMIABLE, PLEASANT. **— good′na′tured·ly** *adv.* **— good′na′tured·ness** *n.*
Good Neighbor Policy A policy of the U.S. government for promoting political and economic amity with the Central and South American countries: first enunciated in 1933 by President Franklin D. Roosevelt.
goods (goodz) *n.* *pl.* **1** Merchandise: dry *goods*, green *goods*; also, property, especially personal property. **2** A fabric: linen *goods*, dress *goods*. **3** *Colloq.* Qualifications; resources; abilities. **4** *Brit.* Freight: a *goods* train. **— to deliver the goods** To produce what was specified, promised, or expected.
good speed Good luck: a wish for a safe journey or for success.
good-tem·pered (good′tem′pərd) *adj.* Of a good disposition. **— good′tem′pered·ly** *adv.*
good usage Standard use: said of diction, phraseology, and idioms acceptable to cultivated speakers and writers of a language. Also **good use.**
good-will (good′wil′) *n.* The prestige and friendly relations with customers built up by a business or member of a profession.
good will 1 A desire for the well-being of others. **2** Benevolence; charity; kindly intent. See synonyms under BENEVOLENCE, FAVOR, FRIENDSHIP.
good·y (good′ē) *n.* A term of civility to women of humble station, formerly used in New England. [<GOODWIFE]
goof (goof) *n.* *Slang* A blockhead; simpleton; stupid, foolish person. **— v.i. & v.t.** To blunder; botch. [Cf. obs. *goff* a stupid person <F *goffe*] **— goof′y** *adj.* **— goof′i·ly** *adv.* **— goof′i·ness** *n.*
goo·gol (goo′gol) *n.* **1** *Math.* The number 10 raised to the hundredth power (10^{100}) or 1 followed by 100 zeros. **2** Any enormous number. [Adopted by E. Kasner, 1878–1955, U.S. mathematician, from a child's word]
goo·gol·plex (goo′gol-pleks′) *n.* *Math.* The number 10 raised to the googol power: this is equivalent to the number 1 followed by a googol of zeros.
goon (goon) *n.* *U.S. Slang* **1** A roughneck; thug; especially, one employed during labor disputes: most commonly used in the phrase **goon squad.** **2** A dolt; stupid person. [after a character created by E. C. Segar, 1894–1938, U.S. cartoonist]
goo·ney (goo′nē) *n.* The black-footed albatross (*Diomedea nigripes*) of Pacific waters, having a sooty-brown plumage, whitish face, and saberlike wings with a spread up to 7 feet: also called *gony*. Also **gooney bird.** [Cf. dial. E *gawney* a fool]

goos·an·der (goos-an′dər) *n.* A merganser. [Origin uncertain]
goose (goos) *n.* *pl.* **geese** (gēs) **1** One of a subfamily (*Anserinae*) of wild or domesticated web-footed birds larger than ducks and smaller than swans. See GRAYLAG. **♦** Collateral adjective: *anserine*. **2** The female of the goose: distinguished from *gander.* **3** *pl.* **goos·es** A tailor's heavy smoothing iron, having a curved handle. **4** A silly creature; ninny. **5** *Obs.* An old game of chance, played with dice and counters. **— Canada goose** The common North American wild goose (*Branta canadensis*), brownish-gray with black neck and head. **— to cook one's goose** *Colloq.* To spoil one's chances; ruin a person. **— the goose hangs** (or **honks**) **high** The prospect is good; everything is favorable. [OE *gōs*]
goose·ber·ry (goos′ber′ē, -bər-ē, gooz′-) *n.* *pl.* **·ries 1** The tart fruit of a spiny shrub (genus *Grossularia* or *Ribes*). **2** This shrub. **3** A casklike portable frame around which barbed wire is wound in forming entanglements.
goose-flesh (goos′flesh′) *n.* A roughened condition of the skin produced by cold, fear, etc. Also **goose′-pim′ples** (-pim′pəlz), **goose′-skin** (-skin′).
goose-foot (goos′foot′) *n.* *pl.* **·foots 1** Any plant of a widely distributed genus (*Chenopodium*) of mealy-leaved shrubs and herbs with small green flowers; the pigweed. **2** A plant of the family (*Chenopodiaceae*) of which the goosefoot is typical.
goose-grass (goos′gras′, -gräs′) *n.* Any of various herbs and grasses, especially the cleavers, the silverweed, and a weed common in the West Indies and warmer parts of the United States (*Eleusine indica*).
goose-herd (goos′hûrd′) *n.* A tender of geese.
goose·neck (goos′nek′) *n.* **1** A mechanical contrivance curved like a goose's neck. **2** *Naut.* A swivel forming the fastening between a boom and a mast. **3** A curved shaft for a seat on a bicycle. **4** A bent pipe or tube having a swivel joint so that its outer end may be revolved.
goose-step (goos′step′) *n.* **1** The act of marking time with the feet. **2** A gymnastic exercise, or setting-up drill for the legs, which are alternately lifted and held straight out. **3** In some European armies, a stiff manner of marching on parade, which suggests this exercise. **— v.i.** To move or march in this manner.
go·pher (gō′fər) *n.* **1** A burrowing American rodent (family *Geomyidae*), especially one with large cheek pouches, as the **pocket gopher** (genera *Thomomys* and *Geomys*). **2** One of various western North American ground squirrels, especially *Citellus columbianus* and related forms. **3** A large, nocturnal, burrowing land tortoise (*Gopherus polyphemus*) of the southern United States. [<F *gaufre* a honeycomb]
gopher snake 1 A nonpoisonous burrowing snake (*Drymarchon corais couperi*) of the southern United States: also called *indigo snake.* **2** Any of several nonpoisonous snakes (genus *Pituophis*) of the United States that feed on gophers and other rodents: also called *bull snake.*
go·pher·wood (gō′fər-wood′) *n.* **1** Yellowwood. **2** The wood of which Noah's ark was made. *Gen.* vi 14. [<Hebrew *gōfer, gōpher*]
go·ral (gō′rəl) *n.* *pl.* **·rals** or **·ral** A Himalayan goat antelope (genus *Nemorhedus*) having a short grayish coat speckled with black, short horns, and a white throat: also spelled *gooral*. [<native name]
Gor·ba·chev (gôr′bə-chof), **Mikhail Sergeyevich,** 1931-, first secretary of the Communist party 1985-
Gordian knot 1 The knot tied by Gordius. **2** A difficulty that can be overcome only by the application of unusual or bold measures.
Gor·di·us (gôr′dē-əs) An ancient king of Phrygia who tied a knot which, according to an oracle, was to be undone only by the man who should rule Asia: Alexander the Great, unable to untie the knot, cut it in two with his sword.
gore¹ (gôr, gōr) *v.t.* **gored, gor·ing** To pierce, as with a tusk or a horn; wound. [ME *goren;* prob. akin to OE *gār* a spear]
gore² (gôr, gōr) *n.* **1** A wedge-shaped or triangular piece, as a tapering or triangular piece of land; also, in Maine and Vermont, a minor civil division. **2** A triangular piece of cloth let into a garment, sail, etc.; also, one of the separate fabric sections of a balloon, airship, or parachute. **3** *Naut.* A triangular piece of plank used in fitting

a vessel. —*v.t.* **gored, gor·ing** To cut into triangular or tapering form, as a garment, or the deck of a vessel. [OE *gāra* triangular piece of land]

gore³ (gôr, gōr) *n.* Blood after effusion, especially clotted blood. [OE *gor* dirt, filth]

gorge (gôrj) *n.* **1** The throat; gullet. **2** A narrow passage between hills; ravine. **3** The act of gorging, or that which is gorged. **4** The part of a garment about the throat. **5** A jam: an ice *gorge*. **6** An entrance into a bastion or similar part of a fortification; hence, the rear of a redan or other work. For illustration see BASTION. **7** Bait used on a gorge hook. **8** *Colloq.* A full meal. **9** In falconry, the crop of a hawk. See synonyms under VALLEY. —*v.* **gorged, gorg·ing** *v.t.* **1** To stuff with food; glut. **2** To swallow gluttonously; gulp down. —*v.i.* **3** To stuff oneself with food. [< OF < L *gurges* a whirlpool]

gorge hook A pair of small fishhooks joined in a heavily leaded shank.

gor·geous (gôr′jəs) *adj.* Conspicuous by splendor of colors; very beautiful; magnificent; resplendent. [< OF *gorgias* elegant; ult. origin uncertain]—**gor′geous·ly** *adv.* —**gor′geous·ness** *n.*

gor·get (gôr′jit) *n.* **1** A piece of armor protecting the junction of the helmet and cuirass. **2** An ornament, often crescent-shaped, worn on the neck or breast. **3** A ruff formerly worn by women. **4** *Zool.* A throat patch distinguished by color or texture. [< OF *gorgete*, dim. of *gorge* throat]

gor·gon (gôr′gən) *n.* Any hideous object, especially a repulsive-looking woman. [< GORGON]

Gor·gon (gôr′gən) In Greek mythology, one of three sisters (Stheno, Euryale, and Medusa) with serpents for hair, so hideous that they turned the beholder to stone. [< L *Gorgo, -onis* < Gk. *Gorgō* < *gorgos* terrible]

gor·go·nei·on (gôr′gə·nē′ən) *n. pl.* **·nei·a** (-nē′ə) In classical mythology, a mask or head of Medusa: an emblem or attribute of Athena, borne as the centerpiece of the aegis and on her shield. Also **gor·go·ne′um** (-nē′əm). [< Gk., neut. of *gorgoneios* of a Gorgon]

gor·gon·ize (gôr′gə·nīz) *v.t.* **·ized, ·iz·ing** To paralyze as if by the Gorgon's spell; petrify or transfix.

GORGONEION
The Gorgon Medusa

Gor·gon·zo·la (gôr′gən·zō′lə) *n.* A white Italian cheese of pressed milk somewhat like Roquefort. [from *Gorgonzola*, a town in Italy]

gor·hen (gôr′hen) *n.* The moorhen; the female red grouse. [See GORCOCK]

go·ril·la (gə·ril′ə) *n.* **1** Any of a dwindling species (*Gorilla gorilla*) of herbivorous great apes native to equatorial Africa, living in a close family groups and having an unearned reputation for aggressiveness due in part to their ritual threat displays, large size, and great strength. **2** *Slang* A tough; a brutal person; especially, a gangster. [< NL < Gk., appar. < native name]

GORILLA

gorse (gôrs) *n. Brit.* Furze. [OE *gors(t)*]—**gors′y** *adj.*

go·ry (gôr′ē, gō′rē) *adj.* **·ri·er, ·ri·est 1** Covered or stained with gore. **2** Resembling gore. See synonyms under BLOODY. [< GORE³]—**go′ri·ness** *n.*

gosh (gosh) *interj.* A minced oath. [Alter. of GOD]

gos·hawk (gos′hôk′, gôs′-) *n.* **1** A powerfully built, short-winged hawk (genus *Accipiter*), formerly used in falconry. **2** The eastern gos-

hawk of North America (*Astur atricapillus*). [OE *gōshafoc* < *gōs* a goose + *hafoc* a hawk]

Go·shen (gō′shən) **1** The district in Egypt occupied by the Israelites. *Gen.* xiv 10. **2** A land of plenty.

gos·ling (goz′ling) *n.* **1** A young goose. **2** The pasqueflower. **3** A catkin or ament. **4** A silly erson.

gos·ling-green (goz′ling·grēn′) *n.* A yellowish-green color.

gos·pel (gos′pəl) *n.* **1** Good news or tidings, especially the message of salvation preached by Jesus Christ and the apostles; the teaching of the Christian church. **2** *Usually cap.* A portion of the Gospels read during the eucharistic services of some churches. **3** Any doctrine concerning human welfare which is considered of great importance. **4** Anything which is regarded as absolutely true. —*v.t.* **·peled** or **·pelled, ·pel·ing** or **·pel·ling** *Obs.* To preach the gospel to. —*adj.* Relating to or agreeing with the gospel; evangelical; veritable. [OE *godspell* good news, trans. of Gk. *euangelion*. See EVANGEL]

Gos·pel (gos′pəl) *n.* A narrative of Christ's life and teaching as given in one of the first four books of the New Testament.

gos·pel·er (gos′pəl·ər) *n.* **1** An ardent adherent of the Reformation, as distinguished from a Roman Catholic. **2** The cleric who reads the Gospel at a church service. **3** An evangelist; missionary. Also **gos′pel·ler**.

gos·sa·mer (gos′ə·mər) *n.* **1** An exceedingly fine thread or web of spider's silk that may float in the air. **2** A fine fabric like gauze. **3** A thin waterproof outer garment. —*adj.* Thin and light as gauze; flimsy: also **gos′sa·mer·y**. [< ME *gossamer* Indian summer, lit. goose summer; appar. so called because often seen in autumn when geese are in season]

gos·san (gos′ən, goz′-) *n. Mining* Decomposed material, usually reddish or ferruginous, forming the upper part of mineral veins and ore deposits. [< Cornish]

gos·sip (gos′əp) *n.* **1** Familiar or idle talk; groundless rumor; mischievous tattle. **2** One who tattles or talks idly: also **gos′sip·er**. **3** *Archaic* A boon companion. —*v.i.* To talk idly, usually about the affairs of others; be a gossip. —*v.t.* To repeat as gossip. See synonyms under BABBLE. [OE *godsibb* a baptismal sponsor < *god* God + *sib* a relative]

got (got) Past tense and past participle of GET. ◆ **have got** In the sense of must, *have got* is in wide colloquial use to add emphasis: I *have* (or I've) *got* to leave. In the sense of possess, *have got* is still more common in informal speech: We *have got* (or We've *got*) plenty and intend to keep it. This usage has long been challenged on the grounds (1) that *have got* properly means "have acquired," and (2) that *got* is superfluous, since *have* alone would convey the same meaning. The usage is now defended as acceptable colloquial idiom on the grounds that *have* is so much used as an auxiliary that it has lost much of its primary sense of possess, and *got* therefore serves to restore and emphasize this meaning. When *have* is dropped, and *got* stands alone in the sense of must or of possess, it is illiterate, or at best dialectal, as in "I *got* rhythm" or "All God's chillun *got* wings."

Goth (goth, gôth) *n.* **1** A member of an ancient East Germanic people, originating in the basin of the Vistula, that overran the Roman Empire in the third and fourth centuries: divided into the Ostrogoths, or **East Goths,** and Visigoths, or **West Goths.** **2** A barbarian; rude or uncivilized person. [< LL *Gothi* the Goths < Gk. *Gothoi* < Gothic]

Goth·ic (goth′ik) *adj.* **1** Of or pertaining to the Goths or to their language. **2** Rude, barbaric. **3** Of or pertaining to Gothic architecture. **4** *Obs.* Germanic or Teutonic. **5** Romantic; medieval: distinguished from *classic*. —*n.* **1** The East Germanic language of the Goths, known chiefly from fragments of a translation of the Bible made by Bishop Ulfilas in the fourth century: extinct by the ninth century. **2** The pointed style in architecture. —**Goth′i·cal·ly** *adv.*

Gothic architecture The pointed type of me-

dieval architecture prevalent in Europe from the full evolution of the Romanesque style until the Renaissance, or roughly from 1200 to 1500.

GOTHIC ARCHITECTURE
Westminster Abbey, London, 13th–15th centuries A.D.

Goth·i·cism (goth′ə·siz′əm) *n.* **1** A Gothic idiom. **2** Imitation of or inclination for Gothic architecture. **3** Rudeness of manners; barbarousness.

Goth·i·cize (goth′ə·sīz) *v.t.* **·cized, ·ciz·ing** To make Gothic.

Gothic novel A type of romance developed in the late 18th and early 19th centuries, characterized by the supernatural and grotesque in a medieval setting: first used by Horace Walpole in "*The Castle of Otranto: A Gothic Story,*" 1764.

gothic type 1 *U.S.* A type face having all the strokes of uniform width and without serifs. **2** *Brit.* Black letter.

got·ten (got′n) Past participle of GET. ◆ *Gotten,* obsolete in British, is current in American English in the sense of "obtained"; We have *gotten* the necessary funds. *Gotten* is also used in the sense of "become": He has *gotten* fat.

gouache (gwàsh) *n.* **1** A method of watercolor painting with opaque colors mixed with water and gum. **2** A painting executed by this method, or the pigment used for it. [< F < Ital. *guazzo* a spray < L *aquatio* a watering < *aqua* water]

Gou·da cheese (gou′də, gōō′-) A mild cheese similar to Edam cheese.

gouge (gouj) *n.* **1** A chisel having a curved cutting edge. **2** A groove made, or as made,

TYPES OF GOUGES
a. Paring. *b.* Turning. *c.* Firmer.

by it. **3** A layer of soft clay or decomposed rock along the wall of a vein; selvage. **4** A tool for stamping metal. **5** *U.S. Colloq.* Stealing or cheating; also, one who cheats or defrauds. —*v.t.* **gouged, goug·ing 1** To cut or scoop out with or as with a gouge. **2** To scoop, force, or tear out as with a gouge: to *gouge* out an eye. **3** *U.S. Colloq.* To cheat in a bargain; swindle. [< F < LL *gulbia*, prob. < Celtic] —**goug′er** *n.*

gou·lash (gōō′läsh, -lash) *n.* A stew made with beef or veal and seasoned with paprika: generally known as **Hungarian goulash.** Also spelled *gulash.* [<Magyar *gulyas (hus)* shepherd's (meat)]

gou·ra·mi (gŏŏr′ə·mē) *n. pl.* **·mis** 1 A large, air-breathing, fresh-water Asian fish (*Osphromenus olfax*) which builds nests and is highly esteemed as food. 2 Any of several related fishes cultivated in home aquaria, as the banded gourami (*Colisa fasciata*), the three-spot gourami (*Trichogaster trichopterus*), and the dwarf gourami (*C. lalia*). [< Malay *gurami*]

gourd (gôrd, gōrd, gŏŏrd) *n.* 1 The melonlike fruit of certain plants of the cucurbit family, having a hard rind, as the pumpkin, squash, etc. 2 The fruit of any of various bottle gourds of the genus *Lagenaria.* 3 The plant that bears this fruit, or a vessel, as a dipper, made of its shell. 4 A hollow die used by gamblers for cheating. [<F *gourde* <L *cucurbita* gourd]

gour·mand (gŏŏr′mənd, *Fr.* gŏŏr·män′) *n.* 1 A glutton. 2 Loosely, an epicure. Also spelled *gormand.* [<F, a glutton]

gour·met (gŏŏr·mā′, *Fr.* gŏŏr·me′) *n.* An epicure. [<F <OF, a winetaster]

gout (gout) *n.* 1 *Pathol.* A disease of metabolism characterized by inflammation of a joint, as of the great toe, paroxysmal recurrent pain, and an excess of uric acid in the blood. Also called *podagra.* 2 A drop; clot. [<F *goutte* a drop <L *gutta*]

gout·y (gou′tē) *adj.* **gout·i·er, gout·i·est** 1 Affected with gout. 2 Of or pertaining to the gout. 3 Swollen; protuberant. — **gout′i·ly** *adv.* — **gout′i·ness** *n.*

gov·ern (guv′ərn) *v.t.* 1 To rule or control by right or authority: to *govern* a kingdom. 2 To control or influence morally or physically; direct: His ideals *govern* his life. 3 To serve as a rule or regulation for; determine: This decision *governed* the case. 4 To hold back; curb, as one's temper. 5 *Gram.* **a** To regulate (a word) as to form: In *Take me home,* the verb *governs* the pronoun. **b** To require (a particular case, mood, or form): In English, a transitive verb *governs* the objective case of a pronoun. — *v.i.* 6 To exercise authority. [<OF *governer* <L *gubernare* steer <Gk. *kubernaein*] — **gov′ern·a·ble** *adj.*

Synonyms: command, control, curb, direct, influence, manage, reign, restrain, rule, sway. A person *commands* another when he has, or claims, the right to make that other do his will, with power of inflicting penalty if not obeyed; he *controls* another whom he can prevent from doing anything contrary to his will; he *governs* one whom he actually does cause to obey his will. A wise mother, by gentle means, *sways* the feelings and *molds* the lives of her children; to be able to *manage* servants is an important element of good housekeeping. The word *reign,* once so absolute, now simply denotes that one holds the official station of sovereign with or without effective power. See COMMAND, REGULATE. *Antonyms:* comply, obey, submit, yield.

gov·ern·ance (guv′ər·nəns) *n.* 1 Exercise of authority; direction; control. 2 Manner or system of government or regulation.

gov·ern·ess (guv′ər·nis) *n.* A woman employed in a private home to train and instruct children. — *v.i.* To act or serve as a governess.

gov·ern·ment (guv′ərn·mənt, -ər-) *n.* 1 The authoritative direction of the affairs of men in a community; rule and administration. 2 The governing body of a community, considered either as a continuous entity or as the group of administrators currently in power. 3 The form by which a community is managed: democratic *government*; ecclesiastical *government.* 4 A governed territory. 5 Management; control: the *government* of one's behavior. 6 *Gram.* A syntactical relation which requires a word to assume a certain case or mood when related to another word.

governor general A governor who has deputy or lieutenant governors under him: the *governor general* of Canada. Also *Brit.* **gov′er·nor-gen′er·al.** — **gov′er·nor-gen′er·al·ship** *n.*

gov·er·nor·ship (guv′ər·nər·ship) *n.* The office of a governor; his term of office; or the territory under his jurisdiction.

gown (goun) *n.* 1 A woman's dress or outer garment, especially when elaborate or costly. 2 A long and loose outer robe worn as a distinctive or official habit, as by clergymen, judges, barristers, professors, or university students, especially in England. See GENEVA GOWN. 3 Any loose outer garment or wrapper, especially when long: a dressing *gown.* 4 *Obs.* Dress; garb: the *gown* of humility. 5 *Obs.* A toga — *v.t.* & *v.i.* To dress in a gown. [<OF *goune* < Med. L *gunna* a loose robe]

gowns·man (gounz′mən) *n. pl.* **·men** (-mən) 1 One who wears a gown professionally, as a clergyman, a graduate or student in a university, or a barrister. 2 *Brit.* A collegian as distinguished from a townsman: also **gown′·man.**

Graaf·i·an follicle (grä′fē·ən) *Anat.* The small sac in which the ova are developed in the ovary. Also **Graafian vesicle.** [after Regnier de *Graaf,* 1641–73, Dutch physician and anatomist]

grab¹ (grab) *v.* **grabbed, grab·bing** *v.t.* 1 To grasp or seize forcibly or suddenly. 2 To take possession of violently or dishonestly. — *v.i.* 3 To make a sudden grasp. See synonyms under GRASP. — *n.* 1 The act of grabbing, or that which is grabbed. 2 A dishonest or unlawful taking possession or acquisition. 3 An apparatus for grappling. [Cf. MDu. *grabben* grip] — **grab′ber** *n.*

grab² (grab) *n.* A coasting vessel of the East Indies, with two or three masts. [<Arabic *ghurāb*]

grab-bag (grab′bag′) *n.* A bag or box filled with miscellaneous articles, from which one draws something unseen on payment of a price for each grab or draw.

grab·ble (grab′əl) *v.i.* **grab·bled, grab·bling** 1 To feel about with the hands; grope. 2 To flounder; sprawl. [Cf. Du. *grabbelen,* freq. of *grabben* grab]

gra·ben (grä′bən) *n. Geol.* A valleylike depression of the land caused by the subsidence of a series of blocks of the earth's crust. [<G, ditch]

grace (grās) *n.* 1 Beauty or harmony of form, attitude, etc.; ease and elegance of speech. 2 Any excellence or attractive characteristic, quality, or endowment. 3 Unmerited favor or good will; clemency; hence, any kindness, favor, or service freely rendered. 4 *Theol.* The unmerited love and favor of God in Christ; hence, free gift; the divine influence acting within the heart, to regenerate, sanctify, and keep it; a state of reconciliation to God through Christ; the power or disposition to exercise saving faith and to live the Christian life; any spiritual gift or attainment. See CHARISMA. 5 A short prayer before or after a meal. 6 Something granted in the exercise of favor or discretion and not as of right. 7 A courteous or gracious demeanor; graciousness; demeanor in general. 8 *Music* An ornament or embellishment, as a trill, turn, or the like. 9 *Obs.* Physical virtue or efficiency. See synonyms under FAVOR, MERCY. — **good graces** Favorable regard; friendship. — *v.t.* **graced, grac·ing** 1 To add grace and beauty to; adorn. 2 To dignify; honor. 3 *Music* To ornament with grace notes or other embellishments. [<OF <L *gratia* favor]

Grace (grās) *n.* Goodness; clemency: a title applied in Great Britain and Ireland to a duke, duchess, or archbishop, formerly to the sovereign, and used with a possessive adjective: His *Grace.*

grace cup A cup passed at the end of a meal for the drinking of the concluding health.

grace·ful (grās′fəl) *adj.* Characterized by grace; elegant; easy; becoming. — **grace′ful·ly** *adv.* — **grace′ful·ness** *n.*

Synonym: beautiful. That which is *graceful* is marked by elegance and harmony, with ease of action, attitude, or posture, or delicacy of form. *Graceful* commonly suggests motion or the possibility of motion; *beautiful* may apply to absolute fixity; a landscape or a blue sky is *beautiful,* but neither is *graceful. Graceful* commonly applies to beauty as addressed to the eye, but we often speak of a *graceful* poem or a *graceful* compliment. *Graceful* applies to the perfection of motion, especially of the lighter motions, which convey no suggestion of stress or strain, and are in harmonious curves. Apart from the thought of motion, *graceful* denotes a pleasing harmony of outline, proportion, etc., with a certain degree of delicacy; a Hercules is massive, an Apollo is *graceful.* We speak of a *graceful* attitude, *graceful* drapery. Compare BEAUTI-

FUL, BECOMING. *Antonyms:* see synonyms for AWKWARD.

graceful tree frog A tiny frog (*Hyla gracilenta*) of Australia, often kept as a pet.

grace note *Music* An ornamental note introduced as an embellishment, but not actually essential to the harmony or melody; an appoggiatura.

Grac·es (grā′siz) In Greek mythology, three sister goddesses: Aglaia (splendor), Euphrosyne (joy), and Thalia (abundance). Also **the three Graces.**

grac·ile (gras′il) *adj.* Gracefully slender or slight. [<L *gracilis* slender] — **grac′ile·ness, gra·cil·i·ty** (grə·sil′ə·tē) *n.*

Gra·cio·sa (grə·syô′zə) An island in the central Azores; 27 square miles.

gra·cious (grā′shəs) *adj.* 1 Disposed to show grace or favor; full of kindness or love. 2 Courteous and condescending; kind; affable. 3 Possessing or exhibiting divine grace. 4 *Obs.* Happy; fortunate. See synonyms under BLAND, HUMANE, MERCIFUL, POLITE, PROPITIOUS. [<OF <L *gratiosus* < *gratia* favor] — **gra′cious·ly** *adv.* — **gra′cious·ness** *n.*

grack·le (grak′əl) *n.* 1 One of various Old World starlinglike birds (family *Sturnidae*), usually black or black and white, as the myna. 2 An American blackbird; especially, the **purple grackle** (*Quiscalus quiscula*), with vivid iridescent plumage. [<NL *Gracula,* name of a genus < *graculus* a jackdaw]

gra·date (grā′dāt) *v.t.* & *v.i.* **·dat·ed, ·dat·ing** To pass or cause to pass imperceptibly from one shade or degree of intensity to another. — *adj.* Graduated according to size.

gra·da·tion (grā·dā′shən) *n.* 1 Orderly or continuous succession, progression, or arrangement, as according to size, quality, state, rank, or proficiency; regular advance upward or downward, as by steps or degrees. 2 A step, degree, rank, or relative position in an order or series; grade. 3 In art and architecture, a relative subordination or arrangement of parts so as to produce a desired effect; such a blending and variation of color and light as will produce effects of depth, relief, etc. 4 *Ling.* Ablaut. [<F <L *gradatio, -onis* a going by steps < *gradus* a step] — **gra·da′tion·al** *adj.* — **gra·da′tion·al·ly** *adv.*

grade (grād) *n.* 1 A degree or step in any scale, as of quality, ability, dignity, etc. 2 A group of persons of the same rank or station: all *grades* of society. 3 Rate or rank in the U.S. armed forces. 4 A class of things of the same quality or value: a high *grade* of wool. 5 *U.S.* **a** One of the divisions of an elementary or secondary school covering a year of work. **b** The pupils in such a division. 6 *pl. U.S.* A grade school. 7 A scholastic rating or mark on an examination or in a course. 8 A part of a road, track, or surface inclined to the horizontal. 9 The degree of inclination of a road or the like as compared with the horizontal. 10 *Agric.* An animal (as a cow or sheep) or a class of animals produced by crossing a common or other breed with a pure or better breed. — **at grade** At the same point of grade or inclination: a road crossing another *at grade.* — *v.* **grad·ed, grad·ing** *v.t.* 1 To arrange or classify by grades or degrees, according to size or quality. 2 To assign a grade to. 3 To gradate. 4 To make level or properly inclined: to *grade* a road. 5 To improve by crossbreeding with better stock: often with *up:* to *grade* up a herd of cattle. — *v.i.* 6 To take rank; be of a grade. [<F <L *gradus* step] — **grad′er** *n.*

-grade *combining form Zool.* Manner of walking: *plantigrade.* [<L *gradi* walk]

grad·ed (grā′did) *adj.* 1 Leveled, as a road or railroad. 2 Improved by crossbreeding.

gra·di·ent (grā′dē·ənt) *adj.* 1 Running on legs; adapted for walking or running: a *gradient* animal or automaton; *gradient* feet. 2 Rising or descending gently or by degrees: a *gradient* road. — *n.* 1 A grade: a *gradient* of 1 to 50. 2 An incline; also, a ramp. 3 *Meteorol.* A rate of change in certain elements affecting weather conditions, as pressure, temperature, etc.: usually with reference to horizontal distance. [<L *gradiens, -entis,* ppr. of *gradi* walk]

gra·din (grā′din, *Fr.* grȧ·daṅ′) *n.* 1 One of a series of rising seats or steps, as in an amphitheater. 2 A raised step back of an altar; superaltar. Also **gra′dine** (-dēn). [<F <Ital. *gradino,* dim. of *grado* <L *gradus* a step]

grad·u·al (graj'ōō·əl) *adj.* 1 Proceeding by steps or degrees; moving or changing slowly and regularly; slow. 2 Divided into degrees; graduated. — *n. Eccl.* 1 An antiphon sung at the Eucharist after the epistle. 2 A book containing the music for the sung parts of the Eucharist. *Ital.* **gra·dua·le** (grä·dwä'lā) *n.* [< Med. L *gradualis* < L *gradus* a step] — **grad'u·al·ly** *adv.* — **grad'u·al·ness** *n.*

Synonyms (adj.): continuous, moderate, progressive, regular, slow. See SLOW. *Antonyms:* instant, instantaneous, momentary, prompt, quick, sudden.

grad·u·ate (graj'ōō·āt) *v.* **·at·ed, ·at·ing** *v.t.* 1 To grant a diploma or degree to upon completion of a course of study, as at a college. 2 To mark in units or degrees, as a thermometer scale; calibrate. 3 To arrange into grades or divisions, as according to size or quality. — *v.i.* 4 To receive a diploma or degree upon completion of a course of study. 5 To change by degrees. — *n.* (graj'ōō·it) 1 One who has been graduated by an institution of learning, or who has completed any prescribed academic or professional course. 2 A graduated vessel used in measuring liquids, etc. — *adj.* (graj'ōō·it) 1 Holding a bachelor's degree: a *graduate* student. 2 Designed for or pertaining to graduate students: a *graduate* school. [< Med. L *graduatus*, pp. of *graduare* < L *gradus* step, degree] — **grad'u·a'tor** *n.*

grad·u·a·tion (graj'ōō·ā'shən) *n.* 1 The act of graduating, as a scale, or state of being graduated, as a series of colors. 2 An equal division or dividing line in a graduated scale. 3 In education, commencement.

gra·dus (grā'dəs) *n.* 1 A dictionary of quantities in prosody. 2 *Music* A collection of graded exercises. [< L *Gradus (ad Parnassum)* step (to Parnassus), title of a Latin dictionary, 1702]

graf·fi·to (grə·fē'tō) *n.* *pl.* **·ti** (-tē) 1 Any design or scribbled motto, etc., drawn on a wall or other exposed surface. 2 *Archeol.* A pictograph scratched on an escarpment, wall, or any other surface. [< Ital. < *graffio* a scratch, ult. < Gk. *graphein* write]

graft¹ (graft, gräft) *n.* 1 *Bot.* **a** A shoot inserted into a tree or plant, so as to become a living part of it. **b** The place where the cion is inserted in a stock. 2 Something amalgamated with a foreign stock: The family was a Spanish *graft* upon an American tree. 3 *Surg.* **a** A juncture between a piece of animal tissue cut from a living person or animal and the tissue of another subject. **b** The piece so implanted. — *v.t.* 1 *Bot.* **a** To insert (a cion or bud) into a tree or plant. **b** To insert a shoot or shoots upon: to *graft* a tree with a new variety. **c** To obtain by such process. 2 *Surg.* To transplant tissue removed from one part, or from one animal, to another. — *v.i.* 3 To insert grafts. 4 To be or become grafted. [Earlier *graff* < OF *grafe* < LL *graphium* stylus < Gk. *grapheion* < *graphein* write] — **graft'age** (-ij) *n.* — **graft'er** *n.*

graft² (graft, gräft) *U.S. n.* 1 The attainment of personal advantage or profit by dishonest or unfair means, especially through one's political or official connections. 2 Anything thus gained. 3 *Austral. Slang* Work. — *v.t.* 1 To obtain by graft. — *v.i.* 2 To practice graft. 3 *Austral. Slang* To work. [Cf. dial. E *graft* work, livelihood] — **graft'er** *n.*

grafting wax A composition of beeswax, tallow, etc., used in grafting to exclude air.

graham flour Unbolted wheat flour. [after Sylvester *Graham*, 1794–1851, U.S. clergyman and vegetarian]

GRAFTING
a. Method of cutting for ligule-grafting, showing shape of ligule.
b. Graft and stock bound together.
c. Protection of the union by a ball of clay.

grail (grāl) *n.* A broad bowl or chalice; specifically, in medieval legend, the **Holy Grail**, or *Sangreal,* the cup used by Jesus at the Last Supper, preserved by Joseph of Arimathea, who received some of Christ's blood into it at the Crucifixion, and brought it to Britain, after which it disappeared because of the impurity of its guardians. Also spelled *graal.* [< OF *graal* < Med. L *gradalis;* ult. origin uncertain]

grain (grān) *n.* 1 Any very small, hard mass: a *grain* of sand; especially, a seed resembling this; a kernel. 2 Any of the common cereals; specifically, the seed or fruit of any cereal, collectively, as wheat, oats, rye, barley, etc. 3 A minute particle. 4 A unit of weight, equal to 1/20 of a scruple apothecary; one troy ounce contains 480 grains; 1 oz. avoirdupois contains 437.5 grains. 5 A unit of weight for pearls, equal to 1/4 of a metric carat or 50 milligrams. 6 The arrangement of the particles of a body of granular texture; hence, degree of coarseness, roughness, fineness of surface, direction or set of fibers, etc.: the *grain* of wood or leather. 7 The innate quality or character of a thing. 8 The cochineal insect, originally mistaken for a seed; hence, a red or purple dye, or any fast color. 9 *pl.* Refuse grain or malt after brewing. 10 Natural disposition; temper. See synonyms under PARTICLE, TEMPER. —**in grain** or **in the grain** 1 Set; fixed: said of dye. 2 Figuratively, innate; deeply rooted; ineradicable. —*v.t.* 1 To form into grains; granulate. 2 To paint or stain in imitation of the grain of wood, marble, etc. 3 In leathermaking: **a** To scrape off hair from with a grainer. **b** To soften or raise the grain or pattern of. —*v.i.* 4 To form grains. [Fusion of OF *grain* a seed and *graine* seed, grain, both < L *granum* a seed]

grain alcohol Alcohol (def. 1), especially if produced by the fermentation of a cereal grain.

graine (grān) *n.* The eggs of the silkworm. [< F, grain]

grain elevator 1 A warehouse or series of storage tanks for the storage, lifting, and distribution of grain. 2 A system of belt conveyors to carry grain to and from storage bins.

grains (grānz) *n. pl. (often construed as singular)* A strong, iron fish spear with a line attached, having several points half-barbed inwardly. [< ON *grein* division]

grains of paradise The seeds of a West African plant (*Aframomum melegueta*) of the ginger family, used in medicine as an aromatic stimulant: also called *guinea grains.*

gral·la·to·ri·al (gral'ə·tôr'ē·əl, -tō'rē-) *adj.* Of or pertaining to a former order (*Grallatores*) of long-legged wading birds, including the herons and snipes. [< L *grallator* a stilt-walker < *grallae* stilts]

gram¹ (gram) *n.* The basic unit of mass (or weight) in the metric system, equal to 15.432 grains: originally defined as the mass of 1 cubic centimeter of water at 4° C., but now as one thousandth of the mass of the kilogram at Sèvres, France. See METRIC SYSTEM. Also **gramme.** [< F *gramme* < LL *gramma* < Gk. *gramma* a small weight]

gram² (gram) *n.* 1 The chickpea of the East Indies: used as food for men, horses, and cattle. 2 One of various kinds of pulse, as **black gram** (*Phaseolus mungo*). [< Pg. *grão* < L *granum* a seed]

-gram¹ *combining form* Something written or drawn: *telegram.* [< Gk. *gramma* a letter, writing < *graphein* write.]

-gram² *combining form* A gram: used in the metric system: *kilogram.* [< GRAM¹]

gra·ma (grä'mə) *n.* Any of various species of low pasture grasses of the western and SW United States, especially **blue grama** (*Bouteloua gracilis*). Also **gram'ma, grama grass, gramma grass.** [< Sp. < L *gramen* grass]

gram-e·quiv·a·lent (gram'i·kwiv'ə·lənt) *n.* The weight in grams of a substance which displaces or otherwise reacts with 1.008 gram of hydrogen or combines with 8 grams of oxygen. —**gram-equivalent** *adj.*

gram·mar (gram'ər) *n.* 1 The systematic analysis of the classes and structure of words (morphology) and of their arrangements and interrelationships in larger constructions (syntax).

2 Formerly, the study of all aspects of language, as phonology, orthography, syntax, etymology, semantics, and prosody. 3 A system of morphological and syntactical rules and principles assumed for a given language. 4 A treatise or book dealing with such rules. 5 Speech or writing considered with regard to current standard of correctness: He employs poor *grammar.* 6 The elements of any science or art, or a book or treatise dealing with them. [< OF *gramaire* < L *grammatica* < Gk. *grammatikē (technē)* literary (art) < *grammata* literature, orig. plural of *gramma* letter < *graphein* write. Related to GLAMOUR.]

gram·mar·i·an (grə·mâr'ē·ən) *n.* 1 One skilled in grammar. 2 A writer or compiler of grammars. 3 Formerly, a learned humanist. 4 A writer on the principles of an art or science.

gram·mat·i·cal (grə·mat'i·kəl) *adj.* 1 Conforming to the principles of grammar. 2 Of or pertaining to grammar. Also **gram·mat'ic.** — **gram·mat'i·cal·ly** *adv.* —**gram·mat'i·cal·ness** *n.*

grammatical gender See under GENDER.

gram-mol·e·cule (gram'mol'ə·kyōōl) *n. Chem.* That quantity of a substance containing a weight in grams numerically equal to its molecular weight: also called *mol, mole.* Also **gram-mo·lec·u·lar weight** (gram'mə·lek'yə·lər).— **gram'-mo·lec'u·lar** *adj.*

gram·pus (gram'pəs) *n. pl.* **·pus·es** 1 A large dolphinlike cetacean (genus *Grampus*) found in North Atlantic and North Pacific waters. 2 The killer whale (genus *Orcinus*). [Alter. of obs. *grapeys* < OF *grapois, graspeis* < Med. L *crassus piscis* fat fish]

GRAMPUS
(Killer whale: from 20 to 30 feet in length)

Gram's method A method for the differentiation and classification of bacteria which depends upon the reaction to treatment, first with aniline gentian violet, then with an iodine solution, followed by immersion in alcohol. Those bacteria which are decolorized by the alcohol are *Gram-negative,* and those which retain the purple dye are *Gram-positive.* [after Hans C. J. *Gram*]

gran (gran) *adj. Scot.* Grand.

Gra·na·da (grə·nä'də, *Sp.* grä·nä'thä) 1 A province of southern Spain; 4,438 square miles. 2 Its capital; site of the Alhambra and former capital of a Moorish kingdom.

gran·a·dil·la (gran'ə·dil'ə) *n.* 1 The edible fruit of various species of passionflower (*Passiflora*) of tropical America, especially the giant granadilla (*P. quadrangularis*), oblong, with a soft pulp of a sweet acid flavor. 2 Any plant yielding this fruit. [< Sp., dim. of *granada* a pomegranate]

gran·a·dil·lo (gran'ə·dil'ō) *n.* 1 Any of a large number of tropical American trees, especially a West Indian tree (*Brya ebenus*) yielding a hard, durable wood used in making flutes, clarinets, recorders, etc. 2 The fine-grained rosewood or cocobolo (*Dalbergia retusa*), valued for furniture and cabinetwork. 3 The wood of such trees, especially that used in making musical instruments. Also called *grenadilla, grenadillo.* [< Sp.]

gran·a·ry (grā'nər·ē, gran'ər-) *n. pl.* **·ries** 1 A storehouse for grain. 2 A country or region where grain grows in abundance. [< L *granarium* < *granum* grain]

grand (grand) *adj.* 1 Of imposing character or aspect; magnificent in proportion, extent, or belongings: *grand* scenery. 2 Characterized by striking excellence or impressive dignity; inspiring: a *grand* oration. 3 Preeminent by reason of great ability or high character; noble; worthy of exalted respect: the *grand* old man. 4 Preeminent in rank or order; also, of prime importance; principal: a *grand* climax. 5 Covering the whole field, or including all details; comprehensive; complete: the *grand* total. 6 *Music* Containing all the parts or movements that belong to a given style of composition. 7 Being one degree of relationship more distant than that ordinarily indicated by the word qualified: used in composition: *grandfather, granduncle, granddaughter, grandniece.* 8 Main; leading: the *grand* hall. —*n. U.S.*

Slang One thousand dollars. [< OF < L *grandis*]
—**grand′ly** *adv.* —**grand′ness** *n.*
 Synonyms *(adj.)*: august, dignified, elevated, exalted, great, illustrious, imposing, impressive, lofty, magnificent, majestic, stately, sublime. Aside from material dimensions,
great is said of that which is more than ordinarily powerful and influential, *grand* of that which is worthily so; a *great* victory may be simply an overwhelming triumph of might over right. We can speak of a *great* bad man, but not of a *grand* bad man; of a *great*, but not of a *grand*, tyrant. Compare AWFUL, IMPERIAL, LARGE, SUBLIME.

Grand Canal 1 A large canal in Venice, Italy, comprising the city's main thoroughfare. **2** The longest canal of China, comprising the main north-south waterway of north China; 1,000 miles long.

Grand Canyon A gorge formed by the Colorado River in NW Arizona; about 250 miles long; width, from 4 to 18 miles; depth, about one mile; partly in **Grand Canyon National Park;** 1,008 square miles; established 1919.

grand·child (grand′chīld′) *n. pl.* **·chil·dren** The child of one's son or daughter.

grand·daugh·ter (gran′dô′tər, grand′-) *n.* The daughter of one's child.

grand duchess 1 The wife or widow of a grand duke. **2** A woman holding sovereign rights over a grand duchy. **3** Formerly, in Russia, a daughter of a czar, or a daughter of any of his descendants in the male line.

grand duchy The domain of a grand duke or grand duchess.

grand duke 1 A sovereign who ranks just below a king. **2** In Russia, formerly, a ruler of a principality; later, any brother, son, uncle, or nephew of a czar.

gran·deur (gran′jər, -jōor) *n.* The quality of being grand; magnificence; sublimity. [< F < *grand* great]

grand·fa·ther (grand′fä′thər) *n.* The father of one's father or mother. Also **grand′pa′** (-pä′), **grand′pa·pa′** (-pə-pä′). —**grand′fa′ther·ly** *adj.*

Grand Forks A city on the Red River in North Dakota.

gran·dil·o·quence (gran-dil′ə-kwəns) *n.* **1** The quality of being grandiloquent. **2** Lofty or bombastic speech.

gran·dil·o·quent (gran-dil′ə-kwənt) *adj.* Speaking in or characterized by a pompous or bombastic style. Also **gran·dil′o·quous** (-kwəs). [< L *grandiloquus* < *grandis* great + *loqui* speak; infl. in form by ELOQUENT] —**gran·dil′o·quent·ly** *adv.*

gran·di·ose (gran′dē-ōs) *adj.* **1** Having an imposing style; impressive; grand. **2** Affecting grandeur; pompous; bombastic. [< F < Ital. *grandioso* < L *grandis* great] —**gran·di·ose·ly** *adv.* —**gran·di·os·i·ty** (gran′dē-os′ə-tē) *n.*

gran·di·o·so (gran′dē-ō′sō) *adj. & adv. Music* In a grand or imposing manner. [< Ital.]

grand mal (grän mál′) *Pathol.* An epileptic seizure characterized by severe convulsions followed by coma, often preceded by warning symptoms: distinguished from *petit mal.* [< F, lit. great sickness]

grand·moth·er (grand′muth′ər) *n.* The mother of one's father or mother. Also **grand′ma′** (-mä′), **grand′ma·ma′** (-mə-mä′). —**grand′moth′er·ly** *adj.*

grand·neph·ew (grand′nef′yōō, -nev′-, gran′-) *n.* A son of one's nephew or niece; grandson of one's brother or sister.

grand·niece (grand′nēs′, gran′-) *n.* A daughter of one's nephew or niece; granddaughter of one's brother or sister.

grand·par·ent (grand′pâr′ənt, gran′-) *n.* The parent of one's parent.

Grand Rapids A city in western Michigan.

gran·drelle (gran-drel′) *n.* **1** Two-ply yarn of contrasting colors. **2** A varicolored fabric made of such yarn.

grand·sire (grand′sīr′) *n.* **1** A grandfather; any male ancestor preceding a father. **2** Any venerable man. Also **grand′sir** (-sûr, gran′-).

grand·son (grand′sun′, gran′-) *n.* The son of one's son or daughter.

grand·stand (grand′stand′, gran′-) *n.* The principal stand on a racecourse; hence, a similar erection for spectators at any public spectacle. —*v.i.* *U.S. Colloq.* To show off in an attempt to win applause.

grand tour See under TOUR.

grand·un·cle (grand′ung′kəl) *n.* The uncle of one's father or mother; brother of one's grandparent.

grange (grānj) *n.* **1** *Brit.* A farm, with its dwelling house and appurtenances; specifically, the residence of a gentleman farmer. **2** *Obs.* A granary. **3** Formerly, a farm establishment belonging to a feudal manor or a monastery: the grain paid in as rent or tithes was stored in its granaries. [< AF *graunge*, OF *grange* < Med. L *granea* < L *granum* grain]

Grange (grānj) *n.* **1** The order of Patrons of Husbandry, a nation-wide association of U.S. farmers, founded in 1867 for the furtherance of agricultural interests. **2** One of the subordinate lodges of the Patrons of Husbandry.

grang·er (grān′jər) *n.* **1** A member of a Grange. **2** A countryman. —**grang′er·ism** *n.*

grang·er·ize (grān′jər-īz) *v.t.* **·ized, ·iz·ing 1** To illustrate (a book) with prints, engravings, etc., taken from other books. **2** To mutilate (a book) by cutting out the illustrations. [after Rev. James Granger, 1723–76, whose *Biographical History of England* (1769) was so illustrated] —**grang′er·ism** *n.* —**grang′er·i·za′tion** *n.* —**grang′er·iz′er** *n.*

grani- *combining form* Grain: *graniform.* [< L *granum* grain]

gra·nif·er·ous (grə-nif′ər-əs) *adj.* Bearing grain.

gran·i·form (gran′ə-fôrm) *adj.* Formed like a grain or a granule.

gran·ite (gran′it) *n.* **1** A hard, coarse-grained, igneous rock composed principally of quartz, feldspar, and mica, of great strength and taking a high polish. **2** Great hardness or rigidity. [< Ital. *granito*, orig. pp. of *granire* make seeds < *grano* a seed < L *granum*] —**gra·nit·ic** (grə-nit′ik) or **·i·cal** *adj.*

granite paper A wove paper containing very short silk threads of different colors.

gran·ite·ware (gran′it-wâr′) *n.* **1** A variety of ironware coated with hard, granite-colored enamel. **2** A fine, hard pottery resembling ironstone china.

gran·it·ite (gran′it-īt) *n.* A variety of granite containing biotite.

gran·it·oid (gran′it-oid) *adj.* Designating any igneous rock of granitelike texture.

gra·niv·o·rous (grə-niv′ər-əs) *adj.* Living on grain or seeds. —**gran·i·vore** (gran′ə-vôr, -vōr) *n.*

gran·ny (gran′ē) *n. pl.* **·nies 1** A grandmother. **2** An old woman. **3** *U.S.* In the South, a nurse. **4** A finical, fussy person. **5** A granny knot. Also **gran′nie.**

granny knot *Naut.* An imperfect sailor's knot, differing from a reef knot in having the second tie crosswise. See illustration under KNOT. Also **granny's knot, granny's bend.**

grano- *combining form* Granitic: *granolith.* [< L *granum* a grain]

gra·no·la (grə-nō′lə) *n.* A mixture of dry cereals, nuts, and raisins, chopped fine and marketed as a health food.

gran·o·lith (gran′ə-lith) *n.* Pulverized granite cement used as artificial stone for paving. —**gran·o·lith·ic** (gran′ə-lith′ik) *adj.*

gran·o·phyre (gran′ə-fīr) *n.* A granite porphyry. [< GRANO- + (POR)PHYRY] —**gran·o·phy·ric** (gran′ə-fī′rik) *adj.*

grant (grant, gränt) *v.t.* **1** To give or accord, as permission, a request, etc. **2** To confer or bestow, as a privilege, charter, favor, etc. **3** To admit as true, especially something not proved, as for the sake of argument; concede. **4** To transfer (property), especially by deed. See synonyms under ACKNOWLEDGE, ALLOT, ALLOW, APPORTION, CONFESS, GIVE. —*n.* **1** The act of granting; a bestowing or conferring. **2** The thing granted; specifically, a piece of land granted to a person, state, etc., by the government. **3** An admission, concession. **4** One of certain tracts of land in New Hampshire, Maine, and Vermont, once belonging to Indian tribes, but allocated to settlers during the 18th century, and the subject of territorial controversy in colonial days. **5** A transfer of real property by deed. See synonyms under GIFT, SUBSIDY. [< AF *graunter, granter,* ult. < L *credens, -entis,* ppr. of *credere* believe] —**grant′a·ble** *adj.* —**grant′er** *n.*

Grant (grant), **Ulysses Simpson,** 1822–85, U.S. general in the Civil War; 18th president of the United States 1869–77.

grant·ee (gran-tē′, grän-) *n. Law* The person to whom property is transferred by deed, or to whom rights are granted by patent or charter.

grant-in-aid (grant′in-ād′, gränt′-) *n.* A grant made by a central to a local government to assist in some public undertaking.

gran·tor (gran′tər, gran-tôr′, grän-) *n. Law* The person by whom a grant is made; maker of a deed.

gran·u·lar (gran′yə-lər) *adj.* Composed of, like, or containing grains or granules. Also **gran′u·lose** (-lōs), **gran′u·lous** (-ləs).

gran·u·lar·i·ty (gran′yə-lar′ə-tē) *n.* **1** The state or condition of being granular. **2** A coarseness in the silver graining of a motion-picture film.

gran·u·late (gran′yə-lāt) *v.t. & v.i.* **·lat·ed, ·lat·ing 1** To make or become granular; form into grains. **2** To become or cause to become rough on the surface by the formation of granules. —**gran′u·lat′ed** *adj.* —**gran′u·la′tor, gran′u·lat′er** *n.*

gran·u·la·tion (gran′yə-lā′shən) *n.* **1** The forming into grains or granules. **2** A granulated surface, or one of the elevations in such surface. **3** *Physiol.* **a** The process of forming new tissue in the healing of wounds. **b** The minute, flesh-colored, breadlike projections so formed. **4** *Astron.* An evanescent mottled appearance observed in the photosphere of the sun, attributed to gaseous convection currents in the outer layers. —**gran′u·la′tive** *adj.*

gran·ule (gran′yōōl) *n.* **1** A small grain; particle; corpuscle. **2** *Biol.* One of the small protoplasmic bodies suspended in the cytoplasm of the cell. [< LL *granulum,* dim. of L *granum* grain]

gran·u·lite (gran′yə-līt) *n.* A finely granulated, crystalline, foliated rock composed mainly of quartz and feldspar, but generally carrying garnet. —**gran·u·lit·ic** (gran′yə-lit′ik) *adj.*

gran·u·lo·cyte (gran′yə-lə-sīt) *n.* Any of several types of leukocyte in which the cytoplasm contains granules. —**gran·u·lo·cytic** (gran′yə-lə-sit′ik) *adj.*

gran·u·lo·ma (gran′yə-lō′mə) *n. Pathol.* A tumor composed of granulation tissue.

gran·u·lose (gran′yə-lōs) *n.* That portion of starch granules capable of being changed into sugar by certain ferments: distinguished from *cellulose.*

grape (grāp) *n.* **1** The smooth-skinned, edible, juicy, berrylike fruit of various species of the grapevine, from which most wines are made. **2** Any grapevine yielding this fruit. **3** Figuratively, wine. **4** Grapeshot. **5** A dark-blue color with a slight reddish tint. **6** *pl.* A cluster of nodular excrescences on a horse's fetlock, caused by a parasitic fungus. [< OF, bunch of grapes < *graper* gather grapes < *grape* a hook < Gmc.]

grape·fruit (grāp′frōōt′) *n.* A large, round, paleyellow citrus fruit of tropical regions (*Citrus paradisi* and varieties), cultivated also in the United States.

grape hyacinth A plant (genus *Muscari*) of the lily family, differing from the common hyacinth in having its small blue flowers ovoid or globular and minutely six-toothed.

graph (graf, gräf) *n.* **1** A diagram indicating any sort of relationship between two or more things by means of a system of dots, curves, bars, or lines. **2** *Math.* The locus of a point moving in relation to coordinates so that all of its values satisfy a function of an equation. —*v.t.* To trace or represent in the form of a graph. [Short for *graphic formula*]

-graph *combining form* **1** One who or that which writes or records: *phonograph.* **2** A writing or record: *monograph.* [< F *-graphe* < L *-graphus* < Gk. *-graphos* < *graphein* write]

Graph·al·loy (graf′ə-loi′) *n.* A composition consisting of graphite into which bronze or Babbitt metal has been forced by hydraulic pressure: a trade name.

-grapher *combining form* A writer or one engaged in a graphic or kindred art: *bibliographer, photographer.*

graph·ic (graf′ik) *adj.* **1** Of or pertaining to the art of writing, or of indicating by letters or written signs. **2** Describing with pictorial effect; portraying with vividness. **3** Written, engraved, or recorded by means of letters or inscriptions. **4** Having the appearance of written or printed signs: *graphic granite.* **5** *Stat.* Indicating or calculating by lines, areas, diagrams, etc. **6** *Math.*

Of or pertaining to the use of plotted

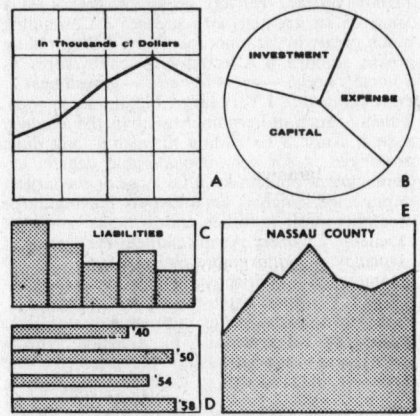

TYPES OF GRAPHS
A. Line graph. B. Pie or sector graph.
C, D. Bar graphs. E. Area graph.

curves to represent or solve an equation 7 *Geol.* Denoting a rock texture produced by a blending of crystalline constituents in such a way as to give a graphic appearance to a freshly cut section. Also **graph′i·cal.** [< L *graphicus* < Gk. *graphikos* of writing < *graphē* writing] — **graph′i·cal·ly, graph′ic·ly** *adv.*

Synonyms: descriptive, forcible, illustrative, pictorial, picturesque, vivid. See VIVID. *Antonyms:* dreary, dull, flat, monotonous, prosy, stupid, uninteresting.

graphic accent A written or printed sign of emphasis, as in many Spanish words.

graphic arts 1 Those arts involving the use of lines or strokes on a flat surface, as painting, drawing, engraving, etc. **2** Those arts which involve impressions printed on flat surfaces, as printing, lithography, etching, wood-engraving, etc.

graph·ics (graf′iks) *n. pl.* The science or art of drawing, particularly of mechanical drawing, or of drawing to mathematical rules as in engineering.

graph·ite (graf′īt) *n.* A soft, black, chemically inert, hexagonal variety of carbon with a metallic luster and oily feel: used as a lubricant and in the making of lead pencils, electrodes, crucibles, etc.: also called *plumbago, black-lead.* [< G *graphit* < Gk. *graphein* write + *-it* -ITE[1]] — **gra·phit·ic** (grə-fit′ik) *adj.*

grapho- *combining form* Of or pertaining to writing: *graphology.* Also, before vowels, **graph-.** [< Gk. *graphē* writing < *graphein* write]

graph·ol·o·gy (graf-ol′ə-jē) *n.* **1** The scientific study and analysis of handwriting, especially with reference to forgeries and questioned documents. **2** The art of interpreting character and personality from the diagnostic peculiarities of handwriting. **3** The study of handwriting as an aid in the diagnosis of diseases of the brain and nervous system. — **graph·o·log·i·cal** (graf′ə-loj′i·kəl) *adj.* — **graph·ol′o·gist** *n.*

-graphy *combining form* A written description: of: *geography, biography.* [< Gk. *-graphia* < *graphein* write]

grap·nel (grap′nəl) *n.* **1** A device for grappling, consisting of several hooks or clamps on one stem, designed to catch hold of any object across which it is thrown or drawn; a grapple. Also *grappling iron.* **2** *Naut.* A boat's anchor with many flukes. See illustration under ANCHOR. [ME *grapenel,* dim. of OF *grapin* a hook]

grap·ple (grap′əl) *v.* **grap·pled, grap·pling** *v.t.* **1** To take hold of; grasp firmly. —*v.i.* **2** To use a grapnel. **3** To seize or come to grips with another, as in wrestling. **4** To deal or contend: with *with:* to *grapple* with a problem. See synonyms under CONTEND, GRASP. [< *n.*] —*n.* **1** A close hold, as in wrestling. **2** A grapnel. [< OF *grappil* < OF *grappil* < OF *grappil*] —**grap′pler** *n.*

grap·pling (grap′ling) *n.* **1** The act of seizing or grasping, or that by which anything is seized and held. **2** A grapnel.

grasp (grasp, gräsp) *v.t.* **1** To lay hold of with or as with the hand; grip. **2** To seize greedily or eagerly; snatch. **3** To take hold of with the mind; understand. —*v.i.* **4** To make grasping motions. —**to grasp at 1** To try to seize. **2** To clutch at eagerly or desperately: to *grasp at* straws. —*n.* **1** The act of seizing or attempting to lay hold of something, as with the hand. **2** The ability to seize and hold; possession taken and kept by force. **3** Power of comprehension, or the exercise of this power. [ME *graspen,* metathetic var. of *grapsen* < LG] —**grasp′er** *n.*

Synonyms (verb): catch, clasp, clutch, comprehend, grab, grapple, grip, gripe, hold, seize, snatch, understand. See CATCH, EMBRACE[1]. *Antonyms:* abandon, fail, loose, lose, miss, release, relinquish.

grasp·ing (gras′ping, gräs′-) *adj.* Avaricious. See synonyms under GREEDY. —**grasp′ing·ly** *adv.* — **grasp′ing·ness** *n.*

grass (gras, gräs) *n.* **1** The green plants on which cattle feed. **2** Any of a large natural family of plants *(Poaceae)* with mostly rounded and hollow jointed stems, sheathing leaves, flowers borne on spikelets, and the fruit a seedlike grain, including all the common cereals, canes, bamboos, and a great variety of pasture plants. **3** *pl.* Spires or sprays of grass. **4** Grassland used for pasture; also, ground covered with grass; lawn. **5** Any of numerous plants with foliage suggesting or resembling the true grasses, as the sedges, the rushes, etc. **6** *Slang* Marihuana. —*v.t.* **1** To cover with grass or turf. **2** To feed with grass; pasture. **3** To spread on grass for bleaching by the sun. —*v.i.* **4** To graze on grass. **5** To produce grass; become covered with grass. [OE *græs.* Akin to GREEN, GROW.]

grass·hop·per (gras′hop′ər, gräs′-) *n.* Any of several orthopterous insects, including the locust and katydid (families *Locustidae* and *Tettigoniidae*), having powerful hind legs adapted for leaping. The males of most species make a chirping sound with their wings or by friction of the hind legs against parts of the wings or wing covers. For illustration, see under INSECT (injurious).

grass·land (gras′land′, gräs′-) *n.* **1** Land reserved for pasturage or mowing. **2** Land in which grasses predominate, as the American prairies. ground covered with grass, sometimes with groups of shrubs, flowers, etc. Also *Obs.* **grass′plat′** (-plat).

grass·quit (gras′kwit, gräs′-) *n.* A small fringilline bird *(Tiaris bicolor* and *T. canora)* of Cuba and the Bahamas.

grass·roots (gras′roots′, -roots′, gräs′-) *n.* The rural sections of the country; the hinterland. — *adj.* Of or pertaining to such sections: a *grass-roots* region.

grass snipe The pectoral sandpiper.

grass tree 1 Any of various Australian plants of the lily family (genus *Xanthorrhoea*) having a thick, woody trunk crowned with long grasslike leaves and yielding a fragrant resin. **2** Any of several Australasian plants with grasslike foliage, as the ti.

grass·y (gras′ē, gräs′ē) *adj.* **grass·i·er, grass·i·est** Abounding in, covered with, consisting of, or resembling grass. —**grass′i·ly** *adv.* —**grass′i·ness** *n.*

grate[1] (grāt) *v.* **grat·ed, grat·ing,** *v.t.* **1** To reduce to small particles by rubbing with a rough surface or through a grate. **2** To rub or grind so as to produce a harsh, scraping sound. **3** To annoy; irritate: to *grate* the nerves. **4** *Archaic* To wear or scrape away. —*v.i.* **5** To sound harshly, from or as from scraping or grinding; creak. **6** To have an irritating effect: with *on* or *upon.* —*n.* A harsh, grinding noise. ◆ Homophone: *great.* [< OF *grater* < Gmc.]

grate[2] (grāt) *n.* **1** A framework of bars, as to close an opening, or to hold fuel in burning. **2** A perforated metallic plate through which the ores pass after being crushed under stamps. **3** A fireplace. **4** *Obs.* A cage furnished with grates; a place of confinement. —*v.t.* **grat·ed, grat·ing** To fit with a grate or grates. ◆ Homophone: *great.* [< Med. L *grata* < Ital. < L *cratis* a lattice]

grate·ful (grāt′fəl) *adj.* **1** Having a due sense of benefits received; thankful. **2** Affording gratification; pleasurable; agreeable. **3** Expressing or denoting thankfulness; indicative of gratitude. [< obs. *grate* pleasing (< L *gratus*) + -FUL] — **grate′ful·ly** *adv.* —**grate′ful·ness** *n.*

Synonyms: obliged, thankful. See AGREEABLE, DELIGHTFUL.

grat·i·fi·ca·tion (grat′ə·fə·kā′shən) *n.* **1** The act of gratifying; a satisfying or pleasing. **2** The state of being gratified; specifically, the satisfaction of sexual craving. **3** *Obs.* That which gratifies; a reward; recompense; gratuity. See synonyms under HAPPINESS, SATISFACTION.

grat·i·fy (grat′ə·fī) *v.t.* **-fied, -fy·ing 1** To give pleasure or satisfaction to. **2** To satisfy or indulge, as a desire or need. **3** *Obs.* To reward. See synonyms under ENTERTAIN, INDULGE, REJOICE. [< MF *gratifier* < L *gratificari* < *gratus* pleasing + *facere* make] —**grat′i·fi′er** *n.* —**grat′i·fy′ing·ly** *adv.*

grat·ing[1] (grā′ting) *n.* **1** A grate. **2** *Physics* An optical device for the dispersion of light waves and the production of spectra, usually consisting of a series of very fine parallel grooves cut in the surface of polished metal or glass, sometimes of a suitably mounted crystal: also called **diffraction grating.**

grat·ing[2] (grā′ting) *adj.* Harsh in sound; rasping; irritating. —*n.* The act or sound of rasping. — **grat′ing·ly** *adv.*

gra·tis (grā′tis, grat′is) *adv.* Without recompense; freely. —*adj.* Given free of charge. [< L, var. of *gratiis* out of kindness, orig. ablative of *gratia* favor]

grat·i·tude (grat′ə·tood, -tyood) *n.* The state of being grateful; thankfulness. [< F < LL *gratitudo* < *gratus* pleasing]

gra·tu·i·tous (grə·too′ə·təs, -tyoo′-) *adj.* **1** Given freely without claim or consideration; voluntary. **2** Without cause, provocation, or warrant; uncalled for; unnecessary. **3** *Law* Imposing no obligation based on a legal or valuable consideration. **4** Freely given by nature, without labor on the part of man: opposed to *onerous.* [< L *gratuitus*] —**gra·tu′i·tous·ly** *adv.* —**gra·tu′i·tous·ness** *n.*

gra·tu·i·ty (grə·too′ə·tē, -tyoo′-) *n. pl.* **-ties 1** That which is given gratuitously; a present. **2** Something given in return for service, etc.; a tip. See synonyms under GIFT.

grat·u·lant (grach′oo·lənt) *adj.* Wishing one joy; congratulatory. [< L *gratulans, -antis,* pp. of *gratulari.* See GRATULATE.]

grau·pel (grou′pəl) *n.* Small, compact pellets of snow: often called *soft hail.* [< G, hailstone]

gra·va·men (grə·vā′men) *n. pl.* **-vam·i·na** (-vam′ə·nə) The essence of a charge or grievance; the burden of a complaint. [< Med. L, grievance < L *gravare* burden < *gravis* heavy]

grave[1] (grāv) *adj.* **1** Of momentous import; solemn; important. **2** Serious, as in mind, manner, or speech; dignified; sedate. **3** Sober in color or fashion. **4** *Phonet.* **a** Having the tonal quality of the grave accent, or marked with it, as the vowel *è.* **b** Unaccented, as a syllable. See synonyms under IMPORTANT, SAD, SEDATE, SERIOUS. —*n.* **1** A mark (`) used in French to indicate the open quality of *e* or a distinction in meaning, as in *ou, où;* in English elocution to indicate a falling inflection or the pronunciation of a final *ed,* as in *preparèd;* in Greek to indicate a lowering of the tone from a higher pitch: also **grave accent.** See ACCENT. **2** *Music* A passage or movement in the slowest tempo. [< F < L *gravis* heavy] — **grave′ly** *adv.* —**grave′ness** *n.*

grave[2] (grāv) *n.* **1** An excavation in the earth for the burial of a dead body; a tomb. **2** Hence, death or ruin. **3** The abode of the dead. [OE *græf.* Related to GRAVE[3].] —**grave′less** *adj.*

grave[3] (grāv) *v.t.* **graved, grav·en, grav·ing 1** To engrave; carve with a chisel. **2** To sculpture. **3** To impress deeply, as on the memory. **4** *Brit. Dial.* To dig. **5** *Archaic* To bury. [OE *grafan* dig. Related to GRAVE[2].]

grave[4] (grāv) *v.t.* **graved, grav·ing** *Naut.* To clean, as a ship's bottom, by scraping or burning off seaweed, etc., and coating with pitch. [< OF. *beach*]

add, āce, câre, pälm; end, ēven; it, īce; odd, ōpen, ôrder; tŏŏk, pool; up, bûrn; ə = a in *above,* e in *sicken,* i in *clarity,* o in *melon,* u in *focus;* yōō = u in *fuse;* oi, oil; ou, pout; ch, check; g, go; ng, ring; th, thin; ŧħ, this; zh, vision. Foreign sounds à, œ, ü, kh, ṅ; and ◆: see page xx. < from; + plus; ? possibly.

gra·ve[5] (grä′vā) *adv. Music* Slowly and solemnly. [< Ital.]

grav·el (grav′əl) *n.* 1 A mixture of sand and small, usually rounded, pebbles or stones. 2 *Pathol.* A disease characterized by formation in the kidneys of granular concretions. 3 *Obs.* Sand. — *v.t.* **grav·eled** or **grav·elled**, **grav·el·ing** or **grav·el·ling** 1 To cover or fill with gravel. 2 To bring up short, as in embarrassment or confusion. 3 *U.S. Colloq.* To irritate; annoy. 4 *Obs.* To run (a vessel) aground. [< OF *gravele*, dim. of *grave* beach] —**grav′el·ly**, **grav′el·y** *adj.*

grave·yard (grāv′yärd′) *n.* A burial place; a cemetery.

graveyard shift A work shift during the late night, generally from midnight to eight in the morning.

grav·id (grav′id) *adj.* Pregnant. [< L *gravidus* < *gravis* heavy] —**grav′id·ly** *adv.* —**grav′id·ness**, **gra·vid·i·ty** (grə·vid′ə·tē) *n.*

gra·vim·e·ter (grə·vim′ə·tər) *n.* An instrument for determining specific gravity, a type of hydrometer. [< L *gravis* heavy + -METER]

grav·i·met·ric (grav′ə·met′rik) *adj.* 1 Determined by weight, or of a kind usually so determined. 2 Pertaining to measurement by weight. —**grav′i·met′ri·cal·ly** *adv.*

gra·vim·e·try (grə·vim′ə·trē) *n.* The measurement of weight or specific gravity with the gravimeter.

grav·i·pause (grav′ə·pôz) *n.* The region in space where the gravitational field of one celestial body ends, or is neutralized by that of another. [< GRAVI(TY) + PAUSE]

grav·i·sphere (grav′ə·sfir) *n.* The spherical area within which the gravitational field of a body is dominant. [< GRAVI(TY) + SPHERE]

grav·i·tate (grav′ə·tāt) *v.i.* **·tat·ed**, **·tat·ing** 1 To tend by or as by force of gravity. 2 To move as though drawn by a powerful force. 3 To sink or fall to the lowest level. [< NL *gravitatus*, pp. of *gravitare* press down < *gravis* heavy] —**grav′i·tat′er** *n.* —**grav′i·ta′tive** *adj.*

grav·i·ta·tion (grav′ə·tā′shən) *n.* 1 *Physics* The force whereby any two bodies attract each other in proportion to the product of their masses and inversely as the square of the distance between them. 2 The act of gravitating or its effect. —**grav′i·ta′tion·al** *adj.* —**grav′i·ta′tion·al·ly** *adv.*

grav·i·ty (grav′ə·tē) *n. pl.* **·ties** 1 The accelerating tendency of bodies toward the center of the earth. 2 A similar tendency toward the center of any heavenly body. 3 Weight. 4 Gravitation. 5 The quality of being charged with or involving great interests; importance. 6 Dignified reserve; sedateness. 7 Lowness of pitch. 8 Something of grave import; a serious subject. See synonyms under WEIGHT. —*adj.* Employing gravity; worked by gravity: the *gravity* feed of an oil burner. [< F *gravité* < L *gravitas, -tatis* heaviness < *gravis* heavy]

gravity cell *Electr.* A primary cell in which the two electrolytes are kept separate by differences in specific gravity.

gravity fault *Geol.* A downward-sloping fault in which the upper portion or hanging wall appears to have moved under gravity to a level lower than that of the lower portion or footwall.

gra·vure (grə·vyŏŏr′) *n.* 1 An engraved copperplate or wooden block used in photogravure. 2 The print made from it. [< F *graver* engrave]

gra·vy (grā′vē) *n. pl.* **·vies** 1 The juice that drips from roasting or baking meat, or a sauce made from it. 2 *U.S. Slang* Any added, easily acquired, or extra payment or income; also, graft; illegally acquired money. —**gravy train** *U.S. Slang* A line of endeavor that is easy and lucrative. [ME *gravey*]

gray (grā) *adj.* 1 Of the color of white and black mixed and without brilliancy. 2 Having gray hair; hoary. 3 Hence, old; aged. 4 Wearing a gray habit: a *Gray* Friar. See synonyms under ANCIENT. —*n.* 1 A gray color; any dull, whitish tint; specifically, an achromatic color; one which may have brilliance but no hue. See COLOR. 2 Something gray; specifically, a gray animal. —*v.t.* & *v.i.* To make or become gray. Also *esp. Brit.* **grey.** [OE *grǣg*] —**gray′ly** *adv.* —**gray′ness** *n.*

Gray (grā) *n.* A soldier of the Confederate Army in the American Civil War; also, collectively, the Confederate Army itself: the Blue and the *Gray.* Compare BLUE.

gray·back (grā′bak′) *n.* 1 One of various animals, as the gray whale, the hooded crow (*Corvus cornix*), the American sandpiper, etc. 2 *Colloq.* A member of the Confederate Army during the Civil War. 3 *Colloq.* The body louse. Also spelled *greyback.*

gray eagle The American bald eagle. See under EAGLE.

gray·fish (grā′fish′) *n. pl.* **·fish** or **·fish·es** The dogfish: also spelled *greyfish.*

gray·lag (grā′lag′) *n. pl.* **·lag** or **·lags** the common wild gray goose (*Anser anser*) of Europe: so called because it migrates late. See GOOSE. Also spelled *greylag.*

gray·ling (grā′ling) *n. pl.* **·ling** or **·lings** 1 A small troutlike fish (genus *Thymallus*), with a richly colored, long, high dorsal fin. 2 A North American butterfly (*Minois alope*), with gray and brown markings (subfamily *Satyrinae*). Also spelled *greyling.*

gray market A trade operation involving the selling of scarce goods at exorbitant prices, a practice considered unethical but not necessarily illegal.

gray matter 1 *Anat.* The grayish substance of the brain, composed largely of ganglionic cell bodies and few fibers. 2 *Colloq.* Brains; intelligence.

gray·out (grā′out′) *n.* A temporary loss or blurring of vision caused by oxygen deficiency: noted especially in aviators subjected to high acceleration.

gray plover A large plover of nearly cosmopolitan range (*Squatarola squatarola*), having a plumage which is gray in winter and black during the breeding season.

gray·wacke (grā′wak, -wak-ə) *n. Geol.* A sedimentary rock composed of rounded or subangular grains of quartz, feldspar, etc., or rock fragments in a siliceous, argillaceous, or calcareous cement: also spelled *greywacke.* [< G *grauwacke* gray wacke]

gray whale A whalebone whale (*Rhachianectes glaucus*) of the northern Pacific coast.

gray wolf A large wolf of northern North America; the timber wolf.

Graz (gräts) The second largest city in Austria, capital of Styria.

graze[1] (grāz) *v.* **grazed**, **graz·ing** *v.i.* 1 To feed upon growing herbage. —*v.t.* 2 To put (cattle, etc.) to feed on growing herbage. 3 To put cattle, etc., to feed on, as a pasture, grass, etc. 4 To tend (cattle, etc.) at pasture. —*n.* The act of cropping or feeding upon growing grass or the like. [OE *grasian* < *grǣs* grass] —**graz′er** *n.*

graze[2] (grāz) *v.* **grazed**, **graz·ing** *v.t.* 1 To touch or rub against lightly in passing. 2 To scrape or cut slightly in passing: The bullet *grazed* his arm. —*v.i.* 3 To touch lightly in passing. 4 To scrape slightly. —*n.* 1 A light or passing touch; a scrape or abrasion. 2 *Mil.* The explosion of a bomb or shell immediately upon impact with the gound. [? < GRAZE[1]] —**graz′er** *n.* —**graz′ing·ly** *adv.*

gra·zier (grā′zhər) *n.* 1 One who is engaged in grazing or pasturing cattle, or in raising them for the market. 2 *Austral.* One who occupies grazing land for sheep farming under a lease or license.

grease (grēs) *n.* 1 Animal fat, especially when soft. 2 A thick, oily or unctuous substance resembling animal fat, derived from the distillation of petroleum. 3 Wool, after shearing and before cleansing: also **grease wool.** 4 The condition of wool or furs before being cleansed: wool in the *grease.* 5 A scabrous inflammation of a horse's pastern and fetlock, characterized by an odorous, oily secretion, and, in the later stages, formation of fungoid masses: also called *grease-heel.* 6 Fat or fatness in an animal, as a deer: a hunting term. 7 *Slang* A bribe; money used for bribery. —*v.t.* (grēs, grēz) **greased**, **greas·ing** 1 To lubricate by smearing with grease; put grease in or on. 2 *Slang* To influence by gifts or bribes: to *grease* the hand or palm. [< OF *graisse*, ult. < L *crassus* fat]

grease cup A receptacle for lubricating oil or grease. Also **grease box**, **grease cock.**

grease-heel (grēs′hēl′) See under GREASE.

grease-paint (grēs′pānt′) *n.* A paste, with a grease base, used in theatrical make-up.

grease·wood (grēs′wŏŏd′) *n.* Any one of various stunted and prickly shrubs of the goosefoot family (genus *Sarcobatus*) found on the alkaline plains of the western United States. Also

grease′bush (-bŏŏsh′).

greas·y (grē′sē, -zē) *adj.* **greas·i·er**, **greas·i·est** 1 Smeared or spotted with grease. 2 Containing much grease or fat; unctuous; oily. 3 Resembling grease; smooth. 4 Affected with scabby sores, as a horse's heels. —**greas′i·ly** *adv.* —**greas′i·ness** *n.*

great (grāt) *adj.* 1 Very large; big; immense; vast. 2 Being much more numerous than the average: a *great* army. 3 Extending through a long time; prolonged. 4 Of very considerable degree; extreme: *great* foolishness. 5 Of large or the largest importance; mighty; foremost. 6 Having large mental, moral, or other endowments; eminent; excellent. 7 *Colloq.* Adept; skilled: He's *great* at carpentry. 8 Important; weighty; momentous. 9 Characterized by or showing elevation, as of feeling, act, or aspect; high-minded; magnanimous. 10 *Archaic* Large in or as in pregnancy; teeming; gravid. 11 More remote by a single generation than the relationship indicated by the word qualified: used in combination with a hyphen: *great*-uncle, *great*-grandson. 12 *Colloq.* Excellent: We had a *great* time. 13 Intimately acquainted: *great* friends. See synonyms under GRAND, LARGE, SERIOUS. —*n.* 1 One who is or those who are powerful, noble, influential, or rich: usually with *the.* 2 *pl.* Great go. 3 The mass, lump, or job; the whole: to do work by the *great.* ◆ Homophone: *grate.* [OE *grēat*] —**great′ness** *n.*

great ape Any of the large anthropoid apes; a chimpanzee, gorilla, or orangutan.

Great Britain The principal island of the United Kingdom, comprising England, Scotland, and Wales; 88,745 square miles; capital, London.

great calorie See under CALORIE.

great circle *Geom.* A circle formed on the surface of a sphere by a plane which passes through the center of the sphere, dividing it into two equal parts.

great-cir·cle course (grāt′sûr′kəl) A course, as of a ship or aircraft, plotted along a great circle of the earth.

great·coat (grāt′kōt′) *n.* A heavy overcoat.

Great Dane One of a breed of close-haired dogs of large size and great strength.

greater glider A flying phalanger (*Schoinobates volans*) of Australia: also called *dusky glider.*

great go In British universities, the final examination for a degree.

great-grand·child (grāt′grand′chīld′) *n.* A child of a grandchild.

great-grand·daughter (grāt′gran′dô′tər) *n.* A daughter of a grandchild.

great-grand·father (grāt′grand′fä′thər) *n.* The father of a grandparent.

great-grand·mother (grāt′grand′muth′ər) *n.* The mother of a grandparent.

great gray owl See under OWL.

great gross Twelve gross, as a unit.

great-heart·ed (grāt′här′tid) *adj.* High-spirited; courageous; also, magnanimous.

great horned owl A large American owl (*Bubo virginianus*) with tufted ears that resemble horns: also called *cat owl.*

Great Lakes A chain of five lakes, the largest group of fresh-water lakes in the world, in central North America on the Canada-United States border: Lakes Superior, Michigan, Huron, Erie, and Ontario; total 94,710 square miles; drained by the Saint Lawrence River.

great laurel The rosebay rhododendron.

great·ly (grāt′lē) *adv.* 1 In a great manner. 2 In or to a great degree.

Great Miami River See MIAMI RIVER.

Great Mogul See under MOGUL.

great northern diver See under LOON.

Great Plains A sloping plateau, generally 400 miles wide, in western North America bordering the eastern base of the Rocky Mountains from Canada to New Mexico and Texas.

great power One of the countries exercising a predominant influence in world affairs.

great primer *Printing* A size of type (18-point).

great Pyr·e·nees (pir′ə·nēz) One of a breed of large dog with a heavy, bearlike head, broad straight back, and long thick coat.

Great Salt Lake A salt lake in NW Utah having no outlet and fluctuating in size from 1,000 to 2,000 square miles: also *Salt Lake.*

Great Schism The division in the Roman Catholic Church, 1378–1417, when rival popes ruled at Rome and Avignon.

Great Seal 1 The chief seal of a government, used to authenticate important documents and commissions in the name of the sovereign or highest executive of the government. 2 The Lord Chancellor of England, custodian of the British Great Seal, or his office. See SEAL[1].

great-un·cle (grāt′ung′kəl) *n.* A granduncle.

Great Wall of China A monumental wall in northern China, extending 1,500 miles between China proper and Mongolia; 20 feet wide at the base, 12 feet wide at the top; from 15 to 50 feet high; constructed 246–209 B.C.: also *Chinese Wall.*

Great War See WORLD WAR I in table under WAR.

Great Week In the Greek Orthodox Church, the week before Easter.

Great White Father A name used by American Indians for the president of the United States.

great white heron 1 A large white heron (*Ardea occidentalis*) of southern North America. 2 An egret (*Casmerodius albus*) of America and the Old World.

Great White Way The brightly lighted theater district of New York City; specifically, the section near Broadway and Times Square.

great year See PRECESSION OF THE EQUINOXES.

greave (grēv) *n.* Armor to protect the leg from knee to ankle. [< OF *greve*; ult. origin unknown]

greaves (grēvz) *n. pl.* Pieces of boiled tallow scrap; cracklings; also, dregs of melted tallow: also spelled *graves.* [Akin to LG *greve* refuse of tallow]

grebe (grēb) *n.* Any of a family (*Colymbidae*) of four-toed swimming and diving birds, smaller than loons and of fresh-water habitat, as the **horned grebe** (*Colymbus auritus*) and the **pied-billed grebe**, or dabchick of America. [< F *grebe*; ult. origin uncertain]

Gre·cian (grē′shən) *adj.* Greek. —*n.* 1 A Greek. 2 A scholar of Greek.

Greco– *combining form* Greek: *Greco–Roman.* Also spelled *Graeco–.* [< L *Graecus* a Greek]

Gre·co–Per·sian Wars (grē′kō–pûr′zhən) See table under WAR.

Gre·co–Ro·man (grē′kō–rō′mən) *adj.* Of or pertaining to Greece and Rome together: *Greco–Roman* art, *Greco–Roman* style of wrestling.

Greece (grēs) A kingdom of SE Europe; 51,182 square miles; capital, Athens: Greek *Hellas.*

greed (grēd) *n.* Eager and selfish desire; greediness; avarice. [Back formation < GREEDY]

greed·y (grē′dē) *adj.* **greed·i·er, greed·i·est** 1 Eager to obtain; avaricious; grasping. 2 Having excessive appetite for food or drink. [OE *grǣdig*] —**greed′i·ly** *adv.* —**greed′i·ness** *n.* *Synonyms:* gluttonous, grasping, insatiable, insatiate, ravenous, selfish, voracious. See AVARICIOUS.

gree·gree (grē′grē) See GRIGRI.

Greek (grēk) *adj.* Pertaining to Greece, its inhabitants, their language, or culture; Grecian; resembling the people of Greece. —*n.* 1 One of the people of ancient Greece; specifically, a member of one of the four major tribes: Achaean, Aeolian, Dorian, and Ionian. 2 One of the people of modern Greece, descended, with admixture, from the ancient Greeks. 3 The Indo-European, Hellenic language of ancient or modern Greece. Ancient, or classical, Greek, from Homer to about A.D. 200, is divided into four literary dialects: Aeolic, Attic, Doric, and Ionic. Abbr. *Gk.* —**Late Greek,** the language from

about A.D. 200 to 600, including the patristic writings. See KOINE. Abbr. *LGk.* —**Medieval Greek,** the language of the Byzantine period, from 600 to 1500. Abbr. *Med. Gk.* —**Modern Greek,** the language of Greece since 1500, in its literary form retaining many classical features: also called *Romaic,* especially in its spoken form. 4 Language or things not understood: It's all *Greek* to me. 5 A member of the Greek Church. 6 *Colloq.* A tricky fellow; sharper; rogue. 7 *Archaic* A gay fellow; roisterer: a merry *Greek.* 8 *U.S. Slang* A member of a student fraternity designated by a combination of Greek letters. [< L *Graecus* < Gk. *Graikos* Greek] —**Greek′ish** *adj.*

Greek calends See CALENDS.

Greek Catholic A member of the Greek Church.

Greek Church 1 The Eastern or Oriental Church (officially, the Holy Oriental Orthodox Catholic Apostolic Church), which finally separated from the Roman or Western Church in the 15th century, on doctrinal and liturgical grounds: also **Greek Orthodox Church.** 2 The Oriental Church in communion with Rome.

Greek cross See under CROSS.

Greek fire See under FIRE.

Greek Revival A style of architecture developed in the 18th and early 19th centuries, depending for its effect on the use of modified Greek motifs and structural elements.

green (grēn) *adj.* 1 Having the spectrum color between blue and yellow. 2 In leaf; grass-covered; verdant: *green* hills. 3 Not arrived at perfect or mature form or condition; unripe. 4 Of or due to immature or unskilled judgment or lack of knowledge; inexperienced; also, gullible. 5 Not seasoned or made ready for use; new; fresh; unrefined; raw. 6 Pale-greenish; pale; sickly; wan. 7 Characterized by strength or youthful vigor; flourishing. See synonyms under FRESH. —*n.* 1 The color of spring foliage; the color in the solar spectrum between the blue and the yellow. 2 A grassy level or piece of ground covered with herbage; a common; specifically, a golf putting green, or a whole golf course. 3 A green pigment or substance. 4 *pl.* The leaves and stems of young plants, as dandelion and spinach, used as food: usually boiled. 5 *pl.* Leaves or branches of trees; wreaths. 6 Something green used as an emblem. —*v.t. & v.i.* To become or cause to become green. [OE *grēne.* Akin to GRASS, GROW.] —**green′ly** *adv.* —**green′ness** *n.*

green algae A class (*Chlorophyceae*) of algae in which the chlorophyll-bearing cells are dominant; especially, *Protococcus viridis,* found as a coating on rocks, trees, fence posts, etc.

green·back (grēn′bak′) *n.* 1 One of a class of legal-tender notes of the United States: so called because the back is printed in green. 2 The golden plover.

Greenback party A U.S. political party, 1874–84, that advocated the restriction of the currency to Treasury notes. —**Green′back′er** *n.*

Green Bay A city in eastern Wisconsin on the Fox River at the head of **Green Bay,** an inlet of Lake Michigan in Michigan and Wisconsin.

green·belt (grēn′belt′) *n.* A strip of recreational or unoccupied land, encircling a community as a protection against objectionable property uses.

Green Berets The nickname of an elite unit of the U.S. Army, officially called Special Forces.

green·bri·er (grēn′brī′ər) *n.* Any of a genus (*Smilax*) of plants, especially a thorny vine (*S. rotundifolia*) of the United States and Canada, having small greenish flowers.

green comma A butterfly of North America (*Polygonia faunus*), so called from the greenish color and comma-shaped markings on the under side of its hind wings.

green corn Indian corn in the unripe, milky stage: boiled or roasted on the cob for eating.

green crop Green manure.

green dragon An American herb (*Arisaema dracontium*) related to the jack-in-the-pulpit: also called *dragonroot.*

Greene (grēn), **Graham,** born 1904, English novelist. —**Nathanael,** 1742–86, American

general in the Revolutionary War. —**Robert,** 1558?–92, English dramatist and pamphleteer.

green earth Native clay containing small amounts of manganese and iron: used as a pigment in dyeing and as a base for some green lakes.

green·er·y (grē′nər·ē) *n. pl.* **·er·ies** 1 A place where plants are grown. 2 A verdant mass of plants; verdure.

green–eyed (grēn′īd′) *adj.* 1 Having green eyes. 2 Influenced by jealousy.

green felt A cluster of green algae (genus *Vaucheria*).

green·finch (grēn′finch′) *n.* 1 An Old World finch (*Chloris chloris*), the male of which has green-and-gold plumage. 2 The Texas sparrow (*Arremonops rufivirgatus*).

green fingers Green thumb. —**green′-fin′-gered** *adj.*

green flash A vivid green hue sometimes seen on the upper edge of the sun's disk during sunrise or sunset.

green·fly (grēn′flī′) *n. pl.* **·flies** A green plant louse; an aphid.

green·gage (grēn′gāj′) *n.* A small, green-fleshed plum, originally developed in France. [< GREEN + GAGE[3]]

green gland *Zool.* One of two excretory organs near the head in decapod crustaceans.

green glass The viscid melted glass used for making bottles: also called *bottle glass.*

green gold An alloy of gold, silver, and copper in varying proportions, ranging from 14 to 18 karats in fineness, the deepest shade of green being 18 karats: used in jewelry.

green·gro·cer (grēn′grō′sər) *n. Brit.* A retailer of fresh vegetables, fruit, etc. —**green′gro′cer·y** *n.*

green·head (grēn′hed′) *n. pl.* **·heads** or **·head** 1 The striped bass. 2 Any of various American horseflies with green eyes (*Tabanus lineola* or *T. costalis*). 3 The male mallard duck 4 The scaup duck. 5 The golden plover. 6 The black-bellied plover.

green·heart (grēn′härt′) *n.* A large hardwood tree (*Ocotea rodiaei*) of Guyana and the Pacific coast of the United States, with a tough, durable wood ranging in color from yellowish-green to black: used in shipbuilding: also called *bebeeru.*

green heron A small, wide-ranging American heron (*Butorides virescens*) with a greenish-black head and a white throat.

green·horn (grēn′hôrn′) *n. Colloq.* An inexperienced person. [< GREEN (*adj.* def. 3) + HORN; with ref. to an immature animal]

green·house (grēn′hous′) *n.* A building having glass walls and roof, for the protection or propagation of plants.

greenhouse effect A postulated warming of the earth due to an increase in atmospheric carbon dioxide, which is relatively transparent to incident solar radiation but opaque to reflected radiation at thermal wavelengths.

Green·land (grēn′lənd) The largest island in the world, off NE North America, comprising a Danish colony; 840,000 square miles. *Danish* **Grön·land** (grœn′län′).

Greenland Sea The southern Arctic Ocean off NE Greenland and north of Iceland.

green·let (grēn'lit) *n.* A vireo.

green·ling (grēn'ling) *n.* Any of a genus *(Hexagrammos)* of large, carnivorous food fishes, found in North Pacific waters.

green lizard 1 A small, harmless, insectivorous lizard *(Anolis carolinensis)* of the southern United States. **2** A slender, long-tailed bright-green lizard *(Lacerta viridis)* of Europe and Asia Minor.

green manure 1 A crop, as of beans, clover, etc., plowed under before ripening to improve the fertility of the soil: also **green crop, green dressing. 2** Unaged stable manure.

green mold See BLUE MOLD.

green monkey A monkey *(Cercopithecus sabaeus)* of West Africa having an olive-greenish coat and a white ruff.

Green Mountain Boys Vermont soldiers of the American Revolution, led by Ethan Allen.

green pepper The unripe fruit of the red pepper (genus *Capsicum*): eaten as a vegetable.

green revolution The large-scale development of inexpensive varieties of wheat, rice, and other grains, esp. to improve the economy of underdeveloped countries.

green·room (grēn'rōōm', -rōōm') *n.* The common waiting room for performers in a theater when they are off stage.

green·sand (grēn'sand') *n. Geol.* Either of two sandstone strata of the Cretaceous system: so called from the color imparted to it by the glauconite with which it is mingled: often used as a fertilizer and water softener. See MARL[2].

Greens·bor·o (grēnz'bûr·ō) A city in north central North Carolina.

green·shank (grēn'shangk') *n.* A European sandpiper *(Tringa nebularia)* with greenish-gray legs and feet.

green·sick·ness (grēn'sik'nis) *n.* Chlorosis.

green·stone (grēn'stōn') *n.* One of various kinds of compact, igneous rocks to which a green color has been imparted by chlorite, such as diabase and diorite.

green·sward (grēn'swôrd') *n.* Turf green with grass.

green tea Tea leaves withered and rolled but not allowed to undergo fermentation.

green thumb Success or skill in making plants grow easily.

Green·ville (grēn'vil) A city in NW South Carolina.

green vitriol Copperas.

Green·wich (grēn'ich, -ij, grin-) A metropolitan borough of SE London on the Thames, England; former site of the Royal Observatory; location of the prime meridian.

Greenwich time See under TIME.

green woodpecker A European woodpecker *(Picus viridis)* with greenish upper plumage, a scarlet crown, and a fringed band on the cheek. Also called *hickwall, yaffle.*

greet[1] (grēt) *v.t.* **1** To address words of friendliness, courtesy, respect, etc., to, as in speaking or writing. **2** To receive or meet in a specified manner: He was *greeted* with a chorus of boos. **3** To come into the sight or awareness of; appear to: The sea *greeted* their eyes. See synonyms under ADDRESS. [OE *grētan*] —**greet'er** *n.*

greet[2] (grēt) *Scot. v.i.* **grat, greet·ing** To weep. —*n.* A crying; weeping. —**greet'ing** *n.*

greg·a·rine (greg'ə·rēn, -rin) One of an order *(Gregarinina)* of sporozoans, parasitic in arthropods, insects, crustaceans, etc. [< NL < L *garius* gregarious]

gre·gar·i·ous (gri·gâr'ē·əs) *adj.* **1** Having the habit of associating in flocks, herds, or companies; not habitually solitary or living alone. **2** Of or pertaining to a flock; characteristic of a crowd or aggregation. **3** *Bot.* Growing in association, but not matted together, as certain mosses; clustered. [< L *gregarius* < *grex, gregis* a flock] —**gre·gar'i·ous·ly** *adv.* —**gre·gar'i·ous·ness** *n.*

gre·go (grē'gō, grā'-) *n.* A short, hooded cloak of coarse cloth, worn in the Levant. [< Ital. *greco* Greek < L *Graecus*]

Gregorian calendar See under CALENDAR.

Gregorian chant 1 The system of church music ascribed to Gregory I, used as ritual music in the Roman Catholic and some other churches. **2** Any of the traditional melodies of this music.

Greifs·wald (grīfs'vält') A university city in Mecklenburg, northern East Germany.

greige (grā, gräzh) *n.* Cotton, linen, silk, rayon, or wool fabric before dyeing, sizing, or other processing: named for its gray unfinished appearance: also called *gray goods.* [< F *grège* raw, finished; infl. in form by *beige*]

grei·sen (grī'zən) *n.* A crystalline mixture of quartz and mica. [< G]

gre·mi·al (grē'mē·əl) *n.* A silken apron laid on the lap of a bishop when celebrating the Eucharist or anointing. [< L *gremium* lap]

grem·lin (grem'lin) *n.* A mischievous, invisible imp said to ride airplanes and cause mechanical trouble: a coinage of British aviators in World War II. [Origin uncertain]

Gre·na·da (gri·nā'də) An island republic in the West Indies, a member of the Commonwealth of Nations; the southernmost of the Windward Islands; with its dependencies in the Grenadines, 133 sq. mi.; capital, St. George's.

gre·nade (gri·nād') *n.* **1** A small bomb designed to be thrown by hand **(hand grenade)** or fired from a rifle or launching device, exploding on impact or by the action of a time fuze. **2** A glass bottle containing chemicals for extinguishing a fire. —**frangible grenade** A glass bottle filled with inflammable fluid, as gasoline, which is ignited on striking any object, as an armored vehicle or tank: popularly called *Molotov cocktail* or *gasoline bomb.* [< F, a pomegranate < Sp. *granada* < L *granatus* having seeds < *granum* a eed]

gre·nade-launch·er (gri·nād'lôn'chər) *n.* An attachment to the muzzle of a rifle or other weapon by which grenades are fired.

gren·a·dier (gren'ə·dir') *n.* **1** Formerly, a soldier assigned to throw grenades. **2** A member of a specially constituted corps or regiment, as the British Grenadier Guards. **3** Any of a family *(Macrouridae)* of deep-sea, soft-finned fishes related to the cod. [< F < *grenade.* See GRENADE.]

gren·a·dil·la (gren'ə·dil'ə), **gren·a·dil·lo** (-dil'ō) See GRANADILLO.

gren·a·dine[1] (gren'ə·dēn', gren'ə·dēn) *n.* **1** A silk or woolen, loosely woven fabric, usually mixed with cotton: used for curtains. **2** Silk cord made of several twisted strands braided together. [< F, ? after Grenada]

gren·a·dine[2] (gren'ə·dēn', gren'ə·dēn) *n.* A beverage sirup made from currants or pomegranates. [< F < *grenade* a pomegranate]

Gre·no·ble (grə·nō'bəl, *Fr.* grə·nō'bl') A city in SE France.

Gren·ville (gren'vil), **George**, 1712–70, English statesman; premier 1763–65. —**Sir Richard**, 1541?–91, English vice admiral: also **Greyn'ville.**

Gresh·am's law (gresh'əmz) In political economy, the law that of two forms of currency the inferior or more depreciated tends to drive the other from circulation, owing to the hoarding and exportation of the better form: as commonly stated, "bad money drives out good." Also **Gresham's theorem.** [after Sir Thomas *Gresham*]

gres·so·ri·al (gre·sôr'ē·əl, -sō'rē-) *adj. Zool.* Having legs or feet adapted for walking; ambulatory: a *gressorial* bird or insect. Also **gres·so'ri·ous** (-sôr'ē-, -sō'rē) [< L *gressus,* pp. of *gradi* walk]

grew (grōō) Past tense of GROW.

grew·some (grōō'səm) See GRUESOME.

grey (grā) *adj. Brit.* Gray.

grey·hound (grā'hound') *n.* **1** One of a breed of tall, slender dogs with a long narrow head and smooth short coat: used for hunting and racing. **2** A fast ocean vessel. [OE *grighund*]

GREYHOUND

Grey·lock (grā'lok), **Mount** The highest point in Massachusetts, in the Berkshires; 3,505 eet.

grib·ble (grib'əl) *n.* A small isopod, as *Limnoria terebrans* or *L. lignorum,* that bores into and destroys submerged timber. [? Akin to GRUB]

grice (grīs) *n. Scot.* A pig; especially, a suckling pig.

grid (grid) *n.* **1** A grating of parallel bars. **2** A gridiron. **3** *Electr.* A metallic framework employed in a storage cell or battery for conducting the electric current and supporting the active material. **4** *Electronics* An electrode mounted between the cathode and anode of a vacuum tube for the control of electrons: usually in the form of a screen. **5** A system of coordinate lines superimposed upon a map and used as a basis for reference from a designated point. **6** A network of catwalks suspended from the ceiling of a motion-picture studio or other enclosure. **7** *Brit.* A network of high-tension lines for distributing electric power throughout a large area. [Short for GRIDIRON]

grid bias *Electronics* The direct-current potential applied to the grid of a vacuum tube to make it negative with respect to the filament or the cathode: also called *C-bias.*

grid circuit *Electronics* The part of a circuit between the cathode and grid of a vacuum tube.

grid condenser *Electronics* A small condenser connected in series with the grid or control circuit of a vacuum tube.

grid current *Electronics* The current flowing between the grid of a vacuum tube and the cathode.

grid·dle (grid'l) *n.* **1** A shallow pan for baking or frying thin cakes. **2** A cover for a hole in a cookstove. —*v.t.* **grid·dled, grid·dling** To cook on a griddle. [< AF *grédil,* var. of OF *greil* < LL *craticulum,* dim. of *cratis* wickerwork]

gride (grīd) *v.t. & v.i.* **grid·ed, grid·ing 1** To grind or scrape harshly; grate. **2** To cut; pierce. —*n.* A harsh cutting, grinding, or hacking. [Metathetic var. of GIRD[2]]

grid·i·ron (grid'ī'ərn) *n.* **1** A grated utensil for broiling. **2** Any object resembling or likened to a gridiron, as a football field prepared for the game, or a network of pipe lines, railroad tracks, or the like. **3** The framework above a theater stage supporting the pulleys that raise and lower scenery; a storage space for scenery. [ME *gredire,* var. of *gredile* < AF *grédil* GRIDDLE; infl. by IRON]

grid leak *Electronics* A high-resistance unit connected directly or indirectly between the grid and cathode of a vacuum tube to allow escape of excess negative charges from the grid.

grid line One of the reference lines forming part of the grid on a map or chart.

grid·lock (grid'lok') *n.* A clogged traffic situation which prevents vehicles from moving in any direction.

grid meridian A grid line extending in a north–south direction on the grid: the prime grid meridian usually coincides with the zero meridian of Greenwich.

grid return *Electronics* The connection which allows electrons to flow from the grid to the cathode of a vacuum tube.

grid road *Canadian* A road following a grid line of the original survey.

grid variation The angle between the magnetic and grid meridian at any place, expressed in degrees east or west to show the variation of the magnetic compass-card axis from grid north. Also called *grivation.*

grief (grēf) *n.* **1** Sorrow or mental suffering resulting from loss, affliction, regret, etc. **2** A cause of sorrow; an affliction; grievance. **3** An accident, as in hunting or racing; a mishap. **4** *Obs.* Physical pain; distress; also, a cause of pain. —**to come to grief** To have misfortune; fail. [< OF < *grever* GRIEVE] —**grief'less** *adj.* —**grief'less·ness** *n.*

Synonyms: affliction, agony, distress, melancholy, mourning, regret, sadness, sorrow, tribulation, trouble, woe. *Grief* is acute mental pain resulting from loss, misfortune, or deep disappointment. *Grief* is more acute and less enduring than *sorrow. Sorrow* and *grief* are for definite cause; *sadness* and *melancholy* may arise from a vague sense of want or loss, from a low state of health, or other ill-defined cause; *sadness* may be momentary; *melancholy* is more enduring, and may become chronic. *Affliction* is a deep *sorrow* and is applied also to the misfortune producing such *sorrow; mourning* most frequently denotes *sorrow* publicly expressed. *Antonyms:* see synonyms for HAPPINESS.

griev·ance (grē'vəns) *n.* **1** That which oppresses, injures, or causes grief and a sense of wrong; a cause of annoyance. **2** A complaint, or a cause for complaint, because of a wrong suffered. **3**

Obs. Mental or physical pain; also, anger; grief. See synonyms under INJUSTICE.

grieve (grēv) *v.* **grieved, griev·ing** *v.t.* **1** To cause great sorrow or grief to; make sad. **2** *Obs.* To injure or offend. —*v.i.* **3** To feel sorrow or grief; mourn; lament. See synonyms under HURT, MOURN. [< OF *grever* < L *gravare* oppress < *gravis* heavy]—**griev'er** *n.* —**griev'ing** *adj.* —**griev'ing·ly** *adv.*

griev·ous (grē'vəs) *adj.* **1** Causing grief or sorrow; hard to be borne; oppressive. **2** Causing mischief or destruction; hurtful; injurious. **3** Expressive of or connected with grief or distress: a *grievous* complaint. **4** Severe: a *grievous* pain or illness. **5** Atrocious; heinous: *grievous* sin. See synonyms under HARD, HEAVY. —**griev'ous·ly** *adv.* —**griev'ous·ness** *n.*

griff (grif) *n.* **1** A series of horizontal blades in a reciprocating frame, to raise and lower the shedding mechanism of a Jacquard loom in forming the pattern. **2** Griffe[1]. **3** A claw. [< F *griffe* a claw. See GRIFFE[1].]

griffe (grif) *n. Archit.* An ornament in the form of a claw at an angle of the base of a column: also spelled *griff*: also called *spur*. [< F, claw < *griffer* grasp]

grif·fin[1] (grif'in) *n.* In Greek mythology, a creature with the head and wings of an eagle and the body of a lion: also spelled *griffon*. [< OF *grifoun* < L *gryphus* < Gk. *gryps* griffin]—**grif·fin·esque'** (-esk') *adj.*

STYLIZED HERALDIC GRIFFIN

grif·fin[2] (grif'in) *n.* Anglo-Indian A newcomer to India from England; greenhorn. [Origin uncertain]

grif·fon (grif'ən) *n.* **1** A griffin. **2** A breed of large sporting dog of European origin, having a gray, wiry coat and long head: also *wire-haired griffon*. Compare BRUSSELS GRIFFON, BELGIAN GRIFFON, BRABANÇON GRIFFON. [< F]

grift·er (grif'tər) *n. U.S. Colloq.* A person given a concession with a circus or carnival to run a freak show or refreshment stand, or operate games of chance, etc. [? < GRAFTER]

grill (gril) *v.t.* **1** To cook on a gridiron; broil. **2** To torment with heat. **3** *U.S. Colloq.* To cross-examine persistently and searchingly. —*v.i.* To be cooked on a gridiron. —*n.* **1** A gridiron. **2** That which is broiled on a gridiron. **3** A grillroom. **4** The action of grilling. **5** A grille or grating of any kind. [< F *griler* < *gril* < OF *greil*. See GRIDDLE.]—**grill'er** *n.*

grill·age (gril'ij) *n.* A heavy framework of crossed timbers or steel beams to sustain a foundation, especially on yielding soil. [< F < *grille*, var. of *gril* a grill]

grille (gril) *n.* **1** A grating or screen; especially one of wrought metal, as in a grate for shielding an open door or window. **2** In court tennis, a square opening at the rear of the hazard court. Also **grill**. [< F, var. of *gril*. See GRILL.]

grill·room (gril'rōōm', -rŏŏm') *n.* A restaurant or eating place where grilling is done or grilled food is served.

grill·work (gril'wûrk') *n.* **1** A grille (def. 1). **2** The design or structure of a grille.

grilse (grils) *n. pl.* **grilse** or **grils·es** A young salmon after its first return to fresh water: also called *graul*. [Origin unknown]

grim (grim) *adj.* **1** Stern and forbidding in aspect or nature; fierce; ferocious. **2** Harsh; severe; dreadful. **3** Unyielding; formidable. [OE]—**grim'ly** *adv.* —**grim'ness** *n.*

Synonyms: ferocious, fierce, hideous, savage, stern, sullen, terrible. *Grim* expresses or suggests a silent but most determined ferocity; as, the *grim* aspect of the executioner. Compare FIERCE. *Antonyms:* benign, genial, gentle, kind, mild, placid, sweet, tender.

gri·mace (gri-mās') *n.* A distortion of the features, either habitual or occasioned by annoyance,

disgust, contempt, etc.; a wry face. —*v.i.* **-maced, -mac·ing** To make grimaces. [< MF < Sp. *grimazo*, prob. < Gmc.]—**gri·mac'er** *n.*

Grimaldi man *Anthropol.* A type of early man represented by skeletons found in the caves of Grimaldi near Menton, on the French–Italian border: variously interpreted as ancestral to the Caucasoid or Negroid type.

gri·mal·kin (gri-mal'kin, -môl-) *n.* **1** A cat, particularly an old female cat. **2** A malevolent old woman. [< GRAY + MALKIN]

grime (grīm) *n.* That which soils; soot; dirt ground into a surface. —*v.t.* **grimed, grim·ing** To make dirty; begrime. [< Flemish *grijm*]

Grimes Golden A variety of golden-yellow eating apple. [after T. P. *Grimes*, c. 1790, who first grew it in W. Virginia]

Grimm's Law A statement by J. L. K. Grimm (earlier enunciated by Rasmus Rask) of the development of the consonants from Indo-European into Germanic. Among the commonest consonantal changes are: Indo-European voiceless plosives *(p, t, k)*, represented by Sanskrit *pitár*, Greek *treis*, Latin *centum*, becoming voiceless fricatives *(f, th, h)*, as seen in English *father*, *three*, *hundred*; Indo-European aspirated voiced plosives *(bh, dh, gh)*, represented by Sanskrit *bhrātar*, Sanskrit *dhā*, Latin *hostis* (IE **ghosti-s*), to unaspirated voiced plosives *(b, d, g)*, as in English *brother*, *do*, *guest*; Indo-European voiced plosives *(b, d, g)*, represented by Latin *cannabis*, Greek *damaein*, Latin *ager*, to voiceless plosives *(p, t, k)*, as in English *hemp*, *tame*, *acre*. A further development in High German accounts for the difference between English *pound*, German *pfund*; English *ten*, German *zehn*, English *make*, German *machen*; English *that*, German *das*. See VERNER'S LAW.

grim·y (grī'mē) *adj.* **grim·i·er, grim·i·est** Full of or covered with grime; dirty. —**grim'i·ly** *adv.* —**grim'i·ness** *n.*

grin (grin) *v.* **grinned, grin·ning** *v.i.* **1** To smile broadly. **2** To draw back the lips so as to show the teeth, as in pain, rage, or foolish laughter. —*v.t.* **3** To express by grinning. —*n.* The act of grinning; a broad smile. [OE *grennian*]—**grin'ner** *n.* —**grin'ning·ly** *adv.*

grind (grīnd) *v.* **ground, grind·ing** *v.t.* **1** To sharpen, polish, or shape by friction. **2** To reduce to fine particles, as by crushing or friction; triturate. **3** To rub or press gratingly or harshly: to *grind* one's teeth. **4** To oppress; harass cruelly. **5** To operate by turning a crank, as a coffee mill. **6** To produce by or as by grinding. **7** *Colloq.* To teach laboriously. —*v.i.* **8** To perform the operation of grinding. **9** To undergo grinding; become ground. **10** To rub; grate. **11** *Colloq.* To study or work steadily; drudge. —*n.* **1** The act of grinding, or the sound made by grinding. **2** *Colloq.* Work or study that is tediously and laboriously performed. **3** *Colloq.* A laborious student. [OE *grindan*]—**grind'ing** *adj. & n.* —**grind'ing·ly** *adv.*

grin·de·li·a (grin-dē'lē·ə) *n.* **1** Any plant of an American genus *(Grindelia)* of coarse herbaceous or shrubby plants with sessile, rigid leaves and large heads of yellow flowers. **2** The dried leaves and flowering tops of certain species of this plant *(G. camporum* or *G. humilis)*, yielding a balsam used in the treatment of asthma, bronchitis, and ivy poisoning. Also called *gum plant*. [< NL, after D. H. *Grindel*, Russian botanist]

grind·stone (grīnd'stōn') *n.* **1** A flat circular stone so hung that it can be rotated upon an axis: used for sharpening tools, abrading, etc. **2** A millstone.

grip (grip) *n.* **1** The act of grasping firmly; a holding fast; clutch; a firm grasp. **2** A particular mode of grasping hands, as among members of a secret society, for mutual recognition. **3** *U.S.* A valise; gripsack. **4** That part of a thing by which it is grasped. **5** One of various mechanical grasping devices. **6** Ability to seize and hold physically or mentally; intellectual grasping power. **7** *Slang* A stagehand; a scene-shifter. **8** A twinge of pain. —*v.* **gripped** or **gript, grip·ping** *v.t.* **1** To take firm hold of with or as with the hand; hold onto tightly. **2** To join or attach securely with a grip (def. 5). **3** To seize or

capture, as the mind; attract and hold the attention or imagination of. —*v.i.* **4** To take firm hold. **5** To take hold of the attention, imagination, etc. See synonyms under CATCH, GRASP. [Fusion of OE *gripe* a grasp and *gripa* handful, both < *gripan* seize. Akin to GROPE.] —**grip'per** *n.* —**grip'ping** *adj.* —**grip'ping·ly** *adv.*

gripe (grīp) *v.* **griped, grip·ing** *v.t.* **1** To seize and hold firmly; grasp; grip. **2** To cause pain in the bowels of, as if by sudden constriction. **3** To cause mental pain to; oppress; grieve. —*v.i.* **4** *U.S. Colloq.* To grumble; complain. **5** To suffer pains in the bowels. **6** *Obs.* To reach for or clutch something firmly. **7** *Naut.* To tend to come up into the wind. See synonyms under CATCH, GRASP. —*n.* **1** A fast or firm hold; grip; control. **2** *pl.* Intermittent pains in the bowels. [OE *gripan*] —**grip'er** *n.* —**grip'y** *adj.*

grippe (grip) *n.* Influenza. Also *grip.* [< F < *gripper* seize] —**grip'py** *adj.*

gri·saille (gri-zāl', *Fr.* grē-zä'y') *n.* **1** A style of painting in grayish monochrome, in imitation of bas-relief: especially adapted for decoration. **2** Any object, especially glass, thus painted. [< F < *gris* gray]

gris·e·ous (gris'ē·əs, griz'-) *adj.* Bluish-gray; having a mottled or grizzled grayish color. [< Med. L *griseus*]

gri·sette (gri-zet') *n.* **1** A Parisian working-girl, especially one of easy, gay manners. **2** A gray woolen dress fabric worn by French workingwomen. [< F, orig. a gray woolen fabric < *gris* gray]

gris·ly (griz'lē) *adj.* **·li·er, ·li·est** Savage-looking; fear-inspiring; horrifying. ◆ Homophone: *grizzly.* [OE *grislic*] —**gris'li·ness** *n.*

gri·son (grī'sən, griz'·ən) *n.* A South American carnivore *(Grison vittata)* resembling a weasel. [< F *grison* < *gris* gray]

GRISON

grist (grist) *n.* **1** A portion of grain brought to a mill to be ground; hence, that which is ground. **2** A supply; provision. **3** *U.S. Colloq.* A number or quantity of anything: a *grist* of flies. [OE < *grindan* grind]

gris·tle (gris'əl) *n.* Cartilage, especially in meat. [OE] —**gris'tled, gris'tly, gris'ly** *adj.* —**gris'tli·ness, gris'li·ness** *n.*

grist·mill (grist'mil') *n.* A mill for grinding grain.

grit[1] (grit) *n.* **1** Rough, hard particles; sand or fine gravel. **2** A coarse compact sandstone adapted for grindstones. **3** *U.S.* Firmness of character, especially in pain or danger; pluck; courage. **4** Degree of hardness with openness of texture or composition: applied to burrstone, etc. —*v.* **grit·ted, grit·ting** *v.t.* To grind or press (the teeth) together, as in anger or determination. —*v.i.* To give forth a grating sound. [OE *grēot*]

grit[2] (grit) *n.* **1** Coarse meal. **2** *pl. U.S.* Coarsely ground hominy. [OE *grytte*]

grit·ty (grit'ē) *adj.* **·ti·er, ·ti·est** **1** Like, containing, or consisting of grit. **2** *U.S.* Full of pluck. —**grit'ti·ly** *adv.* —**grit'ti·ness** *n.*

gri·va·tion (gri-vā'shən) *n.* Grid variation.

griv·et (griv'it) *n.* A small monkey *(Cercopithecus aethiops)* of Abyssinia, greenish above, whitish below. [Origin unknown]

griz·zle[1] (griz'əl) *v.t. & v.i.* **griz·zled, griz·zling** To become or cause to become gray. [< *adj.*] —*n.* **1** A mixture of white and black; gray. **2** A gray wig. **3** *Obs.* A gray-haired person. —*adj.* Gray. [< OF *grisel* < *gris* gray] —**griz'zled** *adj.*

griz·zle[2] (griz'əl) *v.i.* **griz·zled, griz·zling** *Brit. Colloq.* To grumble or fret continuously. [Freq. of dial. E *grize* grind the teeth]

griz·zly (griz'lē) *adj.* **·zli·er, ·zli·est** Grayish; somewhat gray: also spelled *grisly.* ◆ Homophone: *grisly[1].* —*n. pl.* **·zlies** A grizzly bear.

grizzly bear A large, powerful, yellowish or brownish bear *(Ursus horribilis)* of western North America.

groan (grōn) *v.i.* **1** To utter a low, prolonged sound of or as of pain, sorrow, etc.; moan. **2** To be oppressed or overburdened: The people *groaned* under the heavy taxes. —*v.t.*

3 To utter or express with groans. — *n.* A low moaning sound uttered in anguish, distress, or derision. [OE *grānian*] — **groan'er** *n.* — **groan'ing** *adj.* & *n.* — **groan'ing·ly** *adv.*

groat (grōt) *n.* **1** A former English silver coin of the 14th–17th centuries; fourpence. **2** A trifle. [<MDu. *groot*, orig. great, large]

groats (grōts) *n. pl.* Hulled and crushed oats or wheat; fragments of wheat larger than grits. [OE *grotan*]

gro·cer (grō'sər) *n.* One who deals in supplies for the table, as sugar, tea, coffee, spices, country produce, etc., and in other household articles. [<OF *grossier*, lit., one who trades in grosses, a wholesaler <Med. L *grossarius* <*grossus* gross, great]

gro·cer·y (grō'sər·ē) *n. pl.* **·cer·ies** **1** *U.S.* A grocer's store or shop. **2** *pl.* Supplies sold by a grocer.

Grod·no (grôd'nô) A city on the Nieman in western Belorussia; formerly in Poland.

grog (grog) *n.* A mixture of spirits and water; especially, rum and water; hence, any intoxicating drink. [after Old *Grog*, nickname (with ref. to his grogram cloak) of Admiral E. Vernon, 1684–1757, who first rationed it to English sailors]

grog·ger·y (grog'ər·ē) *n. pl.* **·ger·ies** *U.S. Slang* A low drinking place; a grogshop.

grog·gy (grog'ē) *adj.* **·gi·er, ·gi·est** **1** Unsteady on the feet or not fully conscious; dazed, as from weakness or exhaustion. **2** Drunk. — **grog'gi·ly** *adv.* — **grog'gi·ness** *n.*

grog·ram (grog'rəm) *n.* Grosgrain. [<F *gros grain*. See GROSGRAIN.]

groin (groin) *n.* **1** *Anat.* The fleshy hollow where the thigh joins the abdomen. ◆ Collateral adjective: *inguinal.* **2** *Archit.* The line of intersection of two vaults. — *v.t.* To build with or form into groins. [? OE *grynde* abyss, hollow]

grom·met (grom'it) *n.* **1** *Naut.* A ring of rope, as on the peak of a sail. **2** A metallic eyelet, as for a mailbag. Also spelled *grummet.* [<F *gromette* <*gourmer* curb]

grom·well (grom'wəl) *n.* **1** A rough grayish herb (*Lithospermum officinale*) of the borage family. **2** Any plant of this genus. [<OF *gromil* <L *gruinum milium* <*gruinum* a crane + *milium* millet]

Gro·ning·en (grō'ning·ən, *Du.* khrō'ning·ən) A city in northern Netherlands.

groom (grōōm, grŏŏm) *n.* **1** A person who cares for horses in the stable; hostler. **2** A bridegroom. **3** *Archaic* A menial; page; servitor. **4** A dignitary in an English royal household under the chamberlain, having nominal offices to perform. — *v.t.* **1** To take care of; especially, to clean, curry, and brush (a horse). **2** To make neat, clean, and smart. **3** *U.S.* To prepare by training and developing, as for political office: to *groom* a candidate. [ME *grom.* Cf. OF *gromet* a servant.]

groomed (grōōmd, grŏŏmd) *adj.* Brushed and cleaned; cared for: often in combination: ill-*groomed*, well-*groomed*.

grooms·man (grōōmz'mən, grŏŏmz'-) *n. pl.* **·men** (-mən) The best man at a wedding.

groove (grōōv) *n.* **1** A furrow, channel, or long hollow, especially one cut by a tool for something to fit into or work in. **2** A fixed routine in the affairs of life. **3** *U.S. Slang* A satisfying or delightful experience. — **in the groove** *Slang* Acting or performing deftly and smoothly. — *v.* **grooved, groov·ing** *v.t.* **1** To form a groove in. **2** To fix in a groove. **3** *U.S. Slang* To take satisfaction or delight in; dig. — *v.i.* **4** *U.S. Slang* To find satisfaction or delight. [<Du. *groeve.* Akin to GRAVE², GRAVE³.] — **groov'er** *n.*

grope (grōp) *v.* **groped, grop·ing** *v.i.* To feel about with or as with the hands, as in the dark; feel one's way. — *v.t.* To seek out or find by or as by groping. [OE *grāpian.* Akin to GRIP.] — **grop'er** *n.* — **grop'ing** *adj.*

gros·beak (grōs'bēk') *n.* Any of certain species of finches or of other small birds allied to the finches and having a large stout beak, including the **rose-breasted grosbeak** (*Hedymeles ludovicianus*) and the **pine grosbeak** (*Pinicola enucleator*) of North America. [<F *grosbec* large beak]

gro·schen (grō'shən) *n. pl.* **·schen** A former silver coin of Germany and Austria, of small value; also a current Austrian coin, a hundredth part of a schilling.

gros·grain (grō'grān) *n.* A closely woven corded silk or rayon fabric, often having a cotton filling, and of dull luster: used for ribbons, collar facings, etc.: also called *grogram.* [<F, large grain]

gross (grōs) *adj.* **1** Conspicuous by reason of size or openness; glaring; flagrant: said of errors, wrongs, faults, untruths, etc. **2** Undiminished by deduction; entire: opposed to *net*: *gross* earnings, *gross* weight. **3** Coarse in meaning or sense; indelicate; obscene: *gross* epithets. **4** Of excessive or repulsive size combined with coarseness; big; fat; bulky: a *gross* woman. **5** Wanting in fineness; coarse in composition or structure: *gross* material. **6** Closely compacted, so as to be thick or dense: *gross* vapors. **7** Wanting in delicacy of perception or sensibility; dull of apprehension or feeling; stupid. **8** Not specific or detailed; general. **9** *Obs.* Palpable; obvious. See synonyms under CORPULENT, FOUL, IMMODEST, THICK, VULGAR. — *n. pl.* **gross 1** Twelve dozen, as a unit. **2** The greater part; mass; entire amount. — **in gross** or **in the gross** In bulk; all together. — *v.t.* & *v.i.* To make or earn (total profit) before deduction of expenses, taxes, etc. [<OF *gros* <LL *grossus* thick] — **gross'ly** *adv.* — **gross'ness** *n.*

gross national product The total market value of a nation's goods and services, before any deductions or allowances are made.

grosz (grôsh) *n. pl.* **grosz·y** (grôsh'ē) A hundredth part of a zloty. [<Polish]

gro·tesque (grō·tesk') *adj.* **1** The incongruous, fantastic, or uncouth in art; specifically, painting or sculpture combining human and animal forms with foliage, wreaths, etc. **2** Any disproportionate or ludicrous person, figure, or design. — *adj.* **1** Incongruously composed or ill-proportioned; fantastic; ludicrously or whimsically odd or extravagant. **2** Containing or comprised of incongruous or fantastic details; pertaining to grotesques. See synonyms under FANCIFUL, ODD, RIDICULOUS. [<F <Ital. *grottesco* <*grotta* a grotto, excavation; with ref. to works of art found in excavations of ancient houses] — **gro·tesque'ness** *n.*

grot·to (grot'ō) *n. pl.* **·toes** or **·tos** A small cave; an artificial cavernlike retreat. [<Ital. *grotta* <L *crypta.* Doublet of CRYPT.]

grouch (grouch) *U.S. Colloq.* *v.i.* To grumble; be surly or discontented. — *n.* **1** A discontented, grumbling person. **2** A grumbling, sulky mood. [<OF *groucher* murmur] — **grouch'er** *n.* — **grouch'i·ly** *adv.* — **grouch'i·ness** *n.* — **grouch'y** *adj.*

ground¹ (ground) *n.* **1** The firm, solid portion of the earth at and near its surface. **2** Hence, soil; earth; dirt. **3** Any region or tract of land, especially a portion put to special use: a parade *ground*, hunting *ground*, etc. **4** *Often pl.* A starting point; good reason; basis; sufficient cause: On what *ground* is the argument based?; also, pretext. **5** Position or distance: to gain, hold, or lose *ground.* **6** *pl.* The particles that settle at the bottom of a liquid preparation; dregs. **7** In various arts, some preparative work or part, as a surface to be worked on; in painting, a first coat or color or a surface prepared therewith. **8** *Music* The plain song or air as a basis for development and variation. **9** *Electr.* **a** A connection of a circuit with the earth. **b** An object or place to which a ground wire is attached. **10** *Often pl.* Private land; landed estate; especially in the plural, the enclosed spaces immediately appertaining to a mansion. **11** *Often pl.* The base or foundation, as of belief or knowledge. **12** The bottom, as of a lake or the ocean; lowest depth. See synonyms under LAND, REASON. — **to gain ground 1** To conquer land. **2** To make progress; win favor, position, influence, etc. — **to stand one's ground** To maintain an argument or a purpose. — *adj.* **1** Being on the ground or on a level with it. **2** Fundamental: the *ground* form of a word. **3** Terrestrial: said of birds: the *ground* sparrow, *ground* warbler. **4** Burrowing: the *ground* squirrel, *ground* snake. **5** Growing on the ground; trailing or dwarfed: *ground* ivy, *ground* hemlock. — *v.t.* **1** To put, place, or set on the ground. **2** To fix firmly on a basis; found; establish. **3** To train (someone) in first principles or elements, as of Latin or science. **4** *Aeron.* To cause to stay on the ground. **5** *Naut.* To cause to run aground, as a ship. **6** To furnish (a surface) with a ground or background for painting, etc. **7** *Electr.* To place in connection with the earth, as a circuit. — *v.i.* **8** To come or fall to the ground. **9** In baseball, to be retired on a grounder batted to an opposing player: usually with *out.* **10** *Naut.* To run aground. **11** To sink to the bottom: The bait *grounds.* [OE *grund*]

ground² (ground) Past tense and past participle of GRIND.

ground bass *Music* A short bass part or phrase repeated continually against varied melody and harmony in the upper parts.

ground beetle Any of various insectivorous beetles of the family *Carabidae*, often found under logs, stones, etc. For illustration see under INSECT (beneficial).

ground cherry Any of several plants of the nightshade family (genus *Physalis*), as the Cape gooseberry (*P. peruviana*), having yellow, edible berries, or the common strawberry tomato (*P. pruinosa*).

ground fog *Meteorol.* A narrow layer of fog formed over a cool land surface, and not exceeding the height of a man.

ground frost A ground temperature low enough to cause injury to growing plants: usually reckoned at 30° F.

ground gear *Aeron.* The apparatus and equipment needed for the landing of aircraft and their handling while on the ground.

ground hemlock A low, evergreen shrub (*Taxus canadensis*) of the northern United States with long, straggling branches and a red fruit; the American yew: also called *moosegrass.*

ground hog 1 The woodchuck. **2** The aardvark. **3** A sandhog.

ground-hog day (ground'hôg', -hog') February 2, Candlemas: according to rural tradition, if the ground hog, emerging after hibernation, sees his shadow on this day, he retreats to his hole, thus indicating six weeks more of winter; if he does not see his shadow it is a sign of an early spring.

ground ivy A creeping herb (*Nepeta hederacea*) with roundish, kidney-shaped, scalloped leaves and bluish-purple flowers.

ground·less (ground'lis) *adj.* Without foundation, reason, or cause. — **ground'less·ly** *adv.* — **ground'less·ness** *n.*

ground·ling (ground'ling) *n.* **1** An animal of terrestrial habits. **2** A plant which creeps on the ground. **3** A fish that keeps to the bottom. **4** Formerly, one of the audience in the pit of a theater; hence, a person of unrefined tastes.

ground·mass (ground'mas') *n. Geol.* A compact and fine-grained or glassy portion of porphyritic igneous rock, in which the phenocrysts, or larger, distinct crystals, are embedded.

ground owl A small, long-legged, terrestrial owl (*Speotyto cunicularia*) common in the western United States, where it digs extensive nesting burrows in open prairie country: also called *burrowing owl.*

ground pine 1 An evergreen, generally creeping plant (*Lycopodium obscurum*); clubmoss. **2** An evergreen European herb (*Ajuga chamaepitys*): so called from its resinous odor.

ground pink The moss pink.

ground plate 1 A groundsill. **2** A bedplate, as for railroad ties. **3** *Electr.* A metal plate in the ground forming the earth connection of a circuit.

ground plum 1 A plant (*Astragalus crassicarpus*) of the bean family, found in the western Mississippi valley from Minnesota to Texas. **2** Its thick, fleshy, plum-shaped pod. Also called *milkvetch.*

ground speed *Aeron.* The speed of an airplane with relation to the earth. See AIR SPEED.

ground state *Physics* That condition of an atom which corresponds to its lowest level of energy and, hence, to its maximum stability.

ground swell A broad, deep swell or heaving of the sea caused by prolonged storm, continuing into calm weather, and frequently reaching open stretches of coast remote from the area of the storm.

ground water Free subsurface water, the top of which is the water table; all water in and saturating the soil.

ground wave A radio wave which travels along the surface of the ground.

ground·work (ground'wûrk') *n.* A fundamental part; basis.

ground zero The point on the ground vertically beneath or above the point of detonation of an atomic or thermonuclear bomb.

group (grōōp) *n.* **1** A number of persons, animals, or things existing or brought together; an assemblage; cluster. **2** In painting or sculpture, an assemblage of figures or objects affording a harmonious unit or design. **3** A number of plants or animals classed together because of certain common characteristics. **4** In the U.S. Air Force, a tactical, maintenance, medical, or administrative subdivision of a wing. **5** In the U.S. Army or Marine Corps, a tactical unit consisting of two or more battalions. **6** *Chem.* **a** A number of connected atoms constituting a part of a molecule: the hydroxyl *group* (OH). **b** A set of elements having similar properties, as in the periodic table. **7** *Geol.* A rock system of highest rank, corresponding with an era in the time scale. **8** An ethnological or linguistic division ranking below a branch. —*v.t. & v.i.* To gather or form into a group or groups. [< F *groupe* < Ital. *groppo* knot, lump < Gmc.]

group·er (grōō'pər) *n.* Any of certain serranoid food fishes of warm seas, of *Mycteroperca, Epinephalus,* and related genera. [< Pg. *garupa,* appar. < S. Am. Ind.]

grouse[1] (grous) *n. pl.* **grouse** Any of a family (*Tetraonidae*) of game birds of the northern hemisphere, related to the pheasants, smaller than the domestic hen, and having mottled plumage; especially, the **red grouse** (*Lagopus scoticus*) of the British Isles, the **ruffed grouse** or **partridge** (*Bonasa umbellus*) of the United States, the **pinnated grouse** or **prairie chicken** (*Tympanuchus cupido*), the **sage grouse** or cock of the plains, the **spruce grouse** or spruce partridge (*Canachites canadensis*), and the capercaillie. [Origin uncertain]

RUFFED GROUSE
(From 12 to 17 inches tall)

grouse[2] (grous) *Slang v.i.* **groused, grous·ing** To grumble; grouch. [< OF *grousser* murmur] — **grous'er** *n.* —**grous'ing** *n.*

grout (grout) *n.* **1** A light, semi-liquid cement mortar used to fill joints between stones, bricks or tiles. **2** A finishing coat for surfaces. **3** Coarse meal. **4** *pl.* Groats. **5** *pl.* Dregs; lees; grounds. **6** A wall coating of rough plaster studded with small stones. —*v.t.* To fill, surround, or finish with grout. [OE *grūt* coarse meal] —**grout'er** *n.*

grove (grōv) *n.* A group of trees, smaller than a forest; a small wood, especially when cleared of underbrush. ◆ Collateral adjective: *nemoral.* [OE *grāf*]

grov·el (gruv'əl, grov'-) *v.i.* **grov·eled** or **grov·elled, grov·el·ing** or **grov·el·ling 1** To creep or crawl face downward; lie abjectly prostrate. **2** To act with abject humility; abase oneself, as from fear or servility. **3** To take pleasure in what is base or sensual. [Back formation < GROVELING] —**grov'el·er** or **grov'el·ler** *n.*

grow (grō) *v.* **grew, grown, grow·ing** *v.i.* **1** To increase in size by the assimilation of nutriment; progress toward maturity. **2** To sprout and develop to maturity, as from a seed or spore. **3** To flourish; thrive: Moss *grows* in damp places. **4** To become more in size, quantity, or degree: The storm was *growing.* **5** To become; come to be gradually: She was *growing* angry. **6** To become fixed or attached by or as by growth: The vine *grew* to the wall. —*v.t.* **7** To cause to grow; raise by cultivation. **8** To develop: This crab will *grow* a new shell. **9** To cover with a growth: used in the passive: The hull was *grown* with weeds. — **grow on** To become gradually more pleasing or important to. —**grow up** To reach adult maturity. See synonyms under FLOURISH. [OE *grōwan*] —**grow'er** *n.*

grow·ing-pains (grō'ing-pānz') *n. pl.* **1** Pains of a rheumatic or neuralgic character sometimes experienced during the period of growth in children. **2** Problems encountered in the early phases of an enterprise.

growl (groul) *n.* **1** The guttural threatening sound made by an angry animal. **2** Angry fault-finding; grumbling. —*v.i.* **1** To utter a growl, as an angry dog. **2** To grumble or find fault in a surly manner. **3** To rumble, as distant thunder. —*v.t.* **4** To express by growling. See synonyms under COMPLAIN. [? < OF *grouler* mumble

< Gmc.]

growl·er (grou'lər) *n.* **1** One who or that which growls. **2** *U.S. Slang* A vessel in which beer is carried home from the place of sale. **3** *Brit. Slang* A four-wheeled cab. **4** *Electr.* A device which indicates the presence of a short circuit by a growling sound produced by two field poles arranged as in a motor. **5** An irregular fragment of an iceberg or mass of floe ice large enough to be dangerous to ships.

grown (grōn) *adj.* Mature; fully developed.

grown-up (grōn'up') *n.* A mature person. —*adj.* (grōn'up') Adult or like adults.

growth (grōth) *n.* **1** The process of growing; gradual increase of a living organism by natural process; development to maturity or full size. **2** Any gradual increase or development; augmentation; progress. **3** Anything grown or produced, or in the process of growing; product; effect. **4** *Pathol.* A morbid formation: a cancerous *growth.* See synonyms under HARVEST, INCREASE, PROGRESS.

growth industry An industry with a rate of growth or development greater than the rate of growth of the economy as a whole.

growth ring An annual ring.

grub (grub) *v.* **grubbed, grub·bing** *v.i.* **1** To dig in the ground. **2** To do menial labor; toil: to *grub* for a living. **3** To make careful or plodding search; rummage. **4** *Slang* To eat. —*v.t.* **5** To dig from the ground; root out: often with *up* or *out.* **6** To clear (ground) of roots, stumps, etc. **7** *Slang* To provide with food. —*n.* **1** The wormlike larva of certain insects, as of the June beetle and most of the *Hymenoptera.* See illustration under INSECT. **2** One who grubs; a grind or drudge. **3** *Slang* Food. [ME *grubben.* Akin to GRAVE[1], GRAVE[2].]

grub·ber (grub'ər) *n.* **1** One who or that which grubs. **2** A grub hoe. **3** A machine or tool for pulling up stumps.

grub·by (grub'ē) *adj.* **·bi·er, ·bi·est 1** Dirty; unclean. **2** Full of grubs: specifically used in the western United States of cattle or sheep attacked by the larvae of botflies or warbleflies. —**grub'bi·ly** *adv.* — **grub'bi·ness** *n.*

grub hoe A heavy hoe for digging or for grubbing out stumps; a mattock. See illustration under HOE.

grudge (gruj) *v.* **grudged, grudg·ing** *v.t.* **1** To envy the possessions or good fortunes of (another). **2** To give or allow unwillingly and resentfully; begrudge. —*v.i.* **3** *Obs.* To be envious or discontented; grumble. —*n.* **1** Ill will cherished for some remembered wrong. **2** Reluctance; unwillingness. See synonyms under HATRED, PIQUE[1]. [< OF *groucher.* Cf. GROUCH.] —**grudg'er** *n.* — **grudg'ing·ly** *adv.*

gru·el (grōō'əl) *n.* A semi-liquid food made by boiling meal in water or milk. — **to take one's gruel** To take one's punishment. —*v.t.* **gru·eled** or **gru·elled, gru·el·ing** or **gru·el·ling** To wear out, disable, or exhaust by hard work, punishment, etc. [< OF, meal, ult. < Med. L *grutum* coarse meal < Gmc.] —**gru'el·er** or **gru'el·ler** *n.* —**gru'el·ly** *adj.*

gru·el·ing (grōō'əl·ing) *adj.* Severe; exhausting; punishing. —*n.* Punishment; exhausting labor; prolonged and relentless questioning, etc. Also **gru'el·ling.**

grue·some (grōō'səm) *adj.* Frightening; grisly: also spelled *grewsome.* [< GRUE + -SOME] — **grue'some·ly** *adv.* — **grue'some·ness** *n.*

gruff (gruf) *adj.* Having a rough or brusque manner, voice, or countenance; harsh; surly. See synonyms under MOROSE. [< Du. *grof* rough] — **gruff'ish, gruff'y** *adj.* — **gruff'ly, gruff'i·ly** *adv.* — **gruff'ness, gruff'i·ness** *n.*

gru-gru (grōō'grōō) *n.* **1** Either of two West Indian palms (*Acrocomia aculeata* or *A. sclerocarpa*) the nuts of which yield a butter-like oil used for scenting toilet soap: also **gru–gru palm.** **2** The larva of a South American palm weevil (*Rhynchophorus palmarum*), destructive to the gru-gru and other palms and sugarcane, and eaten as a delicacy: also **gru–gru worm.** [< Sp. *grugrú* < Cariban]

grum·ble (grum'bəl) *v.* **grum·bled, grum·bling** *v.i.* **1** To complain in a surly manner; mutter. **2** To make growling sounds in the throat. **3** To rumble, as thunder. —*v.t.* **4** To say with a grumble. See synonyms under COMPLAIN. —*n.* **1** A surly, discontented sound or complaint; murmur. **2** *pl.* An ill-tempered, complaining mood. **3** A rumble. [Cf. Du. *grommelen* < *grommen* growl] —**grum'bler** *n.* — **grum'bling·ly** *adv.* — **grum'bly** *adj.*

grume (grōōm) *n.* **1** A viscid, semifluid mass. **2** A clot, as of blood. [< F < L *grumus* little pile]

gru·mose (grōō'mōs) *adj. Bot.* Consisting of clustered grains.

gru·mous (grōō'məs) *adj.* **1** Like grume; clotted. **2** Grumose.

grump·y (grum'pē) *adj.* **grump·i·er, grump·i·est** Exhibiting surliness or gruffness; cranky. Also **grump'ish.** [Blend of GRUNT and DUMP] — **grump'i·ly** *adv.* — **grump'i·ness** *n.*

grun·ion (grun'yən) *n.* A silversides (*Leuresthes tenuis*), common on the coast of California. [Prob. < Sp. *gruñón* grunter]

grunt (grunt) *v.i.* **1** To make the deep, guttural sound of a hog. **2** To make a similar sound, as in annoyance, assent, effort, etc. —*v.t.* **3** To express, as dissent or disapproval, by grunting. See synonyms under COMPLAIN. —*n.* **1** A short, guttural sound, as of a hog. **2** A food fish of warm American seas related to the snappers (*Haemulon* and related genera): so called from the noise it makes when caught. [OE *grunnettan*] —**grunt'er** *n.*

Grus (grus) A constellation, the Crane. See under CONSTELLATION.

Gru·yère (grē-yâr', grōō-; *Fr.* grü-yâr') *n.* A light-yellow, whole-milk Swiss cheese, usually without holes. [from *Gruyère,* a town in Switzerland]

gryl·lid (gril'id) *n.* One of a family (*Gryllidae*) of orthopterous insects having the hind legs specialized for jumping, long, slender antennae, and wings frequently reduced or absent; a cricket. —*adj.* Of or pertaining to the *Gryllidae.* [< NL < L *gryllus* a grasshopper < Gk. *gryllos*]

G-string (jē'string') *n.* **1** A strip of cloth passed between the legs and supported at the waist by a band or cord; a loincloth. **2** A thin strip of cloth, often ornamented with tassels and spangles, worn about the groin and hip by strip-teasers.

gua·cha·ro (gwä'chä·rō) *n.* The oilbird (*Steatornis caripensis*) of South America and Trinidad, of frugivorous and nocturnal habits, from whose young an oil is extracted and used by the natives as butter and for illumination. [< Sp. *guácharo*]

gua·co (gwä'kō) *n.* Any of certain tropical American climbing plants used as antidotes to snake bites; especially, the birthworts (genus *Aristolochia*), closely allied to the Virginia snakeroot, and a climbing Brazilian plant (genus *Mikania*), of the composite family. [< Sp. < native name]

Gua·da·la·ja·ra (gwä'thä·lä·hä'rä) A city of west central Mexico, capital of Jalisco state.

Gua·de·loupe (gô'də·lōōp', *Fr.* gwà·də·lōōp') An overseas department of France in the Lesser Antilles, comprising the twin islands of Basse-Terre (also called *Guadeloupe*) and Grande-Terre; together 583 square miles; with island dependencies, 639 square miles; capital, Basse-Terre.

guai·ac (gwī'ak) *n.* **1** A brown or greenish-brown resin extracted from guaiacum: used in medicine, in making paints and varnishes, etc.: also **guai'a·cum** (-ə·kəm). **2** The Tonka bean.

guai·a·col (gwī'ə·kōl, -kol) *n. Chem.* A colorless fluid or white crystalline compound, $C_7H_8O_2$, obtained by distilling guaiacum, found in hardwood tar, and also made synthetically: its compounds are widely used in medicine. [< GUAIAC(UM) + -OL[2]]

guai·a·cum (gwī'ə·kəm) *n.* **1** Any of a genus (*Guajacum*) of tropical American trees or shrubs of the caltrop family, especially *G. officinale* and *G. sanctum.* **2** The hard, durable, resinous wood of this tree or shrub; lignumvitae. **3** Guaiac. [< NL < Sp. *guayacán* < Taino]

Guam (gwäm) The largest island of the Marianas group, comprising an unincorporated territory of the United States; ceded by Spain in 1898; 217 square miles; capital, Agaña. — **Gua·ma·ni·an** (gwə·mä′nē·ən) *adj. & n.*

guan (gwän) *n.* A Central and South American gallinaceous bird (subfamily *Penelopinae*), related to the currasows, having a long tail. [<Sp. <Cariban]

gua·na·co (gwä·nä′kō) *n. pl.* **·cos** or **·co** A South American ruminant of the llama family (*Lama huanacus*), of light-brown color, passing into white below: also spelled *huanaco*. [<Sp. < Quechua]

Gua·na·jua·to (gwä′nä·hwä′tō) A state in central Mexico; 11,804 square miles; capital Guanajuato.

gua·nase (gwä′nās) *n. Biochem.* An autolytic enzyme capable of changing guanine into xanthine.

GUANACO
(From 4 to 4 1/2 feet high at the shoulder)

gua·ni·dine (gwä′nə·dēn, -din, gwan′ə-) *n. Chem.* A strongly basic crystalline compound, CH_5N_3, formed by the oxidation of guanine: many of its derivatives are used in the making of plastics, resins, explosives, etc. Also **gua′ni·din** (-din).

gua·nine (gwä′nēn) *n. Biochem.* A white amorphous compound, $C_5H_5N_5O$, contained in guano, fish scales, muscle tissue, the pancreas: it is also a decomposition product of nucleoproteins. Also **gua′nin** (-nin). [<GUANO + -INE[2]]

gua·no (gwä′nō) *n. pl.* **·nos** 1 The accumulated excrement of sea birds found in the dry climate of the Peruvian coast and elsewhere: used as a fertilizer. 2 A manufactured nitrogenous fertilizer; also, decomposing animal remains used as a fertilizer. [<Sp. <Quechua *huanu* dung]

Guan·tá·na·mo (gwän·tä′nä·mō) A city near **Guantánamo Bay,** a sheltered Caribbean inlet, site of a U.S. naval station in SE Cuba.

Gua·po·ré (gwä·pô·rä′) 1 A river of central South America, forming part of the boundary between Brazil and NE Bolivia and flowing 750 miles NW to the Mamore: also *Iténez.* 2 The former name of RONDÔNIA.

gua·ra·ni (gwä′rä·nē′) *n.* The basic monetary unit of Paraguay, equal to 100 centavos.

Gua·ra·ni (gwä′rä·nē′) *n. pl.* **·nis** or **·ni** 1 A member of any of a group of South American Indian tribes, comprising the southern branch of the Tupian stock, and formerly occupying the valleys of the Paraná and the Uruguay. 2 The Tupian language of these tribes. [< Tupian, a warrior]

guar·an·tee (gar′ən·tē′) *n.* 1 A pledge or formal assurance that something will meet stated specifications or that a specified act will be performed. 2 Something given as security. 3 A guarantor. 4 Something which assures a certain outcome: Diligence is a *guarantee* of success. — *v.t.* **·teed, ·tee·ing** 1 To certify or vouch for the performance of (something); warrant. 2 To make (oneself) responsible for the obligation of another. 3 To secure against loss or damage. 4 To affirm with certainty; promise; swear: He *guarantees* to be there. [Var. of GUARANTY]

guar·an·tor (gar′ən·tər, -tôr′) *n.* One who or that which guarantees or warrants; one who makes a guaranty or makes himself responsible for the obligation of another.

guar·an·ty (gar′ən·tē) *n. pl.* **·ties** 1 A pledge, made in separate contract, to be responsible for the contract, debt, or duty of another person in case of his default or miscarriage. 2 A deposit or security made in place of such a pledge. 3 The assumption of such responsibility by pledge or security. 4 A guarantor. — *v.t.* **·tied, ·ty·ing** To guarantee. [<OF *guarantie* < *guarantir* warrant < *guarant* a warrant <Gmc. Doublet of WARRANTY.]

guard (gärd) *v.t.* 1 To stand guard over (a door, pass, etc.). 2 To watch over so as to keep from harm, loss, etc.; protect. 3 To watch over so as to keep from escaping. 4 To

keep a check on; restrain: *Guard* your tongue. 5 *Archaic* To escort. — *v.i.* 6 To take precautions; be on guard. See synonyms under KEEP, PRESERVE, SHELTER. — *n.* 1 One who or that which protects, defends, or secures from loss, injury, or attack; hence, defense; protection; watch. 2 Specifically, a man or a body of men occupied in preserving a person or place from attack, or in controlling prisoners or preventing their escape. 3 Precaution against surprise or attack; care; attention. 4 A posture, attitude, or condition of defense. 5 Any of various protective or defensive devices for wearing, or for attaching to an object, as a machine or implement. 6 *Brit.* A railway official in charge of a train; a conductor. 7 *U.S.* An official employed on elevated and subway trains at points of entrance and egress. 8 In football, one of two line players (the **right guard** and **left guard**) who support the center; also, one of two players in basketball with similar positions and titles. See synonyms under DEFENSE, RAMPART. — **on guard** 1 Ready for defense or protection; on the watch, as a military guard. 2 The first position in fencing or in bayonet exercises. Also, *French, en garde.* [<OF *guarder, garder* <Gmc. Akin to WARD.] — **guard′er** *n.*

guard cell *Bot.* A specialized epidermal cell in plants, controlling the pores by which gases enter and pass from the leaves and young stems.

guard·ed (gär′did) *adj.* Exhibiting caution; circumspect; also, protected. — **guard′ed·ly** *adv.* — **guard′ed·ness** *n.*

guard·house (gärd′hous′) *n.* 1 A quarters and headquarters for military guards. 2 A building for confinement of military personnel convicted of minor offenses or awaiting court martial.

guard·i·an (gär′dē·ən) *n.* 1 *Law* A person who legally has the care of the person or property, or both, of one who is incompetent to act for himself, especially of an infant or minor. 2 One to whom anything is committed for safekeeping or preservation. 3 One who guards; a warden. ♦ Collateral adjective: *custodial.* — *adj.* Keeping guard; watching; protecting; tutelary. [<OF *guarden* < *guarder* guard. Doublet of WARDEN.] — **guard′i·an·ship** *n.*

guard·rail (gärd′rāl′) *n.* 1 *Naut.* A timber bolted to a ship's side to serve as a fender. 2 On railroads, a beam or rail parallel to a main rail in a track to prevent the wheels from jumping the track: used on curves and other dangerous places. 3 A protective railing around any dangerous place.

guard·room (gärd′rōōm′, -rōōm′) *n.* 1 The room occupied by a military guard while on duty. 2 A room where prisoners are kept under guard.

guards·man (gärdz′mən) *n. pl.* **·men** (-mən) 1 A man who serves as a guard. 2 *U.S.* A member of the National Guard.

guard·wire (gärd′wīr′) *n. Electr.* A grounded wire erected near a low-voltage circuit or public crossing as a safeguard against accidental contact with a high-voltage overhead conductor.

Guá·ri·co (gwä′rē·kō) A state in central Venezuela; 25,640 square miles; capital, San Juan de los Morros.

Gua·te·ma·la (gwä′tə·mä′lä) A Central American republic south and east of Mexico; 42,042 square miles; capital, Guatemala City. — **Gua′te·ma′lan** *adj. & n.*

gua·va (gwä′və) *n.* 1 A small tropical American tree or shrub of the myrtle family (genus *Psidium*). 2 Its fruit, about the size of a crab apple, chiefly used in making guava jelly. [<Sp. *guayaba*, appar. <S. Am. Ind.]

gua·yu·le (gwä·yōō′lä) *n.* 1 A perennial herb (*Parthenium argentatum*) of the composite family, grown in Mexico, Texas, and California. 2 The resinous latex of this tree, yielding a natural rubber: also **guayule rubber.** [<Sp. <Nahuatl]

gu·ber·na·to·ri·al (gōō′bər·nə·tôr′ē·əl, -tō′rē-, gyōō′-) *adj.* Of or pertaining to a governor or the office of governor. [<L *gubernator* a governor < *gubernare* govern]

gudg·eon[1] (guj′ən) *n.* 1 An Old World, carp-like, fresh-water fish (genus *Gobio*), very easily caught. 2 A minnow. 3 A simpleton. 4 Anything swallowed credulously; bait.

— *v.t.* To impose upon; cheat; dupe. [<OF *goujon* <L *gobio,* var. of *gobios.* See GOBY.]

gudg·eon[2] (guj′ən) *n.* 1 *Mech.* The bearing of a shaft, especially when made of a separate piece. 2 A metallic journal piece let into the end of a wooden shaft. [<OF *gougeon* pin of a pulley]

guel·der·rose (gel′dər·rōz′) *n.* The snowball tree, a cultivated variety of cranberry with white flowers. [from *Guelder(land) rose*]

Guelf (gwelf) *n.* 1 A member of a medieval political faction in Italy that supported the papacy in its struggle against the influence of the German emperors: opposed to the *Ghibellines.* 2 A member of a German princely family, founded in the time of Charlemagne by Welf I in Swabia, from which the Hanoverian line of English kings descended. Also **Guelph.** [<Ital. *Guelfo,* ult. after OHG *Welf,* a family name] — **Guelf′i·an, Guelf′ic** *adj.* — **Guelf′ism** *n.*

gue·non (gə·nôn′, *Fr.* gə·nôn′) *n.* A long-tailed monkey (genus *Cercopithecus*) found in Mozambique, Africa: its banded hairs give it a mottled appearance. [<F; ult. origin unknown]

guer·don (gûr′dən) *n.* An honorable reward; requital. [<OF <Med. L *widerdonum* <OHG *widarlōn* <*widar* in turn + *lōn* reward] — **guer′don·er** *n.*

guern·sey (gûrn′zē) *n.* A knitted shirt; jersey.

Guern·sey (gûrn′zē) *n.* One of a breed of dairy cattle from the island of Guernsey, Channel Islands.

Guer·re·ro (ger·rā′rō) A state in SW Mexico; 24,885 square miles; capital, Chilpancingo.

guer·ril·la (gə·ril′ə) *n.* One of an irregular, independent band of partisan soldiers. Also **gue·ril′la.** [<Sp. *guerrilla,* dim. of *guerra* a war]

guess (ges) *v.t.* 1 To form a judgment or opinion of (something) on uncertain or incomplete knowledge; surmise; conjecture. 2 To conjecture correctly: to *guess* the answer. 3 To believe; think: I *guess* we'll be late. — *v.i.* 4 To form a judgment or opinion on uncertain or incomplete knowledge. 5 To conjecture correctly: How did you *guess?* — *n.* 1 A tentative opinion or conclusion; a supposition; surmise; conjecture. 2 The act of guessing. [ME *gessen,* prob. <Scand. Cf. Sw. *gissa,* Dan. *gisse* guess.] — **guess′er** *n.*

Synonyms (verb): conjecture, divine, fancy, imagine, suppose, surmise, suspect. See SOLVE, SUPPOSE. *Antonyms:* demonstrate, establish, prove.

Synonyms (noun): conjecture, hypothesis, supposition, surmise. A *guess* is a conclusion from data directly at hand, and held as probable or tentative, while one confessedly lacks material for certainty. A *conjecture* is preliminary and tentative, but more methodical than a *guess;* a *supposition* is more nearly final; a *surmise* is an imagination or a suspicion. *Antonyms:* assurance, certainty, confidence, conviction, demonstration, proof.

guess·ti·mate (ges′tə·mit) *n. U.S. Colloq.* A prediction or extrapolation based, in part, on guesswork.

guess·work (ges′wûrk′) *n.* The process of guessing, or the result obtained thereby; a guess, or guesses collectively.

guest (gest) *n.* 1 A person received and entertained at the house of another; a visitor. 2 A lodger or boarder. 3 A parasitic animal; especially, any of various inquilines or insects living or breeding in the nests of other species: *guest* ants, *guest* wasps, etc. 4 *Obs.* A foreigner; stranger. — *v.t.* To entertain as a guest. — *v.i.* To be a guest. [OE *giest;* infl. in form by ON *gastr* stranger. Akin to HOST[1], HOST[2].]

guest room A room, as in a private home or inn, which is used for the lodging of guests.

guest rope *Naut.* 1 A hawser carried and paid out by a boat so as to connect a vessel with an object towards which it is to be warped. 2 A rope used to assist the towline of a boat in towing; also, a line by which a boat is fastened to a vessel or eased into a gangway. Also **guess rope, guess warp, ges·warp** (ges′wôrp′).

Gueux (gœ) *n. pl.* The Dutch nobles and burghers who from 1566 resisted the Inquisition and Philip II in the Netherlands. [<F, beggars]

guff (guf) *n.* 1 A sudden or slight gust of air;

puff. 2 *Slang* Nonsense; buncombe. [Imit.]
guf·faw (gə-fô′) *n.* A shout of boisterous laughter; horselaugh. — *v.i.* To utter such laughter. [Imit.]

gu·ha (gōō′hä, gōō′ä) *n. Pathol.* A type of bronchial asthma endemic on the island of Guam. Also **gu′ja.**

Gui·an·a (gē-an′ə, -ä′nə) A region of NE South America, comprising British and French Guiana, Surinam, and sometimes including northern Brazil and eastern Venezuela. — **the Guianas:** British Guiana, French Guiana, Surinam.

gui·dance (gīd′ns) *n.* 1 The act, process, or result of guiding. 2 A leading; direction. 3 *Mil.* The principles and techniques of assembling, interpreting, and transmitting intelligence necessary to the maneuvering of guided missiles along their flight paths to the designated targets.

guide (gīd) *v.* **guid·ed, guid·ing** *v.t.* 1 To show the way to; lead or accompany as a guide. 2 To direct the motion or action of, as a vehicle, tool, etc. 3 To lead or direct the affairs, standards, opinions, etc., of: Let these principles *guide* your life. — *v.i.* 4 To act as a guide. See synonyms under LEAD¹, REGULATE. — *n.* 1 One who leads or directs another in any path or direction; one who shows the way by accompanying or going in advance; specifically, one who conducts sightseers, or an expert woodsman who conducts hunters, fishermen, etc. 2 Something serving to guide; a guidebook or guidepost. 3 *Mech.* Any device acting as an indicator or serving to keep a part or object in position or to regulate its operation. 4 *Mil.* A soldier on the flank of a line to mark a pivot or regulate an alinement. See synonyms under RULE. [< OF *guider*] — **guid′a·ble** *adj.* — **guid′er** *n.*

guided missile *Mil.* An unmanned aerial missile whose course can be altered during flight by mechanisms within it and sometimes under the control of radio signals transmitted from ground stations or from aircraft.

guide·line (gīd′līn′) *n.* 1 A line, as a rope, for guiding. 2 A word, phrase, etc., often printed as a guide along the upper margin of printed copy. 3 Any indication of the limits or scope of an undertaking.

guide·post (gīd′pōst′) *n.* 1 A post with an attached sign giving directions to travelers, as at a roadside. 2 Anything that guides, directs, or limits; guideline.

guide·rope (gīd′rōp′) *n.* 1 *Aeron.* **a** A long rope suspended from a balloon or dirigible and trailed along the ground as a brake and to maintain altitude. **b** Any similar rope for hauling down and mooring an airship; a grab line: also called *trail rope.* 2 A line attached to a rope to hold it in position.

gui·don (gīd′n) *n.* 1 A forked flag carried by mounted troops. 2 The man who carries it. 3 A small flag carried by a unit of the U.S. Army as a company emblem. [< F < Ital. *guidone*]

guild (gild) *n.* 1 A corporation or association of persons engaged in kindred pursuits for mutual protection, aid, etc., known in England from the seventh century. 2 A church or religious association organized for benevolent and other parish work. 3 *Ecol.* **a** One of four groups of plants having characteristic modes of life, namely, the lianas, epiphytes, saprophytes, and parasites. **b** A group of plants which, under certain ecological conditions, adapt themselves in mass to a new locality. Also spelled *gild.* ◆ Homophone: *gild.* [Fusion of OE *gild* payment, *gegyld* association, and ON *gildi* payment] — **guild′ship** *n.* — **guilds′man** *n.*

Guild·hall (gild′hôl′) The hall of the Corporation of the City of London, England.

guile (gīl) *n.* 1 The act of deceiving, or the disposition to deceive; craft; duplicity; treachery. 2 *Obs.* A stratagem. See synonyms under ARTIFICE, DECEPTION. [< OF < Gmc. ? Akin to WILE.] — **guile′ful** *adj.*

guile·less (gīl′lis) *adj.* Free from guile; artless; frank. See synonyms under CANDID, INNOCENT, PURE. — **guile′less·ly** *adv.* — **guile′less·ness** *n.*

guil·le·mot (gil′ə-mot) *n.* Any of several narrow-billed auks (genera *Uria* and *Cepphus*), found in northern latitudes; specifically, the **black guille-**

mot (*C. grylle*) or cuttie, and the murres, including the **foolish guillemot** (*Uria aalge*). [< F, dim. of *Guillaume* William]

guil·loche (gi-lōsh′) *n.* An ornament formed by two or more intertwining bands or intersecting lines; an ornamental braid. [< F *guillochis*; ult. origin unknown]

guil·lo·tine (gil′ə-tēn) *n.* 1 The instrument of capital punishment in France, consisting of a weighted knife which falls and beheads the victim: invented by Antoine Louis, 1723–92, French physician. 2 A form of papercutting machine. 3 *Surg.* An instrument for cutting the tonsils. — *v.t.* **·tined, ·tin·ing** To behead with the guillotine. [< F, after Dr. J. I. *Guillotin*, 1738–1814, who advocated its use]

GUILLOTINE
Showing the basket for the body and receptacle for the head.

guilt (gilt) *n.* 1 The state of one who, by violation of law, has made himself liable to or deserving of punishment; culpability. 2 Wrongdoing; wickedness. See synonyms under SIN. ◆ Homophone: *gilt.* [OE *gylt*]

guilt·y (gil′tē) *adj.* **guilt·i·er, guilt·i·est** 1 Having violated a law or rule of duty; liable to penalty. 2 Involving, expressing, feeling, or characterized by guilt. See synonyms under CRIMINAL. — **guilt′i·ly** *adv.* — **guilt′i·ness** *n.*

guin·ea (gin′ē) *n.* 1 A former English gold coin, so called because first coined (1663) from Guinea gold: last issued in 1813; now, money of account: equal to 21 shillings. 2 The guinea fowl.

Guin·ea (gin′ē) 1 A term formerly used to describe a coastal region in western Africa, divided by the Niger delta into **Upper Guinea** and **Lower Guinea.** It was broadly considered to consist of the littoral portions of the British, French, and Portuguese equatorial possessions from Senegal to Angola. 2 The littoral portion of the territory extending from the Niger delta to southern Senegal. See PORTUGUESE GUINEA, SPANISH GUINEA. 3 A republic in west Africa, coextensive with former French Guinea; 95,350 square miles; Capital, Conakry.

Guinea, Gulf of An inlet of the Atlantic in the western coast of Africa, south of the great bulge of the continent.

Guinea corn Durra.

guinea fowl A gallinaceous bird (*Numida meleagris*) of African origin, having dark-gray plumage speckled with white spots: long domesticated in Europe and America: also *guinea, guinea hen.*

guinea grains Grains of paradise.

guinea grass A hardy, perennial, erect grass (*Panicum*

GUINEA FOWL
(About 15 inches tall)

maximum) native to Africa: grown in the southern United States for forage.

guinea green A crystalline substance, $C_{37}H_{35}N_2O_6S_2Na$, dark-green in powder form.

guinea hen 1 A female guinea fowl. 2 A guinea fowl.

Guinea pepper Cayenne pepper.

guinea pig 1 A small, domesticated rodent, usually white, variegated with red and black, having short ears and lacking a visible tail, widely used as an experimental animal in biological and medical research. 2 Any object or victim of experimentation.

Guinea worm A slender, threadlike nematode worm (*Dracunculus medinensis*), common in tropical Africa and Asia. The larva parasitically enters the stomach of man or animal, usually in drinking water, and makes its way to the subcutaneous connective tissue, especially, in man, of the legs and feet.

guise (gīz) *n.* 1 The external appearance as produced by garb or costume; outward seeming; mien; aspect; habit; dress. 2 The manner; behavior; also, customary manner; fashion; way. 3 A mask or pretense; cover. — *v.* **guised, guis·ing** *v.t.* 1 *Archaic* To dress; costume. 2 *Brit. Dial.* To disguise. — *v.i.* 3 *Brit. Dial.* To go about in disguise or costume. [< OF < Gmc. Akin to WISE².]

Guise (gēz) A town in northern France.

gui·tar (gi-tär′) *n.* A musical instrument having a fretted fingerboard and usually six strings, played with the fingers. [< Sp. *guitarra* < Gk. *kithara.* Doublet of CITHARA, ZITHER.]

gui·tar·fish (gi-tär′fish′) *n. pl.* **·fish** or **·fish·es** Any of a family (Rhinobatidae) of viviparous, sharklike rays having a long tail and wide body.

guit-guit (gwit′gwit′) *n.* Any of several tropical American birds, the honey creepers. [Imit.]

Gu·ja·rat (gōōj′ə-rät′) A fertile plain in northern Bombay State, India. Also **Gu′ze·rat′** (gōōz′-).

Gu·ja·ra·ti (gōōj′ə-rä′tē) *n.* The language of the natives of Gujarat, Baroda, and the adjoining states, belonging to the Indic branch of Indo-Iranian languages.

GUITAR

Gujarat States A group of former princely states included since 1949 in various districts of Bombay State, India; 7,493 square miles.

gu·la (gyōō′lə) *n. pl.* **·lae** (-lē) 1 *Anat.* The esophagus or gullet. 2 *Ornithol.* The upper part of the throat next the chin, as in a bird. 3 *Entomol.* The ventral part of the neck in insects; also, the submentum in a beetle. [< L, throat] — **gu′lar** *adj.*

gulch (gulch) *n. U.S.* A ravine; hollow; gully. [< dial. *gulch* swallow greedily]

gul·den (gōōl′dən) *n.* 1 The monetary unit of value in the Netherlands. 2 The Austro-Hungarian florin: a former monetary unit. 3 One of various coins formerly current in Germany and the Netherlands. Also *guilder, gilder.* [< Du. and G, lit., golden]

gules (gyōōlz) *n. Her.* The tincture red: in a blazon without color, indicated by parallel vertical lines. [< OF *gueules* red-dyed ermine fur, ? < L *gula* throat]

gulf (gulf) *n.* 1 The tract of water within an indentation or curve of the coastline, in size between a bay and a sea. 2 An abyss; chasm. 3 That which engulfs irretrievably; a whirlpool. 4 A wide or impassable space; a separation not easily bridged. — *v.t.* To swallow up as in a gulf; engulf. [< OF *golfe* < Ital. *golfo* < LGk. *kolphos* < Gk. *kolpos* a bay]

Gulf Stream The largest of the warm ocean current systems, flowing from the Gulf of Mexico along the coast of the United States to Nantucket, and thence eastward as far as Norway.

gulf·weed (gulf′wēd′) *n.* Any of a genus (*Sargassum*) of brown algae that grow in warm seas and are found drifting in the Gulf Stream and the Sargasso Sea. Also called *sargasso.*

gull¹ (gul) *n.* 1 A long-winged, usually white,

web-footed swimming bird (family *Laridae*) having the upper mandible hooked. **2** One of various sea birds related to the gull, as a tern or gannet. [ME < Celtic. Cf. Welsh *gwylan* a gull.]

gull[2] (gul) *n.* **1** A simple, credulous person; dupe. **2** A deceit; fraud; trick. —*v.t.* To deceive; outwit; cheat. [? < obs. *gull* swallow; infl. by ME *goll* a gosling]

gul·let (gul′it) *n.* **1** *Anat.* The passage from the mouth to the stomach; the esophagus. **2** The throat or neck. **3** A channel for water; ravine; gully. [< OF *goulet*, dim. of *goule* throat < L *gula*]

gul·li·ble (gul′ə-bəl) *adj.* Capable of being easily gulled, duped, or deceived; simple; credulous. Also **gul′la·ble.** —**gul′li·bil′i·ty, gul′la·bil′i·ty** *n.*

gul·ly (gul′ē) *n. pl.* **·lies** **1** A channel or ravine cut in the earth by running water; narrow ravine. **2** A watercourse. —*v.t.* **gul·lied, gul·ly·ing** To cut or wear a gully in. [Var. of GULLET]

gulp (gulp) *v.t.* **1** To swallow eagerly and in large amounts: usually with *down.* **2** To keep back as if by swallowing: to *gulp* down a retort. —*v.i.* **3** To gasp or choke as if taking a large drink of liquid. —*n.* The act of gulping, or something gulped down; a swallow; also, the amount swallowed: a *gulp* of milk. [< Du. *gulpen;* of imit. origin] — **gulp′er** *n.* —**gulp′ing·ly** *adv.*

gum[1] (gum) *n.* **1** An amorphous, brittle, colloidal mass resulting from the drying of the exuded sap of trees or shrubs. True gums are complex hydrocarbons; they are usually soluble in water, but not in alcohol, ether, and the oils; but the name is popularly applied also to true resins and to gum resins, especially when used as mucilage, etc. **2** The gum tree. **3** Rubber. **4** *pl. U.S. Dial.* Rubber overshoes; also, automobile tires. **5** A preparation of some natural gum (as cherry gum or balsam of Tolu), or some other tenacious substance, flavored and sweetened for use as a masticatory: also **chewing gum. 6** *U.S. Dial.* A section of a gum tree made into a well-curb, a watering trough, a bin, etc.; also, a beehive made of a similar hollow log. **7** Any sticky, viscous substance. **8** The adhesive wash on the reverse side of postage stamps. —*v.* **gummed, gum·ming** *v.t.* **1** To smear with gum. **2** To stiffen or unite with gum. —*v.i.* **3** To exude or form gum. **4** To become stiff and sticky. —**to gum up** *U.S. Slang* To bungle or ruin. [< OF *gomme* < L *gummi* < Gk. *kommi*] —**gum′mer** *n.*

gum[2] (gum) *n. Anat.* The fleshy tissue that covers the alveolar arches of the jaws and invests the necks of the teeth. ◆ Collateral adjective: *gingival.* —*v.t.* **gummed, gum·ming** To chew with the gums: He *gums* his food. [OE *goma* inside of mouth]

gum arabic The dried, yellowish-white or amber gum from various species of *Acacia*, especially *A. senegal* and *A. arabica*, composed chiefly of the salts of arabic acid: widely used in medicine and the arts.

gum·bo (gum′bō) *n.* **1** Okra. **2** The stratified portion of the lower till of the Mississippi Valley; especially, those soils which form a sticky or soapy mud when wet. **3** Clay encountered in drilling for oil or sulfur. —*adj.* Resembling or pertaining to gumbo soil (see *n.* def. 3). [< Bantu language of Angola]

gum·bo·til (gum′bō-til) *n. Geol.* A gray or brown plastic clay resulting from the prolonged weathering of glacial deposits; the varying thicknesses of its layers sometimes give indications of the length of interglacial periods. [< GUMBO + TILL[4]]

gum·ma (gum′ə) *n. pl.* **gum·ma·ta** (gum′ə-tə) or **gum·mas** *Pathol.* A soft tumor occurring in tertiary syphilis. [< NL < L *gummi* gum] — **gum′ma·tous** *adj.*

gum·mite (gum′īt) *n.* A greasy, viscid material of red or yellow color, formed as an alteration product of pitchblende.

gum·mo·sis (gu·mō′sis) *n. Bot.* The extensive change of tissue into gum, as in cherry gum.

gum·my (gum′ē) *adj.* **·mi·er, ·mi·est** Like or covered with gum; sticky; viscous. Also **gum′mous.** See synonyms under ADHESIVE. —**gum′mi·ness** *n.*

gum plant Any of several plants of the western United States (genus *Grindelia*), covered with a glutinous varnish when young. Also **gum weed.**

gump·tion (gump′shən) *n. Colloq.* **1** Ready perception; quick-wittedness; initiative. **2** Shrewd common sense. [< dial. E (Scottish). Cf. ME *gome* care, heed.]

gum resin Any of a kind of combined gum and

resin which oozes as a milky juice from incisions in the stems, roots, or branches of certain plants and gradually solidifies in the air.

gum-shoe (gum′shoō′) *n.* **1** *U.S. Slang* A detective. **2** *Pl.* Sneakers. **3** A rubber shoe or overshoe. —*adj. U.S. Slang* **1** Done secretly; undercover. **2** Pertaining to detectives. —*v.i.* **·shoed, ·shoe·ing** *U.S. Slang* To go stealthily and noiselessly; sneak.

gum·tree (gum′trē′) *n.* Any of various species of Australian eucalyptus trees.

gum tree An American gum-producing and hardwood lumber tree, as the sour or black gum and the tupelo.

gum·wood (gum′wŏŏd′) *n.* The wood of several Australasian trees (genus *Eucalyptus*), especially the blue gum (*E. globulus*) and the salmon gum (*E. salmonophloia*), now grown in the United States: used for construction and furniture.

gun (gun) *n.* **1** A metal tube for firing projectiles by the force of an explosive, by compressed air, or a spring, together with its stock and other attachments. **2** A piece of ordnance with a flat trajectory. **3** Any portable firearm except a pistol or revolver, as a rifle, musket, carbine, etc. **4** *U.S. Colloq.* A pistol or revolver. **5** The discharge of a cannon, as in firing salutes or signaling. **6** The throttle controlling the action of an internal-combustion engine, as in an automobile or airplane. **7** Any device resembling a gun in shape or operation: a grease *gun.* —*v.* **gunned, gun·ning** *v.i.* **1** To go hunting with a gun. **2** To shoot with a gun. **3** To seek with intent to harm or kill: with *for.* **4** To seek eagerly: with *for:* to *gun* for votes. **5** *U.S. Colloq.* To go or drive at great speed. — *v.t.* **6** *U.S. Colloq.* To shoot (someone). **7** *U.S. Colloq.* To open the throttle of, as an engine, so as to increase the speed of operation. [ME *gonne, gunne* < ON *gunna*, orig. a nickname for *Gunnhildr,* fem. personal name]

gun·cot·ton (gun′kot′n) *n.* A highly explosive compound prepared by treating cotton with nitric and sulfuric acids: also called *nitrocotton.*

gun deck A covered deck carrying the principal battery of a warship.

gun·fire (gun′fīr′) *n.* **1** The firing or discharge of a gun or guns. **2** *Mil.* **a** An artillery action in which guns fire independently of each other, with or without ordered interval. **b** The use of artillery or small arms in warfare, as distinguished from bayonets, or from charge tactics.

gun·flint (gun′flint′) *n.* A piece of flint fitted to the hammer of a flintlock musket.

gun·lock (gun′lok′) *n.* The mechanism of a gun by which the hammer or needle is driven and the charge exploded. See RIFLE.

gun metal **1** A bronze alloy, composed of nine parts copper to one part tin, formerly much used for smaller cannon, and still used for other purposes. **2** Any other material used in making guns, as gun iron, steel, certain kinds of brass, etc. **3** Any of various alloys treated with sulfur or the like to imitate the color of gun metal: used for metal novelties. **4** A neutral gray color with a bluish tinge: also **gun-met·al gray** (gun′met′l).

gun·nel (gun′əl) *n. pl.* **·nels** or **·nel** A blenny (fish) of the North Atlantic (*Pholis gunnellus*). [Origin unknown]

gun·ny (gun′ē) *n. pl.* **·nies** **1** Coarse sacking of jute or hemp. **2** A bag or sack made of it: also **gunny bag** or **gunny sack.** [< Hind. *gonī* gunny sack]

gun·pa·per (gun′pā′pər) *n.* A cellulose compound used as an absorbent foundation for the preparation of a form of guncotton.

gun·pow·der (gun′pou′dər) *n.* An explosive mixture of potassium nitrate, charcoal, and sulfur, black or brown in color, used especially in gunnery.

gunpowder tea A fine green tea, each leaf of which is rolled into a tiny round pellet.

gun·room (gun′rŏŏm′, -rŏŏm′) *n.* **1** A room in which guns are kept. **2** In the British navy, a room for the accommodation of junior officers.

gun·run·ner (gun′run′ər) *n.* One who smuggles

or carries on illegal traffic in firearms and ammunition. —**gun′run′ning** *n.*

gun-shot (gun′shot′) *n.* **1** The range or reach of a gun. **2** The act of discharging a firearm. —*adj.* Made by the shot of a gun: a *gunshot* wound.

gun·sight (gun′sīt′) *n.* A device on a gun which assists in aiming; a sight.

gun·smith (gun′smith′) *n.* One who makes or repairs firearms.

gun·stock (gun′stok′) *n.* The wooden part of a firearm, as a rifle, etc., holding the lock and the barrel.

gun·wale (gun′əl) *n. Naut.* **1** The upper wale of a war vessel with apertures for guns. **2** The strake which tops a ship's side or bounds the top plank of the side of a vessel: also spelled *gunnel.* [< GUN + WALE (plank)]

Günz (günts) See GLACIAL EPOCH.

gup·py (gup′ē) *n. pl.* **·pies** A small, tropical, fresh-water fish (genus *Lebistes*), valued as an aquarium fish for the brilliant coloring of the males, and for mosquito control. [after R. J. L. *Guppy*, British scientist]

Gup·ta (gŏŏp′tə) A dynasty, 320?–544?, of North India, founded by Chandragupta II.

gur·gle (gûr′gəl) *v.i.* **·gled, ·gling** **1** To flow with a bubbling, liquid sound. **2** To make such a sound. —*v.t.* **3** To utter with a gurgling sound. —*n.* A gurgling flow or sound: also **gur′gling.** [Var. of GARGLE]

gur·glet (gûr′glit) See GOGLET.

Gur·kha (gŏŏr′kə) *n.* One of a warlike Rajput people of Hindu religion in Nepal.

gur·nard (gûr′nərd) *n. pl.* **·nards** or **·nard** One of various spiny-finned marine fishes (family *Triglidae*) with mailed cheeks: some species are called *sea robins.* [< F *grognard* grumbler < *grogner* grunt < L *grunnire*]

gur·ney (gûr′nē) *n. pl.* **·neys** A stretcher mounted on wheels. [Origin uncertain]

gu·ru (gŏŏ′rŏŏ) *n. pl.* **·rus** **1** One who provides instruction or spiritual leadership in Hindu mysticism. **2** A teacher or leader regarded as having special knowledge, powers, etc. [< Hind.]

gush (gush) *v.i.* **1** To flow out suddenly and in volume, as tears or blood. **2** To produce a sudden flood, as of blood, tears, etc.: Her eyes *gushed* with tears. **3** *Colloq.* To express oneself with extravagant and affected emotion; be overly enthusiastic. —*v.t.* **4** To pour forth (blood, tears, etc.). —*n.* **1** A sudden outpouring of fluid or of something likened to it, as of sound, or the thing thus emitted. **2** *Colloq.* An extravagant display of sentiment. [ME *guschen*, prob. < Scand. Cf. ON *gusa* gush.] —**gush′i·ness** *n.* —**gush′y** *adj.*

gush·er (gush′ər) *n.* **1** One who or that which gushes. **2** A free-flowing oil well.

gush·ing (gush′ing) *adj.* Flowing freely; sentimental. —**gush′ing·ly** *adv.* —**gush′ing·ness** *n.*

gus·set (gus′it) *n.* **1** A small triangular piece of cloth fitted into a garment to fill an open angle or to give added strength or more room. **2** In metalworking, an angle-iron or bracket for stiffening an angle in construction. **3** A chain-mail connection between two armor plates. —*v.t.* To furnish with a gusset. [< OF *gousset,* dim. of *gousse* a pod, shell]

gust[1] (gust) *n.* **1** A violent blast of wind; rapid fluctuations in the force of a wind near the earth's surface. **2** A sudden outburst of feeling. [< ON *gustr*] —**gust′i·ly** *adv.* —**gust′i·ness** *n.* —**gust′y** *adj.*

gust[2] (gust) *n.* **1** Taste; relish; gratification; gusto. **2** Flavor, as of food. [< L *gustus* taste] —**gust′a·ble** *adj.*

gus·ta·tion (gus·tā′shən) *n.* The act or power of tasting. —**gus·ta·tive** (gus′tə-tiv) *adj.* —**gus′ta·tive·ness** *n.* —**gus·ta·to·ry** (-tôr′ē, -tō′rē) *adj.*

Gus·ta·vus (gus·tā′vəs, -tä′-) A masculine personal name. Also *Du.* **Gus·taaf** (khŏŏs′täf), *Fr.* **Gus·tave** (güs·täv′), *Ger.* **Gus·tav** (gŏŏs′-täf), *Ital., Sp.* **Gus·ta·vo** (gŏŏs·tä′vō), *Sw.* **Gus·taf** (gŏŏs′täf). [< Gmc., divine staff]
— **Gustavus I,** 1496–1560, king of Sweden who defeated the Danes (king, 1523–60): known as *Gustavus Vasa.*
— **Gustavus II,** 1594–1632, prominent in the Thirty Years' War: known as *Gustavus Adolphus.*
— **Gustavus V,** 1858–1950, king of Sweden 1907–50: known as *Gustaf.*
— **Gustavus VI,** 1882–1973, king of Sweden 1950–1973: known as *Gustaf Adolf.*

gus·to (gus'tō) n. 1 Keen enjoyment; relish; zest. 2 Individual taste. See synonyms under RELISH. [<Ital. <L *gustus* taste]

gut (gut) n. 1 pl. The alimentary canal; an intestine: regarded as indelicate usage. 2 The dried entrails of an animal, used for strings for musical instruments, etc.; catgut. 3 A contracted strait connecting two bodies of water. 4 A strong cord made from fiber drawn out of a silkworm when ready to spin its cocoon, used like catgut for snells, etc. 5 pl. *Slang* Stamina; courage; grit. — v.t. **gut·ted, gut·ting** 1 To take out the intestines of; eviscerate. 2 To plunder. 3 To remove or destroy the contents of: The fire *gutted* the interior of the building. — adj. *Slang* 1 Central; basic; fundamental: *gut* issues. 2 Deeply felt, as though physically experienced: a *gut* conviction. [OE *guttas* viscera] — **gut'·ter** n.

gut·sy (gut'sē) adj. **gut·si·er, gut·si·est** *Slang* Courageous; dauntless; gritty.

gut·ta (gut'ə) n. pl. **·tae** (-ē) 1 In pharmacy, a drop. 2 *Archit.* One of the small droplike ornaments, usually in the form of truncated cones, enriching the under part of mutules and regulae of the Doric entablature. [<L]

gut·ta–per·cha (gut'ə-pûr'chə) n. The purified and coagulated exudate, grayish-white to red in color, from various sapotaceous Malayan trees (genera *Palaquium* and *Payena*): used as an electrical insulator, a dental plastic, etc. [<Malay *getah* gum + *percha* gum tree]

gut·tate (gut'āt) adj. 1 Spotted, as if by colored drops. 2 Containing drops or little round masses likened to drops. Also **gut'tat·ed.** [<L *guttatus* speckled <*gutta* a drop]

gut·té (gŏo-tā') adj. *Her.* Covered with drops. Also **gut·tée', gut'ty.** [<AF *gutté* <L *guttatus.* See GUTTATE.]

gut·ter (gut'ər) n. 1 A channel along the eaves of a house to carry off rain water. 2 A waterway for carrying off surface water, constructed generally at the side of a road or street. 3 Slum areas of a community: language of the *gutter.* 4 Any slight channel, trench, or trough. — v.t. 1 To form channels or grooves

GUSSET *(def. 1)*

in. 2 To furnish with gutters, as a house. 3 To conduct or lead as through a gutter. — v.i. 4 To flow in channels, as water. 5 To melt rapidly into streams of wax: said of candles. [<OF *goutiere* <*goute* a drop <L *gutta*] — **gut'ter·y** adj.

gut·ter·bird (gut'ər·bûrd') n. 1 A sparrow. 2 A mean or contemptible person.

gut·ter·snipe (gut'ər·snīp') n. A neglected child who runs loose on the streets; a slum child; a street Arab.

gut·tur·al (gut'ər·əl) adj. 1 Pertaining to the throat. 2 Produced or formed in the throat; hence, harsh; grating: a *guttural* sound. 3 *Phonet.* Velar. — n. *Phonet.* A velar sound. [<NL *gutturalis* <*guttur* throat] — **gut·tur·al·i·ty** (gut'ə·ral'ə·tē), **gut'tur·al·ness** n. — **gut'·tur·al·ly** adv.

gut·tur·al·ize (gut'ər·əl·īz') v.t. & v.i. **·ized, ·iz·ing** 1 To speak or utter gutturally. 2 *Phonet.* To velarize. — **gut'tur·al·i·za'tion** n.

guy² (gī) n. 1 *Slang* A person; fellow; man. 2 *Brit.* A person of grotesque appearance. 3 An effigy of Guy Fawkes. See GUY FAWKES DAY. — v.t. **guyed, guy·ing** *Slang* To ridicule; make fun of. [after *Guy* Fawkes] — **guy'er** n.

guy·ot (gē'ō) n. A seamount having a flat top: also called *tablemount.* [after A. H. *Guyot,* 1807–84, Swiss-born U.S. geographer]

guz·zle (guz'əl) v.t. & v.i. **guz·zled, guz·zling** To drink immoderately or frequently. [? <OF *gosiller* <*gosier* throat] — **guz'zler** n.

gybe (jīb) See JIBE¹.

Gy·ges (gī'jēz, jī'-) 1 One of the Hecatoncheires. 2 A king of Lydia, 716–678 B.C., said by Plato to possess a magic ring that could make the wearer invisible.

gym (jim) n. *U.S. Colloq.* 1 A gymnasium. 2 A course in physical training. [Short for GYMNASIUM]

gym·bals (jim'bəlz, gim'-) See GIMBALS.

gym·kha·na (jim·kä'nə) n. *Brit.* An athletic meet, especially for racing; the meeting place. [<Hind. *gend-khana* a racket court; infl. by *gymnastics*]

gym·na·si·arch (jim·nā'zē·ärk) n. An official in ancient Greece entrusted with the management of the gymnasia. [<L *gymnasiarchus* <Gk. *gymnasiarchos* <*gymnasion* a gymnasium + *archein* rule]

gym·na·si·um (jim·nā'zē·əm) n. pl. **·si·ums** or **·si·a** (-zē·ə) 1 A building or room used for physical education activities and sports, and usually having gymnastic equipment. 2 In ancient Greece, a place where youths met for physical exercise and discussion. [<L <Gk. *gymnasion* <*gymnazein* exercise, train naked <*gymnos* naked]

Gym·na·si·um (gim·nä'zē·ŏŏm) n. In continental Europe, especially Germany, a classical school preparatory to the universities.

gym·nast (jim'nast) n. One expert in gymnastics. [<Gk. *gymnastēs* a trainer <*gymnazein.* See GYMNASIUM.]

gym·nas·tic (jim·nas'tik) adj. Relating to gymnastics. — **gym·nas'ti·cal·ly** adv.

gym·nas·tics (jim·nas'tiks) n. 1 Gymnastic exercises for the development of bodily strength and agility. 2 Exercises in a gymnasium, as distinguished from outdoor athletics. 3 Feats of bodily skill.

gymno- *combining form* Naked: *gymnosperm.* Also, before vowels, **gymn-.** [<Gk. *gymnos* naked]

gym·no·bac·te·ri·um (jim'nō·bak·tir'ē·əm) n. pl. **·ri·a** (-ē·ə) A type of bacterium without flagella: distinguished from *trichobacterium.*

gym·no·car·pous (jim'nə·kär'pəs) adj. *Bot.* Provided with naked fruits in flowering plants: said of a fruit without pubescence. Also **gym'·no·car'pic.**

gym·no·sperm (jim'nə·spûrm') n. One of a class of plants (the *Gymnospermae*) having their ovules and seeds naked, as certain evergreens: distinguished from *angiosperm.* — **gym'no·sper'mous, gym'no·sper'mic** adj.

gyn- Var. of GYNO-.

gynaeco- See GYNECO-.

gy·nan·der (jī·nan'dər, ji-, gī-) n. 1 *Biol.* An organism exhibiting bisexual characteristics, usually localized on one or the other side of the midline of the body, as certain insects: also **gy·nan·dro·morph** (jī·nan'drə·môrf, ji-, gī-). 2 A masculine woman. [<Gk. *gynandros* of doubtful sex <*gynē* woman + *anēr, andros* man]

gy·nan·droid (jī·nan'droid, ji-, gī-) n. A hermaphrodite with predominantly female characteristics.

gy·nan·dro·mor·phism (jī·nan'drō·môr'fiz·əm, ji-, gī-) n. *Biol.* The occurrence of male and female characteristics in the same individual. — **gy·nan'dro·mor'phic, gy·nan'dro·mor'phous** adj.

gy·nan·drous (jī·nan'drəs, ji-, gī-) adj. 1 *Bot.* Having the stamens united with or seemingly borne upon the pistil. 2 Exhibiting gynandry.

gy·nan·dry (jī·nan'drē, ji-, gī-) n. Hermaphroditism. Also **gy·nan'drism.**

gy·nar·chy (jī'när·kē, jin'är-) n. pl. **·chies** Female authority or domination; the supremacy of women; government by a woman or by women. — **gy·nar'chic** adj.

gyne (jīn) n. The female or queen ant. [<NL <Gk. *gynē* a woman]

gy·ne·ce·um (jī'nə·sē'əm, jin'ə-) n. pl. **·ce·a** (-sē'ə) 1 The part of a Greek house reserved for the women, usually the rear. 2 The gynoecium. Also **gynaeceum.** [<L *gynacium* <Gk. *gynaikeion* <*gynē, gynaikos* a woman]

gyneco- *combining form* Female; pertaining to women: *gynecomorphous:* also spelled *gynaeco-.* Also, before vowels, **gynec-.** [<Gk. *gynē, gynaikos* a woman]

gy·ne·coc·ra·cy (jī'nə·kok'rə·sē, jin'ə-) n. pl. **·cies** Rule by a woman or by women; female supremacy. [<Gk. *gynaikokratia* <*gynē, gynaikos* a woman + *krateein* rule] — **gy·ne·co·crat** (jī·nē'kə·krat, ji-) n. — **gy·ne·co·crat·ic** (jī'nə·kō·krat'ik, jin'ə-) adj.

gy·ne·coid (jī'nə·koid, jin'ə-) n. A worker ant capable of laying eggs.

gy·ne·col·o·gy (gī'nə·kol'ə·jē, jī'nə-, jin'ə-) n. The study of the female reproductive system and the disorders peculiar to it. — **gy·ne·co·log'i·cal** adj. — **gy·ne·col'o·gist** n.

gy·ne·co·mor·phous (jī'nē·kō·môr'fəs, jin'ə·kō-, gī-) adj. Having the characteristics, shape, or appearance of a female.

gy·ni·at·rics (jī'nē·at'riks, jin'ē-) n. The diagnosis and treatment of women's diseases. Also **gy·ni·at·ry** (jī'nē·at'rē, jin'ē-, ji·nī'ə·trē).

gyno- *combining form* 1 Woman; female: *gynophobia.* 2 *Bot. & Med.* Female reproductive organ; ovary; pistil: *gynophore.* Also, before vowels, **gyn-.** [<Gk. *gynē* a woman]

gy·no·base (jī'nə·bās, jin'ə-) n. *Bot.* The conical or flat enlargement of the receptacle of a flower, bearing the gynaecium. — **gy'no·ba'sic, gy'no·ba'seous** (-bā'shəs) adj.

gy·noe·ci·um (jī·nē'sē·əm, ji-) n. *Bot.* The female parts of a flower; the pistil or pistils taken as a unit. Compare ANDROECIUM. [<NL <L *gynaeceum.* See GYNECEUM.]

gy·no·gen·e·sis (jī'nō·jen'ə·sis, jin'ō-) n. *Biol.* The development of an egg after fertilization by a sperm whose nucleus is either absent or inactive, as in certain nematodes. — **gy'no·gen'ic** adj.

gy·nop·a·thy (jī·nop'ə·thē, ji-) n. Any disease of women. — **gy·no·path·ic** (jī'nə·path'ik, jin'ə-) adj.

gy·no·phore (jī'nə·fôr, -fōr, jin'ə-) n. *Bot.* A stalk supporting the ovary of certain plants, as in the cleome and some crucifers.

-gynous *combining form* 1 Female; of women: *philogynous.* 2 *Bot.* Denoting location, number, etc., of the pistils: *acrogynous.* [<Gk. *gynē* a woman]

gyp·soph·i·la (jip·sof'ə·lə) n. Any of a large genus (*Gypsophila*) of hardy annual and perennial herbs with sparse foliage and small rosy or white flowers; babysbreath. [<NL <Gk. *gypsos* chalk + *philein* love]

gypsy moth A European moth with mottled light brown or near-white wings (*Porthetria dispar*), which has become established as a destructive pest in the Eastern United States and Canada, its hairy caterpillar devouring the leaves of deciduous trees.

gy·ral (jī'rəl) adj. 1 Having a circular, revolving, or whirling motion. 2 Of or pertaining to the convolutions of the brain. — **gy'ral·ly** adv.

gy·rate (jī'rāt) v.i. **gy·rat·ed, gy·rat·ing** 1 To rotate or revolve. 2 To move in a spiral path; whirl, as a cyclone. — adj. *Zool.* Having spiral or convoluted parts. [<L *gyratus,* pp. of *gyrare* gyrate <*gyrus* a circle <Gk. *gyros*]

gy·ro (jī'rō) n. A gyroscope or gyrocompass.

gyro- *combining form* Circle, ring, or spiral: *gyroscope.* Also, before vowels, **gyr-.**

gy·ro·com·pass (jī'rō·kum'pəs, -kom'-) n. A compass operating on the principle of a gyroscope; an instrument of navigation indicating a change in the direction of a ship or an aircraft by the resistance of a gyroscope to such change.

gy·ro·scope (jī'rə·skōp) n. A heavy rotating wheel, the axis of which is free to turn in any direction, and which can be set to rotate in any plane, independently of forces tending to change the position of the axis. [<F] — **gy'ro·scop'ic** (-skop'ik) adj.

gyro stabilizer A gyroscopic device which operates to maintain a structural unit in a steady position, as a gun, despite the rolling of a ship or the motion of the vehicle upon which it is mounted.

GYROSCOPE
Showing possible directional movements

H

h, H (āch) *n. pl.* **h's, H's** or **hs, Hs, aitch·es** (ā′chiz) **1** The eighth letter of the English alphabet, from Phoenician *cheth,* which eventually developed into Greek *eta,* Roman *H.* **2** The sound of the letter *h,* a voiceless, glottal fricative. In a few English words of French origin, as heir, honor, hour, etc., initial *h* is still written but not pronounced; usage varies in certain other words, as herb, homage, etc., in which some persons pronounce the *h* and some do not. See ALPHABET. —*symbol Chem.* Hydrogen (symbol H).

ha·be·as cor·pus (hā′bē·əs kôr′pəs) *Law* A writ commanding a person having another in custody to produce the detained person before a court. [<L, (you) have the body]

ha·ben·dum (hə·ben′dəm) *n. pl.* **·da** (-də) *Law* The clause in a deed beginning "to have and to hold" (in Latin, *habendum et tenendum*), which determines what interest or estate is granted by the deed. [<L, gerundive of *habere* have]

hab·er·dash·er (hab′ər·dash′ər) *n.* **1** A dealer in men's furnishings. **2** *Brit.* A dealer in or peddler of ribbons, trimmings, thread, needles, and other small wares. [Prob. <AF *hapertas* kind of fabric]

hab·er·geon (hab′ər·jən) *n.* A coat of mail for the breast and neck, shorter than a hauberk. [<OF *haubergeon,* dim. of *hauberc.* See HAUBERK.]

hab·ile (hab′il) *adj.* Skilful; able. [Var. of ABLE; infl. in form by F *habile* able or L *habilis* apt]

hab·il·i·ment (hə·bil′ə·mənt) *n.* **1** An article of clothing. **2** *pl.* Clothes; garb. See synonyms under DRESS. [<OF *habillement* <*habiller* dress, make fit <L *habilis* fit, apt]

ha·bil·i·tate (hə·bil′ə·tāt) *v.t.* **·tat·ed, ·tat·ing** **1** *U.S.* In the West, to furnish with suitable means of equipment, to work (a mine). **2** *Rare* To dress: clothe. [<Med. L *habilitatus,* pp. of *habilitare* enable < *habilis* fit] —**ha·bil′·i·ta′tion** *n.*

hab·it (hab′it) *n.* **1** A tendency toward an action or condition, which by repetition has become spontaneous. **2** An action so induced; habitual course of action or conduct. **3** Habitual condition, appearance, or temperament; physical or mental make-up. **4** *Biol.* A characteristic mode of growth or aspect of a plant or animal. **5** An outer garment or garments; costume; especially, a woman's dress or costume for horseback riding. **6** The distinctive garment of a religious order. **7** *Psychol.* An acquired response or set of responses; a cultivated tendency. Compare INSTINCT. **8** *Obs.* Intimate acquaintance; familiarity. —*v.t.* **1** To furnish with a habit; clothe; dress. **2** *Obs.* To inhabit. [<OF <L *habitus* condition, dress <*habere* have]

Synonyms (noun): custom, fashion, habitude, practice, routine, rule, system, usage, use, wont. *Habit* is a tendency or inclination toward an action or condition, which by repetition has become easy, spontaneous, or even unconscious, or an action or regular series of actions, or a condition so induced. *Habitude* is habitual relation or association. *Custom* is the uniform doing of the same act in the same circumstance, usually, at least in the origin of the *custom,* for a definite reason; *routine* is the doing of customary acts in a regular and uniform sequence and is more mechanical than *custom.* It is the *custom* of shopkeepers to open at a uniform hour, and to follow a regular *routine* of business until closing time. *Custom* is chiefly used of the action of many; *habit* of the action of one; we speak of the *customs* of society, the *habits* of an individual. *Fashion* is the generally recognized *custom* in the smaller matters, especially in dress. A *rule* is prescribed either by some external authority or by one's own will; as, It is the *rule* of the house; or, my invariable *rule. Practice* is the active doing of something in a systematic way; we do not speak of the *practice,* but of the *habit* of going

to sleep. *Wont* is established *usage* or *custom* and now chiefly poetical. Compare CUSTOM, DRESS, MANNER, PRACTICE, USE.

hab·it·able (hab′it·ə·bəl) *adj.* Fit to be inhabited. [<L *habitabilis* <*habitare* inhabit] —**hab·it·a·bil·i·ty** (hab′it·ə·bil′ə·tē), **hab′it·a·ble·ness** *n.* —**hab′it·a·bly** *adv.*

hab·i·tant (hab′ə·tənt) *n.* **1** An inhabitant. **2** (*Fr.* à·bē·täň′) A small rural proprietor, or resident, of French descent, in Canada or Louisiana: also **ha·bi·tan′.** [<F <L *habitans, -antis,* ppr. of *habitare* dwell]

hab·i·tat (hab′ə·tat) *n.* **1** The region where a race, species, or individual naturally or usually lives or is found. **2** Natural environment. [<NL, it dwells]

hab·i·ta·tion (hab′ə·tā′shən) *n.* **1** A place of abode. **2** The act or state of inhabiting. See synonyms under HOME, HOUSE.

hab·it·ed (hab′ə·tid) *adj.* **1** Clothed; arrayed; wearing a habit. **2** *Obs* Habituated.

ha·bit·u·al (hə·bich′ōō·əl) *adj.* **1** Of, pertaining to, or constituting a habit. **2** Acquired by or resulting from habit, repeated use, or continued causes. **3** Characterized by repeated or constant practice or indulgence; inveterate: a *habitual* liar. [<Med. L *habitualis* <*habitus.* See HABIT.] —**ha·bit′u·al·ly** *adv.* —**ha·bit′u·al·ness** *n.*

Synonyms: accustomed, common, customary, familiar, general, ordinary, regular, stated, usual, wonted. See COMMON, GENERAL, USUAL. Compare synonyms for HABIT. *Antonyms:* exceptional, extraordinary, infrequent, irregular, occasional, rare, unusual, unwonted.

ha·bit·u·ate (hə·bich′ōō·āt) *v.t.* **·at·ed, ·at·ing** **1** To make familiar by repetition or use; accustom. **2** *U.S. Colloq.* To frequent. [<L *habituatus,* pp. of *habituare* condition] —**ha·bit′u·at′ed** *adj.* —**ha·bit′u·a′tion** *n.*

ha·bu (hä·bōō) *n.* A very poisonous crotaline snake (genus *Trimeresurus*) of Okinawa and the Ryukyu archipelago, patterned in green and yellow: related to the American rattlesnake and copperhead. [<Japanese]

ha·chure (ha·shōōr′, hash′ōōr) *n.* **1** In art, a hatching. **2** In mapmaking, the shading or lines used to indicate hills or elevations. —*v.t.* (ha·shōōr′) **·chured, ·chur·ing** To mark or indicate with hatchings. [<F *hacher* HATCH³]

ha·ci·en·da (hä′sē·en′də, *Sp.* ä·syen′dä) *n.* In Spanish America: **1** A landed estate; a country house. **2** A farming, mining, or manufacturing establishment in the country. [<Am. Sp. <L *facienda* things to be done < *facere* do, make]

hack¹ (hak) *v.t.* **1** To cut or chop crudely or irregularly, as with an ax or sword. **2** To break up, as clods of earth. **3** In basketball, to strike (an opposing player) on the arm. **4** In Rugby football, to kick (an opposing player) in the shins. —*v.i.* **5** To make cuts or notches with heavy, crude blows. **6** To emit short, dry coughs. See synonyms under CUT. —**to hack it** *Slang* To cope with it; do it. —*n.* **1** A gash, cut, or nick made by or as by a sharp instrument. **2** An ax or other tool for hacking. **3** A kick on the shins, as in Rugby football. **4** A short, dry cough. [OE *haccian* cut] —**hack′er** *n.*

hack² (hak) *n.* **1** A horse for hire. **2** A horse used for general work or for ordinary riding, as distinguished from one bred or trained for special use. **3** An old, worn-out horse. **4** A hackney coach. **5** A taxicab. **6** A writer who hires himself out for any kind of writing jobs; a literary drudge. —*v.t.* **1** To let out for hire, as a horse. **2** To make stale or trite by constant use; hackney. —*v.i.* **3** *Colloq.* To drive a taxicab. **4** *Brit.* To ride on or move at the pace of a hack (*n.* def. 2). —*adj.* **1** Of or designated for a hack: a *hack* stand. **2** For hire or drudging work: a *hack* horse; a *hack* writer. **3** Done by a hack; requiring drudgery: a *hack* job. **4** Trite; hackneyed. [<HACKNEY]

hack³ (hak) *n.* **1** A frame or rack on which to dry cheese, fish, bricks, etc. **2** A row of bricks laid out to dry. **3** A pile of green brick. [Var. of HATCH¹]

hack·a·more (hak′ə·môr, -mōr) *n. U.S.* A

special headstall of a halter of rawhide or horsehair used to break colts to respond to a bridle. [Alter. of Sp. *jaquima* halter]

hack·ber·ry (hak′ber′ē, -bər·ē) *n. pl.* **·ries** **1** An American tree (genus *Celtis*) resembling the elm and having small, sweet, edible fruit. **2** The fruit or wood of this tree. Also called *hagberry.* [Var. of *hagberry* <ON *heggr* hedge + BERRY]

hack·ham·mer (hak′ham′ər) *n.* An implement for dressing grindstones.

hack·le¹ (hak′əl) *n.* **1** One of the long narrow feathers on the neck of a cock, used by anglers in making artificial flies; also, a similar feather on other birds. **2** An artificial feather fly for angling: also **hackle fly. 3** *pl.* The erectile hairs on the neck and back of a dog: also spelled *heckle.* **4** A hatchel. **5** Unspun fiber, as raw silk. —*v.t.* **hack·led, hack·ling** **1** To furnish (a fly) with a hackle. **2** To hatchel. [See HATCHEL] —**hack′ler** *n.*

hack·le² (hak′əl) *v.t.* & *v.i.* **hack·led, hack·ling** To cut or chop roughly or crudely; mangle; hack. [Freq. of HACK¹]

hack·ma·tack (hak′mə·tak) *n.* The American larch; tamarack. [<N. Am. Ind.]

hack·ney (hak′nē) *n. pl.* **·neys** **1** One of a breed of driving and saddle horses. **2** A horse kept for hire. **3** A hackney coach. **4** A drudge. —*v.t.* **1** To make trite by constant use. **2** To let out or use as a hackney. —*adj.* Let out for hire; common. [<OF *haquenée* a horse; ult. origin unknown] —**hack′ney·ism** *n.*

hackney coach A coach kept for hire.

hack·neyed (hak′nēd) *adj.* Worn out; made commonplace by frequent use; trite. See synonyms under TRITE.

hack·saw (hak′sô′) *n.* A narrow-bladed, close-toothed saw for cutting metal.

hack work The work of a literary hack.

HACKSAW

had (had) Past tense and past participle of HAVE.

had better, had liefer, had rather See usage note under HAVE.

had·dock (had′ək) *n. pl.* **·dock** or **·docks** A food fish (*Melanogrammus aeglefinus*) of the North Atlantic, allied to the cod and with a black lateral line and blackish shoulder spot. [ME; origin unknown]

hade (hād) *n. Geol.* The inclination of a fault plane or vein from the vertical; an underlay: also **had′ing.** See FAULT (def. 3). —*v.i.* **had·ed, had·ing** To incline from a vertical position, as a fault plane. [Cf. dial. E *hade* slope]

hadj (haj) *n.* The pilgrimage to Mecca required of every free Mohammedan at least once in his life. Also spelled *haj, hajj.* See HEGIRA. [<Turkish <Arabic *hajj* pilgrimage. Akin to HEGIRA.]

hadj·i (haj′ē) *n.* **1** A Mohammedan who has made the pilgrimage to Mecca: used also before a name as a title. **2** An Armenian or a Greek who has made a pilgrimage to the holy sepulcher at Jerusalem. Also **hadj′ee.** [<Arabic *hajj* pilgrim]

had·n't (had′nt) Contraction of HAD NOT.

Ha·dri·an (hā′drē·ən), 76–138, Roman emperor 117–138: full name *Publius Aelius Hadrianus:* sometimes called "Adrian."

Hadrian's Wall A wall extending from Solway Firth to the Tyne, built by Hadrian, 122–128, to protect Roman Britain from the Picts and Scots.

Had·ru·me·tum (had′rə·mē′təm) The ancient name for SOUSSE.

haem-, haemo- See HEMO-.

haema- See HEMA-.

haemat-, haemato- See HEMATO-.

hae·ma·to·cry·al (hē′mə·tō·krī′əl) See HEMATOCRYAL.

hae·ma·to·therm·al (hē′mə·tō·thûr′məl) See HEMATOTHERMAL.

hae·ma·tox·y·lon (hē′mə·tok′sə·lon, hem′ə-) *n.* **1** Any of a genus (*Haematoxylon*) of tropical American trees, especially the logwood or bloodwood tree (*H. campechianum*), whose heartwood supplies a purple-red coloring matter. **2** The wood of this tree. [< NL < Gk. *haima, -atos* blood + *xylon* wood]

haem·or·rhoid (hem′ə·roid), **haem·or·rhoi·dal** See HEMORRHOID, etc.

haf·fet (hăf′it) *n. Scot.* Side of the head; temple.

ha·fiz (hä′fiz) *n.* One who has memorized the Koran: a Moslem title of respect. [< Arabic *hāfiz* one who remembers]

Ha·fiz (hä′fiz) Pseudonym of Shams ud-din Mohammed, Persian poet and philosopher of the 14th century.

haf·ni·um (hăf′nē·əm) *n.* A metallic element (symbol Hf, atomic number 72) found combined in zirconium ores and used to control fission in nuclear reactors. See PERIODIC TABLE. [< NL, from L *Hafnia* Copenhagen]

haft (haft, häft) *n.* A handle; specifically, the handle of a cutting weapon. —*v.t.* To supply with or set in a haft or handle. Also spelled *heft*. [OE *hæft* handle < *habban* hold, have]

hag (hag) *n.* **1** A forbidding or malicious old woman; an ugly crone. **2** A witch; sorceress; she-devil; a woman in league with the devil. **3** A hagfish. [OE *hægtes* witch] —**hag′gish** *adj.*

hag·ber·ry (hag′ber·ē, -bər·ē) *n. pl.* **·ries** The hackberry. [See HACKBERRY]

hag·bush (hag′boŏsh′) *n.* The azedarach. [? OE *haga* hedge + BUSH]

hag·but (hag′but) *n.* A hackbut.

hag·don (hag′dən) *n.* The shearwater: also calle *haglet, haglin*. Also **hag′del** (-dəl), **hag′den** (-dən). [? < HAG² v.]

Ha·gen (hä′gən) A city in North Rhine-Westphalia, Germany. Also **Ha·gen-in-West·fal·en** (in vest·fäl′ən).

hag·fish (hag′fish′) *n. pl.* **·fish** or **·fish·es** A primitive eel-like marine cyclostome (order or subclass *Myxinoidea*), allied to the lamprey, which bores its way into the bodies of living fishes by means of a rasping suctorial mouth. [< HAG², v. + FISH]

Hag·ga·dah (hə·gä′də, *Hebrew* hä·gô′dô) *n. pl.* **·doth** (-dōth) **1** A free interpretation or application: specifically, an illustrative anecdote or parable of the Midrash: distinguished from *halacha*. **2** The ritual, including the exposition of the story of the Exodus, read during the Seder on the first two nights of Passover. Also **Ha·ga′dah**, **Hag·ga′da**. [< Hebrew < *higgid* tell]

hag·gad·ic (hə·gad′ik, -gäd′-) *adj.* Of or pertaining to the Haggadah. Also **ha·gad′ic**, **hag·gad′i·cal**.

hag·ga·dist (hə·gä′dist) *n.* A haggadic writer or scholar. Also **ha·ga′dist**. —**hag·ga·dis′tic** (hag′ə·dis′tik), **hag·a·dis′tic** *adj.*

hag·gard (hag′ərd) *adj.* **1** Worn and gaunt in appearance. **2** Wild or intractable, as a hawk. —*n.* **1** In falconry, a wild hawk caught in its adult plumage. **2** Hence, an untamed fierce creature. [< OF *hagard* wild < MHG *hag* hedge] —**hag′gard·ly** *adv.* —**hag′gard·ness** *n.*

hag·gish (hag′ish) *adj.* Resembling or characteristic of a hag.

hag·gle (hag′əl) *v.* **hag·gled, hag·gling** *v.t.* **1** To cut unskilfully; mangle. **2** To tire or confuse, as by wrangling. —*v.i.* **3** To argue about price or terms. —*n.* The act of haggling or higgling. [Freq. of HAG²] —**hag′gler** *n.*

hag·i·ar·chy (hag′ē·är′kē, hä′jē-) *n. pl.* **·chies** A government, or the principle of government, by priests; sacerdotal government. Also **hag·i·oc·ra·cy** (hag′ē·ok′rə·sē, hä′jē-).

hagio- *combining form* Sacred: *hagiography*. Also, before vowels, **hagi-**. [< Gk. *hagios* sacred]

Hag·i·og·ra·pha (hag′ē·og′rə·fə, hä′jē-) *n. pl.* The third of the three ancient divisions of the Old Testament, comprising all books not reckoned in the Law or the Prophets. [< Gk. < *hagios* sacred + *graphein* write]

hag·i·og·ra·phy (hag′ē·og′rə·fē, hä′jē-) *n. pl.* **·phies 1** The writing or study of saints' lives. **2** A collection of biographies of saints. — **hag·i·og′ra·phal** *adj.* —**hag·i·og′ra·pher** *n.* — **hag·i·o·graph·ic** (hag′ē·ə·graf′ik, hä′jē-) *or* **·i·cal** *adj.*

hag·i·ol·a·try (hag′ē·ol′ə·trē, hä′jē-) *n.* The veneration or invocation of saints. —**hag·i·ol′a·ter** *n.* —**hag·i·ol′a·trous** *adj.*

hag·i·ol·o·gy (hag′ē·ol′ə·jē, hä′jē-) *n. pl.* **·gies 1** A

list of saints. **2** A treatise on saints' lives; sacred writings. —**hag·i·o·log·ic** (hag′ē·ə·loj′ik, hä′jē-) *adj.* —**hag·i·ol′o·gist** *n.*

hag·i·o·scope (hag′ē·ə·skōp′, hä′jē-) *n.* An oblique opening in the screen or chancel wall of a medieval church, to permit those in a side chapel or aisle to see the main altar. — **hag·i·o·scop·ic** (-skop′ik) *adj.*

hag·let (hag′lit), **hag·lin** (hag′lin) See HAGDON.

hag·rid·den (hag′rid′n) *adj.* **1** Ridden by a hag or witch. **2** Tormented or distressed by or as by nightmares or hallucinations. **3** By extension, tormented by a woman.

Hague (hāg), **The** The de facto capital of the Netherlands: Dutch *'s Gravenhage*.

—**Hague Conferences** The first international peace conferences, held at The Hague in 1899 (26 states) and 1907 (44 states). The **Hague Conventions**, relating to the conduct of war and to the arbitration of international disputes, were adopted by the conferences, and the **Hague Tribunal** was created by the first. See PERMANENT COURT OF ARBITRATION under COURT.

Hah·ne·mann·ism (hä′nə·män·iz′əm) *n.* The original homeopathy. —**Hah·ne·man·i·an** (hä′nə·man′ē·ən, -män′ē-), **Hah·ne·man′ni·an** *adj.*

Hai·da (hī′də) *n.* **1** A member of any of the tribes of North American Indians inhabiting the Queen Charlotte Islands, British Columbia, and Prince of Wales Island, Alaska. **2** The family of languages spoken by these tribes.

Hai·dar·a·bad (hī′dər·ə·bäd′) See HYDERABAD.

Hai·dar A·li (hī′dər ä′lē) See HYDER ALI.

Hai·duk (hī′dook) *n.* **1** One of a body of Hungarian mercenaries of the 16th century, of Magyar race, who served the Protestant cause. **2** One of the bandit mountaineers of the Balkans who took part in the struggle for independence against Turkey. Also spelled *Heyduck*. Also **Hai′duck**. [< Hungarian *hajduk* drover]

Hai·fa (hī′fə) A port of NW Israel on the Bay of Acre.

haik (hīk, häk) *n.* An Oriental outside garment made of an oblong woolen cloth. Also **haick**. [< Arabic *hayk* < *hāk* to weave]

hai·ku (hī·kōō) *n.* A poem in imitation of a Japanese verse form, consisting of three lines of five, seven, five syllables respectively. Also *hokku*. [< Japanese *haikai*]

hai·kwan (hī′kwän′) *n.* The maritime custom duties of China. [< Chinese < *hai* sea + *kuan* gate]

hail¹ (hāl) *n.* **1** Frozen rain or congealed vapor, often falling in pellets during thunderstorms. **2** Figuratively, anything falling thickly and with violence: a *hail* of blows. **3** A hailstorm. —*v.i.* To pour down hail: used impersonally. — *v.t.* To hurl or pour down like hail: to *hail* curses on someone. ◆Homophone: *hale*. [OE *hægel*] —**hail′y** *adj.*

hail² (hāl) *v.t.* **1** To call loudly to in greeting; salute. **2** To call to so as to attract attention: to *hail* a cab. **3** To name as; designate: They *hailed* him captain. —*v.i.* **4** To call out so as to attract attention or give greeting. —**to hail from** To come from; have as one's original home or residence. See synonyms under ADDRESS. —*n.* **1** A call to attract attention; greeting. **2** The distance a shout can be heard: within *hail*. —*interj.* An exclamation of greeting. ◆Homophone: *hale*. [ME *hailen, heilen* < ON *heilla* < *heill* whole, hale. Akin to HALE².] —**hail′er** *n.*

hail³ (hāl) *adj. Scot.* Healthy; hale; whole.

Hai·le Se·las·sie (hī′lē sə·las′ē, -lä′sē), 1891–1975, emperor of Ethiopia 1930–74; in exile 1936–41.

hail-fel·low (hāl′fel′ō) *adj.* On very familiar or cordial terms. —*n.* A close companion. Also **hail′-fel′low-well′-met′**.

Hail Mary See AVE MARIA.

hail·stone (hāl′stōn′) *n.* A pellet of hail.

hail·storm (hāl′stôrm′) *n.* A storm in which hail falls: also **hail storm**.

Hai·phong (hī′fong′) A port of North Vietnam.

hair (hâr) *n.* **1** One of the filaments of modified epidermal tissue growing from the skin or outer covering of a mammal. ◆ Collateral adjectives: *capillary*, *pilar*. **2** Any mass of such filaments, especially that which grows upon the head. **3** Any filamentous process. **4** *Bot.* An outgrowth of the epidermis in plants. **5** Haircloth; specifically, mats woven from horsehair, used in expressing oils, etc.

HAIR
Section through the skin:
a. Shaft.   *e.* Root
b. Root.   sheath.
c. Sebaceous   *f.* Follicle.
    gland.   *g.* Bulb.
d. Erector   *h.* Papilla.
    pili muscle.   *i.* Fat–cells.

6 Figuratively, an exceedingly minute, slight, or delicate thing, space, etc. —*adj.* Like, or made of, hair. —**to a hair line** With the utmost exactness. —**to split hairs** To quibble; make petty or excessive distinctions. —**to let down one's hair** To disclose the actual state of one's affairs. —**not to turn a hair** To show or reveal no sign of exhaustion nor a lack of composure. ◆Homophone: *hare*. [OE *hær*] —**hair′less** *adj.*

hair·bird (hâr′bûrd′) *n.* The chipping sparrow: so called because it lines its nest with hair.

hair·breadth (hâr′bredth′) *n.* A hair's breadth; an extremely small space or distance. —*adj.* Having only the breadth of a hair; very narrow. Also **hairs′–breadth′**, **hair′s–breadth′**.

hair·brush (hâr′brush′) *n.* A brush used for the hair.

hair cell *Anat.* One of the delicate filamentous cells situated in the organ of Corti in the cochlea, and responsible for the transmission of sound vibrations.

hair·cloth (hâr′klôth′, -kloth′) *n.* A fabric having a warp of either cotton or linen yarn with a horsehair filling.

hair·cut (hâr′kut′) *n.* The act of cutting the hair or the style in which it is cut. —**hair′cut·ter** *n.* —**hair′cut·ting** *adj. & n.*

hair·do (hâr′dōō′) *n.* A style of dressing the hair; coiffure.

hair·dress·er (hâr′dres′ər) *n.* One who arranges the hair, especially women's hair. —**hair′dress·ing** *n.*

hair·line (hâr′līn′) *n.* **1** *Printing* **a** A very thin line on a type face; also, the type itself. **b** A thin rule. **2** A narrow stripe in textile fabrics. **3** The outline of hair on the head.

hair·pin (hâr′pin′) *n.* A U–shaped pin made of wire, bone, celluloid, or the like, for supporting the hair or headdress.

hair-rais·ing (hâr′rā′zing) *adj.* Causing fright or shock. —**hair′-rais′er** *n.*

hair seal The eared seal or sea lion, not valued for its fur.

hair shirt A rough cloth garment of goats' hair worn as a shirt or as a girdle for penance or mortification.

hair space *Printing* The thinnest of the metal spaces for separating letters and words.

hair-split·ting (hâr′split′ing) *n.* Insistence upon minute or trivial distinctions. See synonyms under SOPHISTRY. —*adj.* Drawing excessively nice distinctions. —**hair′-split′ter** *n.*

hair·spring (hâr′spring′) *n.* The fine spring of the balance wheel of a watch.

hair·streak (hâr′strēk′) *n.* A small butterfly (family *Lycaenidae*) with narrow stripes on the underside of the wings.

hair·stroke (hâr′strōk′) *n.* **1** A very fine stroke in writing. **2** A serif.

hair-trig·ger (hâr′trig′ər) *n.* **1** A trigger so delicately adjusted that a very slight pressure discharges the firearm. **2** A pistol or revolver having such a trigger. —*adj.* Stimulated or set in operation by the slightest provocation.

hair·worm (hâr′wûrm′) *n.* Any of various nematode worms (families *Gordiidae* and *Mermithidae*) which inhabit running water and whose larvae are parasitic in insects: sometimes called *horsehair–snake*.

hair·y (hâr′ē) *adj.* **hair·i·er, hair·i·est 1** Covered with, made of, or like hair. **2** *Slang* **a** Troublesome; difficult. **b** Dangerous; harrow-

HAIK

ing. —**hair′i·ness** n.

Hai·ti (hā′tē) **1** A republic comprising the western portion of Hispaniola; 10,714 square miles; capital, Port-au-Prince. **2** Former name of HISPANIOLA. French **Ha·i·ti** (à·ē·tē′). **Hai·ti·an** (hā′tē·ən, -shən) adj. Of or pertaining to Haiti, its people, or their culture. —n. **1** A native or inhabitant of Haiti. **2** A French patois spoken by the Haitians: also **Haitian Creole. 3** Taino.

haj (haj), **hajj** See HADJ.

ha·je (hä′jē) n. The African cobra or asp (Naja haje). See also illustration under URAEUS. [<Arabic ḥayyah snake] **haj·i** (haj′ē), **haj·ji** See HADJI.

hake (hāk) n. pl. **hake** or **hakes 1** A fish (genus Merluccius) having a short first dorsal fin, and long, sinuated second dorsal and anal fins; especially, the European hake (M. smiridus) and the American silver hake or whiting (M. bilinearis). **2** A North American food fish (genus Phycis), the codling. Also spelled haak. [OE hacod pike <haca hook]

Ha·ken·kreuz (hä′kən·kroits) n. A swastika: especially as the symbol of Nazism. [<G, lit., hooked cross]

ha·kim (hä·kēm′) n. In Moslem countries, a governor; also, a sage or physician. Also **ha·keem′, ha·kem′.** [<Arabic, wise, learned]

hal- Var. of HALO-.

ha·la·cha (hä′lä·khä′, Hebrew hä·lô′khô) n. pl. **·choth** (-khōth) In the Talmud, Jewish traditional law embracing minute precepts not found in the written law; the legal part of the Midrash. Compare HAGGADAH. Also **ha′la·kah′.** [<Hebrew halakāh a rule to go by <hālak walk, go] —**ha·lach·ic** (hə·lak′ik) adj.

ha·la·chist (hä′lə·kist, hə·lä′kist) n. One who frames from the Biblical laws precepts of the halacha. Also **ha′la·kist.**

ha·la·tion (hä·lā′shən, ha-) n. Phot. An appearance somewhat like a halo: caused by the radiation of light from a window or other object in the scene of a photograph, or by reflection of light from the plate; ghost. [< HALO]

hal·berd (hal′bərd) n. A weapon in the form of a battle-ax and pike at the end of a long staff. Also **hal′bard, hal′bert** (-bərt). [<OF hallebarde <MHG helmbarte <helm handle + barte broad-ax]

hal·ber·dier (hal′bər·dir′) n. A soldier armed with a halberd.

hal·cy·on (hal′sē·ən) n. **1** A mythical bird, identified with the kingfisher, said to have nested on the sea at the time of the winter solstice, when the sea was supposed to become calm. **2** Any kingfisher of the genus Halcyon of Australasia. —adj. **1** Of or pertaining to the halcyon. **2** Calm; peaceful. [<L halcyon, var. of alcyon <Gk. alkyōn kingfisher]

halcyon days 1 The seven days before and the seven days after the winter solstice, when the halcyon bred and brought calm, peaceful weather. **2** Any period of peace and tranquillity.

Hal·cy·o·ne (hal·sī′ə·nē) See ALCYONE.

hale[1] (hāl) v.t. **haled, hal·ing 1** To drag by force; haul; pull. **2** To compel to go: to hale someone into court. ◆ Homophone: hail. [Var. of HAUL] —**hal′er** n.

hale[2] (hāl) adj. **1** Of sound and vigorous health; robust. **2** Scot. Free from defect or injury. See synonyms under HEALTHY. ◆ Homophone: hail. [OE hāl. Related to WHOLE.] —**hale′ly** adv. —**hale′ness** n.

Ha·le·a·ka·la (hä′lä·ä·kä·lä′) The largest extinct volcanic crater in the world, on eastern Maui island, Hawaii; 10,032 feet high; 19 square miles; 2,000 feet deep.

Ha·le·mau·mau (hä′lä·mou′mou) The fiery pit in the Kilauea crater of Mauna Loa, Hawaii.

half (haf, häf) n. pl. **halves** (havz, hävz) One of two equal parts into which a thing is or may

---

be divided, or a quantity equal to such a part. —**to, for, at,** or **on halves** For half the crop or profits: for rent at halves, to farm on halves. —adj. **1** Being one of two equal parts of a thing. **2** Partial; approximately one half of, in amount or value. —adv. To the degree or extent of a half; partially. —**not half bad** Brit. Actually quite good, don't you know! [OE half]

half-and-half (haf′ənd·haf′, häf′ənd·häf′) adj. Half of one thing and half of another. —n. A mixture of two liquors; specifically, beer and ale. —adv. Equally; in two equal divisions.

half·back (haf′bak′, häf′-) n. In American football, either of two players in the backfield, originally stationed half-way between the line and the fullback.

halfbeak (haf′bēk′, häf′-) n. A fish (genus Hemiramphus), related to the saury, having the lower jaw prolonged into a flat, narrow extension.

half-bind·ing (haf′bīn′ding, häf′-) n. A style of bookbinding in which only the back and corners of the volume are covered with leather. —**half′-bound′** (-bound′) adj.

half blood 1 Law The relationship between persons who have one parent only in common. **2** The condition of being of mixed stock: an Indian of half blood.

half-blood (haf′blud′) n. **1** A person having only one parent of a specified stock; one whose parents are of different stocks; a half-breed. **2** An animal, as a cow, sheep, etc., of crossed inferior and superior stock. **3** A person of Indian and white, or Negro and white parentage. —adj. Being a half-blood or half-breed; in a loose sense, of mixed blood or breed: also **half′-blood′ed.**

half-breed (haf′brēd′, häf′-) n. **1** One having parents of different blood or ethnic stock: a Canadian half-breed. **2** One having a white father and an American Indian mother. **3** An adherent of President Garfield in the factional struggles of 1881 within the Republican party. See STALWART. —adj. Half of one breed and half of another; coming of mixed ethnic or racial stock: also **half′-bred′** (-bred′).

half-breed buffalo A catalo.

half-broth·er (haf′bruth′ər, häf′-) n. A brother related through only one parent.

half-case (haf′kās′, häf′-) n. Printing A type case about half the width of the standard upper case.

half-caste (haf′kast′, häf′käst′) n. One born of mixed European and Asian blood; also, any half-breed. —adj. Of mixed European and other blood.

half-cock (haf′kok′, häf′-) n. The position of the hammer of a firearm when partly raised, but not releasable by the trigger. —**to go off at half-cock 1** To be discharged prematurely. **2** Hence, to act or speak hastily or without deliberation. Also **to go off half-cocked.** —v.t. To raise the hammer of (a gun) to the position of half-cock.

half-dol·lar (haf′dol′ər, häf′-) n. A U.S. silver coin worth fifty cents: first minted, 1794.

half-ea·gle (haf′ē′gəl, häf′-) n. A gold coin of the United States having a value of five dollars.

half gainer A backward somersault from the standing position of a front dive.

half hatchet A hatchet, the blade of which is trimmed flush with the wedge of the shaft. See illustration under HATCHET.

half-heart·ed (haf′här′tid, häf′-) adj. Showing little interest or enthusiasm. See synonyms under FAINT, IRRESOLUTE. —**half′-heart′ed·ly** adv. —**half′-heart′ed·ness** n.

half-hitch (haf′hich′, häf′-) n. A hitch formed by an overhand knot. See illustration under HITCH.

half-hour (haf′our′, häf′-) n. **1** A period of thirty minutes. **2** The point midway between the hours. —**half′-hour′ly** adv.

half leather A style of bookbinding in which the volume has a leather back and muslin sides.

half-length (haf′length′, häf′-) adj. Of half the full length, as of a portrait. —n. A portrait showing only the upper half of the body.

half-life (haf′līf′, häf′-) n. Physics The period of time during which half the atoms of a radioactive element or isotope will disintegrate. The half-life of radium is about 1,620 years, at the end of which period the amount

---

remaining will require another 1,620 years to decline by half. Also called half-value period. Also **half period.**

half-lift (haf′lift′, häf′-) n. A layer of heel leather split to half the standard thickness, and used for close adjustment in built-up heels.

half-light (haf′līt′, häf′-) n. A dim, grayish light, as at evening.

half-mast (haf′mast′, häf′mäst′) n. The position of a flag when half-way up the staff, as a tribute of respect to the dead or as a signal of distress. —v.t. To put, as a flag, at half-mast. Also called half-staff.

half-meas·ure (haf′mezh′ər, häf′-) n. An imperfect or inadequate measure or plan.

half-mitt (haf′mit′, häf′-) n. A type of mitten extending only to the knuckles. Also **half′-mit′ten.**

half-moon (haf′mōōn′, häf′-) n. **1** The moon when half its disk is illuminated. **2** Something similar in shape to a half-moon.

half-nel·son (haf′nel′sən, häf′-) n. A wrestling hold in which one arm is passed below the opponent's armpit and the hand is pressed against the back of his neck.

half note Music A note held half the measure of a whole note; a minim.

half-pace (haf′pās′, häf′-) n. Brit. **1** A floor raised above the adjoining level, in a bay window or the like; the raised place at the head of steps on which an altar stands; a dais. **2** A resting place at the end of a flight of stairs; a footpace.

half-pay (haf′pā′, häf′-) n. Literally, half of full pay; most commonly, the reduced pay of an officer not in regular service or on the retired list, generally more than half.

half-pen·ny (hā′pən·ē, hāp′nē) n. pl. **half-pence** (hā′pəns) or **half-pen·nies** (hā′pən·ēz, hāp′nēz) A British copper coin equivalent to one half of a penny.

half-pike (haf′pīk′, häf′-) n. A spearing weapon having a staff about half as long as that of the pike.

half pint 1 A measure of capacity equal to one half of a pint. **2** Slang A small person.

half relief Mezzo-relievo.

half rime Near rime.

half-sec·tion (haf′sek′shən, häf′-) n. Half a square mile, or 320 acres of land.

half-sis·ter (haf′sis′tər, häf′-) n. A sister related through only one parent.

half-sole (haf′sōl′, häf′-) n. A tap sole on a shoe, extending only to the shank. —v.t. **·soled, ·sol·ing** To repair by attaching a half-sole.

half-step (haf′step′, häf′-) n. **1** Music. A semitone. **2** Mil. A step of fifteen inches at quick time; in double time, one of eighteen inches.

half-tim·bered (haf′tim′bərd, häf′-) adj. Built of heavy timbers, with the spaces between filled with masonry or plaster: said of the framework of a house.

half time The middle break in a field or court game played in definite time intervals.

half-time (haf′tīm′, häf′-) adj. Requiring half a person's usual working hours.

half-tint (haf′tint′, häf′-) n. A tint or tone of color intermediate between two strong tones of different values.

half-ti·tle (haf′tīt′l, häf′-) n. **1** The title of a book, usually abridged, printed on the leaf preceding the title page. **2** The title of any part or section of a book printed on the leaf preceding the text proper: often called mock title.

halftone (haf′tōn′, häf′-) n. **1** An illustration made from a relief plate obtained by photographing an original through a finely ruled glass screen, the lights and shadows appearing when printed as minutely lined or dotted surfaces. **2** A half-tint. **3** Music A semitone. —adj. Made by the process of printing halftones.

half-track (haf′trak′, häf′-) adj. Designating a type of military vehicle propelled by endless tracks, but steered by a pair of wheels in front. —n. A half-track vehicle. Compare FULL-TRACK.

half-truth (haf′trōōth′, häf′-) n. An assertion that is true as far as it goes, but that omits or conceals part of the truth.

half-year (haf′yir′, häf′-) n. **1** Half of a calendar year, or six months. **2** Half the

---

HAJE

The royal serpent of ancient Egypt; widely represented as a religious symbol and in the royal headdress (a) as sign of the royal power. (From 3 to 4 feet long, with neck skin dilatable)

time regularly used in a year, as of a school year. —**half'-year'ly** adj. & adv.

hal·i·but (hal'ə·bət, hol'-) n. pl. ·but or ·buts A large flatfish (Hippoglossus hippoglossus) of northern seas, much esteemed as food, sometimes attaining a weight of 400 pounds: also spelled **holibut**. [ME halybutte, OE halig holy + BUT²]

hal·ic (hal'ik, hā'lik) adj. Ecol. Of or pertaining to plant communities associated with saline soils.

hal·ide (hal'īd, -id, hā'līd, -lid) n. Chem. Any compound of a halogen with an element or radical, as a bromide, chloride, etc. —adj. Resembling sea salt; haloid. Also **hal·id** (hal'·id, hā'lid).

hal·i·dom (hal'ə·dəm) n. Archaic 1 Holiness. 2 A holy relic. 3 A holy place; sanctuary. [OE haligdom < halig holy + -DOM]

Hal·i·fax (hal'ə·faks) 1 The capital of Nova Scotia province, Canada; the principal Atlantic port in Canada. 2 A county borough in SW Yorkshire, England. — **Hal·i·go·ni·an** (hal'i·gō'nē·ən) adj. & n.

hal·i·plank·ton (hal'ə·plangk'tən) n. Marine plankton, as opposed to lacustrine plankton.

hal·ite (hal'īt, hā'līt) n. A massive or granular, white or variously colored sodium chloride, NaCl; rock salt.

hal·i·to·sis (hal'ə·tō'sis) n. A malodorous condition of the breath. [< L halitus breath + -OSIS]

hal·i·tus (hal'ə·təs) n. 1 The breath. 2 The vapor from a living body or from blood newly drawn. [< L]

hall (hôl) n. 1 A passage or corridor in a building. 2 A small room or enclosure at the entry of a house; a vestibule; lobby. 3 A large building or room devoted to public or semipublic business or entertainments. 4 In a university or college, a large building used as a dormitory, classroom building, laboratory, etc. 5 A meeting place for a fraternity or society; also the society itself: Tammany Hall. 6 Brit. A college dining-room; also, the dinner served there. 7 In medieval times, the large main room of a castle or other great house, used for dining, entertaining, and, often, sleeping. 8 The country residence of a baron, squire, etc. See synonyms under HOUSE.— Homophone: haul. [OE heall]

Hal·le (häl'ə) A city in SW East Germany, capital of former Saxony-Anhalt state. Also **Hal·le-an-der-Saa·le** (häl'ə·än·dər·zä'lə).

hal·lel (häl'el, hə·lāl') n. In Jewish religious observances, the Psalms from cxiii to cxviii inclusive, chanted at the Passover, Pentecost, and Sukkoth. [< Hebrew hallēl praise]

hal·le·lu·jah (hal'ə·lōō'yə) interj. Praise ye the Lord! —n. 1 A musical composition whose principal theme is found in the word hallelujah. 2 A flower of the wood sorrel family (Oxalidaceae). Also **hal'le·lu'iah**. [< Gk. < Hebrew hallēlū praise + yāh Jehovah]

hall·mark (hôl'märk') n. 1 An official mark stamped on gold and silver articles in England to guarantee their purity. 2 Any mark or proof of genuineness or excellence. —v.t. To stamp with a hallmark. [< Goldsmiths' Hall, London, where the assaying and stamping were formerly exclusively done + MARK]

hal·loo (hə·lōō') interj. 1 An exclamation to attract attention, express surprise, etc. 2 A shout to incite hounds to the chase. —n. A cry of "halloo." —v.i. To shout "halloo"; cry out. —v.t. 1 To incite or encourage with shouts. 2 To shout to; hail. 3 To shout (something). Also **hal·lo, hal·loa** (hə·lō): also spelled holla, hollo, holloa, hillo, hilloa, hullo. [< OF halloer pursue noisily]

hal·low (hal'ō) v.t. 1 To make holy; consecrate. 2 To look upon as holy; reverence. [OE halgian < halig holy] —**hal·lowed** (hal'ōd, in liturgical use hal'ō·id) adj.

Hal·low·e·en (hal'ō·ēn') n. The evening of Oct. 31, vigil of All Saints' Day. [<(ALL-) HALLOW(s) E(V)EN]

Hall process A process for the electrolytic reduction of aluminum from its ores. [after C. M. Hall, 1863–1914, U.S. inventor]

Hall·statt (häl'shtät) adj. Pertaining to or denoting the earlier of two principal divisions of the prehistoric Iron Age of Europe, extending from about the ninth to the fifth century B.C. — **Hall·statt'i·an** (-ē-ən) adj.

hall tree A clothestree.

hal·lu·ci·nate (hə·lōō'sə·nāt) v.t. ·nat·ed, ·nat·ing To affect or afflict with hallucinations. [< L hallucinatus, pp. of hallucinari, alucinari wander mentally]

hal·lu·ci·na·tion (hə·lōō'sə·nā'shən) n. 1 An apparent perception without any corresponding external object. 2 Psychiatry Any of numerous sensations, auditory, visual, or tactile, experienced without external stimulus, and caused by mental derangement, intoxication, or fever. See ILLUSION. 3 A mistaken notion. See synonyms under DELUSION, DREAM, ERROR. —**hal·lu·ci·na·to·ry** (hə·lōō'sə·nə·tôr'ē, -tō'rē) adj.

hal·lu·ci·no·gen (hə·lōō'sin·ə·jən) n. Any drug or chemical, as peyote, capable of inducing hallucinations.

hal·lu·ci·no·gen·ic (hə·lōō'sə·nə·jen'ik) adj. 1 Causing or having to do with hallucinations or with a distortion of perception or consciousness: hallucinogenic drugs. 2 Of or pertaining to hallucinogens.

hal·lu·ci·no·sis (hə·lōō'sə·nō'sis) n. Psychiatry A mental or nervous disorder characterized by persistent hallucinations.

hal·lux (hal'əks) n. pl. **hal·lu·ces** (hal'yōō·sēz) Biol. 1 The first or innermost digit of the foot; the great toe. 2 In a bird, the hind toe. [< NL < L hallex; infl. by hallus thumb]

hall·way (hôl'wā') n. A passage giving entrance to a building or communicating with its various apartments.

hal·ma (hal'mə) n. In the exercise of the pentathlon, the long jump with weights in the hands. [< Gk. < halesthai leap]

ha·lo (hā'lō) n. pl. ·los or ·loes 1 Meteorol. A luminous circle around the sun or the moon, caused by the refraction of light passing through ice crystals floating in the air. 2 A nimbus; a radiance encircling the head in portrayals of a sacred personage. 3 The ideal brightness with which imagination surrounds an object of affection or sentiment. —v.t. To enclose in a halo. — v.i. To form a halo. [< L < Gk. halos a circular threshing floor]

halo- combining form 1 The sea; of or related to the sea: halophyte. 2 Related to a halogen. Also, before vowels, hal-, as in haloid. [< Gk. hals, halos salt, the sea]

hal·o·bi·os (hal'ə·bī'əs) n. Life in the oceans; marine life collectively. [< HALO- + Gk. bios life] — **hal'o·bi·ot'ic** (-bī·ot'ik) adj.

hal·o·gen (hal'ə·jən) n. Chem. One of certain non-metallic elements belonging to the seventh group in the periodic table, as iodine, fluorine, chlorine, and bromine, which combine directly with metals to form halides. [< Gk. hals sea, salt + -GEN] —**ha·log·e·nous** (hə·loj'ə·nəs) adj.

hal·o·ge·na·tion (hal'ə·jə·nā'shən) n. Chem. The introduction of a halogen into an organic molecule, by substitution or addition.

hal·oid (hal'oid, hā'loid) adj. 1 Resembling sea salt. 2 Pertaining to or derived from a halogen. —n. A haloid salt.

hal·o·man·cy (hal'ə·man'sē) n. Divination by means of salt thrown into a flame: also spelled alomancy.

hal·o·per·i·dol (hal'ō·per'ə·dōl, -dôl) n. An ataractic drug, $C_{21}H_{23}ClFNO_2$.

ha·loph·i·lous (hə·lof'ə·ləs) adj. Bot. Adapted to salt; said of plants growing in saline soil. Also **hal·o·phil** (hal'ə·fil), **hal'o·phile** (-fīl, -fil).

hal·o·phyte (hal'ə·fīt) n. Bot. A plant of saline soil, such as those of the genera Salsola and Salicornia, growing in salt marshes and yielding salt. —**hal'o·phyt'ic** (-fit'ik) adj.

halt¹ (hôlt) n. A complete stop, or cessation of progress in any movement, as of marching troops. —**to call a halt** To put a stop to, or demand that something be stopped. —v.t. & v.i. To stop; bring or come to a halt. See synonyms under REST¹, STAND. [< F halte < G halt, orig. imperative of halten stop]

halt² (hôlt) v.i. 1 To be imperfect; proceed lamely, as verse or logic. 2 To be in doubt; waver. 3 Archaic To walk with a limp; hobble. —adj. Archaic Crippled; limping in gait; lame. —n. Archaic The act of limping; lameness. [OE healt lame] —**halt'ing** adj. —**halt'ing·ly** adv. — **halt'ing·ness** n.

hal·ter¹ (hôl'tər) n. 1 A strap or rope, especially one with a headstall at one end, by which to hold a horse or other animal. 2 A hangman's rope; hence, death by the rope. 3 A woman's waist designed for exposing the back and arms to the sun, fastened around the neck and waist. —v.t. 1 To put a halter on; secure with a halter. 2 To hang (someone). [OE hælftre]

hal·ter² (hal'tər) n. pl. **hal·te·res** (hal·tir'ēz) Entomol. One of a pair of small, knobbed, filamentous appendages on each side of the thorax in dipterous insects, replacing the hind wings; a balancer. [< NL < Gk. haltēres jumping weights (as used in the halma)]

ha·lutz (khä·lōōts') n. pl. **ha·lu·tzim** (khä·lōō·tsēm') A pioneer agriculturist in Israel: also spelled chalutz. [< Hebrew chalutz a warrior]

halve (hav, häv) v.t. **halved, halv·ing** 1 To divide into two equal parts; share equally. 2 To lessen by half; take away half of. 3 In golf, to play (a match or hole) in the same number of strokes as one's opponent. [< HALF]

ham (ham) n. 1 The thigh of an animal, as a hog, prepared for food. 2 pl. The buttocks. 3 The space or region behind the knee joint; the hock of quadrupeds. 4 Slang A third-rate actor; one who overdramatizes scenes, or portrays a character in amateur fashion. 5 An amateur radio operator. [OE hamm] —**ham'my** adj.

ha·mal (hä·mäl', -môl') n. 1 In Oriental countries, one who bears burdens; a porter; a carrier. 2 In India, a man servant: also spelled hammal. Also **ha·maul'**. [< Arabic ḥammāl < ḥamala carry]

Ha·ma·mat·su (hä·mä·mät·sōō) A city on south central Honshu island, Japan.

Ham·a·me·lis (ham'ə·mē'lis) n. A genus of shrubs of the witch hazel family (Hamamelidaceae) having alternate simple leaves and heads or spikes of monoecious or polygamous flowers. H. virginiana is the common witch hazel. [< NL < Gk. hammamēlis tree with pearlike fruit] — **ham·a·me·li·da·ceous** (ham'ə·mē'lə·dā'shəs) adj.

Ha·man (hā'mən) The chief minister of Ahasuerus, whose plot against the Jews recoiled upon himself (Esth. iii–vii), and who was hanged on a gallows fifty cubits high; hence, the phrase **hanged as high as Haman.**

Ham·ble·to·ni·an (ham'bəl·tō'nē·ən) n. 1 One of a famous breed of American trotting horses. 2 The chief harness race for three-year-old trotters, held annually, formerly at Goshen, New York. —adj. Of or pertaining to a horse of the Hambletonian breed. [after Hambletonian, famous American stud, from Black Hambleton, a racecourse in Yorkshire, England]

Ham·burg (ham'bûrg) n. 1 A European variety of the domestic fowl, having lead-gray legs and a rose-colored comb. 2 A black, sweet and juicy grape, indigenous to the Tyrol and widely cultivated in hothouses throughout the northern latitudes. Also **Ham'burgh.**

Ham·burg (ham'bûrg, Ger. häm'bŏŏrkh) A state comprising the chief port and second largest city in Germany, at the head of the Elbe estuary in NW Germany; 288 square miles.

ham·burg·er (ham'bûr'gər) n. 1 Finely ground beef. 2 Such meat fried or broiled in the form of a patty. Also **hamburger steak**: also called Salisbury steak. 3 A sandwich consisting of such meat placed between the halves of a round roll. [from Hamburg, Germany]

hame (hām) n. One of two curved bars fitted to the collar, that hold the traces of a draft harness. [OE hama dress, covering]

Ha·mit·ic (ha·mit'ik) adj. Of or pertaining to Ham, or the Hamites, or their languages. —n. A North African subfamily of the Hamito-Semitic family of languages, divided into three branches — ancient Egyptian, Libyco-Berber (extinct Libyan and the modern Berber dialects), and the Cushitic languages of Ethiopia and Somaliland.

Ham·i·to-Se·mit·ic (ham'ə·tō·sə·mit'ik) n. A large family of languages spoken in northern Africa and part of SW Asia, consisting of the subfamilies Hamitic (ancient Egyptian, Libyan, the modern Berber dialects, and the

Cushitic languages) and *Semitic* (Akkadian, Phoenician, Aramaic, Syriac, Arabic, Hebrew, Amharic, etc.). The family is characterized grammatically by triliteral or biliteral word bases.

ham·let (ham'lit) *n.* **1** A little village; a cluster of houses in the country. **2** *Brit.* A village without a church of its own. [<OF *hamelet*, dim. of *hamel* <LL *hamellum* village <Gmc.]

Ham·let (ham'lit) In Shakespeare's play of this name, the hero, prince of Denmark, who seeks to avenge the murder of his father at the bidding of his father's ghost.

ham·mer (ham'ər) *n.* **1** A hand implement with a head at right angles to the handle, used for driving nails, pounding, swaging, etc. See under CLAW HAMMER, TACK HAMMER. **2** A machine, as a steam hammer or trip hammer, performing functions similar to those of a heavy hand hammer. **3** A part or piece of a machine or apparatus performing functions similar to those of a hammer: especially, the piece by which a gong or the like is struck. **4** That part of a gunlock which strikes the cap or cartridge. **5** A padded piece that strikes the string of a pianoforte. **6** An auctioneer's mallet. **7** A lever in an internal combustion engine which controls the exhaust. **8** *Anat.* The malleus of the middle ear. **9** A metal ball weighing 16 pounds with a long wire or wooden handle: used for throwing in track meets. — **under the hammer** For sale at auction. — *v.t.* **1** To strike or beat with or as with a hammer; drive, as a nail. **2** To shape or fasten with a hammer. **3** To form or force as if with hammer blows: to *hammer* an idea into his head. — *v.i.* **4** To strike blows with or as with a hammer. [OE *hamer*] — **ham'mer·er** *n.*

ham·mer·cloth (ham'ər·klôth', -kloth') *n.* The cloth covering a coachman's box. [? Alter. of *hamper cloth*]

hammered work Work in thin metal having the design hammered or beaten by hand, as in repoussé work.

ham·mer·har·den (ham'ər·här'dən) *v.t.* To harden (metals) by beating with a hammer.

ham·mer·head (ham'ər·hed') *n.* **1** The head of a hammer. **2** A heronlike wading bird (order *Ciconiiformes*) native to Africa and Madagascar, with a blunt-pointed beak, clove-

brown plumage, and a large crest. **3** A voracious shark (family *Sphynidae*) of warm seas, having a transversely elongated head with the eyes at each end. **4** The hogsucker. **5** An African fruit bat (family *Pteropidae*) with an elongated snout, related to the flying fox.

ham·mer·less (ham'ər·lis) *adj.* Having no hammer visible: said of firearms.

hammer lock A wrestling grip in which the arm is twisted behind the back and upwards.

ham·mer·smith (ham'ər·smith') *n.* One who works metal with a hammer.

ham·mer·toe (ham'ər·tō') *n.* *Pathol.* A deformity of the toe, usually the second, in which the joint nearest the foot is bent downward.

ham·mock[1] (ham'ək) *n.* A couch of canvas or netting, swung by the ends. [<Sp. *hamaca* < native name]

ham·mock[2] (ham'ək) *n.* *U.S.* In the South, a thickly wooded tract of fertile land, often elevated: also called *hummock*. [Var. of HUMMOCK]

ham·per[1] (ham'pər) *v.t.* To hinder the movements of; encumber; restrain. — *n.* **1** *Naut.* Necessary but encumbering equipment of a ship, as the rigging. **2** A fetter. See synonyms under EMBARRASS, HINDER. [ME *hampren*; origin uncertain]

ham·per[2] (ham'pər) *n.* A large packing basket, as for food. — *v.t.* To put into hampers. [<OF *hanapier* case to hold a cup or goblet < *hanap* cup <LG. Doublet of HANAPER.]

Hamp·shire (hamp'shir) A county in southern England; 1,650 square miles; capital, Winchester; including the administrative counties of Southampton and the Isle of Wight: shortened form *Hants*.

Hamp·stead (hamp'sted, -stid) A metropolitan borough of London north of the Thames, including **Hampstead Heath**, a public common, once the resort of highwaymen.

ham·shack·le (ham'shak'əl) *v.t.* **·led**, **·ling** **1** To hobble, as a horse, by connecting the head and forelegs with a short rope or strap, so as to impede movement. **2** To restrain or impede. Also spelled *hapshackle*. [<HAM[1] + SHACKLE]

ham·ster (ham'stər) *n.* A sturdy burrowing rodent. The common hamster (*Cricetus cricetus*) of Europe and Asia has very large cheek pouches and a short tail; it stores up grain in subterranean galleries. [<G]

ham·string (ham'string') *n.* **1** A tendon of the thigh, back of the knee. **2** The large sinew at the back of the hock of the hind leg of a quadruped. — *v.t.* **·strung**, **·string·ing** **1** To cut the hamstring of; cripple; disable. **2** To cripple (a whale) by cutting the fluke-tendons.

Ham·tramck (ham·tram'ik) A city of SE Michigan, entirely surrounded by Detroit.

ham·u·late (ham'yə·lāt, -lit) *adj.* **1** Having little hooks, as certain plants. **2** Curved.

ham·u·lus (ham'yə·ləs) *n.* *pl.* **·li** (-lī) **1** A little hook. **2** A hooklike process of a bone. **3** A hooked barbicel of a feather. [<L]

ham·za (ham'zə) *n.* In Arabic orthography, the sign of the glottal stop, transliterated with an apostrophe.

Han (hän) The fifth Chinese dynasty, 207 B.C.–A.D. 220.

Han (hän) **1** A river in east central China, flowing 750 miles SE to the Yangtze. **2** A river in southern China, flowing 210 miles south to the China Sea.

han·a·per (han'ə·pər) *n.* A wicker receptacle for documents or valuables. [<OF *hanapier*. Doublet of HAMPER[2].]

hance (hans) *n.* **1** *Archit.* **a** The haunch of an arch; the lower part of a many-centered arch, above the springing. **b** A small arch joining a straight lintel to its jamb. **2** A break or sudden departure from a natural form; an irregularity, as in a fife rail. [ME, aphetic var. OF ENHANCE.]

Han·cock (han'kok), **John,** 1737–93, American statesman; signer of the Declaration of Independence. — **Winfield Scott,** 1824–86, U.S. general.

hand (hand) *n.* **1** The part of the forelimb in man and other primates that is attached to the lower extremity of the forearm, and is adapted for grasping; it consists of the carpus, metacarpus, and fingers. **2** The end or distal segment of a limb when serving as a prehen-

sile organ, as in bats. **3** Side or direction: At his right *hand* sat the president. **4** A side or viewpoint of a subject or question: on the one *hand* this and on the other *hand* that. **5** A part or role in doing something: They all had a *hand* in it. **6** *pl.* Possession; control; supervision: The work is in my *hands.* **7** Aid; assistance: to lend a *hand.* **8** A pledge of betrothal, or a giving in marriage. **9** A manual laborer: a farm *hand.* **10** A person, as the performer of some action or task: a book written by various *hands.* **11** A person, considered with reference to his skill or ability: He was quite a *hand* with the violin. **12** Skill; ability; touch: The painting showed the *hand* of a master. **13** The members of a group or company: All *hands* joined in the sport. **14** A (specified) remove from a source of supply or information: a story heard at second-*hand.* **15** The cards held by a player at one deal; also, the player. **16** The playing of the cards at one deal. **17** Clapping of hands; a round of applause. **18** Handwriting; style of writing: a legible *hand.* **19** A person's signature. **20** Something resembling a hand in appearance or function. **21** The figure ☞ used as an index; fist. **22** The pointer of a clock. **23** A bunch of tobacco leaves on the stem, tied together. **24** A small cluster of bananas. **25** The approximate width of the palm; specifically, four inches: a horse 16 *hands* high. **26** The part of a gunstock grasped by the hand. **27** *Law* A manus. — **a great hand at** or **for** A person specially fond of or clever at. — **at first hand** At the source. — **at hand** Within reach; nearby; convenient. — **at the hand of** From the hand of; by the operation of. — **by hand** With the hands; not aided by machinery. — **to have one's hands full** To have all or more than one can do. — **in hand 1** Delivered in advance; paid in the hand. **2** In process of execution or under consideration: I have the matter in *hand.* **3** Entirely under control — **laying on of hands** The act or ceremony of laying the hands on the head of another for the purpose of consecrating to a special office, or of blessing or healing. — **to lend a hand** To help. — **off one's hands** Out of one's care or control. — **on hand 1** In present or rightful possession: We have too many goods *on hand.* **2** In place; present: He was promptly *on hand.* — **on one's hands** In one's care or possession; entailing responsibility on one. — **out of hand 1** Unruly; lawless: The rioters got *out of hand.* **2** Immediately; without delay; offhand. — **to hand** At hand; close by; readily accessible. — **to wash one's hands of** To take no further responsibility in; dismiss from consideration. — *v.t.* **1** To give, pass, or deliver with or as with the hand; transmit; transfer. **2** To lead or help with the hand. **3** *Naut.* To furl, as sail. — **to hand down 1** To transmit, as to one's heirs or successors. **2** To deliver, as the decision of a court. — **to hand it to** *U.S. Slang* To acknowledge the abilities, success, etc., of. — **to hand on** To pass on; transmit. — **to hand out** To mete out; distribute. — **to hand over** To give up possession of; surrender. [OE *hand*]

hand·ball (hand'bôl') *n.* **1** A game in which a small ball is struck with the hand and kept bounding against a wall or walls by, usually, two or four players. **2** The rubber ball used in this game.

hand·bill (hand'bil') *n.* A small advertising sheet or public notice, usually distributed by hand.

hand·book (hand'book') *n.* A small guidebook or manual.

hand·breadth (hand'bredth') *n.* The breadth of the hand; a palm. Also *hand's breadth.*

hand car A small open railroad car, propelled by a hand pump or motor, used by section men and other railroad workers.

hand·clasp (hand'klasp', -kläsp') *n.* A clasping of a person's hand in greeting, agreement, farewell, etc.

hand·cuff (hand'kuf') *n.* One of two manacles connected by a chain, and designed to be locked around the wrists. See synonyms under FETTER. — *v.t.* To put handcuffs on; manacle.

HANDCUFFS

hand·gal·lop (hand'gal'əp) *n.* A moderate gallop.

hand glass 1 A mirror intended to be held in the hand. **2** A reading glass. **3** A time glass to mea-

HAMMERS
a. Bricklayer's hammer.
b. Upholsterer's or tack hammer.
c. Machinist's straight-peen.
d. Shoemaker's hammer.
e. Rawhide-faced hammer.
f. Machinist's ball-peen.
g. Riveting hammer.
h. Blacksmith's set-hammer.
i. Claw hammer.
j. Tinner's hammer.

sure a ship's log.

hand·gun (hand′gun′) n. A firearm held and fired in one hand, as a pistol.

hand·i·cap (han′dē·kap′) n. 1 A condition imposed to equalize the chances of competitors in a race or athletic contest, as the carrying of extra weight, or the requirement of a greater distance or a later start than is assigned to an inferior competitor; also, the weight, etc., so required. 2 A race or contest in which such conditions are imposed. 3 Any disadvantage or hindrance making success in an undertaking more difficult. —v.t. ·capped, ·cap·ping 1 To impose a handicap on, as a contestant in a race. 2 To be a handicap to: His leg *handicaps* his movements. [< *hand in cap*, a lottery game in which winners were penalized] —**hand′i·cap′per** n.

hand·i·craft (han′dē·kraft′, -kräft′) n. 1 Skill and expertness in working with the hands. 2 A trade calling for such skill. See synonyms under BUSINESS. [OE *handcrœft*]

hand·i·ly (han′də·lē) adv. 1 In a handy manner; dexterously. 2 Conveniently.

hand·i·work (han′dē·wûrk′) n. Work done by the hands. [OE *handgeweorc*]

hand·ker·chief (hang′kər·chif) n. 1 A kerchief for wiping the face or nose. 2 A neckerchief.

hand·knit (hand′nit′) adj. Knitted by hand: also **hand′·knit′ted.**

han·dle (han′dəl) v. han·dled, han·dling v.t. 1 To touch, feel, etc., with the hands; use the hands upon. 2 To manage or use with the hands; manipulate: to *handle* a rifle. 3 To manage or direct; control. 4 To deal or treat with: to *handle* a disagreement. 5 To trade or deal in; buy and sell: to *handle* cotton. 6 To act toward; treat: They *handled* the matter shamefully. —v.i. 7 To submit or respond to handling: The horse *handles* well. —**to handle with (kid) gloves on** To deal with very carefully and tactfully. —n. That part of an object intended to be grasped with the hand in lifting or using, as a haft, helve, hilt, crank, bail, or knob. —**to fly off the handle** To be suddenly and unreasonably angry; make an emotional scene. [OE *handlian* < *hand* hand]

han·dle·bar (han′dəl·bär′) n. 1 A handle or handles in the form of a bar; specifically, the steering bar of a bicycle, motorcycle, or similar vehicle. 2 pl. U.S. Colloq. A long mustache curved like a handlebar.

han·dler (hand′lər) n. 1 One who or that which handles; specifically, one who trains, breaks in, or manages certain animals, as dogs, colts, fighting cocks, etc. 2 The trainer of a pugilist.

hand level A telescopic hand instrument used in surveying to find approximate elevations.

han·dling (hand′ling) n. 1 The act of touching or turning with the hands. 2 Manner of treatment, as in writing, drawing, arguing, etc.

hand·maid (hand′mād′) n. A female servant or attendant. Also **hand′maid′en.**

hand organ A musical instrument consisting of a boxed revolving cylinder turned by a hand crank; a portable barrel organ.

hand·pick (hand′pik′) v.t. 1 To pick by hand. 2 To select with care. 3 To choose for an ulterior purpose: to *hand-pick* a candidate.

hand pump Any pump worked by hand; especially, an auxiliary fuel pump used to start an engine or for emergency: also called *wobble pump.*

hand rail A rail that can be grasped by the hand, as at the edge of a gallery or along the outer edge of a stairway.

hand·sel (hand′səl, han′-) n. 1 A gift as a token of good will or to secure good luck. 2 Earnest money on a contract. 3 A bridegroom's gift to a bride. 4 Money given as a gift at New Year's. —v.t. ·seled or ·selled, ·sel·ing or ·sel·ling 1 To give handsel to. 2 To do or use for the first time. 3 To inaugurate, as with a ceremony. Also spelled *hansel.* [OE *handselen* < *hand* hand + *selen* gift]

hand·set (hand′set′) n. An apparatus, device, or instrument, especially a telephone, designed to be held in or operated by one hand.

hand·shake (hand′shāk′) n. A clasping and shaking of a person's hand, as in greeting, agreement, parting, etc.

hand·some (han′səm) adj. 1 Agreeable to the eye

or to good taste; of pleasing aspect. 2 Of liberal dimensions or proportions. 3 Marked by magnanimity, generosity, or liberality. 4 Marked by propriety. 5 Obs. Handy; convenient; dexterous. See synonyms under BEAUTIFUL, FINE. ◆ Homophone: *hansom.* [< HAND+-SOME, orig. with sense "easy to handle"] —**hand′some·ness** n.

hands-on (handz′on′; -ôn′) adj. Designating an action that requires active participation; *hands-on techniques.*

hand·spike (hand′spīk′) n. A bar used as a lever.

hand·spring (hand′spring′) n. A somersault in which only the hands, when the feet are in the air, touch the ground.

hand·work (hand′wûrk′) n. Work done by hand, not by machine.

hand·writ·ing (hand′rī′ting) n. 1 The form of writing peculiar to a given person. 2 Penmanship. 3 Written matter.

hand·y (han′dē) adj. hand·i·er, hand·i·est 1 Ready at hand or convenient for use; nearby. 2 Skilful with the hands. 3 Easy to handle: said of a ship or a tool. See synonyms under CONVENIENT, SKILFUL.

handy man One good at odd jobs; a jack-of-all-trades.

hang (hang) v. hung or (esp. for v. defs. 3 and 9) hanged, hang·ing v.t. 1 To fasten or attach to something above; suspend. 2 To attach, as upon hinges, so as to allow some motion. 3 To put (someone) to death by suspending from a gallows, cross, etc.; execute on a gallows. 4 To ornament, cover, or furnish by or as by something suspended: to *hang* walls with tapestry. 5 To fasten in position or at the correct angle: to *hang* a scythe. 6 U.S. To cause, as a jury, to come to or remain in deadlock, as one juror by refusing to vote with the rest. —v.i. 7 To be suspended; swing; dangle. 8 To be suspended without visible support; float, as in the air. 9 To be put to death on the gallows. 10 To project out; overhang. 11 To droop; incline downward. 12 To be imminent or impending: War *hangs* over the world. 13 To be dependent or contingent, as on a decision. 14 To be uncertain or in doubt. 15 To watch or attend closely: to *hang* on someone's words. 16 U.S. To be or remain in deadlock, as a jury. —**to hang around** (or **about**) 1 To linger or loiter. 2 To group around. —**to hang back** To be reluctant or unwilling. —**to hang fire** 1 To fail to fire promptly, as a firearm. 2 To be delayed, as an event. 3 To be undecided, as a business agreement. —**to hang in** Slang To stay; persevere; hold on. —**to hang out** 1 To lean out. 2 To suspend out in the open: to *hang out* the wash. 3 Slang To reside or spend one's time: usually with *at* or *in.* —**to hang together** 1 To stay together. 2 To be coherent or consistent, as an explanation. —**to hang up** 1 To place on hooks or hangers. 2 To place a telephone receiver on the hook and thus break off communication. —**to let it all hang out** Slang 1 To make no effort to conceal one's motives, fears, desires, etc. 2 To be altogether free of restraint or inhibition. —n. 1 The way a thing hangs: the *hang* of a drape. 2 U.S. Colloq. Familiar knowledge or wont; knack. 3 A bit: I don't give a *hang:* euphemism for *damn.* 4 Rake, as of a mast. —**to get the hang of** U.S. Colloq. To come to understand or be able to do. [Fusion of ME *hangen* (OE *hangian* hang down), OE *hon* suspend, and ME *henge* cause or condemn to hang (< ON *hengjan*)]

han·gar (hang′ər, -gär) n. A shelter or shed, especially one for the maintenance and storage of aircraft. [< F]

hang·er (hang′ər) n. 1 One who hangs, as a hangman. 2 A device on which something is hung. 3 A shaped frame on which a garment is suspended or draped.

hang glider A kitelike metal and cloth frame to which a person is harnessed while soaring through the air.

hang·ing (hang′ing) adj. 1 Suspended from something; dangling. 2 Involving or suggesting death on the gallows. 3 Lying on a steep slope: a *hanging* garden. 4 Drooping and dejected: said of the countenance. 5 Held in abeyance. —n. 1 The act of suspending. 2 Execution on the gal-

lows. 3 pl. Drapery for a room, as tapestry.

hang·man (hang′mən) n. pl. ·men (-mən) A public executioner.

hang·nail (hang′nāl′) n. Skin partially torn loose at the side or root of a fingernail. [Alter. of AGNAIL; infl. by HANG]

hang·out (hang′out′) n. Slang A habitual meeting place or resort.

hang·o·ver (hang′ō′vər) n. U.S. Colloq. 1 A person or thing remaining from something that is past; a survival, as of a tradition. 2 The aftereffects of alcoholic dissipation, as headache and nausea.

hang·up (hang′up′) n. Slang 1 A psychological difficulty; especially, a neurotic preoccupation or obsession. 2 Anything blocking a natural or normal process.

hank (hangk) n. 1 A bundle of two or more skeins of yarn tied together; also, a single skein. 2 A measure of yarn varying for different materials: a hank of No. 1 cotton is 840 yards long and weighs 1 pound; a hank of woolen yarn is 560 yards long. 3 Naut. a A rope, string, coil, or tie. b Any fastening; specifically, a ring of rope or iron on the edge of a jib or staysail, used for fastening it. [ME < Scand. Cf. Icel. *hankar*, genitive of *hönk* a skein, coil.]

han·ker (hang′kər) v.i. To yearn; have desire: with *after, for,* or an infinitive. [Cf. Flemish *hankeren* long for] —**han′ker·er** n. —**han′ker·ing** n.

han·ky-pan·ky (hang′kē-pang′kē) n. Slang 1 Trickery. 2 Jugglery; sleight-of-hand. [An arbitrary formation, ? < HAND]

Ha·noi (hä·noi′) A city in North Vietnam, capital of the Democratic Republic of Vietnam (Vietminh).

hanse (hans) n. 1 A guild of medieval merchants. 2 An entrance fee; especially, one paid by merchants not members of a guild. [< OF < OHG *hansa* band]

han·som (han′səm) n. A low, two-wheeled, one-horse cab, with the driver mounted back of the top: also **hansom cab.** ◆ Homophone: *handsome.* [after J. A. *Hansom*, 1803–82, English inventor]

HANSOM

Ha·nuk·kah (khä′nŏŏ·kə) A Jewish festival lasting eight days from Kislew 25th (early December), in memory of the rededication of the temple at Jerusalem under the Maccabees in 164 B.C. It is also known, usually by Christians, as the *Feast of Dedication.* Also **Ha′nu·kah;** also spelled *Chanuca.* [< Hebrew *hanukkah* dedication]

hap (hap) Archaic n. 1 A casual occurrence; happening; chance. 2 Luck; good fortune. See synonyms under ACCIDENT. —v.i. happed, hap·ping To happen; chance. [< ON *happ*]

hap·haz·ard (hap′haz′ərd) adj. Accidental; happening by chance. —n. Mere chance; hazard. —adv. By chance; at random. [< HAP + HAZARD] —**hap′haz′ard·ly** adv.

hap·less (hap′lis) adj. Having no luck; unfortunate; unlucky. —**hap′less·ly** adv. —**hap′less·ness** n.

hap·lite (hap′līt) n. A fine-grained, acid granite, composed mostly of quartz and feldspar and occurring in dikes. Its micaceous constituent, when present, is usually muscovite. Also called *aplite.* [< HAPL(O)- + -ITE[1]] —**hap·lit·ic** (hap·lit′ik) adj.

hap·loid (hap′loid) adj. Biol. Having the character of gametes with a reduced number of chromosomes, in contradistinction to the diploid with the doubled number found in somatic cells. Also **hap·loid′ic.**

hap·ly (hap′lē) *adv.* By chance.

hap·pen (hap′ən) *v.i.* **1** To take place or occur; come to pass. **2** To come about or occur by chance or without expectation or design. **3** To chance; have the fortune: We *happened* to be there. **4** To come by chance: to *happen* upon the answer. **5** To come or go by chance: with *in*, *along*, *by*, etc. **—to happen to 1** To befall. **2** To become of: What *happened* to your old friend? [<HAP]

Synonyms: bechance, betide, chance, fall, occur, supervene. A thing is said to *happen* when no design is manifest or thought of; it is said to *chance* when it appears to be the result of accident (compare synonyms for ACCIDENT). An incident *happens* or *occurs;* something external or actual *happens* to one; a thought or fancy *occurs* to him. *Befall* and *betide* are transitive; *happen* is intransitive; something *befalls* or *betides* a person or *happens* to him. *Betide* is especially used for anticipated evil, thought of as waiting and coming at its appointed time; as, Woe *betide* him. One event *supervenes* upon another event, one disease upon another, etc.

hap·pen·ing (hap′ən·ing) *n.* **1** Something that happens; an event. See synonyms under ACCIDENT. **2** A staged but usually partly improvised event, often bizarre or spectacular, intended to engage the attention or elicit a response through shock or novelty.

hap·pen·stance (hap′ən·stans, -stəns) *n. U.S. Colloq.* A chance occurrence. [<HAPPEN + (CIR-CUM)STANCE]

hap·per (hap′ər) *n. Scot.* The hopper of a mill.

hap·pi·ness (hap′ē·nis) *n.* **1** The state or quality of being happy; the pleasurable experience that springs from possession of good or the gratification of desires; enjoyment; blessedness. **2** Good fortune; luck; prosperity. **3** Unstudied grace; aptness or felicitousness, as of a remark or turn of phrase.

Synonyms: blessedness, bliss, cheer, comfort, contentment, delight, ecstasy, enjoyment, felicity, gaiety, gladness, gratification, joy, merriment, mirth, pleasure, rapture, rejoicing, satisfaction, triumph. *Comfort* may be almost wholly negative, being found in security or relief from that which pains or annoys. *Enjoyment* is more positive and *pleasure* still more vivid; *satisfaction* is more tranquil than *pleasure;* when a worthy *pleasure* is past, a worthy *satisfaction* remains. *Happiness* is more complete than *comfort, enjoyment,* or *satisfaction,* more serene and rational than *pleasure. Felicity* is a colder and more formal term than *happiness. Gladness* is *happiness* that overflows. *Joy* is more intense than *happiness,* deeper than *gladness,* to which it is akin, nobler and more enduring than *pleasure. Bliss* is ecstatic, perfected *happiness.* See RAPTURE.

hap·py (hap′ē) *adj.* **·pi·er, ·pi·est 1** Enjoying, giving or indicating pleasure; joyous; blessed. **2** Dexterously or fortunately effective; opportune; felicitous. **3** Yielding or marked by happiness: *happy* moments. [<HAP]

Synonyms: blessed, blissful, blithe, blithesome, bright, buoyant, cheerful, cheering, cheery, delighted, delightful, dexterous, felicitous, fortunate, gay, glad, jocund, jolly, joyful, joyous, lucky, merry, mirthful, pleased, prosperous, rapturous, rejoiced, rejoicing, smiling, sprightly, successful, sunny. *Happy* primarily refers to something that comes "by good hap," a chance that brings prosperity, benefit, or success. In its most frequent present use, *happy* is applied to the state of one enjoying happiness, or to that by which happiness is expressed; as, a *happy* heart, *happy* laughter. (Compare synonyms for HAPPINESS.) *Cheerful* applies to the possession or expression of a moderate and tranquil happiness. A *cheery* word spontaneously gives cheer to others; a *cheering* word is more distinctly planned to cheer and encourage. *Gay* applies to an effusive and superficial happiness perhaps resulting largely from abundant animal spirits. A *buoyant* spirit is, as it were, borne up by joy and hope. A *sunny* disposition has a tranquil brightness that irradiates all who come within its influence. See AUSPICIOUS, CHEERFUL, CLEVER, FORTUNATE, SKILFUL, WELL. *Antonyms*: despondent, gloomy, melancholy, miserable, mournful, regretful, sad, sorrowful, woeful, wretched.

hap·py-go-luck·y (hap′ē·gō·luk′ē) *adj.* Trusting easily to luck; improvident; haphazard. *—adv.* As one pleases; anyhow; at will.

ha·rangue (hə·rang′) *n.* An oration; especially, a loud and vehement speech. *—v.* **·rangued, ·rangu·ing** *v.t.* To address in a harangue. *—v.i.* To deliver a harangue. See synonyms under SPEECH. [<F <Med. L *harenga* <OHG *hari* host + *hringa* ring] **—ha·rangu′er** *n.*

har·ass (har′əs, hə·ras′) *v.t.* **1** To trouble or worry persistently with cares, annoyances, etc.; torment. **2** *Mil.* To worry (an enemy) by raids and small attacks. **3** *Obs.* To ravage; raid. See synonyms under PERSECUTE, PERPLEX, TIRE[1]. [<OF *harasser* <*harer* set dogs on, prob. <OHG *haren* cry out] **—har′ass·er** *n.* **—har′ass·ment** *n.*

har·bin·ger (här′bin·jər) *n.* **1** One who or that which foreruns and announces the coming of something. **2** Formerly, a courier who rode in advance of a party to arrange for their lodging and entertainment. See synonyms under HERALD. *—v.t.* To act as a harbinger to; presage. [<OF *herbergeor* provider of shelter <*herberge* shelter <Gmc.]

har·bor (här′bər) *n.* **1** A port or haven so protected, naturally or artificially, as to provide shelter for ships. **2** Any place of refuge or rest. See synonyms under REFUGE, SHELTER. *—v.t.* **1** To give refuge to; shelter; protect. **2** To entertain in the mind; cherish, as a grudge. *—v.i.* **3** To take shelter in or as in a harbor. See synonyms under CHERISH, SHELTER. Also, *Brit.,* **har′bour.** [ME *herberwe* <OE *here* army + *beorg* refuge] **—har′bor·er** *n.*

har·bor·age (här′bər·ij) *n.* **1** A port or place of shelter for ships. **2** Shelter; entertainment.

hard (härd) *adj.* **1** Solid and firm in substance and consistency; not easily receiving indentation or impression: opposed to *soft.* **2** Capable of endurance; hardy. **3** Difficult of accomplishment, management, or solution; troublesome: opposed to *easy.* **4** Obdurate or callous in character or demeanor; hard-hearted. **5** Harsh or cruel: He was too *hard* on her; *hard* words. **6** Shrewd and obstinate. **7** Oppressive; difficult to endure: a *hard* life; *hard* times. **8** Strict or exacting in terms: a *hard* bargain. **9** Vigorous; persistent; energetic: *hard* study; a *hard* worker. **10** Sound; trustworthy. **11** Esthetically harsh or unpleasant: a *hard* face. **12** Stormy; inclement; rigorous: a *hard* winter. **13** Indisputable; definite: *hard* facts. **14** Strictly factual: *hard* news. **15** In specie; metallic: said of money. **16** Containing certain mineral salts in solution which interfere with the cleansing action of soap: said of water. **17** Containing much alcohol; strong: said of liquor. **18** Addictive: said of drugs. **19** *Agric.* High in gluten content: said of wheat. **20** Denoting *c* or *g* when articulated as a stop, as in *cod* and *god,* rather than as a fricative or an affricate. *—adv.* **1** With great energy or force; vigorously: to work *hard;* to rain *hard.* **2** Intently; earnestly: to look *hard* for something. **3** Harshly or severely. **4** With effort or difficulty. **5** Securely; tightly: to hold on *hard.* **6** So as to become hard: It was frozen *hard.* **7** In close proximity; near: often with *after, by,* or *upon.* [OE *heard*]

Synonyms (adj.): arduous, austere, bad, callous, compact, cruel, dense, difficult, distressing, exacting, firm, flinty, grievous, hardened, harsh, impenetrable, obdurate, oppressive, rigid, severe, solid, stern, stubborn, unfeeling, unforgiving, unrelenting, unyielding. See ARDUOUS, AUSTERE, BAD, COMPACT, DIFFICULT, FIRM, IMPENETRABLE, TROUBLESOME. *Antonyms*: easy, facile, fluid, genial, gentle, intelligible, kind, lenient, meek, mild, penetrable, soft, submissive, tender, yielding.

hard-and-fast (härd′ən·fast′, -fäst′) *adj.* Absolutely binding; fixed and unalterable.

hard·back (härd′bak′) *adj.* Hard-cover. *—n.* A hard-cover book.

hard·ball (härd′bôl′) *n.* **1** A baseball. *—adj. U.S. Colloq.* Tough; intense: a *hardball* confrontation.

hard·boiled (härd′boild′) *adj.* **1** Boiled until cooked through; said of an egg. **2** *Colloq.* Hardened or unyielding in character; tough.

hard·bound (härd′bound′) *adj.* Hard-cover.

hard cash Actual money as distinguished from debts or claims to be collected or settled.

hard-core (härd′kôr′) *adj.* **1** Thoroughly dedicated, determined, loyal, etc., to a cause or movement: *hard-core* radicals. **2** Extremely ex-

plicit: *hard-core* pornography. **3** Of or pertaining to the hard core.

hard core 1 The basic, central, or most important part; nucleus. **2** Unemployed or underemployed people not trained for any job.

hard-earned (härd′ûrnd′) *adj.* Earned or gained with difficulty; obtained by hard work.

hard·en (här′dən) *v.t.* **1** To make hard or harder; make solid. **2** To make unyielding, pitiless, or indifferent. **3** To strengthen or make firm in any element of character, disposition, etc. **4** To make tough, strong, or hardy; inure. *—v.i.* **5** To become hard. **6** In commerce: **a** To become higher, as prices. **b** To become stable. [<ON *harthna*]

hard·en·ing (här′dən·ing) *n.* Any substance or material that hardens another; specifically, any metal added to iron to make steel.

hard-fea·tured (härd′fē′chərd) *adj.* Stern or forbidding in countenance or aspect.

hard-hand·ed (härd′han′did) *adj.* **1** Having hard or horny hands. **2** Governing with severity or cruelty; despotic; tyrannical.

hard-hat (härd′hat′) *n. U.S. Colloq.* A construction worker.

hard·head (härd′hed′) *n. pl.* **·heads** *for defs.* **1, 2;** **·head** or **·heads** *for defs.* **3, 4. 1** A shrewd, tough-minded person. **2** An obstinate or stupid person. **3** The menhaden. **4** The alewife.

hard-heart·ed (härd′här′tid) *adj.* Lacking pity or sympathy; unfeeling; obdurate. **—hard′-heart′ed·ly** *adv.* **—hard′-heart′ed·ness** *n.*

har·di·hood (här′dē·hood) *n.* **1** Sturdy courage. **2** Rash or foolish daring; presumptuous boldness; audacity; effrontery. **3** The quality of being hardy; physical endurance. See synonyms under COURAGE, EFFRONTERY, TEMERITY.

har·di·ly (här′də·lē) *adv.* With hardihood; boldly.

har·di·ness (här′dē·nis) *n.* **1** The state of being hardy or physically strong. **2** Stout-heartedness; intrepidity.

hard line An unyielding position, as in negotiation. **—hard′-line′** *adj.* **—hard′-lin′er** *n.*

hard·ly (härd′lē) *adv.* **1** Scarcely; not quite: She was *hardly* aware of what she was doing. **2** With difficulty or great pains. **3** Improbably. **4** Rigorously; harshly; severly.

hard·ness (härd′nis) *n.* **1** The state of being hard. **2** Unyieldingness of spirit; insensitivity; callousness. **3** A property of water that contains mineral salts. **4** *Med.* Tension: said of the pulse. **5** In art, harsh effect or treatment. **6** That quality of a mineral that resists scratching: see MOHS SCALE. **7** The toughness of a metal or alloy: see BRINELL HARDNESS. **8** *Physics* A high-penetrating power of X-rays or other forms of radiant energy.

hard-nosed (härd′nōzd′) *adj. Slang* Hard-bitten, unyielding, or firmly businesslike: a *hard-nosed* approach to government spending. Also **hard-nose** (härd′nōz′).

hard of hearing Deaf or partially deaf.

hard sauce Butter, sugar, and flavorings creamed together and used as a sauce with puddings, etc.

hard sell *U.S. Colloq.* The use of aggressive methods of salesmanship.

hard-set (härd′set′) *adj.* **1** In a difficult situation; beset. **2** Firmly resolved; obstinate.

Hardshell Baptist A Primitive or Old School Baptist.

hard·ship (härd′ship) *n.* **1** Something hard to endure, as injustice. **2** *Obs.* Rigor; severity. See synonyms under MISFORTUNE.

hard-spun (härd′spun′) *adj.* Spun with a fine twist.

hard·stand (härd′stand′) *n. Aeron.* A paved, hard-surfaced area adjacent to a runway, for the parking of aircraft and ground vehicles.

hard up 1 In need or want, as of money. **2** Having a meager choice.

hard·ware (härd′wâr′) *n.* **1** Manufactured articles of metal, as utensils or tools. **2** Weapons: military *hardware.* **3** Mechanical, electronic, or other devices or materials, as distinguished from people, planning, operational procedures, etc. **4** Any of the machinery that makes up a computer installation: distinguished from *software.*

hard·wood (härd′wood′) *n.* **1** Wood from broad-leaved deciduous trees as distinguished from the wood of coniferous or needle-leaved trees. 2 Any such tree.

har·dy[1] (här′dē) *adj.* **·di·er, ·di·est** 1 Inured to hardship; robust. 2 Showing hardihood; bold; audacious; strenuous. 3 Able to survive the winter in the open air; perennial: said of plants. 4 Rigid; strong; durable. See synonyms under STRONG. [< OF *hardi*, pp. of *hardir* embolden < OHG *hartjan* make hard]

har·dy[2] (här′dē) *n. pl.* **·dies** A square-shanked chisel or fuller for insertion in a hardy-hole. [< HARD + -Y[1]]

hare (hâr) *n. pl.* **hares** or **hare** 1 A rodent (genus *Lepus*) with cleft upper lip, long ears, and long hind legs: proverbial for its timidity and swiftness. 2 The common American rabbit. ◆ Collateral adjective: *leporine.* ◆ Homophone: *hair.* [OE *hara*]

hare·brained (hâr′brānd′) *adj.* Foolish; flighty; giddy.

hare·lip (hâr′lip′) *n.* A congenital fissure of the upper lip a short distance from the median line.

har·em (hâr′əm, har′-) *n.* 1 The apartments of a Moslem household reserved for females. 2 The wives, concubines, etc., occupying the harem. 3 A Moslem holy place forbidden to all but the faithful. Also **ha·reem** (hä·rēm′). [< Arabic *harim* (something) forbidden, sacred < *harama* forbid]

har·i·cot (har′ə·kō) *n.* 1 A stew of meat, especially mutton, and vegetables. 2 The ripe seeds or green pods of the kidney bean and other string beans; also, the kidney bean. [< F < Nahuatl *ayecotl*]

hark (härk) *v.i.* To listen; harken: usually in the imperative. —*v.t. Archaic* To hear; listen to. —**to hark back** 1 In hunting, to retrace the trail so as to find again a lost scent: said of hounds. 2 To return to some previous point, as after a digression. —*n.* The cry "hark" as used to urge on or guide hounds in the chase. [ME *herkien*]

hark·en (här′kən) *v.t. Archaic* To hear; listen to; heed. —*v.i. Poetic* To listen; give heed. Also spelled *hearken.* See synonyms under LISTEN. [OE *heorcnian*]

har·le·quin (här′lə·kwin, -kin) *n.* A buffoon. —*adj.* 1 Comic; buffoonlike. 2 Parti-colored, like the dress of a Harlequin. —*v.i. Rare* To play the harlequin. —**har′le·quin·esque′** (-esk′) *adj.*

harlequin bug A shiny, black or blue bug with red or red and yellow spots (*Murgantia histrionica*) which feeds on cabbage and related plants: also called *cabbage bug, fire bug.*

harlequin duck A northern sea duck (*Histrionicus histrionicus*) the male of which is brilliantly and variously colored.

harlequin snake One of the coral snakes.

har·lot (här′lət) *n.* 1 A lewd woman; prostitute. 2 *Obs.* A knave or vagabond. [< OF *herlot* fellow, rogue]

har·lot·ry (här′lət·rē) *n.* The trade of a harlot; habitual lewdness.

harm (härm) *n.* 1 That which inflicts injury or loss. 2 The injury inflicted; hurt. 3 Offense against right or morality; wrong. See synonyms under INJURY, MISFORTUNE. —*v.t.* To do harm to; damage; hurt. See synonyms under ABUSE, HURT. [OE *hearm* insult]

harm·ful (härm′fəl) *adj.* Having power to injure; noxious. See synonyms under INIMICAL, NOISOME, PERNICIOUS. —**harm′ful·ly** *adv.* — **harm′ful·ness** *n.*

harm·less (härm′lis) *adj.* 1 Not harmful; innoxious. 2 Without hurt, loss, or liability. See synonyms under INNOCENT. —**harm′less·ly** *adv.* — **harm′less·ness** *n.*

har·mon·ic (här·mon′ik) *adj.* 1 Producing, characterized by, or pertaining to harmony; consonant; harmonious. 2 *Music* **a** Pertaining to harmony, as distinguished from melody or rhythm. **b** Pertaining to a tone whose rate of vibration is an exact multiple of a given primary tone. 3 *Math.* Derived from or originally suggested by the numerical relations between the vibrations of the musical harmonics or overtones of the same fundamental tone: *harmonic* functions. —*n.* 1 An attendant or secondary tone, produced by the vibration in aliquot parts of the same body

or string which gives, by its complete simultaneous vibration, the primary or fundamental tone; overtone. 2 *Music* A note on a stringed instrument produced by stopping a string at a specific point. 3 *Physics* Any component of a periodic quantity which is an integral multiple of the fundamental frequency. Also **har·mon′i·cal.** [< L *harmonicus* < Gk. *harmonikos* < *harmonia* harmony] —**har·mon′i·cal·ly** *adv.*

har·mon·i·ca (här·mon′i·kə) *n.* 1 A musical instrument consisting of small metal reeds fixed within a series of slots in a narrow case, and played by blowing through the slots. 2 An instrument composed of a series of glass tubes, goblets, or the like, graduated to a musical scale and played by rubbing the rims. 3 An instrument composed of glass or metal strips struck by hammers. [< L, fem. of *harmonicus* harmonic]

harmonic analyzer *Physics* An instrument which separates the components of a complex sound wave into the corresponding sine waves.

harmonic distortion *Physics* A wave form distortion which contains both fundamental and harmonic frequencies.

har·mon·i·con (här·mon′i·kən) *n.* 1 An orchestrion. 2 A mouth organ; harmonica. [< Gk. *harmonikon,* neuter of *harmonikos* harmonic]

har·mon·ics (här·mon′iks) *n. pl.* 1 That branch of acoustics dealing with musical sounds: construed as singular. 2 The overtones or partials of a fundamental: construed as plural.

har·mo·ni·ous (här·mō′nē·əs) *adj.* 1 Characterized by harmony or agreement; free from discord. 2 Having the parts related in pleasing combination; symmetrical; congruous. 3 Melodious; pleasing to the ear.

har·mo·nist (här′mə·nist) *n.* 1 A master of the principles of musical harmony. 2 A student or expounder of the harmony of different writings, as of the Christian Gospels. 3 A musician. 4 A harmonizer.

har·mo·nis·tic (här′mə·nis′tik) *adj.* Pertaining or relating to harmony, specifically to the work of literary harmonists.

har·mo·ni·um (här·mō′nē·əm) *n.* A reed organ. [< F < L *harmonia*]

har·mo·nize (här′mə·nīz) *v.t. & v.i.* **·nized, ·niz·ing** 1 To make or become harmonious or suitable. 2 To arrange or sing in musical harmony. Also, *Brit.,* **har′mo·nise.** See synonyms under ACCOMMODATE, ADAPT, AGREE. —**har′mo·ni·za′tion** *n.* —**har′mo·niz′er** *n.*

har·mo·ny (här′mə·nē) *n. pl.* **·nies** 1 Accord or agreement in feeling, manner, or action: the *harmony* of a loving family. 2 A state of order, agreement, or completeness in the relations of things or of parts of a whole to each other. 3 Pleasing sounds; music. 4 *Music* **a** Any agreeable combination of simultaneous tones. **b** The science or study of the relations of combinations of tones or chords, their progressions, resolutions, modulations, etc., as distinguished from melody and rhythm. 5 A literary work to display the agreement of different books: a *harmony* of the Gospels. [< OF *armonie* < L *harmonia* < Gk. < *harmos* joint < *harmozein* join]

Synonyms: accord, accordance, agreement, amity, concord, concurrence, conformity, congruity, consent, consistency, consonance, symmetry, unanimity, uniformity, union, unison, unity. When tones, thoughts, or feelings, individually different, combine to form a consistent and pleasing whole, there is *harmony. Harmony* is deeper and more essential than *agreement. Concord* implies more volition than *accord. Conformity* is submission to authority or necessity. *Congruity* involves the element of suitableness; *consent* and *concurrence* refer to decision or action, but *consent* is more passive than *concurrence.* See MELODY, TUNE, SYMMETRY. *Antonyms:* antagonism, conflict, controversy, disagreement, discord, disproportion, dissension, disunion, hostility, incongruity, inconsistency, opposition, schism, variance.

har·ness (här′nis) *n.* 1 The combination of traces, straps, and other pieces forming the gear of a draft animal and used to attach it for work to a wheeled vehicle or plow. 2 *Archaic* The defensive armor of a soldier or

NOMENCLATURE OF HARNESS
A. Single harness. *B.* Double harness.

a.	Runner.	*o.*	Terrets.
b.	Blinder.	*p.*	Saddle.
c.	Throatlatch.	*q.*	Pole chain.
d.	Browband or front piece.	*r.*	Bellyband strap.
e.	Bit.	*s.*	Breeching strap.
f.	Curb bit.	*t.*	Hipstrap.
g.	Nose piece.	*u.*	Backstrap.
h.	Crownpiece.	*v.*	Crupper.
i.	Curb chain.	*w.*	Breeching.
k.	Checkrein.	*x.*	Traces.
l.	Breech stay.	*y.*	Whiffletree or swingletree.
m.	Hame.	*z.*	Martingale.
n.	Collar showing afterwale.		

of his horse. 3 Any arrangement of straps, cords, etc., as for lifting or performing some mechanical operation. 4 A device on a loom comprising the heddles which shift the sets of warp threads alternately. 5 The routine or obligations of work or business. —*v.t.* 1 To put harness on, as a horse. 2 To make use of the power or potential of: to *harness* a waterfall. 3 *Archaic* To dress in or equip with armor. [< OF *harneis;* ult. origin unknown] —**har′ness·er** *n.*

harness race A race for pacers or trotters harnessed to sulkies.

harp (härp) *n.* 1 A stringed musical instrument, nearly triangular in modern form, played with the fingers. 2 One of several old Irish coins of various values. 3 A harplike part in a mechanism. —*v.i.* 1 To play on a harp. 2 To speak or write persistently; dwell tediously: with *on* or *upon.* —*v.t.* 3 *Archaic* To give utterance to; express. 4 *Poetic* To affect in some way by playing the harp: to *harp* one to sleep. [OE *hearpe*]

Harp (härp) The constellation Lyra.

harp·er (här′pər) *n.* One who plays the harp; a harpist.

harp·ings (här′pingz) *n. pl. Naut.* 1 The foreparts of the wales surrounding the bow of a ship. 2 Extensions of the ribbands. Also **harp′ins.** [Prob. < F *harper* grip]

harp·ist (här′pist) *n.* One who plays the harp; a minstrel.

TOGGLED HAND HARPOON

har·poon (här·pōōn′) *n.* A barbed missile weapon, carrying a long cord, for striking whales or large fish. —*v.t.* To strike, take, or kill with a harpoon. [< F *harpon* grappling iron

< *harper* grip < *harpe* claw] — **har·poon′er,
har′poon·eer′** (-ir′) *n.*

harpoon gun A small cannon which fires a harpoon: used in whaling.

HARPSICHORD

harp·si·chord (härp′sə·kôrd) *n.* A keyboard instrument in wide-spread use from the 16th to the 18th century, and revived in the 20th, precursor of the piano, but having the strings plucked by quills instead of struck. [<MF *harpechorde* <Ital. *arpicordo* <LL *harpa* harp + L *chorda* string <Gk. *chordē*]
har·py (här′pē) *n. pl.* **·pies** 1 Any rapacious person; a plunderer; extortioner. 2 A very large, crested, voracious tropical American eagle, the **harpy eagle** (*Thrasaetus harpyia*): also called *winged wolf.* [<HARPY]
har·ri·dan (har′ə·dən) *n.* A vixenish old woman; a hag. [<OF *haridelle* jade]
har·ri·er[1] (har′ē·ər) *n.* 1 One who or that which harries. 2 The marsh hawk.
har·ri·er[2] (har′ē·ər) *n.* 1 A small hound used for hunting hares. 2 *Brit.* A member of a hare-and-hounds team. [<HARE + -IER]
Har·ris·burg (har′is·bûrg) The capital of Pennsylvania, on the Susquehanna River.
har·row (har′ō) *n.* A farm implement, commonly a frame set with spikes or teeth, or disks, for leveling plowed ground, breaking clods, etc. — *v.t.* 1 To draw a harrow over (a field, etc.). 2 To disturb the mind or feelings of painfully; distress. — *v.i.* 3 To undergo harrowing. [ME *harwe,* prob. <Scand. Cf. ON *herfi.*] — **har′row·er** *n.*
har·row·ing (har′ō·ing) *adj.* Lacerating or tormenting to the feelings. — **har′row·ing·ly** *adv.*
har·ry (har′ē) *v.* **har·ried, har·ry·ing** *v.t.* 1 To lay waste, as in war or invasion; pillage; sack. 2 To harass in any way. 3 *Scot.* To carry off in a raid; seize. — *v.i.* 4 To make raids for plunder. Also *Obs.* **har′row.** See synonyms under PERSECUTE. [OE *hergian* ravage]
harsh (härsh) *adj.* 1 Grating or rough to any of the senses; violently disagreeable; discordant; rasping; irritating. 2 Irritating to the mind; offensive. 3 Rigorous; severe; also, unfeeling: a *harsh* judge, a *harsh* sentence. See synonyms under ARBITRARY, AUSTERE, BITTER, HARD, ROUGH. [ME *harsk,* prob. < Scand. Cf. Sw. *härsk,* Dan. *harsk* rancid.] — **harsh′ly** *adv.* — **harsh′ness** *n.*
harsh·en (här′shən) *v.t.* To make harsh, rough, or severe.
hart (härt) *n.* The male of the red deer, especially after it has passed its fifth year. ◆ Homophone: *heart.* [OE *heort*]
harte·beest (härt′bēst, här′tə-) *n.* 1 A large antelope of Africa (genera *Bubalis* and *Alcelaphus*), grayish-brown above and whitish below. 2 The bontebok. Also **hart′beest.** [< Afrikaans <Du. *hert* hart + *beest* beast]
Hart·ford (härt′fərd) The capital of Connecticut, on the Connecticut River.
harts·horn (härts′hôrn′) *n.* 1 A volatile preparation of ammonia, used as smelling salts, formerly distilled from deer horns. 2 Sal volatile. 3 The antler of a hart.
hart's-tongue (härts′tung′) *n.* A fern (*Phyllitis scolopendrium*) having bright green fronds, found throughout the temperate zone.
har·um-scar·um (hâr′əm·skâr′əm) *adj.* Reckless; irresponsible. — *n.* A wild, reckless, or thoughtless person. [<obs. *hare* frighten + SCARE]

har·vest (här′vist) *n.* 1 A crop, as of grain, gathered or ready for gathering. 2 The time of gathering. 3 The product of any toil or effort. — *v.t. & v.i.* 1 To gather (a crop). 2 To gather the crop of (a field, etc.). [OE *hærfest* autumn, harvest]
   Synonyms (noun): crop, fruit, growth, harvesting, harvest time, increase, ingathering, proceeds, produce, product, reaping, result, return, yield. *Harvest* is the generic word; *crop* is the common and commercial expression; we say a man sells his *crop,* but we should not speak of his selling his *harvest;* we speak of an ample or abundant *harvest,* a good *crop. Harvest* is applied almost wholly to grain; *crop* applies to almost anything that is gathered in; we speak of the potato *crop,* not the potato *harvest;* we may say either the wheat *crop* or the wheat *harvest.* We speak of *produce* collectively, but of a *product* or various *products;* vegetables, fruits, eggs, butter, etc., may be termed farm *produce,* or the *products* of the farm. *Product* is a word of wider application than *produce;* we speak of the *products* of manufacturing, the *product* obtained by multiplying one number by another, etc. The word *proceeds* is chiefly used of the *return* from an investment; we speak of the *produce* of a farm, but of the *proceeds* of the money invested in farming. The *yield* is what the land gives up to the farmer's demand, as the *yield* of corn or oats. *Harvest* has also a figurative use; as, The result of lax enforcement of law is a *harvest* of crime. See INCREASE, PRODUCT.
har·vest·er (här′vis·tər) *n.* 1 One who harvests 2 A reaping machine.
harvest moon The full moon that occurs near the autumnal equinox.
harvest tick An acaridan mite (genus *Trombicula*), mostly red, that attaches itself to the skin, being especially abundant about harvest time; a chigger.
has (haz) Present indicative, third person singular, of HAVE.
has-been (haz′bin′) *n. Colloq.* A person or thing no longer popular or effective.
hash (hash) *n.* 1 A dish of chopped and cooked meat and vegetables, usually sautéed. 2 A mess; a jumble. 3 A rehash; any old thing brought forth in new form. 4 *Scot.* A wasteful or slovenly person; blockhead; dunce. — **to make a hash of** *Colloq.* To bungle; spoil. — **to settle (one's) hash** *Colloq.* To silence, finish off, or put down (a person). — *v.t.* 1 To cut or chop into small pieces; mince. 2 *U.S. Colloq.* To make a mess of; bungle. — **to hash over** *U.S. Colloq.* To talk or think about carefully; mull. [<OF *hacher* chop. See HATCH[1].]
hash·ish (häsh′esh, -ish) *n.* 1 The tops and sprouts of Indian hemp, used as a narcotic and intoxicant. 2 An intoxicating preparation of this plant. Also **hash′eesh.** [<Arabic *hashish* hemp]
hash mark *Mil. Slang* A service stripe worn on the uniform sleeve.
has·n't (haz′ənt) Contraction of HAS NOT.
hasp (hasp, häsp) *n.* A fastening passing over a staple and secured as by a padlock. See synonyms under LOCK. — *v.t.* To shut or fasten with or as with a hasp. [OE *hæpse*]

HASP

has·sle (has′əl) *Slang n.* An argument; squabble. — *v.i.* **·sled, ·sling** To argue. Also **has′sel.** [? <HAGGLE + TUSSLE]
has·sock (has′ok) *n.* 1 An upholstered footstool. 2 *Scot.* A rank tuft of coarse or boggy grass. 3 A shock of hair. [OE *hassuc* coarse grass <Celtic]

haste (hāst) *n.* 1 Celerity of movement or action; speed; dispatch. 2 Necessity for speed; urgency. 3 Hurry; precipitancy; unpremeditated or impulsive action. — *v.t. & v.i.* **hast·ed, hast·ing** *Poetic* To hasten. [<OF <Gmc.]
hast·en (hā′sən) *v.t.* To cause to hurry or move quickly; expedite. — *v.i.* To move with speed or haste; be quick; hurry. See synonyms under FLY, PUSH, QUICKEN. — **hast′en·er** *n.*

hast·y (has′tē) *adj.* **hast·i·er, hast·i·est** 1 Acting with, or done with haste. 2 Acting or done without due consideration; rash. 3 Quick-tempered; impetuous; irascible. 4 *Obs.*

Eager; in a hurry. See synonyms under IMPETUOUS, SWIFT. — **hast′i·ly** *adv.* — **hast′i·ness** *n.*
hasty pudding 1 Pudding made of meal, seasoning, and boiling water or milk. 2 *U.S.* Cornmeal mush.
hat (hat) *n.* 1 A covering for the head, generally with a crown and brim; also, any piece of millinery worn for a hat. 2 A cardinal's red hat; hence, the rank or dignity of a cardinal. — **to pass the hat** To take up a collection. — **to talk through one's hat** *Colloq.* To talk nonsense; also, to bluff. — **under one's hat** *Colloq.* Secret; private: Keep it *under your hat.* [OE *hæt.* Akin to HOOD.]
hat·band (hat′band′) *n.* A narrow ribbon or other band of silk or cloth surrounding a hat just above the brim.
hat·box (hat′boks′) *n.* A case, often of leather, for a hat; also, a small compartment in a trunk for a hat.
hatch[1] (hach) *n.* 1 *Naut.* **a** An opening in the deck of a vessel affording passage to the hold, as for cargo, etc.: also called *hatchway.* **b** The cover over a hatch. 2 Any similar opening in the floor or roof of a warehouse or other building, or the cover or grating for such an opening. 3 A door or gate with an opening above; a divided door; wicket. 4 A sluice gate. [OE *hæcc* grating]
hatch[2] (hach) *v.t.* 1 To bring forth (young) from the egg by incubation. 2 To bring forth young from (the egg). 3 To devise, as a plan; contrive secretly, as a plot. — *v.i.* 4 To emerge from the egg. 5 To produce young. — *n.* 1 The act of hatching. 2 The brood hatched at one time. 3 The result or outcome of any plan. [ME *hacchen;* origin uncertain]
hatch[3] (hach) *v.t.* To mark with hatchings. — *n.* A shade line in drawing or engraving. [< OF *hacher* chop <*hache* an ax <Gmc.]
hatch·back (hach′bak′) *n.* An automobile having a hatch or door at the back of the sloping roof.
hatch·el (hach′əl) *n.* An implement for cleaning flax or hemp, consisting of a set of teeth fastened in a board: also *hackle.* — *v.t.* **hatch·eled** or **·elled, hatch·el·ing** or **·el·ing** 1 To comb or clean with a hatchel, as flax or hemp: also *hackle.* 2 *Rare* To irritate; heckle. [ME *hechele*] — **hatch′el·er, hatch′el·ler** *n.*
hatch·er (hach′ər) *n.* 1 A bird that incubates; also, an incubator. 2 One who hatches or contrives.
hatch·er·y (hach′ər·ē) *n. pl.* **·er·ies** A place where eggs are hatched; especially, a place for producing poultry on a large scale, or a place for hatching fish to restock streams.
hatch·et (hach′it) *n.* A small short-handled ax, for use with one hand. — **to bury the hatchet** To cease from hostilities; forget injuries; make peace. [<F *hachette,* dim. of *hache* an ax <Gmc.]
hatch·et-face (hach′it-fās′) *n.* A thin sharp-featured face. — **hatch′et-faced′** *adj.*
hatch·ing (hach′ing) *n.* In drawing or engraving, the marking with fine parallel lines for shading; also, the result of such lines or shading.
hatch·ment (hach′mənt) *n. Her.* The armorial bearings of a deceased person, so blazoned as to indicate the rank, sex, etc.: usually in a lozenge-shaped panel, as over a tomb. [Alter. of ACHIEVEMENT]

HATCHETS
a. Broad.
b. Lathing.
c. Half.
d. Claw.

hate (hāt) *v.* **hat·ed, hat·ing** *v.t.* 1 To regard with extreme aversion; have great dislike for; detest. 2 To be unwilling; dislike: with a clause or an infinitive as object: I *hate* doing that. — *v.i.* 3 To feel hatred. See synonyms under ABHOR. — *n.* 1 Intense aversion; animosity; malignity. 2 A person or thing detested. See synonyms under HATRED. [OE *hatian*] — **hat′a·ble** *adj.* — **hat′er** *n.*
hate·ful (hāt′fəl) *adj.* 1 Exciting strong aversion; odious. 2 Feeling or manifesting hatred. — **hate′ful·ly** *adv.* — **hate′ful·ness** *n.*
Ha·thor·ic (hə·thôr′ik, -thor′-) *adj. Archit.*

Denoting columns with sculptures on the capitals representing the head of Hathor.

ha·tred (hā'trid) *n.* Bitter dislike or aversion; antipathy; animosity; enmity.

Synonyms: abhorrence, anger, animosity, antipathy, aversion, detestation, dislike, enmity, grudge, hate, hostility, malevolence, malice, malignity, odium, rancor, repugnance, resentment, revenge, spite. *Repugnance* applies to that which one feels when summoned or impelled to do or to endure something from which he instinctively draws back. *Aversion* is the turning away of the mind or feelings from some person or thing, or from some course of action, etc. *Hate,* or *hatred,* as applied to persons, is intense and continued *aversion,* usually with disposition to injure; *anger* is sudden and brief, *hatred* is lingering and enduring. As applied to things, *hatred* is intense *aversion,* with desire to destroy or remove; *hatred* of evil is a righteous passion, akin to *abhorrence,* but more vehement. *Malice* involves the active intent to injure; *malignity* is deep, lingering, and venomous, while often impotent to act; *rancor* (akin to *rancid*) is cherished *malignity* that has soured and festered and is virulent and implacable. *Spite* is petty *malice* that delights to inflict stinging pain; *grudge* is deeper than *spite;* it is sinister and bitter; *resentment* always holds itself to be justifiable, but looks less certainly to action than *grudge* or *revenge.* Compare ABOMINATION, ANGER, ANTIPATHY, ENMITY, REVENGE. *Antonyms:* see synonyms for FRIENDSHIP, LOVE.

hat·ter (hat'ər) *n.* **1** One who makes or deals in hats. **2** *Austral.* A person who lives alone, especially in a remote area.

hat-tree (hat'trē') *n.* A frame with hooks or pegs on which to hang hats.

hau·berk (hô'bûrk) *n.* A coat of chain mail. [<OF *hauberc* <OHG *halsberc* neck-protector]

haugh·ty (hô'tē) *adj.* **·ti·er, ·ti·est** **1** Proud and disdainful; arrogant. **2** *Obs.* Lofty; bold. [<OF *haut* high] — **haugh'ti·ly** *adv.* — **haugh'ti·ness** *n.*

Synonyms: austere, churlish, cold, contemptuous, disdainful, distant, high, insolent, proud, reserved, stately, supercilious, surly, unapproachable, uncivil, unsociable. Compare ABSOLUTE, ARROGANT, IMPERIOUS, PROUD.

haul (hôl) *v.t.* **1** To pull or draw with force; drag. **2** To transport as if by pulling, as in a truck or cart. **3** *Naut.* To shift the course of (a ship), especially so as to sail nearer the wind. — *v.i.* **4** To drag or pull. **5** To shift in direction: said of the wind. **6** To change one's views or course of action. **7** *Naut.* To change course, especially so as to sail nearer the wind. See synonyms under DRAW. — **to haul off** **1** To draw back the arm so as to deliver a blow. **2** *Naut.* To change course so as to move further away from an object. — **to haul up** **1** To come to a stop. **2** *Naut.* To sail nearer the wind. — *n.* **1** A pulling with force. **2** That which is obtained by hauling. **3** The drawing of a fish net. **4** The amount of fish caught in a single drawing of a net. **5** The distance over which anything is hauled. ♦ Homophone: *hall.* [<OF *haler* <Gmc.]

haul·age (hô'lij) *n.* **1** The act, process, or operation of hauling. **2** A charge for hauling. **3** The charge made by a railroad company for the use of a line or track.

haul·er (hô'lər) *n.* **1** One who or that which hauls; specifically a carter: also *Brit.* **haul·ier** (hôl'yər). **2** A fish-hauling apparatus.

haulm (hôm) *n.* **1** The stalks or stems of any of the grains, or of hops, beans, etc. **2** Any plant stem. Also spelled *halm.* [OE *healm*] — **haulm'y** *adj.*

haul·yard (hôl'yərd) See HALYARD.

haunch (hônch, hänch) *n.* **1** The fleshy part of the hip and buttock; the hip or a hindquarter: a *haunch* of venison. **2** *Archit.* The part of an arch on either side of its crown: also spelled *hanch.* [<OF *hanche* <Gmc.] — **haunched** *adj.*

haunch bone The innominate bone.

haunt (hônt, hänt) *v.t.* **1** To visit frequently or customarily in disembodied form; appear to as a ghost or other spirit. **2** To recur persistently to the mind or memory of: The

---

face *haunts* me. **3** To visit often; frequent, as a saloon. — *v.i.* **4** To make ghostly appearances. **5** *Rare* To be present often. — *n.* **1** A place often visited; specifically, a place where wild animals come habitually to feed. **2** *Dial.* A ghost. [<OF *hanter*]

haunt·ed (hôn'tid, hän'-) *adj.* Frequently visited or resorted to, especially by ghosts or apparitions.

haunt·ing (hôn'ting, hän'-) *adj.* Difficult to forget; frequently occurring to memory: a *haunting* melody. — **haunt'ing·ly** *adv.*

hau·sen (hô'zən, *Ger.* hou'zən) *n.* The Russian sturgeon (genus *Acipenser*). [<G]

haus·mann·ite (hous'mən-īt) *n.* A submetallic brownish-black manganese oxide, Mn_3O_4, crystallizing in the tetragonal system. [after J. F. L. *Hausmann,* 1782–1859, German metallurgist]

haus·tel·lum (hôs-tel'əm) *n.* *pl.* **·tel·la** (-tel'ə) *Zool.* The proboscis or sucking organ of certain insects and crustaceans. [<NL, dim of L *haustrum* water-drawing machine <*haurire* draw]

haut·boy (hō'boi, ō'-) *n.* A woodwind instrument; oboe. [<F *hautbois* <*haut* high (in tone) + *bois* wood]

hau·teur (hō-tûr', *Fr.* ō-tœr') *n.* Haughty manner or spirit; haughtiness. [<F]

have (hav) *v.t.* Present indicative: I, you, we, they **have** (*Archaic* **thou hast**), he, she, it **has** (*Archaic* **hath**); past indicative **had** (*Archaic* **thou hadst**); present subjunctive **have;** past subjunctive **had;** *pp.* **had;** *ppr.* **hav·ing** **1** To hold as a possession; own. **2** To possess as a characteristic, attribute, etc.: He *has* only one leg; The very walls *have* ears. **3** To receive; get: I *had* a letter this morning. **4** To hold in the mind; entertain, as an opinion or a doubt. **5** To manifest or exercise: *Have* patience! **6** To experience; undergo: to *have* an operation. **7** To be affected with: to *have* a cold. **8** To carry on; engage in: to *have* a party. **9** To cause to be: to *have* someone shot; *Have* him leave. **10** To allow or permit; tolerate: I will *have* no interference. **11** To possess a certain relation to: to *have* the wind at one's back. **12** To be in relationship to or association with: to *have* three children. **13** To bring forth or beget (young): to *have* a baby. **14** To maintain or declare: so rumor *has* it. **15** *Colloq.* To gain or possess an advantage over; baffle: He *had* me there. **16** *Colloq.* To trick; cheat: I've been *had!* **17** To engage in sexual intercourse with. — *auxiliary* As an auxiliary *have* is used: **a** With past participles to form perfect tenses expressing completed action: often with the addition of other auxiliary verbs: I *have* gone; I *have* been given; I shall *have* gone. **b** With the infinitive to express obligation or compulsion: I *have* to go. — **to have at** To attack. — **to have done** To stop; desist. — **to have it in for** *Colloq.* To hold a grudge against. — **to have it out** To continue a fight or discussion to a final settlement. — **to have on** To be wearing; be clothed in. ♦ *Have* is used in the form *had* (early *hadde,* past subjunctive) in certain phrases of preference: you *had better* hurry = You would be wiser to hurry; I *had rather* (or *liefer*) die = I would prefer to die. — *n.* A person or country possessing relatively much wealth. [OE *habban*]

Synonyms: hold, occupy, own, possess. *Have* is applied to whatever belongs to or is connected with one; a man may be said to *have* what is his own, what he has borrowed, what has been entrusted to him, or what he has stolen. To *possess* a thing is to *have* the ownership with control and enjoyment of it. To *hold* is to *have* in one's hand, or securely in one's control; a man *holds* his friend's coat for a moment, or he *holds* a struggling horse; he *holds* a promissory note, or *holds* an office. To *own* is to *have* the right of property in; to *possess* is to *have* that right in actual exercise; to *occupy* is to *have* possession and use with or without ownership. A man *occupies* his own house or a room in a hotel; he may *own* a farm of which he is not in possession because a tenant *occupies* it and is determined to *hold* it. To be in possession differs from *possess* in that to *possess* denotes both right and

---

fact, while to be in possession denotes simply the fact with no affirmation as to the right. To *have* reason is to be endowed with the faculty; to be in possession of one's reason denotes that the faculty is in actual present exercise.

ha·ven (hā'vən) *n.* **1** A place of anchorage for ships; a harbor; port. **2** A refuge; shelter. See synonyms under SHELTER. — *v.t.* To shelter (a vessel, etc.) in or as in a haven. [OE *hæfen*]

have–not (hav'not') *n.* A person or country relatively lacking in wealth: the haves and *have-nots.*

ha·ver·el (hā'vər·əl, ā'-) *adj.* Half-witted; silly. Also **hav·rel** (hav'rəl).

hav·er·sack (hav'ər-sak) *n.* A bag, slung from the shoulder, for a soldier's rations. [<F *havresac* <G *habersack* oat sack]

hav·er·sine (hav'ər·sīn) *n.* *Trig.* Half of a versed sine.

hav·oc (hav'ək) *n.* **1** General carnage or destruction; ruin. **2** Tumultuous disorder, confusion, or uproar. See synonyms under MASSACRE — **to cry havoc** To give a signal for pillage and destruction. — *v.t.* **hav·ocked, hav·ock·ing** *Rare* To lay waste; destroy. [<OF *havot* plunder <Gmc.]

haw[1] (hô) *interj.* A meaningless utterance occurring in hesitating or drawling speech. — *v.i.* To hesitate in speaking.

haw[2] (hô) *n.* The fruit of the hawthorn. [OE *haga*]

haw[3] (hô) *n.* **1** The nictitating membrane or third eyelid of certain animals. **2** *pl.* A disease of this membrane. [Origin uncertain]

haw[4] (hô) *n. & interj.* An order to turn to the left or near side in driving, usually to a yoked team without reins: opposed to *gee.* — *v.t. & v.i.* To turn to the left. [Origin uncertain]

Ha·wai·i (hə-wä'ē, hə-wī'yə) **1** A State of the United States comprising the Hawaiian Islands; 6,435 square miles; capital, Honolulu; entered the Union Aug. 21, 1959: nickname, *Aloha State:* Abbr. HI **2** The largest of the Hawaiian Islands; 4,030 square miles; chief town, Hilo.

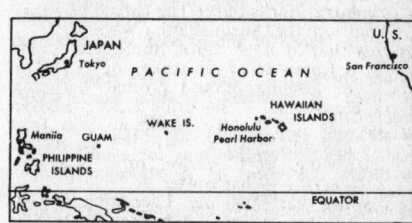

Ha·wai·ian (hə-wī'yən) *adj.* Of or pertaining to Hawaii or its inhabitants. — *n.* **1** A native or naturalized inhabitant of Hawaii. **2** The Polynesian language of the aboriginal inhabitants of Hawaii.

haw·finch (hô'finch') *n.* The European grosbeak (genus *Coccothraustes*), having a very large beak.

hawk[1] (hôk) *n.* **1** A diurnal bird of prey (family *Accipitridae*) with relatively short rounded wings, a hooked beak, and strong claws; including the North American species, Cooper's hawk (*Accipiter cooperi*) and the sharp–shinned hawk (*A. velox*). **2** The goshawk (genus *Astur*) and the red–tailed hawk (genus *Buteo*). **3** Any falconine bird except a vulture or an eagle, as a falcon, buzzard, or kite. **4** One who seeks to resolve a war primarily by means of military force: opposed to *dove*[1] (def. 4). — *v.i.* **1** To hunt game with hawks; practice falconry. **2** To fly in search of prey; soar, as a hawk. [OE *hafoc, hafuc*]

AMERICAN ROUGH–LEGGED HAWK (About 20 to 23 inches)

hawk[2] (hôk) *v.t. & v.i.* To cry (goods) for sale in the streets or in public places; peddle;

[Back formation <HAWKER²]

hawk³ (hôk) v.t. To cough up (phlegm). —v.i. To clear the throat with a coughing sound. —n. A forcible effort to raise phlegm from the throat; also, the sound of this. [Imit.]

hawk⁴ (hôk) n. A small square board with a handle underneath, used to hold plaster or mortar. [Origin uncertain]

hawk·bill (hôk′bil′) n. A small tropical marine turtle (Eretmochelys imbricata) which furnishes the best grade of tortoise shell used in commerce: also **hawk's-bill.**

hawk·er¹ (hô′kər) n. One who hunts with hawks; a falconer.

hawk·er² (hô′kər) n. A street peddler; one who cries goods for sale in the streets. [< MLG hoker a peddler, huckster]

Hawk·eye (hôk′ī′) n. A native or inhabitant of Iowa.

hawk·eyed (hôk′īd′) adj. Having keen, piercing eyes; keen-sighted.

Hawkeye State Nickname of IOWA.

hawk·ing (hô′king) n. The sport of hunting small game with hawks or falcons; falconry.

hawk·ish (hôk′ish) adj. Disposed to rely on military force to resolve a war: opposed to dovish.

hawk moth A large stout-bodied moth (family Sphingidae) which flies by twilight and sucks the nectar from flowers: also called hummingbird moth.

hawk's-beard (hôks′bird′) n. Any species of a genus (Crepis) of European herbs: so called from the long bristly pappus.

hawk's-eye (hôks′ī′) n. 1 The American golden plover (Pluvialis dominica). 2 The tigereye.

hawk·weed (hôk′wēd′) n. Any species of a genus (Hieracium) of weedy perennial herbs of the composite family having small yellow or orange flowers.

hawse (hôz) n. Naut. 1 The part of a vessel's bow having openings, usually steel-lined, for the passage of cables. 2 A hawsehole. 3 The situation of the cables that lead from a moored vessel to her anchors. 4 The horizontal distance between the vessel and her anchors. [<ON hals neck, bow of a ship]

hawse·hole (hôz′hōl′) n. Naut. A hole in the bow of a vessel for the passage of a cable or hawser.

haw·ser (hô′zər) n. Naut. A large rope or cable used in mooring, towing, etc. [<OF haucier lift]

haw·ser-laid (hô′zər-lād′) adj. Made of three small ropes laid up into one; cable-laid.

haw·thorn (hô′thôrn) n. A thorny, spring-flowering, ornamental shrub or small tree of the rose family (genus Crataegus) with white or pink flowers and small pome fruits called haws. The American downy hawthorn is the State flower of Missouri. [OE haguthorn]

hay¹ (hā) n. Grass, clover, or the like, cut and dried for fodder. —to hit the hay U.S. Slang To go to bed. —to make hay while the sun shines To take full advantage of an opportunity. —v.t. 1 To make, as clover, into hay. 2 To feed with hay. 3 To plant (land) with hay. —v.i. 4 To make hay. [OE hēg]

hay² (hā) n. Obs. A net or snare, especially a net enclosing the burrow, hole, or haunt of an animal. [<AF haie; ult. origin uncertain]

hay³ (hā) n. Obs. A hedge, palisade, or fence; also, a place enclosed by such. [OE hege]

hay⁴ (hā) n. A country dance with a winding in-and-out movement. [<MF haye]

hay·cock (hā′kok′) n. A dome-shaped pile of hay in the field

hay fever Pathol. An annually recurring catarrhal affection of the mucous membranes of the eyes and air passages, caused chiefly by the pollen of certain plants.

hay foot One of the alternate marching steps in military drill, as in the phrase hayfoot, straw foot: from the alleged use of hay and straw to help country recruits tell the difference between right and left.

hay·fork (hā′fôrk′) n. 1 A long-handled fork for turning or pitching hay by hand. 2 A large power-driven fork for moving hay.

hay·ing (hā′ing) n. The act or process of cutting, curing, and storing hay.

hay·loft (hā′lôft′, -loft′) n. A loft in a barn or stable for storing hay.

hay·mak·er (hā′mā′kər) n. 1 One who makes hay, especially one who spreads it to dry. 2 A haytedder. 3 A rustic dance. 4 Colloq. A

wide, swinging blow of the fist; in boxing, a knockout punch.

hay·mow (hā′mou′) n. 1 A mass of hay; especially, one stored in a loft or bay. 2 A hayloft.

hay·rack (hā′rak′) n. 1 A broad, long, open frame or rack mounted on wheels or placed on a wagon body, in which hay, straw, etc., are hauled. 2 A framework for holding hay to feed cattle, horses, etc.

hay·seed (hā′sēd′) n. U.S. Slang A country person; a rustic.

hay·stack (hā′stak′) n. A conical pile of hay, stacked in the open air, and sometimes covered. Also **hay′rick′.**

hay·ted·der (hā′ted′ər) n. One who or that which teds hay; especially, a wheeled farm implement for stirring and spreading newly cut hay.

hay·ward (hā′wôrd′, -wərd) n. Obs. An officer of a parish, township, or manor charged with inspecting fences and enclosures for cattle or impounding strays. [<HAY¹ + WARD]

hay·wire (hā′wir′) n. Wire for baling hay. —adj. U.S. Slang 1 Confused; mixed up; scrambled. 2 Crazy: to go haywire. [Slang sense <haywire outfit, loggers' term for a camp with poor or broken equipment which had to be mended with haywire]

haz·ard (haz′ərd) n. 1 Exposure to the chance of loss or injury; risk; peril. 2 A chance or fortuitous event or consequence, as the result of dice; a chance. 3 That which is hazarded, risked, or staked; the stake in gambling. 4 A gambling game played with a dice box and two dice by any number of players. 5 An obstacle on a golf course, such as a bunker, water (except casual water), sand trap, path, etc. 6 In English billiards, the pocketing of a ball, or the stroke that puts a ball into a pocket. When the object ball is forced into a pocket the stroke is called a winning hazard; when the striker's ball falls into a pocket after contact with the object ball it is a losing hazard. 7 In court tennis, a stroke in which the server drives the ball, either direct from the racket or on the first bound, into the grille or the winning gallery. —moral hazard The element of personal character of a property-owner as it affects the willingness of an insurance company to insure his property. —v.t. 1 To put to hazard; imperil. 2 To venture; to take the risk involved in; risk. [<OF hasard <Arabic al-zahr the die]

Synonyms (noun): accident, casualty, chance, contingency, danger, fortuity, jeopardy, peril, risk, venture. Hazard is the incurring of the possibility of loss or harm for the possibility of gain; danger may have no compensating alternative. In hazard the possibilities of gain or loss are nearly balanced; in risk the possibility of loss is the chief thought; in chance and venture the hope of good predominates; we speak of a merchant's venture, but of an insurance company's risk; one may be driven by circumstances to run a risk; he freely seeks a venture; we speak of the chance of winning, the hazard or risk of losing. A contingency is simply an indeterminable future event, which may or may not be attended with danger or risk. See ACCIDENT, DANGER. Antonyms: assurance, certainty, necessity, plan, protection, safeguard, safety, security, surety.

haz·ard·ous (haz′ər-dəs) adj. 1 Exposed to, exposing to, or involving danger of risk or loss. 2 Dependent on chance; fortuitous. See synonyms under PRECARIOUS. —haz′ard·ous·ly adv. —haz′ard·ous·ness n.

haze¹ (hāz) n. 1 Very fine suspended particles in the air, often with little or no moisture. 2 Dimness, as of perception or knowledge. [? Back formation <HAZY]

haze² (hāz) v.t. hazed, haz·ing 1 U.S. To subject (new students) to pranks and humiliating horseplay. 2 Naut. To punish or harass by the imposition of heavy or disagreeable tasks. [<OF haser irritate] —haz′er n.

ha·zel (hā′zəl) n. 1 A bushy shrub or small tree of the birch family (genus Corylus) yielding a hard-shelled edible nut enclosed in a leafy involucre. 2 The wood or nut of the hazel. 3 The color of the hazelnut shell, a medium yellowish-brown. —adj. 1 Made of hazel wood. 2 Of the color of hazel. [OE hæsel] —ha′zel·ly adj.

ha·zel·nut (hā′zəl-nut′) n. 1 The nut of the hazel: also called filbert. 2 The hazel shrub or tree.

haz·ing (hā′zing) n. 1 Imposition of heavy or disagreeable tasks. 2 U.S. The subjection (of new students or initiates) to pranks and humiliating ordeals. 3 A thorough beating.

H-beam (āch′bēm′) n. A structural member having a cross-section resembling an H: also called H-girder.

H-bomb (āch′bom′) n. The hydrogen bomb.

he (hē) pron. 1 The male person or being previously mentioned or understood, in the nominative case. 2 Anyone; any man: He who hesitates is lost. —n. A male, as a man, boy, bull, etc. [OE]

He Chem. Helium (symbol He).

head (hed) n. 1 The part of the body of an animal that contains the brain and the organs of special sense, the ears, eyes, mouth, and nose. ♦ Collateral adjective: cephalic. 2 Something having the shape or position of a head, or being in some way analogous to a head, as a barrel top. 3 The length of the head: taller by a head. 4 Mind; intelligence: He used his head. 5 Mental aptitude: a good head for mathematics. 6 Mental poise; self-possession: He kept his head. 7 A person: crowned heads; learned heads. 8 An individual or single entity, considered as a unit of counting: a price of two dollars a head. In this sense head may appear as a plural: six head of cattle. 9 The end regarded as the uppermost or higher part of something: the head of a valley, bed, table, etc. 10 The source, as of a river. 11 The fore or forward part of anything: the head of a column of troops. 12 The bow of a ship. 13 A headland; cape: chiefly in place names: Beachy Head. 14 A leader; chief; director. 15 The position or rank of a leader: the head of one's profession. 16 The top or summit of something: the head of the stairs; the head of a page. 17 The heading of a book, composition, chapter, etc. 18 The headlines of a single newspaper item. 19 A division of a subject, discourse, composition, or the like: He had little to say on that head. 20 Culmination: climax: to come to a head. 21 The maturated part of a boil or abscess before breaking. 22 Advance in the face of opposition: to make head against the storm. 23 A compact cluster of leaves or leaf stalks, as a head of cabbage, lettuce, or celery. 24 A rounded, compact bud, as a head of cauliflower. 25 A capitulum. 26 A cluster of cereal grain at the top of a stem. 27 The foam that rises to the surface of a fermenting liquid, as of beer or ale. 28 The measure of stored-up force or capacity, as of steam. 29 The height of a column or body of fluid above a certain point, considered as causing pressure: a head of water driving a turbine. 30 The striking or pounding part of a hammer, ax, golf club, etc. 31 The obverse of a coin. 32 Mining A heading. 33 Naut. A toilet. 34 The membrane stretched over a drum or tambourine. 35 The part of a violin, lute, etc., above the neck. 36 Gram. The part of an endocentric construction that functions in the same manner as the construction itself. In the man holding the flag, man is the head: also called head word. 37 Slang One who uses or is addicted to a drug. See synonyms under CHIEF, MASTER. —v.t. 1 To be first or most prominent on: to head the list. 2 To be chief or leader of; command. 3 To furnish with a head. 4 To cut off the head or top of, as a person or tree. 5 To turn or direct the course of: to head a vessel toward shore. 6 To pass around the head of: to head a stream. 7 To excel; beat, as in sports. 8 In soccer, to bunt (the ball) with the head. —v.i. 9 To move in a specified direction or toward a specified point. 10 To come to or form a head. 11 To originate; rise: said of rivers and streams. —to head off To intercept the course of: We'll head him off at the pass. —to head up Colloq. To be the leader or manager of; command. See synonyms under LEAD, PRECEDE. —adj. 1 Principal; chief. 2 Situated at the top or front. 3 Bearing against the front: a head wind. [OE hēafod]

head·ache (hed′āk′) n. 1 A pain in the head. 2 Colloq. A source of vexation or trouble. —head′a′chy (-ā′kē) adj.

head·band (hed′band′) n. 1 A band worn on the

head. **2** A decorative terminal cord or roll forming the end of the inner back of a book. **3** A decorative band at the head of a page or chapter in a printed book.

head·board (hed'bôrd', -bōrd') *n.* A board placed at or forming the head, as of a bed.

head·cheese (hed'chēz') *n.* A pressed and jellied cheeselike mass made of small pieces of the head and feet of a hog or calf.

head·dress (hed'dres') *n.* **1** A covering or ornament for the head. **2** The style in which the hair is arranged; coiffure.

head·first (hed'fûrst') *adv.* With the head first; precipitately. Also **head'fore'most** (-fôr'mōst', -məst, -fōr'-).

head gate The upstream gate of a canal lock; a watergate or floodgate of any race or sluice.

head·gear (hed'gir') *n.* **1** A headdress or the like. **2** That part of the hoisting apparatus at the top of a mine shaft. **3** The parts of the harness that belong about the horse's head. **4** *Naut.* The running rigging of headsails.

head·hunt·ing (hed'hun'ting) *n.* Among certain savage tribes, the custom of decapitating slain enemies and preserving the heads as trophies. —**head'·hunt'er** *n.*

head·ing (hed'ing) *n.* **1** Something located at the head, as a title. **2** *Mining* A driftway in the line of a tunnel; also, any place where work is done in driving a horizontal passage. **3** The action of providing with a head. **4** Boards or other material from which the heads of casks, barrels, etc., are made. **5** A strip along the edge of a piece of lace; also, the part of a ruffle above the gathering line.

head·land (hed'lənd *for def. 1;* hed'land' *for def. 2*) *n.* **1** A cliff projecting into the sea. **2** A strip of unplowed land at the ends of furrows or near a fence.

head·light (hed'līt') *n.* A powerful light, as at the front of a locomotive, motor vehicle, or street car.

head·line (hed'līn') *n.* **1** A word or words set in bold type at the head of a newspaper column or news story, indicating or summarizing the content, especially the heading of the main front-page story. **2** A line at the head of a page, containing title, page number, etc. **3** A line inside a hat where the brim joins the crown. **4** A rope attached to an animal's head. **5** *Naut.* A rope used to fasten the bow of a vessel to a pier or shore.

head·lin·er (hed'lī'nər) *n.* The main attraction at a theatrical performance; the actor or performer whose name appears in large letters.

head·lock (hed'lok') *n.* A wrestling grip in which the head is held between the opponent's arm and body.

head·long (hed'lông', -long') *adv.* **1** Headfirst. **2** Without deliberation; rashly; recklessly. **3** With unbridled speed or force. —*adj.* Precipitate; impetuous; rash.

head·mas·ter (hed'mas'tər, -mäs'-) *n.* The principal of a school. —**head'mas'ter·ly** *adj.* — **head'mas'ter·ship** *n.*

head·mis·tress (hed'mis'tris) *n. fem.* The female principal of a school. —**head'mis'tress·ship** *n.*

head·most (hed'mōst') *adj.* Most advanced; foremost.

head·on (hed'on', -ôn') *adj. & adv.* Front end to front end; a *head-on* collision.

head over heels 1 Somersaulting or tumbling heels over head. **2** Completely: *head over heels* in love. **3** Rashly; impetuously.

head·phone (hed'fōn') *n.* A device for telephone or radio reception, single or paired, usually attached by a band passing over the head.

head·piece (hed'pēs') *n.* **1** A piece of armor to protect the head. **2** A decorative design at the top of a printed page. **3** The head; hence, the wits.

head·pin (hed'pin') *n.* In tenpins, a kingpin.

head·quar·ters (hed'kwôr'tərz) *n. sing. & pl.* **1** The quarters or operating base of an officer in command, as of an army unit, police force, etc. **2** Any center of operations.

head·race (hed'rās') *n.* The channel by which water is led to a water wheel, or to any machinery. [< HEAD + RACE²]

head·rest (hed'rest') *n.* Any device to support the head.

head·right (hed'rīt') *n.* **1** The right of ownership to a piece of public land granted by a government to a head of a family settling on it; also, the land so granted. **2** In the State of Texas, a similar grant; also, the land so granted, usually 640 acres. **3** The right of a North American Indian to a share of the tribal property.

head·sail (hed'sāl', -səl) *n. Naut.* A sail set forward of the foremast, as a jib; also, one set on the foremast.

head·set (hed'set') *n.* A radio or telephone headphone.

head·ship (hed'ship) *n.* The office of a chief; chief authority.

head·spin (hed'spin') *n.* A wrestling movement used to break away from a half-nelson.

head·spring (hed'spring') *n.* **1** The fountainhead; source. **2** A gymnastic feat in which the performer springs, without using his hands and using his head as lever, from a supine position to his feet.

head·stall (hed'stôl') *n.* The part of a bridle that fits over the horse's head.

head·stand (hed'stand') *n.* The act of holding one's body upside-down in a vertical position, with one's weight resting on one's head and, usually, on one's hands or arms.

head·stone (hed'stōn') *n.* **1** The stone at the head of a grave. **2** The cornerstone or keystone of a structure: also **head stone.**

head·strong (hed'strông', -strong') *adj.* **1** Stubbornly bent on having one's own way; obstinate; determined. **2** Involving or proceeding from wilfulness or obstinacy. —**head'strong·ly** *adv.* — **head'strong'ness** *n.*

head·wa·ters (hed'wô'tərz, -wot'ərz) *n. pl.* The waters at or near the source of any stream, river, or the like: sometimes in the singular.

head·way (hed'wā') *n.* **1** Forward motion; momentum; progress. **2** The interval of time between consecutive trains, etc. **3** The clear distance under a girder arch, etc.

head wind A wind from ahead, blowing directly opposite to the course of a ship, airplane, etc.

head·work (hed'wûrk') *n.* Mental labor. — **head'work'er** *n.* —**head'work'ing** *n.*

head·y (hed'ē) *adj.* **head·i·er, head·i·est 1** Headstrong. **2** Tending to affect the head, as liquor. —**head'i·ly** *adv.* —**head'i·ness** *n.*

heal (hēl) *v.t.* **1** To restore to health or soundness; make healthy again; cure. **2** To bring about the remedy or cure of, as a wound or disease. **3** To remedy, repair, or counteract, as a quarrel, breach, etc. **4** To free from sin, grief, worry, etc.; purify: to *heal* the spirit. —*v.i.* **5** To become well or sound. **6** To perform a cure or cures. See synonyms under RECOVER. ◆ Homophone: *heel.* [OE *halan*] —**heal'a·ble** *adj.* —**heal'ing** *adj. & n.* —**heal'ing·ly** *adv.*

heald (held) *n.* In weaving, a device for holding and guiding the heddles in a loom. [OE *hefeld*]

heal·er (hē'lər) *n.* **1** Someone or something that heals. **2** One who undertakes to heal through prayer and faith.

health (helth) *n.* **1** Soundness of any living organism. **2** General condition of body or mind, as to vigor and soundness. **3** A toast wishing health. —*adj.* **1** Pertaining to, connected with, or engaged in public-health work: *health* education, *health* inspector. **2** Conducive to good health: a *health* food. [OE *hælth* < *hāl* whole]

neap (hēp) *n.* **1** A collection of things piled up; a pile; mass. **2** A large number; lot. **3** A crowd. **4** *Slang* An old, broken-down automobile. —*v.t.* **1** To pile into a heap; make a mound or mass of. **2** To fill or pile (a container) full or more than full. **3** To strew with heaps: to *heap* a field with bodies. **4** To give or bestow in great quantities: to *heap* insults on someone. **5** To give or bestow great quantities upon: to *heap* someone with riches. —*v.i.* **6** To form or rise in a heap or pile. —*adv.* Very; very much: North American Indian term. [OE *hēap* a crowd]

Synonyms (*noun*): accumulation, agglomeration, aggregate, aggregation, collection, drift, hoard, mass, pile, store. See COLLECTION. MASS.

hear (hir) *v.* **heard** (hûrd), **hear·ing** *v.t.* **1** To perceive by means of the ear. **2** To listen to; give audience to: *Hear* what I say! **3** To attend as part

of the audience: to *hear* a concert. **4** To learn or be informed of: I *hear* you are leaving town. **5** To listen to officially, judicially, or by way of examination: to *hear* a case in court; to *hear* a lesson. **6** To respond or accede to; grant: to *hear* a prayer. —*v.i.* **7** To perceive or be capable of perceiving sound by means of the ear. **8** To be informed or made aware; receive information: with *of, about,* or *from.* See synonyms under LISTEN. —**hear! hear!** *Brit.* Listen! An expression of approval accorded a public speaker. —**to hear of** To approve of: usually in the negative: He will not *hear of* it. [OE *hēran*] —**hear'er** *n.*

hear·ing (hir'ing) *n.* **1** The capacity to hear. **2** The special sense by which sounds are perceived. **3** An opportunity to be heard; audience. **4** The distance or space within which sound may be heard. **5** The examination of a person charged with an offense, and of the witnesses; a judicial trial, especially without a jury, as in an equity suit.

hearing aid Any of various portable instruments for the improvement of hearing, especially those which amplify sound waves by the use of microphones connected with transistors or vacuum tubes operated by small batteries.

hear·say (hir'sā') *n.* Information received indirectly; common talk; report; rumor; also, hearsay evidence.

hearse (hûrs) *n.* **1** A vehicle for carrying the dead to the grave. **2** A symbolical triangular frame set with spikes, resembling teeth of a harrow, on which lighted candles are placed during the singing of Tenebrae in Holy Week. —*v.t.* **hearsed, hears·ing 1** To put in or on a hearse. **2** To bury. [< F *herse* a harrow < L *hirpex, -icis*; so called because the frame for candles about a coffin resembled a harrow]

heart (härt) *n.* **1** The central organ of the

HEART
a. Right atrium.
b. Right ventricle.
c. Left ventricle.
d. Aorta.
e. Pulmonary artery.
f. Inferior vena cava.
g. Superior vena cava.
h. Anterior coronary artery, with vein.
i. Posterior coronary artery, with vein.

vascular system of animals; a hollow muscular structure which maintains the circulation of the blood by alternate contraction (systole) and dilatation (diastole). ◆ Collateral adjective: *cardiac.* **2** The breast regarded as the seat of the heart. **3** The seat of the affections and emotions, as distinguished from the head as the center of intellect and will. **4** One's inmost thoughts or feelings: to pour out one's *heart.* **5** Affection; love: to win one's *heart.* **6** Tenderness; capacity for sympathy: to have no *heart.* **7** Courage; resolution; firmness of will: The men lost *heart.* **8** Ardor; enthusiasm; energy: He put his whole *heart* into the task. **9** Mood; spirit: a heavy *heart.* **10** A person, especially a dear or courageous one: a brave *heart.* **11** The central part of anything; the core: the *heart* of the city. **12** The inner part or core of a tree, plant, vegetable, etc. **13** The vital or essential part; the essence: the *heart* of the matter. **14** Anything represented as or shaped like a heart; especially the conventional roundish figure with a point opposite two lobes. **15** A playing card bearing red, heart-shaped spots or pips. **16** *pl.* The suit of such playing cards. **17** *pl.* A game of cards played with a full pack, in which the object is to take no hearts. — **after one's own heart** Suiting one perfectly; conforming to one's ideas; to one's taste: a man *after one's own heart.* —**at heart** At the center or bottom; essentially; substantially; in fact. —**athletic heart** Enlargement of the heart induced by excessive participation in athletic sports. —**by heart** By rote, so as to be memorized perfectly: said of recitations. —**from one's heart** With all sincerity. —**to have at heart** To cherish; be concerned for earnestly. —**to have one's heart in one's mouth** To be excessively excited or frightened. —**to have the heart** To be callous or cruel enough. —**to take to heart** To consider seriously. —**to wear one's heart on one's sleeve** To show one's feelings plainly. —**with all one's heart** Intensely; thoroughly; completely; wholly. —*v.t.* Rare **1** To hearten. **2** To place in the heart. —*v.i.* **3** To form a heart. ◆ Homophone: *hart.* [OE *heorte*]

heart·ache (härt'āk') *n.* Mental anguish; grief; sorrow.

heart and soul Entirely; wholly; enthusiastically.

heart·beat (härt'bēt') *n.* A pulsation of the heart.

heart·block (härt'blok') *n. Pathol.* A condition in which the ventricular beats of the heart do not regularly follow the atrial also called *Adams-Stokes disease.*

heart·break (härt'brāk') *n.* Deep grief; overwhelming sorrow. —**heart'·break'ing** *adj. & n.* —**heart'·break'er** *n.*

heart·bro·ken (härt'brō'kən) *adj.* Overwhelmingly grieved: also *heart-stricken.* —**heart'·bro'ken·ly** *adv.* —**heart'·bro'ken·ness** *n.*

heart·burn (härt'bûrn') *n.* **1** A burning sensation in the esophagus, due to acidity of the stomach. **2** Discontent; jealousy.

heart·burn·ing (härt'bûr'ning) *n.* Gnawing discontent or rancor, as from envy or jealousy. —*adj.* Deeply felt; distressful.

heart·en (här'tən) *v.t.* To give heart or courage to; strengthen. See synonyms under ENCOURAGE.

heart·felt (härt'felt') *adj.* Deeply felt; most sincere.

hearth (härth) *n.* **1** The floor of a fireplace, furnace, or the like. **2** The fireside; home. **3** *Metall.* That part of a reverberatory furnace upon which the ore is laid to be subjected to the action of fire; in a blast furnace, the lowest part, through which the melted metal flows. **4** A bloomery. See synonyms under HOME. [OE *heorth*]

hearth·stone (härth'stōn') *n.* **1** A stone forming a hearth. **2** Figuratively, a fireside. **3** A soft stone used for scouring floors, doorsteps, etc. See synonyms under HOME.

heart·i·ly (här'tə·lē) *adv.* **1** With sincerity or cordiality. **2** Earnestly; enthusiastically. **3** Abundantly and with good appetite: to eat *heartily.* **4** Completely; thoroughly: to be *heartily* beaten.

heart·land (härt'land') *n.* **1** That portion of a country essential to the maintenance of its defensive and offensive strength in wartime. **2** The interior of a country as distinguished from its more exposed peripheral areas. **3** Any large geographic area supposed to give the nation controlling it decisive strategic advantage in any struggle for world domination: compare GEOPOLITICS.

heart·less (härt'lis) *adj.* **1** Without sympathy or affection; hard-hearted; pitiless. **2** Without courage; cowardly; craven. —**heart'less·ly** *adv.* —**heart'less·ness** *n.*

heart·rend·ing (härt'ren'ding) *adj.* Extremely distressing; causing anguish.

hearts·ease (härts'ēz') *n.* **1** The pansy or violet. **2** Freedom from sorrow or care. Also **heart's'·ease'.**

heart·sick (härt'sik') *adj.* Deeply disappointed or despondent. Also **heart'sore'** (-sôr', -sōr').

heart·some (härt'səm) *adj.* Cheerful or animated; lively; merry; gay. —**heart'some·ly** *adv.*

heart·strick·en (härt'strik'ən) *adj.* Overwhelmed with grief or fear.

heart·strings (härt'stringz') *n. pl.* The strongest feelings or affections.

heart·struck (härt'struk') *adj.* **1** Heart-stricken. **2** Ineradicable.

heart-to-heart (härt'tə·härt') *adj.* Marked by frankness, intimacy, and sincerity.

heart·whole (härt'hōl') *adj.* **1** Having the affections free; not in love. **2** Undaunted; sincere. —**heart'whole'ness** *n.*

heart·worm (härt'wûrm') *n.* A nematode worm (genus *Filaria*) parasitic in the heart and blood stream of dogs, occasionally of cats and other animals.

heart-worn (härt'wôrn') *adj.* Worn with care and trouble.

heart·y (här'tē) *adj.* **heart·i·er, heart·i·est 1** Full of affection or cordiality; genial. **2** Strongly felt; vigorous: a *hearty* dislike. **3** Healthy and strong. **4** Supplying abundant nourishment: a *hearty* meal. **5** Enjoying or requiring abundant nourishment: a *hearty* appetite. **6** Fertile: said of land. —*n. pl.* **heart·ies** A hearty fellow or sailor.

heat (hēt) *n.* **1** That which raises the temperature of a body or substance or any material system; also the rise itself, however produced. **2** *Physics* A form of energy directly associated with and proportional to the random molecular motions of a substance or body; it may be variously generated (as by combustion, friction, chemical action, radiation, etc.), converted by suitable processes into other forms of energy, and its total absence corresponds with that complete cessation of all translational molecular motion known as absolute zero. ◆ Collateral adjective: *thermal.* **3** The sensation produced by a rise in temperature. **4** The state of being hot; a temperature high as compared with a mean, standard, or normal temperature: summer *heat.* **5** Color, appearance, or condition indicating high temperature; high color; redness; flush. **6** *Metall.* A single heating, melting, or smelting operation, as in working iron or steel; also, the material heated, melted, etc., at one time: The foundry runs three *heats* a day. **7** A single effort or action, or one of an interrupted series of such efforts; especially, a single course or division of a race: to run several *heats.* **8** Greatest vehemence or fury; excitement or agitation; unusual animation; ardor; fervency: the *heat* of battle. **9** Sexual excitement in animals, especially in females; estrus. **10** *Physiol.* The sensation of warmth experienced when certain receptors in the skin are stimulated. **11** A fundamental quality of elements, humors, and bodies in general: opposed to *cold.* See synonyms under WARMTH. —*v.t. & v.i.* **1** To make or become hot or warm. **2** To excite or become excited; arouse. See synonyms under INCENSE. [OE *hatu*] —**heat'ed** *adj.* —**heat'ed·ly** *adv.*

heat·er (hē'tər) *n.* **1** Any device, apparatus, or contrivance designed to generate, impart, transmit, or conserve heat, as a stove, radiator, etc. **2** One who attends to the heating of something: often in combination: a rivet *heater.* **3** *Electronics* An element which supplies current for heating the cathode of a vacuum tube. **4** *Colloq.* A pistol or revolver.

heath (hēth) *n.* **1** A low, hardy, evergreen shrub of a large genus (*Erica*) with narrow, usually whorled leaves and small tubular or globose, rose, white, or yellow flowers. Two of the most durable species are the fine-leaved heath (*E. cinerea*) and the cross-leaved heath (*E. tetralix*). **2** The common heather. **3** *Brit.* An area of open land overgrown with heath or with coarse herbage. **4** In Coverdale's and later versions of the Old Testament, a desert plant; identified both as tamarisk and savin. *Jer.* xvii 6; xlviii 6. [OE *hath*]

hea·then (hē'thən) *n. pl.* **·thens** or **·then 1** One who is not a believer in the God of the Bible; one who is neither Christian, Jew, nor Mohammedan; a pagan; Gentile; idolater. **2** Any irreligious, rude, or uncultured person. —*adj.* **1** Unbelieving; Gentile; pagan. **2** Irreligious; uncultured. **3** Of or pertaining to the heathen or their customs. [OE *haethen.* Akin to HEATH.]

hea·then·dom (hē'thən·dəm) *n.* **1** Heathenism. **2** The regions of the world, collectively, inhabited by heathen peoples. **3** Heathen peoples collectively.

heath·er (heth'ər) *n.* **1** A hardy evergreen shrub related to the heath; especially, the true heather of Scotland (*Calluna vulgaris*), with minute leaves and close, one-sided, spikelike racemes of pinkish-lavender flowers. **2** The heath. **3** A dull, grayish-red color. [ME *hadder*; origin unknown; infl. in form by HEATH]

heath grass A perennial grass (*Sieglingia decumbens*) found growing on heaths and moors in Europe. Also **heather grass.**

heath grouse A European grouse (*Tetrao tetrix*) found in the heath country of Great

Britain, the male of which is mostly black, with a lyre-shaped tail: also called *heath bird.*

heath hen An American grouse (*Tympanuchus cupido cupido*) related to the prairie chicken of western North America: now extinct.

heat index An index expressing the heating value of an oil, determined by the rise in temperature from mixing 50 cc. of a specified oil with 10 cc. of concentrated sulfuric acid. Also **heat number.**

heat lightning A fitful play of lightning unattended by thunder, usually seen near the horizon at the close of a hot day, due to the reflection from distant clouds of far-off flashes, causing a diffused glow.

heat of formation The quantity of heat absorbed or evolved in the formation of a gram-molecule of a compound from its constituents at constant volume. Also **heat of combination.**

heat of fusion The quantity of heat required to convert into the liquid state a given mass of a solid which has already been brought to the melting point.

heat of vaporization The latent heat required to vaporize one gram of a liquid.

hea·tron·ic (hē·tron'ik) *adj.* Of or pertaining to the subjection of a material to a required uniform temperature through the application of high-frequency radio waves: applied in the rapid and accurate molding of plastics. [<HEAT + (ELECT)RONIC]

heat stroke The state of exhaustion and collapse caused by prolonged exposure to heat, as in furnace rooms, foundries, or from the sun's rays. Also **heat prostration.**

heat treatment *Metall.* The application of heat to metals and alloys under such conditions of temperature, time, range of variation, etc., as will give the desired properties, as hardness, to the product.

heave (hēv) *v.* **heaved** or **hove, heav·ing** *v.t.* **1** To raise with effort; lift; hoist. **2** To lift and throw, especially with effort; hurl. **3** To cause to swell, rise, or bulge out, as the chest in breathing. **4** To cause to rise and fall repeatedly: The waves *heaved* the ship up and down. **5** To emit or bring forth (a sigh, groan, etc.) as with effort or pain. **6** *Naut.* **a** To raise or haul up (the anchor); pull on (a cable, etc.). **b** To cause (a ship) to move in a specified direction by or as by hauling on cables or ropes. **7** *Geol.* To fracture and displace (a vein or stratum). —*v.i.* **8** To rise or swell up; bulge. **9** To rise and fall repeatedly. **10** To breathe with effort; gasp; pant. **11** To vomit or make an effort to vomit; retch. **12** *Naut.* **a** To move or proceed: said of ships. **b** To haul or pull, as on a rope; push, as on a capstan. —**heave, ho!** *Naut.* Pull (or push) hard together! —**to heave in** (or **into**) **sight** To come into view, as a ship at sea. —**to heave to** *Naut.* **1** To bring (a ship) to a standstill by heading into the wind with one or more sails aback. **2** To cause a ship to lie to, as in a storm. —*n.* **1** An upward and onward throw; an effort to lift or raise. **2** A rising or an upward movement. **3** A swell or an expansion, as of sea waves, or the earth in an earthquake. **4** *Geol.* The amount of actual displacement of the parts of a fractured mineral vein or stratum, vertically or horizontally or in both directions combined. [OE *hebban* lift]

heav·en (hev'ən) *n.* **1** *Theol.* The abode of God and of blest spirits; the dwelling place or state of existence of righteous souls after their life on earth. **2** *Usually pl.* The region or regions surrounding the earth; especially, the domelike expanse over the earth; the sky; firmament. **3** Any place or condition of supreme happiness; a state of bliss. **4** In Christian Science, harmony; the atmosphere of Soul. **5** Climate, especially as regards the sky of a particular place. [OE *heofon*] —**heav'en·li·ness** *n.* —**heav'en·ward** *adj. & adv.* —**heav'en·wards** *adv.*

heave offering An offering of the Jewish service: so called because heaved or lifted up.

heaves (hēvz) *n. pl.* An asthmatic disease of horses; quick, labored breathing; broken wind. [Plural of HEAVE]

heav·y (hev'ē) *adj.* **heav·i·er, heav·i·est 1** Hard to lift or carry; weighty: opposed to *light.* **2** Having great specific gravity; hence, of dense or concentrated weight: *heavy* as lead. **3** Over the usual weight: *heavy* luggage; *heavy* woolens. **4** Of great quantity or amount; abundant: a *heavy* crop; a *heavy* vote. **5** Dealing in large amounts: *heavy* trade; a *heavy* investor. **6** Laden or weighted: an atmosphere *heavy* with moisture. **7** Permeating; diffuse: a *heavy* odor. **8** Forceful; powerful: *heavy* gunfire; a *heavy* blow. **9** Tempestuous; violent: a *heavy* sea, storm, etc. **10** *Mil.* **a** Of large size: said of weapons. **b** Heavily armed: *heavy* infantry. **11** Clayey; cloggy: said of soils, roads, etc. **12** Doughy; dense and compact: said of bread, pastries, etc. **13** Not easily digested: *heavy* food. **14** Thick; massive; coarse: *heavy* lines, features, etc. **15** Slow and cumbrous: a *heavy* step. **16** Loud and intense: *heavy* applause. **17** Hard to do or accomplish; laborious: *heavy* work. **18** Hard to bear or suffer; oppressive: *heavy* taxes; *heavy* sorrow. **19** Weary; sleepy. **20** Tedious; dull: a *heavy* style. **21** Profound; intense: a *heavy* silence. **22** Gloomy; overcast: a *heavy* sky. **23** Feeling or expressing sorrow or grief; sad; despondent: a *heavy* heart. **24** Serious; grave: a *heavy* role; a *heavy* offense. **25** Pregnant. **26** Steep: a *heavy* grade. — *adv.* Heavily. — *n. pl.* **heav·ies 1** A serious role in a play, representing dignity or self-importance in middle life or vigorous age; often the villain. **2** An actor who interprets such a role. [OE *hefig*]

Synonyms (adj.): burdensome, crushing, cumbrous, dull, grievous, inert, oppressive, ponderous, slow, sluggish, stolid, stupid, weighty. See DROWSY, SAD. *Antonyms*: airy, buoyant, ethereal, light, lively, subtile, trifling, trivial, volatile.

heav·y-dut·y (hev′ē·dōō′tē, -dyōō′-) *adj.* Stoutly constructed so as to bear up under severe or long strain, usage, etc.

heav·y-foot·ed (hev′ē·fŏŏt′id) *adj.* Clumsy or plodding in gait. — **heav′y-foot′ed·ly** *adv.* — **heav′y-foot′ed·ness** *n.*

heav·y-hand·ed (hev′ē·han′did) *adj.* **1** Lacking lightness of touch; clumsy. **2** Oppressive; overbearing; dogmatic. — **heav′y-hand′ed·ly** *adv.* — **heav′y-hand′ed·ness** *n.*

heav·y-heart·ed (hev′ē·här′tid) *adj.* Sad; melancholy. — **heav′y-heart′ed·ly** *adv.* — **heav′y-heart′ed·ness** *n.*

heav·y-lad·en (hev′ē·lād′n) *adj.* **1** Bearing a heavy burden. **2** Troubled; oppressed.

heavy metal 1. Any metal with a specific gravity greater than 4. **2.** Form of rock music.

heav·y-weight (hev′ē·wāt′) *n.* A person of more than average weight; specifically, a boxer or wrestler over 175 pounds in weight. — *adj.* Of more than average weight or thickness.

heb·do·mad (heb′də·mad) *n.* The number seven; any seven things; especially, a period of seven days; a week. [< L *hebdomas, -adis* < Gk. *hebdomas* < *hepta* seven]

heb·dom·a·dal (heb·dom′ə·dəl) *adj.* **1** Composed of seven days. **2** Occurring weekly. — **heb·dom′a·dal·ly** *adv.*

heb·dom·a·dar·y (heb·dom′ə·der′ē) *n. pl.* **·dar·ies** *Eccl.* A member of a chapter or monastic choir who presides over the recitation of the breviary for the week.

he·be·phre·ni·a (hē′bə·frē′nē·ə) *n. Psychiatry* A type of dementia precox occurring at puberty. [< NL < Gk. *hēbē* youth + *phrēn* mind] — **he′be·phre′nic** (-frē′nik, -fren′ik) *adj.*

heb·e·tate (heb′ə·tāt) *v.i. & v.t.* **·tat·ed, ·tat·ing** To make or become blunt or dull. — *adj.* **1** *Bot.* Having a blunt, soft point, as certain plants. **2** Stupid; dull. [< L *hebetatus,* pp. of *hebetare* be dull < *hebes* dull] — **heb′e·ta′tion** *n.* — **heb′e·ta′tive** *adj.*

heb·e·tude (heb′ə·tōōd, -tyōōd) *n.* Stupidity and dulness of the senses, especially as noted in grave fevers. [< LL *hebetudo* < *hebes, -etis* dull]

He·bra·ic (hi·brā′ik) *adj.* Relating to or characteristic of the Hebrews. Also **He·bra′i·cal.** [< LL *Hebraicus* < Gk. *Hebraios* < *Hebraios* a Hebrew] — **He·bra′i·cal·ly** *adv.*

He·bra·ism (hē′brā·iz′əm, -brə-) *n.* **1** A distinctive characteristic of the Hebrews. **2** A Hebrew idiom. **3** The religion of the Hebrews; Judaism.

He·bra·ist (hē′brā·ist, -brə-) *n.* **1** One proficient in or a student of Hebrew. **2** One who

conforms to Hebraic thought and traditions. **3** Among the early Jews, one who upheld the Hebrew language and traditions in opposition to the Hellenists. Also **He′brew·ist.**

He·brew (hē′brōō) *n.* **1** A member of one of a group of Semitic tribes; especially, an Israelite. **2** The Semitic language of the ancient Hebrews, used in the Old Testament: retained as a scholarly and religious language after its decline as a vernacular about the fourth century B.C. **3** The modern descendant of ancient Hebrew, the official language of the republic of Israel. — **Epistle to the Hebrews** A New Testament book of uncertain authorship, addressed to Hebrew Christians: also **Hebrews.** — *adj.* Relating or belonging to the Hebrews; Hebraic. [< OF *Hebreu* < L *Hebraeus* < Gk. *Hebraios* < Hebrew *'ibhri,* lit., one from beyond (Jordan)]

hec·a·tomb (hek′ə·tōm, -tōōm) *n.* A great sacrifice, originally of a hundred oxen. [< L *hecatombe* < Gk. *hecatombē* < *hekaton* a hundred + *bous* an ox]

heck (hek) *interj. Slang* An exclamation: euphemism for hell.

heck·le (hek′əl) *v.t.* **heck·led, heck·ling 1** To try to confuse or annoy (a speaker) with taunts, questions, etc. **2** To hackle (flax, etc.). — *n.* A hackle or hatchel. [ME *hechelen* < *hechele* a hatchel] — **heck′ler** *n.*

hec·tare (hek′târ) *n.* A unit of area in the metric system; 100 ares; equal to 10,000 square meters, or 2.471 acres: also spelled *hektare.* See METRIC SYSTEM. [< F < Gk. *hekaton* a hundred + F *are* ARE²]

hec·tic (hek′tik) *adj.* **1** Characterized by intense excitement or wild feeling. **2** Characterized by or denoting a wasting habit or condition of body. **3** Pertaining to or affected with hectic fever; consumptive. Also **hec′ti·cal.** [< F *hectique* < LL *hecticus* < Gk. *hektikos* consumptive < *hexis* state of the body < *echein* have] — **hec′ti·cal·ly** *adv.*

hectic fever *Pathol.* A fever connected with some organic disease, as pulmonary tuberculosis.

hectic flush A flush on the cheek in hectic fever.

hecto- *combining form* A hundred: *hectogram.* Also, before vowels, **hect-.** For words beginning thus see below or under METRIC SYSTEM. [< F < Gk. *hekaton* a hundred]

hec·to·gram (hek′tə·gram) *n.* A measure of weight equal to 100 grams or 3.527 ounces avoirdupois: also spelled *hektogram.* See METRIC SYSTEM. Also **hec′to·gramme.**

hec·to·graph (hek′tə·graf, -gräf) *n.* A gelatin pad for making multiple copies of a writing or drawing. — *v.t.* To copy by hectograph. — **hec′to·graph′ic** *adj.*

hec·to·li·ter (hek′tə·lē′tər) *n.* A measure of capacity equal to 100 liters or 2.838 U.S. bushels. See METRIC SYSTEM. Also **hec′to·li′tre.**

hec·to·me·ter (hek′tə·mē′tər, hek·tom′ə·tər) *n.* A measure of length equal to 100 meters or 328.08 feet. See METRIC SYSTEM. Also **hec′to·me′tre.**

hec·tor (hek′tər) *v.t. & v.i.* **1** To bully; bluster. **2** To tease; torment. [< *n.*] — *n.* A quarrelsome, domineering fellow; bully. [after HECTOR]

hec·to·stere (hek′tə·stir) *n.* A measure of volume equal to 100 steres.

hed·dle (hed′l) *n.* In weaving, the parallel vertical cords or wires of a loom through which the warp is threaded: used to separate, raise, or lower the warp. See illustration under LOOM. [OE *hefeld* thread for weaving]

hedge (hej) *n.* **1** A fence or barrier formed by bushes set close together. **2** Any barrier or boundary. **3** The act of hedging. — *v.* **hedged, hedg·ing** *v.t.* **1** To surround or border with a hedge; separate with a hedge. **2** To surround, guard, or hem in with or as with obstructions or barriers: usually with *in.* **3** To try to compensate for possible loss from (a bet, investment, etc.) by making offsetting bets or investments. — *v.i.* **4** To hide, as in or behind a hedge; skulk. **5** To make offsetting bets, investments, etc. **6** To avoid definite statement or involvement; refuse to commit oneself. [OE *hegg*] — **hedg′er** *n.* — **hedg′y** *adj.*

hedge apple The Osage orange.

hedge bill A tool used in pruning hedges; billhook. Also **hedging bill.**

hedge garlic A tall hedge weed (*Sisymbrium alliaria*) of the mustard family, with heart-shaped leaves, white flowers, erect pods, and a garlicky odor.

hedge·hog (hej′hôg′, -hog′) *n.* **1** A small, nocturnal, insectivorous mammal of the Old World (family *Erinaceidae*), having the back and sides covered with stout spines; also **hedge′pig′.** **2** The porcupine. **3** *Mil.* **a** One of a chain of strongly fortified villages. **b** A wooden rack or frame, on which barbed wire is strung: used in trench warfare.

EUROPEAN HEDGEHOG
(Average length: 10 inches)

hedge·hop (hej′hop′) *v.i.* **·hopped, ·hop·ping** To fly close to the ground in an airplane, rising over houses, trees, etc., as in spraying insecticide or strafing enemy positions. — **hedge′hop′per** *n.* — **hedge′hop′ping** *n. & adj.*

hedge hyssop 1 A European perennial herb (*Gratiola officinalis*) of the figwort family, once used medicinally as an emetic and purgative. **2** The skullcap (genus *Scutellaria*).

hedge·row (hej′rō′) *n.* A row of shrubs, planted as a hedge.

hedge sparrow A small brownish European warbler (*Prunella modularis*) that frequents hedges.

he·don·ics (hē·don′iks) *n. pl. (construed as singular)* **1** The science of pleasure or positive enjoyment: as a branch of ethics it treats of pleasure in its relation to duty. **2** That branch of psychology which considers pleasurable sensations in their bearing on life.

he·don·ism (hē′dən·iz′əm) *n.* **1** The doctrine of certain Greek philosophers (Aristippus and the Cyrenaics) that pleasure, of whatever kind, is the only good. **2** In ethics, gross self-interest; self-indulgence. **3** A tendency to exaggerate and dwell upon pleasurable sensations. — **he′don·ist** *n.* — **he′don·is′tic** *adj.* — **he′don·is′ti·cal·ly** *adv.*

-hedral *combining form* Having a (given) form or number of sides: *octahedral*: used in adjectives corresponding to nouns in *-hedron.* [< -HEDR(ON) + -AL]

-hedron *combining form Geom. & Mineral.* A figure or crystal having a (given) form or a (specific) number of surfaces: *octahedron.* [< Gk. *hedra* side, surface]

hee·bie-jee·bies (hē′bē-jē′bēz) *n. pl. U.S. Slang* A fit of nervousness. [Coined by Billy de Beck, U.S. comic cartoonist, died 1942]

heed (hēd) *v.t.* To take notice of; pay attention to. — *v.i.* To pay attention. — *n.* Careful attention or consideration. [OE *hēdan*] — **heed′er** *n.*

heed·ful (hēd′fəl) *adj.* Attentive. See synonyms under THOUGHTFUL. — **heed′ful·ly** *adv.* — **heed′ful·ness** *n.*

heed·less (hēd′lis) *adj.* Careless, thoughtless. See synonyms under IMPRUDENT, INATTENTIVE. — **heed′less·ly** *adv.* — **heed′less·ness** *n.*

hee-haw (hē′hô′) *n.* **1** The braying sound of an ass. **2** Loud, rude laughter. — *v.i.* **1** To bray, as an ass. **2** To laugh in a loud, rude manner. [Imit.]

heel¹ (hēl) *n.* **1** In man, the rounded posterior part of the foot; the calcaneum with its associated structures. **2** The corresponding part of the foot or tarsus in any other animal. **3** The part of a shoe, or other foot covering, that surrounds or lies just beneath or around this part of the foot; in a boot or shoe, the built-up portion on which the rear of the foot rests; in hosiery, the separately knitted rear part of the foot. **4** The whole foot, as seen from the rear; sometimes, *pl.,* the hind feet of an animal. **5** Something resembling a heel or located like a heel, as cyma reversa, a form of molding; the lower end of a stud or rafter. **6** *Naut.* **a** The hindmost part of a vessel's keel. **b** The lower end of a mast. **7** That part of the head of a golf club that is nearest to the neck; also, that part of a tool that is nearest to the handle. **8** The last part or remainder: the *heel* of tobacco in a pipe. **9** *Colloq.* A cad. — **down at the heel** Presenting a seedy or slovenly appearance. — **to be at, on,** or **upon the heels of** To follow closely. — **to heel** To a position close behind a master: said of dogs. — *v.t.* **1** To supply with a heel. **2** To follow at the heels of; pursue closely. **3** To touch or strike with the heel. **4** To arm (a fighting cock) with steel spurs. **5** In golf, to strike (the ball) with the heel of the club. **6** *Slang* To supply with money, etc. — *v.i.* **7** To follow at the heels of someone. **8** To touch the ground with or move the heels, as in dancing. ◆ Homophone: *heal.* [OE *hela*] — **heel′less** *adj.*

heel² (hēl) *v.t. & v.i. Naut.* To lean or cause to lean to one side; cant, as a ship. — *n.* The act of heeling or inclining laterally from an upright position; a cant; list: also **heel′ing.** ◆ Homophone: *heal.* [Earlier *heeld,* OE *hieldan*]

heel–and–toe (hēl′ən-tō′) *adj.* Designating a manner of walking in which the heel of one foot touches the ground before the toes of the other foot leave it.

heeled (hēld) *adj.* **1** Having heels; fitted with heels. **2** *Slang* **a** Supplied with money. **b** Armed, as with a gun.

heel·er (hē′lər) *n.* **1** *U.S. Slang* A disreputable political retainer: often called **ward heeler. 2** One who heels shoes.

heel·piece (hēl′pēs′) *n.* **1** That part of a stocking which encloses the heel. **2** One thickness of leather in making the heel of a shoe. **3** The bar of iron which connects the soft iron cores in an electromagnet.

heel·post (hēl′pōst′) *n.* The post in a doorframe to which the door is hinged.

heel·tap (hēl′tap′) *n.* **1** A thickness of leather on the heel of a shoe. **2** A small quantity of liquor left in a glass.

Hef·ner lamp (hef′nər) See STANDARD LAMP.

heft·y (hef′tē) *adj.* **heft·i·er, heft·i·est** *Colloq.* **1** Heavy; weighty. **2** Big and powerful; muscular.

He·ge·li·an (hā-gā′lē-ən, hə-jēl′yən) *adj.* According with or pertaining to the philosophical system of Hegel. — *n.* An adherent of this system.

He·ge·li·an·ism (hā-gā′lē-ən-iz′əm, hə-jēl′yən-) *n.* The philosophical system of Hegel. Its controlling assumption was the so-called Hegelian *dialectic,* or principle which enables reflective thinking to arrange all the categories, or necessary conceptions of reason, in an order of development that corresponds to the actual order, in development, of all reality. The system is customarily characterized as *absolute idealism.* Also **He·gel·ism** (hā′gəl·iz′əm).

he·gem·o·ny (hə-jem′ə-nē, hej′ə-mō′nē, hē′jə-) *n. pl.* **·nies 1** Predominant influence of one state over others as in a league or alliance. **2** Leadership, or supreme command. [< Gk. *hēgemonia* < *hēgeesthai* lead] — **heg·e·mon·ic** (hej′ə-mon′ik) *adj.*

he·gi·ra (hə-jī′rə, hej′ə-rə) *n.* Any precipitate flight or departure: also spelled *hejira.* [< Med. L < Arabic *hijrah* departure < *hajara* go away]

He·gi·ra (hi-jī′rə, hej′ə-rə) *n.* **1** The flight of Mohammed from Mecca to Medina in 622; now taken as the beginning of the Mohammedan era. **2** The Mohammedan era. Also spelled *Hejira.*

he·gu·men (hə-gyōō′mən) *n.* In the Eastern Church, the head of a body of monks: an office of dignity rather than jurisdiction. See ARCHIMANDRITE. Also **he·gu·me·nos** (-nos), **he·gou′me·nos.** [< Med. L *hegumenus* < Gk. *hēgoumenos,* var. of *hēgeomenos,* ppr. of *hēgeesthai* lead]

he·gu·me·ne (hə-gyōō′mə-nē) *n.* In the Eastern Church, the head of a nunnery: similar to an abbess in the Western Church. [< Gk. *hēgoumenē,* fem. var. of *hēgeomenos.* See HEGUMEN.]

he·gu·me·ny (hə-gyōō′mə-nē) *n. pl.* **·nies** The office or position of a hegumen.

Hei·del·berg (hī′dəl-bûrg, *Ger.* hī′dəl·berkh) A city in Baden-Württemberg, Germany.

heif·er (hef′ər) *n.* A young cow. [OE *heahfore*]

heigh (hā, hī) *interj.* An exclamation to attract attention, or to encourage, as a race horse.

heigh-ho (hī′hō′, hā′-) *interj.* An exclamation of varying significance, as of weariness, disappointment, surprise, etc.

height (hīt) *n.* **1** Distance above a base; altitude; highness. **2** An eminence. **3** The acme; culmination. [OE *hiehtho*]
Synonyms: acclivity, altitude, elevation, emin-

ence, exaltation, loftiness. See SUMMIT. Compare HIGH. *Antonyms:* depression, depth, descent, lowliness, lowness.

height·en (hīt′n) *v.t. & v.i.* **1** To make or become high or higher; raise or lift. **2** To make or become more in degree, amount, size, etc.; intensify. — **height′en·er** *n.*
Synonyms: elevate, enhance, exalt, lift, raise, uplift. See AGGRAVATE. INCREASE. *Antonyms:* abase, debase, depress, deteriorate, diminish, lower, reduce.

height-find·er (hīt′fīn′dər) *n. Aeron.* An optical instrument used to determine the height of aircraft.

height-to-pa·per (hīt′tə-pā′pər) *n. Printing* The standard height of type: in the United States, 0.9186 inch; in England, 0.9175 inch. Compare TYPE-HIGH.

Heim·lich maneuver (hīm′lik) A life-saving method of preventing a person's choking on food lodged in the windpipe by firmly grasping the victim around the midsection from behind, and pressing a fist hard against the diaphragm to produce a burst of air up through the throat.

hei·nous (hā′nəs) *adj.* Extremely wicked; atrocious; odiously sinful. See synonyms under FLAGRANT, INFAMOUS. [< OF *haïnos* < *haine* hatred < *hair* hate] — **hei′nous·ly** *adv.* — **hei′nous·ness** *n.*

heir (âr) *n.* **1** *Law* One who on the death of another becomes entitled by operation of law to succeed to the deceased person's estate, as an estate of inheritance: also **heir at law. 2** In states and countries which have adopted the civil law, all persons called to the succession. **3** Anyone inheriting from a deceased person. **4** One who or that which succeeds to any qualities of another by reason of community of origin, or inherits anything by transmission. **5** *Obs.* Offspring. ◆ Homophone: *air.* [< OF < L *heres*] — **heir′ess** *n. fem.* — **heir′less** *adj.*

heir apparent One who must by course of law become the heir if he survives his ancestor.

heir·loom (âr′lōōm) *n.* **1** Any movable chattel that descends to an heir; especially, something that has been handed down for generations. **2** Any personal quality, endowment, or family characteristic inherited from ancestors. [< HEIR + LOOM, in obs. sense "tool"]

heir presumptive One who is at present heir to another but whose claims may become void by birth of a nearer relative.

heir·ship (âr′ship) *n.* **1** The state or condition of an heir. **2** Succession by inheritance. Also **heir′dom** (-dəm).

hek·is·to·ther·mic (hek′is-tə-thûr′mik) *adj. Ecol.* Of or designating plants adapted for living beyond the limits of tree growth and in the prolonged absence of light and warmth. Also spelled *hecistothermic.* [< Gk. *hēkistos* least + *thermē* heat]

hek·tare (hek′târ), **hek·to·gram** (hek′tə-gram), etc. See HECTARE, etc.

hel·co·sis (hel-kō′sis) *n. Pathol.* The development of an ulcer. [< Gk. *helkos* an ulcer + -OSIS] — **hel·cot′ic** (-kot′ik) *adj.*

held (held) Past tense of HOLD.

Hel·e·na (hel′ə-nə) The capital of Montana.

Hel·e·na (hel′ə-nə), **Saint,** 247?–327?, mother of Constantine the Great.

he·li·a·cal (hi-lī′ə-kəl) *adj. Astron.* **1** Pertaining to the sun. **2** Designating those risings and settings of the stars that take place as near the sun as they can be observed. Also **he·li·ac** (hē′lē-ak). [< LL *heliacus* < Gk. *hēliakos* < *hēlios* the sun] — **he·li′a·cal·ly** *adv.*

He·li·an·thus (hē′lē-an′thəs) *n.* A large genus of mainly North American annual or perennial plants of the composite family, the sunflowers, with usually opposite leaves and large heads of yellow flowers. [< NL < Gk. *hēlios* sun + *anthos* a flower]

he·li·ast (hē′lē-ast) *n.* A dicast. [< Gk. *heliastēs* < *heliazesthai* sit in court]

hel·i·cal (hel′i-kəl) *adj.* Pertaining to or shaped like a helix. — **hel′i·cal·ly** *adv.*

helical gear *Mech.* A gear wheel whose teeth are cut across the face at an angle with the axis.

hel·i·cline (hel′ə-klīn) *n.* A ramp with a curving or spiral passageway. [< HELI(X) + (IN)CLINE]

helico- *combining form* Spiral; helical: *helicodromic.* Also, before vowels, **helic-.** [< Gk. *helix* a spiral]

hel·i·co·dro·mic (hel′i-kō-drō′mik, -drom′ik) *adj.* Having a flight path curving like a corkscrew or a bent skew spiral: said of guided missiles. [< HELICO- + -DROM(OUS) + -IC]

hel·i·coid (hel′ə-koid) *adj.* Coiled spirally, as certain univalve shells: also **hel′i·coi′dal.** — *n.* A geometrical surface resembling that of a screw. — **hel′i·coi′dal·ly** *adv.*

hel·i·con (hel′i-kon, -kən) *n.* A horn-shaped bass or contrabass tuba. [< Gk. *Helikōn,* the mountain of the Muses; infl. by HELIX]

hel·i·cop·ter (hel′ə-kop′tər, hē′lə-) *n. Aeron.* A type of aircraft whose aerodynamic support is obtained from propellers rotating on a vertical axis and which is capable of rising and descending vertically. [< F *hélicoptère* < Gk. *helix, -ikos* a spiral + *pteron* a wing]

FOUR–PASSENGER HELICOPTER
A. Pitch control mechanism. *B.* Torque control rotor.

hel·i·co·tre·ma (hel′ə-kō-trē′mə) *n. Anat.* The opening in the inner ear which connects the inner and outer spiral canals at the apex of the cochlea. [< NL < Gk. *helix, -ikos* a spiral + *trēma* hole]

he·li·o (hē′lē-ō) *n. pl.* **-os** *Colloq.* A heliograph.

helio- *combining form* Sun; of the sun: *heliotropic.* [< Gk. *hēlios* the sun]

he·li·o·cen·tric (hē′lē-ə-sen′trik) *adj.* Having reference to the sun as a center: a *heliocentric* system. Also **he′li·o·cen′tri·cal.**

he·li·o·chrome (hē′lē-ə-krōm′) *n.* A photograph in natural colors. — **he′li·o·chro′mic** *adj.*

he·li·o·gram (hē′lē-ə-gram′) *n.* A message sent by means of a heliograph.

he·li·o·graph (hē′lē-ə-graf, -gräf) *n.* **1** An instrument for taking photographs of the sun. **2** A photograph taken by sunlight. **3** A mirror for signaling by flashes of light. — *v.t. & v.i.* To signal with a heliograph. — **he·li·og·ra·pher** (hē′lē-og′rə-fər) *n.* — **he′li·o·graph′ic** *adj.* — **he′li·og′ra·phy** *n.*

he·li·o·gra·vure (hē′lē-ō-grə-vyoor′) *n.* Photoengraving, or a print or plate produced by it. See PHOTOGRAVURE.

he·li·ol·a·try (hē′lē-ol′ə-trē) *n.* Worship of the sun. — **he′li·ol′a·ter** *n.* — **he′li·ol′a·trous** *adj.*

he·li·o·lith·ic (hē′lē-ə-lith′ik) *adj.* Denoting a culture characterized by sun-worship and megaliths. [< HELIO- + (MEGA)LITHIC]

he·li·ol·o·gy (hē′lē-ol′ə-jē) *n. Obs.* The science of the sun's energy and action. — **he′li·ol′o·gist** *n.*

he·li·om·e·ter (hē′lē-om′ə-tər) *n. Astron.* An instrument for the accurate measurement of small angles in the heavens. — **he·li·o·met·ric** (hē′lē-ə-met′rik) or **·ri·cal** *adj.* — **he′li·om′e·try** *n.*

he·li·oph·i·lous (hē′lē-of′ə-ləs) *adj. Bot.* Fond of or turning toward the sun, as the sunflower. [< HELIO- + Gk. *philos* loving]

he·li·o·pho·bi·a (hē′lē-ə-fō′bē-ə) *n.* Morbid aversion to sunlight.

he·li·o·phyte (hē′lē-ə-fīt′) *n. Bot.* A plant growing in the light.

he·li·o·scope (hē′lē-ə-skōp′) *n. Astron.* A telescope in which the eyes are protected during observations of the sun.

he·li·o·stat (hē′lē-ə-stat′) *n. Astron.* An instrument consisting of a mirror moved by clockwork so that the rays of the sun shall be reflected from it in a fixed direction.

he·li·o·tax·is (hē′lē-ə-tak′sis) *n.* Phototaxis resulting from the effect of the sun's rays. [< HE-LIO- + (PHOTO)TAXIS] **—he'li·o·tac'tic** (-tak'tik) *adj.*

he·li·o·ther·a·py (hē'lē·ō·ther'ə·pē) *n. Med.* Exposure to the sun for remedial purposes.

he·li·o·trope (hē'lē·ə·trōp', hēl'yə-) *n.* **1** An herb (genus *Heliotropium*) with small white or purplish fragrant flowers. **2** Any plant which turns toward the sun. **3** The garden heliotrope or common valerian (*Valeriana officinalis*); also, the winter heliotrope or butterburr (*Petasites fragrans*). **4** A variety of quartz, the bloodstone. **5** A soft rosy-purple, the color of flowers of *Heliotropium arborescens*. [< F *héliotrope* < L *heliotropium* < Gk. *hēliotropion* < *hēlios* sun + *trepein* turn]

he·li·o·tropic (hē'lē·ə·trop'ik, -trō'pik, hēl'yə-) *adj.* Characterized by or pertaining to heliotropism. **—he'li·o·trop'i·cal·ly** *adv.*

he·li·ot·ro·pism (hē'lē·ot'rə·piz'əm) *n. Biol.* That property of an organism by virtue of which it tends, when not symmetrically illuminated on all sides, to move either toward or away from the source of light. Also **he'li·ot'ro·py.**

he·li·o·type (hē'lē·ə·tīp') *n.* A photoengraving from which impressions can be taken by a printing press; an impression so taken. *—adj.* Of or pertaining to such photoengravings, or to the process of making them. Also **he'li·o·typ'ic** (-tip'ik). **—he'li·o·ty'py** (-tī'pē) *n.*

he·li·port (hel'ə·pôrt', -pōrt', hēl'ə-) *n.* An airport for helicopters. [< HELI(COPTER) + PORT[1] a harbor]

hel·i·spher·ic (hel'ə·sfer'ik) *adj.* Turning spirally on a sphere. See HELIX, SPHERIC. Also **hel'i·spher'i·cal.** [< Gk. *helix* a spiral + SPHERE]

he·li·um (hē'lē·əm) *n.* A chemically inert, odorless, colorless, gaseous element (symbol He, atomic number 2) having a boiling point near absolute zero, found in natural gas deposits and comprising only about 5 parts per million of the atmosphere but the second most abundant element, after hydrogen, in the universe. See PERIODIC TABLE. [< NL < Gk. *hēlios* sun]

he·lix (hē'liks) *n. pl.* **he·lix·es** or **hel·i·ces** (hel'ə·sēz) **1** *Geom.* A line, thread, wire, or the like, curved into a shape such as it would assume if wound in a single layer round a cylinder; a form like a screw thread. **2** Any spiral. **3** *Anat.* The recurved border of the external ear. **4** *Archit.* A small volute. [< L, a spiral < Gk.]

hell (hel) *n.* **1** The abode of evil spirits; infernal regions; place of eternal punishment, of extreme torment, etc. See GEHENNA, INFERNO, TARTARUS. **2** Any condition of extreme physical or mental suffering. **3** In ancient times, the place of departed spirits; called by the Greeks *Hades,* by the Hebrews *Sheol,* and by the Scandinavians *Hel.* **4** A place of evil, as a gambling house; also, a place for rejected things or refuse. **5** In Christian Science, mortal belief; error; lust; remorse; hatred; revenge; sin. **6** Hellbox. [OE *hel*]

he'll (hēl) Contraction of HE WILL.

hell-bent (hel'bent') *adj. U.S. Slang* Determined; recklessly eager: *hell-bent* for election.

hell-cat (hel'kat') *n.* **1** A furious or spiteful woman. **2** A witch; hag.

hell-div·er (hel'dī'vər) *n.* The dabchick.

hel·le·bo·ras·ter (hel'ə·bə·ras'tər) *n.* An English species of hellebore (*Helleborus foetidus*) with numerous globular flowers, often cultivated for ornament: also called *bear's-foot, stinking* or *fetid hellebore.*

hel·le·bore (hel'ə·bôr, -bōr) *n.* **1** A perennial herb (genus *Helleborus*) of the crowfoot family having serrated leaves and large flowers. Cultivated species are, in the United States, the green hellebore (*H. viridis*), and in Europe, the black hellebore or *Christmas rose (H. niger),* the black roots of which are a powerful cathartic. **2** Any of certain herbs (genus *Veratrum*) of the lily family whose dried rootstocks yield poisonous alkaloids of use in medicine and as insecticides; especially the American or green hellebore (*V. viride*) and the European white hellebore (*V. album*): also called *false hellebore.* **3** The powdered root of the American hellebore, used to destroy plant vermin. [< L *helleborus* < Gk. *helleboros*]

hel·le·bo·re·in (hel'ə·bôr'ē·in, -bō'rē-) *n. Chem.* A toxic glucoside, $C_{37}H_{56}O_{18}$, from the rhizome of *Helleborus niger* and *H. viridis:* a powerful cardiac stimulant.

hel·leb·o·rin (hə·leb'ə·rin, hel'ə·bôr'in, -bō'rin) *n. Chem.* A colorless crystalline glucoside, $C_{28}H_{36}O_6$, from the same sources as helleborein: a powerful cathartic and emmenagog.

Hel·len (hel'ən) In Greek legend, son of Deucalion and Pyrrha and progenitor, through his sons Aeolus, Dorus, and Xuthus, of the Greek race.

Hel·len·ic (he·len'ik, -lē'nik) *adj.* Greek; Grecian. *—n.* A subfamily of the Indo-European languages, consisting of the Greek language and its dialects, ancient and modern. See GREEK.

Hel·len·ism (hel'ə·niz'əm) *n.* **1** Ancient Greek character, ideals, or civilization. **2** A Greek idiom or phrase. **3** Assimilation of Greek speech, manners, and culture, as by the Romans or the Jews of the Diaspora.

hell-fire (hel'fīr') *n.* One of the torments of the damned; the flames of hell.

hell·gram·mite (hel'grə·mīt) *n.* The large aquatic larva of a megalopterous insect, the four-winged dobson fly, much used as a bait for black bass and other fish: also called *dobson.* See DOBSON FLY. [Origin unknown]

hell·hound (hel'hound') *n.* A hound of hell; a fierce and cruel pursuer.

HELLGRAMMITE
Dobson fly (*a*)
and larva (*b*).

hell-ion (hel'yən) *n. Colloq.* A mischievous person; one given to wild and unpredictable actions. Also called *hallion.* [< HELL]

hell-ish (hel'ish) *adj.* Of or like hell; diabolical; also, wicked; malignant; horrible. See synonyms under INFERNAL. **—hell'ish·ly** *adv.* **—hell'ish·ness** *n.*

hell-kite (hel'kīt') *n.* **1** A fierce bird of prey. **2** A wantonly malignant or cruel person.

hel·lo (hə·lō') *interj.* **1** An exclamation used in calling the attention and in greeting, especially over the telephone. **2** An exclamation of surpise. *—n. pl.* **hel·loes** The call "hello." *—v.t. & v.i.* **·loed, ·lo·ing** To call "hello" to.

helm[1] (helm) *n.* **1** *Naut.* The steering apparatus of a vessel, especially the tiller. **2** Metaphorically, any place of control or responsibility; administration. *—v.t.* To manage the helm of; steer; direct. [OE *helma* rudder]

helm[2] (helm) *n. Archaic & Poetic* A helmet; covering. *—v.t.* To cover or supply with a helmet. [OE *helm* covering]

hel·met (hel'mit) *n.* **1** A covering of defensive or protective armor for the head, made of metal, as worn by soldiers of all times, or of leather, as worn by football players. **2** Something resembling head armor in shape, position, or function: as, protective headgear, etc.; the metal head covering of a diving suit, or the wire-mesh headguard worn by fencers. [< OF, dim. of *helme* a helmet < Gmc.] **—hel'met·ed** *adj.*

TYPES OF HELMETS

a. Helmet of Grecian warrior.
b. Casque, 16th century knight.
c. German, World War II.
d. Aviator's with headphone.
e. Football player.
f. Space pilot.

helms·man (helmz'mən) *n. pl.* **·men** (-mən) A steersman; one who guides a ship.

helm roof *Archit.* A pointed roof with four inclined faces, gabled at the apex.

he·lo·phyte (hē'lə·fīt) *n. Bot.* A plant growing in marshes and adapted to an amphibious life. [< Gk. *helos* marsh + -PHYTE]

hel·ot (hel'ət, hē'lət) *n.* **1** One of a class of serfs of ancient Sparta, bound to the soil, and in most cases descended from prisoners of war. **2** Any slave. [< L *helotes* < Gk. *heilōs, heilōtos;* appar. from *Helos,* a Laconian town enslaved by Sparta]

hel·ot·ism (hel'ət·iz'əm, hē'lət-) *n.* **1** Serfdom, as that of ancient Sparta. **2** *Bot.* A type of symbiosis, especially the relation between algae and fungi in forming lichens.

hel·ot·ry (hel'ət·rē, hē'lət-) *n.* **1** Serfdom. **2** Helots as a class.

help (help) *v.t.* **1** To give or provide assistance to; aid. **2** To assist in some action, motion, etc.: with *on, into, out of, up, down,* etc. **3** To rescue, as from death or danger. **4** To give relief to; ease; comfort: to *help* a cold. **5** To be responsible for: He can't *help* it if he's lame. **6** To avoid; refrain from: I couldn't *help* seeing her. **7** To serve; wait on as a waiter, clerk, etc. *—v.i.* **8** To give assistance; be of service. *—n.* **1** Assistance afforded toward the promotion of an object or the attainment of an end. **2** Remedy or relief. **3** Rescue or succor. **4** One who or that which aids; a helper. **5** *U.S.* A hired servant; domestic: often used collectively: The *help* are on strike. **6** *Dial.* A portion of food. [OE *helpan*] **—help'er** *n.*

Synonyms (verb): abet, aid, assist, befriend, cooperate, encourage, foster, relieve, second, succor, support, sustain, uphold. *Help* expresses greater dependence and deeper need than *aid.* In extremity we say "God *help* me" rather than "God *aid* me." In time of danger we cry "*Help! Help!*" rather than "*Aid! Aid!*" To *aid* is to *second* another's own exertions. We speak of *helping* the helpless, rather than of *aiding* them. *Help* includes *aid,* but *aid* may fall short of the meaning of *help.* In law to *aid* or *abet* makes one a principal. (Compare synonyms for ACCESSORY.) To *cooperate* is to *aid* as an equal; to *assist* implies a subordinate and secondary relation. One *assists* a fallen friend to rise; he *cooperates* with him in helping others. *Encourage,* and usually *uphold,* refer to mental *aid; succor* and *support,* oftenest to material assistance. We *encourage* the timid or despondent, *succor* the endangered, *support* the weak, *uphold* those who else might be shaken or cast down. Compare ABET, AID, PROMOTE, SERVE. *Antonyms:* see synonyms for HINDER.

help·ful (help'fəl) *adj.* Affording aid; beneficial. **—help'ful·ly** *adv.* **—help'ful·ness** *n.*

help·ing (hel'ping) *n.* **1** A giving of aid. **2** A portion of food.

helping verb An auxiliary verb. See *auxiliary* (*n.,* def. 2a).

help·less (help'lis) *adj.* **1** Unable to help oneself; feeble. **2** Incompetent; incapable. **3** Destitute of help.

help·mate (help'māt) *n.* **1** A helper; partner. **2** A wife. See synonyms under ASSOCIATE.

help·meet (help'mēt) *n.* A helpmate.

Hel·sin·ki (hel'sing·kē) The capital of Finland, on the Gulf of Finland. *Swedish* **Hel·sing·fors** (hel'sing·fôrz).

hel·ter-skel·ter (hel'tər·skel'tər) *adv.* In a hurried and confused manner. *— adj.* Hurried and confused. *— n.* Disorderly hurry; confused and hasty action. [Imit.]

helve (helv) *n.* The handle, as of an ax or hatchet. [OE *helfe*]

hem[1] (hem) *n.* A finished edge made on a fabric by turning over the raw edge (usually twice) and sewing down the first fold: done to prevent raveling or as an ornament. *— v.t.* **hemmed, hem·ming 1** To make a hem on; border; edge. **2** To shut in; enclose; restrict: usually with *in, about,* etc. [OE] **—hem'mer** *n.*

hem[2] (hem) *n. & interj.* A sound made as in clearing the throat; ahem. *—v.i.* **hemmed, hem·ming 1** To make the sound "hem." **2** To hesitate in speaking. [Imit.]

he·ma·ba·rom·e·ter (hē'mə·bə·rom'ə·tər, hem'-

ə-) *n. Med.* An instrument for determining the specific gravity of the blood.

he·ma·chrome (hē′mə·krōm, hem′ə-) *n. Biochem.* The red coloring matter of the blood.

he·ma·cy·tom·e·ter (hē′mə·sī·tom′ə·tər, hem′ə-) *n.* An instrument used in counting blood cells and micro-organisms. — **he′ma·cy·tom′e·try** *n.*

he·ma·gog (hē′mə·gôg, -gog, hem′ə-) *n. Med.* An agent which promotes or favors the discharge of blood. Also **he′ma·gogue.** [<HEM- + -AGOG] — **he′ma·gog′ic** (-goj′ik) *adj.*

he·mal (hē′məl) *adj.* **1** Pertaining to blood or the vascular system; of the nature of blood. **2** Pertaining to or situated on the side of the body that contains the heart. Also spelled *haemal.* [<Gk. *haima* blood + -AL]

he·man (hē′man′) *n. pl.* **·men** (-men′) *Slang* A virile, muscular man.

Hem·ans (hem′ənz, hē′mənz), **Felicia Dorothea**, 1793–1835, *née* Browne, English poet.

he·ma·pho·bi·a (hē′mə·fō′bē·ə, hem′ə-) See HEMOPHOBIA.

he·ma·poi·e·sis (hē′mə·poi·ē′sis, hem′ə-) *n.* The promotion or production of blood. Also called *hematopoiesis.* [<HEMA- + Gk. *poiēsis* a making < *poieein* make] — **he′ma·poi·et′ic** (-poi·et′ik) *adj.*

he·ma·tal·los·co·py (hē′mə·təl·os′kə·pē, hem′ə-) *n.* The scientific analysis of blood to determine the blood type to which it belongs. [HEMAT- + ALLO- (def. 3) + -SCOPY]

he·ma·tem·e·sis (hē′mə·tem′ə·sis, hem′ə-) *n. Pathol.* Vomiting of blood; gastric hemorrhage.

he·mat·ic (hi·mat′ik) *adj.* **1** Of, pertaining to, or contained in blood. **2** Effecting a change in the blood. — *n.* A medicine that produces a change in the blood.

he·ma·tin·ic (hem′ə·tin′ik, hē′mə-) *n. Med.* Any agent which increases the number of red corpuscles in the blood. — *adj.* Of or pertaining to hematin.

hem·a·to·blast (hem′ə·tō·blast′, hē′mə-) *n. Biol.* A cell in the bone marrow or liver which produces the red corpuscles of the blood; a blood platelet.

hem·a·to·cele (hem′ə·tō·sēl′, hē′mə-) *n. Pathol.* A tumor containing blood.

hem·a·to·crit (hem′ə·tō·krit′, hē′mə-) *n.* An instrument which, by centrifugal action, separates the corpuscles and the serum in blood in order to determine the relative amounts. Also spelled *haematokrit.* [<HEMATO- + Gk. *kritēs* a judge < *krinein* judge]

hem·a·toc·ry·al (hem′ə·tok′rē·əl, hē′mə-) *adj. Zool.* Cold-blooded, as fishes and reptiles: also spelled *haematocryal.* [<HEMATO- + Gk. *kryos* cold]

hem·a·to·gen·e·sis (hem′ə·tō·jen′ə·sis, hē′mə-) *n.* The formation of blood. — **hem′a·to·gen′ic** or **hem′a·to·ge·net′ic** (-jə·net′ik) *adj.*

he·ma·toid (hē′mə·toid, hem′ə-) *adj.* Bloody, or resembling blood.

he·ma·tol·o·gy (hē′mə·tol′ə·jē, hem′ə-) *n.* The branch of medical science that treats of the blood, its formation, functions, and diseases: also spelled *haematology.* Also **he′ma·to·lo′gi·a** (-tə·lō′jē·ə).

he·ma·to·ma (hē′mə·tō′mə, hem′ə-) *n. pl.* **·to·ma·ta** (-tō′mə·tə) *Pathol.* A blood tumor. [<HEMAT- + -OMA]

he·ma·tom·e·ter (hē′mə·tom′ə·tər, hem′ə-) *n.* An instrument for determining the number of corpuscles in a given quantity of blood. — **he′ma·tom′e·try** *n.*

he·ma·tose (hē′mə·tōs, hem′ə-) *adj.* Fully or abnormally charged with blood.

he·ma·to·sis (hē′mə·tō′sis, hem′ə-) *n. Physiol.* The formation of blood; conversion of chyle or venous blood into arterial blood. [<NL <Gk. *haimatōsis* < *haimatoein* make into blood]

he·ma·to·ther·mal (hē′mə·tō·thûr′məl, hem′ə-) *adj. Zool.* Warm-blooded, as mammals and birds: also spelled *haematothermal.*

hem·a·to·zo·on (hem′ə·tō·zō′on, hē′mə-) *n. pl.* **·zo·a** (-zō′ə) An animal parasite living in the blood. [<HEMATO- + Gk. *zōon* animal]

hem·a·tu·ri·a (hem′ə·tŏŏr′ē·ə, -tyŏŏr′-, hē′mə-) *n. Pathol.* Bloody urine. [<HEMAT- + -URIA]

hem·er·a·lo·pi·a (hem′ər·ə·lō′pē·ə) *n. Pathol.* Day blindness, in which sight is less distinct by daylight than by night or by artificial light. See NYCTALOPIA. [<NL <Gk. *hēmera* day + *alaos* blind + *ōps* eye] — **hem′er·a·lo′pic** *adj.*

hem·er·o·phyte (hem′ər·ə·fīt′) *n. Bot.* A plant introduced through the agency of man. [<Gk. *hēmeros* cultivated + -PHYTE]

hem·i·al·gi·a (hem′ē·al′jē·ə) *n. Pathol.* Pain, especially in the head, confined to one side; unilateral pain. [<HEMI- on one side + -ALGIA]

hem·i·a·nop·si·a (hem′ē·ə·nop′sē·ə) *n. Pathol.* A paralysis, partial or total, of some of the fibers of the optic nerve, with the result that part of the field of vision is obscured or obliterated in one or both eyes. Also **hem′i·a·no′pi·a** (-nō′pē·ə). [<NL <Gk. *hēmi-* half + *an-* without + *ōps* eye] — **hem′i·a·nop′tic** (-nop′tik) *adj.*

hem·i·at·ro·phy (hem′ē·at′rə·fē) *n. Pathol.* The wasting away of one side, as of the face.

he·mic (hē′mik, hem′ik) *adj.* Pertaining or relating to blood: hemic diseases. Also spelled *haemic.*

hem·i·chor·date (hem′i·kôr′dāt) *adj.* Of, pertaining to or belonging to a division of chordates (*Hemichordata*) characterized by paired gill slits and a primitive notochord including many small marine forms. — *n.* A member of this division; a tongue worm. [<NL <Gk. *hēmi-* half + *chordata* chordate]

hem·i·cra·ny (hem′i·krā′nē) *n. Pathol.* Migraine, or nervous headache. Also **hem′i·cra′ni·a** (-nē·ə). [<F *hemicraine* <LL *hemicrania* <Gk. *hēmikrania* < *hēmi-* half + *kranion* skull]

hem·i·cy·cle (hem′i·sī′kəl) *n.* **1** A semicircular arena, as in a theater. **2** A semicircle, or objects arranged in a semicircle. — **hem′i·cy′clic** (-sī′klik, -sik′lik) *adj.*

hem·i·dem·i·sem·i·qua·ver (hem′ē·dem′ē·sem′·ē·kwā′vər) *n. Music* A sixty-fourth note.

hem·i·dome (hem′i·dōm) *n. Mineral.* That form in a crystal composed of two parallel domed planes in the triclinic, or of two parallel orthodomic planes in the monoclinic system of crystallization.

hem·i·he·dral (hem′i·hē′drəl) *adj. Mineral.* Pertaining to crystal forms that possess only one half as many planes as are required for complete symmetry in the class to which they belong. [<HEMI- + Gk. *hedra* seat, surface] — **hem′i·he′dral·ly** *adv.*

hem·i·he·dron (hem′i·hē′drən) *n. pl.* **·dra** (-drə) A hemihedral crystal form.

hem·i·met·a·bol·ic (hem′i·met′ə·bol′ik) *adj. Entomol.* Designating those insects whose larvae have an incomplete metamorphosis, developing gradually into the adult stage: opposed to *holometabolic.* Also **hem·i·me·tab·o·lous** (-hem′i·mə·tab′ə·ləs). — **hem′i·me·tab′o·lism** (-tab′ə·liz′əm) *n.*

hem·i·mor·phic (hem′i·môr′fik) *adj. Mineral.* **1** Pertaining to crystals that are unsymmetric with reference to the opposite ends of a symmetry axis. **2** Pertaining to a class in the monoclinic system. — **hem′i·mor′phism** (-fiz′əm) *n.*

Hem·ing·way (hem′ing·wā), **Ernest**, 1899–1961, U.S. novelist.

hem·i·par·a·site (hem′i·par′ə·sīt) *n. Bot.* A plant partly parasitic, as the mistletoe. — **hem′i·par′a·sit′ic** (-par′ə·sit′ik) *adj.*

hem·i·ple·gi·a (hem′i·plē′jē·ə) *n. Pathol.* Paralysis of one side of the body. Also **hem′i·ple′gy.** — **hem′i·ple′gic** (-plē′jik, -plej′ik) *adj.*

hem·i·sphere (hem′i·sfir) *n.* **1** A half-sphere, formed by a plane passing through the center of the sphere. **2** A half of the terrestrial or of the celestial globe, or a map or projection of the half of either on a plane surface. The world is usually considered as divided either at the equator into the *northern* and *southern* hemispheres, or at some meridian between Europe and America into the *eastern* and *western*, usually at the twentieth meridian west of Greenwich. **3** *Anat.* One of two large convoluted, semiovoid masses forming the bulk of the cerebrum. [<F *hémisphère* <L *hemisphaerium* <Gk. *hēmisphairion* < *hēmi-* half + *sphaira* a sphere] — **hem·i·spher·ic** (hem′ə·sfer′ik) or **·i·cal** *adj.*

hem·i·sphe·roid (hem′ə·sfir′oid) *n.* A half of a spheroid. — **hem′i·sphe·roi′dal** (-sfi·roid′l) *adj.*

hem·i·stich (hem′i·stik) *n.* A half of a poetic line; an incomplete poetic line. [<LL *hemistichium* <Gk. *hēmistichion* < *hēmi-* half + *stichos* a row, line of poetry]

hem·i·sys·to·le (hem′i·sis′tə·lē) *n. Med.* Contraction of only one of the heart ventricles, producing only one pulse beat for every two heartbeats.

hem·i·trope (hem′i·trōp) *n.* A twin crystal. — *adj.* **1** Having one part in reverse position with reference to the other: said of a crystal form. **2** Half inverted. Also **hem′i·trop′ic** (-trop′ik, -trō′pik) *adj.* [<F *hémitrope* <Gk. *hēmi-* half + *tropē* a turning < *trepein* turn]

hem·line (hem′līn′) *n.* The line formed by the lower edge of a garment, as a dress.

hem·lock (hem′lok) *n.* **1** An evergreen tree (genus *Tsuga*) of North America and Asia. **2** The wood of this tree. **3** The hemlock spruce. **4** The spotted hemlock (*Conium maculatum*), a large biennial herb of the parsley or carrot family, yielding coniine: also **poison hemlock. 5** A poison made from the unripe dried fruit of this herb: Socrates drank the *hemlock*. **6** Any of several related herbs, as the water hemlock (*Cicuta maculata*). [OE *hymlice*]

hemlock spruce A North American coniferous tree of the pine family (*Tsuga canadense*), having a coarse non–resinous wood used for paper pulp and packing boxes, and a bark which yields an important tanning material.

he·mo·dy·nam·ics (hē′mō·dī·nam′iks, hem′ō-) *n.* The study of the movements of the blood and the dynamics of blood pressure.

he·mo·flag·el·late (hē′mə·flaj′ə·lāt, hem′ə-) *n.* A flagellate protozoan parasitic in the blood.

he·mo·glo·bin (hē′mə·glō′bin, hem′ə-) *n. Biochem.* The complex respiratory pigment in the red blood corpuscles of vertebrates. It is composed of globin in union with hematin, and serves as a carrier of oxygen, with which it combines freely.

he·moid (hē′moid) *adj.* Resembling blood; hematoid: also spelled *haemoid.*

he·mo·leu·ko·cyte (hē′mə·lōō′kə·sīt, hem′ə-) *n.* A white blood corpuscle. Also **he′mo·leu′·co·cyte.**

he·mo·ly·sin (hē′mə·lī′sin, hem′ə-, hi·mol′ə·sin) *n. Biochem.* A substance contained or formed in the blood and having the power to liberate hemoglobin from the red blood corpuscles.

he·mol·y·sis (hi·mol′ə·sis) *n.* Dissolution or breakdown of red blood corpuscles with liberation of their contained hemoglobin: also called *hematolysis.* — **he·mo·lyt·ic** (hē′mə·lit′ik, hem′ə-) *adj.*

he·mo·phil·i·a (hē′mə·fil′ē·ə, -fil′yə, hem′ə-) *n. Pathol.* A disorder characterized by profuse and excessive bleeding even from slight injuries: typically affecting only males, who inherit it as a sex–linked genetic factor transmitted through the mother; the bleeder's disease. Also spelled *haemophilia.* [<NL <Gk. *haima* blood + *philia* fondness]

he·mo·phil·i·ac (hē′mə·fil′ē·ak, hem′ə-) *n.* One afflicted with hemophilia; a bleeder. Also **he′mo·phile** (-fil).

he·mo·phil·ic (hē′mə·fil′ik, hem′ə-) *adj.* **1** Pertaining to hemophilia. **2** Thriving in blood, as certain bacteria.

he·mo·pho·bi·a (hē′mə·fō′bē·ə, hem′ə-) *n.* A morbid fear of blood: also *hemaphobia, hematophobia.* — **he′mo·pho′bic** *adj.*

hem·op·ty·sis (hem·op′tə·sis) *n. Pathol.* Bleeding from the lungs or bronchial tubes. [<HEMO- + *ptysis* spitting <Gk. *ptyein* spit]

hem·or·rhage (hem′ər·ij, hem′rij) *n.* Discharge of blood from a ruptured blood vessel. — *v.i.* **hem·or·rhaged, hem·or·rhag·ing** To bleed copiously. Also spelled *haemorrhage.* [<L *haemorrhagia* <Gk. *haimorrhagia* < *haima* blood + -*rhagia* < *rhēgnynai* burst] — **hem·or·rhag·ic** (hem′ə·raj′ik) *adj.*

hem·or·rhoid (hem′ə·roid) *n. Often pl.* A swollen mass of varicose veins in the rectal mucous membrane: also called (in the plural) *piles.* Also spelled *haemorrhoid.* [<F <L <Gk. *haimorrhoides* (*phlebes*) bleeding (veins) < *haima* blood + *rheein* flow] — **hem·or·rhoi·dal** (hem′ə·roid′l) *adj.*

he·mo·sta·sia (hē′mə·stā′zhə, -zhē·ə, hem′ə-) *n.* **1** Congestion of blood in a part. **2** The checking of hemorrhage. Also **he·mos·ta·sis** (hi·mos′tə·sis). [<NL <Gk. *haima* blood + *stasis* a standing]

he·mo·stat (hē′mə·stat, hem′ə-) *n. Med.* A device or drug for checking the flow of blood.

he·mo·stat·ic (hē′mə·stat′ik, hem′ə-) *adj. Med.*

1 Stopping the flow of blood. **2** Preventive of bleeding. —*n.* A hemostat.

he·mo·ther·a·py (hē′mə·ther′ə·pē, hem′ə-) *n. Med.* The treatment of disease by the administration of blood or blood preparations: also called *hematotherapy.*

he·mo·tho·rax (hē′mə·thôr′aks, -thō′raks, hem′ə-) *n.* Effusion of blood into the chest.

he·mo·thy·mi·a (hē′mə·thī′mē·ə, hem′ə-) *n. Psychiatry* A morbid craving for blood; impulse to murder. [< NL < Gk. *haima* blood + *thymos* passion < *thyein* rage] —**he′mo·thy′mic** *adj.*

hemp (hemp) *n.* **1** A tall, annual Asian herb (*Cannabis sativa*) of the mulberry family, with small green flowers and a tough bark; Indian hemp. **2** The tough and strong fiber obtained from this plant, used for cloth and cordage. **3** A narcotic prepared from the plant, as bhang or hashish. **4** *Colloq.* The hangman's rope. —**Bengal, Bombay, Madras,** or **sunn hemp** See SUNN. [OE *henep*]

hemp agrimony A coarse European herb (*Eupatorium cannabinum*) resembling the boneset of the United States.

hemp dogbane See INDIAN HEMP (def. 2).

hemp·en (hemp′pən) *adj.* **1** Made of hemp. **2** Of or pertaining to hemp.

hemp nettle A common weed (*Galeopsis tetrahit*) of the mint family, having stems covered with prickly deflexed bristles and leaves hairy on both sides.

HEMP
(Plant 4 to 8 feet tall)

hemp·seed (hemp′sēd′) *n.* The seed of hemp.

hem·stitch (hem′stich′) *n.* The ornamental finishing of the inner edge of a hem, made by pulling out several threads adjoining it and drawing the cross-threads together in groups by successive stitches. —*v.t.* To embroider with a hemstitch. —**hem′stitch′er** *n.*

hen (hen) *n.* **1** The mature female of the common domestic fowl. **2** Any female bird. **3** The female of the lobster and certain fishes. [OE *henn*]

hen-and-chickens (hen′ən·chik′ənz) *n.* A plant which propagates by means of offshoots, runners, and other ground parts, as the ground ivy and the European houseleek.

A B C

HEMSTITCH
A. Threads pulled.
B. Cross-threads drawn together at one edge.
C. Cross-threads drawn together at both edges.

hen·bane (hen′bān′) *n.* A poisonous, Old World herb (*Hyoscyamus niger*) of the nightshade family, with sticky, malodorous foliage and reddish-brown flowers: the source of hyoscyamine.

hen·bit (hen′bit′) *n.* **1** A low herb (*Lamium amplexicaule*) of the mint family; deadnettle. **2** The ivy-leaved speedwell (*Veronica hederaefolia*). [Trans. of MLG *hoenderbeet*]

hence (hens) *adv.* **1** Away from this place. **2** In the future. **3** From this cause or source; consequently; therefore. See synonyms under THEREFORE. —*interj.* Depart! [ME *hennes* < *henne* (OE *heonan* from here) + -*s,* adverbial suffix]

hence·forth (hens′fôrth′, -fōrth′, hens′fôrth′, -fōrth′) *adv.* From this time on. Also **hence′for′ward** (-fôr′wərd).

hench·man (hench′mən) *n. pl.* ·**men** (-mən) **1** A servile assistant. **2** A faithful follower. **3** A male servant. See synonyms under ACCESSORY. [ME *henxstman* < OE *hengst* horse + *man* a groom]

hen·coop (hen′kōōp, -kōōp) *n.* A cage or crib for confining poultry.

hen·dec·a·gon (hen·dek′ə·gon) *n.* A plane figure, with eleven sides and eleven angles: also spelled *endecagon.* [< Gk. *hendeka* eleven + -GON] —**hen·de·cag·o·nal** (hen′də·kag′ə·nəl) *adj.*

hen·dec·a·syl·lab·ic (hen′dek·ə·si·lab′ik) *adj.*

Containing eleven syllables. —*n.* A metrical line containing eleven syllables: also **hen′dec·a·syl′la·ble.** [< L *hendecasyllabus* < Gk. *hendekasyllabos* + -IC]

hen·di·a·dys (hen·dī′ə·dis) *n.* In rhetoric, the use of two words connected by a conjunction to express the same idea as a single word with a qualifier; as, with *might and main* instead of by *main strength.* [< LL < Gk. *hen dia dyoin* one through two]

hen·e·quen (hen′ə·kin) *n.* **1** A tough fiber obtained from the leaves of the Mexican plant *Agave fourcroydes,* or from the related *A. sisalana;* Mexican sisal. **2** The plant from which this fiber is obtained. Also **hen′e·quin.** [< Sp. < Taino]

hen·na (hen′ə) *n.* **1** An Oriental shrub or small tree (*Lawsonia inermis*) with lance-shaped, entire leaves. **2** A cosmetic preparation from the leaves of this plant: used for dyeing the fingernails, hair, etc. **3** The color of this dye, varying from reddish-orange to coppery-brown. [< Arabic *henna*]

hen·ner·y (hen′ər·ē) *n. pl.* ·**ner·ies** A place where hens are kept.

hen·o·the·ism (hen′ō·thē·iz′əm) *n.* The doctrine that ascribes supreme power to some one of several gods in turn; also, the belief in a special supreme god for each region, race, or nation. [< Gk. *hen* one + THEISM] —**hen′o·the′ist** *n.* —**hen′o·the·is′tic** *adj.*

hen·peck (hen′pek′) *v.t.* To harass or domineer over (the husband): said of wives.

hen·roost (hen′rōōst′) *n.* A place where poultry roost.

hen·ry (hen′rē) *n. Electr.* The practical unit of inductance; the inductance of a circuit in which the variation of the current at the rate of one ampere per second induces an electromotive force of one volt. [after Joseph *Henry*]

hep (hep) *adj. U.S. Slang* Aware; informed; cognizant: often with *to.* [? Alter. of STEP, as pronounced in counting time for marching]

he·par (hē′pär) *n. Med.* A liver-brown alkaline sulfide formed by fusing an alkaline carbonate, as potash, with sulfur: used as an antacid and alterative: also called *liver of sulfur.* [< Med. L < Gk. *hēpar* the liver]

hep·a·rin (hep′ə·rin) *n. Biochem.* A polysaccharide found in liver and other animal tissues and having the power to prevent the coagulation of blood: used in medicine and surgery. [< Gk. *hēpar* liver + -IN]

he·pat·ic (hi·pat′ik) *adj.* **1** Of, pertaining to, or resembling the liver. **2** Occurring in, affecting, or acting upon the liver. **3** *Bot.* Pertaining to or resembling a class of plants, the liverworts. **4** Liver-colored. —*n.* **1** A drug acting on the liver. **2** A liverwort. Also **he·pat′i·cal.** [< L *hepaticus* < Gk. *hēpatikos* < *hēpar* the liver]

he·pat·i·ca (hi·pat′ə·kə) *n. pl.* ·**cas** or ·**cae** (-sē) Any of a genus (*Hepatica*) of small perennial herbs of the crowfoot family, with three-lobed leaves and delicate, variously colored flowers; the liverleaf. [< NL < L *hepaticus* of the liver]

hepatic cells The functional cells of the liver.

hep·a·ti·tis (hep′ə·tī′tis) *n. Pathol.* Inflammation of the liver.

hep·a·ti·za·tion (hep′ə·tə·zā′shən, -tī·zā′-) *n.* The conversion of any tissue into a substance resembling liver. Also *Brit.* **hep′a·ti·sa′tion.**

hepato- *combining form* Pertaining to the liver: *hepatogenic.* Also, before vowels, **hepat-.** [< Gk. *hēpar, hēpatos* the liver]

hep·a·to·gen·ic (hep′ə·tō·jen′ik) *adj.* Produced by or proceeding from the liver. Also **hep·a·tog·e·nous** (hep′ə·toj′ə·nəs).

hep·a·to·pan·cre·as (hep′ə·tō·pan′krē·əs) *n. Zool.* A glandular organ of many invertebrates, supposed to have the function of the liver and the pancreas.

hep·a·tos·co·py (hep′ə·tos′kə·pē) *n.* **1** Divination by inspecting the livers of animals. **2** Inspection of the liver.

hep·cat (hep′kat′) *n. Slang* A jazz expert or enthusiast. [< HEP + CAT (def. 11)]

He·phaes·tus (hi·fes′təs) In Greek mythology, the ugly, lame god of fire and of metallurgy; son of Zeus and Hera, and, in the *Odyssey,* the husband of Aphrodite: identified with the Roman *Vulcan:* also called the *Lemnian smith.* Greek

He·phais′tos. Also **He·phæs′tus.**

Hep·ple·white (hep′əl·hwit) *adj.* Denoting an English style of furniture characterized by graceful curves and light, slender woodwork: developed in the reign of George III. [after G. *Hepplewhite,* died 1786, the designer]

HEPPLEWHITE CHAIR

hepta- *combining form* Seven: *heptachord.* Also, before vowels, **hept-.** [< Gk. *hepta-* < *hepta* seven]

hep·ta·chlor (hep′tə·klôr, -klōr) *n.* A chlorinated hydrocarbon, $C_{10}H_7Cl_7$, toxic to humans and used as an insecticide.

hep·ta·chord (hep′tə·kôrd) *n. Music* **1** A diatonic octave considered without the upper note. **2** An instrument with seven strings. **3** The interval of the major seventh. [< Gk. *heptachordos* < *hepta-* seven + *chordē* a string]

hep·tad (hep′tad) *adj.* Having a combining power of seven; of or belonging to a heptad. —*n.* **1** A collection of seven things. **2** *Chem.* An atom, radical, or element that has a valence of seven. [< Gk. *heptas, -ados* a group of seven]

hep·ta·glot (hep′tə·glot) *adj.* Written in seven languages. —*n.* A book in seven languages.

hep·ta·gon (hep′tə·gon) *n.* A plane figure having seven sides and seven angles. —**hep·tag·o·nal** (hep·tag′ə·nəl) *adj.*

hep·ta·he·dron (hep′tə·hē′drən) *n.* A solid bounded by seven plane faces. —**hep′ta·he′dral** (-drəl) *adj.*

hep·tam·er·ous (hep·tam′ər·əs) *adj.* **1** Having seven parts. **2** *Bot.* Having seven members in each whorl: said of flowers. [< HEPTA- + -MEROUS]

HEPTAGON

hep·tam·e·ter (hep·tam′ə·tər) *n.* A verse of seven feet or measures.

hep·tane (hep′tān) *n.* A colorless, inflammable, liquid hydrocarbon of the methane series, C_7H_{16}: used as a solvent and in the determination of the octane number of motor fuels. [< HEPT(A)- + -ANE²]

hep·tan·gu·lar (hep·tang′gyə·lər) *adj.* Having seven angles.

hep·tar·chy (hep′tär·kē) *n. pl.* ·**chies 1** A group of seven kingdoms or governments; specifically, the seven Saxon kingdoms in England (fifth to ninth century). **2** Government by seven persons.

hep·ta·stich (hep′tə·stik) *n.* A heptameter.

Hep·ta·teuch (hep′tə·tōōk, -tyōōk) *n.* The first seven books of the Old Testament. [< HEPTA- + Gk. *teuchos* book]

hep·tode (hep′tōd) *n. Electronics* A seven-electrode vacuum tube containing an anode, cathode, control electrode, and four additional electrodes ordinarily acting as grids. [< HEPT(A)- + -ODE¹]

her (hûr) *pron.* The objective case of *she.* —*pronominal adj.* Belonging or pertaining to a female person, animal, etc.: the form of the possessive case of the pronoun *she* when used attributively: *her* garden. [OE *hire*]

He·ra (hir′ə) In Greek mythology, the queen of the gods and goddess of women and marriage, sister and wife of Zeus: identified with the Roman *Juno.* Also spelled *Here.*

her·ald (her′əld) *n.* **1** Formerly, an officer whose business it was to bear messages, challenges, etc., from a sovereign or from the commander of an army. **2** *Brit.* An official whose duty and profession it is to grant or record arms, trace and record genealogies, record the creation of peers, etc. **3** An official bearer of important tidings; hence, any bearer of news. **4** A precursor; harbinger. —*v.t.* To announce publicly; usher in; proclaim. See synonyms under ANNOUNCE, PRECEDE. [< OF *heralt,* ? < OHG *heren* call]

—he·ral·dic (hi·ral′dik) *adj.*
Synonyms (*noun*): ambassador, courier, forerunner, harbinger, pioneer, precursor.
her·ald·ry (her′əl·drē) *n.* **1** The science that treats of blazoning or describing armorial bearings, etc. **2** An emblazonment. **3** The symbolism of heraldic bearings. **4** The ceremony attendant upon heraldry.
herb (ûrb, hûrb) *n.* **1** A seed plant devoid of woody tissue which dies completely, or down to the ground, after flowering. **2** A herbaceous plant valued for its medicinal qualities or for its smell or taste. **3** *Rare* Herbage. [<L *herba* grass, herbage]
herb·a·ceous (hûr·bā′shəs) *adj.* **1** Pertaining to, having the character of, or similar to herbs. **2** Having the semblance, color, or structure of an ordinary leaf.
herb·age (ûr′bij, hûr′-) *n.* **1** Herbs collectively. **2** Pasturage. **3** The leaves, stems, and other succulent parts of herbaceous plants.
herb·al (hûr′bəl, ûr′-) *adj.* Of or pertaining to herbs. —*n.* **1** A book containing classifications and descriptions of herbs or plants. **2** A herbarium.
herb·al·ist (hûr′bəl·ist, ûr′-) *n.* **1** A dealer in herbs, especially medicinal herbs. **2** Formerly, one skilled in the study of herbs or plants. Also **herb′ist.**
her·bar·i·um (hûr·bâr′ē·əm) *n.* *pl.* **·bar·i·ums** or **·bar·i·a** (-bâr′ē·ə) **1** A collection of dried plants scientifically arranged. **2** A room or building containing such a collection. [<LL <L *herba* grass]
herb·a·ry (hûr′bə·rē) *n.* *pl.* **·ries** A garden containing only herbs or vegetables.
herb-ben·net (ûrb′ben′it, hûrb′-) *n.* A European herb of the rose family (*Geum urbanum*); avens. [<OF *herbe beneite* <Med. L *herba benedicta*, lit., blessed herb]
her·bi·cide (hûr′bə·sīd) *n.* A weed-killer.
her·bif·er·ous (hûr·bif′ər·əs) *adj.* Producing herbs or vegetation. [<L *herbifer* <*herba* grass + *ferre* bear]
her·bi·vore (hûr′bə·vôr, -vōr) *n.* A herbivorous animal.
her·biv·o·rous (hûr·biv′ər·əs) *adj.* **1** Feeding on vegetable matter. **2** Belonging to a group or division (*Herbivora*) of mammals (now generally called *Ungulata*) that feed mainly on herbage, as cows, horses, camels, etc. [<L *herba* grass + -VOROUS]
herb-Par·is (ûrb′par′is, hûrb′-) *n.* A European herb of the lily family (*Paris quadrifolia*) closely allied to the wakerobin: also called *paris.*
herb-rob·ert (ûrb′rob′ərt, hûrb′-) *n.* A species of cranebill or geranium (*Geranium robertianum*).
herb·y (ûr′bē, hûr′-) *adj.* **1** Of the nature of herbs. **2** Relating to or abounding with herbs.
her·cu·le·an (hûr·kyōō′lē·ən, hûr′kyə·lē′ən) *adj.* Possessing or requiring great strength; laborious; mighty.
Her·cu·les (hûr′kyə·lēz) **1** In Greek mythology, the son of Alcmene and Zeus, renowned for his strength and endurance: also spelled *Heracles.* **2** Any man of great size and strength. **3** A large northern constellation. See CONSTELLATION. — **labors of Hercules** A series of twelve great tasks imposed by Eurystheus upon Hercules, because of the hostility of Hera: the killing of the Nemean lion; the killing of the Hydra of Lerna; the capture of the Erymanthian boar; the capture of the stag of Ceryneia; the killing of the man-eating birds of Stymphalus; the cleansing of the stables of Augeas; the capture of the Cretan bull; the capture of the horses of Diomedes; the theft of the girdle of Hippolyta; the capture of the cattle of Geryon; the theft of the apples of the Hesperides; and the capture of Cerberus from Hades.
Her·cu·les-club (hûr′kyə·lēz·klub′) *n.* **1** One of several small trees or shrubs, as the prickly ash, the spikenard, etc.: also called *angelicatree.* **2** A large variety of the common gourd.
her·cy·nite (hûr′sə·nīt) *n.* A vitreous, black iron spinel, $FeAl_2O_4$, crystallizing in the isometric system. [<L *Hercynia* (*silva*) the Bohemian (forest) + -ITE[1]]
herd[1] (hûrd) *n.* **1** A number of animals feeding or traveling together. **2** A large crowd; especially, the common people; rabble. —*v.t.* & *v.i.* To bring or group together in or as in a herd. [OE *heord*]
herd[2] (hûrd) *n.* *Scot.* & *Brit. Dial.* A herds-

man; shepherd. —*v.t.* To care for or drive (sheep, cattle, etc.).
-herd *combining form* Herdsman: *swineherd, cowherd,* etc. [OE *hirde* herdsman]
herd·book (hûrd′book′) *n.* A record of the pedigrees of cattle in important herds.
herd·er (hûr′dər) *n.* **1** A herdsman. **2** *U.S.* One who looks after a herd of cattle or a flock of sheep.
her·dic (hûr′dik) *n.* A carriage, usually two-wheeled, with low-hung body, back entrance, and side seats. [after Peter *Herdic,* 1824–88, its inventor]
here (hir) *adv.* **1** In or at this place. **2** To this place; hither. **3** At this point of time or stage of proceedings; now. **4** At a place indicated. **5** In the present life. ✦ Homophone: *hear.* [OE *hēr*]
here·a·bout (hir′ə·bout′) *adv.* About this place; in this vicinity. Also **here′a·bouts′.**
here·af·ter (hir·af′tər, -äf′-) *adv.* **1** At some future time. **2** From this time forth. **3** In the state of life after death; after the present life. —*n.* A future state or existence. [OE *hēræfter*]
here·at (hir·at′) *adv.* **1** At this time. **2** By reason of this; because of this.
here·by (hir·bī′) *adv.* **1** By means or by virtue of this. **2** Near this.
he·red·i·ta·bil·i·ty (hə·red′i·tə·bil′ə·tē), **he·red·i·ta·ble** (hə·red′i·tə·bəl), etc. See HERITABILITY, etc.
her·e·dit·a·ment (her′ə·dit′ə·mənt) *n.* *Law* That capable of being inherited. — **corporeal hereditament** Property of such a nature as to be cognizable by the senses and in, any way connected with land. — **incorporeal hereditament** An inheritable right issuing out of and annexed to some corporeal inheritance, as the right of way over another's land, or the right to the use of running water. [<Med. L *hereditamentum* <L *heres, -edis* an heir]
he·red·i·tar·y (hə·red′ə·ter′ē) *adj.* **1** *Law* Passing, capable of passing, or that must necessarily pass by inheritance, or from an ancestor, to an heir; deriving by inheritance. **2** Passing naturally from parent to child. **3** *Biol.* Transmitted or transmissible directly from a plant or animal to its offspring: distinguished from *congenital.* **4** Endowed with certain qualities derived from an ancestor. **5** Of or pertaining to heredity or inheritance. [<L *hereditarius* <*hereditas.* See HEREDITY.] — **he·red′i·tar′i·ly** *adv.* — **he·red′i·tar′i·ness** *n.*
he·red·i·tist (hə·red′ə·tist) *n.* An adherent of the theory that individuality is determined by heredity.
he·red·i·ty (hə·red′ə·tē) *n.* *pl.* **·ties 1** Transmission of physical characteristics, mental traits, tendency to disease, etc., from parents to offspring. **2** *Biol.* The tendency manifested by an organism to develop in the likeness of a progenitor, because of the transmission of genetic factors in the reproductive process. **3** The sum total of an individual's inherited characteristics. [<F *hérédité* <L *hereditas, -tatis* an inheritance <*heres, -edis* an heir]
Her·e·ford (her′ə·fərd) *n.* One of a breed of cattle, commonly red with a white face and markings. [from HEREFORD]
here·in (hir·in′) *adv.* In this; in this place, circumstance, etc. [OE *hērinne*]
here·in·af·ter (hir′in·af′tər, -äf′-) *adv.* In a subsequent part of this (document).
here·in·be·fore (hir′in·bi·fôr′, -fōr′) *adv.* In a preceding part of this (document).
here·in·to (hir·in′tōō) *adv.* Into this.
here·of (hir·uv′) *adv.* **1** Of this; about this. **2** From this; because of this.
here·on (hir·on′, -ôn′) *adv.* On this; hereupon.
her·e·si·arch (hi·rē′sē·ärk, her′ə·sē·ärk′) *n.* The chief exponent of a heresy. See synonyms under HERETIC. [<LL *haeresiarcha* <Gk. *hairesiarchēs* <*hairesis* a sect + *archēs* leader <*archein* rule]
her·e·sy (her′ə·sē) *n.* *pl.* **·sies 1** A doctrinal view or belief at variance with the recognized tenets of a system, church, school, or party. **2** The maintenance of such a doctrinal view or tenet. **3** *Obs.* Any course of conduct or instruction tending to produce dissension and schism in the church. [<OF *heresie,* ult. <Gk. *hairesis* a sect, lit., a choosing <*hairesthai* choose]
her·e·tic (her′ə·tik) *n.* **1** One who holds a heresy. **2** An actual or former member of a

church, or one whose allegiance is claimed by it, who holds religious opinions contrary to the fundamental doctrines and tenets of that church. [<MF *hérétique* <LL *haereticus* <Gk. *hairetikos* able to choose <*hairesthai* choose] — **he·ret·i·cal** (hə·ret′i·kəl) *adj.* — **he·ret′i·cal·ly** *adv.*
Synonyms: dissenter, heresiarch, nonconformist, schismatic. Etymologically, a *heretic* is one who takes or chooses his own belief, instead of the belief of his church; a *schismatic* is primarily one who produces a split or rent in the church. A *heretic* differs in doctrine from the religious body with which he is connected; a *schismatic* differs in doctrine or practice, or in both. A *heretic* may be reticent, or even silent; a *schismatic* introduces divisions. A *heresiarch* is the author of a heresy or the leader of a heretical party, and is thus at once a *heretic* and a *schismatic.* With advancing ideas of religious liberty, the odious sense once attached to these words is largely modified, and *heretic* is often used playfully. *Dissenter* and *nonconformist* are terms specifically applied to English subjects who hold themselves aloof from the Church of England.
here·to (hir·tōō′) *adv.* To this time, place, or end.
here·to·fore (hir′tə·fôr′, -fōr′) *adv.* Previously; hitherto.
here·un·to (hir′un·tōō′) *adv.* To this; hereto; up to this point, or to this end or result.
here·up·on (hir′ə·pon′, -pôn′) *adv.* Upon this; following immediately after this.
here·with (hir·with′, -with′) *adv.* Along with this.
Her·ing window (her′ing) *Optics* An apparatus for demonstrating color contrast by means of a shutter whose two openings contain samples of the desired colors. [after Ewald *Hering,* 1834–1918, German psychologist]
her·i·ot (her′ē·ət) *n.* In feudal law, a tribute or contribution to the lord of the manor from the heir of a tenant upon succeeding his father. [OE *heregeatwa* <*here* army + *geatwa* equipment]
her·i·ta·ble (her′ə·tə·bəl) *adj.* **1** That can be inherited. **2** Capable of inheriting. [<OF <*heriter* inherit] — **her′i·ta·bil′i·ty** *n.* — **her′i·ta·bly** *adv.*
her·i·tage (her′ə·tij) *n.* **1** Property that is or can be inherited. **2** Any condition or culture which is allotted or handed down to one, as by ancestors. **3** The chosen people of God, as the Israelites or the Christian elect. [<OF <*heriter* inherit <L *hereditare* <*heres, -edis* an heir]
her·i·tor (her′ə·tər) *n.* An inheritor. [<AF *heriter,* OF *heritier* <L *hereditarius.* See HEREDITARY.] — **her′i·trix** (-triks) *n. fem.*
herl (hûrl) *n.* **1** A barb of a feather, used in making artificial flies for angling. **2** A fly so made. [<MLG *herle* a fiber]
her·ma (hûr′mə) *n.* *pl.* **·mae** (-mē) or **·mai** (-mī) In ancient Greece, a rough square stone, broader at the base than above, with a sculptured head of Hermes or some other deity on the top, placed in front of houses and to mark boundaries of estates, streets, etc.; also, such a stone with the head of a mortal. [<L <Gk. *Hermēs* Hermes]
her·maph·ro·dite (hûr·maf′rə·dīt) *adj.* **1** Having the characteristics of both sexes; bisexual. **2** *Naut.* Denoting a type of ship which is square-rigged forward and schooner-rigged aft. **3** *Bot.* Monoclinous. —*n.* **1** *Biol.* A plant or animal organism that combines the characteristics of both sexes. **2** *Naut.* A hermaphrodite brig. [<L *hermaphroditus* <Gk. *hermaphroditos,* after *Hermaphroditos* HERMAPHRODITUS] — **her·maph′ro·dit′ic** (-dit′ik) or **·i·cal** *adj.* — **her·maph′ro·dit′i·cal·ly** *adv.* — **her·maph′ro·dit·ism, her·maph′ro·dism** *n.*
hermaphrodite brig A brigantine.
her·me·neu·tics (hûr′mə·nōō′tiks, -nyōō′-) *n.* The science or art of interpretation, especially of the Scriptures. [<Gk. *hermēneutikē* (*technē*) interpretive (art) <*hermēneutēs* an interpreter] — **her′me·neu′tic** or **·ti·cal** *adj.* — **her′me·neu′ti·cal·ly** *adv.*
Her·mes (hûr′mēz) In Greek mythology, the son of Zeus and Maia, messenger and herald of the gods, god of science, eloquence, and cunning, patron of thieves, travelers, and commerce, protector of boundaries, and guide of souls on their way to Hades: identified with the Roman *Mercury.*

her·met·ic (hûr·met'ik) *adj.* Made airtight; impervious to air and liquids, as by fusion. Also **her·met'i·cal.** [<Med. L *hermeticus* < *Hermes (Trismegistus)*; with ref. to alchemy]

her·met·i·cal·ly (hûr·met'ik·lē) *adv.* So as to be airtight or impervious.

hermetic art Alchemy.

her·mit (hûr'mit) *n.* **1** A person who abandons society and lives alone, especially for religious contemplation; an anchorite. **2** A molasses cooky containing spice and sometimes raisins. **3** *Obs.* A beadsman. Also *Obs.* **ermyte.** [<OF *hermite* <L *eremita* <Gk. *erēmitēs* < *erēmia* a desert < *erēmos* solitary] — **her·mit'ic** or **·i·cal** *adj.* — **her·mit'i·cal·ly** *adv.* — **her'mit·like'** *adj.*

her·mit·age (hûr'mə·tij) *n.* The retreat or cell of a hermit. See synonyms under CLOISTER.

hermit crab A decapod crustacean (genus *Pagurus*) usually having a soft abdomen which for protection is thrust into the empty shell of a univalve mollusk.

hermit thrush A thrush (*Hylocichla guttata*) of eastern North America, having a spotted breast and reddish tail.

hermit warbler A brilliantly colored songbird (*Dendroica occidentalis*) of the Sierra Nevadas.

her·ni·a (hûr'nē·ə) *n. Pathol.* Protrusion, as of an intestine or other organ from its normal position; rupture. [<L] — **her'ni·al** *adj.*

hernio- *combining form* Hernia: *hernioplasty.* [<L *hernia*]

her·ni·o·plas·ty (hûr'nē·ə·plas'tē) *n. Surg.* An operation for the radical cure of hernia. — **her'ni·o·plas'tic** *adj.*

her·ni·ot·o·my (hûr'nē·ot'ə·mē) *n. pl.* **·mies** *Surg.* The operation of cutting down to and severing the constricting part in strangulated hernia.

hern·shaw (hûrn'shô) *n.* **1** A heron. **2** *Her.* The representation of a heron or similar bird. [Var. of HERONSEW]

he·ro (hir'ō) *n. pl.* **·roes** **1** A person distinguished for valor, fortitude, or bold enterprise; anyone regarded as having displayed great courage or exceptionally noble qualities. **2** In classical mythology, the son of a god or goddess and a mortal: the eponymous founder of a city or family, as Cadmus, was sometimes locally worshiped as a hero. **3** The central male figure of a poem, play, romance, or the like; in modern fiction, the male character in whom the principal interest centers. [<L *heros* <Gk. *hērōs*]

Her·od (her'əd), 73?–4 B.C., king of Judea 37–4 B.C.: known as **Herod the Great.** — **Herod Agrippa I,** 10? B.C.–A.D. 44, king of Judea 41–44. — **Herod Antipas,** 4 B.C.–A.D. 39, tetrarch of Galilee; son of Herod the Great. — **He·ro·di·an** (hi·rō'dē·ən) *adj. & n.*

He·rod·o·tus (hi·rod'ə·təs), 484?–424? B.C., Greek historian: called the "Father of History."

he·ro·ic (hi·rō'ik) *adj.* **1** Characteristic of a hero; brave; noble: *heroic* courage; a *heroic* death. **2** Of or involving the heroes of antiquity: a *heroic* age. **3** Describing heroes and their deeds: a *heroic* poem. **4** Like heroic poetry in style; magniloquent; highflown: *heroic* language. **5** Bold; daring; extreme: a *heroic* attempt. **6** In art and sculpture, larger than life and smaller than colossal. Also **he·ro'i·cal.** —*n.* **1** *pl.* Heroic verse. **2** *pl.* High-flown or extravagant language, sentiments, or actions: Cut out the *heroics.* — **he·ro'i·cal·ly** *adv.*

heroic age The mythical age when heroes and demigods lived on earth.

heroic couplet An English verse form consisting of two riming lines of iambic pentameter, often epigrammatic in character.

heroic poetry Epic poetry, especially as dealing with heroes and demigods.

heroic verse A verse form adapted to heroic or lofty themes, and used especially in epic and dramatic poetry, as the hexameter in Greek and Latin, the hendecasyllabic ottava rima in Italian, the Alexandrine in French drama, and the heroic couplet and blank verse, with various other combinations of iambic verse, in English.

her·o·in (her'ō·in) *n.* Diacetylmorphine, $C_{21}H_{23}O_5N$, a white, odorless, crystalline derivative of morphine with a bitter taste: a powerful, habit-forming narcotic of which the manufacture is prohibited in the United States. [<G]

her·o·ine (her'ō·in) *n. fem.* **1** A woman of heroic character. **2** The chief female character in a story, play, or the like. [<L *heroina* <Gk. *hērōinē,* fem. of *hērōs* a hero]

her·o·ism (her'ō·iz'əm) *n.* **1** Heroic character or qualities. **2** A heroic act. See synonyms under FORTITUDE, PROWESS.

her·on (her'ən) *n.* A long-necked and long-legged wading bird; specifically, one of a family (*Ardeidae*) of birds with 12 stiff tail feathers and the outer toe as long as or longer than the inner. See EGRET. — **great blue heron** A large, bluish-gray American heron (*Ardea herodias*). [<OF *hairon,* ult. <Gmc.]

GREAT BLUE HERON
(About 4 feet tall)

her·on·bill (her'ən·bil') *n.* Any of a genus (*Erodium*) of annual or perennial herbs with toothed leaves, widely distributed in temperate regions. Also **her·on's-bill', her'ons·bill'.**

her·on·ry (her'ən·rē) *n. pl.* **·ries** A place where herons congregate and breed.

he·ro-wor·ship (hir'ō·wûr'ship) *n.* Enthusiastic or extravagant admiration for heroes or other distinguished personages.

her·pes (hûr'pēz) *n. Pathol.* An inflammatory eruption on the skin, forming groups of small blisters which tend to spread. [<L <Gk. *herpēs* < *herpein* creep]

herpes sim·plex (sim'pleks) Cold sore.

herpes zos·ter (zos'tər) Shingles.

her·pet·ic (hûr·pet'ik) *adj.* Relating to or like herpes. Also **her·pet'i·cal.** — **her·pe·tism** (hûr'pə·tiz'əm) *n.*

her·pe·tol·o·gy (hûr'pə·tol'ə·jē) *n.* The branch of zoology that treats of reptiles and amphibians. [<Gk. *herpeton* a reptile <*herpein* creep + -LOGY] — **her·pe·to·log·i·cal** (hûr'pə·tə·loj'i·kəl) *adj.* — **her'pe·tol'o·gist** *n.*

her·ring (her'ing) *n. pl.* **·rings** or **·ring** **1** A small food fish (*Clupea harengus*) frequenting moderate depths of the North Atlantic in great numbers. The young are canned as sardines and the adults are smoked or salted. **2** A fish allied to the herring (family *Clupeidae*), especially *Clupea cacruteus* of Pacific waters and the pilchard or sardine. [OE *hæring*]

her·ring·bone (her'ing·bōn') *adj.* Similar to the spinal structure of a herring; especially, laid out, arranged, woven, or stitched in rows of parallel lines with the lines of adjoining rows slanting in opposite directions: said of masonry, textiles, etc. — *n.* Anything made or arranged in such a pattern. — *v.t. & v.i.* **·boned, ·bon·ing** **1** To ornament with or arrange in herringbone stitches, patterns, etc. **2** To walk on skis (up an incline) with the toes pointed out: so called from the herringbone tracks made by the skis.

her·ring·bone-work (her'ing·bōn·wûrk') *n.* **1** Masonry in which the stones are laid slanting in opposite directions alternately. **2** A cross-stitch made of rows of diagonal stitches.

herring gull A small American gull (*Larus argentatus smithsonianus*) of the Atlantic coast that feeds on herring.

her·ry (her'ē) *v.t. Scot.* To harry. — **her'ri·ment** (-mənt) or **her'ry·ment** *n.*

hers (hûrz) *pron.* **1** Belonging or pertaining to her: the form of the possessive case of *she* when used in predicative position, without a following noun, or after *of*: That book is *hers;* those eyes of *hers.* **2** The things or persons belonging to or relating to her: John's story is funnier than *hers;* She provides for herself and *hers.* [OE *hire* + *-s* (after *his*)]

her·self (hər·self') *pron.* **1** Reflexive form of *her.* **2** Emphatic or intensive form of *she.*

hertz (hûrts) *n. Physics* A unit of electromag-

netic wave frequency, equal to one cycle per second. [after Heinrich *Hertz*]

hes·i·tan·cy (hez'ə·tən·sē) *n. pl.* **·cies** **1** The act or manner of one who falters or is uncertain; hesitation; vacillation. **2** A faltering in speech. Also **hes'i·tance.** See synonyms under DOUBT.

hes·i·tant (hez'ə·tənt) *adj.* Hesitating; uncertain. [<L *haesitans, -antis,* ppr. of *haesitare.* See HESITATE.] — **hes'i·tant·ly** *adv.*

hes·i·tate (hez'ə·tāt) *v.i.* **·tat·ed, ·tat·ing** **1** To be uncertain as to decision or action; waver. **2** To pause. **3** To be slow or faltering in speech. [<L *haesitatus,* pp. of *haesitare,* freq. of *haerere* stick] — **hes'i·ta'tive** *adj.* — **hes'i·ta'tive·ly** *adv.*

hes·i·ta·tion (hez'ə·tā'shən) *n.* **1** The act of hesitating; a delay caused by indecision or uncertainty. **2** A state of uncertainty; doubt. **3** A pause or faltering in speech.

Hes·pe·ri·an (hes·pir'ē·ən) *adj.* **1** *Poetic* In or of the west; western. **2** Of or pertaining to the Hesperides. [<L *hesperius* <Gk. *hesperios* western]

hes·per·i·din (hes·per'ə·din) *n.* A glycoside, $C_{28}H_{34}O_{15}$, obtained from citrus fruits as a white, tasteless, odorless, crystalline powder. [<HESPERIDIUM + -IN]

hes·per·id·i·um (hes'pə·rid'ē·əm) *n. pl.* **·i·a** (-ē·ə) *Bot.* An indehiscent, many-celled, fleshy fruit with a spongy or leathery rind; a berry with a hard rind, as the lemon. [<NL <Gk. *Hesperides* the Hesperides; with ref. to the golden apples]

Hes·per·or·nis (hes'pər·ôr'nis) *n.* One of a genus (*Hesperornis*) of extinct swimming birds from the Cretaceous of Kansas with pointed teeth and serpentlike jaws. The type species was six feet long. [<NL <Gk. *hesperos* western + *ornis* a bird]

Hes·pe·rus (hes'pər·əs) The evening star, especially Venus. Also **Hes'per.** [<L <Gk. *Hesperos*]

hes·sian (hesh'ən) *n.* A strong coarse hempen cloth. [from *Hesse*]

Hes·sian (hesh'ən) *n.* **1** A native or citizen of Hesse. **2** A soldier from Hesse hired by the British to fight in the American Revolution. **3** *pl.* Hessian boots. — *adj.* Of or pertaining to Hesse or its inhabitants.

Hessian boots High boots, reaching to the knees, worn early in the 19th century.

Hessian fly A small blackish fly or midge (*Mayetiola* or *Phytophaga destructor*) with red lines on the upper surface, very destructive to wheat, barley, and rye: supposedly introduced into America by the Hessian troops during the Revolutionary War.

hess·ite (hes'īt) *n.* A metallic, lead-gray, silver telluride, Ag_2Te, crystallizing in the isometric system. [after G. H. *Hess,* 1802–50, Swiss chemist]

hes·son·ite (hes'ən·īt) See ESSONITE.

Hes·van (hes'van) See HESHWAN.

Hes·y·chast (hes'i·kast) *n.* A quietist; especially, one of a mystic and quietistic sect that originated in the Greek Church among the monks of Mt. Athos in the 14th century. See ILLUMINATI. [<Med. L *hesychasta* <Gk. *hēsychastēs* < *hēsychazein* be still < *hēsychos* quiet] — **hes'y·chas'tic** *adj.*

he·tae·ra (hi·tir'ə) *n. pl.* **·tae·rae** (-tir'ē) In ancient Greece, one of a class of professional entertainers or courtesans: composed of slaves, freedwomen, and foreigners. Also **he·tai·ra** (hi·tī'rə). [<Gk. *hetaira,* fem. of *hetairos* a companion]

he·tae·rism (hi·tir'iz·əm) *n.* **1** Promiscuous concubinage. **2** The theory that this condition characterized all primitive society. Also **he·tai·rism** (hi·tī'riz·əm).

hetero- *combining form* Other; different: *heterogeneous:* opposed to *homo-*. Also, before vowels, **heter-.** [<Gk. *hetero-* < *heteros* other]

het·er·o·cer·cy (het'ər·ə·sûr'sē) *n. Zool.* Inequality of the caudal fin of a fish produced by the extension of the vertebral column upward and consequent enlargement of one of the lobes, as in sharks, sturgeons, etc. [<HETERO- + Gk. *kerkos* tail] — **het'er·o·cer'cal** (-sûr'kəl) *adj.*

het·er·o·chro·mat·ic (het'ər·ə·krō·mat'ik) *adj.*

Of, pertaining to, characterized by, or designating an array or pattern of different colors. Also **het'er·o·chrome'** (-krōm'), **het'er·o·chro'·mous** (-krō'məs).

het·er·o·chro·mo·some ·(het'ər·ə·krō'mə·sōm) *n.* **1** Sex chromosome. **2** Any aberrant chromosome.

het·er·o·chron·ic (het'ər·ə·kron'ik) *adj. Med.* Occurring at irregular or abnormal times: said of an illness. Also **het·er·och·ro·nous** (het'ər·ok'rə·nəs).

het·er·och·tho·nous (het'ər·ok'thə·nəs) *adj.* Foreign; not indigenous or native. [< HETERO- + Gk. *chthōn* land, country]

het·er·o·clite (het'ər·ə·klīt') *n.* **1** *Gram.* A word that varies or is irregular in inflection; particularly, a noun inflected from more than one stem, as Latin *domus*. **2** A person or thing deviating from the ordinary or correct form. —*adj.* **1** Anomalous. **2** *Gram.* With an irregular inflection: also **het'er·o·clit'ic** (-klit'ik) or **·i·cal.** [< F *hétéroclite* < L *heteroclitus* < Gk. *heteroklitos* irregular < *hetero-* other + *klinein* bend]

het·er·o·cy·clic (het'ər·ə·sī'klik, -sik'lik) *adj. Chem.* Pertaining to or designating an organic ring compound containing one or more types of atoms other than carbon: opposed to *homocyclic.*

het·er·o·cyst (het'ər·ə·sist') *n. Bot.* A cell of doubtful function, larger than its neighbors, developed in some blue-green algae.

het·er·o·dox (het'ər·ə·doks') *adj.* **1** At variance with a commonly accepted doctrine in religion. **2** In general, at variance with any commonly accepted doctrine or opinion: opposed to *orthodox.* [< Gk. *heterodoxos* < *hetero-* other + *doxa* opinion]

het·er·o·dyne (het'ər·ə·dīn') *adj. Telecom.* Describing the manner by which oscillations of a frequency almost equal to that of the transmitted waves are developed in a separate tube of a radio receiving set, the two oscillations forming beats. —*v.t.* **·dyned, ·dyn·ing** To effect such oscillations.

het·er·oe·cism (het'ə·rē'siz·əm) *n. Bot.* A type of parasitism associated with certain fungi and characterized by the development of different stages of the parasite ·on different hosts: also called *metoxeny.* [< HETER(O)- + Gk. *oikos* house] —**het·er·oe'cious** (-shəs) *adj.*

het·er·o·gam·ete (het'ər·ə·gam'ēt, -gə·mēt') *n. Biol.* A gamete sexually or otherwise differentiated: also called *anisogamete.*

het·er·og·a·mous (het'ər·og'ə·məs) *adj.* **1** *Bot.* Bearing flowers that are sexually of two kinds: opposed to *homogamous.* **2** *Biol.* Having unlike gametes: opposed to *isogamous.*

het·er·og·a·my (het'ər·og'ə·mē) *n.* The character or condition of being heterogamous. — **het·er·o·gam·ic** (het'ər·ə·gam'ik) *adj.*

het·er·o·ge·ne·ous (het'ər·ə·jē'nē·əs) *adj.* Consisting of dissimilar elements or ingredients. [< Med. L *heterogeneus* < Gk. *heterogenēs* < *hetero-* other + *genos* kind] —**het·er·o·ge·ne·i·ty** (het'ər·ə·jə·nē'ə·tē) *n.* —**het·er·o·ge'ne·ous·ly** *adv.*
Synonyms: confused, conglomerate, discordant, dissimilar, mingled, miscellaneous, mixed, nonhomogeneous, unhomogeneous, unlike, variant, various. Substances quite *unlike* are *heterogeneous* as regards each other. A *heterogeneous* mixture is one whose constituents are not only *unlike* in kind, but unevenly distributed; cement is composed of substances such as lime, sand, and clay, which are *heterogeneous* as regards each other, but the cement is said to be homogeneous if the different constituents are evenly *mixed* throughout, so that any one portion of the mixture is exactly like any other. A substance may fail of being homogeneous and yet not be *heterogeneous*, in which case it is said to be *non-homogeneous* or *unhomogeneous*; a bar of iron that contains flaws, air bubbles, etc., or for any reason is not of uniform structure and density throughout, even if no foreign substance be *mixed* with the iron, is said to be *non-homogeneous.* A *miscellaneous* mixture may or may not be *heterogeneous*; if the objects are alike in kind, but different in size, quality, use, etc., and without special order or relation, the collection is *miscellaneous*; if the objects differ in kind, such a mixture is also, and more strictly, *heterogeneous.* See COMPLEX. *Antonyms:* alike, homogeneous, identical, like, pure, same, similar, uniform.

het·er·o·gen·e·sis (het'ər·ə·jen'ə·sis) *n. Biol.* **1** Asexual generation. **2** Metagenesis. —**het·er·o·ge·net·ic** (het'ər·ə·jə·net'ik) *adj.*

het·er·og·o·ny (het'ər·og'ə·nē) *n.* **1** *Bot.* The state of having flowers differing in kind, length of stamens and styles: opposed to *homogony.* **2** Metagenesis. —**het·er·og'o·nous** *adj.* —**het·er·og'o·nous·ly** *adv.*

het·er·o·grade (het'ər·ə·grād') *adj. Stat.* Having or denoting a variable magnitude, grade, or intensity. Compare HOMOGRADE.

het·er·og·ra·phy (het'ər·og'rə·fē) *n.* **1** Orthography in which the same letter represents different sounds in different words or syllables, as *c* in *camp* and *cent.* **2** Spelling varying from the standard everyday usage. —**het·er·o·graph·ic** (het'ər·ə·graf'ik) or **·i·cal** *adj.*

het·er·og·y·nous (het'ə·roj'ə·nəs) *adj. Biol.* Having the females differentiated into sexual and neuter forms, as a bee or an ant.

het·er·o·ki·ne·sis (het'ər·ə·ki·nē'sis, -kī-) *n. Biol.* A differential distribution of the sex chromosomes in meiosis. —**het·er·o·ki·net·ic** (-net'ik) *adj.*

het·er·ol·o·gy (het'ə·rol'ə·jē) *n. Biol.* **1** Difference of structure as compared with a type; lack of homology; abnormality. **2** Analogy between unrelated organisms: contrasted with *homology* between related organisms. —**het·er·ol'o·gous** (-gəs) *adj.*

het·er·ol·y·sis (het'ə·rol'ə·sis) *n. Biochem.* Dissolution effected by an outside agent; specifically, the destruction of a cell by external enzymes or lysins: opposed to *autolysis.* —**het·er·o·lyt·ic** (het'ə·rə·lit'ik) *adj.*

het·er·om·er·ous (het'ə·rom'ər·əs) *adj. Bot.* Possessing parts that differ in number, form, or composition, as the whorls of a flower: opposed to *isomerous.*

het·er·o·mor·phic (het'ər·ə·môr'fik) *adj. Biol.* **1** Deviating from the normal form or standard type. **2** Undergoing complete metamorphosis, as certain insects. Also **het'er·o·mor'phous** (-fəs). —**het·er·o·mor'phism** (-fiz·əm) *n.*

het·er·on·o·mous (het'ə·ron'ə·məs) *adj.* **1** *Biol.* Divergent or differing from the common type: said of one of a series of related things, as the somites of an arthropod. **2** Subject to the law or rule of another. [< HETERO- + Gk. *nomos* law, rule] —**het·er·on'o·my** *n.*

het·er·o·nym (het'ər·ə·nim') *n.* **1** A word spelled like another, but having a different sound and meaning, as *bass* (a male voice) and *bass* (a fish). **2** Another name for the same thing; especially, one of two precisely equivalent terms in different languages: "Water" is a *heteronym* of the French word "eau." Compare HOMONYM. [< HETER(O)- + Gk. *onyma*, var. of *onoma* name; on analogy with *synonym*]

het·er·on·y·mous het'ə·ron'ə·məs) *adj.* **1** Relating to, having the nature of, or containing a heteronym. **2** *Optics* Appearing on the side opposite to that of the eye that produced it: said of double images of an object when the image seen by the right eye is on the left side and vice versa.

het·er·o·pha·sia (het'ər·ə·fā'zhə, -zhē·ə) *n. Psychiatry* A form of aphasia in which the patient says or writes one thing when he means another. [< NL < Gk. *hetero-* other + *-phasia* < *phanai* speak]

het·er·o·phyl·lous (het'ər·ə·fil'əs) *adj. Bot.* Having leaves that differ, as in size, form, or function, on the same plant. —**het'er·o·phyl'ly** (-fil'ē) *n.*

het·er·o·pla·sia (het'ər·ə·plā'zhə, -zhē·ə) *n. Pathol.* The development of abnormal tissue by diseased action where the cells of the abnormal tissues differ from the normal ones. [< NL]

het·er·o·plas·ty (het'ər·ə·plas'tē) *n. Surg.* A plastic operation in which the portion grafted is taken from an organism or person other than the patient.

het·er·o·po·lar (het'ər·ə·pō'lər) *adj. Electr.* Designating an unequal distribution of an electric charge: opposed to *homopolar.*

het·er·o·sex·u·al (het'ər·ə·sek'shoo·əl) *adj.* **1** Pertaining to or characterized by sexual attraction toward a person of the opposite sex. **2** *Biol.* Pertaining to different sexes. —*n.* A heterosexual person. Compare BISEXUAL, HOMOSEXUAL. —**het·er·o·sex'u·al·i·ty** (-sek'shoo·al·ə·tē) *n.*

het·er·o·sis (het'ə·rō'sis) *n. Biol.* Exceptional vigor of plant and animal organisms through crossbreeding between two different types; hybrid vigor. [< NL < Gk. *heterōsis* alteration < *heteros* other]

het·er·os·po·rous (het'ə·ros'pər·əs, het'ər·ə·spôr'əs, -spō'rəs) *adj. Bot.* **1** Producing both large and small spores. **2** Producing spores of more than one sex. Also **het·er·o·spor·ic** (het'ər·ə·spôr'ik, -spor'ik).

het·er·o·stat·ic (het'ər·ə·stat'ik) *adj. Electr.* Measuring by the aid of a charge other than the one to be measured: applied to an electrometer, thus distinguishing it from an *idiostatic* one.

het·er·os·ty·ly (het'ər·ə·stī'lē) *n. Bot.* A difference in the length of the styles in flowers of the same species, whereby certain plants insure cross-pollination. Also **het·er·o·sty'lism** (-stī'liz·əm). [< HETERO- + STYLE[2]]

het·er·o·tax·is (het'ər·ə·tak'sis) *n.* **1** *Pathol.* A malformation caused by displacement or lateral transposition of organs. **2** Any irregular or abnormal arrangement of parts, as of rock strata, geographic features, etc.: opposed to *homotaxis.* Also **het·er·o·tax·i·a** (-tak'sē·ə), **het·er·o·tax'y** (-tak'sē). [< NL < Gk. *hetero-* other + *taxis* arrangement] —**het'er·o·tac'tic** (-tak'tik), **het'er·o·tax'ic** (-tak'sik) *adj.*

het·er·o·thal·lism (het'ər·ə·thal'iz·əm) *n. Bot.* A form of sexual differentiation in certain fungi, as the bread mold (*Rhizopus nigricans*), characterized by the possession of two types of mycelia whose hyphae conjugate to produce zygotes. [< HETERO- + Gk. *thallos* sprout] —**het'er·o·thal'lic** *adj.*

het·er·o·to·pi·a (het'ər·ə·tō'pē·ə) *n. Pathol.* A misplacement of an organ, or a growth abnormally situated in the body. Also **het·er·ot'o·py** (-ot'ə·pē). [< NL < Gk. *hetero-* other + *topos* place] —**het'er·o·top'ic** (-top'ik), **het'er·ot'o·pous** (-ot'ə·pəs) *adj.*

het·er·ot·ri·chous (het'ə·rot'rə·kəs) *adj.* **1** Having unlike cilia. **2** Of or pertaining to an order (*Heterotrichida*) of ciliate infusorians. [< HETERO- + Gk. *trichos* hair]

het·er·ot·ro·phy (het'ə·rot'rə·fē) *n.* **1** Any disorder of nutrition. **2** *Bot.* An abnormal manner of obtaining nourishment: applied to certain plants having no true root hairs, and obtaining all nourishment by a fungus, the hyphae of which closely invest the roots and take the place of root hairs. [< HETERO- + Gk. *trophē* nurture < *trephein* feed] —**het'er·o·troph'ic** (-ə·trof'ik, -trōf'ik) *adj.*

het·er·o·tro·pi·a (het'ər·ə·trō'pē·ə) *n. Pathol.* A deviation of the eyes in which the two visual lines so diverge that binocular vision is impaired; a form of strabismus. [< HETERO- + -TROP(E) + -IA]

het·er·o·typ·ic (het'ər·ə·tip'ik) *adj. Biol.* Denoting a form of meiosis in which the chromosomes split at an early period, the halves remaining united at the ends and opening out into rings, each of which represents two chromosomes: contrasted with *homeotypic.* Also **het'er·o·typ'i·cal.**

het·er·ou·si·a (het'ə·rōō'sē·ə, -rou'sē-) *n.* Difference in substance or essence: a theological term. [< LGk. *heterousia* < *heterousios* of different essence < *heteros* other + *ousia* being] —**het'er·ou'si·ous, het'er·ou'si·an** *adj.*

het·er·o·zy·go·sis (het'ə·rə·zi·gō'sis, -zi-) *n. Biol.* The descent of an organism from two different races, species, or varieties; hybridism. [< NL]

het·er·o·zy·gote (het'ər·ə·zī'gōt, -zig'ōt) *n. Biol.* A hybrid resulting from the fusion of two gametes that bear different allelomorphs of the same character and which in consequence does not breed true; a heterozygous individual: contrasted with *homozygote.*

het·er·o·zy·gous (het'ər·ə·zī'gəs) *adj. Biol.* Designating that condition of an individual in which any given genetic factor has been derived from only one of the two generating gametes.

het·man (het'mən) *n. pl.* **·mans** (-mənz) The chieftain of the Cossacks. See ATAMAN. [< Polish < G. *hauptmann* head man, captain]

heu·land·ite (hyōō'lən·dīt) *n.* A pearly, variously colored, transparent, hydrous silicate of aluminum and calcium, belonging to the group of zeolites. [after H. *Heuland,* 19th c. English mineralogist]

heu·ris·tic (hyōō·ris'tik) *adj.* **1** Aiding or guiding in discovery. **2** Inciting to find out. [< Gk. *heuriskein* find out]

hew (hyōō) *v.* **hewed, hewn** or **hewed, hew·ing** *v.t.*

1 To make or shape with or as with blows of an ax: often with *out.* **2** To cut with blows of an ax, sword, etc.; chop; hack. **3** To bring down or fell with or as with blows of an ax: usually with *down.* —*v.i.* **4** To make cutting and repeated blows, as with an ax or sword. ✦ Homophone: *hue.* [OE *hēawan*] —**hew'er** *n.*

hex (heks) *U.S. Colloq. v.t.* To bewitch; enchant. —*n.* **1** A witch; sorceress; specifically, a witch doctor. **2** A bewitchment; enchantment: to put a *hex* on one. [< G *hexe* witch]

hexa- *combining form* Six: *hexagon.* Also, before vowels, **hex-.** [< Gk. *hexa-* < *hex* six]

hex·a·ba·sic (hek'sə·bā'sik) *adj. Chem.* **1** Denoting an acid in which six hydrogen atoms can be replaced by a basic radical. **2** Any compound containing six atoms of a univalent metal or their equivalent.

hex·a·chlo·ro·eth·ane (hek'sə·klôr'ō·eth'ān, -klōrō-) *n. Chem.* A white crystalline trichloride of carbon, C_2Cl_6, used in the manufacture of explosives, dyestuffs, disinfectants, and smoke screens.

hex·a·chlo·ro·phene (hek'sə·klôr'ə·fēn) *n.* An antibacterial agent used in some soaps.

hex·a·chord (hek'sə·kôrd) *n. Music* A series of six tones with a half-step between the third and fourth tones, and whole steps between the others.

hex·ad (hek'sad) *n.* **1** The number six. **2** A group or series of six. [< LL *hexas, hexadis* the number six < Gk. *hexas, hexados*]

hex·a·em·er·on (hek'sə·em'ər·on) *n.* **1** A period of six days, usually applied specifically to those of the creation. **2** An account of the creation. Also **hex'a·hem'er·on** (-hem'-). [< LL < Gk. *hexaēmeros* the six days' work, lit., of six days < *hex* six + *hēmera* day] —**hex'a·em'er·ic, hex'a·hem'er·ic** *adj.*

hex·a·gon (hek'sə·gon) *n.* A figure with six sides and six angles. [< L *hexagonum* < Gk. *hexagonos* six-cornered < *hex* six + *gōnia* angle]

hex·ag·o·nal (hek·sag'ə·nəl) *adj.* **1** Having the form of a hexagon. **2** Having its section a hexagon; six-sided. — **hex·ag'o·nal·ly** *adv.*

hexagonal system A crystal system having three equal axes intersecting in one plane at 60°, and one of different length intersecting the others at right angles. See CRYSTAL.

HEXAGON

hex·a·gram (hek'sə·gram) *n.* One of various figures formed by six intersecting lines, especially one made by completing the equilateral triangles based on the sides of a regular hexagon.

hex·a·he·dron (hek'sə·hē'drən) *n. pl.* **·drons** or **·dra** (-drə) A solid bounded by six plane faces. [< NL] —**hex'a·he'dral** *adj.*

hex·a·hy·drate (hek'sə·hī'drāt) *n. Chem.* A hydrate with six molecules of water.

hex·a·hy·dric (hek'sə·hī'drik) *adj. Chem.* Composed of six hydroxyl groups.

hex·am·er·ous (hek·sam'ər·əs) *adj.* **1** *Bot.* Having a six-parted floral whorl: generally written 6-*merous.* **2** *Zool.* Having six parts or divisions; arranged in sixes or multiples of sixes, as in corals. Also **hex·am'er·al.** [< HEXA- + -MEROUS]

hex·am·e·ter (hek·sam'ə·tər) *n.* A verse of six feet or measures, especially the dactylic verse of the Greek and Latin epics. —*adj.* Having six metrical feet in a verse. [< L < Gk. *hexametros*] —**hex·a·met·ric** (hek'sə·met'rik), **hex·am'e·tral** (-ə·trəl), **hex·a·met'ri·cal** *adj.*

hex·ane (hek'sān) *n. Chem.* One of five isomers, C_6H_{14}, of the methane series of saturated hydrocarbon compounds; especially, a volatile colorless oil contained in petroleum. [< HEX(A)- + -ANE]

hex·an·gu·lar (hek·sang'gyə·lər) *adj.* Having six angles.

hex·a·pod (hek'sə·pod) *adj.* Having six feet. —*n.* One of the true or six-legged insects (*Hexapoda*). [< Gk. *hexapous, hexapodos* six-footed] —**hex·ap·o·dous** (hek·sap'ə·dəs) *adj.*

hex·ap·o·dy (hek·sap'ə·dē) *n. pl.* **·dies** Six metrical feet taken together, or a verse or line con-

sisting of six feet.

hex·arch·y (hek'sär·kē) *n. pl.* **·arch·ies** **1** A group of six states. **2** Government by six persons.

hex·a·stich (hek'sə·stik) *n.* In Greek or Latin prosody, a section or stanza of six lines. Also **hex·as·ti·chon** (heks·as'tə·kon). [< L *hexastichus* < Gk. *hexastichos* < *hex* six + *stichos* line] —**hex·a·stich'ic** *adj.*

hex·a·style (hek'sə·stil) *adj. Archit.* Having a front with six columns, as a temple. [< L *hexastylus* < Gk. *hexastylos* having six columns in front < *hex* six + *stylos* column] —**hex'a·sty'los** (-stī'ləs) *n.*

hex·en·be·sen (hek'sən·bā'zən) *n.* A compact broomlike growth of various trees; witches'-broom. [< G, witches'-broom]

hex·oc·ta·he·dron (heks·ok'tə·hē'drən) *n.* A form of the isometric crystal system consisting of 48 similar triangular planes. [< HEX- + OCTA- + -HEDRON] —**hex·oc'ta·he'dral** (-drəl) *adj.*

hex·one (hek'sōn) *n. Chem.* A colorless liquid ketone compound, $C_6H_{12}O$, used as a solvent for gums and resins.

hex·o·san (hek'sə·san) *n. Biochem.* Any of a group of polysaccharides which hydrolyze to a hexose. [< HEXOSE + -AN]

hex·ose (hek'sōs) *n. Biochem.* Any simple sugar containing six oxygen atoms to the molecule.

hex·tet·ra·he·dron (heks·tet'rə·hē'drən) *n.* A variety of crystal in the isometric system consisting of 24 similar triangular faces. —**hex·tet'ra·he'dral** (-drəl) *adj.*

hex·yl (hek'səl) *n. Chem.* The univalent hydrocarbon radical, C_6H_{13}, of hexane and its derivatives.

hex·yl·re·sor·ci·nol (hek'səl·rə·zôr'sə·nōl) *n.* A yellowish-white compound, $C_{12}H_{18}O_2$, with a pungent odor and astringent taste, used as a germicide and antiseptic.

hey (hā) *interj.* An exclamation of surprise, pleasure, inquiry, incitement, etc., or calling for attention. [Imit.]

hey·day (hā'dā') *n.* **1** The time of greatest vitality and vigor. **2** Exuberant spirits; wildness. [Prob. < HIGH DAY]

hey·day (hā'dā') *interj.* An exclamation of surprise, joy, etc. [< Du. *heida!* hey there!]

Hg *Chem.* Mercury (symbol Hg). [L *hydrargyrum*]

H-hinge (āch'hinj') *n.* A hinge with long, narrow leaves, which, when open, resembles the letter H. See illustration under HINGE.

H-hour (āch'our') *n.* The hour appointed for a military operation to begin: also called *zero hour.*

hi (hī) *interj. Colloq.* Hello: an exclamation of greeting. [Contraction of *how are you?*]

hi·a·tus (hī·ā'təs) *n. pl.* **·tus·es** or **·tus** **1** A gap or opening; break, with a part missing; lacuna; interruption. **2** A pause or break due to the concurrence of two separate vowels without an intervening consonant.

Hi·a·wath·a (hī'ə·woth'ə, -wôth'ə, hē'ə-) Mohawk chief and venerated counselor of the League of the Iroquois, shortly before the advent of the Europeans: name used by Longfellow for the hero of his poem *Hiawatha.*

hi·ba·chi (hi·bä'chē) *n. pl.* **·chis** A charcoal-burning brazier, used for cooking food, etc. [< Jap. *hi* fire + *bachi* bowl]

hi·ber·nac·le (hī'bər·nak'əl) *n.* Hibernaculum (def. 3). [< L *hibernaculum* < *hibernare* pass the winter + -CULUM dim. suffix]

hi·ber·nac·u·lum (hī'bər·nak'yə·ləm) *n. pl.* **·la** (-lə) *Biol.* **1** An encysted winter polyzoon bud capable of germinating in the spring. **2** A hibernating case constructed of foreign materials by certain insects. A den or shelter occupied by a hibernating animal. [< NL]

hi·ber·nal (hī·bûr'nəl) *adj.* Pertaining to winter; wintry. [< L *hibernalis* < *hibernus* wintry]

hi·ber·nate (hī'bər·nāt) *v.i.* **·nat·ed, ·nat·ing** **1** To pass the winter, especially in a torpid state, as certain animals. **2** To pass the time in seclusion. [< L *hibernatus,* pp. of *hibernare* < *hiems* winter] —**hi'ber·na'tion** *n.*

hi·bis·cus (hi·bis'kəs, hī-) *n.* Any of various malvaceous herbs, shrubs and trees of the genus *Hibiscus,* having large, showy flowers of various colors. [< L < Gk. *hibiskos* mallow]

hic·cup (hik'əp) *n.* A short, catching sound,

caused by spasmodic contraction of the diaphragm and windpipe. —*v.i.* **1** To have the hiccups; make a hiccup. —*v.t.* **2** To utter with hiccups. Also **hic·cough** (hik'əp): also spelled *hickup.* [Imit.]

hick (hik) *n. Slang* One characterized by countrified manners, speech, or dress. [Alter. of RICHARD]

hick·ey (hik'ē) *n. pl.* **·eys** **1** *Mech.* A T-shaped device of iron pipe used for bending a conduit. **2** *Electr.* A small fitting employed to secure an electric fixture to an outlet box. [Origin unknown]

hick·o·ry (hik'ər·ē) *n. pl.* **·ries** **1** An American tree of the walnut family (genus *Carya*), yielding an edible nut and having hard, tough, heavy wood: also called *shellbark.* **2** Something made of this wood, as a walking stick or a switch. **3** A strong cotton fabric, usually twilled: used for men's trousers and shirts.

hick·wall (hik'wôl) *n.* The green woodpecker. [ME *hyghwhele*; prob. imit.]

hid (hid) Past tense and alternative past participle of HIDE. —*adj.* Hidden.

hid·den (hid'n) Past participle of HIDE. —*adj.* Put out of sight; secreted; not known; unseen: also *hid.* See synonyms under SECRET.

hide (hīd) *v.* **hid, hid·den** or **hid, hid·ing** *v.t.* **1** To put or keep out of sight; conceal. **2** To keep secret; withhold from knowledge: to *hide* one's fears. **3** To block or obstruct the sight of; keep from view: The smoke *hid* the buildings. **4** To turn away, as from shame or so as to ignore: *Hide* not thy face from me. —*v.i.* **5** To keep oneself out of sight; remain concealed. —**to hide out** To go into hiding. [OE *hȳdan*] —**hid'er** *n.*

Synonyms: bury, cloak, conceal, cover, disguise, dissemble, entomb, inter, mask, overwhelm, screen, secrete, suppress, veil. Hide is the general term, including all the rest, signifying to put out of sight or beyond ready observation or approach; a thing may be *hidden* by intention, by accident, or by the imperfection of the faculties of the one from whom it is *hidden.* As an act of persons, to *conceal* is always intentional; one may *hide* his face in anger, grief, or abstraction; he *conceals* his face when he fears recognition. A house is *hidden* by foliage; the bird's nest is artfully *concealed.* A thing is *covered* by putting something over or around it, by accident or design; it is *screened* by putting something before it, always for protection from observation, inconvenience, attack, censure, etc. In the figurative use, a person may *hide* honorable feelings; he *conceals* an evil or hostile intent. Compare BURY, MASK, PALLIATE. *Antonyms:* admit, advertise, avow, betray, confess, disclose, discover, disinter, divulge, exhibit, exhume, expose, manifest, promulgate, publish, raise, reveal, show, tell, uncover, unmask, unveil.

hide (hīd) *n.* **1** The skin of a large animal, as an ox, especially as material for leather. **2** The human skin: humorously or with contempt. —*v.t.* **hid·ed, hid·ing** **1** To whip; flog severely. **2** To remove the hide from. [OE *hȳd* skin]

hide (hīd) *n.* In Old English law, a measure of land, originally about 120 acres, considered enough to support a family. [OE *hīd, hīgid*]

hide-and-seek (hīd'ən·sēk') *n.* A children's game in which those who hide are sought by one who is "it." Also **hide'-and-go-seek'.**

hide·bound (hīd'bound') *adj.* **1** Obstinately fixed in opinion; narrow-minded; bigoted. **2** Having the bark so closely adherent that it impedes growth: said of trees.

hid·e·ous (hid'ē·əs) *adj.* Shocking or dreadful, especially in looks; ghastly; revolting. See synonyms under FRIGHTFUL, GHASTLY, GRIM. [< AF *hidous,* OF *hideus* < *hisde, hide* fright; ult. origin unknown] —**hid'e·ous·ly** *adv.* —**hid'e·ous·ness** *n.*

hide-out (hīd'out') *n.* A place of concealment and safety; hiding place.

hid·ing (hī'ding) *n.* The act of secreting, or the state of being secreted; concealment.

hid·ing (hī'ding) *n. Colloq.* A flogging.

hiding power **1** The opacity of a paint. **2** The ability of a paint to reduce the contrast of a black-and-white surface.

hi·dro·sis (hi·drō'sis) *n.* **1** *Med.* The formation

and excretion of sweat. **2** *Pathol.* **a** Any skin disease characterized by sweating. **b** Profuse sweating. [<NL <Gk. *hidroein* sweat <*hidrōs* sweat]

hi·drot·ic (hi·drot′ik) *n.* A drug or other substance to promote sweating; a sudorific. [<Med. L *hidroticus* <Gk. *hidrōtikos*]

hie·la·man (hē′lə·mən) *n.* A shield of wood or bark about 3 feet long and 4 inches wide, used by Australian aborigines. [<native word]

hi·er·arch (hi′ər·ärk) *n.* **1** An ecclesiastical chief ruler. **2** An official of ancient Greece who had charge of the votive offerings in a temple. [<Med. L *hierarcha* <*hierarchēs* <*hieros* sacred + *archos* ruler <*archein* rule]

hi·er·ar·chism (hi′ər·är′kiz·əm) *n.* The principles, character, and rule of a hierarchy. —**hi′er·ar′chist** *n.*

hi·er·ar·chy (hi′ər·är′kē) *n. pl.* **·chies 1** A body of persons, especially ecclesiastics, ranked according to successive orders or classes. **2** Government or rule by a body of ecclesiastics organized in ranks or orders. **3** *Theol.* **a** Any of three ranks of angels. See ANGEL. **b** The body of angels collectively. **4** In science and logic, a series of systematic groups, as kingdoms, classes, orders, families, genera, and species. [<LL *hierarchia* <Gk. *hierarchia* rule of a *hierarch*] —**hi′er·ar′chic, hi′er·ar′chi·cal, hi′er·ar′chal** *adj.*

hi·er·at·ic (hi′ə·rat′ik) *adj.* **1** Of or pertaining to priests; devoted to sacred uses; sacerdotal; consecrated. **2** Of or pertaining to a cursive form of ancient Egyptian hieroglyphs, more complex than the demotic or popular cursive; employed for state papers, rituals, etc. Also **hi′er·at′i·cal.** [<L *hieraticus* <Gk. *hieratikos* of a priest's office <*hieros* sacred]

hi·er·oc·ra·cy (hi′ə·rok′rə·sē) *n. pl.* **·cies** Ecclesiastical rule or supremacy. [<HIERO- + -CRACY] —**hi·er·o·crat·ic** (hi′ər·ə·krat′ik) or **·i·cal** *adj.*

hi·er·o·glyph (hi′ər·ə·glif′, hi′rə·glif′) *n.* **1** Picture writing, especially of the ancient Egyptians: usually in the plural. **2** A character or word supposed to convey a hidden meaning. **3** *pl.* Humorously, illegible handwriting; unintelligible scribbling. Also **hi′er·o·glyph′ic.** [<LL *hieroglyphicus* <Gk. *hieroglyphikos* hieroglyphic <*hieros* sacred + *glyphein* carve] —**hi·er·o·glyph′ic** or **·i·cal** *adj.* —**hi·er·o·glyph′i·cal·ly** *adv.*

hi·er·og·ly·phist (hi′ər·og′lə·fist, hi·rog′-) *n.* One skilled in the art of reading hieroglyphs.

hi·er·o·gram (hi′ər·ə·gram′, hi′rə-) *n.* **1** A sacred writing. **2** A character or symbol of sacred significance.

HIEROGLYPHS (n. def. 1)

hi·er·ol·o·gy (hi′ə·rol′ə·jē, hi·rol′-) *n.* **1** The science of or a treatise on ancient Egyptian writings and inscriptions. **2** The scientific study and comparison of religions. [<HIERO- + -LOGY] —**hi·er·o·log·ic** (hi′ə·r·ə·loj′ik, hi′rə-) or **·i·cal** *adj.* —**hi·er·ol′o·gist** *n.*

hi·er·o·man·cy (hi′ər·ə·man′sē, hi′rə-) *n.* The act of divining by observing things offered in sacrifice.

hi·er·o·phant (hi′ər·ə·fant′, hi·er′-) *n.* **1** In ancient Greece, an official expounder of religious mysteries or rites. **2** One who expounds any esoteric cult or doctrine. [<LL *hierophanta* <Gk. *hierophantes* <*hieros* sacred + *phainein* show] —**hi′er·o·phan′tic** *adj.*

hi·er·o·pho·bi·a (hi′ər·ə·fō′bē·ə) *n.* Morbid fear of sacred and religious things.

hi·er·o·ther·a·py (hi′ər·ə·ther′ə·pē) *n.* Treatment of disease by religious symbolism and exercises. —**hi′er·o·ther′a·pist** *n.*

hi-fi (hi′fi′) *adj.* High-fidelity. —*n.* A radio receiver or phonograph capable of reproducing high-fidelity sound.

hig·gle·dy-pig·gle·dy (hig′əl·dē·pig′əl·dē) *adj.* In a disordered state; jumbled; muddled. —*n.* Great confusion; a jumble. —*adv.* In a confused manner. [<obs. *higle-pigle*, a varied reduplication, ? <*pig*]

high (hi) *adj.* **1** Greatly elevated; lofty. **2** Having a (specified) elevation: an inch *high*. **3** Of or pertaining to an elevated, or inland, district: *High* German. **4** Extending to or performed from a height: *high* jump; *high*

dive. **5** *Geog.* Far from the equator: said of latitudes. **6** Remote; old: *high* antiquity. **7** Of exalted rank or estimation: *high* heaven. **8** Of superior character or kind: *high* art. **9** Important; serious: *high* crimes. **10** Expensive; costly: Rent is *high*. **11** Intensified; of great degree, measure, force, etc.: *high* wind; *high* explosives. **12** Fully advanced or culminated: *high* noon. **13** Haughty; arrogant: *high* words. **14** Strict, as in opinion or doctrine: *high* Tory. **15** Elated; merry: *high* spirits. **16** Complex: usually in the comparative degree: *higher* mathematics, *higher* mammals. **17** Slightly tainted: said of meat. **18** *Music* Acute in pitch; shrill. **19** *Phonet.* Produced with the tongue raised close to the roof of the mouth; close: said of vowel sounds, as the (ē) in *bead*: opposed to *low*. **20** *Mech.* Designating a step-up gear mechanism operating at its greatest speed transmission. **21** *Colloq.* Feeling the effects of liquor, drugs, etc.; intoxicated. —*adv.* **1** To or at a high level, position, degree, etc. **2** At a high manner. **3** At a high pitch. —*n.* **1** A high level, position, etc. **2** *Meteorol.* An anti-cyclone. **3** *Mech.* An arrangement of gears for the greatest speed transmission. —**on high 1** High above. **2** In heaven. [OE *hēah*] —**high′ly** *adv.* —**high′ness** *n.*

Synonyms (adj.): elevated, eminent, exalted, lofty, noble, proud, steep, tall, towering, uplifted. *Deep,* while an antonym of *high* in usage, may apply to the very same distance simply measured in an opposite direction, *high* applying to vertical distance measured from below upward, and *deep* to vertical distance measured from above downward; as, a *deep* valley nestling between *high* mountains. *High* is a relative term signifying greatly raised above any object, base, or surface, in comparison with what is usual, or with some standard; a table is *high* if it exceeds thirty inches; a hill is not *high* at a hundred feet. That is *tall* whose height is greatly in excess of its breadth or diameter, and whose actual height is great for an object of its kind; as, a *tall* tree; a *tall* man; *tall* grass. That is *lofty* which is imposing or majestic in height; we term a spire *tall* with reference to its altitude, or *lofty* with reference to its majestic appearance. That is *elevated* which is raised somewhat above its surroundings; that is *eminent* which is far above them; as, an *elevated* platform; an *eminent* promontory. In the figurative sense, *elevated* is less than *eminent,* and this less than *exalted;* we speak of *high, lofty,* or *elevated* thoughts, aims, etc., in the good sense, but sometimes of *high* feelings, looks, words, etc., in the invidious sense of haughty or arrogant. A *high* ambition may be merely selfish; a *lofty* ambition is worthy and *noble.* Compare HAUGHTY. STEEP¹. *Antonyms:* base, deep, degraded, depressed, dwarfed, inferior, low, mean, short, stunted.

high and dry 1 On shore above the reach of water. **2** Stranded; helpless.

high and low Everywhere.

high and mighty Haughty; imperious.

high·ball¹ (hi′bôl′) *n.* An alcoholic drink, consisting of whisky to which is added soda water, mineral water, or ginger ale, served with ice in a tall glass. [Prob. <HIGH + *ball* whisky glass (in bartender's slang)]

high·ball² (hi′bôl′) *n.* A railroad signal meaning to "go ahead." —*v.i. U.S. Slang* To go at great speed. [From a large ball that could be raised or lowered, once used as a semaphore]

high-born (hi′bôrn′) *adj.* Of noble birth or extraction.

high·boy (hi′boi′) *n.* A tall chest of drawers usually in two sections, the lower a tablelike structure: called *tallboy* in England. See LOWBOY. [Origin unknown]

high-bred (hi′bred′) *adj.* **1** Of a fine pedigree. **2** Characterized by fine manners or good breeding.

high·brow (hi′brou′) *Colloq. n.* A person of cultivated or intellectual tastes: sometimes a term of derision. —*adj.* Of or suitable for such a person: also

HIGHBOY

high′browed′. —**high′brow′ism** *n.*

high-chair (hi′châr′) *n.* A baby's chair provided with an eating tray and standing on tall legs.

high-class (hi′klas′, -kläs′) *adj. Colloq.* Superior; of high quality.

high comedy Comedy presenting the world of polite society and relying chiefly on witty dialog.

high day A holiday; feast day.

higher criticism The scientific and historical study of literature, especially the Bible. Compare LOWER CRITICISM.

higher education 1 College education. **2** Any education beyond secondary schooling, giving advanced opportunities in general or special fields of learning.

high·er-up (hi′ər·up′) *n. Colloq.* A person of superior rank or position.

high explosive 1 A bursting charge that explodes by detonation and with extreme rapidity. **2** A shell charged with high explosive.

high-fa·lu·tin (hi′fə·lōōt′n) *Colloq. adj.* Highflown in manner or speech. —*n.* High-sounding language or writing; pompous speech. Also **high′fa·lu′ting.** [? <HIGH-FLOWN]

high-fi·del·i·ty (hi′fi·del′ə·tē) *adj. Electronics* Capable of reproducing sound with a minimum of distortion: said of certain radio and phonographic equipment: also *hi-fi.*

high-fli·er (hi′fli′ər) *n.* **1** One who or that which flies high. **2** One who goes to extremes or lives extravagantly. Also **high′-fly′er.**

high-flown (hi′flōn′) *adj.* **1** Pretentious. **2** Extravagant in style.

high-fly·ing (hi′fli′ing) *adj.* **1** That flies high, as a bird or airplane. **2** Having pretentious ideas and aims; extravagant in claims or opinions.

high-fre·quen·cy (hi′frē′kwən·sē) *adj. Physics* Of or pertaining to a band of wave frequencies, usually from 3 to 30 megacycles.

high-grade (hi′grād′) *adj.* Of superior quality.

high-hand·ed (hi′han′did) *adj.* Carried on in an overbearing manner.

high-hole (hi′hōl′) *n.* A bird, the flicker. Also **high′-hold′er.**

high jump An athletic event in which the contestants jump for height over a horizontal bar.

high-keyed (hi′kēd′) *adj.* **1** With high musical pitch. **2** Sensitive; spirited.

high·land (hi′lənd) *n.* An elevation of land.

Highland fling A lively Scotch dance.

high life The life of fashionable society.

high·light (hi′lit′) *n.* **1** *pl.* The white or bright spots in a photograph or picture; conversely, the dark spots on the negative of a photograph. **2** A part or detail of special importance or vividness: That touchdown was the *highlight* of the game. —*v.t.* To give special emphasis to; feature.

high living A luxurious manner of life, as in diet.

high mass In the Roman Catholic Church, a mass that is sung and accompanied by full ceremonial.

high-mind·ed (hi′min′did) *adj.* **1** Showing an elevated mind; with lofty ethics or feelings. **2** Haughty; arrogant. —**high′-mind′ed·ly** *adv.* —**high′-mind′ed·ness** *n.*

High·ness (hi′nis) *n.* A title of honor belonging to persons of royal rank: with *His, Her,* or *Your.*

high-oc·tane (hi′ok′tān) *adj.* Having a high octane number, indicating superior antiknock properties.

high-pitched (hi′picht′) *adj.* **1** Shrill. **2** Having a steep slope: said of roofs.

high-pres·sure (hi′presh′ər) *adj.* **1** Having or using a high steam pressure: said of steam engines. **2** Exerting vigorous tactics, pressing; urgent: *high-pressure* salesmanship. —*v.t.* **·sured, ·sur·ing** To persuade or influence by such methods.

high priest A chief priest.

high-proof (hi′prōōf′) *adj.* Containing a high percentage of alcohol: *high-proof* whisky.

high-rise (hi′riz′) *adj.* Describing a relatively tall building or structure. —*n.* A tall building, as a many-storied apartment house: also **high rise.**

high-road (hi′rōd′) *n.* **1** A main road. **2** A common or easy method or course. See synonyms under WAY.

high school See under SCHOOL. —**high′-school′** *adj.*

high seas The unenclosed waters of the ocean or sea, especially those beyond the territorial jurisdiction of any one country or nation.

high-sea·soned (hi′sē′zənd) *adj.* **1** Made rich in

flavor, as by the addition of spices. **2** Racy; sparkling; lively.

high·sign (hī′sīn′) *n. Colloq.* An informing or warning gesture or grimace.

high·sound·ing (hī′soun′ding) *adj.* Ostentatious or imposing in sound or import.

high·spir·it·ed (hī′spir′ə·tid) *adj.* Full of spirit; not brooking restraint.

high·strung (hī′strung′) *adj.* Strung to a high pitch; strained; highly sensitive.

high·tail (hī′tāl′) *v.i. U.S. Slang* To depart hastily, especially in fright.

high tea A substantial afternoon or early evening meal at which meat is served.

high-ten·sion (hī′ten′shən) *adj. Electr.* Pertaining to, characterized by, or operating under very high voltage, usually in excess of 1,000 volts.

high-test (hī′test′) *adj.* **1** Designating a material or substance which has passed severe tests of fitness. **2** Denoting a grade of gasoline with a low boiling-point range.

high tide 1 The maximum tidal elevation of the water at any point; also, the time of its occurrence. **2** Any culminating point in a series of events. Also **high water.**

high time 1 About time; past the proper time. **2** *Slang* An occasion of revelry and excitement.

high-toned (hī′tōnd′) *adj.* **1** Of high principles; honorable. **2** Having a high pitch. **3** *U.S. Colloq.* Aristocratic; fashionable.

high treason Treason against the sovereign or state.

high-up (hī′up′) *adj.* In a high or superior position.

High Veld (velt) See NORTHERN KARROO.

high-water (hī′wô′tər, -wot′ər) *adj.* Pertaining to high tide or to its time or highest elevation.

high·way (hī′wā′) *n.* **1** A public thoroughfare; specified line of travel. **2** A common or open way or course. See synonyms under ROAD, WAY.

high·way·man (hī′wā′mən) *n. pl.* **·men** (-mən) One who practices robbery on the highway. See synonyms under ROBBER.

high wine Grain spirits distilled to a high percentage of alcohol; usually in the plural.

high-wrought (hī′rôt′) *adj.* **1** Skilfully or finely wrought. **2** Highly agitated; impassioned.

hi·jack (hī′jak′) *v.t. U.S. Colloq.* **1** To steal a shipment of (goods, bootleg liquor, etc.) by force. **2** To rob or steal (a truck, etc., carrying such goods). **3** To seize control of (an aircraft) in flight by the threat or use of force and redirect it to a different destination; skyjack. **4** To rob, swindle, etc., by force or coercion. [Origin unknown] **—hi′jack·er** *n.*

hike (hīk) *v.* **hiked, hik·ing** *v.i.* To go on foot, as for pleasure or on a military march; tramp. **—***v.t.* To raise or lift: usually with *up* **—n. 1** A weary journey on foot; a long walk. **2** *Colloq.* An increase: a price *hike.* [? Var. of HITCH]

hi·lar·i·ous (hi·lâr′ē·əs, hī-) *adj.* Boisterously merry; romping. See synonyms under MERRY. **—hi·lar′i·ous·ly** *adv.*

hi·lar·i·ty (hi·lar′ə·tē, hī-) *n.* Boisterous mirth. See synonyms under LAUGHTER. [< OF *hilarité* < L *hilaritas, -tatis* < *hilaris* < Gk. *hilaros* cheerful]

Gregory VII. **— Hil′de·bran·dine** (-din, -dīn) *adj.*

hill (hil) *n.* **1** A conspicuous natural elevation rising above the earth's surface and smaller than a mountain. **2** A heap or pile: a *molehill.* **3** A small mound of earth placed over or around certain plants and tubers. **4** The plants and tubers so surrounded. **— the Hill** Capitol Hill. **—***v.t.* **1** To surround or cover with hills, as potatoes. **2** To form a hill or heap of. **—***adj.* Living in, or coming from, a hilly country: *hill* folk, *hill* songs; also, having many hills: *hill* country. [OE *hyll*]

hill–and–dale (hil′ən–dāl′) *adj.* Designating a method of phonograph recording by making the cuts perpendicular to the surface of the disk, the varying depth corresponding with the sound values. Compare LATERAL–CUT.

hill·bil·ly (hil′bil′ē) *n. pl.* **·lies** *Colloq.* A person inhabiting or from the mountains or a backwoods area, especially of the southern United States: originally a derogatory term. **— adj. Colloq.** Of or characteristic of hillbillies: *hillbilly* music. [< HILL + BILLY²]

hill·er (hil′ər) *n.* **1** One who makes hills about seeding plants. **2** A mechanical appliance for this purpose.

hill mi·na (mī′nə) An East Indian starlinglike bird (*Eulabes religiosa*) that can be taught to speak. Also **hill my′na.**

hill·ock (hil′ək) *n.* A small hill; a mound. **— hill′ock·y** *adj.*

hill·side (hil′sīd′) *n.* The side of a hill; a slope or rise of ground.

hill·top (hil′top′) *n.* The summit of a hill.

hill·y (hil′ē) *adj.* **hill·i·er, hill·i·est 1** Full of hills; swelling; rounded. **2** Like a hill; steep. **— hill′i·ness** *n.*

hilt (hilt) *n.* The handle and guard of a sword or dagger. **— to the hilt** Thoroughly; completely. **—***v.t.* To provide with a hilt. [OE]

hi·lum (hī′ləm) *n. pl.* **·la** (-lə) **1** *Bot.* The scar on a seed indicating its point of attachment; also, the nucleus of a starch grain or the eye of a bean. **2** *Anat.* The fissurelike interval where ducts, vessels, and nerves enter and leave an organ. Also **hi′lus** (-ləs). [< L, a trifle]

him (him) *pron.* The objective case of *he.* [OE]

Hi·ma·la·yas (hi·mäl′yəz, -mä′lə·yəz, him′ə·lā′əz) A mountain chain between Tibet and India and in Nepal; highest point, 29,002 feet, world's highest point. Also **the Hi·ma′·la·ya.** **— Hi·ma′la·yan** *adj.*

hi·ma·ti·on (hi·mat′ē·on) *n. pl.* **·i·a** (-ē·ə) A large square or oblong piece of cloth worn as a mantle by ancient Greeks. [< Gk.]

him·self (him·self′) *pron.* **1** A reflexive and usually intensive or emphatic form of the third-person pronoun, masculine gender. **2** One's normal physical or mental condition; one's consciousness; one's individuality: He stumbled, but soon recovered *himself.* **3** *Dial.* He: used as nominative alone without noun or pronoun: The dagger which *himself* gave Edith was lost; *himself* has said so.

hind¹ (hīnd) *adj.* **hind·er, hind·most** or **hind·er·most** Belonging to the rear. [OE *hindan* behind]

hind² (hīnd) *n.* The female of the red deer or stag. [OE]

hind³ (hīnd) *n. Archaic* A farm laborer; also, a peasant. [OE *hina, higna,* genitive pl. of *higan* domestics]

hind·brain (hīnd′brān′) *n. Anat.* That part of the brain which develops from the posterior or third embryonic vesicle, including the cerebellum and pons, the medulla oblongata and its membranous roof, or the epencephalon, metencephalon, etc.

hin·der¹ (hin′dər) *v.t.* **1** To keep back or delay; check. **2** To prevent; obstruct. **—***v.i.* **3** To be an obstruction or obstacle. [OE *hindrian* < *hinder* behind] **—hin′der·er** *n.*

Synonyms: baffle, balk, bar, block, check, clog, counteract, delay, embarrass, encumber, foil, frustrate, hamper, impede, obstruct, prevent, resist, retard, stay, stop, thwart. A railroad train may be *hindered* by a snowstorm from arriving on time; it may by special order be *prevented* from starting. To *retard* is simply to make slow by any means whatever. To *obstruct* is to *hinder,* or possibly to *prevent* advance or passage by putting something in the way; to *oppose* or *resist* is to *hinder,* or possibly to *prevent,* by directly contrary or hostile action, *resist* being the stronger term and having more suggestion of physical force; *obstructed* roads *hinder* the march of an enemy, though there may be no force strong enough to *oppose* it. Compare EMBARRASS, IMPEDE, LIMIT, PROHIBIT, RESTRAIN, SUSPEND. *Antonyms:* see synonyms for HELP, QUICKEN.

hind·er² (hīn′dər) *adj.* Pertaining to or constituting the rear. [OE]

hind·gut (hīnd′gut′) *n. Anat.* The embryonic structure from which the colon develops.

Hin·di (hin′dē) *n.* The principal language of northern India, belonging to the Indic branch of the Indo-Iranian languages. It includes **Western Hindi,** of which Hindustani is the major dialect, and **Eastern Hindi.** [< Hind. *hindī* < *Hind* India < Persian < OPersian *Hindu* land on the Indus < Skt. *sindhu* river, the Indus]

hind·most (hīnd′mōst′) *adj.* Situated in the extreme rear. Also **hind′er·most** (hīn′dər-).

hind·quar·ter (hīnd′kwôr′tər) *n.* One of the two back parts into which the sagittal half of a carcass of a quadruped is usually divided, including a hind leg.

hin·drance (hin′drəns) *n.* **1** The act of hindering. **2** An obstacle or check. See synonyms under IMPEDIMENT.

hind·sight (hīnd′sīt′, hīn′sīt′) *n.* **1** Insight into the nature and difficulties of a situation after the event or after the difficulties have been resolved. **2** The rear sight of a gun or rifle.

Hin·du (hin′dōō) *n.* **1** A member of the native Aryan race of India. **2** Any native of India who professes Hinduism. **— adj.** Of or pertaining to the people or religion of India. Also *Hindoo.* [< Persian *Hindū* < *Hind.* See HINDI.]

Hin·du·ism (hin′dōō·iz′əm) *n.* The popular religion of India, consisting of the ancient religion of the Brahmans, with an admixture of Buddhism and other philosophies: its supreme deities are the triad of Brahma, Vishnu, and Siva, while numberless inferior divinities and natural objects, as trees, serpents, etc., are objects of worship. Also *Hindooism.*

Hin·du·sta·ni (hin′dōō·stä′nē, -stan′ē) *n.* The principal dialect of Western Hindi: the official language and general medium of communication in India. See URDU. **— adj.** Of or pertaining to Hindustan, its people, or to Hindustani. *Abbr. Hind.*

hinge (hinj) *n.* **1** A device allowing one part to turn upon another: the hook or joint on which a door or shutter swings or turns.

HINGES
a. Spring hinge.   *d.* Plate hinge.   *g.* Gate hinge.
b. Blind hinge.   *e.* T-hinge.   *h.* Butt hinge.
c. Strap hinge.   *f.* Link hinge.   *i.* H-hinge.

2 A device consisting of two metal plates joined by a rod, used as to connect a lid to a box. **3** A natural articulation; a joint, as in the shell of an oyster. **4** A pivotal point on which anything depends for its effect or course. — *v.* **hinged, hing·ing** *v.i.* **1** To have one's course determined by an action or eventuality; be dependent: with *on* or *upon*: The deal *hinged* on his acceptance of the offer. — *v.t.* **2** To attach by or equip with a hinge or hinges. [ME *hengen*, prob. <ON *hengja* hang. Related to HANG.]

hinge joint *Anat.* A joint in which angular motion occurs in but one plane, as the elbow joint.

hin·ny[1] (hin′ē) *n. pl.* **·nies** The offspring of a stallion and a she–ass. [<L *hinnus* <Gk. *ginnos*]

hin·ny[2] (hin′ē) *v.i.* **·nied, ·ny·ing** To whinny; neigh. [Var. of WHINNY]

hint (hint) *n.* **1** An indirect suggestion or implication in avoidance of or allusion to a direct statement. **2** A small amount or part: a *hint* of rain. **3** *Obs.* An opportunity; occasion. See synonyms under SUGGESTION. — *v.t.* To suggest indirectly; imply. — *v.i.* To make hints: often with *at*. See synonyms under ALLUDE. [OE *hentan* seize, grasp]

hip[1] (hip) *n.* **1** The lateral part of the body between the brim of the pelvis and the free part of the thigh. ◆ Collateral adjective: *coxal.* **2** The hip joint. **3** The coxa in insects. **4** *Archit.* The external angle in which adjacent roof slopes meet each other. — **on** (or **upon**) **the hip** In a position prejudicial to success: in allusion to a wrestler's trick. — *v.t.* **hipped, hip·ping 1** To fracture or sprain the hip of (an animal). **2** *Archit.* To build with a hip or hips, as a roof. [OE *hype*]

hip[2] (hip) *n.* The fruit of a rose, especially of the dogrose. [OE *hēope*]

hip[3] (hip) *interj.* An exclamation used to introduce a hurrah, or to give the signal for it. [Origin unknown]

hip[4] (hip) *adj. U.S. Slang* Aware; informed: often followed by *to*. [? Alter. of HEP]

hip bone The innominate bone.

hip joint *Anat.* The joint between the hip bone and the thigh bone or femur.

hip·parch (hip′ärk) *n.* In ancient Greek history, a cavalry commander. [<Gk. *hipparchos* < *hippos* horse + *archein* rule]

Hip·par·chus (hi·pär′kəs), 160?–125? B.C., Greek astronomer.

hipped[1] (hipt) *adj.* Having hips of a stated kind: heavy–*hipped.*

hipped[2] (hipt) *adj.* **1** *U.S. Slang* Unduly interested or engrossed by something; obsessed: *hipped* on socialism. **2** *Brit.* Affected with hypochondria or depression. [<HYP(OCHONDRIA) + -ED]

hip·pet·y-hop (hip′ə·tē·hop′) *n.* A hopping gait. — *adv.* With a hop and a skip: also **hip′pet·y-hop·pet·y** (-hop′ə·tē).

hip·pie (hip′ē) *n.* One of a group of young people whose alienation from conventional society is expressed by informal and eccentric clothing, a preoccupation with drugs and mysticism, and an interest in communal living. [Var. of HIPSTER]

Hip·poc·ra·tes (hi·pok′rə·tēz), 460?–377 B.C., Greek physician: called the "Father of Medicine."

Hip·po·crat·ic (hip′ə·krat′ik) *adj.* Of or pertaining to Hippocrates.

Hippocratic oath An oath administered to those entering the practice of medicine in early days and credited to Hippocrates, and still administered to graduates about to receive a medical degree.

hip·po·drome (hip′ə·drōm) *n.* **1** An arena, stadium, or large structure for equestrian exhibitions, circuses, etc. **2** In ancient Greece and Rome, a course or track for horse races and chariot races. [<F <L *hippodromos* < Gk. <*hippos* horse + *dromos* running, course < *dramein* run]

hip·po·griff (hip′ə·grif) *n.* A mythological beast with the wings, head, and claws of a griffin, and the hoofs and tail of a horse. Also **hip′po·gryph.** [<F *hippogriffe* < Ital. *ippogrifo* <Gk. *hippos* horse + LL *gryphus* GRIFFIN]

hip·poph·a·gist (hi·pof′ə·jist) *n.* An eater of horseflesh. Also **hip·poph′a·gus** (-ə·gəs). [< HIPPO- + Gk. *phagein* eat] — **hip·poph′a·gous** (-gəs) *adj.*

hip·poph·a·gy (hi·pof′ə·jē) *n.* The act or habit of eating horseflesh. [<HIPPO- + -PHAGY]

hip·po·pot·a·mus (hip′ə·pot′ə·məs) *n. pl.* **·mus·es** or **·mi** (-mī) A large, amphibious, short–legged, thick–skinned African pachyderm related to the pigs (*Hippopotamus amphibius*), having a massive body and very broad obtuse muzzle; river horse. Among living quadrupeds it ranks next to the elephant in size. [<L <Gk. *hippopotamos* < *hippos* horse + *potamos* river]

HIPPOPOTAMUS
(From 4 1/2 to 5 feet at shoulder; length about 12 feet)

hip·pus (hip′əs) *n. Pathol.* A disorder of the eyes characterized by rapid, spasmodic changes in size of the pupil when exposed to light. [<NL <Gk. *hippos* horse; from the movement of the eye]

-hippus *combining form Paleontol.* Horse: *Eohippus.* [<Gk. *hippos* horse]

hip roof *Archit.* **1** A roof rising directly from the wall plate on all sides, and thus having no gable. **2** A short portion of a roof over a truncated gable. Also called *hipped roof.*

hip-shot (hip′shot′) *adj.* **1** Having the hip joint dislocated. **2** Lame; awkward.

hip·ster (hip′stər) *n. U.S. Slang* One who is hip, as one versed in jazz. [<HIP[4] + -STER]

hi·ran (hī′ran) *n. Telecom.* A form of radar designed for operations requiring extreme precision and accuracy in the location of positions. [<HI(GH PRECISION SHO)RAN]

hir·cine (hûr′sin, -sīn) *adj.* Like a goat; especially, having a goatlike smell. [<L *hircinus* < *hircus* goat]

hire (hīr) *v.t.* **hired, hir·ing 1** To obtain the services of (a person) or the use of (a thing) for a compensation; employ; rent. **2** To grant the use of (a thing) or the services of (a person) for a compensation; let: often with *out.* See synonyms under EMPLOY, RETAIN. — **to hire out** To give one's services for a compensation. — *n.* **1** Compensation for labor, services, etc. **2** The act of hiring. See synonyms under SALARY. — **for hire** Offered for use or rent for a compensation. [OE *hȳr*] — **hir′a·ble, hire′a·ble** *adj.* — **hir′er** *n.*

hired girl A woman hired to do household or farm chores.

hired hand A person employed on a farm.

hired man A man hired to do odd jobs, especially about a farm.

hire-ling (hīr′ling) *adj.* Serving for hire; venal. See synonyms under VENAL. — *n.* One who serves for or only for hire.

Hi·ro·hi·to (hir·ō·hē·tō), born 1901, emperor of Japan 1926–.

Hi·ro·shi·ma (hir′ō·shē′mä, hē·rō′shē·mä) A port in SW Honshu island, Japan; devastated by first atomic bomb used in warfare, August 6, 1945.

hir·sute (hûr′sōot, hûr·sōot′) *adj.* **1** Having a hairy covering; set with bristles; shaggy. **2** Covered with coarse hairs or hairlike processes. **3** Covered with fine hairlike feathers, as the feet of certain birds. [<L *hirsutus* rough] — **hir′sute·ness** *n.*

Hir·u·din·e·a (hir′ə·din′ē·ə) *n. pl.* A class of annelids which includes the leeches. [<NL <L *hirudo, -inis* leech]

hi·ru·di·noid (hi·rōo′də·noid) *adj.* Pertaining to or resembling a leech.

hi·run·dine (hi·run′din, -dīn) *adj.* Of, pertaining to, or resembling the swallow; swallowlike. [<L *hirundo, -dinis* a swallow]

his (hiz) *pron.* **1** Belonging or pertaining to him: the possessive case of *he* used predicatively or after *of*: This room is *his*; that laugh of *his.* **2** The things, persons, etc., belonging or pertaining to him: Her book is better than *his*; He protects himself and *his.* — *pronominal adj.* Belonging or relating to him: the possessive case of *he* used attributively: *his* book. [OE]

his'n (hiz′ən) *pron. Archaic* or *Dial.* His. Also **hisn.**

His·pan·ic (his·pan′ik) *adj.* Of or pertaining to the countries or people of Spain, Portugal, and

Latin America, or to their languages, customs, or culture. — *n.* *U.S.* A native or inhabitant of Spanish America; Spanish American.

Hispanic America See SPANISH AMERICA.

His·pan·i·cism (his·pan′ə·siz′əm) *n.* A turn of phrase peculiar to the Spanish.

His·pa·ni·o·la (his′pə·nyō′lə) An island of the West Indies; 30,000 square miles; formerly *Haiti*; divided into Haiti and the Dominican Republic. *Spanish* **Es·pa·ño·la** (es′pä·nyō′lä).

His·pa·no-Mo·resque (his·pä′nō-mô·resk′) *adj.* Pertaining to or naming the art of Spain having Moorish characteristics.

his·pid (his′pid) *adj. Biol.* Rough with stiff hairs or bristles; bristly. [<L *hispidus* hairy] — **his·pid′i·ty** (his·pid′ə·tē) *n.*

hiss (his) *n.* **1** The prolonged sound of *s*, as that made by escaping air. **2** Such a sound made to express disapproval, hatred, etc. — *v.i.* **1** To make or emit a hiss or hisses. **2** To express disapproval or hatred by hissing. — *v.t.* **3** To express disapproval or hatred of by hissing. **4** To express by means of a hiss or hisses. **5** To pursue, drive off, silence, etc., by hissing: usually with *off, down,* etc. [OE *hyscan* jeer at]

hiss·ing (his′ing) *n.* **1** The act of uttering a hiss. **2** *Archaic* An object of scorn or contempt.

his·ti·oid (his′tē·oid) *adj.* Appearing like a normal tissue. Also **his·toid** (his′toid). [<Gk. *histos* web + -OID]

his·to·blast (his′tə·blast) *n.* A tissue-forming cell.

his·to·chem·is·try (his′tə·kem′is·trē) *n.* The chemistry of tissue structures in organisms.

his·to·gen·e·sis (his′tə·jen′ə·sis) *n.* The formation and development of tissues. Also **his·tog·e·ny** (his·toj′ə·nē). — **his′to·gen′ic** *adj.*

his·to·gram (his′tə·gram) *n. Stat.* A graph of frequency distribution in the form of a series of rectangles whose width and area correspond to the range of the class interval and the quantities represented. See HISTORIGRAM.

his·tol·o·gy (his·tol′ə·jē) *n.* **1** The branch of biology treating of the structure of the tissues of organized bodies; microscopic anatomy. **2** The tissue structure of a plant or animal organism. [<HISTO- + -LOGY] — **his·to·log·i·cal** (his′tə·loj′i·kəl) *adj.* — **his·tol′o·gist** *n.*

his·tol·y·sis (his·tol′ə·sis) *n.* **1** *Biol.* The degeneration and dissolution of the organic tissue. **2** *Entomol.* The process by which the larval organs of many insects dissolve into a creamy consistency during the pupa stage, save for certain cell groups which develop into the organs of the future imago. [<HISTO- + -LYSIS]

his·to·ri·an (his·tôr′ē·ən, -tō′rē-) *n.* **1** One who writes a history; a chronicler. **2** One versed in history.

his·to·ri·at·ed (his·tôr′ē·ā′tid, -tō′rē-) *adj.* Adorned with figures or designs, especially human or animal figures, as the illuminated manuscripts and capitals of columns of the Middle Ages. [<LL *historiatus*, pp. of *historiare* relate a history < *historia* a history]

his·tor·ic (his·tôr′ik, -tor′-) *adj.* **1** Mentioned or celebrated in history; notable. **2** Historical.

his·tor·i·cal (his·tôr′i·kəl, -tor′-) *adj.* **1** Belonging or relating to history or historians; containing the record or representation of facts. **2** Relating to the past. **3** Pertaining to things as known by testimony, or purely as matters of fact: Memory is the *historical* faculty. **4** Phylogenetic. **5** Historic. — **his·tor′i·cal·ly** *adv.* — **his·tor′i·cal·ness** *n.*

historical geology That branch of geology which treats of the chronological succession of earth events, including past forms of plant and animal life as revealed in fossils, etc.

historical method The method which would found conclusions on a detailed and critical study of the history of the development of the object under consideration.

historical present *Gram.* The present tense used to narrate a past event as if it were happening contemporaneously with the narrative.

historical school Followers of and believers in the historical method.

his·tor·i·cism (his·tôr′ə·siz′əm, -tor′ə-) *n.* The conception that the history of anything sufficiently accounts for its nature or values. — **his·tor′i·cist** *n.*

his·to·ric·i·ty (his′tə·ris′ə·tē) *n.* Historical authenticity.

his·to·ried (his′tə·rēd) *adj. Rare* Rich in historic

his·tor·i·fy (his·tôr′ə·fī, -tor′-) **·fied, ·fy·ing** To write the history of; chronicle.

his·tor·i·gram (his·tôr′ə·gram, -tor′-) *n. Stat.* A graph illustrating the changes of a given variable as a function of the time: distinguished from *histogram*. [< HISTORY + -GRAM]

his·to·ri·og·ra·pher (his·tôr′ē·og′rə·fər, -tō′rē-) *n.* One who writes history, especially in an official capacity.

his·to·ri·og·ra·phy (his·tôr′ē·og′rə·fē, -tō′rē-) *n.* 1 The writing of history. 2 History that is written. —**his·to·ri·o·graph·ic** (his·tôr′ē·ə·graf′ik, -tō′rē-) or **·i·cal** *adj.* —**his·to′ri·o·graph′i·cal·ly** *adv.*

his·to·ry (his′tə·rē, his′trē) *n. pl.* **·ries** 1 A recorded narrative of past events, especially those concerning a particular period, nation, individual, etc. 2 The branch of knowledge dealing with the records of the past, especially those involving human affairs. 3 The aggregate of events concerning a given subject, recorded or unrecorded. 4 Past events in general: in the course of *history*. 5 A past worthy of notice; an eventful career. 6 Something in the past: This is all *history* now. 7 *Med.* The facts received from a patient concerning his health, past and present, together with current symptoms: in full, **medical history.** 8 A historical drama. [< L *historia* < Gk., knowledge, narrative < *histōr* knowing. Doublet of STORY.]

Synonyms: account, annals, archives, autobiography, biography, chronicle, memoir, memorial, muniment, narration, narrative, recital, record, register, story. *History* is a systematic *record* of past events. *Annals* and *chronicles* relate events with little regard to their relative importance, and with complete subserviency to their succession in time. *Annals* (L *annus,* year) are yearly records; *chronicles* (Gk. *chronos,* time) follow the order of time. Both necessarily lack emphasis, selection, and perspective. *Archives* are public *records,* which may be *annals,* or *chronicles,* or deeds of property, etc. *Memoirs* generally record the lives of individuals or facts pertaining to individual lives. A *biography* is distinctively a written *account* of one person's life and actions; an *autobiography* is a *biography* written by the person whose life it records. *Annals, archives, chronicles, biographies,* and *memoirs* and other *records* furnish the materials of *history. History* recounts events with careful attention to their importance, their mutual relations, their causes and consequences, selecting and grouping events on the ground of interest or importance. *History* is usually applied to such an *account* of events affecting communities and nations, yet sometimes we speak of the *history* of a single eminent life. Compare RECORD. *Antonyms:* see synonyms for FICTION.

his·tri·on·ic (his′trē·on′ik) *adj.* 1 Pertaining to the stage; theatrical. 2 Having a theatrical manner; artificial; affected. Also **his′tri·on′i·cal.** [< L *histrionicus* < *histrio* actor] —**his′tri·on′i·cal·ly** *adv.*

his·tri·on·ics (his′trē·on′iks) *n. pl.* 1 The art of dramatic representation. 2 Theatrical affectations.

his·tri·on·i·cism (his′trē·on′ə·siz′əm) *n.* A use of histrionic art; stage effect.

hit (hit) *v.* **hit, hit·ting** *v.t.* 1 To come against or in contact with, usually with impact or force. 2 To inflict (a blow, etc.). 3 To strike with a blow: She *hit* him too hard. 4 To strike with or as with a missile: He *hit* the robber in the leg. 5 To move or propel by striking: He *hit* the ball over the fence. 6 To arrive at or achieve, as after effort or search: often with *upon:* to *hit* upon the right answer. 7 To suit; be in accordance with: The idea *hit* her fancy. 8 To affect the emotion, well-being, etc.: Of: His father's death *hit* him hard. 9 *Colloq.* To go at vigorously or to excess: to *hit* the bottle. 10 In baseball, to make a (specified base) hit: to *hit* a triple. —*v.i.* 11 To deliver a blow or blows: often with *out.* 12 To strike with force; bump: often with *against.* 13 To fire the cylinder charges of an internal-combustion engine: The car was *hitting* on all eight cylinders. See synonyms under REACH. —**to hit it off** *Colloq.* To take pleasure in one another's company; be congenial. —**to hit off** 1 To imitate. 2 To express or describe exactly. —*n.* 1 A striking against something; a stroke; blow. 2 A stroke of wit or sarcasm; repartee. 3 A stroke of luck; success. 4 Anything enjoying quick public acclaim: The play was a *hit.* 5 In baseball, a base hit. 6 In backgammon, a move that throws one of the opponent's men back to the entering point, or a game won after one or more men are thrown off by the opponent. See synonyms under BLOW. —**clean hit** In baseball, a hit which drives the ball so that it cannot be fielded in time to prevent the earning of a base. [OE *hittan* < ON *hitta* come upon]

hit-and-run (hit′ən·run′) *adj.* 1 Designating an automobile operator who hits a pedestrian and drives away without stopping. 2 Describing the tactics of a military force which makes small harassing attacks on a larger force without venturing a major engagement. 3 In baseball, describing a maneuver in which the batter and the base runners work together by a prearranged plan.

hitch (hich) *n.* 1 A stop or sudden halt; obstruction; hence, an obstacle to an enterprise. 2 The act of catching or fastening, as by a rope, hook, etc.; also a connection so made. 3 *Naut.* Any of various knots made with

HITCHES
A. Half hitch. *B.* Clove hitch. *C.* Rolling hitch.

rope, rigging, etc. 4 A quick or sudden push or pull; a jerk. 5 A limp; halt; hobble. 6 *U.S. Colloq.* A period of enlistment in military service, especially in the U.S. Navy. —*v.t.* 1 To fasten or tie, especially temporarily, with a knot, rope, strap, etc. 2 To harness to a vehicle: often with *up:* to *hitch* a horse to a buggy. 3 To move or shift with a jerk or jerks: He *hitched* himself around in his chair. 4 To marry: often with *up.* 5 *U.S. Slang* To obtain (a ride) by hitchhiking. —*v.i.* 6 To move with jerks: to *hitch* forward. 7 To become caught or entangled. 8 To strike the feet together, as in trotting: said of horses. 9 *U.S. Colloq.* To get on together; agree: He and I don't *hitch.* 10 *U.S. Slang* To travel by hitchhiking. [ME *hicchen;* origin uncertain]

hitch·hike (hich′hīk′) *v.i. U.S. Colloq.* To travel on foot and by asking rides from passing vehicles. —**hitch′hik′er** *n.*

hitching post A post having iron loops or rings to which a horse, team, etc., may be hitched.

hith·er (hith′ər) *adj.* Near to or toward the person speaking: opposed to *farther.* —*adv.* In this direction; toward this place. [OE *hider*]

hith·er·most (hith′ər·mōst′) *adj.* Nearest.

hith·er·to (hith′ər·tōō′, hith′ər·tōō′) *adv.* 1 Till now. 2 *Archaic* Thus far. See synonyms under YET.

hith·er·ward (hith′ər·wərd) *adv.* Hither. Also **hith′er·wards.**

Hit·ler (hit′lər), **Adolf,** 1889–1945, head of the Nazi party and dictator, officially chancellor, of Germany 1933–45; born in Austria: called "der Führer." —**Hit′ler·ism** (hit·lir′ē·ən) *adj.* —**Hit′ler·ism** *n.*

hit-or-miss (hit′ər·mis′) *adj.* 1 Heedless; haphazard: to live a *hit-or-miss* life. 2 Varicolored. —*adv.* Haphazardly.

hit·ter (hit′ər) *n.* One who strikes or hits.

Hit·tite (hit′īt) *n.* 1 One of an ancient people who established a powerful empire in Asia Minor and Northern Syria about 2000–1200 B.C. 2 The language of the Hittites, known from cuneiform inscriptions discovered in Asia Minor which date from about 1400 B.C. (**Cuneiform Hittite**). Hieroglyphic inscriptions from about 1000 B.C., found in Asia Minor and Northern Syria, have also been attributed to the Hittites (**Hieroglyphic Hittite**). Although Hittite has been established as having a definite connection with Indo-European, it exhibits characteristics which distinguish it so markedly from the rest of the Indo-European family that the exact nature of the relationship remains uncertain.

H.I.V. (human immuno deficiency virus) human retro virus which causes AIDS *abbr.* H.I.V.

hive (hīv) *n.* 1 A structure in which bees may dwell. 2 A colony of bees. 3 A place full of activity. —*v.* **hived, hiv·ing** *v.t.* 1 To cause (bees) to enter a hive; gather into a hive. 2 To store (honey) in a hive. 3 To store (anything) for future use. —*v.i.* 4 To enter or dwell in or as in a hive. [OE *hȳf*]

hives (hīvz) *n.* Any of various skin diseases, especially urticaria. [Origin unknown]

ho (hō) *interj.* 1 A call to excite attention. 2 An exclamation expressing surprise, exultation, or, when repeated, derision. 3 An exclamation directing attention to some distant point: Land *ho!* Westward *ho!* Also **hoa.** [Imit.]

hoar (hôr, hōr) *adj.* 1 White or gray with age; hoary. 2 White or grayish-white in color. 3 Ancient. 4 *Obs.* Musty; moldy. —*n.* 1 Hoarfrost. 2 The condition of being white with age or frost; hoariness. ◆ Homophone: *whore.* [OE *hār* grayhaired]

hoard (hôrd, hōrd) *n.* An accumulation stored away for safeguarding or for future use. See synonyms under HEAP, STOCK. —*v.t.* To gather and store away or hide for future use. —*v.i.* To gather and store away food, jewels, etc. ◆ Homophone: *horde.* [OE *hord* treasure] —**hoard′er** *n.*

hoard·ing (hôr′ding, hōr′-) *n.* 1 The act of accumulating a hoard. 2 *pl.* Treasure laid by; savings.

hoar·frost (hôr′frôst′, -frost′, hōr′-) *n.* Frost having the form of silvery ice needles. [ME *horfrost*]

hoar·hound (hôr′hound′, hōr′-) *n.* Horehound.

hoarse (hôrs, hōrs) *adj.* 1 Harsh and rough in sound. 2 Having the voice harsh and rough. [OE *hā(r)s*] —**hoarse′ly** *adv.* —**hoarse′ness** *n.*

hoars·en (hôr′sən, hōr′-) *v.t. & v.i.* To make or become hoarse or harsh.

hoar·y (hôr′ē, hō′rē) *adj.* **hoar·i·er, hoar·i·est** 1 White, as from age. 2 Ancient. 3 Covered with short and dense grayish-white hairs, as certain animals. See synonyms under ANCIENT. —**hoar′i·ness** *n.*

ho·at·zin (hō·at′sin) *n.* A South American bird (genus *Opisthocomus*) resembling the curassow in appearance, prevailingly olive, with a yellowish crest and a pair of hooked claws on each wing: also called *hoactzin.* Also **ho·az′in.** [< Sp. Am. < Nahuatl *uatzin*]

hoax (hōks) *v.t.* To deceive by a trick. —*n.* 1 A deception practiced for sport. 2 A practical joke or fraud. [< HOCUS(-POCUS)] —**hoax′er** *n.*

hob[1] (hob) *n.* 1 A projection on the side of a fireplace; also, its top, serving as a shelf. 2 The nave of a wheel. 3 A hardened fluted steel mandrel for cutting screw threads. 4 A steel punch with a design in relief. 5 A game in which quoits or other objects are tossed at a stake; also, the stake. [? Var. of HUB]

hob[2] (hob) *n.* A fairy; hobgoblin; elf. —**to play hob** with To throw into confusion; upset; ruin. [Orig., a nickname for ROBERT, ROBIN]

Hobb·ism (hob′iz·əm) *n.* The philosophy of Thomas Hobbes; especially his theory that an absolute monarch is necessary to control the antagonisms of individual interests. Also **Hob·bi·an·ism** (hob′ē·ən·iz′əm). —**Hobbes·i·an** (hobz′ē·ən), **Hob·bi·an** (hob′ē·ən) *adj.* —**Hob·bist** (hob′ist) *n.*

hob·ble (hob′əl) *v.* **hob·bled, hob·bling** *v.i.* 1 walk with or as with a limp; go lamely or on crutches. 2 To move or proceed in an irregular or clumsy manner. —*v.t.* 3 To hamper the free movement of (a horse, etc.), as by tying the legs together. 4 To cause to move lamely or awkwardly. —*n.* 1 A limping gait. 2 A fetter for the legs; specifically, a rope, strap, or pair of linked rings used to fetter the forelegs of an animal. 3 An embarrassment; difficulty. [? Freq. of HOP. Cf. G *hoppeln* hobble.] —**hob′bler** *n.*

hob·ble-bush (hob′əl·bŏŏsh′) *n.* A straggling shrub (*Viburnum alnifolium*) of the honeysuckle family, having flowers resembling those of hydrangea, and the fruit coral-red drupes.

hob·ble·de·hoy (hob'əl·dē·hoi') n. 1 An awkward youth. 2 An adolescent boy. Also **hob'be·de·hoy'** (hob'ə·dē-). [Origin uncertain]

hob·by (hob'ē) n. pl. **·bies** 1 A subject or pursuit in which one takes absorbing interest. 2 A hobbyhorse. 3 An ambling nag. 4 A small falcon (*Falco subbuteo*) with long wings. [from *Robin*, a personal name]

hob·by·horse (hob'ē·hôrs') n. 1 A rocking-horse; also, a toy consisting of a stick with a wooden horse's head attached. 2 The figure of a horse attached to a person's waist so that he appears to be riding it: used in morris dances, pantomimes, etc.

hob·gob·lin (hob'gob'lin) n. 1 A mischievous imp. 2 Anything that causes superstitious terror, particularly anything imagined. See synonyms under SCARECROW. [< HOB² + GOBLIN]

hob·nail (hob'nāl') n. A nail for studding the soles of heavy shoes.

hob·nailed (hob'nāld') adj. 1 Provided or armed with hobnails. 2 Wearing hobnailed boots or shoes; clownish. 3 Ornamented with knobs, as glassware.

hobnail liver The liver in an advanced stage of cirrhosis, characterized by warty surface projections resembling hobnails.

hob·nob (hob'nob) v.i. **·nobbed, ·nob·bing** 1 To drink together familiarly and convivially. 2 To be on familiar terms; chat socially. —n. A friendly talk. Also **hob-or-nob** (hob'ər·nob'). [OE *habban* have + *nabban* have not]

ho·bo (hō'bō) n. pl. **·boes** or **·bos** U.S. 1 A migratory, unskilled workman. 2 A professional idler; a tramp. —v.i. To live or wander as a hobo. [< *Hey, Bo*, a vagrant's greeting] —**ho'bo·ism** n.

Ho Chi Minh (hō' chē' min'), 1890?–1969, leader of the Viet Minh; president of North Vietnam 1945–1969.

hock¹ (hok) n. 1 The joint of the hind leg in digitigrade mammals, as the horse and ox, corresponding to the ankle in man. 2 The knee joint of a fowl. 3 In man, the back part of the knee joint. —v.t. To disable by cutting the tendons of the hock; hamstring. [OE *hōh* heel]

hock² (hok) n. Any white Rhine wine; originally, that known as *Hochheimer*. [Contraction of *hockamore* < G *Hochheimer* < *Hochheim*, a German town where it was first produced]

hock³ (hok) v.t. & n. U.S. Slang Pawn. —**in hock** Slang 1 In pawn. 2 In prison. [Du. *hok* prison, debt]

hock·ey (hok'ē) n. 1 A game played either on a field or on ice, in which opposing players, equipped with curved or hooked sticks, try to drive a small block (puck) or ball into or past the opposite goals. 2 A hockey stick. [< *hock* bent stick, var. of HOOK]

hockey stick The curved stick used to hit the ball or puck in hockey.

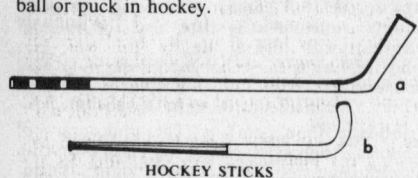

HOCKEY STICKS
a. Ice hockey. *b.* Field hockey.

ho·cus (hō'kəs) v.t. **·cused** or **·cussed, ·cus·ing** or **·cus·sing** 1 To deceive by a trick; impose upon. 2 To drug. 3 To add drugs to, as a drink. [Abbreviation of HOCUS-POCUS]

ho·cus-po·cus (hō'kəs·pō'kəs) n. 1 A verbal formula used in conjuring or juggling. 2 A conjurer's trick, or deception wrought as if by the conjurer's art. —v.t. & v.i. To cheat; trick. [A sham Latin phrase, ? alter. of *hoc est corpus* this is my body, a eucharistic formula]

hod (hod) n. 1 A long-handled receptacle for holding bricks and mortar, carried on the shoulder. 2 A coal scuttle or a box for coals. [< obs. *hot* < OF *hotte* pannier < Gmc. Cf. MDu. *hodde*.]

hodge-podge (hoj'poj') n. 1 A stew of mixed

---

meats and vegetables. 2 A jumbled mixture; conglomeration. Also **hotch-potch**. [Var. of HOTCH-POTCH]

Hodg·kin's disease (hoj'kinz) *Pathol.* A progressive and fatal enlargement of the lymph nodes, lymphoid tissue, and spleen; a form of granuloma. [after Dr. Thomas *Hodgkin*, 1798–1866, English physician, who first described it]

ho·di·er·nal (hō'dī·ûr'nəl) adj. Of or pertaining to the present day. [< L *hodiernus* < *hoc die* (on) this day]

ho·do·graph (hō'də·graf, -gräf) n. Math. The curve traced by the terminal point of a vector drawn from a fixed origin and representing the acceleration of a particle moving at a known velocity along any given path. [< Gk. *hodos* way + GRAPH]

ho·do·scope (hō'də·skōp) n. Physics A device for indicating the path of cosmic rays, consisting of a series of Geiger counters connected with a neon lamp to record the passage of the separate particles. [< Gk. *hodos* way + -SCOPE]

hoe (hō) n. A flat-bladed implement for digging, scraping, and tilling, having in the simplest form a flat and thin blade set nearly at

TYPES OF HOES
a. Warren hoe.   *c.* Grub hoe.   *e.* Garden hoe.
b. Mortar hoe.   *d.* Scuffle hoe.   *f.* Weeding hoe.

a right angle to a long handle. —v.t. & v.i. **hoed, hoe·ing** To dig, scrape, or till with a hoe. [< OF *houe* < OHG *houwa* < *houwan* cut] —**ho'er** n.

hoe-cake (hō'kāk') n. U.S. A thin cake of Indian meal: originally baked on a hoe.

hoe-down (hō'doun') n. U.S. 1 A lively, shuffling dance: originally Southern. 2 The music for such a dance. [Origin uncertain]

hog (hôg, hog) n. 1 An omnivorous ungulate having a long mobile snout with flat, expanded end containing the nostrils; especially, any domestic variety of the wild boar (family *Suidae*) bred and raised for its meat, called *pork*. 2 Some animal like the foregoing, as the peccary, warthog, etc. 3 *Colloq.* A filthy, gluttonous person. 4 A stirrer in a paper-pulp vat. —v. **hogged, hog·ging** v.t. 1 U.S. Slang To take more than one's share of; grab selfishly. 2 To arch (the back) upward like a hog's. 3 To cut short, as a horse's mane. —v.i. 4 To sag at both ends: said of ships. [OE *hogg*]

ho·gan (hō'gən) n. The rude hut of the Navaho and other roving tribes of the SW United States. [< Navaho *qoghan* house]

hog·back (hôg'bak', hog'-) n. 1 A back humped like that of certain hogs. 2 A sandy or rocky ridge caused by unequal erosion or the outcropping edge of tilted strata. Also called *hog's-back*.

hog-backed (hôg'bakt', hog'-) adj. Elevated toward the middle, like the back of a hog.

hog·chain (hôg'chān', hog'-) n. Naut. A tension chain passing from bow to stern of a vessel and fastened to posts amidships: used to prevent the ends from sagging.

hog cholera A highly infectious and contagious disease of swine caused by a filtrable virus, characterized by loss of appetite, fever, exhaustion, and high mortality.

hog-nose (hôg'nōz', hog'-) n. Any North American non-venomous colubrine snake (genus *Heterodon*) with a flattened head and prominent snout, known for its formidable appearance and contorted movements when disturbed. Also **hog'-nosed' snake**.

---

hog·nut (hôg'nut', hog'-) n. 1 The nut of the pignut hickory. 2 *Brit.* The earth chestnut.

hog peanut A slender vine (*Amphicarpa bracteata*) of the bean family bearing usually a one-seeded pod: also called *earth pea*.

hog pen A pigsty.

hog's-back (hôgz'bak', hogz'-) n. A hogback.

hog-score (hôg'skôr', -skōr', hog'-) n. A line drawn across the rink in curling, one sixth of the way from each tee to the other.

hogs·head (hôgz'hed', hogz'-) n. 1 A large cask. 2 A liquid measure of varying capacity: in the United States and Great Britain ordinarily 63 gallons, or 0.238 cubic meter, or 52 1/2 imperial gallons.

hog·suck·er (hôg'suk'ər, hog'-) n. A freshwater fish (*Catostomus nigricans*) of central United States.

hog-tie (hôg'tī', hog'-) v.t. **·tied, ·ty·ing** or **·tie·ing** 1 To tie all four feet or the hands and feet of. 2 Colloq. To bind fast; keep from taking action.

hog-tight (hôg'tīt', hog'-) adj. Strong enough to keep swine in or out: said of a fence.

hog·wal·low (hôg'wol'ō, hog'-) n. 1 A damp, muddy place in which hogs wallow. 2 A depression in a prairie that remains damp and grassy.

hog·wash (hôg'wosh', -wôsh', hog'-) n. 1 Kitchen refuse, swill, etc., fed to hogs. 2 Any worthless rubbish; nonsense; foolishness.

hog·weed (hôg'wēd', hog'-) n. Any of numerous coarse weeds of persistent growth, including the ragweeds, knotweed, dogfennel, etc.

hog wild *U. S. Slang* Wildly excited.

hoick (hoik) *Aeron.* v.t. To throw (an aircraft) into sharp, sudden changes of direction, as in making a steep climb. —v.i. To engage in this kind of maneuver or operation: usually with *about* or *around*. [Origin unknown]

hoicks (hoiks) interj. A cry used to stir up the hounds in hunting. Also *yoicks*.

hoi pol·loi (hoi' pə·loi') The common people; the masses; the herd: usually used contemptuously, and preceded by a redundant *the*. [< Gk., the many]

hoist (hoist) v.t. To raise to a higher position; lift or heave up, especially by some mechanical means. —n. 1 A hoisting machine; lift. 2 The act of hoisting; a boost. 3 The vertical dimension of a flag or the like, measured along the pole or halyard: distinguished from the *fly*. 4 Naut. a The length of a sail between the boom and the peak or the jaws of the gaff. b The midship depth of a square sail set by hoisting the yard. [? < Du. *hijschen*] —**hoist'er** n.

hoi·ty-toi·ty (hoi'tē·toi'tē) interj. Think of that! what now! —adj. 1 Self-important; putting on airs. 2 Flighty; giddy. 3 Petulant; huffy. Also spelled *highty-tighty*. [Reduplication of obs. *hoit* romp; infl. in meaning by HIGH]

ho·key-po·key (hō'kē·pō'kē) n. 1 Ice-cream sold by street peddlers in small quantities: also **ho'ky-po'ky**. 2 Hocus-pocus.

ho·kum (hō'kəm) n. Slang 1 A phrase or device deliberately used by an actor, writer, or speaker to win a laugh or catch attention. 2 Contrived sentimental or pathetic effects in a play or story. 3 Nonsense; bunk. [Alter. of HOCUS]

ho·lard (hō'lərd) n. The total quantity of water found in the soil. See CHRESARD, ECHARD. [< HOL- + Gk. *ardeia* irrigation]

hol·co·dont (hol'kə·dont) adj. Zool. Having teeth set in a continuous groove. [< Gk. *holkos* furrow + *odous, odontos* tooth]

hold¹ (hōld) v. **held, held** or in legal use **hold·en, hold·ing** v.t. 1 To take and keep in the hand; retain. 2 To prevent the movement or escape of: He *held* her so that she could not move. 3 To restrain from acting or speaking: *Hold* your tongue! 4 To keep in a specified state: to *hold* us a prisoner. 5 To regard in a specified manner; consider: to *hold* someone dear. 6 To require to fulfil, as the conditions of a contract; obligate. 7 To support or keep in position: Ropes *held* the tower in position. 8 To be capable of enclosing or containing: The barrel *holds* ten gallons. 9 To maintain in the mind; believe: to *hold* an opinion or a grudge. 10 To conduct or engage in; carry on: to *hold* court or services. 11 To have and retain ownership or control of; keep as one's own; occupy:

to *hold* the chair. **12** To retain possession or control of, as against an enemy: They *held* the town against the enemy. — *v.i.* **13** To maintain a grip or grasp. **14** To remain firm or unbroken: if the rope *holds*; He *held* to his purpose. **15** To remain or continue unchanged: The breeze *held* all day. **16** To be relevant; remain true, correct, etc.: This decision *holds* for all such cases. **17** To check or restrain oneself; forbear: usually used in the imperative. See synonyms under ARREST, EMBRACE, ESTEEM, GRASP, HAVE, INTEREST, KEEP, OCCUPY, RESTRAIN, RETAIN. — **to hold back 1** To prevent from acting or doing. **2** To refrain. **3** To keep apart or aside; retain, as for an undisclosed purpose. — **to hold down 1** To suppress; keep under control. **2** *Colloq.* To occupy (a job, etc.) successfully. — **to hold forth** To harangue; preach or speak at length. — **to hold in** To keep in check; restrain. — **to hold off 1** To keep at a distance. **2** To refrain. — **to hold on 1** To maintain a grip or hold. **2** To persist; continue. **3** *Colloq.* To stop or wait: used in the imperative. — **to hold one's own** To maintain one's position, as in a contest; lose no ground. — **to hold out 1** To stretch forth; offer. **2** To last to the end: Our supplies *held out*. **3** To continue resistance; endure; persist. **4** *U.S. Slang* To keep back part or all of (something). — **to hold out for** *Colloq.* To insist upon as a condition of an agreement: He *held out for* a higher salary. — **to hold over 1** To put off to a later date; delay. **2** To remain beyond the expected time or limit; extend. — **to hold up 1** To support; prop. **2** To exhibit to view. **3** *Colloq.* To last; endure. **4** To delay; stop. **5** *Colloq.* To stop and rob; also, to rob. — *n.* **1** The act of holding, as with the hands; a seizure; figuratively, a controlling force or influence; restraint. **2** A place to grasp. **3** A place of security; a fortified place; stronghold; refuge. **4** The state of being held; possession. **5** *Law* A holding or tenure: in composition: *copyhold, freehold*. **6** *Music* A character (⌢) indicating the sustention of a tone. **7** A cell in jail. **8** Something to hold articles; a receptacle. **9** A lock or latch. [OE *haldan*]

hold² (hōld) *n. Naut.* The space below the decks of a vessel where cargo is stowed. [<HOLE or <MDu. *hol*]

hold-all (hōld'ôl') *n.* A general receptacle; especially, a sort of bag used by travelers.

hold-back (hōld'bak') *n.* **1** That which keeps back; a check. **2** A strap passing from the shafts of a horse-drawn vehicle and through the breeching harness, permitting the horse to hold back the vehicle or to push it back.

hold-en (hōld'n) Alternative past participle of HOLD, obsolete except in legal use.

hold-er (hōl'dər) *n.* **1** One who or that which holds. **2** An owner; possessor: chiefly in compounds: *householder*. **3** *Law* One who has legal possession of a bill of exchange, check, or promissory note for which he is entitled to receive payment.

hold-fast (hōld'fast', -fäst') *n.* **1** That by which something is held securely in place. **2** Something to cling to; a support. **3** A firm grasp. **4** *Bot.* A specialized organ of attachment at the base of certain algae: also **holdfast cell**.

hold-ing (hōl'ding) *n.* **1** The action of someone or something that holds. **2** A tenure or right of possession. **3** *Often pl.* Property held by legal right, especially stocks or bonds. **4** In football, basketball, etc., the act of obstructing an opponent, as with the arms or hands, contrary to the rules of the game.

holding company A company that holds stock in one or more companies for investment or operating purposes, or both.

hold-o-ver (hōld'ō'vər) *n.* **1** Something remaining from a previous time or situation. **2** A place of detention for prisoners awaiting trial. **3** One who continues in office after his term has expired, or after a change of administration. **4** One who is kept on from one engagement to another.

hold-up (hōld'up') *n.* **1** Stoppage, delay, or obstruction of some activity. **2** A forcible stoppage to commit robbery, especially of a traveler, a train, etc. **3** An overcharge, extortion.

hole (hōl) *n.* **1** A cavity extending into any solid body; a pit; hollow; cave. **2** An opening running or made through a body; aperture or orifice; perforation. **3** An animal's burrow or den. **4** Hence, a vile place; also, a place of hiding. **5** In golf, a cavity in a putting green into which the ball must be played; the distance within bounds between the teeing ground and the flag marking the hole toward which the play is moving; also, one of the points in the game of golf scored by the player who holes out, hole by hole, in the fewest strokes. **6** In various other games, a cavity into which a ball is played, or a point thus scored. **7** *Colloq.* A dilemma. **8** A fault; defect: to expose the *holes* in an argument. — **in the hole** *Colloq.* In debt. — *v.* **holed, hol-ing** *v.t.* **1** To make a hole or holes in; perforate. **2** To drive or put into a hole, as in billiards or golf. **3** To dig (a shaft, tunnel, etc.). — *v.i.* **4** To make a hole or holes. — **to hole out** In golf, to hit the ball into a hole. — **to hole up 1** To hibernate. **2** To take refuge in hiding. ◆ Homophone: *whole*. [OE *hol*. Appar. related to HOLLOW.]

Synonyms (noun): aperture, bore, breach, cave, cavern, cavity, chasm, concavity, den, dent, dungeon, excavation, gap, hollow, indentation, kennel, lair, notch, opening, orifice, perforation, rent, A *hole* is an *opening* in a solid body; it may extend entirely through it, forming a passageway or vent, or only partly through it, forming a *cavity*, and may be of any shape, provided the axes are not greatly unequal. An *opening* very long in proportion to its width is more commonly called a crack, fissure, slit, etc., or on the surface of the earth such an opening is designated as a *chasm*, gorge, or ravine; a *rent* in a garment is made by tearing, a slit by cutting. An *orifice* is the mouth of a *hole* or tube. *Aperture* is a very general word; the crack of a partly opened door is an *aperture*, but not a *hole*. The noun *hollow* denotes a shallow *concavity* on the outer surface of a solid, usually round or oval. A *dent* is a depression on the surface of a solid, usually sharp or angular, as if beaten in. A *breach* is roughly broken, generally from the top or edge down through a wall or other object; a *gap* may be between portions that never were joined. See BREACH, BREAK.

hole in one In golf, the act of sinking the ball into a hole in one drive.

hol-e-y (hō'lē) *adj.* Having holes.

hol-i-day (hol'ə-dā) *n.* **1** A day appointed by law or custom for the suspension of general business, usually in commemoration of some person or event. **2** Any day of rest or exemption from work. ◆ Collateral adjective: *ferial.* **3** A period of festivity or leisure; a vacation. **4** *Archaic* A day for special religious observance: now usually spelled *holy day*. — *adj.* Suitable for a holiday; festive. — *v.i.* To vacation. [OE *hālig dæg* holy day]

ho-li-er-than-thou (hō'lē-ər-than-thou') *adj.* Affecting an attitude of superior goodness or virtue; sanctimonious.

ho-li-ly (hō'lə-lē) *adv.* In a holy manner; piously; sacredly.

ho-li-ness (hō'lē-nis) *n.* **1** The state of being holy; piety. **2** *Theol.* Completeness of moral and spiritual purity. **3** The state of anything hallowed or consecrated to God. See synonyms under SANCTITY. — **His (or Your) Holiness** A title of the pope.

ho-lism (hō'liz-əm, hol'iz-) *n. Philos.* The theory that nature tends to synthesize units into organized wholes. [<HOL- + -ISM] — **ho-lis-tic** (hō-lis'tik) *adj.* — **ho-lis'ti-cal-ly** *adv.*

hol-land (hol'ənd) *n.* **1** Unbleached linen, glazed or unglazed: used sometimes in the plural, but construed as a singular. **2** In dressmaking, a form-fitting foundation used as a guide to size. **3** *pl.* Spirit flavored with juniper alone, especially that made in the Netherlands; gin: also **Holland gin** or **Hol'-lands**. [from HOLLAND, where first made]

hol-lan-daise sauce (hol'ən-dāz') A creamy sauce made of butter, yolks of eggs, lemon juice or vinegar, and seasoning. [<F, fem. of *hollandais* of Holland]

Hol-land-er (hol'ən-dər) *n.* A native of the Netherlands; a Dutchman.

hol-ler (hol'ər) *v.t. & v.i.* To call out loudly; shout; yell. — *n.* A loud shout; yell. [Imit.]

hol-low (hol'ō) *adj.* **1** Having a cavity or depression scooped out; not solid: a *hollow* tree. **2** Sunken; fallen: *hollow* cheeks. **3** Empty; vacant; hence, worthless; fruitless; insincere. **4** Sounding like the reverberation from an empty vessel or cavity; deep; murmuring. — *n.* **1** Any depression in a body; a cavity. **2** A valley. **3** A concave tool for making grooves and moldings. See synonyms under HOLE. — *v.t. & v.i.* To make or become hollow: usually with *out*. — *adv. Colloq.* Completely; thoroughly. — **to beat all hollow** To surpass completely. [OE *holh*] — **hol'low-ly** *adv.* — **hol'low-ness** *n.*

hol-low-eyed (hol'ō-īd') *adj.* Having sunken eyes surrounded by dark areas, as a result of sickness or sleeplessness.

hol-low-heart-ed (hol'ō-här'tid) *adj.* Insincere; deceitful. — **hol'low-heart'ed-ness** *n.*

hol-low-ware (hol'ō-wâr') *n.* Silver serving dishes that are more or less hollow, as bowls and pitchers, taken collectively: distinguished from *flatware*.

hol-lus-chick (hol'əs-chik) *n.* pl. **-chick-ie** (-chik'ē) A male fur seal six years old or younger; a bachelor (def. 5). [? <Russian *golyshka* childless <*golyi* naked]

hol-ly (hol'ē) *n.* pl. **-lies** **1** A tree or shrub (genus *Ilex*) with alternate leaves, white flowers, and the fruit a red berry. **2** The holm oak: also **holly oak**. [OE *holen*]

hol-ly-hock (hol'ē-hok') *n.* A tall biennial herb (*Althaea rosea*) of the mallow family, with large flowers of numerous shades. It was originally a native of China. [ME *holihoc* <*holi* holy + *hoc* mallow]

Hol-ly-wood (hol'ē-wŏŏd') *n.* The American motion-picture industry, its character, life, etc. — *adj.* Of, pertaining to, or characteristic of Hollywood.

Hol-ly-wood (hol'ē-wŏŏd') A NW section of Los Angeles, California, considered the center of the motion-picture industry.

holm¹ (hōm) *n.* **1** An island in a river. **2** *Brit.* Low-lying land by a stream. [OE; infl. in meaning by ON *holmr* land by water, island]

holm (hōm) *n.* A European evergreen oak (*Quercus ilex*). Also **holly oak, holm oak**. [OE *holen* holly. Doublet of HOLLY.]

holo- combining form Whole; wholly: *holograph*. Also, before vowels, *hol-*. [<Gk. *holos* whole]

hol-o-caust (hol'ə-kôst) *n.* **1** A sacrifice wholly consumed by fire. **2** Wholesale destruction or loss of life by fire, war, etc. [<F *holocauste* <LL *holocaustum* <Gk. *holokauston*, neut. of *holokaustos* <*holos* whole + *kaustos* burnt] — **hol'o-caus'tal, hol'-o-caus'tic** *adj.*

Hol-o-cene (hol'ə-sēn) *Geol. n.* The epoch following the Pleistocene and extending to the present time. — *adj.* Pertaining to the epoch following the Pleistocene. [<HOLO- + Gk. *kainos* recent]

Hol-o-fer-nes (hol'ə-fûr'nēz) In the book of Judith in the Apocrypha, an Assyrian general slain by Judith.

hol-o-gram (hol'ə-gram) *n.* Photosensitive film containing a three-dimensional image produced by holography. [<HOLO- + -GRAM¹]

hol-o-graph (hol'ə-graf, -gräf) *adj.* Denoting a document wholly in the handwriting of the person whose signature it bears. — *n.* A document so written. [<F *holographe* <Gk. *holographos* <*holos* entire + *graphein* write] — **hol-o-graph-ic** (hol'ə-graf'ik, -gräf'-) *adj.* **1** Holograph. **2** Of or pertaining to holography. Also **hol'o-graph'i-cal**.

ho-log-ra-phy (hə-log'rə-fē) *n.* A photographic

HOLLYHOCK
a. Single.
b. Double.

process utilizing a split beam of laser light to produce on a photographic plate, without the use of a lens, the interference pattern of light waves, thus recording a three-dimensional image that can be reconstructed and viewed. [<HOLO- + -GRAPHY]

hol·o·he·dron (hol′ə·hē′drən) n. A crystal form having the full number of symmetrically arranged planes crystallographically possible. — **hol′o·he′dral** (-drəl) adj.

hol·o·me·tab·o·lism (hol′ə·mə·tab′ə·liz′əm) n. Entomol. The condition of having a complete metamorphosis, with a larval and pupal stage preceding the adult: opposed to hemimetabolism. — **hol′o·met′a·bol′ic** (-met′ə·bol′·ik), **hol′o·me·tab′o·lous** adj.

hol·o·mor·phic (hol′ə·môr′fik) adj. Denoting likeness of form at the ends, as of crystals.

hol·o·phote (hol′ə·fōt) n. A lamp for a lighthouse, etc., so arranged that all light is utilized and thrown in the desired direction by reflectors, refracting lenses, or both. [<HOLO- + Gk. phos, phōtos light] — **hol′o·pho′tal** adj.

ho·loph·ra·sis (hə·lof′rə·sis) n. Expression of a sentence or a complex idea in the form of a single word, as in some American Indian languages. [<HOLO- + Gk. phrasis phrase] — **hol·o·phras·tic** (hol′ə·fras′tik) adj.

hol·o·phyte (hol′ə·fīt) n. Bot. A plant possessing chlorophyll, and therefore capable of manufacturing its own food. — **hol·o·phyt·ic** (hol′ə·fit′ik) adj.

hol·o·sym·met·ric (hol′ə·si·met′rik) adj. Wholly symmetrical. — **hol′o·sym′me·try** (-sim′ə·trē) n.

hol·o·thu·ri·an (hol′ə·thŏŏr′ē·ən) n. Any of a class (Holothurioidea) of echinoderms with generally wormlike shape, skinlike integument, and tentacles about the mouth: including trepangs, sea cucumbers, sea slugs, etc. [<L holothurium, a kind of zoophyte <Gk. holothurion]

Hol·o·trich·i·da (hol′ə·trik′ə·də) n. An order of ciliate infusorians with cilia nearly uniformly disposed over the surface of the body. [<NL <HOLO- + Gk. trix, trichos hair] — **ho·lot·ri·chal** (hə·lot′ri·kəl), **ho·lot′ri·chous** adj.

hol·o·type (hol′ō·tīp) n. In taxonomy, the single specimen of a plant or animal which is taken as representative of a new species.

hol·o·zo·ic (hol′ə·zō′ik) adj. Wholly like an animal: distinguished from holophytic.

Hol·stein (hōl′stīn, -stēn) n. One of a breed of cattle originally developed in the Netherlands province of Friesland and adjoining German provinces: valued for both beef and milk: also **Hol′stein–Frie′sian** (-frē′zhən).

hol·ster (hōl′stər) n. A pistol case. [<Du.]

ho·lus-bo·lus (hō′ləs·bō′ləs) n. The whole lot or quantity. — adv. All together; at a gulp. [Dog Latin <WHOLE + BOLUS]

ho·ly (hō′lē) adj. **·li·er, ·li·est** 1 Devoted to religious or sacred use; consecrated; hallowed. 2 Of highest spiritual purity; saintly: a holy martyr. 3 Befitting a saintly character; devout: holy fear. 4 Of divine nature or origin. 5 Worthy of veneration because associated with something divine. — n. pl. **holies** A holy thing or quality. [OE hālig]

Synonyms (adj.): blessed, consecrated, devoted, devout, divine, hallowed, sacred, saintly. Sacred is applied to that which is to be regarded as inviolable on any account, and so is not restricted to divine things; therefore in its lower applications it is less than holy. That which is sacred may be made so by institution, decree, or association; that which is holy is so by its own nature, possessing intrinsic moral purity, and, in the highest sense, absolute moral perfection. God is holy; his commands are sacred. Holy may be applied also to that which is hallowed; as, "the place whereon thou standest is holy ground," Ex. iii 5. In such use holy is more than sacred, as if the very qualities of a spiritual or divine presence were imparted to the place or object. Divine has been used with great looseness, denoting goodness or power in eloquence, music, etc., but the tendency is to restrict its use to attributes of the Divine Being. See PERFECT, PURE. Antonyms: abominable, common, cursed, impure, polluted, secular, unconsecrated, unhallowed, unholy, unsanctified, wicked, worldly.

Holy Communion The Eucharist or Lord's Supper.

holy day A sacred day, as the Sabbath, or

one set apart for religious uses.

Holy Father A title of the pope.

Holy Ghost See HOLY SPIRIT.

Holy Grail See GRAIL.

Holy Land Palestine.

Holy Mother The Virgin Mary.

holy of holies The innermost and most sacred shrine of the Jewish tabernacle.

holy orders The state of being ordained to the ministry of a church: a term used chiefly in the Anglican, Eastern, and Roman Catholic churches. See also under ORDER.

Holy Roller One belonging to a Protestant sect whose members express religious emotion by violent bodily movements and shouting: a humorous or derogatory term.

Holy Roman Empire An empire in central and western Europe, established in 962 and lasting until 1806: regarded as an extension of the Western Roman Empire and as the temporal form of the dominion of which the pope was spiritual head: sometimes considered as established with the crowning of Charlemagne. See map below; extent in 11th cent.

holy rood The cross over the entrance to the chancel of many churches and cathedrals.

Holy Sepulcher See under SEPULCHER.

Holy Spirit The third person of the Trinity: also called Holy Ghost.

ho·ly·stone (hō′lē·stōn′) n. A flat piece of soft sandstone used for cleaning the wood decks of a vessel. — v.t. **·stoned, ·ston·ing** To scrub with a holystone. [Said to be so called because used to clean decks for Sunday]

Holy Synod The supreme governing body in any of the Greek Catholic churches.

ho·ly·tide (hō′lē·tīd′) n. A holy season.

holy water Water regarded as sacred; especially, in the Eastern and Roman Catholic churches, water blessed by a priest.

hom·age (hom′ij, om′-) n. 1 Reverential regard or worship; deference. 2 In feudal law, formal acknowledgment of tenure by a tenant to his lord. 3 An act evincing deference or vassalage. See synonyms under ALLEGIANCE, REVERENCE. — v.t. Obs. **·aged, ·ag·ing** To pay respect or allegiance to. [<OF <LL hominaticum < homo, -inis vassal, client, man]

hom·ag·er (hom′ə·jər, om′-) n. One who does homage or holds land under tenure of homage.

Hom·burg (hom′bûrg) n. 1 A man's hat of soft felt with slightly rolled-up brim and crown dented lengthwise: so called because originally worn by men in Homburg, Germany. 2 A woman's hat styled after this.

home (hōm) n. 1 One's fixed place of abode; the family residence. 2 A family circle; household: a happy home. 3 The place of abode of one's affections, peace, or rest: He found a home in the church. 4 One's native place or country. 5 The seat or habitat of something; the place of origin: New Orleans is the home of jazz. 6 An establishment for the shelter and care of the needy or infirm. 7 In some games, the goal that must be reached in order to win or score. — **at home**

1 In one's own house, place, or country. 2 At ease, as if in familiar surroundings. 3 Prepared to receive callers. — adj. 1 Of or pertaining to one's home or country. 2 At the place regarded as the base of operations: the home office; a home game. 3 Going to the point; effective: a home thrust. — adv. 1 To or at home. 2 To the place or point intended: to thrust the dagger home. 3 Deeply and intimately; to the heart: Her words struck home. — v. homed, hom·ing v.t. 1 To carry or send to a home. 2 To furnish with a home. — v.i. 3 To go to a home; fly home, as homing pigeons. 4 To have residence. — **to home on** (or **in on**) 1 Mil. To direct toward, seek, or find the target, as a guided missile. 2 Aeron. To direct (an aircraft) to or toward a given spot by radio or other signals. [OE hām]

Synonyms (noun): abode, domicile, dwelling, fireside, habitation, hearth, hearthstone, house, ingleside, residence. See HOUSE.

Home may appear as a combining form in hyphemes or solidemes, or as the first element in two-word phrases, with the following meanings:

1 Of or pertaining to one's home or country:

home address	homekeeper	homemaking
home base	homekeeping	home–owner

2 At or in the home:

home–fed	home–staying
home–grown	home–woven

3 To or toward the home:

home–bound	home letter
homecomer	home–longing
home correspondent	home–wind

4 Relating to, produced or carried on in, one's home or country; domestic; hence, also, belonging to headquarters:

home affairs	home market

home·bod·y (hōm′bod′ē) n. pl. **·bod·ies** A person who habitually stays at home.

home·born (hōm′bôrn′) adj. Native to the home; derived through the home.

home·bred (hōm′bred′) adj. 1 Bred at home; native; domestic. 2 Uncultivated.

home–brew (hōm′brōō′) n. Spirituous or malt liquor distilled or brewed at home. — **home′-brewed′** adj.

home·com·ing (hōm′kum′ing) n. 1 A return home. 2 U.S. In colleges, an annual celebration for visiting alumni.

home economics The science that treats of the economic and social interests and activities of the home: food, clothing, hygiene, heating and ventilation, thrifty management, etc.

home guard Local volunteers organized to defend the home region or country when the standing army is afield.

home·land (hōm′land′) n. The country of one's birth or allegiance.

home·less (hōm′lis) adj. Having no home. — **home′less·ness** n.

home·like (hōm′līk′) adj. Like home; reminding of home. — **home′like′ness** n.

home·ly (hōm′lē) adj. **·li·er, ·li·est** 1 Having a familiar everyday character; unpretentious. 2 U.S. Having plain features; not good-looking. 3 Domestic. — **home′li·ness** n.

home–made (hōm′mād′) adj. 1 Of household or domestic manufacture, as distinguished from factory or foreign make. 2 Simple; homely.

homeo– combining form Like; similar: homeothermal: also spelled homoeo-. Also, before vowels, **home–**. [<Gk. homoios similar]

ho·me·o·path·ic (hō′mē·ə·path′ik, hom′ē-) adj. 1 Relating to homeopathy. 2 Extremely small in quantity. Also spelled homoeopathic.

ho·me·op·a·thist (hō′mē·op′ə·thist, hom′ē-) n. One who advocates or practices homeopathy. Also **ho·me·o·path** (hō′mē·ə·path′, hom′ē-).

ho·me·op·a·thy (hō′mē·op′ə·thē, hom′ē-) n. A system of medicine formulated by Dr. Samuel Hahnemann, 1755–1843. It is founded on the principle that "like cures like," and prescribes minute doses of such medicines as would produce in a healthy person the symptoms of the disease treated. Also spelled homoeopathy. [<HOMEO- + -PATHY]

ho·me·o·pla·sia (hō′mē·ə·plā′zhə, -zhē·ə, hom′·ē-) n. Med. The formation of tissue similar in appearance to the adjacent tissue. — **ho′me·o·plas′tic** (-plas′tik) adj.

ho·me·o·sta·sis (hō′mē·ə·stā′sis, hom′ē-) *n.* The tendency of an organism to maintain a uniform and beneficial physiological stability within and between its parts; organic equilibrium. — **ho′me·o·stat′ic** (-stat′ik) *adj.*

home plate In baseball, the base at which the batter stands when batting: a run is scored when the batter touches first, second, and third base, and home plate consecutively without being retired. See illustration under BASEBALL.

hom·er¹ (hō′mər) *n. U.S. Colloq.* A home run.

ho·mer² (hō′mər) *n.* 1 In Jewish antiquity, a liquid measure of 10 baths. See BATH². 2 A dry measure of 10 ephahs. [<Hebrew *hōmer* <*hāmar* swell up]

home·room (hōm′rōōm′, -rōom′) *n.* The schoolroom in which a class meets daily for attendance check, hearing of bulletins, guidance, etc.

home rule 1 Self-government in local affairs within the framework of state or national laws. 2 A political movement, begun about 1870, to gain autonomy for Ireland.

home-rul·er (hōm′rōō′lər) *n.* One who favors home rule.

home run In baseball, a base hit in which the ball is driven beyond reach of the opposing fielders, thus allowing the batter to touch all bases and score a run.

home·sick (hōm′sik′) *adj.* Suffering because of absence from home; ill in mind or body through longing for home; nostalgic. — **home′sick′ness** *n.*

home·spun (hōm′spun′) *adj.* 1 Of domestic manufacture. 2 Plain and homely in character. — *n.* 1 Fabric woven at home. 2 A loose, rough fabric having the appearance of tweed.

home·stake (hōm′stāk′) *n.* Enough money to get back home.

home·stead (hōm′sted) *n.* 1 The place of a home; the house, subsidiary buildings, and adjacent land occupied as a home. 2 *U.S.* A tract of land occupied by a settler under the Homestead Act (1862) or its revisions. — *v.i. U.S.* To become a settler on a homestead under the Homestead Act. — *v.t. U.S.* To settle on land under the Homestead Act.

home·stead·er (hōm′sted′ər) *n.* 1 One who has a homestead. 2 One who holds lands acquired under the Homestead Act of Congress.

homestead law *U.S.* A law in many States exempting a homestead from seizure or sale to satisfy general debts of a certain amount. Also **homestead exemption law.**

home·stretch (hōm′strech′) *n.* 1 The last part of a racecourse before the winning post is reached; the last part of a horse race. 2 The last part of any journey or endeavor.

home·ward (hōm′wərd) *adj.* Directed toward home. — *adv.* Toward home. Also **home′wards.**

home·work (hōm′wûrk′) *n.* Work performed or assigned for performance at home; work done at home by wage-earners, or lessons assigned to students for home study.

hom·ey (hō′mē) *adj.* **hom·i·er, hom·i·est** *Colloq.* Reminding of home; homelike: also spelled *homy.* — **home′y·ness, hom′i·ness** *n.*

hom·i·cide (hom′ə·sīd, hō′mə-) *n.* 1 The killing of one human being by another. 2 A person who has killed another. [<F <L *homicidium* <*homicida* murderer <*homo* man + *-cidere* <*caedere* cut, kill] — **hom′i·ci′dal** *adj.* — **hom′i·ci′dal·ly** *adv.*

hom·i·let·ics (hom′ə·let′iks) *n.* The branch of rhetoric that treats the composition and delivery of sermons. [<Gk. *homilētikos* sociable <*homileein* be in company with <*homilos* assembly]

hom·i·list (hom′ə·list) *n.* 1 A writer of homilies. 2 One who delivers homilies or preaches to a congregation.

hom·i·ly (hom′ə·lē) *n. pl.* **·lies** 1 A didactic sermon on some text or topic from the Bible. 2 A serious admonition, especially upon morals or conduct. 3 A tedious, moralizing discourse. [<OF *omelie* <LL *homilia* <Gk. *homilia* <*homilos* crowd <*homos* the same + *ilē* crowd] — **hom′i·let′ic** or **·i·cal** *adj.*

hom·i·nal (hom′ə·nəl) *adj.* Pertaining to man.

[<L *homo, hominis* man]

hom·ing (hō′ming) *adj.* 1 Readily finding the way home, returning home. 2 Pertaining to any of various methods and devices for directing an aircraft or guided missile to a specified spot: a *homing* beacon. — *n.* The act of heading for or reaching home.

homing pigeon A pigeon with remarkable capability of making its way home from great distances: used for conveying messages. Also called *carrier pigeon.*

hom·i·nid (hom′ə·nid, hō′mə-) *n. Zool.* A member of the family *Hominidae* of the primate order, now represented by only one living species, *Homo sapiens.* — *adj.* Of or pertaining to any member of this group. [<NL <L *homo, hominis* man]

hom·i·noid (hom′ə·noid, hō′mə-) *adj.* 1 Manlike. 2 *Zool.* Pertaining to or describing any member of the superfamily or group *Hominoidea* of the primate order, including the large tailless apes, as the gibbons, orangutans, gorillas, and chimpanzees, and the genus *Homo* as its most advanced form. — *n.* 1 An animal resembling man. 2 Any primate of the superfamily *Hominoidea.* [<NL <L *homo, hominis* man]

hom·i·ny (hom′ə·nē) *n.* Hulled corn (maize), broken up or coarsely ground, boiled in water or milk for food. Also **hominy grits.** [<Algonquian *rockahominie* parched corn]

Ho·mo (hō′mō) *n.* 1 *Man.* 2 *Zool.* Generic name of various species of erect, large-brained anthropoids belonging to the family *Hominidae* of the primate order of vertebrates, now represented only by *Homo sapiens.* [<L]

homo- *combining form* Same; similar; equal: *homogeneous:* opposed to *hetero-.* [<Gk. *homo-* <*homos* same]

ho·mo·cen·tric (hō′mə·sen′trik, hom′ə-) *adj.* Having a common center. Also **ho′mo·cen′tri·cal.**

ho·mo·cer·cal (hō′mə·sûr′kəl, hom′ə-) *adj. Zool.* Characterized by a similarity of the upper and lower halves of the caudal fin in fishes, due to the straight, central position of the caudal vertebrae. [<HOMO- + Gk. *kerkos* tail] — **ho′mo·cer′cy** (-sûr′sē) *n.*

ho·mo·chro·mat·ic (hō′mə·krō·mat′ik, hom′ə-) *adj.* Pertaining to or consisting of one color; monochromatic. Also **ho·mo·chrome** (hō′mə·krōm, hom′ə-). — **ho·mo·chro·ma·tism** (hō′mə·krō′mə·tiz′əm, hom′ə-) *n.*

ho·mo·chro·mous (hō′mə·krō′məs, hom′ə-) *adj. Bot.* Of one color, as a flower head with similar florets. [<HOMO- + Gk. *chrōma* color]

ho·mo·dyne (hō′mə·dīn, hom′ə-) *adj. Electronics* Pertaining to or designating a system of radio reception by the aid of a locally generated voltage of carrier frequency; zero-beat in reception. Compare HETERODYNE. [< HOMO- + Gk. *dynamos* power]

ho·mo·er·o·tism (hō′mō·er′ə·tiz′əm) *n.* Sexual attraction to members of the same sex, normally well sublimated. Also **ho·mo·e·rot·i·cism** (hō′mō·i·rot′ə·siz′əm). — **ho′mo·e·rot′ic** *adj.*

ho·mo·ga·mous (hō·mog′ə·məs) *adj. Bot.* 1 Having but one kind of flowers; opposed to *heterogamous.* 2 Having pistils and stamens which ripen at the same time: opposed to *dichogamous.* Also **ho·mo·gam·ic** (hō′mə·gam′ik). [<HOMO- + -GAMOUS]

ho·mo·ga·my (hō·mog′ə·mē) *n.* 1 *Bot.* a The simultaneous maturity of stamens and pistils in a flower: distinguished from *dichogamy.* b The condition in which all flowers alike: distinguished from *heterogamy.* 2 *Biol.* Interbreeding among an isolated group of individuals having similar characters, or characters different from those from which they are isolated. [<HOMO- + -GAMY]

ho·mo·ge·ne·i·ty (hō′mə·jə·nē′ə·tē, hom′ə-) *n.* Identity or similarity of kind or structure.

ho·mo·ge·ne·ous (hō′mə·jē′nē·əs, hom′ə-) *adj.* 1 Of the same composition or character throughout. 2 Of the same kind, nature, etc. (with another); like; similar: opposed to *heterogeneous.* 3 *Math.* Having all its terms of the same degree, as an algebraic equation. Also **ho·mo·gene** (hō′mə·jēn), **ho′mo·ge′ne·al.** See synonyms under ALIKE. [< Med. L *homogeneus* <Gk. *homogenēs* of the same race <*homos* the same + *genos* race] — **ho′mo·ge′ne·ous·ly** *adv.* — **ho′mo·**

ge′ne·ous·ness *n.*

ho·mo·gen·e·sis (hō′mə·jen′ə·sis, hom′ə-) *n. Biol.* 1 A mode of reproduction in which the offspring are like the parent and have the same cycle of existence: opposed to *heterogenesis.* 2 Homogeny.

ho·mog·en·ize (hə·moj′ə·nīz, hō′mə·jə·nīz′) *v.t.* **·ized, ·iz·ing** 1 To make or render homogeneous. 2 To process, as milk, by subjecting to high temperature and pressure so as to break up fat globules and disperse them uniformly throughout; emulsify. — **ho·mog′en·ized** *adj.* — **ho·mog′en·i·za′tion** *n.* — **ho·mog′en·iz′er** *n.*

ho·mog·e·nous (hə·moj′ə·nəs) *adj. Biol.* Having a similarity in structure due to descent from a common ancestor or development from a common stock.

ho·mog·e·ny (hə·moj′ə·nē) *n. Biol.* Homology of structures genetically related through a common ancestor: opposed to *homoplasy.* [< Gk. *homogeneia* community of birth <*homos* the same + *genos* race]

ho·mo·grade (hom′ə·grād) *adj. Stat.* Expressed in one or the other of two contrasting categories, as male or female. Compare HETEROGRADE.

hom·o·graph (hom′ə·graf, -gräf, hō′mə-) *n.* A word identical with another in spelling, but differing from it in origin and meaning, and sometimes in pronunciation, as *bass,* a fish, and *bass,* a male voice: also called *homonym.* ◆ See note under HOMONYM. [< Gk. *homographos* having the same letters <*homos* same + *graphein* to write] — **hom′o·graph′ic** *adj.*

ho·moi·o·ther·mal (hə·moi′ə·thûr′məl) *adj.* Preserving a uniform temperature, as warm-blooded animals: opposed to *poikilothermal.* Also **homothermal.**

ho·moi·ou·sian (hō′moi·ōō′sē·ən, -ou′sē-) *adj.* Alike in nature or characteristics. Also **ho′moi·ou′si·ous.**

hom·o·log (hom′ə·lôg, -log) *n.* 1 Something that answers in position, proportion, or type to, or has structural affinity with, something else; a member or form of a homologous series: Ethane is a *homolog* of methane. 2 *Biol.* A structure or part of an organism showing homology: The wing of a bat is the *homolog* of the arm of a man: distinguished from *analog.* Also **hom′o·logue.**

ho·mol·o·gate (hō·mol′ə·gāt) *v.* **·gat·ed, ·gat·ing** *v.t.* 1 To acknowledge; express approval of. 2 In Scots law, to make valid; ratify. — *v.i.* 3 To agree; to express assent. [< Med. L *homologatus,* pp. of *homologare* < Gk. *homologein* agree]

ho·mol·o·gize (hō·mol′ə·jīz) *v.* **·gized, ·giz·ing** *v.t.* 1 To make homologous. 2 To demonstrate the homologies of. — *v.i.* 3 To be homologous; correspond in structure or value.

ho·mol·o·gous (hō·mol′ə·gəs) *adj.* 1 Having a similar structure, proportion, value, or position. 2 Proportional to each other. 3 Identical in nature, relation, or the like. 4 *Biol.* Denoting either of a pair of sexually differentiated chromosomes which unite at meiosis. 5 *Med.* Pertaining to or designating a serum protecting against the same bacterium from which it was prepared. [< Gk. *homologos* agreeing <*homos* the same + *logos* speech < *legein* speak]

homolographic projection A method of map drawing by which the relative areas of different countries are accurately indicated.

homo·log·ra·phy (hom′ə·log′rə·fē) *n.* The study or presentation of proportions, anatomical or geodetic. [< Gk. *homalos* even + *graphein* write]

ho·mol·o·gy (hō·mol′ə·jē) *n.* 1 The state or quality of being homologous; correspondence in structure and properties. 2 *Biol.* The correspondence of a part or organ of one animal with a similar part or organ of another, determined by agreement in derivation and development from a like primitive origin, as the foreleg of a quadruped, the wing of a bird, and the pectoral fin of a fish: distinguished from *analogy* and contrasted with *heterology.* 3 *Chem.* A similarity in compounds having the same fundamental structure but differing in constituents by a regular succession of changes, as the alcohols. 4 *Bacteriol.* A relationship between a bacterium and the serum

obtained from it. [< HOMO- + -LOGY]

ho·mol·o·sine (hə·mol′ə·sin, -sīn) *adj.* Designating a world map combining two homolographic projections so as to portray continents with the least distortion possible. [< Gk. *homalas* even + L *sinus* curve]

ho·mo·mor·phism (hō′mə·môr′fiz·əm, hom′ə-) *n.* **1** *Biol.* Resemblance in form, as among the members of a zoophytic colony. **2** *Entomol.* The exhibition of imperfect metamorphosis in insects; resemblance of larva to adult. **3** *Bot.* The possession of perfect flowers of only one form or kind. Compare HETEROMORPHISM. —**ho′mo·mor′phic, ho′mo·mor′phous** *adj.*

ho·mo·mor·phy (hō′mə·môr′fē, hom′ə-) *n. Biol.* Imitative resemblance between unrelated organisms; adaptive mimicry without structural similarity.

hom·o·nym (hom′ə·nim, hō′mə-) *n.* **1** A word identical with another in pronunciation, but differing from it in spelling and meaning, as *fair* and *fare, read* and *reed:* also called *homophone.* **2** A homograph. **3** A word identical with another in spelling and pronunciation, but differing from it in origin and meaning, as *butter,* the food, and *butter,* one who butts. **4** One who has the same name as another; namesake. **5** *Biol.* A generic or specific name rejected because of previous application to another animal or plant. [< Gk. *homos* same + *onyma* name] —**hom·o·nym·ic** (hom′ə·nim′ik, hō′mə-) or **-i·cal** *adj.*

◆ *Homonym* is used with a variety of meanings, the most common sense being that of definition 1 above. Although *homophone* is etymologically more precise and is unambiguous in meaning, *homonym* is nevertheless the more commonly used form in this sense. *Homonym* is also, but less commonly, used interchangeably with *homograph.*

ho·mon·y·mous (hō·mon′ə·məs) *adj.* **1** Of the nature of a homonym; ambiguous. **2** Indicated by the same name because occupying the same relation.

ho·mon·y·my (hō·mon′ə·mē) *n.* Identity of sound or name with diversity of sense; ambiguity.

ho·mo·ou·si·an (hō′mō·ōō′sē·ən, -ou′sē-, hom′·ō-) *adj.* Identical in nature. Also **ho′mo·ou′si·ous.**

ho·mo·phile (hō′mō·fīl) *n.* A homosexual.

ho·mo·pho·bi·a (hō′mō·fō′bē·ə) *n.* Extreme hatred or fear of either homosexuals or of homosexuality.

hom·o·phone (hom′ə·fōn, hō′mə-) *n.* A homonym (def. 1). ◆ See note under HOMONYM. [< Gk. *homophōnos* of the same sound < *homos* same + *phōnē* sound]

hom·o·phon·ic (hom′ə·fon′ik, hō′mə-) *adj.* **1** *Music* **a** Consisting of sounds having the same pitch; in unison: said of ancient music. **b** Having one predominant part carrying the melody, with the other parts used for harmonic rather than for contrapuntal effect: opposed to *polyphonic.* **2** Of or pertaining to homophones; having the same sound. Also **ho·moph·o·nous** (hō·mof′ə·nəs).

ho·moph·o·ny (hō·mof′ə·nē) *n.* **1** Identity of sound, with difference of meaning. **2** *Music* The condition or quality of being homophonic.

ho·mo·plas·tic (hō′mə·plas′tik, hom′ə-) *adj. Biol.* Pertaining to a resemblance (in forms or organs) not traceable to homogeny: opposed to *homogenous.*

ho·mor·gan·ic (hō′môr·gan′ik) *adj. Phonet.* Describing speech sounds which are produced in a similar position in the mouth, as (p) and (b).

Ho·mo sa·pi·ens (sā′pē·enz) *n.* See HOMO.

ho·mo·sex·u·al (hō′mə·sek′shōō·əl, hom′ə-) *adj.* Pertaining to or characterized by homosexuality. —*n.* A homosexual person. Compare BISEXUAL, HETEROSEXUAL.

ho·mo·sex·u·al·i·ty (hō′mə·sek′shōō·al′ə·tē, hom′ə-) *n.* **1** Sexual attraction toward a person of the same sex. **2** Sexual relations between persons of the same sex.

ho·mo·tax·is (hō′mə·tak′sis, hom′ə-) *n.* **1** Classification in the same category. **2** *Geol.* The assignment to the same period in the life history of the earth of those groups of strata exhibiting the same general faunal characteristics, however widely separated from one another geographically; similarity of fossil formations. —**ho′mo·tax′i·al, ho′mo·tax′ic** *adj.* —**ho′mo·tax′i·al·ly** *adv.*

ho·mo·ther·mal (hō′mə·thûr′məl, hom′ə-) *adj.* Homoiothermal.

ho·mo·type (hō′mə·tīp) *n. Biol.* A part or organ similar to a preceeding, succeeding, or opposite one in the same animal, as one of the legs or arms. —**ho′mo·typ′ic** (-tip′ik) or **-i·cal** *adj.*

ho·mo·ty·py (hō′mə·tī′pē) *n. Biol.* The correspondence of a part or organ of one region with that of another in the same animal.

ho·mo·zy·go·sis (hō′mə·zī·gō′sis, -zi-, hom′ə-) *n. Biol.* The formation of a homozygote by the union of gametes.

ho·mo·zy·gote (hō′mə·zī′gōt, -zig′ōt, hom′ə-) *n. Biol.* A zygote formed by the conjugation of two gametes having the same genetic factors; a homozygous individual. See HETEROZYGOTE.

ho·mo·zy·gous (hō′mə·zī′gəs, hom′ə-) *adj. Biol.* Designating that condition of an individual in which any given genetic factor is doubly present, due usually to conjugating gametes which were alike in respect to this factor. [< HOMO- + Gk. *zygōsis* joining < *zygon* a yoke]

ho·mun·cu·lus (hō·mung′kyə·ləs) *n. pl.* **·li** (-lī) **1** According to Paracelsus, a tiny man produced artificially and endowed with magic power. **2** An undersized man; dwarf; manikin. **3** The human fetus. [< L, dim. of *homo* man] —**ho·mun′cu·lar** *adj.*

Ho·nan (hō′nän′) *n.* A fine Chinese silk, sometimes distinguished by blue edges.

Hon·du·ran (hon·dōōr′ən, -dyōōr′-) *adj.* Of or relating to Honduras. —*n.* A native or inhabitant of Honduras.

Hon·du·ras (hon·dōōr′əs, -dyōōr′-) A republic of NE Central America; 43,278 square miles; capital, Tegucigalpa.

hone¹ (hōn) *n.* A block of fine compact stone for sharpening edged tools, razors, etc. — *v.t.* **honed, hon·ing** To sharpen, as a razor, on a hone. [OE *hān* stone]

hone² (hōn) *v.i.* **honed, hon·ing** *Dial.* **1** To pine; long for. **2** To moan; grumble. [< F *hogner* mutter]

hon·est (on′ist) *adj.* **1** Fair and candid in dealing with others; true; just; upright; trustworthy. **2** Chaste; virtuous. **3** Free from fraud; equitable; fair. **4** Of respectable quality or appearance; creditable; unimpeached. **5** Characterized by openness or sincerity; frank. [< OF *honeste* < L *honestus* < *honos* honor] —**hon′est·ly** *adv.*

Synonyms: candid, equitable, fair, faithful, frank, genuine, good, honorable, ingenuous, just, sincere, straightforward, true, trustworthy, trusty, upright. One who is *honest* in the ordinary sense is disposed to act with regard for the rights of others, especially in matters of business or property; one who is *honorable* scrupulously observes the dictates of a personal honor that is higher than any demands of mercantile law or public opinion. Compare CANDID, JUST, MORAL, RIGHT, VIRTUOUS. *Antonyms:* deceitful, dishonest, disingenuous, faithless, false, fraudulent, hypocritical, lying, mendacious, perfidious, traitorous, treacherous, unfaithful, unscrupulous, untrue.

hone·stone (hōn′stōn′) *n.* **1** Any fine-grained stone from which hones are made, as novaculite. **2** A hone.

hon·es·ty (on′is·tē) *n.* **1** The character or quality of being honest; uprightness of conduct in general; justice; fairness. **2** Chastity; virtue. **3** An ornamental garden plant (*Lundria annua*) of the mustard family.

hone·wort (hōn′wûrt′) *n.* Any of a number of plants formerly believed to have medicinal properties, as the stone parsley, goldenrod, etc.

hon·ey (hun′ē) *n.* **1** A sweet, sirupy secretion, deposited by bees and derived chiefly from the nectaries of flowers. **2** Sweetness or lusciousness in general. **3** Sweet one: a pet name. — *v.* **hon·eyed** or **hon·ied, hon·ey·ing** — *v.t.* **1** To talk in an endearing or flattering manner to. **2** To sweeten. — *v.i.* **3** To talk fondly or in a coaxing manner. — *adj.* Honeylike; sweet. [OE *hunig*]

hon·ey—balls (hun′ē·bôlz′) *n. pl. U.S. Dial.* The spherical, white flower heads of the buttonbush.

honey bee A bee that collects honey; specifically, the common hive bee (*Apis mellifera*).

hon·ey·comb (hun′ē·kōm′) *n.* **1** A structure of hexagonal waxen cells, made by bees to contain honey, eggs, etc. **2** Anything full of small holes or cells. — *v.t.* **1** To fill with small holes or passages. **2** To pervade; corrupt. — *v.i.* **3** To become full of holes or passages. [OE *hunigcamb*] —**hon′ey·combed′** *adj.*

HONEYCOMB

honeycomb moth A moth (*Galleria melonella*) that infests beehives; bee moth. Also called *waxworm.*

hon·ey·dew (hun′ē·dōō′, -dyōō′) *n.* **1** A sweet secretion of plants or insects, as of aphids. **2** A honeydew melon. **3** A light pinkish orange. —**hon′ey·dewed′** *adj.*

honeydew melon A variety of muskmelon with a smooth white skin and sweet pulp.

hon·ey—eat·er (hun′ē·ē′tər) *n.* One of several Australian oscine birds (family *Meliphagidae*) which extract honey from flowers.

hon·eyed (hun′ēd) *adj.* **1** Covered with or full of honey. **2** Sweet; hence, soothing; agreeable; sweetly flattering. Also spelled *honied.* —**hon′eyed·ly** *adv.* —**hon′eyed·ness** *n.*

hon·ey·moon (hun′ē·mōōn) *n.* **1** A wedding trip. **2** The first month or so after marriage.

hon·ey·pot (hun′ē·pot′) *n.* A receptacle, of wax or other substance, made by many species of wild bees to store their honey.

hon·ey·stone (hun′ē·stōn′) *n.* A soft, yellowish or reddish aluminum mineral having a resinous appearance and crystallizing in the octahedral system: also called *mellite.*

hon·ey·suck·le (hun′ē·suk′əl) *n.* **1** Any of a genus (*Lonicera*) of ornamental erect or climbing shrubs having tubular white, buff, or crimson flowers. **2** Any one of a number of other plants, as the bush honeysuckle. [OE *hunisūce*]

honey yellow A soft yellow, as of honey.

hong (hong, hông) *n.* **1** A mercantile warehouse in China, comprising a number of connecting rooms; also, a connected row of warehouses. **2** A foreign trading establishment in China. [< Chinese *hang* row of houses, mercantile association]

Hong Kong (hong′ kong′, hông′ kông′) A British crown colony in SE China; 391 square miles, comprising Hong Kong Island (32 square miles), Kowloon peninsula, and the New Territories; capital, Victoria on Hong Kong Island; under Japanese occupation, 1941–45.

honk (hôngk, hongk) *n.* The cry of a wild goose or a sound imitating it, as that of an automobile horn. — *v.i.* To utter or make a honk or honks. — *v.t.* To cause to emit a honk or honks, as an automobile horn. [Imit.]

honk·er (hông′kər, hong′-) *n.* **1** A wild goose. **2** One who honks.

hon·ky (hông′kē, hungk′ē) *n. pl.* **·kies** *U.S. Slang* A white man: an offensive term. Also **hon′kie.** [? < HUNKY. See BOHUNK.]

hon·ky—tonk (hông′kē·tôngk′, hong′kē·tongk′) *n. Slang* A noisy, low-class barroom or night club. [Prob. imit.]

Hon·o·lu·lu (hon′ə·lōō′lōō) A port on SE Oahu; capital of Hawaii.

hon·or (on′ər) *n.* **1** Consideration due or paid, as to worth; respectful regard. **2** Any outward token of such feeling, such as college distinctions. **3** A nice sense of what is right. **4** That to which respect is due; a cause of esteem. **5** A title used in addressing judges, mayors, etc.: used with a possessive pronoun: *his honor,* the mayor. **6** In whist, one of the four highest trump cards; in bridge, one of the five highest cards of the trump suit, or one of the four aces when there are no trumps. **7** In golf, the privilege of playing first from the tee. See synonyms under FAME, JUSTICE, REVERENCE, VIRTUE. —**to do the honors** To act as host. —*v.t.* **1** To regard with honor or respect; treat with courtesy or respect. **2** To worship. **3** To do honor to; dignify; ennoble. **4** To accept or pay, as a check or draft. See synonyms under ADMIRE, VENERATE, WORSHIP. —*adj.* Having received recognition for outstanding academic work: an *honor* student. Also, *Brit.,* **hon′our.** [<OF <L] —**hon′or·er.**

hon·or·a·ble (on′ər·ə·bəl) *adj.* **1** Worthy of honor, in any degree from simple respectability to eminence; creditable; estimable; illustrious. **2** Conferring honor. **3** Consistent with or acting in accordance with principles of honor; conforming to a code of honor. **4** Betokening honor; accompanied by marks or testimonials of honor: *honorable* burial. **5** Entitled to honor: formal epithet of respect prefixed to the names of persons holding important offices. See synonyms under GOOD, HONEST, ILLUSTRIOUS, JUST, MORAL. Also *Brit.* **hon′our·a·ble.** —**hon′or·a·ble·ness** *n.* —**hon′or·a·bly** *adv.*

hon·o·rar·i·um (on′ə·râr′ē·əm) *n.* *pl.* **·i·ums** or **·i·a** A gratuity given, as to a professional man, for services rendered when law, custom, or propriety forbids a set fee. See synonyms under SALARY. [<L *honorarium (donum)* honorary (gift), neut. of *honorarius* honorary]

hon·or·ar·y (on′ə·rer′ē) *adj.* **1** Done, conferred, or held merely as an honor. **2** Designating an office or title bestowed as a sign of honor, without emoluments or without powers or duties. **3** Depending solely on one's honor: said of a debt or other obligation not legally binding. [<L *honorarius*]

hon·or·if·ic (on′ə·rif′ik) *adj.* **1** Conferring or implying honor or respect. **2** Denoting certain phrases, words, or word elements, as in Oriental languages, used in respectful address. —*n.* Any honorific title, word, phrase, etc. [<L *honorificus* <*honor* + *facere* make] —**hon′or·if′i·cal·ly** *adv.*

honors of war Marks of respect or honorable terms granted to a capitulating force.

honors system In some colleges and universities, a plan of advanced study for selected students, in which the student is excused from classroom routine to undertake individual, specialized work.

honor system A system of administering examinations and schoolwork without supervision and relying upon the honor of the students not to cheat.

hooch (hōōch) *n.* *U.S. Slang* Intoxicating liquor. Also spelled **hootch.** [<*hoochinoo,* alter. of *Hutanuwu,* name of Alaskan Indian tribe that made liquor]

hood¹ (hōōd) *n.* **1** A soft or flexible covering for the head and the back of the neck. **2** Anything of similar form or character. **3** A monk's cowl. **4** An ornamental fold attached to the back of an academic gown. **5** In falconry, a cover for the entire head of a hawk. **6** A projecting cover to a hearth, forge, or ventilator. **7** The movable cover of a machine, as of the engine of an automobile. **8** *Biol.* A concave expansion of any organ, resembling a hood; a crest. —*v.t.* To cover or furnish with or as with a hood. [OE *hōd*]

hood² (hōōd) *n.* *U.S. Slang* A hoodlum. [< HOODLUM]

-hood *suffix of nouns* **1** Condition of; state of being: *babyhood, falsehood.* **2** Class or totality of those having a certain character: *priesthood.* [OE *hād* state, condition]

hood·ed (hōōd′id) *adj.* **1** Wearing or having a hood. **2** Shaped like a hood. **3** Having a hoodlike part. **4** *Ornithol.* A conspicuous patch of feathers on the head of a bird. **5** *Zool.* The folds of skin near the head of certain animals and capable of voluntary expansion, as in the cobra and certain other snakes.

hooded seal One of the more abundant seals of the North Atlantic (*Cystophora cristata*). The males have an inflatable bag on the top of the head.

hood·lum (hōōd′ləm) *n.* *U.S.* One of a class of street rowdies; any ruffian or rowdy. [? < dial. G *hodalum* a rowdy] —**hood′lum·ism** *n.*

hood·man (hōōd′mən) *n.* *pl.* **·men** (-mən) The person blindfolded in the game of **hoodman-blind,** an old form of blindman's-buff.

hoo·doo (hōō′dōō) *n.* **1** Voodoo. **2** *Colloq.* A person or thing that brings bad luck; a jinx. —*v.t.* *Colloq.* To bring bad luck to; bewitch. [Var. of VOODOO] —**hoo′doo·ism** *n.*

hood·wink (hōōd′wingk) *v.t.* **1** To deceive as if by blinding; impose upon; delude. **2** To blindfold. **3** *Obs.* To cover; conceal. [<HOOD + WINK] —**hood′wink′er** *n.*

hoof (hōōf, hōōf) *n.* *pl.* **hoofs** (*Rare* **hooves**) **1** The horny sheath incasing the ends of the digits or foot in various mammals. ◆ Collateral adjective: *ungular.* **2** An animal with hoofs. —**cloven hoof** The sign of Satan. —**on the hoof** Alive; not butchered: said of cattle. —*v.t.* & *v.i.* **1** To trample with the hoofs. **2** *Colloq.* To walk or dance: usually with *it.* [OE *hōf*] —**hoofed** (hōōft, hōōft) *adj.*

hoof-and-mouth disease (hōōf′ən·mouth′) See FOOT-AND-MOUTH DISEASE.

hoof-bound (hōōf′bound′, hōōf′-) *adj.* Having a contraction of the hoof, causing pain and lameness.

hoof-print (hōōf′print′, hōōf′-) *n.* The print left by a hoof on the ground; a track.

hook (hōōk) *n.* **1** A curved or bent piece serving to catch or hold another object. **2** A tool in hooked form; especially, a sickle. **3** *Music* The flag-shaped projection from the stem of an eighth note, or one of still shorter duration. **4** A hook-shaped part, as of a written character. **5** The act of hooking. **6** Something that catches or snares; a trap. **7** In golf, a shot in which the ball deviates to the side on which the player stands. **8** In baseball, a sharp-breaking curve. **9** In boxing, a short blow delivered in a swinging manner crosswise and with the elbow bent and rigid. **10** A bend in a river; a point of land; a cape: *Sandy Hook.* See synonyms under LOCK. —**by hook or by crook** In one way or another. —**on one's own hook 1** By oneself. **2** On one's own authority. —*v.t.* **1** To fasten, attach, or take hold of with or as with a hook. **2** To catch on or with a hook, as fish. **3** To trick; take in: I've been *hooked.* **4** To make or bend in the shape of a hook; crook. **5** To catch on or toss with the horns: said of bulls, etc. **6** To make, as a rug, by looping thread, yarn, etc., through burlap with a hook. **7** *Slang* To steal; pilfer. **8** In baseball, to throw (a ball) with a hook. **9** In boxing, to strike with a hook. **10** In golf, to drive (the ball) in a hook. —*v.i.* **11** To curve like a hook; bend. **12** To be fastened with a hook. —**to hook up 1** To fasten or attach with hooks. **2** To put together, as the parts of a machine. —**to hook up to** To connect (apparatus) to a source of power: The trailer was *hooked up* to the car. —**to hook up with** *Colloq.* To join; become a companion or adherent of. [OE *hōc*]

HOOKS
a. Box hook.   c. Eyehook.   e. Boat hook.
b. Coat hook.   d. Ice hook.

hook·ah (hōōk′ə) *n.* In India and Iran, a form of tobacco pipe by which the smoke is drawn through water; a narghile. Also **hook′a.** [< Arabic *ḥuqqah*]

hook-and-lad·der (hōōk′ən·lad′ər) *n.* A vehicle, equipped with ladders for effecting rescues, and hooks, axes, etc., for tearing down walls, used by fire departments. Also **hook-and-ladder truck.**

hooked (hōōkt) *adj.* **1** Curved like a hook. **2** Supplied with a hook. **3** Made with a hook. —**hook′ed·ness** (hōōk′id·nis) *n.*

hook·er¹ (hōōk′ər) *n.* **1** A two-masted Dutch vessel. **2** A fishing boat used on the English and Irish coasts. **3** An old or clumsy craft. [< Du. *hoeker* < *hoek* hook]

hook·er² (hōōk′ər) *n.* *Slang* A drink, especially an alcoholic one. [<HOOK, prob. with ref. to the bend of the arm in drinking]

hook·er³ (hōōk′ər) *n.* *Slang* A prostitute. [from Corlears *Hook,* formerly a notorious waterfront district in Manhattan]

hook, line, and sinker Completely; without question or reservation.

hook-nose (hōōk′nōz′) *n.* An aquiline nose, or a person having such a nose. —**hook′-nosed′** *adj.*

hook-up (hōōk′up′) *n.* **1** *Telecom.* **a** The assembled apparatus for a radio broadcast or other electrical transmission. **b** The diagram giving the connections for such transmission. **2** A mechanical connection, as of gas or water lines. **3** *Colloq.* An alliance or pact between governments, organizations, etc.

hook·worm (hōōk′wûrm′) *n.* Any of various nematode worms of the genera *Ancylostoma, Necator,* etc., infesting man and several animals, such as sheep, dogs, cattle, etc.

hookworm disease Ancylostomiasis.

hook·y¹ (hōōk′ē) *adj.* Full of hooks, pertaining to hooks, or like a hook.

hook·y² (hōōk′ē) *n.* *U.S. Colloq.* The condition of being illegitimately absent; truant, etc.: used only in the phrase **to play hooky,** to be a truant. [<HOOK, in dial. sense of "make off"]

hoo·li·gan (hōō′lə·gən) *n.* A hoodlum; a gangster. [after *Hooligan,* name of an Irish family in London] —**hoo′li·gan·ism** *n.*

hoop¹ (hōōp, hōōp) *n.* **1** A circular band of stiff material, especially one used to confine the staves of a barrel, cask, etc. **2** A child's toy in the shape of a large circular ring of metal or wood that is trundled along the ground. **3** A large ring of flexible material used for expanding a woman's skirt. **4** The band of a finger ring. **5** An arched wicket in croquet. **6** Anything shaped like a ring or band. —*v.t.* **1** To surround or fasten with hoops, as a cask. **2** To encircle. [OE *hōp*]

hoop² (hōōp) *n.* **1** A whoop; shout. **2** The sound made in whooping cough. —*v.t.* & *v.i.* To whoop. [Var. of WHOOP]

hoop·er (hōō′pər, hōōp′ər) *n.* One who hoops casks or tubs; a cooper.

hoo·poe (hōō′pōō) *n.* An Old World bird (family *Upupidae*), having a long, pointed, curved bill and an erectile crest. Also **hoo′poo.** [<F *huppe* <L *upupa*]

HOOPOE
(About 12 inches long; bill: 2 1/2 inches)

hoop skirt A framework of hoops or crinoline for expanding a skirt; also, the skirt itself.

hoop snake A harmless snake of the southern United States (*Abastor erythrogrammus*): formerly believed to take its tail in its mouth and roll like a hoop.

hoo·ray (hōō·rā′, hə-, hōō-) See HURRAH.

hoot (hōōt) *v.i.* **1** To jeer or call out, as in contempt or disapproval. **2** To utter the low, hollow cry of an owl. —*v.t.* **3** To jeer at or mock with hooting cries. **4** To drive off with shouts of contempt, disapproval, etc. **5** To express by hooting. —*n.* **1** A cry uttered in derision. **2** The cry of an owl. **3** *Slang* A whit: not worth a *hoot.* [<Scand. Cf. Sw. *huta.*]

hootch (hōōch) See HOOCH.

hoot·chy-koot·chy (hōō′chē-kōō′chē) *n.* *U.S. Slang* A suggestive dance involving much hip and abdominal movement. [Origin unknown]

hoot-en-an-ny (hōōt′n·an′ē) *n.* *Slang* A gathering of folk singers. [Origin unknown]

hoot owl An owl that hoots, especially the American northern barred owl (*Strix varia*).

Hoo·ver (hōō′vər), **Herbert Clark,** 1874–1964, president of the United States 1929–33. — **J(ohn) Edgar,** 1895–1972, U.S. criminologist: director of the Federal Bureau of Investigation 1924–1972.

hooves (hōōvz, hōōvz) Alternative plural of HOOF.

hop¹ (hop) v. **hopped, hop·ping** v.i. **1** To move in short leaps with the feet off the ground. **2** To jump about on one foot. — v.t. **3** To jump over, as a fence. **4** To board or catch; get on: to *hop* a train. See synonyms under LEAP. — n. **1** The act or result of hopping. **2** *Colloq.* A dance or dancing party. **3** *Colloq.* An ascent, flight, or trip in an airplane. [OE *hoppian*]

hop² (hop) n. **1** A perennial climbing herb (*Humulus lupulus*) with opposite lobed leaves and scaly fruit. **2** *pl.* The ripe and carefully dried multiple fruit of this plant: used in the brewing of beer and in medicine as an aromatic bitter stomachic. [<MDu. *hoppe*]

hop·cal·ite (hop′kəl·īt) n. A granular mixture of the oxides of copper, cobalt, manganese, and silver: effective as a catalyzing material to protect against carbon monoxide. [< (*Johns*) *Hop*(*kins University*) + (*University of*) *Cal*(*ifornia*) + -ITE¹]

hop clover Yellow clover (*Trifolium procumbens*) whose dried flowers resemble hops.

hope (hōp) v. **hoped, hop·ing** v.t. **1** To desire with expectation of fulfilment: I *hope* to be able to join you. **2** To wish; want: I *hope* that you will be happy. — v.i. **3** To have desire or expectation: usually with *for:* to *hope* for the best. See synonyms under ANTICIPATE, TRUST. — n. **1** Desire accompanied by expectation. **2** The cause of hopeful expectation. **3** The thing confidently desired or hoped for. — **in hopes** Having hope. See synonyms under TRUST. [OE *hopa*]

hope chest A box or chest used by young women to hold linen, clothing, etc., in anticipation of marriage.

hope·ful (hōp′fəl) adj. **1** Full of hope; promising. **2** Having qualities that excite hope. See synonyms under AUSPICIOUS, SANGUINE. — n. A young person who seems likely to succeed in life: a humorous or ironic use. — **hope′ful·ness** n.

hope·ful·ly (hōp′fə·lē) adv. **1** In a hopeful manner. **2** It is hoped; one hopes: *Hopefully,* a strike can be averted.

Ho·peh (hō′pā′) A province in NE China; 50,000 square miles; capital, Paoting: formerly *Chihli.* Also **Ho′pei′.**

hope·less (hōp′lis) adj. **1** Without hope; despairing. **2** Affording no ground of hope. — **hope′less·ly** adv. — **hope′less·ness** n.

hope·sick (hōp′sik′) adj. Sick at heart with unfulfilled hope or ungratified longing.

Ho·pi (hō′pē) n. **1** One of a group of North American Pueblo Indians of Shoshonean linguistic stock: now on a reservation in NE Arizona: also called *Moqui* or *Moki.* **2** Their Shoshonean language. [<Hopi *hópitu,* lit., peaceful ones]

hop·lite (hop′līt) n. In ancient Greece, a heavily armed foot soldier. [<Gk. *hoplitēs* < *hoplon* a shield]

hop-o′-my-thumb (hop′ə·mī·thum′) n. A very small person. [after *Hop-o′-my-thumb,* tiny hero of a fairy tale by Perrault]

hopped-up (hopt′up′) adj. *U.S. Slang* **1** Stimulated by a narcotic drug. **2** Excited; exhilarated. **3** Supercharged for high speed: said of an automobile. [? <HOP²]

hop·per (hop′ər) n. **1** One who or that which hops. **2** A saltatorial insect or larva, as a grasshopper or the larva of a fly that infests cheese. **3** A shaking or conveying receiver, funnel, or trough in which something is placed to be passed or fed, as to a mill. **4** A funnel-shaped spout or tank with a movable bottom or no bottom, as for conveying grain to cars. **5** A tilting, dumping, or discharging bottom or receptacle, as in a car or boat. **6** A tank or boxlike receptacle for holding water, grain, sugar, etc., which may be emptied by opening its bottom.

hopper car A car for coal, gravel, etc., with an opening to discharge the contents.

hop·ple (hop′əl) v.t. **·pled, ·pling** To hamper; hobble. — n. A fetter for the legs of a horse, etc. [Var. of HOBBLE]

hop·sack·ing (hop′sak′ing) n. A coarse fabric with rough surface: used for dresses, etc. [<HOP² + SACK]

hop·scotch (hop′skoch′) n. A child's game in which the player hops on one foot over a diagram marked (scotched) on the ground to recover the block or pebble previously tossed into successive sections of the diagram.

hop, skip (or step), and jump **1** An athletic

feat in which the contestants strive to cover as much distance as possible in a successive hop, step, and jump. **2** A short distance or interval.

ho·ral (hō′rəl) adj. Pertaining to an hour; hourly. [<L *hora* hour]

ho·rar·i·ous (hō·râr′ē·əs) adj. *Bot.* Lasting but one or two hours: said of flowers. [<L *hor(a)* hour + -ARIOUS]

ho·ra·ry (hō′rə·rē) adj. **1** Pertaining to an hour; designating the hours. **2** Continuing only an hour; occurring hourly. **3** In astrology, referring to propitious or specific times. [<L *hora* hour]

horde (hôrd, hōrd) n. **1** A clan or tribe of Mongolian, especially Tatar, nomads; hence, any nomadic group. **2** A multitude; a pack or swarm, as of men, animals, or insects. — **Golden Horde** A fierce and powerful Mongol horde, named from the golden tent of Batu Khan, under whose lead they laid waste eastern Europe in the 13th century; the Kipchaks. — v.i. **hord·ed, hord·ing** To gather in a horde. ◆ Homophone: *hoard.* [<F <G <Polish *horda* <Turkish *ordŭ* camp. Related to URDU.]

hor·de·nine (hôr′də·nēn, -nin, hôr′-) n. A white, crystalline, almost tasteless alkaloid, $C_{10}H_{15}ON$, obtained from malt sprouts: its sulfate is used in the treatment of diarrhea and as a heart stimulant. [<L *hordeum* barley + -INE²]

hore·hound (hôr′hound′, hōr′-) n. **1** A whitish, bitter, perennial herb of the mint family (genus *Marrubium*): used as a remedy for colds. **2** A candy flavored with an extract of this herb. **3** One of various allied plants. Also spelled *hoarhound.* [OE *harhune*]

ho·ri·zon (hə·rī′zən) n. **1** The line of the apparent meeting of earth or sea and sky: called the **local** or **visible horizon. 2** The bounds of observation or experience. **3** *Astron.* **a** The plane passing through a position on the earth's surface at right angles to the line of gravity: called the **sensible horizon. b** The great circle in which the sensible horizon cuts the celestial sphere: called the **celestial, geometric, rational,** or **true horizon. 4** *Geol.* **a** A definite position in the stratigraphic column, or in the scheme of classification of strata according to age. **b** A bed or limited number of beds characterized by one or more distinctive fossils; a zone. **5** One of the layers in a cross-section of soil. **6** The imaginary line, taking the place of the natural horizon, in a picture of a landscape, on which is projected the point of sight of the viewer. See PERSPECTIVE. [<OF *orizonte* <L *horizon* <Gk. *horizōn* (*kyklos*) bounding (circle), ppr. of *horizein* bound <*horos* limit, bound]

horizon blue A soft gray-blue.

hor·i·zon·tal (hôr′ə·zon′təl, hor′-) adj. **1** Parallel to the horizon; on a level. **2** Included or measured in a plane of the horizon. **3** Of, pertaining to, on, or close to the horizon. **4** Equal and uniform: a *horizontal* tariff. **5** Made up of similar units: a *horizontal* trust. — n. A line or plane assumed, for the purpose of measurement or description, to be parallel with the horizon. — **hor′i·zon′tal·ly** adv.

Synonyms (adj.): flat, level, plain, plane. For practical purposes *level* and *horizontal* are identical, but *level* is more loosely used of that which has no especially noticeable elevations or inequalities; as, a *level* road. *Flat* applies to a surface only, and, in the first, most usual sense, to a surface that is *horizontal* or *level* in all directions; *flat* is also applied to any *plane* surface without irregularities or elevations, as a picture may be painted on the *flat* surface of a perpendicular wall. *Plane* applies only to a surface, and is used with more mathematical exactness than *flat. Plain,* originally the same word as *plane,* is now rarely used except in senses pertaining to *level* ground. We speak of a *horizontal* line, a *flat* morass, a *level* road, a *plain* country, a *plane* surface (especially in the scientific sense). See FLAT, LEVEL. *Antonyms:* broken, hilly, inclined, irregular, rolling, rough, rugged, slanting, sloping, uneven.

hor·i·zon·tal·ism (hôr′ə·zon′təl·iz′əm, hor′-) n. The character of being horizontal; horizontal extension. — **hor′i·zon·tal′i·ty** (-zon·tal′ə·tē) n.

hor·mone (hôr′mōn) n. *Physiol.* An internal secretion, produced in and by one of the en-

docrine glands; specifically, one of a group of complex chemical compounds evolved in one part of an organism and carried thence by the blood stream or body fluids to other parts, on which it exercises a specific physiological action. Many important hormones are now made synthetically. Compare COLYONE. See ENDOCRINE. [<Gk. *hormōn,* ppr. of *hormaein* excite] — **hor·mo·nal** (hôr·mō′nəl), **hor·mon·ic** (hôr·mon′ik) adj.

horn (hôrn) n. **1** A hard bonelike growth projecting from the head of various hoofed mammals, as oxen, sheep, cattle, etc.; also, the antler of a deer, shed annually. **2** Any hardened and thickened outgrowth of epidermal tissue, as a feeler, antenna, tentacle, etc. **3** A feather tuft, as on the head of some birds. **4** The appendage like an animal's horn attributed to demons, deities, etc. **5** An imaginary projection from the forehead of a cuckold. **6** The substance of which animal horn consists, as keratin, calcium phosphate, etc. **7** A vessel or implement formed from or shaped like a horn: a powder *horn.* **8** A wind instrument, made formerly of animal horn, now of brass, in the shape of a long tube constricted at one end and widening out to a large bell at the other. **9** *Slang* A trumpet. **10** Any pointed or tapering projection. **11** One of the extremities of a crescent moon. **12** One of the branches forming the delta of a stream. **13** A cape or peninsula. **14** The pommel of a saddle. **15** The point of an anvil. **16** *Aeron.* The lever which operates the wire connecting with the rudder, aileron, or elevator of an aircraft. **17** A hollow conical device with a bell-shaped aperture, for collecting sound waves, as in a sound locator. **18** A device for sounding warning signals: an automobile *horn.* — **on the horns of a dilemma** Forced to choose between two painful alternatives. — **to haul (or pull or draw) in one's horns** To check one's anger, zeal, pretensions, etc. — adj. Of horn or horns. — v.t. **1** To provide with horns. **2** To shape like a horn. **3** To attack with the horns; gore. **4** *Obs.* To cuckold. — **horn in** To enter without invitation. [OE. Akin to CORN².] — **horn′less** adj. — **horn′like′** adj.

horn angle *Geom.* The angle formed by two curved lines tangent to each other at one point.

horn·beam (hôrn′bēm′) n. A small tree of the birch family (genus *Carpinus*), resembling the beech, with white, hard wood.

horn·bill (hôrn′bil′) n. A large bird of tropical Asia and Africa, related to the kingfishers (family *Bucerotidae*) and having a large bill surmounted by a hornlike extension.

horn·book (hôrn′book′) n. **1** A leaf or page containing a printed alphabet, etc., covered with transparent horn and framed: formerly used in teaching reading to children. **2** A primer or book of rudimentary knowledge.

horned (hôrnd, *Poetic* hôr′nid) adj. Having a horn or horns.

horned owl Any of various American owls with conspicuous ear tufts; especially, the great horned owl or the screech owl.

horned toad A harmless, flat-bodied, spiny lizard (*Phrynosoma cornutum*) with a very short tail and toadlike appearance: common in semiarid regions of the western part of the United States: also *horn toad.*

horned viper A venomous African or Indian viper (*Cerastes cornutus*) with a horn over each eye.

HORNED TOAD (From 3 to 7 inches long)

hor·net (hôr′nit) n. Any of various strong-bodied social wasps (family *Vespidae*) capable of inflicting a severe sting; especially, the American bald-faced hornet (*Dolichovespula maculata*) and the European giant hornet (*Vespa crabo*). [OE *hyrnet*]

horn·ing (hôr′ning) n. **1** *U.S. Dial.* A charivari. **2** The act of one who or that which horns.

horn–mad (hôrn′mad′) *adj.* **1** Mad enough to gore: said of a bull. **2** Crazy; insane; wild. — **horn′–mad′ness** *n.*

horn of plenty 1 In Greek mythology, the horn of Amalthea. **2** A symbol of abundance in general, represented in art as a curved horn filled with fruit, etc.: also called *cornucopia.*

horn·pipe (hôrn′pīp′) *n.* **1** A lively English country dance. **2** The music of such a dance, or similar music. **3** A musical instrument resembling the clarinet formerly used in England and Wales.

horn–rimmed (hôrn′rimd′) *adj.* Having frames of horn or of dark–colored plastic, often relatively thick and heavy: said of spectacles or eyeglasses.

horn·work (hôrn′wûrk′) *n.* **1** The art of working horn. **2** Objects collectively that are made of horn. **3** *Mil.* A fortification outwork made up of two half bastions connected by a curtain.

horn·y–hand·ed (hôr′nē-han′did) *adj.* Having hard or calloused hands.

hor·o·loge (hôr′ə-lōj, hor′-) *n.* **1** A timepiece. **2** A clock tower. [< OF *horloge* < L *horologium* < Gk. *hōrologion* < *hōra* time + *legein* tell]

ho·rol·o·ger (hō-rol′ə-jər, hō-) *n.* One skilled in horology; also, one who makes or sells timepieces. Also **ho·rol′o·gist.**

hor·o·log·ic (hôr′ə-loj′ik, hor′-) *adj.* **1** Pertaining to horology or to a horologe. **2** *Bot.* Opening and closing at certain hours, as some flowers. Also **hor′o·log′i·cal.**

Hor·o·lo·gi·um (hôr′ə-lō′jē-əm, hor′-) A southern constellation, the Clock. See CONSTELLATION.

ho·rol·o·gy (hō-rol′ə-jē, hō-) *n.* The science of time-measurement or of the construction of timepieces.

hor·o·scope (hôr′ə-skōp, hor′-) *n.* **1** In astrology, the aspect of the heavens, with special reference to the positions of the planets at any instant. **2** A figure or statement showing such aspect, from which astrologers profess to foretell the future of an individual. **3** The diagram of the twelve divisions or houses of the heavens, used by astrologers in predicting the future. [< L *horoscopus* < Gk. *hōroskopos* observer of hour of nativity < *hōra* hour + *skopos* watcher < *skopeein* watch]

ho·ros·co·py (hō-ros′kə-pē, hō-) *n.* **1** The art of casting horoscopes or of determining the future from the positions of the heavenly bodies. **2** In astrology, the situation of the heavenly bodies at the time of a person's birth; a horoscope.

hor·ren·dous (hô-ren′dəs, ho-) *adj.* Frightful; fearful. [< L *horrendus,* gerundive of *horrere* bristle] — **hor·ren′dous·ly** *adv.*

hor·rent (hôr′ənt, hor′-) *adj.* **1** Standing erect like bristles; bristling. **2** Causing terror and abhorrence. **3** Feeling or expressing horror. [< L *horrens, -entis,* ppr. of *horrere* bristle]

hor·ri·ble (hôr′ə-bəl, hor′-) *adj.* Exciting abhorrence; terrible. See synonyms under AWFUL, FRIGHTFUL. [< F < L *horribilis* < *horrere* bristle] — **hor′ri·ble·ness** *n.* — **hor′ri·bly** *adv.*

hor·rid (hôr′id, hor′-) *adj.* **1** Fitted to inspire horror; dreadful. **2** *Colloq.* Highly obnoxious; outrageous. See synonyms under FRIGHTFUL. [< L *horridus* bristling < *horrere* bristle] — **hor′rid·ly** *adv.* — **hor′rid·ness** *n.*

hor·rif·ic (hô-rif′ik, ho-) *adj.* Causing horror.

hor·ri·fy (hôr′ə-fī, hor′-) *v.t.* **·fied, ·fy·ing** To affect or fill with horror. — **hor′ri·fi·ca′tion** *n.*

hor·rip·i·la·tion (hô-rip′ə-lā′shən, ho-) *n.* A chilliness accompanied by the appearance of goose-pimples and bristling of the hair over the body, preceding fever; goose-flesh. [< L *horripilatio, -onis* < *horripilare* < *horrere* bristle + *pilus* hair]

hor·ror (hôr′ər, hor′-) *n.* **1** The painful emotion of extreme fear or abhorrence; dread. **2** Extreme repugnance. **3** That which excites fear or dread; especially, some great accident or calamity. **4** *Obs.* The shivering fit that precedes a fever. See synonyms under ABOMINATION, FEAR, FRIGHT. — **the horrors** *Colloq.* **1** The blues. **2** Delirium tremens. [< L]

hors d'oeuvre (ôr dûrv′, *Fr.* ôr dœ′vr′) An appetizer served before a meal. ◆ This form is both singular and plural in French. An

English plural, **hors d'oeuvres,** is also seen. [< F]

horse (hôrs) *n. pl.* **hors·es** or **horse 1** A large, solid–hoofed quadruped (*Equus caballus*) with coarse mane and tail: commonly, in the domestic state, employed as a beast of draught and burden and especially for riding upon.

HORSE
Nomenclature for anatomical parts.

◆ Collateral adjective: *equine.* **2** Any of various extinct mammals related to or supposed to be of the ancestral line of the horse, as the eohippus. **3** A male horse, especially when castrated; a gelding. **4** Cavalry: a regiment of *horse.* **5** A device used to support anything or suggesting the uses of a horse: usually used in combination: a *clotheshorse.* **6** *Mining* A mass of rock, similar to the wall rock, found in a vein of ore. **7** *U.S. Slang* A translation or other similar aid used by pupils in working out lessons; pony; crib. **8** A man: a friendly, joking, or opprobrious term. **9** *U.S. Slang* Horseplay; foolery. **10** *Colloq.* In chess, a knight. **11** In gymnastics, a wooden block on four legs used for vaulting and other exercises. — **a horse of another (or different) color** A completely different matter. — **to hold one's horses** To be patient; curb one's impetuosity; wait; take things easy. — **to horse 1** The bugle call summoning mounted troops to saddle and stand equipped at their horses' heads. **2** A signal to mount. — *v.* **horsed, hors·ing** *v.t.* **1** To furnish with horses; mount. **2** To put on another's back or on a sawhorse for flogging. **3** To flog. **4** *Aeron.* To jerk violently at (the controls of an aircraft). **5** *U.S. Slang* To subject to pranks or horseplay. — *v.i.* **6** To mount or ride on a horse. **7** *U.S. Slang* To engage in horseplay: usually with *around.* — *adj.* Coarse; large for its kind: *horse* chestnut, *horselaugh.* [OE *hors*]

horse·back (hôrs′bak′) *n.* **1** A horse's back. **2** An object shaped like a horse's back. — *adv.* On a horse's back.

horse balm Richweed.

horse·block (hôrs′blok′) *n.* **1** A block or platform used in mounting a horse. **2** A frame of boards used as a support.

horse·boat (hôrs′bōt′) *n.* **1** A boat moved by horsepower. **2** A boat for carrying horses.

horse·boot (hôrs′bōōt′) *n.* A leather covering to protect a horse's pastern against injury.

horse·bot (hôrs′bot′) *n.* A botfly or its larva that infests the stomach and intestines of the horse.

horse·boy (hôrs′boi′) *n.* A stableboy.

horse·break·er (hôrs′brā′kər) *n.* One who trains horses to work in harness or under the saddle.

horse·brush (hôrs′brush′) *n.* Any of a genus (*Tetradymia*) of low, tough, hoary, sometimes spiny shrubs of the western United States, especially the little-leaf horsebrush (*T. glabrata*), considered poisonous to sheep.

horse car 1 A car drawn by horses; tramcar. **2** A car for transporting horses by rail.

horse chestnut 1 A tree (*Aesculus hippocastanum*) of Asian origin, having digitate leaves, clusters of flowers, and large chestnutlike fruits: in the United States some species are known as *buckeyes.* **2** The fruit of this tree.

horse·cloth (hôrs′klôth′, -kloth′) *n.* A cloth to cover a horse.

horse collar A stuffed collar for a horse's neck, used to support the hames of a draft harness and to ease the pressure on the

shoulders in drawing.

horse·drench (hôrs′drench′) *n.* A medicinal dose for a horse, or the instrument with which it is administered.

horse·fish (hôrs′fish′) *n. pl.* **·fish** or **·fish·es** The moonfish.

horse·fly (hôrs′flī′) *n. pl.* **·flies 1** A large bloodsucking fly of the family *Tabanidae,* especially of the genus *Tabanus.* **2** The forest fly. **3** A botfly.

horse·foot (hôrs′fŏot′) *n.* **1** Coltsfoot. **2** The king crab.

horse furniture The harness or housing of a horse.

horse·gear (hôrs′gir′) *n.* Horse furniture; also, horsepower.

horse gentian A perennial weedy herb (genus *Triosteum*) of the honeysuckle family, especially the feverwort.

horse·head (hôrs′hed′) *n.* A tropical American moonfish (*Selene vomer*).

horse latitudes *Naut.* A belt of high pressure at about 35° north or south latitude, characterized by calms and light variable winds, with diminishing to prevailing westerlies toward the poles and trade winds toward the equator.

horse·laugh (hôrs′laf′, -läf′) *n.* A loud, boisterous laugh.

horse mackerel 1 A carangoid fish of Pacific waters (*Trachurus symmetricus*). **2** The tunny.

horse·man (hôrs′mən) *n. pl.* **·men** (-mən) **1** One who rides a horse. **2** A cavalryman. **3** A man who is skilled in riding or managing horses.

horse·man·ship (hôrs′mən·ship) *n.* Equestrian skill.

horse marine 1 A member of an imaginary corps of mounted marines. **2** One who is as awkward and out of place as a mounted marine would be aboard ship. **3** A mounted marine or sailor on duty ashore.

horse·mint (hôrs′mint′) *n.* **1** An erect American herb (*Monarda punctata*) of the mint family; wild bergamot. **2** Either of two European woodland mints (*Mentha longifolia* and *M. aquatica*), both naturalized in the United States.

horse·net·tle (hôrs′net′l) *n.* A rough roadside weed (*Solanum carolinense*) with straw-colored prickles, white flowers, and yellow berries, found in the central and southern United States.

horse pistol A large pistol formerly carried in a holster by horsemen.

horse·play (hôrs′plā′) *n.* Rough, boisterous play.

horse·pond (hôrs′pond′) *n.* A pond for watering horses.

horse·post (hôrs′pōst′) *n.* A system of sending mail by a carrier on horseback; also, the carrier. See PONY EXPRESS.

horse post A hitching post.

horse·pow·er (hôrs′pou′ər) *n.* **1** The force exerted by, or rate of work maintained by, an average dray horse. **2** *Mech.* The standard theoretical unit of the rate of work, equal to 33,000 pounds lifted one foot in one minute, or 550 foot-pounds per second. **3** A mechanical arrangement for utilizing a horse's power.

horse·pow·er–hour (hôrs′pou′ər·our′) *n.* A measure of work performed at the rate of one horsepower in one hour. Expressed in foot-pounds it is equal to 33,000 × 60, or 1,980,000 foot-pounds.

horse rack A long pole supported by posts to which horses are hitched.

horse·rad·ish (hôrs′rad′ish) *n.* **1** A coarse, tall, common garden herb (*Armoracia lapathifolia*) of the mustard family. **2** Its pungent root, used as a condiment.

horse·rake (hôrs′rāk′) *n.* A large mechanical rake worked by horsepower.

horse sense *Colloq.* Innate practical intelligence; common sense; shrewdness.

horse·shoe (hôrs′shōō′, hôrs′-) *n.* **1** A metal shoe for a horse, U-shaped like the edge of a horse's hoof, to which it is nailed. **2** Something roughly U-shaped, especially if the opening is narrower than the sweep of the curve. **3** The horseshoe crab. — *v.t.* **·shoed, ·shoe·ing** To furnish with horseshoes.

horseshoe crab A king crab.

horse·shoes (hôr′shōōz′, hôrs′-) *n.* A game, similar to quoits, originally played with discarded horseshoes, now often with new or imitation horseshoes.

horse sugar The sweetleaf, a shrub (*Symplocos tinctoria*) of the southern United States: eaten by cattle and horses.

horse·weed (hôrs′wēd′) *n.* **1** A common weed (*Erigeron canadensis*) of the composite family, found in most parts of North America. **2** The wild lettuce. **3** The great ragweed.

horse·whip (hôrs′hwip′) *n.* A whip for driving or managing horses. —*v.t.* **·whipped**, **·whip·ping** To chastise with a horsewhip.

horse·wom·an (hôrs′wōom′ən) *n. pl.* **·wom·en** (-wim′in) **1** A woman who rides on horseback. **2** A woman who is skilled in riding or managing horses.

horst (hôrst) *n. Geol.* A portion of the earth's crust slightly elevated from the surrounding tracts by faults. Also **horste**. [<G]

hors·y (hôr′sē) *adj.* **hors·i·er, hors·i·est** **1** Pertaining to or suggestive of horses. **2** Devoted to horses or horse-racing. **3** *Slang* Coarse or gross in appearance. Also **hors′ey**. —**hors′i·ly** *adv.* —**hors′i·ness** *n.*

hor·ta·tive (hôr′tə·tiv) *adj.* Hortatory. [<L *hortativus* < *hortari* urge] —**hor′ta·tive·ly** *adv.*

hor·ta·to·ry (hôr′tə·tôr′ē, -tō′rē) *adj.* **1** Giving exhortation. **2** *Ling.* Pertaining to a mood used in some languages to express exhortation, encouragement, etc., or to the imperative or subjunctive moods when used in this manner. [<L *hortatorius*]

hor·ti·cul·ture (hôr′tə·kul′chər) *n.* **1** The cultivation of a garden, or the mode of cultivation employed in a garden. **2** That department of the science of agriculture which relates to the cultivation of gardens or orchards, including the growing of vegetables, fruits, flowers, and ornamental shrubs and trees. See synonyms under AGRICULTURE. [<L *hortus* garden + *cultura* cultivation] —**hor′ti·cul′tor** (-kul′tər) *n.* —**hor′ti·cul′tur·al** *adj.* —**hor′ti·cul′tur·ist, hor′ti·cul′tist, hor′ti·cul′tur·al·ist** *n.*

hor·tus sic·cus (hôr′təs sik′əs) *Latin* Literally, a dry garden; a herbarium.

Ho·rus (hō′rəs) In Egyptian mythology, the hawk-headed god of the sun.

ho·san·na (hō·zan′ə) *interj.* An exclamation of praise to God. —*n.* A cry of hosanna; hence, any exultant acclamation in praise of the Almighty. [<LL < Gk. *hōsanna* <Hebrew *hōshī′āhnnā* save, I pray]

hose (hōz) *n. pl.* **hose** (*Archaic* **hos·en**) **1** *Usually pl.* Formerly, a garment worn by men, covering the legs and the lower part of the body, like very tight trousers. **2** *pl.* Stockings; socks. **3** *pl.* **hos·es** A flexible tube or pipe, of leather, rubber, cotton, etc., for conveying water and other fluids. —*v.t.* **hosed, hos·ing** To drench or douse with a hose. [OE *hosa*]

hose company A group of men who convey and man the hose for extinguishing fires.

ho·sier (hō′zhər) *n.* A dealer in hose, etc.

ho·sier·y (hō′zhər·ē) *n.* Hosiers' wares; stockings; hose; the hosier's business.

hos·pice (hos′pis) *n.* A place of entertainment or shelter, as a monastery in an Alpine pass. [<F <L *hospitium* inn, hospitality <*hospes* host, guest]

hos·pi·ta·ble (hos′pi·tə·bəl, hos·pit′ə·bəl) *adj.* **1** Disposed to behave in a warm manner or to entertain with generous kindness. **2** Characterized by hospitality. **3** Figuratively, very receptive. [<OF <L *hospitare* entertain] —**hos′pi·ta·ble·ness** *n.* —**hos′pi·ta·bly** *adv.*

hos·pi·tal (hos′pi·təl) *n.* **1** An institution for the reception, care, and medical treatment of the sick or wounded; also, the building used for that purpose. **2** *Obs.* An inn or hospice. **3** Formerly, a place of hospitality for those in need of shelter and maintenance: foundling *hospital*, Greenwich *Hospital* (a home for retired seamen in London). [<OF <L *hospitalis* of a guest <*hospes* guest. Doublet of HOTEL, HOSTEL.]

hos·pi·tal·i·ty (hos′pə·tal′ə·tē) *n. pl.* **·ties** The spirit, practice, or act of being hospitable. ◆ Collateral adjective: xenial.

hos·pi·tal·ize (hos′pi·təl·īz′) *v.t.* **·ized, ·iz·ing** To put in a hospital for treatment. —**hos′pi·tal·i·za′tion** *n.*

hos·pi·ti·um (hos·pish′ē·əm) *n. pl.* **·ti·a** (-ē·ə) *Archaic* **1** A monastic inn. **2** An inn; hostel. [<L <*hospes* guest]

hos·po·dar (hos′pə·där) *n.* A title of dignity formerly borne by the princes of Lithuania and the kings of Poland, later by the princes or governors of Moldavia and Wallachia and the emperor of Russia. [<Rumanian, ult. <Slavic]

host[1] (hōst) *n.* **1** One who entertains guests in private life. **2** The landlord of a hotel. **3** *Biol.* Any living plant or animal that harbors another as a parasite. —*v.t. Colloq.* To conduct or entertain in the role of a host. [<OF *hoste* <L *hospes* guest, host. Akin to GUEST, HOST[2].]

host[2] (hōst) *n.* **1** An army. **2** A large body of men; a multitude. See synonyms under ARMY, ASSEMBLY, COMPANY, THRONG. [<OF <L *hostis* enemy. Akin to GUEST, HOST[1].]

host[3] (hōst) *n.* **1** *Usually cap.* In the Roman Catholic, Greek, Lutheran, and some other churches, the eucharistic bread or wafer before or after consecration. **2** *Obs.* An offering; sacrifice. [<OF *hoiste* <L *hostia* sacrificial victim]

hos·tage (hos′tij) *n.* **1** A person held as a pledge, as in war, for the performance of some stipulation. **2** Hence, anything given as a pledge. [<OF]

hos·tel (hos′təl) *n.* An inn; a lodging house; especially, a **youth hostel**, a supervised shelter for the use of young people on walking trips. Also **hos′tel·ry** (-təl·rē), **hos·tler·y** (hos′lər·ē). [<OF <LL *hospitale* inn <*hospes* guest. Doublet of HOTEL, HOSPITAL.]

host·ess (hōs′tis) *n.* A female host.

hos·tile (hos′təl, *esp. Brit.* hos′tīl) *adj.* **1** Having a spirit of enmity. **2** Pertaining to an enemy. See synonyms under ALIEN, MALICIOUS. —*n.* An enemy; antagonist. [<F <L *hostilis*] —**hos′tile·ly** *adv.*

hos·til·i·ty (hos·til′ə·tē) *n. pl.* **·ties** **1** The state of being hostile. **2** *Obs.* Hostile action. **3** *pl.* Warlike measures. See synonyms under ANTIPATHY, ENMITY, FEUD, HATRED.

host·ing (hōs′ting) *n. Obs.* **1** The gathering of an armed host; a muster. **2** An encounter.

hos·tler (hos′lər, os′-) *n.* **1** A stableman; groom: also spelled **ostler**. **2** A man who prepares locomotives for their succeeding trips. [<OF *hostelier* innkeeper]

hot (hot) *adj.* **hot·ter, hot·test** **1** Having or giving heat; of high temperature: opposed to *cold* and exceeding *warm* in degree. **2** Producing a burning or biting sensation to the taste or touch: *hot* pepper; *hot* acid. **3** Marked by passion or zeal; fiery; fervent: *hot* words. **4** *Slang* Excited with sexual desire. **5** Violent; intense; raging: a *hot* battle. **6** *Slang* So new as not to have lost its freshness, currency, excitement, etc. **7** *Slang* Recently stolen or smuggled: *hot* goods. **8** *Music Slang* **a** In jazz, characterized by fervent and exciting rhythm and spirit, a lively tempo, and improvised variations on the original score. **b** Performing such music. **9** Following very closely: in *hot* pursuit. **10** In games, near to the subject or solution sought. **11** In hunting, distinct; strong: said of a scent. **12** Having an electrical charge, especially of high voltage: a *hot* wire. **13** Dangerously radioactive, as the fall-out of an atomic bomb. —**to make it hot for** *Slang* To make the situation extremely uncomfortable for. —*adv.* In a hot manner. [OE *hāt*] —**hot′ly** *adv.* —**hot′ness** *n.*

Synonyms: burning, choleric, fervent, fervid, fiery, glowing, heated, irascible, passionate, peppery, pungent, stinging, vehement, violent. See ARDENT, EAGER[1]. *Antonyms:* arctic, bleak, boreal, chill, chilly, cold, cool, freezing, frigid, frosty, frozen, gelid, icy, polar, wintry.

hot-air (hot′âr′) *adj.* **1** Heating by means of hot air: a *hot-air* furnace. **2** Inflated with hot air: a *hot-air* balloon.

hot·bed (hot′bed′) *n.* **1** A bed of rich earth, protected by glass, and warmed for promoting the growth of plants. **2** A place or condition favoring rapid growth or heated activity.

hot blast A blast of hot air blown into a smelting furnace. —**hot′-blast′** *adj.*

hot-blood·ed (hot′blud′id) *adj.* Being of hot blood; passionate; amorous.

hot·box (hot′boks′) *n.* The overheated journal box of a railroad car or other fast-moving wheeled vehicle: caused by friction.

hot cake A pancake or fritter.

hotch·pot (hoch′pot) *n. Law* A commixture of property made in order to secure an equable division. [<OF *hochepot* <MDu. *hutspot*]

hot cross bun A circular cake or bun marked with a cross of frosting, eaten especially during Lent.

hot dog *Colloq.* A cooked frankfurter, usually grilled and served in a split roll.

ho·tel (hō·tel′) *n.* **1** An establishment or building providing lodging, food, etc., for travelers and others; an inn. **2** In French usage: **a** An official residence or private dwelling in a city or town. **b** A building for the transaction of public business in a city or town. [<F *hôtel* <OF *hostel* inn. Doublet of HOSTEL, HOSPITAL.]

ho·tel·ier (hō′təl·ir′) *n.* A hotel-keeper; hotelman. [<F]

hot·foot (hot′fōot′) *v.i. Colloq.* To hurry; go hastily. —*adv. Colloq.* In all haste; hastily. —*n. Slang* The prank of furtively wedging a match between the upper and sole of a victim's shoe, lighting it, and letting it burn down.

hot·head (hot′hed′) *n.* A hasty, impetuous, or quick-tempered person. —**hot′-head′ed** *adj.* —**hot′-head′ed·ly** *adv.* —**hot′-head′ed·ness** *n.*

hot·house (hot′hous′) *n.* **1** A structure kept warm artificially, as for the forced growth of flowers, etc. **2** *Obs.* A brothel.

hot line A direct means of communication; specifically, a telephone line for emergency use by heads of state of nuclear powers, or for immediate communication between an official and his chief subordinates.

hot plate **1** A heated metal plate for maintaining at a uniform temperature anything set upon it. **2** A small portable gas or electric stove.

hot·pot (hot′pot′) *n.* A dish of meat stewed with potatoes in a covered pot.

hot·press (hot′pres′) *v.t.* To subject to heat and mechanical pressure, as for calendering or to extract oil. —*n.* A machine for hotpressing. —**hot′pressed′** *adj.* —**hot′press′er** *n.* —**hot′press′ing** *n.*

hot rod *Slang* An automobile, popularly a jalopy, with a motor modified for speed.

hot spring A natural spring, the waters of which issue forth at 98° F. or above.

hot·spur (hot′spûr′) *n.* A person who pushes on, heedless of advice or warning; a hot-headed person. —*adj.* Impetuous; reckless: also **hot′spurred′**.

hound (hound) *n.* **1** A hunting dog which hunts by scent; specifically, in Great Britain, a foxhound. **2** A dastardly fellow. **3** In the game of hare-and-hounds, one who acts the part of a hound. **4** *pl. Naut.* Projections at the head of a mast which support the top trestletrees and the lower rigging. **5** *Mech.* A brace to strengthen the running gear of a vehicle: if between the reach and hinder axle, called **hind hound**; if between the tongue and forward axle, **fore hound**. —*v.t.* **1** To hunt with or as with hounds; nag persistently. **2** To incite to pursue; set on the chase. [OE *hund* dog]

hound's-tongue (houndz′tung′) *n.* **1** A coarse hairy weed (*Cynoglossum officinale*) found in pastures and waste grounds, with tongue-shaped leaves, dull-red flowers, and prickly nutlets. **2** The vanilla plant.

hound's-tooth check (houndz′tōoth′) A design of small broken checks in cloth.

hour (our) *n.* **1** A space of time equal to one twenty-fourth of a day; sixty minutes; before the general use of timepieces, one twelfth of the interval from sunrise to sunset (called *hour of the day*), or one twelfth that from sunset to sunrise (called *hour of the night*). **2** A measure of time as indicated by the sun in relation to the horizon: the sun was two *hours* high. **3** The point of time indicated by a chronometer, watch, or clock; the time of day. **4** A set, appointed, or definite time; specifically, the time of death. **5** *pl.* Prayers to be repeated at stated times of the day; also, the time for these devotions, or the book containing them. **6** An hour's journey; commonly a league or three miles. **7** A sidereal hour. See SIDEREAL (def. 2). **8** *Astron.* An angular measure of right ascension or longitude, being 15 degrees or the 24th part of a great circle of the sphere. **— after hours** After the prescribed hours for school, business, etc. **— the small hours** The early morning hours. ◆ Collateral adjective: *horal.* [<L *hora* <Gk. *hōra* time, period]

hour angle *Astron.* The angle subtended by a place on the celestial sphere between the meridian and the hour circle passing through the object: used in determining time.

hour circle *Astron.* A great circle which passes through the celestial pole: used in the determination of the hour angle.

hour·glass (our′glas′, -gläs′) *n.* A glass vessel having two globular parts connected by a narrow neck: used for measuring time by the running of sand from the upper into the lower compartment, the passage taking a full hour.

HOURGLASS

hou·ri (hōō′rē) *n.* A nymph of the Moslem Paradise. [<F <Persian *ḥuri* <Arabic *ḥūriyah* black-eyed woman]

hour·ly (our′lē) *adj.* Happening every hour. *— adv.* At intervals of an hour.

house (hous) *n.* **1** A building intended for human habitation, especially one used as the residence of a family or single tenant. **2** A household; family. **3** A building used for any purpose: a coffee *house*; a *house* of worship. **4** The abode of a fraternity, order, etc.: a sorority *house.* **5** A dormitory or residence hall in a college or university; also, its resident students, collectively. **6** *Brit.* A college in a university; also, its member students, collectively. **7** A legislative body; also, the chamber it occupies. **8** *Eccl.* The deliberative body of a congregation or convocation. **9** A place of business. **10** A business firm: the *house* of Morgan. **11** A theater. **12** An audience at a public entertainment or service: to speak to a full *house.* **13** A line of ancestors and descendants regarded as forming a single family: the *House* of Tudor. **14** In astrology, one of the twelve divisions of the heavens, made by projecting great circles through the north and south points of the horizon. Each division, having special significance, is used in casting horoscopes. See ZODIAC. **15** A sign of the zodiac considered as the seat of greatest influence of a particular planet. **— on the house** At the expense of the proprietor; gratis. **— to bring down the house** To receive loud and enthusiastic applause. **— to clean house** *Colloq.* To get rid of undesirable conditions or persons in an organization. **— to keep house** To manage the affairs or work of a home. *— v.* (houz) **housed, hous·ing** *v.t.* **1** To take or put into a house; furnish with a house; lodge. **2** To store in a house or building. **3** To fit into a mortise, joint, etc. **4** *Naut.* To place in a secure or safe position, as in time of storms. *— v.i.* **5** To take shelter or lodgings; dwell. [OE *hūs*] **— house′ful** *n.*

Synonyms (noun): abode, building, cabin, cot, cottage, domicile, dwelling, dwelling place, edifice, habitation, hall, home, hovel, hut, manor, mansion, palace, residence, shanty, villa. See EDIFICE, HOME.

house arrest Detention in one's own house by authority of law.

house-boat (hous′bōt′) *n.* A boat or barge fitted out as a dwelling.

house-boy (hous′boi′) *n.* A houseman.

house-break·er (hous′brā′kər) *n.* One who breaks into a house to rob. **— house′break′. ing** *n.*

house-bro·ken (hous′brō′kən) *adj.* Trained to

live cleanly in a house: said of animals.

house-carl (hous′kärl) *n.* A member of the bodyguard or household troops of a Danish or early English king or noble.

house coat A long, loose-skirted garment designed for informal indoor wear.

house-fly (hous′flī′) *n. pl.* **-flies** The common fly (*Musca domestica*), found in nearly all parts of the world: an agent in transmitting certain diseases. For illustration see under INSECTS (injurious).

house guest A guest invited to stay one or more nights.

house-hold (hous′hōld) *n.* A number of persons dwelling under the same roof. *— adj.* Domestic. [<HOUSE + HOLD, *n.*]

household arts See under ART.

house-hold·er (hous′hōl′dər) *n.* The head of a family; specifically, in England, one who inhabits a dwelling or tenement of such a nature as to qualify him for the exercise of the franchise.

household goods The furniture, utensils, and supplies necessary for keeping house.

household linen See FLATWORK.

household troops A special body of soldiers detailed for the protection of a sovereign, his family, and residence.

house-keep·er (hous′kē′pər) *n.* One who directs the affairs or work of a household either as mistress or as an upper servant. **— house′keep′ing** *n.*

hou·sel (hou′zəl) *n. Obs.* The Eucharist. [OE *hūsel*]

house-leek (hous′lēk′) *n.* An Old World garden plant (*Sempervivum tectorum*) of the orpine family, with pink flowers and thick fleshy leaves that grow on walls and roofs.

house-line (hous′līn′) *n. Naut.* A small three-stranded line of fine-dressed hemp, used for seizings, etc.: sometimes called *housing.* Also spelled *houslin.*

house-maid (hous′mād′) *n.* A girl employed to do housework.

housemaid's knee *Pathol.* A chronic inflammation of the bursa in front of the knee, afflicting housemaids and others who kneel in working.

house-man (hous′mən) *n.* A handy man employed to do heavy work about a house, hotel, etc.: also called *houseboy.*

house-mas·ter (hous′mas′tər, -mäs′-) *n.* The master having charge of a school residence, specifically in a British school.

house of cards Any weak, unstable organization, plan, etc.

House of Commons The lower house of the British Parliament.

house of correction An institution for minor criminals; reform school.

House of Lords The upper house of the British Parliament.

House of Representatives 1 The lower, larger branch of the United States Congress, and of many State legislatures, composed of members elected popularly on the basis of population. **2** A similar legislative body, as in Australia, Japan, or Mexico.

house organ A publication issued by a commercial enterprise to promote the interest of customers in its products, or to maintain efficiency among its employees.

house party An entertainment of guests for several days, usually in a country house or a college fraternity; also, the guests.

house physician A physician resident by appointment in a hospital or other institution.

house-room (hous′rōōm′, -rōōm′) *n.* Room or lodging in a house or hotel; accommodation.

house snake A harmless snake (*Lampropeltis triangulum*) of the northern United States that frequents houses and preys on rats and mice: also called *milk snake* and *spotted adder.*

house sparrow See under SPARROW (def. 1).

house-top (hous′top′) *n.* **1** The top or roof of a house. **2** Figuratively, an exposed or public place: to cry it from the *housetops.*

house-ware (hous′wâr′) *n.* Kitchen equipment and other wares used in a home.

house-warm·ing (hous′wôr′ming) *n.* A festivity on entering a new home.

house-wife (hous′wīf′) *n. pl.* **·wives** (-wīvz′)

1 A married woman who manages the affairs of her own household as a full-time occupation. **2** (hous′wif′, *esp. Brit.* huz′if) A receptable for small articles required in sewing. **— house′wife′ly** *adj. & adv.* **— house′. wife·li·ness** *n.*

house-wife·ry (hous′wif′rē) *n.* The part of household management under a woman's direction; housekeeping processes. Also **house′. wife′ship** (-ship).

house-work (hous′wûrk′) *n.* Work in keeping house, especially the more menial tasks.

house wren See under WREN.

hous·ing[1] (hou′zing) *n.* **1** The act of providing with a house or shelter. **2** The act of bringing into a house, or putting under cover. **3** Shelter from the weather. **4** *Mech.* **a** A hollow made in one member of an engine or machine to receive a portion of another member. **b** That part of a frame of a machine which sustains a journal box; a jaw. **c** The casing containing either the differential gear or a set of ball bearings in the transmission of an automobile. **5** A niche for a statue. **6** *Naut.* **a** A houseline. **b** A hoarding to protect a ship's deck when in repair dock. **c** That part of a mast or bowsprit below the deck or abaft the knightheads. **7** A mortise in a timber, for receiving the end of another timber.

hous·ing[2] (hou′zing) *n.* The ornamental trappings of a horse, especially the saddlecloth: usually in the plural. See synonyms under CAPARISON. [<OF *houce*; of uncertain origin]

Hous·to·ni·a (hōōs·tō′nē·ə) *n.* A genus of low, slender North American plants of the madder family, including the bluet. [after Dr. William *Houston*, 1695-1733, English naturalist]

hove[1] (hōv) *v.t. & v.i. Obs.* **1** To raise or move upward. **2** To inflate. [<HEAVE]

hove[2] (hōv) Past tense of HEAVE.

hov·el (huv′əl, hov′-) *n.* **1** A wretched dwelling; hut. **2** An open shed for sheltering cattle, tools, or produce. See synonyms under HOUSE, HUT. *— v.t.* **hov·eled** or **hov·elled, hov·el·ing** or **hov·el·ling 1** To shelter in a hovel. **2** To build like a hovel. [? Dim. of OE *hof* building]

hov·er (huv′ər, hov′-) *v.i.* **1** To remain suspended in or near one place in the air, as by fluttering the wings. **2** To linger; be nearby, as if waiting or watching: with *around, near,* etc. **3** To remain in an uncertain or irresolute state: with *between.* *— n.* **1** A shelter or retreat. **2** The act of hovering. [< obs. *hove* float] **— hov′er·er** *n.*

Hov·er·craft (huv′ər·kraft′, hov′-, -kräft′) A vehicle traveling on a thin cushion of air produced by fans directed downward: a trade name. Also **hov′er·craft.**

how[1] (hou) *adv.* **1** In what way or manner: I knew *how* it was done. **2** To what degree, extent, or amount; in what proportion: showing *how* great was the concentration of ions. **3** In what state or condition: Let me see *how* the account stands. **4** For what reason or purpose: I can't see *how* he came to do it. **5** For what price; at what sum: I inquired *how* the stock sold. **6** By what name or designation: We know *how* he is called among his own people. **7** To what effect; with what meaning: *How* do you intend that remark to be taken? **8** *Colloq.* What? *— n.* Way of doing or becoming; means: Teach me the *how* of it. [OE *hū*]

how[2] (hou) *adj. Scot.* Hollow or deep; also, hollow in sound. *— n.* A valley; glen. Also spelled *howe.*

how[3] (hou) *interj.* An expression of greeting attributed to and used humorously in imitation of American Indians.

how·be·it (hou·bē′it) *adv.* Nevertheless. *— conj. Obs.* Although; be that as it may. See synonyms under NOTWITHSTANDING.

how·dah (hou′də) *n.* A railed or canopied seat on the back of an elephant: also spelled *houdah.* [<Hind. *haudah*]

how·dy (hou′dē) *interj. Colloq.* An expression of greeting. [Contraction of HOW DO YOU (DO)?]

how·el (hou′əl) *n.* A cooper's plane for smoothing the inside of casks. *— v.t.* To make smooth with a howel. [<MLG *hövel*]

---

add,āce,câre,pälm; end,ēven; it,īce; odd,ōpen,ôrder; tŏŏk,pōōl; up,bûrn; ə = a in *above*, e in *sicken*, i in *clarity*, o in *melon*, u in *focus*; yōō = u in *fuse*; oi,oil; ou,pout; ch,check; g,go; ng,ring; th,thin; ħ,this; zh,vision. Foreign sounds á,œ,ü,kh,ṅ; and ◆: see page xx. < from; + plus; ? possibly.

how·ev·er (hou·ev′ər) *adv.* **1** In whatever manner; by whatever means. **2** To whatever degree or extent: Spend *however* much it costs. **3** How; in what manner: *However* did it happen? — *conj.* Notwithstanding; still; yet. See synonyms under BUT, NOTWITHSTANDING. Also **how·e′er′** (-âr′).

how·it·zer (hou′it·sər) *n.* A piece of artillery having a barrel longer than a mortar's, and firing at angles up to 65° with medium muzzle velocity. [Appar. <Du. *houwitzer*, ult. <Czech *houfnice* catapult]

HOWITZER—BRITISH ARMY, 1914

howk (hōk) *v.t.* & *v.i. Brit. Dial.* To dig; burrow: also spelled *holk*. — **howk′it** (-it) *adj.*

howl (houl) *v.i.* **1** To utter the loud, mournful wail of a wolf or dog. **2** To utter such a cry in rage, grief, etc. **3** To make such a sound: The storm *howled*. — *v.t.* **4** To utter or express with a howl or howls. **5** To drive or effect with a howl or howls. — *n.* **1** The cry of a wolf or dog. **2** Any resonant cry expressive of grief or rage. **3** An undesirable sound distortion in radio reception, due to acoustic or electrical feedback. [Imit.]

howl·er (hou′lər) *n.* **1** One who or that which howls. **2** A siren for signaling, or, when attached to a military airplane, for creating confusion or panic among the enemy. **3** A tropical American monkey having a long, prehensile tail and great vocal power: the ursine *howler* (*Alouatta ursinus*): also **howling monkey**. **4** *Colloq.* Gross exaggeration; also, an absurd mistake or blunder.

howl·et (hou′lit) *n. Obs.* An owl; owlet. [<F *hulotte*]

howl·ing (hou′ling) *adj.* **1** Filled with or abounding in howls; dismal: the *howling* wilderness. **2** *Slang* Prodigious; tremendous; enormous: a *howling* success, a *howling* lie.

how·so·ev·er (hou′sō·ev′ər) *adv.* In whatever manner; to whatever extent.

hoy[1] (hoi) *n.* **1** A barge used to convey bulky cargo to ships in port. **2** A single-masted, heavy, coastwise vessel or tender of obsolete type. [<MDu. *hoei*]

hoy[2] (hoi) *interj.* Ho; hallo: a cry to attract attention. Compare AHOY. Also spelled *hoigh*, *hooy*. [Imit. Cf. Du. *hui!*]

hoy·den (hoid′n) *n.* A romping or bold girl; tomboy. — *adj.* Inelegant or unseemly; bold. — *v.i.* To romp rudely or indecently. Also spelled *hoiden*. [? <obs. *hoit* romp] — **hoy′den·ish** *adj.*

hua·ra·che (wä·rä′chä) *n.* A Mexican sandal woven of strips of leather and having leather heel straps. Also **hua·ra′cho** (-chō). [<Am. Sp. <Quechua *huaraca* leather thong]

hub (hub) *n.* **1** The central part of a wheel. **2** Anything central; a center of traffic. — **the Hub** Boston, Massachusetts. [Prob. var. of HOB]

hub·ba hub·ba (hub′ə hub′ə) *Colloq.* An exclamation expressing emphatic approval. [Imit.]

hub·ble (hub′əl) *n.* A small protuberance or lump, as in a road; roughness. [Dim. of HUB] — **hub′bly** (-lē) *adj.*

hub·ble-bub·ble (hub′əl·bub′əl) *n.* **1** A continuous bubbling or gurgling sound. **2** A hookah or water pipe. [Reduplication of BUBBLE]

hub·bub (hub′ub) *n.* A confused noise; uproar. See synonyms under NOISE, TUMULT. [Said to be an Irish cry]

hu·bris (hyoo′bris) *n.* Wanton arrogance. [<Gk.]

huck·a·back (huk′ə·bak) *n.* A coarse, durable linen or cotton cloth used for towels. Also **huck**, **huck′a·buck** (-buk). [Origin uncertain]

huck·le (huk′əl) *n.* The hip; also, a hump or projection resembling the hip. [Dim. of obs. *huck* hip; ult. origin unknown]

huck·le·ber·ry (huk′əl·ber′ē) *n. pl.* **·ries** The edible black or dark-blue berry of a species of heath (genus *Gaylussacia*), often confused with the blueberry. **2** The European whortleberry. **3** The shrub producing either of these berries. Also called *hurtleberry, whortleberry*. [Prob. alter. of HURTLEBERRY]

huckle bone The innominate bone; hip bone.

huck·ster (huk′stər) *n.* **1** One who retails small wares, provisions, or the like; a peddler; hawker; especially, one who raises and sells garden products. **2** A mean, venal fellow; a petty jobber or trickster. **3** *U.S. Slang* An advertising man. — *v.t.* **1** To put up for sale; peddle. **2** To haggle over. — *v.i.* **3** To haggle. [<MDu. *hoekster* < *heuken* retail] — **huck′ster·ism** *n.*

hud·dle (hud′l) *v.* **hud·dled**, **hud·dling** *v.i.* **1** To crowd closely together, as from fear or for warmth. **2** To draw or hunch oneself together, as from cold. **3** In football, to gather in a huddle. — *v.t.* **4** To bring together in a group or mass. **5** To draw or hunch (oneself) together. **6** To make or do hurriedly or carelessly. **7** To push or put hastily or confusedly. — *n.* **1** A confused crowd or collection. **2** In football, the grouping of a team before each play, in which signals and instructions are given. **3** Any small, intimate conference. [Origin uncertain]

Hudson Bay An inland sea in northern Canada; 850 miles long; 600 miles wide.

Hudson River A river in eastern New York State, flowing 306 miles south to New York Bay.

Hudson seal Muskrat fur dyed and trimmed to resemble Alaskan sealskin.

hue[1] (hyoo) *n.* **1** The particular shade of a color; that in which one color or shade differs from another; color; tint. **2** That attribute of a chromatic color, as red, green, blue, which determines the character of its difference from the nearest achromatic color. Compare BRIGHTNESS, LIGHTNESS, SATURATION. See COLOR. **3** A compound color, especially one in which one or more of the primary colors is predominant. **4** *Obs.* Appearance; form. ◆ Homophone: *hew*. [OE *heow* appearance]

hue[2] (hyoo) *n.* A vociferous cry; shouting. ◆ Homophone: *hew*. [<OF *hu* cry <*huer*]

Hué (hwä, hyoo·ā′) A port, capital of Central Vietnam.

hue and cry **1** A great stir and clamor about any matter. **2** Formerly, the common-law process of pursuing felons by shouts and cries until taken.

hued (hyood) *adj.* Having a hue or color: usually in combination: dark-*hued*.

huff (huf) *v.t.* **1** To offend; make angry. **2** To treat insolently or arrogantly; bully; hector. **3** *Obs.* To cause to swell; blow up. **4** In checkers, to remove (an opponent's piece) from the board as a forfeit for neglecting to capture an opposing piece. — *v.i.* **5** To be offended. **6** To puff; blow. **7** *Obs.* To puff or swell with anger or pride; bluster. — *n.* **1** Offense suddenly taken. **2** In checkers, the act of huffing. [Imit.]

huff·ish (huf′ish) *adj.* Petulant; irascible. — **huff′ish·ly** *adv.* — **huff′ish·ness** *n.*

huff·y (huf′ē) *adj.* **huff·i·er**, **huff·i·est** **1** Easily offended. **2** Puffed up. — **huff′i·ly** *adv.* — **huff′i·ness** *n.*

hug (hug) *v.* **hugged**, **hug·ging** *v.t.* **1** To clasp tightly within the arms, as from affection. **2** To keep fondly in the mind; cherish, as a belief or opinion. **3** To keep close to, as a shore. — *v.i.* **4** To lie close; nestle. See synonyms under EMBRACE. — *n.* A close embrace. [Prob. <ON *hugga* console]

huge (hyooj) *adj.* Having great bulk; vast. See synonyms under IMMENSE, LARGE. Also *Colloq.* **huge′ous**. [<OF *ahuge* high] — **huge′ly** *adv.* — **huge′ness** *n.*

hug·ger-mug·ger (hug′ər·mug′ər) *n.* **1** Secrecy; privacy. **2** Confusion and disorder. — *adj.* **1** Secret; sly. **2** Slovenly. [<obs. *hoker-moker*, prob. reduplication of ME *mokern* conceal]

Hu·gue·not (hyoo′gə·not) *n.* A French Protestant of the 16th and 17th centuries: persecuted during the religious wars of the time. [<F <G *Eidgenoss* confederate] — **Hu′gue·not′ic** *adj.*

Hu·gue·not·ism (hyoo′gə·not·iz′əm) *n.* The doctrines of the Huguenots; French Protestantism.

huh (hu) *interj.* An exclamation of inquiry, surprise, contempt, etc. [Imit.]

hu·la (hoo′lə) *n.* A native Hawaiian dance performed by women, with intricate arm movements that tell a story in pantomime. Also **hu′la-hu′la**. [<Hawaiian]

hulk (hulk) *n.* **1** The body of a ship or decked vessel, especially of an old, unseaworthy vessel, or of one wrecked. **2** An old ship used for a prison or for purposes other than seagoing. **3** Any bulky or unwieldy object or person. **4** A heavy, clumsy ship. — *v.i.* **1** To rise or loom bulkily: usually with *up*. **2** *Brit. Dial.* To lounge or slouch in a lazy, clumsy manner. [OE *hulc* ship, prob. < Med. L *hulcus* <Gk. *holkas* towed vessel < *hēlkein* drag]

hulk·ing (hul′king) *adj.* Bulky; unwieldy. Also **hulk′y**.

hull (hul) *n.* **1** The outer covering, as of a kernel of grain or of a nut; husk; pod; also, any outer covering; specifically, in the plural, garments, clothes. **2** *Naut.* The body of a ship, exclusive of the masts, sails, yards, and rigging. **3** *Aeron.* The main covered structure of a rigid airship; also, that part of a flying boat which rests upon the water. — *v.t.* **1** To shell; free from the hull. **2** To strike or pierce the hull of (a vessel). [OE *hulu* a covering] — **hull′er** *n.*

hul·la·ba·loo (hul′ə·bə·loo′) *n.* A loud and confused noise; uproar; tumult. Also **hul′la·bal·loo′**. [Imit. reduplication of HULLO]

hum[1] (hum) *v.* **hummed**, **hum·ming** *v.i.* **1** To make a low, continuous, buzzing sound, as a bee. **2** To sing with the lips closed, not articulating the words. **3** To give forth a confused, indistinct sound, as of mingled voices. **4** To pause in speaking, as from confusion; hem. **5** *Colloq.* To be busily active: The office *hummed*. — *v.t.* **6** To sing, as a tune, with the lips closed. **7** To put into a specified state or condition by humming: to *hum* someone to sleep. See synonyms under SING. — *n.* A low, monotonous, or inarticulate sound as of *h'm*). **2** A sound as of *h'm* or *hem*. [Imit.] — **hum′mer** *n.*

hu·man (hyoo′mən) *adj.* **1** Pertaining to or characterizing man or mankind. See synonyms under HUMANE. **2** Possessed by or suitable for man. — *n. Colloq.* One of the human race; a human being. [<OF *humain* <L *humanus*] — **hu′man·ness** *n.*

hu·mane (hyoo·mān′) *adj.* **1** Having or showing kindness and tenderness; compassionate. **2** Tending to refine; polite; elegant. [Var. of HUMAN] — **hu·mane′ly** *adv.* — **hu·mane′ness** *n.*

Synonyms: benevolent, benignant, charitable, clement, compassionate, forgiving, gentle, gracious, human, kind, kind-hearted, merciful, pitying, sympathetic, tender, tenderhearted. *Human* denotes what pertains to mankind, with no suggestion as to its being good or evil. *Humane* denotes what may rightly be expected of mankind at its best in the treatment of sentient beings; a *humane* enterprise or endeavor is one that is intended to prevent or relieve suffering. The *humane* man will not needlessly inflict pain upon the meanest thing that lives; a *merciful* man is disposed to withhold or mitigate the suffering even of the guilty. The *compassionate* man sympathizes with and desires to relieve actual suffering, while one who is *humane* would forestall and prevent the suffering which he sees to be possible. Compare GOOD, PITIFUL. Antonyms: barbarous, brutal, cruel, fierce, ferocious, inhuman, merciless, pitiless, ruthless, savage, selfish, unmerciful, unpitying.

hu·man·ism (hyoo′mən·iz′əm) *n.* **1** Culture derived from classical training; polite learning. **2** A system of thinking in which man, his interests and development are made central and dominant, tending to exalt the cultural and practical rather than the scientific and speculative. **3** Humanity.

Hu·man·ism (hyoo′mən·iz′əm) *n.* The intellectual, scientific, and literary movement of the 14th to 16th centuries which exalted Greek and Roman culture and learning: opposed to *Scholasticism*.

hu·man·ist (hyoo′mən·ist) *n.* **1** One versed in the study of humanities; a classical scholar. **2** One who is versed in human nature. — **hu′man·is′tic** *adj.* — **hu′man·is′ti·cal·ly** *adv.*

hu·man·i·tar·i·an (hyōō·man'ə·târ'ē·ən) n. 1 One who is broadly philanthropic and humane: a philanthropist. 2 One who seeks to forward the welfare of humanity by ameliorating pain and suffering in any of their manifestations. 3 One who believes that Christ was a mere man; an anti–Trinitarian. 4 One who holds that the perfectibility of the human race is attainable without superhuman aid. — adj. Of or pertaining to humanitarianism or the humanitarians.

hu·man·i·tar·i·an·ism (hyōō·man'ə·târ'ē·ən·iz'əm) n. 1 The doctrines, principles, or practices of humanitarians, in any sense. 2 In Comtism, the theory that humanity is the ultimate reality.

hu·man·i·ty (hyōō·man'ə·tē) n. pl. ·ties 1 Mankind collectively. 2 Human nature. 3 The state or quality of being human. 4 The state or quality of being humane; also, a humane act. 5 pl. The branches of learning including literature, language, and philosophy, especially as distinguished from the natural and social sciences. [<OF humanité <L humanitas, -tatis <humanus human] — Synonyms: civilization, culture, refinement; (pl. the humanities) belles–lettres. See BENEVOLENCE, MANKIND. Antonyms: barbarism, boorishness, coarseness, rudeness.

hu·man·ize (hyōō'mən·īz) v.t. & v.i. ·ized, ·iz·ing To make or become humane or human. Also Brit. hu'man·ise. — hu'man·i·za'tion (-ə·zā'shən, -ī·zā'-) n.

hu·man·kind (hyōō'mən·kīnd') n. The human race. See synonyms under MANKIND.

hu·man·ly (hyōō'mən·lē) adv. 1 In accordance with man's nature. 2 Within human power or experience. 3 In a humane or kindly manner.

hu·ma·noid (hyōō'mə·noid) adj. 1 Resembling a human being in structure, function, and general appearance. 2 Imperfectly or deceptively human. — n. An imaginary creature having some resemblance to a human being.

hum·ble (hum'bəl) adj. ·bler, ·blest 1 Having or expressing a sense of inferiority, dependence, or unworthiness; meek. 2 Lowly in condition; unpretending; obscure. 3 Lowly in feeling or manner; submissive; deferential. — v.t. hum·bled, hum·bling 1 To reduce the pride of; make meek; humiliate. 2 To lower in rank or dignity; abase. [<F <L humilis low <humus ground] — hum'ble·ness n. — hum'bler n. — hum'bling n. — hum'bling·ly adv. — hum'bly adv. — Synonyms (adj.): low, lowly, meek, modest, obscure, poor, submissive, unassuming, unobtrusive, unpretending, unpretentious. See MODEST. Antonyms: arrogant, boastful, exalted, haughty, high, lofty, presuming, pretentious, proud.

humble pie A pie made of the humbles of a deer, formerly served to the huntsmen and servants at hunting feasts. — to eat humble pie To make humble apologies; be humiliated: also to eat umble pie.

hum·bles (hum'bəlz) n. pl. The entrails, etc., of a deer. [<OF numbles <L lumbulus, dim. of lumbus loin]

hum·bug (hum'bug) n. 1 Anything intended or calculated to deceive; a sham. 2 An impostor. 3 The spirit or practice of deception; sham. See synonyms under QUACK[2]. — v. ·bugged, ·bug·ging v.t. To impose upon; deceive. — v.i. To practice deceit. [Origin unknown] — hum'bug·ger n. — hum'bug·ger·y n.

hum·ding·er (hum·ding'ər) n. Slang One who or that which excels.

hum·drum (hum'drum') adj. Without interest; tedious. — n. 1 Monotonous existence; tedious talk; anything tiresome. 2 A dull or tedious fellow; bore. [<HUM + DRUM]

hu·mec·tant (hyōō·mek'tənt) adj. Moistening. — n. A moistening preparation or drug; a diluent. [<L humectans, -antis, ppr. of humectare moisten]

hu·mer·al (hyōō'mər·əl) adj. 1 Of or pertaining to the humerus. 2 Of or pertaining to the shoulder. [<L humerus shoulder]

humeral veil Eccl. A veil or scarf worn round the shoulders by the subdeacon at high mass from the offertory to the paternoster, and also by the officiating priest in processions and at benediction of the sacrament.

hu·mer·us (hyōō'mər·əs) n. pl. ·mer·i (-mər·ī) 1 Anat. The bone of the upper part of the arm or forelimb; also, the upper arm or brachium. 2 Entomol. a The front upper corner or angle of the thorax of a wing cover or elytron. b The subcostal nervure in the forewings of certain Hymenoptera, or femur of a foreleg in Orthoptera. ◆ Homophone: humorous. [<L, shoulder]

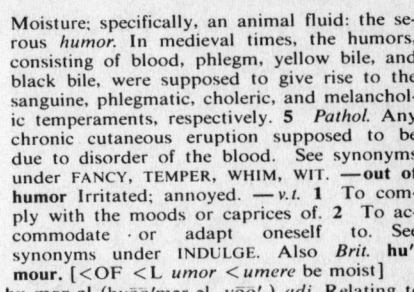

HUMERUS

Hum·fried (hōōm'frēt) Dutch and German form of HUMPHREY. Also Sw. Hum'frid.

hu·mic (hyōō'mik) adj. Of, pertaining to, or derived from humus. [<L humus ground, soil]

hu·mic·o·lous (hyōō·mik'ə·ləs) adj. Bot. Of or pertaining to plants growing on medium–dry soil. [<L humus soil + colere dwell]

hu·mid (hyōō'mid) adj. Containing sensible moisture; damp. [<L humidus <humere, umere be moist] — hu'mid·ly adv.

hu·mid·i·fy (hyōō·mid'ə·fī) v.t. ·fied, ·fy·ing To make moist or humid, as the atmosphere of a room. — hu·mid'i·fi·ca'tion n.

hu·mid·i·stat (hyōō·mid'ə·stat) n. A device for measuring the relative humidity of air.

hu·mid·i·ty (hyōō·mid'ə·tē) n. 1 Moisture; dampness. 2 Meteorol. The percentage of water vapor in the air to the total amount possible at the same temperature (relative humidity). The actual amount of water vapor per unit of volume is known as absolute humidity. Also hu'mid·ness. [<OF humidité <L humiditas <humidus humid]

hu·mi·dor (hyōō'mə·dôr) n. 1 A place for storing cigars or tobacco where the percentage of moisture is regulated; also, a small box fitted for the same purpose. 2 Printing A cabinet in which mats are stored to keep them sufficiently moist for proper impression by type.

hu·mil·i·ate (hyōō·mil'ē·āt) v.t. ·at·ed, ·at·ing To lower or offend the pride or self–respect of. See synonyms under ABASE, ABASH. [<L humiliatus, pp. of humiliare <humilis lowly] — hu·mil'i·at·ing, hu·mil'i·a·to'ry (-tôr'ē, -tō'rē) adj.

hu·mil·i·a·tion (hyōō·mil'ē·ā'shən) n. The act of humiliating, or the state of being humiliated; abasement; mortification; also, that which humiliates. See synonyms under CHAGRIN.

hu·mil·i·ty (hyōō·mil'ə·tē) n. pl. ·ties 1 The quality of being humble. 2 Deference; courtesy; kindness. 3 An act of submission or of humbleness. [<L humilitas, -tatis lowness]

hu·mit (hyōō'mit) n. One degree in the measurement of humiture.

hu·mi·ture (hyōō'mə·chər) n. The combined effect of humidity and temperature: expressed quantitatively by adding the values of the relative humidity and the temperature and dividing by 2. [<HUMI(DITY) + (TEMPERA)TURE; coined (1937) by O. F. Hevener, U.S. banker]

hum·ming (hum'ing) adj. 1 Making a low murmuring or buzzing. 2 Lively; frothing; hence, strong or stimulating. 3 Colloq. Speedy; spirited. — hum'ming·ly adv.

hum·ming·bird (hum'ing·bûrd') n. A small, brilliantly colored bird of the New World (family Trochilidae), mostly tropical, related to the swifts. They feed chiefly upon insects and the sweets of flowers, and are named from the humming sound produced by the rapid motion of their wings as they hover over the flowers. The common hummingbird of the eastern United States is known as the rubythroat.

hum·mock (hum'ək) n. 1 A small elevation; hillock. See HAMMOCK[2]. 2 A pile or ridge of ice on an ice field. [Origin unknown] — hum'mock·y adj.

hu·mor (hyōō'mər, yōō'-) n. 1 Disposition of mind or feeling; caprice; freak; whim. 2 A facetious turn of thought; playful fancy; jocularity; drollery. 3 The capacity to perceive, appreciate, or express what is funny, amusing, incongruous, ludicrous, etc.; also, the capacity to make something seem funny, amusing, ludicrous, etc.; specifically in literature, the expression of this in speech or action. 4 Moisture; specifically, an animal fluid: the serous humor. In medieval times, the humors, consisting of blood, phlegm, yellow bile, and black bile, were supposed to give rise to the sanguine, phlegmatic, choleric, and melancholic temperaments, respectively. 5 Pathol. Any chronic cutaneous eruption supposed to be due to disorder of the blood. See synonyms under FANCY, TEMPER, WHIM, WIT. — out of humor Irritated; annoyed. — v.t. 1 To comply with the moods or caprices of. 2 To accommodate · or adapt oneself to. See synonyms under INDULGE. Also Brit. hu'mour. [<OF <L umor <umere be moist]

hu·mor·al (hyōō'mər·əl, yōō'-) adj. Relating to or arising from the humors of the body.

hu·mor·esque (hyōō'mə·resk') n. Music A lively or fanciful instrumental composition. [<G humoreske]

hu·mor·ism (hyōō'mər·iz'əm, yōō'-) n. 1 The theory that disease proceeds from vitiated humors in the body. 2 The spirit of a humorist. Also hu·mor·al·ism (hyōō'mər·əl·iz'əm)

hu·mor·ist (hyōō'mər·ist, yōō'-) n. 1 One who displays or exercises humor; a wag. 2 A professional writer or entertainer whose work is humorous. — hu'mor·is'tic adj.

hu·mor·ous (hyōō'mər·əs, yōō'-) adj. 1 Adapted to excite merriment; amusing. 2 Moved by caprice; whimsical; also, irritable; peevish. 3 Obs. Humid; watery; moist. ◆ Homophone: humerus. — hu'mor·ous·ly adv. — hu'mor·ous·ness n. — Synonyms: amusing, comic, comical, droll, facetious, funny, jocose, jocular, ludicrous, sportive, witty. See JOCOSE. Antonyms: dreary, dull, grave, melancholy, mournful, sad, serious, sober, solemn.

hu·mor·some (hyōō'mər·səm, yōō'-) adj. 1 Full of humor or whims. 2 Characterized by humor; droll. — hu'mor·some·ly adv. — hu'mor·some·ness n.

hu·mous (hyōō'məs) adj. Relating to or derived from the ground or humus. [<HUMUS]

hump (hump) n. 1 A protuberance, especially that formed by a curved spine or a fleshy growth on the back: the hump of a camel or bison. 2 A mound in a railroad switchyard up one side of which cars are taken by an engine and then allowed to coast down the other; hence, any obstacle. 3 Brit. Slang An attack of ill temper; blues. 4 Colloq. A long tramp or hike, especially with a load on the back. — over the hump Beyond the point where force or effort is needed; at the point where all is easy going. — The Hump The Himalayas: name applied by aviators in World War II. — v.t. 1 To bend or round (the back) in a hump; hunch. 2 U.S. Slang To put forth great effort: used reflexively: Hump yourself. 3 Austral. Slang To carry on the shoulders or back; also, to carry. [Origin uncertain]

hump·back (hump'bak') n. 1 A crooked back. 2 A hunchback. 3 A whalebone whale (genus Megaptera) with a low humplike dorsal fin. — hump'backed' adj.

humph (humf) interj. An exclamation of doubt or dissatisfaction. [<HUM[1]]

hu·mus (hyōō'məs) n. The organic matter of the soil, usually leaf mold and other materials, in which decomposition is well advanced. [<L, ground]

hunch (hunch) n. 1 A hump. 2 A lump or hunk. 3 A sudden shove. 4 U.S. Colloq. A premonition: from the belief that good luck attends the touching of a hunchback's hunch. — v.t. 1 To bend, as the back, so as to form a hump; arch. 2 Obs. To push or jostle. — v.i. 3 To move or thrust oneself forward. [Origin uncertain]

hunch·back (hunch'bak') n. A person having a crooked or deformed back. — hunch'backed' adj.

hun·dred (hun'drid) adj. Being one more than ninety–nine; ten times ten. — n. 1 The product of ten multiplied by ten; the number following ninety–nine; also, the symbols (100, c, C) representing it. ◆ Collateral adjective: cental. 2 An ancient subdivision of a county, common in England and Ireland and still used in the State of Delaware. [OE]

hun·dred·fold (hun′drid·fōld′) *n.* An amount or number a hundred times as great as a given unit. —*adj.* Indicating a hundred times as much or as many; centuplicate. —*adv.* By a hundred: now always used with *a* (in British usage, with *an*).

hun·dred-per·cent·er (hun′drid·pər·sen′tər) *n. Colloq.* An overpatriotic person; a Jingo.

hun·dredth (hun′dridth) *n.* **1** The last in a series of a hundred. **2** One of a hundred equal parts of anything; the quotient of a unit divided by one hundred. —*adj.* **1** Being the tenth group of ten in order after the ninetieth: the ordinal of *one hundred.* **2** Being one of a hundred equal parts.

hun·dred·weight (hun′drid·wāt′) *n.* A weight commonly reckoned in the United States at 100 pounds avoirdupois, in England at 112 pounds. Abbreviated *cwt.*

hung (hung) Past tense and past participle of HANG.

Hun·gar·i·an (hung·gâr′ē·ən) *adj.* Of or pertaining to Hungary, its people, or their language. —*n.* **1** A native or citizen of Hungary; one of a people formerly Magyar, Ruthenian, Slovak, Serbo–Croatian, German, etc., existing side by side: now dominantly Magyar; hence, a Magyar. **2** The Finno–Ugric language of the Hungarians: also called *Magyar.* [< Med. L *Hungarus*]

Hun·ga·ry (hung′gə·rē) A state in central Europe; 35,902 square miles; capital, Budapest: Hungarian *Magyarország.* Officially **Hungarian People's Republic.**

hun·ger (hung′gər) *n.* **1** Craving for food; also, the weakness caused by the lack of it. **2** Any strong desire. —*v.i.* **1** To feel hunger; be hungry. **2** To have a craving or desire: with *for* or *after.* —*v.t.* **3** To starve; famish. [OE]

hun·ger-strike (hung′gər·strīk′) *n.* Persistent abstention from food in order to obtain concessions from authority: sometimes practiced by prisoners with the object of securing release or a melioration of punishment.

hun·gry (hung′grē) *adj.* ·gri·er, ·gri·est **1** Having a keen appetite; suffering from want of food. **2** Eagerly desiring; craving. **3** Indicating hunger. **4** Poor or barren. See synonyms under GAUNT. [OE *hungrig* < *hunger*] —**hun′gri·ly** *adv.* —**hun′gri·ness** *n.*

hung up *Slang* **1** Psychologically disturbed; especially, preoccupied or obsessed. **2** Sidetracked or impeded, as from a natural or normal process: *hung up* on legal technicalities.

hunk (hungk) *n. Colloq.* A large piece; lump. [Prob. < Flemish *hunke*]

hun·ker (hung′kər) *v.i.* To squat or stoop so that the body rests on the calves of the legs. —*n. pl.* The buttocks resting on the calves of the legs. —**on one's hunkers** In a stooping or squatting position.

hun·ker·ish (hung′kər·ish) *adj.* Extremely conservative. —**hun′ker·ism** *n.*

hunks (hungks) *n. sing. & pl.* A niggardly fellow; miser. [Origin unknown]

hunk·y (hung′kē) See BOHUNK.

hun·ky-do·ry (hung′kē·dôr′ē, -dō′rē) *adj. U.S. Slang* Done satisfactorily or in a satisfactory condition; all right. Also **hunk′y.** [Fanciful extension of slang *hunky* safe, satisfactory]

hunt (hunt) *v.t.* **1** To pursue (game or other wild animals) for the purpose of killing or catching. **2 a** To search (a region) for game. **b** To search (a place): to *hunt* a room. **3** To search for diligently; look for. **4** To manage or use in hunting: to *hunt* a pack of hounds. **5** To chase or drive away; pursue. **6** To persecute; harass. —*v.i.* **7** To pursue game or other wild animals; follow the chase. **8** To make a search; seek. **9** *Aeron.* To make weaving motions about its normal flight path, as an aircraft or guided missile. **10** *Mech.* To run alternately fast and slow owing to unsteady action in the governor: said of stationary engines, etc. —**to hunt down 1** To pursue until caught or killed. **2** To search for until found. —**to hunt up 1** To search for until found. **2** To go in search of. —*n.* **1** The act of hunting game; chase. **2** A search. **3** An association of huntsmen; the participants in a hunt. **4** A district hunted over. —**still hunt 1** A hunting for game in quiet manner. **2** Any quiet and cautious hunt for something. [OE *huntian*]

Synonyms (noun): chase, hunting, inquisition, pursuit, search. A *hunt* may be either the act

of pursuing or the act of seeking, or a combination of the two. A *chase* or *pursuit* is after that which is fleeing or departing; a *search* is for that which is hidden; a *hunt* may be for that which is either hidden or fleeing; a *search* is a minute and careful seeking, and is especially applied to a locality; we make a *search* of or through a house, for an object, in which connection it would be colloquial to say a *hunt.* *Hunt* never quite loses its association with field sports, where it includes both *search* and *chase*; the *search* till the game is hunted out, and the *chase* till it is hunted down. Figuratively, we speak of literary *pursuits*, or of the *pursuit* of knowledge; a *search* for reasons; the *chase* of fame or honor; *hunt*, in figurative use, inclines to the unfavorable sense of *inquisition*, but with aggressiveness; as, a *hunt* for heresy.

hunt·er (hun′tər) *n.* **1** A person who hunts in any way; especially, one who hunts game. **2** A horse or dog used in hunting. **3** A hunting watch.

hunting knife A long, sharp, single- or double-edged knife used by hunters and campers.

hunting watch A watch having the dial side as well as the reverse protected by a metal cap or lid.

hunt·ress (hun′tris) *n.* A woman who hunts.

hunts·man (hunts′mən) *n. pl.* ·men (-mən) **1** One who practices hunting. **2** The attendant who has charge of the pack of hounds in a hunt.

hunts·man's-cup (hunts′mənz·kup′) *n.* The common American pitcherplant.

hur·dle (hûr′dəl) *n.* **1** A movable framework wattled together and used for making fences, etc. **2** A framework to be leaped over in racing. **3** Formerly, a sledge for conveying criminals to execution. **4** *pl.* A race over hurdles. —*v.* ·dled, ·dling *v.t.* **1** To leap over, as an obstacle in a race. **2** To make, cover, or enclose with hurdles. **3** To surmount (a difficulty, etc.). —*v.i.* **4** To leap over hurdles, obstacles, etc. [OE *hyrdel*] —**hur′dler** *n.*

HURDLE *(def. 2)*

hur·dy-gur·dy (hûr′dē·gûr′dē) *n. pl.* ·dies One of various musical instruments played by turning a crank; specifically, a hand organ played by street musicians. [Appar. imit. of the instrument]

hurl (hûrl) *v.t.* **1** To throw with violence; fling. **2** To throw down; overthrow. **3** To utter with vehemence. —*v.i.* **4** *Rare* To throw a missile. **5** In baseball, to pitch. See synonyms under SEND. —*n.* The act of throwing with violence; a cast. [ME *hurlen,* ? < Scand. Cf. Dan. *hurle* whirl, Norw. *hurla* buzz.]

hur·ley (hûr′lē) *n. Irish* The game of hurling.

hur·ley-hack·et (hûr′lē·hak′it) *n.* A small trough or sledge for sliding down a steep hill or an inclined plane. [Origin uncertain]

hurl·ing (hûr′ling) *n.* **1** A former game similar to football. **2** In Ireland, the game of hockey. [< HURL]

hur·ly (hûr′lē) *n. pl.* ·lies Confusion; noise; uproar.

hur·ly-bur·ly (hûr′lē·bûr′lē) *n. pl.* ·lies Tumult; uproar. See synonyms under TUMULT. [Origin uncertain]

Hu·ron (hyŏor′on) *n.* A member of any one of four confederated tribes of North American Indians of Iroquoian stock, originally occupying the territory between Lakes Huron and Ontario: destroyed or dispersed by Iroquois tribes to the south of them, 1648–50. [< F, *ruffian*]

Hu·ron (hyŏor′ən), **Lake** The second largest of the Great Lakes of North America, between Michigan and Ontario; 23,200 square miles.

hur·rah (hŏo·rô′, hə·rä′) *interj.* An exclamation expressing triumph or joy. —*n.* A shout of triumph. —*v.t.* To cheer, as a speaker, with hurrahs. —*v.i.* To shout a hurrah or hurrahs: sometimes spelled *hooray.* Also **hur·ra′.**

[Imit. Cf. Sw., Dan. *hurra!* and Du. *hoera!*]

hur·rah's-nest (hŏo·rôz′nest′, hə·räz′-) *n.* A disorderly, untidy mess; wild confusion. [Origin unknown]

hur·ri·cane (hûr′ə·kān) *n. Meteorol.* **1** A tropical cyclone, especially one originating in the West Indies. **2** In the Beaufort scale, a wind force of the 12th or highest degree, moving at more than 75 miles an hour. Also *Obs.* **hur′ri·ca·no** (-kā′nō). See synonyms under CYCLONE. [< Sp. *huracán* < Cariban]

hurricane deck *Naut.* The upper deck of a passenger steamer, as those on the larger rivers of the United States.

hur·ry (hûr′ē) *v.* **hur·ried, hur·ry·ing** *v.i.* **1** To act or move rapidly or in haste; hasten. —*v.t.* **2** To cause or urge to act or move more rapidly: often with *up.* **3** To cause to act or move too hastily: I was *hurried* into it. **4** To hasten the progress, completion, etc., of, often unduly: to *hurry* a decision. See synonyms under HUSTLE, QUICKEN. —*n. pl.* **hur·ries 1** Haste; precipitation. **2** The act of hurrying. [Origin uncertain] —**hur′ried** *adj.* —**hur′ried·ly** *adv.* —**hur′ried·ness** *n.*

hur·ry-scur·ry (hûr′ē-skûr′ē) *v.i.* To rush in haste and confusion; act hurriedly. —*adj.* Hurried; confused. —*n.* Hasty, confused, or disorderly movement; bustling haste. —*adv.* With disorderly haste; pell-mell; confusedly.

hurt (hûrt) *v.* **hurt, hurt·ing** *v.t.* **1** To cause physical harm or suffering to; injure. **2** To cause material damage to; mark; score. **3** To have a bad effect on; do harm to: Another drink won't *hurt* you. **4** To cause mental suffering to; grieve; worry. —*v.i.* **5** To cause suffering: My feet *hurt.* **6** To cause damage, hurt, etc. —*n.* **1** An injury, especially one causing pain, as a bruise. **2** Damage; detriment. **3** An injury to the feelings; a slight. [< OF *hurter* hit] —**hurt′er** *n.*

Synonyms (verb): afflict, damage, grieve, harm, impair, injure, mar, pain, wound. See VIOLATE. *Antonyms:* benefit, comfort, console, delight, heal, help, please, profit, rejoice, relieve, repair, soothe.

hur·ter (hûr′tər) *n.* **1** The shoulder of the axle of a vehicle, or a reenforcing piece thereon. **2** A buffer, to check the motion of a gun carriage. [< F *heurtoir* knocker]

hurt·ful (hûrt′fəl) *adj.* Causing hurt. See synonyms under BAD, INIMICAL, NOISOME, PERNICIOUS. —**hurt′ful·ly** *adv.* —**hurt′ful·ness** *n.*

hur·tle (hûr′təl) *v.* **hur·tled, hur·tling** *v.i.* **1** To come with violence or noise; crash: with *against* or *together.* **2** To make a crashing, rushing sound; move with noisy speed: The shell *hurtled* through the air. **3** To move or rush headlong or impetuously: He *hurtled* from the room. —*v.t.* **4** To drive, shoot, or throw violently. **5** *Archaic* To strike against; collide with. [Freq. of ME *hurten* hit, hurt]

hus·band (huz′bənd) *n.* **1** A married man; man with a wife. **2** *Obs.* A thrifty manager. **3** *Obs.* A husbandman. —*v.t.* **1** To use or spend wisely; economize on; conserve. **2** To be a husband to; marry. **3** *Archaic* To provide with a husband. **4** *Archaic* To till; cultivate. [OE *hūsbonda < hūs* house + *bonda* freeholder] —**hus′band·less** *adj.* —**hus′band·like′** *adj.* —**hus′band·ly** *adj.*

hus·band·man (huz′bənd·mən) *n. pl.* ·men (-mən) A farmer.

hus·band·ry (huz′bən·drē) *n.* **1** Agriculture. **2** Economical management; also, any management, good or bad. See synonyms under AGRICULTURE. —**Patrons of Husbandry** See GRANGE.

hush (hush) *v.t.* **1** To make silent; repress the noise of. **2** To suppress mention of; keep from being public. **3** To soothe; allay, as fears. —*v.i.* **4** To be or become silent or still. [< *adj.*] —*n.* Deep silence; stillness; quiet. —*adj. Obs.* Quiet; still; silent. —*interj.* Be still; calm yourself. [ME *hussht* quiet]

hush-a·by (hush′ə·bī) *interj.* Hush: an expression used to lull a child to sleep.

hush-hush (hush′hush′) *adj. Colloq.* Secret.

hush money A bribe to secure silence or secrecy.

hush-pup·py (hush′pup′ē) *n. pl.* ·pies *U.S.* In the South, a fried ball of cornmeal dough.

husk (husk) *n.* **1** The outer covering of certain fruits or seeds; rind; hull; especially, that of an ear of maize or Indian corn. **2** The carob pod. *Luke* xv 16. **3** Any covering, especially when comparatively worthless. — *v.t.* To remove the husk of. [ME *huske*, ? OE *hosu* husk] — **husk′er** *n.*

husk·ing (hus′king) *n.* **1** The act of stripping off husks, as from maize. **2** A gathering of friends to aid in husking corn: also **husking bee.**

husk·y[1] (hus′kē) *adj.* **husk·i·er, husk·i·est** **1** Abounding in husks; like husks. **2** Dry as a husk; hoarse: said of the voice. [<HUSK] — **husk′i·ly** *adv.* — **husk′i·ness** *n.*

husk·y[2] (hus′kē) *U.S. Colloq. adj.* **husk·i·er, husk·i·est** Strong; burly. — *n.* A strong or powerfully built person. [Special use of HUSKY[1], with ref. to toughness of husks]

Husk·y (hus′kē) *n.* *pl.* **Husk·ies** A heavy-furred Eskimo dog. See SIBERIAN HUSKY. Also **husk′y.** [? Alter. of ESKIMO]

hus·sar (hŏŏ-zär′) *n.* Originally, a light-armed horse trooper of the Hungarian army; later, a member of any light-armed cavalry regiment in other European armies, usually with brilliant dress uniforms. [<Hungarian *huszár* <Serbian *gusar* <Ital. *corsaro* <Med. L *corsarius.* Doublet of CORSAIR.]

hus·sy (huz′ē, hus′ē) *n.* *pl.* **-sies** **1** A pert or forward girl; jade: in reproach or playfully. Also *huzzy.* **2** A case or bag. See HOUSEWIFE (def. 2). [Alter. of HOUSEWIFE]

hust·ing (hus′ting) *n.* **1** A British court formerly held in the larger cities (and still in existence in London): now more commonly in the plural. **2** *pl.* The temporary platform on which the nomination of parliamentary candidates was made prior to the Ballot Act of 1872; hence, the proceedings at an election; now, any platform or place where political speeches are made; hence, a political campaign. [OE *hūsting* council <ON *hūsthing* <*hūs* house + *thing* assembly]

hus·tle (hus′əl) *v.* **hus·tled, hus·tling** *v.t.* **1** To push or knock about roughly or rudely; jostle. **2** To force or impel roughly and hurriedly: to *hustle* a man from a room. **3** *U.S. Colloq.* To hurry; cause to proceed rapidly. **4** *U.S. Slang* **a** To sell aggressively, as for quick profit. **b** To obtain by aggressive action. **c** To dupe; victimize. — *v.i.* **5** To push one's way; shove; elbow. **6** *U.S. Colloq.* To act or work with energy and speed. **7** *U.S. Slang* To be a prostitute. **8** *U.S. Slang* To live by one's wits, as by gambling, petty thievery, etc. **9** In sports, to put forth extra effort. — *n.* **1** The act of hustling. **2** *Colloq.* Energetic activity; push. **3** *U.S. Slang* A way of getting money illegitimately, as by fraud or thievery; a racket. [<Du *hutselen* shake, toss]
Synonyms (verb): crowd, elbow, hasten, hurry, jam, jostle, push, rush, shove. *Antonyms:* dally, dawdle, delay, hold back, loaf.

hus·tler (hus′lər, hus′əl·ər) *n.* **1** *U.S. Colloq.* An aggressive, energetic person; go-getter. **2** *U.S. Slang* A prostitute. **3** *U.S. Slang* One who lives by his wits, as a gambler, confidence man, petty thief, etc.

hut (hut) *n.* A small rude dwelling. — *v.t.* & *v.i.* **hut·ted, hut·ting** To shelter or live in a hut. [<OF *hutte* <OHG *hutta*]
Synonyms (noun): cabin, cot, cottage, hovel, shanty, shed. See HOUSE. *Antonyms:* castle, hall, mansion, palace.

hutch (huch) *n.* **1** A place for storing anything. **2** A small or dark room. **3** A coop or pen for rabbits, etc. **4** A chest or locker. **5** A measure; also, a basket. — *v.t.* To store up or hoard. [<F *huche* <LL *hutica*]

hy·a·cinth (hī′ə·sinth) *n.* **1** A bulbous plant of the lily family (genus *Hyacinthus*) cultivated for its spikelike cluster of flowers. **2** The bulb or flower of this plant. **3** A gem, anciently bluish-violet, probably the sapphire, now a brownish, reddish, or orange zircon. **4** A plant frequently alluded to by the Greek poets, fabled to have sprung from the blood of Hyacinthus, beloved of Apollo, and to have borne on its petals the words of grief, *Ai, Ai:* sometimes

HYACINTH (*def. 1*)

identified as the iris, larkspur, or gladiolus. [Var. of older *jacynth* <OF *jacincte* <L *hyacinthus* <Gk. *hyakinthos.* Doublet of JACINTH.]

hyacinth blue A medium purplish-blue, the color of certain hyacinths.

hy·a·cin·thine (hī′ə·sin′thin, -thīn) *adj.* Pertaining to or like the hyacinth.

hy·ae·na (hī·ē′nə) See HYENA.

hy·a·line (hī′ə·lin, -līn) *n.* **1** A glassy surface, as of the sea; something transparent. **2** *Biochem.* A nitrogenous compound, related to chitin, the chief constituent of hydatid cysts, which on decomposition yields a reducing sugar. **3** *Anat.* The hyaloid membrane. Also **hy′a·lin** (-lin). — *adj.* Consisting of or resembling glass; transparent: the *hyaline* substance of a cell. [<L *hyalinus* <Gk. *hyalos* glass]

hyaline cartilage *Anat.* That form of cartilage in which the cells are embedded in a homogeneous translucent matrix.

hy·a·lite (hī′ə·līt) *n.* A pellucid glassy variety of opal.

hyalo– *combining form* Glass; of or resembling glass: *hyaloplasm.* Also, before vowels, **hyal–.** [<Gk. *hyalos* glass]

hy·al·o·gen (hī·al′ə·jən) *n.* *Biochem.* Any of various insoluble substances found in animal tissues and related to mucin; it yields hyaline on hydrolysis.

hy·a·loid (hī′ə·loid) *adj.* Like glass; pellucid: the *hyaloid* membrane. [<Gk. *hyaloeidēs* glassy]

hyaloid membrane *Anat.* A delicate membrane enveloping the vitreous humor of the eye.

hy·a·lo·plasm (hī′ə·lō·plaz′əm) *n.* *Biol.* The clear, fluid or semifluid ground substance of protoplasm, as distinguished from the granular substance. Also **hy′a·lo·plas′ma** (-plaz′mə). — **hy′a·lo·plas′mic** *adj.*

hy·brid (hī′brid) *adj.* **1** Produced by interbreeding or cross-fertilization. **2** Derived from incongruous sources; mixed. — *n.* **1** An animal or plant of mixed parentage; a mongrel. **2** Anything of heterogeneous origin or incongruous parts. **3** *Ling.* A word composed of elements from more than one language, as *genocide.* [<L *hybrida* offspring of tame sow and wild boar]

hy·brid·ism (hī′brid·iz′əm) *n.* **1** The state of being hybrid: also **hy·brid·i·ty** (hī·brid′ə·tē). **2** The act of interbreeding, or of inducing hybridization. **3** *Ling.* The mingling in one word of elements from more than one language.

hy·brid·ize (hī′brid·īz) *v.t.* & *v.i.* **-ized, -iz·ing** To produce or cause to produce hybrids; crossbreed. Also *Brit.* **hy′brid·ise.** — **hy·brid·i·za·tion** (hī′brid·ə·zā′shən, -i·zā′-) *n.* — **hy′brid·iz′er** *n.* — **hy′brid·ous** *adj.*

hybrid vigor Heterosis.

hy·dan·to·in (hī·dan′tō·in) *n.* A white crystalline derivative of allantoin, C_3H_4ON. [<Gk. *hydōr, hydatos* water + (ALL)ANTOIN]

hy·da·thode (hī′də·thōd) *n.* *Bot.* An epidermal cellular structure, as a gland, that exudes water: found in plants. [<Gk. *hydōr, hydatos* water + *hodos* way]

hy·da·tid (hī′də·tid) *n.* **1** An encysted vesicle containing an aqueous fluid. **2** An encysted larval stage of a tapeworm. — *adj.* Of or pertaining to a water-containing cyst. [<Gk. *hydatis* drop of water]

hy·da·to·gen·e·sis (hī′də·tō·jen′ə·sis) *n.* Formation of water, as in the tissues and cavities of the body. [<Gk. *hydōr, hydatos* water + GENESIS]

hyd·no·car·pate (hid′nə·kär′pāt) *n.* *Chem.* A salt or ester of hydnocarpic acid, especially the sodium salt or ethyl ester, used in the treatment of leprosy.

hyd·no·car·pic (hid′nə·kär′pik) *adj.* *Chem.* Denoting an acid, $C_{16}H_{28}O_2$, extracted from the seeds and oil of the chaulmoogra tree, and used in the treatment of leprosy. [<Gk. *hydnon* truffle + *karpos* fruit]

hy·dra (hī′drə) *n.* *pl.* **·dras** or **·drae** (-drē) **1** Any evil having many forms. **2** A freshwater polyp (genus *Hydra*). [<Gk. *hydra* water serpent]

hy·drac·id (hī·dras′id) *n.* *Chem.* An acid that contains no oxygen, as hydrochloric acid:

contrasted with *oxyacid.*

hy·dra·gog (hī′drə·gôg, -gog) *n.* Any medicine that causes abundant watery evacuations. Also **hy′dra·gogue.** [<F <L *hydragogus* <Gk. *hydragōgos* <*hydōr* water + *agein* lead]

hy·dra–head·ed (hī′drə-hed′id) *adj.* Having many heads; hard to destroy.

hy·dran·ge·a (hī·drān′jē·ə, -jə) *n.* A plant of a genus (*Hydrangea*) of trees and shrubs of the saxifrage family, with opposite, usually serrate, leaves and cymose clusters of large, showy flowers. [<NL <Gk. *hydōr* water + *angeion* vessel]

hy·drant (hī′drənt) *n.* A valved discharge pipe connected with a water main; a plug. [<Gk. *hydōr* water]

hy·drar·gyr·ic (hī′drär·jir′ik) *adj.* Of, pertaining to, or containing mercury.

hy·drar·gy·rism (hī·drär′jə·riz′əm) *n.* Mercury poisoning; mercurialism.

hy·drar·gy·rum (hī·drär′jə·rəm) *n.* Mercury: especially so called in pharmacy. [<NL <L *hydrargyrus* <Gk. *hydrargyros* <*hydōr* water + *argyros* silver]

hy·drate (hī′drāt) *n.* *Chem.* Any of a class of compounds formed by the union of molecules of water with other molecules or atoms. — *v.t.* **·drat·ed, ·drat·ing** To combine with water or its elements to form a hydrate. [<HYDR- + -ATE[3]] — **hy′drat·ed** *adj.* — **hy·dra·tion** (hī·drā′shən) *n.*

hy·drau·lic (hī·drô′lik) *adj.* **1** Pertaining to hydraulics, involving the moving of water, or force exerted by water: *hydraulic* engineering, mining, etc. **2** Denoting any of various machines and structures operating by means of water or other liquid under pressure: a *hydraulic* elevator, crane, ram, press, etc. **3** Hardening under water: *hydraulic* cement. Also **hy·drau′li·cal.** [<L *hydraulicus* <Gk. *hydraulikos* of a water organ <*hydraulos* water organ <*hydōr* water + *aulos* pipe] — **hy·drau′li·cal·ly** *adv.*

hydraulic brake A brake actuated by fluids under pressure in cylinders and tubular connecting lines.

hydraulic press A machine which operates by means of fluid under pressure to exert a large force over an extended area: used in forming steel dies, in baling, etc.

hydraulic ram An automatic device by which the fall of a comparatively large quantity of water furnishes the power to raise a smaller quantity to a height above that of the source.

HYDRAULIC RAM
a. Air chamber.
b. Water chamber.
c. Air inlet.
d. Check valve.
e. Clack valve.
f. Supply pipe.
g. Delivery pipe.

hy·drau·lics (hī·drô′liks) *n. pl.* (*construed as singular*) The science of the laws of motion of water and other liquids and of their practical applications.

hydraulic transmission See FLUID DRIVE.

hy·dric (hī′drik) *adj.* Of or pertaining to hydrogen in combination.

hydro– *combining form* **1** Water; of, related to, or resembling water: *hydrophone.* **2** *Chem.* Denoting a compound of hydrogen: *hydrochloric.* Also, before vowels, **hydr–.** [<Gk. *hydro-* <*hydōr* water]

hy·dro·air·plane (hī′drō·âr′plān′) See HYDROPLANE (def. 1).

hy·dro·car·bon (hī′drə·kär′bən) *n.* *Chem.* One of a large and important group of compounds that contain hydrogen and carbon only. There are many types and classes, including the aliphatic, aromatic, saturated, and unsaturated hydrocarbons.

hy·dro·cele (hī′drə·sēl) *n.* *Pathol.* A localized accumulation of fluid surrounding the testicles or along the spermatic cord. [<L <Gk. *hydrokēlē* <*hydōr* water + *kēlē* tumor]

hy·dro·ceph·a·lus (hī′drə·sef′ə·ləs) *n. Pathol.* An accumulation of watery fluid within the ventricles or between the membranes of the brain. [<HYDRO- + Gk. *kephalē* head] — **hy′·dro·ceph′a·loid** (-loid), **hy′dro·ceph′a·lous** *adj.*

hy·dro·chlo·ric (hī′drə·klôr′ik, -klō′rik) *adj. Chem.* Pertaining to or designating a colorless, corrosive, fuming acid, HCl, exceedingly soluble in water, in which form it is largely used in manufactures and sometimes called *muriatic acid.*

hy·dro·chlo·ride (hī′drə·klôr′īd, -klō′rīd) *n. Chem.* A compound produced by the union of hydrochloric acid with an element or radical.

hy·dro·dy·nam·ic (hī′drō·dī·nam′ik) *adj.* Of or pertaining to the force or pressure of water or other fluids. Also **hy′dro·dy·nam′i·cal.**

hy·dro·dy·nam·ics (hī′drō·dī·nam′iks) *n. pl.* (*construed as singular*) The branch of mechanics that treats of the dynamics of fluids, chiefly water and other liquids.

hy·dro·e·lec·tric (hī′drō·i·lek′trik) *adj.* Of or pertaining to electricity developed by water power, or by the escape of steam under high pressure, etc. — **hy·dro·e·lec·tric·i·ty** (hī′drō·i·lek·tris′ə·tē) *n.*

hy·dro·flu·or·ic (hī′drō·flŏŏ·ôr′ik, -or′-) *adj. Chem.* Pertaining to or designating a volatile, colorless, hygroscopic, corrosive acid, HF, formed by decomposing metallic fluorides. It readily attacks silica, hence is used for etching on glass.

hy·dro·foil (hī′drə·foil) *n.* A streamlined surface designed to provide support in or obtain a reaction from the water through which it moves, as an attachment to a boat, submarine, or hydroplane.

hy·dro·gel (hī′drə·jel) *n. Chem.* A colloid which has assumed a jellylike form in the presence of water.

hy·dro·gen (hī′drə·jən) *n.* The lightest of the elements (symbol H) occurring chiefly in combination with oxygen as water, and in hydrocarbons and other organic compounds. When isolated it is usually a colorless, odorless, tasteless, inflammable gas, lighter than air and liquefying under great pressure and low temperature. — **heavy hydrogen** See DEUTERIUM. [<F *hydrogène* <Gk. *hydōr* water + *gen-*, stem of *gignesthai* be born; so called with ref. to the water formed by its combustion] — **hy·drog·e·nous** (hī·droj′ə·nəs) *adj.*

hy·dro·gen·ate (hī′drə·jə·nāt′) *v.t.* **·at·ed, ·at·ing** *Chem.* **1** To cause to combine with hydrogen. **2** To expose to hydrogen, or to effect chemical action of by the use of or by exposure to hydrogen: to *hydrogenate* fats and oils. Also **hy′dro·gen·ize′** (-īz′).

hy·dro·gen·a·tion (hī′drə·jə·nā′shən) *n. Chem.* The act or process of subjecting to the action of hydrogen, usually in the presence of a catalyst: the *hydrogenation* of coal to form liquid hydrocarbons.

hydrogen bomb A bomb of great destructive power, releasing enormous quantities of energy by the fusion, under extremely high temperatures, of deuterium or tritium atoms, with the formation of helium.

hydrogen cyanide Hydrocyanic acid.

hydrogen ion *Chem.* The positively charged hydrogen ion (H⁺) present in all acids. The number of hydrogen ions per unit volume of an aqueous solution is known as the **hydrogen ion concentration,** or *pH* value.

hydrogen peroxide *Chem.* A sirupy liquid, H_2O_2, whose aqueous solutions are important as antiseptics and bleaching agents, the usual solution being a slightly acid one containing about 3 percent by weight of pure hydrogen peroxide. Also called *peroxide.*

hydrogen sulfide *Chem.* A colorless, gaseous compound, H_2S, having a characteristic odor of rotten eggs, made by decomposing certain metallic sulfides, chiefly iron, by means of acids. It is poisonous and is a valuable laboratory reagent.

hy·dro·glid·er (hī′drə·glī′dər) *n.* A glider with floats attached to permit it to land on or take off from water.

hy·drog·ra·phy (hī·drog′rə·fē) *n.* The science of determining and making known the conditions of navigable waters, charting rivers, coasts, etc. — **hy·drog′ra·pher** *n.* — **hy′dro·graph′ic** or **·i·cal** *adj.*

hy·droid (hī′droid) *adj.* **1** Of or pertaining to

a class (*Hydrozoa*) of mostly marine coelenterates resembling the hydra; like a polyp. **2** Designating a reproductive phase in the development of certain hydrozoans characterized by the formation of colonies. — *n.* A hydrozoan.

hy·dro·ki·net·ic (hī′drō·ki·net′ik) *adj.* Relating to the motion and kinetic energy of fluids. Also **hy′dro·ki·net′i·cal.**

hy·dro·ki·net·ics (hī′drō·ki·net′iks) *n. pl.* (*construed as singular*) The branch of hydrodynamics that treats of fluids in motion.

hy·drol·o·gy (hī·drol′ə·jē) *n.* The branch of physical geography that treats of the waters of the earth, their distribution, characteristics, and effects. [<HYDRO- + -LOGY] — **hy·dro·log·ic** (hī′drə·loj′ik) or **·i·cal** *adj.* — **hy·drol·og′i·cal·ly** *adv.* — **hy·drol′o·gist** *n.*

hy·drol·y·sis (hī·drol′ə·sis) *n. Chem.* Any decomposition involving the addition of water; specifically, a double decomposition reaction between water and some other compound, as phosphorus trichloride. [<HYDRO- + -LYSIS] — **hy·dro·lyt·ic** (hī′drə·lit′ik) *adj.*

hy·dro·lyte (hī′drə·līt) *n.* Any substance affected by hydrolysis.

hy·dro·lyze (hī′drə·līz) *v.t. & v.i.* **·lyzed, ·lyz·ing** To undergo or cause to undergo the process of hydrolysis. — **hy′dro·lyz′a·ble** *adj.* — **hy·dro·ly·za·tion** (hī′drə·lə·zā′shən, -li·zā′-) *n.*

hy·dro·man·cy (hī′drə·man′sē) *n.* Divination by means of water. — **hy′dro·manc′er** *n.* — **hy′dro·man′tic** (-tik) *adj.*

hy·dro·me·chan·ics (hī′drō·mə·kan′iks) *n.* The mechanics of fluids, including hydrostatics, hydrodynamics, hydrokinetics, and pneumatics. — **hy′dro·me·chan′i·cal** *adj.*

hy·dro·me·du·sa (hī′drō·mə·dōō′sə, -dyōō′-) *n. pl.* **·sae** (-sē) A type of coelenterate produced by budding from an individual, as the jellyfish and medusa.

hy·dro·mel (hī′drə·mel) *n.* A liquor, usually unfermented, consisting of honey diluted with water; when fermented, it is called *mead.* [<L <Gk. *hydromeli* <*hydōr* water + *meli* honey]

hy·dro·met·al·lur·gy (hī′drō·met′əl·ûr′jē) *n.* The process of assaying or reducing ore by means of liquid reagents. — **hy′dro·met′al·lur′gi·cal** *adj.*

hy·dro·me·te·or (hī′drō·mē′tē·ər) *n. Meteorol.* A watery or aqueous meteor; any of the conditions or effects produced by water, as rain, snow, hail, etc.

hy·dro·me·te·or·ol·o·gy (hī′drō·mē′tē·ə·rol′ə·jē) *n.* The branch of meteorology that treats of hydrometeors or of water in the atmosphere.

hy·drom·e·ter (hī·drom′ə·tər) *n.* **1** A calibrated sealed tube weighted at one end for determining the density or specific gravity, especially of liquids and solutions: also called *densimeter.* **2** A current gage. — **hy·dro·met·ric** (hī′drə·met′rik) or **·ri·cal** *adj.* — **hy·drom′e·try** *n.*

hy·drop·a·thy (hī·drop′ə·thē) *n.* The treatment of diseases by the use of water; water cure. — **hy·dro·path·ic** (hī′drə·path′ik) or **·i·cal** *adj.* — **hy·drop′a·thist, hy′dro·path** *n.*

hy·dro·phane (hī′drə·fān) *n.* A whitish or light-colored opal, opaque when dry, but translucent when wet. — **hy·droph·a·nous** (hī·drof′ə·nəs) *adj.*

hy·droph·i·lous (hī·drof′ə·ləs) *adj. Bot.* Having the flowers pollinated by the agency of water: said of certain higher plants. [<HYDRO- + Gk. *philos* loving]

hy·dro·pho·bi·a (hī′drə·fō′bē·ə) *n.* **1** Rabies. **2** Any morbid dread of water. [<L <Gk., <*hydōr* water + *phobos* fear] — **hy′dro·pho′bic** *adj.*

hy·dro·phone (hī′drə·fōn) *n.* **1** An electrical instrument for detecting underwater sounds, especially of enemy submarines. **2** A device used for the purpose of detecting leaks in water pipes.

hy·dro·phyte (hī′drə·fīt) *n. Bot.* A plant living in water or in wet ground. — **hy·dro·phyt·ic** (hī′drə·fit′ik) *adj.*

hy·drop·ic (hī·drop′ik) *adj.* Dropsical; affected with dropsy. Also **hy·drop′i·cal.** [<OF *idropique* <L *hydropicus* <Gk. *hydrōpikos* <*hydrōps* dropsy <*hydōr* water] — **hy·drop′i·cal·ly** *adv.*

hy·dro·plane (hī′drə·plān) *n.* **1** An airplane constructed for alighting upon or rising from the water: also called *hydroairplane.* **2** A motorboat of extremely light construction

driven either by submerged screws or by aerial propellers. **3** A hydrofoil. — *v.i.* **·planed, ·plan·ing 1** To move on water at a speed sufficient to give support through hydrodynamic and aerodynamic forces alone. **2** To drive or ride in a hydroplane.

hy·dro·pon·ics (hī′drə·pon′iks) *n. pl.* (*construed as singular*) Soilless agriculture; the raising of plants in nutrient mineral solutions without earth around the roots: also called *water culture, tank farming.* [<HYDRO- + Gk. *ponos* labor] — **hy′dro·pon′ic** *adj.*

hy·drop·sy (hī′drop′sē) *n.* Dropsy. Also **hy′·drops, hy·drop′si·a.**

hy·dro·scope (hī′drə·skōp) *n.* **1** An instrument for detecting moisture, especially in the air. **2** An instrument for seeing through considerable depths of water. — **hy′dro·scop′ic** (-skop′ik) or **·i·cal** *adj.*

hy·dro·sere (hī′drə·sir) *n. Ecol.* In plant succession, the series of changes in vegetation which take place in the water. [<HYDRO- + SERE²]

hy·dro·some (hī′drə·sōm) *n. Zool.* A hydroid colony as a whole. Also **hy′dro·so′ma** (-sō′mə). [<HYDRO- + -SOME²]

hy·dro·sphere (hī′drə·sfir) *n.* **1** The total water surrounding the earth. **2** The atmospheric moisture enveloping the globe, in distinction from the atmosphere itself.

hy·dro·stat (hī′drə·stat) *n.* **1** A contrivance for preventing the explosion of steam boilers. **2** An electrical device for making known the presence of water, as a protection against leakage, overflow, etc.

hy·dro·stat·ic (hī′drə·stat′ik) *adj.* Pertaining to hydrostatics. Also **hy′dro·stat′i·cal.**

hy·dro·stat·ics (hī′drə·stat′iks) *n. pl.* (*construed as singular*) The science of the pressure and equilibrium of fluids, as water.

hy·dro·sul·fate (hī′drə·sul′fāt) *n. Chem.* A compound of sulfuric acid and an alkaloid or other organic base.

hy·dro·sul·fide (hī′drə·sul′fīd) *n. Chem.* A compound derived from hydrogen sulfide, by replacing one of the hydrogen atoms with a basic radical or a base.

hy·dro·sul·fite (hī′drə·sul′fīt) *n.* Sodium hydrosulfite.

hy·dro·tax·is (hī′drə·tak′sis) *n. Biol.* **1** The irritable response or turning of organisms under the influence of humidity or water. **2** The action of moisture in determining the direction of motion, as in protoplasm. — **hy′dro·tac′tic** (-tak′tik) *adj.*

hy·dro·ther·mal (hī′drə·thûr′məl) *adj. Geol.* Of, pertaining to, or produced by action of heated or superheated water, especially the action of such water in dissolving, transporting, and redepositing mineral matter.

hy·dro·tho·rax (hī′drə·thôr′aks, -thō′raks) *n. Pathol.* An accumulation of fluid in the pleural cavity; dropsy of the chest. — **hy·dro·tho·rac·ic** (hī′drō·thə·ras′ik) *adj.*

hy·drot·ro·pism (hī·drot′rə·piz′əm) *n. Bot.* The phenomena of curvature induced in a growing plant organ by the stimulation of moisture. — **hy·dro·trop·ic** (hī′drə·trop′ik) *adj.*

hy·drous (hī′drəs) *adj. Chem.* **1** Watery; containing water of crystallization or hydration. **2** Containing hydrogen.

Hy·dro·vize (hī′drə·vīz) *v.t.* **·vized, ·viz·ing** To make (a textile fabric) rainproof and resistant to stains, winds, and perspiration by the application to its surface of a water repellent: a trade name.

hy·drox·ide (hī·drok′sīd) *n. Chem.* A compound containing hydroxyl.

hy·drox·y (hī·drok′sē) *adj. Chem.* Any of a class of compounds containing the hydroxyl radical: a *hydroxy* acid.

hy·e·na (hī·ē′nə) *n.* A catlike carnivorous mammal of Africa and Asia (family *Hyaenidae*) with very strong, large teeth, striped or spotted body, and skulking habits, as the African laughing hyena (*Hyaena brunnea*) and the spotted hyena (*Crocuta crocuta*): also spelled *hyaena.* [<L *hyaena* <Gk. *hyaina* <*hys* pig]

HYENA
(About 2 feet high at the shoulder)

hy·e·tal (hī′ə·təl) *adj. Meteorol.* **1** Of or pertaining to rain or the amount of the rainfall at different places and seasons. **2** Rainy.

hyeto– *combining form* Rain: *hyetograph.* Also, before vowels, **hyet–**. [<Gk. *hyetos* rain < *hyein* rain]

hy·e·to·graph (hī′i·tə·graf′, -gräf′) *n. Meteorol.* A chart showing the distribution of rainfall over the earth, or over any part of it.

hy·e·to·graph·ic (hī′i·tə·graf′ik) *adj. Meteorol.* Relating to or showing the amount of rainfall: a *hyetographic* map. Also **hy′e·to·graph′i·cal.**

hy·e·tog·ra·phy (hī′i·tog′rə·fē) *n.* The branch of meteorology that treats of the distribution of rainfall, and of the exhibition of it graphically in charts, maps, etc.

hy·e·tol·o·gy (hī′i·tol′ə·jē) *n.* That branch of meteorology which treats of precipitation. [<HYETO– + -LOGY] — **hy·e·to·log·i·cal** (hī′i·tə·loj′i·kəl) *adj.*

hy·giene (hī′jēn, -ji·ēn) *n.* The branch of medical science that relates to the preservation of health; sanitary science. [<F *hygiène* <Gk. *hygienios* healthful]

hy·gi·en·ic (hī′jē·en′ik, hī·jē′nik) *adj.* Pertaining to hygiene; sanitary. See synonyms under HEALTHY. — **hy′gi·en′i·cal·ly** *adv.*

hy·gi·en·ics (hī′jē·en′iks, hī·jē′niks) *n.* The science of preserving and promoting health.

hy·gi·en·ist (hī′jē·ən·ist) *n.* One who studies or is versed in the principles of hygiene. Also **hy′ge·ist** (-jē·ist), **hy′gie·ist.**

hygro– *combining form* Wet; denoting relation to moisture. [<Gk. *hygros* wet]

hy·gro·graph (hī′grə·graf, -gräf) *n.* A recording hygrometer.

hy·grom·e·ter (hī·grom′ə·tər) *n.* An instrument for ascertaining the humidity or degree of moisture in the atmosphere. [<HYGRO– + -METER]

hy·gro·met·ric (hī′grə·met′rik) *adj.* **1** Pertaining to hygrometry or to the state of the atmosphere as to moisture. **2** Readily absorbing and retaining moisture. Also **hy′gro·met′ri·cal.**

hy·grom·e·try (hī·grom′ə·trē) *n.* The branch of physics that treats of the measurement of degrees of moisture, especially the moisture of the air.

hy·gro·scope (hī′grə·skōp) *n.* A device for approximating the humidity of the air.

hy·gro·scop·ic (hī′grə·skop′ik) *adj.* **1** Pertaining to the hygroscope, or capable of being detected by it. **2** Able to absorb or condense moisture from the atmosphere, as glycerol. **3** Expanding or shrinking according to the amount of moisture: said of plants.

hy·la (hī′lə) *n.* The tree frog (genus *Hyla*). [<NL <Gk. *hyle* wood]

hy·lic (hī′lik) *adj.* Relating to or of the nature of matter; material. — **hy′li·cism** (-lə·siz′əm) *n.*

hy·li·cist (hī′lə·sist) *n.* A believer or teacher of materialism; specifically, one of the early Ionic philosophers.

hy·lism (hī′liz·əm) *n.* **1** Materialism. **2** The theory that matter is the principle or source of evil.

hylo– *combining form* Related to matter; material: *hylotropic.* Also, before vowels, **hyl–**. [<Gk. *hylē* wood]

hy·lo·the·ism (hī′lə·thē′iz·əm) *n.* The doctrine of belief that the material universe is God; pantheism.

hy·lo·trop·ic (hī′lə·trop′ik, -trō′pik) *adj.* Having the capacity to change in form without a change in composition; as ice, water, and steam.

hy·lo·zo·ism (hī′lə·zō′iz·əm) *n.* The doctrine that life and matter are inseparable. [<HYLO– + Gk. *zōē* life] — **hy′lo·zo′ic** *adj.* — **hy′lo·zo′ist** *n.* — **hy′lo·zo·is′tic** *adj.*

hy·men (hī′mən) *n.* **1** *Anat.* A thin mucous membrane partially covering the entrance of the vagina; the virginal membrane or maidenhead. **2** The wedded state; marriage. [<Gk. *hymēn* membrane]

hy·me·ne·al (hī′mə·nē′əl) *adj.* Pertaining to marriage: also **hy′me·ne′an.** See synonyms under MATRIMONIAL. — *n.* A wedding song.

hy·me·ni·um (hī·mē′nē·əm) *n. pl.* **·ni·a** (-nē·ə) or **·ni·ums** *Bot.* The fruit-bearing surface or stratum in the higher fungi of the *Ascomycetes* or *Basidiomycetes*, as the two vertical faces on the gills of the common mushroom. It consists of a collection of basidia, sometimes interspersed with sterile cells in a layer or stratum. [<NL <Gk. *hymenion*, dim. of *hymen* membrane]

hymeno– *combining form* Membrane: *hymenophore.* Also, before vowels, **hymen–**. [<Gk. *hymēn* skin, membrane]

Hy·men·o·my·ce·tes (hī′mən·ō·mī·sē′tēz) *n. pl.* A subgroup of fleshy, leathery, or woody fungi, having an exposed hymenium, including the common edible mushroom, *Agaricus campestris.* — **hy′men·o·my·ce′tal** or **·tous** *adj.*

hy·men·o·phore (hī′mən·ō·fôr′, -fōr′) *n. Bot.* The stem and pileus of a hymenomycetous fungus; more specifically, that part of the sporophore which bears the hymenium. Also **hy·men·i·o·phore** (hī·men′ē·ō·fôr′, -fōr′), **hy′men·o·pho′rum** (-fôr′əm, -fō′rəm).

hymn (him) *n.* A song expressive of praise, adoration, or elevated emotion; specifically, a metrical composition, divided into stanzas or verses, intended to be sung in religious worship; also, a religious or patriotic ode, song, lyric, or other poem. — *v.* **hymned, hymn·ing** *v.t.* **1** To praise or worship in hymns. **2** To express by singing: to *hymn* praises. — *v.i.* **3** To sing hymns or praises. See synonyms under SONG. [Fusion of OE *hymen* and OF *ymne,* both <LL *ymnus, hymnus* <Gk. *hymnos* a song, ode] — **hym′nic** (-nik) *adj.*

hym·nal (him′nəl) *n.* A book of hymns: also **hymn book.** — *adj.* Of or concerning a hymn or hymns.

hymnal stanza Common measure.

hym·nist (him′nist) *n.* A writer of hymns. Also **hym′no·dist** (-nə·dist).

hym·no·dy (him′nə·dē) *n. pl.* **·dies 1** Hymns collectively; hymnology. **2** The practice of singing hymns. [<LL *hymnodia* <Gk. *hymnōidia* <*hymnos* hymn + *ōidē* singing]

hym·nog·ra·phy (him·nog′rə·fē) *n.* The art of composing hymns.

hym·nol·o·gy (him·nol′ə·jē) *n.* **1** The study or science of hymns, including their history, use, and classification. **2** A treatise on hymns, or hymns collectively. [<HYMN + -(O)LOGY] — **hym·no·log·ic** (him′nə·loj′ik) or **·i·cal** *adj.* — **hym·nol′o·gist** *n.*

hy·oid (hī′oid) *n. Anat.* A U-shaped bone at the base of the tongue, for the attachment of the muscles of deglutition: also **hyoid bone.** — *adj.* **1** Pertaining to the hyoid bone. **2** Having the form of the Greek letter upsilon (Υ, υ). [<F *hyoïde* <Gk. *hyoeidēs* <Υ upsilon + *eidos* form]

hy·os·cine (hī′ə·sēn) *n.* Scopolamine. [<HYOSC(YAMUS) + -INE]

hy·os·cy·a·mine (hī′ə·sī′ə·mēn, -min) *n. Chem.* A white, crystalline, poisonous alkaloid, $C_{17}H_{23}NO_3$, contained in henbane, thorn apple, deadly nightshade, and other plants: used medicinally. Also **hy′os·cy′a·min** (-min).

hy·os·cy·a·mus (hī′ə·sī′ə·məs) *n.* The henbane, containing alkaloids used for their anodyne and antispasmodic properties. [<Gk. *hyoskyamos* henbane < *hys* hog + *kyamos* bean]

hyp– Var. of HYPO–.

hyp·a·bys·sal (hip′ə·bis′əl) *adj. Geol.* Pertaining to or designating igneous rocks which form minor intrusions, such as dikes and sills; also, the intrusions themselves. [<HYP– + ABYSSAL]

hyp·aes·the·si·a (hip′əs·thē′zhē·ə, -zhə), **hy·pae·thral** (hi·pē′thrəl), etc. See HYPESTHESIA, etc.

hype (hīp) *Slang v.t.* **hyped, hyp·ing 1** To deceive; fool. **2** To stimulate with or as with drugs: with *up.* — *n.* **1** A deception; fraud. **2** A promotional talk or message. [<HYPODERMIC, with ref. to the injection of drugs]

hyper– *prefix* **1** Over; above; excessive: *hypertension:* opposed to *hypo–*. **2** *Chem.* Denoting the highest in a series of compounds: now generally replaced by *per–*. [<Gk. *hyper* <*hyper* beyond]

hy·per·ac·id (hī′pər·as′id) *adj.* Excessively acid. — **hy′per·a·cid′i·ty** (-ə·sid′ə·tē) *n.*

hy·per·a·cu·si·a (hī′pər·ə·kyōō′zhē·ə) *n. Pathol.* Morbid acuteness of hearing. Also **hy′per·a·cu′sis** (-sis). [<HYPER– + Gk. *akousis* hearing]

hy·per·a·dre·ni·a (hī′pər·ə·drē′nē·ə) *n. Pathol.* A disorder caused by excessive secretory activity of the adrenal glands, and characterized by sudden increases in blood pressure. Also **hy·per·ad·re·nal·ism** (hī′pər·ə·drē′nəl·iz′əm).

hy·per·ae·mi·a (hī′pər·ē′mē·ə), **hy·per·aes·the·si·a** (hī′pər·es·thē′zhē·ə, -zhə) See HYPEREMIA, etc.

hy·per·al·ge·si·a (hī′pər·al·jē′zē·ə, -sē·ə) *n. Pathol.* Excessive sensitiveness to pain. Also **hy′per·al·ge′sis.** [<HYPER– + Gk. *algēsis* sense of pain < *algos* pain] — **hy′per·al·ge′sic** (-zik, -sik) *adj.*

hy·per·bar·ic (hī′pər·bar′ik) *adj. Med.* **1** Of, pertaining to, or affected by hyperbarism. **2** Designating a spinal anesthetic solution having a density greater than that of the spinal fluid.

hy·per·bar·ism (hī·per′bə·riz′əm) *n. Med.* A disturbed condition caused by an atmospheric pressure which is greater than the pressure within the tissues, fluids, or cavities of the body: occurs in a sudden descent from a high to a low altitude. Opposed to *hypobarism.* [<HYPER– + Gk. *baros* weight]

hy·per·bo·la (hī·pûr′bə·lə) *n. Math.* A curve traced by a point moving so that the difference between its distances from two fixed points, or foci, remains constant; the curves traced by the edges where a plane intersects the nappes of a right circular cone. [<NL <Gk. *hyperbolē* a throwing beyond, excess. See HYPERBOLE.]

hy·per·bo·le (hī·pûr′bə·lē) *n.* Poetic or rhetorical overstatement; exaggeration. [<L <Gk. *hyperbolē* a throwing beyond, excess < *hyper–* over + *ballein* throw]

hy·per·bol·ic (hī′pər·bol′ik) *adj.* **1** Relating to or containing hyperbole; exaggerating. **2** Of, pertaining to, or having the shape of a hyperbola. Also **hy′per·bol′i·cal.** — **hy′per·bol′i·cal·ly** *adv.*

hyperbolic paraboloid *Math.* A quadric surface generated in such a way that, parallel to one plane, its sections are hyperbolas, and, parallel to the other planes, all sections are parabolas.

hyperbolic sine curve *Math.* A sine curve with hyperbolic convolutions.

hyperbolic spiral *Math.* A polar curve traced by a point moving so that its distance from the pole varies inversely as its polar angle: it is asymptotic to a line parallel to the polar axis.

hy·per·bo·lize (hī·pûr′bə·līz) *v.t. & v.i.* **·lized, ·liz·ing** To express in or use hyperbole; exaggerate. Also *Brit.* **hy·per′bo·lise.** — **hy·per′bo·lism** (-liz′əm) *n.*

hy·per·bo·loid (hī·pûr′bə·loid) *n. Math.* A quadratic surface generated by a hyperbola revolving about a fixed line: also called a **hyperboloid of one sheet.** A **hyperboloid of two sheets** is a quadratic surface generated by an ellipse moving so as to remain parallel to a common transverse axis, and varying so that the ends of its axes coincide with given hyperbolas having the same transverse axis.

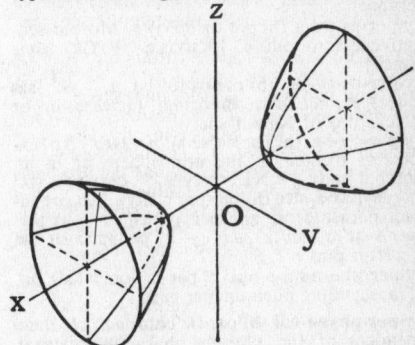

HYPERBOLOID OF TWO SHEETS
O. Origin. *x.* Transverse axis. *y, z.* Coordinate axes.

hy·per·bo·re·an (hī′pər·bôr′ē·ən, -bō′rē-) *adj.* Of the far north; frigid.

hy·per·cat·a·lec·tic (hī′pər·kat′ə·lek′tik) *adj.* Having one or two syllables beyond the final regular measure: said of a line of poetry; hypermetric. [<L *hypercatalecticus* <Gk. *hyperkatalēktikos* < *hyper–* beyond + *katalēktikos* CATALECTIC] — **hy′per·cat′a·lex′is** (-lek′-

sis) *n.*

hy·per·crit·ic (hī'pər·krit'ik) *n.* A very severe critic.

hy·per·crit·i·cal (hī'pər·krit'i·kəl) *adj.* **1** Given to strained or captious criticism. **2** Excessively exact or precise. See synonyms under CAPTIOUS. — **hy'per·crit'i·cal·ly** *adv.* — **hy'per·crit'i·cism** (-siz'əm) *n.*

hy·per·cube (hī'pər·kyōōb) *n.* A tesseract.

hy·per·du·li·a (hī'pər·dōō'lē·ə, -dyōō'-) *n. Eccl.* Worship given to the Virgin Mary as the most sacred of mortal creatures: superior to *dulia.* Compare LATRIA. [< Med. L < *hyper-* beyond + *dulia* service]

hy·per·e·mi·a (hī'pər·ē'mē·ə) *n. Pathol.* Abnormal accumulation of blood in any part of the body: also spelled *hyperaemia.* — **hy'·per·e'mic** *adj.*

hy·per·es·the·si·a (hī'pər·es·thē'zhē·ə, -zhə) *n.* Exaggerated sensitiveness to touch, heat, pain, etc.: also spelled *hyperaesthesia.*

hy·per·es·thet·ic (hī'pər·es·thet'ik) *adj.* **1** Morbidly sensitive. **2** Immoderately esthetic. Also spelled *hyperaesthetic.*

hy·per·ex·ten·sion (hī'pər·ik·sten'shən) *n. Physiol.* The maximum extension of an arm or leg beyond the plane of the body.

hy·per·fine (hī'pər·fīn') *adj. Physics* Of, pertaining to, or characterized by very closely spaced lines, as in the spectra of certain elements and isotopes.

hy·per·fo·cal (hī'pər·fō'kəl) *adj. Phot.* Designating that distance in front of a given camera lens under specified conditions, at and beyond which all objects are in substantially clear focus.

hy·per·gol·ic (hī'pər·gol'ik) *adj.* Pertaining to or describing a type of rocket propellant that ignites spontaneously on contact with an oxidizer. [HYPER- + G *gola* a code word used in German rocketry]

hy·per·hi·dro·sis (hī'pər·hī·drō'sis) *n.* Abnormal sweating. Also **hy'per·i·dro'sis** (-ī·drō'sis).

hy·per·ki·ne·si·a (hī'pər·ki·nē'zhē·ə, -zhə) *n. Pathol.* Exaggerated muscular action; spasm. Also **hy'per·ki·ne'sis** (-nē'sis). — **hy'per·ki·net'·ic** (-net'ik) *adj.*

hy·per·me·ter (hī·pûr'mə·tər) *n.* A hypercatalectic line; also, a period containing a redundant syllable. — **hy·per·met·ric** (hī'pər·met'·rik) or **·ri·cal** *adj.*

hy·per·me·tro·pi·a (hī'pər·mə·trō'pē·ə) *n. Pathol.* An abnormal condition of the eye in which objects at a distance are seen more plainly than those near at hand; far-sightedness. Also **hy'per·met'ro·py** (-met'rə·pē), **hy'·per·o'pi·a** (-ō'pē·ə). [< NL < Gk. *hypermetros* excessive + *ōps* eye] — **hy'per·me·trop'ic** (-mə·trop'ik, -trō'pik) *adj.*

hy·perm·ne·si·a (hī'pərm·nē'zhē·ə, -zhə) *n.* A condition marked by an abnormal retentivity and acuteness of memory; total recall: distinguished from *amnesia.* Also **hy'perm·ne'sis** (-nē'sis). [< HYPER- + Gk. *mnesis* remembrance]

hy·per·os·mi·a (hī'pər·oz'mē·ə) *n.* Morbid sensitiveness to odors. [< HYPER- + Gk. *osmē* smell]

hy·per·os·to·sis (hī'pər·os·tō'sis) *n. pl.* **·ses** (-sēz) *Pathol.* An abnormal increase in or thickening of bony tissue.

hy·per·ox·i·a (hī'pər·ok'sē·ə) *n. Med.* An excess of oxygen in the atmosphere or in an animal body. [< NL < HYPER- + OX(Y)- + -IA]

hy·per·par·a·site (hī'pər·par'ə·sīt) *n.* An organism parasitic on another parasite. — **hy'per·par·a·sit'ic** (-sit'ik) *adj.* — **hy'per·par'a·sit·ism** (-ə·sit·iz'əm) *n.*

hy·per·phe·nom·e·nal (hī'pər·fə·nom'ə·nəl) *adj.* Transcending phenomena; real.

hy·per·phys·i·cal (hī'pər·fiz'i·kəl) *adj.* **1** Independent of the physical. **2** Supernatural. — **hy'per·phys'i·cal·ly** *adv.*

hy·per·pi·e·si·a (hī'pər·pī·ē'zhē·ə, -zhə) *n. Pathol.* Abnormally high blood pressure. Also **hy'per·pi·e'sis** (-sis). [< NL < Gk. *hyper-* beyond + *piesis* pressure < *piezein* press]

hy·per·pi·tu·i·ta·rism (hī'pər·pi·tōō'i·tə·riz'əm, -tyōō'-) *n. Pathol.* Abnormal functioning of the pituitary gland; also, the disorders resulting from it.

hy·per·pla·si·a (hī'pər·plā'zhē·ə, -zhə) *n. Pathol.* Excessive production of cells in a part; enlargement from quantitative increase produced by cell division: distinguished from *hypertrophy.* — **hy·per·plas'ic** (-plas'ik), **hy'·**

per·plas'tic (-plas'tik) *adj.*

hy·perp·ne·a (hī'pərp·nē'ə) *n. Pathol.* Violent or labored breathing caused by a deficiency of oxygen in the blood. Also **hy'perp·noe'a.** [< NL < Gk. *hyper-* above + *pnoē* breathing < *pneein* breathe]

hy·per·pro·sex·i·a (hī'pər·prō·sek'sē·ə) *n. Psychiatry* An inordinate and exaggerated attention to certain things, as the symptoms of an illness or mental disorder. [< HYPER- + Gk. *prosexis* attention]

hy·per·py·rex·i·a (hī'pər·pī·rek'sē·ə) *n. Pathol.* Very high fever. — **hy'per·py·ret'ic** (-ret'ik), **hy'per·py·rex'i·al** *adj.*

hy·per·sen·si·tive (hī'pər·sen'sə·tiv) *adj.* **1** Excessively sensitive. **2** Allergic. — **hy'per·sen'si·tive·ness, hy'per·sen'si·tiv'i·ty** (-sen'sə·tiv'ə·tē) *n.*

hy·per·sen·si·tize (hī'pər·sen'sə·tīz) *v.t.* **·tized, ·tiz·ing** *Phot.* To increase the sensitiveness or speed of, as a plate or film, usually by immersion in a suitable solution or by exposure to mercury vapor. — **hy'per'sen'si·tiz'ing** *n.*

hy·per·son·ic (hī'pər·son'ik) *adj.* Of, pertaining to, or characterized by supersonic speeds of mach 5 or greater.

hy·per·son·ics (hī'pər·son'iks) *n. pl. (construed as singular)* That branch of dynamics which studies the design, characteristics, and performance of objects moving at supersonic speeds of mach 5 or greater: applied especially to jet planes, guided missiles, rockets, and the like.

hy·per·space (hī'pər·spās') *n.* Space regarded as having more than three dimensions.

hy·per·sthe·ni·a (hī'pər·sthē'nē·ə) *n.* Excessive physical vigor and tone. [< HYPER- + Gk. *sthenos* strength] — **hy'per·sthen'ic** (-sthen'ik) *adj.*

hy·per·ten·sion (hī'pər·ten'shən) *n. Pathol.* **1** Excessively high blood pressure. **2** A disease of the arteries caused by or associated with such pressure.

hy·per·ther·mi·a (hī'pər·thûr'mē·ə) *n. Med.* **1** An abnormally high temperature. **2** Therapeutic treatment by means of artifically induced fever. Also **hy'per·ther'my.** [< HYPER- + Gk. *thermē* heat] — **hy'per·ther'mal** *adj.*

hy·per·thy·mic (hī'pər·thī'mik) *adj.* **1** *Psychiatry* Denoting a state of morbidly exaggerated activity of mind or body. **2** Designating a constitutional type associated with persistent overdevelopment of the thymus gland. [< HYPER- + Gk. *thymos* spirit, passion]

hy·per·thy·roid (hī'pər·thī'roid) *adj.* Marked by hyperthyroidism. — *n.* One affected by hyperthyroidism.

hy·per·thy·roid·ism (hī'pər·thī'roid·iz'əm) *n. Pathol.* **1** Abnormal activity of the thyroid gland. **2** Any disorder caused by such activity: opposed to *hypothyroidism.*

hy·per·ton·ic (hī'pər·ton'ik) *adj. Pathol.* Pertaining to or designating a higher osmotic pressure than the normal, as of blood: opposed to *isotonic.* — **hy'per·to·nic'i·ty** (-tō·nis'ə·tē) *n.*

hy·per·tro·phy (hī·pûr'trə·fē) *n. Pathol.* **1** The excessive development of an organ or part. **2** The morbid enlargement of a part from increased nutrition without increase of waste: opposed to *atrophy.* — *v.i.* **·phied, ·phy·ing** To grow excessively; develop abnormally. — **hy·per·troph·ic** (hī'pər·trof'ik, -trō'fik) or **·i·cal** *adj.*

hy·per·ven·ti·la·tion (hī'pər·ven'tə·lā'shən) *n.* **1** An excess supply of air to the lungs, as when airplane pilots resort to deep and rapid breathing to ensure adequate oxygen: often resulting in lowering carbon dioxide content of the blood. **2** Physical therapy by exposure of the body to drafts of air.

hy·per·vi·ta·mi·no·sis (hī'pər·vī'tə·mi·nō'sis) *n. Pathol.* A condition due to an excess of vitamins, either in the diet or in prepared form: opposed to *avitaminosis.*

hyp·es·the·si·a (hip'əs·thē'zhē·ə, -zhə) *n. Pathol.* Diminished sensitiveness; partial loss of capacity for sensation: also spelled *hypaesthesia.* — **hyp'es·the'sic** (-sik) or **·thet'ic** (-thet'ik) *adj.*

hy·pe·thral (hi·pē'thrəl, hī-) *adj.* Roofless, as a building open to the sky: said of a building whose roof has been destroyed or never completed, or of a sanctuary, etc., never intended to be roofed. Also spelled *hypaethral.* [< L *hypaethrus* < Gk. *hypaithros* < *hypo-* under + *aithēr* ether, clear sky]

hy·pheme (hī'fēm) *n.* A hyphened compound word. Compare SOLIDEME. [< HYPH(EN) + (PHON)EME]

hy·phe·mi·a (hī·fē'mē·ə) *n. Pathol.* **1** Deficiency of blood, or a lack of supply of the red corpuscles in the blood. **2** Extravasation of the blood into a surrounding tissue, especially in the eye. Also **hy·phae'mi·a.** [< HYPO- + -HEMIA]

hy·phen (hī'fən) *n.* A mark (- or - or ⁼) indicating connection: used to connect the elements of certain compound words, to show division of a word at the end of a line, and to indicate a unit modifier: a *hit-and-run* driver. — *v.t.* To hyphenate. [< LL < Gk. *hyph' hen* under one, together < *hypo-* under + *hen* one]

hy·phen·ate (hī'fən·āt) *v.t.* **·at·ed, ·at·ing** **1** To connect by a hyphen. **2** To print or write with a hyphen. Also **hy'phen·ize.** — **hy'phen·a'tion, hy'phen·i·za'tion** (-ə·zā'shən, -ī·zā'-) *n.*

hy·phen·at·ed (hī'fən·ā'tid) *adj.* Implying or relating to a naturalized person of foreign birth, especially to one whose sympathies are with the land of his birth.

hyp·na·gog·ic (hip'nə·goj'ik) *adj.* **1** Inducing or promoting sleep, as by a drug or by hypnosis. **2** Of or pertaining to the mental condition occurring just before sleep; dreamlike; visionary. [< HYPN(O)- + -AGOG]

hyp·na·pa·gog·ic (hip'nə·pə·goj'ik) *adj.* Preventing or inhibiting sleep. [< HYPN(O)- + AP(O)- + -AGOG]

hyp·nic (hip'nik) *adj.* Calculated to induce sleep; pertaining to sleep. — *n.* A soporific.

hyp·no·a·nal·y·sis (hip'nō·ə·nal'ə·sis) *n.* A psychoanalytic technique which utilizes data obtained by or under the conditions resulting from hypnosis. — **hyp'no·an'a·lyt'ic** (-an'ə·lit'ik) *adj.*

hyp·no·gen·e·sis (hip'nō·jen'ə·sis) *n.* The production of hypnotic sleep. — **hyp'no·ge·net'ic** (-jə·net'ik), **hyp'no·ge·net'i·cal, hyp·nog·e·nous** (hip·noj'ə·nəs) *adj.*

hyp·nol·o·gy (hip·nol'ə·jē) *n.* The science of the phenomena of sleep. — **hyp·no·log·ic** (hip'nə·loj'ik) or **·i·cal** *adj.* — **hyp·nol'o·gist** *n.*

hyp·no·pho·bi·a (hip'nə·fō'bē·ə) *n.* A morbid fear of sleep or of falling asleep. — **hyp'no·pho'bic** *adj.*

hyp·no·pom·pic (hip'nə·pom'pik) *adj. Psychol.* Persisting after or emerging from sleep: describing the semiconscious state between sleep and waking often marked by visions and fantasies. [< HYPNO- + Gk. *pompaios* accompanying]

hyp·no·sis (hip·nō'sis) *n. pl.* **·ses** (-sēz) *Psychol.* **1** A trancelike condition that may be psychically induced by another person, characterized by loss of consciousness and a greater or lesser degree of responsiveness to the suggestions of the hypnotist. **2** The causing of such a condition.

hyp·no·ther·a·py (hip'nə·ther'ə·pē) *n. Med.* The use of hypnotism in treating disease.

hyp·not·ic (hip·not'ik) *adj.* **1** Pertaining to hypnotism or tending to produce hypnosis. **2** Tending to produce sleep. — *n.* **1** An agent efficacious in producing sleep. **2** A hypnotized person. [< Gk. *hypnōtikos* < *hypnos* sleep] — **hyp·not'i·cal·ly** *adv.*

hyp·no·tism (hip'nə·tiz'əm) *n.* The theory and practice of hypnosis. — **hyp'no·tist, hyp'no·tiz'er** *n.*

hyp·no·tize (hip'nə·tīz) *v.t.* **·tized, ·tiz·ing** **1** To produce hypnosis in. **2** *Colloq.* To fascinate; entrance. Also *Brit.* **hyp'no·tise.** — **hyp'·no·tiz'a·ble** *adj.* — **hyp'no·ti·za'tion** (-tə·zā'·shən, -tī·zā'-) *n.*

hy·po·a·cid·i·ty (hī'pō·ə·sid'ə·tē) *n. Med.* Deficient or subnormal acidity, as of the gastric juices.

hy·po·bar·ic (hī'pə·bar'ik) *adj. Med.* **1** Pertaining to or affected by hypobarism. **2** Denoting a spinal anesthetic solution whose density is less than that of the spinal fluid. Opposed to *hyperbaric.*

hy·po·bar·ism (hī'pə·bär'iz·əm) *n. Med.* A condition brought about when the pressure of the gases within the body is in excess of the atmospheric pressure: opposed to *hyperbarism.* Compare *aeroembolism.* [< HYPO- + Gk. *baros* weight]

hy·po·cap·ni·a (hī'pə·kap'nē·ə) *n. Med.* A deficiency of carbon dioxide in the blood, often due to hyperventilation. [< HYPO- + Gk. *kapnos* smoke] — **hy'po·cap'nic** *adj.*

hy·po·cen·ter (hī'pə·sen'tər) *n.* That point on the earth's surface directly beneath or above the burst of an atomic or thermonuclear bomb; ground zero.

hy·po·chon·dri·a (hī'pə·kon'drē·ə, hip'ə-) *n. Psychiatry* **1** A morbid melancholy and depression of mind or spirits. **2** A morbidly extreme anxiety about one's health, usually associated with one or another part of the body, and accompanied by imagined symptoms of illness. Also **hy·po·chon·dri·a·sis** (hī'pō·kən·drī'ə·sis). [<L, abdomen (once taken to be the seat of this condition) <Gk. *hypochondria*, neut. pl. from *hypochondrios* under the cartilage < *hypo-* under + *chondros* cartilage]

hy·po·chon·dri·ac (hī'pə·kon'drē·ak, hip'ə-) *adj.* **1** Pertaining to or affected by hypochondria. **2** Of, pertaining to, or situated in the hypochondrium. Also **hy·po·chon·dri·a·cal** (hī'pō·kən·drī'ə·kəl). — *n.* A person subject to or afflicted by hypochondria. — **hy'po·chon·dri'a·cal·ly** *adv.*

hy·po·chon·dri·um (hī'pə·kon'drē·əm, hip'ə-) *n. pl.* **·dri·a** (-drē·ə) *Anat.* That region of the abdomen situated on either side under the costal cartilages and short ribs. [<NL <Gk. *hypochondrion.* See HYPOCHONDRIA.]

hy·po·co·ris·tic (hī'pō·kə·ris'tik) *adj.* Of or pertaining to an endearing diminutive or pet name. [<Gk. *hypokoristikos* < *hypo-* under + *korizesthai* caress < *koros* child]

hy·poc·ri·sy (hi·pok'rə·sē) *n. pl.* **·sies** The feigning to be what one is not; extreme insincerity; dissimulation. [<OF *ypocrisie* <L *hypocrisis* <Gk. *hypokrisis* acting a part, feigning < *hypo-* under + *krinein* decide]
— **Synonyms**: affectation, cant, dissimulation, formalism, pharisaism, pietism, pretense, sanctimoniousness, sanctimony, sham. *Pretense* (L. *praetendo*) primarily signifies the holding something forward as having certain rights or claims, whether truly or falsely; in the good sense, it is now rarely used except with a negative; as, There can be no *pretense* that this is due; a false *pretense* implies the possibility of a true *pretense*; but, alone and unlimited, *pretense* commonly signifies the offering of something for what it is not. *Hypocrisy* is the false *pretense* of moral excellence, either as a cover for actual wrong, or for the sake of the credit and advantage attaching to virtue. *Cant* (L. *cantus*, a song), primarily the singsong iteration of the language of any party, school, or sect, denotes the mechanical and pretentious use of religious phraseology, without corresponding feeling or character; *sanctimoniousness* is the assumption of a saintly manner without a saintly character. *Affectation* is in matters of intellect, taste, etc., much what *hypocrisy* is in morals and religion: *affectation* might be termed petty *hypocrisy*. Compare DECEPTION. — **Antonyms**: candor, frankness, genuineness, honesty, ingenuousness, openness, sincerity, transparency, truth, truthfulness.

hyp·o·crite (hip'ə·krit) *n.* One who acts a false part or makes false professions. [<Gk. *hypokritēs* an actor. See HYPOCRISY.] — **hyp'o·crit'i·cal** *adj.* — **hyp'o·crit'i·cal·ly** *adv.*
— **Synonyms**: cheat, deceiver, dissembler, impostor, pretender. A *hypocrite* is one who acts a false part, or assumes a character other than the real. The *deceiver* seeks to give false impressions of any matter where he has an end to gain; the *dissembler* or *hypocrite* seeks to give false impressions in regard to himself. The *dissembler* is content if he can keep some base conduct or evil purpose from being discovered; the *hypocrite* seeks not merely to cover his vices, but to gain credit for virtue. The *cheat* and *impostor* endeavor to make something out of those whom they may deceive. The *cheat* is the inferior and more mercenary, as the thimblerig gambler; the *impostor* may aspire to a fortune or a throne. Compare HYPOCRISY.

hy·po·der·ma (hī'pə·dûr'mə) *n.* **1** *Bot.* The distinct sheath of strengthening tissue beneath the epidermis of stems in plants. **2** The hypoderm. **3** Any of a genus (*Hypoderma*) of dipterous insects, the botflies. [<NL <Gk. *hypo-* under + *derma* skin]
hy·po·der·mal (hī'pə·dûr'məl) *adj.* **1** Pertain-

ing to the hypoderma; situated below the epidermis. **2** Hypodermic.

hy·po·der·mic (hī'pə·dûr'mik) *adj.* **1** Of or pertaining to the area under the skin. **2** Of or pertaining to the hypoderma. — *n.* A hypodermic injection or syringe.

hypodermic injection An injection under the skin.

hypodermic medication Medical treatment by subcutaneous means, as by hypodermic injection.

hypodermic needle The needle of a hypodermic syringe.

hypodermic syringe A syringe having a sharp, hollow needle for injection of substances beneath the skin.

hy·po·der·mis (hī'pə·dûr'məs) *n.* The hypoderm. [<NL]

hy·po·gas·tri·um (hī'pə·gas'trē·əm) *n. pl.* **·tri·a** (-trē·ə) *Anat.* The region at the lower part of the abdomen on the middle line. [<NL <Gk. *hypogastrion* < *hypo-* below + *gastēr* belly] — **hy'po·gas'tric** *adj.*

hy·po·ge·al (hī'pə·jē'əl, hip'ə-) *adj.* **1** *Geol.* Situated beneath the surface of the earth, or underlying the superficial outcropping strata. **2** Hypogeous. [<HYPO- + Gk. *gē* earth]

hyp·o·gene (hip'ə·jēn) *adj. Geol.* **1** Formed beneath the earth's surface, as granite. **2** Pertaining to or caused by subterranean agencies; plutonic: contrasted with *epigene* and *volcanic.*

hy·pog·e·nous (hī·poj'ə·nəs, hi-) *adj. Bot.* Growing beneath, as fungi on the under surface of a leaf. Compare EPIGENOUS. [<HYPO- + -GENOUS]

hyp·o·ge·ous (hip'ə·jē'əs, hī'pə-) *adj.* **1** Underground. **2** *Bot.* Growing or fruiting underground, as truffles and other fungi. [<L *hypogeus* <Gk. *hypogeios* < *hypo-* under + *gē* earth]

hyp·o·ge·um (hip'ə·jē'əm, hī'pə-) *n. pl.* **·ge·a** (-jē'ə) **1** *Archit.* The part of a building below the ground. **2** Any underground structure; an artificial cave. [<L <Gk. *hypogeios* subterranean]

hy·po·glos·sal (hī'pə·glos'əl, hip'ə-) *adj. Biol.* Of or pertaining to a nerve situated under the tongue in birds, reptiles, and mammals; underneath the tongue. — *n.* A hypoglossal nerve. [<HYPO- + Gk. *glōssa* tongue]

hy·pog·y·nous (hī·poj'ə·nəs, hi-) *adj. Bot.* Situated on or growing from the receptacle of the flower beneath the ovary or pistil. [<HYPO- + GYNOUS] — **hy·pog'y·ny** *n.*

hy·po·ma·ni·a (hī'pə·mā'nē·ə, -mān'yə, hip'ə-) *n.* A mild form of mania; a condition of moderate elation and overactivity.

hy·poph·y·ge (hī·pof'ə·jē, hi-) *n. Archit.* A horizontal rounded groove under a structural member, as in the case of archaic Doric capitals. [<Gk. *hypophygē* refuge, recess < *hypo-* under + *pheugein* flee]

hy·poph·y·sis (hī·pof'ə·sis, hi-) *n. pl.* **·ses** (-sēz) *Anat.* A process or outgrowth. [<NL <Gk., an undergrowth < *hypo-* under + *physis* nature < *phyein* grow]

hypophysis cer·e·bri (ser'ə·brī) *Anat.* The pituitary gland. [<NL, outgrowth of the brain]

hy·po·pi·tu·i·ta·rism (hī'pō·pi·tōo'i·tə·riz'əm, -tyōo'-) *n. Pathol.* **1** Diminished activity of the pituitary gland. **2** Any condition produced by this, marked by excessive fat and by adolescent traits.

hy·po·pla·si·a (hī'pə·plā'zhē·ə, -zhə, hip'ə-) *n. Pathol.* The condition of arrested development. — **hy'po·plas'tic** (-plas'tik) *adj.*

hy·po·pne·a (hī'pə·nē'ə, hip'ə-) *n. Med.* Abnormal rapidity and shallowness of breathing, as from hypoventilation. Also **hy·po·pnoe'a.** [<NL <Gk. *hypo-* under + *pnoē* breathing < *pneein* breathe]

hy·po·po·di·um (hī'pə·pō'dē·əm, hip'ə-) *n. pl.* **·di·a** (-dē·ə) *Bot.* The basal portion of a leaf, including the stalk; a supporting structure in plants. [<NL <Gk. *hypo-* under + *podion*, dim. of *pous, podos* a foot]

hy·po·scope (hī'pə·skōp) *n.* A form of altiscope for military use, as a sighting attachment to a rifle, etc.

hy·pos·ta·sis (hī·pos'tə·sis, hi-) *n.* **1** That which forms, either in fact or hypothesis, a groundwork or support for anything; a basis. **2** *Philos.* A distinct individual subsistence;

also, a logical substance. **3** *Theol.* Any one of the persons of the Trinity; also, the separate personal subsistence of each of the three persons of the Trinity in one divine substance. **4** *Med.* A settling down of a fluid of the body. **5** *Pathol.* A morbid deposition of sedimentary matter within the body. [<Gk. *hypostasis* substance, subsistence < *hypo-* under + *histhastai* stand, middle voice of *histanai* cause to stand]

hy·po·stat·ic (hī'pə·stat'ik, hip'ə-) *adj.* **1** Of, pertaining to, or constituting a distinct personality or substance; distinctly personal. **2** Of, relating to, or proceeding from hypostasis; elemental. **3** *Med.* Resulting from downward pressure or deposition of sediment in the body: *hypostatic congestion.* **4** *Genetics* Denoting a factor hidden or masked by another which is not an allelomorph. Also **hy'po·stat'i·cal.** [<Gk. *hypostatikos*] — **hy'po·stat'i·cal·ly** *adv.*

hypostatic union *Theol.* The union of two natures in the one person or hypostasis of Christ.

hy·pos·ta·tize (hī·pos'tə·tīz, hi-) *v.t.* **·tized, ·tiz·ing** To treat as real; ascribe substantial or distinct existence to. — **hy·pos'ta·ti·za'tion** (-tə·ti·zā'shən, -tə·tī·zā'-) *n.*

hy·po·sthe·ni·a (hī'pə·sthē'nē·ə) *n. Pathol.* Deficient vitality. Compare HYPERSTHENIA. [< HYPO- + Gk. *sthenos* strength] — **hy'po·sthen'ic** (-sthen'ik) *adj.*

hy·pos·to·ma (hī·pos'tə·mə, hi-) *n. pl.* **hy·po·sto·ma·ta** (hī'pə·stō'mə·tə) *Zool.* A part or organ lying below the mouth, as in certain crustaceans and coelenterates. Also **hyp·o·stome** (hip'ə·stōm). [<NL <Gk. *hypo-* under + *stoma* mouth] — **hy'po·sto'mi·al** *adj.*

hyp·o·style (hip'ə·stīl, hī'pə-) *n. Archit.* **1** Any structure having a ceiling resting upon columns; a pillared hall. **2** One of the halls with huge pillars characteristic of Egyptian architecture. — *adj.* Of, similar to, or pertaining to such a structure. [<HYPO- + Gk. *stylos* pillar]

hy·po·sul·fite (hī'pə·sul'fīt) *n. Chem.* **1** Sodium thiosulfate. **2** A salt of hyposulfurous acid.

hy·po·sul·fur·ic (hī'pō·sul·fyoōr'ik, hī'pə·sul'fər·ik) *adj. Chem.* Of or pertaining to an unstable, colorless acid, $H_2S_2O_6$, having no odor and forming soluble salts with certain bases: also *dithionic.*

HYPOSTYLE

hy·po·tax·is (hī'pə·tak'sis, hip'ə-) *n. Gram.* Subordinate or dependent arrangement of clauses, phrases, etc.: opposed to *parataxis.* — **hy'po·tac'tic** (-tak'tik) or **·ti·cal** *adj.* — **hy'po·tac'ti·cal·ly** *adv.*

hy·pot·e·nuse (hī·pot'ə·nōos, -nyōos, hi-) *n. Geom.* The side of a right-angled triangle opposite the right angle. Also **hy·poth'e·nuse** (-poth'-). [<L *hypotenusa* <Gk. *hypoteinousa* (*grammē*) a subtending (line) < *hypo-* under + *teinein* stretch]

hy·po·thal·a·mus (hī'pə·thal'ə·məs, hip'ə-) *n. Anat.* The region below the thalamus, controlling visceral activities. — **hy·po·tha·lam·ic** (hī'pə·thə·lam'ik) *adj.*

hy·poth·ec (hī·poth'ik, hi-) *n.* A pledge or mortgage of either lands or goods as security for debt where the property pledged remains in possession of the debtor. [<F *hypothèque* <LL *hypotheca* <Gk. *hypothēkē* pledge < *hypotithenai* deposit as a pledge < *hypo-* under + *tithenai* put] — **hy·poth'e·car'y** (-ə·ker'ē) *adj.*

hy·poth·e·cate (hī·poth'ə·kāt, hi-) *v.t.* **·cat·ed, ·cat·ing** To give (personal property) in pledge as security for debt. [<Med. L *hypothecatus*, pp. of *hypothecare* <LL *hypotheca* pledge] — **hy·poth'e·ca'tion** *n.* — **hy·poth'e·ca'tor** *n.*

hy·poth·e·nar (hī·poth'ə·nər, hi-) *n. Biol.* The ridge on the palm at the base of the little finger, or at a corresponding part in the forefoot of a quadruped. [<HYPO- + Gk. *thenar* palm]

hy·po·ther·mal (hī'pō·thûr'məl, hip'ō-) *adj.* Tepid; moderately warm.

hy·po·ther·mi·a (hī'pə·thûr'mē·ə, hip'ō-) *n. Med.* **1** An abnormally low temperature. **2** Therapeutic anesthesia produced by gradually reducing body temperature to as low as 75° F.; frozen sleep. Also **hy'po·ther'my.** [<HYPO- + Gk. *thermē* heat] — **hy'po·ther'. mal** *adj.*

hy·poth·e·sis (hī·poth'ə·sis, hi-) *n. pl.* **·ses** (-sēz) **1** A set of assumptions provisionally accepted as a basis of reasoning, experiment, or investigation. **2** An unsupported or ill-supported theory. [<NL <Gk., foundation, supposition < *hypotithenai* put under < *hypo-* under + *tithenai* put]
Synonyms: conjecture, guess, scheme, speculation, supposition, surmise, system, theory. A *hypothesis* is a statement of what is deemed possibly true, assumed and reasoned upon as if certainly true, with a view of reaching truth not yet surely known; especially, in the sciences, a *hypothesis* is a comprehensive tentative explanation of certain phenomena, which is meant to include all other facts of the same class, and which is assumed as true till there has been opportunity to bring all related facts into comparison; if the *hypothesis* explains all the facts, it is regarded as verified; till then it is regarded as a working *hypothesis*, that is, one that may answer for present practical purposes. A *hypothesis* may be termed a comprehensive *guess*. Compare GUESS, SYSTEM, THEORY. *Antonyms:* certainty, demonstration, discovery, evidence, fact, proof.

hy·poth·e·size (hī·poth'ə·sīz, hi-) *v.* **·sized, ·siz·ing** *v.t.* To make a hypothesis of. — *v.i.* To conceive or suggest hypotheses.
hy·po·thet·ic (hī'pə·thet'ik) *adj.* **1** Having the nature of or based on hypothesis; assumed conditionally or tentatively as a basis for argument or investigation; also, involving a formal hypothesis. **2** Given to using hypotheses. Also **hy'po·thet'i·cal.** See synonyms under IMAGINARY. [<L *hypotheticus* <Gk. *hypothetikos*] — **hy'po·thet'i·cal·ly** *adv.*
hy·po·thy·roid (hī'pō·thī'roid) *adj.* Manifesting hypothyroidism. — *n.* One affected by hypothyroidism.
hy·po·thy·roid·ism (hī'pō·thī'roid·iz'əm) *n. Pathol.* **1** Deficient functioning of the thyroid gland. **2** The resulting psychosomatic disorders: sometimes called *cretinism,* and opposed to *hyperthyroidism.*
hy·po·ton·ic (hī'po·ton'ik) *adj.* **1** Deficient in body tone. **2** Below the osmotic pressure

of an isotonic fluid. — **hy'po·to·nic'i·ty** (-tō·nis'ə·tē) *n.*
hy·po·tro·phy (hī'pə·trō'fē) *n. Med.* Abiotrophy.
hy·po·ven·ti·la·tion (hī'pō·ven'tə·lā'shən) *n.* Deficient or inadequate ventilation.
hy·po·xe·mi·a (hī'pok·sē'mē·ə) *n. Med.* Deficient oxygenation of the blood, as from hypoxia. [<HYP- + OX(Y)- + -EMIA]
hy·pox·i·a (hī·pok'sē·ə) *n. Med.* Low oxygen intake by the body, especially as resulting from decreased pressure at high altitudes. [<HYP- + OX(Y)- + -IA]

hyp·sog·ra·phy (hip·sog'rə·fē) *n.* **1** The science of observing or describing the topographical features of the earth's surface above sea level. **2** Topographic relief. [<HYPSO- + -GRAPHY] — **hyp·so·graph·ic** (hip'sə·graf'ik) or **·i·cal** *adj.*
hyp·som·e·ter (hip·som'ə·tər) *n.* An instrument for the measurement of heights above sea level by determining the atmospheric pressure through observation of the boiling point of water. [<HYPSO- + -METER]
hyp·som·e·try (hip·som'ə·trē) *n.* The art of measuring, by any method, the heights of points upon the earth's surface above sea level. — **hyp·so·met·ric** (hip'sə·met'rik) or **·ri·cal** *adj.* — **hyp'so·met'ri·cal·ly** *adv.* — **hyp·som'e·trist** *n.*
hy·son (hī'sən) *n.* A grade of green tea from China. The early crop is known as **young hyson.** [<Chinese *hsi-ch'un,* lit., blooming spring]

hys·ter·ec·to·my (his'tə·rek'tə·mē) *n. Surg.* Complete removal of the uterus by excision.
hys·ter·e·sis (his'tə·rē'sis) *n.* **1** *Physics* **a** The tendency of a magnetic substance to persist in any state of magnetization; that property of a medium by virtue of which work is done in changing the direction or intensity of magnetic force among its parts. **b** Some analogous phenomenon, as in dielectrics. When there has been a decrease in magnetization it is called *hysteretic loss,* and the hysteretic loss in ergs per cubic centimeter per cycle is called the *hysteretic constant.* **2** *Biochem.* The influence of the past history of a colloid upon its present condition and behavior. **3** Any state of a material or substance which can be adequately described only

in terms of its previous history. [<Gk. *hysterēsis* deficiency <*hystereein* lag] — **hys·ter·et·ic** (his'tə·ret'ik) *adj.*
hys·te·ri·a (his·tir'ē·ə, -ter'-) *n.* **1** *Psychiatry* A psychoneurotic condition characterized by violent emotional paroxysms, anxiety, and morbid effects, as of the sensory and motor functions. **2** Abnormal excitement; morbid emotionalism, as in wild outbursts of alternate laughing and crying. Also **hys·ter·ics** (his·ter'iks). [<NL <Gk. *hystera* the womb; because the condition was thought to affect women more than men] — **hys·ter·i·cal** (his·ter'i·kəl), **hys·ter'ic** *adj.* — **hys·ter'i·cal·ly** *adv.*
hys·ter·i·tis (his'tə·rī'tis) *n. Pathol.* Inflammation of the womb.
hystero- *combining form* **1** The womb; uterine: *hysteropexy.* **2** Hysteria; hysteric: *hysterogenic.* Also, before vowels, **hyster-.** [< Gk. *hystera* the womb]
hys·ter·o·gen·ic (his'tər·ə·jen'ik) *adj.* Producing or concerned in the production of hysteria.
hys·ter·oid (his'tər·oid) *adj.* Resembling hysteria.
hys·ter·on prot·er·on (his'tər·on prot'ər·on) **1** A figure of speech that reverses the natural order of words or clauses. Example: "Is your father well? is he yet alive?" **2** That form of fallacy in which one asserts a consequent and then infers the antecedent. [<LL <Gk., the latter (put) first]
hys·ter·o·pex·y (his'tər·ə·pek'sē) *n. Surg.* The operation of fixing the uterus to the abdominal wall to relieve prolapsus. [<HYSTERO- + Gk. *pēxis* fixing]
hys·ter·o·phyte (his'tər·ə·fīt') *n.* A plant included in an obsolete group (*Hysterophyta*) embracing fungi. — **hys·ter·o·phyt·ic** (-fit'ik) *adj.*
hys·ter·ot·o·my (his'tə·rot'ə·mē) *n. Surg.* **1** The operation of cutting into the womb. **2** Caesarean section. [<HYSTERO- + -TOMY]
hys·tri·co·mor·phic (his'tri·kō·môr'fik) *adj.* Of or pertaining to a division (*Hystricomorpha*) of rodents, including porcupines, cavies, etc. [<Gk. *hystrix* porcupine + -MORPHIC]
hy·ther (hī'thər) *n. Biol.* The combined effect of moisture and heat on an organism. [<Gk. *hy(dōr)* water + *ther(mē)* heat]
hy·zone (hī'zōn) *n.* Tritium. [<HY(DROGEN) + Gk. *ozein* smell; with ref. to its strong odor]

I

i, I (ī) *n. pl.* **i's, I's** or **Is,** eyes (īz) **1** The ninth letter of the English alphabet: from Phoenician *yod,* Greek *iota,* Roman *I.* **2** Any sound of the letter *i.* See ALPHABET. — *symbol* **1** The Roman numeral one: written I or i. See under NUMERAL. **2** *Chem.* Iodine (symbol I).
I¹ (ī) *pron.* The person speaking or writing, as he denotes himself in the nominative case. — *n.* **1** The self; the pronoun *I* employed as a noun. **2** *Philos.* The ego. [OE *ic*]
I² (ī) *adj.* Shaped like the letter I: an *I*-beam, *I*-rail.
I³ (ī) *interj. Obs.* See AYE or AY.
i-¹ Reduced var. of IN-¹.
i-² See Y-.
i·am·bic (ī·am'bik) *adj.* **1** Pertaining to or employing the iambus: *iambic* poetry. **2** Having characteristics of iambics. — *n.* **1** An iambus. **2** A verse, line, or stanza composed of iambic feet. **3** A satire or invective poem in iambic verse. [<L *iambicus* <Gk. *iambikos*]
i·am·bus (ī·am'bəs) *n. pl.* **·bi** (-bī) A foot of two syllables, a short or unaccented followed by a long or accented one. Also **i·amb** (ī'amb). [<L <Gk. *iambos* < *iambein* assail verbally; because orig. utilized by satiric poets]
i·at·ric (ī·at'rik) *adj.* Relating to physicians and the healing art; medical. Also **i·at'ri·cal.** [<Gk. *iatrikos* healing < *iatros* physician < *iasthai* heal]

i·at·ro·gen·ic (ī·at'rə·jen'ik) *adj. Med.* Generated or induced by the physician; said especially of disorders resulting from autosuggestion based on the physician's manner of handling or discussing a case.
-iatry *combining form* Medical or curative treatment: *psychiatry.* [<Gk. *iatreia* healing]
I·be·ri·a (ī·bir'ē·ə) **1** The part of SW Europe comprising Spain and Portugal: also **Iberian Peninsula. 2** An ancient country between the Caucasus and Armenia, corresponding to modern Georgia.
i·bex (ī'beks) *n. pl.* **i·bex·es** or **i·bi·ces** (ī'bə·sēz, ib'ə-) One of various wild goats of Europe and Asia, with long, recurved horns, especially the Alpine ibex (*Capra ibex*) and the Cretan ibex (*C. hircus*). [<L]
I·bi·cuí (ē·bē·kwē') A river in southern Brazil, flowing 300 miles west to the Uruguay.
i·bi·dem (i·bī'dem) *adv. Latin* In the same place. Abbr. *ibid.*

IBEX

I·bo (ē'bō) *n. pl.* **I·bo 1** A member of a group of Negro tribes of western Africa. **2** The Sudanic language of these tribes. [< the native name]
i·bo·ga (i·bō'gə) *n.* A cultivated shrub (genus *Tabernaemontana,* formerly *Tabernanthe iboga*) of the dogbane family, of central Africa. [< native name]
i·bo·gaine (i·bō'gān, -gə·ēn) *n. Chem.* A poisonous alkaloid, $C_{52}H_{66}O_2N_6$, from the root, bark, and leaves of the iboga: similar in action to cocaine.
Ib·ra·him Pa·sha (ib·rä·hēm' pä'shə), 1789–1848, Egyptian commander and viceroy.
Ib·sen (ib'sən), **Henrik,** 1828–1906, Norwegian dramatist and poet.
Ib·sen·ism (ib'sən·iz'əm) *n.* A theory or doctrine concerning Ibsen's plays, which were conceived by his imitators and critics, though not by Ibsen himself, as problem plays in which social conventions and attitudes were criticized.
-ic *suffix* Of adjectives: **1** Of or pertaining to: *volcanic.* **2** Like; resembling; characteristic of: *angelic.* **3** Consisting of; containing: *alcoholic.* **4** Produced or caused by: *Homeric.* **5** Related to; connected with: *domestic.* **6** *Chem.* Having a higher valence than that indicated by *-ous:* said of elements in compounds: *cupric* oxide, *sulfuric* acid. — Of nouns: **1** By the conversion of adjectives in any of the above senses: *Stoic, public.* **2** The

art or knowledge of: *rhetoric, music.* [<F -*ique* <L -*icus* <Gk. -*ikos*]

◆ -**ic,** -**icly** A few adjectives in -*ic* form adverbs in -*icly,* as, *publicly,* but the adverb is usually formed by adding -*ally: musically, rhythmically, volcanically.* See also note under -ICAL, -ICS.

I·çá (ē·sä') The Putumayo in its lower courses in Brazil.

-**ical** *suffix* **1** Like; pertaining to: *ethical:* used in adjectives derived from nouns in -*ic,* -*ics.* **2** With the same general meaning as -*ic: comical;* sometimes with extended or special meaning: *economical.* [<LL -*icalis* <-*icus* -IC + <-*alis* -AL]

◆ -**ic,** -**ical** In cases where both forms exist and do not differ greatly in meaning, there is no set rule governing usage. Euphony and past usage alone generally determine the choice of one form over the other.

I·car·i·a (i·kâr′ē·ə, ī-) A Greek Aegean island SW of Samos; 99 square miles: formerly *Nicaria:* also *Ikaria.*

ice (īs) *n.* **1** Congealed or frozen water; the solid condition assumed by water at or below 32° F. or 0° C. ◆ Collateral adjective: *glacial.* **2** A frozen dessert made without cream, as a sherbet, water ice, or frappé. **3** Something resembling ice in appearance: camphor *ice.* **4** Frosting or icing for cake. **5** Chilly reserve; a very formal or dignified attitude. **6** *Slang* A diamond; also, diamonds collectively. — **to break the ice** To break through reserve or formality. — **to cut no ice** *U.S. Slang* To have no importance. — **on ice** *U.S. Slang* **1** Set aside or reserved for future action. **2** In prison. **3** Sure; already determined. — *v.* **iced, ic·ing** *v.t.* **1** To cause to freeze; congeal into ice. **2** To cover with ice. **3** To chill with or as with ice. **4** To frost, as cake, with icing. — *v.i.* **5** To freeze; congeal into ice. — *adj.* Made of ice; to be used on ice: *ice skates.* [OE *īs*]

-**ice** *suffix of nouns* Condition, quality, or state of: *justice.* [<OF -*ice* <L -*itius, -itia, -itium*]

ice age The glacial epoch.

ice ax An ax used by mountaineers for cutting steps in the ice: usually equipped with a spiked butt.

ice·berg (īs′bûrg′) *n.* **1** A thick mass of ice found floating in the sea at high latitudes; a portion of a glacier discharged into the sea: distinguished from *field ice.* **2** A cold, unemotional person. [<Du. *ijsberg*]

ice·blink (īs′blingk′) *n.* A shining whiteness on the horizon produced by the reflection of distant masses of ice. [Cf. Du. *ijsblin,* Dan. *iisblink*]

ice·boat (īs′bōt′) *n.* **1** A framework with skatelike runners and sails for sailing over ice. **2** An icebreaker (def. 2).

ice·bone (īs′bōn′) *n.* The aitchbone. [Prob. <L *ischium* ischium + BONE. Cf. MDu. *yschbeen.*]

ICEBOAT

ice boulder A boulder transported and deposited through glacial action.

ice·bound (īs′bound′) *adj.* Surrounded, beset, or obstructed by ice; frozen in: an *icebound* ship, an *icebound* harbor.

ice·box (īs′boks′) *n.* A refrigerator. Also **ice′-chest′** (-chest′).

ice·break·er (īs′brā′kər) *n.* **1** A structure for deflecting ice from a bridge pier or the like: also **ice′-a′pron** (-ā′prən). **2** A specially constructed ship having a strong prow and powerful engines, used to break up ice in navigable channels of icebound waters and harbors.

ice cap An extensive covering of ice and snow permanently overlying a tract of land and moving in all directions from a center. See ICE SHEET.

ice-cream (īs′krēm′) *n.* A mixture of cream or butterfat, flavoring, sweetening, and often eggs, beaten to a uniform consistency and frozen. Also **ice cream.** [Orig., *iced cream*]

iced (īst) *adj.* **1** Coated or covered with ice

or sleet. **2** Made cold with ice. **3** Covered with icing, as cake.

ice·fall (īs′fôl′) *n.* The steepest part or the precipice of a glacier, resembling a frozen waterfall.

ice fishing Fishing through holes cut in the ice.

ice-foot (īs′fŏŏt′) *n.* A wall of ice formed by sea water and snow frozen along the shore in polar regions. [Trans. of Dan. *isfod*]

ice hook **1** A hook attached to a pole: used in handling large blocks of ice. See illustration under HOOK. **2** An S-shaped iron bar sharpened at one point: used with a hawser to secure a vessel to ice: also *ice anchor.*

ice·house (īs′hous′) *n.* A building for storing ice.

Ice·land (īs′lənd) The westernmost state of Europe, comprising an independent island republic in the North Atlantic; 39,709 square miles; capital, Reykjavik; a Danish possession until 1944. *Icelandic* **Ís·land** (ēs′länt).

Ice·land·er (īs′lan′dər) *n.* A native or naturalized inhabitant of Iceland.

Ice·land·ic (īs·lan′dik) *adj.* Of or pertaining to Iceland. — *n.* The North Germanic language of Iceland; strictly, this language since the 16th century. — **Old Icelandic** The language of Iceland before the 16th century, exemplified in the Eddas: the best literary representative of Old Norse, and sometimes used synonymously for it.

ice-man (īs′man′, -mən) *n. pl.* **-men** (-men′, -mən) **1** One who gathers and stores or deals in ice; also, one who carts and delivers ice to consumers. **2** One skilled in traveling upon ice or navigating among masses of ice.

ice needle *Meteorol.* A thin crystal of ice, so light that it floats suspended in the air.

ice pack **1** A large tract of floating ice cakes closely compacted and held together. **2** A container for cracked ice, used for medical applications.

ice pick An awl-like tool for breaking ice into small pieces.

ice plant A fig marigold of southern Africa, the Mediterranean region, and southern California (*Mesembryanthemum crystallinum*) having leaves covered with glistening frostlike protuberances.

ice point *Physics* The melting point of ice at standard atmospheric pressure, 0.0° C: one of the fixed points of the international temperature scale.

ice·quake (īs′kwāk′) *n.* The disturbance attending the rupture of masses of ice.

ice rain **1** A rain that congeals quickly in a deposit of glaze. **2** Falling pellets of clear ice; sleet.

ice sheet A large ice cap; a continental glacier.

ice-skate (īs′skāt′) *v.i.* **-skat·ed, -skat·ing** To skate on ice.

ice skate A skate with a metal runner for skating on ice.

ice-up (īs′up′) *n. Aeron.* The formation of ice on the leading edges or other exposed surfaces of airplanes when passing through moist air at low temperatures. Also **ic′ing.**

ichneumon fly A hymenopterous insect (family *Ichneumonidae*) that deposits its eggs upon in or other insects which its larvae will feed upon. For illustration see under INSECT (beneficial).

ich·nite (ik′nīt) *n. Paleontol.* A fossil footprint. Also **ich′no·lite** (-nə·līt). [<Gk. *ichnos* footprint]

ich·no·graph (ik′nə·graf, -gräf) *n.* A ground plan.

ich·nog·ra·phy (ik·nog′rə·fē) *n.* **1** The art of drawing by means of compass and rule, or of tracing plans, etc. **2** The plan drawn. [<LL *ichnografia* <Gk. < *ichnos* trace + *graphein* write] — **ich·no·graph·ic** (ik′nə·graf′ik) or **-i·cal** *adj.*

ich·thy·ic (ik′thē·ik) *adj.* Fishlike.

ichthyo- *combining form* Fish: *ichthyology.* Also, before vowels, **ichthy-.** [<Gk. *ichthys* fish]

ich·thy·o·cen·taur (ik′thē·ə·sen′tôr) *n.* A fabulous monster, combining the form of man and fish.

ich·thy·oid (ik′thē·oid) *adj.* Of or like a fish:

also **ich·thy·oi′dal.** — *n.* A fishlike vertebrate.

Ich·thy·ol (ik′thē·ōl, -ol) *n.* Proprietary name for a compound of sulfonated hydrocarbons obtained by the distillation of certain shales: used mainly in skin diseases.

ich·thy·o·lite (ik′thē·ə·līt′) *n. Paleontol.* A fossil fish.

ich·thy·ol·o·gy (ik′thē·ol′ə·jē) *n.* The branch of zoology that treats of fishes. [<ICHTHYO- + -LOGY] — **ich·thy·o·log·ic** (ik′thē·ə·loj′ik) *adj.* — **ich·thy·ol′o·gist** *n.*

ich·thy·oph·a·gist (ik′thē·of′ə·jist) *n.* One who feeds on fish.

ich·thy·oph·a·gous (ik′thē·of′ə·gəs) *adj.* Fish-eating.

ich·thy·oph·a·gy (ik′thē·of′ə·jē) *n.* The practice of feeding on fish.

ich·thy·or·nis (ik′thē·ôr′nis) *n. Paleontol.* One of a genus (*Ichthyornis*) of extinct toothed birds of the Cretaceous having fishlike vertebrae. [<ICHTHY- + Gk. *ornis* bird]

ich·thy·o·sau·rus (ik′thē·ə·sôr′əs) *n. pl.* **·sau·ri** (-sôr′ī) *Paleontol.* Any of an order (*Ichthyosauria*) of extinct marine reptiles of the Mesozoic era, having a porpoise-like form with four paddlelike limbs, a large, elongated head, long tail, and

ICHTHYOSAURUS
(The largest are thought to have been about 30 feet long)

broad vertebrae resembling those of fishes. Also **ich′thy·o·saur′.** [<ICHTHYO- + Gk. *sauros* lizard]

ich·thy·o·sis (ik′thē·ō′sis) *n. Pathol.* A congenital skin disease characterized by dry, scaly or horny formations. — **ich·thy·ot′ic** (-ot′ik) *adj.*

i·con (ī′kon) *n. pl.* **i·cons** or **i·con·es** (ī′kə·nēz) **1** An image or likeness. **2** In the Greek Church, a holy picture, mosaic, etc.: also spelled *ikon.* **3** Formerly, any book illustration. Also called *eikon.* See synonyms under IMAGE. [<Gk. *eikōn* image]

i·con·ic (ī·kon′ik) *adj.* **1** Relating to or of the nature of an icon. **2** Relating to portraiture. **3** Customary or conventional, in art: applied originally to the portraits or statues of athletes who had been victorious in the contests, and later to memorial busts, etc., made after conventional types. Also **i·con′i·cal.**

i·ci·cle (ī′si·kal) *n.* A pendent, tapering mass or rod of ice formed by the freezing of drops of dripping water. [OE *īsgicel* <*īs* ice + *gicel* piece of ice, icicle] — **i′ci·cled** *adj.*

i·ci·ly (ī′sə·lē) *adv.* In an icy manner; frigidly; frostily.

ic·ing (ī′sing) *n.* A glazing or coating of sugar, usually mixed with white of egg or cream, for a cake; frosting.

i·ci on parle fran·çais (ē·sē′ ôṅ pårl′ frän·se′) *French* French is spoken here.

i·con·o·clast (ī·kon′ə·klast) *n.* **1** An image breaker. **2** One of certain religious parties devoted to the destruction of images that were venerated or worshiped. **3** One who assails traditional beliefs. [<LL *iconoclastes* <Gk. *eikonoklastēs* <*eikōn* image + -*klastēs* breaker <*klaein* break, destroy] — **i·con′o·clas′tic** *adj.*

i·con·o·ge·net·ic (ī·kon′ə·jə·net′ik) *adj.* **1** Image-forming. **2** *Biol.* Capable of gathering visual information about external objects, as the eyes of animals.

i·co·nog·ra·phy (ī′kə·nog′rə·fē) *n. pl.* **·phies 1** The science of the description and study of paintings, sculptures, portraits, busts, statues, emblems, and symbolism: Christian *iconography.* **2** The art of illustration by figures; pictorial representation. **3** *Obs.* A picture or other representation, or a collection of representations. [<Med. L *iconografia* <Gk. *eikonografia* <*eikōn* icon + *graphein* write] — **i·con·o·graph·ic** (ī·kon′ə·graf′ik) or **-i·cal** *adj.*

i·co·nol·a·ter (ī′kə·nol′ə·tər) *n.* A worshiper of images; an idolater. [<ICONO-+ -LATRY] — **i′co·nol′a·try** *n.*

i·co·nol·o·gy (ī′kə·nol′ə·jē) *n. pl.* **·gies 1** The science of pictorial or emblematic representation. **2** A study or description of works of art, emblematic figures, and particularly the attributes of religious, mythological and historical personages. [<ICONO- + -LOGY] —i·con·o·log·i·cal (ī·kon'ə·loj'i·kəl) adj.

i·con·o·ma·ni·a (ī·kon'ə·mā'nē·ə, -mān'yə) n. A morbid interest in, or obsession with, images, fancied or real.

i·con·o·scope (ī·kon'ə·skōp) n. Telecom. A scanning device used in television, consisting of an evacuated glass bulb containing a photosensitive screen from whose surface the image is picked up by a narrow, intense, swiftly moving beam of electrons.

i·co·nos·ta·sis (ī'kə·nos'tə·sis) n. pl. ·ses (-sēz) In the Eastern Church, the screen separating the sacristy, bema, and chapel of prothesis from the rest of the church. Also i·con·o·stas (ī·kon'ə·stas). [<NL <NGk. eikonostasis < eikōn icon + stasis standing]

i·co·sa·he·dron (ī'kō·sə·hē'drən) n. pl. ·dra (-drə) Geom. A solid bounded by 20 plane faces. [<Gk. eikosaedron] —i'co·sa·he'dral (-drəl) adj.

ic·ter·ic (ik·ter'ik) adj. Pathol. Affected with jaundice. Also ic·ter'i·cal. [<Gk. ikterikos]

ic·ter·us (ik'tər·əs) n. 1 Pathol. Jaundice. 2 Bot. Yellowness in the leaves of plants, caused by protracted wet or cold weather. [<LL <Gk. ikteros jaundice]

ic·tus (ik'təs) n. pl. ·tus·es or ·tus 1 Pathol. a A stroke or blow. b A sudden attack or fit. 2 The sting of an insect. 3 A metrical stress or a syllable. [<L, pp. of icere strike]

i·cy (ī'sē) adj. i·ci·er, i·ci·est 1 Pertaining to ice; frigid; as cold as ice; full of or like ice. 2 Marked by coldness of manner, aspect, etc.; chilling. [OE īsig] —i'ci·ness, i'cy·ness n.

id (id) n. 1 Biol. In Weismann's theory of heredity, a unit of germ plasm representing the characteristics of an ancestral member of the species: supposedly composed of determinants, which are made up of biophores. 2 Psychoanal. The concealed, inaccessible part of the psyche, seated in the unconscious, independent of a sense of reality, logic, and morality, but actuated by fundamental impulses towards fulfilling instinctual needs; the reservoir of psychic energy or libido. [Def. 1, short for IDIOPLASM; def. 2, <NL <L id it, trans. of G es]

I'd (īd) 1 I would. 2 I had.

I·da·ho (ī'də·hō) A NW State of the United States; 83,557 square miles; capital, Boise; entered the Union July 3, 1890; nickname, Gem State: abbr. ID —I'da·ho'an adj. & n.

i·de·a (ī·dē'ə) n. 1 Any notion or thought: the idea of a horse or of happiness. 2 The result of thinking; a definitely formulated thought; an opinion: a clear idea of social justice. 3 A plan or project: to have an idea of going into business. 4 A concept; a mental representation of something perceived through the senses. 5 A vague thought or fancy; supposition: I had no idea you'd come. 6 Colloq. Meaning; aim: What's the idea? 7 In Platonic philosophy, the archetype or external pattern of which all existing things are imperfect representations. 8 Obs. The embodiment of a conception, belief, or view. [<L <Gk. < idein see]
Synonyms: apprehension, archetype, belief, conceit, concept, conception, design, fancy, fantasy, ideal, image, imagination, impression, judgment, model, notion, opinion, pattern, plan, purpose, sentiment, supposition, theory, thought. Idea is in Greek a form or an image. The sense implied by early Platonic philosophy has nearly disappeared and has been largely appropriated by ideal, but something of the original meaning still appears when in theological or philosophical language we speak of the ideas of God. The present popular use of idea makes it signify any product of mental apprehension or activity, considered as an object of knowledge or thought; this coincides with the primitive sense at but a single point—that an idea is mental as opposed to anything substantial or physical; thus, almost any mental product, as a belief, conception, design, opinion, etc., may now be called an idea. Compare FANCY, IDEAL, IMAGE, THOUGHT[1]. Antonyms: actuality, fact, reality, substance.

i·de·al (ī·dē'əl, ī·dēl') adj. 1 Pertaining to or existing in ideas; conceptional. 2 Of or pertaining to an ideal or perfection. 3 Conceived

as perfect, supremely excellent, or very desirable. 4 Existing only in imagination or notion; of such perfection as to be practically unattainable. 5 In philosophy, existing as an archetypal idea or pattern. —n. 1 That which is taken as a standard of excellence or beauty; an ultimate object of attainment; model; type. 2 That which exists only in imagination. [<L idealis]
Synonyms (adj.): fancied, fanciful, imaginary, unreal, visionary. Compare IMAGINARY, ROMANTIC. See also PERFECT. Antonyms: actual, material, palpable, physical, real, substantial, tangible, visible.
Synonyms (noun): archetype, idea, model, original, pattern, prototype, standard. An ideal is that which is conceived or taken as the highest type of excellence or ultimate object of attainment. The archetype is the primal form, actual or imaginary, according to which any existing thing is constructed; the prototype has or has had actual existence; in the derived sense, as in metrology, a prototype may not be the original form, but one having equal authority with that as a standard. An ideal may be primal, or may be slowly developed even from failures and by negations; an ideal is meant to be perfect, the best conceivable thing that could by possibility be attained. The artist's ideal is his own mental image, of which his finished work is but an imperfect expression. The original is the first specimen, good or bad; the original of a master is superior to all copies. The standard may be below the ideal. The ideal is ordinarily unattainable; the standard is concrete, and ordinarily attainable, being a measure to which all else of its kind must conform; as, the standard of weights and measures, of corn, or of cotton. The idea of virtue is the mental concept or image of virtue in general: the ideal of virtue is the mental concept or image of virtue in its highest conceivable perfection. Compare EXAMPLE, IDEA. Antonyms: accomplishment, achievement, act, action, attainment, development, doing, embodiment, execution, fact, incarnation, performance, practice, reality, realization.

i·de·al·ism (ī·dē'əl·iz'əm) n. 1 Any of several philosophical theories that there is no reality, no world of objects or "thing–in–itself" apart from a reacting mind or consciousness; that only the mental is knowable, and therefore that reality is essentially spiritual or mental: variously developed by Berkeley, Kant, Hegel. 2 In literature, the development of subject matter following an imaginative or preconceived idea of perfection instead of adhering strictly to facts: opposed to realism. 3 The quest of the ideal; the habit of forming ideals and of striving after their realization, by extension, that which is so realized; the attainment of an ideal. 4 In art, the endeavor to attain perfection by improving and uniting in one form all the best qualities to be found in different individual forms. Idealism creates in conformity with a preconceived ideal; realism restricts the imaginative faculty.

i·de·al·ist (ī·dē'əl·ist) n. 1 One who idealizes, or seeks an ideal or ideal conditions; a visionary; a romantic. 2 An exponent of idealism in art or literature. 3 One who holds the doctrines of any philosophic idealism. —i·de'·al·is'tic or ·ti·cal adj.—i·de·al·is'ti·cal·ly adv.

i·de·al·i·ty (ī'dē·al'ə·tē) n. pl. ·ties 1 The condition or character of being ideal; existence only in the mind 2 The power or tendency to form ideals; imagination.

i·de·al·ize (ī·dē'əl·īz) v. ·ized, ·iz·ing v.t. To represent or think of as conforming to some standard of perfection or beauty; make ideal; exalt. —v.i. To form an ideal or ideals. —i·de·al·i·za·tion (ī·dē'əl·ə·zā'shən, -ī·zā'-) n. —i·de'al·iz'er n.

i·de·al·ly (ī·dē'əl·ē) adv. 1 Conforming to an ideal. 2 In idea or imagination; mentally; intellectually.

i·de·ate (ī·dē'āt) v. ·at·ed, ·at·ing v.t. To form an idea of; frame in the mind; conceive. —v.i. To form ideas; think. —n. Philos. The object corresponding to an idea: so distinguished by those who regard the object not simply as perceived, but as the product of perception: also i·de·a·tum (ī'dē·ā'təm).

i·de·a·tion (ī'dē·ā'shən) n. 1 The mental power to form ideas. 2 The mental process of forming and using ideas. —i'de·a'tion·al adj.

i·den·tic (ī·den'tik) adj. 1 Identical. 2 In diplomatic correspondence, identical in form: said of notes sent by two governments dealing with a third.

i·den·ti·cal (ī·den'ti·kəl) adj. 1 Absolutely the same; the very same. 2 Uniform with something else in quality, condition, execution, appearance, etc. [<Med. L identicus < idem the same] —i·den'ti·cal·ly adv. —i·den'ti·cal·ness n.
Synonyms: alike, equivalent, interchangeable, same, selfsame. Strictly, no two persons or things can be identical or the same. In looser usage, two volumes may be said to be identical or the same in contents; a carbon copy is identical in substance with the original, but it is not the same document. Two synonyms, as "begin" and "commence," may be in most cases equivalent and interchangeable, but one is not the same as the other, and at some point they will be found to draw apart, either in meaning or use. A check may be equivalent to the money specified, but it is not the same as cash. When a person or thing is surely recognized as the very one referred to, and no other, we say, "This is the identical man, the identical document," or "the same man, document." See SYNONYMOUS. Antonyms: contrary, different, dissimilar, distinct, unlike.

identical twin Genetics One of a pair of human offspring which develop from a division of a single fertilized egg cell. They are invariably of the same sex and exhibit similarities due to participation in the same genetic factors: distinguished from fraternal twin.

i·den·ti·fi·ca·tion (ī·den'tə·fə·kā'shən) n. 1 The act or process of showing to be the same. 2 The state of being shown or proved to be identical. 3 Anything by which identity can be established. 4 Psychoanal. A process by which an individual, usually subconsciously, behaves or imagines himself behaving as if he were a person with whom he has formed an emotional tie. 5 The act or state of feeling sympathy for a fictitious or dramatic character, sometimes extending to projection of the image of the self into the character. See EMPATHY.

identification tag 1 Mil. Either of two metal disks worn by a soldier, and bearing his name, serial number, and other personal data: popularly called dog tag. 2 Any tag affixed, as to a suitcase or trunk, for purpose of identification.

i·den·ti·fy (ī·den'tə·fī) v.t. ·fied, ·fy·ing 1 To determine or establish as a particular person or thing; ascertain the nature or supposed identity of. 2 To consider or treat as the same; make the same or identical: He identifies money with happiness. 3 To serve as a means of recognition or identification of: The teeth identified the skull. 4 To join or associate in interest, action, etc.: usually with with: He identified his name with a well-known charity. 5 Biol. To determine the proper genus, order, etc., of. 6 Psychoanal. To make identification of (oneself) with someone else. [<LL identificare] —i·den'ti·fi'a·ble adj. —i·den'ti·fi'er n.

i·den·ti·ty (ī·den'tə·tē) n. pl. ·ties 1 The state of being identical or absolutely the same; selfsameness. 2 Sameness of character or quality. Identity may be of two sorts: absolute, which involves exact equality with itself, or selfsameness, as the equation $a = a$; and relative, a less rigid sense, which implies a close material resemblance or similarity, as that of the green of two leaves. 3 The distinctive character belonging to an individual; personality; individuality. 4 The state of being what is asserted or described. [<LL identitas, -tatis < idem the same]

i·de·o·graph (ī'dē·ə·graf', -gräf', id'ē-) n. 1 A picture symbol or sign of an object, or the graphic representation of a thought, as distinguished from a representation of the sound of a word in the given language. 2 A symbol, as +, =, ¶, $, etc. Also i'de·o·gram' (-gram'). —i'de·o·graph'ic or ·i·cal adj. —i'de·o·graph'i·cal·ly adv.

i·de·og·ra·phy (ī'dē·og'rə·fē, id'ē-) n. The graphic representation of ideas by symbolic characters: use of ideographs. [<IDEO- + -GRAPHY]

i·de·ol·o·gist (ī'dē·ol'ə·jist, id'ē-) n. 1 One who formulates or is expert in an ideology. 2 A visionary.

i·de·ol·o·gize (ī′dē·ol′ə·jīz, id′ē-) *v.t.* To imbue, as a person, group, or nation, with a certain ideology; to indoctrinate.

i·de·o·logue (ī′dē·ə·lôg, -log, id′ē-) *n.* One who is committed to an ideology. [< F]

i·de·ol·o·gy (ī′dē·ol′ə·jē, id′ē-) *n.* **1** The ideas or kind of thinking characteristic of an individual or group; specifically, the ideas and objectives that influence a whole group or national culture, shaping especially their political and social procedure: German *ideology*. **2** The science that treats of the evolution of human ideas. [< -LOGY] — **i·de·o·log·ic** (ī′dē·ə·loj′ik, id′ē-) or **-i·cal** *adj.*

i·de·o·phone (ī′dē·ə·fōn′, id′ē-) *n.* A sound or combination of sounds representing a thought or an idea; an uttered word or phrase.

id·i·o·cy (id′ē·ə·sē) *n. pl.* **·cies** **1** The condition of being an idiot; mental deficiency amounting almost to total absence of understanding, caused by non-development or abnormality of the brain tissue. **2** *Psychiatry* The lowest grade of mental capacity and intelligence, often accompanied by physical abnormalities. **3** An idiotic utterance or act. [< IDIOT]

Synonyms: fatuity, folly, foolishness, imbecility, incapacity, senselessness, stupidity. *Idiocy* is a state of mental deficiency amounting almost or quite to total absence of understanding. *Imbecility* is a condition of mental weakness, which incapacitates for the serious duties of life. *Incapacity*, or lack of legal qualification for certain acts, necessarily results from *imbecility*, but may also result from other causes, as from insanity or from age, sex, etc.; as, the *incapacity* of a minor to make a contract. *Idiocy* or *imbecility* is deficiency of mind, while insanity is disorder or abnormal action of the brain. *Folly* and *foolishness* denote a want of mental and often of moral balance. *Fatuity* is sometimes used as equivalent to *idiocy*, but more frequently signifies conceited and excessive *folly*. *Stupidity* is dulness and slowness of mental action which may range all the way from lack of normal readiness to absolute *imbecility*. Compare INSANITY.

id·i·o·glos·si·a (id′ē·ō·glos′ē·ə, -glôs′-) *n. Psychiatry* Defective speech, characterized by a succession of meaningless sounds. [< IDIO- + Gk. *glossa* tongue]

id·i·o·graph (id′ē·ə·graf, -gräf′) *n.* One's private mark or signature; a trademark. — **id′i·o·graph′ic** or **-i·cal** *adj.*

id·i·om (id′ē·əm) *n.* **1** An expression peculiar to a language, not readily analyzable from its grammatical construction or from the meaning of its component parts, as *to put up with* (tolerate; endure). **2** A speech pattern, dialect, or language characteristic of a certain group, class, trade, region, etc.: legal *idiom*. **3** The peculiar genius or spirit of a language. **4** Specific character, peculiarity, or style, as in art or literature. See synonyms under LANGUAGE. [< L *idioma* < Gk. *idiōma* peculiarity, property < *idioein* appropriate < *idios* one's own]

id·i·o·mat·ic (id′ē·ə·mat′ik) *adj.* **1** Full of idiom; vernacular. **2** Peculiar to or characteristic of a certain language or dialect. Also **id′i·o·mat′i·cal.** [< Gk. *idiōmatikos* characteristic < *idiōma*. See IDIOM.] — **id′i·o·mat′i·cal·ly** *adv.*

id·i·op·a·thy (id′ē·op′ə·thē) *n. pl.* **·thies** *Pathol.* **1** A disease of unknown or indeterminate origin. **2** A disease generated by an allergy or by some forms of eczema and gastrointestinal disorder. [< IDIO- + -PATHY] — **id·i·o·path·ic** (id′ē·ō·path′ik) or **-i·cal** *adj.*

id·i·o·syn·cra·sy (id′ē·ō·sing′krə·sē) *n. pl.* **·sies** **1** A constitutional peculiarity, as of susceptibility or aversion. **2** Any quality, characteristic, tendency, or mode of expression peculiar to an individual; quirk. [< Gk. *idiosynkrasia* < *idios* peculiar + *synkrasis* a mixing together < *syn* together + *krasis* mixing] — **id′i·o·syn·crat′ic** (-sin·krat′ik) — **id′i·o·syn·crat′i·cal·ly** *adv.*

id·i·ot (id′ē·ət) *n.* **1** A human being conspicuously deficient in mental powers and in the capacity for self-protection. **2** *Psychiatry* A person exhibiting the lowest grade of mental development. **3** A foolish fellow; a simple-

ton. [< OF *idiot* < L *idiota* < Gk. *idiōtēs* private person < *idios* one's own]

id·i·ot·ic (id′ē-ot′ik) *adj.* Like or pertaining to an idiot; senseless; stupid. Also **id′i·ot′i·cal.** — **id′i·ot′i·cal·ly** *adv.*

id·i·ot·ism (id′ē·ət·iz′əm) *n.* **1** Excessive stupidity; a senseless course of action. **2** Idiocy. **3** *Obs.* An idiom. [< F *idiotisme*]

i·dle (īd′l) *adj.* **1** Not occupied; doing nothing. **2** Averse to labor; lazy. **3** Affording leisure. **4** Without effect; useless; unavailing: *idle* talk, *idle* rage. — *v.* **i·dled, i·dling** *v.i.* **1** To spend time in idleness. **2** To saunter or move idly; loaf. **3** *Mech.* To operate without transmitting power, usually at reduced speed: said of motors and machines. — *v.t.* **4** To pass in idleness; waste, as a day. **5** To cause to be idle, as a person or an industry. ◆ Homophones: *idol, idyl*. [OE *īdel* empty, useless]

Synonyms (*adj.*): inactive, indolent, inert, lazy, slothful, sluggish, trifling, unemployed, unoccupied, vacant. *Idle* etymologically denotes not the absence of action, but vain, useless action—the absence of useful, effective action; the *idle* schoolboy may be very actively whittling his desk or tormenting his neighbors. Doing nothing whatever is the secondary meaning of *idle*. A *lazy* person may chance to be employed in useful work, but he acts without energy or impetus. We speak figuratively of a *lazy* stream. *Slothful* belongs in the moral realm, denoting a self-indulgent aversion to exertion. *Indolent* is a milder term for the same quality. See INSIGNIFICANT. *Antonyms:* active, busy, diligent, employed, industrious, occupied, working.

i·dle·ness (īd′l·nis) *n.* The state of being idle in any sense; slothfulness; inactivity. [OE *īdelnes*]

idle pulley *Mech.* A pulley to guide a driving belt, increase its tension, or increase its arc of contact on one of the working pulleys.

i·dler (īd′lər) *n.* **1** One who idles; a lazy person; a loafer. **2** An idle wheel. **3** One of a ship's crew who stands no night watches, having special day duties.

idle wheel *Mech.* **1** A gear wheel to convey motion from one wheel to another, all three being upon different axes. **2** An idle pulley. Also **idler.**

IDLE WHEEL

i·dly (īd′lē) *adv.* **1** In an idle manner. **2** Uselessly; vainly; without effect.

I·do (ē′dō) *n.* An artificial language, a simplification of the principles of Esperanto: developed in 1907. [< Esperanto, offspring]

id·o·crase (id′ō·krās, ī′dō-) *n.* Vesuvianite. [< IDIO- + Gk. *krasis* mixture]

i·dol (īd′l) *n.* **1** An image of a god or saint, or an object to which or through which worship is offered. **2** The image of a heathen god. **3** That on which the affections are passionately set. **4** A source of error; a fallacy. **5** An unsubstantial apparition; a phantom due to reflection, as in a mirror. **6** *Obs.* An impostor; counterfeit. See synonyms under IMAGE. ◆ Homophones: *idle, idyl*. [< OF *idele* < L *idolum* < Gk. *eidōlon* image, phantom < *eidos* form, shape]

i·dol·a·ter (ī·dol′ə·tər) *n.* **1** An adorer of images. **2** One who is inordinately fond of some person or thing. [< OF *idolatre* < LL *idolatres* < Gk. *eidōlolatrēs* < *eidōlon* an idol + *latreuein* worship] — **i·dol′a·tress** *n. fem.*

i·dol·a·trize (ī·dol′ə·trīz) *v.* **·trized, ·triz·ing** *v.t.* To make an idol of; idolize. — *v.i.* To practice idolatry.

i·dol·a·trous (ī·dol′ə·trəs) *adj.* **1** Pertaining to idolatry. **2** Extravagant in admiration. — **i·dol′a·trous·ly** *adv.* — **i·dol′a·trous·ness** *n.*

i·dol·a·try (ī·dol′ə·trē) *n. pl.* **·tries** **1** The worship of idols. **2** Idolatrous admiration. [< OF *idolatrie* < LL *idololatria* < Gk. *eidōlolatreia* < *eidolon* an idol + *latreuein* worship]

i·dol·ism (ī′dəl·iz′əm) *n.* **1** A fanciful or false notion. **2** Idol-worship.

i·dol·ize (ī′dəl·īz) *v.* **ized, ·iz·ing** *v.t.* **1** To have inordinate love for; adore. **2** To worship as an idol. — *v.i.* **3** To worship idols. Also *Brit.* **i′dol·ise.** See synonyms under WORSHIP.

i·dol·i·za·tion (ī′dəl·ə·zā′shən, -ī·zā′-) *n.* — **i′dol·iz′er** *n.*

i·dol·o·clast (ī·dol′ə·klast) *n.* A breaker of images. [< IDOL + (ICON)OCLAST]

i·dol·o·clas·tic (ī·dol′ə·klas′tik) *adj.* Of or pertaining to the breaking of images.

i·do·ne·ous (ī·dō′nē·əs) *adj.* Proper; suitable; proportionate. [< L *idoneus* fitting]

i·dyl (īd′l) *n.* **1** A short poem or prose piece depicting simple scenes of pastoral, domestic, or country life; also, a more extended descriptive or narrative poem. **2** Any event, scene, or circumstance of a kind suitable for such a work. **3** *Music* A composition of simple or pastoral character. Also **i′dyll.** ◆ Homophones: *idle, idol*. [< L *idyllium* < Gk. *eidyllion*, dim. of *eidos* form] — **i′dyl·ist, i′dyl·list** *n.*

i·dyl·lic (ī·dil′ik) *adj.* Of or pertaining to the idyl; having the essential qualities of an idyl or pastoral poem. Also **i·dyl′li·cal.** — **i·dyl′li·cal·ly** *adv.*

if (if) *conj.* **1** On the supposition or condition that: We'll go by plane *if* the weather permits. **2** Allowing that; although: *If* he was there, I didn't see him. **3** Whether: I am not sure *if* he is at home. ◆ *If* is also used in exclamatory clauses to introduce (a) a wish or determination: *If* I had only thought of that!; and (b) surprise or irritation: Well, *if* he hasn't run away again! — *n.* **1** The word *if* itself. **2** A condition; supposition. [OE *gif*]

ig·loo (ig′lōō) *n. pl.* **·loos** **1** An Eskimo house, dome-shaped and usually built of blocks of packed snow. **2** A conical mound, for protecting munitions, made of earth and concrete. Also **ig′lu.** [< Eskimo *igdlu*]

ig·ne·ous (ig′nē·əs) *adj.* **1** Pertaining to or resembling fire. **2** *Geol.* Formed by the action of a fusing heat within the earth: said especially of rocks consolidated from a molten state: distinguished from *sedimentary*. [< L *igneus* < *ignis* fire]

ig·nes·cent (ig·nes′ənt) *adj.* **1** Emitting sparks of fire when struck with steel or iron. **2** Coruscating. [< L *ignescere* < *ignis* fire]

ig·ni·fy (ig′nə·fī) *v.t.* **·fied, ·fy·ing** *Rare* **1** To set on fire; burn. **2** To fuse or melt. [Cf. LL *ignifacere* to set on fire]

ig·nis fat·u·us (ig′nis fach′ōō·əs) *pl.* **ig·nes fat·u·i** (ig′nēz fach′ōō·ī) **1** A phosphorescent light seen in the air over marshy places; jack-o′-lantern; will-o′-the-wisp. **2** Figuratively, a delusion; deceptive attraction. [< Med. L, foolish fire]

ig·nite (ig·nīt′) *v.* **ig·nit·ed, ig·nit·ing** *v.t.* **1** To set on fire; cause to burn. **2** To cause to glow with intense heat; make incandescent. **3** *Chem.* To bring to the point of combustion. — *v.i.* **4** To take fire; start burning. See synonyms under BURN. [< L *ignitus*, pp. of *ignire* set on fire] — **ig·nit′i·ble, ig·nit′a·ble** *adj.* — **ig·nit′i·bil·i·ty, ig·nit′a·bil·i·ty** *n.*

ig·nit·er (ig·nī′tər) *n.* **1** One who or that which ignites. **2** A device for exploding a shell or torpedo, for setting off a blasting charge, etc. **3** An ignitor.

ig·ni·tion (ig·nish′ən) *n.* **1** The act of, or system employed in, igniting. **2** The act of exploding the charge of gases in the cylinder of an internal-combustion engine. **3** The electrical apparatus that fires these gases. [< Med. L *ignitio, -onis* burning < *ignire* burn]

ig·ni·tor (ig·nī′tər) *n. Electronics* A silicon carbide electrode used to initiate the action of an Ignitron. Also spelled *igniter.*

ig·no·ble (ig·nō′bəl) *adj.* **1** Unworthy or degraded in character. **2** *Rare* Low-born. **3** Of inferior kind; specifically, in falconry, said of the short-winged hawks, which chase their prey, as distinguished from the *noble* falcons which attack by a single swoop. See synonyms under BASE, VULGAR. [< F < L *ignobilis* < *in*- not + *gnobilis* noble, known] — **ig·no·bil·i·ty** (ig′nə·bil′ə·tē), **ig·no′ble·ness** *n.* — **ig·no′bly** *adv.*

ig·no·min·i·ous (ig′nə·min′ē·əs) *adj.* **1** Entailing or implying dishonor or disgrace. **2** Deserving ignominy; despicable. **3** Abasing; humiliating. See synonyms under INFAMOUS. [< L *ignominiosus* < *ignominia* IGNOMINY] — **ig′no·min′i·ous·ly** *adv.* — **ig′no·min′i·ous·ness** *n.*

ig·no·min·y (ig′nə·min′ē) *n. pl.* **·min·ies** **1** Disgrace or dishonor. **2** That which causes disgrace; disgraceful action or conduct. [<L *ignominia* < *in-* not + *nomen* name, reputation]

ig·no·ra·mus (ig'nə·rā'məs, -ram'əs) *n.* An ignorant pretender to knowledge. [<L, we do not know]

ig·no·rance (ig'nər·əns) *n.* **1** The state of being ignorant; the condition of not being informed; lack of knowledge. **2** An act, offense, or sin due to ignorance. [<F <L *ignorantia*]

ig·no·rant (ig'nər·ənt) *adj.* **1** Destitute of education or knowledge. **2** Unacquainted; unaware. **3** Manifesting or characterized by ignorance. [<OF <L *ignorans, -antis,* ppr. of *ignorare* not to know. See IGNORE.] —**ig'no·rant·ly** *adv.*

Synonyms (adj.): ill-informed, illiterate, uneducated, unenlightened, uninformed, uninstructed, unlearned, unlettered, unskilled, untaught, untutored. *Ignorant* signifies destitute of education or knowledge, or lacking knowledge or information; it is thus a relative term. The most learned man is still *ignorant* of many things; persons are spoken of as *ignorant* who have not the knowledge that has become generally diffused in the world; the *ignorant* savage may be well-instructed in matters of the field and the chase, and is thus more properly *untutored* than *ignorant*. *Illiterate* is without letters and the knowledge that comes through reading. *Unlettered* is similar in meaning to *illiterate,* but less absolute; the *unlettered* man may have acquired the art of reading and writing and some elementary knowledge; the *uneducated* man has never taken any systematic course of mental training. *Ignorance* is relative; *illiteracy* is absolute; we have statistics of *illiteracy*; no statistics of *ignorance* are possible. See BRUTISH. *Antonyms*: educated, instructed, learned, sage, skilled, trained, well-informed, wise.

ig·nore (ig·nôr', -nōr') *v.t.* **·nored, ·nor·ing** **1** To refuse to notice or recognize; disregard intentionally. **2** *Law* To reject (a bill of indictment) for insufficient evidence. [<F *ignorer* <L *ignorare* < *in-* not + *gno-,* stem of *gnoscere* know] —**ig·nor'er** *n.*

i·gua·na (i·gwä'nə) *n.* **1** An edible, tropical American lizard (family *Iguanidae*); especially *Iguana iguana,* which sometimes attains a length of 6 feet: it is partly arboreal, partly herbivorous, and, unless attacked, is harmless. **2** Any one of several lizards related to the iguana. [<Sp. <Cariban]

COMMON IGUANA
Grass-green in color with black and white markings; the dewlap and spiny crest are characteristic of the true iguana.

i·guan·o·don (i·gwan'ə·don) *n.* A large, powerfully built, herbivorous, bipedal dinosaur (order *Ornithischia*), associated with the Lower Cretaceous period in Belgium. [<NL < IGUANA + Gk. *odón* tooth]

il·e·ac (il'ē·ak) *adj.* Of or pertaining to the ileum. Also **il'e·al.** [A refashioning of ILIAC]

il·e·i·tis (il'ē·ī'tis) *n. Pathol.* Inflammation of the ileum.

ileo- *combining form* Of or pertaining to the ileum: *ileostomy.* Also, before vowels, **ile-.** [< L *ileum* the ileum]

il·e·os·to·my (il'ē·os'tə·mē) *n. Surg.* The operation of forming an artificial opening into the ileum. [<ILEO- + -STOMY]

il·e·um (il'ē·əm) *n. Anat.* The lower three fifths of the small intestine from the jejunum to the cecum, excluding the duodenum. [< L <Gk. *eilein* roll, twist]

il·e·us (il'ē·əs) *n. Pathol.* An obstruction of the intestines, variously caused and resulting in severe colic. [<L <Gk. *eileos* colic <*eilein* twist]

i·lex (ī'leks) *n.* **1** A tree or shrub (genus *Ilex*) of the holly family. **2** The holm oak. **3** The holly. [<L holm oak]

il·i·ac (il'ē·ak) *adj.* Pertaining to or near the ilium. [<LL *iliacus* suffering from colic <*ileus* colic]

il·i·um (il'ē·əm) *n. pl.* **·i·a** (-ē·ə) *Anat.* The large upper portion of the innominate bone. [<L, flank]

ilk (ilk) *adj. & n. Obs.* Same. —**of that ilk** Of that same: a phrase denoting that a person's surname and the name of his estate are the same: Kent *of that ilk*—that is, Kent of Kent. **2** Of that race, class, or kind. [OE *ilka* the same]

ill (il) *adj.* **1** Disordered in physical condition; diseased; unwell; sick. **2** Evil in effect or tendency; baneful; harmful; unjust; unkind. **3** Of inferior quality; wretched. **4** Lacking skill; ineffective. **5** Evil; malevolent; wrong: *ill* wind, *ill* repute. **6** *Scot.* Difficult; also, grieved; afflicted with sorrow. See synonyms under BAD¹, SICKLY.—*n.* Anything that prevents or impairs what is good or desirable, as sickness, misfortune, or bad luck. See synonyms under MISFORTUNE. —*adv.* **1** Not well. **2** With difficulty; hardly. **3** Badly; unfavorably. —**ill at ease** Uneasy; uncomfortable. [<ON *illr*]

I'll (īl) **1** I will. **2** I shall.

il·la·tion (i·lā'shən) *n.* **1** The act of inferring. **2** That which is inferred; deduction. [<L *illatio, -onis* <*illatus,* pp. of *inferre* bring in, infer]

il·la·tive (il'ə·tiv) *adj.* Pertaining to, denoting, or derived by inference, especially legitimate inference. —*n.* A word denoting an inference, as *therefore.* —**il'la·tive·ly** *adv.*

il·laud·a·ble (i·lô'də·bəl) *adj.* Blameworthy.

ill–be·ing (il'bē'ing) *n.* The condition of being ill or evil: opposed to *well–being.*

ill–bod·ing (il'bō'ding) *adj.* Ill-omened; inauspicious.

ill–bred (il'bred') *adj.* Badly taught, reared, or trained; rude.

il·le·gal (i·lē'gəl) *adj.* Contrary to the law; not legal. See synonyms under CRIMINAL. —**il·le'gal·ly** *adv.*

il·le·gal·i·ty (il'ē·gal'ə·tē) *n. pl.* **·ties** **1** The state of being illegal. **2** Something unlawful.

il·le·gal·ize (i·lē'gəl·īz) *v.t.* **·ized, ·iz·ing** To make illegal or unlawful.

il·leg·i·ble (i·lej'ə·bəl) *adj.* Not legible; undecipherable. —**il·leg·i·bil'i·ty, il·leg'i·ble·ness** *n.* —**il·leg'i·bly** *adv.*

il·le·git·i·ma·cy (il'i·jit'ə·mə·sē) *n. pl.* **·cies** **1** The character or condition of being born out of lawful wedlock; bastardy. **2** Unsoundness, spuriousness, or irregularity, as of an argument; illogicality.

il·le·git·i·mate (il'i·jit'ə·mit) *adj.* **1** Not legitimate; contrary to law. **2** Born out of wedlock. **3** Illogical; unsound. **4** Contrary to good usage; irregular. [<L *illegitimus* < *in-* not +*legitimus.* See LEGITIMATE.] —**il'le·git'i·ma'tion** *n.* —**il'le·git'i·mate·ly** *adv.*

ill fame Bad repute.

ill–fa·vored (il'fā'vərd) *adj.* **1** Repulsive; ugly. **2** Objectionable. Also *Brit.* **ill'–fa'voured.**

ill–got·ten (il'got'n) *adj.* Obtained dishonestly.

ill–hu·mor (il'hyōō'mər) *n.* A morose, disagreeable, or choleric state of mind; sullenness. —**ill'–hu'mored** *adj.*

il·lib·er·al (i·lib'ər·əl) *adj.* **1** Not liberal; not generous in giving; parsimonious. **2** Narrow-minded. **3** Lacking breadth of culture; vulgar. —**il·lib'er·al·ism** (-iz'əm) *n.* —**il·lib'er·al'i·ty** (-al'ə·tē) *n.* —**il·lib'er·al·ly** *adv.* —**il·lib'er·al·ness** *n.*

il·lic·it (i·lis'it) *adj.* **1** Not permitted; unlawful. **2** Having to do with unlawful things or actions. [<F *illicite* <L *illicitus* < *in-* not + *licitus.* See LICIT.] —**il·lic'it·ly** *adv.* —**il·lic'it·ness** *n.*

il·lim·it·a·ble (i·lim'i·tə·bəl) *adj.* That can not be limited; boundless. See synonyms under INFINITE. —**il·lim'it·a·bil'i·ty, il·lim'it·a·ble·ness, il·lim'i·ta'tion** (-ə·tā'shən) *n.* —**il·lim'it·a·bly** *adv.*

Il·li·nois (il'ə·noi', -noiz') *n. pl.* **·nois** A North American Indian belonging to any one of the Algonquian tribes of the Illinois Confederacy. [<F <N. Am. Ind.]

Il·li·nois (il'ə·noi', -noiz') A north central State of the United States; 56,400 square miles; capital, Springfield; entered the Union Dec. 3, 1818; nickname, *Prairie State*: abbr. IL. —**Il'li·nois'an** (-noi'ən, -noi'zən) *adj. & n.*

il·liq·uid (i·lik'wid) *adj. Law* Not clearly manifest or proved: said of a debt, right, or claim which has no legal standing. [<IL- + LIQUID]

il·lit·er·a·cy (i·lit'ər·ə·sē) *n. pl.* **·cies** **1** The state of being illiterate or untaught; lack of

culture; ignorance of letters; especially, as in census statistics, inability to read or to read and write. **2** A literary blunder or series of such blunders.

il·lit·er·ate (i·lit'ər·it) *adj.* **1** Unable to read or write. **2** Ignorant of letters; not literate; manifesting want of culture; uneducated. See synonyms under IGNORANT. —*n.* An illiterate person; especially, one who cannot read or write. [<L *illiteratus* < *in-* not + *literatus.* See LITERATE.] —**il·lit'er·ate·ly** *adv.* —**il·lit'er·ate·ness** *n.*

ill–look·ing (il'look'ing) *adj.* Looking ill; homely; uncomely.

ill nature Peevishness; surliness; sullenness.

ill–na·tured (il'nā'chərd) *adj.* Surly; cross. See synonyms under MALICIOUS, MOROSE. —**ill'–na'tured·ly** *adv.* —**ill'–na'tured·ness** *n.*

ill·ness (il'nis) *n.* **1** The state of being out of health. **2** An ailment; sickness. **3** *Obs.* Badness; evil.

Synonyms: ailment, complaint, disease, disorder, distemper, indisposition, infirmity, sickness. See DISEASE. *Antonyms*: health, soundness, strength, vigor.

il·lo·cal (i·lō'kəl) *adj.* Having no location in space; without place. [<LL *illocalis* < *in-* not + *localis.* See LOCAL.] —**il·lo·cal'i·ty** (il'ō·kal'ə·tē) *n.*

il·log·ic (i·loj'ik) *n.* That which is not logical.

il·log·i·cal (i·loj'i·kəl) *adj.* Not logical; contrary to or neglectful of the rules of logic; not reasonable. —**il·log'i·cal'i·ty, il·log'i·cal·ness** *n.* —**il·log'i·cal·ly** *adv.*

ill–set (il'set') *adj.* Incorrectly or improperly set.

ill–sort·ed (il'sôr'tid) *adj.* Not well sorted; unharmonious; unsuitably matched.

ill–starred (il'stärd') *adj.* Unfortunate; as if under an evil star.

ill temper Irritability; moroseness.

ill–tem·pered (il'tem'pərd) *adj.* **1** Characterized by bad temper. **2** *Obs.* In an unhealthy condition.

ill–treat (il'trēt') *v.t.* To treat badly; maltreat. See synonyms under ABUSE. —**ill'–treat'ment** *n.*

ill turn An act of unkindness or hostility.

il·lude (i·lōōd') *v.t. Obs.* To trick; cheat. [<L *illudere* make sport of < *in-* toward, against + *ludere* play]

il·lume (i·lōōm') *v.t.* **·lumed, ·lum·ing** *Poetic* To illumine; illuminate. [<ILLUMINE, prob. influenced in form by F *rallumer* light]

il·lu·mi·nance (i·lōō'mə·nəns) *n. Physics* The luminous flux per unit area of a uniformly illuminated surface.

il·lu·mi·nant (i·lōō'mə·nənt) *adj.* Giving light; illuminating. —*n.* Any material used for illuminating. [<L *illuminans, -antis,* ppr. of *illuminare* give light]

il·lu·mi·nate (i·lōō'mə·nāt) *v.* **·nat·ed, ·nat·ing** *v.t.* **1** To give light to; light up. **2** To explain; make clear. **3** To enlighten, as the mind. **4** To make illustrious or resplendent. **5** To decorate with lights. **6** To decorate (a manuscript, letter, etc.) with ornamental borders, figures, etc., of gold or other colors. —*v.i.* **7** To light up. —*adj.* **1** Lighted up. **2** *Obs.* Enlightened. —*n.* One of the illuminati. [<L *illuminatus,* pp. of *illuminare* < *in-* thoroughly+ *luminare* light <*lumen* light]

il·lu·mi·na·ti (i·lōō'mə·nā'tī, -nä'tē) *n. pl. sing.* **·na·to** (-nä'tō, -nä'tō) **1** Those who have or profess to have remarkable discernment or spiritual enlightenment. **2** In early church usage, baptized persons, to whom in the ceremony a lighted taper was given as a symbol of spiritual enlightenment. [<L, pl. of *illuminatus,* pp of *illuminare* light up]

Il·lu·mi·na·ti (i·lōō'mə·nä'tī, -nä'tē) *n. pl.* **1** Any of various European religious sects which claimed to have received a special religious enlightenment. **2** A select, secret, deistic and republican society founded by Adam Weishaupt at Ingolstadt, Bavaria, in 1776, aiming at emancipation from despotism: also called *Perfectibilists.*

il·lu·mi·nat·ing gas (i·lōō'mə·nā'ting) Gas consisting of hydrogen mixed with carbon monoxide, methane, ethylene, and other hydrocarbons (as well as impurities such as carbon dioxide, nitrogen, etc.): used for lighting purposes.

il·lu·mi·na·tion (i·lōō'mə·nā'shən) *n.* **1** The act of illuminating. **2** The fact or state of being illuminated. **3** A lighting up, especially for festal purposes. **4** Illuminance. **5** Mental enlightenment; imparted light; spiritual enlightenment. **6** *Often cap.* The specific doctrines held by the Illuminati. **7** Embellishment of manuscript, with colors and gold, or a particular figure or design in such ornamentation. See synonyms under LIGHT. [<L *illuminatio, -onis*]

il·lu·mi·na·tive (i·lōō'mə·nā'tiv) *adj.* **1** Having power or tending to illuminate; illustrative. **2** Relating to adornment or decoration of books or manuscripts.

il·lu·mi·na·tor (i·lōō'mə·nā'tər) *n.* **1** One who or that which gives light. **2** A lamp, lens, etc., for throwing light on particular objects or places. **3** One who executes illuminations on manuscripts. [<L *illuminator*]

il·lu·mine (i·lōō'min) *v.t. & v.i.* **·mined, ·min·ing** To illumine or be illuminated. [<F *illuminer* <L *illuminare* illuminate. Related to LIMN.] — **il·lu'mi·na·ble** *adj.*

Il·lu·mi·nism (i·lōō'mə·niz'əm) *n.* The principles of the Illuminati.

il·lu·mi·nist (i·lōō'mə·nist) *n.* **1** One aspiring to or claiming high spiritual enlightenment. **2** One who professionally illuminates manuscripts, etc.; an illuminator.

Il·lu·mi·nist (i·lōō'mə·nist) *n.* One of the Illuminati.

ill–use (il'yōōz') *v.t.* **·used, ·us·ing** To treat roughly, cruelly, or unjustly; misuse; abuse. — *n.* (-yōōs') Bad treatment; misuse. — **ill'·us'age** (-yōō'sij, -yōō'zij) *n.*

il·lu·sion (i·lōō'zhən) *n.* **1** An unreal image seemingly presented to the senses; any misleading appearance; a false show. **2** *Psychol.* A sensory impression which misrepresents the true character of the object perceived; false perception. See HALLUCINATION. **3** The act of deceiving or misleading by a false appearance. **4** The state of being deceived; delusion; false impression. **5** A thin material resembling tulle, usually of silk: used for veils and garments. **6** An artistic effect giving the appearance of reality to a painting. See synonyms under DELUSION, DREAM. [<OF <L *illusio, -onis* mocking, deceit <*illudere* make sport of. See ILLUDE.] — **il·lu'sion·al** *adj.*

il·lu·sion·ism (i·lōō'zhən·iz'əm) *n.* Any doctrine that treats the material world as an illusion of the senses.

il·lu·sion·ist (i·lōō'zhən·ist) *n.* **1** One given to illusions; a visionary; a dreamer. **2** One who creates illusions; a sleight–of–hand performer. **3** A believer in illusionism.

il·lu·sive (i·lōō'siv) *adj.* Misleading; deceptive; unreal. Also **il·lu'so·ry** (-sər·ē). See synonyms under DECEPTIVE, IMAGINARY. — **il·lu'sive·ly** *adv.* — **il·lu'sive·ness** *n.*

il·lus·trate (il'əs·trāt, i·lus'trāt) *v.t.* **·trat·ed, ·trat·ing** **1** To explain or make clear by means of figures, examples, etc.; exemplify. **2** To furnish with drawings, pictures, etc., for decoration or explanation, as a book or article. **3** *Obs.* To make luminous or bright. **4** *Obs.* To make illustrious. See synonyms under ADORN. [<L *illustratus,* pp. of *illustrare* light up <*in-* thoroughly + *lustrare* illuminate] — **il'lus·tra'tor** *n.*

il·lus·tra·tive (i·lus'trə·tiv, il'əs·trā'tiv) *adj.* Serving to illustrate or exemplify. — **il·lus'tra·tive·ly** *adv.*

il·lus·tra·tion (il'əs·trā'shən) *n.* **1** That which illustrates, as an example, comparison, anecdote, etc., by which a subject or statement is elucidated or explained. **2** A print, drawing, or picture of any kind inserted in written or printed text to elucidate or adorn it. **3** The act or art of illustrating. See synonyms under ALLEGORY, SAMPLE, SIMILE. [<L *illustratio, -onis*]

il·lus·tri·ous (i·lus'trē·əs) *adj.* **1** Greatly distinguished; renowned. **2** Conferring luster. **3** *Obs.* Luminous; bright. [<L *illustris* <*in-* in + *lustrum* light] — **il·lus'tri·ous·ly** *adv.* — **il·lus'tri·ous·ness** *n.*

Synonyms: celebrated, distinguished, eminent, famed, famous, glorious, honorable, honored, noble, noted, renowned. See GRAND. *Antonyms:* base, besmirched, degraded, despised, disgraced, dishonored, disreputable, ignominious, infamous, inglorious, notorious, stained, sullied, unhonored, unknown.

---

ill will Enmity; malevolence.

il·ly (il'lē) *adv.* In an ill or evil manner; not well; ill. ◆ While *illy* is regularly formed from the adjective *ill,* discriminating writers prefer to use *ill* as the adverb as well.

il·men·ite (il'mən·īt) *n.* An iron–black, opaque titanium–iron oxide, FeTiO₃, crystallizing in the hexagonal system. [from Lake *Ilmen*]

I'm (īm) I am.

im·age (im'ij) *n.* **1** A visible representation of something; a statue, picture, idol, etc. **2** *Optics* The picture or counterpart of an object produced by reflection or refraction, or the passage of rays through a small aperture. If such an image can be actually thrown on a surface as in a camera, it is a **real image;** but if it is visible only as in a mirror, it is a **virtual image. 3** A natural resemblance; also, that which resembles something; counterpart. **4** A representation in the mind of something not perceived at the moment through the senses; a product of the reproductive imagination or memory, of things seen, heard, touched, etc., including the accompanying emotion. **5** A mental picture or idea: a false *image* of oneself. **6** The way in which a person or thing is popularly perceived or regarded, especially through the agency of the mass media, as television, magazines, etc.; public impression: a politician striving to improve his *image;* a distorted *image* of the U.S. **7** A metaphor or a simile that reproduces or suggests in words the form, color, aspect, or semblance of an object. **6** A symbol of anything; embodiment; type. **7** *Telecom.* The optical replica of a scene produced by a television camera. **8** *Obs.* An apparition. — *v.t.* **·aged, ·ag·ing 1** To form a mental picture of; imagine. **2** To make a visible representation of; portray; delineate. **3** To mirror; reflect. **4** To describe vividly in speech or writing, as with images, figures of speech, etc. **5** To symbolize. [<OF <L *imago* <the base of *imitari* imitate]

Synonyms (noun): conception, copy, effigy, emblem, figure, icon, idea, idol, likeness, picture, representation, semblance, similitude, shadow, statue. See FANCY, FIGURE, IDEA, MODEL, PICTURE, SIMILE.

image point The point whose depth below ground zero is equal to the height of an exploding atomic or hydrogen bomb: it is considered as a source of radiating reflected shock.

im·age·ry (im'ij·rē) *n. pl.* **·ries 1** The act of forming images; images collectively. **2** Figurative description in speech or writing. See synonyms under SIMILE.

im·ag·i·na·ble (i·maj'ə·nə·bəl) *adj.* Conceivable. [<LL *imaginabilis*] — **im·ag'i·na·bly** *adv.*

im·ag·i·nar·y (i·maj'ə·ner'ē) *adj.* Existing only in imagination; unreal. — *n. Math.* An algebraic quantity or value that involves the square root of a negative quantity. — **im·ag'i·nar·i·ly** *adv.* — **im·ag'i·nar·i·ness** *n.*

Synonyms (adj.): airy, chimerical, dreamy, fancied, fanciful, hypothetical, ideal, illusive, illusory, quixotic, shadowy, utopian, visionary. See IDEAL. *Antonyms:* actual, material, palpable, physical, real, realized, substantial, tangible, visible.

im·ag·i·na·tion (i·maj'ə·nā'shən) *n.* **1** The picturing power or act of the mind. **2** *Psychol.* The constructive or creative faculty, expressed in terms of images which either reproduce past experiences or recombine them in ideal or creative forms. **3** That which is imagined; a mental image; a fantasy. **4** An irrational notion or belief. **5** *Archaic* Planning, plotting, or scheming, as involving mental construction. [<L *imaginatio, -onis* <*imaginatus,* pp. of *imaginari* IMAGINE]

Synonyms: fancy, fantasy. *Fancy* and *imagination* both belong to the productive or, more properly, the constructive faculty. Both recombine and modify mental images; the one great distinction between them is that *fancy* is superficial, while *imagination* is deep, essential, spiritual. *Fantasy* in ordinary usage simply denotes capricious or erratic *fancy,* as appears in the adjective *fantastic.* Compare FANCY, IDEA, THOUGHT¹.

im·ag·i·na·tion·al (i·maj'ə·nā'shən·əl) *adj.* Pertaining to, resulting from, or affected by the imagination.

---

im·ag·i·na·tive (i·maj'ə·nə·tiv, -nā'tiv) *adj.* **1** Creative or constructive; having capacity for imagining. **2** Characterized by or proceeding from imagination. See synonyms under FANCIFUL, ROMANTIC. [<L *imaginatus,* pp. of *imaginari* IMAGINE] — **im·ag'i·na·tive·ly** *adv.* — **im·ag'i·na·tive·ness** *n.*

im·ag·ine (i·maj'in) *v.* **·ined, ·in·ing** *v.t.* **1** To form a mental image of; conceive or create in the mind. **2** To suppose or conjecture; think. — *v.i.* **3** To use the imagination. **4** To make conjectures; suppose. See synonyms under GUESS, SUPPOSE. [<L *imaginari* <*imago* image]

im·bal·ance (im·bal'əns) *n.* **1** A lack of balance. **2** Inability to maintain an erect position. **3** Defective coordination of the eye muscles, endocrine glands, etc.

im·be·cile (im'bə·sil) *adj.* **1** Having the mental faculties feeble or defective; feeble–minded. **2** Characterized by stupidity. — *n. Psychiatry* A person of feeble mind; one intermediate between an idiot and a moron. See IDIOT. [<F *imbécile* <L *imbecillus* weak]

im·be·cil·i·ty (im'bə·sil'ə·tē) *n. pl.* **·ties 1** The condition or quality of being imbecile or impotent; feebleness, especially of the mind. **2** *Psychiatry* The next to the lowest grade of mental capacity and intelligence. See IDIOCY. **3** Any expression of character or opinion that indicates mental feebleness. **4** Incompetency; inability. **5** Absurdity; folly; silliness. [<MF *imbécillité* <L *imbecillitas* feebleness]

im·bibe (im·bīb') *v.* **·bibed, ·bib·ing** *v.t.* **1** To drink in; drink. **2** To take in as if drinking; absorb. **3** To receive into the mind or character: to *imbibe* good principles. **4** *Obs.* To saturate; imbue. — *v.i.* **5** To drink. See synonyms under ABSORB. [<F *imbiber* <L *imbibere* <*in-* in + *bibere* drink] — **im·bib'er** *n.*

im·bi·bi·tion (im'bi·bish'ən) *n.* **1** The act or process of imbibing, drinking in, or absorbing. **2** The absorption of moisture by any porous body.

im·bri·cate (im'brə·kāt) *v.* **·cat·ed, ·cat·ing** *v.t.* To lay or arrange regularly so as to overlap, as tiles on a roof. — *v.i.* To overlap. — *adj.* (-brə·kit) **1** Lying regularly over one another like shingles or slates, so as to break joints. **2** *Biol.* Overlapping with the extremities or margins, as the scales of fishes, the feathers of birds, or flower petals in the bud. **3** Decorated with overlapping scales, or so as to represent a surface of overlapping scales or tiles. Also **im'bri·cat'ed, im'bri·ca'tive.** [<L *imbricatus,* pp. of *imbricare* cover with gutter tiles <*imbrex* gutter tile <*imber* rain] — **im'bri·ca'tive·ly** *adv.*

im·bri·ca·tion (im'brə·kā'shən) *n.* **1** The condition of being imbricate: especially applied to shingles or tiles. **2** An imbricated organ, part, or structure.

im·brue (im·brōō') *v.t.* **·brued, ·bru·ing** To stain or wet; moisten, especially with blood. [<OF *embreuver* <L *imbibere* drink]

im·brute (im·brōōt') *v.t. & v.i.* **·brut·ed, ·brut·ing** To make or become brutal or brutish; brutalize.

im·bue (im·byōō') *v.t.* **·bued, ·bu·ing 1** To wet thoroughly; saturate. **2** To impregnate with color; dye; imbrue. **3** To impregnate or fill, as the mind, with emotions, principles, etc. [<OF *imbuer* <L *imbuere* wet, soak]

im·i·tate (im'ə·tāt) *v.t.* **·tat·ed, ·tat·ing 1** To do or try to do after the manner of; try to be the same as. **2** To mimic; counterfeit, as a tone of voice. **3** To make a copy or reproduction of; duplicate. **4** To use as a pattern or model. **5** To assume the appearance of; look like: lead painted to *imitate* gold. See IMITATION. [<L *imitatus,* pp. of *imitari* imitate] — **im·i·ta·ble** (im'ə·tə·bəl) *adj.* — **im'·i·ta·bil'i·ty** *n.* — **im'i·ta'tor** *n.*

Synonyms: ape, copy, counterfeit, duplicate, follow, impersonate, mimic, mock, pattern, personate, portray, repeat, represent, resemble, simulate. See FOLLOW. *Antonyms:* alter, change, differentiate, distort, misrepresent, modify, pervert, remodel, transform, vary.

im·i·ta·tion (im'ə·tā'shən) *n.* **1** The act of imitating. **2** Something done or made in resemblance of something else; a likeness; also, a counterfeit: *imitation* of money. **3**

Music The repetition of a phrase or subject in another voice or a different key. **4** *Biol.* Mimicry of environment or of another animal, plant, etc., for concealment or protection. See synonyms under CARICATURE, DUPLICATE, MODEL. —*adj.* Counterfeit; imitating something genuine or superior: *imitation* diamonds. [<L *imitatio, -onis*]

im·i·ta·tive (im′ə·tā′tiv) *adj.* **1** Inclined to imitate; given to or characterized by imitation. **2** Formed after a copy or model; resembling an original. **3** Fictitious; counterfeit. **4** *Ling.* Designating a word that approximates a natural sound, as *buzz, clink, swish.* Abbr. *imit.* —**im′i·ta·tive·ly** *adv.* —**im′i·ta′·tive·ness** *n.*

im·mac·u·late (i·mak′yə·lit) *adj.* **1** Without spot or blemish; pure; without taint of evil or sin. **2** Faultless; flawless. **3** Of one color; not spotted. See synonyms under GOOD, INNOCENT, PERFECT, PURE. [<L *immaculatus* <*in-* not + *maculatus* spotted] —**im·mac′u·late·ly** *adv.* —**im·mac′u·late·ness** *n.*

Immaculate Conception In the Roman Catholic Church, the doctrine that the Virgin Mary was conceived in her mother's womb without the stain of original sin: distinguished from *Virgin Birth.*

im·man·a·cle (i·man′ə·kəl) *v.t.* *Rare* To put manacles on; fetter.

im·ma·nence (im′ə·nəns) *n.* **1** A permanent abiding within; an indwelling. **2** The doctrine that the ultimate principle of the universe is not to be distinguished from the universe itself, that God dwells in all things and permeates the spirit of man. Also **im′ma·nen·cy.**

im·ma·nent (im′ə·nənt) *adj.* **1** Remaining within; indwelling; inherent: opposed to *transeunt, transcendent.* **2** Pertaining to the philosophical or the theological doctrine of immanence. See synonyms under INHERENT. [<L *immanens, -entis,* ppr. of *immanere* remain in <*in-* in + *manere* stay] —**im′ma·nent·ly** *adv.*

im·ma·te·ri·al (im′ə·tir′ē·əl) *adj.* **1** Not material; incorporeal: opposed to corporeal. **2** Unimportant. See synonyms under INSIGNIFICANT. [<Med. L *immaterialis*] —**im′ma·te′ri·al·ly** *adv.* —**im′ma·te′ri·al·ness** *n.*

im·ma·te·ri·al·ism (im′ə·tir′ē·əl·iz′əm) *n.* The doctrine that the objective world has no existence apart from perception by the consciousness; specifically, the idealism of Berkeley. —**im′ma·te′ri·al·ist** *n.*

im·ma·te·ri·al·i·ty (im′ə·tir′ē·al′ə·tē) *n.* *pl.* **·ties** **1** The state or quality of being immaterial. **2** That which has no material existence or essence.

im·ma·te·ri·al·ize (im′ə·tir′ē·əl·īz) *v.t.* **·ized, ·iz·ing** To make immaterial or incorporeal.

im·ma·ture (im′ə·choŏr′, -tyŏor′, -tŏor′) *adj.* **1** Not mature or ripe; not full-grown; undeveloped. **2** Not brought to a complete state; imperfect. **3** In physical geography, not in accordance with or thoroughly adapted to surrounding or local conditions, particularly of base level: *immature* topography. **4** *Obs.* Too early; premature. [<L *immaturus*] —**im′·ma·ture′ly** *adv.* —**im′ma·tur′i·ty, im′ma·ture′·ness** *n.*

im·meas·ur·a·ble (i·mezh′ər·ə·bəl) *adj.* Not capable of being measured; indefinitely extensive; boundless. See synonyms under INFINITE. —**im·meas′ur·a·ble·ness, im·meas′ur·a·bil′i·ty** *n.* —**im·meas′ur·a·bly** *adv.*

im·me·di·a·cy (i·mē′dē·ə·sē) *n.* **1** The state or quality of being immediate; freedom from the intervention of any intermediate person or thing. **2** In the feudal system, the condition of being next in rank to the suzerain. **3** *Philos.* **a** Independent or non–relative existence or being. **b** Consciousness or direct awareness, apart from memory or reasoning. **c** Intuitive knowledge as distinguished from that arrived at by proof or reasoning.

im·me·di·ate (i·mē′dē·it) *adj.* **1** Without delay; instant. **2** Separated by no appreciable space; nearly related; close. **3** Acting without the intervention of anything; direct: opposed to *mediate.* **4** Pertaining to a direct perception; intuitive. **5** Directly concerning; having a direct bearing. [<Med. L *immediatus*] —**im·me′di·ate·ness** *n.*

Synonyms: close, contiguous, direct, instant, intimate, next, present, proximate. *Antonyms:* distant, far, remote. See synonyms under PROXIMATE.

im·me·di·ate·ly (i·mē′dē·it·lē) *adv.* **1** In an immediate manner; without lapse of time;

instantly; at once. **2** Without the intervention of anything; directly. —*conj.* As soon as.

Synonyms (*adv.*): directly, forthwith, instanter, instantly, now, presently, straightway. *Immediately* primarily signifies without the intervention of anything as a medium, hence without the intervention of any, even the briefest, interval or lapse of time. *Directly,* which once meant with no intervening time, now means after some little while; *presently* no longer means in this very present, but before very long. Even *immediately* is sliding from its instantaneousness, so that we are fain to substitute *at once, instantly,* etc., when we would make promptness emphatic.

im·med·i·ca·ble (i·med′i·kə·bəl) *adj.* Incurable. [<L *immedicabilis* <*in-* not + *medicabilis* curable]

im·me·mo·ri·al (im′ə·môr′ē·əl, -mō′rē-) *adj.* Reaching back beyond memory; having its origin in the indefinite past. See synonyms under PRIMEVAL. [<Med. L *immemorialis*] —**im′me·mo′ri·al·ly** *adv.*

im·mense (i·mens′) *adj.* **1** Very great in degree or size; vast; huge. **2** Infinite. —*n.* The limitless void; infinity. [<F *immensus* <*in-* not + *mensus,* pp. of *metiri* measure] —**im·mense′ly** *adj.*

Synonyms (*adj.*): colossal, enormous, gigantic, huge, prodigious, stupendous, vast. See LARGE.

im·men·si·ty (i·men′sə·tē) *n.* *pl.* **·ties** **1** The state or quality of being immense; vastness. **2** Boundless space. See synonyms under MAGNITUDE. Also **im·mense′ness.** [<MF *immensité* <L *immensitas* <*immensus* IMMENSE]

im·men·sur·a·ble (i·men′shŏŏr·ə·bəl) *adj.* Immeasurable. [<MF <L *immensurabilis* <*in-* not + *mensurabilis* MENSURABLE] —**im·men′sur·a·bil′i·ty** *n.*

im·merge (i·mûrj′) *v.* **·merged, ·merg·ing** *v.t.* To immerse. —*v.i.* To plunge, as into a liquid; sink. [<L *immergere* <*in-* in + *mergere* dip] —**im·mer′gence** *n.*

im·merse (i·mûrs′) *v.t.* **·mersed, ·mers·ing** **1** To plunge or dip entirely in water or other fluid. **2** To involve deeply; engross: He *immersed* himself in study. **3** To baptize by immersion. [<L *immersus,* pp. of *immergere* dip]

Synonyms: bury, dip, douse, duck, immerge, plunge, sink, submerge. *Dip* is a native word, while *immerse* is a Latin borrowing; *dip* is accordingly the more popular and commonplace, *immerse* the more elegant and dignified expression in many cases. To speak of baptism by immersion as *dipping* now seems rude, but was entirely proper and usual in early English. Baptists now universally use the word *immerse.* To *dip* and to *immerse* alike signify to *bury* or *submerge* some object in a liquid; but *dip* implies that the object *dipped* is at once removed from the liquid. *Immerse* suggests more absolute completeness of the action; one may *dip* his sleeve or *dip* a sponge in a liquid, if he but touches the edge; if he *immerses* it, he completely *sinks* it under, and covers it with the liquid. *Submerge* implies that the object cannot readily be removed, if at all; as, a *submerged* wreck. To *plunge* is to *immerse* suddenly and violently, for which *douse* and *duck* are colloquial terms. *Dip* is used, also, unlike the other words, to denote the putting of a hollow vessel into a liquid in order to remove a portion of it; in this sense we say *dip up, dip out.* Compare synonyms for BURY[1].

im·mer·sion (i·mûr′zhən, -shən) *n.* **1** The act of immersing or the state of being immersed; specifically, baptism by submersion in water. **2** The state of being overwhelmed or deeply engaged; absorption: *immersion* in business. **3** *Astron.* The disappearance of a heavenly body, either by passing behind another or by entering into the light of the sun or the shadow of the earth. [<L *immersio, -onis*]

im·mer·sion·ism (i·mûr′zhən·iz′əm, -shən-) *n.* **1** The theological doctrine of immersion. **2** The custom of baptizing by immersion.

im·mew (i·myōo′) *v.t.* *Obs.* To coop up; imprison. [See MEW[1].]

im·mi·grant (im′ə·grənt) *n.* **1** One who or that which immigrates. **2** A foreigner who enters a country to settle there. Compare EMIGRANT. —*adj.* Immigrating.

im·mi·grate (im′ə·grāt) *v.* **·grat·ed, ·grat·ing** *v.i.* To come into a new country or region for the purpose of settling there. —*v.t.* To bring in as an immigrant or settler. See synonyms under

EMIGRATE. [<L *immigratus,* pp. of *immigrare* go into <*in-* in + *migrare* migrate] —**im′mi·gra·to′ry** (-tôr′ē, -tō′rē) *adj.*

im·mi·gra·tion (im′ə·grā′shən) *n.* **1** The act of immigrating; entrance of a settler or settlers from a foreign country. **2** The total number of aliens entering a country for permanent residence during a stated period. **3** Immigrants collectively.

im·mi·nence (im′ə·nəns) *n.* **1** The state or quality of being imminent. **2** Impending evil. Also **im′mi·nen·cy.** [<LL *imminentia*]

im·mi·nent (im′ə·nənt) *adj.* **1** About to happen; impending; said especially of danger or evil. **2** Overhanging as if about to fall. [<L *imminens, -entis* <*imminere* lean over, impend <*in-* on + *-minere* project]—**im′mi·nent·ly** *adv.*

Synonyms: impending, threatening. *Imminent,* from the Latin, with the sense of projecting over, signifies liable to happen at once, as some calamity, dangerous and close at hand. *Impending,* also from the Latin, with the sense of hanging over, is closely akin to *imminent,* but somewhat less emphatic. *Imminent* is more immediate, *impending* more remote, *threatening* more contingent. An *impending* evil is almost sure to happen at some uncertain time, near or remote; an *imminent* peril is one liable to befall very speedily; a *threatening* peril may be near or remote, but always with hope that it may be averted. *Antonyms:* chimerical, contingent, doubtful, improbable, problematical, unexpected, unlikely.

im·min·gle (i·ming′gəl) *v.t. & v.i.* **·gled, ·gling** To mix thoroughly; mingle.

im·mis·ci·ble (i·mis′ə·bəl) *adj.* Not capable of mixing, as oil and water. Also **im·mix′a·ble** (-mik′sə-). [? <L *immiscibilis* <*in-* not + *miscere* mix] —**im·mis′ci·bil′i·ty** *n.*

im·mit (i·mit′) *v.t. Obs.* To send in; inject. [<L *immittere* <*in-* in + *mittere* send] —**im·mis′sion** (i·mish′ən) *n.*

im·mit·i·ga·ble (i·mit′ə·gə·bəl) *adj.* That cannot be mitigated. [<L *immitigabilis*] —**im·mit′i·ga·bly** *adv.*

im·mix (i·miks′) *v.t.* To mingle; mix in. [<L *immixtus,* pp. of *immiscere* <*in-* in + *miscere* mix]

im·mix·ture (i·miks′chər) *n.* An intermingling; association with; commingling.

im·mo·bile (i·mō′bəl, -bēl) *adj.* **1** Unmovable; stable. **2** Not to be touched through the emotions. [<OF < L *immobilis*]

im·mo·bil·i·ty (im′ō·bil′ə·tē) *n.* The condition of being immovable or immobile; fixedness. See synonyms under APATHY.

im·mo·bi·lize (i·mō′bə·līz) *v.t.* **·lized, ·liz·ing** **1** To make immovable; fix in place, as a limb by splints or bandages. **2** To make unable to move or mobilize, as a fleet or body of troops. **3** To withdraw (specie) from circulation and hold as security for banknotes. [<F *immobiliser*] —**im·mo·bi·li·za′tion** (-lə·zā′shən, -lī·zā′-) *n.*

im·mod·er·ate (i·mod′ər·it) *adj.* Not moderate; exceeding reasonable bounds. [<L *immoderatus*] —**im·mod′er·ate·ly** *adv.* —**im·mod′er·ate·ness** *n.*

Synonyms: excessive, exorbitant, extravagant, inordinate, intemperate, unreasonable, violent. Compare IRREGULAR, VIOLENT. *Antonyms:* see synonyms for MODERATE.

im·mod·er·a·tion (i·mod′ə·rā′shən) *n.* Want of moderation; excess. Also **im·mod′er·a·cy** (-ə·sē). [<L *immoderatio, -onis*]

im·mod·est (i·mod′ist) *adj.* **1** Wanting in modesty; indelicate or indecent. **2** Impudent; bold. [<L *immodestus*] —**im·mod′est·ly** *adv.* —**im·mod′es·ty** *n.*

Synonyms: bold, brazen, coarse, forward, gross, impure, indecent, indecorous, indelicate, lewd, obscene, shameless, unchaste, wanton. Compare synonyms for IMPUDENT. *Antonyms:* see synonyms for PURE.

im·mo·late (im′ə·lāt) *v.t.* **·lat·ed, ·lat·ing** To sacrifice; especially, to kill as a sacrifice. [<L *immolatus,* pp. of *immolare* sprinkle with sacrificial meal <*in-* on + *mola* meal] **im′mo·la′tor** *n.*

im·mo·la·tion (im′ə·lā′shən) *n.* **1** The act of immolating. **2** The state of being immolated. **3** That which is immolated or sacrificed. [<L *immolatio, -onis*]

im·mor·al (i·môr′əl, i·mor′-) *adj.* **1** Violating the moral law; contrary to rectitude or public morality. **2** Habitually licentious. —**im-**

mor′al·ly *adv.*

Synonyms : bad, corrupt, criminal, depraved, dishonest, dissolute, evil, loose, profligate, sinful, unprincipled, vicious, vile, wicked, wrong. See BAD[1], CRIMINAL, SINFUL. *Antonyms* : chaste, devout, dutiful, godly, good, just, moral, pious, pure, religious, righteous, upright, virtuous, worthy.

im·mor·al·i·ty (im′ə·ral′ə·tē) *n. pl.* **·ties 1** The quality or condition of being immoral; vice; wickedness; licentiousness. **2** An act of licentiousness. **3** An immoral act. See synonyms under SIN.

im·mor·tal (i·môr′təl) *adj.* Having unending existence; deathless; enduring. —*n.* **1** A person considered worthy of immortality. **2** In mythology, a god. —**the Immortals 1** The members of the French Academy, forty in number: also called **the Forty Immortals. 2** The royal guard of ancient Persia; hence, any band or group that has conducted itself with marked gallantry in the face of extraordinary perils (especially of war). [< L *immortalis*] — **im·mor′tal·ly** *adv.*

Synonyms (*adj.*): deathless, endless, eternal, everlasting, imperishable, incorruptible, indestructible, indissoluble, never-dying, never-fading, never-failing, sempiternal, undying, unfading, unfailing. See ETERNAL. *Antonyms* : dying, ephemeral, fading, failing, fleeting, mortal, perishable, perishing, transient, transitory.

im·mor·tal·i·ty (im′ôr·tal′ə·tē) *n.* **1** Exemption from death or oblivion; eternal life. **2** Eternal fame. [< OF *immortalité* < L *immortalitas*]

im·mor·tal·ize (i·môr′təl·īz) *v.t.* **·ized, ·iz·ing** To make immortal; give perpetual fame or life to.

im·mo·tile (i·mō′til) *adj.* Not motile; stationary.

im·mov·a·ble (i·mōō′və·bəl) *adj.* **1** That cannot be moved or stirred from its place; fixed: an *immovable* foundation. **2** Steadfast; unchangeable: an *immovable* purpose. **3** Not having the feelings easily roused; impassive. **4** *Law* Not liable to be removed; permanent in place: *immovable* property. See synonyms under FIRM, INFLEXIBLE, OBSTINATE. —*n.* **1** That which cannot be moved. **2** *Law* Any piece of land, together with trees, buildings, etc., strictly appertaining to it, either naturally or otherwise, so as not to be movable: opposed to *movable*. —**im·mov′a·bil′i·ty, im·mov′a·ble·ness** *n.* —**im·mov′a·bly** *adv.*

im·mune (i·myōōn′) *adj.* **1** Exempt from taxation. **2** *Med.* Protected from disease by inoculation. —*n.* A person not susceptible to some particular disease. [< F < L *immunis*]

im·mu·ni·ty (i·myōō′nə·tē) *n. pl.* **·ties 1** Freedom or exemption, as from a penalty, burden, duty, or evil, such as the exemption of ecclesiastical persons and places from duties and burdens thought unbecoming their sacred character: followed by *from*. **2** *Med.* Exemption from contagion or infection or from liability to suffer from epidemic or endemic disease. It may be *active* through the formation of specific antibodies in the organism, or *passive* through the effect of a serum injected from another organism. See synonyms under RIGHT. [< OF *immunité* < L *immunitas* < *immunis* exempt < *in-* not < *munis* serviceable < *munus* service, duty]

im·mu·nize (im′yə·nīz) *v.t.* **·nized, ·niz·ing** To make immune; protect, as from infection. — **im·mu·ni·za·tion** (im′yə·nə·zā′shən, -nī·zā′-) *n.*

im·mu·no·ge·net·ics (i·myōō′nō·jə·net′iks) *n.* The study of immunity to disease as conditioned by and associated with the transmission of specific genetic factors.

im·mu·nol·o·gy (im′yə·nol′ə·jē) *n.* The science which treats of the phenomena and techniques of immunity from disease. [< IMMUNO- + -LOGY] —**im·mu·no·log·i·cal** (i·myōō′nə·loj′i·kəl) *adj.*

im·mu·no·sup·pres·sive (i·myōō′nō·sə·pres′iv) *adj.* Preventing the action of an antibody in order to permit an organism to accept foreign material, such as an organ transplant.

im·mure (i·myōōr′) *v.t.* **·mured, ·mur·ing** To shut up within or as within walls; imprison. [< Med. L *immurare* < *in-* in + LL *murare* wall < *murus* wall] —**im·mure′ment** *n.*

im·mu·ta·bil·i·ty (i·myōō′tə·bil′ə·tē) *n.* The state or quality of being immutable or unchangeable. Also **im·mu′ta·ble·ness.** [< L *immutabilitas, -tatis*]

im·mu·ta·ble (i·myōō′tə·bəl) *adj.* Not mutable; unchangeable. See synonyms under FIRM, PERMANENT. [< L *immutabilis*] —**im·mu′ta·bly** *adv.*

imp (imp) *n.* **1** An evil spirit; a little devil; a child of the devil. **2** A mischievous or malicious person: especially applied to a child. **3** *Obs.* Progeny; offspring. —*v.t.* **1** To mend or repair by something inserted or added. **2** To furnish with wings. **3** In falconry, to repair or improve powers of flight by grafting feathers to (a falcon, a falcon's wing, tail, etc.); to graft (a feather or feathers). **4** *Obs.* To graft; implant [OE *impa* a graft < *impian* ingraft < LL *impotus* a shoot < Gk. *emphytos* < *emphyein* implant < *en-* in + *phyein* produce]

im·pact (im·pakt′) *v.t.* To press or drive firmly together; pack; wedge. —*n.* (im′pakt) **1** The act of striking; collision. **2** The forcible momentary contact of a moving body with another either moving or at rest: the *impact* of a bullet against a target. **3** A continuing, powerful influence: the *impact* of science on culture. See synonyms under COLLISION. [< L *impactus,* pp. of *impingere.* See IMPINGE]

im·pact·ed (im·pak′tid) *adj.* **1** Packed firmly. **2** *Dent.* Denoting a tooth wedged between the jawbone and another tooth in such a way as to prevent its emergence through the gums.

im·pac·tion (im·pak′shən) *n.* **1** An overloading of an organ, as of the intestine. **2** A wedging of one part into another. **3** *Dent.* An impacted tooth. [< L *impactio, -onis* a striking]

im·pair (im·pâr′) *v.t.* To diminish in quality, strength, or value; injure. [< OF *empeirer* < LL *in-* thoroughly + *pejorare* make worse < L *pejor* worse]

Synonyms : debase, decrease, deteriorate, diminish, enervate, enfeeble, lessen, reduce, weaken. See HURT, WEAKEN, WEAR. *Antonyms* : see synonyms for AMEND, INCREASE.

im·pair·ment (im·pâr′mənt) *n.* **1** The act of impairing. **2** The state of being impaired. **3** Deterioration; injury. [< OF *empeirement*]

im·pale (im·pāl′) *v.t.* **·paled, ·pal·ing 1** To fix upon a pale or sharp stake. **2** To torture or put to death by thrusting a sharp stake through the body. **3** To make helpless as if by fixing upon a stake; transfix: to *impale* someone with a glance. **4** *Her.* To place (two coats of arms) side by side on an escutcheon. Also spelled *empale.* [< OF *empaler* < LL *impalare* < *in-* in + *palus* a stake]

im·pale·ment (im·pāl′mənt) *n.* **1** The act of impaling. **2** That which impales, or the space impaled; an enclosure. **3** The displaying of two coats of arms side by side on one escutcheon. Also spelled *empalement.*

im·pal·pa·ble (im·pal′pə·bəl) *adj.* **1** Imperceptible to the touch; specifically, ground so fine that no grit can be felt. **2** Intangible unreal. **3** Immaterial: incorporeal. [< Med. L *impalpabilis*] —**im·pal′pa·bil′i·ty** *n.* —**im·pal′pa·bly** *adv.*

im·pa·na·tion (im′pə·nā′shən) *n.* The doctrine that the body and blood of Christ are united into one substance with the consecrated bread and wine: distinguished from *transubstantiation.* [< Med. L *impanatus,* pp. of *impanare* embody in bread < *in-* in + *panis* bread] — **im·pa·nate** (im·pā′nit, -nāt), **im·pa·nat·ed** (im·pā′nā·tid) *adj.*

im·par (im·pär′) *adj.* Odd or unequal; without a corresponding part; not paired. [< L < *in-* not + *par* equal]

im·par·a·dise (im·par′ə·dīs) *v.t.* **·dised, ·dis·ing** To place in or as in paradise; make supremely happy.

im·par·i·ty (im·par′ə·tē) *n. pl.* **·ties** Lack of correspondence; inequality; diversity. [< LL *imparitas, -tatis*]

im·part (im·pärt′) *v.t.* **1** To make known; tell; communicate. **2** To give a portion of; give. —*v.i.* **3** To give a part; share. See synonyms under GIVE, INFORM, PUBLISH. [< OF *empartir* < L *impartire* < *in-* on + *partire* share < *pars, partis* part, share] —**im·part′er** *n.*

im·par·ta·tion (im′pär·tā′shən) *n.* The act of imparting, as knowledge. Also **im·part′ment.**

im·par·tial (im·pär′shəl) *adj.* Not partial; unbiased; just. See synonyms under CANDID,

JUST. —**im·par′tial·ly** *adv.*

im·par·ti·al·i·ty (im′pär·shē·al′ə·tē, im·pär′-) *n.* The quality or character of being impartial; fairness. Also **im·par′tial·ness.**

im·part·i·ble[1] (im·pär′tə·bəl) *adj.* Not subject to partition; not dividable. [< LL *impartibilis*] —**im·part′i·bil′i·ty** *n.* —**im·part′i·bly** *adv.*

im·part·i·ble[2] (im·pär′tə·bəl) *adj. Obs.* Capable of being imparted, shared, or made known.

im·pass·a·ble (im·pas′ə·bəl, -päs′-) *adj.* Not passable. See synonyms under IMPENETRABLE. —**im·pass′a·bil′i·ty, im·pass′a·ble·ness** *n.* —**im·pass′a·bly** *adv.*

im·passe (im′pas, im·pas′; *Fr.* aṅ·päs′) *n.* **1** A blind alley, or passage open only at one end; cul-de-sac. **2** Any serious and insurmountable obstacle or problem. [< F]

im·pas·si·bil·i·ty (im·pas′ə·bil′ə·tē) *n.* **1** Essential incapacity for suffering. **2** The state of being unfeeling or apathetic. Also **im·pas′si·ble·ness.** [< OF *impassibilité* < L *impassibilitas* < *impassibilis* impassible]

im·pas·si·ble (im·pas′ə·bəl) *adj.* **1** Incapable of suffering or sympathizing. **2** Not affected by feeling; apathetic. [< OF *impassible* < Med. L *impassibilis* < *in-* not + *passibilis.* See PASSIBLE.] —**im·pas′si·bly** *adv.*

im·pas·sion (im·pash′ən) *v.t.* To affect with passion; inflame. [< Ital. *impassionare*]

im·pas·sion·ate (im·pash′ən·it) *adj.* Without passion: dispassionate.

im·pas·sive (im·pas′iv) *adj.* **1** Insensible to or unaffected by suffering or pain; unimpressionable. **2** Unmoved by or not exhibiting feeling; apathetic. **3** Not susceptible of injury. **4** Lifeless; insensible; also, unconscious. —**im·pas′sive·ly** *adv.* —**im·pas′sive·ness, im·pas·siv·i·ty** (im′pa·siv′ə·tē) *n.*

im·pa·tience (im·pā′shəns) *n.* **1** Lack of patience; unwillingness to brook delay. **2** Intolerance of opposition or control. [< OF *impacience* < L *impatientia*]

Synonyms : fretfulness, irritation, peevishness, pettishness, petulance, vexation. These words express the slighter forms of anger. *Irritation, petulance,* and *vexation* are temporary and for immediate cause. *Fretfulness, pettishness,* and *peevishness* are chronic states finding in any petty matter an occasion for their exercise. Compare ACRIMONY, ANGER. *Antonyms*: amiability, benignity, forbearance, gentleness, leniency, lenity, long-suffering, mildness, patience, peace, peaceableness, peacefulness, self-control, self-restraint.

im·pa·tient (im·pā′shənt) *adj.* **1** Not possessed of or not exercising patience; intolerant; disturbed by or complaining about pain, delay, strain, etc. **2** Exhibiting or expressing impatience. See synonyms under EAGER, FRETFUL, RESTIVE. [< OF *impacient* < L *impatiens, -entis* < *in-* not + *patiens.* See PATIENT.] — **im·pa′tient·ly** *adv.*

im·pav·id (im·pav′id) *adj.* Without fear; intrepid; bold. [< L *impavidus* < *in-* not + *pavidus* timid] —**im·pa·vid·i·ty** (im′pə·vid′ə·tē) *n.* —**im·pav′id·ly** *adv.*

im·peach (im·pēch′) *v.t.* **1** To bring discredit upon; challenge: to *impeach* one's honesty. **2** To charge with crime or misdemeanor in office; arraign (a public official) before a competent tribunal on such a charge. See synonyms under ARRAIGN. [< OF *empescher* hinder < LL *impedicare* entangle < *in-* in + *pedica* fetter < *pes, pedis* foot] —**im·peach′er** *n.*

im·peach·a·ble (im·pē′chə·bəl) *adj.* Liable to be impeached; censurable. —**im·peach′a·bil′i·ty** *n.*

im·peach·ment (im·pēch′mənt) *n.* **1** A discrediting. **2** The act of impeaching; especially the arraignment of a high civil officer. [< OF *empeschement* obstruction]

im·pec·ca·ble (im·pek′ə·bəl) *adj.* **1** Not liable to commit sin or wrong. **2** Faultless. —*n.* An impeccable person. [< LL *impeccabilis* < *in-* not + *peccare* sin] —**im·pec′ca·bil′i·ty** *n.* —**im·pec′ca·bly** *adv.*

im·pec·cant (im·pek′ənt) *adj.* Free from sin or error; blameless. —**im·pec′cance, im·pec′can·cy** *n.*

im·pe·cu·ni·ous (im′pə·kyōō′nē·əs) *adj.* Having no money; habitually poor. [< F *impécunieux*] —**im·pe·cu·ni·os·i·ty** (-kyōō′nē·os′ə·tē) *n.* —**im′pe·cu′ni·ous·ly** *adv.* —**im′pe·cu′ni·ous·ness** *n.*

impede (im·pēd') v.t. **·ped·ed, ·ped·ing** To retard or hinder in progress or action; obstruct. See synonyms under EMBARRASS, HINDER¹, LIMIT, OBSTRUCT. [<L impedire, lit., shackle the feet < in- in + pes, pedis foot] — **im·ped'er** n.
im·pe·di·ent (im·pē'dē·ənt) adj. That impedes. — n. That which impedes. [<L impediens, -ientis, ppr. of impedire. See IMPEDE.]
im·ped·i·ment (im·ped'ə·mənt) n. **1** That which hinders or impedes; an obstruction. **2** An organic hindrance to easy speech; a stammer. **3** Law Anything that prevents the contraction of a valid marriage. — **absolute impediment** Law A condition which makes it impossible for a person to contract a valid marriage. — **prohibitive impediment** Law A condition under which persons who have contracted marriage are subject to punishment for having done so. — **relative impediment** Law A state of facts which bars only people of a certain degree of consanguinity from contracting marriage with each other, as a brother with a sister. See also DIRIMENT IMPEDIMENT OF MARRIAGE. [<L impedimentum]
Synonyms: bar, barrier, clog, difficulty, encumbrance, hindrance, obstacle, obstruction. *Difficulty* makes an undertaking not easy. That which rests upon one as a burden is an *encumbrance.* A *hindrance* (kindred with *hind, behind*) is anything that makes one come behind or short of his purpose. An *impediment* (literally, that which checks the foot) may be either what one finds in his way or what he carries with him; *impedimenta* was the Latin name for the baggage of a soldier or of an army. The tendency is to view an *impediment* as something constant or, at least for a time, continuous; as, an *impediment* in one's speech. A *difficulty* or a *hindrance* may be either within one or without; a speaker may find *difficulty* in expressing himself, or *difficulty* in holding the attention of restless children. An *encumbrance* is always what one carries with him; an *obstacle* or an *obstruction* is always without. To an infantryman the steepness of a mountain path is a *difficulty,* loose stones are *impediments,* a fence is an *obstruction,* a cliff or a boulder across the way is an *obstacle,* a bedroll is an *encumbrance.* *Antonyms:* advantage, aid, assistance, benefit, help, relief, succor.
im·ped·i·tive (im·ped'ə·tiv) adj. Causing hindrance; obstructive.
im·pel (im·pel') v.t. **·pelled, ·pel·ling 1** To drive or push (something) forward or onward. **2** To urge or force (someone) to an action, course, etc.; incite; compel. See synonyms under ACTUATE, DRIVE, ENCOURAGE, INFLUENCE, PERSUADE, PUSH, SEND¹, SPUR. [<L impellere < in- on + pellere drive]
im·pel·lent (im·pel'ənt) adj. Tending to impel. — n. An impelling person, thing, or force. [<L impellens, -entis, ppr. of impellere. See IMPEL.]
im·pend (im·pend') v.i. **1** To be imminent; threaten, as something evil or destructive. **2** To be suspended; hang: with *over.* [<L impendere overhang < in- on + pendere hang] — **im·pen'dence, im·pen'den·cy** n.
im·pen·dent (im·pen'dənt) adj. Imminent; threatening. [<L impendens, -entis, ppr. of impendere. See IMPEND.]
im·pend·ing (im·pen'ding) adj. Hanging over; threatening; about to happen. See synonyms under IMMINENT.
im·pen·e·tra·bil·i·ty (im·pen'ə·trə·bil'ə·tē) n. **1** The quality of being impenetrable. **2** Physics The property of matter which prevents two bodies from occupying the same space at the same time. Also **im·pen'e·tra·ble·ness.**
im·pen·e·tra·ble (im·pen'ə·trə·bəl) adj. **1** That cannot be penetrated or pierced: said of material things. **2** That cannot be penetrated by the eye or mind; abstruse; dense: an *impenetrable* darkness or mystery. **3** Not to be affected by moral considerations: an *impenetrable* conscience. **4** Possessing the property of impenetrability. [<OF impenetrable <L impenetrabilis] — **im·pen'e·tra·bly** adv.
Synonyms: close, dense, hard, impassable, impermeable, impervious, solid. See HARD. *Antonyms:* fluid, loose, open, penetrable, pervious, soft, yielding.
im·pen·i·tence (im·pen'ə·təns) n. Want of penitence or repentance; hardness of heart. Also

im·pen'i·ten·cy. [<LL impaenitentia]
im·pen·i·tent (im·pen'ə·tənt) adj. Not penitent; hardened; obdurate. [<LL impaenitens, -entis < in- not + paenitens. See PENITENT.] — **im·pen'i·tent·ly** adv. — **im·pen'i·tent·ness** n.
im·per·a·tive (im·per'ə·tiv) adj. **1** Expressive of or containing positive, as distinguished from advisory or discretionary, command; authoritative; peremptory. **2** Gram. Designating that mood of the verb which expresses command, entreaty, or exhortation. **3** Not to be evaded or avoided; obligatory. — n. **1** That which is imperative. **2** Gram. The mood of the verb which expresses command; also, a verb in this mood. [<L imperativus <imperare command] — **im·per'a·tive·ly** adv. — **im·per'a·tive·ness** n.
im·per·cep·ti·ble (im'pər·sep'tə·bəl) adj. That cannot be perceived, as by reason of smallness, extreme tenuity or delicacy, distance or gradual progress; inappreciable by the mind or sense; undiscernible: an *imperceptible* change. [<F <L imperceptibilis] — **im'per·cep'ti·ble·ness, im'per·cep'ti·bil'i·ty** n. — **im'·per·cep'ti·bly** adv.
im·per·cep·tive (im'pər·sep'tiv) adj. Not perceptive; deficient in perception. — **im·per·cep·tiv·i·ty** (im'pər·sep·tiv'ə·tē), **im'per·cep'tive·ness** n.
im·per·fect (im·pûr'fikt) adj. **1** Not perfect; incomplete; defective. **2** Gram. Pertaining to a tense of the verb that indicates past action as uncompleted, continuous, or synchronous with some other action. **3** Law Without binding force; not enforceable by law. **4** Music Diminished: an *imperfect* interval. **5** Bot. Lacking certain parts normally present; diclinous. See synonyms under BAD¹. — n. Gram. The imperfect tense, or a verb or verbal form expressing this tense. [<OF imparfait <L imperfectus; refashioned after L] — **im·per'fect·ly** adv. — **im·per'fect·ness** n.
im·per·fec·tion (im'pər·fek'shən) n. **1** Lack of perfection: also **im·per'fect·ness. 2** A defect. See synonyms under BLEMISH, FOIBLE. [<OF imperfection <LL imperfectio, -onis <L imperfectus incomplete]
im·per·fec·tive (im'pər·fek'tiv) Gram. adj. Of or pertaining to an aspect of the verb which expresses continuing action or repetition; durative. — n. The imperfective aspect, or a verb in this aspect. — **im'per·fec'tive·ly** adv.
im·per·fo·ra·ble (im·pûr'fər·ə·bəl) adj. That cannot be perforated.
im·per·fo·rate (im·pûr'fər·it) adj. **1** Without perforations; not perforated. **2** Not separated by a line of perforations, as stamps. Also **im·per'fo·rat'ed** (-rā'tid). — n. An unperforated stamp.
im·per·fo·ra·tion (im·pûr'fə·rā'shən) n. The state of being imperforate.
im·pe·ri·al (im·pir'ē·əl) adj. **1** Of or pertaining to an empire, or to an emperor or an empress. **2** Designating the legal weights and measures of the United Kingdom. **3** Of or pertaining to a state as supreme over colonies or the like. **4** Possessing commanding power or dignity; predominant. **5** Superior in size or quality. — n. **1** A pointed tuft of hair on the chin: from the emperor Napoleon III, who wore such a beard. **2** Anything of more than usual size of the class to which it belongs, or of superior excellence. **3** A size of paper: in the United States, 23 in. × 31 in.; in Great Britain, 22 in. × 30 in. **4** A size of slate 24 inches wide and from 12 to 30 inches long. **5** A former Russian gold coin worth 15 rubles. **6** The top of a carriage, as of a diligence. [<OF <L imperialis <imperium rule] — **im·pe'ri·al·ly** adv.
Synonyms (adj.): exalted, grand, kingly, magnificent, majestic, noble, queenly, regal, royal, sovereign, supreme. *Antonyms:* base, beggarly, cowering, cringing, ignoble, inferior, mean, paltry, poor, servile, slavish.
im·pe·ri·al·ism (im·pir'ē·əl·iz'əm) n. **1** A policy that aims at creating, maintaining, or extending an empire or superstate, comprising many nations and areas, all controlled by a central government. **2** A governmental policy of developing foreign trade and exploiting the raw materials of backward countries through the use of political and military pressures, without necessarily assuming direct political control of the nations affected. **3** A system of imperial government. **4** Imperial

im·pe·ri·al·ist (im·pir'ē·əl·ist) n. **1** One who advocates or upholds imperialism. **2** A partisan or supporter of an emperor. — adj. Imperialistic.
im·per·il (im·per'il) v.t. **·iled** or **·illed, ·il·ing** or **·il·ling** To place in peril; endanger.
im·pe·ri·ous (im·pir'ē·əs) adj. **1** Assuming and determined to command; domineering; arrogant. **2** Urgent; imperative. **3** Obs. Imperial; lordly. [<L imperiosus] — **im·pe'ri·ous·ly** adv. — **im·pe'ri·ous·ness** n.
Synonyms: arbitrary, arrogant, authoritative, commanding, controlling, despotic, dictatorial, dogmatic, domineering, exacting, haughty, imperative, irresistible, lordly, overbearing. An *imperious* demand or requirement may have in it nothing offensive; it is simply one that resolutely insists upon compliance, and will not brook refusal; an *arrogant* demand is offensive by its tone of superiority, an *arbitrary* demand by its unreasonableness; an *imperious* disposition is liable to become *arbitrary* and *arrogant.* A person of an independent spirit is inclined to resent an *imperious* manner in anyone, especially in one whose superiority or authority is not clearly recognized. *Commanding* is always used in a good sense; as, a *commanding* appearance; a *commanding* eminence. See ARBITRARY, DOGMATIC. *Antonyms:* complaisant, compliant, docile, ductile, gentle, humble, lenient, lowly, meek, mild, submissive.
im·per·ish·a·ble (im·per'ish·ə·bəl) adj. Not perishable or subject to decay. See synonyms under ETERNAL, IMMORTAL. — **im·per'ish·a·bil'i·ty, im·per'ish·a·ble·ness** n. — **im·per'ish·a·bly** adv.
im·pe·ri·um (im·pir'ē·əm) n. pl. **·ri·a** (-ē·ə) **1** Command not subject to definition or limitation of function; absolute command. **2** Law The right to command, which includes authority to use the force of the state to enforce its laws. [<L. See EMPIRE.]
im·per·ma·nence (im·pûr'mə·nəns) n. The state or quality of being impermanent; also, something impermanent. Also **im·per'ma·nen·cy.**
im·per·ma·nent (im·pûr'mə·nənt) adj. Not permanent.
im·per·me·a·ble (im·pûr'mē·ə·bəl) adj. **1** Not permeable. **2** Impervious to moisture. See synonyms under IMPENETRABLE. [<LL impermeabilis] — **im·per'me·a·bil'i·ty** n. — **im·per'me·a·bly** adv.
im·per·son·al (im·pûr'sən·əl) adj. **1** Not having personality: an *impersonal* deity. **2** Not relating to a particular person or thing: an *impersonal* statement. **3** Gram. Having or containing an indeterminate subject: an *impersonal* verb. In English the subject of an impersonal verb is usually the pronoun *it,* as *it thunders:* often in apposition with a following clause or phrase, as *it is fun to swim.* — n. That which lacks personality; especially, an impersonal verb. [<LL impersonalis] — **im·per'son·al'i·ty** (-al'ə·tē) n. — **im·per'son·al·ly** adv.
im·per·son·al·ize (im·pûr'sən·əl·īz') v.t. **·ized, ·iz·ing** To render impersonal.
im·per·son·ate (im·pûr'sən·āt) v.t. **·at·ed, ·at·ing 1** To adopt or mimic the appearance, mannerisms, etc., of. **2** To act or play the part of. **3** To represent in human form; personify: He *impersonates* the quality of virtue. See synonyms under IMITATE. — adj. (-it) Embodied in a person; having personality.
im·per·son·a·tion (im·pûr'sən·ā'shən) n. **1** The act of impersonating. **2** Personification.
im·per·son·a·tor (im·pûr'sən·ā'tər) n. One who impersonates or plays a character part.
im·per·ti·nence (im·pûr'tə·nəns) n. **1** The state, quality, or instance of being impertinent. **2** Improper intrusion: rudeness. **3** Irrelevancy; inappropriateness. Also **im·per'ti·nen·cy.**
im·per·ti·nent (im·pûr'tə·nənt) adj. **1** Rude; impudent. **2** Irrelevant; not to the point. **3** Not suitable or fitting. See synonyms under IMPUDENT, MEDDLESOME. [<F <L impertinens, -entis < in- not + pertinens. See PERTINENT.] — **im·per'ti·nent·ly** adv.
im·per·turb·a·ble (im'pər·tûr'bə·bəl) adj. Incapable of being agitated. See synonyms under CALM. [<LL imperturbabilis] — **im'per·turb'a·bil'i·ty, im'per·turb'a·ble·ness** n. — **im'·per·turb'a·bly** adv.
im·per·tur·ba·tion (im·pûr'tər·bā'shən) n. Free-

dom from agitation; calmness.

im·per·turbed (im'pər·tûrbd') *adj.* Not perturbed or agitated.

im·per·vi·ous (im·pûr'vē·əs) *adj.* 1 Permitting no passage into or through; impenetrable; impermeable. 2 Not permeable by fluids, light rays, etc. 3 Not capable of being influenced by; deaf to: a mind *impervious* to reason. See synonyms under IMPENETRABLE. [<L *impervius* < *in-* not + *per-* through + *via* way, road] — **im·per'vi·ous·ly** *adv.* — **im·per'vi·ous·ness** *n.*

im·pe·trate (im'pə·trāt) *v.t.* ·trat·ed, ·trat·ing 1 To obtain by request or entreaty. 2 *Rare* To importune; beseech. [<L *impetratus*, pp. of *impetrare* obtain by request < *in-* to + *patrare* bring to pass] — **im'pe·tra'tion** *n.* — **im'pe·tra'tor** *n.*

im·pe·tra·tive (im'pə·trā'tiv) *adj.* Using prayer or entreaty, or tending to obtain by entreaty. [<L *impetrativus*]

im·pet·u·ous (im·pech'ōō·əs) *adj.* 1 Characterized by impetus, energy, or violent force: *impetuous* haste. 2 Characterized by spontaneous or vehement impulse of action or emotion: *impetuous* affection. [<MF *impétueux* <L *impetuosus*] — **im·pet'u·os'i·ty** (-os'ə·tē) *n.* — **im·pet'u·ous·ly** *adv.* — **im·pet'u·ous·ness** *n.*

Synonyms: excitable, fiery, hasty, headlong, impulsive, passionate, precipitate, quick, rash, sudden, swift. See EAGER, FIERCE, VIOLENT. *Antonyms:* calm, careful, cautious, circumspect, considerate, deliberate, lazy, leisurely, slow, sluggish, steady.

im·pe·tus (im'pə·təs) *n.* 1 The energy with which anything moves or is driven. 2 Momentum. 3 Any impulse or incentive. See synonyms under IMPULSE. [<L < *impetere* rush upon < *in-* upon + *petere* seek]

im·pi·e·ty (im·pī'ə·tē) *n. pl.* ·ties 1 Ungodliness; irreverence. 2 An impious act. 3 Want of natural dutifulness toward parents. [<OF *impieté* <L *impietas, -tatis*]

imp·ing (im'ping) *n.* The process of grafting; a graft, as of feathers on a hawk's wing. [OE *impian* graft. See IMP.]

im·pinge (im·pinj') *v.i.* ·pinged, ·ping·ing 1 To come into contact; strike; collide, especially sharply: with *on, upon,* or *against.* 2 To encroach; infringe: with *on* or *upon.* [<L *impingere* < *in-* against + *pangere* strike] — **im·pinge'ment** *n.* — **im·ping'er** *n.*

im·pi·ous (im'pē·əs) *adj.* 1 Destitute of reverence for the divine character or will; ungodly; wicked. 2 Characterized by irreverence; blasphemous. 3 Unfilial; lacking reverence, especially to one's parents. See synonyms under PROFANE. [<L *impius* < *in-* not + *pius* reverent] — **im'pi·ous·ly** *adv.* — **im'pi·ous·ness** *n.*

imp·ish (im'pish) *adj.* Implike. — **imp'ish·ly** *adv.* — **imp·ish·ness** *n.*

im·pla·ca·ble (im·plā'kə·bəl, -plak'ə-) *adj.* That cannot be placated; inexorable. [<F <L *implacabilis* < *in-* not + *placare* please] — **im·pla'ca·bil'i·ty, im·pla'ca·ble·ness** *n.* — **im·pla'ca·bly** *adv.*

Synonyms: cruel, inexorable, irreconcilable, merciless, pitiless, relentless, severe, unappeasable, unforgiving, unrelenting. *Antonyms:* forgiving, gentle, mild, placable, tender, yielding.

im·plant (im·plant', -plänt') *v.t.* 1 To insert or graft, as living tissue. 2 To inculcate or instil, as principles. 3 To plant, as seeds. — *n.* (im'plant', -plänt') *Med.* 1 A tissue implanted in the body. 2 A small tube containing radon or other radioactive material, embedded in tissue for therapeutic or remedial purposes. [<F *implanter*] — **im·plant'er** *n.*

im·plau·si·ble (im·plô'zə·bəl) *adj.* Not plausible. — **im·plau'si·bly** *adv.*

im·plead (im·plēd') *v.t. Law* 1 To sue in a court of justice. 2 To accuse; arraign. 3 To plead, as a cause. — *v.i.* 4 To bring a suit at law. [<AF *enpleder,* OF *empleidier*] — **im·plead'a·ble** *adj.*

im·ple·ment (im'plə·mənt) *n.* 1 A thing used in work, especially in manual work; a utensil; tool. 2 Originally, that which supplies a want; any means or agent for the accomplishment of a purpose. See synonyms under TOOL. — *v.t.* (-ment) 1 To carry into effect; fulfil;

accomplish. 2 To provide what is needed for; supplement. 3 To furnish with implements. [<L *implementum* a filling up < *implere* fill up < *in-* in + *plere* fill] — **im'ple·men'tal** *adj.*

im·ple·men·ta·tion (im'plə·men·tā'shən) *n.* A putting into effect, fulfilment, or carrying through, as of ideas, a program, etc.

im·ple·tion (im·plē'shən) *n.* The act of filling, or the state of being full; also, that which fills. [<LL *impletio, -onis* < *implere.* See IMPLEMENT.]

im·pli·cate (im'plə·kāt) *v.t.* ·cat·ed, ·cat·ing 1 To show to be involved or concerned, as in a plot or crime. 2 To imply. 3 To fold or twist together; entangle; intertwine. See synonyms under INVOLVE. [<L *implicatus,* pp. of *implicare* involve < *in-* in + *plicare* fold]

im·pli·ca·tion (im'plə·kā'shən) *n.* 1 The act of implying; something implied; especially, something that leads to a deduction. 2 An entanglement. — **im'pli·ca'tion·al** *adj.*

im·plic·it (im·plis'it) *adj.* 1 Fairly to be understood, but not specifically stated; implied. 2 Arising from thorough confidence in another; unquestioning: *implicit* trust. 3 Virtually contained in; essential, though not apparent; potential: The man is *implicit* in the child. 4 *Obs.* Infolded; entangled. [<F *implicite* <L *implicitus,* later form of *implicatus,* pp. of *implicare* involve. See IMPLICATE.] — **im·plic'it·ly** *adv.* — **im·plic'it·ness** *n.*

Synonyms: absolute, blind, complete, firm, full, perfect, steadfast, submissive, undoubting, unhesitating, unquestioning, unreserved, unshaken. *Implicit* primarily signifies "implied." *Implicit* faith assumes all reasons for belief or action to be "implied" in the fact that a statement, for instance, comes from some trusted source, as the Scriptures or the church; *implicit* obedience assumes that all reasons for action are "implied" in the mere command given by adequate authority. As contrasted with *explicit, implicit* belief is given to an *explicit* statement, *implicit* obedience rendered to an *explicit* command. Compare EXPLICIT; see, also, TACIT.

im·plied (im·plīd') *adj.* Contained or included, but not directly stated. See synonyms under TACIT. — **im·pli·ed·ly** (im·plī'id·lē) *adv.*

im·plode (im·plōd') *v.t.* & *v.i.* ·plod·ed, ·plod·ing 1 To burst inward. 2 *Phonet.* To pronounce by implosion. [<IM- + (EX)PLODE]

im·plore (im·plôr', -plōr') *v.* ·plored, ·plor·ing *v.t.* 1 To call upon in supplication; beseech; entreat. 2 To beg for urgently; pray for. — *v.i.* 3 To make urgent supplication. See synonyms under ASK, PLEAD, PRAY. [<L *implorare* < *in-* thoroughly + *plorare* cry out]

im·plo·sion (im·plō'zhən) *n.* 1 A bursting inward; sudden collapse: opposed to *explosion.* 2 *Phonet.* The initial, sudden blockage of the breath stream in the production of a stop consonant: opposed to *plosion.* [<IM-PLODE, on analogy with *explosion*] — **im·plo'sive** (-siv) *adj.*

im·ply (im·plī') *v.t.* ·plied, ·ply·ing 1 To involve necessarily as a circumstance, condition, effect, etc.: An action *implies* an agent. 2 To indicate (a meaning not expressed); hint at; intimate. 3 *Obs.* To entangle; infold. See synonyms under ALLUDE, IMPORT, INVOLVE. [<OF *emplier* <L *implicare* involve < *in-* in + *plicare* fold. Doublet of EMPLOY.]

im·pol·i·cy (im·pol'ə·sē) *n.* Unsuitableness to the end proposed; inexpediency. [<IMPOLITIC, on analogy with *policy*]

im·po·lite (im'pə·līt') *adj.* Lacking in politeness; rude. See synonyms under BLUFF. [<L *impolitus* < *in-* not + *politus.* See POLITE.] — **im'po·lite'ly** *adv.* — **im'po·lite'ness** *n.*

im·pol·i·tic (im·pol'ə·tik) *adj.* 1 Pursuing unwise measures. 2 Adapted to injure the interests involved; inexpedient; injudicious. See synonyms under IMPRUDENT. Also **im·po·lit·i·cal** (im'pə·lit'i·kəl). — **im·pol'i·tic·ly, im'po·lit'i·cal·ly** *adv.*

im·pon·der·a·ble (im·pon'dər·ə·bəl) *adj.* 1 Without weight. 2 Impossible of reckoning. — *n.* A factor in a situation which cannot be definitely foreseen. — **im·pon'der·a·bil'i·ty, im·pon'der·a·ble·ness** *n.* — **im·pon'der·a·bly** *adv.*

im·port (im·pôrt', -pōrt', im'pôrt, -pōrt) *v.t.* 1 To bring (goods) into one country from a

foreign country in commerce: opposed to *export.* 2 To bring in; introduce: to *import* acrimony into a debate. 3 To mean; signify: His expression *imports* no good for me. 4 To be of importance or significance to; concern. — *v.i.* 5 To be of importance or significance; matter: The argument does not *import.* — *n.* (im'pôrt, -pōrt) 1 That which is implied; meaning; significance. 2 That which is brought from one country into another. 3 Importance. See synonyms under WEIGHT. [<F *importer* <L *importare* bring in < *in-* in + *portare* carry; prob. infl. in meaning by L *oportet* it is necessary] — **im·port'a·ble** *adj.*

Synonyms (verb): betoken, denote, imply, mean, purport, signify, suggest. See INTEREST.

im·por·tance (im·pôr'təns) *n.* 1 The quality of being important or momentous. 2 Weight or consequence, as in public estimation or in self-esteem. 3 Consequential manner; pretentiousness. 4 *Obs.* Significance; meaning; also, urgency. Also *Obs.* **im·por'tan·cy.** [<F <Med. L *importantia*]

im·por·tant (im·pôr'tənt) *adj.* 1 Of great import, consequence, prominence, or value. 2 Mattering greatly: with *to:* evidence *important* to the case. 3 Pompous; pretentious. 4 *Obs.* Importunate; urgent. [<F <L *importans, -antis,* ppr. of *importare.* See IMPORT.] — **im·por'tant·ly** *adv.*

Synonyms: grave, influential, material, momentous, prominent, serious, significant, valuable, weighty. See SERIOUS. *Antonyms:* empty, idle, inconsiderable, irrelevant, mean, petty, slight, trifling, trivial, unimportant, useless, worthless.

im·por·ta·tion (im'pôr·tā'shən, -pōr-) *n.* 1 The act of importing, or bringing from one country into another merchandise for sale, processing, etc. 2 That which is imported.

im·por·tu·nate (im·pôr'chə·nit) *adj.* 1 Urgent in character, request, or demand; insistent; pertinacious. 2 *Obs.* Vexatious. See synonyms under EAGER[1], TROUBLESOME, URGENT. [<Med. L *importunatus,* pp. of *importunari.* See IMPORTUNE.] — **im·por'tu·nate·ly** *adv.* — **im·por'tu·nate·ness** *n.*

im·por·tune (im'pôr·tōōn', -tyōōn', im·pôr'chən) *v.* ·tuned, ·tun·ing *v.t.* 1 To beset with persistent requests or demands. 2 To ask for persistently or urgently. 3 *Obs.* To annoy. 4 *Obs.* To impel; urge. — *v.i.* 5 To make persistent requests or demands. — *adj.* Persistent; importunate. [<F *importuner* < Med. L *importunari* be troublesome <L *importunus* having no access, vexatious < *in-* without + *portus* a port] — **im'por·tune'ly** *adv.* — **im'por·tun'er** *n.*

im·por·tu·ni·ty (im'pôr·tōō'nə·tē, -tyōō'-) *n. pl.* ·ties 1 The act of importuning. 2 The state of being importunate. 3 *pl.* Importunate demands. Also **im·por·tu·na·cy** (im·pôr'chə·nə·sē). [<L *importunitas, -tatis*]

im·pose (im·pōz') *v.t.* ·posed, ·pos·ing 1 To place or lay by authority, as something to be borne, endured, or obeyed: to *impose* a tax or penalty. 2 To place by or as by force: to *impose* opinions on another. 3 To obtrude or force (oneself, one's presence, etc.) upon others. 4 To palm off (something) as true or genuine; foist. 5 *Printing* To arrange in a form, as pages of type. 6 *Eccl.* To lay on (hands), as in confirmation or ordination. 7 *Obs.* To lay down; deposit. — **to impose on** (or **upon**) 1 To take advantage of; presume. 2 To cheat or deceive by trickery or false representation. 3 To make an impression; influence. — *n. Obs.* An injunction; command. [<F *imposer* < *im-* on + *poser.* See POSE[1].] — **im·pos'a·ble** *adj.* — **im·pos'er** *n.*

im·pos·ing (im·pō'zing) *adj.* Adapted to make an impression; grand; elegant.

im·po·si·tion (im'pə·zish'ən) *n.* 1 The act of imposing, in any sense of the word. 2 An unjust requirement. 3 A trick of deception; imposture. 4 *Printing* The arrangement of pages of type or plates, in the right order for printing. 5 The act of laying on hands, as in confirmation or ordination. 6 A tax, toll, or duty. See synonyms under DECEPTION, FRAUD. [<L *impositio, -onis* < *impositus.* See IMPOST.]

im·pos·si·bil·i·ty (im·pos'ə·bil'ə·tē) *n. pl.* ·ties 1 The fact or state of being impossible. 2

That which is impossible; something that cannot exist or be done. [<L *impossibilitas, -tatis*]

im·pos·si·ble (im·pos′ə·bəl) *adj.* **1** Not possible. **2** *Law* Impracticable in the nature of the case. **3** Unimaginable; hopelessly objectionable; intolerable; absurd. See synonyms under IMPRACTICABLE. [<F] — **im·pos′·si·bly** *adv.*

im·post (im′pōst) *n.* **1** That which is imposed; specifically, a customs duty. **2** *Archit.* A projecting band or block placed at the top of a column or pier, and from which an arch springs. See illustration under ARCH. **3** A weight carried by a horse in a handicap race. See synonyms under TAX. — *v.t.* To classify so as to fix the customs duty: said of imported goods. [<OF <Med. L *impostum* <L *impositus*, pp. of *imponere* lay on <*in-* on + *ponere* lay, place]

im·pos·tor (im·pos′tər) *n.* One who deceives by false pretenses, especially under an assumed name or character. See synonyms under HYPOCRITE, QUACK[2]. [<F *imposteur* <LL *impostor* <*impositus*, pp. of *imponere* lay on, impose]

im·pos·ture (im·pos′chər) *n.* Deception by means of false pretenses. See synonyms under ARTIFICE, FRAUD. [<F <LL *impostura*]

im·po·tence (im′pə·təns) *n.* **1** The state or quality of being impotent; feebleness. **2** Loss or lack of capacity for sexual intercourse: said of men. Compare FRIGIDITY. Also **im′·po·ten·cy.** [<OF <L *impotentia*]

im·po·tent (im′pə·tənt) *adj.* **1** Destitute of or lacking in power, physical, moral, or intellectual; not potent; weak; feeble. **2** Destitute of sexual power: said usually of the male; also, occasionally, barren; sterile. **3** Lacking in self-control. [<OF <L *impotens, -entis* <*in-* not + *potens*. See POTENT.] — **im′po·tent·ly** *adv.*

im·pound (im·pound′) *v.t.* **1** To shut up in a pound, as a stray dog. **2** To place in custody of a court of law. **3** To collect (water) in a pond, reservoir, etc., as for irrigation. — **im·pound′age** (-poun′dij) *n.* — **im·pound′er** *n.*

im·pov·er·ish (im·pov′ər·ish) *v.t.* **1** To reduce to poverty. **2** To exhaust the fertility or quality of, as soil; deteriorate. Also spelled EMPOVERISH. [<OF *empovrir* <*em-* thoroughly + L *pauperare* impoverish <*pauper* poor]

im·pov·er·ish·ment (im·pov′ər·ish·mənt) *n.* The act of impoverishing, or the state of being impoverished.

im·prac·ti·ca·ble (im·prak′ti·kə·bəl) *adj.* **1** Impossible or unreasonably difficult of performance. **2** Unserviceable. **3** Hard to get on with; unreasonable; intractable: said of persons. — **im·prac′ti·ca·bil′i·ty, im·prac′ti·ca·ble·ness** *n.* — **im·prac′ti·ca·bly** *adv.*

Synonyms: impossible, impractical, intractable. That which is *impossible* cannot be done at all; that which is *impracticable* is theoretically possible, but cannot be done under existing conditions. *Impractical*, which strictly means not practical, is coming into frequent popular use as the equivalent of *impracticable*, but the difference should be maintained; an *impractical* man lacks practical judgment or efficiency; an *impracticable* man is difficult to deal with (compare OBSTINATE, PERVERSE); an *impractical* scheme lacks practical fitness, is theoretic or visionary; an *impracticable* scheme has some inherent difficulties that would insure its failure in action. *Antonyms:* easy, feasible, possible, practicable.

im·prac·ti·cal (im·prak′ti·kəl) *adj.* Not practical; unpractical. See synonyms under IMPRACTICABLE. — **im·prac′ti·cal′i·ty** (-kal′ə·tē) *n.*

im·pre·cate (im′prə·kāt) *v.t.* **·cat·ed, ·cat·ing** To invoke or call down, as a judgment, calamity, or curse. [<L *imprecatus*, pp. of *imprecare* pray to <*in-* + *precari* pray <*prex, precis* prayer] — **im′pre·ca′tor** *n.* — **im′pre·ca·to·ry** (-kə·tôr′ē, -tō′rē) *adj.*

im·pre·ca·tion (im′prə·kā′shən) *n.* A malediction; curse. [<L *imprecatio, -onis*]

Synonyms: anathema, curse, execration, malediction. See OATH. *Antonyms:* benediction, benison, blessing, praise.

im·pre·ci·sion (im′pri·sizh′ən) *n.* Want of precision.

im·preg·na·ble (im·preg′nə·bəl) *adj.* **1** Proof against attack; that cannot be taken. **2** Not

to be overcome by temptation. See synonyms under INCONTESTABLE, SECURE. [<OF *imprenable* <*im-* not (<L *in-*) + *prenable* pregnable <*prendre* take <L *prehendere*] — **im·preg′na·bil′i·ty** *n.* — **im·preg′na·bly** *adv.*

im·preg·nate (im·preg′nāt) *v.t.* **·nat·ed, ·nat·ing** **1** To make pregnant; get with child. **2** To fertilize. **3** To saturate or permeate with another substance. **4** To fill or imbue with emotion, ideas, principles, etc.: to *impregnate* a book with religious feeling. — *adj.* Made pregnant. [<LL *impraegnatus*, pp. of *impraegnare* impregnate <*in-* in + *praegnans* pregnant] — **im·preg′na·ble** (-nə·bəl) *adj.* — **im·preg′na·tor** *n.*

im·pre·scrip·ti·ble (im′pri·skrip′tə·bəl) *adj.* **1** Incapable of being either lost or acquired by usage or prescription. **2** Inalienable. [<F] — **im′pre·scrip′ti·bil′i·ty** *n.* — **im′pre·scrip′ti·bly** *adv.*

im·press[1] (im·pres′) *v.t.* **1** To produce a marked effect upon, as the mind; influence: His proposal *impressed* me. **2** To fix firmly in the mind, as ideas, beliefs, etc.: to *impress* a fact on the memory. **3** To form or make (an imprint or mark) by pressure; stamp: to *impress* a design on metal. **4** To form or make an imprint or mark upon. **5** To apply with pressure; press: to *impress* one's hand into the mud. **6** *Electr.* To create or establish (a difference of potential) in a conductor by means of a dynamo, battery, or other source of electrical energy. — *n.* (im′pres) **1** A mark or indentation produced by pressure. **2** The effect of a force. **3** The act or process of making an impression. **4** Peculiar character or form; stamp. [<L *impressus*, pp. of *imprimere* impress <*in-* on + *premere* press]

Synonyms (verb): imprint, inculcate, press, print, stamp. *Antonyms:* see synonyms for CANCEL.

im·press[2] (im·pres′) *v.t.* **1** To compel to enter public service: to *impress* seamen. **2** To seize (property) for public use. — *n.* Impressment. [<IM-[1] in + PRESS[1]] — **im·press′er** *n.*

im·pres·sion (im·presh′ən) *n.* **1** The act of impressing or imprinting; the imparting of a distinguishing mark, form, or character. **2** The result of exterior influence, as impressment; a stamp, mark, or figure made by pressure. **3** An effect produced on the senses, the mind, the feelings, or the conscience. **4** A slight or indistinct remembrance; a notion or belief held by the mind without adequate grounds. **5** An effect left upon the mind, which resembles in any way, or bears the marks of, some past experience; specifically, any mental effect regarded as the resultant of a previous experience. **6** *Printing* **a** The imprint of types, illustrations, etc., on a page or sheet. **b** All the copies of a book printed at one time: especially, an unaltered reprint from standing type or from plates, as distinguished from *edition.* **c** One copy of a book, engraving, etching, etc. See synonyms under FEELING, IDEA, MARK[1]. [<OF <L *impressio, -onis*] — **im·pres′sion·al** *adj.*

im·pres·sion·a·ble (im·presh′ən·ə·bəl) *adj.* Subject to or susceptible of impression; easily molded; plastic. [<F] — **im·pres′sion·a·bil′i·ty, im·pres′sion·a·ble·ness** *n.*

im·pres·sive (im·pres′iv) *adj.* Producing or tending to produce an impression; holding the attention; exciting emotion or admiration. See synonyms under GRAND. [<IMPRESS[1]] — **im·pres′sive·ly** *adv.* — **im·pres′sive·ness** *n.*

im·press·ment (im·pres′mənt) *n.* **1** The act of impressing into the public service, or of seizing property for public use. **2** The seizure of civilians for service in the navy or the seizure of members of a ship's crew by a foreign vessel.

im·pres·sure (im·presh′ər) *n.* An impression.

im·prest (im·prest′) *adj. Obs.* Given as a loan in advance: said of money given, as to soldiers, sailors, or government employees. — *n.* A prepayment of money, especially to carry on some public service. [< *in prest* on loan, after Ital. *impresto* loan. See PREST.]

im·print (im·print′) *v.t.* **1** To produce or reproduce (a figure, mark, etc.) by pressure: to *imprint* a design on wax. **2** To mark (something), as with a stamp or seal. **3** To fix firmly in the heart, mind, etc. See synonyms under IMPRESS[1], INSCRIBE. — *n.* (im′print) **1** A mark or character made by printing, stamping, or pressing. **2** The effect left by

impression. **3** A publisher's or printer's name, place of publication, date, etc., printed in a book or other publication. **4** An impression, as of a medal, etc. [<OF *empreinte*, pp. of *empreinter* <L *imprimere* <*in-* in + *premere* press]

im·pris·on (im·priz′ən) *v.t.* **1** To put into or keep in a prison. **2** To confine or restrain in any way. See synonyms under SHUT. [<OF *emprisoner* <*en-* in + *prison*. See PRISON.]

im·pris·on·ment (im·priz′ən·mənt) *n.* **1** The act of imprisoning. **2** Confinement in, or as in a prison.

im·prob·a·ble (im·prob′ə·bəl) *adj.* Not likely to be true; not reasonably to be expected. [<L *improbabilis*] — **im·prob·a·bil′i·ty** (im′prob·ə·bil′ə·tē, im·prob′-), **im·prob′a·ble·ness** *n.* — **im·prob′a·bly** *adv.*

im·prob·i·ty (im·prō′bə·tē) *n. pl.* **·ties** Want of probity; dishonesty. [<L *improbitas, -tatis* <*improbus* wicked <*in-* not + *probus* honest]

im·promp·tu (im·promp′tōō, -tyōō) *adj.* Made, done, or uttered on the spur of the moment; extempore; offhand. See synonyms under EXTEMPORANEOUS. — *n.* Anything done on the impulse of the moment. — *adv.* Without preparation. [<F <L *in promptu* in readiness]

im·prop·er (im·prop′ər) *adj.* **1** Not proper; not strictly belonging or appropriate; inapplicable. **2** Not in accord with the proprieties of speech, manners, or conduct; indecorous. **3** Unsuitable; inappropriate. **4** Irregular or abnormal. [<OF *impropre* <L *improprius*] — **im·prop′er·ly** *adv.*

im·pro·pri·ate (im·prō′prē·āt) *v.t.* **·at·ed, ·at·ing** To transfer (ecclesiastical property or revenues) to laymen. — *adj.* (-prē·it) Vested or placed in the hands of a layman; impropriated. [<Med. L *impropriatus*, pp. of *impropriare* take as one's own <L *in-* on + *proprius* one's own] — **im·pro′pri·a′tion** *n.* — **im·pro′pri·a′tor** *n.*

im·pro·pri·e·ty (im′prə·prī′ə·tē) *n. pl.* **·ties** **1** The state or quality of being improper. **2** Anything that is improper, as an act. **3** A violation of good usage in speech or writing. See synonyms under INDECENCY. [<L *improprietas, -tatis*]

im·prove (im·prōōv′) *v.* **·proved, ·prov·ing** *v.t.* **1** To make better the quality, condition, etc., of. **2** To use to good advantage; utilize: to *improve* one's opportunities. **3** *U.S.* To increase the value or profit of, as land by cultivation or lots by construction of buildings. — *v.i.* **4** To become better. **5** To make improvements: with *on* or *upon*. See synonyms under AMEND. [<AF *emprower* <OF *en-* into + *prou* profit] — **im·prov′a·bil′i·ty, im·prov′a·ble·ness** *n.* — **im·prov′a·ble** *adj.* — **im·prov′a·bly** *adv.* — **im·prov′er** *n.*

im·prove·ment (im·prōōv′mənt) *n.* **1** The act or process of improving; betterment; amelioration. **2** Something that is better than (something previous): Diesel power is an *improvement* over steam. **3** A beneficial change or addition; an advance. **4** *U.S.* A tract of land developed by cultivation, buildings, enclosures, etc. **5** *pl. U.S.* The enclosures, buildings, clearings, etc., produced on a piece of land. See synonyms under INCREASE, PROFIT, PROGRESS.

im·prov·i·dent (im·prov′ə·dənt) *adj.* **1** Lacking foresight; incautious. **2** Taking no thought for future needs. — **im·prov′i·dence** *n.* — **im·prov′i·dent·ly** *adv.*

Synonyms: careless, imprudent, prodigal, reckless, shiftless, thoughtless, thriftless, unthrifty. See IMPRUDENT. *Antonyms:* careful, economical, provident, prudent, saving, thoughtful, thrifty.

im·pro·vise (im′prə·vīz) *v.t. & v.i.* **·vised, ·vis·ing** **1** To compose, recite, sing, etc., without previous preparation; extemporize. **2** To make or devise on the spur of the moment, especially from what is at hand: to *improvise* a raft from driftwood. Also **im·prov′i·sate** (im·prov′ə·zāt). [<F *improviser* <Ital. *improvvisare* <*improvviso* unforeseen <L *improvisus* <*in-* not + *provisus* foreseen] — **im·prov′i·sa·tion** (im·prov′ə·zā′shən, im′prə·vī·zā′shən) *n.* — **im′pro·vis′er, im·prov′i·sa′tor** *n.* — **im·prov′i·sa·to·ri·al** (im·prov′ə·zə·tôr′ē·əl, -tō′rē·əl), **im·prov′i·sa·to·ry** (-tôr′ē, -tō′rē) *adj.*

im·pru·dent (im·prōō′dənt) *adj.* Not prudent; lacking discretion. [<L *imprudens, -entis* <*in-* not + *prudens* PRUDENT] — **im·pru′dent·ly** *adv.* — **im·pru′dence** *n.*

Synonyms: careless, toolhardy, heedless, ill–advised, ill–judged, impolitic, improvident, incautious, inconsiderate, indiscreet, injudicious, rash, reckless, short–sighted, thoughtless, thriftless, unthinking, unthrifty, venturesome, venturous. *Improvident* is chiefly used of lack of provision for future need, supply, support, etc.; *imprudent*, of a lack of provision against future danger, loss, or harm. Each word has also acquired a positive meaning: *improvident* referring to *careless* or *reckless* waste of present resources without thought of future need; *imprudent*, to *thoughtless* or *reckless* disregard of possible or probable future dangers. See IMPROVIDENT. *Antonyms*: see synonyms for ASTUTE.

im·pu·dence (im′pyə-dəns) n. **1** Effrontery; insolence. **2** Insolent language or behavior. **3** *Obs.* Shamelessness; immodesty. Also **im′·pu·den·cy.** [<OF <L *impudentia*]
Synonyms: assurance, boldness, effrontery, forwardness, impertinence, incivility, insolence, intrusiveness, officiousness, pertness, presumption, rudeness, sauciness. *Impertinence* primarily denotes what does not pertain or belong to the occasion or the person, and hence comes to signify interference by word or act not consistent with the age, position, or relation of the person interfered with or of the one who interferes; especially, forward, presumptuous, or meddlesome speech. *Impudence* is shameless *impertinence*. What would be arrogance in a superior becomes *impertinence* or *impudence* in an inferior. *Impertinence* has less of intent and determination than *impudence*. We speak of thoughtless *impertinence*, shameless *impudence*. *Insolence* is literally that which is against custom, that is, the violation of customary respect and courtesy. *Officiousness* is thrusting upon others unasked and undesired service, and is often as well–meant as it is annoying. *Rudeness* is the behavior that might be expected from a thoroughly uncultured person, and may be either deliberate and insulting or unintentional and even unconscious. Compare ARROGANCE, ASSURANCE, EFFRONTERY. *Antonyms*: bashfulness, coyness, diffidence, humility, lowliness, meekness, modesty, submissiveness.

im·pu·dent (im′pyə-dənt) adj. **1** Offensively bold; insolently assured. **2** *Obs.* Immodest; shameless. [<OF <L *impudens* <*in-* not + *pudens* modest, orig. ppr. of *pudere* feel shame] — **im′pu·dent·ly** adv.
Synonyms: bold, bold–faced, brazen, brazen-faced, forward, immodest, impertinent, insolent, pert, rude, saucy, shameless. Compare synonyms for IMPUDENCE. *Antonyms*: bashful, deferential, diffident, modest, obsequious, retiring, shrinking, shy, timid.

im·pu·dic·i·ty (im′pyə-dis′ə-tē) n. Immodesty; shamelessness. [<F *impudicité* <L *impudicitia* <*impudicus* shameless <*in-* not + *pudicus* modest <*pudor* shame]

im·pugn (im·pyōōn′) v.t. To assail by words or arguments; attack as false or untrustworthy; challenge. [<OF *impugner* <L *impugnare* <*in-* against + *pugnare* fight <*pugna* battle <*pugnus* fist] — **im·pugn′a·ble** adj. — **im·pug·na·tion** (im′pəg-nā′shən) n. — **im·pugn′er** n. — **im·pugn′ment** n.

im·pu·is·sance (im-pyōō′ə-səns) n. Want of power or ability; impotence. [<F] — **im·pu′is·sant** adj.

im·pulse (im′puls) n. **1** An impelling force, especially one that acts suddenly and produces motion; impulsion. **2** The motion produced by a sudden impelling force; impetus. **3** A sudden or transient mental urge resulting in undeliberated action, caused by the feelings or by some objective stimulus. **4** Any natural, unreasoned motive or tendency to act: a kind *impulse*. **5** An instinctive or reactive craving for action; a desire to act resulting from instantaneous judgments as to how to meet an emergency. **6** *Physiol.* A stimulus. **7** *Mech.* A great force acting for a very short time; also, the momentum due to a force. **8** *Electr.* A surge of current flowing in one direction. [<L *impulsus*, pp. of *impellere*. See IMPEL.]
Synonyms: feeling, force, impetus, incentive, incitement, influence, instigation, motive. See INFLUENCE.

im·pul·sion (im-pul′shən) n. **1** The act of impelling. **2** The state of being impelled. **3** An impulse or motion suddenly communicated; impetus. **4** That which impels, whether a force or motive. **5** Mental impetus. **6** Incitement; instigation. [<OF <L *impulsio, -onis*]

im·pul·sive (im-pul′siv) adj. **1** Actuated by impulse. **2** Having the power of impelling. **3** Acting by instantaneous or intermittent force or impulse. See synonyms under IMPETUOUS. [<OF *impulsif* <Med. L *impulsivus*] — **im·pul′sive·ly** adv. — **im·pul′sive·ness** n.

im·pu·ni·ty (im-pyōō′nə-tē) n. pl. ·ties Freedom from punishment or from injurious consequences. [<L *impunitas, -tatis* <*impunis* unpunished <*in-* not + *poena* punishment]

im·pure (im-pyoor′) adj. **1** Not pure; containing some foreign substance; adulterated. **2** Unchaste. **3** Containing foreign idioms or grammatical blemishes. **4** Unfit for religious use; unhallowed. **5** Mixed with or having a tendency toward extraneous, corporeal, or foreign matter. See synonyms under FOUL, IMMODEST. [<L *impurus*] — **im·pure′ly** adv. — **im·pure′ness** n.

im·pu·ri·ty (im-pyoor′ə-tē) n. pl. ·ties **1** The state of being impure. **2** Adulteration. **3** Moral pollution. **4** That which is impure or polluting. See synonyms under INDECENCY. [<OF *impurité* <L *impuritas, -tatis* <*in-* not + *purus* pure]

im·pu·ta·tive (im-pyōō′tə-tiv) adj. **1** Transferred or transmitted by imputation; imputed. **2** Addicted to making imputations. [<LL *imputativus*] — **im·pu′ta·tive·ly** adv.

im·pute (im-pyōōt′) v.t. ·put·ed, ·put·ing **1** To attribute, as a fault or crime, to a person; ascribe. **2** *Theol.* To attribute, as righteousness or guilt, vicariously. See synonyms under ATTRIBUTE. [<OF *emputer* <L *imputare* enter into the account <*in-* in + *putare* reckon, think] — **im·put′a·bil′i·ty, im·put′a·ble·ness** n. — **im·put′a·ble** adj. — **im·put′er** n.

in (in) prep. **1** Within the bounds of; contained or included within: six rooms *in* the house. **2** Amidst; surrounded by: *in* the rain; buried *in* sand. **3** Within the class or group of; being a worker at, investor *in*, etc.: a man *in* a thousand; He is *in* munitions. **4** Occupied or concerned with: *in* search of truth. **5** Wearing, decorated with, etc.: that girl *in* blue; a room *in* green. **6** Made out of: I can show you this watch *in* gold. **7** So as to form or constitute: ornaments arranged *in* a spiral. **8** So as to enter into or remain within: sinking *in* the mud; putting his hands *in* his pockets. **9** As a part or function of; belonging to: We knew you had it *in* you. **10** According to or within the scope or range of: *In* my opinion you're mistaken; to come *in* hearing. **11** During; throughout the course of: a concert given *in* the evening. **12** At or before the end or expiration of: the note due *in* three days; I'll be there *in* no time. **13** With regard or respect to: Students vary *in* talent. **14** Affected by; under the influence of: *in* doubt as to the outcome. **15** By means of; with the use of: speaking *in* whispers; painted *in* water colors. **16** For the purpose of: to run *in* pursuit. **17** By reason of or as a result of: to run *in* fear. —adv. **1** To or toward the interior or inside from the exterior or outside: Please come *in*. **2** So as to be part of, contained by, or included with: to join *in*; to stir *in* flour. —**all in** *Colloq.* Exhausted; worn out. —**in that** Because; since: *In that* you're here already, you might as well stay. —**in with** In association or friendship with. —**to be in for** *Colloq.* To have the certain expectation of receiving (usually something unpleasant). —**to have it in for** *Colloq.* To resent; bear ill toward. —adj. **1** That is successful; having control or authority. **2** On the inside; inner. **3** Leading or going in: the *in* train. **4** *Colloq.* **a** Privileged or in status. **b** Much publicized and often admired. **5** *Colloq.* Understandable only to a select few: *in* jokes. —n. **1** A member of a party in office or power, a team at bat, etc. **2** *Colloq.* A door or other means of entrance or access. **3** *Colloq.* Favored position or influence: an *in* with the boss. **4** A nook or corner. —**ins and outs 1** All the twists and turns, nooks and corners, etc. **2** The full complexities, details, etc.: the *ins and outs* of a question. — v.t. **inned, in·ning 1** To gather, as hay. **2** *Dial.* To enclose, as land. [OE]

in-[1] prefix Not; without; un–; non–. Also: *i*- before *gn*, as in *ignore*; *il*- before *l*, as in *illiterate*; *im*- before *b, m, p*, as in *imbalance*, *immiscible*, *impecunious*; *ir*- before *r*, as in *irrefragable*. [<L]
There follows a list of self–defining words with this prefix, most of them being variants of words beginning with *un-*. *In-* as here used has the meaning of "want or lack of," "not" (as *incivility*, lack of civility; *indevout*, not devout). See the foot of this page, etc.

in-[2] prefix In; into; on; within; toward: *include*, *incur*, *invade*: also used intensively, as in *inflame*, or without perceptible force. Also *il*- before *l*, as in *illuminate*; *im*- before *b, m, p*, as in *imbibe*, *immigrate*, *impress*; *ir*- before *r*, as in *irradiate*. The form generally remains unassimilated in words formed in English, as in *inbreed*. [Fusion of IN, prep. & adv. + L *in-*]

in-[3] prefix In, into; within: *inlet*. [OE]

in·a·bil·i·ty (in′ə-bil′ə-tē) n. The state of being unable; lack of necessary power.

in·ac·ces·si·ble (in′ak-ses′ə-bəl) adj. Not accessible; incapable of being reached. — **in′ac·ces′si·bil′i·ty** n.

in·ac·cu·ra·cy (in-ak′yər-ə-sē) n. pl. ·cies **1** The state or condition of being inaccurate. **2** Something which is inaccurate.

in·ac·cu·rate (in-ak′yər-it) adj. Wanting in accuracy. — **in·ac′cu·rate·ly** adv. — **in·ac′cu·rate·ness** n.

in·ac·tion (in-ak′shən) n. A state of inactivity; forbearance from action; idleness.

in·ac·ti·vate (in-ak′tə-vāt) v.t. ·vat·ed, ·vat·ing **1** To render inactive. **2** *Med.* To stop the activity of (a serum or its complement) by heat or other means. — **in·ac′ti·va′tion** n.

in·ac·tive (in-ak′tiv) adj. **1** Characterized by inaction; not making special exertion or effort. **2** Marked by absence of effort or desire for action; indolent. **3** Without power to act. **4** *Physics* Having no effect or action upon polarized light. See synonyms under IDLE, PASSIVE, SLOW. — **in·ac′tive·ly** adv. — **in·ac·tiv·i·ty** (in·ak·tiv′ə-tē), n. pl. ·ties.

in·ad·e·quate (in-ad′ə-kwit) adj. Not equal to that which is required; inapt; insufficient; imperfect. — **in·ad′e·qua·cy, in·ad′e·quate·ness** n. — **in·ad′e·quate·ly** adv.

in·ad·ver·tence (in′əd-vûr′təns) n. **1** The quality of being inadvertent; want of care or circumspection. **2** An effect of inattention; oversight: This error was a mere *inadvertence*. Also **in′ad·ver′ten·cy.** [<Med. L *inadvertentia*]

in·ad·ver·tent (in′əd-vûr′tənt) adj. **1** Done without consideration. **2** Habitually heedless. **3** Unintentional. — **in′ad·ver′tent·ly** adv.

in·ad·vis·a·ble (in′əd-vī′zə-bəl) adj. Not advisable. — **in′ad·vis′a·bil′i·ty** n.

in·af·fa·ble (in-af′ə-bəl) adj. Not affable; austere; disagreeable.

in·al·ien·a·ble (in-āl′yən-ə-bəl) adj. Not transferable; that cannot be rightfully taken away. — **in·al′ien·a·bil′i·ty, in·al′ien·a·ble·ness** n. — **in·al′ien·a·bly** adv.

in·al·ter·a·ble (in-ôl′tər-ə-bəl) adj. That cannot be altered; unalterable. — **in·al′ter·a·bil′i·ty, in·al′ter·a·ble·ness** n. — **in·al′ter·a·bly** adv.

in·ane (in-ān′) adj. **1** Wanting in understanding; silly. **2** Having no substance or contents; vacant. —n. That which is void; any vacuity; infinite space. [<L *inanis* empty]

in·an·i·mate (in-an′ə-mit) adj. Wanting in life and animation; not animate: opposed to *sentient*. [<LL *inanimatus*] — **in·an′i·mate·ly** adv. — **in·an′i·mate·ness** n.

in·a·ni·tion (in′ə-nish′ən) n. **1** The state of being void or empty. **2** Exhaustion from lack of nourishment. [<F <LL *inanitio, -onis* <*inanitus*, pp. of *inanire* empty <*inanis* empty]

in·an·i·ty (in-an′ə-tē) n. pl. ·ties **1** The condition of being inane or empty; inanition; lack of sense. **2** A frivolous or silly thing. **3** A stupid or trite remark. [<OF *inanité* <L *inanitas* <*inanis* empty]

in·ap·peas·a·ble (in′ə-pē′zə-bəl) adj. That cannot be appeased; not to be appeased.

in·ap·pe·tence (in-ap′ə-təns) n. A lack of appetite or desire. Also **in·ap'pe·ten·cy.** — **in·ap'pe·tent** *adj.*

in·ap·pro·pri·ate (in'ə·prō'prē·it) *adj.* Not appropriate; unsuitable; unfitting.

in·arm (in·ärm') *v.t.* To encircle with or as with the arms; embrace.

in·ar·tic·u·late (in'är·tik'yə·lit) *adj.* 1 Indistinctly or unintelligibly uttered by the speech organs. 2 Incapable of speech; dumb. 3 Unable to speak coherently or to express oneself fully. 4 Unspoken; unexpressed. 5 *Anat.* Not jointed or segmented, as certain worms; also, not hinged. — **in'ar·tic'u·late·ly** *adv.* — **in'ar·tic'u·late·ness** *n.*

in·as·much as (in'əz·much' az') 1 Since; because; seeing that. 2 *Archaic* In the measure that; to the degree that.

in·at·ten·tion (in'ə·ten'shən) *n.* Lack of or failure to give attention; heedlessness; negligence; disregard.

in·at·ten·tive (in'ə·ten'tiv) *adj.* Neglecting or failing to pay attention; careless. — **in'at·ten'tive·ly** *adv.* — **in'at·ten'tive·ness** *n.*

Synonyms: absent, absent-minded, careless, heedless, inconsiderate, listless, neglectful, negligent, regardless, remiss, restless, unmindful, unobservant. See ABSTRACTED. *Antonyms:* attentive, careful, considerate, heedful, listening, noticing, noting, observing, regardful, studious, thoughtful, watchful.

in·au·di·ble (in·ô'də·bəl) *adj.* That cannot be heard; beyond the range of hearing. — **in·au'di·bil'i·ty** *n.* — **in·au'di·bly** *adv.*

in·au·gu·rate (in·ô'gyə·rāt) *v.t.* **·rat·ed, ·rat·ing** 1 To induct into office with formal ceremony; invest. 2 To begin or commence upon formally; initiate: to *inaugurate* a reform. 3 To celebrate the public opening or first use of: to *inaugurate* a bridge. See synonyms under INSTALL. [<L *inauguratus*, pp. of *inaugurare* take omens, consecrate, install. See AUGUR.] — **in·au'gu·ral** (-rəl) *adj.* — **in·au'gu·ra'tor** *n.* — **in·au'gu·ra·to·ry** (-tôr'ē, -tō'rē) *adj.*

in·au·gu·ra·tion (in·ô'gyə·rā'shən) *n.* The act or ceremony of inaugurating. See synonyms under ACCESSION, BEGINNING. [<L *inauguratio, -onis*]

in·be·ing (in'bē'ing) *n.* 1 Inherent existence. 2 Essential nature; what a thing is in itself.

in·board (in'bôrd', -bōrd) *adj.* 1 *Naut.* Inside the hull or bulwarks of a ship: used also adverbially. 2 *Mech.* Toward the inside.

in·born (in'bôrn') *adj.* Implanted by nature; innate. See synonyms under INHERENT.

in·bound (in'bound') *adj.* Bound inward: an *inbound* ship.

in·bred (in'bred') *adj.* 1 Bred within; innate. 2 Bred from closely related parents. See synonyms under INHERENT.

in·breed (in'brēd', in'brēd') *v.t.* **·bred, ·breed·ing** 1 To develop or produce within. 2 To breed by continual mating of closely related stock.

in·can·desce (in'kən·des') *v.t. & v.i.* **·desced, ·desc·ing** To be or become, or cause to become luminous with heat. [<L *incandescere*] — **in'can·des'cence, in'can·des'cen·cy** *n.*

in·can·des·cent (in'kən·des'ənt) *adj.* 1 Made luminous by heat; white or glowing with heat. 2 Of or pertaining to a lamp the light of which is derived from incandescing material, such as the filament in an electric lamp or the mantle in a Welsbach burner. [<L *incandescens, -entis*, ppr. of *incandescere* grow hot < *in-* in + *candescere*, inceptive of *candere* glow white] — **in'can·des'cent·ly** *adv.*

in·can·ta·tion (in'kan·tā'shən) 1 The utterance of magical words for enchantment or exorcism. 2 The formula so used. 3 Any magic or sorcery. See synonyms under SORCERY. [<F <L *incantatio, -onis* < *incantare* make an incantation. See ENCHANT.] — **in'can·ta'tor** *n.* — **in·can·ta·to·ry** (in·kan'tə·tôr'ē, -tō'rē) *adj.*

in·ca·pa·ble (in·kā'pə·bəl) *adj.* 1 Not capable; lacking power, capacity or abil-

INCANDESCENT
LIGHT BULB
a. Base.
b. Stem.
c. Leading-in wires.
d. Stem seal.
e, h. Anchors.
f. Hub.
g. Filament.
i. Bulb.

ity: with *of*; incompetent. 2 Without legal qualifications or eligibility. — *n.* A totally incompetent person. — **in·ca·pa·bil'i·ty, in·ca'pa·ble·ness** *n.* — **in·ca'pa·bly** *adv.*

in·ca·pac·i·tate (in'kə·pas'ə·tāt) *v.t.* **·tat·ed, ·tat·ing** 1 To make incapable or unfit; deprive of capacity; disable. 2 *Law* To deprive of legal or political capacity; disqualify. — **in'ca·pac'i·ta'tion** *n.*

in·ca·pac·i·ty (in'kə·pas'ə·tē) *n. pl.* **·ties** 1 Lack of capacity; incapability. 2 *Law* Want of competency. See synonyms under IDIOCY.

in·cap·su·late (in·kap'sə·lāt, -syoo-) *v.t.* **·lat·ed, ·lat·ing** To enclose as in a capsule. [<IN- + CAPSUL(E) + -ATE[1]]

in·car·cer·ate (in·kär'sər·āt) *v.t.* **·at·ed, ·at·ing** 1 To imprison; put in jail. 2 To confine; enclose. — *adj.* Imprisoned. [<Med. L *incarceratus*, pp. of *incarcerare* imprison < *in-* in + *carcer* jail] — **in·car'cer·a'tion** *n.* — **in·car'cer·a'tor** *n.*

in·car·di·nate (in·kär'də·nāt) *v.t.* **·nat·ed, ·nat·ing** In the Roman Catholic Church: 1 To establish in a particular church, diocese, or place as principal priest, deacon, etc. 2 To make a cardinal. [<Med. L *incardinatus*, pp. of *incardinare* install a priest < *in-* in + *cardinalis* a chief priest] — **in·car'di·na'tion** *n.*

in·car·nant (in·kär'nənt) *adj. Med.* Promoting the granulation of wounds. — *n.* An agent that promotes the healing of wounds. Also **in·car'na·tive.** [< earlier *incarn* cover with flesh, heal over <LL *incarnare* INCARNATE]

in·car·nate (in·kär'nāt) *v.t.* **·nat·ed, ·nat·ing** 1 To embody in flesh; give bodily form to. 2 To give concrete shape or form to; actualize: a doctrine *incarnated* in institutions. 3 To be the embodiment of; typify: The warrior *incarnates* the spirit of battle. — *adj.* (-nit) 1 Invested with flesh. 2 Embodied in human form: a fiend *incarnate*. 3 Personified or epitomized: savagery *incarnate*. 4 Flesh-colored; roseate. [<LL *incarnatus*, pp. of *incarnare* embody in flesh < *in-* in + *caro, carnis* flesh]

in·car·na·tion (in'kär·nā'shən) *n.* 1 The act of becoming incarnate. 2 *Often cap.* The assumption of the human nature by Jesus Christ as the second person of the Trinity. 3 That which is personified by, or embodied in or as in human form; personification; embodiment of a quality, idea, principle, etc.; specifically, an avatar. [<AF *incarnaciun* < LL *incarnatio, -onis*]

in·case (in·kās') *v.t.* **·cased, ·cas·ing** To place or enclose in or as in a case or cases: often spelled *encase*.

in·case·ment (in·kās'mənt) *n.* 1 The act of incasing, or the state of being incased. 2 That which incases. — **theory of incasement** *Biol.* An old theory of reproduction that assumes each ovum to contain a fully formed organism in miniature; preformation.

in·ca·va·tion (in'kə·vā'shən) *n.* 1 The act of making hollow. 2 The hollow itself. [<L *incavatus*, pp. of *incavare* < *in-* in + *cavare* make hollow < *cavus* hollow]

in·cen·di·ar·y (in·sen'dē·er'ē) *adj.* 1 Pertaining to malicious setting on fire. 2 Tending to inflame passion. 3 Capable of generating intense heat, as any of various substances such as magnesium, thermit, or white phosphorus. 4 Pertaining to or containing such a substance: an *incendiary* bomb. — *n. pl.* **·ries** 1 One who maliciously sets a building on fire; one who commits arson. 2 One who excites to sedition, inflames evil passions, or the like. 3 An incendiary bomb or shell. [<L *incendiarius* < *incendium* a fire < *incendere* set on fire] — **in·cen'di·a·rism** (-ə·riz'əm) *n.*

in·cense[1] (in·sens') *v.t.* **·censed, ·cens·ing** To excite or arouse the wrath of; inflame to anger; enrage. [<OF *incenser* <L *incendere* set on fire < *in-* in + *candere* glow] — **in·cense'ment** *n.* — **in·cen'sor** *n.*

Synonyms: anger, chafe, enrage, exasperate, fire, gall, goad, heat, inflame, irritate, provoke, sting. *Antonyms:* allay, appease, conciliate, mollify, pacify, placate, soothe.

in·cense[2] (in·sens') *n.* 1 An aromatic substance that exhales perfume during combustion, as certain gums and spices. 2 The odor or fumes of spices, etc., burnt as an act of worship. 3 Any agreeable perfume. 4 Figuratively, pleasing attention; praise. — *v.* **·censed, ·cens·ing** *v.t.* 1 To perfume with incense. 2 To burn incense to. — *v.i.* 3 To burn incense.

[<OF *encens* <L *incensus*, pp. of *incendere* set on fire]

in·cen·tive (in·sen'tiv) *adj.* Encouraging or impelling. — *n.* That which incites, or tends to incite, to action. See synonyms under IMPULSE, MOTIVE. [<L *incentivus* < *incentus*, pp. of *incinere* set the tune < *in-* in + *canere* sing] — **in·cen'tive·ly** *adv.*

in·cept (in·sept') *v.t.* 1 *Biol.* To take in, as a cell or organism. 2 *Obs.* To begin; undertake. [<L *inceptus*, pp. of *incipere* begin < *in-* on + *capere* take]

in·cep·tion (in·sep'shən) *n.* 1 The act of beginning. 2 The state of being begun. 3 The initial period, as of an undertaking. See synonyms under BEGINNING. [<L *inceptio, -onis* < *inceptus*, pp. of *incipere*. See INCEPT.]

in·cep·tive (in·sep'tiv) *adj.* 1 Noting the beginning or commencement of an action or occurrence; initial. 2 *Gram.* Referring to a class of verbs or to the aspect of a verb denoting the commencement of an action; inchoative; ingressive. In Latin, for example, such verbs are formed by the addition of *-scere* to the present stem, as *cale(scere)*, to grow warm, from *cale(re)*, to be hot. — *n.* 1 That which tends to commence, as an inceptive word or construction. 2 *Gram.* An inceptive word or construction. [<OF *inceptif* <L *inceptus*, pp. of *incipere*. See INCEPT.] — **in·cep'tive·ly** *adv.*

in·cer·ti·tude (in·sûr'tə·tood, -tyood) *n.* 1 The state of being uncertain; uncertainty; doubtfulness. 2 Insecurity. [<F <Med. L *incertitudo* <L *incertus* uncertain]

in·ces·sant (in·ses'ənt) *adj.* Continued or repeated without cessation. See synonyms under CONTINUAL, PERPETUAL. [<F <LL *incessans, -antis* < *in-* not + *cessare* cease] — **in·ces'san·cy** (-ən·sē) *n.* — **in·ces'sant·ly** *adv.*

in·cest (in'sest) *n.* 1 Sexual intercourse between persons too closely related for legal marriage. 2 *Theol.* Spiritual incest. [<L *incestum* < *incestus* unchaste < *in-* not + *castus* chaste]

in·ces·tu·ous (in·ses'choo·əs) *adj.* 1 Guilty of incest. 2 Of the nature of incest. [<L *incestuosus*] — **in·ces'tu·ous·ly** *adv.*

inch (inch) *n.* 1 A linear measure: the twelfth part of a foot or 2.54 centimeters. 2 *Meteorol.* The amount of snow or rain which would cover a surface to the depth of an inch. 3 *Physics* The unit of pressure equivalent to the weight of a fluid column, as of mercury, having a height of one inch. 4 An exceedingly small distance, amount of time, or quantity of material. — **by inches** Gradually; very slowly. — *v.t. & v.i.* To move by inches or small degrees. [OE *ynce* <L *uncia* the twelfth part, inch, ounce. Doublet of OUNCE.]

inch·meal (inch'mēl') *adv.* Inch by inch; piecemeal. — *n.* A fragment an inch long; a little piece. [<INCH + -MEAL]

in·ci·dence (in'sə·dəns) *n.* 1 A falling, or the direction or manner of falling. 2 *Physics* The angle which the path of a body or of any form of radiant energy makes with the perpendicular of a surface at the point of impact. 3 The fact or the manner of being incident. 4 The degree of occurrence or effect of something: a high *incidence* of typhus. 5 *Geom.* Partial coincidence in the position of two figures, as a line and a point on it.

in·ci·dent (in'sə·dənt) *n.* 1 Anything that takes place as part of an action or in connection with an event; a subordinate or concomitant event or act. 2 A happening in general, especially one of little importance; any event; an occurrence. 3 Something characteristically, naturally, or legally depending upon, connected with, or contained in another thing as its principal. See synonyms under ACCIDENT, CIRCUMSTANCE, EVENT, SCENE, STORY. — *adj.* 1 Falling or striking upon; impinging from without: *incident* rays. 2 Likely to befall; naturally or usually appertaining or attending: danger *incident* to travel. 3 Of the nature of an incident or concomitant; belonging subsidiarily; appurtenant: The right of alienation is *incident* to a title in fee simple. 4 *Obs.* Incidental. [<F <L *incidens, -entis*, ppr. of *incidere* fall upon < *in-* on + *cadere* fall]

in·ci·den·tal (in'sə·den'təl) *adj.* 1 Occurring in the course of something else; contingent. 2 Happening without regularity or design; casual. — *n.* 1 Something that is incidental, contingent, or fortuitous; a subordinate or minor occurrence, circumstance, or result. **2** *Music* In the tonic sol-fa system, a tone foreign to a chord. **3** *Usually pl.* Minor or casual expenses or items. — **in·ci·den·tal·ly** *adv.* — *Synonyms (adj.):* accessory, accidental, casual, chance, collateral, concomitant, concurrent, contingent, fortuitous, occasional. That is *incidental* which comes in the regular course of things, but is not viewed as primary or important; as, an *incidental* allusion, reference, or mention. That which is *incidental* is subordinate to the main design; that which is *accidental* occurs without design. Compare ACCIDENT. *Antonyms:* essential, fundamental, independent, inherent, invariable, regular, systematic, underlying.

in·cin·er·ate (in·sin′ər·āt) *v.t.* **·at·ed, ·at·ing** To consume with fire; reduce to ashes; cremate. See synonyms under BURN. [<Med. L *incineratus,* pp. of *incinerare* <*in-* in + *cinis, cineris* ashes]

in·cin·er·a·tor (in·sin′ə·rā′tər) *n.* **1** One who or that which incinerates. **2** A furnace or apparatus for reducing any substance to ashes, as for consuming refuse or for cremating.

in·cip·i·ent (in·sip′ē·ənt) *adj.* Belonging to the first stages. [<L *incipiens, -entis,* ppr. of *incipere.* See INCEPT.] — **in·cip′i·ent·ly** *adv.*

in·cise (in·sīz′) *v.t.* **·cised, ·cis·ing** **1** To cut into with a sharp instrument; gash. **2** To make (designs, marks, etc.) by cutting; engrave; carve. [<MF *inciser* <L *incidere* cut into <*in-* in + *caedere* cut]

in·ci·sion (in·sizh′ən) *n.* **1** The act of incising. **2** An opening made with a cutting instrument: a cut; gash. **3** *Surg.* A division of soft parts with a cutting instrument, as in an operation. **4** Sharpness; incisiveness; trenchancy. **5** A slit or notch, having the appearance of a cut, as in the margin of a leaf, a butterfly's wing, etc. [<OF <L *incisio, -onis*]

in·ci·sive (in·sī′siv) *adj.* **1** Having the power of incising. **2** Cutting; trenchant; acute: *incisive* wit. **3** Pertaining to an incisor. Also **in·ci′so·ry** (-sər·ē). [<Med. L *incisivus*] — **in·ci′sive·ly** *adv.* — **in·ci′sive·ness** *n.*

in·ci·sor (in·sī′zər) *adj.* Adapted for cutting. — *n.* A front or cutting tooth; in man, one of eight such teeth, four in each jaw. [<NL]

in·ci·sure (in·sizh′ər) *n.* An incision; cut. [<L *incisura*]

in·ci·tant (in·sī′tənt) *adj.* Inciting; instigating. — *n.* One who or that which incites. [<L *incitans, -antis,* ppr. of *incitare.* See INCITE.]

in·ci·ta·tion (in′sī·tā′shən) *n.* **1** Incitement. **2** An incentive. [<OF <L *incitatio, -onis*]

in·cite (in·sīt′) *v.t.* **·cit·ed, ·cit·ing** To urge to a particular action; instigate; stir up. See synonyms under ABET, ACTUATE, INFLUENCE, PERSUADE, SPUR, STIR. [<OF *inciter* <L *incitare* <*in-* thoroughly + *citare* rouse, freq. of *ciere* set in motion] — **in·ci′ta·tive** (-tə·tiv) *adj.* — **in·cit′er** *n.*

in·cite·ment (in·sīt′mənt) *n.* **1** The act of inciting. **2** That which incites; incentive; motive. See synonyms under IMPULSE.

in·ci·vil·i·ty (in′sə·vil′ə·tē) *n. pl.* **·ties** **1** The state of being uncivil; discourteous manner. **2** An uncivil or rude act.

in·clem·ent (in·klem′ənt) *adj.* Not clement; harsh; severe; rigorous, as weather; unpropitious or untoward. [<L *inclemens, -entis*] — **in·clem′en·cy** *n.*

in·cli·na·tion (in′klə·nā′shən) *n.* **1** Deviation from a given direction, especially from the vertical or horizontal. **2** The act of inclining or state of being inclined. **3** A slope or declivity. **4** A mental bent or tendency; predilection. **5** *Geom.* The angle between two lines, planes, etc. **6** *Astron.* The angle formed between the orbital plane of a planet and the ecliptic. [<F <L *inclinatio, -onis*] — **in·cli·na·to·ry** (in·klī′nə·tôr′ē, -tō′rē) *adj.* — *Synonyms:* appetite, attraction, bent, bias, desire, direction, disposition, drift, fancy, predilection, prepossession, proclivity, proneness, propensity, tendency. See AIM, APPETITE, ATTACHMENT, DESIRE, DIRECTION, FANCY, RELISH, WILL. *Antonyms:* aversion, disinclination, dislike, opposition, repulsion, resistance.

in·cline (in·klīn′) *v.* **·clined, ·clin·ing** *v.i.* **1** To deviate from the horizontal or vertical; slant; slope. **2** To have a tendency or disposition of the mind; be disposed or biased. **3** To tend in some quality or degree: purple *inclining* toward blue. **4** To bow or bend the head or body, as in courtesy. — *v.t.* **5** To cause to bend, lean, or slope. **6** To give a tendency or leaning to; influence. **7** To bow, as the head. See synonyms under ACTUATE, DRAW, INFLUENCE, LEAN[1], PERSUADE, TIP. — **to incline one's ear** To hear with favor; heed. — *n.* (in′klīn, in·klīn′) That which inclines from the horizontal; a gradient; slope. [<OF *encliner* <L *inclinare* <*in-* on + *clinare* lean] — **in·clin′a·ble** *adj.* — **in·clin′er** *n.*

in·clined (in·klīnd′) *adj.* **1** Bent out of line, or making an angle with some standard. **2** Having a tendency in some (specified) direction. **3** *Bot.* Bent out of the perpendicular, or with convex side up. **4** Toward the horizontal.

inclined plane A plane forming any but a right angle with a horizontal plane.

in·cli·nom·e·ter (in′klə·nom′ə·tər) *n.* **1** *Aeron.* An instrument for measuring inclination or slope of an aircraft with relation to the horizontal. **2** A magnetic needle pivoted to swing vertically in order to indicate the inclination of the earth's magnetic field; a dip needle. [<IN·CLIN(E) + -(O)METER]

INCLINED PLANE
ab. Base.
bc. Height.
ac. Inclined plane.
bac. Angle formed by plane.

in·close (in·klōz′), **in·clo·sure** (in·klō′zhər) See ENCLOSE, etc.

in·clude (in·klood′) *v.t.* **·clud·ed, ·clud·ing** **1** To have as a component part; contain. **2** To have or involve as a subordinate part, quality, element, etc.; imply: Religion *includes* morality. **3** To place in a general category, aggregate, etc. **4** To enclose within; confine. [<L *includere* <*in-* in + *claudere* shut] — **in·clud′a·ble, in·clud′i·ble** *adj.*

in·clu·sion (in·kloo′zhən) *n.* **1** The act of including. **2** That which is included. **3** *Mineral.* A substance either gaseous (as air), liquid (as water), or solid (as crystal), enclosed in a mineral, usually in a crystal. **4** *Biol.* Any inactive particle lodged in a living cell. [<L *inclusio, -onis* <*includere.* See INCLUDE.]

in·clu·sive (in·kloo′siv) *adj.* **1** Including the things, times, places, limits, or extremes mentioned: from A to Z *inclusive.* **2** Including within; surrounding: often with *of:* The list is *inclusive of* all the items. [<Med. L *inclusivus*] — **in·clu′sive·ly** *adv.* — **in·clu′sive·ness** *n.*

in·co·er·ci·ble (in′kō·ûr′sə·bəl) *adj.* **1** That cannot be coerced. **2** *Physics* Resistant to forces tending to change the form or properties of a substance or material.

in·cog·i·ta·ble (in·koj′ə·tə·bəl) *adj.* Not capable of being thought of; inconceivable. [<LL *incogitabilis*] — **in·cog′i·ta·bil′i·ty** *n.*

in·cog·i·tant (in·koj′ə·tənt) *adj.* Unthinking; thoughtless. [<L *incogitans, -antis*]

in·cog·ni·to (in·kog′nə·tō, in′käg·nē′tō) *adj. & adv.* Unknown; under an assumed name, so as to avoid notice or ceremony. — *n. pl.* **·tos** (-tōz) **1** The state of being incognito. **2** One who passes under an assumed name. **3** The assumed name. [<Ital. <L *incognitus* unknown < *in-* not + *cognitus,* pp. of *cognoscere* know] — **in·cog′ni·ta** (-tə) *n. & adj. fem.*

in·co·her·ence (in′kō·hir′əns) *n.* **1** Want of coherence. **2** Looseness or separateness of material particles. **3** That which is incoherent. Also **in′co·her′en·cy.**

in·co·her·ent (in′kō·hir′ənt) *adj.* **1** Having little or no coherence; incongruous; unconnected. **2** Manifesting incoherence in thought, speech, or action. **3** Without physical coherence of parts. — **in′co·her′ent·ly** *adv.*

in·com·bus·ti·ble (in·kəm·bus′tə·bəl) *adj.* Incapable of burning or of being burned. — *n.* That which does not burn; an incombustible substance or material. — **in′com·bus′ti·bil′i·ty, in′com·bus′ti·ble·ness** *n.* — **in′com·bus′ti·bly** *adv.*

in·come (in′kum) *n.* **1** Money, or other benefit, periodically received; the amount so received. **2** The gain derived from capital, or

labor, or both, inclusive of profit gained through the sale or conversion of capital assets. **3** *Obs.* The act of coming in; an incoming; specifically, the influx of divine grace into the soul. — **earned income** Income from labor, professional work, or business. — **unearned income** Income from capital investments, etc.

income tax See under TAX.

in·com·ing (in′kum′ing) *adj.* Coming in or about to come in: an *incoming* tenant, *incoming* profits. — *n.* The act of coming in; entrance or arrival.

in·com·men·su·ra·ble (in′kə·men′shər·ə·bəl, -sər·ə-) *adj.* **1** Lacking a common measure or standard of comparison. **2** *Math.* Not expressible in terms of a common measure or unit: *incommensurable* numbers. **3** Conspicuously disproportionate. — *n.* That which is incommensurable. — **in′com·men′su·ra·bil′i·ty, in′com·men′su·ra·ble·ness** *n.* — **in′com·men′su·ra·bly** *adv.*

in·com·men·su·rate (in′kə·men′shər·it) *adj.* **1** Incommensurable. **2** Inadequate; disproportionate. — **in′com·men′su·rate·ly** *adv.* — **in′com·men′su·rate·ness** *n.*

in·com·mode (in′kə·mōd′) *v.t.* **·mod·ed, ·mod·ing** To cause inconvenience to; disturb. [<F *incommoder* <L *incommodare* <*incommodus* inconvenient <*in-* not + *commodus* proper measure]

in·com·mo·di·ous (in′kə·mō′dē·əs) *adj.* Not commodious; not affording sufficient accommodation; inconvenient. — **in′com·mo′di·ous·ly** *adv.* — **in′com·mo′di·ous·ness** *n.* — **in′com·mod′i·ty** (-mod′ə·tē) *n.*

in·com·mu·ni·ca·ble (in′kə·myōō′nə·kə·bəl) *adj.* **1** Not capable of being communicated or imparted. **2** Incommunicative. — **in′com·mu′ni·ca·bil′i·ty** *n.*

in·com·mu·ni·ca·do (in′kə·myōō′nə·kä′dō) *adj. & adv.* Confined without the opportunity to communicate, as a prisoner. [<Sp.]

in·com·mu·ni·ca·tive (in′kə·myōō′nə·kā′tiv, -kə·tiv) *adj.* Reserved; guarded in speech and manner. — **in′com·mu′ni·ca′tive·ly** *adv.* — **in′com·mu′ni·ca′tive·ness** *n.*

in·com·pa·ra·ble (in·kom′pər·ə·bəl) *adj.* **1** Not admitting of comparison, as being inapproachable; peerless. **2** Unsuitable for comparison. See synonyms under RARE[1]. [<F] — **in·com′pa·ra·bil′i·ty, in·com′pa·ra·ble·ness** *n.* — **in·com′pa·ra·bly** *adv.*

in·com·pat·i·ble (in′kəm·pat′ə·bəl) *adj.* **1** Not compatible; incapable of existing together in agreement or harmony; discordant. **2** Incapable of coexisting. **3** *Med.* **a** Incapable of use in combination, as certain drugs. **b** Mutually antagonistic, as different blood types. **4** *Logic* Incapable of being true simultaneously: said of two or more propositions. — *n. Usually pl.* Incompatible persons or things. See synonyms under CONTRARY, INCONGRUOUS. — **in′com·pat′i·bly** *adv.*

in·com·pat·i·bil·i·ty (in′kəm·pat′ə·bil′ə·tē) *n. pl.* **·ties** **1** The quality of being incompatible: also **in′com·pat′i·ble·ness.** **2** That which is incompatible. [<F *incompatibilité*]

in·com·pe·tent (in·kom′pə·tənt) *adj.* **1** Not competent; unable to do what is required. **2** Not legally qualified. See synonyms under BAD. — *n.* An incompetent person. [<F *incompétent*] — **in·com′pe·tence, in·com′pe·ten·cy** *n.* — **in·com′pe·tent·ly** *adv.*

in·com·plete (in′kəm·plēt′) *adj.* **1** Not complete; imperfect. **2** Lacking in certain parts, as some flowers. — **in′com·plete′ly** *adv.* — **in′com·plete′ness** *n.* — **in′com·ple′tion** *n.*

in·com·pre·hen·si·ble (in′kom·pri·hen′sə·bəl, in·kom′-) *adj.* **1** Not comprehensible; not understandable; inconceivable. **2** *Archaic* That cannot be included or confined within limits. See synonyms under MYSTERIOUS. [<L *incomprehensibilis*] — **in·com′pre·hen·si·bil′i·ty, in·com′pre·hen′si·ble·ness** *n.* — **in·com′pre·hen′si·bly** *adv.*

in·com·pre·hen·sion (in′kom·pri·hen′shən, in·kom′-) *n.* Lack of understanding.

in·com·pre·hen·sive (in′kom·pri·hen′siv, in·kom′-) *adj.* Not comprehensive; limited.

in·con·ceiv·a·ble (in′kən·sē′və·bəl) *adj.* **1** That cannot be conceived; incomprehensible. **2** Incredible; impossible. **3** *Philos.* Involving a

---

add,āce,câre,pälm; end,ēven; it,īce; odd,ōpen,ôrder; tŏŏk,pōōl; up,bûrn; ə = a in *above,* e in *sicken,* i in *clarity,* o in *melon,* u in *focus* ; yōō = u in *fuse,* oi,oil; ou,pout; ch,check; g,go; ng,ring; th,thin; th,this; zh,vision. Foreign sounds à,œ,ü,kh,ṅ; and ◆: see page xx. <from; + plus; ? possibly.

contradiction in terms; inherently contradictory. — **in·con·ceiv′a·ble·ness, in′con·ceiv′a·bil′i·ty** *n.* — **in′con·ceiv′a·bly** *adv.*

in·con·clu·sive (in′kən·kloō′siv) *adj.* **1** Not leading to an ultimate conclusion; indecisive. **2** Not achieving a definite result; ineffective: *inconclusive* efforts.

in·con·dite (in·kon′dit) *adj.* Badly constructed; irregular. [<L *inconditus* < *in-* not + *conditus,* pp. of *condere* put together]

in·con·gru·ent (in·kong′groō·ənt) *adj.* Incongruous. — **in·con′gru·ence** *n.* — **in·con′gru·ent·ly** *adv.*

in·con·gru·i·ty (in′kən·groō′ə·tē) *n.* *pl.* **·ties 1** The state of being incongruous; lack of harmony or suitableness. **2** That which is incongruous. [<Med. L *incongruitas, -tatis*]

in·con·gru·ous (in·kon′groō·əs) *adj.* **1** Not congruous. **2** Composed of inharmonious elements. — **in·con′gru·ous·ly** *adv.* — **in·con′gru·ous·ness** *n.*

Synonyms: absurd, conflicting, contradictory, contrary, discordant, discrepant, ill-matched, inapposite, inappropriate, incommensurable, incompatible, inconsistent, inharmonious, irreconcilable, mismatched, mismated, repugnant, unsuitable. Two or more things that do not fit well together, or are not adapted to each other, are said to be *incongruous;* a thing is said to be *incongruous* that is not adapted to the time, place, or occasion; the term is also applied to a thing made up of ill-assorted parts or *inharmonious* elements. *Discordant* is applied to all things that jar like musical notes that are not in accord; *inharmonious* has the same original sense, but is a milder term. Things are *incompatible* which cannot exist together in harmonious relations, and whose action when associated tends to ultimate extinction of one by the other. *Inconsistent* applies to things that cannot be made to agree in thought with each other, or with some standard of truth or right; slavery and freedom are *inconsistent* with each other in theory, and *incompatible* in fact. *Incongruous* applies to relations, *unsuitable* to purpose or use; two colors are *incongruous* which cannot be agreeably associated: either may be *unsuitable* for a person, a room, or an occasion. *Incommensurable* is a mathematical term, applying to two or more quantities that have no common measure or aliquot part. See CONTRARY. *Antonyms:* accordant, agreeing, compatible, consistent, harmonious, suitable.

in·con·se·quent (in·kon′sə·kwənt) *adj.* **1** Contrary to reasonable inference. **2** Not according to sequence; hence, irrelevant. **3** Illogical in thought or action; eccentric. — **in·con′se·quence** *n.* — **in·con′se·quent·ly** *adv.*

in·con·se·quen·tial (in′kon·sə·kwen′shəl, in·kon′-) *adj.* **1** Of little consequence; trivial. **2** Irrelevant. — **in·con′se·quen′ti·al·i·ty** (-kwen′shē·al′ə·tē) *n.* — **in·con′se·quen′tial·ly** *adv.*

in·con·sid·er·ate (in′kən·sid′ər·it) *adj.* **1** Not considerate; thoughtless. **2** Showing want of consideration. See synonyms under BLUFF, IMPRUDENT, INATTENTIVE. — **in′con·sid′er·ate·ly** *adv.* — **in′con·sid′er·ate·ness** *n.* — **in′con·sid′·er·a′tion** *n.*

in·con·sis·ten·cy (in′kən·sis′tən·sē) *n.* *pl.* **·cies 1** The state or quality of being inconsistent; logical incompatibility; lack of uniformity or coherence in thought or conduct. **2** That which is inconsistent. Also **in′con·sis′tence.**

in·con·sis·tent (in′kən·sis′tənt) *adj.* **1** Logically incompatible. **2** Self-contradictory. **3** Not consistent; capricious. See synonyms under CONTRARY, INCONGRUOUS. — **in′con·sis′tent·ly** *adv.*

in·con·spic·u·ous (in′kən·spik′yoō·əs) *adj.* **1** Not conspicuous; not prominent. **2** Not attracting attention to oneself.

in·con·stant (in·kon′stənt) *adj.* Not constant; fickle; variable. See synonyms under FICKLE, VAIN. [<F <L *inconstans, -antis*] — **in·con′stan·cy** *n.* — **in·con′stant·ly** *adv.*

in·con·test·a·ble (in′kən·tes′tə·bəl) *adj.* Not admitting of controversy. [<F]

Synonyms: certain, impregnable, incontrovertible, indisputable, indubitable, irrefragable, unassailable, undeniable, undoubted, unquestionable. *Antonyms:* apocryphal, doubtful, dubious, fictitious, hypothetical, problematical, questionable, uncertain, unsustained, unverified.

in·con·ti·nent (in·kon′tə·nənt) *adj.* **1** Not continent; exercising no control over the

appetites, especially sexual passion; unchaste. **2** Unrestrained: an *incontinent* passion. **3** *Pathol.* Unable to hold back bodily discharges or evacuations. **4** *Obs.* Immediate. — *adv. Archaic* Immediately. [<OF <L *incontinens, -entis.* See IN-¹, CONTINENT.] — **in·con′ti·nence, in·con′ti·nen·cy** *n.* — **in·con′ti·nent·ly** *adv.*

in·con·ven·ience (in′kən·vēn′yəns) *n.* **1** The state of being inconvenient. **2** A disadvantage; embarrassment. Also **in′con·ven′ien·cy.** — *v.t.* **·ienced, ·ienc·ing** To cause inconvenience to; incommode; trouble. [<OF]

in·con·ven·ient (in′kən·vēn′yənt) *adj.* **1** Not convenient; incommodious; embarrassing. **2** Not expedient; unsuitable. [<OF *inconvenient* <L *inconveniens, -entis.* See IN-¹, CONVENIENT.] — **in′con·ven′ient·ly** *adv.*

in·con·vert·i·ble (in′kən·vûr′tə·bəl) *adj.* Not interchangeable, as paper money into specie. — **in′con·vert′i·bil′i·ty** *n.*

in·cor·po·rate¹ (in·kôr′pə·rāt) *v.* **·rat·ed, ·rat·ing** *v.t.* **1** To take into or include as part of a mass or whole: His philosophy *incorporates* the ideas of Hegel. **2** To form into a legal corporation. **3** To combine or unite into one body or whole; blend; mix. **4** *Rare* To give material form to; embody. — *v.i.* **5** To become combined or united as one body or whole. **6** To form a legal corporation. See synonyms under ENROL, MIX, UNITE. — *adj.* (-pər·it) **1** Joined, or intimately associated. **2** Incorporated. [<LL *incorporatus,* pp. of *incorporare* embody <*in-* + *corporare.* See CORPORATE.] — **in·cor′po·ra′tive** *adj.*

in·cor·po·rate² (in·kôr′pər·it) *adj.* **1** Not consisting of matter; incorporeal. **2** Not formed into a corporation. [<L *incorporatus*]

in·cor·po·rat·ed (in·kôr′pə·rā′tid) *adj.* **1** Constituting a legal corporation. **2** Combined.

in·cor·po·ra·tion (in·kôr′pə·rā′shən) *n.* **1** The act of incorporating. **2** A corporation. **3** The combining of elements.

in·cor·po·re·al (in′kôr·pôr′ē·əl, -pō′rē-) *adj.* **1** Not consisting of matter; immaterial. **2** Pertaining to the immaterial world. **3** Not appreciable by the senses. **4** *Law* Having no material existence, but regarded as existing by the law; intangible: *incorporeal* rights. Also *Obs.* **in·cor′po·ral** (in·kôr′pər·əl). [<L *incorporeus*] — **in′cor·po′re·al·ism** *n.* — **in′cor·po′re·al·ly** *adv.*

in·cor·rect (in′kə·rekt′) *adj.* **1** Inaccurate or untrue. **2** Not proper; unsuitable. **3** Erroneous; faulty. — **in′cor·rect′ly** *adv.*

in·cor·ri·gi·ble (in·kôr′ə·jə·bəl, -kor′-) *adj.* **1** That cannot be corrected. **2** Depraved beyond reform. — *n.* One who is beyond correction. [<MF <*in-* not + *corrigible.* See CORRIGIBLE.] — **in·cor′ri·gi·ble·ness, in·cor′ri·gi·bil′i·ty** *n.* — **in·cor′ri·gi·bly** *adv.*

in·cor·rupt (in′kə·rupt′) *adj.* **1** Not depraved nor defiled morally; above the power of bribes; pure. **2** Not marred in physical substance; not acted upon by decay. **3** Not tainted by other idioms: free from error, as a language. **4** Unchanged; unaltered, as a text. Also **in′cor·rupt′ed.** [<L *incorruptus* <*in-* not + *corruptus.* See CORRUPT.] — **in′cor·rupt′ly** *adv.* — **in′cor·rupt′ness** *n.* — **in′cor·rup′tion** (-rup′shən) *n.* — **in′cor·rup′tive** *adj.*

in·cor·rupt·i·ble (in′kə·rup′tə·bəl) *adj.* Incapable of corruption; especially, not accessible to bribery. See synonyms under FAITHFUL, IMMORTAL, JUST, MORAL. — **in′cor·rupt′i·bil′i·ty, in′cor·rupt′i·ble·ness** *n.* — **in′cor·rupt′i·bly** *adv.*

in·cras·sate (in·kras′āt) *v.t. & v.i.* **·sat·ed, ·sat·ing 1** To make or become thick or thicker. **2** To thicken (a fluid), as by mixing or evaporation. — *adj. Biol.* Thickened, as the antennae or femora of certain insects: also **in·cras′sat·ed.** [<L *incrassatus,* pp. of *incrassare* <*in-* very + *crassus* thick]

in·crease (in·krēs′) *v.* **·creased, ·creas·ing** *v.i.* **1** To become greater, as in amount, size, degree, etc.; grow. **2** To grow in numbers, especially by reproduction: May your tribe *increase.* — *v.t.* **3** To make greater, as in amount, size, degree, etc.; augment; enlarge. — *n.* (in′krēs) **1** The act or process of growing larger, as in quantity, size, degree, etc.; augmentation; enlargement; extension. **2** An added or increased amount; increment: an *increase* in pay. **3** A production of offspring; propagation: blessed with a large *increase.* **4** Offspring; progeny. **5** *Archaic.* Crops of the earth. [<OF *encreistre* <L *increscere* <*in-* in + *crescere* grow <*creare* create]

— **in·creas′a·ble** *adj.* — **in·creas′ing·ly** *adv.*

Synonyms (verb): advance, aggravate, augment, enhance, enlarge, exaggerate, extend, heighten, intensify, magnify, prolong, raise. See ADD, AGGRAVATE, AMPLIFY, FLOURISH, PROPAGATE, SWELL. *Antonyms:* abbreviate, abridge, contract, curtail, decrease, diminish. *Synonyms (noun):* access, accession, accretion, addendum, addition, aggravation, amplification, appendage, augmentation, complement, enhancement, enlargement, expansion, extension, growth, harvest, improvement, increment, product, reenforcement, return. See ACCESSION, HARVEST, PROGRESS. *Antonyms:* abbreviation, contraction, deduction, diminution, expenditure, loss, subtraction, waste.

in·cred·i·bil·i·ty (in·kred′ə·bil′ə·tē) *n.* *pl.* **·ties 1** The state or quality of being unbelievable or hard to believe. **2** An unbelievable thing.

in·cred·i·ble (in·kred′ə·bəl) *adj.* **1** Seeming too far-fetched or extraordinary to be possible. **2** Beyond or difficult of belief. — **in·cred′i·ble·ness** *n.* — **in·cred′i·bly** *adv.*

in·cre·du·li·ty (in′krə·doō′lə·tē, -dyoō′-) *n.* Indisposition or refusal to believe. See synonyms under DOUBT. Also **in·cred·u·lous·ness** (in·krej′ə·ləs·nis). [<OF *incredulité*]

in·cred·u·lous (in·krej′ə·ləs) *adj.* **1** Refusing belief; skeptical. **2** Characterized by, caused by, or manifesting doubt. **3** *Obs.* Incredible. [<L *incredulus* <*in-* not + *credulus.* See CREDULOUS.] — **in·cred′u·lous·ly** *adv.*

in·cre·mate (in′krə·māt) *v.t. Obs.* **·mat·ed, ·mat·ing** To cremate.

in·cre·ment (in′krə·mənt) *n.* **1** The act of increasing; enlargement. **2** That which is added; increase: opposed to *decrement.* **3** *Math.* The amount by which a varying quantity increases between two of its stages. **4** *Mil.* The quantity of powder added to, or subtracted from, the propelling charge of separate loaded artillery ammunition to compensate for differences in range. See synonyms under INCREASE. — **unearned increment** Any increase of value produced by forces independent of the person who receives it; specifically, increase of value in land that springs from the increase of population or other cause independent of the land itself and of its owner. [<L *incrementum* <*increscere* INCREASE] — **in′cre·men′tal** (-men′təl) *adj.*

in·cres·cent (in·kres′ənt) *adj.* Characterized by increase; growing: said especially of the moon. [<L *increscens, -entis,* ppr. *of increscere* INCREASE]

in·cre·tion (in·krē′shən) *n.* Internal secretion or its product; a hormone. [<IN-² + (SE)CRETION]

in·crim·i·nate (in·krim′ə·nāt) *v.t.* **·nat·ed, ·nat·ing 1** To charge with a crime or fault; accuse. **2** To show or appear to show the guilt or error of. [<Med. L *incriminatus,* pp. of *incriminare* <*in-* + *criminare* accuse one of a crime] — **in·crim′i·na′tion** *n.* — **in·crim′i·na·to′ry** (-nə·tôr′ē, -tō′rē) *adj.*

in·crust (in·krust′) *v.t.* **1** To cover with a crust or hard coat. **2** To decorate, as with jewels. Also spelled *encrust.* [<OF *encrouster* <L *incrustare* <*in-* on + *crustare* form a crust]

in·cu·bate (in′kyə·bāt, ing′-) *v.* **·bat·ed, ·bat·ing** *v.t.* **1** To sit upon (eggs) in order to hatch; brood. **2** To hatch (eggs) in this manner or by artificial heat. **3** To maintain under conditions favoring optimum growth or development, as bacterial cultures. — *v.i.* **4** To sit on eggs; brood. **5** To undergo incubation. [<L *incubatus,* pp. of *incubare* <*in-* on + *cubare* lie] — **in′cu·ba′tive** *adj.*

in·cu·ba·tion (in′kyə·bā′shən, ing′-) *n.* **1** The act of hatching. **2** State of being hatched. **3** A planning or producing. **4** Figuratively, a brooding upon, especially that of the Spirit of God over chaos at the Creation (*Gen.* i 2). **5** *Med.* The period between the time of exposure to an infectious disease and its development. [<L *incubatio, -onis*]

in·cu·bus (in′kyə·bəs, ing′-) *n.* *pl.* **·bus·es or ·bi** (-bī) **1** Anything that tends to weigh down or discourage. **2** A nightmare. **3** A demon supposed to descend upon sleeping persons with whom it sought to have sexual intercourse. Compare SUCCUBUS. See synonyms under LOAD. [<Med. L, a demon that causes nightmare <LL, nightmare <L *incubare* lie on]

in·cul·cate (in·kul′kāt, in′kul-) *v.t.* ·cat·ed, ·cat·ing To impress upon the mind by frequent and emphatic repetition; instil. See synonyms under IMPRESS. [<L *inculcatus*, pp. of *inculcare* tread on < *in-* on + *calcare* tread < *calx, calcis* heel] — **in·cul·ca·tion** (in′kul·kā′shən) *n.* — **in′cul·ca′tor** *n.*

in·cul·pa·ble (in·kul′pə·bəl) *adj.* Not culpable.

in·cul·pate (in·kul′pāt, in′kul-) *v.t.* ·pat·ed, ·pat·ing 1 To charge with fault; blame. 2 To involve in guilt; implicate. [<Med. L *inculpatus*, pp. of *inculpare* blame < *in-* in + *culpa* fault] — **in′cul·pa′tion** *n.* — **in·cul′pa·to′ry** (-pə·tôr′ē, -tō′rē) *adj.*

in·cum·ben·cy (in·kum′bən·sē) *n. pl.* ·cies 1 The state of holding an office or discharging its duties or functions. 2 The period during which an office is held. 3 The state of being incumbent, or that which is incumbent, as a mental or physical burden. 4 *Rare* An obligation.

in·cum·bent (in·kum′bənt) *adj.* 1 Resting upon one as a moral obligation, or as necessary under the circumstances; obligatory. 2 Resting, leaning, or weighing wholly or partly upon something. — *n.* One who holds an office or performs official duties. [<L *incumbens, -entis,* ppr. of *incumbere* recline < *in-* on + *cubare* lie down]

in·cur (in·kûr′) *v.t.* ·curred, ·cur·ring To meet with or become subject to, as unpleasant consequences, especially through one's own action; bring upon oneself. [<L *incurrere* run into < *in-* in + *currere* run]

in·cur·rent (in·kûr′ənt) *adj.* Having or characterized by an inward-flowing current. [<L *incurrens, -entis,* ppr. of *incurrere* INCUR]

in·cur·sion (in·kûr′zhən, -shən) *n.* A hostile entrance into a territory; a temporary invasion; raid. See synonyms under AGGRESSION, ATTACK, INVASION. [<L *incursio, -onis* < *incurrere* INCUR] — **in·cur′sive** *adj.*

in·curve (in·kûrv′) *v.t.* & *v.i.* To curve inward. — *n.* (in′kûrv′) In baseball, a pitched ball that curves inward toward the batter.

in·cus (ing′kəs) *n. pl.* **in·cu·des** (in·kyōō′dēz) 1 *Anat.* The central one of three small bones in the tympanum or middle ear; so called from its fancied resemblance to an anvil. See illustration under EAR. 2 *Meteorol.* The anvil-shaped upper part of a cumulonimbus cloud; an anviltop. [<L, anvil] — **in′cu·dal** *adj.*

in·cuse (in·kyōōz′) *adj.* Formed by hammering or stamping. — *n.* An impression made by striking a coin with or against a die. [<L *incusus,* pp. of *incudere* forge with a hammer < *in-* on + *cudere* beat]

in·da·gate (in′də·gāt) *v.t. Obs.* ·gat·ed, ·gat·ing To investigate. [<L *indagatus,* pp. of *indagare* investigate] — **in′da·ga′tion** *n.* — **in′da·ga′tor** *n.*

in·debt·ed (in·det′id) *adj.* 1 Having contracted a debt. 2 Owing gratitude; beholden. [<OF *endetté,* pp. of *endetter* < *en-* on + *dette* debt. See DEBT.]

in·debt·ed·ness (in·det′id·nis) *n.* 1 The state of being indebted. 2 The amount of one's debts.

in·de·cen·cy (in·dē′sən·sē) *n. pl.* ·cies 1 The condition of being indecent; especially, vulgarity or immorality in actions, spoken or printed words, pictures, etc. 2 An indecent act. 3 Obscenity.
Synonyms: coarseness, filthiness, foulness, grossness, immodesty, impropriety, impurity, indecorum, indelicacy, obscenity, offensiveness, uncleanness, unseemliness, vileness. See OUTRAGE. *Antonyms:* delicacy, modesty, nicety, propriety, purity, refinement.

in·de·cent (in·dē′sənt) *adj.* 1 Offensive to decency or propriety; immodest; gross. 2 Contrary to what is fit and proper. See synonyms under IMMODEST. — **in·de′cent·ly** *adv.*

in·de·ci·sive (in′də·sī′siv) *adj.* 1 Not decisive. 2 Hesitant; irresolute. — **in′de·ci′sive·ly** *adv.* — **in′de·ci′sion** *n.*

in·deed (in·dēd′) *adv.* In fact; in truth: used to emphasize an affirmation, to mark a qualifying word or clause, to denote a concession,

or interrogatively for the purpose of drawing forth confirmation of a fact stated. — *interj.* An exclamation of surprise, irony, incredulity, etc. [<IN + DEED]

in·de·fat·i·ga·ble (in′də·fat′ə·gə·bəl) *adj.* Not yielding readily to fatigue; tireless; unflagging. [<MF *indéfatigable* <L *indefatigabilis* < *in-* not + *defatigare* tire out] — **in′de·fat′i·ga·bil′i·ty, in′de·fat′i·ga·ble·ness** *n.* — **in′de·fat′i·ga·bly** *adv.*
Synonyms: assiduous, indomitable, industrious, never-failing, never-tiring, persevering, persistent, tireless, unfailing, unfaltering, unflagging, untiring, unwearied. *Antonyms:* defeated, despondent, discouraged, fainting, faltering, flagging, indolent, negligent, remiss, wearied.

in·de·fea·si·ble (in′də·fē′zə·bəl) *adj.* Not defeasible; incapable of being annulled, set aside, or made void. — **in′de·fea′si·bil′i·ty** *n.* — **in′de·fea′si·bly** *adv.*

in·de·fen·si·ble (in′di·fen′sə·bəl) *adj.* 1 Incapable of being justified, excused, etc. 2 Incapable of being defended.

in·de·fin·a·ble (in′di·fī′nə·bəl) *adj.* That cannot be defined or described; vague; subtle. — **in′de·fin′a·ble·ness** *n.* — **in′de·fin′a·bly** *adv.*

in·def·i·nite (in·def′ə·nit) *adj.* 1 Not definite or precise. 2 Indeterminate; without fixed boundaries; incapable of measurement. 3 So large as to have no definite or particular limit; also, infinite. 4 *Bot.* Uncertain: said of stamens when too many to be counted easily, and of inflorescence when not terminated absolutely by a flower. 5 *Gram.* Not defining or determining; tending to generalize, as the *indefinite* articles *a* and *an.* See synonyms under EQUIVOCAL, VAGUE. — **in·def′i·nite·ly** *adv.* — **in·def′i·nite·ness** *n.*

indefinite pronoun See under PRONOUN.

in·del·i·ble (in·del′ə·bəl) *adj.* That cannot be blotted out; ineffaceable. [<L *indelibilis* < *in-* not + *delibilis* perishable < *delere* destroy] — **in·del′i·bil′i·ty, in·del′i·ble·ness** *n.* — **in·del′i·bly** *adv.*

in·del·i·ca·cy (in·del′ə·kə·sē) *n. pl.* ·cies 1 The quality of being indelicate; coarseness. 2 An act offensive to propriety or refined feeling.

in·del·i·cate (in·del′ə·kit) *adj.* Not delicate; offensive to propriety; immodest. See synonyms under IMMODEST. — **in·del′i·cate·ly** *adv.*

in·dem·ni·fy (in·dem′nə·fī) *v.t.* ·fied, ·fy·ing 1 To compensate for loss or damage sustained. 2 To make good (a loss). 3 To give security against future loss or punishment to. See synonyms under PAY. [<L *indemnis* unhurt (< *in-* not + *damnum* harm) + -FY] — **in·dem′ni·fi·ca′tion** *n.* — **in·dem′ni·tor** (-nə·tər) *n.*

in·dem·ni·ty (in·dem′nə·tē) *n. pl.* ·ties 1 That which is given as compensation for a loss or for damage. 2 An undertaking to remunerate another for loss or to protect him against liability. 3 Exemption from penalties or liabilities incurred. See synonyms under RECOMPENSE, RESTITUTION, SUBSIDY. [<F *indemnité* <L *indemnitas* < *indemnis.* See INDEMNIFY.]

in·dent (in·dent′) *v.t.* 1 To set, as the first line of a paragraph, in from the margin. 2 To cut or mark the edge of with toothlike hollows or notches; serrate. 3 To make an order for goods upon. 4 To make an order for (goods). 5 To cut or tear (a document drawn in duplicate) along an irregular line in order to identify the halves when fitted together. 6 To cut or tear the edge or top of (a document) in an irregular line. 7 To indenture, as an apprentice. — *v.i.* 8 To be notched or cut; form a recess. 9 To set a line, etc., in from the margin. 10 To make out an order in duplicate; make a requisition. 11 *Archaic* To enter into a bargain or covenant. — *n.* (in′dent, in·dent′) 1 A cut or notch in the edge of anything; an opening like a notch; an indentation or impression. 2 An indented contract; indenture. 3 An indented certificate issued by the United States government at the close of the American Revolution, for principal or in-

terest due on the public debt. 4 An official order for supplies. 5 In commerce, a foreign order for goods, with or without specified particulars as to quality, price, mode of shipment, etc. 6 An indention. [<OF *endenter* <Med. L *indentare* < *in-* in + *dens, dentis* tooth]

in·den·ta·tion (in′den·tā′shən) *n.* 1 The act of denting. 2 A cut or notch in an edge or border. 3 An indention. See synonyms under HOLE.

in·dent·ed (in·den′tid) *adj.* 1 *Archit.* a Notched or serrated. b Formed into several angles: said of a parapet. 2 *Her.* Toothed like a saw. 3 In printing or typewriting, set in from the margin. 4 Indentured.

in·den·tion (in·den′shən) *n.* 1 A dent. 2 *Printing* a The setting in of a line or body of type at the left side. b The space thus left blank.
—**hanging indention** *Printing* Equal indention of all lines of a paragraph except the first, which is not indented.

in·den·ture (in·den′chər) *n.* 1 *Law* An instrument of contract under seal; an instrument in duplicate between parties, each party keeping a counterpart. 2 *Often pl.* A legal instrument for binding an apprentice or a servant to his master. 3 The act of indenting, or the state of being indented. — *v.t.* ·tured, ·tur·ing 1 To bind by indenture, as an apprentice. 2 To indent; furrow. [<OF *endenture* <Med. L *indentare.* See INDENT.]

in·de·pen·dence (in′di·pen′dəns) *n.* 1 Freedom from dependence upon others, as for government or financial support. 2 A competency. 3 A spirit of self-reliance. See synonyms under LIBERTY, WEALTH. See DECLARATION OF INDEPENDENCE.

Independence Day The Fourth of July: so called in the United States in commemoration of the Declaration of Independence, adopted July 4, 1776.

in·de·pen·den·cy (in′di·pen′dən·sē) *n. pl.* ·cies 1 Independence. 2 An independent state or territory.

In·de·pen·den·cy (in′di·pen′dən·sē) *n. Eccl.* The doctrine that each congregation of the Christian church is an entity independent of central ecclesiastical control.

in·de·pen·dent (in′di·pen′dənt) *adj.* 1 Not subordinate or subject to nor dependent for support upon another government, person, or thing. 2 Affording means of independence or freedom of action. 3 Indicating self-reliance; resentful of, or uninfluenced by, advice or assistance. 4 Separate or disconnected. 5 Pertaining to the Independents or Congregationalists. 6 Not identified with any political party. 7 Possessing sufficient means to live without labor. 8 *Math.* a Capable of taking any value without regard to the variation of other quantities. b Denoting two or more quantities such that the value of none of them depends upon that of the others. — *n.* 1 One who exercises his own will or judgment without the guidance or control of others. 2 *Often cap.* One who is not an adherent of any political party. — **in′de·pen′dent·ly** *adv.*

In·de·pen·dent (in′di·pen′dənt) *n.* 1 A believer in Independency. 2 In England, a Congregationalist.

independent clause *Gram.* A clause capable of constituting a sentence.

in-depth (in′depth′) *adj.* Extensive and thorough; not superficial; penetrating or profound: an *in-depth* study of world-wide intelligence operations.

in·de·ter·mi·na·ble (in′di·tûr′mi·nə·bəl) *adj.* 1 Not capable of exact determination or measurement. 2 Not decided or clearly established. — **in′de·ter′mi·na·bly** *adv.*

in·de·ter·mi·na·cy (in′di·tûr′mə·nə·sē) *n.* The state of being indefinite or undetermined; lack of certainty.

indeterminacy principle The uncertainty principle.

in·de·ter·mi·nate (in′di·tûr′mə·nit) *adj.* 1 Not

definite in extent, amount, or nature. **2** Not clear or precise; vague. **3** Not decided; unsettled. **4** *Bot.* Not definitely terminated, as a raceme. **5** *Math.* Designating any of a class of undefined expressions, as infinity minus infinity, zero divided by infinity, zero to the zero power, etc. — **in·de·ter′mi·nate·ly** *adv.* — **in′de·ter′mi·nate·ness** *n.*

in·de·ter·mi·na·tion (in′di·tûr′mə·nā′shən) *n.* **1** Lack of determination. **2** The state of being indeterminate.

in·de·ter·min·ism (in′di·tûr′mə·niz′əm) *n.* The doctrine that the will, while influenced, is not absolutely determined by motives or environment. — **in′de·ter′min·ist** *n.*

in·dex (in′deks) *n. pl.* **·dex·es** or **·di·ces** (-də·sēz) **1** Anything used to indicate, point out, or guide, as the index finger, or forefinger, the hand of a clock, a pointer, etc. **2** Anything that manifests or denotes: an *index* of character. **3** An alphabetic list of matters or references, as in a book. **4** *Math.* An exponent. **5** A mark [☞] employed to direct attention. **6** A numerical expression of the ratio between one dimension or magnitude and another with which it is regarded as comparable: the cephalic *index.* **7** *Obs.* A prolog; prelude. — *v.t.* **1** To provide with an index. **2** To enter in an index. **3** To indicate; mark. [< L. See INDICATE.] — **in′dex·er** *n.* — **in·dex′i·cal** *adj.*

index finger The forefinger: so called from its universal use as a pointer or indicator.

index number *Stat.* Any of a series of numbers indicating the quantitative time changes in a given statistical aggregate, as prices, costs, etc., with reference to an arbitrary base (usually 100) which represents the status of the aggregate at a specified previous time or period.

In·di·a (in′dē·ə) The central peninsula of southern Asia, south of the Himalayas; 1,581,000 square miles: ancient *Bharat;* divided into: (1) the **Republic of India,** a self-governing member of the Commonwealth of Nations; 1,138,814 square miles; capital, New Delhi; (2) Pakistan; (3) several smaller states unaffiliated with the Commonwealth.

India ink 1 A black pigment composed of a mixture of lampblack or burnt cork with gelatin and water, originally made in India, China, and Japan and molded in sticks or cakes. **2** A liquid ink made from this pigment. **3** Any of various heavy drawing inks in different colors, especially one containing sepia. Also called *Chinese ink.*

In·di·an (in′dē·ən) *adj.* **1** Pertaining to India or the East Indies or to Indians. **2** Pertaining to the American aboriginal race or to the West Indies. **3** Made from maize. — *n.* **1** A native of India or of the East Indies. **2** A member of the aboriginal race of America (American Indian) or of the West Indies. **3** Loosely, any of the languages of the American Indians. [< L *India* < Gk. < *Indos* the Indus river < OPersian *Hindu* India < Skt. *sindhu* river. Cf. HINDI.

In·di·an·a (in′dē·an′ə) A north central State of the United States; 36,291 square miles; capital, Indianapolis; entered the Union Dec. 11, 1816; nickname, *Hoosier State:* abbr. IN — **In′di·an′i·an** *adj. & n.*

In·di·an·ap·o·lis (in′dē·ə·nap′ə·lis) The capital of Indiana.

Indian hemp 1 The common Asian hemp (*Cannabis sativa*). **2** A perennial American herb (*Apocynum cannabinum*) of the dogbane family, with a tough bark, greenish–white flowers, and a milky juice: its dried roots have medicinal properties: also called *Canada hemp, hemp dogbane, Indian physic.*

Indian meal Cornmeal.

Indian Ocean The smallest of the three great oceans of the world, bounded by Africa, Asia, Australia, and Antarctica; 28,357,000 square miles.

Indian physic **1** Either of two perennial herbs (genus *Gillenia*) common in the woods of the United States, and reputed to be emetic, cathartic, or tonic, according to the dose. **2** Indian hemp (def. 2).

Indian red 1 A pure native iron oxide found in India and used as a pigment. **2** A red earth used by the American Indian and by early American painters.

Indian summer See under SUMMER.

India rubber A soft and elastic substance derived from the sap of various tropical plants and having many uses in industry and the arts; caoutchouc. See RUBBER.

in·di·can (in′də·kən) *n.* **1** *Chem.* A colorless, crystalline, toxic glycoside, $C_{14}H_{17}O_6N$, contained in several species of indigo plants. **2** *Biochem.* Potassium indoxyl sulfate, $C_8H_6NSO_4K$, contained in the urine and other body fluids of certain animals, including man:
also called *uroxanthin.* [< L *indicum* INDIGO + -AN]

in·di·cant (in′də·kənt) *adj.* Indicating.. — *n.* An indicator.

in·di·cate (in′də·kāt) *v.t.* **·cat·ed,** **·cat·ing** **1** To be or give a sign of; betoken: Those clouds *indicate* rain. **2** To point out; direct attention to: to *indicate* the correct page. **3** To express or make known, especially briefly or indirectly: His smile *indicates* his approval. **4** *Med.* To show or suggest, as a disease or its remedy: said of symptoms, etc. [< L *indicatus,* pp. of *indicare* < *in-* in + *dicare* point out, proclaim] — **in′di·ca′to·ry** (-kə·tôr′ē, -tō′rē) *adj.*

in·di·ca·tion (in′də·kā′shən) *n.* **1** The act of indicating, in any sense; manifestation; prediction. **2** That which indicates or suggests; a token; sign; symptom. **3** *Med.* The manifestation afforded by the symptoms of a disease as to the course of treatment. See synonyms under CHARACTERISTIC, MARK[1], SIGN. [< F]

in·dic·a·tive (in·dik′ə·tiv) *adj.* **1** Suggestive; giving intimation. **2** *Gram.* Of or pertaining to a mood in which an act or condition is stated or questioned as an actual fact, rather than as a potentiality or an unrealized condition. — *n. Gram.* The indicative mood, or a verb in this mood. — **in·dic′a·tive·ly** *adv.*

in·di·ca·tor (in′də·kā′tər) *n.* **1** One who or that which indicates or points out. **2** Any contrivance or apparatus, automatic or otherwise, which makes a mark, record, or sign to indicate the condition or position of something: a water gage; a speed indicator; a dial showing the position of elevators, cages, etc.; a device for recording the arrival and departure of trains, the number of fares collected in street cars, etc. **3** An instrument attached to a steam engine which, by the action of the steam itself, draws an **indicator–diagram** from which may be ascertained the gross power, the correct adjustment of the distribution valves, the ratio of the pressure in the cylinder to the boiler pressure, etc. **4** *Chem.* A substance, as litmus, potassium permanganate, etc., which colors a solution and by its disappearance, reappearance, or change of color when a reagent is added, indicates alkalinity, acidity, etc. **5** *Ecol.* A type of vegetation or plant growth serving to indicate the general character of a habitat. [< LL]

in·di·ca·tor–reg·u·la·tor (in′də·kā′tər·reg′yə·lā′tər) *n. Mil.* A device which supplies data on the various elements, as timing, elevation, etc., required for accurate firing of a gun.

in·di·ces (in′də·sēz) Plural of INDEX: used especially in mathematical or other abstract works.

in·di·cia (in·dish′ə) *n. pl. sing.,* **·di·cium** (-dish′əm) Discriminating marks; indications; badges; tokens; symptoms. [< L, pl. of *indicium* sign]

in·dict (in·dīt′) *v.t.* **1** *Law* To prefer an indictment against: said of the action of grand juries. **2** To charge with a crime. See synonyms under ARRAIGN. ◆ Homophone: *indite.* [< AF *enditer* make known, inform; later infl. in form by Med. L *dictare* accuse. Related to INDITE.] — **in·dict′a·ble** *adj.* — **in·dict·ee** (in·dī·tē′) *n.* — **indict′er, in·dict′or** *n.*

in·dic·tion (in·dik′shən) *n.* **1** A cycle of fifteen years, introduced by Constantine as a fiscal term, and adopted by the popes as part of their chronological system. **2** The number of one of these cycles, or that of any particular year in its cycle. [< OF < L *indictio, -onis* < *indicere* announce < *in-* in + *dicere* say, tell]

in·dict·ment (in·dīt′mənt) *n.* **1** The act of indicting, or the state of being indicted; formal charge or accusation in general. **2** A formal written charge of crime, preferred at the suit of the government and presented by a grand jury on oath to the court in which it is impaneled, as the basis for trial of the accused; the legal document itself. [< AF *enditement*]

In·dies (in′dēz) **1** The East Indies. **2** The East Indies, India, and Indochina. **3** The West Indies.

in·dif·fer·ence (in·dif′ər·əns) *n.* **1** The state of being unconcerned or indifferent; lack of interest or feeling; apathy; freedom from prejudice or bias. **2** The quality of not arousing interest or approval; a low degree of excellence; immateriality; slight importance. See synonyms under APATHY, NEGLECT. Also **in·dif′fer·en·cy.**

in·dif·fer·ent (in·dif′ər·ənt) *adj.* **1** Having no inclination or interest; apathetic. **2** Only passably or tolerably good or large; mediocre; ordinary. **3** Awakening no concern or preference; unimportant. **4** Unprejudiced; with no predominating tendency; impartial. **5** *Biol.* **a** Undifferentiated; not specialized, as plant or animal tissue. **b** Denoting a species of plants or animals found in diversified habitats. **6** Not active; neutral: said of chemical compounds, parts of magnets, etc. — *n.* **1** An apathetic person. **2** An object of indifference. — *adv. Obs.* Tolerably. [< OF *indifferent* < L *indifferens.* See IN-[1], DIFFERENT.] — **in·dif′fer·ent·ly** *adv.*

in·dif·fer·ent·ism (in·dif′ər·ən·tiz′əm) *n.* **1** The doctrine that the differences in religious faiths are of no importance. **2** The doctrine that to be in thought and in reality are one and the same thing; the doctrine of absolute identity. **3** Habitual or systematic indifference. — **in·dif′fer·ent·ist** *n.*

in·di·gen (in′də·jən) *n.* A person, animal, or thing native to the soil; aboriginal; autochthon: distinguished from *cultigen.* Also **in′de·gene** (-jēn). [< F *indigène*]

in·dig·e·nous (in·dij′ə·nəs) *adj.* **1** Originating in a (specified) place or country; not exotic; native. **2** Innate; inherent. See synonyms under NATIVE, PRIMEVAL. Also **in·dig′e·nal.** [< LL *indigenus* < L *indigena* native < *indu-* within + *gen-*, root of *gignere* beget] — **in·dig′e·nous·ly** *adv.* — **in·dig′e·nous·ness** *n.*

in·di·gent (in′də·jənt) *adj.* Destitute of property; poor. [< F < L *indigens, -entis,* ppr. of *indigere* lack, want < *indu-* within + *egere* need] — **in′di·gence, in′di·gen·cy** *n.*

in·di·gest (in′də·jest′) *Obs. adj.* Undigested; confused. — *n.* A disordered mass. [< L *indigestus*] — **in′di·gest′ed** *adj.*

in·di·gest·i·ble (in′də·jes′tə·bəl) *adj.* Not digestible; difficult to digest. — **in′di·gest′i·bil′i·ty, in′di·gest′i·ble·ness** *n.* — **in′di·gest′i·bly** *adv.*

in·di·ges·tion (in′də·jes′chən) *n.* Defective digestion; dyspepsia. [< F]

in·dign (in·dīn′) *adj. Obs.* Unworthy. [< MF *indigne* < L *indignus*]

in·dig·nant (in·dig′nənt) *adj.* **1** Having just anger and scorn. **2** Manifesting or provoked by such a feeling. [< L *indignans, -antis,* ppr. of *indignari* regard as unworthy < *indignus* unworthy] — **in·dig′nant·ly** *adv.*

in·dig·na·tion (in′dig·nā′shən) *n.* Just resentment. See synonyms under ANGER. [< OF < *indignatio, -onis* < *indignari* think unworthy]

in·dig·ni·ty (in·dig′nə·tē) *n. pl.* **·ties** **1** An act tending to degrade or mortify; an insult; affront. **2** *Obs.* Base character or conduct; also, anger aroused thereby. See synonyms under OFFENSE, OUTRAGE. [< L *indignitas, -tatis* < *indignus*]

in·di·go (in′də·gō) *n.* **1** A blue coloring substance, $C_{16}H_{10}N_2O_2$, obtained by the decomposition of indican, contained in the indigo plant and now synthetically produced from various aromatic hydrocarbons. Mixed with oil, it forms a paint of great body, but one easily decomposed by impure air. **2** A deep violet blue: often used adjectivally. **3** The indigo plant. [< Sp. < L *indicum* < Gk. *Indikon (pharmakon)* Indian (dye), neut. of *Indikos* Indian]

indigo blue 1 The blue coloring substance of crude indigo; indigotin. **2** Any similar dark–blue color.

in·di·rect (in′də·rekt′) *adj.* **1** Deviating from a direct line in space. **2** Not in the direct line of derivation or succession: *indirect* descent. **3** Not in direct relation; not tending to a result by the shortest or plainest course; inferential. **4** Designating gunfire aimed at a target which cannot be seen by sighting at a known aiming point. **5** Not morally direct; tending to mislead or deceive: *indirect* conduct. **6** Not in the exact words of the speaker. — **in′di·rect′ly** *adv.* — **in′di·rect′ness** *n.*

in·di·rec·tion (in′də·rek′shən) *n.* **1** Indirect course of practice. **2** Dishonest means;

deceit.

indirect object See under OBJECT.

in·dis·creet (in'dis·krēt') *adj.* Lacking discretion; imprudent. See synonyms under IMPRUDENT. — **in'dis·creet'ly** *adv.* — **in'dis·creet'·ness** *n.*

in·dis·cre·tion (in'dis·kresh'ən) *n.* 1 The state of being indiscreet. 2 An indiscreet act.

in·dis·crim·i·nate (in'dis·krim'ə·nit) *adj.* 1 Showing no discrimination. 2 Mingled in confusion. — **in'dis·crim'i·nate·ly** *adv.* — **in'·dis·crim'i·nate·ness** *n.* — **in'dis·crim'i·nat'ing** *adj.* — **in'dis·crim'i·na'tion** *n.*

in·dis·pen·sa·ble (in'dis·pen'sə·bəl) *adj.* Not to be dispensed with; necessary or requisite for a purpose. See synonyms under INHERENT, NECESSARY. *n.* An indispensable person or thing. — **in'dis·pen'sa·bil'i·ty, in'dis·pen'sa·ble·ness** *n.* — **in'dis·pen'sa·bly** *adv.*

in·dis·pose (in'dis·pōz') *v.t.* **·posed, ·pos·ing** 1 To render unwilling or averse; disincline. 2 To render unfit; disqualify. 3 To make ill or ailing.

in·dis·posed (in'dis·pōzd') *adj.* 1 Ill; unwell. 2 Disinclined. See synonyms under RELUCTANT. — **in'dis·posed'ness** (-pōzd'-, -pō'zid-) *n.*

in·dis·po·si·tion (in'dis·pə·zish'ən) *n.* 1 Slight illness. 2 The state of being mentally disinclined. See synonyms under ILLNESS.

in·dis·put·a·ble (in'dis·pyōō'tə·bəl, in·dis'pyōō·tə·bəl) *adj.* Incapable of being disputed; unquestionable. See synonyms under INCONTESTABLE, SURE. [<LL *indisputabilis*] — **in'·dis·put'a·bil'i·ty, in'dis·put'a·ble·ness** *n.* — **in'·dis·put'a·bly** *adv.*

in·dis·sol·u·ble (in'di·sol'yə·bəl, in·dis'ə·lyə·bəl) *adj.* 1 That cannot be dissolved, liquefied, or melted. 2 Perpetually binding. Also **in·dis·solv·a·ble** (in'di·zol'və·bəl). See synonyms under IMMORTAL. [<L *indissolubilis*] — **in'dis·sol'u·bil'i·ty, in'dis·sol'u·ble·ness** *n.* — **in'dis·sol'u·bly** *adv.*

in·dis·tinct (in'dis·tingkt') *adj.* 1 Not clearly distinguishable or separable by senses or intellect; not distinct; confused; dim; vague; obscure. 2 Not presenting clear and well-defined images or impressions; obscured. 3 Indiscriminate. See synonyms under EQUIVOCAL, OBSCURE. [<L *indistinctus*] — **in'dis·tinct'ly** *adv.*

in·dis·tinc·tion (in'dis·tingk'shən) *n.* 1 Want of distinction; indiscrimination; confusion. 2 Equality of rank or condition. 3 Indistinctness.

in·dis·tinc·tive (in'dis·tingk'tiv) *adj.* 1 Having no distinguishing quality. 2 Incapable of distinguishing. — **in'dis·tinc'tive·ly** *adv.* — **in'·dis·tinc'tive·ness** *n.*

in·dis·tinct·ness (in'dis·tingkt'nis) *n.* 1 Lack of distinctness; obscurity; faintness. 2 Lack of mental qualities necessary for the purpose of making a clear distinction; indistinguishableness.

in·dite (in·dīt') *v.t.* **·dit·ed, ·dit·ing** 1 To put into words or writing; write; compose. 2 *Obs.* To dictate. ◆ Homophone: *indict.* [<AF *enditer* make known, inform <L *in-* in + *dictare* declare. Related to INDICT.] — **in·dite'·ment** *n.* — **in·dit'er** *n.*

in·di·vid·u·al (in'də·vij'ōō·əl) *adj.* 1 Existing as an entity; single; particular. 2 Not divisible; not capable of actual division without loss of something essential to its existence. 3 Pertaining, belonging, or peculiar to one particular person or thing. 4 Differentiated from others by peculiar or distinctive characteristics: an *individual* style. See synonyms under PARTICULAR. — *n.* 1 A single person, animal, or thing; especially, a human being; a person with distinctive or marked peculiarities. 2 Anything that cannot be divided or separated into parts without losing its identity. [<Med. L *individualis* <L *individuus* indivisible <*in-* not + *dividuus* divisible] — **in'di·vid'u·al·ly** *adv.*

in·di·vid·u·al·ism (in'də·vij'ōō·əl·iz'əm) *n.* 1 The quality of being separate. 2 Personal independence in action, character, or interest. 3 A personal peculiarity; idiosyncrasy. 4 A tendency or attitude, in religion, ethics, or politics, favoring the liberty of the individual: opposed to *socialism, totalitarianism,* etc. 5 Excessive self-interest; selfishness. 6 *Philos.*

Egoism. — **in'di·vid'u·al·ist** *n.* — **in'di·vid'u·al·is'tic** *adj.*

in·di·vid·u·al·i·ty (in'də·vij'ōō·al'ə·tē) *n.* *pl.* **·ties** 1 Something that distinguishes one person or thing from others. 2 Distinctive character or personality. 3 The quality or state of existing separately. 4 An individual; a personality. 5 *Archaic* State or quality of inseparability; indivisibility.

in·di·vid·u·al·ize (in'də·vij'ōō·əl·īz') *v.t.* **·ized, ·iz·ing** 1 To make individual; give individual characteristics to; distinguish. 2 To treat, mention, or consider individually; particularize. — **in'di·vid'u·al·i·za'tion** (-ə·zā'shən, -ī·zā'-) *n.*

in·di·vid·u·ate (in'də·vij'ōō·āt) *v.t.* **·at·ed, ·at·ing** 1 To distinguish from others; individualize. 2 To bring into existence as an individual. [<Med. L *individuatus,* pp. of *individuare* <*individuus* individual]

in·di·vid·u·a·tion (in'də·vij'ōō·ā'shən) *n.* 1 The action or process of rendering individual. 2 State of being individualized. 3 Personal identity; individuality. 4 *Zool.* The development of separate units in a colony of protozoans. 5 *Philos.* The differentiation of the individual from the species and from every other individual. [<Med. L *individuatio, -onis*]

in·di·vis·i·ble (in'də·viz'ə·bəl) *adj.* Not divisible; incapable of being divided. — **in'di·vis'i·bil'i·ty** *n.* — **in'di·vis'i·bly** *adv.*

In·do-Af·ri·can (in'dō-af'ri·kən) *adj.* Of or pertaining to both India and Africa.

In·do-Ar·y·an (in'dō-âr'ē·ən) *adj.* Of the Indic branch of the Indo-Iranian subfamily. — *n.* An Aryan of India. See ARYAN.

In·do·chi·na (in'dō-chī'nə) 1 The SE peninsula of Asia, comprising the Union of Burma, Cambodia, Laos, the Federation of Malaya, Thailand, North Vietnam and South Vietnam: sometimes *Farther India.* 2 The states of Cambodia, Laos, North Vietnam and South Vietnam: formerly *French Indochina.* Also **Indo-China.**

In·do·chi·nese (in'dō-chī·nēz', -nēs') *adj.* Of or pertaining to Indochina or its inhabitants. — *n.* 1 A member of one of the native Mongoloid races inhabiting Indochina. 2 The Sino-Tibetan family of languages.

in·doc·tri·nate (in·dok'trə·nāt) *v.t.* **·nat·ed, ·nat·ing** 1 To instruct in doctrines, principles, etc. 2 To instruct; teach. See synonyms under TEACH. [<Med. L *in-* into + *doctrinare* teach <*doctrina* teaching <*doctor* a teacher <*docere* teach] — **in·doc'tri·na'tion** *n.*

In·do-Eu·ro·pe·an (in'dō-yōōr'ə·pē'ən) *n.* 1 The largest family of languages in the world, assumed to have descended from an unrecorded common ancestor and comprising most of the languages of Europe and many languages of India and SW Asia. These languages are conventionally divided into two classifications, *centum* and *satem* (from the Latin and Avestan words for 'hundred'), primarily according to the representation of the proto-Indo-European palatalized velar (k) as velar stops in the *centum* (mainly western) division, and as sibilants in the *satem* (mainly eastern) division. The principal *centum* subfamilies are Hellenic, Italic, Celtic, and Germanic. The principal *satem* subfamilies are Indo-Iranian, Armenian, Albanian, and Balto-Slavic. Among the lesser-known, extinct languages which have been established as belonging to the Indo-European family are Hittite and Tocharian. Cuneiform Hittite is grouped with the *centum* languages, while Hieroglyphic Hittite is thought by some to be a *satem* language. Tocharian is generally classed with the *centum* languages. See also THRACIAN, PHRYGIAN, LIGURIAN, SICEL, ILLYRIAN, MESSAPIAN, and VENETIC. 2 The assumed prehistoric parent language of this family of languages: now fairly well reconstructed by linguists. — *adj.* Of or pertaining to the Indo-European family of languages, or to the peoples speaking them. Also *Aryan, Indo-Germanic.*

In·do-I·ra·ni·an (in'dō-i·rā'nē·ən) *n.* A subfamily of the Indo-European family of languages, consisting of Indic and Iranian branches. — *adj.* Of or pertaining to this subfamily. Also *Aryan.*

in·do·lence (in'də·ləns) *n.* Habitual idleness; laziness. Also **in'do·len·cy.** [<L *indolentia* freedom from pain]

in·do·lent (in'də·lənt) *adj.* 1 Averse to exertion; habitually inactive or idle. 2 Without pain; sluggish. See synonyms under IDLE. [<LL *indolens, -entis* <*in-* not + *dolens,* ppr. of *dolere* feel pain] — **in'do·lent·ly** *adv.*

in·dom·i·ta·ble (in·dom'i·tə·bəl) *adj.* Not to be subdued. See synonyms under INDEFATIGABLE, OBSTINATE. [<LL *indomitabilis* <L *indomitus* untamed <*in-* not + *domitus* tamed, pp. of *domitare,* intens. of *domare* subdue] — **in·dom'i·ta·bly** *adv.*

In·do·ne·sia (in'dō-nē'zhə, -shə) Since 1950 a republic, the **Republic of Indonesia,** comprising Java, Sumatra, most of Borneo, half of Timor, Celebes, the Moluccas, and other islands of the Malay Archipelago: 575,893 square miles; capital, Jakarta: formerly *Netherlands East Indies.*

in·door (in'dôr', -dōr') *adj.* Being or done within doors; pertaining to the interior of a building.

in·doors (in'dôrz', -dōrz') *adv.* Inside or toward the inside of a building.

In·dra (in'drə) In early Hindu mythology, the god of the firmament and of rain. In the Vedas he is a god of the first rank: in later mythology he falls to a second rank.

in·draft (in'draft', -dräft') *n.* The act of drawing in or that which is drawn in; an inward flow. Also **in'draught'.**

in·drawn (in'drôn') *adj.* 1 Drawn in; uttered with suppressed breath. 2 Abstracted; preoccupied.

in·dri (in'drē) *n.* A lemur of Madagascar; especially, a species (*Indris brevicaudata*) about two feet long, with erect ears, rudimentary tail, and usually prevailingly black in color. [<F <Malagasy *indry lo,* there he goes: mistaken for the name of the animal]

INDRA

in·du·bi·ta·ble (in·dōō'bə·tə·bəl, -dyōō'-) *adj.* Not open to doubt or question; unquestionable; certain. See synonyms under EVIDENT, INCONTESTABLE, MANIFEST. [<F] — **in·du'bi·ta·ble·ness** *n.* — **in·du'bi·ta·bly** *adv.*

in·duce (in·dōōs', -dyōōs') *v.t.* **·duced, ·duc·ing** 1 To lead on to a specific action, belief, etc., by persuasion or influence; prevail on. 2 To bring on; produce; cause: a sickness *induced* by fatigue. 3 *Physics* To produce, as by exposure to electric, magnetic, or radioactive influences. 4 To reach as a conclusion by an inductive process of reasoning. 5 *Obs.* To lead in; introduce. [<L *inducere* introduce <*in-* in + *ducere* lead] — **in·duc'er** *n.* — **in·duc'i·ble** *adj.*

induced drag *Aeron.* That portion of the drag of an aircraft induced by the lift. Compare PARASITE DRAG, PROFILE DRAG.

---

add, āce, câre, pälm; end, ēven; it, īce; odd, ōpen, ôrder; tŏŏk, pōōl; up, bûrn; ə = a in *above,* e in *sicken,* i in *clarity,* o in *melon,* u in *focus;* yōō = u in *fuse;* oi, oil; ou, pout; ch, check; g, go; ng, ring; th, thin; ŧħ, this; zh, vision. Foreign sounds å, œ, ü, kh, ṅ; and ◆: see page xx. < from; + plus; ? possibly.

in·duce·ment (in·dōōs′mənt, -dyōōs′-) *n.* **1** An incentive; motive. **2** The act of inducing. **3** *Law* In pleading, the preamble, or explanatory introduction to the particular charges and allegations.

in·duct (in·dukt′) *v.t.* **1** To bring into or install in an office, benefice, etc., especially with formal ceremony. **2** To bring or lead in; introduce; initiate. **3** *U.S.* To bring (one who has been conscripted) into a military service. [< L *inductus,* pp. of *inducere.* See INDUCE.]

in·duc·tance (in·duk′təns) *n. Electr.* **1** The capacity of an electric circuit for responding to a magnetoelectrically induced current. **2** Self-induction in an electrical circuit or its equivalent, for purposes of measurement in terms of henries.

in·duc·tee (in′duk·tē′) *n.* One inducted into military service.

in·duc·tion (in·duk′shən) *n.* **1** The process of causing an event or bringing about a conclusion by some particular path or course of reasoning. **2** *Logic* The process of inferring or aiming at the general from observation of the particular; specifically, the inference of a specific law of causational connection from the observation and analysis of some particular instance or instances. **3** Any conclusion reached by inductive reasoning. **4** In English ecclesiastical law, the formal installation of a person into an office or church living. **5** An introduction; especially, a preamble, prolog, or prelude foreshadowing the argument or character of a literary work. **6** The bringing forward of separate facts as evidence in order to prove a general statement. **7** *Electr.* The production of magnetization or electrification in a body by the mere proximity of a magnetic field or electric charge, or of an electric current in a conductor by the variation of the magnetic field in its vicinity. **8** *Physiol.* The stimulating effect of one tissue upon the growth or alteration of another. **9** The act or process of inducting, as for military service; initiation; installation. **10** *Obs.* A beginning or introduction to anything; that which leads to or induces a thing. — **magnetic induction** The magnetization of iron, steel, etc., by its introduction into a magnetic field. [< OF < L *inductio, -onis*] — **in·duc′tion·al** *adj.*

Synonyms: deduction, inference. *Deduction* is reasoning from the general to the particular; *induction* is reasoning from the particular to the general. In *deduction,* if the general rule is true, and the special case falls under the rule, the conclusion is certain; *induction* can ordinarily give no more than a probable conclusion, because we can never be sure that we have collated all instances. An *induction* is of the nature of an *inference,* but while an *inference* may be partial and hasty, an *induction* is careful, and aims to be complete. Compare DEMONSTRATION, INFERENCE.

induction coil *Electr.* An apparatus for generating currents by electromagnetic induction, consisting usually of two concentric coils of insulated wire enclosing an iron core. One of the coils, called the *primary,* is usually short and of thick wire, and the *secondary* long and of thin wire. An alternating current of high tension is induced in the secondary coil by rapid automatic making and breaking of the circuit in the primary.

INDUCTION COIL

in·duc·tive (in·duk′tiv) *adj.* **1** Pertaining to or proceeding by induction. **2** Produced by induction. **3** Introductory. [< LL *inductivus*] — **in·duc′tive·ly** *adv.* — **in·duc′tive·ness** *n.*

in·duc·tiv·i·ty (in′duk·tiv′ə·tē) *n. Electr.* Specific capacity for induction.

in·duc·tor (in·duk′tər) *n.* **1** One who or that which inducts. **2** *Electr.* Any part of an electrical apparatus which acts inductively upon another. [< L]

in·due (in·dōō′, -dyōō′) *v.t.* **·dued, ·du·ing** To endue. [See ENDUE.]

in·dulge (in·dulj′) *v.* **·dulged, ·dulg·ing** *v.t.* **1** To yield to or gratify, as desires or whims.

2 To yield to or gratify the desires, whims, etc., of. **3** *Eccl.* To grant a dispensation or indulgence to. **4** *Obs.* To grant as a privilege or favor. **5** In business: **a** To grant more time to (someone) to meet a bill. **b** To grant more time for (a bill) to be met. — *v.i.* **6** To yield to or gratify desires; indulge oneself; with *in.* [< L *indulgere* be kind to, concede] — **in·dulg′er** *n.*

Synonyms: content, favor, gratify, humor, pamper, please, satisfy, spoil. See PAMPER. *Antonyms:* check, contradict, control, deny, disappoint, discipline, displease, oppose, refuse, thwart.

in·dul·gence (in·dul′jəns) *n.* **1** The act of indulging; hence, excess; self-gratification. **2** That with which a person is indulged or indulges himself; an act of compliance, grace, or favor. **3** Permission to defer payment, as of a note. **4** In the Roman Catholic Church, remission, by those authorized, of the temporal punishment still due to sin after sacramental absolution, either in this world or in purgatory; also, a relaxation, in a person's favor, of a particular rule of ecclesiastical law: properly called *dispensation.* **5** The granting of special favors by the Declaration of Indulgence. Also **in·dul′gen·cy.** — **Declaration of Indulgence** In English history, a royal proclamation granting a larger measure of religious freedom to nonconformists: especially those of Charles II, 1671, and James II, 1687. [< OF < L *indulgentia*]

in·dul·gent (in·dul′jənt) *adj.* Prone to indulge; lenient. See synonyms under CHARITABLE. [< L *indulgens, -entis,* ppr. of *indulgere* concede] — **in·dul′gent·ly** *adv.*

in·dul·gen·tial (in′dul·jen′shəl) *adj.* Pertaining to ecclesiastical indulgences.

in·du·rate (in′dŏŏ·rāt, -dyŏŏ-) *v.t. & v.i.* **·rat·ed, ·rat·ing** To make or become hard, hardy, or callous; harden; inure. — *adj.* (-rit) Hard or hardened: also **in′du·rat′ed.** [< L *induratus,* pp. of *indurare* make hard. See ENDURE.] — **in′du·ra·tive** *adj.*

in·du·ra·tion (in′dŏŏ·rā′shən, -dyŏŏ-) *n.* **1** The act or process of indurating, or the state of being indurated. **2** Hardening of the heart; obduracy. **3** An indurated part. [< OF < Med. L *induratio, -onis*]

In·dus (in′dəs) A southern constellation, the Indian. See CONSTELLATION. [< L, an Indian]

in·dus·tri·al (in·dus′trē·əl) *adj.* **1** Pertaining to or engaged in industry. **2** Denoting the processes or products of manufacture. — *n.* **1** One engaged in industry. **2** A stock or security based upon an established manufacture. [< F *industriel* and Med. L *industrialis*] — **in·dus′tri·al·ly** *adv.*

industrial arts See under ART[1].

industrial democracy **1** Control, or equal participation in the control, of an industry by the workers in that industry. **2** Nondiscrimination among employees in an industry, as for race or religion.

industrial insurance Insurance for small amounts, usually for low-income groups, the premium being paid in weekly instalments.

in·dus·tri·al·ism (in·dus′trē·əl·iz′əm) *n.* **1** The modern industrial system, especially with reference to large-scale manufacturing industries; the organization of industries. **2** A condition of society in which the highest aim is success in peaceful industries. See CAPITALISM. — **in·dus′tri·al·ist** *adj. & n.*

in·dus·tri·al·ize (in·dus′trē·əl·īz′) *v.t.* **·ized, ·iz·ing** To render industrial; affect with or devote to industrialism: to *industrialize* a village. — **in·dus′tri·al·i·za′tion** (-ə·zā′shən, -ī·zā′-) *n.*

industrial relations The relationships between employers and employees.

industrial union A labor union in which membership is open to all workers in a particular industry. Compare CRAFT UNION.

in·dus·tri·ous (in·dus′trē·əs) *adj.* **1** Assiduously or habitually occupied in any work, business, or pursuit. **2** Indicating diligence. **3** Industrial. [< F *industrieux* < L *industriosus*] — **in·dus′tri·ous·ly** *adv.* — **in·dus′tri·ous·ness** *n.*

Synonyms: active, assiduous, busy, diligent, employed, engaged, occupied, sedulous. *Industrious* signifies zealously or habitually applying oneself to any work or business. *Busy* applies to an activity which may be tem-

porary, *industrious* to a habit of life. We say a man is *busy* just now; that is, *occupied* at the moment with something that takes his full attention. It would be ridiculous or satirical to say, He is *industrious* just now. But *busy* can be used in the sense of *industrious,* as when we say he is a *busy* man. *Diligent* indicates also a disposition, which is ordinarily habitual, and suggests more of heartiness and volition than *industrious.* We say one is a *diligent,* rather than an *industrious,* reader of the Bible. Compare ACTIVE, BUSY, INDEFATIGABLE.

in·dus·try (in′dəs·trē) *n. pl.* **·tries** **1** Earnest or constant application to work or business. **2** Useful labor in general. **3** A special branch of productive work, or the capital or workers employed in it: the steel *industry,* the farming *industry.* **4** The mechanical and manufacturing branches of productive activity, as distinguished from agricultural. **5** *Obs.* Skill, dexterity; also, a clever device or contrivance. [< F *industrie* < L *industria* diligence < *industrius* diligent]

Synonyms: application, assiduity, attention, constancy, diligence, effort, exertion, intentness, labor, pains, patience, perseverance, persistence, sedulousness. *Industry* is the quality, action, or habit of earnest, steady, and continued attention or devotion to any useful or productive work or task, manual or mental. *Assiduity* (L *ad,* to, and *sedere,* sit), as the etymology suggests, sits down to a task until it is done. *Diligence* (L *diligere,* love, choose) invests more effort and exertion, with love of the work or deep interest in its accomplishment; *application* (L *ad,* to, and *plicare,* fold) bends to its work and concentrates all one's powers upon it with utmost intensity; hence, *application* can hardly be as unremitting as *assiduity.* *Constancy* is a steady devotion of heart and principle. *Patience* works on in spite of annoyances; *perseverance* overcomes hindrances and difficulties; *persistence* strives relentlessly against opposition; *persistence* has very frequently an unfavorable meaning, implying that one persists in spite of considerations that should induce him to desist. *Industry* is *diligence* applied to some vocation, business, or profession; hence, by derived use, the occupation itself. *Labor* and *pains* refer to the *exertions* of the worker and the tax upon him, while *assiduity, perseverance,* etc., refer to his continuance in the work. See BUSINESS. *Antonyms:* idleness, inattention, inconstancy, indolence, neglect, negligence, remissness, sloth.

in·e·bri·ant (in·ē′brē·ənt) *adj.* Intoxicating. — *n.* Anything that intoxicates.

in·e·bri·ate (in·ē′brē·āt) *v.t.* **·at·ed, ·at·ing** **1** To make drunk; intoxicate. **2** To exhilarate; excite. — *n.* (-it, -āt) A habitual drunkard. — *adj.* (-it, -āt) Intoxicated: also **in·e′bri·at′ed.** [< L *inebriatus,* pp. of *inebriare* intoxicate < *in-* thoroughly + *ebriare* make drunk < *ebrius* drunk]

in·e·bri·a·tion (in·ē′brē·ā′shən) *n.* **1** Drunkenness; habitual intoxication. **2** Exhilaration. Also **in·e·bri·e·ty** (in′ē·brī′ə·tē).

in·ed·i·ble (in·ed′ə·bəl) *adj.* Not edible; not fit to eat. — **in·ed′i·bil′i·ty** *n.*

in·ef·fa·ble (in·ef′ə·bəl) *adj.* **1** That cannot be expressed in speech. **2** That must not be spoken; too lofty or sacred for expression. [< F < L *ineffabilis* < *in-* not + *effabilis* utterable < *effari* speak < *ex-* out + *fari* speak] — **in·ef′fa·bil′i·ty** *n.* — **in·ef′fa·bly** *adv.*

in·ef·fec·tive (in′i·fek′tiv) *adj.* **1** Not effective; not producing the effect expected. **2** Incompetent. — **in′ef·fec′tive·ly** *adv.* — **in′ef·fec′tive·ness** *n.*

in·ef·fec·tu·al (in′i·fek′chŏŏ·əl) *adj.* **1** Not effectual; not able to produce an intended effect. **2** Unsuccessful; fruitless. — **in′ef·fec′tu·al·ly** *adv.*

in·ef·fi·cient (in′i·fish′ənt) *adj.* **1** Not efficient; uneconomical or wasteful. **2** Not capable; incompetent. — **in′ef·fi′cien·cy** *n.* — **in′·ef·fi′cient·ly** *adv.*

in·e·las·tic (in′i·las′tik) *adj.* Not elastic; inflexible; unyielding; unadaptable. — **in·e·las·tic·i·ty** (in′i·las′tis′ə·tē) *n.*

in·el·e·gant (in·el′ə·gənt) *adj.* **1** Not elegant; lacking in beauty, polish, grace, refinement, good taste, or the like. **2** Coarse; crude.

in·el·i·gi·ble (in·el′ə·jə·bəl) *adj.* Not eligible; disqualified; unsuitable; inexpedient. — **in·el′i-**

gi·bil·i·ty n. — **in·el'i·gi·bly** adv.

in·e·luc·ta·ble (in'i·luk'tə·bəl) adj. Not to be escaped; impossible to struggle against; irresistible. [<L *ineluctabilis* < *in-* not + *eluctabilis* surmountable < *eluctari* surmount] — **in'e·luc·ta·bil'i·ty** n. — **in'e·luc'ta·bly** adv.

in·ept (in·ept') adj. **1** Not suitable or qualified; out of place. **2** Absurd; foolish. **3** Clumsy; awkward. [<L *ineptus* < *in-* not + *aptus* fit] — **in·ep'ti·tude** n. — **in·ept'ly** adv. — **in·ept'ness** n.

in·e·qual·i·ty (in'i·kwol'ə·tē) n. pl. **·ties 1** The condition of being unequal; disparity. **2** Lack of evenness or proportion; variableness: *inequalities* of surface; *inequalities* of climate. **3** Inadequacy; incompetency. **4** *Math.* A statement that two quantities are not equal, made by placing the sign ≠ between them; or by the sign < or >, the angle being toward the symbol of smaller quantity. **5** The daily variation in rise of the tides due to varying lunar influences. See synonyms under DIFFERENCE.

in·eq·ui·ty (in·ek'wə·tē) n. pl. **·ties 1** Want of equity; injustice. **2** An unfair act.

in·er·ran·cy (in·er'ən·sē, -ûr'-) n. **1** The state of being free from error. **2** As applied to Scripture, plenary inspiration.

in·ert (in·ûrt') adj. **1** Destitute of inherent power to move; possessing inertia; inactive. **2** Sluggish. **3** *Chem.* Devoid of active properties; incapable of or resisting combination: the *inert* gases. See synonyms under HEAVY, IDLE, LIFELESS, PASSIVE, SLOW. [<L *iners, inertis* < *in-* not + *ars* art] — **in·ert'ly** adv. — **in·ert'ness** n. — **in·er'tion** (-ûr'shən) n.

in·er·tia (in·ûr'shə) n. **1** The state of being inert; sluggishness. **2** *Physics* **a** That property of matter by virtue of which any physical body persists in its state of rest or of uniform motion until acted upon by some external force; its quantitative expression is *mass*. **b** A similar property noted in certain forms of energy, as electricity and quanta. [<L, idleness] — **in·er'tial** adj.

in·es·cap·a·ble (in'ə·skā'pə·bəl) adj. Inevitable; unavoidable. — **in'es·cap'a·bly** adv.

in·es·sen·tial (in'i·sen'shəl) adj. **1** Unessential; not essential. **2** Immaterial. — **in'es·sen'·ti·al'i·ty** n.

in·es·ti·ma·ble (in·es'tə·mə·bəl) adj. Above price; very valuable. — **in·es'ti·ma·bly** adv.

in·ev·i·ta·ble (in·ev'ə·tə·bəl) adj. **1** That cannot be prevented; unavoidable. **2** Hence, customary; usual: a humorous usage. See synonyms under NECESSARY. [<L *inevitabilis* < *in-* not + *evitare* avoid < *ex-* completely + *vitare* avoid] — **in·ev'i·ta·ble·ness, in·ev'i·ta·bil'i·ty** n. — **in·ev'i·ta·bly** adv.

in·ex·act (in'ig·zakt') adj. Not exact, accurate, or true. — **in'ex·act'ly** adv. — **in'ex·act'ness, in'ex·act'i·tude** n.

in·ex·cus·a·ble (in'ik·skyōō'zə·bəl) adj. Not excusable; impossible to excuse or justify. — **in'·ex·cus'a·bly** adv.

in·ex·haust·i·ble (in'ig·zôs'tə·bəl) adj. **1** Incapable of being exhausted or used up. **2** Incapable of fatigue; tireless.

in·ex·o·ra·ble (in·ek'sər·ə·bəl) adj. Not to be moved by entreaty; unyielding. See synonyms under IMPLACABLE, INFLEXIBLE. [<L *inexorabilis*. See IN-², EXORABLE.] — **in·ex'o·ra·bil'i·ty, in·ex'o·ra·ble·ness** n. — **in·ex'o·ra·bly** adv.

in·ex·pen·sive (in'ik·spen'siv) adj. Not expensive; costing little.

in·ex·pe·ri·enced (in'ik·spir'ē·ənst) adj. Not experienced; lacking in the skill and knowledge derived from experience.

in·ex·plic·a·ble (in·eks'pli·kə·bəl, in'iks·plik'ə·bəl) adj. Not explicable; impossible to explain; inexplainable. — **in'ex·pli·ca·bil'i·ty, in'ex·plic'·a·ble·ness** n. — **in·ex'pli·ca·bly** adv.

in·ex·press·i·ble (in'iks·pres'ə·bəl) adj. Incapable of being expressed; especially, that cannot be expressed in words; unutterable: often used loosely for *great*. — **in'ex·press·i·bil'i·ty, in'ex·press'i·ble·ness** n. — **in'ex·press'i·bly** adv.

in·ex·pug·na·ble (in'iks·pug'nə·bəl) adj. Impregnable; unconquerable. [<F <L *inexpugnabilis* < *in-* not + *ex-* out + *pugnare* fight] — **in'ex·pug'na·bil'i·ty, in'ex·pug'na·ble·ness** n. — **in'ex·pug'na·bly** adv.

in·ex·tri·ca·ble (in·eks'tri·kə·bəl) adj. So in-volved that extrication is impossible. [<L *inextricabilis* < *in-* not + *extricare*. See EXTRICATE.] — **in·ex'tri·ca·bil'i·ty, in·ex'tri·ca·ble·ness** n. — **in·ex'tri·ca·bly** adv.

in·fal·li·ble (in·fal'ə·bəl) adj. **1** Exempt from fallacy or error of judgment. **2** Exempt from uncertainty or liability to error. **3** In Roman Catholic theology, insusceptible of error in matters relating to faith and morals: said of the pope speaking *ex cathedra*. — n. One who or that which is infallible. — **in·fal'li·bil'i·ty, in·fal'li·ble·ness** n. — **in·fal'li·bly** adv.

in·fa·mous (in'fə·məs) adj. **1** Having an odious reputation; notorious. **2** Involving infamy. **3** *Law* Convicted of infamy. [< Med. L *infamosus* <L *infamis* < *in-* not + *fama* fame < *fari* speak] — **in'fa·mous·ly** adv. — **in'fa·mous·ness** n.

Synonyms: atrocious, base, detestable, disgraceful, dishonorable, disreputable, heinous, ignominious, ill-famed, nefarious, odious, outrageous, scandalous, shameful, shameless, vile, villainous, wicked. See BASE.

in·fa·my (in'fə·mē) n. pl. **·mies 1** Total lack of honor or reputation. **2** That which is odious; depravity; an infamous act. **3** *Law* The legal status of a person convicted of serious crimes which, in the United States, disqualify him as a witness or juror. [<F *infamie* <L *infamia*. See INFAMOUS.]

in·fan·cy (in'fən·sē) n. pl. **·cies 1** The state of being an infant. **2** *Law* Minority. **3** The earliest period in the history of a thing.

in·fant (in'fənt) n. **1** A baby; a child under seven years of age. **2** *Law* A minor; in most States of the United States, a person under 21 years of age. — adj. **1** Babyish; infantile. **2** *Law* Minor; not yet of age. [<OF *enfant* <L *infans, -antis* not speaking < *in-* not + *fans, fantis*, ppr. of *fari* talk]

in·fan·ti·cide (in·fan'tə·sīd) n. **1** Child murder. **2** One who murders a child. [<F <LL *infanticidium* <L *infans, -antis* child + *caedere* kill; def. 2 <L *infanticida*]

in·fan·tile (in'fən·tīl, -til) adj. **1** Pertaining to or characteristic of infants or infancy. **2** *Geol.* In an early period of development succeeding an upheaval of the earth's crust or other change affecting basic level. See synonyms under CHILDISH. Also **in'an·tine** (-tīn, -tin).

infantile paralysis Poliomyelitis.

in·fan·til·ism (in'fən·təl·iz'əm) n. **1** Abnormal prolonging of an infantile condition as to sex and body in adults. **2** Backwardness in physical and mental development.

in·fan·try (in'fən·trē) n. pl. **·tries** Soldiers or units of an army that fight on foot and are equipped with small arms. [<F *infanterie* < Ital. *infanteria* < *infante* boy, page, foot soldier <L *infans, infantis* child]

in·fan·try·man (in'fən·trē·mən) n. pl. **·men** (-mən) A foot soldier.

in·fat·u·ate (in·fach'ōō·āt) v.t. **·at·ed, ·at·ing 1** To make foolish or fatuous; deprive of sound judgment. **2** To inspire with foolish and unreasoning passion. [<L *infatuatus*, pp. of *infatuare* make a fool of < *in-* very + *fatuus* foolish] — **in·fat'u·at'ed** adj. — **in·fat'u·a'tion** n.

in·fect (in·fekt') v.t. **1** To introduce pathogenic micro-organisms into, as a wound; communicate disease to, as a person, etc. **2** To contaminate, as a scalpel, with disease-bearing matter. **3** To affect or influence, as with emotion, beliefs, etc., especially harmfully; taint. **4** *Law* To taint with illegality; render subject to seizure or penalty. See synonyms under DEFILE, POLLUTE. [<L *infectus*, pp. of *inficere* dip into, stain < *in-* in + *facere* do, make] — **in·fect'er, in·fec'tor** n.

in·fec·tion (in·fek'shən) n. **1** The act of infecting, as with disease, attitude, mood, ideas, etc. **2** Communication of disease, as by entrance of pathogenic germs into an organism in any manner. **3** Any diseased condition so produced. **4** The instilation of a quality, usually evil, by influence or communication. **5** *Law* Taint of illegality. **6** That which infects; especially, infectious morbific matter. **7** *Rare* Liking; affection: in humorous use. See synonyms under CONTAGION. [<F] — **focal infection** A bacterial infection localized in certain body tissues, as the tonsils or a tooth, from which toxins are sent to other areas.

in·fec·tious (in·fek'shəs) adj. **1** That may be communicated by infection. **2** Able to communicate infection. **3** *Law* Tainting with illegality. **4** Having the quality of being transmitted from one to another: *infectious* laughter. **5** *Obs.* Infected. — **in·fec'tious·ly** adv. — **in·fec'tious·ness** n.

in·fec·tive (in·fek'tiv) adj. Infectious.

in·fe·lic·i·tous (in'fə·lis'ə·təs) adj. Not felicitous, happy, or suitable in application, condition, or result. — **in'fe·lic'i·tous·ly** adv. — **in'·fe·lic'i·tous·ness** n.

in·fe·lic·i·ty (in'fə·lis'ə·tē) n. pl. **·ties 1** The state of being infelicitous; unhappiness. **2** That which is infelicitous; an inappropriate or inapt remark, act, etc. [<L *infelicitas, -tatis*]

in·felt (in'felt') adj. Felt inwardly or deeply.

in·fer (in·fûr') v. **·ferred, ·fer·ring** v.t. **1** To derive by reasoning; conclude or accept from evidence or premises; deduce. Compare POSIT. **2** To involve or imply as a conclusion; give evidence of: said of facts, statements, etc.: His actions *infer* a motive. **3** Loosely, to imply; hint. **4** *Obs.* To bring in; advance; also, to cause. — v.i. **5** To draw inferences. [<L *inferre* bring into < *in-* in + *ferre* bring, carry] — **in·fer'a·ble, in·fer'ri·ble** adj.

in·fer·ence (in'fər·əns) n. **1** The act of inferring. **2** That which is inferred; a deduction or conclusion. **3** Loosely, a conjecture. [< Med. L *inferentia* <L *inferens, -entis*, ppr. of *inferre*. See INFER.]

Synonyms: conclusion, consequence, deduction, demonstration, induction. A *conclusion* is the absolute and necessary result of the admission of certain premises; an *inference* is a probable *conclusion*, toward which known facts, statements, or admissions point, but which they do not absolutely establish; sound premises together with their necessary *conclusion* constitute a *demonstration*. See DEMONSTRATION, INDUCTION.

in·fer·en·tial (in'fə·ren'shəl) adj. Deducible by inference. — **in'fer·en'tial·ly** adv.

in·fe·ri·or (in·fîr'ē·ər) adj. **1** Lower in quality, merit, importance, or rank. **2** *Biol.* Situated or placed lower, as certain parts of the body relative to others; in animals, situated on or pertaining to the lower or ventral side. **3** Later in point of time: the *inferior* limit of a year. **4** In music, having a lower pitch. **5** *Bot.* Below some other organ; in a blossom, anterior. **6** *Astron.* **a** Between the earth and the sun: an *inferior* planet. **b** Below the horizon; below the celestial pole. **7** *Printing* Set below the level of the line, as small characters without a shoulder below, used in chemical formulas. See synonyms under BAD¹. — n. One who or that which is classed lower than others; a subordinate. [<L, lower, compar. of *inferus* low]

in·fe·ri·or·i·ty (in·fîr'ē·ôr'ə·tē, -or'-) n. The state of being inferior; low condition.

inferiority complex *Psychol.* An emotional trend or state of mind characterized by a morbidly exaggerated sense of one's own limitations and incapacities, and sometimes compensated for by aggressive behavior.

in·fer·nal (in·fûr'nəl) adj. **1** Belonging to hell; diabolical: often used colloquially to express indignation or emphasis: an *infernal* rascal. **2** Pertaining to Tartarus. [<OF <L *infernalis* < *infernus* situated below < *inferus* below] — **in·fer'nal·ly** adv.

Synonyms: demoniac, demoniacal, devilish, diabolic, diabolical, fiendish, hellish, satanic.

in·fer·no (in·fûr'nō) n. pl. **·nos 1** The infernal regions; hell. **2** Any place comparable to hell; especially, a hot or fiery place. [<Ital.]

in·fer·o·lat·er·al (in'fər·ō·lat'ər·əl) adj. Below and on one side.

in·fer·tile (in·fûr'til) adj. Not fertile or productive; sterile; barren. — **in·fer'til'i·ty** n.

in·fest (in·fest') v.t. To overrun or haunt in large numbers, especially so as to render unpleasant or unsafe: The barn is *infested* with rats. [<MF *infester* <L *infestare* assail < *infestus* hostile] — **in·fest'er** n.

in·fes·ta·tion (in'fes·tā'shən) n. **1** The act of infesting. **2** The state of being infested, as with parasites or vermin. [<LL *infestatio, -onis*]

in·feu·da·tion (in′fyoo·dā′shən) *n.* **1** In feudal law, the granting or the putting in possession of an estate in fee; also, the feudal relation. **2** The granting of tithes to laymen. [<Med. L *infeudatio, -onis* < *infeudare* enfeoff < *in-* in + *feudum* FEUD[2]]

in·fi·del (in′fi·dəl) *n.* **1** One who denies the existence of God. **2** An unbeliever, as viewed from the standpoint of a believer in any particular religion or belief. See synonyms under SKEPTIC. — *adj.* **1** Lacking the true faith; especially, rejecting the Christian religion. **2** Faithless; recreant. **3** Of, relating to, or characteristic of infidels or infidelity. [<OF *infidèle* <L *infidelis* unfaithful < *in-* not + *fidelis* faithful]

in·fi·del·i·ty (in′fi·del′ə·tē) *n. pl.* **·ties 1** The state of being an infidel; lack of belief. **2** Lack of fidelity; specifically, violation of the marriage vow by adultery.

in·field (in′fēld′) *n.* **1 a** The space thirty yards square enclosed within the base lines of a baseball field: distinguished from *outfield.* **b** The infielders collectively. See illustration under BASEBALL. **2** Land under tillage; distinguished from *outfield.*

in·field·er (in′fēl′dər) *n.* In baseball, a defensive player in the infield: the first, second, and third basemen, the shortstop, and, when fielding the ball, the pitcher and catcher: distinguished from *outfielder.*

in·fil·ter (in·fil′tər) *v.t.* & *v.i.* To enter by infiltration.

in·fil·trate (in·fil′trāt; *esp. for v. defs. 2, 3* in′fil·trāt) *v.* **·trat·ed, ·trat·ing** *v.t.* **1** To cause (a liquid or gas) to pass into or through pores or interstices. **2** To filter through or into; permeate. **3** *Mil.* To pass through, as enemy lines, singly or in small groups so as to attack from the rear or on the flanks. — *v.i.* **4** To pass into or through a substance, as in filtering. — *n.* **1** That which infiltrates or has infiltrated. **2** Any morbid substance that passes into the tissues of the body.

in·fil·tra·tion (in′fil·trā′shən) *n.* **1** The act or process of infiltrating. **2** That which infiltrates. — **in·fil·tra·tive** (in·fil′trā·tiv) *adj.*

in·fi·nite (in′fə·nit) *adj.* **1** So great as to be immeasurable and unbounded; limitless: *infinite* power or space. **2** All-embracing; perfect; absolute: the *infinite* God. **3** *Math.* **a** Of, pertaining to, or designating a quantity conceived as always increasing so as to exceed any other assignable quantity in value. **b** Consisting of as many elements as a proper part of a total assemblage. **4** In music, composed so that it can be repeated over and over, without finale. **5** Very numerous; very great: to take *infinite* pains. — *n.* That which is infinite; an infinite quantity or magnitude; infinity. — **the Infinite** God; Eternity; the Absolute. [<L *infinitus* unlimited < *in-* not + *finitus* finite < *finis* limit] — **in′fi·nite·ly** *adv.* — **in′fi·nite·ness** *n.*

Synonyms: absolute, boundless, countless, eternal, illimitable, immeasurable, innumerable, interminable, limitless, measureless, numberless, unbounded, unconditioned, unfathomable, unlimited, unmeasured. *Infinite* signifies without bounds or limits in any way, and may be applied to space, time, quantity, or number. *Countless, innumerable,* and *numberless,* which should be the same as *infinite,* are in common usage vaguely employed to denote what it is difficult or practically impossible to count or number, but still perhaps falling far short of *infinite;* as, *countless* leaves, the *countless* sands on the seashore, *numberless* battles, *innumerable* delays. So, too, *boundless, illimitable, limitless, measureless,* and *unlimited* are loosely used in reference to what has no apparent or readily determinable limits in space or time; as, we speak of the *boundless* ocean. *Infinite* space is without bounds, not only in fact, but in thought; *infinite* time is truly *eternal.* Compare ETERNAL, PERFECT. *Antonyms:* bounded, brief, circumscribed, evanescent, finite, limited, little, measurable, moderate, narrow, restricted, shallow, short, small, transient, transitory.

in·fin·i·tes·i·mal (in′fin·ə·tes′ə·məl) *adj.* **1** Infinitely small. **2** So small as to be incalculable and insignificant for all practical purposes. **3** *Math.* Denoting a quantity conceived as continually diminishing toward zero as a limit. — *n.* An infinitesimal quantity. [<NL

infinitesimus < *infinitus* infinite + *-esimus* (after *centesimus* hundredth)] — **in′fin·i·tes′i·mal·ly** *adv.*

in·fin·i·tive (in·fin′ə·tiv) *Gram. adj.* **1** Without limitation of person or number: opposed to *finite.* **2** Of, pertaining to, or using the infinitive mood. — *n.* In many languages, a mood of the verb expressing action or condition without the limitation of person or number, as *to run.* In English, its sign *to* is omitted after the auxiliaries *can, could, do, may, might, must, shall, should, will, would,* and after such phrases as *had better, had rather,* and is used optionally after *bid, dare, help, let, make, need, please, see,* etc. The infinitive may also function as a noun while retaining the ability of the verb to take objects and adverbial modifiers. Example: *To ride horses* was his favorite sport. Also **infinitive mood. — split infinitive** An expression in which the sign of the infinitive "to" is separated from its verb by an intervening word, usually an adverb, as in the phrase "to quickly return." Although the construction is often condemned, it is sometimes justified to escape ambiguity. [<LL *infinitivus*]

in·fin·i·ty (in·fin′ə·tē) *n. pl.* **·ties 1** The quality or state of being infinite; boundlessness; perfection. **2** Something, as space, regarded as boundless. **3** The portion of space that lies at an infinite distance. **4** *Math.* **a** An infinite number or quantity: denoted by ∞. **b** The point or series of points in space that by supposition lie at an infinite distance from the definite point in question. [<OF *infinité* <L *infinitas, -tatis* < *infinitus* INFINITE]

in·firm (in·fûrm′) *adj.* **1** Feeble or weak from age. **2** Lacking soundness, resolution, stability, or firmness. **3** Not legally secure; voidable. See synonyms under FRAGILE, SICKLY. [<OF *enferm* <L *infirmus*] — **in·firm′ly** *adv.* — **in·firm′ness** *n.*

in·fir·ma·ry (in·fûr′mər·ē) *n. pl.* **·ries 1** A place for the treatment of the sick; a dispensary. **2** A small hospital. [<Med. L *infirmaria* < *infirmus* infirm]

in·fir·mi·ty (in·fûr′mə·tē) *n. pl.* **·ties 1** A physical, mental, or moral weakness or flaw. **2** Infirm condition. See synonyms under DISEASE, FOIBLE, ILLNESS.

in·fix (in·fiks′) *v.t.* **1** To fix or drive in, as by thrusting. **2** To implant firmly; instil; inculcate. **3** *Gram.* To insert (an infix) within a word. — *n.* (in′fiks) *Gram.* A modifying addition inserted in the body of a word. Compare PREFIX, SUFFIX. — **in·fix′ion** *n.*

in·flame (in·flām′) *v.* **·flamed, ·flam·ing** *v.t.* **1** To set on fire; kindle. **2** To excite to violent emotion or activity; arouse the fury of. **3** To excite or make more intense, as anger or lust. **4** To make red or florid, as with rage. **5** To cause inflammation in; heat morbidly. — *v.i.* **6** To catch fire; burst into flame. **7** To become excited or aroused. **8** To become inflamed by infection, etc. See synonyms under INCENSE[1]. [<OF *enflammer* <L *inflammare* < *in-* in + *flammare* flame < *flamma* flame] — **in·flam′er** *n.*

in·flam·ma·ble (in·flam′ə·bəl) *adj.* **1** Readily set on fire; combustible: also *flammable.* **2** Easily excited or roused to passion. — *n.* A combustible substance or material. See synonyms under ARDENT. [<F] — **in·flam′ma·bil′i·ty, in·flam′ma·ble·ness** *n.* — **in·flam′ma·bly** *adv.*

in·flam·ma·tion (in′flə·mā′shən) *n.* **1** *Pathol.* A morbid process in some tissue, organ, or part of the body characterized by heat, redness, swelling, and pain. **2** The act of inflaming.

in·flam·ma·to·ry (in·flam′ə·tôr′ē, -tō′rē) *adj.* **1** Tending to produce heat or excitement. **2** Calculated to arouse evil passions, riot, etc.; seditious. **3** Characterized by or pertaining to inflammation. **4** Inducing or provoking inflammation.

in·flate (in·flāt′) *v.* **·flat·ed, ·flat·ing** *v.t.* **1** To fill with gas or air so as to distend or expand; blow up; dilate. **2** To increase the proportions of; puff up: to *inflate* one's pride. **3** To increase unduly, especially so that the nominal value exceeds the real: to *inflate* currency or prices. — *v.i.* **4** To become distended or inflated. See synonyms under PUFF, SWELL. [<L *inflatus,* pp. of *inflare* blow into < *in-* in + *flare* blow] — **in·flat′a·ble** *adj.*

in·flat·ed (in·flā′tid) *adj.* **1** Puffed out; distended; swollen, as by air or gas. **2** Hollowed or puffed out, as a plant stem or capsule; bulbous; dilated. **3** Overloaded with figures of speech and high-sounding words; pompous; bombastic; magniloquent. **4** Enhanced or swollen abnormally or improperly; increased unjustifiably: *inflated* values. **5** Puffed up with conceit.

in·flat·er (in·flā′tər) *n.* One who or that which inflates; especially, any mechanical device, as an air pump, for inflating. Also **in·fla′tor.**

in·fla·tion (in·flā′shən) *n.* **1** The act of inflating, or the state of being inflated; distention: the *inflation* of a bubble or a balloon. **2** Bombast; conceit. **3** Expansion or extension beyond natural or proper limits or so as to exceed normal or just value; specifically, overissue of currency, or the state resulting therefrom; also, increase in price levels arising from mounting effective demand without corresponding increase in commodity supply. **4** That which is inflated or puffed up. — **in·fla′tion·ar′y** *adj.*

in·fla·tion·ist (in·flā′shən·ist) *n.* An advocate of or believer in the issuing of an abnormally large amount of currency.

in·fleet (in·flekt′) *v.t.* **1** *Gram.* To give or recite the inflections of (a word); conjugate; decline. **2** To modulate, as the voice. **3** To turn inward or aside; deflect; curve. — *v.i.* **4** To take grammatical inflection. [<L *inflectere* < *in-* in + *flectere* bend] **in·flec·tion** (in·flek′shən) *n.* **1** The act of inflecting, the state of being inflected, or that which is inflected; a bending or bend; curvature; angle. **2** *Gram.* **a** A pattern of change undergone by words to express grammatical and syntactical relations, as of case, number, gender, person, tense, etc. The inflection of nouns, pronouns and adjectives is called *declension;* that of verbs, *conjugation.* **b** An element denoting the grammatical function of a word, as the use of *'s* to signify possession in *boy's.* **c** An inflected form. **3** Modulation or change of pitch in the voice. **4** *Geom.* A change in the nature of a curve, as from convex to concave. Also *Brit.* **in·flex′ion:** sometimes called *flection.*

◆ The few inflections surviving in English include: *s* for the regular plural of nouns, and for the third person singular present indicative of verbs; *'s* for the possessive: *-er* for the comparative, and *-est* for the superlative, of many adjectives and adverbs; *-ed* for the past and past participle of regular (or weak) verbs, and *-ing* for the present participle.

in·flec·tion·al (in·flek′shən·əl) *adj. Ling.* **1** Belonging to, relating to, or showing grammatical inflection. **2** Designating a language, such as Latin, that expresses grammatical relationships by means of inflections, rather than by auxiliary words; synthetic: opposed to *analytic.* Also *Brit.* **in·flex′ion·al. — in·flec′tion·al·ly** *adv.*

in·flexed (in·flekst′) *adj. Bot.* Abruptly turned or bent inward, as the petals of a flower.

in·flex·i·ble (in·flek′sə·bəl) *adj.* **1** Not to be turned from a purpose; unyielding; firm; inexorable: *inflexible* resolves, an *inflexible* will. **2** Incapable of being physically bent; unbending; rigid; not flexible. **3** That cannot be altered or varied: the *inflexible* laws of nature. [<L *inflexibilis*] — **in·flex′i·bil′i·ty, in·flex′i·ble·ness** *n.* — **in·flex′i·bly** *adv.*

Synonyms: immovable, inexorable, obstinate, persistent, pertinacious, resolute, rigid, steadfast, stiff, stubborn, unbending, unrelenting, unyielding. See OBSTINATE. *Antonyms:* ductile, elastic, flexible, indulgent, lithe, pliable, pliant, supple, yielding.

in·flict (in·flikt′) *v.t.* **1** To cause another to suffer or endure, as a blow or wound. **2** To impose, as punishment. **3** To impose as if by force or against opposition: to *inflict* one's views on the public. [<L *inflictus,* pp. of *infligere* strike on < *in-* on + *fligere* strike] — **in·flict′er, in·flic′tor** *n.* — **in·flic′tive** *adj.*

in·flic·tion (in·flik′shən) *n.* **1** The act or process of inflicting or imposing: the *infliction* of a penalty. **2** That which is inflicted, as pain or punishment.

in·flo·res·cence (in′flə·res′əns) *n. Bot.* **1** The act of flowering; the expanding of blossoms. **2** The mode of disposition of flowers: racemose and cymose *inflorescence.* **3** Flowers collectively: said of certain plants or of a tree or a group of trees: the *inflorescence* of the horse chestnut. **4** An axis along which all the buds are flower buds. [<NL *inflorescentia* <LL *inflorescens*, ppr. of *inflorescere* come into flower. See IN-², FLORESCENCE.] — **in'flo·res'cent** *adj.*

in·flow (in'flō') *n.* The act of flowing in, or that which flows in.

in·flu·ence (in'flŏŏ·əns) *n.* **1** The power or process of producing an effect upon a person, by imperceptible or intangible means. **2** Power arising from social, financial, moral, or similar authority. **3** A person, group, or the like possessing such power. **4** *Electr.* Electrostatic induction. **5** In astrology, originally, an ethereal fluid flowing from the stars and affecting the character and actions of men; later, an occult force of the stars exercising a similar control. See synonyms under IM-PULSE, OPERATION. — *v.t.* **·enced, ·enc·ing 1** To exert mental or moral influence upon or over; sway; persuade. **2** To act upon physically; affect the nature or condition of; modify: Fatigue often *influences* the eyesight. [<F <LL *influentia* <*influens, -entis*, ppr. of *influere* flow in + *fluere* flow. Doublet of INFLUENZA.] — **in'flu·enc'er** *n.*

Synonyms (verb): activate, actuate, affect, command, compel, dispose, draw, drive, excite, impel, incite, incline, induce, instigate, lead, mold, move, persuade, prompt, stir, sway, urge. To *influence* is to affect, modify, or act upon by physical, mental, or moral power, especially in some gentle, subtle, and gradual way; as, Vegetation is *influenced* by light; Everyone is *influenced* to some extent by public opinion; *influence* is chiefly used of power acting from without, but it may be used of motives regarded as forces acting upon the will. *Activate* means to put or go into action, to make capable of acting. *Actuate* refers to that which initiates the action of a mechanism or apparatus, as well as to mental or moral power *impelling* one from within. One may *influence*, but cannot directly *actuate* another; but one may be *actuated* to cruelty by hatred. *Prompt* and *stir* are words of mere suggestion toward some course of action; *dispose, draw, incline, influence,* and *lead* refer to the use of mild means to awaken in another a purpose or disposition to act. To *excite* is to arouse one from lethargy or indifference to action. *Incite* and *instigate,* to spur or goad to action, differ in the fact that *incite* may be good, while *instigate* is usually to evil (compare ABET). To *urge* and *impel* signify to produce strong excitation toward some act. *Drive* and *compel* imply irresistible influence accomplishing its object. One may be *driven* either by his own passions or by external force or urgency; one is *compelled* only by some external power; as, The owner was *compelled* by his misfortunes to sell his estate. Compare ACTUATE, BEND, COMPEL, DRIVE, GOVERN, PERSUADE. *Antonyms*: deter, discourage, dissuade, hinder, impede, inhibit, prevent, restrain, retard.

influence fuze A proximity fuze.

in·flu·ent (in'flŏŏ·ənt) *adj.* **1** Flowing in. **2** Relating to a channel through which either air or any fluid passes into a receptacle. — *n.* An inflow; a tributary stream or river; affluent. [<L *influens, -entis*, ppr. of *influere.* See INFLUENCE.]

in·flu·en·tial (in'flŏŏ·en'shəl) *adj.* **1** Having or exercising influence. **2** Having or exercising a great influence or power; effective. — **in'flu·en'tial·ly** *adv.*

in·flu·en·za (in'flŏŏ·en'zə) *n.* **1** *Pathol.* A contagious, infective, sometimes epidemic disease generally caused by a filtrable virus and commonly characterized by inflammation of the upper air passages, attended by fever and nervous and muscular prostration. **2** A contagious disease common among horses: characterized by its attack upon the mucous membranes of the throat and eyelids. [<Ital. <*influire* influence <L *influere* flow in. Doublet of INFLUENCE.] — **in'flu·en'zal** *adj.* — **in'flu·en'za·like'** *adj.*

in·flux (in'fluks') *n.* **1** The act of flowing in; a continuous flowing in. **2** A pouring in or instilling. **3** The mouth of a river. **4** The place or point at which one stream flows into

another. See synonyms under ACCESSION. [<F <LL *influxus*, pp. of *influere* flow in]

in·fold (in·fōld') *v.t.* **1** To wrap in folds; enclose. **2** To embrace in or as in the arms; contain. **3** To turn or fold inward; make a fold in. Also *enfold.* — **in·fold'er** *n.*

in·form¹ (in·fôrm') *v.t.* **1** To tell (someone) facts or information previously unknown; make something known to; notify: He *informed* me of the outcome. **2** To give character to; inspire; animate. **3** *Obs.* To give form or vitality to; shape. **4** *Rare* To teach; instruct. — *v.i.* **5** To give information, especially concerning infractions of the law: with *on* or *against.* [<OF *enformer* <L *informare* give form to, describe <*in-* in + *forma* form]

Synonyms: advertise, advise, apprise, communicate, disclose, divulge, impart, instruct, intimate, mention, notify, reveal, teach, tell. See LEARN, TEACH.

in·form² (in·fôrm') *adj.* **1** Shapeless; unformed. **2** Deformed. [<F *informe* <L *informis* <*in-* not + *forma* form]

in·for·mal (in·fôr'məl) *adj.* **1** Not in the usual or prescribed form; unofficial: an *informal* truce. **2** Without ceremony or formality: an *informal* dinner. **3** Describing a manner of speech or writing characteristic of familiar conversation; colloquial. — **in·for'mal·ly** *adv.*

in·for·mal·i·ty (in'fôr·mal'ə·tē) *n.* *pl.* **·ties 1** Absence of regular form; the state of being informal. **2** An informal act or proceeding.

in·form·ant (in·fôr'mənt) *n.* **1** One who imparts information. **2** *Ling.* A native speaker of a language whose speech is used by linguists in recording and studying linguistic forms, sounds, etc.

in·for·ma·tion (in'fər·mā'shən) *n.* **1** Knowledge acquired or derived. **2** Timely or specific knowledge. **3** *Law* An accusation or complaint made without the intervention of a grand jury. **4** The act of informing. **5** Any distinct signal element forming part of a message or communication, especially one assembled and made available for use by automatic machines, as a digital computer: usually measured in bits. [<OF *enformacion*] — **in'for·ma'tion·al** *adj.* See synonyms under EDU-CATION, KNOWLEDGE, TIDINGS, WISDOM.

information theory The scientific study of the characteristics, properties, and functions of any signal system designed to transmit information, with special emphasis on the number of bits that can be sent on a given power in a given time over a communication system operating under given conditions: also called *communication theory.*

in·form·a·tive (in·fôr'mə·tiv) *adj.* Instructive; affording information. Also **in·form'a·to·ry.** [<L *informatus*, pp. of *informare* describe]

in·formed (in·fôrmd') *adj.* Having a high degree of knowledge, information, or education.

in·form·er (in·fôr'mər) *n.* **1** One who informs against others; specifically, with regard to infractions of the law; a stool pigeon; a spy. **2** One who imparts information. **3** A telltale.

in·for·tune (in·fôr'chən) *n. Obs.* **1** Misfortune: also **in·for·tu'ni·ty.** **2** In astrology, an unlucky or ill-disposed planet: particularly applicable to Saturn and Mars; also, sometimes, Mercury. [<OF <L *infortunium*]

in·fra·ba·sal (in'frə·bā'səl) *n. Zool.* Any one of a circle of plates of a crinoid cup which lie next to the stalk and beneath the natural basal plates.

in·fra·cos·tal (in'frə·kos'təl) *adj. Anat.* **1** Situated below a rib (costa): an *infracostal* nerve. **2** Indicating numerous minor muscles below the surface of the ribs. — *n. pl.* **·kos·ta·les** (-kos·tā'lēz) An infracostal muscle.

in·fract (in·frakt') *v.t.* To break; infringe; violate (a law, pledge, etc.). [<L *infractus*, pp. of *infringere* INFRINGE] — **in·frac'tor** *n.*

in·frac·tion (in·frak'shən) *n.* **1** The act of breaking or violating. **2** A fracture. [<L *infractio, -onis*]

in·fra·lap·sar·i·an·ism (in'frə·lap·sâr'ē·ən·iz'əm) *n. Theol.* The doctrine respecting the order of decrees that places the decree of election and predestination after that of the fall of man; sublapsarianism; moderate Calvinism. See SUPRALAPSARIAN. [<INFRA- + L *lapsus*, pp. of *labi* slip, fall + -ARIAN + -ISM] — **in'fra·lap·sar'i·an** *adj. & n.*

in·fra·max·il·lar·y (in'frə·mak'sə·ler'ē) *adj. Anat.* Of or pertaining to the lower jaw or inferior maxillary bone. — *n. pl.* **·lar·ies** The lower jaw bone.

in·fra·me·di·an (in'frə·mē'dē·ən) *n.* That interval or zone along the sea bottom which is between 50 and 100 fathoms in depth. — *adj.* Of or pertaining to this zone.

in·fran·gi·ble (in·fran'jə·bəl) *adj.* **1** Not breakable or capable of being broken into parts. **2** Inviolable. — **in·fran'gi·bil'i·ty, in·fran'gi·ble·ness** *n.* — **in·fran'gi·bly** *adv.*

in·fra·o·ral (in'frə·ôr'əl, -ō'rəl) *adj. Anat.* Placed beneath the mouth.

in·fra·or·bit·al (in'frə·ôr'bit·əl) *adj. Anat.* Situated below the orbit of the eye.

in·fra·red (in'frə·red') *adj. Physics* **1** Situated beyond the red end of the visible spectrum, as certain heat rays. **2** Designating radiations of wavelength in excess of about 7,600 angstroms but less than radio waves.

in·fra·son·ic (in'frə·son'ik) *adj.* Of, pertaining to, or characterized by a sound frequency below the range of audibility: also called *subsonic.* Compare ULTRASONIC.

in·fra·struc·ture (in'frə·struk'chər) *n.* The permanent foundation or essential elements of a structure, system, plan of operations, etc.; especially, the essential installations of a community, as schools, hospitals, transportation facilities, power plants, etc.

in·fre·quent (in·frē'kwənt) *adj.* Occurring at widely separate intervals; uncommon. — **in·fre'quent·ly** *adv.* — **in·fre'quen·cy** *n.*

in·fringe (in·frinj') *v.t.* **·fringed, ·fring·ing** To break or disregard the terms or requirements of, as an oath or law; violate. — *v.i.* **infringe on** (or **upon**) To transgress or trespass on rights or privileges; encroach: to *infringe on* a liberty or a patent. [<L *infringere* <*in-* in + *frangere* break] — **in·fring'er** *n.*

in·fringe·ment (in·frinj'mənt) *n.* **1** The act of infringing. **2** Any breaking in upon or violation of a right, privilege, regulation, law, contract, etc. **3** The wrongful use of trademarks or trade names.

in·fun·dib·u·li·form (in'fən·dib'yə·lə·fôrm') *adj.* **1** Funnel-shaped. **2** *Bot.* Having a tube below and gradually enlarged above.

in·fun·dib·u·lum (in'fən·dib'yə·ləm) *n. pl.* **·la** (-lə) **1** *Anat.* **a** A structure or conduit shaped like a funnel, as that connecting the third ventricle of the brain with the pituitary body, passing through the hypothalamus. **b** An expanded end of a bronchial tubule or of a ureter, etc. **2** *Biol.* **a** A depression on the crown of the head of tapeworms. **b** The siphon or funnel of a cephalopod. See INFUSE.] [<L, funnel <*infundere* pour into. See INFUSE.] — **in'fun·dib'u·lar, in'fun·dib'u·late** *adj.*

in·fu·ri·ate (in·fyŏŏr'ē·āt) *v.t.* **·at·ed, ·at·ing** To make furious. — *adj.* Infuriated; enraged; mad. [<Med. L *infuriatus*, pp. of *infuriare* madden <*in-* in + *furia* rage] — **in·fu'ri·at'ed** *adj.* — **in·fu'ri·ate·ly, in·fu'ri·at'ed·ly** *adv.* — **in·fu'ri·at'ing·ly** *adv.* — **in·fu'ri·a'tion** *n.*

in·fus·cate (in·fus'kit) *adj. Entomol.* Tinged or darkened with brown, as part of an insect's wing. Also **in·fus'cat·ed.** [<L *infuscatus*, pp. of *infuscare* make dark <*in-* thoroughly + *fuscare* darken <*fuscus* dark]

in·fuse (in·fyŏŏz') *v.t.* **·fused, ·fus·ing 1** To instil or inculcate, as principles or qualities. **2** To inspire; imbue: with *with.* **3** To pour in. **4** To steep, so as to make an extract or infusion. [<L *infusus*, pp. of *infunder* pour in <*in-* in + *fundere* pour] — **in·fus'er** *n.*

in·fus·i·ble¹ (in·fyŏŏ'zə·bəl) *adj.* Incapable of or resisting fusion or melting. [<IN-¹ not + FUSIBLE] — **in·fus'i·bil'i·ty, in·fus'i·ble·ness** *n.*

in·fus·i·ble² (in·fyŏŏ'zə·bəl) *adj.* That can be infused or poured in. [<INFUSE + -IBLE] — **in·fus'i·bil'i·ty, in·fus'i·ble·ness** *n.*

in·fu·sion (in·fyŏŏ'zhən) *n.* **1** The act of infusing, imbuing, or pouring in; instilation. **2** That which is infused; an admixture; tincture. **3** A pouring out or upon, as in baptism; an affusion. **4** The process of steeping or soaking any substance, as a vegetable or powder, in a liquid for the purpose of extracting its medicinal properties without boiling: distinguished from *decoction.* **5** The liquid extract so obtained: an *infusion* of tobacco. **6** *Med.* The operation of introducing saline or other solutions into the veins.

in·fu·sion·ism (in-fyōō'zhən-iz'əm) *n. Theol.* The doctrine that the human soul emanates from the divine substance, and is infused into the body at conception or birth: distinguished from *creationism* and *traducianism.* — **in·fu'sion·ist** *n.*

in·fu·sive (in-fyōō'siv) *adj.* Having the power of infusing; inspiring.

In·fu·so·ri·a (in'fyōō·sôr'ē·ə, -sō'rē·ə) *n. pl.* **1** Formerly, a division of the animal kingdom, including especially those microscopic protozoans found in infusions of decaying matter. **2** A class of the phylum *Protozoa*, characterized by ciliated bodies and free-living aquatic habits, including *Paramecium* and *Stentor:* also called *Ciliata.* — **in'fu·so'ri·an** *adj.* & *n.* [<NL *infusus,* pp. of *infundere* pour into]

in·fu·so·ri·al (in'fyōō·sôr'ē·əl, -sō'rē-) *adj.* **1** Of or pertaining to infusorians. **2** Containing or composed of infusorians.

in·gem·i·nate (in·jem'ə·nāt) *v.t.* **·nat·ed, ·nat·ing** To repeat or redouble; reiterate. — *adj.* (-it) Repeated; redoubled. [<L *ingeminatus,* pp. of *ingeminare* double. See IN-¹, GERMINATE.] — **in·gem'i·na'tion** *n.*

in·gen·er·ate¹ (in·jen'ər·āt) *v.t.* **·at·ed, ·at·ing** To generate or produce within. — *adj.* (-it) Inborn. [<L *ingeneratus,* pp. of *ingenerare* ENGENDER] — **in·gen'er·a'tion** *n.*

in·gen·er·ate² (in·jen'ər·it) *adj.* Not brought into being by generation. [<LL *ingeneratus* self-existent]

in·gen·ious (in·jēn'yəs) *adj.* **1** Possessed of or manifesting inventive faculty. **2** Characterized by ingenuity; well conceived; apt. **3** *Obs.* Of clever mind or genius, or displaying exceptional mental qualities. See synonyms under CLEVER. [<MF *ingénieux* <L *ingeniosus* talented <*ingenium* natural quality, ability < *in-* in + *gignere* beget] — **in·gen'ious·ly** *adv.* — **in·gen'ious·ness** *n.*

in·gen·i·tal (in·jen'ə·təl) *adj. Obs.* That is natural to one; inherent. [<L *ingenitus,* pp. of *ingignere* implant, beget]

in·ge·nu·i·ty (in'jə·nōō'ə·tē, -nyōō'-) *n.* **1** The quality of having inventive power; cleverness in contriving or originating. **2** Ingeniousness of execution or design. **3** *Obs.* Ingeniousness; candor.

Synonyms: acuteness, cleverness, cunning, dexterity, genius, ingeniousness, invention, inventiveness, readiness, skill. *Ingenuity* is inferior to *genius,* being rather mechanical than creative, and is shown in devising expedients, overcoming difficulties, inventing appliances, adapting means to ends. *Dexterity* is chiefly of the hand; *cleverness* may be either of the hand or of the mind, but chiefly of the latter. See ADDRESS. *Antonyms:* awkwardness, clumsiness, dulness, stupidity, unskilfulness.

in·gen·u·ous (in·jen'yōō·əs) *adj.* **1** Free from disguise or dissimulation; frank; artless. **2** High-minded; sincere. **3** Ingenious: an incorrect use. See synonyms under CANDID, HONEST. [<L *ingenuus* inborn, natural, frank <*ingignere* beget, engender] — **in·gen'u·ous·ly** *adv.* — **in·gen'u·ous·ness** *n.*

in·gest (in·jest') *v.t.* To take in (food) for digestion. [<L *ingestus,* pp. of *ingere* carry in < *in-* in + *gerere* carry] — **in·ges'tion** *n.* — **in·ges'tive** *adj.*

in·gle·nook (ing'gəl·nŏŏk') *n.* A corner by the fire.

in·glo·ri·ous (in·glôr'ē·əs, -glō'rē-) *adj.* **1** Characterized by failure or disgrace. **2** Without glory; obscure; humble. [<L *ingloriosus*] — **in·glo'ri·ous·ly** *adv.* — **in·glo'ri·ous·ness** *n.*

in·go·ing (in'gō'ing) *adj.* Entering; going in.

in·grain (in·grān') *v.t.* **1** To fix deeply; impress indelibly upon the mind or character. **2** To dye before weaving; dye with "grain" or scarlet. Also spelled *engrain.* — *n.* (in'grān') A carpet made of ingrained worsted; also, the ingrained wool or other material of which it is made. — *adj.* (in'grān') Dyed in the yarn before manufacture; hence, thoroughly inwrought. [Var. of ENGRAIN]

in·grained (in·grānd') *adj.* **1** Dyed in the wool; deeply rooted or worked in. **2** Thorough; inveterate.

in·grate (in'grāt) *adj. Obs.* Ungrateful. Also **in·grate'ful.** — *n.* One who is ungrateful. [<OF *ingrat* <L *ingratus* unpleasant, ungrateful < *in-* not + *gratus* pleasing]

in·gra·ti·ate (in·grā'shē·āt) *v.t.* **·at·ed, ·at·ing** To bring (oneself) into the favor or confidence of others. — **in·gra'ti·at'ing·ly** *adv.* — **in·gra'ti·a'tion** *n.* — **in·gra'ti·a·to'ry** (-ə·tôr'ē, -tō'rē) *adj.* [<Ital. *ingraziare* <L *in gratiam* in favor]

in·grat·i·tude (in·grat'ə·tōōd, -tyōōd) *n.* Lack of gratitude; insensibility to kindness; thanklessness.

in·gre·di·ent (in·grē'dē·ənt) *n.* **1** That which enters into the composition of a mixture: usually distinguished from the *constituent* of a chemical compound. **2** A component part of anything. See synonyms under PART. [<F *ingrédient* <L *ingrediens, -entis,* ppr. of *ingredi* entering into < *in-* in + *gradi* walk]

in·gress (in'gres) *n.* **1** Means or power of effecting entrance. **2** A place of entrance. **3** The act of entering. See synonyms under ENTRANCE¹. [<L *ingressus,* pp. of *ingredi* enter]

in·gres·sion (in·gresh'ən) *n.* The act of entering, or an entrance into something.

in·gres·sive (in·gres'iv) *adj.* **1** Pertaining to entrance; entering. **2** *Gram.* Inceptive. — **in·gres'sive·ness** *n.*

in-group (in'grōōp') *n. Sociol.* Any group considered by any of its members to have a certain exclusiveness: contrasted with *out-group.*

in·grown (in'grōn) *adj.* **1** Grown into the flesh, as a toe nail. **2** Growing inward or within. — **in'grow'ing** *adj.*

in·growth (in'grōth') *n.* An inward growth, or a thing that grows inward.

in·gui·nal (ing'gwə·nəl) *adj.* Of, pertaining to, or near the groin. See illustration under ABDOMINAL. [<L *inguinalis*]

in·gui·no-ab·dom·i·nal (ing'gwə·nō-ab·dom'ə·nəl) *adj.* Related to the groin and the abdomen.

in·gur·gi·tate (in·gûr'jə·tāt) *v.t.* & *v.i.* **·tat·ed, ·tat·ing** To eat or drink greedily or to excess; gorge; swill. [<L *ingurgitatus,* pp. of *ingurgitare* pour in, gorge oneself < *in-* in + *gurges, -ites* whirlpool] — **in·gur'gi·ta'tion** *n.*

in·hab·it (in·hab'it) *v.t.* To live or dwell in; occupy as a home. — *v.i. Archaic* To dwell; abide. [<OF *enhabiter* <L *inhabitare* < *in-* in + *habitare* dwell, freq. of *habere* have] — **in·hab'it·a·bil'i·ty** *n.* — **in·hab'it·a·ble** *adj.* — **in·hab'it·er** *n.* — **in·hab'i·ta'tion** *n.*

in·hab·i·tance (in·hab'ə·təns) *n.* **1** The act of dwelling; state of being inhabited; residence, as distinguished from sojourn. **2** A habitation; abode. Also **in·hab'i·tan·cy.**

in·hab·i·tant (in·hab'ə·tənt) *n.* One making his home or dwelling permanently in a place, as distinguished from a lodger or visitor; a resident. [<AF <L *inhabitans -antis,* pp. of *inhabitare*]

in·ha·lant (in·hā'lənt) *adj.* **1** That inhales or draws in. **2** Used for inhaling. — *n.* **1** An apparatus used for inhaling. **2** That which is to be inhaled. Also **in·ha'lent.**

in·ha·la·tion (in'hə·lā'shən) *n.* **1** The act of inhaling. **2** That which is inhaled; an inhalant.

in·hale (in·hāl') *v.* **·haled, ·hal·ing** *v.t.* To draw into the lungs, as breath or tobacco smoke; breathe in. — *v.i.* To draw breath, tobacco smoke, etc., into the lungs. Opposed to *exhale.* [<L *inhalare* < *in-* in + *halare* breathe]

in·hal·er (in·hā'lər) *n.* **1** One who inhales. **2** Something from or through which one inhales; specifically an appliance or apparatus enabling one to inhale air, medicinal vapors, anesthetics, etc.

in·har·mo·ni·ous (in'här·mō'nē·əs) *adj.* Lacking in, or not in, harmony; discordant. Also **in'har·mon'ic** (-mon'ik), **in'har·mon'i·cal.** See synonyms under INCONGRUOUS. — **in'har·mo'ni·ous·ly** *adv.* — **in'har·mo'ni·ous·ness** *n.*

in·haul (in'hôl') *n. Naut.* A rope or rigging for bringing in a sail or spar, as the jib boom. Also **in'haul'er.**

in·here (in·hir') *v.i.* **·hered, ·her·ing** To be a permanent or essential part: with *in.* [<L *inhaerere* < *in-* in + *haerere* stick] — **in·her'ence,** **in·her'en·cy** *n.*

in·her·ent (in·hir'ənt, -her'-) *adj.* **1** Permanently united; intrinsic; innate; essential. **2** Pertaining as a property or attribute. Also **in·he·ren·tial** (in'hi·ren'shəl). [<L *inhaerens, -entis,* ppr. of *inhaerere* INHERE] — **in·her'ent·ly** *adv.*

Synonyms: congenital, essential, immanent, inborn, inbred, indispensable, indwelling, infixed, ingrained, innate, inseparable, internal, intrinsic, inwrought, native, natural, subjective. *Immanent* is a philosophic word, to de-

note that which dwells in or pervades any substance or spirit without necessarily being a part of it. That which is *inherent* is an *inseparable* part of that in which it inheres, and is usually thought of with reference to some outworking or effect; as, an *inherent* difficulty. God is said to be *immanent* (not *inherent*) in the universe. Frequently *intrinsic* and *inherent* can be interchanged, but *inherent* applies to qualities, while *intrinsic* applies to essence, so that to speak of *intrinsic* excellence conveys higher praise than if we say *inherent* excellence. *Inherent* and *intrinsic* may be said of persons or things; *congenital, inborn, inbred, innate,* apply to living beings. *Congenital* is frequent in medical and legal use with special application to defects; as, *congenital* idiocy. *Innate* and *inborn* are almost identical, but *innate* is preferred in philosophic use, as when we speak of *innate* ideas; that which is *inborn, congenital,* or *innate* may be original with the individual, but that which is *inbred* is inherited. *Ingrained* signifies dyed in the grain, and denotes that which is deeply wrought into substance or character. See NATURAL. *Antonyms:* accidental, casual, external, extrinsic, fortuitous, incidental, outward, subsidiary, superadded, superficial, superfluous, superimposed, supplemental, transient, unconnected.

in·her·it (in·her'it) *v.t.* **1** To receive, as property or a title, by succession or will; fall heir to. **2** To receive (traits, qualities, etc.) as if by succession or will; have as hereditary traits. **3** *Obs.* To make heir; place (an heir) in possession: usually with *of.* — *v.i.* **4** To come into or possess an inheritance. **5** To receive traits, qualities, etc.: with *from.* [<OF *enheriter* <LL *inhereditare* inherit < *in-* in + *heres* heir]

in·her·i·tance (in·her'ə·təns) *n.* **1** Anything acquired or possessed by descent or succession; something which is or can be inherited, as property or title acquired by an heir at the owner's death. **2** A heritage, especially in the sense of mental, cultural or spiritual legacies left by past generations to succeeding generations. **3** Physical or mental characteristics derived from ancestry. **4** Act or fact of inheriting.

inherited character *Genetics* A modification of an organism considered as having been transmitted by inheritance: distinguished from *acquired character.*

in·her·i·tor (in·her'ə·tər) *n.* An heir. — **in·her'i·tress** (-tris), **in·her'i·trix** (-triks) *n. fem.*

in·he·sion (in·hē'zhən) *n.* The condition of inhering or being fixed in something; inherence. [<LL *inhaesio, -onis* <*inhaerere.* See INHERE.]

in·hib·it (in·hib'it) *v.t.* **1** To hold back; restrain, as an impulse. **2** To forbid (a cleric) to perform religious functions. **3** To check or block (one mental or nervous process) by another, nearly simultaneous, opposed process. See synonyms under PROHIBIT. [<L *inhibitus,* pp. of *inhibere* check < *in-* in + *habere* have, hold] — **in·hib'it·er, in·hib'i·tor** *n.* — **in·hib'it·a·ble** *adj.* — **in·hib'i·tive, in·hib'i·to'ry** (-tôr'ē, -tō'rē) *adj.*

in·hi·bi·tion (in'hi·bish'ən, in'i-) *n.* **1** The act of inhibiting or the state of being inhibited; restriction; repression; embargo; ban. **2** *Physiol.* **a** The checking of one stimulus or reflex by another acting in opposition. **b** A state of diminished activity at the synapses of the nerves. **3** *Psychol.* **a** The blocking of one mental impulse or process by another. **b** The restraint of will over the impulsive tendencies to habitual or strongly stimulated reactions. **c** Any mental or emotional block.

in·hib·i·tor (in·hib'ə·tər) *n.* **1** That which causes inhibitory action; especially, an inhibitory nerve. **2** A medicinal agent that tends or operates to check organic activity.

in hoc sig·no vin·ces (in hok sig'nō vin'sēz) *Latin* By this sign (i.e., of the cross) thou wilt conquer: motto of the emperor Constantine.

in·hos·pi·ta·ble (in·hos'pi·tə·bəl, in'hos·pit'ə·bəl) *adj.* **1** Not hospitable. **2** Barren; wild; cheerless; affording no shelter or subsistence. — **in·hos'pi·ta·ble·ness** *n.* — **in·hos'pi·ta·bly** *adv.* — **in·hos'pi·tal'i·ty** (-tal'ə·tē) *n.*

in·hu·man (in·hyōō'mən) *adj.* **1** Not possessed of human qualities; cruel; savage; barbarous. **2** Characterized by cruelty; manifesting lack of humanity. **3** Not of the ordinary human type. See synonyms under BARBAROUS, SANGUINARY. [<F *inhumain* <L *inhumanus*] — **in-**

hu·man·ly adv. — **in·hu·man·ness** n.

in·hu·mane (in′hyōō·mān′) adj. Not humane; not kind; inhuman. — **in′hu·mane′ly** adv.

in·hu·man·i·ty (in′hyōō·man′ə·tē) n. pl. ·ties The state of lacking human or humane qualities; cruelty; also, a cruel act, word, etc. [<F inhumanité <L inhumanitas]

in·hu·ma·tion (in′hyōō·mā′shən) n. Burial.

in·hume (in·hyōōm′) v.t. ·humed, ·hum·ing To place in the earth, as a dead body; bury; inter. [<L inhumare <in- in + humus soil, earth] — **in·hum′er** n.

in·im·i·cal (in·im′i·kəl) adj. 1 Of a character regarded as hurtful in tendency or opposed in influence; antagonistic. 2 Unfriendly; hostile. [<LL inimicalis <inimicus unfriendly <in- not + amicus friend] — **in·im′i·cal′i·ty** (-kal′ə·tē) n. — **in·im′i·cal·ly** adv.
Synonyms: adverse, antagonistic, averse, contradictory, contrary, disaffected, harmful, hurtful, noxious, opposed, pernicious, repugnant, unfriendly, unwilling.

in·im·i·ta·ble (in·im′ə·tə·bəl) adj. That cannot be imitated; matchless; incomparable. [<L inimitabilis <in- not + imitabilis imitable] — **in·im′i·ta·bil′i·ty, in·im′i·ta·ble·ness** n. — **in·im′i·ta·bly** adv.

in·iq·ui·tous (in·ik′wə·təs) adj. Wicked; unjust. See synonyms under CRIMINAL, SINFUL. — **in·iq′ui·tous·ly** adv. — **in·iq′ui·tous·ness** n.

in·iq·ui·ty (in·ik′wə·tē) n. pl. ·ties 1 Deviation from right; wickedness; gross injustice. 2 A wrongful act; unjust thing or deed. See synonyms under ABOMINATION, INJUSTICE, SIN. [<OF iniquité <L iniquitas < iniquus unequal <in- not + aequus equal]

in·i·tial (in·ish′əl) adj. 1 Standing at the beginning or head. 2 Pertaining to the first stage. —n. 1 The first letter of a word, name, etc. 2 In a book or manuscript, the first letter of a chapter, division of a chapter, or verse: often elaborately painted and gilded. —v.t. ·tialed or ·tialled, ·tial·ing or ·tial·ling To mark or sign with initials. [<F <L initialis <initium beginning <initus, pp. of inire go into, enter upon <in- in + ire go] — **in·i′tial·ly** adv.

in·i·ti·ate (in·ish′ē·āt) v.t. ·at·ed, ·at·ing 1 To begin; originate. 2 To introduce, as into a position or club, usually with rites or ceremony. 3 To instruct in fundamentals or principles. See synonyms under ENROL, INSTALL, TEACH. —adj. (-it, -āt) 1 Instructed in the rudiments or secrets; initiated; newly admitted, as into a secret society. 2 Initial; begun; commenced; new. 3 Characteristic of an inexperienced person or of one newly initiated. —n. (-it, -āt) One who has been initiated; also, a beginner. [<L initiatus, pp. of initiare enter upon <initium beginning. See INITIAL.] — **in·i′ti·a′tor** n.

in·i·ti·a·tion (in·ish′ē·ā′shən) n. ·1 The act of initiating. 2 Ceremonial admission, as into a society; the rites or ceremonies which have to be undergone. See synonyms under BEGINNING.

in·i·ti·a·tive (in·ish′ē·ə·tiv) n. 1 A first move. 2 The power of initiating; ability for original conception and independent action. 3 The process by which the electorate initiates or enacts legislation. See REFERENDUM. —adj. Pertaining to initiation; serving to initiate; preliminary. —**in·i′ti·a·tive·ly** adv.

in·i·ti·a·to·ry (in·ish′ē·ə·tôr′ē, -tō′rē) adj. 1 Introductory. 2 Serving to initiate.

in·ject (in·jekt′) v.t. 1 To drive or force in: to inject gas into a carburetor. 2 To force a fluid into, as for anesthetizing, preserving, etc., especially by means of a syringe or hypodermic needle. 3 To introduce (something new or lacking): with into: to inject life into a play. 4 To throw in or interject, as a remark or comment, usually by way of interruption. [<L injectus, pp. of inicere, injicere throw, cast in <in- in + jacere throw]

in·jec·tion (in·jek′shən) n. 1 The act of injecting, the state of being injected, or that which is injected. 2 Med. The introduction by instruments of a fluid into some cavity or tissue of the body. 3 The similar introduction of a substance into a cadaver to facilitate dissection or anatomical demonstration. 4 Any liquid or substance so introduced. 5 An enema. 6 The state of being hyperemic.

in·ju·di·cious (in′jōō·dish′əs) adj. 1 Not judicious; indiscreet; ill-advised. 2 Wanting in judgment. See synonyms under IMPRUDENT. — **in′ju·di′cious·ly** adv. — **in′ju·di′cious·ness** n.

in·junc·tion (in·jungk′shən) n. 1 The act of enjoining. 2 An admonition or order given with authority. 3 Law A judicial order requiring the party enjoined to take or (usually) to refrain from some specified action. See synonyms under ORDER. [<LL injunctio, -onis <injunctum, pp. of injungere join to, enjoin. See IN-², JUNCTION.]

in·jure (in′jər) v.t. ·jured, ·jur·ing 1 To do harm or hurt to; wound; damage; impair. 2 To do wrong to; treat with injustice. See synonyms under ABUSE, HURT, VIOLATE. [<F injurier <L injurari <injuria INJURY] — **in′jur·er** n.

in·ju·ri·ous (in·jōōr′ē·əs) adj. 1 Hurtful, deleterious, or detrimental in any way. 2 Obs. Disposed to inflict injury; inimical. 3 Slanderous; abusive. See synonyms under BAD, PERNICIOUS. Compare INJURY. [<F injurieux <L injuriosus] — **in·ju′ri·ous·ly** adv. — **in·ju′ri·ous·ness** n.

in·ju·ry (in′jər·ē) n. pl. ·ries 1 Any wrong, damage, or mischief done or suffered. 2 A source of harm. 3 A wrong or damage done to another; the unlawful infringement or privation of rights. 4 Obs. Abuse; insult. [<AF injurie <L injuria <injurius injust <in- not + jus, juris right, law]
Synonyms: blemish, damage, detriment, disadvantage, evil, harm, hurt, impairment, injustice, loss, mischief, outrage, prejudice, wrong. Injury is the general term including all the rest. Whatever reduces the value, utility, beauty, or desirableness of anything is an injury to that thing; of persons, whatever is so done as to operate adversely to one in his person, rights, property, or reputation is an injury. Damage (L damnum, loss) is that which occasions loss to the possessor; hence, damage reduces value, utility, or beauty; detriment (L deterere, to rub or wear away) is similar in meaning, but far milder. As a rule, the slightest use of an article by a purchaser operates to its detriment if again offered for sale, even when the article may not have received the slightest damage. Damage is partial; loss is properly absolute as far as it is predicted at all; the loss of a ship implies that it is gone beyond recovery; the loss of the rudder is a damage to the ship; but since the loss of a part still leaves a part, we may speak of a partial or total loss. Evil commonly suggests suffering or sin, or both; as, the evils of poverty, the social evil. Harm is closely synonymous with injury; it may apply to body, mind, or estate, but always affects real worth, while injury may concern only estimated value. A hurt is an injury that causes pain, physical or mental; a slight hurt may be no real harm. Mischief is disarrangement, trouble, or harm usually caused by some voluntary agent, with or without injurious intent; a child's thoughtless sport may do great mischief; wrong is harm done with evil intent. An outrage combines insult and injury. Compare synonyms for BLEMISH, INJUSTICE, LOSS, OUTRAGE, VIOLENCE. *Antonyms:* advantage, amelioration, benefit, blessing, boon, help, improvement, remedy, service, utility.

in·jus·tice (in·jus′tis) n. 1 The violation or denial of justice. 2 An unjust act; a wrong. [<OF <L injustitia]
Synonyms: grievance, inequity, iniquity, injury, unfairness, unrighteousness, wrong. Injustice is a violation or denial of justice, an act or omission that is contrary to equity or justice; as, the injustice of unequal taxes. In legal usage a wrong involves injury to person, property, or reputation, as the result of evil intent; injustice applies to civil damage or loss, not necessarily involving injury to person or property, as by misrepresentation of goods which does not amount to a legal warranty. In popular usage, injustice may involve no direct injury to person, property, interest, or character, and no harmful intent, while wrong always involves both; one who attributes another's truly generous act to a selfish motive does him an injustice. Compare synonyms for INJURY, SIN. *Antonyms:* equity, fairness, faithfulness, honesty, honor, impartiality, integrity, justice, lawfulness, rectitude, right, righteousness, uprightness.

ink (ingk) n. 1 A colored liquid or viscous substance, used in writing, printing, etc. ◆ Collateral adjective: atramental. 2 The dark fluid secreted by a cuttlefish and ejected so as to color the water and thus assist in escaping an enemy. —v.t. To spread ink upon; mark or color with ink. [<OF enque <LL encaustum purple ink used by the Caesars <Gk. enkauston, neut. of enkaustos burned out. See ENCAUSTIC.] — **ink′er** n.

ink·horn (ingk′hôrn′) n. An inkholder: so called because formerly made of horn.

ink·ling (ingk′ling) n. A slight intimation; a faint notion; hint. [ME inkle hint, ? <OE inca suspicion]

ink·stand (ingk′stand′) n. A vessel to hold ink for writing: often combined with a rack for pens, etc. Also **ink′well′** (-wel′).

in·laid (in′lād, in·lād′) adj. 1 Decorated by the insertion of wood, ivory, or other material. 2 Inserted to form such decoration. See INLAY.

in·land (in′lənd) adj. 1 Remote from the sea. 2 Located in or limited to the interior of a country. 3 Not foreign; domestic. —n. (in′lənd, -land′) The interior of a country. —adv. (in′lənd, -land′) Toward the interior of a land.

in·land·er (in′lən·dər, -lan′dər) n. One living inland or from inland.

in-law (in′lô) n. Colloq. A member of the family of one's husband or wife, or the spouse of one's child.

in·lay (in·lā′, in′lā′) v.t. in·laid, in·lay·ing 1 To set decorative patterns or designs of (ivory, gold, etc.) into the surface of an object. 2 To decorate, as a piece of furniture, by inserting such patterns or designs. 3 To attach (a page, illustration, etc.) in a place cut for it in a larger or heavier sheet, either for framing or enlarging the margin. —n. (in′lā) 1 That which is inlaid. 2 A pattern or design so produced. 3 Dent. A filling for a tooth, of gold, porcelain, etc., cemented into a cavity so as to be even with the surface. 4 An inlay graft. — **in′lay′er** n.

in·let (in·let′) v.t. ·let, ·let·ting 1 To insert; inlay. 2 Obs. To admit. —n. (in′lit) 1 A small body of water leading into a larger, as a small bay or creek or a tributary of a lake. 2 An entrance, as to a culvert. 3 Something inserted. 4 Obs. The act of admitting. See synonyms under ENTRANCE¹.

in·li·er (in′lī·ər) n. Geol. An underlying uneroded formation of rock imbedded in a later deposit: opposed to outlier.

in·mate (in′māt′) n. 1 One who lives in a place with others; an associate or mate in occupancy. 2 One who is kept or confined in a prison, asylum, or similar institution. 3 Obs. An alien; a stranger; one not properly belonging to the place where he dwells. [? <INN + MATE]

in·mi·grant (in′mi′grənt) n. A person who has moved from one locality to another in the same country. — **in′-mi·gra′tion** (-grā′shən) n.

in·most (in′mōst′, -məst) adj. 1 Farthest from the exterior. 2 Figuratively, deepest, most secret, or most intimate. [OE innemest, a double superlative of inne in]

inn (in) n. 1 A public house for the entertainment of travelers; a place where meals and lodging are obtainable; hostelry; tavern. 2 Brit. A house of residence for students: now only in the names of such residences, as Inns of Court. 3 Obs. A dwelling place; abode. [OE <inn in]

in·nards (in′ərdz) n.pl. Dial. or Colloq. Inner or interior parts or organs; the insides. [<INWARDS, n.]

in·nate (in′āt, i·nāt′) adj. 1 Native to or original with the individual; inborn; natural. 2 Immediately in or from the mind or intellect rather than acquired by experience; intuitive: innate truths. 3 Bot. Attached by its base to the apex of a filament: said of an anther. 4 Endogenous. Compare ADNATE. See synonyms under INHERENT, NATIVE, RADICAL. [<L innatus, pp. of innasci be born in <in- in + nasci be born] — **in′nate·ly** adv. — **in′nate·ness** n.

in·ner (in′ər) adj. 1 At a point farther in or

inward; interior; nearer a center. **2** Pertaining to that which is within; specifically, denoting the spiritual or immaterial. **3** Not easily discerned or understood; esoteric; hidden. — *n.* **1** The inside of something. **2** The section of a target between the center and the outer. **3** A shot striking this section. [OE *innerra,* compar. of *inne*]

inner city A central part of a large city, usually characterized by poverty and often populated by minority groups. — **in′ner-cit′y** *adj.*

in-ner-most (in′ər-mōst′) *adj.* Inmost; farthest within. — *n.* The inmost part, thing, or place.

in-ner-sole (in′ər-sōl′) *n.* A continuous piece of leather or other material cut to the contour of a shoe last and placed inside to give a smooth surface.

inner tube A flexible, inflatable tube, usually of rubber, which together with an outer casing comprises a pneumatic tire.

in-ner-vate (i-nûr′vāt, in′ər-vāt) *v.t.* **-vat-ed, -vat-ing** *Physiol.* **1** To supply with nerves or nervous filaments. **2** To give stimulus to (a nerve); innerve. [<INNERVE]

in-ner-va-tion (in′ər-vā′shən) *n.* **1** *Physiol.* The act of innervating. **2** *Anat.* The arrangement of nervous filaments in any part of the body.

in-nerve (i-nûrv′) *v.t.* **-nerved, -nerv-ing** To impart nervous energy to; invigorate; animate; stimulate. [<IN-² + NERVE]

in-ning (in′ing) *n.* **1** The period during which a party or person is in power, control, or action. **2** In baseball and other games, a turn at the bat; the period during which one side is at the bat, or the period when each side takes one turn at the bat. **3** *pl.* In cricket, the play of, or score made by, either side while batting or by any one batsman during his turn: construed in the singular. **4** Reclamation (of marsh or swamp land). **5** *pl.* Lands reclaimed from the sea. **6** An ingathering, as of grain into a barn; a harvest. [OE *innung,* gerund of *innian* get it, put in]

inn-keep-er (in′kē′pər) *n.* The proprietor or keeper of an inn. Also **inn′hold′er** (-hōl′dər).

in-no-cence (in′ə-səns) *n.* **1** The state of being innocent; the condition of being free from evil or guile, or from that which corrupts or vitiates; purity of heart; freedom from taint. **2** Freedom from guilt, as of some specific crime or charge; absence of legal guilt. **3** Freedom from harmful or noxious qualities; harmlessness; innocuousness. **4** Simplicity or ignorance through lack of intellect or imperfect development; hence, weak-mindedness. **5** Freedom from illegal taint, as violation of an embargo or blockade by conveying goods to a belligerent. **6** A bluet. **7** A slender-stemmed, erect herb (*Collinsia verna*) with a blue and white corolla; also a related California herb (*C. bicolor*). [<OF <L *innocentia*]
Synonyms: blamelessness, goodness, guilelessness, guiltlessness, harmlessness, innocuousness, inoffensiveness, purity, simplicity, sincerity, sinlessness, stainlessness, virtue. *Innocence,* which is *goodness* without temptation or trial, or perhaps without knowledge of evil, is less than *virtue* which is *goodness* that resists and overcomes temptation. Compare synonyms for INNOCENT. *Antonyms:* contamination, corruption, crime, criminality, evil, fault, guile, guilt, harm, harmfulness, hurt, hurtfulness, impurity, ruin, sin, sinfulness, stain, wrong.

in-no-cent (in′ə-sənt) *adj.* **1** Not tainted with sin; pure; ignorant of evil; blameless: an *innocent* babe. **2** Free from the guilt of a particular evil action or crime. **3** Free from qualities that can harm or injure; innocuous; harmless. **4** Of artless or ingenuous disposition; naive. **5** Not maliciously intended: an *innocent* lie, an *innocent* remark. **6** Free from liability to forfeiture; not contraband; lawful; permitted. **7** Lacking in knowledge or sense; simple or ignorant; imbecile. **8** Lacking in worldly knowledge: an *innocent* girl. **9** Entirely lacking; devoid: with *of*: *innocent* of grammar. — *n.* **1** One unstained by sin. **2** A young child. **3** A simpleton. **4** The bluet. — **the Innocents** The children put to death by Herod: commemorated Dec. 28. Matt. *ii* 16. [<OF <L *innocens, -entis* <*in-* not + *nocens,* ppr. of *nocere* harm] — **in′no-cent-ly** *adv.*
Synonyms (adj.): blameless, clean, clear, faultless, guileless, guiltless, harmless, immaculate, innocuous, innoxious, inoffensive,

pure, right, righteous, sinless, spotless, stainless, upright, virtuous. *Innocent,* in the full sense, signifies not tainted with sin; not having done wrong or violated legal or moral precept or duty; as, an *innocent* babe. *Innocent* is a negative word, expressing less than *righteous, upright,* or *virtuous,* which imply knowledge of good and evil, with free choice of the good. A little child or a lamb is *innocent;* a tried and faithful man is *righteous, upright, virtuous. Immaculate, pure,* and *sinless* may be used either of one who has never known the possibility of evil or of one who has perfectly and triumphantly resisted it. *Innocent,* in a specific case, signifies free from the guilt of a particular act, even when the total character may be very evil; as, The thief was found to be *innocent* of the murder. See CANDID, PURE. *Antonyms:* compare synonyms for CRIMINAL.

in-noc-u-ous (i-nok′yōō-əs) *adj.* **1** Having no harmful qualities. **2** Non-poisonous: said of plants and animals, especially snakes. See synonyms under INNOCENT. [<L *innocuus* <*in-* not + *nocuus* harmful <*nocere* harm] — **in-noc′u-ous-ly** *adv.* — **in-noc′u-ous-ness** *n.*

in-nom-i-nate (i-nom′ə-nit) *adj.* **1** Without specific name. **2** Anonymous. [<LL *innominatus* <*in-* not + *nominatus,* pp. of *nominare* name. See NOMINATE.]

innominate artery *Anat.* A large but short trunk springing from the arch of the aorta near the heart.

innominate bone *Anat.* A large, irregular bone resulting from the consolidation of the ilium, ischium, and pubis to form one of the sides of the pelvis in adult mammals; the hip bone; haunch bone; huckle bone: also called *os innominatum.*

in-no-vate (in′ə-vāt) *v.* **-vat-ed, -vat-ing** *v.i.* To make changes or alterations in anything established; bring in new ideas, methods, etc.: often with *in, on,* or *upon.* — *v.t.* To bring in as an innovation. [<L *innovatus,* pp. of *innovare* renew <*in-* in + *novare* make new, alter <*novus* new] — **in′no-va′tor** *n.*

in-no-va-tion (in′ə-vā′shən) *n.* **1** The making of a change in something established. **2** A novelty. See synonyms under CHANGE. [<LL *innovatio, -onis*]

in-no-va-tive (in′ə-vā′tiv) *adj.* Characterized by or tending to introduce innovations.

in-no-va-to-ry (in′ə-vā′tər-ē) *adj.* Having the character of innovation.

in-nox-ious (i-nok′shəs) *adj.* Free from harmful qualities; not noxious. [<L *innoxius* <*in-* not + *noxius* NOXIOUS. Related to INNOCENT, INNOCUOUS.]

in-nu-en-do (in′yōō-en′dō) *n. pl.* **-dos** or **-does** **1** A suggestion or hint about some person or thing; an indirect aspersion; insinuation: usually in derogation. **2** *Law* In pleading, an explanatory phrase employed to make a previous phrase more explicit, as in saying "the perjured villain, meaning the plaintiff," in which the phrase "meaning the plaintiff" is an innuendo. Also spelled *inuendo.* See synonyms under SUGGESTION. [<L, by nodding at, intimating, ablative gerund of *innuere* nod to, signify <*in-* to + *-nuere* nod]

in-nu-mer-a-ble (i-nōō′mər-ə-bəl, i-nyōō′-) *adj.* Too numerous to be counted; very numerous; countless. Also **in-nu′mer-ous.** See synonyms under INFINITE. [<L *innumerabilis*] — **in-nu′mer-a-bil′i-ty, in-nu′mer-a-ble-ness** *n.* — **in-nu′mer-a-bly** *adv.*

in-nu-tri-tion (in′nōō-trish′ən, -yōō-) *n.* Lack of nutrition; failure of nourishment. — **in′nu-tri′tious** *adj.*

in-ob-serv-ance (in′əb-zûr′vəns) *n.* Non-observance; inattention.

in-oc-u-la-ble (in-ok′yə-lə-bəl) *adj.* That can be inoculated or communicated by inoculation. — **in-oc′u-la-bil′i-ty** *n.* — **in-oc′u-la′tor** (-lā′tər) *n.*

in-oc-u-late (in-ok′yə-lāt) *v.t.* **-lat-ed, -lat-ing** **1** To communicate a disease to (a person or animal) by inoculation. **2** To inject an immunizing serum into. **3** To implant ideas, opinions, etc., in the mind of. **4** *Bot.* To insert a bud in, as a tree, for propagation. [<L *inoculatus,* pp. of *inoculare* engraft an eye or bud <*in-* in + *oculus* bud, eye]

in-oc-u-la-tion (in-ok′yə-lā′shən) *n.* **1** *Med.* The introduction of specific disease organisms into the living tissues of animals and man, as a means of securing immunity through induc-

ing a mild form of the disease. Inoculation may be *curative,* when an antitoxin is injected as a remedy, or *protective,* when the substance injected aims to secure immunity from disease. **2** *Bot.* The operation of inserting a bud in a tree for propagation. **3** Contamination; infection: the *inoculation* of vice. **4** The improvement of soils by introducing special micro-organisms: practiced especially in the cultivation of leguminous crops.

in-oc-u-lum (in-ok′yə-ləm) *n.* The prepared material, as bacteria, viruses, spores, etc., used in making an inoculation. [<NL <INOCULATE]

in-o-dor-ous (in-ō′dər-əs) *adj.* Having no odor; emitting no scent.

in-of-fen-sive (in′ə-fen′siv) *adj.* Giving no offense; unobjectionable; causing nothing displeasing, disturbing, or harmful. See synonyms under INNOCENT. — **in′of-fen′sive-ly** *adv.* — **in′of-fen′sive-ness** *n.*

in-of-fi-cious (in′ə-fish′əs) *adj.* **1** *Law* Without consideration of duty or natural obligation; regardless of office or duty: an *inofficious* will neglects to provide for those naturally dependent on the testator. **2** Without office; inoperative. **3** *Obs.* Not civil or attentive. [<L *inofficiosus*] — **in′of-fi′cious-ly** *adv.*

in-op-er-a-ble (in-op′ər-ə-bəl) *adj.* **1** *Surg.* Not suitable for operative procedures without undue risk: an *inoperable* cancer. **2** Not practicable.

in-op-er-a-tive (in-op′ər-ə-tiv) *adj.* Not operative; having no effect or result; ineffectual. — **in-op′er-a-tive-ness** *n.*

in-op-por-tune (in-op′ər-tōōn′, -tyōōn′) *adj.* Unseasonable or inappropriate; unsuitable or inconvenient, especially as to time; not opportune. [<L *inopportunus*] — **in-op′por-tune′ly** *adv.* — **in-op′por-tune′ness** *n.*

in-or-di-nate (in-ôr′də-nit) *adj.* Not restrained by prescribed rules or bounds; immoderate; excessive. See synonyms under IMMODERATE, IRREGULAR. — **in-or′di-na-cy** (-nə-sē), **in-or′di-nate-ness** *n.* — **in-or′di-nate-ly** *adv.*

in-or-gan-ic (in′ôr-gan′ik) *adj.* **1** Devoid of organized vital structure; not organic; not being animal or vegetable; inanimate. **2** Not the result of living or organic processes. **3** Of, pertaining to, or designating the branch of chemistry that treats of substances lacking carbon, but including the carbonates and cyanides. **4** *Ling.* Not belonging to the normal development of a word; extraneous, as the final *t* in *against.* — **in′or-gan′i-cal-ly** *adv.*

in-os-cu-late (in-os′kyə-lāt) *v.t.* & *v.i.* **-lat-ed, -lat-ing** **1** To unite by contact of openings, as two blood vessels. **2** To unite or join together, as in continuity.

in-os-cu-la-tion (in-os′kyə-lā′shən) *n.* **1** Union by tubelike passages; intercommunication. **2** A union that implies continuity.

in-ot-ro-pism (in-ot′rə-piz′əm, ī-not′-) *n. Med.* Any interference with the contractility of muscle. — **in-o-trop-ic** (in′ō-trop′ik, -trō′pik, ī′nō-) *adj.* [<Gk. *is, inos* muscle + -TROPISM]

in-ox-i-dize (in-ok′sə-dīz) *v.t.* **-dized, -diz-ing** To render incapable of oxidation.

in-pa-tient (in′pā′shənt) *n.* A patient who is lodged, fed, and receives treatment in a hospital or the like: distinguished from *outpatient.*

in-phase (in′fāz′) *adj. Electr.* Being of the same phase: said of currents. See PHASE.

in-put (in′pŏŏt′) *n.* **1** Something put into a system or device, as energy into a machine, food into the body, data into a computer, or a signal into an electronic device. **2** A place or point of introduction, as of data into a computer. **3** An effect or influence resulting from contributing opinions, information, suggestions, etc.: The staff had real *input* in the directive.

in-quest (in′kwest) *n.* **1** A judicial inquiry, aided by a jury, into a special matter, as a sudden death. **2** The body of men making such inquiry. **3** Inquiry; investigation. [<OF *enqueste* <L *inquisita (res)* (thing) inquired (into), fem. of *inquisitus, inquestus,* pp. of *inquirere* INQUIRE]

in-qui-e-tude (in-kwī′ə-tōōd, -tyōōd) *n.* **1** A state of restlessness; uneasiness. **2** *pl.* Anxieties; disquieting thoughts. [<F *inquiétude* <LL *inquietudo*] — **in-qui′et** *adj.* — **in-qui′et-ly** *adv.*

in-qui-line (in′kwə-līn, -lin) *adj. Zool.* Living in the abode of another, as an insect in a gall made by another: also **in-quil-i-nous** (in-kwil′ə-nəs). — *n.* An animal that lives in the abode of another; a commensal. [<L *inquilinus* lodger < *in-* in + *colere* dwell]

in·qui·nate (in'kwə·nāt) *v.t.* **·nat·ed, ·nat·ing** To pollute; corrupt. [<L *inquinatus,* pp. of *inquinare* pollute < *in-* in + *cunire* void excrement]

in·qui·na·tion (in'kwə·nā'shən) *n.* **1** The state of being defiled; corruption. **2** Pollution; infection. [<L *inquinatio, -onis*]

in·quire (in·kwīr') *v.* **·quired, ·quir·ing** *v.t.* **1** To ask information about: They *inquired* the way. — *v.i.* **2** To seek information by asking questions: to *inquire* about one's health. **3** To make investigation, search, or inquiry: with *into.* Also spelled *enquire.* [<L *inquirere* inquire into < *in-* into + *quaerere* seek] — **in·quir'a·ble** *adj.* — **in·quir'er** *n.* — **in·quir'ing** *adj.* — **in·quir'ing·ly** *adv.*

Synonyms: ask, examine, interrogate, query, question. One may either *ask* or *inquire* one's way. In this sense *ask* and *inquire* are nearly interchangeable, chiefly differing in the fact that *ask* is the popular and *inquire* the more formal word, although *ask* has place in the best literary use. Also, *ask* has more reference to the presence of a second person; the solitary investigator *inquires* rather than *asks* the cause of some phenomenon: in this sense *ask* is often used reflexively; as, "I *asked* myself why this happened." *Inquire into* thus becomes a natural synonym for *examine, investigate,* etc. Compare ASK, EXAMINE, QUESTION.

in·quir·y (in·kwīr'ē, in'kwə·rē) *n.* *pl.* **·quir·ies** **1** The act of inquiring. **2** Investigation; research; search for knowledge. **3** A query. [ME *enquere*]

Synonyms: examination, interrogation, investigation, query, question, research, scrutiny, study. See QUESTION. *Antonyms:* see synonyms for ANSWER.

in·qui·si·tion (in'kwə·zish'ən) *n.* **1** The proceedings and findings of a jury of inquest. **2** The jury or other body making judicial inquiry into some particular matter. **3** Investigation. See synonyms under HUNT, QUESTION. [<OF <L *inquisitio, -onis* < *inquisitus.* See INQUIRE.]

in·quis·i·tive (in·kwiz'ə·tiv) *adj.* **1** Given to questioning, especially for the gratification of curiosity; prying: an *inquisitive* busybody. **2** Inclined to the pursuit of knowledge. [<L *inquisitus*] — **in·quis'i·tive·ly** *adv.* — **in·quis'i·tive·ness** *n.*

Synonyms: curious, inquiring, intrusive, meddlesome, meddling, peeping, prying, scrutinizing, searching. An *inquisitive* person is one who is bent on finding out all that can be found out by inquiry, especially of little and personal matters, and hence is generally *meddlesome* and *prying. Inquisitive* may be used in a good sense, but in such connection *inquiring* is to be preferred; as, an *inquiring* mind. As applied to a state of mind, *curious* denotes a keen and rather pleasurable desire to know fully something to which one's attention has been called, but without the active tendency that *inquisitive* implies; a well-bred person may be *curious* to know, but will not be *inquisitive* in trying to ascertain what is of interest in the affairs of another. *Antonyms:* apathetic, careless, heedless, inattentive, indifferent, unconcerned, uninterested.

in·quis·i·tor (in·kwiz'ə·tər) *n.* **1** One who inquires or investigates; specifically, an official whose duty it is to investigate or examine. **2** A member of the Inquisition. [<OF *inquisiteur* <L *inquisitor*]

in·road (in'rōd') *n.* **1** A hostile entrance into a country; raid; any forcible encroachment. **2** Any illegal, destructive, or wasteful encroachment: *inroads* upon one's health, time, savings, etc. See synonyms under INVASION. [<IN-³ + obs. *road* riding]

in·rush (in'rush') *n.* A sudden rushing in; invasion.

in·sal·i·vate (in·sal'ə·vāt) *v.t.* **·vat·ed, ·vat·ing** To mix with saliva, as food, in eating. — **in·sal'i·va'tion** *n.*

in·sa·lu·bri·ous (in'sə·lōō'brē·əs) *adj.* Not wholesome; not healthful. [<L *insalubris*] — **in'sa·lu'bri·ous·ly** *adv.* — **in'sa·lu'bri·ty** *n.*

in·sane (in·sān') *adj.* **1** Not sane; mentally deranged or unsound; crazy; irrational. **2** Set apart for or used by the insane. **3** Characteristic of those who are mentally deranged; insensate. **4** Foolish, extravagant, or impractical: *insane* hopes. [<L *insanus* < *in-* not + *sanus* whole] — **in·sane'ly** *adv.* — **in·sane'ness** *n.*

Synonyms: absurd, cracked, crazed, crazy, delirious, demented, deranged, distracted, frantic, frenzied, irrational, lunatic, mad, maniac, maniacal, monomaniac, wandering, wild. *Antonyms:* clear, collected, level-headed, sage, sane, sensible, sober, sound, wise.

in·san·i·ty (in·san'ə·tē) *n.* **1** Any mental disorder characterized by temporary or permanent irrational or violent deviations from normal thinking, feeling, and behavior: not a technical term in medicine or psychiatry. **2** *Law* Any degree of mental unsoundness resulting in inability to distinguish between right and wrong, to control the will, foresee the consequences of an act, make a valid contract, or manage one's own affairs. **3** Lack of sound sense; extreme folly.

Synonyms: alienation, craziness, delirium, dementia, derangement, frenzy, lunacy, madness, mania, monomania. Of these terms *insanity* is the most comprehensive, including in a loose sense all morbid conditions of mind due to diseased action of the brain or nervous system. *Craziness* is a vague popular term for any sort of disordered mental action, or for conduct suggesting it. *Lunacy,* originally denoted intermittent *insanity,* supposed to be dependent on the changes of the moon (L *luna*). *Madness* is the old popular term, now suggesting excitement akin to *mania. Derangement* is a common euphemism for *insanity. Delirium* is always temporary, and is specifically the *insanity* of disease, as in acute fevers. *Dementia* is a general weakening of the mental powers: the word is specifically applied to the mental incapacities of senility. *Monomania* is mental *derangement* as to one subject or object. *Frenzy* and *mania* are forms of raving and furious *insanity.* Compare DELUSION, FRENZY, IDIOCY. *Antonyms:* clearness, lucidity, rationality, sanity.

in·sa·tia·ble (in·sā'shə·bəl, -shē·ə·bəl) *adj.* Not satiable; not to be sated or satisfied; unappeasable. Also **in·sa'ti·ate** (-it). See synonyms under GREEDY. [<OF *insaciable*] — **in·sa'ti·a·bil'i·ty, in·sa'tia·ble·ness** *n.* — **in·sa'tia·bly, in·sa'ti·ate·ly** *adv.* — **in·sa'ti·ate·ness** *n.*

in·sa·ti·e·ty (in'sə·tī'ə·tē) *n.* Lack of satiety or surfeit; unsatisfied wish or appetite. [<L *insatietas, -tatis*]

in·scribe (in·skrīb') *v.t.* **·scribed, ·scrib·ing** **1** To write or engrave (signs, words, names, etc.). **2** To mark the surface of with engraved or written characters, especially in a durable or conspicuous way. **3** To dedicate, as a book, usually by an informal, written note. **4** To enter the name of on a list; enrol. **5** *Brit.* To register or record the names of holders of (stocks, securities, etc.). **6** *Geom.* To draw (one figure) in another so that the latter circumscribes the former. [<L *inscribere* < *in-* on, in + *scribere* write] — **in·scrib'er** *n.*

Synonyms: address, dedicate, engrave, impress, imprint, mark, stamp, write.

in·scrip·tion (in·skrip'shən) *n.* **1** The act or operation of inscribing, or that which is inscribed. **2** Incised or relief lettering; any legend or record marked in lasting characters on a solid and durable object. **3** Entry in a roll or the like. **4** *Brit.* A registry, as of securities. **5** The lettering on a print or similar work. **6** An address in a book; a dedication. See synonyms under RECORD, SUPERSCRIPTION. [<L *inscriptio, -onis* < *inscriptus,* pp. of *inscribere* INSCRIBE] — **in·scrip'tion·al, in·scrip'tive** *adj.*

in·scru·ta·ble (in·skrōō'tə·bəl) *adj.* That cannot be searched into; incomprehensible; unfathomable; impenetrable. See synonyms under MYSTERIOUS. [<LL *inscrutabilis* < *in-* not + *scrutare* look at] — **in·scru'ta·bil'i·ty, in·scru'ta·ble·ness** *n.* — **in·scru'ta·bly** *adv.*

in·sect (in'sekt) *n.* **1** A minute invertebrate animal; one of the class *Insecta.* The true insects or hexapods have the body divided into a head, a thorax of 3 segments, each of which bears a pair of legs, and an abdomen

of 7 to 11 segments, and in development usually pass through a metamorphosis. There are usually 2 pairs of wings, sometimes one pair or none. **2** Loosely, any small, air-breathing invertebrate resembling or suggesting an insect, as spiders, centipedes, ticks, etc. [<L *(animal) insectum* (animal) notched or cut into < *insectus,* pp. of *insecare* cut into, notch] — **in·sec'te·an** (-sek'tē·ən) *adj.* — **in'sect·like'** *adj.*

in·sec·tar·i·um (in'sek·târ'ē·əm) *n.* *pl.* **·i·ums** or **·i·a** (-ē·ə) A place for keeping and breeding insects, as for the purpose of studying economic entomology. Also **in·sec·tar·y** (in'sek·ter'ē). [<NL]

in·sec·ti·cide (in·sek'tə·sīd) *n.* A substance which kills insects, usually in powder, paste, or liquid form. [<INSECT + -CIDE]

in·sec·tion (in·sek'shən) *n.* A cutting into; incision. [<L *insectus,* pp. of *insecare* cut up]

in·sec·ti·val (in'sek·tī'vəl, in·sek'tə-) *adj.* Pertaining to, or like, insects.

in·sec·ti·vore (in·sek'tə·vôr, -vōr) *n.* **1** Any of an order (*Insectivora*) of insect-eating mammals, as shrews, moles, and hedgehogs. **2** An insectivorous animal or plant. [<F <L *insectum* insect + -*vorus* devouring < *vorare* devour]

in·se·cure (in'sə·kyōōr') *adj.* **1** Not secure or safe; in danger of breaking or failing; infirm. **2** Not assured of safety; liable to suffer loss or harm. — **in'se·cure'ly** *adv.* — **in'se·cure'ness** *n.*

in·se·cu·ri·ty (in'sə·kyōōr'ə·tē) *n.* The condition of being unsafe; liability to injury, loss or failure; uncertainty; instability.

in·sem·i·nate (in·sem'ə·nāt) *v.t.* **·nat·ed, ·nat·ing** **1** To impregnate; make pregnant. **2** To sow seed in, as soil. [<L *inseminatus,* pp. of *inseminare* sow < *in-* in + *seminare* sow < *semen* seed] — **in·sem'i·na'tion** *n.*

in·se·nes·cence (in'sə·nes'əns) *n.* The process of becoming old, especially in a normal manner and without undue loss of vigor. [<IN-² + SENESCENCE] — **in'se·nes'cent** *adj.*

in·sen·sate (in·sen'sāt, -sit) *adj.* **1** Manifesting or marked by a lack of sense or reason; brutish; mad. **2** Destitute of sensibility. **3** Inanimate. [<LL *insensatus*] — **in·sen'sate·ly** *adv.* — **in·sen'sate·ness** *n.*

in·sen·si·ble (in·sen'sə·bəl) *adj.* **1** That is not or cannot be felt or perceived by the sense; an *insensible* motion or change. **2** Blunted in feeling or perception: to be *insensible* to pity. **3** Deprived of sensation or perception; senseless. **4** Insensate; inanimate: *insensible* earth. **5** *Obs.* Without intelligent meaning; senseless. **6** Devoid of passion, emotion, or sensitiveness; apathetic; unaware. See synonyms under BRUTISH, NUMB. [<L *insensibilis*] — **in·sen'si·bil'i·ty, in·sen'si·ble·ness** *n.* — **in·sen'si·bly** *adv.*

in·sen·si·tive (in·sen'sə·tiv) *adj.* Not sensitive to impressions, whether physical, mental, or emotional. — **in·sen'si·tiv'i·ty, in·sen'si·tive·ness** *n.*

in·sen·ti·ent (in·sen'shē·ənt, -shənt) *adj.* Inanimate. — **in·sen'ti·ence, in·sen'ti·en·cy** *n.*

in·sep·a·ra·ble (in·sep'ər·ə·bəl) *adj.* Incapable of being separated or disjoined: *inseparable* friends. — **in·sep'a·ra·ble·ness** *n.* — **in·sep'a·ra·bly** *adv.*

in·sert (in·sûrt') *v.t.* To put or place into something else; put between or among other things; introduce. — *n.* (in'sûrt) That which is inserted; an addition made by insertion; specifically, in bookbinding, an inset; also, a circular or the like placed within a newspaper or book for mailing. [<L *insertus,* pp. of *inserere* < *in-* in + *serere* place, join] — **in·sert'er** *n.*

in·ser·tion (in·sûr'shən) *n.* **1** The act of inserting, or the state of being inserted. **2** That which is inserted, as lace or embroidery placed between pieces of plain fabric. **3** *Bot.* Place or mode of attachment, as of a leaf to a branch. **4** *Anat.* The end of a muscle that is attached to the bone or part which it moves. **5** A word, paragraph, or written material inserted in a written or printed page; also, an advertisement in a newspaper. See INSERT.

---

add, āce, câre, pälm; end, ēven; it, īce; odd, ōpen, ôrder; tŏŏk, pōōl; up, bûrn; ə = a in *above,* e in *sicken,* i in *clarity,* o in *melon,* u in *focus;* yōō = u in *fuse;* oi, oil; ou, pout; ch, check; g, go; ng, ring; th, thin; th, this; zh, vision. Foreign sounds à, œ, ü, kh, ṅ; and ◆: see page xx. < from; + plus; ? possibly.

in·set (in·set′) *v.t.* To set in; implant; insert. — *n.* (in′set′) **1** A leaf or leaves inserted, as in a book or newspaper. **2** A small diagram, map, etc., inserted in the border of a larger one. **3** A piece of material let or set into a garment. **4** Influx, as of the tide.

in·sheathe (in·shēth′) *v.t.* **·sheathed, ·sheath·ing** To place or enclose in or as in a sheath.

in·shore (in′shôr′, -shōr′, in′shôr′, -shōr′) *adj.* **1** Being or occurring near the shore: *inshore* fishing. **2** Coming toward the shore: an *inshore* wind. — *adv.* Toward the shore.

in·side (in′sīd′, -sīd′) *n.* **1** The side, surface, or part that is within; interior. **2** That which is contained; contents. **3** Inner thoughts or feelings: One cannot know the *inside* of a man's mind. **4** *pl. Colloq.* Inner organs; entrails. **5** *Printing* **a** *pl.* Sheets of paper that do not include any of the outer or soiled sheets of a ream or package. **b** The side of a sheet containing the second page. **6** An inside passenger or place for a passenger, as in a vehicle. — *adj.* **1** Situated or occurring on or in the inside; internal. **2** Suited for or pertaining to the inside. **3** For use indoors: *inside* paint. **4** Private; confidential; known only within a certain group or organization: *inside* reports. — *adv.* (in′sīd′) **1** In or into the interior; within. **2** Indoors. — **inside out** Reversed so that the inside is exposed. — *prep.* (in′sīd′) In or into the interior of; within. — **inside of** *Colloq.* Within the time or distance of: a house *inside of* a mile away.

in·sid·er (in′sī′dər) *n.* One who is inside; hence, one who has special information or advantages.

inside track The inner and shorter way around a race track; hence, a position of advantage; the favored position.

in·sid·i·ous (in·sid′ē·əs) *adj.* **1** Designed to entrap; full of wiles. **2** Doing or contriving harm. **3** Awaiting a chance to harm. **4** Causing harm by slow, stealthy, usually imperceptible means: an *insidious* disease. [< L *insidiosus* < *insidiae* ambush < *insidere* sit in, lie in wait] — **in·sid′i·ous·ly** *adv.* — **in·sid′i·ous·ness** *n.*

Synonyms: artful, crafty, cunning, deceitful, designing, guileful, intriguing, sly, subtle, treacherous, tricky, wily.

in·sight (in′sīt′) *n.* **1** Intellectual discernment. **2** A perception of the inner nature of a thing; intuition. See synonyms under ACUMEN, WISDOM.

in·sig·ni·a (in·sig′nē·ə) *n. pl. of* **in·sig·ne** (in·sig′nē) **1** Badges, emblems, etc., used as marks of office or distinction. **2** Things significant or indicative of a calling. See illustration under SHOULDER PATCH. [< L, neut pl. of *insignis* eminent < *in-* in + *signum* sign, emblem, badge]

in·sig·nif·i·cance (in′sig·nif′ə·kəns) *n.* The state of being insignificant; lack of import or of importance; triviality. Also **in′sig·nif′·i·can·cy.**

in·sig·nif·i·cant (in′sig·nif′ə·kənt) *adj.* **1** Not significant; without import, meaning, or bearing; without importance; trivial. **2** Small, little. — **in′sig·nif′i·cant·ly** *adv.*

Synonyms: idle, immaterial, irrelevant, little, mean, meaningless, paltry, petty, slight, small, trifling, trivial. See LITTLE. *Antonyms:* considerable, essential, grand, grave, great, immense, influential, large, mighty, significant.

in·sin·cere (in′sin·sir′) *adj.* Not sincere, honest, or genuine; hypocritical. — **in′sin·cere′ly** *adv.* — **in′sin·cer′i·ty** (-ser′ə·tē) *n.*

in·sin·u·ate (in·sin′yōō·āt) *v.t.* **·at·ed, ·at·ing** **1** To indicate slyly or deviously; imply; intimate. **2** To infuse or instil gradually or subtly into the mind: to *insinuate* distrust. **3** To introduce (someone) gradually or artfully into a position or relation: to *insinuate* oneself into another's confidence. See synonyms under ALLUDE. [< L *insinuatus,* pp. of *insinuare* curve < *in-* in + *sinus* bosom, curved surface]

in·sin·u·at·ing (in·sin′yōō·ā′ting) *adj.* Characterized by insinuation; winding, or creeping in; insensibly or subtly winning favor and confidence; ingratiating.

in·sin·u·a·tion (in·sin′yōō·ā′shən) *n.* **1** The act of insinuating; indirect suggestion; implication; specifically, an injurious suggestion. **2** That which is insinuated; hint; a subtly ingratiating act, remark, etc. **3** Gradual or sly introduction. **4** Power or faculty of

gaining affection, favor, or confidence. See synonyms under SUGGESTION.

in·sin·u·a·tive (in·sin′yōō·ā′tiv) *adj.* **1** Making use of insinuation, as to gain favor or confidence. **2** Tending to instil into the mind. **3** Characterized by or necessitating insinuation; suggestive.

in·sin·u·a·tor (in·sin′yōō·ā·tər) *n.* **1** One who worms his way into favor. **2** One who subtly hints or intimates (something usually malicious).

in·sip·id (in·sip′id) *adj.* **1** Without flavor; unsavory; tasteless. **2** Not qualified to interest; vapid; lacking in energy or ambition; dull. See synonyms under FLAT. [< F *insipide* < LL *insipidus* < *in-* not + *sapidus* savory < *sapere* savor, taste] — **in·si·pid′i·ty** (in′si·pid′ə·tē), **in·sip′id·ness** *n.* — **in·sip′id·ly** *adv.*

in·sip·i·ence (in·sip′ē·əns) *n.* Lack of wisdom; foolishness. ◆ Homophone: *incipience.* [< OF < L *insipientia* < *insipiens, -entis* unwise]

in·sip·i·ent (in·sip′i·ənt) *adj.* Foolish; unwise.

in·sist (in·sist′) *v.i.* To make emphatic or repeated assertion, demand, or request: often with *on* or *upon*: He *insisted* on the correctness of his theory. — *v.t.* To state or demand emphatically: with a clause as object: He *insisted* that he was right. [< F *insister* < L *insistere* dwell upon, persist < *in-* on + *sistere* stand] — **in·sis′tence, in·sis′ten·cy** *n.*

Synonyms: persevere, persist. *Insist* implies some alleged authority or right; *persist* implies simply determination of will; we *insist* upon the action of others; we *persist* in our own. *Insist* is used of any urgency, good or bad, but largely in the good sense; *persist* is used chiefly in a bad sense, *persevere* being preferred for the better meaning. See PERSIST.

in·sis·tent (in·sis′tənt) *adj.* **1** Insisting; persistent; urgent. **2** Standing out prominently; conspicuous: *insistent* colors. — **in·sis′tent·ly** *adv.*

in si·tu (in sī′tyōō) *Latin* In its original site or position.

in·snare (in·snâr′) See ENSNARE.

in·so·bri·e·ty (in′sə·brī′ə·tē) *n.* Lack of moderation; intemperance, especially in drinking.

in·so·far as (in′sō·fär′ az′) To the extent that; in such measure as. Also **in so far as.**

in·so·late (in′sō·lāt) *v.t.* **·lat·ed, ·lat·ing** To expose to the rays of the sun, as for bleaching, drying, maturing, etc. [< L *insolatus,* pp. of *insolare* expose to the sun < *in-* in + *sol* sun]

in·so·la·tion (in′sō·lā′shən) *n.* **1** The act of insolating; exposure to the rays of the sun. **2** Sunstroke. **3** A method of treating disease by exposure to the rays of the sun. **4** A disease in plants caused by exposure to the sun. **5** *Meteorol.* **a** Solar radiation received by the earth or other planets. **b** The rate of delivery of such radiant energy per unit of horizontal surface.

in·sole (in′sōl′) *n.* **1** The fixed inner sole of a boot or shoe. **2** A removable inner sole placed within a shoe to improve its fit or as a protection against dampness.

in·so·lence (in′sə·ləns) *n.* **1** The quality of being insolent; pride or haughtiness exhibited in contemptuous and overbearing treatment of others; offensive impertinence. **2** An insult. See synonyms under ARROGANCE, IMPUDENCE. [< OF < L *insolentia* < *insolens, -entis* unwonted]

in·so·lent (in′sə·lənt) *adj.* **1** Presumptuously or defiantly offensive in language or manner; impudent. **2** Grossly disrespectful; characterized by insolence. See synonyms under HAUGHTY, IMPUDENT. [< L *insolens, -entis* unusual, haughty, insolent < *in-* not + *solens, -entis,* ppr. of *solere* be wont, accustomed] — **in′so·lent·ly** *adv.*

in·sol·u·ble (in·sol′yə·bəl) *adj.* **1** Not capable of being dissolved, as in a liquid; not soluble. **2** That cannot be explained or solved; insolvable. **3** Impossible to pay or discharge, as a debt or obligation. [< OF < L *insolubilis*] — **in·sol′u·bil′i·ty, in·sol′u·ble·ness** *n.* — **in·sol′u·bly** *adv.*

in·solv·a·ble (in·sol′və·bəl) *adj.* **1** Not admitting of explanation; insoluble. **2** *Obs.* That cannot be untied or loosened.

in·sol·ven·cy (in·sol′vən·sē) *n. pl.* **·cies** Bankruptcy.

in·sol·vent (in·sol′vənt) *adj.* **1** Unable to meet the claims of creditors; not solvent; bankrupt. **2** Inadequate for the payment of debts.

3 Pertaining to insolvency. — *n.* A debtor who is not solvent; a bankrupt; specifically, a debtor whose property is taken to be divided among his creditors by a court under the operation of bankruptcy law.

in·som·ni·a (in·som′nē·ə) *n.* Chronic inability to sleep. [< L < *insomnis* sleepless]

in·som·ni·ac (in·som′nē·ak) *n.* One who suffers from sleeplessness.

in·som·ni·ous (in·som′nē·əs) *adj.* Affected with insomnia; sleepless.

in·som·no·lence (in·som′nə·ləns) *n.* Sleeplessness.

in·so·much (in′sō·much′) *adv.* **1** To such a degree or extent: with *that* or *as.* **2** Inasmuch: with *as.*

in·so·nate (in′sə·nāt) *v.t.* **·nat·ed, ·nat·ing** To expose or subject to the action of sound waves, especially those of very high frequency. [< IN-² + L *sonatus,* pp. of *sonare* sound] — **in′so·na′tion** *n.*

in·sou·ci·ance (in·sōō′sē·əns, *Fr.* aṅ·sōō·syäṅs′) *n.* Careless unconcern; indifference; heedlessness. [< F]

in·sou·ci·ant (in·sōō′sē·ənt, *Fr.* aṅ·sōō·syäṅ′) *adj.* Without concern or care; heedless; unmindful. [< F < *in-* not + *souciant,* ppr. of *soucier* care < OF *solcier* < L *sollicitare* disturb] — **in·sou′ci·ant·ly** (in·sōō′sē·ənt·lē) *adv.*

in·soul (in·sōl′) See ENSOUL.

in·span (in·span′) *v.t.* & *v.i.* **·spanned, ·span·ning** To harness or yoke (animals) to a vehicle. [< Afrikaans < Du. *inspannen*]

in·spect (in·spekt′) *v.t.* **1** To look at or examine carefully and critically. **2** To examine or review officially and with ceremony, as troops. See synonyms under EXAMINE, LOOK. [< L *inspectus,* pp. of *inspicere* look into < *in-* into + *specere* look]

in·spec·tion (in·spek′shən) *n.* Critical viewing or investigation; especially, an official examination. See synonyms under OVERSIGHT. [< OF < L *inspectio, -onis*] — **in·spec′tion·al** *adj.*

in·spec·tive (in·spek′tiv) *adj.* Of or pertaining to inspection; tending to inspect, or that may be inspected.

in·spec·tor (in·spek′tər) *n.* **1** One who inspects. **2** An official designated to carry out inspection; a supervisor. **3** An officer of police usually ranking next below the superintendent. See synonyms under SUPERINTENDENT. [< L]

in·spec·tor·ate (in·spek′tər·it) *n.* The office or district of an inspector. Also **in·spec′tor·ship** (-ship).

Inspector General A military, air, or naval officer responsible for the conduct of inspections and investigations of the economy, discipline, and efficiency of the branch of the armed forces in which he serves; also an officer of his department serving on the staff of a division or higher unit.

in·spir·a·ble (in·spīr′ə·bəl) *adj.* **1** That can be breathed; inhalable. **2** Capable of being inspired. — **in·spir′a·bil′i·ty** *n.*

in·spi·ra·tion (in′spə·rā′shən) *n.* **1** The infusion or imparting of an idea, an emotion, or a mental or spiritual influence. **2** That which is so infused or imparted. **3** An actuating or exalting influence; a stimulus to creativity in thought or action. **4** State of being inspired. **5** Divine or supernatural influence considered as exerted upon men so that their writings have divine authority; attributed by the Society of Friends to the direct teaching of the mind of man by the Holy Spirit. **6** A person or thing that inspires. **7** The act of drawing air into the lungs, inbreathing, or inspiring; inhalation: opposite of *expiration.* See synonyms under ENTHUSIASM. [< OF < LL *inspiratio, -onis*]

in·spi·ra·tion·al (in′spə·rā′shən·əl) *adj.* Of or pertaining to inspiration; bestowing or influenced by inspiration; inspiring. — **in′spi·ra′tion·al·ly** *adv.*

in·spi·ra·tion·al·ist (in′spə·rā′shən·əl·ist) *n.* One who inspires others, whether by speech, writing, or conduct.

in·spir·a·to·ry (in·spīr′ə·tôr′ē, -tō′rē) *adj.* Of or pertaining to inspiration or inhalation. [< L *inspiratus* + -ORY]

in·spire (in·spīr′) *v.* **·spired, ·spir·ing** *v.t.* **1** To stir or affect by some mental or spiritual influence; stimulate; animate: A brave leader *inspires* his followers. **2** To affect or imbue with a specified idea or feeling: to *inspire* survivors with hope. **3** To arouse or give rise to;

generate: Fear *inspires* hatred. **4** To motivate or cause by supernatural influence or guidance. **5** To draw into the lungs; inhale. **6** To prompt the saying or writing of indirectly so as to avoid responsibility: This rumor was *inspired* by my enemies. **7** *Obs.* To blow or breathe into or upon. — *v.i.* **8** To draw in breath; inhale. **9** To give or provide inspiration. See synonyms under ENCOURAGE. [<OF *enspirer* <L *inspirare* breathe into <*in-* into + *spirare* breathe] — **in·spir′er** *n.*

in·spired (in·spīrd′) *adj.* **1** Communicated, imparted, or guided by inspiration: the *inspired* writings (Scriptures). **2** Prompted or kindled by ideas, emotions, etc.: an *inspired* speech. **3** Officially motivated or shaped: an *inspired* editorial. — **in·spir·ed·ly** (in·spīr′id·lē, -spīrd′lē) *adv.*

in·spir·it (in·spir′it) *v.t.* To fill with spirit or life; animate; exhilarate; enliven. See synonyms under ENCOURAGE. — **in·spir′it·ing·ly** *adv.*

in·spis·sate (in·spis′āt) *v.t. & v.i.* ·sat·ed, ·sat·ing To thicken, as by evaporation. — *adj.* Thickened; inspissated. See synonyms under THICK. [<LL *inspissatus*, pp. of *inspissare* thicken <*in-* thoroughly + *spissare* thicken <*spissus* thick] — **in·spis·sa·tion** (in′spi·sā′shən) *n.* — **in′spis·sa·tor** *n.*

in·sta·bil·i·ty (in′stə·bil′ə·tē) *n.* *pl.* ·ties **1** Lack of stability or firmness. **2** Mutability of opinion or conduct; inconstancy; changeableness. **3** Flimsiness of construction; liability to give way; insecurity: the *instability* of a bridge. *Synonyms:* changeableness, fickleness, flightiness, inconstancy, mutability, unstableness, unsteadiness. *Antonyms:* certainty, constancy, firmness, persistence, stability, steadiness.

in·sta·ble (in·stā′bəl) *adj.* Unstable.

in·stall (in·stôl′) *v.t.* **1** To place in office, etc., with formal ceremony. **2** To establish in a place or position. **3** To place in position for service or use: to *install* a hot-water system. [<F *installer* <Med. L *installare* <*in-* in + *stallare* seat <OHG *stal* a seat] — **in·stall′er** *n.* *Synonyms:* inaugurate, induct, initiate, ordain. *Antonyms:* break, cashier, depose, dismiss.

in·stal·la·tion (in′stə·lā′shən) *n.* **1** The act or ceremony of inducting into an office or place of honor. **2** An installing or being installed; especially, the introduction of apparatus or machines for use. **3** Such a machine or apparatus fixed for use: a ventilating *installation.* **4** Any large, fixed base of the armed service.

in·stal·ment (in·stôl′mənt) *n.* **1** A partial payment of a price due; a payment on account. **2** One of several parts of anything furnished at different times; especially a section of a novel or other writing running serially in a magazine, newspaper, etc. **3** The act of installing. Also **in·stall′ment.** [< obs. *estall* arrange payments <OF *estaler* stop <OHG *stal* seat, place]

instalment plan The purchase of goods or services by means of deferred payments at regular intervals.

in·stance (in′stəns) *n.* **1** Something offered or occurring as an exemplification. **2** A case. **3** Illustration, evidence, or proof: an *instance* of her forthrightness. **4** *Archaic* Urgency. **5** The act of asking, soliciting, suggesting or urging: They took action at the *instance* of aroused taxpayers. **6** *Obs.* An impelling motive. **7** A step in proceeding: in the first *instance.* **8** *Law* The institution of a process or suit. — **for instance** For example. — *v.t.* ·stanced, ·stanc·ing **1** To refer to as illustration or example. **2** *Rare* To manifest or show. **3** *Rare* To cite an instance, or as an instance. [<OF <L *instantia* a standing near, urgent supplication <*instans, -antis* standing. See INSTANT.]

in·stan·cy (in′stən·sē) *n.* **1** Urgency; solicitation. **2** Immediateness.

in·stant (in′stənt) *adj.* **1** Immediately impending. **2** Now passing; current; present: the 10th *instant* the 10th day of the month now passing). See PROXIMO, ULTIMO. **3** Direct; immediate. **4** Eager and active; urgent; importunate. See synonyms under IMMEDIATE.

— *n.* **1** A particular point of time; the moment which in passing may be called now. **2** A very brief portion of time; moment. — *adv. Poetic* Instantaneously; instantly. [<OF <L *instans, -antis,* ppr. of *instare* stand near, urge <*in-* upon + *stare* stand]

in·stan·ta·ne·ous (in′stən·tā′nē·əs) *adj.* **1** Acting or done instantly. **2** Relating to a particular instant. [<INSTANT, on analogy with *simultaneous*] — **in′stan·ta·ne·ous·ly** *adv.* — **in′stan·ta′ne·ous·ness** *n.*

in·stan·ter (in·stan′tər) *adv.* Without an instant of delay. See synonyms under IMMEDIATELY. [<L]

in·stant·ly (in′stənt·lē) *adv.* **1** On the instant; at once. **2** *Archaic* With urgency; insistently. — *conj.* As soon as. See synonyms under IMMEDIATELY.

in·star¹ (in·stär′) *v.t.* ·starred, ·star·ring **1** To adorn or stud with or as with stars. **2** To set as a star; make a star of.

in·star² (in′stär) *n. Entomol.* **1** Any stage in the metamorphosis of an insect or other arthropod between successive molts: the pupal *instar* of a butterfly. **2** The insect or arthropod while undergoing any of these stages. [<L, form, likeness]

in·state (in·stāt′) *v.t.* ·stat·ed, ·stat·ing **1** To place or establish in a certain office or rank; induct. **2** *Obs.* To endow.

in·stau·rate (in·stôr′āt) *v.t.* ·rat·ed, ·rat·ing *Rare* To renew; renovate; restore. [<L *instauratus,* pp. of *instaurare* renew] — **in·stau·ra·tion** (in′stô·rā′shən) *n.*

in·stead (in·sted′) *adv.* **1** In place or room; in lieu: with *of:* a friend *instead* of an enemy. **2** In one's (its, their, etc.) stead or place: They went prospecting for silver and found gold *instead.*

in·step (in′step′) *n.* **1** *Anat.* The arched upper part of the human foot, extending from the toes to the ankle. ◆ Collateral adjective: *tarsal.* **2** The front part of the hind leg of a horse, extending from the ham, or hock, to the pastern joint. **3** That part of a shoe or of a stocking that covers the instep.

in·sti·gate (in′stə·gāt) *v.t.* ·gat·ed, ·gat·ing **1** To bring about by inciting; foment. **2** To urge or incite to an action or course: to *instigate* someone to treason. See synonyms under ABET, ENCOURAGE, INFLUENCE, SPUR, STIR. [<L *instigatus,* pp. of *instigare* <*in-* against + the root *-stig-* prick, goad] — **in′sti·ga′tive** *adj.* — **in′sti·ga′tor** *n.*

in·sti·ga·tion (in′stə·gā′shən) *n.* **1** The act of instigating, inciting, or urging, especially to evil. **2** That in which instigating is embodied; an incitement; stimulus.

in·stil (in·stil′) *v.t.* ·stilled, ·stil·ling **1** To put into the mind gradually, as if drop by drop. **2** To pour in by drops. Also **in·still′.** [<L *instillare* drop, drip <*in-* in + *stillare* drop <*stilla* a drop] — **in·stil·la·tion** (in′stə·lā′shən) or **in·stil·la′tion, in·stil′ment** or **in·still′ment** *n.* — **in·still′er** *n.*

in·stinct (in′stingkt) *n.* **1** A natural impulse or innate propensity that incites animals (including man) to the actions that are essential to their existence, preservation, and development; animal intuition. **2** *Psychol.* **a** A strong, innate tendency to certain actions and forms of behavior, often accompanied by emotional excitement. **b** A complex, unlearned, adaptive response to some situation or experience. **3** A natural aptitude. — *adj.* (in·stingkt′) Animated from within; moved by or imbued with inward impulse; filled; alive: usually with *with.* [<L *instinctus,* pp. of *instinguere* impel]

in·stinc·tive (in·stingk′tiv) *adj.* Of the nature of, or prompted by, instinct; spontaneous; innate. Also **in·stinc′tu·al** (-chōō·al). See synonyms under SPONTANEOUS. — **in·stinc′tive·ly, in·stinct′ly** *adv.*

in·sti·tute (in′stə·tōōt, -tyōōt) *v.t.* ·tut·ed, ·tut·ing **1** To set up or establish; found. **2** To set in operation; initiate. **3** To appoint to an office, position, etc.; place in a benefice. **4** *Law* To nominate as heir or executor. — *n.* **1** An established organization or society pledged to some special purpose and work, or the building devoted to its use; an institution. **2** *pl.* Fundamental principles of law, or a digest of them, as for beginners. **3** An es-

tablished principle, rule, or order. — **farmers′ institute** An organization of farmers addressed by experts in agriculture for the purpose of disseminating knowledge in farming. — **naval institute** A society having as its object the development of naval knowledge. — **teachers′ institute** A meeting of the schoolteachers of a state or county for the discussion of methods of teaching and problems which arise within a certain period. [<L *institutus,* pp. of *instituere* erect, establish <*in-* in, on + *statuere* set up, stand] *Synonyms (verb):* appoint, begin, commence, erect, establish, found, ordain, organize, originate, start. *Antonyms:* see synonyms for ABOLISH.

in·sti·tu·tion (in′stə·tōō′shən, -tyōō′-) *n.* **1** That which is instituted or established; an established order, principle, law, or usage as an element of organized society or of civilization: the *institution* of chivalry. **2** A corporate body or establishment instituted and organized for an educational, medical, charitable, or similar purpose, or the building occupied by such a corporate body: the Smithsonian *Institution.* **3** The act of instituting, establishing, or setting on foot: *institution* of an investigation. **4** *Eccl.* **a** The investment of a clergyman by a competent authority with the spiritualities of his office: contrasted with *induction,* which confers the temporalities. **b** The establishment of a sacrament, especially of the Eucharist. **c** That part of the ritual in baptism or the Eucharist at which the words used by Christ in establishing the sacrament are recited. **5** *Law* The formal designation by one person of another to be his heir. **6** *Colloq.* A well-established custom, object, or person: The postman was one of the *institutions* of the place. **7** *Obs.* Instruction, or a book of instruction. [<OF <L *institutio, -onis*]

in·sti·tu·tion·al (in′stə·tōō′shən·əl, -tyōō′-) *adj.* **1** Pertaining to or enjoined by institutions: *institutional* principles. **2** Relating to first principles or elements; rudimentary: *institutional* instruction. **3** Pertaining to investiture in office. **4** Designating a form of advertising intended to promote good will and prestige, as for an institution, rather than to get immediate sales. — **in′sti·tu′tion·al·ly** *adv.*

in·sti·tu·tion·al·ism (in′stə·tōō′shən·əl·iz′əm, -tyōō′-) *n.* **1** The system of institutions. **2** Belief in and support of the usefulness and authority of institutions. **3** The spirit that exalts established institutions, especially in religion: opposed to *individualism.*

in·sti·tu·tion·al·ize (in′stə·tōō′shen·əl·īz′, -tyōō′-) *v.t.* ·ized, ·iz·ing **1** To make institutional. **2** To turn into or regard as an institution. **3** *U.S. Colloq.* To put (someone) in an institution (def. 2).

in·sti·tu·tion·ar·y (in′stə·tōō′shən·er′ē, -tyōō′-) *adj.* Of or pertaining to legal or ecclesiastical institutions or to institutions of learning.

in·sti·tu·tive (in′stə·tōō′tiv, -tyōō′-) *adj.* **1** Tending or intended to institute or establish; having power to ordain. **2** Established by authority; instituted. — **in′sti·tu′tive·ly** *adv.*

in·sti·tu·tor (in′stə·tōō′tər, -tyōō′-) *n.* **1** One who establishes, organizes, or sets in operation; a founder. **2** *U.S.* In the Protestant Episcopal Church, one who institutes a clergyman into a church or parish. **3** *Obs.* An educator. Also **in′sti·tut′er.**

in·stroke (in′strōk′) *n.* **1** An inwardly directed stroke. **2** *Mech.* The thrust of an engine's piston away from the crankshaft. Compare OUTSTROKE.

in·struct (in·strukt′) *v.t.* **1** To impart knowledge or skill to, especially by systematic method; educate; teach. **2** To give specific orders or directions to; order: He *instructed* his men to break camp. **3** To give information or explanation to; inform. See synonyms under INFORM¹, LEARN, TEACH. [<L *instructus,* pp. of *instruere* <*in-* in + *struere* build]

in·struc·tion (in·struk′shən) *n.* **1** The act of instructing; teaching. **2** Imparted knowledge; precept. **3** The act of giving specific directions or commands. **4** The directions given. **5** *pl.* In English law, directions given to a solicitor or counsel. See synonyms under EDUCATION, LEARNING, NURTURE, ORDER. [<

OF *enstruccion* <L *instructio, -onis*]

in·struc·tion·al (in·struk'shən·əl) *adj.* Pertaining or relating to instruction; educational; containing information.

in·struc·tive (in·struk'tiv) *adj.* Serving to instruct; conveying knowledge. — **in·struc'tive·ly** *adv.* — **in·struc'tive·ness** *n.*

in·struc·tor (in·struk'tər) *n.* **1** One who instructs; a teacher. **2** *U.S.* A college teacher of lower rank than the lowest professorial grade. Also **in·struct'er.** [<L]

in·struc·tor·ship (in·struk'tər·ship) *n.* The position or office of an instructor.

in·stru·ment (in'strə·mənt) *n.* **1** A means by which work is done; an implement or tool, especially a device or mechanism for scientific or professional purposes, as distinguished from an apparatus, tool, or machine for industrial use. **2** Any means of accomplishment: The hands are *instruments* of the will. **3** A mechanical or other contrivance for the production of musical sounds. **4** A person doing the will of another. **5** *Law* A formal document, as a contract, deed, etc. See synonyms under AGENT, RECORD, TOOL. — *v.t.* **1** *Law* To draw up an instrument. **2** *Music* To orchestrate. [<L *instrumentum* < *instruere* fit out, INSTRUCT]

in·stru·men·tal (in'strə·men'təl) *adj.* **1** Serving as a means or instrument; serviceable. **2** Fitted for or produced by musical instruments. **3** Traceable to a mechanical instrument, as errors in observation or measurement. **4** *Gram.* Pertaining to a case of the noun, as in Sanskrit, indicating the means or instrument by or with which something is done. — *n. Gram.* **1** The instrumental case. **2** A word in this case.

in·stru·men·tal·ism (in'strə·men'təl·iz'əm) *n. Philos.* The doctrine that experience (or use) determines the value of anything; hence, the doctrine that ideas are true or valid according to their usefulness; pragmatism.

in·stru·men·tal·ist (in'strə·men'təl·ist) *n.* **1** *Music* One who plays an instrument, as distinguished from a vocalist. **2** A believer in instrumentalism.

in·stru·men·tal·i·ty (in'strə·men·tal'ə·tē) *n. pl.* **·ties** **1** The condition of being instrumental; subordinate agency. **2** That which is instrumental; means.

in·stru·men·tal·ly (in'strə·men'təl·ē) *adv.* **1** By means of an instrument or agency; not directly. **2** With musical instruments.

in·stru·men·ta·tion (in'strə·men·tā'shən) *n.* **1** *Music* **a** The act or art of arranging compositions for performance by instruments; orchestration. **b** The use of an instrument, as for producing special or peculiar effects. **2** The art and technique of using instruments of precision. **3** Instrumentality; agency.

instrument board The panel containing the gages and other indicators of performance in an automobile, airplane, or other complex apparatus. Also **instrument panel.**

instrument flight *Aeron.* Control of the course of an aircraft by reference to instruments within the craft rather than by observation of landmarks: contrasted to *contact flight.*

in·sub·or·di·nate (in'sə·bôr'də·nit) *adj.* **1** Not subordinate or obedient; not submitting to authority; rebellious; mutinous. **2** Not lower or inferior in height: an *insubordinate* hill. — *n.* A disobedient or unsubmissive person. — **in'sub·or'di·nate·ly** *adv.*

in·sub·or·di·na·tion (in'sə·bôr'də·nā'shən) *n.* The state of being insubordinate; disobedience to constituted authorities; unruliness.

in·sub·stan·tial (in'səb·stan'shəl) *adj.* Unsubstantial; not material; illusive. — **in'sub·stan'ti·al'i·ty** (-shē·al'ə·tē) *n.*

in·suf·fer·a·ble (in·suf'ər·ə·bəl) *adj.* Not to be endured; intolerable. — **in·suf'fer·a·ble·ness** *n.* — **in·suf'fer·a·bly** *adv.*

in·suf·fi·cien·cy (in'sə·fish'ən·sē) *n. pl.* **·cies** **1** Lack of sufficiency; inadequacy in amount, value, power, fitness, etc.; deficiency; also, mental inability. **2** Anything that is not enough. [<F *insuffisance* <LL *insufficientia*]

in·suf·fi·cient (in'sə·fish'ənt) *adj.* **1** Inadequate for some need, purpose, or use. **2** Mentally or physically unfit. — **in·suf·fi'cient·ly** *adv.*

in·suf·flate (in·suf'lāt, in'sə·flāt) *v.t.* **·flat·ed, ·flat·ing** **1** To blow or breathe into or upon. **2** To blow a substance into: to *insufflate* a room with disinfectant. **3** *Med.* **a** To blow (air, medicinal gas, etc.) into an opening or

upon some part of the body. **b** To treat by insufflation, as an asphyxiated person. **4** *Eccl.* To breathe upon, as at baptism. [<L *insufflatus*, pp. of *insufflare* < *in-* + *sufflare* < blow from below < *sub-* under + *flare* blow] — **in·suf'fla·tor** *n.*

in·suf·fla·tion (in'sə·flā'shən) *n.* **1** The act or process of blowing or breathing upon or into. **2** *Eccl.* A breathing upon a person or thing as symbolic of the operation and entrance of the Holy Spirit, or the casting out of unclean spirits, as in some churches in the ordinance of baptism for the purification of catechumens. **3** *Med.* A forcible blowing, as of air into the lungs, or of a gas, vapor, or powder into some opening or cavity of the body. [<LL *insufflatio, -onis*]

in·su·la (in'sə·lə) *n. pl.* **·lae** (-lē) **1** *Anat.* Any detached or isolated area in an organ of the body, as the central lobe of the cerebral cortex. **2** In ancient Rome, a block of houses. [<L, island]

in·su·lar (in'sə·lər) *adj.* **1** Of or pertaining to, like, living on or characteristic of an island. **2** Standing alone; isolated. **3** *Biol.* Having an island as its habitat. **4** Of or pertaining to people inhabiting an island or otherwise isolated, or to their customs, opinions, etc. **5** Not broad, liberal, nor cosmopolitan; narrow: *insular* ideas or prejudices. **6** *Med.* **a** Breaking out or appearing sporadically in spots, as a rash on the body. **b** Characterized by spots appearing singly here and there. **7** *Anat.* Pertaining to an insula or to the islands of Langerhans in the pancreas. [<L *insularis* <*insula* island]

in·su·lar·i·ty (in'sə·lar'ə·tē) *n.* **1** The state or quality of being insular or belonging to an island. **2** Insular position, character, or condition. **3** Narrowness or illiberality. Compare PENINSULARITY. Also **in'su·lar·ism.**

in·su·late (in'sə·lāt) *v.t.* **·lat·ed, ·lat·ing** **1** To place in a detached state or situation; isolate. **2** To change into an island; surround by water. **3** *Physics* To separate from conducting bodies, as by a covering or support of a non-conducting substance, usually in order to prevent or lessen the leakage of an electric current, heat, sound, radiation, etc. [<L *insulatus* formed like an island <*insula* island]

in·su·la·tion (in'sə·lā'shən) *n.* **1** The act of insulating; isolation. **2** The act of surrounding a body with non-conductors. **3** Material used in insulating.

in·su·la·tor (in'sə·lā'tər) *n.* **1** One who or that which insulates. **2** *Electr.* A dielectric substance or material, as glass or porcelain, adapted to minimize leakage from a charged conductor which it supports.

in·su·lin (in'sə·lin) *n.* A protein hormone secreted by and obtained from the pancreas: used in the form of a standardized aqueous solution, it checks the accumulation of glucose in the blood and promotes the utilization of sugar in the treatment of diabetes. [<L *insula* island (of Langerhans) + -IN]

in·su·lize (in'sə·līz) *v.t.* **·lized, ·liz·ing** To inject insulin into; treat with insulin.

in·sult (in·sult') *v.t.* **1** To treat with insolence or contempt; affront. **2** *Obs.* To attack suddenly; assault. — *v.i.* **3** *Obs.* To exult or behave insolently. See synonyms under AFFRONT, MOCK, OUTRAGE. — *n.* (in'sult) **1** Something offensive said or done; an indignity or affront. **2** Contumelious treatment; abuse; outrage. **3** *Obs.* A sudden attack or assault. See synonyms under OFFENSE. [<F *insulter* <L *insultare* leap at, insult, freq. of *insilire* leap upon <*in-* on + *salire* leap] — **in·sult'er** *n.*

in·sult·ing (in·sul'ting) *adj.* Conveying or intending to insult. — **in·sult'ing·ly** *adv.*

in·su·per·a·ble (in·sōō'pər·ə·bəl) *adj.* Not to be surmounted or overcome; insurmountable. [<L *insuperabilis*] — **in·su'per·a·bil'i·ty, in·su'per·a·ble·ness** *n.* — **in·su'per·a·bly** *adv.*

in·sup·port·a·ble (in'sə·pôr'tə·bəl, -pôr'-) *adj.* **1** Intolerable; insufferable. **2** Without grounds; unjustifiable. — **in'sup·port'a·bly** *adv.*

in·sup·press·i·ble (in'sə·pres'ə·bəl) *adj.* Incapable of being suppressed or concealed; irrepressible. Also **in'sup·pres'sive** (-pres'iv).

in·sur·ance (in·shoor'əns) *n.* **1** An act, business, or system by which pecuniary indemnity is guaranteed by one party (as a company) to another party in certain contingencies, as of death, accident, damage, disaster, injury, loss, old age, risk, sickness, unemployment,

etc., upon specified terms: in Great Britain, often *assurance.* **2** A contract made under such a system. **3** The consideration paid for insuring; premium. **4** The sum that the insurer has agreed to pay in case of the occurrence of the specified contingency. **5** The act of making safe or secure. **6** Something that provides protection or security.

in·sur·ant (in·shoor'ənt) *n.* One to whom an insurance policy is issued; also, the beneficiary.

in·sure (in·shoor') *v.* **·sured, ·sur·ing** *v.t.* **1** To contract to pay or be paid an indemnity in the event of harm to or the loss or death of; issue or take out a policy of insurance on. **2** To make safe; guard or protect: with *against* or *from*: Only vigilance *insures* freedom against tyranny. **3** To make sure or certain; guarantee: His researches *insure* the accuracy of the report. — *v.i.* **4** To issue or take out a policy of insurance. Also spelled *ensure.* [<OF *enseurer* make sure < *en-* in + *seur* sure] — **in·sur'a·bil'i·ty** *n.* — **in·sur'a·ble** *adj.*

in·sured (in·shoord') *n.* **1** The person or persons to whom insurance (as fire or marine) is to be paid after loss or damage. **2** The person or persons upon whose death or disability insurance (life or accident) becomes due.

in·sur·er (in·shoor'ər) *n.* One who or that which insures; especially, a company or individual that undertakes, for compensation, to guarantee against loss; an underwriter.

in·sur·gence (in·sûr'jəns) *n.* The act of rising in insurrection; insurrection; uprising.

in·sur·gen·cy (in·sûr'jən·sē) *n.* **1** The state of being insurgent. **2** In international law, any uprising against a government of less gravity than a revolution.

in·sur·gent (in·sûr'jənt) *adj.* .Rebellious; rising in rebellion against an existing government. See synonyms under TURBULENT. — *n.* One who takes part in active and forcible opposition or resistance to the constituted authorities; also, a rebel to whom belligerent rights have not been accorded. [<L *insurgens, -entis*, ppr. of *insurgere* rise up against < *in-* against + *surgere* rise]

in·sur·mount·a·ble (in'sər·moun'tə·bəl) *adj.* That cannot be surmounted, passed over, or overcome; insuperable. — **in'sur·mount'a·bly** *adv.*

in·sur·rec·tion (in'sə·rek'shən) *n.* An organized resistance to established government. See synonyms under REVOLUTION. [<F <LL *insurrectio, -onis* <*insurrectus*, pp. of *insurgere* rise up against. See INSURGENT.] — **in'sur·rec'tion·al** *adj.* — **in'sur·rec'tion·ar'y** *adj. & n.* — **in'sur·rec'tion·ism** *n.* — **in'sur·rec'tion·ist** *n.*

in·sus·cep·ti·ble (in'sə·sep'tə·bəl) *adj.* Not susceptible; incapable of being moved or impressed. — **in'sus·cep'ti·bil'i·ty** *n.*

in·swept (in'swept') *adj.* Narrowed or tapering in front, as an airplane wing.

in·tact (in·takt') *adj.* Left complete or unimpaired. [<L *intactus* untouched < *in-* not + *tactus*, pp. of *tangere* touch] — **in·tact'ness** *n.*

in·take (in'tāk') *n.* **1** That which is taken in; also, a taking in. **2** A point at which a knit or woven article is narrowed. **3** The area in which a water supply is formed. **4** The point at which a fluid is taken into a pipe or channel, as distinguished from the outlet. **5** The current flowing in such a pipe. **6** The amount so taken in. **7** The amount of energy or power taken into a machine or system.

in·tan·gi·ble (in·tan'jə·bəl) *adj.* **1** Not capable of being touched; not tangible; impalpable. **2** Not directly appreciable by the mind; unfathomable. — *n.* Something intangible but often noteworthy or influential nevertheless. [<Med. L *intangibilis*] — **in·tan'gi·bil'i·ty, in·tan'gi·ble·ness** *n.* — **in·tan'gi·bly** *adv.*

in·tar·si·a (in·tär'sē·ə) *n.* Mosaic woodwork of tinted and natural woods. [<Ital. *intarsio* < *intarsiare* inlay, encrust < *in-* in + Arabic *tarsi* incrustation]

in·te·ger (in'tə·jər) *n.* **1** A whole. **2** A number that is not a fraction; a whole number. [<L < *in-* not + root *tag-*, of *tangere.* Doublet of ENTIRE.]

in·te·ger vi·tae (in'tə·jər vī'tē) *Latin* Innocent; pure: literally, blameless in life.

in·te·gra·ble (in'tə·grə·bəl) *adj.* Capable of being integrated.

in·te·gral (in'tə·grəl) *adj.* **1** Constituting a completed whole. **2** Constituting an essential part of a whole necessary for completeness; intrinsic. **3** *Math.* **a** Pertaining to an integer. **b** Produced by integration. — *n.* **1** An entire thing; a whole. **2** *Math.* The result of integration. [<LL *integralis*] — **in·te·gral′i·ty** (-gral′ə·tē) *n.* — **in′te·gral·ly** *adv.*

integral calculus See under CALCULUS.

in·te·grand (in′tə·grand) *n. Math.* An expression to be integrated, or whose integration is indicated. [<L *integrandus*, gerundive of *integrare* make whole]

in·te·grant (in′tə·grənt) *adj.* Contributing or essential to the making up of a whole; integral. — *n.* A component. [<L *integrans, -antis,* ppr. of *integrare* make whole]

in·te·grate (in′tə·grāt) *v.* **·grat·ed, ·grat·ing** *v.t.* **1** To make whole by the bringing together or addition of parts. **2** To give the sum total or mean value of. **3** *Math.* To find the integral of. **4** *U.S.* **a** To make (schools, housing, public facilities, etc.) available to people of all races and ethnic groups on an equal basis. **b** To remove any barriers imposing segregation upon (religious, racial, or other groups). — *v.i.* **5** To become integrated. [<L *integratus,* pp. of *integrare* make whole, renew <*integer* whole, intact] — **in′te·gra′tive** (-grā′tiv) *adj.*

in·te·grat·ed (in′tə·grā′tid) *adj.* **1** Made whole by combining in systematic order or arrangement the component parts or factors: an *integrated* curriculum. **2** Well adjusted: an *integrated* personality. **3** *Econ.* Organized and equipped to produce all materials (usually excluding the raw materials) and components required by a manufacturing process without recourse to independent suppliers; a fully *integrated* plant. **4** *U.S.* Made up of individuals or groups of various cultural, economic, racial, etc., backgrounds functioning as a unit: an *integrated* school.

in·te·gra·tion (in′tə·grā′shən) *n.* **1** The act or operation of integrating; the bringing together of parts into a whole. **2** *Math.* The process of determining a function from its derivative; the inverse of *differentiation.* **3** *Physiol.* The combination of different nervous processes or reflexes so that they cooperate in a larger activity and thus unify the bodily functions. **4** *Psychol.* The orderly arrangement of the physical, emotional, and mental components of the personality into a more or less stable and harmonious pattern of behavior. **5** *U.S.* The act or process of integrating, especially racially, an institution, place, or group. — **in′·te·gra′tion·ist** (*especially for def. 5*) *n.* [<L *integratio, -onis*]

in·te·gra·tor (in′tə·grā′tər) *n.* **1** One who or that which integrates. **2** Any mechanical device for obtaining the numerical value of an integral, especially the area of an irregular figure. **3** An integrating instrument, as a planimeter.

in·teg·ri·ty (in·teg′rə·tē) *n.* **1** Uprightness of character; probity; honesty. **2** Unimpaired state; soundness. **3** Undivided or unbroken state; completeness. See synonyms under FIDELITY, JUSTICE, VIRTUE, WORTH. [<L *integritas, -tatis* <*integer* whole]

in·teg·u·ment (in·teg′yə·mənt) *n.* **1** A covering; coating; investment. **2** *Biol.* Any natural outer covering or envelope, as the skin of an animal, coat of a seed, etc. [<L *integumentum* covering <*integere* cover <*in-* thoroughly + *tegere* cover] — **in·teg·u·men·ta·ry** (in·teg′·yə·men′tə·rē) *adj.*

in·tel·lect (in′tə·lekt) *n.* **1** The faculty or power of perception or thought; intelligence; mind; sometimes, the higher thinking powers, as distinguished from the senses and memory: *Intellect* distinguishes man from brutes. **2** Intelligent people collectively: The *intellect* of the age is enlisted in these inquiries. **3** The faculty or power of understanding, whether of the objects immediately presented in sense perception, or of those known by processes of reasoning. **4** Formerly, in the archaic threefold division of psychology, the faculty of knowing, as distinguished from sensibility and will. **5** The power to perceive things in a rational way, as involving a more than ordinary comprehension of their relations, laws, and profounder meanings; the scientific or philosophical mind: Aristotle was a man

of mighty *intellect.* **6** The sum of the mental powers by which knowledge is acquired, retained, and extended, as distinguished from the senses; the understanding. [<L *intellectus* perception, understanding, sense <*intelligere* understand. See INTELLIGENT.]

Synonyms: intelligence, reason, reasoning, understanding. According to the long-established division of the mental powers into the *intellect,* the sensibilities, and the will, the *intellect* is that assemblage of faculties which is concerned with knowledge, as distinguished from emotion and volition. *Understanding* is the Saxon word of the same general import, but is chiefly used of the reasoning powers. See MIND, UNDERSTANDING. *Antonyms:* body, matter, passion, sensation, sense.

in·tel·lec·tion (in′tə·lek′shən) *n.* Exercise of the intellect; thought. [<Med. L *intellectio, -onis*]

in·tel·lec·tive (in′tə·lek′tiv) *adj.* Of or pertaining to the intellect; intelligent. [<OF *intellectif* <LL *intellectivus*] — **in′tel·lec′tive·ly** *adv.*

in·tel·lec·tu·al (in′tə·lek′chōō·əl) *adj.* **1** Pertaining to the intellect; bringing into action the intellect or higher capacities; mental. **2** Possessing intellect or intelligence; characterized by a high degree of intelligence. **3** Requiring intelligence or study: *intellectual* pursuits. See synonyms under CLEVER, WISE. — *n.* **1** An intellectual person. **2** *pl. Archaic* The mental faculties; intellect: often in the plural. [<L *intellectualis*] — **in′tel·lec′tu·al·ly** *adv.*

in·tel·lec·tu·al·ism (in′tə·lek′chōō·əl·iz′əm) *n.* **1** Intellectual quality or power; intellectuality. **2** Devotion to intellectual occupation. **3** Belief in the supremacy of the intellect among human faculties. **4** The doctrine that the ultimate principle of all reality is intellect or reason. — **in′tel·lec′tu·al·ist** *n.* — **in′tel·lec′tu·al·is′tic** *adj.*

in·tel·lec·tu·al·i·ty (in′tə·lek′chōō·al′ə·tē) *n.* The quality or state of being intellectual; possession of intellectual force or endowment.

in·tel·lec·tu·al·ize (in′tə·lek′chōō·əl·īz′) *v.t.* & *v.i.* **·ized, ·iz·ing** To make or become intellectual.

in·tel·li·gence (in·tel′ə·jəns) *n.* **1** The quality, exercise, or product of active intellect; intellect; knowledge; ability to exercise the higher mental functions; readiness of comprehension. **2** The capacity to meet situations, especially if new or unforeseen, by a rapid and effective adjustment of behavior; also, the native ability to grasp the significant factors of a complex problem or situation. **3** Information acquired or communicated; notification; news; especially, secret information, political, military, etc. **4** Mutual understanding; interchange of information or thought: to exchange a look of *intelligence.* **5** An intelligent being; especially, a spirit not embodied: the Supreme *Intelligence.* See synonyms under INTELLECT, KNOWLEDGE, MIND, TIDINGS, UNDERSTANDING. [<OF <L *intelligentia* <*intelligens, -entis,* ppr. of *intelligere* understand]

intelligence department A department charged with getting information for a government, an army, or a navy, as by means of spies.

intelligence office **1** An office where information may be obtained. **2** *U.S.* Formerly, an employment bureau, especially for servants.

intelligence officer An officer in the service of an intelligence department.

intelligence quotient *Psychol.* A numerical quotient obtained by multiplying the mental age of a person by 100, and dividing the result by his chronological age. Abbr. *I.Q.* or *IQ.*

in·tel·li·genc·er (in·tel′ə·jən·sər) *n.* A sender or conveyor of intelligence or news; a messenger; spy.

intelligence test *Psychol.* Any test designed to show the relative mental capacity of a person.

in·tel·li·gent (in·tel′ə·jənt) *adj.* **1** Distinguished for intelligence; of active mind; discerning; acute: an *intelligent* reader. **2** Marked by intelligence: an *intelligent* reply. **3** Endowed with intellect; reasoning: Man is an *intelligent* animal. **4** *Archaic* Informed; cognizant: with *of.* **5** *Obs.* Communicating information. [<L *intelligens, -entis,* ppr. of *intelligere* understand, perceive <*inter-* between + *legere*

choose, pick] — **in·tel′li·gent·ly** *adv.*

Synonyms: acute, astute, bright, clear-headed, clear-sighted, clever, discerning, educated, instructed, keen, keen-sighted, knowing, long-headed, quick-sighted, sensible, sharp-sighted, sharp-witted, shrewd, well-informed. *Antonyms:* see synonyms for IGNORANT.

in·tel·li·gen·tial (in·tel′ə·jen′shəl) *adj.* **1** Exercising or characterized by intelligence; rational. **2** Conveying intelligence.

in·tel·li·gent·si·a (in·tel′ə·jent′sē·ə, -gent′-) *n. pl.* Intellectual or learned people, collectively; especially those capable of thinking for themselves: sometimes used derisively: a term adopted during the Russian Revolution to differentiate the intellectual classes as such from the bourgeoisie and proletariat. Also **in·tel′li·gent′zi·a.** [<Russian *intelligentsiya* < Ital. *intelligenza* <L *intelligentia*]

in·tel·li·gi·bil·i·ty (in·tel′ə·jə·bil′ə·tē) *n. pl.* **·ties 1** Clearness; understandableness. **2** That which is intelligible.

in·tel·li·gi·ble (in·tel′ə·jə·bəl) *adj.* **1** Capable of being understood. **2** *Philos.* Capable of being apprehended only by the intellect, not by the senses. Compare SENSIBLE. See synonyms under CLEAR, PLAIN. [<L *intelligibilis*] — **in·tel′li·gi·bly** *adv.*

in·tem·er·ate (in·tem′ər·it) *adj.* Undefiled; pure. [<L *intemeratus* <*in-* not + *temeratus,* pp. of *temerare* violate <*temere* rashly, by chance]

in·tem·per·ance (in·tem′pər·əns) *n.* **1** Lack of moderation or due restraint. **2** Excess in speech or action, especially in the use of alcoholic drinks. **3** An intemperate act. See synonyms under EXCESS. [<OF <L *intemperantia*]

in·tem·per·ate (in·tem′pər·it) *adj.* **1** Characterized by lack of moderation, as in speech or action; unrestrained, as in indulgence or exertion. **2** Given to or characterized by excessive use of alcoholic drinks: *intemperate* habits. **3** Excessive in character or degree: inordinate; inclement: *intemperate* weather. — **in·tem′per·ate·ly** *adv.* — **in·tem′per·ate·ness** *n.*

in·tend (in·tend′) *v.t.* **1** To have in mind to accomplish or do; purpose: He *intends* to go. **2** To make or destine for a purpose, use, etc.: Was that gift *intended* for me? **3** To have the purpose of meaning or expressing; mean: She *intended* nothing by the remark. **4** *Obs.* To direct, as one's course or thoughts. — *v.i.* **5** *Rare* To have intention; mean: to *intend* well. **6** *Obs.* To tend; incline. See synonyms under PURPOSE. [<OF *entendre* <L *intendere* stretch out (for) <*in-* in, at + *tendere* stretch] — **in·tend′er** *n.*

in·ten·dance (in·ten′dəns) *n.* **1** Business management or superintendence. **2** An intendancy. [<F]

in·ten·dan·cy (in·ten′dən·sē) *n. pl.* **·cies 1** The office or work of an intendant; intendants collectively. **2** An administrative district in Spanish America. Also **in·ten′den·cy.**

in·ten·dant (in·ten′dənt) *n.* **1** A superintendent; provincial administrator, as under the Bourbons in France. **2** A Spanish or Mexican district administrator or treasurer. Also **in·ten′dent,** *Spanish* **in·ten·den·te** (ēn′ten·den′tā). See synonyms under SUPERINTENDENT. [<F]

in·tend·ed (in·ten′did) *adj.* **1** Made the object of design or intent; designed. **2** Betrothed. — *n. Colloq.* One who is betrothed.

in·tend·ment (in·tend′mənt) *n.* **1** The true intent or meaning, or correct understanding, of the law, or of a legal instrument; also, a general presumption of law. **2** *Obs.* Intention; object, as of an action; purpose; design. [<OF *entendement*]

in·ten·er·ate (in·ten′ər·āt) *v.t.* **·at·ed, ·at·ing** *Rare* To make tender; soften. [<L *in-* very + *tener* tender + -ATE[1]] — **in·ten′er·a′tion** *n.*

in·tense (in·tens′) *adj.* **in·tens·er, in·tens·est 1** Strained or exerted to a high degree; ardent; unremitting; fervid: *intense* study. **2** Extreme in degree; very deep or strong; severe; violent; excessive: *intense* light or pain. **3** Putting forth strenuous effort; intent. **4** Susceptible to or exhibiting deep emotion, earnestness, or application: said of a person. **5** *Phot.* Having strength or marked contrast; dense: said of a negative. See synonyms under ARDENT,

EAGER, VIOLENT, VIVID. [<OF <L *intensus*, pp. of *intendere* stretch out] — **in·tense′ly** *adv.* — **in·tense′ness** *n.*

in·ten·si·fi·ca·tion (in·ten′sə·fə·kā′shən) *n.* **1** The act or result of intensifying or of making intense. **2** *Phot.* The process of increasing the density of a negative.

in·ten·si·fi·er (in·ten′sə·fī′ər) *n.* **1** One who or that which intensifies. **2** *Phot.* A chemical solution used to effect intensification. **3** A device by which fluid pressure is intensified.

in·ten·si·fy (in·ten′sə·fī) *v.* **·fied, ·fy·ing** *v.t.* **1** To make intense; increase in intensity. **2** *Phot.* To increase the density of (a film) so as to obtain stronger contrast between light and shadow. — *v.i.* **3** To become intense or more intense. See synonyms under AGGRAVATE, INCREASE.

in·ten·sion (in·ten′shən) *n.* **1** The act of straining or stretching, or state of being strained or made tense; tension. **2** Increase of energy or power; intensification. **3** *Logic* All the implications in a concept or term; connotation: distinguished from *extension.* **4** Intensity; degree. **5** Intense exertion of the mind or the will. [<L *intensio, -onis*]

in·ten·si·ty (in·ten′sə·tē) *n.* *pl.* **·ties 1** The state or quality of being intense; relative strength or degree of a quality or force; intenseness. **2** *Physics* The force, energy, or quantity of action of any physical agent, generally estimated by its ratio to the space within which it acts, or to the quantity of matter on which it acts: the *intensity* of pressure of a fluid, the *intensity* of gravity. **3** *Electr.* **a** The strength of an electric or magnetic field as measured by the number of force lines that pass through unit area of cross-section. **b** Current strength or density. **c** Potential or electromotive force. **4** *Phot.* Strong contrast between light and shade in a negative; density; also, opacity. See synonyms under ENTHUSIASM, VIOLENCE, WARMTH.

in·ten·sive (in·ten′siv) *adj.* **1** Serving or tending to intensify. **2** Admitting of increase of force or degree; capable of being intensified. **3** Thorough, as contrasted with *extensive.* **4** *Logic* Relating to intension or content. See CONTENT. **5** *Agric.* Of or pertaining to the tillage of land by the application of much labor and costly fertilization to a given area (usually small) which is thereby brought to a high degree of productiveness. **6** Of or relating to a way of making any industry more lucrative by perfecting methods and appliances without enlarging the scale of operations. **7** *Med.* **a** Characterizing a method of inoculation wherein the injections are successively increased in strength. **b** A method of administering increasingly strong remedies or doses. **8** *Gram.* Adding emphasis or force. **9** Intense; assiduous; concentrated: *intensive* research; *intensive* warfare. **10** Characterized by a relatively heavy investment in (something specified) as compared with other factors: used in combination: an *energy–intensive* method of heating; a *labor–intensive* industry. — *n.* **1** Whatever gives intensity or emphasis. **2** *Gram.* An intensive particle, word, or phrase. [<F *intensif*] — **in·ten′sive·ly** *adv.* — **in·ten′sive·ness** *n.*

intensive particle A particle or prefix expressing heightened meaning: as *be-* in *besmirch*; *for-* in *forlorn*; *de-* in *desiccate*; *per-* in *perjure.* Also **intensive prefix.**

in·tent (in·tent′) *adj.* **1** Having the mind earnestly bent or fixed; attentive; earnest. **2** Firmly, constantly, or assiduously directed. See synonyms under EAGER. — *n.* **1** That which is designed; intention; meaning; connotation; aim; purpose. **2** *Law* The state of mind in which or the purpose with which one does an act; also, the character that the law imputes to an act. See synonyms under DESIGN, PURPOSE. [<OF *entent, entente* <L *intentus*, pp. of *intendere* stretch out, endeavor] — **in·tent′ly** *adv.* — **in·tent′ness** *n.*

in·ten·tion (in·ten′shən) *n.* **1** A settled direction of the mind toward the doing of a certain act. **2** That upon which the mind is set or which it wishes to express or achieve; meaning; purpose conceived. **3** *pl. Colloq.* Purpose with regard to marriage. **4** *Law* An intelligent purpose to do a criminal act; intent; purpose: an essential element in a criminal offense. **5** *Med.* Natural course, operation, or process, as in the healing of a wound.

6 *Logic* In scholasticism: **a** First intention, a general concept of an object, kind of object, or notion formed from something outside the mind, as *man, house, integrity, word, to run.* **b** Second intention, a general concept formed from or extended to abstractions of other concepts of objects and their relationships, as *genus* and *species, property, ethics, language* and *meaning, physiological functions.* Compare CONSTRUCT *n.* (def. 2). **7** *Eccl.* **a** The inward intent or purpose on the part of the minister of a sacrament to do what the church requires to be done: considered essential to the validity of a sacrament. **b** The purpose for which a person offers up prayers or other devotions: often with *special* or *particular.* **8** Earnest attention; application. See synonyms under AIM, DESIGN, PURPOSE. [<OF *entencion* <L *intentio, -onis*]

in·ten·tion·al (in·ten′shən·əl) *adj.* Done with intention; designed. [<Med. L *intentionalis*] — **in·ten′tion·al·ly** *adv.*

in·ten·tioned (in·ten′shənd) *adj.* Having designs or intentions: used in composition with a qualifying adverb: well–*intentioned.*

in·ter (in·tûr′) *v.t.* **·terred, ·ter·ring** To place in a grave or tomb; bury. See synonyms under BURY, HIDE. [<OF *enterrer* <LL *interrare* <*in-* in + *terra* earth]

in·ter·act (in′tər·akt′) *v.i.* To act on each other. — **in′ter·ac′tive** *adj.*

in·ter·ac·tion (in′tər·ak′shən) *n.* Reciprocal action or influence: the *interaction* between the executive and legislative branches of government. — **in′ter·ac′tion·al** *adj.*

in·ter·ac·tion·ism (in′tər·ak′shən·iz′əm) *n. Psychol.* The theory that physical occurrences are the causes of mental modifications and that mental modifications give rise to physical changes.

in·ter a·li·a (in′tər ā′lē·ə) *Latin* Among other things.

in·ter a·li·os (in′tər ā′lē·ōs) *Latin* Among other persons.

in·ter·bed·ded (in′tər·bed′id) *adj. Geol.* Occurring between beds: said of rocks.

in·ter·bor·ough (in′tər·bûr′ō) *adj.* Pertaining to, situated in, or running in two or more boroughs: an *interborough* railroad.

in·ter·brain (in′tər·brān′) *n. Anat.* The portion of the brain that is derived from the second cerebral vesicle; the diencephalon.

in·ter·breed (in′tər·brēd′) *v.* **·bred, ·breed·ing** *v.t.* **1** To breed by crossing different stocks, varieties, etc.; crossbreed. **2** To cause (animals or plants) to breed by crossing. — *v.i.* **3** To breed with another: said of different varieties, stocks, etc.

in·ter·ca·lar·y (in·tûr′kə·ler′ē) *adj.* **1** Added to the calendar. **2** Containing an added day. **3** Interposed; inserted. [<L *intercalarius*]

in·ter·ca·late (in·tûr′kə·lāt) *v.t.* **·lat·ed, ·lat·ing 1** To insert or interpolate. **2** To insert, as an additional day or month, into the calendar. [<L *intercalatus*, pp. of *intercalare* insert <*inter-* between +*calare* proclaim, call]

in·ter·ca·la·tion (in·tûr′kə·lā′shən) *n.* **1** The insertion of one thing between other things, especially in an irregular manner. **2** An insertion of a day or days in the calendar. — **in·ter′ca·la·tive** *adj.*

in·ter·car·di·nal (in′tər·kär′də·nəl) *adj. Naut.* Between the cardinal points of the compass, as northeast, southwest, etc. — *n.* One of the intercardinal points of the compass.

in·ter·cede (in′tər·sēd′) *v.i.* **·ced·ed, ·ced·ing 1** To plead in behalf of another; make intercession. **2** To interpose a veto: said of the ancient Roman tribunes. See synonyms under INTERPOSE. [<L *intercedere* come between <*inter-* between +*cedere* pass, go] — **in′ter·ced′er** *n.*

in·ter·cel·lu·lar (in′tər·sel′yə·lər) *adj. Biol.* Situated between or among cells: the *intercellular* substance or matrix of cartilage.

in·ter·cept (in′tər·sept′) *v.t.* **1** To seize or stop on the way to a destination; arrest in passage: to *intercept* a messenger. **2** To stop, interrupt, or prevent: to *intercept* the flow of water. **3** To cut off from connection, sight, etc. **4** *Math.* To contain or include between two points of a curve. See synonyms under INTERPOSE, SHUT. — *n.* (in′tər·sept) **1** That which is cut off or intercepted. **2** *Math.* The part of a curve contained between two points of intersection with other curves. [<L *interceptus*, pp. of *intercipere*

<*inter-* between +*capere* seize] — **in′ter·cep′tion** *n.* — **in′ter·cep′tive** *adj.*

in·ter·cep·tor (in′tər·sep′tər) *n.* **1** One who or that which intercepts. **2** *Aeron.* **a** A lateral control device in an airplane. **b** An airplane adapted to the pursuit and interception of enemy aircraft. Also **in′ter·cept′er.** [<L]

in·ter·ces·sion (in′tər·sesh′ən) *n.* **1** The act of interceding between persons; entreaty in behalf of others. **2** A prayer, or series of prayers. [<L *intercessio, -onis* <*intercessus*, pp. of *intercedere* INTERCEDE] — **in′ter·ces′sion·al** *adj.*

in·ter·ces·sor (in′tər·ses′ər) *n.* One who intercedes; a mediator. [<L] — **in′ter·ces′so·ry** *adj.*

in·ter·change (in′tər·chānj′) *v.* **·changed, ·chang·ing** *v.t.* **1** To put each of (two things) in the place of the other. **2** To give and receive in return, as gifts; exchange. **3** To alternate: to *interchange* work and rest. — *v.i.* **4** To make an interchange. — *n.* (in′tər·chānj) **1** Exchange. **2** Alternation. See synonyms under INTERCOURSE. [<OF *entrechangier* <*entre-* between (<L *inter-*) +*changier* <LL *cambiare* exchange] — **in′ter·chang′er** *n.*

in·ter·change·a·ble (in′tər·chān′jə·bəl) *adj.* Capable of being interchanged or substituted one for the other; permitting transposition. [<OF *entrechangeable*] — **in′ter·change′a·ble·ness, in′ter·change′a·bil′i·ty** *n.* — **in′ter·change′a·bly** *adv.*

in·ter·cip·i·ent (in′tər·sip′ē·ənt) *adj.* Intercepting; stopping. — *n.* One who or that which intercepts. [<L *intercipiens, -entis*, ppr. of *intercipere.* See INTERCEPT.]

in·ter·clude (in′tər·klood′) *v.t.* **·clud·ed, ·clud·ing** *Obs.* To shut out; cut off; intercept. [<L *intercludere* <*inter-* between +*claudere* close] — **in′ter·clu′sion** (-zhən) *n.*

in·ter·col·le·giate (in′tər·kə·lē′jit, -jē·it) *adj.* Existing, representing, or conducted between, two or more colleges: an *intercollegiate* committee, *intercollegiate* rules, games, etc.

in·ter·co·lum·ni·a·tion (in′tər·kə·lum′nē·ā′shən) *n. Archit.* **1** The space or method of spacing between columns. **2** The space between two consecutive columns. [<L *intercolumnium* space between columns +-ATION] — **in′ter·co·lum′nar** *adj.*

in·ter·com (in′tər·kom) *n. Colloq.* A system for intercommunication.

in·ter·com·mon (in′tər·kom′ən) *v.i. Brit. Law* To share the use of a common with a nearby town, village, etc. [<AF *entrecomuner* <*entre-* between (<L *inter-*) +*comuner* share <L *communis* common]

in·ter·com·mu·ni·cate (in′tər·kə·myoo′nə·kāt) *v.t.* **·cat·ed, ·cat·ing** To communicate mutually, as between individuals, rooms, different units of an organization, factory, etc. — **in′ter·com·mu′ni·ca′tion** *n.* — **in′ter·com·mu′ni·ca′tive** *adj.*

in·ter·com·mu·ni·ty (in′tər·kə·myoo′nə·tē) *n.* Mutual community or participation.

in·ter·con·nect (in′tər·kə·nekt′) *v.t. & v.i.* To connect with one another.

in·ter·con·nect·ed (in′tər·kə·nek′tid) *adj.* So joined as to move in unison; geared: said of mechanical parts. — **in′ter·con·nec′tion** *n.*

in·ter·con·ti·nen·tal (in′tər·kon′tə·nen′təl) *adj.* Being or operating between continents: an *intercontinental* ballistic missile.

in·ter·cos·tal (in′tər·kos′təl) *adj. Anat.* Being or occurring between the ribs. — *n.* An intercostal muscle. [<NL *intercostalis* <L *inter-* between +*costa* rib] — **in′ter·cos′tal·ly** *adv.*

in·ter·course (in′tər·kôrs, -kōrs) *n.* **1** Mutual exchange; commerce; communication. **2** The interchange of ideas. **3** Sexual connection; coitus. [<OF *entrecours* <L *intercursus*, pp. of *intercurrere* run between <*inter-* between +*currere* run]

Synonyms: association, commerce, communication, communion, connection, conversation, converse, correspondence, dealing, exchange, fellowship, interchange, intercommunication, intercommunion, reciprocation, reciprocity. See CONVERSATION. *Antonyms:* alienation, avoidance, boycotting, estrangement, ostracism, reserve, reticence, silence.

in·ter·crop (in′tər·krop′) *Agric. v.t. & v.i.* **·cropped, ·crop·ping 1** To raise (one crop) between the rows of another. **2** To raise (a quick-growing crop) between the harvesting and planting of the regular crops. —*n.* (in'·tər·krop') **1** A crop cultivated between the rows of another crop. **2** A quickly maturing crop raised when ground is unoccupied by the crops grown in regular rotation.

in·ter·cur·rent (in'tər·kûr'ənt) *adj. Med.* Coming or taking place between: an *intercurrent* disease. [< L *intercurrens, -entis,* ppr. of *intercurrere* run between]

in·ter·den·tal (in'tər·den'təl) *adj.* **1** Situated between the teeth. **2** *Phonet.* Produced with the tip of the tongue between the teeth, as *th* in *thin:* also *dentilingual, linguadental.* —*n. Phonet.* An interdental consonant.

in·ter·dict (in'tər·dikt') *v.t.* **1** To prohibit or restrain authoritatively. **2** *Eccl.* To exclude from religious privileges. —*n.* **1** A prohibitive order; ban. **2** A ban formerly declared by the pope, forbidding the clergy to perform religious services or administer the sacraments under certain circumstances. **3** In ancient Roman law, an interlocutory edict of the pretor, in matters affecting right of possession. **4** In Scots law, a judicial injunction. See synonyms under PROHIBIT. [< OF *entredit* < L *interdictum,* pp. of *interdicere* forbid < *inter-* between +*dicere* say; refashioned after L] —**in·ter·dic'tion** *n.* —**in·ter·dic'tive** *adj.* —**in·ter·dic'tive·ly** *adv.* —**in·ter·dic'tor** *n.* —**in·ter·dic'to·ry** *adj.*

in·ter·est (in'tər·ist, -trist) *n.* **1** Attention with a sense of concern; lively sympathy or curiosity; also, the power to excite or hold such attention. **2** That which is of advantage or profit; benefit; also, selfish or private advantage. **3** Payment for the use of money, or money so paid; an agreed or statutory compensation accruing to a creditor during the time that a loan or debt remains unpaid, reckoned usually as a yearly percentage of the sum owed. **4** Something added in making a return; something more than is due. **5** Proprietary right or share; part ownership; participation in profit: sometimes used in the plural. **6** The persons interested in some department of work or business. **7** Power to procure favorable regard; influence. —*v.t.* (*also* in'tə·rest) **1** To excite or hold the curiosity or attention of. **2** To cause to have a share or interest in; induce to participate. **3** *Obs.* To relate to; affect; concern. [< OF < L *interest* it is of concern or advantage; 3rd person sing. of *interesse* lie between, be important < *inter-* between +*esse* be]

Synonyms (verb): amuse, attract, concern, engage, entertain, excite, hold, import, matter, occupy. *Interest* is used absolutely without a preposition, and with or without other qualification; *import* is now commonly used with a preposition and with some word or phrase indicating measure or estimate of value; as, It *imports* much to me. A matter may *interest* one financially or intellectually; in this sense the noun is commonly used; as, It is of *interest* to me. See AMUSE, CONCERN, ENTERTAIN. *Antonyms:* bore, disturb, fatigue, tire, weary, worry.

in·ter·est·ed (in'tər·is·tid, -tris-, -təres'-) *adj.* **1** Having the attention attracted or the feelings engaged. **2** Biased; not impartial. **3** Being a part owner. —**in'ter·est·ed·ly** *adv.* —**in'ter·est·ed·ness** *n.*

in·ter·est·ing (in'tər·is·ting, -tris-, -tə·res'-) *adj.* Possessing or exciting interest; attractive. —**in'ter·est·ing·ly** *adv.* —**in'ter·est·ing·ness** *n.*

in·ter·face (in'tər·fās) *n.* A surface, usually a plane surface, forming the boundary between adjacent solids, spaces, or immiscible liquids.

in·ter·fere (in'tər·fir') *v.i.* **·fered, ·fer·ing 1** To come into mutual conflict or opposition; clash. **2** To get in the way; be an obstacle or obstruction; intervene: The noise *interferes* with concentration. **3** To enter into or take part unasked in the concerns of others; meddle. **4** To strike one foot against the opposite foot or fetlock in walking or running: said of horses. **5** *Physics* To counteract one another, as waves of light, sound, or electricity. **6** In sports, to obstruct the actions of an opponent in an illegal manner. **7** In patent law, to claim priority for an invention: distinguished from *infringe.* See synonyms under INTERPOSE. [< OF (s')*entreferir* strike each other < L *inter-* between +*ferire* strike] —**in'-**

ter·fer'er *n.* —**in·ter·fer'ing·ly** *adv.*

in·ter·fer·ence (in'tər·fir'əns) *n.* **1** The act of interfering; conflict; collision. **2** *Physics* The action of two or more wave trains, as of

A   B

PATTERNS OF LIGHT INTERFERENCE
A. Interference pattern of a uniaxial crystal. *B.* Interference patterns of a biaxial crystal when the axes of the polarizer and analyzer are at right angles to each other.

light, sound, electricity, radiation, etc., which on meeting tend to neutralize or to augment each other by a combination of dissimilar or like phases. With light rays, interference may produce alternate dark and bright bands; with sound, intervals of silence, or increased volume; in radio, a disturbance in reception due to conflict of signals, etc. **3** *Aeron.* The aerodynamic influence of two or more bodies on one another. **4** In patent law, the conflict created by an application for a patent, covering, wholly or partly, any pending application or unexpired patent. **5** In sports, obstruction of the actions of an opponent in an illegal manner. **6** In football: **a** The protecting of the ball carrier from opposing tacklers. **b** The players providing this protection. See synonyms under FRICTION.

in·ter·fe·ren·tial (in'tər·fə·ren'shəl) *adj.* Of or pertaining to interference.

in·ter·fe·rom·e·ter (in'tər·fə·rom'ə·tər) *n. Physics* An instrument which utilizes the interference of light rays for the comparison of wavelengths and the measurement of very small distances: largely developed by A. A. Michelson, of Chicago. [<INTERFER(E) + -(O)METER] —**in'ter·fe·rom'e·try** *n.*

in·ter·fer·on (in'tər·fir'on) *n. Biochem.* A protein produced by virus-infected cells that halts the multiplication of the virus.

in·ter·fer·tile (in'tər·fûr'til) *adj. Biol.* Having the power to interbreed, as individuals of the same species.

in·ter·flu·ent (in·tûr'floo·ənt) *adj.* **1** Flowing between. **2** Flowing together; blending. Also **in·ter'flu·ous** (-əs). [<L *interfluens, -entis,* ppr. of *interfluere* flow between] —**in·ter'flu·ence** *n.*

in·ter·fluve (in'tər·floov) *n. Geog.* The area between two neighboring rivers or river valleys. [<INTER- + L *fluvius* stream]

in·ter·ga·lac·tic (in'tər·gə·lak'tik) *adj. Astron.* Between or among the galaxies: *intergalactic* space.

in·ter·gla·cial (in'tər·glā'shəl) *adj. Geol.* Pertaining to, or occurring in, the interval between periods of continental glaciation.

In·ter·glos·sa (in'tər·glôs'ə, -glos'ə) *n.* An international language based chiefly on Greek and Latin roots and having few grammatical inflections. [<INTER- + Gk. *glôssa* tongue]

in·ter·gra·da·tion (in'tər·grā·dā'shən) *n. Biol.* A stage or grade between two types, varieties, genetic characters, or the like.

in·ter·grade (in'tər·grād') *v.i.* **·grad·ed, ·grad·ing** To merge gradually with each other, as two varieties. —*n.* (in'tər·grād') A form transitional or intermediate between others in a graded series. —**in'ter·gra'di·ent** (-grā'dē·ənt) *adj.*

in·ter·im (in'tər·im) *n.* **1** An intermediate season; time between periods or events. **2** An interval of time; the meantime. —*adj.* For or during an intervening period of time; temporary: an *interim* appointment. [<L, meanwhile]

in·te·ri·or (in·tir'ē·ər) *adj.* **1** Existing, pertaining to, or occurring within something or between limits; internal; inner: opposed to *exterior.* **2** Inland. **3** Of a private or confidential nature. **4** Of or pertaining to spiri-

tual matters; not worldly. **5** *Astron.* Having an orbit within the earth's, as Mercury and Venus. —*n.* **1** The internal part; inside. **2** The inland or central region of a country. **3** A painted scene or drop representing the inside of a dwelling, etc. **4** The domestic affairs of a country; home ministry. **5** The spiritual nature or basic character. —**Department of the Interior** An executive department of the U.S. government (established in 1849), headed by the Secretary of the Interior, dealing with mines, government lands, parks and reservations, Indian affairs, wildlife, geological survey, etc. [<OF *interieur* <L *interior,* compar. of *inter* within] —**in·te'ri·or'i·ty** (-ôr'ə·tē, -or'-) *n.* —**in·te'ri·or·ly** *adv.*

interior angle See under ANGLE.

interior decorator One whose occupation is the furnishing and decorating of interiors of houses, offices, etc.

interior drainage Drainage whose waters are confined to and evaporate within a land area not connected with the ocean.

in·ter·ja·cent (in'tər·jā'sənt) *adj.* Situated between; intermediate. [<L *interjacens, -entis* lying between, pp. of *interjacere* <*inter-* between + *jacere* lie]

in·ter·ject (in'tər·jekt') *v.t.* To throw between other things; introduce abruptly; insert; interpose. [<L *interjectus,* pp. of *interjicere* < *inter-* between + *jacere* throw]

in·ter·jec·tion (in'tər·jek'shən) *n.* **1** *Gram.* A word expressing emotion or simple exclamation, as *oh! alas! look!:* one of the eight traditional parts of speech. **2** The act of ejaculating. **3** A sudden interposition. [<OF <L *interjectio, -onis*] —**in'ter·jec'tion·al** *adj.* —**in'·ter·jec'tion·al·ly** *adv.*

in·ter·jec·to·ry (in'tər·jek'tər·ē) *adj.* Full of interjections; also, interposed. —**in'ter·jec'·to·ri·ly** *adv.*

in·ter·ki·ne·sis (in'tər·ki·nē'sis) *n. Biol.* The pause or interval of relative quiescence between two meiotic divisions of the cell: applied particularly to the vegetative stage of the nucleus. —**in'ter·ki·net'ic** (-net'ik) *adj.*

in·ter·lace (in'tər·lās') *v.* **·laced, ·lac·ing** *v.t.* **1** To pass (branches, strips, etc.) over and under one another; interlock; lace; weave. **2** To blend; combine. **3** To mingle or cross; intersperse. —*v.i.* **4** To pass over and under one another. [<OF *entrelacier*] —**in'ter·lace'·ment** *n.*

in·ter·lam·i·nate (in'tər·lam'ə·nāt) *v.t.* **·nat·ed, ·nat·ing** To lay or insert between laminae; arrange in layers. —**in'ter·lam'i·na'tion** *n.* —**in'ter·lam'i·nar** (-nər) *adj.*

in·ter·lard (in'tər·lärd') *v.t.* **1** To scatter throughout with something different from or irrelevant to the subject or material: to *interlard* a conversation with sarcasms. **2** To insert fat, bacon, etc., into (meat) for cooking. [<MF *entrelarder*]

in·ter·leaf (in'tər·lēf') *n. pl.* **·leaves** (-lēvz') A blank leaf inserted or bound between others; also, the printed or written matter on a leaf so inserted.

in·ter·leave (in'tər·lēv') *v.t.* **·leaved, ·leav·ing 1** To insert interleaves into (a book). **2** To insert an interleaf or interleaves between (printed leaves).

in·ter·line' (in'tər·līn') *v.t.* **·lined, ·lin·ing 1** To write or print between the lines of. **2** To insert between lines. [OF *entreligner* < Med. L *interlineare* <L *inter-* between + *linea* line] —**in'ter·lin'er** *n.*

in·ter·line² (in'tər·līn') *v.t.* **·lined, ·lin·ing** To put a lining between the usual lining and the outer fabric of (a garment).

in·ter·lin·e·al (in'tər·lin'ē·əl) *adj.* **1** Interlinear. **2** Arranged in alternate lines. —**in'·ter·lin'e·al·ly** *adv.*

in·ter·lin·e·ar (in'tər·lin'ē·ər) *adj.* **1** Situated or occurring between lines: *interlinear* annotations. **2** Having translations or glosses inserted between the lines of the text. [<Med. L *interlinearis*]

in·ter·lin·e·ate (in'tər·lin'ē·āt) *v.t.* **·at·ed, ·at·ing** To interline (a book, etc.). [<Med. L *interlineatus,* pp. of *interlineare.* See INTERLINE¹.]

in·ter·lin·e·a·tion (in'tər·lin'ē·ā'shən) *n.* **1** The act or process of interlining. **2** An interpolation between lines.

in·ter·lin·ing (in'tər·lī'ning) *n.* **1** Interlineation. **2** An intermediate lining in a garment; also, the material of which it is made.

in·ter·lock (in'tər·lok') *v.t.* & *v.i.* **1** To join together; link with one another. **2** *Mech.* To connect or engage so that the operation of any part of a machine, apparatus, or system is interrelated with the operation of one or more other parts. — *n.* (in'tər·lok') The action of interlocking, or the state of being interlocked.

interlocking directorates *Econ.* Boards of directors which, through shared membership, assume dominant control of and responsibility for the operation of many separately organized and legally distinct corporations, especially when in related fields of activity.

in·ter·lo·cu·tion (in'tər·lō·kyōō'shən) *n.* Interchange of speech; dialog. [<L *interlocutio, -onis* < *interlocutus,* pp. of *interloqui* speak between < *inter-* between + *loqui* speak]

in·ter·loc·u·tor (in'tər·lok'yə·tər) *n.* **1** One who takes part in a conversation; an interpreter; questioner. **2** The center man in a minstrel troupe. [<L *interlocutus,* pp. of *interloqui* speak between, converse] — **in'ter·loc·u·tress** (-tris) *n. fem.*

in·ter·loc·u·to·ry (in'tər·lok'yə·tôr'ē, -tō'rē) *adj.* **1** Consisting of or pertaining to dialog; conversational. **2** Interposed, as in a narrative. **3** *Law* Done during pendency of a lawsuit, but not final.

in·ter·lope (in'tər·lōp') *v.i.* **·loped, ·lop·ing** **1** Originally, to engage in a commerce, trade, etc., legally belonging to others. **2** To intrude in the affairs of others. [<INTER- + *lope,* Du. *loopen* run]

in·ter·lop·er (in'tər·lō'pər) *n.* **1** One who thrusts himself into a place without right. **2** One who traffics in a trade legally belonging to others.

in·ter·lude (in'tər·lōōd) *n.* **1** An action or event considered as coming between others of greater length or importance; a differing and intervening time or space. **2** A song of the chorus in Greek drama without dialog. **3** An independent performance, usually light or humorous, introduced between the acts of a play or the parts of a performance. **4** A short passage of music played to bridge a transition; an intermezzo; also, an instrumental passage between stanzas of a hymn, between portions of a formal church service, between the acts of a play or opera, or the like. **5** Anything introduced or inserted, breaking the regular order or aspect; any intervening time or act. [<Med. L *interludium* <L *inter-* between + *ludus* a game, play < *ludere* play]

in·ter·lu·nar (in'tər·lōō'nər) *adj. Astron.* Pertaining to the period, generally about four days, between old and new moon, during which the moon is invisible, owing to its proximity to the sun. Also **in'ter·lu'na·ry.** [<L *interlunium* period between old and new moon]

in·ter·mar·riage (in'tər·mar'ij) *n.* **1** Marriage between persons of different families, races, etc. **2** Marriage between blood kindred.

in·ter·mar·ry (in'tər·mar'ē) *v.i.* **·ried, ·ry·ing** **1** To become connected by marriage: said of different clans, families, etc. **2** To marry each other: said of members of the same clan, family, etc.

in·ter·max·il·lar·y (in'tər·mak'sə·ler'ē) *adj.* **1** *Anat.* **a** Situated between the two maxillae or bones of the upper jaw. **b** Of or pertaining to one of two or more bones at the anterior and median part of the upper jaw, carrying the incisor teeth. **2** *Zool.* Situated between the maxillary lobes, as in crustaceans.

in·ter·med·dle (in'tər·med'l) *v.i.* **·dled ·dling** To interfere unduly in the affairs of others; meddle. See synonyms under INTERPOSE. [< AF *entremedler*] — **in'ter·med'dler** *n.*

in·ter·me·di·a·cy (in'tər·mē'dē·ə·sē) *n.* The state or character of being intermediate; intermediate action or agency.

in·ter·me·di·ar·y (in'tər·mē'dē·er'ē) *adj.* **1** Situated, acting, or coming between; having an intermediate function. **2** Acting as a mediator; mediatory. — *n.* **1** An intermediate agent or medium. **2** A form, stage, or product intermediate between others. [<F *intermédiaire*]

in·ter·me·di·ate (in'tər·mē'dē·it) *adj.* **1** Being in a middle place or degree. **2** Situated or occurring between limits or extremes. — *n.* (-it) **1** An intermediator; adjuster. **2** Something

intermediate. **3** A substance formed at a state between the raw material and the finished product. **4** *Chem.* An organic compound derived from coal tar or petroleum crude oil and used as a starting point in the manufacture of a wide range of drugs, cosmetics, plastics, and dyestuffs. — *v.i.* (-āt) **·at·ed, ·at·ing** To act as an intermediary; mediate. [<Med. L *intermediatus* < *intermedius*] — **in'ter·me'di·ate·ly** *adv.* — **in'ter·me'di·ate·ness** *n.*

in·ter·me·di·a·tion (in'tər·mē'dē·ā'shən) *n.* The act of intermediating; intervention.

in·ter·me·di·a·tor (in'tər·mē'dē·ā'tər) *n.* One who adjusts differences; a mediator; also, an intervening agent; intermediary. — **in'ter·me'di·a·to·ry** (-tôr'ē, -tō'rē) *adj.*

in·ter·ment (in·tûr'mənt) *n.* The act of interring; burial.

in·ter·mez·zo (in'tər·met'sō, -med'zō) *n.* *pl.* **·zos** or **·zi** (-sē, -zē) **1** A song, chorus, or short ballet given between the acts of a play or opera. **2** A short light movement connecting the main divisions of a large musical composition; also, a short piece of instrumental music composed in this style to be played independently. [<Ital. <L *intermedius* intermediate]

in·ter·mi·na·ble (in·tûr'mə·nə·bəl) *adj.* Having no limit or end; continuing for a very long time; endless. See synonyms under ETERNAL, INFINITE, PERPETUAL. [<OF] — **in·ter'mi·na·bly** *adv.*

in·ter·min·gle (in'tər·ming'gəl) *v.t.* & *v.i.* **·gled, ·gling** To mingle together; mix.

in·ter·mis·sion (in'tər·mish'ən) *n.* **1** Temporary cessation; interruption. **2** A recess; interval, as between acts in the theater; entr'acte. [<L *intermissio, -onis* < *intermissus,* pp. of *intermittere.* See INTERMIT.] — **in'ter·mis'sive** *adj.*

in·ter·mit (in'tər·mit') *v.t.* & *v.i.* **·mit·ted, ·mit·ting** To stop temporarily or at intervals; cease or interrupt; pause. See synonyms under CEASE, SUSPEND. [<L *intermittere* < *inter-* between + *mittere* send, put] — **in'ter·mit'·tence** *n.*

in·ter·mit·tent (in'tər·mit'ənt) *adj.* **1** Having periods of intermission. **2** Alternately ceasing and beginning: an *intermittent* fever. — **in'·ter·mit'tent·ly** *adv.*

intermittent current *Electr.* An interrupted current flowing in one direction.

intermittent fever *Pathol.* A fever in which the paroxysms occur at regular intervals, as in malaria. See AGUE.

in·ter·mix (in'tər·miks') *v.t.* & *v.i.* To mix together; intermingle.

in·ter·mix·ture (in'tər·miks'chər) *n.* **1** The act of mixing together, or the state of being so mixed. **2** A mass of mixed ingredients. **3** An additional ingredient; admixture.

in·ter·mod·u·late (in'tər·moj'ŏŏ·lāt) *v.t.* & *v.i.* **·lat·ed, ·lat·ing** *Electronics* To cause a reciprocal modulation of (the components of a complex wave), with the production of new waves having frequencies equal to the sums and differences of integral multiples of the original complex wave. — **in'ter·mod'u·la'tion** *n.*

in·ter·mon·tane (in'tər·mon'tān) *adj.* Situated between mountains: *intermontane* silt. Also **in'ter·moun'tain** (-moun'tən). [<INTER- + L *montanus* mountainous < *mons, montis* mountain]

in·tern (in·tûrn') *v.t.* To confine or detain within the limits of a country or area, as enemy aliens, or, in neutral countries, soldiers, ships, etc., of warring countries. — *v.i.* To undergo resident training in medicine or surgery in a hospital; be an intern. — *adj. Archaic* Internal. — *n.* (in'tûrn) **1** An advanced medical student or graduate undergoing resident training in a hospital: opposed to *extern.* **2** A person confined and segregated in wartime as a prisoner of war or enemy alien. Also **in'terne.** [<F *interne* resident within <L *internus* internal] — **in'tern·ship** (-ship) *n.*

in·ter·nal (in·tûr'nəl) *adj.* **1** Situated in or applicable to the inside; interior: opposed to *external.* **2** Pertaining to or derived from the inside; based on the thing itself; inherent. **3** Pertaining to the inner self or the mind; subjective. **4** Pertaining to the domestic affairs of a country: opposed to *external* or *foreign.* **5** *Anat.* **a** Situated relatively nearer to the median plane of the body or farther from the

surface. **b** Supplying the interior of an organ or region. See synonyms under INHERENT. — *n.* **1** A remedy to be taken internally. **2** *pl.* The internal bodily organs; entrails. **3** *pl.* The essential qualities of anything. [<LL *internalis* < *internus* < *in* in]

in·ter·nal-com·bus·tion (in·tûr'nəl·kəm·bus'chən) *adj.* Designating a type of engine in which the energy is produced by burning or exploding a mixture of compressed air and fuel, as gasoline, in one or more of its cylinders.

in·ter·nal·i·ty (in'tər·nal'ə·tē) *n.* The quality or state of lying within; inwardness; interiority.

in·ter·nal·ly (in·tûr'nəl·ē) *adv.* **1** As to the interior or inner part; interiorly: cold on the surface but hot *internally.* **2** Mentally or spiritually: *internally* content. **3** In respect to internal affairs.

internal medicine The branch of medicine which is concerned with diagnosis and treatment of internal diseases.

internal revenue See under REVENUE.

internal rime The riming of a word or group of syllables in a line of verse, as the word before the caesura, with a word or group of syllables at the end of the line or another line: also called *leonine rime.*

internal secretion *Physiol.* **1** A secretion of any one of the endocrine glands. **2** A hormone.

in·ter·na·sal (in'tər·nā'zəl) *n. Zool.* One of a pair of dermal scutes of some reptiles lying between the nasals.

in·ter·na·tion·al (in'tər·nash'ən·əl) *adj.* Pertaining to two or more nations; affecting nations generally. — *n.* A person who is a citizen of more than one nation. — **in'ter·na'·tion·al·ly** *adv.*

In·ter·na·tion·al (in'tər·nash'ən·əl) *n.* **1** One of several international organizations of socialist workers. **2** A society formed in London in 1864 for the international political organization of workingmen, in the socialistic conflict with capital, of which Karl Marx was the dominant spirit; its full title was the **International Workingmen's Association:** last convention in Philadelphia, 1876. **3** See INTERNATIONALE. —**Second International** An organization, formed in 1889, to replace the First International, from which the Third International seceded: also called **Socialist International.** —**Third** or **Red International** A socialist workers' organization proclaimed in Russia March 5, 1919, representing twelve countries: dissolved in 1943: also called *Comintern.*

international candle A candela.

In·ter·na·tio·nale (in'tər·nash'ən·əl, *Fr.* an·ter·nà·syô·nàl') A French song written by Eugene Pottier in 1871 and adopted as a revolutionary hymn by French Socialists and those of other European countries: the national anthem of Soviet Russia until 1944, and still popular as a workers' song: usually written *L'Internationale.* [<F]

in·ter·na·tion·al·ism (in'tər·nash'ən·əl·iz'əm) *n.* **1** The character of being related to more nations than one or to nations generally. **2** The doctrine that common interest, mutual understanding, and friendly dependence among nations can be the foundation of world-wide equality, justice, and peace: opposed to *nationalism.* **3** The doctrine of a workers' international socialistic organization for the betterment of workers throughout the world. — **in'ter·na'tion·al·ist** *n.* — **in'ter·na'·tion·al'i·ty** *n.*

in·ter·na·tion·al·ize (in'tər·nash'ən·əl·īz') *v.t.* **·ized, ·iz·ing** To make international, as in character or administration. — **in'ter·na'tion·al·i·za'tion** *n.*

International Labor Organization A permanent administrative association of 77 nations including the United States, constituting a specialized agency of the United Nations, with tripartite representation of workers, employers, and governments, working for the improvement of labor conditions in member nations, and functioning through the **International Labor Conference** and the **International Labor Office.** Commonly known as the ILO.

International Morse code A variation, differing in eleven letters, of the telegraphic code devised by S. F. B. Morse: also called **continental Morse code.**

International News Service An organization for collecting news and distributing it to member newspapers. Abbr. *INS, I.N.S.*

International Phonetic Alphabet The alphabet of the International Phonetic Association (a society founded in 1886), in which the speech sounds of a language can be transcribed. Each of the symbols of this alphabet represents a specific sound, distinguished as to place and manner of articulation, regardless of the language being recorded. *Abbr. IPA.* See chart on page 665.

in·terne (in'tûrn) *n.* **1** Intern. **2** The inner nature: poetical usage. [<F]

in·ter·ne·cine (in'tər·nē'sin, -sīn) *adj.* Involving mutual slaughter; sanguinary. [<L *inter necinus* < *internecare* kill, slaughter < *inter-* among + *necare* kill]

in·tern·ee (in'tûr·nē') *n.* An interned person. [<INTERN + -EE]

in·tern·ist (in·tûr'nist) *n.* A specialist in internal medicine. [<INTERN(AL) + -IST]

in·tern·ment (in·tûrn'mənt) *n.* The act of interning; the state of being interned.

internment camp A military station for the detention of prisoners of war and enemy aliens.

in·ter·no·dal (in'tər·nōd'l) *adj.* **1** Of or pertaining to an internode. **2** Situated between two nodes or joints. — *n.* An internodal joint.

in·ter·node (in'tər·nōd') *n.* **1** *Anat.* A part situated between two joints or nodes, as a phalanx or other segment of a limb. **2** *Bot.* The part of a plant stem between the nodes or places from which the leaves grow. **3** *Ornithol.* In a feather, the contracted part between the roots of the barbs. **4** The part of a vibrating string between two nodes. [<L *internodium* < *inter-* between + *nodus* node]

in·ter nos (in'tər nōs') *Latin* Between ourselves.

in·ter·nun·ci·o (in'tər·nun'shē·ō) *n.* *pl.* **·ci·os** **1** A diplomatic representative of the pope in countries not represented by a papal nuncio. **2** A go-between; messenger between two parties. [<Ital. <L *inter-* between + *nuntius* messenger] — **in'ter·nun'cial** (-shəl) *adj.*

in·ter·o·cep·tor (in'tər·ə·sep'tər) *n.* *Physiol.* A peripheral sense organ excited by internal stimuli arising chiefly within the viscera: also spelled *enteroceptor.* Compare EXTEROCEPTOR. [< *intero-* <INTERNAL + (RE)CEPTOR] — **in'ter·o·cep'tive** *adj.*

in·ter·or·bi·tal (in'tər·ôr'bə·təl) *adj.* *Anat.* Situated between the orbits of the eyes.

in·ter·os·cu·late (in'tər·os'kyə·lāt) *v.i.* **1** To form a connecting link, as between objects, genera, etc.; osculate. **2** To inosculate with each other; interpenetrate. — **in'ter·os'cu·la'·tion** *n.*

in·ter·os·se·ous (in'tər·os'ē·əs) *adj.* *Anat.* Pertaining to structures situated between bones: an *interosseous* membrane.

in·ter·pel·lant (in'tər·pel'ənt) *adj.* Causing interpellation. — *n.* One who interpellates: also **in·ter·pel·la·tor** (in'tər·pə·lā'tər, in·tûr'pə·lā'tər). [<L *interpellans, -antis,* ppr. of *interpellare.* See INTERPELLATE.]

in·ter·pel·late (in'tər·pel'āt, in·tûr'pə·lāt) *v.t.* **·lat·ed, ·lat·ing** To subject to an interpellation. [<L *interpellatus,* pp. of *interpellare* interrupt by speaking < *inter-* between + *pellere* drive]

in·ter·pel·la·tion (in'tər·pə·lā'shən, in·tûr'-) *n.* A formal demand upon a member of a government to explain an official action or policy. [<L *interpellatio, -onis*]

in·ter·pen·e·trate (in'tər·pen'ə·trāt) *v.* **·trat·ed, ·trat·ing** *v.t.* **1** To penetrate thoroughly; pervade; permeate. **2** To penetrate mutually. — *v.i.* **3** To penetrate each other. **4** To penetrate between or among parts or things. — **in'ter·pen'e·tra'tion** *n.*

in·ter·per·son·al (in'tər·pûr'sən·əl) *adj.* Existing between people: *interpersonal* relations.

in·ter·phone (in'tər·fōn') *n.* A telephone for use exclusively within a building, office, ship, airplane, etc.

in·ter·plane (in'tər·plān') *adj.* *Aeron.* Situated or placed between the wings of an airplane.

in·ter·plan·e·tary (in'tər·plan'ə·ter'ē) *adj.* Between or among planets: *interplanetary* travel.

in·ter·play (in'tər·plā') *n.* Action or movement between parts of something, as parts of a machine; mutual or reciprocal action or influence. — *v.i.* (in'tər·plā') To exert influence reciprocally.

in·ter·plead (in'tər·plēd') *v.i.* *Law* To litigate adverse claims by bill of interpleader. [<AF *entrepleder*]

in·ter·plead·er (in'tər·plē'dər) *n.* *Law* A proceeding in which one who has money or goods claimed by two or more persons may ask that the claimants be required to litigate the title between themselves.

in·ter·po·late (in·tûr'pə·lāt) *v.* **·lat·ed, ·lat·ing** *v.t.* **1** To alter, as a manuscript, by the insertion of new or unauthorized matter; corrupt. **2** To insert (such matter). **3** To put (something different or irrelevant) between other things; intercalate; interpose. **4** *Math.* **a** To compute intermediate values of a quantity between a series of given values: distinguished

---

THE INTERNATIONAL PHONETIC ALPHABET.
(Revised to 1951.)

		Bi-labial	Labio-dental	Dental and Alveolar	Retroflex	Palato-alveolar	Alveolo-palatal	Palatal	Velar	Uvular	Pharyngal	Glottal
CONSONANTS	Plosive . . .	p b		t d	ʈ ɖ			c ɟ	k g	q ɢ		ʔ
	Nasal . . .	m	ɱ	n	ɳ			ɲ	ŋ	N		
	Lateral Fricative .			ɬ ɮ								
	Lateral Non-fricative .			l	ɭ			ʎ				
	Rolled . . .			r						R		
	Flapped . . .			ɾ	ɽ					R		
	Fricative . . .	ɸ β	f v	θ ð s z ɹ	ʂ ʐ	ʃ ʒ	ɕ ʑ	ç j	x ɣ	χ ʁ	ħ ʕ	h ɦ
	Frictionless Continuants and Semi-vowels	w ɥ	ʋ	ɹ				j (ɥ)	(w)	ʁ		

		Front		Central		Back	
VOWELS	Close . . . . (y ʉ u)	i y		ɨ ʉ		ɯ u	
	Half-close . . . (ø o)	e ø				ɤ o	
				ə			
	Half-open . . . (œ ɔ)	ɛ œ		ɜ		ʌ ɔ	
				æ	ɐ		
	Open . . . . (ɒ)			a		ɑ ɒ	

(Secondary articulations are shown by symbols in brackets.)

OTHER SOUNDS.—Palatalized consonants: ţ, ḑ, etc.; palatalized ʃ, ʒ: ʆ, ʓ. Velarized or pharyngalized consonants: ɫ, đ, ʐ, etc. Ejective consonants (with simultaneous glottal stop): p', t', etc. Implosive voiced consonants: ɓ, ɗ, etc. ɼ fricative trill. σ, ʚ (labialized θ, ð, or s, z). ʃ, ʒ (labialized ʃ, ʒ). ɿ, ʅ, ʮ (clicks, Zulu c, q, x). ɹ (a sound between r and l). ŋ Japanese syllabic nasal. ʓ (combination of x and ʃ). ʍ (voiceless w). ɪ, ʏ, ʊ (lowered varieties of i, y, u). з (a variety of ə). ɵ (a vowel between ø and o).

Affricates are normally represented by groups of two consonants (ts, tʃ, dʒ, etc.), but, when necessary, ligatures are used (ʦ, ʧ, ʤ, etc.), or the marks ◠ or ◡ (t͡s or t͜s, etc.). ◠ ◡ also denote synchronic articulation (m͡ŋ = simultaneous m and ŋ). ɕ, ʝ may occasionally be used in place of tʃ, dʒ, and ʃ, ʒ for ts, dz. Aspirated plosives: ph, th, etc. r-coloured vowels: ɛɹ, aɹ, ɔɹ, etc., or ɛ˞, a˞, ɔ˞, etc., or ɚ, a̱, ə, etc.; r-coloured ə: ɹ or ə˞ or ɹ or ɐ or ə.

LENGTH, STRESS, PITCH.— : (full length). · (half length). ' (stress, placed at beginning of the stressed syllable). ˌ (secondary stress). ˉ (high level pitch); ˍ (low level); ´ (high rising); ˏ (low rising); ˋ (high falling); ˎ (low falling); ^ (rise-fall); ˅ (fall-rise).

MODIFIERS.— ˜ nasality. ˳ breath (l̥ = breathed l). ˬ voice (ş = z). ' slight aspiration following p, t, etc. ˷ labialization (n̫ = labialized n). ˵ dental articulation (ţ = dental t). ˙ palatalization (ż = ʑ). ˴ specially close vowel (e̝ = a very close e). ˛ specially open vowel (e̞ = a rather open e). ꓸ tongue raised (e꓿ or e̝ = ẹ). ꓹ tongue lowered (e꓿ or e̞ = e̜). + tongue advanced (u+ or ṵ = an advanced u, ţ = t̪). - or ꓺ tongue retracted (i- or i꓿ = ɨ, t̠ = alveolar t). ꓹ lips more rounded. ꓻ lips more spread. Central vowels: ɪ(= ɨ), ʊ(= ʉ), ë(= ə꓿), ö(= ɵ), ɛ̈, ö̞. ˌ (e.g. ŋ̩) syllabic consonant. ˘ consonantal vowel. ʆ variety of ʃ resembling s, etc.

Courtesy, Association Phonétique Internationale

---

from *extrapolate*. **b** To insert (an intermediate term or terms) in a series. — *v.i.* **5** To make interpolations. [<L *interpolatus*, pp. of *interpolare* polish, form anew <*interpolis* refurbished, vamped up <*inter-* between + root of *polire* polish] — **in·ter·po·la·tion** *n.* — **in·ter·po·la·tive** *adj.* — **in·ter·po·la·tor, in·ter·po·lat·er** *n.*

in·ter·pose (in'tər·pōz') *v.* **·posed, ·pos·ing** *v.t.* **1** To place between other things; insert. **2** To put forward or introduce by way of intervention or interference: He *interposed* his authority. **3** To put in or inject, as a remark, into a conversation, argument, etc. — *v.i.* **4** To come between; intervene. **5** To put in a remark; interrupt. [<F *interposer* place between <*inter-* between (<L) + *poser*. See POSE¹.] — **in·ter·po'sal** *n.* — **in·ter·pos'er** *n.* — **in·ter·pos'ing·ly** *adv.*

Synonyms: arbitrate, intercede, intercept, interfere, intermeddle, interrupt, meddle, mediate. To *interpose* is to place or come between other things or persons, usually as a means of obstruction or prevention of some effect or result that might otherwise occur. *Intercede* and *interpose* are used in a good sense; *intermeddle* always in a bad sense, and *interfere* frequently so. To *intercede* is to come between persons who are at variance, and plead with the stronger in behalf of the weaker. To *intermeddle* is to thrust oneself into the concerns of others with officiousness; *meddling* commonly arises from idle curiosity. To *interfere* is to intrude into others' affairs with more serious purpose, with or without acknowledged right or propriety. *Intercept* is applied to an object that may be seized or stopped while in transit; as, to *intercept* a letter or a messenger; *interrupt* is applied to an action which might or should be continuous, but is broken in upon (L *rumpere* to break) by some disturbing power. One who *arbitrates* or *mediates* must do so by the request or at least with the consent of the contending parties; the other words of the group imply that he steps in of his own accord. *Antonyms*: avoid, retire, withdraw.

in·ter·po·si·tion (in'tər·pə·zish'ən) *n.* **1** The act of interposing. **2** That which is interposed. **3** In U.S. political theory, the doctrine and practice of interposing the sovereign powers of a State between the people of that State and the enforcement of a Federal statute or judicial ruling that is deemed by the State government to infringe upon its sovereignty and the autonomy of its institutions. [<OF]

in·ter·pret (in·tûr'prit) *v.t.* **1** To give the meaning of; explain or make clear; elucidate: to *interpret* Scripture. **2** To derive a particular understanding of; give a certain explanation to; construe: We *interpreted* his silence as pride. **3** To bring out the meaning of by artistic representation or performance. **4** To translate. — *v.i.* **5** To act as interpreter. **6** To explain. [<F *interpréter* <L *interpretatus*, pp. of *interpretari* <*interpres* agent, interpreter] — **in·ter'pret·a·ble** *adj.* — **in·ter'pret·a·bil'i·ty, in·ter'pret·a·ble·ness** *n.*

Synonyms: construe, decipher, define, elucidate, explain, explicate, expound, render, translate, unfold, unravel. See synonyms for DEFINITION, SOLVE. *Antonyms*: confound, confuse, darken, distort, falsify, involve, jumble, mingle, misinterpret, misread, misrepresent, mistake, misunderstand, mix, perplex.

in·ter·pre·ta·tion (in·tûr'prə·tā'shən) *n.* **1** The act of interpreting. **2** The sense given by an interpreter or an expositor; meaning. **3** Histrionic or artistic representation. See synonyms under DEFINITION. — **authentic interpretation** *Law* An interpretation made by the author himself. — **close interpretation** *Law* One in which the words are taken in their narrowest meaning. — **extravagant interpretation** *Law* One which substitutes a broader meaning for the true one. — **free interpretation** *Law* One made in good faith but uncontrolled by any specific principle. — **judicial interpretation** *Law* Judge-made rulings construing the meaning and purport of a statute; the act of making such rulings. [<F] — **in·ter'pre·ta'tion·al** *adj.*

in·ter·pre·ta·tive (in·tûr'prə·tā'tiv) *adj.* **1** Designed or fitted to interpret; explanatory; defining. **2** Containing an interpretation; embodying ideas or facts; significative. **3**

Admitting of interpretation; constructive. Also **in·ter'pre·tive.** — **in·ter'pre·ta'tive·ly** *adv.*

in·ter·pret·er (in·tûr'prit·ər) *n.* One who interprets or translates; specifically, one who serves as oral translator between people speaking different languages. [<OF *interpreteur* <LL *interpretor*]

in·ter·ra·di·al (in'tər·rā'dē·əl) *adj.* Between rays or radii.

in·ter·reg·num (in'tər·reg'nəm) *n.* **1** The time during which a throne is vacant. **2** A suspension of executive authority through a change of government. **3** Any period of abeyance or derangement.· **4** In Roman history, the interval filled by an interrex. [<L *interregnum* <*inter-* between + *regnum* reign]

in·ter·re·late (in'tər·ri·lāt') *v.t.* & *v.i.* **·lat·ed ·lat·ing** To bring or come into reciprocal relation.

in·ter·re·lat·ed (in'tər·ri·lā'tid) *adj.* Reciprocally related.

in·ter·re·la·tion (in'tər·ri·lā'shən) *n.* Mutual or reciprocal relation. — **in'ter·re·la'tion·ship** *n.*

in·ter·rex (in'tər·reks) *n.* *pl.* **in·ter·re·ges** (in'·tər·rē'jēz) One who governs during an interregnum; specifically, in Roman history, one of the magistrates appointed to govern during a vacancy on the throne or in the consulate. [<L *interrex* <*inter-* between + *rex* king]

in·ter·ro·gate (in·ter'ə·gāt) *v.* **·gat·ed, ·gat·ing** *v.t.* To put questions to; question. — *v.i.* To ask questions. See synonyms under EXAMINE, INQUIRE, QUESTION. [<L *interrogatus*, pp. of *interrogare* <*inter-* between + *rogare* ask]

in·ter·ro·ga·tion (in·ter'ə·gā'shən) *n.* **1** The act of interrogating. **2** A question; query. **3** An interrogation point. **4** *Telecom.* The transmission of a signal pulse or combination of such pulses by an interrogator. See synonyms under INQUIRY, QUESTION.

interrogation point A mark of punctuation (?) indicating that the foregoing sentence asks a direct question: sometimes called *question mark.* Also **interrogation mark.**

in·ter·rog·a·tive (in'tə·rog'ə·tiv) *adj.* **1** Denoting inquiry; questioning. **2** *Gram.* Of or pertaining to a word, phrase, or sentence which asks a question. — *n. Gram.* A word, phrase, or sentence used to ask a question, as *who, whose book, Who is there?* [<L *interrogativus*] — **in'ter·rog'a·tive·ly** *adv.*

in·ter·ro·ga·tor (in·ter'ə·gā'tər) *n.* **1** One who or that which interrogates. **2** *Telecom.* A device for transmitting pulses of challenge or inquiry to a transponder: usually connected with a responser for receiving and displaying the return pulses.

in·ter·rog·a·to·ry (in'tə·rog'ə·tôr'ē, -tō'rē) *adj.* Pertaining to, expressing, or implying a question; interrogative. — *n.* A question; interrogation. See synonyms under INQUIRY, QUESTION. — **in'ter·rog'a·to·ri·ly** (-tôr'ə·lē, -tō'rə-) *adv.*

in·ter·rupt (in'tə·rupt') *v.t.* **1** To cause a delay or break in: to *interrupt* service; hinder the doing or completion of: to *interrupt* a speech. **2** To break the continuity, course, or sameness of: to *interrupt* work or a speech. **3** To break in on (someone) talking, working, etc. — *v.i.* **4** To break in upon an action or speech. See synonyms under HINDER¹, INTERPOSE, OBSTRUCT, SUSPEND. [<L *interruptus*, pp. of *interrumpere* <*inter-* between + *rumpere* break]

in·ter·rupt·ed (in'tə·rup'tid) *adj.* **1** Broken in upon; irregular; intermittent. **2** *Bot.* Suddenly or abruptly stopped. — **in'ter·rupt'ed·ly** *adv.*

in·ter·rup·tion (in'tə·rup'shən) *n.* **1** The act of interrupting. **2** The state of being interrupted; breach in continuity; an interval. **3** Obstruction caused by breaking in upon any course, progress, or motion; hindrance; stop; check. **4** In Scots law, the legal step necessary to terminate a period of prescription; exception or reply against prescription. **5** An intermission; a temporary cessation.

in·ter·rup·tive (in'tə·rup'tiv) *adj.* Tending to interrupt; interrupting. — **in'ter·rup'tive·ly** *adv.*

in·ter se (in'tər sē') *Latin* Between (or among) themselves.

in·ter·sect (in'tər·sekt') *v.t.* To pass across; cut through or into so as to divide. — *v.i.* To cross each other. [<L *intersectus*, pp. of *intersecare* <*inter-* between + *secare* cut]

in·ter·sec·tion (in'tər·sek'shən) *n.* **1** The act of intersecting. **2** A place of crossing. [<L

intersectio, -onis]

in·ter·sex (in'tər·seks') *n. Biol.* An individual, usually sterile, showing biological characteristics of both sexes. — **in'ter·sex'u·al** *adj.* — **in'ter·sex'u·al'i·ty** *n.*

in·ter·space (in'tər·spās') *v.t.* **·spaced, ·spac·ing 1** To make spaces between. **2** To occupy spaces between. — *n.* (in'tər·spās') Intervening room; space between.

in·ter·sperse (in'tər·spûrs') *v.t.* **·spersed, ·spers·ing 1** To scatter among other things; set here and there. **2** To diversify or adorn with other things scattered here and there. [<L *interspersus*, pp. of *interspergere* <*inter-* among + *spargere* scatter] — **in'ter·spers'ed·ly** *adv.* — **in'ter·sper'sion** (-spûr'zhən) *n.*

in·ter·state (in'tər·stāt') *adj.* Between different States, as of the United States, or their citizens: *interstate* commerce.

in·ter·stice (in·tûr'stis) *n.* **1** An opening in anything. **2** A narrow space between adjoining parts or things. **3** A crack; crevice; chink; cranny. **4** An interval of time; specifically, the interval that canon law requires between promotions from one order to another in the Roman Catholic Church. [<F <L *interstitium* <*interstitus*, pp. of *intersistere* stand between <*inter-* between + *sistere* cause to stand <*stare* stand]

in·ter·sti·tial (in'tər·stish'əl) *adj.* **1** Pertaining to, existing in, or forming an interstice. **2** *Biol.* Situated within the tissues of an organ or part; interstitial cells. [<L *interstitus*] — **in'ter·sti'tial·ly** *adv.*

in·ter·tex·ture (in'tər·teks'chər) *n.* **1** The act of interweaving. **2** The web or tissue interwoven.

in·ter·twine (in'tər·twīn') *v.t.* & *v.i.* **·twined, ·twin·ing** To unite by twisting or interlacing.

in·ter·ur·ban (in'tər·ûr'bən) *adj.* Between cities.

in·ter·val (in'tər·vəl) *n.* **1** An open space between two objects; distance between points; intervening room. **2** The degree of difference between objects. **3** The time that intervenes between two events or periods or between a state or condition and its recurrence. **4** *U.S. & Can.* Intervale. **5** *Music* **a** The difference in pitch between two tones sounded in succession.

MUSICAL INTERVALS

1. Prime or unison. 2. Augmented prime. 3. Minor second. 4. Major second. 5. Augmented second. 6. Minor third. 7. Major third. 8. Perfect fourth. 9. Augmented fourth. 10. Diminished fifth. 11. Perfect fifth. 12. Augmented fifth. 13. Minor sixth. 14. Major sixth. 15. Augmented sixth. 16. Minor seventh. 17. Major seventh. 18. Diminished octave. 19. Octave. On a keyboard instrument where mechanical limitations make it necessary to make one tone serve for two slightly different ones, some of the intervals above appear identical, as 5 and 6.

b The difference in pitch of tones sounded at or near the same time. — **augmented interval** A musical interval longer than the indicated standard by a half-step or semitone. — **diminished interval** An interval that is a half-step shorter than the perfect or minor interval indicated. — **harmonic interval** An interval in which the tones are simultaneous. — **inverted interval** A simple interval in which the lower tone is transposed an octave upward, or the upper tone an octave downward. — **melodic interval** An interval in which the tones are successive. — **perfect interval.** An interval admitting of no change without destroying the consonance, as the prime, fourth, fifth, and octave. [<OF *entreval, intervalle* <L *intervallum* between the ramparts <*inter-* between + *vallum* rampart]

Pertaining to or designating a cross between two varieties, strains, or breeds of the same species.

in·ter·vene (in′tər·vēn′) *v.i.* **·vened, ·ven·ing** **1** To come between by action or authority; interfere or mediate: The king *intervened* in the quarrel. **2** To occur, as something irrelevant or unexpected, so as to influence or modify an action, result, etc.: I will come if nothing *intervenes*. **3** To be located between; lie between. **4** To take place between other events or times; happen in the meantime: Many years *intervened*. **5** *Law* To interpose in a lawsuit so as to become a party to it. [<L *intervenire* <*inter-* between + *venire* come] — **in′ter·ven′er** *n.* — **in′ter·ven′ient** (-vēn′yənt) *adj.*

in·ter·ven·tion (in′tər·ven′shən) *n.* **1** The act of intervening or coming between. **2** Interference with the acts of others. **3** *Law* The becoming or applying to become a party to a suit in which the applicant has an interest. **4** In international law, interference in the affairs of one country by another by force or threat of force. **5** An intervening time, event, or thing. [<LL *interventio, -onis* <*interventus*, pp. of *intervenire* intervene] — **in′ter·ven′tion·al** *adj.*

in·ter·ven·tion·ist (in′tər·ven′shən·ist) *n.* One who advocates intervention, as in the affairs of another state.

in·ter·view (in′tər·vyōō) *n.* **1** A meeting of two persons, as by appointment. **2** Specifically, in journalism, a colloquy with one whose views are sought for publication. **3** The report of such a colloquy. — *v.t.* To have an interview with. [<MF *entrevu*, pp. of *entrevoir* glimpse, *s'entrevoir* see each other <L *inter-* between + *videre* see] — **in′ter·view′er** *n.*

in·ter·volve (in′tər·volv′) *v.t.* & *v.i.* **·volved, ·volv·ing** To wind or coil one within another; involve or be involved with each other. [<INTER- + L *volvere* roll]

in·ter·weave (in′tər·wēv′) *v.t.* & *v.i.* **·wove** or **·weaved, ·wo·ven** (*Obs.* ·wove), **·weav·ing** To weave together; intermingle or connect closely; interlace; blend.

in·tes·ta·ble (in·tes′tə·bəl) *adj.* Legally disqualified from making a will, as a lunatic. [<LL *intestabilis.* See INTESTATE.]

in·tes·ta·cy (in·tes′tə·sē) The condition resulting from one's dying intestate: opposed to *testacy.*

in·tes·tate (in·tes′tāt) *adj.* **1** Not having made a valid will. **2** Not legally devised or disposed of by will. — *n.* A person who dies intestate. [<L *intestatus* <*in-* not + *testatus*, pp. of *testari* make a will <*testis* witness]

in·tes·ta·tion (in′tes·tā′shən) *n.* *Law* **1** Testamentary incapacity. **2** Withdrawal of the right to make a will.

in·tes·tine (in·tes′tin) *n.* *Anat.* That part of the alimentary canal between the pylorus and the anus; bowel. In man the small intestine, divided into *duodenum, jejunum*, and *ileum*, is the upper part, and is much convoluted; the large intestine is of greater caliber, and is divided into *cecum, colon*, and *rectum.*

HUMAN INTESTINES
a. Duodenum. *b.* Small intestine. *c.* Colon. *d.* Vermiform appendix.

◆ Collateral adjective: *alvine.* — *adj.* **1** Internal with regard to state or community; domestic; civil. **2** Pertaining to the interior. [<L *intestinus* internal <*intus* within <*in* in] — **in·tes′ti·nal** *adj.*

in·ti·ma (in′tə·mə) *n. pl.* **·mae** (-mē) **1** *Anat.* The internal coat of a·part or organ, as of a lymphatic, blood vessel, intestine, or artery. **2** *Entomol.* The lining membrane of the trachea of an insect. [<NL <L *intimus* innermost. See INTIMATE[1].] — **in′ti·mal** *adj.*

in·ti·ma·cy (in′tə·mə·sē) *n. pl.* **·cies** **1** Close or confidential friendship. **2** An intimate act; especially, illicit sexual connection: a euphemistic use. See synonyms under ACQUAINTANCE.

in·ti·mate[1] (in′tə·mit) *adj.* **1** Closely connected

by friendship or association; personal; confidential. **2** Pertaining to the inmost being; innermost; indwelling; *intimate* knowledge. **3** Adhering closely; close: *intimate* union. **4** Proceeding from within; inward; internal: an *intimate* impulse. **5** Having illicit sexual relations (with): a euphemism. — *n.* A close or confidential friend. [<F *intime* <L *intimus*, superl. of *intus* within] — **in′ti·mate·ly** *adv.*

in·ti·mate[2] (in′tə·māt) *v.t.* **·mat·ed, ·mat·ing** **1** To make known without direct statement; hint; imply. **2** *Rare* To make known formally; declare. [<L *intimatus*, pp. of *intimare* announce <*intimus*, superl. of *intus* within]

in·ti·ma·tion (in′tə·mā′shən) *n.* **1** Information communicated indirectly; a hint. **2** A declaration or notification. See synonyms under SUGGESTION. [<F]

in·tim·i·date (in·tim′ə·dāt) *v.t.* **·dat·ed, ·dat·ing** **1** To make timid; cause fear in; cow. **2** To force or restrain by threats or violence. See synonyms under FRIGHTEN. [<Med. L *intimidatus*, pp. of *intimidare* <L *in-* very + *timidus* afraid] — **in·tim′i·da′tor** *n.*

in·tim·i·da·tion (in·tim′ə·dā′shən) *n.* **1** The use of violence or threats to influence the conduct of another. **2** The state of being intimidated.

in·tinc·tion (in·tingk′shən) *n. Eccl.* A method of administering both elements of the Eucharist at once, by dipping the bread into the wine. [<L *intinctio, -onis* <*intinctus*, pp. of *intingere* dip in <*in-* in + *tingere* tinge]

in·tine (in′tin, -tīn) *n. Bot.* The inner coating of the wall of a pollen grain. [<L *intus* within]

in·ti·tle (in·tīt′l) See ENTITLE.

in·tit·ule (in·tit′yōōl) *v.t.* **·uled, ·ul·ing** To give a title or designation to. [<F *intituler* <LL *intitulare* <L *in-* in, on + *titulus* title]

in·to (in′tōō) *prep.* **1** To or toward the inside of; penetrating or entering within: Come *into* the house. **2** Extending within (a period of time): talking well *into* the night. **3** So as to become: Boiling changes water *into* steam. **4** *Math.* Dividing: Two *into* six is three. **5** As an addition to: *into* the bargain. **6** In the direction of: *into* the northwest. **7** To the practice or study of: to go *into* medicine. **8** *Slang* Actively engaged or involved with, as an interest or enthusiasm: He's *into* oriental religion. [OE]

Synonyms: in, to. *Into* is the preposition of tendency, direction, destination, etc.; *in* is that of condition, state, position, or situation. *Into* should be used and not *in*, when entrance or insertion is intended; *into* indicates motion, change, entrance, in a more marked degree than *in*. "I throw the stone *into* the water, and it lies *in* the water." Used adverbially *in* follows verbs of motion, as *come, go, walk*, and such use has established certain phrases as idioms. One says, "Come *in* the house" but the preferred expression is "Come *into* the house." Where no object is expressed, we say "come *in*," "go *in*." *Antonyms:* beyond, by, from, out, past, through.

in·tol·er·a·ble (in·tol′ər·ə·bəl) *adj.* Not tolerable; that cannot be borne or endured; insufferable. — *adv. Obs.* Intolerably. — **in·tol′er·a·bil′i·ty, in·tol′er·a·ble·ness** *n.* — **in·tol′er·a·bly** *adv.*

in·tol·er·ance (in·tol′ər·əns) *n.* **1** Refusal to tolerate opposing beliefs; bigotry. **2** Incapacity or unwillingness to bear or endure. Also **in·tol′er·an·cy.** See synonyms under FANATICISM.

in·tol·er·ant (in·tol′ər·ənt) *adj.* **1** Not disposed to tolerate contrary beliefs or opinions; bigoted. **2** Unable or unwilling to bear or endure: with *of: intolerant* of opposition. — **in·tol′er·ant·ly** *adv.*

in·tomb (in·tōōm′), **in·tomb·ment** (in·tōōm′mənt), etc. See ENTOMB, etc.

in·to·nate (in′tō·nāt) *v.t.* **·nat·ed, ·nat·ing** **1** To intone. **2** To sound the tones of the musical scale, as in sol-faing. [<Med. L *intonatus*, pp. of *intonare* intone, thunder <*in-* in + L *tonus* tone]

in·to·na·tion (in′tō·nā′shən) *n.* **1** The modulation of the voice in speaking: distinguished from *articulation*: Her *intonation* is soft and sweet. **2** The act of intoning, as of the church service by a priest. **3** *Music* Production of tones, as by the voice, especially in regard to precision of tone. **4** In plain song, the notes

leading up to the reciting tone: commonly sung by a single voice.

in·tone (in·tōn′) *v.* **·toned, ·ton·ing** *v.t.* **1** To utter or recite in a musical monotone: chant. **2** To give particular tones or intonation to. — *v.i.* **3** To utter a musical monotone; chant. [<MF *entonner* <Med. L *intonare*. See INTONATE.] — **in·ton′er** *n.*

in·tox·i·cate (in·tok′sə·kāt) *v.t.* **·cat·ed, ·cat·ing** **1** To make drunk; inebriate. **2** To elate or excite to a degree of frenzy. **3** To poison, as by bacterial toxins, serum injections, drugs, alcohol, etc. — *adj.* (-kit) Drunk; intoxicated. [<Med. L *intoxicatus*, pp. of *intoxicare* poison, drug <L *toxicum* poison] — **in·tox′i·cant** *adj.* & *n.* — **in·tox′i·ca′tion** *n.* — **in·tox′i·ca′tive** *adj.*

intra– *prefix* Within; inside of. [<L *intra-* <*intra* within]

in·tra–a·tom·ic (in′trə·ə·tom′ik) *adj. Physics* Within an atom or atoms; pertaining to atomic structure.

in·trac·ta·ble (in·trak′tə·bəl) *adj.* **1** Not tractable; refractory; unruly. **2** Lacking plastic quality; difficult to treat or work. See synonyms under IMPRACTICABLE, OBSTINATE, PERVERSE, REBELLIOUS, RESTIVE. — **in·trac′ta·bil′i·ty, in·trac′ta·ble·ness** *n.* — **in·trac′ta·bly** *adv.*

in·tra·dos (in·trā′dos) *n. Archit.* The interior or lower surface of an arch or vault. See illustration under ARCH. [<F *intrados* <L *intra-* within + F *dos* back <L *dorsum*]

in·tra·mo·lec·u·lar (in′trə·mə·lek′yə·lər) *adj. Chem.* Pertaining to or occurring in the interior of a molecule.

in·tra·mu·ral (in′trə·myōōr′əl) *adj.* **1** Situated within the walls of a city. **2** *Anat.* Situated within the walls of a hollow organ. **3** Taking place within the confines of an educational institution: *intramural* football: opposed to *extramural.*

in·tra·mus·cu·lar (in′trə·mus′kyə·lər) *adj. Anat.* Within a muscle or muscular tissue, as an injection.

in·tra·na·tion·al (in′trə·nash′ən·əl) *adj.* Situated within or relating to matters within a nation: opposed to *international.*

in·tran·si·gent (in·tran′sə·jənt) *adj.* Refusing to agree or compromise; irreconcilable. — *n.* One who is intransigent; a radical or revolutionary: also **in·tran′si·gent·ist.** Also *French* **in·tran·si·geant** (aṅ·trän·sē·zhäṅ′). [<F *intransigeant* <Sp. *intransigente* <L *in-* not + *transigens, -entis*, ppr. of *transigere* agree. See TRANSACT.] — **in·tran′si·gence** *n.*

in·tran·si·tive (in·tran′sə·tiv) *Gram. adj.* **1** Not taking or requiring an object, as certain verbs. **2** Of or pertaining to such verbs. — *n.* An intransitive verb. — **in·tran′si·tive·ly** *adv.*

intransitive verb A verb whose action is not transferred to an object but terminates in the subject or doer. *Waits, sleeps, dreams, grows*, are intransitive in the following: the man waits, he sleeps, he dreams, the grass grows. Intransitive verbs become transitive only with a cognate object: I dreamed a dream; to sleep the sleep of the just; to die a soldier's death.

in·trant (in′trənt) *adj.* Entering. — *n.* An entrant; especially, one entering an association or institution. [<L *intrans, -antis*, ppr. of *intrare* enter. See ENTER.]

in·tra·nu·cle·ar (in′trə·nōō′klē·ər, -nyōō′-) *adj.* Within the nucleus, as of an atom or a cell.

in·tra·state (in′trə·stāt′) *adj.* Confined within or pertaining to a single state.

in·tra·tel·lu·ric (in′trə·tə·lōōr′ik) *adj. Geol.* **1** Formed or occurring within the earth. **2** Pertaining to the constituents of an effusive rock formed prior to their appearance on the surface, or to the period of their formation.

in·tra·ve·nous (in′trə·vē′nəs) *adj. Med.* Into or within a vein: an *intravenous* injection. — **in·tra·ve′nous·ly** *adv.*

in·tra·vi·tel·line (in′trə·vi·tel′in, -vī-) *adj. Biol.* Within the yolk of an egg.

in·trench·ant (in·tren′chənt) *adj. Obs.* Indivisible.

in·trep·id (in·trep′id) *adj.* Unshaken in the presence of danger; dauntless. See synonyms under BRAVE. [<L *intrepidus* <*in-* not + *trepidus* agitated] — **in·tre·pid·i·ty** (in′trə·pid′ə·tē) *n.* — **in·trep′id·ly** *adv.*

---

in·tri·ca·cy (in'tri·kə·sē) *n. pl.* **·cies 1** The quality of being complicated or entangled. **2** A complication; complexity.

in·tri·cate (in'tri·kit) *adj.* **1** Exceedingly or perplexingly entangled, complicated, or involved. **2** Difficult to follow or understand. See synonyms under COMPLEX. [<L *intricatus,* pp. of *intricare* entangle < *in-* in + *tricae* difficulties] **— in'tri·cate·ly** *adv.* **— in'tri·cate·ness** *n.*

in·tri·gant (in'trə·gənt, *Fr.* aṅ·trē·gäṅ') *n. pl.* **·gants** (-gənts, *Fr.* -gäṅ') One given to intrigue. [<F <Ital. *intrigante,* ppr. of *intrigare* intrigue <L *intricare* entangle. See INTRICATE.] **— in·tri·gante** (in'trə·gant', -gänt'; *Fr.* aṅ·trē·gäṅt') *n. fem.*

in·trigue (in·trēg', in'trēg) *n.* **1** The working for an end by secret or underhand means; a plot or scheme. **2** A clandestine and illicit love affair; liaison. **3** The plot of a play, poem, or story, or the complications in which the characters are involved. **— v. ·trigued, ·tri·guing** *v.t.* **1** To arouse and hold the interest or curiosity of; beguile; allure. **2** To plot for; bring on or get by secret or underhand means. **3** *Rare* To puzzle; perplex. **—v.i. 4** To use secret or underhand means; make plots. **5** To carry on a secret or illicit love affair. [<F *intriguer* <Ital. *intrigare* <L *intricare.* See INTRICATE.] **— in·tri'guer** *n.*

in·trin·sic (in·trin'sik) *adj.* **1** Pertaining to the nature of a thing or person; inherent; real; true: opposed to *extrinsic.* **2** Contained or being within. **3** *Anat.* Contained within a certain portion of the body as nerves or muscles. Also **in·trin'si·cal.** See synonyms under INHERENT. [<OF *intrinseque* <Med. L <L *intrinsecus* internally] **— in·trin'si·cal·ly** *adv.*

intro- *prefix* In; into; within: *introvert.* [<L *intro- < intro* inwardly]

in·tro·cep·tion (in'trə·sep'shən) *n. Psychol.* The thorough acceptance by an individual of the fundamental moral standards and conventions of society; social conformity in motives and purpose. [<INTRO- + (RE)CEPTION]

in·tro·duce (in'trə·dōōs', -dyōōs') *v.t.* **·duced, ·duc·ing 1** To bring (someone) to acquaintance with another; cause to become acquainted: He *introduced* me to his cousin; He *introduced* the women to each other. **2** To present formally: to *introduce* one to society. **3** To bring (someone) to acquaintance with or knowledge of something: with *to:* to *introduce* someone to gambling. **4** To bring into notice, use, or practice: to *introduce* a new fashion. **5** To bring, lead, or put into; insert: to *introduce* a probe into a wound. **6** To bring forward for notice or consideration: to *introduce* a resolution. **7** To begin; start: to *introduce* a new line of questioning. See synonyms under ALLEGE. [<L *introducere < in-* within + *ducere* lead] **— in'tro·duc'er** *n.* **— in'tro·duc'i·ble** *adj.*

in·tro·duc·tion (in'trə·duk'shən) *n.* **1** The act of introducing, as inserting, bringing into notice or use, or making acquainted. **2** The means of introducing one person to another, as by letter, card, etc. **3** Something that leads up to and tends to explain something else; specifically, a preliminary statement made by an author or speaker in explanation of the subject or design of his writing or discourse. **4** Hence, an elementary treatise in any branch of study: an *introduction* to chemistry. **5** *Music* A preparatory movement intended to foreshadow or lead up to the theme. See synonyms under ENTRANCE. [<OF] **— in'tro·duc'tor** *n.*

in·tro·duc·to·ry (in'trə·duk'tər·ē) *adj.* Serving as an introduction; prefatory; preliminary. Also **in'tro·duc'tive.** [<LL *introductorius*] **— in'tro·duc'to·ri·ly** *adv.*

in·tro·ject (in'trə·jekt') *v.t. Psychoanal.* To transform external realities, as persons and objects, into mental replicas or images with which one may enter into direct emotional relations. [<INTRO- + (PRO)JECT]

in·tro·jec·tion (in'trə·jek'shən) *n.* **1** *Psychoanal.* The incorporation into the ego of mental images of persons and objects to the extent of being emotionally affected by them: compare PROJECTION. **2** *Psychol.* The attribution of sentient qualities to inanimate objects; personification. [<intro- + (PRO)JECTION]

in·tro·mit (in'trə·mit') *v.t.* **·mit·ted, ·mit·ting 1** To send or place in; insert. **2** To permit to enter; admit. [<L *intromittere < intro-* within

+ *mittere* send] **— in'tro·mis'sion** (-mish'ən) *n.* **— in'tro·mis'sive** (-mis'iv), **in'tro·mit'tent** *adj.*

in·tro·spect (in'trə·spekt') *v.t.* To look into; examine the interior of. **— v.i.** *Psychol.* To examine and analyze one's own thoughts and emotions; practice self-examination. [<L *introspectus,* pp. of *introspicere < intro-* within + *specere* look] **— in'tro·spec'tive** *adj.* **— in'tro·spec'tive·ly** *adv.* **— in'tro·spec'tive·ness** *n.*

in·tro·spec·tion (in'trə·spek'shən) *n.* **1** The act of looking within. **2** *Psychol.* The contemplation of one's own mental processes and emotional states; self-examination.

in·tro·ver·sion (in'trə·vûr'zhən, -shən) *n.* **1** The act or process of introverting. **2** *Psychol.* The direction or concentration of one's interest upon oneself. **3** *Psychoanal.* The concentration of the libido upon inwardly derived activities or satisfactions. Compare EXTROVERSION. [<NL *introversio, -onis* <L *introwithin + versio, -onis* a turning] **— in'tro·ver'sive** (-vûr'siv) *adj.*

in·tro·vert (in'trə·vûrt) *n.* **1** *Psychol.* An individual with strongly self-centered patterns of emotion, fantasy, and thought: opposed to *extrovert.* **2** *Biol.* An organ capable of being turned inward, as the eye tentacle of a land snail or the proboscis of a gastropod. **—v.t. 1** To turn within; cause to take an inward direction, as the mind or one's thoughts. **2** *Biol.* To turn (an organ) inward upon itself. **— adj.** Characterized by or tending to introversion: *introvert* habits. [<INTRO- + L *vertere* turn]

in·trude (in·trōōd') *v.* **·trud·ed, ·trud·ing** *v.t.* **1** To thrust or force in without leave or excuse: to *intrude* one's views. **2** *Geol.* To cause to enter by intrusion. **— v.i. 3** To come in without leave or invitation; thrust oneself in. [<L *intrudere < in-* in + *trudere* thrust] **— in·trud'er** *n.*

in·tru·sion (in·trōō'zhən) *n.* **1** The act of intruding; encroachment. **2** *Geol.* **a** The thrusting of molten rock within an earlier formation. **b** An intrusive rock.

in·tru·sive (in·trōō'siv) *adj.* **1** Coming without warrant; intruding; obtrusive; prone to intrude. **2** *Geol.* Formed by solidification before reaching the surface of the earth, as certain igneous rocks; plutonic. **3** *Phonet.* Referring to speech sounds in a word which do not have etymological basis, but result from the adjustment of the vocal organs to the sounds preceding and following, as the *d* in spindle (Old English *spinel*). **—intrusive r** An *r* sound sometimes heard between a word ending in a vowel and a following word beginning with a vowel, as in law*r* office. [<L *intrusus,* pp. of *intrudere.* See INTRUDE.] **— in·tru'sive·ly** *adv.* **— in·tru'sive·ness** *n.*

in·tu·it (in'tyōō·it, in·tōō'it) *v.t. & v.i.* To know by intuition. [<L *intuitus,* pp. of *intueri* look upon < *in-* on + *tueri* look]

in·tu·i·tion (in'tōō·ish'ən, -tyōō-) *n.* **1** Quick perception of truth without conscious attention or reasoning. **2** Knowledge from within; instinctive knowledge or feeling. **3** *Philos.* **a** An immediate knowledge, or envisagement, of an object, truth, or principle, whether of a physical, rational, artistic, or ethical nature: a conception derived by analogy from the act and result of clear and concentrated vision. **b** That which is known intuitively; truth obtained by internal apprehension without the aid of perception or the reasoning powers. See synonyms under KNOWLEDGE. [<Med. L *intuitio, -onis < intuitus,* pp. of *intueri* look upon. See INTUIT.] **— in'tu·i'tion·al** *adj.* **— in'tu·i'tion·al·ly** *adv.*

intuitional ethics The teaching of that school of ethics which holds that man has an intuitive apprehension and intrinsically valid judgment of moral values.

in·tu·i·tion·al·ism (in'tōō·ish'ən·əl·iz'əm, -tyōō-) *n.* The doctrine that certain truths are immediately, and without discursive argument, cognized as fundamental and incontestable and are the foundation of all knowledge. Also **in'tu·i'tion·ism. — in'tu·i'tion·al·ist, in'tu·i'tion·ist** *n.*

in·tu·i·tive (in·tōō'ə·tiv, -tyōō'-) *adj.* **1** Perceived by the mind without the intervention of any process of thought: *intuitive* evidence. **2** Discovering truth or reaching a just conclusion without resort to the powers of reason: the *intuitive* faculty. **— in·tu'i·tive·ly** *adv.* **— in·tu'i·tive·ness** *n.*

in·tu·i·tiv·ism (in·tōō'ə·tiv·iz'əm, -tyōō'-) *n.* **1** The doctrine that all ethical principles are intuitive. **2** Intuitive faculty; insight; instinct. **— in·tu'i·tiv·ist** *n.*

in·tu·mesce (in'tōō·mes', -tyōō-) *v.i.* **·mesced, ·mesc·ing 1** To enlarge or expand, as from heat or congestion. **2** To swell or bubble up; become tumid. [<L *intumescere,* intens. of *tumescere,* inceptive of *tumere* swell]

in·tu·mes·cence (in'tōō·mes'əns, -tyōō-) *n.* **1** A tumid state or process. **2** A tumid growth; a swelling. **3** The bubbling up of a molten mass. **4** Excited feeling or language. Also **in'tu·mes'cen·cy. — in'tu·mes'cent** *adj.*

in·turn (in'tûrn) *n.* **1** The act of turning inward, or the state of being so turned, as of the toes. **2** A dancing step. Also **in'turn'ing.**

in·twine (in·twīn'), **in·twist** (in·twist'), etc. See ENTWINE, etc.

in·unc·tion (in·ungk'shən) *n.* **1** The act of anointing. **2** *Med.* The process of rubbing into the skin, as an ointment or liniment. [<L *inunctio, -onis < inunctus,* pp. of *inungere* anoint]

in·un·dant (in·un'dənt) *adj.* Inundating; overflowing.

in·un·date (in'un·dāt) *v.t.* **·dat·ed, ·dat·ing** To cover by overflowing; flood; fill to overflowing. [<L *inundatus,* pp. of *inundare < in-* in, on + *undare* overflow < *unda* wave] **— in'un·da'tor** *n.* **— in·un·da·to·ry** (in·un'də·tôr'ē, -tō'rē) *adj.*

Synonyms: deluge, flood, overflow, overwhelm, submerge. *Antonyms:* drain, dry, parch, scorch.

in·un·da·tion (in'un·dā'shən) *n.* **1** A flood. **2** A condition of superabundance.

in·ure (in·yōōr') *v.* **·ured, ·ur·ing** *v.t.* To harden or toughen by use or exercise; accustom; habituate. **— v.i.** To have or take effect; be applied. Also spelled *enure.* [<IN² + obs. *ure* work, use <OF *eure* <L *opera* work] **— in·ure'ment** *n.*

in·urn (in·ûrn') *v.t.* To put into a cinerary urn; bury; entomb.

in·u·tile (in·yōō'til) *adj.* Useless. [<F <L *inutilis*] **— in·u'tile·ly** *adv.* **— in·u·til'i·ty** *n.*

in va·cu·o (in vak'yōō·ō) *Latin* In a vacuum.

in·vade (in·vād') *v.* **·vad·ed, ·vad·ing** *v.t.* **1** To enter with or as with hostile intent, as for conquering or plundering. **2** To encroach upon; trespass on: to *invade* privacy. **3** To spread over or penetrate injuriously: Disease *invaded* the lungs. **— v.i. 4** To make an invasion. [<L *invadere < in-* in + *vadere* go] **— in·vad'er** *n.*

in·vag·i·nate (in·vaj'ə·nāt) *v.* **·nat·ed, ·nat·ing** *v.t.* **1** To put or receive into a sheath. **2** To turn back within itself, as a tubular organ or part. **— v.i. 3** To undergo invagination. [<L *in-* in + *vagina* sheath + -ATE²] **— in·vag'i·nat'ed** *adj.*

in·vag·i·na·tion (in·vaj'ə·nā'shən) *n.* **1** The act of invaginating, or the state of being invaginated; intussusception. **2** *Biol.* **a** The differentiation of the germinal layers by a pushing in of the wall of the blastula to form the gastrula, or by the growth of the epiblast cells as a thin layer over the hypoblast. **b** That which is invaginated; specifically, a pouch formed by an infolding of a membrane: the buccal *invagination.*

in·va·lid¹ (in'və·lid) *n.* A sickly person, or one disabled, as by wounds, disease, etc. **— adj. 1** Enfeebled by ill health. **2** Pertaining to or for the use of sick persons. **— v.t. 1** To cause to become an invalid; disable. **2** To classify, or release (a soldier, sailor, etc.) from active service as an invalid. **— v.i. 3** To become an invalid. **4** To retire from active service because of ill health: said of soldiers, sailors, etc. [<F *invalide* <L *invalidus* not strong] **— in'va·lid·ism** *n.*

in·val·id² (in·val'id) *adj.* Having no force, weight, or cogency; null; void. [<L *invalidus*] **— in·va·lid·i·ty** (in'və·lid'ə·tē) *n.* **— in·val'id·ly** *adv.*

in·val·i·date (in·val'ə·dāt) *v.t.* **·dat·ed, ·dat·ing** To weaken or destroy the force or validity of; render invalid; annul. [<INVALID² + -ATE¹] **— in·val'i·da'tion** *n.* **— in·val'i·da'tor** *n.*

in·val·u·a·ble (in·val'yōō·ə·bəl, -yōō·bəl) *adj.* Of a value beyond estimation; very precious. **— in·val'u·a·bly** *adv.*

in·var·i·a·ble (in·vâr'ē·ə·bəl) *adj.* That does not or can not vary or be varied; always uniform. See synonyms under CONTINUAL, PERMANENT.

— in·var'i·a·bil'i·ty, in·var'i·a·ble·ness *n.* — in·var'i·a·bly *adv.*

in·var·i·ance (in·vâr'ē·əns) *n.* The property or condition of being invariant.

in·var·i·ant (in·vâr'ē·ənt) *adj.* Constant; not subject to variation. — *n. Math.* A quantity which remains unchanged; a constant.

in·va·sion (in·vā'zhən) *n.* **1** The act of invading; a military inroad or incursion for conquest, reconquest, or plunder. **2** Hence, any attack with harmful intent or result: an *invasion* of disease. **3** Encroachment, as by an act of intrusion or trespass: the *invasion* of privacy. [<LL *invasio, -onis* < *invasum,* pp. of *invadere.* See INVADE.]
  Synonyms: aggression, encroachment, foray, incursion, inroad, irruption, raid. See AGGRESSION, ATTACK.

in·va·sive (in·vā'siv) *adj.* Having the character or effect of an invasion; encroaching; aggressive.

in·vec·tive (in·vek'tiv) *n.* Railing accusation; vituperation; abuse. — *adj.* Using or characterized by vituperation or abuse. [<OF *invectif* <LL *invectivus* <L *invectus,* pp. of *invehere.* See INVEIGH.] — in·vec'tive·ly *adv.* — in·vec'tive·ness *n.*

in·veigh (in·vā') *v.i.* To utter vehement censure or invective: with *against.* [<L *invehere* carry into < *in-* into + *vehere* carry] — in·veigh'er *n.*

in·vent (in·vent') *v.t.* **1** To create the idea, form, or existence of by original thought or effort; devise: to *invent* a better mousetrap. **2** To fabricate in the mind; make up, as something untrue or contrary to fact: He *invented* an excuse. **3** *Obs.* To come or chance upon; find. See synonyms under DISCOVER, PLAN. [<L *inventus,* pp. of *invenire* come upon, discover < *in-* on + *venire* come] — in·vent'i·ble *adj.*

in·ven·tion (in·ven'shən) *n.* **1** The act or process of inventing. **2** That which is invented: a useful *invention.* **3** Skill or ingenuity in contriving. **4** Mental fabrication or concoction. **5** In literature or ,art, creation by the exercise of imaginative powers: poetic *invention.* **6** In rhetoric, the finding out or selection of topics to be treated, or arguments to be used. **7** *Archaic* A finding; discovery. **8** *Law* **a** The process of devising and producing by independent investigation and experiment something not previously known or existing. **b** The article, device, or composition thus created. See synonyms under ARTIFICE, FICTION, INGENUITY, PROJECT. [<OF *invencion*]

in·ven·tive (in·ven'tiv) *adj.* Able to invent; quick at contrivance. — in·ven'tive·ly *adv.* — in·ven'tive·ness *n.*

in·ven·tor (in·ven'tər) *n.* One who invents; especially, one who has originated some method, process, or mechanical device, or who devotes his time to invention. Also in·vent'er. [<L]

in·ven·to·ry (in'vən·tôr'ē, -tō'rē) *n. pl.* ·ries **1** An itemized list of articles, with the number and value of each. **2** The items so listed or to be listed, as the stock of goods of a business. **3** The process of listing articles, supplies, or materials with the description, quantity, and value of each. **4** The value of the goods or stock of a business. **5** A detailed account of the property of a deceased person. **6** A list of articles, with valuations, covered by an insurance policy. See synonyms under RECORD. — *v.t.* ·ried, ·ry·ing **1** To make an inventory of; to list in detail. **2** To insert in an inventory. **3** To take stock of; appraise. [<Med. L *inventarium,* L *inventorium.* See INVENT.] — in'ven·to'ri·al (-tôr'ē·əl, -tō'rē-) *adj.* — in'ven·to'ri·al·ly *adv.*

in·ve·rac·i·ty (in'və·ras'ə·tē) *n. pl.* ·ties **1** Lack of veracity; untruthfulness. **2** An untruth; lie.

in·verse (in·vûrs', in'vûrs) *adj.* Opposite in order or effect; inverted; reciprocal. — *n.* That which is inverted. — in·verse'ly *adv.*

in·ver·sion (in·vûr'zhən, -shən) *n.* **1** The act of inverting. **2** The state of being inverted; a reversal of the natural order of things. **3** In rhetoric: **a** A reversal of the natural order of words. **b** A form of discussion that makes use of a speaker's own argument against himself.

4 *Music* The alteration of a harmony or melody by inverting the relations of its intervals; also, the arrangement resulting from such change. **5** In marching, a reversal of the order of companies in line, so as to bring the left to the right, and vice versa. **6** *Chem.* A rearrangement of the molecular structure of compounds, with the forming of two new compounds whose effects on the plane of polarization are opposed to each other: Sucrose, by acid hydrolysis, is an *inversion* of glucose and fructose. **7** *Meteorol.* An increase of temperature with elevation often noted in anticyclones. **8** *Phonet.* A tongue position in which the tip is turned up and back. **9** Homosexuality. [<L *inversio, -onis* < *inversus,* pp. of *invertere.* See INVERT.] — in·ver'sive *adj.*

in·vert (in·vûrt') *v.t.* **1** To turn upside down or inside out. **2** To reverse the position, order, or sequence of; turn in the opposite direction. **3** To change to the opposite: to *invert* a meaning. **4** *Music* To transpose, as an interval, phrase, or vocal part. **5** *Chem.* To alter, as a compound, by inversion. **6** *Phonet.* To articulate with inversion of the tongue. — *v.i.* **7** To undergo inversion. — *adj.* (in'vûrt) Inverted. — *n.* (in'vûrt) A homosexual. [<L *invertere* < *in-* in + *vertere* turn] — in·vert'i·ble *adj.* — in·ver'tor *n.*

in·ver·te·brate (in·vûr'tə·brit, -brāt) *adj.* **1** Destitute of a backbone; not vertebrate. **2** Of or pertaining to the *Invertebrata.* **3** Lacking force or firmness; irresolute: also in·ver'te·bral. — *n.* **1** An invertebrate animal; one of the *Invertebrata.* **2** One who lacks resolution.

in·vert·ed (in·vûr'tid) *adj.* **1** Turned in a contrary direction, or turned upside down; reversed in order or position. **2** Having a position the opposite of the usual or normal one: an *inverted* ovule in plants, *inverted* commas, etc. **3** *Phonet.* Cacuminal. — in·vert'ed·ly *adv.*

in·vert·er (in·vûr'tər) *n. Electr.* A device for converting direct current into alternating current; a converter.

invert sugar A mixture of fructose and glucose occurring in some fruits and artificially produced by the hydrolysis of cane sugar.

in·vest (in·vest') *v.t.* **1** To use (money or capital) for the purchase of property, stocks, securities, etc., with the expectation of future profit or income. **2** To place in office formally; install. **3** To give power, authority, or rank to. **4** To cover or surround as if with a garment: Mystery *invested* the whole affair. **5** To surround or hem in; lay siege to. **6** *Rare* To confer or settle (a right, power, etc.): with *in.* **7** *Obs.* To clothe; also, to don. — *v.i.* **8** To make an investment or .investments. [<L *investire* clothe, enshroud < *in-* on + *vestire* clothe < *vestis* clothing; infl. in meaning by Ital. *investire* invest] — in·ves'tor *n.*

in·ves·ti·gate (in·ves'tə·gāt) *v.* ·gat·ed, ·gat·ing To search or inquire into; examine in detail. — *v.i.* To make an investigation. See synonyms under EXAMINE, QUESTION. [<L *investigatus,* pp. of *investigare* < *in-* in + *vestigare* track, trace < *vestigium* track] — in·ves'ti·ga·ble (-tə·gə·bəl) *adj.* — in·ves'ti·ga'tive *adj.* — in·ves'ti·ga'tor *n.*

in·ves·ti·ga·tion (in·ves'tə·gā'shən) *n.* **1** The act of investigating; careful inquiry or research. **2** An inquiry by authority, as by a legislative committee, into certain facts. **3** A systematic examination of some scientific question, whether by experiment or mathematical treatment. [<F]

in·ves·ti·tive (in·ves'tə·tiv) *adj.* **1** Of or pertaining to investiture. **2** Having the function of investing; serving to invest. [<L *investitus,* pp. of *investire.* See INVEST.]

in·ves·ti·ture (in·ves'tə·chər) *n.* **1** The act or ceremony of investing with something, as robes of office. **2** That which invests or clothes. **3** In feudal law, the delivery of possession of lands in the presence of witnesses. **4** *Eccl.* The ceremony of inducting an abbot or bishop into his office by placing the symbols of the office in his hands and receiving his oath of fealty. **5** *Obs.* Clothing. [<Med. L *investitura.*]

in·vest·ment (in·vest'mənt) *n.* **1** The placing of money, capital, or other resources to gain

a profit, as in interest. **2** That which is invested. **3** That in which one invests. **4** Investiture. **5** *Biol.* An outer covering. **6** *Archaic* Clothing; a garment. **7** *Mil.* The surrounding of a fort or town by an enemy force to create a state of siege; a blockade.

investment trust A company that invests its capital in other companies.

in·vid·i·ous (in·vid'ē·əs) *adj.* **1** Expressing, prompted by, or provoking envy or ill will; unjustly discriminating; hence, displeasing. **2** *Obs.* Showing envy. See synonyms under MALICIOUS. [<L *invidiosus* < *invidia* envy. Doublet of ENVIOUS.] — in·vid'i·ous·ly *adv.* — in·vid'i·ous·ness *n.*

in·vig·or·ate (in·vig'ər·āt) *v.t.* ·at·ed, ·at·ing To give vigor and energy to; animate. [<L *in-* in + *vigor* vigor + -ATE²] — in·vig'or·at'ing·ly *adv.* — in·vig'or·a'tion *n.*

in·vin·ci·ble (in·vin'sə·bəl) *adj.* Not to be overcome; unconquerable. [<F <L *invincibilis.* See IN-¹, VINCIBLE.] — in·vin'ci·bil'i·ty, in·vin'ci·ble·ness *n.* — in·vin'ci·bly *adv.*

in·vi·o·la·ble (in·vī'ə·lə·bəl) *adj.* That must not or can not be violated. [<L *inviolabilis*] — in·vi'o·la·bil'i·ty, in·vi'o·la·ble·ness *n.* — in·vi'o·la·bly *adv.*

in·vi·o·late (in·vī'ə·lit) *adj.* **1** Not violated; unprofaned; pure; unbroken. **2** Inviolable; not to be violated. — in·vi'o·late·ly *adv.* — in·vi'o·late·ness *n.*

in·vis·i·ble (in·viz'ə·bəl) *adj.* **1** Not visible; not capable of being seen. **2** Not in sight; concealed. **3** *Econ.* Referring to resources or reserves that do not appear in regular processes or in financial statements: *invisible* products, *invisible* revenue, *invisible* assets. — *n.* **1** One who or that which is invisible. **2** *Often cap.* One of a sect of Protestants in the 16th century who denied the visibility of the church. **3** A Rosicrucian, as belonging to a secret fraternity. — the Invisible The Supreme Being; God. [<OF] — in·vis'i·bil'i·ty, in·vis'i·ble·ness *n.* — in·vis'i·bly *adv.*

in·vi·ta·tion (in'və·tā'shən) *n.* **1** The act of inviting; courteous solicitation to come to some place or to do some act; especially, a requesting of another's company: a standing *invitation* to dinner. **2** The means of inviting; the words by which one is invited: a written *invitation.* **3** The act of alluring; incitement; attraction. **4** In the Anglican Church, the hortatory introduction preceding the confession in the communion office; the invitatory. [<L *invitatio, -onis*]

in·vite (in·vīt') *v.* ·vit·ed, ·vit·ing *v.t.* **1** To ask (someone) politely or graciously to be present in some place, to attend some event, or to perform some action. **2** To make formal or polite request for: to *invite* suggestions. **3** To present opportunity or inducement for; attract: The situation *invites* criticism. **4** To tempt; entice. — *v.i.* **5** To give invitation; entice. — *n.* (in'vīt) *Slang* An invitation. [<F *inviter* <L *invitare* entertain] — in·vit'er *n.*

in·vit·ing (in·vī'ting) *adj.* That invites or allures. — in·vit'ing·ly *adv.* —in·vit'ing·ness *n.*

in·vo·ca·tion (in'vō·kā'shən) *n.* **1** The act of invoking. **2** A judicial order. **3** *Eccl.* A form of prayer, as at the opening of a service. **4** An appeal invoking the Muses or some divine being, at the beginning of an epic or other work. **5** The act of conjuring an evil spirit. **6** The formula or incantation thus used. See synonyms under PRAYER. [<OF <L *invocatio, -onis* < *invocare.* See INVOKE.]

in·voc·a·to·ry (in·vok'ə·tôr'ē, -tō'rē) *adj.* Having the nature of, expressive of, or employed in invocation.

in·voice (in'vois) *n.* **1** A list sent to a purchaser, etc., containing the items and charges of merchandise. **2** The goods so listed. — *v.t.* ·voiced, ·voic·ing To itemize; make an invoice of. [<F *envois,* pl. of *envoi* a thing sent < *envoyer* send. See ENVOY¹.]

in·voke (in·vōk') *v.t.* ·voked, ·vok·ing **1** To call on for aid, protection, etc.; address, as in prayer. **2** To call for, as in supplication: to *invoke* a blessing. **3** To summon or conjure by incantation, as evil spirits. **4** To appeal to for confirmation; quote as an authority. See synonyms under PRAY. [<F *invoquer* <L *invocare* call upon < *in-* on + *vocare* call]

— **in·vok′er** *n.*

in·vol·un·tar·y (in·vol′ən·ter′ē) *adj.* **1** Contrary to one's will or wish. **2** Not under the control of the will. **3** Unintentional. **4** *Physiol.* Describing those muscles, glands, and other bodily organs which act independently of conscious control. See synonyms under SPONTANEOUS. — **in·vol′un·tar′i·ly** *adv.* — **in·vol′un·tar′i·ness** *n.*

in·vo·lute (in′və·lōōt) *adj.* **1** Complicated by reason of the intertwinings or the interrelation of parts or elements. **2** *Bot.* Having the edges rolled inward, as a leaf. **3** *Zool.* Having the whorls nearly or quite concealing the axis, as a shell; also, coiled spirally, as certain antennae. Also **in′vo·lut′ed.** — *n. Geom.* The curve traced by a point on a line as the line unrolls from a fixed curve. [< L *involutus,* pp. of *involvere* involve]

in·vo·lu·tion (in′və·lōō′shən) *n.* **1** The act of involving, infolding, or rolling up, or the state of being involved or rolled up; complication; entanglement. **2** Something involved, rolled up, or entangled. **3** *Physiol.* **a** The return of an organ to its normal condition after a physiological increase in its size and structure: the *involution* of the womb after childbirth. **b** Retrograde development; the physiological decline preceding and accompanying old age. **4** *Math.* The multiplication of a quantity by itself any number of times; the raising of a quantity to any power. **5** In rhetoric, complicated or cumbrous arrangement of words, clauses, or phrases, caused by the insertion of qualifying or modifying phrases between words that belong together. **6** *Biol.* Degeneration; retrograde evolution.

in·volve (in·volv′) *v.t.* **·volved, ·volv·ing 1** To have as a necessary circumstance, condition, or implication. **2** To have effect on; affect: The law will *involve* many people. **3** To draw within itself; swallow up; overwhelm: The whirlpool *involved* ten persons. **4** To draw into entanglement, trouble, etc.; implicate; entangle. **5** To make intricate or difficult; complicate. **6** To hold the attention of; engross: He was *involved* in his work. **7** To wrap up or infold; cover or conceal; envelop: to *involve* a place in darkness. **8** To wind in spirals or curves; coil, especially intricately. **9** *Math.* To raise (a number) to a given power. [< L *involvere* roll into or up < *in-* in + *volvere* roll] — **in·volve′ment** *n.*

Synonyms: complicate, embarrass, embroil, entangle, implicate, imply, include, overwhelm. To *involve* is to roll or wind up with or in, so as to combine inextricably or very nearly inseparably; as, The nation is *involved* in war; The bookkeeper's accounts, or the writer's sentences, are *involved. Involve* is a stronger word than *implicate,* denoting more complete entanglement. As applied to persons, *implicate* applies only to that which is wrong, while *involve* is more commonly used of that which is unfortunate; one is *implicated* in a crime, *involved* in embarrassments, misfortunes, or perplexities. One is *embroiled* in a serious conflict, *entangled* in a conspiracy, which, once the situation is *complicated* by treachery, may *overwhelm* the participants who are *involved.* As regards logical connection, that which is *included* is usually expressly stated; that which is *implied* is not stated, but is naturally to be inferred; that which is *involved* is necessarily to be inferred, as, a slate roof is *included* in the contract; that the roof shall be watertight is *implied*; the contrary supposition *involves* an absurdity. Compare COMPLEX, PERPLEX. *Antonyms:* disconnect, disentangle, distinguish, explicate, extricate, remove, separate.

in·volved (in·volvd′) *adj.* Intricate; complicated; not easily comprehended. — **in·volv·ed·ness** (in·vol′vid·nis) *n.*

in·vul·ner·a·ble (in·vul′nər·ə·bəl) *adj.* Not capable of being wounded; not to be overcome; having no weak point; unconquerable. — **in·vul′ner·a·bil′i·ty, in·vul′ner·a·ble·ness** *n.* — **in·vul′ner·a·bly** *adv.*

in·ward (in′wərd) *adv.* **1** Toward the inside, center, or interior. **2** In or on the inside. **3** Into the spirit or mind. Also **inwards.** — *adj.* **1** Situated within, especially with reference to the body; inner: opposed to *outward.* **2** Pertaining to the mind or spirit: an *inward* light. **3** Muffled; low, as the voice. **4** Proceeding toward the inside. **5** Inland. **6** In-

herent; intrinsic. — *n. Obs.* An intimate. [OE *inweard*]

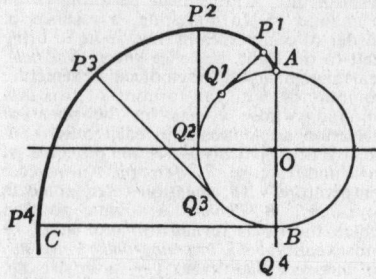

INVOLUTE

Involute *AC* is formed by the locus of point *P* (at P^1, P^2, P^3, P^4) as line *BC* unrolls from curve *BA.* Length of the tangent to the curve (P^1 Q^1, P^2 Q^2, etc.) from any point on the involute *AC* is equal to the length of the curve to the point of tangency ($AQ^1 = P^1Q^1$; $AQ^2 = P^2Q^2$; etc.).

in·ward·ly (in′wərd·lē) *adv.* **1** In an inward manner; especially, in one's thoughts and feelings; with no outward manifestation; secretly. **2** *Rare* Toward the center or interior; inward: to turn *inwardly.* **3** Essentially; inherently; intrinsically. [OE *inweardlíce*]

in·ward·ness (in′wərd·nis) *n.* **1** The inner quality or meaning; true nature or import. **2** The state of being inward or internal, mentally or physically, actually or figuratively. **3** Collectively, the ideas and interests which belong to the life of the mind or spirit, and to its true development. **4** *Obs.* Intimacy.

in·wards (in′wərdz) *adv.* **1** Inward. **2** With respect to taxable imports: duties paid *inwards.* — *n. pl.* Inner or interior parts.

in·weave (in·wēv′) *v.t.* **·wove** or **·weaved, ·woven** (*Obs.* **·wove**), **·weav·ing** To weave in or together; introduce into a fabric as a component part.

in·wind (in·wīnd′) *v.t.* **·wound, ·wind·ing** To wind in or around; entwine.

in·wo·ven (in·wō′vən) *adj.* Woven in; entwined.

in·wrap (in·rap′) See ENWRAP.

in·wreathe (in·rēth′) See ENWREATHE.

in·wrought (in·rôt′) *adj.* Worked into, as a fabric or metalwork, so as to form part of it. See synonyms under INHERENT.

iod— Var. of IODO–.

i·o·date (ī′ə·dāt) *v.t.* **·dat·ed, ·dat·ing** To iodize. — *n. Chem.* A salt of iodic acid. [< IOD- + -ATE³] — **i′o·da′tion** *n.*

i·od·ic (ī·od′ik) *adj. Chem.* **1** Of, pertaining to, or containing iodine. **2** Designating a white crystalline acid, HIO_3, used as an oxidizing agent.

i·o·dide (ī′ə·dīd) *n. Chem.* **1** A binary compound of iodine. **2** A salt or compound in which iodine is the acid radical. **3** A salt of hydriodic acid: potassium *iodide.* Also **i′o·did** (-did). [< IOD- + -IDE]

i·o·dine (ī′ə·dīn, -din, -dēn) *n.* A bluish-black crystalline element (symbol I) of the halogen group, having a metallic luster and yielding, when heated, corrosive fumes of a rich violet color. It is valuable for its powerful antiseptic properties, and is applied externally as a counterirritant. It is also extensively used in photography and organic synthesis. See ELEMENT. Also **i·o·din** (ī′ə·din). [< F *iode* < Gk. *iṓdēs* violetlike (< *ion* a violet + *eidos* form) + -INE² (as in *chlorine*); from its violet-colored vapor]

i·o·dize (ī′ə·dīz) *v.t.* **·dized, ·diz·ing 1** To treat with or bring under the influence of iodine. **2** To add iodine to: to *iodize* collodion. **3** To expose to the vapor of iodine. [< IOD- + -IZE] — **i′o·diz′er** *n.* — **i·o·di·za′tion** *n.*

iodo– *combining form* Denoting the presence of, or relation to, iodine: *iodoform.* Also, before vowels, *iod–.*

i·o·do·form (ī·ō′də·fôrm) *n. Chem.* A light-yellow crystalline compound, CHI_3, formed by the action of iodine on alcohol in an alkaline solution: used in medicine as an antiseptic. [< IODO- + FORM(YL)]

i·o·dom·e·try (ī′ə·dom′ə·trē) *n. Chem.* **1** The determination of iodine by volumetric methods. **2** The art of making quantitative determination by the use of standard solutions of iodine, or by the liberation of iodine from an

iodide. Also *iodimetry.* [< IODO- + -METRY] — **i·o·do·met·ric** (ī′ə·dō·met′rik) or **·ri·cal** *adj.*

i·o·dous (ī′ə·dəs) *adj. Chem.* **1** Of, pertaining to, or like iodine. **2** Containing iodine in its lower valency. [< IOD- + -OUS]

i·o moth (ī′ō) A large American moth (*Automeris io*) having conspicuous eyelike spots on the hind wings. The caterpillar has stinging spines. [See IO]

IO MOTH

i·on (ī′ən, ī′on) *n. Physics* **1** An electrically charged atom, radical, or molecule, formed by the dissolution of an electrolyte and becoming a *cation* with a positive (+) charge if electrons are lost, or an *anion* with a negative (−) charge if electrons are gained. Thus, a molecule of sodium chloride, NaCl, in aqueous solution, dissociates into the sodium cation Na⁺, with a deficiency of one electron, and the chlorine anion Cl⁻, with an excess of one electron. **2** In a gas, an electrified particle produced in various ways, as by the action of an electric current or of rays such as the ultraviolet and certain radium emanations. See HYDROGEN ION. [< Gk. *ion,* neut. of *iōn,* ppr. of *ienai* go]

–ion *suffix of nouns* **1** Action or process of: *communion.* **2** Condition or state of being: *union.* **3** Result of: *opinion.* Also *–ation, –tion.* [< F *ion* < L *-io, -ionis*]

ion engine A reaction engine producing a small but sustained thrust by emission of positive ions accelerated in an electrical field. Compare PLASMA ENGINE.

ion exchange *Chem.* **1** A process whereby ions may be reversibly interchanged at the boundary of a liquid and solid in contact, the composition of the solid not being altered: used especially in water softening with zeolites and in the purification of solutions. **2** A similar process occurring between immiscible electrolytes.

ion exchange resin *Chem.* Any of a class of substances which yield cations and anions in the ion–exchange process.

i·on·ic (ī·on′ik) *adj. Chem.* **1** Of, pertaining to, or containing ions. **2** Designating the theory of electrolytic dissociation, according to which the molecules of all acids, bases, and salts dissociate in varying degrees when they are dissolved in water and certain other solvents.

I·on·ic (ī·on′ik) *adj.* **1** Ionian. **2** *Archit.* Of or pertaining to an order of Greek architecture characterized by scroll–like ornaments of the capital. See illustration under CAPITAL. **3** In prosody, designating a metrical foot, consisting either of two long and two short syllables (- - ˘ ˘) and called **greater Ionic,** or *Ionic a majore,* or of two short and two long (˘ ˘ - -), when it is called **lesser Ionic** or *Ionic a minore.* — *n.* **1** In prosody, an Ionic foot; also, a verse composed of Ionic feet. **2** A dialect of ancient Greek spoken in Ionia and in most of the Aegean Islands, divided into **Old Ionic** or **Epic,** the language of the Homeric poems, and **New Ionic,** of the fifth century B.C., used by Herodotus and Hippocrates. **3** *Printing* A style of type with a large, heavy roman face. [< L *Ionicus* < Gk. *Iōnikos*]

i·o·ni·um (ī·ō′nē·əm) *n. Physics* The immediate precursor of radium in the radioactive disintegration of uranium: it is an isotope of thorium, of mass 230 and a half-life of about 80,000 years. [< ION + (URAN)IUM; from its ionizing action]

i·on·i·za·tion (ī′ən·ə·zā′shən, -ī·zā′-) *n.* **1** *Chem.* The breaking apart of electrolytes into anions and cations, by solution or other process, mechanical or chemical; electrolytic dissociation. **2** *Physics* The generation of ions by radioactivity. **—degree of ionization** The fraction of the molecules of an electrolyte dissociated or ionized at a given temperature and concentration of solution, usually expressed as a percentage.

ionization potential *Physics* The energy, expressed in electron volts, required to remove an electron from an atom by impact: 5.13 is the *ionization potential* for sodium.

i·on·ize (ī′ən·īz) *v.t.* **·ized, ·iz·ing 1** To convert, totally or in part, into ions. **2** To divide into ions. — **i′on·iz′a·ble** *adj.* — **i′on·iz′er** *n.*

i·on·o·pause (ī·on′ə·pôz) *n.* The zone of transition between the ionosphere and the exosphere, beginning at a height of about 400 miles beyond the earth's surface. [<IONO- (< ION)+ PAUSE]

i·on·o·sphere (ī·on′ə·sfir) *n.* An upper layer of the earth's atmosphere above the mesosphere consisting of several layers subject to ionization, with seasonal variations: it is a part of the Heaviside layer responsible for the reflection of radio waves [<IONO- (<ION) + SPHERE]

i·on·to·pho·re·sis (ī·on·to·fə·rē′sis) *n. Med.* Treatment by the introduction of ions into the body; therapeutic ionization of affected organs and tissues. Also **i·on·o·ther·a·py** (ī′ən·ō·ther′·ə·pē). [<*ionto-*, combining form of ION + PHORESIS]

i·o·ta (ī·ō′tə) *n.* **1** The ninth letter and fourth vowel in the Greek alphabet (I, ι): corresponding to English I, i. As a numeral it denotes 10. **2** A small or insignificant mark or part. See synonyms under PARTICLE. [<L < Gk. *iōta.* Doublet of JOT.]

I O U 1 A paper having on it these letters (meaning *I owe you*) followed by a named sum and duly signed. **2** A symbol and acknowledgment of indebtedness. Also **I.O.U.**

I·o·wa (ī′ə·wə) *n. pl.* **·was** or **·wa 1** One of a North American tribe of Siouan Indians, formerly living in Minnesota, and now on reservations in Oklahoma and Kansas. **2** The Siouan language of this tribe.

I·o·wa (ī′ə·wə, ī′ə·wä) A north central State of the United States; 56,280 square miles; capital, Des Moines; entered the Union Dec. 28, 1846; nickname *Hawkeye State*: abbr. IA — **I′o·wan** *adj. & n.*

ip·e·cac (ip′ə·kak) *n.* **1** A South American creeping or shrubby plant (*Cephaelis ipecacuanha*) of the madder family, yielding the medicinal alkaloids emetine and cephaeline. **2** An extract or tincture of the root of this plant, generally used as an emetic, but also having cathartic properties; also, the root itself. Also **ip·e·cac·u·an·ha** (ip′ə·kak′yŏo·ä′nə). [<Pg. *ipecacuanha* <Tupian *ipi–kaa–guéne* < *ipe* little + *kaa* tree, herb + *guéne* causing sickness]

Iph·i·ge·ni·a (if′ə·jə·nī′ə) In Greek legend, the daughter of Agamemnon and Clytemnestra, sacrificed by her father at Aulis to Artemis, who rescued her and made her a priestess in Tauris: here she later rescued her brother Orestes and fled with him to Greece.

ip·o·moe·a (ip′ə·mē′ə) *n.* Any of a large genus (*Ipomoea*) of mainly tropical herbs, or, rarely, shrubs or trees, of the convolvulus family, with trumpet–shaped flowers, including the morning–glory and sweet potato. Also **ip′o·me′a.** [<NL <Gk. *ips, ipos* sort of horn + *homoios* like]

IPOMOEA

ip·so fac·to (ip′sō fak′tō) *Latin* By the fact itself, or in or by the very fact or act: *ipso facto* outlawed. [<L]

ir– Assimilated var. of IN-¹ and IN-².

i·ra·cund (ī′rə·kund) *adj.* Angry, or easily angered; choleric; passionate. [<L *iracundus < ira* anger] — **i′ra·cun′di·ty** *n.*

I·ran (i·ran′, ē·rän′) A kingdom of SW Asia; 630,000 square miles; capital, Teheran: officially called *Persia* until March, 1935.

I·ra·ni·an (i·rā′nē·ən) *adj.* Belonging or relating to Iran or Persia. — *n.* **1** A modern Persian. **2** A member of the ancient Persian or Iranian race. **3** A branch of the Indo–Iranian subfamily of Indo–European languages, embracing Afghan or Pushtu in the east and, in the west, Avestan, Old Persian, Middle Persian, Scythian, etc., modern Per-

sian, Kurdish, and other ancient and modern tongues of Persia, Caucasia, etc. — **I·ran·ic** (ī·ran′ik) *adj.*

I·raq (i·rak′, ē·räk′) A kingdom approximately coextensive with ancient Mesopotamia in SW Asia; 168,040 square miles; capital, Baghdad; with Jordan, formed the Arab Federation, 1958. Also **I·rak′.**

I·ra·qi (ē·rä′kē) *adj.* Of or pertaining to Iraq, its inhabitants, or their language. — *n.* **1** A native or inhabitant of the kingdom of Iraq. **2** The dialect of Arabic spoken in Iraq.

i·ras·ci·ble (i·ras′ə·bəl, ī-) *adj.* **1** Prone to anger; choleric. **2** Caused by anger. See synonyms under HOT. [<F <LL *irascibilis < irasci* be angry < *ira* anger] — **i·ras′ci·bil′i·ty, i·ras′·ci·ble·ness** *n.* — **i·ras′ci·bly** *adv.*

i·ra·ta·men·te (ē·rä′tä·men′tä) *adv. Music* Angrily; indignantly; passionately: a direction as to the style of playing a composition or passage. [<Ital.]

i·rate (ī′rāt, ī·rāt′) *adj.* Moved to anger; wrathful. See synonyms under BITTER. [<L *iratus,* pp. of *irasci* be angry] — **i′rate·ly** *adv.*

ire (īr) *n.* Strong resentment; wrath; anger. See synonyms under ANGER. [<OF <L *ira* , anger]

ire·ful (īr′fəl) *adj.* Full of ire; wrathful; angry. — **ire′ful·ly** *adv.* — **ire′ful·ness** *n.*

Ire·land (īr′lənd) The westernmost and second largest of the British Isles; 31,838 square miles; divided into: **1 Northern Ireland,** a part of the United Kingdom comprising six counties and two boroughs of the former province of Ulster in the north; 5,237 square miles; capital, Belfast; and **2** the **Republic of Ireland,** independent (1949) of the Commonwealth of Nations and comprising 26 southern counties; 26,600 square miles; capital, Dublin; formerly *Irish Free State* (Irish *Saorstat Eireann*), 1922–37; *Eire,* 1937–49.

i·ren·ic (ī·ren′ik) *adj.* Tending to promote peace; conciliatory. Also **i·ren′i·cal.** [<Gk. *eirēnikos < eirēnē* peace]

i·ren·ics (ī·ren′iks) *n.* Irenical theology; theology concerned with promoting Christian unity.

ir·i·dec·to·my (ir′ə·dek′tə·mē, ī′rə-) *n. Surg.* The operation of removing a part of the iris. [<IRID(O)- + -ECTOMY]

ir·i·des·cence (ir′ə·des′əns) *n. Optics* The many–colored appearance caused by the interference effect of light rays striking the outer and inner surface layers of various bodies, as clouds, mother–of–pearl, oil films, etc. [< IRIDESCENT <Gk. *iris, iridos* rainbow + -ESCENCE] — **ir′i·des′cent** *adj.* — **ir′i·des′cent·ly** *adv.*

i·rid·ic (i·rid′ik, ī-) *adj. Chem.* Of, pertaining to, or containing iridium in its higher valence: *iridic* bromide, IrBr₄. [<IRID(IUM) + -IC]

i·rid·i·um (i·rid′ē·əm, ī-) *n.* A brittle, silver–gray, metallic element (symbol Ir) of extreme hardness belonging to the platinum group: discovered by William Tennant in 1904. It is used in certain alloys, for penpoints, jewelry, etc. [<NL <L *iris, iridis* rainbow <Gk. *Iris* goddess of the rainbow + -IUM; from the iridescence of some of its salts]

irido– *combining form Med.* Iris of the eye: *iridotomy.* Also, before vowels, **irid–.** [<Gk. *iris, iridos* the iris]

ir·i·do·cyte (i·rid′ə·sīt, ī-) *n. Biol.* A cell having the power to produce color in an organism, especially a cell containing guanine and located in the integument of the cuttlefish. [<L *iris, iridos* rainbow <Gk. *iris* + -CYTE]

ir·i·do·ple·gi·a (ir′ə·dō·plē′jē·ə, ī′rə-) *n. Pathol.* Paralysis of the sphincter of the iris, resulting in an inability of the pupil to contract. — **ir′i·do·pleg′ic** (-plej′ik, -plē′jik) *adj.*

ir·i·dos·mi·um (ir′ə·doz′mē·əm, -dos′-, ī′rə-) *n.* Osmiridium. Also **ir·i·dos·mine** (ir′ə·doz′·min, -dos′-, ī′rə-). [<IRID(IUM) + OSMIUM]

iris diaphragm An adjustable diaphragm, like the iris of the eye, designed for regulating the size of an aperture, as in a camera lens.

i·rised (ī′rist) *adj.* Having colors like those of the rainbow.

I·rish (ī′rish) *adj.* Pertaining to Ireland, its people, or their language. — *n.* **1** The people of Ireland collectively: with *the.* **2** The an-

cient or modern language of Ireland, belonging to the Goidelic branch of the Celtic languages; Irish Gaelic: sometimes called *Erse.* Historically, the language is divided into **Old Irish,** from approximately 700 to 1100; **Middle Irish,** from 1100 to 1600; and **Modern Irish,** after 1600. **3** The dialect of English spoken in Ireland; Irish English. **4** *Colloq.* Temper: He got his *Irish* up. [ME *Irisc,* OE *Iras* <ON *Irar* the Irish <OIrish *Eriu* Ireland. Cf. EIRE.]

Irish bridge *Engin.* A surface of reinforced concrete laid on the bed of a river, over which flood waters may run without causing damage.

Irish moss A seaweed (*Chondrus crispus*) found off the coasts of Ireland and North America: used as a food, especially in blanc-mange, and in medicine and industry; carrageen.

Irish Republican Army An anti–British secret organization originally organized in behalf of Irish independence and outlawed by the Irish government in 1936, but continuing terrorist activities to force annexation of Northern Ireland.

Irish stew A stew made originally with mutton, potatoes, and onions; now with almost any meat and vegetables.

irk (ûrk) *v.t.* To annoy or weary; irritate; disgust; vex. [ME *irken*; origin uncertain]

irk·some (ûrk′səm) *adj.* Troublesome or tiresome; tedious. See synonyms under TEDIOUS, TROUBLESOME, WEARISOME. — **irk′some·ly** *adv.* — **irk′some·ness** *n.*

i·ron (ī′ərn) *n.* **1** A tough, abundant, malleable, ductile, and strongly magnetic metallic element (symbol Fe). Easily oxidized in moist air and attacked by many reagents, iron is seldom obtained in its pure, silver–white form, but occurs widely in both ferrous and ferric compounds, and combines in varying proportions with carbon, phosphorus, silicon, sulfur, etc. Typical commercial varieties are: cast iron, pig iron, steel, and wrought iron. **2** An iron tool, weapon, utensil, or anything composed of iron. **3** *pl.* Fetters, especially shackles for the feet. **4** A metal–headed golf club with the face slightly laid back. **5** In the leather industry, a unit of thickness, equal to one forty–eighth of an inch. **6** A flatiron. — **in irons 1** Fettered. **2** *Naut.* Unable to cast away on either side; in stays: said of a vessel coming about into the wind. — *adj.* **1** Made of iron. **2** Resembling iron; hard; rude; heavy; also, firm; unyielding: an *iron* will. **3** Of or pertaining to the Iron Age. — *v.t.* **1** To smooth or press with an iron implement, as cloth or clothing. **2** To fetter. **3** To furnish or arm with iron. — *v.i.* **4** To smooth or press cloth, clothing, etc., with an iron implement. — **to iron out** To smooth out; remove. [OE *īren, īsen, īsern*] — **i′ron·er** *n.*

Iron Age *Archeol.* The last and most advanced of the three roughly classified prehistoric stages of human progress, preceded by the Stone Age and Bronze Age.

iron black Finely divided antimony.

i·ron·bound (ī′ərn·bound′) *adj.* **1** Bound with iron. **2** Faced or surrounded with rocks; rugged. **3** Hard to change; unyielding.

i·ron·clad (ī′ərn·klad′) *adj.* **1** Protected by iron or steel armor, as warships. **2** Not to be evaded; rigorous. **3** Strong. — *n.* A warship sheathed with armor: a term not common since the Spanish–American War.

iron curtain An impenetrable barrier of secrecy and censorship: a term made current by Winston Churchill in a speech in Fulton, Missouri (1946), to describe the dividing line between Western Europe and the Soviet sphere of influence.

i·rone (ī·rōn′) *n. Chem.* A colorless, volatile, aromatic oil, C₁₄H₂₂O, extracted from orris–root and used in perfumery. [<IR(IS) + -ONE]

iron glance A crystallized variety of hematite.

iron gray The color of freshly cut or broken iron. Also **iron grey.** — **i′ron–gray′** *adj.*

i·ron–hand·ed (ī′ərn·han′did) *adj.* Severe and rigorous; despotic.

i·ron·ic (ī·ron′ik) *adj.* **1** Conveying a meaning that contradicts the literal sense of the words used: an *ironic* comment. **2** Being the reverse of what was expected: an *ironic* event. **3** Of the nature of or given to the use of irony. Also **i·ron'i·cal** (-i·kəl). — **i·ron'i·cal·ly** *adv.* — **i·ron'·i·cal·ness** *n.*

i·ron·ing (ī'ər·ning) *n.* The process of pressing and smoothing with flatirons.

iron lung A cabinetlike enclosure used in the treatment of pulmonary disorders, fitted with automatically operated bellows, in order to promote the rhythmic action of the impaired lungs and thus maintain respiration in the patient who lies within it, his head only exposed: also called *Drinker respirator.*

i·ron·mas·ter (ī'ərn·mas'ter, -mäs'-) *n.* A manufacturer of iron.

iron pyrites 1 Ordinary pyrites; fool's-gold. **2** Marcasite. **3** Pyrrhotite.

i·ron·side (ī'ərn·sīd') *n.* A person or thing of tremendous strength or endurance.

i·ron·smith (ī'ərn·smith') *n.* A worker in iron; a blacksmith.

i·ron·stone (ī'ərn·stōn') *n.* Any mineral or rock containing iron; iron ore.

i·ron·weed (ī'ərn·wēd') *n.* An herb or shrub (genus *Vernonia*) of the composite family, from three to six feet high, with alternate leaves, and heads of perfect, tubular, mostly purple or reddish flowers.

i·ron·wood (ī'ərn·wŏŏd') *n.* Any of various trees of unusually hard, heavy, or strong wood; especially, the Catalina ironwood (*Lyonothamnus floribundus*) of southern California and the hop hornbeam (*Ostrya virginiana*) of the eastern United States.

i·ron·work (ī'ərn·wûrk') *n.* Anything made of iron, as parts of a building. — **i'ron·work'er** *n.*

i·ron·works (ī'ərn·wûrks') *n. sing. & pl.* An establishment for the manufacture of iron or of heavy ironwork.

i·ron·wort (ī'ərn·wûrt') *n.* Any of various plants of the mint family, especially the red hemp nettle.

i·ro·ny¹ (ī'rə·nē) *n. pl.* **·nies 1** The use of words to signify the opposite of what they usually express; ridicule disguised as praise or compliment; covert sarcasm or satire. **2** The feigning of ignorance, as in the Socratic method of questions and answers: hence **Socratic irony. 3** A condition of affairs or events exactly the reverse of what was expected: the *irony* of fate. [<L *ironia* <Gk. *eirōneia* < *eirōn* dissembler < *erein* question, ask]

i·ron·y² (ī'ər·nē) *adj.* Of or like iron.

Ir·o·quoi·an (ir'ə·kwoi'ən) *n.* **1** A large North American Indian linguistic stock including the Cayuga, Cherokee, Conestoga, Erie, Mohawk, Oneida, Onondaga, Seneca, Tuscarora, Wyandot, and certain other tribes. **2** A member of any of the Iroquoian tribes. — *adj.* Of or pertaining to the Iroquois Indians, or to any of their languages.

Ir·o·quois (ir'ə·kwoi, -kwoiz) *n. pl.* **·quois 1** A member of any of the powerful North American Indian tribes comprising the confederacy known as the Five Nations. See FIVE NATIONS. **2** A member of any tribe belonging to the Iroquoian linguistic stock. [<F <Algonquian *Irinakoiw*, lit., real adders]

ir·ra·di·ant (i·rā'dē·ənt) *adj.* Sending out rays of light. [<L *irradians, -antis,* ppr. of *irradiare* shine] — **ir·ra'di·ance, ir·ra'di·an·cy** *n.*

ir·ra·di·ate (i·rā'dē·āt) *v.* **·at·ed, ·at·ing** *v.t.* **1** To direct light upon; light up; illuminate. **2** To make clear or understandable; enlighten. **3** To send forth in or as in rays of light; diffuse; radiate. **4** To treat with or subject to X-rays, ultraviolet light, or other radiant energy. **5** To heat with radiant energy. — *v.i.* **6** To emit rays; shine. **7** To become radiant. [<L *irradiatus,* pp. of *irradiare* <*in-* thoroughly + *radiare* shine <*radius* ray] — **ir·ra'di·a·tive** *adj.* — **ir·ra'di·a'tor** *n.*

ir·ra·di·a·tion (i·rā'dē·ā'shən) *n.* **1** The act of irradiating. **2** The state of being irradiated. **3** Rays emitted: the *irradiation* of a candle. **4** *Optics* An apparent enlargement of a bright object, when seen against a dark background, due to the fact that the rays of light do not converge accurately to a focus upon the retina. **5** The application, to a person, substance, or object, of any form of radiant energy, for therapeutic, preservative, or other purposes. **6** The amount or intensity of radiation falling on a surface in a given time. **7** *Physiol.* A diffusion or branching out of

afferent nerve impulses or of conditioned reflexes.

ir·ra·tion·al (i·rash'ən·əl) *adj.* **1** Not possessed of or not exercising reasoning powers. **2** *Math.* **a** Pertaining to an irrational number. **b** Denoting an algebraic expression containing variables that are irreducible, as $\sqrt{-1}$, $\sqrt{x^3}$. Compare RATIONAL. **3** Contrary to reason; absurd. **4** In Greek and Latin prosody, not keeping the proper ratio between thesis and arsis, as a long syllable used in place of a short one. See synonyms under ABSURD, INSANE. [<L *irrationalis*] — **ir·ra'tion·al·ly** *adv.*

ir·ra·tion·al·ism (i·rash'ən·əl·iz'əm) *n.* A belief or philosophy that is not grounded in reason.

ir·ra·tion·al·i·ty (i·rash'ə·nal'ə·tē) *n. pl.* **·ties 1** The state of lacking reason or understanding. **2** Something irrational or absurd. Also **ir·ra'tion·al·ness.**

irrational number See under NUMBER.

ir·re·cip·ro·cal (ir'i·sip'rə·kəl) *adj.* **1** Not reciprocal; wanting in mutual interaction, assistance, or exchange. **2** Designating a type of colony or group whose members do not contribute equally to the general welfare.

ir·re·claim·a·ble (ir'i·klā'mə·bəl) *adj.* That cannot be reclaimed or redeemed. — **ir're·claim'a·bil'i·ty, ir're·claim'a·ble·ness** *n.* — **ir'·re·claim'a·bly** *adv.*

ir·rec·on·cil·a·ble (i·rek'ən·sī'lə·bəl, i·rek'ən·sī'lə·bəl) *adj.* That cannot be reconciled: *irreconcilable* enemies. — *n.* One who will not agree or become reconciled: said especially of political factionists. — **ir·rec'on·cil'a·bil'i·ty, ir·rec'on·cil'a·ble·ness** *n.* — **ir·rec'on·cil'a·bly** *adv.*

ir·re·cov·er·a·ble (ir'i·kuv'er·ə·bəl) *adj.* That cannot be recovered or regained; irredeemable; lost beyond recall. — **ir're·cov'er·a·ble·ness** *n.* — **ir're·cov'er·a·bly** *adv.*

ir·re·cu·sa·ble (ir'i·kyōō'zə·bəl) *adj.* That cannot be rejected. [<F *irrécusable* <LL *irrecusabilis* <*in-* not + *recusabilis* that should be rejected < *recusare* reject] — **ir're·cu'sa·bly** *adv.*

ir·re·deem·a·ble (ir'i·dē'mə·bəl) *adj.* **1** Not to be redeemed or replaced by an equivalent. **2** That cannot be reclaimed; not to be atoned for or escaped from: an *irredeemable* scoundrel, crime, or slavery. **3** Not ended by payment of principal: an *irredeemable* annuity. — **ir're·deem'a·bly** *adv.*

ir·re·duc·i·ble (ir'i·dōō'sə·bəl, -dyōō'-) *adj.* Not reducible.

ir·ref·ra·ga·ble (i·ref'rə·gə·bəl) *adj.* That cannot be refuted or disproved. [<LL *irrefragabilis* <*in-* not + *refragari* oppose] — **ir·ref'·ra·ga·bil'i·ty, ir·ref'ra·ga·ble·ness** *n.* — **ir·ref'ra·ga·bly** *adv.*

ir·re·fran·gi·ble (ir'i·fran'jə·bəl) *adj.* **1** That cannot be broken or violated: an *irrefrangible* law. **2** Not susceptible of refraction: said of light rays. — **ir're·fran'gi·bly** *adv.*

ir·ref·u·ta·ble (i·ref'yə·tə·bəl, ir'i·fyōō'tə·bəl) *adj.* Not refutable; that cannot be disproved; irrefragable, as an argument. — **ir·ref'u·ta·bil'i·ty** *n.* — **ir·ref'u·ta·bly** *adv.*

ir·re·gard·less (ir'i·gärd'lis) *adj. & adv. Illit.* Regardless: an incorrect or humorous usage.

ir·reg·u·lar (i·reg'yə·lər) *adj.* **1** Not regular; departing from or being out of the usual or proper form, order, course, method, proportion, etc. **2** Not conforming in action or character to rule, duty, discipline, etc.; lawless: *irregular* habits. **3** *Bot.* Exhibiting a want of symmetry in form and size: said of flowers in which the members of the various whorls differ from one another in size or shape. **4** Laboring under an ecclesiastical irregularity. See IRREGULARITY (def. 2). **5** Not belonging to a regular military force: *irregular* troops. **6** *Gram.* Not inflected or conjugated according to the most prevalent pattern: *irregular* verbs. See STRONG (def. 28). **7** *Law* Not according to rule; improper; not complying with legal formalities. — *n.* A person exercising a calling or profession without belonging to its regular organization or conforming to its regulations, as a soldier not in a regular military force. [<OF *irreguler* <Med. L *irregularis*] — **ir·reg'u·lar·ly** *adv.*

Synonyms (adj.): abnormal, anomalous, confused, crooked, desultory, devious, disorderly, dissolute, eccentric, erratic, exceptional, fitful, immoderate, inordinate, uneven, unnatural, unsettled, unsymmetrical, unsystematic, unusual, variable, vicious, wandering,

wild. *Antonyms:* common, constant, established, fixed, formal, methodical, natural, normal, orderly, ordinary, periodical, punctual, regular, stated, steady, systematic, uniform, universal, unvarying, usual.

ir·reg·u·lar·i·ty (i·reg'yə·lar'ə·tē) *n. pl.* **·ties 1** The condition of being irregular; an aberration, inconsistency, etc. **2** In the Roman Catholic and Anglican churches, an impediment to the taking or performing the functions of orders. See synonyms under DISORDER.

ir·rel·e·vant (i·rel'ə·vənt) *adj.* Not relevant; not apposite; impertinent. See synonyms under ALIEN, INSIGNIFICANT. — **ir·rel'e·vance, ir·rel'e·van·cy** *n.* — **ir·rel'e·vant·ly** *adv.*

ir·re·lig·ion (ir'i·lij'ən) *n.* The state of being without or opposed to religion; unbelief; godliness. [<F *irréligion*] — **ir're·lig'ion·ist** *n.*

ir·re·lig·ious (ir'i·lij'əs) *adj.* **1** Not religious; indifferent or hostile to religion. **2** Profane or sinful; ungodly. — **ir're·lig'ious·ly** *adv.* — **ir'·re·lig'ious·ness** *n.*

ir·rem·e·a·ble (i·rem'ē·ə·bəl, i·rē'mē-) *adj.* Admitting no return, irretraceable. [<L *irremeabilis* < *in-* not + *remeabilis* returning <*remeare* return <*re-* back + *meare* go] — **ir·rem'e·a·bly** *adv.*

ir·re·me·di·a·ble (ir'i·mē'dē·ə·bəl) *adj.* Not to be remedied; incurable; irreparable. [<L *irremediabilis*] — **ir're·me'di·a·ble·ness** *n.* — **ir're·me'di·a·bly** *adv.*

ir·re·mis·si·bil·i·ty (ir'i·mis'ə·bil'ə·tē) *n.* Impossibility of being forgiven; the state of being without remission. — **ir're·mis'si·ble** *adj.* — **ir're·mis'si·ble·ness** *n.* — **ir're·mis'si·bly** *adv.*

ir·re·mov·a·ble (ir'i·mōō'və·bəl) *adj.* Not removable; permanent. — **ir're·mov'a·bly** *adv.*

ir·rep·a·ra·ble (i·rep'ər·ə·bəl) *adj.* That cannot be repaired, rectified, or made amends for. — **ir·rep'a·ra·bil'i·ty, ir·rep'a·ra·ble·ness** *n.* — **ir·rep'a·ra·bly** *adv.*

ir·re·peal·a·ble (ir'i·pē'lə·bəl) *adj.* Not repealable.

ir·re·place·a·ble (ir'i·plā'sə·bəl) *adj.* Not capable of being replaced.

ir·re·pres·si·ble (ir'i·pres'ə·bəl) *adj.* Not repressible; that cannot be restrained. — **ir're·pres'si·ble·ness, ir're·pres'si·bil'i·ty** *n.* — **ir're·pres'si·bly** *adv.*

ir·re·proach·a·ble (ir'i·prō'chə·bəl) *adj.* Not reproachable; blameless. [<F *irréprochable*] — **ir're·proach'a·ble·ness** *n.* — **ir're·proach'a·bly** *adv.*

ir·re·sis·ti·ble (ir'i·zis'tə·bəl) *adj.* Not resistible; that cannot be successfully withstood or opposed. — **ir're·sis'ti·bil'i·ty, ir're·sis'ti·ble·ness** *n.* — **ir're·sis'ti·bly** *adv.*

ir·res·o·lu·ble (i·rez'ə·lōō·bəl) *adj.* **1** Not resoluble. **2** Not to be relieved; beyond help. **3** Not solvable; insoluble.

ir·res·o·lute (i·rez'ə·lōōt) *adj.* Not resolute or resolved; wavering; hesitating. — **ir·res'o·lute'·ly** *adv.* — **ir·res'o·lute'ness, ir·res'o·lu'tion** *n.*

Synonyms: capricious, doubtful, faint-hearted, faltering, fickle, fitful, half-hearted, hesitant, hesitating, indecisive, undecided, vacillating, wavering. Indecision denotes lack of intellectual conviction; irresolution denotes defect of volition, weakness of will. A thoughtful man may be *undecided* as to the course to take in perplexing circumstances; yet when decided he may act with promptness; an *irresolute* man lacks the nerve to act. Indecision commonly denotes a temporary state or condition, irresolution a trait of character. See FAINT, FICKLE. *Antonyms:* decided, determined, firm, persistent, resolute, resolved.

ir·re·solv·a·ble (ir'i·zol'və·bəl) *adj.* Not separable into parts; incapable of being resolved; not analyzable.

ir·re·spec·tive (ir'i·spek'tiv) *adj.* Lacking respect or relation; regardless: now used mostly with *of,* often adverbially. — **ir're·spec'tive·ly** *adv.*

ir·re·spon·si·ble (ir'i·spon'sə·bəl) *adj.* **1** Not accountable or amenable; not of sound mind. **2** Careless of responsibilities; unreliable. See synonyms under ARBITRARY. — *n.* A person who is irresponsible. — **ir're·spon'si·bil'i·ty, ir're·spon'si·ble·ness** *n.* — **ir're·spon'si·bly** *adv.* — **ir're·spon'sive** *adj.* — **ir're·spon'sive·ness** *n.*

ir·re·trace·a·ble (ir'i·trā'sə·bəl) *adj.* Not retraceable.

ir·re·triev·a·ble (ir'i·trē'və·bəl) *adj.* Not retrievable; irreparable. — **ir're·triev'a·ble·ness, ir're·triev'a·bil'i·ty** *n.* — **ir're·triev'a·bly** *adv.*

ir·rev·er·ence (i·rev′ər·əns) *n.* **1** The quality or condition of being irreverent. **2** The condition of not being reverenced; lack of honor.

ir·rev·er·ent (i·rev′ər·ənt) *adj.* Lacking in proper reverence; without deep respect or veneration. — **ir·rev′er·ent·ly** *adv.*

ir·re·vers·i·ble (ir′i·vûr′sə·bəl) *adj.* **1** That cannot be reversed or inverted. **2** Of, pertaining to, or designating a chemical or biological process which can continue only in one direction, as the coagulation of the white of a raw egg by heat, a degenerative disease, or the path of a stimulus along the nerves. — **ir′re·vers′i·bil′i·ty**, **ir′re·vers′i·ble·ness** *n.* — **ir′re·vers′i·bly** *adv.*

ir·rev·o·ca·ble (i·rev′ə·kə·bəl) *adj.* Incapable of being revoked or repealed; unalterable. — **ir·rev′o·ca·bil′i·ty**, **ir·rev′o·ca·ble·ness** *n.* — **ir·rev′o·ca·bly** *adv.*

ir·ri·gate (ir′ə·gāt) *v.t.* **·gat·ed**, **·gat·ing** **1** To supply (land) with water by means of ditches or other artificial channels. **2** *Med.* To moisten, as a wound, with dropping water, or spray, jet, etc. **3** *Rare* To moisten; wet. [< L *irrigatus*, pp. of *irrigare* bring water to < *in-* to + *rigare* water] — **ir′ri·ga·ble** (ir′ə·gə·bəl) *adj.* — **ir′ri·ga′tor** *n.*

ir·ri·ga·tion (ir′ə·gā′shən) *n.* **1** The artificial watering of land. **2** The condition of being irrigated. **3** *Med.* The steady maintenance of a flow of water over an affected part, for cleansing or therapeutic purposes. — **ir′ri·ga′tion·al** *adj.*

ir·rig·u·ous (i·rig′yŏŏ·əs) *adj.* **1** Watered or watery. **2** Supplying water. [< L *irriguus* < *in-* very + *riguus* watered < *rigare* wet, water]

ir·ri·ta·bil·i·ty (ir′ə·tə·bil′ə·tē) *n.* *pl.* **·ties** **1** The state of being irritable. **2** Susceptibility to anger or impatience. **3** *Biol.* **a** The responsiveness of living matter or protoplasm in general to changes in external conditions, manifested by motion, change of form, and in other ways; specifically, the response to stimuli characterizing certain tissues or organs of plants and animals. Compare STIMULUS. **b** A morbid condition of an organ, manifested by undue excitability under the action of a stimulant. Also **ir′ri·ta·ble·ness**.

ir·ri·ta·ble (ir′ə·tə·bəl) *adj.* **1** Showing impatience or ill temper on little provocation; irascible; petulant. **2** *Biol.* Responding easily to the action of external stimuli. **3** *Pathol.* Influenced to an abnormal degree by the action of stimulants or irritants. See synonyms under FRETFUL. [< L *irritabilis* < *irritare*] — **ir′ri·ta·bly** *adv.*

ir·ri·tant (ir′ə·tənt) *adj.* **1** Causing irritation. **2** *Med.* Irritating the eyes, nose, or digestive system: an *irritant* gas or smoke. — *n.* **1** *Pathol.* An agent of inflammation, pain, etc. **2** A provocation; spur. [< L *irritans*, *-antis*, ppr. of *irritare*] — **ir′ri·tan·cy** *n.*

ir·ri·tate (ir′ə·tāt) *v.t.* **·tat·ed**, **·tat·ing** **1** To excite ill temper or impatience in; fret; exasperate. **2** To make sore or inflamed. **3** *Biol.* To excite, as organic tissue, to a characteristic function or action. See synonyms under AFFRONT, INCENSE[1], PIQUE[1]. [< L *irritatus*, pp. of *irritare* irritate]

ir·ri·ta·tion (ir′ə·tā′shən) *n.* **1** The act of irritating. **2** The state of being irritated. **3** *Pathol.* A condition of morbid irritability in an organ or part of the body.

ir·ri·ta·tive (ir′ə·tā′tiv) *adj.* **1** Serving to produce irritation. **2** Accompanied by irritation.

ir·ro·ta·tion·al (ir′rō·tā′shən·əl) *adj.* Without rotatory motion.

ir·rup·tion (i·rup′shən) *n.* **1** A breaking or rushing in. **2** A violent incursion. See synonyms under INVASION. [< L *irruptio*, *-onis* < *irruptus*, pp. of *irrumpere* burst in < *in-* in + *rumpere* break] — **ir·rup′tive** *adj.*

is (iz) Present tense, third person singular of BE. [OE]

is– Var. of ISO-.

I·saac (ī′zek, *Fr.* ē·zȧk′) A masculine personal name. Also *Ger.* **I·saak** (ē′zäk), *Latin* **I·sa·a·cus** (ī·sā′ə·kəs), *Ital.* **I·sac·co** (ē·zäk′kō), *Dan., Sw.* **I·sak** (ē′säk). [< Hebrew, laughter] — **Isaac** A Hebrew patriarch; son of Abraham and Sarah, and father of Esau and Jacob. *Gen.* xxi 3.

i·sa·go·ge (ī′sə·gō′jē) *n.* An introduction, as to a work of scholarship. [< L < Gk. *eisagōgē* < *eisagein* introduce < *eis-* into + *agein* lead] — **i′sa·gog′ic** (-goj′ik) *adj.*

i·sa·gog·ics (ī′sə·goj′iks) *n. pl. (construed as sing.)* That part of exegetical theology which has to do with the literary history of the books of the Bible, their inspiration, authorship, genuineness, and time and place of composition; Biblical introduction.

i·sal·lo·bar (ī·sal′ə·bär) *n. Meteorol.* A contour line on a chart connecting places which show equal changes in barometric pressure over a specified interval. [< IS- + ALLO- + Gk. *baros* weight] — **i·sal′lo·bar′ic** *adj.*

i·san·drous (ī·san′drəs) *adj. Bot.* Having the stamens all similar and of the same number as the petals. [< IS- + -ANDROUS]

i·sa·nom·al (ī′sə·nom′əl) *n. Meteorol.* A line on a map or chart, connecting all those places which exhibit the same types or degrees of meteorological anomaly, as of pressure, temperature, wind, etc. [< IS- + ANOM(ALOUS)] — **i′sa·nom′a·lous** *adj.*

i·san·ther·ous (ī·san′thər·əs) *adj. Bot.* Having equal anthers. [< IS- + Gk. *anthēros* flowery < *anthos* flower]

i·san·thous (ī·san′thəs) *adj. Bot.* Having regular flowers. [< IS- + Gk. *anthos* flower]

i·sa·tin (ī′sə·tin) *n. Chem.* A yellowish or brownish-red crystalline compound with a bitter taste, $C_8H_5NO_2$, obtained by oxidizing indigo: used as a reagent and in the manufacture of vat dyes. Also **i′sa·tine** (-tēn, -tin). [< L *isatis* woad < Gk. + -IN] — **i′sa·tin′ic** *adj.*

is·chi·um (is′kē·əm) *n. pl.* **·chi·a** (-kē-ə) **1** *Anat.* The posterior part of the pelvic arch; in man, the part of the hip bone on which the body rests when sitting. **2** *Zool.* The third joint of any limb or lateral appendage in crustaceans. **3** *Entomol.* A side of the thorax in insects. Also **is·chi·on** (is′kē·ən). [< L < Gk. *ischion* hip joint < *ischys* strong] — **is·chi·at·ic** (is′kē·at′ik) or **·ad·ic** (-ad′ik), **is′chi·ac** (-ak) or **is′ki·al** (-əl) *adj.*

-ise Var. of -IZE.

is·en·trop·ic (īs′en·trop′ik, -trō′pik) *adj. Physics* Without change in entropy.

-ish[1] *suffix* **1** Of or belonging to (a national group): *Polish*; *Danish*. **2** Of the nature of; like: *boyish*; *clownish*. **3** Verging toward the character of: *feverish*; *bookish*. **4** Somewhat; rather: *bluish*; *tallish*. **5** *Colloq.* Approximately: *fortyish*. [OE *-isc*, adjectival suffix]

-ish[2] *suffix of verbs* Found in verbs of French origin: *brandish*, *demolish*. [< F *-iss-*, stem ending of *-ir* verbs < L *-isc-*, stem ending of inceptives]

i·sin·glass (ē′zing·glas, -gläs, ī′zən-) *n.* **1** A preparation of nearly pure gelatin made from the swim bladders of certain fishes, as sturgeons, cod, and carp. **2** Mica, chiefly in the form of thin sheets. [< MDu. *huysenblas* sturgeon bladder < *huysen* sturgeon + *blase* bladder; infl. in form by GLASS]

I·sis (ī′sis) In Egyptian mythology, the goddess of fertility, sister and wife of Osiris.

Is·lam (is′ləm, iz′-, is·läm′) *n.* **1** The religion of the Muslims, which maintains that there is but one God, Allah, and that Mohammed is his prophet; Mohammedanism. **2** The body of Muslim believers, their culture, and the countries they inhabit. [< Arabic *islām* submission < *salama* to be resigned]

Is·lam·a·bad (iz·läm′ə·bäd) The capital of Pakistan.

Is·lam·ic (is·lam′ik, -läm′-, iz-) *adj.* Muslim.

Is·lam·ism (is′ləm·iz′əm, iz′-) *n.* Islam. — **Is′lam·is′tic**, **Is·lam′it′ic** *adj.*

Is·lam·ite (is′ləm·īt, iz′-) *n.* A Muslim; Mussulman.

Is·lam·ize (is′ləm·īz, iz′-) *v.t. & v.i.* **·ized**, **·iz·ing** To convert or conform to Islam.

is·land (ī′lənd) *n.* **1** A tract of land, usually of moderate extent, surrounded by water. **2** Anything isolated or like an island; anything set distinctly apart from its surroundings, as a piece of elevated woodland surrounded by prairie. **3** A patch of land differentiated from the surrounding area by a certain kind of vegetation: They walked to the oak *island*. **4** A cultivated or settled spot, especially a big farm in the woods or other

unsettled area: often used as a place name. **5** *Anat.* Any of various isolated structures of the body; an insula. — *v.t.* **1** To make into an island or islands; insulate. **2** To isolate; set apart. **3** To intersperse with or as with islands. [OE *īgland*, lit., island land < *īg*, *īeg* isle + *land*; the *s* was added to the spelling in the 16th c. on a mistaken association from *isle*]

is·land·er (ī′lən·dər) *n.* An inhabitant of an island. Also **isles·man** (īlz′mən).

islands of Lang·er·hans (läng′ər·häns) *Anat.* Clusters of cells dispersed within the tissues of the pancreas and involved in the secretion of insulin. [after E. R. *Langerhans*, 1847–1888, German histologist]

Islands of the Blessed In Greek mythology, islands in the Western Ocean where the favorites of the gods lived after death.

isle (īl) *n.* **1** A small island. **2** *Poetic* An island. — *v.* **isled**, **isl·ing 1** To make into or place on an isle or island. — *v.i.* To live on an isle or island. ◆ Homophone: *aisle*. [< OF < L *insula* island]

is·let (ī′lit) *n.* A little island. [< OF *islette*, dim. of *isle*]

ism (iz′əm) *n.* A doctrine or system: often applied satirically or with derogatory force. [< -ISM]

-ism *suffix of nouns* **1** The act, process, or result of: *ostracism*. **2** The condition of being: *skepticism*. **3** The characteristic action or behavior of: *heroism*. **4** The beliefs, teachings, or system of: *Calvinism*. **5** Devotion to; adherence to the teachings of: *nationalism*. **6** A characteristic or peculiarity of: said of language or idiom: *Americanism*. **7** *Med.* An abnormal condition resulting from an excess of: *alcoholism*. [< L *-ismus* < Gk. *-ismos*]

is·n't (iz′ənt) Is not: a contraction.

iso– *combining form* **1** Equal; the same; identical. **2** *Chem.* Isomeric with, or an isomer of (the compound named): *isoprene*. Also, before vowels, *is-*. [< Gk. *isos* equal]

i·so·ag·glu·ti·na·tion (ī′sō·ə·glŏŏ′tə·nā′shən) *n. Med.* The agglutination of the red blood corpuscles of an animal by a serum taken from another individual of the same species.

i·so·ag·glu·tin·in (ī′sō·ə·glŏŏ′tə·nin) *n. Physiol.* An agglutinin having the power to agglutinate the red blood corpuscles of another individual of the same species.

i·so·am·yl (ī′sō·am′il) *n. Chem.* The univalent radical C_5H_{11} which enters into many organic compounds: *isoamyl* acetate (pear oil), *isoamyl* alcohol (fusel oil), etc.

i·so·bar (ī′sə·bär) *n.* **1** *Meteorol.* A line on a chart or diagram connecting places on the earth's surface having the same barometric pressure for a specified time or period. **2** *Physics* Any of two or more atoms having the same atomic weights but different atomic numbers and chemical properties. [< ISO- + Gk. *baros* weight] — **i′so·bar′ic** (-bar′ik) *adj.* — **i′so·bar′o·met′ric** (-bar′ə·met′rik) *adj.*

i·so·bath (ī′sə·bath) *n.* A contour line connecting points of equal depth beneath the earth or along the ocean floor. [< ISO- + Gk. *bathys* deep]

i·so·bront (ī′sə·bront) *n. Meteorol.* A line joining points at which any specified phase of a thunderstorm occurs at the same time. [< ISO- + Gk. *brontē* thunder]

i·so·can·dle (ī′sə·kan′dəl) *adj. Physics* **1** Designating a curve drawn through those points about a source of light at which the candlepower is the same. **2** Denoting a diagram comprising several sets of such curves.

i·so·chasm (ī′sə·kaz′əm) *n.* An isogram indicating the same average frequency of auroral displays. [< ISO- + Gk. *chasma* gap]

i·so·cheim (ī′sə·kīm) *n. Meteorol.* A line joining points on the earth's surface which have the same mean winter temperature. Also **i′so·chime**. [< ISO- + Gk. *cheima* winter] — **i′so·chei′mal** *adj.*

i·so·chore (ī′sə·kôr) *n. Physics* An isogram for which volume is the constant quantity. Also **i′so·chor**. [< ISO- + Gk. *chōra* space] — **i′so·chor′ic** *adj.*

i·so·chro·mat·ic (ī′sō·krō·mat′ik) *adj.* **1** *Optics* Having or denoting identity of color. **2** Orthochromatic.

i·so·chron (ī′sə·kron) *n. Biol.* In studies of

growth, a mathematical function equal to one percent of the time required to attain maturity. Also **i'so·chrone** (-krōn). [< ISO- + Gk. *chronos* time]

i·soch·ro·nal (ī·sok'rə·nəl) *adj.* Relating to or characterized by equal intervals of time, as a pendulum that always vibrates in the same period. Also **i·so·chron·ic** (ī'sə·kron'ik), **isoch'ro·nous.** — **i·soch'ro·nous·ly** *adv.*

i·so·cli·nal (ī'sə·klī'nəl) *adj.* 1 Dipping at the same angle and in the same direction. 2 Designating a line projected on the earth's surface connecting places that have the same inclination to the earth's magnetic field. 3 *Geol.* Pertaining to an isocline. — *n.* An isoclinal line.

i·so·cline (ī'sə·klīn) *n. Geol.* A rock fold in which the strata are so closely appressed that the sides are parallel. [< ISO- + Gk. *klinein* bend] — **i'so·clin'ic** (-klin'ik) *adj.*

i·so·cosm (ī'sə·koz'əm) *n. Physics* A line connecting points on the earth's surface showing an equal cosmic ray intensity. [< ISO- + Gk. *kosmos* world]

ISOCLINE
Vertical isoclinal folds.

i·soc·ra·cy (ī·sok'rə·sē) *n. pl.* **·cies** Equality in government; government in which all have equal power. [< Gk. *isokratia* < *iso-* same + *-kratia* rule < *kratos* power] — **i·so·crat** (ī'sə·krat) *n.* — **i'so·crat'ic** *adj.*

I·soc·ra·tes (ī·sok'rə·tēz), 436–338 B.C., Athenian orator.

i·so·cy·clic (ī'sō·sī'klik, -sik'lik) *adj.* 1 *Chem.* Pertaining to or designating any of two or more closed-chain hydrocarbon compounds containing the same number of atoms. 2 *Bot.* Denoting a flower whose whorls have an equal number of parts.

i·so·def (ī'sə·def) *n.* An isogram joining points that show an equal percentage deviation from the mean of some specified phenomenon or characteristic. [< ISO- + DEF(ICIENCY)]

i·so·des·mic (ī'sō·dez'mik) *adj. Physics* Pertaining to or denoting an ionic crystal structure in which all the bonds are of equal strength. [< ISO- + Gk. *desmos* chain]

i·so·di·a·met·ric (ī'sō·dī'ə·met'rik) *adj.* 1 Equal in the three dimensions. 2 Having only the lateral axes equal, as crystals of the tetragonal and hexagonal systems.

i·so·di·mor·phism (ī'sō·dī·môr'fiz·əm) *n.* The phenomenon in which two or more similar crystals are at the same time isomorphous and dimorphous. — **i'so·di·mor'phous** *adj.*

i·so·dose (ī'sə·dōs) *n.* The same or an equal dose, as of drugs, X-rays or other forms of radioactivity.

i·so·dy·nam·ic (ī'sō·dī·nam'ik) *adj.* 1 Relating to or characterized by equality of force. 2 Designating any line on the earth's surface at all points of which the intensity of terrestrial magnetism is the same. Also **i'so·dy·nam'i·cal.**

i·so·e·lec·tric (ī'sō·i·lek'trik) *adj.* 1 Exhibiting the same electric potential. 2 *Chem.* Designating the *p*H value at which a colloidal suspension is electrically neutral with respect to the surrounding medium. [< ISO- + ELECTRIC]

i·so·e·lec·tron·ic (ī'sō·i·lek·tron'ik) *adj. Physics* Pertaining to or denoting atoms having the same number of valence electrons and similar physical properties.

i·so·eu·ge·nol (ī'sō·yōō'jə·nōl, -nol) *n. Chem.* A colorless oily liquid, $C_{10}H_{12}O_2$, derived from ylang-ylang and used in the manufacture of vanillin. [< ISO- + EUGENOL]

i·so·gam·ete (ī'sō·gam'ēt, -gə·mēt') *n. Biol.* One of a pair of uniting gametes similar in size, form, and structure: opposed to *heterogamete.*

i·sog·a·my (ī·sog'ə·mē) *n. Biol.* That form of sexual reproduction in which there is a union of two similarly formed sexual cells, or gametes. Compare OOGAMY. [< ISO- + -GAMY] — **i·sog'a·mous** *adj.*

i·sog·e·nous (ī·soj'ə·nəs) *adj.* 1 Having a similarity of origin. 2 *Biol.* Developed from the same cells or tissues. [< ISO- + -GENOUS] — **i·so·gen·e·sis** (ī'sō·jen'ə·sis), **i·sog'e·ny** *n.*

i·so·ge·o·therm (ī'sō·jē'ə·thərm) *n. Geol.* A line or surface along which the earth, below its surface, has the same temperature. [< ISO- + GEO- + Gk. *thermē* heat] — **i'so·ge·o·ther'mal, i'so·ge'o·ther'mic** *adj.*

i·so·gloss (ī'sə·glôs, -glos) *n. Ling.* A line on a map in a dialect atlas delimiting areas within which certain linguistic features, as pronunciation, vocabulary, etc., are exhibited in common.

i·so·gon (ī'sə·gon) *n.* A polygon whose angles are all equal. [< ISOGONIC]

i·so·late (ī'sə·lāt, is'ə-) *v.t.* **·lat·ed, ·lat·ing** 1 To place in a detached or separate situation; set apart. 2 *Electr.* To insulate. 3 *Chem.* To obtain in a free or uncombined state, as an element or compound. 4 *Med.* To set apart from others, as a person with a communicable disease. 5 *Bacteriol.* To obtain a pure bacterial culture of (a specified disease or bacterium). — *n.* 1 A definite constituent or factor of some natural phenomenon, or aspect of experience, set apart from the whole for purposes of study, experiment, and analysis. 2 *Chem.* A pure compound, as one derived from an essential oil. [Back formation of ISOLATED < Ital. *isolato*, pp. of *isolare* isolate < *isola* island < L *insula* island] — **i'so·la'tor** *n.*

i·so·lat·ing (ī'sə·lā'ting, is'ə-) *adj. Ling.* Describing a language, such as Chinese, in which there is no distinction in form between the parts of speech, with meaning being determined primarily by word order.

i·so·la·tion·ism (ī'sə·lā'shən·iz'əm) *n.* The advocacy of national self-sufficiency and freedom from foreign political and economic alliances. — **i'so·la'tion·ist** *n.*

i·so·lead (ī'sə·lēd) *n. Mil.* A curved line drawn on a chart which indicates instantly the required lead of a gun in relation to a moving target. Also **isolead curve.**

i·so·lec·i·thal (ī'sō·les'ə·thəl) *adj. Biol.* Having the yolk evenly distributed through the protoplasm of an egg. [< ISO- + Gk. *lekithos* yolk of an egg]

i·so·leu·cine (ī'sə·lōō'sēn) *n. Biochem.* An amino acid, $C_6H_{13}NO_2$, found in body tissues and believed to be essential in nutrition.

i·so·log (ī'sə·lôg, -log) *n. Chem.* An isologous compound. Also **i'so·logue.** [< ISOLOGOUS]

i·sol·o·gous (ī·sol'ə·gəs) *adj. Chem.* Having similar molecular structure but different atoms of the same valency: applied especially to those groups of hydrocarbon compounds that have a constant difference of two hydrogen atoms in their composition. [< ISO- + Gk. *logos* proportion]

i·so·lux (ī'sə·luks) *n. Optics* 1 A line plotted on an appropriate set of coordinates to connect points of equal illumination. 2 A diagram containing sets of such lines. [< ISO- + L *lux* light]

i·so·mag·net·ic (ī'sō·mag·net'ik) *adj.* Relating to or designating lines connecting points of equal magnetic force. — *n.* An isomagnetic line.

i·so·mer (ī'sə·mər) *n. Chem.* A compound having the same molecular weight and formula as another but with a different spatial arrangement of its atoms, resulting in different properties. [< Gk. *isomerēs* equally divided < *isos* equal + *meros* part] — **i'so·mer'ic** (-mer'ik) *adj.*

i·so·mer·ism (ī·som'ər·iz'əm) *n. Chem.* The condition of having different chemical or physical properties, or both, but identical molecular composition.

i·so·mer·ous (ī·som'ər·əs) *adj.* 1 *Bot.* Equal in number, as the members of the successive circles or whorls of a flower: opposed to *heteromerous.* 2 *Entomol.* Having an equal number of tarsal joints on all feet: said of certain coleopterous insects. 3 Isomeric.

i·so·met·ric (ī'sō·met'rik) *adj.* 1 Having equality in dimensions or measurements. 2 Pertaining to that system of crystallization in which the three axes are equal in length and at right angles to each other. 3 *Physics* Indicating or maintaining the same proportions, measure, dimensions, etc., as a constant volume in a gas. Also **i'so·met'ri·cal.** 4 Based upon the forceful contraction of muscles against immovable resistance without shortening muscle fibers, a means of strengthening muscles: *isometric* exercises. — *n.* An isometric line. [< Gk. *isometros*

< *isos* equal + *metron* measure] — **i'so·met'ri·cal·ly** *adv.*

i·so·me·tro·pi·a (ī'sō·mə·trō'pē·ə) *n. Optics* Equality of the focal length of the two eyes. [< ISO- + Gk. *metron* measure + -OPIA]

i·som·e·try (ī·som'ə·trē) *n.* 1 Equality in measured parts or proportions. 2 *Geog.* Equality of elevation, as of mountain peaks. [< Gk. *isometria* equality of measure < *isos* same + *metros* measure]

i·so·morph (ī'sə·môrf) *n.* An organism or crystal superficially like another but morphologically different. [< ISO- + Gk. *morphē* form] — **i'so·mor'phic** *adj.*

i·so·mor·phism (ī'sə·môr'fiz·əm) *n.* 1 The property shown by two substances of analogous chemical composition that crystallize in identical or nearly identical forms. 2 *Biol.* The possession of like characters by organisms of different groups, resulting usually from like environmental influences. — **i'so·mor'phous** *adj.*

i·son·o·my (ī·son'ə·mē) *n.* 1 Equality of civil rights. 2 Equality in rank, kind, or grade, in classification. [< Gk. *isonomia* < *isos* same + *nomos* law] — **i'so·nom·ic** (ī'sō·nom'ik) *adj.*

i·sop·a·thy (ī·sop'ə·thē) *n. Med.* 1 The theory that a contagious disease contains in its own causative agent the means for its cure. 2 Treatment by the application or use of diseased matter. — **i·so·path·ic** (ī'sō·path'ik) *adj.*

i·so·phyl·ly (ī'sō·fil'ē) *n. Bot.* The condition in which a plant bears only one kind of leaf. [< ISO- + Gk. *phyllon* leaf] — **i'so·phyl'lous** *adj.*

i·so·pi·es·tic (ī'sō·pī·es'tik) *adj.* Showing equal pressure; isobaric. — *n.* An isobar. [< ISO- + Gk. *piezein* press]

i·so·pod (ī'sə·pod) *n.* Any of a large and varied order (*Isopoda*) of terrestrial and aquatic crustaceans, having sessile eyes, flattened bodies lacking a carapace, and seven free thoracic segments, of which each carries a pair of closely similar legs. — *adj.* Of or pertaining to the *Isopoda.* [< NL < Gk. *isos* equal + *pous, podos* foot] — **i·sop·o·dan** (ī·sop'ə·dən) *adj.*

i·so·pol·i·ty (ī'sō·pol'ə·tē) *n.* Reciprocity of civil rights.

i·so·por (ī'sə·pôr, -pōr) *n.* An isogram indicating an equal rate of change in any element of the earth's magnetic field. [< ISO- + Gk. *poros* passage] — **i'so·por'ic** *adj.*

i·so·pract (ī'sə·prakt) *n.* A boundary enclosing areas of equal frequency or value of specified physical conditions, as population, snowfall, etc. [< ISO- + Gk. *praktikos* of action]

i·so·prene (ī'sə·prēn) *n. Chem.* A volatile liquid hydrocarbon of the terpene group, C_5H_8, obtained when caoutchouc and gutta-percha are subjected to dry distillation. [Appar. an arbitrary coinage]

i·so·pro·pyl (ī'sə·prō'pil) *n. Chem.* The univalent radical $(CH_3)_2CH$, an important constituent of many organic compounds, as isopropyl alcohol, $(CH_3)_2CHOH$, used as a solvent and in perfumery. Also called **i'so·pro'pa·nol** (-pə·nōl, -nol).

i·sop·ter·ous (ī·sop'tər·əs) *adj.* Of or pertaining to an order (*Isoptera*) of small and medium-sized social insects having soft bodies, strong mandibles, and well-developed claws, the workers and soldiers being wingless and sterile. See WHITE ANT. [< ISO- + -PTEROUS]

i·so·pyc·nic (ī'sə·pik'nik) *adj.* Of, pertaining to, or having equal density, as sea water or air masses. — *n.* A line connecting points of equal density. [< ISO- + Gk. *pyknos* thick, dense]

i·so·pyre (ī'sə·pīr) *n.* A variety of impure opal.

i·sos·ce·les (ī·sos'ə·lēz) *adj. Geom.* Pertaining to or designating a triangle having two sides of equal length. [< LL < Gk. *isoskelēs* equal-legged < *iso-* equal + *skelos* leg]

ISOSCELES
TRIANGLE

i·so·seis·mic (ī'sə·sīz'mik, -sīs'-) *adj.* Pertaining to or designating equal intensities of earthquake shocks. — *n.* A coseismal.

i·sos·ta·sy (ī·sos'tə·sē) *n.* 1 *Geol.* The theoretical condition of equilibrium which the earth's surface tends to assume under the action of terrestrial gravitation, as affected by the transference of material from regions of denudation to those of deposition, and by differences in density in various portions of the earth's mass near the surface. 2 Equilibrium resulting from equal pressure on all sides. [<ISO- + Gk. *stasis* a standing still] — **i·so·stat·ic** (ī′sə·stat′ik) *adj.*

i·so·stem·o·nous (ī′sə·stem′ə·nəs) *adj. Bot.* Having the stamens in a single series and of the same number as the petals and sepals. [<ISO- + Gk. *stēmōn* thread + -OUS] — **i′so·stem′o·ny** *n.*

i·so·stere (ī′sə·stir) *n.* 1 *Meteorol.* A line connecting points of equal atmospheric density. 2 *Chem.* A compound or radical which exhibits isosterism. [<ISO- + Gk. *stereos* solid]

i·sos·ter·ism (ī·sos′tər·iz′əm) *n. Chem.* A similarity in the physical properties of certain compounds, radicals, and elements, due to their having the same number and arrangement of electrons. — **i·so·ster·ic** (ī′sə·ster′ik) *adj.*

i·so·ther·mal (ī′sə·thûr′məl) *adj.* 1 Having the same temperature. 2 Designating a layer of the atmosphere lying above the region of convection: also called *stratospheric.* 3 Of or pertaining to an isotherm. — *n.* An isotherm.

i·so·tone (ī′sə·tōn) *n. Physics* One of two or more atomic nuclei having the same number of neutrons. [<ISOTONIC]

i·so·ton·ic (ī′sə·ton′ik) *adj.* 1 Having the same tonicity. 2 *Physiol.* **a** Having the same osmotic pressure on opposite sides of a membrane: said of solutions, especially blood or plasma: distinguished from *hypertonic:* also *isosmotic.* **b** Denoting a muscle which contracts against a small but uniform tension or the curve of such a contraction. 3 *Music* Pertaining to, characterized by, or having equal tones. [<Gk. *isotonos* having equal accent or tone < *iso-* equal + *tonos* accent, tone] — **i·so·ton·ic·i·ty** (ī′sə·tō·nis′ə·tē) *n.*

i·so·tope (ī′sə·tōp) *n. Physics* Any of two or more forms of an element having the same atomic number and similar chemical properties but differing in atomic weight and radioactive behavior. The accepted atomic weight of an element is the average of the nuclear masses of all the isotopes it may contain. [<ISO- + Gk. *topos* place] — **i·so·top·ic** (ī′sə·top′ik, -tō′pik) *adj.* — **i·sot·o·py** (ī·sot′ə·pē) *n.*

i·so·tron (ī′sə·tron) *n.* An apparatus for the electromagnetic separation of uranium isotopes, especially in the generation of atomic energy. [<ISO(TOPE) + (ELEC)TRON]

i·so·trop·ic (ī′sə·trop′ik, -trō′pik) *adj.* 1 *Physics* Exhibiting the same physical properties in every direction. 2 *Biol.* Having indifferent structure, as various eggs. Also **i′so·trope**, **i·sot·ro·pous** (ī·sot′rə·pəs).

i·sot·ro·pism (ī·sot′rə·piz′əm) *n.* 1 The quality of being isotropic. 2 *Biol.* An ability in an unsegmented egg to develop an embryo from any part. Also **i·sot·ro·py** (ī·sot′rə·pē). [<ISO- + -TROPISM]

Is·ra·el (iz′rē·əl) *n.* 1 The Jewish people, traditionally regarded as descended from Israel (Jacob). 2 The kingdom in the northern part of ancient Palestine formed by the ten tribes of Israel.

Is·ra·el (iz′rē·əl) A republic comprising parts of Palestine, proclaimed as a Jewish national state in May, 1948; 8,040 square miles; capital, Jerusalem. — **Is·rae·li** (iz·rā′lē) *adj. & n.*

Is·ra·el·ite (iz′rē·əl·īt′) *n.* 1 Any of the people of Israel or their descendants; a Hebrew; a Jew. 2 One of God's chosen people. — **Is′·ra·el·it′ish** (-ī′tish), **Is′ra·el·it′ic** (-it′ik) *adj.*

is·su·a·ble (ish′ōō·ə·bəl, -yōō-) *adj.* 1 That can issue or be issued. 2 *Law* Tending to an issue. — **is′su·a·bly** *adv.*

is·su·ance (ish′ōō·əns, -yōō-) *n.* The act of putting, sending, or giving out; promulgation; distribution.

is·su·ant (ish′ōō·ənt, -yōō-) *adj.* 1 Issuing or emerging. 2 *Her.* Denoting a beast of which the upper half only is seen.

is·sue (ish′ōō, -yōō) *v.* **·sued, ·su·ing** *v.t.* 1 To

give out or deliver in a public or official manner; put into circulation; publish: to *issue* a new stamp; to *issue* a magazine. 2 To deal out or distribute: to *issue* ammunition. 3 To send forth or emit; let out; discharge. — *v.i.* 4 To come forth or flow out; emerge: Water *issued* from the pipe. 5 To come as a result or consequence; proceed: His charity *issues* from his good character. 6 To come to a specified end: with *in:* The argument *issued* in a duel. 7 To be given out or published; appear. 8 To come as profit or revenue; accrue: with *out of.* 9 *Rare* or *Law* To be born or descended. — *n.* 1 The act of going out; outflow. 2 A place or way of egress. 3 Result; outcome; upshot. 4 The action of giving out or supplying officially or publicly. 5 An item or amount which is issued. 6 Offspring; progeny. 7 Profits; proceeds. 8 *Med.* **a** A suppurating sore, produced and maintained by artificial means. **b** A discharge, as of blood. 9 *Law* The point in question between parties to an action. 10 A subject of discussion or interest. See synonyms under CONSEQUENCE, END, EVENT, TOPIC. [<F *issue* < *issir, eissir* <L *exire* <*ex-* out of + *ire* go] — **at issue** Under dispute; in question. — **to take issue** To disagree. — **is′su·er** *n.*

-ist *suffix of nouns* 1 One who or that which does or has to do with: often used with verbs in *-ize: catechist.* 2 One whose profession is; one who practices: *pharmacist.* 3 A student or devotee of: *genealogist.* 4 One who advocates or adheres to: in extension from nouns ending in *-ism: socialist.* [<L *-ista* <Gk. *-istēs*]

Is·tan·bul (is′tan·bōōl′, -tän-, Turkish is·täm′·bōōl) The largest city of Turkey, a port on both sides of the Bosporus at its entrance into the Sea of Marmara: formerly *Byzantium* and, as *Constantinople,* capital of Turkey until 1923: also *Stambul.* Also **Is′tan·boul′**.

isth·mi·an (is′mē·ən, *rarely* isth′-) *adj.* Of or pertaining to an isthmus. — *n.* An inhabitant of an isthmus.

isth·mus (is′məs, *rarely* isth′-) *n.* *pl.* **·mus·es** or **·mi** (-mī) 1 A narrow body of land connecting two larger bodies. 2 *Anat.* A contracted passage or portion of an organ between two larger cavities or parts: the portion of the brain which joins the pons Varolii with the interbrain and hemisphere. 3 *Bot.* The constricted or contracted part of the cells of desmids connecting the two hemicells. [<L <Gk. *isthmos* narrow passage]

it (it) *pron.* The neuter pronoun, nominative (pl. *they*) and objective (pl. *them*), of the third person singular, used: 1 As a substitute for things or for infants and animals when the sex is unspecified. 2 As the subject of an impersonal verb: *It* rained. 3 As the subject or object of a clause regarding a general condition or state of affairs: How was *it? It* was warm. 4 As the subject or predicate nominative of a verb whose logical subject is anticipated: Who was *it? It* was John. 5 As the indefinite subject of a verb introducing a clause or phrase: *It* seems that he knew. 6 *Colloq.* As the indefinite object after certain verbs in idiomatic expressions: to lord *it* over; to face *it.* — *n.* In certain children's games, the player required to perform some specified act. [OE *hit*]

i·tab·i·rite (i·tab′ə·rīt) *n.* A schist containing hematite in grains or scales. Also **i·tab′i·ryte.** [from *Itabira,* Brazil]

it·a·col·u·mite (it′ə·kol′yə·mīt) *n.* A laminated, granular, friable sandstone which is flexible in thin slabs. [from *Itacolumi,* mountain in eastern Brazil]

I·tal·ian (i·tal′yən) *adj.* Pertaining to Italy, its people, culture or language. — *n.* 1 A native or naturalized inhabitant of Italy. 2 The Romance language of modern Italy. [<L *Italianus* < *Italia* Italy]

I·tal·ian·ize (i·tal′yən·īz) *v.t. & v.i.* **·ized, ·iz·ing** To make or become Italian in manner, customs, language, etc. — **I·tal′ian·i·za′tion** *n.*

Italian sonnet See under SONNET.

i·tal·ic (i·tal′ik) *Printing n.* A style of type in which the letters slope, as *these:* also **i·tal′ics.** — *adj.* Designating, or printed in, italic. Compare ROMAN.

I·tal·ic (i·tal′ik) *adj.* Relating to any of the peoples of ancient Italy. — *n.* A subfamily of the Indo-European languages, comprising three branches—Falisco-Latinian (including Latin and the Romance languages), Osco-Umbrian, and Sabellian. [<L *Italicus*]

i·tal·i·cize (i·tal′ə·sīz) *v.t. & v.i.* **·cized, ·ciz·ing** 1 To print in italics. 2 To underscore (written words or phrases) with a single line to indicate italics. Also **i·tal′i·cise.**

I·tal·i·ote (i·tal′ē·ōt) *n.* One of the Greek inhabitants of Italy. Also **I·tal′i·ot** (-ot). [<Gk. *Italiōtēs* <*Italia* Italy]

It·a·ly (it′ə·lē) A republic in southern Europe; 116,224 square miles; capital, Rome. *Italian* **I·ta·lia** (ē·täl′yä).

itch (ich) *v.i.* 1 To feel a peculiar irritation of the skin which inclines one to scratch the part affected. 2 To have a desire or longing; crave. — *n.* 1 Any of various usually contagious skin diseases accompanied by itching, as scabies. 2 An itching of the skin. 3 A restless desire or yearning. [OE *giccan*] — **itch′i·ness** *n.* — **itch′ing** *n.* — **itch′y** *adj.*

itch mite A mite (*Sarcoptes scabiei*), the female of which burrows and lays eggs under the scarfskin, causing inflammation and intense itching.

-ite[1] *suffix of nouns* 1 A native of: *Brooklynite.* 2 An adherent of: *Darwinite.* 3 A descendant of: *Israelite.* 4 *Mineral.* A rock or mineral: *graphite.* 5 *Zool.* A part of the body or of an organ: *somite.* 6 *Paleontol.* A fossil: *ammonite.* 7 Like; resembling; related to: often used in the names of commercial products: *dynamite.* [<F *-ite* <L *-ita* <Gk. *-itēs*]

-ite[2] *suffix Chem.* A salt or ester of an acid whose name ends in *-ous: sulfite.* [<F *-ite;* arbitrarily coined (1787) from *-ate* -ATE[3]]

-ite[3] *suffix* Used in adjectives and verbs formed on the past participial stems of Latin verbs in the second, third, and fourth conjugations: *finite, unite.* [<L *-itus*]

i·tem (ī′təm) *n.* 1 A separate article or entry in an account, etc. 2 A newspaper paragraph. 3 *Obs.* An admonition; hint; especially, a maxim or saying, formerly introduced by the word *item.* See synonyms under CIRCUMSTANCE. — *v.t.* 1 To set down by items. 2 To make a note or memorandum of. — *adv.* Likewise. [<L, likewise]

i·tem·ize (ī′təm·īz) *v.t.* **·ized, ·iz·ing** To set down or specify by items. — **i′tem·iz′er** *n.* — **i′tem·i·za′tion** *n.*

item veto The power of a government executive to veto parts of a bill without vetoing the entire bill.

it·er·ate (it′ə·rāt) *v.t.* **·at·ed, ·at·ing** 1 To utter or do again. 2 To utter or do repeatedly. [<L *iteratus,* pp. of *iterare* repeat < *iterum* again] — **it′er·a·ble** (it′ər·ə·bəl) *adj.* — **it′er·ant** *adj.* — **it′er·ance, it′er·a′tion** *n.*

it·er·a·tive (it′ə·rā′tiv, it′ər·ə·tiv) *adj.* 1 Characterized by repetition; repetitious. 2 *Gram.* Frequentative.

i·te·rum (it′ər·əm) *adv. Latin* Again; once more.

ith·y·phal·lic (ith′ə·fal′ik) *adj.* 1 Relating to the phallus used in the festivals of Bacchus; hence, obscene; lewd. 2 In classical prosody, describing a trochaic tripody: used in verse sung in the phallic processions. [<L *ithyphallicus* <Gk. *ithyphallikos* < *ithyphallos* < *ithys* erect, rigid + *phallos* a phallus]

i·tin·er·a·cy (ī·tin′ər·ə·sē, i·tin′-) *n.* A passing from place to place in circuit, as in the discharge of ministerial duties. Also **i·tin′er·an·cy.**

i·tin·er·ant (ī·tin′ər·ənt, i·tin′-) *adj.* Going from place to place. — *n.* One who travels from place to place, as a minister serving a circuit of churches. [<LL *itinerans, -antis,* ppr. of *itinerari* make a journey < *iter, itineris* journey] — **i·tin′er·ant·ly** *adv.*

i·tin·er·ar·y (ī·tin′ər·rer′ē, i·tin′-) *n.* *pl.* **·ar·ies** 1 A detailed account or diary of a journey. 2 A plan of a proposed tour. 3 An exploring tour, or its record. 4 A route pursued in traveling. 5 Originally, a book or chart giving the roads, places, and distances of a region or along a route. 6 A guidebook. 7 In the Roman Catholic Church, a form of prayer for clergy departing on a journey. — *adj.* 1 Pertaining to or done on a journey. 2 Itinerant.

[<LL *itinerarium*, neut. of *itinerarius* pertaining to a journey < *iter, itineris* journey, route]

i·tin·er·ate (ī·tin′ər·āt, i·tin′-) *v.i.* **·at·ed, ·at·ing** To journey from place to place in or on circuit; to roam; wander. [<LL *itineratus*, pp. of *itinerari* make a journey. See ITINERANT.] — **i·tin′er·a′tion** *n.*

-itis *suffix* Inflammation of: *peritonitis, laryngitis.* [<Gk.]

it'll (it′l) **1** It will. **2** It shall.

its (its) *pronominal adj.* (possessive case of the pronoun *it*) Belonging or pertaining to it: *its* color. [<IT + ′s, possessive case ending; written *it's* until the 19th century]

it's (its) **1** It is. **2** It has.

it·self (it·self′) *pron.* It: an intensive or reflexive use. Also *Scot.* **it·sel′.**

I·van·hoe (ī′vən·hō) A historical romance by Sir Walter Scott based on the Norman–Saxon conflict in England at the time of Richard I.

I've (īv) I have.

-ive *suffix of adjectives* **1** Having a tendency or predisposition to: *disruptive.* **2** Having the nature, character, or quality of: *massive.* Also *-ative.* [<F *-if* <L *-ivus,* suffix of adjectives]

i·vied (ī′vēd) *adj.* Covered or overgrown with ivy.

i·vo·ry (ī′vər·ē) *n. pl.* **·ries 1** The hard, creamy-white, fine–grained, opaque dentine that constitutes the greater part of the tusks of certain animals, as the elephant, walrus, etc. ◆ Collateral adjective: *eburnean.* **2** Any form of dentine. **3** Some ivorylike substance. **4** *pl.* Things made of, consisting of, or similar to ivory; especially, in slang use, the teeth, billiard balls, dice, keys of a piano. **5** The ivory nut. **6** The color of ivory. — *adj.* Made of or resembling ivory. [<OF *ivurie* <L *eboreus* of ivory < *ebur* ivory]

i·vo·ry·bill (ī′vər·ē·bil′) *n.* A large North American woodpecker (*Campephilus principalis*), now rare, having a white or ivory-like bill.

ivory black A deep–black pigment made by charring bones or ivory scraps; carbon black.

Ivory Coast The coastal region of western Africa along the Gulf of Guinea.

ivory gull The white arctic gull (*Pagophila alba*).

ivory nut The hard, ivorylike seed of the ivory palm, used for small carvings, buttons, etc.; vegetable ivory.

ivory palm The South American palm (*Phytelephas macrocarpa*) that bears ivory nuts.

ivory tower A place or condition of seclusion from the world and worldly attitudes, reality, action, etc.

i·vo·ry·type (ī′vər·ē·tīp′) *n. Phot.* A picture made by fixing a translucent photograph over another.

i·vy (ī′vē) *n. pl.* **i·vies 1** A European, evergreen, climbing or creeping shrub (*Hedera helix*) of the ginseng or ivy family, bearing glossy leaves, small yellowish flowers, and black berries: also called **English ivy. 2** One of various other climbing plants, as the **Japanese** or **Boston ivy** (*Parthenocissus tricuspidata*) and the **ground ivy** (*Nepeta hederacea*). [OE *ifig*]

IVY

a. Poison ivy (*Rhus radicans*).
b. Poison sumac (*Rhus vernix*).

i·vy·ber·ry (ī′vē·ber′ē) *n. pl.* **·ries** Wintergreen.

Ivy League An association, primarily athletic, of colleges in the NE United States, comprising Brown, Columbia, Cornell, Dartmouth, Harvard, Princeton, the University of Pennsylvania, and Yale: often used attributively to denote the fashions or manners characteristic of students in these colleges: *Ivy League* clothes.

ivy vine 1 An American vitaceous plant (*Ampelopsis cordata*) with cordate leaves. **2** The Virginia creeper.

ix·o·di·a·sis (ik′sə·dī′ə·sis) *n. Pathol.* Skin disease caused by ticks of the genus *Ixodes;* tick fever. [<NL *Ixodes,* genus of ticks + -IASIS]

iz·ar (iz′ər) *n. Arabic* A piece of white cotton fabric worn as the chief outer garment of Moslem women.

-ization *suffix* State or process of: used to form nouns from verbs in *-ize: oxidization.* [<-IZE + -ATION]

-ize *suffix of verbs* **1** To make; cause to become or resemble: *Christianize, concretize, Americanize.* **2** Subject to the action of; affect with: *oxidize.* **3** Change into; become: *mineralize.* **4** To act in the manner of; to practice: *sympathize.* Also *-ise.* [<F *-iser* <L *-izare* <Gk. *-izein*]

I·zhevsk (ē·zhefsk′) The capital of the Udmurt Autonomous S.S.R.

Iz·ma·il (ēz·mä·ēl′) A city on the Danube in Ukrainian S.S.R.

Iz·mir (ēz·mir′) The Turkish name for SMYRNA.

Iz·nik (ēz·nēk′) A village of NW Turkey on the site of ancient Nicaea. Also **Is·nik′.**

iz·zard (iz′ərd) *n. Colloq.* The letter Z. — **from A to izzard** From beginning to end. [Earlier *ezed,* var. of ZED]

J

j, J (jā) *n. pl.* **j's, J's** or **js, Js, jays** (jāz) **1** The tenth letter of the English alphabet: originally identical with Roman *I.* In the 17th century, the calligraphic practice of carrying initial *I* (which usually had consonant value) both above and below the line gradually developed into a graphic distinction between *i* the vowel and *i* or *j* the consonant. **2** A sound of the letter *j,* usually a voiced affricate, as in *judge* (juj); in borrowings from Modern French, often a voiced, alveolar fricative, as in *jabot.* See ALPHABET. — *symbol* **1** In Roman numerals, one: used as a variant of *i* at the end of a number, as *vij,* especially in medical prescriptions. **2** Anything shaped like a J, as a bolt or hook.

jab (jab) *v.t. & v.i.* **jabbed, jab·bing 1** To poke or thrust sharply, as with the point of something. **2** To punch or strike with sharp blows. — *n.* A sharp thrust or poke: punch. [Var. of JOB²]

jab·ber (jab′ər) *v.t. & v.i.* To speak rapidly or unintelligibly; chatter. See synonyms under BABBLE. — *n.* Rapid or unintelligible talk; chatter. [Prob. imit.] — **jab′ber·er** *n.*

jab·i·ru (jab′ə·rōō) *n.* A large tropical American wading bird (*Jabiru mycteria*) of the stork family, with white plumage and a scarlet inflatable pouch. [<Tupian]

jab·o·ran·di (jab′ō·ran′dē) *n.* **1** Any of a genus (*Pilocarpus*) of numerous South American shrubs of the rue family, especially *P. jaborandi.* **2** The dried leaves of this and allied plants, which yield pilocarpine and other medicinal alkaloids. [<Tupian]

ja·bot (zha·bō′, jab′ō; *Fr.* zha·bō′) *n. pl.* **·bots** (-bōz′, *Fr.* -bō′) A lace frill worn by women on the bodice; formerly, a ruffle on a man's shirt bosom. [<F, lit., a gizzard]

ja·bot·i·ca·ba (jə·bot′ə·kä′bə) *n.* A semitropical evergreen tree (*Myrciaria cauliflora*) of the myrtle family, with edible, grapelike fruit:

cultivated in Florida and California. [< Tupian *jabuti* a tortoise + *caba* fat]

jab·o·ty (jab′ə·tē) *n.* **1** An oil–bearing seed from a tropical American tree (genus *Erisma*). **2** The oil from this seed, sometimes used as a substitute for cocoa butter. [<Tupian]

ja·cal (hä·käl′) *n. pl.* **·ca·les** (-kä′lās) A one-room Mexican hut built of upright poles laced together with wicker and plastered with mud or adobe. [<Sp. <Nahuatl]

jac·a·mar (jak′ə·mär) *n.* A tropical American insectivorous bird (family *Galbulidae*) of various genera, having golden–green or coppery plumage. [<F <Tupian *jacamaciri*]

ja·ça·na (zhä′sə·nä′) *n.* Any of a family (*Jacanidae*) of small tropical wading birds with long, straight claws by which they walk over the floating leaves of aquatic plants. [<Pg. <Tupian]

jac·a·ran·da (jak′ə·ran′də) *n.* **1** Any of a genus (*Jacaranda*) of tropical American trees and shrubs of the bignonia family, with a hard, fine–textured wood: some species, as *J. caroba,* are used in medicine. **2** Brazilian rosewood (*Dalbergia nigra*): used for making tool handles, radio cabinets, etc. [<Tupian]

ja·cinth (jā′sinth, jas′inth) *n.* **1** A reddish-orange variety of zircon: used as a gemstone. **2** *Obs.* A hyacinth. [<OF *iacinte* <L *hyacinthus.* Doublet of HYACINTH.]

jack (jak) *n.* **1** *Mech.* **a** A device, appliance, or part of a machine: so called from its serving to supply the place of an assistant. **b** A portable device, operating by lever, screw, or other mechanical principle, for exerting considerable energy through a short distance: used in raising weights. **2** The male of the ass or of certain other animals. **3** A flag showing the canton or union of the national ensign without the fly, as of the United States or or Great Britain. See UNION JACK. **4** A playing card; in most games, the lowest of the face

cards; a knave. **5** *U.S. Slang* Money. **6** *Electr.* A spring clip to which the wires of a circuit may be attached and which is arranged for the insertion of a plug. **7** A bootjack. **8** A jacklight. **9** A device to prevent back draft in a chimney or vent pipe. **10** *Naut.* An iron crosstree at the topgallant-masthead: also **jack crosstree. 11** An automatic figure of a man which strikes the time bell of a clock. **12** A small white ball used as the object played for in the game of bowls. **13** The hopper of a pianoforte; in a harpsichord, the piece of wood holding the quill which strikes the string. **14** One of various fishes, as a pike or pickerel. **15** *pl.* The game played with jackstones. — **hydraulic jack** A device for lifting heavy weights or exerting great force by fluid pressure from a hand pump connected with a large–bore cylinder and a piston: also **hydrostatic jack.** — *v.t.* **1** To raise or lift with or as with a jack. **2** *Colloq.* To advance, as a price or charge: often with *up.* **3** *U.S.* To jack–light. [from *Jack,* a personal name]

jack–a–dan·dy (jak′ə·dan′dē) *n. pl.* **·dies** A ridiculous fop.

jack·al (jak′ôl, -əl) *n.* **1** One of various dog-like carnivorous mammals (family *Canidae*), smaller than the wolf, with a long bushy tail, feeding on small animals and on carrion. **2** One who does base work to serve another's purpose: from the erroneous notion that the jackal finds prey for the lion. Also **jack′all.** — *v.i.* To do menial work. [<Turkish *chakal* <Persian *shaghal*]

jack–a–napes (jak′ə·nāps) *n.* An impertinent fellow; an upstart. [<*Jack Napes,* nickname of William de la Pole, 15th c. Duke of Suffolk]

jack·ass (jak′as′) *n.* **1** The male ass. **2** A foolish person; blockhead.

jackass brig A brigantine.

jack bean A three-leaved climber of the bean family (*Canavalia ensiformis*) having purple flowers in auxiliary racemes and long pods: grown for stock feed in the southern United States: also called *overlook*.

jack·boots (jak′bōōts′) *n. pl.* Heavy topboots reaching above the knees.

jack box A unit for plugging a loudspeaker or individual headphone into a radio receiving system: used in airplanes, etc.

jack·daw (jak′dô′) *n.* **1** A small, glossy-black, crowlike bird (*Corvus monedual*) of Europe, often tamed as a pet. **2** Any of various American grackles, especially the boat-tailed grackle (*Cassidix mexicanus*).

jack·er (jak′ər) *n.* One who or that which jacks.

jack·et (jak′it) *n.* **1** A short coat, usually not extending below the hips. **2** Anything resembling a jacket. **3** A covering for a steam cylinder, to prevent radiation of heat. **4** A removable paper wrapper or cover for a bound book. **5** An open envelope or folder, used for filing letters, documents, papers, etc. **6** A covering of hard metal on a bullet or shell. **7** The skin of a potato. — *v.t.* To cover with a jacket. [<OF *jaquette*, dim. of *jaque* a coat] — **jack′et·ed** *adj.*

Jack Frost A personification of wintry or frosty weather.

jack·ham·mer (jak′ham′ər) A rock drill operated by compressed air.

jack-in-a-box (jak′in·ə·boks′) *n.* **1** A toy consisting of a grotesque figure in a box, springing up when the lid is unfastened. **2** A tropical tree (*Hernandia sonora*) yielding a fruit that when shaken makes a rattling sound. **3** A rogue; swindler. Also **jack′-in-the-box′**.

jack-in-the-pul·pit (jak′in-thə·pŏōl′pit) *n.* A common American herb (*Arisaema triphyllum*) of the arum family, growing from a turnip-shaped bulb, with an intensely acrid juice and a curious spike of flowers enclosed in a greenish-purple spathe: also called *Indian turnip*.

JACK-IN-THE-PULPIT

jack·knife (jak′nīf′) *n. pl.* **·knives** (-nīvz) **1** A large pocket knife with recessed handle into which the blade is folded. **2** A dive during which the body is doubled from the hips with the hands touching the ankles, and then straightened before entering the water.

jack·light (jak′līt′) *n. U.S.* A torch or light used in hunting or fishing at night to attract and dazzle game or fish.

jack·light (jak′līt′) *v.t. & v.i.* To seek (game or fish) with a jacklight.

jack oak A black-barked oak of the eastern United States (*Quercus marilandica*).

jack-of-all-trades (jak′əv·ôl′trādz) *n.* One who is able to do many kinds of work.

jack-o'-lan·tern (jak′ə-lan′tərn) *n.* **1** A will-o'-the-wisp; ignis fatuus. **2** A lantern made of a pumpkin hollowed and carved into a grotesque face, or an imitation of this. Also **jack′-ə-lan′tern**.

jack pine The gray pine (*Pinus banksiana*), growing chiefly on barren tracts of North America.

jack·plane (jak′plān′) *n.* A carpenter's roughing plane.

jack·pot (jak′pot′) *n.* **1** In poker, a pot that must accumulate till one of the players gets a pair of jacks or cards of higher value on the deal; also, a game or part of it in which this rule is observed. **2** Hence, any pot or pool in which contributions accumulate. — **to hit the jackpot** *U.S. Colloq.* To win the biggest possible prize; to achieve a major success.

jack rabbit One of a genus (*Lepus*) of large American hares with long hind legs and long ears.

jack·screw (jak′skrōō′) *n.* A mechanical jack in which pressure is transmitted by the action of a screw.

jack·shaft (jak′shaft′, -shäft′) *n.* **1** A shaft sunk in a mine. **2** A bar or crosspiece for supporting a mechanical drill, held in place by jackscrews.

jack snipe **1** A small European snipe. **2** The pectoral sandpiper.

Jack·son (jak′sən), **Andrew**, 1767–1845, president of the United States 1829–37: called "Old Hickory." — **Chevalier**, born 1865, U.S. laryngologist. — **Helen Hunt**, 1831–85, *née* Maria Fiske, U.S. novelist. — **Thomas Jonathan**, 1824–63, Confederate general: known as *Stonewall Jackson* from the firm stand of his command at the first battle of Bull Run, 1861.

jack·stay (jak′stā′) *n. Naut.* **1** A rope or rod along the upper surface of a yard, to which to fasten a sail. **2** A rope or rod running up and down on the forward side of a mast, on which a yard travels; a traveler.

jack·stone (jak′stōn′) *n.* **1** One of a set of stones or knobbed metal pieces used in a child's game: also *jack*. **2** *pl.* The game so played; jacks.

jack towel A long coarse towel hanging on a roller.

jac·o·bin (jak′ə·bin) *n.* A pigeon with neck feathers ruffed so as to form a hood.

Jac·o·bin (jak′ə·bin) *n.* **1** A member of a French revolutionary society that inaugurated the Reign of Terror, 1793; dissolved, 1799. **2** Hence, an extreme revolutionist. **3** *pl.* Dominican friars before the French Revolution. [<F *Jacobin* of St. James <Med. L *Jacobinus* <LL *Jacobus* James; with ref. to the church of St. James, in Paris, where they first met]

Jac·o·bin·i·cal (jak′ə·bin′i·kəl) *adj.* **1** Belonging to the French Jacobins. **2** Turbulently democratic; revolutionary; radical. Also **Jac′·o·bin′ic**. — **Jac′o·bin′i·cal·ly** *adv.*

Jac·o·bin·ism (jak′ə·bin·iz′əm) *n.* **1** Unreasonable or violent opposition to legitimate government; popular turbulence. **2** A Jacobinical characteristic or idea.

jac·o·net (jak′ə·net) *n.* **1** A soft, thin, white cotton cloth. **2** A cotton fabric with one side glazed. [from *Jagganath* (now Puri) in India, where first made]

jac·ta·tion (jak·tā′shən) *n.* **1** The act of throwing. **2** Jactitation (def. 2). **3** Exercise, as in riding. **4** Boasting. [<L *jactatio, -onis* <*jactare*, freq. of *jacere* throw]

jac·ti·ta·tion (jak′tə·tā′shən) *n.* **1** A public boasting; bragging. **2** *Pathol.* A morbid restlessness, as in acute disease. **3** *Law* A false assertion, as of marriage, repeated to the injury of another; an action to enjoin such false pretension. [<Med. L *jactitatio, -onis* <L *jactitare* say publicly, freq. of *jactare* hurl]

jac·u·late (jak′yə·lāt) *v.t.* **·lat·ed**, **·lat·ing** *Rare* To hurl, as a dart. [<L *jaculatus*, pp. of *jaculare* throw] — **jac′u·la′tion** *n.*

jac·u·la·to·ry (jak′yə·lə·tôr′ē, -tō′rē) *adj.* Darting or thrown out suddenly.

jade[1] (jād) *n.* **1** A hard, tough, greenish or white silicate, used for making ornaments and including chiefly two species: jadeite and nephrite. **2** The greenish color of jade; jade green. [<F *jade*, var. of *ejade* <Sp. (*piedra de*) *ijada* (stone for) colic, lit., the side, ribs]

jade[2] (jād) *n.* **1** An old, worn-out horse. **2** A worthless person; specifically, a hussy. **3** A woman: ironical usage. — *v.t. & v.i.* **jad·ed, jad·ing** To weary or become weary by hard service; tire. See synonyms under TIRE[1]. [Origin uncertain]

jad·ed (jā′did) *adj.* **1** Worn-out; exhausted. **2** Satiated; sated, as from overindulgence. — **jad′ed·ly** *adv.* — **jad′ed·ness** *n.*

jade green Any of several shades of green characteristic of jade.

jade·ite (jā′dīt) *n.* A translucent sodium-aluminum silicate of the pyroxene group. [<JADE[1] + -ITE[1]]

jad·ish (jā′dish) *adj.* **1** Vicious: said of a horse. **2** Unchaste or wanton: said of a woman. Also **jad′y**. — **jad′ish·ly** *adv.* — **jad′ish·ness** *n.*

jae·ger (yā′gər) *n.* **1** (*also* jā′gər) Any of a genus (*Stercorarius*) of sea birds which pursue and harass gulls and terns until they drop or disgorge their prey. **2** A huntsman or hunting attendant. **3** *Obs.* A soldier of the German or Austrian army especially trained in scouting, sharpshooting, and forestry: hired by England during the American Revolution. Also spelled *yager*. Also **jä′ger**. [<G, hunter <*jagen* hunt]

jag[1] (jag) *n.* **1** A projecting point; notch; tooth. **2** A bolt with barbed point. **3** *Brit. Dial.* A stab or jab, as of a dirk. — *v.t.* **jagged, jagging 1** To cut notches or jags in. **2** To cut unevenly or with slashing strokes, as a garment. Also **jagg**. [ME *jagge*; origin unknown]

jag[2] (jag) *n.* **1** A load for one horse; small load. **2** *Slang* Enough liquor to intoxicate; also, intoxication: to have a *jag* on. Also **jagg**. [Origin unknown]

jag·ged (jag′id) *adj.* Having jags or notches. Also **jaggy**. See synonyms under ROUGH. — **jag′ged·ly** *adv.* — **jag′ged·ness** *n.*

jag·ger·y (jag′ər·ē) *n.* **1** A coarse sugar made in the East Indies from the sap of the date palm or from sugarcane. **2** A wine made from the coconut palm. Also **jag′gar·y, jag′gher·y, jag′ra** (jag′rə). [<Hind. *jágrī* <Skt. *çarkara* sugar]

jag·gy (jag′ē) *adj.* **·gi·er**, **·gi·est** Having notches; jagged.

jag·uar (jag′wär, jag′yoo·är) *n.* A large, tawny, spotted feline (*Panthera onca*) of tropical America. [<Tupian *jaguara*]

JAGUAR
(Up to 9 feet in length; tail: about 2 1/2 feet)

ja·gua·run·di (jä′gwə·run′dē) *n.* A carnivorous, weasel-like wildcat (genus *Felis*) of tropical America, having grayish-brown fur: also called *yaguarundi*. Also **ja′gua·ron′di**. [<Tupian]

Jah (jä, yä) *Hebrew* Jehovah. *Psalms* lxviii 4.

Jah·veh, Jah·we (yä′ve), **Jah·vism, Jah·wism** (yä′viz·əm), etc. See YAHWEH, etc.

jai a·lai (hī ə·lī′) A Spanish game, popular in Latin America, played by two opposed couples in a court called a *frontón*: the ball is served against a wall, and each player wears a gauntlet from which projects a long, curved wicker racket, called the *cesta*, in which he alternately receives the ball and hurls it back against the wall. The first to miss loses the point. Compare PELOTA. [<Sp. <Basque, jolly festival]

jail (jāl) *n.* A building or place for the confinement of arrested persons or those guilty of minor offenses. — *v.t.* To put or hold in jail; imprison. Also, *Brit.,* gaol. [<OF *jaiole*, ult. <L *cavea* cave]

jail·bird (jāl′bûrd′) *n. Colloq.* **1** One sentenced to or confined in prison. **2** A habitual lawbreaker; one often confined in jail. Also, *Brit.,* gaolbird.

jail-de·liv·er·y (jāl′di·liv′ər·ē) *n.* **1** *Law* The legal disposal, as by trial and condemnation or acquittal, of the cases of all prisoners awaiting trial. **2** The escape or forcible liberation of prisoners from jail.

jail·er (jā′lər) *n.* The officer in charge of a jail: also, *Brit.,* gaoler. Also **jail′or**.

Jain (jīn) *n.* An adherent of Jainism. — *adj.* Of or pertaining to Jainism. Also **Jai·na** (jī′nə). [<Hind. *Jaina* <*jina* victorious]

Jain·ism (jī′niz·əm) *n.* A Hindu religious system, founded about 500 B.C., which combines certain elements of Brahmanism and Buddhism, its principal distinctive features being the worship of sages or saints, known as *jinas*, and the great respect for the lives of animals.

jake (jāk) *adj. Slang* All right; fine.

jal·a·pin (jal′ə·pin) *n.* A resinous glycoside contained in several convolvulaceous plants: used in medicine as a cathartic. [<JALAP + -IN]

ja·lop·y (jə·lop′ē) *n. pl.* **·lop·ies** *U.S. Colloq.* A decrepit automobile. [Origin uncertain]

ja·lou·sie (jal′ŏŏ·sē, zhal′ŏŏ·zē′) *n.* A Venetian blind. [<F, lit., jealousy]

jam[1] (jam) *v.* **jammed, jam·ming** *v.t.* **1** To press or force into a tight place or position; wedge or squeeze in. **2** To fill and block up by crowding: to *jam* a corridor. **3** To bruise or crush by violent pressure. **4** To cause (a machine, part, etc.) to become wedged or stuck fast so that it cannot work. **5** In radio, to interfere with (a broadcast, station, etc.) by transmitting on the same wavelength. — *v.i.* **6** To become wedged; stick fast.

7 To press or wedge; push: The crowd *jammed* into the room. **8** In jazz music, to improvise; also, to take part in a jam session. —*n.* **1** A number of people or objects closely crowded; a crush; the act of jamming. **2** A mass of logs, ice, etc., blocked in a stream. See synonyms under THRONG. —*adv.* Completely: *jam* full. ◆ Homophone: *jamb*. [Related to CHAMP¹]

Synonyms (verb): crowd, crush, force, pack, press, push, squeeze, throng. See HUSTLE. *Antonyms*: ease, free, liberate, loosen, release, relieve.

jam² (jam) *n.* A pulpy, sweet conserve of fruit boiled with sugar: distinguished from *jelly*. ◆ Homophone: *jamb*. [? <JAM¹, *v.*]

Ja·mai·ca (jə·mā′kə) An independent member of the Commonwealth of nations comprising the island of Jamaica, SE of Cuba; 4,411 square miles; capital, Kingston; and its dependencies, the Cayman Islands and Turks and Caicos Islands; total, 4,705 square miles. —**Ja·mai′can** *adj.* & *n.*

jamb (jam) *n.* **1** A side post or side of a doorway, window, etc. **2** A jambeau. ◆ Homophone: *jam.* [<OF *jambe* leg, support <LL *gamba* hoof, leg <Celtic]

jam·ba·la·ya (jam′bə·lä′yə, zham′-) *n.* A traditional Creole dish of rice cooked with seafood and fowl. [<Provençal *jambalaia*]

jam·beau (jam·bō′) *n.* *pl.* ·**beaux** (-bōz′) A piece of armor for the leg. Also **jambe** (jam). [<OF *jambe* a leg]

jam·bo·ree (jam′bə·rē′) *n.* **1** *Colloq.* A boisterous frolic or spree. **2** A large, especially international, assembly of Boy Scouts. **3** In euchre, a lone hand consisting of the five highest cards. [<JAM¹; on analogy with *corroboree, chivaree*]

James (jāmz), **Henry**, 1843–1916, U.S. novelist and critic active in England. —**Jesse (Woodson)**, 1847–82, U.S. outlaw. —**William**, 1842–1910, U.S. psychologist; brother of Henry James.

James·town (jāmz′toun) **1** A restored village in eastern Virginia: the first permanent English settlement within the limits of the United States, 1607. **2** A port and the capital of St. Helena.

jam–packed (jam′pakt′) *adj.* *Colloq.* Crowded to capacity; as tightly packed as possible.

jam session An informal gathering of jazz musicians performing improvisations on various themes, each exploring the possibilities of his instrument while following no set musical form other than a motif mutually evolved.

jan·gle (jang′gəl) *v.* ·**gled**, ·**gling** *v.i.* **1** To make harsh, unmusical sounds. **2** To wrangle; bicker. —*v.t.* **3** To cause to sound discordantly. —*n.* Discordant sound; wrangling. See synonyms under NOISE, QUARREL. [<OF *jangler*] —**jan′gler** *n.* —**jan′gling** *n.*

jan·i·tor (jan′i·tər) *n.* **1** One who has the care of a building, offices, etc. **2** A doorkeeper; porter. [<L <*janua* door]

jan·i·zar·y (jan′ə·zer′ē) *n.* *pl.* ·**zar·ies** One of the former bodyguards of the Turkish sultans, originally composed of young prisoners trained to arms: suppressed in 1826; also, sometimes, any Turkish soldier. Also **jan′i·sar·y, jan′is·sar·y.** [<F *janissaire* <Turkish *yenicheri* new army]

Jan·u·ar·y (jan′yŏŏ·er′ē) The first month of the year, containing 31 days. [<L *Januarius* < *Janus* Janus]

Ja·nus (jā′nəs) In Roman mythology, the god of portals and beginnings, having two faces, one on each side of his head.

Ja·nus–faced (jā′-nəs·fāst′) *adj.* Two-faced; looking both ways; deceitful.

Jap (jap) *adj.* & *n.* *Slang* Japanese: an opprobrious usage.

jap·a·con·i·tine (jap′-ə·kon′ə·tēn) *n.* *Chem.* A white, crystalline, extremely poisonous alkaloid, $C_{24}H_{47}O_{11}N$, from the root of the Japanese aconite (*Aconitum japonicum*). [<JAP(ANESE) + ACONIT(E) + -INE²]

JANUS

ja·pan (jə·pan′) *n.* **1** A varnish used as a medium in which to grind colors, and as a drier for pigments. **2** A hard jet-black lacquer for coating sheet metal; Brunswick-black. —*adj.* Pertaining to or lacquered with japan. —*v.t.* ·**panned, ·pan·ning** To lacquer with or as with japan. [from JAPAN] —**ja·pan′ner** *n.*

Ja·pan (jə·pan′) A constitutional empire of eastern Asia, comprising the four main islands of Honshu, Hokkaido, Kyushu, and Shikoku with many adjacent smaller islands; 147,692 square miles; capital, Tokyo: also *Nihon, Nippon, Dai Nippon.*

Japan clover A perennial, cloverlike herb (*Lespedeza striata*) of the bean family, from eastern Asia, naturalized in the United States and used for feeding horses and cattle. Also **Japanese clover.**

Jap·a·nese (jap′ə·nēz′, -nēs′) *adj.* Belonging or relating to Japan, its language, or its people. —*n.* **1** A native of Japan. **2** The agglutinative language of Japan, showing a slight similarity to Korean, but generally considered to be unrelated to any language: see KANA.

Japanese beetle A small green and brown beetle (*Popillia japonica*) with a metallic luster introduced into this country from Japan and first noted in 1916. The adults eat the leaves and fruits of various plants; the larvae feed on grass roots. See illustration under INSECT (injurious).

Japanese ivy A climbing shrub (*Parthenocissus tricuspidata*) closely related to the Virginia creeper.

Japanese tissue A fine silky paper, originally made from the bark of the paper mulberry.

Japanese vellum A smooth, creamy, handmade paper of exceptional strength, originally made from the paper mulberry.

Jap·a·nesque (jap′ə·nesk′) *adj.* In the style of Japanese art or industry. —*n.* An article made in such style. —**Jap′a·nesque′ly** *adv.* —**Jap′a·nesque′ry** *n.*

Japan rose Any of several true roses native to Japan; specifically, *Rosa multiflora* and *Rosa rugosa*, both widely cultivated garden plants in the United States.

Japan wax A vegetable fat containing palmitic acid and extracted from the berries of certain species of sumac (genus *Rhus*): used largely for adulterating beeswax: also called *Japan tallow.*

jape (jāp) *v.* **japed, jap·ing** *v.i. Archaic* To joke; make jests. —*v.t. Obs.* To mock; jibe at. —*n.* A jest; jibe. [ME *jappen*; origin uncertain] —**jap′er** *n.* —**jap′er·y** *n.*

Ja·pon·ic (jə·pon′ik) *adj.* Of, pertaining to, or from Japan. [<*Japon*, obs. var. of *Japan* + -IC]

ja·pon·i·ca (jə·pon′i·kə) *n.* **1** An eastern-Asian shrub (*Chaenomeles lagenaria*) with toothed leaves and bright scarlet flowers; the Japanese quince. **2** The camellia (*Camellia japonica*). [<NL, Japanese]

Ja·ques (jā′kwēz, -kwiz) In Shakespeare's *As You Like It*, a lord, melancholy and cynical, attending on the banished duke.

jar¹ (jär) *n.* **1** A deep, wide-mouthed vessel of earthenware or glass. **2** The quantity which a jar contains; jarful. [<F *jarre* < Arabic *jarrah*]

jar² (jär) *v.* **jarred, jar·ring** *v.i.* **1** To shake or rattle, as from a shock or blow. **2** To make

a harsh, discordant sound. **3** To have an unpleasant or painful effect: Her manner *jarred* on my nerves. **4** To disagree or conflict; quarrel. —*v.t.* **5** To cause to shake or rattle, as by a shock or blow. **6** To affect unpleasantly or painfully, as one's nerves or feelings; shock. **7** To cause to make a harsh, discordant sound. See synonyms under SHAKE. —*n.* **1** A shaking, as from a sudden shock. **2** A discordant sound. **3** Discord; strife. See synonyms under QUARREL. [Imit.]

jar³ (jär) *n.* A swinging, as of a door on its hinges: used only in the phrases **on a jar** and **on the jar**, meaning slightly opened. [OE *cerr*. See AJAR¹.]

ja·ra·be (hä·rä′bä) *n.* A Mexican dance. [<Sp., lit., sirup]

jar·di·nière (jär′də·nir′, *Fr.* zhàr·dē·nyâr′) *n.* An ornamental pot or stand, as of porcelain, for flowers or plants. [<F, fem. of *jardinier* a gardener]

jar·fly (jär′flī′) *n. pl.* ·**flies** A cicada or harvest fly: so called because of the jarring noise it makes.

jar·gon¹ (jär′gən) *n.* **1** Confused, unintelligible speech; gibberish. **2** Any language thought to be meaningless or excessively confused. **3** The technical or specialized language characteristic of a particular sect, profession, or similarly restrictive group; cant; lingo: the *jargon* of the law courts. **4** A mixture of two or more dissimilar languages, often used as a lingua franca, as the Chinook *jargon*; pidgin. See synonyms under SLANG. —*v.i.* To talk in jargon; gabble. [<OF]

jar·gon² (jär′gon) *n.* A transparent, adamantine, colorless, yellowish, leaf-green, or smoky zircon found in Ceylon. Also **jar·goon′** (-gōōn′). [<F, ult. <Persian *zargūn* gold-colored]

jar·go·nelle (jär′gə·nel′) *n.* An early variety of pear. Also **jar′go·nel′, jar′gon·elle′.** [<F, dim. of *jargon* JARGON²]

jar·gon·ize (jär′gən·īz) *v.* ·**ized, ·iz·ing** *v.t.* To translate into jargon. —*v.i.* To speak in jargon.

ja·ri·na (jä·rē′nə) *n.* The ivory nut.

jar·o·site (jar′ə·sīt, jə·rō′-) *n.* A hydrous sulfate of iron and potassium, occurring massive or in brown or yellow crystals. [from Barranco *Jarosa*, in Spain]

jas·mine (jas′min, jaz′-) *n.* **1** An ornamental plant of the olive family (genus *Jasminum*) with fragrant, generally white, flowers. **2** One of various other plants, as the **Cape Jasmine** (*Gardenia jasminoides*), the **Carolina** or **yellow jasmine** (*Gelsemium sempervirens*), etc. **3** Frangipani. **4** Papaw. Also spelled *jessamine.* [<F *jasmin* <Persian *yāsmīn*]

jas·pé (zhas·pā′) *adj.* Veined or clouded on the surface in imitation of jasper; streaked. —*n.* A variety of plain-weave shaded cloth, usually printed or embroidered. [<F, like jasper]

jas·per (jas′pər) *n.* **1** An impure, opaque, usually red, brown, or yellow variety of quartz, admitting of a high polish and used for vases and other articles: also **jas′per·ite.** **2** A stone in the breastplate of the high priest. *Exod.* xxviii 20. [<MF *jaspre*, var. of *jaspe* <L *jaspis* <Gk. <Semitic. Cf. Hebrew *yashpeh.*]

Jat·ro·pha (jat′rə·fə) *n.* A genus of tropical American herbs, shrubs, and trees of the spurge family, the seeds of which yield alkaloids having medicinal properties. [<NL < Gk. *iatros* physician + *trophē* food]

jaun·dice (jôn′dis, jän′-) *n.* **1** *Pathol.* A morbid condition due to excretion of bile pigments in the blood, characterized by yellowness of the skin, lassitude, and anorexia; icterus. **2** A mental condition, as in jealousy or prejudice, in which the judgment is warped. —*v.t.* ·**diced, ·dic·ing** **1** To affect with jaundice. **2** To affect with prejudice or envy. [<OF *jaunisse* <*jaune* yellow <L *galbinus* yellowish <*galbus* yellow]

jaun·diced (jôn′dist, jän′-) *adj.* **1** Affected with jaundice. **2** Yellow-colored. **3** Prejudiced because of envy or jealousy.

jaunt (jônt, jänt) *n.* **1** A short journey; pleasure trip; excursion. **2** A tiresome journey. **3** *Obs.* A jolting; jounce. —*v.i.* To make a short trip, especially for pleasure. [Cf. obs. *jaunce* prance]

Ja·va (jä′və, jav′ə) *n.* **1** A type of coffee. **2** Coffee: a cup of *Java.* **3** A domestic fowl. [from *Java*, where first grown]

Ja·va (jä′və, jav′ə) An Indonesian island SE

of Sumatra; with Madura and adjacent islands, 51,032 square miles; capital, Jakarta.

Java man Pithecanthropus.

Jav·a·nese (jav′ə·nēz′, -nēs′) *adj.* Of or pertaining to Java, its language, or its people. — *n. pl.* **·nese** 1 A native or naturalized inhabitant of Java. 2 The Indonesian language of central Java, closely related to Malay, and containing some elements of Sanskrit.

Java sparrow A seed-eating bird (*Munia oryzivora*) of Java: a common cage bird.

jave·lin (jav′lin, jav′ə·lin) *n.* 1 A short, light spear, used as a missile weapon for hunting or in war. 2 A long spear with wooden shaft, thrown for distance in an athletic contest. [<F, prob. <Celtic]

Ja·velle water (zhə·vel′) A solution of chlorinated potash or of sodium hypochlorite, used as an antiseptic and as a bleaching agent. Also **Ja·vel′ water.**

jaw (jô) *n.* 1 *Anat.* One of the two bony structures forming the framework of the mouth; a maxilla or a mandible. 2 The mouth. 3 Anything like or suggesting a jaw, as one of the gripping parts of a vise: often used figuratively: *jaws* of death. 4 *Slang* Needless talk; scolding; abuse. — *v.i. Slang* 1 To talk; jabber. 2 To scold. — *v.t.* 3 *Slang* To scold. [Earlier *jowe, chawe.* ? Akin to *chew*, infl. by F *joue* cheek.]

HUMAN
JAW

jaw·bone (jô′bōn′) *n.* One of the bones of the jaw; especially, the mandible. — *v.t.* **·boned**, **·bon·ing** *U.S. Slang* 1 To urge vigorously; especially, to urge to abide voluntarily by price or wage guidelines fixed by government. — *v.i.* 2 To argue vigorously. — *adj. U.S. Slang* Based on voluntary compliance.

jaw·break·er (jô′brā′kər) *n.* 1 Very hard candy. 2 A machine that crushes ore: also **jaw′crush′er.** 3 A word hard to pronounce.

jay (jā) *n.* 1 A small crowlike bird, usually of brilliant coloring, as the **European jay** (*Garrulus glandarius*), the **blue jay** (*Cyanocitta cristata*), the **Canada jay** (*Perisoreus canadensis*), etc. 2 *Slang* A poor actor; also, a country bumpkin; greenhorn. 3 An unscrupulous chatterbox. 4 *Obs.* A coarse or loud woman. [<OF; ult. origin unknown]

jay·walk (jā′wôk′) *v.i. Colloq.* To cross a street without observing the traffic regulations. [<JAY (def. 2) + WALK] — **jay′walk′er** *n.* — **jay′walk′ing** *n.*

jazz (jaz) *n.* 1 A kind of music, generally improvised but sometimes arranged, achieving its effects by syncopation, heavily accented rhythms, dissonance, melodic variation, and particular tonal qualities of the saxophone, trumpet, clarinet, and other instruments. It was originated by New Orleans Negro musicians. 2 Popular dance music. 3 *Slang* Nonsense; claptrap. — *adj.* Of or pertaining to jazz. — *v.t.* To play or arrange (music) as jazz. — *v.i.* To dance to or play jazz. — **to jazz up** *Slang* To make exciting or more exciting. [< Creole *jass* coition; from its origin in the brothels of New Orleans]

jazz age *U.S.* The 1920's regarded as a period of relaxed morality and gay, irresponsible behavior.

jazz·y (jaz′ē) *adj.* **jazz·i·er, jazz·i·est** 1 Resembling or characteristic of jazz. 2 *Slang* Showy or loud, as clothes; also, lively or swinging. — **jazz′i·ly** *adv.*

jeal·ous (jel′əs) *adj.* 1 Apprehensive of being displaced by a rival in affection or favor; revengeful on account of fickle treatment or the like. 2 Earnestly and anxiously suspicious; vigilant in guarding; watchful. 3 Demanding exclusive worship and love: applied to God. *Ex.* xx 5. 4 *Obs.* Zealous. 5 *Obs.* Fearful; doubtful. See synonyms under ENVIOUS. [<OF *gelos* <Med. L *zelosus* <LL *zelus* <Gk. *zēlos* zeal. Doublet of ZEALOUS.] — **jeal′ous·ly** *adv.* — **jeal′ous·ness** *n.*

jeal·ous·y (jel′əs·ē) *n. pl.* **·ous·ies** The state or quality of being jealous in any sense.

jean (jēn) *n.* 1 A sturdy, twilled cotton cloth, used especially in work clothes or for casual wear. 2 *pl.* Trousers made of jean, denim,

or a similar fabric. 3 *pl. U.S. Colloq.* Trousers. [Orig. *jene fustian* <ME *Jene, Gene* Genoa, where it was made]

Jeep (jēp) *n.* A military motor vehicle with four-wheel drive and a carrying capacity of one quarter of a ton, used for reconnaissance and for the transportation of passengers and light cargo: a trade name. [Alter. of *G.P.*, for *General Purpose* Vehicle, its military designation]

jeer¹ (jir) *v.i.* To speak or shout in a derisive, mocking manner; scoff. — *v.t.* To treat with derision or mockery; scoff at. See synonyms under MOCK, SCOFF. — *n.* A derisive and flouting word or speech. See synonyms under SNEER. [? OE *cēir* clamor] — **jeer′er** *n.* — **jeer′ing·ly** *adv.*

jeer² (jir) *n. Naut.* A tackle for raising or lowering a lower yard of a sailing ship. [? <GEE² + -ER¹]

Jef·fer·son (jef′ər·sən), **Joseph,** 1829–1905, U. S. actor. — **Thomas,** 1743–1826, American statesman: drafted the Declaration of Independence; president of the United States 1801–1809.

Jef·fer·so·ni·an (jef′ər·sō′nē·ən) *adj.* Of or relating to Thomas Jefferson or his political opinions; democratic. — **Jef′fer·so′ni·an·ism** *n.*

Je·ho·vah (ji·hō′və) In the Old Testament, God; the Lord: the common transliteration of the Tetragrammaton. See YAHWEH. [<Hebrew *JHVH* Yahweh, with the substitution of vowels from *'adhonay* my Lord] — **Je·ho′vi·an, Je·ho′vic** *adj.*

je·june (jə·jōōn′) *adj.* 1 Lifeless; dry; dull. 2 Wanting in substance; barren. 3 Not mature; puerile; childish. See synonyms under MEAGER. [<L *jejunus* hungry] — **je·june′ly** *adv.* — **je·june′ness** *n.*

je·ju·num (jə·jōō′nəm) *n. pl.* **·na** (-nə) *Anat.* That portion of the small intestine that extends from the duodenum to the ileum. [<NL <L *jejunus* hungry, empty]

Je·kyll (jē′kəl, jek′əl), **Doctor** In Robert Louis Stevenson's *Strange Case of Doctor Jekyll and Mr. Hyde,* one half of the dual personality consisting of a kindly physician (Jekyll) and a criminal ruffian (Hyde).

jell (jel) *v.i. & v.t.* 1 To jelly. 2 To assume or cause to assume definite form. [Back formation <JELLY]

jel·lied (jel′ēd) *adj.* Brought to a jelly.

jel·li·fy (jel′ə·fī) *v.t. & v.i.* **·fied, ·fy·ing** To make or turn into jelly. — **jel′li·fi·ca′tion** *n.*

jel·lo (jel′ō) *n.* A fruit-flavored gelatin dessert. [<*Jell-O,* a trade name]

jel·ly (jel′ē) *n. pl.* **·lies** 1 Any semisolid gelatinous substance that will quiver when shaken, but will not flow, as fruit juice boiled with sugar or meat juice boiled down. 2 Any food preparation having the consistency of jelly. 3 A gelatin filter placed in front of electric lamps to change their color values; used with motion-picture cameras. — *v.t. & v.i.* **·lied, ·ly·ing** To bring or turn to jelly. [<OF *gelee* <L *gelata,* orig. pp. fem. of *gelare* freeze]

jel·ly·bean (jel′ē·bēn′) *n.* A bean-shaped candy consisting of a hard, often colored coating over a gelatinous center.

jel·ly·fish (jel′ē·fish′) *n. pl.* **·fish** or **·fish·es** 1 Any of a number of marine coelenterates (classes *Hydrozoa* and *Scyphozoa*) of jellylike appearance, and usually umbrella-shaped bodies with trailing tentacles, as the medusa and the Portuguese man-of-war. 2 *Colloq.* A person without energy, determination, or stamina.

jen·net (jen′it) *n.* 1 A small Spanish horse, a cross of Arabian and native stock. 2 A female donkey: also spelled *genet.* [<OF *genet* <Sp. *jinete* a light horseman <Arabic *Zenāta,* a Barbary tribe]

jeof·ail (jef′āl) *n. Law* An oversight; a mistake; the acknowledgment of an error in pleading. Also **jeof′aile.** [<AF *jeo fail* I am wrong]

jeop·ard·ize (jep′ər·dīz) *v.t.* **·ized, ·iz·ing** To put in jeopardy; expose to loss or injury; imperil. Also **jeop′ard.**

jeop·ard·y (jep′ər·dē) *n.* 1 Exposure to or chance of death, loss, or injury; danger; peril. 2 The peril in which a defendant is put when placed on trial for a crime. See synonyms under DANGER, HAZARD. [<OF *jeu parti* even

chance]

je·quir·i·ty (ji·kwir′ə·tē) *n.* 1 A twining, tropical shrub (*Abrus praecatorius*), the Indian or wild licorice. 2 One of the handsome, poisonous seeds, **jequirity beans,** of this plant used in India as weights, ornaments, and in medicine: often called *jumble-beads.* Also **je·quer′i·ty.** [<F *jéquirity* <Tupian]

jer·bo·a (jər·bō′ə) *n.* An Old World, nocturnal, social rodent (family *Dipodidae*) with the hind legs much elongated for jumping, especially *Jaculus jaculus* of North Africa. [<NL <Arabic *yarbu'*]

JERBOA
Can make a jump of 6 feet.
(About 3 inches long;
tail: 5 inches)

je·reed (je·rēd′) *n.* A javelin of Moslem countries; also, a game in which it is used: also spelled *jerreed, jerrid.* Also **je·rid′.** [<Arabic *jerid*]

jer·e·mi·ad (jer′ə·mī′ad) *n.* A lament; tale of woe; a denunciation of existing conditions. [<F *jérémiade* <*Jérémie* Jeremiah]

jerk¹ (jûrk) *v.t.* 1 To give a sharp, sudden pull, tug, or twist to. 2 To throw or move with a sharp, suddenly arrested motion. 3 To utter in broken or abrupt manner. — *v.i.* 4 To give a jerk or jerks. 5 To move with sharp, sudden motions; twitch. — *n.* 1 A short, sharp pull, twitch, or fling. 2 *Physiol.* An involuntary contraction of some muscle, due to the reflex action of nerves; specifically, an involuntary muscular spasm or twitching caused by religious excitement. 3 *Slang* A railroad local branch line. 4 *Slang* A stupid or unsophisticated person. [Prob. imit.] — **jerk′y** *adj.* — **jerk′i·ly** *adv.* — **jerk′i·ness** *n.*

jerk² (jûrk) *v.t.* To cure (meat) by cutting into strips and drying. — *n.* Jerky². [Alter. of Sp. *charquear* < *charqui.* See CHARQUI.]

jer·kin (jûr′kin) *n.* A waistcoat; short coat; jacket; doublet: often made of leather. — **buff jerkin** A jerkin of buff leather or, later, of buff-colored cloth. [Origin unknown]

jerk·wa·ter (jûrk′wô′tər, -wot′ər) *adj. U.S. Colloq.* 1 Not on the main line: a *jerkwater* train or station. 2 Insignificant; small: a *jerkwater* college. — *n.* A train serving a branch line. [<JERK¹, v. + WATER]

jerk·y (jûr′kē) *n.* Jerked meat: also called *charqui.* Also **jerked beef.** [Alter. of CHARQUI]

jer·o·bo·am (jer′ə·bō′əm) *n.* 1 An oversized champagne bottle holding about four quarts. 2 A drinking cup of great size. [after JEROBOAM]

jer·ry¹ (jer′ē) *n. pl.* **·ries** 1 One who erects buildings or does work in an unsubstantial and mean manner: also **jer′ry·build′er** (-bil′dər). 2 Work that is inferior or fraudulent in material or construction. — *adj.* Cheaply and fraudulently constructed; flimsy. [Origin unknown]

jer·ry² (jer′ē) *n. pl.* **·ries** *Slang* A German; especially, a German soldier. [Alter. of GERMAN]

jer·ry·build (jer′ē·bild′) *v.t.* **·built, ·build·ing** To build flimsily and of inferior materials. — **jer′ry·build′ing** *n.* — **jer′ry·built′** *adj.*

jer·sey (jûr′zē) *n.* 1 A plain-knitted, elastic, ribbed fabric of wool, cotton, rayon, etc. 2 A close-fitting knit shirt as worn by athletes; hence, any close-fitting upper garment of knitted material. 3 Fine woolen yarn, or fine-combed wool, as spun in the island of Jersey. [from *Jersey*]

Jer·sey (jûr′zē) *n.* One of a breed of cattle, usually fawn-colored, originating in the island of Jersey or the Channel Islands, noted for milk rich in butterfat content. — *adj.* Of or pertaining to the island of Jersey or to the State of New Jersey.

Je·ru·sa·lem (ji·rōō′sə·ləm, -lem) A holy city of Judaism and Christianity in central Palestine, partly in Israel (of which it is the capital) and partly in Jordan: identified with the Old Testament *Salem.* Ancient *Hierosolyma.* Arabic **El Quds esh She·rif** (al kōōts′ ash sha·rēf′).

jer·vine (jûr′vēn) *n. Chem.* A white, crystalline, toxic alkaloid, $C_{26}H_{37}O_3N$, obtained from the rhizome of the white hellebore (*Veratrum* *album*). [<Sp. *yerva*, the root of the hellebore + -INE²]

jess (jes) *n.* **1** A short strap fastened to the leg of a hawk: used in falconry. **2** A ribbon hanging from a garland or crown. [<OF *ges* <L *jactus* a throw <*jacere* throw] — **jessed** *adj.*

jes·sant (jes'ənt) *adj. Her.* **1** Shooting forth as a plant. **2** Issuing, as an animal, from the middle of an ordinary. Compare ISSUANT. [<OF *issant*, ppr. of *isser* spring forth]

jest (jest) *n.* **1** Something said or done in joke, plesantary, or raillery; a joke. **2** The object of laughter, sport, or raillery; a laughingstock. **3** *Obs.* An exploit, tale of exploits; a masquerade; pageant. See synonyms under WIT. —*v.i.* **1** To speak or act an a playful or trifling manner. **2** To scoff; jeer. —*v.t.* **3** To scoff at; ridicule. [<OF *geste, jeste* <L *gesta* deeds <*gerere* do]

jest·er (jes'tər) *n.* **1** One who jests; specifically. a medieval cort fool. **2** *Archaic* In the Middle Ages, a professional teller of romances.

jest·ing (jes'ting) *n.* The action of one who jokes; fun; raillery; —*adj.* Of the nature of a jest; prone to humor; mirthful; jocose. —**jest'ing·ly** *adv.*

Jes·u·ate (jezh'o͞o·āt, jez'yo͞o-) *n. pl.* **Jes·u·ates** or **Jes·u·a·ti** (jezh'o͞o·ā'tī, jez'yo͞o-) One of the order or congregation of *Jesuati*, founded by St. John Colombini of Siena in the 14th century, and suppressed by Pope Clement IX in 1688. Their chief occupation was care of the sick, especially the plague-stricken. Also **Jes'u·et.** [<Ital. *Gesuato* <*Gesù Jesus*]

Jes·u·it (jezh'o͞o·at, jez'yo͞o-) *n.* **1** A member of the Society of Jesus, a Roman Catholic religious order founded in 1534 by Ignatius Loyola to combat the Reformation and propagate the faith among the heathen. Abbr. *S.J.* [<NL *Jesuita* <L *Jesus Jesus*]

Je·sus (jē'zəs) A masculine personal name. [<Hebrew, the Lord is salvation] —**Jesus** The source of Christianity; probably living from 6 B.C. to A.D. 29 or 30; son of Mary; regarded in all Christian faiths as Christ, the Messiah. Hence, also **Jesus Christ.** —**Jesus** The son of Sirach; lived about the third or fourth century B.C.; author of *Ecclesiasticus.*

jet¹ (jet) *n.* **1** A rich black variety of lignite, used for ornaments. **2** The color of jet; a deep, glossy black. **3** *Obs.* Black marble. —*adj.* Made of or having the appearance of jet. [<OF *jaiet* <L *gagates* <Gk. *gagatēs*, from *Gagai*, a Lycian town where it was mined] —**jet'-black'** (-blak') *adj. & n.*

jet² (jet) *n.* **1** That which spurts from a narrow orifice; a gushing flow. **2** A spout or nozzle. **3** A projecting or overhanging course of bricks or the like; jut. **3** A jet plane. [<*v.*] —*v.t. & v.i.* **jet·ted, jet·ting** To spurt forth or emit in a stream; spout. [<F *jeter* throw, ult. <L *jactare,* freq. of *jacere* throw]

je·té (zhə·tā') *n.* In ballet, a wide leap with one leg forward and the other back. [<F, p.p. of *jeter,* to jump]

jet engine An engine that takes in outside air to oxidize fuel which is coverted into the energy of a powerful jet of heated gas expelled to the rear under high pressure: a special form of reaction engine.

jet lag A disruption of the body's accustomed rhythms of sleep, hunger, etc. owing to the change of time zones when traveling long distances by jet aircraft.

jet·lin·er (jet'lī'nər) *n.* A large, commercial jet aircraft.

jet·port (jet'pôrt', -pōrt') *n.* An airport designed to accomodate jet aircraft.

jet propulsion 1 Propulsion by means of a jet of gas or other fluid. **2** *Aeron.* Aircraft propulsion by means of jet engines. —**jet'-pro·pul'sion** *adj.*

jet rotor The rotor unit of a helicopter powerored by jet engines mounted on the blades.

jet·sam (jet'səm) *n.* **1** Unbuoyed goods cast from a vessel in peril, and which sink: distinguished from *flotsam* and *lagan.* **2** Jettison [Earlier *jetson,* short for JETTISON]

jet set A group of wealthy, international celebrities who frequently travel long distances, as by jet aircraft, for social events, etc. —**jet-set·ter** (jet'set'ər) *n.*

jet stream 1 The strong flow of gas or other fluid expelled from a jet engine, rocket motor, and the like. **2** *Meteorol.* A high-velocity circumpolar wind circulating, usually from west to east,

near the base of the stratosphere.

jet·ti·son (jet'ə·sən) *n.* **1** The throwing overboard of goods, or cargo, especially from a ship in danger of foundering. **2** Jetsam. —*v.t.* **1** To throw overboard, as goods or cargo. **2** Hence, to discard or abandon something that hampers. [<AF *getteson* <L *jactatio, -onis* a throwing <*jactare.* See JET².]

jet·ton (jet'ən) *n.* A counter or token. Also **jet'on.** [<MF *jeton* <*jeter* throw. See JET².]

jet·ty¹ (jet'ē) *n. pl.* **·ties 1** A structure in a body of water serving to control or divert a current, protect a harbor or the like, or as a wharf or pier. **2** A part of a building projecting or overhanging. Also, *Obs. jutty.* [<OF *jetee,* jetee, orig. pp. of *jeter* throw. See JET².]

jet·ty² (jet'ē) *adj.* Like or made of jet; black as jet. —**jet'ti·ness** *n.*

jet vane A fixed or adjustable vane of heat-resistant material placed in a jet stream for purposes of stability and control.

jet wash *Aeron.* The backwash caused by a jet engine, rocket, guided missle, and the like.

Jew (jo͞o) *n.* **1** A member of the ancient Near Eastern Hebrew people, the Israelites, or one tracing descent from them by genealogy or conversion. **2** Any person professing Judaism. **3** Originally, a member of the tribe or the kingdom of Judah. —**Wandering Jew** The shoemaker Ahasuerus, fabled to be condemned to wander perpetually for driving Christ from his door; hence, a restless wanderer. —*adj.* Jewish; relating to Jews. [OF *gui, jeu* <L *Judaeus* <Gk. *Ioudaios* <Hebrew *y'hudi* descendant of Judah.

jew·el (jo͞o'əl) *n.* **1** A precious stone; gem, especially one set in precious metal. **2** Anything or rare excellence or special value. **3** A bit of precious stone, crystal, or glass used to form a durable bearing, as for a watch pivot. **4** One dearly beloved. —*v.t.* **·eled** or **·elled, ·el·ing** or **·el·ling** To adorn with jewels; set jewels in. [<OF *jouel,* ult. <L *jocus* a joke, sport]

jew·el·er (jo͞o'əl·ər) *n.* A dealer or maker of jewelry. Also **jew'el·ler.**

jew·el·ry (jo͞o'əl·rē) *n.* **1** Jewels collectively. **2** The art of mounting precious stones; trade of a jeweler. Also *Brit.* **jew'el·ler·y.**

jew·el·weed (jo͞o'əl·wēd') *n.* Either of two American plants of the genus *Impatiens,* the touch-me-nots (*I. biflora* or *I. pallida*).

jew·fish (jo͞o'fish') *n. pl.* **·fish** or **·fishes 1** One of various large groupers of American waters, especially *Stereolepis gigas* of the California coast. **2** The giant grouper (*Promicrops itaiara*) of the Florida coast. **3** The tarpon.

Jew·ish (jo͞o'ish) *Adj.* Belonging to, like, or characteristic of the Jews, their customs, religion, etc.; Hebrew. —**Jew'ish·ness** *n.*

Jew·ry (jo͞o'rē) *n.* **1** The country of the Jews; Judea. **2** The Jewish people or race.

jew's-harp (jo͞oz'härp') *n.* **1** A small musical instrument with a lyre-shaped metal frame and a bent metallic tounge. **2** *Naut.* The shackle that connects the chain cable with the anchor ring.

JEW'S-HARP

Jez·e·bel (jez'ə·bel) The wife of Ahab, notorious for her evil life (I *Kings* xvi 31); hence, a bold, vicious or cruel woman.

jib¹ (jib) *n.* **1** *Naut.* A triangular sail, set on a stay and extending from the foretopmast head to the jib boom or the bowspirit. **2** The swinging boom of a crane or derrick. —**flying jib** A jib set out beyond the standing jib, or an extended boom, called the **flying-jib boom.** —**the cut of one's jib** One's appearance. —*v.t. & v.i.* **jibbed, jib·bing** *Naut.* To shift or swing; jibe. Also **jibb.** [? Short for GIBBET]

jib² (jib) *v.t.* **jibbed, jib·bing 1** To move restively sidewise and backward; refuse to go forward, as a horse. **2** To refuse to do something; balk. —*n.* A horse that jibs; also **jib'ber** [Cf. OF *giber* kick]

jib boom *Naut.* A spar forming a continuation of the bowsprit.

jib crane A crane having a swinging boom.

jibe¹ (jīb) *v.* **jibed, jib·ing** *v.t.* **1** *Naut.* To swing from one side of a vessel to the other; said of a fore-and-aft sail or its boom. **2** To change course so that the sails shift in this manner. —*v.t.* **3** To cause to swing from one side of a vessel to the other. Also spelled *gibe, gybe, jib.* [<Du.

gijben]

jibe² (jīb) See GIBE¹.

jibe³ (jīb) *v.i.* **jibed, jib·bing** *U.S. Colloq.* To agree; be in accordance. [Origin uncertain]

ji·ca·ma (hē'kə·mə) *n.* A tropical plant with edible tuberous roots and with seeds that yield rotenone and oils [<Nahuatl *xicama*]

jif·fy (jif'ē) *n. pl.* **·fies** *Colloq.* An instant; moment. Also **jiff.** [Origin unknown]

jig (jig) *n.* **1** A light, gay dance to a rapid tune, usually in triple time, or the music for it. **2** A practical joke. **3** *Mech.* A tool or fixture used to guide cutting tools. **4** A fish hook having a loaded shank. **5** *Mining* A wire sieve or system of sieves used in separating ore by vibration. —**the jig is up** *Colloq.* All is over and done. —*v.* jigged, jig·ging *v.i.* **1** To dance or play a jig. **2** To move with quick, jerky motions. **3** To fish with a jig. **4** *Mech.* To use a jig. —*v.t.* **5** To sing or play to the time of a jig. **6** To dance, as a jig. **7** To jerk up and down or to and fro. **8** To catch (fish) by hooking through the body with a jig. **9** *Mech.* To form or produce with the aid of jigs. [Cf. OF *gigue* a fiddle]

JIG
a. A drill jig.
b. Matter to be drilled.
c. Support block.

jig·ger¹ (jig'ər) *n.* **1** One who or that which jigs. **2** One of various jolting mechanisms: an apparatus for separating ores by jolting in sieves in water. **3** A potter's wheel. **4** *Naut.* A small spanker sail set on a short mast in the stern of a canoe; also, a small smacklike boat carrying such a sail. **5** Jiggermast. **6** A short, lofting, iron-headed golf club used for approaching. **7** A support for a billiard cue when about to strike a ball in an awkward position; a bridge. **8** A small glass or cup for measuring liquor, holding about one ounce; also, the amount of liquor so measured. **9** *Colloq.* Any small indefinite device.

jig·ger² (jig'ər) *n.* **1** A chigger or chigoe: also **jigger flea. 2** Some other insect of similar habits to the chigoe, as a harvest tick. [Alter. of CHIGGER]

jig·ger·mast (jig'ər·mast', -mäst') *n. Naut.* The aftermast in a yawl or a four-masted vessel.

jig·gle (jig'əl) *v.t. & v.i.* **·gled, ·gling** To move with slight, quick jerks. —*n.* An up-and-down unsteady movement. [Freq. of JIG, *v.*]

jig·saw (jig'sô') *n.* A fine, narrow saw set vertically in a frame, so as to be moved rapidly up and down.

jigsaw puzzle A puzzle, the object of which is to reassemble into the original pattern a mounted picture which has been cut by a jigsaw into numerous irregularly shaped, and often interlocking pieces.

ji·had (ji·häd') *n.* **1** A religious war of Moslems against the enemies of their faith. **2** Any war for a faith. Also spelled *jehad.* [<Arabic *jihād*]

jilt (jilt) *v.t.* To cast off or discard (a previously favored lover or sweetheart); deceive in love. —*n.* One who capriciously discards a lover. [Cf. dial. E (Scottish) *jillet* a giddy girl] — **jilt'er** *n.*

jim-crow (jim'krō') *U.S. Colloq. adj.* Segregating Negroes: *jim-crow* buses; *jim-crow* laws. —*v.t.* To subject to Negro segregation. Also **Jim'-Crow'.**

Jim Crow *U.S. Colloq.* **1** A Negro: a term of contempt, from a Negro character in an old Negro song. **2** The segregation of Negroes. —**Jim-Crow·ism** (jim'krō'iz·əm) *n.*

jim·my (jim'ē) *n. pl.* **·mies** A burglar's crowbar: sometimes made in sections. —*v.t.* **·mied, ·my·ing** To break or pry open with a jimmy. Also, *Brit., jemmy.* [from *Jimmy,* dim. of *James,* a personal name]

jim·son·weed (jim'sən·wēd') *n.* **1** A tall, coarse, evil-smelling, very poisonous annual weed of the nightshade family (*Datura stramonium*): it yields several important alkaloids, as atropine and scopolamine. **2** Apple of Peru. Also **jimp·son weed** (jimp′sən). [Alter. of *Jamestown weed,* so called because first observed in Jamestown, Va.]

jin·gle (jing′gəl) v. **·gled, ·gling** *v.i.* **1** To make light, ringing sounds, as keys striking together. **2** To sound regularly or pleasingly on the ear, as verse, tunes, etc. — *v.t.* **3** To cause to jingle. — *n.* **1** A tinkling or clinking sound; also, that which produces it. **2** Any pleasing succession of rhythmical sounds in a verse; also, such a verse. **3** A one-horse, two-wheeled carriage or car, once used in Ireland and Australia. [Imit.] — **jin′gly** *adj.*

jin·glet (jing′glit) n. **1** A small, free, metallic ball used as the clapper of a globular sleigh bell. **2** Any small jingling appendage.

Jin·go (jing′gō) n. pl. **·goes 1** One who boasts of his patriotism and favors an aggressive foreign policy. **2** *Brit.* Originally, one of a party supporting Disraeli's Near Eastern policy. — **by Jingo!** A meaningless oath or ejaculation expressing strong conviction, surprise, etc. — *adj.* Of, pertaining to, or characteristic of the Jingoes. [Origin uncertain] — **Jin′go·ish** *adj.* — **Jin′go·ism** *n.* — **Jin′go·ist** *n.* — **Jin′go·is′tic** *adj.*

jin·ni (ji·nē′) n. pl. **jinn** In Moslem mythology, an order of supernatural beings able to assume animal or human form, and often at the call and service of men through some magical controlling object: the plural form is often erroneously used as a singular: sometimes spelled **djinni, genie.** Also **jin·nee′.** [< Arabic *jinni*]

jin·ny (jin′ē) n. pl. **·nies 1** An incline in a mine, upon which loaded cars descend by gravity: also **jinny road. 2** *Mech.* The traveler on the arm of a crane: also *jenny.* [Cf. JENNY]

jinx (jingks) n. A person or thing supposed to bring bad luck; a hoodoo. — *v.t.* To bring bad luck to. [< Earlier *jynx* < Gk. *iynx* the wryneck (a bird anciently used in witchcraft)]

ji·pi·ja·pa (hē′pē·hä′pä) n. A shrubby, stemless, palmlike plant (*Carludovica palmata*), native to South America; the fan-shaped leaves provide the fiber of which Panama hats are made. [from *Jipijapa,* town in Ecuador]

jit·ter (jit′ər) v.i. *Colloq.* To talk or act nervously. [Var. of CHITTER]

jit·ter·bug (jit′ər·bug′) U.S. *Slang* n. A person who responds to swing or jazz music by dancing in a fast, violent manner. — *v.i.* **·bugged, ·bug·ging** To dance to swing or jazz music in a fast, violent manner.

jit·ters (jit′ərz) n. pl. *Colloq.* Intense nervousness or a spell of nerves. — **jit′ter·y** *adj.*

jiu·jit·su (jōō·jit′sōō) n. A Japanese system of unarmed self-defense in which one's opponent is compelled to use his strength to his own disadvantage: also spelled **jujitsu, jujutsu.** Also **jiu·jut·su** (jōō·jit′sōō, -jōōt′sōō). Compare JUDO. [< Japanese *jiu, ju* gentle, pliant + *jitsu* art]

jive (jīv) n. *Slang* **1** The jargon of jazz music and musicians. **2** Jazz music. [Origin uncertain]

joad (jōd) n. A migratory worker. [after the *Joad* family in John Steinbeck's *Grapes of Wrath*]

Jo·ash (jō′ash) Name of two Jewish kings: Joash, king of Judah 837–797 B.C., and Joash, king of Israel 800–785 B.C. Also called *Jehoash.*

job¹ (job) n. **1** A piece of work of a definite extent or character, especially one done in the course of one's profession or occupation. **2** A specific piece of work done for a certain fee. **3** Anything to be done. **4** *Colloq.* A situation or position of employment. **5** A material thing to be worked on. **6** A public service or transaction done ostensibly for the public good but actually for private or partisan gain. **7** *Colloq.* An affair; circumstance: to make the best of a bad *job.* **8** *Slang* A theft; robbery. **9** *Printing* The printing of small or miscellaneous circulars, cards, posters, etc. See synonyms under BUSINESS, TASK. — v. **jobbed, job·bing** *v.i.* **1** To work by the job or piece. **2** To be a jobber. **3** To turn a position of public trust improperly to private advantage. — *v.t.* **4** To buy in bulk from the importers or manufacturers and

resell in lots to dealers. **5** To sublet (work) among separate contractors. — *adj.* That may be bought, sold, or used by the job: a *job* lot. [Origin unknown]

job² (job) v.t. & v.i. **jobbed, job·bing** To jab. — *n.* The act of thrusting, poking, or stabbing suddenly; a jab. [ME *jobben*]

Job (jōb; *Fr.* zhōb, *Sw.* yōb) A masculine personal name. Also *Lat.* **Jo·bus** (jō′bəs). [< Hebrew, persecuted] — **Job** The chief personage of the Old Testament book of Job: often referred to as the symbol of patience on account of his many afflictions; also this book itself.

job·ber (job′ər) n. **1** One who buys goods in bulk from the manufacturer or importer and sells to the retailer. **2** *Brit.* A middleman, as among stockbrokers. **3** An intriguer, as in politics. **4** One who works by the job, or on small jobs.

job·ber·y (job′ər·ē) n. pl. **·ber·ies** Corrupt use of a public office or trust for private or partisan gain.

job·less (job′lis) adj. **1** Without a job. **2** Of or pertaining to those without a job. — **job′·less·ness** *n.*

job lot A collection of miscellaneous goods sold as a lot.

job printer One who does miscellaneous printing. — **job printing.**

Job's comforter One who, like the friends of Job, professes to console or comfort, but actually increases one's wretchedness.

Job's-tears (jōbz′tirz′) n. **1** A hardy, annual, tropical grass (*Coix lacryma–jobi*). **2** The white, pearly seeds of this plant, sometimes used as beads.

Jo·cas·ta (jō·kas′tə) In Greek legend, the wife of Laius, who unwittingly married her own son Oedipus and killed herself when she discovered it.

jock (jok) n. **1** *Colloq.* A jockstrap. **2** *Slang* An athlete. [< JOCK(STRAP)]

jock·ey (jok′ē) n. **1** One employed to ride horses, especially at races. **2** One who takes undue advantage in trade. **3** *Obs.* A strolling minstrel. **4** *Obs.* A lad; boy. **5** *Obs.* A horse dealer. — v. **·eyed, ·ey·ing** *v.i.* **1** To maneuver for an advantage: to *jockey* for position. **2** To be tricky; cheat. **3** To ride as a jockey. — *v.t.* **4** To put or guide by skilful handling or control. **5** To trick; cheat. **6** To ride (a horse) in a race. [Dim. of JOCK]

jock·o (jok′ō) n. **1** A chimpanzee. **2** Any ape or monkey. Also called *jacko.*

jock·strap (jok′strap) n. An elastic support for the genitals worn by male athletes. [< cant *jock* the male genitals + STRAP]

jo·cose (jō·kōs′) adj. Of the nature of a joke; jocular. [< L *jocosus* < *jocus* joke] — **jo·cose′ly** *adv.* — **jo·cose′ness** *n.*

Synonyms: droll, facetious, funny, humorous, jocular, merry, sportive, waggish. See HUMOROUS, MERRY, VIVACIOUS. Antonyms: careworn, cheerless, doleful, dreary, dull, grave, lugubrious, melancholy, miserable, mordant, mournful, rueful, sad, serious, solemn, sorrowful, woeful.

jo·cos·i·ty (jō·kos′ə·tē) n. pl. **·ties 1** Jocularity; jocoseness; mirthfulness. **2** A joke.

joc·u·lar (jok′yə·lər) adj. **1** Being in a joking mood; making jokes. **2** Having the nature of, intended as, or appropriate to a joke or joking; comic; funny. Also **joc′u·la·to·ry** (-tôr′ē, -tō′rē). See synonyms under HUMOROUS, JOCOSE. [< L *jocularis* < *joculus,* dim. of *jocus* a joke] — **joc·u·lar′i·ty** (-lar′ə·tē) n. — **joc′u·lar·ly** *adv.*

joc·und (jok′ənd, jō′kənd) adj. Having a blithe or gay disposition or appearance; jovial; sportive. [< OF *jocund* < LL *jocundus,* alter. of L *jucundus* pleasant < *juvare* delight] — **joc′und·ly** *adv.* — **joc′und·ness** *n.*

jo·cun·di·ty (jō·kun′də·tē) n. pl. **·ties** The state or quality of being jocund; sportiveness; mirth.

Jodh·pur (jōd·poor′, jōd′poor) **1** A former princely state in the Rajputana States, India: also *Marwar.* **2** A city in central Rajasthan; formerly the capital of Jodhpur state.

jodh·pur boots (jōd′pər) Riding shoes that end just above the ankle, buckled on the sides.

jodh·purs (jōd′pərz) n. pl. Wide riding breeches, close-fitting from knee to ankle, designed to be worn with jodhpur boots. Also **jodhpur breeches.** [from *Jodhpur,* India]

joe-pye weed (jō′pī′) Either of two tall American herbs, *Eupatorium purpureum* or *E. maculatum,* with pale–purple flowers.

jog (jog) v. **jogged, jog·ging** *v.t.* **1** To push or touch with a slight jar; shake. **2** To nudge; arouse the attention of. **3** To give a slight reminder to; stimulate: to *jog* the memory. — *v.i.* **4** To move with a slow, jolting pace or trot. **5** To proceed slowly or monotonously: with *on* or *along.* — *n.* **1** A slight push, as with the elbow; any slight incentive. **2** A slow, jolting motion or pace. **3** Any angle or break in a line or surface. **4** In the theater, a narrow flat used with other scenery to form a corner or projection in the stage set. [Prob. imit. Akin to SHOG.] — **jog′ger** *n.*

jog·ging (jog′ing) n. The exercise of running at a slow, regular pace, often alternately with walking.

jog·gle (jog′əl) v. **·gled, ·gling** *v.t.* **1** To shake slightly; jog; jolt. **2** To fasten or join together by a joggle or joggles. — *v.i.* **3** To have an irregular or jolting motion; shake. See synonyms under SHAKE. — *n.* **1** An irregular shake; jog; jolt. **2** A joint by means of which a piece, as of stone, is fitted to another. **3** A dowel. **4** A shoulder to receive the thrust of a brace or strut. [Freq. of JOG, v.]

joggle post 1 A post having shoulders to receive the feet of struts; kingpost. **2** A post built of timbers joggled together.

jog trot 1 A slow, easy trot, as of a horse. **2** A slow, humdrum habit of living or doing the daily tasks.

jo·han·nes (jō·han′ēz) n. A former gold coin of Portugal: also *joannes.* [after *Joannes V* of Portugal]

Jo·han·nes·burg (jō·han′is·bûrg, yō·hän′is-) A city in NE Republic of South Africa.

Jo·hans·son gage (yō·hän′sən) One of a series of metallurgically perfect, flat, steel blocks with parallel surfaces: used in precision measurements. [after C. E. *Johansson,* Swedish engineer]

john (jon) n. *Slang* **1** A toilet. **2** A man who patronizes a prostitute.

John (jon) A masculine personal name: often used, especially in phrases or compounds, to denote a man or boy in general. [< Hebrew, the grace of the Lord] — **John** One of the twelve apostles, son of Zebedee and brother of James: also, the Gospel according to this apostle, or one of the three Epistles written by him: also called "Saint John the Evangelist." — **John** Son of Zacharias; the forerunner of Jesus; beheaded by Herod Antipas: known as *John the Baptist.* — **John,** 1166?–1216, king of England 1199–1216; signed Magna Carta, 1215: called "John Lackland."

John Bull The Englishman personified: a nickname; hence, the English people. Also **Johnny Bull.** [after a character in a satire (1712) by Dr. Arbuthnot] — **John-Bul·lism** (jon·bool′iz·əm) *n.*

John Doe (dō) A name commonly used to designate a fictitious or real personage: from the fictitious plaintiff in the action at common law for ejectment, the fictitious defendant being *Richard Roe.*

John Hancock U.S. *Colloq.* A person's autograph. [after *John Hancock,* whose large signature is the first on the Declaration of Independence]

Johnny Appleseed See APPLESEED, JOHNNY.

john·ny·cake (jon′ē·kāk′) n. A flat cake of Indian meal, baked on a griddle; also, cornbread: often spelled *jonnycake.* [? < obs. *jonikin,* a type of bread (< N. Am. Ind.) + CAKE]

John·ny-come-late·ly (jon′ē·kum′·lāt′lē) n. *Colloq.* A person who has recently arrived on the scene.

john·ny-jump-up (jon′ē·jump′up′) n. **1** A naturalized variety of the pansy (*Viola kitaibeliana*). **2** The bird's-foot violet. **3** The wild pansy. Also **john′ny–jump′er.**

Johnny on the spot *Colloq.* One who is always on hand and ready for anything. — **John·ny-on-the-spot** (jon′ē·on·thə·spot′) *adj.*

Johnny red *Pathol.* Kwashiorkor.

John Paul Appellation of two popes. — **John Paul I,** 1912–1978, real name Albino

Luciani; pope 1978.
— **John Paul II**, born 1920, real name Karol Wojtyla, pope 1978–
John·son (jon'sǝn), **Andrew**, 1808–75, president of the United States 1865–69. — **James Weldon**, 1871–1938, U.S. lawyer and author. — **Lyndon Baines**, 1908–1973, 36th president of the United States 1963–1969. — **Samuel**, 1709–84, English author, critic, and lexicographer: known as *Doctor Johnson*. — **Sir William**, 1715–74, English official in the American colonies.

Johnson grass A perennial pasture grass (*Sorghum halepense*) also valued for hay, but considered a weed in cultivated land: also called *Arabian millet*. [after Wm. *Johnson*, Alabama planter]

join (join) *v.t.* **1** To set or bring together; connect; combine: to *join* girders. **2** To come to a junction with; become part of: The path *joins* the road here. **3** To become a member of, as a club. **4** To unite in act or purpose: to *join* forces. **5** To come to as a companion or participant; meet and accompany: When will you *join* us? **6** To unite in marriage. **7** To engage in (battle, etc.). **8** *Colloq.* To adjoin. **9** *Geom.* To draw a straight line or curve between. — *v.i.* **10** To come together; connect; unite: The roads *joined*. **11** To enter into association or agreement. **12** To take part: usually with *in*. — **to join up** To enlist in a military service. — *n.* A place of junction or contact; joint. [<OF *joign-*, stem of *joindre* <L *jungere*]

join·der (join'dǝr) *n.* **1** The act of joining. **2** *Law* A joining of causes of action or defense; a joining of parties in an action; also, the acceptance of an issue tendered. [<F *joindre* join]

join·er (joi'nǝr) **1** One who or that which joins. **2** An artisan who finishes woodwork in houses; also, loosely, any mechanic who puts together pieces of wood.

join·er·y (joi'nǝr·ē) *n.* **1** The art or work of a joiner. **2** The articles constructed by a joiner.

joint (joint) *n.* **1** The place, point, line, or surface where two or more things are joined together; a junction or mode of junction; hinge. **2** An articulation or place of natural or easy separation between two parts, as of a machine, animal, or plant; a node; also, an internode or portion between two nodes or joints. **3** *Anat.* A place of union of two bones or separate parts of the skeleton; an articulation. **4** *Geol.* One of a series of approximately parallel divisional planes occurring in many rocks. **5** One of the pieces into which a carcass is divided by the butcher. **6** *U.S. Slang* A marihuana cigarette. **7** *U.S. Slang* A place of low resort, as for gambling. **8** *U.S. Slang* Any place of dwelling or gathering. — **out of joint 1** Not fitted at the joint; dislocated. **2** Disordered; disorganized. — *adj.* **1** Produced by combined action. **2** Sharing together. **3** Participated in or used by two or more; held or shared in common. **4** *Law* Joined together in unity of interest or of liability: opposed to *several*. **5** Of or relating to both branches of a legislature: a *joint* session. See synonyms under MUTUAL. — *v.t.* **1** To fasten by means of a joint or joints. **2** To form or shape with a joint or joints, as a board. **3** To separate into joints, as meat. [<OF <L *junctus*, pp. of *jungere* join] — **joint'less** *adj.*

joint account An account in the name of two or more persons.

joint committee A committee of representatives from both houses of a legislative body.

joint convention 1 A session of both houses of a legislature. **2** An assembly of delegates representing two or more political parties. Also **joint session.**

joint·ed (join'tid) *adj.* Having joints, knots, or nodes; articulated.

joint·er (join'tǝr) *n.* **1** One who or that which joints; especially, one of several instruments for constructing joints. **2** An edged part, triangular in shape, attached to the beam of a plow. **3** A trying plane.

joint evil *Pathol.* A form of leprosy which is anesthetic in its later stages, especially as known in the West Indies.

joint fir Any of a genus of shrubs (*Ephedra*) growing in dry or desert regions, with jointed green branches and red berries; especially, ma huang.

joint·grass (joint'gras', -gräs') *n.* A creeping

grass (*Paspalum distichum*) of the southern United States, which roots at the joints: used as fodder.

joint·ly (joint'lē) *adv.* In a joint manner; unitedly.

joint-mouse (joint'mous') *n.* A movable cartilage, calculus, or other foreign body in a joint.

joint·ress (join'tris) *n.* **1** A woman who has a jointure: also **join·tur·ess** (join'chǝr·is). **2** A woman who is a joint ruler or owner.

joint snake The glass snake.

joint stock Capital or stock that is held jointly.

joint-stock company (joint'stok') A company or partnership whose capital is divided into shares (usually transferable), some of which are held by each of the members. Also **joint'stock' association.**

join·ture (join'chǝr) *n.* **1** *Law* A settlement, as of land, made to a woman in place of dower. **2** *Obs.* A joining together. — *v.t.* **join·tured**, **join·tur·ing** To settle a jointure on. [<F <L *junctura* <*jungere* join]

joint·weed (joint'wēd') *n.* A slender, erect American annual herb (*Polygonella articulata*) with small, white flowers on jointed stems.

joint·worm (joint'wûrm') *n.* The larva of a plant-feeding chalcidid hymenopterous fly (genus *Harmolita*), especially *H. tritici*, that does great damage to wheat, barley, etc., by causing a gall-like excrescence at the joints of the stalk.

joist (joist) *n.* A horizontal timber in a floor or ceiling. See synonyms under STICK. — *v.t.* To furnish with joists. [<OF *giste* <*gesir* lie <L *jacere*]

JOIST
a. Joists.
b. Floor boards.

Jó·kai (yō'koi), **Mau·rus**, 1825–1904, Hungarian novelist.

joke (jōk) *n.* **1** Something said or done for the purpose of creating amusement; a jest. **2** A subject of merriment. **3** Something not said or done in earnest; sport. See synonyms under WIT. — *v.* **joked**, **jok·ing** *v.t.* To make merry with. — *v.i.* To make jokes; jest. [<L *jocus*] — **jok'ing·ly** *adv.*

jok·er (jō'kǝr) *n.* **1** One who jokes. **2** In certain card games, as euchre, an extra card that counts as the highest trump, or, in poker, as any card the holder names. **3** *U.S.* An ambiguous or inconspicuous clause, inserted in a legislative bill to render it ineffectual or cause it to serve some purpose other than the original intention of the bill. **4** Any hidden device or ruse used for purposes of trickery or deception.

jol·li·fi·ca·tion (jol'ǝ·fǝ·kā'shǝn) *n.* An act or occasion of festivity; a merrymaking.

jol·li·fy (jol'ǝ·fī) *v.t. & v.i.* **·fied**, **·fy·ing** To be or cause to be merry or jolly.

jol·li·ness (jol'ē·nis) *n.* The state or quality of being jolly; gaiety. Also **jol·li·ty** (jol'ǝ·tē).

jol·ly (jol'ē) *adj.* **·li·er**, **·li·est 1** Full of life and mirth; jovial. **2** Expressing, inspiring, or characterized by mirth; exciting gaiety. **3** *Obs.* Exhilarated. See synonyms under HAPPY, MERRY. — *adv. Brit. Colloq.* Extremely; very: a *jolly* good time. — *n. pl.* **·lies 1** Fun; banter; flattery. **2** *Brit. Slang* A British marine. **3** *Brit. Colloq.* A merry or festive gathering. — *v.t.* **·lied**, **·ly·ing** *Colloq.* **1** To attempt to put or keep in good humor by agreeable or flattering attentions: often with *along* or *up*. **2** To make fun of; joke; rally. [<OF *joli*] — **jol'li·er** *n.* — **jol'li·ly** *adv.*

Jolly balance A spring balance used in the determination of specific gravities. [after Philip von *Jolly*, 1809–84, German physicist]

jol·ly-boat (jol'ē-bōt') *n.* A small boat belonging to a ship. [<Dan. *jolle* yawl + BOAT]

Jolly Roger See BLACK FLAG under FLAG[1].

Jo·lo (hō'lō, hō-lō') **1** The chief island in the Sulu archipelago, Philippines; 345 square miles. **2** Its chief city, capital of Sulu province.

jolt (jōlt) *v.t.* **1** To strike or knock against with a jarring shock. **2** To shake about with such shock. — *v.i.* To move with jolts or bumps, as over a rough road. See synonyms under SHAKE. — *n.* A sudden, slight shock. [? Blend of ME *jot* bump and *joll* bump] — **jolt'er** *n.* — **jolt'y** *adj.*

Jo·ma·da (jō-mä'dä) The name of two Mohammedan months. See under CALENDAR (Mohammedan). Also spelled *Jumada.*

Jo·nah (jō'nǝ) A masculine personal name. Also **Jo·nas** (jō'nǝs; *Fr.* zhô·näs', *Ger.* yō'näs). [<Hebrew, dove]
— **Jonah 1** A Hebrew prophet of the eighth or ninth century B.C., who was cast overboard during a tempest sent because he had defied God: he was swallowed by a large fish, lived in its belly for three days, and was vomited up on shore alive. **2** The minor book of the Old Testament named for him and telling his story. **3** Any person or thing regarded as bringing bad luck: in allusion to the bad luck brought upon the sailors of the vessel the prophet traveled on. *Jonah* i 13–17. Also **Jo·nas** (jō'nǝs).

jon·quil (jon'kwil, jong'-) *n.* **1** An ornamental bulbous plant (*Narcissus jonquilla*) related to the daffodil, having long, linear leaves and fragrant, white or yellow flowers. **2** The bulb or flower of this plant. **3** One of several other species of *Narcissus*. **4** A light–yellow color used in staining porcelains. Also **jon'quille.** [<F *jonquille*, ult. <L *juncus* a rush]

Jon·son (jon'sǝn), **Ben(jamin)**, 1573–1637, English poet and dramatist.

Jor·dan (jôr'dǝn) The chief river of Palestine, flowing over 200 miles south to the Dead Sea.

Jordan, Hashemite Kingdom of the A constitutional monarchy comprising the territories of Trans–Jordan and Arab Palestine; formed, with Iraq, The Arab Federation, 1958, but remains a sovereign state; 37,758 square miles: capital, Amman. *Arabic* **Al Ur·du·ni·yah** (al ŏŏr·dŏŏ·nē'yä). Also **Jordan.** — **Jor·da·ni·an** (jôr·dā'nē·ǝn) *adj. & n.*

Jordan almond A large Spanish almond, frequently sugar–coated as a confection.

jor·na·da (hôr·nä'thä) *n. SW U.S.* A stretch of desert land that can be crossed in a day's journey. [<Sp., ult. <L *diurnus* of a day]

jo·seph (jō'zef) *n.* A long coat formerly worn by men; also, a similar garment formerly worn as a riding habit by women. [In allusion to the coat of *Joseph* (*Gen.* xxxvii 3)]

Jo·seph·ite (jō'zǝf·īt) *n.* A member of the Reorganized church of Jesus Christ of Latter-day Saints (the Mormon Church), established about 1860 by the followers of Joseph Smith.

josh (josh) *U.S. Slang v.t. & v.i.* To make good–humored fun of (someone); tease; banter. — *n.* A hoax; a good–natured joke. [Blend of JOKE and BOSH] — **josh'er** *n.*

Joshua tree A tall, treelike desert plant (*Yucca brevifolia*) with forking branches that end in a cluster of leaves.

joss (jos) *n.* A Chinese god. [Pidgin English <Pg. *deos* God]

joss house A Chinese temple or place for idols.

joss paper Gold or silver paper burnt by the Chinese at funerals, etc.

joss stick A stick of perfumed paste burnt as incense.

jos·tle (jos'ǝl) *v.t. & v.i.* **·tled**, **·tling** To push or crowd; elbow; hustle; bump. See synonyms under HUSTLE. — *n.* A collision, bumping against, or rough shaking. Also spelled *justle.* [Freq. of JOUST] — **jos'tler** *n.*

jot (jot) *v.t.* **jot·ted**, **jot·ting** To make a hasty note of: usually with *down*. — *n.* The least bit; an iota. See synonyms under PARTICLE. [<IOTA]

jo·ta (hō'tä) *n.* A lively Spanish dance in 3/4 time danced by a man and a woman with castanets.

jot·tings (jot'ingz) *n. pl.* Items of news, or memoranda.

Jö·tun (yœ'tŏŏn) In Norse mythology, one of the giants personifying the hostile powers of nature. Also **Jo·tun** (yô'tŏŏn, yō'-), **Jo'tunn.**

joule (joul, jōōl) *n. Physics* The mks unit of work or energy: equivalent to the work done, or heat generated, in one second by an electric current of one ampere against a resistance of one ohm, or in raising the potential of one coulomb by one volt: equal to 10,000,000 ergs or .737324 foot–pounds. [after James Prescott *Joule*]

jour·nal (jûr'nǝl) *n.* **1** A record of daily occurrences of personal interest; a diary. **2** An official record of the daily proceedings of a legislature or other deliberative body. **3** A periodical recording

JOURNAL (*def.* 7)
a. Journal. *b.* Bearing.

news or other events of current interest. **4** A daily chronicle of a voyage. **5** *Naut.* A log or logbook. **6** In bookkeeping: **a** A daybook. **b** In double entry, a book in which transactions of the day are entered in systematic form, either as original entries or as transfers from the daybook, in order to facilitate later posting in the ledger. **7** *Mech.* That part of a shaft or axle which rotates in or against a bearing. [<OF <L *diurnalis.* Doublet of DIURNAL.]

journal box *Mech.* The box or bearing for a rotating axle or shaft.

jour·nal·ese (jûr′nəl·ēz′, -ēs′) *n.* A style of writing supposedly characteristic of newspapers; facile and sensational writing, hackneyed phrases and effects, etc.

jour·nal·ism (jûr′nəl·iz′əm) *n.* **1** The occupation of a journalist; the writing, editing, or publishing of newspapers or other periodicals. **2** Newspapers collectively.

jour·nal·ist (jûr′nəl·ist) *n.* One who manages, edits, or writes for a journal or newspaper.

jour·nal·is·tic (jûr′nəl·is′tik) *adj.* Pertaining to journalists or journalism. — **jour′nal·is′ti·cal·ly** *adv.*

jour·nal·ize (jûr′nəl·īz) *v.* **·ized**, **·iz·ing** *v.t.* **1** To enter in a journal. **2** To write or describe in a journal. — *v.i.* **3** To keep a journal or diary. Also *Brit.* **jour′nal·ise.**

jour·ney (jûr′nē) *n.* **1** Passage from one place to another, especially by land: sometimes applied figuratively to the passage through life. **2** The distance traversed, or traversable, in a specified time: a week's *journey* away. **3** In glassmaking, the round of work or the time taken in making raw material into glass. — *v.i.* To travel; go on a journey. [<OF *journee* a day's travel <L *diurnum,* orig. neut. sing. of *diurnus* daily <*dies* a day] — **jour′ney·er** *n.*
Synonyms (noun): excursion, expedition, pilgrimage, tour, transit, travel, trip, voyage. A *journey* is a direct going from a starting point to a destination, ordinarily over a considerable distance; we speak of a day's *journey,* or the *journey* of life. *Travel* is a passing from place to place, not necessarily in a direct line or with a fixed destination. A *voyage,* which was formerly a *journey* of any kind, is now a going to a considerable distance by water, especially by sea. A *trip* is a short and direct *journey.* A *tour* is a *journey* that returns to the starting point, generally over a considerable distance; as, a bridal *tour,* or business *tour.* An *excursion* is a brief *tour* or *journey* taken for pleasure, often by many persons at once; as, an *excursion* to West Point. *Passage* is a general word for a *journey* by any conveyance, especially by water; as, rough *passage* across the Atlantic. *Transit,* literally the act of passing over or through, is used specifically of the conveyance of passengers or merchandise; rapid *transit* is demanded for suburban residents or perishable goods. *Pilgrimage,* once always of a sacred character, retains in derived uses something of that sense; as, a *pilgrimage* to Monticello.

jour·ney·man (jûr′nē·mən) *n.* *pl.* **·men** (-mən) A mechanic who has learned his trade and who works at it for another.

jour·ney·work (jûr′nē·wûrk′) *n.* Work done by a journeyman.

joust (just, joust, jōōst) *n.* A tilting match between mounted knights, usually with blunt lances and in single combat. — *v.i.* To engage in a joust. Also spelled *just.* [<OF *jouste* <*jouster* <LL *juxtare* approach <*juxta* nearby] — **joust′er** *n.*

Jove (jōv) Jupiter. — **by Jove!** A mild oath expressing surprise, emphasis, etc.

jo·vi·al (jō′vē·əl) *adj.* Possessing or expressive of good-natured mirth or gaiety; jolly. See synonyms under MERRY. [<F <LL *Jovialis* born under the influence of Jupiter] — **jo′vi·al·ly** *adv.* — **jo′vi·al·ness** *n.*

Jo·vi·al (jō′vē·əl) *adj.* **1** In astrology, pertaining to the influence of the planet Jupiter; favorable; benignant. **2** *Obs.* Of or pertaining to the god Jupiter; Jovelike; majestic.

jo·vi·al·i·ty (jō′vē·al′ə·tē) *n.* **1** The quality of being jovial. **2** Merriment; conviviality; mirth. Also **jo·vi·al·ty** (jō′vē·əl·tē). See synonyms under SPORT.

jo·vi·al·ize (jō′vē·əl·īz′) *v.t.* **·ized**, **·iz·ing** To make jovial.

Jo·vi·an (jō′vē·ən) *adj.* Of or pertaining to Jove

or Jupiter.

Jo·vi·a·nus (jō′vē·ā′nəs), **Flavius Claudius,** 331?–364, Roman emperor 363–364. Also **Jo′vi·an** (-ən).

jowl[1] (joul, jōl) *n.* **1** The fleshy part of the lower jaw, especially when fat and pendulous. **2** The wattle of fowls. **3** The dewlap of cattle. Also spelled *jole.* [ME *cholle,* ? OE *coeulr* throat]

jowl[2] (joul, jōl) *n.* The cheek or jaw. Also spelled *jole.* [OE *ceafl*] — **jowled** *adj.*

jowl·er (jou′lər) *n.* A heavy-jawed hound.

joy (joi) *n.* **1** A lively emotion of happiness; gladness. **2** Anything which causes delight. **3** An expression or manifestation of this. **4** *Obs.* Festivity. See synonyms under HAPPINESS, RAPTURE. — *v.i.* To be glad; rejoice. — *v.t. Obs.* To gladden. See synonyms under REJOICE. [<OF *joie* <L *gaudium* <*gaudere* rejoice]

Joyce (jois), **James,** 1882–1941, Irish novelist and poet. — **William** See HAW-HAW, LORD.

joy·ful (joi′fəl) *adj.* **1** Full of joy. **2** Manifesting or causing joy. See synonyms under HAPPY. — **joy′ful·ly** *adv.* — **joy′ful·ness** *n.*

joy·less (joi′lis) *adj.* Destitute of joy; having or causing no joy. — **joy′less·ly** *adv.* — **joy′·less·ness** *n.*

joy·ous (joi′əs) *adj.* Joyful. See synonyms under AIRY, CHEERFUL, HAPPY, MERRY. — **joy′ous·ly** *adv.* — **joy′ous·ness** *n.*

joy-ride (joi′rīd′) *n. Colloq.* An automobile ride taken exclusively for pleasure: often with the idea of reckless driving in a stolen car. — **joy′-rid′er** *n.* — **joy′-rid′ing** *n.*

joy-stick (joi′stik′) *n. Slang* The control stick in an airplane.

ju·ba (jōō′bə) *n.* A lively Southern Negro dance. — **to pat juba** To keep time to the juba by patting with the hands and feet. [Of African origin]

Ju·bal (jōō′bəl) A descendant of Cain; a musician or inventor of musical instruments. *Gen.* iv 21.

ju·bate (jōō′bāt) *adj.* Having a manelike growth. [<L *jubatus* <*juba* a mane]

ju·be (jōō′bē) *n.* **1** *Archit.* A rood loft or screen and gallery at the entrance of the choir of a church. **2** *Obs.* An ambo. [<L *jube,* imperative of *jubere* bid; from the first word of a prayer anciently recited from this gallery]

ju·bi·lance (jōō′bə·ləns) *n.* Jubilation. Also **ju′bi·lan·cy.**

ju·bi·lant (jōō′bə·lənt) *adj.* **1** Manifesting great joy; exultingly glad. **2** Expressing triumph. [<L *jubilans, -antis,* ppr. of *jubilare* exult] — **ju′bi·lant·ly** *adv.*

ju·bi·late (jōō′bə·lāt) *v.t. & v.i.* **·lat·ed**, **·lat·ing** To rejoice; exult. [<L *jubilatus,* pp. of *jubilare* exult]

Ju·bi·la·te (jōō′bə·lā′tē, -lä′-) *n.* **1** The 100th (in the Vulgate and Douai versions, the 99th) Psalm, or the music to which it may be set: from its opening word in the Latin version. **2** The third Sunday after Easter, whose introit begins *Jubilate.* [<L, imperative of *jubilare* exult, be joyful]

Ju·bi·la·te De·o (jōō′bə·lä′tē dē′ō, jōō′bə·lä′tē dā′ō) *Latin* Be joyful in the Lord.

ju·bi·la·tion (jōō′bə·lā′shən) *n.* Rejoicing; exultation.

ju·bi·lee (jōō′bə·lē) *n.* **1** In Jewish history, every fiftieth year, from the entrance of the Hebrews into Canaan. At its recurrence, all Hebrew slaves were emancipated and all alienated lands reverted to their former owners or their heirs. **2** In the Roman Catholic Church, a year of special indulgence, appointed by the Pope, during which compliance with certain conditions of confession, communion, good works, etc., will secure remission from the penal consequences of sin: also called *Annus Sanctus.* **3** The fiftieth or the twenty-fifth anniversary of an event; also, the celebration of this. **4** Any season of rejoicing or festivity. **5** *Obs.* A state or manifestation of exultation or delight. Also **ju′bi·le.** [<OF *jubile* <LL *jubilaeus* (infl. by *jubilum* a shout of joy) <Gk. *iōbēlaios* <Hebrew *yōbēl* ram's horn, trumpet]

jubilee singer One, especially a Negro, who sings jubilee songs.

jubilee song A Negro folk song or spiritual; originally, one of rejoicing over emancipation

from slavery.

ju chin (jōō′ chin′) **1** A creamy gold emulsion made by rubbing gold leaf under water with a circular motion of the fingers: used in Chinese and Japanese painting to outline rocks in landscapes, to impart bright highlights to birds and flowers, and to decorate the garments in Buddhistic portraits. **2** A brush technique for applying this emulsion. [<Chinese, lit., milk gold]

Ju·da·ic (jōō·dā′ik) *adj.* Pertaining to the Jews. Also **Ju·da′i·cal.** [<L *Judaicus* <Gk. *Ioudaikos* <*Ioudaios.* See JEW.] — **Ju·da′i·cal·ly** *adv.*

Ju·da·ism (jōō′dē·iz′əm) *n.* **1** The religious beliefs or practices of the Jews. **2** The acceptance of Jewish rites or doctrines. — **Ju′da·ist** *n.* — **Ju′da·is′tic** *adj.*

Ju·das (jōō′dəs) See JUDAH.
— **Judas** The disciple of Jesus who betrayed him with a kiss, thus identifying him to the Roman captors; hence, one who betrays another under the guise of friendship: also **Judas Iscariot.**
— **Judas** A brother of Jesus. *Matt.* xiii 55.
— **Judas Maccabeus** See under MACCABEUS.

Judas kiss A treacherous kiss or other gesture simulating friendliness.

Judas tree Any of a genus (*Cercis*) of trees, as *C. siliquastrum,* a European species, or the redbud (*C. canadensis*) with profuse, reddish-purple flowers, of the central and western United States. [From a tradition that Judas hanged himself upon a tree of this kind]

JUDAS TREE
a. Leaves.
b. Blossom.
c. Fruit.

Jude (jōōd) See JUDAH.
— **Jude** One of the apostles, the brother of James, and possibly of Jesus: sometimes identified with Thaddeus (*Luke* vi 16); also, a New Testament epistle attributed to him.

judge (juj) *n.* **1** An officer invested with authority to administer justice. **2** One who decides upon the merits of things, as in contests. **3** One who is competent to decide upon the merits of persons, animals, things, etc.; a connoisseur. **4** In Jewish history, one of the Israelitish rulers from the death of Joshua to the anointing of Saul. — *v.* **judged**, **judg·ing** *v.t.* **1** To hear and decide in an official capacity the merits of (a case) or the guilt of (a person); examine and pass judgment on; try. **2** To form an opinion or judgment concerning; evaluate; estimate: to *judge* a painting. **3** To hold as judgment or opinion; consider; suppose: We *judged* it the proper time. **4** To govern: said of the ancient Hebrew judges. — *v.i.* **5** To act as a judge; sit in judgment. **6** To form a judgment or estimate. **7** To make a judgment or decision. [<OF *juge* <L *judex, -icis* <*jus* right + *dic-,* root of *dicere* speak] — **judg′er** *n.*
Synonyms (noun): arbiter, arbitrator, justice, referee, umpire. A *judge,* in the legal sense, is a judicial officer appointed or elected to preside in courts of law, and to decide legal questions duly brought before him; the name is sometimes given to other legally constituted officers; as, the *judges* of election; in other relations, any person duly appointed to pass upon the merits of contestants or of competing articles may be called a *judge.* In various sports the *judge* is called an *umpire,* or in some cases the *referee,* as, the *umpire* of a ball game. In law, a *referee* is appointed by a court to decide disputed matters between litigants; an *arbitrator* is chosen by the contending parties to decide matters in dispute without action by a court. In certain cases, an *umpire* is appointed by a court to decide where *arbitrators* disagree. *Arbiter,* with its suggestion of final and absolute decision, has come to be used only in a high or sacred sense; as, war must now be the *arbiter;* the Supreme *Arbiter* of our destinies. The *judges* of certain courts, as the United States Supreme Court, are technically known as *justices.*

judge advocate *Mil.* **1** A commissioned officer of the U. S. Army belonging to the Judge Advocate General's Department. **2** The legal staff officer for a commander. **3** The prosecutor in a general or special court martial.

Judg·es (juj′iz) The seventh book of the Old Testament.

judge·ship (juj′ship) *n.* The office, or period in office, of a judge.

judg·mat·ic (juj·mat′ik) *adj. Colloq.* Evincing good judgment; skilful. Also **judg·mat′i·cal.** [<*judge*; on analogy with *dogmatic*] — **judg·mat′i·cal·ly** *adv.*

judg·ment (juj′mənt) *n.* **1** The act or faculty of affirming or denying a conclusion, whether as based upon a direct comparison of objects or ideas, or derived by a process of reasoning. **2** The result of judging; the decision or conclusion reached, as after consideration or deliberation. **3** *Law* The sentence or final order of a court in a civil or criminal proceeding; the sentence of the law; the final determination or adjudication of the rights of the parties to an action; decision; award; also, the obligation or debt created by the decision or verdict of a court, or the official certificate or record of such decision, which constitutes a lien on leviable property. **4** A disaster or affliction regarded as inflicted by God as a punishment for sin. **5** *Theol.* The final award or sentence of the human race; also, the time of this: also **Judgment** or **Last Judgment.** **6** *Psychol.* The mental act or attitude of decision with which the process of observation, comparison, or ratiocination is terminated; also, loosely, the rational faculty; thought. **7** *Logic* That form of thought in which two terms are compared and their fitness to be joined under a given relation is affirmed or denied; also, the result of judging, the verbal expression of which is called an assertion or proposition. **8** *Obs.* Uprightness; rectitude. Also *Brit.* **judge′ment.** See synonyms under IDEA, PRUDENCE, THOUGHT[1], UNDERSTANDING, WISDOM. — **general judgment** *Theol.* The final judgment of all men after the dissolution of the world. — **particular judgment** *Theol.* The judgment of the soul immediately after death.

Judgment Day *Theol.* The day or time of the Last Judgment.

judgment debtor *Law* A debtor against whom judgment of indebtedness has been recorded.

judgment of God Trial by single combat or by ordeal or the like, supposed to be under direct divine control.

ju·di·ca·ble (jōō′də·kə·bəl) *adj.* That can be tried or judged. Also **ju·di·ci·a·ble** (jōō·dish′ē·ə·bəl).

ju·di·ca·tive (jōō′də·kā′tiv, -kə-) *adj.* Competent to judge; judicial. [<L *judicatus*, pp. of *judicare* judge]

ju·di·ca·tor (jōō′də·kā′tər) *n.* One who performs the office of a judge.

ju·di·ca·to·ry (jōō′də·kə·tôr′ē, -tō′rē) *adj.* Pertaining to the administration of justice. — *n. pl.* **·ries** **1** A tribunal. **2** The judiciary. **3** *Obs.* Judicial power; justice.

ju·di·ca·ture (jōō′də·kə·chŏŏr) *n.* **1** The power of administering justice. **2** The jurisdiction of a court. **3** A court of justice; also, judges collectively. **4** *Obs.* Established right; legality; lawfulness.

ju·di·cial (jōō·dish′əl) *adj.* **1** Pertaining to the administration of justice. **2** Of, pertaining to, or connected with a court or judge. **3** Discriminating; impartial. **4** Serving to decide or determine; judging: *judicial* duels. **5** *Obs.* Established by formal enactment or positive law. [<L *judicialis* <*judex, -icis* a judge] — **ju·di′cial·ly** *adv.*

ju·di·ci·ar·y (jōō·dish′ē·er′ē, -dish′ə·rē) *adj.* Pertaining to courts of justice or to a judge. — *n. pl.* **·ar·ies** **1** That department of government which administers the law. **2** The judges of the courts considered collectively.

ju·di·cious (jōō·dish′əs) *adj.* **1** Having or acting on sound judgment; proceeding with discretion; manifesting forethought and sense; wise; prudent. **2** Done with sound judgment; well-calculated; planned or arranged with discretion. See synonyms under POLITIC, SAGACIOUS, WISE[1]. [<F *judicieux* <L *judicium* a judgment] — **ju·di′cious·ly** *adv.* — **ju·di′cious·ness** *n.*

ju·do (jōō′dō) *n.* A Japanese system of mental and physical conditioning based upon jiujitsu and often practiced as a sport. Compare JIUJITSU. [<Japanese *ju* gentle, pliant + *do* way of life]

jug (jug) *n.* **1** A narrow-necked, stout, bulg-ing vessel with a cork, for keeping or carrying liquids. **2** A deep vessel for holding or serving liquids; a drinking vessel; pitcher. **3** A pint of ale or beer. **4** *Slang* A prison; jail. — *v.t.* **jugged, jug·ging** **1** To put into a jug. **2** To cook in a jug. **3** *Slang* To imprison; jail. [from *Jug*, a nickname for *Joan*]

jug (jug) *v.i.* **jugged, jug·ging** To collect together and nestle in a flock or covey: said of partridges. [Cf. OF *jouquier* be at rest]

ju·gal (jōō′gəl) *adj. Anat.* Of or pertaining to a bone of the zygomatic arch or malar bone. [<L *jugalis* <*jugum* a yoke]

ju·gate (jōō′git, -gāt) *adj.* **1** Occurring in pairs. **2** *Bot.* Having paired leaves, as certain plants. [<L *jugatus*, pp. of *jugare* bind together <*jugum* a yoke]

jug·ger·naut (jug′ər·nôt) *n.* **1** Anything to which one makes unquestioning sacrifices. **2** Any irresistible force. [after JUGGERNAUT]

Jug·ger·naut (jug′ər·nôt) The eighth avatar of Vishnu whose idol at Puri, India, was drawn on a heavy car under the wheels of which devotees were said to have thrown themselves to be crushed. Also spelled **Jaganath, Jag·anatha, Jaggurnath.** [<Hind. *jagannāth* lord of the universe]

jug·gle (jug′əl) *v.* **·gled, ·gling** *v.t.* **1** To toss (a number of balls, plates, etc.) into the air, keeping them in continuous motion by successively catching and tossing them up again. **2** To perform tricks of sleight of hand with. **3** To manipulate for the purpose of deception or trickery: to *juggle* financial accounts. — *v.i.* **4** To perform as a juggler. **5** To practice deception or trickery. — *n.* **1** A feat of legerdemain. **2** A trick or deception. [<OF *jogler* <L *joculari* jest]

jug·gler (jug′lər) *n.* **1** One who juggles; a prestidigitator. **2** One who deceives by cheating; an impostor. [<OF *joglere* <L *joculator* jester]

jug·gling (jug′ling) *adj.* Deceiving; cheating; relating to tricks of magic. — *n.* Jugglery.

jug·head (jug′hed′) *n. U.S. Slang* **1** A slow-witted horse. **2** A slow or stupid person.

ju·glan·da·ceous (jōō′glan·dā′shəs) *adj.* Designating a family (*Juglandaceae*) of trees with odd-pinnate leaves and monoecious flowers, including the walnut and hickory. [<NL *Juglandaceae*, the walnut family <L *juglans* a walnut]

ju·glone (jōō′glōn) *n.* A brownish-red crystal-line compound, $C_{10}H_6O_3$, extracted from the bark or unripe fruit of the walnut tree (*Juglans cinerea*). [<L *juglans* walnut + -ONE]

jug·u·lar (jug′yə·lər, jōō′gyə-) *adj.* **1** *Anat.* Pertaining to the throat or to the jugular vein. **2** *Biol.* **a** Situated in front of the pectoral fins. **b** Having the ventral fins at the throat, as a fish. — *n.* One of the jugular veins. [<NL *jugularis* <L *jugulum* a collar bone]

jugular vein *Anat.* One of the large veins on either side of the neck that returns blood from the brain, face, and neck.

ju·gu·late (jōō′gyə·lāt) *v.t.* **·lat·ed, ·lat·ing** **1** *Med.* To arrest the course of (a disease) by drastic therapeutic measures. **2** *Obs.* To cut the throat of. [<L *jugulatus*, pp. of *jugulare* slay, cut the throat of <*jugulum* a collar bone] — **ju′gu·la′tion** *n.*

juice (jōōs) *n.* **1** The fluid part of vegetable or animal matter; especially, the expressible watery matter in fruits, containing usually the characteristic flavor. **2** *Usually pl.* The fluids of the body. **3** The essence of anything. **4** *Slang* Electric current, or other means of generating power, as oil, gasoline, etc. **5** The liquid extracted from anything. [<OF *jus* <L] — **juice′less** *adj.*

juic·y (jōō′sē) *adj.* **juic·i·er, juic·i·est** **1** Abounding with juice; moist. **2** Full of interest; colorful; spicy. — **juic′i·ly** *adv.* — **juic′i·ness** *n.*

ju·ju (jōō′jōō) *n.* An African fetish or talisman; an object of religious veneration or awe; hence, anything inexplicable, mysterious, or magical; also, the charm said to be worked by a juju. [<native West African name, ? ult. <F *joujou* a toy] — **ju′ju·ism** *n.*

ju·jube (jōō′jōōb) *n.* **1** Any of a genus (*Zizyphus*) of several Old World trees or shrubs of the buckthorn family; especially, the common jujube (*Z. jujuba*), the lotus tree. **2** Its edible fruit. **3** A lozenge. [<F <Med. L *jujuba*, alter. of L *zizyphum* <Gk. *zizyphon* <Persian

zīzafūn]

juke box A large automatic phonograph, usually coin-operated and permitting selection of the records to be played.

juke joint *U.S. Slang* A roadhouse or barroom for drinking and dancing. [<Gullah *juke*, orig. a brothel (of West African origin) + JOINT (*n.* def. 6)]

Jukes, the A pseudonym used for the members of an actual New York family whose history, as investigated over several generations by 19th century sociologists, showed abnormal incidence of crime, disease, and pauperism. See KALLIKAK.

ju·lep (jōō′lip) *n.* **1** A drink composed usually of brandy or whisky, sugar, cracked ice, and some flavoring, commonly fresh green mint: also **mint julep.** **2** A subacid, mucilaginous, sweetened drink, often used as a vehicle for the administration of medicine. **3** A cool drink made with herbs. Also **ju′lap.** [<MF <Persian *gulāb* rose-water]

ju·li·enne (jōō′lē·en′) *n.* A clear meat soup containing vegetables chopped or cut into thin strips. — *adj.* Cut into thin strips: *julienne* potatoes. [<F, from *Julienne*, a personal name]

Ju·ly (jōō·lī′, jōō-) The seventh month of the calendar year, having 31 days. [<OF *Julie* <L (*mensis*) *Julius* (month) of Julius; because inserted in the calendar by Julius Caesar]

jum·ble (jum′bəl) *v.* **·bled, ·bling** *v.t.* **1** To mix in a confused mass; put or throw together without order. **2** To confuse in the mind. — *v.i.* **3** To meet or unite confusedly. See synonyms under DISPLACE. — *n.* **1** A confused mixture or collection: also **jum′ble·ment.** **2** A thin sweet cake. [Origin uncertain]

jum·ble-beads (jum′bəl·bēdz′) *n. pl.* The seeds of the jequirity.

jum·bo (jum′bō) *n. pl.* **·bos** A very large person, animal, or thing. — *adj.* Very large; especially, larger than usual. [after JUMBO]

Jum·bo (jum′bō) An elephant exhibited by P. T. Barnum: the largest ever captured; killed by accident, 1885.

jump (jump) *v.i.* **1** To spring from the ground, floor, etc., by the action of the muscles of the feet and legs. **2** To move abruptly as by bounds or leaps. **3** To rise abruptly: The temperature *jumped.* **4** In checkers, to capture an opponent's piece by passing a man over it to a vacant square beyond. — *v.t.* **5** To leap over. **6** To cause to leap: to *jump* a horse over a barrier. **7** To cause to rise, as prices. **8** To pass over; leave out: to *jump* a stage in explaining a process. **9** To leave or move from abruptly: to *jump* the track. **10** To take possession of illegally: to *jump* a claim. **11** *U.S. Colloq.* To get on or off (a train, etc.) by or as by jumping. **12** *Colloq.* To assault; attack. **13** *Colloq.* To leave or quit abruptly or secretly: to *jump* town. **14** In checkers, to capture (an opponent's piece) by passing a man over it. **15** In bridge, to raise (the bid) in a partner's suit more than necessary, as in indicating a strong hand. **16** In hunting, to cause (game) to leave cover; start; flush. — **to jump at** To accept quickly or eagerly. **2** To reach (a conclusion) hastily and illogically. — **to jump bail** *U.S. Slang* To forfeit by violating the terms of. — **to jump on** To scold; castigate. — **to jump ship** To desert a ship. — **to jump the gun** *Colloq.* **1** To begin before the starting signal is given. **2** To begin prematurely. — *n.* **1** The act of jumping; a leap; spring. **2** The length or height of a leap; also, that which is jumped over. **3** *Colloq.* A head start; advantage: He has the *jump* on me. **4** An involuntary twitch or movement, as when startled. **5** *pl.* Convulsive starts, as in delirium tremens. **6** *Mining* A fault or dislocation, as of a vein. **7** An abrupt break in a level course of masonry. **8** *Obs.* An effort; attempt. — **on the jump** *Colloq.* Hurrying from one thing to another; on the go; working hard and fast. [Origin uncertain]

jump area *Mil.* A locality, usually behind enemy lines, assigned for the landing of parachute troops: also called *landing area.*

jump ball In basketball, a ball tossed between two opposing players by the referee, as in beginning or resuming play.

jump bid In bridge, a bid higher than needed to beat or raise a previous declaration.

jump·er[1] (jum'pər) *n.* **1** One who or that which jumps. **2** The larva of a cheese fly. **3** A piece of mechanism or a tool having a jumping motion. **4** A rude sled. **5** *Electr.* A wire used to cut out part of a circuit, or to close a temporary gap in it.

jum·per[2] (jum'pər) *n.* **1** *Chiefly Brit.* A loose outer jacket, often of coarse cloth, worn over or instead of other clothes, as to protect them from getting soiled. **2** A hooded fur jacket used by Eskimos and Arctic explorers. **3** A one-piece, sleeveless dress, usually worn with a blouse or sweater by women and children: also **jumper dress.** [Prob. alter. of OF *juppe* a jacket, ult. <Arabic *jubbah* a short coat]

JUMPER
(def. 3)

jumping bean The seed of certain tropical shrubs (genera *Sebastiania* and *Sapium*) of the spurge family, which jumps about owing to the movements of the larva of a small moth (*Carpocapsa saltitans*) inside.

jumping mouse A small, hibernating mouse of North America (*Zapus hudsonius*) having long hind legs and tail: able to leap 9 to 15 feet.

jump seat An extra seat that folds up, as in the rear of a limousine or taxi.

jump shot In basketball, a shot attempted at the height of a leap.

jump spark A spark produced by electricity jumping across a fixed gap.

jump suit **1** A one-piece garment consisting of pants with a blouse or shirt attached. **2** A kind of coverall worn by parachutists, mechanics, etc.

jump weld A weld of metal effected by hammering together the butt ends of two pieces heated to the welding point.

jump·y (jum'pē) *adj.* **jump·i·er, jump·i·est** **1** Subject to sudden changes; fluctuating. **2** Characterized by nervous, spasmodic movements; apprehensive. — **jump'i·ness** *n.*

jun·ca·ceous (jung·kā'shəs) *adj. Bot.* Pertaining or belonging to a family (*Juncaceae*) of widely distributed grasslike plants, the rush family, mostly growing in moist places. [<NL *Juncaceae,* the rush family <L *juncus* bulrush]

jun·co (jung'kō) *n.* *pl.* **·cos** Any of a genus (*Junco*) of North American finches, mainly gray with white underparts: also called *snowbird.* [<Sp., a rush]

junc·tion (jungk'shən) *n.* **1** The act of joining, or condition of being joined. **2** A place of union or meeting, as of railroads. See synonyms under UNION. [<L *junctio, -onis* <*jungere* join] — **junc'tion·al** *adj.*

junc·ture (jungk'chər) *n.* **1** An act of joining; junction. **2** A point or line of junction, as of two bodies; an articulation, joint, or seam. **3** A coincidence of two chains of events; a crisis, exigency. See synonyms under UNION. [<L *junctura* <*jungere* join]

June (jōon) The sixth month of the calendar year, having 30 days. [<OF *Juin* <L (*mensis*) *Junius* (month) of the Junii, a Roman gens]

Ju·neau (jōo'nō) The capital of Alaska, a port on the SE coast.

June beetle **1** A large, brightly colored scarabaeid beetle (genus *Polyphylla*) that begins to fly early in June: often called *Maybug.* Also **June bug.** For illustrations see under INSECT (injurious). **2** The fig-eater of the southern United States.

June·ber·ry (jōon'ber'ē) *n.* *pl.* **·ries** **1** A small tree (*Amelanchier canadensis*) bearing racemes of white flowers followed by purple edible berries. **2** One of the berries. Also called *shadbush, serviceberry, service tree.*

June·teenth (jōon'tēnth') *n.* June 19, a holiday observed especially in Texas by Negroes in commemoration of the freeing of Texas slaves on June 19, 1865.

Jung (yŏong), **Carl Gustav,** 1875–1961, Swiss psychologist and psychiatrist.

jun·gle (jung'gəl) *n.* **1** A dense tropical thicket of high grass, reeds, vines, brush, or trees choked with undergrowth; hence, any similar tangled growth. **2** *U.S. Slang* A gathering place for hoboes and tramps. [<Hind. *jangal* a desert, forest <Skt. *jangala* dry, desert] — **jun'gly** *adj.*

jungle fever **1** A malarial or intermittent fever characteristic of the jungles of the East Indies. **2** Yellow fever.

jungle fowl One of a genus (*Gallus*) of East Indian gallinaceous birds: one species (*G. gallus*) resembles a black-breasted red game fowl and is held to be the original of the domestic fowl.

jun·ior (jōon'yər) *adj.* **1** Younger in years or lower in rank. **2** Denoting the younger of two: opposed to *senior* and distinguishing a father from a son, usually abbreviated *Jr.* **3** Belonging to youth or earlier life. **4** Later in point of existence or occurrence: *junior* securities. **5** Pertaining to the third year of a high-school or collegiate course of four years. — *n.* **1** The younger of two; one later or lower in service or standing; a younger person. **2** A student in the third or junior year of a high-school, college, or university course. [<L *junior,* comp. of *juvenis* young]

junior college A college giving academic courses up to and including the sophomore year.

jun·ior·i·ty (jōon·yôr'ə·tē, -yor'-) *n.* The state or rank of being a junior.

ju·ni·per (jōo'nə·pər) *n.* **1** Any of a genus (*Juniperus*) of evergreen pinaceous shrubs; especially the common juniper (*J. communis*) of Europe and America. It has dark-blue berries of a pungent taste, which are used in making gin. **2** The dried berries of the juniper plant. **3** A leafless shrub (*Retama*) mentioned in the Old Testament. **4** Loosely, the American larch or tamarack. [<L *juniperus*]

junk[1] (jungk) *n.* **1** A sea term for discarded cable or cordage. **2** Salt meat supplied to ships. **3** Cast-off materials of little or no value. **4** A chunk; small mass. **5** *Surg.* A type of cushion used in dressing wounds. — *v.t. Colloq.* To scrap; to demolish or cast aside. [<OF *jonc* <L *juncus* rush]

junk[2] (jungk) *n.* A large Chinese vessel with high poop, prominent stem, full stern and lug sails. [<Sp. and Pg. *junco* <Malay *djong* a ship]

CHINESE JUNK

Jun·ker (yŏong'kər) *n.* **1** A younger member of a German noble family. **2** One of the reactionary aristocracy of Prussia seeking to maintain social and political supremacy. [<G <*jung* young + *herr* master] — **Jun'ker·dom** *n.* — **Jun'ker·ism** *n.*

jun·ket (jung'kit) *n.* **1** A feast, banquet, picnic, or pleasure trip. **2** A trip taken with all expenses paid, usually from public funds: also **jun'ket·ing.** **3** A delicacy made of curds or of sweetened milk and rennet. — *v.i.* **1** To have a feast; banquet. **2** To go on a pleasure trip, especially at public expense. — *v.t.* **3** To entertain by feasting; regale. [<AF *jonquette* rush basket <L *juncus* rush]

junk·ie (jung'kē) *n. Slang* One addicted to narcotic drugs, especially to heroin.

junk·man (jungk'man') *n.* *pl.* **·men** (-men') One who purchases, collects, and sells junk.

junk·yard (jungk'yärd') *n.* A place where junk is thrown or collected.

jun·ta (jun'tə) *n.* **1** A Central or South American legislative council. **2** A junto. [<Sp. <L *juncta,* pp. fem. of *jungere* join]

jun·to (jun'tō) *n.* *pl.* **·tos** A faction; a cabal. See synonyms under CABAL. [<JUNTA]

Ju·pi·ter (jōo'pə·tər) **1** In Roman mythology, the god ruling over all the other gods and all men: identified with the Greek *Zeus:* also called *Jove.* **2** *Astron.* The fifth planet from the sun; its mean diameter is 87,000 miles, and it revolves around the sun in about 11 7/8 years at a mean distance of 483,000,000 miles. See PLANET.

ju·ra (jŏor'ə) Plural of JUS.

ju·ral (jŏor'əl) *adj.* Relating to rights and obligations as subjects of jurisprudence. [<L *jus, juris* law]

Ju·ras·sic (jŏo·ras'ik) *adj. Geol.* Of or pertaining to a period of the Mesozoic era succeeding the Triassic and followed by the Cretaceous: it was characterized by the dominance of dinosaurian reptiles and the earliest bird forms. — *n.* The Jurassic period or corresponding rock system. [<F *jurassique,* from *Jura*]

ju·rat (jŏor'at) *n.* **1** One sworn to the faithful performance of a duty, as a magistrate or juror. **2** An officer with duties similar to those of an alderman, as in the English Cinque Ports. **3** A magistrate in the Channel Islands. **4** *Law* The clause in an official certificate testifying that the deposition has been duly sworn to at a stated time before a competent authority. [<L *juratus,* pp. of *jurare* swear]

ju·ra·to·ry (jŏor'ə·tôr'ē, -tō'rē) *adj. Law* Pertaining to an oath.

ju·rid·i·cal (jŏo·rid'i·kəl) *adj.* **1** Relating to law and judicial proceedings. **2** Pertaining to the judicial office, or to jurisprudence. Also **ju·rid'ic.** [<L *juridicus* <*jus, juris* law + *dicere* declare] — **ju·rid'i·cal·ly** *adv.*

ju·ris·con·sult (jŏor'is·kən·sult', -kon'sult) *n.* One learned in the law; a jurist. [<L *jurisconsultus* <*jus, juris* law + *consultus* skilled]

ju·ris·dic·tion (jŏor'is·dik'shən) *n.* **1** Lawful right to exercise official authority, whether executive, legislative, or judicial. **2** The territory within or the matter over which such authority may be lawfully exercised. **3** A judicature; a court, or series of courts, of justice. **4** Power of those in authority; control. [<OF *juridiction* <L *jurisdictio, -onis* <*jus, juris* law + *dicere* declare] — **ju'ris·dic'tion·al** *adj.* — **ju'ris·dic'tion·al·ly** *adv.*

ju·ris·pru·dence (jŏor'is·prŏod'ns) *n.* **1** The philosophy of positive law and its administration; the science of law. **2** A system of laws, as of a particular country. See synonyms under LEGISLATION. — **analytical jurisprudence** Jurisprudence formed by analysis and comparison of legal conceptions. — **comparative jurisprudence** The analytical comparison of systems of law prevailing in different countries and nations, ancient and modern. — **medical jurisprudence** The branch of jurisprudence that pertains to questions involving wounds, poisons, insanity, and presumption of survivorship. [<L *jurisprudentia* <*jus, juris* law + *prudentia* knowledge]

ju·ris·pru·dent (jŏor'is·prŏod'nt) *adj.* Skilled in jurisprudence. — *n.* A person learned in the law. — **ju'ris·pru·den'tial** (-prŏo·den'shəl) *adj.*

ju·rist (jŏor'ist) *n.* One versed in the science of laws. [<F *juriste* <Med. L *jurista* <L *jus, juris* law]

ju·ris·tic (jŏo·ris'tik) *adj.* Of or pertaining to a jurist or the profession of law. Also **ju·ris'ti·cal.** — **ju·ris'ti·cal·ly** *adv.*

juristic act A proceeding intended to have a legal result and having the necessary qualifications.

ju·ror (jŏor'ər) *n.* One who serves on a jury or is sworn in for jury duty. [<AF *jurour* <L *jurator* <*jurare* swear]

ju·ry[1] (jŏor'ē) *n.* *pl.* **·ries** **1** A body of persons (usually twelve) legally qualified and summoned to serve on a judicial tribunal, there sworn to try well and truly a cause and give a true verdict according to the evidence. **2** A committee of award in a competition. — **coroner's jury** A body of persons selected to attend a coroner's investigation and determine the causes of deaths not obviously due to natural causes. — **grand jury** A jury called to hear complaints of the commission of offenses and to ascertain whether there is prima–facie ground for a criminal accusation. — **petit jury** The jury that sits at a trial in civil and criminal cases: also **petty jury.** [<AF *juree* an oath <Med. L *jurata*, orig. pp. of L *jurare* swear <*jus, juris* law]

ju·ry² (jŏŏr′ē) *adj. Naut.* Rigged up temporarily, for relief, replacement, or emergency use: a *jury* mast. [Prob. <OF *ajurie* aid <L *adjutare* help]

ju·ry·man (jŏŏr′ē·mən) *n.* *pl.* **·men** (-mən) A juror.

jury mast 1 *Naut.* A temporary mast. 2 *Med.* An iron rod used for supporting the weight of the head in spinal disease or injury.

jus (jus) *n.* *pl.* **ju·ra** (jŏŏr′ə) 1 Law in its abstract sense distinguished from statute law; right; justice. 2 Any right that is enforceable by law. [<L, law]

just (just) *adj.* 1 Actuated by or doing justice; righteous; upright; honest: *just* to all concerned. 2 Based on or conforming to the principles of justice; impartial; legitimate. 3 Agreeing with a required standard; true. 4 Consistent with what is proper or reasonable: *just* in one's dealings. 5 Morally pure; perfect; righteous before God. 6 *Obs.* Faithful; true; exact. — *adv.* 1 To the exact point, instant, or degree; without lack, excess, or variation; exactly; precisely. 2 But now; this moment. 3 A moment ago; very lately: He has *just* left. 4 By very little; barely; only. 5 *Colloq.* Actually; positively: That gift is *just* wonderful. [<L *justus* <*jus* law] — **just′ly** *adv.*

Synonyms (adj.): equitable, even, exact, fair, fitting, honest, honorable, impartial, incorrupt, incorruptible, lawful, reasonable, right, righteous, rightful, square, straightforward, true, trusty, upright, virtuous. See HONEST, MORAL, RIGHT, VIRTUOUS. Compare synonyms for JUSTICE. *Antonyms:* corrupt, dishonest, dishonorable, faithless, false, inequitable, one–sided, partial, perfidious, treacherous, unfair, unfaithful, unjust, unreasonable, unrighteous, venal.

jus·tice (jus′tis) *n.* 1 Conformity in conduct or practice to the principles of right or of positive law; regard for or fulfilment of obligations; rectitude; honesty. 2 The moral principle by which actions are determined as just or unjust. 3 Adherence to truth of fact; impartiality. 4 The rendering of what is due or merited; that which is due or merited; just requital or consideration. 5 The quality of being just or reasonable; rightness; equitableness. 6 A judge, as of the U.S. Supreme Court, etc. 7 Administration of law; the forms and processes by which it is made effective. 8 Right of authority; also, formerly, jurisdiction. 9 *Theol.* One of God's attributes, by virtue of which he wills equal laws and makes just awards. 10 *Obs.* Exactness or precision; justness. — **bed of justice** The seat occupied by the French king when attending the deliberations of the parliament; also, the session itself. — **Department of Justice** An executive department of the U.S. government (established in 1870) under the direction of the Attorney General: it supervises enforcement of Federal laws, directs the activities of U.S. judicial districts, and represents the

government in legal matters generally. Also **Justice Department.** [<OF <L *justitia* < *justus* JUST]

Synonyms: equity, fairness, faithfulness, honor, impartiality, integrity, justness, law, lawfulness, legality, propriety, rectitude, right, righteousness, rightfulness, truth, uprightness, virtue. In its governmental relations, *justice* is the giving to every person exactly what he deserves, not necessarily involving any consideration of what any other may deserve; *equity* (the quality of being equal) is giving every one as much advantage, privilege, or consideration as is given to any other; it is that which is equally right or just to all concerned; *equity* is a close synonym for *fairness* and *impartiality,* but it has a legal precision that those words have not. In legal proceedings, the system of *equity,* devised to supply the insufficiencies of *law,* deals with cases to which the *law* by reason of its universality cannot apply. *Integrity, rectitude, right, righteousness,* and *virtue* denote conformity of personal conduct to the moral law, and thus necessarily include *justice,* which is giving others that which is their due. *Lawfulness* is an ambiguous word, meaning in its narrower sense mere *legality,* which may be far from *justice,* but in its higher sense signifying accordance with the supreme *law* or *right,* and thus including perfect *justice. Justness* refers rather to logical relations than to practical matters; as, we speak of the *justness* of a statement or of a criticism. See JUDGE, VIRTUE. *Antonyms:* dishonesty, inequity, injustice, partiality, unfairness, unlawfulness, unreasonableness, untruth, wrong.

justice of the peace An inferior magistrate elected or appointed to prevent breaches of the peace within a county or township, to punish violators of the law, and to discharge various other local magisterial duties.

jus·tic·er (jus′tis·ər) *n.* *Obs.* A magistrate; justice of the peace.

jus·tice·ship (jus′tis·ship) *n.* A justice's office or dignity.

jus·ti·ci·a·ble (jus·tish′ə·bəl) *adj.* Proper to be examined in a court of justice. — *n.* A person subject to the jurisdiction of another. [<AF <*justicier* try in court]

jus·ti·ci·ar (jus·tish′ē·ər) *n.* A justiciary (def. 2). Also **jus·ti′ci·er.**

jus·ti·ci·ar·y (jus·tish′ē·er′ē) *adj.* Pertaining to law or the administration of justice. — *n.* *pl.* **·ar·ies** 1 A high judicial officer; a judge. 2 In medieval England, a high officer, or king's deputy, who, during the time of the Norman kings, exercised both administrative and judicial powers. [<Med. L *justiciarius* a judge <*justicia* JUSTICE]

jus·ti·fi·a·ble (jus′tə·fī′ə·bəl) *adj.* Capable of being justified. — **jus′ti·fi′a·bil′i·ty, jus′ti·fi·a·ble·ness** *n.* — **jus′ti·fi′a·bly** *adv.*

jus·ti·fi·ca·tion (jus′tə·fə·kā′shən) *n.* 1 The state of being justified. 2 The ground of justifying, or that which justifies. 3 *Theol.* The forensic, juridical, or gracious act of God by which the sinner is declared righteous, or justly free from obligation to penalty, and fully restored to divine favor. 4 *Printing* The even spacing of type within a fixed measure. 5 *Law* A plea in bar to a plaintiff's action alleging and showing the rightfulness or lawfulness of the act complained of and

sued for: in slander, to plead the truth of the words spoken in *justification* of the speaking. See synonyms under APOLOGY, DEFENSE. [<LL *justificatio, -onis* <*justificare* JUSTIFY]

jus·ti·fi·ca·tive (jus′tə·fə·kā′tiv) *adj.* Tending to justify, or capable of justifying; vindicatory. Also, **jus·tif·i·ca·tor·y** (jus·tif′ə·kə·tôr′ē, -tō′rē)

jus·ti·fy (jus′tə·fī) *v.* **·fied, ·fy·ing** *v.t.* 1 To show to be just, right, or proper. 2 To declare or prove guiltless or blameless; exonerate; acquit. 3 *Law* To show sufficient reason for (something done). 4 *Printing* To adjust (lines) to the proper length by spacing. — *v.i.* 5 *Law* a To show sufficient reason for something done. b To qualify as a bondsman. 6 *Printing* To be properly spaced; fit. [<OF *justifier* <LL *justificare* pardon <*justus* just + *facere* make]

Synonyms: absolve, acquit, approve, authorize, clear, defend, endorse, exculpate, excuse, exonerate, maintain, sustain, uphold, vindicate, warrant. That may sometimes be *excused* which cannot be *justified;* that which can be *justified* does not need to be *excused.* See RATIFY. *Antonyms:* arraign, blame, censure, chide, condemn, convict, criminate, denounce, reprehend, reprobate, reprove.

just·ness (just′nis) *n.* The quality of being just; justice. See synonyms under JUSTICE.

just now Scarcely a moment ago.

jut (jut) *v.i.* **jut·ted, jut·ting** To extend beyond the main portion; project: often with *out.* — *n.* Anything that juts; a projection. [Var. of JET²]

jute (jŏŏt) *n.* 1 A tall annual Asian herb (*Corchorus capsularis* or *C. olitorius*) of the linden family. 2 The soft, lustrous fiber obtained from the inner bark of this plant, used for bags, cordage, etc. [<Bengali *jhuto* <Skt. *jūṭa* a braid of hair]

jut·ty (jut′ē) See JETTY.

ju·ve·nal (jŏŏ′və·nəl) *n.* 1 *Obs.* A youth; young man. 2 *Ornithol.* The plumage acquired by a bird subsequent to leaving the nest. [<L *juvenalis* young]

ju·ve·nes·cent (jŏŏ′və·nes′ənt) *adj.* Becoming young; also, rejuvenating. [<L *juvenescens, -entis,* ppr. of *juvenescere* grow younger] — **ju′ve·nes′cence** *n.*

ju·ve·nile (jŏŏ′və·nīl, -nil) *adj.* 1 Characteristic of youth; young. 2 Adapted to youth. — *n.* 1 A young person; a youth. 2 An actor who interprets youthful roles. 3 A book for children or youth. See synonyms under YOUTHFUL. [<L *juvenilis* <*juvenis* young]

ju·ve·nil·i·a (jŏŏ′və·nil′ē·ə, -nil′yə) *n. pl.* Youthful writings. [<L, orig. neut. pl. of *juvenalis* young]

ju·ve·nil·i·ty (jŏŏ′və·nil′ə·tē) *n.* *pl.* **·ties** 1 A youthful act or character; juvenile character or manner. 2 Youthfulness; youth; the state of being juvenile. Also **ju′ve·nile·ness.**

juxta- *prefix* Near; next to: *juxtamarine,* bordering on the sea. [<L *juxta* near]

jux·ta·pose (juks′tə·pōz′) *v.t.* **·posed, ·pos·ing** To place close together; put side by side. [<F *juxtaposer* <L *juxta* near + *poser.* See POSE¹.]

jux·ta·po·si·tion (juks′tə·pə·zish′ən) *n.* A placing close together or side by side; contiguity.

K

k, K (kā) *n.* *pl.* **k's, K's** or **ks, Ks** or **kays** (kāz) 1 The eleventh letter of the English alphabet: from Phoenician *kaph,* Greek *kappa,* Roman *K.* 2 The sound of the letter *k,* a voiceless plosive which varies from velar to alveolar position according to the place of articulation of the accompanying vowel, as in *coop* and *keep.* It is normally not pronounced when initial before *n,* as in *knee, knight, know,* etc. See ALPHABET. — *symbol Chem.* Potassium (K for *kalium*).

K2 (kā′tŏŏ′) The world's second highest mountain peak, in the Karakoram range, northern Kashmir, India; 28,250 feet: also *Dapsang, Godwin Austen.*

ka (kä) *n.* In Egyptian religion, the genius or spiritual self: believed to dwell in man and images and to survive in the tomb. [< Egyptian]

Ka·a·ba (kä′ə·bə, kä′bə) *n.* The Moslem shrine at Mecca enclosing a sacred black stone, supposedly given to Abraham by the angel

Gabriel, toward which worshipers face when praying: also spelled *Caaba.*

kab·a·la (kab′ə·lə, kə·bä′lə), **kab·ba·la,** etc. See CABALA, etc.

ka·bar (kä′bär) See CABER.

ka·bob (kə·bob′) *n.* 1 A dish of small pieces of meat roasted or broiled on skewers and served with various condiments. 2 In India, any roast meat. Also **ka·bab′:** sometimes spelled *cabob.* [<Arabic *kabāb*]

ka·bu·ki (kä·bōō′kē) *n.* A kind of Japanese play

on popular or comic themes, employing elaborate costume, stylized gesture, music, and dancing. Compare NO². [<Japanese]

kad·dish (kä′dish) n. Often cap. In Judaism, a daily prayer recited in the synagogue service, in one form used by mourners. [<Aramaic *qaddîsh* holy]

Kadiak bear A very large brown bear (*Ursus middendorffi*) found on Kodiak and adjacent islands off the Alaskan coast: also *Kodiak bear.*

kaf·fee·klatsch (kôf′ē·klach′, -kläch′, kof′-) n. A social gathering for conversation while coffee and refreshments are served. [<G, lit., coffee + gossip]

kaf·ir (kaf′ər) n. A variety of sorghum grown in dry regions as a grain and forage plant; East Indian millet. Also **kaf′ir:** erroneously **kaffir corn.** [after the *Kaffirs*]

Kaf·fir (kaf′ər) n. **1** A member of a powerful group of South African Bantu tribes. **2** Xhosa, the language of these tribes. **3** A non-Moslem: term used contemptuously by Arab Moslems. Also **Kaf′ir:** sometimes spelled *Caffer, Caffre.* [<Arabic *kâfir* unbeliever]

Kaf·ka (käf′kä), **Franz,** 1883–1924, Austrian novelist and writer of short stories.

Kaf·ka·esque (käf′kə·esk′) adj. Characteristic of the novels of Franz Kafka; especially, bizarre or absurd, and often marked by the ineffectuality of the individual.

ka·go (kä′gō) n. A form of palanquin. [<Japanese *kango*]

kain (kän) n. Rental or tax paid in land produce, livestock, eggs, etc.: also spelled *cain, kane.* [<OIrish *cáin* law]

kai·nite (kī′nīt, kā′ə·nīt) n. A colorless to dark flesh-red hydrous sulfate of potassium and magnesium and magnesium chloride, crystallizing in the monoclinic system: used as a fertilizer. [<G *kainit* <Gk. *kainos* recent]

kai·ser (kī′zər) n. Emperor: the German title applied to the emperors of the Holy Roman Empire, as successors to those of the old Roman Empire. [<G <L *Caesar* Caesar]

ka·ka (kä′kə) n. A New Zealand parrot (genus *Nestor*), typically with olive-green body, gray crown, and crimson-red on the rump and abdomen. [<Maori]

ka·ka·po (kä′kə·pō′) n. A nocturnal, flightless, greenish-brown New Zealand parrot (*Strigops habroptilus*). [<Maori *kaka* a parrot + *po* night]

ka·ke·mo·no (kä′ke·mō′nō) n. A picture on paper or silk attached to a roller and used as a wall hanging. [<Japanese <*kake* hang + *mono* thing]

ka·ki (kä′kē) n. An Asian tree (*Diospyros kaki*) of the ebony family, with yellowish-white flowers and an edible orange or yellow fruit; cultivated in southern and western United States: also called *Japanese persimmon.* [<Japanese, persimmon]

ka·la–a·zar (kä′lä·ä·zär′, -az′ər) n. Pathol. An infectious fever of India, China, and Egypt characterized by enlarged spleen, anemia, and emaciation: caused by a protozoan parasite (*Leishmania donovani*). [<Hind. *kālā–āzār* black disease]

Kal·a·ma·zoo (kal′ə·mə·zōō′) A city in SW Michigan.

Kalb (kalb, Ger. kälp), **Johann,** 1721–80, German general in the American Revolution; known as *Baron de Kalb.*

kale (käl) n. **1** A variety of headless cabbage yielding curled leaves. **2** Scot. Cabbage of any kind; also, broth of kale; broth. **3** U.S. Slang Money. Also spelled *kail.* [Var. of COLE]

ka·lei·do·scope (kə·lī′də·skōp) n. An instrument which, by means of mirrors, presents bits of colored glass, viewed through it, in ever-changing symmetrical patterns, as the tube is rotated. [<Gk. *kalos* beautiful + *eidos* form + -SCOPE]

ka·lei·do·scop·ic (kə·lī′də·skop′ik) adj. Pertaining to a kaleidoscope; picturesquely diversified. Also **ka·lei′do·scop′i·cal.** — **ka·lei′do·scop′i·cal·ly** adv.

kal·ends (kal′əndz) See CALENDS.

kale·wife (käl′wīf) n. pl. ·**wives** (-wīvz′) Scot. A woman who sells vegetables.

kaleyard school A late 19th century school of

fiction writers, including J. M. Barrie and Ian Maclaren, who described Scottish life with much use of dialect. Also *kailyard school.*

kal·i (kal′e, kä′le) n. The common saltwort. [<Arabic *qali.* See ALKALI.]

Ka·li (kä′le) In Hindu mythology, the goddess of destruction and wife of Siva: worshiped with bloody sacrifices.

kal·ian (käl·yän′) n. The hookah of Persia. [<Persian *kalián*]

ka·lif (kä′lif, kal′if) See CALIPH.

ka·li·um (kä′le·əm) n. Potassium: from this name, used by pharmacists and German chemists, its symbol K is derived. [<KALI]

kal·li·type (kal′ə·tip) n. A photoprinting process by which ferric salts are reduced to ferrous salts, which in turn act upon soluble silver salts. [<Gk. *kalli-* beautiful + TYPE]

kal·mi·a (kal′me·ə) Any plant of a genus (*Kalmia*) of North American shrubs of the heath family, with evergreen leaves and umbellate clusters of rose, purple, or white flowers. [<NL, after Peter *Kalm,* 1716–79, Swedish botanist]

Kal·muck (kal′muk) n. **1** A member of one of the western Buddhistic Mongol tribes extending from western China to the valley of the Volga river. **2** The Mongolian language of these tribes. Also **Kal′muk.**

ka·long (kä′lông) n. A fruit–eating bat (family *Pteropodidae*) of Africa, Asia, and Australia. [<Malay *kalong*]

kal·pac (kal′pak) See CALPAC.

kal·so·mine (kal′sə·mine) See CALCIMINE.

ka·lyp·tra (kə·lip′trə) n. A thin veil worn by women of ancient Greece over the face and as a headdress. [<Gk. <*kalyptein* hide]

kam·a·cite (kam′ə·sīt) n. A variety of meteoric iron containing nickel and showing, when polished, a fine network of bands. [<G *kamacit* <Gk. *kamax, -akos* a vine pole]

ka·ma·la (kə·mä′lə, kam′ə-) n. **1** An Indian tree (*Mallotus philippinensis*) of the spurge family. **2** The fine orange-red powder from its capsular fruit, used as a purgative and in dyeing. [<Skt.]

kame (kam) n. Geol. A conical hill or short ridge of stratified sand and gravel formed by glacier deposition. [See COOMB]

ka·mi (kä′mē) n. Japanese **1** The gods collectively of the first and second mythological dynasties of Japan; also, their descendants, the mikados. **2** The deified spirits of the heroes and famous men of Japan.

ka·mi·ka·ze (kä′mi·kä′zē) n. In World War II, a Japanese pilot pledged to die in crashing his bomb-laden plane against the target; also, the airplane itself on such a mission. [<Japanese, divine wind <*kami* a god + *kaze* the wind]

kam·pong (käm·pong′, käm′pong) n. An enclosed space; a compound. [<Malay]

kam·sin (kam′sin) See KHAMSIN.

ka·na (kä′nə) n. Japanese syllabic writing: a system of 46 phonetic symbols normally used for foreign words, and used collaterally with Chinese ideographs to indicate Japanese grammatical inflections. [<Japanese]

Ka·nak·a (kə·nak′ə, kan′ə·kə) n. **1** A native of Hawaii. **2** Any South Sea Islander. [<Polynesian, man]

Kan·chen·jun·ga (kun′chən·joong′gə) The third highest mountain in the world, in the eastern Nepal Himalayas; 28,146 feet: formerly *Kinchi*

kane (kän) See KAIN.

kan·ga·roo (kang′gə·rōō′) n. Any of a large family (*Macropodidae*) of herbivorous marsupials of the Australian region, having weak forelimbs and strong hind limbs, with stout tail, moving by leaping bounds, and ranging in size from nine feet long to about the size of a rat. [Australian]

KANGAROO
(Standing height, male adult, up to 6 feet)

kangaroo court 1 An unofficial court in which the law is disregarded or wilfully misinterpreted. **2** A mock court or trial. **3** A frontier or backwoods court.

kangaroo rat 1 One of various pouched rodents (*Dipodomys agilis*) of the SW United States and Mexico, with elongated hind limbs and tail. **2** Any of several Australian rodents (genus *Notomys*) noted for their leaping habits.

K'ang–hsi (käng′shē′), 1654–1722, also called Sheng-tsu. First Manchu emperor of China, 1662–1722; annexed Tibet and made the first Chinese treaty with a European power (Russia, 1689).

ka·noon (ka·nōōn′) A kind of dulcimer having fifty or sixty strings and played with the fingers. Also **ka·nun.** [<Persian *qānūn*]

Kan·sas (kan′zəs) A north central State of the United States; 82,276 square miles; capital, Topeka; entered the Union Jan. 29, 1861; nickname, *Sunflower State.* Abbr. KS — **Kan′san** (-zən) adj. & n.

Kansas City 1 A city on the Missouri River in NE Kansas. **2** A city on the Missouri River in western Missouri.

Kant (kant, Ger. känt), **Immanuel,** 1724–1804, German philosopher; author of *Critique of Pure Reason* (1781).

kan·tar (kän·tär′) See CANTAR.

Kant·i·an (kan′te·ən) adj. Of or pertaining to Kant or his philosophy. — n. A follower of Kantianism.

Kant·i·an·ism (kan′te·ən·iz′əm) n. The critical philosophy of Immanuel Kant that sets forth the doctrine of a priori knowledge: man experiences the material world through sense perception, but its form is determined by the mind alone. Also **Kant′ism.**

ka·o·lin (kä′ə·lin) n. A claylike, friable, hydrous aluminum silicate used in making porcelain. Also **ka′o·line.** [from Chinese *Kao Ling* High Ridge, a mountain range where first mined]

ka·o·lin·ite (kä′ə·lin·it′) n. A highly purified form of kaolin.

kap·a (kap′ə) n. pl. **kap·a–kap·a** Tapa cloth. [<Hawaiian]

Ka·pell·meis·ter (kä·pel′mis′tər) n. The musical director of a choir, orchestra, etc.: also called *chapelmaster.* [<G, bandmaster]

kaph (käf) n. The eleventh Hebrew letter: also spelled *caph.* See ALPHABET.

ka·pok (kä′pok) n. A cottony or silky fiber covering the seeds of a tropical tree (*Ceiba pentandra*) of the silk–cotton family: used for mattresses, life–savers, insulation material, etc. [<Malay *kāpoq*]

kap·pa (kap′ə) n. Greek The tenth letter in the Greek alphabet (Κ, κ), equivalent to English k. See under ALPHABET.

kappa curve Math. A plane, kappa–shaped curve, symmetrical with respect to the coordinate axes and the origin, and having two cusps at the origin.

ka·put (kä·pŏŏt′) adj. Slang Ruined; done for; finished. [<G]

Ka·ra (kä′rə) A river in northern European Russian S.F.S.R., flowing 130 miles north from the northern Urals.

kar·a·bi·ner (kar′ə·bē′nər) n. An article of mountaineering equipment: a steel loop or ring snapped into a piton, through which a rope may be passed, to hold climbers. [Short for G *karabinerhaken* carbine snap]

KARABINER
a. Closed.
b. Open.

kar·a·kul (kar′ə·kəl) n. **1** A breed of sheep of Bokhara. **2** Astrakhan of the best quality, obtained from the black, lustrous, tightly curled coat of young lambs of the karakul sheep. Also spelled *caracul.* [from *Kara Kul,* lake in central Siberia]

kar·at (kar′ət) n. The twenty-fourth part by weight of gold in an article; thus, 18–karat gold means an article 18/24 or 3/4 gold by weight; distinguished from *carat.* [Var. of CARAT]

ka·ra·te (kä·rä′tä, -tē) n. An Oriental style of hand-to-hand fighting using sudden forceful blows, as with the side of the hand or with the fingertips. [<Japanese]

kar·ma (kär′mə, kûr′-) n. The effect of any act, religious or otherwise; the law of cause and effect regulating one's future life; inevitable retribution: a Brahmanic idea developed by the Buddhists. [<Sanskrit, *action*]

karn (kärn) *n. Brit.* A cairn.

ka·ross (kə·ros') *n. Afrikaans* 1 A native garment made of skins sewed together in the form of a square. 2 A rug made of skins.

kar·roo (kə·rōō', ka-) *n. pl.* **-roos** A dry plateau or tableland of South Africa. Also **ka·roo'**. See GREAT KARROO, SOUTHERN KARROO, NORTHERN KARROO. [<Hottentot]

Kar·roo (kə·rōō', ka-) *adj. Geol.* Belonging to or designating a period or rock system of the Paleozoic and Mesozoic eras, developed in South Africa. Also **Ka·roo'**.

kart (kärt) *n.* A small, low, motorized vehicle for one person, used especially in racing. [Var. of CART] — **kart'ing** *n.*

karyo- *combining form Biol.* Nucleus: *karyoplasm.* Also, before vowels, **kary-**: also spelled *caryo-.* [<Gk. *karyon* a nut]

kar·y·og·a·my (kar'ē·og'ə·mē) *n. Biol.* The merging or close union of the nuclei of two gametes to form the primary nucleus of the embryo. [<KARYO- + -GAMY]

kar·y·o·ki·ne·sis (kar'ē·ō·ki·nē'sis) *n. Biol.* 1 The series of changes which the nucleus goes through in indirect or mitotic cell division. 2 Such cell division; mitosis. Also spelled *caryokinesis.* [<KARYO- + Gk. *kinēsis* movement] — **kar'y·o·ki·net'ic** (-net'ik) *adj.*

kar·y·o·lymph (kar'ē·ə·limf') *n. Biol.* The clear protoplasmic fluid surrounding the structures of the cell nucleus.

kar·y·o·mere (kar'ē·ə·mir') *n. Biol.* One of the small vesicles formed in chromosomes in certain types of mitosis. Also **kar'y·om'er·ite** (-om'ər·it).

kar·y·o·plasm (kar'ē·ə·plaz'əm) *n. Biol.* The protoplasm of the nucleus of a cell: also called *nucleoplasm.* — **kar'y·o·plas'mic** *adj.*

kar·y·o·some (kar'ē·ə·sōm') *n. Biol.* 1 A chromosome. 2 A mass of chromatin in the resting nucleus of the cell. 3 The cell nucleus itself. Also **kar'y·o·so'ma** (-sō'mə).

kar·y·o·tin (kar'ē·ō'tin) *n. Biol.* The stainable, usually reticulated substance of the cell nucleus; chromatin: also spelled *caryotin.* [<KARYO- + (CHROMA)TIN]

kar·y·o·type (kar'ē·ə·tīp') *n. Genetics* The particular chromosome number and gene arrangement in the gametes of any given species, type, or strain of organism.

Kas·bah (käz'bä) See CASBAH.

ka·sher (kä'shər) *v.t.* To make or pronounce kosher. — *adj. & n.* See KOSHER.

Kash·mir (kash·mir', kash'mir) 1 See JAMMU AND KASHMIR. 2 A province of Jammu and Kashmir; 8,539 square miles; capital, Srinagar; containing the **Vale of Kashmir**, a valley in the Himalayas in western Kashmir province. Formerly *Cashmere.*

Kash·mi·ri (kash·mir'ē) *n.* The Indic language of the Kashmirians.

Kash·mi·ri·an (kash·mir'ē·ən) *adj.* Of or pertaining to Kashmir or its people. — *n.* A native of Kashmir. Also spelled *Cashmerian.*

kata- See CATA-.

ka·tab·a·sis (kə·tab'ə·sis) *n.* 1 The march back to the sea of the Greek mercenaries who followed Cyrus against Artaxerxes. See ANABASIS. 2 Any retreat. [<Gk., a going down]

kat·a·bat·ic (kat'ə·bat'ik) *adj. Meteorol.* Pertaining to or designating a down-flowing wind cooled by radiation, as one reaching a valley from high ground.

kat·a·bol·ic (kat'ə·bol'ik), **ka·tab·o·lism** (kə·tab'ə·liz'əm), etc. See CATABOLIC, etc.

ka·tal·y·sis (kə·tal'ə·sis), **kat·a·lyt·ic** (kat'ə·lit'ik), etc. See CATALYSIS, etc.

kat·a·mor·phism (kat'ə·môr'fiz·əm) *n.* Metamorphism.

kath·ode (kath'ōd), etc. See CATHODE, etc.

kat·i·on (kat'i'ən) See CATION.

Kat·mai National Monument (kat'mī) A region of the NE Alaska Peninsula, southern Alaska; 14,214 square miles; contains **Katmai Volcano**; 7,000 feet; last eruption, 1912; and the Valley of the Ten Thousand Smokes.

Kat·man·du (kät'män·dōō') The capital of Nepal. Also **Kath'man·du'.**

ka·ty·did (kā'tē·did) *n.* An arboreal, green, long-horned insect allied to the grasshoppers and crickets (family *Tettigoniidae*): named from the sound produced by the stridulating organs at the base of the wing covers in the male.

kau·ri (kou'rē) *n.* 1 A large timber tree (*Agathis australis*) of New Zealand. 2 The wood of this tree. 3 Any other species of the genus *Agathis.* 4 Kauri gum. Also **kau'ry.** [<Maori]

kauri gum A colorless to amber or brown resinous exudation of the kauri tree, used in varnishes, for oilcloth, linoleum, etc. Also **kauri copal, kauri resin.**

ka·va (kä'vä) *n.* 1 A shrub (*Piper methysticum*) of the pepper family. 2 An intoxicating and narcotic beverage made from the roots of this plant by the Polynesians: also **ka'va·ka'va.** [<Maori *kawa* bitter]

ka·vass (kä·väs') *n.* A guard or military courier attending Turkish dignitaries; also, a Turkish police officer. [<Turkish *qawwās* a maker of bows <*qaws* a bow]

Ka·vi (kä'vē) *n.* The extinct language of Java from which modern Javanese developed: preserved in ancient Buddhist writings.

Kay (kā), **Sir** A braggart and spiteful knight of the Round Table; foster brother and seneschal of King Arthur. Also spelled *Kai* and, in French romances, *Queux.*

kay·ak (kī'ak) *n.* The hunting canoe of arctic America, made of sealskins stretched over a pointed frame, leaving a hole amidships where the navigator sits, excluding the water by fastening the deck covering around him. Also spelled *kaiak.* [<Eskimo]

KAYAK
A. Side view. B. Top view. C. Paddle.

kayles (kālz) *n. pl. Brit. Dial.* 1 A game of ninepins or skittles. 2 The pins used in the game.

kay·o (kā'ō) *Slang v.t.* **kay·oed, kay·o·ing** In boxing, to knock out. — *n.* A knockout (def. 1). Also **KO.** [<*k(nock) o(ut)*]

Ka·zakh (kä·zäk', *Russian* kä·zäkh') *n.* 1 One of a Turkic people, formerly largely nomadic, dwelling in the Kazakh S.S.R. 2 A long-piled rug, usually in geometrical patterns, made by the Kazakhs.

ka·zoo (kə·zōō') *n.* A toy musical instrument: a wooden or metal tube to which is attached a piece of stretched catgut or paper which vibrates when the tube is sung or hummed into. [Origin uncertain]

ke·a (kā'ə, kē'ə) *n.* A large New Zealand parrot (*Nestor notabilis*), olive-brown variegated with blue and green, which feeds on carrion in addition to fruits, etc., and even attacks live sheep. [Maori]

Ke·a (kā'ä) See KEOS.

Kean (kēn), **Edmund,** 1787–1833, English actor.

Kear·ny (kär'nē), **Philip,** 1815?–62, U. S. general; served in Mexican and Civil wars.

Keats (kēts), **John,** 1795–1821, English poet.

ke·bar (kē'bär) See CABER.

keb·bie (keb'ē) *n. Scot.* A cudgel, or rude walking stick.

Ke·ble (kē'bəl), **John,** 1792–1866, English divine and poet; one of the founders of the Oxford movement.

Kech·ua (kech'wä), **Kech·uan** (kech'wən) See QUECHUA, QUECHUAN.

keck[1] (kek) *v.i.* 1 To heave as in vomiting; retch. 2 To show or feel great disgust. — *n.* Nausea. [Prob. imit.]

keck[2] (kek) *n.* A hollow stalk of a plant. [Back formation <KEX, mistaken as a plural]

keck·le (kek'əl) *v.t.* **keck·led, keck·ling** *Naut.* To wrap or serve, as a cable, with canvas, rope, etc., as a protection from chafing. [Origin unknown]

Ke·dar (kē'dər) A son of Ishmael; also, a tribe or confederacy of Arabian tent-dwellers descending from him. — **Ke'dar·ite** *adj.*

ked·dah (ked'ə) *n.* An enclosure or corral for the capture of wild elephants: also spelled *khedah.* [<Hind. *khedā*]

kedge (kej) *Naut. n.* A light anchor used in warping, freeing a vessel from shoals, etc.: also **kedge anchor.** — *v.i.* 1 To move a vessel by hauling up to a kedge anchor placed at a distance. 2 To be moved in this way. — *v.t.* 3 To move (a vessel) in this way. [<*kedge (anchor)* <CADGE]

ke·ef (kē·ef') See KEF.

keek (kēk) *Scot.* To peep; pry. — *n.* A peep.

keel[1] (kēl) *n.* 1 *Naut.* The lowest lengthwise member of the framework of a vessel, serving to stiffen it and, when it projects below the planking or plating, as is usually the case, giving it stability. 2 Figuratively, a ship. 3 *Aeron.* **a** A vertical fin which extends longitudinally for a considerable length at the bottom of an airship. **b** The center bottom of an airplane fuselage. 4 Any keel-shaped part or object. 5 *Ornithol.* A median longitudinal ridge or process, as of the breast bone of a fowl. — **fin keel** An extension of a yacht's keel downward, suggesting the back fin of a fish: commonly of metal, and serving to ballast and prevent lateral drifting. — *v.t. & v.i.* To turn over with the keel uppermost; capsize. — **to keel over** 1 To turn bottom up; capsize. 2 To fall over or be felled, as from an injury. [<ON *kjolr* keel]

keel[2] (kēl) *n.* 1 A coal barge used on the Tyne in England. 2 The quantity of coal in a barge load. 3 A former British unit of weight for coal, equal to 21.54 metric tons. [<MDu. *kiel* ship]

keel[3] (kēl) *v.t. Obs.* To cool. [OE *cēlan*]

keel·age (kē'lij) *n. Naut.* The sum paid for anchoring a vessel in a harbor.

keel·boat (kēl'bōt') *n.* A covered freight boat of shallow draft having a keel but no sails, usually propelled by poles or the current: used on rivers in the western United States.

keel·er (kē'lər) *n.* 1 A shallow tub. 2 A box used to hold salt in salting fish. [<KEEL[3]]

Kee·ley cure (kē'lē) A proprietary system for the treatment of drug addiction and alcoholism by the administration of gold chloride. [after Leslie J. *Keeley*, 1832–1900, American physician]

keel·haul (kēl'hôl') *v.t.* 1 *Naut.* To haul (a man) through the water under a ship from one side to the other or from stem to stern: a former punishment. 2 To reprove severely; castigate. Also **keel·hale** (kēl'hāl').

keel·son (kēl'sən) *n.* 1 *Naut.* A beam running lengthwise above the keel of a ship. 2 A similar structural member running above the keel of a flying boat. Also spelled *kelson.* [Related to KEEL[1]]

keen[1] (kēn) *adj.* 1 Very sharp, as a knife. 2 Cutting; piercing, as wit. 3 Vivid; pungent. 4 Having or exhibiting sharpness or penetration; shrewd. 5 Acute: *keen* sight. 6 Exceptionally intelligent. 7 Characterized by intensity, force, or zest: a *keen* appetite. See synonyms under ACUTE, ARDENT, ASTUTE, CLEVER, EAGER[1], FINE[1], KNOWING, SAGACIOUS, SHARP, VIVID. [OE *cēne*] — **keen'ly** *adv.* — **keen'ness** *n.*

keen[2] (kēn) *n.* A wailing cry; dirge. — *v.i.* To wail with lamentation for the dead. [<Irish *caoine* <*caoinim* I wail] — **keen'er** *n.*

keep (kēp) *v.* **kept, keep·ing** *v.t.* 1 To have and retain possession or control of; hold. 2 To withhold knowledge of, as a secret. 3 To manage or conduct: to *keep* a shop. 4 To have charge of; tend: to *keep* bar. 5 To care for; guard or defend from harm: May God *keep* you. 6 To be faithful to the conditions of; fulfil, as a promise or contract. 7 To maintain by action or conduct: to *keep* silence. 8 To cause to continue in some condition or state; preserve unchanged: *Keep* the home fires burning. 9 To make regular entries in: to *keep* a diary. 10 To set down in writing; maintain a written record of: to *keep* accounts. 11 To have regularly for sale: to *keep* groceries. 12 To provide for or maintain, as with food or lodging. 13 To have in one's employ or for one's use or pleasure. 14 To celebrate or observe, especially with rites or ceremony, as a holiday. 15 To conduct, as a meeting. 16 To detain or restrain; prevent: What *kept* you? 17 To hold prisoner; confine. 18 To remain; hold to: *Keep* your present course. 19 To hold or maintain in the same position or state as before: *Keep* your seat. — *v.i.* 20 To continue in a condition, place, or action: They *kept* firing; *Keep* to the right-hand side. 21 To remain; stay:

often with *up, down, in, out, off, away,* etc. **22** To remain sound, fresh, etc.: This fruit *keeps* till spring. **23** *Colloq.* To be in session: School *keeps* till three o'clock. — **to keep back 1** To restrain. **2** To withhold. — **to keep in with** *Colloq.* To remain in the good graces of. — **to keep on** To continue; persist. — **to keep time 1** To indicate time correctly, as a clock. **2** To make movements in unison or concord with others. **3** To count or observe rhythmic accents. — **to keep track of** (or **tabs on**) To continue to be informed about. — **to keep up 1** To keep pace with; not fall behind. **2** To maintain in good condition or repair. **3** To continue; go on with. **4** To maintain and renew knowledge or information concerning: usually with *with* or *on*. **5** To cause to stay awake or out of bed. — *n.* **1** Means of subsistence; livelihood. **2** The donjon of a medieval castle; hence, a castle; fortress. **3** That in which something is kept. — **for keeps** *Colloq.* For permanent keeping; for good; for ever. [OE *cēpan* observe]

Synonyms (verb): carry, celebrate, conduct, continue, defend, detain, fulfil, guard, hold, maintain, obey, observe, preserve, protect, refrain, restrain, retain, support, sustain, withhold. *Keep,* signifying generally to have and *retain* in possession, is the terse, strong Old English term for many acts which are more exactly discriminated by other words. We *keep, observe,* or *celebrate* a festival; we *keep* or *hold* a prisoner in custody; we *keep* or *preserve* silence, *keep* the peace, *preserve* order—*preserve* being the more formal word; we *keep* or *maintain* a horse, a servant, etc.; a man *supports* his family; we *keep* or *obey* a commandment, *keep* or *fulfil* a promise. In the expressions to *keep* a secret, *keep* one's own counsel, *keep* faith or *keep* the faith, such words as *preserve* or *maintain* could not be substituted without loss. A person *keeps* a shop or store, *conducts* or carries on a business; he *keeps* or *carries* a certain line of goods; we may *keep* or *restrain* one from folly, crime, or violence; we *keep* from or *refrain* from evil, ourselves. *Keep* in the sense of *guard* or *defend* implies that the defense is effectual. Compare CELEBRATE, OCCUPY, PRESERVE, RESTRAIN, RETAIN. *Antonyms:* see synonyms for ABANDON.

keep·er (kē'pər) *n.* **1** One who or that which keeps; specifically, the overseer of a prison; the guardian of an insane person; the caretaker of a wild animal; any guardian. **2** A device for keeping something in place, as the socket into which a bolt slides. **3** One who observes or obeys: a *keeper* of promises. **4** That which keeps well, without spoiling, as fruit. **5** The armature of a magnet; also, the soft iron bar placed across the poles of a horseshoe magnet to prevent loss of magnetism.

keep·ing (kē'ping) *n.* **1** Custody, charge, or possession. **2** Right relation or proportion; harmony; congruity: The act was in *keeping* with his mood. **3** Maintenance; support.

keep·sake (kēp'sāk') *n.* Anything kept, or given to be kept, for the sake of the giver; a memento.

kees·hond (kās'hond, kēs'-) *n. pl.* **·hond·en** (-hon'dən) A breed of dog of Arctic or sub-Arctic origin, long popular in Holland, ash-gray in color and having a short, closely knit body, straight legs, wedge-shaped head, thick feathery coat, and curly tail. [< Du. *Kees,* a nickname for Cornelius + *hond* a dog; so called from the first breeder]

KEESHOND
(About 20 inches high at the shoulder)

keeve (kēv) *n.* A large vat. [OE *cȳf*]

kef (kāf) *n.* **1** A condition marked by voluptuous and dreamy repose and the passive enjoyment of languor. **2** Indian hemp, smoked to produce this condition: also spelled *keef, kief.* [< Arabic *kaif* good humor]

kef·ir (kef'ər) *n.* A kind of fermented milk resembling kumiss: used in the Caucasus. Also spelled *kephir.* [< Caucasian]

keg (keg) *n.* A small, strong barrel, usually of 5- to 10-gallon capacity. [< earlier *cag* < ON *kaggi*]

keir (kir) See KIER.

keit·lo·a (kīt'lō·ə, kāt'-) *n.* A South African two–horned rhinoceros. [< native name]

Kel·lar (kel'ər), **Harry,** 1849–1922, U.S. magician.

Kel·ler (kel'ər), **Helen Adams,** 1880–1968, U.S. writer and lecturer; blind and deaf from infancy.

ke·loid (kē'loid) *n. Pathol.* A fibrous tumor in the connective tissue of the skin, of various shapes and sizes, and usually caused by injury: also spelled *cheloid.* [< Gk. *kēlē* tumor + -OID]

kelp (kelp) *n.* **1** Any large coarse seaweed (family *Laminariaceae*); specifically, the California sea palm (*Postelsia palmaeformis*). **2** The ashes of seaweeds: formerly the source of soda as used in glassmaking and soapmaking, now a source chiefly of iodine. — **giant kelp** A very large, tough, and massive seaweed (*Macrocystis pyrifera*), belonging to the brown algae: it is found mainly on the Pacific coast of the United States, and has been known to reach a length of 700 feet. [ME *culp;* origin uncertain]

kel·son (kel'sən) See KEELSON.

Kelt (kelt), **Kelt·ic** (kel'tik) See CELT, etc.

kel·ter (kel'tər) *n. Brit. Dial.* Working order; kilter.

Kel·vin scale (kel'vin) *Physics* The absolute scale of temperature, based on the average kinetic energy per molecule of a perfect gas. Zero is equal to −273° Celsius or −459.4° Fahrenheit. [after William Thompson, 1824–1907, Lord *Kelvin,* English physicist]

Kem·ble (kem'bəl), **Frances Anne,** 1809–93, English actress: called "Fanny Kemble." — **John Philip,** 1757–1823, English tragedian; uncle of the preceding.

Kem·pis (kem'pis), **Thomas à,** 1380–1471, German mystic, reputed author of the *Imitation of Christ.*

ken (ken) *v.* **kenned** or **kent, ken·ning** *v.t.* **1** *Scot.* To know; have knowledge of. **2** *Scot. Law* To recognize as heir. **3** *Obs.* To see. — *v.i.* **4** *Scot. & Brit. Dial.* To have understanding. — *n.* Reach of sight or knowledge; cognizance.

kench (kench) *n.* A bin for salting fish or skins. — *v.t. Dial.* To place in a salting bin. [Var. of dial. E *canch* a trench]

Ken·dal (ken'dəl) *n.* A coarse woolen cloth of green color made at Kendal, England; also, the color of this cloth. Also **Kendal green.**

Kenilworth ivy A scrophulariaceous herb (*Cymbalaria muralis*) of delicate growth.

Ken·nan (ken'ən), **George Frost,** born 1904, U.S. diplomat; writer on Russian affairs.

Ken·ne·dy (ken'ə·de), **John Fitzgerald,** 1917–1963, 35th president of the United States, 1961–63; assassinated. — **Robert Francis,** 1925–68, U.S. Senator; assassinated.

Kennedy, Cape A cape of eastern Florida, site of a rocket and missile launching installation: formerly *Cape Canaveral.*

ken·nel[1] (ken'əl) *n.* **1** A house for a dog or for a pack of hounds; also, the pack. **2** *pl.* A professional establishment where dogs are bred, raised, boarded, trained, etc. **3** The hole or lair of a fox or like beast. **4** A vile lodging. — *v.* **·neled** or **·nelled, ·nel·ing** or **·nel·ling** *v.t.* To keep or confine in or as in a kennel. — *v.i.* To lodge or take shelter in a kennel. [< F *chenil* < L *canis* a dog; formed on analogy with *ovile* a sheepfold < *ovis* a sheep]

ken·nel[2] (ken'əl) *n.* The gutter of a street; channel. [Var. of obs. *cannel* a channel]

ken·nel[3] (ken'əl) See CANNEL.

Ken·nel·ly–Heav·i·side layer (ken'əl·ē·hev'ē·sīd) See HEAVISIDE LAYER.

ke·no (kē'nō) *n.* A game of chance played by drawing numbers from a container and covering with counters the corresponding numbers on cards. The player who first covers a row of five numbers is the winner. Also called *bin-*

go, lotto. [< F *quine* five winners]

ken·o·gen·e·sis (ken'ə·jen'ə·sis, kēnə-) See CENOGENESIS.

ke·no·sis (ki·nō'sis) *n. Theol.* Christ's action in putting aside his divinity during the Incarnation, *Phil.* ii 5–8. [< Gk. *kenōsis* an emptying < *kenoein* empty]

ke·not·ic (ki·not'ik) *adj.* Of or pertaining to the doctrine of kenosis. — *n.* One who believes in the doctrine of kenosis.

ken·o·tron (ken'ə·tron) *n.* A unidirectional, two–electrode thermionic tube, which acts as a rectifier of high–voltage alternating currents. [< Gk. *kenōsis* emptying + (ELEC)TRON]

Kent (kent) A county in SE England; 1,525 square miles; county town, Maidstone.

Kent·ish (ken'tish) *adj.* Of or pertaining to Kent. — *n.* The Old English and Middle English dialects of Kent.

kent·ledge (kent'lej) *n. Naut.* Permanent pig-iron ballast. [? < QUINTAL + -AGE]

Ken·tuck·y (kən·tuk'ē) A south central State of the United States; 40,395 square miles; capital, Frankfort; entered the Union June 1, 1792: nickname *Bluegrass State.* Abbr. KY. — **Ken·tuck'i·an** *adj. & n.*

Kentucky bluegrass A grass (*Poa pratensis*) common in temperate and cold regions: valuable for forage.

Kentucky boat A large flat–bottomed river boat, usually towed or propelled by oars, formerly used for transporting freight. Also **Kentucky ark, Kentucky flat.**

Kentucky coffee tree A tall leguminous tree (*Gymnocladus dioicus*) having seeds, called **Kentucky coffee beans,** often used as a substitute for coffee.

Kentucky Derby A famous American horse race, run at Churchill Downs, Louisville, Ky., since 1875.

Ken·ya (kēn'yə, ken'-) A republic of the Commonwealth of Nations in eastern Africa; 224,960 square miles; capital, Nairobi: formerly *East African Protectorate.*

kep (kep) *v.t. Scot.* To catch; stop.

keph·a·lin (kef'ə·lin) See CEPHALIN.

keph·ir (kef'ər) See KEFIR.

kep·i (kep'ē) *n.* A flat–topped military cap with vizor. [< F *képi* < dial. G *käppi,* dim. of *kappe* a cap]

Kep·ler (kep'lər), **Johannes,** 1571–1630, German astronomer; formulated **Kepler's laws,** relative to the motions of planets.

kept (kept) Past tense and past participle of KEEP.

ker (kûr) *n.* **1** In Greek religion, a spirit or soul of one dead; sometimes, a malignant spirit. **2** The personification of fate. [< Gk. *Kēr*]

Ker·ak (ker'äk) A town of south central Jordan, near the Dead Sea.

ke·ram·ic (kə·ram'ik), **ke·ram·ics** See CERAMIC, etc.

ker·a·tin (ker'ə·tin) *n. Biochem.* A highly insoluble albuminous compound containing sulfur that forms the essential ingredient of horny tissue, as of horns, claws, nails, etc. — **ke·rat·i·nous** (kə·rat'ə·nəs) *adj.*

ker·a·ti·tis (ker'ə·tī'tis) *n. Pathol.* Inflammation of the cornea.

kerato– *combining form* **1** Horn: *keratogenous.* **2** Cornea of the eye: *keratoplasty.* Also, before vowels, **kerat–.** [< Gk. *keras, keratos* horn]

ker·a·to–con·junc·ti·vi·tis (ker'ə·tō·kən·jungk'·tə·vī'tis) *n. Pathol.* Inflammation of the cornea and conjunctiva; shipyard eye.

ker·a·tog·e·nous (ker'ə·toj'ə·nəs) *adj.* Promoting the growth of horn.

ker·a·toid (ker'ə·toid) *adj.* Resembling keratin or horn; horny.

Ker·a·tol (ker'ə·tōl, -tol) *n.* A pyroxylin-coated waterproof cloth resembling leather: a trade name.

ker·a·to·plas·ty (ker'ə·tō·plas'tē) *n. Surg.* The operation of transplanting corneal tissue; plastic surgery of the cornea. — **ker'a·to·plas'tic** *adj.*

ker·a·tose (ker'ə·tōs) *adj.* Pertaining to or characterized by horny tissue, as certain sponges.

kerb (kûrb), **kerb·stone** (-stōn) See CURB, etc.

ker·chief (kûr'chif) *n.* A square of linen, silk, or other fabric used to cover the head or neck, or as a handkerchief. [ME *keverchef, kerchef* <OF *couvrechef* <*covrir* cover + *chef* head] — **ker'chiefed** *adj.*

kerf (kûrf) *n.* **1** The channel made by a saw, or the width of such a channel. **2** A cut of a cloth-shearing machine. **3** The act or process of cutting. [OE *cyrf* a cutting]

Ke·rin·chi (kə·rin'chē), **Mount** A peak of western Sumatra; 12,467 feet: also *Indrapura.*

Ker·ky·ra (ker'kē·rä) The Greek name for CORFU.

kermes oak A small evergreen oak (*Quercus coccifera*) of the Mediterranean region, infested by the kermes insect. Also **ker'mes.**

ker·mess (kûr'mis) *n.* **1** In Flanders, etc., a periodical outdoor festival. **2** An indoor or outdoor festival imitative of the Flemish. Often spelled *kirmess.* Also **ker'mis.** [<Du. *kermis* <*kerk misse* church mass]

kern¹ (kûrn) *n.* **1** *Archaic* An Irish irregular, light-armed foot soldier. **2** *Archaic* A body of such soldiers. **3** A peasant; churl. Also **kerne.** [<Irish *ceithern* a band of soldiers]

kern² (kûrn) *n. Printing* That part of a type which overhangs the shaft or shank, as of an italic *f.* — *v.t.* To make (type) with a kern. [<F *carne* projecting angle]

Kern (kûrn), **Jerome David,** 1885–1945, U.S. composer.

ker·nel (kûr'nəl) *n.* **1** A grain or seed; the edible part of a nut. **2** A hard concretion of flesh. **3** The central part of anything; nucleus; gist. — *v.i.* To envelop as a kernel. ◆ Homophone: *colonel.* [OE *cyrnel,* dim. of *corn* a seed]

ker·o·sene (ker'ə·sēn) *n.* A mixture of hydrocarbons distilled from crude petroleum and used for burning in lamps: also called *coal oil.* [<Gk. *kēros* wax + -ENE]

Ker·ry (ker'ē) *n. pl.* **·ries** One of an Irish breed of cattle raised in County Kerry.

Kerry blue terrier See under TERRIER.

ker·sey (kûr'zē) *n.* **1** A smooth, lightweight, ribbed woolen cloth. **2** *pl.* Kinds of kersey; also trousers of kersey. [from *Kersey,* village in England]

kes·trel (kes'trəl) *n.* A European falcon (*Falco tinnunculus*), resembling the American sparrow hawk and noted for its hovering habits. [Var. of ME *castrel* <OF *cresserelle*]

ketch¹ (kech) *n.* A fore-and-aft rigged, two-masted vessel: similar to a yawl but having the mizzen- or jiggermast forward of the rudder post. [Earlier *cache.* Related to CATCH, *v.*]

GAFF–RIGGED KETCH

ketch² (kech) *n.* A hangman. [after Jack *Ketch*]

ketch·up (kech'əp) *n.* A spiced condiment for meats: also spelled *catchup, catsup.* [Appar. <Chinese *ke–tsiap* brine of pickled fish]

ke·tene (kē'tēn) *n. Chem.* **1** A pungent, colorless gas, $H_2C:CO$, obtained by decomposing acetone, ethyl acetate, or acetic anhydride with intense heat. **2** Any of a group of organic compounds of the form $R_2C:CO$. [<KET(ONE) + -ENE]

keto– *combining form Chem.* Ketone; related to ketone bodies. Also, before vowels, **ket–,** as in *ketosis.* [<KETONE]

ke·to·e·nol tautomerism (kē'tō·ē'nôl) *Chem.* Tautomerism in which certain organic compounds may occur in both the keto and enol forms.

ke·tone (kē'tōn) *n. Chem.* One of a class of reactive organic compounds in which the carbonyl group unites with two hydrocarbon radicals, a single bivalent radical, or derivatives. The simplest member of the class is acetic ketone or acetone. [<G *keton* <F *acétone* acetone] — **ke·ton·ic** (ki·ton'ik) *adj.*

ke·tose (kē'tōs) *n. Chem.* Any of a class of monosaccharides containing a ketone group.

ke·to·sis (kē·tō'sis) *n. Pathol.* Excessive formation or secretion of ketones in the body, as in acidosis, diabetes, etc.

Ket·ter·ing (ket'ər·ing), **Charles Franklin,** 1876–1958, U.S. electrical engineer and inventor.

ket·tle (ket'l) *n.* **1** A metallic vessel for stewing or boiling; a teakettle. **2** A tin pail. **3** A hole in the bottom of a stream or pond where carp lie in winter. **4** A kettle-shaped cavity, as in rock or glacial drift: also **kettle hole. 5** A kettledrum. [OE *cetel*]

ket·tle·drum (ket'l·drum') *n.* **1** A drum having a brass hemispherical shell and parchment head, and sounded by soft-headed elastic-drumsticks. **2** An informal afternoon party.

kev·el (kev'əl) *n. Naut.* A belaying cleat or peg: usually in pairs. [<AF *keville* a pin, peg <LL *clavicula* bar of a door, orig. dim. of L *clavis* a key]

Ke·wee·naw Peninsula (kē'wə·nô) A Michigan headland extending 60 miles NE into Lake Superior to form **Keweenaw Bay.**

Kew·pie (kyōō'pē) *n.* A chubby, cherubic doll, made of chalkstone or plastic: a trade name.

kex (keks) *n.* A hollow stalk; a weed. [Origin unknown]

key¹ (kē) *n.* **1** A detachable instrument for turning the catch or bolt of a lock forwards or backwards in order to lock or unlock. **2** An instrument for holding and turning a screw, nut, valve, or the like, as for winding a clock. **3** Anything serving to disclose, open, or solve something. **4** Something that opens or prepares a way. **5** A gloss, table, or group of notes interpreting certain symbols, ciphers, problems, etc. **6** Any one of the finger levers in typewriters, typesetting machines, etc. **7** *Electr.* A circuit-breaker or -opener operated by the fingers, as in a telegraph-sending apparatus. **8** *Music* **a** In musical instruments, a lever to be pressed by the finger. **b** A system of tones, according to which a piece of music is written, in which all the notes of a scale bear a definite and recognized relationship to some particular note (the keynote or tonic): the *key* of C. **9** Tone or pitch of the voice. **10** Tone or style of expression. **11** *Mech.* **a** A wedge, cotter, bolt, or pin used to secure various parts together. **b** One of various implements, as a tightening wedge, for fixing a collar to a shaft. **12** *Archit.* A keystone (def. 1). **13** In building, any special surfacing or surface for holding plaster in place. **14** The roughness on the unfinished face of a veneer giving stronger adherence to the glue. **15** *Bot.* A key fruit; samara. — *v.t.* **1** To fasten with or as with a key. **2** To wedge tightly or support firmly with a key, wedge, etc. **3** To complete (an arch) by adding the keystone. **4** To provide with keys. **5** *Music* To regulate the pitch or tone of. — **to key up 1** To raise the pitch of. **2** To cause excitement, anticipation, etc., in. — *adj.* Of chief or decisive importance: a *key* position. ◆ Homophone: *quay.* [OE *cæg*]

key² (kē) *n.* A low island, especially one of coral, along a coast: usually *cay* in the Gulf of Mexico and the West Indies: rarely *kay.* ◆ Homophone: *quay.* [Var. of CAY]

Key (kē), **Francis Scott,** 1780?–1843, American lawyer; wrote *The Star-Spangled Banner.*

key·board (kē'bôrd', -bōrd') *n.* A row of keys as in a piano or typewriter; also, the range or arrangement of the keys, as of an organ, piano, etc.

key bugle A bugle having keys, and a compass of two octaves including semitones.

keyed (kēd) *adj.* **1** Having keys: said of musical instruments, etc. **2** Brought to a tension, as a musical string. **3** Tuned, as a musical instrument. **4** Secured by a keystone or key.

key·hole (kē'hōl') *n.* A hole for a key, as in a door or lock.

key log The log caught or wedged in a log jam that must be released to break the jam.

key man 1 A person without whose work or direction something could not go on; an indispensable person. **2** A telegraph operator.

Keynes (kānz), **John Maynard,** 1883–1946, English economist.

key·note (kē'nōt') *n.* **1** *Music* The tonic of a key, from which it is named: also **key tone. 2** A basic idea, fact, principle, or sentiment. — *v.t.* **·not·ed, ·not·ing 1** To sound the keynote of. **2** To give the essential points of, as a political platform.

key·not·er (kē'nō'tər) *n.* The person selected to present the basic issues, especially of a political platform.

key·plug (kē'plug') *n.* That part of a cylinder lock which receives the key, permitting it to turn when all the tumblers are in the release

position. See illustration under LOCK.

key signature *Music* The number of sharps or flats following the clef sign at the beginning of each staff, to indicate in what key the music is to be played.

keyst·er (kēs'tər) See KEISTER.

key·stone (kē'stōn') *n.* **1** *Archit.* The uppermost and last-set stone of an arch, which completes it and locks its members together. **2** The fundamental element, as of a science or doctrine.

KEYSTONE (*k*) OF AN ARCH

K.G.B. In the former Soviet Union, a division of the Ministry of State Security. The K.G.B. was created in 1954. K.G.B. and renowned for its meticulous and far-reaching methods of information gathering. There were 17 divisions within the K.G.B., including the border guard. counterintelligence, and the secret police. [*Russian* K(omitet) G(osudarstvenaoy) B(ezopasnosti)]

khad·dar (kud'ər) *n.* Homespun cotton cloth made in India: also **khadi** (kä'dē). [< Hind. *khādar*]

Khai·ber Pass (kī'bər) See KHYBER PASS.

khak·i (kak'ē, kä'kē) *adj.* Of the color of dust; having a neutral tannish-brown or olive-drab color. — *n.* A light olive-drab or brownish cotton cloth. [< Hind. *khākī* dusty]

kha·lif (kā'lif, kal'if) See CALIPH.

kham·sin (kam'sin, kam·sēn') *n. Meteorol.* A hot wind from the Sahara that prevails in Egypt before the vernal equinox; simoom. Also **kamsean': sometimes spelled** *kamsin.* [< Arabic *khamsīn* < *khamsūn* fifty; so called because it occurs for a period of 50 days]

khan¹ (kän, kan) *n.* An Oriental inn surrounding a courtyard. [< Arabic *khān* an inn]

khan² (kän, kan) *n.* In various Oriental countries, a ruler, chief, etc.; now a title of respect for any dignitary. See CHAM. [< Persian *khān* prince]

khan·ate (kän'āt, kan'-) *n.* The jurisdiction of a khan; a principality.

Khar·toum (kär·tōōm') A city near the confluence of the Blue Nile with the White Nile; capital of Sudan. Also **Khar·tum'.**

Khay·yám (kī·äm'), **Omar** See OMAR KHAYYAM.

khed·ah (ked'ə) See KEDDAH.

khe·dive (kə·dēv') *n.* The title of the Turkish viceroy of Egypt from 1867 to 1914. [< Persian *khidīv* king]

Khe·lat (kə·lät') See KALAT.

khen·em stone (ken'əm) In ancient Egyptian practice, the inscribed amulet placed on the body of the deceased, while passages were recited from the Book of the Dead.

khet·em (ket'əm) *n.* In ancient Egypt, the cylinder seal worn as a pendant around the neck, which was dipped into a colored substance and rolled across the surface on which the seal was to appear.

Khi·u·ma The former name of the island province of Hiiumaa, Estonia; 14 miles from the mainland on the Baltic Sea; 395 square miles; pop. 11,500.

Khmer *n.* **1** One of the ethnic groups of Cambodia accounting for 95 % of the pop. of the country. The other ethnic groups in Cambodia are the Chinese, Cham, and other Asian nationalities. **2** The traditional language of the Khmer population and the official language of Cambodia.

Khmer Republic The former name of Cambodia (1970-1975) a republic in SW Indochina; 53,668 square miles; capital, Phnom Penh; Also the State of Kampuchia.

Khnum (khnōōm) The ram-headed god associated with ancient Elephantine in Egypt; in early Egypt, the ram and other animals were considered as actual gods associated with particular cities.

Khoi·san (koi'sän) *n.* A family of languages spoken by Negroid tribes in SW Africa, including Bushman and Hottentot.

Kholm (khôlm) The Russian name for CHELM.

Khond (kond) *n.* **1** A member of an aboriginal hill people of India, of Dravidian stock. **2** Their Dravidian language.

Khrush·chev (khrōōsh'chef), **Nikita,** 1894–1971, U.S.S.R. official; first secretary of the Communist Party 1953–1964; chairman of the Council of Ministers (premier) 1958–1964.

Khu·fu (kōō'fōō) See CHEOPS.

Khy·ber Pass (kī'bər) A mountain pass on the

India-Pakistan border; over 30 miles long: also *Khaiber Pass.*

Kia·yi (jyä'yē) See CHIAYI.

kib·blings (kib'lingz) *n. pl.* Small bits or strips cut from fish, used as bait by Newfoundland fishermen. [Cf. dial. E *kibble* grind coarsely]

kib·butz (ki-bŏŏts) *n. pl.* **·butz·im** (-bŏŏ tsēm') An Israeli collective or communal settlement, esp. a cooperative farm.

kibe (kīb) *n.* 1 A chap or crack in the flesh; an ulcerated chilblain. 2 A sore on the hoof of a sheep. [Cf. Welsh *cibi* a chilblain]

Ki·bei (kē'bā') *n. pl.* **·bei** A citizen or citizens of the United States of Japanese parentage, born in America but educated in Japan. Compare ISSEI, NISEI. [< Japanese]

kib·itz (kib'its) *v.i.* Colloq. To act as a kibitzer. [Back formation < KIBITZER]

kib·itz·er (kib'it·sər) *n.* Colloq. One who meddles with other persons' affairs; specifically, a person who, although not a player, makes suggestions and gives gratuitous advice to card-players. [< Yiddish]

kib·lah (kib'lä) *n.* The direction toward which Moslems kneel and bow in prayer indicated by a niche on the wall in each mosque in Islam. See KAABA. [Arabic *qiblah* something placed opposite < *qabala* be opposite]

ki·bosh (kī'bosh) *n.* Slang Nonsense or humbug. **—to put the kibosh on** To put a stop to; do for. [Prob. < Yiddish]

kick (kik) *v.i.* 1 To strike out with the foot or feet; give a blow with the foot, as in swimming, propelling the ball in football, etc. 2 To strike out with the foot habitually: This horse *kicks*. 3 To recoil, as a firearm. 4 Colloq. To object; complain. **—v.t.** 5 To strike with the foot. 6 To drive or impel by striking with the foot. 7 To strike in recoiling. 8 In football, to score (a goal) by a kick. **—to kick about (or around)** 1 To abuse; neglect. 2 Colloq. To roam from place to place. 3 To be neglected; go unnoticed. 4 Colloq. To give thought or consideration to; discuss. **—to kick back** 1 To recoil violently or unexpectedly, as a gun. 2 Colloq. To pay (part of a commission, salary, etc.) to someone in a position to grant privilege, power, etc., usually as a bribe. **—to kick in** 1 Colloq. To contribute or participate by contributing. 2 Slang To die. **—to kick off** 1 In football, to put the ball in play by kicking it toward the opposing team. 2 Slang To die. **—to kick oneself** To have remorse or regret. **—to kick out** Colloq. To exclude or eject violently or suddenly, as with a kick. **—to kick the bucket** Slang To die. **—to kick up** Slang To make or stir up (trouble, confusion, etc.). **—to kick upstairs** To give an apparent promotion to (someone) in order to remove from a position of actual power. **—n.** 1 A blow with the foot; also, ability or power to kick. 2 The recoil of a firearm. 3 In football, one who kicks; also, a turn at kicking. 4 Slang An act of violent opposition or objection. 5 Something that stimulates or excites, as the alcoholic content of drink. 6 Effective action or power; energy; vim; pep. 7 Slang Stimulation; pleasure; thrill. 8 The depression in the bottom of a molded bottle. 9 Slang A pocket. **—on a kick** Slang Intensely but temporarily interested in a particular subject or activity; He's on a silent-movie *kick*. [ME *kike*; origin unknown]

Kick·a·poo (kik'ə·pōō) *n.* One of a tribe of Algonquian Indians, formerly of northern Illinois: now on reservations in Kansas, Oklahoma, and Mexico.

kick·back (kik'bak') *n.* 1 A recoil; repercussion; any reaction to something said or done. 2 Money comprising part of a commission, fee, etc., returned by prior agreement or coercion, often illegal or unethical.

kick·er (kik'ər) *n.* 1 One who or that which kicks. 2 Slang A surprising element or turn of events.

kick·off (kik'ôf', -of') *n.* 1 In football, the kick with which a game or half is begun. 2 Any beginning.

kick plate A metal plate affixed to the bottom portion of a door to protect its surface. Also **kicking plate.**

kick·shaw (kik'shô) *n.* 1 Something fantastic or trifling; a nameless trifle. 2 Any unsubstantial, fancy, or unrecognizable dish of food. Also **kick'shaws.** [Alter. of F *quelque chose* some-

thing]

kick·y (kik'ē) *adj.* **kick·i·er, kick·i·est** Slang Stimulating; exciting.

kid¹ (kid) *n.* 1 A young goat. 2 Leather, or, in the plural, gloves or shoes made from goatskin. 3 The meat of a young goat. 4 Colloq. A child or infant; youngster. 5 Formerly, a white servant in the American colonies indentured for four or five years. **—adj.** 1 Made of kidskin. 2 Colloq. Younger: my *kid* brother. **—v.t. & v.i. kid·ded, kid·ding** 1 To give birth to (young): said of goats. 2 Slang To make fun of (someone); tease jokingly. 3 Slang To deceive or try to deceive (someone); humbug. [< ON *kidh*] **—kid'der** *n.*

kid² (kid) *n.* 1 A small tub for sailors' rations. 2 On fishing vessels, a small wooden tub to hold fish when caught. [? Var. of KIT¹]

Kidd (kid), **William,** 1650?–1701, British sea captain and pirate; hanged: called "Captain Kidd."

Kid·der·min·ster (kid'ər·min'stər) *n.* A two-ply ingrain carpet, showing warp and filling on each side. [from *Kidderminster,* England, where first made]

kid·dy (kid'ē) *n. pl.* **kid·dies** Slang A small child.

kid glove A glove made of kidskin or similar material. **—with kid gloves** In a tactful or gingerly manner.

kid-glove (kid'gluv') *adj.* 1 Wearing or requiring kid gloves; hence, socially formal. 2 Over-nice; too fastidious to use the hands for work.

kid·nap (kid'nap) *v.t.* **·naped** or **·napped, ·nap·ing** or **·nap·ping** 1 To seize and carry off (someone) by force or fraud, usually so as to demand a ransom. 2 To steal (a child). [< KID¹ (def. 4) + *nap,* dial. var. of NAB] **—kid'nap·er, kid'nap·per** *n.*

kid·ney (kid'nē) *n.* 1 Biol. One of a pair of bean–shaped glandular organs situated at the back of the abdominal cavity, close to the spinal column in man and other vertebrates. The kidneys serve in the excretion of waste products through a fine network of tubules to the ureters and thence to the bladder. ◆ Collateral adjective: *renal.* 2 Temperament. [Origin uncertain]

HUMAN KIDNEY
Longitudinal Section
p. Pyramids.   *u.* Ureter.
g. Papillae.   *d.* Pelvis.
c. Cortical portion.
b. Bertin's columns.

kidney bean 1 The kidney–shaped seed of a plant of the bean family (*Phaseolus vulgaris*); French bean; haricot. 2 The plant itself. 3 The scarlet runner.

kidney ore A variety of hematite found in compact, kidney–shaped masses.

kidney stone 1 Nephrite. 2 A hard mineral formed in the kidney or bladder.

kidney vetch A European herb (*Anthyllis vulneraria*) having cloverlike flower heads, commonly yellow: once reputed useful in kidney troubles and for stanching wounds.

kid·skin (kid'skin') *n.* 1 Leather tanned from the skin of a young goat, used for gloves, shoes, etc. 2 The fur, used for coats.

kier (kir) *n.* A cylindrical tank or vat in which fabric materials are boiled, cleaned, and bleached: also spelled *keir.* [Prob. < ON *ker* tub]

Kier·ke·gaard (kir'kə·gôr), **Sören Aabye,** 1813–55, Danish philosopher and theologian.

kie·sel·guhr (kē'zəl·gŏŏr) *n.* A fine, variously colored earth, derived from the accumulated deposits of the cell walls of diatoms, used as an absorbent for dynamite, as a polishing powder, etc.; diatomite. [< G *kiesel* flint + *guhr* sediment]

kie·ser·ite (kē'zər·īt) *n.* A white, friable, slightly soluble hydrous magnesium sulfate, MgSO₄·H₂O. [after D. G. *Kieser,* German mineralogist]

kiest·er (kēs'tər) See KEISTER.

kil·der·kin (kil'dər·kin) *n.* 1 A cask with the capacity of half a barrel. 2 An old English measure of 18 gallons. [< MDu. *kinderkin*

little child]

ki·lim (ki·lēm') *n.* A tapestry–woven type of rug or spread made in the Caucasus, Turkey, and other parts of the Near East. [< Turkish *kilim* < Persian]

Kil·i·man·ja·ro (kil'i·män·jä'rō) The highest mountain of Africa, in NE Tanganyika; 19,565 feet.

Kilkenny cats In Irish legend, two cats said to have fought till only their tails remained: supposed to refer to a contest between Kilkenny and Irishtown.

kill¹ (kil) *v.t.* 1 To deprive of life; cause the death of; slay. 2 To slaughter for food; butcher. 3 To destroy; put an end to: to *kill* love with hatred. 4 To destroy the active qualities of; neutralize: to *kill* lye. 5 To spoil the effect of; offset, as a color. 6 To cancel; cross out: to *kill* a paragraph. 7 To stop, as an engine or electric current. 8 To pass (time) aimlessly. 9 Colloq. To overwhelm with strong emotion, laughter, etc. 10 In tennis, to strike (the ball) to the opponent's court with such force that it cannot be returned. **—v.i.** 11 To slay or murder. 12 To suffer or undergo death; die: These plants *kill* easily. **—n.** 1 An animal killed as prey. 2 The act of killing, especially in hunting. **—in at the kill** Present at the climax of a chase or other undertaking. [ME *cullen, killen,* origin uncertain]

Synonyms (verb): assassinate, butcher, destroy, dispatch, execute, massacre, murder, slaughter, slay. To *kill* is simply to *destroy* life, whether human, animal, or vegetable, with no suggestion of how or why. *Assassinate, execute, murder,* apply only to the taking of human life; to *murder* is to *kill* with premeditation and malicious intent; to *execute* is to *kill* in fulfilment of a legal sentence; to *assassinate* is to *kill* by assault; this word is chiefly applied to the *killing* of public or eminent persons through political motives, whether secretly or openly To *slay* is to *kill* by a blow, or by a weapon. *Butcher* and *slaughter* apply primarily to the *killing* of cattle; to *butcher* when the *killing* is especially brutal; soldiers mown down in a hopeless charge are said to be *slaughtered* when no brutality on the enemy's part is implied. To *dispatch* is to *kill* swiftly and in general quietly, always with intention, with or without right.

kill² (kil) *n.* A creek, stream, or channel: an element in many U.S. geographical names: *Schuylkill.* [< Du. *kil*]

kill·deer (kil'dir) *n. pl.* **·deers** or **·deer** A North American ring plover (*Oxyechus vociferus*), common in the Mississippi Valley. Also **kill'dee** (-dē). [Imit.; from its cry]

kill·er (kil'ər) *n.* 1 A destroyer of life; a slayer. 2 A murderer or an assassin. 3 A delphinoid cetacean of the genus *Orcinus*; the killer whale of northern seas, especially *Orcinus orca* of the North Atlantic.

kil·li·fish (kil'i·fish') *n. pl.* **·fish** or **·fish·es** One of a family (*Cyprinodontidae*) of widely distributed small fishes (*Fundulus* and related genera), found in fresh or brackish waters. [Appar. KILL² + FISH]

kil·li·ki·nick (kil'ē·ki·nik') See KINNIKINIC.

kill·ing (kil'ing) *n.* 1 The act of taking life; murder. 2 Colloq. A phenomenal profit resulting from bold speculation; a financial coup. 3 Any great success. **—adj.** 1 Slaying; that kills. 2 Slang Very amusing.

kill-kid (kil'kid') *n.* Lambkill.

kill·joy (kil'joi') *n.* One who spoils pleasure; a gloomy person.

kil·lock (kil'ək) *n.* Naut. A small anchor; specifically, a heavy stone in a wooden frame used as an anchor by small boats. Also **kil'lick.** [Origin unknown]

Kil·mer (kil'mər), **Joyce,** 1886–1918, U.S. poet and editor; killed in World War I.

kiln (kil, kiln) *n.* An oven or furnace for baking, burning, or drying industrial products, as for burning bricks. [OE *cylne* < L *culina* kitchen]

kiln-dry (kil'drī', kiln'-) *v.t.* **·dried, ·dry·ing** To dry in a kiln.

kil·o (kil'ō, kē'lō) *n. pl.* **kil·os** Kilogram: an abbreviated form.

kilo- *prefix* One thousand (times a given unit): used chiefly in the metric system of weights and measures: *kilogram, kilocalorie.* [<F <Gk. *chilioi* a thousand]

kil·o·cal·o·rie (kil′ə·kal′ə·rē) *n.* A great calorie: equal to one thousand calories.

kil·o·gram (kil′ə·gram) *n.* A measure of weight equal to 1,000 grams. See METRIC SYSTEM. Also **kil′o·gramme.**

kil·o·gram-me·ter (kil′ə·gram·mē′tər) *n.* A unit of work, the equivalent of the force expended in raising one kilogram one meter vertically: about 7.2 foot-pounds. Also **kil′o·gram-me′tre.**

kil·o·hertz (kil′ə·hûrts) *n.* The unit of electrical frequency equal to one thousand cycles per second: formerly called *kilocycle.*

kil·o·li·ter (kil′ə·lē′tər) *n.* A measure of capacity equal to 1,000 liters. See METRIC SYSTEM. Also **kil′o·li′tre.**

kil·o·me·ter (kil′ə·mē′tər, ki·lom′ə·tar) *n.* A measure of length equal to 1,000 meters. See METRIC SYSTEM. Also **kil′o·me′tre.**

kil·o·met·ric (kil′ə·met′rik) *adj.* Of, pertaining to, or expressed in terms of kilometers. Also **kil′o·met′ri·cal.**

kil·o·ton (kil′ə·tun) *n.* **1** A weight of 1,000 tons. **2** A unit equivalent to the explosive power of 1,000 tons of TNT; used in expressing the energy of atomic and thermonuclear weapons.

kil·o·watt (kil′ə·wät) *n.* One thousand watts: a unit of electrical power.

kil·o·watt-hour (kil′ə·wät·our′) *n.* The work done or the energy resulting from one kilowatt acting for one hour: equal to approximately 1.34 horsepower-hours.

kilt (kilt) *n.* A short pleated skirt worn by Scottish Highland men. —*v.* **1** To make broad, vertical pleats in; pleat. **2** *Scot.* To tuck up, as the skirts of a dress. [Prob. <Scand. Cf. Dan. *kilte* tuck up.] —**kilt′ing** *n.*

kilt·ed (kil′tid) *adj.* **1** Attired in a kilt. **2** Made with pleats, as a dress. **3** Tucked up, as a skirt.

kil·ter (kil′tər) *n. U.S. Dial.* Proper or working order: My radio is out of *kilter.* Also, *Brit. Dial., kelter.*

KILT
a. Tartan. *b.* Kilt. *c.* Sporran.

kilt·ie (kil′tē) *n. Scot.* **1** One wearing a kilt. **2** A Highland soldier. Also **kilt′y.**

kilt·ing (kil′ting) *n.* A series of flat pleats, each of which partly overlaps the preceding one.

kim·ber·lite (kim′bər·līt) *n.* A biotite-bearing, commonly porphyritic, variety of peridotite. The residual clay resulting from its decomposition is the diamond-bearing "blue ground" of Kimberley.

ki·mo·no (kə·mō′nə, ki·mō′nō) *n.pl.* **·nos** A Japanese loose robe fastened with a sash: imitated as an Occidental woman's negligée. [< Japanese]

kin (kin) *n.* **1** Relationship; consanguinity. **2** Collectively, relatives by blood. **3** *Obs.* A group of persons having a common ancestor; clan; tribe. —*adj.* Of the same blood or ancestry; hence, related; kindred. [OE *cyn.* Akin to KIND[2].]

Synonyms (noun): affinity, alliance, birth, blood, consanguinity, descent, family, kind, kindred, race, relationship. *Kind* is broader than *kin,* denoting the most general *relationship,* as the whole human species in *mankind, humankind,* etc; *kin* denotes direct *relationship* that can be traced through either blood or marriage, preferably the former; either of these words may signify collectively all persons of the same blood or members of the same family, relatives, or relations. *Affinity* denotes *relationship* by marriage, *consanguinity* denotes *relationship* by blood. There are no true antonyms of *kin* or *kindred,* except those by negatives, since strangers, aliens, foreigners, and foes may still be *kin* or *kindred.* See KINDRED.

-kin *suffix* Little; small: *lambkin.* [<MDu. *-kijn, -ken*]

kin·aes·the·sia (kin′is·thē′zhə, -zhē·ə), **kin·aes·the·sis** (kin′is·thē′sis) See KINESTHESIA, etc.

kin·ase (kin′ās, kī′nās) *n. Biochem.* A ferment capable of activating another ferment, as zymogen. [<KIN(ETIC) + -ASE]

kind[1] (kīnd) *adj.* **1** Having gentleness, tenderness, or goodness of heart; humane; kindly; also, proceeding from or expressing good-heartedness: *kind* words. **2** Gentle or tractable, as an animal. **3** *Archaic* Affectionate; loving. **4** *Obs.* Characteristic; native. See synonyms under AMIABLE, AMICABLE, CHARITABLE, FRIENDLY, GOOD, HUMANE, PLEASANT, PROPITIOUS. [OE *gecynde*]

kind[2] (kīnd) *n.* **1** Essential or distinguishing quality; sort. **2** A number of persons or things of the same character; a class. **3** A modification or variety of a given sort of thing; a species. **4** *Obs.* Nature in general, or natural disposition. See synonyms under AFFINITY, KIN, SORT. — **in kind 1** With something of the same sort: to repay a blow *in kind.* **2** Specifically, in produce instead of money: to pay taxes *in kind.* — **of a kind 1** Of the same sort or variety. **2** Of imperfect quality; of sorts; poetry *of a kind.* [OE *cynd.* Akin to KIN.]

kin·der·gar·ten (kin′dər·gär′tən) *n.* A school for little children in which instructive diversions, object lessons, and healthful games are prominent features. [<G <*kinder* children + *garten* garden]

kin·der·gart·ner (kin′dər·gärt′nər) *n.* A kindergarten teacher or pupil. Also **kin′der·gar′ten·er** (-gär′tən·ər). [<G]

kind-heart·ed (kīnd′här′tid) *adj.* Having a kind and sympathetic nature. — **kind′-heart′ed·ly** *adv.* — **kind′-heart′ed·ness** *n.*

kin·dle (kin′dəl) *v.* **·dled, ·dling** *v.t.* **1** To cause (a flame, fire, etc.) to burn; light. **2** To set fire to; ignite. **3** To excite or inflame, as the feelings or passions. **4** To make bright or glowing as if with flame. —*v.i.* **5** To take fire; start burning. **6** To become excited or inflamed. **7** To become bright or glowing. See synonyms under BURN[1]. [ON *kynda*]

kin·dler (kind′lər) *n.* **1** One who or that which kindles, illumines, or animates. **2** A piece of light wood or artificial composition used in kindling fires.

kind·less (kīnd′lis) *adj.* **1** *Poetic* Heartless; unkind. **2** *Obs.* Unnatural. — **kind′less·ly** *adv.*

kin·dling (kind′ling) *n.* **1** Material with which a fire is started or kindled. **2** The act of starting a fire or causing to burn. **3** The act of arousing emotion, ambition, etc.

kind·ly (kīnd′lē) *adj.* **·li·er, ·li·est 1** Having or manifesting kindness; sympathetic. **2** Having a favorable or grateful effect; beneficial. **3** *Obs.* Proper to its kind; natural; native; akin. —*adv.* **1** In a kind manner or spirit; goodnaturedly. **2** *Obs.* By nature; naturally. See synonyms under FRIENDLY, PLEASANT, PROPITIOUS. — **kind′li·ness** *n.*

kind·ness (kīnd′nis) *n.* **1** The quality of being kind; good will; kindly disposition. **2** A kind act; a favor. **3** A kindly feeling. See synonyms under BENEVOLENCE, MERCY.

kin·dred (kin′drid) *adj.* **1** Of the same family; related by blood; akin. **2** Of a like nature or character; congenial. —*n.* **1** Relationship; consanguinity. **2** Collectively: relatives by blood; kind. **3** Affinity. [Earlier *kynred* <OE *cyn* family + *-raeden* state]

Synonyms (noun): kin, kinfolk, kinsmen, relations, relatives. *Kin* and *kindred* are used to denote both relationship and the persons related. See AFFINITY, KIN. Compare FAMILY.

kine (kīn) *n. Archaic* Cattle: plural of COW[1].

kin·e·mat·ics (kin′ə·mat′iks) *n.* *pl. (construed as singular)* That branch of mechanics treating of the motion of bodies in the abstract and without reference to the action of forces. [<Gk. *kinēma, -atos* movement < *kineein* move] — **kin′e·mat′ic** or **·i·cal** *adj.* — **kin′e·mat′i·cal·ly** *adv.*

kin·e·phan·tom (kin′ə·fan′təm) *n.* The illusion of reversed motion in a fast-moving object, as the spokes of a wheel in a motion picture. [<KINE(MATOGRAPH) + PHANTOM]

kin·e·scope (kin′ə·skōp) *n.* **1** A vacuum tube attached to a prepared screen against which a beam of electrons reproduces the images sent out from a television transmitter. **2** A filmed record of a television program made with such a device: also **kin·e** (kin′ē). [<KINE(MATOGRAPH) + -SCOPE]

ki·ne·si·at·rics (ki·nē′sē·at′riks) *n.* The treatment of disease by muscular movement or exercise. [<Gk. *kinēsis* motion + -IATRICS]

ki·ne·sim·e·ter (ki·nə·sim′ə·tər) *n.* An instrument for measuring the motion of a part. Also **ki·ne·si·om·e·ter** (ki·nē′sē·om′ə·tər).

ki·ne·si·ther·a·py (ki·nē′si·ther′ə·pē) *n. Med.*

A mode of treating disease by muscular movements. [<Gk. *kinēsis* motion + THERAPY]

kin·es·the·si·a (kin′is·thē′zhə, -zhē·ə) *n. Psychol.* The perception or consciousness of one's own muscular movements: often spelled *kinaesthesia.* Also **kin′es·the′sis** (-thē′sis). [<NL <Gk. *kineein* move + *aisthēsis* perception] — **kin′es·thet′ic** (-thet′ik) *adj.*

ki·net·ic (ki·net′ik) *adj.* **1** Producing motion; motor. **2** Consisting in or depending upon motion; active: distinguished from *potential: kinetic* energy. [<Gk. *kinētikos* < *kineein* move]

kinetic lead *Mil.* In gunnery, the correction made for the relative motion of a target when the lead angle is computed.

ki·net·ics (ki·net′iks) *n. pl. (construed as singular)* That branch of dynamics treating of the production or modification of motion in bodies.

kinetic theory *Physics* Any theory of the constitution of bodies which explains their properties by the motion of their particles, especially that according to which the elasticity of gases is due to the rapid motion of their molecules, which dart about in straight lines with an average velocity that increases with the temperature, until deflected by encounters with one another or with the walls of the containing vessel. This theory has been found capable of explaining nearly all the phenomena of gases, and is now generally accepted.

kin·folk (kin′fōk′) *n. pl.* Relatives collectively; kin. Also **kin′folks:** also *kinsfolk, kinspeople.* See synonyms under KINDRED.

king (king) *n.* **1** The sovereign male ruler of a kingdom. ◆ Collateral adjective: *regal.* **2** One who or that which is preeminent among others of the same kind or class; a leader; chief; head. **3** A person or thing of great importance, position, or power: a *king* of finance. **4** A playing card bearing the semblance of a king. **5** In chess, the principal piece; in checkers, a piece that has reached the adversary's king row, and may then be moved in any direction. [OE *cyng*]

king·bird (king′bûrd′) *n.* An American tyrant flycatcher (genus *Tyrannus*).

king·bolt (king′bōlt′) *n.* A vertical central bolt attaching the body of a vehicle to the fore axle and serving as a pivot in turning.

king crab A large marine arachnid (*Limulus polyphemus*) having a horseshoe-shaped carapace, a posterior shield composed of the abdominal segments, and a long telson: also called *horseshoe crab.*

KING CRAB
A. Shell, or carapace, seen from above.
B. Under side, showing legs and telson.

king·cup (king′kup′) *n.* **1** Any of several buttercups, especially the bulbous buttercup (*Ranunculus bulbosus*) and the creeping buttercup (*R. repens*). **2** The common marsh marigold.

king·dom (king′dəm) *n.* **1** The territory, people, state, or realm ruled by a king or a queen; a monarchy. **2** The spiritual dominion of God on earth. **3** Any separate field of independent authority, action, or influence; sphere. **4** One of the three primary divisions of natural objects known as the *animal, vegetable,* and *mineral* kingdoms.

king·fish (king′fish′) *n. pl.* **·fish** or **·fish·es 1** One of various American food fishes (genus *Menticirrhus*), especially *M. saxatilis,* common on the northern Atlantic coast. **2** The opah. **3** The cero. **4** *U.S. Slang* A vainglorious person.

king·fish·er (king′fish′ər) *n.* Any of several non-passerine birds (family *Alcedinidae*), generally crested, with straight, deeply cleft bill, which feed on fish; especially, the **eastern belted kingfisher** of the United States (*Megaceryle alcyon*).

king·let (king′lit) *n.* **1** A little or unimportant king. **2** Any of several small birds, resembling the warblers, especially the American **golden-crowned kinglet** (*Regulus satrapa*) and the **ruby-crowned kinglet** (*Regulus calendula*).

king·ly (king′lē) *adj.* **·li·er, ·li·est** Pertaining to or worthy of a king; regal; kinglike. —*adv.* In a regal or kingly way; royally. — **king′li-**

ness *n.*

Synonyms (adj.): august, kinglike, majestic, princely, regal, royal. *Royal* denotes that which actually belongs or pertains to a monarch; *regal* denotes that which in outward state is appropriate for a king; a subject may assume *regal* magnificence in residence, dress, and equipage. *Kingly* denotes that which is worthy of a king in personal qualities, especially of character and conduct; *princely* is especially used of treasure, expenditure, gifts, etc., as *princely* munificence, a *princely* fortune, where *royal* would change the sense. See IMPERIAL. *Antonyms:* beggarly, contemptible, inferior, mean, poor, servile, slavish, vile.

king·palm (king′päm′) *n.* Any of a genus (*Archontophoenix*) of tropical and subtropical forest feather palms.

king·pin (king′pin′) *n.* **1** A kingbolt. **2** In tenpins, the foremost pin of a set arranged in order for playing: also called *headpin.* **3** In ninepins, the center pin. **4** *Slang* A person of first importance.

king·post (king′pōst′) *n.* A single vertical strut supporting the apex of a triangular truss and resting on a crossbeam. Also **king post.**

king salmon The quinnat, or North Pacific salmon.

king's bench See under COURT.

king's counsel In the British Empire, barristers who are designated as counsel of the crown and cannot afterward plead against the crown without permission: also *queen's counsel.*

king's English See under ENGLISH.

king's evil Scrofula: once supposed to be curable by a monarch's touch.

king·ship (king′ship) *n.* **1** Royal state; kinghood. **2** Government by a king. **3** The person of a king.

king snake A large harmless colubrine snake (*Lampropeltis getulus*) of the southern United States that kills other snakes and feeds largely on rats and mice.

king's silver A soft, very pure silver formerly used for costly dishes and plate.

King·ston (king′stən, kingz′tən) **1** A port, capital of Jamaica, British West Indies. **2** A city on the Hudson River in SE New York. **3** A city in SE Ontario, Canada.

Kings·town (king′stən, kingz′toun) Capital of St. Vincent in the Windward Islands.

king's yellow A vivid yellow pigment, formerly obtained from orpiment, now also made synthetically from arsenic trisulfide: also called *Chinese yellow.*

king·truss (king′trus′) *n.* A truss, as in roofing, having a kingpost.

king·wood (king′wŏŏd′) *n.* **1** A Brazilian tree (*Dalbergia cearensis*) prized for its wood of fine texture having handsome dark–violet stripings. **2** The wood of this tree.

kink[1] (kingk) *n.* **1** An abrupt bend, twist, loop, or tangle, as in a wire rope. **2** A tightly twisted curl, as in hair or wool. **3** A mental quirk or prejudice. **4** An original, novel, or clever way of doing something. **5** A fashion or fad. **6** A hindrance, obstruction, or difficulty. **7** A crick; cramp. See synonyms under WHIM. —*v.t. & v.i.* To form or cause to form a kink or kinks. [< Du., twist, curl]

kink[2] (kingk) *n. Scot.* **1** A violent or convulsive laughing fit. **2** The whoop in whooping cough. —*v.i.* **1** To laugh violently or convulsively. **2** To gasp, as in laughing or coughing.

kink·a·jou (king′kə·jōō) *n.* A nocturnal, arboreal, raccoon-like carnivore (genus *Potos*, family *Procyonidae*) of the warmer parts of South and Central America, having large eyes, soft woolly fur, and a long prehensile tail. [< F *quincajou* < Tupian]

KINKAJOU
(Up to 3 feet long including the tail)

kink·y (king′kē) *adj.* **kink·i·er, kink·i·est 1** Full of kinks; snarled. **2** Closely or tightly curled, as hair. **3** *Slang* Odd; queer; eccen-

tric. **4** *Slang* Involving or appealing to unconventional or perverted sexual tastes. **5** *Slang* Unconventional in a sophisticated way. —**kink′i·ly** *adv.* —**kink′i·ness** *n.*

kin·ni·ki·nic (kin′ē·kə·nik′) *n.* **1** The leaves or bark of certain plants, as the willow and sumac, prepared for smoking. **2** Any plant so used. Also **kin′ni·kin·nic′, kin′ni·kin·nick′:** sometimes **killikinnick.** [< Algonquian, that which is mixed]

Kin·sey (kin′zē), **Alfred,** 1894–1956, U.S. zoologist; especially known for his statistical reports on sexual behavior in the United States.

kins·folk (kinz′fōk′), **kins·peo·ple** (kinz′pē′pəl) See KINFOLK.

Kin·sha·sa (kēn·shä′sä) The capital of the Republic of the Congo.

kin·ship (kin′ship) *n.* Relationship, especially by blood.

kins·man (kinz′mən) *n. pl.* **-men** (-mən) A blood relation. —**kins′wom′an** (-wŏŏm′ən) *n. fem.*

Synonyms: connection, relative, relation. *Kinsman* is preferred in certain cases, on the ground of greater clearness, to *relative, relation, connection.* A man's *relative* or *relation* is one who is related to him, either by blood, as a brother (a *kinsman*), or by law, as a brother-in-law (not a *kinsman*), or, loosely, by some other bond. *Connection* is still more vague and unsatisfactory. The same applies to *kinswoman.* See KINDRED.

ki·osk (kē·osk′, kē′osk, kī′-) *n.* An open ornamental summerhouse in Turkey now imitated in other countries and modified to serve as a booth, news–stand, bandstand, or the like. [< Turkish *kiüshk*]

Ki·o·wa (kī′ə·wä, -wə) *n.* One of a fierce tribe of Plains Indians of the Kiowan linguistic stock, formerly inhabiting parts of Nebraska and Wyoming. Also **Ki′o·way** (-wā).

Ki·o·wan (kī′ə·wən) *n.* A North American Indian linguistic stock consisting of the Kiowas.

kip (kip) *n.* **1** The untanned skin of a calf. **2** The untanned skin of an adult of any small breed of cattle. **3** A collection of such skins composed of a specific number. Also **kip′. skin′** (-skin′). [Origin uncertain]

Kip·ling (kip′ling), **Rudyard,** 1865–1936, English author and poet.

kip·per (kip′ər) *n.* **1** A salmon or herring cured by kippering. **2** The male salmon during the spawning season. —*v.t.* To cure, as fish, by splitting, salting, and drying or smoking. [? OE *cypera* spawning salmon]

Kir·ghiz *n. pl.* **·ghiz** or **·ghiz·es** (also **Kyr·gyz**) **1** One of a Turkic people of Mongolian descent, dwelling in the Asian region, south of Kazakhstan. **2** The Turkic language of the Kirghiz.

Kir·man (kir·män′) *n.* A type of Persian rug having naturalistic floral patterns and soft, rich coloring. [from *Kerman,* Iran, where originally made]

Kirsch (kirsh) *n.* A brandy distilled from the fermented juice of cherries and their pits, originally from Germany and Alsace. Also **Kirsch′. was′ser** (-väs′ər)

kir·tle (kûrt′l) *n.* A garment with a skirt; a frock or mantle. [OE *cyrtel,* prob. ult. < L *curtus* short] —**kir′tled** *adj.*

kish (kish) *n.* Graphite which forms on the top of molten iron high in carbon. [< G *kies* gravel, pyrites]

Ki·shi·nev (kish′i·nef, *Russian* kē·shē·nyôf′) The capital of the Moldavian S.S.R.: Rumanian *Chişinău.*

kis·met (kiz′met, kis′-) *n.* Appointed lot; fate. [< Turkish < Arabic *qisma* < *qasama* divide]

kiss (kis) *n.* **1** An affectionate salutation by contact of the lips. **2** A gentle touch. **3** One of various forms of confectionery. [< *v.*] —*v.t. & v.i.* **1** To touch with the lips, as in greeting or love. **2** To touch slightly. **3** *Printing* To touch: said of printed characters. See synonyms under CARESS. [OE *cyssan* kiss] —**kiss′er** *n.*

kissing bug 1 A hemipterous insect (*Reduvius personatus*) which occasionally bites man on the lips or cheeks: also called *masked hunter.*

2 One of several other bloodsucking insects, as the sharp–beaked *Melanolestes picipes.*

kist·vaen (kist′vīn) *n.* An ancient, box–shaped sepulchral chamber smaller than a dolmen, made of flat stones: sometimes spelled *cistvaen.* Also **kist.** [Welsh *cist faen* < *cist* coffin + *faen* stone]

kit[1] (kit) *n.* **1** A tub, pail, or box for packing. **2** A small pail. **3** A collection of articles and appliances for any special purpose; an outfit; also, a group of persons; especially, a political constituency. **4** A collection of persons or things; the whole lot: the whole *kit* and caboodle of them. Compare CABOODLE. [< MDu. *kitte*]

kit[2] (kit) *n.* A kitten.

kit[3] (kit) *n.* A small, three–stringed violin, used from the 16th to the 18th century: also *kit violin.* [Origin unknown]

Ki·ta·za·to (kē·tä·zä·tō), **Shibamiro,** 1852–1931, Japanese bacteriologist and pathologist; discoverer of the bacilli of bubonic plague and of dysentery. Also **Ki·ta·sa·to.**

kitch·en (kich′ən) *n.* **1** A room specially set apart and containing the necessary utensils for cooking food. **2** A culinary department. [OE *cycene,* ult. < L *coquina* < *coquere* cook]

kitch·en·ette (kich′ən·et′) *n.* A small kitchen.

kitchen garden A garden in which vegetables and, sometimes, fruits are grown for home use.

kitchen midden *Anthropol.* A mound composed of shells, bones, rude stone implements, and other refuse of primitive or prehistoric dwellings. [Trans. of Dan. *kökkenmödding*]

kitchen police *Mil.* Enlisted men detailed to perform routine kitchen chores; also, such duty. Abbr. *K.P.*

kitch·en·ware (kich′ən·wâr′) *n.* Kitchen utensils.

kite (kīt) **1** Any of certain birds of prey of the hawk family (*Falconidae*), having long, pointed wings and a forked tail. Some species are scavengers, as the **pariah kite** (genus *Milvus*) of India. **2** A light frame, usually of wood, covered with paper or some light fabric, to be flown in the air at the end of a long string. **3** *Naut.* One of several light

TYPES OF KITES *(def. 2)*

sails for use in a very light wind, as skysails. **4** In commerce, any negotiable paper not representing a genuine transaction but so employed as to obtain money, sustain credit, etc.; also, a bank check which is drawn with insufficient funds on deposit to secure the advantage of the time period prior to collection: considered to be a malpractice. **5** A shrewd and greedy bargainer; a sharper. —**to fly one's own kite** To tend to one's own affairs. —*v.* **kit·ed, kit·ing** *v.i.* **1** To soar or fly like a kite; move along swiftly. **2** In commerce, to obtain money or credit by the use of kites. **3** In commerce, to issue as a kite. [OE *cȳta*]

kith (kith) *n. Scot. & Brit. Dial.* One's friends, acquaintances, or associates.

kith and kin Friends and relatives.

kith·a·ra (kith′ə·rə) *n.* A cithara.

kitsch (kich) *n.* Art or literary works, etc., having broad popular appeal and little aesthetic merit. [< G]

kit·tel (kit′l) *n.* A white cotton gown worn by orthodox Jews for solemn occasions and as a burial garment. [< G, a smock]

kit·ten (kit′n) *n.* A young cat or other feline animal. —*v.t. & v.i.* **·tened, ·ten·ing** To give birth to (kittens). [<OF *chitoun*, dim. of *chat* a cat]

kit·ten·ish (kit′ən-ish) · *adj.* Playfully coy. — **kit′ten·ish·ly** *adv.* — **kit′ten·ish·ness** *n.*

kit·ti·wake (kit′ē-wāk) *n.* A gull of northern seas (genus *Rissa*), having the hind toe rudimentary. [Imit.]

kit·tool (ki·tōōl′) *n.* A stiff, elastic fiber from the leaves of the fishtail palm (*Caryota urens*) of Ceylon and India: used for machine brushes. Also **kit·tul′**. [<Singhalese *kitūl* <Skt. *hintāla* marshy date tree]

Kitt·redge (kit′rij), **George Lyman,** 1860–1941, U.S. educator, author, editor, and scholar.

kit·ty[1] (kit′ē) *n. pl.* **·ties** 1 In certain card games, the pool to which each player contributes a percentage of his winnings, used to cover expenses, the cost of refreshments, etc.: also called *widow.* 2 Hence, money pooled for any specific purpose. 3 In certain card games, a hand or part of a hand left over after a deal, which may be used by the highest bidder. [Cf. obs. *kidcote* a prison]

kit·ty[2] (kit′ē) *n. pl.* **·ties** 1 A kitten. 2 A pet name for a cat.

kit·ty-cor·nered (kit′ē-kôr′nərd) See CATER-CORNERED.

Kitty Hawk A village on Albermarle Sound, North Carolina: here Wilbur and Orville Wright made the first sustained airplane flight in the United States, December, 1903.

kit violin See KIT[3].

ki·va (kē′və) *n.* A room built in a Pueblo dwelling or beneath it, devoted to secret religious ceremonies, tribal councils, etc., entered by an opening in the roof. [<Hopi]

ki·wi (kē′wē) *n.* 1 A flightless bird of New Zealand, the apteryx: named from its cry. 2 *Mil. Slang* An air force officer who does not make flights. 3 *Austral.* A New Zealander. [Imit.]

Klam·ath (klam′əth) *n.* 1 One of a tribe of North American Indians of Lutuamian linguistic stock, formerly occupying the Klamath Lake and River region in Oregon, now on Klamath reservation, Oregon. 2 The language of the Klamath Indians: term usually extended also to the Modoc dialect.

Klan (klan) See KU KLUX.

Klans·man (klanz′mən) *n. pl.* **·men** (-mən) A member of the Ku Klux Klan.

klax·on (klak′sən) *n.* 1 An early type of automobile horn. 2 A low horn, especially one used on shipboard for sounding an alarm. Also **klaxon horn.** [<Gk. *klazein* make a harsh sound]

Klebs–Löff·ler bacillus (klebz′lœf′lər) The diphtheria bacillus. [after Edwin *Klebs,* 1834–1913, and Friedrich August Johannes *Löffler,* 1852–1915, German bacteriologists]

Klee (klā, klē), **Paul,** 1879–1940, Swiss painter.

Kleen·ex (klē′neks) *n.* A soft paper tissue, used as a handkerchief, etc.: a trade name.

Klein bottle *Math.* A surface having only one side and no edges, constructed by inserting the smaller end of a tapering tube through one side of its larger end, then spreading the smaller end to join and coincide with the larger. [after Felix *Klein*]

klepht (kleft) *n.* One of a group of patriotic Greek mountaineers who organized into brigand bands and carried out robberies to aid the cause of Greek independence from Turkish rule. [<Gk. *kleptēs* a thief <*kleptein* steal]

klep·to·ma·ni·a (klep′tə-mā′nē-ə) *n.* An uncontrollable, morbid propensity to steal: also spelled *cleptomania.* [<Gk. *kleptein* steal + -MANIA] — **klep′to·ma′ni·ac** (-mā′nē-ak) *n.*

klieg light (klēg) A powerful incandescent floodlight, rich in actinic rays: used in making motion pictures. [after A. *Kliegl,* 1872–1927, and his brother John, 1869–1959, U.S. stage-lighting pioneers born in Germany]

Kling·sor (kling′zôr, -zōr) In Wagner's *Parsifal,* a magician who in revenge for his exclusion from the knighthood of the Grail attempts to corrupt the knights by his arts, and, after failing to tempt Parsifal, is destroyed.

klip·spring·er (klip′spring·ər) *n.* A small, agile African antelope (*Oreotragus oreotragus*) inhabiting mountainous regions from Ethiopia to the Cape of Good Hope. [<Du., lit., cliff-springer]

Klon·dike (klon′dīk) A region in NW Canada

in the basin of the **Klondike River,** a tributary of the Yukon River, flowing 100 miles west.

klys·tron (klis′tron, -trən, klī′stron, -strən) *n.* A vacuum tube for generating a powerful, high-frequency radio beam by means of a flow of electrons rhythmically accelerated and retarded between cavities within which electrical oscillations are produced. [<Gk. *kleistos* closed + (ELEC)TRON]

knack (nak) *n.* 1 The trick of doing a thing readily and well. 2 Cleverness; adroitness. 3 A clever device. — *v.t. & v.i. Rare* To strike sharply. [Cf. ME *knack* a sharp blow]

knack·er (nak′ər) *n. Brit.* A dealer in, and slaughterer of, old horses. [Origin uncertain]

knack·wurst (näk′wûrst) *n.* A short, thick sausage, often highly seasoned: also *knockwurst.* [<G <*knacken* sputter, crackle + *wurst* sausage]

knag·gy (nag′ē) *adj.* **·gi·er, ·gi·est** Full of knots; rough.

knap (nap) *v.t. & v.i.* **knapped, knap·ping** 1 *Archaic* To break in pieces; snap. 2 *Rare* To bite sharply; nibble. — *n.* A sharp cracking noise. [Imit.]

knave (nāv) *n.* 1 A dishonest person; rogue. 2 A playing card, the jack. 3 *Archaic* A male servant. ♦ Homophone: *nave.* [OE *cnafa* servant]

knav·er·y (nā′vər·ē) *n. pl.* **·er·ies** 1 Deceitfulness; trickery. 2 An instance of this; knavish action or behavior. 3 *Archaic* Mischievous quality; roguery.

knav·ish (nā′vish) *adj.* Of, pertaining to, or characteristic of a knave. — **knav′ish·ly** *adv.*

knead (nēd) *v.t.* 1 To mix and. work, as dough or clay, into a uniform mass, usually by pressing, turning, etc., with the hands. 2 To work upon by thumps or squeezes of the hands; massage. 3 To make by or as by kneading. ♦ Homophone: *need.* [OE *cnedan*] — **knead′er** *n.*

knee (nē) *n.* 1 *Anat.* The joint, or the region about the joint of the human leg, midway between the hip joint and the ankle. 2 A region considered similar to the knee of man: in the hind leg of horses, dogs, and similar animals, the stifle joint; in the foreleg, the carpal joint at the top of the cannon bone: said of hoofed beasts. 3 In birds, the joint at the top of the tarsus. 4 A plate, usually triangular, for connecting or joining structural members. 5 Anything like or suggesting a knee; also, in clothing, the part covering the knee. 6 Any of the upward projections, spurlike or angular, from the roots of swamp trees, especially the bald cypress. — *v.t.* To touch or strike with the knee. — *v.i. Obs.* To kneel. [OE *cnēow*]

knee breeches Breeches extending from the waist to a point just below the knee. Also **knee-smalls** (nē′smôlz′).

knee·cap (nē′kap′) *n.* 1 The patella. 2 A protective covering or padding for the knee: also **knee′pad′.**

knee-jerk (nē′jûrk′) *adj. Colloq.* Acting in a way that displays unthinking acceptance of preconceived ideas or stereotypes: *knee-jerk liberals.*

knee jerk A reflex action of the lower leg caused by a sudden, brisk tapping of the tendon just below the kneecap.

knee joint 1 *Anat.* The articulation between the femur and the tibia, which includes the patella. 2 A joint made or stiffened by a knee, as in shipbuilding. 3 A toggle joint.

kneel (nēl) *v.i.* **knelt** or **kneeled, kneeling** To fall or rest on the bent knee or knees. [OE *cnēowlian*] — **kneel′er** *n.*

knee·pad (nē′pad′) *n.* A protective covering for the knee or for the stocking at the knee.

knee·piece (nē′pēs′) *n.* In medieval armor, a covering strapped to the leg as protection for the knee and adjacent parts.

KNEE JOINT
c. Crucial ligament.
f. Femur.
lp. Ligamentum patellae.
p. Patellae.
pl. Posterior ligament.
t. Tibia.

knell (nel) *n.* 1 The tolling of a bell, as in announcing a death. 2 An omen of death, rain, or failure. — *v.i.* 1 To sound a knell; toll, as mourning. 2 To give a sad or warning sound. — *v.t.* 3 To summon or proclaim by or as by a knell. [OE *cnyll* <*cnyllan* knock]

knew (nōō, nyōō) Past tense of KNOW.

Knick·er·bock·er (nik′ər-bok′ər) *n.* 1 A descendant of one of the early Dutch settlers in New York State. 2 A New Yorker. [after Diedrich *Knickerbocker,* typical Dutch character, fictitious author of Irving's *History of New York*]

knick·er·bock·ers (nik′ər-bok′ərz) *n. pl.* Wide short breeches gathered below the knee; knickers.

knick·ers (nik′ərz) *n. pl.* 1 Knickerbockers. 2 A woman's or girl's undergarment, similar to bloomers.

knick-knack (nik′nak) *n.* A trifling article; trinket; trifle: also spelled *nick-nack.* [Varied reduplication of KNACK]

knife (nīf) *n. pl.* **knives** (nīvz) 1 A cutting instrument with one or more sharp-edged, often pointed, blades, commonly set in a handle. 2 An edged blade forming a part of an implement or machine. 3 A weapon such as a cutlas or sword. — *v.t.* **knifed, knif·ing** 1 To stab or cut with a knife. 2 *U.S. Slang* To work against with underhand methods. [OE *cnīf*]

KNIVES

A. Saw–back fish knife.	G. Blade of mat–knife.
B. Hacking knife.	H. Felt knife.
C. Paperhanger's knife.	I. Paring knife.
D. Oilcloth knife.	J. Hunting knife.
E. Putty knife.	K. Table knife.
F. Woodcarver's knife.	L. Paring or fruit knife.
M. Folding pocket knife or penknife.	

knife-edge (nīf′ej′) *n.* 1 An edge sharpened like that of a knife. 2 A wedge of steel with a fine edge, serving as a fulcrum, as for a balance beam or a pendulum. 3 The girdle of a gem.

knife switch *Electr.* A switch consisting of one or more knifelike blades which make contact between flat springs.

knight (nīt) *n.* 1 In medieval times, a gentleman bred to the profession of arms, and admitted with special ceremonies to honorable military rank. 2 *Brit.* The holder of a title next below that of baronet, entitling him to use *Sir* before his given name. 3 A champion or devoted follower, as of a cause; any man devoted to the service of a woman, principle, etc. 4 A member of any society in which the official title of knight obtains. 5 A chessman bearing a horse's head and moving one square in any direction, then one diagonally, without regard to intervening pieces. — *v.t.* To make (someone) a knight. ♦ Homophone: *night.* [OE *cniht* boy, servant] — **knight′age** *n.* ♦ Such terms as *knight banneret, knight baronet, knight companion,* and *Knight Templar* are each two nouns in apposition. In the plural each word often takes the inflection: *Knights Templars,* etc.

knight bachelor *pl.* **knights bachelors** In England, a member of the most ancient but lowest order of knighthood.

knight errant *pl.* **knights errant** A medieval knight who went forth to redress wrongs or seek adventures.

knight-er·rant·ry (nīt′er′ən-trē) *n. pl.* **·ries** 1 The customs and practices of the knights errant; chivalry. **2** Quixotic behavior.

knight·head (nīt′hed′) *n. Naut.* One of two timbers rising from the keel of a vessel and supporting the bowsprit between them.

knight·hood (nīt′hŏŏd) *n.* **1** The character, dignity, rank, or vocation of a knight. **2** Knights collectively. **3** Chivalry.

Knights of the Round Table The body of knights comprising King Arthur's court. See ROUND TABLE.

knish (kə-nish′) *n.* A small square or round of dough filled with potatoes, meat, kasha, etc., and baked or fried. [<Yiddish]

knit (nit) *v.* **knit** or **knit·ted, knit·ting** *v.t.* **1** To form (a fabric or garment) by interlocking loops of a single yarn or thread by means of needles. **2** To fasten or unite closely and firmly. **3** To draw (the brows) together into wrinkles; contract. —*v.i.* **4** To make a fabric by interweaving a yarn or thread. **5** To become closely and firmly united; grow together, as broken bones. **6** To come together in wrinkles; contract. [OE *cnyttan.* Akin to KNOT.]

knit·ting (nit′ing) *n.* **1** The act of one who or that which knits. **2** The fabric produced by knitting.

knitting needle A straight, slender rod, pointed at one or both ends, used in hand knitting.

knob (nob) *n.* **1** A rounded protuberance, bunch, or boss. **2** A rounded handle, as of a door. **3** A rounded mountain; knoll. [ME *knobbe,* prob. <MLG. Cf. Flemish *knobbe.*] —**knobbed** (nobd) *adj.* —**knob′like′** *adj.*

knob·by (nob′ē) *adj.* **·bi·er, ·bi·est** Full of knobs; also, knoblike. —**knob′bi·ness** *n.*

knock (nok) *v.t.* **1** To give a heavy blow to; hit. **2** To strike (one thing) against another; bring into collision. **3** To drive or impel by striking: to *knock* a ball over a fence. **4** To make or cause by striking: to *knock* a hole in a wall. **5** *U.S. Slang* To find fault with; carp at. —*v.i.* **6** To strike a blow or blows, as with the fist or a club. **7** To come into collision; bump. **8** To make a pounding or clanking noise, as an engine. **9** *U.S. Slang* To find fault; carp. —**to knock about (or around) 1** To strike repeatedly; hit from side to side. **2** To wander from place to place. **3** To treat neglectfully; abuse. —**to knock down 1** To take apart for convenience in shipping or storing. **2** In auctions, to sell to the highest bidder. **3** *U.S. Slang* To embezzle a part of money passing through one's hands. —**to knock off 1** To leave off; stop, as work, talking, etc. **2** To deduct. **3** To do or make quickly or easily. **4** *U.S. Slang* To kill; also, to overwhelm or defeat. —**to knock out 1** In boxing, to defeat (an opponent) by striking him to the ground for a count of ten. **2** To render unconscious or exhausted. —**to knock out of the box** In baseball, to hit the pitches of (an opposing pitcher) so often as to cause his removal from the game. —**to knock together** To build or make roughly or hurriedly. —**to knock up 1** *Brit.* To rouse, as by knocking on the door. **2** *Brit. Colloq.* To tire out; exhaust. **3** *U.S. Slang* To make pregnant. —*n.* **1** A sharp blow; a rap; also, a knocking. **2** *Mech.* **a** The noise produced in machinery or in engines when the operating parts are defective, badly worn, or poorly adjusted. **b** In an internal–combustion engine, the metallic explosive sounds due to uneven or improperly timed combustion. **3** *U.S. Colloq.* Hostile criticism; an adverse comment. [OE *cnocian.*]

knock·a·bout (nok′ə-bout′) *adj.* **1** Characterized by knocking about, noisiness, or roughness. **2** Adapted for or suitable to any kind of rough usage. **3** Adaptable to all kinds of labor. —*n. Naut.* A small, partially decked yacht, carrying a mainsail and jib rigged fore-and-aft. Compare RACE–ABOUT.

knock·down (nok′doun′) *adj.* **1** Having sufficient force to fell or overthrow. **2** Constructed so as to be easily taken down, or apart, or so that the parts can be readily put together. —*n.* **1** A blow that fells; also, the act of felling. **2** Any prefabricated unassembled article.

knocked-on-at·om (nokt′on·at′əm) *n. Physics* An atom in a solid substance which recoils

after the impact of a high–energy particle, often with sufficient energy to displace other atoms.

knock·er (nok′ər) *n.* **1** One who knocks. **2** A hinged metal hammer fastened to a door as a means of signaling for admittance.

knock-knee (nok′nē′) *n.* **1** An inward curvature of the legs that causes the knees to knock together in walking. **2** *pl.* Such knees. —**knock′-kneed′** *adj.*

knock-off hub (nok′ôf′, -of′) In automobiles, the system by which a wheel is affixed to an axle by an eared screw cap, enabling rapid removal and replacement of the wheel.

knock-out (nok′out′) *adj.* Rendering insensible, as a blow at the angle of the jaw; overpowering. —*n.* **1** A knockout blow; also, a prizefight that has been ended by such a blow. **2** *Slang.* An overwhelmingly attractive or successful person or thing.

knockout drops Drops of some powerful narcotic, as chloral hydrate, used to produce unconsciousness, often for criminal purposes.

knock-wurst (näk′wûrst) See KNACKWURST.

knoll¹ (nōl) *n.* A small round hill; a mound; also, a hilltop. [OE *cnoll* hill]

knoll² (nōl) *Archaic v.t.* **1** To proclaim or call by ringing a bell. **2** To sound, as a knell. —*v.i.* **3** To sound a knell; toll. —*n.* The tolling of a bell; knell. [Var. of KNELL]

knop (nop) *n.* A knob; an ornamental boss or stud. [Prob. var. of KNOB]

knosp (nosp) *n. Archit.* A flower bud, or a budlike ornament. [<MHG *knospe* bud]

knot¹ (not) *n.* **1** An intertwining of the parts of one or more ropes, cords, etc., so that they will not slip. **2** An ornamental bow of silk, lace, etc. **3** Anything that resembles a knot. **4** A hard, gnarled portion of the trunk of a tree at the insertion of a branch; especially, such a gnarled knob of a pine tree, used for kindling or firewood. **5** *Bot.* **a** A node or joint in a stem; also, a protuberance or swelling. **b** *pl.* Any of several diseases of trees, characterized by such swellings. **6** A cluster or group, as of persons. **7** *Naut.* **a** A division of a log line, marked by pieces of cloth or knotted string at equal distances, and used to determine the rate of a ship's motion. **b** A speed of a nautical mile in an hour. **c** A nautical mile. **8** A knob. **9** A bond or association or union. **10** Something not easily solved; a difficulty; problem. **11** An enlargement of a muscle or of the bone beneath it; a swollen gland or nerve. **12** The red-breasted sandpiper. See REDBREAST. —**French knot** A decorative knot made by twisting or winding a thread several times around a needle and then pushing the latter through the coil. —*v.* **knot·ted, knot·ting** *v.t.* **1** To tie in a knot; form a knot or knots in. **2** To secure or fasten by a knot. **3** To form knobs, bosses, etc., in. —*v.i.* **4** To form a knot or knots. **5** To tie knots for fringe. [OE *cnotta*]

KNOTS

a. Square or reef knot.	*e.* Single bowknot.
b. Granny knot.	*f.* Double bowknot.
c. Overhand knot.	*g.* Boat knot.
d. Figure-8 knot.	*h.* Surgeon's knot.

knot² (not) *n.* A migratory sandpiper (*Calidris Canutis*) breeding in Arctic regions. [Origin unknown]

knot·grass (not′gras′, -gräs′) *n.* **1** A widely distributed polygonaceous herb (*Polygonum aviculare*) with jointed stems and small greenish flowers. **2** Any of several other grasses, as the wild oat (*Avena fatua*). Also called *birdgrass.*

knot·hole (not′hōl′) *n.* A hole, as in a plank, left by the falling out of a knot.

knot·ted (not′id) *adj.* **1** Tied with a knot or into knots. **2** Having knots; knotty. **3** Ornamented with knotwork.

knot·ter (not′ər) *n.* **1** A person or machine employed for removing knots. **2** One who or

that which knots. **3** Tangled; intricate. **4** Puzzling; confusing.

knot·ty (not′ē) *adj.* **·ti·er, ·ti·est 1** Knotted; full of, or tied in, knots; like a knot. **2** Difficult; puzzling; intricate. —**knot′ti·ness** *n.*

knot·weed (not′wēd′) *n.* **1** Knotgrass. **2** Knapweed. Also called *persicary, smartweed.*

knout (nout) *n.* A whip or scourge used formerly for flogging in Russia: often a bundle of thongs twisted with wire. —*v.t.* To flog with the knout. [<F <Russian *knut* knot, whip, prob. <Scand. Cf. Sw. *knut.*]

know (nō) *v.* **knew, known, know·ing** *v.t.* **1** To perceive or understand clearly or with certainty; apprehend as objectively true: to *know* the truth. **2** To have information or intelligence of: to *know* the enemy's plans. **3** To be acquainted with; have experience of or familiarity with: Do you *know* each other? **4** To recognize; identify; also, to distinguish between: to *know* peas from beans. **5** To have practical skill in or knowledge of: often with *how:* Do you *know* how to ski? **6** *Archaic* To have sexual intercourse with. —*v.i.* **7** To have knowledge: often with *of:* Do you *know* of any better reason? **8** To be or become aware or cognizant. —*n.* The fact or condition of knowing; knowledge. —**in the know** *Colloq.* Having full, or more than usual, information. [OE *cnāwan*] —**know′a·ble** *adj.* & *n.* —**know′er** *n.*

Synonyms (verb): apprehend, ascertain, cognize, comprehend, discern, discover, discriminate, distinguish, experience, learn, perceive, realize, recognize, understand. See LEARN. Compare synonyms for KNOWLEDGE. *Antonyms:* Compare synonyms for IGNORANT.

know-how (nō′hou′) *n. Colloq.* Knowledge of how to perform a complicated operation or procedure; technical skill.

know·ing (nō′ing) *adj.* **1** Perceptive; astute; shrewd; also, possessing sly, covert, or secret knowledge: a *knowing* look. **2** Conscious; intentional. **3** Having knowledge or information. —**know′ing·ness** *n.*

Synonyms: acute, astute, clever, cunning, discerning, intelligent, keen, penetrating, sagacious, sharp, shrewd. A *knowing* look, air, etc., indicates the possession of reserved knowledge which the person could impart if he chose. *Knowing* has often a slightly invidious sense. We speak of a *knowing* rascal, meaning *cunning* or *shrewd* within a narrow range, but a *knowing* child has more knowledge than would be looked for at his years, perhaps more than is quite desirable, although to speak of a child as *intelligent* is altogether complimentary. See ASTUTE, CLEVER, INTELLIGENT, WISE². *Antonyms:* dull, gullible, senseless, silly, simple, stolid, stupid, undiscerning, unintelligent.

know·ing·ly (nō′ing·lē) *adv.* **1** With knowledge. **2** Shrewdly; slyly. **3** Intentionally; on purpose: Who would *knowingly* commit a crime?

know-it-all (nō′it·ôl′) *n. Colloq.* A person affecting knowledge in almost all subjects. Also **know′-all′.**

knowl·edge (nol′ij) *n.* **1** A result or product of knowing; information or understanding acquired through experience; practical ability or skill. **2** Information; learning; specifically, the cumulative culture of the human race. **3** The clear and certain apprehension of truth; assured rational conviction. **4** The act, process, or state of knowing; cognition. **5** Any object of knowing or mental apprehension; that which is or may be known; the knowable; also actual or possible range of information. **6** Specific information; notification; notice. **7** *Archaic* Sexual intercourse. [OE *cnawlæc* < *cnāwan* know]

Synonyms: acquaintance, apprehension, cognition, cognizance, comprehension, erudition, experience, information, intelligence, intuition, learning, light, lore, perception, recognition, scholarship, science, wisdom. *Knowledge* is all that the mind knows, from whatever source derived or obtained, or by whatever process; the aggregate facts, truths, or principles acquired or retained by the mind, including alike the *intuitions* native to the mind and all that has been learned respecting phenomena, causes, laws, principles, literature, etc. We say of a studious man that he has a great store of *knowledge*, or of an intelligent man of the world, that he has a fund of varied *information*. We speak of *perception* of external objects, *apprehension* of intellectual truth. Simple *perception* gives a limited *knowledge* of external objects, merely as such; the *cognition* of the same objects is a *knowledge* of them in some relation; *cognizance* is the formal or official *recognition* of something as an object of *knowledge*; we take *cognizance* of it. *Intuition* is primary *knowledge* antecedent to all teaching or reasoning; *experience* is *knowledge* that has entered directly into one's own life; as, a child's *experience* that fire will burn. See ACQUAINTANCE, EDUCATION, LEARNING, SCIENCE, WISDOM. *Antonyms:* ignorance, illiteracy, inexperience, misapprehension, misconception, misunderstanding, rudeness, unfamiliarity.

knowl·edge·a·ble (nol′ij·ə·bəl) *adj. Colloq.* Having knowledge; knowing; shrewd.

known (nōn) Past participle of KNOW. — *adj.* Apprehended mentally; recognized; understood; especially, recognized by all as the truth.

know–noth·ing (nō′nuth′ing) *n.* An uneducated or ignorant person; an ignoramus.

known quantity *Math.* A quantity whose value is stated: generally denoted by one of the earlier letters of the alphabet, *a, b, c,* etc.

knub·bly (nub′lē) *adj.* Having protuberances; gnarled. [< *knubble,* dim. of *knub,* var. of KNOB]

knuck·le (nuk′əl) *n.* **1** One of the joints of the fingers, or the region about it; especially, one of the joints connecting the fingers to the rest of the hand. **2** The knee or ankle joint of certain animals, used as foods. **3** The central tubular projection of a hinge through which the pin passes. **4** In shipbuilding, an angular fitting of timbers. **5** *pl. U.S.* A children's game of marbles. — **brass knuckles** A device of metal, fitting over the knuckles, used as a protection for them in striking and to add force to the blow; also **knuck′le–dust′er.** — *v.i.* **knuckled, knuck·ling** To hold the knuckles on the ground in shooting a marble. — **to knuckle down 1** To apply oneself seriously and assiduously. **2** To yield; submit; give in: also **knuckle under.** [ME *knokel* < LG. Cf. G *knöchel,* dim. of *knochen* bone.]

knuckle bone 1 A huckle bone, as of a sheep; also, in man, one of the bones of the fingers. **2** *pl.* A children's game.

knur (nûr) *n.* A knot or knob. [ME *knorre, knurre* < MDu. knorre]

knurl (nûrl) *n.* **1** A hard substance or protuberance; knot; lump. **2** One of a series of small ridges on the edge of a thumbscrew to facilitate manual turning. **3** *Scot.* A hunchbacked dwarf. [? Dim. of KNUR] — **knurled, knurl′y** *adj.*

KO (kā′ō′) See KAYO.

ko·a·la (kō·ä′lə) *n.* An arboreal marsupial of Australia (*Phascolarctos cinereus*), having cheek pouches, large ears, gray woolly fur, and no external tail. It feeds on the leaves and buds of the eucalyptus, but descends at night to dig up and eat roots. [< native Australian name]

KOALA

kob (kob, kōb) *n.* **1** A large antelope (genus *Kobus* or *Adenota*), with elongated horns, ringed at the base, and a long tufted tail, like the waterbuck. **2** Any of the several smaller related antelopes, as a reedbuck: all natives of southern Africa. Also **ko·ba** (kō′bə). [< Senegalese]

Ko·be (kō′be) A port in southern Honshu, Japan.

KOB (*Kobus kob*)

ko·bold (kō′bold, -bōld) *n.* In German folklore, an underground being inhabiting mines and caves; goblin; gnome. [< G; ult. origin unknown]

physician and bacteriologist; discovered pathogenic bacteria of tuberculosis and cholera.

Kock (kôk), **Paul de,** 1794–1871, French novelist and dramatist.

Ko·da·chrome (kō′də·krōm) *n.* A full-color photographic film: a trade name.

Ko·dak (kō′dak) *n.* A small portable camera carrying a roll of sensitized film upon which a series of negatives can be quickly made: a trade name. — *v.t. & v.i.* To photograph with a Kodak.

Ko·di·ak bear (kō′dē·ak) See KADIAK BEAR.

ko·el (kō′əl) *n.* A cuckoo (genus *Eudanamys*) native to Australia, India, and the East Indies; the coee bird. [< Hind. < Skt. *kokila*]

Ko·hel·eth (kō·hel′ith) **1** The preacher: often identified with Solomon. *Eccles.* i 1–2. **2** The book of Ecclesiastes. [< Hebrew *qōheleth*]

Koh·i·nor (kō′i·nŏŏr′) A famous Indian diamond, weight (cut) about 106 carats; one of the British crown jewels since the annexation of Punjab, 1849. Also **Koh′i·noor′, Koh′i·nur′.** [< Persian *kōhinūr* mountain of light]

kohl (kōl) *n.* In Eastern countries, a powder of antimony used to darken the edges of the eyes. [< Arabic *kuhl.* Akin to ALCOHOL.]

kohl·ra·bi (kōl′rä·bē, kōl·rä′-) *n. pl.* **·bies** A variety of cabbage with an edible turnip-shaped stem. [< G < Ital. *cavoli rape (pl.)* < L *caulis* cabbage + *rapa* turnip]

Koi·ne (koi·nā′) *n.* **1** The common form of Greek, an outgrowth of the Attic dialect with many Ionic elements, used throughout the Greek world from the time of the conquests of Alexander to the sixth century A.D. Koine was the literary language of Aristotle and Plutarch, and was used in the Septuagint and the New Testament; in its spoken form it became the basis of virtually all modern Greek dialects. **2** Any mixed language that becomes the lingua franca of a region: also *koine.* [< Gk. *koinē (dialektos)* common (language)]

kok–sa·ghyz (kōk′sa·gēz′) *n.* A dandelionlike plant (*Taraxacum kok–saghyz*) native to Turkestan, the roots of which yield latex and inulin: cultivated as a source of rubber. [< Russian < Turkish *kök* a root + *sagīz* rubber]

ko·lin·sky (kə·lin′skē, kō-) *n.* Any of several minks of northern China and Russia; especially, *Mustela siberica,* the Siberian mink; also, the fur of any of these: sometimes called *Tartar Sable.* [< Russian *kolinski* of Kola, a peninsula abounding in minks]

kol·khoz (kôl·khôz′) *n.* A collective farm in the U.S.S.R. [< Russian *kol(lektivnoe)* collective + *khoz(aistvo)* farm, household]

Ko·lusch·an (kə·lush′ən) *n.* A linguistic stock of North American Indians of SE Alaska, consisting of the 18 Tlingit tribes. Also **Ko·lush′.** [< Russian *kalyuschka* piece of wood (inserted in the nether lip)]

ko·mon·dor (kō′mon·dôr′) *n.* A breed of working dog used in Hungary for ten centuries; tall, sturdy, and having a wide muzzle and long, thick, white coat. [< Magyar]

koo·doo (kōō′dōō) *n.* A large, striped African antelope (genus *Strepsiceros*), grayish-brown in color: also spelled *kudu.* [< Hottentot *kudu*]

kook (kōōk) *n. Slang* An unconventional, eccentric, or unbalanced person. [? < CUCKOO] — **kook′i·ness** *n.* — **kook′y** *adj.*

GREATER KOODOO

kook·a·bur·ra (kōōk′ə·bûr′ə) *n.* A large, insectivorous Australian kingfisher; the laughing jackass. [< native Australian]

koo·ra·jong (kōō′rə·jong) See KURRAJONG.

ko·peck (kō′pek) *n.* A small copper coin of Russia; one one-hundredth of a ruble: also spelled *copeck.* Also **ko′pek.** [< Russian *kopeïka* < *kopye* lance]

Ko·ran (kō·rän′, -ran′) *n.* The Moslem sacred scripture, written in Arabic and professing to record the revelations of Allah (God) to Mohammed: also *Alcoran, Alkoran.* [< Arabic

Qur'ān, lit., book < *quar'a* read]

Ko·re·a (kô·rē′ə, kō-) A peninsula of eastern Asia; 85,228 square miles; 1910–45 Japanese *Chosen;* divided (1948) into: **1** the **Republic of Korea (South Korea);** 36,760 square miles; capital, Seoul; and **2** the **Democratic People's Republic of Korea (North Korea);** 46,968 square miles; capital, Pyongyang.

Ko·re·an (kô·rē′ən, kō-) *adj.* Belonging or relating to Korea (Chosen) or its inhabitants. — *n.* **1** An inhabitant or a native of Korea. **2** The agglutinative language of Korea, somewhat similar to Japanese.

ko·ru·na (kô·rōō′nä) *n.* The monetary unit of Czechoslovakia. See CROWN (money). [< Czech < L *corona* crown]

Ko·rze·niow·ski (kô′zhe·nyôf′skē), **Teodor Józef Konrad** See CONRAD, JOSEPH.

Kor·zyb·ski (kôr·zib′skē), **Alfred Habdank,** 1879–1950, U.S. scientist and originator of general semantics; born in Poland.

kos (kos) *n.* A Hebrew measure of capacity of about four cubic inches. [< Hebrew, cup]

ko·sher (kō′shər) *adj.* **1** Permitted by the Jewish ceremonial law; clean; pure: said usually of food. **2** *Slang* All right; good; legitimate. — *n.* A kosher shop, also, the food sold there. — *v.t.* (kosh′ər) To make kosher. Also spelled *kasher.* [< Hebrew *kāshēr* fit, proper]

Ko·sy·gin (ko·sig′in), **Alexei Nikolayevich,** born 1904, Soviet statesman; chairman of the Council of Ministers (premier) 1964–

Ko·ta·ba·ru (kō′tə·bä′rōō) The capital of West Irian, a port in the NE part: formerly *Hollandia.*

Ko·ta Bha·ru (kō′tə bä′rōō) The capital of Kelantan, a State of Malaya. Also **Kota Ba′roe** or **Ba′ru.**

ko·to (kō′tō) *n.* A Japanese musical instrument with 13 strings, plucked with 3 plectra fastened to the thumb, index, and middle finger of the right hand, while the left adjusts the strings. [< Japanese]

Kot·ze·bue (kôt′sə·bōō), **August Friedrich Ferdinand von,** 1761–1819, German dramatist.

Kous·se·vitz·ky (kōō′sə·vit′skē), **Serge,** 1874–1951, Russian orchestral conductor active in the United States.

kow·tow (kou′tou′, kō′-) *n.* A Chinese form of obeisance: kneeling and touching the forehead to the ground before a superior. — *v.i.* **1** To make such obeisance. **2** To act in an obsequious or servile manner. Also **ko·tow** (kō′tou′). [< Chinese *k'o–t'ou,* lit., knock the head]

kraal (kräl) *n.* **1** A village or group of native huts in South Africa, usually surrounded by a stockade. **2** The social unit such a community represents. **3** An enclosure for cattle. Also spelled *craal.* [< Afrikaans, village, pen < Pg. *curral* pen for cattle. Related to CORRAL.]

kraft (kraft, kräft) *n.* A tough, usually dark-brown paper, made from high-grade sulfate wood pulp. [< G, strength]

Krag (krag) *n.* A bolt-action repeating rifle formerly used in the U.S. Army: in full, **Krag–Jör·gen·sen rifle** (-jûr′gən·sən). [after O. *Krag* and E. *Jörgensen,* Norwegian inventors]

krait (krīt) *n.* An extremely venomous dull-bluish snake (genus *Bungarus*), especially the **banded krait** (*B. fasciatus*) of the Malay Peninsula, India, and Borneo. [< Hind. *karait*]

Kra·ka·to·a (krä′kə·tō′ä) A volcanic island in the Strait of Sunda, between Java and Sumatra, Malay Archipelago; major eruption, 1883. Also **Kra′ka·tau′** (-tou′).

kra·ken (krä′kən, krä′-) *n.* A fabulous sea monster of Norwegian seas. [< Norw.]

K–ra·tion (kā′rash′ən, -rā′shən) *n.* A highly condensed emergency ration provided for soldiers of the U.S. Army.

krem·lin (krem′lin) *n.* The citadel of a Russian town. [< F < Russian *kreml'* citadel]

Krem·lin (krem′lin) **1** The citadel of Moscow, enclosing the former palace of the Czar. **2** The government of the U.S.S.R.

kreu·zer (kroit′sər) *n.* Any of several former small silver or copper coins of Austria and Germany. Also **kreut′zer.** [< G < *kreuz* cross]

krieg·spiel (krēg′spēl) *n.* A game in which figures representing troops, guns, etc., are moved about a model of the terrain in simulation of actual military maneuvers: used in the instruction or practice of military tactics. [<G *kriegspiel*, lit., war game]

Kriem·hild (krēm′hild, *Ger.* krēm′hilt) In the *Nibelungenlied*, the wife of Siegfried and sister of King Gunther; rival of Brunhild. Also **Kriem·hil·de** (krēm·hil′də).

krim·mer (krim′ər) *n.* A fur resembling Persian lamb prepared from fleece of lambs raised mostly in the Crimean Peninsula. [<G *krimmer* <*Krim* Crimea]

kris (krēs) *n.* A dagger with a wavy blade used in Malaysia: also spelled *crease, creese, cris*. [<Malay]

KRIS WITH SHEATH

Krish·na (krish′nə) 1 A celebrated Hindu deity, an incarnation of Vishnu. 2 See KISTNA. — **Krish′na·ism** *n.*

Kriss Krin·gle (kris kring′gəl) St. Nicholas; Santa Claus. [<G *Christkindl*, dim. of *Christkind* Christ child]

Kris·ti·a·ni·a (kris′chē·a′nē·ə) The former name of OSLO.

kro·na (krō′nə, *Sw.* krōō′nə) *n. pl.* **kro·nor** (krō′nôr) The Swedish monetary unit, equivalent to 100 öre. [<Sw.]

kro·ne (krō′nə) *n.* 1 *pl.* **kro·ner** (krō′nər) A gold coin, the monetary unit of Norway and Denmark, equivalent to 100 öre: also called *crown*. 2 *pl.* **kro·nen** (krō′nən) Any of several former European gold coins, equivalent in Germany to 10 marks, in Austria–Hungary to 100 heller. [<Dan.]

Kro·nos (krō′nos) In Greek mythology, the youngest of the Titans, son of Uranus and Gaea, who deposed his father, married his sister, Rhea, and was himself deposed by his son Zeus, who threw him into Tartarus with the other Titans: identified with the Roman *Saturn*: also spelled *Cronus*.

kroon (krōōn) *n. pl.* **kroons** or **kroo·ni** (krōō′nē) The monetary unit of Estonia. [<Estonian *kron*]

Kro·pot·kin (krə·pot′kin, *Russian* krô·pôt′·kēn), **Prince Peter Alexeivich**, 1842–1921, Russian geographer, anarchist, and author.

kru·bi (krōō′bē) *n.* A giant plant (*Amorphophallus titanum*) of the arum family native in Sumatra, with tuberous roots and a malodorous vaselike spathe that may grow to a diameter of 8 feet and a height of 12 feet or more: regarded as the largest flower in the world: also called *grubi*. Also **kru′but** (-but). [<native name]

kry·o·lite (krī′ə·līt), **kry·o·lith** (-lith) See CRYOLITE.

kryp·ton (krip′ton) *n.* A colorless, inert, gaseous element (symbol Kr) of the zero group in the periodic table, isolated by Ramsay in 1898. See ELEMENT. [<NL <Gk. *krypton*, neut. of *kryptos* hidden]

K–se·ries (kā′sir′ēz) *Physics* The group of shorter wavelengths in the typical X-ray spectrum of an element, believed to be caused by the transition of electrons to the quantum number of one.

Kshat·ri·ya (kshat′rē·yə) *n.* The warrior caste of the Aryan Hindus; a member of the caste. Also **Kshat′ru·ya** (-rōō-). [<Skt. *kṣatriya* <*kṣatra* rule]

Kuan Yin (kwän yin) A Chinese Buddhistic goddess: often called the Goddess of Mercy: also spelled *Kwan Yin*, or, in Japanese, *Kwannon*.

Ku·blai Khan (kōō′blī kän′), 1214–94, founder of the Mongol dynasty of China. Also *Kubla Khan*.

ku·chen (kōō′khən) *n.* A yeast dough coffee cake. [<G]

Ku·ching (kōō′ching) The capital of Sarawak, Malaysia.

ku·dos (kyōō′dos) *n.* Glory; credit; praise. [<Gk. *kydos* glory]

ku·du (kōō′dōō) See KOODOO.

kud·zu-vine (kŏŏd′zōō-vīn′) *n.* A hairy, fragrant climbing vine of China and Japan (*Pueraria thunbergiana*). A fiber from the inner bark is used by the Japanese for fabrics and cordage. [<Japanese]

Kuen·lun (kōōn′lōōn′) See KUNLUN.

Ku·fic (kyōō′fik) *adj.* Relating to Kufa, an ancient Arabian city on the Euphrates, or to the primitive Arabic characters used by its writers, and in which the Koran was originally written. — *n.* The Arabic alphabet, as written at Kufa. Also spelled *Cufic*.

Ku·fra (kōō′frä) A group of oases in the center of the Libyan Desert, southern Cyrenaica, Libya. *Italian* **Cu′fra**.

Ku Klux Klan (kyōō′ kluks′ klan′) *n.* 1 A secret society in the southern United States after the Civil War, aiming to prevent Negro ascendency. 2 A modern secret society, founded in 1915 at Atlanta, Ga., aiming at arbitrary regulation of life by white Protestants: also **Ku–Klux Klan**. 3 A member of either society. [Alter. of Gk. *kyklos* a circle] — **Ku′ Klux′ Klan′ner**.

ku·lak (kōō′lak, kyōō′-, kōō·lak′, kyōō-) *n.* A well-to-do Russian peasant employing hired labor: the object of particular liquidation by the Soviet government after the Bolshevik revolution. [<Russian, lit., fist, tight-fisted man <Estonian]

Kul·tur (kŏŏl·tōōr′) *n.* Progress, achievement, and efficiency, in all phases, practical or theoretical, of political, economic, social, scientific, or artistic life. [<G]

ku·miss (kōō′mis) *n.* Fermented mare's milk, used by the Tatar tribes of central Asia, or a drink made in imitation of it: often spelled *koumiss, koumys*. Also **ku′mys**. [<Russian *kumys* <Tatar *kumix*]

küm·mel (kim′əl, *Ger.* kü′məl) *n.* A German or Russian liqueur flavored with aniseed, cumin, or caraway. [<G, caraway seed <L *cuminum*]

kum·mer·bund (kum′ər·bund) See CUMMERBUND.

kum·quat (kum′kwot) *n.* 1 A small citrus tree (genus *Fortunella*) cultivated in China, Japan, and the United States. 2 Its acid, plumlike, orange-colored fruit. Also spelled *cumquat*. [Cantonese alter. of Mandarin *chinchü*, lit., golden orange]

Kun (kōōn), **Béla**, 1886–1938?, Hungarian Communist leader; premier 1919.

Kun·dry (kōōn′drē) In Wagner's *Parsifal*, a beautiful woman, slave of Klingsor, doomed to eternal penitence for having laughed at Christ while he carried the cross. She is redeemed from sin by Parsifal.

K'ung Fu–tse (kŏŏng′ fōō′tse′) See CONFUCIUS.

Ku·ni·yo·shi (kōō·nē·yō·shē), **Yasuo**, 1893–1953, U. S. painter born in Japan.

Kun·lun (kōōn′lōōn′) A series of mountain ranges in northern Tibet and southern Sinkiang; highest altitude, 25,340 feet: also *Kuenlun*.

Kun·ming (kōōn′ming′) The capital of Yunnan province, China: formerly *Yunnan*.

kunz·ite (kōōnts′īt) *n.* A lilac-colored variety of spodumene, used as a gemstone: found at Pala, California. [after G. F. *Kunz*, 1856–1932, U. S. mineralogist]

Kuo·min·tang (kwō′min′tang′) *n.* The nationalist party of China, founded in 1912 by Sun Yat-sen and led since 1927 by Chiang Kai-shek; defeated and ousted by the Chinese Communists following the Chinese civil war (1945–49). It retains control of Taiwan. [< Chinese *kuo* nationalist + *min* people's + *tang* party]

kur·bash (kōōr′bash) *n.* A whip of heavy hide, used as an instrument of torture by the Turks. [<Turkish *qirbāch*]

Kurd (kûrd, kōōrd) *n.* One of a Moslem people dwelling chiefly in Kurdistan.

Kurd·ish (kûr′dish, kōōr′-) *adj.* Of or pertaining to the Kurds, their culture, or language. — *n.* The Iranian language of the Kurds.

Kur·di·stan (kûr′di·stan, kōōr′di·stän) A region in NW Iran, NE Iraq, and SE Turkey in Asia.

kur·ra·jong (kûr′ə·jong) *n.* Any of various Australian trees of the families *Sterculiaceae* and *Malvaceae* whose leaves are valued as fodder; especially, the black **kurrajong** (*Brachychiton populneum*), whose bark yields a durable, tough fiber: also spelled *currajong, koorajong*. [< native name]

kur·to·sis (kər·tō′sis) *n. Stat.* The relative degree of curvature near the mode of a frequency curve, as compared with that of a normal curve of the same variance. [<Gk. *kyrtos* curved + -OSIS]

Ku·tu·zov (kōō·tōō′zôf), **Mikhail Ilarionovich**, 1745–1813, Russian field marshal; defeated Napoleon at Smolensk (1812).

ku·vasz (kōō′väsh) *n.* A breed of large, powerful working dog with a thick, white coat. [<Magyar]

Ku·wait (kōō·wīt′) A sheikdom in NE Arabia; 1,930 square miles; capital, Kuwait: also *Koweit*. — **Ku·wait′i** *n. & adj.*

Kuz·netsk Basin (kōōz·nyetsk′) The richest coal basin in the U.S.S.R., comprising a region along the Tom in the south central Russian S.F.S.R. in Asia. Shortened form **Kuz·bas** (kōōz·bäs′).

kvass (kväs, kvas) *n.* A Russian fermented drink resembling sour beer, made from rye, barley, etc. [<Russian *kvas*]

kwash·i·or·kor (kwäsh′ē·ôr′kôr) *n. Pathol.* A nutritional disease prevalent among children in South Africa and elsewhere, characterized by swelling of the hands, feet, and face and the appearance of discolored blotches on the body. It is associated with a carbohydrate diet low in proteins and amino acids. Also called *Johnny red.* [< native name]

Kwei·lin (kwä′lin′, *Chinese* gwä′lin′) The capital of Kwangsi province, China.

Kwei·sui (kwä′swä′, *Chinese* gwä′swä′) The capital of Suiyuan province, northern China.

Kwei·yang (kwä′yang′, *Chinese* gwä′yäng′) The capital of Kweichow province, China.

ky·a·nite (kī′ə·nīt) See CYANITE.

ky·an·ize (kī′ən·īz) *v.t.* **-ized, -iz·ing** To impregnate, as wood, with mercuric chloride so as to prevent decay. Also, *Brit.* **ky′an·ise**. [< after J. H. *Kyan*, 1774–1850, Irish inventor] — **ky′an·i·za′tion** (-ə·zā′shən, -ī·zā′-) *n.*

kyar (kyär) See COIR.

Kyd (kid), **Thomas**, 1558–94, English dramatist.

ky·lix (kī′liks) *n. pl.* **ky·li·kes** (kī′li·kēz) A shallow, circular, earthenware drinking cup, having small handles at the sides and resting on a slender, moderately high foot: used chiefly at banquets in ancient Greece: also spelled *cylix*. [<Gk., cup]

KYLIX

ky·mo·graph (kī′mə·graf, -gräf) *n.* 1 *Med.* An instrument for recording wavelike oscillations, composed of a revolving tambour on which a stylus records pulse waves, muscular contractions, respiratory movements, and the like. 2 *Aeron.* A device for recording the oscillations of an aircraft in flight. Also **ky′mo·graph′i·on** (-ē·on): sometimes spelled *cymograph*. [<Gk. *kyma* wave + -GRAPH] — **ky′mo·graph′ic** *adj.*

Kym·ric (kim′rik), **Kym·ry** (kim′rē) See CYMRIC, etc.

Kyn·e·wulf (kin′ə·wŏŏlf, kün′-) See CYNEWULF.

Kyo·ga (kyō′gə), **Lake** A lake in central Uganda in the middle course of the Victoria Nile: also *Kioga*.

Kyong·song (kyông·sông) See SEOUL.

Kyo·to (kyō·tō) A city on SW Honshu island, Japan; the third largest city and the capital of the Japanese Empire until 1868: also *Kioto*.

ky·pho·sis (kī·fō′sis) *n. Pathol.* Backward curvature of the spine; humpback. [<NL <Gk. *kyphōsis* <*kyphos* humpbacked] — **ky·phot·ic** (kī·fot′ik) *adj.*

Kyr·i·e e·le·i·son (kir′i·ē i·lā′i·sən) *Eccl.* 1 An ancient petition used in eucharistic rites and other offices: **a** In the Greek Church, a response made by the people to prayers said in the liturgy. **b** In the Roman Catholic Church, a part of a short litany said or chanted immediately after the introit of the mass. 2 In the Anglican Church, a translation of this, said or chanted during the Eucharist. 3 A musical setting for this petition. [<LL <Gk. *Kyrie eleēson* Lord, have mercy]

kyr·i·o·log·ic (kir′ē·ə·loj′ik) See CURIOLOGIC.

kyte (kīt) *n. Scot.* The belly.

L

l, L (el) *n.* *pl.* **l's, L's** or **ls, Ls** or **ells** (elz) **1** The 12th letter of the English alphabet: from Phoenician *lamed*, Greek *lambda*, Roman *L.* **2** The sound of the letter *l*, normally a voiced alveolar continuant. See ALPHABET. —*symbol* **1** The Roman numeral 50: see under NUMERAL. **2** *Chem.* Lithium (L). **3** Anything shaped like an л.

la¹ (lä) *n.* *Music* The sixth tone of the diatonic scale. [<Ital. <Med. L. See GAMUT.]

la² (lä, lô) *interj.* Look! O!: an exclamation expressing surprise, emphasis, etc. Also spelled *law.* [OE *lā.* Doublet of LO.]

L.A. (el'ā') *Colloq.* Los Angeles.

laa·ger (lä'gər) *n.* A defensive enclosure formed by wagons or otherwise; camp. —*v.t.* & *v.i.* To camp in or form into a laager. Also spelled *lager.* [<Afrikaans <Du. *leger* a camp]

lab·a·rum (lab'ə·rəm) *n.* *pl.* **·ra** (-rə) **1** The form of the Roman military standard adopted by Constantine, bearing the cross and the monogram of Christ. **2** An ecclesiastical banner borne in processions. [<LL <Gk. *labaron*; ult. origin unknown]

lab·da·num (lab'də·nəm) See LADANUM.

lab·e·fac·tion (lab'ə·fak'shən) *n.* The act of making or becoming weak or tottering; decay; downfall. Also *Archaic* **lab'e·fac·ta'tion** (-fak-tā'shən). [<L *labefactus*, pp. of *labefacere* cause to totter <*labare* totter, fall to pieces + *facere* make]

la·bel (lā'bəl) *n.* **1** A slip, as of paper, affixed to something and bearing an inscription to indicate its character, ownership, etc. **2** *Archit.* A projecting molding or dripstone over a wall opening. —*v.t.* **·beled** or **·belled**, **·bel·ing** or **·bel·ling 1** To mark with a label; attach a label to. **2** To classify; designate. [<OF, a ribbon, ? <OHG *lappa* a rag] —**la'bel·er** or **la'bel·ler** *n.*

la·bel·lum (lə·bel'əm) *n.* *pl.* **·la** (-ə) **1** *Bot.* The lip or lower petal of an orchid, often enlarged or variously shaped. **2** *Entomol.* Part of the proboscis of a dipterous insect. [<NL <L, dim. of *labrum* a lip]

la·bi·a (lā'bē·ə) Plural of LABIUM.

la·bi·al (lā'bē·əl) *adj.* **1** Of or pertaining to the lips: a *labial* vein. **2** *Phonet.* Formed, articulated, or modified by the lips, as (p), (b), (m), (w), or the rounded vowels (ō) and (ōō). **3** Having edges or lips, as an organ pipe. **4** Pertaining to the labia. —*n.* **1** *Phonet.* A labial sound. **2** An appliance designed to correct stammering. **3** An organ pipe with lips. [<Med. L *labialis* <L *labium* a lip]

la·bi·al·ize (lā'bē·əl·īz') *v.t.* **·ized**, **·iz·ing** *Phonet.* **1** To make labial; give a labial sound to. **2** To modify (a vowel) by rounding the lips; round. —**la'bi·al·ism, la'bi·al·i·za'tion** *n.*

la·bi·a ma·jo·ra (lā'bē·ə mə·jō'rə) *Anat.* The external mucous folds of the vulva. [<NL <L, lit., the larger lips]

labia mi·no·ra (mi·nō'rə) *Anat.* The inner mucous folds of the vulva. [<NL <L, lit., the smaller lips]

La·bi·a·tae (lā'bē·ā'tē) *n. pl.* A family of widely distributed herbs and shrubs with characteristically square stems, opposite leaves, and whorled flowers: it includes mint, hyssop, thyme, and many other aromatic and medicinal plants. [<NL <*labiatus* LABIATE]

la·bi·ate (lā'bē·āt, -it) *adj.* *Bot.* **1** Having lips or liplike parts, as a calyx or corolla. **2** Belonging to the Labiatae. Also **la'bi·at'ed.** [<NL *labiatus* <L *labium* a lip]

La·biche (lȧ·bēsh'), **Eugène Marin**, 1815–88, French dramatist.

la·bile (lā'bil) *adj.* **1** Prone to undergo chemical change or alteration of atomic structure; unstable. **2** Having a tendency to glide from place to place; smoothly flowing or passing along. **3** Liable to err, slip, or fall. **4** Being free and uncontrolled: said of the emotions. [<L *labilis* <*labi* slip, fall] —**la·bil'i·ty** *n.*

labio– *combining form* Related to, or formed by the lips and (another organ): *labiodental.* [<L *labium* a lip]

la·bi·o·den·tal (lā'bē·ō·den'təl) *Phonet.* *adj.* Formed with the lower lip and the upper front

teeth, as *f* and *v* in English. —*n.* A sound so formed. Also *dentilabial.*

la·bi·o·na·sal (lā'bē·ō·nā'zəl) *Phonet.* *adj.* Produced with the lips closed and the voiced breath passing through the nose, as *m.* —*n.* A sound so formed.

la·bi·o·ve·lar (lā'bē·ō·vē'lər) *Phonet.* *adj.* Produced with the lips rounded and partially closed and the back of the tongue near or against the velum, as *w.* —*n.* A sound so formed.

la·bi·um (lā'bē·əm) *n.* *pl.* **·bi·a** (-bē·ə) **1** A lip or liplike organ or part. **2** *pl.* The folds of the external genitals of the mammalian female. **3** *Entomol.* A movable sclerite between the maxillae of an insect, forming the lower surface of the mouth; the lower lip. [<L, a lip]

la·bor (lā'bər) *n.* **1** Physical or mental exertion, particularly for some useful or desired end; toil; work. **2** That which requires exertion or effort; a task. **3** The working class collectively. **4** Parturition; travail. **5** Any stress or difficulty. **6** *Naut.* Heavy rolling and pitching of a vessel. — **Department of Labor** An executive department of the U. S. government, since 1913 (from 1903 to 1913 part of the Department of Commerce and Labor) headed by the Secretary of Labor and charged with matters pertaining to the welfare of wage earners, especially in regard to wages, working conditions, and opportunities for employment. Also **Labor Department.** See synonyms under BUSINESS, INDUSTRY, TASK, TOIL¹, WORK. —*v.i.* **1** To do work; toil; strive to accomplish a work or purpose. **2** To move with difficulty or painful exertion. **3** To roll or pitch, as a ship in a heavy sea. **4** To be hindered, burdened, or oppressed: to *labor* under a misapprehension. **5** To suffer the pains of childbirth; be in travail. —*v.t.* **6** To work at laboriously; develop in great detail: to *labor* a point. **7** *Archaic* or *Poetic* To till; cultivate. Also, *Brit.* **labour.** [<OF *labor, labour* <L *labor, -oris* toil, distress]

lab·o·ra·to·ry (lab'rə·tôr'ē, -tō'rē; *Brit.* lə·bor'ə·trē) *n.* *pl.* **·ries 1** A building or room fitted up for conducting scientific experiments, analyses, or similar work. **2** A department, as in a factory, for research, testing, and experimental technical work. [<Med. L *laboratorium* <L *laborare* labor <*labor, -oris* labor]

Labor Day In most States of the United States, a legal holiday, usually the first Monday in September, originally set aside as a holiday in honor of labor.

la·bored (lā'bərd) *adj.* Performed laboriously; elaborate; strained: a *labored* joke.

la·bor·er (lā'bər·ər) *n.* One who performs physical or manual, especially unskilled, labor.

la·bo·ri·ous (lə·bôr'ē·əs, -bō'rē·əs) *adj.* **1** Requiring much labor; toilsome. **2** Diligent; industrious. See synonyms under ARDUOUS, DIFFICULT, WEARISOME. —**la·bo'ri·ous·ly** *adv.* —**la·bo'ri·ous·ness** *n.* [<OF *laborios* <L *laboriosus* <*labor* labor]

la·bor·ite (lā'bər·īt) *n.* One who supports labor interests, especially in politics. Also *Brit.* **la'bour·ite.**

labor union A union of workers organized to better working conditions and advance mutual interests; a trade union.

la·bour (lā'bər), **la·bour·er** (lā'bər·ər), etc. British spelling of LABOR, etc.

La·bour·ite (lā'bər·īt) *n.* A member of a Labour party in Great Britain or the Commonwealth.

Labour Party 1 In Great Britain, a political party drawing its chief support from the working class and committed to socialistic reform. Organized in the later 19th century, by the 1920's it had supplanted the Liberal Party as the chief opposition to the Conservative Party. **2** A similar party in other members of the Commonwealth.

Labrador auk See PUFFIN.

lab·ra·dor·ite (lab'rə·dôr'īt) *n.* A triclinic lime-soda feldspar exhibiting a brilliant play of colors. [from *Labrador*, where originally found + -ITE¹]

la·bret (lā'bret) *n.* A stud or plug of hard material, as stone, worn as an ornament in a hole pierced in the lip by various primitive peoples. [Dim. of LABRUM]

la·broid (lā'broid) *adj.* Of or pertaining to a family (*Labridae*) of fishes including the wrasses, tautog, etc. —*n.* A labroid fish. [< NL *Labroidea* <*Labrus* a genus of the family *Labridae* <L *labrus* a kind of fish <*labrum* a lip]

la·brum (lā'brəm, lab'rəm) *n.* *pl.* **·bra** (-brə) **1** A lip (especially an outer lip) or a liplike part. **2** *Entomol.* A usually movable sclerite situated between the mandibles of an insect; the upper lip. **3** *Zool.* The outer lip of a univalve shell. [<L, a lip]

la·bur·num (lə·bûr'nəm) *n.* Any of a genus (*Laburnum*) of deciduous Old World trees, especially the **golden–chain laburnum** (*L. anagyroides*), having pendulous racemes of yellow flowers and hard, dark wood: it yields a poisonous alkaloid used in medicine as a purgative and emetic. [<NL <L; ult. origin unknown]

lab·y·rinth (lab'ə·rinth) *n.* **1** A confusing network of passages, as in a building; a maze of intricate paths, as in a park or garden. **2** Hence, any perplexing combination. **3** *Anat.* The winding passages of the internal ear. [<LABYRINTH] —**lab'y·rin'thine** (-thin, -thēn) or **thi·an** or **·thic** or **·thi·cal** *adj.* —**lab'y·rin'thi·cal·ly** *adv.*

THE LABYRINTH OF MINOS

Lab·y·rinth (lab'ə·rinth) In Greek mythology, the maze used to confine the Minotaur, constructed by Daedalus for Minos of Crete. [<L *labyrinthus* <Gk. *labyrinthos*; ult. origin unknown]

lac (lak) *n.* **1** A resinous substance exuded from an East Indian lac insect (*Tachardia lacca*) and used in making varnishes, etc. Compare SHELLAC. **2** The sap of certain trees or plants used for varnish. **3** Lacquer. [< Hind. *lākh* <Prakrit *lakkha* <Skt. *lākshā*]

lac·case (lak'ās) *n.* A copper–protein enzyme which oxidizes phenols, found in the lacquer tree and other plants. [< NL *lacc(a)* lacquer + -ASE]

lac·cate (lak'āt) *adj.* *Bot.* Having a varnished appearance, as the leaves of certain plants. [<NL *lacc(a)* lacquer + -ATE¹]

lace (lās) *n.* **1** A cord or string for fastening together the parts of a shoe, a corset, etc.; any string. **2** A delicate network of threads of linen, silk, cotton, etc., arranged in figures

TYPES OF LACE
Alencon   Battenberg   Blonde   Pointe
   Mechlin   Honiton   d'Angleterre

or patterns; also, any ornamental cord or braid. **3** A dash of spirits, as in tea or coffee. —*v.* **laced, lac·ing** *v.t.* **1** To fasten or draw together by tying the lace or laces of. **2** To pass (a cord or string) through hooks, eyelets, etc., as a lace. **3** To trim with or as with lace. **4** To compress the waist of (a person) by tightening laces, as of a corset. **5** To intertwine or interlace. **6** To streak, as with color. **7** To add a dash of spirits to. **8** *Colloq.* To beat; thrash. —*v.i.* **9** To be fastened by means of a lace. — **to lace into** To strike or attack with or as with a heavy blow or blows. [<OF *laz, las* orig. a noose <L *laqueus* a noose, trap. Akin to LASH, LATCH.]

Lac·e·dae·mon (las′ə·dē′mən) See SPARTA.

Lac·e·dae·mo·ni·an (las′ə·di·mō′nē·ən) *adj.* & *n.* Spartan; Laconian.

lace-ground (lās′ground′) *n.* A foundation of lacelike net; a réseau.

lac·er·ate (las′ər·āt) *v.t.* **·at·ed**, **·at·ing** **1** To tear raggedly, as the flesh. **2** To hurt; injure, as the feelings. See synonyms under REND. — *adj.* Rent; jagged; torn. [<L *laceratus*, pp. of *lacerare* < *lacer* mangled] — **lac′er·a·ble** *adj.* — **lac′er·a′tion** *n.* — **lac′er·a′tive** *adj.*

lac·er·til·i·an (las′ər·til′ē·ən) *n.* One of a suborder of reptiles (*Lacertilia*) which includes lizards, chameleons, and related limbless forms. — *adj.* Of or pertaining to the *Lacertilia*: also **la·cer·ti·an** (lə·sûr′shē·ən, ·shən). [<NL *Lacertilia* <L *lacertus, lacerta* a lizard]

lace·wing (lās′wing′) *n.* Any of certain insects (order *Neuroptera*) having four lacy wings and shiny eyes, especially the green lacewing (genus *Chrysopa*) or the brown lacewing (genus *Hemerobius*), the larvae of which destroy insects. For illustration see INSECT (beneficial).

lace·wood (lās′wŏŏd′) *n.* **1** The American sycamore. **2** The silky oak (*Cardwellia sublimis*) of Queensland, Australia. **3** The wood of either of these trees, used for furniture, cabinetwork, and veneering.

lace·work (lās′wûrk′) *n.* **1** Lace. **2** Any openwork resembling lace.

lach·es (lach′iz) *n. Law* Inexcusable delay in asserting a right. [<AF *laches, lachesse,* OF *laschesse* < *lasche* negligent < *laschier* slacken <L *laxare* < *laxus* lax]

lac·ing (lā′sing) *n.* **1** The act of fastening, as with a lace. **2** Lace (def. 1). **3** A connecting or strengthening member; crosspiece. **4** *Colloq.* A thrashing. **5** Any ornamental braid, as of gold or silver.

la·cin·i·ate (lə·sin′ē·āt, ·it) *adj.* **1** Bordered with fringe; fringed. **2** *Bot.* Slashed or cut irregularly into narrow lobes or segments; fringed; incised, as flower petals. Also **la·cin′i·at·ed**, **la·cin′i·ose** (·ōs). [<NL *lacinia* a slash in a leaf or petal (<L, a flap) + ·ATE[1]]

lack (lak) *v.t.* **1** To be without; have none or too little of. **2** To be short by; require: It *lacks* two months till summer. — *v.i.* **3** To be wanting or deficient; be missing. — *n.* **1** The state of being needy. **2** Want; deficiency; failure. [ME *lac,* prob. <MLG *lak* deficiency]

lack·a·dai·si·cal (lak′ə·dā′zi·kəl) *adj.* Affectedly sentimental; languishing; listless. Also **lack′a·dai′sy** (·dā′zē). [<*lackadaisy,* alter. of LACKADAY.] — **lack′a·dai′si·cal·ly** *adv.* — **lack′a·dai′si·cal·ness** *n.*

lack·a·day (lak′ə·dā′) *interj. Archaic* Alack!: an exclamation expressing grief or regret. [Aphetic var. of ALACKADAY. See ALACK.]

lack·ey (lak′ē) *n.* **1** A male servant; a footman; menial. **2** Any servile attendant or follower. — *v.t.* & *v.i.* To attend or act as a lackey. Also LACQUEY. [<OF *laquay* <Sp. *lacayo,* ? <Arabic *luka′* servile]

lack·lus·ter (lak′lus′tər) *adj.* Wanting luster; dim. — *n.* A lack of luster; dullness; also, that which wants luster. Also *Brit.* **lack′lus′tre.**

La·co·ni·a (lə·kō′nē·ə) A region and ancient country in the SE Peloponnesus, Greece; 1,500 square miles; capital, Sparta: Modern Greek *Lakonía.* Also **La·con·i·ca** (lə·kon′i·kə). — **La·co′ni·an** *adj.* & *n.*

la·con·ic (lə·kon′ik) *adj.* Using or consisting of few words; short and forceful; concise; pithy. Also **la·con′i·cal.** See synonyms under TERSE. [<L *Laconicus* <Gk. *Lakonikos* <*Lakon* a Spartan; with ref. to the habitual terseness of Spartan speech] — **la·con′i·cal·ly** *adv.*

lac·o·nism (lak′ə·niz′əm) *n.* **1** A brief and sententious manner of expression. **2** A terse, pointed phrase; laconic expression. Also **la·con·i·cism** (lə·kon′ə·siz′əm).

lac·quer (lak′ər) *n.* **1** A quick-drying varnish made from pyroxylin or other resin, nitrocellulose, and sometimes a pigment, dissolved in a volatile solvent. **2** Varnished woodwork, often inlaid: Chinese *lacquer,* Japanese *lacquer*: also **lac′quer·work′**. **3** A resinous varnish susceptible of a fine polish, obtained from the lacquer tree (*Toxicodendron verniciffuum*) of China and Japan. **4** Decorative work, as on leather lacquered in imitation of enamel. — *v.t.* To coat or varnish with lacquer. Also **lack′er.** [<MF *lacre* a kind of sealing wax <Pg. <*lacca* gum lac <Hind. *lākh* LAC[1]; infl. in form by F *lacque* LAC[1]] — **lac′quer·er** *n.*

lac·ri·mal (lak′rə·məl) *adj.* **1** Of or pertaining to tears. **2** Pertaining to or related to tear-producing organs. — *n.* A lacrimatory. Also spelled *lachrymal.* [<Med. L *lacrimalis, lacrymalis* <L *lacrima* a tear]

lac·ri·mar·y (lak′rə·mer′ē) *adj.* Pertaining to, containing, or meant to contain tears: also *lacrimatory.* Also spelled *lachrymary.* [<L *lacrima*]

lac·ri·ma·tion (lak′rə·mā′shən) *n.* **1** The act of shedding tears. **2** The secretion of tears. [<L *lacrimatio, -onis* <*lacrimatus,* pp. of *lacrimare* shed tears <*lacrima* a tear]

lac·ri·ma·tor (lak′rə·mā′tər) *n.* Any of various chemicals which, on being released from shells, bombs, or other containers, provoke a copious flow of tears, with irritation of the eyes: also called *tear gas.* [<L *lacrima* a tear + ·ATOR]

lac·ri·ma·to·ry (lak′rə·mə·tôr′ē, ·tō′rē) *n. pl.* **·ries** A small, narrow-necked glass bottle of a type found in ancient tombs, formerly supposed to have contained the tears of mourners. — *adj.* Lacrimary. Also spelled *lachrymatory.* [<Med. L *lacrimatorium* <L, neut. of *lacrimatorius* of tears <*lacrima* a tear]

LACRIMATORY

lac·ri·mose (lak′rə·mōs) *adj.* Shedding, or given to shedding, tears; tearful: also spelled *lachrymose.* [<L *lacrimosus* <*lacrima* a tear] — **lac′ri·mose′ly** *adv.*

la·crosse (lə·krôs′, ·kros′) *n.* A ball game of American Indian origin, played by two teams of ten men each: the object of each side is to advance the ball across the field with a long, racketlike implement (the *crosse*) between the opponents' goal posts. [<F *la crosse,* lit., the crozier, hooked stick]

lac·tam (lak′tam) *n. Chem.* Any of a series of organic ring compounds containing the CO·NH group and formed by the elimination of water from the carboxyl and amino groups. [<LACT- + AM(INO)]

lac·ta·ry (lak′tər·ē) *adj.* Of or pertaining to milk. [<L *lactarius* <*lac, lactis* milk]

lac·tase (lak′tās) *n. Biochem.* An enzyme present in the digestive juices, in certain yeasts, etc., and capable of changing lactose into glucose and galactose.

lac·tate (lak′tāt) *v.i.* **·tat·ed**, **·tat·ing** **1** To form or secrete milk. **2** To suckle young. — *n.* A salt or ester of lactic acid. — **lac·ta′tion** *n.*

lac·te·al (lak′tē·əl) *adj.* Pertaining to or like milk; conveying a milklike fluid: also **lac′te·an, lac′te·ous.** — *n. Anat.* One of the lymphatic vessels that take up and convey the chyle. [<L *lacteus* <*lac, lactis* milk]

lac·tes·cence (lak·tes′əns) *n.* The quality of being milklike; milkiness. Also **lac·tes′cen·cy.**

lac·tes·cent (lak·tes′ənt) *adj.* **1** Milklike; becoming milky. **2** Having or secreting a milky juice. [<L *lactescens, -entis,* ppr. of *lactescere,* inceptive of *lactere* be milky <*lac, lactis* milk]

lac·tic (lak′tik) *adj.* **1** Of, pertaining to, or derived from milk. **2** *Chem.* Designating a limpid sirupy acid, **lactic acid,** $C_3H_6O_3$, with a very bitter taste, contained in sour milk, and the result of lactic fermentation in many compounds.

lac·tif·er·ous (lak·tif′ər·əs) *adj.* **1** Conveying or containing milk or milky fluid; lacteal. **2** Yielding a milky juice, as certain plants. [<LL *lactifer* milk-bearing <L *lac, lactis* milk + *-fer* -FEROUS]

lacto- *combining form* Milk: lactogenic. Also, before vowels, **lact-.** [<L *lac, lactis* milk]

lac·to·ba·cil·lus (lak′tō·bə·sil′əs) *n. pl.* **·cil·li** (·sil′ī) Any aerobic, rod-shaped bacterium of a genus (*Lactobacillus*) which forms lactic acid, especially *L. acidophilus,* used in the dairy industry and in fermentation processes. [<NL <L *lac, lactis* milk + BACILLUS]

lac·to·fla·vin (lak′tō·flā′vin) See RIBOFLAVIN.

lac·to·gen·ic (lak′tō·jen′ik) *adj.* **1** Stimulating the milk glands. **2** Designating a hormone, as prolactin, which stimulates the secretion of milk.

lac·to·glob·u·lin (lak′tō·glob′yə·lin) *n.* A globulin of milk.

lac·tom·e·ter (lak·tom′ə·tər) *n.* A hydrometer for determining the density or richness of milk.

lac·tone (lak′tōn) *n. Chem.* One of a class of organic anhydrides in which the molecule of water is derived from hydroxyl and carboxyl, both contained in the same radical, with the etherification of the acid part by the alcoholic part. [<LACT- + -ONE] — **lac·ton·ic** (lak·ton′ik) *adj.*

lac·to·pro·te·in (lak′tō·prō′tē·in, ·tēn) *n.* A protein derived from milk.

lac·to·scope (lak′tə·skōp) *n.* An instrument for determining the purity or richness of milk.

lac·tose (lak′tōs) *n. Biochem.* A white, odorless, crystalline disaccharide, $C_{12}H_{22}O_{11} \cdot H_2O$, present in milk; milk sugar. [<LACT(O)- + -OSE[2]]

lac·tu·ca·ri·um (lak′tŏŏ·kâr′ē·əm) *n.* The wild lettuce (*Lactuca virosa*) or its inspissated milky juice, used as a sedative. [<NL <L *lactuca* lettuce]

La Cum·bre (lä kŏŏm′brä) See USPALLATA.

la·cu·na (lə·kyōō′nə) *n. pl.* **·nas** or **·nae** (·nē) **1** A space from which something is wanting or has been omitted; hiatus; gap. **2** A small pit, hollow, or depression; a gap or small opening. **3** *Anat.* One of the cavities in which lie the osteoblasts of bone. Also **la·cune** (·kyōōn′). [<L, a hole, pool <*lacus* a basin, pond]

la·cu·nar (lə·kyōō′nər) *adj.* **1** Of or pertaining to a lacuna. **2** Containing or having lacunae: also **la·cu′nal.** — *n. pl.* **la·cu·nars** or **la·cu·nar·i·a** (lak′yŏŏ·nâr′ē·ə) *Archit.* **1** A sunken panel or coffer in a ceiling or a soffit. **2** A ceiling or a soffit having sunken panels or compartments. — **lac·u·nar·y** (lak′yŏŏ·ner′ē) *adj.*

la·cu·nose (lə·kyōō′nōs) *adj.* Marked by shallow depressions. [<L *lacunosus* <*lacuna.* See LACUNA.]

la·cus·trine (lə·kus′trin) *adj.* **1** Of or pertaining to a lake. **2** Found in or growing in lakes, as certain plants. **3** Formed in or near lakes, as geological deposits. Also **la·cus′tral, la·cus′tri·an.** [<L *lacus* a lake]

lac·y (lā′sē) *adj.* **lac·i·er, lac·i·est 1** Lacelike. **2** Of lace. — **lac′i·ly** *adv.* — **lac′i·ness** *n.*

lad (lad) *n.* A boy or youth; companion; fellow. Also **lad′die.** [<ME *ladde,* ? ult. <ON]

lad·a·num (lad′ə·nəm) *n.* A dark-colored, brittle, bitter resin from various species of the rockrose (genus *Cistus*): often spelled *labdanum.* See LAUDANUM. [<L *ladanum, ledanum* <Gk. *ladanon, lēdanon* <*lēdon* mastic]

lad·der (lad′ər) *n.* **1** A device of wood, rope, etc., for climbing and descending: usually a series of rounds, supported at their ends by long sidepieces; also, any means of ascending. **2** A run in a stocking or other knit fabric. **3** *Mil.* A three-round burst fired rapidly from a gun pointing in the same direction but with the second and third rounds at a decreased range. [OE *hlǽdder*]

lad·der·back (lad′ər·bak′) *n.* A chair back constructed with two posts connected by horizontal slats; also, a chair having such a back.

ladder stitch An embroidery stitch giving a ladder effect.

lade (lād) *v.* **lad·ed, lad·ed** or **lad·en, lad·ing** *v.t.* **1** To load with a burden or cargo; also, to load as a cargo. **2** To weigh down; burden; oppress. **3** To dip or lift (a liquid) in or out with a ladle or dipper. — *v.i.* **4** To receive cargo. **5** To dip or lift a liquid. See synonyms under LOAD. [OE *hladan* load]

lad·en[1] (lād′n) Alternative past participle of LADE. — *adj.* Burdened: *laden* with care.

lad·en[2] (lād′n) *v.t.* & *v.i.* **lad·ened, lad·en·ing** To lade. [Var. of LADE]

ladies' room In a public building, a room or rooms provided with toilet facilities for women.

lad·ing (lā′ding) *n.* **1** The act of loading. **2** A load or cargo.

la·di·no (lə·dē′nō) *n. SW U.S.* A horse that is cunning as well as vicious and unmanageable. [<Sp., cunning, crafty]

La·di·no (lä·dē′nō) *n.* **1** A Spanish dialect, with many Hebrew elements, spoken by Turkish and other Sephardic Jews. **2** In Latin America, a mestizo. [<Sp., wise, learned, <L *Latinus* Latin]

la·dle (lād′l) *n.* **1** A cup-shaped vessel, with a long handle, for dipping or conveying liquids. **2** A millwheel float. —*v.t.* **·dled, ·dling** To dip up and carry in a ladle. [OE *hlædel* <*hladan* lade] —**la′dler** *n.*

La·do·ga (lä′dô·gä), **Lake** The largest lake in Europe, in NW European U.S.S.R.; 7,100 square miles. *Finnish* **Laa·tok·ka** (lä′tôk·kä).

La·don (lā′dən) In Greek mythology, the never-sleeping dragon guarding the golden apples of the Hesperides.

la·drone (lə·drōn′) *n.* A mercenary soldier; robber; rascal. [<Sp. *ladrón* <L *latro, -onis* a robber]

la·dro·nism (lə·drō′niz·əm) *n.* **1** Brigandage; plunder. **2** Resistance by ladrones.

la·dy (lā′dē) *n. pl.* **·dies 1** A refined and well-bred woman; a gentlewoman. **2** A woman of superior position in society; a woman of good family and recognized social standing. **3** Any woman: in the plural, used as a form of address. **4** The woman who is at the head of or has authority over a household or an estate: the *lady* of the house; the mistress of a family or manor. **5** A sweetheart; ladylove. **6** *Colloq.* Wife: the colonel's *lady.* —*adj.* **1** Of or like a lady; becoming to a lady. **2** Female: a *lady* doctor. ◆ *Lady* is here a genteelism, as it is in such compounds as *saleslady. Woman* is the more appropriate word to indicate the feminine gender of these occupational terms: a *woman* doctor, a *saleswoman,* etc. [OE *hlæfdīge,* lit., bread-kneader <*hlāf* bread, loaf + *-dige,* a stem akin to *dāh* dough]

La·dy (lā′dē) *n.* **1** In Great Britain, the title belonging to the wife of any peer below the rank of duke; also given by courtesy to the daughters of dukes, marquises, and earls, and to the wives of lords, baronets, and knights: correlative to *Lord* or *Sir.* **2** The Virgin Mary: usually with *Our.*

la·dy·bell (lā′dē·bel′) *n.* An erect perennial herb (genus *Adenophora*) having fleshy roots and bell-shaped, usually violet, flowers: often confused with the bellflower.

la·dy·bird (lā′dē·bûrd′) *n.* A small, convex, brightly-colored beetle (*Adalia bipunctata*), usually red spotted with black, or black spotted with red. It feeds on aphids and other small insects. Also **lady beetle, la′dy·bug′** (-bug′). For illustration see INSECT (beneficial).

Lady Day A day observed in honor of the Virgin Mary; specifically, the feast of the Annunciation, March 25: one of the quarter days in England.

la·dy·fin·ger (lā′dē·fing′gər) *n.* **1** A small sponge cake: so called from its shape. **2** A very small firecracker.

la·dy-in-wait·ing (lā′dē·in·wā′ting) *n. pl.* **la·dies-in-wait·ing** A lady of the British royal household in attendance at court.

la·dy-kill·er (lā′dē·kil′ər) *n. Colloq.* A man supposed to be peculiarly fascinating to women. —**la′dy·kill′ing** *adj. & n.*

la·dy·kin (lā′di·kin) *n.* A little lady. [Dim. of LADY]

la·dy·like (lā′dē·līk′) *adj.* **1** Like or suitable to a lady; gentle; delicate. **2** Effeminate.

la·dy·love (lā′dē·luv′) *n.* A woman who is beloved; sweetheart.

Lady of the Lake See VIVIEN.

la·dy-palm (lā′dē·päm′) *n.* A low, reedlike fan palm (genus *Rhapis*) with broad leaves and yellowish flowers, native to southern China.

la·dy-ship (lā′dē·ship) *n.* The rank or condition of a lady: used as a title, with *her* or *your.*

la·dy's-thumb (lā′dēz·thum′) *n.* Persicary.

la·dy-tress·es (lā′dē·tres′iz) *n.* A hardy terrestrial orchid (genus *Spiranthes*) of wide distribution, having slender stems and small flowers in more or less twisted spikes: also spelled *ladies-tresses.* Also **la′dy's-tress′es.**

La·er·tes (lā·ûr′tēz) **1** In the *Odyssey,* a king of Ithaca; father of Odysseus. **2** In Shakespeare's *Hamlet,* brother of Ophelia and son of Polonius.

Lae·ta·re Sunday (lē·tär′ē) *n.* The fourth Sunday in Lent; Mid-Lent Sunday: so called from the first word in the introit of the mass of that day. [<L, imperative sing. of *laetari* rejoice <*laetus* joyful]

laevo– See LEVO-.

La Farge (lə färj′), **John,** 1835-1910, U.S. painter.

La Fon·taine (lä fon·tān′, *Fr.* lä fôn′ten′), **Jean de,** 1621-95, French fabulist and poet.

lag[1] (lag) *v.i.* **lagged, lag·ging 1** To move slowly; stay or fall behind; loiter. **2** In billiards, to shoot one's cue ball to the end rail so that it will rebound to the head rail, the player whose ball stops nearest the end rail winning first place in the order of play. **3** In marbles, to throw one's taw as near as possible to a line on the ground in order to decide the order of play. See synonyms under LINGER. —*n.* **1** Retardation of movement for any cause. **2** The retardation of magnetization in respect of a magnetizing force. **3** In billiards and marbles, an act of lagging. [? Var. of LACK]

lag[2] (lag) *n.* **1** A stave of a barrel, cask, drum, etc. **2** A piece forming part of a lagging. —*v.t.* **lagged, lag·ging** To provide or cover with lags or lagging. [Prob. <ON *lögg* rim of a barrel]

lag[3] (lag) *v.t.* **lagged, lag·ging** *Slang* **1** To arrest. **2** To send to penal servitude. —*n. Slang* **1** A convict. **2** A period of penal servitude. [Prob. <LEG, with ref. to fetters]

lag·an (lag′ən) *n.* In maritime law, goods cast from a vessel in peril, but to which a buoy or float is attached as evidence of ownership: also spelled *ligan.* Compare FLOTSAM, JETSAM. [<AF <Gmc.: prob. akin to ON *lögn* a net laid in the sea]

La·gash (lā′gash) An ancient Sumerian city in southern Babylonia: also *Shirpula.*

la·ger (lä′gər) *n.* **1** Beer containing few hops, and stored for several months before use: also **lager beer. 2** Laager. [<G *lager-bier,* lit., store beer, <*lager* a storehouse + *bier* beer]

lag·gard (lag′ərd) *n.* One who lags; a loiterer. —*adj.* Falling behind; loitering; slow; tardy. [<LAG[1] + -ARD] —**lag′gard·ly** *adv.* —**lag′gard·ness** *n.*

lag·ger (lag′ər) *n.* **1** One who lags. **2** *Slang* A convict serving or having served a term of penal servitude.

lag·ging (lag′ing) *n.* **1** Strips of wood used for various purposes, as to form a jacketing for a steam cylinder, to support an arch of masonry while in construction, to brace the beams of a floor, etc. **2** The action of covering. [<LAG[2]]

La Gio·con·da (lä jō·kôn′dä) See MONA LISA.

La·go·a dos Pa·tos (lə·gō′ə thoosh pä′toos) See PATOS, LAGOA DOS.

Lag·o·mor·pha (lag′ə·môr′fə) *n. pl.* An order of gnawing mammals regarded as differing from the rodents in dentition and in structure of the jaws, including rabbits, hares, and pikas. [<NL <Gk. *lagōs* a hare + *morphē* form]

la·goon (lə·goon′) *n. Geog.* **1** A body of shallow salt water, as a bay or inlet, separated from but connecting with the sea. **2** A body of shallow fresh water, as a pond or lake, usually connecting with a river or lake. **3** A depression in high tablelands of the western United States. Also **la·gune′.** [<F *lagune* <Ital. *laguna* <L *lacuna* lake; see LACUNA.]

lag·oph·thal·mos (lag′əf·thal′məs) *n. Pathol.* A morbid condition in which the eyes cannot be completely closed; also called *hare's-eye.* [<NL <Gk. *lagophthalmos* hare-eyed, unable to close the eyes <*lagōs* a hare + *ophthalmos* an eye] —**lag′oph·thal′mic** *adj.*

La·gos (lā′gos, lä′gos) **1** A port on the Gulf of Guinea, capital of Nigeria. **2** A former British colony, amalgamated with Nigeria since 1906.

La Guar·di·a (lə gwär′dē·ə), **Fiorello,** 1882-1947, U.S. politician and mayor of New York 1934-45.

la·ic (lā′ik) *adj.* Pertaining to the laity: also **la′i·cal.** —*n.* A layman. [<LL *laicus* <Gk. *laikos* <*laos* the people] —**la′i·cal·ly** *adv.*

la·i·cize (lā′ə·sīz) *v.t.* **·cized, ·ciz·ing** To secularize. —**la′i·ci·za′tion** *n.*

laid (lād) Past tense and past participle of LAY[1]. —*adj.* Covered with close, fine, parallel watermarked lines: *laid* paper.

laigh (lākh) *Scot. adj.* Low. —*n.* A hollow. Also **laich.**

l'Ai·glon (lā·glôn′) Son of Napoleon I. [<F, lit., the eaglet]

Lai·ka (lī′kə) *n.* **1** A breed of dog of Siberian Arctic origin, of medium size and white or gray coloring, noted for its sturdiness and intelligence. **2** The name of a dog of this breed sent aloft in the second U.S.S.R. artificial earth satellite in November, 1957.

lain (lān) Past participle of LIE[1].

lair (lâr) *n.* **1** The resting place or den of a wild animal. **2** *Scot.* Any place for resting; a bed. **3** A burial plot. —*v.i.* **1** To rest in a lair; make a lair. —*v.t.* **2** To place in a lair. **3** To serve as a lair for. [OE *leger* bed. Akin to LIE[1].]

lais·sez-faire (les′ā·fâr′) *n.* **1** The let-alone principle; in economics, absolutely uncontrolled industrial and commercial competition; non-interference. **2** Indifference. Also **lais′ser-faire′.** [<F, lit., let do <*laissez,* imperative of *laisser* let + *faire* do, make]

lais·sez-pas·ser (les′ā pä·sā′) *n.* A permit. [<F, lit., let pass <*laissez,* imperative of *laisser* let + *passer* pass]

la·i·ty (lā′ə·tē) *n. pl.* **·ties 1** The people as distinguished from the clergy. **2** Those outside a certain profession. [<LAY[2] + -ITY]

La·ius (lā′yəs) In Greek legend, a king of Thebes, husband of Jocasta, who was unwittingly killed by his son Oedipus. He is said to have introduced homosexual love into Greece.

lake[1] (lāk) *n.* **1** A considerable inland body of water or natural enclosed basin serving to drain the surrounding country. ◆ Collateral adjective: *lacustrine.* **2** A small artificial pond; also, a pool of any liquid: a *lake* of wine. [Fusion of OE *lac* a stream, pool and OF *lac* a basin, pond, lake <L *lacus.* Akin to LEACH, LEAK.]

lake[2] (lāk) *n.* **1** A deep red pigment made by combining some animal (as cochineal) or vegetable (as madder) coloring matter with a metallic oxide, usually that of aluminum or tin. **2** The color of this pigment. **3** Any insoluble metallic compound yielding variously colored pigments by the chemical interaction of mordant and dye. [Var. of LAC[1]]

lake[3] (lāk) *v.t.* **laked, lak·ing 1** To separate the hemoglobin from the red corpuscles of (blood). **2** To make red in color, as the blood. [<LAKE[2] (from the red color of the corpuscles)] —**lak′ing** *n.*

Lake District A region in Cumberland, Lancashire, and Westmoreland counties, England, containing the principal English lakes. Also **Lake Country, Lake Land.**

lake dweller An inhabitant of a lake dwelling; a lacustrian.

lake dwelling A habitation erected on piles over the waters of a lake, as in prehistoric Switzerland.

lake herring A herringlike whitefish or cisco (genus *Leucichthys*) of the Great Lakes.

Lake Poets The English poets Coleridge, Wordsworth, and Southey, who lived for a while in the English Lake District.

lak·er (lā′kər) *n.* **1** A lake fish; especially, the lake trout of America. **2** One connected with a lake, or lakes, as a visitor to a lake, or a vessel engaged in lake trade. [<LAKE[1]]

lake trout Any of various salmonoid fishes, especially, in North America, the namaycush. Also **lake salmon.**

lakh (lak) *n.* The sum of 100,000; 100,000 rupees; a great number: also spelled *lac.* [<Hind. *lākh* <Skt. *laksha* 100,000]

lak·y[1] (lā′kē) *adj.* Like a lake. [<LAKE[1]]

lak·y[2] (lā′kē) *adj.* Of or pertaining to the pigment lake. [<LAKE[2]]

lak·y[3] (lā′kē) *adj.* Transparent: said of blood in which the red corpuscles have been made colorless. [<LAKE[3]]

la·li·a·try (lə·lī′ə·trē) *n.* The branch of medicine which studies disorders of speech. [<NL <Gk. *lalia* speech + -IATRY]

lal·la·tion (la·lā′shən) *n.* An imperfect pronunciation of *r* which makes it sound like *l*; lambdacism; babbling speech. [<L *lallatus,* pp. of *lallare* sing "la la" or a lullaby]

l'Al·le·gro (lä·lā′grō) *Italian* The merry or cheerful one; the joyous man: title of a poem by Milton.

lal·o·neu·ro·sis (lal′ō·nŏŏ·rō′sis, -nyŏŏ-) *n. Psychiatry* A nervous disorder affecting speech.

[<NL <Gk. *laleein* talk, chatter + NEUROSIS]
lal·o·pa·thol·o·gy (lal'ō·pa·thol'ə·jē) *n.* The branch of medicine which deals with speech disorders. [<Gk. *laleein* talk, chatter + PATHOLOGY]
lal·o·pho·bi·a (lal'ō·fō'bē·ə) *n.* A morbid fear of speaking. [<NL <Gk. *laleein* talk, chatter + -PHOBIA]
lam[1] (lam) *v.t.* **lammed, lam·ming** *Slang* To beat; thrash; punish. [? <ON *lamdha*, pt. of *lemja* thrash. Akin to LAME.]
lam[2] (lam) *Slang v.i.* **lammed, lam·ming** To run away; flee hastily. — *n.* Sudden flight. — **on the lam** In flight; fleeing. — **to take it on the lam** To flee hastily; run away. [Prob. < *lammas*, alter. of *nammus*, ? alter. of Sp. *vamos* let us be off, infl. in form by G *nehmen* take]
la·ma[1] (lä'mə) *n.* **1** A priest or monk of Lamaism ranking high in the hierarchy. **2** A title of courtesy given to all monks of Lamaism. See DALAI LAMA. [<Tibetan *blama* < *bla* above]
la·ma[2] (lä'mə) See LLAMA: an erroneous use.
La·ma·ism (lä'mə·iz'əm) *n.* The religious system of Tibet and Mongolia, a variety of Northern Buddhism, introduced into Tibet in the 7th century, and essentially modified by Sivaism and native Shamanistic beliefs and practices. [<LAMA[1] + -ISM] — **La'ma·ist** *n.* — **La·ma·is'tic** *adj.*
La·marck (là·märk'), **Chevalier de,** 1744–1829, Jean Baptiste Pierre Antoine de Monet, French naturalist; pioneer of the theory of evolution of species by adaptation to environments and by the inheritance of acquired characteristics.
La·marck·i·an (lə·märk'ē·ən) *adj.* Of or pertaining to Jean de Lamarck, or to Lamarckism. — *n.* A believer in Lamarckism.
La·marck·ism (lə·märk'iz·əm) *n. Biol.* The theory of descent or evolution propounded by Lamarck, which assumes that species have become developed by the efforts of an organism to adapt itself to new conditions, and by the inheritance of the changes thus produced: often applied to belief in the inheritability of acquired characteristics.
La·mar·tine (là·màr·tēn'), **Alphonse Marie Louis de Prat de,** 1790–1869, French poet.
la·ma·ser·y (lä'mə·ser'ē) *n. pl.* **·ser·ies** A Buddhist monastery or convent of Tibet or Mongolia. [<F *lamaserie* < *lama* a lama]
lamb (lam) *n.* **1** A young sheep; also, its flesh. **2** Any gentle or innocent person. **3** An unsophisticated person; simpleton. **4** An inexperienced and gullible speculator in stocks. — **the Lamb** Christ. — **to give birth:** said of sheep. [OE] — **lamb'like', lamb'ish** *adj.*
lam·baste (lam·bāst') *v.t.* **·bast·ed, ·bast·ing** *Slang* **1** To beat or thrash. **2** To scold; castigate. [<LAM[1] + BASTE[3]] — **lam·bast'ing** *n.*
lamb·da (lam'də) *n.* The eleventh letter and seventh consonant of the Greek alphabet (Λ, λ). See ALPHABET. [<Phoenician *lamed*]
lamb·da·cism (lam'də·siz'əm) *n.* A disorder of speech in which the sufferer cannot pronounce the letter *l* correctly. See LALLATION. [<L *lambdacismus* <Gk. *lambdakismos* < *lambdakizein* pronounce lambda imperfectly < *lambda* LAMBDA]
lamb·doid (lam'doid) *adj.* Resembling in form the Greek letter lambda (Λ): said of the suture between the occipital and the two parietal bones of the skull. Also **lamb·doi'dal.**
lam·bent (lam'bənt) *adj.* **1** Playing with a soft, undulatory movement; gliding; flickering. **2** Softly radiant. **3** Touching lightly but brilliantly: *lambent* wit. [<L *lambens, -entis,* ppr. of *lambere* lick] — **lam'ben·cy, lam'bent·ness** *n.* — **lam'bent·ly** *adv.*
lam·bert (lam'bərt) *n. Physics* The cgs unit of brightness; the uniform brightness of a perfect diffusing surface emitting or reflecting light at the rate of one lumen per square centimeter. [after J. H. *Lambert,* 1728–1777, German physicist]
Lam·beth (lam'bəth) A metropolitan borough of SW London.
Lambeth Palace The official London residence of the archbishop of Canterbury.
lamb·kill (lam'kil') *n.* A North American shrub (*Kalmia angustifolia*) with deep-pink flowers and narrow leaves said to be poisonous to

animals: also called *killikid, sheep laurel.*
lamb·kin (lam'kin) *n.* A little lamb; figuratively, a cherished child. Also **lamb'ie.** [Dim. of LAMB]
lamb lettuce Corn salad.
Lamb of God Christ, by analogy with the paschal lamb. *John* i 29.
lam·boys (lam'boiz) *n. pl.* Flexible steel plates worn skirtlike from the waist of 15th century armor. [? Alter. of JAMBEAUX]
lam·bre·quin (lam'-bər·kin, -brə-) *n.* **1** A draped strip, as of cloth or leather, hanging from the casing above a window, doorway, etc. **2** An ornamental covering for a helmet. [<F <Du. *lam-perkin,* dim. of *lamper* a veil]

LAMBREQUIN *(def. 1)*

lamb·skin (lam'skin') *n.* A lamb's skin, especially when dressed, as for glovemaking.
lamb's wool The wool of lambs used in the manufacture of various textile fabrics.
lamb's–wool (lamz'wool') *n.* A drink made of hot ale with sugar, nutmeg, and roasted apples.
lam·dan (läm'dən) *n.* A person learned in Jewish lore. [<Hebrew]
lame[1] (lām) *adj.* **1** Crippled or disabled, especially in the legs. **2** Hence, inefficient; halting. **3** Sore; painful: a *lame* back. — *v.t.* **lamed, lam·ing** To make lame; cripple. [OE *lama.* Akin to LAM[1].] — **lame'ly** *adv.* — **lame'·ness** *n.*
lame[2] (lām) *n.* A thin plate of metal; specifically one used in making armor. [<F <L *lamina* a lamina]
la·mé (la·mā') *n.* A fabric woven of flat gold or silver thread, often brocaded, sometimes mixed with silk or other fiber. [<F, orig. pp. of *lamer* laminate < *lame* a lame[2]]
lame duck *Colloq.* **1** A helpless or disabled person. **2** On the stock exchange, one who cannot fulfil his contracts. **3** *U.S.* A member of a legislature, especially of Congress, whose term continues some time after his defeat for reelection.
la·mel·la (lə·mel'ə) *n. pl.* **·lae** (-ē) **1** A thin plate, scale, or lamina, as in the gills of bivalves, or in bone. **2** *Bot.* A gill of a mushroom, one of the thin plates attached to the under side of the cap. [<NL <L, dim. of *lamina* a lamina]
lam·el·lar (lə·mel'ər, lam'ə·lər) *adj.* Scalelike; composed of thin layers or scales. Also **lam·el·late** (lam'ə·lāt, lə·mel'āt), **lam'el·lat'ed.** — **lam'el·la'tion** *n.*
la·mel·li·branch (lə·mel'i·brangk) *n.* One of a class (*Pelecypoda,* formerly *Lamellibranchiata*) of mollusks, having bivalve shells enclosing a mantle within which is the compressed body of the organism, including clams, mussels, and oysters. — *adj.* Of or pertaining to this class. [<NL *lamellibranchia,* name of this class <L *lamella* LAMELLA + Gk. *branchia* gills, pl. of *branchion* a fin] — **la·mel'li·bran'chi·ate** (-brang'kē·āt, -it) *adj. & n.*
la·mel·li·corn (lə·mel'i·kôrn) *adj. Entomol.* **1** Terminating in leaflike joints, as the antennae of certain beetles. **2** Having such antennae. **3** Of or pertaining to a division of beetles (*Lamellicornia*) having a lateral leaflike expansion on each of the terminal antennal segments, as the scarab beetle. — *n.* One of the lamellicorn beetles. [<NL *lamellicornis* <L *lamella* LAMELLA + *cornu* a horn]
la·mel·li·form (lə·mel'i·fôrm) *adj.* Having the form of a thin plate, scale, or lamella; scalelike; lamellar.
la·mel·li·ros·tral (lə·mel'i·ros'trəl) *adj. Ornithol.* Of or pertaining to a group of birds having lamellar ridges on the inner edges of the bills, as ducks, swans, and geese. Also **la·mel'li·ros'trate** (-trāt). [<NL *lamellirostris* <L *lamella* LAMELLA + *rostrum* a beak]
lamelli– *combining form* Lamellae; resembling lamellae: *lamellibranch.* [<L *lamella* a plate]
la·mel·loid (lə·mel'oid, lam'ə·loid) *adj.* Of or resembling a plate or lamella. [<LAMELL(A) + -OID]
la·mel·lose (lə·mel'ōs, lam'ə·lōs) *adj.* Composed

of or full of thin plates, scales, or lamellae; lamelliform. [<LAMELL(A) + -OSE[1]]
la·ment (lə·ment') *v.t.* To feel or express sorrow for; bewail. — *v.i.* To feel or express sorrow; mourn; grieve. — *n.* **1** The expression of grief; lamentation. **2** A plaintive song or melody. See synonyms under MOURN. [<L *lamentari* < *lamentum* a wailing, weeping] — **la·ment'er** *n.*
lam·en·ta·ble (lam'ən·tə·bəl) *adj.* **1** Expressing sorrow; mournful: a *lamentable* cry. **2** Exciting regret or dissatisfaction; despicable; deplorable: a *lamentable* failure. See synonyms under PITIFUL. — **lam'en·ta·bly** *adv.*
lam·en·ta·tion (lam'ən·tā'shən) *n.* The act of lamenting or bewailing; utterance of profound regret or grief; a wailing cry.
Lam·en·ta·tions (lam'ən·tā'shəns) A lyrical poetic book of the Old Testament, attributed to Jeremiah the prophet; also, the music to which a portion of it is sung in the Roman Catholic Church at Tenebrae.
la·mi·a (lā'mē·ə) *n.* A female demon or vampire; witch. [<L, a witch sucking children's blood <Gk., a fabulous monster]
lam·i·na (lam'ə·nə) *n. pl.* **·nae** (-nē) or **·nas** **1** A thin scale or sheet. **2** A layer or coat lying over another, as in bone, minerals, armor, etc. **3** *Bot.* The blade or flat expanded portion of a leaf, or the blade of a petal. [<L]
lam·i·nar·i·a (lam'ə·nâr'ē·ə) *n.* Any member of a genus (*Laminaria*) of brown algae, especially the giant kelp. [<NL <L *lamina* a leaf] — **lam·i·nar·i·a·ceous** (lam'ə·nâr'ē·ā'shəs) *adj.*
lam·i·nate (lam'ə·nāt) *v.* **·nat·ed, ·nat·ing** *v.t.* **1** To beat, roll, or press, as metal, into thin sheets. **2** To cut or separate into thin sheets. **3** To make, as plastic materials or plywood, of layers united by the action of heat and pressure. **4** To cover with thin sheets or laminae. — *v.i.* **5** To become separated into sheets or laminae. — *adj.* Consisting of or disposed in laminae: also **lam'i·nal, lam'i·nar, lam'i·nar'y, lam'i·nat'ed.** [<NL *laminatus* laminated <L *lamina* a leaf] — **lam'i·na·ble** *adj.* — **lam'i·na'tion** *n.*
lam·i·nif·er·ous (lam'ə·nif'ər·əs) *adj.* Bearing or composed of laminae.
lam·i·ni·tis (lam'ə·nī'tis) *n.* Inflammation of the laminae of a horse's hoof; founder. [<NL <L *lamina* a leaf, layer + -*itis* -ITIS]
lam·i·nose (lam'ə·nōs) *adj.* Laminate. Also **lam'i·nous** (-nəs). [<LAMIN(A) + -OSE[1]]
lam·mer·gei·er (lam'ər·gī'ər) *n.* The great bearded vulture (*Gypaëtus barbatus*), native to the mountains of Asia, southern Europe, and North Africa. Also **lam'mer·geir** (-gīr), **lam'mer·gey'er.** [<G *lämmergeier,* lit., lamb-vulture <*lämmer,* pl. of *lamm* a lamb + *geier* a vulture]
Lam·mer·muir Hills (lam'ər·moōr', lam'ər·moōr) A range of low hills in SE Scotland; highest point, 1,733 feet. Also **Lam'mer·moor Hills.**
lam·my (lam'ē) *n. pl.* **·mies** A sailor's quilted woolen jumper. Also **lam'mie.** [? <*lammy,* var. of *lambie,* affectionate dim. of LAMB]
La·mont (lə·mont'), **Thomas William,** 1870–1948, U. S. banker.
lamp (lamp) *n.* **1** A vessel in which oil is burnt through a wick; hence, any device employing a flame, incandescent wire, or the like, for furnishing an artificial light, or a similar device for heating. ◆ Collateral adjective: *lucernal.* **2** Anything that gives out light, actually or metaphorically. **3** A flash, as of lightning. **4** A heavenly body. **5** A torch. **6** *pl. Slang* The eyes. — *v.t. Slang* To look at. [<OF *lampe* <L *lampas* <Gk. <*lampein* shine]
lam·pad (lam'pad) *n.* A lamp or torch; candlestick. [<Gk. *lampas, lampados* <*lampein* shine]
lam·pas[1] (lam'pəs) *n.* Inflammation and swelling of the fleshy bars in the roof of a horse's mouth. Also **lam'pers** (-pərs). [<F <OF, throat]
lam·pas[2] (lam'pəs) *n.* Any elaborately patterned fabric; specifically, a fabric similar to damask, but in many colors, used as furniture covering. [<F; origin uncertain]
lamp·black (lamp'blak') *n.* Fine carbon deposited from smoke or smoky flame: used as

a pigment, in printer's ink, etc.: also called *carbon black.*

lam·per-eel (lam′pər-ēl′) *n.* **1** A lamprey: also **lam′preel** (-prēl). **2** An eelpout or mutton fish. [? < *lampre,* var. of LAMPREY + EEL]

lam·pi·on (lam′pē·ən) *n.* A small lamp. [<F <Ital. *lampione* a carriage or street lamp, aug. of *lampa* <L *lampas* LAMP]

lamp·light (lamp′līt′) *n.* Light emitted by lamps; artificial light.

lamp·light·er (lamp′līt′ər) *n.* **1** A person who lights lamps, especially gas street lamps. **2** That by which a lamp is lighted, as a torch, or an electric device.

lam·poon (lam·pōōn′) *n.* A written satire designed to bring a person into ridicule or contempt; a pasquinade. See synonyms under RIDICULE. — *v.t.* To abuse or satirize in a lampoon. [<MF *lampon* <*lampons* let's drink (a drinking-song refrain) <*lamper* guzzle] — **lampoon′er, lam·poon′ist** *n.* — **lam·poon′er·y** *n.*

lamp·post (lamp′pōst′) *n.* A post supporting a lamp in a street, park, etc.

lam·prey (lam′prē) *n.* An eel-like carnivorous cyclostome (*Petromyzon* and related genera) having in the adult stages a circular suctorial mouth, with sharp rasping teeth on its inner surface, and well-developed eyes. [<OF *lampreie* <Med. L. *lampreda, lampetra* <L *lambere* lick + *petra* rock <Gk.; supposedly so called because they cling to rocks with their mouths]

lamp shell *Zool.* A brachiopod: so called from its resemblance to an old Roman oil lamp.

lamp·wick (lamp′wik′) *n.* A wick for a lamp.

lam·yik (läm′yik) *n.* A piece of parchment issued by the Dalai Lama of Tibet to serve as a passport permitting a Westerner to enter the Forbidden City of Lhasa: also called *red arrow letter.* [<Tibetan]

la·na·ry (lā′nə·rē) *n. pl.* **·ries** A place for storing wool. [<L *lanaria,* fem. of *lanarius* of wool <*lana* wool]

la·nate (lā′nāt) *adj.* **1** Woolly. **2** *Bot.* Provided or covered with long, fine, wool-like hairs. Also **la′nat·ed.** [<L *lanatus* <*lana* wool]

Lan·cas·ter (lang′kəs·tər) A royal house of England, reigning from 1399 to 1461, and descended from John of Gaunt, fourth son of Edward III. The three Lancastrian kings were Henry IV, Henry V, and Henry VI. See YORK, and WARS OF THE ROSES in table under WAR.

Lan·cas·te·ri·an (lang′kəs·tir′ē·ən) *adj.* Pertaining to the system introduced in primary schools by Joseph Lancaster, 1778–1838, of England, in which advanced pupils taught those below them.

Lan·cas·tri·an (lang·kas′trē·ən) *adj.* Belonging to or relating to the House of Lancaster. — *n.* **1** An adherent of the House of Lancaster, as opposed to the Yorkists, especially in the Wars of the Roses. **2** A native or inhabitant of Lancashire.

lance (lans, läns) *n.* **1** A long shaft with a spearhead, used as a thrusting weapon; any long, slender spear, or something resembling one. **2** A lancet. **3** A thrust with a lance or lancet. **4** One who uses a lance; lancer. **5** In pyrotechnics, a small paper case for white or colored fire. **6** A whaler's spear for killing the whale after its capture with the harpoon and line. — *v.t.* **lanced, lanc·ing 1** To pierce with a lance. **2** To cut or open with a lancet. [<OF <L *lancea* a light spear <Celtic]

lance corporal See under CORPORAL².

lance·let (lans′lit, läns′-) *n.* Any of several species of small fishlike translucent animals (genus *Branchiostoma*) having a notochord and other vertebrate characteristics, which burrow in the sand of warm sea beaches; an amphioxus. [Dim. of LANCE]

Lan·ce·lot (lan′sə·lot, län′-; *Fr.* län·slō′) A masculine personal name: often spelled *Launcelot.* Also *Pg.* **Lan·ce·lo·te** (län·sə·lō′tē).
— **Lancelot of the Lake** In Arthurian romance, the bravest and ablest of the knights of the Round Table; lover of Guinevere; father of Galahad. Also **Lancelot du Lac.** [<F, servant]

lan·ce·o·late (lan′sē·ə·lit, -lāt) *adj.* **1** Shaped like the head of a lance or spear. **2** *Bot.* Tapering, as some leaves. Also **lan′ce·o·lar** (-lər), **lan′ce·o·lat′ed.** [<LL *lanceolatus* <*lanceola* a small

---

lance, dim. of *lancea* LANCE]

lanc·er (lan′sər, län′-) **1** One who lances; a cavalry soldier armed with a lance. **2** *pl.* A quadrille, or square dance for eight or sixteen couples; also, the music for it: also **lan′ciers** (-sərz).

lance sergeant See under SERGEANT.

lan·cet (lan′sit, län′-) *n.* **1** A surgeon's two-edged cutting or bloodletting instrument with one or more small blades. **2** *Archit.* **a** A lancet-shaped or acutely pointed window: also **lancet window. b** An acutely pointed arch: also **lancet arch. 3** A small lance. [<F *lancette,* dim. of *lance* <OF, LANCE]

lan·cet·ed (lan′sit·id, län′-) *adj.* Having lancet windows or arches.

LANCET WINDOWS

lancet fish 1 An ocean fish (genus *Alepisaurus*) with large, lancetlike teeth. **2** A surgeon fish.

lance·wood (lans′wŏŏd′, läns′-) *n.* **1** A tough, elastic wood from Cuba, Guiana, or Brazil, used for carriage shafts, fishing rods, billiard cues, etc. **2** Any of the various trees yielding this wood, especially *Oxandra lanceolata.*

lan·ci·nate (lan′sə·nāt) *v.t.* **·nat·ed, ·nat·ing** To strike through; pierce, as with pain. [<L *lancinatus,* pp. of *lancinare* tear to pieces]

lan·ci·na·tion (lan′sə·nā′shən) *n.* **1** Shooting or acute pain. **2** A tearing away; laceration.

land (land) *n.* **1** The solid substance composing the material part of the earth, considered in its entirety. **2** A country or district, large or small, especially considered as a place of human habitation, or as distinguished by events or facts of interest. **3** Ground or soil considered with reference to its use, value, condition, etc.: real estate: farm *land* ; coal *land.* **4** *Law* Any tract of ground whatever, together with all its appurtenances; also, a share or interest in land, tenements, or any hereditament, both corporeal and incorporeal. ◆ Collateral adjective: *predial.* **5** Any unindented space in a surface marked with indentations, as a level space between the furrows of a millstone, or a space on the bore of a rifle between two grooves. **6** In economic discussion, those resources which are supplied by nature, as distinguished from the developments and improvements resulting from human labor. — *v.t.* **1** To put ashore; transfer from a vessel to the shore. **2** To bring to rest on land or water: He *landed* the plane at Washington. **3** To bring to some point, condition, or state: His words *landed* him in trouble. **4** In fishing, to bring (a fish) from the water or into a net, boat, etc.; catch. **5** *Colloq.* To obtain or secure; win, as a position. **6** *Colloq.* To deliver, as a blow. — *v.i.* **7** To go or come ashore, as from a boat. **8** To touch at a port; come to land: said of ships. **9** To descend and come to rest, as' after flight; come down: The bird *landed* in the tree. **10** To come to some place, condition, or state; arrive; end: The swindlers soon *landed* in jail. See synonyms under ARRIVE, REACH. [OE]

Synonyms (noun): continent, country, district, earth, ground, region, shore, soil. *Antonyms*: deep, flood, ocean, sea, surge, water, wave.

-land *combining form* **1** A region of a certain kind: *woodland.* **2** The country of: *Scotland.* **3** A specified place or realm: *cloudland.* An inhabitant of any of these places is denoted by the combining form **-lander.** [<LAND]

land agent 1 A real-estate agent. **2** One who helps settlers get title to their claims.

lan·dau (lan′dô, -dou) *n.* **1** A type of closed automobile body the rear top of which may be raised or lowered. **2** A four-wheeled covered carriage with a double top that can be removed or folded back. [from *Landau,* a Bavarian city where it was first made]

TWO TYPES OF THE LANDAU
a. Closed top.
b. Open top.

---

land bank 1 A bank taking mortgages on land in exchange for currency notes; especially, the **Massachusetts Land Bank** of 1740. **2** One of twelve U.S. government banks organized in 1916 to make mortgage loans on land.

land claim 1 A claim to a piece of land based on conformity to the legal requirements for settlement and title. **2** The land claimed, and the paper entitling the claimant to the land.

lande (land) *n.* A level sandy region unfit for cultivation and covered with heath or broom, as along the seacoast in SW France. [<F <OF *launde* <Breton *lann* <Celtic. Doublet of LAWN.]

land·ed (lan′did) *adj.* **1** Having an estate in land. **2** Consisting in land.

land·fall (land′fôl′) *n.* **1** Property in land immediately transferred by the death of its owner. **2** A landslide. **3** A sighting of or coming to land.

land·fill (land′fil′) *n.* **1** The disposal of garbage, trash, excavated earth, etc., by depositing in a site, often used to build up swampy or shoreline areas. **2** Materials so used. **3** A site where such deposits are made.

land·form (land′fôrm′) *n.* A physical feature of the earth's surface, such as a plateau, an isthmus, a mountain, etc.

land·grant (land′grant′, -gränt′) *n.* Government land granted to a railroad, educational institution, etc.

land·hold·er (land′hōl′dər) *n.* A landowner.

land·ing (lan′ding) *n.* **1** The act of going or placing ashore from any kind of craft or vessel: the *landing* of passengers; also, the act of coming or falling to earth, as of an airplane. **2** The place where any kind of craft lands; a wharf; pier. **3** *Archit.* The place at the head of a staircase, or a platform interrupting a flight of stairs.

landing area 1 A landing field. **2** A jump area.

landing beam *Aeron.* A short-wave radio beam transmitted from a landing field to an aircraft pilot in order to facilitate safe landing.

landing craft One of several types of military vessels especially designed for the landing of men and materiel upon a hostile shore.

landing field A tract of ground properly surfaced for the landing and take-off of aircraft.

landing gear *Aeron.* The under-structure of an aircraft designed to carry the load when resting or running on the surface of land or water, and also to buffer the shock of landing.

landing ramp A broad gangplank to permit the rapid landing of men and supplies from a landing craft.

landing strip A narrow, surfaced runway for the landing and take-off of aircraft.

Lan·dis (lan′dis), **Kenesaw Mountain,** 1866–1944, U.S. jurist and baseball commissioner.

land·la·dy (land′lā′dē) *n. pl.* **·dies** A woman who keeps an inn or boarding house, or who lets her property; also, the wife of a landlord.

land·locked (land′lokt) *adj.* **1** Surrounded and protected by land. **2** Living in or confined to landlocked water: said especially of a normally anadromous fish: *landlocked* salmon.

land·lord (land′lôrd′) *n.* **1** A man who keeps an inn or hotel. **2** A man who owns and lets real estate. **3** In England, the lord of a manor. [OE *landhlāford* <*land* land + *hlāford* lord]

land·lord·ism (land′lôrd·iz·əm) *n.* **1** Action, conduct, or opinions peculiar to a landlord; a landlord's authority, or the view that landed interests should be paramount. **2** The system under which land is owned by persons to whom tenants pay a fixed rent.

land·lub·ber (land′lub′ər) *n.* An awkward or inexperienced person on board a ship; a raw sailor. [<LAND + LUBBER]

land·mark (land′märk′) *n.* **1** A fixed object serving as a boundary mark to a tract of land, or as a guide to seamen, etc. **2** A prominent or memorable object in the landscape. **3** A distinguishing fact, event, etc. See synonyms under BOUNDARY. [OE *landmearc* <*land* land + *mearc* boundary]

landmark beacon A beacon light, other than an airport or airway beacon, that serves to indicate a definite geographical location.

land mine See under MINE¹.

land office A U.S. government office of the Department of the Interior for the transaction of business pertaining to the public lands. Officially, **General Land Office.**

land-of·fice business (land'ô'fis, -of'is) *U. S. Colloq.* A flourishing business conducted at a rapid pace.

Land of Nod (nod) See NOD, LAND OF.

Land of Promise 1 Canaan, promised to Abraham by God. *Gen.* xv 18. 2 Any longed-for place of happiness or improvement.

Land of the Midnight Sun Norway.

Land of the Rising Sun Japan.

Lan·dor (lan'dər, -dôr), **Walter Savage,** 1775–1864, English poet and prose writer.

land·own·er (land'ō'nər) *n.* One who owns real estate. — **land'own'er·ship** *n.* — **land'own'ing** *n. & adj.*

land pike *U.S.* 1 The hellbender (def. 1). 2 An inferior breed of hog.

land·plane (land'plān') *n. Aeron.* An airplane designed to rise from and alight on land.

land·poor (land'pōŏr') *adj.* Owning much land which yields an income insufficient to meet its expenses.

land power A nation having military strength on land: opposed to *sea power.*

land·scape (land'skāp) *n.* 1 A stretch of country as seen from a single point. 2 A picture representing natural scenery. Also *Obs.* **land'skip** (-skip) — *v.* ·scaped, ·scap·ing *v.t.* To improve or change the natural features or appearance of, as a park or garden. — *v.i.* To be a landscape gardener. [<Du. *landschap* < *land* land + *-schap* -SHIP]

landscape architect One who draws up, coordinates, and supervises the execution of plans for converting a given area of land into a unified ornamental development.

land·scap·ist (land'skā·pist) *n.* 1 A painter of landscapes. 2 A landscape gardener.

land scrip *U.S.* 1 A landholding certificate issued to a person or company. 2 In connection with land grants made for higher education, a certificate granted to a State having insufficient public lands, entitling it to its share of such lands in other States.

land·side (land'sīd') *n.* The flat side of a plowshare, away from the furrow.

land·slide (land'slīd') *n.* 1 The slipping of a mass of land from a higher to a lower level. 2 The land that has slipped down: also **land'slip'.** 3 *Colloq.* An overwhelming plurality of votes for one political party or candidate in an election.

Lands·mål (läns'môl) *n.* One of the two official forms of Norwegian, based on an arbitrary consolidation of Norwegian dialects: also called *New Norwegian.* Compare RIKSMÅL. [<Norw., lit., country's language < *land* country + *mål* language]

lands·man (landz'mən) *n. pl.* ·men (-mən) 1 One who lives on the land. 2 *Naut.* An inexperienced sailor, as one on his first voyage or one rated below an ordinary seaman: opposed to *seaman.*

land speculator One who buys and sells land; specifically, one who profits illegally in the buying and selling of unsettled government lands.

Land·sturm (länt'shtŏŏrm) *n.* 1 A general levy in time of war, as made in various European countries. 2 The final reserve forces of a nation, called out in cases of great emergency or for home-defense. [<G, lit., land-storm < dial. G (Swiss), trans. of F *levée en masse,* general levy of troops]

land·ward (land'wərd) *adj. & adv.* Being, facing, or going toward the land. Also **land'wards.**

Land·wehr (länt'vär) *n.* An emergency military force of various European countries. [<G < *land* land + *wehr* defense < *wehren* defend]

lane (lān) *n.* 1 A narrow way or path, confined between fences, walls, hedges, or similar boundaries: distinguished from an *alley,* which is ordinarily between buildings and in city or town, while the *lane* is rural. 2 Any narrow way, passage, or similar course; a prescribed route or passage, as for steamers: a shipping *lane.* See synonyms under ROAD. [OE *lanu* lāne]

lane route One of the routes prescribed for trans-Atlantic steamers in northern waters, being different for eastward- and westward-

bound vessels to avoid collisions: also called *ocean-lane route.*

Lan·franc (lan'frangk), 1005–89, Benedictine prior; archbishop of Canterbury.

Lang (lang), **Andrew,** 1844–1912, Scottish critic, essayist, historian, poet, and translator. — **Cosmo Gordon,** 1864–1945, English prelate; archbishop of Canterbury, 1928–42.

Lang·land (lang'land), **William,** 1330?–1400?, English poet. Also **Lang'ley** (-lē).

lang·lauf (läng'louf) *n.* A cross-country run, especially in skiing. [<G < *lang* long + *lauf* a course < *laufen* run]

lang·läuf·er (läng'loi·fər) *n.* A cross-country skier. [<G < *langlauf* LANGLAUF]

lang·ley (lang'lē) *n.* A unit of solar radiation, equal to 1 small calorie per square centimeter of surface per unit of time. [after S. P. *Langley*]

Lan·go·bar·di (lang'gō·bär'dē) *n. pl.* The Lombards. [<L, prob. <OHG *lang* long + *bart* beard] — **Lan'go·bar'dic** *adj.*

lang·shan (lang'shan) *n.* A breed of large domestic fowl introduced from China. [< Chinese, from *Langshan,* lit., wolf hill, a town near Shanghai]

lang·syne (lang'sīn', -zīn') *adv. Scot.* Long since; long ago: used also as a noun. See AULD LANG SYNE.

Lang·ton (lang'tən), **Stephen,** died 1228, English patriot and archbishop of Canterbury.

Lang·try (lang'trē), **Lily,** 1852–1929, *née* Emily Charlotte Le Breton, English actress: called the "Jersey Lily."

lan·guage (lang'gwij) *n.* 1 The expression and communication of emotions or ideas between human beings by means of speech and hearing, the sounds spoken or heard being systematized and confirmed by usage among a given people over a period of time. 2 Transmission of emotions or ideas between any living creatures by any means. 3 The words forming the means of communication among members of a single nation or group at a given period; tongue: the French *language.* 4 The impulses, capacities, and powers which induce and make possible the creation and use of all forms of human communication by speech and hearing. 5 The vocabulary or technical expressions used in a specific business, science, etc.: the *language* of mathematics. 6 One's characteristic manner of expression or use of speech. [<OF *langage* < *langue* tongue <L *lingua* tongue, language. Akin to TONGUE.]

Synonyms: barbarism, dialect, diction, expression, gibberish, idiom, patois, speech, tongue, vernacular. *Language* originally signified only the *expression* of thought by spoken words; it has now acquired the broader interpretation of the *expression* of thought by any means. *Speech* denotes the power of articulate utterance; we can speak of the *language* of animals, but not of their *speech.* A *tongue* is the *speech* or *language* of some one people, country, or race. A *dialect* is a special mode of speaking a *language* peculiar to some locality or class; a *barbarism* is a usage that is felt to be substandard. *Idiom* refers to the construction of phrases and sentences, and the way of forming or using words; it is the peculiar mold in which each *language* casts its thought. The great difficulty of translation lies in giving the thought expressed in one *language* in the *idiom* of another. A *dialect* may be used by the highest as well as the lowest within its range; a *patois* is usually illiterate, belonging to the lower classes; those who speak a *patois* understand the cultured form of their own *language,* but speak only their own form; often a *patois* is a kind of linguistic enclave, as the dialect of the French-Canadians in rural Quebec, or the speech of the Cajuns in Louisiana.

language arts Those elementary-school subjects, especially, reading, spelling, literature, and composition, both written and oral, that deal with the acquisition of facility in one's native language.

Langue·doc (läng·dôk') A region and former province in southern France, between the Loire and the Pyrenees.

langue d'oc (läng dôk') The form of Old French spoken south of the Loire in the

Middle Ages, surviving in modern Provençal: so called from the use of the word *oc* for "yes." [<OF, lit., language of *oc* <Provençal: *oc* yes <L *hoc* this (thing)]

lan·guet (lang'gwet) *n.* A little tongue or something resembling a tongue in structure or function. Also **lan'guette.** [<F *languette,* dim. of *langue* tongue. See LANGUAGE.]

lan·guid (lang'gwid) *adj.* 1 Indisposed to physical exertion; affected by weakness or fatigue. 2 Wanting in interest or animation; listless. 3 Lacking in force or quickness of movement. See synonyms under FAINT, SICKLY. [<L *languidus* faint, weak < *languere* languish] — **lan'guid·ly** *adv.* — **lan'guid·ness** *n.*

lan·guish (lang'gwish) *v.i.* 1 To become weak or feeble; be or grow faint or listless. 2 To live or be in unfavorable circumstances so as to be weakened by them: to languish in a dungeon. 3 To affect a look of sentimental longing or melancholy. 4 To pine with love or desire. — *n.* 1 A tender look. 2 The act or state of languishing. [<OF *languiss-,* stem of *languir* <L *languescere,* inceptive of *languere* be weary, languish] — **lan'guish·er** *n.*

lan·guish·ing (lang'gwish·ing) *adj.* 1 Lacking interest or force. 2 Sentimentally pensive. 3 Becoming weak or listless. — **lan'guish·ing·ly** *adv.*

lan·guish·ment (lang'gwish·mənt) *n.* 1 The state of being languid. 2 Sentimental languor or tenderness.

lan·guor (lang'gər) *n.* 1 Lassitude of body or depression of mind, as from exertion; weakness. 2 An atonic debility or prostration. 3 Amorous dreaminess. 4 The absence of activity; dulness. 5 A state of premature decay in plants. [<OF <L *languor, languoris* < *languere* languish] — **lan'·guor·ous** *adj.* — **lan'·guor·ous·ly** *adv.* — **lan'·guor·ous·ness** *n.*

lan·gur (lung·gŏŏr') *n.* A long-tailed Asian monkey (genus *Presbytis*), noted for its remarkable leaping power; as, the common langur or hanuman and the Himalayan langur. [<Hind. *langur* <Skt. *lāṅgūlin,* lit., having a tail]

lan·iard (lan'yərd) See LANYARD.

la·ni·ar·y (lā'nē·er'ē, lan'ē-) *adj.* Adapted for tearing, as the canine teeth. — *n. pl.* ·ar·ies A canine tooth. [< L *laniarius* pertaining to a butcher < *lanius* a butcher < *laniare* tear]

La·nier (lə·nir'), **Sidney,** 1842–81, U.S. poet.

la·nif·er·ous (lə·nif'ər·əs) *adj.* Bearing wool: often **la·nig'er·ous** (-nij'-). [< L *lanifer* < *lana* wool + *-fer* -FEROUS]

lan·i·tal (lan'ə·tal) *n.* A substance originally produced in Italy from casein, similar to wool in chemical composition and use. [< Ital. *lan(a)* wool + *Ital(ia)* Italy]

lank (langk) *adj.* 1 Lean; shrunken. 2 Long, straight, and thin: *lank* hair. 3 *Obs.* Languid. See synonyms under GAUNT, MEAGER. [OE *hlanc* flexible] — **lank'ly** *adv.* — **lank'ness** *n.*

lank·y (lang'kē) *adj.* lank·i·er, lank·i·est Tall; thin; shrunken. [< LANK + -Y] — **lank'i·ly** *adv.* — **lank'i·ness** *n.*

lan·ner (lan'ər) *n.* 1 A falcon of southern Europe and Asia, especially *Falco biarmicus.* 2 In falconry, the female of this falcon. [< OF *lanier,* ? ult. < L *laniarius.* See LANIARY.]

lan·ner·et (lan'ər·et) *n.* In falconry, the male of the lanner. [< OF *laneret,* dim. of *lanier* LANNER]

lan·o·lin (lan'ə·lin) *n.* An unctuous fatty mixture of the ethers of cholesterin with fatty acids, obtained from various keratin tissues, as the wool of sheep, valuable in pharmacy as a vehicle for substances intended to be applied to the skin: also called *wool fat.* Also **lan'o·line** (-lin, -lēn). [< L *lan(a)* wool + *ol(eum)* oil + -IN]

la·nose (lā'nōs) *adj.* Woolly; resembling wool. [< L *lanosus* < *lana* wool]

lans·downe (lanz'doun) *n.* A material made of silk or similar fiber and wool mixed. [? from *Lansdown,* a town in England]

Lan·sing (lan'sing) The capital of Michigan.

lans·que·net (lans'kə·net) *n.* A card game for any number of players, in which all bets are made on single cards and must be covered by the banker. [< F < G *landsknecht* a (mercenary) foot soldier < *land* country + *knecht* servant]

---

add,āce,câre,pälm; end,ēven; it,īce; odd,ōpen,ôrder; tŏŏk,pōol; up,bûrn; ə = a in *above,* e in *sicken,* i in *clarity,* o in *melon,* u in *focus;* yōō = u in *fuse;* oi,oil; ou,pout; ch,check; g,go; ng,ring; th,thin; ṯẖ,this; zh,vision. Foreign sounds á,œ,ü,kh,ṅ; and ◆: see page xx. <from; + plus; ? possibly.

lant (lant) *n.* Urine, particularly if stale: used as a detergent in wool-scouring. [OE *hland* urine]

lan·ta·na (lan·tā'nə, -tä'-) *n.* Any of a genus(*Lantana*) of mainly tropical American shrubs of the verbena family bearing spikes or umbels of red, orange, lilac, or white flowers. [< NL, viburnum]

lan·tern (lan'tərn) *n.* **1** A transparent case, as on a lamp post or of portable character, for enclosing and protecting a light. **2** *Archit.* A tower or the like, as on a roof or dome, open below and admitting light from the sides; also, a small tower, pavilion, or pinnacle placed on the apex of a dome or crowning another tower. **3** One of various mechanisms likened to a lantern. **4** A lighthouse. **5** A magic lantern. **6** One of the street lamps of Paris, used as gallows during the French Revolution. Also *Obs.* **lant·horn** (lant'hôrn', lan'tərn). [< F *lanterne* < L *lanterna* < Gk. *lamptēr* < *lampein* shine]

LANTERN ON CHURCH TOWER

lantern fish Any of various small, large-eyed marine fishes bearing rows of phosphorescent organs along the under parts of their bodies.

lantern fly A homopterous insect (family *Fulgoridae*) formerly supposed to produce light from a large protuberant snout.

lan·tern-jawed (lan'tərn·jôd') *adj.* Having long, thin jaws; hence, having a thin visage.

lantern wheel *Mech.* A lantern-shaped device performing the work of a pinion, in which a circle of bars between two heads takes the place of pinion teeth: sometimes called *trundle.* Also **lantern horn.**

lan·tha·nide series (lan'thə·nīd) *Physics* The group of rare-earth elements beginning with lanthanum and ending with lutetium, atomic numbers 57 to 71, characterized by closely related properties and great difficulty of separation. [< LANTHAN(UM) + -*ide*, var. of -ID[2]]

lan·tha·num (lan'thə·nəm) *n.* A dark lead-gray metallic element (symbol La). See ELEMENT.[< NL < Gk. *lanthanein* lie concealed]

lan·tho·pine (lan'thə·pēn) *n.* A white crystalline alkaloid, $C_{23}H_{25}O_4N$, obtained from opium. [< Gk. *lanth(anein)* lie hidden + OP(IUM) + -INE[2]]

la·nu·gi·nous (lə·nōō'jə·nəs, -nyōō'-) *adj.* Woolly or downy. Also **la·nu'gi·nose** (-nōs). [< L *lanuginosus* < *lanugo, -inis* down < *lana* wool]

la·nu·go (lə·nōō'gō, -nyōō'-) *n.* *Biol.* A downy growth; specifically, the soft, rudimentary hair found on the body of a child at birth. [< L, down < *lana* wool]

lan·yard (lan'yərd) *n.* **1** *Naut.* A small rope used on a ship, especially, a four-stranded hemp rope, especially one rove through deadeyes and used in setting up riggings. **2** A cord used in firing certain kinds of cannon. **3** A stout cord worn around the neck, especially by sailors, and used for attaching a knife: called a **knife lanyard.** Also spelled *laniard.* [Alter. of obs. *lanyer* < OF *lasniere* a thong < *lasne* a noose; infl. in form by *yard* [1] a spar]

La·o (lä'ō) *n.* **1** A Buddhistic people living in Laos and northern and eastern Thailand. **2** Their Thai language.

La·oc·o·on (lā·ok'ō·won, -ō·won) In Greek legend, a priest of Apollo who warned the Trojans against the wooden horse of the Greeks, and was destroyed with his two sons by two serpents sent by Athena or Apollo.

La·o·da·mi·a (lā·od'ə·mī'ə) In the *Iliad,* the wife of Protesilaus, the first Greek killed at Troy, who died from grief at his loss, after persuading the gods to grant him three more hours of life in which to be with her. Also **La·o·da·mei·a** (lā'ō·də·mī'ə).

La·od·i·ce·a (lā·od'ə·sē'ə) **1** Any of several Greek cities in Asia and Asia Minor, especially that in Phrygia, seat of one of the seven churches mentioned in the Apocalypse. **2** The ancient name for LATAKIA.

La·od·i·ce·an (lā·od'ə·sē'ən) *adj.* Of or pertaining to Laodicea; hence, indifferent or lukewarm, as in religion *Rev.* iii 14–22. — *n.* **1** An inhabitant of one of the eight Greek cities named Laodicea. **2** An indifferent or lukewarm Christian; hence, any indifferent or lukewarm person.

La·om·e·don (lā·om'ə·don) In Greek legend, the founder of Troy and father of Priam.

La·os (lā'os, lä'ōs) A constitutional monarchy in NW Indochina; 91,400 square miles; capital, Vientiane; royal residence, Luang Prabang.

Lao-tse (lou'dzu'), 604?–531? B.C., Chinese philosopher and mystic, founder of Taoism; also **Lao-tze** and **Lao-tzu.**

lap[1] (lap) *n.* **1** That part of the body below the waist on which, when in a sitting posture, one may conveniently support anything; the upper and front surface of the thighs or knees: to hold a child on one's *lap.* **2** The clothing that covers the front of the thighs when one sits down. **3** By extension, a place for supporting or fostering: fortune's *lap.* **4** A loose fold or flap of a garment; a skirt. **5** That part of a substance which extends over another; also, the length of such extension: the *lap* of a shingle. **6** One course around a race track, usually an even fraction of a mile. **7** A piece of soft metal, wood, or leather, usually in the form of a rotating disk, used in cutting gems and polishing hard metal. **8** The state of overlapping. — *v.* **lapped, lap·ping** *v.t.* **1** To fold and lay over; wrap around something. **2** To lay (one thing) partly over or beyond another: to *lap* weatherboards. **3** To reach or extend partly over or beyond; overlap: These doors *lap* each other. **4** To take upon or as upon the lap; surround with love, care, etc.: *lapped* in idleness and luxury. **5** To grind or polish (a gem) with a lap. **6** To get one or more laps ahead of (an opponent) in a race. — *v.i.* **7** To be folded; wrap. **8** To lie partly upon or beside something else; overlap. **9** To lie beyond or into something else: One wall *laps* into the other. [OE *læpa, lappa* a fold or hanging part of a garment]

lap[2] (lap) *v.t.* & *v.i.* **lapped, lap·ping** **1** To take (a liquid) into the mouth with the tongue: said of animals. **2** To wash against (the shore, etc.) with a slight, rippling sound: said of water. — *n.* **1** The act of lapping, as with the tongue; a lick. **2** The sound of lapping, or a similar sound. **3** *Colloq.* That which is licked up, as pap or a drink, especially a weak or diluted drink. [Prob. fusion of OE *lapian* lap and OF *laper* lick < Gmc.] — **lap'per** *n.*

La Pal·ma (lä päl'mä) See PALMA (sense 2).

laparo- *combining form Med.* The flanks or loins; the wall of the abdomen. Also, before vowels, **lapar-.** [< Gk. *lapara* flank]

lap·a·ros·co·py (lap'ə·ros'kə·pē) *n. Surg.* The examination of the abdominal cavity by means of a narrow instrument inserted through an incision.

lap·a·rot·o·my (lap'ə·rot'ə·mē) *n. Surg.* The operation of opening the abdomen by incision in the loin. [< LAPARO- + -TOMY]

La Paz (lä päz', *Sp.* lä päs') A city in western Bolivia; the de facto capital, although Sucre is nominally the capital.

lap·board (lap'bôrd', -bōrd') *n.* A flat wide board sometimes having a cavity on one edge hollowed out to fit the waist: used especially by tailors, etc., or over the arms of a chair, as a table.

lap·dis·solve (lap'di·zolv') *n.* In motion pictures, the gradual change of one scene into another, as by lapping two exposures on the same strip of film.

lap dog A dog small enough to be held on the lap.

la·pel (lə·pel') *n.* The part of the front of a coat, attached to the collar, which is folded back: usually plural. [Dim. of LAP[1]]

lap·ful (lap'fŏŏl') *n.* As much as the lap can hold.

lap·i·dar·i·an (lap'ə·dâr'ē·ən) *adj.* Of or relating to stones; written on stones: a *lapidarian* inscription. [< L *lapidarius* < *lapis, -idis* a stone]

lap·i·dar·y (lap'ə·der'ē) *adj.* **1** Pertaining to stones or the art of working in precious stones. **2** Inscribed upon or cut in stone. — *n. pl.* **·dar·ies 1** One who cuts, engraves, and sets precious stones. **2** A connoisseur in lapidary work or gems; lapidist. [< L *lapidarius* LAPIDARIAN]

lap·i·date (lap'ə·dāt) *v.t.* **·dat·ed, ·dat·ing 1** To hurl stones at. **2** To stone to death. [< L *lapidatus,* pp. of *lapidare* < *lapis, -idis* a stone] — **lap'i·da'tion** *n.*

la·pid·i·fy (lə·pid'ə·fī) *v.t.* & *v.i.* **·fied, ·fy·ing** To turn to stone; petrify. [< F *lapidifier* < Med. L *lapidificare* < L *lapis, -idis* a stone + *facere* make] — **lap·i·dif·ic** (lap'ə·dif'ik) or **·i·cal** *adj.* — **la·pid'i·fi·ca'tion** *n.*

la·pil·lus (lə·pil'əs) *n. pl.* **·li** (-ī) A small fragment of lava ejected from a volcano. [< L, dim. of *lapis* a stone]

lap·in (lap'in, *Fr.* lȧ·paṅ') *n.* A rabbit; also, its fur. [< F]

la·pis (lā'pis, lap'is) *n. pl.* **lap·i·des** (lap'ə·dēz) A stone: used in Latin phrases. [< L]

lap·is laz·u·li (lap'is laz'yōō·lī) **1** A rich blue complex mixture of minerals, originally used to produce ultramarine and by the ancients for decoration, and believed to be their sapphire. **2** The color of this substance. [< NL < L *lapis* a stone + Med. L *lazuli,* genitive of *lazulus* azure < Arabic *lāzaward.* See AZURE.]

Lap·i·thae (lap'ə·thē) *n. pl.* of **Lap·ith** (lap'ith) In Greek mythology, a wild tribe of Thessaly who, at the wedding of their king Pirithous, fought and overcame the centaurs, after the latter had attempted to carry off the bride and other women present at the feast. Also **Lap'i·thæ.**

lap–joint (lap'joint') *v.t.* To join together by a lap joint.

lap joint A joint in which a layer of material laps over another, as in shingling. — **lap-joint·ed** (lap'join'tid) *adj.*

Lap·land (lap'land) A region of northern Europe on the Barents Sea, largely within the Arctic Circle. See LAPP. — **Lap'land·er** *n.*

Lapp (lap) *n.* **1** One of a Mongoloid people inhabiting Lapland, of short stature, and markedly brachycephalic: also called *Saami.* Formerly nomadic and dependent upon reindeer herds for food and clothing, the Lapps are now settled largely in Sweden and Norway. Also **Lap'land'er. 2** The Finno–Ugric language of the Lapps. [< Sw.]

lap·per (lap'ər) *n.* **1** One who laps or folds. **2** One who polishes with a lap. **3** A lapping machine.

lap·pet (lap'it) *n.* **1** A small lap or flap used for ornamenting a garment, etc. **2** *Ornithol.* A fleshy process pendent from the head of a bird; a wattle. **3** A lobe, as of the ear. **4** A portion of anything that hangs loose. **5** The guard of a keyhole. [Dim. of LAP[1]]

lap·sa·tion (lap·sā'shən) *n.* In insurance, a lapsing.

lapse (laps) *v.i.* **lapsed, laps·ing 1** To pass slowly or by degrees; slip; sink: to *lapse* into a coma. **2** To deviate from virtue or truth; fail in duty or accuracy. **3** To pass or elapse, as time. **4** To become void, usually by disuse or neglect: The agreement *lapsed.* **5** *Law* To pass or be forfeited to another because of the negligence, failure, or death of the holder. See synonyms under FALL. — *n.* **1** An insensible or gradual slipping, gliding, or passing away; imperceptible movement onward or downward: the *lapse* of ages. **2** A fall to a lower form or state; a falling into decay or ruin, as a building: used also figuratively. **3** A slight deviation from what is right, proper, or just; a slip or mistake through lack of care or attention: a *lapse* in conduct; *lapse* of the pen. **4** Failure or miscarriage, as through fault or negligence: a *lapse* of justice. **5** *Law* The defeat of a right or privilege through fault, failure, or neglect, as, to perform certain conditions of a testamentary bequest. **6** Apostasy. [< L *lapsus* a slip < *labi* glide, slip] — **laps'a·ble, laps'i·ble** *adj.* — **laps'er** *n.*

lapse rate *Meteorol.* The rate of decrease of temperature with vertical height above the earth.

lap·stone (lap'stōn') *n.* A stone, held in the lap, on which a shoemaker hammers leather.

lap·strake (lap'strāk') *adj.* Built with planks overlapping and riveted together; clinker-built, as a boat. — *n.* A boat so built. Also **lap'streak'** (-strēk'). [< LAP[1] + STRAKE]

LAPSTRAKE
Flat-bottom rowboat.

La·pu·ta (lə·pyōō'tə) In Swift's *Gulliver's Trav-*

els, a flying island peopled by philosophers.

lap·wing (lap'wing') *n.* A ploverlike bird (*Vanellus vanellus*) having the plumage of the upper parts lustrous or metallic and the head crested. Its flight is heavy and flopping; its shrill note resembles the sound *pee–weet*. [OE *hlēapwince* < *hleapan* leap + *wince*, prob. < *wincan* totter; so called from its awkward manner of flight; infl. in form by LAP¹ and WING]

Lar·a·mie (lar'ə-mē) A city in SE Wyoming on the **Laramie River,** a river flowing 216 miles NE to the North Platte through northern Colorado and SE Wyoming.

lar·board (lär'bərd, -bôrd', -bord') *adj & adv. Naut.* Being or going on or toward the left side of a ship as one faces the bow. —*n.* The left-hand side of a ship: now replaced by *port.* [ME *laddebord,* lit., prob., lading side < OE *hladan* lade + *bord* side; infl. in form by STARBOARD]

lar·ce·ner (lär'sə-nər) *n.* A thief; one who commits larceny. Also **lar'ce·nist.**

lar·ce·ny (lär'sə-nē) *n. pl.* **·nies** *Law* The unlawful abstraction, without claim of right, of the personal goods of another with intent to defraud the owner; theft. The distinction between **grand larceny** and **petit** (or **petty**) **larceny,** based on the value of the stolen property, has been abolished in England and most of the United States. [< AF *larcin,* OF *larrecin* < L *latrocinium* theft < *latrocinari* rob < *latro* robber] —**lar'ce·nous** *adj.* —**lar'ce·nous·ly** *adv.*

larch (lärch) *n.* **1** Any of several cone-bearing, deciduous trees of the pine family (genus *Larix*). **2** The strong, durable wood of this tree. [< G *lärche* < MHG *lerche* < L *larix, laricis*]

lard (lärd) *n.* The semisolid oil of hog's fat after rendering. —*v.t.* **1** To prepare lean meat or poultry by inserting strips of bacon or fat before cooking. **2** To cover or smear with lard or grease. **3** To mix with something so as to enrich or improve; interlard. [< OF, bacon < L *lardum* lard] —**lard'y** *adj.*

lar·da·ce·in (lär-dā'sē·in, -sēn) *n.* A fatty protein compound produced in waxy or albuminoid degeneration. [< LARD + -ACE(OUS) + -IN]

lar·der (lär'dər) *n.* A room where articles of food are kept before cooking; pantry; hence, the provisions of a household. [< AF *larder,* OF *lardier* < Med. L *lardarium,* orig., a storehouse for bacon < L *lardum* lard]

larder beetle A small, blackish-and-gray beetle (*Dermestes lardarius*) about 1/3 inch long, whose larva feeds on dried meats, etc. For illustration see INSECT (injurious).

Lard·ner (lärd'nər), **Ring(gold) (Wilmer),** 1885–1933, U. S. author.

lar·don (lär'dən) *n.* A thin slice of bacon or pork for larding meat. Also **lar·doon** (lär-dōōn'). [< F < *lard.* See LARD.]

Lar·es (lâr'ēz, lā'rēz) *n. pl.* of Lar (lär) Tutelary deities of ancient Rome, adopted from the Etruscans, and worshiped as spirits of departed ancestors presiding over the households of their descendants: associated with the *Penates.*

lares and pe·na·tes (pə-nā'tēz) The household gods; hence, one's home and cherished belongings.

large (lärj) *adj.* **larg·er, larg·est 1** Absolutely or relatively great or ample as regards size, dimensions, quantity, number, extent, range, etc.; big; great; spacious; ample; extensive: opposed to *little* or *small.* **2** Having unusual breadth of sympathy or comprehension: a *large* heart or mind. **3** Favorable in direction; fair: said of a wind when it is abeam. **4** Characterized by fullness: said of the pulse. **5** *Obs.* Prodigal of words, gifts, or money; lavish. **6** *Obs.* Unrestrained in liberty or morals. **7** *Obs.* Complete; full. — **at large** (Formerly with the possessive pronoun: *at his large.*) **1** To the fullest extent; in full. **2** Free or unrestrained in movement; at liberty: The thief is still *at large.* **3** Not included within particular limitations; in general; for all. **4** Elected from a State as a whole rather than from a particular congressional or electoral district: a congressman *at large.* —*adv.*

1 *Naut.* Before the wind, or with the wind on the quarter. **2** *Colloq.* Boastfully. [< OF < L *larga,* fem. of *largus* abundant] —**large'· ness** *n.*

Synonyms (*adj.*): abundant, ample, big, broad, bulky, capacious, coarse, colossal, commodious, considerable, enormous, extensive, gigantic, grand, great, huge, immense, long, massive, spacious, vast, wide. *Large* denotes extension in more than one direction, and beyond the average of the class to which the object belongs; we speak of a *large* surface or a *large* solid, but of a *long* line. A *large* man is a man of more than ordinary size; a *great* man is a man of remarkable ability. *Big* is a more emphatic word than *large,* but ordinarily less elegant. *Antonyms:* diminutive, inconsiderable, infinitesimal, insignificant, limited, little, mean, microscopic, minute, narrow, paltry, petty, scanty, slender, slight, small, tiny, trifling, trivial.

large–heart·ed (lärj'här'tid) *adj.* Generous. —**large'–heart'ed·ness** *n.*

large·ly (lärj'lē) *adv.* **1** In a large manner. **2** To a great extent; generally. **3** Generously; abundantly; copiously. **4** Pompously.

large–mind·ed (lärj'mīn'did) *adj.* Liberal in ideas; not narrow-minded. —**large'–mind'ed· ness** *n.*

lar·gess (lär'jis, -jes) *n.* **1** A gift; gratuity. **2** Liberality; bounty. Also **lar'gesse.** See synonyms under GIFT. [< F *largesse* < L *largus* abundant]

lar·ghet·to (lär-get'ō) *Music adj.* Slow; in a time not quite so slow as *largo:* a direction to the performer. —*n.* A musical movement requiring moderately slow time. [< Ital., dim. of *largo* LARGO]

lar·ghis·si·mo (lär-gis'i·mō) *adj. Music* Very slow. [< Ital., superl. of *largo* LARGO]

larg·ish (lär'jish) *adj.* Somewhat large.

lar·go (lär'gō) *adj. & adv. Music* Slow; broad; majestic. —*n. pl.* **·gos** A movement in slow time. [< Ital., slow, large < L *largus* abundant]

lar·i·at (lar'ē·ət) *n.* **1** A rope, especially of horsehair, for tethering animals. **2** A lasso. —*v.t.* To fasten or catch with a lariat. [< Sp. *la reata* < *la* the + *reata* rope]

lar·ine (lar'in, lā'rin) *n.* One of a subfamily (*Larinae*) of longipennate birds, having the upper mandible as long as the lower and with a single sheath; a gull or tern. —*adj.* Of or pertaining to the *Larinae.* [< NL < LL *larus* a gull < Gk. *laros*]

la·rith·mics (lə-rith'miks) *n.* The scientific study and analysis of human populations in their quantitative aspects: distinguished from *eugenics.* [< Gk. *laos* people + *arithmos* a number] —**la·rith'mic** *adj.*

lark¹ (lärk) *n.* **1** Any of numerous small singing birds (family *Alaudidae*), as the European skylark (*Alauda arvensis*). **2** One of various other birds, as a titlark or meadowlark. [OE *lāferce, lāwerce*]

lark² (lärk) *n.* A hilarious time; frolic; humorous adventure. —*v.i.* To play pranks; frolic. [< dial. E (Northern) *lake* play, fusion of ON *leika* leap and OE *lācan* frolic; infl. in form by LARK¹] —**lark'er** *n.* —**lark'some** *adj.*

lark·spur (lärk'spûr) *n.* Any of several showy herbs of the crowfoot family (genus *Delphinium*) with alternate, palmately divided leaves, and loose, terminal clusters of irregular, spurred, white, pink, lavender, or blue flowers. — **scarlet larkspur** A species of larkspur (*Delphinium cardinale*) that grows wild in California. [< LARK¹ + SPUR]

larkspur blue A light, bright blue, the color of some larkspurs.

lark·y (lär'kē) *adj.* **lark·i·er, lark·i·est** *Colloq.* High-spirited and carefree; frolicsome: a *larky* adventure.

La Ro·chelle (là rō·shel') A port city of western France on the Bay of Biscay; Huguenot stronghold, besieged and taken by Cardinal Richelieu, 1627–28.

La·rousse (là·rōōs'), **Pierre Athanase,** 1817– 1875, French grammarian and encyclopedist.

lar·ri·gan (lar'ə·gən) *n.* A moccasin made of prepared oiled leather: used chiefly by lumbermen. [< dial. E (Canadian); origin unknown]

lar·va (lär'və) *n. pl.* **·vae** (-vē) **1** *Biol.* The early form of any animal when it is unlike

the parent, or undergoes a metamorphosis. **2** *Entomol.* The first stage of an insect after leaving the egg, preceding the pupa, as a caterpillar, a grub, or a maggot. **3** In ancient Roman superstition, an evil spirit. [< L, a ghost, a mask] —**lar'val** *adj.*

lar·vate (lär'vāt, -vit) *adj.* Clothed or concealed as if with a mask: said of certain diseases. Also **lar'vat·ed.** [< L *larvatus* < *larva* a mask]

lar·vi·pos·i·tor (lär'və·poz'ə·tər) *n. Entomol.* In certain dipterous insects, the modified ovipositor. [< LARVA + L *positor* a placer < *positus,* pp. of *ponere* put, place]

la·ryn·gal (lə·ring'gəl) *adj.* Originating in the larynx.

la·ryn·ga·phone (lə·ring'gə·fōn) *n.* A type of microphone which picks up and transmits voice vibrations by direct contact with the throat of the speaker: used to minimize interference by external sounds. [< *larynga-,* var. of LARYNGO- + -PHONE]

la·ryn·ge·al (lə·rin'je·əl, -jəl) *adj.* **1** Of, pertaining to, or near the larynx: also **la·ryn'· ge·an. 2** Attacking the larynx, as a disease. **3** Adapted or used for treating the larynx, as an instrument. [< NL *laryngeus* < Gk. *larynx, laryngos* larynx]

lar·yn·gis·mus (lar'ən·jiz'məs) *n.* **1** *Pathol.* Spasm of the muscles of the glottis. **2** A disease of horses caused by paralysis of muscles of the larynx; roaring. [< NL < Gk. *laryngismos* shouting < *laryngizein* shout < *larynx, laryngos* larynx] —**lar'yn·gis'mal** *adj.*

laryngismus strid·u·lus (strid'yə·ləs) *Pathol.* A disease of children marked by laryngeal spasms and a strident breathing; false or spasmodic croup. [< NL, lit., rattling laryngismus]

lar·yn·gi·tis (lar'ən·jī'tis) *n. Pathol.* Inflammation of the larynx. —**lar'yn·git'ic** (-jit'ik) *adj.*

laryngo– combining form The larynx; pertaining to the larynx: *laryngoscope.* Also, before vowels, **laryng–.** [< Gk. *larynx, laryngos* the larynx]

lar·yn·gol·o·gy (lar'ing·gol'ə·jē) *n.* Scientific knowledge of the larynx, its functions and diseases. —**la·ryn·go·log·i·cal** (lə·ring'gō·loj'i· kəl) *adj.* —**lar'yn·gol'o·gist** *n.*

lar·yn·got·o·my (lar'ing·got'ə·mē) *n. Surg.* The operation of cutting into the larynx. [< Gk. *laryngotomia* < *larynx, laryngos* the larynx + *tomē* a cutting < *temnein* cut]

lar·ynx (lar'ingks) *n. pl.* **la·ryn·ges** (lə·rin'jēz) or **lar·ynx·es** *Anat.* The organ of voice in mammals and most other vertebrates, situated at the upper part of the trachea, consisting of a cartilaginous box across which are stretched the vocal cords whose vibrations produce sound. [< Gk. *larynx, laryngos* the larynx]

HUMAN LARYNX

Left: front view.   Right: side view.
a. Hyoid bone.   *f.* Epiglottis.
b. Thyrohyoid ligament. *g.* Thyrohyoid membrane.
c. Thyroid cartilage.   *h.* Vocal chord.
d. Cricothyroid ligament. *i.* Vocal chord.
e. Cricoid cartilage.   *j.* Laryngeal ventricle.
                          k. Trachea.

Las Ca·sas (läs kä'säs), **Bartolomé de,** 1474– 1566, Spanish historian and missionary to the American Indians: called "Apostle of the Indies."

las·civ·i·ous (lə·siv'ē·əs) *adj.* **1** Having wanton desires; lustful; lewd. **2** Tending to produce sensual desires. See synonyms under BRUTISH.

[<LL *lasciviosus* <L *lascivia* wantonness < *lascivus* sportive, lustful] — **las·civ'i·ous·ly** *adv.* — **las·civ'i·ous·ness** *n.*

la·ser (lā'zər) *n.* An optical maser.

lash (lash) *n.* **1** A thong on a whip handle; a whip. **2** A stroke with or as with a whip. **3** A sharp, sarcastic remark. **4** An eyelash. **5** Any heavy blow, as of waves beating the shore. — *v.t.* **1** To strike, punish, or urge forward with or as with a whip. **2** To throw or move quickly or suddenly, as from side to side: to *lash* the tail. **3** To beat or dash against with force or violence: The waves *lashed* the pier. **4** To attack or criticize severely; berate. **5** To arouse the emotions of, as with words. **6** To bind or tie with or as with a lashing. — *v.i.* **7** To move quickly or violently; dash. — **to lash out 1** To strike out violently or wildly. **2** To break into angry or vehement speech. [<Prob. fusion of MLG *lasch* a flap and OF *laz* a cord; infl. in form and sense by OF *lachier* fasten. Akin to LACE, LATCH.]

lash·er[1] (lash'ər) *n.* One who or that which lashes.

lash·er[2] (lash'ər) *n.* **1** Slack water, as above a weir. **2** The weir itself. [<LASH (*v.* def. 7) + -ER[1]]

lash·ing (lash'ing) *n.* **1** A fastening made by passing a rope, cord, or the like, around two or more objects. **2** The rope used to do this. **3** A whipping.

Las Pal·mas (läs päl'mäs) See PALMAS, LAS.

La Spe·zia (lä spā'tsyä) A port on the Gulf of Spezia: also *Spezia.*

lass (las) *n.* **1** A young woman; girl. **2** A sweetheart. **3** *Scot.* A servant–girl; maid. [<Scand. Cf. OSw. *lösk kona* an unmarried woman.]

las·sie (las'ē) *n.* A little girl; a lass. Also **las'sock** (-ək). [Dim. of LASS]

las·si·tude (las'ə·tood, -tyood) *n.* A state of disinclination to exertion; languor; weariness; debility. [<F <L *lassitudo* <*lassus* faint]

las·so (las'ō) *n. pl.* **·sos** or **·soes** A long rope or leather thong, with a running noose, for catching horses and cattle. — *v.t.* To catch with a lasso. [<Sp. *lazo* <L *laqueus* a snare] — **las'so·er** *n.*

lasso cell A nematocyst.

last[1] (last, läst) *adj.* **1** Being at the end; latest; hindmost; final. **2** Next before the present; most recent. **3** Least fit or likely; most remote. **4** Beyond or above all others; utmost. **5** Beneath all others. — *adv.* **1** After all others in time or order. **2** At a time next preceding the present: He was *last* seen heading west. **3** In conclusion; finally. — *n.* **1** The end; conclusion. **2** The final appearance, experience, or mention: We'll never hear the *last* of this. — **at last** At length; at the end; finally. [OE *latost,* superl. of *læt* late, slow] — **last'ly** *adv.*

last[2] (last, läst) *v.i.* **1** To remain in existence; continue to be; endure. **2** To continue unchanged or unaltered; persevere. **3** To be as much as or more than needed; hold out: Will our supplies *last* through the winter? — *n.* Ability to endure; stamina. [OE *læsten* follow a track, continue, accomplish. Akin to LAST[3].] — **last'er** *n.*

last[3] (last, läst) *n.* A shaped form, usually of wood, on which to make a boot or shoe. — *v.t.* To fit to or form on a last. [OE *læst* a boot, shoemaker's last <*last* a footstep, track. Akin to LAST[2].] — **last'er** *n.*

last[4] (last, läst) *n.* **1** A weight or measure varying for different articles, but often reckoned as 80 bushels. **2** One or two tons, usually 4,000 pounds: a unit in estimating ship capacity. [OE *hlæst* a load <*hladan* lade]

last·ing[1] (las'ting, läs'-) *adj.* Continuing; durable; permanent. See synonyms under PERMANENT, PERPETUAL. — *n.* Endurance; continuance. [<LAST[2]] — **last'ing·ly** *adv.* — **last'ing·ness** *n.*

last·ing[2] (las'ting, läs'-) *n.* **1** A fabric used for the uppers of shoes, etc. **2** The operation of stretching an upper on a shoemaker's last. [<LAST[3]]

Last Judgment See under JUDGMENT.

Last Supper The last meal of Jesus Christ with his disciples before the Crucifixion.

last word 1 The final say, as in a dispute. **2** The latest or most modern fashion, style, advancement, etc.

Las Ve·gas (läs vā'gəs) The second largest city of Nevada, in the SE part; famous for its gambling casinos.

la·ta·ni·a (lə·tā'nē·ə) *n.* The palmetto or cabbage palm of the southern United States. [<NL <F *lattanier* <Cariban *aláttani*]

latch[1] (lach) *n.* A catch for fastening a door, lid, shutter, etc., commonly not requiring any special key. See synonyms under LOCK[1] — *v.t. & v.i.* To fasten by means of a latch; close. — **to latch on to** *Slang* **1** To fasten (oneself) to. **2** To obtain; get. [OE *laeccan, laeccean* seize. Akin to LACE, LASH.]

latch[2] (lach) *v.t.* See LEACH.

latch·et (lach'it) *n.* A lace, thong, or strap that fastens a shoe or sandal. Also **shoe latchet.** [<OF *lachet,* dial. var. of *lacet,* dim. of *las, laz.* See LACE.]

latch·key (lach'kē) *n.* A key for releasing a latch, especially on an outside or front door.

latchkey child A child who comes home after school to an empty house, the parent or parents being still at work.

latch·string (lach'string') *n.* A string fastened to a latch and passed through a hole above it to the outside: used for lifting a latch.

late (lāt) *adj.* **lat·er** or **lat·ter, lat·est** or **last 1** Coming after the appointed time; tardy. **2** Far advanced toward the end or close; at or continuing to an advanced hour. **3** Recent or comparatively recent: often implying a subsequent change. **4** Deceased, especially recently deceased. — *adv.* **1** After or beyond the usual proper or appointed time; after delay; at or until an advanced hour. **2** Not long ago; recently. **3** After a while; in course of time: contrasted with *soon* or *early*: We rue our follies soon or *late*: more frequently used in the comparative degree. — **of late** In time not long past or near present; recently. [OE *lœt* late, slow] — **late'ness** *n.*

lat·ed (lā'tid) *adj.* Belated.

la·teen (la·tēn') *adj. Naut.* Designating a rig common in the Mediterranean, having a triangular sail (**lateen sail**) suspended from a long yard set obliquely to the mast. [<F (*voile*) *latine* Latin (sail), fem. of *latin* <L *Latinus*]

la·teen-rigged (la·tēn'rigd') *adj. Naut.* Having a lateen sail or sails.

late·ly (lāt'lē) *adv.* Not long ago; recently.

LATEEN SAIL

la·ten·si·fi·ca·tion (lə·ten'sə·fə·kā'shən) *n. Phot.* The technique of making a fogging exposure after the initial exposure, in order to bring out shadow details and increase the effective emulsion speed of some negative materials. [<LATEN(CY) + INTEN)SIFICATION]

la·tent (lā'tənt) *adj.* **1** Not visible or apparent; hidden; dormant. **2** *Psychol.* Potentially capable of being expressed, as an emotion or attitude. **3** *Bot.* Undeveloped, as a concealed bud. [<L *latens, -entis,* ppr. of *latere* be hidden] — **la'ten·cy** *n.* — **la'tent·ly** *adv.*

latent heat *Physics* The amount of heat required to change the state of a unit mass of a body, either from solid to liquid or from liquid to vapor, without changing the temperature of the body.

latent image *Phot.* The invisible image produced by the action of light on the silver halide or other grains of a photographic emulsion before development of the film.

latent period 1 *Pathol.* The interval between the incubation period of a disease and its outbreak. **2** *Physiol.* Elapsed time between a stimulus and its response.

lat·er (lā'tər) *adv.* At a subsequent time; hereafter.

lat·er·al (lat'ər·əl) *adj.* **1** Pertaining to, proceeding from, or directed toward the side. **2** *Biol.* Situated on one or both sides of the median plane of a body, limb, or organ: opposed to *medial.* [<L *lateralis* <*latus, lateris* a side] — **lat'er·al·ly** *adv.*

lat·er·ite (lat'ər·īt) *n.* A red, ferruginous, porous clay of tropical regions. [<L *later* a brick + -ITE[1]] — **lat'er·it'ic** (-it'ik) *adj.*

lat·er·i·tious (lat'ər·ish'əs) *adj.* Pertaining to or resembling brick; brick-red in color. [<L *lateritius* <*later* a brick]

la·tes·cent (lə·tes'ənt) *adj.* Becoming obscure, latent, or hidden. [<L *latescens, -entis,* ppr. of *latescere,* inceptive of *latere* be hidden] — **la·tes'cence** *n.*

lat·est (lā'tist) Alternative superlative of LATE. — *adj. & adv.* **1** Most recent. **2** *Archaic & Poetic* Last.

la·tex (lā'teks) *n. pl.* **lat·i·ces** (lat'ə·sēz) or **la·tex·es** The viscid, milky, complex emulsion of proteins, alkaloids, starches, resins, and other substances secreted by the cells of certain plants, as the milkweed, rubber tree, poppy, dandelion, etc. [<L, a liquid]

lath (lath, läth) *n.* **1** A thin strip of wood or metal, as one of a number nailed to studs or beams and serving to support a coat of plaster, or on rafters to support shingles or slates. **2** An angle-iron forming the support for an iron roof. **3** Laths taken collectively; lathwork. **4** Figuratively, a thin, slender, or delicate person or thing. — *v.t.* To cover or line with laths. [Prob. fusion of OE *lætt* and OE *læth* (assumed); ? infl. in form by Welsh *llath*] — **lath'er** *n.*

lathe[1] (lāth) *n.* **1** A machine for shaping articles in which an object is mounted and rotated, while a tool is thrust against the work, shaping it down, usually to some circular form. **2** In a loom, the swinging beam which beats up the weft. **3** A potter's wheel. — *v.t.* **lathed, lath·ing** To form or shape on a lathe. [Prob. <MDu. *lade*]

lath·er (lath'ər) *n.* **1** Foam or froth of soapsuds. **2** Foam of profuse sweating, as of a horse. — **in a lather** *Colloq.* In a state of intense excitement or agitation. — *v.t.* **1** To cover with lather. **2** *Colloq.* To flog; thrash. — *v.i.* **3** To become covered with lather. **4** To form lather. [OE *léathor* washing soda, soap. Akin to LAVE.] — **lath'er·er** *n.* — **lath'er·y** *adj.*

lath·ing (lath'ing, läth'-) *n.* **1** The act or process of covering with laths. **2** The foundation of laths on which plaster may be laid; the material for such foundation. **3** Any work with laths or like material.

lathing hatchet A hatchet with a narrow blade, for cutting and attaching wooden laths. See illustration under HATCHET.

lath·work (lath'wûrk', läth'-) *n.* Lathing.

lath·y (lath'ē, läth'ē) *adj.* **lath·i·er, lath·i·est** Like a lath; long and slender.

La·tian (lā'shən) *adj.* Of or pertaining to ancient Latium in Italy; Latin.

lat·i·ces (lat'ə·sēz) Plural of LATEX.

lat·i·cif·er·ous (lat'ə·sif'ər·əs) *adj.* Containing or conveying latex. [<L *latex, laticis* a liquid + -FEROUS]

lat·i·clave (lat'ə·klāv) *n.* **1** A broad vertical purple stripe down the tunics of ancient Romans of senatorial rank. **2** A tunic thus marked. [<LL *laticlavium, laticlavus* <*latus* broad + *clavus* a purple stripe]

lat·i·fo·li·ate (lat'ə·fō'lē·it, -āt) *adj. Bot.* Having broad leaves. Also **lat·i·fo'li·ous.** [<NL *latifoliatus* <L *latus* broad + *folia* a leaf]

lat·i·fun·di·um (lat'ə·fun'dē·əm) *n. pl.* **·di·a** (-dē·ə) A large landed property. [<L <*latus* wide + *fundus* an estate]

Lat·in (lat'n) *adj.* **1** Pertaining to ancient Latium, its inhabitants, their culture, or language. **2** Pertaining to or denoting the peoples or countries, as France, Italy, and Spain, whose languages and cultures are derived from the ancient Roman civilization. **3** Of or belonging to the Western or, since the Reformation, the Roman Catholic Church, as distinguished from the Greek Church. — *n.* **1** One of the people of ancient Latium. **2** A member of any of the modern Latin peoples. **3** A member of the Western or Roman Catholic Church: used especially in the Greek Church. **4** The Indo-European, Italic language of ancient Latium and Rome: extensively used in western Europe until modern times as a language of learning, and still retained as the official language of the Roman Catholic Church. — **Old Latin,** the language before the first century B.C., as preserved in early inscriptions and the comedies of Plautus. — **Classical Latin,** the literary language of the period 80 B.C. to A.D. 200, standardized by such writers as Cicero, Caesar, Livy, Vergil, Tacitus, and Juvenal. Abbr. *L* —**Late Latin,** the language from 200–600, including the patristic writings. Abbr. *LL* —**Low Latin,** the language of any period after the classical, as Medieval Latin, especially as influenced and modified by other continental languages. —**Medieval Latin,** the language used by the writers of the Middle Ages, from 600-1500: also called *Middle Latin.* Abbr. *Med. L* —**New Latin,** a form of the language, based on Latin and Greek elements, developed since the Renaissance and used chiefly in scientific and taxonomic terms. Abbr. *NL* —**Vulgar Latin,** the popular speech of the Romans in all stages of the language from about A.D. 200 through the medieval period: the chief source of the Romance languages. [< L *Latinus* of Latium, Latin]

Latin alphabet A set of letters containing, originally, 20 characters derived from the Western Greek alphabet (in turn, developed from the Phoenician) with the later addition of G, Y, and Z. The English alphabet, descendent from the Latin, has the added characters J, U, and W. Also called *Roman alphabet.*

Latin America Those countries of the western hemisphere south of the Rio Grande, in which the official languages are derived from Latin. See SPANISH AMERICA. —**Lat′in·A·mer′·i·can** *adj.*

Latin American A native or inhabitant of Latin America.

Lat·in·ate (lat′ən·āt) *adj.* Resembling or derived from Latin.

Latin Church That part of the Catholic Church which accepts the pope as supreme authority on earth, and uses Latin for the liturgy of the mass. Compare UNIAT.

Latin cross See under CROSS.

La·tin·ic (lə·tin′ik) *adj.* Of Latin.

Lat·in·ism (lat′ən·iz′əm) *n.* An idiom peculiar to or imitating Latin. —**Lat′in·is′tic** *adj.*

Lat·in·ize (lat′ən·īz) *v.* ·**ized,** ·**iz·ing** *v.t.* 1 To translate into Latin. 2 To make Latin in customs, thought, etc. 3 To cause to resemble the Roman Catholic Church, as in dogma or ritual. 4 To transliterate into Latin characters, as a Greek word. —*v.i.* 5 To use Latin words, forms, etc. [< L *latinizare* < *Latinus* Latin] —**Lat′in·i·za′tion** *n.* —**Lat′in·iz′er** *n.*

la·ti·no (la·tē′nō) *n. pl.* ·**nos** *Often cap.* A Latin American. [< Am. Sp. < Sp., L]

Latin Quarter A section of Paris on the left (south) bank of the Seine, known for the large number of artists and students who live there.

lat·i·ros·tral (lat′ə·ros′trəl) *adj. Ornithol.* Having a broad beak, as certain birds. [< NL *Latirostres,* former group name for the swallows < L *latus* broad + *rostrum* a beak]

lat·ish (lā′tish) *adj.* Rather late.

lat·i·tude (lat′ə·tōod, -tyōod) *n.* 1 *Geog.* Distance on the earth's surface northward or southward from the equator measured in degrees of the meridian; angular distance reckoned on a meridian. 2 *Astron.* The angular distance of a heavenly body above the plane of the ecliptic, as viewed from some point. 3 A region or place with reference to its distance north or south of the equator. 4 Figuratively, one's proper place or environment. 5 Extent of deviation from what is regular or customary; independence or liberty of action or conduct. 6 Laxity. 7 Strength of application; range or scope. [< L *latitudo* breadth < *latus* broad] —**lat′i·tu′di·nal** *adj.*

lat·i·tu·di·nar·i·an (lat′ə·tōo′də·nâr′ē·ən,-tyōo′-) *adj.* Broad, tolerant, or lax in religious principles. —*n.* 1 One who is extremely tolerant or lax in religious principles; a freethinker; liberal. 2 One who departs from the strict standards of orthodoxy. [< L *latitudo,* -*inis* LATITUDE + -ARIAN] —**lat′i·tu′di·nar′i·an·ism** *n.*

La·to·na (lə·tō′nə) In Roman mythology, the mother of Diana and Apollo: identified with the Greek *Leto.*

la·tri·a (lə·trī′ə) *n.* In the Roman Catholic Church, that supreme worship which can be lawfully given to God only: distinguished from *dulia* and *hyperdulia.* [< LL *latria* < Gk. *latreia* service, worship < *latreuein* work for hire, worship < *latris* a hired servant]

la·trine (lə·trēn′) *n.* A privy, especially in a camp, barracks, hospital, etc. [< F < L *latrina* a bath, a privy < *lavatrina* < *lavare* wash]

lat·ten (lat′n) *n.* Metal in thin sheets, especially (and originally) brass. [< OF *laton, leiton,* prob. < MHG *latta* a thin plate, a lath. Akin to LATH.]

lat·ter (lat′ər) *adj.* 1 Of more recent date; modern. 2 *Obs.* Latest or last. —**the latter** The second of two mentioned persons or things: opposed to *the former.* [OE *lætra,* compar. of *læt* late] —**lat′ter·ly** *adv.*

lat·ter–day (lat′ər·dā′) *adj.* Belonging to the present; recent; modern.

Latter–day Saint A Mormon.

lat·ter·most (lat′ər·mōst′) *adj.* Last; latest.

lat·tice (lat′is) *n.* 1 Openwork of metal or wood, formed by crossing or interlacing strips or bars; also, anything made of such work, as a window, a blind, or a screen: also called *latticework.* 2 That which resembles a lattice: a *lattice* of branches. 3 *Her.* A bearing of vertical and horizontal bars crossing one another. 4 *Physics* A space lattice. 5 *Telecom.* A network of lines indicating fixed positions in a radio or radar system. —*v.t.* **lat·ticed, lat·tic·ing** 1 To furnish or enclose with a lattice. 2 To arrange or interlace like latticework. [<OF *lattis* < *latte* a lath <MHG. Akin to LATH.]

LATTICE

lat·tice·work (lat′is·wûrk′) *n.* 1 Lattice (def. 1). 2 In embroidery, stitching in an outline resembling a lattice: done on solid material, and used as a background.

lat·tic·ing (lat′is·ing) *n.* 1 The act of making or furnishing with lattice. 2 In bridge-building, a system of timbers or bars crossing in such a manner as to connect and strengthen the two channels of a strut and cause them to act as one construction.

la·tus rec·tum (lā′təs rek′təm) *Math.* The chord drawn through a focus of a plane curve perpendicular to its major axis. [<NL, a straight line <L, lit., a right side]

Lat·vi·a A republic on the Baltic Sea in NE Europe; 24,900 square miles, capital, Riga; pop. 2,700,000. Formerly the **Latvian Soviet Socialist Republic** (1940-1991).

Lat·vi·an (lat′vē·ən) *adj.* Of or pertaining to Latvia, its inhabitants, or their language. —*n.* 1 A Lett. 2 The Lettish language.

laud (lôd) *n.* 1 Praise or commendation; extolment. 2 The part of divine worship that consists chiefly of praise; also, a song of praise or honor. 3 *pl.* A religious service consisting of the psalms immediately following matins, and constituting with the latter the first of the seven canonical hours: sometimes Lauds. See synonyms under PRAISE. —*v.t.* To praise; extol. [<OF *laude* <L *laus, laudis* praise] —**laud′er** *n.*

laud·a·ble (lô′də·bəl) *adj.* 1 Worthy of approval; praiseworthy. 2 Healthy or promotive of health or healing; salubrious; normal: said of pus or bodily juices. —**laud′a·ble·ness, laud·a·bil′i·ty** *n.* —**laud′a·bly** *adv.*

lau·da·nine (lô′də·nēn) *n. Chem.* A white, crystalline alkaloid from opium, $C_{20}H_{25}O_4N$, belonging pharmacologically to the codeine group. [<LAUDAN(UM) + -INE²]

lau·da·num (lô′də·nəm) *n.* 1 Tincture of opium. 2 Formerly, a preparation in which opium predominated. [<NL <Med. L, var. of L *ladanum* LADANUM]

lau·da·tion (lô·dā′shən) *n.* The act of praising; praise.

laud·a·to·ry (lô′də·tôr′ē, -tō′rē) *adj.* Eulogizing; praising: also **laud′a·tive.** —*n. pl.* ·**ries** A panegyric. [<L *laudatorius* <L *laudare* praise, celebrate]

laugh (laf, läf) *v.i.* 1 To express amusement, hilarity, derision, etc., by expressions of the face and by a series of explosive sounds made in the chest and throat. 2 To be or appear gay or lively. —*v.t.* 3 To express by laughter. 4 To move or influence by laughter or ridicule: He *laughed* himself out of his worries. —**to laugh at** 1 To express amusement concerning. 2 To make light of; belittle. —**to laugh away** To drive off or away by laughter. —**to laugh in** (or **up**) **one's sleeve** To be secretly amused although outwardly serious. —**to laugh off** To dismiss with a laugh; treat lightly or scornfully. —**to laugh on** (or **out of**) **the other** (or **wrong**) **side of the mouth** To feel

sudden disappointment or annoyance after mirth or supposed triumph. —*n.* 1 The act or sound of laughter. 2 *Colloq.* Anything provoking or producing laughter. [OE *hlæhhan*] —**laugh′er** *n.*

laugh·a·ble (laf′ə·bəl, läf′-) *adj.* Ridiculous; exciting laughter; humorous; ludicrous. —**laugh′a·ble·ness** *n.* —**laugh′a·bly** *adv.*

laugh·ing (laf′ing, läf′-) *adj.* Fit to be laughed at: a *laughing* matter.

laughing gas Nitrous oxide, N_2O, an anesthetic with exhilarating effect when inhaled: used in dental surgery.

laughing goose The white-fronted goose (*Anser albifrons*) of western North America: also called *harlequin brant.*

laughing gull The black-headed gull (*Larus atricilla*) of the Atlantic coast of North America.

laughing jackass The kookaburra.

laugh·ing·ly (laf′ing·lē, läf′-) *adv.* With a laugh, laughter, or merriment.

laugh·ing·stock (laf′ing·stok′, läf′-) *n.* A butt for ridicule.

laugh·ter (laf′tər, läf′-) *n.* 1 The sound or action of laughing. 2 Any exclamation or expression indicating merriment or derision. ♦ Collateral adjective: *risible.* [OE *hleahtor* < root of *hlæhhan* laugh]
Synonyms: cachinnation, fun, giggling, glee, hilarity, jollity, merriment, mirth, rejoicing, snickering, tittering. *Antonyms:* distress, frowning, gloom, glowering, groaning, lowering, mourning, sadness, sorrow, tears, wailing, weeping.

launce (lôns) *n.* The sand eel: also spelled *lance.*

Laun·ce·lot (lôn′sə·lot, län′-) See LANCELOT.

launch¹ (lônch, länch) *v.t.* 1 To cause to move from land into water for the first time, as a ship on completion of its hull. 2 To put into the water; set afloat, as a boat or log. 3 To make a beginning of; set in motion: to *launch* an enterprise. 4 To start (someone) on a career, course, etc. 5 To give a start to the flight or course of, as a rocket, torpedo, or airplane. 6 To hurl or throw, as a spear. —*v.i.* 7 To put or go to sea: usually with *out* or *forth.* 8 To start on a career, course, etc. 9 To begin something with vehemence or urgency; plunge: He *launched* into a tirade. —**to launch out** 1 To strike out suddenly or wildly. 2 To be vehement or reckless. 3 To start; commence. —*n.* 1 The act of launching. 2 The movement of a ship, boat, etc., from the land into the water; especially, the sliding over ways of a newly built vessel from the stocks into the water; also, the spot where a ship is built, and the tackle used in launching it. 3 The start of a bird for flight. [<AF *lancher,* OF *lancier* < *lance* LANCE]

launch² (lônch, länch) *n.* 1 The largest of the boats carried by a warship, used for transporting men and supplies. 2 A large, open boat, propelled by steam or electricity, and used as a pleasure craft. [<Sp. *lancha,* prob. <Malay *lanca* a three-masted boat < *lancãr* speedy]

launch·er (lôn′chər, län′-) *n.* 1 One who or that which launches. 2 Any mechanical device or installation for launching rockets, guided missiles, satellites, etc.

launching pad The platform from which a rocket or guided missile is fired.

laun·der (lôn′dər, län′-) *v.t.* 1 To wash and iron, as clothing. —*v.i.* 2 To wash and iron laundry. 3 To undergo washing and ironing. —*n.* A trough or gutter, as of wood, for conveying water. [Contraction of ME *lavender* a laundress <OF *lavendier* a washerwoman < LL *lavandarius,* ult. <L *lavare* wash] —**laun′der·er** *n.*

laun·dress (lôn′dris, län′-) *n.* A woman who works in a laundry; washerwoman.

laun·dro·mat (lôn′drə·mat, län-) *n. U.S.* A commercial establishment where the customer brings laundry to be washed and dried in coin-operated automatic machines. [<*Laundromat,* a trade name]

laun·dry (lôn′drē, län′-) *n. pl.* ·**dries** 1 A place for washing and ironing clothes. 2 Articles sent to a laundry for washing and ironing. 3 *Obs.* A laundress. [Alter. of obs. *lavendry*

<OF *lavenderie* < *lavendier.* See LAUNDER.]
— **laun′dry·man** (-mən) *n.* — **laun′dry·wom′an** (-wŏŏm′ən) *n. fem.*

lau·ra·ceous (lô-rā′shəs) *adj.* Belonging to a family (*Lauraceae*) of aromatic and medicinal trees and shrubs, the laurels, which includes sassafras and cinnamon, mostly natives of warm climates. [<NL <L *laurus* the laurel]

lau·re·ate (lô′rē-it) *adj.* **1** Crowned or decked with laurel, as a mark of distinction or honor. **2** Deserving of distinction; preeminent, especially as a poet; also, relating to or distinctive of poets. **3** Made of laurel or in imitation of laurel. — *n.* **1** In England, the poet officially invested with the title of poet laureate by the crown. **2** In former times, a poet publicly crowned with laurel in recognition of his merit. See under POET. — *v.t.* (-rē·āt) ·**at·ed,** ·**at·ing 1** To crown with a laurel wreath. **2** To make poet laureate. [<L *laureatus* crowned with laurel < *laurea* a laurel tree or crown, orig. fem. of *laureus* made of laurel < *laurus* laurel] — **lau′re·ate·ship′** *n.* — **lau′re·a′tion** *n.*

lau·rel (lôr′əl, lor′-) *n.* **1** An evergreen shrub (*Laurus nobilis*) of the Mediterranean area, with aromatic, lance-shaped leaves, yellowish flowers, and succulent, cherrylike fruit: also called **bay laurel, Grecian laurel, noble laurel:** also called **bay. 2** Any other species of the genus *Laurus.* **3** An American evergreen shrub of either of two genera, as the mountain laurel (*Kalmia latifolia*) or the great laurel (*Rhododendron maximum*). **4** In England, a species of evergreen cherry tree (genus *Prunus*) with flowers in racemes and inedible fruit. **5** *pl.* A crown or wreath of laurel, indicating honor or high merit; hence, honor or distinction. **6** A salmon that has passed the summer in fresh water. — **to rest on one's laurels** To be content with what one has already achieved or accomplished. — *v.t.* ·**reled** or ·**relled,** ·**rel·ing** or ·**rel·ling 1** To wreathe or crown with laurel. **2** To honor. [<OF *laurier, lorier* < *lor* <L *laurus* a laurel]

lau·ric (lô′rik) *adj. Biochem.* Designating a fatty acid, $C_{11}H_{23}COOH$, found as a glyceride in spermaceti, laurel oil, etc. [<L *laurus* laurel + -IC]

Lau·rus (lô′rəs) *n.* A genus of evergreen trees of the family *Lauraceae.* [<L, laurel tree]

lau·rus·tine (lô′rəs·tin) *n.* A southern European shrub (*Viburnum tinus*) having oblong leaves hairy on the underside and fragrant white or pink flowers appearing in winter. Also **lau·rus·ti·nus** (lô′rəs·tī′nəs). [<NL *laurustinus* <L *laurus tinus* < *laurus* laurel + *tinus* a plant]

Lau·sanne (lō·zàn′) A Swiss city on the northern shore of Lake Geneva, capital of Vaud canton.

laus De·o (lôs dē′ō) *Latin* Praise be to God.

la·va (lä′və, lav′ə) *n.* **1** Melted rock, issuing from a volcanic crater or a fissure in the earth's surface. **2** Such rock when solidified. [<Ital., orig. a stream of rain < *lavare* wash <L]

la·va·bo (lə·vā′bō) *n. pl.* ·**boes 1** In the Anglican and Roman Catholic churches, the washing of the hands by the celebrant after the offertory, during the Eucharist. **2** That part of Psalm xxvi which is recited by the priest while washing the hands: from the opening word. **3** A small linen towel used to wipe the priest's hands in this rite. **4** A stationary washbowl or lavatory with running water; also, in monasteries, the room in which this is placed. [<L, I shall wash, 1st person sing. future of *lavare* wash]

lav·age (lav′ij, *Fr.* là·vàzh′) *n. Med.* A cleansing, especially the washing out or irrigation of an organ, as the stomach. [<F < *laver* wash <L *lavare*]

la·va-la·va (lä′və·lä′və) *n.* A loincloth or waistcloth of printed calico worn by natives of Samoa and other islands of the Pacific. [<Samoan]

lav·a·liere (lav′ə·lir′) *n.* A piece of jewelry, consisting of a necklace and pendant. Also **lav′a·lier′.** [<F *la vallière* a sort of necktie, ? after Louise de *La Vallière,* 1644–1710, mistress of Louis XIV]

la·va·tion (la·vā′shən) *n.* A washing. Also **lave·ment** (lāv′mənt). [<L *lavatio, -onis* < *lavare* wash]

lav·a·to·ry (lav′ə·tôr′ē, -tō′rē) *n. pl.* ·**ries 1** An apartment for washing; a place where

anything is washed; specifically, a room in a public or semipublic place, as in a school or hotel, provided with appliances for washing and usually with urinals and toilets. **2** *Med.* A wash for a diseased part; lotion. **3** *Eccl.* A piscina; also, a water drain in a sacristy where the priest washes his hands before vesting. — *adj.* Washing. [<LL *lavatorium* a place for washing < *lavare* wash]

lave¹ (lāv) *v.t.* & *v.i.* **laved, lav·ing 1** To wash; bathe. **2** To flow along or against as if washing. [Fusion of OE *lafian* wash, pour and OF *laver* wash, both <L *lavare* wash. Akin to LATHER.]

lave² (lāv) *n. Scot.* The rest; remainder. [OE *laf*]

lav·en·der (lav′ən·dər) *n.* **1** An aromatic shrub (genus *Lavandula*) of the mint family, especially the Old World **spike lavender** (*L. officinalis*), the source of oil of lavender. '**2** Its characteristic perfume. **3** The dried flowers and leaves of this plant, used to scent linen, etc. **4** The color of lavender flowers, a pale lilac. — *adj.* Of, pertaining to, or like lavender. [<AF *lavendre* <Med. L *lavendula, livendula,* ? <L *livere* be bluish < *lividus* blue; infl. in form by *lavare* wash, because used as a perfume in baths]

SPIKE
LAVENDER
(Plant from 2
to 3 feet tall)

la·ver¹ (lā′vər) *n.* **1** A large basin or other receptacle to wash in; specifically, in Solomon's temple and the ancient Jewish tabernacle, a large vessel of bronze at which the priests washed their hands and feet before sacrifices. **2** That which laves. [<LAVE¹]

la·ver² (lā′vər) *n.* Any edible purple seaweed (genus *Porphyra*) or a dish prepared from it. Also **red laver.** [<L, a water plant]

lav·ish (lav′ish) *adj.* **1** Bestowed, expended, or existing in profusion; superabundant. **2** Spending extravagantly; prodigal. **3** Wild or unrestrained. — *v.t.* To give or bestow profusely or generously; squander. See synonyms under SQUANDER. [<OF *lavasse, lavache* a downpour of rain <Provençal *lavaci* <L *lavatio* a lavation] — **lav′ish·er** *n.* — **lav′ish·ly** *adv.* — **lav′ish·ness** *n.*

lav·ish·ment (lav′ish·mənt) *n.* A lavishing prodigality.

la·vol·ta (lə·vol′tə) *n.* An old dance for two persons consisting of lively, bounding steps. Also **la·volt′, la·vol′to.** [<Ital. < *la* the + *volta* a turn <L *volutus,* pp. of *volvere* turn]

law (lô) *n.* **1** A rule of conduct, recognized by custom or by formal enactment, which a community considers as binding upon its members. **2** A system or body of such rules. **3** The condition of society when such rules are observed: to establish *law* and order. **4** The body of rules relating to a specified subject: criminal *law;* statute *law.* **5** Statute and common law, as opposed to equity. **6** An enactment of a legislature, as opposed to a constitution. **7** Remedial justice as administered by the courts: to resort to the *law.* **8** The branch of knowledge concerned with jurisprudence: to study *law.* **9** The vocation of an attorney, solicitor, etc.: to practice *law.* **10** The legal profession as a whole. **11** The Mosaic system of rules recorded in the Pentateuch. **12** A rule of conduct having divine origin; also such rules, collectively. **13** An imperative rule or command: His word is *law.* **14** Any rule of conduct or procedure: the *laws* of hospitality; the *laws* of poetry. **15** In science and philosophy, a statement of the manner or order in which a defined group of natural phenomena occur under certain conditions: also called *law of nature.* **16** *Math.* The rule or formula by which certain functions vary or according to which certain operations are performed. **17** An allowance made or a start given to a competitor in a race or to a hunted animal. — **the law** The police, personifying legal force. — *v.t.* & *v.i.* To proceed against (someone) at law. — *adj.* Of or pertaining to law or the law. [OE *lagu* <ON *lag* something laid or fixed, in pl., law. Akin to LAY¹.]

Synonyms (noun): canon, code, command, commandment, decree, edict, enactment, formula, mandate, order, ordinance, princi-

ple, regulation, rule, statute. *Law* in its ideal is the statement of a *principle* of right in mandatory form, by competent authority, with adequate penalty for disobedience; in common use the term is applied to any legislative act, however imperfect or unjust. *Command* and *commandment* are personal and particular; as, the *commands* of a parent; the Ten *Commandments.* An *edict* is the act of an absolute sovereign or other authority; we speak of the *edict* of an emperor, the *decree* of a court. A *mandate* is specific for an occasion or a purpose; a superior court issues its *mandate* to an inferior court to send up its records (see MANDATE). *Statute* is the recognized legal term for a specific *law; enactment* is the more vague and general expression. We speak of algebraic or chemical *formulas,* municipal *ordinances,* military *orders,* army *regulations,* ecclesiastical *canons,* the *rules* of a business house. *Law* is often used, also, for a recognized *principle,* whose violation is attended with injury or loss that acts like a penalty; as, the *laws* of business; the *laws* of nature. In more strictly scientific use, a natural *law* is simply a recognized system of sequences or relations; as Kepler's *laws* of planetary distances. See JUSTICE, LEGISLATION.

— **canon law** See CANON LAW.

— **ceremonial law** Law pertaining to the religious ceremonies of the Jews, as given in the Old Testament.

— **civil law 1** The body or system of jurisprudence which the people of a state or nation establish for their government as citizens. **2** The body of Roman law, received by the governments of continental Europe as the foundation of their jurisprudence; also so received in the State of Louisiana.

— **common law** A system of jurisprudence originating in custom or usage, as distinguished from statutory law: the *common law* of England.

— **criminal law** The branch or department of jurisprudence which relates to crimes, their repression and punishment.

— **international law** The rules of conduct generally recognized by civilized states as binding them in their conduct toward each other: also LAW OF NATIONS.

— **maritime law** The body of principles and usages recognized by commercial nations as just and equitable in regulating affairs on the sea.

— **moral law** The divinely prescribed law regarding moral conduct; the law of right; especially, the Decalog.

— **Mosaic law** The Law of Moses.

— **natural law 1** The rule of civil conduct deducible from the common reason and conscience of mankind: the *natural law* of self-defense. **2** A law of nature. See LAW (def. 15).

— **organic law** The fundamental law of a state; a constitution.

— **parliamentary law** The body of rules recognized or ordained for preserving order and regulating the modes of procedure and course of debate in legislative or deliberative bodies.

— **Roman Law** See CIVIL LAW.

law-a-bid·ing (lô′ə·bī′ding) *adj.* Obedient to or abiding by the law.

law-break·er (lô′brā′kər) *n.* One who violates the law; a criminal. — **law′-break′ing** *n.* & *adj.*

law·ful (lô′fəl) *adj.* **1** Permitted or not forbidden by law; legitimate: *lawful* acts. **2** Constituted by law; enforceable at law: *lawful* claims. **3** Valid, or regarded as valid: said of a marriage; also, born of such a marriage: said of offspring. **4** Having full legal rights. See synonyms under JUST, RIGHT. — **law′ful·ly** *adv.* — **law′ful·ness** *n.*

law·giv·er (lô′giv′ər) *n.* One who makes or enacts a law or laws; a legislator. — **law′giv·ing** *adj.* & *n.*

law-hand (lô′hand′) *n.* The handwriting used in or characteristic of old legal documents; also, manuscripts written in this hand.

la·wi·ne (lä·vē′nə) *n. pl.* ·**nen** (-nən) An avalanche. Also **lauwine.** [<G <LL *labina.* See AVALANCHE.]

law·less (lô′lis) *adj.* **1** Not subject or obedient to law of any sort; unruly; disobedient. **2** Without the sanction or authority of law; contrary to law: *lawless* measures. **3** Not formed or constructed according to law or rule; irregular: *lawless* verses. **4** Beyond the reach, or not within the province, of law. **5** Without the protection of law; outlawed: a *lawless* fugitive. — **law'less·ly** *adv.* — **law'less·ness** *n.*

law merchant 1 The body of commercial usages or rules recognized by civilized nations as regulating the rights of persons engaged in trade. **2** Commercial and mercantile law.

lawn[1] (lôn) *n.* **1** A piece of ground with grass kept closely mown. **2** A glade between woods. [Var. of LAUNDE] — **lawn'y** *adj.*

lawn[2] (lôn) *n.* **1** Fine thin linen or cotton fabric. **2** A fine clay sieve. [Earlier *laune* (*lynen*) Laon (linen) <*Laon* Laon, where it was formerly made]

Law of Moses The Pentateuch; Mosaic law.

law of nations International law.

law of parsimony *Philos.* A regulative principle in the interpretation of scientific data, requiring that of several equiprobable assumptions, hypotheses, or theories regarding a given phenomenon or group of phenomena, the simplest and least cumbersome is to be preferred. Also called *Ockham's razor.*

Law·rence (lôr'əns, lor'-) **D(avid) H(erbert)**, 1885-1930, English novelist and poet. — **Ernest Orlando**, 1901-58, U.S. physicist. — **Sir Thomas**, 1769-1835, English painter. — **T(homas) E(dward)**, 1888-1935, English soldier, archeologist, adventurer, and writer: known as *Lawrence of Arabia*: changed his surname to *Shaw* after 1927.

law·ren·ci·um (lô·ren'sē·əm) *n.* A very short-lived radioactive element (symbol Lw), originally produced by bombarding californium with the nuclei of a boron isotope.

law·sone (lô'sōn) *n.* The red coloring matter extracted from the leaves and twigs of the henna plant: used as a hair dye and as a constituent of henna. [after Dr. John *Lawson*, died about 1712, Scottish naturalist]

law·suit (lô'sōot') *n.* A proceeding in a court of law for redress of wrongs, or for enforcement of right.

law·yer (lô'yər) *n.* **1** One who practices law; an attorney or solicitor. **2** A member of any branch of the legal profession. **3** In the New Testament, an expositor of the Mosaic law. **4** *U.S.* The black-necked stilt (*Himantopus mexicanus*): also called *longshanks.* **5** The American burbot. **6** The bowfin: also called *mudfish* and *grindle.* **7** *Brit. Dial.* A long briar or bramble. [<LAW[1] + -YER]

lax (laks) *adj.* **1** Lacking tenseness or firmness; slack; yielding. **2** Not stringent or energetic; remiss; weak in control. **3** Wanting exactness of meaning or application. **4** *Med.* Loose: said of the bowels. **5** *Bot.* Not having the parts close together: a *lax* flower cluster. **6** *Phonet.* Formed with a relatively relaxed tongue and jaw, as (i) and (oo); wide: opposed to *tense.* See synonyms under VAGUE. [<L *laxus* loose] — **lax'i·ty, lax'ness** *n.* — **lax'ly** *adv.*

lax·a·tion (lak·sā'shən) *n.* The act of loosening, or the state of being loosed; relaxation.

lax·a·tive (lak'sə·tiv) *n. Med.* A gentle purgative. — *adj. Med.* **1** Having power to open or loosen the bowels, as a medicine; gently purgative. **2** Subject to or characterized by diarrhea: *laxative* bowels, a *laxative* disease. [<F, fem. of *laxatif* <L *laxativus* <*laxare.* See LAXATION.]

lay[1] (lā) *v.* **laid**, **lay·ing** *v.t.* **1** To cause to lie; place prostrate or at length; deposit. **2** To put or place: Don't *lay* a hand on me. **3** To strike or beat down; overthrow; destroy: to *lay* a city in ashes. **4** To cause to settle or subside, as dust, a storm, etc. **5** To calm or allay, as doubts. **6** To place in regular order or proper position: to *lay* title. **7** To think out; devise; arrange: to *lay* plans. **8** To attribute or ascribe: to *lay* blame. **9** To give importance to; put: to *lay* emphasis on something. **10** To bring forward; advance, as a claim. **11** To bring forth from the body and deposit, as an egg. **12** To construct; build, as a foundation. **13** To make (a table) ready for a meal. **14** To bury; inter. **15** To impose, as taxes, punishment, etc.; assess. **16** To spread over a surface: to *lay* a fixative. **17** To strike with or apply, as in punishment: He *laid* the whip across the culprit's back. **18** To locate: The scene is *laid* in the boudoir. **19** To set or prepare, as a trap. **20** To place as a wager

or bet. **21** To twist strands so as to form (rope). **22** *Mil.* To aim (a cannon). **23** *U.S. Slang* To have sexual intercourse with; seduce. — *v.i.* **24** To bring forth and deposit eggs. **25** To make a bet or bets. **26** *Naut.* To go to a specified position: *Lay* aloft to hand sail! **27** To lie; recline: an incorrect use. See synonyms under PUT[1]. — **to lay about one 1** To deal blows on all sides. **2** To exert oneself to the utmost. — **to lay away 1** To store up; save. **2** To bury. — **to lay before** To put forward or present, as a report. — **to lay by** To lay away (def. 1). — **to lay down 1** To give up or relinquish; sacrifice. **2** To state or proclaim: to *lay down* the law. **3** To bet. — **to lay for** To wait to attack or harm. — **to lay hold of** To seize or grasp. — **to lay in** To procure and store. — **to lay into** To attack vigorously. — **to lay it on** *Colloq.* To be extravagant or exorbitant, as in praise or demands. — **to lay off 1** To take off and put aside, as clothes. **2** To survey; mark off. **3** *U.S. Colloq.* To dismiss from a job, usually temporarily. **4** *U.S. Colloq.* To take a rest; stop working. **5** *U.S. Slang* To stop annoying, teasing, etc. — **to lay on 1** To put on; apply, as color. **2** To beat or strike; attack. — **to lay out 1** To spend. **2** To prepare for burial. **3** *Slang* To strike prostrate or unconscious. **4** To set forth the details of: to *lay out* the plot of a novel. — **to lay over** To stop, as for a rest, on a journey. — **to lay siege to** To besiege. — **to lay up 1** To make a store of. **2** To confine, as by illness or injury. — *n.* **1** The manner in which something lies or is placed; relative arrangement: the *lay* of the land. **2** *Slang* A line of work; particular business or field of activity. **3** A definite quantity of yarn or thread. **4** The swinging beam or batten of a loom. **5** The direction or amount of twist given to the strands of a rope. **6** A profit or share of profits; a price; specifically, a share of the profits of a whaling or sealing voyage, according to an arrangement made before sailing. [OE *lecgan* make lie < pt. of *licgan* lie[1]. Akin to LAW[1].]

lay[2] (lā) *adj.* Pertaining to the laity; non-professional; inexperienced. [<OF *lai* <Med. L *laicus* <Gk. *laikos* <*laos* the people]

lay[3] (lā) Past tense of LIE[1].

lay·a·bout (lā'ə·bout') *n. Chiefly Brit.* A lazy, idle person; a good-for-nothing.

lay·a·way (lā'ə·wā') *n.* An agreement to make a series of payments to buy merchandise that is delivered when fully paid for. Also **layaway plan.**

lay brother 1 A layman. **2** A brother in a monastery, serving under vows and wearing the dress of the order, but not in holy orders.

lay communion 1 The communion of the laity at the Lord's table. **2** The condition of being in communion with the church as a layman only.

lay-days (lā'dāz') *n. pl.* **1** In commerce, the days allowed a ship's lessee for loading and discharging cargo. **2** In marine insurance, the days (usually not beyond 30) while a ship lies idle in port without fires, for which return of insurance premium may be demanded. [<LAY[1] + pl. of DAY]

lay·er (lā'ər) *n.* **1** One who or that which lays. **2** A single horizontal thickness of a course, stratum, or coat. **3** *Bot.* A shoot or twig laid in the ground to take root without being detached from the parent plant. **4** In leatherwork, a welt. **5** In tanning, a pit in which hides are soaked in layers.

LAYER (*def. 3*)
A method of securing new plants from old stock.

6 An artificial oyster bed. — *v.t. Bot.* To propagate by layers. [<LAY[1] + -ER[1]] — **lay'er·ing** *n.*

lay·er·age (lā'ər·ij) *n. Bot.* The propagation of plants by rooting parts of them.

lay·ered (lā'ərd) *adj.* Having or covered with layers; arranged in layers.

lay·ette (lā·et') *n.* A full equipment of clothes, bedding, etc., for a newly born child. [<F,

dim. of *laie* a packing box, drawer <Flemish *laeye* <MDu. *lade* a chest, trunk. Akin to LADE.]

lay figure 1 A jointed model of the human body that can be arranged, as by artists, to hang drapery upon. **2** A mere puppet; a tool of others. [<Earlier *layman* (<Du. *leeman* <*led* a limb + *man* man) + FIGURE]

lay·man (lā'mən) *n.* *pl.* **·men** (-mən) One of the laity; a man not belonging to the clergy or other profession or body of experts. — **lay'wom·an** (-wŏom'ən) *n. fem.* [<LAY[2] + MAN]

lay-off (lā'ôf', -of') *n.* The act of discharging or firing workmen or employees; also, a discontinuance, as of work.

lay-out (lā'out') *n.* **1** *Slang* That which is laid out; a set of articles set out or provided; an outfit; a spread. **2** The space dragged over by a seine in fishing. **3** A laying out or planning, as of a piece of work, a campaign, etc.; a design; an arrangement. **4** In faro, the thirteen cards of a suit laid face upward at the beginning of the game. **5** The make-up of a book, magazine, etc. Also **lay·out.**

lay·o·ver (lā'ō'vər) *n.* A stopover.

la·zar (lā'zər, laz'ər) *n.* One afflicted with a loathsome disease; a leper. [<Med. L *lazarus*, after LAZARUS (*Luke* xiv 20)]

laz·a·ret·to (laz'ə·ret'ō) *n.* *pl.* **·tos 1** A pesthouse or pest ship; also, a hospital. **2** A quarantine building. **3** A storeroom near a vessel's stern. Also **laz'a·ret', laz'a·rette', la·zar·house** (lā'zər·hous', laz'ər-). [<Ital. *lazzaretto* <*led* a limb + FIGURE] dial. Ital. (Venetian) *lazareto, nazareto* < (Santa Madonna di) *Nazaret,* a Venetian church used as a plague hospital in the 15th c.; infl. in form by *lazzaro* a leper <Med. L *lazarus.* See LAZAR.]

Laz·a·rist (laz'ə·rist) *n.* A member of a Roman Catholic order founded in 1624 by St. Vincent de Paul for rural mission work in France. Called *Vincentian* in the United States. Also **Laz'a·rite** (-rīt). [<F *lazariste,* from (*Collège de St.*) *Lazare,* a school at Paris, where the order was established <L *Lazarus* Lazarus]

la·zar·like (lā'zər·līk', laz'ər-) *adj.* Covered with sores; leprous. Also **la'zar·ly.**

laze (lāz) *v.* **lazed, laz·ing** *v.i.* To be lazy; loaf; idle. — *v.t.* To pass (time) in idleness. — *n.* Idleness; laziness. [Back formation <LAZY]

laz·u·li (laz'yŏo·lī) See LAPIS LAZULI.

lazuli finch The indigo bunting.

laz·u·lite (laz'yŏo·līt) *n.* A vitreous, azure-blue, brittle phosphate of aluminum and magnesium, crystallizing in the monoclinic system. [<Med. L *lazulus* lazuli + -ITE[1]]

laz·u·rite (laz'yŏo·rīt) *n. Mineral.* A silicate of sodium and aluminum containing sulfur and occurring in deep-blue crystals: the principal constituent of lapis lazuli. [<Med. L *lazur* azure + -ITE[1]]

la·zy (lā'zē) *adj.* **·zi·er, ·zi·est 1** Indisposed to exertion; indolent; slothful. **2** Moving or acting slowly or heavily; sluggish. See synonyms under IDLE. [Prob. <MLG *lasich* loose, feeble] — **la'zi·ly** *adv.* — **la'zi·ness** *n.*

la·zy·bones (lā'zē·bōnz') *n. Colloq.* A lazy person; an idler.

La·zy-Su·san (lā'zē·sōo'zən) *n.* A revolving stand for condiments, bread, butter, etc., usually placed in the center of the table.

–le *suffix* Repeatedly: used to form frequentative verbs, but often without appreciable force: *sparkle, haggle.* [OE *-lian*]

lea[1] (lē) *n.* A grassy field or plain. ◆ Homophone: *lee.* [OE *lēah,* orig. open ground in a wood]

lea[2] (lē) *n.* A varying measure of yarn: 80 yards in worsted, 120 yards in cotton and silk, and 300 yards in linen: also spelled *lay.* ◆ Homophone: *lee.* [Back formation <earlier *leas,* taken as pl., prob. <F *lier* <L *ligare* bind]

leach (lēch) *v.t.* **1** To cause (a liquid) to percolate through something. **2** To percolate a liquid through (ashes, etc.) so as to remove the soluble portions. **3** To remove (soluble portions) by means of a percolating liquid. **4** *Metall.* To dissolve (metals or minerals) out of ore by cyanide or chlorine solutions, acids, etc. — *v.i.* **5** To lose soluble matter by percolation. **6** To be removed by percolations. — *n.* **1** Wood ashes, through which water is passed to carry away the soluble portions. **2** The vessel in which ashes, etc., are leached: also **leach tub. 3** The act or process of leaching. **4** The solution obtained by leaching. Also spelled *latch.* ◆ Homophone: *leech.* [OE *leccan* wet, irrigate. Akin to LAKE[1], LEAK.] — **leach′er** *n.*

leach·y (lē′chē) *adj.* **leach·i·er, leach·i·est** Pervious; porous.

lead[1] (lēd) *v.* **led, lead·ing** *v.t.* **1** To go with or ahead of so as to show the way; guide. **2** To draw along; guide by or as by pulling: to *lead* a person by the hand. **3** To serve as a direction or route for: The path *led* them to a valley. **4** To cause to go in a certain course of direction, as wire, water, etc. **5 a** To direct the affairs or actions of; be the leader of, as an army or expedition. **b** To direct the playing or performance of: to *lead* an orchestra. **6** To have the first or foremost place among: He *led* the field by ten feet. **7** To influence or control the opinions, thoughts, actions, etc., of; induce: His experiments *led* him to these conclusions. **8** To live or experience; pass: to *lead* a happy life. **9** To begin or open: to *lead* a discussion. **10** In card games, to begin a round of play with: He *led* the ace. **11** In hunting, to aim a weapon or missile ahead of (a moving target). — *v.i.* **12** To act as guide; conduct. **13** To have leadership or command; be in control. **14** To be guided: The horse *leads* easily. **15** To be first or in advance. **16** To afford a way or passage; reach or extend: The road *led* into a swamp. **17** In card games, to make the first play. **18** In boxing, to strike at an opponent, especially in testing his defense: to *lead* with a left. — **to lead off** To make a beginning; start. — **to lead on** To entice or tempt, especially to extravagance or error. — **to lead one a merry chase** (or **dance**) To cause someone trouble or confusion by unpredictable actions. — **to lead the way 1** To act as guide. **2** To take the initiative. — **to lead to** To result in; cause: His carelessness *led* to his downfall. — **to lead with one's chin** *U.S. Slang* To expose oneself to unnecessary harm. — *n.* **1** Position in advance or at the head; priority. **2** The distance, time, etc., by which anything precedes. **3** The act of leading or conducting; guidance: to give a novice a *lead* in hunting; a clue or hint. **4** In cards, etc., the right to play first in a round; the card, piece, or suit played first. **5** A way or passage; especially, an open channel or passage through ice. **6** A lode or vein of ore; also, an old river bed where gold has been found. **7** In drama, the principal part; the actor who performs in such a part. **8** *Naut.* The course of a rope. **9** *Electr.* A main electrical conductor. **10** In shooting a gun, the act of aiming ahead of a moving target. **11** In baseball, the distance from base of a runner ready to run to the next base. **12** A leash for leading a dog. **13** In journalism, the opening of a news story with a summary of its contents. — *adj.* Acting as leader: the *lead* dog. [OE *lǣden* cause to go]

Synonyms (*verb*): conduct, convey, direct, escort, excel, guide, head, outstrip, precede, surpass. See ACTUATE, DRAW, INFLUENCE, PERSUADE, PRECEDE. *Antonyms:* ape, chase, copy, follow, imitate, obey, pursue, succeed.

lead[2] (led) *n.* **1** A soft, heavy, inelastic, malleable, ductile, bluish-gray metallic element (symbol Pb) in the fourth group of the periodic table, most commonly occurring in the sulfide mineral, galena. **2** Any one of various articles made of lead or its alloys. **3** *Printing* A thin strip of type metal or brass used in composition. **4** *Naut.* A weight of lead used in sounding at sea. **5** Leaden sheets or plates used for covering roofs. **6** One of the cames in a diamond-paned window. **7** Graphite: also called **black lead. 8** A mixture of lead carbonate and hydrated lead oxide: also called **white lead. 9** *Colloq.* Projectiles from firearms; bullets. — *v.t.* **1** To cover, weight, fasten, treat, or fill with lead. **2** To glaze, as porcelain, with powdered metallic ore. **3** *Printing* To separate (lines of type) with leads. **4** To construct (a window) with leaden cames. — *v.i.* **5** To become filled or clogged with lead: said of rifle grooves. [OE *lēad*, prob. <Celtic] — **lead′y** *adj.*

lead acetate *Chem.* A white, soluble, crystalline salt, $Pb(C_2H_3O_2)_2 \cdot 3H_2O$, made by the action of acetic acid on litharge. From the sweet taste of the solution it is named *sugar of lead.*

lead arsenate *Chem.* A white, heavy, poisonous crystalline compound, $Pb_3(AsO_4)_2$: used as a constituent of insecticides.

lead azide *Chem.* A white to brownish crystalline compound, PbN_6: used as a substitute for mercury fulminate in explosives.

Lead-beat·er's possum (lēd′bē′tərz) An arboreal marsupial (*Gymnobelideus leadbeateri*) of Australia, related to the flying phalangers; thought to be extinct until rediscovered in 1961.

lead carbonate Cerusite.

lead chromate Chrome yellow.

lead dioxide *Chem.* The compound PbO_2 prepared as a dark-brown, amorphous powder: used in the manufacture of storage batteries.

lead·en (led′n) *adj.* **1** Made of lead; also, of the dull-gray color of lead. **2** Heavy; dull or sluggish; also, base in quality. — **lead′en·ly** *adv.* — **lead′en·ness** *n.*

lead·er (lē′dər) *n.* **1** One who leads or conducts; a guide; commander. **2** *Music* A director or conductor of an orchestra; also, the player of the first or principal instrument in an orchestra or band; in an orchestra, usually the head of the first violins. **3** That which leads, or occupies a chief place, as the foremost horse of a team, etc. **4** A tendon or sinew. **5** In journalism, the chief editorial article of a newspaper. **6** An article of merchandise offered at a special price to attract customers. **7** *Printing* A horizontal row of printed dots or hyphens, or a dot or hyphen of such a row, used to guide the eye, as from one side of a page to the other. **8** In fishing, a short line of gut, nylon, etc., attaching the hook or lure to the line. **9** A pipe to carry water from the roof or upper part of a building to the ground. See synonyms under CHIEF, MASTER.

lead·er·ship (lē′dər·ship) *n.* The office or position of a leader; guidance. See synonyms under PRECEDENCE.

lead glass (led) Flint glass. See under GLASS.

lead-in (lēd′in′) *n.* A wire connecting the antenna of a radio with the receiving set: also, *Brit.*, *down-lead.*

lead·ing (lē′ding) *adj.* **1** Having priority or influence; chief. **2** Attention-getting, as, a *leading* display. **3** Furnishing a lead or precedence. See synonyms under FIRST. — *n.* A directing or guiding influence; specifically, spiritual guidance. — **lead′ing·ly** *adv.*

leading article 1 An editorial; also, the first article, as in a magazine. **2** Leader (def. 6).

leading edge *Aeron.* The forward edge of an airfoil or propeller blade.

lead line (led) A line for taking soundings.

lead-off (lēd′ôf′, -of′) *n.* **1** A beginning; the first of a succession or series. **2** The opening or attacking movement in any bout of skill or strength, competitive game, etc. **3** The player who leads off.

lead plant (led) A low shrub (*Amorpha canescens*) of the southern and southwestern United States, with lead-gray leaves and twigs.

lead poisoning (led) *Pathol.* Poisoning caused by the slow, continuous absorption of lead by the tissues of the body: marked by nutritional disturbances, anemia, paralysis, and cerebral disorders: also called *plumbism.*

leads·man (ledz′mən) *n.* *pl.* **·men** (-mən) *Naut.* A sailor who heaves the lead.

lead tetraethyl *Chem.* A colorless, heavy, inflammable, extremely poisonous, liquid hydrocarbon, $Pb(C_2H_5)_4$, prepared by the action of ethyl chloride on a lead sodium alloy: used as an anti-knock agent in internal-combustion engines.

lead time (lēd) **1** *Mil.* **a** The time required to move from the planning and development stage of a new aircraft, ship, weapon, etc., to active production for use. **b** The calculation based on target distance and speed that determines the point of aim of a projectile or missile. **2** The interval between one stage in a sequence of industrial operations or commercial procedures and a subsequent one.

lead·wort (led′wûrt′) *n.* Plumbago.

leaf (lēf) *n.* *pl.* **leaves** (lēvz) **1** A lateral photosynthetic appendage of the stem of a plant, commonly broad, flat, thin, and of a green color. ◆ Collateral adjective: *foliar.* **2** Foliage collectively; leafage; specifically, the leaves of the tobacco or the tea plant when gathered for curing or sale. **3** A single division of a folded sheet of paper or the like, as in a book, or a single unfolded piece; also, what is written or printed on a leaf. **4** A hinged, folding, sliding, or removable part or section, as of a table, door, gate, screen, or folding fan. **5** A very thin sheet or plate of metal, as gold; also, one of marble, horn, etc. **6** A layer or fold of fat, especially over the kidneys of a hog. **7** One of the thin, flat strips of metal composing a spring of an automobile. **8** A petal: incorrect, but popularly used. — **to turn over a new leaf** To change one's ways or conduct, especially for the better. — *adj.* Of, pertaining to, suggestive of, or occurring in, a leaf or leaves. — *v.i.* To put forth or produce leaves. — *v.t.* To turn or run through the pages of a book: often with *through.* ◆ Homophone: *lief.* [OE *lēaf*]

Linear Lanceolate Acuminate Acute

Spatulate Obtuse Ovate Serrate

Sagittate Binate Amplexicaul Decussate

Digitate Compound

TYPES OF TREE LEAVES

leaf·age (lē′fij) *n.* Leaves collectively; foliage.

leaf beet Chard (def. 2).

leaf beetle Any of a family (*Chrysomelidae*) of usually small, bright-colored beetles which are found, both in the larval and the adult stages, on leaves.

leaf blight Any of various plant diseases, chiefly of fungous origin, having a conspicuously damaging effect on leaves, especially those affecting pome fruits.

leaf bud A bud that develops into a leafy branch without flowers.

leaf curl A destructive plant disease caused by various fungi of the family *Exoascaceae,* which attack certain forest and fruit trees, as the oak, poplar, and peach, with serious deformation of the leaves: also called *witch broom.* Also **leaf blister.**

leaf fat 1 A layer of fat about the kidneys of swine, from which is obtained leaf lard. **2** Folds of fat over the kidneys of other animals.

leaf·hop·per (lēf′hop′ər) *n.* Any of a family (*Cicadellidae*) of homopterous leaping insects which suck the juices of various plants.

leaf insect Phyllium.

leaf lard Lard made from leaf fat; also, the leaves themselves.

leaf·less (lēf′lis) *adj.* Having or bearing no leaves.

leaf·let (lēf′lit) *n.* **1** A little leaf. **2** *Bot.* One of the separate divisions of a compound leaf. **3** A small printed leaf; a tract; also, a folding circular having several unsewed or unstitched pages in one strip; a folder. **4** A leaflike part. [Dim. of LEAF]

leaf miner The larva of a tineid moth, or of a beetle, fly, or other insect, which feeds on the leaves of plants and trees.

leaf roll 1 A virus disease of the potato, characterized by a pronounced upward curling of the leaves and by a reduction in the size of the tubers. 2 Any of various other plant diseases having a similar effect upon the leaves.

leaf roller The larva of certain small moths, especially of the family *Tortricidae*, that rolls itself up in the leaves of the plant it attacks.

leaf spot A disease of apples, pears, quinces, and other fruits, caused by a sac fungus (*Physalospora malorum*) and resulting in widespread damage: also called *black rot*, *fruit rot*.

leaf spring *Mech.* A spring made of one or more flat plates or strips: distinguished from a spiral spring.

LEAF SPRING

leaf·stalk (lēf′stôk′) *n.* A petiole.

leaf·y (lē′fē) *adj.* **leaf·i·er, leaf·i·est** 1 Having or full of leaves; consisting of or characterized by leaves. 2 Producing broad leaves. 3 Like a leaf or leaves. 4 Existing in thin sheets or layers; laminate.

league¹ (lēg) *n.* 1 A measure of distance, varying from about 2.42 to 4.6 English statute miles. The English **land league** contains approximately 3 statute miles, or 4.82 kilometers; the **marine league** in common use equals 3 geographic miles, or 5.56 kilometers. 2 In Texas, an old Spanish land measure equaling about 4,438 acres; a square league. [<OF *legue* <LL *leuga, leuca* a Gaulish mile <Celtic]

league² (lēg) *n.* 1 An alliance of persons or states for mutual support in a common cause. 2 Any close connection or union; as, a commercial *league*. 3 An association of baseball, football, basketball, or other teams which play among themselves. See synonyms under ALLIANCE. —*v.t.* & *v.i.* **leagued, lea·guing** To join in a league; combine. [<OF *ligue* <Ital. *liga, lega* < *legare* bind <L *ligare*] — **lea·guer** (lē′gər) *n.*

League of Nations An international organization established January 10, 1920, primarily for the preservation of peace under the Covenant of the League in the Treaty of Versailles; formally dissolved April 18, 1946, when its functions, library, and buildings were turned over to the United Nations.

lea·guer (lē′gər) *Archaic n.* 1 A siege. 2 The camp of a besieging force; also, any military camp. —*v.t.* To beleaguer; besiege. [<Du. *leger* a camp]

leak (lēk) *n.* 1 An opening, mechanical or otherwise, that permits the unintended entrance or escape of a fluid, of electric current, etc. 2 Hence, anything which permits the unintentional loss or accrual of something: a *leak* in the espionage system. 3 Leakage. —**to spring a leak** To spring open, part, or crack, so as to let a fluid in or out. —*v.i.* 1 To let a liquid, etc., enter or escape undesignedly, as through a hole or crack. 2 To pass in or out accidentally: often with *in* or *out*. 3 To become known despite efforts at secrecy: usually with *out*: Our plans *leaked* out. —*v.t.* 4 To let (a liquid, etc.) enter or escape undesignedly. 5 To disclose (information, etc.) without authorization. ◆ Homophone: *leek.* [<ON *leka* drip. Akin to LEACH, LAKE¹.] — **leak′y** *adj.*

leak·age (lē′kij) *n.* 1 The act of leaking. 2 The quantity that leaks. 3 An allowance for loss by leaking.

leakage current *Electr.* A stray current, generally weak, which escapes through inadequate or defective insulation.

lean¹ (lēn) *v.* **leaned** or **leant, lean·ing** *v.i.* 1 To incline from an erect position: The tower is *leaning*. 2 To incline against or rest on something for support: to *lean* against a tree. 3 To depend or rely: with *on* or *upon*: to *lean* on friendship. 4 To have a mental tendency or inclination: to *lean* toward an opinion. —*v.t.* 5 To cause to incline from an erect position. 6 To place (one thing) against another for support: to *lean* a ladder against a house. —*n.* A leaning; inclination. ◆ Homophone: *lien.* [Fusion of OE *hleonian* lean and OE *hlænen* cause to lean]

Synonyms (verb): bear, confide, depend, recline, rely, repose, rest, trust. See REST¹.

lean² (lēn) *adj.* 1 Free from or lacking fat; lank; thin. 2 Lacking in richness, productiveness, or other desirable qualities: *lean* ore, a *lean* harvest. 3 Manifesting thinness, or attended by want. See synonyms under MEAGER. —*n.* Flesh or muscle without fat: *lean* meat. ◆ Homophone: *lien.* [OE *hlæne* thin] — **lean′ly** *adv.* — **lean′ness** *n.*

lean·ing (lē′ning) *adj.* Inclining from the vertical: a *leaning* tower. —*n.* An inclination; bias; tendency.

leant (lent) Alternative past tense and past participle of LEAN.

lean-to (lēn′tōō′) *n.* *pl.* **-tos** (-tōōz′) 1 A building having a single-pitched roof with its apex against an adjoining wall. 2 A rude shelter consisting of branches or planks which slope from a crossbar to the ground. —*adj.* Having rafters, as a roof, which slope in only one direction.

leap (lēp) *v.* **leaped** or **leapt, leap·ing** *v.i.* 1 To jump from the ground with the feet in the air, as from one place or position to another. 2 To move suddenly by or as by jumps or jumping: to *leap* aboard; to *leap* to a conclusion. —*v.t.* 3 To clear by jumping over: to *leap* a barrier. 4 To cause to leap: to *leap* a horse over a hedge. —*n.* 1 The act of leaping; a bound. 2 The space passed over in leaping. [OE *hléapan*] — **leap′er** *n.*

Synonyms (verb): bounce, bound, caper, dance, frisk, gambol, hop, jump, skip, spring, vault.

leap·frog (lēp′frôg′, -frog′) *n.* A game in which one player puts his hands on the back of another, who is stooping over, and leaps over him. —*v.* **-frogged, -frog·ging** *v.t.* 1 To jump over as in the game of leapfrog. 2 *Mil.* To bypass (an enemy position), the capture of which is considered strategically unnecessary. —*v.i.* 3 To jump as in the game of leapfrog.

leaping evil Louping ill.

leapt (lept, lēpt) Alternative past tense and past participle of LEAP.

leap year In the Julian and Gregorian calendars, a year of 366 days, an additional day being added to February to allow for the difference in length between the common and the astronomical years. Every year exactly divisible by four, or, in centesimal years, exactly divisible by 400, is a leap year.

Lear (lir) Legendary king of Britain mentioned by Geoffrey of Monmouth, Layamon, Holinshed, etc.; hero of Shakespeare's *King Lear.*

learn (lûrn) *v.* **learned** or **learnt, learn·ing** *v.t.* 1 To acquire knowledge of or skill in by observation, study, instruction, etc. 2 To find out; gain acquaintance with; ascertain: to *learn* the facts. 3 To fix in the mind; memorize. 4 To become practiced in: to *learn* bad habits. —*v.i.* 5 To gain knowledge; acquire skill. 6 To be informed; hear. [OE *leornian.* Akin to LORE¹.] — **learn′er** *n.*

Synonyms: acquire, commit, get, inform, instruct, know, master, memorize, perceive, teach, train. *Learn* refers to the process of getting knowledge, *know* to the result. What we once thoroughly *learn* we *know.* See ACQUIRE, GAIN, KNOW. Compare KNOWLEDGE. *Antonyms:* forget, lose, miss, pass.

learn·ed (lûr′nid) *adj.* Possessed of learning; erudite. — **learn′ed·ly** *adv.*

learn·ing (lûr′ning) *n.* 1 Knowledge obtained by study or from instruction; scholarship; erudition. 2 The act of acquiring knowledge or skill. 3 *Psychol.* The modification of behavior following upon and induced by interaction with the environment and as a result of experiences leading to the establishment of new patterns of response to external stimuli.

Synonyms: education, erudition, instruction, knowledge, lore, scholarship, study, training, tuition. *Learning* may be acquired by one's unaided industry, but any full *education* must be the result in great part of *instruction, training,* and personal association. *Study* is emphatically what one does for himself, and in which *instruction* and *tuition* can only point the way. *Lore* is used only in poetic style, for accumulated *knowledge,* as of a people or age, or in a general sense for *learning* or *erudition. Information* is *knowledge* of fact, real or supposed, derived from persons, books, or observation; it is regarded as casual and haphazard. *Learning* is much higher, being wide and systematic *knowledge,* the result of long, assiduous *study; erudition* is recondite *learning* secured only by extraordinary industry, opportunity, and ability. See EDUCATION, KNOWLEDGE, SCIENCE, WISDOM. *Antonyms:* ignorance, illiteracy. See synonyms for IGNORANT.

lease¹ (lēs) *n.* The system of crossing warp threads during weaving. [Appar. var. of LEASH, in this sense]

lease² (lēs) *v.t.* **leased, leas·ing** 1 To grant the temporary possession and profits of, as lands or tenements, usually for a specified rent; let. 2 To take possession of or hold under a lease. —*n.* 1 A contract for the letting of land, etc., for rent; also, such letting. 2 Any tenure by permission, or its duration. [<AF *les,* OF *lais* a letting < *laissier* let, leave <L *laxare* loosen < *laxus* loose] — **leas′a·ble** *adj.*

lease·back (lēs′bak′) *n.* The sale of real property to a buyer who as part of the same transaction leases it to the seller: short for *sale and lease back.*

lease·hold (lēs′hōld′) *adj.* Held by lease. —*n.* A tenure held by a lease. — **lease′hold′er** *n.*

leash (lēsh) *n.* 1 A line or thong, as for holding a dog, etc. 2 A brace and a half; three creatures of like kind, as greyhounds; three in general. —*v.t.* To hold or secure by a leash. [<OF *lesse, laisse* <L *laxa,* fem. of *laxus* loose]

leas·ing (lē′sing) *n.* *Brit. Dial.* Lying or a lie; falsehood. [OE *léasung* < *léasian* tell lies < *léas* destitute of, false]

least (lēst) *adj.* Smallest in size, value, etc.; minimal. —*n.* That which is least. —*adv.* In the lowest or smallest degree. [OE *læst, læsest,* superl. of *læssa* less]

least action *Physics* That property of a dynamic system having a constant total energy whereby any change in its configuration will take place with a minimum of action among and between its constituent particles.

least common denominator See under DENOMINATOR.

least energy *Physics* The tendency of a dynamic system to remain in stable equilibrium only under those conditions for which the potential energy of the system is at a minimum.

least squares *Math.* A method of deducing the most probable value of a quantity from a set of observations or measurements, in accordance with the principle that the sum of the squares of all the errors is at a minimum.

least·wise (lēst′wīz′) *adv.* *Colloq.* At least. Also **least′ways′** (-wāz′).

leath·er (leth′ər) *n.* 1 The skin or hide of an animal, when tanned or dressed for use. 2 A piece, part, or article consisting or made of leather, as a football. —*v.t.* 1 To cover or furnish with leather. 2 *Colloq.* To beat or flog with or as with a leather strap. [OE *lether*] — **leath′er·y** *adj.* — **leath′er·i·ness** *n.*

leath·er·back (leth′ər·bak′) *n.* The soft-shelled turtle (*Dermochelys coriacea*) living in warm seas, and notable for its flexible, leathery carapace. It sometimes exceeds 1,000 pounds in weight.

leath·er·board (leth′ər·bôrd′, -bōrd′) *n.* An imitation leather sole made from scraps of leather assembled and pressed into sheets: also called *fiber leather.*

leath·er·coat (leth′ər·kōt′) *n.* A russet apple.

leath·er·craft (leth′ər·kraft′, -kräft′) *n.* The handicraft of designing and making things of leather.

Leath·er·ette (leth′ər·et′) *n.* An imitation leather, used chiefly in bookbinding, upholstering, etc.: a trade name.

leath·ern (leth'ərn) *adj.* Made of leather. [OE *letheren* < *lether* leather]

leath·er·neck (leth'ər·nek') *n. Slang* A member of the U.S. Marine Corps.

leath·er·oid (leth'ər·oid') *n.* A material with leatherlike qualities, made by treating vegetable fiber with certain chemicals.

leath·er·stock·ing (leth'ər·stok'ing) *n.* A person who wears leather stockings; hence, a frontiersman. — *adj.* Characteristic of, or about, pioneers and pioneer life: *leatherstocking* customs or stories.

leath·er·wood (leth'ər·wood') *n.* A low, thymelaeaceous, North American shrub or bush (*Dirca palustris*) with white, soft wood, tough, fibrous bark, and small, yellow flowers: also called *moosewood*.

leath·er·work·er (leth'ər·wûr'kər) *n.* One who prepares or ornaments leather. — **leath'er·work'ing** *n.*

leave[1] (lēv) *v.* **left, leav·ing** *v.t.* **1** To go or depart from; quit. **2** To allow to remain behind or continue as specified; abandon: to *leave* work undone; to *leave* a plow in a field. **3** To place or deposit so as to allow to remain behind: to *leave* word. **4** To cause to remain after departure, cessation, healing, etc.: The war *left* its mark. **5** To refer or entrust to another for doing, deciding, etc.: I *leave* the matter to you. **6** To sever or terminate connection, employment, etc., with: to *leave* a job. **7** To have as a remainder: Three minus two *leaves* one. **8** To have remaining after death: to *leave* a large family. **9** To give by will; bequeath. **10** To desist from; stop: usually with *off*. — *v.i.* **11** To depart or go away; set out. **12** To desist; cease: with *off*: He *left* off where I began. See synonyms under ABANDON. — **to leave out** To omit from consideration; fail to include. [OE *lǣfan,* lit., let remain] — **leav'er** *n.*

◆ **leave, let** *Leave* and *let,* often confused, are not synonyms. *Leave* means to go away or depart, *let* to permit. Perhaps because the noun *leave* has "permission" as one of its meanings, popular usage endows the verb *leave* with the sense "permit," and tries to make it interchangeable with *let* in such expressions as *Let me go.* But the substitution of *leave* for *let* violates established idiom, for while *let* can be followed by the infinitive without "to," *leave* cannot: *Leave it to him to decide* or *Leave the decision to him,* but never *Leave him decide. Leave me go* is readily recognized as violating both sense and idiom, and is hence considered illiterate. So with *Leave me be.* This last is synonymous with *Leave me alone,* widespread in children's speech as a replacement for the standard English *Let me alone,* which has the idiomatic meaning "Don't bother me" or "Stop bothering me." In this case, and in this case only, *Leave it alone* may be regarded as having acquired fair colloquial standing, with two reservations. It is only in the imperative that *leave* is here admissible as a substitute for *let*; in declined forms, the substitution sense does not carry over. *They left him alone* does not mean *They let him alone.* The second reservation follows from this. In formal English, *Leave me alone* means "Go away so that I may be alone." Solitude may insure freedom from annoyance, but asking *to be left alone* is not the same as demanding *to be let alone.*

leave[2] (lēv) *n.* **1** Permission given to do something otherwise forbidden or unlawful. **2** Liberty to go or to be absent. **3** A departure; parting. **4** Permission granted an officer of a military service or to enlisted naval personnel to be absent from duty: also **leave of absence.** See synonyms under PERMISSION. — **to take leave 1** To depart; go away. **2** To abandon; quit: with *of*: He *took leave* of his senses. [OE *lēaf* permission]

leave[3] (lēv) *v.i.* **leaved, leav·ing** To put forth leaves.

leaved (lēvd) *adj.* Having a leaf, leaves, or folds: usually in composition: *four-leaved* clover.

leav·en (lev'ən) *n.* **1** Fermenting dough, or anything that causes fermentation, as yeast. **2** Any influence or addition that causes general change or modification of the whole. — *v.t.* **1** To produce fermentation in; make light by fermentation. **2** To affect in char-

acter; imbue. [< OF *levain* < L *levamen* alleviation < *levare* raise] — **leav'en·ing** *n.*

leaves (lēvz) Plural of LEAF.

leave-tak·ing (lēv'tā'king) *n.* A taking leave; a parting; a farewell.

leav·ing (lē'ving) *n.* **1** The act of departure. **2** *pl.* Things left; scraps; refuse; offal. See synonyms under WASTE.

Leb·a·non (leb'ə·nən) An Arab republic on the east coast of the Mediterranean, between Israel and Syria; 3,880 square miles; capital, Beirut; formerly a French mandate. French **Li·ban** (lē·bän'). — **Leb'a·nese'** (-nēz', -nēs') *adj.* & *n.*

leb·en (leb'ən) *n.* An Arabian beverage of fermented milk, similar to the Turkish matzoon: also spelled *laban.* [< Arabic *laban*]

Le·bens·raum (lā'bəns·roum) *n. German* Territory into which a nation claims it must expand to fulfill its economic needs. A term of Nazi ideology; literally, space for living. See GEOPOLITICS.

lech·er (lech'ər) *n.* A habitually lewd or excessively sensual man. [< OF *lecheor* < *lechier* live in debauchery, lick < OHG *leccōn* lick]

lech·er·ous (lech'ər·əs) *adj.* Given to or characterized by lewdness or lust. — **lech'er·ous·ly** *adv.* — **lech'er·ous·ness** *n.*

lech·er·y (lech'ər·ē) *n.* **1** Free indulgence in lust; gross sensuality. **2** Selfish pleasure. [< OF *lecherie, licherie* < *lecheor* LECHER]

lec·i·thin (les'ə·thin) *n. Biochem.* A brownish-yellow, waxy, phosphorized fat contained in the cell tissue of many plants and animals, especially the brain, nerves, egg yolk, and protoplasm: used in medicine as a tonic and nutrient. [< Gk. *lekithos* an egg's yolk + -IN]

lec·i·thin·ase (les'ə·thin·ās') *n.* Any of several enzymes capable of hydrolyzing lecithin. [< LECITHIN + -ASE]

Le·conte de Lisle (lə·kônt' də lēl'), **Charles Marie René,** 1818–94, French poet.

lec·tern (lek'tərn) *n.* **1** A reading desk, in some churches, from which various services are chanted or read. **2** A reading stand, as on a rostrum. [< OF *lettrun* < LL *lectrum* < L *lectus,* pp. of *legere* read]

lec·tion (lek'shən) *n.* **1** A lesson appointed to be read in church service. **2** A variation in the text of an author. [< OF *lectiun* < L *lectio, -onis* < *lectus,* pp. of *legere* read]

lec·tion·ar·y (lek'shən·er'ē) *n.* *pl.* ·**ar·ies** A book or a table of lessons for church service. [< Med. L *lectionarium* < L *lectio* LECTION]

lec·tor (lek'tər) *n.* A reader; specifically, one who reads lessons in a church or lectures in a university. [< L, a reader < *lectus,* pp. of *legere* read]

lec·tu·al (lek'chōō·əl) *adj.* **1** Of or pertaining to a bed or couch. **2** Confining one to his bed: a *lectual* disease. [< LL *lectualis* < L *lectus* a bed, couch]

lec·ture (lek'chər) *n.* **1** A discourse delivered aloud for instruction or entertainment. **2** A formal reproof; reprimand. — *v.* ·**tured, ·turing** *v.t.* **1** To deliver lectures to; instruct by lecturing. **2** To rebuke or castigate authoritatively or at length. — *v.i.* **3** To give a lecture. [< L *lectura* an act of reading < *lectus,* pp. of *legere* read] — **lec'tur·er** *n.*

lec·ture·ship (lek'chər·ship) *n.* The office or rank of lecturer.

led (led) Past tense and past participle of LEAD[1].

Le·da (lē'də) In Greek mythology, the wife of Tyndareus and by him mother of Clytemnestra; by Zeus, who appeared to her in the form of a swan, she was the mother of Helen and of Castor and Pollux.

ledge (lej) *n.* **1** A shelf upon which articles can be laid. **2** Something resembling a shelf, as a shelflike ridge of rock, or a shelflike projection from a building. **3** A rocky outcrop or reef. **4** A metal-bearing rock stratum; a lode or vein. [ME *legge,* prob. < root of *leggen* LAY[1]] — **ledg'y** *adj.*

ledg·er[1] (lej'ər) *n.* **1** The principal book of accounts of a business establishment, in which all the transactions of each day are entered under appropriate heads so as to show the debits and credits of each account. **2** A bar, stone, or the like, that is made to lie flat or stay in a fixed position. **3** A horizontal piece fastened to a timber scaffolding to sustain the putlogs. **4** A horizontal stone slab over a grave. **5** Ledger tackle or ledger bait:

also spelled *leger.* [ME *legger,* prob. < *leggen* LAY[1]; infl. by MDu. *legger* lay]

ledg·er[2] (lej'ər) *adj.* Remaining or lying in a place: *ledger* bait. Also *leger.* [See LEDGER[1]]

ledger bait A fishing bait lying at the bottom of the water: also spelled *leger bait.*

ledger board The horizontal board forming the top rail of a fence, the handrail of a stairway, etc.

ledger tackle Any form of floating tackle the lower portion of which lies on the bottom: also *leger line, leger tackle.* Also **ledger line.**

lee (lē) *n.* **1** The direction opposite that from which the wind comes; the side sheltered, or that shelters, from wind. **2** A shelter afforded by any object in a wind. — *adj.* Pertaining to the side opposite to that from which the wind comes: a *lee* shore. ◆ Homophone: *lea.* [OE *hlēo* a shelter]

Lee (lē), **T(sung) D(ao),** born 1926, U.S. physicist born in China.

lee·board (lē'bôrd', -bōrd') *n. Naut.* A board lowered on the lee side of a vessel and acting as a keel or centerboard to keep it from drifting to leeward.

LEECH
a. Common. *b.* Medicinal.
(Vary in size from 1 to 18 inches)

leech[1] (lēch) *n.* **1** Any one of a class (*Hirudinea*) of carnivorous, aquatic, bloodsucking annelid worms; especially, the **medicinal leech** (*Hirudo medicinalis*), formerly used for drawing blood, which can ingest three times its weight in blood. **2** Hence, one who appropriates or filches the substance or wealth of others. **3** *Archaic* A physician; doctor. **4** A blood-drawing apparatus: also **artificial leech.** — *v.t.* **1** To bleed with leeches. **2** *Obs.* To treat with medicine; heal. ◆ Homophone: *leach.* [OE *lǣce,* orig. a physician] — **leech'er** *n.*

leech[2] (lēch) *n. Naut.* **1** The edge of a square sail. **2** The after edge of a fore-and-aft sail. ◆ Homophone: *leach.* [ME *lich,* ? < Scand. Cf. ON *lik* a boltrope.]

leek (lēk) *n.* A culinary herb (*Allium porrum*) of the lily family, closely allied to the onion. ◆ Homophone: *leak.* [OE *lēac*]

leer[1] (lir) *n.* A sly look or glance expressing immodest desire, malicious intent, etc. — *v.i.* To look with a leer. [OE *hlēor* a cheek, face; hence "a glance over one's cheek"]

leer[2] (lir) *n.* An oven for annealing glass: also spelled *lear, lehr.* [Origin unknown]

leer·ing·ly (lir'ing·lē) *adv.* With a leer. [< LEER[1]]

leer·y (lir'ē) *adj. Slang* Shrewd and sly; suspicious; wary. [< LEER[1] + -Y]

lees (lēz) *n. pl.* The settlings of liquor; sediment; dregs. [Pl. of obs. *lee* < OF *lie* < Med. L *lia,* prob. < Celtic]

lee shore The shore on the lee side of a ship, toward which the wind blows the ship. — **on a lee shore** In danger or difficulties.

lee·ward (lē'wərd, lōō'ərd) *adj. Naut.* Pertaining to the direction in which the wind blows. — *n.* The direction toward which the wind blows: opposed to *windward.* — *adv.* Toward the lee: also **lee'ward·ly.**

Lee·ward Islands (lē'wərd) **1** A northern group of West Indian islands in the Lesser Antilles, extending SE from Puerto Rico into the Windward Islands. **2** A former British colony in this group, divided into the four colonies (former federated presidencies) of (1) Antigua, (2) St. Christopher, Nevis and Anguilla, (3) Montserrat, these three being members of The West Indies, and (4) the British Virgin Islands; 422.5 square miles; former capital, St. John's, on Antigua. **3** See SOCIETY ISLANDS.

lee·way (lē'wā') *n.* **1** *Naut.* The lateral drift of a vessel to leeward. **2** The falling behind or away from a set course. **3** *Colloq.* Extra margin, space, time, money, etc.

left[1] (left) Past tense and past participle of LEAVE[1].

left[2] (left) *adj.* **1** Pertaining to that side of the body which is toward the north when one faces the rising sun: opposite to *right.* **2** Situated on the left-hand side; sinistral.

3 Designating that side or bank of a river which is on the left facing the direction of flow. — *n.* **1** The left side. **2** Anything on or toward that side of the human body which normally contains the lower portion of the heart. **3** In European countries, the more radical political parties, seated to the left of the presiding officer in a deliberative assembly: also **The Left.** — *adv.* On or to the left. [OE (Kentish), weak, worthless, as in *lyftādl* paralysis]

Left Bank A district of Paris along the left (south) bank of the Seine, famous for its many artist and student inhabitants.

left–hand (left′hand′) *adj.* **1** Situated on the left side; sinistral. **2** Turning, opening, or swinging to the left.

left–hand·ed (left′han′did) *adj.* **1** Having the left hand or arm stronger or more dexterous than the right. **2** Done with the left hand; turning or moving from right to left or oppositely to the motion of the hands of a clock: a *left–handed* screw. **3** Adapted for use by the left hand, as a tool. **4** Clumsy; awkward. **5** Without sincerity; indirect: a *left–handed* compliment. **6** Morganatic: from the giving to the bride of the left hand instead of the right by the bridegroom in a morganatic marriage. — **left′–hand′ed·ly** *adv.* — **left′–hand′·ed·ness** *n.*

left·ism (lef′tiz·əm) *n.* The advocacy of radical or ultraliberal policies. — **left′ist** *n.* & *adj.*

left·o·ver (left′ō′vər) *n.* A part not used or consumed. — *adj.* Remaining unconsumed.

left wing 1 A political party or group advocating radical or liberal politics. **2** That part of any group advocating radical liberal policies. Also **Left Wing.** — **left′–wing′** *adj.* — **left′–wing′er** *n.*

left·y (lef′tē) *n. Slang* A left–handed person: especially applied to a baseball pitcher or batter.

leg (leg) *n.* **1** A limb of an animal used for supporting the body and for walking; especially, in man, the part of the lower limb between knee and ankle. ◆ Collateral adjective: *crural.* **2** Something that resembles a leg: the *leg* of a table, etc. **3** Hence, anything that gives support. **4** That portion of a garment or stocking which covers the leg. **5** *Naut.* The distance run by a vessel on one tack. **6** Any appreciable section of a journey. **7** That portion of a cricket field which would be included between an imaginary line drawn at right angles from the batsman's left leg to the boundary and a line drawn from the batsman's middle wicket to the boundary. **8** *Archaic* An obeisance. — **a leg to stand on** A tenable or logical basis for argument. — **to pull one's leg** *Slang* To fool or make fun of someone. — **on one's last legs** On the verge of death or collapse. — **to shake a leg** *Slang* To make haste; hurry. — *v.i.* **legged, leg·ging** *Colloq.* To walk; run: often with *it.* [< ON *leggr*]

leg·a·cy (leg′ə·sē) *n. pl.* **·cies 1** Something left by will; a bequest. **2** Hence, anything, as a characteristic, derived from an ancestor. [< OF *legacie,* orig. a legateship < Med. L *legatia* the district of a legate < L *legatus.* See LEGATE.]

le·gal (lē′gəl) *adj.* **1** Created or permitted by law. **2** Of, pertaining to, or connected with law: the *legal* mind. **3** In conformity with law; lawful: a *legal* rate of interest. **4** Capable of being remedied by a resort to law, as distinguished from equity. **5** Characteristic of those who practice law: He has a *legal* approach to all situations. **6** *Theol.* **a** Relating to or founded upon the Mosaic law. **b** Pertaining to the doctrine of salvation by works rather than by grace. — *n. pl.* Investments legally open to trustees, fiduciaries, etc. [< OF *legal* < L *legalis* < *lex, legis* law. Doublet of LOYAL.]

legal cap Ruled writing paper, about 8 1/2 x 13 inches, made up in pads gummed at the top for lawyers' use.

le·gal·ism (lē′gəl·iz′əm) *n.* **1** Close adherence to law; strict conformity to law. **2** *Theol.* The doctrine of salvation by works, as distinguished from that by grace. **3** The tendency to observe the letter rather than the

spirit of the law. — **le′gal·ist** *n.* — **le′gal·is′tic** *adj.*

le·gal·i·ty (li·gal′ə·tē) *n. pl.* **·ties 1** The condition of being legal. **2** The distinctive spirit of the legal profession. **3** Adherence or conformity to law.

le·gal·ize (lē′gəl·īz) *v.t.* **·ized, ·iz·ing** To make legal; sanction. Also *Brit.* **le′gal·ise.** — **le′gal·i·za′tion** (-ə·zā′shən, -ī·sā′-) *n.*

legal memory *Law* The period through which things past are accepted in law as definitely affecting present rights or principles.

legal tender Coin or other money that may legally be offered in payment of a debt, and that may not be refused by a creditor.

leg·ate (leg′it) *n.* **1** A person accredited by one state or nation as its diplomatic representative to the court or government of another state or nation; an ambassador; envoy. **2** A representative of the pope in various functions, political or ecclesiastical. **3** In ancient Roman history: **a** An ambassador sent from ancient Rome to a foreign nation, or one sent by a foreign nation to Rome. **b** A person accompanying a Roman general into the field as adviser, or a subordinate in command. **c** A governor of a province **4** A district governed by a legate; specifically, formerly one of the six provinces of the Romagna. See synonyms under DELEGATE. [< OF *legat* < L *legatus,* pp. of *legare* send as a deputy, bequeath] — **leg′ate·ship** *n.* — **leg′a·tine** (-tin, -tīn), **leg·an·tine** (-ən·tin, -tīn) *adj.*

leg·a·tee (leg′ə·tē′) *n.* The recipient of a legacy. [< *legate, v.* bequeath < L *legatus,* pp. of *legare* bequeath]

le·ga·tion (li·gā′shən) *n.* **1** The act of deputing or delegating. **2** A diplomatic mission, or the persons composing it. **3** The official residence or place of business of the chief of a diplomatic mission. **4** The office or rank of a legate. [< L *legatio, -onis* < *legare* send]

le·ga·to (li·gä′tō) *adj.* & *adv. Music* In a smooth, connected manner: opposed to *staccato.* [< Ital., lit., bound, pp. of *legare* bind < L *ligare*]

le·ga·tor (li·gā′tər, leg′ə·tôr′) *n.* One who makes a will; a testator. [< L < *legatus,* pp. of *legare* bequeath]

leg·end (lej′ənd) *n.* **1** An unauthenticated story from early times, preserved by tradition and popularly thought to be historical. **2** Such narratives, collectively. **3** A chronicle of the life of a saint, originally to be read aloud in religious services or at meals. **4** Loosely, the fame of a person or place: the Woodrow Wilson *legend.* **5** An inscription or motto on a coin or monument. **6** A caption for an illustration; an explanatory description or key to a map or chart. **7** *Music* A composition intended to describe or relate a story, without words. See synonyms under FICTION. — **local legend** A story, current in a definite region, which explains some local custom, geographical feature, name, etc., as of lovers' leaps, outlaws, haunted places, buried treasure, etc. [< OF *legende* < Med. L *legenda* things read, neut. pl. of L *legendus* to be read, gerundive of *legere* read]

leg·en·dar·y (lej′ən·der′ē) *adj.* **1** Of or pertaining to a legend. **2** Quasi-historical or traditional. **3** Celebrated in or known from legends.

leg·er (lej′ər) See LEDGER[2].

Lé·ger (lā·zhā′), **Fernand,** 1881-1955, French painter.

leger bait, etc. See LEDGER BAIT, etc.

leg·er·de·main (lej′ər·də·mān′) *n.* **1** Sleight of hand. **2** Any deceptive adroitness; any artful trick. [< F *léger de main,* lit., light of hand < *léger* light (< L *levis*) + *de* of (< L, from) + *main* hand (< L *manus*)] — **leg′er·de·main′ist** *n.*

leger lines Short lines added above or below a musical staff to increase its range. [< *leger,* var. of LEDGER[1] + *lines,* pl. of LINE]

le·ges (lē′jēz) Plural of LEX.

leg·ged (leg′id, legd) *adj.* Having a specified kind or number of legs: usually in combination: *bow–legged, two–legged,* etc.

leg·ging (leg′ing) *n. Usually pl.* A covering for the leg; long gaiter.

leg·gy (leg′ē) *adj.* **·gi·er, ·gi·est** Having disproportionately long or conspicuous legs.

leg·horn[1] (leg′ərn, -hôrn) *n.* **1** A fine plait of leghorn straw, used for making bonnets and hats. **2** A bonnet or hat made of this plait. — *adj.* Made of leghorn straw. [from *Leghorn*]

leg·horn[2] (leg′hôrn, leg′ərn) *n.* A hardy Mediterranean breed of domestic fowls. [from *Leghorn*]

leghorn straw The straw of a variety of wheat (*Triticum aestivum*) or of spelt.

leg·i·ble (lej′ə·bəl) *adj.* **1** That can be deciphered or read with ease. **2** That can be discovered or discerned from evident indications. [< LL *legibilis* < L *legere* read] — **leg′i·bil′i·ty, leg′i·ble·ness** *n.* — **leg′i·bly** *adv.*

le·gion (lē′jən) *n.* **1** A division of the ancient Roman army, consisting of ten cohorts of infantry, with an auxiliary force of 300 cavalry: altogether between 4,200 and 6,000 men. **2** One of various other military organizations of other countries. **3** *pl.* Military force. **4** A great number; multitude. **5** *Zool.* A taxonomic category, no longer used. [< OF *legiun* < L *legio -onis* < *legere* choose, levy an army]

le·gion·ar·y (lē′jən·er′ē) *adj.* **1** Pertaining to a legion. **2** Innumerable. — *n. pl.* **·ar·ies** A soldier of a legion.

legionary ant See DRIVER ANT.

le·gion·naire (lē′jən·âr′) *n.* **1** A legionary. **2** A member of the American Legion. Also *Fr.* **lé·gion·naire** (lā·zhə·nâr′). [< F *légionnaire* < *légion* (< OF *legiun* LEGION) + *-aire* -ARY]

leg·is·late (lej′is·lāt) *v.* **·lat·ed, ·lat·ing** *v.i.* To make a law or laws. — *v.t.* To bring about or effect by legislation. [Back formation < LEGISLATOR]

leg·is·la·tion (lej′is·lā′shən) *n.* **1** Enactment of laws, or business incidental thereto. **2** The laws enacted by a legislative power. [< LL *legislatio, -onis* < *legis,* genitive of *lex* a law + *latio, -onis* a bringing, proposing < *latus,* pp. to *ferre* bring]

Synonyms: code, economy, jurisprudence, law, polity. A *code* is a system of *laws; jurisprudence* is the science of *law,* or a system of *laws* scientifically considered, classed, and interpreted; *legislation,* primarily the act of legislating, denotes also the body of statutes enacted by a legislative body; an *economy* is a body of *laws* and regulations, with the entire system, political or religious, especially the latter, of which they form a part; as, the *code* of Draco, Roman *jurisprudence,* British *legislation,* the Mosaic *economy.* The Mosaic *economy* is known also as the Mosaic *law,* and we speak of the English common *law,* or the *law* of nations. *Polity* differs from *economy* as applying to the system itself, while *economy* applies to the method of administration or to the system as administered. See LAW[1].

leg·is·la·tive (lej′is·lā′tiv) *adj.* **1** Having the power to legislate; that makes or enacts laws: distinguished from *administrative* and *judicial.* **2** Of, pertaining to, or suitable to legislation. **3** Of or pertaining to a legislature. — *n.* The law–making power in government. — **leg′is·la′tive·ly** *adv.*

leg·is·la·tor (lej′is·lā′tər) *n.* **1** One who legislates; a lawgiver. **2** A member of a legislature. [L, proposer of a law < *lex, legis* a law + *lator* < *latus,* pp. to *ferre* bring] — **leg·is·la·to·ri·al** (lej′is·lə·tôr′ē·əl, -tō′rē-) *adj.* — **leg′is·la′tress** (-tris), **leg′is·la′trix** (-triks) *n. fem.*

leg·is·la·ture (lej′is·lā′chər) *n.* A body of men empowered to make laws for a country or state; the legislative body of a state or territory. See CONGRESS.

le·git·i·mate (lə·jit′ə·mit) *adj.* **1** Having the sanction of law or custom; authorized; lawful; also, genuine. **2** Born in wedlock. **3** Based strictly on hereditary rights or sovereignty. **4** Following in regular or natural sequence; logically deduced. See synonyms under AUTHENTIC. — *v.t.* (lə·jit′ə·māt) **·mat·ed, ·mat·ing 1** To make legitimate. **2** To justify. [< Med. L *legitimatus,* pp. of *legitimare* declare to be lawful < L *legitimus* lawful < *lex, legis* a law] — **le·git′i·ma·cy, le·git′i·mate·ness** *n.* — **le·git′i·mate·ly** *adv.* — **le·git′i·ma′tion** *n.*

legitimate drama 1 Any drama spoken and acted on the stage: opposed to motion pictures, television, etc. **2** Formerly, drama conforming to certain literary and dramatic principles; not burlesque or melodrama.

le·git·i·mist (lə·jit′ə·mist) *n.* One who supports legitimate authority or supports a certain authority as legitimate; specifically, in France, a supporter of the claims of the elder branch of the Bourbon family. Also **le·git′i·ma·tist.** [<F *légitimiste* < *légitime* legitimate <L *legitimus.* See LEGITIMATE.] — **le·git′i·mism** *n.*

le·git·i·mize (lə·jit′ə·mīz) *v.t.* **-mized, ·miz·ing** **1** To make legitimate. **2** To make acceptable or tolerable: to assert that some TV programs *legitimize* violence. Also **le·git′i·ma·tize.** — **le·git′i·mi·za′tion** *n.*

leg·man (leg′man′) *n.* *pl.* **·men** (-men′) **1** A reporter who collects data for a news story outside the editorial offices, as from interviews, obtaining official statements and documents, etc. **2** An office assistant or subordinate employed to do various errands.

leg·ume (leg′yōom, lə·gyōom′) *n.* **1** The fruit or seed of any leguminous plant, as peas and beans. **2** A one-celled, two-valved seed vessel formed of a single dehiscent carpel having the seeds arranged along the inner or ventral suture. [<F *légume* <L *legumen,* lit., a gatherable thing < *legere* gather]

le·gu·min (lə·gyōo′min) *n.* *Biochem.* A globulin present in peas and other leguminous seeds. [<LEGUM(E) + -IN]

le·gu·mi·nous (lə·gyōo′mə·nəs) *adj.* **1** Of or pertaining to legumes, or to a large, widely distributed family (*Leguminosae*) of plants, the pea or bean family, bearing legumes. **2** Producing legumes. Also **le·gu′mi·nose** (-nōs). [<L *legumen, -inis* a legume + -OUS]

leg·work (leg′wûrk′) *n.* *Colloq.* The physical activity incidental to doing research.

le·hu·a (lā·hōo′ä) *n.* **1** A tree (*Metrosideros tremuloides*) of the myrtle family, native in the Pacific Islands, having vivid red flowers and a hard wood. **2** The blossom of this tree. **3** Its wood. [<Hawaiian]

lei[1] (lā, lā′ē) *n.* In the Hawaiian Islands, a garland or wreath of showy flowers and leaves, as hibiscus blossoms, or of feathers: usually worn around the neck or as an ornamental headdress. [<Hawaiian]

lei[2] (lā) Plural of LEU.

Leib·nitz (līp′nits), **Baron Gottfried Wilhelm von,** 1646–1716, German philosopher and mathematician. Also **Leib′niz.** — **Leib·nitz′·i·an** *adj.* & *n.*

lei·ot·ri·chous (lī·ot′rə·kəs) *adj.* Lissotrichous. [<NL *Leiotrichi* the smooth-haired (division of mankind) <Gk. *leios* smooth + *thrix, trichos* hair]

leish·man·i·a·sis (līsh′mən·ī′ə·sis) *n.* *Pathol.* Any disease caused by parasitic protozoans of the genus *Leishmania,* especially the tropical disease kala-azar. Also **leish′man·i′o·sis.** [after Sir William B. *Leishman,* 1865–1926, English army surgeon]

leis·ter (lēs′tər) *n.* A three-pronged fishing spear. — *v.t.* To spear with a leister. [<ON *liōstr* < *liōsta* strike] — **leis′ter·er** *n.*

lei·sure (lē′zhər, lezh′ər) *n.* **1** Freedom from the demands of work or duty. **2** Spare time; time available for some particular purpose. — *adj.* **1** Free or unoccupied. **2** Having leisure: the *leisure* class. [<OF *leisir* be permitted <L *licere*]

lei·sure·ly (lē′zhər·lē, lezh′ər-) *adj.* Done at leisure; deliberate; slow. — *adv.* At leisure; deliberately. — **lei′sure·li·ness** *n.*

leit·mo·tif (līt′mō·tēf′) *n.* *Music* A representative theme used to indicate a certain person, attribute, or idea, in an opera or other composition. Also **leit′mo·tiv** (-tēf). [<G *leitmotiv* < *leiten* lead + *motiv* <Med. L *motivus.* See MOTIVE.]

Le Mans start In automobile racing, a method of starting contestants by lining the cars diagonally on one side of the track, the drivers standing on the other; at a signal the drivers run to their cars, start them, and proceed onto the track. [from *Le Mans;* because traditionally used at an annual automobile race held there]

lem·ma[1] (lem′ə) *n.* *pl.* **lem·mas** or **lem·ma·ta** (lem′ə·tə) **1** A subject or theme assumed for treatment, as in verse. **2** *Logic* **a** A subsidiary proposition employed as auxiliary in demonstrating another one. **b** A proposition assumed to be true. [<L <Gk. *lēmma* something taken, a premise < *lēmm-,* stem of *lambanein* take]

lem·ma[2] (lem′ə) *n.* *Bot.* A small, chaffy bract

inside and above the glumes in a spikelet of grass. [<Gk. *lemma* a husk < *lepein* peel]

lem·ming (lem′ing) *n.* Any of several small arctic rodents (genera *Lemmus, Dicrostonyx,* and *Myopus*) with a short tail and furry feet. One European species is noted for recurrent migrations in vast numbers, often terminated by drowning in the ocean. [<Norw.]

LEMMING

Lemnian bole A white or grayish-yellow variety of aluminous earth. Also **Lemnian earth.**

lem·nis·cate (lem′nis·kāt, -kit) *n.* *Math.* The plane curve in the shape of a figure eight traced by the foot of a perpendicular drawn from the origin to a tangent to a rectangular hyperbola: the locus of the vertex of a triangle when the product of the two adjacent sides is maintained equal to 1/4 of the fixed, opposite side. Also called **Bernoulli's lemniscate.** [<NL *lemniscata,* orig. fem. of L *lemniscatus* adorned with ribbons < *lemniscus.* See LEMNISCUS.]

LEMNISCATE
A symmetrical tracing in polar coordinates.

lem·nis·cus (lem·nis′kəs) *n.* *pl.* **·nis·ci** (-nis′ī) **1** *Anat.* A bundle or fillet of nerve fibers in the medulla and pons. **2** *Zool.* One of a pair of club-shaped organs at the base of the proboscis of certain parasitic worms (class *Acanthocephala*). [<NL <L, a ribbon <Gk. *lēmniskos*]

lem·on (lem′ən) *n.* **1** An oval citrus fruit with a bright-yellow skin containing the essential **oil of lemon,** and very acid pulp and juice. **2** The small or medium-sized evergreen tree (*Citrus medica* and *C. lemon*) of the rue family that produces this fruit. **3** The color of the rind of lemon; bright yellow. **4** *U.S. Slang* Something disappointing, worthless, or unpleasant. — *adj.* **1** Flavored with or containing lemon: *lemon* pie. **2** Lemon-colored. [<OF *limon* <Sp. *limón* <Arabic *laimūn* <Persian *līmūn.* Related to LIME[2].]

lem·on·ade (lem′ən·ād′) *n.* A drink made of lemon juice, water, and sugar. [<F *limonade* < *limon* LEMON]

lemon geranium A common garden flower (*Pelargonium limoneum*) related to the geranium, having the odor of lemons.

lemon grass An Old World tropical grass (*Cymbopogon citratus*) whose leaves yield an oil used as a flavoring and in perfumery.

lemon squash *Brit.* Lemonade.

lemon verbena A tropical American shrub (*Lippia citriodora*) with white flowers and lanceolate leaves having an odor of lemon.

lem·on·wood (lem′ən·wŏod′) *n.* **1** The yellowish-white, tough, flexible wood of a Central American tree (*Calycophyllum candidissimum*), used for fishing rods, bow staves, etc. **2** The tree itself. Also called *degame.*

lemon yellow **1** A pigment consisting of a mixture of barium and chromic acid ground in water or oil. **2** Lead chromate.

lem·pi·ra (lem·pē′rä) *n.* The gold monetary unit of Honduras. [<Am. Sp., after *Lempira,* an Indian chief who fought the Spanish]

lem·u·res (lem′yŏo·rēz) *n. pl.* In Roman religion, the shades or spirits of the dead; ghosts; specters. On the ninth of May a festival, the **Le·mu·ri·a** (lə·myŏor′ē·ə), was held to appease these departed spirits. [<L]

Le·mu·ri·a (lə·myŏor′ē·ə) A hypothetical continent, supposedly submerged beneath the Indian Ocean, thought by E. Haeckel to be the original home of lemuroid primates.

lem·u·roid (lem′yŏo·roid) *adj.* Of or pertaining to the lemurs. — *n.* A lemur. Also **lem′u·rine** (-rīn, -rin).

Le·nard rays (lā′närt) *Physics* Cathode rays that stream into the atmosphere through a metallic window of a vacuum tube known as a **Lenard tube** or a Coolidge cathode-ray tube. [after Philipp von *Lenard,* 1862–1947, German physicist]

Len·clos (län·klō′), **Ninon de,** 1620–1705, French beauty and wit: real name *Anne L'Enclos.*

lend (lend) *v.* **lent, lend·ing** *v.t.* **1** To grant the temporary use of without further compensation than the understanding that the thing or its equivalent will be returned. **2** To grant the temporary use of, as money, for a compensation. **3** To impart; furnish: The thought *lends* beauty to the poem. **4** To accommodate (oneself or itself): The statement *lends* itself to interpretation. — *v.i.* **5** To make a loan or loans. — **to lend a hand** To give assistance. — **to lend an ear** To hearken. [OE *lǣnan* < *lǣn* a loan. Akin to LOAN.] — **lend′er** *n.*

lend–lease (lend′lēs′) *n.* In World War II, the furnishing of goods and services to any country whose defense was deemed vital to the defense of the United States, under the terms of the **Lend–Lease Act** passed by Congress March 11, 1941.

le·net·ic (lə·net′ik) *adj.* *Ecol.* Of, pertaining to, or designating plant or animal communities inhabiting still waters. Also **le·nit′ic** (-nit′-). [<L *lenis* smooth]

length (lengkth) *n.* **1** Extension from end to end; hence, usually, the greatest dimension of a surface or body, as distinguished from *breadth* or *width.* **2** Distance measured along a line from end to end. **3** The state of being long. **4** Extent in point of time. **5** A specific or understood distance; a thing of known extent: a boat's *length.* **6** Power of extension; reach; extent; the distance reached or that may be reached. **7** In classical prosody, quantity. **8** *Phonet.* **a** The period required for the pronunciation of a vowel. **b** The quality of a vowel. — **at length 1** After an interval of expectation; finally; at last. **2** At full length; without omission or contraction. [OE *lengthu* < *lang* long]

length·en (lengk′thən) *v.t.* & *v.i.* To make or become longer. See synonyms under PROTRACT, STRETCH.

length·wise (lengkth′wīz′) *adv.* In a longitudinal direction. Also **length′ways′** (-wāz′).

length·y (lengk′thē) *adj.* **length·i·er, length·i·est** Having length; unduly long. — **length′i·ly** *adv.* — **length′i·ness** *n.*

le·ni·ent (lē′nē·ənt, lēn′yənt) *adj.* **1** Of merciful disposition; gentle; mild; indulgent. **2** *Archaic* Soothing; emollient. See synonyms under CHARITABLE. [<L *leniens, -entis,* ppr. of *lenire* soothe < *lenis* soft, mild] — **le′ni·ence** *n.* — **le′ni·en·cy** *n.* — **le′ni·ent·ly** *adv.*

Le·nin (len′in, *Russian* lye′nyin), **Nikolai,** 1870–1924, Russian revolutionary; leader of Bolshevik party; chief leader of the Russian Revolution and head of the Soviet government 1917–24: real name *Vladimir Ilyich Ulianov.*

Len·in·ism (len′in·iz′əm) Social doctrine based upon the teachings of Lenin. — **Len′in·ist, Len′in·ite** *n.* & *adj.*

le·nis (lē′nis) *adj.* *Phonet.* Weakly articulated, with little or no aspiration: said especially of stop consonants, and opposed to *fortis.* — *n. pl.* **le·nes** (lē′nēz) **1** A lenis consonant. **2** In Greek grammar, the smooth breathing (*spiritus lenis*). Also **le·ne** (lē′nē). [<L, smooth, soft]

len·i·tive (len′ə·tiv) *adj.* Having the power or tendency to allay pain or mitigate suffering. — *n.* That which soothes or mitigates; an aperient medicine; a laxative. [<Med. L *lenitivus* <L *lenitus,* pp. of *lenire* soothe]

len·i·ty (len′ə·tē) *n.* The state or quality of being lenient. [<OF *lenité* <L *lenitas, -tatis* softness < *lenis* soft]

le·no (lē′nō) *n.* **1** A type of weave with paired and twisted warp yarns. **2** A loose, open fabric of such a weave. [<F *linon* < *lin* flax]

lens (lenz) *n.* **1** A piece of glass or other transparent substance, bounded by two surfaces, of different curvature, generally spherical, or by one spherical or curved, and one plane surface, by which rays of light may be made to converge or to diverge. ◆ Collateral adjective:

lenticular. **2** Any device for concentrating or dispersing radiation by refraction. **3** A biconvex transparent body situated behind the iris of the eye. See illustration under EYE. **— crown lens** The convex portion in an achromatic lens. [<L *lens, lentis* a lentil; so called from the similarity in form]

LENS
a. Convexo-convex.   *d.* Concavo-concave.
b. Plano-convex.   *e.* Plano-concave.
c. Convexo-concave.   *f.* Concavo-convex.

lent (lent) Past tense and past participle of LEND.

Lent (lent) *n.* **1** *Eccl.* A fast of forty days (excluding Sundays), observed annually from Ash Wednesday till Easter as a season of penitence and self-denial. **2** *Obs.* In the Middle Ages, a period of fasting at any time of the year: St. Martin's *Lent,* observed from Martinmas (November 11) till Christmas. [Short for *Lenten,* OE *lencten, lengten* the spring] **— Lent'en** *adj.*

len·ta·men·te (len'tä·men'tā) *adv. Music* Slowly. [<Ital. <*lento* LENTO]

len·tan·do (len·tän'dō) *adj. & adv. Music* Becoming slower by degrees; rallentando. [<Ital., ppr. of *lentare* become slow <*lento* LENTO]

lent·en (len'tən) *adj.* **1** Plain; spare; meager. **2** Cold or chary. [OE *lencten* spring, Lent; with ref. to the traditional meagerness of Lenten fare]

len·ti·cel (len'tə·sel) *n. Bot.* A loose, lens-shaped mass of cells belonging to the corky layer of plants, constituting a break in the continuity of the epidermis and permitting an interchange between gases within the plant and the external air. [<F *lenticelle* <NL *lenticella,* dim. of L *lens, lentis* a lentil]

len·tic·u·lar (len·tik'yə·lər) *adj.* **1** Resembling a double-convex lens; lens-shaped. **2** Of or pertaining to a lens. **3** *Meteorol.* Designating an ovoid-shaped cloud with usually clean edges, found at all levels and characterized by a tendency to remain stationary for long intervals, despite constant evaporation. [<L *lenticularis* <*lenticula,* dim. of L *lens, lentis* a lentil. See LENS.]

len·ti·form (len'tə·fôrm) *adj.* Lens-shaped. [<L *lens, lentis* a lentil + -FORM. See LENS.]

len·tig·i·nose (len·tij'ə·nōs) *adj.* Pertaining to lentigo; freckled; dusty. Also **len·tig'i·nous** (-nəs). [<LL *lentiginosus* <L *lentigo, -ginis* a freckle <*lens, lentis* a lentil]

len·ti·go (len·tī'gō) *n. pl.* **·tig·i·nes** (-tij'ə·nēz) **1** A freckle. **2** *Med.* A freckly condition of the skin. [<L <*lens, lentis* a lentil]

len·til (len'təl) *n.* **1** An Old World leguminous plant (*Lens culinaris*) with pale-blue flowers and broad pods containing edible seeds. **2** The seed itself. [<F *lentille* <L *lenticula,* dim. of *lens, lentis* a lentil]

len·tis·si·mo (len·tis'i·mō) *adj. & adv. Music* Very slow; very slowly. [<Ital., superl. of *lento* LENTO]

len·to (len'tō) *adj. & adv. Music* Slow; slowly. [<Ital. <L *lentus*]

len·toid (len'toid) *adj.* Lens-shaped; lenticular. [<L *lens, lentis* a lentil + -OID. See LENS.]

len·tor (len'tôr) *n.* Extreme slowness of movement or function; sluggishness: heart *lentor.* [<F *lenteur* <L *lentor* <*lentus* slow]

Le·o (lē'ō) **1** The fifth sign of the zodiac, which the sun enters about July 21. **2** A constellation containing the Sickle and the bright star Regulus. See CONSTELLATION. [<NL <L, a lion]

Le·o·nar·desque (lē'ə·när·desk') *adj.* Resembling or pertaining to the style of Leonardo da Vinci.

Le·o·nar·do da Vin·ci (lā'ō·när'dō dä vēn'chē), 1452–1519, Italian painter, sculptor, architect, engineer, musician, scientist, and

natural philosopher.

Le·o·nid (lē'ə·nid) *n.* One of the meteors that form a shower about November 14 in a modified form every year, but especially brilliant at intervals of approximately 33 years: their radiant point is in the constellation Leo. [<F <NL *Leo, Leonis* the constellation LEO + -*id* -ID[1]]

le·o·nine (lē'ə·nīn, -nin) *adj.* Pertaining to or like a lion; fierce; powerful; majestic. [<OF *leonin* <L *leoninus* <*leo, leonis* a lion]

le·on·ti·a·sis (lē'on·tī'ə·sis) *n. Pathol.* A morbid thickening of the facial bones, giving a leonine appearance: seen in leprosy, elephantiasis, and certain other diseases. [<NL <Gk. <*leōn, leontos* a lion + -IASIS]

leop·ard (lep'ərd) *n.*
1 A ferocious, carnivorous mammal of the cat family (*Felis* or *Panthera pardus*) of Asia and Africa, of a pale fawn color, spotted with dark brown or black. A black variety, but having detectable spots, is often called a *panther.* **2** Any similar cat, such as the **American leopard** or jaguar, the **hunting leopard** or cheetah, the **snow leopard** or ounce. **3** *Her.* A lion passant gardant. **4** *Brit.* A gold coin of the reign of Edward III; a half-florin. [<OF <LL *leopardus* <Gk. *leopardos* <*leōn* a lion + *pardos* a panther] **— leop'ard·ess** *n. fem.*

LEOPARD
(About 2 1/2 feet high at the shoulder; length: 7 feet over–all)

leopard cat The American ocelot (*Felis pardalis*).

leopard moth A European moth (*Zeuzera pyrina*) introduced into the United States; its larvae are destructive borers in trees and shrubs.

le·o·tard (lē'ə·tärd) *n.* **1** A short, close-fitting, sleeveless garment, low at the neck, and fitted between the legs: worn by acrobats, etc. **2** A modern adaptation of this, having a high neck and covering the body to the wrist and ankle: used by dancers as practice clothes. [after *Léotard,* 19th c. French aerialist]

lep·er (lep'ər) *n.* One afflicted with leprosy. [<obs. *leper* leprosy <OF *lepre, liepre* <L *lepra* <Gk., orig. fem. of *lepros* scaly <*lepos* a scale <*lepein* peel]

lepido– *combining form* Scale or flake: *lepidolite.* Also, before vowels, **lepid–.** [<Gk. *lepis, lepidos* a scale]

le·pid·o·lite (li·pid'ə·līt, lep'ə·dō·līt') *n.* A lithium-bearing variety of mica. [<Gk. *lepis, -idos* a scale + -LITE]

lep·i·dop·ter·an (lep'ə·dop'tər·ən) *n.* Any of an order (*Lepidoptera*) of insects having four wings covered with minute scales, and undergoing a complete metamorphosis through the egg, caterpillar, pupa, and imago stages; butterflies and moths. — *adj.* Of or pertaining to the *Lepidoptera.* [<NL, order name < *lepidopteron* LEPIDOPTERON] **— lep'i·dop'ter·al, lep'i·dop'ter·ous** *adj.*

lep·i·dop·ter·on (lep'ə·dop'tər·on) *n. pl.* **·ter·a** (-tər·ə) Any lepidopterous insect; a moth or butterfly. [<NL <Gk. *lepis, -idos* a scale + *pteron* a wing]

lep·i·do·si·ren (lep'ə·dō·sī'rən) *n.* One of a genus (*Lepidosiren*) of primitive, eel-like lungfishes, as *L. paradoxa* of South America. [<LEPIDO- + SIREN (def. 3)]

lep·i·dote (lep'ə·dōt) *adj. Bot.* Scurfy with minute scales. [<NL *lepidotus* <Gk. *lepidōtos* <*lepis, lepidos* a scale]

Lep·i·dus (lep'ə·dəs), **Marcus Aemilius,** died 13 B.C., Roman triumvir with Antony and Octavian (Augustus).

lep·o·rid (lep'ə·rid) *n.* One of a family (*Leporidae*) of gnawing mammals belonging to the order *Lagomorpha* or suborder *Duplicidentata;* a rabbit or hare. — *adj.* Of or pertaining to the *Leporidae.* [<NL *Leporidae,* family name <L *lepus, leporis* a hare]

lep·o·ride (lep'ə·rid) *n.* The hybrid offspring of the European hare and rabbit; a Belgian hare. [<F *léporide* <L *lepus, leporis* a hare]

lep·o·rine (lep'ə·rīn, -rin) *adj.* Like or pertain-

ing to hares. [<L *leporinus* <*lepus, leporis* a hare]

lep·re·chaun (lep'rə·kôn) *n.* In Irish folklore, a fairy cobbler who, if caught and held, must reveal the location of treasure. [<Irish *lupracān* <OIrish *luchorpan* <*lu* little + *corpān,* dim. of *corp* body <L *corpus, -oris*]

lep·ro·sar·i·um (lep'rə·sâr'ē·əm) *n.* A leper colony or hospital. [<NL <LEPROS(Y) + (SANIT)ARIUM]

lep·rose (lep'rōs) *adj. Bot.* Having a scurfy appearance; scalelike; leprous: usually said of crustaceous lichens. [<L *leprosus* <*lepra.* See LEPER.]

lep·ro·sy (lep'rə·sē) *n. Pathol.* A chronic, endemic, communicable disease characterized by nodular skin lesions, nerve paralysis, and physical mutilation: caused by the microorganism *Mycobacterium* or *Bacillus leprae.* Also *Hansen's disease.* [<OF *leprosie,* prob. <LL *leprosus* <L *lepra.* See LEPER.]

lep·rous (lep'rəs) *adj.* **1** Affected with leprosy; unclean. **2** Scalelike; scurfy; covered with scales; leprose. Also **lep'er·ous** (-ər·əs). [<OF *lepros, leprous* <LL *leprosus* <L *lepra.* See LEPER.] **— lep'rous·ly** *adv.* **— lep'rous·ness** *n.*

-lepsy *combining form* Seizure; attack: *catalepsy.* Also **-lepsia.** [<Gk. *lepsis* a seizure <*lambanein* seize]

lepto– *combining form Biol.* Fine; slender; small: *leptorrhine.* Also, before vowels, **lept–.** [<Gk. *leptos* slender]

lep·tome (lep'tōm) *n.* Phloem. [<Gk. *leptos* fine, delicate]

lep·ton[1] (lep'ton) *n. pl.* **·ta** (-tə) A coin of modern Greece, valued at 1/100 drachma. [<Gk. *lepton (nomisma),* lit., a small coin, neut. of *leptos* small, fine]

lep·ton[2] (lep'ton) *n. Physics* An atomic particle of very small mass as the electron, positron, neutrino, or antineutron. [<Gk., neut. of *leptos* fine]

lep·tor·rhine (lep'tə·rīn, -rin) *adj.* Having a narrow or slender nose. [<LEPTO- + Gk. *rhis, rhinos* nose]

lep·to·so·mat·ic (lep'tə·sō·mat'ik) *adj.* Denoting a person having a light, lean, narrow body.

lep·to·tene (lep'tə·tēn) *adj. Biol.* Designating a stage in cell meiosis in which the nuclear substance assumes the form of delicate threads. [<LEPTO- + Gk. *tainia* a ribbon]

Le·pus (lē'pəs) *n.* **1** The genus of mammals (family *Leporidae*) which includes most of the hares and rabbits. **2** A southern constellation, the Hare. See CONSTELLATION. [<L, a hare]

Les·bi·an (lez'bē·ən) *n.* **1** A native or inhabitant of Lesbos. **2** A homosexual woman: so called from the alleged homosexuality of Sappho and her followers. — *adj.* **1** Of or pertaining to Lesbos or to Lesbians. **2** *Rare* Erotic. [<L *Lesbius* <Gk. *Lesbios* <*Lesbos,* the home of Sappho]

Les·bi·an·ism (lez'bē·ən·iz'əm) *n.* Homosexuality among women.

Les·bos (lez'bəs, -bos) A Greek island off NW Turkey; 623 square miles: also *Mytilene.*

le·sion (lē'zhən) *n.* **1** A hurt; loss; injury. **2** *Pathol.* Any morbid change in function or structure of an organ or tissue. [<F *lésion* <L *laesio, -onis* <*laesus,* pp. of *laedere* injure]

Le·so·tho (le·sōō'tōō, -sō'thō) An independent member of the Commonwealth of Nations consisting of an enclave in the eastern part of South Africa; 11,716 sq. mi.; capital, Maseru: formerly *Basutoland.*

less (les) Comparative of LITTLE. — *adj.* **1** Smaller; not as large or much. **2** Of slighter consequence; inferior in age, rank, etc. **3** Fewer: used with collective nouns. *Less* refers to quantity, measure, or degree; *fewer* refers to number. — *n.* **1** A smaller part or quantity. **2** The smaller (of things compared); the younger (of persons). — *adv.* In an inferior degree; not as much. — *prep.* Minus; by the subtraction or omission of: a year *less* a month, nine *less* six. [OE *lǣssa*]

-less *suffix* **1** Deprived or destitute of; without: *harmless.* **2** Beyond the range of (the action of the main element): *countless.* [OE *-leas* <*leas* free from]

les·see (les·ē') *n.* One to whom a lease is made:

one holding property by lease. [<AF *lessee*, OF *lessé*, pp. of *lesser*, *laissier*. See LEASE².]

less·en¹ (les'ən) *v.t.* **1** To make less; decrease. **2** To make little of; disparage. — *v.i.* **3** To become less. ◆ Homophone: *lesson*. See synonyms under ABATE, ALLAY, ALLEVIATE, IMPAIR. — **less'en·er.** — **less'en·ing** *adj. & n.*

less·en² (les'ən) *conj. Dial.* Unless.

less·er (les'ər) *adj.* Less; smaller; inferior.

les·son (les'ən) *n.* **1** A specific exercise to be learned or recited at one time; task assigned by a teacher. **2** Instruction; an instance of instruction. **3** *pl.* A course of instruction. **4** A set portion of any work or writing suitable for reading at one time; a reading; specifically, a portion of Scripture read or appointed to be read in divine service. **5** Knowledge gained by experience. **6** A reprimand; lecture. See synonyms under TASK. — *v.t.* **1** To give a lesson or lessons to. **2** To rebuke; scold. ◆ Homophone: *lessen*. [<OF *lecon* <L *lectio*, *-onis* a reading. Doublet of LECTION.]

les·sor (les'ôr, les·ôr') *n.* One who grants a lease or demises a property. [<AF <*lesser*, *laissier.* See LESSEE.]

lest (lest) *conj.* **1** In order that . . . not; so that . . . not; for fear that: We hid it *lest* he should see it. **2** That: following expressions indicating alarm or anxiety: We were worried *lest* the money run out. [OE *(thy) læs the* (by the) less that]

let¹ (let) *v.* **let, let·ting** *v.t.* **1** To allow; permit: He won't *let* her do it. **2** To allow to go, come, or pass: They would not *let* us on board. **3** To cause; make: She disliked him and *let* him know it. **4** To cause to escape or be released: to *let* blood. **5** To grant the temporary possession or occupancy of, as a room or house, for rent or other compensation: often with *out.* **6** To assign, as a contract, for performance. **7** As an auxiliary verb, *let* is used to express command or suggestion: *Let* him come. — *v.i.* **8** To be rented or leased. — **to let alone** (or **be**) To refrain from disturbing, bothering, or tampering with. See note under LEAVE. — **to let down 1** To allow to descend; lower. **2** To relax; reduce effort or concentration. **3** *Colloq.* To disappoint. — **to let fly** To hurl, as a missile. — **to let loose 1** To free; liberate. **2** *Colloq.* To act unrestrainedly. — **to let off 1** To discharge or reduce, as pressure. **2** *Colloq.* To excuse from an engagement, duty, or penalty; dismiss. — **to let on** *Colloq.* **1** To pretend. **2** To reveal; allow to be known. — **to let out 1** To release; allow to go, escape, etc. **2** To reveal; divulge. **3** To make larger by releasing a part previously fastened: to *let out* a seam. **4** *Colloq.* To dismiss or be dismissed, as a school. — **to let up** To slacken; abate. — **to let up on** *Colloq.* To reduce or cease applying pressure or harsh measures to. — **to let well enough alone** To refrain from tampering with what is regarded as unfavorable to change or already satisfactory. [OE *lætan*]

let² (let) *n.* **1** Anything that obstructs or hinders; an obstacle; impediment: usually in the phrase "without *let* or hindrance." **2** In tennis, rackets, fives, ping-pong, etc., a served ball which touches the net in passing over. — *v.t. Archaic* let or let·ted, let·ting To hinder or impede; obstruct. [OE *lettan*, lit., make late]

-let *suffix of nouns* **1** Small; little: *kinglet.* **2** A band or small article for: *bracelet.* [<OF *-let*, *-lette* <*-el* (<L *-ellus*) + *-et*, dim. suffixes]

let alone Without mentioning; to say nothing of: He can't even float, *let alone* swim.

let-down (let'doun') *n.* **1** Abatement or slackening; decrease, as of speed or energy. **2** *Colloq.* Disillusionment; disappointment.

le·thal (lē'thəl) *adj.* **1** Causing death; deadly; fatal. **2** Pertaining to death. [<L *lethalis* <*lethum*, *letum* death] — **le'thal·ly** *adv.*

le·thal·i·ty (lē·thal'ə·tē) *n.* **1** The quality of being lethal. **2** The degree of destructiveness produced by the action of a bomb, warhead, or similar weapon.

le·thar·gic (li·thär'jik) *adj.* Pertaining to, resembling, or affected by lethargy; drowsy; apathetic; dull; sleepy. Also **le·thar'gi·cal.** — **le·thar'gi·cal·ly** *adv.*

leth·ar·gize (leth'ər·jīz) *v.t.* **·gized, ·giz·ing** To make lethargic.

leth·ar·gy (leth'ər·jē) *n. pl.* **·gies 1** *Pathol.* A state of morbid and prolonged sleep; stupor. **2** A state of inaction, indifference, or dulness; apathy. See synonyms under APATHY, STUPOR. [<OF *lethargie* <LL *lethargia* <Gk. *lēthargia* < *lēthargos* forgetful < *lēthē* oblivion]

Le·the (lē'thē) **1** In Greek and Roman mythology, the river of forgetfulness, one of the five rivers surrounding Hades. **2** Oblivion; forgetfulness. [<Gk. *lēthē* oblivion] — **Le·the·an** (li·thē'ən) *adj.*

le·thif·er·ous (li·thif'ər·əs) *adj.* Deadly; lethal; fatal. [<L *lethifer* <*lethum*, *letum* death + *ferre* carry]

Lett (let) *n.* **1** One of a people inhabiting Latvia and adjacent Baltic regions. **2** Lettish.

let·ter (let'ər) *n.* **1** A mark or character used to represent a sound or articulation of human speech; a character of the alphabet; a primary element of written speech; also, a type bearing such a character, or, collectively, printer's type or a style of type. **2** A school insigne of cloth to be worn on a sweater, customarily awarded by a school or college to its distinguished athletes. **3** A written or printed communication from one person to another; especially, a missive longer than a note; an epistle. **4** A document certifying a grant of authority, right, privilege, or the like, made to the person named therein: often in the plural: *letters* dimissory, *letters* patent. **5** The literal or exact meaning or requirement of the words used: the *letter* of the law. **6** *pl.* Literary culture; learning; knowledge; erudition; also, literature in the aggregate or in general: the domain of *letters.* **7** *Music* A tone, note, key, or degree designated or symbolized by a letter of the alphabet. — **man of letters** A man who follows literature as a profession; also, a man of learning; a scholar. — *v.t.* To inscribe or write with letters. [<OF *lettre* <L *littera* a letter of the alphabet, in pl., an epistle] — **let'ter·er** *n.*

Synonyms (noun): character, emblem, mark, sign, symbol, type.

let·ter-drop (let'ər·drop') *n.* A small opening in a mailbox, post office, etc., through which letters are dropped.

let·tered (let'ərd) *adj.* **1** Versed in letters; learned; literary; educated. **2** Inscribed or marked with letters.

let·ter·gram (let'ər·gram) *n.* A telegraphic communication, slower than a regular telegram and sent at a reduced rate. See DAY LETTER, NIGHT LETTER. [<LETTER + (TELE)GRAM]

let·ter·head (let'ər·hed') *n.* A printed heading at the top of a sheet of letter paper, or a sheet that bears such a heading.

let·ter-high (let'ər·hī') *adj.* Type-high.

let·ter·ing (let'ər·ing) *n.* **1** The act, process, or business of marking or stamping with letters or of making letters. **2** Letters collectively; an inscription.

let·ter·man (let'ər·man') *n. pl.* **·men** (-men') *U.S.* An athlete to whom a letter has been awarded.

letter of advice A letter giving special information, as from a consignor to a consignee, from an agent to a principal, or from drawer to drawee of a bill of exchange.

letter of credence The document accrediting an envoy to a foreign power.

letter of credit A commercial instrument issued by a merchant or banker authorizing the bearer to draw money or obtain goods up to a certain amount from other bankers or merchants.

letter of marque A commission issued by a government authorizing a private person to take the property of a foreign state; especially, a document licensing an individual to arm a vessel and prey upon enemy merchant shipping. Also **letter of marque and reprisal.**

let·ter-per·fect (let'ər·pûr'fikt) *adj.* **1** Having thoroughly memorized (something, as a speech, dramatic role, etc.); knowing by heart. **2** Accurate as to spelling, etc.: said of a manuscript, proof, etc.

let·ter·press (let'ər·pres') *n.* Letters and words printed; the printed text of a book. — *adj.* Printed from type or plates with a raised surface, as distinguished from matter printed by lithography, gravure, and offset printing.

let·ter·shop (let'ər·shop') *n.* An establishment that furnishes a service for duplicating, addressing, or mailing letters in quantity.

letters of administration *Law* A document issued by a court authorizing a certain person named therein to administer or settle the estate of one who has died without making a will.

letters patent An open document, under seal of the government, granting some special right, authority, privilege, or property, or conferring some title; especially, a document giving to the person named the exclusive right to use, make, or sell some invention.

letters testamentary *Law* A document issued to an executor of a will authorizing him to be executor.

Let·tic (let'ik) *adj.* Of or pertaining to the language of the Letts. — *n.* Lettish.

Let·tish (let'ish) *adj.* Of or pertaining to the Letts or their language. — *n.* The language of the Letts, belonging to the Baltic branch of the Balto-Slavic languages; Latvian: spoken in Latvia, Lithuania, and East Prussia.

let·tuce (let'is) *n.* **1** A garden herb (*Lactuca sativa*) whose crisp, edible leaves are used as a salad. **2** Any of several similar plants. [<OF *laituës*, pl. of *laituë* <L *lactuca* <*lac*, *lactis* milk; with ref. to its milky juice]

let-up (let'up') *n. Colloq.* Abatement; cessation; intermission.

le·u (lā'ōō) *n. pl.* **lei** (lā) A silver coin, the monetary unit of Rumania, equivalent to 100 bani. Also **ley.** [<Rumanian, lit., a lion <L *leo*]

leu·cine (lōō'sin, -sēn) *n. Biochem.* A white, crystalline amino acid, $C_6H_{13}NO_2$, produced in the decomposition of proteins during pancreatic digestion. Also **leu'cin** (-sin). [<Gk. *leukos* white + -INE²]

leu·cite (lōō'sīt) *n.* A white potassium-aluminum silicate found in igneous rocks. [<Gk. *leukos* white + -ITE¹]

leuco- See LEUKO-.

leu·co·crat·ic (lōō'kō·krat'ik) *adj. Geol.* Characterized by the predominance of light-colored minerals, as certain igneous rocks: opposed to *melanocratic.* [<LEUCO- + Gk. *krat(eein)* rule + -IC]

leu·co·cyte (lōō'kə·sīt) *n. Biol.* The most commonly occurring type of the white or colorless blood corpuscle: a large, nucleated ameboid cell formed in red bone marrow, constituting an important agent in protection against infectious diseases. Also *leukocyte.* [<LEUCO- + -CYTE] — **leu'co·cyt'ic** (-sit'ik) *adj.*

leu·co·ma·ine (lōō·kō'mə·ēn, -in) *n. Biochem.* One of various nitrogen compounds normally present in animal tissues as products of metabolism: related to uric acid and creatine, and sometimes toxic. [<LEUCO- + (PTO)MAINE]

leu·co·mel·a·nous (lōō'kō·mel'ə·nəs) *adj.* Having a light or fair complexion, with dark eyes and hair. Also **leu'co·me·lan'ic** (-mə·lan'ik). [<LEUCO- + Gk. *melas*, *melanos* black]

leu·co·plas·tid (lōō'kō·plas'tid) *n. Bot.* One of the colorless granules embedded in the protoplasmic mass of active vegetable cells, forming points about which the starch accumulates. Also **leu'co·plast.**

leu·co·poi·e·sis (lōō'kō·poi·ē'sis) *n. Physiol.* The production of leucocytes. [<NL <LEUCO(CYTE) + Gk. *poiēsis* a making < *poieein* make] — **leu'co·poi·et'ic** (-et'ik) *adj.*

leu·co·sin (lōō'kə·sin) *n. Biochem.* A simple protein found in wheat. [<Gk. *leukos* white + -IN]

leu·co·stic·te (lōō'kō·stik'tē) *n.* A fringilline bird (*Leucosticte tephrocotis littoralis*), the rosy finch of the NW United States. [<NL *Leucosticte*, genus name <Gk. *leukos* white + *stiktos* pricked]

Leuc·tra (lōōk'trə) An ancient city of Boeotia, Greece, SW of Thebes; scene of the Theban defeat of the Spartans, 371 B.C.

leud (lōōd) *n. pl.* **leuds** or **leu·des** (lōō'dēz) A feudal vassal in the Frankish kingdoms. [< Med. L *leudes* <OHG *liudi*, *liuti*]

leuk (lōōk) *v.t. & v.i. Scot.* To look.

leu·ke·mi·a (lōō·kē'mē·ə) *n. Pathol.* A disordered and generally fatal condition of the blood and bloodmaking tissues, characterized by a marked and persistent excess in the number of leucocytes, accompanied by hyperactivity of the lymph glands, internal hemorrhage, anemia, and exhaustion. Also

leu·kae′mi·a. — leu·ke′mic *adj.*

leuko- *combining form* Whiteness; lack of color: *leukoderma*: also spelled *leuco-*. Also, before vowels, **leuk-**. [< Gk. *leukos* white] ◆ *Leuko-*, though used interchangeably with *leuco-*, is preferred for most medical and many biological terms.

leu·ko·cyte (loo′kə·sit) See LEUCOCYTE.

leu·ko·cy·the·mi·a (loo′kō·sī·thē′mē·ə) *n.* Leukemia. [< Gk. *leukos* white + *kytos* vessel + *haima* blood]

leu·ko·cy·to·sis (loo′kō·sī·tō′sis) *n. Pathol.* An abnormal increase in the number of leucocytes in the blood. — **leu′ko·cy·tot′ic** (-tot′ik) *adj.*

leu·ko·der·ma (loo′kō·dûr′mə) *n. Pathol.* Defective pigmentation of the skin, occurring in white patches. [< LEUKO- + Gk. *derma* skin] — **leu′ko·der′mic** *adj.*

leu·ko·ma (loo·kō′mə) *n. Pathol.* An opaque and whitish condition of the cornea. [< NL < Gk. *leukōma* < *leukos* white]

leu·ko·pe·ni·a (loo′kō·pē′nē·ə) *n. Pathol.* An abnormal reduction in the number of white blood corpuscles in the blood. [< NL < Gk. *leukos* white + *penia* poverty < *penesthai* be poor] — **leu·ko·pe′nic** *adj.*

leu·kor·rhe·a (loo′kə·rē′ə) *n. Pathol.* A whitish morbid discharge from the vagina. Also **leu′cor·rhe′a, leu′cor·rhoe′a.** [< NL < Gk. *leukos* white + *rheein* flow]

lev (lef) *n. pl.* **lev·a** (lev′ə) A copper coin, the monetary unit of Bulgaria, equivalent to 100 stotinki. [< Bulgarian, lit., a lion < OSlavic *livu*, ult. < Gk. *leōn, -ontos*]

Lev·al·loi·si·an (lev′ə·loi′zē·ən) *adj. Anthropol.* Denoting a culture stage of the Lower Paleolithic following the Acheulean and merging with the Mousterian. [after the *Levallois* flake, a type of flint tool first found near Levallois–Perret]

le·vant (lə·vant′) *n.* **1** Morocco leather from the Levant: also **Levant morocco.** **2** Levanter. — *adj.* Made of Levant morocco.

Le·vant (lə·vant′) **1** The coast of the eastern Mediterranean from western Greece to western Egypt. **2** The non-European coastlands along the eastern shore of the Mediterranean. [< F < Ital. *levante* < L *levans, -antis*, pp. of *levare* raise]

le·vant·er (lə·van′tər) *n.* An easterly gale in the Mediterranean: also called *levant.*

le·van·tine (lə·van′tin, lev′ən·tin, -tēn) *n.* A stout, closely woven, reversible silk fabric.

Le·van·tine (lə·van′tin, lev′ən·tīn, -tēn) *adj.* **1** Pertaining to the Levant; eastern; Oriental. **2** Pertaining to the descendants of Europeans in the East. — *n.* A native or naturalized inhabitant of the Levant, especially one of European descent.

le·va·tor (lə·vā′tər) *n. pl.* **le·va·to·res** (lev′ə·tôr′ēz, -tō′rēz) or **le·va·tors 1** *Anat.* A muscle that raises an organ or part. **2** *Surg.* An instrument for lifting up the depressed part in a fracture of the skull or in trephining. [< LL, a raiser < L *levare* raise]

lev·ee[1] (lev′ē) *n.* **1** An embankment beside a stream, to prevent overflow. **2** A steep natural bank. — *v.t.* To furnish with a levee or levees; embank. [< F *levée*, pp. fem. of *lever* raise < L *levare*]

lev·ee[2] (lev′ē, lə·vē′) *n.* **1** A morning reception or assembly at the house of a sovereign or great personage. **2** In Great Britain, a formal reception held shortly after midday by the sovereign at which only men are received. **3** A reception or promiscuous assembly of callers or guests; especially, a reception given by the president of the United States. [< F *levé*, an arising, var. of *lever* < *se lever* arise < L *levare* raise]

lev·el (lev′əl) *adj.* **1** Having a flat and even surface; without inequalities; strictly conforming to the surface of a body of still water; also, approximately flat. **2** Conforming to a horizontal plane; not sloping. **3** Being in the same line or plane with something else. **4** Equal to something or someone else in importance, rank, or degree. **5** Aimed or moving in a direct line; hence, straightforward; honest. **6** Well-balanced; having good judgment. **7** Even in tone, color, etc. **8** Denoting a surface everywhere at right angles to the line in which a force acts, so that

motion upon it causes no gain or loss of energy. — **one's level best** *Colloq.* One's very best. — *n.* **1** A line or surface wholly at right angles to the vertical. **2** A horizontal line, surface, plane, or position; also, an approximately horizontal surface, as a plain. **3** The mean altitude of something: *sea level.* **4** Degree of moral, intellectual, or social elevation; rank; specifically, an equal rank: The men were on a *level* mentally. **5** The line in which anything is aimed. **6** A device for ascertaining, or for adjusting something to, a horizontal line or plane by noting the position of a bubble contained within a sealed tube of alcohol or other liquid: used by builders and surveyors, with or without a microscope. **7** Differences in altitude thus measured. **8** A section of a canal from one lock to another. — **on the level** *U.S. Colloq.* Without equivocation; in a fair, honest manner. — *v.* **lev·eled** or **lev·elled, lev·el·ing** or **lev·el·ling** *v.t.* **1** To make flat; give a flat or horizontal surface to: often with *off.* **2** To reduce to the ground; demolish; raze. **3** To bring or reduce to a common condition, state, etc. **4** To make horizontal, as with a level (def. 6). **5** To aim or direct, as a rifle, the eyes, etc. **6** To make even and uniform, as colors. **7** In surveying, to ascertain the vertical contours of (ground). — *v.i.* **8** To aim a weapon directly at a mark or target. **9** To bring persons or things to a common state or condition. — **to level off** *Aeron.* To fly a plane parallel with the ground, as before landing. — *adv.* **1** In a right or level line; direct; straight. **2** In an even manner; steadily. [< OF *livel, nivel* < L *libella*, dim. of *libra*, balance] — **lev′el·ly** *adv.* — **lev′el·ness** *n.*

Synonyms (adj.): even, flat, horizontal, plain, plane, smooth. We speak of a *horizontal* line, a *flat* morass, a *level* road, a *plain* country, a *plane* surface (especially in the scientific sense). That which is *level* may not be *even,* and that which is *even* may not be *level*; a *level* road may be very rough; a slope may be *even.* See FLAT, HORIZONTAL, SMOOTH. *Antonyms:* broken, hilly, inclined, irregular, rolling, rugged, slanting, sloping, uneven.

lev·el·er (lev′əl·ər) *n.* **1** One who or that which levels. **2** One who would destroy social distinctions; specifically, **Leveler,** a member of an English political body during the rule of Oliver Cromwell. **3** A scraping implement used in grading, or a device for leveling. Also **lev′el·ler.**

lev·el–head·ed (lev′əl·hed′id) *adj.* **1** Having sound common sense; not flighty or impulsive. **2** Steady; reliable: said of a horse. — **lev′el–head′ed·ness** *n.*

lev·el·ing (lev′əl·ing) *n.* **1** The reduction of uneven surfaces to a level. **2** The reduction of unequal ranks or conditions to a common level. **3** In surveying, the operation of ascertaining the comparative levels of different points of land, so as to lay out a grade. Also **lev′el·ling.**

leveling rod A graduated pole bearing a marker: used by surveyors to mark a level, being sighted through a leveling instrument. Also **levelling rod.**

lev·er (lev′ər, lē′vər) *n.* **1** A mechanical device, consisting of a rigid structure, often a straight bar, turning freely on a fixed point or fulcrum, and serving to impart pressure or motion from a source of power to a resistance; one of the six so-called mechanical powers. **2** Any one of various tools on the principle defined above, as a starting bar for a marine engine. **3** Any means of exerting effective power. — *v.t. & v.i.* To move with or use a lever. [< OF *leveour*, lit.,

TWO PRINCIPAL TYPES OF LEVERS
Above: First class.
Below: Second class.

a lifter < *lever* raise < L *levare*]

lev·er·age (lev′ər·ij, lē′vər-) *n.* **1** The mechanical advantage gained by use of a lever. **2** Increased power or advantage. **3** The arrangement by which the power of a lever is controlled.

lev·er·et (lev′ər·it) *n.* A young hare; a hare less than a year old. [< AF, OF *levrete*, dim. of *levre* a hare < L *lepus, leporis*]

lev·i·a·ble (lev′ē·ə·bəl) *adj.* That may be levied or levied upon or seized. [< LEVY[1] + -ABLE]

le·vi·a·than (lə·vī′ə·thən) *n.* **1** A large aquatic but unidentified animal mentioned in the Scriptures: possibly a crocodile or other large reptile (*Job* xli 1), a serpent (*Isa.* xxvii 1), or a whale (*Ps.* civ 26). **2** Hence, any large animal, as a whale. **3** By extension, something huge and colossal, as a ship of unusual size. [< LL < Hebrew *liwyāthān*]

Le·vi·a·than (lə·vī′ə·thən) The title of a work by Thomas Hobbes which develops the analogy between the human body and human society and expounds the monarchic principle; hence, the political organism; the state.

lev·i·gate (lev′ə·gāt) *v.t.* **·gat·ed, ·gat·ing 1** To reduce to a fine powder, as by grinding between hard surfaces. **2** To make a smooth paste of. — *adj.* Made smooth; polished. [< L *levigatus,* pp. of *levigare* polish < *levis* smooth + *agere* make] — **lev′i·ga′tion** *n.* — **lev′i·ga′tor** *n.*

lev·i·rate (lev′ə·rāt, lē′və·rit) *n.* The ancient custom of marriage between a man and the widow of his brother, required by the Mosaic law when there was no male issue and when the two brothers had been residing on the same family estate. [< L *levir* a husband's brother + -ATE[1]] — **lev′i·rat′i·cal** (-rat′i·kəl) *adj.*

Le·vis (lē′vīz) *n. pl.* Tight-fitting, heavy denim trousers, with narrow legs and with rivets inserted at points of greatest strain: a trade name. Also **Levi Strauss·es** (strou′siz). [after *Levi* Strauss, U. S. manufacturer]

lev·i·tate (lev′ə·tāt) *v.* **·tat·ed, ·tat·ing** *v.i.* To rise and float in the air, as from lightness or buoyancy. — *v.t.* To cause to rise and float in the air. [< L *levis* light, on analogy with *gravitate*] — **lev′i·ta′tor** *n.*

lev·i·ta·tion (lev′ə·tā′shən) *n.* **1** The act of making light, or the state of being light; buoyancy, whether physical or spiritual. **2** The illusion of suspending heavy objects or the human body in the air without support.

Le·vite (lē′vīt) *n.* One of the tribe or family of Levi, especially a descendant of Levi, acting as assistant to the priests of the tribe in the services of the sanctuary. *Num.* xviii 6.

Le·vit·i·cal (lə·vit′i·kəl) *adj.* Pertaining to the Levites, to the law, or the book of Leviticus. Also **Le·vit′ic.**

Le·vit·i·cus (lə·vit′i·kəs) The third book of the Old Testament, containing ceremonial laws. [< L *Leviticus (liber)* < Gk. *Leuitikon (biblion),* lit., the Levitical (book)]

lev·i·ty (lev′ə·tē) *n.* **1** Lightness of humor or temperament; lack of mental gravity; want of seriousness or earnestness. **2** Frivolity; volatility; also, fickleness. **3** The state or quality of being light; especially, the quality of relative lightness. **4** A supposed tendency to rise in spite of gravity. [< L *levitas, -tatis* < *levis* light]

Synonyms: flightiness, frivolity, giddiness, inconstancy, lightness, thoughtlessness, vanity. *Antonyms:* earnestness, gravity, seriousness, sobriety, steadiness, thoughtfulness.

levo- *combining form* Turned or turning to the left: used especially in chemistry and physics: *levorotatory.* Also spelled *laevo-.* [< L *laevus* left]

le·vo·duc·tion (lē′vō·duk′shən) *n.* Movement toward the left: said of the eye. [< LEVO- + L *ductus,* pp. of *ducere* lead]

le·vo·ro·ta·to·ry (lē′vō·rō′tə·tôr′ē, -tō′rē) *adj. Physics* Rotating the plane of polarization from right to left: opposed to *dextrorotatory:* also called **le′vo·gy′rate** (-jī′rāt). — **le′vo·ro·ta′tion** *n.*

lev·u·lin (lev′yə·lin) *n. Biochem.* A colorless amorphous compound resembling starch. It readily decomposes into levulose. [< LEVUL-(OSE) + -IN]

lev·u·lin·ic (lev′yə·lin′ik) *adj. Chem.* Denoting

an odorless, colorless acid, $C_5H_8O_3$, extracted from the nucleic acid of the thymus gland and also obtained synthetically by heating levulose and certain other sugars with concentrated hydrochloric acid.

lev·u·lose (lev′yə·lōs) *n.* Fructose. [<L *laevus* left + -UL(E) + -OSE²]

lev·y¹ (lev′ē) *v.* **lev·ied, lev·y·ing** *v.t.* **1** To impose and collect by authority or force, as a tax, fine, etc. **2** To enlist or call up (troops, etc.) for military service. **3** To prepare for, begin, or wage (war). — *v.i.* **4** To make a levy. **5** *Law* To seize property by judicial writ in order to fulfil a judgment: usually with *on*. — *n. pl.* **lev·ies 1** The act of exacting or collecting by compulsion. **2** That which is levied, as money or troops. [<OF *levée*, pp. fem. of *lever* raise <L *levare*] — **lev′i·er** *n.*

lev·y² (lev′ē) *n. pl.* **lev·ies** The Spanish real, equal to 12 1/2 cents: once current in the United States as *elevenpence*. [Short for ELEVENPENCE]

levy in mass A levy of all men capable of military service and within the control of the power making the levy.

lev·y·ist (lev′ē·ist) *n.* One who advocates a levy on capital.

lewd (lood) *adj.* **1** Characterized by lust; lustful; carnal; licentious. **2** Morally depraved; vicious; wicked. **3** *Obs.* Low; unlearned. See synonyms under IMMODEST. [OE *lǣwede* lay, unlearned, ? fusion of L *laicus* LAY² and OE *lǣwan* betray] — **lewd′ly** *adv.* — **lewd′ness** *n.*

lew·is·ite (loo′is·īt) *n. Chem.* An oily, colorless to light–amber liquid, $C_2H_2Cl_3As$, having a faint odor of geraniums. Used in chemical warfare it combines the vesicant effects of mustard gas with the toxic action of arsenic. Also called *chlorvinylchlorarsine*. [after W. L. Lewis, 1878–1943, U.S. chemist]

lex (leks) *n. pl.* **le·ges** (lē′jēz) Law: used in numerous Latin phrases. [<L]

lex·i·cal (lek′si·kəl) *adj.* **1** *Ling.* Relating to the meaning of the words of a language, as distinguished from their syntactical function. **2** Pertaining to a lexicon or to lexicography. [<Gk. *lexikos* pertaining to words <*lexikon* LEXICON]

lex·i·cog·ra·phy (lek′sə·kog′rə·fē) *n.* The art or process of compiling lexicons or dictionaries. [<NL *lexicografia* <Gk. *lexikographos* one who writes a lexicon <*lexikon* lexicon + *graphein* write] — **lex′i·cog′ra·pher** *n.* — **lex′i·co·graph′ic** (-kō·graf′ik) or **·i·cal** *adj.*

lex·i·con (lek′sə·kon) *n.* **1** An alphabetically arranged book setting forth the meanings and etymology of the words of a language; a dictionary: specifically applied to dictionaries of Latin, Greek, or Hebrew. **2** All the morphemes in any language. [<Gk. *lexikon*, neut. of *lexikos* pertaining to words <*lexis* way of speaking <*legein* say, speak]

Leyden jar *Electr.* A condenser for static electricity, consisting of a glass jar coated inside and out with tinfoil nearly to the top. Also **Leyden vial.** [from *Leyden*, where it was invented]

LEYDEN JAR

Ley·ton (lāt′n) A municipal borough in SW Essex county, England.

Lez·ghi·an (lez′gē·ən) See LESGHIAN.

Lha·sa (lä′sä) The capital of Tibet, near the southern border; seat of the Dalai Lama: Chinese *Lasa.* Also **Lhas′sa.**

Lhasa ap·so (äp′sō) A small, long–haired, ancient breed of dog, native to Tibet, used as watchdogs in lamaseries: also called *Tibetan lion dog.* [<LHASA + Tibetan *abso seng kye* bark lion sentinel dog]

li (lē) *n.* A Chinese unit of length, approximately one–third of a mile. [<Chinese *li*]

li·a·bil·i·ty (lī′ə·bil′ə·tē) *n. pl.* **·ties 1** The state of being liable, or exposed to some accidental or incidental result or occurrence: *liability* to disease. **2** The condition of being responsible for a possible or actual loss, penalty, evil, expense, or burden: *liability* for damages. **3** That for which one is liable; in the plural, debts as opposed to *assets.*

li·a·ble (lī′ə·bəl) *adj.* **1** Exposed, as to damage, penalty, expense, burden, etc.: with *to.* **2**

Justly or legally responsible. **3** Having a tendency, inclination, or likelihood; likely: with unfavorable sense. See synonyms under APT, LIKELY. [<F *lier* <L *ligare* bind]

li·ai·son (lē′ā·zon′, lē·ā′zon, lē′ə·zon; *Fr.* lē·ā·zôn′) *n.* **1** An illicit intimacy between two persons of opposite sex; intrigue. **2** A bond or union: a *liaison* of the intellect. **3** In cookery, a thickening used in sauces, soups, etc., as yolks of eggs beaten with cream. **4** In speaking or reading French, the carrying over in pronunciation of a final consonant to a succeeding word beginning with a vowel or silent *h*, as in *Est–il un homme?* Applied also to such sound–unions in certain other languages. **5** Unity of action, as between distant fighting forces or between an executive officer and his subordinates, maintained by various forms of contact and communication. — *adj.* Pertaining to one who or that which serves to maintain unity of action, as between an executive officer and his subordinates, or between parts of an army, etc.: a *liaison* officer. [<F <L *ligatio* <*ligare* bind]

li·an·a (lē·an′ə, -ä′nə) *n.* A twining or climbing plant of tropical forests, with ropelike, woody stems. Also **li·ane** (lē·än′). [<F *liane*, earlier *viorne* <L *viburnum* viburnum; infl. in F by *lier* bind <L *ligare*]

li·ar (lī′ər) *n.* One who intentionally utters falsehood, or is given to lying. [OE *leogere*]

Li·as (lī′əs) *n. Geol.* The lowest of the rock series comprised in the Jurassic system of Europe. [<F *liais*, kind of limestone; ult. origin unknown] — **Li·as·sic** (lī·as′ik) *adj. & n.*

lib (lib) *n. Slang* Liberation (def. 2). — **lib′ber** *n.*

li·ba·tion (lī·bā′shən) *n.* **1** Liquid poured out, as in honor of a deity; also, the act of so pouring liquid. **2** Humorously, a drinking; potation. [<F <L *libatio, -onis* <*libare* pour out (as an offering)]

li·bec·cio (lē·bet′chō) *n.* A Mediterranean wind blowing from the southwest. Also *Obs.* **li·bec′chio** (-bek′yō). [<Ital. <L *Libs, Libis* <Gk. *Lips, Libos* southwest wind]

li·bel (lī′bəl) *n.* **1** Anything tending to degrade or asperse character or reputation. **2** *Law* Slander written and published; the act or crime of publishing it; also, a false publication damaging to property or business. **3** *Law* The written allegation of the plaintiff in a suit before a court of admiralty or an ecclesiastical court. **4** Any publicly circulated slanderous document. — *v.t.* **·beled** or **·belled, ·bel·ing** or **·bel·ling 1** To publish a libel concerning; defame. **2** In admiralty law, to bring suit against, as a ship or cargo. See synonyms under ASPERSE. [<OF <L *libellus*, dim. of *liber* book] — **li′bel·er** or **li′bel·ler, li′bel·ist** or **li′bel·list** *n.*

li·bel·ant (lī′bəl·ənt) *n.* One who institutes a libel or suit in admiralty. Also **li′bel·lant.** [<F *libellant*, ppr. of *libeller* institute a suit]

li·bel·ee (lī′bəl·ē′) *n.* The party against whom a suit in admiralty is filed. Also **li′bel·lee′.**

li·bel·lu·la (lī·bel′yoo·lə) *n.* Any of a genus (*Libellula*) of typical dragonflies. [<NL <L *libellulus*, reduplicated dim. of *liber* book; from its resemblance to a book when in flight]

li·bel·ous (lī′bəl·əs) *adj.* Containing that which defames or libels; defamatory; slanderous. Also **li′bel·lous.**

li·ber (lī′bər) *n. pl.* **li·bri** (lī′brī) **1** A book, as a volume of public records of deeds, mortgages, etc. **2** *Bot.* The bast or inner bark of exogenous plants. [<L, book, inner bark (which was once used to write upon)]

lib·er·al (lib′ər·əl, lib′rəl) *adj.* **1** Possessing or manifesting a free and generous heart; bountiful. **2** Appropriate or fitting for a broad and enlightened mind: a *liberal* education; *liberal* arts. **3** Free from narrowness, bigotry, or bondage to authority or creed, as in religion; inclined to democratic or republican ideas, as opposed to monarchical or aristocratic, as in politics; broad; popular; progressive. **4** Bestowed without stint; abundant. **5** Not restricted to the literal meaning: a *liberal* construction. **6** Free by or from birth; hence, of high character; refined; independent. **7** *Obs.* Unduly free; licentious. See synonyms under AMPLE, CHARITABLE, GENEROUS. — *n.* Any person who advocates liberty of thought, speech, or action; one who is opposed to conservatism: distinguished from *radical*. Also **lib′er·al·ist.** [<OF <L

liberalis pertaining to a freeman < *liber* free] — **lib′er·al·is′tic** *adj.* — **lib′er·al·ly** *adj.*

liberal arts See under ART¹.

lib·er·al·ism (lib′ər·əl·iz′əm) *n.* **1** An attitude toward social, economic, political, and ecclesiastical policies, favoring gradual reform and ordered change rather than reaction or revolution and opposed equally to arbitrary censorship and undue license in dealing with ideas. **2** A doctrine often equated with laissez–faire economics, holding to free trade and to minimum interference by the state with economic activities: contrasted to SOCIALISM, SYNDICALISM, and COMMUNISM. **3** In political theory, adherence to policies of gradual reform through parliamentary procedure, the upholding of civil liberties as central in a free society, and a belief in the doctrine of progress: opposed to *conservatism.* **4** *Eccl.* **a** In 19th century Roman Catholic church polity, a movement opposed to ultramontanism, and favoring the formulation of doctrines and practices governing the relation of theology to social ethics; opposing promulgation of the infallibility doctrine with broad participation by laity, clergy, and prelacy in formulating the social and economic policies of the state. **b** In Protestant church bodies, an attitude favoring the use of the methods of historical criticism on the Bible, wide leeway for individual interpretation of creeds, doctrines, and ritual, and latitude as to methods of church government and congregational organization: opposed to *fundamentalism.* **5** Loosely, general opposition to conservatism and reaction in any field.

lib·er·al·i·ty (lib′ə·ral′ə·tē) *n. pl.* **·ties 1** The quality of being liberal or generous. **2** A gift; donation. See synonyms under BENEVOLENCE.

lib·er·al·ize (lib′ər·əl·īz′) *v.t. & v.i.* **·ized, ·iz·ing** To make or become liberal. — **lib′er·al·i·za′tion** (lib′ər·əl·ə·zā′shən, -ī·zā′, lib′rəl-) *n.* — **lib′er·al·iz′er** *n.*

lib·er·ate (lib′ə·rāt) *v.t.* **·at·ed, ·at·ing 1** To set free; release from bondage. **2** To release from chemical combination. **3** *Colloq.* To free from oppression or from conventions considered oppressive. [<L *liberatus*, pp. of *liberare* free < *liber* free] — **lib′er·a′tor** *n.*

lib·er·a·tion (lib′ər·ā′shən) *n.* **1** The act of liberating, or the state of being liberated. **2** A political and social movement formed to promote the interests of a group regarded as the object of unfair discrimination or bias: women's *liberation.* — **lib′er·a′tion·ist** *n.*

Li·be·ri·a (lī·bir′ē·ə) A republic on the west coast of Africa; 43,000 square miles; capital, Monrovia. — **Li·be′ri·an** *adj. & n.*

lib·er·tar·i·an (lib′ər·târ′ē·ən) *n.* **1** One who believes in the freedom of the will. **2** One who maintains the principles and doctrines of liberty, particularly in thought and conduct. **3** An adherent of libertarianism. — *adj.* Of or pertaining to the doctrine of the libertarians.

lib·er·tar·i·an·ism (lib′ər·târ′ē·ən·iz′əm) *n.* A theory of government which holds that the state is subordinate to the individual. It may range from anarchism to democracy.

lib·er·tine (lib′ər·tēn) *n.* **1** One who does not restrain his desires or appetites; a debauchee. **2** In ancient Rome, a manumitted slave, a freedman, or the child of such a person. — *adj.* **1** Dissolute; licentious. **2** Freed from slavery; manumitted. [<L *libertinus* < *libertus* freedman < *liber* free]

lib·er·tin·ism (lib′ər·tēn·iz′əm) *n.* **1** Unrestrained indulgence in licentious practices. **2** An extreme exercise of freedom in thought or opinion, especially on religious subjects. Also **lib′er·tin·age** (-ij).

lib·er·ty (lib′ər·tē) *n. pl.* **·ties 1** The state of being exempt from the domination of others or from restricting circumstances; freedom. **2** A special exemption; franchise; privilege; in the U.S. Navy, permission to be absent from one's ship or station for a short period. **3** Unusual or undue freedom or familiarity. **4** The possession and exercise of the right of self–government. **5** The power of voluntary choice; freedom from necessity. **6** A place or district within which certain immunities or privileges are enjoyed; specifically, in England, a district within a county, exempt from the jurisdiction of the sheriff. — **at**

liberty Free; unconfined; having permission (to do something). — **civil liberty** Freedom of the individual citizen from government control, restraint of, or interference with, his property, opinions, or affairs, except as the public good may require. — **individual liberty** Freedom from restraint in the performance of rights outside of government control. — **political liberty** The right to participate in the election of rulers and the making and administration of laws. [<F *liberté* <L *libertas, -tatis* <*liber* free]
   Synonyms: emancipation, freedom, independence, license. In general terms, it may be said that *freedom* is absolute, *liberty* relative; *freedom* is the absence of restraint, *liberty* is the removal or avoidance of restraint. The two words are constantly interchanged; the slave is set at *liberty*, or gains his *freedom*. *Independence* is said of states or nations, *freedom* and *liberty* of individuals. *Liberty* keeps strictly to the thought of being clear from restraint or compulsion; *freedom* takes a wider range, applying to other oppressive influences; we speak of *freedom* from annoyance or intrusion. *License* is a permission or privilege granted by adequate authority, a bounded *liberty*; in the wider sense, *license* is an ignoring and defiance of all that should restrain. See PERMISSION, RIGHT. *Antonyms*: captivity, compulsion, constraint, imprisonment, necessity, obligation, oppression, serfdom, servitude, slavery, superstition.

Liberty Bell The bell in Independence Hall, Philadelphia, rung July 4, 1776, when the Declaration of Independence was adopted; cracked 1835.

liberty cap A close-fitting, soft cap, with elongated crown, usually folded over: originally worn by freedmen in ancient Rome, and adopted as a symbol of liberty in the French Revolution: also called *Phrygian cap.*

li·bid·i·nous (li·bid′ə·nəs) *adj.* Lustful; lewd. [<F *libidineux* <L *libidinosus* <*libido, -inis* lust < *libet, lubet* it pleases] — **li·bid′i·nous·ly** *adv.* — **li·bid′i·nous·ness** *n.*

li·bi·do (li·bī′dō, -bē′-) *n. Psychoanal.* **1** The instinctual craving or drive behind all human activities, the repression of which leads to psychoneuroses. **2** Psychic energy, especially that associated with sexual instinct. [<L, lust] — **li·bid′i·nal** (-bid′ə·nəl) *adj.*

Li·bra (lī′brə) **1** The Balance, the seventh sign of the zodiac which the sun enters about Sept. 21. **2** *Astron.* A zodiacal constellation. See CONSTELLATION. [<L, a balance]

li·brar·i·an (lī·brâr′ē·ən) *n.* **1** A person in charge of a library. **2** A person qualified by training for library service. — **li·brar′i·an·ship′** *n.*

li·brar·y (lī′brer·ē, -brə·rē) *n. pl.* **·brar·ies 1** A collection of books, pamphlets, etc., kept for reading and consultation; especially, such a collection arranged to facilitate reference, as by classification and indexing. **2** A building, an apartment, or a series of apartments containing such a collection: the *Library* of Congress. **3** A series of books having some characteristic in common issued by the same publisher. **4** A collection of books for recreation or study belonging to a private individual: a doctor's *library.* **5** A commercial establishment for selling or hiring out books. — **circulating library** A library from which books can be taken away under certain restrictions: also **lending library**: distinguished from a **reference library**, where books may be consulted but not carried away. [<OF *librarie* <L *librarium* <*liber, libri* book]

Library of Congress The national library of the United States in Washington, D.C.; established 1800.

li·brate (lī′brāt) *v.i.* **·brat·ed, ·brat·ing 1** To move back and forth, as a balance before coming to rest; oscillate. **2** To be poised; hover. [<L *libratus,* ppr. of *librare* balance < *libra* balance] — **li′bra·to·ry** (-brə·tôr′ē, -tō′rē) *adj.*

li·bra·tion (lī·brā′shən) *n.* **1** The act of balancing or librating; balance; equipoise. **2** *Astron.* An apparent slow swinging motion of a body on each side of its mean position, as in the *libration* of the moon.

li·bret·tist (li·bret′ist) *n.* A writer of librettos.

li·bret·to (li·bret′ō) *n. pl.* **·tos** or **·ti** (-ē) A book containing the words of an opera, or the words themselves. [<Ital., little book, dim. of *libro* <L *liber*]

li·bri·form (lī′brə·fôrm) *adj. Bot.* Having the form of liber or bast. [<L *liber, libri* liber (def. 2) + -FORM]

Lib·y·a (lib′ē·ə) **1** The ancient Greek and Roman name for all of North Africa except Egypt. **2** A constitutional monarchy (1951) in North Africa on the Mediterranean; formerly an Italian colony; 679,358 square miles; capitals, Tripoli and Bengasi. *Italian* Lib**′i·a.**

Lib·y·an (lib′ē·ən) *adj.* Pertaining to Libya, its inhabitants, or their language. — *n.* **1** A native or inhabitant of Libya. **2** The extinct Hamitic language spoken in ancient Libya, including the Numidian and Mauretanian dialects.

lice (līs) Plural of LOUSE.

li·cense (lī′səns) *n.* **1** Authority or liberty granted to do or omit an act; specifically, in law, a permission, as for manufacturing a patented article or for the sale of intoxicants. **2** A written or printed certificate of a legal permit. **3** Unrestrained liberty of action; abuse of privilege; disregard of propriety. **4** Allowable deviation from established rule; variation from a standard for a purpose: poetic *license.* See synonyms under LIBERTY, PERMISSION, RIGHT. — *v.t.* **·censed, ·cens·ing** To grant a license to or for; give permission to; authorize. See synonyms under PERMIT. Also **li′cence.** [<OF *licence* <L *licentia* <*licens, licentis,* ppr. of *licere* be permitted] — **li′cens·a·ble** *adj.* — **li′cens·er** or **li′cenc·er** or *Law* **li′cen·sor** *n.*

li·cen·see (lī′sən·sē′) *n.* One to whom a license is granted. Also **li′cen·cee′.**

li·cen·ti·ate (lī·sen′shē·it, -āt) *n.* **1** A person licensed, as by a university, to practice a certain profession: a *licentiate* in dental surgery. **2** In some Continental universities, a person holding a degree intermediate between bachelor and doctor. [<Med. L *licentiatus,* pp. of *licentiare* allow, license <L *licentia* LICENSE]

li·cen·tious (lī·sen′shəs) *adj.* **1** Exceeding the limits of propriety; wanton; lewd. **2** Careless of rule and accuracy, especially in literary matters. [<F *licentieux* <L *licentiosus*] — **li·cen′tious·ly** *adv.* — **li·cen′tious·ness** *n.*

li·chen (lī′kən) *n.* **1** A flowerless plant (class or group *Lichenes*) commonly growing flat upon a surface, as of a rock, and composed of loose cellular tissue, a slender white–celled epiphytic ascomycetous or (rarely) basidiomycetous fungus, and a number of globular greenish or bluish algal cells upon which the fungal cells prey. **2** *Pathol.* Any of several papular skin diseases. — *v.t.* To cover with lichens. [<L <Gk. *leichēn,* prob. <*leichein* lick] — **li′chen·a′ceous** (-ā′shəs), **li′chen·ous,** **li′chen·ose** (-ōs) *adj.*

li·chen·ol·o·gy (lī′kən·ol′ə·jē) *n.* The science or study of lichens. — **li′chen·ol′o·gist** *n.*

lich·gate (lich′gāt′) *n.* A churchyard gate covered with a roof under which a bier may stand. [OE *līc* corpse + GATE]

LICHGATE

lic·it (lis′it) *adj.* Lawful. [<L *licitus* <*licere* be allowed] — **lic′it·ly** *adv.*

lick (lik) *v.t.* **1** To pass the tongue over the surface of. **2** To bring to a specified state or condition by passing the tongue over: to *lick* a surface clean. **3** To take in by the tongue; lap up. **4** To move or pass lightly over or about: The waves *licked* the base of the cliff. **5** *Colloq.* **a** To defeat; overcome. **b** To thrash; beat. — *v.i.* **6** To move quickly or lightly: The flame *licked* up in the grate. — **to lick into shape** *Colloq.* To put in proper form or condition. — **to lick one's chops** To show pleased anticipation. — **to lick up** To consume or devour entirely. — *n.* **1** A stroke of the tongue in licking. **2** The application of something, as if by a stroke of the tongue, or something so applied: a *lick* of paint. **3** As much as can be taken up by the tongue at one stroke or lap. **4** A deposit of salt frequented

by animals that lick it. **5** A camping place along a trail near a pond, pool, or creek. **6** *Colloq.* A stroke, blow, or whack: a *lick* on the ear; also, in the plural, in baseball, an inning at bat. **7** *Slang* A spurt of speed or energy; exertion. [OE *liccian* lick]

lick·e·ty–split (lik′ə·tē·split′) *adv. Slang* At full speed. Also **lick′e·ty–cut′** (-kut′).

lick·ing (lik′ing) *n.* **1** A lapping with the tongue. **2** *Colloq.* A whipping; castigation; also, a defeat.

lick·spit·tle (lik′spit′l) *n.* A servile flatterer.

lic·o·rice (lik′ə·ris, -rish) *n.* **1** A perennial leguminous herb (*Glycyrrhiza glabra*) of southern and central Europe. **2** Its root, used in medicine and confection. **3** The inspissated juice of the root. Also spelled *liquorice.* [<AF *licorys,* OF *licoresse* <LL *liquiritia,* alter. of Gk. *glycyrrhiza* <*glykys* sweet + *rhiza* root]

lic·tor (lik′tər) *n.* One of the officers or guards attending the chief Roman magistrates: they bore the fasces as a symbol of office. [<L, prob. <*ligare* tie]

lid (lid) *n.* **1** A cover closing an aperture, as of a receptacle, movable to afford access to the inside. **2** An eyelid. **3** *Bot.* A top, as that of a pyxis or the capsule of a moss, which separates by a transverse dividing line: an operculum. **4** *Slang* A hat. [OE *hlid*] — **lid′ded** *adj.*

ROMAN LICTOR

lid·less (lid′lis) *adj.* **1** Having no lid, as a pot or kettle. **2** Without eyelids; hence, watchful; sleepless.

lie¹ (lī) *v.i.* **lay, lain, ly·ing 1** To rest or place oneself prone or at full length, as on a bed: often with *down*: He is *lying* down. **2** To be on or rest against a surface: The sign is *lying* next to the wall. **3** To be or continue in or as in a specified condition or position: to *lie* in ambush: to *lie* at a disadvantage. **4** To be situated: Rome *lies* in a plain of central Italy. **5** To extend in some direction: Our route *lies* northward. **6** To have source or cause; exist: usually with *in*: His trouble *lies* in his carelessness. **7** To be buried, as in a tomb. **8** *Law* To be maintainable, as a criminal charge. — **to lie (or lay) down on the job** *U.S. Colloq.* To loaf; do something in a desultory manner. — **to lie in** To be in childbed. — **to lie in wait (for)** To wait in ambush (for). — **to lie low** *Slang* To go into hiding. — **to lie to** *Naut.* To remain nearly stationary with the bow as near the wind as possible. — **to lie with** *Archaic* To have sexual intercourse with. — *n.* **1** The position or arrangement in which a thing lies; manner of lying; lay. **2** The lair of an animal. [OE *licgan*]

lie² (lī) *n.* **1** An untruth; falsehood. **2** Anything that deceives or creates a false impression. **3** An accusation of lying: to give him the *lie.* — **white lie** An untruth uttered or implied in deference to conventionality, expediency, or courtesy; a fib. — **to give the lie to 1** To accuse of lying. **2** To expose as false; belie. — *v.* **lied, ly·ing** *v.i.* **1** To make untrue statements knowingly, especially with intent to deceive. **2** To give an erroneous or misleading impression: Figures do not *lie.* — *v.t.* **3** To bring or obtain by lying: He *lied* his way out of trouble. [OE *lyge*]
   Synonyms (noun): deceit, deception, fabrication, falsehood, untruth. A *lie* is the uttering of what one knows to be false with intent to deceive. The novel or drama is not a *lie,* because not meant to deceive; the ancient teaching that the earth was flat was not a *lie,* because not then known to be false. *Untruth* is more than lack of accuracy, implying always lack of veracity; but it is a somewhat milder and more dignified word than *lie.* See DECEPTION, FRAUD. *Antonyms*: fact, truth, veracity.

Liech·ten·stein (lik′tən·stīn, *Ger.* lēkh′tən·shtīn) A sovereign principality of central Europe between Switzerland and Austria; 62 square miles; capital, Vaduz.

lie detector A psychogalvanometer or similar instrument whose records are assumed to indicate the guilt or innocence of the person under questioning to whom it is applied.

lief (lēf) *adv.* Willingly; freely; as willingly as not: I had as *lief* stay as go: often used to imply preference: as *lief* die as live dishonored. —*adj. Archaic* 1 Dear; dearly loved; pleasing. 2 Willing; glad. ◆ Homophone: *leaf.* [OE *lēof* dear]

lief·er (lē'fər) *adv.* More gladly or willingly; rather.

liege (lēj) *adj.* 1 Bound in vassalage to a lord. 2 Having the right to the service and allegiance of a vassal; sovereign; supreme. 3 Faithful; loyal. —*n.* 1 A vassal; also, a citizen. 2 A liege lord; a feudal sovereign or superior. [<OF <Med. L *ligius* free <*laeticus* free <*letus* freedman <OHG *ledig* free]

lien (lēn, lē'ən) *n.* A legal claim on property, as security for a debt. ◆ Homophone: *lean.* [<F, band <L *ligamen* <*ligare* tie]

li·e·nal (lī-ē'nəl) *adj.* Of or pertaining to the spleen. [<L *lien* spleen]

li·en·ter·y (lī'ən·ter·ē) *n. Pathol.* Diarrhea characterized by the discharge of undigested food. [<Med. L *lienteria* <Gk. *leienteria* <*leios* smooth + *enteron* intestine] —**li'en·ter'ic** *adj.*

li·erne (lē·ûrn') *n. Archit.* A crossrib or a branch rib in Gothic vaulting. [<F]

lieu (loō) *n.* Place; stead: in the phrase *in lieu of.* [<F <L *locus.* Doublet of LOCUS.]

lieu·ten·ant (loō·ten'ənt, *Brit. Army* lef·ten'-ənt) *n.* 1 An officer who fills the place of a superior in the latter's absence or acts for him under his direction; deputy. 2 In the U.S. Army, Air Force, and Marine Corps, a commissioned officer holding either of two ranks, **first** or **second lieutenant,** the former ranking next below a captain. 3 In the U.S. Navy and Coast Guard, a commissioned officer holding either of two ranks, **lieutenant** or **lieutenant (junior grade),** the former ranking next below a lieutenant commander and the latter next above an ensign. 4 A police officer next above a sergeant and below a captain. [<F *lieutenant* < *lieu* place + *tenant,* ppr. of *tenir* hold] —**lieu·ten'an·cy** *n.*

lieutenant colonel, lieutenant commander, lieutenant general See under COLONEL, etc.

lieutenant governor 1 An officer authorized to perform the duties of a governor during his absence or disability, or to take his place in case of death or resignation. 2 Occasionally, in the British Empire, a subordinate governor, who is acting governor of a territory under a governor general. —**lieu·ten'ant-gov'er·nor·ship'** *n.*

life (līf) *n. pl.* **lives** (līvz) 1 That state in which animals and plants exist which distinguishes them from inorganic substances and from dead organisms: characterized by metabolism and growth, reproduction, and internally initiated adaptations to the environment. 2 That vital existence, the loss of which means death: to give one's *life.* 3 The period of animate existence from birth until death, or a part of it. 4 Any conscious and intelligent existence: the *life* here and hereafter. 5 Energy and animation; spirit; vivacity: to put *life* into an enterprise. 6 A source of liveliness, animation, etc.: to be the *life* of the party. 7 That which keeps something alive; the source or essence of existence. 8 A living being; a person: Many *lives* were lost. 9 Living things in the aggregate: plant *life.* 10 In art, a living figure or semblance: a picture drawn from *life.* 11 The course of active human existence; human affairs: daily *life* in the city. 12 A certain manner or way of living: the *life* of a recluse. 13 *Theol.* A state of spiritual attainment or awareness following conversion. 14 A biography. 15 The duration of efficiency or usefulness of anything: the *life* of a machine. —**for life** For the remainder of one's existence, until death: to hold office *for life.* —*adj.* 1 Of or pertaining to life or a life. 2 Lasting for a lifetime, or from a given point until death: a *life* sentence. 3 In art, studying from a living model: a *life* class. [OE *līf*]

    Synonym: vitality. *Life* is the state of actual living; *vitality* is the power of living or the capacity of maintaining *life;* as, Reptiles have remarkable *vitality. Life* may also be used for the vital principle; as, the *life* of a seed. See WARMTH. *Antonyms:* death, decease, dissolution.

life-blood (līf'blud') *n.* 1 The blood necessary to life; vital blood. 2 Anything giving strength or energy or as indispensable as blood.

life-boat (līf'bōt') *n.* A strong, buoyant boat used in abandoning ship, saving castaways, etc.

life-buoy (līf'boi', -boō'ē) *n.* A life preserver, usually in the shape of a ring: also *life ring.*

life cycle The entire series of processes comprehended in the life of an organism from the ovum.

life expectancy The probable length of life of a person, varying according to age, sex, physical condition, occupation, and prevailing environmental factors. Compare LIFE SPAN.

life-guard (līf'gärd') *n.* An expert swimmer hired by a bathing resort, pool, etc., to protect the safety of bathers.

life history *Biol.* The complete train of phenomena characterizing the existence and growth of an organism from its inception to its decease.

life insurance Insurance on the life of oneself or of another. Also **life assurance.** See under INSURANCE.

life jacket A life preserver in the form of a jacket.

life·less (līf'lis) *adj.* 1 Destitute of life, either naturally or by deprivation; dead; inanimate. 2 Wanting in energy, vigor, or spirit; torpid; dull. 3 Exhibiting none of the signs of life; apparently dead: He fell *lifeless* at his feet. 4 Uninhabited by men or animals. —**life'less·ly** *adv.* —**life'less·ness** *n.*

    Synonyms: dead, deceased, defunct, dull, extinct, inanimate, inert, spiritless, torpid. *Dead* primarily applies to a once-living organism from which life has departed: this original meaning controls the derived senses; *inanimate* primarily applies to that which never had life. *Lifeless* may be used in either connection, and may be used of that which exhibits none of the signs of life. The derived meanings of these words are many. A picture, a statue, a poem, an actor's rendering of his part may be spoken of as *lifeless;* we speak of a *dead* book, *dead* capital, a *dead* wall, and even of a *dead* (that is, a dull or non-resonant) sound. *Deceased* is in formal and approved use as a euphemism for *dead; defunct* is used to mean finished or *extinct* as well as *dead. Extinct* implies cessation of vitality or force: an *extinct* volcano. See DEAD, FLAT. *Antonyms:* active, alive, animated, live, stirring, vigorous.

life preserver 1 A buoyant device, often inflatable, in the form of a belt, jacket, ring, etc., used to keep a person afloat in water. 2 *Brit.* A loaded cane or other weapon for self-defense.

LIFE PRESERVERS
A. Solid block cork. *B.* Cork ring buoy.
C. Collar-type life jacket.

life-sav·er (līf'sā'vər) *n.* 1 One who saves a life; especially, a trained person stationed at a bathing beach, or the like, to prevent loss of life by drowning. 2 A life preserver. —**life'-sav'ing** *n. & adj.*

life span The extreme length of life regarded as biologically possible in any plant or animal, or in the species to which it belongs. Compare LIFE EXPECTANCY.

lift (lift) *v.t.* 1 To raise from a lower to a higher position or place; hoist; elevate. 2 To hold up; support or display in the air. 3 To raise to a higher degree or condition; exalt. 4 To make clearly audible; shout: to *lift* a cry. 5 To subject (the face) to plastic surgery, usually so as to impart beauty or restore an appearance of youth: She had her face *lifted.* 6 *Colloq.* To take surreptitiously; steal; plagiarize. 7 *U.S.* To pay off, as a mortgage. 8 In golf, to pick up (the ball), as from an unfavorable position, and concede the prescribed penalty. —*v.i.* 9 To put forth effort in order to raise something: All together now, *lift!* 10 To rise; yield to upward pres-

sure. 11 To rise or disperse; dissipate: The fog *lifted.* —*n.* 1 The act of lifting or raising. 2 The distance through which something rises or is raised. 3 The amount of weight lifted. 4 Exaltation or stimulation of the mind or feelings. 5 A rise in condition; promotion. 6 Elevated carriage or position: the *lift* of her chin. 7 Assistance by lifting or raising. 8 A ride in a vehicle offered to a pedestrian, taking him part or all of the way to his destination. 9 A machine, device, or the like that lifts or assists in lifting, as a hoisting machine. 10 *Brit.* An elevator in a building. 11 *Mining* **a** A set of pumps. **b** A vertical slice of ore removed in one series of operations. **c** The difference in height between one level and another. 12 In shoemaking, any layer of leather or other material forming the heel. 13 *Aeron.* The vertical component of the aerodynamic pressure upon an aircraft. 14 An elevation of ground. [<ON *lypta* raise in the air. Akin to LOFT.] —**lift'-er** *n.*

lig·a·ment (lig'ə·mənt) *n.* 1 *Anat.* A band or sheet of firm, compact, fibrous tissue, closely binding related structures, as bones, etc., together; especially one connecting or investing the opposed surfaces of a joint. 2 A band or connecting tie; that which binds together. [<L *ligamentum* band <*ligare* bind] —**lig'a·men'tous, lig'a·men'tal, lig'a·men'ta·ry** *adj.*

lig·a·ture (lig'ə·chər) *n.* 1 Anything that constricts, or serves for binding or tying. 2 *Surg.* A thread or wire tied around a blood vessel to arrest bleeding or used for removing a tumor. 3 A ligation; the act of binding. 4 *Printing* Two or more connected letters, as *fi, ffi, æ;* also, in writing, the character used to indicate the connection (⌢). Compare DIGRAPH. 5 *Music* A slur; notes joined by a slur. —*v.t.* **·tured, ·tur·ing** To bind or compress with a ligature. [<F <L *ligatura* <*ligatus,* pp. of *ligare* bind]

light[1] (līt) *n.* 1 *Physics* **a** That form of radiant energy that stimulates the organs of sight, having wavelengths ranging from about 3900 to 7700 angstrom units and propagated at a speed of about 186,300 miles a second. **b** Ultraviolet or infrared light. Also called *luminous energy.* 2 The natural condition or medium that permits vision; luminosity: opposed to *darkness.* 3 The sensation produced by exciting the organs of vision, as the eye, optical nerves, and visual centers of the brain. 4 Mental or spiritual illumination. 5 A source of light, as the sun, moon, a flame, lamp, beacon, etc.; also, an emission of light. 6 That which admits light; a window or pane. 7 The state of being visible, known, or exposed: to come to *light.* 8 Daytime; daylight; dawn. 9 The point of view from which, or circumstances in which, a thing is seen or considered; aspect. 10 A part of a picture representing an illuminated object. 11 The power of vision; perception by eyesight. 12 Something with which to enkindle or make a blaze or light: a *light* for a pipe. 13 One who is noteworthy or eminent; a model. —**accidental light** In art, light coming from some other source than that of the chief light; a cross light. —**in the light of** In view of; considering. —**pick-up light** An anti-aircraft searchlight working alone or in coordination with a locator system to spot aircraft targets. —*adj.* 1 Full of light; not dark; bright. 2 Of a faint or pale color. —*v.* **light·ed** or **lit, light·ing** *v.t.* 1 To set burning, as wood, a lamp, etc.; ignite; kindle, as a fire. 2 To make light; illuminate. 3 To brighten or animate. 4 To guide or conduct with light: The fires *lighted* him home. —*v.i.* 5 To take fire; start burning. 6 To become bright or luminous: usually with *up.* [OE *lēoht*] —**light'er** *n.* —**light'less** *adj.*

    ◆ **lighted, lit** Either form is acceptable as the past tense and past participle of *light,* but *lighted* is probably more common as the past participle and is the usual form for the attributive adjective: The moon *lighted* (or *lit*) my path; I have already *lighted* (or *lit*) the oven; a *lighted* cigarette. In figurative use, the more common form is *lit:* Her face was *lit* with joy.

    Synonyms (noun): blaze, flame, flare, flash, flicker, glare, gleam, glimmer, glisten, glistening, glitter, glow, illumination, incandescence, scintillation, sheen, shimmer, shine, shining, sparkle, twinkle, twinkling. A *flame* is both hot and luminous; if it contains few solid particles it will yield little *light*, but it may afford intense heat, as in the case of a hydrogen *flame*. A *blaze* is an extensive, brilliant *flame*. *Light* is the general term for any luminous effect discernible by the eye, from the faintest phosphorescence to the *blaze* of the sun. A *flare* is a wavering *flame* or *blaze*, a *flash* is a *light* that appears and disappears in an instant. The *glare* and *glow* are steady, the *glare* painfully bright, the *glow* subdued. *Shine* and *shining* refer to a steady or continuous emission of *light*; *sheen* is faint *shining*, usually by reflection. *Glimmer*, *glitter*, and *shimmer* denote wavering *light*. A *gleam* is not wavering, but transient or intermittent; a *glitter* is a hard *light*: the *glitter* of burnished arms. A *sparkle* is a sudden *light*, as of sparks thrown out; *scintillation* is the more exact and scientific term for the actual emission of sparks, also the figurative term for what suggests such emission: *scintillations* of wit or of genius. *Illumination* is wide-spread, brilliant *light*, as when all the windows of a house are lighted. The *light of incandescence* is intense and white like that from metal at a white heat. See KNOWLEDGE. *Antonyms:* blackness, dark, darkness, dimness, dusk, gloom, gloominess, obscurity, shade, shadow.

light² (līt) *adj.* **1** Having little weight; of small weight by comparison; not heavy: *light* as air. **2** Easy to carry, handle, move, etc.; not taxing to the muscles or digestive organs; not burdensome: a *light* task; *light* food. **3** Free from that which encumbers; not heavily loaded: *light* troops. **4** Of no great consequence; lacking gravity; trivial. **5** Lacking in intensity or effect; moderate. **6** Free from anxiety, trouble or distress; cheerful. **7** Not in full possession of the senses; flighty; delirious: *light* in the head. **8** Below the proper or usual weight: *light* coin. **9** Well-leavened and raised; not soggy: *light* bread. **10** Loose or sandy: a *light* soil. **11** Characterized by levity; without dignity or substantial character; also, loose in morals. **12** Handling or touching with slight force; hence, easy; graceful; active; nimble: a *light* touch; a *light* style. **13** Suitable for easy work. **14** Free from clumsiness or heaviness in appearance or construction: *light* tracery. **15** Having no metrical stress: said of a syllable or vowel. **16** In Sanskrit grammar, having a short vowel: said of a syllable. **17** *Meteorol.* Designating air (No. 1) or a breeze (No. 2) on the Beaufort scale. — **to make light of** To treat or consider as trifling. — *v.i.* **light·ed** or **lit**, **light·ing** **1** To descend and settle down after flight, as a bird; land. **2** To happen or come, as by chance or accident: with *on* or *upon*. **3** To get down, as from a horse or carriage; dismount. **4** To fall; strike, as a blow. — **to light into** *Slang* **1** To attack; assail. **2** To scold; castigate. — **to light out** *U.S. Slang* To depart in haste. — *adv.* Lightly; cheaply; easily. [OE *lēoht*, *līht*] — **light'ly** *adv.*

light·en¹ (līt'n) *v.t.* **1** To make light or more light. **2** To enlighten, as the mind. **3** *Rare* To send forth like lightning. — *v.i.* **4** To become light or more light. **5** To flash or shine. **6** To flash lightning.

light·en² (līt'n) *v.t.* **1** To make less heavy. **2** To reduce the load of: to *lighten* ship. **3** To make less burdensome or oppressive. **4** To relieve from distress; gladden. — *v.i.* **5** To become less heavy. See synonyms under ALLAY, ALLEVIATE.

light·er-than-air (līt'tər-thən-âr') *adj.* *Aeron.* Having a specific gravity less than that of air: said especially of aircraft of the aerostat type, as a balloon or dirigible.

light-foot·ed (līt'fʊt'id) *adj.* Nimble in running or dancing; having a light step. — **light'- foot'ed·ly** *adv.*

light-head·ed (līt'hed'id) *adj.* **1** Silly; frivolous. **2** Dizzy; delirious. — **light'-head'ed·ly** *adv.* — **light'-head'ed·ness** *n.*

light-heart·ed (līt'här'tid) *adj.* Free from care; gay. See synonyms under MERRY. — **light'- heart'ed·ly** *adv.* — **light'-heart'ed·ness** *n.*

light·house (līt'- hous') *n.* A tower equipped with high-powered lamps, erected at a point of danger to guide seamen by night.

LIGHTHOUSE
a. Stone and steel construction.
b. Screwpile ocean lighthouse.

light·ing (līt'ting) *n.* **1** Illumination. **2** A distribution of light, as on a face or in a picture. **3** An arrangement of lights, especially on a stage.

light·ly (līt'lē) *adv.* **1** With little weight, force, pressure, or effect. **2** Without heaviness of spirit; airily; cheerily. **3** With levity; carelessly; heedlessly; also, frivolously, wantonly, or irreverently. **4** In a slight degree; slightly; mildly. **5** For slight reasons. **6** Nimbly; with light or swift step or motion. **7** Easily; readily. — *v.t. Scot.* To make light of; slight.

light-mind·ed (līt'mīn'did) *adj.* Lacking seriousness or strength of mind; foolish. — **light'-mind'ed·ly** *adv.* — **light'-mind'ed·ness** *n.*

light·ness (līt'nis) *n.* **1** The state, quality, or condition of being light. **2** That attribute of a color which identifies it as equivalent to some member of the series of grays between black and white: also called *brilliance*. Compare BRIGHTNESS, HUE, SATURATION. See COLOR.

light·ning (līt'ning) *n.* **1** A sudden flash of light caused by the discharge of electricity between two electrified regions of cloud, or between a cloud and the earth. **2** The discharge itself. — **ball lightning** A luminous, electrically charged sphere, usually less than a foot across, which sometimes appears during a thunderstorm, moving slowly and generally discharging on contact. — **chain lightning** Lightning discharged in swift, long strokes, forked or jagged in appearance. — *adj.* Fast; rapid: a *lightning* movement. [Earlier *lightening* < *lighten* flash]

lightning arrester A device for preventing damage to electrical equipment by carrying off excess voltage due to lightning or other electric disturbance.

lightning bug A firefly.

lightning rod A sharp-pointed metallic conductor used to protect buildings from lightning by carrying an electric current harmlessly to the ground. Also **lightning conductor**.

light ratio *Astron.* The constant numerical factor 2.512 by which stars of successive apparent magnitudes differ from each other in brightness.

light red High-quality burnt ocher, used as a permanent pigment; loosely, any calcined ocher or certain iron oxides. — **light-red** *adj.*

lights (līts) *n. pl.* Lungs, especially of mammals. [ME *lihtes*; so called from their light weight]

light·ship (līt'ship') *n.* A vessel, having warning lights, signals, etc., moored in dangerous waters as a guide to ships.

light·some¹ (līt'səm) *adj.* **1** Light; playful. **2** Graceful. **3** Nimble. **4** Frivolous. — **light'- some·ly** *adv.* — **light'some·ness** *n.*

light·some² (līt'səm) *adj.* Full of light; luminous. — **light'some·ly** *adv.* — **light'some·ness** *n.*

light·stand (līt'stand') *n.* A small table on which to set a light.

light-struck (līt'struk') *adj.* Exhibiting a light-fog.

light·wood (līt'wʊd') *n.* **1** Resinous pine, commonly the heart of the yellow pine. **2** The resinous knots of pine used for kindling.

light-year (līt'yir') *n.* *Astron.* The distance that light traverses in one year, approximately six trillion miles: used as a unit in measuring the distance of stars. Compare PARSEC.

lign-al·oes (līn-al'ōz, lig-nal'-) *n.* **1** A fragrant, resinous Oriental wood (*Aquilaria agallocha*); aloe weed. **2** Aloes, the drug. [< OF < L *lignum aloes* wood of aloes]

lig·ne·ous (lig'nē-əs) *adj.* Composed of or like wood; woody. [< L *ligneus* < *lignum* wood]

ligni– *combining form* Wood: *lignivorous*. Also, before vowels, **lign-**. Also **ligno-**. [< L *lignum* wood]

lig·ni·form (lig'nə-fôrm) *adj.* Having the form or appearance of wood.

lig·ni·fy (lig'nə·fī) *v.t.* & *v.i.* **·fied**, **·fy·ing** To convert into or become wood. [< LIGNI- + -FY] — **lig'ni·fi·ca'tion** *n.*

lig·nin (lig'nin) *n.* *Bot.* An organic substance which, with cellulose, forms the chief part of woody tissue. Also **lig'nose** (-nōs). [< LIGN(I)- + -IN]

lig·nite (lig'nīt) *n.* A compact, carbonized vegetable substance often retaining fibrous structure, forming an imperfect fuel intermediate between peat and true coal; brown coal. [< F] — **lig·nit'ic** (-nit'ik) *adj.*

lig·niv·o·rous (lig·niv'ə·rəs) *adj.* Wood-eating, as certain insects. [< LIGNI- + -VOROUS]

lig·no·cel·lu·lose (lig'nō·sel'yə·lōs) *n. Bot.* The substance making up the woody and fibrous parts of plants, consisting of lignin combined with cellulose.

lig·num·vi·tae (lig'nəm·vī'tē) *n.* **1** A small tropical American tree (*Guaiacum officinale*). **2** Its greenish-brown, hard, heavy wood. **3** Any of certain related American trees, as the **bastard lignumvitae** (*G. sanctum*). [< NL < L, wood of life]

lig·ro·in (lig'rō·in) *n. Chem.* A distillate of petroleum used as a solvent and illuminant; petroleum naphtha. Also **lig'ro·ine**. [Origin unknown]

lig·ule (lig'yōol) *n.* **1** *Biol.* A strap-shaped organ or part. **2** *Bot.* **a** An appendage at the junction of the petiole and blade in grasses. **b** A strap-shaped corolla of certain flowers in the composite family. Also **lig'u·la** (-yə·lə). [< L *ligula*, dim. of *lingua* tongue; infl. in meaning by L *ligare* bind]

like¹ (līk) *v.* **liked**, **lik·ing** *v.t.* **1** To take pleasure in; enjoy. **2** To regard favorably; have affection or kindly feeling for. **3** To wish or desire; prefer: He would *like* us to do it. — *v.i.* **4** To feel inclined; choose: Do as you *like*! **5** *Archaic* To be agreeable or pleasing to: with the dative: It *likes* me not. — *n.* Liking; preference; inclination: common in the phrase *likes and dislikes*. [OE *līcian*] — **lik'a· ble, like'a·ble** *adj.* — **lik'er** *n.* — **lik'a·ble·ness, like'a·ble·ness** *n.*

Synonyms (verb): affect, approve, enjoy, esteem, fancy, love, relish. See LOVE. *Antonyms:* see synonyms under ABHOR.

like² (līk) *adj.* **1** Resembling; similar in qualities, appearance, etc. **2** Bearing a close or faithful resemblance, as a portrait. **3** *Math.* Identical: *like* angles. **4** Nearly identical; equivalent: Take a *like* amount of plaster. **5** In golf, having played the same number of strokes: said of competing players. **6** *Dial.* Likely to; expected: We are *like* to meet no more. **7** *Dial.* On the point or verge of; about to: I am *like* to cry when I think of her. — **like..., like...** As the one is, so the other will be: *like* father, *like* son. — *adv.* **1** In the manner of; as if: To run *like* mad. **2** *Colloq.* Likely: *Like* as not we'll meet again. — *prep.* **1** Similar to; resembling: You look *like* your father. **2** Characteristic of; expected from: That's just *like* your impudence! **3** In the mood or frame of mind for: to feel *like* sleeping. **4** So as to indicate, promise, or presage: to look *like* rain. — **like anything** (or **blazes, the devil**, etc.) *Colloq.* With great speed, force, violence, or vehemence. — *n.* That which is similar or equivalent to, or of the same nature as, something else. — **the like** (or **likes**) of: *Colloq.* Any thing or person like. — *v.i. Dial.* To come near or be on the point of: used in the past and past perfect tenses with the perfect infinitive: He *liked* (or *had liked*) to have died. — *conj.* **1** *Colloq.* As; in the manner that: It all happened *like* you said. **2** *Colloq.* As if: It looks *like* he's going to fall. [OE *gelīc*]

♦ **like, as, as if** *Like* is unacceptable as a conjunction at the formal level of writing, where factual clauses of comparison are introduced by *as*, contrary-to-fact ones by *as if* with the subjunctive. At the informal level, because it signals a coming comparison much more strongly than the rather neutral *as, like* is in widespread use. It has good colloquial standing, except with die–hard sticklers for correctness, in idiomatic expressions where it serves both as an adverb to round out a phrasal verb, and as a conjunction governing a finite verb: It looks *like* we're in for trouble; It sounds *like* a train's coming, and I'll have to run for it. In the last, the almost imperceptible gradation from the formally correct *That sounds like a train coming* to the informal *It sounds like a train's coming* shows why any ironclad prohibition of *like* as a conjunction at the informal level is ill–advised. The effort to ban it has frightened the timid into substituting *as* for *like* in adjectival or prepositional uses where *like* is idiomatic. Nor has the attempted ban deterred novelists and playwrights, whose trade demands a good ear for the way people actually speak, from representing their literate characters as making rather free use in dialog of *like* as a conjunction, usually, however, with a regard for idiom.

–like *suffix of adjectives* Resembling or similar to: *childlike, wavelike.* [<LIKE]
◆ Compounds containing *–like* are usually written solid, but hyphenated when three *l*'s occur together, as in *shell–like,* or when two *l*'s occur in a confusing sequence of letters, as in *eel–like.*

like·li·hood (līk′lē·hŏŏd) *n.* **1** The character of being likely. **2** Probability or a probability: There is some *likelihood* of his coming. Also **like′li·ness.** See synonyms under PROBABILITY.
like·ly (līk′lē) *adj.* **·li·er, ·li·est 1** Apparently true or real; plausible; probable. **2** Reasonably to be expected; liable. **3** Apt to please; promising. **4** Well adapted for the purpose. — *adv.* Probably.
Synonyms: (*adj.*): apt, credible, liable, presumable, probable, reasonable. *Apt* implies a natural fitness or tendency: An impetuous person is *apt* to speak hastily. *Liable* refers to a contingency regarded as unfavorable: The ship was *liable* to founder at any moment. *Likely* refers to a contingent event regarded as very probable: An industrious worker is *likely* to succeed. *Credible* signifies readily to be believed: a *credible* narrative; *likely* in such connection is used ironically to signify the reverse: a *likely* story! A thing is *presumable* which, from what is known, may be taken for granted in advance of proof. *Reasonable* in this connection signifies such as the reason can be satisfied with, independently of external grounds for belief or disbelief. Compare APPARENT, PROBABLE. *Antonyms:* doubtful, dubious, improbable, incredible, questionable, unlikely.
like·mind·ed (līk′mīn′did) *adj.* Similarly disposed in opinion or tastes.
lik·en (lī′kən) *v.t.* To represent as similar; compare. See synonyms under COMPARE.
like·ness (līk′nis) *n.* **1** The state or quality of being like; a resemblance. **2** A portrait; representation. **3** Counterfeit form; guise. See synonyms under ANALOGY, APPROXIMATION, DUPLICATE, IMAGE, PICTURE.
like·wise (līk′wīz′) *adv.* **1** In like manner. **2** Also; moreover.
lik·ing (lī′king) *n.* Inclination due to some attraction; preference.
li·lac (lī′lak, -lŏk) *n.* **1** An ornamental flowering shrub (genus *Syringa*) having fragrant purplish or white flowers. The species best known in America are the **common lilac** (*S. vulgaris*), which has light rosy–purple flowers and is the State flower of New Hampshire, and the **Persian lilac** (*S. persica*), a smaller shrub with white or purplish flowers. **2** The light rosy–purple color of the common lilac flower. [<Sp. <Arabic *līlak, laylak* <Persian *līlak* bluish, var. of *nīlak,* dim. of *nīl* blue]
lil·i·a·ceous (lil′ē·ā′shəs) *adj.* Of or pertaining to a large, widely distributed family (*Liliaceae*) of monocotyledonous, mostly perennial herbs and shrubs, characterized by radially symmetrical flowers and bulbous rootstocks; designating the lily family. [<LL *liliaceus* <L *lilium* lily]
lilt (lilt) *n.* **1** A brisk, merry song. **2** Rhythmic movement or flow. **3** A buoyant manner of walking. — *v.t.* & *v.i.* To sing or speak in a light, rhythmic manner. [ME *lulte.* Cf. Du. *lul* pipe.]
lil·y (lil′ē) *n.* *pl.* **lil·ies 1** Any of numerous ornamental liliaceous plants (genus *Lilium*)

having a bulbous root, erect stem, and large, showy, erect or nodding flowers; especially, the **madonna lily** (*L. candidum*) and the **gold–band lily** (*L. auratum*). **2** A fleur-de-lis. **3** Any of numerous plants resembling the true lilies: *waterlily; daylily.* — *adj.* White and soft; pale and delicate, like a lily. [OE *lilie* <L *lilium,* prob. <Gk. *leirion*]
lil·y–liv·ered (lil′ē-liv′ərd) *adj.* Cowardly.
lil·y–of–the–Nile (lil′ē·uv·thə·nīl′) *n.* **1** The calla. **2** The African lily.
lil·y–of–the–val·ley (lil′ē·uv·thə·val′ē) *n.* *pl.* **lil·ies–of–the–val·ley** A low, smooth, stemless lilywort (*Convallaria majalis*) with two oblong leaves and nodding, fragrant, cup–shaped flowers.
lil·y·wort (lil′ē·wûrt′) *n.* Any plant of the lily family.
Li·ma (lē′mə) **1** A department in west central Peru; 15,048 square miles. **2** Its capital, the capital and largest city of Peru.
Li·ma bean (lī′mə) **1** A variety of climbing bean (*Phaseolus limensis*). **2** Its large flat seeds, a common article of food. [after Lima, Peru]
lim·a·cine (lim′ə·sīn, -sin) *adj.* **1** Of or pertaining to a family (*Limacidae*) of gastropods; the slug family. **2** Sluglike. [<L *limax, limacis* slug]
lim·a·çon (lim′ə·son) *n. Math.* The curve traced by a point fixed on a secant of a fixed circle, the circumference of which touches the origin, as the secant revolves about the origin. Also called **Pascal's limaçon.**
limb¹ (lim) *n.* **1** One of the jointed parts of the animal body, as a leg, arm, or wing. **2** A branch of a tree. **3** A person or thing forming a part of something else; an arm or branch of anything; member: *limb* of the law. **4** *Colloq.* A roguish young person; a mischievous child. — **out on a limb** *Colloq.* At a great disadvantage. — *v.t.* To dismember. ◆ Homophone: *limn.* [OE *lim*] — **limb′less** *adj.*
limb² (lim) *n.* **1** An edge or part, as of a disk; specifically, the edge of the disk of the moon or other heavenly body. **2** The graduated portion of a leveling rod or instrument for determining angles. ◆ Homophone: *limn.* [<F *limbe* <L *limbus* edge]
lim·bate (lim′bāt) *adj. Bot.* Bordered, as a leaf or flower having the margin of a different color from the rest. [<LL *limbatus* <L *limbus* border]
lim·ber (lim′bər) *adj.* **1** Easily bent; pliant; flexible. **2** Lithe and agile; nimble; supple: said of persons or their movements. See synonyms under SUPPLE. — *v.t.* & *v.i.* To make or become limber: often with *up.* [Origin uncertain] — **lim′ber·ly** *adv.* — **lim′ber·ness** *n.*
lim·bo (lim′bō) *n.* **1** *Theol.* A region on the edge of hell to which are consigned the souls of the righteous who died before the coming of Christ (**limbo patrum,** or **limbo of the fathers**) and the souls of infants who died before baptism (**limbo infantum,** or **limbo of the infants**). **2** A place of neglect or oblivion to which unwanted or worthless persons or things are relegated and forgotten. **3** A place of confinement; a prison. [<L *limbus* border, *in limbo* on the border]
lim·bus (lim′bəs) *n.* A border or interface, especially if marked by a difference in color or structure between the adjoining parts. [<L, border]
lime¹ (līm) *n.* **1** A white, earthlike calcium oxide, CaO. It is produced artificially by calcining calcium carbonate, as limestone, marble, or seashells, yielding the anhydrous calcium–oxide quicklime, which with water forms **slaked lime.** It also readily absorbs moisture from the air, forming **air–slaked lime.** — *v.t.* **limed, lim·ing 1** To apply lime to. **2** To catch with or as with birdlime; ensnare. **3** To cement. [OE *līm*]
lime² (līm) *n.* **1** A small tree (*Citrus aurantifolia*) of the rue family, native in tropical regions. **2** Its small, green, lemonlike, acid fruit. [<F <Sp. *lima* <Arabic *limah.* Related to LEMON.]
lime·ade (līm·ād′) *n.* A drink made of lime juice, water, and sugar.
lime·kiln (līm′kil′, -kiln′) *n.* A kiln for burning lime from limestone or seashells. Also **lime kiln.**
lime·light (līm′līt′) *n.* **1** A powerful light originally produced by burning lime, now

often replaced by the electric spotlight: thrown on the stage to make actors more prominent. **2** That part of a theater stage illuminated by a limelight or spotlight. **3** Publicity; notoriety.
li·men (lī′mən) *n.* *pl.* **li·mens** or **lim·i·na** (lim′ə·nə) A threshold (def. 3). [<L, threshold]
lim·er·ick (lim′ər·ik) *n.* A humorous verse of five anapestic lines, of which the first, second, and fifth lines are three–stress and rime, and the third and fourth lines are two–stress and rime. [after LIMERICK]
lime·stone (līm′stōn′) *n.* A rock composed wholly or in part of calcium carbonate. When containing magnesium carbonate, it is *dolomitic* or *magnesian;* when clayey, *argillaceous;* when sandy or quartzose, *siliceous.* Crystalline limestone is called *marble.*
lime tree 1 The linden. **2** The tupelo or sourgum tree (*Nyssa ogeche*) of Florida and Texas. [Earlier *line* <OE *lind* linden]
lime·wa·ter (līm′wô′tər, -wot′ər) *n.* **1** A saturated solution of lime in water. **2** Water in which slaked lime has been dissolved. Also **lime water.**
li·mic·o·line (lī·mik′ə·līn) *adj.* Shore–dwelling: said of certain wading birds, as plovers and snipes. Also **li·mic′o·lous.** [<LL *limicola* dweller in mud < *limus* mud + *colere* dwell]
lim·i·nal (lim′ə·nəl) *adj.* Relating to or at the threshold, entrance, or beginning. [<L *limen* threshold]
lim·it (lim′it) *n.* **1** A line, point, or boundary beyond which something ceases to extend, operate, avail, etc. **2** That which is limited or has bounds; a district; period. **3** That which impedes or hinders; a check. **4** *Math.* A definite quantity or value which a series is conceived or proved to approach but never reach. **5** In certain games, as of cards, the largest amount which may be wagered at one time: used with the definite article, especially in poker. See synonyms under BOUNDARY, END, MARGIN. — **off limits** A locality or area forbidden to military personnel except on official business. — **three–mile limit** A distance of three geographic miles from the shore line seaward, allowed by international law for territorial jurisdiction. — *v.t.* To set a bound or bounds to; keep within a limit; restrict. [<L *limes, limites*] — **lim′it·a·ble** *adj.* — **lim·i·ta·tive** (lim′ə·tā′tiv) *adj.* — **lim′it·er** *n.* — **lim′it·less** *adj.*
Synonyms (*verb*): bound, check, circumscribe, confine, define, hinder, impede, repress, restrain, restrict. See CIRCUMSCRIBE, SCRIMP.
lim·i·tar·y (lim′ə·ter′ē) *adj.* **1** Forming or marking a limit or boundary; limiting. **2** Limited.
lim·i·ta·tion (lim′ə·tā′shən) *n.* **1** The act of limiting. **2** Restriction; circumscription. **3** *Law* A restrictive condition or stipulation; also, a period of time fixed by law within which certain acts are to be performed to render them valid. [<L *limitatio, -onis*]
lim·it·ed (lim′it·id) *adj.* **1** Confined to certain limits; in law, restricted within prescribed limits. **2** Circumscribed, as a government, a monarchy, etc.; held in check by a constitution. **3** Making only a few specific stops, carrying only a certain number of passengers, and usually charging extra fare: a *limited* train. **4** Restricted to use on or within certain dates: a *limited* ticket. **5** *Brit.* Restricted in liability to the amount invested in stock of a business: a *limited* company.
lim·it·ed–slip differential (lim′it·id·slip′) An automobile differential–gear system so designed that in the event of one driving wheel losing its traction, the power is transmitted to the other wheel.
limit load *Engin.* The load which may safely be carried by a given structure under normal conditions.
limn (lim) *v.t.* **1** To draw or paint; delineate. **2** To describe in words. **3** To decorate, as manuscripts; illuminate. ◆ Homophone: *limb.* [ME *limnen* < *luminen* <OF *enluminer* <L *illuminare.* Doublet of ILLUMINATE.] — **lim·ner** (lim′nər) *n.* — **lim·ning** (lim′ning) *n.*
lim·net·ic (lim·net′ik) *adj. Ecol.* Pertaining to or dwelling in lakes, as certain plants and animals. Also **lim·nic·o·lous** (lim·nik′ə·ləs). [<Gk. *limnētēs* marsh–dwelling < *limnē* pool]
lim·nol·o·gy (lim·nol′ə·jē) *n.* The scientific study of bodies of fresh water in all their aspects, with special reference to plant and

animal life. [<Gk. *limnē* pool + -LOGY]

Lim·nos (lēm'nôs) See LEMNOS.

lim·o·nene (lim'ə·nēn) *n. Chem.* One of three isomeric terpenes, $C_{10}H_{16}$, occurring in various essential oils, and having a lemonlike odor. [<NL *Limonum* lemon + -ENE]

li·mo·nite (lī'mə·nīt) *n.* A stalactitic, fibrous, silky, brown or yellow ferric hydroxide; bog ore. [<Gk. *leimōn* meadow + -ITE²] — **li'mo·nit'ic** (-nit'ik) *adj.*

li·mo·sis (li·mō'sis) *n.* Morbid or excessive hunger. [<Gk. *līmos* hunger]

lim·ou·sine (lim'ə·zēn', lim'ə·zēn) *n.* A large automobile, originally with a closed compartment for three to five passengers, and the roof projecting over the driver's seat; later, with each compartment separately enclosed. [<F, from *Limousin*]

limp¹ (limp) *v.i.* **1** To walk with a halting or irregular gait, as in favoring an injured leg or foot. **2** To proceed in a defective or irregular manner: His logic *limps*. — *n.* The step of a lame person; a halt. [Prob. OE *limpan* occur, walk lamely. Cf. OE *lemphealt* lame.] — **limp'er** *n.*

limp² (limp) *adj.* **1** Lacking stiffness; limber. **2** Lacking positiveness or firmness. [Origin uncertain. Cf. ON *limpa* indisposition, weakness.] — **limp'ly** *adv.* — **limp'ness** *n.*

lim·pet (lim'pit) *n.* A small, edible gastropod with a spirally coiled shell, found clinging to rocks. [OE *lempedu* <LL *lampreda* lamprey]

lim·pid (lim'pid) *adj.* Characterized by liquid clearness; transparent; lucid; clear. See synonyms under CLEAR, TRANSPARENT. [<L *limpidus* clear] — **lim·pid·i·ty** (lim·pid'ə·tē), **lim'pid·ness** *n.* — **lim'pid·ly** *adv.*

limp·kin (limp'kin) *n.* A courlan of Florida and tropical America. [<LIMP¹ + -KIN; from its walk]

lim·u·lus (lim'yə·ləs) *n. pl.* ·li (-lī) A king crab. [<L, dim. of *limus* sidelong, askance]

lim·y (lī'mē) *adj.* lim·i·er, lim·i·est **1** Containing or covered with lime. **2** Resembling lime. **3** Smeared with birdlime.

lin·age (lī'nij) *n.* **1** The number of printed lines, as of text or advertising matter, contained in a book or magazine. **2** Alinement. Also spelled *lineage*.

lin·al·o·ol (lin·al'ō·ôl, lin'ə·lōol') *n. Chem.* An unsaturated, open-chain alcohol, $C_{10}H_{17}OH$, found in the essential oils of certain plants, as the bergamot. [<*linaloa*, a scented Mexican wood <Sp. *linaloe*. Cf. LIGNALOES.]

linch·pin (linch'pin') *n.* A pin through the end of an axle, to keep a wheel in place. [OE *lynis* linchpin + PIN]

Lin·coln (ling'kən), **Abraham**, 1809–1865, president of the United States during the Civil War, 1861–65; issued Proclamation of Emancipation; assassinated. — **Benjamin**, 1733–1810, American Revolutionary general and statesman.

Lind·bergh (lind'bûrg), **Charles Augustus**, 1902–74, U.S. aviator; made the first nonstop solo flight from New York to Paris, 1927.

lin·den (lin'dən) *n.* A tree (genus *Tilia*) with soft white wood, cordate leaves, and cream-colored flowers; especially, the **American linden** (*T. americana*), used for making furniture. Also called *basswood, lime tree*. [OE, orig. adj. <*lind* linden, lime tree]

line¹ (līn) *n.* **1** A string or cord. **2** *Naut.* A rope, cord, or wire used for a specific purpose. **3** A wire or cable conducting power or telecommunication signals between two stations. **4** A fishing line. **5** Any slender mark or stroke, as drawn with a pen, pencil, tool, etc. **6** Something resembling the long mark or trace made by a pen or tool; band; seam; furrow. **7** In art: **a** The representation of form by the use of strokes, instead of by shading or coloring. **b** *pl.* The distinguishing features of the composition of a painting or drawing. **8** *Music* One of the parallel horizontal strokes that form a musical staff. **9** In various games, as football, baseball, tennis, etc., a mark of division or outline on the field, diamond, court, etc. **10** In television, one horizontal trace of the electron beam across the screen. **11** A thin furrow or wrinkle on the face or hands. **12** *Geom.* The trace, straight or curved, made by a moving point; an extent of

length conceived without breadth or thickness. **13** A boundary or limit: the Mason–Dixon *Line*. **14** Contour; outline: the broken *line* of the shore. **15** *Geog.* **a** The equator. **b** Any circle, arc, or boundary conceived for purposes of plotting the earth's surface: the date *line*. **16** A row of persons or things: The people stood in *line*. **17** Agreement; accord: to bring all the factions into *line*. **18** A course of action, thought, procedure, etc.: a *line* of argument; the *line* of duty. **19** Plan of construction or procedure: an argument based on political *lines*. **20** A course of movement; route: the *line* of march. **21** A branch of activity; a business or vocation: the advertising *line*. **22** The compass of one's ability, talent, etc.: Such jokes are not in his *line*. **23** A series of persons each of whom is the next descendant or heir of the one preceding. **24** A row of printed or written words bounded by the margins of a page or column. **25** A short letter; a note. **26** A verse (def. 1). **27** *pl.* The words of a play or of an actor's part. **28** In advertising, a measure of column space equaling 1/14 inch. **29** A railroad track or roadbed. **30** Any system of public transportation: a steamship *line*. **31** A pipe or system of pipes conveying a fluid: a gas *line*. **32** *Mil.* **a** A series of fortifications presenting an extended front: Maginot *line*. **b** A trench or rampart. **c** A row of soldiers standing abreast, as distinguished from *column*. **33** *Naut.* An arrangement of ships in a certain order. **34** *Mil.* The combatant forces, as distinguished from the special services and the staff. **35** *Nav.* The class of officers having command of combat operations. **36** In football: **a** The linemen, collectively. **b** The line of scrimmage: see LINE OF SCRIMMAGE under SCRIMMAGE. **37** A variety of goods of a certain class or type, carried by a store or offered by an advertiser. **38** *pl. Colloq.* Marriage-lines. **39** *Colloq.* **a** A glib manner of speech. **b** A few words or a speech intended to sway or influence. See synonyms under BOUNDARY, MARK. — **in line for** In succession; ready for. — **in line with** In accord with. — *v.* **lined, lin·ing** *v.t.* **1** To mark with lines; put lines upon. **2** To place in a line; bring into alinement or conformity: often with *up*. **3** To form a line along: Police *lined* the side of the road. **4** To place something in a line along: to *line* a wall with archers. **5** In baseball, to bat (the ball) in a line drive. — *v.i.* **6** To form a line; assume position or place: usually with *up*. — **to line out** In baseball: **a** To be retired by batting a line drive to a fielder. **b** To get (a hit) by batting a line drive which is not caught or fielded. — **to line up 1** To form a line. **2** To bring into line. **3** To organize for or against some activity, issue, etc. [OE *līne* cord; infl. by F *ligne* <L *linea* linen thread < *linum* flax]

line² (līn) *v.t.* **lined, lin·ing 1** To apply a covering or layer, usually of different material, to the inside surface of. **2** To serve as an inner covering or layer for: Lockers *lined* the wall. **3** To fill or supply: to *line* one's pockets with bribes. — *n.* **1** The fiber of flax. **2** Linen. [OE *līn* flax]

lin·e·age (lin'ē·ij) *n.* Ancestral line of consanguinity; pedigree; family. [<OF *lignage* <L *linea* line]

lin·e·al (lin'ē·əl) *adj.* **1** Of the nature of an ancestral line or lineage; ascending or descending in a direct line: distinguished from *collateral*. **2** Made with lines. [<L *linealis* <*linea* line] — **lin'e·al·ly** *adv.*

lin·e·a·ment (lin'ē·ə·mənt) *n.* A distinguishing line or mark; a feature. [<L *lineamentum* <*linea* line]

lin·e·ar (lin'ē·ər) *adj.* **1** Pertaining to or composed of lines. **2** Very narrow and elongate: a *linear* leaf. **3** Denoting a measurement in one dimension. **4** *Math.* Pertaining to an equation of the first degree. [<L *linearis* <*linea* line]

linear measure Measurement by length; a unit or system of units for measuring length, as in the following table of the principal customary standards. See also METRIC SYSTEM.

1 mil	=	0.001 inch (in.)
12 inches	=	1 foot (ft.)
3 feet	=	1 yard (yd., yds.)
6 feet	=	1 fathom (fath.)
5.5 yards	=	1 rod (rd.)
40 rods	=	1 furlong (fur.)
5280 feet	=	1 mile (mi.)
1760 yards	=	1 mile

lin·e·a·tion (lin'ē·ā'shən) *n.* **1** A drawing of lines; delineation. **2** A contour or outline.

line·back·er (līn'bak'ər) *n.* In football, a defensive player whose normal position is just behind the line of scrimmage.

line–breed (līn'brēd') *v.t. Genetics* To interbreed (successive generations) to one ancestor of a given line in order to develop selected characteristics. — **line'–breed'ing** *n.*

line·man (līn'mən) *n. pl.* ·men (-mən) **1** In surveying, a man who carries the tape, line, or chain. **2** A man employed about the line of a railway, telegraph, or telephone, especially in making repairs. **3** In football, one of the players stationed along the line of scrimmage, consisting of the center and the right and left guards, tackles, and ends.

lin·en (lin'in) *n.* **1** A fabric woven from the fibers of flax. **2** Articles made of linen, or made formerly of linen but now often of cotton: bed *linen*, table *linen*, body *linen*. — *adj.* Made of the textile fiber of flax: *linen* cloth. [OE *līnen* made of flax < *līn* flax]

line of force *Physics* A line in a field of force every point on which coincides with the field intensity.

line of vision The straight line joining the central fovea of the retina and the point to which vision is directed.

lin·er¹ (lī'nər) *n.* **1** A ship, aircraft, etc., operated commercially by a specific line. **2** A person or thing that marks or traces lines. **3** In baseball, a line drive.

lin·er² (lī'nər) *n.* **1** One who makes linings. **2** A lining, or a piece used in forming a lining.

lines·man (līnz'mən) *n. pl.* ·men (-mən) **1** In many games, as in tennis, the official watching the lines of the court. **2** In football, the official supervising the sidelines and marking the distances gained or lost in each play.

line·up (līn'up') *n.* **1** The formation of players in any game, such as football, hockey, etc., when drawn up for action. **2** An array of people united by some aim. **3** A mustering of criminal suspects by police for identification and questioning.

ling¹ (ling) *n.* **1** A codlike food fish (*Molva molva*) of the North Atlantic. **2** The Lake Ontario burbot (*Lota maculosa*). [? <Du. *leng* or OE *lengu* length]

ling² (ling) *n.* The heath or heather. [<ON *lyng*]

–ling¹ *suffix of nouns* **1** Little; young; petty: *duckling*: often used contemptuously: *princeling*. **2** A person or thing related to or characterized by: *worldling*. [OE]

–ling² *suffix* Forming adverbs: **1** (from nouns) Toward: *sideling*. **2** (from adjectives) Being; becoming: *darkling*. Also **–lings.** [OE *-ling*, *-linga*]

lin·ger (ling'gər) *v.i.* **1** To stay on as if reluctant to leave; delay going. **2** To move slowly; saunter; loiter: to *linger* on the way. **3** To dwell upon, as from enjoyment or persistence. **4** To continue in life or existence; endure: often with *on*: The sound *lingers* on in my memory. — *v.t.* **5** To protract; drag out. **6** To pass (time) in lingering: with *away* or *out*. [Earlier *lenger*, freq. of OE *lengen* delay. Akin to LONG.] — **lin'ger·er** *n.*

Synonyms: crawl, creep, dawdle, delay, drag, flag, halt, hesitate, lag, loiter, saunter, wait. *Antonyms:* see synonyms for ACCELERATE.

lin·go (ling'gō) *n. pl.* lin·goes **1** Language, especially if strange or unintelligible. **2** The specialized vocabulary and idiom of a profession, class, etc.: medical *lingo*. See synonyms under SLANG. [<Pg. <L *lingua* tongue]

lin·gua (ling'gwə) *n. pl.* ·guae (-gwē) **1** The tongue. **2** A language. [<L]

lin·gua fran·ca (ling'gwə frang'kə) **1** A mixture of French, Spanish, Italian, Greek, and Arabic, spoken in the Mediterranean ports: often called *Sabir*. **2** Any mixed jargon used as a commercial or trade language, such as pidgin English, Chinook jargon, etc. [<Ital., lit., language of the Franks; prob. infl. by *franco* rough and ready]

---

add,āce,câre,pälm; end,ēven; it,īce; odd,ōpen,ôrder; tŏŏk,pōōl; up,bûrn; ə = a in *above*, e in *sicken*, i in *clarity*, o in *melon*, u in *focus*; yōō = u in *fuse*; oi,oil; ou,pout; ch,check; g,go; ng,ring; th,thin; ŧh,this; zh,vision. Foreign sounds à,œ,ü,kh,ṅ; and ✦: see page xx. < from; + plus; ? possibly.

lin·gual (ling′gwəl) *adj.* Pertaining to the tongue or the use of the tongue in utterance. —*n. Phonet.* A sound pronounced chiefly with the tongue, as (t), (d), and (l). [<Med. L *lingualis*]

lin·gui·form (ling′gwi·fôrm) *adj.* Tongue-shaped. [<L *lingua* + -FORM]

lin·guist (ling′gwist) *n.* 1 One who knows many languages. 2 An authority in linguistics. [<L *lingua* + -IST]

lin·guis·tic (ling·gwis′tik) *adj.* 1 Of or pertaining to language. 2 Pertaining to linguistics. Also **lin·guis′ti·cal. —lin·guis′ti·cal·ly** *adv.*

lin·guis·tics (ling·gwis′tiks) *n.* The science of language, its origin, structure, modifications, etc., including among its studies the fields of phonetics, phonemics, morphology, syntax, and semantics: usually divided into **historical** (or *diachronic*) **linguistics**, the study of the evolution of languages and linguistic phenomena; **descriptive** (or *synchronic*) **linguistics**, the study of a language or languages at a given stage of development; **comparative linguistics**, the comparison and contrast of related languages; **geographical linguistics** (or **linguistic geography**), the classification of the distribution of languages and dialects on a regional basis.

linguistic stock 1 An original language and all the languages and dialects derived from it. 2 All the people speaking languages or dialects derived from one original: The Shawnee Indians belong to the Algonquian *linguistic stock.*

lin·i·ment (lin′ə·mənt) *n.* A liquid preparation for external use, for bruises, inflammation, etc. [<LL *linimentum* <L *linire* anoint]

li·nin (lī′nin) *n.* 1 *Chem.* A white, bitter, crystalline compound, $C_{23}H_{22}O_9$, found in the purging flax (*Linum catharticum*). 2 *Biol.* A fiber of the nuclear reticulum of the cell that has little affinity for dyes; an achromatic thread of the nucleus: contrasted with *chromatin.* [<L *linum* + -IN]

link¹ (lingk) *n.* 1 One of the loops of which a chain is made; hence, something which connects separate things; a tie. 2 A hinge. 3 A single constituent part of a continuous series. 4 *Mech.* A connecting rod which transmits power from one part of a machine to another. 5 A length of 7.92 inches, or 20.11 centimeters, used in surveying. 6 *Colloq.* A section of a chain of sausages. 7 One of the component parts of a mechanical device formed of a number of identical or similar units. 8 *Chem.* A bond. 9 Links (def. 2). —*v.t. & v.i.* To join or connect by or as by links; unite. See synonyms under UNITE. [ME *linke* <Scand.; cf. Icel. *hlekkr*, Sw. *länk* a link. Akin to OE *hlencan* twist.]

link² (lingk) *n.* A torch. [Origin uncertain]

link·age (ling′kij) *n.* 1 The act of linking, or the state of being linked. 2 *Mech.* A series or system of links and connecting rods for transmitting power, especially as used in automotive vehicles. 3 *Electr.* A relation between a magnetic line of force and the conductive coil that forms its vehicle. 4 *Biol.* Inheritance of the kind in which the genes, usually in the same chromosome, tend to act together as a unit or **linkage group** in the general process of segregation. 5 A pantograph.

linked (lingkt) *adj.* 1 Joined together. 2 *Biol.* Exhibiting linkage.

link hinge *Mech.* A hinge having the two leaves permanently attached to a link permitting free rotation. See illustration under HINGE.

link motion *Mech.* An assemblage of parts for operating the valves of locomotive and similar engines, its essential feature being a slotted bar, which is driven by one or two eccentrics.

links (lingks) *n. pl.* 1 Flat or undulating land. 2 A golf course: sometimes construed as singular. [OE *hlinc* slope]

link-up (lingk′up′) *n.* 1 A linking together; contact; the *linkup* of space vehicles. 2 A pooling or combining, as of resources or efforts.

link·work (lingk′wûrk′) *n.* A fabric consisting of links joined together; a chain.

linn (lin) *n.* The linden tree. [<LINDEN]

lin·net (lin′it) *n.* 1 One of various singing birds, as the common European **gray** or **gorse linnet** (genus *Carduelis*), the male of which in summer has the breast and crown bright crimson. 2 The house finch (*Carpodacus mexicana*) of the western United States. [<OF *linette* <L *linum* flax; from its feeding on flax seeds]

lin·o·le·ic (lin′ə·lē′ik, li·nō′lē·ik) *adj. Chem.* Of or denoting a colorless to yellow, oily, fatty acid, $C_{18}H_{32}O_2$, found in linseed oil, cottonseed oil, and other vegetable oils. [<LINOLEUM]

li·no·le·um (li·nō′lē·əm) *n.* A preparation of linseed oil hardened by oxidizing. When mixed with ground cork and pressed upon canvas or burlap, it is used as a floor covering. [<L *linum* flax + *oleum* oil]

lin·sang (lin′sang) *n.* A long-tailed, East Indian viverrine mammal (genus *Prionodon*) related to but smaller than the genet. [< Javanese *linsang*]

lin·seed (lin′sēd′) *n.* Flaxseed. [OE *līnsǣd*]

linseed oil A yellowish drying oil made from flaxseed.

lin·sey-wool·sey (lin′zē·wool′zē) *n.* 1 A cloth made of linen and wool or cotton and wool mixed. 2 *Obs.* Nonsense; jargon. —*adj.* Made of linen and wool. [ME *lynsy—wolsye* < *lynsy* (? <*lin* linen + *saye* cloth) + WOOL]

lin·stock (lin′stok) *n.* Formerly, an iron-shod pike with a crotch designed to hold a rope match for firing a gun. [<Du. *lontstok* <*lont* match + *stok* stick]

lint (lint) *n.* 1 The soft down of raveled or scraped linen; also, downy feathers. 2 A net; netting. 3 Cotton fiber. [<L *linteum* linen cloth < *linum* flax] —**lint′y** *adj.*

lin·tel (lin′təl) *n.* A horizontal top piece, as of a doorway or window opening. [<OF <LL *lintellus, limitellus,* dim. of *limes, limites* limit]

lint·er (lin′tər) *n.* A machine for removing linters from cotton seeds after they have been ginned.

lint·ers (lin′tərz) *n. pl.* A mixture of cotton fuzz and fibers left behind on the cotton gin; used as batting, for stuffing upholstery, and in the manufacture of rayon.

lint-white (lint′hwīt′) *n.* The European gray linnet. [OE *līnetwige,* lit., flax-plucker]

lin·y (lī′nē) *adj.* **lin·i·er, lin·i·est** 1 Like a line. 2 Full of, or marked with, lines or streaks. Also spelled *liney.*

li·on (lī′ən) *n.* 1 A large, yellowish-brown or tawny, carnivorous mammal (*Panthera leo*) of the cat family, native to Africa and SW Asia, the adult male having a long mane. 2 Figuratively, a man of conspicuous courage; one of leonine character or mien. 3 An object of peculiar interest and curiosity; a prominent or notable person. 4 A former gold coin of Scotland. —**mountain lion** The puma. —**to twist the lion's tail** To make anti-British statements: from the lion on the heraldic shield of England. [<F <L *leo* <Gk. *leōn*]

LION
(About 3 feet high at the shoulder; length: 10 feet over-all)

lion dog 1 In Chinese and Japanese art and sculpture, a stylized lion, distorted so that the body resembles that of a dog, used as a symbol of good luck: also **Foo dog.** 2 Any of several breeds of small dog, as the Lhasa apso or Pekingese, having a leonine head.

li·on·ess (lī′ən·is) *n.* A female lion. [<OF *lionnesse*]

li·on·et (lī′ən·et) *n.* A small or young lion; a lion cub. [<OF]

li·on·heart (lī′ən·härt′) *n.* A person of exceptional bravery; especially, **Lionheart,** as a nickname of Richard I of England. See COEUR DE LION. —**lion′heart′ed** *adj.*

li·on·ize (lī′ən·īz) *v.t.* **ized, ·iz·ing** To treat or regard as a celebrity. —**li′on·i·za′tion** *n.*

lip (lip) *n.* 1 One of the two folds of flesh that bound the mouth and cover the teeth. ◆ Collateral adjective: *labial.* 2 Hence, from the use of these organs in speaking, speech; especially, impertinent speech; sauciness. 3 Anything having the appearance or purpose of a lip, as of a cup, bell, crater, wound, etc. 4 An embouchure. 5 Any structure that bounds an orifice, slit, or groove. 6 *Bot.* Either of the two large lobes of a bilabiate corolla or calyx; also, in orchids, a labium. —**to keep a stiff upper lip** To keep up one's courage; be stoical. —*v.* **lipped, lip·ping** *v.t.* 1 To touch with the lips; apply the lips to. 2 *Archaic* To utter with the lips; whisper. 3 In golf, to hit the ball so that it strikes the edge of (the cup) without dropping in. —*v.i.* 4 To adjust the lips to the mouthpiece of a wind instrument for playing. —*adj.* 1 Of or pertaining to the lips or a lip. 2 Characterized by or made with the lips. 3 Made with the lips only; superficial; insincere: *lip* service. [OE *lippa*]

lip·a·roid (lip′ə·roid) *adj.* Fatty; resembling fat. [<Gk. *l;paros* fat, greasy +-OID]

lip·ase (lip′ās, lī′pās) *n.* A fat-splitting enzyme.

li·pec·to·my (li·pek′tə·mē) *n. Surg.* An operation for the removal of excess fatty tissue. [<LIP(O)- + -ECTOMY]

lip·id (lip′id, lī′pid) *n. Biochem.* Any of a large class of organic substances which include the true fats and certain related compounds, as waxes and sterols. They are insoluble in water and have a typical greasy feel. Also **lip·ide** (lip′īd, lī′pīd).

lip·o·ca·ic (lip′ō·kā′ik) *n. Biochem.* A hormonelike substance extracted from raw pancreas and having the power to regulate the fat metabolism of the liver. [<LIPO- + Gk. *kaiein* burn]

lip·o·chrome (lip′ō·krōm) *n. Biochem.* Any of a class of pigments, including the carotenoids, found in natural fats, as butter or egg yolk.

lip·o·cyte (lip′ō·sīt) *n. Biol.* A fat-bearing cell.

lip·oid (lip′oid) *n. Biochem.* A fat that is not decomposed by alkalis, as cholesterol.

li·pol·y·sis (li·pol′ə·sis) *n.* The breakdown and decomposition of fat. [<LIPO- + -LYSIS] —**lip·o·lyt·ic** (lip′ō·lit′ik) *adj.*

li·po·ma (li·pō′mə) *n. Pathol.* A tumor, generally painless and benign, made up of fat cells. [<LIP(O)- + -OMA] —**li·pom·a·tous** (li·pom′ə·təs) *adj.*

lip·o·pro·te·in (lip′ō·prō′tē·in, -tēn) *n. Biochem.* Any of a class of proteins found in combination with lipids, as in blood, egg yolk, milk, etc.

li·pot·ro·py (li·pot′rə·pē) *n.* An affinity for fats or oils or for fatty tissue. Also **li·pot′ro·pism.** —**li·po·trop·ic** (lip′ō·trop′ik) *adj.*

Lip·pi·zan·er (lip′it·sä′nər) *n.* One of a breed of generally white horses developed in Austria and often ridden in dressage exhibitions.

lip-read (lip′rēd′) *v.t. & v.i.* **-read, -read·ing** To interpret (speech) from the position assumed by the lips and mouth for each word.

lip service Service that is professed but not intended or performed.

lip·stick (lip′stik′) *n.* A small, colored cosmetic stick of creamy texture, used to tint lips.

li·quate (lī′kwāt) *v.t.* **quat·ed, ·quat·ing** 1 To liquefy; melt. 2 *Metall.* To separate (a metal) from its impurities by the application of heat. [<L *liquatus,* pp. of *liquare* melt] —**li·qua·tion** (lī·kwā′shən) *n.*

liq·ue·fac·tion (lik′wə·fak′shən) *n.* 1 The operation of liquefying. 2 The state of being liquefied. —**liq·ue·fa′cient** (-fā′shənt) *adj. & n.*

liq·ue·fi·er (lik′wə·fī′ər) *n.* An apparatus devised for the liquefaction of gases.

liq·ue·fy (lik′wə·fī) *v.t. & v.i.* **·fied, ·fy·ing** To convert into or become liquid; melt. See synonyms under MELT. [<L *liquefacere* < *liquere* be liquid + *facere* make] —**liq′ue·fi′a·ble** *adj.*

li·ques·cent (li·kwes′ənt) *adj.* 1 Melting. 2 Having a tendency to melt or to become liquid. [<L *liquescens, -entis,* ppr. of *liquescere,* incept. of *liquere* become liquid] —**li·ques′cence, li·ques′cen·cy** *n.*

li·queur (li·kûr′) *n.* A sweetened alcoholic beverage, usually served after dinner, made by flavoring a spirit with aromatic ingredients, such as fruit, seeds, or herbs, before the distillation process; a cordial. [<F <OF *licur.* Doublet of LIQUOR.]

liq·uid (lik′wid) *adj.* 1 Flowing, or capable of flowing; being a liquid. 2 Limpid; clear. 3 *Physics* Composed of molecules having free movement among themselves, but without a separative tendency like that of gases. 4 Flowing smoothly; mellifluous: *liquid* tones. 5 Containing or suggesting liquid; watery. 6 *Phonet.* Pronounced with a smoothly flowing sound; vowel-like, as (l) and (r). **7** Easily or quickly converted into cash: *liquid* assets. See synonyms for FLUID. — *n.* **1** *Physics* A substance in that state in which the particles move freely among themselves and remain in one mass; a fluid which differs from a gas in not diffusing through the entire volume of a containing vessel. **2** *Phonet.* The consonants (l) and (r). [<F *liquide* <L *liquidus* < *liquere* be liquid] — **li·quid·i·ty** (li·kwid′-ə·tē), **liq′uid·ness** *n.* — **liq′uid·ly** *adv.*

liquid air An intensely cold mixture of nitrogen and oxygen, existing only at temperatures below the boiling point of its components, and brought to a liquid condition by a reduction of temperature and an increase of pressure: chiefly used as a refrigerant.

liq·uid·am·bar (lik′wid·am′bər) *n.* **1** Any of a genus (*Liquidambar*) of balsamiferous trees of eastern Asia and Atlantic North America; especially, the American sweetgum. **2** The balsam yielded by such trees: used in medicine and the arts; copalm. [<NL]

liq·ui·date (lik′wə·dāt) *v.* **·dat·ed, ·dat·ing** *v.t.* **1** *Law* **a** To determine and settle the liabilities of (an estate, firm, etc.) and apportion the assets. **b** To determine and settle the amount of, as indebtedness or damages. **2** To pay or settle, as a debt. **3** To convert into cash. **4** To destroy or annihilate; to away with. **5** *Slang* To murder. — *v.i.* **6** To settle one's debts; go into liquidation. [< Med. L *liquidatus*, pp. of *liquidare* make liquid or clear <L *liquidus* liquid] — **liq′ui·da′·tor** *n.*

liquid crystal *Chem.* A substance intermediate in state between liquid and solid, having the fluidity of a liquid and the optical anisotropy of a crystalline solid.

liquid fire Burning oil or other inflammable chemicals: used in warfare, as from flamethrowers.

liquid measure A unit or system of units for measuring liquids, as in the following table of principal customary standards. See also METRIC SYSTEM.

4 gills	=	1 pint (pt., pts.)
2 pints	=	1 quart (qt., qts.)
4 quarts	=	1 gallon (gal., gals.)
60 minims (min., ♏)	=	1 fluid dram (fl. dr., ʒ)
8 fluid drams	=	1 fluid ounce (fl. oz., ʒ)
16 fluid ounces	=	1 pint

liq·uo·crys·tal·line (lik′wō·kris′tə·lin, -līn) *adj.* Designating that state of a liquid which exhibits properties similar to those of a crystal; mesomorphic.

liq·uor (lik′ər) *n.* **1** Any alcoholic or intoxicating liquid; especially, one that is distilled. **2** One of various solutions; specifically, an aqueous solution of a non-volatile substance: distinguished from a sirup, infusion, or decoction. **3** A liquid of any sort, as blood, milk, etc. — *v.t.* **1** To treat with liquor (def. 2). **2** *Slang* To supply or ply with alcoholic liquor: often with *up.* — *v.i.* **3** *Slang* To drink alcoholic liquor, especially in quantity: usually with *up.* [<OF *licor, licur* <L *liquor.* Doublet of LIQUEUR.]

lir·i·o·den·dron (lir′ē·ō·den′drən) *n.* *pl.* **·dra** (-drə) Any of a genus (*Liriodendron*) of Asian and North American trees of the magnolia family; especially, the tuliptree of the United States. [<NL <Gk. *leirion* lily + *dendron* tree]

lir·i·pipe (lir′ə·pīp) *n.* In medieval dress, the long tail of a clerical tippet; hence, any long scarf or streamer attached to a headdress. Also **lir′i·poop** (-pōōp). [<Med. L *liripipium*; ult. origin uncertain]

Li·sa (lē′sə, -zə, lī′-) Diminutive of ELIZABETH. Also **Li′za.**

Lis·bon (liz′bən) A port on the Tagus, capital of Portugal. *Portuguese* **Lis·bo·a** (lēzh·bō′ə).

LIRIPIPE

lisle (līl) *n.* **1** A fine, hard-twisted cotton thread, formerly linen: used in knitting gloves, stockings, etc. **2** Any fabric made of lisle thread. [from *Lisle*, now Lille, in France]

lisp (lisp) *n.* **1** A speech defect or affectation

in which the sibilants (s) and (z) are pronounced with the tongue between the teeth so that the sounds produced are like (th) in *thank* and (th) in *this*. **2** The act or habit of speaking with a lisp. **3** The sound of a lisp. — *v.t.* & *v.i.* **1** To pronounce or speak with a lisp. **2** To speak imperfectly or in a childlike manner. [OE *wlispian*] — **lisp′er** *n.*

lis·sot·ri·chous (li·sot′rə·kəs) *adj.* Having straight hair. [<Gk. *lissos* smooth + *thrix, trichos* hair]

list¹ (list) *n.* A series of words, numbers, names, etc., as on a strip of paper; a roll or catalog. — *v.t.* To place on or in a list or catalog, especially in alphabetical or numerical order. [<OF *liste* <OHG *līsta*]

list² (list) *n.* **1** The selvage or edge of a woven textile fabric. **2** Selvages, collectively. **3** A strip of fabric. **4** A colored stripe. **5** A narrow strip of wood cut from a plank. **6** *Agric.* A ridge or furrow made with a lister in cultivating corn. **7** *pl.* The palisades bounding a piece of ground used as a jousting field; hence, the field itself. — **to enter the lists** To accept a challenge; enter a contest or discussion. — *v.t.* **1** To cover with lists of cloth. **2** To sew or arrange in strips or stripes. **3** *Agric.* **a** To plow by means of a lister. **b** To plant by means of a lister. **4** In carpentry, to remove the rough edge of, as a board. [OE *līste*]

list³ (list) *v.t.* & *v.i.* **1** To lean or incline to one side; careen, as a ship. **2** *Archaic* To wish or choose; please. — *n.* **1** A careening; leaning or inclination of a ship to one side. **2** *Archaic* Desire; wish. [OE *lystan* < *lust* desire]

list⁴ (list) *v.t.* & *v.i.* *Poetic* To listen to or listen. See synonyms under LISTEN. [OE *hlystan* < *hlyst* hearing]

listed security A stock or bond that has been admitted to the roster of approved securities by a stock exchange, thus becoming available for trading on the exchange.

lis·tel (lis′təl) *n.* *Archit.* A small square molding; a list. [<F <Ital. *listello*, dim. of *lista* list²]

lis·ten (lis′ən) *v.i.* **1** To make an effort to hear; give ear. **2** To pay attention; give heed or compliance, as to warning or advice. — *n.* The act of listening. [OE *hlysnan*] — **lis′ten·er** *n.*

Synonyms (verb): attend, hark, harken, hear, heed, list⁴. To *hear* is simply to become conscious of sound, to *listen* is to make a conscious effort to *hear*. We may *hear* without *listening*, as words suddenly uttered in an adjoining room; or we may *listen* without *hearing*, as to a distant speaker. In *listening* the ear is intent upon the sound; in *attending* the mind is intent upon the thought, but *listening* implies some attention to the meaning or import of the sound. To *heed* is not only to *attend*, but to remember and observe. *Harken* is nearly obsolete. *Antonyms:* ignore, neglect, scorn, slight.

listening post 1 A concealed position near enemy lines from which an observer may transmit to his own forces information or warning of hostile action. **2** A station equipped with sound-locating devices for warning against the approach of enemy aircraft or sea vessels. **3** A radio station equipped to pick up short-wave messages from different countries.

list·er¹ (lis′tər) *n.* *Agric.* A double-moldboard plow for throwing up ridges, as in beet- or corn-culture: it simultaneously throws a deep furrow, plants the seed, and covers it with earth. Also called *middle-breaker.* [<LIST² + -ER¹]

list·er² (lis′tər) *n.* One who makes a list or lists; specifically, a tax appraiser.

list·less (list′lis) *adj.* Inattentive; heedless of what is passing; indifferent; languid; lacking energy. See synonyms under FAINT, INATTENTIVE. [OE *lust* desire + -LESS] — **list′·less·ly** *adv.* — **list′less·ness** *n.*

list mill A power-driven wheel covered with cloth on which gemstones are buffed or polished.

Liszt (list), **Franz**, 1811–86, Hungarian composer and pianist.

lit·a·ny (lit′ə·nē) *n.* *pl.* **·nies** **1** *Eccl.* A

liturgical form of prayer, consisting of a series of different supplications said by the clergy, to which the choir or people repeat the same response. **2** Any solemn prayer. See synonyms under prayer. — **the Litany** In the Book of Common Prayer, a general supplication in this form. [<OF *letanie* <LL *litania* <Gk. *litaneia* < *litaneuein* pray]

li·tchi (lē′chē) *n.* **1** A Chinese tree (*Litchi chinensis*) of the soapberry family, producing small, thin-shelled, edible fruits called **litchi nuts**. **2** The fruit of this tree. Also spelled *lichee, lychee.* [<Chinese *li-chih*]

-lite *combining form* Mineral. Stone; stonelike: *cryolite.* Also spelled *-lyte.* [<F, var. of *-lithe* <Gk. *lithos* stone]

li·ter (lē′tər) *n.* A measure of capacity in the metric system, equal to the volume of one kilogram of water at 4° C. and 760 mm. atmospheric pressure, or to 1.0567 liquid quarts. See METRIC SYSTEM. Also *litre.* [<F *litre* <Gk. *litra* pound]

lit·er·al (lit′ər·əl) *adj.* **1** According to the letter or verbal statement; not figurative or metaphorical. **2** Following the exact words or construction: a *literal* translation. **3** Consisting of or expressed by letters. **4** Matter-of-fact; unimaginative: said of persons. **5** Exact as to fact or detail; not exaggerated. See synonyms under VERBAL. ◆ Homophone: *littoral.* [<OF <LL *literalis, litteralis* < *littera* letter]

lit·er·al·ism (lit′ər·əl·iz′əm) *n.* **1** Close adherence to the exact word or sense, often to the point of unimaginativeness. **2** In the fine arts, a tendency to represent without idealizing; realistic representation or depiction. — **lit′er·al·ist** *n.*

lit·er·al·ize (lit′ər·əl·īz′) *v.t.* **·ized, ·iz·ing** To make literal; interpret or accept literally.

lit·er·ar·y (lit′ə·rer′ē) *adj.* **1** Of or pertaining to letters or used in literature. **2** Versed in or devoted to literature. **3** Engaged or occupied in the field of literature: a *literary* man. [<L *litterarius*]

lit·er·ate (lit′ər·it) *adj.* **1** Able to read and write. **2** Having a knowledge of letters or literature; educated. **3** Literary. — *n.* **1** Anyone able to read and write. **2** One versed in letters or literature. [<L *litteratus* < *littera* letter]

lit·e·ra·tim (lit′ə·rā′tim, -rä′-) *adv.* Letter for letter; with exact literalness; literally. [<L]

lit·er·a·ture (lit′ər·ə·chŏŏr, lit′rə·chər) *n.* **1** The written or printed productions of the human mind collectively. **2** Written works which deal with themes of permanent and universal interest, characterized by creativeness and grace of expression, as poetry, fiction, essays, etc.: distinguished from works of scientific, technical, or journalistic nature; belles-lettres. **3** The writings that pertain to a particular epoch, country, language, subject, or branch of learning: ancient *literature;* the *literature* of chemistry. **4** The act or occupation of a literary man; literary work. **5** Acquaintance with letters or books; learning. **6** *Music* The total number of compositions for a particular instrument or ensemble. **7** Any printed matter used or distributed for advertising or political purposes, etc.: campaign *literature.* [<L *litteratura* < *littera* letter]

Synonyms: belles-lettres, books, publications, writings. *Literature* is collective, referring to all that has been written in some land or age, or in some department of human knowledge: the *literature* of Greece; the *literature* of art. *Literature*, used absolutely, denotes *belles-lettres, i.e.,* the works collectively that embody taste, feeling, loftiness of thought, and purity and beauty of style, as poetry, history, fiction, and dramatic compositions. In the broad sense we speak of the *literature* of science; in the narrower sense, we speak of *literature* and science as distinct departments of knowledge. *Literature* is also used to signify literary pursuits or occupations: to devote one's life to *literature.* Compare KNOWLEDGE.

-lith *combining form* Stone; rock: *monolith.* [<Gk. *lithos* a stone]

lith·arge (lith′ärj, li·thärj′) *n.* Yellow lead monoxide, PbO, made by heating lead in a current of air: used in glassmaking, as a pigment, cement, etc. [<F *litarge* <L *lithargyrus* <Gk. *lithargyros* silver scum < *lithos* stone + *argyros* silver]

lithe (līth) *adj.* Bending easily or gracefully; supple. See synonyms under SUPPLE. [OE, soft] —**lithe′ly** *adv.* —**lithe′ness** *n.*

li·the·mi·a (li·thē′mē·ə) *n. Pathol.* An excess of urates and uric acid in the blood. Also **li·thae′mi·a.** [<LITH(O)- + -EMIA] —**li·the′mic** *adj.*

lithe·some (līth′səm) *adj.* Lithe; nimble; lissome.

lith·i·a (lith′ē·ə) *n.* A white, caustic compound, Li_2O, that dissolves slowly in water to form lithium hydrate; lithium oxide. [<NL <Gk. *lithos* stone]

li·thi·a·sis (li·thī′ə·sis) *n. Pathol.* The formation of stones or calculi in the body. [<NL <Gk. *lithos* stone]

lithia water A natural mineral water containing lithium salts.

lith·ic (lith′ik) *adj.* 1 Of, pertaining to, or having calculus or stone in the bladder. 2 Of or pertaining to stone. 3 *Chem.* Of or pertaining to lithium. [<Gk. *lithikos* of stone]

lith·i·um (lith′ē·əm) *n.* A soft, silver-white, metallic element (symbol Li) belonging to the first group of the periodic table. It is the lightest of the metals and is found only in combination. See ELEMENT. [<NL <Gk. *lithos* stone]

litho– *combining form* Stone; related to stone; *lithophilous.* Also, before vowels, **lith–.** [<Gk. *lithos* stone]

li·thog·ra·phy (li·thog′rə·fē) *n.* The art of producing printed matter from a stone or stones on which the design or matter to be printed has been made in a soapy ink, grease pencil, or other suitable material. Zinc and aluminum are now widely substituted for stone.

lithographic stone A yellowish, compact, fine-grained, slaty limestone used in lithography. Also **lithographic slate.**

lith·oid (lith′oid) *adj.* Of or resembling stone; having stony structure or texture. Also **li·thoi·dal** (li·thoid′l).

li·thol·o·gy (li·thol′ə·jē) *n.* 1 The science that treats of rocks as mineral masses, especially with reference to their structure. 2 The branch of medicine which treats of calculi in the body. [<LITHO- + -LOGY] —**lith·o·log·ic** (lith′ə·loj′ik) or **·i·cal** *adj.* —**li·thol′o·gist** *n.*

lith·o·marge (lith′ə·märj) *n.* A mixture of hydrous aluminum silicates, related to kaolin. [<LITHO- + L *marga* marl]

li·thoph·i·lous (li·thof′ə·ləs) *adj.* 1 Stoneloving. 2 *Ecol.* Living among, beneath, or on stones: said of insects and plants preferring a stony habitat. [<LITHO- + -PHILOUS]

lith·o·phyte (lith′ə·fīt) *n.* 1 *Zool.* A calcareous or stony polyp or plantlike organism, as a coral. 2 *Bot.* A plant that lives on stony or rocky surfaces in air or under water. —**lith′o·phyt′ic** (-fit′ik) *adj.*

lith·o·pone (lith′ə·pōn) *n.* A mixture of barium sulfate and zinc sulfide, used as a white paint and in the manufacture of rubber tires, linoleums, etc. [<LITHO- + L *ponere* place]

lith·o·sphere (lith′ə·sfir) *n.* The rigid crust of rock surrounding the inner viscous material of the earth and similar bodies in the solar system.

li·thot·o·my (li·thot′ə·mē) *n. Surg.* The operation of removing stones from the bladder by incision into the organ. [<LL *lithotomia* <Gk. < *lithos* stone + *temnein* cut] —**lith·o·tom·ic** (lith′ə·tom′ik) or **·i·cal** *adj.* —**li·thot′o·mist** *n.*

lith·o·tint (lith′ə·tint) *n.* 1 The art of producing pictures in color tints from lithographic stones. 2 A picture so produced.

li·thot·ri·ty (li·thot′rə·tē) *n. Surg.* The operation of reducing stone in the bladder to fine, easily voided fragments. Also **li·thot′rip·sy** (-rip·sē). [<LITHO- + L *tritus*, pp. of *terere* rub, grind]

Lith·u·a·ni·a (lith′ōō·ā′nē·ə) Southernmost of the Baltic States of NE Europe; since 1940 formally **Lithuanian Soviet Socialist Republic,** a constituent republic of the U.S.S.R.; 25,200 square miles; capital, Vilna. *Lithuanian* **Lie·tu·va** (lye·tōō′vä).

Lith·u·a·ni·an (lith′ōō·ā′nē·ən) *adj.* Of or pertaining to Lithuania, its people, or their language. —*n.* 1 A native or inhabitant of Lithuania. 2 The Balto-Slavic language of

the Lithuanians, belonging to the Baltic branch.

lit·i·gate (lit′ə·gāt) *v.* **·gat·ed, ·gat·ing** *v.t.* To bring before a court of law for decision or settlement; contest at law. —*v.i.* To carry on a lawsuit. [<L *litigatus*, pp. of *litigare* < *lis, litis* lawsuit + *agere* do, act] —**lit′i·ga·ble** (-gə·bəl) *adj.* —**lit′i·ga′tor** *n.*

lit·i·ga·tion (lit′ə·gā′shən) *n.* The act of carrying on a suit in a law court; a judicial contest; hence, any controversy that must be decided upon evidence.

li·ti·gious (li·tij′əs) *adj.* 1 Inclined to litigation; hence, quarrelsome. 2 Subject to litigation or contention; controvertible; disputable: a *litigious* right. 3 Of or pertaining to litigation: *litigious* form. [<F *litigieux* <L *litigiosus* < *litigium* litigation] —**li·tig′ious·ly** *adv.* —**li·tig′ious·ness** *n.*

lit·mus (lit′məs) *n.* A blue dyestuff made by fermenting certain coarsely powdered lichens. It is turned red by acids and remains blue when treated with an alkali. Also called *lacmus.* [<AF *lytemoise* <ON *litmose* lichen used in dyeing < *litr* color + *mosi* moss]

li·to·tes (lī′tə·tēz, -tō-, lit′ə-) *n.* A rhetorical figure in which an assertion is made by means of negation or understatement; ironic understatement. Example: a fact of no small importance (*i.e.*, of very great importance). See MEIOSIS. [<NL <Gk. *litotēs* < *litos* simple, spare]

lit·ter (lit′ər) *n.* 1 The offspring borne at one time by a cat, sow, or other multiparous animal. 2 A stretcher used for conveying sick or wounded. 3 A couch carried on shafts protruding at each end, and used for the transportation of people of wealth or impor-

LITTER
Late Roman period.

tance. 4 Straw, hay, or other similar material, used as bedding for horses, cattle, etc. 5 Waste materials, shreds, and fragments scattered about; a clutter; a state of disorder. 6 The upper part of a forest floor which is not in an advanced state of decomposition. See synonyms under FLOCK. —*v.t.* 1 To bring forth young: said of animals. 2 To furnish, as cattle, with litter. 3 To cover or strew with or as with litter: often with *up*: to *litter* a room with toys. 4 To throw or spread about carelessly. —*v.i.* 5 To give birth to a litter of young. [<OF *litiere* < Med. L *lectaria* <L *lectus* bed] —**lit′ter·y** *adj.*

lit·ter·a·teur (lit′ər·ə·tûr′) *n.* One who is by profession engaged in literature. [<F]

lit·tle (lit′l) *adj.* **less** or *Colloq.* **lit·tler, least** or *Colloq.* **lit·tlest** 1 Of a size, amount, quantity, etc., below the ordinary; diminutive; small. 2 Below the usual amount; restricted. 3 Below the normal distance or time; short; brief. 4 Below the standard in respect to dignity or consequence; insignificant; petty; hence, mean; narrow: a *little* quarrel, a *little* nature. 5 Lacking in ability, efficiency, or force; weak. 6 Smaller than other like things. 7 Being in the early years of life: when I was *little*. —*n.* A small quantity, space, time, degree, etc. —*adv.* **less, least** 1 In a small degree; slightly. 2 Not at all: used before a verb: She *little* knows how much I care. [OE *lȳtel* < *lȳt* small] —**lit′tle·ness** *n.*

Synonyms (*adj.*): brief, contemptible, diminutive, feeble, inconsiderable, insignificant, mean, microscopic, minute, narrow, paltry, petty, short, slender, slight, small, tiny, trifling, trivial, unimportant. See INSIGNIFICANT, MINUTE², SMALL.

lit·tle·neck clam (lit′l·nek′) The young of the hardshell clam or quahaug: much esteemed as a food. Also **lit′tle·neck′.** [from *Little Neck*, Long Island]

little theater A small theater, usually composed of an artists' group, college students, etc., producing plays which are often experimental and innovative: often used attributively to denote a movement in the 1920's involving the growth of these theaters.

lit·to·ral (lit′ər·əl) *n.* A shore and the country contiguous to the shore. —*adj.* Pertaining to the

shore. Also spelled *litoral.* ◆ Homophone: *literal.* [<L *littoralis* < *litus, -oris* seashore]

lit·ur·gist (lit′ər·jist) *n.* 1 One who uses or advocates liturgical forms of worship. 2 One versed in liturgics. 3 One who leads in reciting the liturgy.

lit·ur·gy (lit′ər·jē) *n. pl.* **·gies** 1 A collection of prescribed forms for public worship; a ritual; specifically, in the Roman Catholic Church, the mass. 2 In the Greek Church, the Eucharist: also **Divine Liturgy.** [<F *liturgie* <Med. L *liturgia* <Gk. *leitourgia* public duty, ult. < *laos* people + *ergon* work] —**li·tur·gic** (li·tûr′jik) or **·gi·cal** *adj.* —**li·tur′gi·cal·ly** *adv.*

lit·u·us (lit′yōō·əs) *n. pl.* **lit·u·i** (lit′yōō·ī) *Math.* A polar curve traced by a point moving so that the square of its distance from the pole varies inversely as its polar angle: it is trumpet-shaped, asymptotic to the polar axis, and approaches the pole as a limit. [<L, crooked staff, curved trumpet]

LITUUS

liv·a·ble (liv′ə·bəl) *adj.* 1 Worth living; fit to be lived. 2 Agreeable or fit for living in or with. Also **live·a·ble.**

live (liv) *v.* **lived, liv·ing** *v.i.* 1 To be alive; have life. 2 To continue in life; remain alive: As long as you *live.* 3 To endure or persist; last: This day will *live* in infamy. 4 To maintain life; subsist: to *live* on a pittance. 5 To depend for food; feed: with *on* or *upon*: to *live* on carrion. 6 To dwell; abide. 7 To pass life in a specified manner: to *live* frugally. 8 To enjoy a varied and active life. 9 To escape destruction; stay afloat: No boat can *live* in that surf. —*v.t.* 10 To pass: to *live* the life of a saint. 11 To manifest or practice in one's life: to *live* a lie. —**to live down** To live in such a manner as to expiate (a crime), forget or cause to be forgotten (shame), or mature beyond (folly). —**to live high** To live luxuriously. —**to live in** To reside at one's place of employment. —**to live on** To depend on parasitically, as for one's maintenance. —**to live out** To reside away from one's place of employment. —**to live through** To have experience of and survive. —**to live up to** To fulfil the hopes, terms, or character of. —**to live well** 1 To live luxuriously. 2 To live virtuously. —**to live with** 1 To dwell with as a lodger or companion. 2 To cohabit with: also **to live together.** —*adj.* (līv) 1 Possessing life; living; alive; quick: opposed to *dead* and *inanimate*; hence, ready for use; operative; effective. 2 Burning or glowing: a *live* coal. 3 Of present interest and importance; vital: a *live* book or topic. 4 Possessing liveliness, interest, or animation; alert; energetic: a *live* man of business. 5 *Printing* Ready for printing; kept for use: *live* copy. 6 Of or pertaining to living beings. 7 Containing an unexploded charge: said of munitions, etc.: a *live* shell. 8 Swarming with, or caused by a great number of living creatures. 9 Charged with electricity; carrying a current: a *live* wire. 10 Unwrought; pure; vivid: *live* rock or color. 11 Having motion or power to impart motion, as a part of a machine. See synonyms under ALIVE. [OE *lifian* live]

Synonyms (*verb*): continue, endure, exist, feed (with *on* or *upon*), subsist, survive. See ABIDE. *Antonyms*: see synonyms for DIE.

-lived *combining form* Having a (specified kind of) life or life span or (a given number of) lives: long-*lived*, nine-*lived*. [<LIFE]

live-for-ev-er (liv′fər·ev′ər) *n.* A garden herb (*Sedum telephium*) of the orpine family, with greenish-white or purple flowers: naturalized in the United States.

live·li·hood (līv′lē·hood) *n.* Means of subsistence; regular maintenance; employment; living.

live·long (liv′lông′, -long′) *adj.* That lives long or is tediously slow in passing; whole; entire: the *livelong* day. [ME *lefe longe*, lit., lief long; *lief*, here orig. intens., was later confused with *live*]

live·ly (līv′lē) *adj.* **·li·er, ·li·est** **1** Full of energy or of animation; stimulating; brisk; vivacious. **2** Intensely alive or active in the mind; animated; also, enlivening. **3** Striking to the senses; forcible; vivid. **4** In games, reactive; responsive to impact; rebounding: said of a ball: opposed to *dead*. **5** *Obs.* Lifelike. See synonyms under ACTIVE, AIRY, ALIVE, CHEERFUL, GOOD, MERRY, NIMBLE, RACY, SPRIGHTLY, VIVACIOUS, VIVID. — *adv.* Briskly. [OE *līflīce*] — **live′li·ly** *adv.* — **live′li·ness** *n.*
li·ven (lī′vən) *v.t. & v.i.* To make or become lively or cheerful: often with *up.*
live oak 1 One of several evergreen trees of the oak family native in the United States, especially *Quercus virginiana.* **2** The hard, durable wood of this tree.
liv·er¹ (liv′ər) *n.* **1** The largest glandular organ of vertebrates, in man situated just under the diaphragm and on the right side: it secretes bile, and is of great importance in metabolism. ◆ Collateral adjective: *hepatic.* **2** A digestive gland in invertebrates usually functioning as a pancreas, and consisting of cecal tubes. **3** The liver of certain animals, used as food. [OE *lifer*]
liv·er² (liv′ər) *n.* One who lives; a dweller.
liver extract A concentrated extract of mammalian liver, used in the treatment of anemia.
liver fluke Any of various trematode worms parasitic in the bile ducts of sheep, cows, pigs, and sometimes man, especially *Fasciola hepatica,* associated with the black disease of sheep.
liv·er·ied (liv′ər·ēd) *adj.* Dressed in livery, as a servant.
liv·er·ish (liv′ər·ish) *adj.* Feeling or exhibiting symptoms of disordered liver.
liv·er·leaf (liv′ər·lēf′) *n.* Hepatica.
liver ore 1 A variety of cinnabar. **2** A brownish variety of cuprite.
liv·er·stone (liv′ər·stōn′) *n.* A form of barite which yields an unpleasant odor when heated or rubbed.
liv·er·wort (liv′ər·wûrt′) *n.* Any mosslike plant belonging to the family *Hepaticae,* but differing from true mosses in always having bilateral stems, vertically ranked leaves, and a capsule which opens by two or four valves.
liv·er·wurst (liv′ər·wûrst′) *n.* A sausage made of or containing ground liver. [< G *leberwurst*]
liv·er·y (liv′ər·ē) *n. pl.* **·er·ies 1** A particular dress or uniform worn by servants. **2** The distinguishing dress of any association or organization. **3** Formerly, the dress or badge peculiar to a retainer of a feudal baron or knight. **4** Any characteristic dress, covering, or outward appearance: trees in the *livery* of spring. **5** The stabling and care of horses for compensation, as at a boarding stable. **6** *Law* Delivery, as of lands. **7** *U.S.* A livery stable. [< OF *livree* gift of clothes by a master to a servant < *livrer* deliver, free < L *liberare* free < *liber* free]
livery cupboard A cupboard or stand formerly used in a dining-room to hold the liveries or rations.
livery stable A stable where horses and vehicles are kept for hire.
lives (līvz) Plural of LIFE.
live steam Steam supplied direct from a boiler, before doing or while doing its work in a cylinder: distinguished from *exhaust steam.*
live·stock (līv′stok′) *n.* Domestic animals kept for farm purposes, especially marketable animals, as cattle, horses, and sheep.
live wire 1 A wire carrying an electric current. **2** *Colloq.* An energetic person; a hustler.
liv·id (liv′id) *adj.* Black-and-blue, as contused flesh; lead-colored; ashy-pale. [< F *livide* < L *lividus* < *livere* be livid] — **liv′id·ly** *adv.* — **liv′id·ness, li·vid·i·ty** (li·vid′ə·tē) *n.*
liv·ing (liv′ing) *adj.* **1** Having life or vitality; live: opposed to *dead;* pertaining to the living. **2** Actually operative or efficient; also, quickening or vivifying. **3** Flowing, as water: distinguished from *stagnant.* **4** Ignited; flaming: said of coal, etc. **5** Filled with or true to life; vivacious; lively; animated. **6** Enough to sustain life or live on: a *living* wage. See synonyms under ALIVE. — *n.* **1** Livelihood. **2** In the Church of England, a benefice, or the

revenue derived from it. **3** Manner of life. **4** Those who live; formerly, also, he who lives: with the definite article. **5** The fact of existing, or of dwelling in a certain place. **6** The action of existing or of passing one's life in a specified manner. **7** *Obs.* An estate; property; possessions.
liv·ing-room (liv′ing·rōōm′, -rōom′) *n.* A room designed and furnished for the general occupancy of a family.
lix·iv·i·ate (lik·siv′ē·āt) *v.t.* **·at·ed, ·at·ing** To leach. [< L *lixivius* made into lye < *lix* ashes, lye] — **lix·iv′i·al** *adj.*
lix·iv·i·a·tion (lik·siv′ē·ā′shən) *n.* The process of extracting a soluble alkali or saline compound from a mixture by washing; leaching.
lix·iv·i·um (lik·siv′ē·əm) *n.* **1** A solution of alkaline salts, as lye. **2** A solution obtained by leaching. [< L < *lix* ashes, lye]
liz·ard (liz′ərd) *n.* **1** Any of various reptiles (suborder *Sauria*), as an agama, basilisk, chameleon, gecko, glass snake, horned toad, iguana, monitor, or skink. Lizards commonly have an elongate, scaly body, a long tail, and four legs, but the latter may be reduced to two or may be rudimentary or absent. **2** Any four-legged reptile of similar form. **3** A kind of low sledge for hauling logs, stones, etc. [< OF *laisard* < L *lacerta*]

LIZARD
a. Varanus (from 4 to 12 feet in length).
b. Chameleon (up to 18 inches in length).

lla·ma (lä′mə, *Sp.* lyä′mä) *n.* A South American woolly-haired, humpless, cameloid ruminant (genus *Auchenia* or *Lama*), usually white or spotted with brown or black; the guanaco: used as a beast of burden in the Andes. [< Sp. < Quechua]

LLAMA

lla·no (lä′nō, *Sp.* lyä′nō) *n. pl.* **·nos** A flat, treeless plain, as the wide, grassy tracts of northern South America. [< Sp., plain, flat < L *planus*]
loach (lōch) *n.* A small, fresh-water, cyprinoid fish of the Old World (family *Cobitidae*), related to the minnow. [< F *loche*]
load (lōd) *n.* **1** That which is laid upon anything for conveyance; a burden; specifically, as much as can be carried, or as is customarily carried. **2** That which is borne with difficulty; hence, figuratively, a grievous mental burden. **3** The charge of a firearm. **4** A weight of various amounts. **5** The resistance overcome by a motor or engine in driving machinery. **6** Downward pressure on a structure: when caused by gravity alone, it is called **dead load;** when caused by gravity

increased by the stresses of transverse motion, it is called **live load.** **7** The power delivered by a machine or apparatus, especially an electric generator. **8** *Slang* An excess of alcoholic liquor. **9** *pl. Colloq.* A great plenty; abundance: *loads* of time. — **to get a load of** *U.S. Slang* To listen to or look at. — *v.t.* **1** To put something on or into to be carried. **2** To place (a load) in or on a carrier. **3** To supply with something excessively or in abundance: to *load* one with honors. **4** To weigh down or oppress; burden. **5** To charge (a firearm) with ammunition. **6** To take on (a load, cargo, etc.). **7** To make heavy on one side or end by adding extra weight: to *load* dice or a whip. **8** To add a substance to for the purpose of falsifying; adulterate; doctor: to *load* silk with gum. **9** In insurance, to increase (a premium) by the addition of loading. See LOADING (def. 4). — *v.i.* **10** To take on or put on a load or cargo. **11** To charge a firearm with ammunition. **12** To be charged with ammunition: The new gun *loads* through the breech. ◆ Homophone: *lode.* [OE *lād* way, journey, act of carrying goods. Doublet of LODE.] — **load′er** *n.*
Synonyms (noun): burden, cargo, charge, clog, encumbrance, freight, incubus, pack, weight. A *burden* is what one has to bear, and is used chiefly of that which is borne by a living agent. A *load* is what is laid upon a person, animal, or conveyance, or what is customarily so imposed: as, a *load* of coal. *Weight* measures the pressure due to gravity. A ship's *load* is called distinctively a *cargo,* or it may be known as *freight* or *lading. Freight* denotes merchandise in or for transportation. A *load* to be fastened upon a horse or mule is called a *pack.* See WEIGHT. *Synonyms (verb):* burden, charge, cumber, lade, oppress.
load displacement *Naut.* A ship's displacement when fully loaded.
load·ed (lō′did) *adj.* **1** Filled or laden. **2** Weighted, as fraudulent dice. **3** Charged with ammunition. **4** Charged with special implication: a *loaded* question. **5** *Slang* Intoxicated. **6** *Slang* Wealthy.
load factor *Electr.* The ratio of the average load of a generating station to the maximum or peak load.
load·ing (lō′ding) *adj.* Arranged so that it may be loaded (in a specified way): used in compounds: a *breechloading* cannon. — *n.* **1** Anything added to a substance for the purpose of giving it weight or body. **2** In art, a heavy charge of opaque color. **3** A load or burden; lading. **4** In insurance, an addition to the premium to cover expenses, fluctuations in the death rate, etc. **5** The act or operation of furnishing with a load.
loading coil *Electr.* An inductance coil connected in a circuit to increase its period of oscillation.
load line *Naut.* **1** A line drawn on the plan of a ship to indicate the maximum mean draft to which it may be submerged by the weight of its cargo or under various conditions. **2** The Plimsoll mark. **3** The line of intersection of the surface of the water with a ship's side under any given load.
loaf¹ (lōf) *v.i.* **1** To hang about or saunter lazily or aimlessly; idle time away. **2** To neglect one's work. — *v.t.* **3** To spend (time) idly: with away. [Back formation < LOAFER]
loaf² (lōf) *n. pl.* **loaves** (lōvz) A shaped mass, as of bread, cake, etc., intended to be cut. [OE *hlāf* bread]
loaf·er (lō′fər) *n.* **1** One who loafs; an idler. **2** A casual shoe resembling a moccasin. [Cf. G *landläufer* an idler, loiterer, Du. *landloper* a vagrant]
loam (lōm) *n.* **1** A non-coherent mixture of sand and clay, containing organic matter. **2** A mixture of sand and clay, usually with straw or the like: used in foundry work to make molds, in plastering walls, plugging holes, etc. **3** *Archaic* Any soil; especially, fertile earth. — *v.t.* To coat or fill with loam. [OE *lām*] — **loam′y** *adj.*
loan (lōn) *n.* **1** Something lent, especially a sum of money lent at interest. **2** The act of lending; a lending. **3** Permission to use: a *loan* of credit. — *v.t. & v.i.* To lend. ◆ Homo-

phone: *lone.* [OE *lān*]

loan office 1 A pawnshop. **2** An office where loans are arranged, the accounts kept, and interest paid to lenders. **3** Formerly, an office set up in certain states by the Revolutionary Continental government to handle subscriptions to government loans.

lo·a·sis (lō′ə·sis) *n. Pathol.* A species of filariasis common in West Africa, caused by a wandering parasitic roundworm (*Loa loa*) which often invades the orbit and conjunctiva of the eye: also called *loiasis.* [<NL <*loa* a trematode worm <African native name + -(o)SIS]

loath (lōth) *adj.* Strongly disinclined; reluctant; averse: often with *to.* Also spelled *loth.* See synonyms under RELUCTANT. [OE *lāth* hateful] — **loath′ness** *n.*

loathe (lōth) *v.t.* **loathed, loath·ing** To feel great hatred or disgust for; abhor; detest. See synonyms under ABHOR. [OE *lāthian* be hateful] — **loath′er** *n.*

loath·ful (lōth′fəl) *adj.* Exciting abhorrence; hateful; detestable. — **loath′ful·ly** *adv.* — **loath′ful·ness** *n.*

loath·ing (lō′thing) *n.* Extreme dislike or disgust; aversion. See synonyms under ANTIPATHY.

loath·some (lōth′səm) *adj.* Exciting revulsion or disgust. — **loath′some·ly** *adv.* — **loath′some·ness** *n.*

loaves (lōvz) Plural of LOAF.

lob (lob) *v.* **lobbed, lob·bing** *v.t.* **1** To pitch or strike (a ball, etc.) in a high, arching curve, as in tennis or cricket. — *v.i.* **2** To move clumsily or heavily. **3** To lob a ball. — *n.* **1** In tennis, a stroke that sends the ball high into the air. **2** In cricket, a slow, underhand ball. **3** A soft, thick, lumpy mixture. **4** A worm for bait. [? Imit.] — **lob′ber** *n.*

lo·bar (lō′bər, -bär) *adj.* **1** Of a lobe or lobes. **2** *Pathol.* Of, pertaining to, or describing acute febrile pneumonia affecting one or more lobes of the lungs. [<NL *lobaris*]

lo·bate (lō′bāt) *adj.* Composed of lobes; lobelike. Also **lo′bat·ed.** [<NL *lobatus*] — **lo′bate·ly** *adv.* — **lo·ba′tion** *n.*

lob·by (lob′ē) *n. pl.* **·bies** **1** A hall, vestibule, or corridor on the main floor of a large public building, as a theater or hotel; a lounge; foyer. **2** The part of an assembly-room of a legislative or deliberative body not appropriated to the official use of members, and to which outsiders have free entry. **3** *U.S.* The persons or groups of persons who accost or solicit legislators in order to influence the action of a legislative body in the interest of a special group, industry, etc.: so called because supposed to frequent lobbies. **4** A cold-storage chamber for the temporary storage of ice. — *v.* **·bied, ·by·ing** *v.i.* To attempt to influence a legislator or legislators in favor of one's own interests. — *v.t.* To attempt to obtain passage or defeat of (a bill, etc.) by such means. [<Med. L *lobia.* Doublet of LODGE, *n.*, LOGE, LOGGIA.]

lob·by·ism (lob′ē·iz′əm) *n. U.S.* The practice of lobbying. — **lob′by·ist** *n.*

lobe (lōb) *n.* **1** A protuberance, especially globular, as of an organ or part. **2** The soft lower extension of the external ear. **3** A principal division of a molar tooth. [<F <Gk. *lobos*]

lo·bec·to·my (lō·bek′tə·mē) *n. Surg.* The operation of removing a lobe, as of the brain, lung, etc. [<LOBE + -ECTOMY]

lobed (lōbd) *adj.* **1** Lobate; having lobes. **2** *Bot.* Having divisions that extend not more than half-way from the margin to the center and rounded lobes or sinuses: said of leaves, petals, etc.

lo·be·li·a (lō·bē′lē·ə, -bēl′yə) *n.* Any of a large genus (*Lobelia*) of herbaceous plants with showy flowers either axillary or in bracted racemes. [<NL, after Matthias de *Lobel,* 1538–1616, Flemish botanist]

lo·be·line (lō′bə·lēn) *n. Chem.* A white, crystalline alkaloid, $C_{22}H_{27}O_2N$, from the seeds of Indian tobacco. Its hydrochloride is used as a respiratory stimulant. [<LOBEL(IA) + -INE²]

loblolly bay A tree (*Gordonia lasianthus*) with smooth, shining, lanceolate leaves and showy white flowers, growing in southern U.S. coastal swamps.

lo·bo (lō′bō) *n. pl.* **·bos** The timber wolf (*Canis nubilus*), of the western United States. [<Sp.,

wolf]

lo·bot·o·my (lō·bot′ə·mē) *n. Surg.* The operation of cutting into or across a lobe, especially of the brain. [<Gk. *lobos* a lobe + -TOMY]

lob·scouse (lob′skous) *n.* A dish consisting of salt meat, vegetables, and biscuit. Also **lob·scourse** (-skôrs, -skōrs). [Origin unknown]

lob·ster (lob′stər) *n.* **1** A marine crustacean (genus *Homarus*) much used as food, having a large first pair of ambulatory legs, which form the claws, and compound eyes carried on flexible stalks. **2** One of various other long-tailed crustaceans, as a spiny lobster or crayfish. [OE *loppestre* lobster, grasshopper <L *locusta* lobster, locust; infl. in form by *loppe* spider. Doublet of LOCUST.]

lobster pot A trap consisting of a cage with netting at the ends for catching lobsters.

lobster shift A work shift during the latter part of the night; a graveyard shift.

lob·ule (lob′yōol) *n.* A small lobe, or lobe made small by separation from a larger lobe. [<NL *lobulus,* dim. of *lobus* a lobe] — **lob′u·lar,** **lob′u·late** (-lit, -lāt) *adj.*

lo·cal (lō′kəl) *adj.* **1** Pertaining to a prescribed place or a limited portion of space. **2** Restricted to or characteristic of a particular place. **3** Pertaining to place in general. **4** *Med.* Relating to or affecting a specific part or organ of the body: said of a disease or injury, or of the remedies used. **5** Relating to a locus. — *n.* **1** A subway or suburban train that stops at all the stations. **2** A local branch or unit of a trade union or fraternal organization. **3** An item of local interest in a newspaper. [<F <L *localis* <*locus* place] — **lo′cal·ly** *adv.*

local government 1 Independent government in local affairs by the small political entity of a limited region. **2** The governing head or body of such a locality.

lo·cal·ism (lō′kəl·iz′əm) *n.* **1** A manner of acting or speaking particular to a place; local custom or idiom. **2** A word, a meaning of a word, a pronunciation, etc., peculiar to a locality, rather than in general usage. **3** Provincialism. **4** The state or condition of being local; influence exerted by a particular place.

lo·cal·i·ty (lō·kal′ə·tē) *n. pl.* **·ties** **1** A definite region in any part of space; geographical position. **2** Restriction to a particular place. See synonyms under NEIGHBORHOOD, PLACE. [<F *localité* <LL *localitas, -tatis*]

lo·cal·ize (lō′kəl·īz) *v.t.* **·ized, ·iz·ing** **1** To make local; limit or assign to a specific area or locality. **2** To determine the place of origin of. Also *Brit.* **lo′cal·ise.** — **lo′cal·i·za′tion** *n.*

lo·cate (lō′kāt, lō·kāt′) *v.* **·cat·ed, ·cat·ing** *v.t.* **1** To discover the position or source of; find. **2** To assign place or locality to: to *locate* a scene in a valley. **3** *U.S.* To establish in a place; situate: My office is *located* in Portland. **4** *U.S.* To survey, set, or designate the site or boundaries of, as a mining claim. — *v.i.* **5** *Colloq.* To establish oneself or take up residence; settle. See synonyms under SET. [<L *locatus,* pp. of *locare* <*locus* place]

lo·ca·tion (lō·kā′shən) *n.* **1** The act of locating, or the state of being located. **2** The exact position in space; place. **3** A plot of ground defined by boundaries; a mining claim. **4** *Law* A renting or letting for hire; also, the establishment or fixing of the boundaries of a tract of land. **5** A site selected for staging a scene in a motion picture. **6** Any one of five minor civil divisions in New Hampshire. See synonyms under PLACE. [<L *locatio, -onis*]

loc·a·tive (lok′ə·tiv) *adj.* In certain inflected languages, as Latin, Greek, and Sanskrit, designating the case of the noun denoting place where or at which. **2** *Anat.* & *Zool.* Indicating relative position in a series. — *n. Gram.* **1** The locative case. **2** A word in this case. [<L *locatus,* pp. of *locare* locate; on analogy with L *vocativus* vocative]

lo·chi·a (lō′kē·ə, lok′ē·ə) *n. pl. Med.* The discharges from the vaginal passages after childbirth, continuing from two to three weeks. [<NL <Gk. *lochia,* neut. pl. of *lochios* pertaining to childbirth <*lochos* childbirth] — **lo′chi·al** *adj.*

lock¹ (lok) *n.* **1** A device to fasten an object; specifically, one for so securing a door, drawer, or the like, as to prevent its being opened, except by a special key or combination. **2** A

spring mechanism for exploding the charge of a firearm. **3** A section of a canal, etc., enclosed by gates at either end, within which the water level may be varied to raise or lower vessels from one level to another. **4** An intermingling or fastening together; hence, a hold, hug, or grapple in wrestling. **5** A lockup. **6** One of various mechanical devices for fixing something so that it may remain in place. **7** An airlock. **8** A device to prevent a carriage wheel from turning, as in descending a hill. **9** The oblique position of the fore axle with relation to the hind axle of a vehicle when turning or swerving. — **combination lock** A lock which can be opened only by combining its dial-operated tumblers in a certain sequence. — **cylinder lock** A lock fitted with a cylinder having a control element which can be actuated only by a key whose particularly shaped surface engages with the tumblers and sets them to the exact position

CYLINDER LOCK
Insertion of the proper key raises all the tumblers (*a*) to the exact position required to release the key-plug (*b*), thus permitting the key to turn (here partly inserted).

for unlocking. — *v.t.* **1** To secure or fasten by means of a lock. **2** To shut, confine, or exclude by means of a lock: with *in, up,* or *out.* **3** To join or unite securely; interlock; link: to *lock* arms. **4** To make immovable, as by jamming or by a lock. **5** To provide (a canal, etc.) with a lock or locks. **6** To move (a ship) through a waterway by means of locks. — *v.i.* **7** To become locked or fastened. **8** To become joined or linked. **9** To become jammed immovably. **10** To proceed by means of locks: said of ships. **11** To turn (wheels) under a carriage body. [OE *loc* fastening, enclosure]

Synonyms (noun): bar, bolt, catch, clasp, fastening, hasp, hook, latch. A *bar* is a piece of wood or metal, usually of considerable size, by which an opening is obstructed, a door held fast, etc. A *bar* may be movable or permanent; a *bolt* is a movable rod or pin of metal sliding in a socket, and adapted for securing a door or window. A *lock* is an arrangement by which an enclosed *bolt* is shot forward or backward by a key, or other device; the *bolt* is the essential part of the *lock.* A *latch* or *catch* is an accessible *fastening* designed to be easily movable, and simply to secure against accidental opening of the door, cover, etc. A *hasp* is a metallic strap that fits over a staple, calculated to be secured by a padlock; a simple *hook* that fits into a staple is also called a *hasp.* A *clasp* is a *fastening* that can be sprung into place, to draw and hold the parts of some object firmly together, as the *clasp* of a book.

lock² (lok) *n.* **1** A tuft of hair; ringlet; tress. **2** *pl.* A head of hair. **3** A small quantity of hay, wool, etc. [OE *locc*]

lock·age (lok′ij) *n.* **1** Material going to form the lock of a canal. **2** The difference in level between the locks of a canal. **3** The toll levied for passing through a lock.

lock·er (lok′ər) *n.* **1** One who or that which locks. **2** A closet or receptacle fastened with a lock.

lock·et (lok′it) *n.* A small case, suspended on a necklace or chain, often holding a portrait. [<OF *locquet,* dim. of *loc* latch <Gmc.]

lock·fast (lok′fast′, -fäst′) *adj.* Securely held by some locked contrivance.

lock·jaw (lok′jô′) *n. Pathol.* A spasmodic contraction of the muscles of the lower jaw; trismus. See TETANUS.

lock nut *Mech.* **1** An auxiliary nut used to prevent the loosening of another. **2** A nut that automatically locks when screwed tight.

lock-out (lok′out′) *n.* The closing of a factory or other place of business by employers to bring employees on strike to terms. Also **lock′out′**. Compare STRIKE.

lock·ram (lok′rəm) *n.* A coarse, cheap linen. [after *Locronan*, a village in Brittany]

locks·man (loks′mən) *n.* *pl.* **·men** (-mən) A warden; turnkey.

lock·smith (lok′smith′) *n.* A maker or repairer of locks. — **lock′smith′er·y, lock′smith′ing** *n.*

lock step A marching step in which each marcher follows as closely as possible the one in front of him.

lock stitch A stitch made by two interlocking threads, as on some sewing machines.

lock, stock, and barrel Altogether; completely; in its entirety.

lock·up (lok′up′) *n.* **1** A prison. **2** The act of locking up; the condition of being locked up; imprisonment.

loco (lō′kō) *n.* **1** Any one of several plants of the bean family (genera *Astragalus* and *Oxytropis*), often poisonous to livestock, and found in the western and SW United States: also called *crazyweed.* **2** Loco disease. — *adj. Slang* Crazy; insane. — *v.t.* **1** To poison with locoweed. **2** *U.S. Slang* To render insane. [< Sp., insane]

LOCO
(About 12 inches tall)

loco disease An ailment attacking horses or other animals that have eaten the loco. It affects the brain, causing slowness of gait, loss of flesh, defective vision, delirium, and eventually, death: generally curable by careful and prolonged dieting.

lo·co·mo·bile (lō′kə·mō′bil) *adj.* Self-propelling.

lo·co·mo·tion (lō′kə·mō′shən) *n.* The act or power of moving from one place to another. [< L *loco* from a place + *motio, -onis* movement]

lo·co·mo·tive (lō′kə·mō′tiv) *adj.* **1** Pertaining to locomotion. **2** Moving from one place to another. **3** Possessed of the power of moving. — *n.* A self-propelling electric, diesel, or steam engine on wheels, especially one for use on a railway.

lo·co·mo·tor (lō′kə·mō′tər) *adj.* Of or pertaining to locomotion. — *n.* One who or that which has the power of locomotion.

locomotor ataxia *Pathol.* A disease of the spinal cord, characterized by unsteadiness and inability to coordinate locomotor and other voluntary movements; tabes dorsalis.

loc·u·lus (lok′yə·ləs) *n.* *pl.* **·li** (-lī) A small cavity or chamber; a cell. [< L, dim. of *locus* place] — **loc′u·lar, loc′u·late** (-lāt, -lit), **loc′u·lat′ed** *adj.*

lo·cus (lō′kəs) *n.* *pl.* **·ci** (-sī) **1** A place; locality; area. **2** *Math.* A surface or curve regarded as traced by a line or point moving under specified conditions; any figure made up wholly of points or lines that satisfy given conditions. **3** A figure formed by the foci of a series of pencils of light. **4** A passage in a writing. **5** *pl.* A series of passages, as from the Scriptures, classified for reading or study; any book containing such passages. **6** *Genetics* The linear position of a gene on a chromosome. [< L. Doublet of LIEU.]

lo·cust¹ (lō′kəst) *n.* **1** Any of a family (*Locustidae*) of widely distributed orthopterous insects resembling grasshoppers but having short antennae, especially those of migratory habits (*Locusta, Pachytylus, Melanoplus,* and related genera), which are destructive of grain and vegetation in many parts of the world. **2** A cicada or harvest fly. [< OF *locuste* < L *locusta.* Doublet of LOBSTER.]

lo·cust² (lō′kəst) *n.* **1** A North American tree (*Robinia pseudoacacia*) of the bean family, with a rough bark, odd-pinnate leaves, and loose, slender racemes of fragrant, white flowers; also, its wood. **2** Any of several other trees with similar pods, as the carob

tree. **3** The honey locust. [< NL *locusta;* orig. applied to the carob pod from its fancied resemblance to the insect]

lo·cus·ta (lō·kus′tə) *n.* *Bot.* A spikelet in grasses. [< NL. See LOCUST².]

lo·cu·tion (lō·kyōō′shən) *n.* **1** A mode of speech. **2** An idiom; phrase. [< L *locutio, -onis* a speaking < *loqui* speak]

loc·u·to·ry (lok′yə·tôr′ē, -tō′rē) *n.* *pl.* **·ries** A place for conversation; specifically, a reception room in a monastery or convent. [< Med. L *locutorium* < L *locutor* speaker < *loqui* talk]

lode (lōd) *n.* **1** A somewhat continuous, unstratified, metal-bearing vein. **2** A tabular deposit of valuable mineral between definite boundaries of associated rock. **3** A reach of water, as in a canal. ◆ Homophone: *load.* [OE *lād* way, journey. Doublet of LOAD.]

lode·star (lōd′stär′) *n.* A guiding star; the polestar: also spelled *loadstar.*

lode·stone (lōd′stōn′) *n.* A variety of magnetite that shows polarity and acts like a magnet when freely suspended: also spelled *loadstone.*

lodge (loj) *v.* **lodged, lodg·ing** *v.t.* **1** To furnish with temporary living quarters; house. **2** To rent a room or rooms to; take as a paying guest. **3** To serve as a shelter or dwelling for. **4** To deposit for safekeeping or storage. **5** To place or implant, as by throwing, thrusting, etc.: I *lodged* an arrow in the tree. **6** To place (a complaint, information, etc.) before proper authority. **7** To confer or invest (power, etc.). **8** To beat down (crops): said of rain, storms, etc. — *v.i.* **9** To take temporary shelter or quarters; pass the night. **10** To live in a rented room or rooms. **11** To become fixed in some place or position: The bullet *lodged* in his leg. See synonyms under ABIDE, ACCOMMODATE. — *n.* **1** A small house affording temporary accommodations; a hut. **2** A small dwelling appurtenant to a manor house, park, or the like. **3** The lair of a wild animal, especially of a group of beavers; also, collectively, the beavers themselves. **4** A local subdivision of a secret society, or its meeting place. **5** *U.S.* Among the American Indians, a small hut or tepee of skins, bark, and poles; also, its inhabitants. [< OF *logier* < *loge* < Med. L *lobia, laubia* porch, gallery < OHG *louba* < *loub* foliage; *n.,* doublet of LOBBY, LOGE, LOGGIA]

lodge pole A pole used in building an American Indian lodge.

lodge-pole pine (loj′pōl′) A tall, slender tree (*Pinus contorta latifolia*) of the western United States.

lodg·er (loj′ər) *n.* Something or someone that lodges; especially, one who occupies a rented room or rooms in the house of another.

lodg·ing (loj′ing) *n.* **1** A place of temporary abode. **2** *pl.* A room or rooms hired as a place of residence in the house of another. **3** Accommodation, as a room: to include board and *lodging.*

lodging house A house other than a hotel where lodgings are let.

lodg·ment (loj′mənt) *n.* **1** The act of lodging or the state of being lodged. **2** A foothold gained in some place. **3** Lodgings; accommodation; a lodging house. Also **lodge′ment.**

loess (lō′is, lœs) *n.* *Geol.* A pale, yellowish clay or loam forming deposits along river valleys, etc., in Asia, Europe, and North America. [< G < *lösen* pour, dissolve]

loft (lôft, loft) *n.* **1** A low story directly under a roof. **2** A large storeroom. **3** An elevated floor or gallery within a large building, as a church or barn. **4** An incline on the face of a golf club tending to cause elevation in the trajectory of the ball; also, a stroke which lifts the ball high in the air. **5** A place for keeping pigeons; hence, a flock of pigeons. — *v.t.* **1** To provide with a loft. **2** In golf: **a** To give loft to (a club). **b** To strike (a ball) so that it rises or travels in a high arc. — *v.i.* **3** In golf, to strike the ball so that it rises in a high arc. [OE < ON, upper room, air, sky. Akin to LIFT.]

loft·er (lôf′tər, lof′-) *n.* In golf, an iron club used for lofting the ball. Also **lofting iron.**

loft·y (lôf′tē, lof′-) *adj.* **loft·i·er, loft·i·est** Elevated, as in position, character, language,

or quality; exalted; haughty; stately. See synonyms under EMINENT, GRAND, HIGH, SUBLIME. — **loft′i·ly** *adj.* — **loft′i·ness** *n.*

log (lôg, log) *n.* **1** A bulky piece of timber cut down and cleared of branches. **2** Figuratively, a dull, stupid person. **3** *Naut.* A device for showing the speed of a vessel, consisting of a triangular board, the **log chip** or **ship,** weighted on one edge and attached to a line, the **log line,** that runs out from a reel, the **log reel,** on shipboard. **4** A record of the daily progress of a vessel and of the events of a voyage. **5** Any record of performance, as of an engine, oil well, aircraft, etc. — *v.* **logged, log·ging** *v.t.* **1** To cut (trees) into logs. **2** To cut down the trees of (a region) for timber. **3** *Naut.* **a** To enter in a logbook. **b** To travel (a specified distance) as shown by a log. **c** To travel at (a specified speed). — *v.i.* **4** To cut down trees and transport logs for sawing into lumber. [ME *logge,* prob. < Scand. Cf. ON *lāg,* Dan. *laag* felled tree.]

log– Var. of LOGO-.

lo·ga·ni·a·ceous (lō·gā′nē·ā′shəs) *adj.* Designating or pertaining to a family (*Loganiaceae*) of poisonous herbs, shrubs, and trees, with opposite, entire, stipulate leaves and a cymose inflorescence of regular, perfect, four- or five-parted flowers. [< NL, after James *Logan,* 1674–1751, Irish botanist]

lo·gan·ber·ry (lō′gən·ber′ē) *n.* *pl.* **·ries** **1** A hybrid plant (*Rubus loganobaccus*) obtained by crossing the red raspberry with the blackberry: cultivated for its edible fruit. **2** The fruit itself. [after J. H. *Logan* of California, the originator]

log·a·oe·dic (lôg′ə·ē′dik, log′-) *adj.* Prose-poetic; partaking of the nature of prose and poetry: applied to a meter composed of cyclic dactyls and trochees. — *n.* A logaoedic verse. [< LL *logaoedicus* < Gk. *logaoidikos* < *logos* speech + *aoidē* song]

log·a·rithm (lôg′ə·rith′əm, log′-) *n.* *Math.* **1** The exponent of the power to which a fixed number, called the base, must be raised in order to produce a given number. For example, in decimal logarithms the base is 10 and the logarithm of 100 is 2 because 10 raised to the second power is 100; the logarithm of 1000 is 3 because 10 raised to the third power is 1000, and so on. **2** In a former and broader sense, one of any series of numbers whose members correspond, each to each, with the natural numbers, but are in arithmetical progression when the latter are in geometrical, so that, if the products of two sets of numbers are equal, the sums of the corresponding logarithms are also equal. [< NL < Gk. *logos* word, ratio + *arithmos* number] — **log′a·rith′mic** or **·mi·cal** *adj.* — **log′a·rith′mi·cal·ly** *adv.*

logarithmic curve *Math.* A curve traced by a point with ordinates increasing arithmetically and abscissas increasing geometrically. It is asymptotic to the negative axis of the dependent variable and passes through the coordinate (1,0) or (0,1) depending on which coordinate is assumed as the variable.

logarithmic spiral *Math.* The polar curve traced by a point moving so that the angle subtended between its radius vector and a tangent to the curve is equal to the modulus; a polar curve traced by a point with a polar angle proportional to the logarithm of the distance from the point to the pole: also called *equiangular spiral, logistic spiral.*

LOGARITHMIC SPIRAL
*o.*Origin.
x.,y. x-axis,*y*-axis.

log·book (lôg′book′, log′-) *n.* The book in which the official record of a ship or aircraft is entered; also, a book containing a similar record of performance of a small military unit. Also **log book.**

log cabin A small, rough house built of logs. Also **log house, log hut.**

log carriage The carriage in a sawing machine

that moves the log back and forth before the saw.

loge (lōzh) *n.* A box in a theater; booth; stall. [<F <OF. Doublet of LOBBY, LODGE, *n.*, LOGGIA.]

log·gan (lôg'ən, log'-) *n.* A large boulder so balanced as to rock easily; a rocking stone. Also **lo·gan** (lō'gən), **loggan stone.** [<dial. E rock, move to and fro]

log·ger·head (lôg'ər·hed', log'-) *n.* 1 A blockhead; dunce. 2 A large marine turtle (*genus Caretta*) of tropical Atlantic waters. 3 The loggerhead shrike. See under SHRIKE. 4 A post on the gunwale of a whaleboat around which the line is turned to retard the motion of a harpooned whale. — **at loggerheads** Engaged in a quarrel; unable to agree. [<dial. E *logger* log tied to a horse's leg to impede movement + HEAD]

log·gi·a (loj'ē·ə, lô'jə; *Ital.* lôd'jä) *n.* A covered gallery or portico having a colonnade on one or more sides, open to the air: compare PORCH, VERANDA. [<Ital. <OF *loge.* Doublet of LOBBY, LODGE, *n.*, LOGE.]

LOGGIA

log·ging (lôg'ing, log'-) *n.* The business or occupation of felling timber and transporting logs to a mill or market.

log·i·a (log'ē·ə) *n. pl.* of **log·i·on** (log'ē·on) Collections of sayings attributed to a religious leader; especially, **Logia,** the maxims, doctrines, or truths ascribed to Jesus in the four Gospels; also, the agrapha, or collection of sayings ascribed to Jesus, but not found in the Bible. [<Gk., pl. of *logos* word]

log·ic (loj'ik) *n.* 1 The normative science which investigates the principles of valid reasoning and correct inference, either from the general to the particular, **deductive logic;** or from the particular to the general, **inductive logic.** Compare FORMAL LOGIC, SYMBOLIC LOGIC. 2 The basic principles of reasoning developed by and applicable to any field of knowledge: the *logic* of science. 3 Effective or convincing force: The *logic* of his argument is unassailable. 4 The system of thought or ideas governing conduct, belief, behavior, etc.: the *logic* of business enterprise. [<F *logique* <L *logica* <Gk. *logikē* (*technē*) logical (art) < *logikos* of speaking or reason < *logos* word, speech, thought]

log·i·cal (loj'i·kəl) *adj.* 1 Relating to or of the nature of logic. 2 Conformed to the laws of logic; consistent in point of reasoning: a *logical* conclusion. 3 Capable of or characterized by clear reasoning; versed in the principles of logic: a *logical* writer. — **log'i·cal·ly** *adv.* — **log'i·cal'i·ty** (-kal'ə·tē), **log'i·cal·ness** *n.*

-logical *combining form* Of or related to a (specified) science or study: *biological, geological, zoological.* [<-LOG(Y) + -ICAL]

logical positivism A movement in philosophy devoted to unifying the sciences, chiefly by creation of a unified terminology in which the statements of any science are expressible. Also called **logical empiricism.**

lo·gi·cian (lō·jish'ən) *n.* One versed in logic.

lo·gis·tic (lō·jis'tik) *adj.* 1 Of, pertaining to, or skilled in calculation. 2 Of or pertaining to proportion. 3 Sexagesimal. 4 Of or pertaining to logistics. Also **lo·gis'ti·cal.** — *n.* 1 The art of calculation; common practical arithmetic. 2 Sexagesimal arithmetic. [< Med. L *logisticus* <Gk. *logistikos* < *logizesthai* reckon < *logos* word, calculation]

lo·gis·tics (lō·jis'tiks) *n. pl.* (construed as *singular*) 1 The branch of military science that embraces the details of moving, evacuating, and supplying armies. 2 Logistic. [<F *logistique* < *logis* quarters, lodging < *loger* quarter <OF *logier.* See LODGE.]

logo- *combining form* Word; speech: *logomachy.* Also, before vowels, *log-.* [<Gk. *logos* word, speech]

log·o·gram (lôg'ə·gram, log'-) *n.* 1 An abbreviation or other sign representing a word,

as \$ for *dollar.* 2 A form of versified word puzzle. — **log'o·gram·mat'ic** *adj.*

log·o·graph (lôg'ə·graf, -gräf, log'-) *n.* 1 A character, or combination of characters, used to represent a word; logogram. 2 A logotype. — **log'o·graph'ic** or **-i·cal** *adj.*

lo·gog·ra·phy (lō·gog'rə·fē) *n.* 1 *Printing* The use of logotypes. 2 The art of reporting speeches in longhand by several reporters, each taking down a few words in succession.

log·o·griph (lôg'ə·grif, log'-) *n.* 1 A word riddle, in which it is required to discover some word by a recombination of the letters or elements of various given words or by guessing and combining other words which (when correctly arranged) form the word to be guessed. 2 Any anagram or puzzle which involves an anagram. [<LOGO- + Gk. *griphos* riddle] — **log'o·griph'ic** *adj.*

log·on (lôg'on, log'-) *n.* An elementary tone signal, of whatever frequency and intensity, distinguishable as such by the human ear: used especially in the quantitative study and analysis of auditory capacity. [<Gk. *logon,* accusative of *logos* word, utterance]

lo·gop·a·thy (lō·gop'ə·thē) *n. Pathol.* Any disorder affecting the speech. [<LOGO- + -PATHY]

log·o·tech·nics (lō'gō·tek'niks) *n.* The theory, art, and practice of forming new words, especially with reference to specific requirements in science, technology, medicine, etc. [<Gk. *logotechnēs* an artificer of words + -ICS; coined (1954) by R. W. Brown, U. S. geologist] — **lo'go·tech'ni·cal** *adj.*

log·o·type (lôg'ə·tīp, log'-) *n. Printing* A type bearing a syllable, a word, or words. Compare LIGATURE (def. 4).

log·o·typ·y (lôg'ə·tī'pē, log'-) *n.* The use of logotypes.

log-roll (lôg'rōl', log'-) *v.t.* To obtain passage of (a bill) by log-rolling. — *v.i.* To engage in log-rolling. Also **log'roll.** [Back formation <LOG-ROLLING]

log-rolling (lôg'rō'ling, log'-) *n.* 1 Handling and removing of logs, as in clearing land. 2 *U.S.* A combining of politicians for mutual assistance on their separate projects. 3 Birling. — **log'-roll'er** *n.*

log scale A table showing the amount of lumber in board measure one inch thick contained in a round log of given length and diameter.

-logue *combining form* Speech; recitation; discourse: *monologue.* Also **-log.** [<Gk. *logos* word, speech]

log·way (lôg'wā', log'-) *n.* 1 An inclined chute or slide up which logs are moved from the water to the sawmill: also called *gangway.* 2 A corduroy road.

log·wood (lôg'wood', log'-) *n.* 1 A Central American tree (*Haematoxylon campechianum*). 2 Its heavy, reddish wood: used as a dyestuff.

log·work (lôg'wûrk', log'-) *n.* 1 The service of keeping a ship's log. 2 A structure of logs.

-logy *combining form* 1 The science or study of: *biology, conchology.* 2 A list or compilation of: *anthology, martyrology.* [<Gk. *-logia* < *logos* word, study < *legein* speak]

loin (loin) *n.* 1 The part of the body between the lower rib and hip bone. ◆ Collateral adjective: *lumbar.* 2 The forepart of the hindquarters of beef, lamb, veal, etc., with the flank removed. — **to gird one's loins** To prepare for action. [<OF *loigne, logne* <L *lumbus*]

loir (lwär) *n.* A large European dormouse (*Glis glis*). [<F <L *glis, gliris*]

loi·ter (loi'tər) *v.i.* 1 To remain or pause idly or aimlessly; loaf. 2 To travel in a leisurely manner and with frequent pauses; linger on the way; dawdle. — *v.t.* 3 To pass (time) idly: with *away.* [<Du. *leuteren* shake, totter, dawdle]— **loi'ter·er** *n.* — **loi'ter·ing** *adj. & n.*

loll (lol) *v.i.* 1 To lie or lean in a relaxed or languid manner; lounge. 2 To hang loosely; droop. — *v.t.* 3 To permit to droop or hang, as the tongue. — *n.* 1 The act of lolling. 2 An indolent person. [Cf. MDu. *lollen* sleep]— **loll'er** *n.*

lol·li·pop (lol'ē·pop) *n.* A lump or piece of hard candy attached to the end of a stick. Also **lol'ly·pop.** [Prob.<dial. E *lolly* tongue + POP[1]]

Lombardy poplar See under POPLAR.

Lo·mé (lō·mā') A port on the Gulf of Guinea, capital of Togo.

lo·ment (lō'ment) *n. Bot.* An indehiscent legume with constrictions or transverse articulations between the seeds, as a peanut. Also **lo·men·tum** (lō·men'təm). [<L *lomentum* bean meal < *lotum,* pp. of *lavare* wash; because used as a cosmetic wash in antiquity]— **lo'men·ta'ceous** (-tā'shəs) *adj.*

Lon·don (lun'dən), **Jack,** 1876–1916, U.S. author.

Lon·don (lun'dən) 1 A city and administrative county near the mouth of the Thames, England, capital of the United Kingdom and chief city of the British Empire. The **City of London** represents London within its ancient boundaries and is the business and financial center: often called *the City,* 1 square mile. The **County of London** comprises the cities of London and Westminster and 28 metropolitan boroughs; administered by the **London County Council;** 117 square miles. **Greater London,** embracing the City and Metropolitan Police Districts, comprises the County of London, County of Middlesex, and parts of Surrey, Hertford, Essex, and Kent, an area roughly within a radius of 15 miles from Charing Cross; 693 square miles. *Ancient* **Lon·din·i·um** (lən·din'ē·əm). 2 A city on the Thames in SW Ontario, Canada.

lone (lōn) *adj.* 1 Standing by itself; isolated. 2 Unaccompanied; solitary. 3 Single; unmarried; widowed. 4 Lonesome. 5 Lonely; unfrequented. ◆ Homophone: *loan.* [Aphetic var. of ALONE] — **lone'ness** *n.*

lone hand *n.* In some card games, a person playing without aid from a partner; also, the hand he plays.

lone·ly (lōn'lē) *adj.* **·li·er, ·li·est** 1 Deserted or unfrequented by human beings; sequestered: a *lonely* dell or gorge. 2 Solitary or addicted to solitude; living in seclusion. 3 Sad from lack of sympathy or friendship; lonesome; forlorn. See synonyms under SOLITARY. — **lone'li·ly** *adv.* — **lone'li·ness** *n.*

lon·er (lō'nər) *n. U.S. Colloq.* One who prefers to live or work alone.

lone·some (lōn'səm) *adj.* 1 Depressed or sad because of loneliness. 2 Lonely or secluded; so sequestered as to cause uneasiness: a *lonesome* forest. See synonyms under SOLITARY. — **lone'some·ly** *adv.* — **lone'some·ness** *n.*

Lone Star State Nickname of TEXAS.

long[1] (lông, long) *adj.* 1 Having relatively great linear extension; not short: opposed to *short,* and distinguished from *broad* and *wide.* 2 Having relatively great extension in time; lasting. 3 Extended either in space or time to a specified degree: an hour *long,* a foot *long.* 4 Continued in a series to a great extent: a *long* list of grievances. 5 Delayed unexpectedly or unduly; dilatory. 6 Far-reaching; extending far in prospect or into the future; far away in time. 7 Holding for a rise, as stocks. 8 Denoting measure, weight, quantity, etc., in excess of a standard: a *long* five minutes. 9 *Phonet.* a Relatively more prolonged in sound: The sound (ē) is *longer* in *seed* than in *seat.* b Conventionally, indicating the sounds of *a, e, i, o, u* as they are pronounced in *mate, scene, nice, dote, fuse* (in diacritical systems, often written with a macron), as opposed to the "short" sounds of *bat, fed, pit, rot, cup:* in the early Old English period, each of these letters indicated a long or a short vowel sound of similar quality but different duration; this distinction no longer exists and the designation is now an arbitrary one. 10 In classical prosody, requiring relatively more time to pronounce: said of syllables containing a long vowel (*eta, omega,* etc.), a diphthong, or a vowel followed by two consonants or a double consonant. 11 In English prosody, accented. — *n.* 1 The whole extent of a thing; something that is characterized by length: used elliptically. 2 In medieval music, a note equal to four or sometimes six whole notes. 3 A long syllable. 4 *pl.* Those who have purchased securities or commodities and are holding them for an advance in price: opposed to *shorts.* — **the long and the short** The whole; the entire sum and substance. — *adv.* 1 To or at a great extent or period. 2 For a length of time. 3 Through the whole extent or duration. 4 At a point of duration far distant: *long* before or after. — **as** (or **so**) **long as** Under condition that; since. — **before long** Soon. — **for long** For a long time. — **so long** *Colloq.* Good-by. [OE *lang, long*]

long² (lông, long) *v.i.* To have a strong or yearning desire; wish earnestly. [OE *langian* grow long]

long³ (lông, long) *v.i. Obs.* **1** To be fitting or proper. **2** To belong. [Aphetic form of OE *gelang* dependent on]

lon·gan (long'gən) *n.* **1** A Chinese and East Indian tree (*Euphoria longan*) of the soapberry family. **2** Its small, edible fruit, resembling the litchi. [<NL *longanum* <Chinese *lung–yen* dragon's–eye]

lon·ga·nim·i·ty (long'gə-nim'ə-tē) *n.* Disposition to endure patiently. [<LL *longanimitas* <*longus* long + *animus* mind]

long·boat (lông'bōt', long'-) *n. Naut.* The largest boat carried on a sailing vessel.

long·bow (lông'bō', long'-) *n.* A bow of great length drawn and discharged by hand: distinguished from the *crossbow.*—**to draw, use,** or **pull the longbow** To overstate; exaggerate.

LONGBOW AND ARROWS

long·cloth (lông'klôth', long'kloth) *n.* A fine, soft, cotton cloth garment.

long–dis·tance (lông'dis'təns, long'-) *adj. & adv.* **1** Connecting distant places: a *long–distance* telephone. **2** To or from a distant place.

long distance The telephone exchange or operator dealing with other than local or suburban connections.

long–drawn (lông'drôn', long'-) *adj.* Protracted; prolonged; tedious. Also **long'–drawn'–out'** (-out').

longe (lunj, *Fr.* lônzh) *n.* A long rein used in training horses. —*v.t.* **longed, longe·ing** To cause (a horse) to circle at the end of a longe. Also spelled *lunge.* [<F]

long–eared owl (lông'ird', long'-) See under OWL.

lon·ge·ron (lon'jər·ən, *Fr.* lônzh·rôn) *n. Aeron.* A main longitudinal member of the body of an airplane. [<F]

lon·gev·i·ty (lon·jev'ə·tē) *n.* **1** Great age, or length of life. **2** The tendency to live long. [<L *longaevitas, -tatis* < *longaevus* long–lived < *longus* long + *aevum* age]

longevity pay Additional pay for long service given to members of the U.S. armed forces. Also called *fogy pay.*

long face An expression of the face indicating exaggerated sadness. —**long–faced** (lông'fāst', long'-) *adj.*

Long·fel·low (lông'fel·ō, long'-), **Henry Wadsworth,** 1807–82, U.S. poet.

long–hand (lông'hand', long'-) *n.* Ordinary handwriting with the words spelled in full: distinguished from *shorthand.*

long·head (lông'hed', long'-) *n.* A dolichocephalic person. —**long'head'ed** *adj.* —**long'head'ed·ly** *adv.* —**long'head'ed·ness** *n.*

long head *Colloq.* Shrewdness; foresight; common sense. —**long'–head'ed** *adj.*

long·horn (lông'-hôrn', long'-) *n.* **1** One of a breed of domestic cattle with long horns: also Texas longhorn. **2** *Entomol.* A longicorn beetle. **3** In the western United States, a seasoned inhabitant who knows the ways and cannot be tricked: opposed to *tenderfoot.*

TEXAS LONGHORN

long house Among North American Indians, especially the Iroquois, a council house or community dwelling sometimes 100 to 200 feet long.

longi– *combining form* Long: *longipennate.* [<L *longus* long]

lon·gi·corn (lon'ji·kôrn) *n. adj.* **1** Having long antennae. **2** Of or pertaining to a family of beetles (*Cerambycidae*), usually with long, filiform antennae: the larvae are woodborers. [<LONGI- + L *cornu* horn]

lon·gi·lin·e·al (lon'ji·lin'ē·əl) *adj. Anthropol.* Designating a physical type characterized by length and relative slenderness of body; dolichomorphic: opposed to *brevilineal.*

long·ing (lông'ing, long'-) *n.* An eager, strong, or earnest craving. See synonyms under APPETITE, DESIRE. —**long'ing·ly** *adv.*

lon·gi·pen·nate (lon'ji·pen'āt) *adj. Ornithol.* Having long wings or feathers, as certain birds. Also **lon'gi·pen'nine** (-pen'ēn, -īn).

lon·gi·ros·tral (lon'ji·ros'trəl) *adj. Ornithol.* Having a long bill, as the ibis and related birds. Also **lon'gi·ros'trate** (-trāt, -trit).

lon·gi·tude (lon'ji·tōōd, -tyōōd) *n.* **1** *Geog.* Distance east or west on the earth's surface, measured by the angle which the meridian through a place makes with some standard meridian, as that of Greenwich or Paris. Longitude may be expressed either in time (**longitude in time**) or in degrees (**longitude in arc**). **2** *Astron.* The angular distance from the vernal equinox to the intersection with the ecliptic of the perpendicular from a heavenly body: usually termed **celestial longitude**, and distinguished as *geocentric* when the earth's center is assumed as the central point, and *heliocentric* when the sun's center is taken as the central point. **3** *Math.* The angle the radius vector makes with the initial meridian axis in the spherical coordinate system. [<F <L *longitudo* <*longus* long]

lon·gi·tu·di·nal (lon'ji·tōō'də·nəl, -tyōō'-) *adj.* **1** Pertaining to longitude or length. **2** Running lengthwise. **3** *Biol.* Of, pertaining to, or extending along the cephalocaudal axis. —**lon'gi·tu'di·nal·ly** *adv.*

long johns (jonz) *Slang* Ankle–length, fitted underdrawers of knitted fabric.

long jump In sports, the broad jump.

long·leaf pine (lông'lēf', long'-) The southern yellow or Georgia pine (*Pinus palustris*), important as a source of turpentine.

long–lived (lông'livd', -livd', long'-) *adj.* Having a long life. —**long'–lived'ness** *n.*

long measure Linear measure.

long moss Spanish moss.

long·neck (lông'nek', long'-) *n.* The pintail duck.

long–range (lông'rānj', long'-) *adj.* **1** Designed to shoot or move over distances: a *long–range* projectile. **2** Taking account of, or extending over, a long span of future time: *long–range* plans.

long run An extended series of occurrences. —**in the long run** After the whole course of events; eventually.

long·shanks (lông'shangks', long'-) *n.* The black–necked stilt (*Himantopus mexicanus*).

long·shore (lông'shôr', -shōr', long'-) *adj.* Belonging, living, or working along a shore or waterside. [Aphetic var. of ALONGSHORE]

long·shore·man (lông'shôr'mən, -shōr'-, long'-) *n. pl.* **·men** (-mən) One who loads and unloads vessels; a stevedore.

long shot *Colloq.* **1** A bet made with little chance of winning and hence at great odds. **2** Something backed at great odds, as a horse. —**not by a long shot** Decidedly not; not at all.

long–sight·ed (lông'sī'tid, long'-) *adj.* **1** Seeing far or to a great distance; sagacious. **2** Far–sighted; hypermetropic. —**long'–sight'·ed·ness** *n.*

long·some (lông'səm, long'-) *adj.* Very long; hence, irksome; tedious. [OE *langsum*]

long·spur (lông'spûr', long'-) *n.* A fringilline bird (genera *Calcarius* and *Rhynchophanes*) with elongated hind claws, found in the arctic regions and Great Plains of North America.

long–sta·ple (lông'stā'pəl, long'-) *adj.* Having a long fiber: said of cotton.

long–suf·fer·ing (lông'suf'ər·ing, long'-) *adj.* Enduring injuries for a long time; patient; forbearing. —*n.* Patient and forbearing endurance of injuries or offense: also **long'–suf'fer·ance.**

long–wind·ed (lông'win'did, long'-) *adj.* Continuing for a long time in speaking or writing; hence, tedious; lacking conciseness. —**long'wind'ed·ly** *adv.* —**long'wind'ed·ness** *n.*

long·wise (lông'wīz', long'-) *adv.* Lengthwise. Also **long'ways'** (-wāz').

loo·fah (lōō'fə) *n.* **1** Any of a genus (*Luffa*) of Old World, tropical, cucurbitaceous herbs with the male flowers in racemes and the female solitary. **2** The ovate or oblong fruit of this herb, fibrous within, and often used to filter oil and grease from condensed steam, as well as for cleaning and scrubbing. Also **loo'fa.** Also called *dishcloth gourd, vegetable sponge, luffa.* [<Arabic *lūfah*]

look (lōōk) *v.i.* **1** To direct the eyes toward something in order to see. **2** To direct or turn one's attention or consideration. **3** To search; make examination or inquiry: to *look* through a desk. **4** To appear to be; seem: He *looks* trustworthy. **5** To have a specified direction or view; front: This house *looks* over the park. **6** To expect: with an infinitive: I didn't *look* to find you home. —*v.t.* **7** To turn or direct the eyes upon: He *looked* her up and down. **8** To express by looks: to *look* one's hatred. **9** To give the appearance of being (a specified age). **10** To influence by looks: to *look* someone into silence. —**to look after** To take care of. —**to look daggers (at)** To scowl; glare (at). —**to look down on** To regard condescendingly or contemptuously. —**to look for 1** To search for. **2** To expect. —**to look forward to** To anticipate pleasurably. —**to look in** (or **in on**) To make a short visit to. —**to look into** To examine; make inquiry. —**to look like 1** To have the appearance of being; resemble. **2** To indicate the probability of: It *looks like* rain. —**to look on 1** To be a spectator. **2** To consider; regard. —**to look out** To be on the watch; take care. —**to look over** To examine; scrutinize. —**to look to 1** To attend to. **2** To turn to, as for help, advice, etc. —**to look up 1** To search for and find, as in a file, dictionary, etc. **2** *Colloq.* To discover the whereabouts of and make a visit to. **3** *Colloq.* To improve; become better. —**to look up to** To have respect for. —*n.* **1** The act of looking or seeing with voluntary attention: I will take a *look* at it. **2** *pl.* The appearance of the face or figure; cast of countenance. **3** Aspect; expression. **4** Appearance in general, either to the eye or understanding: I do not like the *look* of the thing. See synonyms under AIR, MANNER. [OE *locian*]

  Synonyms (verb): behold, contemplate, descry, discern, gaze, glance, inspect, regard, scan, see, stare, survey, view, watch. To *see* is simply to become conscious of an object of vision; to *look* is to make a conscious and direct endeavor to *see.* To *behold* is to fix the sight and the mind with distinctness and consideration upon something that has come to be clearly before the eyes. We may *look* without *seeing,* as in darkness, and we may *see* without *looking,* as in the case of a flash of lightning. To *gaze* is to *look* intently, long, and steadily. To *glance* is to *look* casually or momentarily. To *stare* is to *look* with a fixed intensity. To *scan* is to *look* at minutely, to note every visible feature. To *inspect* is to go below the surface, study item by item. *View* and *survey* are comprehensive, *survey* expressing the greater exactness of measurement. *Watch* brings in the element of time; we *watch* for a movement or change.

look·er (lōōk'ər) *n.* **1** One who looks or watches. **2** *U.S. Slang* A handsome or good–looking person.

look·er–on (lōōk'ər·on') *n. pl.* **look·ers–on** A spectator; onlooker.

look·ing–glass (lōōk'ing·glas', -gläs') *n.* A mirror.

look·out (lōōk'out') *n.* **1** The act of watching or looking out; especially, careful or alert watchfulness. **2** A post of observation; also, the person or the group on watch in or at such a post. **3** One engaged in the U.S. Forest Service to detect fires. **4** One assigned to watch for enemy aircraft, tanks, or troop movements. **5** Prospect; outlook; chances of good or bad to come: a good *look–out* ahead. **6** *Colloq.* Concern; care: It's your own *look-out.*

loom¹ (lōōm) *v.i.* **1** To appear or come into view indistinctly, as from below the horizon or through a mist, especially so as to seem large or ominous. **2** To appear to the mind as threatening or portentous: Great difficulties *loom* ahead. **3** To shine. —*n.* A gradual, vague appearance of something, as of a ship in the fog. [Origin uncertain. Cf. Sw. *loma* move slowly (toward).]

loom² (lōōm) *n.* **1** A machine in which yarn or thread is woven into a fabric, by the crossing of threads called chain or warp, running lengthwise, with others called weft, woof, or filling. See illustration on page following. **2** The art or technique of working with a loom; the occupation of a weaver; weaving. **3** *Naut.* **a** The shaft of an oar, as distinguished from the blade. **b** That part of an oar between the rowlock and the handle. [OE *gelōma* tool]

loom³ (lōōm) *n.* **1** A guillemot. **2** A loon (def. 1). [<ON *lomr*]

loom·ing (lōō'ming) *n.* A mirage that elevates and elongates a figure, especially when viewed across the water.

loon¹ (lōōn) *n.* **1** A diving, fish-eating waterfowl (genus *Gavia*), with short tail feathers and webbed feet. **2** A guillemot. — **common loon** The great northern diver (*Gavia immer*). [See LOOM³]

LOON
(Length 31 to 36 inches)

loon² (lōōn) *n.* **1** A worthless, demented, or stupid person; a lout; dolt. **2** A rogue; scamp. **3** *Obs.* A menial. Also *Obs. & Scot. loun, lown.* [Cf. Du. *loen* stupid fellow G *lümmel* lout]

HAND LOOM
The two sets of warp threads (*a, a*), alternately raised and lowered by the heddle (*b, b*), form between them a tunnel of threads called the shed (*c*). Through this shed the shuttle (*d*) is passed, carrying across the weft thread (*e*), which is beaten against the finished fabric by the movable comblike frame or reed (*f*). When the heddle is shifted, the two sets of warp reverse position, binding the weft into the fabric and opening another shed.

loop¹ (lōōp) *n.* **1** A fold or doubling, as of a string or rope, so as to form an eye or a bend through which something may be passed; a noose; bight; hence, a curve or bend of any kind. **2** A stitch used in crocheting and knitting. **3** *Electr.* A complete magnetic or electrical circuit. **4** A curve in a railroad, carried completely around to reach a different level; also, a branch from the main line, returning to it after making a detour. **5** One of the basic patterns by which fingerprints are classified and identified, consisting of one or more ridges whose terminal points are on or toward the same side of the design. **6** *Aeron.* A complete, vertical, circular turn made by an airplane in flight. **7** *Physics* The part of a vibrating string, column of air, or standing wave system which is between two nodes; an antinode. — **to loop the loop** To make a vertical, circular turn, as an airplane in flight. — *v.t.* **1** To form a loop or loops in or of. **2** To fasten, connect, or encircle by means of a loop or loops. **3** *Aeron.* To fly (an aircraft) in a loop or loops. — *v.i.* **4** To make a loop or loops. **5** To move by forming loops, as a measuring worm. [Cf. Irish *lub* loop]

loop² (lōōp) *n.* Iron of pasty consistency ready for rolling. [<F *loupe*]

loop³ (lōōp) *n.* Any small window or aperture; a loophole. [Cf. MDu. *lupen* lie in wait, peer]

loop·er (lōō'pər) *n.* **1** A bodkinlike instrument for making loops. **2** A measuring worm.

loop·hole (lōōp'hōl') *n.* **1** A narrow opening through which small arms are fired. **2** A means of escape, or place of observation. — *v.t.* ·**holed**, ·**hol·ing** To furnish with loopholes. [<LOOP² + HOLE]

loose (lōōs) *adj.* **loos·er**, **loos·est** **1** Not fastened or confined; not bound or attached; unbound or untied; freed from normal bonds or restraint: *loose* tresses; to be *loose* from old habits. **2** Lax in power, character, quality, principle, or conduct; careless; slovenly; slack; relaxed; wanton; dissolute: *loose* bond; *loose* conduct. **3** Not precise or exact; vague; indefinite; rambling; unconnected: *loose* reasoning; a *loose* style. **4** Not close, compact, dense, tight, or crowded; lacking union of parts; slackly joined or tied; not compact in frame: a *loose* knot or bond; a *loose* array; a fabric of *loose* texture; a man of *loose* build. **5** Not tight; open: said of a cough when expectoration is without difficulty, or of an abnormal laxity of the bowels. **6** Designating a stable or stall in which the animals are kept untied. See synonyms under IMMORAL, VAGUE, VULGAR, WANTON. — **on the loose** At liberty; at large; unconfined. — *adv.* In a loose manner: to play fast and loose. — *v.* **loosed**, **loos·ing** *v.t.* **1** To set free, as from bondage, penalty, etc. **2** To untie or undo, as a knot or rope. **3** To make less tight; loosen; slacken. **4** *Naut.* To cast off; release, as a boat from its moorings. **5** To let fly; shoot or discharge, as arrows. — *v.i.* **6** To become loose. **7** To loose something. [<ON *lauss*] — **loose'ly** *adv.* — **loose'ness** *n.*

loos·en (lōō'sən) *v.t.* **1** To untie or undo, as bonds or chains. **2** To set free; release. **3** To make less tight, firm, or compact: to *loosen* the stones of a wall. **4** To effect laxity in the action of (the bowels). **5** To relax the strictness of, as discipline. — *v.i.* **6** To become loose or looser. See synonyms under RELAX. — **loos'en·er** *n.*

loose·strife (lōōs'strīf') *n.* **1** Any one of various plants, mostly with four-cornered branches and regular or irregular flowers, as the **common loosestrife** (*Lysimachia vulgaris*) of the primrose family or the **purple loosestrife** (*Lythrum salicaria*) of the family Lythraceae. **2** Any plant of the loosestrife family. [<LOOSE + STRIFE; direct trans. of L *lysimachia* <Gk. *lysimachion* <*lyein* loose + *mache* battle]

loot (lōōt) *v.t.* **1** To plunder, as a conquered city; pillage. **2** To carry off as plunder. — *v.i.* **3** To engage in plundering. — *n.* **1** Booty taken from a sacked city by a victorious army; plunder. **2** Anything unlawfully taken, as by one in an official position. [<Hind. *lūt* <Skt. *luṇṭ*] — **loot'er** *n.*

looves (lōōvz) Plural of LOOF.

lop¹ (lop) *v.t.* **lopped**, **lop·ping** **1** To cut or trim the branches, twigs, etc., from, as a tree. **2** To cut off, as branches or twigs. — *n.* A cutting from a tree; specifically, the trimmings or small twigs and branches not measured as timber; fagot. [Origin unknown] — **lop'per** *n.*

lop² (lop) *v.* **lopped**, **lop·ping** *v.i.* **1** To droop or hang down. **2** To hang or move about in an awkward or slouching manner. — *v.t.* **3** To permit to droop or hang down. — *adj.* Drooping. [Origin unknown]

lope (lōp) *v.t. & v.i.* **loped**, **lop·ing** To run or cause to run with a steady, swinging stride. — *n.* A slow, easy gallop. [<ON *hlaupa* leap, run] — **lop'er** *n.*

lo·pho·branch (lō'fō·brangk, lof'ō-) *adj.* Of or pertaining to a division of teleost fishes (*Lophobranchii*), especially an order with imperfect branchial arches and tuftlike gill elements, including pipefishes and sea horses. — *n.* One of the *Lophobranchii*. [<LOPHO- + Gk. *branchion* gill] — **lo'pho·bran'chi·ate** (-kē·it, -āt) *adj. & n.*

lo·phot·ri·chous (lō·fot'ri·kəs) *adj. Zool.* Having a tuft of cilia at one pole of the cell: characteristic of some micro-organisms. Also **lo·pho·trich·ic** (lō'fō·trik'ik, lof'ō-). [<LOPHO- + Gk. *thrix, trichos* hair]

lop·py (lop'ē) *adj.* **·pi·er**, **·pi·est** **1** Limp; pendulous; hanging down. **2** Choppy: said of

water.

lo·qua·cious (lō·kwā'shəs) *adj.* Given to continual talking; chattering. See synonyms under GARRULOUS. [<L *loquax, loquacis* <*loqui* talk] — **lo·qua'cious·ly** *adv.* — **lo·qua'cious·ness, lo·quac'i·ty** (lō·kwas'ə·tē) *n.*

lo·quat (lō'kwot, -kwat) *n.* **1** A low-growing, pomaceous tree (*Eriobotrya japonica*), cultivated for its fruit, a small, yellow pome. **2** This fruit. [Cantonese alter. of Chinese *lu-chü* rush orange]

lord (lôrd) *n.* **1** One possessing supreme power and authority; a ruler. **2** A title of respect, formerly given to any superior, as by a wife to a husband: still sometimes humorously so used. **3** In feudal law, the owner of a manor under grant from the crown; a landlord. **4** A title of honor or nobility in Great Britain, given generally to men noble by birth or ennobled by patent. This includes **lords spiritual** (archbishops and bishops), who are members of the House of Lords, and also **lords temporal**: marquises, earls, viscounts, and barons. The formal titles are as follows: *Baron* X, the *Marquis* of X, the *Earl* of X, *Viscount* X; informally all are addressed *Lord* X. The given name is mentioned only to distinguish holders of the same title at different periods. Where the names are homonymous, the locality of the peerage is stated, as *Viscount Grey of Fallodon*, who was spoken of as *Lord Grey*. The title is given by courtesy to the eldest sons of dukes, marquises, and earls, who each take by courtesy also an inferior title held by the father, frequently the second title, and to the younger sons of dukes and marquises, prefixed to their Christian name and surname; in these cases the Christian names must always be mentioned, coming after "Lord," to distinguish among brothers: *Lord* Robert Cecil. It is also a title of office, such as the *Lord* Lieutenant, the *Lord* Chancellor, *Lord* Privy Seal, *Lords* of the Treasury, Admiralty, Bedchamber. **5** In astrology, a controlling planet. — *v.t.* To invest with the title of lord. — **to lord it** (**over**) To act in a domineering or arrogant manner. [OE *hlāford, hlāfweard*, lit., bread keeper <*hlāf* loaf + *weard* keeper, ward] — **lord'less** *adj.* — **lord'like** *adj.*

Lord (lôrd) **1** God. **2** Jesus Christ. Also *Our Lord.*

lord·ling (lôrd'ling) *n.* A little lord; petty chieftain: generally used contemptuously.

lord·ly (lôrd'lē) *adj.* **·li·er, ·li·est** **1** Of, pertaining to, or like a lord; becoming a lord; lofty; noble; insisting on compliance: a *lordly* presence. **2** Characterized by undue loftiness; insolent: a *lordly* air or demeanor. See synonyms under IMPERIOUS. — *adv.* In a lordly manner. — **lord'li·ness** *n.*

Lord of Hosts Jehovah; God.

lor·do·sis (lôr·dō'sis) *n. Pathol.* Inward curvature of a bone; specifically, curvature of the spine with the convexity forward. Also **lor·do'ma** (-mə). [<NL <Gk. *lordōsis* <*lordos* bent backward] — **lor·dot'ic** (-dot'ik) *adj.*

lords–and–la·dies (lôrdz'ənd·lā'dēz) *n.* **1** The cuckoo pint or wakerobin. **2** The jack-in-the-pulpit.

lord·ship (lôrd'ship) *n.* **1** The state or quality of a lord; hence, the title by which noblemen (excluding dukes), bishops, and judges in England are addressed or spoken of, preceded by *your* or *his*. **2** The jurisdiction of a lord; seigniory; domain; manor. **3** The dominion, power, or authority of a lord; hence, sovereignty in general; supremacy. [OE *hlafordscipe*. See LORD.]

Lord's Prayer The prayer taught by Jesus to his disciples. *Matt.* vi 9–13.

Lord's Supper *Eccl.* **1** The Eucharist; the Holy Communion. **2** The Last Supper.

Lord's Table The altar or table on which the elements of the Eucharist are laid during and after consecration.

lore¹ (lôr, lōr) *n.* **1** The body of traditional, popular, often anecdotal knowledge about a particular subject. **2** Learning or erudition. **3** *Archaic* Any special instruction; also, a lesson or the act of teaching. See synonyms under LEARNING, WISDOM. [OE *lar*]

lore² (lôr, lōr) *n.* **1** *Ornithol.* The side of a bird's head between the eye and the beak. **2** *Zool.* A corresponding part in fishes and reptiles. [<L *lorum* strap, thong]

lor·gnette (lôr′nyet′) *n.* **1** A pair of eyeglasses with an ornamental handle into which they may be folded when not in use. **2** A long-handled opera glass. [<F <*lorgner* spy, peer <OF *lorgne* squinting]

lo·ri·ca (lō·rī′kə) *n. pl.* **·cae** (-kē) **1** An ancient Roman cuirass or corselet. **2** *Zool.* A protective covering or shell, as in infusorians or rotifers. [<L <*lorum* thong]

lor·i·cate (lôr′ə·kāt, lôr′-) *v.t.* **·cat·ed**, **·cat·ing** To cover with a protective coating. —*adj.* Covered with a lorica or shell. [<L *loricatus,* pp. of *loricare* clothe in mail, harness <*lorica* corselet] —**lor′i·ca′tion** *n.*

lor·i·keet (lôr′ə·kēt, lôr′-) *n.* Any of certain small Polynesian parrots resembling the lory. [<LORY + (PARA)KEET]

lo·ris (lôr′is, lō′ris) *n.* A small, arboreal, nocturnal, Asian lemur (genera *Loris* and *Nycticebus*), having the index finger small. *Loris gracilis* is the **slender loris** of southern India and Ceylon; *Nycticebus tardigradus* is the **slow lemur** or **East Indian loris**. [<F <Flemish *lorrias* lazy, ′the sloth]

lor·ry (lôr′ē, lor′ē) *n. pl.* **·ries** **1** A low, four-wheeled, platform wagon. **2** *Brit.* A similar motor vehicle for carrying heavy loads; a truck. [Prob. dial. E *lurry* pull, tug]

lo·ry (lō′rē, lôr′ē) *n. pl.* **·ries** Any of certain parrots of Australasia (genera *Lorius, Apnosmictus,* and others) with brilliant, scarlet plumage, long bill, and tongue ending in a form of brush. [<Malay *lūrī*]

Lo·schmidt number (lō′shmit) *Physics* **1** The number of molecules in 1 cubic centimeter of an ideal gas at 0°C. and normal atmospheric pressure, equal to 2.687×10^{19}. **2** The Avogadro number. [after Joseph *Loschmidt,* 1821–95, Austrian physicist]

lose (lōōz) *v.* **lost, los·ing** *v.t.* **1** To part with, as by accident or negligence, and be unable to find; mislay. **2** To fail to keep, control, or maintain: to *lose* one's footing; to *lose* one's mind. **3** To be deprived of; suffer the loss of, as by accident, death, removal, etc.: to *lose* a leg. **4** To fail to gain or win: to *lose* a prize; to *lose* a battle. **5** To fail to utilize or take advantage of; miss: to *lose* a chance. **6** To fail to see or hear; miss: I *lost* not a word of the speech. **7** To fail to keep in sight, memory, etc.: We *lost* him in the crowd. **8** To cease to have: to *lose* one's sense of duty. **9** To squander; waste, as time. **10** To wander from so as to be unable to find: to *lose* the path. **11** To outdistance or elude, as runners or pursuers. **12** To cause the loss of: His rashness *lost* him his opportunity. **13** To bring to destruction or death; ruin: usually in the passive: All hands were *lost.* —*v.i.* **14** To suffer loss. **15** To be defeated. —**to lose heart** To become discouraged. —**to lose oneself** **1** To lose one's way, as in a wood. **2** To disappear or hide: The thief *lost himself* in the crowd. **3** To become engrossed. **4** To become confused or bewildered. —**to lose one's heart (to)** To fall in love (with). —**to lose out** *U.S. Colloq.* To fail or be defeated. —**to lose sight of** **1** To fail to keep in sight. **2** To take no notice of; ignore or forget. [Fusion of OE *losian* be lost and *lēosan* lose] —**los′a·ble** *adj.*

lo·sel (lō′zəl, lōō′zəl, loz′əl) *adj.* Inclined to idleness and waste. —*n.* A worthless fellow. [OE *losen,* pp. of *losian* be lost]

los·er (lōō′zər) *n.* One who loses or fails to win in any transaction; a defeated contestant.

los·ing (lōō′zing) *n.* **1** The act or fact of letting go, missing, lacking, or being deprived. **2** *pl.* Money lost, especially in gambling. —*adj.* **1** That incurs loss: a *losing* business. **2** Not winning; defeated: the *losing* team.

loss (lôs, los) *n.* **1** The act or state of losing; failure to keep or win; privation: *loss* of fortune or friends. **2** *Usually pl.* That which is lost, or its amount: His *losses* were great; The *losses* of the army were severe. **3** The state of being lost, or of having suffered destruction: the *loss* of a ship at sea. **4** Useless application; futile expenditure; waste. **5** Injury or diminution of value within the limits provided in an insurance policy, or the sum payable on that account. **6** *Physics*

That part of electrical or mechanical energy which is expended in overcoming friction, etc., and from which no productive work is obtained. —**at a loss** **1** At so low a price as to result in a loss. **2** In confusion or doubt; perplexed. —**dead loss** An irremediable loss; one without hope of salvage, insurance, or any mitigation. —**to bear a loss** **1** To sustain a loss bravely. **2** To make good a loss. [OE *los*]
Synonyms: damage, defeat, deprivation, destruction, detriment, disadvantage, failure, forfeiture, injury, misfortune, privation, waste. See INJURY.

lost (lôst, lost) *adj.* **1** Not to be found or recovered; parted with; missing; left, as by accident, in a forgotten place: *lost* goods or friends. **2** Not won, gained, used, or enjoyed; missed; wasted: *lost* opportunity. **3** Ruined physically, morally, or spiritually; damned; destroyed. **4** Having wandered from the way; also, abstracted: *lost* in thought; bewildered; perplexed. **5** No longer known or used: a *lost* art. —**to be lost upon** (or on) To have no effect upon (a person).

lost cause Any cause that cannot possibly succeed; specifically, in American history, the cause of the Confederate States.

lost motion Slackness in a mechanical connection resulting in an appreciable difference between the travel of the driving and the driven elements.

lost tribes Those members of the ten northern, or Israelitish, Hebrew tribes that were taken into Assyrian captivity (II *Kings* xvii 6), believed never to have returned.

lot (lot) *n.* **1** Anything, as a die or piece of paper, used in determining something by chance; also, the fact or process of deciding something in such manner. **2** The share that comes to one as the result of drawing lots. **3** The part in life that comes to one without his planning; chance; fate. **4** A collection or parcel of things separated from others: The auctioneer sold the goods in ten *lots.* **5** A parcel or quantity of land, as surveyed and apportioned for sale or other special purpose: a city *lot,* a wood *lot.* **6** *Colloq.* A kind of person: He is a bad *lot.* **7** *Often pl. Colloq.* A great quantity or amount; a number of things, collectively: a *lot* of money, *lots* of trouble. ◆ *Lot* or *lots* is construed as a singular if attributed to a singular word, plural if to a plural word: A *lot* of money was hidden, but, A *lot* of diamonds were hidden. **8** A proportion of taxes allotted to one. **9** A motion-picture studio and the space it uses. See synonyms under FLOCK. —*adv.* Very much: a *lot* worse. —*v.* **lot·ted, lot·ting** *v.t.* **1** To divide, as land, into lots. **2** To apportion by lots; allot. —*v.i.* **3** To cast lots. [OE *hlot*]

lo·tah (lō′tə) *n. Anglo-Indian* A small, round pot, usually of brass or copper, used in India for drinking and ablution. Also **lo′ta.**

loth (lōth) *adj.* Loath.

lo·tion (lō′shən) *n.* **1** A medicated liquid for the skin, eyes, or any diseased or bruised part, for cleansing or healing. **2** *Archaic* A bathing òr washing. [<L *lotio, -onis* washing <*lavare* wash]

lot·ter·y (lot′ər·ē) *n. pl.* **·ter·ies** A distribution of, or scheme for distributing, prizes as determined by chance or lot, especially where such chances are allotted by sale of tickets; hence, any chance disposition of any matter. [<Ital. *lotteria* <*lotto* lottery, lot <F *lot* <Gmc.]

lot·to (lot′ō) *n.* A game of chance played with cards and disks: also called *keno.* Also **lo·to** (lō′tō). [<Ital. See LOTTERY.]

lo·tus (lō′təs) *n.* **1** One of various Old World plants of the waterlily family, noted for their large floating leaves and showy flowers; especially, the **white** and **blue lotus** of the Nile (respectively *Nymphaea lotus,* and *N. caerulea*); also, the

LOTUS

lotus tree The common jujube.

loud (loud) *adj.* **1** Striking the auditory nerves with great force; having great volume or intensity of sound; noisy. **2** Making a great noise. **3** Pressing or urgent; clamorous: a *loud* demand. **4** Conspicuous or ostentatious without taste or refinement; vulgarly showy; flashy. —*adv.* With loudness; loudly. [OE *hlūd*] —**loud′ly** *adv.* —**loud′ness** *n.*

loud·en (loud′n) *v.t. & v.i.* To make or become louder.

loud–mouthed (loud′mouthd, -moutht′) *adj.* Possessed of a loud voice; offensively clamorous or talkative.

loud·speak·er (loud′spē′kər) *n.* An electromagnetic device for amplifying the sounds transmitted by radio, public–address system, or the like.

Lou·is (lōō′is), Joe, born 1914, U.S. heavyweight boxing champion 1937–49; real name *Joseph Louis Barrow.*

Lou·i·si·an·a (lōō·ē′zē·an′ə) One of the United States, fronting south on the Gulf of Mexico; 48,523 square miles; capital, Baton Rouge; comprised of portions of West Florida and of the Louisiana Purchase of 1803, it entered the Union April 8, 1812; nickname, *Pelican State* or *Creole State:* abbr. LA —**Lou·i′si·an′an, Lou·i′si·an·an** *adj. & n.*

Louisiana Purchase The French colonial territory in west central North America, purchased from France by the United States in 1803 for $15,000,000: the land between the Mississippi River and the Rocky Mountains, the Gulf of Mexico and Canada.

Lou·is–Qua·torze (lōō′ē·ká·tôrz′) *adj.* Designating the style of architecture, interior decoration, and furniture which characterized the period of Louis XIV in France (1643–1715), marked by baroque architectural forms and ornate and grandiose decorative treatment employing animal and mythological forms richly carved. [<F]

Lou·is–Quinze (lōō′ē·kaṅz′) *adj.* Designating the style of architecture, decoration, and furniture characteristic of the period of Louis XV (1715–74), marked by the culmination of the rococo as expressed in flowing lines, rounded forms, and graceful shell, flower, and other ornaments. [<F]

Lou·is–Seize (lōō′ē·sez′) *adj.* Designating the style of architecture, decoration, and furniture which characterized the period of Louis XVI (1774–93): a reaction against the Louis–Quinze period, marked by simple, rectilinear forms, and using symmetrical Greco–Roman wreaths, birds, etc., as ornaments, or Greek egg–and–anchor or leaf motifs, achieving a plain internal decoration. [<F]

Lou·is–Treize (lōō′ē·trez′) *adj.* Designating the style of architecture, decoration, and furniture which characterized the period of Louis XIII (1610–43), marked by Renaissance forms, rich inlaid ornaments, geometric panels and deep moldings, and carving in the Flemish style. [<F]

PERIOD STYLES ILLUSTRATED BY CHAIR LEGS
a. Louis XIII. *b.* Louis XIV. *c.* Louis XV.
d. Louis XVI.

loun (loun) *adj. Scot.* Lown.
lounge (lounj) *v.* **lounged, loung·ing** *v.i.* **1** To

lie, lean, move, etc., in an idle or lazy manner. **2** To pass time indolently. — *v.t.* **3** To spend or pass indolently, as time. — *n.* **1** act of lounging. **2** A room in a hotel, club, etc., for lounging. **3** A couch with little or no back; any sofa. [Origin unknown]

loung·er (loun'jər) *n.* One who lounges; an idler.

loup (lōō) *n.* A light mask or half–mask made of silk: worn at masquerades. [<F]

loupe (lōōp) *n.* A small magnifying glass; a lens, especially one adapted for the use of jewelers and watchmakers. [<F]

loup·ga·rou (lōō·gá·rōō′) *n.* *pl.* **loups·ga·rous** (lōō·gá·rōō′) A werewolf. [<F *loup* wolf (<L *lupus*) + *garou* were·wolf <Gmc.]

LOUPE

Lou·ren·ço Mar·ques (lō·ren′sō mär′kəs, *Pg.* lō·rän′sōō mär′kish) A port on Delagoa Bay, capital of Mozambique.

louse (lous) *n.* *pl.* **lice** (līs) **1** A small, flat–bodied, wingless insect (order *Anoplura*) living as an external parasite on birds or mammals, especially the crab louse (*Phthirus pubis*) and the human body louse (genus *Pediculus*). **2** One of various other insects parasitic on other animals or plants, as the biting bird louse (order *Mallophaga*) and the plant louse. For illustrations see under INSECTS (injurious). **3** *Slang* A contemptible person. — *v.t. & v.i.* *U.S. Slang* To ruin; bungle: with *up.* [OE *lūs*]

louse·wort (lous′wûrt′) *n.* Any one of a genus (*Pedicularis*) of scrophulariaceous woodland herbs; wood betony.

lous·y (lou′zē) *adj.* **lous·i·er, lous·i·est 1** Infested with lice; pedicular. **2** *Slang* Dirty. **3** *Slang* Contemptible; foul; mean. **4** *Slang* Having plenty (of): usually with *with*: *lousy* with money.

lout[1] (lout) *n.* An awkward fellow; clown; boor. [? <ON *lutr* bent, stooped]

lout[2] (lout) *v.i. Obs.* To bow or curtsy; bend; stoop. [OE *lūtan* bow]

lout·ish (lou′tish) *adj.* Clumsy; awkward; boorish. — **lout′ish·ly** *adv.* — **lout′ish·ness** *n.*

lou·ver (lōō′vər) *n.* **1** A window, as in a belfry tower, designed for ventilation and having slats (**louver boards**) sloped to keep out the rain: also **lou′ver–win′dow** (-win′dō). **2** A lantern-like cupola or turret on the roof of a medieval dwelling. **3** Any of several narrow openings, or the slatted piece having these, serving as outlets for heated air. [<OF *lover*]

LOUVER
a. Construction set in gable (*b*).

Lou·vre (lōō′vr′) An ancient royal palace in Paris, made a museum in the 18th century.

lov·a·ble (luv′ə·bəl) *adj.* Worthy of love; amiable; also, evoking love. See synonyms under AMIABLE, LOVELY. Also **love′a·ble.** — **lov′a·bil′i·ty, lov′a·ble·ness** *n.* — **lov′a·bly** *adv.*

lov·age (luv′ij) *n.* A European herb (*Levisticum officinale*) of the parsley family: used sometimes as a domestic remedy. [<OF *luvesche* <LL *levisticum*, alter. of L *ligusticum*, neut. of *ligusticus* Ligurian]

love (luv) *n.* **1** A strong, complex emotion or feeling causing one to appreciate, delight in, and crave the presence or possession of another and to please or promote the welfare of the other; devoted affection or attachment. **2** Specifically, such feeling between husband and wife or lover and sweetheart. **3** One who is beloved; a sweetheart. **4** Sexual passion, or the gratification of it. **5** A very great interest or fondness: *love* of learning. **6** In tennis, a score of nothing. — **for the love of** For the sake of; in loving remembrance of: used in adjurations, solemn oaths, etc. — **for love or money** For any consideration; under any circumstances. — **in love** Experiencing love; enamored. — **no love lost between** No affection or liking between. — *v.* **loved, lov·ing** *v.t.* **1** To feel love or affection for. **2** To take pleasure or delight in; like very much. **3** To caress. — *v.i.* **4** To feel love, especially for one of the opposite sex; be in love. See synonyms under ADMIRE, LIKE. [OE *lufu*]

Synonyms (*noun*): affection, attachment, attraction, charity, devotion, esteem, feeling, fondness, friendship, liking, passion, regard, tenderness. *Affection* is kindly feeling, deep, tender, and constant, going out to some person or object, being less fervent and ardent than *love.* *Love* is the yearning or outgoing of soul toward something that is regarded as excellent, beautiful, or desirable; *love* may be briefly defined as strong and absorbing *affection* for and *attraction* toward a person or object. *Love* is more intense, absorbing, and tender than *friendship*, more intense, impulsive, and perhaps passionate than *affection*; we speak of fervent *love*, but of deep or tender *affection*, or of close, firm, strong *friendship*. *Love* is used specifically for personal *affection* between the sexes, and can never properly denote mere animal passion, which is expressed by such words as appetite, desire, lust. One may have *love* for animals, inanimate objects, or for abstract qualities that enlist the affections, as we speak of *love* for a horse or a dog, for mountains, woods, ocean, or of *love* of nature, and *love* of virtue. *Love* of articles of food is better expressed by *liking*, as *love*, in its full sense, denotes something spiritual and reciprocal, such as can have no place in connection with objects that minister merely to the senses. See ATTACHMENT, FRIENDSHIP. *Antonyms*: see synonyms for ANTIPATHY, ENMITY, HATRED.

love affair A romantic attachment between two people not married to each other.

love apple The tomato.

love·bird (luv′bûrd′) *n.* One of several small parrots (genera *Agapornis* and *Psitta*) often kept as cage birds: so called from the affection they appear to show for their mates.

love feast 1 A common devotional meal partaken of by early Christians, originally culminating in the Eucharist; agape. **2** A somewhat similar celebration observed in some modern churches, as the Methodist and Moravian. **3** A banquet held in common rejoicing over something.

love game In tennis, a game in which the winner has lost no point.

love–in–a–mist (luv′in·ə·mist′) *n.* A European ranunculaceous garden plant (*Nigella damascena*) with blue flowers.

love–in–i·dle·ness (luv′in·ī′dəl·nis) *n.* The pansy.

love·knot (luv′not′) *n.* A knot tied in pledge of love and constancy, or representation of it, as in jewelry.

love·less (luv′lis) *adj.* Having no love; unloving; also, not lovable. — **love′less·ly** *adv.* — **love′less·ness** *n.*

love–lies–bleed·ing (luv′līz′blē′ding) *n.* Any of several species of amaranth.

love·lock (luv′lok′) *n.* A separate lock of hair worn curled and tied with ribbons; especially such a lock as worn formerly by courtiers.

love·lorn (luv′lôrn′) *adj.* Forsaken by or pining for a lover.

love·ly (luv′lē) *adj.* **·li·er, ·li·est 1** Possessing mental or physical qualities that inspire admiration and love; charming. **2** Beautiful. **3** Attractive; inviting. **4** *Colloq.* Delightful; pleasing: We had a *lovely* visit with them. **5** *Obs.* Affectionate; loving. [OE *luflic*] — **love′li·ness** *n.*

Synonyms: amiable, beautiful, charming, delectable, delightful, enchanting, lovable, pleasing, sweet, winning, winsome. See AMIABLE, BEAUTIFUL.

love·mak·ing (luv′mā′king) *n.* The act of making love; wooing; courtship.

love potion A magic draft or drink designed to arouse love toward a certain person in the one who drinks.

lov·er (luv′ər) *n.* **1** One who loves; a warm admirer; devoted friend. **2** One who is in love; specifically, a paramour: in the singular now used only of the man. **3** One who enjoys or is strongly attracted by some object or diversion. — **lov′er·ly** *adj. & adv.*

love seat A double chair or small sofa for two persons in Queen Anne and later styles.

love set In tennis, a set in which the winner has not lost a game.

love·sick (luv′sik′) *adj.* **1** Languishing with love. **2** Indicating or expressing such a condition: a *lovesick* serenade. — **love′sick′ness** *n.*

love·some (luv′səm) *adj. Obs.* **1** Inspiring

love; lovable. **2** Expressing love; loving.

love·vine (luv′vīn′) *n.* The dodder.

lov·ing (luv′ing) *adj.* **1** Affectionate; devoted; kind: *loving* friends or brothers. **2** Indicative of love or kind feeling: *loving* looks and words. See synonyms under AMIABLE, CHARITABLE. — **lov′ing·ly** *adv.* — **lov′ing·ness** *n.*

loving cup 1 A wine cup, usually with two or more handles, meant to be passed from hand to hand around a circle of friends; a parting cup. **2** A trophy presented to the winner of an athletic or other kind of contest.

lov·ing–kind·ness (luv′ing·kīnd′nis) *n.* Kindness that comes from personal attachment; specifically, the loving care of God for his people.

low[1] (lō) *adj.* **1** Having relatively little upward extension; not high or tall. **2** Having relatively little elevation; raised only slightly above a recognized level: a *low* bridge; near the horizon: a *low* moon. **3** Situated below a recognized level; deep; depressed. **4** Having less than the normal or regular height, or less height than something taken as a standard; descending from the usual level. **5** Cut so as to expose the neck; décolleté. **6** Of sounds having low depth of pitch; deep; also, having little volume or strength; soft. **7** Being less than the usual rate, amount, or reckoning; scant: *low* wages or interest. **8** Being little in degree, number, grade, station, quality, character, etc.; humble; moderate. **9** Being below the proper standard in refinement, moral character, principle, or condition; lacking pride, principle, force, dignity, or worth; vulgar; weak: *low* spirits; *low* standards of morality. **10** Dead; prostrate: He lies *low*. **11** *Phonet.* Pronounced with the tongue low and flat; open: said of vowels: opposed to *high*. **12** Little advanced in civilization or organic evolution. **13** Badly nourished; lacking in vigor; also, not nourishing; plain: a *low* diet. **14** *Mech.* Giving the least speed: *low* gear. **15** *Geog.* Pertaining to latitudes near the equator. **16** *Eccl.* **a** Pertaining to broad evangelical doctrine. **b** Denoting a service shorn of elaborate ritual: a *low* mass. **17** *Bot.* Growing close to the ground: a *low* herb. See synonyms under BASE, COMMON, HUMBLE, VULGAR. — *adv.* **1** In a low way; in or to a low position; not on high. **2** At a low price; cheap. **3** In a humble rank or degraded condition. **4** So as not to be loud in sound; softly; also, at a low pitch. **5** In such a path that the declination or the altitude is small; near the equator or the horizon. — **to lie low 1** To be dead or prostrate. **2** To be or remain in hiding. **3** To hold one's tongue till the proper moment; wait. — *n.* **1** A low area. **2** The first gear or speed of an automobile: Put it in *low*. [OE *lah* <ON *lagr*] — **low′ness** *n.*

low[2] (lō) *n.* The moo or bellow of cattle: also **low′ing.** — *v.i.* To bellow, as cattle; moo. — *v.t.* To utter by lowing. [OE *hlowan*]

low area *Meteorol.* A region of low atmospheric pressure.

low–ar·e·a storm (lō′âr′ē·ə) A cyclone.

low–born (lō′bôrn′) *adj.* Of humble birth.

low·boy (lō′boi′) *n.* A table, often a dressing table, with drawers, similar to the lower part of a highboy.

low–bred (lō′bred′) *adj.* Vulgar; ill-bred.

low–brow (lō′brou′) *Colloq. n.* A person of uncultivated tastes; a non-intellectual: an uncomplimentary term. — *adj.* Of or suitable for such a person: also **low′browed′.** — **low′brow′·ism** *n.*

Low–Church (lō′chûrch′) *adj.* Of or belonging to a group (**Low Church**) in the Anglican Church which stresses evangelical doctrine and is, in general, opposed to extreme ritualism. — **Low–Church·man** (lō′chûrch′mən) *n.*

low comedy Comedy in which both subject matter and presentation are in the broad style of farce or burlesque; comedy characterized by slapstick and lively physical action rather than by witty dialog.

low·er[1] (lou′ər) *v.i.* **1** To look angry or sullen; scowl. **2** To appear dark and threatening, as the weather. — *n.* A scowl; a gloomy aspect. Also spelled *lour.* [Cf. G *lauern* lurk]

low·er[2] (lō′ər) Comparative of LOW. — *adj.* **1** Inferior in position, in value or rank; situated below something else: a *lower* berth. **2** *Geol.* Older; designating strata normally beneath the newer (and upper) rock formations. — *n.* That which is beneath something above; specifically, a lower berth. — *v.t.* **1** To bring to a lower position or level; let down, as a window. **2** To reduce in degree, quality, amount, etc.: to *lower* prices. **3** To bring down in estimation, rank, etc.; humble or degrade. **4** To change, as a sound, to a lower pitch or volume. — *v.i.* **5** To become lower; sink; decrease. See synonyms under ABASE, ABATE, DISPARAGE, WEAKEN.

low·er-case (lō'ər·kās') *adj. Printing* Describing the small letters of a font of type which are kept in the low case (see CASE); small letters. — *v.t.* -cased, -cas·ing To set as or change to lower-case letters. [From their being kept in the lower two cases of type]

lower class The socially or economically inferior group in society. — **low·er-class** (lō'ər·klas', -kläs') *adj.*

low·er-class·man (lō'ər·klas'mən, -kläs'-) *n. pl.* **·men** (-mən) A freshman or a sophomore.

Lower Cretaceous *Geol.* The older part of the Cretaceous period, or its representative rocks or fossils. See CRETACEOUS.

lower criticism The method of critical investigation which seeks to determine the original wording of a text: also called *textual criticism.* Compare HIGHER CRITICISM.

Lower House The popular division of a legislative body; in the United States, the House of Representatives, as opposed to the Upper House or Senate; in Great Britain, the House of Commons, as opposed to the House of Lords.

low·er·ing (lou'ər·ing) *adj.* **1** Overcast with clouds; gloomy; threatening. **2** Frowning or sullen. Also spelled *louring.* — **low'er·ing·ly** *adv.* — **low'er·ing·ness** *n.*

low·er·most (lō'ər·mōst') *adj.* Lowest.

Lower Silurian *Geol.* The former name for ORDOVICIAN.

lower world 1 The abode of the dead; hell; Hades. Also **lower regions. 2** The earth.

low·er·y (lou'ər·ē) *adj.* Cloudy; threatening storm: also spelled *loury.*

Low German See under GERMAN.

low-key (lō'kē') *adj.* Having a low degree of intensity; relatively pale or quiet; understated. Also **low-keyed** (lō'kēd').

low·land (lō'lənd) *adj.* Pertaining to or characteristic of a low or level country. — *n.* (*also* lō'land') *Usually pl.* Land lower than the adjacent country; level land. — **The Lowlands** The less elevated districts lying in the south and west of Scotland. — **Low'land·er** *n.*

low·ly (lō'lē) *adj.* **·li·er, ·li·est 1** Situated or lying low, as land. **2** Having low rank or importance; unpretending; humble. See synonyms under HUMBLE. — *adv.* **1** In a manner appropriate to humble life; rudely; meanly. **2** In a meek or modest manner. — **low'li·ness** *n.*

low mass The ordinary form of mass without music.

low-mind·ed (lō'mīn'did) *adj.* Having low or mean thoughts, sentiments, or motives; base.

low-necked (lō'nekt') *adj.* Cut low in the neck; décolleté: said of a garment.

low-pitched (lō'picht') *adj.* **1** Low in tone, key, or range of tone, as a voice. **2** Having little angular elevation: said of a roof.

low-pres·sure (lō'presh'ər) *adj.* **1** Requiring a low degree of pressure. **2** Having a condenser, as an engine. **3** *Meteorol.* Designating an atmospheric pressure below that which is normal at sea level.

low relief Bas-relief.

low-spir·it·ed (lō'spir'it·id) *adj.* Lacking spirit or animation; despondent; melancholy. — **low'-spir'it·ed·ly** *adv.* — **low'-spir'it·ed·ness** *n.*

Low Sunday The Sunday following Easter.

low-ten·sion (lō'ten'shən) *adj. Electr.* Having or characterized by a low electric potential, as a battery, magneto, or vacuum tube.

low-test (lō'test') *adj.* Possessing a relatively high boiling point, as gasoline.

low tide The furthest recession of the tide at any point; also, the time of its occurrence. Also **low water.**

low-wa·ter (lō'wô'tər, -wot'ər) *adj.* Pertaining to low tide or its time or measure of recession.

lox¹ (loks) *n.* Smoked salmon. [<Yiddish <G *lachs* salmon]

lox², **LOX** (loks) *n.* Liquid oxygen.

lox·o·drom·ic (lok'sə·drom'ik) *adj.* Pertaining to oblique sailing on the rhumb line. Also **lox'o·drom'i·cal.** [<Gk. *loxos* oblique + *dromos* a running]

lox·o·drom·ics (lok'sə·drom'iks) *n. pl.* (construed as singular) The art of oblique sailing. Also **lox·od·ro·my** (lok·sod'rə·mē).

loy·al (loi'əl) *adj.* **1** Constant and faithful in any relation implying trust or confidence; bearing true allegiance to constituted authority. **2** Professing or indicative of faithful devotion. **3** *Obs.* Legitimate. See synonyms under FAITHFUL. [<OF *loial, leial* <L *legalis.* Doublet of LEGAL.] — **loy'al·ism** *n.* — **loy'al·ly** *adv.*

loy·al·ist (loi'əl·ist) *n.* One who adheres to and defends his sovereign or state.

Loy·al·ist (loi'əl·ist) *n.* **1** One who was loyal to the British crown during the American Revolution. **2** One who was loyal to the Union during the Civil War. **3** One who was loyal to the Republican Constitution during the Spanish Civil War.

loy·al·ty (loi'əl·tē) *n. pl.* **·ties** Devoted allegiance. See synonyms under ALLEGIANCE, FIDELITY. [<OF *loialte*]

Lo·yo·la (loi·ō'lə, *Sp.* lō·yō'lä), **Ignatius of,** 1491–1556, Spanish soldier and priest; founder, with Francisco Xavier, of the Society of Jesus (the Jesuits); canonized in 1622: original name *Iñigo de Oñez y Loyola.* — **Loy·o·lism** (loi'ə·liz'əm) *n.*

loz·enge (loz'inj) *n.* **1** *Math.* A rhombus with all sides equal, having two acute and two obtuse angles. **2** A small medicated or sweetened tablet, originally diamond-shaped. [<OF *losenge,* ?<L *lapis, -idis* stone]

LP (el'pē') *adj.* Designating a phonograph record pressed with microgrooves and played at a speed of 33¹/₃ revolutions per minute. — *n.* A long-playing phonograph record: a trade name. [<l(ong)-p(laying)]

LSD (el'es'dē') *n.* A drug that produces states similar to those of schizophrenia, used in medicine and illicitly as a hallucinogen. See LYSERGIC ACID. Also **LSD-25.** [<l(y)s(ergic acid) d(iethylamide)]

Lu·an·da (lōō·än'də) A port, capital of Angola: formerly *Loanda, São Paulo de Loanda.*

lu·au (lōō'ou) *n.* A Hawaiian outdoor feast, esp. one that features roast pig. [<Hawaiian *lu'au*]

lub·ber (lub'ər) *n.* An awkward, ungainly fellow; specifically, a landsman on shipboard. [Origin uncertain. Cf. ON *lubba* short.] — **lub'ber·li·ness** *n.* — **lub'ber·ly** *adj. & adv.*

lubber line *Aeron.* A fixed line in an aircraft compass, gyro, direction finder, or similar instrument, parallel to the longitudinal axis of the aircraft and used as a base line.

lubber's hole *Naut.* A hole through the floor of a platform or top at the head of a lower mast by which sailors can go aloft without climbing over the rim by the futtock shrouds.

lu·bri·cant (lōō'brə·kənt) *adj.* Lubricating. — *n.* Anything that lubricates, as grease.

lu·bri·cate (lōō'brə·kāt) *v.t.* **·cat·ed, ·cat·ing 1** To apply grease, oil, or other lubricant to so as to reduce friction and wear. **2** To make slippery or smooth. [<L *lubricatus,* pp. of *lubricare* make slippery <*lubricus* slippery] — **lu'bri·ca'tion** *n.* — **lu'bri·ca'tive** *adj.*

lu·bri·ca·tor (lōō'brə·kā'tər) *n.* **1** One who or that which lubricates. **2** A device, as an oil cup, by which a lubricant is fed or applied to a bearing surface.

lu·bric·i·ty (lōō·bris'ə·tē) *n.* **1** The state of being slippery; hence, shiftiness; instability; evanescence. **2** Lewdness. **3** Power for lubrication. [<F *lubricité* <L *lubricitas* <*lubricus* slippery]

lu·bri·cous (lōō'brə·kəs) *adj.* **1** Smooth and slippery. **2** Elusive; unstable. **3** Lascivious; lewd; wanton. Also **lu·bri·cious** (lōō·brish'əs). [<L *lubricus*]

lu·bri·fac·tion (lōō'brə·fak'shən) *n.* The act or process of lubricating or making slippery or smooth. [<L *lubricus* smooth + *factus,* pp. of *facere* make]

lu·carne (lōō·kärn') *n.* A dormer or garret window; also, a small window or light in a spire. [<F; ult. origin uncertain. Cf. OHG *lukka* opening.]

luce (lōōs) *n.* A fish, the pike, especially when fully grown. [<OF *lus* <L *lucius*]

lu·cent (lōō'sənt) *adj.* Showing radiance or brilliance; shining; luminous. [<L *lucens, -entis,* ppr. of *lucere* shine] — **lu'cen·cy** *n.*

lu·cer·nal (lōō·sûr'nəl) *adj.* Relating to a lamp or to any artificial light. [<L *lucerna* lamp < *lux* light]

lu·cerne (lōō·sûrn') *n.* A tall, cloverlike herb of the pea family (*Medicago sativa*), used for forage: now commonly called *alfalfa, purple medic.* Also **lu·cern'.** [<F *luzerne*; ult. origin unknown]

lu·cid (lōō'sid) *adj.* **1** Intellectually bright and clear; mentally sound; sane. **2** Easily understood; perspicuous; clear. **3** Giving forth light; shining. **4** Translucent; pellucid. **5** Smooth and shining. See synonyms under CLEAR, SANE, TRANSPARENT. [<L *lucidus* < *lucere* shine] — **lu·cid·i·ty** (lōō·sid'ə·tē), **lu'cid·ness** *n.* — **lu'cid·ly** *adv.*

lu·ci·fer (lōō'sə·fər) *n.* A friction match. — *adj.* Emitting light. [after *Lucifer*]

Lu·ci·fer (lōō'sə·fər) *n.* **1** The planet Venus as the morning star. **2** Satan, especially as the leader of the revolt of the angels before his fall from heaven. [<L, light-bearer < *lux, lucis* light + *ferre* bear] — **Lu·cif·er·ous** (lōō·sif'ər·əs) *adj.*

lu·cif·er·ase (lōō·sif'ə·rās) *n. Biochem.* An enzyme present in fireflies and in certain other luminous organisms: it oxidizes luciferin to produce light. [<L *lucifer* light-bearing + -ASE]

lu·cif·er·in (lōō·sif'ər·in) *n. Biochem.* A water-soluble, heat-stable protein which produces heatless light, as in fireflies. [<L *lucifer* light-bearing + -IN]

lu·cif·er·ous (lōō·sif'ər·əs) *adj.* Emitting light. [<L *lucifer* light-bearing + -OUS]

lu·ci·form (lōō'sə·fôrm) *adj.* Having the nature or appearance of light. [<L *lux, lucis* light + -FORM]

Lu·cite (lōō'sīt) *n.* A thermoplastic, transparent acrylic resin, easily machined into various shapes and having the property of transmitting light around curves and corners: a trade name.

lu·ci·vee (lōō'sə·vē) *n.* The loup-cervier. Also **lu'ci·fee** (-fē). [Alter. of LOUP-CERVIER]

luck (luk) *n.* **1** That which happens by chance; fortune or lot. **2** Happy chance; good fortune; success. [Prob. <MDu. *luk, geluk*]

luck·less (luk'lis) *adj.* Having no luck. — **luck'less·ly** *adv.*

luck·y (luk'ē) *adj.* **luck·i·er, luck·i·est 1** Favored by fortune; fortunate; successful. **2** Productive of luck; auspicious; favorable: said of events and things: a *lucky* penny or circumstance. See synonyms under AUSPICIOUS, FORTUNATE, HAPPY, WELL. — **luck'i·ly** *adv.* — **luck'i·ness** *n.*

lu·cra·tive (lōō'krə·tiv) *adj.* Productive of wealth; highly profitable. See synonyms under PROFITABLE. [<L *lucrativus* <*lucratus,* pp. of *lucrari* gain <*lucrum* wealth] — **lu'cra·tive·ly** *adv.* — **lu'cra·tive·ness** *n.*

lu·cre (lōō'kər) *n.* Money, especially as the object of greed; gain. See synonyms under WEALTH. [<F <L *lucrum* gain]

lu·cu·brate (lōō'kyōō·brāt) *v.i.* **·brat·ed, ·brat·ing 1** To study or write laboriously, as at night. **2** To write in a learned manner. [<L *lucubratus,* pp. of *lucubrare* work by artificial light <*lux, lucis* light]

lu·cu·bra·tion (lōō'kyōō·brā'shən) *n.* **1** Close and earnest meditation or study. **2** The product of deep meditation or earnest study; a literary composition; often, a pedantic or over-elaborated work. [<L *lucubratio, -onis*] — **lu'cu·bra'tor** *n.* — **lu'cu·bra·to'ry** (-brə·tôr'ē, -tō'rē) *adj.*

lu·cu·lent (lōō'kyōō·lənt) *adj.* **1** Full of light; brilliant. **2** Clearly evident; lucid. [<L *luculentus*]

Lud·dite (lud'īt) *n.* One of a band of workmen who joined in riots (1811–16) for the destruction of machinery, under the belief that its introduction reduced wages and increased unemployment: called after Ned Lud, a feeble-witted mechanic who destroyed several stocking-frames: in English industrial history.

lu·di·crous (lōō'də·krəs) *adj.* Calculated to excite laughter; incongruous; droll; ridiculous. See synonyms under ABSURD, HUMOROUS, QUEER, RIDICULOUS. [<L *ludicrus* <*ludere* play] — **lu'di·crous·ly** *adv.* — **lu'di·crous·ness** *n.*

lu·es (lōō'ēz) *n.* **1** Formerly, an infectious or pestilential disease. **2** Plague. **3** Syphilis. [<L, plague, discharge <*luere* flow] — **lu·et·ic** (lōō·et'ik) *adj.*

luff (luf) *n. Naut.* **1** The sailing of a ship close to the wind. **2** The rounded part of a vessel's bow. **3** The foremost edge of a fore–and–aft sail. — *v.i. Naut.* **1** To bring the head of a vessel nearer the wind; sail near the wind. **2** To bring the head of a vessel into the wind, with the sails shaking. Also spelled *loof.*

Luft·waf·fe (lōoft'väf'ə) *n. German* The German air force, as organized by the Nazi regime in 1939. [<G, lit., air weapon]

lug[1] (lug) *n.* **1** The lobe of the ear; the ear. **2** Hence, an earlike projection such as an ear or handle for carrying or supporting, or for insertion of a handle, ring, pole, etc.: the *lugs* of a kettle. **3** The loop at the side of the saddle of a harness which holds the shaft. [Origin uncertain. Cf. Sw. *lugg* forelock.]

lug[2] (lug) *n.* **1** The act or exertion of lugging; anything that is moved with slowness and difficulty. **2** A shallow box or container, 13 1/2 by 16 inches inside dimensions, for carrying fruit or vegetables. **3** *Naut.* A square sail bent to a yard and having no boom: also *lugsail.* **4** *Slang* An exaction, especially of money for political uses. — *v.t.* **lugged, lug·ging 1** To carry or pull with effort; drag. **2** *Colloq.* To bring, as irrelevant topics, into a conversation, discussion, etc.; introduce unreasonably. [Prob. <Scand. Cf. Sw. *lugga* pull by the hair.]

lug[3] (lug) *n.* A lugworm. [Origin uncertain. Cf. LG *lug* slow, heavy.]

luge (lōōj) *n.* A short, stout sled: also called *toboggan.* [<F <dial. F]

Lu·ger (lōō'gər) *n.* A German automatic pistol widely used in Europe as a military sidearm: manufactured in various calibers, most commonly 7.65 mm. and 9 mm.: also called *Parabellum* in Europe. [after Georg *Luger,* 19th c. German engineer]

lug·gage (lug'ij) *n.* **1** Anything burdensome or heavy to carry. **2** Baggage. [<LUG[2]]

lug·ger (lug'ər) *n.* A one-, two-, or three- masted vessel hav- ing lugsails only. [<LUG(SAIL) + -ER[2]]

LUGGER

lug·sail (lug'səl, -sāl') *n.* Lug[2] (def. 3).

lu·gu·bri·ous (lōo- gōō'brē·əs, -gyōō'-) *adj.* **1** Exhibiting or producing sadness; doleful. **2** Exag- geratedly solemn or sad. See synonyms under SAD. [<L *lugubris* <*lugere* mourn] — **lu·gu'- bri·ous·ly** *adv.* — **lu·gu'bri·ous·ness** *n.*

lug·worm (lug'wûrm') *n.* An annelid worm (genus *Arenicola*) with two rows of tufted gills on the back, living in the sand of sea- shores: much used for bait: also called *lob- worm.*

luke·warm (lōōk'wôrm') *adj.* **1** Moderately warm; tepid. **2** Hence, not ardent or hearty; indifferent. [Prob. OE *hlēow* warm. Cf. LG *luk* tepid.] — **luke'warm'ly** *adv.* — **luke'warm'- ness** *n.*

lull (lul) *v.t.* **1** To soothe or quiet; put to sleep. **2** To calm; allay, as suspicions. — *v.i.* **3** To become calm. — *n.* **1** An abatement of noise or violence; an interval of calm or quiet. **2** That which lulls or soothes. See synonyms under TRANQUILIZE. [Prob. <Sw. *lulla* sing to sleep; ult. imit.]

lull·a·by (lul'ə·bī) *n. pl.* **·bies 1** A song to lull a child to sleep; a cradlesong; also, the music for such a song. **2** *Obs.* A goodnight or fare- well. [<LULL]

lu·lu (lōō'lōō) *n. Slang* Anything of an excep- tional or outstanding nature, as a difficult examination, a beautiful person, etc. [Prob. reduplication of *Lou,* the familiar form of LOUISE]

lu·ma·chelle (lōō'mə·kel) *n.* A variety of lime- stone containing fragments of shells, fossils, etc., sometimes brilliantly iridescent. Also **lu'ma·chel, lu'ma·chel'la** (-kel'ə). [<Ital. *lumachella,* dim. of *lumaca* snail <L *limax, limacis*]

lum·ba·go (lum·bā'gō) *n. Pathol.* Rheumatic pain in the lumbar region of the back; back- ache. [<L <*lumbus* loin]

lum·bar (lum'bər, -bär) *adj.* Pertaining to or situated near the loins. — *n.* A lumbar ver- tebra or nerve. [<NL *lumbaris* <L *lumbus* loin]

lum·ber[1] (lum'bər) *n.* **1** *U.S. & Can.* Timber sawed into boards, planks, etc. **2** Disused articles laid aside. **3** Hence, rubbish. — *adj.* Made of, pertaining to, or dealing in, lumber. — *v.t.* **1** *U.S. & Can.* To cut down (timber); also, to cut down the timber of (an area). **2** To fill or obstruct with useless articles. **3** To heap in disorder. — *v.i.* **4** *U.S. & Can.* To cut down or saw timber for marketing. [Var. of *Lombard* in obs. sense of "money- lender, pawnshop"; hence, stored articles] — **lum'ber·er** *n.*

lum·ber[2] (lum'bər) *v.i.* **1** To move or pro- ceed in a heavy or awkward manner. **2** To move with a rumbling noise. — *n.* A rumbling noise. [Origin uncertain. Cf. Sw. *lomra* re- sound, *loma* walk heavily.]

lum·bered (lum'bərd) *adj.* Having the timber cut off: said of land.

lum·ber·ing[1] (lum'bər·ing) *n.* The business of felling and shaping timber into logs, boards, etc.

lum·ber·ing[2] (lum'bər·ing) *adj.* Clumsily huge and heavy; moving heavily; rumbling. — **lum'ber·ing·ly** *adv.* — **lum'ber·ing·ness** *n.*

lum·ber·jack (lum'bər·jak) *n.* **1** A lumberman. **2** A boy's or man's short, straight jacket of heavy warm material: originally made in imi- tation of coats worn by lumbermen: also **lum'ber·jack'et** (-jak'it). [<LUMBER[1] + *jack* man, boy]

lum·ber·man (lum'bər·mən) *n. pl.* **·men** (-mən) A person engaged in the business of lumbering.

lum·ber–room (lum'bər·rōōm', -rōōm') *n.* A room for lumber or useless articles.

lum·ber·some (lum'bər·səm) *adj.* Cumbersome.

lum·ber·yard (lum'bər·yärd) *n.* A yard for the storage or sale of lumber.

lum·bri·ca·lis (lum'brə·kā'lis) *n. pl.* **·les** (-lēz) *Anat.* **1** One of the four vermiform muscles in the palm of the hand. **2** One of four simi- lar muscles in the sole of the foot. [<NL <L *lumbricus* worm] — **lum'bri·cal** *adj.*

lum·bri·coid (lum'brə·koid) *adj.* **1** Of or per- taining to the common earthworm (genus *Lumbricus*). **2** Pertaining to or designating a roundworm (*Ascaris lumbricoides*) parasitic in the intestines of man. — *n.* The roundworm. [<L *lumbricus* earthworm + -OID]

lu·men (lōō'mən) *n. pl.* **·mens** or **·mi·na** (-mə·nə) **1** A passageway or opening. **2** *Biol.* The inner cavity of a cell or tubular organ, as a gland. **3** *Physics* A unit for measuring luminous flux, equal to the flow through a steradian from a uniform point source of one international candle. [<L, light]

Lu·mi·nal (lōō'mə·nəl, -nōl) Proprietary name for a brand of phenobarbital.

lu·mi·nance (lōō'mə·nəns) See BRIGHTNESS (def. 2).

lu·mi·nar·y (lōō'mə·ner'ē) *n. pl.* **·nar·ies 1** Any body that gives light; specifically, one of the heavenly bodies as a source of light. **2** One who enlightens men or makes clear any sub- ject. **3** Any light or source of illumination. [<OF *luminaire* <LL *luminarium* candle, torch <*lumen* light]

lu·mi·nesce (lōō'mə·nes') *v.i.* **·nesced, ·nesc- ing** To become luminescent. [Back formation <LUMINESCENT]

lu·mi·nes·cence (lōō'mə·nes'əns) *n.* A light– emission not directly attributable to the heat that produces incandescence, as *biolumines- cence.*

lu·mi·nes·cent (lōō'mə·nes'ənt) *adj.* Emitting or capable of emitting light apart from incan- descence or high temperature. [<L *lumen* light + -ESCENT]

lu·mi·nif·er·ous (lōō'mə·nif'ər·əs) *adj.* Produc- ing or conveying light. [<L *lumen* light + -FEROUS]

lu·mi·nos·i·ty (lōō'mə·nos'ə·tē) *n. pl.* **·ties 1** The quality of being luminous. **2** Some- thing luminous. **3** *Physics* The ratio of the luminous flux of an object to the corresponding radiant flux, expressed in lumens per watt.

lu·mi·nous (lōō'mə·nəs) *adj.* **1** Giving or emit- ting light; shining. **2** Full of light; well lighted; bright. **3** Perspicuous; lucid. See synonyms under BRIGHT, VIVID. [<L *luminosus* <*lumen*

light] — **lu'mi·nous·ly** *adj.* — **lu'mi·nous·ness** *n.*

luminous energy Light.

luminous flux *Physics* The time rate of the flow of visible light, expressed in lumens.

luminous intensity *Physics* The luminous flux emitted from a point source of light per spheradian.

lu·mis·ter·ol (lōō·mis'tər·ōl) *n.* A sterol, $C_{28}H_{44}O$, resulting from the ultraviolet irradia- tion of ergosterol. [<*lumi-* (<L *lumen* light) + (ERGO)STEROL]

lum·mox (lum'əks) *n. U.S. Colloq.* A stupid, heavy, clumsy person. [Cf. G *lümmel* lout]

lump[1] (lump) *n.* **1** A shapeless mass of inert matter, especially a small mass. **2** A mass of things thrown together. **3** A protuberance. **4** A stupid person. **5** A heavy, ungainly per- son. See synonyms under MASS. — **in a** (or **the**) **lump** All together; with no distinction. — *v.t.* **1** To put together in one mass, group, etc. **2** To consider or treat collectively: to *lump* facts. **3** To make lumps in or on. — *v.i.* **4** To become lumpy; raise in lumps. **5** To move or fall heavily. [<ME, prob. <Scand. Cf. Dan. *lumpe* a lump.]

lump[2] (lump) *v.t. Colloq.* To put up with; en- dure (something disagreeable); You may like it or *lump* it. [Origin uncertain]

lump·fish (lump'fish') *n. pl.* **·fish** or **·fish·es** A fish of northern seas (*Cyclopterus lumpus*), oval in shape and with the skin studded with three lateral rows of tubercles. Also **lump'suck'- er** (-suk'ər). [So called from its bulk]

lump·ish (lum'pish) *adj.* Like a lump; stupid. — **lump'ish·ly** *adv.* — **lump'ish·ness** *n.*

lump sum A full and single sum.

lump·y (lum'pē) *adj.* **lump·i·er, lump·i·est 1** Full of lumps. **2** Lumpish or gross. **3** Running in confused, pounding waves that do not break: a *lumpy* sea. — **lump'i·ly** *adv.* — **lump'i·ness** *n.*

lumpy jaw Actinomycosis.

lu·na (lōō'nə) *n.* In alchemy, silver. [<L, the moon]

lu·na·cy (lōō'nə·sē) *n. pl.* **·cies 1** An intermit- tent form of insanity: formerly supposed to depend on the changes of the moon. **2** In forensic psychiatry and law, mental unsound- ness to the point of irresponsibility. **3** Wild foolishness; wanton and senseless conduct. See synonyms under INSANITY. [<LUNATIC]

Luna moth A large North American moth (*Tropaea luna*), having light-green wings with long tails and lunate spots. [So called from the crescent- shaped spots on its wings]

lu·nar (lōō'nər) *adj.* **1** Of or pertaining to the moon; cres- cented or orbed; like the moon. **2** Measured by revo- lutions of the moon. **3** In alchemy and medi- cine, of or pertaining to silver. [<L *lunaris* <*luna* the moon]

LUNA MOTH
(Wingspread from 4 1/2 to 6 inches)

lunar caustic *Chem.* Silver nitrate formed into pencils and used for cauterizing. [<LUNA]

lunar day The period of the moon's rotation on its axis.

lu·nar·i·an (lōō·nâr'ē·ən) *adj.* Pertaining to the moon. — *n.* **1** A supposed inhabitant of the moon. **2** An investigator of the moon. [<L *lunaris*]

lunar module *Aerospace* A part of a space ve- hicle designed to land astronauts on the moon and lift them off to link up with the com- mand module. Also **lunar excursion module.**

lunar month See under MONTH.

lu·na·ry (lōō'nər·ē) *adj.* Connected with the moon; lunar. — *n.* A fern, the moonwort. [<L *lunaris*]

lunar year Twelve lunar months.

lu·nate (lōō'nāt) *adj.* Crescent-shaped. Also **lu'nat·ed.** [<L *lunatus*]

lu·na·tic (lōō'nə·tik) *adj.* **1** Affected with lunacy. **2** Characteristic of or resembling lunacy; crazy; insane. Also **lu·nat·i·cal** (lōō- nat'i·kəl). See synonyms under INSANE. — *n.* An insane person. [<LL *lunaticus* <L *luna* moon]

lu·na·tion (lōō·nā'shən) *n. Astron.* The interval between two returns of the new moon, averag- ing 29.53059 days. [<Med. L *lunatio, -onis*

<L *luna* the moon]

lunch (lunch) *n.* **1** A light meal between other meals, as between breakfast and dinner. **2** Food provided for a lunch. — *v.i.* To eat lunch. — *v.t.* To furnish lunch for. [Short for LUNCHEON] — **lunch′er** *n.*

lunch·eon (lun′chən) *n.* **1** A bit of food taken between meals. **2** A lunch. [? Blend of dial. E *lunch* a lump of food + obs. *nuncheon* afternoon snack]

lunch·eon·ette (lun′chən·et′) *n.* A place or counter where light lunches can be obtained.

lunch·room (lunch′rōōm′, -rōōm′) *n.* A restaurant serving light meals and refreshments.

lune¹ (lōōn) *n.* **1** *Geom.* A figure bounded by two arcs of circles. **2** The moon. ◆ Homophone: *loon*. [<F <L *luna* the moon]

lune² (lōōn) *n.* A leash used in hawking. ◆ Homophone: *loon*. [<OF *loigne* leash < Med. L *longea* <L *longus* long]

lu·nette (lōō·net′) *n.* **1** Something shaped like a half-moon. **2** *Mil.* A fieldwork or a detached work formed by two parallel flanks, two faces meeting in a salient angle, with an open gorge. **3** *Archit.* An arched opening in the side of a long vault formed by the intersection with it of a smaller vault, as for a window. **4** A ring on the tongue or trail plate of a vehicle, for attaching to a limber, motor truck, or other towing vehicle. Also **lu·net** (lōō′nit). [<F, dim. of *lune* moon]

lung (lung) *n. Anat.* **1** Either of the two sac-like organs of respiration in air-breathing vertebrates. ◆ Collateral adjective: *pulmonary*. **2** An analogous organ in invertebrates. [OE *lungen*]

lunge (lunj) *n.* **1** A sudden pass or thrust; specifically, a long thrust with a sword or a bayonet. **2** A sudden forward lurch; plunge. — *v.* **lunged, lung·ing** — *v.i.* **1** To make a lunge or pass; thrust. **2** To move with a lunge. — *v.t.* **3** To thrust with or as with a lunge. [Aphetic var. of obs. *allonge* <F *allonger* prolong <L *ad* to + *longus* long]

lung·fish (lung′fish′) *n. pl.* **·fish** or **·fish·es** A dipnoan.

lung·worm (lung′wûrm′) *n.* Any of several nematode worms parasitic in the lungs of animals, especially the common lungworm (genus *Dictyocaulus*) of horses, cattle, and sheep.

lung·wort (lung′wûrt′) *n.* **1** A European herb (genus *Pulmonaria*) of the borage family, having white blotches on the leaves. **2** The Virginia cowslip.

luni- *combining form* Of or pertaining to the moon; lunar. [<L *luna* moon]

lu·ni·so·lar (lōō′ni·sō′lər) *adj.* Of or resulting from the combined action of the sun and moon.

lu·ni·ti·dal (lōō′ni·tīd′l) *adj.* Relating to the tides as produced by the moon's attraction. **lunitidal interval** The interval between the moon's passage of the meridian and lunar high tide.

lunk·head (lungk′hed′) *n. Slang* A slow-witted person. [Prob. alter. of LUMP + HEAD] — **lunk′head·ed** *adj.*

lu·nu·la (lōō′nyə·lə) *n. pl.* **·lae** (-lē) **1** A crescentic structure or appearance. **2** The whitish area at the base of the nails: also **lu′nule** (-nyōōl). **3** A lune (arc). [<L, diminutive of *luna* the moon]

lu·nu·lar (lōō′nyə·lər) *adj.* Having the form of a small crescent. [<LUNULA]

lu·nu·late (lōō′nyə·lāt, -lit) *adj.* **1** Having or approaching a crescent form. **2** Having crescentic markings. Also **lu′nu·lat′ed.**

lu·pine¹ (lōō′pīn) *adj.* **1** Of or pertaining to a wolf; like a wolf; wolfish. **2** Pertaining to the group of canines that includes dogs and wolves. [<L *lupinus* <*lupus* wolf]

lu·pine² (lōō′pin) *n.* A plant of the bean family (genus *Lupinus*) bearing terminal racemes of mostly blue or purple flowers, as the **white lupine** of the Old World (*L. albus*) whose seeds are edible. Also **lu′pin** (-pin). [<F *lupin* <L *lupinus* wolflike; reason for the name unknown]

lu·pu·lin (lōō′pyə·lin) *n.* **1** A brittle crystalline compound forming the active principle of hops. **2** A yellow aromatic powder contained in the fruit of hops, and used medicinally as a sedative. [<NL *lupulus* the hop, dim. of L *lupus*]

lu·pus (lōō′pəs) *n. Pathol.* A chronic tuberculous skin disease with warty nodules, generally about the nose. Also **lupus vul·ga·ris** (vul·gar′is). [<L, wolf]

lurch¹ (lûrch) *v.i.* **1** To roll suddenly to one side, as a ship at sea. **2** To move unsteadily; stagger. — *n.* A sudden swaying or rolling to one side; hence; any sudden swinging movement. [Origin uncertain]

lurch² (lûrch) *n.* **1** In cribbage, the state of a player who has made 30 holes or less while his opponent has won with 61; also a game thus won. — **to leave in the lurch** To leave in an embarrassing position. — *v.i.* In cribbage, piquet, and similar games, to win a double game. [<F *lourche*, name of a game < *lourche* deceived <Gmc. Cf. MDu. *lurz* left-handed, unlucky.]

lurch·er (lûr′chər) *n.* **1** One who lies in wait or lurks; a lurking thief; poacher. **2** A cross-bred dog that hunts by scent and in silence.

lure (lōōr) *n.* **1** A device resembling a bird and sometimes baited with food: fastened to a falconer's wrist and used to recall the hawk. **2** In angling, an artificial bait; also, a decoy for animals. **3** Anything that invites by the prospect of advantage or pleasure. — *v.t.* **lured, lur·ing 1** To attract or entice; allure. **2** To recall (a hawk) with a lure. See synonyms under ALLURE, DRAW. [<OF *leurre* <MHG *luoder* bait] — **lur′er** *n.*

LURES

a. Wood or plastic lure.   *c.* Feather lure.
b. Floating cork lure.   *d.* Dry fly.

lu·rid (lōōr′id) *adj.* **1** Giving a ghastly or dull-red light; dismal. **2** Of a dingy, dirty-brown color. **3** Violent; terrible; sensational: a *lurid* crime. **4** Pale; wan; sallow; ghastly. [<L *luridus* sallow] — **lu′rid·ly** *adv.* — **lu′rid·ness** *n.*

lurk (lûrk) *v.i.* **1** To lie hidden, as in ambush. **2** To exist unnoticed or unsuspected. **3** To move secretly or furtively; slink. — *n. Austral. Slang* A dodge; scheme; racket. [Origin uncertain. Cf. Norw. *lurka* sneak off.] — **lurk′er** *n.* — **lurk′ing·ly** *adv.*

Lu·sa·tia (lōō·sā′shə) A region of SE Germany and SW Poland between the Elbe and the Oder. German **Lau·sitz** (lou′zits).

lus·cious (lush′əs) *adj.* **1** Very grateful to the sense of taste; rich, sweet, and delicious; pleasing to any sense or to the mind. **2** Sweet and rich to excess. See synonyms under DELICIOUS, SWEET. [? Blend of LUSH and DELICIOUS] — **lus′cious·ly** *adv.* — **lus′cious·ness** *n.*

lush¹ (lush) *adj.* **1** Full of juice or succulence; fresh and luxuriant; also, having abundant growth. **2** Easily plowed and mellow, as ground. [? Var. of dial. E *lash* soft and watery <OF *lasche* <L *laxus* loose] — **lush′ness** *n.*

lush² (lush) *Slang n.* **1** Intoxicating, or strong alcoholic beverage. **2** A drunken man: also **lush′er.** — *v.t. & v.i.* To drink (alcoholic liquor). [Origin unknown]

Lu·si·ta·ni·a (lōō′sə·tā′nē·ə) *n.* A British passenger ship torpedoed and sunk by a German submarine off the coast of Ireland May 7, 1915, with loss of 1,198 lives including 128 Americans.

lust (lust) *n.* **1** Vehement or longing affection or desire. **2** Inordinate desire for carnal pleasure. **3** *Obs.* Pleasure; inclination. See synonyms under APPETITE. — *v.i.* To have passionate or inordinate desire, especially sexual desire. [OE, pleasure]

lus·ter (lus′tər) *n.* **1** Natural or artificial brilliancy or sheen; refulgence; gloss. **2** Brilliancy of beauty, of character, or of achievements; splendor. **3** A glaze, varnish, or enamel applied to porcelain in a thin layer, and giving it a smooth, glistening surface: common in the phrase *metallic luster.* **4** A dress material having a highly finished surface. **5** A source or center of light; specifically, a branched candelabrum, chandelier, or the like. **6** *Mineral.* The quality of the surface of a mineral as regards the kind and intensity of the light it reflects. — *v.* **·tered** or **·tred, ·ter·ing** or **·tring** *v.t.* To give a luster or gloss to. — *v.i.* To be or become lustrous. Also **lus′tre.** [<F *lustre* <Ital. *lustro* <*lustrare* shine <L < *lustrum* purification]

lus·ter·ware (lus′tər·wâr′) *n.* Pottery treated with metallic luster.

lust·ful (lust′fəl) *adj.* **1** Having carnal or sensual desire. **2** *Archaic* Vigorous; lusty. — **lust′ful·ly** *adv.* — **lust′ful·ness** *n.*

lus·tral (lus′trəl) *adj.* **1** Pertaining to or used in purification. **2** Pertaining to a lustrum. [<L *lustralis* <*lustrum* purification]

lus·trate (lus′trāt) *v.t.* **·trat·ed, ·trat·ing** To make pure by propitiatory offering or ceremony. [<L *lustratus*, pp. of *lustrare* purify by propitiatory offerings <*lustrum* purification]

lus·tra·tion (lus·trā′shən) *n.* The ancient rite of purification and expiation. [<L *lustratio, -onis*]

lus·trous (lus′trəs) *adj.* Having luster; shining; also, illustrious. See synonyms under BRIGHT. — **lus′trous·ly** *adv.* — **lus′trous·ness** *n.*

lus·trum (lus′trəm) *n.* **1** A lustration or purification; the solemn ceremony of purification of the entire Roman people made every five years. **2** A period of five years. [<L, ? < *luere* wash]

lust·y (lus′tē) *adj.* **lust·i·er, lust·i·est 1** Full of vigor and health; able-bodied; robust. **2** *Obs.* Jolly; merry. **3** *Obs.* Agreeable; delightful. **4** *Obs.* Lustful. — **lust′i·ly** *adv.* — **lust′i·ness** *n.*

lu·ta·nist (lōō′tə·nist) *n.* One who plays the lute. Also **lu′te·nist.**

lute¹ (lōōt) *n.* A stringed musical instrument having a large, pear-shaped body like a mandolin, played by plucking the strings with the fingers. — *v.t. & v.i.* To play on the lute. [<OF *leüt* < Pg. *laut* <Arabic *al′ūd* the piece of wood]

lute² (lōōt) *n.* **1** A cementlike composition used to exclude air, as around pipe joints. **2** In brickmaking, a scraper having a cutting edge to smooth the surface of a drying yard. Also **lut′ing.** — *v.t.* **lut·ed, lut·ing** To seal with lute. [<OF *lut* <L *lutum* mud] — **lu·ta′tion** *n.*

lu·te·al (lōō′tē·əl) *adj. Anat.* Pertaining to or similar to the cells of the corpus luteum. [<L *luteus* yellow]

lu·te·in (lōō′tē·in, -tēn) *n. Biochem.* A yellow pigment, $C_{48}H_{56}O_2$, found in egg yolks, fat cells, and in the corpus luteum. [<L *luteum* egg yolk <*luteus* yellow] — **lu′te·in′ic** *adj.*

lu·te·o·lin (lōō′tē·ə·lin) *n. Chem.* A yellow crystalline compound, $C_{15}H_{10}O_6$, obtained from dyer's-broom, and used as a dyestuff. [<F *lutéoline* <NL (*Reseda*) *luteola* dyer's weed <L *luteolus* yellowish <*luteus* yellow]

lu·te·ous (lōō′tē·əs) *adj.* Of golden-yellowish color. [<L *luteus* <*lutum* weed used by dyers]

Lu·te·tia (lōō·tē′shə) Ancient name for PARIS. Also **Lu·te′tia Pa·ri·si·o·rum** (pa·rē′sē·ō′rəm).

lu·te·tium (lōō·tē′shəm) *n.* A metallic element (symbol Lu) of the lanthanide series, isolated from ytterbium. See ELEMENT. [from LUTETIA]

Lu·ther (lōō′thər), **Martin,** 1483–1546, German monk, theologian, and leader of the Reformation; excommunicated in 1520 by Pope Leo X; composed many Lutheran hymns and translated the Bible into German. **Lu·ther·an** (lōō′thər·ən) *n.* A follower or disciple of Luther; a member of the Lutheran Church. —*adj.* **1** Pertaining to or believing in Martin Luther or his doctrines. **2** Pertaining to the Lutheran Church or its doctrines. —**Lu′ther·an·ism** *n.*

Lutheran Church A Protestant denomination founded in Germany by Martin Luther in the 16th century. Its chief doctrine is justification by faith alone. The Lutheran churches in America are grouped in three principal bodies: the **American Lutheran Church, Evangelical Lutheran Synodical Conference of North America,** and **United Lutheran Church in America.** See also MISSOURI SYNOD.

lu·thern (loo′thərn) *n.* A lucarne. [? Alter. of LUCARNE]

lux (luks) *n.* *pl.* **lux·es** or **lu·ces** (loo′sēz) *Physics* The unit of illumination in the metric system, equivalent to the illumination on a surface of one square meter on which there is a uniformly distributed flux of one lumen. [<L, light]

lux·ate (luk′sāt) *v.t.* **·at·ed, ·at·ing** To put out of joint; dislocate. [<L *luxatus,* pp. of *luxare* dislocate <*luxus* dislocated] —**lux·a′tion** *n.*

luxe (looks, luks; *Fr.* lüks) *n.* Superfine quality; luxury: usually with *de:* edition *de luxe.* [<F <L *luxus* extravagance]

Lux·em·burg (luk′səm·bûrg, *Fr.* lük·sän·bòòr′) **1** A constitutional grand duchy between Belgium, France, and Germany; 999 square miles; capital, Luxemburg. **2** A province of SE Belgium; 1,705 square miles; capital, Arlon. Also **Lux′em·bourg.**

lux·me·ter (luks′mē′tər) *n.* An instrument that measures illumination in terms of luxes.

lux·u·ri·ance (lug·zhŏŏr′ē·əns, luk·shŏŏr′-) *n.* Excessive growth; exuberance; lushness. Also **lux·u′ri·an·cy.**

lux·u·ri·ant (lug·zhŏŏr′ē·ənt, luk·shŏŏr′-) *adj.* **1** Exhibiting or characterized by luxuriance in growth; also, fertile, as soil. **2** Exuberant in fancy, invention, etc.; abundant, extravagant, or excessive in action or speech; ornate, florid, or rich in design. See synonyms under FERTILE. [<L *luxurians, -antis,* ppr. of *luxuriare.* See LUXURIATE.] —**lux·u′ri·ant·ly** *adv.*

lux·u·ri·ate (lug·zhŏŏr′ē·āt, luk·shŏŏr′-) *v.i.* **·at·ed, ·at·ing** **1** To take great pleasure; indulge oneself fully. **2** To live sumptuously. **3** To grow profusely. [<L *luxuriatus,* pp. of *luxuriare* be fruitful, abound <*luxuria.* See LUXURY.] —**lux·u′ri·a′tion** *n.*

lux·u·ri·ous (lug·zhŏŏr′ē·əs, luk·shŏŏr′-) *adj.* **1** Pertaining or administering to luxury; voluptuous. **2** Supplied with luxuries. [<L *luxuriosus*] —**lux·u′ri·ous·ly** *adv.* —**lux·u′ri·ous·ness** *n.*

lux·u·ry (luk′shər·ē, *occasionally* lug′zhər·ē) *n.* *pl.* **·ries** **1** A free indulgence in the pleasures that gratify the senses. **2** Anything that ministers to comfort or pleasure that is expensive or rare, but is not necessary to life, health, subsistence, etc.; a delicacy. [<OF *luxurie* <L *luxuria* <*luxus* extravagance]

-ly¹ suffix of adjectives Like; characteristic of; pertaining to: *manly, godly.* Compare -LIKE. [OE -*lic*]

-ly² suffix of adverbs **1** In a (specified) manner: used to form adverbs from adjectives, or (rarely) from nouns: *brightly, busily.* **2** Occurring every (specified interval): *hourly, yearly.* [OE -*lice* <-*lic* -LY¹]

◆ In cases where an adjective already ends in -*ly,* the forms of the adjective and adverb are often identical: He spoke *kindly.* Occasionally, -*ly* is added to -*ly* (which is then changed to -*li*), as in *surlily,* but this is generally avoided as awkward. In the case of words derived from French adjectives in -*le,* the ending is dropped before adding -*ly,* as in *nobly, possibly.*

ly·can·thrope (lī′kən·thrōp, lī·kan′thrōp) *n.* **1** A werewolf. **2** One afflicted with lycanthropy. [<Gk. *lykanthrōpos* <*lykos* wolf + *anthrōpos* a man]

ly·can·thro·py (lī·kan′thrə·pē) *n.* **1** The supposed power of turning a human being into a wolf or of becoming a wolf, by magic or witchcraft. **2** Belief in werewolves. **3** *Psychiatry* A mania in which the patient imagines himself to be a wolf or some other wild animal. [<Gk. *lykanthrōpia*] —**ly′can·throp′ic** (-thrŏp′ik) *adj.*

Ly·ca·on (lī·kā′on) In Greek mythology, a king of Arcadia and father of Callisto, who, when

Zeus sought his hospitality disguised as a poor man, tested the god's divinity by offering him human flesh as food: Zeus transformed him into a wolf. [<Gk. *Lykaōn* <*lykos* wolf]

ly·ce·um (lī·sē′əm) *n.* *pl.* **·ce·ums** or **·ce·a** (-sē′ə) **1** An association for popular instruction by lectures, a library, debates, etc.; **lych·nis** (lik′nis) *n.* Any plant of the genus *Lychnis* of erect ornamental herbs. *L. chalcedonica* is the scarlet lychnis, and *L. coronaria* the rose campion. [<L <Gk.]

lyd·dite (lid′īt) *n.* A high explosive, chiefly of picric acid: used for torpedo and other shells which on explosion kill by shock or suffocation from its deadly fumes. [from *Lydd,* town in England, where first manufactured]

Ly·co·me·des (lī′kə·mē′dēz) In Greek legend, a king of Scyros; son of Apollo and guardian of Achilles.

ly·co·pod (lī′kə·pod) *n.* A plant of the clubmoss family. [<Gk. *lykos* wolf + -POD; after the resemblance of the root to a claw]

ly·co·po·di·um (lī′kə·pō′dē·əm) *n.* **1** A plant (genus *Lycopodium*) of erect or creeping evergreen pteridophytes, the clubmosses. **2** An inflammable fine yellow powder, the spores of clubmosses. [<NL]

lye (lī) *n.* **1** A solution leached from ashes, or derived from a substance containing alkali: used in making soap, preparing hominy, etc. **2** A lixivium. [OE *lēah*]

ly·ing¹ (lī′ing) *n.* The practice of telling lies; untruthfulness. See synonyms under DECEPTION. —*adj.* Addicted to, conveying, or constituting falsehood; mendacious; false. —**ly′ing·ly** *adv.*

ly·ing² (lī′ing) Present participle of LIE¹. —*adj.* Being in a horizontal position; prostrate.

ly·ing-in (lī′ing·in′) *n.* The confinement of women during childbirth; parturition. —*adj.* Of or pertaining to childbirth: a *lying-in* home or hospital.

lymph (limf) *n.* **1** A transparent, colorless, alkaline fluid which circulates in the lymph vessels of vertebrates. It consists of a plasma resembling that of the blood and of corpuscles like the white blood corpuscles. **2** The coagulable exudation from the blood vessels in inflammation. **3** The virus, or a culture of the virus, of a disease, used in vaccination or similar treatment. **4** *Obs.* A spring; water. [<L *lympha,* var. of *limpa* water, ? <Gk. *nymphē* nymph, goddess of moisture]

lym·phad·e·ni·tis (lim·fad′ə·nī′tis, lim′fə·də-) *n.* *Pathol.* Inflammation of the lymphatic glands. [<NL <LYMPH(O)- + ADEN(O)- + -ITIS]

lym·phan·gi·al (lim·fan′jē·əl) *adj.* Of or pertaining to the lymphatic vessels; lymphatic. [<LYMPH(O)- + ANGI(O)- + -AL¹]

lym·phat·ic (lim·fat′ik) *adj.* **1** Pertaining to, containing, or conveying lymph. **2** Caused by or affecting the lymphatic glands. **3** Having a phlegmatic temperament. —*n.* A vessel that conveys lymph into the veins; an absorbent vessel. [<NL <L *lymphaticus* frantic, frenzied, trans. of Gk. *nympholēptos* caught by nymphs]

lym·pha·tism (lim′fə·tiz′əm) *n.* **1** Lymphatic temperament. **2** *Pathol.* An unhealthy condition due to an excess of lymphatic tissue. [<LYMPHATIC]

lym·pha·ti·tis (lim′fə·tī′tis) *n.* *Pathol.* Inflammation in any part of the lymphatic system. [<LYMPHAT(O)- + -ITIS]

lymphato- *combining form* Lymphatic. Also, before vowels, **lymphat-.**

lym·pha·tol·y·sis (lim′fə·tol′ə·sis) *n.* *Pathol.* Dissolution or breakdown of lymphatic tissue. [<LYMPHATO- + -LYSIS] —**lym·pha·to·lyt·ic** (lim′fə·tō·lit′ik) *adj.*

lymph cell A lymphocyte.

lymph gland *Anat.* One of the nodular bodies about the size of a pea, found in the course of the lymphatic vessels, composed of a reticulum containing lymphoid cells.

lympho- *combining form* Lymph; of or pertaining to lymph or the lymphatic system: *lymphocyte.* Also, before vowels, **lymph-.** [See LYMPH]

lym·pho·cyte (lim′fə·sīt) *n.* *Anat.* A variety of nucleated, colorless leucocyte in the lymphatic glands of all vertebrate animals, resembling a small white blood corpuscle.

lym·pho·cy·to·sis (lim′fə·sī·tō′sis) *n.* *Pathol.*

An excess of lymphocytes in the blood. —**lym′pho·cy·tot′ic** (-tot′ik) *adj.*

lym·phoid (lim′foid) *adj.* Of, pertaining to, or resembling lymph or a lymphatic gland. [<LYMPH + -OID]

lymphoid tissue Tissue constituting the lymph glands; adenoid tissue.

lym·phor·rhe·a (lim′fə·rē′ə) *n.* *Pathol.* A flow of lymph from ruptured lymph vessels.

lyn·ce·an (lin·sē′ən) *adj.* **1** Pertaining to or characteristic of the lynx. **2** Lynx-eyed; sharp-sighted. [<L *lynceus* <Gk. *lynkeios* <*lynx* lynx]

lynch (linch) *v.t.* To kill by mob action, as by hanging or burning. —*adj.* Of or relating to lynching. [<LYNCH LAW] —**lynch′er** *n.* —**lynch′ing** *n.*

lynch law The practice of administering punishment, usually by hanging, for alleged crimes without trial by law. [? after Capt. Wm. *Lynch,* 1742–1820, Virginia magistrate]

lynx (lingks) *n.* Any of several wildcats (genus *Lynx*) of Europe and North America; with short tails, tufted ears, and relatively long limbs; especially, the Canadian lynx (*L. canadensis*) and the North American bay lynx (*L. rufus*). [<L *lynx, lyncis* <Gk. *lynx*]

Lynx (lingks) A northern constellation. See CONSTELLATION.

lynx-eyed (lingks′īd′) *adj.* Having acute sight.

lyo- *combining form* A loosening; dissolution: *lyophilic.* Also, before vowels, **ly-.** [<Gk. *lyein* loosen]

ly·on·naise (lī′ə·nāz′, *Fr.* lē·ô·nez′) *adj.* Made with finely sliced onions; especially, designating a method of preparing potatoes with fried onions. [<F, fem. of *lyonnais* of Lyon]

Ly·ons (lī′ənz, *Fr.* lē·ôn′) A city of east central France at the confluence of the Rhône and the Saône; the third largest city of France. Also **Ly·on′.** —**Ly·on·nais′** *adj.*

ly·o·phil·ic (lī′ə·fil′ik) *adj.* *Chem.* Pertaining to or designating a colloidal system either phase of which is more or less freely soluble in the other. [<LYO- + Gk. *philos* loving]

ly·o·pho·bic (lī′ə·fō′bik) *adj.* *Chem.* Resisting solution: said of colloidal systems neither phase of which will freely dissolve in the other. [<LYO- + Gk. *phobos* fear]

ly·o·sorp·tion (lī′ə·sôrp′shən) *n.* *Chem.* The adsorption of a solvent film upon the surface of suspended particles. [<LYO- + (AD)SORPTION]

ly·o·trop·ic (lī′ə·trop′ik, -trō′pik) *adj.* *Chem.* **1** Designating a series of ions, radicals, or salts arranged according to their influence on certain colloidal, physiological, or catalytic phenomena. **2** Having an affinity for entering into solution.

Ly·ra (lī′rə) An ancient constellation representing the lyre of Hermes or of Orpheus; the Harp. It contains the bright star Vega. See CONSTELLATION. [<L <Gk.]

ly·rate (lī′rāt) *adj.* *Bot.* Lyre-shaped, as a pinnatifid leaf having its upper lobes largest. Also **ly′rat·ed.** [<NL *lyratus*] —**ly′rate·ly** *adv.*

lyre (līr) *n.* An ancient harplike stringed instrument, having a hollow body and two horns bearing a crosspiece between which and the body were stretched the strings, generally seven. [<L *lyra* <Gk.]

LYRES

Lyre (līr) The constellation Lyra.

lyre·bird (līr′bûrd′) *n.* An Australian passerine bird (genera *Menura* and *Harriwhitea*) having the tail feathers of the males arranged in lyre shape.

lyr·ic (lir′ik) *adj.* **1** Originally, belonging to a lyre; hence, adapted for singing to a lyre. **2** Characterizing verse expressing the poet's personal emotions or sentiments; songlike: distinguished from *epic, dramatic.* **3** Pertaining to the writing of such verse; having written lyric poetry. **4** Musical; singing or to be sung. **5** *Music* Light, graceful, and having a flexible quality: opposed to *dramatic:* said of the voice in singing. Also **lyr′i·cal.** —*n.* **1** A lyric poem; a song. **2** *Usually pl.* The words of a song, especially as distinguished from the music. [<L *lyricus* <Gk. *lyrikos* <*lyra* a lyre] —**lyr′i·cal·ly** *adv.*

lyr·i·cism (lir'ə·siz'əm) *n.* **1** Lyrical quality; a lyric composition. **2** Emotional expression, as of enthusiasm.

lyr·i·cist (lir'ə·sist) *n.* **1** One who writes the words of a song or the lyrics for a musical play. **2** A lyric poet.

lyric poetry Any form of poetry giving expression to the poet's personal emotions or sentiments. It includes the *sonnet,* the *elegy, ode, song, psalm, hymn,* etc.

ly·ri·form (lī'rə·fôrm) *adj.* Shaped like a lyre.

lyr·ism (līr'iz·əm) *n.* **1** Lyre–playing; hence, the singing of lyrics, or music in general. **2** Lyricism. [<F *lyrisme*]

lyr·ist (līr'ist) *n.* **1** One who plays the lyre. **2** A lyric poet. [<L *lyristes* <Gk. *lyristēs* <*lyrixein* play on a lyre]

lyse (līs) *v.t. & v.i.* **lysed, lys·ing** To undergo or cause to undergo lysis. [<Gk. *lysis* loosening]

ly·ser·gic acid (lī·sûr'jik) *n. Biochem.* A crystalline alkaloid, $C_{16}H_{16}N_2O_2$, derived from ergot, of which it is the chief toxic principle, and forming the base of **lysergic acid di·eth·**

yl·am·ide–25 (dī'eth·əl·am'īd), or LSD. [<LYS- + *erg(ot)* + -IC]

lysi– *combining form* A loosening: *lysigenetic.* Also, before vowels, **lys–.** [<Gk. *lysis* a loosening]

ly·si·ge·net·ic (lī'sə·jə·net'ik) *adj. Biol.* Produced or producing by the breakdown or absorption of intermediate or contiguous cells: said of certain intercellular spaces or of their mode of formation. Also **ly'si·gen'ic, ly·sig·e·nous** (lī·sij'ə·nəs). —**ly'si·ge·net'i·cal·ly** *adv.*

ly·sim·e·ter (lī·sim'ə·tər) *n.* An instrument for determining the solubility of substances.

ly·sin (lī'sin) *n.* A substance capable of destroying bacteria, blood corpuscles, etc. [<LYS(I)- + -IN]

ly·sine (lī'sēn, -sin) *n. Biochem.* An important amino acid, $C_6H_{14}O_2N_2$, produced on hydrolysis of various proteins. Also **ly'sin.** [<LYS(I)- + -INE[2]]

ly·sis (lī'sis) *n.* **1** *Pathol.* The gradual disappearing of a disease. Compare CRISIS. **2** *Biochem.* The process of disintegration or destruction of cells. [<NL <Gk., loosening

<Gk. *lyein* loose, dissolve]

–lysis *combining form* A loosing, dissolving, etc.: *hydrolysis, paralysis.* [<Gk., loosening]

lys·sa (lis'ə) *n.* Hydrophobia; rabies. [<Gk., frenzy, madness]

lys·so·pho·bi·a (lis·ə·fō'bē·ə) *n. Psychiatry* A morbid fear of insanity. [<Gk. *lyssa* madness + -PHOBIA] —**lys'so·pho'bic** *adj.*

Lys·ter bag (lis'tər) A portable, waterproof bag for supplying disinfected drinking water to troops: also spelled *Lister bag.* [after W.J.L. *Lyster,* 1869–1947, U. S. Army surgeon]

–lyte[1] *combining form* A substance decomposed by a (specified) process: *electrolyte.* [<Gk. *lytos* loosened, dissolved < *lyein* loosen]

–lyte[2] See –LITE.

–lytic *combining form* Loosing; dissolving: used in adjectives corresponding to nouns in *–lysis: hydrolytic paralytic.* [<Gk. *lytikos* loosing < *lysis* a loosening]

lyt·ta (lit'ə) *n. pl.* **lyt·tae** (lit'ē) *Anat.* A vermiform cartilage or fibrous band on the under surface of the tongue in carnivores, as the dog. [<L, a worm said to grow under a dog's tongue and cause madness <Gk., madness]

M

m, M (em) *n. pl.* **m's, M's** or **ms, Ms** or **ems** (emz) **1** The 13th letter of the English alphabet: from Phoenician *mem,* Greek *mu,* Roman *M.* **2** The sound of the letter *m,* usually a voiced, bilabial nasal. See ALPHABET. —*symbol* **1** The Roman numeral 1,000. See under NUMERAL. **2** *Printing* An em.

ma (mä, mô) *n.* Mama; mother. [Short for MAMA]

ma'am (mam, mäm, *unstressed* məm) *n.* **1** A respectful address to women, corresponding to *sir* in the case of men. **2** A dame; mistress: used in combination: a *schoolma'am.* **3** *Brit.* A term of respectful address used to the queen or to a royal princess. [Contraction of MADAM]

Mab (mab), **Queen** In English folklore, the queen of the fairies.

tion of eleven medieval Welsh romances translated by Lady Charlotte Guest in 1838–1849. [<Welsh *mabinogion,* pl. of *mabinogi* bardic instructional material < *mabinog* a bard's apprentice]

Mac– *prefix* In Scottish and Irish names, son of: *MacDougal,* son of Dougal: abbr. *Mc, M[c],* or *M'.* See also MC–. [<Scottish Gaelic and Irish, son]

ma·ca·bre (mə·kä'brə, -bər) *adj.* Suggestive of death; gruesome; frightful. Also **ma·ca'ber.** [<F <OF (*danse*) *macabré* (dance) of death, prob. alter. of *Macabé* <LL *Maccabaeus,* ? a character in a morality play]

ma·ca·co (mə·kä'kō) *n. pl.* **·cos** Any one of various lemurs, especially the black lemur of Madagascar (*Lemur macaco*). [<Pg. < Tupian *macaco, macaca* a monkey]

mac·ad·am (mə·kad'əm) *n.* **1** Broken stone for macadamizing a road. **2** A macadamized road. [after John L. *McAdam,* 1756–1836, British engineer]

mac·ad·am·ize (mə·kad'ə·mīz) *v.t.* **·ized, ·iz·ing** To pave with small consolidated broken stone on a soft or hard, but drained and convex, substratum. —**mac·ad'am·i·za'tion** *n.* —**mac·ad'am·iz'er** *n.*

ma·caque (mə·käk') *n.* An Old World monkey (genus *Macaca*) with stout body, short tail, cheek pouches, and pronounced muzzle. [<F <Pg. *macaco.* See MACACO.]

MACAQUE

Ital. *maccaroni, maccheroni,* pl. of *macherone* groats <LGk. *makaria* a broth with barley groats <Gk., blessedness < *makar* blessed]

mac·a·ron·ic (mak'ə·ron'ik) *adj.* **1** Consisting of a burlesque medley of real or coined words from various languages; hence, jumbled; mixed. **2** Pertaining to or like macaroni. Also **mac'a·ron'i·cal.** [<NL *macaronicus* <Ital. *maccheronico* <*maccheroni* MACARONI]

mac·a·roon (mak'ə·rōōn') *n.* A small cooky of ground almonds or almond paste, white of egg, and sugar; also, an imitation of this made with coconut. [<MF *macaron* <Ital. *maccarone,* var. of *macherone* MACARONI]

Mac·Ar·thur (mək·är'thər), **Douglas,** 1880–1964, U.S. general in World War II; commander in chief in the Pacific and in Japan.

ma·caw (mə·kô') *n.* A large tropical American parrot (genus *Ara*), with a long tail, harsh voice, and brilliant plumage. [<Pg. *macao,* prob. <Tupian *maca(vuana)*]

Mac·beth (mək·beth'), died 1057, king of Scotland; hero of Shakespeare's tragedy of the same name.

mac·chia (mak'yə) See MAQUIS.

Mac·Duff (mək·duf') A character in Shakespeare's *Macbeth,* who kills Macbeth.

mace[1] (mās) *n.* **1** A club–shaped staff of office borne before officials or displayed on the table of a legislative body. **2** A medieval steel war club, often with spiked metal head, for use against armor. **3** A person who carries a mace, as in a ceremony. **4** A curriers' knobbed mallet for softening hides. **5** A flat-headed form of billiard cue, formerly used on pocket tables. [<OF *masse, mace.* Cf. LL *matteola* a mallet.]

mace[2] (mās) *n.* An aromatic spice made from the covering of nutmeg seed. [<OF *macis* <L *macir* <Gk. *maker* a spicy bark from India]

Mace (mās) *n.* A chemical solution similar to tear gas that temporarily blinds or incapacitates one when sprayed in the face, used as a weapon. —*v.t.* **Maced, Mac·ing** To spray with Mace. [<Chemical *Mace,* a trade name]

mac·é·doine (mas'i·dwän', *Fr.* mà-sā·dwän') *n.* A dish of mixed vegetables or fruits, served as a salad or dessert; also, any mixture; medley; olio. [<F, a type of parsley <OF (*perresel*) *macedoine* Macedonian (parsley)]

MACES

mac·er (mā'sər) *n.* **1** A macebearer. **2** In Scotland, an officer who attends the courts and executes their orders. [<OF *maissier* < *masse, mace* mace]

mac·er·ate (mas'ə·rāt) *v.* **·at·ed, ·at·ing** *v.t.* **1 a** To reduce to a soft mass by soaking. **b** To separate the soft parts of by soaking; digest. **2** To make thin; emaciate. —*v.i.* **3** To undergo maceration. [<L *maceratus,* pp. of *macerare* make soft, knead] —**mac'er·at'er, mac'er·a'tor** *n.*

mac·er·a·tion (mas'ə·rā'shən) *n.* The process or action of steeping a solid material in liquid so as to soften it or break down its structure; digestion.

mach (mak, mäk) See MACH NUMBER.

mach effect (mak, mäk) *Physics* **1** Any effect produced by an object moving at transonic or supersonic speeds, as a shock wave. **2** The aggregate of such effects.

ma·chet·e (mə·shet'ē, mə·shet'; *Sp.* mä-chā'tā) *n.* A heavy knife or cutlas used both as an implement and as a weapon by the natives of tropical America. [<Sp., dim. of *macho* an ax, a hammer <L *marculus,* dim. of *marcus* a hammer]

SPANISH MACHETES

Mach·i·a·vel·li (mäk'ē·ə·vel'ē, *Ital.* mä'kyä·vel'lē), **Niccolò,** 1469–1527, Florentine statesman and writer on government.

Mach·i·a·vel·li·an (mak'ē·ə·vel'ē·ən) *adj.* Of or pertaining to Niccolò Machiavelli, or to the unscrupulous doctrines of political opportunism associated with his name. —*n.* A follower of Machiavelli.

Mach·i·a·vel·li·an·ism (mak'ē·ə·vel'ē·ən·iz'əm) *n.* The theory and practice of power politics elaborated from Machiavelli's *The Prince:* envisaging (1) seizure, maintenance, and extension of absolute power by the nicely graduated use of guile, fraud, force, and terror; (2) control by the ruler of all avenues of communication, thus facilitating the deliberate molding of public opinion; (3) the employment for surveillance and terrorist activities of subordinates who can be disowned and liquidated by the ruler, who thus escapes the blame for their atrocities.

mach·i·co·late (mə·chik'ə·lāt) *v.t.* **·lat·ed, ·lat·ing** To furnish with machicolations. [<Med. L *machicolatus,* pp. of *machicolare*]

ma·chic·o·la·tion (mə·chik'ə·lā'shən) *n.* **1**

Archit. An opening between a wall and a parapet, to permit missiles or boiling liquids to be dropped upon an assailing enemy. **2** The act of showering missiles on an attacking party through such openings.

ma·chin·a·ble (mə·shē′nə·bəl) *adj. Metall.* Capable of being shaped, cut, or polished by high-speed machine tools, as certain metals and alloys. — **ma·chin′a·bil′i·ty** *n.*

mach·i·nate (mak′ə·nāt) *v.t. & v.i.* **·nat·ed, ·nat·ing** To plan or devise; scheme, especially with evil intent. [<L *machinatus,* pp. of *machinari* contrive <*machina* MACHINE]

mach·i·na·tion (mak′ə·nā′shən) *n.* The act of contriving a secret or hostile plan; also, such a plan; plot. See synonyms under ARTIFICE. — **mach′i·na′tor** *n.*

ma·chine (mə·shēn′) *n.* **1** Any combination of mechanisms for utilizing, modifying, applying, or transmitting energy, whether simple, as a lever and fulcrum, pulley, etc., or complex, as a Fourdrinier papermaking apparatus. **2** An automobile; also, any other mechanical vehicle, as a bicycle, airplane, etc. **3** In many trades or vocations, the construction principally used or typical of the trade. **4** One who acts in a mechanical manner; a robot. **5** An ancient theatrical contrivance, originating in Greece, for the creation of stage effects: also applied to such portions of the plot of a work of fiction as are introduced for the sake of effect. **6** The organization of the powers of any complex body: the *machine* of government; specifically, an organization within a political party, controlled by practical politicians, in which discipline and subordination are maintained chiefly by the use of patronage, as in the distribution of offices and contracts. **7** Formerly, a military engine. — *adj.* **1** Pertaining to, for, produced by, or producing a machine or machinery: *machine* knitting, *machine* shop, etc. **2** Typified by the application or predominance of machines: *machine* age. **3** Mechanical; lacking in originality or uniqueness. — *v.t.* **·chined, ·chin·ing** To shape, mill, make, etc., by machinery. [<F <L *machina* <Gk. *mēchanē* < *mēchos* a contrivance] — **ma·chin′al** *adj.*

machine element One of various simple mechanisms, as the lever, pulley, cam, gearwheel, etc., which, alone or in combination, facilitate conversion of energy to useful work. See illustration, page 763. Also **simple machine.**

ma·chine-gun (mə·shēn′gun′) *n.* An automatic gun that discharges small-arms ammunition in a rapid, continuous fire: also **machine gun.** — *v.t.* **-gunned, -gun·ning** To fire at or shoot with a machine-gun. — **ma·chine′-gun′ner** *n.*

ma·chin·er·y (mə·shē′nər·ē) *n. pl.* **·er·ies 1** The parts of a machine or a number of machines and kindred appliances collectively. **2** Any combination of means working together; a complex system of appliances; the arrangements for effecting a specific end. **3** The supernatural or other means by which the catastrophe of a classical drama was brought about; hence, the incidents and events introduced to build up the plot in a work of fiction.

machine shop A workshop for making or repairing machines.

machine tool A power-driven tool, partly or wholly automatic in action, as a lathe, used for cutting and shaping the parts of a machine.

ma·chin·ist (mə·shē′nist) *n.* A maker or repairer of machines; one expert in their design or construction, or in using metalworking tools.

ma·chis·mo (mä·chēz′mō, -chiz′-) *n.* Maleness or masculinity, especially when associated with strong or exaggerated pride in or a conspicuous display of the qualities, attitudes, etc., considered characteristically masculine. [<Sp. < *macho* male]

mach·me·ter (mak′mē′tər, mäk′-) *n. Aeron.* An instrument for determining the speed of airplanes, especially with reference to the mach number. [<MACH (NUMBER) + -METER]

mach number (mak, mäk) A number expressing the speed of an object moving through a fluid medium in relation to the speed of sound in the same medium: in aeronautics it is the ratio of the air speed to the speed of sound in the undisturbed medium, a mach number of 1 indicating a speed equal to the speed of sound. Also *mach.* [after Ernst *Mach,* 1838–1916, Austrian physicist]

ma·cho (mä′chō) *n. pl.* **·chos** (-chōs) A virile man, especially one who takes excessive pride in his virility. — *adj.* Of or characteristic of a macho. [<Sp., male]

ma·chree (mə·krē′) *n.* My heart; my love: a term of endearment. [<Irish <*mo* my + *croidhe* heart <OIrish *cride*]

-machy *combining form* A fight between, or by means of: *logomachy.* [<Gk. -*machia* < *machē* a battle]

mac·in·tosh (mak′ən·tosh) See MACKINTOSH.

mack·er·el (mak′ər·əl) *n.* **1** An Atlantic food fish (*Scomber scombrus*), steel-blue above with blackish bars, and silvery beneath. **2** Some scombroid fish resembling it, as the Spanish mackerel (*Scomberomorus maculatus*). [<OF *makerel;* ult. origin unknown]

mackerel gull The common tern.

mackerel sky *Meteorol.* A cloud formation with numerous detached cloudlets resembling the markings on a mackerel's back.

Mack·i·nac Island (mak′ə·nô) A resort city on the southern end of Mackinac Island in the Straits of Mackinac. Also **Mackinac.**

mack·i·naw (mak′ə·nô) A shortened form of MACKINAW BLANKET, MACKINAW BOAT, MACKINAW COAT. [<dial. F (Canadian) *Mackinac* <*Michilimackinac* Mackinac Island <Algonquian (Ojibwa) *mitchimakinak* a large turtle]

Mackinaw blanket A thick, heavy blanket formerly used by Indians and traders of the western United States.

Mackinaw boat A large, sharp-ended, flat-bottomed bateau, sometimes equipped with sails, and formerly used on the northern Great Lakes.

Mackinaw cloth A heavy-napped woolen fabric, or one having cotton or rayon mixed in the yarns: the two sides may be different colors, sometimes in plaids: used for lumbermen's jackets, sport clothes, windbreakers, etc.

Mackinaw coat A thick, short, double-breasted coat with a plaid pattern.

mack·in·tosh (mak′ən·tosh) *n.* **1** A waterproof overgarment or cloak. **2** Thin rubber-coated cloth. Also *macintosh.* [after Charles *Macintosh,* 1766–1843, Scottish chemist, inventor of the cloth]

mack·le (mak′əl) *n.* A spot or blemish; also, a blurred impression. — *v.t. & v.i.* **mack·led, mack·ling** To print with a blurred or double image; blur; blot. Also spelled *macule.* [<F *macule* <L *macula* a spot]

mac·le (mak′əl) *n.* **1** A twin crystal, espe-

Toggle Joint

Cam

Lever

Worm Gear

Link Motion

Crank Motion

Gears

Belt Drive

Ball Bearing

Universal Joint

Ratchet and Double Pawl

MACHINE ELEMENTS

cially of a diamond. **2** Chiastolite. **3** A mackle. **4** Mascle. [<F <OF *mascle* <Med. L *mascula* mesh of net <L *macula* spot]

Mâ·con (mà·kôṅ′) *n.* A wine produced in the neighborhood of Mâcon, France.

mac·ra·mé (mak′rə·mā) *n.* A fringe, lace, or trimming of knotted thread or cord; knotted work. [Appar. <Turkish *maqramah* a towel <Arabic *miqramah* a veil]

mac·ren·ceph·a·ly (mak′ren·sef′ə·lē) *n. Pathol.* Hypertrophy of the brain. [<MACR(O)- + EN-CEPHAL(O)- + -Y¹] — **mac′ren·ce·phal′ic** (-sə·fal′ik), **mac′ren·ceph′a·lous** *adj.*

macro- *combining form* Large or long in size or duration: *macrocephaly, macrobiosis.* Also, before vowels, **macr-.** [<Gk. *makros* large]

mac·ro·bi·o·sis (mak′rō·bī·ō′sis) *n.* Longevity. [<NL <Gk. *makros* long + *bios* life] — **mac′·ro·bi·ot′ic** (-ot′ik) *adj.*

mac·ro·bi·ot·ics (mak′rō·bī·ot′iks) *n.pl.* (*construed as sing.*) A dietetic regimen advocating the use of whole-grain cereals, the avoidance of meat, etc. [<MACRO- + BIOTIC]

mac·ro·ceph·a·ly (mak′rō·sef′ə·lē) *n.* Excessive size of the head. [<MACRO- + Gk. *kephalē* head] — **mac′ro·ce·phal′ic** (-sə·fal′ik) *adj.* & *n.* — **mac′ro·ceph′a·lous** *adj.*

mac·ro·chem·is·try (mak′rō·kem′is·trē) *n.* The chemistry of large-scale operations or of reactions visible to the naked eye. — **mac′·ro·chem′i·cal** (-i·kəl) *adj.*

mac·ro·cli·mate (mak′rō·klī′mit) *n. Meteorol.* The general climate prevailing over a large area considered as a unit. Compare MICRO-CLIMATE. — **mac′ro·cli·mat′ic** (-klī·mat′ik) *adj.*

mac·ro·cosm (mak′rə·koz′əm) *n.* **1** The great world; the universe: opposed to *microcosm.* **2** The whole of any sphere or department of nature or knowledge to which man is related. [<OF *macrocosme* <Med. L *macrocosmus* <Gk. *makros* long, great + *kosmos* world] — **mac′ro·cos′mic** *adj.*

mac·ro·cyst (mak′rə·sist) *n. Biol.* **1** An enlarged cyst. **2** *Bot.* A large reproductive cell in certain fungi.

mac·ro·cyte (mak′rə·sīt) *n.* An abnormally large erythrocyte. [<MACRO- + (ERYTHRO)-CYTE]

mac·ro·dome (mak′rə·dōm) See under DOME.

mac·ro·e·co·nom·ics (mak′rō·ē′kə·nom′iks, -ek′ə-) *n.* Economics studied in terms of large aggregates of data whose mutual relationships are interpreted with reference to the behavior of the system as a whole: developed by John Maynard Keynes. — **mac′ro·e′co·nom′ic** *adj.*

mac·ro·ga·mete (mak′rō·gə·mēt′, -gam′ēt) *n. Biol.* The female of two conjugating gametes: so called from its being the larger. Compare MICROGAMETE. [<MACRO- + GAMETE]

ma·crog·a·my (mə·krog′ə·mē) *n. Biol.* Conjugation between gametes similar in structure to the original vegetative cells.

mac·ro·graph (mak′rə·graf, -gräf) *n.* A drawing or illustration of an object as seen with the unaided eye.

ma·crog·ra·phy (mə·krog′rə·fē) *n.* **1** Examination with the unaided eye. **2** Extremely large writing: contrasted with *micrography.*

ma·crom·e·ter (mə·krom′ə·tər) *n.* A range-finding instrument similar to a sextant, for measuring distant objects.

mac·ro·me·te·or·ol·o·gy (mak′rō·mē′tē·ə·rol′ə·jē) *n.* The meteorology of large areas; world meteorology; also, the study of climatic phenomena over extended periods of time. Compare MICROMETEOROLOGY.

mac·ro·mol·e·cule (mak′rə·mol′ə·kyōōl) *n.* A giant molecule, as that of a protein, rubber, cellulose, starch, etc. — **mac′ro·mo·lec′u·lar** (-yə·lər) *adj.*

mac·ro·mor·phol·o·gy (mak′rō·môr·fol′ə·jē) *n.* The gross anatomy of plants.

ma·cron (mā′krən, -kron) *n.* A straight line (-) over a vowel to show that it has a long sound, as, ā: opposed to *breve* (˘). [<Gk. *makron,* neut. of *makros* long]

mac·ro·nu·cle·us (mak′rō·nōō′klē·əs, -nyōō′-) *n. pl.* **-cle·i** (-klē·ī) *Biol.* The larger of two nuclei in certain protozoans, as *Paramecium.*

mac·ro·nu·tri·ent (mak′rō·nōō′trē·ənt, -nyōō′-) *n.* A chemical nutrient required in large amounts for plant growth and vitality.

mac·ro·phys·ics (mak′rə·fiz′iks) *n.* The physics

of masses, or of large bodies. — **mac′ro·phys′i·cal** *adj.*

mac·ro·po·di·an (mak′rə·pō′dē·ən) *n.* Any of a family (*Macropodidae*) of marsupials, especially those having six sharp upper incisors and two larger lower ones, enlarged saltatorial hind legs, and long tail: including wallabies and kangaroos. — *adj.* Of or pertaining to the *Macropodidae:* also **ma·crop·o·dine** (mə·krop′ə·din, -dīn), [<NL <Gk. *makropous, -podos* long–footed <*makros* long + *pous, podos* a foot]

ma·crop·si·a (mə·krop′sē·ə) *n. Pathol.* A condition of the eyes in which objects appear larger than they really are: often called *megalopsia.* Also **ma·cro′pi·a** (-krō′pē·ə). [<NL <Gk. *makros* large + *ōps, ōpos* eye]

mac·ro·scop·ic (mak′rə·skop′ik) *adj.* Visible to the naked eye. Also **mac′ro·scop′i·cal.**

mac·ro·spe·cies (mak′rə·spē′shēz) *n. Biol.* A species of which the members exhibit a large range of variation. Compare MICROSPECIES.

mac·ro·spore (mak′rə·spôr, -spōr) *n.* **1** *Bot.* A megaspore. **2** *Biol.* One of the larger of the two kinds of anisospores in ameboid protozoans.

mac·ro·struc·ture (mak′rə·struk′chər) *n.* The structure of metal as observed with the naked eye or under low magnification on a polished or etched surface. — **mac′ro·struc′tur·al** *adj.*

mac·ro·therm (mak′rə·thûrm) *n.* A tropical plant, or one requiring much heat and moisture for survival: also called *megatherm.*

ma·cru·ran (mə·krŏŏr′ən) *n.* One of a suborder (*Macrura*) of crustaceans with well-developed, elongated abdomens, including shrimps, prawns, lobsters, and crayfishes. [<NL <Gk. *makros* long + *oura* tail] — **ma·cru′ral, ma·cru′roid, ma·cru′rous** *adj.*

mac·ta·tion (mak·tā′shən) *n.* The killing of a sacrificial victim. [<L *mactatio, -onis* < *mactatus,* pp. of *mactare* kill]

mac·u·la (mak′yə·lə) *n. pl.* **-lae** (-lē) **1** A spot, as of color on the skin. **2** *Astron.* A dark spot on the sun's surface. **3** A fleck; blotch. [<L, a spot]

mac·u·late (mak′yə·lāt) *v.t.* **-lat·ed, -lat·ing** To spot or blemish; stain. — *adj.* (-lit) Spotted; stained. [<L *maculatus,* pp. of *maculare* < *macula* a spot]

mac·u·la·tion (mak′yə·lā′shən) *n.* **1** The act of spotting, or a spotty condition. **2** The marking of a spotted animal or plant. **3** A soiling; defilement.

mad (mad) *adj.* **mad·der, mad·dest 1** Mentally deranged; insane. **2** Subject to an overpowering emotion; excited intensely or beyond self-control: *mad* with jealousy or grief. **3** *Colloq.* Angry; furious; enraged. **4** Rabid; having hydrophobia; hence, uncontrollable. **5** Proceeding from or indicating a disordered mind; rash: a *mad* project. **6** Tumultuous or uncontrollable in movement or action: said of things: a *mad* torrent. **7** Reckless; heedless. — *n. Slang* Anger; a fit of temper. — **to have a mad on** *Slang* To be angry. [Apheptic var. of OE *gemǣd, gemǣded,* pp. of *gemǣdan* make mad <*gemād* insane] — **mad′ly** *adv.* — **mad′·ness** *n.*

Mad·a·gas·car A country off the east coast of Africa, and the world's fourth largest island., in the Indian Ocean;227,600 square miles; capital, Antananarivo; pop. 13,000,000. French Grande-Ile, Grande-Terre. Formerly Malagasy Republic. - *adj.* & *N.* Madagasean, Malagasy.

mad·am (mad′əm) *n. pl.* **mes·dames** (mā·däm′, Fr. mā·dàm′) *for def.* 1; **mad·ams** *for def.* 2. **1** My lady; mistress: a title of courtesy originally addressed to a woman of rank or high position, but now used to any woman, as at the beginning of a letter. Compare SIR. See MA′AM. **2** The mistress of a brothel. [<OF *ma dame* <*ma* my (<L *meus*) + *dame* lady <L *domina.* Doublet of MADONNA, MADAME.]

mad·ame (mad′əm, Fr. mà·dàm′) *n. pl.* **mes·dames** (mā·däm′, Fr. mā·dàm′) The French title of courtesy for a married woman, equivalent to the English *Mrs.:* abbreviated *Mme.;* often used in English, especially in the plural. [<F <OF *ma dame.* Doublet of MAD-AM, MADONNA.]

mad·cap (mad′kap′) *adj.* Wild; rattle-brained. — *n.* One who acts wildly or rashly.

mad·den (mad′n) *v.t.* & *v.i.* To make or become mad or insane; inflame with anger; enrage. — **mad′den·ing** *adj.* — **mad′den·ing·ly** *adv.*

mad·der¹ (mad′ər) Comparative of MAD.

mad·der² (mad′ər) *n.* **1** Any plant of the genus *Rubia* (family *Rubiaceae*); especially, an Old World shrubby, perennial, hairy herb (*R. tinctorum*), resembling the common bedstraw. **2** A brilliant red tinctorial extract from the root of the madder plant, used in dyeing and as a pigment in many lakes: the coloring principle, alizarin, is now made also synthetically. — *v.t.* To dye with madder. [OE *mædere, mæddre*]

madder lake A pigment and dyestuff formerly made from the madder plant, now largely replaced by alizarin.

mad·ding (mad′ing) *adj.* Being or growing mad; delirious; raging.

mad·dish (mad′ish) *adj.* Rather mad.

mad–dog skullcap (mad′dôg′, -dog′) A common American plant (*Scutellaria lateriflora*) having blue flowers: formerly believed to cure hydrophobia.

made (mād) Past tense and past participle of MAKE. — *adj.* **1** Fabricated; produced, especially artificially. **2** Assured of fortune. **3** Filled in: *made* land.

Ma·dei·ra (mə·dir′ə, Pg. mə·thā′rə) *n.* A fortified wine made in the Madeira islands.

Madeira vine A vine (*Boussingaultia baselloides*) having a bulbous root, shiny leaves, and clusters of white flowers.

mad·e·moi·selle (mad′ə·mə·zel′, Fr. màd·mwà·zel′) *n. pl.* **mad·e·moi·selles,** Fr. **mes·de·moi·selles** (mād·mwà·zel′) **1** The French title of courtesy for unmarried women, equivalent to the English *Miss:* abbreviated *Mlle.* **2** A French nurse or governess. [<F <*ma* my + *demoiselle.* See DEMOISELLE.]

made–up (mād′up′) *adj.* **1** Artificial; fictitious. **2** Complete; finished. **3** With make–up or cosmetics applied.

mad·house (mad′hous′) *n.* **1** A lunatic asylum. **2** A place of confusion, turmoil, and uproar; bedlam.

Mad·i·son (mad′ə·sən) The capital of Wisconsin.

Mad·i·son (mad′ə·sən), **Dolly,** 1768–1849, *née* Payne, wife of James; celebrated as a hostess. —**James,** 1751–1836, president of the United States 1809–17.

Madison Avenue 1 A street running north and south through Manhattan borough of New York City, center of a commercial district containing many advertising agencies and offices of mass media. **2** The world of American advertising and mass media, its power, influence, policies, etc.

Madison's War The War of 1812.

mad·man (mad′man′, -mən) *n. pl.* **·men** (-men′, -mən) A lunatic; maniac.

Ma·don·na (mə·don′ə) *n.* **1** My lady; madam: an Italian title of respect now replaced by *Signora.* **2** The Virgin Mary; also, a painting or statue of the Virgin Mary. [<Ital. <*ma* my (<L *meus*) + *donna* lady <L *domina.* Doublet of MADAM, MADAME.]

ma·dras (mə·dras′, -dräs′, mad′rəs) *n.* **1** A kind of cotton cloth, with thick strands at intervals throughout its weave, giving either a striped, corded, or checked effect. **2** A large, brightly colored kerchief, formerly worn as a headdress [from *Madras,* India, because originally made there]

mad·re·po·rar·i·an (mad′rə·pô·râr′ē·ən) *n.* One of a suborder (*Madreporaria*) of anthozoans with a calcareous skeleton secreted by cells; one of the reef–forming stony corals of tropical seas. — *adj.* Of or pertaining to the *Madreporaria:* also **mad′re·po′ral** (-pô′rəl, -pō′rəl). [<NL <Ital. *madrepora* MADREPORE]

mad·re·pore (mad′rə·pôr, -pōr) *n.* **1** A branched reef coral (family *Acroporidae*); also, any perforate stone coral. **2** The animal which produces madrepore coral. **3** Limestone consisting of fossil madrepores. Also **mad′re·po′ra** (-pôr′ə, -pō′rə). [<F <Ital. *madrepora,* lit., mother stone <*madre* mother (<L *mater*) + *poro,* ? calcareous stone <L *porus* <Gk. *pōros*] — **mad′re·por′ic** (-pôr′ik, -por′ik) *adj.*

mad·re·po·rite (mad′rə·pô·rīt′) *n. Zool.* In starfishes and certain other echinoderms, the circular perforated plate by which the internal ambulacral system communicates with the outside. Also **madreporic plate.** [<MADREPOR(E) + -ITE¹]

Ma·drid (mə·drid', *Sp.* mä·thrēth') The capital of Spain, in the central part.

mad·ri·gal (mad'rə·gəl) *n.* **1** A short lyric poem, usually dealing with a pastoral or amatory subject. **2** A musical setting for such a poem; an a capella part song characterized by elaborate rhythm and contrapuntal imitation. **3** Any part song **4** Any song. [<Ital. *madrigale, mandrigale* <LL *matricale* original, chief <L *matrix* womb; infl. in form by Ital. *mandra* a flock <L, a herd <Gk., a stable, fold]

mad·ri·gal·ist (mad'rə·gəl·ist) *n.* One who writes, or performs in, madrigals.

ma·dri·lène (mad'rə·len', *Fr.* mä·drē·len') *n.* A consommé flavored with tomato and served hot or cold. [<F <Sp. *Madrileño* of Madrid]

ma·dro·ña (mə·drō'nyə) *n.* A large evergreen tree *(Arbutus menziesii)* of northern California with shining oval or oblong leaves, dense racemes of white flowers, and dry, yellow, edible berries, called **madroña apples.** Also **ma·dro'ño** (-nyō). [<Sp. *madroño*]

mad·stone (mad'stōn') *n.* A stone formerly believed to cure hydrophobia.

Madura foot Mycetoma.

Ma·du·ro (mə·dŏŏr'ō) *adj.* Matured; that is, of full strength and color: said of cigars. — *n.* Such a cigar. [<Sp. <L *maturus*]

mad·wom·an (mad'wŏŏm'ən) *n.* *pl.* **·wom·en** (-wim'in) An insane woman; lunatic.

mad·wort (mad'wûrt') *n.* Any of various shrubs or herbs of the mustard family (genera *Alyssum* or *Lobularia*) with small alternate leaves and small yellow or white flowers in terminal racemes or clusters. [? Trans. of NL *Alyssum,* genus name <L <Gk. *alysson* <a- not + *lyssa* rabies]

mael·strom (māl'strəm) *n.* Any irresistible movement or influence: from the **Maelstrom,** a whirlpool or current off the NW coast of Norway. [<Du. *maelstrom, maalstroom* < *malen* grind, whirl round + *stroom* a stream]

mae·nad (mē'nad) *n.* **1** A female votary or priestess of Dionysius; a bacchante. **2** Any woman beside herself with frenzy or excitement. Also spelled *menad.* [<L *Maenas, -adis* <Gk. *mainas* frenzied < *mainesthai* rave] — **mae·nad'ic** *adj.*

ma·es·to·so (mä'es·tō'sō) *adj. & adv. Music* With majesty; stately. [<Ital., majestic <L *majestas* greatness]

ma·es·tro (mä·es'trō, mī'strō) *n.* A master in any art, especially in music. [<Ital., a master <L *magister*]

Ma·fi·a (mä'fē·ä, maf'ē·ə) *n.* A Sicilian secret society, characterized by hostility to and deliberate flouting of the law and its representatives; also, any similar organization of Italians and Sicilians believed to exist in other countries; Black Hand. Also **Maf'fi·a.** Compare CAMORRA. [<Ital. *maffia;* ult. origin uncertain]

ma·fi·o·so (mä'fē·ō'sō, -zō, maf'ē-) *n.* *pl.* **·si** (-sē, -zē) *Sometimes cap.* A member of the Mafia. [<Ital. <MAFIA]

mag·a·zine (mag'ə·zēn', mag'ə·zēn) *n.* **1** A house, room, or receptacle in which anything is stored; a depot; warehouse; specifically, a strong building for storing gunpowder and other military stores; also, a storeroom for gunpowder and shells aboard ship. **2** A receptacle in which the supply of reserve cartridges of a repeating rifle is placed; also, a case in which cartridges are carried. **3** A periodical publication containing sketches, stories, essays, etc. **4** A reservoir or supply chamber in a battery, camera, or the like. — *v.t.* **·zined, ·zin·ing** To store up for future use. [<MF *magasin* <OF *magazin* <Arabic *makhāzin,* pl. of *makhzan* a storehouse < *khazana* store up]

magazine gun A quick-firing small arm fitted with a case carrying a supply of reserve cartridges. See MAGAZINE (def. 2). Also **magazine pistol** or **rifle.**

mag·a·zin·ist (mag'ə·zē'nist) *n.* A contributor to or editor of a magazine. — **mag'a·zin'ism** *n.*

mag·da·len (mag'də·lin) *n.* A reformed prostitute. Also **mag'da·lene** (-lēn). [after *Mary Magdalene*]

Mag·da·lene (mag'də·lēn, *Ger.* mäg'dä·lā'nə) A feminine personal name. Also **Mag'da·len,**

Mag·da·le·na (mag'də·lē'nə, *Du., Pg., Sp., Sw.* mäg'dä·lā'nä). [<LL <Gk. *Magdalēnē,* lit., of Magdala <*Magdala* Magdala, a town on the Sea of Galilee]
— **the Magdalene** Mary Magdalene.

Mag·da·le·ni·an (mag'də·lē'nē·ən) *adj. Anthropol.* Describing an advanced culture stage of the upper Paleolithic in western Europe, immediately preceding the Mesolithic period: it is noted especially for its delicate carvings in bone and ivory and for the brilliant realism of its polychrome cave paintings. [<F *magdalenien,* from *La Madeleine* in west central France, where artifacts were found]

mage (māj) *n.* A magician. [<F <L *magus.* See MAGI.]

Ma·gel·lan (mə·jel'ən), **Fernando,** 1480–1521, Portuguese navigator in the Spanish service.
— **Mag·el·lan·ic** (maj'ə·lan'ik) *adj.*

Magellan, Strait of The channel between the Atlantic and the Pacific separating the South American mainland from Tierra del Fuego.

ma·gen·ta (mə·jen'tə) *n.* **1** A somewhat glaring red coal-tar dyestuff derived from aniline: also called *aniline red* and *fuchsin.* **2** The color given by the pigment, a strong purplish-rose or purplish-red. [from *Magenta;* so called because discovered just after the French victory (1859)]

mag·got (mag'ət) *n.* **1** The larva of a fly; a footless insect larva; a grub. **2** A whim; fancy. [Prob. alter. of ME *maddock, mathek* <ON *mathkr* a worm]

mag·got·y (mag'ət·ē) *adj.* **1** Infested with maggots; flyblown. **2** Whimsical.

mag·ic (maj'ik) *n.* **1** Any supernatural art; sorcery; necromancy. **2** Sleight of hand. **3** Any agency that works with wonderful effect. See synonyms under SORCERY. — **black magic** Any of the branches of magic which invoke the aid of demons or spirits, as witchcraft or diabolism. — **like magic** As if by magic; instantly. — *adj.* **1** Of the nature of magic; used in magic; possessing supernatural powers; sorcerous. **2** Acting like magic. [<OF *magique* <LL *magica (ars)* magic (art) <Gk. *magikē (technē)* < *magikos* of the Magi]

mag·i·cal (maj'i·kəl) *adj.* Pertaining to or produced by or as by magic. ◆ The adjective *magic* is applied more commonly to the powers, influences, or practices, while *magical* is more frequently used of the effects of magic: *magic* arts, a *magic* wand, but *magical* effect, a *magical* result. — **mag'i·cal·ly** *adv.*

ma·gi·cian (mə·jish'ən) *n.* An expert in magic arts; sorcerer; wizard.

magic lantern A device for throwing magnified pictures upon a screen in a darkened room by means of a light placed behind a lens or lenses.

ma·gilp (mə·gilp') *n.* A mixture used as a vehicle for oil colors, usually composed of a pale drying oil and a turpentine varnish, such as mastic: also spelled *megilp.* Also **ma·gilph'** (-gilf'). [? after *McGilp,* a surname]

Ma·gi·not line (mazh'ə·nō, *Fr.* mà·zhē·nō') A system of French fortifications along the German frontier, built during 1925–1935. [after André *Maginot,* 1877–1932, French statesman]

mag·is·te·ri·al (maj'is·tir'ē·əl) *adj.* **1** Of or pertaining to a magistrate or magistracy; like or befitting a master; commanding; authoritative. **2** Hence, having an air of authority; dictatorial. **3** Domineering; pompous. **4** Pertaining to a chemist's or alchemist's magistery. See synonyms under DOGMATIC. [<Med. L *magisterialis* <LL *magisterius* <L *magister* a master] — **mag'is·te'ri·al·ly** *adv.* — **mag'is·te'ri·al·ness** *n.*

mag·is·te·ri·um (maj'is·tir'ē·əm) *n.* The authority of the church to teach dogmatically: a Roman Catholic usage. [<L, the office of a master <*magister* a master]

mag·is·ter·y (maj'is·ter'ē, -tər·ē) *n.* *pl.* **·ter·ies 1** An authoritative statement or exposition; a magisterial decree. **2** A fundamental master principle of nature; also, a panacea. **3** In alchemy, the power to transmute metals or the product of transmutation. **4** A compound, as a precipitate, formed when two liquids are mixed, and differing in character from either: a term used by the older chemists and preserved in the phrase *magistery of bismuth.* [<Med. L *magisterium* the philosopher's stone <L. See MAGISTERIUM.]

mag·is·tra·cy (maj'is·trə·sē) *n.* *pl.* **·cies 1** The office or dignity of a magistrate. **2** The district under a magistrate's jurisdiction. **3** Magistrates collectively.

mag·is·tral (maj'is·trəl) *adj.* **1** Like a magistrate; imperious or pedagogical; magisterial. **2** In pharmacy, specially compounded or prescribed; not kept in stock. **3** Having sovereign power as a medicine. **4** Chief; main: the *magistral* line. — *n. Mil.* The line from which the positions of the various members of a fortification are determined: also **magistral line.** [<F <L *magistralis* <*magister* a master]

mag·is·trate (maj'is·trāt, -trit) *n.* **1** One clothed with public civil authority; an executive or judicial officer. **2** Usually, when unqualified, a minor local justice. [<L *magistratus* magisterial office <L *magister* a master]

mag·is·tra·ture (maj'is·trə·chŏŏr) *n.* **1** Magistracy; government. **2** The term of a magistrate's office. **3** Magistrates collectively. [<F <*magistrat* <L *magistratus.* See MAGISTRATE.]

mag·ma (mag'mə) *n.* *pl.* **·ma·ta** (-mə·tə) **1** Any soft, doughy mixture of organic and mineral materials. **2** *Geol.* The molten mass from which igneous rocks are formed. **3** The residue obtained after expressing the juice from fruits. [<L <Gk. < root of *massein* knead] — **mag·mat·ic** (mag·mat'ik) *adj.*

Mag·na Car·ta (mag'nə kär'tə) **1** The Great Charter of English liberties, delivered June 19, 1215, by King John, at Runnymede, on the demand of the English barons: first document of the English constitution. **2** Any fundamental constitution that secures personal liberty and civil rights. Also **Mag'na Char'ta,** the erroneous but common form. [<Med. L, lit., Great Charter]

mag·na·flux test (mag'nə·fluks) A method for the detection of defects in metals and in engine parts by noting the arrangement of the particles of a magnetic powder scattered over the magnetized surface. [<MAGN(ETIC) + -a- + FLUX]

mag·nan·i·mous (mag·nan'ə·məs) *adj.* **1** Elevated in soul; scorning what is mean or base. **2** Dictated by magnanimity; unselfish: *magnanimous* candor. See synonyms under GENEROUS. [<L *magnanimus* < *magnus* great + *animus* mind, soul] — **mag·nan'i·mous·ly** *adv.* — **mag·nan'i·mous·ness** *n.*

mag·nate (mag'nāt) *n.* A person of rank or importance; a noble or grandee; one notable or powerful in any sphere: an industrial *magnate.* [<LL *magnas, -atis* <*magnus* great]

mag·ne·sia (mag·nē'zhə, -shə, -zē·ə) *n. Chem.* Magnesium oxide, MgO, a light, white, earthy powder, used in medicine as an antacid laxative, in glassmaking, etc. It can be made by burning magnesium or by igniting certain of the magnesium salts. — **milk of magnesia** A milk-white aqueous suspension of magnesium hydroxide, Mg(OH)₂: used as a laxative and antacid. [<Med. L <Gk. *Magnēsia (lithos)* (stone) of Magnesia <*Magnēsia* Magnesia (def. 2)] — **mag·ne'sian, mag·ne'sic** *adj.*

mag·ne·site (mag'nə·sīt) *n.* A massive, granular carbonate of magnesium, MgCO₃. [<MAGNES(IA) + -ITE¹]

mag·ne·si·um (mag·nē'zē·əm, -zhē-, -shē-) *n.* A light, malleable, ductile, silver-white, metallic element (symbol Mg), used to produce a brilliant light by its combustion, and also as an alloy metal. It occurs abundantly in combination, as in magnesite and dolomite. See ELEMENT. [<NL, magnesia]

mag·net (mag'nit) *n.* **1** A lodestone. **2** Any mass of a material capable of attracting magnetic or magnetized bodies. Magnets are natural when, like lodestones, they are found already magnetized, or artificial when magnetism has been given to them by placing them in the field of another magnet or in that caused by an electric current. See ELECTRO-MAGNET. 3 Figuratively, a person or thing exercising a strong attraction. [<OF *magnete* <L *magnes, magnetis* <Gk. *Magnēs (lithos)* Magnesian (stone), i.e., a magnet <*Magnēsia* Magnesia (def. 2)]

magnetic chart A chart indicating the variations in the earth's magnetic field for a given area.

magnetic equator An irregular, unstable line on the earth's surface, encircling it nearly midway between the magnetic poles, where a free magnetic needle has no tendency to dip; the aclinic line. It coincides nearly with the terrestrial equator. See ACLINIC.

magnetic field That region in the neighborhood of a magnet or current-carrying body in which magnetic forces are observable.

magnetic flux *Physics* The flux of magnetic intensity through a surface: expressed in maxwells or webers.

magnetic head *Electronics* A device for recording and playback by which magnetized particles on a moving tape are impressed with a pattern analogous to that of incident sound waves.

magnetic latitude Latitude as measured from the magnetic equator.

magnetic lens *Physics* An assembly of coils and electromagnets so arranged as to produce a magnetic field which will constrain a stream of charged particles to follow a prescribed path.

magnetic meridian A grid line indicating any of the horizontal components of the earth's magnetic field and which passes through the magnetic poles.

magnetic moment A measure of the magnetizing force exerted by a magnetized body or electric current.

magnetic needle A freely movable, needle-shaped piece of magnetized material which tends to point to the north and south (magnetic) poles of the earth.

magnetic north That direction on the earth's surface toward which one end of the magnetic needle tends to point.

MAGNETIC NEEDLE
a. Magnetic north.
b. True north.
c. Magnetic needle.
d. Angle of variation.

magnetic pole 1 Either of the poles of a magnet; more specifically, those points on the earth's surface where the lines of magnetic force are vertical, called the **North** and **South Magnetic Poles.** These slowly change position and do not coincide with the geographical poles. 2 A pole of a magnet.

mag·net·ics (mag·net'iks) *n. pl. (construed as singular)* The science of magnetism.

magnetic signature The specific magnetic susceptibility of a material, product, or structure: said especially of the change of field in the neighborhood of ships exposed to the danger of sensitive magnetic mines.

magnetic speaker A loudspeaker.

magnetic storm A sudden disturbance of the magnetic field surrounding the earth, occurring simultaneously over areas of the earth and apparently connected with sunspots.

magnetic tape *Electronics* A thin ribbon of paper or plastic, one side of which is coated with particles of iron oxide which form magnetic patterns corresponding to the electromagnetic impulses of a tape recorder.

mag·net·ism (mag'nə·tiz'əm) *n.* 1 The specific properties of a magnet, regarded as an effect of molecular interaction. 2 The science that treats of the laws and conditions of magnetic phenomena: also *magnetics.* 3 The amount of magnetic moment in a magnetized body. 4 The sympathetic personal quality that attracts or interests. 5 Mesmerism. Com-

pare ANIMAL MAGNETISM.

mag·net·ite (mag'nə·tīt) *n.* A massive, granular, isometric, black iron oxide, Fe_3O_4; lodestone; an important ore of iron. [<MAGNET + -ITE[1]] — **mag'net·it'ic** (-tit'ik) *adj.*

mag·net·i·za·tion (mag'nə·tə·zā'shən) *n.* The amount of magnetism in or the magnetic moment of a material.

mag·net·ize (mag'nə·tīz) *v.t.* **·ized, ·iz·ing** 1 To communicate magnetic properties to. 2 To attract by strong personal influence; captivate. 3 *Obs.* To hypnotize. Also *Brit.,* **mag'net·ise.** — **mag'net·iz'a·bil'i·ty** *n.* — **mag'net·iz'a·ble** *adj.* — **mag'net·iz'er** *n.*

magnetizing force A vector quantity that measures the capacity of magnetized bodies or electric currents to produce magnetic induction. Symbol, H.

mag·ne·to (mag·nē'tō) *n. pl.* **·tos** Any magnetoelectric machine in which the rotation of a coil of wire between the poles of a permanent magnet induces a current of electricity in the coil; especially, a type of alternator, widely used as a means of igniting the explosive mixtures used in internal-combustion engines, as in automobiles. Also **mag·ne·to·dy·na·mo** (mag·nē'tō·dī'nə·mō), **mag·ne·to·gen·er·a·tor** (mag·nē'tō·jen'ə·rā'tər). [Short for *magnetoelectric machine*]

magneto- *combining form* Magnetic; magnetism: *magnetomotive.*

mag·ne·to·chem·is·try (mag·nē'tō·kem'is·trē) *n.* The science which treats of the interrelations between magnetic and chemical phenomena. — **mag'ne·to·chem'i·cal** *adj.*

mag·ne·to·e·lec·tric·i·ty (mag·nē'tō·i·lek·tris'ə·tē) *n.* 1 Electricity generated by the inductive action of a magnet. 2 The science that treats of the principles and phenomena of such electricity. — **mag·ne·to·e·lec'tric, mag·ne·to·e·lec'tri·cal** *adj.*

mag·ne·to·hy·dro·dy·nam·ic (mag·nē'tō·hī'drō·dī·nam'ik) *adj. Physics* Of, pertaining to, or characterized by the interaction of electromagnetic, mechanical, thermal, and hydrodynamic forces, as by an electric arc in the generation of a plasma jet.

mag·ne·tol·y·sis (mag'nə·tol'ə·sis) *n.* Chemical action in a substance placed in a magnetic field: analogous to electrolysis. [<MAGNETO- + -LYSIS] — **mag·net·o·lyt·ic** (mag·net'ə·lit'ik) *adj.*

mag·ne·tom·e·ter (mag'nə·tom'ə·tər) *n.* An instrument for measuring the intensity and direction of magnetic forces. — **mag'ne·tom'e·try** *n.*

mag·ne·to·mo·tive (mag·nē'tō·mō'tiv, mag'nə·tō-) *adj.* 1 Acting magnetically. 2 Characterizing a force producing magnetic flux: distinguished from *electromotive.*

mag·ne·to·op·tics (mag·nē'tō·op'tiks) *n.* The study of the behavior of light waves in a magnetic field. — **mag·ne·to·op'tic, mag·ne·to·op'ti·cal** *adj.*

mag·ne·to·scope (mag·nē'tə·skōp, -net'ə-) *n.* An instrument designed to indicate the presence of magnetic force lines without measuring them.

mag·ne·to·sphere (mag·nē'tə·sfir) *n.* A region of the atmosphere extending beyond the exosphere to about 40,000 miles and forming a continuous band of ionized particles trapped by the earth's magnetic field. Compare VAN ALLEN RADIATION.

mag·ne·to·stric·tion (mag·nē'tō·strik'shən) *n. Physics* The mechanical deformation produced in certain materials when subjected to the action of a magnetic field.

mag·ne·tron (mag'nə·tron) *n. Electronics* A vacuum tube in which the flow of electrons is subject to the control of an external magnetic field. [<MAGNET + (ELEC)TRON]

magni- *combining form* 1 Great; large: *magnirostrate,* large-beaked. 2 *Zool.* Long: *magnicaudate,* long-tailed. [<L *magnus* great]

mag·nif·ic (mag·nif'ik) *adj.* 1 Illustrious; magnificent; sumptuous. 2 Strikingly vast or dignified; imposing. 3 Of language, exalted; sublime; also, pompous; grandiloquent. Also **mag·nif'i·cal.** [<F *magnifique* <L *magnificus* <*magnus* great + *fic-,* stem of *facere* make] — **mag·nif'i·cal·ly** *adv.*

Mag·nif·i·cat (mag·nif'ə·kat) *n.* The hymn or canticle of the Virgin Mary, beginning with

the word *Magnificat* in the Latin version. *Luke* i 46–55. [<L, it magnifies]

mag·ni·fi·ca·tion (mag'nə·fə·kā'shən) *n.* 1 The act, process, or degree of magnifying. 2 The state of being magnified. 3 Magnifying power. 4 The act of extolling or glorifying. [<L *magnificatio, -onis* <*magnificare* <*magnificus.* See MAGNIFIC.]

mag·nif·i·cence (mag·nif'ə·səns) *n.* 1 The state or quality of being magnificent; the exhibition of greatness of action, character, intellect, wealth, or power; brilliant or imposing appearance; display of splendor. 2 A title of courtesy in medieval Rome. [<OF <L *magnificentia* <*magnificus* noble. See MAGNIFIC.]

mag·nif·i·cent (mag·nif'ə·sənt) *adj.* 1 Grand or majestic in appearance, quality, character, or action; extremely fine or good; befitting the great, as in deeds, manners, or surroundings; great in effect, promise, or import: a *magnificent* prospect, pearl, plan, etc.; also, exalted; imposing: *magnificent* language. 2 Exhibiting magnificence; characterized by splendor: sometimes used as a title: Suleiman the *Magnificent.* See synonyms under GRAND, IMPERIAL, SUBLIME. [<OF <LL *magnificens,* var. of *magnificus.* See MAGNIFIC.] — **mag·nif'i·cent·ly** *adv.*

mag·nif·i·co (mag·nif'ə·kō) *n. pl.* **·coes** 1 A noble of the Venetian republic: an old title. 2 A lordly personage; one who affects state or splendor. [<Ital. <L *magnificus.* See MAGNIFICENCE.]

mag·ni·fy (mag'nə·fī) *v.t.* **·fied, ·fy·ing** 1 To increase the apparent size of, as by a microscope. 2 To increase the size of; enlarge. 3 To cause to seem greater or more important. 4 *Archaic* To extol; exalt. See synonyms under AGGRAVATE, INCREASE, PRAISE. [<OF *magnifier* <L *magnificare* <*magnificus.* See MAGNIFICENCE.] — **mag·ni·fi'a·ble** *adj.* — **mag'ni·fi'er** *n.*

mag·nil·o·quent (mag·nil'ə·kwənt) *adj.* Of bombastic, pompous style; vainglorious. [<L *magnus* great + *loquens, -entis,* ppr. of *loqui* speak] — **mag·nil'o·quence** *n.* — **mag·nil'o·quent·ly** *adv.*

mag·ni·tude (mag'nə·tōōd, -tyōōd) *n.* 1 Great size or extent; grandeur; importance. 2 *Math.* That which is conceived of as measurable. 3 The property of having size or extent. 4 *Astron.* A measure of the relative brightness of a star, ranging from one for the brightest to six for those just visible to the naked eye. The standard of reference is the polestar, with a brightness 2.512 times greater than the one next below it; magnitudes greater than one on the scale are expressed as minus quantities. Compare LIGHT RATIO. 5 Largeness in respect to relation or effect. [<L *magnitudo* <*magnus* large]
Synonyms: bigness, bulk, dimension, extent, greatness, hugeness, immensity, largeness, size, vastness. *Antonyms:* diminutiveness, littleness, pettiness, slightness, smallness.

mag·no·li·a (mag·nō'lē·ə, -nōl'yə) *n.* 1 Any of a genus (*Magnolia*) of trees or shrubs with large, fragrant, and often showy flowers. 2 The blossom of the evergreen magnolia (*M. grandiflora*), the State flower of Louisiana and of Mississippi. [<NL, genus name, after Pierre *Magnol,* 1638–1715, French botanist]

mag·no·li·a·ceous (mag·nō'lē·ā'shəs) *adj.* Of or pertaining to a family (*Magnoliaceae*) of polypetalous trees or shrubs, the magnolia family, often aromatic, with alternate, undivided, feather-veined leaves, and large, solitary, axillary or terminal flowers with calyx and corolla colored alike, in three or more rows of three each. [<NL *Magnoliaceae,* family name <*Magnolia* MAGNOLIA]

magnolia warbler The black-and-yellow warbler (*Dendroica magnolia*) of North America.

mag·num (mag'nəm) *n.* A wine bottle of twice the ordinary size, holding about two quarts; also, the quantity such a bottle will hold. [<L, neut of *magnus* great]

Mag·nus effect (mag'nəs) *Physics* The deflecting effect upon the normal path of a rotating cylinder or sphere caused by the transverse forces of wind or air currents circulating around it. [after H. G. *Magnus,*

1802–70, German physicist]

mag·nus hitch (mag′nəs) A knot used to fasten a rope to a spar, etc., similar to a clove–hitch but having one more turn. [Prob. <L *magnus* large]

ma·got (mà·gō′) *n.* The Barbary ape. [<F, ? <*Magog* MAGOG]

Mag·ot·ty–bay bean (mag′ə·tē·bā′) A leguminous vine (*Chamaecrista fasciculata*) common on eastern American shores. [? from *Magothy* River, Maryland]

mag·pie (mag′pī) *n.* **1** A corvine bird (genus *Pica*), having a long, graduated tail. The common **European magpie** (*P. pica* or *caudata*) has iridescent black plumage with white scapulars, belly, sides, flanks, and inner web of flight feathers: often tamed and taught to speak words, and noted for its thievishness. The **American magpie** (*P. hudsonia*) is a variety of the European magpie. *P. nuttali* is the **yellow–billed magpie** of California. **2** An Australian crow shrike resembling a magpie. **3** A chatterbox; a garrulous gossip. [<*Mag*, diminutive of MARGARET, + PIE²]

mag·uey (mag′wā, *Sp.* mä·gā′ē) *n.* **1** Any of various Mexican agave plants with fleshy leaves and edible cabbage-like heads, especially the century plant (*Agave americana*) and the pulque agave (*A. atrovirens*). **2** A fiber plant (genus *Furcraea*) related to the agave. **3** The fiber of these plants. [<Sp., prob. <Taino]

MAGUEY
(Leaves up to 6 feet long; 8 to 10 inches broad)

ma·hal·a (mə·hal′ə) *n.* In the western United States and Canada, an Indian squaw. [<N. Am. Ind. *muk′ela*]

ma·ha·ra·ja (mä′hə·rä′jə, *Hind.* mə·hä′rä′jə) *n.* **1** A great Hindu prince; the title of some native rulers. **2** A prominent religious teacher of the Hindus. Also **ma′ha·ra′jah.** [<Hind. <Skt. *mahārāja* <*maha* great + *rājā* a king]

ma·ha·ra·ni (mä′hə·rä′nē, *Hind.* mə·hä′rä′nē) *n.* A Hindu princess; the wife of a maharaja. Also **ma′ha·ra′nee.** [<Hind. <*maha* great + *rānī* a queen]

ma·hat·ma (mə·hat′mə, -hät′-) *n.* In theosophy or esoteric Buddhism, an adept of the highest order; literally, great–souled one: a title of respect. [<Skt. *mahātman* <*maha* great + *ātman* soul] — **ma·hat′ma·ism** *n.*

Mah·di (mä′dē) *n.* The Moslem messiah, or one claiming the title; specifically, Mohammed Ahmed, 1843–85, who led a revolt in the Sudan, 1883. [<Arabic *mahdīy*, lit., he who is guided aright, pp. of *hadā* lead rightly] — **Mah′dism** *n.* — **Mah′dist** *adj.* & *n.*

Ma·hi·can (mə·hē′kən) *n.* One of a tribe of North American Indians of Algonquian linguistic stock formerly occupying the territory from the Hudson River to Lake Champlain; later, one of an Algonquian tribe between the Hudson River and Narragansett Bay, dialectally divided into the *Mohegans* of the Thames and lower Connecticut rivers, and the *Mohicans*, occupying both banks of the Hudson. [<Algonquian, lit., a wolf]

mah jong (mä′jong′, jông′) A game of Chinese origin, usually for four persons, played with 144 tiles marked in suits, dice, and counters. Also **mah jongg.** [<dial. Chinese <Chinese *ma ch′iao*, lit., a house sparrow; from the design on one of the tiles]

Mah·ler (mä′lər), **Gustav,** 1860–1911, Austrian composer and conductor.

mahl·stick (mäl′stik′, môl′) *n.* A staff with a ball at one end, used by painters to steady the hand while using the brush. Also spelled *maulstick.* [<Du. *maalstok* <*malen* paint + *stok* a stick]

ma·hog·a·ny (mə·hog′ə·nē) *n.* **1** A large tropical American tree (genus *Swietenia*), with fine-grained, hard, reddish wood much used for cabinetwork. **2** The wood itself. **3** One of various trees yielding a similar wood, as African mahogany (*Khaya ivorensis*); also its wood. **4** Acajou. **5** Any of the various shades of brownish–red or reddish–brown of the finished wood. — *adj.* **1** Of or pertaining to, or consisting of mahogany. **2** Of

a mahogany color. [<obs. Sp. *mahogani*, prob. <Arawakan]

Ma·hound (mə·hound′, -hōōnd′) *n.* **1** The prophet Mohammed. **2** *Scot.* Satan; an evil spirit. [<OF *Mahon, Mahum* <*Mahomet* Mohammed]

ma·hout (mə·hout′) *n.* The keeper and driver of an elephant. [<Hind. *mahaut, mahavat* <Skt. *mahāmātra*, lit., great in measure]

ma huang (mä hwäng′) A Chinese species of joint fir. [<Chinese]

maid (mād) *n.* **1** Any unmarried woman; virgin; girl; lass. **2** A female servant: also **maidservant.** [Short for MAIDEN]

mai·dan (mī·dän′) *n.* In Persia and India, a public plaza or parade ground; hence, an open space. [<Persian *maidān*]

Mai·da·nek (mī′də·nek) During World War II, a Nazi concentration and extermination camp near Lublin, Poland.

maid·en (mād′n) *n.* **1** An unmarried woman, especially if young; a maid; virgin. **2** Something untried or unused, as a race horse that has never won an event. **3** A rude kind of beheading machine used in Scotland in the 16th and 17th centuries. — *adj.* **1** Pertaining to or suitable for a maiden. **2** Virgin; unmarried. **3** Initiatory; unused; untried. **4** Of or pertaining to the first use or experience: a *maiden* voyage. **5** Pure; sinless. [OE *mægden*, prob. dim. of *mægeth* a virgin] — **maid′en·li·ness** *n.* — **maid′en·ly** *adj.* & *adv.*

maid·en·hair (mād′n·hâr′) *n.* A very delicate and graceful fern (genus *Adiantum*) with an erect black stem, common in damp, rocky woods. Also **maidenhair fern.**

maidenhair tree The ginkgo.

maid·en·head (mād′n·hed′) *n.* **1** The hymen. **2** Maidenhood; virginity.

maid·en·hood (mād′n·hŏŏd′) *n.* The state of being a maiden; freshness; purity; virginity. Also **maid′hood.**

maiden name A woman's surname before marriage.

maid of honor 1 An unmarried lady attendant upon an empress, queen, or princess: usually of noble birth. **2** The chief unmarried attendant of a bride at a wedding ceremony.

maid·ser·vant (mād′sûr′vənt) *n.* A female servant.

ma·ieu·tic (mā·yōō′tik) *adj.* Helping to bring forth ideas and truths from the mind of a pupil by a series of pertinent questions: said of the Socratic method. Also **ma·ieu′ti·cal.** [<Gk. *maieutikos*, lit., obstetric <*maieuesthai* act as a midwife <*maia* a midwife]

mai·gre (mā′gər) *adj.* Not consisting of flesh or its juices: said of dishes used by Roman Catholics on days of abstinence; hence, of or appropriate for a fast. — *n.* A large marine food fish, the European *Sciaena aquila*. [<OF. See MEAGER.]

mai·hem (mā′hem) See MAYHEM.

mail¹ (māl) *n.* **1** The governmental system for handling letters, etc., by post. **2** Letters, magazines and other printed matter, parcels, etc., consigned and sent from place to place under a governmental post–office system. **3** The collection or delivery of postal matter at a specified time: My letter missed the *mail.* **4** Letters, papers, etc., received by, or for, a person: Your *mail* is on the table. **5** A conveyance, as a train, plane, etc., for carrying postal matter. — *adj.* Pertaining to or used in the process of conveying or handling mail. — *v.t.* To send by mail, as letters; deposit in a mailbox or at a post office; post. ◆ Homophone: *male.* [<OF *male* <OHG *malha* a wallet] — **mail′a·ble** *adj.*

mail² (māl) *n.* **1** Armor of chains, rings, or scales: often called **chain mail. 2** Any strong covering or defense, as the shell of a turtle. — **coat of mail** A hauberk. — *v.t.* To cover with or as with mail. ◆ Homophone: *male.* [<OF *maille* <L *macula* spot, mesh of a net]

mail³ (māl) *n. Scot. & Brit. Dial.* That which is paid; rent; wages. Also **maill.** ◆ Homophone: *male.* [OE *māl* <ON, speech, agreement; infl. in sense by ON *māle′* contract; stipend]

CHAIN MAIL
ARMOR

mail·box (māl′boks′) *n.* **1** A box in which letters, etc., are posted for collection. **2** A box into which private mail is put when delivered. Also **mail box.**

mail·catch·er (māl′kach′ər) *n.* A mechanical device for transferring mailbags to or from a moving train.

mailed (māld) *adj.* **1** Covered or armed with mail. **2** *Zool.* Having a defensive armor, as scales. [<MAIL²]

mailed fist Menace of attack or violence; especially, menace of aggressive war.

mail·er (mā′lər) *n.* **1** A mail boat. **2** An addressing machine: also **mailing machine. 3** One who mails a letter.

mail·gram (māl′gram′) *n. U.S.* A message transmitted electronically between place of origin and destination, converted to written form, and delivered in the next scheduled distribution of mail. [<MAIL + (TELE)GRAM]

mail·ing (mā′ling) *n.* **1** The act of sending mail. **2** The mail sent at one time. **3** *Scot.* A rented piece of ground; farm; homestead: also **mail′en.**

mailing list A list of names, as of individuals, organizations, etc., to which advertising circulars, announcements, solicitations, and the like, are sent.

mail·lot (mī·yō′) *n.* A tightly fitting garment which covers the torso, used by dancers, acrobats, and swimmers. [<F, dim. of *máille* knitted material, lit., mail²]

mail·man (māl′man′, -mən) *n. pl.* **·men** (-men′, -mən) A letter–carrier; postman.

mail order An order for goods, sent and filled through the agency of the mail. — **mail–or·der** (ôr′dər) *adj.*

maim (mām) *v.t.* To deprive of the use of a bodily part; mutilate; disable. — *n. Rare* A crippling; mutilation; maiming. See MAYHEM. [<OF *mahaigner, mayner*; ult. origin uncertain] — **maim′er** *n.*

main¹ (mān) *n.* **1** A chief conduit or conductor, as for conveying gas, water, etc. **2** The mainland. **3** *Poetic* The ocean. **4** Violent effort; strength: chiefly in the phrase *with might and main.* **5** The chief part; the most important point. — **in** (or **for**) **the main** For the most part; on the whole. — *adj.* **1** First or chief in size, rank, importance, strength, extent, etc.; principal; chief; leading: the *main* building, the *main* line of a railroad, with which branch lines connect. **2** undivided; unqualified; full: by *main* force. **3** Designating any broad extent or expanse, as of land or sea. **4** *Naut.* Near or connected with the mainsail or mainmast. **5** *Brit. Dial.* Considerable; remarkable. **6** *Obs.* Vast; mighty; powerful. — *adv. Brit. Dial.* Very; greatly; extremely. ◆ Homophone: *mane.* [OE *mægen*] — **main′ly** *adv.*

main² (mān) *n.* **1** A match of several battles at cockfighting. **2** A hand or throw of dice; also, a number selected by the caster before he throws the dice in games of hazard and craps. ◆ Homophone: *mane.* [? <MAIN¹, as in *main chance*]

main deck *Naut.* The chief deck of a vessel; on a warship, the topmost deck stretching from stem to stern; on a merchantman, the deck between and below the poop and forecastle decks.

main drag *U.S. Slang* The principal street or section of a city.

Maine (mān) **1** A State of the NE United States bordering on Canada and the Atlantic; 32,562 square miles; capital, Augusta; entered the Union March 15, 1820; nickname, *Pine-Tree State*: abbr. ME **2** An ancient province of western France.

Maine (mān) A U.S. battleship, blown up in Havana harbor, Feb. 15, 1898, with the loss of 260 lives: one of the events precipitating the Spanish–American War.

main·land (mān′land′, -lənd) *n.* A principal body of land; a continent, as distinguished from an island. — **main′land′er** *n.*

main·line (mān′līn′) *n.* A main road, railroad line, etc. — *v.t. & v.i.* **·lined, ·lin·ing** *Slang* To inject (a narcotic drug, especially heroin) directly into a vein. — **main′lin′er** *n.*

main·mast (mān′məst, -mast′, -mäst′) *n. Naut.* The principal mast of a vessel: ordinarily, the second mast from the bow.

main·sail (mān′səl, -sāl′) *n. Naut.* A sail bent to the main yard, or one carried on the mainmast: in a square–rigged vessel, called the **main course.**

main sequence *Astron.* The area of the Hertzsprung–Russell diagram that includes the sun and the majority of stars.

main·sheet (mān'shēt') *n. Naut.* The sheet by which the mainsail is trimmed and set.

main·spring (mān'spring') *n.* **1** The principal spring of a mechanism, as of a watch. **2** The most efficient cause or motive.

main·stay (mān'stā') *n.* **1** *Naut.* The rope from the mainmast head forward, used to steady the mast in that direction. **2** A chief support or dependence.

main·stream (mān'strēm') *n.* The main or middle course or direction: in the *mainstream* of American political thought.

Main Street The principal business street of a small town: a symbol of its manners, customs, culture, typical thinking, etc.

main·tain (mān·tān') *v.t.* **1** To carry on or continue; engage in, as a correspondence. **2** To keep unimpaired or in proper condition: to *maintain* roads; to *maintain* a reputation. **3** To supply with food or livelihood; support; pay for. **4** To uphold; claim to be true. **5** To assert or state; affirm. **6** To hold or defend, as against attack. See synonyms under AFFIRM, ALLEGE, ASSERT, JUSTIFY, KEEP, PRESERVE, RETAIN, SUPPORT. [<OF *maintenir* < L *manu tenere*, lit., hold in one's hand < *manu*, ablative of *manus* hand + *tenere* hold]

main·te·nance (mān'tə·nəns) *n.* **1** The act of maintaining. **2** Means of support. **3** *Law* The officious intermeddling in a suit, by assisting or maintaining either party, with money or otherwise. [<OF *maintenance* < *maintenir* MAINTAIN]

main·top (mān'top') *n. Naut.* A platform at the head of the lower section of the mainmast.

main·top·gal·lant·mast (mān'tə·gal'ənt·məst, mast', -mäst', -top-) *n. Naut.* On a square–rigged vessel, the mast next above the main-mast.

main·top·mast (mān'top'məst) *n. Naut.* **1** On a square–rigged vessel, the mast next above the maintopgallantmast. **2** On a fore–and–aft–rigged ship, the mast next above the mainmast.

main yard *Naut.* The lower yard on the main-mast.

ma·iol·i·ca (mä·yol'ē·kä) See MAJOLICA.

mai·o·sis (mī·ō'sis) See MEIOSIS (def. 1).

maî·tre d' (mā'trə dē') *pl.* **maî·tre d's** (dēz) A headwaiter. [Short for MAÎTRE D'HOTEL]

maître d'hô·tel (dô·tel') *French* **1** The proprietor or manager of a hotel. **2** A headwaiter, steward. **3** A sauce of melted butter, parsley, and lemon juice or vinegar.

maize (māz) *n.* **1** A tall, stout food and forage plant (*Zea mays*). **2** Its grain; Indian corn. **3** A light, soft shade of yellow; any of the various yellow tints of ripe corn. ◆ Homophone: *maze.* [<Sp. *maíz* <Taino *mahiz*]

maize–bird (māz'bûrd') *n.* A bird that feeds on Indian corn, as the red–winged blackbird.

ma·jes·tic (mə·jes'tik) *adj.* Having or exhibiting majesty; stately; royal, august. Also **ma·jes'ti·cal.** See synonyms under AWFUL, GRAND, IMPERIAL, KINGLY, SUBLIME. — **ma·jes'ti·cal·ly** *adv.* — **ma·jes'ti·cal·ness** *n.*

maj·es·ty (maj'is·tē) *n. pl.* **·ties** Exalted dignity; stateliness; grandeur; especially, **His, Her,** or **Your Majesty,** a title given to monarchs. [<OF *majesté* <L *majestas, -tatis* (related to *majus*, neut. compar. of *magnus* great)]

ma·jol·i·ca (mə·jol'i·kə, -yol'-) *n.* A kind of Italian pottery, glazed and decorated, usually in rich colors and Renaissance designs; any glazed Italian pottery; faience. Also spelled *maiolica.* [<Ital. *maiolica*, prob. < *Majolica*, early name of MAJORCA, where formerly made]

ma·jor (mā'jər) *adj.* **1** Greater in number, quantity, or extent. **2** Greater in dignity or importance; of primary consideration; principal; leading. **3** *Music* **a** Designating a chord or interval greater by a half–step than the preceding minor. **b** Containing a major third, sixth, and seventh. See INTERVAL. **4** *Logic* Designating the first premise of a syllogism, or the premise containing the first proposi-

tion. **5** *Law* Being of legal age. — *n.* **1** An officer in the U.S. Army, Air Force, or Marine Corps ranking next above a captain and next below a lieutenant colonel. **2** *Law* One who is of legal age. **3** *Music* A major key, chord, or interval. **4** *U.S.* The specialized course of study in a definite field which a college or university student follows to obtain his degree. **5** *U.S.* A student who follows a (specified) course of study: an English *major.* — *v.i.* To pursue a definite field of study: with *in*: to *major* in history. [<L, compar. of *magnus* great. Doublet of MAYOR.]

ma·jor·do·mo (mā'jər·dō'mō) *n. pl.* **·mos** **1** The chief steward of a royal household. **2** A butler. **3** *SW U.S.* The overseer of a ranch. [<Sp. *mayordomo* <Med. L *major domus* chief of a house < *major* an elder (<L, greater) + *domus* a house]

major general See under GENERAL.

ma·jor·i·ty (mə·jôr'ə·tē, -jor'-) *n. pl.* **·ties** **1** More than half of a given number or group; the greater part. **2** The amount or number by which one group of things exceeds another group; excess. **3** The age at which the laws of a country permit a person to manage his or her own affairs: in most States of the United States, the age of 21 years. **4** The rank or commission of a major. **5** In U.S. politics, more than half of the people; more than half of the votes cast. **6** The number of votes cast for a candidate over and above the number cast for his nearest opponent; a plurality. **7** The party having the most power in a legislature. [<MF *majorité* <L *majoritas, -tatis* < *major.* See MAJOR.]

major key *Music* A key based on the tones of a major scale, the intervals being a half–step larger than minor intervals.

major league In baseball, either of the two main groups of professional teams in the United States. — **ma'jor–league'** *adj.*

major mode See under MODE.

major scale See under SCALE.

major suit In bridge, either of the sets of spades and hearts: so called from their higher point value.

major term See under TERM.

ma·jus·cule (mə·jus'kyōōl) *n.* A capital letter; especially, a large initial letter, as in old manuscripts. [<F <L *majuscula (littera)*, fem. of *majusculus* somewhat larger, dim. of *major.* See MAJOR.] — **ma·jus'cu·lar** *adj.*

make (māk) *v.* **made, mak·ing** *v.t.* **1** To bring about the existence of by the shaping or combining of materials; produce; build; construct; fashion. **2** To bring about; cause: Don't *make* trouble. **3** To bring to some state or condition; cause to be: The wind *made* him cold. **4** To appoint or assign; elect: They *made* him captain. **5** To form or create in the mind, as a plan. **6** To compose or create, as a poem or piece of music. **7** To understand or infer to be the meaning or significance; interpret; think: What do you *make* of it? **8** To put forward; advance: to *make* an offer. **9** To present, as for record; utter or express: to *make* a declaration. **10** To obtain for oneself; earn; accumulate: to *make* a fortune. **11** To amount to; add up to: Four quarts *make* a gallon. **12** To bring the total to: That *makes* five attempts. **13** To develop into; become: He *made* a good soldier. **14** To accomplish; effect or form: to *make* an agreement. **15** To estimate to be; reckon: He *made* the height twenty feet. **16** To induce or force; compel: He *made* me do it! **17** To draw up, enact, or frame, as laws, testaments, etc. **18** To prepare for use, as a bed. **19** To afford or provide: This brandy *makes* good drinking. **20** To be the essential element or determinant of: Stone walls do not a prison *make.* **21** To cause the success of: His speech *made* him politically. **22** To traverse; cover: to *make* fifty miles before noon. **23** To travel at the rate of: to *make* fifty miles per hour. **24** To arrive at; reach: to *make* Boston. **25** To board before departure: to *make* a train. **26** To earn so as to count on a score: to *make* a touchdown. **27** *Electr.* To complete (a circuit). **28** *Colloq.* To win a place on: to

make the team. **29** In card games: **a** To declare as trump. **b** To capture a trick with (a card). **c** To shuffle: to *make* the deck. **30** In bridge, to win (a bid). **31** *U. S. Slang.* To seduce. — *v.i.* **32** To cause something to assume a specified condition: to *make* ready; to *make* fast. **33** To act or behave in a certain manner: to *make* merry. **34** To start: They *made* to go. **35** To go or extend in some direction: with *to* or *toward.* **36** To flow, as the tide; rise, as water. — **to make as if** (or **as though**) To pretend. — **to make away with** **1** To carry off; steal. **2** To get rid of; destroy. — **to make believe** To pretend. — **to make do** To get along with what is available, especially with an inferior substitute. — **to make for 1** To go toward. **2** To attack; assail. **3** To have effect on; contribute to. — **to make heavy weather** *Naut.* To roll and pitch, as a ship in a storm. — **to make it** To succeed in doing something. — **to make off** To leave suddenly; run away. — **to make off with** To steal. — **to make out 1** To see; discern. **2** To comprehend; understand. **3** To establish by evidence. **4** To fill out; draw up, as a bank draft. **5** To be successful; manage. — **to make over 1** To put into new form; renovate. **2** To transfer title or possession of. — **to make up 1** To compose; compound, as a prescription. **2** To be the parts of; comprise: These elements *make up* the structure. **3** To settle differences and become friendly again: to kiss and *make up.* **4** To devise; invent; fabricate: to *make up* an answer. **5** To supply what is lacking in. **6** To compensate for; atone for. **7** To settle; decide: to *make up* one's mind. **8** *Printing* To arrange, as lines, into columns or pages. **9** To put cosmetics on (the face). **10** In education, to repeat (an examination or course one has failed), or take (an examination) one has missed. — **to make up to** *Colloq.* To make a show of friendliness and affection toward; flatter. — *n.* **1** The manner in which parts or qualities are grouped to constitute a whole; constitution; structure; shape. **2** The operation or product of manufacture; brand: a new *make* of automobile. **3** The amount produced; yield. **4** The closing or completion of an electrical circuit. **5** A declaration (def. 3). — **on the make** *Slang* **1** Greedy for profit; interested only in making money. **2** Eager for amorous conquest. [OE *macian*] *Synonyms (verb):* become, cause, compel, compose, constitute, constrain, construct, create, do, effect, establish, execute, fabricate, fashion, force, frame, get, manufacture, occasion, perform, reach, require, shape. *Make* is essentially causative; to the idea of cause all its various senses may be traced (compare synonyms for CAUSE *noun*). To *make* is to *cause* to exist, or to *cause* to exist in a certain form or in certain relations; it thus includes the idea of *create. Make* includes also the idea of *compose, constitute;* as, The parts *make up* the whole. Similarly, to *cause* a voluntary agent to do a certain act is to *make* him do it, or *compel* him to do it, *compel* fixing the attention more on the process, *make* on the accomplished fact. See COMPEL, GET, PRODUCE, REACH. *Antonyms:* see synonyms for ABOLISH, BREAK, DEMOLISH.

make–and–break (māk'ənd·brāk') *n. Electr.* A device for making and breaking an electrical circuit.

make–be·lieve (māk'bi·lēv') *adj.* Pretended; unreal. — *n.* A mere pretense; sham. Also **make'–be·lief'** (-lēf').

make–fast (māk'fast', -fäst') *n. Naut.* An iron ring or other object to which a boat is made fast.

make·peace (māk'pēs') *n.* A peacemaker.

mak·er (mā'kər) *n.* **1** One who makes. **2** A manufacturer. **3** *Law* One who signs a promissory note. **4** *Archaic* A poet.

Mak·er (mā'kər) *n.* God, as the creator of the universe.

–maker *combining form* One who or that which produces: *glassmaker.* [<MAKE]

make·shift (māk'shift') *adj.* Having the character of or being a temporary resource: also **make'shift'y.** — *n.* Something adopted as a temporary contrivance in any emergency.

make–up (māk'up') *n.* **1** The arrangement or combination of the parts of which anything is composed; an aggregate of qualities. **2** *Printing* The arrangement of composed type in pages, columns, or forms, as in imposition. **3** The costumes, wigs, cosmetics, etc., used to assume a theatrical role; also, the art of applying or assuming them. **4** Lipstick, powder, rouge, etc., applied to a woman's face.

make·weight (māk′wāt′) *n.* **1** That which is thrown into a scale to increase weight. **2** Any person or thing made use of to fill up a deficiency.

mak·ing (mā′king) *n.* **1** The act of causing, fashioning, or constructing; workmanship. **2** That which contributes to improvement or success: He has the *making* of a fine character. **3** A quantity of anything made at one time; batch. **4** *Often pl.* The materials or ingredients required to make something. **5** Composition; structure; make.

-making *combining form* Act of causing or producing; creating or causing to be: *paper-making.* [<MAKE]

mal- *prefix* Bad; ill; evil; wrong; defective; imperfect; uneven: signifying also simple negation, and forming words directly from Latin and mediately through French: opposed to *bene-, eu-.* [<F *mal-* <L *male-* < *malus* bad]

Malacca cane A walking stick made from the wood of an Asian rattan palm (*Calamus rotang*). [from *Malacca*]

ma·la·ceous (mə·lā′shəs) *adj.* Designating a family (*Malaceae*) of trees, including the apple, pear, quince, etc. See POMACEOUS. [<NL, family name <L *malum* an apple <Gk. *mēlon*]

Mal·a·chi (mal′ə·kī) A masculine personal name. [<Hebrew *malākhī*, lit., my messenger] —Malachi A minor Hebrew prophet of the fifth century B.C.; also, the book containing his prophecies.

mal·a·chite (mal′ə·kīt) *n.* A green basic cupric carbonate, $CuCO_3 \cdot Cu(OH)_2$, found usually massive, rarely in crystals, and sometimes as an incrustation. It is one of the ores of copper. [< OF *melochite*, ult. <L *malache* a mallow < Gk. *malachē*; so called because resembling mallow leaves in color]

malachite green A pigment made of malachite, having an intense bluish–green color. Compare BICE GREEN.

malaco- *combining form* Soft; mucilaginous: *malacopterous.* Also, before vowels, **malac-.** [< Gk. *malakos* soft]

mal·a·coid (mal′ə·koid) *adj.* Having a soft texture.[<MALAC(O)- + -OID]

mal·a·col·o·gy (mal′ə·kol′ə·jē) *n.* The branch of zoology that treats of mollusks. [MALACO- + -LOGY]

mal·a·cop·ter·ous (mal′ə·kop′tər·əs) *adj.* Having soft fins, as certain fishes. [<MALACO- + -PTEROUS]

mal·a·cos·tra·can (mal′·ə·kos′trə·kən) *n.* Any of a division or subclass (*Malacostraca*) of crustaceans, embracing crabs, lobsters, crayfish, etc. —*adj.* Of or pertaining to the *Malacostraca:* also **mal′a·cos′tra·cous.** [<NL *Malacostraca*, subclass name <Gk. *malakostrakos* soft–shelled <*malakos* soft + *ostrakon* a shell]

mal·ad·dress (mal′ə·dres′) *n.* Awkwardness or rudeness in speech or manner; lack of politeness or tact. [<F *maladresse* <*maladroit* MALADROIT]

mal·ad·just·ed (mal′ə·jus′tid) *adj.* **1** Imperfectly adjusted. **2** *Psychol.* Poorly adapted to one's environment through conflict between personal desires and external circumstances. —**mal′ad·just′ment** *n.*

mal·ad·min·is·ter (mal′ad·min′is·tər) *v.t.* To administer badly or dishonestly.

mal·ad·min·is·tra·tion (mal′ad·min′is·trā′shən) *n.* Bad management, as of public affairs.

mal·a·droit (mal′ə·droit′) *adj.* Clumsy or blundering. See synonyms under AWKWARD. [<F <*mal-* MAL- +*adroit* clever] —**mal′a·droit′ly** *adv.* —**mal′a·droit′ness** *n.*

mal·a·dy (mal′ə·dē) *n. pl.* **·dies 1** A disease, especially when chronic or deep–seated; sickness; illness. **2** Any disordered condition. See synonyms under DISEASE. [<OF *maladie* <LL *male habitus* <L *male* ill + *habitus*, pp. of *habere* have]

ma·la fi·de (mā′lə fī′dē) *Latin* In bad faith.

Mal·a·ga (mal′ə·gə) *n.* **1** A rich, sweet white wine made in Málaga, Spain. **2** A white, sweet grape of the muscat variety, grown in Spain and California.

Mal·a·gas·y (mal′ə·gas′ē) *adj.* Of or pertaining to Madagascar, its inhabitants, or their language. —*n.* **1** A native of Madagascar. **2** The Indonesian language of Madagascar.

Malagasy Republic An independent republic of the French Community comprising the island of Madagascar; 227,-602 square miles; capital, Tananarive.

ESKIMO MALAMUTE
(From 22 to 25 inches high at the shoulder)

mal·aise (mal·āz′, *Fr.* má·lez′) *n.* Uneasiness; indisposition. [<F <*mal* ill + *aise* EASE]

ma·la·mute (mä′lə·myōōt, mal′ə-) *n.* A large sled dog of Alaska, having a compact body, a thick, long coat, usually gray or black–and–white, a broad head, straight, big–boned forelegs, and well–cushioned feet. Also spelled *malemute, malemiut.* [Orig., name of an Innuit tribe, alter. of Eskimo (Malamute) *Mahlemut* < *Mahle*, the tribe's name +*mut* a village]

mal·an·ders (mal′ən·dərz) *n. pl.* A scaly disease on the hock and at the bend of the knee of the foreleg of a horse: also spelled *mallenders.* Compare SALLENDERS. [<OF *malandre* a sore in a horse's knee <L *malandria*]

mal·a·pert (mal′ə·pûrt) *adj.* Bold or forward; impudent; saucy. —*n.* A saucy person. [<OF <*mal-* MAL- + *apert, espert* clever, able <L *expertus.* See EXPERT.] —**mal′a·pert′ly** *adv.* —**mal′a·pert′ness** *n.*

mal·ap·por·tion·ment (mal′ə·pôr′shən·mənt, -pōr′-) *n.* Unfair apportionment of representatives in a legislature.

Mal·a·prop (mal′ə·prop), **Mrs.** A character in Sheridan's *The Rivals,* who uses words inappropriately. [<MALAPROPOS]

mal·a·prop·ism (mal′ə·prop·iz′əm) *n.* The incorrect or inappropriate use of a word; a verbal blunder. [after Mrs. *Malaprop*] —**mal′a·pro′pi·an** (-prō′pē·ən) *adj.*

mal·ap·ro·pos (mal′ap·rə·pō′) *adj.* Out of place; not appropriate. [<F *mal à propos* not to the point <*mal* ill + *à* to + *propos* purpose] —**mal′ap·ro·po′ism** *n.*

ma·lar (mā′lər) *adj. Anat.* Relating to or being in or near the cheek. —*n.* The cheek bone. [< NL *malaris* <L *mala* jaw, cheek]

ma·lar·i·a (mə·lâr′ē·ə) *n.* **1** *Pathol.* A disease caused by any of certain animal parasites (genus *Plasmodium*), which are introduced into the system by the bite of the infected anopheles mosquito and invade the red corpuscles of the blood, causing intermittent chills and fever. **2** Any foul or unwholesome air, as from decomposition; miasma; mephitis. [<Ital. *mal'aria, mala aria,* lit., bad air] —**ma·lar′i·al, ma·lar′i·an, ma·lar′i·ous** *adj.*

ma·lar·i·o·ther·a·py (mə·lâr′ē·ō·ther′ə·pē) *n. Med.* The treatment of cerebrospinal syphilis by inoculation with the parasite causing tertian malaria. [MALARI(A) + -o- +THERAPY]

ma·lar·ky (mə·lär′kē) *n. Slang* Insincere or senseless talk; bunk. Also **ma·lar′key.** [? <an Irish personal name]

mal·as·sim·i·la·tion (mal′ə·sim′ə·lā′shən) *n.* Imperfect or faulty assimilation.

mal·ate (mal′āt, mā′lāt) *n. Chem.* A salt or ester of malic acid. [<MAL(IC) + -ATE³]

Ma·la·wi (mä′lä·wē) An independent member of the Commonwealth of Nations in SE Africa; 49,177 square miles; capital, Zomba: formerly *Nyasaland.*

Ma·lay (mā′lā, mə·lā′) *n.* **1** A member of the dominant race in Malaysia; a Malayan. **2** The language spoken on the Malay Peninsula and widely used as a lingua franca throughout the East Indies, belonging to the Indonesian subfamily of Austronesian languages. **3** A variety of domestic fowl. —*adj.* Of or pertaining to the Malays; Malayan.

Ma·lay·a (mə·lā′ə) A federation of eleven states in the Commonwealth of Nations, now incorporated in Malaysia, including the former Federated Malay States and Unfederated Malay States, the two settlements of Malacca and Penang on the southern Malay Peninsula, and adjacent islands; 50,600 square miles; capital, Kuala Lumpur: formerly **Malayan Union.** Also **Malaya.**

Mal·a·ya·lam (mal′ə·yä′ləm) *n.* The language of the Malabar coast, India, related to Tamil, and belonging to the Dravidian family of languages.

Ma·lay·an (mə·lā′ən) *adj.* **1** Malay. **2** Indonesian. —*n.* **1** A Malay (def. 1). **2** An Indonesian. **3** The Indonesian subfamily of Austronesian languages.

Malay Peninsula The southernmost peninsula of Asia, including the Federation of Malaya and part of Thailand.

Ma·lay·sia (mə·lā′zhə, -shə) **1** A federation of fourteen states in the Commonwealth of Nations, including Malaya, Sabah, and Sarawak; 127,334 square miles; capital, Kuala Lumpur. **2** The Malay Archipelago. —**Ma·lay′sian** *adj. & n.*

Mal·colm X (mal′kəm eks) Name adopted by *Malcolm Little,* 1925–65, U.S. political and religious leader, active in the Black Muslim movement; assassinated.

mal·con·tent (mal′kən·tent) *adj.* Discontented, as with a government or economic system; dissatisfied; uneasy. —*n.* A person dissatisfied with the existing state of affairs; one rebellious against authority. [<OF <*mal-* MAL- + *content* CONTENT]

mal·dis·tri·bu·tion (mal′dis·trə·byōō′shən) *n.* Unfair or uneven distribution of people or goods.

Mal·dive Islands (môl′dīv, mal′-) An independent republic in the Indian Ocean; 12 islands SW of Sri Lanka; 115 square miles; capital, Malé.

male (māl) *adj.* **1** Pertaining to the sex that begets young; masculine. **2** Made up of men or boys. **3** *Bot.* Having stamens, but no pistil; also, adapted to fertilize, but not to produce fruit, as stamens. **4** Denoting some implement or object, as a gage or plug, which fits into a corresponding part known as *female.* **5** Indicating superiority of strength and quality of anything. See synonyms under MASCULINE. —*n.* **1** An organism that produces sperm cells; a male person or animal. **2** *Bot.* A plant with only staminate flowers. ◆ Homophone: *mail.* [<OF *male, mascle* <L *masculus.* Doublet of MASCULINE.]

mal·e·dic·tion (mal′ə·dik′shən) *n.* **1** An invocation of evil; a cursing: opposed to *benediction.* **2** Slander. **3** The state of being reviled. See synonyms under IMPRECATION, OATH. [<L *maledictio, -onis* <*maledictus,* pp. of *maledicere* <*male* ill + *dicere* speak] —**mal′e·dic′to·ry** *adj.*

mal·e·fac·tor (mal′ə·fak′tər) *n.* One who commits a crime. [<L <*malefactus,* pp. of *malefacere* <*male* ill + *facere* do] —**mal′e·fac′tion** *n.* —**mal′e·fac′tress** *n. fem.*

male fern A fern (*Dryopteris filixmas*) used in medicine as a vermifuge.

ma·lef·ic (mə·lef′ik) *adj.* Occasioning evil or disaster. [<L *maleficus* <*malefacere.* See MALEFACTOR.]

ma·lef·i·cent (mə·lef′ə·sənt) *adj.* Causing or doing evil or mischief; harmful: opposed to *beneficent.*[<L *maleficus* MALEFIC]

ma·le·ic (mə·lē′ik) *adj. Chem.* Pertaining to or designating a white, crystalline, astringent acid, $C_4H_4O_4$, prepared by the catalytic oxidation of benzene: used as a dye for fabrics, etc. [<F *maléique* < *malique* MALIC]

ma·le·mute (mä′lə·myōōt, mal′ə-), **ma·le·miut** See MALAMUTE.

ma·lev·o·lent (mə·lev′ə·lənt) *adj.* Having an evil disposition toward others; ill-disposed. See synonyms under MALICIOUS. [<OF <L *malevolens, -entis* <*male* ill + *volens, -entis,* ppr. of *velle* wish, will] —**ma·lev′o·lence** *n.* —**ma·lev′o·lent·ly** *adv.*

mal·fea·sance (mal·fē′zəns) *n. Law* The performance of some act which is unlawful or wrongful or which one has specifically contracted not to perform: said usually of official misconduct. Compare MISFEASANCE, NONFEASANCE. [<AF *malfaisance* <OF *malfaisant* < *mal* ill + *faisant,* ppr. of *faire* do <L *facere*] **mal·fea·sant** (mal·fē′zənt) *adj.* Guilty of malfeasance. —*n.* A person guilty of malfeasance.

mal·for·ma·tion (mal′fôr·mā′shən) *n.* Any irregularity, anomaly, or abnormal deformation in the structure of an organism. [<MAL- + FORMATION]

mal·formed (mal·fôrmd′) *adj.* Badly formed or made; deformed.

mal·func·tion (mal·fungk′shən) *n. Physiol.* Impairment or disturbance of any bodily function; dysfunction.

Ma·li (mä′lē) A landlocked, independent republic in west Africa; 464,873 miles; capital, Bamako; formerly French Sudan, an overseas territory. —**Ma′li** *adj.* & *n.*

mal·ic (mal′ik, mā′lik) *adj.* **1** Of, pertaining to, or obtained from apples. **2** *Chem.* Pertaining to or designating a deliquescent crystalline acid, $C_4H_6O_5$, with a pleasant taste: contained in the juice of many sour fruits and some plants, and also made synthetically. [< F *malique* <L *malum* an apple]

mal·ice (mal′is) *n.* **1** A disposition to injure another; evil intent; spite; ill will. **2** *Law* A wilfully formed design to do another an injury: also **malice aforethought**. See synonyms under ENMITY, HATRED. [<OF <L *malitia* < *malus* bad]

ma·li·cious (mə·lish′əs) *adj.* **1** Harboring malice, ill will, or enmity; spiteful. **2** Resulting from or prompted by malice. [<OF *malicios* <L *malitiosus* <*malitia* MALICE] —**ma·li′·cious·ly** *adv.* —**ma·li′cious·ness** *n.*
Synonyms: bitter, evil-disposed, evil-minded, hostile, ill-disposed, ill-natured, invidious, rancorous, resentful, spiteful, venomous, virulent. The *malevolent* person wishes ill to another; the *malicious* person has the desire and intent to do evil, if possible, to another. The *malign* or *malignant* spirit has a deep, intense, and insatiable hostility, such as is indicated by *rancorous* or *venomous*, with or without active desire or intent to injure. *Spiteful* is a feeble word indicating the desire or intent to inflict petty, exasperating annoyance or injury. Compare ACRIMONY, BITTER, ENMITY, HATRED. *Antonyms:* amiable, amicable, beneficent, benevolent, benign, benignant, friendly, good-natured, kind, kind-hearted, kindly, sympathetic, tender, well-disposed.

ma·lign (mə·līn′) *v.t.* To speak slander of. See synonyms under ABUSE, ASPERSE, REVILE. —*adj.* **1** Having an evil disposition toward others; ill-disposed; malevolent: opposed to *benign*. **2** Tending to injure; pernicious. See synonyms under MALICIOUS. [<OF *malignier, maliner* plot, deceive <L *malignare* contrive maliciously <*malignus* evil-disposed <*malus* evil] —**ma·lign′ly** *adv.* —**ma·lign′er** *n.*

ma·lig·nant (mə·lig′nənt) *adj.* **1** Having or manifesting extreme malevolence or enmity. **2** Evil in nature, or tending to do great harm; also, malcontent. **3** *Pathol.* So aggravated as to threaten life: opposed to *benign:* a *malignant* tumor. **4** Boding ill; baleful; threatening. —*n.* A person of extreme enmity or evil intentions. [<L *malignans, -antis,* ppr. of *malignare.* See MALIGN.] —**ma·lig′nance, ma·lig′nan·cy** *n.* —**ma·lig′nant·ly** *adv.*

ma·lig·ni·ty (mə·lig′nə·tē) *n. pl.* ·**ties 1** The state or quality of being malign; violent animosity. **2** Destructive tendency; virulence. **3** *Often pl.* An evil thing or event. See synonyms under ACRIMONY, ENMITY, HATRED.

ma·lines (mə·lēn′, *Fr.* má·lēn′) *n.* **1** Lace made in Mechlin, Belgium: also called *Mechlin lace.* **2** A gauzelike veiling for trimming hats: also **ma·line′**. [<F, from *Malines* Mechlin]

ma·lin·ger (mə·ling′gər) *v.i.* To feign sickness or incapacity, especially so as to avoid work or duty. [<F *malingre* sickly <*mal* bad (<L *malus*) + OF *heingre* lean] —**ma·lin′ger·er** *n.*

mall[1] (môl, mal) *n.* **1** A maul. **2** A war hammer. —*v.t.* To maul. [Var. of MAUL]

mall[2] (môl, mal, mel) *n.* **1** The game pall-mall, or a place in which it is played. **2** A level, shaded walk. [Short for PALL-MALL]

mal·lard (mal′ərd) *n.* **1** The common wild duck (*Anas platyrhynchos*), or, formerly, its drake. **2** Any wild duck. **3** *Obs.* The domesticated duck. [<OF *malart* <*masle* MALE]

mal·le·a·ble (mal′ē·ə·bəl) *adj.* **1** Capable of being hammered or rolled out without breaking; ductile. **2** Hence, susceptible to the shaping power of surrounding influences; pliant. [<OF <L *malleare* MALLEATE] —**mal′le·a·bil′i·ty, mal′le·a·ble·ness** *n.* —**mal′le·a·bly** *adv.*

malleable iron 1 Cast iron that has been rendered tough and malleable by long-continued high heating and slow cooling. **2** Wrought iron; forged iron.

mal·le·ate (mal′ē·āt) *v.t.* ·**at·ed, ·at·ing** To shape into a plate or leaf by beating; hammer. [<L *malleatus,* pp. of *malleare* <*malleus* a hammer] —**mal′le·a′tion** *n.*

mal·lee (mal′ē) *n. Austral.* **1** Any one of several scrubby species of eucalyptus of South Australia and Victoria; especially, *Eucalyptus dumosa* and *E. oleosa.* **2** Brushwood composed of such trees.

mal·le·in (mal′ē·in) *n. Biochem.* A poisonous, yellowish-white compound, obtained from the active metabolic products of the bacillus of glanders, used for the diagnosis of that disease. Also **mal′le·ine** (-in, -ēn). [<L *malle(us)* glanders + -IN]

mal·le·muck (mal′ə·muk) *n.* The southern albatross, fulmar, petrel, or other closely related bird. [<Du. *mallemok* <*mol* foolish + *mok* a gull]

mal·le·o·lus (mə·lē′ə·ləs) *n. pl.* ·**o·li** (-ə·lī) *Anat.* A hammer-shaped bony process on each side of the ankle. [<L, dim. of *malleus* a hammer] —**mal·le′o·lar** *adj.*

mal·let (mal′it) *n.* **1** A wooden hammer or light maul. **2** A light hammer, frequently of metal. **3** A long-handled wooden hammer used in the game of croquet. **4** A wooden-headed Malacca cane or stick used in the game of polo. [<OF *maillet,* dim. of *mail* a MAUL]

MALLETS
a. Mason's mallet.   *b.* Bossing mallet.
c. Carpenter's mallet.   *d.* Tinsmith's mallet.
e. Calking mallet.

mal·le·us (mal′ē·əs) *n. pl.* ·**le·i** (-lē·ī) *Anat.* The club-shaped outermost ossicle of the middle ear, articulating with the incus. See illustration under EAR. [<L, a hammer]

mal·low (mal′ō) *n.* **1** Any plant of the genus *Malva.* The most common in the United States is the **running** or **dwarf mallow** (*M. rotundifolia*), a spreading herb with roundish leaves, small, pale-pink flowers, and flat, disklike fruit: the leaves are used in brewing a medicinal tea. **2** Any plant of the mallow family: Indian *mallow.* [OE *mealuwe* <L *malva.* Double of MAUVE.]

malm (mäm) *n.* **1** A soft, friable, whitish limestone. **2** A whitish calcareous loam occurring in the southern counties of England; marl. [OE *mealm(stan)* sandstone or limestone]

malm·sey (mäm′zē) *n.* A rich sweet wine made in the Canary Islands, Madeira, Spain, and Greece. [<Med. L *malmasia* <Gk. *Monembasia* Monemvasia, Greece, a small Laconian coastal town formerly exporting wine]

mal·nu·tri·tion (mal′nōō·trish′ən, -nyōō-) *n.* Faulty or inadequate nutrition.

ma·lo (mä′lō) *n.* A loin cloth or girdle worn by Hawaiian men, formerly made of tapa, now of brightly dyed cotton fabrics. [<Hawaiian, cloth]

mal·oc·clu·sion (mal′ə·klōō′zhən) *n. Dent.* Faulty closure of the upper and lower teeth. [<MAL- + OCCLUSION]

mal·o·dor (mal·ō′dər) *n.* An offensive odor.

mal·o·dor·ous (mal·ō′dər·əs) *adj.* Having a disagreeable smell, literally or figuratively; obnoxious. —**mal·o′dor·ous·ly** *adv.* —**mal·o′·dor·ous·ness** *n.*

ma·lon·ic (mə·lon′ik, -lō′nik) *adj. Chem.* Of, pertaining to, or designating a white, crystalline acid, $CH_2(CO_2H)_2$ obtained chiefly by oxidizing malic acid. [<F *malonique* <*malique* MALIC]

mal·o·nyl·u·re·a (mal′ə·nil·yoor′ē·ə) *n.* Barbituric acid. [<MALON(IC) + -YL + UREA]

mal·pais (mal′pīs) *n. SW U.S.* Bad land; specifically, land having an under layer of basaltic lava. [<Sp. *mal, malo* bad (<L *malus*) +

país a country <L *patria*]

mal·pigh·i·a·ceous (mal·pig′ē·ā′shəs) *adj.* Of or pertaining to a family (*Malpighiaceae*) of trees, shrubs, or, more rarely, herbs, with hermaphrodite flowers, mostly native to the tropics. [<NL *Malpighiaceae,* family name < *Malpighia,* genus name, after Marcello *Malpighi*]

Malpighian bodies *Anat.* A tuft of blood vessels at the commencement of the uriniferous tubules in the kidney. Also **Malpighian capsules** or **corpuscles.** [after Marcello *Malpighi*]

Malpighian layer *Anat.* The deeper, softer layer of the epidermis, comprising the active cells.

Malpighian tubes *Entomol.* The tubular portions of the excretory organ of an insect. Also **Malpighian vessels.**

mal·po·si·tion (mal′pə·zish′ən) *n. Pathol.* A wrong or faulty position, as of the fetus. —**mal·posed** (-pōzd′) *adj.*

mal·prac·tice (mal·prak′tis) *n.* **1** Improper or illegal practice, as in medicine or surgery. **2** Improper or immoral conduct. —**mal·prac·ti·tion·er** (mal′prak·tish′ən·ər) *n.*

malt (môlt) *n.* **1** Grain, usually barley, softened by water, artificially germinated and then dried: rich in carbohydrates and proteins and essential in brewing and as a nutrient. **2** *Slang* Malt liquor; beer or ale. —*v.t.* **1** To cause (grain) to germinate artificially, by moisture and heat, and become malt. **2** To treat with malt, or extract of malt. —*v.i.* **3** To be changed into or become malt: said of grain. **4** To convert grain into malt. [OE *mealt.* Akin to MELT.]

Mal·ta (môl′tə) **1** A republic in the Mediterranean, comprising the **Maltese Islands;** Malta, Gozo, and Comino; 122 square miles; capital, Valletta. **2** The largest of these islands; 95 square miles: ancient *Melita.*

mal·tase (môl′tās) *n. Biochem.* A digestive enzyme which hydrolyzes maltose into dextrose. [<MALT + -ASE]

malted milk 1 A powder made of dehydrated milk and malted cereals, soluble in milk or water. **2** The beverage made with this powder.

Mal·tese (môl·tēz′, -tēs′) *adj.* Of or pertaining to Malta, its inhabitants, or their language, or to the Knights of Malta. —*n. pl.* ·**tese 1** A native of Malta; the people of Malta collectively. **2** The language of Malta, a dialectal Arabic with elements of Italian. **3** A Maltese cat or dog.

malt house A building in which grains are malted and other preparations made for use in the brewer's trade.

malt liquor A fermented liquor, esp. beer or ale made from malt.

malt·ose (môl′tōs) *n. Biochem.* A hard, white, dextrorotatory, crystalline sugar, $C_{12}H_{22}O_{11}·H_2O$, formed by the action of amylase on starch. [<MALT + -OSE[2]]

mal·treat (mal·trēt′) *v.t.* To treat badly or unkindly; abuse. See synonyms under ABUSE. [< F *maltraiter* <*mal-* MAL- + *traiter* <OF *traitier* TREAT] —**mal·treat′ment** *n.*

malt·ster (môlt′stər) *n.* A maker of or dealer in malt.

malt·y (môl′tē) *adj.* **malt·i·er, malt·i·est** Of, pertaining to, containing, or resembling malt.

mal·va·ceous (mal·vā′shəs) *adj.* Pertaining or belonging to the mallow family (*Malvaceae*) of herbs, shrubs, or trees, with alternate palmately nerved leaves and regular flowers, including althea, cotton, okra, etc. [<LL *malvaceus* <*malva* a mallow]

mal·ver·sa·tion (mal′vər·sā′shən) *n.* Evil or corrupt conduct; misconduct, as in public office. [<MF <*malverser* <L *male versari* < *male* wrongly, ill + *versari* behave, passive freq. of *vertere* turn]

ma·ma (mä′mə, mə·mä′) *n.* Mother: a term of familiar address and endearment. Also **mam′·ma.** [Repetition of infantile syllable *ma*]

mam·ba (mäm′bə) *n.* Any of certain long, venomous, arboreal snakes (genus *Dendraspis*) of southern Africa; especially, the common olive-green or black mamba (*D. angusticeps*). [< Zulu *in-amba*]

mam·bo (mäm′bō) *n. pl.* ·**bos** A form of popular music, derived from Cuban Negro styles, achieving its effects by syncopation of a four-beat rhythmic pattern, with accents on the second and fourth beats.

ma·melle (ma-mel′) n. In western United States, a rounded hillock. [F, breast]

ma·mey (mä-mā′, -mē′) n. 1 A tropical American tree (Mamea americana) bearing edible, yellow fruits resembling the pomelo in size and shape: also mamey de Santo Domingo. 2 A fruit of this tree: also mamey apple. 3 The sapodilla or marmalade tree. Also mam·mee (mä-mä′, -mē′). [<Sp.<Taino]

mam·ma (mam′ə) n. pl. ·mae (-ē) The milk-secreting organ of a mammal; a breast, udder, or bag. [<L, breast]

mam·mal (mam′əl) n. A vertebrate animal whose female suckles its young. [< MAMMALIA]

Mam·ma·li·a (ma-mā′lē-ə) n. pl. A class of vertebrates whose females have milk-secreting mammae to nourish their young, including man, all warm-blooded quadrupeds, seals, cetaceans, and sirenians. [<NL <LL mammalis of the breast <L mamma breast]

mam·ma·lif·er·ous (mam′ə-lif′ər-əs) adj. Containing remains of mammals, as geological strata. [<MAMMALI(A) + -FEROUS]

mam·mal·o·gy (ma-mal′ə-jē) n. The branch of zoology that treats of the Mammalia. [< MAMMAL + -LOGY]

mam·ma·ry (mam′ər-ē) adj. Of, pertaining to, or of the nature of a mamma or breast, or the mammae.

mammary gland The milk gland, which in a female forms the bulk of the breast or mamma. The mammary glands occur in both the male and female in all mammals, but are rudimentary in the male.

mam·mate (mam′āt) adj. Having mammae or breasts. Also mam′me·at·ed (-ē-ā′tid). [<L mammatus <mamma breast]

mam·ma·tus (ma-mā′təs) n. Meteorol. A cloud form characterized by pouchlike protuberances along the lower surface: noted especially in stratocumulus and cumulonimbus clouds. [< L. See MAMMATE.]

mam·mer·ing (mam′ər-ing) n. A state of doubt or perplexity.

mam·mie (mam′ē) See MAMMY.

mam·mif·er·ous (ma-mif′ər-əs) adj. Having mammae or breasts; mammalian. [<MAMM(A) + -(I)FEROUS]

mam·mil·la (ma-mil′ə) n. pl. ·lae (-ē) Anat. A nipple or teat, or some nipplelike or teat-shaped structure or protuberance. [<L mamilla, mammilla, dim. of mamma breast]

mam·mil·lar·y (mam′ə-ler′ē) adj. 1 Of, pertaining to, or resembling a mammilla or a mamma. 2 Studded with or composed of breast-shaped or rounded protuberances: a mammillary mineral, a mammillary prairie.

mam·mil·late (mam′ə-lāt) v.t. ·lat·ed, ·lat·ing To shape like a breast or a nipple. —adj. 1 Having a mammilla, mammillae, or nipplelike processes. 2 Shaped like a nipple. Also **mam′mil·lat·ed.** [<MAMMILL(A) + -ATE¹]

mam·mil·li·form (ma-mil′ə-fôrm) adj. Shaped like or resembling a mammilla. Also **mam·mil·loid** (mam′ə-loid). [MAMMILL(A) + -(I)FORM]

mam·mi·tis (ma-mī′tis) n. Mastitis. [<MAMM(A) + -ITIS]

mam·mo·gram (mam′ə-gram) n. An X-ray photograph of the breast or breasts.

mam·mog·ra·phy (mə-mog′rə-fē) n. X-ray examination of the breast or breasts. [<L mamma breast + Gk. graphein write]

mam·mol·o·gy (mam′ə-mol′ə-jē) n. Mammalogy. [<MAMM(ALIA) + -(O)LOGY]

mam·mon (mam′ən) n. 1 Riches; wealth. 2 Worldliness; avarice. Matt. vi 24; Luke xvi 9. [<LL <Gk. mammōnas <Aramaic māmōnā riches, prob. ult. <'āman trust]

Mam·mon (mam′ən) 1 The personification of riches, avarice, and worldly gain. 2 In Milton's Paradise Lost, one of the fallen angels.

mam·mon·ism (mam′ən-iz′əm) n. Devotion to the acquisition of wealth; worldliness. —**mam′·mon·ist, mam′mon·ite** n.

mam·my (mam′ē) n. pl. ·mies 1 Mother; mama. 2 A Negro nurse or foster mother of white children, especially in the Southern U.S. Also spelled **mammie.** [Dim. of MAMA]

man (man) n. pl. **men** (men) 1 A member of the genus Homo (family Hominidae, class Mammalia), the most highly developed of the primates, differing from other animals in having erect posture, extraordinary development of the brain, and the power of articulate language: only existing species, Homo sapiens. Earlier forms include the following: CRO-MAGNON MAN, GRIMALDI MAN, HEIDELBERG MAN, MIDLAND MAN, MODJOKERTO MAN, NEANDERTHAL MAN, RHODESIAN MAN, SOLO MAN, WADJAK MAN. 2 The human race. 3 Any one, indefinitely. 4 An adult male of the human kind: distinguished from woman, boy, and youth. 5 The male part of the race collectively. 6 A male person who is manly; also, manhood. 7 An adult male servant, dependent, or vassal. 8 A piece, figure, disk, etc., used in playing certain games, as chess or checkers. 9 A ship or vessel: used in composition: a man-of-war; an Indiaman. 10 A husband; lover; man and wife; Her man is dead. 11 Fellow: used in direct address: Hey, man, look at this! —**the Man** U.S. Slang A white man regarded as a representative of the establishment, as a police officer or a boss. —**to a man** Every one. —**to be one's own man** To be independent. —v.t. **manned, man·ning** 1 To supply with men: to man a fort. 2 To take stations at, on, or in for work, defense, etc.: Man the pumps! —**to man oneself** To prepare or brace oneself, as for an ordeal. [OE mann]

ma·na (mä′nə) n. Among Pacific islanders, the supernatural power or force that works through a person or an inanimate object.

man–a·bout–town (man′ə·bout′toun′) n. A man who frequents night clubs, theaters, restaurants, bars, etc.; hence, a sophisticate.

man·a·cle (man′ə-kəl) n. 1 Usually pl. One of a connected pair of metallic instruments for confining or restraining the hands; a handcuff. 2 Anything that constrains or fetters. —v.t. ·cled, ·cling 1 To put manacles on. 2 To hamper; constrain. [< OF manicle < manicula, dim. of manus hand]

man·age (man′ij) v. ·aged, ·ag·ing v.t. 1 To direct or conduct the affairs or interests of: to manage a business. 2 To control the direction, operation, etc., of, as a machine. 3 To cause to do one's bidding, as by persuasion or flattery. 4 To bring about or contrive: to manage to do something. 5 To handle or wield, as a weapon or implement. 6 To train (a horse) in the exercises of a manège. —v.i. 7 To carry on or conduct business or affairs. 8 To contrive to get along: I'll manage. See synonyms under GOVERN, REGULATE. —n. Obs. 1 Management. 2 Behavior. 3 Manège; a riding school. [<Ital. maneggiare handle, train horses, ult. <L manus a hand]

man·age·a·ble (man′ij-ə-bəl) adj. Capable of being managed; tractable; docile. See synonyms under DOCILE. —**man′age·a·bil′i·ty, man′age·a·ble·ness** n. —**man′age·a·bly** adv.

man·age·ment (man′ij-mənt) n. 1 The act, art, or manner of managing, controlling, or conducting. 2 The skilful use of means to accomplish a purpose. 3 Managers or directors collectively. See synonyms under CARE, OVERSIGHT.

man·ag·er (man′ij-ər) n. 1 One who manages; especially, one who has the control of a business or a business establishment; a director. 2 An adroit schemer; intriguer. See synonyms under MASTER, SUPERINTENDENT. —**man′ag·er·ship** n.

man·a·ge·ri·al (man′ə-jir′ē-əl) adj. Of, pertaining to, or characteristic of a manager or management. —**man′a·ge′ri·al·ly** adv.

man–at–arms (man′ət-ärmz′) n. pl. **men–at–arms** (men′-) A soldier; especially, a heavily armed soldier of medieval times.

man·a·tee (man′ə-tē′) n. A sirenian (genus Trichechus) of the tropical Atlantic shores and rivers; a sea cow. [<Sp. manati <Cariban manattoui]

MANATEE
(From 8 to 12 feet in length over-all)

ma·nav·e·lins (mə-nav′ə-linz) n. pl. Naut. Slang Odds and ends; leftover scraps. Also **ma·nav′i·lins.** [Var. of nautical slang manarvelings <manarvel steal small stores]

man·chi·neel (man′chi-nēl′) n. A tropical American tree (Hippomane mancinella) having an acrid, milky, poisonous sap. [<F mancenille <Sp. manzanilla, dim. of manzana an apple <L (mala) matiana (apples) of Matius <Matius, a Roman culinary author]

Man·chu·kuo (man′chōō′kwō′, Chinese män′·jō′kwō′) A former empire in NE Asia, 1932-45, established under Japanese auspices; comprising Manchuria and the Chinese province of Jehol and part of Chahar in Inner Mongolia; about 503,013 square miles; capital, Hsinking. Also **Man′chou′kuo′.**

Man·chu·ri·a (man-chŏŏr′ē-ə) A major division of NE China; 585,000 square miles; capital, Mukden. See MANCHUKUO. —**Man·chu′ri·an** adj. & n.

man·ci·ple (man′sə-pəl) n. A steward, as of an English college. [<OF manciple, mancipe <L mancipium MANCIPIUM]

-mancy combining form Divining, foretelling, or discovering by means of: necromancy. [<Gk. manteia power of divination]

man·da·mus (man-dā′məs) n. Law A writ originally (in England) of royal prerogative, now a writ of right, issued by courts of superior jurisdiction and directed to subordinate courts, corporations, or the like, commanding them to do something therein specified: modified by statute from the ordinary common law form in jurisdiction. —v.t. Colloq. To command by or serve with a mandamus. [<L, we command <mandare. See MANDATE.]

Man·dan (man′dan) n. 1 One of a tribe of North American Indians of Siouan stock. of the NW United States. 2 The Siouan language of this tribe.

man·da·rin (man′də-rin) n. 1 An official of the Chinese Empire, either civil or military: a title used by foreigners indiscriminately. The recognized official grades under the Empire were nine, each rank being distinguished by its official specific regalia, a conspicuous part of which is the **mandarin button.** 2 Any of certain small Chinese oranges, having a loose skin and very sweet pulp; a tangerine. 3 An orange or reddish-yellow dye. [<Pg. mandarim <Malay mantri a minister of state <Hind. <Skt. mantrin a counselor <mantra counsel]

Man·da·rin (man′də-rin) n. 1 (l)The Chinese language of north China, in the Peking dialect now the official language of the country. 2 Formerly, the court language of the Chinese Empire.

mandarin duck A crested duck (Aix galericulata), with variously colored plumage.

man·da·tar·y (man′də-ter′ē) n. pl. ·tar·ies One to whom a charge is given; an agent. See MANDATE (def. 2).

man·date (man′dāt, -dit) n. 1 An authoritative requirement, as of a sovereign; a command; order; charge. 2 A charge to a nation, authorizing the government, administration, and development of conquered territory, given by a congress or league of nations, to which the grantee is responsible; also, the territory given in charge. 3 A judicial command directed to an officer of the court to enforce an order of that court; a precept from an appellate court directing what a subordinate court shall do in an appealed case. 4 A rescript of the pope ordering that the person named shall have the first vacant benefice in the gift of the person addressed. 5 An instruction from an electorate to the legislative body, or its representative, to follow a certain course of action. See synonyms under LAW. —v.t. (-dāt) ·dat·ed, ·dat·ing To assign (a colony or other territory) to a specific nation under a mandate. [<L mandatum, pp. neut. of mandare command <manus hand + dare give (to)]

man·da·tor (man-dā′tər) n. One who gives a mandate; a director. [<L <mandatus, pp. of mandare. See MANDATE.]

man·da·to·ry (man′də-tôr′ē, -tō′rē) adj. Expressive of positive command; obligatory. —n. pl. ·ries 1 A mandatary. 2 A mandate.

man·del·ic (man·del′ik) adj. Pertaining to or designating a white crystalline acid, $C_8H_8O_3$, used in medicine as a urinary antiseptic. [<G mandel an almond]

man·di·ble (man′də-bəl) n. Biol. 1 The lower jaw bone, or its equivalent. 2 Either the upper or the lower part of the beak of a bird, or of the beak of a cephalopod. 3 Either one

of the upper or outer pair of jaws in an insect.
4 The operculum of a polyzoan. [<LL *mandibula* jaw <L *mandere* chew]
man·dib·u·lar (man·dib'yə·lər) *adj.* Of, pertaining to, or formed by a mandible: the *mandibular* arch of the fetal skull. Also **man·dib'u·lar'y** (-ler'ē). — *n.* The lower jaw, or mandible. [<LL *mandibul(a)* MANDIBLE + -AR]
man·dib·u·late (man·dib'yə·lit, -lāt) *adj.* Having mandibles adapted for biting and chewing: said of certain insects. — *n.* Any insect having chewing jaws.
man·do·la (man·dō'lə) *n.* A large mandolin. [<Ital. *mandola, mandora* <L *pandura.* See BANDORE.]
man·do·lin (man'də·lin, man'də·lin') *n.* A stringed musical instrument with an almond-shaped body and metal strings arranged like those of a violin. [<F *mandoline* <Ital. *mandolino,* dim. of *mandola* MANDOLA] — **man'do·lin'ist** *n.*
man·drake (man'drāk) *n.* **1** A short-stemmed Old World plant (*Mandragora officinarum*) of the nightshade family, with narcotic properties. **2** Its fleshy roots, sometimes having a fancied resemblance to the human form. **3** The May apple. Also **man·drag·o·ra** (man·drag'ə·rə). [Alter. of ME *mandrag(g)e* <OE *mandragora* <LL *mandragoras* <Gk.; infl. in form by folk etymology <MAN + DRAKE² a dragon]
man·drel (man'drəl) *n. Mech.* **1** A shaft or spindle on which an object may be fixed for rotation. **2** A smooth, hard, cylindrical or conical core about which wire may be coiled or metal or glass forged. **3** A pattern or form against which metalwork is pressed in spinning. Also **man'dril.** [Prob. alter. of F *mandrin* a lathe]
man·drill (man'dril) *n.* A large, ferocious West African baboon (genus *Papio*), having large canine teeth and bony prominences on the cheeks striped with blue and scarlet. [<MAN + DRILL³]

MANDRILL
(About 30 inches at the shoulder; length 3 to 4 feet)

man·du·cate (man'jŏŏ·kāt) *v.t.* **·cat·ed, ·cat·ing** *Rare* To chew; masticate. [<L *manducatus,* pp. of *manducare* chew]
mane (mān) *n.* The long hair growing on and about the neck of some animals, as the horse, lion, etc. ◆ Homophone: *main.* [OE *manu*] — **maned** *adj.* — **mane'less** *adj.*
ma·nège (ma·nezh') *n.* **1** The art of training and riding horses. **2** A school of horsemanship; riding school; also, a school for the training of horses. **3** The style and movements of a trained horse. Also **ma·nege'.** [<F <Ital. *maneggio* <*maneggiare.* See MANAGE.]
Ma·net (ma·nā', *Fr.* ma·ne'), **Édouard,** 1832–1883, French painter.
ma·neu·ver (mə·nōō'vər, -nyōō'-) *n.* **1** A movement or change of position, as of troops or war vessels. **2** Any dexterous or artful proceeding. — *v.t.* **1** To put, as troops, through a maneuver or maneuvers. **2** To put, bring, make, etc., by a maneuver or maneuvers. **3** To manipulate; conduct adroitly. — *v.i.* **4** To perform a maneuver or maneuvers. **5** To use tricks or stratagems; manage adroitly. Also spelled *manoeuver, manoeuvre.* [<F *manoeuvre* <OF *maneuvre* <LL *manopera* <*manoperare* <L *manu operari* work with the hand <*manus* hand + *operari.* See OPERATE. Doublet of MAINOR, MANURE.] — **ma·neu'ver·a·bil'i·ty** or **·vra·bil'i·ty** *n.* — **ma·neu'ver·a·ble** or **·vra·ble** *adj.* — **ma·neu'ver·er** *n.*
ma·neu·vers (mə·nōō'vərz, -nyōō'-) *n. pl.* Large-scale military exercises involving the use of great numbers of troops under conditions simulating actual battle conditions; war games.
man·ful (man'fəl) *adj.* Having a manly spirit; characterized by courage and perseverance; sturdy. See synonyms under MANLY, MASCULINE. — **man'ful·ly** *adv.* — **man'ful·ness** *n.*
man·ga·nate (mang'gə·nāt) *n. Chem.* A salt

of manganic acid, such as those of sodium, potassium, and barium. [<MANGAN(IC) + -ATE³]
man·ga·nese (mang'gə·nēs, -nēz) *n. Chem.* A hard, brittle, metallic element (symbol Mn). In color, it is grayish-white tinged with red; it rusts like iron, but is not magnetic; it is widely distributed (in combination) in nature, and forms an important component of certain alloys, such as manganese steel. See ELEMENT. [<F *manganèse* <Ital. *manganese,* alter. of Med. L *magnesia* MAGNESIA]
manganese dioxide Pyrolusite.
manganese spar 1 Rhodonite. **2** Rhodochrosite.
manganese steel A very hard, ductile steel containing from 12 to 14 percent of manganese.
man·gan·ic (mang·gan'ik) *adj. Chem.* Of, pertaining to, containing, or obtained from manganese in its highest valence, as manganic acid, H₂MnO₄, known chiefly by its salts. [<MANGAN(ESE) + -IC]
man·ga·nite (mang'gə·nīt) *n.* **1** A dark, steel-gray to iron-black orthorhombic manganese hydroxide, MnO(OH). **2** *Chem.* Any salt obtained from certain hydroxides of manganese, and regarded as an acid.
man·ga·nous (mang'gə·nəs) *adj.* Of, pertaining to, or containing manganese in its lowest valence.
mange (mānj) *n.* An itching skin disease of dogs and other domestic animals, caused by burrowing parasitic mites. Also **the mange.** [<OF *manjue* an itch, eating <*manjuer, mangier.* See MANGER.]
man·gel-wur·zel (mang'gəl-wûr'zəl, -wûrt'səl) *n.* A large-rooted European beet (*Beta vulgaris*), fed to cattle. Also **man'gel.** [<G <*mangoldwurzel* <*mangold* a beet + *wurzel* a root]
man·ger (mān'jər) *n.* A trough or box, for feeding horses or cattle. [<OF *mangeoire, mangeure* <*mangier* eat <L *manducare* chew]
man·gle¹ (mang'gəl) *v.t.* **·gled, ·gling 1** To disfigure or mutilate, as by cutting, bruising, or crushing; lacerate. **2** To mar or ruin; spoil: to *mangle* a word. See synonyms under REND. [<AF *mangler, mahangler,* appar. freq. of OF *mahaigher* MAIM]
man·gle² (mang'gəl) *n.* A machine for smoothing fabrics by pressing them between rollers. — *v.t.* **gled, ·gling** To smooth with a mangle. [<Du. *mangel* <MDu. *mange* <Ital. *mangano* <LL *manganum* <Gk. *manganon* a pulley, a war machine. Doublet of MANGONEL.]
man·gler (mang'glər) *n.* One who or that which mangles.
man·go (mang'gō) *n. pl.* **·goes** or **·gos 1** The edible, fleshy fruit of a tropical tree allied to the sumac. **2** The tree (*Mangifera indica,* family *Anacardiaceae*) producing the fruit. **3** A pickled green muskmelon. [<Pg. *manga* <Malay *mangga* <Tamil *mān-kāy* <*mān* a mango tree + *kāy* a fruit]
man·go·nel (mang'gə·nel) *n.* A military engine formerly used for throwing stones and other missiles. [<OF, dim. of LL *manganum.* Doublet of MANGLE².]
man·go·steen (mang'gə·stēn) *n.* **1** The reddish-brown fruit of an East Indian tree, about the size of an apple, having a thick, fleshy rind, and a white, juicy pulp. **2** The tree (*Garcinia mangostana*) producing this fruit. [<Malay *mangustan*]
man·grove (mang'grōv, man'-) *n.* **1** A tropical tree (genus *Rhizophora,* especially *R. mangle*) which throws out many aerial roots from the lower branches and stem, forming dense thickets. **2** A shrub of the vervain family, as the **black mangrove** (*Avicennia marina*). [<Sp. *mangle* <Taino; infl. in form by GROVE]
mangrove cuckoo A cuckoo (*Coccyzus minor*) frequenting mangroves of the West Indies, Florida, etc.
man·gy (mān'jē) *adj.* **·gi·er, ·gi·est 1** Affected with the mange. **2** Figuratively, poverty-stricken; squalid. — **man'gi·ly** *adv.* — **man'gi·ness** *n.*
man·han·dle (man'han'dəl) *v.t.* **·dled, ·dling 1** To move by manpower without mechanical aids. **2** To handle with roughness, as in

anger.
Man·hat·tan (mən·hat'ən, man-) *n.* **1** A cocktail made of whisky and vermouth, often with a dash of bitters and a cherry. **2** One of a tribe of Algonquian North American Indians, formerly inhabiting Manhattan Island.
Man·hat·tan Island (mən·hat'ən, man-) An island in SE New York at the mouth of the Hudson River; 22 square miles; comprising **Manhattan** borough of New York City.
man·hole (man'hōl') *n.* An opening through which a man may enter a boiler, conduit, sewer, etc., for making repairs.
man·hood (man'hŏŏd) *n.* **1** Manly qualities collectively; manliness; courage. **2** The state of being of age; man's estate. **3** The state of being a man, or a human being as distinguished from other animals or beings. **4** Men collectively: the *manhood* of the nation.
ma·ni·a (mā'nē·ə, mān'yə) *n.* **1** Madness. **2** *Psychiatry* Exaggerated melancholia alternating periodically with an exaggerated sense of well-being, accompanied by excessive activity (both mental and physical): also called manic-depressive psychosis. **3** A strong, ungovernable desire; also, colloquially, a craze: a *mania* for rare books. See synonyms under FRENZY, INSANITY. [<L <Gk., madness < *mainesthai* rage. Akin to MANTIC.]
-mania *combining form* An exaggerated, persistent, or irrational craving for or infatuation with. [<Gk. *mania* madness]
ma·ni·ac (mā'nē·ak) *adj.* Having a mania; raving. See synonyms under INSANE. — *n.* A person wildly or violently insane; a madman. [<LL *maniacus* <L *mania* MANIA] — **ma·ni·a·cal** (mə·nī'ə·kəl) *adj.* — **ma·ni'a·cal·ly** *adv.*
-maniac *combining form* Forming adjectives (often used as nouns) from nouns in *-mania:* kleptomaniac.
man·ic (man'ik, mā'nik) *adj.* Pertaining to, like, or affected by mania. [<MAN(IA) + -IC]
man·ic-de·pres·sive (man'ik·di·pres'iv) *adj. Psychiatry* Denoting a mental disorder characterized by sudden fluctuations of depression and excitement. — *n.* One who suffers from this disorder.
man·i·cure (man'ə·kyŏŏr) *n.* **1** The care or treatment of the hands and fingernails. **2** *Obs.* A manicurist. — *v.t.* & *v.i.* **·cured, ·curing** To take care of or treat (the hands and nails). [<F <L *manus* hand + *cura* care]
man·i·cur·ist (man'ə·kyŏŏr'ist) *n.* One who cares for or treats the hands and fingernails.
man·i·fest (man'ə·fest) *n.* **1** In shipping and transportation: **a** An itemized account of a carrier's cargo, showing ports of lading, consignees, etc. **b** The list of passengers, cargo, etc., for an airplane flight. **c** A detailed list of the cars of a train. **d** A fast freight train, or perishable goods on it. **2** *Obs.* A manifesto. — *v.t.* **1** To make plain to sight or understanding; reveal; display. **2** To prove; be evidence of. **3** To show the manifest of (a shipment). — *adj.* Plainly apparent to sight or understanding; evident; plain. [<L *manifestus* evident, lit., struck by the hand] — **man'i·fest'ly** *adv.*
Synonyms (adj.): apparent, bare, clear, conspicuous, distinct, evident, glaring, indubitable, obvious, open, overt, palpable, patent, plain, transparent, unmistakable, visible. See CLEAR, EVIDENT, NOTORIOUS, OVERT. *Antonyms:* concealed, covert, dark, hidden, impalpable, impenetrable, imperceptible, invisible, latent, obscure, occult, secret, undiscovered, unimagined, unknown, unseen.
man·i·fes·ta·tion (man'ə·fes·tā'shən) *n.* **1** The act of manifesting or making plain; the state or fact of being manifested; disclosure or display; a revelation. **2** Hence, a public or collective act by a government or party in order to emphasize its power, determination, or special views. **3** A revealing agency. **4** In spiritualism, the materialization of a spirit. See synonyms under MARK¹, SIGN. — **man'i·fes'tant** *n.*
man·i·fes·to (man'ə·fes'tō) *n. pl.* **·toes** A public, official, and authoritative declaration making announcement or explanation of intentions, motives, or principles of actions. [<Ital. <L *manifestus.* See MANIFEST.]

man·i·fold (man'ə·fōld) v.t. **1** To make more than one copy of at once, as with carbon paper on a typewriter. **2** To multiply. — adj. **1** Of great variety; numerous. **2** Manifested in many ways, or including many acts or elements; complex; being so in many ways or for many reasons. **3** Existing in great abundance. **4** Comprising or uniting several parts or channels of the same kind, as a pipe with several outlets. See synonyms under COMPLEX, MANY. — n. **1** A copy made by manifolding. **2** Math. A number of objects related under one system. **3** A tube with one or more inlets and two or more outlets; a T branch, as the pipe between carburetor and engine, in internal-combustion engines with more than one cylinder. [OE manigfeald varied, numerous] — **man'i·fold·ly** adv. — **man'i·fold·ness** n.

man·i·fold·er (man'ə·fōl'dər) n. **1** One who or that which manifolds. **2** A machine or apparatus for making manifold copies, as of a document.

man·i·hot (man'ē·hot) n. Any of a large genus (Manihot) of tropical American, mainly Brazilian, herbs or woody plants of the spurge family. Brazilian or Ceará rubber is the product of M. glaziovi. [<NL <F <Tupian mandioca manioc root]

man·i·kin (man'ə·kin) n. **1** A model of the human body, showing its structure. **2** A dressmaker's assistant or lay figure wearing new costumes so as to display them for sale: also spelled mannequin. **3** A little man; dwarf. Also spelled manakin, mannikin. [<Du. manneken, dim. of man man]

ma·nil·a (mə·nil'ə) n. **1** A cheroot made in Manila. **2** The fiber of the abaca (Musa textilis), a tall, perennial herb of the same genus as the banana: also **Manila hemp, ma·nil'la.**

Manila paper A heavy, light-brown paper originally made of Manila hemp, now made of various fibers.

Manila rope Rope made of Manila hemp.

man·i·oc (man'ē·ok, mä'nē-) n. The bitter or sweet cassava. [<F <Tupian mandioca manioc root]

man·i·ple (man'ə·pəl) n. **1** Eccl. A band worn on the left arm as a vestment by the clergy of the Roman Catholic and sometimes the Anglican Church. **2** A subdivision of the Roman legion containing 60 or 120 men. [<OF maniple, manipule <L manipulus a handful <manus hand + base of plere fill]

ma·nip·u·lar (mə·nip'yə·lər) adj. **1** Pertaining to manipulation or handling. **2** Pertaining to a maniple. [<L manipularis <manipulus a MANIPLE; infl. in sense by MANIPULATION]

ma·nip·u·late (mə·nip'yə·lāt) v.t. ·lat·ed, ·lat·ing **1** To handle, operate, or use with or as with the hands, especially with skill. **2** To influence or control artfully or deceptively: to manipulate stocks. **3** To change or alter (figures, accounts, etc.), usually fraudulently. [Back formation <MANIPULATION <F, ult. <L manipulus a MANIPLE] — **ma·nip'u·la'tion** n. — **ma·nip'u·la'tive, ma·nip'u·la·to'ry** adj. — **ma·nip'u·la'tor** n.

ma·nis (mā'nis) n. A pangolin. [<NL, sing. <L manes MANES]

Man·i·to·ba (man'ə·tō'bə, -tō·bä') A province in central Canada; 246,512 square miles; capital, Winnipeg. — **Man'i·to'ban** adj. & n.

man·kind (man'kīnd', man'kīnd') n. **1** The whole human species. **2** (man'kīnd') Men collectively as distinguished from women. Synonyms: humanity, humankind, man, men. See HUMANITY.

man·like (man'līk') adj. Like a man; having the qualities proper to the human race, or to the male sex, to manly character. See synonyms under MANLY, MASCULINE.

man·ly (man'lē) adj. ·li·er, ·li·est Possessing the characteristics of a true man, as strength, frankness, and intrepidity. — adv. Archaic In a manner befitting a man. — **man'li·ly** adv. — **man'li·ness** n.
Synonyms: manful, manlike, mannish. Manlike may mean only having the outward appearance or semblance of a man, or it may be substantially equivalent to manly. Manly refers to all the qualities and traits worthy of a man; manful especially to the valor and prowess that become a man; we speak of a manful struggle; manly decision; we say manly gentleness, or tenderness; we could not say

manful tenderness. Mannish is a depreciatory word referring to the mimicry or parade of some superficial qualities of manhood; as, a mannish woman. See MASCULINE.

man·na (man'ə) n. **1** The miraculously supplied food on which the Israelites subsisted in the wilderness. Exodus xvi 14–36. **2** Divine or spiritual nourishment. **3** A sweetish substance obtained from incisions in the stems of various trees or shrubs, especially the stems of the flowering ash (Fraxinus ornus and F. rotundifolia) of southern Europe. It is a mild laxative. [OE <LL <Gk. <Aramaic mannā <Hebrew mān]

man·ne·quin (man'ə·kin) See MANIKIN (def. 2).

man·ner (man'ər) n. **1** The way of doing anything; method of procedure; mode. **2** The demeanor or bearing peculiar to one; personal carriage; mien; address. **3** pl. General modes of life or conduct; especially, social behavior. **4** pl. Polite, civil, or well-bred behavior. **5** Usual or ordinary practice; habit; custom; also, characteristic style in literature or art. **6** Sort or kind. **7** Character; guise. — **to the manner born** Familiar with something from birth. ◆ Homophone: manor. [<AF manere, OF maniere, ult. <L manuarius of the hand <manus hand]
Synonyms: appearance, aspect, carriage, demeanor, deportment, fashion, habit, look, mien, mode, practice, style, way. See ADDRESS, AIR, BEHAVIOR, CUSTOM, SYSTEM.

man·nered (man'ərd) adj. **1** Having (specified) manners: often used in combination: ill-mannered. **2** Affected.

man·ner·ism (man'ər·iz'əm) n. **1** Characteristic or marked adherence to an unusual or affected manner, style, or peculiarity. **2** A peculiarity of manner, as in behavior or speech.

man·ner·ist (man'ər·ist) n. A person addicted to mannerism; an imitator; specifically, an artist or writer whose work is marked by a persistent or extreme adherence to some style, manner, etc., as one of the school of painters of the 16th and 17th centuries who unduly emphasized and imitated the style of Michelangelo and other Italian painters.

man·ner·less (man'ər·lis) adj. Lacking manners; ill-mannered.

man·ner·ly (man'ər·lē) adj. Well-behaved; polite. — adv. With good manners; politely. — **man'ner·li·ness** n.

man·ners-bit (man'ərz·bit') n. A small amount left on a plate by a guest at table, for the sake of good manners, as indicating that the serving was abundant.

man·ni·tol (man'ə·tōl, -tol) n. Biochem. A slightly sweet crystalline alcohol, $C_6H_{14}O_6$, found widely distributed in nature, as in celery, sponges, sea grasses, and especially in the dried sap of the flowering ash. Also **man'nite** (-īt). [<MANNA (def. 3) + -ITE³ + -OL¹] — **man·nit·ic** (mə·nit'ik) adj.

man·nose (man'ōs) n. A hexose, $C_6H_{12}O_6$, obtained by the oxidation of mannitol. [< MANN(ITOL) + -OSE]

man·o·cry·om·e·ter (man'ō·krī·om'ə·tər) n. An instrument for determining the variations in the freezing or melting point of substances with changes in pressure. [<Gk. manos thin, rare + kryos an icy cold + -METER]

ma·noeu·ver (mə·nōō'vər, -nyōō'-), **ma·noeu·vre** See MANEUVER.

Man of Destiny Napoleon I: so regarded by himself.

man of God **1** A saint, prophet, etc.; a holy man. **2** A clergyman.

Man of Sorrows A name supposed to allude to the Messiah (Isa. liii 3); hence, Jesus Christ.

man of straw One put forward as an irresponsible tool or as a fraudulent surety.

man-of-war (man'əv·wôr', man'ə-) n. pl. **men-of-war** (men'-) **1** A naval vessel armed for active hostilities. **2** The Portuguese man-of-war. Also **man'-o'-war'.**

man-of-war bird or **hawk** A frigate bird.

ma·nom·e·ter (mə·nom'ə·tər) n. An instrument for measuring pressure, as of gases and vapors; usually, a U-tube. [<Gk. manos thin, rare + -METER] — **man·o·met·ric** (man'ə·met'rik) or **·ri·cal** adj.

man·or (man'ər) n. **1** Brit. A nobleman's or gentleman's landed estate. **2** In old English law, a tract or district of land granted by the

king to one as lord, with authority to exercise jurisdiction over it by a court-baron. **3** In Anglo-Saxon times, a thane's or lord's estate, composed of the land and of a part of the agricultural capital employed to till it, as well as the laborers, beasts, implements, etc., and having on it a community of serfs or villeins; later, an estate complying with the minimum requirements entitling the lord of the manor to hold a court-baron. **4** U.S. A tract of land originally granted as a manor and let by the proprietor to tenants in perpetuity or for a long term. See synonyms under HOUSE. ◆ Homophone: manner. [<OF manoir a dwelling, orig. a verb <L manere remain] — **ma·no·ri·al** (mə·nôr'ē·əl, -nō'rē-) adj.

man·or-house (man'ər·hous') n. The residence of the lord of the manor. Also **man'or-seat'** (-sēt').

man·pow·er (man'pou'ər) n. **1** Power supplied by the physical strength of a man or men. **2** The normal rate at which a man can work, generally equal to 1/10 horsepower. **3** The strength of all the men available for any service; specifically, the warpower of a nation in terms of the number of men available for military service, industry, agriculture, etc.

man·rope (man'rōp') n. Naut. A rope serving as a hand railing to a gangway, ladder, etc., on board ship.

man·sard (man'särd) n. **1** A roof with a double pitch on all sides: also **mansard roof. 2** A room within such a roof; an attic. [<F mansarde, after François Mansard, 1598–1666, French architect who revived it]

MANSARD ROOF

manse (mans) n. **1** A clergyman's house, especially a Scottish Presbyterian minister's house; a parsonage. **2** A landholder's residence. [<Med. L mansa, mansus. See MANSION.]

man·ser·vant (man'sûr'vənt) n. An adult male servant.

man·sion (man'shən) n. **1** A large or handsome dwelling; specifically, the house of the lord of a manor; a manor-house. **2** In astrology, one of the 12 divisions of the heavens; a house. **3** According to Oriental and medieval astronomers, one of the 28 divisions of the heavens occupied by the moon on successive days. **4** Archaic Any place of abode. **5** A small compartment, abode, or dwelling in a larger house or enclosure. **6** pl. Brit. An apartment house. See synonyms under HOUSE. [<OF <L mansio, -onis a dwelling <mansus, pp. of manere remain, dwell. Doublet of MENAGE.]

man·slaugh·ter (man'slô'tər) n. The killing of man by man; especially, such killing without malice.

man·slay·er (man'slā'ər) n. One who commits homicide. — **man'slay'ing** n.

man·sue·tude (man'swə·tōōd, -tyōōd) n. Accustomed gentleness or mildness; tameness. [<L mansuetudo, -inis <mansuetus, pp. of mansuesere tame <manus hand + suescere accustom]

man·swear (man'swâr') v.i. ·swore, ·sworn, ·swear·ing Obs. To swear falsely. [OE mānswerian <mān wickedness + swerian swear]

man·teau (man'tō, Fr. män·tō') n. pl. ·teaus (-tōz) or ·teaux (Fr. -tō) **1** A cloak or mantle worn by women; any mantle. **2** Obs. A woman's gown; a mantua. [<F <OF mantel MANTLE]

man·tel (man'təl) n. The facing about a fireplace, including the shelf above it; also, the shelf. ◆ Homophone: mantle. [Var. of MANTLE; infl. in meaning by F manteau a mantelpiece]

MANTEL

man·tel·et (man'təl·et, mant'lit) n. **1** A small mantle or short cloak. **2** Mil. A screen or shield, as in an embrasure, to protect the defenders;

a movable roof to protect a besieging party; also, a shield or protection, made of metal, rope, or wood, placed at openings, portholes, etc., to protect the gunner from bullets or smoke. **3** In target-shooting, a bulletproof enclosure for observation. **4** A movable shelter used by hunters. Also spelled *mantlet*. [<OF, dim. of *mantel*. See MANTLE.]

man·tel·let·ta (man'tə·let'ə) *n.* In the Roman Catholic Church, a sleeveless vestment reaching almost to the knees, worn by bishops and various church dignitaries. [<Ital., dim. of *mantello* <L *mantellum*. See MANTLE.]

man·tel·piece (man'təl·pēs') *n.* A mantel shelf.

man·tel·tree (man'təl·trē') *n.* A wooden mantel; also, the arch of a mantel.

man·tic (man'tik) *adj.* Relating to divination, soothsaying, or the supposed inspired condition of a soothsayer; prophetic: *mantic frenzy.* [<Gk. *mantikos* <*mantis* a prophet. Akin to MANIA.]

-mantic *combining form* Used to form adjectives corresponding to nouns ending in *-mancy*: *necromantic*. [<Gk. *mantikos* prophetic <*manteia* divination]

man·til·la (man·til'ə) *n.* **1** A woman's light scarf or head covering of lace, as worn in Spain, Mexico, Italy, etc. **2** Any short mantle. [<Sp., dim. of *manta* MANTA]

man·tis (man'tis) *n. pl.* **·tis·es** or **·tes** (-tēz) A carnivorous, orthopterous, long-bodied insect (family *Mantidae*) with large eyes and movable head, which assumes a position with its forelegs folded as if in prayer. Also called *praying mantis*. For illustration see INSECTS (beneficial). [<Gk., a prophet, also a kind of insect]

PRAYING MANTIS
(From 3 to 6 inches long)

man·tis·sa (man·tis'ə) *n. Math.* The decimal or fractional part of a logarithm: so named as being added to the integral part or characteristic. [<L, a makeweight, trifling addition, ? <Etruscan]

mantis shrimp A squill. Also **mantis crab**.

man·tle (man'təl) *n.* **1** A loose garment, usually without sleeves, worn over the other garments; a cloak. **2** Anything that clothes or envelops; hence, whatever covers or conceals: a *mantle* of darkness. **3** *Zool.* **a** The variously modified flap or folds of the membranous covering of a mollusk. It secretes the shell. **b** The back, scapulars, and folded wings of a bird, when distinguished by color, as in gulls. **c** The soft external body-wall in the tunic of ascidians. **4** The outer covering of a wall. **5** The outer masonry of a blast furnace. **6** A sheath of clay laid over a wax model, forming a mold when the wax is melted out. **7** A mantel. **8** A hood of network fabric, generally cylindrical, of the salts of certain rare refractory earths with high radiating power, as cerium oxide, intended to give light by incandescence, as in the flame of a Bunsen burner, or in the Welsbach burner. —*v.* **·tled**, **·tling** *v.t.* **1** To cover with or as with a mantle; conceal. —*v.i.* **2** To overspread or cover the surface of something. **3** To be or become covered, overspread, or suffused. **4** To spread out one wing at a time over the corresponding outstretched leg: said of hawks. ◆ Homophone: *mantel*. [Fusion of OE *mentel* and OF *mantel*, both <L *mantellum*, *mantelum* a cloak, cloth, towel]

mant·let (mant'lit) See MANTELET.

man·u·al (man'yŏŏ·əl) *adj.* **1** Done, made, or used by the hand; of, relating to, or affecting the hand: *manual* employments. **2** *Law* Actually possessed; in one's own hands. **3** Resembling a manual; designed to be retained for reference: said of a book. —*n.* **1** A compact volume; handbook of instruction or directions. **2** A keyboard, as of an organ. **3** A systematic exercise in the handling of some military weapon. [<OF *manuel* <L *manualis* <L *manus* hand] —**man'u·al·ly** *adv.*

manual alphabet A series of manual signs or gestures representing the letters of the writ-

ten alphabet, used by the deaf and by deaf-mutes as a substitute for vocal speech: sometimes called *deaf-and-dumb alphabet*. For illustration see DEAF-AND-DUMB ALPHABET.

man·u·fac·to·ry (man'yə·fak'tər·ē) *n. pl.* **·ries** A place or establishment where anything is manufactured; a factory. [<MANUFACTURE; on analogy with FACTORY]

man·u·fac·ture (man'yə·fak'chər) *v.t.* **·tured**, **·tur·ing** **1** To make or fashion by hand or machinery, especially in large quantities. **2** To work into useful form, as wool or steel. **3** To create by artifice; invent falsely; concoct. **4** To produce in a mechanical way, as art, poetry, etc. See synonyms under MAKE[1], PRODUCE. —*n.* **1** The production of goods by hand or by industrial art or processes. **2** Anything made by industrial art or processes; manufactured articles collectively. **3** The making or contriving of anything. [<MF <Med. L *manufactura* <L *manus* hand + *factura* a making <*factus*, pp. of *facere* make] —**man'u·fac'tur·er** *n.* —**man'u·fac'tur·ing** *adj.*

man·u·mit (man'yə·mit') *v.t.* **·mit·ted**, **·mit·ting** To free from bondage, as a slave; emancipate; liberate. [<L *manumittere* <*manu emittere*, lit., send forth from one's hand <*manus* hand + *emittere* <*ex* away from + *mittere* send] —**man'u·mis'sion** (-mish'ən) *n.*

ma·nure (mə·nŏŏr', -nyŏŏr') *n.* Any substance, as dung, decaying animal or vegetable matter, or certain minerals, applied to fertilize soil. —*v.t.* **·nured**, **·nur·ing** To apply manure or other fertilizer to, as soil. [<AF *maynoverer* work with the hands, OF *manouvrer* <LL *manoperare*. Doublet of MANEUVER, MAINOR.] —**ma·nur'er** *n.*

man·u·script (man'yə·skript) *n.* **1** Matter written by hand with a pen or the like; a composition in handwriting or typewriting, as distinguished from a printed one. Abbr. *MS.*, plural *MSS.* **2** A roll or book written before the invention of printing. —*adj.* Written by hand. [<Med. L *manuscriptus* <L *manus* hand + *scriptus*, pp. of *scribere* write]

Manx cat (mangks) A variety of domestic cat having no tail.

Manx·man (mangks'mən) *n. pl.* **·men** (-mən) A native of the Isle of Man.

man·y (men'ē) *adj.* **more**, **most** Constituting a large number; numerous. —*n.* **1** A large number: *Many* of those present left early. **2** The masses; crowd; multitude: with *the*. —*pron.* A large number of persons or things. [OE *manig*]

◆ *Many* followed by *a*, *an*, or *another* indicates a great number thought of singly: *Many a man has had to find this out for himself.* The phrase *a great many* is idiomatic; it resembles a collective noun, but takes only a plural verb: *A great many* are involved.
  Synonyms (adj.): divers, frequent, manifold, multifarious, multiplied, multitudinous, numerous, sundry, various. *Antonyms:* few, infrequent, rare, scarce, uncommon.

man·y·plies (men'i·plīz') *n. Zool.* The third stomach of a ruminant, whose lining membrane is raised into many closely set, longitudinal folds; omasum. [<MANY + *plies*, pl. of PLY[1], n.]

man·za·nil·la (man'zə·nil'ə, *Sp.* män'thä·nē'lyä) *n.* **1** A pale, dry sherry with low alcoholic content. **2** A bitter olive usually stuffed with pimentos. [<Sp., orig. name of several carduaceous plants, dim. of *manzana* an apple. See MANCHINEEL.]

man·za·ni·ta (man'zə·nē'tə, *Sp.* män'sä·nē'tä) *n.* Any one of several shrubs or small trees (genus *Arctostaphylos*) of the western United States, including the bearberry. [<Sp., dim. of *manzana* an apple. See MANCHINEEL.]

Mao·ism (mou'iz'əm) *n.* The militant communist doctrines or practices of Mao Tse-tung,

MANX CAT
Named after the Isle of Man, this cat is common throughout Russia and the Far East.

characterized especially by a rejection of the possibility of coexistence with capitalistic states. —**Mao'ist** *n.*

Mao Tse-tung (mou' dzu'dŏŏng'), 1893–1976, Chinese Communist leader; chairman of the People's Republic of China 1949–59.

map (map) *n.* **1** A representation on a plane surface of any region, as of the earth's surface; a chart. **2** Figuratively, any exact delineation. **3** *Slang* The face. —**off the map** Out of existence; out of the running. —*v.t.* **mapped**, **map·ping** **1** To make a map of. **2** To plan in detail: often with *out*. [<OF *mappe-(monde)* <Med. L *mappa (mundi)* map (of the world) <L, cloth, napkin]

ma·ple (mā'pəl) *n.* **1** Any of a large genus (*Acer*) of deciduous trees of the north temperate zone, with opposite leaves and a fruit of two joined samaras. **2** Its wood, which is hard, light in color, and of close grain. **3** The amber-yellow color of the finished wood. **4** The flavor of the sap of the sugar maple. —**hard maple 1** The sugar maple. **2** The black maple (*A. nigrum*). [OE *mapel(trēow)*, *mapul(der)* a maple (tree)]

ma·qui (mä'kē) *n.* An ornamental evergreen shrub (*Aristotelia macqui*), used in Chile in making musical instruments. A medicinal wine is made from its purple acid berries. [< Sp. <Araucan]

ma·quis (mä·kē') *n.* A zone of shrubby, mostly evergreen plants in the Mediterranean region, transitional between steppe and forest growths: known as cover for game or bandits: also called *macchia*. [<F <Ital. *macchia* a thicket, orig. a spot <L *macula* a spot]

mar (mär) *v.t.* **marred**, **mar·ring 1** To do harm to; impair or ruin. **2** To injure so as to deface; disfigure. See synonyms under HURT. —*n.* A disfiguring mark; blemish; injury. [OE *merran*, *mierran* hinder, injure] —**mar'rer** *n.*

mar·a·bou (mar'ə·bŏŏ) *n.* **1** A stork of the genus *Leptoptilos*, especially the African marabou (*L. crumeniferus*), whose soft, white, lower tail and wing feathers are used in millinery. **2** The adjutant bird. **3** A plume from the marabou. **4** A delicate white silk that can be dyed without being freed from gum. Also **mar'a·bout** (-bŏŏt). [<F *marabou*, *marabout*. See MARABOUT.]

MARABOU

ma·ra·ca (mə·rä'kə, *Pg.* mä·rä'kä) *n.* A percussion instrument made of a gourd or gourd-shaped rattle with beans or beads inside it. [< *Pg. maracá* <Tupian]

Mar·a·can·da (mar'ə·kan'də) Ancient name for SAMARKAND.

ma·ran·ta (mə·ran'tə) *n.* Starch from arrowroot. [after Bartolommeo *Maranta*, died 1554, Italian physician and botanist]

ma·ras·ca (mə·ras'kə) *n.* A small, wild cherry (*Prunus cerasus marasca*) of the Dalmatian mountains. [<Ital., aphetic var. of *amarasca* < *amaro* bitter <L *amarus*]

mar·a·schi·no (mar'ə·skē'nō) *n.* A cordial distilled from the fermented juice of the marasca and flavored with the cracked pits. [<Ital. < *marasca* MARASCA]

maraschino cherries Cherries preserved in maraschino liqueur.

ma·ras·mus (mə·raz'məs) *n. Pathol.* A gradual and continuous wasting away of the body; emaciation, especially in infants and the aged. [<NL <Gk. *marasmos* <*marainein* waste]— **ma·ras'mic** *adj.*

mar·a·thon (mar'ə·thon) *n.* **1** A footrace of 26 miles, 385 yards: a feature of the Olympic games: so called from a messenger's legendary run from Marathon to Athens to announce the Athenian victory over the Persians, 490 B.C. **2** Any endurance contest.

ma·raud (mə·rôd′) *v.i.* To rove in search of plunder; make raids for booty. —*v.t.* To invade for plunder; raid. —*n.* A foray. [<F *marauder* <*maraud* a rogue]—**ma·raud′er** *n.*

mar·ble (mär′bəl) *n.* **1** A compact, granular, partly crystallized limestone, occurring in many colors, valuable for building or ornamental purposes. ◆ Collateral adjective: *marmoreal.* **2** A sculptured or inscribed piece of this stone. **3** A small ball made of this stone, or of baked clay, glass, or porcelain. **4** *pl.* A boys' game played with such balls. **5** Marbling (def. 1). —*v.t.* **·bled, ·bling** To color or vein in imitation of marble, as book edges.—*adj.* **1** Made of or like marble. **2** Without feeling; cold. See synonyms under PALE[2]. [<OF *marble, marbre* <L *marmor* <Gk. *marmaros*, lit., sparkling-stone, orig. stone; infl. in sense by *marmairein* sparkle]

marble cake A cake made of light and dark batter mixed to give a marblelike appearance.

mar·bled (mär′bəld) *adj.* Veined, clouded, or variegated like marble.

mar·ble·wood (mär′bəl·wood′) *n.* **1** A large East Indian tree *(Diospyros marmorata)* of the ebony family, yielding a variegated wood. **2** Its wood.

mar·bling (mär′bling) *n.* **1** A marking, mottling, or coloring resembling that of marble. **2** The act or method of imitating marble.

mar·bly (mär′blē) *adj.* **1** Resembling or containing marble. **2** Still or rigid like marble.

marc (märk) *n.* **1** Solid refuse remaining from grapes or other fruit after pressing. **2** A brandy distilled from this. **3** Any insoluble residue after a substance has been treated with a solvent. [<F, prob. <*marcher* tread, press (grapes). See MARCH[1].]

mar·ca·site (mär′kə·sīt) *n.* **1** A pale, bronze-yellow, orthorhombic iron disulfide, FeS$_2$; white iron pyrites. It is a dimorphous form of pyrites. **2** An ornament made of crystallized white pyrites or of highly polished steel. [<Med. L *marcasita*, prob. <Arabic *marqashīta*<Aramaic]

mar·cel (mär·sel′) *v.t.* **·celled, ·cel·ling** To dress (the hair) in even, continuous waves by means of special irons. [after M. *Marcel*, 19th c. French hairdresser] —**mar·cel′ler** *n.*

marcel wave In hairdressing, a style of dressing the hair in tiers of even, continuous waves.

mar·ces·cent (mär·ses′ənt) *adj.* **1** Withering; withered. **2** *Bot.* Withering without falling off, as the corollas of heaths, etc. [<L *marcescens, -entis*, ppr. of *marcescere*, inceptive of *marcere* be faint, languid] —**mar·ces′cence** *n.*

march[1] (märch) *n.* **1** Movement together on foot and in time, as of soldiers; a stately, dignified walk. **2** A movement, as of soldiers, from one stopping place to another. **3** The distance thus passed over. **4** Onward progress: the *march* of events. **5** A piece of music suitable for regulating the movements of persons marching. —*v.i.* **1** To move with measured, regular steps, as a soldier; proceed in step, as troops. **2** To walk in a solemn or dignified manner. **3** To proceed steadily; advance. —*v.t.* **4** To cause to march. [<MF*marche* <*marcher* walk, orig. trample, ult. <LL *marcus* a hammer <L *marculus*] —**march′er** *n.*

march[2] (märch) *n.* **1** A region or district lying along a boundary line; frontier. **2** *pl.* The border regions of England and Wales, or of England and Scotland. **3** *Scot.* The boundary or boundary marks between lands or estates. See synonyms under BOUNDARY. [<OF *marche* <Gmc. Akin to MARK[1], MARGIN.]

March The third month of the year, containing 31 days. [<AF *marche*, OF *marz* <L *Martius (mensis)* (month) of Mars <*Mars* the god Mars]

march·er (mär′chər) *n.* **1** An officer who defended a march. **2** One who resides in a march. [<MARCH[2]]

March hare A hare in the breeding season: regarded as a symbol of madness from the supposed wildness of hares at this time.

mar·chion·ess (mär′shən·is) *n.* **1** The wife or widow of a marquis. **2** A woman having in her own right the rank corresponding to that of a marquis. [<Med. L *marchionissa*, fem. of *marchio, -onis* a captain of the marches <*marca* march[2] <Gmc.]

march·land (märch′land′) *n.* Land along the boundaries of adjacent countries; borderland. [<MARCH[2] + LAND]

march·pane (märch′pān) *n.* Marzipan. [<MF *marcepain* <Ital. *marzapane* MARZIPAN]

Mar·co Po·lo (mär′kō pō′lō) See POLO, MARCO.

Marconi rig In yachting, a type of rig consisting of a triangular sail mounted on a tall mast and having no gaff and a relatively short boom: so called from the resemblance of the mast and its stays to a radio mast. Compare GAFF RIG.

mar·cot·tage (mär′kō·täzh′) *n.* A method for the vegetative propagation of plants in which a part of the stem or branch is packed with moss until roots have formed and the treated part is ready for independent growth. [<F *marcotter* plant layers <*marcotte* a layer (def. 3) <L *mergus* a vine layer, a diver <*mergere* dip, bury]

Mar·di gras (mär′dē grä′) Shrove Tuesday; last day before Lent: celebrated as a carnival in certain cities. [<F., lit., fat Tuesday]

mare[1] (mâr) *n.* The female of the horse and other equine animals. [OE *mēre*, fem. of *mearh* a horse]

mare[2] (mâr) *n.* A hag or goblin supposed to produce nightmare; also, nightmare. [OE. Akin to MAR.]

mar·e[3] (mâr′ē) *n. pl.* **mar·i·a** (mâr′ē·ə) Any of a number of dark, seemingly flat areas of the moon's surface. [<L, sea; because of their resemblance to seas]

ma·rem·ma (mə·rem′ə) *n. pl.* **·me** (-ē) **1** A fertile, marshy, but unhealthful piedmont region near the sea, as in Tuscany, Italy. **2** The miasmatic exhalations of such a region. [<Ital. <L *maritimus* MARITIME]

mare's-nest (mârz′nest′) *n.* A seemingly important discovery that proves worthless, imaginary, or false.

mare's-tail (mârz′tāl′) *n.* **1** *Meteorol.* Long, fibrous, cirrus clouds, supposed to indicate rain. **2** A perennial aquatic herb *(Hippuris vulgaris)* with entire lineal leaves in whorls.

mar·gar·ic (mär·gar′ik, -gär′-) *adj.* Of, pertaining to, or resembling pearl; pearly. Also **mar·ga·rit·ic** (mär′gə·rit′ik). [<F *margarique* <Gk. *margaron* a pearl]

margaric acid A white, crystalline, fatty acid, C$_{17}$H$_{34}$O$_2$, obtained from the wax of lichens or made synthetically. [<F *margarique* MARGARIC; with ref. to the pearly luster of its crystals]

mar·ga·rine (mär′jə·rin, -rēn, -gə-) *n.* A blend of refined, edible vegetable oil or meat fat, or a combination of both, churned with cultured skim milk to the consistency of butter. Also called *oleomargarine.* [<the early mistaken belief that it contained a derivative of margaric acid]

mar·ga·ri·ta (mar′gə·rē′tə) *n.* A cocktail made of tequila, lime or lemon juice, and an orange liqueur.

mar·ga·rite (mär′gə·rit) *n.* **1** A hydrated silicate of calcium and aluminum. **2** Minute spherical crystals arranged as a beadlike pattern in glassy igneous rocks. **3** *Obs.* A pearl. [<OF <L *margarita* a pearl]

mar·gay (mär′gā) *n.* One of various South and Central American striped and spotted wild cats; especially, the long-tailed *Felis tigrina* [<F <*margaia* <Pg. *maracajá* <Tupian *mbaracaïa*]

mar·gin (mär′jin) *n.* **1** A bounding line; border; verge; brink; edge. **2** An allowance, provision, or reservation for contingencies or changes, as of time or money. **3** Range or scope; provision for increase or progress. **4** The difference between the cost of an article and its selling price. **5** A sum of money or other security deposited with a broker to protect him against loss in buying and selling for his principal; also, the difference in value between the security and the loan. **6** The difference between price and cost of production; in the adjustment of the relations of capital and labor, the minimum profit which will enable an undertaking to continue active. **7** The part of a page left blank around the body of printed or written text. —*v.t.* **1** To furnish with a margin; form a margin or border to; border. **2** To enter, place, or specify on the margin of a page, as a note or comment. **3** In commerce, to deposit a margin upon; hold by giving an addition to or a deposit upon a

margin. [<L *margo, -inis.* Akin to MARK[1], MARCH[2].]
   Synonyms (noun): beach, border, boundary, brim, brink, confines, edge, limit, lip, marge, shore, skirt, verge. See BANK, BOUNDARY.

mar·gi·nal (mär′jə·nəl) *adj.* **1** Pertaining to or constituting a margin. **2** Written, printed, or placed on the margin. **3** *Psychol.* Relating to the fringe of consciousness. **4** *Econ.* Operating or furnishing goods at a rate barely meeting the costs of production. **5** Of a nature that barely qualifies as useful, productive, or necessary. —**mar′gi·nal·ly** *adv.*

mar·gi·na·li·a (mär′jə·nā′lē·ə, nāl′yə) *n. pl.* **1** Marginal notes. **2** *Zool.* Spicules forming a collar around the osculum of a sponge. [<NL, neut. pl. of *marginalis* marginal <L *margo, -inis* a margin]

mar·gi·nate (mär′jə·nāt) *v.t.* **·nat·ed, ·nat·ing** To provide with a margin or margins. —*adj. Biol.* Having a margin, especially one of a distinct character, appearance, or color: also **mar′gi·nat·ed.** [<L *marginatus,* pp. of *marginare* <*margo, -inis* a margin] —**mar·gi·na′tion** *n.*

mar·grave (mär′grāv) *n.* **1** A hereditary German title of nobility, corresponding to *marquis.* **2** Formerly, the lord or governor of a German mark, march, or border. **3** A hereditary title of certain princes of the Holy Roman Empire. [<MDu. *markgrave* <MHG *marcgrave* <*mark* a march[2] + *graf* a count]

mar·gra·vi·ate (mär·grā′vē·it) *n.* The territory of a margrave. Also **mar·gra·vate** (mär′grə·vāt). [<Med. L *margravius,* ? <MHG *marcgrave* a margrave]

mar·gra·vine (mär′grə·vēn) *n.* The wife or widow of a margrave. [<Du. *markgravin,* fem. of *markgraaf* <MDu. *markgrave* a margrave]

mar·gue·rite (mär′gə·rēt′) *n.* A flower of the composite family, as the common garden daisy and the oxeye daisy of the fields; also, a chrysanthemum, *Chrysanthemum frutescens.* [<F, a pearl, daisy, from a proper name. See MARGARET.]

ma·ri·a·chi (mär·ē·ä′chē) *n.* **1** A wandering band of Mexican street musicians. **2** The musicians, usually made up of singers and guitarists. **3** The music they play. [<Mexican Sp.]

Mar·i·an (mâr′ē·ən) *n.* **1** A worshiper or devotee of the Virgin Mary. **2** An adherent of Mary I, queen of England, or a defender of Mary Queen of Scots. —*adj.* **1** Of or pertaining to the Virgin Mary, or characterized by a special devotion to her. **2** Pertaining to Queen Mary of England, or to Mary Queen of Scots.

mar·i·gold (mar′ə·gōld) *n.* **1** A plant of the composite family (genus *Tagetes*), with golden-yellow flowers; especially, the French marigold *(T. patula),* and the Aztec or African marigold *(T. erecta).* **2** The calendula. **3** The marsh marigold. [<MARY, prob. with ref. to the Virgin Mary + GOLD]

marigold yellow The bright orange-yellow color of various marigolds.

mar·i·hua·na (mar′ə·wä′nə, *Sp.* mä′rē·hwä′nä) *n.* The hemp plant *(Cannabis sativa),* whose dried leaves and flower tops yield a narcotic smoked in cigarettes. Also **ma′ri·jua′na.** [<Am. Sp. *marihuana, mariguana,* ? blend of N. Am. Ind. name and Sp. *Maria Juana* Mary Jane, a personal name]

MODERN MARIMBA

ma·rim·ba (mə·rim′bə) *n.* A form of xylophone sometimes having calabash resonators. [<Bantu *marimba, malimba,* pl. of *limba,* a kind of musical instrument]

ma·ri·na (mə·rē′nə) *n. Naut.* A basin or safe anchorage for small vessels; especially, one at which provisions, supplies, etc., may be obtained. [<Ital., a seacoast <L *marinus* MARINE]

mar·i·nade (mar′ə·nād′) *n.* **1** A brine pickle sometimes flavored with wine, spices, and herbs, in which meat or fish are placed before cooking, to improve their flavor. **2** Pickled meat or fish. [<F <Sp. *marinada* < *marinar* pickle in brine < *marino* marine <L *marinus* MARINE]

mar·i·nate (mar′ə·nāt) *v.t.* **·nat·ed**, **·nat·ing** **1** To soak in oil and vinegar or brine preparatory to cooking; prepare with marinade. **2** To allow, as salad, to soak in French dressing before serving. [<MARIN(ADE) + -ATE¹]

ma·rine (mə·rēn′) *adj.* **1** Of or pertaining to the sea or matters connected with the sea; maritime. **2** Native to, existing in, or formed by the sea. **3** Intended for use at sea or in navigation; nautical; naval: *marine* currents, *marine* law, a *marine* almanac. **4** Employed on shipboard. See synonyms under NAUTICAL. — *n.* **1** A soldier trained for service at sea and on land; a member of the Marine Corps: also **Marine.** **2** Shipping, or shipping interests generally. See MERCHANT MARINE. **3** A picture or painting of the sea. [<OF *marin* <L *marinus* < *mare, maris* a sea]

Marine Corps A branch of the U.S. Navy made up of combat troops, air forces, etc., under their own officers: the oldest organized military or naval body in the United States, authorized 1775: officially, the *United States Marine Corps.*

mar·i·ner (mar′ə·nər) *n.* One who navigates or assists in navigating a ship; a sailor. [<AF <L *marinus* marine]

Mariner's Medal A medal awarded to any seaman who is wounded or suffers from exposure owing to enemy action while serving on a ship during a war.

Ma·ri·nism (mar′ə·niz′əm) *n.* An ornate and flamboyant literary style, of the type cultivated by the Italian poet **Giambattista Ma·ri·ni** (mä·rē′nē), 1569–1625.

Mar·i·ol·a·try (mâr′ē·ol′ə·trē) *n.* Worship of the Virgin Mary: an opprobrious term: also spelled *Maryolatry.* [<*Mario-* (<MARY) + -LATRY] — **Mar′i·ol′a·trous** *adj.*

Mar·i·ol·o·gy (mâr′ē·ol′ə·jē) *n.* The whole body of religious belief and dogma relating to the Virgin Mary. Also spelled *Maryology.* [<*Mario-* (<MARY) + -LOGY]

mar·i·o·nette (mar′ē·ə·net′) *n.* A puppet moved by strings. [<F *marionnette,* dim. of *Marion,* dim. of *Marie* MARY; prob. orig. a small image of the Virgin Mary]

Mariposa lily Any of a genus (*Calochortus*) of showy, colorful, liliaceous Mexican and Californian plants. Also **Mariposa tulip.**

mar·ish (mar′ish) *Obs. adj.* Marshy; boggy; growing in marshes, as plants. — *n.* A marsh; fen. [<OF *marais, mareis* <Med. L *mariscus* a marsh <Gmc.]

Mar·ist (mâr′ist) *adj.* **1** Of, pertaining to, or dedicated to the Virgin Mary. **2** Of or pertaining to the Marist Fathers, or to institutions founded by them. — *n.* A member of a Roman Catholic order devoted specifically to instruction and foreign missions: also **Marist Fathers.** [<(the VIRGIN) MAR(Y) + -IST]

mar·i·tal (mar′ə·təl) *adj.* **1** Of or pertaining to marriage. **2** Of or pertaining to a husband. [<L *maritalis* < *maritus* a husband, orig. married] — **mar′i·tal·ly** *adv.*

mar·i·time (mar′ə·tīm) *adj.* **1** Situated on or near the sea. **2** Pertaining to the sea or matters connected with the sea; marine. **3** Characterized by pursuits, interests, or power at sea; nautical. See synonyms under NAUTICAL. [<F <L *maritimus* < *mare, maris* a sea]

mar·jo·ram (mär′jər·əm) *n.* Any of several perennial herbs of the mint family (genus *Majorana*), with nearly entire leaves, dense oblong spikes of flowers, and colored bracts. *M. hortensis* is the **sweet marjoram,** used for seasoning in cookery. [<OF *majorane* <Med. L *majorana,* ? ult. <L *amaracus* <Gk. *amarakos*]

mark (märk) *n.* **1** A visible trace, impression, or sign produced or left on any substance, as a line, scratch, dot, scar, spot, stain, or blemish; any physical peculiarity produced by drawing, indenting, stamping, or other process or agency. **2** A symbol or character, as a stamp, brand, or device, made on or attached to something to identify, distinguish, or call attention; a trademark. **3** A cross or other character made instead of a signature by one who cannot write. **4** A letter of the alphabet, number, or character by which excellence, defect, or quality is registered, as on a student's paper or record. **5** A symbol, written or printed: a *mark* of interrogation. **6** An object serving to guide, direct, or point out, as a boundary, a course, or a place in a book. **7** That which indicates the presence or existence of something; a characteristic; an evidence; a symptom. **8** That which is aimed at, or toward which effort is directed; something shot, fired, or thrown at, as a target; that which one strives to attain or achieve; a goal. **9** A proper bound or limit; standard. **10** Distinction; eminence: a person of *mark.* **11** A license to make reprisals. See LETTER OF MARQUE. **12** A person easily duped: an easy *mark.* **13** *Naut.* A strip of cloth or the like knotted or twisted into a lead line at intervals to indicate fathoms of depth. **14** An observing or noting; heed. **15** In medieval times, a piece of land held in common by a body of kindred freemen. **16** *Archaic* A boundary; limit. — **beside the mark** Pointless. — **bless the mark! save the mark!** Ejaculations of deprecation, irony, scorn, or humorous surprise: used originally of a good, then ironically of a bad, marksman. — **to make one's mark** To succeed. — **of mark** Famous; noteworthy; important. — **up to the mark** Up to standard; in good health or condition, etc. — *v.t.* **1** To make a mark or marks on. **2** To trace the boundaries of; limit. **3** To indicate by a mark or sign: X *marks* the spot. **4** To make or produce by writing, drawing, etc. **5** To be a characteristic of; typify. **6** To designate as if by marking; destine: He was *marked* for death. **7** To pay attention to; notice; remark. **8** To make known; manifest; show: to *mark* displeasure with a frown. **9** To apply a price, identification, etc., to. **10** To give marks or grades to; grade. — *v.i.* **11** To take notice; pay attention. **12** To keep score or count. **13** To make a mark or marks. See synonyms under INSCRIBE. Compare CIRCUMSCRIBE. — **to mark down** **1** To note down by writing or making marks. **2** To put a lower price on, as for a sale. — **to mark time** **1** To keep time by moving the feet but not advancing. **2** To pause in action or progress temporarily, as while awaiting developments. — **to mark up** **1** To make marks on; scar. **2** To increase the price of. [OE *mearc,* orig. boundary. Akin to MARGIN, MARCH².]

Synonyms (noun): badge, characteristic, fingerprint, footprint, impress, impression, indication, line, manifestation, print, sign, stamp, symbol, token, trace, track, vestige. See AIM, CHARACTERISTIC, LETTER, SIGN, TRACE.

notice; distinguished; prominent. — **mark·ed·ly** (mär′kid·lē) *adv.* — **mark′ed·ness** *n.*

marked man One who is singled out by others, as for suspicion, vengeance, etc.

mark·er (mär′kər) *n.* **1** That which marks; specifically, a bookmark, a milestone, a gravestone, etc. **2** A scorekeeper. **3** A device for tracing the lines of a tennis court or other playing ground. **4** *Slang* A written promise to pay a specified amount, used as currency in gambling, speculation, etc.

mar·ket (mär′kit) *n.* **1** A place where merchandise is exposed for sale; specifically, an open space or a large building in a town or city, generally with stalls or designated positions occupied by different dealers, especially such a place for the sale of provisions: also **market place.** **2** A private store for the sale of provisions: a meat *market.* **3** The state of trade as determined by prices, supply, and demand; traffic: a brisk *market.* **4** A locality or country where anything can be bought or sold; a place where any commodity is in demand: the South American *markets.* **5** A gathering of people for selling and buying, especially of a particular commodity: the wheat *market.* **6** The value of a thing as determined by the price it will bring; value in general; worth. — *v.t.* **1** To take or send to market for sale; sell. — *v.i.* **2** To deal in a market; sell or buy. **3** To buy food. [OE <AF <L *mercatus,* orig. pp. of *mercari* trade < *merx, mercis* merchandise. Doublet of MART¹.]

nar·ket·a·ble (mär′kit·ə·bəl) *adj.* **1** Suitable for sale; in demand. **2** Current in markets. **3** Of or pertaining to trading. — **mar′ket·a·bil′i·ty** *n.*

mar·ket·er (mär′kit·ər) *n.* One who buys or sells in a market.

market order An order to a broker to buy or sell at the current market price.

market price See under PRICE.

mar·ket·ripe (mär′kit·rīp′) *adj.* Not quite ripe: said of slightly unripe fruits picked to reach the market in salable condition.

market value The price which may be expected for a given commodity, security, or service under the conditions of a given market: distinguished from *normal value,* which is the average of values over a long period.

mark·ing (mär′king) *n.* **1** A mark or an arrangement of marks; characteristic coloring. **2** The act of making a mark.

marks·man (märks′mən) *n. pl.* **·men** (-mən) **1** One skilled in hitting the mark, as with a rifle or other weapon. **2** In the U.S. Army, the lowest of three grades for skill in the use of small arms. **3** The soldier having this grade. Compare SHARPSHOOTER, EXPERT. — **marks′man·ship** *n.* — **marks′wom′an** *n. fem.*

Mark Twain (märk twān) Pseudonym of Samuel Langhorne Clemens, 1835–1910, U.S. humorist and novelist.

mark–up (märk′up′) *n.* **1** A raising of price. **2** The amount of price increase. **3** The sum added to cost, in computing selling price, to cover overhead and profit. **4** *Printing* The placement on copy of editorial directions for the printer or engraver.

marl¹ (märl) *v.t. Naut.* To wrap with marline, tying each turn with a hitch. [<Du. *marlen,* appar. freq. <MDu. *merren* tie]

marl² (märl) *n.* **1** An earthy deposit containing lime, clay, and sand, used as fertilizer. **2** A soft, earthy, crumbling stratum of varying composition. — *v.t.* To fertilize or spread with marl. [<OF *marle* <LL *margila,* dim. of L *marga,* ? <Celtic]

mar·lin¹ (mär′lin) *n.* Any of various deep–sea game fishes of the genus *Makaira;* especially, *M. ampla* of the Atlantic and the black or striped marlins of the Pacific. [<MARLINE-(SPIKE); so called because of its shape]

mar·lin (mär′lin) *n. U.S. Dial.* A curlew. [Alter. of obs. *marling,* var. of MERLIN]

mar·line (mär′lin) *n. Naut.* A small rope of two strands loosely twisted together: used for winding ropes, cables, etc. [<Prob. fusion of Du. *marlijn* (< *marren* tie + *lijn* a line) and E *marling* a binding <Du. <*marlen,* freq. of *marren*]

mar·line·spike (mär′lin·spīk′) *n. Naut.* A sharp–pointed iron pin used in splicing ropes. Also **mar′lin·spike′, mar′ling·spike′** *n.*

MARLINESPIKES

mar·lite (märl′īt) *n.* A variety of marl that differs from common marl by remaining solid on exposure to air. [<MARL² + -ITE¹] — **mar·lit·ic** (mär·lit′ik) *adj.*

marl·y (mär′lē) *adj.* Resembling or of the nature of marl; abounding in marl. Also **mar·la·ceous** (mär·lā′shəs).

mar·ma·lade (mär′mə·lād) *n.* A preserve made by boiling the pulp and part of the rind or skin of fruits, usually citrus fruits, with sugar to the consistency of jam. [<MF *marmelade* <Pg. *marmelada* < *marmelo* a quince <L *melimelum* <Gk. *melimēlon* < *meli* honey + *mēlon* an apple]

marmalade tree A tall, tropical American, sapotaceous evergreen tree (*Achras zapota*).

It bears plumlike fruits used chiefly for preserving. Also called *sapodilla*.

mar·mite (mär·mēt') *n.* A small, lidded ceramic or enameled cooking pot. [<F, a pot, kettle]

mar·mo·re·al (mär·môr'ē·əl, -mō'rē-) *adj.* Pertaining to, made of, or resembling marble. Also **mar·mo're·an** (-môr'ē-, -mō'rē-). [<L *marmoreus* < *marmor* MARBLE]

mar·mo·set (mär'mə·zet) *n.*
1 A small Central and South American monkey (family *Callithricidae*) with soft, woolly hair and a long hairy tail. **2** A related species, Goeldi's marmoset (*Callimico goeldii*). **3** The tamarin. **4** The ouistiti. [<OF *marmouset* a grotesque figure, prob. ult. <Gk. *mormō, -ous* a she-monster, bogey; with ref. to its appearance]

MARMOSET
(About the size of
a large squirrel)

mar·mot (mär'mət) *n.* **1** A stout, short-tailed, burrowing rodent of mountain regions (genus *Marmota*). The species found in North America is known as a *woodchuck* or *ground hog*. **2** A related rodent, as the prairie dog. [<F *marmotte*, fusion of OF *marmotte* a monkey and Romansch *murmont* a marmot <L *mus, muris* a mouse + *mons, montis* a mountain]

Marne (märn) A river in NE France, flowing 325 miles NW to the Seine; scene of two decisive battles of World War I, 1914, 1918.

Ma·roc (må·rôk') The French name for MOROCCO.

ma·roon[1] (mə·rōōn') *v.t.* **1** To put ashore and abandon on a desolate island or coast. **2** To abandon; leave helpless. [< *n.* (def. 1)] — *n.* **1** One of a class of Negroes, chiefly fugitive slaves or their descendants, living wild in the mountains of some West Indies islands and of Guiana. **2** *Rare* A person left alone on an island; a marooned person. [<F *marron* a maroon (def. 1) <Sp. *cimarron* wild]

ma·roon[2] (mə·rōōn') *n.* **1** A dull, dark-red color. **2** A coal-tar dyestuff. — *adj.* Having a dull, dark-red color. [<F *marron* a chestnut, chestnut color <Ital. *marrone*]

mar·plot (mär'plot') *n.* One who, by meddling, mars or frustrates a design or plan.

marque (märk) *n.* A license of reprisal upon an enemy, as at sea in wartime: chiefly in the phrase *letter of marque*. [<F, mark, imprint, stamp <Provençal *marca* seizure < *marcar* seize as a pledge < *marc* a pledge <Gmc. Akin to MARK[1].]

mar·quee (mär·kē') *n.* **1** A large field tent, especially one for an officer, or one used at lawn entertainments. **2** An awning or rooflike structure over the entrance to a hotel, theater, or other building. [<MARQUISE a canopy, mistaken as pl. <F]

mar·quess (mär'kwis) See MARQUIS.

mar·que·try (mär'kə·trē) *n.* Inlaid work of wood often interspersed with stones, ivory, etc., especially as used in the decoration of furniture. Also **mar'que·te·rie**. [<MF *marqueterie* < *marqueter* variegate, inlay < *marque* a mark[1], ult. <Gmc.]

mar·quis (mär'kwis, *Fr.* mår·kē') *n.* The title of a nobleman next in rank below a duke. Also, *Brit.*, *marquess*. [<OF *marchis, marquis* <Med.L *marchensis* a commander of the marches < *marca* a march[2] <Gmc.]

Mar·quis (mär'kwis) *n.* An important variety of wheat, first developed in Canada, widely grown in the United States.

mar·quis·ate (mär'kwiz·it) *n.* The rank of a marquis.

mar·quise (mär·kēz') *n.* **1** The wife or widow of a French marquis. **2** An ornamental hood over a door; a marquee. **3** In gem-cutting, a pointed oval form, especially for diamonds. **4** A ring set with an oval cluster of gemstones. [<F, fem. of *marquis* a marquis]

mar·qui·sette (mär'ki·zet', -kwi-) *n.* A lightweight, open-mesh fabric of cotton, silk, rayon, or nylon, or a combination of these, used for curtains and women's and children's garments. [<F, dim. of *marquise* a marquise]

Marquis of Queensberry Rules A widely observed boxing code devised in 1869 by John Sholto Douglas (1844–1900), eighth Marquis of Queensberry.

mar·ram (mar'əm) *n.* **1** Beachgrass. **2** A dune overgrown and bound together by this grass. [<ON *maralmr* < *marr* a sea + *halmr* haulm]

mar·riage (mar'ij) *n.* **1** The act of marrying, or the state of being married; specifically, a compact entered into by a man and a woman, to live together as husband and wife; wedlock. ◆ Collateral adjectives: *hymeneal, marital.* **2** A wedding; a nuptial celebration: with *of* or *between*. **3** Figuratively, any close union. **4** In pinochle, the king and queen of any suit. [<OF *mariage*, ult. <L *maritus* a husband] *Synonyms:* matrimony, nuptials, union, wedding, wedlock. *Matrimony* denotes the state of those united in the *marriage* relation; *marriage* denotes primarily the act of so uniting, but is much used also for the state. *Wedlock*, a word of specific legal use, is the Saxon term for the state or relation denoted by *matrimony*. *Wedding* denotes the ceremony, with any attendant festivities, by which two persons are united as husband and wife, *nuptials* being the more formal and stately term to express the same idea. *Antonyms:* bachelorhood, celibacy, divorce, maidenhood, virginity, widowhood.

mar·riage·a·ble (mar'ij·ə·bəl) *adj.* Fitted by age, physical condition, etc., for marriage; nubile. — **mar'riage·a·bil'i·ty, mar'riage·a·ble·ness** *n.*

mar·ried (mar'ēd) *adj.* **1** Pertaining to marriage; connubial; conjugal: the *married* state. **2** Having a spouse; united by or as by matrimony; wedded: a *married* man.

mar·ron (mar'ən, *Fr.* må·rôñ') *n.* A chestnut, especially when used as food and in confectionery. [<F. See MAROON[2].]

mar·row (mar'ō) *n.* **1** A soft vascular tissue found in the central cavities of bones. **2** The interior substance of anything; essence; pith. [OE *mearg, mearh*] — **mar'row·y** *adj.*

mar·row·bone (mar'ō·bōn') *n.* **1** A bone containing marrow. **2** *pl.* One's knees: used humorously. **3** *pl.* Crossbones, the piratical emblem.

mar·row·fat (mar'ō·fat') *n.* A large, rich pea. Also **marrow pea.**

marrow squash A variety of squash having an ovoid, fine-grained body; vegetable marrow.

Mar·rue·cos (mär·rwā'kōs) The Spanish name for MOROCCO.

mar·ry (mar'ē) *v.* **·ried, ·ry·ing** *v.t.* **1** To join as husband and wife in marriage. **2** To take in marriage. **3** To give in marriage. **4** To unite closely. **5** *Naut.* To fasten end to end, as ropes, without increasing the diameter. — *v.i.* **6** To take a husband or wife. [<OF *marier* <L *maritare* < *maritus* a husband, married] — **mar'ri·er** *n.*

Mars (märz) **1** In Roman mythology, the god of war: identified with the Greek *Ares*: formerly called *Mavors*. **2** *Astron.* The fourth planet in order of distance from the sun, from which its mean distance is 141,500,000 miles, its least distance from the earth being about 35,000,000 miles. Mars has two satellites, a diameter of about 4,230 miles, a diurnal rotation of 24 hours, 37 minutes, 22.67 seconds, and a year of 686.9 days.

Marseillaise The national anthem of the French Republic, written in 1792 by Rouget de Lisle. [<F, fem. of *Marseillais* MARSEILLAIS]

mar·seille (mär·sāl') *n.* A thick cotton fabric having a raised weave, similar to piqué. Also **mar·seilles** (mär·sālz'). [from *Marseille*, France]

marsh (märsh) *n.* A tract of low, wet land; swamp. ◆ Collateral adjective: *paludal.* [OE *mersc, merisc.* Akin to MORASS.] — **marsh'y** *adj.* — **marsh'i·ness** *n.*

mar·shal (mär'shəl) *n.* **1** An officer authorized to regulate ceremonies, preserve order, etc. **2** An official of the United States courts; also, the head of the police force or fire department in some cities. **3** In some European countries, a military officer of high rank; a field marshal. **4** In medieval times, a groom or master of the horse; later, as an officer of the king, a judge in courts of chivalry, etc. — *v.t.* **·shaled** or **·shalled, ·shal·ing** or **·shal·ling 1** To arrange or dispose in order, as facts. **2** To array or draw up, as troops for battle. **3** To lead; usher. ◆ Homophone: *martial.* [<OF *mareschal* <Med.L *mariscalcus* <OHG *marahscalh*, lit., a horse-servant < *marah* a horse + *scalh* a servant] — **mar'shal·cy, mar'shal·ship** *n.* — **mar'shal·er, mar'shal·ler** *n.*

Marshall Plan A post-World War II recovery program of U.S. financial aid to certain European countries, initiated June, 1947.

marsh bluebill A ring-necked duck.

marsh elder 1 Any of a genus (*Iva*) of American salt-marsh plants, especially the high-water shrub (*I. frutescens*) of the SE United States: also called *sumpweed*. **2** The guelder-rose.

marsh frog A pickerel frog.

marsh gas Methane.

marsh hare In Louisiana, the muskrat.

marsh harrier An Old World hawk (*Circus aeruginosus*) with a yellowish head and predominantly dark-brown plumage: it nests on swampy ground and feeds largely on frogs, snakes, and small waterfowl.

marsh hawk An American hawk (*Circus hudsonius*) inhabiting marshes where it preys on snakes, frogs, etc.

marsh hen 1 The northern clapper rail (*Rallus longirostris crepitans*), which inhabits saltwater marshes along the American Atlantic coast. **2** The American coot (*Fulica americana*).

marsh·mal·low (marsh'mal'ō, -mel'ō) *n.* **1** A plant of the mallow family (*Althaea officinalis*) growing in marshy places. **2** A sweetmeat formerly made from the root of this plant; now a confection made of starch, corn sirup, and gelatin, coated with powdered sugar.

marsh marigold A showy swamp plant (*Caltha palustris*) of the crowfoot family, having bright-yellow flowers, found in swamps and wet meadows: also called *cowslip*.

marsh poisoning Impaludism.

marsh rosemary 1 A seaside perennial herb (*Limonium carolinianum*), with a strongly astringent root: used medicinally. **2** The moorwort.

mar·su·pi·al (mär·sōō'pē·əl) *n.* Any member of an order (*Marsupialia*) of mammals, as the kangaroos, opossums, wombats, etc., whose females typically lack a placenta, carrying their young in a marsupium. — *adj.* **1** Having a marsupium. **2** Of or pertaining to the *Marsupialia*, or of the nature of a marsupium or pouch. [<NL *marsupialis* <L *marsupium*. See MARSUPIUM.] — **mar·su'pi·a'li·an** (-ā'lē·ən), **mar·su'pi·an** *adj. & n.*

marsupial mouse Any of several small marsupials of Australia, as the **fat-tailed marsupial mouse** (*Sminthopsis crassicaudata*), or the **yellow-footed marsupial mouse** (*Antechinus flavipes*).

mar·su·pi·um (mär·sōō'pē·əm) *n.* *pl.* **·pi·a** (-pē·ə) A pouchlike invagination; specifically, a brood pouch or external receptacle for carrying young, as on the abdomen of marsupials. [<L, a pouch, purse <Gk. *marsypion*, dim. of *marsipos*]

Mars yellow A pigment consisting chiefly of hydrous oxide of iron and aluminum; iron yellow. Other pigments in the same group are **Mars orange, Mars red, Mars violet.**

Mar·sy·as (mär'sē·əs) In Greek mythology, a satyr and flute-player, who was defeated in a musical contest and flayed alive by Apollo.

mart (märt) *n.* **1** A market. **2** *Archaic* A fair; also, traffic; trading. [<MDu. *markt, mart* <L *mercatus*. Doublet of MARKET.]

mar·tel·lo tower (mär·tel'ō) A circular tower of masonry, formerly erected on coasts for defense against invasion. Also **mar·tel'lo.** [from Cape *Mortella*, in Corsica, where such a tower was erected; infl. in form by Ital. *martello* a hammer]

mar·tens·ite (mär'tənz·īt) *n.* *Metall.* A constituent of rapidly quenched steel, consisting of iron and up to two percent of carbon.

MARQUISE

[after Prof. A. *Martens,* German metallurgist + -ITE¹] —**mar·ten·sit·ic** (-tən-zit′ik) *adj.*

mar·tial (mär′shəl) *adj.* **1** Pertaining to, connected with, or suggestive of war or military operations: opposed to *civil: court martial.* **2** Warlike; brave; characteristic of a warlike person. See synonyms under WARLIKE. ◆ Homophone: *marshal.* [<OF <L *martialis* pertaining to Mars <*Mars, Martis* Mars] —**mar′tial·ism** *n.* —**mar′tial·ist** *n.* —**mar′tial·ly** *adv.*

martial law Military jurisdiction exercised by a government temporarily governing the civil population of a locality through its military forces, without the authority of written law, as necessity may require.

Mar·tian (mär′shʌn) *adj.* **1** *Astron.* Pertaining to the planet Mars. **2** Martial (defs. 1 and 2). —*n.* One of the supposed inhabitants of Mars. [<L *Mars, Martis* Mars]

mar·tin (mär′tən) *n.* **1** Any of certain birds of the swallow family, having a tail less forked than the common swallows; specifically, the **purple martin** (*Progne subis*), the **sand martin** or bank swallow (*Riparia riparia*), etc. **2** Some bird likened to a true martin, as a kingbird or chimney swift. [<F, prob. <*Martin* MARTIN]

mar·ti·net (mär′tə·net′) *n.* A strict disciplinarian, especially military or naval: often used in derogatory sense. [after General *Martinet,* 17th c. French drillmaster]

mar·tin·gale (mär′tən·gāl) *n.* **1** A forked strap for holding down a horse's head by connecting the head gear with the bellyband. **2** *Naut.* A vertical spar under the bowsprit used in guying the stays. Also **mar′tin·gal** (-gal). [<F <Provençal *martengalo,* appar. fem. of *martengo* an inhabitant of Martigues, a town in Provence; ? with ref. to tight hose or breeches worn there]

mar·ti·ni (mär·tē′nē) *n.* A cocktail made of gin and dry vermouth, usually served with a green olive or a twist of lemon peel. [after *Martini* and Rossi, a company making vermouth]

Mar·tin·mas (mär′tən·məs) *n.* The feast of St. Martin, November 11. [<Saint *Martin* + -MAS]

mart·let (märt′lit) *n.* **1** A martin. **2** *Her.* A martin or swallow without feet: used as a bearing, crest, or mark of cadency. [<F *martelet,* alter. of *martinet,* dim. of *martin* a martin; ? infl. in form by *roitelet* a wren]

mar·ton·ite (mär′tən·īt) *n.* Bromacetone.

mar·tyr (mär′tər) *n.* **1** One who submits to death rather than forswear his religion; specifically, one of the early Christians who suffered death for their religious principles. **2** One who dies or suffers for principles, or sacrifices all for a cause: a *martyr* to science. **3** One who suffers much or long, as from ill health or misfortune: a *martyr* to rheumatism. —*v.t.* **1** To put to death as a martyr. **2** To torture; persecute or torment. [OE <LL < Gk. *martyr,* Aeolic form of *martys, martyros* a witness]

mar·tyr·dom (mär′tər·dəm) *n.* **1** The condition or fate of a martyr. **2** Protracted or extreme suffering. [OE *martyrdōm*]

mar·tyr·ize (mär′tər·īz) *v.* ·ized, ·iz·ing *v.t.* To make a martyr of. —*v.i.* To become a martyr. —**mar′tyr·i·za′tion** *n.* —**mar′tyr·iz′er** *n.*

mar·tyr·ol·o·gy (mär′tə·rol′ə·jē) *n. pl.* ·gies A historical record of martyrs. [<Med. L *martyrologium* <LGk. *martyrologion* <*martyr* martyr + Gk. *logos* word, account] —**mar·tyr·o·log·ic** (mär′tə·rə·loj′ik) or ·i·cal *adj.* —**mar·tyr·ol′o·gist** *n.*

mar·vel (mär′vəl) *v.* ·veled or ·velled, ·vel·ing or ·vel·ling *v.i.* To be filled with wonder, surprise, etc.: *We marveled* at the young pianist's precocious brilliance. —*v.t.* To wonder at or about: with a clause as object. —*n.* **1** That which excites wonder; a prodigy. **2** The emotion of wonder. **3** A miracle. See synonyms under PRODIGY. [<OF *merveillier* <*merveille* a wonder <L *mirabilia,* neut. pl. of *mirabilis* wonderful <*mirari* wonder at]

Mar·vell (mär′vəl), **Andrew**, 1621–78, English poet and satirist.

mar·vel·ous (mär′vəl·əs) *adj.* **1** Exciting astonishment; singular; wonderful. **2** Pertaining

to the supernatural; miraculous. Also **mar′vel·lous.** See synonyms under EXTRAORDINARY. —**mar′vel·ous·ly, mar′vel·lous·ly** *adv.* —**mar′vel·ous·ness, mar′vel·lous·ness** *n.*

Marx (märks), **Karl**, 1818–83, German socialist, revolutionary leader and writer on economics; author of *Das Kapital.* —**Marx′i·an** *adj. & n.*

Marx·ism (märk′siz·əm) *n.* The body of doctrine formulated by Karl Marx and Friedrich Engels in systematic form, including economic determinism, class conflicts leading inevitably to revolution in the transition from feudalism to capitalism and thence to communism under the dictatorship of the proletariat, and the predicted ultimate triumph of world communism as a result of destructive rivalries among the capitalist–imperialist powers.

Marx·ism–Len·in·ism (märk′siz·əm·len′in·iz′əm) *n.* The philosophy of history and politics based upon the works of Karl Marx and Nikolai Lenin, stressing Lenin's recension of Marxism in order to make it applicable to backward agrarian countries. —**Marx′ist–Len′in·ist** *n.*

Marx·ist (märk′sist) *adj.* **1** Of or pertaining to Karl Marx or his theories; Marxian. **2** Like or developed from the theories of Karl Marx: *Marxist* socialism. —*n.* A follower of Karl Marx; specifically, an adherent of Marxist socialism.

Mar·y (mâr′ē) A feminine personal name. Also *Polish* **Mar·ya** (mär′yä). See also MARIA. [< Hebrew, bitter]
—**Mary** The mother of Jesus: also *Virgin Mary.*
—**Mary** The sister of Lazarus and Martha.
—**Mary I**, 1516–58, queen of England, 1553–1558: known as *Mary Tudor* or *Bloody Mary.*
—**Mary II**, 1662–94, queen of England 1689–1694, ruling jointly with her husband, William III.
—**Mary Magdalene** A disciple from Magdala out of whom Jesus cast seven devils. *Luke* viii 2. She is often identified with the penitent sinner whom Jesus forgave. *Luke* vii 36–50.
—**Mary Queen of Scots,** 1542–87, queen of Scotland 1542–67; beheaded: also *Mary Stuart.*

Mary Jane (jān) **1** A low–heeled, usually patent–leather slipper with an ankle strap, worn especially by young girls. **2** *Slang* Marihuana. [def. 2 <folk etymology]

Mar·y·land (mâr′i·lənd, mer′i-) An eastern State of the United States, on Chesapeake Bay; 12,327 square miles; capital, Annapolis; entered the Union April 28, 1788, one of the original thirteen States; nickname, *Cockade State* or *Old Line State:* abbr. MD

Maryland yellowthroat See under YELLOWTHROAT.

mar·zi·pan (mär′zə·pan) *n.* A confection of grated almonds, sugar, and white of eggs, usually made into a paste and molded into various shapes: formerly known as *marchpane.* [<G <Ital. *marzapane,* orig. a small box, a dry measure, a weight <Med. L *matapanus* a Venetian coin stamped with an enthroned Christ <Arabic *mauthabān* a seated king, a coin <*wathaba* sit]

—**mas** *combining form* Mass; a (specified) festival or its celebration: *Christmas.* [<MASS²]

mas·ca·longe (mas′kə·lonj) See MUSKELLUNGE.

mas·car·a (mas·kar′ə) *n.* A cosmetic preparation used to darken the eyelashes, usually black, brown, or blue. [<Sp. *máscara* a mask <Arabic *maskharah* a buffoon]

mas·cle (mas′kəl) *n.* **1** A lozenge–shaped plate used in scale armor. **2** *Her.* A lozenge voided. Also spelled *macle.* [<OF. See MACLE.]

mas·con (mas′kon, mäs-) *n.* Any of the dense concentrations of mass in the moon's lithosphere which cause irregularities in the gravitational field surrounding the moon. [<MAS(S) + CON(CENTRATION)]

mas·cot (mas′kot, -kət) *n.* **1** A person, animal, or thing thought to bring good luck. **2** *Brit.* An ornament on the radiator of an automobile. [<F *mascotte* <Provençal *mascot,* dim. of *masco* a sorcerer, lit., a mask]

mas·cu·line (mas′kyə·lin) *adj.* **1** Having the distinguishing qualities of the male sex, or

pertaining to males; specially suitable for men; manly: opposed to *feminine.* **2** *Gram.* Being of the male gender. **3** *Bot.* Male; staminate. —*n.* **1** A male person; that which is of the male sex. **2** *Gram.* The masculine gender or a word of this gender: opposed to *feminine* and *neuter.* [<OF *masculin* <L *masculinus* <*masculus* male <*mas.* Doublet of MALE.] —**mas′cu·line·ly** *adv.* —**mas′cu·lin′i·ty, mas′cu·line·ness** *n.*

Synonyms (adj.): male, manful, manlike, manly, mannish, virile. *Male* is applied to the sex, *masculine* to the qualities, especially to the stronger, hardier, and more imperious qualities that distinguish the *male* sex; as applied to women, *masculine* has often the depreciatory sense of unwomanly, rude, or harsh; as, a *masculine* face or voice, or the like; still one may say in a commendatory way, she acted with *masculine* courage or decision. *Masculine* may apply to the distinctive qualities of the *male* sex at any age; *virile* applies to the distinctive qualities of mature manhood only, as opposed not only to *feminine* or *womanly* but to *childish,* and is thus an emphatic word for *sturdy, intrepid,* etc. See also under MANLY. *Antonyms:* see synonyms for FEMININE.

ma·ser (mā′zər) *n. Physics* Any of various devices that generate electromagnetic waves of precise frequency or that amplify such waves while maintaining frequency and phase, by using the excess energy of a resonant atomic or molecular system. [Acronym derived from *m*(icrowave) *a*(mplification by) *s*(timulated) *e*(mission of) *r*(adiation)]

mash (mash) *n.* **1** A soft, pulpy mass. **2** A mixture of meal, bran, etc., and water, fed warm to cattle. **3** Crushed or ground grain or malt, infused in hot water to produce wort. **4** In winemaking, the crushed grapes before fermentation begins. —*v.t.* **1** To crush or beat into a mash or pulp. **2** To convert into mash, as malt or grain, by infusing in hot water. [OE *māsc(wyrt)* mashwort, infused malt]

mash·er (mash′ər) *n.* **1** One who or that which mashes. **2** *Slang* A man who persistently annoys women unacquainted with him, as by attempting familiarities, etc.

mash·ie (mash′ē) *n.* An iron golf club with a deep, short blade and much loft: used in approaching. See illustration under GOLF CLUB. Also **mash′y.** [? Alter. of F *massue* a club < LL *mattiuca* (assumed), prob. <Celtic]

mask (mask, mäsk) *n.* **1** A cover or disguise, as for the features; a protective appliance for the face or head: a gas *mask.* **2** A subterfuge. **3** A cast of the face taken just after death. **4** A play or dramatic performance, in vogue in the 16th and 17th centuries, in which the actors were masked and represented allegorical or mythological subjects, originally in dumb show, but later in dialog, poetry, and song; also, a dramatic composition written for such a play: also spelled *masque.* **5** A masquerade: also spelled *masque.* **6** A masker. **7** An artistic covering for the face, used by Greek and Roman actors in comedy and tragedy. **8** *Archit.* A reproduction of a face or a face and neck, used as a gargoyle, a keystone of an arch, etc. **9** *Mil.* A screen of brush or the like for hiding a battery or any military operation from the enemy; camouflage. **10** *Zool.* Any formation about the head suggesting a mask; specifically, the enlarged lower lip of a larval dragonfly. **11** A fox's or dog's head. See synonyms under PRETENSE. —*v.t.* **1** To cover (the face, head, etc.) with a

MASKS
a. Greek tragedy.   c. Tibetan ceremonial.
b. Greek comedy.   d. Ancient Shinto.
e. Domino.

mask. 2 To hide or conceal with or as with a mask; disguise. —*v.i.* 3 To put on a mask; assume a disguise. [<F *masque* <Ital. *maschera, mascara* <Arabic *maskharah* a buffoon]

Synonyms (verb): cloak, conceal, cover, disguise, dissemble, hide, masquerade, pretend, screen, shroud, veil. See HIDE. *Antonyms:* betray, communicate, declare, disclose, divulge, exhibit, expose, publish, reveal, show, tell.

masked (maskt, mäskt) *adj.* 1 Having the face covered with or as with a mask; disguised. 2 Personate. 3 *Zool.* Having markings resembling a mask, as various pupae of insects.

masked or **mask ball** A ball at which the dancers wear masks or dominos.

masked hunter The kissing bug.

mask·er (mas′kər, mäs′-) *n.* One who wears a mask: also spelled *masquer.*

masking tape An adhesive tape used to protect those parts of a surface not to be painted, sprayed, or otherwise treated.

mas·ki·nonge (mas′kə·nonj) See MUSKELLUNGE.

mas·o·chism (mas′ə·kiz′əm) *n. Psychiatry* A condition in which sexual gratification depends on being dominated, cruelly treated, beaten, etc. [after Leopold von Sacher-*Masoch,* 1835–95, Austrian novelist, who described this condition] —**mas′o·chist** *n.* —**mas′o·chis′tic** *adj.*

ma·son (mā′sən) *n.* One who lays brick and stone in building; also, a stonecutter. —*v.t.* To build of masonry. [<OF *masson, maçon* <Med. L *matio, macio, -onis,* prob. <Gmc.]

Ma·son (mā′sən) *n.* A member of the order of Freemasons. —**Ma·son·ic** (mə·son′ik) *adj.*

mason bee A solitary bee (*Chalicodoma muraria*) of southern Europe which builds its nest of sand, clay, etc.

Ma·son–Dix·on line (mā′sən·dik′sən) The boundary between Pennsylvania and Maryland as surveyed by the Englishmen Charles Mason and Jeremiah Dixon in 1763–67: before the Civil War it was regarded as dividing Slave States from Free States, and is still used to distinguish the North from the South. Also **Mason and Dixon's line.**

Ma·son·ite (mā′sən·īt) *n.* A tough, dense, moisture–resistant fiberboard made from wood fibers exploded under high steam pressure: widely used as a building and construction material: a trade name.

Mason jar A glass jar having a tightly fitting screw top, used for canning and preserving: patented by John L. Mason of New York in 1857.

ma·son·ry (mā′sən·rē) *n. pl.* **·ries** 1 The art or work of building with brick or stone. 2 That which is built by masons or of materials which masons use.

Ma·son·ry (mā′sən·rē) *n.* Freemasonry.

Ma·so·ra (mə·sō′rə) *n.* 1 A collection of criticisms and marginal notes to the Old Testament, made by Jewish writers before the tenth century. 2 The tradition relied on by the Jews to preserve the Old Testament text from corruption. Also **Ma·so′rah.** [<Hebrew (modern) *māsōrah* <Hebrew *māsōreth* tradition, orig., bond (of the covenant)] —**Mas·o·ret·ic** (mas′ə·ret′ik) or **·i·cal,** *adj.* —**Mas′o·rete** (-rēt), **Mas′o·rite** (-rīt) *n.*

Mas·qat (mus′kat, mäs′kät) See MUSCAT.

masque (mask, mäsk), **mas·quer** (mas′kər, mäs′-) See MASK[1] (defs. 4 and 5), MASKER.

mas·quer·ade (mas′kə·rād′, mäs′-) *n.* 1 A social party composed of persons masked and costumed; also, the costumes and disguises worn on such an occasion. 2 A false show or disguise. 3 Formerly, a form of dramatic representation. —*v.i.* **·ad·ed, ·ad·ing** 1 To take part in a masquerade. 2 To wear a mask or disguise. 3 To disguise one's true character; assume a false appearance. See synonyms under MASK[1]. [Alter. of F *mascarade* <Sp. *mascarada* <*máscara* a mask. See MASCARA.] —**mas′quer·ad′er** *n.*

mass[1] (mas, mäs) *n.* 1 An assemblage of things that collectively make one quantity. 2 A body of concrete matter; a lump. 3 The principal part of anything. 4 Extent of volume; bulk; size. 5 *Physics* The measure or expression of the inertia of a body, as indicated by the acceleration imparted to it when acted upon by a given force: it is the quotient of the weight of a body divided by the acceleration

due to gravity. —*adj.* 1 Of, for, or consisting of the public in general. 2 Done on a large scale: *mass* production. —**the masses** The common people. See synonyms under MOB[1]. —*v.t. & v.i.* To form into a mass; assemble. [<OF *masse* <L *massa,* prob. <Gk. *maza* a barley cake]

Synonyms (noun): aggregate, body, bulk, heap, lump, matter, substance, total, totality, whole. See AGGREGATE, HEAP, THRONG.

mass[2] (mas, mäs) *n. Eccl.* 1 The eucharistic liturgy in the Roman Catholic and some Anglican churches, regarded as a commemoration or repetition of Christ's sacrifice on Calvary. 2 A celebration of this. See HIGH MASS, LOW MASS. 3 A musical setting for the fixed portions of this liturgy, as the Credo, Sanctus, Kyrie eleison, etc. Also **Mass.** —**black mass** 1 A mass for the dead: so called because the celebrant wears black vestments. 2 A ceremony performed in so–called worship of Satan as a burlesque of the Christian mass. [OE *mæsse* <LL *messa* dismissal <L *missa,* pp. fem. of *mittere* send, dismiss < *ite, missa est* go, you are dismissed; said by the priest after the Eucharist is ended]

Mas·sa·chu·set (mas′ə·chōō′sit) *n.* 1 One of a large and important tribe of North American Indians of Algonquian linguistic stock, formerly inhabiting the region around Massachusetts Bay. 2 The language of this tribe. Also **Mas′sa·chu′sett.** [<Algonquian (Massachuset) *Massa–adchu–es–et,* lit., at the big hill <*massa* big + *wadchu* hill + *es,* dim. suffix + *et* at the]

Mas·sa·chu·setts (mas′ə·chōō′sits) A NE State of the United States on the Atlantic; 8,266 square miles; capital, Boston; entered the Union Feb. 6, 1788, one of the thirteen original States; nickname, *Bay State:* abbr. MA

Massachusetts Bay A wide inlet of the Atlantic on the eastern coast of Massachusetts, extending from Cape Ann to Cape Cod.

mas·sa·cre (mas′ə·kər) *n.* The indiscriminate killing of human beings, as in savage warfare; slaughter. —*v.t.* **·cred** (-kərd), **·cring** To kill indiscriminately or in great numbers; slaughter. [<MF <OF *maçacre, macecle,* ? < *mache–col* butcher <*macher* smash + *col* neck <L *collum*] —**mas′sa·crer** *n.*

Synonyms (noun): butchery, carnage, havoc, slaughter. A *massacre* is the indiscriminate killing in numbers of the unresisting or defenseless; *butchery* is the killing of men rudely and ruthlessly as cattle are killed in the shambles. *Havoc* may not be so complete as *massacre,* nor so coldly brutal as *butchery,* but is more widely spread and furious; it is destruction let loose, and may be applied to organizations, interests, etc., as well as to human life. *Carnage* refers to widely scattered or heaped up corpses of the slain; *slaughter* is similar in meaning, but refers more to the process, and *carnage* to the result.

mas·sage (mə·säzh′) *n.* A system of remedial treatment consisting of kneading, rubbing, and otherwise manipulating a part or the whole of the body with the hands. —*v.t.* **·saged, ·sag·ing** To treat by massage. [<F *masser* massage <*masse* mass <L *massa,* ? < Gk. *massein* knead] —**mas·sag′er, mas·sag′ist** *n.* —**mas·sa·geuse** (mas′ə·zhœz′) *n. fem.*

mas·sa·sau·ga (mas′ə·sô′gə) *n.* The pigmy rattlesnake (*Sistrurus miliarius*) of the southern United States, seldom exceeding 20 inches in length, and living in dry, warm areas: also called *ground rattlesnake.* [<Ojibwa name of a river in Ontario, Canada]

Mas·sa·soit (mas′ə·soit), died 1661, American Indian chief of Massachusetts; friendly with the Pilgrims of Plymouth Colony.

mass bell The Sanctus bell.

mass communication The simultaneous dissemination of a single item of information, advertising, propaganda, etc., to the largest possible audience by the use of mass media.

mass defect *Physics* The difference between the mass number of a nuclide and its nucleon mass.

mas·sé (ma·sā′) *n.* In billiards, a stroke with a cue held perpendicularly, causing the cue ball to return in a straight line or to describe a curve. Also **massé shot.** [<F <*masser* make a massé shot <*masse* billiard cue, lit., a mace]

mas·se·ter (ma·sē′tər) *n. Anat.* A masticatory muscle connected with the lower jaw. [<NL

<Gk. *masētēr* chewer <*masasthai* chew] — **mas·se·ter·ic** (mas′ə·ter′ik), **mas′se·ter′ine** (-ēn, -īn) *adj.*

mas·si·cot (mas′ə·kot) *n.* 1 Lead monoxide: a rare mineral associated with galena. 2 A yellowish paint pigment similar to litharge. [< F <Sp. *mexacote* <Arabic *shabb qubṭi* Coptic alum]

mas·sif (mas′if, *Fr.* mä·sēf′) *n. Geol.* 1 The dominant, central mass of a mountain ridge more or less defined by longitudinal and transverse valleys. 2 A diastrophic block of the earth's crust, isolated by boundary faults. [<F]

mas·sive (mas′iv) *adj.* 1 Constituting a large mass; ponderous; large: a *massive* forehead. 2 Belonging to the total mass of anything. 3 Being without definite form, as a mineral; amorphous. 4 *Geol.* Homogeneous: said of certain rock formations. 5 Figuratively, imposing in scope or degree; having considerable magnitude. See synonyms under LARGE. [<F *massif*] —**mas′sive·ly** *adv.* —**mas′sive·ness** *n.*

mass media Newspapers, magazines, paperbound books, radio, television, and motion pictures, considered as means of reaching a very wide public audience.

mass meeting A large public gathering for the discussion of some topic, usually political.

mass number *Physics* 1 The whole number nearest the mass of any isotope of an element: 3 and 4 are *mass numbers* of the isotopes of helium. 2 The number of protons and neutrons in an atom: distinguished from *atomic number.*

mas·so·ther·a·py (mas′ō·ther′ə·pē) *n.* Treatment by massage. [<Gk. *massein* knead + THERAPY] —**mas′so·ther′a·peu′tic** (-ther′ə·pyōō′tik) *adj.*

mass–pro·duce (mas′prə·dōōs′, -dyōōs′) *v.t.* **·duced, ·duc·ing** To manufacture or produce by machinery (goods or articles) in great numbers or quantities. —**mass production**

mass ratio The ratio of the total mass of a rocket to its mass after the expenditure of fuel, calculated at approximately 2.72 to 1 for a rocket designed to travel at the exhaust velocity of its fuel.

mass spectrograph *Physics* An instrument for determining the relative masses of electrically charged particles by passing a stream of them through a magnetic field and noting the variable deflections from a straight path.

mass·y (mas′ē) *adj.* **mass·i·er, mass·i·est** Consisting of a mass or masses; big; bulky. —**mass′i·ness** *n.*

mast[1] (mast, mäst) *n.* 1 *Naut.* A pole or spar of round timber or tubular iron or steel, set upright in a sailing vessel to sustain the yards, sails, etc. 2 The upright pole of a derrick. 3 Any large, upright pole. —**before the mast** Occupying the position of, or serving as, a common sailor: from the fact that common sailors were quartered forward of the foremast. —*v.t.* To furnish with a mast or masts. [OE *mæst*] —**mast′less** *adj.*

mast[2] (mast, mäst) *n.* The fruit of the oak, beech, and other trees; acorns, etc. [OE *mæst* mast, fodder]

mast– Var. of MASTO–.

mas·ta·ba (mas′tə·bə) *n.* In ancient Egypt, an oblong building used as a mortuary chapel and place of offerings, with sloping sides and flat top, covering the mouth of a sepulchral pit. Also **mas′ta·bah.** [<Arabic *maṣṭabah* bench]

MASTABA
Of solid masonry, except for a small chapel and (unconnected) shaft to the mummy chamber.

mas·tax (mas′taks) *n. Zool.* The pharynx or gizzard of a rotifer. [<Gk., mouth, jaws <*masasthai* chew]

mas·tec·to·my (mas·tek′tə·mē) *n. Surg.* The operation of removing the breast. [<MAST– + -ECTOMY]

mas·ter (mas′tər, mäs′-) *n.* 1 A male person who has authority over others, as the principal of a school, an employer, the head of a household, the owner of a domestic animal, etc. 2 One who has control or disposal of something; an owner. 3 In the U.S. merchant marine, the captain of a vessel. 4 One who

is familiar with all the details of an art, profession, science, or trade. **5** One who has charge of some special thing, place, or business. **6** A young gentleman. **7** An honorary title; specifically, **Master**, a scholastic title and rank between bachelor and doctor. **8** *Law* Any of various officers of the court who assist the judges by hearing evidence, reporting, etc.: a *master* in chancery. **9** *Scot.* The courtesy title of a viscount's (or baron's) eldest son. **10** One who has disciples or followers; a religious leader. **11** One who gains the victory; a victor. — **the** (or **our**) **Master** Christ. —*v.t.* **1** To overcome or subdue; bring under control; defeat. **2** To become expert in: to *master* Greek. **3** To control or govern as a master. See synonyms under CONQUER, GAIN, LEARN, SUBDUE. — *adj.* Having the mastery; chief; controlling. [Fusion of OE *magister* and OF *maistre*, both <L *magister*, orig. a double compar. of *magnus* great] — **mas′ter·dom** *n.* — **mas′ter·hood** *n.* — **mas′·ter·less** *adj.*
Synonyms (noun): boss, captain, chief, commander, despot, director, employer, foreman, governor, head, leader, lord, manager, monarch, overseer, owner, prince, principal, proprietor, schoolmaster, sovereign, teacher. See CHIEF, SUPERINTENDENT, VICTOR. *Antonyms*: assistant, attendant, dependent, drudge, inferior, menial, retainer, serf, servant, servitor, slave, subaltern, subordinate, valet, waiter.
mas·ter-at-arms (mas′tər·ət·ärmz′, mäs′-) *n. pl.* **mas·ters-at-arms** A petty officer who maintains discipline and order on a naval vessel.
master builder **1** A contractor who employs men to build. **2** One who has charge of building operations; a foreman or architect.
mas·ter·ful (mas′tər·fəl, mäs′-) *adj.* **1** Having the power or characteristics of a master; domineering; arbitrary. **2** Showing mastery, as of an art, science, situation, etc. — **mas′ter·ful·ly** *adv.* — **mas′ter·ful·ness** *n.*
master hand **1** One skilled in his craft; an expert. **2** Great skill; expertness.
master key A key that will unlock two or more locks each of which has its own key that fits no other lock.
mas·ter·ly (mas′tər·lē, mäs′-) *adj.* Characteristic of a master; befitting a master. — *adv.* In a masterly manner; as befits a master. — **mas′ter·li·ness** *n.*
master mason A skilled mason.
mas·ter·mind (mas′tər·mīnd′, mäs′-) *n.* A person of great intelligence and executive ability. — *v.t.* To plan and direct (a project) skilfully: to *mastermind* a plot.
Master of Arts **1** A degree given by a college or university to a person who has completed a prescribed course of graduate study in the humanities, social sciences, etc. **2** A person who has received this degree. Abbr. *M.A., A.M.*
master of ceremonies A person presiding over an entertainment or dinner and introducing the performers or speakers: also, *emcee.*
Master of Science **1** A degree given by a college or university to a person who has completed a prescribed course of graduate study in science. **2** A person who has received this degree. Abbr. *M.S., M.Sc.*
mas·ter·piece (mas′tər·pēs′, mäs′-) *n.* A work or piece of art or literature done with consummate skill or showing the hand of a master; a supreme accomplishment; chef-d'oeuvre. [after G *meisterstück*]
mas·ter·stroke (mas′tər·strōk′, mäs′-) *n.* A masterly or decisive action or achievement.
mas·ter·work (mas′tər·wûrk′, mäs′-) *n.* A masterpiece.
mas·ter·work·man (mas′tər·wûrk′mən, mäs′-) *n. pl.* **-men** (-mən) A skilled workman, craftsman, or artist; also, a foreman or overseer over workmen.
mas·ter·wort (mas′tər·wûrt′, mäs′-) *n.* **1** Any of several herbs of the parsley family, especially those of the genus *Astrantia.* **2** A European plant (*Peucedanum ostruthium*), formerly used as a pot herb.
mas·ter·y (mas′tər·ē, mäs′-) *n.* **1** The condition of having power and control; dominion. **2** The knowledge or skill of a master. **3** Superiority in a contest; victory. See syno-

nyms under VICTORY.
mast·head (mast′hed′, mäst′-) *n.* **1** *Naut.* **a** The top of a lower mast. **b** The head or top of a mast to which a flag is raised. **c** A sailor acting as look-out at the masthead. **2** That section of a newspaper or other periodical, published in each edition, stating the ownership, officers, and staff conducting it, the advertising, editorial, and publishing offices, etc. —*v.t.* **1** To raise to or display at the masthead, as a flag. **2** To send to a masthead for punishment.
mas·tic (mas′tik) *n.* **1** A small Mediterranean evergreen tree (*Pistacia lentiscus*) of the cashew family. **2** The aromatic resin obtained from this tree, used as a varnish and in medicine as a styptic. **3** A quick-drying cement. [<F <LL *mastichum* <Gk. *mastichē*]
mas·ti·cate (mas′tə·kāt) *v.t.* **·cat·ed, ·cat·ing** **1** To crush or grind (food) for swallowing; chew. **2** To reduce, as rubber, to a pulp by crushing or kneading. [<LL *masticatus*, pp. of *masticare* chew <Gk. *mastichaein* gnash the teeth <*mastax* jaw] — **mas′ti·ca′tion** *n.* — **mas′ti·ca′tor** *n.*
mas·ti·ca·to·ry (mas′tə·kə·tôr′ē, -tō′rē) *adj.* **1** Of, pertaining to, or used in mastication. **2** Adapted for chewing: the *masticatory* mouth of a bee. — *n. pl.* **·ries** A substance chewed to increase the secretion of saliva.
mas·tiff (mas′tif, mäs′-) *n.* One of an old English breed of large hunting dogs, with a thick-set, heavy body, straight forelegs, a broad skull, drooping ears, and pendulous lips. [<OF *mastin* <L *mansuetus* gentle < pp. of *mansuescere* tame < *manus* hand; infl. in form by OF *mestif* mongrel]

MASTIFF
(About 30 inches high at the shoulder)

mas·ti·goph·o·ran (mas′ti·gof′ər·ən) *n.* Any one of a class of protozoa (*Mastigophora*), many of which are parasitic in man and other animals, characterized by the presence of one or more whiplike organs of locomotion called flagellae. — *adj.* Of or pertaining to the *Mastigophora*. [<Gk. *mastix, mastigos* whip + *phoros* bearing <*pherein* bear]
mas·ti·tis (mas·tī′tis) *n.* **1** *Pathol.* Inflammation of the mammary gland. **2** Garget. [< MAST- + -ITIS]
masto- *combining form Med.* The breast or the mammary gland. Also, before vowels, *mast-*, as in *mastitis.* [<Gk. *mastos* the breast]
mas·to·don (mas′tə·don) *n.* A primitive elephantlike mammal (order *Proboscidea*), distinguished from elephants and mammoths chiefly by its molar teeth; especially, the extinct, shaggy-haired *Mammut americanus* once common in North America. [< NL <MAST- + Gk. *odous, odontos* tooth; from the nipple-shaped projections on its teeth]

MASTODON
(About 9 feet high at the shoulder)

mas·toid (mas′toid) *adj. Anat.* **1** Designating a process of the temporal bone behind the ear for the attachment of muscles. **2** Pertaining to or situated near this process. **3** Nipplelike; breastlike. — *n.* The mastoid process. [<Gk. *mastoeidēs* <*mastos* breast + *eidos* form]
mas·toid·ec·to·my (mas′toid·ek′tə·mē) *n. Surg.* Excision of mastoid cells or of the mastoid process. [<MASTOID + -ECTOMY]
mas·toid·i·tis (mas′toid·ī′tis) *n. Pathol.* Inflammation of the mastoid process. [<MASTOID + -ITIS]
mas·tur·bate (mas′tər·bāt) *v.i.* **·bat·ed, ·bat·ing** To perform masturbation. [<L *masturbatus*, pp. of *masturbari*; ult. origin uncertain]
mas·tur·ba·tion (mas′tər·bā′shən) *n.* Sexual self-gratification; onanism: also called *self-*

abuse. [<L *masturbatio, -onis*] — **mas′tur·ba′tor** *n.*
mat[1] (mat) *n.* **1** A flat article, woven or plaited, or made of some perforated or corrugated material, to be laid on a floor, and on which to wipe one's shoes or feet. **2** Any flat piece of lace, plaited straw, leather, etc., used as a floor covering, table protection, ornament, etc. **3** Any dense or twisted growth, as of hair or rushes. — *v.* **mat·ted, mat·ting** *v.t.* **1** To cover with or as with mats. **2** To knot or entangle into a mat. — *v.i.* **3** To become knotted or entangled together. [OE *matt(e)* <LL *matta*]
mat[2] (mat) *n.* **1** A lusterless, dull, or roughened surface; also, a tool for producing such a surface. **2** *Printing* A sheet of papier-mâché or wood fiber for recording the impression of type or cuts in stereotyping; a matrix. **3** A border of white cardboard, serving as the frame, or part of the frame, of a picture. — *v.t.* **mat·ted, mat·ting** To produce a dull surface on, as metal or glass. — *adj.* Presenting a lusterless surface. Also *matte.* [OF, defeated, overcome <Arabic *māt*]
mat·a·dor (mat′ə·dôr) *n.* **1** In bullfighting, the man who kills the bull with a thrust of a sword. **2** In various card games, one of the highest trumps. [<Sp., killer <*matar* slay]
match[1] (mach) *n.* **1** One similar or equal in appearance, position, quality, or character; a suitable or fit associate; also, a possible mate. **2** A person or thing that is the equal of another in ability, strength, character, position, etc.; one able to cope with or oppose another; a peer. **3** A contest of skill, strength, etc., between persons or animals. **4** A counterpart; facsimile; also, either of two things harmonizing or corresponding. **5** A marriage or mating, or an agreement to marry or pair; a pairing or coupling. — *v.t.* **1** To be similar to or in accord with in quality, degree, etc.: His looks *match* his mood; The hat *matches* the coat. **2** To make or select as equals or as suitable for one another: to *match* pearls. **3** To place together as mates or companions; marry. **4** To cause to correspond; adapt: *Match* your efforts to your salary. **5** To compare so as to decide superiority; test: to *match* wits. **6** To set (equal opponents) in opposition: to *match* boxers. **7** To equal; oppose successfully: No one could *match* him. — *v.i.* **8** To be equal, similar, or corresponding; suit. **9** To be married; mate. [OE *gemæcca* companion] — **match′a·ble** *adj.* — **match′er** *n.*
match[2] (mach) *n.* **1** Any article manufactured for the purpose of starting or communicating a fire; specifically, a splinter of soft wood or a piece of waxed thread or cardboard tipped with a combustible composition that ignites by friction. **2** A fuse of cotton wicking prepared to burn quickly or slowly, and used for firing cannon. [<OF *mesche* wick, prob. <L *myxa* wick of a candle]
match·board (mach′bôrd′, -bōrd′) *n.* A board, specially cut with a groove along one edge and a tongue along the other, for close joining on floors, ceilings, etc.
match·book (mach′bŏŏk′) *n.* A small paper folder containing safety matches, with a strip of specially prepared surface at one end for striking them.
match·box (mach′boks′) *n.* A small box for containing matches.
matched (macht) *adj.* Having a tongue on one edge and a groove on the other: said of boards.
match·less (mach′lis) *adj.* That cannot be matched or equaled; peerless. — **match′less·ly** *adv.* — **match′less·ness** *n.*
match·lock (mach′lok′) *n.* **1** An old type of musket fired by placing a lighted match against the powder in the pan. **2** The gunlock on such a musket.
match·mak·er[1] (mach′mā′kər) *n.* **1** One who makes plans, or schemes, to bring about a marriage. **2** One who arranges matched games or contests. — **match′mak′ing** *adj. & n.*
match·mak·er[2] (mach′mā′kər) *n.* One who makes matches for lighting. — **match′mak′ing** *adj. & n.*
match·mark (mach′märk′) *n.* A distinguishing mark placed on separable parts of machinery

as a guide for assembling. — *v.t.* To put a matchmark upon.

match play In golf, a form of competitive play in which the score is computed by totaling the number of holes won or lost by each side.

match player A golfer who competes in match play.

match point In tennis and similar games, the final point needed to win a match.

match·stick (mach'stik') *n.* A piece of wood tipped with sulfur and used as a match.

mate[1] (māt) *n.* **1** A companion or associate; comrade. **2** One that is paired or coupled with another, as in matrimony; also, the male or female of animals paired for propagation. **3** An equal in a contest; a match. **4** An officer of a merchant vessel, ranking next below the captain. **5** *Nav.* An assistant to a warrant officer; a petty officer: the boatswain's *mate.* See synonyms under ASSOCIATE. — *v.* **mat·ed, mat·ing** *v.t.* **1** To join as mates or a pair; match; marry. **2** To pair for breeding, as animals. **3** To associate; couple. — *v.i.* **4** To match; marry. **5** **6** To consort; associate. [<MLG < *gemate* < *ge-* together + *mat* meat, food. Prob. akin to MEAT.] — **mate'less** *adj.*

mate[2] (māt) *v.t.* **mat·ed, mat·ing** **1** In chess, to checkmate. **2** To defeat or confound. — *n.* A checkmate. — *interj.* Checkmate. [<CHECKMATE]

ma·te·ri·al (mə·tir'ē·əl) *n.* **1** That of which anything is composed or may be constructed; matter considered as a component part of something. **2** Collected facts, impressions, ideas, or notes containing them, and sketches, etc., that may be used in completing a literary or an artistic production. **3** Matter regarded as the amorphous substratum of reality. **4** The tools, instruments, articles, etc., for doing something. See also MATERIEL. **5** A cloth or fabric. — *adj.* **1** Pertaining to matter; having a corporeal existence; physical. **2** Pertaining to matter in a corporeal relation; affecting the physical nature; also, pertaining to the body or the appetites; corporeal; sensuous; sensual. **3** Pertaining to the subject matter; essential; important. **4** Pertaining to matter as opposed to form. **5** Consisting of, relating to, or composed of matter regarded as the primary substance of the physical universe. **6** Replete with matter or good sense. See synonyms under IMPORTANT, PHYSICAL. [<LL *materialis* <L *materia* matter, stuff]

ma·te·ri·al·ism (mə·tir'ē·əl·iz'əm) *n.* **1** The doctrine that the facts of experience are all to be explained by reference to the reality, activities, and laws of physical or material substance. **2** Undue regard for material interests.

ma·te·ri·al·ist (mə·tir'ē·əl·ist) *n.* **1** A believer in the doctrine of materialism; also, a believer in the existence of matter. **2** One who takes interest exclusively, chiefly, or excessively in the material or bodily necessities and comforts of life. — **ma·te·ri·al·is·tic** *adj.* — **ma·te·ri·al·is·ti·cal·ly** *adv.*

ma·te·ri·al·i·ty (mə·tir'ē·al'ə·tē) *n.* *pl.* **·ties** **1** The quality or state of being material; physical as distinguished from psychical being. **2** Substance; matter; a material thing; a body. Also **ma·te'ri·al·ness.**

ma·te·ri·al·ize (mə·tir'ē·əl·īz') *v.* **·ized, ·iz·ing** *v.t.* **1** To give material or actual form to; represent as material. **2** To cause (a spirit, etc.) to appear in visible form. **3** To make materialistic. — *v.i.* **4** To assume material or visible form; appear. **5** To take form or shape; be realized: Our plans never *materialized.* — **ma·te'ri·al·i·za'tion** *n.* — **ma·te'ri·al·iz'er** *n.*

ma·te·ri·al·ly (mə·tir'ē·əl·ē) *adv.* **1** In a material and important manner. **2** In essence or substance. **3** From a physical point of view; physically.

ma·te·ri·el (mə·tir'ē·el') *n. Mil.* **1** All nonexpendable ordnance, transport, and equipment of an army. **2** All material things of an army except personnel. Also *French* **ma·té·riel** (mȧ·tā·ryel'). [<F, material]

ma·ter·nal (mə·tûr'nəl) *adj.* **1** Pertaining to a mother; motherly. **2** Connected with or inherited from one's mother; coming through the relationship of a mother. [<F *maternel*

<L *maternus* < *mater* a mother] — **ma·ter'nal·ly** *adv.*

ma·ter·ni·ty (mə·tûr'nə·tē) *n. pl.* **·ties** **1** The condition of being a mother. **2** The qualities of a mother; motherliness. [<F *maternité* <L *maternitas*]

mate·ship (māt'ship) *n.* **1** The state or condition of being a mate or companion. **2** The position or authority of one holding the office of mate.

math[1] (math) *n.* A mowing, or that obtained by mowing: now rare except in *aftermath.* [OE *mǣth*]

math[2] (math) *n. Colloq.* Mathematics.

math·e·mat·i·cal (math'ə·mat'i·kəl) *adj.* **1** Pertaining to or of the nature of mathematics. **2** Rigidly exact or precise. Also **math'e·mat'ic.** [<L *mathematicus* <Gk. *mathēmatikos* disposed to learn, mathematical < *mathēma* learning < *manthanein* learn] — **math'e·mat'i·cal·ly** *adv.*

mathematical expectation *Stat.* The probability of the occurrence of a given event multiplied by the amount of money offered or wagered on its occurrence.

mathematical logic Symbolic logic.

math·e·ma·ti·cian (math'ə·mə·tish'ən) *n.* One versed in mathematics.

math·e·mat·ics (math'ə·mat'iks) *n.* The logical study of quantity, form, arrangement, and magnitude; especially, the methods for disclosing, by the use of rigorously defined concepts and self-consistent symbols, the properties and exact relations of quantities and magnitudes, whether in the abstract, **pure mathematics,** or in their practical connections, **applied mathematics.**

ma·ti·co (mə·tē'kō) *n.* A tropical American shrub (*Piper angustifolium*) of the pepper family: its hairy leaves yield a volatile oil having stimulant and hemostatic properties. [<Sp., dim. of *Mateo* Matthew]

mat·in (mat'in) *n.* **1** *pl. Eccl.* The first of the canonical hours, usually said at midnight. **2** *pl.* In the Anglican Church, Morning Prayer.

3 Figuratively, any morning song, as of a bird. **4** *Obs.* Morning. — *adj.* Of or belonging to the morning: also **mat'in·al.** Also spelled *mattin.* [<OF *matin* early <L *matutinus* (*tempus*) (time) of the morning, appar. <*Matuta* goddess of morning]

mat·i·née (mat'ə·nā') *n.* An entertainment or reception held in the daytime; specifically, a theatrical or cinematic performance given in the afternoon. Also **mat'i·nee'.** [<F <*matin* morning. See MATIN.]

mat·ing (mā'ting) *n.* The act of pairing or matching.

matri– *combining form* Mother: *matricide.* [<L *mater, matris* mother]

ma·tri·arch (mā'trē·ärk) *n.* A woman holding the position corresponding to that of a patriarch in her family or tribe. [<MATRI– (PATRI)ARCH] — **ma'tri·ar'chal** *adj.* — **ma'tri·ar'chal·ism** *n.*

ma·tri·ar·chate (mā'trē·är'kit) *n.* Matriarchal government; a system of matriarchalism. [< MATRIARCH + -ATE[2]]

ma·tri·ar·chy (mā'trē·är'kē) *n. pl.* **·chies** A social organization having the mother as the head of the family, in which descent, kinship, and succession are reckoned through the mother, instead of the father; also, government by women. — **ma'tri·ar'chic** *adj.*

mat·ri·cide (mat'rə·sīd) *n.* **1** The killing of one's mother. **2** One who kills his mother. [<L *matricidium* < *mater, matris* mother + *caedere* kill; def. 2 <L *matricida*] — **mat'ri·ci'dal** *adj.*

mat·ri·cli·nous (mat'rə·klī'nəs) *adj. Biol.* Showing hereditary characteristics inclined to the maternal side: opposed to *patriclinous.* Also **mat'ro·cli'nous, mat'ro·cli'nal.**

ma·tric·u·lant (mə·trik'yə·lənt) *n.* A candidate or applicant for matriculation.

ma·tric·u·late (mə·trik'yə·lāt) *v.t. & v.i.* **·lat·ed, ·lat·ing** To enrol in a college or university as a candidate for a degree. — *n.* One who is so enrolled. [<Med.L *matriculatus*, pp. of *matriculare* enrol < *matricula*, dim. of *matrix*

MATHEMATICAL SYMBOLS

$+$	Plus or positive; sign of addition	$\int$	Integral of
$-$	Minus or negative; sign of subtraction	$\int_b^a$	Integral between limits of a and b
$\pm$	Plus or minus	$\doteq$ or $\rightarrow$	Approaches as a limit
$\mp$	Minus or plus	$f(x), F(x), \phi(x)$	Function of x
$\times$ or $\cdot$	Multiplied by	Δ	Increment of, as Δy
$\div$ or $:$	Divided by	d	Differential, as dy
$=$ or $::$	Equals; is equal to; as	$\dfrac{dy}{dx}$, or $f'(x)$	Derivative of $y = f(x)$ with respect to x
$\neq$ or $\pm$	Does not equal	δ	Variation, as δy
$\cong$	Approximately equal; congruent	π	pi; ratio of circumference of circle to diameter
$>$	Greater than	$n!$ or $\lfloor n$	Factorial n or n factorial
$<$	Less than	$\angle, \measuredangle s$	Angle, angles
$\geq$	Greater than or equal to	$\perp, \perp s$	Perpendicular to, perpendiculars
$\leq$	Less than or equal to		
$\sim$	Similar to; equivalent	$\parallel, \parallel s$	Parallel to, parallels
$\therefore$	Therefore	$\triangle, \triangle$	Triangle, triangles
$\because$	Since or because	$\llcorner, \llcorner$	Right angle, right angles
$\equiv$	Identical; identically equal to	$\square, \square$	Parallelogram, parallelograms
$\propto$	Directly proportional to; varies directly as	$\square, \square$	Rectangle, rectangles
∞	Infinity	$\square, \square$	Square, squares
$\sqrt{\ }$	Square root	$\bigcirc$ or $\odot$	Circle, circumference
$\sqrt[n]{\ }$	nth root	$'$	Minutes of arc; prime; minutes of time; feet
e or ϵ	Base (2.718···) of natural system of logarithms	$''$	Seconds of arc; double prime; seconds of time; inches
Σ	Summation of		

womb, origin, public roll <*mater* mother]
— **ma·tric′u·la′tion** *n.* — **ma·tric′u·la′tor** *n.*
mat·ri·lin·e·al (mat′rə·lin′ē·əl) *adj.* Pertaining to or describing descent or derivation through the female line. Compare PATRILINEAL.
mat·ri·mo·ny (mat′rə·mō′nē) *n.* *pl.* **·nies** 1 The union of a man and a woman in marriage; wedlock. 2 A card game played by any number of persons; also, a combination of king and queen in this and certain other games. See synonyms under MARRIAGE. [<L *matrimonium* <*mater, matris* mother]
matrimony vine The boxthorn.
ma·trix (mā′triks) *n.* *pl.* **ma·tri·ces** (mā′trə·sēz, mat′rə-) 1 That which contains and gives shape or form to anything. 2 The womb. 3 *Biol.* Intercellular substance; hence, the formative cells from which a structure grows. 4 A mold in which anything is cast or shaped, or that which encloses like a mold. 5 *Printing* A papier-mâché, plaster, or other impression of a form, from which a plate for printing may be made. 6 *Geol.* The impression or mold of the exterior of a crystal or other mineral left in the containing rock when the object is removed, or the mass in which a fossil, gemstone, mineral, etc., is embedded. 7 *Math.* A rectangular array of symbols or terms enclosed between parentheses or double vertical bars to facilitate the study of relationships. 8 The material used as a filler between the fragments of a shrapnel projectile. [<L, womb, breeding animal <*mater, matris* mother]
ma·tron (mā′trən) *n.* 1 A married woman; mother; also, a woman of established age and dignity. 2 A housekeeper, or a female superintendent, as of an institution. [<OF *matrone* <L *matrona* <*mater, matris* mother] — **ma′tron·al** *adj.* — **ma′tron·like′** *adj.*
ma·tron·age (mā′trən·ij) *n.* 1 The condition of being a matron. 2 Matronly attention or care. 3 Matrons collectively.
matron of honor A married woman acting as chief attendant to a bride at her wedding. See MAID OF HONOR.
mat·ro·nym·ic (mat′rō·nim′ik) See METRONYMIC.
matte¹ (mat) *n.* *Metall.* An impure metallic product containing sulfur, obtained in smelting sulfide ores, as of copper, lead, etc. [<F]
matte² (mat) See MAT².
mat·ted (mat′id) *adj.* 1 Covered with mats or matting. 2 Tangled like the fibers of a mat. — **mat′ted·ly** *adv.* — **mat′ted·ness** *n.*
mat·ter (mat′ər) *n.* 1 That which makes up the substance of anything, especially of material things. 2 The material of which a thing is composed. 3 *Physics* That aspect of reality conceived as existing prior to and independently of the mind and to have characteristics susceptible to precise measurement in terms of extension, force, mass, radiation, and energy. 4 That which constitutes the essence or substance of a particular thing. 5 Something not exactly conceived or stated; an indefinite, often a comparatively small, amount. 6 A subject for discussion or feeling. 7 Something of moment and importance. 8 A condition of affairs, especially if unpleasant or unfortunate; case; difficulty; trouble: What's the *matter*? 9 The thought, or material of thought. 10 Pus. 11 *Philos.* The as yet undifferentiated substratum of those properties and changes of which the human senses take cognizance and which, by their differentiation and combination in an infinite variety of forms, constitute the separate existences and characteristic qualities of physical things. 12 *Printing* Type that is set or composed; also, material to be set up; copy. 13 Written or printed documents sent by mail. See synonyms under MASS¹, TOPIC. — *v.i.* 1 To be of concern or importance; signify. 2 To form or discharge pus; suppurate. [<F *matière* <L *materia* stuff]
Mat·ter·horn (mat′ər·hôrn, *Ger.* mä′ter·hôrn) A mountain in the Alps on the Swiss-Italian border: 14,780 feet: French *Mont Cervin*.
mat·ter-of-course (mat′ər·əv·kôrs′, -kōrs′) *adj.* Following or accepting as an expected conclusion or as a natural or logical result.
mat·ter-of-fact (mat′ər·əv·fakt′) *adj.* Closely adhering to facts; straightforward.

mat·ter-of-fact·ly (mat′ər·əv·fakt′lē) *adv.* In a matter-of-fact manner; straightforwardly.
— **mat′ter-of-fact′ness** *n.*
mat·tin (mat′in) See MATIN.
mat·ting (mat′ing) *n.* 1 A woven fabric of fiber, straw, etc., used as a floor covering, etc. 2 The act or process of making mats. 3 A dull, flat surface effect, as in gilding, etc.
mat·tock (mat′ək) *n.* A pickaxlike tool for digging and grubbing, having blades instead of points. [OE *mattuc*]

MATTOCK

mat·toid (mat′oid) *n.* A person mentally unbalanced in one way or on one subject. [<Ital. *mattoide* <*matto* mad <L *mattus* intoxicated]
mat·tress (mat′rəs) *n.* 1 A casing of ticking or other strong fabric filled with hair, cotton, or rubber, and used as a bed. 2 A mat woven of brush, poles, etc., used in protecting embankments, forming dikes, jetties, etc. [<OF *materas* <Ital. *materasso* <Arabic *maṭraḥ* place where something is thrown]
mat·u·rate (mach′oo·rāt, mat′yoo-) *v.i.* **·rat·ed, ·rat·ing** 1 To ripen or mature. 2 *Med.* To suppurate; form pus. [<L *maturatus*, pp. of *maturare* ripen <*maturus* ripe, fully developed] — **mat′u·ra′tive** *adj.*
mat·u·ra·tion (mach′oo·rā′shən, mat′yoo-) *n.* 1 *Med.* The formation of pus. 2 The process of ripening or coming to maturity; ripeness. 3 *Biol.* The final stages in the preparation of gametes for fertilization, during which reduction to one half in the number of chromosomes in the germ cells occurs; meiosis.
ma·ture (mə·choor′, -toor′, -tyoor′) *adj.* 1 Completely developed; perfectly ripe: *mature* grain; as applied to persons, fully developed in character and powers: a *mature* thinker. 2 Highly developed; approaching perfection. 3 Thoroughly elaborated or arranged; fully digested or considered; complete in detail: a *mature* scheme. 4 Due and payable; having reached its time limit: a *mature* bond. 5 *Geol.* Designating the maximum complexity and diversity of earth features, as achieved by the forces of erosion at full vigor; also, adjusted to local surroundings, as the course of a river. See synonyms under RIPE. — *v.* **·tured, ·tur·ing** *v.t.* 1 To cause to ripen or come to maturity; bring to full development. 2 To perfect; complete. — *v.i.* 1 To come to maturity or full development; ripen. 2 To become due, as a note. [<L *maturus* of full age] — **ma·ture′ly** *adv.*
ma·tu·ti·nal (mə·too′tə·nəl, -tyoo′-) *adj.* Pertaining to morning; before noon; early. [<L *matutinalis* <*matutinus* early in the morning <*Matuta*, goddess of morning] — **ma·tu′ti·nal·ly** *adv.*
mat·zo (mät′sə, -sō) *n.* *pl.* **mat·zoth** (mät′sōth, -sōs) or **mat·zos** (-səs, -səz) 1 Unleavened bread in the form of wafers, eaten by Jews at Passover. 2 A wafer of unleavened bread. [<Hebrew *matstsōth*, pl. of *matstsāh* unleavened]
mat·zoon (mat·sōōn′) See YOGURT.
maud·lin (môd′lin) *adj.* 1 Made foolish by liquor. 2 Foolishly and tearfully affectionate. [<*Maudlin* <OF *Maudelene, Madeleine* (Mary) Magdalen, who was often depicted with eyes swollen from weeping]

maul (môl) *n.* A heavy mallet for driving wedges, piles, etc. — *v.t.* 1 To beat and bruise; batter. 2 To handle roughly; manhandle; abuse. 3 *U.S.* To split by means of a maul and wedges, as logs or rails. Also spelled *mall*. [<OF *mail* <L *malleus* hammer. ? Akin to L *molere* grind into pieces, crush.] — **maul′er** *n.*
Maul·main (môl′mān′) See MOULMEIN.

maul·stick (môl′stik′) See MAHLSTICK.
maun·der (môn′dər) *v.i.* 1 To talk in a wandering or incoherent manner; drivel. 2 To move dreamily or idly. [? Freq. of obs. *maund* beg; infl. in meaning by MEANDER]

STEEL FENCE-POST MAUL

— **maun′der·er** *n.*
maun·dy (môn′dē) *n.* The religious ceremony of washing the feet of others, especially of inferiors: in commemoration of the washing of the disciples' feet by Christ; hence, **Maundy**, the service connected with such ceremony. [<OF *mandé* <L *mandatum* command; from the use of *mandatum* at the beginning of the ceremony. See MANDATE.]
Maundy Thursday The day before Good Friday, commemorating the Last Supper of Christ with his disciples, at which he washed their feet. [See MAUNDY]
Mau·ri·ta·ni·a (môr′ə·tā′nē·ə), **Islamic Republic of** An independent republic of the French Community, on the coast of west Africa; 418,120 square miles; capital, Nouakchott; formerly a French overseas territory. — **Mau′·ri·ta′ni·an** *adj.* & *n.*
Mau·ri·ti·us (mô·rish′ē·əs) An island in the Indian Ocean east of Madagascar; 720 square miles; comprising with its dependencies a British crown colony (804 square miles); capital, Port Louis. French **Mau·rice** (mô·rēs′). — **Mau·ri′ti·an** *adj.* & *n.*
Mau·ser (mou′zər) *n.* A magazine rifle having great range and high muzzle velocity; also, a type of automatic pistol: a trade name. [after P. P. *Mauser*, 1838–1914, German inventor]
mau·so·le·um (mô′sə·lē′əm) *n.* *pl.* **·le·ums** or **·le·a** (-lē′ə) A large, stately tomb. [<L <Gk. *Mausōleion*, tomb of King Mausolus of Caria, erected by Queen Artemisia at Halicarnassus about 350 B.C. See SEVEN WONDERS OF THE WORLD.] — **mau·so·le′an** *adj.*
mauve (mōv) *n.* 1 A purple pigment and dye derived from mauvein. 2 Any of various purplish-rose shades. [<F, mallow <L *malva.* Doublet of MALLOW.]
mauve·in (mō′vin) *n.* *Chem.* A coal-tar violet dyestuff, $C_{27}H_{24}N_4$, obtained by oxidizing aniline: the first aniline dye of commerce. Also **mauve·ine** (mō′vin, -vēn). [<MAUVE]
mav·er·ick (mav′ər·ik) *n.* 1 *U.S.* An unbranded or orphaned animal, particularly a calf, legitimately belonging to the first one to brand it. 2 *Colloq.* A person with no attachments or affiliations, especially political ones. [after Samuel A. *Maverick*, 1803–1870, Texas lawyer, who did not brand his cattle]
ma·vis (mā′vis) *n.* The European song thrush or throstle (genus *Turdus*). [<F *mauvis*]
Ma·vors (mā′vôrz) An early name for Mars, the Roman god of war.
ma·vour·neen (mə·voor′nēn, -vôr′-) *n.* My darling: an expression of affection. Also **ma·vour′nin.** [<Irish *mo muirnín*]
maw (mô) *n.* 1 The craw of a bird. 2 The stomach. 3 The air bladder of a fish. 4 The gullet, jaws, or mouth of a voracious mammal or fish. [OE *maga* stomach]
mawk·ish (mô′kish) *adj.* 1 Productive of disgust or loathing; sickening or insipid. 2 Characterized by false or feeble sentimentality; lacking in strength or vigor. See synonyms under FLAT. [<obs. *mawk* a maggot] — **mawk′ish·ly** *adv.* — **mawk′ish·ness** *n.*
max·il·la (mak·sil′ə) *n.* *pl.* **·lae** (-ē) 1 *Anat.* The upper jaw bone in vertebrates. 2 *Zool.* One of the pair or pairs of jaws behind the mandibles of an arthropod. [<L, dim. of *mala* jaw]
max·il·lar·y (mak′sə·ler′ē, mak·sil′ər·ē) *adj.* Of, pertaining to, or situated near the jaw or a maxilla: a *maxillary* artery. — *n.* *pl.* **·lar·ies** A maxilla or jaw bone.
max·il·li·ped (mak·sil′ə·ped) *n.* *Zool.* 1 One of the limbs of certain crustaceans, modified to serve as masticatory organs, and situated behind the maxillae. 2 One of a pair of poisonous claws situated near the mouth of a centipede. [<L *maxilla* jaw bone + -PED]
max·im (mak′sim) *n.* A brief statement of a practical principle or proposition; a proverbial saying. See synonyms under ADAGE, RULE. [<F *maxime* <L *maxima* (*sententia, propositio*) greatest (authority, premise), fem. of *maximus.* See MAXIMUM.]
max·i·mal (mak′sə·məl) *adj.* Greatest; highest. See MAXIMUM.
Max·i·mal·ist (mak′sə·məl·ist) *n.* One of a for-

mer party or faction of extremist Russian revolutionists: distinguished from *Minimalist*.

Maxim gun A water-cooled machine-gun which utilizes the recoil of each shot to fire the next: invented by Sir Hiram S. Maxim.

max·im·ite (mak'sim-īt) *n.* A picric-acid high explosive used as a bursting charge for projectiles: invented by Hudson Maxim.

max·i·mize (mak'sə-mīz) *v.t.* **·mized, ·miz·ing** To make as great as possible; increase to the maximum; intensify. — **max'i·mi·za'tion** *n.*

max·i·mum (mak'sə-məm) *n.* *pl.* **·ma** (-mə) **1** The greatest quantity, amount, degree, or magnitude that can be assigned. **2** *Math.* **a** A value of a varying quantity that is greater than any neighboring value. **b** The highest possible of all the values which a variable or a function can express; the point at which a varying quantity ceases to increase and begins to decrease. **3** *Astron.* The moment of greatest brightness in a variable star, or its magnitude at such time. — *adj.* **1** As large or great as possible. **2** Pertaining to a maximum: *maximum* weight. [<L *maximus*, superl. of *magnus* great]

ma·xi·xe (mə-shē'shā, måk·sēks') *n.* A Brazilian dance to the two-step. [<Brazilian Pg.]

max·well (maks'wel) *n.* The practical cgs unit of magnetic flux, equal to the flux through one square centimeter normal to a magnetic field with an intensity of one gauss. [after James Clerk *Maxwell*]

may¹ (mā) *v.* Present: *sing.* **may, may** (*Archaic* **may·est** or **mayst**), **may**, *pl.* **may**; past: **might** A defective verb now used only in the present and past tenses as an auxiliary followed by the infinitive without *to*, or elliptically with the infinitive understood, to express: **1** Permission or allowance: *May* I go? You *may*. **2** Desire or wish: *May* your tribe increase! **3** Contingency, especially in clauses of result, concession, purpose, etc.: He died that we *might* live. **4** Possibility: You *may* be right. **5** *Law* Obligation or duty: the equivalent of *must* or *shall*. **6** *Obs.* Ability; power: now usually *can*. ◆ See usage note under CAN. [OE *mæg*]

may² (mā) *n.* The English hawthorn (*Crataegus oxyacantha*), with white, rose, or crimson flowers. Also **may'bush'** (-bōōsh'). [<MAY, because it blooms in this month]

May (mā) **1** The fifth month of the year, containing 31 days. **2** The prime of life; youth. **3** May Day festivities. [<OF *mai* <L (*mensis*) *Maius* (month of) May, prob. <*Maia*, goddess of growth; so called because regarded as a month of growth]

Ma·ya (mä'yə) **1** In Hindu religion, Devi, mother of the world; the personified active will of the Creator. **2** In Hindu philosophy, illusion, often personified as a maiden. [<Skt. *māyā* illusion]

Ma·ya (mä'yə) *n.* **1** One of a tribe of Central American Indians, the most important tribe of the Mayan linguistic stock, still comprising a large percentage of the population of Yucatán, northern Guatemala, and British Honduras. They were the first Indians to develop writing and an accurate astronomical calendar. **2** The language of the Mayas, in its historical and modern forms. — *adj.* Of or pertaining to the Mayas, their culture, or their language.

Ma·yan (mä'yən) *adj.* Of the Mayas, their culture, or their language. — *n.* **1** A Maya. **2** A family of Central American Indian languages, including Maya and Quiché.

May apple 1 The ovoid, oblong, yellowish fruit of a North American herb (*Podophyllum peltatum*). **2** The herb itself, of which the rhizomes yield podophyllin. Also called *mandrake root*.

Ma·ya·ri iron (mä·yä'rē) An iron made from Cuban ores, containing small percentages of chromium, vanadium, nickel, titanium, and certain other elements: used in high-grade machine castings. [from *Mayari*, a Cuban town]

MAY APPLE
a. Flower.
b. Fruit.

May basket A little basket of flowers left at the door of a friend as a May Day token.

may·be (mā'bē) *adv.* Perhaps; possibly. [<(*it*)

---

may be]

May·bird (mā'bûrd') *n.* **1** In the southern United States, the bobolink. **2** In the eastern United States, the redbreast (def. 3).

May·bug (mā'bug') *n.* **1** The cockchafer. **2** The June beetle. Also **May'bee'tle** (-bēt'l).

May·day (mā'dā') *n.* The international radio-telephone call for immediate help sent out by an aircraft or ship in distress. [<F *m'aidez* help me]

May Day The first day of May, traditionally celebrated as a spring festival by crowning a May Queen, dancing around a Maypole, etc.: commemorated in many countries as a labor holiday.

may·flow·er (mā'flou'ər) *n.* **1** The trailing arbutus, State flower of Massachusetts. **2** *Brit.* The hawthorn or may; also, the marsh marigold. **3** Any of various other plants which blossom in the spring.

Mayflower The ship on which the Pilgrims came to America in 1620.

may·fly (mā'flī') *n.* *pl.* **·flies 1** An ephemerid insect, which in the nymphal state inhabits water and is long-lived, and in the adult state merely propagates its kind and then dies. **2** An artificial fly in imitation of this insect. **3** *Brit.* A caddis fly.

may·hem (mā'hem) *n.* **1** *Law* The offense of depriving a person by violence of any limb, member, or organ, or causing any mutilation of the body. Also spelled *maihem*. **2** Egregious disorder or damage. [<OF *mehaing, mahaigne*. Related to MAIM.]

may·on·naise (mā'ə·nāz', mī'-) *n.* A sauce or dressing made by beating together raw egg yolk, butter or olive oil, lemon juice or vinegar, and condiments. [<F, ? <*Mahón*, Balearic port]

may·or (mā'ər, mâr) *n.* The chief magistrate of a city, borough, or municipal corporation. [<F *maire* <L *major* greater. Doublet of MAJOR.] — **may'or·al** *adj.*

may·or·al·ty (mā'ər·əl·tē, mâr'əl-) *n.* *pl.* **·ties** The office or term of a mayor. [<OF *mairalté*]

May·pole (mā'pōl') *n.* A pole decorated with flowers and ribbons, around which dancing takes place on May Day.

may·pop (mā'pop') *n.* **1** The passionflower (*Passiflora incarnata*) of the southern United States. **2** The small yellow fruit of this plant. [Alter. of N. Am. Ind. *maracock*. Cf. Tupian *maracujá*.]

May·thorn (mā'thôrn') *n.* The hawthorn.

May·time (mā'tīm') *n.* The month of May. Also **May'tide'** (-tīd').

may·weed (mā'wēd') *n.* A strong-scented, acrid weed (*Anthemis cotula*) of the composite family, bearing white-rayed flowers on a yellow disk; stinking camomile. [Alter. of *maidweed* <*maytheweed* <OE *magothe* + WEED]

May wine Any still, white wine flavored with steeped orange and pineapple slices and woodruff: named for the month of May, in which the woodruff flowers.

maz·ard (maz'ərd) *n.* *Obs.* **1** A mazer. **2** The skull; the head. Also **maz'zard**. [Var. of MAZER]

Maz·da·ism (maz'də·iz'əm) *n.* Zoroastrianism. Also **Maz'de·ism**. [<OPersian *Aura mazda* the principle of good]

maze (māz) *n.* **1** An intricate network of paths or passages; a labyrinth. **2** Embarrassment; uncertainty; perplexity. — *v.t.* *Archaic* To daze or stupefy; bewilder. ◆ Homophone: *maize*. [<AMAZE] — **maz'y** *adj.* — **maz'i·ly** *adv.* — **maz'i·ness** *n.*

ma·zer (mā'zər) *n.* A bowl, goblet, or drinking cup made of hard wood. Also *mazard*. [<OF *masere* maple wood <Gmc.]

ma·zur·ka (mə·zûr'kə, -zōōr'-) *n.* **1** A lively Polish round dance resembling the polka. **2** The music for such a dance. Also **ma·zour'·ka**. [<Polish, woman from Mazovia, a province in Poland]

ma·zut (mə·zōōt') *n.* The residue from the distillation of Russian petroleum: used as a fuel oil. Also **ma·zout'**. [<Russian]

maz·zard cherry (maz'ərd) The fruit of the European wild sweet cherry (*Prunus avium*). [Earlier *mazer* maple wood; appar. from the hardness of the wood]

Mc— See also MAC–.

Mc·Car·thy·ism (mə·kär'thē·iz'əm) *n.* **1** The practice of making public and sensational accusations of disloyalty or corruption, usually

---

with little or no proof or with doubtful evidence. **2** The practice of conducting sensational inquisitorial investigations, ostensibly to expose subversion, especially pro–Communist activity. [after Joseph *McCarthy*, 1909–1957, U.S. Senator]

Mc·Coy (mə·koi'), **the (real)** *U.S. Slang* The authentic person or thing. [Appar. from an episode, existing in many versions, in which a celebrated American boxer, Kid McCoy, spectacularly established his identity]

Mc·In·tosh (mak'ən·tosh) *n.* A red variety of early autumn apple. Also **McIntosh red**. [after John *McIntosh* of Ontario, who discovered it in the 18th century]

Mc·Kin·ley (mə·kin'lē), **William**, 1843–1901, president of the United States 1897–1901; assassinated.

M–Day (em'dā') *n.* *Mil.* Mobilization day; the day the Department of Defense orders mobilization for war.

me (mē) *pron.* The objective case of *I*. ◆**It's me, etc.** Anyone who answers the question "Who's there?" by saying "It's me" is using acceptable colloquial idiom. Here *It is I* would seem stilted, although at the formal level of writing it is expected: They have warned me that *it is I*, and not he, who will have to bear the brunt of the criticism. After a finite impersonal form of the verb *to be*, as *it is, it was*, etc., a personal pronoun should, according to prescriptive grammar, be in the same case as the subject: the nominative; accordingly, at the formal level, we find *It is he, It is we, It is they*, etc. Since only the personal and relative pronouns retain different inflected forms for the nominative and objective cases, the rule might appear to be invented to cover this one exceptional situation. The normal subject–verb–object order of the English sentence creates a strong expectation that what follows the verb will be in the objective case, and perhaps for this reason popular usage has long favored *It's me* over the formal *It is I*. British and American playwrights in recent years have also represented their characters, and not only the uneducated speakers among them, as saying *It's him, It's her, It's them*, etc. In spite of the exact parallel in construction with *It's me*, these expressions are not yet condoned to the same extent, even at the colloquial level.

mead¹ (mēd) *n.* A liquor of fermented honey and water to which malt, yeast, and spices are added; metheglin. See HYDROMEL. ◆ Homophone: *meed*. [OE *meodu*]

mead² (mēd) *n.* *Poetic* A meadow. ◆ Homophone: *meed*. [OE *mæd*]

mead·ow (med'ō) *n.* A tract of low or level land, producing grass for hay. [OE *mædwe*, oblique case of *mæd*] — **mead'ow·y** *adj.*

mead·ow·beau·ty (med'ō·byōō'tē) *n.* *pl.* **·ties** Any of a genus (*Rhexia*) of low-growing herbs, usually with four-parted purple flowers; especially, the common species (*R. virginica*).

meadow bird The bobolink.

meadow hen The American bittern.

mead·ow·lark (med'ō·lärk') *n.* An American songbird (genus *Sturnella*) related to the blackbird; especially, the southern meadowlark (*S. magna*), brownish or grayish above, marked with black and yellow beneath.

meadow lily The Canada lily.

meadow mouse The field mouse.

meadow rue Any species of the genus *Thalictrum* of the crowfoot family, having leaves like those of rue.

mead·ow·sweet (med'ō·swēt') *n.* **1** A shrub of the rose family (genus *Spiraea*); especially, *S. salicifolia*, having alternate simple or pinnate leaves and white or rose–colored flowers: also **meadow queen**. **2** Any plant of a related genus (*Filipendula*).

mea·ger (mē'gər) *adj.* **1** Deficient or destitute of quantity or quality; scanty; inadequate. **2** Deficient in or scantily supplied with fertility, strength, or richness. **3** Wanting in flesh; thin; emaciated. Also **mea'gre**. [<OF *maigre* <L *macer* lean] — **mea'ger·ly** *adv.* — **mea'ger·ness** *n.*

Synonyms: barren, emaciated, feeble, gaunt, jejune, lank, lean, poor, skinny, spare, starved, starveling, tame, thin. See GAUNT. *Antonyms*: bonny, bouncing, burly, chubby, corpulent, fat, fleshy, hearty, obese, plump, portly, stout.

meal¹ (mēl) *n.* **1** Comparatively coarsely ground grain. **2** Unbolted wheat flour; chop. **3** A powder produced by grinding; any powdery, meal-like material: sulfur *meal*. [OE *melu*]

meal² (mēl) *n.* **1** The portion of food taken at one time; a repast. **2** Its occasion or time. ◆ Collateral adjective: *prandial*. [OE *mǣl* measure, time, meal]

-meal *suffix* The quantity taken at one time or the unit of measurement: now obsolete except in *piecemeal*. [OE *-mǣlum*, oblique case of *mǣl* measure, time, meal]

meal·ie (mē′lē) *n.* **1** An ear of maize. **2** *pl.* Maize; Indian corn. [<Afrikaans *milje* <Pg. *milho* millet <L *milium*]

meal·worm (mēl′wûrm′) *n.* **1** The larva of a beetle *(Tenebrio molitor)* destructive to flour, meal, etc. **2** A meal-bred grub prepared as bait for ground fishing.

meal·y (mē′lē) *adj.* **meal·i·er**, **meal·i·est** **1** Having a resemblance to or the qualities or taste of meal; farinaceous. **2** Overspread or besprinkled with or as with meal; pale-colored; of anemic appearance. **3** Having the appearance of being covered with meal; farinose. **4** Mealy-mouthed. **5** Friable; floury: said of the endosperm of malt. **6** Flecked with white spots: said of cattle. **7** Smooth-flavored; harsh to the taste: said of tea. — **meal′i·ness** *n.*

meal·y·bug (mē′lē·bug′) *n.* Any of a large cosmopolitan family *(Pseudococcidae)* of coccids whose soft, oval bodies are usually covered with a mealy wax secretion: they include many of the most destructive plant pests.

meal·y-mouthed (mē′lē·mouтht′, -mouтhd′) *adj.* Unwilling to express adverse opinions plainly; euphemistic; insincere.

mean¹ (mēn) *v.* **meant**, **mean·ing** *v.t.* **1** To have in mind as a purpose or intent: I *meant* to visit him. **2** To intend or design for some purpose, destination, etc.: Was that remark *meant* for me? **3** To intend to express or convey: That's not what I *meant*. **4** To have as the particular sense or significance; denote; portend: Those clouds *mean* snow. — *v.i.* **5** To have disposition or intention; be disposed: He *means* well. **6** To be of specified importance or influence: Her beauty *means* everything to her. See synonyms under IMPORT, PURPOSE. ◆ Homophone: *mien*. [OE *mǣnan* tell, wish, intend]

mean² (mēn) *adj.* **1** Low in grade, quality, or condition; of humble antecedents; lowly; also, indicative of or suited to low rank; poor; inferior; shabby. **2** *Colloq.* Disagreeable; unpleasant; unkind; wicked. **3** Ignoble in mind, character, and spirit; lacking magnanimity or honor; base; petty; also, miserly; stingy. **4** Worthy of no respect; slight or contemptible. **5** Of little value or efficiency. **6** Not fit for cultivation: said of land. **7** Vicious or unmanageable: said of horses. **8** *Colloq.* Irritable; ashamed; paltry; also, ill: to feel *mean*. See synonyms under BAD, BASE, COMMON, INSIGNIFICANT, LITTLE, SMALL, VULGAR. ◆ Homophone: *mien*. [OE *(ge)mǣne* common, ordinary] — **mean′ly** *adv.* — **mean′ness** *n.*

mean³ (mēn) *n.* **1** The middle state between two extremes; hence, moderation; avoidance of excess; medium: the happy *mean*. **2** *Math.* A quantity having an intermediate value between two extremes, or between several quantities: the arithmetical *mean*. **3** *pl.* The medium through which anything is done; instrumentality: used often with singular construction: a *means* to an end. **4** *pl.* Money or property as a procuring medium; wealth. **5** A plan of procedure. **6** *Logic* The middle term in a syllogism. **7** *Obs.* An intermediary; mediator. See synonyms under AGENT. — **arithmetical mean** The quotient of the sum of two or more quantities divided by the number of quantities; the average. — **by all means** Without hesitation; certainly. — **by any means** **1** In any manner possible; somehow; at all. **2** By all means. — **by no manner of means** Most certainly not; not for any consideration; on no account whatever: also **by no means.** — **geometric** (or **geometrical**) **mean** The square root of the product of two given numbers. — **golden mean** A wise moderation; the

avoidance of extremes. — *adj.* **1** Intermediate as to position between extremes. **2** Intermediate as to size, degree, or quality; medium; average. **3** Intermediate as to time; intervening. **4** Having an intermediate value between two extremes or among several values; average: the *mean* distance covered daily. ◆ Homophone: *mien*. [<OF *meien* <L *medianus* <*medius* middle. Doublet of MEDIAN, MESNE, MIZZEN.]

me·an·der (mē·an′dər) *v.i.* **1** To wind or turn in a course. **2** To wander aimlessly. — *n.* **1** A tortuous or winding course; hence, a maze; perplexity. **2** The Greek key or fret pattern. [<MEANDER] — **me·an′der·er** *n.* — **me·an′der·ing**, **me·an′drous** *adj.*

mean·ing (mē′ning) *n.* **1** That which is intended; object; intention; aim. **2** That which is signified; significance; sense; acceptation; import; connotation. See synonyms under PURPOSE. — *adj.* **1** Having purpose or intention: usually in combination: well-*meaning*. **2** Significant; suggestive. — **mean′ing·ful** *adj.* — **mean′ing·ful·ly** *adv.* — **mean′ing·less** *adj.* — **mean′ing·less·ly** *adv.* — **mean′ing·less·ness** *n.* — **mean′ing·ly** *adv.*

mean latitude Middle latitude.

mean sun *Astron.* A fictitious sun considered to be moving uniformly with respect to the equator: a concept used to facilitate the computation of time.

meant (ment) Past tense and past participle of MEAN¹.

mean·time (mēn′tīm′) *n.* Intervening time or occasion. — *adv.* In or during the meantime.

mean time See under TIME. Also **mean solar time.**

mean·while (mēn′hwīl′) *n. & adv.* Meantime.

mea·sle (mē′zəl) *n.* **1** The larva *(Cysticercus)* of a certain tapeworm (genus *Taenia*) found in meat and generally producing measles in swine. **2** Any excrescence upon a plant or tree. [See MEASLES]

mea·sled (mē′zəld) *adj.* Affected with measles.

mea·sles (mē′zəlz) *n.* **1** An acute, highly contagious, generally self-immunizing virus disease affecting children and sometimes adults: it is characterized by chills, fever, severe coryza, and an extensive eruption of small red macules; rubeola. **2** Any of various eruptive diseases of a similar character: used with a qualifying adjective: French *measles*. **3** A disease affecting swine and cattle, caused by the presence of larval tapeworms in the flesh. — **French measles, German measles** Rubella. [ME *maseles*, pl. of *masel* a blister <LG. Cf. MDu. *masel* spot on the skin.]

mea·sly (mēz′lē) *adj.* **·sli·er**, **·sli·est** **1** Affected with measles. **2** Containing tapeworm larvae: said of meat. **3** *Slang* Not fit to be touched; beneath contempt; also, mean; skimpy; stingy; scanty.

meas·ur·a·ble (mezh′ər·ə·bəl) *adj.* **1** Capable of being measured or of computation. **2** Limited; moderate: *measurable* severity. — **meas′ur·a·bil′i·ty**, **meas′ur·a·ble·ness** *n.* — **meas′ur·a·bly** *adv.*

meas·ure (mezh′ər) *n.* **1** The extent or dimensions of anything. **2** A standard of measurement. **3** Hence, any standard of criticism, comparison, judgment, or award. **4** A series of measure units; a system of measurements: dry *measure*. See WEIGHT. **5** An instrument or vessel of measurement. **6** The act of measuring; measurement. **7** A quantity measured, or regarded as measured. **8** Reasonable limits; moderation: beyond *measure*; also, degree; reasonable proportion: A *measure* of allowance should be made. **9** A certain proportion; relative extent. **10** A specific act or course; transaction; specifically, a legislative bill. **11** That which makes up a sum or total. **12** Any quantity regarded as a unit and standard of comparison with other quantities; a quantity of which some other given quantity forms an exact multiple. **13** *Music* **a** That division of time by which melody and rhythm are regulated; rate of movement; time. **b** The portion of music contained between two bar lines; bar. **14** In prosody, meter; a rhythmical period. **15** A slow and stately dance or dance movement. **16** *pl. Geol.* A series of related rock strata, having some common feature. — *v.* **·ured**, **·ur·ing** *v.t.* **1** To take or ascertain

the dimensions, quantity, capacity, etc., of, especially by means of a measure. **2** To set apart, mark off, etc., by measuring: often with *off* or *out*. **3** To estimate by comparison; judge; weigh: to *measure* a risk. **4** To serve as the measure of. **5** To bring into competition or comparison. **6** To traverse as if measuring; travel over. **7** To adjust; regulate: *Measure* your actions to your aspirations. — *v.i.* **8** To make or take measurements. **9** To yield a specified measurement: The table *measures* six by four feet. **10** To admit measurement. — **to measure one's length** To fall prostrate at full length. — **to measure out** To distribute or allot by measure. — **to measure swords** **1** To fight with swords. **2** To fight or contend as in a debate. — **to measure up to** To fulfil, as expectations. [<F *mesure* <L *mensura* <*metiri* measure] — **meas′ur·er** *n.*

meas·ured (mezh′ərd) *adj.* **1** Ascertained, adjusted, or proportioned by rule. **2** Uniform; slow and stately; rhythmical; deliberate. **3** In moderation; held in restraint; guarded. — **meas′ured·ly** *adv.* — **meas′ured·ness** *n.*

meas·ure·less (mezh′ər·lis) *adj.* Incapable of measurement; unlimited; immense. See synonyms under INFINITE.

meas·ure·ment (mezh′ər·mənt) *n.* **1** The process or result of measuring anything; mensuration. **2** The amount, capacity, or extent determined by measuring. **3** A system of measuring units.

measuring worm A geometrid.

meat (mēt) *n.* **1** The flesh of animals used as food: sometimes limited to the flesh of mammals, as opposed to fish or fowl; also, any animal killed for food: to hunt one's *meat*. **2** Anything eaten for nourishment; victuals; hence, that which nourishes. **3** The edible part of anything. **4** A meal; especially, dinner; the main meal. **5** The essence, gist, or pith: the *meat* of an essay. **6** *Slang* Anything one does with special ease or pleasure; forte. ◆ Homophones: *meet, mete*. [OE *mete*] — **meat′less** *adj.*

meat packing *U.S.* The commercial slaughtering of meat-producing animals and the processing, packaging, and distribution of meat and meat products. — **meat packer**

me·a·tus (mē·ā′təs) *n. pl.* **·tus** or **·tus·es** *Anat.* A conspicuous passage or canal: the auditory *meatus*. [<L, a passage <*meare* go]

meat·y (mē′tē) *adj.* **meat·i·er**, **meat·i·est** **1** Full of or resembling meat. **2** Having strength; nourishing. **3** Significant; pithy. — **meat′i·ness** *n.*

me·ca·te (mā·kä′tā) *n. SW U.S.* A rope made of maguey fiber, or sometimes of plaited horsehair: used for tying horses. [<Sp. < Nahuatl]

mec·ca (mek′ə) *n.* **1** A place visited by many people; any attraction. **2** The object of one's aspiration, yearning, or effort. [from *Mecca*]

Mec·ca (mek′ə) The capital of Hejaz and one of the capitals of Saudi Arabia; birthplace of Mohammed and a holy city of Islam to which Moslems make pilgrimages: also *Mekka*.

me·chan·ic (mə·kan′ik) *n.* **1** One engaged in mechanical employment; an artisan; handicraftsman. **2** *Obs.* A mean or lowly fellow. See synonyms under ARTIST. — *adj.* **1** Pertaining to mechanics; mechanical. **2** Involving manual labor or skill. [<L *mechanicus* <Gk. *mēchanikos* <*mēchanē* a machine]

me·chan·i·cal (mə·kan′i·kəl) *adj.* **1** Pertaining to mechanics, in accordance with the laws of mechanics. **2** Produced by a machine. **3** Operated by mechanism. **4** Operating as if by a machine or machinery. **5** Doing or done involuntarily, by mere force of habit. **6** Automatic; not instinct with life; artificial. **7** Failing to show independence of thought; slavish. **8** Skilled in the use of tools and mechanisms. — **me·chan′i·cal·ly** *adv.* — **me·chan′i·cal·ness** *n.*

mech·a·ni·cian (mek′ə·nish′ən) *n.* One who understands the science of mechanics; a designer of machinery.

me·chan·ics (mə·kan′iks) *n. pl.* **1** The branch of physics that treats of the phenomena caused by the action of forces on material bodies, including statics and kinetics: construed as singular. **2** The science of machinery and of its practical applications: construed as singular. **3** The mechanical or technical aspects:

mech·a·nism (mek′ə-niz′əm) *n.* **1** The parts of a machine collectively; machinery in general. **2** A system which constitutes a working agency. **3** Technique; mechanical execution or action. **4** The theory that the forces that produce organic growth are the same physical and chemical agencies that operate in the inorganic world, differing from them only in degree: opposed to *vitalism.* **5** *Psychol.* The mental processes, conscious or unconscious, by which certain actions are effected. See synonyms under TOOL. — **mech′·a·nis′tic** *adj.* — **mech′a·nis′ti·cal·ly** *adv.*

mech·a·nist (mek′ə-nist) *n.* **1** A mechanician. **2** A believer in philosophical mechanism.

mech·a·ni·za·tion (mek′ə-nə-zā′shən, -nī-) *n.* **1** The act or process of applying machinery to the performance of specified operations. **2** The aggregate results of such application. **3** *Mil.* The maximum coordinated utilization of power–driven equipment, mechanized armament, and automatic weapons in the service of the combat personnel.

mech·a·nize (mek′ə-nīz) *v.t.* **·nized**, **·niz·ing 1** To make mechanical. **2** To convert (an industry, etc.) to machine production. **3** *Mil.* To equip with tanks, trucks, etc. — **mech′a·nized** *adj.*

mech·a·no·ther·a·py (mek′ə-nō-ther′ə-pē) *n. Med.* The treatment of disease by mechanical means, as massage. [< *mechano-* (<MECHANIC) + THERAPY]

med·al (med′l) *n.* A small piece of metal, bearing a device, usually commemorative of some event or deed of bravery, scientific research, or literary production, etc. — *v.t.* **·aled** or **·alled**, **·al·ing** or **·al·ling** To confer a medal upon. ◆ Homophone: *meddle.* [<F *médaille* <Ital. *medaglia,* ult. <L *metallum.* Doublet of METAL.] — **me·dal·lic** (mə-dal′ik) *adj.*

med·al·ist (med′l-ist) *n.* **1** A collector, engraver, or designer of medals. **2** The recipient of a medal awarded for services or merit. **3** In golf, the winner at medal play. Also **med′·al·ist.**

me·dal·lion (mə-dal′yən) *n.* **1** A large medal; also, a subject painted, engraved, etc., and set in a circular or oval frame or design: used as decorative elements in carpets, lace, etc. **2** Any one of several ancient Greek silver coins. [<F *médaillon* <Ital. *medaglione,* aug. of *medaglia* MEDAL] — **me·dal′lion·ist** *n.*

med·dle (med′l) *v.i.* **·dled**, **·dling 1** To take part in or concern oneself with something without need or request: often with *in* or *with.* **2** *Obs.* To mix; mingle. See synonyms under INTERPOSE, MIX. ◆ Homophone: *medal.* [<OF *medler, mesdler,* var. of *mesler,* ult. <L *miscere* mix] — **med′dler** *n.* — **med′dling** *adj. & n.*

med·dle·some (med′l-səm) *adj.* Given to meddling; officiously inclined; interfering; intrusive. — **med′dle·some·ly** *adv.* — **med′dle·some·ness** *n.*

Synonyms: impertinent, intrusive, meddling, obtrusive, officious. The *meddlesome* person interferes unasked in the affairs of others; the *intrusive* person thrusts himself uninvited into their company or conversation; the *obtrusive* person thrusts himself or his opinions conceitedly and undesirably upon their notice; the *officious* person thrusts his services, unasked and undesired, upon others. Compare ACTIVE, INQUISITIVE, INTERPOSE. *Antonyms:* modest, reserved, retiring, shy, unassuming, unobtrusive.

med·e·vac (med′ə-vak′) *n.* The evacuation of the wounded, as from battle sites, usually by helicopter. [< *med(ical)*+*evac(uation)*]

me·di·a (mē′dē-ə) *n. pl.* of **medium 1** Means of disseminating information, entertainment, etc., such as books, newspapers, radio, television, motion pictures, and magazines. **2** In advertising, all means of communication that carry advertisements, including billboards, direct mail, catalogs, radio, etc.

me·di·a·cy (mē′dē-ə·sē) *n.* **1** The state or quality of being mediate. **2** Mediation.

me·di·al (mē′dē-əl) *adj.* **1** Of or pertaining to the middle, in position or character or in calculation; mean. **2** Nearer the median plane of a body: opposed to *lateral.* **3** Designating a letter neither initial nor final. — *n. Phonet.* Any of a group of voiced stops (b, d, g), conceived as intermediate between the voiceless stops (p, t, k) and the rough or aspirate group (bh, dh, gh, ph, th, kh). [<LL

medialis <L *medius* middle] — **me′di·al·ly** *adv.*

me·di·an (mē′dē-ən) *adj.* **1** Pertaining to the middle, or situated in the median plane. **2** *Stat.* Of, pertaining to, or designating that point in a series of values which divides the series into two groups, each containing the same number of entries: 8 is the *median* point of the series 2, 5, 8, 10, 13. [<L *medianus* <*medius* middle. Doublet of MEAN³, MESNE, MIZZEN.] — **me′di·an·ly** *adv.*

median plane That plane which divides a body longitudinally into symmetrical halves.

me·di·ate (mē′dē-āt) *v.* **·at·ed**, **·at·ing** *v.t.* **1** To settle or reconcile by mediation, as differences. **2** To bring about or effect by mediation. **3** To serve as the medium for effecting (a result) or conveying (an object, information, etc.). — *v.i.* **4** To act between disputing parties in order to bring about a settlement, compromise, etc. **5** To occur or be in an intermediate relation or position. See synonyms under INTERPOSE. — *adj.* (-it) **1** Acting as an intervening agency; indirect. **2** Occurring or effected as a result of indirect or median agency. **3** Intermediate. [<LL *mediatus,* pp. of *mediare* stand between, mediate] — **me′·di·ate·ly** *adv.* — **me′di·ate·ness** *n.* — **me′di·a·tive** *adj.* — **me′di·a′tor** *n.* — **me′di·a·to′ri·al** (-tôr′ē·əl, -tō′rē·əl), **me′di·a·to′ry** *adj.*

me·di·a·tion (mē′dē-ā′shən) *n.* **1** The act of mediating; intercession; interposition. **2** A friendly intervention in the disputes of others, with their consent, for the purpose of adjusting differences. See CONCILIATION.

med·ic¹ (med′ik) *n.* Any one of several plants of the bean family (genus *Medicago*), especially the lucerne or alfalfa. [<L *medicus* <Gk. *Mēdikē (poa)* Median (grass) <*Mēdos* a Mede]

med·ic² (med′ik) *n. Colloq.* **1** A doctor, physician, or intern. **2** A medical corpsman.

med·i·ca·ble (med′ə·kə·bəl) *adj.* Capable of relief by medicine; curable.

Med·i·caid (med′i·kād′) *n. U.S.* A tax–supported health insurance program for low–income people.

med·i·cal (med′i·kəl) *adj.* **1** Pertaining to medicine or its practice. **2** Having curative properties. [<F *médicale* <LL *medicalis* <L *medicus* a physician] — **med′i·cal·ly** *adv.*

medical examiner 1 *Law* An official legally designated to examine the bodies of those dead as a result of violence or crime, to perform autopsies, and to establish the proximate cause and circumstances of the death. **2** A doctor authorized by a life insurance company to determine the physical fitness of a prospective insurant.

medical jurisprudence The branch of medicine and related sciences which deals with questions involving the applications of the civil and criminal law; forensic medicine. See under JURISPRUDENCE.

med·i·ca·ment (med′ə·kə·mənt, mə·dik′ə-) *n.* **1** Any substance for the alleviation of disease or wounds. **2** A healing agency. [<L *medicamentum* <*medicare.* See MEDICATE.] — **med′i·ca·men′tal** *adj.*

med·i·care (med′i·kâr′) *n. Often cap. U.S.* A health insurance program supported in part by government funds, serving especially the aged.

med·i·cate (med′ə·kāt) *v.t.* **·cat·ed**, **·cat·ing 1** To treat medicinally. **2** To tincture or impregnate with medicine. [<L *medicatus,* pp. of *medicare* heal <*medicus* a physician] — **med′i·ca′tive, med′i·ca·to′ry** (-kə·tôr′ē, -tō′rē) *adj.*

med·i·ca·tion (med′ə·kā′shən) *n.* **1** Any substance used to treat disease, heal wounds, etc.; a medicine. **2** The act or process of medicating.

me·dic·i·nal (mə·dis′ə·nəl) *adj.* Adapted to cure or mitigate disease. — **me·dic′i·nal·ly** *adv.*

med·i·cine (med′ə·sin) *n.* **1** A substance possessing, or reputed to possess, curative or remedial properties. **2** The healing art; the science of the preservation of health and of treating disease for the purpose of cure, specifically, as distinguished from surgery or obstetrics. **3** Among North American Indians, any agent or influence used to prevent or cure ills or to invoke supernatural protection or aid, varying from actual remedies (cinchona, etc.) to fetishes, prayers, and symbolic rites (**medicine dance, medicine song,** etc.); specifically, among the Algonquians,

any mystery. See MANITO. **4** *Colloq.* Something distasteful or unpleasant: to give someone a dose of his own *medicine.* **5** *Obs.* Something used for other than healing purposes, as the philosopher's stone, elixirs, poisons, love philters, etc. — **to take one's medicine** To endure necessary hardship, discomfort, or punishment, or to do something unpleasant but required. [<L *medicina* <*medicus* physician <*mederi* heal]

medicine ball A large, heavy, leather–covered ball, thrown and caught for physical exercise.

medicine lodge A lodge in a North American Indian village, used for ritualistic, religious ceremonies.

medicine man Among North American Indians, one professing supernatural powers of healing and of invoking the spirits; a shaman.

medico– *combining form* Pertaining to medical science and: *medico–legal.* Also, before vowels, **medic–.** [<L *medicus* a physician]

me·di·e·val (mē′dē·ē′vəl, med′ē-) *adj.* Belonging to or descriptive or characteristic of the Middle Ages: also spelled *mediaeval.* [<L *medius* middle + *aevum* age] — **me′di·e′val·ly** *adv.*

me·di·e·val·ism (mē′dē·ē′vəl·iz′əm, med′ē-) *n.* The spirit or practices of the Middle Ages; the flavor or general tone of medieval life; devotion to the institutions, ideas, or traits of the Middle Ages; also, any custom, idea, etc., surviving from the Middle Ages. — **me′di·e′val·ist** *n.*

Me·di·na (mə·dē′nə) A Moslem holy city in Hejaz, western Saudi Arabia; goal of Mohammed's Hegira and the place of his tomb.

medio– *combining form* Middle. Also, before vowels, **medi–.** [<L *medius* middle]

me·di·o·cre (mē′dē·ō′kər, mē′dē·ō′kər) *adj.* Of only middle quality; ordinary; commonplace. [<L *mediocris* <*medius* middle]

me·di·oc·ri·ty (mē′dē·ok′rə·tē) *n. pl.* **·ties 1** Commonplace ability or condition. **2** A commonplace person.

med·i·tate (med′ə·tāt) *v.* **·tat·ed**, **·tat·ing** *v.i.* To engage in continuous and contemplative thought; muse; cogitate. — *v.t.* To think about doing; plan; intend: to *meditate* mischief. See synonyms under CONSIDER, DELIBERATE, MUSE. [<L *meditatus,* pp. of *meditari* muse, ponder] — **med′i·tat′er, med′i·ta′tor** *n.* — **med′i·ta′tive** *adj.* — **med′i·ta′tive·ly** *adv.*

med·i·ta·tion (med′ə·tā′shən) *n.* The act of meditating; the turning or revolving of a subject in the mind; continuous thought; contemplation. See synonyms under REFLECTION, THOUGHT.

med·i·ter·ra·ne·an (med′ə·tə·rā′nē·ən) *adj.* Enclosed nearly or wholly by land, as a sea or other large body of water; landlocked. [<L *medius* middle + *terra* earth]

Med·i·ter·ra·ne·an (med′ə·tə·rā′nē·ən) *adj.* **1** Of or pertaining to the Mediterranean Sea. **2** Inhabiting the shores of the Mediterranean. — *n.* **1** The Mediterranean Sea. **2** One who lives in a Mediterranean country, or belongs to the Mediterranean race. — **Key of the Mediterranean** Gibraltar.

Mediterranean Sea An arm of the Atlantic Ocean comprising a great inland sea between Europe, Asia Minor, and Africa; 965,000 square miles.

me·di·um (mē′dē·əm) *n. pl.* **·di·ums** (*always for def 5*) or **me·di·a** (-dē·ə) **1** An intermediate quality, degree, or condition; mean. **2** A surrounding or enveloping element; condition of life; environment. **3** Any substance, as air, through or in which something may move or an effect be produced: Air is a *medium* of sound. **4** An intermediate means or agency; instrument: Radio is an advertising *medium.* **5** A person believed to be in communication with or controlled by the personality of someone deceased. **6** In painting, a liquid which gives fluency to the pigment. **7** A mathematical mean. **8** *Bacteriol.* A substance sterilized by heat in which bacteria, viruses, and other micro–organisms are developed: also **culture medium. 9** A size of paper, usually 18 x 23 inches, between demy and royal. — **circulating medium** A money currency. — *adj.* **1** Intermediate in quantity, quality, position, size, or degree; middle. **2** Mediocre. [<L, orig. neut. sing. of *medius* middle]

med·lar (med′lər) *n.* **1** A small, European tree (*Mespilus germanica*) of the rose family. **2** Its edible fruit, hard and bitter when ripe, but agreeably acid when it begins to decay. [<OF *medler*, var. of *meslier* <*mesle* fruit of the medlar <L *mespila* <Gk. *mespilē*]

med·ley (med′lē) *n.* **1** A mingled and confused mass of ingredients, usually incongruous; a heterogeneous group; jumble. **2** A composition of different songs or parts of songs arranged to run as a continuous whole. **3** A cloth woven from yarn of mingled colors: properly including blue and black. **4** In sports, a relay race in which all legs are not the same, as in distance or in swimming stroke used. —*adj.* **1** Mixed; confused. **2** Of mixed colors; motley. [<OF *medlee*, orig. fem. pp. of *medler*. See MEDDLE.]

me·dul·la (mə·dul′ə) *n. pl.* **·lae** (-ē) **1** *Anat.* **a** The inner portion of an organ or part, distinguished from the cortex. **b** The marrow of long bones. **c** The pith of a hair. **d** The spinal cord: also **medulla spi·na·lis** (spī′nā′lis). **2** The ganglion of the brain which, connecting with the spinal cord, controls breathing, swallowing, circulation, etc.: also **medulla ob·lon·ga·ta** (ob′lông·gä′tə). **3** *Bot.* The inner central columnar mass of parenchymatous tissue in the stems and roots of certain plants; also, in lichens, the middle layer of tissue composing the thallus, and in fungi proper, the central tissue within the rind of the fungus body. [< L <*medius* middle] —**med·ul·lar·y** (med′ə·ler′ē, mi·dul′ər·ē), **me·dul′lar** *adj.*

medullary rays 1 *Anat.* Extensions of the tubules of the kidney into the cortical substance. **2** *Bot.* The vertical bands or plates of cellular (parenchymatous) tissue, proceeding from the pith to the surface, and characteristic of the species of exogenous plants.

medullary sheath Myelin. See illustration under EXOGEN.

med·ul·lat·ed (med′ə·lā′tid, mi·dul′ā·tid) *adj.* Provided with a medullary sheath: said of nerve fibers.

me·du·sa (mə·dōō′sə, -zə, -dyōō′-) *n. pl.* **·sas** or **·sae** (-sē, -zē) A jellyfish. [<L] —**me·du′san** *adj.*

Me·du·sa (mə·dōō′sə, -zə, -dyōō′-) One of the Gorgons, killed by Perseus who gave her head to Athena.

me·du·soid (mə·dōō′soid, -zoid, -dyōō′-) *adj.* Resembling a medusa or jellyfish. —*n.* **1** A medusa–shaped gonophore of a hydrozoan. **2** Any medusa.

meek (mēk) *adj.* **1** Of gentle and long–suffering disposition. **2** Submissive; compliant; lacking spirit or backbone. **3** Humble; lowly. **4** *Obs.* Gentle; indulgent; kind; compassionate. See synonyms under HUMBLE, PACIFIC. —*adv.* Meekly. [<ON *miukr* gentle, soft] —**meek′ly** *adv.* —**meek′ness** *n.*

meer·schaum (mir′shəm, -shôm, -shoum) *n.* **1** A soft, light, compact, heat–resisting magnesium silicate, $H_4Mg_2Si_3O_{10}$, used for carving into tobacco pipes, cigar holders, and the like; sepiolite. It is closely related to talc. **2** A pipe made from this material. [<G <*meer* sea + *schaum* foam]

meet¹ (mēt) *v.* **met, meet·ing** *v.t.* **1** To come upon; encounter. **2** To make the acquaintance of; be introduced to. **3** To be at the place of arrival of: We *met* him at the station. **4** To come into contact, conjunction, or intersection with; join: where the path *meets* the road. **5** To keep an appointment with. **6** To come into the view, hearing, etc., of: A ghastly sight *met* our eyes. **7** To experience; undergo: to *meet* bad weather. **8** To oppose in battle; fight with. **9** To face or counter: to *meet* a blow with a blow. **10** To deal with; refute or cope with: to *meet* an accusation. **11** To comply with; act or result in conformity with, as expectations or wishes. **12** To pay, as a bill. —*v.i.* **13** To come together, as from opposite or different directions. **14** To come together in contact, conjunction, or intersection; join. **15** To assemble. **16** To make acquaintance or be introduced. **17** To come together in conflict or opposition; contend. **18** To agree. — **meet up with** *U.S. Colloq.* **1** To encounter. **2** To experience; undergo. —**to meet with 1** To come upon; encounter. **2** To deal or confer with. **3** To experience. **4** To be the sub-

ject or recipient of. —*n.* **1** An assembling together of huntsmen; also, the company or rendezvous. **2** An athletic contest: a track meet. ◆ Homophones: *meat, mete.* [OE *mētan*]

meet² (mēt) *adj.* Suitable, as to an occasion; adapted; fit. See synonyms under APPROPRIATE, BECOMING. —*adv. Obs.* Meetly; suitably. ◆ Homophones: *meat, mete.* [OE *gemǣte*] —**meet′ly** *adv.* —**meet′ness** *n.*

meet·ing (mē′ting) *n.* **1** A coming together. **2** An assembly of persons; specifically, a congregation of the Friends or Quakers; also, their meeting house. See synonyms under ASSEMBLY, COLLISION, COMPANY.

meeting house 1 A house used for public meetings, especially for public worship. **2** A place of worship used by the Friends.

mega– *combining form* **1** Great; large; powerful: *megaphone.* **2** In the metric system, electricity, etc., a million, or a million times, as in the following:

megabar	mega–erg	megampere
megacycle	megafarad	megavolt
megadyne	megameter	megohm

Also, before vowels, **meg–.** [<Gk.*megas* large]

meg·a·ce·phal·ic (meg′ə·sə·fal′ik) *adj.* Large-headed; specifically, having a cranial capacity above the average. Also **meg′a·ceph′a·lous** (-sef′ə·ləs).

meg·a·death (meg′ə·deth) *n.* The death of one million persons: a term used in reference to nuclear warfare. [<MEGA–+ DEATH]

meg·a·hertz (meg′ə·hûrtz′) *n.* A unit of frequency equal to one million cycles per second.

meg·a·lith (meg′ə·lith) *n. Archeol.* A huge stone, especially one used in prehistoric monuments. —**meg′a·lith′ic** *adj.*

megalo– *combining form* Big; indicating excessive or abnormal size: *megalocephalic.* Also, before vowels, **megal–.** [<Gk. *megas, megalou* big]

meg·a·lo·car·di·a (meg′ə·lō·kär′dē·ə) *n. Pathol.* Morbid enlargement of the heart. [<MEGALO– + Gk. *kardia* heart]

meg·a·lo·ceph·a·ly (meg′ə·lō·sef′ə·lē) *n.* **1** Unusual largeness of the head. **2** *Pathol.* Progressive enlargement of the cranium. Also **meg·a·lo·ce·pha′li·a** (-sə–fā′lē·ə). [<MEGALO– + Gk. *kephalē* head] —**meg·a·lo·ce·phal′ic** (-sə·fal′ik), **meg·a·lo·ceph′a·lous** *adj.*

meg·a·lo·ma·ni·a (meg′ə·lō·mā′nē·ə, -mān′yə) *n.* **1** *Psychiatry* A mental disorder in which the subject thinks himself great or exalted; delusions of grandeur, power, etc. **2** A tendency to magnify and exaggerate. —**meg·a·lo·ma′ni·ac** *adj. & n.* —**meg·a·lo·ma·ni′a·cal** (-mə·nī′ə·kəl) *adj.*

meg·a·lop·o·lis (meg′ə·lop′ə·lis) *n.* A densely populated urban area including one or more major cities. [<MEGALO– + Gk. *polis* city] —**meg·a·lo·pol′i·tan** (meg′ə·lō·pol′ə·tən) *adj. & n.*

meg·a·lop·si·a (meg′ə·lop′sē·ə) *n.* Macropsia.

Meg·a·lop·ter·a (meg′ə·lop′tər·ə) *n. pl.* An order of soft–bodied insects with large wings, long antennae, chewing mouth parts, and aquatic larvae; alderflies and hellgrammites or dobson flies. [<MEGALO– + Gk. *pteron* wing] —**meg·a·lop′ter·ous** *adj.*

meg·a·lo·saur (meg′ə·lə·sôr) *n. Paleontol.* A gigantic, terrestrial, carnivorous dinosaur (genus *Megalosaurus*) of the suborder *Therapoda.* [< MEGALO– + Gk. *sauros* lizard] —**meg·a·lo·saur′i·an** *adj. & n.*

meg·a·phone (meg′ə·fōn) *n.* A funnel–shaped device for amplifying or directing sound. —*v.t. & v.i.* **·phoned, ·phon·ing** To address or speak through a megaphone.

meg·a·pod (meg′ə·pod) *adj.* Having large feet, as certain Australian jungle birds.

meg·a·spore (meg′ə·spôr, -spōr) *n. Bot.* A large, asexual spore developed by certain seed plants, and giving rise always to a female gamete; the embryo sac of a seed plant: also called *macrospore.*

meg·a·spo·ro·phyll (meg′ə·spôr′ə·fil, -spō′rə-) *n. Bot.* A leaf or sporophyll which produces only megasporangia.

me·gass (mə·gas′, -gäs′) *n.* Bagasse. Also **megasse′.**

meg·a·there (meg′ə·thir) *n. Paleontol.* A gigan-

tic, extinct, slothlike edentate (genus *Megatherium*), associated with the Pleistocene in North America. [<MEGA– + Gk. *thērion* wild animal]

MEGATHERE
(Fossils indicate length up to 20 feet)

meg·a·therm (meg′ə·thûrm) *n.* A macrotherm.

meg·a·ton (meg′ə·tun′) *n.* A unit of nuclear explosive power equal to one million tons of TNT.

meg·a·tron (meg′ə·tron) *n.* A compact, sturdy type of vacuum tube designed to increase the range of wave frequencies and power in radio, television, and other electronic fields. [<MEGA– + (ELEC)TRON]

meg·a·vi·ta·min (meg′ə·vī′tə·min) *adj.* Pertaining to the treatment of disease by the administering of very large vitamin dosage: *megavitamin therapy.*

me·grim (mē′grim) *n.* **1** A headache confined to one side of the head, characterized by nausea and vomiting; migraine. **2** *pl.* Dulness; depression of spirits. **3** A whim or fad. [< F *migraine*]

mei·o·sis (mī·ō′sis) *n.* **1** *Biol.* That process in the division of germ cells by which the number of chromosomes is reduced from the double or *diploid* number typical of somatic cells to the halved or *haploid* number characteristic of gametes: distinguished from *mitosis:* also spelled *maiosis.* **2** In rhetoric, understatement, often giving the effect of irony or humor, by representing a fact, thing, deed, etc., as being smaller than it really is: also spelled *miosis.* [<Gk. *meiōsis* lessening] —**mei·ot′ic** (-ot′ik) *adj.*

Mé·ji·co (mā′hē·kō) The Spanish name for MEXICO.

Mek·ka (mek′ə) See MECCA.

mel (mel) *n.* Honey; especially the pure, clarified honey used in the preparation of certain drugs. [<L]

mel·a·mine (mel′ə·mēn, -min) *n. Chem.* A transparent, colorless, crystalline compound, $C_3N_3(NH_2)_3$, the amide of cyanuric acid: combined with cellulose pulp and formaldehyde, it produces a synthetic resin of good qualities. [< *mel(am)*, a chemical compound + AMINE]

melan– Var. of MELANO–.

mel·an·cho·li·a (mel′ən·kō′lē·ə) *n. Psychiatry* Mental disorder characterized by excessive brooding and depression of spirits: typical of manic–depressive psychoses. [<L. See MELANCHOLY.] —**mel′an·cho′li·ac** *adj. & n.*

mel·an·chol·y (mel′ən·kol′ē) *adj.* **1** Morbidly gloomy; sad; dejected. **2** Suggesting or promoting sadness. **3** Somberly thoughtful; pensive. —*n.* **1** Low spirits; despondency; depression. **2** Melancholia. **3** Pensive contemplation; serious and sober reflection. **4** *Archaic* The dark, acrid, and viscous substance once believed to be secreted by the kidneys and to be responsible for gloomy dejection of spirits; one of the humors. [<F *melancolie* <L *melancholia* <Gk. <*melas, -anos* black + *cholē* bile] —**mel′an·chol′ic** *adj.* —**mel′an·chol′i·cal·ly** *adv.*

mel·a·ne·mi·a (mel′ə·nē′mē·ə) *n. Pathol.* A morbid excess of black pigment in the blood: noted chiefly in pernicious anemia. Also **mel′·a·nae′mi·a.** [<MELAN– + Gk. *haima* blood] —**mel′a·ne′mic** *adj.*

Mel·a·ne·sia (mel′ə·nē′zhə, -shə) The islands of the western Pacific south of the Equator, comprising one of the three main divisions of the Pacific Islands; total, 60,000 square miles.

me·la·ni·an (mə·lā′nē·ən) *adj. Anthropol.* Having dark or black pigmentation: said of Negroes, Melanesians, etc. [<F *mélanien* <Gk. *melas, -anos* black]

me·lan·ic (mə·lan′ik) *adj.* 1 Relating to or resembling melanosis or melanism; melanoid. 2 Black; melanian.

mel·a·nin (mel′ə·nin) *n. Biochem.* The brownish-black pigment contained in animal tissues, as the skin and hair, formed by the action of the enzyme tyrosinase upon tyrosine.

mel·a·nism (mel′ə·niz′əm) *n.* 1 Abnormal development of dark coloring matter in the skin, feathers, etc.: opposed to *albinism.* 2 Excessive darkness, as of the eyes, hair, skin, etc., due to extreme pigmentation. — **mel′a·nis′tic** *adj.*

mel·a·nite (mel′ə·nīt) *n.* A black variety of garnet.

melano– *combining form* Black; dark-colored: *melanosis.* Also, before vowels, **melan–.** [< Gk. *melas, melanos* black]

mel·an·o·crat·ic (mel′ən·ō·krat′ik) *adj. Geol.* Of or pertaining to those igneous rocks characterized by a predominance of dark or ferromagnesian minerals: opposed to *leucocratic.*

mel·a·noid (mel′ə·noid) *adj.* 1 Looking black or having a dark appearance. 2 Of the nature of melanosis.

mel·a·no·ma (mel′ə·nō′mə) *n. Pathol.* A black-pigmented tumor. [<MELAN- + -OMA]

mel·a·no·sis (mel′ə·nō′sis) *n. Pathol.* An organic disease in which pigment is deposited in the skin and other tissues; black degeneration. — **mel′a·not′ic** (-not′ik) *adj.*

mel·a·nous (mel′ə·nəs) *adj.* Having dark or black skin and hair: opposed to *xanthous.*

mel·an·tha·ceous (mel′ən·thā′shəs) *adj.* Of or pertaining to a former family (*Melanthaceae*) of monocotyledonous plants in the lily order, distinguished from lilies by the absence of bulbs: it included plants of the genera *Colchicum* and *Veratrum.* [<NL <Gk. *melas, -anos* black + *anthos* flower]

mel·a·phyre (mel′ə·fīr) *n.* Any igneous porphyry with a dark groundmass. [<F <Gk. *melas* black + F (*por*)*phyre* porphyry]

Melba toast Thinly sliced bread toasted until brown and crisp.

meld (meld) *v.t. & v.i.* In pinochle and other card games, to announce or declare (a combination of cards in the hand), for inclusion in one's total score. — *n.* A group of cards to be declared, or the act of declaring them. [<G *melden* announce]

mê·lée (mā′lā, mā·lā′; *Fr.* me·lā′) *n.* A general hand-to-hand fight; an affray. [<F <OF *meslee,* var. of *medlee.* See MEDLEY.]

me·li·a·ceous (mē′lē·ā′shəs) *adj.* Of or pertaining to a family (*Meliaceae*) of trees and shrubs of the order *Geraniales,* mainly native to the warm portions of Asia and America; the mahogany family, including the Spanish cedar (genus *Cedrela*). [<NL <Gk. *melia* an ash tree]

mel·ic (mel′ik) *adj.* Suitable for singing, or meant to be sung: said of poetry. In ancient Greek poetry it is the successor of the elegiac and iambic forms of verse and includes the Aeolian or single-voice lyric, and the Dorian or choral lyric. — *n.* Melic poetry. Compare ELEGIAC and IAMBIC. [<Gk. *melikos* < *melos* song]

mel·i·lot (mel′ə·lot) *n.* Any one of several sweet-smelling, cloverlike herbs of the genus *Melilotus,* especially the **sweet clover** (*M. officinalis*) and the **Bokhara clover** (*M. alba*). [<OF *melilot* <LL *melilotos* <Gk. *melilōtos* < *meli* honey + *lōtos* a lotus]

mel·i·nite (mel′ə·nīt) *n.* An explosive of great power and similar to lyddite, yielded by combining guncotton with picric acid. [<Gk. *mēlinos* yellow]

mel·io·rate (mēl′yə·rāt) *v.t. & v.i.* **·rat·ed, ·rat·ing** To improve, as in quality or condition; ameliorate. See synonyms under AMEND. [<LL *melioratus,* pp. of *meliorare* improve < *melior* better] — **mel′io·ra·ble** *adj.* — **mel′io·ra′tive** *adj.*

mel·io·ra·tion (mēl′yə·rā′shən) *n.* 1 A betterment. 2 *Ling.* An improvement or elevation in the meaning of a word, as in *nice* (formerly "foolish"): opposed to *pejoration.*

mel·io·rism (mēl′yə·riz′əm) *n.* 1 The improvement of society by bettering man's physical being and environment instead of by ethical or religious means. 2 A modified optimism, teaching that the world is neither the best nor the worst possible, but is susceptible of improvement through the increase of good as man evolves. Compare OPTIMISM and PESSIMISM. [<L *melior* better] — **mel′io·rist** *adj. & n.* — **mel′io·ris′tic** *adj.*

mel·ior·i·ty (mēl·yôr′ə·tē, -yor′-) *n.* The state of being better; superiority.

mel·is·mat·ic (mel′is·mat′ik) *adj. Music* Florid and ornate in phrasing. [<NL *melisma* song <Gk.]

mel·lif·er·ous (mə·lif′ər·əs) *adj.* Producing or bearing honey. Also **mel·lif′ic.** [<L *mellifer* honey-bearing < *mel* honey + *ferre* bear]

mel·lif·lu·ous (mə·lif′lōō·əs) *adj.* 1 Sweetly or smoothly flowing; dulcet; honeyed. 2 Flowing like or as with honey. Also **mel·lif′lu·ent.** [<L *mellifluus* < *mel* honey + *fluere* flow] — **mel·lif′lu·ence, mel·lif′lu·ous·ness** *n.* — **mel·lif′lu·ous·ly, mel·lif′lu·ent·ly** *adv.*

mel·liph·a·gous (mə·lif′ə·gəs) *adj.* Feeding on honey, as certain animals and birds: often **mel·liv′o·rous** (-liv′ər·əs). Also **me·liph′a·gous.** [<Gk. *meli* honey + *phagein* to eat]

mel·lite (mel′īt) *n.* 1 Any medicated preparation containing honey. 2 The mineral honeystone. [<L *mel* honey + -ITE¹]

mel·lo·phone (mel′ō·fōn) *n.* A circular althorn. [<MELLOW + -PHONE]

mel·low (mel′ō) *adj.* 1 Soft by reason of ripeness; well-matured; not bitter or acid: *mellow* fruit; *mellow* wine. 2 Of a rich or delicate quality: *mellow* tints; *mellow* tones. 3 Companionable; jolly. 4 Made jovial by liquor. 5 Soft and friable, as soil. See synonyms under RIPE. — *v.t. & v.i.* To make or become mellow; ripen; soften. [ME *melwe,* ? <OE *melu* meal. Akin to Flemish *meluw* soft, tender.] — **mel′low·ly** *adv.* — **mel′low·ness** *n.*

me·lo·de·on (mə·lō′dē·ən) *n.* A small reed organ or harmonium. [<Gk. *melōdia* melody]

me·lo·di·a (mə·lō′dē·ə) *n.* An organ stop having wood pipes and a tone nearly like the clarabella; a stopped diapason. [<LL]

me·lod·ic (mə·lod′ik) *adj.* Pertaining to or containing melody; melodious. — **me·lod′i·cal·ly** *adv.*

me·lod·ics (mə·lod′iks) *n. pl.* (*construed as singular*) The branch of musical science relating to the pitch of tones and the principles of melody.

me·lo·di·ous (mə·lō′dē·əs) *adj.* Agreeable to the ear; producing or characterized by melody; tuneful. — **me·lo′di·ous·ly** *adv.* — **me·lo′di·ous·ness** *n.*

mel·o·dize (mel′ə·dīz) *v.* **·dized, ·diz·ing** *v.t.* 1 To make melodious. 2 To compose melody for. — *v.i.* 3 To make melody or melodies. — **mel′o·diz′er, mel′o·dist** *n.*

mel·o·dra·ma (mel′ə·drä′mə, -dram′ə) *n.* 1 Originally, a drama with a romantic story or plot, sensational incidents, and usually including some music and song. 2 Any sensational and emotional drama, usually having a happy ending. 3 Behavior or language of a theatrical nature. [<F *mélodrame* <Gk. *melos* song + *drama* drama] — **mel′o·dram′a·tist** *n.*

mel·o·dra·mat·ic (mel′ə·drə·mat′ik) *adj.* Of, pertaining to, or like melodrama; sensational. — **mel′o·dra·mat′i·cal·ly** *adv.*

mel·o·dra·mat·ics (mel′ə·drə·mat′iks) *n. pl.* Melodramatic behavior.

mel·o·dy (mel′ə·dē) *n. pl.* **·dies** 1 Pleasing sounds or an agreeable succession of such sounds. 2 Musical sounds or quality, as in the words of a poem. 3 A poem written or suitable for being set to music. 4 *Music* a A succession of simple tones, usually in the same key, constituting, in combination, a rhythmic whole: distinguished as a formal element from *harmony* and *rhythm.* b The chief part or voice in a harmonic composition; the air. [<OF *melodie* <LL *melodia* <Gk. *melōidia* choral song < *melōidos* melodious < *melos* song + *aoidos* singer]

Synonyms: harmony, music, symphony, unison. *Harmony* is simultaneous; *melody* is successive; *harmony* is the correspondence of two or more notes sounded at once, *melody* the succession of a number of notes continuously following one another. A *melody*

may be wholly in one part; *harmony* must be of two or more parts. Accordant notes of different pitch sounded simultaneously produce *harmony; unison* is the simultaneous sounding of two or more notes of the same pitch. Tones sounded at the interval of an octave are also said to be in *unison,* but this is not literally exact. *Music* may denote the simplest *melody* or the most complex and perfect *harmony.* A *symphony* (apart from its technical orchestral sense) is any pleasing consonance of musical sounds, vocal or instrumental. Compare METER², SONG, TUNE. *Antonyms:* discord, dissonance.

Me·lo·i·dae (mə·lō′ə·dē) *n. pl.* A family of coleopterous insects with plump cylindrical bodies; the blister beetles. [<NL <*meloē* oil beetle; ult. origin unknown] — **mel·oid** (mel′oid) *adj. & n.*

Mel·o·lon·thi·nae (mel′ə·lon·thī′nē) *n. pl.* A subfamily of beetles (family *Scarabaeidae*) including the cockchafers and June beetles. [<NL <Gk. *mēlolonthē* cockchafer] — **mel′o·lon′thine** (-thin, -thīn) *adj. & n.*

mel·o·ma·ni·a (mel′ə·mā′nē·ə, -mān′yə) *n.* An excessive or morbid fondness for music. [<Gk. *melos* song + -MANIA] — **mel′o·ma′ni·ac** *n.*

mel·on (mel′ən) *n.* A trailing plant of the gourd family, or its fruit. There are two genera, the muskmelon and the watermelon, each with numerous varieties. [<F <LL *melo, melonis* <L *melopepo* <Gk. *mēlopepōn* apple-shaped melon < *mēlon* apple + *pepōn* melon]

mel·on·ite (mel′ən·īt) *n.* A reddish-white, granular nickel telluride, Ni₂Te₃; telluronickel. [from *Melones* mine, Calif., where found]

melt (melt) *v.t. & v.i.* **melt·ed, melt·ed** (*Archaic* **mol·ten**), **melt·ing** 1 To reduce or change from a solid to a liquid state by heat; fuse. 2 To dissolve, as in water. 3 To disappear or cause to disappear; dissipate: often with *away.* 4 To blend by imperceptible degrees; merge. 5 To make or become softened in feeling or attitude. — *n.* 1 Something melted. 2 A single operation of fusing. 3 The amount of a single fusing. [OE *meltian.* Akin to MALT.] — **melt′a·ble** *adj.* — **melt′a·bil′i·ty** *n.* — **melt′er** *n.*

Synonyms (*verb*): dissolve, fuse, liquefy, thaw. *Antonyms:* congeal, freeze, harden, indurate, solidify.

melt·age (melt′ij) *n.* 1 The process of melting. 2 The amount resulting from melting.

melting point The temperature at which a specified solid substance becomes liquid.

melting pot 1 A vessel in which things are melted; crucible. 2 A country, city, or region in which immigrants of various racial and cultural backgrounds are assimilated.

mel·ton (mel′tən) *n.* A heavy woolen cloth with a short nap: used for overcoats. [after *Melton* Mowbray, England]

melt·wa·ter (melt′wô′tər, -wot′ər) *n.* The whitish water from melting glaciers.

Mel·ville (mel′vil), **Herman,** 1819–91, U.S. novelist and poet.

mem (mem) *n.* The thirteenth Hebrew letter. See ALPHABET. [<Hebrew *mēm,* lit., water]

mem·ber (mem′bər) *n.* 1 A person belonging to an incorporated or organized body, society, etc.: a *Member* of Congress, a *member* of a club. 2 A limb or other functional organ of an animal body. 3 A part or element of a structural or composite whole, distinguishable from other parts or elements, as a part of a sentence, syllogism, period, or discourse, or any necessary part of a structural framework, as a tie rod, post, or strut in the truss of a bridge. 4 A subordinate classificatory part: A species is a *member* of a genus. 5 *Bot.* A part of a plant considered with reference to position and structure, but regardless of function. 6 *Math.* a Either side of an equation. b A set of figures or symbols forming part of a formula or number. c Any one of the items forming a series. See synonyms under PART, TERM. [<OF *membre* <L *membrum* limb]

mem·ber·ship (mem′bər·ship) *n.* 1 The state of being a member. 2 The members of an organization, collectively.

mem·brane (mem′brān) *n.* 1 A thin, pliable, sheetlike layer of animal or vegetable tissue serving as a cover, connection, or lining. 2 A piece of parchment. [<L *membrana* skin, membrane < *membrum* member] — **mem′bra·nous** (-brə·nəs), **mem′bra·na′ceous** (-nā′shəs) *adj.*

membrane bone *Anat.* A bone developed in membrane, as one of those of the vault of the skull.

me·men·to (mə·men′tō) *n.* *pl.* **·toes** or **·tos** **1** A hint or reminder to awaken memory; souvenir; memorial. **2** *Eccl.* Either of the two prayers in the canon of the mass in which the living and the departed are respectively mentioned. [< L, remember, imperative of *meminisse* remember]

mem·o (mem′ō) *n.* *pl.* **mem·os** *Colloq.* A memorandum.

mem·oir (mem′wär) *n.* **1** An account of something deemed worthy of record; especially, one addressed to a public institution or scientific society. **2** *pl.* The reminiscences of a person, either general or relating to a particular period, published together. **3** A biographic memorial. See synonyms under HISTORY. [< F *mémoire* < L *memoria* memory. Doublet of MEMORY.] — **mem′oir·ist** *n.*

mem·o·ra·bil·i·a (mem′ə·rə·bil′ē·ə) *n. pl.* Things worthy of memory, or an account of them. [< L, neut. pl. of *memorabilis* memorable]

mem·o·ra·ble (mem′ər·ə·bəl) *adj.* Worthy to be remembered; noteworthy. [< L *memorabilis*] — **mem′o·ra·bil′i·ty, mem′o·ra·ble·ness** *n.* — **mem′o·ra·bly** *adv.*

mem·o·ran·dum (mem′ə·ran′dəm) *n.* *pl.* **·dums** or **·da** (-də) **1** Something to be remembered; hence, a brief note of a thing or things to be remembered. **2** *Law* A brief written outline of the terms of a transaction. **3** An informal letter. **4** A statement of goods sent from a consignor to a consignee. See synonyms under RECORD. [< L, a thing to be remembered]

me·mo·ri·al (mə·môr′ē·əl, -mō′rē-) *adj.* **1** Commemorating the memory of a deceased person or of any event. **2** Contained within one's memory; distinguished from *immemorial.* — *n.* **1** Something designed to keep in remembrance a person, event, etc. **2** A summary or presentation of facts usually made the ground of a petition or remonstrance. **3** *Law* A memorandum filed for record. See synonyms under HISTORY, RECORD, TRACE. [< OF < L *memorialis*]

Memorial Day Decoration Day.

me·mo·ri·al·ist (mə·môr′ē·əl·ist, -mō′rē-) *n.* **1** One who writes memoirs. **2** One who writes, signs, or presents a memorial.

me·mo·ri·al·ize (mə·môr′ē·əl·īz′, -mō′rē-) *v.t.* **·ized, ·iz·ing** **1** To commemorate. **2** To present a memorial to. Also *Brit.* **me·mo′ri·al·ise′.** — **me·mo′ri·al·i·za′tion** *n.*

mem·o·rize (mem′ə·rīz) *v.t.* **·rized, ·riz·ing** To commit to memory; learn by heart. See synonyms under LEARN. — **mem′o·ri·za′tion** *n.* — **mem′o·riz′er** *n.*

mem·o·ry (mem′ər·ē) *n.* *pl.* **·ries** **1** The mental process or faculty of representing in consciousness an act, experience, or impression, with recognition that it belongs to time past. **2** The experiences of the mind taken in the aggregate, and considered as influencing present and future behavior. **3** The accuracy and ease with which a person can retain and recall past experiences. **4** That which is remembered, as an act, event, person, or thing. **5** The period of time covered by the faculty of remembrance: beyond the *memory* of man. **6** The state of being remembered; posthumous reputation: The *memory* of Washington will endure. **7** That which reminds; a memorial; a memento. **8** The information storage unit of a computer. [< OF *memorie* < L *memoria* < *memor* mindful. Doublet of MEMOIR.]

Synonyms: recollection, remembrance, reminiscence, retrospect, retrospection. *Memory* is the faculty by which knowledge is retained or recalled; *memory* is a retention of knowledge within the grasp of the mind, while *remembrance* is the having what is known consciously before the mind. Either may be voluntary or involuntary. *Recollection* involves volition, the mind making a distinct effort to recall something, or fixing the attention actively upon it when recalled. *Reminiscence* is a half-dreamy *memory* of scenes or events long past; *retrospection* is a distinct turning of the mind back upon the past, bringing long periods under survey. *Antonyms:* forgetfulness, oblivion, obliviousness.

men·ace (men′is) *v.* **·aced, ·ac·ing** *v.t.* **1** To threaten with evil or harm. **2** To make threats of. — *v.i.* **3** To make threats; appear threatening. See synonyms under THREATEN. — *n.* A threat; something which threatens; an impending evil. [< OF *manace* < L *minacia* < *minax, -acis* threatening < *minari* threaten] — **men′ac·er** *n.* — **men′ac·ing·ly** *adv.*

me·nac·me (mə·nak′mē) *n.* *Physiol.* The reproductive period of a woman's life, during which menstruation occurs. [< Gk. *mēn* month + *akmē*peak]

mé·nage (mā·näzh′, *Fr.* mā·nazh′) *n.* **1** The persons of a household, collectively; a domestic establishment. **2** Household management. Also **me·nage′.** [< F < L *mansio, -onis* house. Doublet of MANSION.]

me·nag·er·ie (mə·naj′ər·ē) *n.* **1** A collection of wild animals kept for exhibition. **2** The enclosure in which they are kept. [< F]

me·nar·che (mə·när′kē) *n.* *Physiol.* The commencement of menstrual function in women. [< Gk. *mēn* month + *archē* beginning]

mend (mend) *v.t.* **1** To make sound or serviceable again by repairing; patch. **2** To correct errors or faults in; reform; improve: *Mend* your ways. **3** To correct (some defect). — *v.i.* **4** To become better, as in health; improve. — *n.* **1** The act of repairing or patching. **2** A mended portion of a garment. — **on the mend** Recovering health; recuperating; convalescing. [Aphetic form of AMEND] — **mend′a·ble** *adj.* — **mend′er** *n.*

men·da·cious (men·dā′shəs) *adj.* **1** Addicted to lying; falsifying. **2** Characterized by deceit; false. [< L *mendax, -acis* lying] — **men·da′ci·ous·ly** *adv.* — **men·da′cious·ness** *n.*

men·dac·i·ty (men·das′ə·tē) *n.* Lying; falsity. [< L *mendacitas, -tatis*]

Men·del (men′dəl), **Gregor Johann,** 1822–1884, Austrian monk and botanist; founder of the science of genetics.

men·de·le·vi·um (men′də·lē′vē·əm) *n.* *Chem.* The short-lived radioactive element (symbol Md) of atomic number 101 and mass number 256. [after Dmitri Ivanovich *Mendeleyev*]

Men·de·li·an (men·dē′lē·ən) *adj.* **1** Of or pertaining to Gregor Mendel. **2** Relating to or in accordance with Mendel's laws.

Men·del·ism (men′dəl·iz′əm) *n.* The theory of heredity as put forth by Mendel. Also **Men·de′li·an·ism.**

Mendel's laws *Genetics* Principles formulated by Gregor Mendel as a result of experiments in breeding garden peas. They state that certain contrasting characters of cross-bred parents, as color height, etc., are inherited by the hybrid offspring through determining factors which act as units, and that subsequent cross-bred generations manifest these characters in varying combinations from dominant to recessive, each combination being present in a definite proportion of the total number of offspring.

men·di·cant (men′də·kənt) *adj.* **1** Begging; depending on alms for a living. **2** Pertaining to or like a beggar. — *n.* **1** A beggar. **2** A begging friar. [< L *mendicans, -antis,* ppr. of *mendicare* beg < *mendicus* needy] — **men′di·can·cy, men·dic·i·ty** (men·dis′ə·tē) *n.*

men·di·go (men′di·gō) The splake.

mend·ing (men′ding) *n.* Articles to be mended.

men·ha·den (men·hād′n) *n.* A herringlike fish (*Brevoortia tyrannus*) found along the North Atlantic coast of the United States: it is the source of menhaden oil, used in industry, and of fertilizer. [Alter. of Algonquian *munnawhat* fertilizer]

men·hir (men′hir) *n.* A prehistoric sepulchral or battle monument consisting of a single tall stone, usually left rough. [< F < Celtic (Breton) *men* stone + *hir* long]

me·ni·al (mē′nē·əl, mēn′yəl) *adj.* **1** Pertaining or appropriate to servants. **2** Servile. See synonyms under BASE[2] — *n.* **1** One doing servile work: generally in contempt. **2** Figuratively, a person of low or servile nature. [< AF < OF *meisniee, maisnie* household < LL *mansionata* < L *mansio* house] — **me′ni·al·ly** *adv.*

Mé·nière's disease (mā·nyârz′) *Pathol.* Progressive deafness of one ear, with vertigo, tinnitus, nausea, and vomiting. [after Prosper *Ménière,* 1799–1862, French physician]

me·nin·ges (mə·nin′jez) *n. pl.* of **me·ninx** (mē′

ningks) *Anat.* The membranes (the dura mater, pia mater, and arachnoid) enveloping the brain and spinal cord. [< NL < Gk. *mēninx, mēningos* membrane] — **me·nin′ge·al** *adj.*

men·in·gi·tis (men′ən·jī′tis) *n.* *Pathol.* Inflammation of the enveloping membranes of an organ, especially those of the brain and spinal cord. Certain forms are caused by infection with diplococcus bacterium (*Neisseria intracellularis*). — **men·in·git′ic** (-jit′ik) *adj.*

me·nis·cus (mə·nis′kəs) *n.* *pl.* **·nis·cus·es** or **·nis·ci** (-nis′ī) **1** Any crescent-shaped body. **2** *Optics* A lens convex on one side and concave on the other. **3** *Anat.* A disklike body of fibro-cartilage found in some joints of the body exposed to concussion. **4** *Physics* The surface or upper part of a liquid column made convex or concave by capillarity. [< L < Gk. *mēniskos* crescent, dim. of *mēnē* the moon]

MENISCUS LENSES

men·i·sper·ma·ceous (men′ē·spər·mā′shəs) *adj.* Designating a family (*Menispermaceae*) of mostly tropical, woody or herbaceous climbing plants having alternate leaves and small dioecious flowers, and yielding substances of narcotic and toxic properties; the moonseed family. [< NL *menispermaceae* < Gk. *mēnē* moon + *sperma* seed]

Men·non·ite (men′ən·īt) *n.* A member of a Protestant denomination that grew out of the Anabaptist movement in the 16th century, and still flourishes in Europe and the United States: named after Menno Simons, 1496?–1561, a leader of the sect in the Netherlands. They are opposed to the taking of oaths, the holding of public office, and military service.

me·no (mā′nō) *adv.* *Music* Less. [< Ital. < L *minus*]

me·nol·o·gy (mə·nol′ə·jē) *n.* **1** A calendar of the months; especially, one having a record of events by month. **2** A register or collection of lives of the saints arranged according to months and days of the month, as in the Greek Church. [< Gk. *mēn* month + -LOGY]

me·nom·i·nee (mə·nom′ə·nē) *n.* *Canadian* Wild rice. [< Algonquian (Cree)]

men·o·pause (men′ə·pôz) *n.* *Physiol.* Final cessation of the menses; change of life: opposed to *menarche.* [< Gk. *mēn* month + *pauein* cause to cease]

men·or·rha·gi·a (men′ə·rā′jē·ə) *n.* *Pathol.* Excessive menstruation [< Gk. *mēn* month + -RRHAGIA]

men·sal[1] (men′səl) *adj.* Belonging to or used at the table. [< L *mensalis* < *mensa* table]

men·sal[2] (men′səl) *adj.* Monthly. [< L *mensis* month]

mensch (mensh) *n. pl.* **men·schen** *Colloq.* A genuine, respected, honored person. [< Yiddish < Ger., person]

men·ses (men′sēz) *n. pl.* *Physiol.* A periodical bloody flow from the uterus of a female mammal, resulting when an ovum is not fertilized, and occuring in women about once every lunar month; the menstrual flow. [< L, pl. of *mensis* month]

Men·she·vik (men′shə·vik) *n. pl.* **·vi·ki** (-vē′kē) **·viks** A member of the conservative element in the Russian Social Democratic Party. Compare BOLSHEVIK, MAXIMALIST. Also **Men′she·vist.** [< Russian *menshe* smaller, minority] — **Men′she·vism** *n.*

men·stru·al (men′strōō·əl) *adj.* **1** *Physiol.* Pertaining to the menses or to a menstruum. **2** Continuing a month; occurring monthly. Also **men′stru·ous.**

men·stru·ate (men′strōō·āt) *v.i.* **·at·ed, ·at·ing** To discharge the menses. [< L *menstruatus,* pp. of *menstruare menstruus* monthy < *mensis* month] — **men′stru·a′tion** *n.*

men·stru·um (men′strōō·əm) *n.* *pl.* **·stru·ums** or **·stru·a** (-strōō·ə) The medium in which a substance is dissolved; a solvent.

men·su·ra·ble (men′shər·ə·bəl) *adj.* **1** That can be measured. **2** Mensural. [< LL *mensurabilis* < *mensurare* measure < *mensura.* See MEASURE.] — **men′su·ra·bil′i·ty** *n.*

men·su·ral (men′shər·əl) *adj.* **1** Pertaining to measure. **2** *Music* Characterized by a fixed rhythm and measure.

men·su·rate (men'shə·rāt) v.t. **·rat·ed, ·rat·ing** *Rare* To measure the dimensions or quantity of. [< L *mensuratus*, pp. of *mensurare* < *mensura*. See MEASURE.]

men·su·ra·tion (men'shə·rā'shən) n. **1** The act, art, or process of measuring. **2** The branch of mathematical science that has to do with measurement, as of lines, surfaces, or volume. **3** The result of measuring; measure.
[< LL *mensuratio, -onis*] — **men'su·ra'tive** adj.

-ment suffix of nouns **1** The concrete result of; a thing produced by: *achievement*. **2** The instrument or means of: *atonement*. **3** The process or action of: *government*. **4** The quality, condition, or state of being: *astonishment*. [< F < L *-mentum*]

men·tal[1] (men'təl) adj. **1** Pertaining to the mind: contrasted with *corporeal*. **2** Effected by or due to the mind, especially without the aid of written symbols. [< F < LL *mentalis* < L *mens, mentis* mind] — **men'tal·ly** adv.

men·tal[2] (men'təl) adj. Of, pertaining to, or situated near the chin: the *mental* point. — n. A plate or scale of the chin, as in snakes. [< L *mentum* chin]

mental age See under AGE.

mental blindness A mental condition in which images conveyed by the optic nerves are not properly recognized: also called *mind-blindness, psychic blindness.*

mental deafness A form of deafness in which sounds and words are heard but cannot be interpreted: also called *mind-deafness, psychic deafness.*

mental deficiency *Psychiatry* Lack of one or more mental capacities and functions present in the normal individual, usually to the point of disqualifying from full participation in ordinary life; feeble-mindedness. The principal types, in order of increasing deficiency, are moronism, imbecility, and idiotism.

mental healing The curing of any disorder, ailment, or disease by concentrating the mind either directly on the healing forces in nature, or on the denial of the discomforts experienced.

mental hygiene The scientific study and rational application of all methods that will restore, preserve, promote, and improve mental health, especially in relation to the normal functioning of the personality as a whole.

men·tal·i·ty (men·tal'ə·tē) n. pl. **·ties 1** The sum of the mental faculties or powers; mental activity. **2** Cast or habit of mind.

men·tha·ceous (men·thā'shəs) adj. Designating or pertaining to a genus (*Mentha*) of odorous perennial herbs of the mint family, with opposite leaves and small flowers, including the peppermint, spearmint, etc. [< L *mentha* mint + -ACEOUS]

men·thane (men'thān) n. *Chem.* Any one of three isomeric, saturated hydrocarbons, $C_{10}H_{20}$, corresponding to cymenes: parent substance for several of the terpenes. [< MENTHOL + -ANE[2]]

men·thene (men'thēn) n. *Chem.* A colorless, liquid, oily hydrocarbon, $C_{10}H_{18}$, derived from the oil of peppermint. [< L *mentha* mint + -ENE]

men·thol (men'thōl, -thol, -thol) n. *Chem.* A white, waxy, crystalline alcohol, $C_{10}H_{19}OH$, obtained from and having the odor of oil of peppermint: used as a flavoring agent, in perfumery, and in medicine as an anodyne for neuralgia and similar ailments. [< L *mentha* mint + -OL[1]]

men·tho·lat·ed (men'thə·lā'tid) adj. Treated with, containing, or impregnated with menthol.

men·ti·cide (men'tə·sīd) n. The undermining and destruction of a person's mental powers by deliberate intent and with the use of all available psychological means. [< L *mens, mentis* mind + -CIDE]

men·tion (men'shən) v.t. To speak of incidentally or briefly; refer to in passing; specify or name. See synonyms under ALLUDE, INFORM. — n. The act of mentioning; casual allusion; notice: used especially in the phrase *to make mention of*. [< OF < L *mentio, -onis* < *mens, mentis* mind] — **men'tion·a·ble** adj. — **men'tion·er** n.

men·tor (men'tər, -tôr) n. A wise and trusted teacher, guide, and friend; an elderly monitor or adviser. [< MENTOR] — **men·to'ri·al** (-tôr'ē- əl, -tō'rē-) adj.

Men·tor (men'tər, -tôr) In the *Odyssey*, the sage guardian of Telemachus, appointed by Odysseus before he departed for the Trojan War. [< Gk., lit., adviser]

men·tum (men'təm) n. **1** The chin. **2** *Entomol.* The distal sclerite of the labium or lower lip of insects.

men·u (men'yōō, mān'-; *Fr.* mə·nü') n. A bill of fare or the dishes included in it. [< F, small, detailed < L *minutus*. See MINUTE[2].]

me·per·i·dine hydrochloride (mə·per'ə·dēn, -din) A white, odorless, crystalline compound, $C_{15}H_{22}ClO_2$, used in medicine as an analgesic and sedative; Demerol.

Me·phis·to·phe·le·an (mə·fis'tə·fē'lē·ən) adj. Of, pertaining to, or like Mephistopheles; cynical; crafty; sardonic; fiendish. Also **Me·phis'to·phe'li·an.**

Meph·is·toph·e·les (mef'is·tof'ə·lēz) **1** In medieval legend, a devil to whom Faust sold his soul for wisdom and power. **2** A crafty, sardonic fiend; a diabolical person. Also **Me·phis·to** (mə·fis'tō).

me·phit·ic (mə·fit'ik) adj. Poisonous; pestilential; foul; noxious. Also **me·phit'i·cal.**

me·phi·tis (mə·fī'tis) n. **1** A noxious exhalation caused by the decomposition of organic remains. **2** A pestilential or deadly gas, as from a cave or mine. Also **me·phi'tism.** [< L]

Me·rak (mē'rak) The star Beta in the constellation Ursa Major; the smaller of the two stars composing the Pointers toward the pole-star.

mer·can·tile (mûr'kən·til, -tīl) adj. **1** Pertaining to or characteristic of merchants. **2** Conducted or acting on business principles; commercial. [< F < Ital. < L *mercans, -antis*, pp. of *mercari* traffic. See MERCHANT.]

mercantile agency An institution which collects, records, and furnishes to regular clients full information about the financial standing, credit ratings, etc., of individuals and firms.

mercantile paper Negotiable instruments for the payment of money, given in course of business, as bills of exchange, promissory notes, etc.: also called *commercial paper*.

mercantile system A theory in political economy that wealth consists not in labor and its products, but in the quantity of silver and gold in a country, and hence that mining, the exportation of goods, and the importation of gold should be encouraged by the state.

mer·can·til·ism (mûr'kən·til·iz'əm) n. **1** The spirit or theory of mercantile life or trade in general. **2** The mercantile system. — **mer'can·til·ist** n. & adj. — **mer'can·til·is'tic** adj.

mer·cap·tan (mər·kap'tan) n. Thiol. [< G < Med. L *mer(curium) captan(s)* seizing mercury]

mer·cap·tide (mər·kap'tīd) n. The metal salt of a mercaptan or thiol, obtained by replacing the sulfur hydrogen constituent with a metal.

mer·cap·to (mər·kap'tō) n. Sulfhydryl. [See MERCAPTAN]

MERCATOR'S PROJECTION

Mercator's projection A system of making maps in which the meridians are represented by parallel straight lines, and the parallels of latitude by lines perpendicular to the meridians, and at increasing intervals, so as to preserve the actual ratio between the increments of longitude and latitude at every point. It is accurate at the equator, but areas become increasingly distorted toward the poles.

mer·ce·nar·y (mûr'sə·ner'ē) adj. **1** Influenced by desire for gain or reward; greedy; venal. **2** Serving for pay or profit; hired: *mercenary* soldiers. **3** Pertaining to or resulting from sordidness. See synonyms under VENAL[1]. — n. pl. **·nar·ies** A person working or serving only or chiefly for pay; a hired soldier in foreign service. See synonyms under AUXILIARY. [< L *mercenarius* < *merces* reward, hire] — **mer'ce·nar'i·ly** adv. — **mer'ce·nar'i·ness** n.

mer·cer·ize (mûr'sə·rīz) v.t. **·ized, ·iz·ing** To treat (cotton fabrics) with caustic soda or potash, so as to increase their color-absorbing qualities and impart a silky gloss. [after John Mercer, 1791–1866, English inventor] — **mer·cer·i·za·tion** (mûr'sər·ə·zā'shən, -ī·zā'shən) n.

mer·chan·dise (mûr'chən·dīz, -dīs) n. **1** Anything movable customarily bought and sold for profit. **2** *Obs.* Mercantile dealings; commerce; trade: hence, gain or advantage. — v.t. & v.i. **·dised, ·dis·ing** To barter; trade; buy and sell. **2** To promote the sale of (an article) through advertising, etc. Also **mer'chan·dize.** [< F *marchandise*. See MERCHANT.] — **mer'chan·dis'er** n.

mer·chant (mûr'chənt) n. **1** A person who buys and sells commodities as a business or for profit; a trader. **2** A shopkeeper; storekeeper. — adj. Of or pertaining to merchants or merchandise; commercial. [< OF *marchant* < L *mercari* traffic, buy < *merx, mercis* wares]

mer·chant·a·ble (mûr'chən·tə·bəl) adj. That can be bought or sold.

merchant iron Wrought iron converted into marketable bars or rods of various sizes and shapes: often used for making hooks, chains, and rivets, and in reinforcing concrete.

mer·chant·man (mûr'chənt·mən) n. pl. **·men** (-mən) **1** A trading or merchant vessel. **2** *Archaic* A merchant.

merchant marine 1 All the vessels of a nation, collectively, both publicly and privately owned. engaged in commerce and trade. **2** The officers and men employed on these vessels.

mer·ci·ful (mûr'sə·fəl) adj. **1** Full of mercy; compassionate. **2** Characterized by or indicating mercy. — **mer'ci·ful·ly** adv. — **mer'ci·ful·ness** n.

Synonyms: benignant, clement, compassionate, forgiving, gentle, gracious, humane, pitiful, pitying, tender, tender-hearted. The *merciful* man is disposed to withhold or mitigate the suffering even of the guilty; the *compassionate* man sympathizes with and desires to relieve actual suffering, while one who is *humane* would forestall and prevent the suffering which he sees to be possible. See CHARITABLE, GOOD, HUMANE, PROPITIOUS.

mer·ci·less (mûr'sə·lis) adj. Having or showing no mercy. See synonyms under BARBAROUS, IMPLACABLE. — **mer'ci·less·ly** adv. — **mer'ci·less·ness** n.

mer·cu·ri·al (mər·kyŏor'ē·əl) adj. **1** Pertaining to the god Mercury; hence, lively; volatile. **2** Of or relating to quicksilver. — n. A preparation containing mercury. [< L *mercurialis* < *Mercurius* Mercury] — **mer·cu'ri·al·ly** adv. — **mer·cu'ri·al·ness** n.

mer·cu·ri·al·ism (mər·kyŏor'ē·əl·iz'əm) n. *Pathol.* The condition produced by excessive use of medicines containing mercury; mercury poisoning.

mer·cu·ri·al·ize (mər·kyŏor'ē·əl·īz') v.t. **·ized, ·iz·ing 1** To make mercurial. **2** To treat with mercury. — **mer·cu'ri·al·i·za'tion** n.

mer·cu·ric (mər·kyŏor'ik) adj. *Chem.* Of, pertaining to, or containing mercury in its highest valence.

mercuric chloride Corrosive sublimate. Also **mercury chloride.**

mer·cu·rous (mər·kyŏor'əs) adj. *Chem.* Of, pertaining to, or containing mercury in its lowest valence: *mercurous* chloride, *mercurous* oxide, etc.

mer·cu·ry (mûr'kyə·rē) n. pl. **·ries 1** A heavy, silver-white metallic element (symbol Hg), liquid at ordinary temperatures; quicksilver. See ELEMENT. **2** The quicksilver in a thermometer or barometer, as indicating temperature, etc. **3** A messenger. **4** An Old World plant (genus *Mercurialis*), especially *M. annua*, the **annual** or **French mercury**, used in medicine, and *M. perennis*, the **perennial** (or **dog's**) **mercury**, which is poisonous.

Mer·cu·ry (mûr′kyə·rē) **1** In Roman mythology, the herald and messenger of the gods, god of commerce, eloquence, and skill, and patron of messengers, travelers, merchants, and thieves: identified with the Greek *Hermes.* **2** *Astron.* The planet of the solar system nearest the sun, from which its mean distance is about 36,000,000 miles. It is the smallest of the major planets, having a diameter of about 3,000 miles, and revolving about the sun in 88 of our days.

mer·cy (mûr′sē) *n. pl.* **·cies 1** The act of treating an offender with less severity than he deserves; also, forbearance to injure others when one has power to do so. **2** The act of relieving suffering, or the disposition to relieve it; compassion. **3** A providential blessing. [<OF <L *merces, mercedis* hire, payment, reward; with ref. to the heavenly reward for compassion]
Synonyms: benevolence, benignity, blessing, clemency, compassion, favor, forbearance, forgiveness, gentleness, grace, kindness, lenience, leniency, lenity, mildness, pardon, pity, tenderness. *Mercy* is the exercise of less severity than one deserves, or in a more extended sense, the granting of *kindness* or *favor* beyond what one may rightly claim. *Clemency* is a colder word than *mercy* signifying *mildness* and moderation in the use of power where severity would have legal sanction; it often denotes a habitual *mildness* of disposition on the part of the powerful, and is a matter rather of good nature or policy than of principle. *Leniency* or *lenity* denotes an easy-going avoidance of severity; these words are more general and less magisterial than *clemency. Grace* is *favor, kindness,* or *blessing* shown to the undeserving; *forgiveness, mercy,* and *pardon* are exercised toward the ill-deserving. *Pardon* remits the outward penalty which the offender deserves; *forgiveness* dismisses resentment or displeasure from the heart of the one offended. *Mercy* is also used in the wider sense of refraining from harshness or cruelty toward those who are in one's power without fault of their own; as, They besought the robber to have *mercy.* See LENITY, PITY. *Antonyms:* cruelty, hardness, harshness, implacability, justice, penalty, punishment, revenge, rigor, severity, sternness, vengeance.

mercy killing Euthanasia.

mercy seat 1 In ancient Jewish ritual, the golden lid of the ark of the covenant whence God gave his oracles to the high priest, and upon which was sprinkled the blood of the yearly atonement. **2** Figuratively, the throne of God.

mere[1] (mir) *adj.* **1** Such as is mentioned and no more; nothing but. **2** *Obs.* Absolute; entire; unqualified. See synonyms under PURE. [<L *merus* unmixed, bare]

mere[2] (mir) *n.* **1** A pond; pool. **2** *Scot.* The sea. [OE *mere*]

-mere *combining form Zool.* A part or division: *blastomere.* [<Gk. *meros* part]

mere·ly (mir′lē) *adv.* **1** Without including anything else; only; solely. **2** *Obs.* Absolutely; wholly. See synonyms under BUT[1].

mer·e·tri·cious (mer′ə·trish′əs) *adj.* **1** Deceitfully or artificially attractive; vulgar; tawdry. **2** Pertaining to a harlot; wanton. [<L *meretricius* <*meretrix, -icis* prostitute <*merere* earn, gain] — **mer′e·tri′cious·ly** *adv.* — **mer′e·tri′cious·ness** *n.*

mer·gan·ser (mər·gan′sər) *n.* A fish-eating duck (subfamily *Merginae*), with toothlike processes along the upper edge of the bill, and the head usually crested, as the hooded merganser (*Lophodytes cucullatus*) of North America. [<NL <L *mergus* diver <*mergere* plunge + *anser* goose]

merge (mûrj) *v.t.* & *v.i.* **merged, merg·ing** To combine or be combined so as to lose separate identity; blend. See synonyms under UNITE. [<L *mergere* dip, immerse] — **mer′gence** *n.*

merg·er (mûr′jər) *n.* **1** *Law* The extinguishment of a lesser estate, right, or liability in a greater one. **2** One who or that which merges. **3** A combination of a number of commercial interests or companies in one.

me·rid·i·an (mə·rid′ē·ən) *n.* **1** *Obs.* Noontime; midday. **2** The highest or culminating point

of anything; the zenith: the *meridian* of life. **3** *Astron.* A great circle passing through the poles and zenith of the celestial sphere at any point; the celestial meridian. **4** *Geog.* **a** A great circle drawn from any point on the earth's surface and passing through both poles. **b** The half-circle so drawn between the poles, called a meridian of longitude, or geographic meridian. **5** A line on a surface of revolution in the same plane as its axis. — *adj.* **1** Of or pertaining to noonday: *meridian* heat. **2** Pertaining to or at the highest or culminating point; brightest: *meridian* fame. **3** Of or pertaining to a meridian. [<OF *meridien* <L *meridianus* <*meridies* noon, south <*medidies* <*medius* middle + *dies* day]

me·rid·i·o·nal (mə·rid′ē·ə·nəl) *adj.* **1** Of or pertaining to the meridian. **2** Relating to southern climates or people: *meridional* customs. **3** Approximating a direction north and south. **4** Situated or lying in the south; southerly. — *n.* An inhabitant of a southern country; specifically, a resident of southern France. [<OF <LL *meridionalis* southern] — **me·rid′i·o·nal′i·ty** *n.* — **me·rid′i·o·nal·ly** *adv.*

me·ringue (mə·rang′) *n.* The beaten white of eggs sweetened, baked, and used to garnish pastry; also, pastry so garnished. [<F <G *meringe,* lit., cake of Mehringen (in Germany)]

me·ri·no (mə·rē′nō) *n. pl.* **·nos 1** A superior breed of sheep, originating in Spain, and having very fine, closely set, silky wool. See SHEEP. Also **Merino sheep. 2** The wool of this sheep. **3** A fabric made of merino wool. **4** A kind of knitted goods used for underwear. — *adj.* **1** Pertaining to merino sheep or their wool. **2** Made of merino wool. [<Sp.]

me·ris·tic (mə·ris′tik) *adj.* Divided into parts; segmented. [<Gk. *meristos*]

mer·it (mer′it) *n.* **1** *Often pl.* The quality or fact of deserving, especially of deserving well; desert: Does his *merit* justify the reward? **2** Worth or excellence; quality: A man of *merit.* **3** That which deserves esteem, praise, or reward; a commendable act or quality: the *merit* of silence. **4** *pl.* The actual rights or wrongs of a matter considered exclusively of extraneous details or technicalities: to decide a case on its *merits.* **5** Reward, recompense, or, sometimes, punishment received or deserved; a token or award of excellence. See synonyms under WORTH. — *v.t.* To earn as a reward or punishment; deserve. [<OF *merite* <L *meritum* <*meritus,* pp. of *merere* deserve] — **mer′it·ed** *adj.* — **mer′it·ed·ly** *adv.*

mer·i·toc·ra·cy (mer′ə·tok′rə·sē) *n. pl.* **·ra·cies 1** A system or society in which talent, intellectual achievements, and excellence of performance are considered worthier of reward than race, sex, social status, or wealth. **2** The leaders produced by such a system or society. — **mer·i·to·crat** (mer′ə·tə·krat′) *n.* — **mer·i·to·crat·ic** (mer′ə·tə·krat′ik) *adj.*

mer·i·to·ri·ous (mer′ə·tôr′ē·əs, -tō′rē-) *adj.* Deserving of reward; praiseworthy. — **mer′i·to′ri·ous·ly** *adv.* — **mer′i·to′ri·ous·ness** *n.*

merit system A system adopted in the U.S. Civil Service whereby appointments and promotions are made on the basis of the merit and fitness of the appointee, ascertained through qualifying examinations.

merle (mûrl) *n.* The European blackbird (*Turdus merula*). Also **merl.** [<F <L *merula* blackbird]

mer·lin (mûr′lin) *n.* A small European falcon (*Falco columbarius aesalon*); also, a related American species, the pigeon hawk (*F. columbarius*). [<OF *esmerillon,* dim. of *esmeril*]

mer·maid (mûr′mād′) *n.* A legendary marine creature having as its upper part the head and body of a lovely woman and as its lower part the scaled body and tail of a fish. Also **mer′maid′en.** [<MERE[2] + MAID]

mer·man (mûr′man′) *n. pl.* **·men** (-men′) A legendary marine creature, having as its upper part the head and body of a man and as its lower part the scaled body and tail of a fish. [<MERE[2] + MAN]

mero- *combining form* Part; partial; incomplete: *meroplankton.* Also, before vowels, *mer-.* [<Gk. *meros* a part, division]

mer·o·blast (mer′ə·blast) *n.* A meroblastic

ovum. [<MERO- + Gk. *blastos* sprout]

mer·o·blas·tic (mer′ə·blas′tik) *adj. Biol.* Undergoing partial or incomplete segmentation, with formation of food yolk, as in the eggs of birds: opposed to *holoblastic.* — **mer′o·blas′ti·cal·ly** *adv.*

mer·o·gen·e·sis (mer′ə·jen′ə·sis) *n. Biol.* Segmentation; reproduction by the formation of parts. [<MERO- + GENESIS] — **mer′o·ge·net′ic** (-jə·net′ik) *adj.*

Mer·o·pe (mer′ə·pē) In Greek mythology, one of the Pleiades, not seen by the naked eye with the other six among the stars, supposedly having hidden herself from shame for loving a mortal: called the *lost Pleiad.*

mer·o·plank·ton (mer′ə·plangk′tən) *n. Biol.* Plankton found only at certain times or in certain seasons of the year.

-merous *suffix Zool.* Having (a specified number or kind of) parts: *trimerous, pentamerous* (often written 3-*merous,* 5-*merous,* etc.). [<Gk. *meros* a part, division]

mer·o·zo·ite (mer′ə·zō′īt) *n. Zool.* One of the mature spores liberated in the sporulating stage of certain protozoa, as the parasite causing malaria (*Plasmodium*). [<MERO- + (SPORO)ZO(A) + -ITE[1]]

Mer·ri·mack (mer′ə·mak) *n.* The U.S. first armored warship, a Confederate vessel; fought the *Monitor* at Hampton Roads, 1862: Confederate name *Virginia.*

THE MERRIMACK: 4,636 TONS; DRAFT 23 FEET
Originally the U.S.S. *Merrimack,* later renamed
C.S.S. *Virginia.*

mer·ri·ment (mer′i·mənt) *n.* The act of making merry; mirth; celebration. See synonyms under ENTERTAINMENT, HAPPINESS, LAUGHTER, SPORT.

mer·ry (mer′ē) *adj.* **·ri·er, ·ri·est 1** Inclined to mirth and laughter; full of fun; lively. **2** Of or pertaining to mirth or scenes of mirth; jovial and sportive; mirthful. **3** Inciting to mirth, cheerfulness, and gay spirits; fitted or calculated to enliven; exhilarating; bracing. **4** *Colloq.* Slightly tipsy; high. **5** *Obs.* Jibing; sarcastic. [OE *myrige* pleasant] — **mer′ri·ly** *adv.* — **mer′ri·ness** *n.*
Synonyms: blithe, blithesome, facetious, frolicsome, gay, glad, gladsome, gleeful, hilarious, jocose, jocund, jolly, jovial, joyous, lighthearted, lively, mirthful, sportive. See CHEERFUL, HAPPY, JOCOSE, VIVACIOUS, WANTON. *Antonyms:* see synonyms for SAD.

mer·ry-an·drew (mer′ē·an′drōō) *n.* A clown or buffoon.

mer·ry-go-round (mer′ē·gō·round′) *n.* **1** A revolving platform fitted with wooden horses, boatlike vehicles, etc., on which people ride for amusement, usually to music; a carousel. **2** A whirl, as of pleasure.

mer·ry·mak·ing (mer′ē·mā′king) *adj.* Frolicking. — *n.* Festivity; frolic. See synonyms under FROLIC, REVEL, SPORT. — **mer′ry·mak′er** *n.*

mes- Var. of MESO-.

me·sa (mā′sə, *Sp.* mā′sä) *n.* A high, broad, and flat tableland with sharp, usually rocky, slopes descending to the surrounding plain, common in the SW United States. [<Sp. <L *mensa* table]

mé·sal·li·ance (mā·zal′ē·əns, *Fr.* mā·zà·lyäns′) *n.* A marriage with one of inferior position; misalliance. [<F]

mes·cal (mes·kal′) *n.* **1** A spineless cactus (*Lophophora williamsii*), native to the SW United States and northern Mexico. Its tops, which are often called **mescal buttons,** grow but little above the ground, contain a narcotic stimulating substance, and are chewed by the Indians, especially during the performance of religious ceremonies. **2** A mescal maguey. **3** An intoxicating liquor distilled from pulque. [<Sp. *mezcal* <Nahuatl *mexcalli*]

mes·ca·line (mes′kə·lēn, -lin) *n. Chem.* A white, crystalline alkaloid, $C_{11}H_{17}O_3N$, extracted from mescal buttons. It has narcotic and tetanic properties, and induces powerful color hallucinations: also spelled *mezcaline*. [<MES-CAL]

mescal maguey Any plant from which the liquor mescal is obtained, especially the pulque agave (*Agave atrovirens*).

mes·en·ceph·a·lon (mes'en·sef'ə·lon) *n. Anat.* The central division of the brain; the midbrain. [<NL <MES- + ENCEPHALON] — **mes·en·ce·phal·ic** (mes·en·sə·fal'ik) *adj.*

mes·en·chyme (mes'eng·kim) *n. Biol.* The portion of the mesoderm that produces the connective tissues of the body, the blood vessels, lymphatic system, and heart. It is cellular in structure, and in some of the lower forms of life is the same as *mesoblast.* Also **mes·en·chy·ma** (mes·eng'kə·mə). [<NL *mesenchyma* <MES- + Gk. *en-* in + *chein* pour] — **mes·en'chy·mal, mes·en·chym·a·tous** (-kim'ə·təs) *adj.*

mes·en·ter·i·tis (mes·en'tə·rī'tis) *n. Pathol.* Inflammation of the mesentery. [<MESENTER(ON) + -ITIS]

mes·en·ter·on (mes·en'tər·on) *n. pl.* **·ter·a** (-tər·ə) *Biol.* **1** The middle portion of the primitive intestinal cavity, lined with endoderm: distinguished from the buccal and anal parts, which are lined with ectoderm. **2** The midgut. [<MES- + ENTERON] — **mes·en'ter·on'ic** (-tə·ron'ik) *adj.*

mes·en·ter·y (mes'ən·ter'ē) *n. pl.* **·ter·ies** *Anat.* A fold of the peritoneum that invests an intestine and connects it with the abdominal wall; especially, the fold investing the small intestine. Also **mes·en·te·ri·um** (-tir'ē·əm). [<Med. L *mesenterium* <Gk. *mesenterion* <*mesos* middle + *enteron* intestine] — **mes'·en·ter'ic** *adj.*

mesh (mesh) *n.* **1** One of the open spaces between the cords of a net or the wires of a sieve: often expressed numerically in terms of a unit area: a 100-*mesh* screen. **2** *pl.* Such cords or wires collectively. **3** Anything that entangles or involves. **4** *Mech.* The engagement of gear teeth. — *v.t. & v.i.* **1** To mesh or become entangled, as in a net. **2** To make or become engaged, as gear teeth. [Cf. OE *max* a net and MDu. *maesche* a mesh] — **mesh'y** *adj.*

mesh·work (mesh'wûrk') *n.* A combination of meshes; network.

me·si·al (mē'zē·əl, mes'ē·əl) *adj.* Situated in or directed toward the middle: the *mesial* plane of the body. Also **me'si·an.** [<Gk. *mesos* middle] — **me'si·al·ly** *adv.*

mes·ic¹ (mes'ik, mē'zik) *adj. Bot.* Pertaining to or characterized by a medium moisture supply, as in certain plants. [<Gk. *mesos* middle]

mes·ic² (mes'ik, mē'sik) *adj. Physics* Of, pertaining to, characteristic of, or produced by mesons. [<MESON²]

me·sit·y·lene (mə·sit'ə·lēn, -lin) *n. Chem.* A colorless, liquid hydrocarbon, C_9H_{12}, made by heating acetone with concentrated sulfuric acid. [<*mesityl* a hypothetical organic radical (<Gk. *mesitēs* mediator + -YL) + -ENE]

mes·i·tyl oxide (mes'i·təl) *Chem.* A colorless hydrocarbon, $C_6H_{10}O$, used as a solvent for nitrocellulose and certain gums and resins. [See MESITYLENE]

mes·mer·ism (mes'mə·riz'əm, mez'-) *n.* **1** The theory, as exemplified by Franz Anton Mesmer, 1733–1815, that one person can produce in another an abnormal condition resembling sleep, during which the mind of the subject is passively responsive to the will of the operator: now identified with hypnotism. Compare ANIMAL MAGNETISM. **2** Personal magnetism. — **mes·mer·ic** (mes·mer'ik, mez-), **mes·mer'i·cal** *adj.* — **mes·mer'i·cal·ly** *adv.* — **mes'mer·ist** *n.*

mes·mer·ize (mes'mə·rīz, mez'-) *v.t.* **·ized, ·iz·ing** To hypnotize. Also *Brit.* **mes'mer·ise.** — **mes'mer·i·za'tion** *n.* — **mes'mer·iz'er** *n.*

mesn·al·ty (mē'nəl·tē) *n.* The estate of a mesne lord. Also **mesn·al·i·ty** (mē·nal'ə·tē). [<MF *mesnalte*]

mesne (mēn) *adj. Law* Being between two periods or extremes; intermediate; intervening. [<MF, alter. of AF *meen* <L *medianus* mean. Doublet of MEAN³, MEDIAN, MIZZEN.]

mesne lord One holding lands as an intermediate between a superior lord and a subordinate tenant.

meso– *combining form* **1** Situated in the middle: *mesocarp.* **2** Intermediate in size or degree: *mesognathous.* Also, before vowels,

mes–. [<Gk. *mesos* middle]

mes·o·blast (mes'ə·blast, mē'sə-) *n. Biol.* The middle germinal layer of the embryo. See MESENCHYME. [<MESO- + Gk. *blastos* sprout] — **mes'o·blas'tic** *adj.*

mes·o·carp (mes'ə·kärp, mē'sə-) *n. Bot.* The middle layer of a pericarp.

mes·o·ce·phal·ic (mes'ō·sə·fal'ik, mē'sō-) *adj. Anat.* **1** Intermediate in head form; having a cephalic index of from 76.0 to 80.9. **2** Having a medium cranial capacity. **3** Of or pertaining to the mesocephalon. Also **mes·o·ceph·a·lous** (-sef'ə·ləs). — **mes·o·ceph'a·ly** *n.*

mes·o·crat·ic (mes'ə·krat'ik, mē'sə-) *adj. Geol.* Having the dark constituents slightly in excess of the light ones: said of certain igneous rocks.

mes·o·derm (mes'ə·dûrm, mē'sə-) *n.* **1** *Biol.* The middle germ layer of the embryo, from which are developed the muscular, vascular, and osseous systems. **2** *Bot.* The middle layer of the wall of a moss and capsule. — **mes'o·der'mal, mes'o·der'mic** *adj.*

mes·o·gas·tri·um (mes'ə·gas'trē·əm, mē'sə-) *n. Biol.* One of the two mesenteries in the stomach of an embryo; also, the region of the umbilicus. [<MESO- + Gk. *gastēr* belly] — **mes'o·gas'tric** *adj.*

mes·og·na·thous (mə·sog'nə·thəs) *adj.* Having moderately projecting jaws; also, having a facial profile angle of 98° to 103°. Also **mes·og·nath·ic** (mes'og·nath'ik). [<MESO- + -GNATHOUS] — **mes·og'na·thism, mes·og'na·thy** *n.*

mes·o·kur·to·sis (mes'ō·kər·tō'sis, mē'sō-) *n. Stat.* The symmetrical kurtosis characterizing the region near the mode of a normal probability curve. — **mes·o·kur'tic** (-kûr'tik) *adj.*

Mes·o·lith·ic (mes'ə·lith'ik, mē'sə-) *adj. Anthropol.* Pertaining to or describing that period of human culture immediately following the Magdalenian stage of the Paleolithic, characterized by small, delicately worked microliths and an economy transitional between food gathering and a settled agriculture. Also called *Epipaleolithic, Miolithic.* [<MESO- + LITH(O)- + -IC]

me·sol·o·gy (mə·sol'ə·jē) *n.* The study of the environment in its relations to organisms; ecology. [<MESO- + -LOGY] — **mes'o·log'ic, mes'o·log'i·cal** (mes'ə·loj'i·kəl) *adj.*

mes·o·mor·phic (mes'ə·môr'fik, mē'sə-) *adj.* **1** *Physics* Of or pertaining to a state of matter intermediate between the true liquid and the crystal; liquo–crystalline: also **mes'o·mor'·phous.** **2** Designating a physical type developed predominantly from the mesodermal layer of the embryo; the muscular or athletic type. Compare ECTOMORPHIC, ENDOMORPHIC.

mes·on¹ (mes'on, mē'son) *n.* **1** The plane that divides the body longitudinally into two halves; the median or mesial plane. **2** *Music* Loosely, a tetrachord. [<NL <Gk. *mesos* middle]

mes·on² (mes'on, mē'son) *n. Physics* Any of a group of short–lived, unstable atomic particles having a mass intermediate between that of the electron and the proton. They are believed to be a product of cosmic–ray disintegration and may be electrically neutral or carry either a positive or negative charge. The principal types are the mu–meson and pi–meson. [<Gk. *mesos* middle]

mes·o·neph·ros (mes'ə·nef'rəs, mē'sə-) *n. Biol.* The middle of three tubular organs found in connection with the primitive genitourinary apparatus, and formed later than the pronephros; the mid–kidney or Wolffian body. It is the permanent kidney in some animals, as amphibians. [<NL <MESO- + Gk. *nephros* kidney] — **mes'o·neph'ric** *adj.*

mes·o·pause (mez'ō·pôz) *n.* A transition zone between the mesosphere and the ionosphere, beginning at a height of about 50 miles.

mes·o·phyll (mes'ə·fil, mē'sə-) *n. Bot.* The soft, inner, parenchymatous tissue of a leaf; the cellular portion lying between the upper and lower epidermis. Also **mes'o·phyl, mes'o·phyl'lum.** [<MESO- + Gk. *phyllon* leaf]

mes·o·phyte (mes'ə·fit, mē'sə-) *n. Bot.* A plant requiring medium conditions of moisture and dryness, intermediate between a hydrophyte and a xerophyte. — **mes'o·phyt'ic** (-fit'ik) *adj.*

mes·o·plast (mes'ə·plast, mē'sə-) *n. Biol.* A cell nucleus. [<MESO- + Gk. *plastos* formed] — **mes'o·plas'tic** *adj.*

mes·or·rhine (mes'ə·rīn, -rin, mē'sə-) *adj.* Having a relatively broad, high–bridged nose. [<MESO- + Gk. *rhis, rhinos* nose]

mes·o·sere (mes'ə·sir, mē'sə-) *n. Bot.* The flora and major plant development of the Mesozoic era. [<MESO- + L *serere* sow, plant]

mes·o·sphere (mes'ō·sfir) *n.* A layer of the atmosphere lying between the stratopause and mesopause.

mes·o·the·li·um (mes'ə·thē'lē·əm, mē'sə-) *n. Biol.* **1** The portion of the mesoderm and the tissues derived from it that in vertebrates forms two principal layers, visceral and parietal, and produces the epithelium of the peritoneum and pleurae, the striated muscles, etc. **2** Epithelium when mesoblastic in origin. [<NL <MESO-+ (EPI)THELIUM] — **mes·o·the'li·al** *adj.*

mes·o·ther·mal (mes'ə·thûr'məl, mē'sə-) *adj.* Possessing or pertaining to medium warmth. Also **mes'o·ther'mic.**

mes·o·tho·rax (mes'ə·thôr'aks, -thō'raks, mē'sə-) *n. Entomol.* The middle one of the three segments of the thorax in insects, bearing the anterior wings and the middle legs. — **mes·o·tho·rac·ic** (-thō·ras'ik, -thō·ras'ik) *adj.*

mes·o·tho·ri·um (mes'ə·thôr'ē·əm, -thō'rē·əm, mē'sə-) *n. Physics* Either of two isotopes resulting from the radioactive disintegration of thorium, intermediate between thorium and radiothorium.

mes·o·tron (mes'ə·tron, mē'sə-) *n. Physics* Meson. [<MESO- + (ELEC)TRON]

Mes·o·zo·ic (mes'ə·zō'ik, mē'sə-) *n. Geol.* The era between the Paleozoic and the Cenozoic, including the Triassic, Jurassic, and Cretaceous periods: characterized by the dominance of the reptiles, the rise of flowering plants, and the beginnings of archaic mammals. — *adj.* Of or pertaining to this era. [<MESO- + -ZOIC]

mes·quite (mes·kēt', mes'kēt) *n.* Either of two spiny, deep–rooted shrubs or small trees of the pea family, found in the southwestern United States, and extending southward to Peru. The honey mesquite (*Prosopis glandulosa* or *juliflora*) yields sweet algarroba pods used for cattle fodder; the screw–pod mesquite (*Strombocarpa odorata*), or screwbean, has edible spiral pods. Also spelled *mezquite, muskit.* Also **mes·quit'.** [< Sp. *mezquite* <Nahuatl *mizquitl*]

MESQUITE
a. Flower.
b. Fruit (edible).

mess (mes) *n.* **1** A quantity of food sufficient for one meal or for a particular occasion: a *mess* of beans; also, a portion of soft, partly liquid food, as pottage. **2** A number of persons who habitually take their meals together, as on board ship or in military units; also, a meal taken by them. **3** The sum or total of a haul of fish. **4** A state of disorder; especially, a condition of unclean confusion. **5** A confusing and embarrassing situation. **6** An unpleasant or unclean concoction; confused jumble. — *v.i.* **1** To busy oneself; dabble: often with *around* or *about.* **2** To make a mess; bungle: often with *up.* **3** To interfere; meddle: often with *around.* **4** To eat with a mess (def. 2). — *v.t.* **5** To make a mess of; muddle; botch: often with *up.* **6** To make dirty; to be foul: often with *up.* **7** To provide meals for. [<OF *mes* <L *missus* course at a meal, orig. pp. of *mittere* send] — **mess'y** *adj.* — **mess'i·ly** *adv.* — **mess'i·ness** *n.*

mes·sage (mes'ij) *n.* **1** A communication, as of information, sent in any way. **2** A formal communication from a chief executive to a legislative body, not delivered in person: a *message* from the president to Congress. **3** An errand; the carrying out of a mission; a messenger's business. **4** An utterance divinely inspired; hence, any important communication embodying a truth, principle, or advice. **5** A television or radio commercial. [<OF < Med. L *missaticum* <*missus,* pp. of *mittere*]

message center *Mil.* An agency attached to a headquarters or command post, and charged with the receipt, transmission, and delivery of messages.

mes·sa·line (mes'ə·lēn', mes'ə·lēn) *n.* A lightweight, lustrous, twilled silk fabric.

mes·sen·ger (mes′ən·jər) *n.* **1** One sent with a message or on an errand; one employed to carry messages; specifically, a bearer of official dispatches. **2** A forerunner; herald. [ME *messenger, messanger* < OF *messagier* < *message* MESSAGE: the *n* is non-historic]

mess hall A building or room where meals are regularly eaten, as by a military group.

Mes·si·ah (mə·sī′ə) *n.* **1** The Anointed One; the Christ: the name for the promised deliverer of the Hebrews, assumed by Jesus, and given to him by Christians: with *the.* **2** Loosely, a looked-for liberator of a country or people. Also **Mes·si′as.** [< LL *Messias* < Gk. < Aramaic *měshīhā,* Hebrew *māshīah* anointed] — **Mes·si′ah·ship** *n.* — **Mes·si·an·ic** (mes′ē·an′ik) *adj.*

mes·sieurs (mes′ərz, *Fr.* mā·syœ′) *n. pl.* of *Fr.* **mon·sieur** (mə·syœ′) Sirs; gentlemen: in English in the contracted form *Messrs.,* used as plural of *Mr.*

mess jacket A man's short, tailored jacket, usually white and terminating exactly at the waistline: worn on semiformal occasions.

mess kit A small, compactly arranged unit containing cooking and eating utensils: used by soldiers and campers.

mess·mate (mes′māt′) *n.* An associate at a mess, especially on onboard ship.

mes·suage (mes′wij) *n. Law* A dwelling house with its belongings, outhouses, garden, etc. [< OF *mesuage,* prob. alter. of *mesnage.* See MÉNAGE.]

mes·tee (mes·tē′) *n.* The offspring of a white person and a quadroon; an octoroon: also spelled *mustee.* [< Sp. *mestizo* mongrel, hybrid]

mes·ti·zo (mes·tē′zō) *n. pl.* **·zos** or **·zoes** Any one of mixed blood; in Mexico and the western United States, a person of Spanish and Indian blood. Also **mes·te′so, mes·ti′no** (-nō). [< Sp. < LL *mixticius* < L *mixtus,* pp. of *miscere* mix] — **mes·ti′za** (-zə) *n. fem.*

met (met) Past tense and past participle of MEET[1].

met- Var. of META-.

meta- *prefix* **1** Changed in place or form; reversed; altered: *metamorphosis.* **2** *Anat.* & *Zool.* Behind; after; on the farther side of; later: often equivalent to *post-* or *dorso-*: *metathorax, metaplasis.* **3** With; alongside: *metabiosis.* **4** Beyond; over; transcending: *metaphysics, metapsychology.* **5** *Chem.* **a** A modification, usually polymeric, of. **b** A derivative of: *metaprotein.* **c** A derivative of an acid anhydride, formed by withdrawal of one or more water molecules: distinguished from *ortho-*: *metaphosphoric* acid. **d** A benzene derivative in which the substituted atoms or radicals occupy the positions 1, 3: abbr. *m-.* Compare ORTHO-, PARA-. See BENZENE RING. Also, before vowels and *h, met-.* [< Gk. *meta* after, beside, with]

met·a·bi·o·sis (met′ə·bī·ō′sis) *n. Biol.* The condition of dependence of one organism upon another. [< META- + Gk. *bios* life] — **met′a·bi·ot′ic** (-ot′ik) *adj.*

met·a·bol·ic (met′ə·bol′ik) *adj.* **1** Of, pertaining, to, or exhibiting metabolism: *metabolic* processes. **2** Pertaining to or undergoing change, transformation, or metamorphosis. Also **met′a·bol′i·cal.** [< Gk. *metabolikos*]

me·tab·o·lism (mə·tab′ə·liz′əm) *n. Biol.* The aggregate of all physical and chemical processes constantly taking place in living organisms, including those which use energy to build up assimilated materials (anabolism) and those which release energy by breaking them down (catabolism). Also **me·tab′o·ly** (-ə·lē). [< Gk. *metabolē* < *meta-* beyond + *ballein* throw]

me·tab·o·lite (mə·tab′ə·līt) *n.* A chemical product of metabolism.

me·tab·o·lize (mə·tab′ə·līz) *v.t.* & *v.i.* **·lized, ·liz·ing** To subject to or change by metabolism.

met·a·car·pal (met′ə·kär′pəl) *adj.* Of or pertaining to the metacarpus. — *n.* One of the bones of the metacarpus.

met·a·car·pus (met′ə·kär′pəs) *n. Anat.* The part of the fore- or thoracic limb between the carpus or wrist and the phalanges or bones of the finger. It consists in man of five bones. [< NL < Gk. *metakarpion* < *meta-* beyond +

karpos wrist]

met·a·cen·ter (met′ə·sen′tər) *n. Physics* That point in a floating body slightly displaced from equilibrium through which the resultant upward pressure of the fluid always passes; the center of gravity of the unsubmerged portion of a floating body. Also **met′a·cen′tre.** — **met′a·cen′tric** *adj.*

met·a·chem·is·try (met′ə·kem′is·trē) *n.* The chemistry of elements and compounds which yield exceptionally large amounts of energy in relation to their mass. — **met′a·chem′i·cal** *adj.*

met·a·chro·ma·tism (met′ə·krō′mə·tiz′əm) *n.* An alteration in color; specifically, such alteration due to heating or cooling. — **met′a·chro·mat′ic** (-krō·mat′ik) *adj.*

met·a·gal·ax·y (met′ə·gal′ək·sē) *n. pl.* **·ax·ies** *Astron.* The entire material universe, regarded especially as a system including all the galaxies.

met·age (mē′tij) *n.* **1** Measurement. **2** The price charged for measurement. **3** A general term for the tolls formerly exacted by the corporation of London over a part of the Thames above and below the city. [< METE[1]]

met·a·gen·e·sis (met′ə·jen′ə·sis) *n. Biol.* A type of reproduction in which a series of generations of unlike forms comes between the egg and the parent type; alternation of generations. — **met′a·ge·net′ic** (-jə·net′ik) *adj.*

me·tag·na·thous (mə·tag′nə·thəs) *adj. Ornithol.* Having the points of the mandibles crossing each other, as in the crossbill. [< META- + -GNATHOUS] — **me·tag′na·thism** *n.*

met·ag·nos·tic (met′ag·nos′tik) *adj.* Beyond the knowledge, whether of the sense or the understanding, of man as he is at present constituted; metaphysical. — *n.* A person holding a belief in the existence of a Supreme Being who transcends human knowledge. [< META- + Gk. *gnōstikos* knowing] — **met′ag·nos′ti·cism** *n.*

met·al (met′l) *n.* **1** An element that forms a base by combining with a hydroxyl group or groups. It is usually hard, heavy, lustrous, malleable, ductile, tenacious, and a good conductor of heat and electricity. **2** A composition of some metallic element; also, an alloy: generally with a qualifying word. **3** Cast iron while melted. **4** Broken stone for road surfaces or for railway ballast: also called **road metal.** **5** *Her.* Gold (*or*) or silver (*argent*) tincture. **6** Molten glass. **7** The weight of the projectiles that a warship's guns can throw at once. **8** *Printing* Type metal; also, composed type. **9** The constituent material of anything; essential quality. — **noble metal** A metal that does not readily oxidize in the open air, as gold, silver, and platinum. — **white metal** Any one of the various white alloys, such as pewter, used for making ornaments, small castings, etc; specifically, a soft, smooth, malleable, copper-zinc alloy of exceptional antifrictional properties used to form the bearing surface in the crankshaft and connecting-rod bearings in most internal-combustion engines. — *adj.* Consisting of or pertaining to metal. — *v.t.* **·aled** or **·alled, ·al·ing** or **·al·ling** To furnish or cover with metal. ◆ Homophone: *mettle.* [< OF < L *metallum* mine < Gk. *metallon.* Doublet of MEDAL.]

met·a·lin·guis·tics (met′ə·ling·gwis′tiks) *n.* An area of linguistic study concerned with the interrelationship of the structure and meaning of the language of a society and other aspects of its culture, such as the social system.

met·al·ist (met′l·ist) *n.* **1** One who works with or has special knowledge of metals. **2** An advocate of metallic money as against a paper currency. Also **met′al·list.**

me·tal·lic (mə·tal′ik) *adj.* **1** Being, containing, yielding, or having the characteristics of a metal: a *metallic* voice; *metallic* luster. **2** Pertaining to a metal. — **me·tal′li·cal·ly** *adv.*

metallic soap A soapy, waxlike material made by combining the salts of certain metals, as lead or aluminum, with various fatty acids: used in the textile, varnish, and paint industries.

met·al·lif·er·ous (met′ə·lif′ər·əs) *adj.* Yielding or containing metal.

met·al·line (met′ə·lin, -līn) *adj.* **1** Relating

to, having the properties of, or resembling metal. **2** Impregnated with metals or metallic salts.

met·al·log·ra·phy (met′ə·log′rə·fē) *n.* **1** The science that treats of metallic substances; also, a treatise on metals. **2** Microscopic study of the structure of metals and alloys. [< Gk. *metallon* mine, metal + -GRAPHY] — **me·tal·lo·graph·ic** (mə·tal′ə·graf′ik) *adj.*

met·al·loid (met′ə·loid) *n.* One of those nonmetallic elements that resemble the metals in some of their properties, as arsenic and antimony. — *adj.* **1** Resembling a metal. **2** Of, pertaining to, or having the properties of a metalloid. Also **met′al·loi′dal.**

me·tal·lo·ther·a·py (mə·tal′ō·ther′ə·pē) *n.* Medical treatment by the use of metals, especially metal salts. [< Gk. *metallon* mine, metal + THERAPY]

met·al·lur·gy (met′ə·lûr′jē) *n.* The art or science of extracting a metal or metals from ores, as by smelting, reducing, refining, alloying, electrolysis, etc. [< NL *metallurgia* < Gk. *metallourgos* working in mines < *metallon* mine + *-ergos* working] — **met′al·lur′gic** or **·gi·cal** *adj.* — **met′al·lur′gi·cal·ly** *adv.* — **met′·al·lur′gist** *n.*

met·al·work (met′l·wûrk′) *n.* **1** Articles made of metal. **2** Metalworking.

met·al·work·ing (met′l·wûr′king) *n.* The making or the business of making things out of metal. — **met′al·work′er** *n.*

met·a·math·e·mat·ics (met′ə·math′ə·mat′iks) *n.* That branch of mathematics which is concerned with the formalized and rigorously logical treatment of pure symbols, having regard only to internal consistency and the establishment of absolute proofs of the validity of a given set of axioms, postulates, theorems, etc., within a mathematical system. — **met′a·math′e·mat′i·cal** *adj.*

met·a·mere (met′ə·mir) *n. Biol.* One of the series of homologous segments that form the body of a chordate or articulate animal, as a worm; a somite. Also **me·tam·er·on** (mə·tam′ər·on). [< META- + -MERE] — **me·tam′er·ic, me·tam′er·al** *adj.* — **met′a·mer′i·cal·ly** *adv.*

met·a·mor·phic (met′ə·môr′fik) *adj.* **1** Producing metamorphism. **2** Pertaining to, caused by, or exhibiting metamorphism. Also **met′a·mor′phous.**

met·a·mor·phism (met′ə·môr′fiz·əm) *n.* **1** *Geol.* The changes in the composition and texture of rocks caused by earth forces accompanied by heat, pressure, moisture, etc. **2** Any metamorphosis. [See METAMORPHOSIS.]

met·a·mor·phop·si·a (met′ə·môr·fop′sē·ə) *n. Pathol.* A defect in vision which makes objects appear distorted. [< NL < Gk. *metamorphōsis* transformation + *ōps* eye]

met·a·mor·phose (met′ə·môr′fōz) *v.t.* **·phosed, ·phos·ing** **1** To change the form of; transmute. **2** To change by metamorphism. Also **met′a·mor′phize.** See synonyms under CHANGE. [< F *métamorphoser*]

met·a·mor·pho·sis (met′ə·môr′fə·sis) *n. pl.* **·pho·ses** (-fə·sēz) **1** A passing from one form or shape into another; transformation with or without change of nature: especially applied to change by means of witchcraft, sorcery, etc. **2** Complete transformation of character, purpose, circumstances, etc.; also, a person or thing metamorphosed. **3** *Biol.* A change in form, structure, or function in an organism resulting from development; transformation; specifically, the series of marked external changes through which an individual passes after leaving the egg and before attaining sexual maturity, as the larva, pupa, and imago of an insect. Compare METAGENESIS. **4** *Bot.* The varied development of plant organs of the same morphological value, such development resulting from their adaptations of different functions: also **met′a·mor′phy.** **5** *Pathol.* A morbid change of the elements of tissues into another form of structure. **6** The changes in form going on in living tissues, blood corpuscles, etc. [< L < Gk. *metamorphōsis* < *metamorphoein* transform < *meta-* beyond + *morphē* form]

met·a·phase (met′ə·fāz) *n. Biol.* The middle stage of mitotic cell division, during which the chromosomes split along the equatorial plane between the two poles of the spindle. [<META- + -PHASE]

met·a·phor (met′ə-fôr, -fər) *n.* A figure of speech in which one object is likened to another by speaking of it as if it were that other: distinguished from *simile* by not employing any word of comparison, such as "like" or "as." See synonyms under ALLEGORY, SIMILE. — **mixed metaphor** Figurative language in which incongruous, and often contradictory, metaphors are used; confusion of figurative with plain statement. [<F *métaphore* <L *metaphora* <Gk. <*metapherein* <*meta-* beyond, over + *pherein* carry] — **met′a·phor′ic** (-fôr′ik, -for′ik) or **·i·cal** *adj.* — **met′a·phor′i·cal·ly** *adv.*

met·a·phrase (met′ə-frāz) *v.t.* **·phrased, ·phras·ing 1** To translate word for word. **2** To alter the wording of. — *n.* **1** A literal translation. **2** A phrase in response; retort. **3** A school exercise consisting in the rendering of a piece of poetry into prose or of prose into verse. [<Gk. *metaphrasis* <*metaphrazein* paraphrase <*meta-* beyond + *phrazein* phrase]

met·a·phrast (met′ə-frast) *n.* One who renders poetry into prose or prose into poetry, or changes the meter of verse. [<Gk. *metaphrastēs*] — **met′a·phras′tic** or **·ti·cal** *adj.*

met·a·phys·ic (met′ə-fiz′ik) *n.* Metaphysics. — *adj.* Metaphysical.

met·a·phys·i·cal (met′ə-fiz′i-kəl) *adj.* **1** Of or pertaining to metaphysics. **2** Treating of or versed in metaphysics. **3** Beyond or above the physical or experiential; pertaining to or being of the essential nature of reality; transcendental. **4** Dealing with abstractions; apart from, or opposed to, the practical. **5** Designating certain poets of the 17th century, notably Cowley and Donne, whose verses were characterized by complex, intellectualized imagery: term originating with Dr. Samuel Johnson. [See METAPHYSICS] — **met′a·phys′i·cal·ly** *adv.*

metaphysical healing Christian Science.

met·a·phy·si·cian (met′ə-fi·zish′ən) *n.* One skilled or versed in metaphysics. Also **met′a·phys′i·cist.**

met·a·phys·ics (met′ə-fiz′iks) *n. pl. (construed as singular)* **1** The systematic study or science of the first principles of being and of knowledge; the doctrine of the essential nature and fundamental relations of all that is real. **2** Speculative philosophy in the wide sense. **3** The principles of philosophy as applied to the methodology of any particular science. **4** Mental science in general; psychology. **5** In popular use, abstruse and bewildering discussion. Also **metaphysic.** [<Med. L *metaphysica* <Med. Gk. < *ta meta ta physika* the (works) after the physics; in ref. to Aristotle's ontological treatises, which came after his *Physics*]

met·a·pla·si·a (met′ə-plā′zhē-ə) *n. Biol.* The direct transformation of one kind of tissue into another, as cartilage into bone. [<NL <Gk. *meta-* beyond + *plassein* mold]

me·tap·la·sis (mə-tap′lə-sis) *n. Biol.* The period of completed growth in the life cycle of an organism; maturity. [<NL]

met·a·plasm (met′ə-plaz′əm) *n.* **1** *Biol.* The lifeless, non–protoplasmic material of a cell, as inclusions of fats and carbohydrates. **2** A reversal or change in the order of the letters or syllables of a word. [<L *metaplasmus* <Gk. *metaplasmos* <*meta-* beyond + *plassein* mold] — **met′a·plas′mic** *adj.*

met·a·po·di·um (met′ə-pō′dē-əm) *n. pl.* **·di·a** (-dē-ə) **1** The posterior part of the foot in gastropods and pteropods. **2** The metacarpus and metatarsus of quadrupeds. Also **met′a·pode** (-pōd), **met′a·pod** (-pod).

met·a·pro·te·in (met′ə-prō′tē·in, -tēn) *n. Biochem.* A protein resulting from the action of acids and alkalis and soluble in weak solutions of either but not in solutions of neutral salts.

met·a·psy·chics (met′ə-sī′kiks) *n.* Parapsychology.

met·a·psy·chol·o·gy (met′ə-sī·kol′ə-jē) *n.* **1** Psychology restricted to philosophical speculations on the origin, structure, function, purpose, etc., of the mind. **2** *Psychoanal.* The investigation and study of mental processes from three points of view: the dynamic, topographical, and economic. — **met′a·psy′·cho·log′i·cal** (-sī′kə·loj′i·kəl) *adj.*

met·a·psy·cho·sis (met′ə-sī·kō′sis) *n.* Interchange of mental influence or action without

a recognized physical medium.

met·a·so·ma·to·sis (met′ə-sō′mə-tō′sis) *n. Geol.* That form of metamorphism by means of which a rock or mineral undergoes chemical change through the action of external materials. Also **met′a·so′ma·tism** (-sō′mə-tiz′əm). [<META- + SOMAT(O)- + -OSIS]

met·a·some (met′ə-sōm) *n. Geol.* A mineral which has developed individually within another mineral. [<META- + -SOME²]

met·a·sta·ble (met′ə-stā′bəl) *adj. Physics & Chem.* Denoting an apparent state of equilibrium, as in supersaturated solutions. — **met′a·sta·bil′i·ty** (-stə-bil′ə-tē) *n.*

me·tas·ta·sis (mə-tas′tə-sis) *n. pl.* **·ses** (-sēz) **1** Change of one thing into another. **2** Metabolism. **3** *Pathol.* The transfer of a disease or of its manifestations from one part of the body to another. **4** In rhetoric, a rapid change from one point to another. [<L <Gk. <*methistanai* place differently, change <*meta-* after + *histanai* place] — **met′a·stat′ic** (-stat′-) *adj.* — **met′a·stat′i·cal·ly** *adv.*

me·tas·ta·size (mə-tas′tə-sīz) *v.i.* **·sized, ·siz·ing** *Pathol.* To shift or spread from one part of the body to another: said specifically of malignant growths.

met·as·then·ic (met′əs-then′ik) *adj. Biol.* Having the posterior or lower part of the body well developed, as a kangaroo. [<META- + STHENIC]

met·a·syph·i·lis (met′ə-sif′ə-ləs) *n. Pathol.* **1** Congenital syphilis, with typical degenerative changes, but without localized external lesions. **2** Parasyphilis. — **met′a·syph′i·lit′ic** (-sif′ə-lit′ik) *adj.*

met·a·tar·sal (met′ə-tär′səl) *adj.* Of or pertaining to the metatarsus. — *n.* One of the bones of the metatarsus. See illustration under FOOT.

met·a·tar·sus (met′ə-tär′səs) *n. pl.* **·si** (-sī) *Anat.* The part of the hind or pelvic limb between the tarsus or ankle and the phalanges or bones of the toe. In man it consists of five bones. [<NL <META- + TARSUS]

met·a·the·ri·an (met′ə-thir′ē-ən) *n.* Any one of a subclass (*Metatheria*) of mammals whose young are born immature and are carried in a pouch until fully developed; one of the marsupials, as a kangaroo, opossum, or bandicoot. — *adj.* Of or pertaining to the *Metatheria.* [<META- + Gk. *thērion* beast]

me·tath·e·sis (mə-tath′ə-sis) *n. pl.* **·ses** (-sēz) **1** The transposition of letters, syllables, or sounds in a word. **2** *Chem.* A substitution, as the replacing or exchange of one or more radicals or groups in a compound; double decomposition or mutual exchange. **3** *Surg.* The operation of removing a morbific substance from one place to another for relief, as by pushing a calculus lodged in the urethra back into the bladder. **4** Any change or reversal of conditions. [<LL <Gk. < *metatithenai* transpose <*meta-* over + *tithenai* place] — **met·a·thet·ic** (met′ə-thet′ik) or **·i·cal** *adj.*

met·a·tho·rax (met′ə-thôr′aks, -thō′raks) *n. Entomol.* The hindmost of the three segments of the thorax in insects, bearing the hind wings and the third pair of legs. — **met′a·tho·rac′ic** (-thô-ras′ik, -thō-) *adj.*

met·a·troph·ic (met′ə-trof′ik) *adj.* Saprophytic. [<META- + Gk. *trophikos* feeding, nursing]

me·tat·ro·phy (mə-tat′rə-fē) *n. Pathol.* A wasting away because of disordered nutrition. Also **met·a·tro·phi·a** (met′ə-trō′fē-ə). [<MET- + ATROPHY]

met·a·xy·lem (met′ə-zī′ləm) *n. Bot.* The thick–walled cell portion in the woody tissues of plants, developed outside the primary xylem. [<META- + XYLEM]

met·a·zo·an (met′ə-zō′ən) *n.* Any member of a primary division (*Metazoa*) of the animal kingdom, whose cells become differentiated into at least an outer and an inner wall, including all animals higher than protozoans. Also **met·a·zo′on.** — *adj.* Of or pertaining to the metazoans: also **met′a·zo′ic.** [<META- + Gk. *zōion* animal]

mete¹ (mēt) *v.t.* **met·ed, met·ing 1** To allot or distribute by measure; apportion: usually with *out.* **2** *Obs.* To measure. — *n. Obs.* Measure. ◆ Homophones: *meat, meet.* [OE *metan* measure]

mete² (mēt) *n. Obs.* A boundary line; limit; confine: usually in the phrase *metes and bounds.* ◆ Homophones: *meat, meet.* [<OF <L *meta* goal, boundary]

met·em·pir·i·cal (met′em-pir′i·kəl) *adj.* Lying

beyond the bounds of experience, as intuitive principles; not derived from experience; transcendental; a priori: opposed to *empirical.* Also **met′em·pir′ic.**

met·em·pir·i·cism (met′em-pir′ə-siz′əm) *n.* The science of pure reason; metaphysics proper; hence, with some, transcendental philosophy. Also **met′em·pir′ics.**

me·tem·psy·cho·sis (mə-temp′sə-kō′sis, met′əm-sī-) *n.* Transmigration of souls from body to body. [<LL <Gk. *metempsychōsis* <*metempsychoein* <*meta-* over + *empsychoein* animate <*en-* in + *psychē* soul, life]

met·en·ceph·a·lon (met′ən-sef′ə-lon) *n. pl.* **·la** (-lə) **1** The fifth cerebral vesicle of the brain and the parts derived therefrom, comprising the medulla oblongata and the posterior part of the roof of the fourth ventricle. **2** The part of the brain consisting of the cerebellum and pons Varolii. [<NL <MET- + ENCEPHALON] — **met′en·ce·phal′ic** (-sə-fal′ik) *adj.*

me·te·or (mē′tē-ər, -ôr) *n.* **1** *Astron.* A luminous phenomenon, produced by a small mass of matter from the celestial spaces which strikes the earth's atmosphere with great velocity and is dissipated by heat: when not very brilliant, called a *shooting star.* **2** A meteoroid. **3** *Obs.* Any phenomenon of the atmosphere: **aerial meteors** (winds, hurricanes, etc.), **aqueous meteors** (rain, snow, etc.), **igneous meteors** (lightning, shooting stars, etc.), **luminous meteors** (aurora, rainbow, etc.). [<Med. L *meteorum* <Gk. *meteōron* thing in the air <*meteōros* high in the air <*meta-* beyond + *eōra* suspension]

Meteor Crater A depression caused by a meteor in central Arizona; 600 feet deep, 4,000 feet in diameter: also *Diablo Crater.*

me·te·or·ic (mē′tē-ôr′ik, -or′ik) *adj.* **1** Relating to meteors. **2** Meteorological. **3** Transitorily brilliant: a *meteoric* career. Also **me′·te·or′i·cal.** — **me′te·or′i·cal·ly** *adv.*

me·te·or·ite (mē′tē-ə-rīt′) *n.* **1** A fallen meteor; a mass of stone or iron that has fallen upon the earth from outer space. **2** A meteoroid. — **me′te·or·it′ic** (-ə-rit′ik) *adj.*

me·te·or·o·graph (mē′tē-ər-ə-graf′, -gräf′, mē′·tē-ôr′ə-, -or′ə-) *n.* A self-recording instrument, frequently attached to a kite or balloon, by which several meteorological elements are plotted in the form of a diagram. [<F *météorographe*]

me·te·or·oid (mē′tē-ə-roid) *n. Astron.* One of innumerable small particles of matter moving through the celestial spaces, which, when they encounter the earth's atmosphere, form meteors or shooting stars.

me·te·or·ol·o·gy (mē′tē-ə-rol′ə-jē) *n.* **1** The science that treats of atmospheric phenomena, especially those that relate to weather. **2** The character of the weather and of atmospheric changes of any particular place. [<Gk. *meteōrologia* <*meteōros* high in the air + *logos* discourse] — **me′te·or′o·log′ic** (-ôr′ə-loj′ik), **me′te·or′o·log′i·cal** *adj.* — **me′te·or′o·log′i·cal·ly** *adv.* — **me′te·or·ol′o·gist** *n.*

meteor shower *Astron.* The apparent passage of a group of meteors upon entering the earth's atmosphere.

me·ter¹ (mē′tər) *n.* **1** An instrument, apparatus, or machine for measuring fluids, gases, electric currents, grain, etc., and recording the results obtained. **2** Any person or thing that measures; specifically, one of several officers appointed to measure certain commodities, as for tolls. — *v.t.* To measure or test by means of a meter. [< METE¹]

me·ter² (mē′tər) *n.* **1** The fundamental unit of length in the metric system, originally defined as one ten-millionth of the distance on the earth's surface from the pole to the equator; 39.37 inches. In practice, it is the distance between two fiducial lines marked on the platinum-iridium International Prototype Meter deposited at Sèvres, France. See METRIC SYSTEM. **2** A measured verbal rhythm, the structure of verse; a definite arrangement of groups of syllables in a line, having a time unit and a regular beat; also, a specific arrangement of words, or a specific sequence of such lines in a stanza. **3** The character of a musical composition as being divisible into measures equal in time and length, and similar in rhythmic pattern. Also spelled *metre.* [< F *mètre* <L *metrum* measure <Gk. *metron*]

Synonyms : euphony, measure, rhythm, verse. *Euphony* is agreeable linguistic sound, however produced; *meter, measure,* and *rhythm* denote agreeable succession of sounds in the utterance of connected words; *euphony* may apply to a single word or even a single syllable; the other words apply to lines, sentences, paragraphs, etc.; *rhythm* and *meter* may be produced by accent only, as in English, or by accent and quantity combined, as in Greek or Italian; *rhythm* or *measure* may apply either to prose or to poetry, or to music, dancing, etc.; *meter* is more precise than *rhythm,* applies only to poetry, and denotes a measured *rhythm.* A *verse* is strictly a metrical line, but the word is often used as synonymous with stanza. *Verse,* in the general sense, denotes metrical writing; as, prose and verse. Compare MELODY, POETRY.

-meter *combining form* **1** That (instrument or unit) by which a thing is measured: *calorimeter.* **2** Measure expressing (the main element): *hexameter.* [< L *metrum* < Gk. *metron* measure]

me·ter·age (mē′tər·ij) *n.* **1** The act or result of measuring. **2** The charge for measurement.

met·es·trus (met·es′trəs) *n. Biol.* The period of sexual quiescence following estrus in female mammals: often spelled *metoestrus, metoestrum.* Also **met·es′trum.** [< NL < MET- + ESTRUS] — **met·es′trous** *adj.*

meth·ac·ry·late (meth·ak′rə·lāt) *n. Chem.* An ester of methacrylic acid.

meth·a·cryl·ic acid (meth′ə·kril′ik) *Chem.* A colorless acid, $C_4H_6O_2$, the esters of which are extensively used in the making of plastics. [< METH(YL) + ACRYLIC]

meth·a·done (meth′ə·dōn) *n.* A synthetic opiate used as an analgesic and experimentally as a substitute for heroin in the treatment of addicts. Also **meth′a·don** (-don). [< (*di*)*meth*(*yl*) *a*(*mino*) *d*(*iphenylheptan*)*one*]

meth·am·phet·a·mine (meth′am·fet′ə·mēn,-min) *n. Chem.* A compound, $C_{10}H_{15}N·HCl$, related to the amphetamines, that allays hunger and stimulates the central nervous system. [< METH- + AMPHETAMINE]

meth·ane (meth′ān) *n. Chem.* A colorless, inflammable gas, CH_4, the simplest of the saturated hydrocarbons, formed by decomposition of vegetable matter, or artificially by dry distillation of certain organic matter, or by chemical treatment of certain metal compounds, as aluminum carbide. It is an important component of illuminating gas: often called *marsh gas.* [< METH(YL) + -ANE²]

methane series *Chem.* A group of saturated aliphatic hydrocarbons having the general formula C_nH_{2n+2}, and identified by the ending *-ane* : also called *alkanes.*

meth·a·nol (meth′ə·nōl, -nol) *n. Chem.* Methyl alcohol; a colorless, volatile, inflammable liquid, CH_3OH, obtained by the destructive distillation of wood or by catalytic treatment of hydrogen and carbon monoxide: highly toxic and widely used in industry and the arts: also called *carbinol, wood alcohol.* [< METHANE + -OL¹]

meth·a·qua·lone (meth′ə·kwä′lōn) *n.* An addictive drug, $C_{16}H_{14}N_2O$, used as a sedative; Quaalude.

me·theg·lin (mə·theg′lin) *n.* A fermented drink made of water and honey; mead. [< Welsh *meddyglyn* < *meddyg* doctor (< L *medicus*) + *llyn* juice, liquor]

met·he·mo·glo·bin (met·hē′mə·glō′bin, -hem′ə-) *n. Biochem.* A stable, brown-red, crystalline compound formed by the decomposition of blood and by oxidation of hemoglobin. Also **met·haé·mo·glo′bin.** [< MET- + HEMOGLOBIN]

me·the·na·mine (mə·thē′nə·mēn, -min) *n. Chem.* An organic compound, $C_6H_{12}N_4$, crystallized from a mixture of formalin and ammonia: used in the vulcanization of rubber, in making synthetic resins, and as an antiseptic: also called *Urotropin, hexamethylenamine, hexamethylenetetramine.* [< *methene* (< METHYL + -ENE) + AMINE]

metho- *combining form Chem.* Used to indicate the presence of a methyl group in a compound. Also, before vowels, **meth-,** as in *methane.* [< METHYL]

meth·od (meth′əd) *n.* **1** A general or established way or order of doing anything, or the means or manner by which it is presented or taught. **2** Orderly and systematic arrangement, as of ideas and topics, etc.; the design or plan of a speaker or of an author. **3** The arrangement of natural bodies according to their common characteristics. See synonyms under MANNER, RULE, SYSTEM. [< F *méthode* < L *methodus* < Gk. *methodos* < *meta-* after + *hodos* way]

me·thod·i·cal (mə·thod′i·kəl) *adj.* **1** Given to or characterized by orderly arrangement. **2** Arranged with method. Also **me·thod′ic.** — **me·thod′i·cal·ly** *adv.* — **me·thod′i·cal·ness** *n.*

meth·od·ist (meth′əd·ist) *n.* An observer of method or order. — **meth′od·ism** *n.* — **meth′od·is′tic·al** *adj.*

Meth·od·ist (meth′əd·ist) *n.* A member of any one of the Protestant churches that have grown out of the religious movement begun at Oxford University in the first half of the 18th century, in which John Wesley as a leader was associated with Charles Wesley, George Whitefield, and others. The largest Methodist body in the United States is the **Methodist Church,** formed by the union of the **Methodist Episcopal Church,** the **Methodist Episcopal Church, South,** and the **Methodist Protestant Church.** —*adj.* Pertaining to, belonging to, like, or typical of this church or its doctrines. [< METHOD + -IST] —**Meth′od·ism** *n.* —**Meth′od·is′tic, Meth′od·is′ti·cal** *adj.*

meth·od·ize (meth′əd·īz) *v.t.* **·ized, ·iz·ing** To reduce or subject to method; systematize. Also *Brit.* **meth′od·ise.** See synonyms under REGULATE. — **meth′od·i·za′tion** *n.*

meth·od·ol·o·gy (meth′ə·dol′ə·jē) *n.* **1** The science of method or of arranging in due order. **2** The division of pure logic that treats of the methods of directing the means of thinking to the end of clear and connected thinking. [< Gk. *methodos* method + -LOGY]

meth·yl (meth′əl) *n. Chem.* An organic radical, CH_3, existing only in combination, as in methyl alcohol, etc. It is univalent, and forms esters with acids. [< METHYLENE] — **me·thyl·ic** (mə·thil′ik) *adj.*

meth·yl·am·ine (meth′əl·am′ēn, -in) *n. Chem.* A colorless, gaseous, inflammable amine, CH_3NH_2, with a strong fishy odor, contained in the products of the decomposition of certain organic compounds, and also made synthetically from ammonia by replacement of hydrogen by methyl. [< METHYL + AMINE]

meth·yl·ate (meth′əl·āt) *v.t.* **·at·ed, ·at·ing** *Chem.* To mix or saturate with methyl or methanol. — *n.* A compound derived from methanol by replacing the hydrogen of the hydroxyl group with an element or radical of equal valence: potassium *methylate.* [< METHYL + -ATE] — **meth′yl·a′tion** *n.*

methylated spirit *Chem.* A mixture of ethyl alcohol with ten percent of methanol: used in the arts, unfit for drinking.

methyl chloride *Chem.* A gas, CH_3Cl, which on compression becomes a colorless liquid of ethereal odor yielding a poisonous vapor: used as a refrigerant and fire extinguisher.

meth·yl·cho·lan·threne (meth′əl·kō·lan′thrēn) *n. Biochem.* A yellow, crystalline hydrocarbon, $C_{21}H_{16}$, extracted from bile acids and also prepared synthetically: believed to be strongly carcinogenic. [< METHYL + CHOL(E)- + ANTHR(ACINE) + -ENE]

meth·yl·di·chlor·ar·sine (meth′əl·dī′klôr·är′·sēn, -sin) *n. Chem.* A colorless liquid compound, CH_3AsCl_2, adapted for chemical warfare as a vesicant and lung irritant. [< METHYL + DI- + CHLOR- + ARSINE]

methylene blue *Chem.* A dark, blue-green aniline dye, $C_{16}H_{18}N_3ClS·3H_2O$, having medicinal properties in the treatment of diphtheria, malaria, etc., and as an antidote in cyanide poisoning: used also as a chemical indicator and bacteriological stain.

methyl orange *Chem.* An azo dyestuff used chiefly as an indicator in alkalimetry; a brilliant orange-yellow powder, readily soluble in water, colored red on the addition of acids.

meth·yl·ros·an·i·line (meth′əl·roz·an′ə·lēn, -lin) *n.* Gentian violet. [< METHYL + ROSANILINE]

me·tic·u·lous (mə·tik′yə·ləs) *adj.* Careful about trivial matters; finical; particular. [< F *méticuleux* < L *meticolosus* fearful < *metus* fear] — **me·tic′u·los′i·ty** (-los′ə·tē) *n.* — **me·tic′u·lous·ly**

adv.

met·o·chy (met′ə·kē) *n. Entomol.* The relationship of mutual tolerance without mutual aid existing between ants and their neutral insect guests. [< Gk. *metochē* sharing < *metochein* share in]

met·o·don·ti·a·sis (met′ō·don·tī′ə·sis) *n. Dent.* **1** Abnormal or imperfect dentition. **2** Faulty teething. [< NL < MET- + Gk. *odontiaein* cut teeth + -IASIS]

met·o·nym (met′ə·nim) *n.* A word used as a substitute for another. [See METONYMY]

me·ton·y·my (mə·ton′ə·mē) *n.* A figure of speech that consists in the naming of a thing by one of its attributes, as "the crown prefers" for "the king prefers." [< L *metonymia* < Gk. *metōnymia* < *meta-* altered + *onyma* name] — **met·o·nym·ic** (met′ə·nim′ik), **met·o·nym′i·cal** *adj.* — **met′o·nym′i·cal·ly** *adv.*

me-too·ism (mē′tōō′iz′əm) *n.* The practice of representing as one's own the popular or successful policies of another, especially a political rival. — **me′-too′er** *n.*

met·o·pe¹ (met′ə·pē) *n. Archit.* **1** A square slab, sculptured or plain, between triglyphs in a Doric frieze. **2** Originally, the opening supposed to have been left by primitive Greek builders between the ends of adjoining ceiling beams. [< L *metopa* < Gk. *metopē* < *meta-* between + *opē* opening]

met·o·pe² (met′ə·pē) *n. Anat.* The face, forehead, or frontal surface. [Gk. *metōpon* forehead < *meta-* between + *ōps* eye] — **me·top·ic** (mə·top′ik) *adj.*

me·tral·gi·a (mə·tral′jē·ə) *n. Pathol.* Pain in the womb. [< METR(O)-¹ + -ALGIA]

met·ric (met′rik) *adj.* **1** Pertaining to the meter as a unit of measurement or to the metric system. **2** Metrical (def. 1). [< L *metricus* < Gk. *metrikos*]

met·ri·cal (met′ri·kəl) *adj.* **1** Relating to meter or versification; composed in poetic measures; rhythmical. **2** Metric (def. 1). — **met′ri·cal·ly** *adv.*

metrical stress The emphasis required by the meter of a poem: opposed to *rhetorical stress.*

metric hundredweight A weight of 50 kilograms.

me·tri·cian (mə·trish′ən) *n.* **1** One versed in metrics. **2** A composer of verse.

met·rics (met′riks) *n. pl.* (*construed as singular*) **1** The mathematical theory of measurement. **2** The art of metrical composition.

metric system A decimal system of weights and measures having as fundamental units the gram and the meter. From the *gram* are derived measures of weight, and from the *meter* measures of length; measures of surface are based on the *square meter* and measures of capacity on the *liter.* The table shown on page 618 gives the basic and derived units of the metric system, together with abbreviations and a list of equivalent values in customary U.S. standards; originating in a report to the French Academy (1791) it was legalized in France, Nov. 2, 1801; now universally used in scientific measurement.

metric ton A unit of weight, equal to 1,000 kilograms, 0.984 long ton, or 1.023 short tons.

met·ri·fi·ca·tion (met′rə·fə·kā′shən) *n.* The adoption of the metric system or the conversion to metric units from those of another system. Also *Brit.* **met·ri·ca·tion** (met′rə·kā′shən).

met·ri·fy (met′rə·fī) *v.t.* & *v.i.* **·fied, ·fy·ing 1** To write in meter, versify. **2** To convert to the metric system or metric units.

me·trist (mē′trist, met′rist) *n.* One versed in meters or skilled in metrical composition; a versemaker. [< Med. L *metrista*]

me·tri·tis (mə·trī′tis) *n. Pathol.* Inflammation of the womb. — **me·trit′ic** (-trit′ik) *adj.*

met·ro (met′rō) *n. pl.* **·ros** *Often cap.* In European countries, an underground railway; subway. [< F *métro* < *chemin de fer*) *métro-*(*politain*) metro(politan railroad); in England < METRO(POLITAN DISTRICT RAILWAY)]

metro-¹ *combining form* The uterus; pertaining to the uterus: *metropathic.* Also, before vowels, **metr-.** [< Gk. *metra* the uterus]

metro-² *combining form* Measure: *metrology.* Also, before vowels, **metr-.** [< Gk. *metron* a measure]

me·trol·o·gy (mə·trol′ə·jē) *n.* The science that

METRIC SYSTEM

Length		Equivalents			Weight or Mass		Equivalents			Capacity		Equivalents		
		Metric		U.S.			Metric		U.S.			Metric		U.S.
millimeter	(mm)	.001	m	.03937	in.	milligram	(mg)	.001	g	.0154	gr.	milliliter	(ml)	.001	l	.033	fl. oz.
centimeter	(cm)	.01	m	.3937	in.	centigram	(cg)	.01	g	.1543	gr.	centiliter	(cl)	.01	l	.338	fl. oz.
decimeter	(dm)	.1	m	3.937	in.	decigram	(dg)	.1	g	1.543	gr.	deciliter	(dl)	.1	l	3.38	fl. oz.
METER	(m)	1	m	39.37	in.	GRAM	(g)	1	g	15.43	gr.	LITER	(l)	1	l	1.056	li. qts.
dekameter	(dkm)	10	m	10.93	yds.	dekagram	(dkg)	10	g	.3527	oz. av.	dekaliter	(dkl)	10	l	.283	bu.
hectometer	(hm)	100	m	328.08	ft.	hectogram	(hg)	100	g	3.527	oz. av.	hectoliter	(hl)	100	l	2.837	bu.
kilometer	(km)	1000	m	.6213	mi.	kilogram	(kg)	1000	g	2.2	lbs. av.	kiloliter	(kl)	1000	l	264.18	gal.

Area		Equivalents				Volume		Equivalents			
		Metric		U.S.				Metric		U.S.	
sq. millimeter	(mm²)	.000001	ca	.00155	sq. in.	cu. millimeter	(mm³)	.001	cm³	.016	minim
sq. centimeter	(cm²)	.0001	ca	.155	sq. in.	cu. centimeter	(cc, cm³)	.001	dm³	.061	cu. in.
sq. decimeter	(dm²)	.01	ca	15.5	sq. in.	cu. decimeter	(dm³)	.001	m³	61.023	cu. in.
CENTARE	(ca, m²)	1	m²	10.76	sq. ft.	STERE	(s, m³)	1	m³	1.307	cu. yds.
sq. dekameter	(dkm²)	100	ca	.0247	acre	cu. dekameter	(dkm³)	1000	m³	1307.942	cu. yds.
Also are	(a)			2.47	acres	cu. hectometer	(hm³)	1,000,000	m³	1,307,942.8	cu. yds.
sq. hectometer	(hm²)	10,000	ca	.386	sq. mi.	cu. kilometer	(km³)	1,000,000,000	m³	0.24	cu. mile
Also hectare	(ha)										
sq. kilometer	(km²)	1,000,000	ca								

Other prefixes occasionally used are: MICRO—one millionth; MYRIA—10,000 times; MEGA—1,000,000 times

treats of systems of weights and measures or of measure. [<METRO-² + -LOGY] — **met·ro·log·i·cal** (met′rə-loj′i-kəl) *adj.* — **me·trol′o·gist** *n*

met·ro·nome (met′rə-nōm) *n.* An instrument for indicating and marking exact time in music, consisting usually of a reversed pendulum whose period of vibration is regulated by a shifting weight. [<METRO-² + Gk. *nomos* law] — **met′ro·nom′ic** (-nom′ik) *adj.*

METRONOME

me·tro·nym·ic (mē′trə-nim′ik, met′rə-) *adj.* Pertaining to or derived from the name of one's mother or female ancestors: also **me·tron·y·mous** (mə-tron′ə-məs). — *n.* **1** A name taken from the mother's side or derived from the maternal name: also **me′tro·nym.** Compare PATRONYMIC. **2** A metronymic designation. [<Gk. *mētrōnymikos* <*mētēr* mother + *onyma* name]

met·ro·path·ic (met′rə-path′ik) *adj. Pathol.* Of or pertaining to disorders of the uterus. [< METRO-¹ + Gk. *pathos* suffering] — **me·trop·a·thy** (mə-trop′ə-thē) *n.*

me·trop·o·lis (mə-trop′ə-lis) *n.* **1** A chief city, either the capital or the largest or most important city of a state or country. **2** The seat of a metropolitan bishop. **3** In ancient Greece, the mother city of a colony. [<Gk. *mētropolis* city <*mētēr* mother + *polis* city]

met·ro·pol·i·tan (met′rə-pol′ə-tən) *n.* **1** An archbishop who exercises a limited authority over the bishops of the same ecclesiastical province. **2** A citizen of the mother city, as opposed to a colonist. **3** One who lives in a metropolis; also, one who has the manners and the ideas, or practices the customs, of a metropolis. — *adj.* Pertaining to or peculiar to a metropolis or to a metropolitan. [<LL *metropolitanus*]

-metry *combining form* The process, science, or art of measuring: *geometry.* [<Gk. *me·tria* <*metron* a measure]

met·tle (met′l) *n.* The stuff or material of which a thing is composed; especially, constitutional temperament or disposition; specifically, courage; ardor. See synonyms under COURAGE. — **on one's mettle** Aroused to one's utmost or best efforts. ◆ Homophone: *metal.* [Var. of METAL]

met·tle·some (met′l-səm) *adj.* Having courage or spirit; ardent; fiery. Also **met′tled.**

mew¹ (myōo) *n.* **1** A cage for molting birds; an enclosure; pen for fattening or breeding; also, any place of concealment. **2** *pl.* A stable; specifically, the stables in London in which the royal horses are kept: so called because built on the site of the *mews* or cages of the royal hawks. — *v.t.* **1** To confine in or as in a mew; immure or conceal: often with *up.* **2** *Obs.* To change (feathers); molt. — *v.i.* **3** *Obs.* To molt. [<OF *muer* change <L *mutare*]

mew² (myōo) *v.i.* To cry as a cat. — *n.* The ordinary plaintive cry of a cat. Also spelled *miaou, miaow, meow.* [Imit.]

mew³ (myōo) *n.* A European sea gull. Also **mew gull.** [OE *mæw*; imit.]

mewl (myōol) *v.i.* To cry, as an infant. — *n.* An infant's cry or crying. [Freq. of MEW²]

Mex·i·can (mek′sə-kən) *n.* **1** A native or inhabitant of Mexico. The inhabitants are chiefly of mestizo and native Indian blood, with a minority of white persons of Spanish ancestry. **2** The Nahuatl or Aztec language. — *adj.* Pertaining to Mexico, its inhabitants, or their language.

Mexican bean beetle A ladybird (*Epilachna varivestis*) with spotted wings, which feeds on the leaves and green pods of beans. For illustration see INSECTS (injurious).

Mexican hairless An ancient breed of small dog found in Mexico, hairless excepting a tuft on the head and a fuzzy growth toward the end of the tail: also called *biche.*

Mex·i·co (mek′sə-kō) **1** A republic in southern North America between the Pacific and the Caribbean and the Gulf of Mexico, administratively divided into 29 states; 760,373 square miles. **2** Its capital, the largest city in the republic and capital of the **Federal District of Mexico** (573 square miles) in the center of the country: also **Mexico City. 3** A state in central Republic of Mexico; 8,267 square miles; capital, Toluca. Spanish *Méjico.*

Mexico, Gulf of An arm of the Atlantic; nearly enclosed by the United States, Mexico, and Cuba; 700,000 square miles.

me·ze·re·on (mə-zir′ē-ən) *n.* **1** A low, Old World shrub (*Daphne mezereum*) with clusters of sweet-smelling, lilac-purple flowers: cultivated in the United States. **2** Mezereum (def. 1). [< Med. L < Arabic *māzarivān* camellia]

me·ze·re·um (mə-zir′ē-əm) *n.* **1** The dried bark of any of the *Daphne* species: used in medicine as an irritant and vesicant, and in the treatment of syphilis, rheumatism, and various skin diseases. **2** Mezereon (def. 1).

me·zu·zah (mə-zŏŏ′zə, me·zŏŏ′zä) *n. pl.* **·zoth** (-zōth) In Judaism, a parchment inscribed with the passages *Deut.* vi 4–9 and xi 13–21, to be rolled up in a case or tube and affixed to the doorpost of a dwelling, as the passages command. Also **me·zu′za.** [< Hebrew *mezūzāh* doorpost]

mez·za·nine (mez′ə-nēn, -nin) *n. Archit.* **1** A low-ceilinged story between two main ones, especially between the ground floor and the one above it. Also **mezzanine floor, mezzanine story.** **2** In a theater, the first balcony or the front rows of the first balcony. [< F < Ital. *mezzanino,* dim. of *mezzano* middle < L *medianus*]

mez·zo (met′sō, med′zō, mez′ō) *adj.* Half; medium; moderate. [< Ital. < L *medius* middle]

mez·zo-re·lie·vo (met′sō-ri-lē′vō) *n. pl.* **-vos** Half relief; a piece of sculpture in which the rounded figures project half-way from the background material; demi-relief. See RELIEF. [< Ital. *mezzo rilievo.* See MEZZO and RELIEF.]

mezzo soprano A voice lower than a soprano and higher than a contralto; also, a person possessing, or a part written for, such a voice.

mez·zo·tint (met′sō-tint, med′zō-, mez′ō-) *n.* **1** A method of copperplate engraving, producing an even gradation of tones, like a photograph. **2** An impression so produced. — *v.t.* To engrave in or represent by mezzotint. [< Ital. *mezzotinto* <*mezzo* middle + *tinto* painted] — **mez′zo·tint′er** *n*

Mi·am·i (mī·am′ē) *n.* A member of an Algonquian tribe of North American Indians formerly located between the Miami and Wabash rivers. [< N. Am. Ind.]

mi·a·na bug (mē·ä′nə) The tampan. [from *Miana,* an Iranian town]

mi·as·ma (mī·az′mə, mē-) *n. pl.* **·mas** or **·ma·ta** (-mə·tə) Polluting exhalations; the poisonous effluvium once supposed to rise from putrid matter, swamps, and marshy ground, especially at night. Also **mi′asm.** [< NL < Gk., pollution <*miainein* stain, defile] — **mi·as′mal, mi·as·mat·ic** (mī′az·mat′ik), **mi·as′mic** *adj.*

mib (mib) *n.* **1** A marble. **2** *pl.* The game of marbles. [? Alter. of MARBLE]

mi·ca (mī′kə) *n.* Any of a class of silicates, crystallizing in the monoclinic system and having eminently perfect basal cleavage, affording thin, tough laminae or scales, colorless to jet-black, transparent to translucent, and of widely varying chemical composition. The better grades are extensively used for electrical insulation; the transparent varieties are loosely called *isinglass.* [< L, crumb; infl. by *micare* glitter]

mice (mīs) Plural of MOUSE.

mi·celle (mi·sel′) **1** *Biol.* One of the theoretical structural units which are said to make up organized bodies. **2** *Chem.* The structural unit of a colloid, composed of an aggregate of molecules having crystalline properties and able to change in size without chemical alteration. Also **mi·cell′, mi·cel′la** (-sel′ə). [< NL *micella,* dim. of L *mica* crumb, grain] — **mi·cel′lar** *adj.*

Mich·ael·mas (mik′əl·məs) The feast of St. Michael, Sept. 29; a quarterly rent day in England. [< MICHAEL + -MAS]

Michaelmas daisy 1 A European blue aster (*Aster tripolium*). **2** Any of several North American asters, wild and cultivated.

Mi·chel·an·ge·lo (mī′kel·an′jə·lō), 1475–1564, Italian sculptor, painter, architect, and poet. Also **Mi′chael An′ge·lo:** full name **Mi·chel·an·ge·lo Buo·nar·ro·ti** (mē′kel·än′je·lō bwô′när·rô′tē).

Mich·i·gan (mish′ə·gən) A north central State of the United States: 57,980 square miles; capital, Lansing; entered the Union Jan. 26, 1837; nickname, *Wolverine State:* abbr. MI —**Mich′i·**

MEXICAN HAIRLESS
(From 11 to 13 inches high at the shoulder)

gan·ite´ (-īt´), Mich·i·gan´der (-gan´dər) n.

Michigan, Lake The only one of the Great Lakes entirely within the United States, lying between Michigan and Wisconsin; 22,400 square miles.

Mic·mac (mik´mak) n. pl. **·mac** or **·macs** One of a tribe of North American Indians of Algonquian linguistic stock located in Nova Scotia, New Brunswick, and Newfoundland. [< N. Am. Ind., lit., allies]

mi·cri·fy (mī´krə·fī) v.t. **·fied**, **·fy·ing** To make small or insignificant. [< MICR(O)- + -(I)FY]

micro- combining form **1** In the metric and other systems of measurement, the one-millionth part of (the specified unit):

microampere	microfarad	micromho
microangstrom	microhenry	micromicron
microbar	microhm	microphot
microcoulomb	microjoule	microvolt
microcurie	microlux	microwatt

2 An apparatus or instrument which enlarges in size or volume: microphone. **3** Exceptionally or abnormally small: micro-organism. **4** Microscopic; using or requiring a microscope:

microbotany	micropathology
microgeology	micropetrography
microhistology	micropetrology
micromechanics	microphysiography
micrometallurgy	microphysiology
micromineralogy	microzoology

Also, before vowels, sometimes **micr-**. [< Gk. mikros small]

mi·cro·an·al·y·sis (mī´krō·ə·nal´ə·sis) n. The chemical analysis and identification of minute quantities. —**mi·cro·an·a·lyt´i·cal** (-an´ə·lit´i·kəl) adj. —**mi´cro·an·a·lyt´i·cal·ly** adv.

mi·crobe (mī´krōb) n. A microscopic organism; especially, a pathogenic bacterium. Also **mi·cro·bi·on** (mī·krō´bē·on). [< F < Gk. mikros small + bios life] —**mi·cro´bi·al, mi·cro´bi·an, mi·cro´bic** adj.

mi·cro·bi·cide (mī·krō´bə·sīd) n. Any substance or agent that destroys microbes; a germ-killer. [< MICROBE + -CIDE] —**mi·cro·bi·ci´dal** adj.

mi·cro·bi·ol·o·gy (mī´krō·bī·ol´ə·jē) n. The scientific study of the structure, development, function, and mode of action of micro-organisms, as bacteria, viruses, molds, etc., especially with regard to their significance in health and disease. —**mi·cro·bi·o·log·i·cal** (mī´krō·bī´ə·loj´i·kəl) adj. —**mi·cro·bi·ol´o·gist** n.

mi·cro·bi·o·ta (mī´krō·bī·ō´tə) n. pl. Ecol. The microscopic plant and animal organisms of a region. [< NL < MICRO- + BIOTA] —**mi·cro·bi·ot´ic** (-ot´ik) adj.

mi·cro·ceph·a·ly (mī´krō·sef´ə·lē) n. Abnormal smallness of the head; imperfect development of the cranium. Also **mi´cro·ce·pha´li·a** (-sə·fā´lē·ə). [< MICRO- + Gk. kephalē head] —**mi´cro·ce·phal·ic** (-sə·fal´ik), **mi·cro·ceph´a·lous** adj.

mi·cro·chem·is·try (mī´krō·kem´is·trē) n. The chemistry of very small objects or quantities, especially those requiring the use of the microscope. —**mi·cro·chem´i·cal** adj.

mi·cro·cir·cuit (mī´krō·sûr´kət) n. An electronic circuit made up of very tiny components.

mi·cro·cli·mate (mī´krō·klī´mit) n. Meteorol. The climate of a very small area, as of a forest, meadow, lake, wheat field, etc., with special reference to local variations from the general climate of a region. Compare MACRO-CLIMATE. —**mi·cro·cli·mat·ic** (mī´krō·klī·mat´-ik) adj.

mi·cro·coc·cus (mī´krə·kok´əs) n. pl. **·coc·ci** (-kok´sī) Any member of a genus (Micrococcus) of spherical bacteria occurring in irregular masses or in plates. They are generally Gram-positive, and feed either on living or on dead matter. [< NL]

mi·cro·cop·y (mī´krə·kop´ē) n. pl. **·cop·ies** A reduced photographic copy, as of a letter, manuscript, etc.

mi·cro·cosm (mī´krə·koz´əm) n. **1** A little world; the world or universe on a small scale; hence, man, as if combining in himself all the elements of the great world: opposed to macrocosm. **2** A little community. Also **mi´cro·cos´mos** (-koz´mos), **mi´cro·cos´mus**. [< F microcosme < LL microcosmus < Gk. mikros kosmos, lit., little world] —**mi´cro·cos´mic, mi´cro·cos´mi·cal, mi´cro·cos´mi·an** adj.

mi·cro·cyte (mī´krə·sīt) n. Pathol. A small red blood corpuscle found in cases of anemia.

mi·cro·dis·sec·tion (mī´krō·di·sek´shən) n. Dissection, as of tissue, under the microscope.

mi·cro·dont (mī´krə·dont) adj. Having unusually small teeth. Also **mi´cro·don´tous**. [< MI-CR(O) + Gk. odous, odontos tooth]

mi·cro·e·co·nom·ics (mī´krō·ē´kə·nom´iks, -ek´-ə-) n. Economics studied in terms of individual areas of the economy, esp. a company or a family.

mi·cro·e·lec·tron·ics (mī´krō·i·lek´tron´iks) n. Branch of electronics that deals with the miniaturization of circuits and components.

mi·cro·fiche (mī´krō·fēsh´) n. A sheet of microfilm. [< F < MICRO- + fiche card]

mi·cro·film (mī´krə·film) n. **1** A photograph, as of a printed page, document, or other object, highly reduced for ease in transmission and storage, and capable of reenlargement or reading by suitable optical devices. **2** A microphotograph. —**mi·cro·film´ing** n.

mi·cro·form (mī´krō·fôrm´) n. A method of reproducing images greatly reduced in size, as on microfilm.

mi·cro·fos·sil (mī´krə·fos´əl) n. The fossilized remains of an extremely minute organism, usually of submarine origin and of value in the study of early geological conditions and biological development.

mi·cro·ga·mete (mī´krō·gə·mēt´, -gam´ēt) n. Biol. The male of two conjugating gametes: so called from its being the smaller one. Compare MACROGAMETE.

mi·cro·gram (mī´krə·gram) n. A unit of weight in the metric system, equal to one thousandth of a milligram. Also **mi´cro·gramme**.

mi·cro·graph (mī´krə·graf, -gräf) n. **1** A pantograph instrument for minute writing, drawing, or engraving. **2** A picture of an object as seen through a microscope. **3** An instrument for recording and photographically magnifying very small movements, as those of a diaphragm. —**mi·cro·graph´ic** adj.

mi·crog·ra·phy (mī·krog´rə·fē) n. **1** The description or study of microscopic objects. **2** The art or habit of writing very minutely. **3** Very minute handwriting. Contrasted with macrography.

mi·cro·in·cin·er·a·tion (mī´krō·in·sin´ə·rā´shən) n. A method for the study of the inorganic constituents of cells and tissues by burning the organic materials and examining the residue under the microscope.

mi·cro·li·ter (mī´krə·lē´tər) n. A metric unit of capacity, equal to one thousandth of a milliliter. Also **mi´cro·li´tre**.

mi·crol·o·gy (mī·krol´ə·jē) n. **1** The branch of science that treats of microscopic objects or is dependent on microscopic investigations. **2** Undue attention to minute and unimportant matters. [< MICRO- + -LOGY]

mi·cro·me·te·or·ol·o·gy (mī´krō·mē`tē·ə·rol´ə·jē) n. The study of climatic conditions in very small areas or localities. Compare MAC-ROMETEOROLOGY.

mi·crom·e·ter (mī·krom´ə·tər) n. **1** An instrument for measuring very small distances or dimensions. **2** A caliper or gage arranged to allow of minute measurements. [< MICRO- + -METER] —**mi·cro·met·ri·cal** (mī´krə·met´ri·kəl), **mi´-cro·met´ric** adj. —**mi´cro·met´ri·cal·ly** adv. —**mi·crom´e·try** n.

micrometer screw A screw with fine and very accurately cut threads, and a circular, graduated head, which shows the amount of advancement or retraction of the screw: used in making fine measurements, often to .0001 of an inch.

MICROMETER

mi·cro·min·i·a·tur·ize (mī´krō·min´ē·ə·chər·īz, -min´ə-) v.t. **·ized**, **·iz·ing**. To reduce the size of, as the parts of electronic circuits, to a scale smaller than miniature. —**mi´cro·min´i·a·tur´i·za´tion** n.

mi·cron (mī´kron) n. pl. **·cra** (-krə) The one-thousandth part of a millimeter, or the one-millionth part of a meter (symbol μ). Also spelled mikron. [< NL < Gk. mikron, neut. of mikros small]

mi·cron·ize (mī´krən·īz) v.t. **·ized**, **·iz·ing** To comminute (a substance) into particles not more than a few microns in diameter. [< MI-CRON + -IZE] —**mi´cron·i·za´tion** n.

mi·cro·nu·tri·ent (mī´krō·nōō´trē·ənt, -nyōō´-) n. A substance essential in the nourishment of animals and plants but only in small amounts or in low concentration, as certain minerals. —adj. Of or pertaining to such a substance.

mi·cro·or·gan·ism (mī´krō·ôr´gən·iz´əm) n. Any extremely small plant or animal organism, especially one visible only in an optical or electron microscope, as a bacterium, protozoan, or virus.

mi·cro·pa·le·on·tol·o·gy (mī´krō·pā`lē·ən·tol´-ə·jē) n. The study of microscopic fossils in relation to their geologic and ecological environment, especially those forms found in core samples from submarine depths. —**mi´cro·pa´le·on·to·log´ic** (-pā`lē·on·tə·loj´ik) or **·i·cal** adj. —**mi´cro·pa´le·on·tol´o·gist** n.

mi·cro·par·a·site (mī´krō·par´ə·sīt) n. A parasitic micro-organism.

mi·cro·phone (mī´krə·fōn) n. A device for amplifying sounds by the electromagnetic conversion of sound waves impinging upon a sensitive diaphragm. It forms the principal element of a telephone transmitter, and is the first component of any sound-reproducing system, as in radio broadcasting, sound films, etc. —**mi´cro·phon´ic** (-fon´ik) adj.

mi·cro·pho·to·graph (mī´krō·fō´tə·graf, -gräf) n. **1** A microscopic photograph of any object, as a writing, picture, etc. Compare PHOTOMICROGRAPH. **2** Microfilm. —**mi´cro·pho´to·graph´ic** adj. —**mi´cro·pho·tog´ra·phy** (-fə·tog´rə·fē) n.

mi·cro·pho·tom·e·ter (mī´krō·fō·tom´ə·tər) n. An instrument for the measurement of very small luminous intensities, and for the comparative study of spectral lines. —**mi´cro·pho´-to·met´ric** (-fō´tə·met´rik) adj. —**mi´cro·pho·tom´e·try** n.

mi·cro·phys·ics (mī´krə·fiz´iks) n. **1** That branch of physics which investigates the structure, characteristics, and behavior of microscopic particles of matter. **2** Nucleonics.

mi·cro·phyte (mī´krə·fīt) n. A microscopic plant, generally parasitic. —**mi´cro·phy´tal, mi´·cro·phyt´ic** (-fit´ik) adj.

mi·cro·print (mī´krə·print) n. A microphotograph reproduced in a print that may be examined or read by means of a magnifying glass.

mi·cro·proc·ess·or (mī´krō·pros´əs·ər) n. Electronic processor located in a quarter-inch square silicon chip, which can carry out the functions of an ordinary computer or processor.

mi·crop·si·a (mī·krop´sē·ə) n. Pathol. A defect in vision causing objects to appear unusually small. Also **mi·cro´pi·a** (-krō´pē·ə). [< MICR(O)- + -OPSIS] —**mi·crop´tic** (-tik) adj.

mi·cro·py·rom·e·ter (mī´krō·pī·rom´ə·tər) n. An optical instrument for observing the temperature, etc., of minute light- or heat-radiating bodies.

mi·cro·rock·et (mī´krō·rok´it) n. A miniature rocket used for testing a proposed full-scale model.

mi·cro·scope (mī´krə·skōp) n. An optical instrument consisting of a single lens or a combination of lenses for magnifying objects too small to be seen or clearly observed by the naked eye. [< NL microscopium]

mi·cro·scop·ic (mī´krə·skop´ik) adj. **1** Pertaining to a microscope or to microscopy. **2** Made with or as with a microscope. **3** Exceedingly minute; visible only under the microscope: opposed to macroscopic. See synonyms under LITTLE. Also **mi´cro·scop´i·cal**. —**mi´cro·scop´i·cal·ly** adv.

mi·cro·sec·ond (mī´krə·sek´ənd) n. One millionth of a second: used especially in timing the action of subatomic particles in nuclear physics.

mi·cro·seism (mī´krə·sīz´əm) Geol. A very

slight tremor or vibration of the earth's crust, detectable only by a microseismometer. [< MICRO- + Gk. *seisma* shaking] —**mi'cro·seis'mic, mi'cro·seis'mi·cal** *adj.*

mi·cro·seis·mom·e·ter (mī'krō·sīz·mom'ə·tər, -sīs-) *n.* An apparatus for indicating the direction, duration, and intensity of microseisms. Also **mi'cro·seis'mo·graph** (-sīz'mə·graf, -gräf, -sīs'-). [< MICROSEISM + (O)METER]

mi·cro·some (mī'krə·sōm) *n. Biol.* A minute corpuscle embedded in the protoplasm of an active cell. The great number of these corpuscles contributes to the granular appearance of protoplasm. Also **mi'cro·so'ma** (-sō'mə).

mi·cro·spec·tro·scope (mī'krō·spek'trə·skōp) *n.* A combination of the microscope and spectroscope for observing the absorptive spectrum of a minute body.

mi·cro·spore (mī'krə·spôr, -spōr) *n. Bot.* A small, asexually produced spore in seed plants, male in function.

mi·cros·to·mous (mī·kros'tə·məs) *adj.* Having an unusually small mouth. Also **mi·cro·stom·a·tous** (mī'krō·stom'ə·təs). [< MICRO- + -STOMOUS]

mi·cro·tome (mī'krə·tōm) *n.* An instrument for making very thin sections for microscopic observations. —**mi'cro·tom'ic** (-tom'ik) or **·i·cal** *adj.* —**mi·crot·o·mist** (mī·krot'ə·mist) *n.* —**mi·crot'o·my** *n.*

mi·cro·wave (mī'krə·wāv) *n.* A high-frequency electromagnetic wave having a wavelength of from 1 millimeter to about 30 centimeters.

mi·crur·gy (mī'krûr·jē) *n.* A highly refined precision technique for the microdissection, study, and investigation of living protoplasm, usually in the form of single cells, as bacteria, amebae, etc. [< MICR(O)- + -URGY] —**mi·crur'gic** (mī·krûr'jik) or **·gi·cal** *adj.* —**mi'crur·gist** *n.*

mic·tu·rate (mik'chə·rāt) *v.i.* **·rat·ed, ·rat·ing** To urinate. [< MICTURITION; an erroneous formation]

mic·tu·ri·tion (mik'chə·rish'ən) *n.* The act of urination. [< L *micturitus*, pp. of *micturire*, desiderative of *mingere* pass water]

mid¹ (mid) *adj.* **1** Middle. **2** *Phonet.* Produced with the tongue in a relatively midway position between high and low: said of certain vowels, as (ō) in *boat*. —*n. Archaic* The middle. [OE *midd*]

mid² (mid) *prep.* Amid; among: a poetical usage.

mid- *combining form* Middle; middle point or part of:

mid–act	midmonth
mid–African	midmonthly
midafternoon	midmorning
mid–April	mid–mouth
mid–arctic	mid–movement
mid–Asian	mid–nineteenth
mid–August	mid–November
midautumn	mid–ocean
midaxillary	mid–October
mid–block	mid–oestral
mid–breast	mid–orbital
mid–Cambrian	mid–Pacific
mid–career	mid–part
midcarpal	mid–period
mid–century	mid–periphery
mid–channel	mid–pillar
mid–chest	midpit
mid–continent	mid–Pleistocene
mid–course	mid–position
mid–court	midrange
mid–crowd	mid–refrain
mid–current	mid–region
mid–December	mid–Renaissance
mid–diastolic	mid–river
mid–dish	mid–road
middorsal	mid–sea
mid–eighteenth	midseason
mid–Empire	midsentence
mid–European	mid–September
midevening	mid–Siberian
midfacial	mid–side
mid–February	mid–sky
mid–field	mid–slope
mid–flight	mid–sole
midforenoon	midspace
mid–forty	mid–span
midfrontal	midstory
mid–hour	midstout
mid–ice	midstreet
mid–incisor	mid–stride
mid–Italian	mid–styled
mid–January	mid–sun

mid–July	mid–swing
mid–June	mid–tap
mid–lake	midtarsal
midleg	mid–Tertiary
mid–length	mid–thigh
mid–life	mid–thoracic
mid–line	mid–tide
mid–link	mid–time
mid–lobe	mid–totality
midmandibular	mid–tow
mid–March	mid–town
mid–May	mid–value
midventral	mid–water
mid–volley	midwintry
mid–walk	mid–world
mid–wall	midyear
mid–watch	mid–zone

mid-air (mid'âr') *n.* The middle or midst of the air.

mid-At·lan·tic (mid'ət·lan'tik) *n.* The middle part of the Atlantic Ocean.

mid-brain (mid'brān') *n.* The mesencephalon.

mid-day (mid'dā') *n.* Noon.

mid·dle (mid'l) *adj.* **1** Occupying a position equally distant from the extremes; mean. **2** Occupying any intermediate position. **3** *Gram.* In Greek and Sanskrit, designating a voice of the verb which indicates action by the subject for his own sake. See VOICE. —*n.* **1** The part or point equally distant from the extremities. ◆ Collateral adjective: *median.* **2** Something that is intermediate. **3** The middle voice. See synonyms under CENTER. —*v.t.* **·dled, ·dling** *Naut.* To fold or double in the middle. [OE *middel*]

middle age The time of life between youth and old age, commonly between 40 and 60. —**mid'dle-aged'** (-ājd') *adj.*

Middle Ages The period in European history between classical antiquity and the Renaissance: usually regarded as extending from the downfall of Rome, in 476, to about 1450.

mid·dle-break·er (mid'l·brā'kər) *n. Agric.* A lister. Also **mid'dle-bust'er** (-bus'tər).

mid·dle-brow (mid'l·brou') *n.* A person who has conventional or middle-class tastes, interests, opinions, etc.

middle C *Music* The note written on the first leger line above the bass staff and the first leger line below the treble staff; also, the corresponding tone or key.

middle class The class of a society that occupies a position between the laboring class and the very wealthy or the nobility. —**mid'dle-class'** (-klas', -kläs') *adj.*

middle ear *Anat.* The tympanum: occasionally applied to the tympanum, the mastoid cells, and the Eustachian tube.

middle latitude The latitude midway between two places on the same hemisphere: also called *mean latitude.*

mid·dle·man (mid'l·man') *n. pl.* **·men** (-men') **1** One who acts as an agent; one who buys in bulk from producers and resells. **2** The actor in the middle of a line of minstrel performers who propounds questions to the endmen; the interlocutor. **3** Any intermediary.

mid·dle·most (mid'l·mōst') *adj.* **1** Situated exactly in the middle. **2** Being in the midst of; hence, very intimate. Also *midmost.*

mid·dle-of-the-road (mid'l·ɔv·thə·rōd') *adj.* Tending toward neither side or extreme; moderate, especially in politics. Also **mid·dle-road·ing** (mid'l·rō'ding).

mid·dle-piece (mid'l·pēs') *n. Biol.* The part lying between the nucleus and the flagellum of a spermatozoon.

mid·dling (mid'ling) *adj.* **1** Of middle rank, condition, size, or quality. **2** In tolerable but not good health; in fair health. —*n.* **1** *pl.* The coarser part of ground wheat, as distinguished from flour and bran: formerly used only for feed, but now manufactured into the best brand of flour, since it contains most gluten. **2** Pork or bacon cut from between the shoulder and ham of a hog. **3** A quality of cotton on which prices are based. [< MID + -LING²]

mid·dling·ly (mid'ling·lē) *adj.* Tolerably. Also **mid'dling.**

mid·dy (mid'ē) *n. pl.* **·dies** *Colloq.* A midshipman.

middy blouse A woman's or child's blouse not closely fitted and having a wide collar similar to that of a sailor's blouse.

midge (mij) *n.* **1** A gnat or small fly; espe-

cially, a small, long-legged, dipterous insect of the family *Ceratopogonidae* that does not bite and has aquatic larvae. For illustration see INSECTS (injurious). **2** A small person; dwarf. [OE *mycge*]

midg·et (mij'it) *n.* **1** An extremely small person. **2** Anything very small of its kind. —*adj.* Small; diminutive. [Dim. of MIDGE]

mid·gut (mid'gut') *n. Anat.* The primitive intestinal cavity, formed by the closure of the body walls of the embryo.

mid-i·ron (mid'ī'ərn) *n.* An iron golf club with a loft intermediate between that of the cleek and that of the mashie.

mid·land (mid'lənd) *adj.* **1** In the interior country. **2** Surrounded by the land; mediterranean. —*n.* The interior of a country.

mid·most (mid'mōst') *adj.* Middlemost. —*n.* The midmost part of anything. —*adv.* In the midst or middle. [OE *mydmest*]

mid·night (mid'nīt') *n.* Twelve o'clock at night; the middle of the night. —*adj.* Pertaining to, occurring in, or like the middle of the night; dark.

midnight blue A very dark blue, almost black.

midnight sun The sun visible at midnight as a result of the fact that the latitude of the place from which it is viewed is greater than the polar distance of the sun, or above 66 degrees.

mid·noon (mid'nōon') *n.* The middle of the day; noon.

mid·rib (mid'rib') *n. Bot.* The primary vein, or rib, of a leaf, usually running from apex to base.

mid·riff (mid'rif) *n.* The diaphragm. [OE *midhrif* < *midd* mid + *hrif* belly]

mid·ship (mid'ship') *adj. Naut.* At or pertaining to the middle of a vessel's hull.

mid·ship·man (mid'ship'mən) *n. pl.* **·men** (-mən) **1** A student training at the United States Naval Academy for commissioning as an officer. **2** *Brit.* In the Royal Navy: **a** An officer ranking between a naval cadet and the lowest commissioned officer. **b** Formerly, one of a class of youths performing minor duties on shipboard as training for commissioning as officers. [< *amidshipman*; so called from being amidships when on duty]

mid·ships (mid'ships') *adv.* Amidships. —*n. pl.* The midship timbers.

midst (midst) *n.* The central part; middle: often with the implication of being surrounded, beset, or hard pressed: in the *midst* of duties or dangers. See synonyms under CENTER. Compare synonyms for AMID. —**in our, your, or their midst** In the midst of, or among, us, you, or them. —*prep.* Amidst. —*adv.* In the middle. [OE *midd* + adverbial *-s* + intrusive or superlative *-t*]

mid·sum·mer (mid'sum'ər) *n.* **1** The middle of summer. **2** Popularly, the time of the summer solstice, about June 21. —*adj.* Like, or occurring in, the middle of the summer.

mid·way (mid'wā', -wā') *adj.* Being in the middle of the way or distance. —*n.* (mid'wā') **1** The middle or the middle course. **2** The space, at a fair or exposition, assigned for the display of exhibits and along which the various amusements are situated. —*adv.* Half-way. [OE *midweg*]

mid-wife (mid'wīf') *n. pl.* **·wives** (-wīvz') A woman who assists women in childbirth. [OE *mid* with + *wif* wife]

mid-wife·ry (mid'wī'fər·ē, -wīf'rē) *n.* Obstetrics.

mid-win·ter (mid'win'tər) *n.* **1** The middle of winter. **2** Popularly, the winter solstice, about Dec. 21.

mid·years (mid'yirz') *n. pl.* Examinations given in the middle of a school or college year.

mien (mēn) *n.* The external appearance or manner of a person; carriage; bearing. See synonyms under AIR¹, MANNER. ◆ Homophone: *mean.* [? Aphetic form of DEMEAN; infl. by F *mine* < Celtic (Breton) *min* beak, muzzle]

miff (mif) *Colloq. v.t.* To cause to be irritated or offended. —*v.i.* To take offense. —*n.* A huff. [Origin uncertain. Cf. G *muffen* sulk.]

mif·fy (mif'ē) *adj. Colloq.* **1** Supersensitive; easily offended. **2** Delicate: said of plants. —**mif'fi·ness** *n.*

might¹ (mīt) Past tense of MAY¹. Both *may* and *might* are now considered subjunctives with present or future sense, the difference between the two being one of degree rather than of time.

May implies a greater probability than *might*, the latter indicating possibility but less likelihood: He *might* be on time, but don't depend on it. As a request for permission, *might* is felt to be more hesitant in approach: *Might* we expect your reply by Tuesday? *Might* I come to dinner some evening?

might² (mīt) *n.* **1** Ability to do anything requiring force or power; strength. **2** The possession of great resources; intensity of will; ability. See synonyms under POWER. — **with might and main** With utmost endeavor; with one's whole strength. ◆ Homophone: *mite*. [OE *meaht, miht*]

might·i·ly (mī′tə·lē) *adv.* **1** With might; with great force, energy, or earnestness. **2** To a great degree; greatly; very much: I wanted *mightily* to go.

might·y (mī′tē) *adj.* **might·i·er, might·i·est** **1** Possessed of might; powerful; strong. **2** Of unusual bulk, consequence, etc. **3** Momentous; wonderful: a *mighty* host. See synonyms under POWERFUL. — *adv. Colloq.* Very; to a great degree; very much: a *mighty* fine person.

mi·gnon·ette (min′yən·et′) *n.* A North African annual plant (*Reseda odorata*) having wedge-shaped leaves, greenish, fragrant flowers with fringed petals, and bladdery seed vessels open at the top. [<F]

mi·graine (mī′grān) *n.* A form of recurrent paroxysmal headache, usually confined to one side of the head, and associated with various gastric and nervous disturbances. See MEGRIM. [<F <LL *hemicrania* <Gk. *hēmikrania* <*hēmi* half + *kranion* skull]

mi·grant (mī′grənt) *adj.* Migratory. — *n.* A migratory bird or other animal or person. [<L *migrans, -antis*, ppr. of *migrare* roam]

mi·grate (mī′grāt) *v.i.* **·grat·ed, ·grat·ing** **1** To move from one country, region, etc., to settle in another. **2** To move periodically from one region or climate to another, as birds or fish. See synonyms under EMIGRATE. [<L *migratus*, pp. of *migrare*] — **mi′gra·tor** *n.*

mi·gra·tion (mī·grā′shən) *n.* **1** The act of migrating. **2** The totality of persons or animals migrating, or the time occupied in migrating. **3** *Chem.* The removal or shifting of one or more atoms from one position in the molecule to another. **4** *Physics* The drift or movement of ions, under the influence of electromotive force, toward one or the other electrode. [<L *migratio, -onis*] — **mi·gra′tion·al** *adj.* — **mi·gra′tion·ist** *n.*

mi·gra·to·ry (mī′grə·tôr′ē, -tō′rē) *adj.* **1** Pertaining to migration. **2** Given to migrating. **3** Roving; nomadic.

mike (mīk) *n. Colloq.* A microphone. [Short for MICROPHONE]

mil (mil) *n.* **1** A unit of length or diameter, equal to one thousandth of an inch or to 25.4001 microns. **2** A milliliter, or one cubic centimeter. **3** *Mil.* **a** A unit of angular measure equal to 1/6400 of a circle, or about 0.0560 degree. **b** A unit of angular measure equal to 0.001 radian. **4** A former monetary unit of Palestine, equal to one thousandth of a pound; also, the coin having this value. [<L *mille* thousand]

mi·la·dy (mi·lā′dē) *n.* An English noblewoman; a gentlewoman: a Continental term used of such a woman. Also **mi·la′di.** [<F <E *my lady*]

mil·age (mī′lij) See MILEAGE.

milch (milch) *adj.* Giving milk, as a cow. [OE *milc, meolc* milk]

milch·y (mil′chē) *adj.* Milky.

mild (mīld) *adj.* **1** Moderate in action or disposition. **2** Expressing kindness; calm. **3** Moderate in effect or degree. **4** Not of strong flavor. **5** *Metall.* Designating strong and tough but malleable steel containing only a small percentage of carbon. See synonyms under BLAND, CHARITABLE, PACIFIC. [OE *milde*] — **mild′ly** *adv.* — **mild′ness** *n.*

mild·en (mīl′dən) *v.t. & v.i.* To make or become mild.

mil·dew (mil′dōō, -dyōō) *n.* **1** Any of a family (*Erysiphaceae*) of ascomycetous parasitic fungi that attack a great variety of plants, as hops, cherries, roses, etc. **2** A fungous disease of plants, particularly one caused by a fungus that makes a superficial downy coating on the diseased part of the host plant. **3** Any mold

on walls, food, clothing, etc. — *v.t. & v.i.* To affect or be affected with mildew. [OE *mildēaw* honeydew] — **mil′dew·y** *adj.*

mile (mīl) *n.* A measure of distance (see STATUTE MILE below) in the United States, Great Britain, and Ireland, and in all British possessions; remotely derived from the ancient Roman mile, which was about 1,620 yards or 4,860 feet. — **air mile** A nautical mile by air. — **geographical, nautical,** or **sea mile** One sixtieth of a degree of the earth's equator, or 6,080.2 feet. That of the United States is now the international nautical mile, equal to 6,076.103 feet or 1,852 meters. — **statute mile** The legal mile of the United States, Great Britain, etc., 5,280 feet, or 1,609.35 meters. [OE *mil* <LL *milia, millia* <L *mille passuum* thousand paces]

mile·age (mī′lij) *n.* **1** The entire length or amount of anything that is or may be measured in miles, especially when stated in miles; aggregate number of miles of track, wire, etc., traversed, made, or used. **2** Compensation reckoned at so much a mile, allowed in lieu of expenses of travel. **3** The rate a mile paid by one traveling in a car, or using a car for any purpose. **4** Number of miles traveled by an automobile, etc., as estimated for each gallon of fuel used. **5** Length of service, quality of performance, etc.; use. Also spelled *milage.*

mileage ticket A ticket entitling the holder to transportation for a specific number of miles.

mil·er (mī′lər) *n.* A person or horse trained to race a mile.

mile·stone (mīl′stōn) *n.* **1** A post, pillar, or stone set up to indicate distance in miles from a given point: also **mile′post′** (-pōst′). **2** An important event or turning point in a person's life.

mil·foil (mil′foil) *n.* Yarrow. [<OF <L *millefolium* <*mille* thousand + *folium* leaf]

MILESTONE

mil·i·a·ri·a (mil′ē·âr′ē·ə) *n. Pathol.* An acute inflammatory disease of the sweat glands marked by an eruption of vesicles and papulae of the size of a pinpoint or larger; miliary fever; the millet-seed rash. [<NL, fem. of L *miliarius*. See MILIARY.]

mil·i·ar·y (mil′ē·er′ē, mil′yə·rē) *adj.* **1** Like millet seeds. **2** Accompanied by a rash of pimples the size of a millet seed. **3** *Pathol.* Designating a form of tuberculosis caused by the discharge into one or more organs of minute bacillary tubercles originating elsewhere in the body. [<L *miliarius* <*milium* millet]

mi·lieu (mē·lyœ′) *n.* Surroundings; environment. [<F <OF *mi* middle (<L *medius*) + *lieu* place <L *locus*]

mil·i·tant (mil′ə·tənt) *adj.* **1** Pertaining to conflict with opposing powers or influences. **2** Of a warlike or combative tendency; aggressive. — *n.* A combative person; a soldier. [<L *militans, -antis*, ppr. of *militare* be a soldier] — **mil′i·tan·cy** *n.* — **mil′i·tant·ly** *adv.*

mil·i·ta·rism (mil′ə·tə·riz′əm) *n.* **1** A system emphasizing and aggrandizing the military spirit and the need of constant preparation for war. **2** A desire to foster the maintenance of a powerful military position. — **mil′i·ta·rist** *n.* — **mil′i·ta·ris′tic** *adj.* — **mil′i·ta·ris′ti·cal·ly** *adv.*

mil·i·ta·rize (mil′ə·tə·rīz′) *v.t.* **·rized, ·riz·ing** **1** To imbue with militarism. **2** To convert to a military system. — **mil′i·ta·ri·za′tion** (-rə·zā′shən, -rī-) *n.*

mil·i·tar·y (mil′ə·ter′ē) *adj.* **1** Pertaining to armed forces or to warfare; martial; warlike. **2** Done or carried on by force of arms: distinguished from *civil.* See synonyms under WARLIKE. — *n.* A body of armed men or soldiers; soldiery. See synonyms under ARMY. [<L *militaris* <L *militaris* <*miles, militis* soldier] — **mil′i·tar′i·ly** *adv.*

military attaché An army officer attached to his country's embassy or legation in a foreign country.

military governor An army or navy officer serving (usually temporarily) as the civil governor of a state or territory under martial law.

military intelligence **1** Information, of what-

ever character and however obtained, that is of military value to a country in peace or war. **2** The branch or division of a government engaged in obtaining, interpreting, and using such information.

military mast A strong mastlike structure on a warship, designed to carry a turret, observation tower, etc.

military police *Mil.* A body of soldiers charged with police duties among troops.

mil·i·tate (mil′ə·tāt) *v.i.* **·tat·ed, ·tat·ing** To have influence: with *against*, or, more rarely, *for.* [<L *militatus*, pp. of *militare* be a soldier <*miles, militis*]

mi·li·tia (mə·lish′ə) *n.* **1** A body of citizens enrolled and drilled in military organizations other than the regular military forces, and called out only in emergencies. **2** *U.S.* All able-bodied male citizens between eighteen and forty-five years of age not members of the regular military forces. — **organized militia** *U.S.* The National Guard, Organized Reserves, the Naval Reserve, and the Marine Corps Reserve. [<L, military service <*miles, militis*] — **mi·li′tia·man** (-mən) *n.*

mil·i·um (mil′ē·əm) *n. Pathol.* A skin disease characterized by small yellowish globules. [<L, millet; after the resemblance of the globules to millet seed]

Mil·i·um (mil′ē·əm) *n.* A genus of millet grass. [<NL]

milk (milk) *n.* **1** The opaque, whitish liquid secreted by the mammary glands of female mammals for the nourishment of their young; especially, cow's milk, drunk or used by human beings. ◆ Collateral adjectives: *galactic, lacteal.* **2** The sap of certain plants. **3** Any one of various emulsions. — *v.t.* **1** To draw milk from the mammary glands of. **2** To draw (milk). **3** To draw off as if by milking; extract: to *milk* sap from a tree. **4** To draw or extract something from: to *milk* someone of information. **5** To exploit; take advantage of. — *v.i.* **6** To yield milk. [OE *meolc, milc*]

milk-and-wa·ter (milk′ən·wô′tər, -wot′ər) *adj.* **1** Weak and vacillating; namby-pamby. **2** Mawkish; sentimental.

milk·ber·ry (milk′ber′ē) *n.* The snowberry.

milk·er (mil′kər) *n.* **1** One who or that which milks; specifically, a mechanical device for milking cows. **2** A domestic animal, especially a cow, that is milked or that gives milk.

milk fever **1** *Pathol.* A fever attending the secretion of milk about the third day after childbirth. **2** A similar disease of milk cows.

milk·fish (milk′fish′) *n.* *pl.* **·fish** or **·fish·es** A large, toothless, silvery fish (genus *Chanos*) allied to the herring, especially *C. chanos* of South Pacific waters.

milk-liv·ered (milk′liv′ərd) *adj.* Cowardly; timorous.

milk run *U.S. Slang* In the air force, a regularly repeated mission.

milk shake A drink made of chilled, flavored milk, and sometimes ice-cream, shaken or whipped until frothy.

milk sickness *Pathol.* A disease caused by drinking the milk or eating the dairy products of cows that have fed on certain poisonous plants: marked by vomiting, intestinal disturbances, and trembling.

milk snake The house snake. Also called *milk adder.*

milk·vetch (milk′vech′) *n.* The ground plum: so called from the supposed increase in the secretion of milk by goats feeding upon it.

milk·weed (milk′wēd′) *n.* **1** One of a genus (*Asclepias*) of plants having a milky juice. **2** Any of several similar or related plants.

milkweed butterfly The monarch butterfly.

milk white A bluish-white color, like the color of skimmed milk.

milk·wort (milk′wûrt′) *n.* **1** Any of a genus (*Polygala*) of plants with varicolored, showy flowers: so called from the fancied property of increasing the secretion of milk in nursing women; specifically, the **orange milkwort** (*P. lutea*) of the SE United States. **2** The sea milkwort.

milk·y (mil′kē) *adj.* **milk·i·er, milk·i·est** **1** Containing or like milk. **2** Yielding milk. **3** Very mild; spiritless. **4** Containing young or spawn: said of oysters. Also spelled *milchy.* — **milk′-**

i·ly *adv.* — **milk′i·ness** *n.*
Milky Way *Astron.* A luminous band encircling the heavens, composed of distant stars and nebulae not separately distinguishable to the naked eye; the Galaxy.
mill[1] (mil) *n.* **1** A machine by means of which grain is ground for food. **2** Any one of various kinds of machines that transform raw material by other processes than grinding: often in combination: a *sawmill*; *planing mill.* **3** A machine for reducing to small or smaller proportions hard substances of any kind. **4** A building fitted up with the machinery requisite for a factory: often in combination: *powdermill.* **5** A hardened steel roller, bearing a design in relief, by which a printing plate or a die may be made by pressure. **6** A milling cutter. **7** *Slang* A pugilistic combat; set-to. **8** A raised or ridged edge or surface made by milling. **9** A machine for crushing or grinding vegetable substances in order to express the juice. — **to go through the mill** To receive or undergo the experiences or hardships needed to acquire a certain degree of skill or wisdom. — *v.t.* **1** To grind, shape, polish, roll, etc., in or with a mill. **2** To raise and indent the edge of (a coin). **3** To cause to move with a circular motion. **4** To beat or whip to a froth, as chocolate. **5** *Slang* To strike or thrash; beat. — *v.i.* **6** To move slowly in a circle, as cattle. **7** *Slang* To fight or box. [OE *myln, mylen* <LL *molina* <L *mola* millstone]
mill[2] (mil) *n.* **1** A thousandth part. **2** *U.S.* The thousandth part of a dollar, or the tenth part of a cent. [<L *mille* thousand]
mill·board (mil′bôrd′, -bōrd′) *n.* Heavy pasteboard used for the covers of books; imitation pressboard.
mill·cake (mil′kāk′) *n.* **1** The by-product left after the oil has been extracted from linseed. **2** The cake formed by mixing and pressing together the materials of gunpowder previous to granulation.
mill cinder The slag from the puddling furnaces of a steel-rolling mill.
mill·dam (mil′dam′) *n.* **1** A barrier thrown across a watercourse to raise its level sufficiently to turn a millwheel. **2** The pond formed by such a barrier.
milled (mild) *adj.* **1** Passed through, cut by, or mixed in a mill. **2** Having the edges fluted or grooved: said of coins.
mil·le·nar·i·an (mil′ə·nâr′ē·ən) *adj.* Of or pertaining to a thousand; specifically, relating to the millennium. — *n.* One who believes in the millennium. — **mil′le·nar′i·an·ism** *n.*
mil·le·nar·y (mil′ə·ner′ē) *adj.* Of or pertaining to a thousand; millenarian; millennial. — *n. pl.* **·nar·ies** **1** The space of a thousand years; the millennium. **2** A millenarian. [<LL *millenarius* <L *milleni* a thousand each < *mille* thousand]
mil·len·ni·al (mi·len′ē·əl) *adj.* Of or pertaining to the millennium or to any period of a thousand years. — *n.* A thousandth anniversary. — **mil·len′ni·al·ist** *n.* — **mil·len′ni·al·ly** *adv.*
mil·len·ni·um (mi·len′ē·əm) *n. pl.* **·ni·a** (-ē·ə) **1** A period of a thousand years. **2** The thousand years of the kingdom of Christ on earth. *Rev.* xx 1–5. **3** Hence, by extension, any period of happiness, beneficial government or the like. [<NL <*mille* thousand + *annus* year]
mil·le·ped (mil′ə·ped), **mil·le·pede** (mil′ə·pēd) See MILLIPEDE.
mill·er (mil′ər) *n.* **1** One who keeps or tends a mill, particularly a gristmill. **2** A milling machine. **3** A mothmiller.
mil·ler·ite (mil′ər·īt) *n.* A metallic, brass-yellow, brittle nickel sulfide, NiS, crystallizing in the hexagonal system. [after W. H. *Miller,* 1801–80, English mineralogist]
miller's thumb A small, fresh-water fish (family *Cottidae*) with broad, flattened head and spiny fins.
mil·les·i·mal (mi·les′ə·məl) *adj.* Pertaining to thousandths. — *n.* A thousandth. [<L *millesimus* <*mille* thousand]
mil·let (mil′it) *n.* **1** A grass (*Panicum miliaceum*), or its seed, cultivated in the United States for forage, but in the Old World from earliest times, and still in some parts of Europe, as a cereal. **2** One of various other grasses, or their seed, as the **foxtail** or **Italian millet** (*Setaria italica*), **pearl millet** (*Penni-*

setum glaucum), etc. [<F, dim. of *mil* <L *milium*]
mill finish A surface finish produced on sheet and plate steel characteristic of the ground finish that is present on the rollers used in fabrication.
mill·hand (mil′hand′) *n.* A worker in a mill.
milli– *combining form* **1** A thousand: *millipede.* **2** In the metric and other systems of measurement, the thousandth part of (a specified unit):

milliampere	**millicurie**	**millilux**
milliangstrom	**millifarad**	**milliphot**
milliare	**millihenry**	**millistere**
millibar	**millilambert**	**millivolt**

[<L *mille* a thousand]
mil·liard (mil′yərd) *n.* A thousand millions; usually, in the United States, called a billion. [<F <Pg. *milhar* thousand]
mil·lier (mē·lyä′) *n.* A metric ton, 1,000 kilograms. [<F]
mil·li·gram (mil′ə·gram) *n.* The thousandth part of a gram. See METRIC SYSTEM. Also **mil′·li·gramme.** [<F *milligramme*]
mil·li·li·ter (mil′ə·lē′tər) *n.* The thousandth part of a liter. See METRIC SYSTEM. Also **mil′·li·li′tre.** [<F *millilitre*]
mil·li·me·ter (mil′ə·mē′tər) *n.* The thousandth part of a meter. See METRIC SYSTEM. Also **mil′·li·me′tre.** [<F *millimètre*]
mil·li·mi·cron (mil′ə·mī′kron) *n.* A thousandth of a micron, or a millionth of a millimeter; also, ten angstroms (symbol m, also μ).
mil·li·mol (mil′ə·mol) *n.* The thousandth part of a mol. Also **mil′li·mole** (-mōl). [<MILLI- + MOL]
mil·line (mil·līn′) *n.* The rate of cost for placing an advertisement of one agate line before a million readers. [<MILL(ION) + LINE]
mil·li·ner (mil′ə·nər) *n.* **1** A person employed in making, trimming, or selling bonnets, women's hats, etc. **2** *Obs.* A dealer in small wares: a haberdasher. [<*Milaner* an inhabitant of Milan, in Italy; hence, a man from Milan who imported silks and the like]
mil·li·ner·y (mil′ə·ner′ē, -nər·ē) *n.* **1** The articles made or sold by milliners. **2** The occupation or establishment of a milliner. [<MILLINER]
mill·ing (mil′ing) *n.* **1** The operating of a mill or mills, as in the grinding of meal or metals, the preparation of cloth, etc. **2** A milled surface, as of a coin, or the act or process of producing it: distinguished from *reeding.* **3** The slow, round-and-round motion of or as of a herd of cattle. [<MILL, *v.*]
mil·lion (mil′yən) *n.* **1** The cardinal number equivalent to ten hundred thousand or to a thousand thousand, or the symbols (1,000,000) representing it; ten to the sixth power. **2** Elliptically, a thousand thousand of the ordinary units of account, as dollars, francs, or pounds: He is worth a *million.* **3** An indefinitely great number. — **the million** The common people. [<OF <Ital. *millione* (now *milione*), aug. of *mille* thousand]
mil·lion·aire (mil′yən·âr′) *n.* One whose possessions are valued at a million or more, as of dollars, pounds, etc. Also **mil′lion·naire′.** [<F *millionaire*]
mil·lion·fold (mil′yən·fōld′) *adj.* A million times the quantity. — *adv.* In a millionfold proportion; a million times in amount: with the indefinite article *a,* construed as a plural.
mil·lionth (mil′yənth) *adj.* **1** Being last in a series of a million: an ordinal numeral. **2** Being one of a million equal parts: a *millionth* part. — *n.* One part in a million equal parts; one divided by one million.
mil·li·pede (mil′ə·pēd) *n.* A herbivorous, slow-moving arthropod (class *Diplopoda*) having a rounded body marked by numerous segments, from nearly all of which issue two pairs of appendages: also spelled *milleped, millepede.* Also **mil′li·ped** (-ped). [<L *millepeda* <*mille* thousand + *pes, pedis* foot]
mill·race (mil′rās′) *n.* The sluice through which the water runs to a millwheel.
mill·run (mil′run′) *n.* **1** A millrace. **2** A certain amount of ore tested for content or quality by the process of milling. **3** The mineral yielded by the test.
mill–run (mil′run′) *adj.* Average; just as it comes from the mill; not selected: also *run-of-the-mill.*

mill·stone (mil′stōn′) *n.* **1** One of a pair of thick, heavy, stone disks for grinding something, as grain. **2** That which pulverizes or bears down. **3** A heavy or burdensome weight. *Matt.* xvii 6.
mill town A town whose center of activity is a mill or group of mills, and whose population is employed, for the most part, in the mill or mills.
mill·wheel (mil′hwēl′) *n.* The waterwheel that drives a mill.
mill·work (mil′wûrk′) *n.* Carpentry work delivered from a mill ready for installation or use.
mill·wright (mil′rīt′) *n.* One who plans, builds, or fits out mills; also, a machinist who sets up shafting, etc.
mi·lo (mī′lō) *n.* A non-saccharin sorghum similar to millet. [<Bantu *maili*]
mi·lord (mi·lôrd′) *n.* An English nobleman; a gentleman: a Continental term used of such a man. [<F <E *my lord*]
milt[1] (milt) *n.* The spleen. [OE *milte* spleen]
milt[2] (milt) *n.* **1** The sperm of a fish. **2** The spermatic organs of a fish when filled with seminal fluid; the soft roe. — *v.t.* To impregnate (fish roe) with milt. [OE *milte*]
milt·er (mil′tər) *n.* **1** A male fish. **2** The milt of a fish.
Mil·ton (mil′tən), **John,** 1608–74, English poet.
Mil·ton·ic (mil·ton′ik) *adj.* Of, pertaining to, or like the poet Milton or his works or style; sublime; majestic. Also **Mil·to′ni·an** (-tō′nē·ən).
mime (mīm) *n.* **1** A mimic play or farce or the dialog for this; a dramatic representation, akin to comedy, mimicking real persons or events: a favorite amusement among the Greeks and Romans. **2** An actor in a mime; hence, a mimic; clown, buffoon. — *v.* **mimed, mim·ing** *v.t.* To mimic; imitate. — *v.i.* To play the mimic; play a part with gestures and usually without words. [<L *mimus* <Gk. *mimos*] — **mim′er** *n.*
Mim·e·o·graph (mim′ē·ə·graf′, -gräf′) *n.* An apparatus in which a thin fibrous paper coated with paraffin is used as a stencil for reproducing copies of written or typewritten matter: a trade name. — *v.t.* To reproduce by means of a Mimeograph. [<Gk. *mimeisthai* imitate + -GRAPH]
mi·me·sis (mi·mē′sis, mī-) *n.* **1** Imitation or representation of the supposed speech, characteristic dialect, carriage, or gestures of an individual or a people, as in art and literature. **2** *Biol.* Mimicry. [<NL <Gk. *mimēsis* imitation]
mi·met·ic (mi·met′ik, mī-) *adj.* **1** Quick to mimic; imitative. **2** Relating to mimicry or mimesis. **3** Mimic (*adj.* def. 1). Also **mi·met′i·cal.** [<Gk. *mimētikos*] — **mi·met′i·cal·ly** *adv.*
mim·ic (mim′ik) *v.t.* **·icked, ·ick·ing** **1** To imitate the speech or actions of, as in ridicule. **2** To copy closely; ape. **3** To have or assume the color, shape, etc., of; simulate: Some insects *mimic* leaves. See synonyms under IMITATE. — *n.* **1** One who is given to mimicry; a mimic actor; buffoon. **2** A copy; imitation. — *adj.* **1** Of the nature of mimicry; imitative; mimetic: a *mimic* gesture. **2** Copying the real; simulated; mock: a *mimic* court. [<L *mimicus* <Gk. *mimikos* <*mimos* mime] — **mim′i·cal** *adj.* — **mim′ick·er** *n.*
mim·ic·ry (mim′ik·rē) *n. pl.* **·ries** **1** The act of imitating, especially for sport; also, a thing produced as a copy. **2** *Zool.* An imitative superficial resemblance in one animal to another or to its immediate environment, for purposes of concealment or protection. Compare PROTECTIVE COLORATION. See synonyms under CARICATURE.
mi·mo·sa (mi·mō′sə, -zə) *n.* **1** Any plant of a large genus (*Mimosa*) of tropical herbs, shrubs, or trees of the bean family, with feathery, bipinnate foliage, and clusters of small flowers; especially, the sensitive plant. **2** A light yellow: the color of certain varieties of mimosa. [<NL <L *mimus* mime; from its supposed mimicry of animal life] — **mim·o·sa·ceous** (mim′ō·sā′shəs, mī′mō-) *adj.*
mi·na·cious (mi·nā′shəs) *adj.* Threatening; of a menacing character. [<L *minax, minacis.* See MENACE.] — **mi·na′cious·ly** *adv.* — **mi·na′cious·ness, mi·nac·i·ty** (mi·nas′ə·tē) *n.*
min·a·ret (min′ə·ret′) *n.* A high, slender tower attached to a Moslem mosque, surrounded by one or more balconies, from which is sounded the stated summons to prayer. [<Sp. *minarete*

<Turkish *manārat* <Arabic *manārah* lamp, lighthouse <*minār* candlestick]

MINARET
A. Shown in relation to mosque.
B. Detail showing the balcony.

min·a·to·ry (min′ə·tôr′ē, -tō′rē) *adj.* Threatening, as with destruction or punishment. Also **min′a·to′ri·al.** [<OF *minatoire* <LL *minatorius* <*minatus*, pp. of *minari* threaten] — **min′a·to′ri·al·ly, min′a·to′ri·ly** *adv.*

mince (mins) *v.* **minced, minc·ing** *v.t.* **1** To cut or chop into small bits, as meat. **2** To subdivide minutely. **3** To diminish the force or strength of; moderate: He didn't *mince* words with her. **4** To say or do with affected primness or elegance. — *v.i.* **5** To walk with short steps or affected daintiness. **6** To speak or behave with affected primness. — *n.* **1** Mincemeat. **2** *Rare* An affectation. [<OF *mincier*; ult. <L *minuere* lessen, make smaller] — **minc′er** *n.* — **minc′ing·ly** *adv.*

mince·meat (mins′mēt′) *n.* **1** Meat chopped very fine. **2** A mixture of chopped meat, fruit, spices, etc., used in mince pie.

mince pie A pie made of mincemeat.

minc·ing–horse (min′sing·hôrs′) *n.* A heavy block of hardwood usually mounted on legs, used for chopping meats or vegetables.

mind (mīnd) *n.* **1** The aggregate of all conscious and unconscious processes originating in and associated with the brain, especially those pertaining to cognition, intelligence, and intellect. **2** Memory; remembrance: to bear in *mind.* **3** Opinion; way of thinking: to change one's *mind.* **4** Desire; inclination: to have a *mind* to leave. **5** Mental disposition, character, or temper: a liberal *mind*; a cheerful *mind.* **6** Intellectual power or capacity. **7** The faculty of cognition and intellect, as opposed to the will and emotions: a noble heart and a cultivated *mind.* **8** A person, regarded as having intellect: the great *minds* of our time. **9** Sanity; sound mentality: to lose one's *mind.* **10** *Philos.* The spirit of intelligence pervading the universe: opposed to *matter.* **11** In Christian Science, God: also **Divine Mind. — a month's mind** The monthly commemoration, usually the first, of a person's death. — **on one's mind** Occupying one's thoughts. — **to speak one's mind** To declare one's opinions freely or candidly. — **to take one's mind off** To turn one's thoughts from. — *v.t.* **1** To pay attention to; occupy oneself with: *Mind* your own business. **2** To be careful or wary concerning: *Mind* your step. **3** To give heed to, as commands; obey. **4** To care for; tend. **5** To be concerned about; regard with annoyance; dislike: Do you *mind* the noise? **6** To be aware of; notice; perceive. **7** *Colloq.* To remember: sometimes used reflexively. **8** *Archaic* To remind. **9** *Obs.* To intend; purpose. — *v.i.* **10** To pay attention; take notice; watch. **11** To be obedient. **12** To be concerned; care: I don't *mind.* **13** To be careful. [OE *gemynd*] — **mind′er** *n.*

Synonyms (noun): brain, consciousness, disposition, instinct, intellect, intelligence, reason, sense, soul, spirit, thought, understanding. *Mind* includes all the powers of sentient being apart from the physical factors in bodily faculties and activities; in a limited sense, *mind* is nearly synonymous with *intellect,* but includes *disposition,* or the tendency toward action, as appears in the phrase "to have a *mind* to work." The *intellect* is that assemblage of faculties which is concerned with knowledge, as distinguished from emotion and volition. *Understanding* is chiefly used of the reasoning powers: the *understanding* is distinguished by many philosophers from *reason* in that *reason* is the faculty of the high cognitions or a priori truth. *Thought,* the act, process, or power of thinking, is often used to denote the thinking faculty, and especially the *reason.* The *instinct* of animals is held to be of the same nature as the *intellect* of man, but inferior and limited; yet the apparent difference is very great. Human *instincts* denote tendencies independent of reasoning or instruction. As the seat of mental activity, *brain* is often used as a synonym for *mind, intellect, intelligence. Sense* is used as denoting clear mental action, good judgment, acumen; as, He is a man of *sense,* or, he showed good *sense. Consciousness* includes all that a sentient being perceives, knows, thinks, or feels, from whatever source. See GENIUS, SOUL, UNDERSTANDING. *Antonyms:* body, brawn, matter.

mind–cure (mīnd′kyŏor′) *n.* **1** The treatment and cure of disease, especially of neuroses, by direct influence upon the mind of the patient and without the use of drugs. **2** Psychotherapy.

mind–deaf·ness (mīnd′def′nis) *n.* Mental deafness.

mind·ed (mīn′did) *adj.* **1** Disposed. **2** Having a specified kind of mind: evil–*minded.*

mind·ful (mīnd′fəl) *adj.* Keeping in mind; heeding; having knowledge (of); aware. See synonyms under THOUGHTFUL. — **mind′ful·ly** *adv.* — **mind′ful·ness** *n.*

mind·less (mīnd′lis) *adj.* **1** Devoid of intelligence. **2** Not giving heed or attention; careless. — **mind′less·ly** *adv.* — **mind′less·ness** *n.*

mind–read·ing (mīnd′rē′ding) *n.* **1** The ascertaining of the thoughts or purpose of some other mind by the interpretation of voluntary or involuntary muscle movements or facial expressions. **2** Telepathy. — **mind′–read′er** *n.*

mine¹ (mīn) *n.* **1** An excavation for digging out some useful product, as ore or coal. **2** Any deposit of such material suitable for excavation. **3** An underground tunnel dug beneath an enemy's fortifications, as for the placement of an explosive charge. **4** A case containing such a charge buried in the earth, or floating on or near, or anchored beneath, the surface of the water. **5** Any productive source of supply. **6** A burrow made by an insect. — **bounding mine** A land mine set just beneath the surface of the ground and designed to rise a few feet in the air before exploding its charge of shrapnel and fragments. — **land mine** A high-explosive or chemical mine, actuated by the weight of a person, troops, or vehicles. — *v.* **mined, min·ing** *v.t.* **1** To dig (coal, ores, etc.) from the earth. **2** To dig into (the earth, etc.) for coal, ores, etc. **3** To make by digging, as a tunnel; burrow. **4** To dig a tunnel under, as for placing an explosive mine; sap. **5** To attack or destroy by slow or secret means; undermine. **6** To place an explosive mine or mines in or under: to *mine* a harbor. — *v.i.* **7** To dig in a mine for coal, ores, etc.; work in a mine. **8** To make a tunnel, etc., by digging; burrow. **9** To place explosive mines. [<OF <Celtic. Cf. Irish *mein* vein of metal.] — **min′er** *n.*

mine² (mīn) *pron.* **1** The possessive case of *I* employed predicatively; belonging or pertaining to me: That book is *mine.* **2** The things or persons belonging or pertaining to me: His work is better than *mine*; Fortune has been good to me and *mine.* — **of mine** Belonging or relating to me; my: the double possessive. — *pronominal adj. Archaic* My: *mine* eyes. [OE *mīn*]

mine detector An electromagnetic instrument for detecting the presence and locating the position of mines.

mine field An area in water or on land systematically planted with mines.

mine layer An auxiliary naval vessel, of submarine or surface type, provided with special equipment for the laying of mines.

min·er·al (min′ər·əl) *n.* **1** A naturally occurring, homogeneous substance or material formed by inorganic processes and having a characteristic set of physical properties, a definite range of chemical composition, and a molecular structure usually expressed in crystalline forms. **2** Any inorganic substance, as ore, a rock, or a fossil. — **accessory minerals** Those components or minerals forming so small a part of a rock or occurring so rarely as not to be included in its description. — *adj.* **1** Pertaining to, consisting of, or resembling minerals. **2** Impregnated with mineral constituents. [<OF <Med. L *minerale,* neut. sing. of *mineralis* of a mine <*minera* a mine]

min·er·al·ize (min′ər·əl·īz′) *v.* **·ized, ·iz·ing** *v.t.* **1** To convert from a metal to a mineral, as iron to rust. **2** To convert to a mineral substance; petrify. **3** To impregnate with minerals or other inorganic substances. — *v.i.* **4** To observe, study, and collect minerals. Also **min·er·al·o·gize** (min′ə·ral′ə·jīz), *Brit.* **min′er·al·ise′.** — **min′er·al·i·za′tion** *n.*

min·er·al·iz·er (min′ər·əl·īz′ər) *n.* **1** An element that combines with a metal to form an ore, as sulfur. **2** A volatile or other substance, as boron or water, that facilitates the recrystallization of rocks.

mineral jelly See PETROLATUM.

mineral kingdom The great division of nature which comprises all inorganic and non-living materials, as rocks, metals, minerals, etc. Compare ANIMAL KINGDOM, VEGETABLE KINGDOM.

min·er·al·o·gy (min′ə·ral′ə·jē) *n.* The science of minerals. — **min′er·a·log′i·cal** (-ər-ə-loj′i-kəl) *adj.* — **min′er·a·log′i·cal·ly** *adv.* — **min′er·al′o·gist** *n.*

mineral oil Any of various oils derived from inorganic matter, especially petroleum and its products: used as a fuel, in medicine as a laxative, etc.

mineral pitch Asphalt.

mineral tar Maltha.

mineral water Any natural water containing one or more minerals in solution, especially one impregnated with salts or gases having therapeutic properties.

mineral wax Ozocerite.

mineral wool A fibrous, fluffy material resembling wool in appearance, and made by subjecting molten silicate, molten slag, or other similar materials to a steam blast and cooling rapidly to prevent crystallization: used as packing and as an insulator: also called *rock wool, slag wool.* Compare GLASSWOOL.

min·e·stro·ne (min′ə·strō′nē) *n.* A thick vegetable soup containing vermicelli, barley, etc., in a meat broth.

mine sweeper 1 A naval vessel equipped for the detection, destruction, and removal of marine mines. **2** A heavy roller attached to the front of a tank for exploding land mines.

min·gle (ming′gəl) *v.* **min·gled, min·gling** *v.t.* **1** To mix or unite together; blend. **2** To join or combine; bring into close relation. — *v.i.* **3** To be or become mixed, united, or closely joined. **4** To enter into company; mix or associate, as with a crowd. **5** To take part; become involved, as in a dispute. See synonyms under MIX. [<Freq. of OE *mengan*] — **min′gler** *n.*

min·i (min′ē) *n. pl.* **min·is 1** A miniskirt. **2** *Colloq.* Anything smaller or shorter than others of its class. — *adj.* **·i·er, ·i·est** Very small or miniaturized. [<MINI-]

mini– combining form Small; tiny: *miniskirt.* [<L *minimus* least, smallest]

min·i·a·ture (min′ē·ə·chər, min′ə·chər) *n.* **1** A painting of small dimensions and delicate workmanship, usually a portrait, or the art of executing such paintings on ivory, metal, or vellum, in water-colors or oils. **2** A portrayal of anything on a small scale; hence, reduced dimensions or extent. **3** *Obs.* Lettering in red; rubrication, as of medieval manuscripts. See synonyms under PICTURE. — *adj.* Much smaller than reality; very small. [<F <Ital. *miniatura* <Med. L <L *miniare* paint red <*minium* red lead, ? <Iberian; later infl. in meaning by L *minuere* lessen]

min·i·a·tur·ize (min′ē·ə·chər·īz′, min′ə·chər·īz′) *v.t.* **·ized, ·iz·ing** To reduce the size of, as the parts of an instrument or machine. **—min′· i·a·tur′i·za′tion** *n.*

min·i·bike (min′ē·bīk′) *n.* A small motorcycle with a single seat.

min·i·cam (min′ə·kam) *n.* A small, portable camera, usually one using 35-mm. film.

min·i·com·put·er (min′ē·kəm·pyōō′tər) *n.* A small, inexpensive electronic computer.

min·i·fy (min′ə·fī) *v.t.* **·fied, ·fy·ing 1** To make small or less. **2** To lessen the worth or importance of. [< L *minor* less + -FY]

min·im (min′im) *n.* **1** An apothecaries' fluid measure; roughly, one drop, or one sixtieth of a fluid dram: in the United States, 0.06 cubic centimeter; in England, 0.059 cubic centimeter. **2** *Music* A half note. **3** An extremely small creature; a pigmy. **4** A down-stroke in writing, as in forming the letter *n.* **5** *Printing* A size of type, about 7-point, between nonpareil and brevier. —*adj.* Extremely small. [< F *minime* < L *minimus* least, smallest. Doublet of MINIMUM.] **—min′i·mal** *adj.*

Min·i·mal·ist (min′ə·məl·ist) *n.* One belonging to the more conservative branch of the former Russian Social Democrats: distinguished from *Maximalist.*

min·i·mize (min′ə·mīz) *v.t.* **·mized, ·miz·ing 1** To reduce to the smallest possible amount or degree. **2** To regard or represent at a minimum. Also *Brit.* **min′i·mise.** **—min′i·miz′er** *n.* **— min′i·mi·za′tion** *n.*

min·i·mum (min′ə·məm) *adj.* Consisting of or showing the least possible amount or degree; being a minimum. —*n. pl.* **·ma** (-mə) or **·mums 1** The least possible quantity, amount, or degree. **2** A value of a function that is less than any value which immediately precedes and follows it. **3** The lowest degree, variation, etc., as of temperature, recorded. [< L, neut. of *minimus.* Doublet of MINIM.] **—min′i·mal** *adj.*

minimum wage 1 A wage fixed by law or agreement as the smallest amount an employer may offer an employee in a specific group. **2** A living wage.

min·ing (mī′ning) *n.* **1** The act, process, or business of extracting coal, ores, etc., from mines. **2** The act of laying explosive mines.

mining camp A temporary settlement around or near a mine.

min·ion (min′yən) *n.* **1** A servile favorite or follower: a term of contempt. **2** *Printing* A size of type, about 7-point. **3** A saucy girl or woman; minx. **4** *Obs.* One who is beloved; a paramour. — *adj.* *Rare* Dainty; delicate; fine. [< F *mignon.* Doublet of MIGNON.]

min·i·scule (min′əs·kyōōl) *adj.* Minuscule.

min·i·skirt (min′i·skûrt′) *n.* A short skirt worn by women with the hemline well above the knee. Also **min′i·skirt′.** [< MINI- + SKIRT]

min·is·ter (min′is·tər) *n.* **1** The chief of an executive department of a government. **2** One commissioned to represent his government in diplomatic intercourse with another government. **3** One who is authorized to preach the gospel and administer the ordinances of the church; a clergyman. **4** One who acts in subservience to the will of another; a servant; agent. **5** One who promotes or dispenses. —*v.i.* **1** To give attendance or aid; provide for the wants or needs of someone. **2** To be conducive; contribute. —*v.t.* **3** To administer or apply. **4** *Archaic* To supply; furnish. See synonyms under SERVE. [< OF *ministre* < L *minister* an attendant < *minor* less; after L *magister* master < *magis* greater]

min·is·te·ri·al (min′is·tir′ē·əl) *adj.* **1** Of or pertaining to a minister of the gospel or the ministry; clerical. **2** Of or pertaining to a minister or executive staff in civil government. **3** *Law* Pertaining to an act or duty performed according to the mandate of legal authority, so that the agent is not accountable for its propriety or consequences: opposed to *judicial.* **4** Instrumental; causative. [< F *ministériel*] **—min′is· te′ri·al·ly** *adv.*

min·is·trant (min′is·trənt) *adj.* Ministering. —*n.* One who ministers. [< L *ministrans, -antis,* ppr. of *ministrare* serve]

min·is·tra·tion (min′is·trā′shən) *n.* **1** The act of performing service as a minister. **2** Any religious ceremonial. [< L *ministratio, -onis*] **— min′is·tra′tive** *adj.*

min·is·try (min′is·trē) *n. pl.* **·tries 1** The body of

officials in charge of the administration of the departments of a government. In the United States it is selected by the president with the advice and consent of the Senate, and is called the *Cabinet.* **2** An executive department of government. **3** Ministers of the gospel collectively, or their office. **4** The act of ministering, or the state or office of a minister; ministration; service. [< L *ministerium*]

min·i·ver (min′ə·vər) *n.* **1** A fur or mixture of furs used in the Middle Ages for trimming. **2** Any white fur, as ermine. [< OF *menu vair,* lit., little spotted (fur)]

mink (mingk) *n.* **1** An amphibious, slender-bodied, carnivorous mammal (genus *Mustela*), related to the weasel and valued for its soft, thick, glossy, brown fur. **2** The fur of this mammal. [< Scand. Cf. Sw. *menk.*]

min·ne·sing·er (min′ə·sing′ər) *n.* A lyric poet of medieval Germany. Compare TROUBADOUR. [< G < *minne* love + *singer* singer]

Min·ne·so·ta (min′ə·sō′tə) A State in the north central United States bordering on Canada and Lake Superior; 84,682 square miles; capital, St. Paul; entered the Union May 11, 1858; nickname, *Gopher State:* abbr. MN **—Min′ne·so′tan** *n. & adj.*

min·now (min′ō) *n.* **1** A small European cyprinoid fish *(Phoxinus phoxinus).* **2** One of various other small fishes; especially, in the United States, a fish of the carp family. **3** The young of various fishes. Also **min′nie.** [OE *myne* small fish; prob. infl. in meaning by F *menu* small]

mi·nor (mī′nər) *adj.* **1** Less in number, quantity, or extent: opposed to *major.* **2** Of secondary consideration. **3** *Music* **a** Higher than the corresponding major interval by a semitone. **b** Characterized by minor intervals, scales, or tones. **c** In a minor key; sad; plaintive. **4** *Logic* Designating a minor term. —*n.* **1** One below the age when full civil and personal rights can be exercised. **2** *Logic* A minor term or minor premise. See SYLLOGISM. **3** *Music* A minor key, interval, etc. **4** Hence, a pathetic or plaintive quality, as in literature or art. **5** *U.S.* A branch of study for degree candidates in colleges and universities, usually related to but requiring less time than a major; a secondary subject of study. **6** In English public schools, the younger of two namesakes; junior. ♦ Homophone: *miner.* [< L]

mi·nor·i·ty (mə·nôr′ə·tē, -nor′-, mī-) *n. pl.* **·ties 1** The smaller in number of two parts or parties: opposed to *majority.* **2** The state of being a minor; legal infancy. **3** A group comprising less than half of a population and differing from the others and especially from a larger predominant group, as in race, religion, political affiliation, etc.: also **minority group.** [< F *minorité*]

minor key *Music* A key or mode based on the minor scale and characterized by the use of the minor third, and producing a plaintive or mournful effect. See THIRD *n.*

minor league Any professional sports league not having the standing of a major league. **—mi′nor-league′** *adj.*

minor term *Logic* The subject of both the minor premise and the conclusion of a syllogism.

min·ster (min′stər) *n.* A monastery church; in Great Britain, often a cathedral: often used in combination: *Axminster.* [OE *mynster* < LL *monasterium.* Doublet of MONASTERY.]

min·strel (min′strəl) *n.* **1** Originally, in the Middle Ages, a retainer whose business it was to play musical instruments for the entertainment of his lord. **2** A wandering musician who composed and sang to the harp; one of a class of vagrant musicians and mountebanks, repressed by Henry IV. **3** A performer in a minstrel show. **4** *Poetic* A poet; singer; musician. See synonyms under POET. [< OF *menestrel* < LL *ministerialis* servant, jester < L *minister* attendant]

min·strel·sy (min′strəl·sē) *n. pl.* **·sies 1** The occupation of a minstrel. **2** Ballads or lyrics collectively. **3** A troupe of minstrels. [< AF *menestralcie,* OF *menestralsie*]

mint[1] (mint) *n.* **1** A place where the coin of a country is manufactured. **2** Figuratively, an abundant supply of anything: used especially of money. **3** Figuratively, the source of a fabrication or invention. —*v.t.* **1** To make (money) by stamping; coin. **2** To invent or fabricate, as a

word. —*adj.* Unused; in original condition: a *mint* stamp. [OE *mynet* coin < L *moneta* mint < *Moneta* epithet of Juno, whose temple at Rome was used as a mint. Doublet of MONEY.] **—mint′er** *n.*

mint[2] (mint) *n.* Any one of several aromatic herbs of the genus *Mentha,* of the family *Labiatae;* especially, spearmint and peppermint, used medicinally. [OE *minte* < L *menta, mentha* < Gk. *mintha*]

mint·age (min′tij) *n.* **1** The act of minting, or that which is minted; coinage; also, figuratively, the act of fabricating or coining. **2** The duty paid for coining. **3** The authorized impression placed upon a coin.

mint julep A drink made of brandy or whisky mixed with crushed ice and sugar and flavored with fresh mint.

min·u·end (min′yōō·end) *n.* The number from which another is to be subtracted: opposed to *subtrahend.* [< L *minuendus* to be lessened, gerundive of *minuere* lessen]

min·u·et (min′yōō·et′) *n.* **1** A slow, stately dance for couples in triple measure: introduced in France in the 17th century. **2** A musical composition suited to this dance: often as a movement in a sonata or symphony. [< F *menuet,* dim. of *menu* small < L *minutus*]

mi·nus (mī′nəs) *prep.* **1** Lessened, or requiring to be lessened by; less: 10 *minus* 5. **2** *Colloq.* Deprived of; lacking: *minus* a hat. —*adj.* **1** Lying or reckoned in that one of two opposite directions arbitrarily assumed as negative. **2** Negative: A debt may be treated as a *minus* quantity. —*n.* **1** A minus sign. **2** A minus quantity. [< L, neut. of *minor*]

mi·nus·cule (mi·nus′kyōol) *n.* **1** A semi-uncial cursive script, developed by the monks out of the uncial in the 7th–9th centuries and forming the basis of the modern small Roman and Greek letters; hence, any small or lower-case letter. **2** Any very small thing. —*adj.* **1** Of, pertaining to, like, or composed of minuscules. **2** Very small; miniature. [< L *minusculus,* dim. of *minor* less]

minus sign A sign (−) denoting subtraction, or reckoning or measuring in the negative direction.

min·ute[1] (min′it) *n.* **1** The 60th part of an hour; also, a moment; hence, any short, indefinite period of time. **2** The 60th part of a degree: a unit of angular measure indicated by the sign(′), and called a *minute* of arc. **3** A brief note or summary in writing of something to be remembered; memorandum; specifically, in the plural, an official record of the proceedings of any deliberative body. —*v.t.* **·ut·ed, ·ut·ing 1** To make a minute or brief note of; record. **2** To time to the minute. [< F < Med. L *minuta (pars)* small (part), minute < L *minutus* small]

mi·nute[2] (mī·nōōt′, -nyōōt′, mi-) *adj.* **1** Exceedingly small; hence, unimportant; trifling. **2** Attending to small things; critically careful; very exact. [< L *minutus* small, little, orig. pp. of *minuere* lessen] **—mi·nute′ness** *n.*

Synonyms: circumstantial, comminuted, critical, detailed, diminutive, exact, fine, little, particular, precise, slender, tiny. That is *minute* which is of exceedingly limited dimensions, as a grain of dust. That which is broken up into *minute* particles is said to be *comminuted;* things may be termed *fine* which would not be termed *comminuted;* as, *fine* sand; *fine* gravel; but, in using an adverb, we say a substance is finely *comminuted.* An account extended to very *minute* particulars is *circumstantial, detailed, particular,* and examination so extended is *critical, exact, precise.* See FINE, LITTLE, PRECISE, SMALL. *Antonyms:* see synonyms for LARGE.

minute hand (min′it) The hand of a timepiece that marks the minutes.

min·ute·ly[1] (min′it·lē) *adj. & adv.* At intervals of a minute.

mi·nute·ly[2] (mī·nōōt′lē, -nyōōt′-, mi-) *adv.* In a minute manner; very finely, closely, or exactly.

min·ute·man (min′it·man′) *n. pl.* **·men** (-men′) A man ready for service at a minute's notice: specifically applied to certain militiamen and armed citizens in the American Revolution.

mi·nu·ti·a (mi·nōō′shē·ə, -shə, -nyōō′-) *n. pl.* **·ti·ae** (-shi·ē) *Chiefly pl.* Small or unimportant details. [< L]

mi·o·car·di·a (mī′ə·kär′dē·ə) *n. Physiol.* Contraction of the heart; systole. [< NL < Gk. *meiōn* less + *kardia* heart]

Mi·o·cene (mī'ə·sēn) *adj.* Pertaining to or designating a geological epoch near the end of the Tertiary period, associated with a great development of modern mammals: also **Mi'o·cen'ic** (-sen'ik), See chart under GEOLOGY. —*n.* The Miocene epoch or series. [< Gk. *meiōn* less + *kainos* recent]

mi·o·sis (mī·ō'sis) *n.* **1** *Pathol.* **a** The period in the course of a disease when the symptoms begin to diminish. **b** Excessive contraction of the pupil of the eye: also spelled *myosis*. **2** Meiosis. [< Gk. *myein* close + -OSIS] —**mi·ot'ic** (-ot'ik) *adj.*

mi·o·ther·mic (mī'ə·thûr'mik) *adj.* Of or pertaining to those temperature conditions now prevailing on earth, especially as compared with past geological periods. [< Gk. *meiōn* less + *thermē* heat]

mir·a·cle (mir'ə·kəl) *n.* **1** Any wonderful or amazing thing, fact, or event; a wonder. **2** An event in the natural world, but out of its established order, possible only by the intervention of divine power. **3** A medieval dramatic representation of religious subjects: also **miracle play:** see MYSTERY¹ (def. 10). See synonyms under PRODIGY. [< F < L *miraculum* < *mirari* wonder < *mirus* wonderful]

mi·rac·u·lous (mi·rak'yə·ləs) *adj.* **1** Effected by direct divine agency; supernatural. **2** Surpassingly strange; wonderful. **3** Possessing the power to work miracles; wonder-working. See synonyms under SUPERNATURAL. [< F *miraculeux* < Med. L *miraculosus* < L *miraculum*] —**mi·rac'u·lous·ly** *adv.* —**mi·rac'u·lous·ness** *n.*

mir·a·dor (mir'ə·dôr', -dōr') *n.* *Archit.* A balcony or oriel window. [< Sp. < *mirar* behold < L *mirari* wonder]

mi·rage (mi·räzh') *n.* **1** An optical illusion, as of an oasis or a sheet of water in the desert, or ships seen inverted in the air. It occurs when the lower strata of air are at a very different temperature from the higher strata, so that images are seen as by reflection. **2** Anything that falsely appears to be real. [< F < *se mirer* be reflected, look at oneself < L *mirari* wonder at]

mir·bane oil (mûr'bān) Nitrobenzene. [Prob. a fanciful formation]

mire (mir) *n.* Wet, yielding earth; swampy ground; deep mud or slush. —*v.* **mired, mir·ing** *v.t.* **1** To cause to sink or become stuck in as in mire. **2** To defile; soil. —*v.i.* **3** To sink in mire; bog down. [< ON *myrr* swampy ground] —**mir'y** *adj.* —**mir'i·ness** *n.*

mir·ex (mir'eks) *n.* A persistent, toxic chlorinated hydrocarbon, $C_{10}Cl_{12}$, formerly used widely as a pesticide against fire ants. Also **Mir'ex.**

mir·ror (mir'ər) *n.* **1** An object having a nearly perfect reflecting surface; a looking-glass. **2** *Optics* A speculum. **3** Whatever reflects or clearly represents; an exemplar. **4** A crystal used by diviners. —*v.t.* To reflect or show an image of, as in a mirror. [< OF *mirour* < LL *mirare* look at < L *mirari* wonder at, admire]

mir·ror·scope (mir'ər·skōp) *n.* **1** A mirror used to reflect a design so as to permit of rapid reproduction, as by artists. **2** A projector (def. 3).

mir·ror·stone (mir'ər·stōn') *n.* Mica, especially of the muscovite variety.

mirth (mûrth) *n.* **1** Pleasurable feelings, or gaiety of spirits, manifested in jesting and laughter; social merriment; jollity. **2** *Obs.* Pleasure; joy. See synonyms under HAPPINESS,

LAUGHTER, SPORT. [OE *myrth, myrgth* < *myrig* pleasant, merry]

mirth·ful (mûrth'fəl) *adj.* Merry. See synonyms under CHEERFUL, HAPPY, MERRY, VIVACIOUS. —**mirth'ful·ly** *adv.* —**mirth'ful·ness** *n.*

mirth·less (mûrth'lis) *adj.* Lacking mirth or merriment; joyless. —**mirth'less·ly** *adv.* —**mirth'less·ness** *n.*

mis-¹ *prefix* Bad; amiss; wrongly. [OE *mis-* wrong; infl. in meaning by ME *mes-* MIS-²] *Mis-* may appear as a prefix in hyphemes or solidemes; for examples, see the list of self-explanatory words at the foot of the page.

mis-² *prefix* Bad; amiss; not: found with negative or depreciatory force in words borrowed from Old French; *misadventure, miscreant.* [< OF *mes-* < L *minus* less]

mis-³ Var. of MISO-.

mis·ad·ven·ture (mis'əd·ven'chər) *n.* An unlucky chance; misfortune. See synonyms under ACCIDENT, MISFORTUNE. [< OF *mesaventure*]

mis·al·li·ance (mis'ə·lī'əns) *n.* An undesirable alliance, as marriage with one of inferior station or character. [< F *mésalliance*]

mis·an·thrope (mis'ən·thrōp, miz'-) *n.* One who entertains aversion to or distrust of his fellow men. Also **mis·an·thro·pist** (mis·an'thrə-pist). [< Gk. *misanthrōpos* hating mankind < *misein* hate + *anthrōpos* a man] —**mis'an·throp'ic** (-throp'ik) or **·i·cal** *adj.* —**mis'an·throp'i·cal·ly** *adv.*

mis·an·thro·py (mis·an'thrə·pē) *n.* Hatred or distrust of mankind.

mis·ap·ply (mis'ə·plī') *v.t.* **·plied, ·ply·ing 1** To use or apply incorrectly or inefficiently. **2** To use or apply wrongfully or dishonestly.

mis·ap·pro·pri·ate (mis'ə·prō'prē·āt) *v.t.* **·at·ed, ·at·ing** To use or take improperly or dishonestly; misapply. —**mis'ap·pro'pri·a'tion** *n.*

mis·be·come (mis'bi·kum') *v.t.* **came, ·come, ·com·ing** To be unbecoming or not befitting to.

mis·brand (mis·brand') *v.t.* To label or brand incorrectly or falsely.

mis·call (mis·kôl') *v.t.* **1** To call by a wrong name; misname. **2** *Brit. Dial.* To revile; abuse.

mis·car·riage (mis·kar'ij) *n.* **1** *Med.* A premature delivery of a non-viable fetus; abortion. **2** Failure to reach or to bring to an expected result, destination, or conclusion.

mis·car·ry (mis·kar'ē) *v.i.* **·ried, ·ry·ing 1** To fail of an intended effect; go wrong. **2** To bring forth a fetus prematurely; have a miscarriage; abort.

mis·cel·la·ne·ous (mis'ə·lā'nē·əs) *adj.* Consisting of several kinds; variously mixed; also, many-sided; promiscuous; varied. See synonyms under HETEROGENEOUS. [< L *miscellaneus* < *miscellus* mixed < *miscere* mix] —**mis'cel·la'ne·ous·ly** *adv.* —**mis'cel·la'ne·ous·ness** *n.*

mis·cel·la·ny (mis'ə·lā'nē) *n. pl.* **·nies 1** *Often pl.* A collection of literary compositions on various subjects. **2** Any miscellaneous collection. [Anglicized var. of MISCELLANEA]

mis·chance (mis·chans', -chäns') *n.* An instance of ill-luck; a mishap. See synonyms under CATASTROPHE, MISFORTUNE. [< OF *mescheance*]

mis·chief (mis'chif) *n.* **1** Any occurrence attended with evil or injury; troublesome or damaging action or its result; damage; vexation. **2** Any annoying or vexatious action or course of conduct; a prank; also, the spirit or mood leading to such acts. **3** A prankish person. See synonyms under INJURY. [< OF *meschef* bad result < *meschever* come to grief < *mes-* mis- (< L *minus* less) + *chief*

head, end < L *caput* head]

mis·chie·vous (mis'chi·vəs) *adj.* **1** Inclined to mischief; of a prankish nature. **2** Injurious. See synonyms under BAD, MALICIOUS, NOISOME, PERNICIOUS. —**mis'chie·vous·ly** *adv.* —**mis'chie·vous·ness** *n.* [< AF *meschevous*]

mis·ci·ble (mis'i·bəl) *adj.* **1** Capable of being mixed. **2** Suitable for mixing. [< L *miscere* mix] —**mis'ci·bil'i·ty** *n.*

mis·col·or (mis·kul'ər) *v.t.* **1** To give a wrong color to. **2** To misrepresent. Also *Brit.* **mis·col'our.**

mis·con·ceive (mis'kən·sēv') *v.t. & v.i.* **·ceived, ·ceiv·ing** To conceive wrongly; misunderstand. —**mis'con·ceiv'er** *n.* —**mis'con·cep'tion** (-sep'shən) *n.*

mis·con·duct (mis'kən·dukt') *v.t.* **1** To behave (oneself) improperly. **2** To mismanage. —*n.* (mis·kon'dukt) **1** Improper conduct; bad behavior. **2** *Law* Adultery. **3** Mismanagement.

mis·con·stru·al (mis'kən·strōo'əl) *n.* **1** An erroneous interpretation. **2** The act of putting a false meaning upon something said or done by another. **3** Misunderstanding or the result of a misunderstanding.

mis·con·strue (mis'kən·strōo') *v.t.* **·strued, ·stru·ing** To interpret erroneously; put a false or unwarranted meaning to; misunderstand. —**mis'con·struc'tion** (-struk'shən) *n.*

mis·cre·ant (mis'krē·ənt) *n.* **1** A vile wretch; an evil-doer. **2** *Archaic* An unbeliever; infidel. —*adj.* **1** Villainous; conscienceless. **2** *Archaic* Unbelieving; infidel. [< OF *mescreant* unbelieving]

mis·deed (mis·dēd') *n.* A wrong or improper act. See synonyms under OFFENSE, SIN. [OE *misdǣd*]

mis·de·mean·ant (mis'di·mē'nənt) *n.* One who is guilty of a misdemeanor or misconduct. —**first-class misdemeanant** In English law, one of a class of prisoners guilty of misdemeanor, but not subjected to the same prison regulations as a criminal, nor considered as a person convicted of a crime.

mis·de·mean·or (mis'di·mē'nər) *n.* **1** Misbehavior; a misdeed. **2** *Law* Any offense less than a felony. In England the distinction between a felony and a misdemeanor is still maintained. In the United States this distinction has, in most States, either been abolished or is treated in a manner that makes it of no practical value. Compare FELONY. Also *Brit.* **mis'de·mean'our.** See synonyms under OFFENSE.

mis·do (mis·dōo') *v.t. & v.i.* **·did, ·done, ·do·ing** To do wrongly; bungle. [OE *misdon*] —**mis·do'er** *n.* —**mis·do'ing** *n.*

mise (mīz) *n.* **1** *Law* The issue pleaded in a writ of right. **2** *Law* Expenses; specifically, the costs and charges in an action. **3** The adjustment of a dispute by arbitration or compromise. [< AF < OF *mis* put, laid out, pp. of *mettre* < L *mittere* send]

mi·ser (mī'zər) *n.* One who saves and hoards avariciously. [< L *miser* wretched]

mis·er·a·ble (miz'ər·ə·bəl, miz'rə-) *adj.* **1** Wretchedly unhappy. **2** Of mean quality; bad; valueless: sometimes expressing contempt. **3** Producing, proceeding from, or exhibiting misery; pitiable: *miserable* weather; a *miserable* groan. See synonyms under PITIFUL, SAD. —*n. Obs.* A miserable person. [< OF < L *miserabilis* pitiable < *miserari* pity < *miser* wretched] —**mis'er·a·ble·ness** *n.* —**mis'er·a·bly** *adv.*

mis·e·re·re (miz'ə·râr'ē, -rir'ē) *n.* In church stalls, a small wooden bracket affixed perpendicularly to the bottom of the seat and designed to afford support to the worshiper

misaccent	misadvise	misanalyze	misassay	misbandage	mischaracterization	miscoinage
misaccentuation	misaffection	misanswer	misassent	misbegin	mischaracterize	miscollocation
misachievement	misaffirm	misapparel	misassert	misbelove	mischarge	miscommand
misacknowledge	misagent	misappear	misassign	misbestow	mischristen	miscommit
misact	misaim	misappearance	misassociate	misbetide	miscipher	miscommunicate
misadapt	misalienate	misappellation	misassociation	misbias	miscitation	miscompare
misadaptation	misalinement	misappoint	misatone	misbill	miscite	miscomplain
misadd	misallegation	misappointment	misattribute	misbind	misclaim	miscomplaint
misaddress	misallege	misappraise	misattribution	misbuild	misclaiming	miscompose
misadjust	misallotment	misappraisement	misauthorization	miscanonize	misclass	miscomputation
misadmeasurement	misallowance	misapprehensible	misauthorize	miscensure	misclassification	miscompute
misadministration	misalphabetize	misascribe	misaver	miscenter	misclassify	miscon
misadvice	misalter	misascription	misaward	mischallenge	miscoin	misconclusion

when the seat is turned up: also called *misericorde*.

mis·er·i·corde (miz′ər·i·kôrd′, mi·zer′i·kôrd′) *n.*
1 A small dagger used in the Middle Ages to give the death stroke to a fallen knight.
2 Formerly, a dispensation from fasting given to a member of a monastic order. **3** An apartment in a monastery serving as a refectory for monks who had received such dispensation. **4** Miserere. Also **mis′er·i·cord′**. [<OF <L *misericordia* <*misereri* have pity + *cor, cordis* heart]

mis·er·y (miz′ər·ē) *n. pl.* **·er·ies 1** Extreme distress or suffering, especially as a result of poverty; wretchedness; also, a cause of wretchedness. **2** *Dial.* A cause of pain: a *misery* in the back. See synonyms under MISFORTUNE, PAIN. [<OF *miserie* <L *miseria* < *miser* wretched]

mis·fea·sance (mis·fē′zəns) *n. Law* The performance of a lawful act in an unlawful or culpably negligent manner. Compare MALFEASANCE, NONFEASANCE. [<OF *mesfaisance* <*mesfaire* do wrong <*mes-* mis- + *faire* do <L *facere*] — **mis·fea′sor** *n.*

mis·fire (mis·fīr′) *n.* The failure to discharge or explode when desired: said of a firearm, explosive, or internal-combustion engine. —*v.i.* **·fired, ·fir·ing** To fail to explode or be fired.

mis·fit (mis·fit′) *v.t. & v.i.* **·fit·ted, ·fit·ting** To fail to fit or make fit. —*n.* **1** Something that fits badly. **2** (mis′fit′) A person who does not adjust or adapt himself readily to his surroundings. **3** The act or condition of fitting badly.

mis·for·tune (mis·fôr′chən) *n.* **1** Adverse or ill fortune. **2** An unlucky chance or occurrence; calamity.
Synonyms: adversity, affliction, bereavement, blow, calamity, chastening, chastisement, disappointment, disaster, distress, failure, hardship, harm, ill, misadventure, mischance, misery, mishap, reverse, ruin, sorrow, stroke, trial, tribulation, trouble, visitation. *Misfortune* is usually of lingering character or consequences, and such as the sufferer is not deemed directly responsible for; as, He had the *misfortune* to be born blind. Any considerable *disappointment, failure,* or *misfortune,* as regards outward circumstances, as loss of fortune, position, and the like, when long continued or attended with enduring consequences, constitutes *adversity.* For the loss of friends by death we commonly use *affliction* or *bereavement. Calamity* and *disaster* are used of sudden and severe *misfortunes.* We speak of the *misery* of the poor, the *hardships* of the soldier. *Affliction, chastening, trial,* and *tribulation* all suggest some disciplinary purpose of God with beneficent design. *Affliction* may be keen and bitter, but brief; *tribulation* is long and wearing. Compare ACCIDENT, ADVERSITY, BLOW, CATASTROPHE, LOSS. *Antonyms:* blessing, boon, comfort, consolation, gratification, happiness, joy, pleasure, prosperity, relief, success, triumph.

mis·give (mis·giv′) *v.* **·gave** (-gāv′), **·giv·ing** *v.t.* To make fearful, suspicious, or doubtful: My heart *misgives* me. —*v.i.* To be apprehensive.

mis·guide (mis·gīd′) *v.t.* **·guid·ed, ·guid·ing** To guide wrongly in action or thought; mislead. — **mis·guid′ance** *n.* — **mis·guid′er** *n.*

mis·hap (mis′hap, mis·hap′) *n.* An unfortunate accident; slight misfortune. See synonyms under ACCIDENT, CATASTROPHE, MISFORTUNE. [<MIS-¹ + HAP]

mish·mash (mish′mash′, -mosh′) *n.* A medley; hotch-potch. —*v.t.* To make a hotch-potch of; jumble. Also **mish′-mash′**. [Reduplication of MASH]

or erroneous information to. — **mis′in·for·ma′tion** *n.* — **mis′in·form′er, mis′in·form′ant** *n.*

mis·in·ter·pret (mis′in·tûr′prit) *v.t.* To interpret wrongly; misunderstand. — **mis′in·ter′pre·ta′tion** *n.* — **mis′in·ter′pret·er** *n.*

mis·lay (mis·lā′) *v.t.* **·laid, ·lay·ing** To lay in a place not remembered; misplace. See synonyms under DISPLACE. — **mis·lay′er** *n.*

mis·lead (mis·lēd′) *v.t.* **·led, ·lead·ing** To direct wrongly; lead astray or into error. — **mis·lead′er** *n.* — **mis·lead′ing** *adj.* — **mis·lead′ing·ly** *adv.*

mis·like (mis·līk′) *v.t.* **1** To dislike. **2** To displease. —*n.* Dislike; aversion; disapproval. — **mis·lik′er** *n.* — **mis·lik′ing** *n.* — **mis·lik′ing·ly** *adv.*

mis·man·age (mis·man′ij) *v.t. & v.i.* **·aged, ·ag·ing** To manage badly or improperly. —

mis·no·mer (mis·nō′mər) *n.* **1** A name wrongly applied; an inapplicable designation. **2** A misnaming; specifically, the giving of a wrong name to a person in a legal document. [<AF <OF *mesnommer* call by the wrong name <*mes-* wrongly + *nomer* <L *nominare* name]

miso- *combining form* Hating: *misogynist.* Also, before vowels, *mis-.* [<Gk. *misein* hate]

mis·og·a·my (mis·og′ə·mē) *n.* Hatred of marriage. [<MISO- + -GAMY] — **mis·og′a·mist** *n.*

mis·og·y·ny (mis·oj′ə·nē) *n.* Hatred of woman: opposed to *philogyny.* [<Gk. *misogynia* <*misein* hate + *gynē* woman] — **mis·og′y·nist** *n.* — **mis·og′y·nous** *adj.*

mis·ol·o·gy (mis·ol′ə·jē) *n.* Hatred of discussion or inquiry; aversion to enlightenment. [<Gk. *misologia* <*misein* hate + *logos* discourse] — **mis·ol′o·gist** *n.*

mis·o·ne·ism (mis′ō·nē′iz·əm, mī′sō-) *n.* Hatred of change, innovation or novelty. [<MISO- + Gk. *neos* new] — **mis′o·ne′ist** *n.*

mis·play (mis·plā′) *n.* In games, a wrong play; hence, any bad move.

mis·rep·re·sent (mis′rep·ri·zent′) *v.t.* To give an incorrect or false representation of. See synonyms under PERVERT. — **mis′rep·re·sen·ta′tion** *n.* — **mis′rep·re·sen′ta·tive** *adj. & n.*

mis·rule (mis·rōōl′) *v.t.* **·ruled, ·rul·ing** To rule unwisely or unjustly; misgovern. —*n.* **1** Bad or unjust rule or government. **2** Disorder or confusion.

miss¹ (mis) *n.* **1** A young girl: chiefly colloquial, or in trade use: clothing for *misses.* **2** *Often cap.* A title used in speaking to an unmarried woman or girl: used without the name. [Contraction from MISTRESS]

miss² (mis) *v.t.* **1** To fail to hit or strike. **2** To fail to meet, catch, obtain, accomplish, see, hear, perceive, etc.: to *miss* the point. **3** To fail to attend, keep, perform, etc.: to *miss* church. **4** To overlook or fail to take advantage of, as an opportunity. **5** To discover or feel the loss or absence of. **6** To escape; avoid: He just *missed* being wounded. —*v.i.* **7** To fail to hit; strike wide of the mark. **8** To be unsuccessful; fail. — **to miss fire 1** To fail to discharge: said of firearms. **2** To be unsuccessful; fail. —*n.* **1** The act of missing; a failure to hit, find, attain, succeed, etc. **2** *Obs.* Loss; want. [OE *missan*]

mis·sal (mis′əl) *n.* **1** The book containing the service for the celebration of mass throughout the year; a mass book. **2** Loosely, an illuminated black-letter or manuscript book of early date resembling the old mass books. ◆ Homophone: *missile.* [<Med. L *missale,* neut. of *missalis (liber)* mass (book) <LL *missa* mass]

mis·shape (mis·shāp′) *v.t.* **·shaped, ·shaped** or **·shap·en, ·shap·ing** To shape badly; deform.

mis·sile (mis′əl) *n.* **1** Any object, especially a weapon, intended to be thrown or discharged; a projectile. **2** A guided missile. —*adj.* Such as may be thrown or hurled. ◆ Homophone: *missal.* [<L *missilis* <*missus,*

pp. of *mittere* send]

miss·ing (mis′ing) *adj.* Absent from the proper or accustomed place; lost; gone: said specifically of soldiers who are absent but whose fate has not been definitely ascertained. — **to turn up missing** To be absent; fail to arrive or be found.

missing link 1 Something lacking to make complete a chain or series. **2** *Biol.* A hypothetical form of life assumed to be intermediate in development between man and the anthropoid apes.

mis·sion (mish′ən) *n.* **1** The act of sending, or the state of being sent, as on some errand. **2** The sending forth of men with authority to preach or spread the gospel; authority so given by God or the church. **3** The business or service on which one is sent. **4** That which one is or feels destined to accomplish; the destined or chosen end of one's efforts. **5** An effort to spread, or the work of spreading, religious teaching. **6** A single field or locality covered by missionary work; the body of missionaries there established; a missionary station; also, any educational, religious, or welfare center for the underprivileged in a city. **7** *Eccl.* A regularly organized church and congregation not having the status of a parish in canon law; a quasi-parish. **8** The office of a foreign ambassador or envoy. **9** The persons sent on any errand or service. **10** *Mil.* A definite task assigned to an individual or unit of the armed services. **11** *Aeron.* A flight operation of a single aircraft or formation. —*adj.* **1** Pertaining to or belonging to a mission. **2** Like the early Spanish architecture and simple furniture of the missions of the SW United States. —*v.t.* **1** To send on a mission. **2** To establish a mission in. [<L *missio, -onis* <*missus,* pp. of *mittere* send] — **mis′sion·al** *adj.*

mis·sion·ar·y (mish′ən·er′ē) *n. pl.* **·ar·ies 1** A person sent to propagate religion or to do educational or charitable work in some place where his church has no self-supporting local organization; hence, one who spreads any new system or doctrine. **2** A person sent on a mission; a messenger; ambassador. —*adj.* Pertaining to missions.

Mis·sis·sip·pi (mis′ə·sip′ē) A State in the south central United States on the Gulf of Mexico; 47,716 square miles; capital, Jackson; entered the Union Dec. 10, 1817; nickname *Bayou State.* Abbr. MS

Mississippi River A river in the central United States, flowing 2,350 miles south to the Gulf of Mexico; from the headwaters of the Missouri River, flowing 3,892 miles to the Gulf of Mexico.

mis·sive (mis′iv) *n.* That which is sent; especially a letter; a message in writing. —*adj.* Sent or designed to be sent. [<Med. L

missivus <L *missus*, pp. of *mittere* send]

miss·lick (mis′lik) *n. Colloq.* A cut made by an ax or knife off the true line; hence, any mistake.

Mis·sou·ri (mi-zŏŏr′ē) *n. pl.* **·ri** One of a tribe of North American Indians of the Siouan family, formerly inhabiting northern Missouri, now in Oklahoma with the Otoe.

Mis·sou·ri (mi-zŏŏr′ē, -zŏŏr′ə) A State in the west central United States west of the Mississippi; 69,674 square miles; capital, Jefferson City; entered the Union Aug. 10, 1821: nickname, *Ozark State* or *Show Me State*: abbr. **MO —to be from Missouri** To be on the alert against deception; be skeptical. **—Mis·sou′ri·an** *adj. & n.*

mis·spell (mis-spel′) *v.t. & v.i.* **·spelled** or **·spelt**, **·spell·ing** To spell incorrectly.

mis·state (mis-stāt′) *v.t.* **·stat·ed**, **·stat·ing** To state wrongly or falsely.

mis·step (mis-step′) *n.* A false or wrong step; error.

miss·y (mis′ē) *n. pl.* **miss·ies** Miss: a colloquial or diminutive form.

mist (mist) *n.* **1** An aggregation of fine drops of water in the atmosphere at or near the earth's surface, floating or falling very slowly: used either synonymously with *fog* or distinguished from it, as being less dense, or as consisting of drops large enough to fall perceptibly but slowly. **2** *Meteorol.* A very thin fog in which the horizontal visibility is greater than 1,100 yards. **3** Water vapor condensed on and dimming a surface. **4** Any colloidal suspension of a liquid in a gas. **5** Anything that dims or darkens; that which obscures physical or mental vision. **—v.i. 1** To be or become dim or misty; blur. **2** To rain in very fine drops. **—v.t. 3** To make dim or misty; blur. [OE]

mis·take (mis-tāk′) *n.* An error in action, judgment, perception, or impression; a blunder. See synonyms under ERROR. **—v.** **·took**, **·tak·en**, **·tak·ing** *v.t.* **1** To understand wrongly; acquire a wrong conception of; misinterpret. **2** To take (a person or thing) to be another; fail to identify correctly: to *mistake* friends for enemies. **—v.i. 3** To make a mistake. [<ON *mistaka*] **—mis·tak′a·ble** *adj.*

mis·tak·en (mis-tā′kən) *adj.* **1** Characterized by mistake; incorrect; wrong. **2** Being in error; wrong in opinion or judgment. See synonyms under ABSURD. **—mis·tak′en·ly** *adv.* **—mis·tak′en·ness** *n.*

Mis·ter (mis′tər) *n.* **1** Master: a title of address prefixed to the name and to some official titles of a man: commonly written *Mr.*: *Mr.* Darwin; *Mr.* Chairman. **2** Official salutation in addressing a warrant officer, flight officer, or a cadet in the U.S. Military Academy at West Point, and, in some practice, officers below the rank of captain. In the Navy it is directed to those of all ranks below that of commander; in the Maritime Service it is applicable to all ranks below the captain of the ship. [Var. MASTER]

mist·flow·er (mist′flou′ər) *n.* A tall perennial herb (*Eupatorium coelestinum*) of the composite family, with coarsely toothed leaves and clusters of light–blue or violet flowers.

mis·tral (mis′trəl, *Fr.* mēs·trȧl′) *n.* **1** A cold, dry, and violent northwest Alpine wind blowing from the Ebro to the Gulf of Genoa and also through the southern provinces of France. **2** A worsted dress fabric with twisted warp and weft threads woven so as to give a nubbed effect. [<F, lit., master wind <L *magistralis* <*magister* master]

mis·treat (mis-trēt′) *v.t.* To treat badly or un-

kindly; abuse. **—mis·treat′ment** *n.*

mis·tress (mis′tris) *n.* **1** A woman in authority or control, or to whom service is rendered; a female head, chief, or owner, as of a country household, an institution, or an estate; also a female schoolteacher. **2** A woman who unlawfully, or without marriage, fills the place of a wife; also, a woman beloved and courted; a sweetheart. **3** A woman who is well skilled in or has mastered anything. **4** *Scot.* A married woman or wife. [<OF *maistresse*, fem. of *maistre*. See MASTER.]

Mis·tress (mis′tris) *n.* A title of address formerly applied to both married and unmarried women: now generally supplanted by *Mrs.* for married and *Miss* for unmarried women.

mis·tri·al (mis-trī′əl) *n.* A trial of a lawsuit that is void because of errors; also, a trial of a lawsuit in which the jury cannot agree on a verdict.

mis·trust (mis-trust′) *n.* Lack of trust or confidence. **—v.t. & v.i.** To regard (someone or something) with suspicion or doubt; distrust. See synonyms under DOUBT, SUSPECT. **—mis·trust′er** *n.* **—mis·trust′ful** *adj.* **—mis·trust′ful·ly** *adv.* **—mis·trust′ful·ness** *n.*

mist·y (mis′tē) *adj.* **mist·i·er**, **mist·i·est 1** Containing, characterized by, or accompanied by mist. **2** Dimmed or obscured by or as by mist; hence, lacking clearness or perspicuity; confused; indistinct; vague. See synonyms under THICK. **—mist′i·ly** *adv.* **—mist′i·ness** *n.*

mis·un·der·stand (mis′un-dər-stand′, mis·un′-) *v.t. & v.i.* **·stood**, **·stand·ing** To understand wrongly; misinterpret.

mis·un·der·stand·ing (mis′un-dər-stan′ding, mis·un′-) *n.* **1** A misapprehension; mistake as to meaning or motive. **2** A disagreement; dissension. See synonyms under QUARREL.

mis·un·der·stood (mis′un-dər-stŏŏd′, mis·un′-) *adj.* **1** Not comprehended; wrongly interpreted. **2** Not appreciated at true worth.

mis·use (mis-yōōs′) *n.* **1** Ill–treatment; violence; abuse. **2** Erroneous or improper use; misapplication. Also **mis·us′age**. **—v.t.** (mis-yōōz′) **·used**, **·us·ing 1** To use or apply wrongly or improperly. **2** To subject to ill–treatment; abuse; maltreat. See synonyms under ABUSE.

mis·ven·ture (mis-ven′chər) *n.* An ill venture; a misadventure.

mite[1] (mīt) *n.* Any of various small arachnids (order *Acarina*) of both terrestrial and aquatic habits: many of them are parasitic on men, animals, plants, and stored grain, as the *itch mite*, *cheese mite*, etc. ◆ Homophone: *might*. [OE *mīte*] **—mit′y** *adj.*

mite[2] (mīt) *n.* **1** A very small amount or particle. **2** Any very small coin or sum of money: the widow's *mite*. *Mark* xii 42. See synonyms under PARTICLE. ◆ Homophone: *might*. [<Du. *mijt*]

mi·ter (mī′tər) *n.* **1** A headdress worn by various church dignitaries, as popes, archbishops, bishops, and abbots: a tall ornamental cap terminating in two peaks; hence, the office or dignity of a bishop, etc. **2** The official headdress of the ancient Jewish high priest. **3** A headdress resembling a bishop's miter, worn in the 15th century by women. **4** The junction of two bodies at an equally divided angle, as at the corner of a picture frame: also **miter joint. —v.t. 1** To confer a miter upon;

ECCLESIASTICAL MITER

raise to the rank of bishop. **2** To make or join with a miter joint. Also *mitre*. [<OF *mitre* <L *mitra* <Gk., belt, turban] **—mi′ter·er** *n.*

miter box A box having a bottom and sides, but no top or ends, the sides having kerfs or sawguides in which wooden strips may be sawed to accurate miters.

mi·ter·wort (mī′tər·wûrt′) *n.* Any of a genus (*Mitella*) of low, slender, mainly North American perennial herbs of the saxifrage family, having small miter–shaped flowers. Also **mi′tre·wort′.**

mith·ri·da·tism (mith′rə·dā′tiz·əm) *n.* Immunity against poisons secured by the administration of gradually increasing doses: so called from King Mithridates VI of Pontus, who is said to have immunized himself by this method. [<obs. *mithridate* an antidote against poison <LL *mithridatium* <*Mithridateus* of Mithridates] **—mith′ri·dat′ic** (-dat′ik) *adj.*

mi·ti·cide (mī′tə·sīd) *n.* A chemical agent destructive of mites: also called *acaricide*. [< *miti-* (<MITE[1]) + -CIDE]

mit·i·gate (mit′ə·gāt) *v.t. & v.i.* **·gat·ed**, **·gat·ing** To make or become milder, less harsh, or less severe; moderate. See synonyms under ABATE, ALLAY, ALLEVIATE, AMEND, PALLIATE, RELAX. [<L *mitigatus*, pp. of *mitigare* <*mitis* mild + *agere* do, drive] **—mit′i·ga·ble** *adj.* **—mit′i·gant** *adj. & n.* **—mit′i·ga′tion** *n.* **—mit′i·ga′tive** *adj.* **—mit′i·ga′tor** *n.* **—mit′i·ga·to′ry** (-gə·tôr′ē, -tō′rē) *adj. & n.*

mi·tis casting (mī′tis, mē′-) **1** The process of making castings of wrought iron of which the melting point has been lowered by the addition of a small amount of aluminum. **2** A casting so made. [<L *mitis* mild + CASTING]

mi·to·chon·dri·a (mī′tə·kon′drē·ə) *n.* Chondriosome. [<NL <Gk. *mitos* thread + *chondros* cartilage, granule]

mi·to·sis (mī·tō′sis) *n. Biol.* The series of changes in indirect cell division by which the chromatin of the nucleus is modified into a double set of chromosomes that splits longitudinally, one set going to each nuclear pole of the spindle before final division into two fully mature daughter cells. Compare MEIOSIS. [<NL <Gk. *mitos* thread + -OSIS] **—mi·tot·ic** (mī·tot′ik) *adj.* **—mi·tot′i·cal·ly** *adv.*

mi·trail·leuse (mē·trȧ·yœz′) *n.* **1** A kind of breechloading machine–gun of grouped barrels for the rapid firing of small missiles. **2** Any machine–gun. [<F]

mitral valve *Anat.* A membranous valve between the left auricle and the left ventricle of the heart: it prevents the flow of blood into the auricle.

mi·tre (mī′tər) See MITER.

mitt (mit) *n.* **1** A glove, often of lace or knitwork, that does not extend over the fingers. **2** A mitten; specifically, in baseball, a heavy padded mitten used by the catcher and the first baseman. **3** *pl. Slang* The hands. [<MITTEN]

mit·ten (mit′n) *n.* **1** A covering for the hand, encasing the four fingers together and the thumb separately. **2** A mitt. **3** *pl. Slang* The hands; also, boxing gloves. [<F *mitaine*]

mix (miks) *v.* **mixed** or **mixt**, **mix·ing** *v.t.* **1** To put together in one mass or compound; blend. **2** To make by combining ingredients: to *mix* dough. **3** To combine or join: to *mix* business with pleasure. **4** To cause to associate or mingle: to *mix* social classes together. **5** To crossbreed. **—v.i. 6** To be mixed or blended.

mis–hear	misincite	misinter	mislive	misnatured	mispagination	misphrase
mis–hearer	misinclination	misinterment	mislocate	misnavigation	mispaint	mispoint
mis–heed	misincline	misintimation	mislocation	misnumber	misparse	mispoise
mis–hit	misinfer	misjoin	mislodge	misnurture	mispart	mispolicy
mis–hold	misinference	miskeep	mismark	misnutrition	mispassion	misposition
mishumility	misinflame	miskindle	mismeasure	misobservance	mispatch	mispossessed
misidentification	misingenuity	mislabel	mismeasurement	misobserve	mispen	mispractice
misidentify	misinspired	mislabor	mismeet	misoccupy	misperceive	misprejudiced
misimagination	misinstruct	mislanguage	mismenstruation	misopinion	misperception	mispresent
misimagine	misinstruction	mislearn	misminded	misordination	misperform	misprincipled
misimpression	misinstructive	mislie	mismingle	misorganization	misperformance	misproceeding
misimputation	misintend	mislight	mismotion	misorganize	mispersuade	misproduce
misimpute	misintention	mislikeness	misnarrate	mispage	misperuse	mispronounce

add,āce,câre,pälm; end,ēven; it,īce; odd,ōpen,ôrder; tŏŏk,pōōl; up,bûrn; ə = a in *above*, e in *sicken*, i in *clarity*, o in *melon*, u in *focus*; yōō = u in *fuse*; oi,oil; ou,pout; ch,check; g,go; ng,ring; th,thin; t͡h,this; zh,vision. Foreign sounds à,œ,ü,kh,ṅ; and ◆ : see page xx. <from; + plus; ? possibly.

7 To associate; get along. **8** To take part; become involved. — **to mix up 1** To blend thoroughly. **2** To confuse; bewilder. **3** To implicate or involve. — *n.* **1** The act or effect of mixing. **2** A mixture, expecially a commercial mixture of prepared ingredients: a cake *mix.* **3** A proportion, as of things that make up a mixture; specifically, the proportion of certain substances or raw materials before their subjection to a fabricating or manufacturing process: a *mix* of cement. **3** *Telecom.* The correct blending of the sound input of two or more microphones. **4** A combination of various elements; mixture: a movie providing a heady *mix* of violence, sex, and glamour. [Back formation <MIXED] — **mix′·a·ble, mix′i·ble** *adj.*

Synonyms (verb): amalgamate, associate, blend, combine, commingle, commix, compound, confuse, fuse, incorporate, join, meddle, mingle, unite. Compare COMPLEX, HETEROGENEOUS.

mixed (mikst) *adj.* **1** Mingled in a body or mass; joined together; associated; blended: generally of different or even incongruous elements: a *mixed* metaphor. **2** Containing persons of both sexes: a *mixed* school, *mixed* foursome, etc. **3** Mentally confused, as with liquor. **4** *Law* Designating statutes which concern both persons and property; also, designating property which is not altogether real nor personal, but a compound of both. **5** *Bot.* Denoting inflorescence which combines cymose and racemose. [<F *mixte* <L *mixtus,* pp. of *miscere* mix]

mixed bag A mixture or assortment of miscellaneous elements.

mixed economy A combination of laissez-faire with governmentally planned and/or controlled economy.

mixed-up (mikst′up′) *adj.* Confused or disordered.

mix·er (mik′sər) *n.* **1** One who or that which mixes; a machine or device for mixing. **2** *Colloq.* A person with reference to his ability to mix socially or get along well in groups.

mix·ture (miks′chər) *n.* **1** The act of mixing. **2** Something resulting from mixing; admixture. **3** Something added as an ingredient. **4** A pharmaceutical preparation consisting of an aqueous solution in which is suspended an insoluble compound: intended for internal use. **5** A commingling of two or more substances in varying proportions, in which the ingredients retain their individual chemical properties, and from which they may be separated, unaltered, by mechanical means. Compare COMPOUND. [<F <L *mixtura* <*miscere* mix]

mix-up (miks′up′) *n.* **1** A confusion; muddle. **2** *Colloq.* A fight.

miz·zen·mast (miz′ən·məst, -mast′, -mäst′) *n.* *Naut.* **1** The mast next abaft the mainmast. **2** The shorter of the two masts of a ketch or yawl.

mks The meter-kilogram-second system of units for ·the measurement of physical quantities. It differs from the cgs system in using the international standards of length and mass instead of their submultiples, the centimeter and the gram.

mne·me (nē′mē) *n.* A hypothetical unit of memory assumed to exist in all animal cells. [<Gk. *mnēmē* memory]

mne·mon·ic (ni·mon′ik) *adj.* Pertaining to, aiding, or designed to aid the memory. Also **mne·mon′i·cal.** [<Gk. *mnēmonikos* <*mnēmōn* mindful <*mnasthai* remember]

mne·mon·ics (ni·mon′iks) *n.* The science of memory improvement. Also **mne·mo·tech·nics** (nē′mō·tek′niks).

mo·a (mō′ə) *n.* A large, flightless, extinct bird (family *Dinornithiformes*) of New Zealand, having enormous legs with at least three toes; especially, the largest species (*Dinornis robustus*). [<native name]

Mo·ab (mō′ab) An ancient country in the upland area east of the Dead Sea.

Mo·ab·ite (mō′əb·it) *n.* One of the descendants of Moab, son of Lot. *Gen.* xix 37.

Moabite Stone A stone slab with a Moabite inscription, dating from 850 B.C.; discovered, 1868.

moan (mōn) *n.* **1** A low mournful sound indicative of grief or pain. **2** A similar sound: the *moan* of the wind. **3** *Obs.* Lamentation; complaint. —*v.i.* **1** To utter moans of grief or pain. **2** To make a low, mournful sound, as wind in trees. —*v.t.* **3** To lament; bewail. [Cf. OE *mænan* lament, moan]

moat (mōt) *n.* A defensive ditch on the outside of a fortress wall. —*v.t.* To surround with or as with a moat. ◆Homophone: *mote.* [<OF *mote* embankment]

mob¹ (mob) *n.* **1** A turbulent or lawless crowd or throng; a rabble. **2** The lowest class of people; the masses; populace. **3** *Austral.* A herd, as of sheep or cattle. **4** *Slang* A gang, as of thieves. — *v.t.* **mobbed, mob·bing 1** To attack in a mob; crowd around and annoy. **2** To crowd into, as a hall. [<L *mob(ile vulgus)* movable crowd] — **mob′ber** *n.* —**mob′bish** *adj.* —**mob′bish·ly** *adv.*

Synonyms (noun): canaille, crowd, masses, people, populace, rabble.

mob² (mob) *n.* A cap or headdress formerly worn by women and girls and usually tied under the chin. Also **mob′cap′.** [<Du. *mop* coif, cap]

mo·bile (mō′bəl, -bēl) *adj.* **1** Characterized by freedom of movement; movable. **2** Changing easily in expression or in state of mind; changeable. **3** Moving or flowing freely. **4** That can be easily and quickly moved, as military units. **5** Designating a mobile. —*n.* (mō′bēl) A form of sculpture arranged so that its movable parts, suspended or balanced on rods, wires, etc., describe kinetic rather than static patterns. [<F < L *mobilis* movable] —**mo·bil·i·ty** (mō·bil′ə·tē) *n.*

Synonyms: changeable, changing, expressive, fickle, movable, sensitive, variable, volatile. See ACTIVE. *Antonyms:* dull, fixed, immovable, still, stolid, unchanging, unvarying.

mo·bi·lize (mō′bə·līz) *v.* **·lized, ·liz·ing** *v.t.* **1** To make ready for war, as an army, industry, etc. **2** To assemble for use; organize. **3** To make mobile; put into circulation or use. —*v.i.* **4** To get ready for war. Also *Brit.* **mo′bi·lise.** [<F *mobiliser*] —**mo′bi·li·za′tion** (-lə·zā′shən, -lī·zā′-) *n.*

Mö·bi·us surface (mœ′bē·oŏs) *Geom.* A surface both sides of which may be completely traversed without crossing either edge: made by joining the half-twisted ends of a rectangular strip of paper or other flexible material. Also **Möbius strip.** [after August Ferdinand *Möbius,* 1790–1868, German mathematician and astronomer]

mob law Lynch law.

mob·oc·ra·cy (mob·ok′rə·sē) *n. pl.* **·cies 1** Lawless control of public affairs by the mob or populace. **2** The mob considered as the dominant class. [<MOB¹ + -(O)CRACY]

mob·o·crat (mob′ə·krat) *n.* One who favors mobocracy; a demagog. —**mob′o·crat′ic, mob′o·crat′i·cal** *adj.*

mob·ster (mob′stər) *n. Slang* A gangster.

moc·ca·sin (mok′ə·sin) *n.* **1** A foot covering made of soft leather or buckskin: worn by North American Indians; also, a soft shoe or slipper. **2** A dark-colored, obscurely blotched, venomous snake (genus *Agkistrodon*) of the southern United States. *A. piscivorus* is the water moccasin. [<Algonquian *mohkisson*]

MOCCASIN
(Average length about 4 feet; largest specimens to 6 feet)

moccasin flower Any one of certain orchids of the genus *Cypripedium,* common in the United States, especially the showy ladyslipper (*C. reginae*), State flower of Minnesota.

mo·cha (mō′kə) *n.* **1** A choice coffee, originally grown in Arabia. **2** A rich, coffee-flavored icing, or a cake flavored with it. **3** A fine sheepskin leather used for making gloves. **4** A dark, dull, grayish-brown color. [from *Mocha*]

mock (mok) *v.t.* **1** To treat or address scornfully or derisively; hold up to ridicule. **2** To ridicule by imitation of action or speech; mimic derisively. **3** To deceive; delude. **4** To defy; make futile. **5** *Poetic* To imitate; counterfeit. —*v.i.* **6** To express or show ridicule, scorn, or contempt; scoff. —*adj.* Merely imitating the reality; sham. —*n.* An act of mocking; a jeer; mockery. [<OF *mocquer*] —**mock′er** *n.* —**mock′ing·ly** *adv.*

Synonyms (verb): banter, chaff, deride, flout, gibe, insult, jeer, taunt. See IMITATE, MISLEAD, SCOFF. Compare COUNTERFEIT.

mock·er·y (mok′ər·ē) *n. pl.* **·er·ies 1** Derisive or contemptuous mimicry. **2** A false show; sham. **3** A butt of ridicule. **4** Labor in vain. See synonyms under BANTER, SCORN.

mock-he·ro·ic (mok′hi·rō′ik) *adj.* Imitating or satirizing the heroic manner, style, attitude, or character. —*n.* **1** Any writing using the grand style as a comic expedient. **2** *pl.* Affectation of the grand manner in expressing trivialities.

mock·ing·bird (mok′ing·bûrd′) *n.* **1** A bird (*Mimus polyglottos*) common in the southern and eastern United States, noted for its rich song and powers of imitating the calls of other birds. **2** One of various other birds that mock, as the catbird.

mocking thrush The thrasher.

mock moon A paraselene.

mock sun A parhelion.

mock-tur·tle soup (mok′tûr′təl) Soup prepared from calf's head or other meat, and somewhat resembling green-turtle soup.

mock-up (mok′up′) *n.* **1** A model, usually full-scale, of a proposed structure, machine, apparatus, etc. **2** An airplane, etc., constructed for purposes of study, testing, or training of personnel.

mod (mod) *adj.* Bold, flamboyant, and unconventional, as in dress or behavior. —*n.* Sometimes cap. One who dresses or behaves in a flamboyant or unconventional manner. [<MODERN]

mo·dal (mōd′l) *adj.* **1** Of or denoting a mode or manner, especially a mode of grammar, a mode in music, or a mode of logical statement. **2** Characterized by form or manner without reference to matter or substance. **3** Pertaining to or designating a statistical mode. —**mo′dal·ly** *adv.*

mode (mōd) *n.* **1** Manner of being, doing, etc.; way; method. **2** Prevailing style; common fashion. **3** *Gram.* Mood. **4** *Music* A method of dividing an octave by placing the steps and half-steps of which it is composed in certain arbitrary relations. In the **major mode,** tones are arranged as given in the major scale; in the **minor mode,** as in the minor scale. **5** *Psychol.* A faculty or phenomenon of mind considered as a state of consciousness. **6** *Philos.* The manner of a thing's existence so far as it is not essential. **7** *Logic* **a** The style of the connection between the antecedent and the consequent of a proposition. **b** The arrangement of the propositions of a syllogism according to their quantity and quality. **8** *Stat.* That value, magnitude, or score which occurs the greatest number of times in a given series of observations: also called *norm.* **9** *Geol.* The actual mineral composition of a rock, expressed in percentages by weight: distinguished from *norm.* **10** A light bluish-gray color. **11** *Physics* One of a set of forms of motion of a dynamic system, having the properties that the variation with time is either harmonic or exponential and that any form of motion of the system can be represented as a superposition of members of the set. See synonyms under MANNER, SYSTEM. [< L *modus* measure, manner]

mod·el (mod′l) *n.* **1** An object, usually in miniature, representing accurately something to be made or already existing; more rarely, a plan or drawing: a *model* of a building. **2** A person who poses for painters, sculptors, etc. **3** A thing or person to be imitated or patterned after; that which is taken as a pattern or an example. **4** A person employed to wear articles of clothing to display them to customers. **5** That which strikingly resembles something else; an approximate copy or image. — *v.* **·eled** or **·elled,** **·el·ing** or **·el·ling** *v.t.* **1** To plan or fashion after a model or pattern. **2** To make a model of. **3** To fashion; make. **4** To display by wearing, as a coat or hat. — *v.i.* **5** To make a model or models. **6** To pose or serve as a model (defs. 2 and 4). **7** To assume the appearance of natural form. — *adj.* Serving or used as a model; suitable for a model; worthy to be imitated. [< F *modèle* < Ital. *modello,* dim. of *modo* < L *modus* measure, manner] — **mod′· el·er, mod′el·ler** *n.*

Synonyms (noun): archetype, copy, design, ectype, example, facsimile, image, imitation, mold, original, pattern, prototype, replica, representation, type. A *pattern* must be closely followed in its minutest particulars by a faithful copyist; a *model* may allow a great degree of freedom. A sculptor may idealize his living *model;* his workmen must exactly copy in marble or metal the *model* he has made in clay. The *archetype* is the original form, actual or ideal, in accordance with which existing things are made; a *prototype* is either the original or an authenticated copy that has the authority of the original. See EXAMPLE, IDEA, IDEAL.

Model T An early model of automobile manufactured by Henry Ford in great numbers: also called *tin lizzie.*

mod·er·ate (mod′ər·it) *adj.* **1** Keeping or kept within reasonable limits; not extreme, excessive, or radical; also, mild; temperate; calm; reasonable; gentle. **2** Not strongly partisan: said of political and religious parties, and their tenets or views. **3** Medium; fair; also, mediocre. **4** Slow in thought, speech, or action. **5** *Meteorol.* Designating a breeze (No. 4) or a gale (No. 7) on the Beaufort scale. See synonyms under GRADUAL, MODEST, SLOW, SOBER. — *n.* A person of moderate views, opinions, or practices; especially, a member of a political or religious party which is not strongly partisan. — *v.* (mod′ə·rāt) **·at·ed, ·at·ing** *v.t.* **1** To reduce the violence, severity, etc., of; make less extreme; restrain. **2** To preside over. — *v.i.* **3** To become less intense or violent; abate. **4** To act as moderator. See synonyms under ABATE, ALLAY, ALLEVIATE, TEMPER, TRANQUILIZE. [< L *moderatus,* pp. of *moderare* regulate < *modus* measure] — **mod′er·ate·ly** *adv.* — **mod′er·ate·ness** *n.* — **mod′er·a′tion** *n.*

mod·er·a·tor (mod′ə·rā′tər) *n.* **1** One who restrains or regulates. **2** The presiding officer of a meeting; also, the presiding officer in Presbyterian and Congregational courts. **3** *Physics* A substance, as graphite or beryllium, used to control the rate of a nuclear chain reaction in an atomic-energy reactor. — **mod′er·a′tor·ship** *n.*

mod·ern (mod′ərn) *adj.* **1** Pertaining to the present or recent period; not ancient. **2** *Obs.* Commonplace; common; trite. — *n.* **1** A person of modern times, or modern views or characteristics: also **mod′ern·er.** **2** *Printing* A style of type face characterized by contrasting heavy down-strokes and thin cross-strokes. [< LL *modernus* recent < L *modo* just now] — **mod′ern·ly** *adv.* — **mo·der·ni·ty** (mo·dûr′nə·tē), **mod′ern·ness** *n.*

Synonyms (adj.): fresh, late, new, novel, recent. *Modern* history pertains to any period since the Middle Ages; *modern* literature, *modern* architecture, etc., are not strikingly remote from the styles and types prevalent today. That which is *late* is somewhat removed from the present, but not far enough to be called old. That which is *recent* is very close to the present, but not quite so sharply distinguished from the past as *new.* See NEW.

mod·ern·ism (mod′ərn·iz′əm) *n.* **1** Something characteristic of modern as distinguished from former or classical times; a modern idiom or practice. **2** Modern character, methods, or mental attitude. **3** The humanistic tendency in religious thought to supplement old theological creeds and dogmas by new scientific and philosophical learning and thus to place emphasis on practical ethics and world-wide social justice: distinguished from *fundamentalism.* — **mod′ern·ist** *n.* — **mod′ern·is′tic** *adj.*

mod·ern·ize (mod′ərn·īz) *v.t.* & *v.i.* **·ized, ·iz·ing** To make or become modern in ideas, standards, methods, etc. — **mod′ern·i·za′tion** *n.* — **mod′ern·iz′er** *n.*

mod·est (mod′ist) *adj.* **1** Restrained by a sense of propriety or humility. **2** Characterized by reserve, propriety, or purity; decorous; chaste. **3** Free from excess; moderate. [< F *modeste* < L *modestus* moderate < *modus* measure] — **mod′est·ly** *adv.*

Synonyms: chaste, decent, decorous, humble, moderate, proper, pure, retiring, unassuming, unobtrusive, unostentatious, unpretending, unpretentious, virtuous. See HUMBLE.

mod·es·ty (mod′is·tē) *n.* Decent reserve and propriety; delicacy; decorum.

Synonyms: backwardness, bashfulness, coldness, constraint, coyness, diffidence, reserve, shyness, timidity, unobtrusiveness. *Bashfulness* is a shrinking from notice without assignable reason. *Coyness* is a half encouragement, half avoidance of offered attention, and may be real or affected. *Diffidence* is self-distrust; *modesty,* a humble estimate of oneself in comparison with others or with the demands of some undertaking. *Modesty* has also the specific meaning of a sensitive shrinking from anything indelicate. *Shyness* is a tendency to shrink from observation; *timidity,* a distinct fear of criticism, error, or failure. *Reserve* is holding oneself aloof from others, or holding back one's feelings from expression, or one's affairs from communication to others. Compare ABASH, PRIDE, RESERVE, TACITURN. *Antonyms:* abandon, arrogance, assumption, assurance, boldness, conceit, confidence, egotism, forwardness, frankness, freedom, haughtiness, impudence, indiscretion, loquaciousness, loquacity, pertness, sauciness, self-conceit, self-sufficiency, sociability.

mod·i·cum (mod′i·kəm) *n.* *pl.* **·cums** or **·ca** (-kə) **1** A moderate amount; a little. **2** A small thing or person. [< L *modicum* measure]

mod·i·fi·ca·tion (mod′ə·fə·kā′shən) *n.* **1** The act of modifying, or the state of being modified. **2** *Biol.* Variation in plants and animals, specifically that resulting from localized changes in an organism due to external influences and not inheritable. Compare MUTATION. **3** That which results from modifying. — **mod·i·fi·ca·to·ry** (mod′ə·fə·kā′tər·ē) *adj.*

mod·i·fi·er (mod′ə·fī′ər) *n.* **1** One who or that which qualifies, changes, limits, or varies. **2** *Gram.* A word, phrase, or clause that alters, restricts, or varies the application of another word or group of words, as an adjective or adverb. See also UNIT MODIFIER.

mod·i·fy (mod′ə·fī) *v.* **·fied, ·fy·ing** *v.t.* **1** To make somewhat different in form, character, etc.; vary. **2** To reduce in degree or extent; moderate. **3** *Gram.* To qualify the meaning of; restrict; limit. **4** *Ling.* To alter (a vowel) by umlaut. — *v.i.* **5** To be or become modified; change. See synonyms under CHANGE, TEMPER. [< F *modifier* < L *modificare* < *modus* measure + *facere* make] — **mod′i·fi′a·ble** *adj.*

mo·dil·lion (mō·dil′yən) *n. Archit.* An enriched block or horizontal bracket used in series under a Corinthian or Composite cornice: sometimes, with less ornament, under one of the Roman Ionic order. [< F *modillon* < Ital. *modiglione*]

mo·di·o·lus (mō·dī′ə·ləs) *n. pl.* **·li** (-lī) *Anat.* The central stem round which wind the passages of the cochlea of the internal ear. [< L, bucket on a water wheel < *modus* measure]

mod·ish (mō′dish) *adj.* Conformable to the current mode, fashion, or usage; stylish. — **mod′ish·ly** *adv.* — **mod′ish·ness** *n.*

Mo·doc (mō′dok) *n.* A North American Indian of a small, nearly extinct tribe of Lutuamian linguistic stock, formerly living in California, now on reservations in Oregon and Oklahoma. See LUTUAMIAN.

mod·u·lar (moj′ŏŏ·lər) *adj.* **1** Of, like, or pertaining to a module or modulus. **2** Composed of modules: *modular* homes.

mod·u·late (moj′ŏŏ·lāt) *v.* **·lat·ed, ·lat·ing** *v.t.* **1** To vary the tone, inflection, or pitch of. **2** To regulate or adjust; temper; soften. **3** *Music* To change or cause to change to a different key. **4** To intone or sing. **5** *Electronics* To alter the frequency or amplitude of (a radio carrier wave). — *v.i.* **6** *Electronics* To alter the frequency or amplitude of a carrier wave. **7** *Music* To change from one key to another by using a transitional chord common to both. [< L *modulatus,* pp. of *modulari* regulate < *modulus* MODULE] — **mod′u·la·to·ry** (-lə·tôr′ē, -tō′rē) *adj.*

mod·u·la·tion (moj′ŏŏ·lā′shən) *n.* **1** The act of modulating, or the state of being modulated; specifically, a musical inflection of the voice; change in pitch. **2** *Music* A change from one key to another by the use of a transitional chord common to both. **3** *Telecom.* The process of varying the frequency, amplitude, intensity, or phase of a carrier wave so as to conform with a transmitted signal wave.

mod·u·la·tor (moj′ŏŏ·lā′tər) *n.* **1** One who or that which modulates. **2** *Telecom.* A tube or valve for effecting modulation. **3** A musical chart showing the relations of tones and scales.

mod·ule (moj′ŏōl) *n.* **1** A standard or unit of measurement. **2** *Archit.* A measure of proportion among the parts of a classical order, the size of the diameter or semidiameter of the base of a column shaft usually being taken as a unit. **3** A standard structural component repeatedly used, as in a building, computer, etc.: cubic *modules* used in the design of a table. **4** A preassembled, self-contained unit, often a component or subassembly of a larger structure: a housing *module;* a lunar *module.* **5** *Obs.* A mere image. [< L *modulus* < *modus* measure. Doublet of MOLD[1].]

mod·u·lor (moj′ŏŏ·lôr) *n.* A system of industrial design based upon the ideal proportions of the human body: units derived from the basic dimensions can be assembled to secure maximum harmony and utility. — *adj.* Of or characterized by such design.

mod·u·lus (moj′ŏŏ·ləs) *n. pl.* **·li** (-lī) **1** *Physics* A number, coefficient, or quantity that measures a force, function, or effect: *modulus* of elasticity: sometimes abbreviated to *M* or μ. See CONGRUENT. **2** *Math.* The logarithm of *e* to the base 10 ($\log_{10}e$): Napierian logarithms are multiplied by this factor to convert them to logarithms to the base 10. [< L, dim. of *modus* a measure]

mo·el·lon (mō′əl·on) *n.* **1** A form of rubble masonry used as a filling in the facing walls of a structure. **2** Dégras (def. 1). [< F, alter. of OF *moilon;* ? infl. by F *moelle* pith]

mo·fette (mō·fet′) *n.* **1** A noxious emanation

of gas from a fissure; a gas spring. **2** An opening in the earth from which noxious gas escapes, as from a volcano. Also **mof·fette'.** [<F <Ital. *mofetta* <*muffare* decay <G *muff* mold]

mo·gen Da·vid (mō'gən dā'vid, duv'id) A mystic device formed by the intertwining of two equilateral triangles; the six-pointed star: used as a symbol of Judaism. Also called *star of David, shield of David, Solomon's seal.* [<Hebrew, star of David]

mo·gul (mō'gul, mō·gul') *n.* **1** Any great or pretentious personage; autocrat: also **great mogul. 2** A type of freight locomotive with three pairs of coupled drivers and one pair of leading truck wheels.

Mo·gul (mō'gul, mō·gul') *n.* A Mongol; Mongolian; specifically, one of the Mongol conquerors of Hindustan, or a follower of Genghis Khan in the 13th century. Also **Mo·ghul'.** — **the Great** or **Grand Mogul** The former Mongol emperor of Delhi. [<Persian *mugal* a Mongol]

mo·hair (mō'hâr) *n.* **1** The hair of the Angora goat. **2** A smooth, wiry fabric made of mohair filling and cotton warp: often called *brilliantine.* **3** A fabric of cut or uncut loops with cotton or wool back and mohair pile: used chiefly for upholstery. [Earlier *mocayare* <Arabic *mukhayyar*; infl. in form by *hair*]

Mo·ham·med (mō·ham'id), 570–632, Arabian religious and military leader; founder of Islam and author of the *Koran:* also spelled *Mahomet.* Also **Mo·hom'ed.** — **Mohammed II,** 1430?–81, sultan of Turkey 1451–81; captured Constantinople, 1453.

mo·har·ra (mə·här'ə) See MOJARRA.

Mo·ha·ve (mō·hä'vē) *n.* A member of a tribe of North American Indians of Yuman linguistic stock, formerly living along the Colorado River. — *adj.* Of or pertaining to this tribe. Also spelled *Mojave.*

Mo·hawk (mō'hôk) *n.* **1** One of a tribe of North American Indians of Iroquoian stock, one of the original tribes of the Five Nations, formerly ranging from the Mohawk River Valley, New York, to the St. Lawrence: now in Canada, New York, and Wisconsin. **2** The Iroquoian language of this tribe. **3** A Mohock. [<N. Am. Ind. Cf. Narragansett *mohowaicuck,* lit., they eat animate things, hence, eaters of human flesh; so named by enemy tribes.]

Mo·he·gan (mō·hē'gən) *n.* One of a tribe of North American Indians of Algonquian linguistic stock, the eastern branch of the Mahican group: formerly occupying the region from the lower Connecticut and Thames rivers northward to Massachusetts. See MAHICAN. [<Algonquian *maingan* wolf]

Mo·hi·can (mō·hē'kən) *n.* One of a warlike tribe of North American Indians belonging to the Algonquian linguistic stock, and formerly dwelling along both banks of the Hudson. See MAHICAN.

Mo·hole (mō'hōl') *n.* A hole drilled or to be drilled through the ocean floor to the Mohorovicic discontinuity.

Mo·hor·o·vic·ic discontinuity (mə·hôr'ə·vis'ik, -vich'ik) *n.* Geol. A rock layer forming a boundary between the earth's crust and mantle about 6 to 25 miles deep. Also **Mo·ho** (mō'hō'). [after Andrija *Mohorovic,* Yugoslavian scientist]

Mohs scale (mōz) *Mineral.* A qualitative scale in which the hardness of a mineral is determined by its ability to scratch, or be scratched by, any one of 10 standard minerals arranged in the following increasing order of hardness: 1, talc; 2, gypsum; 3, calcite; 4, fluorite; 5, apatite; 6, feldspar; 7, quartz; 8, topaz; 9, corundum; 10, diamond. [after Friedrich *Mohs,* 1773–1839, German mineralogist who conceived it]

moi·e·ty (moi'ə·tē) *n. pl.* **·ties 1** A half. **2** A small portion. [<F *moitié* <L *medietas* < *medius* half]

moil (moil) *v.i.* To work hard; toil; drudge. — *n.* **1** A soiling; defilement; spot. **2** Confusion; vexation; trouble. **3** *Scot.* Toil; drudgery. [<OF *moillier, muiller* wet <L *mollis* soft; infl. in meaning by *toil*] — **moil'er** *n.* — **moil'ing·ly** *adv.*

moi·ré (mwä·rā') *adj.* Having a wavelike or watered appearance, as certain fabrics. — *n.* **1** A corded silk or rayon fabric, having

a wavy or watered pattern produced by passing the fabric between engraved cylinders which press the design into the material: also **moire** (mwär). **2** The finish or effect of this process on certain fabrics. [<F <*moirer* water silk <*moire* watered silk <MOHAIR]

moist (moist) *adj.* **1** Having slight sensible wetness; damp; humid. **2** Tearful: *moist* eyes. **3** Marked by the presence of pus, phlegm, etc. [<OF *moiste* <a fusion of L *musteus* dew + *mucidus* moldy <*mucus* mucus] — **moist'ly** *adv.* — **moist'ness** *n.*

mois·ten (mois'ən) *v.t. & v.i.* To make or become moist. — **mois'ten·er** *n.*

mois·ture (mois'chər) *n.* Slight sensible wetness; a small amount of liquid exuding from, diffused through, or resting on a substance; dampness. [<OF *moisteur*]

mo·jar·ra (mə·här'ə) *n.* A large salt-water fish (genus *Gerres*), similar to a bass, inhabiting mostly tropical waters: also spelled *moharra.* [<Sp.]

mol (mōl) *n. Chem.* The gram-molecule; that weight of a substance, expressed in grams, which is equal numerically to its molecular weight: also spelled *mole.* [<G]

mo·lal (mō'lal) *adj. Chem.* **1** Pertaining to the mol or gram-molecule. **2** Designating a solution which has a concentration equivalent to one mol of the solute in 1,000 grams of the solvent. Compare MOLAR[1]. [<MOL + -AL] — **mo·lal·i·ty** (mō·lal'ə·tē) *n.*

mo·lar[1] (mō'lər) *adj.* **1** *Physics* Pertaining to a mass; acting on or exerted by a mass, as force. **2** *Chem.* Having or containing a gram-molecular weight or mol; specifically, denoting a solution containing one mol of solute to the liter. Compare MOLAL. [<MOL + -AR] — **mo·lar·i·ty** (mō·lar'ə·tē) *n.*

mo·lar[2] (mō'lər) *n.* A grinding tooth with flattened crown, situated behind the canine and incisor teeth. — *adj.* **1** Grinding, or adapted for grinding. **2** Pertaining to a molar. [<L *molaris* <*mola* mill]

mo·las·ses (mə·las'iz) *n.* A viscid, dark-colored liquor drained off from raw cane or beet sugar; treacle. [<Pg. *melaço* <L *mellaceus* honeylike <*mel* honey]

mold[1] (mōld) *v.t.* **1** To work into a particular shape or form; model; shape. **2** To shape or cast in or as in a mold; make on a mold. **3** In founding, to form a mold of or from. **4** To ornament with molding. See synonyms under BEND, GOVERN, INFLUENCE. [<*n.*] — *n.* **1** A matrix for shaping anything in a fluid or plastic condition: distinguished from *cast.* **2** Hence, that after which something else is patterned, or the thing that is molded. **3** Form; nature; also, kind; character. **4** The physical form; shape: now applied to the human form. **5** A molding, or number of moldings. See synonyms under MODEL. Also spelled *mould.* [<OF *modle* <L *modulus* < *modus* measure, limit. Doublet of MODULE.] — **mold'a·ble** *adj.* — **mold'er** *n.*

IRON-MOLDER'S TOOLS

a. Lifter.
b. Taper and square.
c. Oval or dog-tail.
d. Square corner.
e. Half-round corner.
f. Yankee.
g. Heart and square.
h. Flange and bead.

mold[2] (mōld) *n.* **1** Any fungous growth on food, clothing, walls, etc., especially such growths as form a woolly or furry coating on decaying vegetable matter or in moist, warm places. **2** Any of various fungi producing such growths. **3** Mustiness; decay. — *v.t. & v.i.* To become or cause to become moldy. Also spelled *mould.* [< obs. *moul* grow moldy <Scand. Cf. Dan. *mugle* grow moldy.]

mold[3] (mōld) *n.* **1** Earth that is fine and soft, and rich in organic matter. **2** The constituent material of anything; earthy material; matter. **3** The earth; ground; hence, a grave. — *v.t.* To cover with mold. Also spelled *mould.* [OE *molde* earth]

mol·da·vite (mol'də·vīt) *n.* **1** A dull-green natural glass resembling obsidian and thought to be of meteoritic origin. **2** A variety of ozocerite found in Moravia. [from the *Moldau,* near which it is found]

mold·board (mōld'bôrd', -bōrd') *n.* **1** *Agric.* The curved metal plate of a plow, by which the earth is turned over and pulverized. **2** A similar part of a machine for building roads: also spelled *mouldboard.* [<MOLD[3] + BOARD]

mold·er (mōl'dər) *v.i.* To decay gradually and turn to dust; crumble; waste away. — *v.t.* To cause to crumble. Also spelled *moulder.* See synonyms under DECAY. [Freq. of obs. *mold* crumble]

–mol·der *combining form* One who molds or fashions (a specific thing): *glass-molder, iron-molder.* [<MOLD[1]]

mold fungus A fungus which causes mold; specifically, any of an order (*Mucorales*) of phycomycetous fungi, as the common bread mold (*Rhizopus nigricans*).

mold·ing (mōl'ding) *n.* **1** The act of shaping with or as with a mold. **2** Anything made in or as in a mold. **3** *Archit.* **a** A more or less ornamental strip on some part of a structure. **b** A cornice or other depressed or projecting decorative member on a surface or angle of any part of a building. Also spelled *moulding.*

mold·y (mōl'dē) *adj.* **mold·i·er, mold·i·est** Covered with mold; hence, old; musty: also spelled *mouldy.* — **mold'i·ness** *n.*

mole[1] (mōl) *n.* **1** A small permanent spot on the skin; a birthmark. **2** A stain or spot, as in a garment. [OE *māl*]

mole[2] (mōl) *n.* A small, insectivorous mammal (family *Talpidae*) with velvety fur, minute eyes, and very broad forefeet adapted for digging and forming extensive underground excavations. [ME *molle* <MLG. Cf. MDu. *molle.* Prob. related to MOLD[3].]

COMMON MOLE
(About 5 1/2 inches long, with tail an inch long)

mole[3] (mōl) *n.* A jetty or breakwater, partially enclosing an anchorage or harbor. [<F *môle* <L *moles* great mass]

mole[4] (mōl) *n. Pathol.* A morbid mass formed in the womb by the degeneration of the partly developed ovum, and giving rise to false pregnancy: also spelled *mola.* [<F *môle* <L *mola* millstone, false conception]

mole[5] (mōl) See MOL.

mole cricket 1 A burrowing cricket (family *Gryllotalpidae*) with a soft, cylindrical body and broad, stout, molelike front legs, found in some sandy soils. For illustration see INSECTS (injurious). **2** Any of several related species.

mo·lec·u·lar (mə·lek'yə·lər) *adj.* **1** Of, pertaining to, or consisting of molecules. **2** Resulting from the action of molecules: *molecular* changes. [<NL *molecularis*]

molecular film A layer of a substance having a thickness of one molecule: also called *monolayer.*

molecular volume *Chem.* The molecular weight of a substance divided by its density under specified conditions, usually the boiling point and normal atmospheric pressure.

molecular weight *Chem.* The sum of the weights of the constituent atoms of a molecule; specifically, the weight of a molecule of any gas or vapor as compared with some standard gas, such as oxygen.

mol·e·cule (mol'ə·kyōol) *n.* **1** *Physics* The smallest part of an element, substance, or compound that can exist freely in the solid, liquid, or gaseous state and still retain its composition and properties. **2** Any small particle. See synonyms under PARTICLE. [<F *molécule* <NL *molecula,* dim. of L *moles* mass]

mole·hill (mōl'hil') *n.* A small heap or ridge of earth raised by a burrowing mole.

mole·skin (mōl'skin') *n.* **1** The skin of a mole. **2** A heavy, twill fabric, usually cotton, having a thick, soft nap resembling moleskin: used chiefly for coats, jackets, etc.

mo·lest (mə·lest') *v.t.* To annoy or harm by interference; disturb injuriously. See synonyms under ABUSE, PERSECUTE. [<OF *molester* <L *molestare* <*molestus* troublesome <*moles* mass, burden] **—mo·les·ta·tion** (mō'les·tā'shən, mol'es·tā'shən) *n.* **—mo·lest'er** *n.*

Mo·lière (mō·lyâr') Pseudonym of Jean Baptiste Poquelin, 1622–73, French dramatist.

mol·le (mō·lā') *n.* The sharp, astringent condiment extracted from the drupes of a tropical American pepper tree (*Schinus molle*).

mol·les·cent (mə·les'ənt) *adj.* Producing softness; softening. [< L *mollescens, -entis*] — **mol·les'cence** *n.*

mol·li·fy (mol'ə·fī) *v.t.* **·fied, ·fy·ing 1** To make less angry; soothe; pacify; appease. **2** To reduce the violence or intensity of. See synonyms under ALLAY, TEMPER. [< F *mollifier* < LL *mollificare* < L *mollis* soft + *facere* make] **—mol'li·fi'a·ble** *adj.* **—mol'li·fi·ca'tion** *n.* **—mol'li·fi'er** *n.* **—mol'li·fy'ing·ly** *adv.*

mol·li·ti·es (mə·lish'i·ēz) *n. Pathol.* A softening of an organ or tissue. [< L]

mol·lus·cum (mə·lus'kəm) *n. Pathol.* Any of various skin diseases, especially, **molluscum con·ta·gi·o·sum** (kən·tā'jē·ō'səm), caused by a filtrable virus and characterized by the formation of hard skin tubercles, usually on the face. [< NL]

mol·lusk (mol'əsk) *n.* Any member of a large phylum (*Mollusca*) of mostly marine invertebrates having a soft, unsegmented body protected usually by a calcareous shell and including snails, oysters, cuttlefish, squids, whelks, limpets, etc. Also **mol lusc**. [< F. *mollusque* < L *molluscus (nux)* soft, thin-shelled (nut) < *mollis* soft] **—mol·lus·can** (mə·lus'kən) *adj. & n.* **—mol·lus'cous** *adj.*

mol·ly·cod·dle (mol'ē·kod'l) *n.* Any excessively pampered or protected person; one who is coddled or coddles himself; a sissy. **—v.t. ·dled, ·dling** To pamper; coddle. [< *Molly*, dim. of MARY, + CODDLE] **—mol'ly·cod'dler** *n.*

mo·loch (mō'lok) *n.* A spiny Australian lizard (genus *Moloch*), resembling the horned toad. [< NL *Moloch*, genus name < MOLOCH]

Molotov cocktail See FRANGIBLE GRENADE under GRENADE.

molt (mōlt) *v.t. & v.i.* To cast off or shed (feathers, horns, skin, etc.) in preparation for replacement by new growth. **—n.** The molting process or season. Also spelled **moult**. [ME *mouten*, OE *bimūtian* exchange for < L *mutare* change] **—molt'er** *n.*

mol·ten (mōl'tən) Archaic past participle of MELT. **—adj. 1** Reduced to fluid by heat; melted. **2** Made by molding; cast.

mol·to (mōl'tō) *adv. Music* Much; very: *molto adagio*. [< Ital. < L *multum* much]

lay **Ma·lu·ku** (mä·lōō'kōō). Also **Mo·luc'cas**.

mo·ly (mō'lē) *n. pl.* **·lies 1** A mythical plant of magic virtues, with a white flower and a black root: mentioned in the *Odyssey*. **2** A European wild garlic. **3** Molybdenum. [< L < Gk. *mōly*]

mo·lyb·date (mə·lib'dāt) *n. Chem.* A salt of molybdic acid.

mo·lyb·de·nite (mə·lib'də·nīt) *n.* A scaly, metallic, lead-gray, soft molybdenum disulfide, MoS₂: an important ore of molybdenum.

mo·lyb·de·num (mə·lib'də·nəm, mol'ib·dē'nəm) *n.* A silvery-white, very hard metallic element (symbol Mo, atomic number 42) widely distributed in various minerals, used in alloys and essential in trace amounts to plant nutrition. See PERIODIC TABLE. [< NL < L *molybdaena* lead, galena < Gk. *molybdaina* < *molybdos* lead]

mo·lyb·dic (mə·lib'dik) *adj. Chem.* Of, pertaining to, or containing molybdenum. especially in its higher valence.

mo·lyb·dous (mə·lib'dəs) *adj. Chem.* Of or pertaining to molybdenum, especially in its lower valence.

mom (mom) *n. U.S. Colloq.* Mother. [< MAMA]

mo·ment (mō'mənt) *n.* **1** A very short period of time; an instant; also, a point of time; definite period. **2** The present time. **3** Consequence or importance, as in influencing judgment or action. **4** *Stat.* The arithmetic mean of the deviations in a frequency distribution, each deviation being raised to the same power. **5** *Physics* **a** The product of a quantity and its distance to some significant related point: *moment of area, moment of* mass, etc. **b** The measure of a force with reference to its effect in producing rotation: also called *torque*. **6** The thing originating or causing; principle of movement or development; a moving force. See synonyms under WEIGHT. [< F < L *momentum* movement. Doublet of MOMENTUM.]

mo·men·tar·i·ly (mō'mən·ter'ə·lē, mō'mən·ter'-ə·lē) *adv.* **1** For a moment. **2** From moment to moment. **3** At any moment. Also **mo'ment·ly.**

mo·men·tar·y (mō'mən·ter'ē) *adj.* Lasting but a moment. **—mo'men·tar'i·ness** *n.*

mo·men·tous (mō·men'təs) *adj.* Of great importance; weighty. See synonyms under IMPORTANT, SERIOUS. **—mo·men'tous·ly** *adv.* **—mo·men'tous·ness** *n.*

mo·men·tum (mō·men'təm) *n. pl.* **·ta** (-tə) *or* **·tums 1** *Mech.* The impetus of a moving body. **2** *Physics* The quantity of motion in a body as measured by the product of its mass and velocity. **3** An essential or constituent element. **4** *Music* An eighth rest. [< L. Doublet of MOMENT.] **—mo·men'tal** *adj.*

mom·ism (mom'iz·əm) *n.* Dominance of feminine values in a society, attributed to undue prolongation of maternal influence: a derogatory term. [< MOM + -ISM; coined by Philip Wylie, 1902–1971, U.S. author]

Mom·son lung (mom'sən) A respiratory device to aid persons to escape from a sunken submarine: invented by Rear Admiral Charles B. Momson, born 1896, U.S. Navy.

mon- *combining form* Var. of MONO-.

mon·ac·e·tin (mon·as'ə·tin) *n.* A colorless or pale-yellow, hygroscopic liquid, C₅H₁₀O₄, obtained by heating glycerol with glacial acetic acid: it is used as a solvent for basic dyes, and in making certain explosives: also spelled *monoacetin*. [< MON- + *acetin* a liquid ester of acetic acid]

mon·a·chism (mon'ə·kiz'əm) *n.* The monastic manner of life; monasticism. [< L *monachus* monk + -ISM] **—mon'a·chal** (-kəl) *adj.*

mon·ac·id (mon·as'id) See MONOACID.

Mon·a·co (mon'ə·kō, mə·nä'kō; *Fr.* mô·nà·kō') An independent principality on the Mediterranean in SE France; 370 acres. **—Mon'a·can** *adj.*

mon·ad (mon'ad, mō'nad) *n.* **1** An indestructible unit; a simple and indivisible substance. **2** A minute, simple, single-celled organism, especially a flagellate infusorian. **3** In metaphysics, the one inseparable spirit in mankind manifesting itself in each person; also, the one inseparable spirit in nature. **—adj.** Of, pertaining to, or consisting of a monad: also **mo·nad'ic** *or* **·i·cal.** [< LL *monas, monadis* < Gk. *monas* a unit < *monos* alone]

mon·a·del·phous (mon'ə·del'fəs) *adj. Bot.* Having the stamens united by their filaments into a single set or tube, as in plants of the mallow family. Also **mon'a·del'phi·an.** [< MON- + Gk. *adelphos* brother]

mon·ad·ism (mon'ad·iz'əm, mō'nad-) *n.* A theory of monads in philosophy or physics. **—mon'ad·is'tic** *adj.*

mo·nad·nock (mə·nad'nok) *n. Geog.* An isolated hill or mass of rock rising above a peneplain. [from Mt. *Monadnock*]

Mo·na Li·sa (mō'nə lē'zə) A portrait by Leonardo da Vinci of a Neapolitan woman: also called *La Gioconda*.

mo·nan·drous (mə·nan'drəs) *adj.* **1** Having one male or husband at a time. **2** *Bot.* Having one stamen to the flower. [< Gk. *monandros* < *monos*- single + *anēr, andros* male, man]

mo·nan·dry (mə·nan'·drē) *n.* **1** The custom or practice of having only one husband at a time. **2** *Bot.* The condition of possessing only one perfect stamen, as in certain orchids. [< Gk. *monandria*. See MONANDROUS.]

mo·nan·thous (mə·nan'thəs) *adj. Bot.* Having but one flower: said of a peduncle or a whole plant. [< MON- + Gk. *anthos* flower]

mon·arch (mon'ərk) *n.* **1** A sovereign, as a king or emperor; in modern times, usually, a hereditary constitutional sovereign; originally, the sole ruler of a nation. **2** One who or that which surpasses others of the same kind. **3** A large, orange-brown butterfly (*Danaus menippe*) whose larva feeds on milkweed: also called *milkweed butterfly*. See synonyms under MASTER. [< LL *monarcha* < Gk. *monarchēs* < *monarchos* ruling alone < *monos* alone + *archein* rule] **—mo·nar·chal** (mə·när'kəl) *adj.* **—mo·nar'chal·ly** *adv.*

mo·nar·chi·an·ism (mə·när'kē·ən·iz'əm) *n.* A heretical doctrine of the second and third centuries which denied any real distinction between the persons of the Trinity. [< LL *monarchianus* < *monarchia* sovereignty of a single person < *monarcha* MONARCH] **—mo·nar'chi·an·is'tic** *adj.*

mo·nar·chi·cal (mə·när'ki·kəl) *adj.* Pertaining to, governed by, or favoring a monarch or monarchy. Also **mo·nar'chi·al, mo·nar'chic. —mo·nar'chi·cal·ly** *adv.*

mon·arch·ism (mon'ərk·iz'əm) *n.* Monarchical preferences or principles. **—mon'arch·ist** *n.* **—mon'arch·is'tic** *adj.*

mon·ar·chy (mon'ər·kē) *n. pl.* **·chies 1** Government by a monarch; sovereign control. **2** A government or territory ruled by a monarch. **— absolute monarchy** A government in which the will of the monarch is positive law; a despotism. **—constitutional** *or* **limited monarchy** A monarchy in which the power and prerogative of the sovereign are limited by constitutional provisions. [< LL *monarchia* < Gk.]

Mo·nar·da (mə·när'də) *n.* A genus of aromatic American herbs of the mint family, with toothed leaves and large flowers in showy clusters; including the horsemint and Oswego tea. [< NL, after N. *Monardes*, 1493–1588, Spanish botanist]

mon·as (mon'əs, mō'nəs) *n.* A monad. [< Gk.]

mon·as·ter·y (mon'əs·ter'ē) *n. pl.* **·ter·ies** A dwelling place occupied in common by persons, especially monks, under religious vows of seclusion; also, the community of persons living in such a place. See synonyms under CLOISTER. [< LL *monasterium* < Gk. *monastērion* < *monastēs* a monk < *monazein* be alone < *monos* alone. Doublet of MINSTER.]

mo·nas·tic (mə·nas'tik) *adj.* **1** Pertaining to religious seclusion. **2** Characteristic of monasteries or their inhabitants; monkish. Also **mon·as·te·ri·al** (mon'əs·tir'ē·əl), **mo·nas'ti·cal. —n.** A monk or other religious recluse. [< F *monastique* < Med. L *monasticus* < Gk. *monastikos*] **—mo·nas'ti·cal·ly** *adv.*

mo·nas·ti·cism (mə·nas'tə·siz'əm) *n.* The monastic life; asceticism.

mon·a·tom·ic (mon'ə·tom'ik) *adj. Chem.* **1** Consisting of a single atom, as the molecules of certain elements. **2** Containing one replaceable or reactive atom. **3** Monovalent.

mon·au·ral (män·ôr'əl, mōn'-) *adj.* **1** Pertaining to, designed for, or characterized by the perception of sound by one ear only. **2** Designating the transmission or reproduction of sound through a single channel.

mon·ax·i·al (mon·ak'sē·əl) *adj.* Having but one axis; uniaxial.

mon·a·zite (mon'ə·zīt) *n.* A resinous, brownish-red or brown phosphate of the rare-earth metals, chiefly cerium, lanthanum, and didymium: an important source of thorium. [< G *monazit* < Gk. *monazein* be alone < *monos* alone]

Mon·day (mun'dē, -dā) *n.* The second day of the week. [OE *mōn(an)dæg* day of the moon; trans. of L *lunae dies*]

mo·ne·cious (mə·nē'shəs, mō-) See MONOECIOUS.

mo·ner·on (mə·nir'on) *n. pl.* **·a** An organism that lacks a cellular nucleus, including bacteria and blue-green algae. [< NL < GK. *monos* alone]

Mo·net (mō·ne'), **Claude**, 1840–1926, French painter.

mon·e·tar·ism (mon'ə·tə·riz'əm, mun'-) *n.* The theory that the economy of a country is determined chiefly by the amount of money available. **—mon'e·tar·ist** *adj., n.*

mon·e·tar·y (mon'ə·ter'ē, mun'-) *adj.* Pertaining to money, finance, or currency; consisting of money; pecuniary. See synonyms under FINANCIAL. [< L *monetarius* of a mint < *moneta* mint. See MINT.] **—mon'e·tar·i·ly** *adv.*

mon·e·tize (mon'ə·tīz, mun'-) *v.t.* **·tized, ·tiz·ing 1** To legalize as money. **2** To give a standard value to (a metal) as currency. **3** To coin into money. Also *Brit.* **mon'e·tise.** [< L *moneta* mint, money] —**mon′e·ti·za′tion** n.

mon·ey (mun′ē) n. pl. **mon·eys** or **mon·ies 1** Anything that serves as a common medium of exchange in trade, as coin or notes. ◆Collateral adjective: *pecuniary*. **2** Legal tender for debts. **3** Purchasing power; credit; bank deposits, etc.; a denomination of value or unit of account. **4** Wealth; property. **5** pl. Cash payments or receipts. **6** A system of coinage. —**call money** Money loaned on security, or deposited in a bank, subject to repayment on demand of the lender. —**hard money** Metallic currency or specie. [< OF *moneie* < L *moneta*. Doublet of MINT.]

Synonyms : bills, bullion, capital, cash, coin, currency, funds, gold, notes, property, silver, specie. Money is the authorized medium of exchange; coined *money* is called *coin* or *specie*. What are termed in England *banknotes* are in the United States commonly called *bills* : a five-dollar *bill. Cash* is *specie* or *money* in hand, or paid in hand: the *cash* account; the *cash* price. In the legal sense, *property* is not *money*, and *money* is not *property;* for *property* is that which has inherent value, while *money*, as such, has but representative value, and may or may not have intrinsic value. *Bullion* is either *gold* or *silver* uncoined or the coined metal considered without reference to its coinage, but simply as merchandise, when its value as *bullion* may be very different from its value as *money*. The word *capital* is used chiefly of accumulated *property* or *money* invested in productive enterprises or available for such investment. Compare PROPERTY, WEALTH.

mon·ey-chang·er (mun′ē-chān′jər) n. A person who changes money at a prescribed rate. Also **mon′ey-deal′er** (-dē′lər), **mon′ey-job′ ber** (-job′ ər).

mon·eyed (mun′ēd) adj. **1** Possessed of money; wealthy. **2** In the form of money. Also spelled *monied*.

mon·ey-lend·er (mun′ē-len′dər) n. A person whose business is the lending of money at interest.

mon·ey-mak·ing (mun′ē-mā′king) adj. **1** Bent upon and successful in accumulating wealth. **2** Likely to bring in money; profitable. —n. The acquisition or procurement of money or wealth. —**mon′ey-mak′er** n.

money market The market in which money is the commodity bought and sold; the sphere of financial operations.

money of account A monetary denomination used in keeping accounts, but not represented by a coin, as the mill of the United States.

money order An order for the payment of a specified sum of money; specifically, such an order issued at one post office or telegraph office and payable at another.

mon·ey-wort (mun′ē-wûrt′) n. A trailing herb (*Lysimachia nummularia*) of the primrose family with solitary yellow flowers and rounded leaves. [< MONEY + WORT; trans. of NL *Nummularia* < *nummus* a coin]

Mon·gol (mong′gəl, -gol, -gōl) adj. Of or pertaining to Mongolia or its inhabitants. —n. **1** A member of any of the native tribes of Mongolia; specifically, a Mongol (eastern Mongolia), a Buriat (Siberia), or an Eleut or Kalmuck (western Mongolia). **2** The Mongolian language of any of these peoples. **3** Any member of the Mongoloid race. [< Mongolian *mong* brave]

Mon·go·lia (mong·gō′lē·ə, mon-) A region of east central Asia south of Asiatic Russian S.F.S.R., east and north of China's Sinkiang-Uigur Autonomous Region, west of most of former Manchuria and the rest of NE China, and north of central China; about 1,000,000 square miles; divided into: (1) the **Mongolian People's Republic** (formerly *Outer Mongolia*), an independent country in the northern and western part; 590,966 square miles; capital, Ulan Bator; (2) *Inner Mongolia*, a region of northern China, including the former provinces of Ningsia, Suiyuan, Chahar, and Jehol and western (former) Manchuria, most of which region now comprises: (3) the *Inner Mongolian Autonomous Region*, an autonomous division of central northern China, including parts of western (former) Manchuria, and former Chahar and Jehol provinces and all of former Suiyuan province; over 400,000 square miles; capital, Huhehot (formerly *Kweisui*).

Mon·gol·ic (mong·gol′ik, mon-) adj. Of or pecu-

liar to the Mongols; Mongolian. —n. Any of the Mongolian languages.

Mon·go·loid (mong′gə·loid) adj. **1** Anthropol. Of or pertaining to the racial group native to Asia and North America, including Malaysians, Eskimos, and some Native Americans. Characteristics include broad noses, high cheek bones, and dark eyes with marked epicanthic folds. **2** Resembling a Mongol or a Mongolian.

mon·goose (mong′gōōs, mung′-) n. pl. ·**goos·es** A small, ferretlike mammal (family *Viverridae*) which fearlessly attacks and kills venomous snakes; especially, the **Indian mongoose** (*Herpestes nyula*): often written *mungoose*. [< Marathi *mungūs*]

MONGOOSE

mon·grel (mung′grəl, mong′-) n. **1** The progeny of crossed breeding; sometimes restricted to the progeny of artificial varieties: distinguished from a *hybrid;* specifically, a dog of mixed breed. **2** Any incongruous mixture. —adj. Of mixed breed or origin; specifically, of a word or language made up of other words or languages: often a term of contempt. [? obs. *mong* mixture < OE *gemang* +-rel, dim. suffix]

mon·ied (mun′ēd) See MONEYED.

mon·i·li·a·sis (mon′ə·lī′ə·sis) n. Pathol. A disease caused by infection with any of various gas-forming fungi (family *Moniliaceae*). Also **mon′ i·li′o·sis.** [< NL < L *monile* necklace +-IASIS; from the alternating swellings and constrictions caused by it]

mo·nil·i·form (mō·nil′ə·fôrm) adj. Biol. Resembling a string of beads; contracted or jointed at regular intervals so as to resemble a necklace. [< L *monile* necklace +-FORM]

mon·ism (mon′iz·əm, mō′niz·əm) n. **1** The doctrine of cosmology that attempts to explain the phenomena of the cosmos by one principle of being or ultimate substance: opposed to philosophical *dualism* and *pluralism*. **2** Any theory that refers many different facts to a single principle. **3** See MONOGENESIS (Def. 1). [< NL *monismus* < Gk. *monos* single]—**mon′ist** n. —**mo·nis′tic** or -**ti·cal** adj. —**mo·nis′ti·cal·ly** adv.

mo·ni·tion (mō·nish′ən) n. **1** Friendly counsel given by way of warning and implying caution or reproof; admonition. **2** Indication; notice. **3** *Law* A summons or citation in civil law and admiralty practice. [< F < L *monitio, -onis* < *monitus*, pp. of *monere* warn]—**mon·i·tive** (mon′ə·tiv) adj.

mon·i·tor (mon′ə·tər) n. **1** One who advises or cautions. **2** A senior pupil placed in charge of a dormitory or class. **3** Something that warns or advises; a reminder. **4** Nav. An ironclad vessel having a low, flat deck and low freeboard, and fitted with a blister and with one or more turrets carrying heavy guns; specifically, the first vessel of the type, **"The Monitor."** See MERRIMAC. **5** *Zool.* Any of several large carnivorous lizards (family *Varanidae*) of the Old World tropics; especially, the East Indian kabara-goya (*Varanus salvator*), which reaches a length of seven feet. **6** *Mining* A contrivance, consisting of nozzle and holder, whereby the direction of a stream can be readily changed. **7** *Telecom.* **a** A high-fidelity loudspeaker in the control-room of a radio studio, used to insure adequate sound transmission. **b** A receiver for listening to a station's broadcasts to check on quality and frequency of transmission, compliance with laws, material transmited, etc. —v.t. **1** *Telecom*. To listen to (a station, broadcast, etc.) with or as with a monitor. **2** To have charge of (a person or group) as a monitor. **3** To keep watch over or check as a means of control: to *monitor* tax returns. [< L < *monitus.* See MONITION.]

mon·i·to·ri·al (mon′ə·tôr′ē·əl, -tō′rē-) adj. **1** Pertaining to a monitor or to instruction by monitors. **2** Monitory.

mon·i·to·ry (mon′ə·tôr′ē, -tō′rē) adj. Conveying monition; admonitory: a *monitory* look. —n. An ecclesiastical monition. [< L *monitorius.* See MONITION]

monitory letter A papal letter of monition.

monk (mungk) n. **1** Formerly, a religious hermit. **2** One of a company of men vowed to separation from the world and to poverty, celibacy, and religious duties; a member of a monastic order. **3** *Printing* An area on a printed page or sheet containing too much ink: opposed to *friar*. [OE *munuc* < LL *monachus* < Gk. *monachos* < *monos* alone]—**monk′ish** adj. —**monk′ish·ly** adv.

monk·er·y (mungk′ər·ē) n. pl. ·**er·ies 1** Monastic life, ways, or beliefs: generally used opprobriously. **2** A monastery or its inmates.

mon·key (mung′kē) n. **1** Any of a group of primates (suborder *Anthropoidea*) having elongate limbs, hands and feet adapted for grasping, and a highly developed nervous system, including marmosets, baboons, and macaques, but not the anthropoid apes. **2** Any primate below man, especially the smaller arboreal forms, as lemurs and tarsiers. **3** A person regarded as a monkey, as a mischievous child. **4** One of various small articles or contrivances; especially, an iron block or ram with a catch, used in pile-driving by hoisting and dropping. —v.t. To play or trifle; fool; meddle: often with *with* or *around with*. [? < MLG *Moneke*, name of the son of Martin the Ape in *Reynard the Fox*. Cf. MF *monne*, Sp. *mona* a female ape.]

monkey business *Slang* Foolish tricks; deceitful or mischievous behavior; folly.

monkey cup An East Indian pitcherplant; any species of the genus *Nepenthes*.

monkey flower Any one of various figworts of the genus *Mimulus*, especially the cultivated species, *M. luteus* with yellow flowers, and *M. cardinalis* with red: so called from the gaping and grimacing appearance of the corolla.

monkey gaff *Naut.* A gaff attached to the mizzentopmast of a vessel for the display of signals.

monkey jacket 1 A short jacket of coarse material, worn especially by sailors. **2** *Slang* A dinner jacket.

monkey pot 1 The hard, woody, pot- or urn-shaped fruit of several tropical American trees of the family *Lecythidaceae*, especially *Lecythis ollaria* and *L. zabucajo;* also, the plant, the fruit of which has a circular lid which, when the nut-like seeds are ripe, separates with a cracking sound. **2** A barrel-shaped melting pot used in making flint glass.

monkey puzzle A large Chilean tree (*Araucaria araucana*) yielding a hard, durable, yellowish-white wood and edible seeds.

mon·key-shines (mung′kē-shīnz′) n. pl. U.S. Slang Frolicsome tricks like a monkey's; pranks. [< MONKEY + SHINE, n. (def. 4)]

monkey wrench A wrench having an adjustable jaw for grasping a nut, bolt, or the like.

monk·fish (mungk′fish′) n. pl. ·**fish** or ·**fish·es 1** The angelfish. **2** The angler. [So called from a hoodlike protuberance suggesting a monk's cowl]

monk·hood (mungk′hŏŏd) n. **1** The character or condition of a monk. **2** Monks collectively. [OE *munukhade*]

monks·hood (mungks′hŏŏd′) n. **1** A plant of the genus *Aconitum*, especially the poisonous *A. napellus*, having the upper sepal arched at the back like a hood. **2** Aconite.

Mon·mouth (mon′məth) **1** A county in western England on the border of Wales; 546 square miles; county town, Monmouth. Also **Mon′mouth·shire** (-shir). **2** A county in east central New Jersey; site of the Revolutionary War battle of **Monmouth Courthouse,** June 28, 1778.

mon·o (mon′ō) adj. Monophonic (def. 1). —n. Mononucleosis.

MONKS-HOOD

mono- *combining form* **1** Single; one. **2** *Chem.* Denoting the presence in a compound of a single atom, or an equivalent of the element or radical to the name of which it is prefixed: *monobasic*. Also, before vowels, **mon-**. [< Gk. < *monos* single, alone]

mon·o·ac·e·tin (mon'ō·as'ə·tin) See MONACETIN.

mon·o·ac·id (mon'ō·as'id) *adj. Chem.* Possessing one hydroxyl group that can replace the hydrogen of an acid: said of bases: also spelled *monacid*. Also **mon·o·a·cid·ic** (-ə·sid'ik).

mon·o·ba·sic (mon'ə·bā'sik) *adj. Chem.* Possessing but a single hydrogen atom replaceable by a metal or positive radical: applied to acids.

mon·o·chlo·ride (mon'ə·klôr'īd, -klō'rīd) *n. Chem.* A chloride which contains one chlorine atom in each molecule.

mon·o·chord (mon'ə·kôrd) *n.* **1** A single chord or string on which intervals can be marked in mathematical ratios, the vibrations giving the notes in the musical scale. **2** An acoustical instrument with one string and a movable bridge, used for measuring intervals. [< Med. L *monochordus* < Gk. *mono-* single *chordē* string]

mon·o·chro·mat·ic (mon'ə·krō·mat'ik) *adj.* Of one color. Also **mon·o·chro·ic**. [< Gk. *monochrō matikos*] —**mon·o·chro·mat·i·cal·ly** *adv.*

mon·o·chrome (mon'ə·krōm) *n.* A painting or the art of painting in a single color, or different shades of a single color. —*adj.* Monochromatic. [< Gk. *monochrōmos*] —**mon·o·chro·mic, mon·o·chro·mi·cal** *adj.*

mon·o·cle (mon'ə·kəl) *n.* An eyeglass for one eye. [< F < LL *monoculus* one-eyed < Gk. *monos* single + L *oculus* eye] —**mon·o·cled** *adj.*

mon·o·cli·nal (mon'ə·klī'nəl) *adj. Geol.* Having an inclination in only one direction, or composed of rock strata so inclined. —*n.* A monocline. —**mon·o·cli·nal·ly** *adv.*

mon·o·cline (mon'ə·klīn) *n. Geol.* A stratum or fold of rocks inclined in only one direction. [< MONO- + Gk. *klinein* incline]

mon·o·clin·ic (mon'ə·klin'ik) *adj.* Pertaining to or designating a crystal system having two oblique axes and a third perpendicular to both.

mon·o·cli·nous (mon'ə·klī'nəs) *adj. Bot.* Containing both androecium and gynoecium in the same flower; bisexual; hermaphrodite.

mon·o·clo·nal antibody (mon'ō·clō'nəl) An antibody produced by cloning a specific hybridoma.

mon·o·cot·y·le·don (mon'ə·kot'ə·lēd'n) *n.* Any of a great subclass (*Monocotyledones*) of seed plants (*Angiospermae*) bearing one cotyledon in the embryo, including palms, orchids, lilies, and grasses. Compare DICOTYLEDON. Also **mon'·o·cot.** —**mon·o·cot·y·le·do·nous** *adj.*

mon·o·crat (mon'ə·krat) *n.* A person in favor of rule by a monarch: term used by Thomas Jefferson about 1790 to mean a Federalist sympathizer with England in the war between England and France. —**mon·o·crat·ic** *adj.* —**mo·noc·ra·cy** (mo·nok'rə·sē) *n.*

mo·noc·u·lar (mə·nok'yə·lər) *adj.* **1** One-eyed. **2** Of or pertaining to one eye. Also **mo·noc·u·lous**. [See MONOCLE]

mon·o·cul·ture (mon'ə·kul'chər) *n. Agric.* The use of a given tract of land for the intensive cultivation of only one crop or product, as cotton, wool, tobacco, etc.

mon·o·cy·cle (mon'·ə·sī'kəl) *n.* A one-wheeled vehicle.

mon·o·cyte (mon'ə·sīt) *n. Physiol.* A large, white blood corpuscle with a horseshoe-shaped nucleus surrounded by clear cytoplasm.

mon·o·dac·ty·lous (mon'ə · dak'tə · ləs) *adj. Zool.* Having only one toe, finger, or claw. Also **mon'·o·dac'tyl.** [< Gk. *mono daktylos* < *monos* single + *daktylos* finger]

MONOCYCLE

mon·o·dra·ma (mon'ə·drä'mə, -dram'ə) *n.* A drama written for or acted by a single performer.

mon·o·dy (mon'ə·dē) *n. pl.* **-dies** **1** Any melancholy literary composition with a single emotional motive; especially, a poem on the death of a friend. Compare THRENODY. **2** In Greek tragedy, the lyric solo, usually of a somber character; hence, a dirge. **3** *Music* **a** A composition in which one vocal part predominates, or the style of such a composition; homophony: opposed to *polyphony*. **b** A song for a single voice, with instrumental accompaniment. **4** A monotonous sound; unvarying tone: the *monody* of waves. [< LL *monodia* < Gk. *monōidia* < *monōidos* singing alone < *monos* alone + *aedein* sing] —**mo·nod·ic** (mə·nod'ik), **mo·nod·i·cal** *adj.* —**mo·nod·i·cal·ly** *adv.* —**mon·o·dist** *n.*

mo·noe·cious (mə·nē'shəs) *adj. Bot.* Having male and female organs in the same individual, as stamens and pistils in separate blossoms on the same plant. Also spelled *monecious, monoicous*. Also **mo·ne·cian**. [< MON- + Gk. *oikos* house]

mo·nog·a·mist (mə·nog'ə·mist) *n.* **1** One who has only one living spouse: opposed to *bigamist* and *polygamist*. **2** One who does not practice or believe in second marriage after the death of the first spouse: opposed to *digamist*. —**mo·nog·a·mis·tic** *adj.*

mo·nog·a·mous (mə·nog'ə·məs) *adj.* **1** Pertaining to monogamy: *monogamous* practices. **2** Having only one spouse; holding to monogamy. **3** Having or paired with but one mate, as certain birds. **4** *Biol.* Having flowers with the anthers united. [< LL *monogamus*] —**mo·nog·a·mous·ly** *adv.*

mo·nog·a·my (mə·nog'ə·mē) *n.* **1** The principle or practice of single marriage: opposed to *bigamy* and *polygamy*, and to *digamy*. **2** The habit of pairing with or having but one mate. [< F *monogamie* < LL *monogamia* < Gk. < *monos* single + *gamos* marriage]

mon·o·gen·e·sis (mon'ə·jen'ə·sis) *n. Biol.* **1** Oneness of origin; the doctrine of the descent of all living organisms from a single cell. Compare POLYGENESIS. **2** Asexual reproduction. **3** Direct development of an ovum into an organism which resembles the parent. **4** Monogenism. [< NL]

mon·o·ge·net·ic (mon'ə·jə·net'ik) *adj.* **1** Pertaining to or exhibiting monogenesis or monogenism. **2** Asexual. **3** *Geol.* Resulting from one genetic process, as a group of mountains. **4** Giving only one color to textile fabrics: said of dyestuffs.

mon·o·gen·ic (mon'ə·jen'ik) *adj.* **1** *Biol.* Having but one method of reproduction, specifically asexual reproduction. **2** *Geol.* Having parts all of the same nature: said of certain rocks.

mo·nog·e·nism (mə·noj'ə·niz'əm) *n.* The doctrine that the whole human race is of one blood or species. [< MONO- + -GEN + -ISM] —**mo·nog·e·nist** *n.*

mo·nog·e·nous (mə·noj'ə·nəs) *adj.* Asexual. [< MONO- + -GENOUS]

mon·o·gram (mon'ə·gram) *n.* **1** A character consisting of two or more letters interwoven into one, as the initials of several names. **2** A single character in writing, or a mark representing a word. [< LL *monogramma* < Gk. *monos* single + *gramma* letter] —**mon·o·gram·mat·ic** (-grə·mat'ik) *adj.*

mon·o·graph (mon'ə·graf, -gräf) *n.* A description or systematic exposition of one thing or class of things; a dissertation or treatise written in great detail. —**mo·nog·ra·pher** (mə·nog'rə·fər) *n.* — **mon·o·graph·ic** *adj.* —**mo·nog·ra·phy** *n.*

mo·nog·y·ny (mə·noj'ə·nē) *n.* The custom or practice of having only one wife at a time. Compare MONANDRY. ◆Homophone: *monogeny*. [< MONO- + Gk. *gynē* woman] —**mo·nog·y·nist** *n.* —**mo·nog·y·nous** *adj.*

mo·noi·cous (mə·noi'kəs) See MONOECIOUS.

mo·nol·a·try (mə·nol'ə·trē) *n.* Worship of some one of several gods: distinguished from *monotheism*. [< MONO- + -LATRY] —**mo·nol·a·ter, mo·nol·a·trist** *n.* —**mo·nol·a·trous** *adj.*

mo·no·lay·er (mon'ō·lā'ər) *n.* A molecular film.

mon·o·lith (mon'ə·lith) *n.* **1** A single piece or block of stone fashioned or placed by art, particularly one notable for its size. **2** Something like a monolith, as in size, structure, aspect, or quality.

mon·o·lith·ic (mon'ə·lith'ik) *adj.* **1** Of or resembling a monolith. **2** Single in character, as a political movement or ideology; marked by uniformity.

mon·o·log (mon'ə·lôg, -log) *n.* **1** That which is spoken by one person alone; especially, a dramatic soliloquy, or a story or drama told or performed by one person; also, a lengthy speech by one person, occurring in the course of conversation. **2** A literary composition, or a poem, written as a soliloquy. Also **mon·o·logue**. [< F *monologue* < Gk. *monologos* speaking alone < *monos* alone + *logos* discourse] —**mon·o·log·ic** (-loj'ik) or **-i·cal** *adj.* —**mo·nol·o·gist** (-ə·jist) *n.*

mon·o·ma·ni·a (mon'ə·mā'nē·ə, -mān'yə) *n.* **1** A mental disorder characterized by obsession with one idea. **2** The unreasonable pursuit of one idea; a craze. [< NL] —**mon·o·ma·ni·ac** *n.* —**mon·o·ma·ni·a·cal** (-mə·nī'ə·kəl) *adj.*

mon·o·mer·ic (mon'ə·mer'ik) *adj.* **1** Having or consisting of a single piece. **2** *Zool.* Derived from one segment or part. [< MONOMER]

mo·nom·er·ous (mə·nom'ər·əs) *adj. Bot.* Having a single member in each whorl or circular series: said of a flower. Sometimes written *1-merous*. [< MONO- + -MEROUS]

mon·o·met·al·ism (mon'ō·met'əl·iz'əm) *n.* The theory or system of a single metallic standard in coinage. Also **mon·o·met·al·lism**. —**mon·o·met·al·ist** *n.*

mon·o·me·tal·lic (mon'ō·mə·tal'ik) *adj.* **1** Consisting of a single metal: a *monometallic* currency. **2** Of or pertaining to monometalism.

mo·nom·e·ter (mə·nom'ə·tər) *n.* **1** A line of verse having one metrical foot. **2** Verse consisting of monometers. [< MONO- + METER²]

mo·no·mi·al (mō·nō'mē·əl) *adj.* Consisting of a single term: a *monomial* expression. —*n. Math.* An expression consisting of a single term. [< MONO- + -nomial, as in *binomial*; an irregular formation]

mon·o·mo·lec·u·lar (mon'ō·mə·lek'yə·lər) *adj. Chem.* Having a thickness of one molecule.

mon·o·mor·phic (mon'ə·môr'fik) *adj.* **1** *Biol.* Of the same or an essentially similar type of structure; also, having the same form throughout successive stages of development. **2** *Bot.* Forming similar spores: said of fungi. Also **mon·o·mor·phous**.

mon·o·nu·cle·o·sis (mon'ō·nōō'klē·ō'sis,-nyōō'-) *n. Pathol.* See INFECTIOUS MONONUCLEOSIS. [< NL < MONO- + NUCLE(US) + -OSIS]

mon·o·pet·al·ous (mon'ə·pet'əl·əs) *adj. Bot.* **1** Gamopetalous. **2** Having corollas actually consisting of a single laterally placed petal: applicable to a few flowers.

mo·noph·a·gous (mə·nof'ə·gəs) *adj.* Monotrophic. [< MONO- + -PHAGOUS]

mon·o·pho·bi·a (mon'ə·fō'bē·ə) *n. Psychiatry* Morbid fear of solitude.

mon·o·phon·ic (mon'ə·fon'ik) *adj.* **1** Of, pertaining to, or functioning in the reproduction of sound through a single channel. **2** *Music* Of or pertaining to a monody.

mon·o·phy·let·ic (mon'ō·fī·let'ik) *adj.* **1** *Zool.* Of or pertaining to a single phylum. **2** *Biol.* Derived from one parent form.

mon·o·phyl·lous (mon'ə·fil'əs) *adj. Bot.* Having or composed of one leaf.

mon·o·plane (mon'ə·plān) *n. Aeron.* An airplane with only one supporting surface: distinguished from *biplane* and *triplane*.

mon·o·ple·gi·a (mon'ə·plē'jē·ə) *n. Pathol.* Paralysis of one part of the body. [< NL] —**mon·o·ple·gic** *adj.*

mon·o·pode (mon'ə·pōd) *n.* **1** Anything sustained by one foot; particularly, one of a fabulous Ethiopian race with only one leg. **2** A monopodium. —*adj.* One-footed. **mo·nop·o·dous** (mə·nop'ə·dəs). [< LL *monopodius* < Gk. *monos* single + *pous, podos* foot]

mon·o·po·di·um (mon'ə·pō'dē·əm) *n. pl.* **-di·a** (-dē·ə) *Bot.* A stem or axis of growth, as in the pine and other conifers, formed by the continued development of a terminal bud, all branches originating as lateral appendages.

mo·nop·o·lize (mə·nop'ə·līz) *v.t.* **-lized, -liz·ing** **1** To obtain or exercise a monopoly of. **2** To assume exclusive possession or control of: to *monopolize* one's time. Also *Brit.* **mo·nop'o·lise.** — **mo·nop'o·liz'er** *n.*

of a commodity, as allows prices to be raised. **2** A combination or company controlling a monopoly. **3** Exclusive possession or control of anything. **4** That which is the subject of a monopoly. **5** *Law* An exclusive license from the government for buying, selling, making, or using anything, and now granted only in case of patents and copyrights. [< L *monopolium* < Gk. *monopōlion* < *monos* alone + *pōlein* sell] — **mo·nop'o·lism** *n.* —**mo·nop'o·list** *n.* & *adj.* — **mo·nop'o·lis'tic** *adj.*

mon·o·pro·pel·lant (mon'ō·prə·pel'ənt) *n.* A liquid rocket propellant consisting of fuel and oxidizer mixed and ready for ignition in the combustion chamber: applied also to solid fuels.

mo·nop·so·ny (mə·nop'sə·nē) *n. Econ.* A condition of the market in which there is only one buyer for the product of a number of sellers. [< MON- + Gk. *opson* market]

mon·o·rail (mon'ō·rāl) *n.* **1** A single rail serving as a track for cars either suspended from it or balanced upon it by means of gyroscopes. **2** A railway using such a track.

mon·o·some (mon'ə·sōm) *n. Genetics* The unpaired sex or X-chromosome.

mon·o·sper·mous (mon'ə·spûr'məs) *adj. Bot.* One-seeded. Also **mon'o·sper'mal.**

mon·o·stich (mon'ə·stik) *n.* A composition of one verse; especially, an epigram.

mon·o·stome (mon'ə·stōm) *adj. Zool.* Having a single sucker or mouth: also **mo·nos·to·mous** (mə·nos'tə·məs). —*n.* An animal with but a single mouth or sucker.

mo·nos·tro·phe (mə·nos'trə·fē) *n.* A metrical composition containing only one kind of strophe. [< MONO- + STROPHE] —**mon·o·stroph·ic** (mon'ə·strof'ik) *adj.*

mon·o·syl·la·ble (mon'ə·sil'ə·bəl) *n.* A word of one syllable. —**mon'o·syl·lab'ic** (-si·lab'ik) *adj.* —**mon'o·syl·lab'i·cal·ly** *adv.*

mon·o·the·ism (mon'ə·thē·iz'əm) *n.* The doctrine that there is but one God. [< MONO- + Gk. *theos* god] —**mon'o·the'ist** *n.* —**mon'o·the·is'tic** or **·ti·cal** *adj.* —**mon'o·the·is'ti·cal·ly** *adv.*

mon·o·ther·mi·a (mon'ə·thûr'mē·ə) *n. Med.* A condition of uniform temperature, as in the body. [< NL < Gk. *monos* single + *thermē* heat] —**mon'o·ther'mic** *adj.*

mon·o·tint (mon'ə·tint) *n.* A monochrome.

mon·o·tone (mon'ə·tōn) *n.* **1** Sameness of utterance or tone; monotony in the style of composition or speech, or something composed in such style. **2** A single musical tone unvaried in pitch or key; also, a chant in such a tone; an intoning.

mo·not·o·nous (mə·not'ə·nəs) *adj.* **1** Not varied in inflection, cadence, or pitch. **2** Tiresomely uniform. See synonyms under TEDIOUS. [< Gk. *monotonos*] —**mo·not'o·nous·ly** *adv.* —**mo·not'o·nous·ness** *n.*

mo·not·o·ny (mə·not'ə·nē) *n.* **1** The state or quality of being monotonous; irksome uniformity or lack of variety; also, sameness of tone; want of variety in cadence or inflection. **2** *Math.* **a** Continual increase or decrease of a quantity, function, etc. **b** Absence of either increase or decrease. [< Gk. *monotonia* < *monos* single + *tonos* tone] —**mon·o·ton·ic** (mon'ə·ton'ik) *adj.*

mon·o·treme (mon'ə·trēm) *n.* Any member of the lowest order of mammals (*Monotremata*), without true teeth in the adult stage and having a single opening for the genitourinary and digestive organs, as in duckbills and echidnas. [< MONO- + Gk. *trēma* hole] —**mon'o·trem'a·tous** (-trem'ə·təs), **mon'o·tre'mous** *adj.*

mo·not·ri·chous (mə·not'rə·kəs) *adj.* Having only one polar flagellum, as certain bacteria: also **mon·o·trich·ic** (mon'ə·trik'ik). [< MONO- + Gk. *thrix, trichos* hair]

mon·o·troph·ic (mon'ə·trof'ik) *adj.* Subsisting on or requiring only one kind of food; monophagous. [< MONO- + Gk. *trophē* food]

mo·not·ro·py (mə·not'rə·pē) *n.* The property, possessed by certain substances, tissues, or organs, of occurring in only one stable form. [< MONO- + -TROPY] —**mon·o·trop'ic** (mon'ə·trop'ik) *adj.*

mon·o·type (mon'ə·tīp) *n.* **1** *Biol.* The only representative of its kind, as a species of a genus or

the like. **2** *Printing* A print from a metal plate on which a design, painting, etc., has been made.

mon·o·va·lence (mon'ə·vā'ləns) *n. Chem.* Univalence. Also **mon'o·va'len·cy.** —**mon'o·va'lent** *adj.*

mon·ox·ide (mon·ok'sīd, mə·nok'-) *n. Chem.* A compound containing a single atom of oxygen in each molecule.

Mon·roe (mən·rō') , **James,** 1758–1831, president of the United States 1817–25.

Monroe Doctrine The doctrine, essentially formulated by President Monroe in his message to Congress (December 2, 1823), that any attempt by European powers to interfere in the affairs of the American countries or to acquire territory on the American continents would be regarded by the United States as an unfriendly act.

Mon·ro·vi·a (mən·rō'vē·ə) The capital of Liberia, a port on the Atlantic.

mons (monz) *n. pl.* **mon·tes** (mon'tēz) *Anat.* The rounded fatty eminence at the lower part of the abdomen, covered with hair in the adult: the **mons pu·bis** (pyōō'bis) of the male, or the **mons ven·er·is** (ven'ər·is) of the female. [< L, hill, mountain]

mon·soon (mon·sōōn') *n. Meteorol.* **1** A wind that blows more or less steadily along the Asiatic coast of the Pacific, in winter from the northeast (**dry monsoon**), in summer from the southwest (**wet monsoon**). **2** A trade wind. [< MDu. *monssoen* < Pg. *monção* < Arabic *mausim* season]

mon·ster (mon'stər) *n.* **1** A fabulous animal, compounded of various brute forms. **2** A being that is greatly malformed; anything hideous or abnormal in structure and appearance; a teratism. **3** One abhorred because of his unnatural or inhuman character. **4** A very large person, animal, or thing. See synonyms under PRODIGY. —*adj.* Extraordinary or enormous in size or numbers; huge. [< OF *monstre* < L *monstrum* divine omen, monster < *monere* warn]

mon·strance (mon'strəns) *n.* In Roman Catholic ritual, a sacred vessel in which the consecrated Host is exposed for adoration: also called *ostensorium, ostensory.* [< OF < Med. L *monstrantia* < L *monstrare* show]

mon·stros·i·ty (mon·stros'ə·tē) *n. pl.* **·ties 1** Anything unnaturally huge, malformed, or distorted. **2** The character of being monstrous.

mon·strous (mon'strəs) *adj.* **1** Deviating greatly from the natural or normal; unnatural in form or structure. **2** Of extraordinary size or number; excessive; huge: a *monstrous* beast or multitude. **3** Inspiring abhorrence, hate, incredulity, etc., in a remarkable degree; hateful; hideous; incredible; intolerable: a *monstrous* cruelty. See synonyms under ABSURD, EXTRAORDINARY, FLAGRANT. —*adv. Archaic* Extremely. [< OF *monstreux* < L *monstrosus* < *monstrum.* See MONSTER.] —**mon'strous·ly** *adv.* —**mon'strous·ness** *n.*

mon·tage (mon·täzh') *n.* **1** A picture made by superimposing several different pictures so as to blend into one another, or so as to show figures upon a desired background; a composite picture; also, the process of composing such a picture. **2** In motion pictures, a swiftly run sequence of images or pictures illustrating a sequence of associated ideas; the dizzy revolving of several images around a central, focused image or picture to signify the passage of time or the like. **3** The section of a motion picture using this method. [< F]

Mon·tan·a (mon·tan'ə) A State in the NW United States bordering on Canada; 147,138 square miles; capital, Helena; entered the Union Nov. 8, 1889; nickname, *Treasure State*: abbr. MT —**Mon·tan'an** *adj. & n.*

mon·tan·ic (mon·tan'ik) *adj.* Of or pertaining to mountains; mountainous. Also **mon·tane** (mon'tān). [< L *montan(us)* + -IC]

mon·tan wax (mon'tən) A hydrocarbon wax of high melting point extracted from lignite, used as insulation and in making polishes, candles, phonograph records, etc. [< L *montanus* of the mountain]

mon·te (mon'tē) *n.* **1** A Spanish gambling game of cards. **2** A table on which, or a place where, monte is played. **3** The money stacked in front of the dealer to pay off stakes: also **monte bank** [< Sp., lit., mountain; in ref. to the pile of unplayed cards]

mon·teith (mon·tēth') *n.* An ornamental punch bowl. [from *Monteigh,* a surname]

Montessori method A system of teaching small children by training their sense perceptions, and by guiding rather than controlling their activity.

Mon·te·vid·e·o (mon'tə·vi·dā'ō, -vid'ē·ō; *Sp.* mōn'tā·vē·thā'ō) A port on the Rio de la Plata, capital of Uruguay.

Mon·te·zu·ma (mon'tə·zōō'mə), 1479?–1520, last Aztec emperor of Mexico; dethroned by Cortez: also *Moctezuma.*

mont·gol·fi·er (mont·gol·fē'ər) *n.* A hot–air balloon. [after the *Montgolfier* brothers]

Mont·gom·er·y (mont·gum'ər·ē) **1** The capital of Alabama, in the east central part of the State on the Alabama River. **2** A county in central Wales; 797 square miles; county town, Montgomery: also **Mont·gom'er·y·shire** (-shir).

month (munth) *n.* **1** A unit of time, originally equal to the interval between two new moons, afterward called a **lunar month,** and equal on the average to 29.53 days. **2** One of the 12 parts into which the calendar year is divided, called a **calendar month;** loosely, thirty days or four weeks. **3** The twelfth part of a solar year: also **solar month.** ◆ Collateral adjective: *mensal.* [OE *mōnath.* Akin to MOON.]

month·ly (munth'lē) *adj.* **1** Continuing a month, or done in a month. **2** Happening once a month. **3** Pertaining to the menses. —*adv.* Once a month. —*n. pl.* **·lies 1** A periodical published once a month. **2** *pl.* The menses.

monthly meeting In the Society of Friends, a meeting held once a month, by two or more neighboring congregations, for worship and business; also, the organized unit composed of these congregations.

Mont·pel·ier (mont·pēl'yər) The capital of Vermont.

mon·u·ment (mon'yə·mənt) *n.* **1** Something erected to perpetuate the memory of a person or of an event. **2** A notable structure, deed, production, etc., worthy to be considered as a memorial of the past, or of some event or person. **3** A stone or other permanent mark serving to indicate an angle or boundary. **4** A tomb. **5** *Obs.* A statue; effigy. [< F < L *monumentum* < L *monere* remind]

mon·u·men·tal (mon'yə·men'təl) *adj.* **1** Pertaining to or like a monument. **2** Serving as a monument; memorial; impressive; conspicuous; enduring. **3** Spectacular; excessive: a *monumental* fraud. [< L *monumentalis*] —**mon'u·men'tal·ly** *adv.*

mon·u·men·tal·ize (mon'yə·men'təl·īz) *v.t.* **·ized, ·iz·ing** To establish a lasting record or memorial of.

-mony *suffix of nouns* The condition, state, or thing resulting from: *parsimony.* [< L *-monia, -monium*]

mon·zo·nite (mon'zə·nīt) *n.* A coarse–grained, igneous rock containing approximately equal amounts of orthoclase and plagioclase, with inclusions of colored silicates. [from Mount *Monzoni,* in the Tirol] —**mon'zo·nit'ic** (-nit'-ik) *adj.*

moo (mōō) *v.i.* To low as or like a cow. —*n.* The lowing noise made by a cow. [Imit.]

mooch (mōōch) *Slang v.t.* **1** To obtain without paying; beg; cadge: to *mooch* a drink. **2** To steal. —*v.i.* **3** To loiter about; skulk; sneak. Also spelled *mouch.* [Var. of dial. *miche* pilfer < OF *muchier* hide, skulk] —**mooch'er** *n.*

mood[1] (mōōd) *n.* **1** Temporary or capricious state of mind in regard to passion or feeling; humor; disposition. **2** *pl.* Fits of morose or sullen behavior; the state of being moody: to have *moods.* **3** *Obs.* Anger. See synonyms under FANCY, TEMPER. [OE *mōd*]

mood[2] (mōōd) *n.* **1** *Gram.* The manner in which the action or condition expressed by a verb is stated, whether as actual, doubtful, commanded, etc. The English moods proper are the indicative, subjunctive, and imperative. The infinitive is sometimes also classed as a mood. Certain verb–phrases are likewise loosely called moods, as those formed by *may, might, can, could* (potential), *should, would* (conditional), *must, ought* (obligative). Also *mode.* **2** *Logic* Mode. **3** *Music* Mode. [Var. of MODE]

mood·y (mōō′dē) *adj.* **mood·i·er, mood·i·est** **1**
Given to or expressive of capricious moods. **2**
Petulant; sullen; melancholy. See synonyms
under MOROSE. —**mood′i·ly** *adv.* —**mood′i·
ness** *n.*

moo·ley (mōō′lē) *n.* A cow without horns. See
MULEY.

moon (mōōn) *n.* **1** A celestial body revolving
around the earth from west to east in a lunar
month of 29.53 days or a sidereal month of
27.33 days; mean diameter, 2,160 miles; mean
distance from the earth, 238,900 miles. In
mass, the earth is 81.5 times greater than the
moon; in volume, 49 times greater. **2** A satellite revolving about any planet. See under
PLANET. **3** A lunar month. **4** Something resembling a moon or crescent. **5** Moonlight.
—**dark of the moon** That period of time between the full moon and the new moon. —
man in the moon The fancied appearance of a
face in the disk of the full moon, caused by
the shadows, lines, spots, etc., on its surface.
—*v.i. Colloq.* To stare or wander about in an
abstracted or listless manner. —*v.t.* To pass
(time) thus. [OE *mōna.* Akin to MONTH.]

PHASES OF THE MOON
E. Earth. *S.* Sun.
a. New.   *d.* Gibbous.   *g.* 3rd Quarter.
b. Crescent.   *e.* Full.   *h.* Crescent.
c. 1st Quarter.   *f.* Gibbous.

moon·beam (mōōn′bēm′) *n.* A ray of moonlight.

moon·blind (mōōn′blīnd′) *adj.* **1** Purblind; fee-
ble-sighted. **2** Moon-struck. **3** Affected
with moonblindness.

moon·blind·ness (mōōn′blīnd′nis) *n.* **1** A form
of blindness erroneously attributed to moonlight; nyctalopia. **2** A periodic inflammation
of the eyes of a horse.

moon·calf (mōōn′kaf′, -käf′) *n.* **1** A stupid
person; dolt; idiot. **2** A monster; deformity.
[With ref. to the supposed bad influence of
the moon]

moon·craft (mōōn′kraft′, -kräft′) *n.* A spacecraft designed to travel to the moon.

moon·eye (mōōn′ī′) *n.* **1** An eye affected with
moonblindness. **2** Moonblindness.

moon–eyed (mōōn′īd′) *adj.* **1** Having moon-
eyes. **2** Moonblind (def. 3). **3** Having eyes
wide open, as with amazement, awe, etc.

moon·fish (mōōn′fish′) *n. pl.* **·fish** or **·fish·es 1**
Any of various carangoid fishes found on ei-
ther coast of the western hemisphere, having a
silvery or yellowish, much compressed body,
especially *Vomer setipinnis:* also called
horsefish. **2** The opah. **3** The Mexican top
minnow (*Platypoecilus maculatus*).

moon·flow·er (mōōn′flou′ər) *n.* Any of a genus
(*Calonyction*) of perennial climbing herbs of
the morning–glory family; especially, *C.
aculeatum* (formerly genus *Ipomoea*), bearing
fragrant, white flowers which open at night.

moon·glade (mōōn′glād′) *n.* The silvery reflection of moonlight on water.

moon·light (mōōn′līt′) *n.* The light of the
moon. —*adj.* Pertaining to or illuminated by
moonlight. —*v.i. Colloq.* To work at a job in
addition to one's regular job. —**moon′light·
er, moon′light·ing** *n.*

moon·lit (mōōn′lit′) *adj.* Lighted by the moon.

moon·quake (mōōn′kwāk′) *n.* A trembling or
shaking of the moon's surface analogous to an
earthquake. [<MOON + (EARTH)QUAKE]

moon·rise (mōōn′rīz′) *n.* The appearing of the
moon above the horizon, or the time when it
appears.

moon·seed (mōōn′sēd′) *n.* A North American
climbing plant of the genus *Menispermum,* of

the family *Menispermaceae:* so called from its
crescent–shaped seeds.

moon·set (mōōn′set′) *n.* The setting, or the
time of setting, of the moon; specifically, the
moment at which it passes below the horizon.

moon·shine (mōōn′shīn′) *n.* **1** Moonlight. **2**
Something visionary or unreal; pretence; nonsense. **3** *Colloq.* Smuggled or illicitly distilled
spirits. —**moon′shin′y** *adj.*

moon·stone (mōōn′stōn′) *n.* A whitish, cloudy
feldspar, valued as a gemstone.

moon·struck (mōōn′struk′) *adj.* Affected by or
as by the moon; lunatic; deranged. Also
moon′·strick′en (-strik′ən).

moon·wort (mōōn′wûrt′) *n.* **1** The herb honesty. **2** Any fern of the genus *Botrychium,* especially *B. lunaria.* [Trans. of Med. L
lunaria <L *luna* moon]

moon·y (mōō′nē) *adj.* **moon·i·er, moon·i·est 1**
Moon-struck. **2** Moonlit. **3** Like moonlight, or giving out light resembling moonlight. **4** Round or crescent–shaped. **5**
Absent–minded; dreaming; vacant.

moor[1] (mōōr) *v.t.* **1** To secure (a ship, etc.) in
one place by means of cables attached to
shore, anchors, etc. **2** To secure in place; fix.
—*v.i.* **3** To secure a ship in position; anchor.
4 To be secured by chains or cables. [Cf.
OE *mǣrels* mooring rope]

moor[2] (mōōr) *n.* **1** A tract of wasteland
sometimes covered with heath, often elevated
and frequently marshy and abounding in peat.
2 A tract of land on which game is preserved for shooting. [OE *mōr*] —**moor′ish**
adj.

Moor (mōōr) *n.* **1** A person of mixed Berber
and Arab blood, inhabiting Morocco and the
southern Mediterranean coast. **2** Any North
African native; specifically, a Saracen or a
Spanish descendant of the Saracens. **3** A
Mohammedan of India. [<F *more, maure* <
L *Maurus* Moor, Mauritanian <Gk. *Mauros*]
—**Moor′ish** *adj.*

moor·age (mōōr′ij) *n.* A mooring place.

moor·cock (mōōr′kok′) *n.* The male of the red
grouse.

moor·fowl (mōōr′foul′) *n.* The red grouse.

moor·hen (mōōr′hen′) *n.* **1** The female of the
moorfowl. **2** The water hen (*Gallinula
chloropus*). **3** The American coot.

moor·ing (mōōr′ing) *n.* **1** The act of securing
a vessel. **2** *Chiefly pl.* The place where a vessel is moored. **3** *Chiefly pl.* Anything by
which an object is fastened.

moor·land (mōōr′land′) *n.* A moor or marsh.
—*adj.* Having marshy properties. —**moor′·
land·er** *n.*

moor·wort (mōōr′wûrt′) *n.* A low, smooth
shrub (*Andromeda polifolia*) of the heath family, with narrow, thick, evergreen leaves, growing in wet bogs.

moor·y (mōōr′ē) *adj.* **moor·i·er, moor·i·est** Of
the nature of moor-
land; marshy.

moose (mōōs) *n. pl.*
moose 1 A large,
heavily built mam-
mal (*Alces america-
na*) of the deer fami-
ly, found in north-
ern North America:
the male bears huge,
palmate antlers. **2**
The northern Euro-
pean elk. [<Algon-
quian (Massachuset)
moos he strips off;
because it eats the
bark of trees]

MOOSE
(Up to nearly 7 feet
high at the shoulder;
weight to 1,000 pounds)

moose·bird (mōōs′-
bûrd′) *n.* The Cana-
da jay.

moose·call (mōōs′kôl′) *n.* A small horn or
trumpet made of birch bark or other materials, used by hunters to lure moose within
shooting distance. Also **moose horn.**

moose·flow·er (mōōs′flou′ər) *n.* Trillium: also
called *wakerobin.*

moose·grass (mōōs′gras′, -gräs′) *n.* Ground
hemlock.

moot court A court for the trial of a fictitious
suit by law students.

mop[1] (mop) *n.* **1** A piece of cloth, or the like,
attached to a handle: used for washing floors.

2 Any loosely tangled bunch or mass, as of
hair. —*v.t.* **mopped, mop·ping** To rub or
wipe with or as with a mop. —**to mop up 1**
To take up with or as with a mop. **2** *Mil.*
To wipe out remnants of enemy resistance in
(captured areas). —**to mop (up) the floor
with** *Slang* To defeat easily and decisively.
[Origin uncertain. Cf. F. *mappe* napkin <L
mappa.]

mop[2] (mop) *n.* **1** A wry mouth; grimace. **2**
A pouting or petted young person; a young
girl. [<*v.*] —*v.i.* To make a wry face; grimace. [Cf. Du. *moppen* pout]

mope (mōp) *v.* **moped, mop·ing** *v.i.* To be
gloomy, listless, or dispirited. —*v.t.* To make
gloomy or dispirited.—*n.* **1** One who mopes.
2 *pl.* Dejection; depression. [Prob. <Scand.
Cf. Sw. *mopa* sulk, Dan. *maabe* be stupid, unaware.] —**mop′er** *n.* —**mop′ish** *adj.* —**mop′·
ish·ly** *adv.* —**mop′ish·ness** *n.*

mo·ped (mō′ped) *n.* A heavy–duty bicycle
equipped with an engine. [<*mo(tor)* +*ped
(al)*]

mop·pet (mop′it) *n.* **1** A rag doll or one made
of cloth. **2** A child; youngster. [Dim. of
ME *moppe* rag doll, ? <L *mappa* napkin]

mo·quette (mō·ket′) *n.* A woolen fabric with a
velvety pile, used for carpets and upholstery.
[<F; ult. origin uncertain]

mo·ra·ceous (mô·rā′shəs, mō-) *adj.* Denoting
or belonging to a family (*Moraceae*) of mostly
tropical herbs, shrubs, and trees of the order
Urticales, including the mulberry, common fig,
hop, hemp, etc. [<L *morus* mulberry]

mo·raine (mə·rān′, mō-) *n. Geol.* A ridge or
heap of earth, stones, etc., carried by a glacier
and deposited on adjacent ground, either
along the course or at the edges of the glacier,
as a **medial** or **lateral moraine,** or at its lower
terminus, as a **terminal moraine.** [<dial. F]
—**mo·rain′al, mo·rain′ic** *adj.*

mor·al (môr′əl, mor′-) *adj.* **1** Pertaining to
character and behavior from the point of view
of right and wrong, and obligation of duty;
pertaining to rightness and duty in conduct. **2**
Conforming to right conduct; actuated by a
sense of the good, true, and right; good; righteous; virtuous. **3** Concerned with the principles of right and wrong; ethical: *moral*
philosophy; *moral* values. **4** Acting or suited
to act through man's intellect or sense of
right: often opposed to *physical*: *moral* support. **5** *Logic* Probable as opposed to demonstrative: *moral* proof. **6** Of or pertaining to
the science or doctrine of human nature as fitted for conduct. Most writers on modern
philosophy use the term to cover the entire
sphere of human conduct which comes under
the distinctions of right and wrong. **7**
Attempting or serving to inculcate or convey
a moral; moralizing: a *moral* writer. **8** Of or
influencing morals or morale: *moral* force. **9**
Capable of understanding the difference between right and wrong: a *moral* agent. —*n.*
1 The lesson taught by a fable or the like. **2**
pl. Conduct or behavior; ethics. [<F <L
moralis <*mos, moris* custom; in the pl., manners, morals] —**mor′al·ly** *adv.*

Synonyms (*adj.*): dutiful, ethical, excellent,
faithful, good, honest, honorable, incorruptible, just, pious, religious, right, righteous,
true, upright, virtuous, worthy. Antonyms: see
synonyms for IMMORAL.

mo·rale (mə·ral′, -räl′, mō-) *n.* **1** State of
mind with reference to confidence, courage,
hope, etc.: used especially of a number of persons associated in some enterprise, as troops,
workers, etc. **2** *Obs.* Morality. [<F. See
MORAL.]

moral hazard In insurance, a risk resulting
from doubt as to the honesty of the person
insured.

moral insanity Mental deficiency amounting to
the incapacity to distinguish between right
and wrong, or characterized by compulsions
to perform unsocial, irresponsible, or criminal
acts: a legal term variously interpreted in different statutes.

mor·al·ism (môr′əl·iz′əm, mor′-) *n.* The belief
in a morality divested of all religious character.

mor·al·ist (môr′əl·ist, mor′-) *n.* **1** A teacher
of morals. **2** One who practices morality
without religion. —**mor′al·is′tic** *adj.*

mo·ral·i·ty (mə·ral'ə·tē, mô-) n. pl. ·ties 1 The doctrine of man's moral duties; ethics. 2 Virtuous conduct; rectitude; chastity. 3 The quality of being morally right. 4 A lesson inferred; a moral. 5 Conformity, or degree of conformity, to conventional rules, without or apart from inspiration and guidance by religion or other spiritual influences. 6 A form of allegorical drama of the 15th and 16th centuries in which the characters were personified virtues, vices, mental attributes, etc. See synonyms under VIRTUE. [<L moralitas, -tatis <moralis. See MORAL.]

mor·al·ize (môr'əl·īz, mor'-) v. ·ized, ·iz·ing v.i. 1 To make moral reflections; talk about morality. —v.t. 2 To explain in a moral sense; derive a moral from. 3 To improve the morals of. Also Brit. mor'al·ise.—mor'al·i·za'tion n.—mor'al·iz'er n.

moral philosophy Ethics.

moral victory A defeat that is accounted a victory on the moral level, as when the righteousness of a defeated cause has been clearly established.

mo·rass (mə·ras', mô-, mō-) n. A tract of low-lying, soft, wet ground; marsh. [<Du. moeras, earlier marasch <OF maresc <Med. L mariscus <Gmc. Ult. akin to MARSH.]

mor·a·to·ri·um (môr'ə·tôr'ē·əm, -tō'rē-, mor'-) n. pl. ·ri·a (-ē·ə) or ·ri·ums Law An emergency act of legislation or a government edict authorizing a debtor or bank to suspend payments for a given period; also, the period during which it is, or is to be, in force. [<NL <LL moratorius. See MORATORY.]

mor·a·to·ry (môr'ə·tôr'ē, -tō'rē, mor'-) adj. Pertaining or intended to delay: particularly applied to legislation in the nature of a moratorium. [<LL moratorius <L morari delay <mora delay]

mo·ray (môr'ā, mō·rā') n. A brightly colored, voracious, savage eel of the family Muraenidae, inhabiting tropical and subtropical waters, especially among coral reefs: also called murry. The Mediterranean moray (Muraena helena) is esteemed as a food fish. A related species is the banded moray (Gymnothorax waialuoe) of Hawaiian waters. [? <Pg. moreia <L muraena]

mor·bid (môr'bid) adj. 1 Being in a diseased or abnormal state. 2 Caused by or denoting a diseased condition of body or mind. 3 Taking an excessive interest in matters of a gruesome or unwholesome nature; also, apprehensive; suspicious. 4 Grisly; gruesome: a morbid story. 5 Of or pertaining to disease; pathological: morbid anatomy. [<L morbidus <morbus disease]—mor'bid·ly adv.—mor'bid·ness n.

mor·bid·i·ty (môr·bid'ə·tē) n. 1 The condition of being morbid or diseased. 2 The rate of disease or proportion of diseased persons in a community: compare MORTALITY (def. 3).

mor·bif·ic (môr·bif'ik) adj. Producing disease. Also mor·bif'i·cal.—mor·bif'i·cal·ly adv.

mor·bil·li (môr·bil'ī) n. pl. The measles. [<Med. L, pl. of morbillus, dim. of morbus disease]

mor·bil·li·form (môr·bil'ə·fôrm) adj. Resembling measles. [<MORBILLI + -FORM]

mor·da·cious (môr·dā'shəs) adj. Biting, or given to biting; hence, sarcastic. [<L mordax, -acis <mordere bite]—mor·da'cious·ly adv.—mor·dac'i·ty (-das'ə·tē) n.

mor·dan·cy (môr'dən·sē) n. Pungency; the quality of being biting or sarcastic. 2 Acting as a mordant. —v.t. To treat or imbue with a mordant. [<OF]

mor·dant (môr'dənt) n. 1 Any substance, such as tannic acid or aluminum hydroxide, which, by combining with a dyestuff to form an insoluble compound (lake), serves to produce a fixed color in a textile fiber. 2 The corrosive used in etching. —adj. 1 Biting; pungent; sarcastic. 2 Acting as a mordant. —v.t. To treat or imbue with a mordant. [<OF]

mor·dent (môr'dənt) n. Music The rapid alternation of a tone with the tone immediately below it or the character indicating it: a form of trill. Also mor·den·te (môr'den'tā). —inverted mordent The rapid alternation of a note with one above it. [<G <Ital. mordente, ppr. of mordere bite <L]

more (môr, mōr) adj. superlative most 1 Greater in amount, extent, or degree: comparative of much: more water. 2 Greater in

number: comparative of many. 3 Greater in rank or dignity. 4 Added to some former number; extra. —n. 1 A greater quantity, amount, etc. 2 Something that exceeds something else. —adv. 1 To a greater extent or degree. 2 In addition; further; again: usually qualified by any, never, a numeral, etc.: I cannot walk any more. [OE māra]

mo·reen (mə·rēn') n. A sturdy, ribbed, cotton, wool, or wool and cotton fabric, often with a watered or embossed finish, used for hangings and upholstery. [Prob. <MOIRE + -een, as in velveteen]

mo·rel¹ (mə·rel') n. An edible mushroom of the genus Morchella, somewhat resembling a sponge on the end of a stalk. [<MF morille, ult. <Gmc. Cf. OHG morhila little carrot.]

mo·rel² (mə·rel') n. The black nightshade (Solanum nigrum). Also mo·relle'. [<OF morele <Med. L morella, ? <LL maurella, a kind of plant]

mo·rel·lo (mə·rel'ō) n. A variety of cultivated cherry, with a dark–red skin, flesh, and juice: used in cooking and preserving. [<Flemish marelle, aphetic var. of amarelle <Ital. amarello, dim. of amaro bitter <L amarus]

more·o·ver (môr·ō'vər, mōr-) adv. Beyond what has been said; further; besides; likewise.

mo·res (môr'ēz, mō'rēz) n. pl. Sociol. 1 Those established, traditional customs or folkways regarded by a social group as essential to its preservation and welfare. 2 The accepted conventions of a group or community. [<L, pl. of mos, moris custom]

Mo·resque (mô·resk', mə-) adj. Moorish; decorated in the style of the Moors. —n. Decorative work, by means of interlacings, relief, etc., highly colored and gilded. Compare MORISCO (def. 3). [<F <Ital. moresco <L Maurus Mauritanian]

MORESQUE PANEL DECORATION

mor·ga·nat·ic (môr'gə·nat'ik) adj. Designating a legitimate marriage between a male member of certain royal families of Europe and a woman of inferior rank, in which the titles and estates of the husband are not shared by the wife or their children. Also mor'ga·nat'i·cal. [<NL morganaticus <LL (matrimonium ad) morganaticum (wedding with) morning gift <OHG morgengeba morning gift (in lieu of a share in the estate)]—mor'ga·nat'i·cal·ly adv.

Morgan horse A breed of horse of Arabian strain descendent from the stallion Justin Morgan (died 1821): noted for its powerful frame, gentle disposition, and versatility. [after Justin Morgan, owner of the original horse]

mor·gan·ite (môr'gən·īt) n. A rose–pink variety of beryl, used as a semiprecious gemstone. [after John Pierpont Morgan]

morgue (môrg) n. 1 A place where bodies of the dead are kept until identified or claimed. 2 In a newspaper editorial office, the department in charge of filed items and biographical material: used for obituary notices, etc. [<F, orig., the name of the Paris building used for this purpose]

Dying; at the point of death. [<L moribundus <mori die]—mor'i·bun'di·ty n.—mor'i·bund·ly adv.

mo·rin (môr'in, mō'rin) n. A crystalline compound, $C_{15}H_{10}O_7$, obtained from old fustic: used as a yellow dyestuff and as a reagent for aluminum. [<F morine <L morum mulberry]

mo·ri·on¹ (môr'ē·on, mō'rē-) n. A kind of open helmet without vizor worn by men–at–arms: also spelled morrion. [<OF <Sp. morrión <morra crown of the head]

mo·ri·on² (môr'ē·on, mō'rē-) n. A dark, sometimes nearly black, variety of smoky quartz. [<F <LL, a misreading of L mormorion]

Mo·ris·co (mə·ris'kō) adj. Moorish. —n. pl. ·cos or ·coes 1 One of the Moors who remained in Spain after the conquest of Granada in 1492; a Moor. 2 A morris dance or dancer. 3 The Moresque style of architecture or decoration. [<Sp. <Moro Moor]

Mor·mon (môr'mən) n. 1 A member of a religious sect officially styled "The Church of Jesus Christ of Latter–day Saints," founded in

the U.S. by Joseph Smith in 1830: also Mor'mon·ist, Mor'mon·ite. 2 In Mormon belief, a prophet and sacred historian of the fourth century A.D. who wrote, on golden tablets, a history of an early American people. The tablets, called the Book of Mormon, one of the holy books of the Mormon faith, were found by Joseph Smith near Palmyra, New York, and translated and published by him in 1830. —Mor'mon·ism n.

Mormon Church The Church of Jesus Christ of Latter–day Saints.

Mormon State Nickname of UTAH.

Mormon trail The trail taken by the Mormons, 1847, from Iowa to Utah.

morn (môrn) n. Poetic The morning. [OE morgen]

morn·ing (môr'ning) n. 1 The early part of the day; the time from midnight to noon, or from sunrise to noon; hence, any early stage. 2 The dawn: often personified as Morning, the goddess Eos or Aurora. —adj. Pertaining to or occurring in the early part of the day. ◆ Collateral adjective: matutinal. [<MORN; by analogy with EVENING]

morn·ing–glo·ry (môr'ning·glôr'ē, -glō'rē) n. pl. ·ries 1 A twining plant (genus Ipomoea) with funnel–shaped flowers of various colors. 2 Any one of many convolvulaceous plants.

morning gun A gun fired at reveille on military posts as a signal for raising the flag.

morning sickness Vomiting and nausea in the morning, common in early pregnancy.

Mo·roc·co (mə·rok'ō) 1 A kingdom on the Atlantic and Mediterranean coasts of NW Africa; 160,000 square miles; capital, Rabat: French Maroc, Spanish Marruecos. 2 A former name for MARRAKESH. Arabic El Maghreb el Ag·sa (al mä'greb al äg'sä). —Mo·roc'can adj. & n.

morocco leather A fine leather made from goatskin tanned with sumac. Also mo·roc'co.

mo·ron (môr'on, mō'ron) n. A person whose mental capacity has been arrested during development and who represents mentally the condition of a child of from 8 to 12 years of age. [<Gk. mōron, neut. of mōros dull, sluggish] —mo·ron·ic (mô·ron'ik, mō-) adj. —mo·ron'i·cal·ly adv.

mo·ron·ism (môr'on·iz'əm, mō'ron-) n. The mildest degree of feeble–mindedness, rated above imbecility and idiocy. Also mo·ron·i·ty (mô·ron'ə·tē, mō-).

mo·rose (mə·rōs') adj. Having a surly temper; sullen; gloomy. [<L morosus <mos, moris manner, habit] —mo·rose'ly adv. —mo·rose'ness, mo·ros·i·ty (-ros'ə·tē) n.

Synonyms (adj.): acrimonious, bitter, churlish, crabbed, crusty, dogged, gloomy, gruff, ill-humored, ill-natured, moody, severe, sour, splenetic, sulky, sullen, surly. The sullen and sulky are discontented and resentful; sullen denotes more of pride, sulky more of resentful obstinacy. The morose are bitterly dissatisfied with the world in general, and disposed to vent their ill nature upon others. The sullen and sulky are for the most part silent; the morose growl out bitter speeches. A surly person is in a state of latent anger, resenting approach as intrusion, and ready to take offense at anything. See AUSTERE. Compare ACRIMONY. Antonyms: amiable, benignant, bland, complaisant, friendly, genial, gentle, good–natured, indulgent, kind, mild, pleasant, sympathetic, tender.

mor·phal·lax·is (môr'fə·lak'sis) n. Biol. The regeneration of parts of a living organism by the gradual transformation of other parts. [<Gk. morphē form + allaxis exchange]

mor·phic (môr'fik) adj. Morphologic.

–morphic combining form Having the form or shape of: anthropomorphic. [<Gk. morphē form]

mor·phine (môr'fēn) n. Chem. A bitter, white, crystalline, narcotic alkaloid, $C_{17}H_{19}NO_3 \cdot H_2O$, contained in opium and used for alleviating pain. Also mor'phi·a (-fē·ə). [<F <L Morpheus god of sleep]

morpho– combining form Form; shape: morpholysis. Also, before vowels, morph–. [<Gk. morphē form]

mor·pho·gen·e·sis (môr'fō·jen'ə·sis) n. Biol. 1 The evolution of forms of structure. 2 The development of organic forms. Also mor·phog·e·ny (môr·foj'ə·nē). —mor'pho·ge·net'ic (-jə·net'ik) adj.

mor·phol·o·gy (môr·fol′ə·jē) n. 1 That branch of biology which treats of the form and structure of plants and animals. 2 The form of an organism considered apart from function. 3 *Geog.* The study of the forms of earth features. 4 *Ling.* a The branch of linguistics which deals with morphemes, their arrangement in words, and the changes they undergo in various grammatical constructions. b The arrangement, composition, and inflection of the morphemes of a language. [<MORPHO- + -LOGY] — **mor·pho·log·ic** (môr′fə·loj′ik) or **·i·cal** adj. — **mor′pho·log′i·cal·ly** adv. — **mor·phol′o·gist** n.

mor·phol·y·sis (môr·fol′ə·sis) n. The breakdown of form or structure. [<MORPHO- + -LYSIS]

-morphous combining form Having a (specified) form: often equivalent to *-morphic*: *anthropomorphous.* [<Gk. *morphē* form]

mor·ri·on (môr′ē·on, mō′rē-) See MORION[1].

mor·ris (môr′is, mor′-) n. 1 An old English rustic dance, in which the performers took the part of Robin Hood and other characters in English folklore. 2 A dance by a single dancer with castanets. Also **mor′rice, morris dance.** [Earlier *morys, morish* Moorish]

mor·ro (môr′ō, mō′rō; *Sp.* môr′rō) n. pl. **mor·ros** (môr′ōz, mor′-; *Sp.* môr′rōs) A round hill. [<Sp.]

mor·row (môr′ō, mō′rō) n. 1 The first day after the present or after a day specified; hence, any time following immediately after a specified event. 2 Formerly, morning: good *morrow.* — adj. Next succeeding, as a day. [OE *morgen* morning]

INTERNATIONAL MORSE CODE

LETTERS

a	·—	j	·———	s	···
b	—···	k	—·—	t	—
c	—·—·	l	·—··	u	··—
d	—··	m	——	v	···—
e	·	n	—·	w	·——
f	··—·	o	———	x	—··—
g	——·	p	·——·	y	—·——
h	····	q	——·—	z	——··
i	··	r	·—·		

NUMERALS

1	·————	4	····—	8	———··
2	··———	5	·····	9	————·
3	···——	6	—····	0	—————
		7	——···		

PUNCTUATION

Period	·—·—·—
Comma	——··——
Semicolon	—·—·—·
Question mark	··——··
Exclamation	—·—·——
Colon	———···
Apostrophe	·————·
Hyphen	—····—
Fraction bar	—··—·
Parenthesis	—·——·—
Quotation marks	·—··—·
Double dash	—···—

Morse code 1 A system of telegraphic signals invented by S. F. B. Morse, comprised of dots and dashes or short and long flashes representing the letters of the alphabet and used in transmitting messages. 2 International Morse code. Also **Morse alphabet.**

mor·sel (môr′səl) n. 1 A bit of food; bite. 2 A small piece of anything. [<OF, dim. of *mors* bite <L *morsus* <*mordere*]

Morse telegraph A telegraph employing the dot–and–dash or Morse code, recording the signals on a continuous paper strip. The first commercial system was set up between Baltimore and Washington in 1844.

mor·tal (môr′təl) adj. 1 Subject to death; hence, pertaining to humanity; human. 2 Causing, or that may or will cause, death; fatal. 3 *Theol.* Incurring the penalty of eternal death, as a sin: opposed to *venial.* 4 Marking the end of life. 5 Subject to fatal injury, as a vital organ. 6 *Colloq.* Extreme: a *mortal* fright; also, long and tedious. 7 Deadly in malice or purpose; inveterate; a *mortal* foe. — n. Whatever is mortal or subject to death; a human being. — adv. *Colloq.*

Very; exceedingly: *mortal* tired. [<OF <L *mortalis* <*mors, mortis* death]

mor·tal·i·ty (môr·tal′ə·tē) n. 1 The quality of being mortal. 2 Death. 3 Frequency of death; the proportion of deaths in a specified number of the population; the death rate. 4 Humanity; mankind. [<OF *mortalité* <L *mortalitas*]

mortality table A life table.

mor·tal·ly (môr′təl·ē) adv. 1 Fatally. 2 After the manner of a mortal. 3 Extremely.

mortal mind In Christian Science, nothing, claiming to be something, for Mind is immortal; a belief that life, substance, and intelligence are in and of matter: the opposite of Spirit and therefore the opposite of God, or good.

mor·tar[1] (môr′tər) n. 1 A strong bowl-like vessel in which substances are crushed or pounded with a pestle. 2 *Mil.* A piece of ordnance with a large bore for firing heavy shells at low muzzle velocity and great angles of elevation that they may drop upon the object aimed at. 3 *Mining* A tublike cast-iron receptacle with grated sides, in which ore is stamped. 4 Any of several devices for hurling pyrotechnic shells or bombs and also life lines. [OE *mortere* <L *mortarium*]

mor·tar[2] (môr′tər) n. 1 A building material prepared by mixing lime, plaster of Paris, or cement, with sand, water, and sometimes other materials. It is used in masonry, plastering, etc. 2 Loosely, a cement. — v.t. To plaster or join with mortar. [<OF *mortier* <L *mortarium*]

mor·tar·board (môr′tər·bôrd′, -bōrd′) n. 1 A square board with a handle, on which a mason holds mortar. 2 The academic cap: so called from the four-cornered piece forming its crown.

mortar hoe A hoe with openings in the blade, used for mixing mortar, cement, etc. See illustration under HOE.

mort·gage (môr′gij) n. 1 *Law* An estate in land created by conveyance coupled with a condition of defeasance on the performance of some stipulated condition, as the payment of money. 2 A lien upon land or other property as security for the performance of some obligation, to become void on such performance. 3 The act of conveying, or the instrument effecting the conveyance. 4 A state or condition of being pledged as security for a debt like that of a mortgage of property. — **first mortgage** A mortgage having precedence as a lien over all other mortgages. — v.t. **·gaged, ·gag·ing** 1 To make over or pledge (property) by mortgage. 2 To pledge. [<F, dead pledge]

mort·ga·gee (môr′gi·jē′) n. The person to whom a mortgage is given; the holder of a mortgage.

mort·ga·gor (môr′gi·jər) n. A person who mortgages his property to another as security for a loan. Also **mort′gag·er.**

mor·tice (môr′tis) See MORTISE.

mor·ti·cian (môr·tish′ən) n. A funeral director; undertaker. [<L *mors, mortis* death + -ICIAN]

mor·ti·fi·ca·tion (môr′tə·fə·kā′shən) n. 1 The state of being humbled or depressed by disappointment or chagrin. 2 *Pathol.* The death of one part of an animal body, as from gangrene, while the rest is still alive. 3 In religion, the act of subduing the passions and appetites by fasting, penance, or painful severities inflicted on the body. 4 That which mortifies or causes humiliation. See synonyms under CHAGRIN. [<LL *mortificatio, -onis*]

mor·ti·fy (môr′tə·fī) v. **·fied, ·fy·ing** v.t. 1 To affect with humiliation, shame, or chagrin; humiliate. 2 To discipline or punish (the body, passions, etc.) by fasting, penance, or other ascetic practices. 3 *Pathol.* To cause mortification in (a part of the body). — v.i. 4 To practice ascetic self-discipline. 5 *Pathol.* To undergo mortification; become gangrenous. [<OF *mortifier* <LL *mortificare* <L *mors, mortis* death + *facere* make] — **mor′ti·fi′er** n. — **mor′ti·fy′ing·ly** adv.

mor·tu·ar·y (môr′chōō·er′ē) adj. Pertaining to the burial of the dead; also, relating to or reminiscent of the dead. — n. pl. **·ar·ies** 1 In old English law, a gift claimed by or given to a parish minister on the death of a parishioner. 2 A place for the temporary

reception of the dead; dead house. [<L *mortuarius* belonging to the dead]

mor·u·la (môr′yōō·lə, -ōō-) n. pl. **·lae** (-lē) *Biol.* The compact, spherical mass of cells formed by an ovum in the early stages of its development; the mulberry body. [<NL, dim. of L *morum* mulberry] — **mor′u·lar** adj.

mo·sa·ic (mō·zā′ik) n. 1 Inlaid work composed of bits of stone, glass, etc., forming a pattern or picture. 2 A piece of inlaid work of this kind, or anything resembling such work. 3 *Phot.* An assemblage of aerial photographs pieced together and joined at the margins so as to form a single, continuous picture of a terrain. 4 The plate covered with minute, photosensitive granules which is mounted in the image-scanning element of an electron television camera. — adj. Of, pertaining to, or resembling mosaic; tessellated; inlaid. — v.t. **·icked, ·ick·ing** 1 To make as if by combining in a mosaic. 2 To decorate with mosaic. [<OF *mosaicq* <Med. L *musaicus* <Gk. *mouseios* of the Muses, artistic <*Mousa* Muse] — **mo·sa·i·cist** (mō·zā′ə·sist) n.

mosaic disease One of several destructive and infectious diseases of plants caused by a filtrable virus and characterized by a pale, mottled appearance of the foliage: tobacco *mosaic*; potato *mosaic*.

mosaic gold 1 An alloy of copper and zinc; ormolu varnish. 2 Stannic sulfide.

mos·ca·tel (mos′kə·tel′) See MUSCATEL (def. 2).

mos·chate (mos′kāt, -kit) adj. Having the odor of musk. [<NL *moschatus* <Med. L *moschus* musk]

mos·cha·tel (mos′kə·tel′, mos′kə·tel) n. A low perennial herb (*Adoxa moschatellina*) with greenish flowers and having a musky odor; muskroot. [<F *moscatelle* <Ital. *moscatella*]

Mo·ses (mō′zis, -ziz; *Ger., Sw.* mō′ses) A masculine personal name. [<Egyptian, child, son] — **Moses** In the Old Testament, the younger son of Amram and Jochebed, who led the Israelites out of Egypt into the Promised Land, received the Ten Commandments from God, and gave laws to the people; hence, a leader; legislator.

mo·sey (mō′zē) v.i. *U. S. Slang* 1 To saunter, or stroll; shuffle along. 2 To go away; move off. [? <VAMOOSE]

Mos·lem (moz′ləm, mos′-) n. pl. **·lems** or **·lem** A Muslim. — adj. Muslim. — **Mos′lem·ism** n.

mosque (mosk) n. A Muslim temple of worship. Also **mosk.** [<F *mosquée* <Ital. *moschea* <Arabic *masjid* <*sajada* prostrate oneself, pray]

mos·qui·to (məs·kē′tō) n. pl. **·toes** or **·tos** 1 A two-winged, dipterous insect (family *Culicidae*), having (in the female) a long proboscis capable of puncturing the skin for extracting blood. The infections of malaria and yellow fever are spread by the bite of certain species. For illustration see INSECTS (injurious). 2 Any of various other gnats or flies inflicting a similar puncture. Also spelled *musquito*. [<Sp., dim. of *mosca* fly <L *musca*] — **mos·qui′tal** adj.

mosquito boat A patrol torpedo boat.

mosquito hawk 1 A nighthawk. 2 A dragonfly.

mosquito net A fine netting or gauze placed in windows, over beds, etc., to keep out mosquitoes.

mosquito netting A coarsely meshed fabric used to make mosquito nets.

moss[1] (môs, mos) n. 1 A delicate, bryophytic plant (class *Musci*), growing on the ground, decaying wood, rocks, trees, etc., having a stem and distinct leaves, and producing capsules which open by an operculum and contain spores unmixed with elaters. 2 Any of several other cryptogamous plants, as certain lichens, clubmosses, etc. — v.t. To cover with moss. [<MOSS[2]] — **moss′y** adj. — **moss′i·ness** n.

moss[2] (môs, mos) n. A bog; peat bog. [OE *mos*]

moss agate A variety of quartz containing mineral oxides, as manganese dioxide, arranged in mosslike forms.

moss·back (môs′bak′, mos′-) n. 1 An old fish or turtle on whose back is a growth of algae and the like. 2 One who is out of touch with the progress of the times; a conservative or reactionary person; especially, an extreme conservative in politics. **3** During the American Civil War, in the South, one who avoided conscription by hiding.

moss-backed (môs′bakt′, mos′-) *adj.* **1** Having moss or mosslike growth on the back. **2** Behind the times; reactionary.

Möss·bau·er effect (mœs′bou′ər) The absorption of gamma rays emitted from a radioactive isotope by nuclei of the same isotope, with resonance between the emitting and absorbing nuclei, both of which are anchored in crystals. It is used in the exact determination of wavelengths, time intervals, the red shift, and in testing various concepts of relativity and quantum theory. [after Rudolf L. *Mössbauer*, born 1929, U.S. physicist born in Germany]

moss-board (môs′bôrd′, -bōrd′, mos′-) *n.* A type of pasteboard made principally of peat moss and used in the preparation of surgical dressings.

moss-bunk·er (môs′bungk·ər, mos′-) *n.* The menhaden. Also **moss′bank·er.** [Alter. of Du. *marskanker*]

moss green Any of various shades of dull yellowish green.

moss-grown (môs′grōn′, mos′-) *adj.* Overgrown with moss; hence, very ancient.

mos·so (môs′sō) *adj. Music* Rapid; literally, moved. [<Ital., pp. of *movere* move <L]

moss pink A plant (*Phlox subulata*) of the eastern United States, occurring in several varieties which form mats close to the ground and have white, pink, or purplish flowers. Also **moss phlox.**

moss rose 1 A cultivated variety of the rose (*Rosa centifolia muscosa*) with a mossy calyx and stem. **2** Portulaca.

moss starch Lichenin.

most (mōst) *adj.* **1** Consisting of the greatest number: superlative of *many.* **2** Consisting of the greatest amount or quantity: superlative of *much.* **3** *Obs.* Greatest in size, rank, or age. — *n.* **1** The greater number; the larger part: the *most* of my belongings. **2** Greatest amount, value, or advantage; utmost degree, extent, or effect. — *adv.* **1** In the highest degree, or in the greatest number or quantity. **2** *Dial.* Almost. **3** Greatest, as in amount or degree: used with adjectives and adverbs to form the superlative degree. [OE *mæst*]

-most *suffix* Most: added to adjectives, adverbs, and prepositions to form superlatives: *outmost.* [OE -*mest* <-*ma* + -*est*, superlative suffixes]

most-fa·vored-na·tion clause (mōst′fā′vərd·nā′shən) A provision in many commercial treaties stipulating that the parties shall accord each other treatment as favorable as that granted to any other country.

most·ly (mōst′lē) *adv.* For the most part; principally.

mot[1] (mō) *n.* A witty or pithy saying; bon mot. [<F, word <LL *muttum* uttered sound <*muttire* murmur]

mot[2] (mot) *n.* A bugle note, or its mark in music. [<OF]

mote (mōt) *n.* A minute particle; speck. ✦ Homophone: *moat.* [OE *mot* atom]

mo·tel (mō·tel′) *n.* A hotel for motorists, usually comprising private cabins and garage or parking facilities. [<MO(TOR) + (HO)TEL]

mo·tet (mō·tet′) *n. Music* A contrapuntal, polyphonic song of a sacred nature, usually unaccompanied. Also **mo·tet′to.** [<OF, dim. of *mot* word. See MOT[1].]

moth (môth, moth) *n. pl.* **moths** (môthz, môths, mothz, moths) Any of various typically nocturnal, lepidopterous insects (division *Heterocera*), distinguished from butterflies by their stout bodies and smaller, usually dull-colored wings, which fold laterally across the abdomen. The larvae of the gipsy moth, silkworm, etc., feed on plants; those of the clothes moth (family *Tineidae*) feed on textiles, clothing, and furs. [OE *moththe*]

moth ball A ball of camphor or naphthalene, for the protection of clothing, etc., from moths. — **in moth balls** In protective storage.

moth-eat·en (môth′ēt′n, moth′-) *adj.* Eaten by moths; hence, used up or worn out: also *mothy.*

moth·er[1] (muth′ər) *n.* **1** A female parent. **2** That which has produced or given birth to

anything. **3** An abbess or other nun of rank or dignity. **4** An elderly woman or matron: a familiar title. — *v.t.* **1** To care for as a mother. **2** To bring forth as a mother; produce. **3** To admit or claim parentage, authorship, etc., of. — *adj.* **1** Native: *mother* tongue. **2** Holding a maternal relation. [OE *mōdor*]

moth·er[2] (muth′ər) *n.* **1** A slimy film composed of bacteria and yeast cells that forms on the surface of fermenting liquids and is active in the production of vinegar: also called *mother-of-vinegar.* **2** Dregs; lees. — *v.i.* To become mothery, as vinegar. [Special use of MOTHER[1]] — **moth′er·y** *adj.*

mother cell A cell which by division produces other cells.

Mother Goose 1 The imaginary narrator of a volume of folk tales, compiled in French by Charles Perrault in 1697. **2** The imaginary compiler of a collection of nursery rimes of English folk origin, first published in London about 1760 by John Newbery.

moth·er·hood (muth′ər·hŏŏd) *n.* The state of being a mother.

moth·er-in-law (muth′ər·in-lô′) *n. pl.* **moth·ers-in-law 1** The mother of one's spouse. **2** *Brit. Dial.* A stepmother.

moth·er·land (muth′ər·land′) *n.* The land of one's ancestors; native land; mother country.

moth·er·less (muth′ər·lis) *adj.* Having no mother.

mother liquor The liquid remaining after the substances in solution have been deposited by crystallization or precipitation.

mother lode *Mining* **1** *Cap.* The great gold-bearing quartz vein in California, traced by its outcrop from Mariposa to Amador. **2** Any principal vein in a mining region.

moth·er-of-pearl (muth′ər·əv·pûrl′) *n.* The hard, iridescent internal layer of certain shells, as of pearl oysters, abalones, and mussels; nacre.

mother tongue 1 One's native language. **2** A language from which another language has sprung.

mother wit Inherent, natural, or native intelligence; common sense.

moth·er·wort (muth′ər·wûrt′) *n.* An Old World herb (*Leonurus cardiaca*) of the mint family, with lanceolate, toothed leaves, and small, purplish flowers: now common in the U.S. [So called because once thought to be valuable in the treatment of diseases of the womb]

moth-mill·er (môth′mil′ər, moth′-) *n.* **1** A pale moth with floury wings; a miller. **2** *Colloq.* Any moth.

moth-proof (môth′prŏŏf′, moth′-) *adj.* Resistant to the attack of moths. — *v.t.* **·proofed, ·proof·ing** To render (textiles) resistant to moths.

mo·tif (mō·tēf′) *n.* **1** The underlying idea or main feature or element in literary, musical, or artistic work. **2** In the decorative arts, a distinctive element of design. Also **mo·tive** (mō′tiv). [<F]

mo·tile (mō′til) *adj.* **1** *Biol.* Having the power of spontaneous motion, as certain minute organisms. **2** Causing motion. [<L *motus*, pp. of *movere* move] — **mo·til′i·ty** *n.*

mo·tion (mō′shən) *n.* **1** Change of position in reference to an assumed point or center; a shifting movement. **2** The interaction of parts in a mechanism to produce a particular result. **3** A formal proposition in a deliberative assembly. **4** A significant movement of the limbs, eyes, etc.; a gesture: She made *motions* to him. **5** An impulse to action; incentive. **6** *Music* Melodic progression. **7** *Law* An application to a court to obtain an order or rule directing some act to be done. **8** A mechanism. **9** *Obs.* A puppet or puppet show. — **perpetual motion** Continuous mechanical motion, especially as applied to machines which are claimed to do useful work without the expenditure of equivalent amounts of work upon them. — *v.i.* To make a gesture of direction or intent, as with the hand. — *v.t.* To direct or guide by a gesture. [<F <L *motio, -onis* <*motus*, pp. of *movere* move] — **mo′tion·al** *adj.* — **mo′tion·less** *adj.* — **mo′tion·less·ly** *adv.*

Synonyms (noun): act, action, change, move, movement, passage, transit, transition. *Motion* may be either abstract or concrete, more frequently the former; *movement* is always concrete, that is, considered in connection

with the thing that moves or is moved; thus we speak of the *movements* of the planets, but of the laws of planetary *motion*; of military *movements*, but of perpetual *motion*. *Motion* is *change* of place or position in space; *transition* is a passing from one point or position in space to another. *Move* is used chiefly of contests or competition, as in chess or politics: as, It is your *move*; a shrewd *move* of the opposition. We speak of mental or spiritual *acts* or processes, or of the laws of mental *action*, but a formal proposal of *action* in a deliberative assembly is termed a *motion*. *Action* is a more comprehensive word than *motion*. See ACT, TOPIC. *Antonyms*: quiescence, quiet, repose, rest.

motion picture 1 A sequence of pictures, each slightly different from the last, photographed by a special camera on a single strip of film, for projection on a screen, giving the optical illusion of continuous, ordered movement: also called *cinema, movie, moving picture.* **2** A photoplay. — **mo′tion-pic′ture** *adj.*

motion sickness Nausea and sometimes vomiting caused by the effect of certain complex movements on the semicircular canals of the inner ear, typically experienced in a moving vehicle, ship, or airplane.

motion study The detailed observation and analysis of the different movements involved in the performance of a given repetitive task, with a view to lessening the fatigue and increasing the efficiency of the workers.

mo·ti·vate (mō′tə·vāt) *v.t.* **·vat·ed, ·vat·ing** To provide with a motive; instigate; induce.

mo·ti·va·tion (mō′tə·vā′shən) *n.* Causative factor; incentive; drive. — **mo′ti·va′tion·al** *adj.*

mo·tive (mō′tiv) *n.* **1** That which incites to motion or action. **2** A predominant idea; design. — *adj.* **1** Having power to move; causing motion. **2** Relating to a motive or motives. — *v.t.* **·tived, ·tiv·ing 1** To motivate; prompt. **2** To relate to the leading idea or motif in a work of art, etc. [<OF *motif* <Med. L *motivus* <*motus*, pp. of *movere* move]

Synonyms (noun): consideration, ground, incentive, incitement, inducement, influence, reason. *Motive* may signify either a mental impulse, or something external that is an object of desire, and so an *inducement* or *incitement* to action. Compare CAUSE, IMPULSE, PURPOSE, REASON.

motive power 1 The power, or means of generating power, by which motion is imparted to an object, machine, etc. **2** Figuratively, an impelling force.

mo·tiv·i·ty (mō·tiv′ə·tē) *n.* The power of producing motion; motive energy.

mot·ley (mot′lē) *adj.* **1** Variegated in color; parti-colored. **2** Composed of heterogeneous elements. **3** Clothed in varicolored garments. — *n.* **1** A dress of various colors, such as was formerly worn by court jesters. **2** A jester or fool in motley garments. **3** A medley, as of colors. [ME *motteley*; origin uncertain]

Mot·ley (mot′lē), **John Lothrop,** 1814–77, U.S. historian.

MOTLEY (*n. def. 1*)

mo·tor (mō′tər) *n.* **1** One who or that which produces motion, as a machine, nerve, etc. **2** An internal-combustion engine, especially one operating on gasoline. **3** A motorcar or motorcycle. **4** An electric motor. — **rotary motor** An internal-combustion engine having multiple radial cylinders rotating about a fixed crankshaft. — *adj.* **1** Causing, producing, or imparting motion. **2** Transmitting impulses from the nerve centers to the muscles. **3** Pertaining to consciousness of motion. — *v.i.* To travel or ride in an automobile. [<L *motus*, pp. of *movere*] — **mo′tor·ing** *adj. & n.*

mo·tor·boat (mō′tər·bōt′) *n.* A boat propelled by an internal-combustion engine, or by an electric motor.

mo·tor·bus (mō′tər·bus′) *n.* A power-driven omnibus. Also **motor coach.**

mo·tor·cade (mō′tər·kād) *n.* A procession of motorcycles or automobiles. [<MOTOR + (CAVAL)CADE]

mo·tor·car (mō′tər·kär′) *n.* An automobile.

mo·tor·cy·cle (mō′tər·sī′kəl) *n.* A two-wheeled vehicle, sometimes having an attached sidecar with a third wheel, propelled by an internal-combustion engine. — *v.i.* **·cled, ·cling** To travel or ride on a motorcycle. — **mo′tor·cy′clist** *n.*

motor drive A power unit consisting of an electric motor and auxiliaries, used to operate a machine or group of machines.

mo·tor·drome (mō′tər·drōm) *n.* An enclosure, course, or track where motor-driven vehicles of various kinds are tested in competition or otherwise.

motor generator A device for transforming electrical power by permanently connecting, usually on a common bedplate, a motor and a generator; a dynamotor.

motor home *U.S.* An automotive vehicle equipped with living accommodations and resembling a trailer but built on a single chassis.

mo·tor·ist (mō′tər·ist) *n.* One who drives an automobile; one who travels by automobile.

mo·to·ri·um (mō·tôr′ē·əm, -tō′rē-) *n. Physiol.* 1 That portion of the nervous system which controls the motor apparatus. 2 Any center of a motor function. [<NL <L *motor* a mover]

mo·tor·ize (mō′tər·īz) *v.t.* **·ized, ·iz·ing** 1 To equip with a motor or motors. 2 To equip with motor-propelled vehicles in place of horses and horse-drawn vehicles. — **mo′tor·i·za′tion** *n.*

motor oil A high-grade lubricating oil, designed for the exacting requirements of internal-combustion engines.

motor scooter See SCOOTER (def. 2).

mo·tor·ship (mō′tər·ship′) *n.* A vessel, as a passenger ship, of which the principal motive power is derived from an internal-combustion oil or gas engine.

motor spirit Any fuel adapted for spark-ignition, internal-combustion engines; specifically, coal or petroleum distillates blended with suitable additions, as alcohol.

motor transport *Mil.* Any motor vehicle used for transport only: distinguished from *combat vehicle.*

motor vehicle 1 Any vehicle operated by a motor or engine. 2 A vehicle adapted to be pulled by another, as a trailer.

mot·tle (mot′l) *v.t.* **·tled, ·tling** To mark with spots or streaks of different colors or shades; blotch. — *n.* 1 The spotted, blotched, or variegated appearance of any mottled surface, as of wood or marble. 2 One of a number of spots or blotches on any surface. [<MOTLEY]

mot·tled (mot′ld) *adj.* Marked with spots of different color or shades of color; blotched; variegated.

mot·to (mot′ō) *n. pl.* **·toes** or **·tos** 1 An expressive word or pithy sentence enunciating some guiding principle, rule of conduct, or the like; a phrase inscribed on something or prefixed to a literary composition as somehow indicative of its qualities. 2 A piece of paper printed with a motto or sentiment and wrapped around a small piece of candy; also, the piece of candy enclosed. See synonyms under ADAGE. [<Ital. <F *mot.* See MOT.]

moue (mōō) *n.* A pouting grimace expressive of disdain or distaste. [<F]

mouf·lon (mōōf′lon) *n.* A hairy wild sheep; specifically, *Ovis musimon* of the mountains of Corsica and Sardinia, the males with very large and curved horns. Also **mouf′flon.** [<F < dial. Ital. *muffolo* < *muffione* <LL *mufro, -onis*]

mou·lage (mōō·läzh′) *n.* 1 A cast, in plaster of Paris or other similar material, of an object or of its impressed outlines on a surface: frequently used in criminal identification, as of footprints, tire marks, etc. 2 A synthetic, rubberlike, plastic material used in making casts. [<F]

mould (mōld), **moult** (mōlt), etc. See MOLD, etc.

mould goose The musk duck.

mou·lin (mōō·lan′) *n.* A nearly vertical shaft in a glacier, formed by the surface water trickling through a crevice. [<F, mill <LL *molina.* See MILL.]

mou·line (mōō·lēn′) *n.* 1 The circular swing of a saber. 2 The drum of a winch, capstan, or the like; a windlass mechanism. 3 A form of turnstile. Also **mou·li·net** (mōō′lē·net). [<F, dim. of *moulin* mill]

mound¹ (mound) *n.* 1 A heap or pile of earth, either natural or artificial; hillock. 2 One of the earthworks built by the Mound Builders for burial or fortification. 3 In baseball, the slightly raised ground from which the pitcher pitches the ball. See synonyms under RAMPART. — *v.t.* 1 To fortify or enclose with a mound. 2 To heap up in a mound. [Origin uncertain]

mound² (mound) *n.* A jeweled ball or globe, often surmounted by a cross, forming part of the regalia of a king or emperor: an emblem of sovereignty; an orb. [<F *monde* <L *mundus* world]

MOUND²

Mound Builder One of the aboriginal people who built the burial mounds and fortifications found in the Mississippi basin and adjoining regions: the ancestors of the North American Indians dwelling in that region at the time of the first European explorers.

mount¹ (mount) *v.t.* 1 To ascend by climbing; go up, as stairs. 2 To climb upon; ascend and seat oneself on, as a horse. 3 To put on horseback. 4 To furnish with a horse or horses. 5 To set or place in an elevated position: to *mount* a plaque on a wall. 6 To place in position for use or operation, as a cannon or engine. 7 To put in or on a support, frame, etc., as for exhibition: to *mount* a butterfly. 8 To furnish, as a play, with scenery, costumes, etc. 9 To copulate with a female: said of male animals. 10 In microscopy: **a** To place or fix (a sample) on a slide. **b** To prepare (a slide) for examination. 11 *Mil.* & *Nav.* To carry or be equipped with: a ship *mounting* thirty-two guns. 12 To put on (clothing), especially for display. 13 *Mil.* To stand or post (guard). 14 *Mil.* To prepare for and begin: to *mount* an offensive. — *v.i.* 15 To rise or ascend; go up. 16 To increase in number, amount, or degree: often with *up:* The bills *mounted* up. 17 To get on horseback. 18 To get up on or on top of something. — *n.* 1 That upon or by which anything is prepared or equipped for use, exhibition, ornament, preservation, or examination. 2 The card, etc., upon which a drawing or photograph is mounted. 3 The parts and appliances by which a gun is attached to its carriage. 4 The glass slide and its adjuncts upon which a microscopic subject is secured for examination. 5 A saddle horse or other animal used for riding: by extension, a bicycle. 6 The act of riding a horse in a race; also, the privilege or opportunity of doing so. 7 A style of mounting. [<OF *monter* <L *mons, montis* mountain] — **mount′a·ble** *adj.* — **mount′er** *n.*

mount² (mount) *n.* 1 An elevation of the earth's surface; a mountain; a hill. When used as part of a proper name it usually precedes the specific application: *Mount* Washington. 2 *Obs.* A raised fortification commanding the surrounding country. 3 In palmistry, one of seven fleshy protuberances in the palm of the hand. [OE *munt* <L *mons* mountain]

moun·tain (moun′tən) *n.* 1 A natural elevation of the earth's surface, rising more or less abruptly to a small summit area, attaining an elevation greater than that of a hill, and standing either in a single mass or forming part of a series. 2 Any large heap or pile resembling this. 3 Something of great magnitude. — **the Mountain.** A name given to the ultra-revolutionary party of the French National Assembly or Convention in 1793, from the fact that its members occupied the highest seats in the chamber. — *adj.* 1 Of, pertaining to, or living or growing on mountains. 2 Like or suggesting a mountain or mountains. [<OF *montaigne* <L *montanus* mountainous < *mons, montis* mountain]

mountain ape *Paleontol.* Oreopithecus.

mountain ash 1 Any of various American deciduous shrubs (genus *Sorbus*), having alternate simple or pinnate leaves, white flowers, and vivid red fruit, especially *S. americana.* 2 The rowan.

mountain avens A small evergreen plant (*Dryas octopetala*) of the rose family, growing in arctic and alpine regions.

mountain cat 1 The cougar. 2 The bobcat.

mountain chain A series of mountains connected and having some common characteristics.

mountain cork A variety of asbestos occurring in light, flexible sheets which will float on water. Also **mountain leather.**

mountain cranberry The mountain cowberry (*Vaccinium vitis-idaea minus*), having edible red berries, evergreen leaves, and pink or red flowers.

mountain dew *Slang* Illicitly distilled whiskey.

moun·tain·eer (moun′tən·ir′) *n.* 1 An inhabitant of a mountainous district. 2 One who climbs mountains. — *v.i.* To climb mountains.

mountain goat The Rocky Mountain goat; a goat antelope.

mountain laurel In the eastern United States, the low-growing calicobush (*Kalmia latifolia*), an evergreen shrub with white or pink flowers; State flower of Connecticut and Pennsylvania. The foliage is poisonous to livestock.

ROCKY MOUNTAIN
GOAT
(About 3 1/2 feet high
at the shoulder)

mountain lion The puma or cougar.

moun·tain·ous (moun′tən·əs) *adj.* 1 Full of mountains. 2 Huge. — **moun′tain·ous·ly** *adv.*

mountain range 1 One of the components of a mountain chain, usually a group of more or less parallel ridges of similar origin, structure, etc. 2 A land area dominated by such a group of mountains, characterized by great variations in elevation above sea level.

mountain rat A pack rat.

mountain sheep The bighorn.

mountain sickness *Pathol.* A form of anoxemia accompanied by nausea, due to insufficient oxygen consumption at high altitudes, especially on mountains.

Mountain Standard Time See STANDARD TIME. Abbr. **M.S.T.**

moun·te·bank (moun′tə·bangk) *n.* 1 A vendor of quack medicines at fairs, who usually mounts a platform or wagon to sell his wares. 2 Hence, a charlatan. See synonyms under QUACK. — *v.i.* To play the mountebank. [<Ital. *montimbanco* <*monta* mount + *in* on + *banco* bench]

mount·ed (moun′tid) *adj.* Elevated on or equipped with horses: *mounted* police.

mount·ing (moun′ting) *n.* 1 The act of mounting; elevation. 2 A mount, as of a picture. 3 The act of preparing for use, etc.

Mount Ver·non (vûr′nən) The home and burial place of George Washington; 15 miles below Washington, D.C., on the Potomac River.

mourn (môrn, mōrn) *v.i.* 1 To feel or express grief or sorrow. 2 To display the conventional signs of grief after someone's death; wear mourning. — *v.t.* 3 To grieve or sorrow for (someone dead). 4 To grieve over or lament (misfortune, failure, etc.); bewail; deplore. 5 To utter in a sorrowful manner. [OE *murnan*]

Synonyms: bemoan, bewail, deplore, grieve, lament, regret, rue, sorrow. Mourning is thought of as prolonged; grief or regret may be transient. One may *grieve* or *mourn, regret, rue,* or *sorrow* without a sound; he *bemoans* with suppressed and often inarticulate sounds of grief; *bewails* with passionate utterance, whether of inarticulate cries or of spoken words; he *laments* in plaintive or pathetic words.

mourn·er (môr′nər, mōr′-) *n.* 1 One who mourns; specifically, one who attends a funeral. 2 A penitent at a revival meeting.

mourn·ful (môrn′fəl, mōrn′-) *adj.* 1 Indicating or expressing grief. 2 Oppressed with grief. 3 Exciting sorrow. See synonyms under PITIFUL, SAD. — **mourn′ful·ly** *adv.* — **mourn′ful·ness** *n.*

mourn·ing (môr′ning, mōr′-) *n.* 1 The act of sorrowing or expressing grief; lamentation; sorrow.

2 The symbols or outward manifestations of grief, as the use of symbolical colors in dress, the draping of buildings or doors, and the half-masting of flags. —*adj.* Relating to or expressive of mourning. —**mourn′ing·ly** *adv.*

mourning cloak A brownish-black butterfly (*Nymphalis antiopa*) widely distributed in temperate regions: it has a row of dark spots just inside the yellow border on the upper side of the wings: also called *Camberwell beauty.*

mourning dove The Carolina turtledove (*Zenaidura macroura*), common in North America: so called for its plaintive note.

mourning warbler A warbler of the eastern United States (*Oporonis philadelphia*) also called for its plaintive note.

mouse (mous) *n. pl.* **mice** (mīs) **1** One of various small rodents frequenting human habitations throughout the world, as the common **house mouse** (*Mus musculus*). ◆Collateral adjective: *murine.* **2** Any of various similar animals, as the American **harvest mouse** (genus *Reithrodontomys*), or the **lemming mouse** (genus *Synaptomys*). **3** *Slang* A young woman. **4** *Slang* A discolored swelling of the eye, caused by a blow or bruise. **5** *Naut.* A swelling worked on a rope to prevent its slipping; also, a mousing. —*v.* (mouz) **moused**, **mous·ing** *v.i.* **1** To hunt or catch mice. **2** To hunt for something cautiously and softly; prowl. —*v.t.* **3** To hunt for, as a cat hunts mice. **4** *Naut.* To secure (a hook) with mousing. **5** *Obs.* To rend as a cat does a mouse. [OE *mūs*, pl. *mȳs.*]

mouse·bane (mous′bān′) *n.* Aconite.

mouse·bird (mous′bûrd′) *n.* **1** An African bird (genus *Colius*) with a conical bill, long medial tail feathers, and soft plumage. **2** A shrike.

mouse·ear (mous′ir′) *n.* Any one of various plants whose leaves resemble the ears of a mouse; especially, the European hawkweed (*Hieracium pilosella*). **2** The forget-me-not.

mouse gray A medium shade of gray, the color of the fur of the common house mouse.

mous·er (mou′zər) *n.* **1** An animal that catches mice; especially, a cat. **2** A person who goes about stealthily.

mouse·tail (mous′tāl′) *n.* One of a genus (*Myosurus*) of plants of the crowfoot family: so called from its slender spike.

mouse·trap (mous′trap′) *n.* A trap for catching mice.

mous·ing (mou′zing) *n.* **1** The act of hunting mice. **2** *Naut.* A lashing or shackle passed around the shank and point of a hook, to prevent its spreading or unhooking. —*adj.* **1** Given to catching mice; prowling. **2** Thorough; careful; patient, as a cat hunting a mouse.

mous·sa·ka (mōō′sə·kä′) *n.* A baked dish of the Middle East made of alternating layers of ground meat and eggplant, served with a cheese sauce.

mousse (mōōs) *n.* A light, frozen dessert made of whipped cream, white of egg, sugar, and flavoring extract, sometimes with the beaten yolks of eggs and gelatin; also, a similar dish made with finely ground meat, fish, or vegetables: lobster *mousse.* [< F]

mousse·line (mōōs·lēn′) *n.* **1** Fine French muslin. **2** A thin glass blown to resemble lace. [< F. See MUSLIN.]

mousse·line-de-soie (mōōs·lēn′də·swá′) *n.* French A plain-weave silk chiffon fabric, often figured; silk muslin.

Mous·sorg·sky (mōō·sôrg′skē), **Modest Petrovich**, 1835–81, Russian composer: also *Mussorgsky.*

mous·tache (məs·tash′, mus′tash) See MUSTACHE.

Mous·te·ri·an (mōō·stir′ē·ən) *adj. Anthropol.* Pertaining to or describing the culture stage of the Middle Paleolithic, represented in western Europe by artifacts of stone and other materials believed to indicate the social forms of the Neanderthal race of hunters. [< F *moustérien* < *Le Moustier*, a village in France where such remains were found]

mous·y (mou′sē, -zē) *adj.* **mous·i·er**, **mous·i·est** **1** Infested with or inhabited by mice. **2** Of, pertaining to, or like a mouse; having the color or smell of a mouse. **3** Like a mouse in appearance or manner; pallid; timid. Also

mous′ey.

mouth (mouth) *n. pl.* **mouths** (mouthz) **1** The orifice at which food is taken into the body; the entrance to the alimentary canal; the cavity between the lips and throat. ◆ Collateral adjective: *oral.* **2** The human mouth as the channel of speech. **3** A wry face; grimace. **4** That part of a stream where its waters are discharged; also, the entrance to a harbor. **5** The opening for discharge in the muzzle of a firearm. **6** The slit in an organ pipe, from which the wind passes against the lip; also, the edge of the opening in a flute or similar instrument, against which the performer's breath is directed. **7** The opening of a vessel by which it is emptied or filled. **8** The entrance or opening into a cavity, mine, etc. **9** The space or opening between the jaws of a vice. —**down in** (or **at**) **the mouth** Disconsolate; dejected. —**to fix one's mouth for** To get ready for. —*v.t.* (mouth) **1** To utter in a forced or affected manner; declaim. **2** To seize or take in the mouth. **3** To caress or fondle with the mouth. **4** To accustom (a horse) to the bit. —*v.i.* **5** To speak in a forced or affected manner. **6** To distort the mouth; grimace. [OE *mūth*] —**mouth′er** (mou′thər) *n.*

mouthed (mouthd, moutht) *adj.* **1** Having a mouth: used in composition, to denote a characteristic of the mouth or of speech: a hard-*mouthed* horse. **2** Provided with a mouth.

mouth·ful (mouth′fōōl′) *n. pl.* **-fuls** (-fōōlz′) **1** As much as can be or is usually put into or held in the mouth at one time. **2** A small quantity.

mouth organ 1 A harmonica. **2** A set of panpipes.

mouth·piece (mouth′pēs′) *n.* **1** That part of any instrument, tool, etc., that is applied to the mouth. **2** One who speaks for others. **3** *Slang* A criminal lawyer.

mouth-to-mouth (mouth′tə·mouth′) *adj.* Pertaining to or designating a first-aid technique in which the lungs of a nonbreathing subject are repeatedly and forcibly filled with air from the mouth of the operator, which is closely applied to the mouth of the subject at each insufflation.

mouth·y (mou′thē, -thē) *adj.* **mouth·i·er**, **mouth·i·est 1** Garrulous. **2** Addicted to grimaces in speaking. —**mouth′i·ly** *adv.* —**mouth′i·ness** *n.*

mou·ton (mōō′ton) *n.* Processed lambskin or sheepskin used in various types of apparel, especially coats. [< F, sheep]

mov·a·ble (mōō′və·bəl) *adj.* **1** Capable of being moved in any way, as from one place, position, or posture to another; susceptible of transposition: *movable* property. **2** Capable of being moved in respect of time; recurring at varying intervals. See synonyms under MOBILE. —*n.* **1** Anything that can be moved; especially, anything that may be readily moved or is adapted for moving. **2** *pl.* House furniture of a movable nature; also, personal property, as distinguished from real or fixed property. Also **move′a·ble.** —**mov′a·ble·ness, mov′a·bil′i·ty** *n.* —**mov′a·bly** *adv.*

move (mōōv) *v.* **moved**, **mov·ing** *v.i.* **1** To change place or position; pass or go from one place to another. **2** To change one's residence. **3** To make progress; advance; proceed. **4** To live or associate; be active: to *move* in cultivated circles. **5** To operate or revolve; work: said of machines, etc. **6** *Colloq.* To depart; go or start: often with *on.* **7** To take action; begin to act. **8** To be disposed of by sale. **9** To make an application, appeal, or proposal: to *move* for adjournment. **10** To evacuate: said of the bowels. **11** In chess, checkers, etc., to make a move. —*v.t.* **12** To change the place or position of; carry, push, or pull from one place to another. **13** To set or keep in mo-

HUMAN MOUTH
a. Hard palate.
b. Pharynx.
c. Soft palate.
d. Uvula.
e. Tonsil.
f. Epiglottis.
g. Esophagus.
h. Trachea
i. Tongue.
j. Hyoid bone.
k. Larynx.

tion; stir or shake. **14** To rouse, influence, or impel to some action; prompt; actuate. **15** To affect with passion, sympathy, etc.; stir; excite. **16** To offer for consideration, action, etc.; propose, especially formally. **17** To cause (the bowels) to evacuate. See synonyms under ACTUATE, CARRY, CONVEY, INFLUENCE, PERSUADE, STIR[1]. —*n.* **1** The act of moving; movement. **2** An act in the carrying out of a plan. **3** In games, the changing of the place of a piece. —**to get a move on** To hurry; get going. See synonyms under MOTION. [< AF *mover*, OF *moveir* < L *movere*]

move·ment (mōōv′mənt) *n.* **1** The act of changing place or of moving in any way; any change of position. **2** A series of actions, incidents, or ethical impulses tending toward some end: the temperance *movement.* **3** An effect resembling motion, as in a picture. **4** *Mech.* A particular arrangement of related parts accomplishing a motion: the *movement* of a watch. **5** *Music* **a** The pace or speed at which a piece or section of music sounds best. **b** One of the sections of a larger work, as of a symphony. **c** Melodic progression. **6** Rhythm; meter. **7** The act of emptying the bowels; also, the state of being or the matter so emptied. **8** An elemental part of action in military or naval evolution or maneuver. See synonyms under ACT, MOTION.

mov·er (mōō′vər) *n.* **1** One who or that which moves; specifically, one engaged in the business of moving household goods and other possessions. **2** A tenant farmer who moves away as soon as the soil is exhausted.

mov·ie (mōō′vē) *n. Colloq.* **1** A motion picture. **2** A motion-picture theater. **3** *pl.* The motion-picture industry. **4** *pl.* A showing of motion pictures. [Contraction of *moving picture*]

mov·ing (mōō′ving) *adj.* **1** Causing to move; impelling to act; influencing; instigating; persuading. **2** Exciting the susceptibilities; affecting; touching. —**mov′ing·ly** *adv.* —**mov′ing·ness** *n.*

moving platform A platform operated by an endless belt or several such side by side, moving at graduated speeds, carrying along passengers or merchandise. Also **moving sidewalk.**

moving staircase An escalator.

mow[1] (mō) *v.* **mowed**, **mowed** or **mown**, **mowing** *v.t.* **1** To cut down, as grain, with a scythe or machine. **2** To cut the grain or grass of, as a field or lawn. **3** To cut down or kill rapidly or indiscriminately: with *down.* —*v.i.* **4** To cut down grass or grain. [OE *māwan*] —**mow′er** *n.*

mow[2] (mō, mou) *v.i.* To make faces; grimace. [< *n.*] —*n.* A grimace. [< OF *moue*]

mow[3] (mou) *n.* Hay or grain stored in a barn; also, the place of storage. —*v.t.* To store in a mow. [OE *mūga*]

mown (mōn) *adj.* Cut down, as by mowing.

Mo·zart (mōt′särt, -zärt), **Wolfgang Amadeus**, 1756–91, Austrian composer.

Moz·za·rel·la (môd′dzä·rel′lä) *n.* A soft Italian curd cheese, originally made of buffalo's milk: used mainly in cooking. [< Ital.]

Mr. (mis′tər) *n. pl.* **Messrs.** (mes′ərz) A title prefixed to the name of a man: a contracted form of *Mister.*

Mrs. (mis′iz) *n. pl.* **Mmes.** (mā·däm′) A title prefixed to the name of a married woman: a contracted form of *Mistress.*

Ms. (miz) *n. pl.* **Ms.'s** (miz′əz) A title prefixed to the name of a woman: a contracted form of *Mistress.*

much (much) *adj.* **more**, **most 1** Great in quantity or amount. **2** *Obs.* Many in number. —*n.* **1** A considerable quantity. **2** A remarkable or important thing. —*adv.* **1** In a great degree. **2** For the most part; nearly. [ME *muchel*, OE *mycel*] —**much′ness** *n.*

mu·cid (myōō′sid) *adj.* Moldy; also, slimy; mucilaginous. [< L *mucidus* < *mucere* be moldy] —**mu′cid·ness** *n.*

mu·ci·lage (myōō′sə·lij) *n.* **1** A gummy or slimy substance obtained from the seeds, bark, or roots of various plants by infusion in water. **2** A solution of vegetable gum or mucus in water, especially when intended as an adhesive. [< F < LL *mucilago* < *mucere* be moldy, musty < *mucus* mucus]

mu·ci·lag·i·nous (myōō′si·laj′ə·nəs) *adj.* **1** Of, pertaining to, or like mucilage; soft, slimy, and viscid. 2 Producing mucilage, as glands. [< F *mucilagineux*] —**mu'ci·lag'i·nous·ness** n.

mu·cin (myo͞o'sin) n. *Biochem.* A glycoprotein secreted by the mucous membranes. [< F *mucine* mucus] —**mu'cin·ous** adj.

muck (muk) n. 1 Moist manure containing decomposed vegetable matter. 2 A nasty mess; filth. 3 Vegetable mold combined with earth. — v.t. 1 To fertilize with manure. 2 *Colloq.* To make dirty; pollute. 3 To remove muck from. [ME *muk* < Scand. Cf. ON *myki* dung, *moka* shovel manure.]

muck·rake (muk'rāk') v.i. ·raked, ·rak·ing To search for or expose real or alleged corruption on the part of political officials, businessmen, etc. [Back formation < MUCKRAKER, used in 1906 by President Theodore Roosevelt, in allusion to the "man with the muckrake" in Bunyan's *Pilgrim's Progress*] —**muck'rak'er** n. — **muck'rak'ing** n.

muck rake A rake used in collecting muck or dung.

muck·worm (muk'wûrm') n. 1 The larva of a beetle *(Ligyrus gibbosus)* common in dung heaps. 2 *Slang* A miser.

muck·y (muk'ē) adj. **muck·i·er, muck·i·est** Foul; nasty. —**muck'i·ly** adv. —**muck'i·ness** n.

muco- *combining form* Mucus; mucus and: *mucopurulent*: also, before vowels, *muc-*. Also **muci-**. [< L *mucus* mucus]

mu·coid (myo͞o'koid) adj. Like mucus. —n. *Biochem.* A compound glycoprotein similar to mucin, found in connective tissue, in cysts, in the vitreous humor, etc. [< MUC- + -OID]

mu·co·pro·te·in (myo͞o'kō·prō'tē·in, -tēn) n. *Biochem.* A glycoprotein combining a protein with a carbohydrate group.

mu·co·pu·ru·lent (myo͞o'kō·pyo͞or'ə·lənt, -yə-lənt) adj. Relating to or consisting of both mucus and purulent matter.

Mu·co·ra·les (myo͞o'kō·rā'lēz) n. pl. An order of fungi (class *Phycomycetes*) which includes several mold species, as the common bread mold. [< NL]

mu·co·sa (myo͞o·kō'sə) n. pl. ·sae (-sē) *Anat.* A mucous membrane. [< NL, fem. of L *mucosus* mucous] —**mu·co'sal** adj.

mu·cous (myo͞o'kəs) adj. 1 Secreting mucus. 2 Pertaining to or resembling mucus. Also **mu'cose** (-kōs). [< L *mucosus* slimy < *mucus*] — **mu·cos'i·ty** (-kos'ə·tē) n.

mucous membrane *Anat.* A membrane secreting or producing mucus, that lines passages communicating with the exterior, as the alimentary canal, air passages, etc.

mu·cro (myo͞o'krō) n. pl. **mu·cro·nes** (myo͞o·krō'nēz) *Biol.* A small, sharp process or part, as the point of a leaf; a spine. [< NL < L, point of a sword]

mu·cro·nate (myo͞o'krə·nāt) adj. *Biol.* Having a short, straight point, as a leaf, feather, etc.: also **mu'cro·nat·ed**. [< L *mucronatus* < *mucro* point of a sword]

mu·cus (myo͞o'kəs) n. 1 *Biol.* A viscid animal substance, as that secreted by the mucous membranes. 2 *Bot.* A gummy substance in plants. [< L]

mud (mud) n. 1 Wet and sticky earth; mire. 2 *Colloq.* Slander; abuse; detraction of character: to sling *mud* at someone. —v.t. **mud·ded, mud·ding** To soil or cover with mud. [? < MLG *mudde*]

mud boat 1 A scow or barge used in dredging: also **mud scow**. 2 A kind of low sledge with wide runners used for hauling logs over swampy ground.

mud·cap (mud'kap') v.t. **·capped, ·cap·ping** 1 To cap with mud. 2 To cover (a charge of high explosive) with mud before detonating it above an exposed mass of rock. —**mud'cap'ping** n.

mud·cat (mud'kat') n. A large catfish of the Mississippi valley.

mud dauber 1 Any· of various wasps (family *Sphecidae*) that build mud cells in which their larvae develop. For illustration see INSECTS (beneficial). 2 A swallow that builds a nest of mud.

mud·dle (mud'l) v. **·dled, ·dling** v.t. 1 To mix in confusion; jumble. 2 To confuse mentally; bewilder. 3 To make muddy or turbid; roil. 4 To stir or mix, as a drink. —v.i. 5 To act in a confused or ineffective manner. —**to muddle through**

Brit. To achieve one's object despite one's own confusion and mistakes; succeed despite oneself. —n. 1 A muddy or dirty condition. 2 A mixed or confused condition, as of the mind; a mess. [< MUD + freq. suffix]

mud drum An enclosed container placed at the bottom of any manufacturing or power apparatus, as a boiler, for the purpose of collecting insoluble waste matter, sludge, etc.

mud·dy (mud'ē) adj. **·di·er, ·di·est** 1 Bespattered with mud; turbid. 2 Mentally confused. 3 Consisting of mud; earthy; gross; impure. 4 Dull; cloudy: a *muddy* complexion, *muddy* weather. See synonyms under FOUL, THICK. —v.t. & v.i. **·died, ·dy·ing** To become or cause to become muddy. —**mud'di·ly** adv. —**mud'di·ness** n.

mud eel An eel-shaped amphibian having very small forelegs and no hind legs, that buries itself in the mud; especially, *Siren lacertina* of the swamps of the southern United States: also called *congo* and *siren*.

mud·fish (mud'fish') n. pl. **·fish** or **·fish·es** Any of various fishes that inhabit stagnant or muddy water, as the bowfin, killifish, etc.

mud flat A low-lying strip of ground covered with mud, especially one between high and low tide.

mud·guard (mud'gärd') n. A guard over the wheel of a vehicle to protect from splashing mud.

mud hen 1 The American coot *(Fulica americana)*. 2 The Florida gallinule *(Gallenula chloropus)*. 3 The clapper rail. See under RAIL[2].

mud·pot (mud'pot') n. A geyser which ejects mud. Also **mud geyser**.

mud·pup·py (mud'·pup'ē) n. pl. **·pies** 1 The hellbender. 2 A tailed amphibian with bushy, persistent, external gills, especially *Necturus maculosus*, found in the large lakes of North America.

MUDPUPPY

mud·sling·ing (mud'sling'ing) n. The practice of casting malicious slurs at an opponent, especially in a political campaign. —**mud'sling'er** n.

mud·stone (mud'stōn') n. A gray, sandy shale that readily decomposes into mud.

mud·suck·er (mud'suk'ər) n. A California fish related to the goby *(Gillichthys mirabilis)*, much used as bait.

mud turtle Any of various turtles inhabiting muddy rivers in different parts of the world, especially the small common variety of the United States (genus *Kinosternon*).

mu·ez·zin (myo͞o·ez'in) n. In Moslem countries, a crier from a minaret or other part of the mosque who calls the faithful to prayer. Also **mu·ed'din** (-ed'in). [< Arabic *mu'adhdhin* < *adhana* call]

muff[1] (muf) v.t. & v.i. 1 To perform (some act) clumsily; blunder. 2 In baseball, to fail to hold (the ball) in attempting a catch. —n. 1 A bungling action; in baseball, etc., a failure to catch the ball. 2 A bungler. 3 A stupid fellow; dolt. [Origin unknown]

muff[2] (muf) n. A covering of fur or cloth, usually cylindrical, into which the hands are thrust from opposite ends to keep them warm. [< Du. *mof* < F *moufle*]

muf·fin (muf'in) n. A light, quick bread, baked in small cup-shaped tins, and usually eaten hot with butter; also, a small, flat yeast bread: also called *English muffin*. [Origin uncertain. Cf. OF *moufflet* soft (bread).]

muf·fin·eer (muf'in·ir') 1 A metal cruet with a perforated top for sprinkling salt or sugar on muffins. 2 A covered dish to keep muffins, etc., hot.

muffin stand A small tiered stand used in tea service for holding and passing cakes, sandwiches, etc.

muf·fle (muf'əl) v.t. **·fled, ·fling** 1 To wrap up in a blanket, scarf, etc., as for warmth or concealment. 2 To prevent from seeing, hearing, or speaking by wrapping the head. 3 To deaden the sound of by or as by wrapping:

to *muffle* a cry. 4 To deaden (a sound). —n. 1 Something used for muffling. 2 A clay oven for firing pottery without direct exposure to flame. 3 The naked upper lip and nose of ruminants and certain other mammals. [< OF *moufle* heavy leather or fur mitten]

muf·fler (muf'lər) n. 1 Anything used for wrapping up or muffling; specifically, a scarf worn about the neck; also, a veil or scarf worn by women. 2 A device to reduce noise, as from the exhaust of an internal-combustion engine. 3 A mitten. [< MUFFLE]

muf·ti[1] (muf'tē) n. In Moslem countries, an expounder of religious law. [< Arabic *āftā* expound the law]

muf·ti[2] (muf'tē) n. Civilian dress; plain clothes, especially when worn by one who normally wears a uniform. [< MUFTI[1]; prob. from the fact that a mufti is a civil official]

mug[1] (mug) n. 1 A drinking cup, usually cylindrical, with a handle and no lip. 2 That which is contained in a mug. [Cf. Sw. *mugg*, Norw. *mugga*]

mug[2] (mug) *Slang* n. 1 The human face or mouth. 2 A grimace. 3 A photograph of the face of a suspect: also **mug shot**. 4 A criminal. —v. **mugged, mug·ging** v.t. 1 To photograph (someone), especially for official purposes. 2 To assault, usually with the intent to rob. —v.i. 3 To make faces; grimace. [< MUG[1]; prob. from the fact that drinking mugs were often shaped to resemble a face] —**mug'ger** n.

mug·ger (mug'ər) n. A crocodile *(Crocodilus palustris)* of India and the East Indies, with a broad snout: it grows to a length of about 12 feet. Also **mug'gar, mug'gur**. [< Hind. *magar* < Skt. *makara* sea monster]

mug·ging (mug'ing) n. *Slang* Assault, often with the intention of robbery, usually by attacking the victim from behind and locking an arm around his throat. [< MUG[2]]

mug·gins (mug'inz) n. 1 One of several card games in which exposed cards are matched or suits are built. 2 A variant in the game of dominoes. 3 *Brit. Slang* A foolish person. [Prob. < *Muggins*, a surname used in arbitrary allusion to *mug* (slang) a card-sharper's dupe]

mug·gy (mug'ē) adj. **·gi·er, ·gi·est** Warm, moist, and close; sultry. [< dial. E *mug* drizzle, prob. < ON *mugga* drizzling mist] —**mug'gi·ness** n.

mug·wort (mug'wûrt') n. An aromatic bitter herb *(Artemisia vulgaris)* of the composite family, sometimes used in folk medicine as a diaphoretic and emmenagog.

mug·wump (mug'wump) n. *U.S.* 1 A Republican who bolted the party candidate, James G. Blaine, in the presidential election of 1884. 2 Anyone who claims the right of independent action, especially in politics; an independent. [< Algonquian *mugquomp* great man, chief] —**mug'wump·er·y, mug'wump·ism** n.

muh·ly grass (myo͞o'lē) Any of a genus *(Muhlenbergia)* of mostly perennial, wiry grasses growing in the SW United States and Mexico, as the **ring muhly** *(M. torreyi)*, and **spike muhly** *(M. wrighti)*, valued as forage plants for livestock. [after Dr. G. H. E. *Muhlenberg*, 1753–1815, American botanist]

mu·i·ra·pu·a·ma (mo͞o·ē'rä·po͞o·ä'mä) n. The dried stems and roots of a Brazilian plant *(Liriosma ovata)*, reputed to have properties as a nerve stimulant and aphrodisiac. [< Pg. <Tupian]

muk·luk (muk'luk) n. 1 An Alaskan Eskimo boot of seal or other animal skin, made so that the fur is inside. 2 pl. Sport or lounging shoes of the soft moccasin type. [< Alaskan Eskimo *makliak, muklok* large seal]

mu·lat·to (mə·lat'ō, myo͞o-, -lä'tō) n. pl. **·toes** A person having one white and one Negro parent; loosely, anyone having white and Negro blood. — adj. 1 Of or pertaining to a person of such descent. 2 Of a light-brown color. [< Sp. *mulato* of mixed breed < *mulo* mule < L *mulus*]

mul·ber·ry (mul'ber'ē, -bər·ē) n. pl. **·ries** 1 The edible, berrylike fruit of a tree (genus *Morus*) whose leaves are valued for silkworm culture, especially the white mulberry *(M. alba)*. 2 A deep purplish-red, the color of a mulberry. [ME *mulberie*, dissimilated var. of *murberie*, OE *morberie* <L *morum* mulberry + OE *berie* a berry]

mulberry body   The morula.

mulch (mulch) *n.* Any loose material, as straw, placed about the stalks of plants to protect their roots. —*v.t.* To cover with mulch. [ME *molsh.* Cf. dial. G *molsch* soft, decaying.]

mulct (mulkt) *v.t.* **1** To punish (a person) by a fine or penalty. **2** To deprive of something fraudulently or deceitfully; cheat. —*n.* A fine, or similar penalty. [<L *mulctare* <*mulcta, multa* a fine]

mule[1] (myōol) *n.* **1** A hybrid between the ass and horse, especially between a jackass and a mare, as distinguished from a hinny. **2** Any hybrid or cross, especially one that is sterile. **3** A spinning machine which draws, stretches, and twists at one operation: also called *spinning mule, jenny, spinning jenny*: also **mule′jen′ny** (-jen′ē). **4** A person having the stubborn qualities of a mule. **5** A small electric engine or tractor for towing canal boats. [<F <L *mulus*]

mule[2] (myōol) *n.* A backless lounging slipper. [<MF <L *mulleus* red slipper]

mule deer   The black–tailed deer (genus *Odocoileus*), of the western United States, having long ears.

mule–driv·er (myōol′drī′vər) *n.* One who drives mules.

mu·le·teer (myōo′lə·tir′) *n.* A mule–driver. [<F *muletier* <*mulet* mule]

mule train   A train of mules carrying packs; also, a train of heavy freight wagons drawn by mules.

mu·ley (myōo′lē, mōol′ē, mōo′lē) *adj.* Hornless: said of cattle. —*n.* A hornless cow. Also spelled **mooley, mulley.** [<Irish *maol, moile* hornless, dismantled]

mu·li·eb·ri·ty (myōo′lē·eb′rə·tē) *n.* The state of being a woman; womanliness. [<LL *muliebris* womanly <*mulier* woman]

mul·ish (myōo′lish) *adj.* Resembling a mule; stubborn. See synonyms under OBSTINATE. — **mul′ish·ly** *adv.* — **mul′ish·ness** *n.*

mull[1] (mul) *v.t.* To heat and spice, as wine or beer. [<MULSE]

mull[2] (mul) *v.t.* To ponder; cogitate: usually with *over.* [<obs. *mull* grind, OE *myl* dust]

mull[3] (mul) *n.* **1** A thin, soft, cotton, rayon, or silk dress goods. **2** A variety of soft, thin muslin used as a base for medicated ointments, as mulla. [Short for *mulmull* <Hind. *malmal*]

mull[4] (mul) *n.* A horn snuffbox. [Var. of *mill* (in a Scottish use); orig., a snuffbox in which tobacco could be ground to a powder by a mechanism]

mul·la (mul′ə) *n.* *Med.* An ointment having a base of lard and salt, spread on a piece of mull.

mul·len (mul′ən) *n.* **1** A tall, stout, woolly herb (*Verbascum thapsus*) of the figwort family, the **great mullen.** **2** Any plant of the same genus, as the **moth mullen** (*V. blattaria*). Also **mul′lein.** [<AF *moleine* <OF *mol* soft <L *mollis*]

mull·er (mul′ər) *n.* **1** A pestlelike implement with which to mix paints. **2** A mechanical pulverizer or grinder. [<obs. *mull* pulverize, OE *myl* dust]

mul·let[1] (mul′it) *n. pl.* **·lets** or **·let** **1** A food fish (family *Mugilidae*), usually greenish or copper–colored, with silvery sides, found on warm coasts. *Mugil cephalus* is the **striped mullet** of both coasts of the Atlantic. **2** A food fish (family *Mullidae*): often called *surmullet. Mullus barbatus* is the highly esteemed European **red mullet.** [<OF *mulet* <L *mullus* red mullet]

mul·let[2] (mul′it) *n. Her.* A star of five or more points. [<OF *molette* rowel]

mul·let–head (mul′it·hed′) *n.* A fresh–water fish having a flat head.

mul·ley (mōol′ē, mōo′lē) See MULEY.

mul·li·gan (mul′i·gən) *n. Slang* **1** A stew, originally made by tramps, composed of odds and ends of food: also **mulligan stew.** **2** In golf, an extra shot, especially a tee shot, after an inept first shot. [<*Mulligan*, Irish surname]

mul·li·ga·taw·ny (mul′i·gə·tô′nē) *n.* A strongly flavored soup of meat and curry. [<Tamil *milagu–tannir* pepper water]

mul·li·grubs (mul′ə·grubz) *n. Slang* An acute colicky pain; colic; hence, the blues. [A gro-

tesque arbitrary formation]

Mul·lin·gar (mul′in·gär′) The county town of Westmeath, Ireland.

mul·lion (mul′yən) *n. Archit.* A vertical dividing piece between window lights or panels. —*v.t.* To furnish with or divide by means of mullions. [Prob. metathetic var. of earlier *monial* <OF *moinel, monial;* ult. origin unknown] — **mul′lioned** *adj.*

mul·lock (mul′ək) *n.* An accumulation of waste rock about a mine; refuse earth: a waste dump. [< obs. *mull* dust + -OCK] — **mul′lock·y** *adj.*

MULLIONS

mulse (muls) *n.* Wine heated and sweetened. [<L *mulsum*, pp. of *mulcere* sweeten]

mul·ti·cip·i·tal (mul′ti·sip′ə·təl) *adj. Bot.* Many–headed: said of plants with many stems from one root. [<MULTI- + L *caput* head]

mul·ti·col·ored (mul′ti·kul′ərd) *adj.* Exhibiting or made up of many colors.

mul·ti·far·i·ous (mul′tə·fār′ē·əs) *adj.* Having great diversity or variety. [<L *multifarius*] — **mul′ti·far′i·ous·ly** *adv.* — **mul′ti·far′i·ous·ness** *n.*

mul·ti·fid (mul′tə·fid) *adj. Bot.* Cut into many lobes or segments, as a leaf. Also **mul·tif·i·dous** (mul·tif′ə·dəs). [<MULTI- + -FID]

mul·ti·foil (mul′tə·foil) *n. Geom.* A plane figure made of the congruent arcs of circles which are symmetrically arranged along the sides of a regular polygon.

mul·ti·fold (mul′tə·fōld) *adj.* Many times doubled; manifold.

mul·ti·form (mul′tə·fôrm) *adj.* Having many forms, shapes, or appearances. See synonyms under COMPLEX. [<L *multiformis*] — **mul′ti·form′i·ty** *n.*

mul·ti·lat·er·al (mul′ti·lat′ər·əl) *adj.* **1** Having many sides. **2** *Govt.* Involving more than two nations: a *multilateral* trade agreement.

mul·ti·me·di·a (mul′ti·mē′dē·ə) *adj.* Relating to or using two or more media, especially a combination apprehended by different senses, as sight and hearing.

mul·ti·mil·lion·aire (mul′ti·mil′yən·âr′) *n.* A person having a fortune of several or many millions of dollars, pounds, francs, etc.

mul·ti·na·tion·al corporation   a business enterprise operating in several nations, esp. involved in world market.

mul·ti·no·mi·al (mul′ti·nō′mē·əl) *adj.* Polynomial. [<MULTI- + (BI)NOMIAL]

mul·tip·a·ra (mul·tip′ə·rə) *n. pl.* **·rae** (-rē) A woman who has borne more than one child, or who is parturient the second time. [<NL <L *multiparus*]

mul·tip·a·rous (mul·tip′ə·rəs) *adj.* **1** Giving birth to many at one time. **2** Having borne more than one child. [<MULTI- + -PAROUS]

mul·ti·pede (mul′tə·pēd) *n.* A many–footed animal or insect. —*adj.* Having many feet. Also **mul′ti·ped** (-ped).

mul·ti·phase (mul′tə·fāz) *adj.* Polyphase.

mul·ti·plane (mul′tə·plān) *n. Aeron.* An airplane with two or more supporting surfaces, one above another.

mul·ti·ple (mul′tə·pəl) *adj.* **1** Containing or consisting of more than one; repeated more than once; manifold. **2** *Electr.* Having two or more conductors or pieces of apparatus, such as lamps, connected in parallel: a *multiple* circuit. —*n. Math.* The product of a given number and its factor. — **common multiple** Any number which is exactly divisible by two or more numbers, not including itself. — **lowest common multiple** The smallest number divisible by each of two or more numbers: 12 is the *least common multiple* of 2, 3, 4, and 6: often abbr. *L.C.M.* Also **least common multiple.** [<F <L *multiplex*]

multiple allele *Genetics* One of three or more alleles, only two of which may pass from the parents to a normal diploid offspring.

multiple factors *Genetics* Two or more distinct genes which are believed to act as a unit or with cumulative effect in the transmission of certain plant and animal characteristics,

as size, pigmentation, color of eyes, etc.

multiple fruit *Bot.* A fruit consisting of numerous smaller fruits, each developed from a single flower, as the pineapple: also called *collective fruit.*

multiple myeloma *Pathol.* A malignant tumor of the bone marrow occurring at numerous sites.

multiple neuritis *Pathol.* Neuritis involving several nerves simultaneously.

multiple sclerosis *Pathol.* Sclerosis occurring in patches in the brain or spinal cord or both, and characterized by tremors, failure of coordination, and various nervous and mental symptoms.

multiple star *Astron.* A system of three or more stars revolving around a common gravitational center.

mul·ti·plet (mul′tə·plit) *n. Physics* Two or more spectral lines very close together in an atomic spectrum and associated with different energy characteristics of the atom. [<MULTIPLE]

mul·ti·plex (mul′tə·pleks) *adj.* **1** Multiple; manifold. **2** *Telecom.* Designating a system for the simultaneous transmission of two or more messages in either or both directions over the same wire, as in telegraphy or telephony. **3** *Phot.* Designating a method based upon the stereoscopic principle: three cameras are used, together with auxiliary equipment designed to facilitate the construction of accurate maps. —*v.t. & v.i. Telecom.* To send (two or more messages) at the same time over the same wire. [<L <*multus* much + stem of *plicare* fold]

mul·ti·pli·cand (mul′tə·plə·kand′) *n.* A number multiplied, or to be multiplied, by another. [<L *multiplicandus* to be multiplied, gerundive of *multiplicare.* See MULTIPLY.]

mul·ti·pli·cate (mul′tə·plə·kāt) *adj.* Consisting of or being many or more than one. [<L *multiplicatus*, pp. of *multiplicare* multiply]

mul·ti·pli·ca·tion (mul′tə·plə·kā′shən) *n.* **1** The process of multiplying. **2** The process of finding the sum (the *product*) of a number (the *multiplicand*) repeated a given number of times (the *multiplier*). Opposed to *division.* [<OF <L *multiplicatio, -onis*]

mul·ti·pli·ca·tive (mul′tə·plə·kā′tiv) *adj.* Tending to multiply; indicating multiplication. — **mul′ti·pli·ca′tive·ly** *adv.*

mul·ti·plic·i·ty (mul′tə·plis′ə·tē) *n.* The condition of being manifold or various; hence, a large number. [<LL *multiplicitas, -tatis* <L *multiplex*]

mul·ti·pli·er (mul′tə·plī′ər) *n.* **1** One who or that which multiplies or increases in quantity, or causes something else to multiply or increase. **2** *Math.* The number by which a quantity is multiplied. **3** *Physics* An instrument or mechanical device for increasing or intensifying an effect. **4** *Electr.* An open spiral coil in a wireless telegraph receiver which has the effect of exalting the potential oscillations.

mul·ti·ply (mul′tə·plī) *v.* **·plied, ·ply·ing** *v.t.* **1** To increase the quantity, amount, or degree of; make more numerous. **2** *Math.* To perform the operation of multiplication upon. —*v.i.* **3** To become more in number, amount, or degree; increase. **4** *Math.* To perform the operation of multiplication. See synonyms under PROPAGATE. —*adv.* So as to be numerous; in many ways. [<OF *multiplier* <*multiplicare* <*multiplex.* See MULTIPLEX.] — **mul′ti·pli′a·ble** *adj.*

mul·ti·pro·pel·lant (mul′ti·prə·pel′ənt) *n.* A rocket propellant consisting of two or more chemicals separately fed into the combustion chamber. —*adj.* Of or pertaining to such a propellant.

mul·ti·pur·pose (mul′ti·pûr′pəs) *adj.* Adapted to more than one use or type of service.

mul·ti·range (mul′tə·rānj) *adj.* Having a wide range of operations or performance, as certain precision instruments.

mul·ti·sec·tion (mul′ti·sek′shən) *adj.* Having or occupying more than one section.

mul·ti·stage (mul′tə·stāj) *adj.* **1** Having or characterized by a number of definite stages in the completion of a process or action. **2** Having several sections, each of which fulfils a given task before burnout: said especially of a rocket or ballistic missile.

mul·ti·tude (mul′tə·tōōd, -tyōōd) *n.* **1** The state of being many or numerous. **2** A large gathering; concourse. **3** A large number of things. See synonyms under ARMY, ASSEMBLY, COMPANY, THRONG. — **the multitude** The common people. [<OF <L *multitudo* <*multus* much, many]

mul·ti·tu·di·nous (mul'tə·tŏŏ'də·nəs, -tyŏŏ'-) *adj.* Consisting of a vast number. See synonyms under MANY. [<L *multitudo, -inis* a crowd + -OUS] — **mul'ti·tu'di·nous·ly** *adv.* — **mul'ti·tu'di·nous·ness** *n.*

mul·ti·va·lent (mul'ti·vā'lənt) *adj. Chem.* Having three or more valences. — **mul'ti·va'lence** *n.*

mul·ti·valve (mul'tə·valv) *n.* A shell with many valves. — *adj.* Having many valves. — **mul'·ti·val'vu·lar** (-val'vyə·lər) *adj.*

mul·ti·verse (mul'tə·vûrs) *n. Philos.* The plurality of worlds as conceived in or projected by the mind: contrasted with *universe*. [<MULTI- + (UNI)VERSE]

mul·ti·ver·si·ty (mul'ti·vûr'sə·tē) *n. pl.* ·ties A very large university with a student enrollment of many thousands, offering instruction and graduate study in many fields and often on a number of campuses. [< MULTI- + (UNI)VERSITY]

mul·tiv·o·cal (mul·tiv'ə·kəl) *adj.* Having various meanings. — *n.* A word that has more than one signification. [<MULTI- + VOCAL]

mul·ti·vol·tine (mul'ti·vol'tin, -tēn) *adj. Entomol.* Having many broods of offspring in a year, as certain insects. [<MULTI- + Ital. *volta* turn]

mul·toc·u·lar (mul·tok'yə·lər) *adj.* 1 Having two or more eyes. 2 Having eyes divisible, like those of a fly, into facets. [<MULT(I)- + OCULAR]

mul·ture (mul'chər) *n.* 1 A grinding of grain. 2 The grain ground or the toll paid for the grinding. [<OF *moulture* <Med. L *molitura* <L *molere* grind]

mum[1] (mum) *v.i.* **mummed, mum·ming** *Obs.* To be silent. —*adj.* Silent; saying nothing. —*n.* Silence: *Mum's* the word. —*interj.* Hush! Be quiet! [Imit.]

mum[2] (mum) *v.i.* **mummed, mum·ming** To play or act in a mask, as at Christmas; be a mummer. Also **mumm.** [<MUM[1]. Cf. MDu. *mommen* mask, OF *momer* act in a dumb show.]

mum[3] (mum) *n.* A strong sweet beer, first brewed in Germany by Christian Mumme, 1492.

mum[4] (mum) Corruption of MADAM, MA'AM.

mum·ble (mum'bəl) *v.t.* & *v.i.* **·bled, ·bling** 1 To speak or utter in low, indistinct tones; mutter. 2 *Rare* To chew slowly and ineffectively, as with toothless gums. —*n.* A low, mumbling speech; mutter. [ME *momelen,* freq. of obs. *mum* make inarticulate sounds. Cf. G *mummeln.*] — **mum'bler** *n.* — **mum'bling** *adj.* — **mum'bling·ly** *adv.*

mum·ble-the-peg (mum'bəl·thə·peg') *n.* A boy's game played with a jackknife, which is tossed and flipped in various ways so as to stick into the ground: so called because the player who failed was originally required to draw a peg out of the ground with his teeth. Also **mum'ble-peg',** **mum·ble·ty-peg** (mum'bəl·tē·peg'). [<MUMBLE, *v.* (def. 2) + PEG]

mum·bo jum·bo (mum'bō jum'bō) 1 Any object of superstitious homage; a fetish. 2 Incantation. [<MUMBO JUMBO]

mu·mes·on (myŏŏ'mes'on, -mē'son) *n. Physics.* A muon. [<MU + MESON]

mum·mer (mum'ər) *n.* 1 One who acts or makes sport in a mask. 2 An actor.

mum·mer·y (mum'ər·ē) *n. pl.* ·mer·ies 1 A masked performance. 2 Hypocritical parade of ritual. [<MF *mommerie* dumb show]

mum·mi·fy (mum'ə·fī) *v.* **·fied, ·fy·ing** *v.t.* To make a mummy of; preserve by drying. —*v.i.* To dry up; shrivel. Also **mummy.** [<F *momifier*] — **mum'mi·fi·ca'tion** *n.*

mum·my (mum'ē) *n. pl.* ·mies 1 A body embalmed in the ancient Egyptian manner; also, any dead body which is very well preserved. 2 A person or thing that is dried up and withered. 3 *Obs.* The dried flesh of mummies; dead meat. — *v.t.* & *v.i.* **·mied, ·my·ing** To mummify. [<F *momie* <Med. L *mumia* <Arabic *mūmiyā* <Persian *mūm* wax] — **mum'mi·form** *adj.*

mummy cloth 1 The fabric in which a mummy is enwrapped. 2 A crêpelike fabric of cotton, silk, rayon, or wool.

mump·ish (mum'pish) *adj.* Sullen; sulky; mo-

rose; petulant. [<obs. *mump* mutter, ? <Du. *mompelen* mumble]

mumps (mumps) *n. pl.* (construed as singular) *Pathol.* An acute, contagious, febrile disease of viral origin, characterized by inflammation and swelling of the facial glands, and occasionally of the ovaries and testicles: also called *parotitis.* [Pl. of obs. *mump* grimace]

munch (munch) *v.t.* & *v.i.* To chew steadily and noisily. [ME *monchen, manchen.* Prob. ult. imit.] — **munch'er** *n.*

mun·dane (mun'dān, mun·dān') *adj.* Pertaining to the world; worldly. [<F *mondain* <L *mundanus* <*mundus* world] — **mun'dane·ly** *adv.* — **mun'dane·ness** *n.*

mun·go (mung'gō) *n.* The waste produced from hard-spun or felted cloth. Compare SHODDY. [? <*mung,* var. of obs. *mong* mixture]

mun·goose (mung'gōōs) See MONGOOSE.

mu·nic·i·pal (myŏŏ·nis'ə·pəl) *adj.* 1 Pertaining to a town or city or its local government; also, having local self-government. 2 Pertaining to the internal government of a state or nation. [<L *municipalis* <*municipium* town possessing right of self-government <*municeps* free citizens <*munia* official duties + *capere* take] — **mu·nic'i·pal·ly** *adv.*

municipal borough See under BOROUGH.

municipal corporation An incorporated town.

mu·nic·i·pal·ism (myŏŏ·nis'ə·pəl·iz'əm) *n.* Municipal government as opposed to central government; also, the theory of this.—**mu·nic'i·pal·ist** *n.*

mu·nic·i·pal·i·ty (myŏŏ·nis'ə·pal'ə·tē) *n. pl.* ·ties 1 An incorporated borough, town, or city. 2 In Cuba and some other Latin-American countries, an administrative area somewhat like a county. [<F *municipalité*]

mu·nic·i·pal·ize (myŏŏ·nis'ə·pəl·īz) *v.t.* **·ized, ·iz·ing** 1 To place within municipal authority or transfer to municipal ownership. 2 To make a municipality of. — **mu·nic'i·pal'i·za'tion** *n.*

municipal ownership Ownership by a municipality: said especially of public services, as electricity, waterworks, etc.

mu·nif·i·cent (myŏŏ·nif'ə·sənt) *adj.* Extraordinarily generous or bountiful; liberal. See synonyms under GENEROUS. [<L *munificens, -entis* <*munificus* <*munus* gift + *facere* make] — **mu·nif'i·cence, mu·nif'i·cen·cy** *n.* —**mu·nif'i·cent·ly** *adv.*

mu·ni·ment (myŏŏ'nə·mənt) *n.* 1 That which supports or defends. 2 *Law* Any deed, record, or instrument by which title to property may be defended or evidenced: usually in the plural. 3 Any means of defending. [<OF <L *munimentum* fortification, support <*munire* fortify]

mu·ni·tion (myŏŏ·nish'ən) *n.* 1 Ammunition and all necessary war materiel: usually in the plural. 2 The requisites for any undertaking. 3 *Obs.* A fort; stronghold. —*v.t.* To furnish with munitions. [<F <L *munitio, -onis* <*munire* fortify]

mun·nion (mun'yən) *n.* A mullion.

Mun·sell color system (mun·sel') A system for the classification and identification of colors by means of reference to the three standard factors of hue, chroma (saturation), and value (lightness). [after Albert H. *Munsell,* 1858–1918, U.S. artist]

munt·jac (munt'jak) *n.* Any of various small, short-legged deer (genus *Muntiacus*) of east Asia, the males having short, two-pronged horns on long pedicles; especially, *M. muntjak* of Java. Also **munt'iak.** [<Javanese *měnjaṅan*]

mu·on (myŏŏ'on) *n. Physics* An unstable subatomic particle bearing an electric charge and having a mass approximately 210 times that of an electron.

Muo·nio (mwô'nyô) A river rising in Lapland near the meeting point of the Norwegian, Swedish, and Finnish borders and flowing 180 miles SE and south along the Swedish-Finnish border, to its confluence with the Torne.

mu·rae·na (myŏŏ·rē'nə) *n.* An eel; moray. [<L *muraena,* a fish <Gk. *myraina* sea eel, lamprey]

mu·ral (myŏŏr'əl) *adj.* 1 Pertaining to or supported by a wall. 2 Resembling a wall. —*n.* A

painting or decoration on a wall. [<L *muralis* <*murus* wall]

mu·ral·ist (myŏŏr'əl·ist) *n.* A painter of murals.

mur·der (mûr'dər) *v.t.* 1 To kill (a human being) with premeditated malice. 2 To kill in a barbarous or inhuman manner; slaughter. 3 To spoil by bad performance, etc.; mangle; butcher. See synonyms under KILL. —*n.* The unlawful and intentional killing of one human being by another. —**murder will out** Murder cannot be concealed. [Fusion of OE *morthor* + OF *murdre,* both <Gmc.] —**mur'der·er** *n.* —**mur'der·ess** *n. fem.*

mur·der·ous (mûr'dər·əs) *adj.* 1 Pertaining to murder; destructive. 2 Given to murder. 3 Characterized by murder. See synonyms under SANGUINARY. —**mur'der·ous·ly** *adv.* —**mur'·der·ous·ness** *n.*

mure (myŏŏr) *v.t.* **mured, mur·ing** To immure; confine. —*n. Obs.* A wall. [<F *murer,* ult. <L *murus* wall]

mu·rex (myŏŏr'eks) *n. pl.* **mu·ri·ces** (myŏŏr'ə·sēz) or **·rex·es** A rough-shelled marine gastropod (genus *Murex*) of warm seas, especially *M. trunculus* and *M. brandaris,* from whose large mucus gland a purple dye was obtained in ancient times. [<L, purple fish]

mu·rex·ide (myŏŏ·rek'sīd) *n. Chem.* The ammonium hydrogen salt, $C_8H_8O_6N_6 \cdot H_2O$, of purpuric acid: formerly used to produce pink, purple, or red dyes, now displaced by aniline colors. [<MUREX + -IDE]

mu·ri·at·ed (myŏŏr'ē·ā'tid) *adj.* 1 Salted; pickled. 2 *Archaic* Treated with or containing a chloride or hydrochloric acid.

mu·ri·at·ic (myŏŏr'ē·at'ik) *adj.* Hydrochloric. [<L *muriaticus* pickled <*muria* brine]

mu·ri·cate (myŏŏr'ə·kit) *adj. Biol.* Rough, with short, hard, tubercular excrescences. [<L *muricatus* murex-shaped, pointed <*murex*]

mu·ri·form (myŏŏr'ə·fôrm) *adj. Bot.* Regularly arranged like bricks in a wall: said of cells in plants. Also **mu'rine** (-ēn). [<L *murus* wall + -FORM]

Mu·ril·lo (myŏŏ·ril'ō, *Sp.* mŏŏ·rē'lyō), **Bartolomé Esteban,** 1618–82, Spanish painter.

mu·rine (myŏŏr'īn, -in) *adj.* Of or pertaining to a family (*Muridae*) or a subfamily (*Murinae*) of rodents, embracing true mice and rats. —*n.* One of the *Murinae* or *Muridae.* [<L *murinus* <*mus, muris* a mouse]

murk (mûrk) *adj.* Murky; dark. —*n.* Darkness; gloom. Also spelled **mirk.** [<ON *myrkr* darkness] —**murk'ly** *adv.*

murk·y (mûr'kē) *adj.* **murk·i·er, murk·i·est** Darkened, thickened, or obscured; hazy; gloomy; obscure: also spelled *mirky.* See synonyms under DARK. — **murk'i·ly** *adv.* — **murk'i·ness** *n.*

Mur·mansk (mŏŏr·mänsk') A port of the western Murman Coast; world's largest city north of the Arctic Circle.

mur·mur (mûr'mər) *n.* 1 A low sound continually repeated. 2 A complaint uttered in a half-articulate voice. 3 An abnormal, rasping sound heard in certain morbid conditions: a *heart* murmur. —*v.i.* 1 To make a murmur. 2 To complain in a low tone; mutter. —*v.t.* 3 To utter in a low tone. See synonyms under BABBLE, COMPLAIN. [<OF <L] —**mur'mur·er** *n.* —**mur'mur·ing** *adj.* —**mur'mur·ing·ly** *adv.*

mur·mur·ous (mûr'mər·əs) *adj.* Characterized or accompanied by murmurs. —**mur'mur·ous·ly** *adv.* —**mur'mur·ous·ness** *n.*

mur·rain (mûr'in) *n.* 1 A malignant contagious fever affecting domestic animals, as anthrax. 2 Any plague or pestilence. See RINDERPEST. —*adj.* Affected with murrain. [<OF *morine* <L *mori* die]

Murray River The principal river of Australia, forming part of the boundary between Victoria and New South Wales and flowing 1,600 miles to the Indian Ocean.

murre (mûr) *n. pl.* **murres** or **murre** 1 The foolish guillemot. 2 The razor-billed auk. Also **murr.** [Origin uncertain]

murre·let (mûr'lit) *n.* Any of certain small sea birds (family *Alcidae*) of the islands of the North Pacific. [Dim. of MURRE]

mur·rey (mûr'ē) *adj.* Of a purplish-red or mulberry color. —*n.* 1 *Her.* The tincture sanguine. 2 A dark purplish red. [<OF *moree* <L *mo-*

rum mulberry]

murrine glass Glassware having a transparent ground with embedded flowers, ribbons, etc., of colored glass.

mu·sa·ceous (myōō·zā′shəs) *adj.* Pertaining to or designating a family (*Musaceae*) of monocotyledonous plants including the common banana, proceeding from rootstocks, with stems composed of sheathing leafstalks and flowers bursting through spathes. [<NL *Musaceae* < *Musa*, genus name < Arabic *mawzah* banana]

mus·ca (mus′kə) *n. pl.* **mus·cae** (mus′sē) A fly; any of a genus (*Musca*) of dipterous insects of the family *Muscidae*, including the housefly. [< L, fly] — **mus·cid** (mus′id) *adj. & n.*

Mus·ca (mus′kə) A southern constellation, the Fly. See CONSTELLATION. [<NL]

mus·ca·dine (mus′kə·din, -dīn) *n.* The fox grape or scuppernong (*Vitis* or *Muscadinia rotundifolia*) of the southern United States. [<Provençal *muscade*, fem. of *muscat*. See MUSCAT.]

mus·cae vol·i·tan·tes (mus′sē vol′ə·tan′tēz) Minute specks or motes apparently moving before the eye, caused by defects or impurities in the vitreous humor of the eye, etc. [< L, flying flies]

mus·ca·rine (mus′kə·rēn, -rin) *n. Chem.* A deliquescent, extremely poisonous, white, crystalline alkaloid, $C_8H_{13}O_3N$, found in certain fungi, as the fly agaric, and in putrefying fish. [<NL *muscarius* of flies <L *musca* fly]

mus·cat (mus′kat, -kət) *n.* 1 One of several varieties of musk-flavored Old World grapes. 2 A sweet, white wine made from such grapes. [<F <Provençal <Ital. *moscato* <LL *muscus* musk]

mus·ca·tel (mus′kə·tel′) *n.* 1 A rich, sweet wine made from the muscat grape. 2 The muscat grape: also spelled *moscatel.* Also **mus′ca·del** (-del′). [<OF, dim. of *muscat.* See MUSCAT.]

mus·cle (mus′əl) *n.* 1 *Anat.* An organ composed of tissue arranged in bundles of fibers, by whose contraction bodily movements are effected. Two principal types are known: *striated* (striped), involved in voluntary movements, and *smooth* (unstriped), acting independently of the will. The heart muscle belongs anatomically between the two. 2 The tissue of the muscular organs. 3 Muscular strength. — *v.i.* ·**cled**, ·**cling** To push in or ahead by sheer physical strength. ◆ Homophone: mussel. [<F <L *musculus*, lit., little mouse, dim. of *mus.* Doublet of MUSSEL.]

mus·cle-bound (mus′əl·bound′) *adj.* Affected with a form of muscular hypertrophy characterized by lack of elasticity in a muscle: caused by excessive exercise in training.

mus·cled (mus′əld) *adj.* Having or supplied with muscles.

muscle fiber *Physiol.* A muscle cell consisting of a soft contractile substance enclosed in a tubular sheath.

muscle plasma *Physiol.* The liquid that can be expressed from muscle tissue: it clots spontaneously and is sometimes injected intravenously as a restorative and stimulant.

muscle sense *Physiol.* The perception of muscular movement derived from the functioning of afferent nerves connected with muscle tissue, skin, joints, and tendons.

muscle spindle *Anat.* One of various groups of muscle fibers enclosed in a sheath of connective tissue and terminating in sensory organs.

muscle sugar Inositol.

mus·coid (mus′koid) *adj.* Mosslike. — *n.* A mosslike plant. [<L *muscus* moss + -OID]

mus·co·va·do (mus′kə·vä′dō) *n.* A raw brown sugar obtained by evaporating the juice of sugarcane and draining off the molasses. Also **mus′ca·va′da** (-də), **mus′co·vade** (-vād). [<Sp. *mascabado* unrefined, pp. of *mascabar* diminish, var. of *menoscabar* <*menos* <L *minus* + *cabo* head (<L *caput*)]

mus·co·vite (mus′kə·vīt) *n.* The most common and important white or potash mica, $KAl_2(OH)_2AlSi_3O_{10}$. [<earlier *Muscovy glass*]

mus·co·vy (mus′kə·vē) *n. pl.* ·**vies** A large greenish-black duck (*Cairina moschata*) of America from Mexico to Brazil, now widely domesticated. Also **muscovy duck.** [Alter. of MUSK DUCK]

mus·cu·lar (mus′kyə·lər) *adj.* 1 Pertaining to or depending upon muscles. 2 Possessing strong muscles; powerful. 3 Accomplished by muscle or muscles. — **mus′cu·lar′i·ty** (-lar′ə·tē) *n.* — **mus′cu·lar·ly** *adv.*

muscular dystrophy *Pathol.* One of various diseases of undetermined cause, characterized by wasting of muscles and often terminating in physical helplessness.

mus·cu·la·ture (mus′kyə·lə·chŏŏr) *n.* 1 The disposition or arrangement of muscles in a part or organ. 2 The muscle system as a whole. Also **mus′cu·la′tion.** [<F]

muse¹ (myōōz) *n.* Something regarded as the source of artistic inspiration; the inspiring power of a poet or of poetry. [<MUSE]

muse² (myōōz) *v.t. & v.i.* **mused, mus·ing** To consider thoughtfully or at length; ponder; meditate. — *n.* 1 The act or state of musing; reverie. 2 Wonder. [<OF *muser*] — **mus′er** *n.* — **muse′ful** *adj.*

Synonyms (verb): brood, cogitate, consider, contemplate, deliberate, dream, meditate, ponder, reflect, ruminate, stew, study, think. Compare REFLECTION.

Muse (myōōz) In Greek mythology, any of the nine goddesses presiding over poetry, the arts, sciences, etc.: Calliope, Clio, Erato,

THE MUSES—FROM A SARCOPHAGUS IN THE LOUVRE, PARIS

A. Clio. B. Thalia. C. Erato. D. Euterpe. E. Polyhymnia. F. Calliope. G. Terpsichore. H. Urania. I. Melpomene.

Euterpe, Melpomene, Polyhymnia, Terpsichore, Thalia, and Urania. [<F <L *Musa* <Gk. *Mousa* a Muse, eloquence, music]

mu·sette (myōō·zet′) *n.* 1 Any melody of soft, pastoral character written in imitation of bagpipe airs. 2 A small bagpipe formerly popular in France. 3 A variety of small oboe. 4 A small leather or canvas knapsack or wallet, used especially by soldiers, and carried by a strap worn over the shoulder: also **musette bag.** [<F, dim. of *muse* a bagpipe]

mu·se·um (myōō·zē′əm) *n.* 1 A place preserving and exhibiting works of nature, art, curiosities, etc.; also, any collection of such objects. 2 Any place where curiosities, freaks, monstrosities, etc., are exhibited. [<L <Gk. *mouseion* temple of the Muses < *Mousa*]

mush¹ (mush) *n.* 1 Thick porridge, made by boiling meal or flour in water or milk. 2 Anything soft and pulpy. 3 *Colloq.* Sentimentality. [Var. of MASH]

mush² (mush) *v.i.* In Alaska and the Canadian Arctic, to travel on foot, using snow with a dog sled. — *interj.* Get along! a call of the drivers of a dog team. [Prob. <*mush on*, alter. of F (Canadian) *marchons*, the cry of voyageurs and trappers to their dogs] — **mush′er** *n.*

mush·room (mush′rōōm, -rŏŏm) *n.* 1 A large, rapidly growing fungus of the order *Agaricales*, consisting of an erect stalk and a caplike expansion: certain poisonous varieties are called *toadstools*, but the distinction is not scientifically correct. The best-known edible mushrooms are of the genus *Agaricus*, especially the **field mushroom,** *A. campestris.* 2 An object or excres-

AGARIC MUSHROOM

cence of similar shape. — *v.i.* 1 To grow or spread rapidly, like a mushroom: The town *mushroomed* overnight. 2 To expand at one end into a mushroomlike shape: said of bullets. — *adj.* 1 Pertaining to or made of mushrooms. 2 Sudden in growth and rapid in decay; ephemeral; upstart. [<OF *mouscheron* < *mousse* moss]

mush·y (mush′ē) *adj.* **mush·i·er, mush·i·est** 1 Soft; pulpy. 2 *Colloq.* Sentimental; romantic. — **mush′i·ly** *adv.* — **mush′i·ness** *n.*

mu·sic (myōō′zik) *n.* 1 The science and art of the rhythmic combination of tones, vocal or instrumental, embracing melody and harmony. 2 A composition, or mass of compositions, conceived or executed according to musical rule or spirit. 3 Any rhythmic succession or combination of sounds, especially if pleasing to the ear; also, the sensations or emotions thus produced. 4 A band of musicians; an orchestra. See synonyms under MELODY. — **absolute music** Pure or abstract music wholly self-sufficient without representation or dependence on title, program, etc.: opposed to the pictorial or descriptive **program music.** — **to face the music** To take the consequences courageously and without complaint; accept facts. [<F *musique* <L *musica* <Gk. *mousikē* (*technē*) musical (art) < *Mousa* a Muse]

mu·si·cal (myōō′zi·kəl) *adj.* 1 Pertaining to music. 2 Capable of producing or appreciating music; fond of music. 3 Melodious. — *n.* 1 A musical comedy. 2 *Colloq.* A musicale. — **mu′si·cal·ly** *adv.* — **mu′si·cal·ness** *n.*

musical comedy A kind of theatrical performance, characterized by music, songs, dances, jokes, and elaborate costumes, staging, and settings, usually based on a tenuous plot: also *musical.*

mu·si·cale (myōō′zə·kal′, *Fr.* mü·zē·kál′) *n.* An informal concert or private recital: also *musical.* [<F]

music box A case containing a mechanism that reproduces melodies.

music hall 1 A public hall or building devoted to musical entertainments. 2 *Brit.* A vaudeville house.

mu·si·cian (myōō·zish′ən) *n.* One skilled in music; especially, a professional performer. [<OF *musicien*]

mu·si·cian·ly (myōō·zish′ən·lē) *adj.* Exhibiting musical taste, learning, or skill.

music of the spheres The harmony produced by the movements of the celestial spheres: a conception of Pythagorean philosophy.

mu·si·col·o·gist (myōō′zə·kol′ə·jist) *n.* One engaged in or versed in musicology.

mu·si·col·o·gy (myōō′zə·kol′ə·jē) *n.* The scientific and historical study of music as an art and as a craft.

music stand 1 A rack to hold sheet music for a performer. 2 A bandstand.

mus·ing (myōō′zing) *adj.* Thoughtful; dreamy; preoccupied. — **mus′ing·ly** *adv.*

musk (musk) *n.* 1 A soft, reddish-brown, powdery secretion of a penetrating odor, obtained from the preputial follicles or **musk bag** of the male musk deer. It is used by perfumers and in medicine. 2 A similar substance from some other animals, as the muskrat or civet. 3 *Chem.* Any of several organic compounds used to replace natural musk. 4 Muskroot. 5 The odor of musk. [<OF *musc* <LL *muscus* <Gk. *moschos* <Persian *mushk* (prob. akin to Skt. *mushka* testicle, dim. of *mus* a mouse)]

musk beaver The muskrat.

musk beetle A large European beetle (*Aromia moschata*) of a bronze-green color, and having a musky odor suggesting roses.

musk deer A small hornless deer (*Moschus moschiferus*) of central and eastern Asia, of which the male has a musk-secreting gland.

MUSK DEER
(From 17 to 20 inches high;
color brown speckled with
gray or buff)

musk duck 1 A muscovy. 2 ♦ An Australian duck (*Biziura lobata*), with a disklike appendage on the chin, and having a musky odor in the breeding season: also called *mould goose*.

mus·keg (mus'keg) *n.* 1 A rocky basin filled by successive deposits of unstable material, as leaves, muck, and moss, incapable of sustaining much weight. 2 A swamp. Also spelled *maskeg*. [<Chippewa *muskig* grassy bog]

muskeg moss An absorbent, sterilized swamp moss (genus *Sphagnum*) used as a surgical dressing.

mus·kel·lunge (mus'kə·lunj) *n. pl.* **·lunge** *n.* A large North American pike (*Esox masquinongy*), valued as a game fish: also spelled *mascalonge, maskinonge*. [<Algonquian *maskinonge* < *mas* great + *kinonge* pike]

mus·ket (mus'kit) *n.* A smoothbore military hand gun; specifically, a hand gun for infantry, now superseded by the rifle. [<OF *mosquet* gun, hawk <Ital. *moschetto* hawk <L *musca* fly]

mus·ket·eer (mus'kə·tir') *n.* A soldier armed with a musket; hence, a foot soldier. [<F *mousquetaire*]

Mus·kho·ge·an (mus·kō'gē·ən, mus'kō·gē'ən) *n.* One of the principal North American Indian linguistic stocks, well advanced in culture, including the Chickasaw, Choctaw, Creek, and Seminole tribes, formerly inhabiting the Gulf region of the SE United States. Also **Mus·ko·gi·an** (mus·kō'gē·ən).

mus·kit (mus·kēt') See MESQUITE.

musk·mel·on (musk'mel'ən) *n.* 1 The juicy, edible, gourdlike fruit of a trailing herb (*Cucumis melo*) of the melon family; cantaloup. 2 The plant bearing this fruit. Also, *Colloq.*, *mushmelon*.

musk ox A shaggy, hollow-horned ruminant (*Ovibos moschatus*) combining the characteristics of the sheep and ox and emitting a strong odor of musk: now restricted to Greenland and the North American continent.

MUSK OX
(About 4 feet
high at the shoulder)

musk·rat (musk'rat') *n. pl.* **·rats** or **·rat** A North American aquatic rodent (*Ondatra zibethica*) yielding a valuable fur and secreting a substance with a musky odor: sometimes called *musquash*.

musk·root (musk'rōōt', -rŏŏt') *n.* The musky, spongy root of a plant (*Ferula sumbul*) of the parsley family, from Russian Turkestan: employed medicinally as a stimulant and anti-spasmodic. Also called *sumbul*.

MUSKRAT
(About 22 inches
over-all in length)

musk rose A cultivated climbing rose (*Rosa moschata*) from Europe, with large white flowers in panicled clusters.

musk turtle A small turtle (*Sternotherus odoratus*) of the eastern United States and Canada, distinguished by bright-yellow lines on each side of the head.

Mus·lim (muz'lim, mŏŏz'-, mŏŏs'-) *n. pl.* **·lims** or **·lim** A believer in Islam; Mohammedan. —*adj.* Of or pertaining to Islam or the Muslims. Also called *Moslem*: also **Mus'lem**. [< Arabic, one who submits < *aslama* surrender (to God)] —**Mus'lim·ism** *n.*

mus·lin (muz'lin) *n.* Any of several varieties of plain-weave cotton cloth ranging from thin batiste and nainsook to heavy sheetings such as longcloth and percale. [<F *mousseline* <Ital. *mussolino*, dim. of *mussolo* muslin < *Mussolo* Mosul, city in Iraq where made.

mus·sel (mus'əl) *n.* 1 A small bivalve mollusk, especially the common edible mussel (*Mytilus edulis*). 2 One of several other fresh-water mollusks, of the genera *Anodonta, Unio*, and others, whose shells are made into buttons, etc. ♦ Homophone: *muscle*. [OE *musle* <L *musculus*, dim. of *mus* mouse. Doublet of MUSCLE.]

Mus·so·li·ni (mōōs'ə·lē'nē, *Ital.* mōōs'sō·lē'nē), **Benito**, 1883–1945, Italian Fascist leader; premier 1922–43; executed: called "Il Duce" (the leader).

must[1] (must) *v.* A defective verb now used only as an auxiliary followed by the infinitive without *to*, or elliptically with the infinitive understood, to express: 1 Obligation or compulsion: *Must* you go? I *must.* 2 Requirement: You *must* be healthy to be accepted. 3 Probability or supposition: You *must* be tired. 4 Conviction or certainty: War *must* follow. ♦ A past conditional is formed by placing the following verb in the perfect infinitive: *He must have gone.* —*n.* 1 Anything that is required or vital. 2 A news item or other material that must be printed: usually marked *must.* —*adj.* Important and essential: a *must* book. [OE *moste*, pt. of *mōtan* may]

must[2] (must) *n.* Mustiness; mold. —*v.t.* & *v.i. Obs.* To make or become musty. [Back formation < MUSTY[1]]

must[3] (must) *n.* 1 The expressed unfermented juice of the grape. 2 Unfermented potato pulp. [OE <L *mustum (vinum)* new wine]

must[4] (must) *n.* 1 A state of dangerous frenzy, related to sexual excitement, associated with adult male animals, especially elephants. 2 An elephant in this condition. —*adj.* Being in a state of must. Also spelled *musth.* [< Hind. *mast* drunk, lustful]

mus·tache (məs·tash', mus'tash) *n.* 1 The growth of hair on the upper lip of men: occasionally used in the plural, in reference to its two parts. 2 The hair or bristles growing near the mouth of an animal. 3 An old soldier: a brave old *mustache*: a gallicism. Also **mus·ta'chio** (-tä'shō): sometimes spelled *moustache*. [<F *moustache* <Ital. *mostaccio* face < Med. L *mustacia* <Gk. *mystax* upper lip < *mastax* mouth, jaws] —**mus·tached** (məs·tasht') *adj.*

mus·tang (mus'tang) *n.* 1 The wild horse of the American plains. 2 One of these horses broken to the saddle; a cow pony. [< Sp. *mesteño*, obs. *mestengo*, lit., belonging to a cattlemen's association, wild < *mesta* association, group <L *mixtus*, pp. of *miscere* mix]

mustang grape A vine (*Vitis candicans*) of the SW United States, having light-colored pungent berries or grapes.

mus·tard (mus'tərd) *n.* 1 Either of two species of *Brassica*, **white mustard** (*B. hirta*) and **black mustard** (*B. nigra*), both annual herbs with yellow flowers and pods of roundish seeds. 2 The pungent seed of the mustard, crushed and adapted for use as a condiment or as a medicinal rubefacient and diuretic. 3 A strong, dark-yellow color, the color of ground mustard. [<OF *moustarde* < L *mustum* must[3]; from once having been prepared with must]

mustard gas *Chem.* An oily amber liquid, dichlorethyl sulfide, $C_4H_8Cl_2S$, having an odor of mustard or garlic, and used in warfare because of its powerful blistering effect.

mustard oil A fixed oil of unpleasant odor extracted from mustard seeds and used in making soap, as a lubricant, etc.

mustard plaster A plaster of powdered mustard and flour used as a counterirritant and rubefacient.

mus·ter (mus'tər) *v.t.* 1 To summon or assemble (troops, etc.), as for service, review, or roll call. 2 To collect or summon: often with *up*: to *muster* up one's courage. —*v.i.* 3 To come together or

assemble, as troops for service, review, etc. —**to muster in** To enrol as military recruits. —**to muster out** To collect or assemble, as troops, for discharge from military service. See synonyms under CONVOKE. —*n.* 1 An assemblage, especially of troops for parade or review. 2 A muster roll. 3 A specimen; pattern; sample. 4 An imposing gathering; array. —**to pass muster** To pass inspection; hence, to be acceptable or accepted. [< OF *mostrer* exhibit <L *monstrare* show]

mus·ter·mas·ter (mus'tər·mas'tər, -mäs'-) *n.* An officer who inspects troops, their equipment, etc.

muster roll The official list or roll of officers and men in a military troop or a ship's crew.

must·y[1] (mus'tē) *adj.* **must·i·er, must·i·est** 1 Having a moldy odor; ill-flavored; fetid; stale. 2 Without life, sparkle, or flavor. 3 Without life or energy; listless; apathetic. See synonyms under TRITE. [? Alter. of earlier *moisty* <MOIST] —**must'i·ly** *adv.* —**must'i·ness** *n.*

must·y[2] (mus'tē) *n.* Formerly, a cheap quality of snuff having a musty flavor.

mu·ta·ble (myōō'tə·bəl) *adj.* Capable of changing; liable to change; hence, fickle; unstable. See synonyms under FICKLE. [<L *mutabilis* < *mutare* change] —**mu'ta·ble·ness, mu'ta·bil'i·ty** *n.* —**mu'ta·bly** *adv.*

mu·ta·gen (myōō'tə·jən) *n.* Any agent that increases the incidence of mutation in germ plasm. [<L *mutare* change + -GEN] —**mu·ta·gen·ic** (myōō'tə·jen'ik) *adj.*

mu·ta·gen·e·sis (myōō'tə·jen'ə·sis) *n.* The initiation of mutation.

mu·tant (myōō'tənt) *n.* 1 That which admits of or undergoes mutation or change. 2 *Biol.* A plant or animal organism differing from its parents in one or more characteristics that are inheritable; a sport. [<L *mutans, -antis*, ppr. of *mutare* change]

mu·tate (myōō'tāt) *v.t.* & *v.i.* **·tat·ed, ·tat·ing** To undergo or subject to change, especially by mutation. [<L *mutatus*, pp. of *mutare* change] —**mu'ta·tive** *adj.*

mu·ta·tion (myōō·tā'shən) *n.* 1 The act or process of change; alteration; variation. 2 Modification of one vowel by another; umlaut. See UMLAUT. 3 *Biol.* A sudden, well-marked, transmissible variation in the organism of a plant or animal, especially as resulting from new combinations of genes and chromosomes and as distinguishable from cumulative evolutionary changes over a long period. 4 Change; hence, succession and serial succession; consecutive order. See synonyms under CHANGE. [<L *mutatio, -onis*] —**mu·ta'tion·al** *adj.*

mute (myōōt) *adj.* 1 Uttering no word or sound; silent. 2 *Law* Refusing to plead upon arraignment. 3 Lacking the power of speech; dumb. 4 *Phonet.* Of or pertaining to a stop consonant. See synonyms under TACITURN. —*n.* 1 One who is silent; especially, a person who refuses or is unable to speak; a person who is dumb by reason of deafness or other infirmity: also called *deafmute.* 2 An undertaker's assistant. 3 *Law* A prisoner who refuses to plead on arraignment. 4 *Phonet.* A stop consonant, as (b), (p), (t), (d). 5 A device to silence, muffle, or deaden the tone of a musical instrument. —*v.t.* **mut·ed, mut·ing** To deaden or muffle the sound of (a musical instrument). [<L *mutus* dumb] —**mute'ly** *adv.* —**mute'ness** *n.*

mu·ti·cous (myōō'tə·kəs) *adj. Biol.* Without a point; unarmed; defenseless: said especially of certain plants and animals. Also **mu'tic, mu'ti·cate** (-kāt). [<L *muticus*, var. of *mutilus* docked, curtailed. See MUTILATE.]

mu·ti·late (myōō'tə·lāt) *v.t.* **·lat·ed, ·lat·ing** 1 To deprive (a person, animal, etc.) of a limb or essential part; maim. 2 To damage or injure by the removal of an important part or parts: to *mutilate* a speech. [<L *mutilatus*, pp. of *mutilare* maim < *mutilus* docked, maimed] —**mu'ti·la'tion** *n.* —**mu'ti·la'tive** *adj.* —**mu'ti·la'tor** *n.*

mu·ti·nous (myōō'tə·nəs) *adj.* Disposed to mutiny; seditious. See synonyms under REBELLIOUS, RESTIVE, TURBULENT. —**mu'ti·nous·ly** *adv.* —**mu'ti·nous·ness** *n.*

mu·ti·ny (myōō'tə·nē) *n. pl.* **·nies** 1 Rebellion against constituted authority; insubordination; especially, a revolt of soldiers or sailors against their officers or commander. **2** *Obs.* Tumult; discord; strife. See synonyms under REVOLUTION. —*v.i.* **·nied, ·ny·ing** To revolt against constituted authority, as in the army or navy; take part in a mutiny. [< F *mutiner* rebel < OF *mutin, meutin* riotous < *muete* riot < L *motus*, pp. of *movere*]

mut·ism (myoo′tiz·əm) *n.* **1** Inability or refusal to utter articulate sounds: often associated with certain mental disorders. **2** Muteness. [< F *mutisme*]

mut·ter (mut′ər) *v.i.* **1** To speak in a low, indistinct tone and with compressed lips, as in complaining or talking to oneself. **2** To complain; grumble. **3** To make a low, rumbling sound. —*v.t.* **4** To say in a low, indistinct tone. —*n.* An imperfect utterance; murmur. [Prob. imit. Cf. dial. G *muttern* and L *muttire*.] —**mut′ter·er** *n.* —**mut′ter·ing** *n. & adj.* —**mut′ter·ing·ly** *adv.*

mut·ton (mut′n) *n.* **1** The flesh of sheep as food. **2** Humorously, a sheep. [< F *mouton* < Celtic. Cf. O Irish *molt* ram, Welsh *mollt* Breton *maout*.] —**mut′ton·y** *adj.*

mut·ton·fish (mut′n·fish′) *n. pl.* **·fish** or **·fish·es** **1** The eelpout. **2** An abalone (*Haliotis iris*) said to taste like mutton. **3** The pargo or other snapper found from Florida to Brazil. **4** The mojarra.

mutton ham *Naut.* A small sail shaped like a leg of mutton, used on small fishing boats: also *mutton-leg.*

mut·ton-leg (mut′n·leg′) *n.* **1** A woman's dress sleeve, very full at the top: so called because shaped like a leg of mutton. **2** Mutton ham.

mu·tu·al (myoo′choo·əl) *adj.* **1** Pertaining reciprocally to both of two; reciprocally related or bound; reciprocal in action or effect. **2** Shared or experienced alike; common. [< F *mutuel* < LL *mutualis* < L *mutuus* < *mutare* change] —**mu′tu·al·ly** *adv.* —**mu′tu·al·i·ty** *n.*

Synonyms: common, correlative, interchangeable, joint, reciprocal. That is *common* to which two or more persons have the same or equal claims, or in which they have equal interest or participation; that is *mutual* which is freely interchanged; that is *reciprocal* in respect to which one act or movement is met by a corresponding act or movement in return. *Antonyms:* detached, disconnected, dissociated, distinct, disunited, separate, separated, severed, sundered, unconnected, unreciprocated, unshared.

mu·tu·al·ism (myoo′choo·əl·iz′əm) *n. Biol.* Symbiosis advantageous to both or all parties concerned.

mu·tu·al·ize (myoo′choo·əl·īz) *v.t. & v.i.* **·ized, ·iz·ing** **1** To make or become mutual. **2** To put (a firm or corporation) on the basis of majority employee or consumer ownership of common stock. —**mu′tu·al·i·za′tion** *n.*

muu-muu (moo′moo′) *n.* A long, loose gown for women, originally worn in Hawaii. [< Hawaiian]

muz·zle (muz′əl) *n.* **1** The projecting snout of an animal. **2** A guard or covering for an animal's snout to prevent biting or eating. **3** The front end of a firearm. —*v.t.* **·zled, ·zling** **1** To put a muzzle on. **2** To restrain from speaking, expressing opinions, etc.; gag. [< OF *musel* < Med. L *musellum*, dim. of LL *musus* snout] —**muz′zler** *n.*

muz·zle-load·er (muz′əl·lō′dər) *n.* A firearm loaded through the muzzle. —**muz′zle-load′ing** *adj.*

muzzle velocity The velocity of a bullet or projectile at the instant of leaving the muzzle of a gun.

my (mī) *pronominal adj.* **1** The possessive case of the pronoun *I* employed attributively; belonging or pertaining to me: *my* house. **2** An adjective used in forms of address in customary phrases: *my* lord; also used in expressions of endearment: *my* boy. —*interj.* An exclamation of surprise: oh *my!* [OE *mīn*]

my- Var. of MYO-.

my·a·sis (mī′ə·sis) See MYIASIS.

my·as·the·ni·a (mī′əs·thē′nē·ə) *n. Pathol.* Muscular debility, accompanied by general and usually progressive exhaustion but without marked sensory disturbance or atrophy. [< NL < MY- + ASTHENIA]

my·ce·li·um (mī·sē′lē·əm) *n. Bot.* The thallus or vegetative portion of a fungus, consisting of threadlike tubes, or hyphae. See illustration un-

der MUSHROOM. Also **my′cele** (-sēl). [< NL < Gk. *mykēs* mushroom] —**my·ce′li·al, my·ce′li·an** *adj.* —**my·ce′li·oid, my·ce·loid** (mī′sə·loid) *adj.*

my·ce·to·gen·ic (mī·sē′tō·jen′ik) *adj.* Produced or caused by a fungus. Also **my·ce′to·ge·net′ic** (-jə·net′ik), **my′ce·tog′e·nous** (-toj′ə·nəs). [< Gk. *mykēs, mykētos* mushroom + -GENIC]

my·ce·to·ma (mī′sə·tō′mə) *n. pl.* **·to·ma·ta** (-tō′mə·tə) *Pathol.* A tumor or tumorlike growth caused by a fungus, as Madura foot. [< Gk. *mykēs, mykētos* fungus + -OMA]

my·ce·to·zo·an (mī·sē′tō·zō′ən) A myxomycete. [< Gk. *mykēs, mykētos* fungus + -ZOA]

myco- *combining form* Fungus: *mycology.* Also before vowels, **myc-.** [< Gk. *mykēs* fungus]

my·co·bac·te·ri·um (mī′kō-bak·tir′ē·əm) *n. pl.* **·ri·a** (-ē·ə) One of a genus (*Mycobacterium*) of slender, typically aerobic bacteria difficult to stain, including the bacterium of tuberculosis and that of leprosy. [< MYCO- + BACTERIUM]

my·col·o·gy (mī·kol′ə·jē) *n.* **1** The science of ngi. **2** The fungous life of a region. [< MYCO- + -LOGY] —**my·co·log·ic** (mī′kə·loj′ik) or **·i·cal** *adj.* —**my·col′o·gist** *n.*

my·cor·rhi·za (mī′kə·rī′zə) *n. Bot.* A subterranean hyphal mass or mycelium often found on the roots of certain trees, especially of the oak, heath, and pine families. Also **my′co·rhi′za.** [< MYCO- + Gk. *rhiza* root] —**my′cor·rhi′zic** *adj.*

my·co·sis (mī·kō′sis) *n. Pathol.* **1** A fungous growth within the body. **2** A disease or morbid condition caused by a fungous growth, as ringworm. [< MYC(O) + -OSIS] —**my·cot′ic** (-kot′ik) *adj.*

my·co·tro·phism (mī′kō·trō′fiz·əm) *n. Bot.* The nutrition of the higher plants by the aid of fungi on their roots and in their leaves; nourishment by mycorrhiza. [< MYCO- + Gk. *trophē* nutrition] —**my′co·tro′phic** *adj.*

my·dri·a·sis (mi·drī′ə·sis, mī-) *n. Pathol.* An abnormal or prolonged dilation of the pupil of the eye. [< LL < Gk.]

myd·ri·at·ic (mid′rē·at′ik) *adj. Med.* Relating to or causing dilation of the pupil. —*n.* A drug that dilates the pupil, as belladonna.

my·e·len·ceph·a·lon (mī′ə·len·sef′ə·lon) *n. Anat.* The afterbrain; the posterior part of the rhombencephalon or that portion of the medulla oblongata lying behind the pons Varolii and cerebellum. [< MYEL(O) + ENCEPHALON]

my·e·lin (mī′ə·lin) *n. Biochem.* A semisolid, fatlike substance that surrounds the axillary portion of medullated nerve fibers; the medullary sheath. Also **my′e·line** (-lēn, -lin). [< Gk. *myelos* marrow]

my·e·li·tis (mī′ə·lī′tis) *n. Pathol.* **1** Inflammation of the spinal cord. **2** Inflammation of the bone marrow. [< MYEL(O) + -ITIS]

myelo- *combining form Anat.* **1** The bone marrow. **2** The spinal cord. Also, before vowels, **myel-.** [< Gk. *myelon* marrow]

my·e·loid (mī′ə·loid) *adj. Anat.* **1** Pertaining to, from, or resembling marrow. **2** Of or pertaining to the spinal cord. [< MYEL(O)- + -OID]

my·e·lo·ma (mī′ə·lō′mə) *n. pl.* **·mas** or **·ma·ta** (-mə·tə) *Pathol.* A tumor composed of bone marrow cells. [< MYEL- + -OMA]

my·ia·sis (mī′yə·sis) *n. Pathol.* Any of various diseases caused by flies or maggots. [< NL < Gk. *myia* fly + -(O)SIS]

my·lo·nite (mī′lə·nīt) *n. Geol.* A hard, compact rock having a banded or streaky appearance, produced by the crushing and reforming of earth material under extreme pressure. [< Gk. *mylōn* mill]

my·na (mī′nə) *n.* One of various Oriental, starlinglike birds of the genera *Acridotheres* and *Eulabes. Eulabes religiosa,* the common myna of India, is often tamed and taught to speak words: sometimes spelled *mina, minah.* Also **my′nah.** [< Hind. *mainā*]

MYNA

myo- *combining form* Muscle; of or pertaining to muscle: *myology.* Also, before vowels, **my-.** [< Gk. *mys, myos* a muscle]

my·o·car·di·al (mī′ō·kär′dē·əl) *adj. Anat.* Of or pertaining to the heart muscle. [< MYO- + Gk. *kardia* heart]

my·o·car·di·o·graph (mī′ō·kär′dē·ə·graf, -gräf) *n.* An instrument for registering the muscular action of the heart.

my·o·car·di·tis (mī′ō·kär·dī′tis) *n. Pathol.* Inflammation of the myocardium. [< NL] —**my′o·car·dit′ic** (-dit′ik) *adj.*

my·o·car·di·um (mī′ō·kär′dē·əm) *n. Anat.* The muscular tissue of the heart. [< NL < MYO- + Gk. *kardia* heart]

my·o·ge·net·ic (mī′ō·jə·net′ik) *adj. Physiol.* Originating in muscle or in muscle tissue. Also **my′o·gen′ic, my·og·e·nous** (mī·oj′ə·nəs).

my·o·gram (mī′ə·gram) *n.* The record made by a myograph.

my·o·graph (mī′ə·graf, -gräf) *n.* An instrument for recording and showing muscular movement.

my·oid (mī′oid) *adj.* Resembling a muscle or muscle tissue.

my·ol·o·gy (mī·ol′ə·jē) *n.* The study of the structure, functions, and diseases of the muscles. [< MYO- + -LOGY] —**my·o·log·ic** (mī′ə·loj′ik) or **·i·cal** *adj.* —**my·ol′o·gist** *n.*

my·o·ma (mī·ō′mə) *n. pl.* **·ma·ta** (-mə·tə) *Pathol.* A muscular tumor. [< MY- + -OMA] —**my·om′a·tous** (-om′ə·təs) *adj.*

my·o·mec·to·my (mī′ō·mek′tə·mē). *n. Surg.* The removal of a myoma. [< MYOMA + -ECTOMY]

my·op·a·thy (mī·op′ə·thē) *n. Pathol.* Disease of a muscle. Also **my·o·path·i·a** (mī′ō·path′ē·ə) [< MYO- + -PATHY] —**my·o·path′ic** *adj.*

my·ope (mī′ōp) *n.* One who is near-sighted. Also **my′ops** (-ops). [< F < LL *myops* < Gk. *myōps* < *myein* close + *ōps* an eye]

my·o·pi·a (mī·ō′pē·ə) *n. Pathol.* Defect in vision so that objects can be seen distinctly only when very near the eye; near-sightedness due to focusing of images in front of instead of on the retina. Also **my·o·py** (mī′ə·pē). [< NL] —**my·op′ic** (-op′ik) *adj.*

my·o·scope (mī′ə·skōp) *n. Med.* An instrument for observing the contraction of muscles.

my·o·sin (mī′ə·sin) *n.* A globulin constituting about half of the protein in muscle and combining with actin to form actomyosin. [< Gk. *mys, myos* muscle]

my·o·sis (mī·ō′sis) See MIOSIS.

my·o·so·tis (mī′ə·sō′tis) *n.* Any of a genus of plants (*Myosotis*) of the borage family; especially, *M. scorpioides,* having branched racemes of blue or pink flowers. Also **my′o·sote** (-sōt). [< NL < Gk., lit., mouse ear < *mys, myos* a mouse + *ous, ōtos* ear]

my·ot·ic (mī·ot′ik) *adj.* Of, pertaining to, or having miosis. —*n.* A drug causing contraction of the pupil of the eye.

myria- *combining form* **1** Very many; of great number: *myriapod.* **2** In the metric system, ten thousand: *myriagram.* Also, before vowels, **myri-.** [< Gk. *myrios* < *myrioi* ten thousand]

myr·i·ad (mir′ē·əd) *adj.* Composed of a very large indefinite number; innumerable. —*n.* **1** A vast indefinite number. **2** Ten thousand. [< Gk. *myrias, myriados* < *myrois* numberless]

myr·i·a·gram (mir′ē·ə·gram′), **myr·i·a·li·ter** (-lē′tər), **myr·i·a·me·ter** (me′tər) *n.* In the metric system, 10,000 grams, liters, or meters.

myr·i·a·pod (mir′ē·ə·pod) *n.* One of a class of arthropods (*Myriapoda*) whose bodies are made up of a varying number of segments, each of which bears one or two pairs of jointed appendages: includes the centipedes and millipedes. —**myr·i·ap′o·dan** (mir′ē·ap′ə·dən) *adj. & n.* —**myr·i·ap′o·dous** *adj.*

my·ri·ca (mi·rī′kə) *n.* The dried bark of the waxmyrtle root, used in medicine as an alterative and emetic. [< L < Gk. *myrikē* tamarisk]

myrmeco- *combining form* Ant; pertaining to ants: *myrmecophagous.* Also, before vowels, **myrmec-.** [< Gk. *myrmēx, myrmēkos* ant]

myr·me·col·o·gy (mûr′mə·kol′ə·jē) *n.* The department of entomology that treats of ants. [< MYRMECO- + -LOGY] —**myr′me·co·log′i·cal** (-kə·loj′i·kəl) *adj.* —**myr′me·col′o·gist** *n.*

myr·me·coph·a·gous (mûr′mə·kof′ə·gəs) *adj.* Feeding on ants. [< MYRMECO- + -PHAGOUS]

myr·mi·don (mûr′mə·don, -dən) *n.* A faithful adherent; also, a follower or underling of rough or desperate character, who executes the commands of his master without question or scruple; especially, a petty officer of the law. [< MYRMIDON]

myrrh (mûr) *n.* **1** An aromatic gum resin that exudes from several trees or shrubs of Arabia and Abyssinia: used in medicine. **2** Any shrub or tree that yields this gum, especially *Commiphora myrrha* and *C. abyssinica.* [OE *murra* < L *myr-*

rha <Gk. <Semitic. Cf. Arabic *myrr*, Hebrew *mōr*.]

myr·ta·ceous (mûr·tā′shəs) *adj.* Pertaining to or designating a family (*Myrtaceae*) of trees or shrubs, the myrtle family, widely distributed in tropical and semitropical countries, and including many valuable aromatic resin- and timber-producing genera, as *Pimenta, Eucalyptus, Caryophyllus,* etc. [<NL *Myrtaceae* <L *myrtus* a myrtle tree]

myr·tle (mûr′təl) *n.* **1** A tree or shrub of the genus *Myrtus;* especially, *M. communis* of southern Europe, originally from Asia. It is a bushy shrub or small tree with glossy evergreen leaves, fragrant white or rose-colored flowers, and black berries. **2** One of various other plants like the common myrtle. Among the ancients it was sacred to Venus. **3** The periwinkle (*Vinca minor*); also, the California laurel (*Umbellularia californica*). [<F *myrtille* bilberry <Med. L *myrtillus* myrtle, dim. of L *myrtus* <Gk. *myrtos* <Semitic. Cf. Persian *mūrd*.]

myrtle warbler A small insectivorous bird (*Dendroica coronata*) of North America, with blue-gray or black-and-yellow back.

my·self (mī·self′) *pron.* **1** I; me: the emphatic form of *I* and *me,* and reflexive of *me:* used in the nominative with *I* in apposition: I *myself* will see to it; I'll write it *myself;* also, in poetical nominative use as a simple subject: *Myself* hath often heard; also used as the object of a verb either direct or indirect: I deceived *myself* (reflexive); She invited Helen, Jeff, and *myself* (compound object); I got it for *myself* (object of a preposition). **2** Normal condition of mind or body: I feel *myself* again. [OE *mē sylf*]

mys·ta·gog (mis′tə·gôg, -gog) *n.* An interpreter of religious mysteries; an initiator into mysteries; teacher. Also **mys′ta·gogue.** [<F <L *mystagogus* <Gk. *mystagōgos* <*mystēs* an initiate + *agōgos* leader <*agein.* See MYSTERY.] —**mys′ta·gog′ic** (-goj′ik) *adj.* —**mys′ta·go′gy** (-gō′jē) *n.*

mys·te·ri·ous (mis·tir′ē·əs) *adj.* Involved in or implying mystery; unexplained; obscure. [<L *mysterium*] —**mys·te′ri·ous·ly** *adv.* —**mys·te′ri·ous·ness** *n.*
Synonyms: abstruse, cabalistic, dark, enigmatic, hidden, incomprehensible, inexplicable, inscrutable, mystic, mystical, obscure, occult, recondite, secret, transcendental, unfathomable, unfathomed, unknown. That is *mysterious* in the true sense which is beyond human comprehension; that is *mystic* or *mystical* which has associated with it some *hidden* or *recondite* meaning.

See DARK, SECRET. *Antonyms:* see synonyms for CLEAR.

mys·ter·y (mis′tər·ē) *n. pl.* **·ter·ies 1** Something unknown or incomprehensible in its nature; an inexplicable phenomenon. **2** Secrecy or obscurity: an event wrapped in *mystery.* **3** A secret: the *mysteries* of freemasonry. **4** Any affair or event so concealed or unexplained as to excite awe or curiosity: a murder *mystery.* **5** A literary or dramatic piece relating such an affair. **6** *Theol.* A truth known only through faith or revelation and incomprehensible to the human reason. **7** *Eccl.* **a** A sacrament, especially the Eucharist. **b** *pl.* The eucharistic elements. **8** *pl.* In classical antiquity, certain religious rites to which only selected worshipers were admitted. **9** *pl.* A cult practicing such rites. **10** A medieval dramatic performance based on Scriptural events or characters: also **mystery play.** [<L *mysterium* <Gk. *mystērion* secret worship, secret thing <*mystēs* an initiate into the mysteries <*myein* shut, shut the eyes]

mys·tic (mis′tik) *adj.* **1** Pertaining to a mystery of the faith. **2** Spiritually symbolic. **3** Of or designating an occult or esoteric rite, practice, etc. **4** Of mysterious meaning or character; mysterious. —*n.* **1** One who professes a knowledge of spiritual truth or a feeling of union with the divine, reached through contemplation or intuition. **2** A practicer of occult or mystical rites. [<L *mysticus* <Gk. *mystikos* pertaining to secret rites <*mystēs* an initiate]

mys·ti·cism (mis′tə·siz′əm) *n.* **1** The belief that knowledge of divine truth or the soul's union with the divine is attainable by spiritual insight or ecstatic contemplation without the medium of the senses or reason. **2** Any theory advancing intense meditative and intuitive methods of thought or conduct. **3** Vague or obscure speculation involving confused or fanciful thinking.

mys·ti·fy (mis′tə·fī) *v.t.* **·fied, ·fy·ing 1** To confuse, especially deliberately; perplex or bewilder; hoax. **2** To treat as obscure or mysterious. See synonyms under PERPLEX. [<F *mystifier*] —**mys′ti·fi·ca′tion** *n.* —**mys′ti·fi′er** *n.*—**mys′ti·fy′ing** *adj.* —**mys′ti·fy′ing·ly** *adv.*

myth (mith) *n.* **1** A story, presented as historical, dealing with the cosmological and supernatural traditions of a people, their gods, culture, heroes, religious beliefs, etc. **2** A popular fable or folk tale. **3** A parable; allegory. See synonyms under FICTION. [<LL *mythos* <Gk., word, speech, story]

myth·i·cal (mith′i·kəl) *adj.* **1** Pertaining to myth;

legendary. **2** Fictitious. Also **myth′ic.** —**myth′i·cal·ly** *adv.*

myth·i·cize (mith′ə·sīz) *v.t.* **·cized, ·ciz·ing** To convert into or explain as a myth.

mytho- *combining form* Myth; myth and: *mythography.* Also, before vowels, **myth-.** [<Gk. *mythos* a legend]

my·thog·ra·phy (mi·thog′rə·fē) *n.* **1** The collecting of myths; descriptive mythology. **2** Expression of mythic characters or ideas in art form. [<MYTHO- + -GRAPHY] —**my·thog′ra·pher** *n.*

my·thol·o·gize (mi·thol′ə·jīz) *v.* **·gized, ·giz·ing** *v.i.* To narrate, classify, or explain myths. —*v.t.* To mythicize. Also *Brit.* **my·thol′o·gise.** [<F *mythologiser*] —**my·thol′o·gist, my·thol′o·giz′er** *n.*

my·thol·o·gy (mi·thol′ə·jē) *n. pl.* **·gies 1** The myths and legends of a people concerning creation, gods, and heroes. **2** The scientific collection and study of myths; study of the beliefs of mankind; also, a volume of myths. [<LL *mythologia* <Gk., telling of tales < *mythos* legend + *logos* discourse] —**myth·o·log·i·cal** (mith′ə·loj′i·kəl), **myth′o·log′ic** *adj.* —**myth′o·log′i·cal·ly** *adv.*

myth·o·ma·ni·a (mith′ə·mā′nē·ə, -mān′yə) *n.* A compulsive tendency to tell lies.

myth·o·pe·ic (mith′ə·pē′ik) *adj.* Mythmaking; relating to a supposed stage of human culture when all natural phenomena are explained by myths. Also **myth′o·poe′ic.** [<Gk. *mythopoios* <*mythos* legend + *poieein* make] —**myth′o·pe′ist** *n.*

myx·e·de·ma (mik′sə·dē′mə) *n. Pathol.* A disease associated with hypotrophy of the thyroid gland and characterized by dryness and wrinkling of the skin, swelling of the face, and progressive mental deterioration. Also **myx′oe·de′ma.** [<NL <MYX(O)- + EDEMA] —**myx′e·dem′ic** (-dem′ik), **myx′e·dem′a·tous** (-dem′ə·təs) *adj.*

myxo- *combining form* Slimy; like mucus. Also, before vowels, **myx-.** [<Gk. *myxa* mucus]

myx·o·ma (mik·sō′mə) *n. pl.* **·ma·ta** (-mə·tə) *Pathol.* A soft, elastic tumor composed of mucous tissue. [<NL <MYX(O)- + -OMA] —**myx·om·a·tous** (mik·som′ə·təs) *adj.*

myx·o·my·cete (mik′sō·mī·sēt′) *n.* One of the slime molds (*Myxomycetes*), a class of fungi exhibiting both plant and animal characteristics and classified by some authorities as *Mycetozoa.* They consist of masses of naked protoplasm with ameboid movements, and are chiefly saprophytic, living on dead and decaying matter. [<MYXO- + -MYCETE] —**myx′o·my·ce′tous** *adj.*

N

n, N (en) *n. pl.* **n's, N's** or **ns, Ns, ens** (enz) **1** The 14th letter of the English alphabet: from Phoenician *nun,* Greek *nu,* Roman *N.* **2** The sound of the letter *n,* a voiced, alveolar nasal. See ALPHABET. —*symbol* **1** *Printing* An en: see EN. **2** *Chem.* Nitrogen (symbol N). **3** *Math.* An indefinite number.

Na *Chem.* Sodium (symbol Na). [<NL *natrium*]

nab[1] (nab) *v.t.* **nabbed, nab·bing** *Colloq.* **1** To catch or arrest, as a criminal. **2** To take or seize suddenly. [Cf. Norw., Sw. *nappa* snatch]

nab[2] (nab) *n.* **1** *Geog.* A projecting part of a hill or rock; a peak, promontory, or summit. **2** *Mech.* A projection or spur on the bolt of a lock. [<ON *nabbi* a knoll]

nac·a·rat (nak′ə·rat) *n.* **1** Bright red-orange color. **2** A fine linen or crêpe fabric dyed this color. [<F, appar. <Sp. *nacarado* <*nacar* nacre]

na·celle (nə·sel′) *n. Aeron.* **1** The basket suspended from a balloon. **2** The framework below

the envelope of a dirigible balloon, which carries the motor, passengers, etc. **3** An enclosed shelter for housing the cargo or power plant and sometimes the personnel of an airplane. [<F]

na·cho (nä′chō) *n. pl.* **·chos** A tortilla chip covered with beans, hot peppers, etc., then sprinkled with cheese. [<Sp.]

na·cre (nā′kər) *n.* Mother-of-pearl. [<F]

na·cre·ous (nā′krē·əs) *adj.* **1** Of, like, or producing nacre. **2** Iridescent; pearly.

na·da (nä′də) *n.* In East Indian music, the term for esthetically agreeable sound, as distinct from noise, grinding, clanging, etc.

na·dir (nā′dər, -dir) *n.* **1** The point of the celestial sphere directly beneath the place where one stands: opposed to *zenith.* **2** Figuratively, the lowest possible point: the *nadir* of melancholy. [<F <Arabic *nadir* (*es-semt*) opposite (the zenith)]

nag[1] (nag) *v.* **nagged, nag·ging** *v.t.* To torment with constant faultfinding, scolding, and urging. —*v.i.* To scold, find fault, or urge continually. —*n.* One who nags, especially a woman. [<Scand. Cf. Sw. *nagga* vex.] —**na**-

g′·ger *n.* —**nag′ging** *adj.* —**nag′ging·ly** *adv.*

nag[2] (nag) *n.* **1** A pony or small horse. **2** An old or inferior horse. **3** *Archaic* A worthless person; jade. [ME *nagge;* origin uncertain]

Na·ga Hills (nä′gə) A series of hill ranges between NE India and western Burma.

na·ga·na (nə·gä′nə) *n.* A disease of cattle and horses caused by trypanosomes introduced into the blood by the tsetse fly. [<Zulu]

nai·ad (nā′ad, nī′-) *n. pl.* **·ads** or **·a·des** (-ə·dēz) **1** In classical mythology, one of the water nymphs who were believed to dwell in and preside over fountains, lakes, brooks, and wells. **2** *Bot.* A plant of the pondweed family (genus *Naias*). **3** The nymph stage in the life cycle of certain insects: applied especially to aquatic forms. [<Gk. *Naias, -ados.* Related to Gk. *naein* flow.]

nai·ant (nā′ənt) See NATANT.

Na·i·du (nä′i·dōō), **Sarojini,** 1879–1949, Hindu poet and reformer.

na·if (nä·ēf′) *adj. French* Masculine form of NA-IVE. Also **na·if′.**

naig (nāg) *n. Scot.* A nag; riding horse. Also **naig′ie.**

nail (nāl) *n.* **1** A thin horny plate on the end of a finger or toe. **2** A claw, talon, or hoof. **3** A slender piece of metal having a point and a head, and used for driving into or through wood, etc., as for fastening pieces together. **4** A measure of length, 2 1/4 inches. **5** A callosity on the inner side of a horse's leg. —**on the nail** *Colloq.* **1** Right away; immediately. **2** At the exact spot or moment. **3** Of immediate interest or importance; under discussion. —*v.t.* **1** To fasten or fix in place with a nail or nails. **2** To close up or shut in by means of nails. **3** To secure by decisive or prompt action: to *nail* a contract. **4** To fix firmly or immovably: Terror *nailed* him to the spot. **5** To succeed in hitting or striking. **6** *Colloq.* To catch or seize; intercept. **7** *Colloq.* To detect and expose, as a lie or liar. [OE *nægel*]

nail bed *Anat.* That portion of the true skin upon which the nail rests.

nail·brush (nāl′brush′) *n.* A brush with stiff bristles, used for cleaning the hands and fingernails.

nail file A fine, flat file used for manicuring the fingernails.

nail·fold (nāl′fōld′) *n. Anat.* The duplication of the skin that surrounds the edges of a nail; cuticle.

nail polish A lacquer applied to the nails to give a glossy finish, made from soluble cotton treated with various organic compounds, as toluene, ethyl acetate, ethanol, etc., and usually colored by the addition of dyes. Also **nail enamel**.

nain·sook (nān′sŏŏk, nan′-) *n.* A soft, lightweight cotton fabric, heavier than batiste: used for lingerie and infants' wear. [< Hind. *nainsukh*, lit., pleasure of the eye]

Nai·ro·bi (nī·rō′bē) The capital of Kenya in eastern Africa.

na·ive (nä·ēv′) *adj.* **1** Ingenuous; artless; without sophistication. **2** Not consciously logical; uncritical. Also **na·ïve′**. See synonyms under CANDID. [< F, fem. of *naïf* < L *nativus* natural. Doublet of NATIVE.] —**na·ive′ly** *adv.* —**na·ive′ness** *n.*

na·ive·té (nä·ēv′tā′, nä·ēv′tā) *n.* The state or quality of being naive. Also **na·ïve·té′, na·ive·ty** (nä·ēv′tē).

na·ked (nā′kid) *adj.* **1** Having no clothes or garments on; nude. **2** Having no covering, or lacking the usual covering. **3** Unsheathed; bare, as a sword. **4** Unsaddled, as a horse. **5** Having no defense or protection; exposed. **6** Being without means of sustenance, etc.; destitute; bare; also, stripped. **7** Being without concealment or excuse. **8** Without addition or adornment; plain; evident; mere. **9** Without some accessory, qualification, belonging, etc., which is customary or natural. **10** *Law* Having no consideration or inducement; unconfirmed; not validated. **11** *Bot.* **a** Not enclosed in an ovary or case. **b** Without a pericarp: said of seeds. **c** Destitute of leaves: said of stalks. **d** Having no hairs; smooth: said of leaves. **12** *Zool.* Lacking fur, hair, scales, or feathers. [OE *nacod*] —**na′ked·ly** *adv.* —**na′ked·ness** *n.*

naked eye The eye unaided by optical instruments.

nam (näm, nam) Past tense of NIM.

nam·a·ble (nā′mə·bəl) *adj.* **1** Capable of being named. **2** Memorable; worthy of being mentioned. Also **name′a·ble.** —**nam′a·bil′i·ty, name′a·bil′i·ty** *n.*

nam·ay·cush (nam′ə·kush, -ā-) *n.* The great lake trout (*Cristivomer namaycush*) of North America; the Mackinaw trout: also spelled *naymacush*. [< Algonquian (Cree) *namekus* trout]

nam·by-pam·by (nam′bē·pam′bē) *adj.* Weakly sentimental; insipid; inane. —*n. pl.* **-pam·bies 1**

Writing, talk, or action of a feebly sentimental or finical character. **2** A person given to such talk or action. [< nickname of Ambrose Philips, 1671–1749, English poet; with ref. to his feeble, sentimental verse]

name (nām) *n.* **1** The distinctive appellation by which a person or thing is known. **2** A descriptive or arbitrary appellation; designation; title. **3** General reputation; eminence; fame. **4** A person, cause, thing, or class, or the claims of authority thereof, as represented by the name. **5** An opprobrious appellation. **6** A race or family, as having a common descent and patronymic. **7** A memorable person, character, or thing: great *names* in music. **8** Mere sound or simulation, in distinction from substance or reality: a wife in *name* only. —**by the name of** Named. —*v.t.* **named, nam·ing 1** To give a name to; entitle; style; term. **2** To mention or refer to by name; cite. **3** To designate for some particular purpose or office; nominate; appoint. **4** To give the name of; identify: *Name* the capital of Peru. **5** To set or specify, as a price or requirement. [OE *nama*] —**nam′er** *n.*

Synonyms (noun): agnomen, appellation, cognomen, denomination, designation, epithet, style, title. *Name* in the most general sense includes all other words of this group; in the more limited sense a *name* is personal, an *appellation* is descriptive, a *title* is official. In the phrase William the Conqueror, king of England, William is the man's *name*, which belongs to him personally; Conqueror is the *appellation* which he won by his acquistion of England; king is the *title* denoting his royal rank. An *epithet* is given to mark some assumed characteristic, good or bad. *Designation* may be used in the sense of *appellation*, but is far broader and more general in meaning. One's personal *name*, as John or Mary, given in infancy, and is often called the given, or Christian, or first *name*. The *cognomen* is the family *name* which belongs to one by right of birth or marriage. In modern use, *style* is the legal *designation* by which a person or house is known in official or business relations. A *denomination* is a specific, and especially a collective name; the term is applied to a separate religious organization, also to money or notes of a certain value; as, The sum was in notes of the *denomination* of one thousand dollars. See TERM.

name·less (nām′lis) *adj.* **1** Having no name; unnamed. **2** Having no fame or reputation; illegitimate; obscure; anonymous. **3** Not suitable or fit to be spoken of. **4** Not to be named; inexpressible; indescribable. —**name′less·ly** *adv.* —**name′less·ness** *n.*

name·ly (nām′lē) *adv.* That is to say; to wit; videlicet.

name·sake (nām′sāk) *n.* One who is named after or has the same name as another.

nan·keen (nan·kēn′) *n.* **1** A buff-colored Chinese cotton fabric, or nankeen. **2** *pl.* Clothes made of nankeen. Also **nan·kin′.** [from *Nanking*, where originally made]

Nanking porcelain Any of various types of fine Chinese porcelain painted in blue on white: also called *blue-and-white.* Also **Nankeen porcelain.**

nan·ny (nan′ē) *n. pl.* **·nies** *Colloq.* **1** A female goat: also **nanny goat. 2** *Brit.* A child's nurse. [from *Nanny*, a personal name]

nano- *combining form* **1** One billionth part of: *nanosecond.* **2** Microscopic; very small: *nanoplankton.*

na·no·plank·ton (nā′nə·plangk′tən, nan′ə-) *n.* Floating plant and animal organisms of microscopic size. Also **nan′no·plank′ton** (nan′·ə-). [< Gk. *nanos* dwarf + PLANKTON]

na·no·sec·ond (nan′ə·sek′ənd, nā′nə-) *n.* One billionth of a second.

Nantes (nants, *Fr.* nänt) A city of western France, on the Loire. —**Edict of Nantes** An order granting freedom of conscience to Protestants, issued by Henry IV of France in 1598 and revoked in 1685 by Louis XIV.

na·os (nā′os) *n. Archit.* The principal chamber or body of an ancient Greek temple, usually containing a statue of the deity; a cella. [< Gk., a temple]

nap[1] (nap) *n.* A short sleep; doze. —*v.i.* **napped, nap·ping 1** To take a nap; doze. **2** To be unprepared or off one's guard. [OE *hnappian* doze] —**nap′per** *n.*

nap[2] (nap) *n.* **1** The short fibers on the surface of flannel, etc., forming a soft surface lying smoothly in one direction. **2** A covering resembling this, as upon some plants or insects. —*v.t.* **napped, nap·ping** To raise a nap on. [< MDu. *noppe*]

nap[3] (nap) See NAPOLEON (def. 2).

na·palm (nā′päm) *n.* A jellied mixture of aluminum soap powder and oil or gasoline, used as an incendiary in bombs, flame-throwers, etc. —*v.t. & v.i.* To attack or burn with napalm. [< *na(phthenic)* and *palm(itic) acids*]

nape (nāp) *n.* **1** The back of the neck, especially its upper part. ◆ Collateral adjective: *nuchal.* **2** The back of a fish next to the head. [Origin uncertain]

na·per·y (nā′pər·ē) *n. pl.* **·per·ies** An article of household linen, as napkins, tablecloths, etc., or such linen collectively. [< OF *naperie* < *nape.* See NAPKIN.]

naph·tha (naf′thə, nap′-) *n.* **1** A volatile mixture of low-boiling hydrocarbons between gasoline and benzine, obtained by distilling petroleum: used as a solvent, cleaning fluid, fuel, etc., and in the making of varnishes. **2** Petroleum. [< L < Gk., prob. < Persian *naft* petroleum]

naph·tha·lene (naf′thə·lēn, nap′-) *n. Chem.* A white, solid, aromatic hydrocarbon, $C_{10}H_8$, obtained from coal-tar distillates and crystallizing in white platelets: its derivatives are used in the making of dyestuffs: also called *tar camphor.* Also **naph′tha·line** (-lin, -lēn).

naph·thene (naf′thēn, nap′-) *n. Chem.* Any of a group of saturated ring hydrocarbons having the general formula C_nH_{2n}, especially those obtained from Russian and Galician petroleum.

naph·thol (naf′thol, -thōl, nap′-) *n. Chem.* **1** Either of two isomeric compounds, the alpha and beta, $C_{10}H_7OH$, derived from naphthalene by replacing an atom of hydrogen by the hydroxyl group; specifically, the beta variety. They are used as antiseptics and in the manufacture of synthetic dyes. **2** Any one of a class of naphthalene derivatives containing the hydroxyl group. Also **naph′tol** (-tōl, -tol). [< NAPHTH(ALENE + -OL²]

naph·tho·lism (naf′thə·liz′əm, nap′-) *n. Pathol.* Poisoning caused by excessive or prolonged use of naphthol.

Na·pi·er (nā′pē·ər, nə·pir′), **Sir Charles James,** 1782–1853, British general. —**John,** 1550–1617, Scottish mathematician; invented logarithms. —**Robert Cornelis,** 1810–80, Lord Napier of Magdala, British general.

Na·pier·i·an logarithms (nə·pir′ē·ən) *Math.* The logarithmic system employing the base *e*: (2.71828 . . . .): also called *natural logarithms.* Also **Na·pe′ri·an.**

na·pi·form (nā′pə·fôrm) *adj. Bot.* Turnip-shaped; large above and small or slender below: a *napiform* rootstock. [< L *napus* turnip + -(I)FORM]

nap·kin (nap′kin) *n.* **1** A small cloth, as of linen, for use at table, etc. **2** *Brit.* A diaper. **3** *Scot.* A handkerchief. [ME *napekyn,* dim. of OF *nape* < L *mappa* a cloth]

Na·ples (nā′pəlz) A port in SW Italy on the **Bay of Naples,** a semicircular inlet of the Tyrrhenian Sea in SW Italy. Greek *Parthenope, Neapolis.* Italian **Na·po·li** (nä′pō·lē).

nap·less (nap′lis) *adj.* **1** Made without a nap. **2** Threadbare.

Naples yellow A semi-opaque, permanent pigment in various shades of yellow consisting of lead antimoniate. Inferior grades are mixtures of ocher, zinc oxide, or cadmium yellow.

Na·po (nä′pō) A river in NE Ecuador and north central Peru, flowing 550 miles SE to the Amazon.

na·po·le·on (nə·pō′lē·ən, *Fr.* nà·pô·lā·ôn′) *n.* **1** A former French gold coin, equivalent to 20 francs. **2** A card game: the highest bidder names trumps and, if he takes the tricks he has bid, receives from each adversary one chip for each trick; also, the taking of all the tricks in this game by one player: also called *nap.* **3** A pastry composed of layers of puff paste filled with cream or custard. [after *Napoleon* Bonaparte]

Na·po·le·on (nə·pō′lē·ən) A masculine personal name. Also *Fr.* **Na·po·lé·on** (nà·pô·lā·ôn′), *Ital.* **Na·po·le·o·ne** (nä·pō′lā·ō′nä). [< F < Gk., of the new city] —**Napoleon** See BONAPARTE.

Na·po·le·on·ic (nə-pō'lē-on'ik) *adj.* **1** Belonging or relating to Napoleon Bonaparte, his conquests, etc. **2** Belonging or relating to Napoleon III.

NAPOLEONIC EMPIRE AND DEPENDENT STATES 1803-1810

Napoleonic Wars See table under WAR.

nappe (nap) *n.* **1** *Geol.* A recumbent anticline, a portion of which has been thrust over other rocks. **2** *Engin.* The sheet of water overlying the top of a weir. **3** *Geom.* In a cone, one of the two conical surfaces divided by the vertex. [<F, a sheet]

nap·per (nap'ər) *n.* An implement or machine that raises a nap on fabrics.

nap·py[1] (nap'ē) *adj.* **·pi·er**, **·pi·est** Having or characterized by a nap, or abundance of nap.

nap·py[2] (nap'ē) *adj.* **·pi·er**, **·pi·est** **1** Inclined to fall asleep; drowsy. **2** Tending to produce drowsiness or intoxication; hence, slightly intoxicated. — *n. Scot.* Strong ale or beer.

nap·py[3] (nap'ē) *n. pl.* **·pies** A round earthen or glass dish with flat bottom and sloping sides. Also **nap'pie.** [OE *hnæp* bowl]

na·prap·a·thy (nə-prap'ə-thē) *n.* The treatment of disease by the manipulative correction of the disordered ligaments and connective tissues by which the disease is assumed to be caused. [<Czech *napra(va)* correction + -PATHY] — **nap'ra·path** *n.*

nar·ce·ine (när'si·en, -in) *n. Chem.* A silky, bitter, crystalline alkaloid, $C_{23}H_{27}NO_8$, contained in the aqueous extract of opium from which the morphine has been separated. Also **nar·ce'ia, nar'ce·in.** [<L *narce* torpor (<Gk. *narkē*) + -INE[2]]

nar·cis·sism (när·sis'iz·əm) *n.* **1** *Psychoana.* Sexual excitement or gratification derived from contemplation of the self: an arrested or regressive stage. **2** Self–love; excessive interest in or admiration for oneself. Also **nar·cism** (när'siz·əm). — **nar·cis'sist** *n.* — **nar'·cis·sis'tic** *adj.*

nar·cis·sus (när·sis'əs) *n.* **1** One of a genus (*Narcissus*) of bulbous flowering plants of the amaryllis family, including the daffodil and jonquil. **2** A flower or bulb of this genus. *N. poeticus* is the **poet's narcissus.**

Nar·cis·sus (när·sis'əs) In Greek mythology, a youth who caused the death of Echo by spurning her love: in punishment Nemesis caused him to pine away and die for love of his own image in a pool, and changed him into the narcissus.

narco– *combining form* Torpor; insensibility: *narcomania.* Also, before vowels, **narc–.** [<Gk. *narkē* numbness]

nar·co·lep·sy (när'kō·lep'sē) *n. Pathol.* A condition marked by an uncontrollable desire for sleep or by sudden attacks of drowsiness: sometimes associated with petit mal. — **nar'·co·lep'tic** *adj.*

nar·co·ma·ni·a (när'kō·mā'nē·ə, -mān'yə) *n. Psychiatry* **1** A morbid craving to seek relief from pain, principally through the use of narcotics. **2** Psychotic alcoholism. — **nar'co·ma'ni·ac** *adj.* & *n.*

nar·co·sis (när·kō'sis) *n.* Deep sleep or unconsciousness produced by a drug. Also **nar·co'ma** (-kō'mə).

nar·co·syn·the·sis (när'kō·sin'thə·sis) *n. Psychiatry* A condition of seminarcosis induced by certain drugs to aid in the treatment of abnormal mental conditions by encouraging the patient to talk freely about himself.

nar·cot·ic (när·kot'ik) *n.* **1** Any of various substances, as opium, morphine, and codeine, that in medicinal doses relieve pain, induce sleep, and in excessive or uncontrolled doses may produce convulsions, coma, and death. **2** An individual addicted to the use of narcotics. — *adj.* **1** Having the quality of causing narcosis or stupor. **2** Figuratively, causing sleep or dulness, as a book or sermon. Also **nar·cose** (när'kōs), **nar·cot'i·cal** *adj.* [<Gk. *narkōtikos* <*narkē* torpor] — **nar·cot'i·cal·ly** *adv.*

nar·co·tism (när'kə·tiz'əm) *n.* **1** Stupor due to narcotics. **2** Any method or influence inducing narcosis. **3** A morbid tendency to sleep. **4** Addiction to narcotics.

nar·co·tize (när'kə·tīz) *v.t.* **·tized**, **·tiz·ing** To bring under the influence of a narcotic; stupefy. — **nar'co·ti·za'tion** *n.*

nard (närd) *n.* **1** Spikenard (the plant, oil, or ointment). **2** Any one of several aromatic plants or roots (mostly species of valerian) formerly used in medicine. [<OF *narde* <L *nardus* <Gk. *nardos*, prob. <Semitic] — **nard'ine** (när'dēn, -din) *adj.*

nar·es (nâr'ēz) *n. pl. of* **nar·is** (nâr'is) *Anat.* **1** Openings into the nose or nasal passages. **2** The nostrils. [<L, nostrils]

nar·ghi·le (när'gə·li) *n.* An Oriental tobacco pipe by which the smoke is drawn through water by means of a long tube. See HOOKAH. Also **nar'gi·le, nar'gi·leh.** [<Persian *nārgīleh* < *nārgīl* a coconut; because originally made of coconut shell]

Nar·ra·gan·set (nar'ə·gan'sit) *n.* **1** One of a tribe of North American Indians of Algonquian stock, formerly inhabiting Rhode Island. **2** The Algonquian language of this tribe. **3** One of a breed of small, robust, sure-footed horses, originally bred in Rhode Island, and valued as saddle horses: also **Nar'ra·gan'sett.**

nar·rate (na·rāt', när'āt) *v.t.* **·rat·ed**, **·rat·ing** To tell or relate as a story; give an account of. See synonyms under RELATE. [<L *narratus*, pp. of *narrare* relate] — **nar·ra'tor, nar·rat'er** *n.* — **nar'ra·to'ry** (-tôr'ē, -tō'rē) *adj.*

nar·ra·tion (na·rā'shən) *n.* **1** The act of narrating the particulars of an event or series of events. **2** That which is narrated; narrative. See synonyms under HISTORY, REPORT.

nar·ra·tive (när'ə·tiv) *n.* **1** An orderly, continuous account of an event or series of events. **2** The act or art of narrating. See synonyms under HISTORY, REPORT, STORY[1]. — *adj.* Pertaining to narration. — **nar'ra·tive·ly** *adv.*

nar·row (når'ō) *adj.* **1** Having comparatively little distance from side to side. **2** Limited in extent or duration; circumscribed; small. **3** Illiberal; bigoted. **4** Limited in means or resources; straitened. **5** Niggardly; parsimonious. **6** Barely accomplished, attained, or sufficient: a *narrow* escape. **7** Scrutinizing closely. **8** *Phonet.* Tense. See synonyms under LITTLE, SCANTY, SMALL. — *v.t.* & *v.i.* To make or become narrower, as in width or scope. — *n.* Usually *pl.* A narrow passage; strait; also, the narrowest part of an isthmus or cape. **2** A narrow part of a street, or of a valley or pass. — **The Narrows 1** A strait connecting Upper New York Bay with Lower New York Bay between the western end of Long Island and Staten Island. **2** The narrowest part of the Dardanelles. [OE *nearu*] — **nar'row·ness** *n.*

nar·row-gage (når'ō·gāj') *adj.* **1** Denoting a width of railroad track less than the standard gage. **2** *Colloq.* Petty; illiberal; narrow-minded. — *n.* **1** A railroad having a gage narrower than 4 feet 8 1/2 inches. **2** A train for a narrow-gage railroad.

nar·row·ly (når'ō·lē) *adv.* **1** With little breadth, width, or distance from side to side. **2** With small extent or duration; contractedly; restrictedly. **3** Barely; hardly.

nar·row-mind·ed (når'ō-mīn'did) *adj.* Of contracted mental scope; also, illiberal or bigoted. — **nar'row-mind'ed·ly** *adv.* — **nar'row-mind'ed·ness** *n.*

nar·thex (när'theks) *n. Archit.* A porch, vestibule, or division of a church or basilica before the entrance proper. [<L <Gk. *narthēx*, orig. a plant with a hollow stalk]

nar·whal (när'wəl, -hwəl) *n.* A large, arctic cetacean (*Monodon monoceros*) of the family *Delphinidae*, having in the male a long, straight, spiraled tusk: valued for its oil and ivory. Also **nar'wal, nar'whale'.** [<Dan. or Sw. *narhval*]

NARWHAL
a. Head of male showing tusk.
b. The female.
(From 12 to 16 feet in body length; the spiraled tusk from 6 to 8 feet)

nar·y (nâr'ē) *adj. Dial.* Never a; not one: opposite of *ary.*

na·sal[1] (nā'zəl) *adj.* **1** Of or pertaining to the nose. **2** *Phonet.* Pronounced with the voiced breath passing partially or wholly through the nose, as in (m), (n), and (ng), and the French nasal vowels. — *n. Phonet.* A nasal sound. [<NL *nasalis* <L *nasus* the nose] — **na·sal·i·ty** (nā·zal'ə·tē) *n.*

na·sal[2] (nā'zəl) *n.* A nosepiece. [<OF *nasal*, *nasel* <L *nasus* nose]

nasal index A number expressing the ratio of the greatest breadth of the nose (multiplied by 100) to the length· it is greater when measured on the face than on the skull, and varies with age.

na·sal·ize (nā'zəl·īz) *v.* **·ized**, **·iz·ing** *v.t.* To give a nasal sound to. — *v.i.* To pronounce oral sounds in the manner of nasals; talk through the nose. — **na·sal·i·za'tion** *n.*

nas·cent (nas'ənt, nā'sənt) *adj.* Beginning to exist or develop. [<L *nascens*, ppr. of *nasci* be born] — **nas'cence, nas'cen·cy** *n.*

nascent state *Chem.* The uncombined condition of an atom or radical when recently set free from a compound and ready to enter into combination with some other atom or radical. Also **nascent condition.**

nase·ber·ry (nāz'ber'ē) *n. pl.* **·ries** The plumlike fruit of the sapodilla. [<Sp. *níspero* medlar]

Nash·ville (nash'vil) The capital of Tennessee, on the Cumberland River.

Nashville warbler The common warbler of eastern North America (*Vermivora ruficapilla*), having an olive-green back and yellow breast.

na·si·on (nā'zē·on) *n. Anat.* The point at the root of the nose where the frontal and two nasal bones meet. [<NL <L *nasus* nose] — **na'si·al** *adj.*

naso– *combining form* Nose; nasal and: *nasofrontal.* [<L *nasus* nose]

na·so·fron·tal (nā'zō·frun'təl) *adj. Anat.* Of or pertaining to the nasal and frontal bones.

na·so·phar·ynx (nā'zō·far'ingks) *n. Anat.* The upper part of the pharynx, above and behind the soft palate. — **na'so·pha·ryn'ge·al** (-fə·rin'jē·əl) *adj.*

na·so·scope (nā'zō·skōp) *n.* A small electric lamp for examining the nasal cavity.

nas·tic (nas'tik) *adj. Bot.* Pertaining to or designating an automatic response in plants whose direction and character is determined by internal cellular pressure. [<Gk. *nastos* tight–pressed]

–nastic *combining form* Nastic toward or by: *epinastic.*

na·stur·tium (na·stûr'shəm) *n.* **1** A plant of the geranium family (genus *Tropaeolum*) with funnel–shaped flowers, commonly yellow, orange, scarlet, or crimson. **2** A rich yellow or reddish–orange color. [<L, cress <*nasus* the nose + *tortus*, pp. of *torquere* twist (from the pungent odor of the plant)]

nas·ty (nas'tē) *adj.* **·ti·er**, **·ti·est 1** Filthy or offensively dirty. **2** Morally filthy; indecent. **3** Nauseating; disgusting to the senses; disagreeable: the *nasty* task of cleaning a chicken coop. **4** Difficult to handle or deal with; vexatious; annoying: a *nasty* turn of events. **5** Painful; serious; bad: a *nasty* cut. **6** Ill-natured: a *nasty* brat; a *nasty* trick. See synonyms under FOUL. [Cf. Sw. *naskug* filthy] — **nas′ti·ly** *adv.* — **nas′ti·ness** *n.*

-nasty *combining form* A generalized automatic response to a (specified) stimulus: *epinasty*. [< Gk. *nastos* close-pressed]

na·tal (nāt′l) *adj.* **1** Pertaining to one's birth; dating from birth. **2** *Poetic* Native. [< L *natalis* < *nasci* be born]

na·tal·i·ty (nə·tal′ə·tē) *n.* The birth rate in a given community or place.

na·tant (nā′tənt) *adj.* Floating or swimming at the surface. [< L *natans*, *-antis*, ppr. of *natare* swim]

na·ta·tion (nā·tā′shən) *n.* The art of swimming or floating. [< L *natatio*, *-onis* < *natare* swim] — **na·ta′tion·al** *adj.*

na·ta·to·ri·al (nā′tə·tôr′ē·əl, -tō′rē-) *adj.* Swimming, or adapted for swimming. Also **na′ta·to′ry.**

na·ta·to·ri·um (nā′tə·tôr′ē·əm, -tō′rē-) *n. pl.* **·to·ri·ums** or **·to·ri·a** (-tôr′ē·ə, -tō′rē·ə) A swimming pool.

Natch·ez (nach′iz) *n.* One of a tribe of North American Indians of Muskhogean linguistic stock, formerly occupying the lower Mississippi Valley; overcome by the French in 1729–1730; later merged with Creek.

na·tes (nā′tēz) *n. pl.* The buttocks. [< L]

na·tion (nā′shən) *n.* **1** A people as an organized body politic, usually associated with a particular territory and possessing a distinctive cultural and social way of life. **2** An aggregation of people of common origin and language. **3** A race; tribe; specifically, a tribe of American Indians or the territory occupied by them. See synonyms under PEOPLE. [< F < L *natio*, *-onis* breed, race < *nasci* be born]

na·tion·al (nash′ən·əl) *adj.* **1** Belonging to a nation as a whole: opposed to *local*. **2** Of, pertaining to, or characteristic of a nation as distinguished from other nations. **3** Patriotic. **4** Authorized by a national government. — *n.* One who is a member of a nation. — **na′tion·al·ly** *adv.*

national debt The debt owed by any state; especially, the funded debt.

National Geographic Society A scientific society founded in 1888 in Washington, D.C.

National Guard *U.S.* An organized land or air force maintained by a State, a Territory, or the District of Columbia, usually in conjunction with but not under the direct control of the U.S. Army or Air Force. Its units or personnel operate on a semiactive basis as part of the militia except in national emergencies or under special circumstances, when they may be called into Federal service.

National Guard of the United States Those members and units of the National Guard that have taken an oath of appointment in the Federal service and are thereby constituted as a component part of the United States Army.

na·tion·al·ism (nash′ən·əl·iz′əm) *n.* **1** Devotion to the nation as a whole; patriotism. **2** A system demanding national conduct of all industries. **3** A world order founded on the right of each nation to determine its policies unhindered by others: opposed to *internationalism*. **4** A demand for national independence. **5** A national custom, trait, etc. — **na′tion·al·ist** *adj.* & *n.* — **na′tion·al·is′tic** *adj.* — **na′tion·al·is′ti·cal·ly** *adv.*

na·tion·al·i·ty (nash′ən·al′ə·tē) *n. pl.* **·ties 1** The quality of being national; national independence. **2** A nation. **3** A connection with a particular nation, as by citizenship.

na·tion·al·ize (nash′ən·əl·īz) *v.t.* **·ized, ·iz·ing 1** To place under the control or ownership of a nation. **2** To give a national character to. **3** To make into a nation. Also *Brit.* **na′tion·al·ise.** — **na′tion·al·i·za′tion** *n.* — **na′tion·al·iz′er** *n.*

national park A tract of U.S. government land withdrawn by special Act of Congress from settlement, occupancy, or sale, for the benefit and enjoyment of the public: preserved and maintained by the Federal government because of its historical interest, great natural beauty, or the value of its forests, wildlife, etc.

National Socialism The doctrines of the Nazi party. See NAZI.

Nation of Islam See under BLACK MUSLIM.

na·tion-wide (nā′shən·wīd′) *adj.* Throughout the entire nation.

na·tive (nā′tiv) *adj.* **1** Born or produced in a region or country in which one lives; indigenous: opposed to *foreign, exotic.* **2** Of or pertaining to one's birth or to its place or circumstances. **3** Natural rather than acquired; inborn; inherited. **4** Of or pertaining to natives; conferred by or peculiar to natives: usually applied to non-European peoples. **5** Natural to any one or any thing. **6** Plain, simple, unaffected, unadorned; untouched by art. **7** Occurring in nature in a pure state: *native* copper. **8** *Obs.* Related to birth; near; closely connected. — *n.* **1** One born in, or any product of, a given country or place; an aborigine. **2** Livestock common to a country or region. **3** In astrology, one born under a star or its aspect. [< F *natif* < L *nativus* < *nasci* be born. Doublet of NAIVE.] — **na′tive·ly** *adv.* — **na′tive·ness** *n.*

Synonyms (adj.): indigenous, innate, natal, natural, original. *Native* denotes that which belongs to one by birth; *natal* that which pertains to the event of birth; *natural* denotes that which rests upon inherent qualities of character or being. We speak of one's *native* country, or of his *natal* day; of *natural* ability, *native* genius. See INHERENT, NATURAL, PRIMEVAL, RADICAL. *Antonyms:* acquired, alien, artificial, assumed, foreign.

na·tive-born (nā′tiv·bôrn′) *adj.* Born in the region or country specified.

na·tiv·ism (nā′tiv·iz′əm) *n.* **1** Partiality in favor of native-born citizens in preference to foreign-born. **2** The doctrine of innate ideas. — **na′tiv·ist** *n.* — **na′tiv·is′tic** *adj.*

na·tiv·i·ty (nā·tiv′ə·tē, nə-) *n. pl.* **·ties 1** The coming into life or the world; birth. **2** A horoscope. **3** The condition of being born a serf or villein. **4** The condition of being a native. — **the Nativity** The birth of Jesus.

na·tri·um (nā′trē·əm) *n.* Sodium: so called in pharmacy and formerly in chemistry. [< NL < F *natron* NATRON]

nat·ro·lite (nat′rə·līt, nā′trə-) *n.* A white or colorless, orthorhombic, hydrous sodium-aluminum zeolite occurring in prismatic, needlelike crystals: also called *needlestone.*

na·tron (nā′tron) *n.* A brittle, vitreous, white, alkaline, hydrous sodium carbonate, $Na_2CO_3 \cdot 10H_2O$, crystallizing in the monoclinic system. [< F < Sp. *natrón* < Arabic *natrūn, nitrūn* < Gk. *nitron* niter]

nat·ty (nat′ē) *adj.* **·ti·er, ·ti·est** Smart; spruce; tidy. See synonyms under NEAT[1]. [? Akin to NEAT[1]] — **nat′ti·ly** *adv.* — **nat′ti·ness** *n.*

nat·u·ral (nach′ər·əl) *adj.* **1** Of or pertaining to one's nature or constitution; inherent; inborn; also, indigenous; native. **2** Of or pertaining to a particular nature; derived from nature; hence, exhibiting kindly feeling or affection. **3** Of or pertaining to nature; belonging or pertaining to the existing order of things: *natural* law; normal. **4** Coming within common experience; having to do with objects in the order of nature: opposed to *supernatural*. **5** Not forced or artificial; without affectation or exaggeration; lifelike. **6** Produced by nature; not artificial: a *natural* bridge. **7** Connected by ties of consanguinity; being such by birth: a *natural* brother. **8** Belonging to the inferior nature; not spiritual; animal. **9** Born out of wedlock; illegitimate. **10** *Music* Not sharped nor flatted: G *natural*; specifically, denoting the key of C, which is without flats or sharps in the signature. **11** *Math.* Designating an actual number in contradistinction to a logarithm: a *natural* sine, *natural* cosine, *natural* tangent, etc. See synonyms under INHERENT, NATIVE, NORMAL, PHYSICAL, RADICAL. — *n.* **1** *Music* A note on a line or a space that is affected by neither a sharp nor a flat. **b** A character (♮) which acts upon a sharped degree of the staff as a flat and upon a flatted degree as a sharp. **2** In keyboard musical instruments, a white key. **3** One born without the usual powers of reason or understanding; a born fool. **4** *Colloq.* A person or thing admirably suited for some purpose, or obviously destined for success. [< F *naturel* < L *naturalis* < *natura* nature] — **nat′u·ral·ness** *n.*

natural gas Any gaseous hydrocarbon, consisting chiefly of methane, generated naturally in subterranean oil deposits: used as a fuel.

natural history The observation and study of

the facts of the material universe as distinguished from man: commonly restricted to zoology, botany, geology, mineralogy, etc.

nat·u·ral·ism (nach′ər·əl·iz′əm) *n.* **1** Action or thought derived from or identified with exclusively natural desires and instincts. **2** In literature, art, etc.: **a** Adherence to observed nature; specifically, the principles of Zola, de Maupassant, and others who attempted to apply "scientific" objectivity to their treatment of life, without imposing judgments of value or avoiding what is considered ugly. **b** The qualities of a work of art resulting from such doctrines. **3** *Philos.* The doctrine that phenomena are derived from natural causes and can be explained by scientific laws: opposed to *supernaturalism*. **4** *Theol.* The doctrine that religion does not depend on supernatural revelation, but may be derived from the natural world.

nat·u·ral·ist (nach′ər·əl·ist) *n.* **1** One versed in natural sciences, as a zoologist or botanist. **2** An adherent of naturalism.

nat·u·ral·is·tic (nach′ər·əl·is′tik) *adj.* **1** In accordance with nature; not conventional or ideal. **2** According to the doctrines of naturalism. **3** Pertaining to naturalists.

nat·u·ral·i·za·tion (nach′ər·əl·i·zā′shən, -ī·zā′-) *n.* The act or process of admitting an alien to citizenship.

naturalization papers Documents recording an alien's application for citizenship or verifying the conferment of citizenship.

nat·u·ral·ize (nach′ər·əl·īz) *v.* **·ized, ·iz·ing** *v.t.* **1** To confer the rights and privileges of citizenship upon, as an alien. **2** To adopt (a foreign word, custom, etc.) into the common use of a country or area. **3** To adapt (a foreign plant, animal, etc.) to the environment of a country or area. **4** To explain by natural laws: to *naturalize* a miracle. **5** To make natural; free from conventionality. — *v.i.* **6** To become as if native; adapt. Also *Brit.* **nat′u·ral·ise.** — **nat′u·ral·iz′er** *n.*

natural law A rule of conduct supposed to be inherent in man's nature and discoverable by reason alone.

nat·u·ral·ly (nach′ər·əl·ē) *adv.* **1** Without effort; spontaneously. **2** Without affectation or exaggeration. **3** As might have been expected; of course. **4** In a lifelike or natural manner.

natural philosophy 1 Natural history. **2** The physical sciences taken collectively.

natural resource Any of those sources of wealth provided by nature, as soil, forests, minerals, water supply, water power, and wild game.

natural sciences The sciences treating of the physical universe, taken collectively and in distinction from the mental and moral sciences and from abstract mathematics.

natural selection *Biol.* The process whereby individual variations of peculiarities that are of advantage in a certain environment tend to become perpetuated in the race; survival of the fittest.

na·ture (nā′chər) *n.* **1** The character, constitution, or essential traits of a person, thing, or class, especially if original rather than acquired. **2** The physical or psychic constitution or character of persons or things, whether native or acquired: often personified in poetry or figurative prose. **3** The entire material universe and its phenomena. **4** The system of natural existences, forces, changes, and events, regarded as distinguished from, or exclusive of, the supernatural: Man is included in *nature*. **5** The sum of physical or material existences and forces in the universe. **6** The constitution or inherited or habitual condition and tendencies of man. **7** *Theol.* The unregenerate state; character unchanged by grace. **8** *Obs.* Generative energy; genesis; birth. See synonyms under CHARACTER, SORT, TEMPER. [< F < L *natura* < *natus*, pp. of *nasci* be born]

-natured *combining form* Possessing a (specified) nature, disposition, or temperament: ill-*natured*. [< NATURE (def. 1)]

na·tur·op·a·thy (nā′chə·rop′ə·thē) *n. Med.* A system of therapy which avoids drugs in favor of such physical agencies as sunshine, air, water, exercise, etc. [< NATURE + -(O)PATHY] — **na·tur′o·path** (nə·choŏr′ə·path) *n.* — **na·tur′o·path′ic** *adj.*

naught (nôt) *n.* **1** Not anything; nothing. **2** A cipher; zero; the character 0. — *adj.* **1** Of no value or account. **2** *Obs.* Bad; wicked; also, poor in quality. — *adv.* Not in the least. Also spelled nought. [OE *nāwiht* < *nā* not + *wiht* thing]

naugh·ty (nô'tē) *adj.* **·ti·er, ·ti·est 1** Perverse and disobedient; wayward; mischievous. **2** *Obs.* Corrupt; wicked. See synonyms under BAD. [< NAUGHT] —**naugh'ti·ly** *adv.* —**naugh'ti·ness** *n.*

nau·path·i·a (nô·path'ē·ə) *n.* Seasickness. [< NL < Gk. *naus* a ship + *path-*, stem of *paschein* suffer]

nau·pli·us (nô'plē·əs) *n. pl.* **·pli·i** (-plē·ī) *Zool.* A larval stage of certain crustaceans, with body unsegmented, a median eye, and three pairs of legs which correspond to the anterior and posterior antennae and the mandibles of the adult. [< L, a kind of shellfish]

nau·sea (nô'zhə, -zē·ə, -shə, -sē·ə) *n.* **1** Sickness of the stomach, producing dizziness and an impulse to vomit. **2** A feeling of loathing in general. [< L < Gk. *nausia* < *naus* ship]

nau·se·ate (nô'zhē·āt, -zē, -shē, -sē-) *v.t. & v.i.* **·at·ed, ·at·ing** To affect with or feel nausea or disgust. —**nau'se·a'tion** *n.*

nau·seous (nô'zhəs, -shəs) *adj.* **1** Nauseating; disgusting. **2** *Colloq.* Affected with nausea; queasy. —**nau'seous·ly** *adv.* —**nau'seous·ness** *n.*

nau·ti·cal (nô'ti·kəl) *adj.* Pertaining to ships, seamen, or navigation. Also **nau'tic.** [< Gk. *nautikos* < *naus* ship] —**nau'ti·cal·ly** *adv.*

Synonyms: marine, maritime, naval, ocean, oceanic. *Marine* signifies belonging to the ocean; *maritime* bordering on or connected with the ocean; as, *marine* products; *marine* animals; *maritime* nations; *maritime* laws. *Naval* refers to the armed force of a nation on the sea, and on lakes and rivers; *nautical* denotes primarily anything connected with sailors, or with ships or navigation; as, a *nautical* almanac. *Oceanic* is especially applied to that which is suggestive of an *ocean*.

nautical mile See under MILE.

nau·ti·lus (nô'tə·ləs) *n. pl.* **·lus·es** or **·li** (-lī) **1** Any of a family of cephalopod mollusks containing a single surviving genus (*Nautilus*) found in southern seas and having a natant spiral shell containing a series of empty chambers lined with mother-of-pearl that are successively secreted and then sealed off as the animal outgrows them. **2** The paper nautilus. [< L < Gk. *nautilos*, sailor]

CHAMBERED NAUTILUS
Cross-section
(The shell up to 10 inches across)

Nautilus The first atomic-powered submarine, launched by the U.S. Navy: made the first undersea crossing of the North Pole on August 3, 1958.

Nav·a·ho (nav'ə·hō) *n. pl.* **·hos** or **·hoes** One of a tribe of North American Indians of Athapascan stock, now living on reservations in Arizona, New Mexico, and Utah. Also **Nav'a·jo.**

na·val (nā'vəl) *adj.* **1** Pertaining to ships and a navy: distinguished from *civil.* **2** Having a navy; relating to the navy. See synonyms under NAUTICAL. ◆ Homophone: *navel.* [< L *navalis* < *navis* ship]

naval auxiliary A launch or auxiliary vessel, as a tanker.

naval brass *Metall.* A type of brass containing a small percentage of tin to increase hardness and resistance to corrosion: used for marine fittings, etc.

naval stores Rosin and its products, as turpentine, pine oil, etc.; also, tar, pitch, asphalt, and other similar materials formerly or still used by shipbuilders.

nave¹ (nāv) *n. Archit.* The main body of a cruciform church, between the side aisles, and usually having a clerestory. ◆ Homophone: *knave.* [< OF < L *navis* ship]

nave² (nāv) *n.* **1** The central part or hub of a wheel. **2** *Obs.* The navel. ◆ Homophone: *knave.* [OE *nafu*]

na·vel (nā'vəl) *n.* **1** The depression on the abdomen where the umbilical cord was attached. **2** A central part or point. ◆ Homophone: *naval.* [OE *nafela* < *nafu* nave²]

na·veled (nā'vəld) *adj.* Having a navel; set as in a navel or hollow. Also **na'velled.**

navel orange An orange, usually seedless, having a small secondary fruit and a rind marked at the apex with a navel-like depression.

na·vel·wort (nā'vəl·wûrt') *n.* **1** A low herb (genus *Omphalodes*) of the borage family, native in Europe and Asia, with alternate leaves and blue or white flowers resembling forget-me-nots: also **na'vel·seed'. 2** A succulent herb (*Umbilicus pendulinus*) with yellowish or greenish tubular flowers. **3** Any of various other plants, as the pennywort or the water milfoil.

na·vic·u·lar (nə·vik'yə·lər) *adj.* **1** Boat-shaped; scaphoid. **2** Pertaining to a boat. —*n. Anat.* **1** A bone on the radial side of the wrist; also, the bone in front of the astragalus in the foot: also **na·vic·u·la're** (-lâr'ē). See illustration under FOOT. **2** A large bone behind the joint between the second and third phalanges of a horse's foot. [< LL *navicularis* < L *navis* ship]

na·vic·u·lar·thri·tis (nə·vik'yə·lär·thrī'tis) *n.* Inflammation of the navicular bone of the foot of a horse. Also **navicular disease.**

nav·i·gate (nav'ə·gāt) *v.* **·gat·ed, ·gat·ing** *v.t.* **1** To travel over, across, or on by ship or aircraft. **2** To steer; direct the course of. —*v.i.* **3** To travel by means of ship or aircraft. **4** To steer or manage a ship or aircraft. **5** To plot a course for a ship or aircraft. [< L *navigatus*, pp. of *navigare* < *navis* a boat + *agere* drive] —**nav·i·ga·ble** (nav'ə·gə·bəl) *adj.* —**nav'i·ga·bly** *adv.* —**nav'i·ga·bil'i·ty, nav'i·ga·ble·ness** *n.*

nav·i·ga·tion (nav'ə·gā'shən) *n.* **1** The act of navigating. **2** The art of ascertaining the position and directing the course of vessels at sea or of aircraft in flight. —**nav'i·ga'tion·al** *adj.*

nav·i·ga·tor (nav'ə·gā'tər) *n.* **1** One who navigates, or directs the course of a ship, aircraft, etc. **2** A person skilled in navigation.

na·vy (nā'vē) *n. pl.* **·vies 1** The entire marine military force of a country, under the control of a government department, and including vessels, men in the service, yards, etc. **2** The entire shipping of a country engaged in trade and commerce; the merchant marine. **3** A fleet of ships, as of merchantmen. —**United States Navy** The U.S. naval force administered by the Department of the Navy under the Department of Defense and including the Regular Navy, the Naval Reserve, the United States Marine Corps, and the United States Coast Guard when operating as a component of the Navy. [< OF *navie* < L *navis* ship]

navy bean The common, small, dried, white bean: so called from its common use in the U.S. Navy.

navy blue Any of various shades of dark blue. Also **navy.** —**na'vy-blue'** *adj.*

navy gray A medium bluish-gray: adopted in World War II for the color of work uniforms of officers in the U.S. Navy. —**na'vy-gray'** *adj.*

navy yard A government-owned dockyard for the construction, repair, equipment, or care of warships.

nay (nā) *adv.* **1** No: indicating negation. **2** Not only so, but also: He is a good, *nay,* an excellent man. —*n.* **1** A negative vote or voter: opposed to *yea.* **2** A negative; denial. [< ON *nei* < *ne* not + *ei* ever]

Naz·a·reth (naz'ə·rith) An ancient town in Lower Galilee, northern Israel; scene of Christ's childhood.

Na·zi (nä'tsē, nat'sē, na'zē) *n.* A member of the National Socialist German Workers Party, founded in 1919 on fascist principles and dominant from 1933 to 1945 in Germany under the dictatorship of Hitler, where it followed the principles of extreme nationalism, racism, totalitarian direction of all cultural, political, and economic activity, and militarization, while urging a destiny of world leadership for Germany. —*adj.* Of or pertaining to the Nazis or their party. [< G, short for *Nationalsozialistische (Partei)* National Socialist (Party)]

Na·zi·fy (nä'tsə·fī, nat'sə-) *v.t.* **·fied, ·fy·ing** To subject to Nazi influence or control; cause to be Nazi-like. —**Na'zi·fi·ca'tion** *n.*

Na·zism (nä'tsiz·əm, nat'siz-) *n.* The doctrines or practices of the Nazi party. Also **Na·zi·ism** (nä'tsē·iz'əm, nat'sē-).

Nb *Chem.* Niobium (symbol Nb).

Nd *Chem.* Neodymium (symbol Nd).

Ne *Chem.* Neon (symbol Ne).

Ne·an·der·thal man (nē·an'dər·täl, -thôl, -thol; *Ger.* nā·än'dər·täl) A relatively advanced protohuman species (*Homo neanderthalensis*) first identified from fragments of a fossil skeleton discovered in 1856 in cave deposits of the Neander valley near Düsseldorf. It is regarded as typical of a race of ancient cave-dwellers who preceded modern man, developing the Mousterian stone culture in western Europe. [< G *Neanderthal* Neander valley]

NEANDERTHAL SKULL

neap¹ (nēp) *adj.* Designating the tide occurring one or two days after the first and third quarters of the moon. —*n.* **1** A neap tide. **2** The lowest ebb. [OE *nēp-* in *nēpflod* low tide]

neap² (nēp) *n. U.S. Dial.* A wagon tongue [? < Scand. Cf. dial. Norw. *neip* forked pole.]

near (nir) *adj.* **1** Not distant in place, time, or degree; nigh; contiguous. **2** Closely related by blood or affection; familiar. **3** Closely touching one's interests. **4** In riding or driving, placed on the left: opposed to *off.* **5** Following or imitating closely; literal: a *near* copy; also, resembling or substituted for: *near* beer. **6** Penurious or miserly; stingy. **7** Short or speedy; tending to lessen a distance: a *near* way. **8** Avoiding by a narrow margin; close: a *near* escape. See synonyms under ADJACENT. —*adv.* **1** At little distance; not remote in place, time, or degree. **2** Nearly; almost; approximately. **3** In a close relation; intimately. **4** *Naut.* Close to the wind. **5** Stingily; parsimoniously. —*v.t. & v.i.* To come or draw near (to); approach. —*prep.* Close by or to. See synonyms under AT. [OE *nēar,* comp. of *nēah* NIGH] —**near'ness** *n.*

near beer Any imitation beer of little or no alcoholic content.

near·by (nir'bī') *adj. & adv.* Close at hand; adjacent.

near·ly (nir'lē) *adv.* **1** Within a little; almost. **2** With a close regard to one's interest. **3** At no great distance; closely; narrowly. **4** Stingily.

near rime In prosody, a more or less radical substitute for rime, including such devices as assonance and consonance: also called *paraphone, half rime, oblique rime.*

near·sight·ed (nir'sī'tid) *adj.* Able to see distinctly at short distances only; myopic. —**near'sight'ed·ly** *adv.* —**near'-sight'ed·ness** *n.*

neat (nēt) *adj.* **1** Characterized by strict order, tidiness, and cleanliness. **2** Well-proportioned; trim; shapely. **3** Suited in character to a required purpose; hence, adroit; clever. **4** Clear of extraneous matter; free from admixture; undiluted: a glass of brandy *neat.* **5** Remaining after every deduction; net. [< AF *niet,* OF *net* < L *nitidus* shining] —**neat'ly** *adv.* —**neat'ness** *n.*

Synonyms: clean, cleanly, dapper, natty, nice, orderly, prim, spruce, tidy, trim. That which is *clean* is simply free from soil or defilement of any kind. Things are *orderly* in relation to other things; a room or desk is *orderly* when every article is in place; a person is *orderly* who habitually keeps things so. *Tidy* denotes that which conforms to propriety in general; an unlaced shoe may be perfectly *clean,* but is not *tidy. Neat* refers to that which is *clean* and *tidy,* with nothing superfluous, conspicuous, or showy; we speak of plain but *neat* attire; the same idea of freedom from the superfluous appears in the phrases "a *neat* speech," "a *neat* turn," "a *neat* reply," etc. A *clean* cut has no ragged edges; a *neat* stroke just does what is intended. *Nice* is stronger than *neat*, implying value and beauty; a cheap, coarse dress may be perfectly *neat*, but would not be termed *nice*. *Spruce* is applied to the show and affectation of neatness with a touch of smartness. *Trim* denotes a certain shapely and elegant firmness, often with suppleness and grace. *Prim* applies to a precise, formal, affected nicety. *Dapper* is *spruce* with the suggestion of smallness and slightness; *natty*, a diminutive of *neat*, suggests minute elegance, with a tendency toward the exquisite; as, a *dapper* man in a *natty* business suit. See BECOMING. *Antonyms*: dirty, disorderly, dowdy, negligent, rough, rude, slouchy, slovenly, soiled, untidy.

neat·herd (nēt′hûrd′) *n.* A herdsman.

neat's-foot oil (nēts′foot′) A pale yellow oil obtained by boiling the feet of neat cattle: used as a lubricant and softening agent for leather.

neb (neb) *n.* **1** The beak or bill, as of a bird; nose; snout. **2** The tip end of a thing; nib, as of a pen. **3** *Scot.* The face; also, the mouth. [OE *nebb*]

Ne·bras·ka (nə·bras′kə) A State in the north central United States; 77,237 square miles; capital, Lincoln; entered the Union Feb. 9, 1867; nickname, *Tree Planter State.* abbr. NE —**Ne·bras′kan** *adj. & n.*

neb·u·la (neb′yə·lə) *n. pl.* **·lae** (-lē) or **·las** **1** *Astron.* A luminous celestial body of cloudlike appearance and vast extent, composed of gaseous or stellar matter in various degrees of density. **2** *Pathol.* **a** A speck on the cornea; visual opacity. **b** Cloudiness of the urine. [< L, vapor, mist] —**neb′u·lar** *adj.*

nebular hypothesis *Astron.* A hypothesis that the solar system existed originally in the form of a nebula which, by cooling, condensing, and revolving, was formed into the sun and into rings of matter which later were consolidated into the planetary bodies.

neb·u·lize (neb′yə·līz) *v.t.* **·lized**, **·liz·ing** **1** To spray, as a wound or a morbid surface, with medicated liquid. **2** To reduce to a spray; atomize. —**neb′u·li·za′tion** *n.* —**neb′u·liz′er** *n.*

neb·u·lose (neb′yə·lōs) *adj.* Cloudlike; clouded.

neb·u·lous (neb′yə·ləs) *adj.* **1** Having its parts confused or mixed; hazy; indistinct: a *nebulous* idea. **2** Like a nebula. —**neb′u·lous·ly** *adv.* —**neb′u·lous·ness** *n.*

nec·es·sar·i·an·ism (nes′ə·sâr′ē·ən·iz′əm) *n.* The philosophical doctrine that acts of volition are predetermined by the force of inner motives; determinism; fatalism; necessity. Also **ne·ces′·si·tar′i·an** —**nec′es·sar′i·an**, **ne·ces·si·tar·i·an** (nə·ses′ə·târ′ē·ən) *adj. & n.*

nec·es·sar·y (nes′ə·ser′ē) *adj.* **1** Being such in its nature or conditions that it must exist, occur, or be true; inevitable. **2** Absolutely needed to accomplish a desired result; essential; requisite. **3** Compulsory: a *necessary* action. **4** Being such that it must be believed. **5** *Archaic* Rendering useful and intimate service. —*n. pl.* **·sar·ies** **1** That which is indispensable; an essential requisite: used usually in the plural: the *necessaries* of life. **2** That which is subject to the law of necessity: The *necessary* is opposed to the contingent. **3** A watercloset; privy. [< L *necessarius* necessary] —**nec′es·sar′i·ly** *adv.* —**nec′es·sar′i·ness** *n.*

Synonyms (adj.): compulsory, essential, indispensable, inevitable, needed, needful, required, requisite, unavoidable, undeniable. That which is *essential* belongs to the essence of a thing, so that the thing cannot exist in its completeness without it; that which is *indispensable* may be only an adjunct, but it is one that cannot be spared. That which is *requisite* is so in the judgment of the person requiring it. Food is *necessary*, death is *inevitable*; a *necessary* conclusion satisfies a thinker; an *inevitable* conclusion silences opposition. *Needed* and *needful* are more concrete than *necessary*, and respect an end to be attained, while *necessary* may apply simply to what exists; we speak of a *necessary* inference; *necessary* food is what one cannot live without, while *needful* food is that without which we cannot enjoy comfort, health, and strength. *Antonyms*: casual, contingent, needless, non-essential, optional, unnecessary, useless, worthless.

ne·ces·si·tate (nə·ses′ə·tāt) *v.t.* **·tat·ed**, **·tat·ing** **1** To make necessary, unavoidable, or certain. **2** To

compel. See synonyms under COMPEL. [< Med. L. *necessitatus*, pp. of *necessitare* compel < *necessitas*, *-tatis* necessity] —**ne·ces′si·ta′tion** *n.* —**ne·ces′si·ta′tive** *adj.*

ne·ces·si·tous (nə·ses′ə·təs) *adj.* Extremely needy; destitute; poverty-stricken. —**ne·ces′·si·tous·ly** *adv.* —**ne·ces′si·tous·ness** *n.*

ne·ces·si·ty (nə·ses′ə·tē) *n. pl.* **·ties** **1** The quality of being necessary: Food is a *necessity* for growth. **2** That which is unavoidable or necessary, as in physical, moral, or logical sequence; a state of things rendering something inevitable. **3** That which is indispensably requisite to an end desired: often in the plural: the *necessities* of life; also, the fact of being indispensable; indispensableness. **4** The condition of being in want; poverty. **5** The doctrine that all events are necessarily determined. It embraces physical determinism, or fatalism, and philosophical or rational determinism, thus precluding chance or free will. — **of necessity** Necessarily; unavoidably. [< L *necessitas, -tatis*]

Synonyms: compulsion, destiny, emergency, essential, exigency, extremity, fatality, fate, indispensability, indispensableness, need, requirement, requisite, unavoidableness, urgency, want. An *essential* is something, as a quality or element, that belongs to the essence of something else so as so to be inseparable from it in its normal condition, or in any complete idea or statement of it. *Need* and *want* always imply a lack; but *necessity* simply denotes the exclusion of any alternative either in thought or fact. See PREDESTINATION, WANT. Compare NECESSARY. *Antonyms*: choice, contingency, doubt, doubtfulness, dubiousness, fortuity, freedom, option, possibility, uncertainty.

neck (nek) *n.* **1** *Anat.* **a** The part of an animal that connects the head with the trunk. **b** Any similarly constricted portion of an organ or part: the *neck* of the femur. ◆ Collateral adjective: *cervical.* **2** The narrowed part of an object, particularly if near one end. **3** Something likened to a neck, from its position, shape, etc. **4** The narrow part of a bottle. **5** A narrow passage of water connecting two larger bodies. **6** A peninsula, isthmus, or cape. **7** That part of a garment which is close to the neck. **8** That part of a stringed musical instrument of the banjo class between the head and the body, and bearing the frets, if any. **9** *Archit.* The upper part of the shaft of a column, immediately below the capital. **10** The diminished part of a shaft, axle, etc., where it rests in a bearing. — *v.i.* **1** *U.S. Slang* To make love by kissing and caressing. — *v.t.* **2** *U.S. Slang* To make love to (someone) in such a manner. **3** To behead or strangle, as a chicken. [OE *hnecca*]

neck and neck Keeping evenly abreast; keeping up with each other.

neck·band (nek′band′) *n.* **1** The part of a garment that fits around the neck: the *neckband* of a shirt or dress. **2** A band around the neck.

neck·cloth (nek′klôth′) *n.* A folded cloth worn around the neck and collar; a cravat. Compare STOCK (def. 24).

neck·er·chief (nek′ər·chif) *n.* A kerchief for the neck.

neck·ing (nek′ing) *n.* **1** *Archit.* An ornamental treatment, as a sculptured band, a hollow, etc., of the neck of a column; also, a gorgerin. **2** Any necklike stem. **3** *Slang* Kissing and caressing in lovemaking.

neck·lace (nek′lis) *n.* An ornament, as of precious stones, precious metal, beads, or the like, worn around the neck.

neck of the woods *U.S. Colloq.* A region or neighborhood.

neck–or–noth·ing (nek′ôr·nuth′ing) *adj.* Risking everything; desperate.

neck·tie (nek′tī) *n.* **1** A band or scarf passing round the neck or collar and tying in front under the chin; any bow or tie worn under the chin. **2** *U.S. Slang* A halter. — **necktie sociable** or **party** *U.S. Slang* A lynching.

neck·wear (nek′wâr′) *n.* **1** Any article worn around the throat. **2** Ties, cravats, collars, mufflers, etc., collectively.

neck·yoke (nek′yōk′) *n.* **1** A yoke for the neck. **2** A crosspiece to connect the forward end of the tongue of a vehicle with the harness.

nec·rec·to·my (nek·rek′tə·mē) *n. Surg.* The removal of dead matter. [< NECR(O) + -ECTOMY]

nec·ren·ceph·a·lus (nek′rən·sef′ə·ləs) *n. Pathol.* Softening of the brain. [< NECR(O)- + Gk. *enkephalos* brain]

necro- *combining form* Corpse; dead matter: *necropolis.* Also, before vowels, **necr-**. [< Gk. *nekros* a corpse]

nec·ro·bac·il·lo·sis (nek′rō·bas′ə·lō′sis) *n.* An infective disease of cattle, sheep, horses, elk, and swine due to invasion of the body by a micro-organism (*Actinomyces necrophorus*) which produces large areas of gangrenous and necrotic tissue.

nec·ro·bi·o·sis (nek′rō·bī·ō′sis) *n. Pathol.* Progressive decay and death of an organ or tissue. [< NECRO- + Gk. *bios* life] — **nec′ro·bi·ot′ic** (-ot′ik) *adj.*

nec·ro·gen·ic (nek′rə·jen′ik) *adj.* Originating or living in dead matter. Also **ne·crog·e·nous** (ne·kroj′ə·nəs).

ne·crol·o·gy (ne·krol′ə·jē) *n. pl.* **·gies** **1** A list of persons who have died in a certain place or time. **2** A treatise on or an account of the dead. **3** Formerly, a register of those for whose souls prayer was to be offered. [< NECRO- + Gk. *logos* a list, register] — **nec·ro·log·ic** (nek′rə·loj′ik), **nec′ro·log′i·cal** *adj.* — **nec′ro·log′i·cal·ly** *adv.* — **ne·crol′o·gist** *n.*

nec·ro·man·cy (nek′rə·man′sē) *n.* **1** Divination by means of pretended communication with the dead. **2** Black magic; sorcery. See synonyms under SORCERY. — **nec′ro·man′cer** *n.* — **nec′ro·man′tic** *adj.*

nec·ro·ma·ni·a (nek′rō·mā′nē·ə, -mān′yə) *n.* A morbid preoccupation with death or interest in dead persons. — **nec′ro·ma′ni·ac** (-nē·ak) *n.*

ne·croph·a·gous (ne·krof′ə·gəs) *adj.* Subsisting on carrion. [< NECRO- + -PHAGOUS]

nec·ro·phile (nek′rə·fīl, -fil) *n.* One who has a morbid attraction, usually of an erotic nature, to corpses. — **nec′ro·phil′i·a**, **ne·croph·i·lism** (ne·krof′ə·liz′əm) — **nec′ro·phil·y** *n.*

nec·ro·pho·bi·a (nek′rō·fō′bē·ə) *n.* A morbid fear of death or of dead bodies. — **nec′ro·pho′bic** *adj.*

ne·crop·o·lis (ne·krop′ə·lis) *n.* A cemetery, especially one belonging to an ancient city. [< NECRO- + Gk. *polis* city]

nec·rop·sy (nek′rop·sē) *n. pl.* **·sies** An examination of a dead body; an autopsy. Also **ne·cros·co·py** (ne·kros′kə·pē). [< NECRO- + -OPSY]

ne·crose (ne·krōs′, nek′rōs) *v.t. & v.i.* **·crosed**, **·cros·ing** To affect with or suffer from necrosis.

ne·cro·sis (ne·krō′sis) *n.* **1** *Pathol.* The death of a part of the body, as of a bone; mortification; gangrene. **2** *Bot.* A gradual decay in trees or plants. [< Gk. *nekrōsis* deadness] — **ne·crot′ic** (-krot′ik) *adj.*

ne·crot·o·my (ne·krot′ə·mē) *n.* **1** The dissection of a dead body. **2** *Surg.* The excision of dead bone. [< NECRO- + -TOMY] — **nec·ro·tom·ic** (nek′rə·tom′ik) *adj.* — **ne·crot′o·mist** *n.*

nec·tar (nek′tər) *n.* **1** In Greek mythology, the drink of the gods. **2** Hence, any especially sweet drink: applied specifically to certain spiced or honeyed wines. **3** *Bot.* The saccharine substance secreted by some plants and forming the base of natural honey. [< L < Gk. *nektar*] — **nec·tar·e·an** (nek·târ′ē·ən) *adj.* — **nec·tar′e·ous** *adj.*

nec·tar·ine (nek′tə·rēn′, nek′tə·rēn) *n.* A variety of peach having a smooth, waxy skin without down and a firm, aromatic pulp. — *adj.* Sweet and delicious.

nec·ta·ry (nek′tər·ē) *n. pl.* **·ries** **1** *Bot.* The organ or part of a plant that secretes nectar. **2** *Entomol.* One of the small, abdominal honey tubes of an aphid. — **nec·tar′i·al**, **nec·tar′e·al** (-târ′ē·əl) *adj.*

née (nā) *adj.* Born: noting the maiden name of a married woman: Madame d'Arblay, *née* Burney. [< F, pp. of *naître* be born < L *nasci*]

need (nēd) *v.t.* **1** To have need of or want of; require. — *v.i.* **2** To be in want. **3** *Archaic* To be necessary: It *needs* not. **4** To be obliged or compelled: in this sense *need* is used as an uninflected auxiliary verb only in negative and interrogative sentences, followed by the infinitive without *to*: He *need* not go; *Need* he come? — *n.* **1** A lack of something requisite or desirable; hence, indigence; poverty: He was in *need.* **2** A situation of want or peril. **3** The thing needed. See synonyms under NECESSITY, POVERTY, WANT. ◆ Homophone: *knead.* [OE *nied*, *nēd*] — **need′er** *n.*

need·ful (nēd′fəl) *adj.* **1** Needed; requisite; necessary. **2** Needy. — **need′ful·ly** *adv.* — **need′ful·ness** *n.*

need·i·ness (nē′di·nis) *n.* The state of being in want; poverty.

nee·dle (nēd′l) *n.* **1** A small, slender, pointed instrument containing an eye at the head, or, in sewing machines, at the point, to carry thread through a fabric in sewing. **2** The straight rod, commonly of wire, bone, or wood, used in knitting; also, the hooked rod used in crocheting. **3** Any instrument or object shaped like or used as a needle, as a pinnacle of rock, or a leaf, such as that of the pine. **4** A straight wire, balanced and pivoted, as in a compass: a magnetic needle. **5** In a needle gun, the steel bolt that fires the cartridge. **6** A needle valve. **7** The sharp-pointed end of a hypodermic syringe. **8** *Colloq.* A hypodermic needle. **9** An obelisk. **10** A thin, sharp-pointed piece of steel, etc., often tipped with diamond, etc., to transmit the sound vibrations from a phonograph record. — *v.* **·dled, ·dling** *v.t.* **1** To sew or pierce with a needle. **2** *Colloq.* To heckle or annoy. **3** *Colloq.* To goad; prod. **4** *Colloq.* To increase the alcoholic content of: to *needle* the beer. — *v.i.* **5** To sew or work with a needle. [OE *nǣdl*]

nee·dle·bath (nēd′l·bath′, ·bäth′) *n.* A form of shower bath in which the water is projected with force in fine jets.

nee·dle·fish (nēd′l·fish′) *n.* *pl.* **·fish** or **·fish·es 1** One of the long, slender sea fishes of the family *Belonidae*, superficially resembling the fresh-water gar. **2** The pipefish.

nee·dle·ful (nēd′l·fŏŏl′) *n.* *pl.* **·fuls** The length of thread that can be suitably used in a needle at one time.

needle grass Feather grass.

nee·dle·point (nēd′l·point′) *n.* **1** A sharp-pointed attachment for the leg of a drawing instrument; anything resembling the point of a needle, as spires of cathedrals or crystals of rock. **2** Lace made entirely with a sewing needle rather than bobbins, and worked with buttonhole and blanket stitches on a paper pattern. **3** A stitch used in needle tapestry, or embroidered needle tapestry itself.

need·less (nēd′lis) *adj.* Useless; not required. — **need′less·ly** *adv.* — **need′less·ness** *n.*

needle valve *Mech.* **1** A valve having a conoidal opening closed by a plug of similar shape: designed to control accurately the flow of a liquid, as in a carbureter. **2** A valve with a conoidal plug fitting into a cylindrical opening: designed to give a large increase in opening with a slight increase in lift.

nee·dle·work (nēd′l·wûrk′) *n.* **1** Work done with a needle; sewing; specifically, embroidery. **2** The business of sewing with a needle. — **nee′dle·work′er** *n.*

needs (nēdz) *adv.* Necessarily; indispensably: often with *must.*

need·y (nē′dē) *adj.* **need·i·er, need·i·est** Being in need, want, or poverty; necessitous. — **need′i·ly** *adv.*

ne'er (nâr) *adv.* Never: a contraction.

ne'er–do–well (nâr′dŏŏ·wel′) *n.* A useless, unreliable person. — *adj.* Useless; good-for-nothing. Also **ne'er′–do–good′** (-gŏŏd′), *Scot.* **ne'er′–do–weel′** (-wēl′).

ne·far·i·ous (ni·fâr′ē·əs) *adj.* Wicked in the extreme; heinous. See synonyms under CRIMINAL, FLAGRANT, INFAMOUS, SINFUL. [< L *nefarius* < *nefas* a crime < *ne*- not + *fas* a divine command, right] — **ne·far′i·ous·ly** *adv.* — **ne·far′i·ous·ness** *n.*

ne·gate (ni·gāt′, nē′gāt) *v.t.* **·gat·ed, ·gat·ing 1** To make ineffective; nullify. **2** To deny the existence of. [< L *negatus*, pp. of *negare* deny]

ne·ga·tion (ni·gā′shən) *n.* **1** The act of denying or of asserting the falsity of a proposition; denial in general. **2** Absence of anything affirmative or definite; voidness; nullity.

neg·a·tive (neg′ə·tiv) *adj.* **1** Containing contradiction or denial; expressing negation; opposed to *affirmative.* **2** Characterized by denial or refusal: a *negative* reply. **3** Exhibiting or characterized by absence of that which is essential to positive or affirmative char-

acter: the opposite of *positive.* **4** *Phot.* Exhibiting the reverse; showing dark for light and light for dark: a *negative* plate or film. **5** *Math.* **a** Denoting a direction or quality the opposite of another assumed as positive: usually denoted by the minus sign (–). **b** Less than zero; to be subtracted; minus: said of quantities. **6** *Geom.* Situated or measured downward from the axis of *X* or to the left of the axis of *Y.* **7** *Electr.* Denoting a type of electricity characterized by an excess of electrons on a charged body: opposed to *positive.* It is similar to that produced on a resinous object after rubbing with wool. **8** *Biol.* Describing a plant or animal response directed away from or in opposition to a stimulus. **9** *Med.* Indicating the absence of a suspected condition, or the absence of certain bacteria. See synonyms under PASSIVE. — *n.* **1** A proposition, word, or act expressing refusal or denial: My request received a *negative.* **2** The side of a question that denies; also, a negative decision. **3** The right to veto. **4** A photograph having the lights and shades reversed, used for printing positives. **5** *Gram.* A particle employing or expressing denial. The principal negative is *not.* **6** *Electr.* **a** Negative or frictional electricity. **b** The negative plate of a voltaic cell. **7** *Math.* A negative sign or quantity. — **double negative** *Gram.* The use of two negatives in the same statement, as in "I didn't see nobody." ◆ This usage is a descendant of a formation native to the Germanic languages and was regularly used in Old and Middle English to intensify negation. It survives in Modern English, but is now considered substandard on analogy with Latin, where a double negative becomes an affirmative. Such statements as "I am not unhurt," however, are standard English, and have the effect of weak affirmatives. — *v.t.* **·tived, ·tiv·ing 1** To deny; contradict. **2** To refuse to sanction or enact; veto. **3** To prove to be false; disprove. **4** To neutralize; counteract. [< L *negativus* < *negare* deny] — **neg′a·tive·ly** *adv.* — **neg′a·tive·ness, neg·a·tiv·i·ty** (neg′ə·tiv′ə·tē) *n.*

neg·a·tiv·ism (neg′ə·tiv·iz′əm) *n.* **1** The beliefs or attitude of any negative thinker; atheism, agnosticism, etc. **2** The denial of traditional beliefs without proposing constructive substitutes. **3** *Psychol.* A type of behavior characterized by resistance to suggestion: when the subject fails to do what he is expected or asked to do, such behavior is known as **passive negativism;** when the subject does the opposite, **active** or **command negativism.** — **neg′a·tiv·ist** *n.* — **neg′a·tiv·is′tic** *adj.*

neg·a·to·ry (neg′ə·tôr′ē, -tō′rē) *adj.* Signifying negation.

neg·lect (ni·glekt′) *v.t.* **1** To disregard; ignore. **2** To fail to give proper attention to or take proper care of: to *neglect* one's business. **3** To fail to do or perform through carelessness or oversight; leave undone. — *n.* **1** The act of neglecting, or the state of being neglected. **2** Habitual want of attention or care; negligence. [< L *neglectus,* pp. of *negligere* < *nec-* not + *legere* gather, pick up] — **neg·lect′a·ble** *adj.* — **neg·lect′er** *n.*

Synonyms (noun): carelessness, default, disregard, failure, heedlessness, inadvertence, inattention, indifference, neglectfulness, negligence, oversight, remissness, slackness, slight. *Neglect* is the failing to take such care, show such attention, pay such courtesy, etc., as may be rightfully or reasonably expected. *Negligence* may be used in almost the same sense, but with a slighter force; but it is often used to denote the quality or trait of character of which the act is a manifestation, or to denote the habit of neglecting that which ought to be done. *Negligence* in dress implies want of care as to its arrangement, tidiness, etc.; *neglect* of one's garments would imply leaving them exposed to defacement or injury, as by dust, moths, etc. See SLIGHT. *Antonyms:* see synonyms under CARE.

neg·lect·ful (ni·glekt′fəl) *adj.* Exhibiting or indicating neglect. See synonyms under INATTENTIVE. — **neg·lect′ful·ly, neg·lect′ing·ly** *adv.* — **neg·lect′ful·ness** *n.*

neg·li·gée (neg′li·zhā′, neg′li·zhā; *Fr.* nā·glē·

zhā′) *n.* **1** A woman's soft, flowing, usually decorative dressing gown. **2** Any informal, careless, or incomplete attire. — *adj.* Of a woman, appearing careless in dress. [< F *négligée,* orig. pp. of *négliger* neglect]

neg·li·gence (neg′lə·jəns) *n.* **1** The act of neglecting. **2** An act or instance of neglecting. **3** Disregard for outward appearances or for conventionalities. See synonyms under NEGLECT.

neg·li·gent (neg′lə·jənt) *adj.* **1** Apt to omit what ought to be done; neglectful. **2** Unconventional. See synonyms under INATTENTIVE. [< L *negligens, -entis,* ppr. of *negligere* NEGLECT] — **neg′li·gent·ly** *adv.*

neg·li·gi·ble (neg′lə·jə·bəl) *adj.* That can be disregarded; inconsiderable; trifling; of little importance or size. — **neg′li·gi·bil′i·ty, neg′li·gi·ble·ness** *n.* — **neg′li·gi·bly** *adv.*

ne·go·ti·a·ble (ni·gō′shē·ə·bəl, -shə·bəl) *adj.* **1** That can be negotiated. **2** *Law* Transferable to a third person, as for the payment of debts. **3** That can be managed, overcome, or successfully dealt with. — **ne·go′ti·a·bil′i·ty** *n.* — **ne·go′ti·a·bly** *adv.*

negotiable instruments Instruments, such as bills of exchange, notes, checks, drafts, bills of lading, etc., covered by the Negotiable Instrument Law in effect in most States of the United States.

ne·go·ti·ant (ni·gō′shē·ənt) *n.* One who negotiates; a negotiator.

ne·go·ti·ate (ni·gō′shē·āt) *v.* **·at·ed, ·at·ing** *v.i.* **1** To treat or bargain with others in order to reach an agreement. — *v.t.* **2** To procure, arrange, or conclude by mutual discussion: to *negotiate* an agreement. **3** To transfer for a value received; sell; assign, as a note or bond. **4** To surmount, cross, or cope with (some obstacle). See synonyms under TRANSACT. [< L *negotiatus,* pp. of *negotiari* trade < *negotium* business] — **ne·go′ti·a′tion** *n.* — **ne·go′ti·a′tor** *n.* — **ne·go′ti·a·to′ry** *adj.*

Ne·gro (nē′grō) *n.* *pl.* **·groes 1** A member of the Negroid ethnic division of mankind; specifically, one belonging to the tribes inhabiting the Congo and Sudan regions of Africa. **2** One who is descended from the African Negro, full-blooded or of mixed descent. — *adj.* Of, pertaining to, like, for, or being, a Negro. [< Sp. < L *niger* black]

Ne·groid (nē′groid) *adj.* **1** *Anthropol.* Pertaining to or characteristic of the so-called black race, having skin color varying from light brown to almost black, stature tall to dwarfish, curly or woolly hair, slight body hair, nose usually broad or flat, eyes brown or black, often with a vertical epicanthic fold, and some prognathism. **2** Resembling, related to, or characteristic of Negroes. — *n.* A person of Negro descent or having some Negro characteristics.

ne·gus (nē′gəs) *n.* A drink made of wine, water, and lemon juice, sweetened. [after Col. Francis *Negus,* died 1732, who concocted it]

neigh (nā) *v.i.* To utter the cry of a horse; whinny. — *n.* A whinny. [OE *hnǣgan*]

neigh·bor (nā′bər) *n.* **1** One who lives near another. **2** One who is near by chance. **3** Friend; stranger: a colloquial and friendly term of address. **4** A fellow man. — *adj.* Close at hand; adjacent. — *v.t.* **1** To live or be near to or next to; adjoin: Ohio *neighbors* Indiana. **2** To bring near to or in close association. — *v.i.* **3** To be in proximity; lie close. **4** To live nearby; be neighborly. Also *Brit.* **neigh′bour.** [OE *nēahgebur* < *nēah* near + *gebur* farmer]

neigh·bor·hood (nā′bər·hŏŏd) *n.* **1** The region near where one is or resides; vicinity. **2** The people collectively who dwell in the vicinity. **3** Nearness; the condition of standing in the relation of a neighbor. **4** Friendly relations; neighborliness. **5** A district considered with reference to a given characteristic. — **in the neighborhood of** About; near.

Synonyms: district, locality, vicinage, vicinity. See APPROXIMATION.

neigh·bor·ing (nā′bər·ing) *adj.* Adjacent; near.

neigh·bor·ly (nā′bər·lē) *adj.* Appropriate to a neighbor; sociable. See synonyms under AMICABLE, FRIENDLY. — **neigh′bor·li·ness** *n.*

---

add,āce,câre,pälm; end,ēven; it,īce; odd,ōpen,ôrder; tŏŏk,pōōl; up,bûrn; ə = a in *above,* e in *sicken,* i in *clarity,* o in *melon,* u in *focus* ; yōō = u in *fuse,* oi,oil; ou,pout; ch,check; g,go; ng,ring; th,thin; ᵺ,this; zh,vision. Foreign sounds à,œ,ü,kh,ṅ; and ◆ : see page xx. < from; + plus; ? possibly.

neis·ser·o·sis (nī'sə·rō'sis) n. Pathol. Gonococcus infection. [after A. L. S. *Neisser*]

nei·ther (nē'thər, nī-) adj. Not either. —pron. Not the one nor the other. —conj. 1 Not one nor the other: followed by correlative *nor*: He will neither go nor send. 2 Not at all: an intensive now replaced by *either* except in incorrect usage: He has no strength, nor sense neither. 3 Nor yet. [OE nother; infl. in form by EITHER]

nek·ton (nek'ton) n. The aggregate of marine organisms actively swimming on or near the surface of the sea. [< NL < Gk. *nektos* swimming] —**nek·ton'ic, nek·ter'ic** (-ter'ik) adj.

nel·son (nel'sən) n. A wrestling hold in which the arms are thrust under the opponent's armpits from behind, and the hands gripped at the back of his neck: also called **full nelson**. The **half, quarter,** and **three-quarter nelson** are variants of this fundamental hold.

ne·lum·bo (ni·lum'bō) n. pl. **·bos** One of a genus (*Nelumbium*) of aquatic herbs of the waterlily family. *N. pentapetalum* is the water chinkapin and *N. nelumbo* is the sacred lotus of India. [< NL < Singhalese *nelumbu*]

nem·a·thel·minth (nem'ə·thel'minth) n. One of a phylum or class (*Nemathelminthes*) of worms having a threadlike, unsegmented body with papillae or spines at the anterior extremity, as the nematodes and acanthocephalans; the roundworms. —adj. Pertaining to these worms. Also **nem'a·tel'minth** (-tel'-). [< NL < Gk. *nēma, -atos* thread + *helmins* a worm]

nemato- combining form Thread; filament: *nematocyst*: also, before vowels, **nemat-.** Also **nema-.** [< Gk. *nēma, -matos* thread]

nem·a·to·cyst (nem'ə·tō·sist') n. Zool. One of the stinging cells in jellyfishes, polyps, and other hydrozoans, in the interior of which is coiled a long filament whose instantaneous release causes paralysis of the organism it touches: also called *lasso cell, nettle cell.* —**nem'a·to·cys'tic** adj.

nem·a·tode (nem'ə·tōd) n. Any of a phylum or class (*Nematoda*) of roundworms having a mouth and intestinal canal, some of which, as the hookworm, are intestinal parasites in man and other animals. [< NL < Gk. *nēma, -atos* thread]

ne·mer·te·an (ni·mûr'tē·ən) n. One of a phylum or class (*Nemertea*) of flatworms, mostly marine and non-parasitic, with skin ciliated, proboscis retractile, and muscular, vascular, and nervous systems characteristically developed: often brilliantly colored. —adj. Of or pertaining to the *Nemertea.* [< NL < Gk. *Nēmertēs,* one of the Nereids] —**ne·mer'ti·an, ne·mer'tine, ne'mer·tin'e·an** adj. & n.

nem·e·sis (nem'ə·sis) n. Retributive justice; retribution. [< L < Gk. < *nemein* distribute]

nem·o·ral (nem'ər·əl) adj. Pertaining to a wood, grove, or the like. [< L *nemoralis* < *nemus, nemoris* a grove]

nem·o·rose (nem'ə·rōs) adj. Bot. Inhabiting groves or open woodland places: said especially of plants.

neo- combining form 1 New; recent; a modern or modified form of: *Neo-Platonism.* 2 Geol. Denoting the most recent subdivision of a period: *Neocene.* Also, before vowels, usually **ne-.** [< Gk. < *neos* new]

ne·o·ars·phen·am·ine (nē'ō·ärs'fen·am'in, -fen·ə·mēn') n. Chem. A modified compound of arsphenamine, $C_{13}H_{13}O_4N_2SAs_2Na$, used in the treatment of syphilis and certain other diseases.

Ne·o·cene (nē'ə·sēn) adj. Geol. Of or pertaining to the later of the two epochs into which the Tertiary period was at one time divided, or to the corresponding series of strata. —n. The Neocene epoch. [< NEO- + Gk. *kainos* new]

Ne·o·Chris·ti·an·i·ty (nē'ō·kris'chē·an'ə·tē) n. A rationalistic interpretation of Christianity.

ne·o·clas·sic (nē'ō·klas'ik) adj. Of, pertaining to, or denoting neo-classicism. Also **ne'o·clas'si·cal.**

ne·o·clas·si·cism (nē'ō·klas'ə·siz'əm) n. 1 A revival of classical style in literature, art, etc. 2 In the later 17th and the 18th centuries, an esthetic and philosophical movement which sought to recover the classical spirit of order and moderation, characterized by close adherence to rules and conventional forms, restraint in the expression of emotion, and an emphasis on the typical and general rather than the individual or eccen-

---

tric. —**ne'o·clas'si·cist** n.

ne·o·cul·tu·ra·tion (nē'ō·kul'chə·rā'shən) n. The creation and establishment of new cultural forms, especially as a result of transculturation.

ne·o·dym·i·um (nē'ō·dim'ē·əm) n. A metallic element (symbol Nd, atomic number 60) found in combination with cerium and other elements of the lanthanide series. See PERIODIC TABLE. [< NEO- + (DI)DYMIUM]

Ne·o·gae·a (nē'ō·jē'ə) n. A zoogeographical region including the western hemisphere or New World. [< NEO- + Gk. *gaia* earth] —**Ne'o·gae'an** adj.

ne·o·ge·ic (nē'ō·jē'ik) adj. Of or belonging to the western hemisphere or New World: opposed to *gerontogeic.*

Ne·o·gene (nē'ō·jēn) adj. Geol. Of or pertaining to the Upper Tertiary and the Quaternary periods in the Cenozoic geological era: includes the Miocene, Pliocene, Pleistocene, and Holocene epochs. [< Gk. *neogenēs* newborn]

ne·o·gen·ic (nē'ō·jen'ik) adj. Newly formed: said especially of rocks and minerals. Also **ne'o·ge·net'ic** (-jə·net'ik).

Ne·o·He·bra·ic (nē'ō·hē·brā'ik) n. That form of the Hebrew language used in post-Biblical Jewish literature. —adj. Pertaining to post-Biblical Hebrew.

ne·o·im·pres·sion·ism (nē'ō·im·presh'ən·iz'əm) n. The doctrines and methods of a group of artists of the 19th century, based on a more strictly scientific practice of impressionist technique. Compare IMPRESSIONISM, POINTILLISM, POST-IMPRESSIONISM. —**ne'o·im·pres'sion·ist** n. & adj.

Ne·o·Lat·in (nē'ō·lat'n) n. 1 One of a group of peoples whose language is derived from Latin. 2 New Latin: see under LATIN.

ne·o·lith (nē'ə·lith) n. A Neolithic implement.

Ne·o·lith·ic (nē'ə·lith'ik) adj. Anthropol. Of or pertaining to the period of human culture following the Mesolithic: characterized by a great variety of polished stone implements and the development of new social forms based upon primitive techniques in weaving, spinning, and potterymaking, and the introduction of a settled agriculture exploiting many new domesticated plants. [< Gk. *neos* new + *lithos* stone]

ne·ol·o·gism (nē·ol'ə·jiz'əm) n. 1 A new word or phrase. 2 The use of new words or new meanings for old words. 3 A new doctrine in theology. —**ne·ol'o·gis'tic, ne·ol'o·gis'ti·cal** adj.

ne·ol·o·gist (nē·ol'ə·jist) n. 1 A person who invents or employs new views in theology. 2 A person who adopts new views in theology.

ne·ol·o·gy (nē·ol'ə·jē) n. pl. **·gies** A neologism. [< NEO- + Gk. *logos* word] —**ne·o·log·i·cal** (nē'ə·loj'i·kəl) adj. —**ne'o·log'i·cal·ly** adv.

ne·o·morph (nē'ə·môrf) n. A newly acquired organ or part. Also **ne'o·mor'phism.**

ne·o·my·cin (nē'ə·mī'sin) n. An antibiotic related to streptomycin, used in the local treatment of certain skin and eye infections.

ne·on (nē'on) n. A colorless, odorless, chemically inactive gaseous element (symbol Ne, atomic number 10) found in the atmosphere in a ratio of about 15 parts per million. See PERIODIC TABLE. [< NL < Gk. *neos* new]

ne·o·na·tal (nē'ō·nā'təl) adj. Of or pertaining to newborns: *neonatal* care.

ne·o·nate (nē'ō·nāt) n. A newborn infant. [< NEO- + L *natus* born]

ne·o·pho·bi·a (nē'ə·fō'bē·ə) n. Morbid fear of the new or unfamiliar. —**ne'o·phobe** n. —**ne'o·pho'bic** adj.

ne·o·phyte (nē'ə·fīt) n. 1 A recent convert. 2 A novice of a religious or mystic order. 3 Any novice or beginner. 4 Bot. A new or recently introduced plant species; an exotic. [< Gk. *neophytos* novice]

ne·o·plasm (nē'ə·plaz'əm) n. Pathol. A growth or formation of tissue resulting from morbid action; a tumor.

ne·o·plas·ty (nē'ə·plas'tē) n. Plastic surgery for the restoration of old or the formation of new parts. —**ne'o·plas'tic** adj.

Ne·o·Pla·ton·ism (nē'ō·plā'tən·iz'əm) n. An Alexandrian system of philosophy of the third century, commingling Jewish and Christian ideas with doctrines of Plato and other Greek philosophers and Oriental mysticism. —**Ne'o·Pla·ton'ic** (-plə·ton'ik) adj. —**Ne'o·Pla'ton·ist** n.

---

ne·o·prene (nē'ə·prēn) n. Chem. A synthetic rubber obtained in a variety of types from chloroprene, and produced by the combination of hydrogen with acetylene gas. [< NEO- + (CHLORO)PRENE]

ne·o·style (nē'ə·stīl) n. A contrivance for making several copies of a document; a cyclostyle.

ne·o·ter·ic (nē'ə·ter'ik) adj. Recent in origin; new. Also **ne'o·ter'i·cal.** —n. One of modern times; a modern. [< Gk. *neōterikos* youthful] —**ne'o·ter'i·cal·ly** adv.

ne·ot·er·ism (nē·ot'ə·riz'əm) n. That which is new, modern, or recently introduced; the coinage of new words, or a newly coined word. —**ne·ot'er·ist** n. —**ne·ot'er·is'tic** adj.

Ne·o·trop·i·cal (nē'ō·trop'i·kəl) adj. Of, pertaining to, or designating the zoogeographical region of the New World that includes Central and South America and the adjacent islands.

ne·o·type (nē'ə·tīp) n. In systematics, any specimen of a plant or animal chosen to replace the original specimen when all type material has been lost or destroyed.

Ne·o·zo·ic (nē'ə·zō'ik) adj. Geol. 1 Of or pertaining to the Mesozoic and Cenozoic geological eras, as contrasted with the Paleozoic. 2 The Cenozoic era.

nep (nep) n. Small knots in cotton fiber produced by uneven growth of the plant or by friction in process machinery. [Cf dial. E *nap* a knob, button]

Ne·pal (ni·pôl') An independent kingdom between Tibet and India; 56,000 square miles; capital, Katmandu. —**Nep·a·lese** (nep'ə·lēz', -lēs') adj. & n.

ne·pen·thes (ni·pen'thēz) n. One of a genus (*Nepenthes*) of mainly East Indian herbs or half-shrubby plants, the East Indian pitcher plants. [< NL < Gk. *nēpenthēs* NEPENTHE]

ne·per (nā'pər) n. A unit of power-level difference or of attenuation in electrical communication circuits: equal to 8.686 decibels. [after John Napier]

NEPENTHES

neph·e·lin·ite (nef'ə·lin·īt') n. A dark-gray volcanic rock composed of the minerals nepheline, augite, and magnetite. Also **neph'e·lin·yte.**

neph·e·lom·e·ter (nef'ə·lom'ə·tər) n. An instrument used for the measurement of light transmitted or scattered by translucent substances: also used for the determination of the quantity of matter suspended in a liquid. [< Gk. *nephelē* cloud + -METER] —**neph·e·lo·met·ric** (nef'ə·lō·met'rik) adj. —**neph·e·lom'e·try** n.

neph·ew (nef'yōō, esp. Brit. nev'yōō) n. 1 The son of a sister or a brother; by extension, a grandnephew. 2 An unlawfully begotten son: a euphemism. 3 Obs. A descendant; grandchild; also, a cousin. [< F *neveu* < L *nepos* grandson, nephew]

nepho- combining form Cloud; pertaining to the clouds: *nephology.* Also, before vowels, **neph-.** [< Gk. *nephos* cloud]

neph·o·gram (nef'ə·gram) n. Meteorol. A cloud picture made by a nephograph.

neph·o·graph (nef'ə·graf, -gräf) n. Meteorol. An electrically operated camera for photographing clouds, with special reference to their position in the sky.

ne·phol·o·gy (nē·fol'ə·jē) n. The branch of meteorology that treats of clouds. —**neph·o·log·i·cal** (nef'ə·loj'i·kəl) adj.

neph·o·scope (nef'ə·skōp) n. Meteorol. An instrument for indicating the direction and velocity of winds by observations of cloud drift.

ne·phral·gi·a (ni·fral'jē·ə, -jə) n. Pathol. Pain in the kidney or kidneys. [< NEPHR(O)- + -ALGIA]

ne·phrec·to·my (ni·frek'tə·mē) n. Surg. The excision of a kidney. [< NEPHR(O)- + -ECTOMY]

neph·ric (nef'rik) adj. Of, pertaining to, or situated near the kidneys; renal. [< Gk. *nephros* kidney]

ne·phrid·i·um (ni·frid'ē·əm) n. pl. **·phrid·i·a** (-frid'ē·ə) Biol. 1 One of the series of primitive excretory organs that afterward develop into uriniferous tubules, as in annelid worms, mollusks, and other invertebrates. 2 The embryonic tube which develops into the kidney in vertebrates. [< NL < Gk. *nephridios* pertaining to the kidneys] —**ne·phrid′i·al** *adj.*

neph·rism (nef′riz·əm) *n. Pathol.* General ill health due to chronic kidney disease.

neph·rite (nef′rīt) *n.* A very hard, compact, white to dark-green mineral: formerly worn as a remedy for diseases of the kidney. Compare JADE¹. [< G *nephrit* < Gk. *nephros* a kidney]

ne·phrit·ic (ni-frit′ik) *adj.* **1** Pertaining to, affecting, or affording relief to the kidneys. **2** Affected with nephritis. **3** Of the nature of nephrite. Also **ne·phrit′i·cal.** —*n.* Any medicine applicable to disease of the kidney.

ne·phri·tis (ni-frī′tis) *n. Pathol.* **1** Inflammation of the kidneys. **2** Bright's disease.

nephro- *combining form* A kidney; pertaining to the kidneys: *nephropathy.* Also, before vowels, **nephr-.** [< Gk. *nephros* kidney]

ne·phrog·e·nous (ni-froj′ə-nəs) *adj.* Originating in or caused by the kidney. Also **neph·ro·gen·ic** (nef′rə-jen′ik). [< NEPHRO- + -GENOUS]

neph·roid (nef′roid) *adj.* Shaped like a kidney.

ne·phrop·a·thy (ni-frop′ə-thē) *n.* Any disease of the kidney. —**neph·ro·path·ic** (nef′rə-path′ik) *adj.*

ne·phrot·o·my (ni-frot′ō-mē) *n. Surg.* Incision of the kidney.

nep·o·tism (nep′ə-tiz′əm) *n.* Favoritism, especially governmental patronage, extended toward relatives. [< F *népotisme* < Ital. *nepotismo* < L *nepos* a grandson, nephew] —**ne·pot·ic** (ni-pot′ik) *adj.* —**nep′o·tist** *n.*

Nep·tune (nep′tōōn, -tyōōn) **1** In Roman mythology, son of Saturn and Ops, god of the sea: identified with the Greek *Poseidon.* **2** By personification, the ocean. **3** *Astron.* The eighth planet from the sun, discovered in 1846 by Galle of Berlin. Its mean distance from the sun is 2,793,000,000 miles; period of revolution, about 165 years; diameter, about 27,700 miles. It has two satellites. See PLANET.

Nep·tu·ni·an (nep·tōō′nē·ən, -tyōō′-) *adj.* **1** Of or pertaining to Neptune or his domain, the sea. **2** *Geol.* **a** Formed in or by the agency of water: said of rocks. **b** Of or pertaining to the theory of the aqueous origin of certain rocks: opposed to the *Plutonic* theory. —**Nep′tun·ist** *adj. & n.*

nep·tu·ni·um (nep·tōō′nē·əm, -tyōō′-) *n.* A radioactive element (symbol Np, atomic number 93) existing in minute amount in uranium ores and produced in gram quantities in nuclear reactors. See PERIODIC TABLE.

neptunium series *Physics* A sequence of radioactive elements beginning with plutonium of mass 241 and continuing through successive disintegrations to the stable isotope bismuth 209: named from its longest-lived member, neptunium 237, with a half-life of 2.2×10^6 years.

ne·re·is (nir′ē·is) *n.* Any of a genus (*Nereis*) of burrowing annelid worms having a long, flattened body and a distinct head: common near the seashore: also called *clamworm.* [< NL < Gk., a Nereid]

ne·rit·ic (ni-rit′ik) *adj.* Of or pertaining to the coastline or to shallow water. [< L *nerita* mussel < Gk. *nērītēs*]

ner·o·li (ner′ə-lē) *n.* The essential oil distilled from orange blossoms: an isomer of geraniol used in perfumery. [after Princess *Neroli*, an Italian noblewoman said to have discovered it]

ner·vate (nûr′vāt) *adj.* Provided with nerves or veins; having nerves.

ner·va·tion (nûr·vā′shən) *n.* The arrangement or disposition of nerves, as in plants and insects. Also **ner·va·ture** (nûr′və·chŏŏr).

nerve (nûrv) *n.* **1** A cordlike structure, composed of delicate filaments, by which impulses are transmitted to or from different parts of the body. ♦ Collateral adjective: *neural.* **2** A tendon: used only in the phrase, to strain every *nerve.* **3** Anything likened to a nerve, as a rib or vein of a leaf or of an insect's wing. **4** Active strength or vigor; coolness; intrepidity. **5** *pl.* Nervous excitability; a nervous attack. –*v.t.* **nerved**, **nerv′ing** To give strength, vigor, or courage to. [< L *nervus* sinew] —**nerv′al** *adj.*

nerve-block (nûrv′blok′) *n.* A method of surgical anesthesia in which sensation is cut off from definite nerves.

nerve canal *Dent.* The narrow cavity in a tooth for passage of the nerve to the pulp.

nerve cell *Physiol.* **1** The cell body of a neuron. **2** An individual cell of the nervous system.

nerve center *Anat.* An aggregation of nerve cells controlling a particular sense or function, as hearing, respiration, etc.

nerve fiber One of the essential threadlike units of which a nerve is composed.

nerve impulse *Physiol.* A wave of chemical and electrical change propagated along a nerve fiber and serving as a stimulus to body movements and activities.

nerve·less (nûrv′lis) *adj.* **1** Destitute of nerve or force; strengthless; unnerved. **2** Having no nerves. —**nerve′less·ly** *adv.* —**nerve′less·ness** *n.*

nerve net *Zool.* The primitive, reticulated nervous system of coelenterates, as in the hydra: its reactions to stimuli affect the entire organism.

nerve-rack·ing (nûrv′rak′ing) *adj.* Extremely irritating or exasperating to one's nerves. Also **nerve′wrack′ing.**

ner·vi·duct (nûr′və·dukt) *n. Anat.* A passage in a bone for a nerve. [< L *nervus* a nerve + *ductus,* pp. of *ducere* lead]

ner·vine (nûr′vēn, -vin) *adj.* **1** Pertaining to the nerves. **2** Calming or quieting to the nerves. —*n.* Any medicine acting on the nerves.

nerv·ing (nûr′ving) *n.* A veterinary operation for the excision of a part of a nerve trunk when in a state of chronic inflammation.

ner·vos·i·ty (nûr·vos′ə·tē) *n.* The state of being nervous; the tendency or disposition to exhibit nervous tension.

ner·vous (nûr′vəs) *adj.* **1** Affected or caused by the condition or action of the nerves: *nervous* prostration. **2** Easily disturbed or agitated, owing to weak nerves; excitable; timid. **3** Abounding in nerve or nerve force; vigorous; sinewy; nervy; also, highly strung. **4** Terse; crisp, as literary style. **5** Of or pertaining to the nerves or nervous system. [< L *nervosus* sinewy] —**ner′vous·ly** *adv.* —**ner′vous·ness** *n.*

nervous prostration Neurasthenia.

nervous system *Biol.* The organized aggregate of all the nerve cells and nerve tissues of the higher animals, centralized in the spinal cord and brain of vertebrates. It has the functions of coordinating, controlling, and regulating responses to stimuli, directing behavior, and, in man, conditioning the phenomena of consciousness.

ner·vu·ra·tion (nûr′vyə·rā′shən) *n.* The arrangement or disposition of nervures.

ner·vure (nûr′vyŏŏr) *n. Biol.* A principal vein, as on a leaf or an insect's wing. Also **ner′vule** (-vyōōl). [< F < L *nervus* sinew]

nerv·y (nûr′vē) *adj.* **nerv·i·er, nerv·i·est** **1** Exhibiting force or strength; sinewy. **2** Full of nerve or courage; brave. **3** *Slang* Displaying brazen assurance; cool; impudent. **4** *Brit.* Nervous; jumpy; excitable.

nes·cience (nesh′əns, -ē·əns) *n.* The state of not knowing; ignorance, especially that due either to the nature of the human mind or of external things. [< LL *nescientia* ignorance < *ne-* not + *scire* know] —**nes′cient** *adj. & n.* —**nes′cient·ist** *n.*

ness (nes) *n.* A promontory or cape: frequently used as a termination in the proper name of a headland: *Dungeness; Sheerness.* [OE *næs*]

-ness *suffix of nouns* **1** State or quality of being: *darkness.* **2** An example of this state or quality: to do someone a *kindness.* [OE *-nis(s), -nes(s)*]

Nes·sel·rode pudding (nes′əl·rōd) A custard made with preserved fruits and nuts, and flavored with rum: used as a pie filling. [after Count K. R. *Nesselrode*]

Nessler's reagent (nes′lərz) *Chem.* An aqueous solution of mercuric iodide, potassium iodide, and caustic potash: used in testing for ammonia. Also **Nessler's solution.** [after Julius *Nessler*, 1827–1905, German chemist]

nest (nest) *n.* **1** The habitation prepared by a bird for the hatching of its eggs and the rearing of its young. **2** The bed or home of

TYPES OF NESTS
a. Tailorbird.   *c.* Hummingbird.
b. Hornet.   *d.* Oriole.

certain fish, insects, turtles, mice, etc. **3** Any cozy place or abode; a retreat. **4** A haunt of anything bad, vulgar, or unpleasant; a den; also, those occupying it: a *nest* of brigands. **5** A series or set of similar things fitting into each other: a *nest* of bowls. **6** A connected set of small gearwheels, springs, or the like. **7** An isolated deposit of any ore or mineral in a rock. **8** A center of enemy resistance in battle: a machine-gun *nest.* —*v.t.* **1** To place in or as in a nest. **2** To pack or place one inside another. —*v.i.* **3** To build or occupy a nest. **4** To hunt for nests. [OE]

nest egg 1 A natural or artificial egg kept in a nest to attract a fowl. **2** Something laid by, as a sum of money, as a nucleus for future accumulation or for emergencies.

nes·tle (nes′əl) *v.* **·tled, ·tling** *v.i.* **1** To lie closely or snugly; cuddle; snuggle. **2** To settle down in comfort and pleasure. **3** To lie as if sheltered; be half-hidden. **4** *Rare* To nest. —*v.t.* **5** To place or press lovingly or fondly. **6** To place in or as in a nest. [OE *nestlian*] —**nes′tler** *n.*

nest·ling (nest′ling, nes′-) *n.* A bird too young to leave the nest; hence, a young child. —*adj.* Recently hatched.

Nes·to·ri·an·ism (nes·tôr′ē·ən·iz′əm, -tō′rē-) *n. Theol.* The doctrine that Christ had two distinct natures, the divine and human, subsisting independently. —**Nes·to′ri·an** *n. & adj.*

net¹ (net) *n.* **1** An open fabric, woven or tied with meshes, for the capture of fishes, birds, etc. ♦ Collateral adjective: *reticular.* **2** An openwork fabric, as lace. **3** Something constructed with meshes, as a tennis net. **4** In tennis and similar games, a returned ball which does not go over the net. —*v.t.* **net·ted, net·ting 1** To catch in or as in a net; ensnare. **2** To make into a net. **3** To cover or enclose with a net. **4** In tennis, etc., to hit (the ball) into the net. —*adj.* **1** Manufactured or formed of netting, or resembling netting. **2** Captured or snared in a net. [OE]

net² *adj.* **1** Free from everything extraneous; obtained after deducting all expenses. **2** Not subject to any discount or deduction. —*n.* A net profit, amount, weight, etc. —*v.t.* **net·ted, net·ting** To earn or yield as clear profit. [< F. See NEAT.]

net-ground (net′ground′) *n.* A foundation of net or meshes.

neth·er (neth′ər) *adj.* Situated at the lowest part; especially, pertaining to the parts beneath the heavens or the earth. [OE *neothera* under]

Neth·er·lands (neth′ər·ləndz) A country of NW Europe, first part of the Kingdom of the Netherlands; 12,425 square miles of land, 15,780 square miles with interior waters; capital, Amsterdam; seat of government, The Hague. Also, popularly, *Holland.* Dutch *Nederland.* —**Neth′er·land′er** *n.* —**Neth′er·land′ish** *adj.*

neth·er·most (neth′ər·mōst′) *adj.* Lowest.

neth·er·ward (neth′ər·wərd) *adv.* In a descending course; downward.

nether world The world of the shades or dead; specifically, the world of punishment after death; hell, conceived as being beneath the earth.

net knot *Biol.* A relatively large and thickened mass of chromatin in the nucleus of a cell.

net·ting (net'ing) *n.* **1** A fabric of openwork; a net; network. **2** The act or operation of making net. **3** The act, practice, or right of using nets, as in fishing.

net·tle[1] (net'l) *n.* **1** An herb of the genus *Urtica*, with opposite leaves, inconspicuous, greenish, imperfect flowers, and minute stinging hairs. The stinging is due to the irritating watery juice discharged by the hairs when broken. **2** Any of the various plants of some other genus of the nettle family. **3** Any of various plants of the same or some other family, having some real or fancied resemblance to the nettle genus. **4** A condition of irritation. —*v.t.* **·tled, ·tling** **1** To sting as the nettle does. **2** To annoy or irritate; provoke. See synonyms under PIQUE[1]. [OE *netle*] —**net'tler** *n.*

net·tle[2] (net'l) *n. Naut.* A small rope made by tightly twisting two or three yarns. Also **net'·tle·stuff'** (-stuf'). [Var. of *knettle* < *knit*]

nettle cell A nematocyst.

net ton A short ton.

net·work (net'wûrk') *n.* **1** A fabric of openwork; netting. **2** A system of interlacing lines, tracks, or channels. **3** Any complex arrangement of interconnected electrical circuits. **4** *Telecom.* A chain of broadcasting stations.

Neuf·châ·tel (noo'shə·tel', *Fr.* nœ·shä·tel') *n.* A soft, white cheese produced in Neufchâtel, a town in northern France.

neume (noom, nyoom) *n. Music* **1** One of various symbols in a system of notation first devised to aid rote singers of the Gregorian chants, indicating direction of the melody and later including the musical pitch and accents: also spelled **neum.** **2** *pl.* This system. [< LL *neuma* song < Gk. *pneuma* breath, sigh]

neur– Var. of NEURO–.

neu·ral (noor'əl, nyoor'-) *adj.* **1** Of or pertaining to the nerves or nervous system: the *neural* axis. **2** Of, pertaining to, or situated on the side that contains the axis of the central nervous system; in vertebrates, the dorsal side. [< Gk. *neuron* nerve]

neu·ral·gi·a (noo·ral'jē·ə, -jə, nyoo-) *n. Pathol.* An acute, paroxysmal pain along the course and over the local distribution of a nerve. [< NEUR– + -ALGIA] —**neu·ral'gic** *adj.*

neu·ras·the·ni·a (noor'əs·thē'nē·ə, -thēn'yə, nyoor'-) *n.* **1** *Pathol.* Derangement of the nervous system with depression of vital force; nervous prostration. **2** *Psychoanal.* A neurosis characterized by physical disorder, as headache, constipation, etc., originated by inadequate expression of the libido. [< NL < Gk. *neuron* a nerve + *asthenia* weakness] —**neu·ras·then·ic** (-then'ik) *adj.* & *n.*

neu·rax·is (noo·rak'sis, nyoo-) *n. Anat.* The brain and spinal cord; the axon. [< NEUR– + AXIS] —**neu·rax'i·al** *adj.*

neu·rax·on (noo·rak'sən, nyoo-) *n. Anat.* The process of a nerve cell that forms the axial cylinder of a nerve; axon. [< NEUR– + AXON]

neu·rec·to·my (noo·rek'tə·mē, nyoo-) *n. Surg.* The excision of a nerve. [< NEUR– + -ECTOMY]

neu·ren·ter·ic (noor'ən·ter'ik, nyoor'-) *adj. Biol.* Of or pertaining to the neural and the enteric tubes of the embryo: the *neurenteric* canal, the tube connecting the caudal end of the neural tube with the digestive tract of the embryo.

neu·ri·lem·ma (noor'ə·lem'ə, nyoor'-) *n. Anat.* The delicate sheath of a nerve fiber: also spelled *neurolemma.* Also **neu'ri·lem'a.** [< NL < Gk. *neuros* nerve + *eilēma* sheath]

neu·ri·tis (noo·rī'tis, nyoo-) *n. Pathol.* Inflammation of a nerve. —**neu·rit'ic** (-rit'ik) *adj.*

neuro– *combining form* Nerve; pertaining to a nerve: *neurocyte* : also, before vowels, *neur–.* Also **neuri–.** [< Gk. *neuron* sinew, nerve]

neu·ro·cele (noor'ə·sēl, nyoor'-) *n. Anat.* The system of central communicating cavities (ventricles and passages) found in the spinal cord and brain. Also **neu'ro·coele.**

neu·ro·chem·is·try (noor'ō·kem'ə·strē) *n.* That branch of chemistry that has to do with chemicals, esp. the neurotransmitters, that affect the nervous system.

neu·ro·cyte (noor'ə·sīt, nyoor'-) *n.* A nerve cell together with its processes.

neu·rog·li·a (noo·rog'lē·ə, nyoo-) *n. Anat.* The supporting tissue of the central nervous system, composed of finely branched ectodermic cells within thin interlacing processes. [< NL < Gk.

neuro– nerve + *glia* glue]

neu·ro·hy·po·phy·sis (noor'ō·hī·pof'ə·sis, nyoor'-) *n. pl.* **·ses** (-sēz). The posterior lobe of the pituitary gland together with the stalk of gray matter that connects it with the brain.

neu·roid (noor'oid, nyoor'-) *adj.* Nervelike.

neu·ro·lem·ma (noor'ə·lem'ə, nyoor'-) *n.* **1** The retina. **2** Neurilemma.

neu·rol·o·gy (noo·rol'ə·jē, nyoo-) *n.* The science of the nervous system in health and disease. —**neu·ro·log·i·cal** (noor'ə·loj'i·kəl, nyoor'-) *adj.* —**neu·rol'o·gist** *n.*

neu·rol·y·sis (noo·rol'ə·sis, nyoo-) *n.* **1** The destruction of nerve tissue. **2** Liberation of a nerve from morbid adhesions. **3** Relief of nerve tension by stretching. **4** Nervous exhaustion through over stimulation. —**neu·ro·lyt·ic** (noor'ə·lit'ik, nyoor'-) *adj.*

neu·ro·ma (noo·rō'mə, nyoo-) *n. pl.* **·ma·ta** (-mə·tə) *Pathol.* A tumor developing from a nerve. [< NL < Gk. *neuros* nerve + -ōma growth]

neu·ro·path (noor'ə·path, nyoor'-) *n. Psychiatry* One suffering from or subject to nervous disorders; a neurotic. —**neu·ro·path'ic, neu·ro·pa·th'i·cal** *adj.* —**neu·ro·path'i·cal·ly** *adv.*

neu·ro·pa·thol·o·gy (noor'ō·pə·thol'ə·jē, nyoor'-) *n.* The pathology of the nervous system. —**neu·ro·pa·thol'o·gist** *n.*

neu·ro·phys·i·ol·o·gy (noor'ō·fiz'ē·ol'ə·jē, nyoor'-) *n.* The physiology of the nervous system. —**neu·ro·phys·i·o·log·i·cal** (-fiz'ē·ə·loj'i·kəl) *adj.* —**neu·ro·phys·i·ol'o·gist** *n.*

neu·ro·psy·chi·a·try (noor'ō·sī·kī'ə·trē, nyoor'-) *n.* The study and treatment of diseases involving both neurological and mental factors; the pathology of nervous disorders combined with psychiatry. —**neu·ro·psy·chi·at·ric** (-sī'kē·at'rik) *adj.* —**neu·ro·psy·chi·a·trist** (-sī·kī'ə·trist) *n.*

neu·ro·psy·chol·o·gy (noor'ō·sī·kol'ə·jē, nyoor'-) *n.* The study of the relationships existing between the mind and the nervous system. —**neu·ro·psy·cho·log·i·cal** (-sī'kə·loj'i·kəl) *adj.*

neu·ro·psy·cho·sis (noor'ō·sī·kō'sis, nyoor'-) *n. Psychiatry* Mental disorder arising from a nervous disorder.

neu·rop·ter (noo·rop'tər, nyoo-) *n.* Any of an order (*Neuroptera*) of insects having four similar, net-veined wings, chewing mouth parts, and active carnivorous larvae, as ant-lions, etc. [< NL < Gk. *neuros* sinew, nerve + *pteron* wing] —**neu·rop'ter·al** *adj.* —**neu·rop'·ter·an** *adj.* & *n.*

neu·rop·ter·oid (noo·rop'tə·roid, nyoo-) *adj.* Like the *Neuroptera.* —*n.* A neuropteroid insect.

neu·rop·ter·ous (noo·rop'tər·əs, nyoo-) *adj.* **1** Of or pertaining to the *Neuroptera.* **2** Having net-veined wings.

neu·ro·sis (noo·rō'sis, nyoo-) *n. pl.* **·ses** (-sēz) *Psychiatry* A disorder of the psychic or mental functions without lesion of nerves and of less severity than a psychosis. —**neu·ro'sal** *adj.*

neu·rot·ic (noo·rot'ik, nyoo-) *adj.* **1** Pertaining to or suffering from neurosis. **2** *Colloq.* Having a morbid nature or tendency. **3** Pertaining to a nerve or the nervous system. —*n.* **1** A person afflicted with neurosis. **2** Disease of the nerves.

neu·rot·o·my (noo·rot'ə·mē, nyoo-) *n.* **1** *Surg.* The division or severing of a nerve, to relieve pain. **2** The dissection of the nervous system, as for study. [< NEURO– + -TOMY] —**neu·ro·tom·ic** (noor'ə·tom'ik, nyoor'-) *adj.* —**neu·rot'o·mist** *n.*

neu·ro·trans·mit·ter (noor'ō·tranz·mit'ər, nyoor'-) *n.* A chemical agent (such as acetylcholine, norepinephrine) which transmits a nerve impulse across a synapse.

neu·ter (noo'tər, nyoo'-) *adj.* **1** *Gram.* **a** Neither masculine nor feminine in gender. Compare GENDER. **b** *Rare* Intransitive; neither active nor passive; middle: said of verbs in classical languages. **2** *Biol.* Sexless; having functionless or imperfectly developed sex organs, as certain plants and animals. **3** *Obs.* Neutral. —*n.* **1** An animal of no apparent sex, as a worker bee. **2** A eunuch. **3** A castrated animal. **4** *Gram.* **a** The neuter gender. **b** A word in this gender. **5** A neutral in warfare or other conflict. [< MF *neutre* < L *neuter* < *ne*–not + *uter* either]

neu·tral (noo'trəl, nyoo'-) *adj.* **1** Refraining from interference in a contest; not taking the part of either or any belligerent: a *neutral* power. **2** Be-

longing to neither of two contestants; belonging to a neutral power: *neutral* forces. **3** Having no decided character; indefinite; middling. **4** Having no decided color; predominantly brownish or grayish. **5** *Biol.* Sexless; neuter. **6** *Bot.* Lacking pistils or stamens. **7** *Chem.* Lacking decided acid or alkaline qualities. **8** *Electr.* Neither positive nor negative. **9** *Phonet.* Pronounced with the tongue in a relaxed, mid-central position, as the *a* in *about.* —*n.* One who or that which is neutral. [< L *neutralis* < *neuter* neuter] —**neu'tral·ly** *adv.*

neu·tral·ism (noo'trəl·iz'əm, nyoo'-) *n.* A political doctrine holding that abstention from alliance with ideologic or economic power blocs in international relations serves a country's best interests. —**neu'tral·ist** *n.*

neu·tral·i·ty (noo·tral'ə·tē, nyoo-) *n. pl.* **·ties 1** The state of being a neutral nation during a war. **2** The state of being neither good nor bad; indifference. **3** *Chem.* The condition of being neither acid nor basic. **4** The character of being neutral: the *neutrality* of a ship.

neu·tral·i·za·tion (noo'trəl·ə·zā'shən, -ī·zā'-, nyoo'-) *n.* **1** Act of neutralizing or state of being neutralized. **2** *Ling.* The temporary suspension of a relevant feature in two phonemes, as /t/ and /d/ in *latter* and *ladder.*

neu·tral·ize (noo'trəl·īz, nyoo'-) *v.t.* **·ized, ·iz·ing 1** To counteract or destroy by opposite force or influence; nullify; counterbalance. **2** To declare (a nation, area, etc.) to be neutral and not involved in hostilities. **3** *Chem.* To make neutral or inert. **4** *Electr.* To render electrically inert; void of electricity. **5** *Mil.* To render incapable of effective action. Also *Brit.* **neu'tral·ise.** —**neu'tral·iz'er** *n.*

neu·tron (noo'tron, nyoo'-) *n. Physics* An electrically neutral particle of the atom, having a mass approximately equal to that of the proton.

neutron bomb A thermonuclear bomb designed to release intense radiation in order to destroy life and spare property.

neutron star A hypothetical celestial body of small radius and great density representing a terminal stage in the evolution of a star of mass comparable to that of the sun.

Ne·vad·a (nə·vad'ə, -vä'də) A State in the western United States; 110,540 square miles; capital, Carson City; entered the Union Oct. 31, 1864; nickname, *Sagebrush State* : abbr. NV —**Ne·vad'an** *adj.* & *n.*

né·vé (nā·vā') *n.* The consolidated snow on the summit of a mountain, composed of roundish grains, resembling sand: a transition stage in the formation of glacier ice. [< dial. F (Swiss), glacier, ult. < L *nix, nivis* snow]

nev·er (nev'ər) *adv.* **1** Not at any time: also used in composition to form adjectives: *never-ending.* **2** Not at all; positively not: used emphatically: *Never* fear. [OE *nœfre* < *ne* not + *œfre* ever]

nev·er·more (nev'ər·môr', -mōr') *adv.* Never again.

never so To an extent or degree beyond the actual or conceivable; no matter how: *never so* great.

nev·er·the·less (nev'ər·thə·les') *conj.* & *adv.* None the less; however; yet. See synonyms under BUT[1], NOTWITHSTANDING.

ne·vus (nē'vəs) *n. pl.* **·vi** (-vī) A birthmark, or congenital mole on man or animal: also spelled *naevus.* [< L *naevus* blemish] —**ne'·void** (-void) *adj.*

new (noo, nyoo) *adj.* **1** Recently come into existence or use; lately made; recently settled or recently opened to settlement: *new* country. **2** Lately discovered; also, recently become important or well known. **3** Beginning or recurring afresh; renewed: the *new* moon. **4** Changed in essence, constitution, force, etc.: usually for the better: I feel a *new* man. **5** Another; different from that heretofore known or used. **6** Recently come from any place or out of any condition. **7** Unaccustomed; unfamiliar: a horse *new* to the saddle. **8** Specifically, named for another: used in place names, to distinguish a place from its namesake: *New* Zealand, *New* Orleans. —*adv.* Newly; recently. [OE *nēowe*] —**new'ness** *n.*

new·born (noo'bôrn', nyoo'-) *adj.* Newly born; in the first few days or weeks of life. —*n.* A newborn infant or animal.

New Brunswick A province of SE Canada on

the Bay of Fundy; 27,985 square miles; capital, Fredericton: abbr. *N.B.*

new·com·er (nōō'kum'ər, nyōō'-) *n.* One who has recently arrived.

new deal 1 A dealing of cards with a new deck. **2** Any new system designed to do away with old ills and to promote reform.

New Deal The policies and principles of the administration under President Franklin D. Roosevelt, embracing various social, economic, and political measures through legislative and administrative change; also, the Roosevelt administration.

New Dealer A supporter of the measures advocated by the New Deal.

New Delhi The capital of India in Delhi State, and administrative center just SW of Delhi.

new·el (nōō'əl, nyōō'-) *n.* **1** A post from which the steps of a winding stair radiate. **2** A post at the end of a stair or hand rail. [< OF *nouel* stone of a fruit < LL *nucale* <L nut]

New England The NE section of the United States, including Maine, New Hampshire, Vermont, Massachusetts, Rhode Island, and Connecticut. —**New Englander**

NEWEL

New England aster A perennial aster (*Aster novae-angliae*) having purple flowers and growing wild throughout eastern North America.

new-fan·gled (nōō'fang'gəld, nyōō'-) *adj.* **1** Of new fashion: generally in depreciation: *new-fangled* notions **2** *Rare* Fond of novelty. —**new'-fan'gled·ness** *n.*

new-fash·ioned (nōō'fash'ənd, nyōō'-) *adj.* Made in a new style; recently become fashionable.

neutral oil A light lubricating oil from petroleum, generally mixed with animal or vegetable oils.

New·found·land (nōō'fənd·lənd, nyōō'-) *n.* A large dog of a breed originating in Newfoundland, characterized by a broad head, square muzzle, and thick, usually black coat.

New·found·land (nōō'fənd·land', nyōō'-) The easternmost province of Canada, comprising the island of Newfoundland (42,734 square miles) and its dependency, Labrador, on the mainland; total, 152,734 square miles; capital, St. John's—**New·found'land·er** (-found'-) *n.*

New Guin·ea (gin'ē) The world's second largest island, north of Australia in the Malay Archipelago; 304,200 square miles: also *Papua*: Indonesian **I·ri·an** (ē'rē·än); divided into West Irian, and Territory of Papua and New Guinea.

New Hampshire A State of the NE United States; 9,304 square miles; capital, Concord; entered the Union June 21, 1788, one of the thirteen original States; nickname, *Granite State*: abbr. NH

New Haven A city on Long Island Sound in Connecticut; site of Yale University.

new·ish (nōō'ish, nyōō'-) *adj.* Rather new.

New Jersey A State of the eastern United States on the Atlantic; 7,836 square miles; capital, Trenton; entered the Union Dec. 18, 1787, one of the thirteen original States; nickname, *Garden State*: abbr. NJ —**New Jerseyite**

new·ly (nōō'lē, nyōō'-) *adv.* **1** In a new or recent manner; lately. **2** In a different way; so as to be or appear new; afresh.

new·ly-wed (nōō'lē·wed', nyōō'-) *n.* A person recently married.

new·mar·ket (nōō'mär·kit, nyōō'-) *n.* **1** A long, close-fitting coat for outdoor wear: also **Newmarket coat. 2** A game of cards resembling the game of *stops.*

New Mexico A State of the SW United States on the Mexican border; 121,666 square miles; capital, Santa Fe; entered the Union Jan. 6, 1912; nickname, *Sunshine State*: abbr. NM —**New Mexican**

new moon That phase of the moon when it is directly between the earth and the sun, its disk then being invisible; also, the first visible

crescent of the disk.

new-mown (nōō'mōn', nyōō'-) *adj.* Recently cut or mown.

new-rich (nōō'rich', nyōō'-) *adj.* Newly rich; hence, showy; pretentious.

new rich Those who have recently acquired riches. Also, *French, nouveaux riches.*

news (nōōz, nyōōz) *n. pl. (construed as singular)* **1** Fresh information concerning something that has recently taken place. **2** A newspaper. **3** Anything new or strange. See synonyms under TIDINGS. [Trans. of OF *noveles* <LL *nova* new (things)]

news agency 1 A business concern that deals in and distributes newspapers and other periodicals. **2** An agency that sells news items to newspapers, etc.: also called **news bureau.**

news·boy (nōōz'boi', nyōōz'-) *n.* A boy who sells or delivers newspapers.

news·cast (nōōz'kast', -käst', nyōōz'-) *n.* A radio news program. —*v.t. & v.i.* To broadcast (news). —**news'cast'er** *n.*

news·gath·er·er (nōōz'gath'ər·ər, nyōōz'-) *n.* One who collects news.

news·hawk (nōōz'hôk', nyōōz'-) *n.* U.S. Colloq. A journalist with a sharp eye for news.

news·mag·a·zine (nōōz'mag·ə·zēn, nyōōz'-) *n.* A periodical, especially a weekly, that summarizes the news and reports current events of general interest.

news·man (nōōz'man', -mən, nyōōz'-) *n. pl.* **·men** (-men', -mən) A man who delivers or sells newspapers; also, a newspaper reporter.

news·pa·per (nōōz'pā'pər, nyōōz'-) *n.* A publication issued for general circulation at frequent intervals; a public print that circulates news, etc. —**news'pa'per·man** (-man', -mən) *n.*

news·print (nōōz'print', nyōōz'-) *n.* The thin, unsized paper on which the ordinary daily or weekly newspaper is printed.

news·reel ((nōōz'rēl', nyōōz'-) *n.* A motion picture, usually of short duration, showing events of current interest.

news-stand (nōōz'stand', nyōōz'-) *n.* A stand or stall at which newspapers and periodicals are offered for sale.

news·worth·y (nōōz'wûr'thē, nyōōz'-) *adj.* Important enough to be written up in a newspaper; considered to be of current interest.

news·y (nōō'zē, nyōō'-) *adj. Colloq.* Full of news.

newt (nōōt, nyōōt) *n.* One of various small, semiaquatic, salamander–like amphibians, chiefly of the genus *Triturus.* [Earlier *ewt, evet,* OE *efete;* in ME *an ewt* was taken as *a newt*]

NEWT
(From 3 1/2 to 20 inches in length, varying with the species)

New Testament 1 The promises of God to man as revealed in the life and teachings of Christ. **2** That portion of the Bible containing the life and teachings of Christ, including the Gospels, the Epistles, the Acts of the Apostles, and the Revelation of St. John the Divine.

New Thought A modern religious philosophy stressing "God in man" and the power of right thinking over disease and failure: also called *Higher Thought, Mental Science, Practical Christianity.*

new·ton (nōō'tən, nyōō'-) *n. Physics* A unit of force in the mks system, equal to 100,000 dynes, or that force which will impart to a mass of 1 kilogram an acceleration of 1 meter per second per second. [after Isaac *Newton*]

New·ton (nōō'tən, nyōō'-), **Sir Isaac,** 1642–1727, English philosopher, mathematician, and physicist; formulated the basic laws of dynamics, the law of gravitation, and the elements of differential calculus. —**New·to·ni·an** (nōō·tō'nē·ən, nyōō'-) *adj.*

new wave 1. (cinema) art form using new photographic techniques to create abstract and symbolic images, often improvised, exemplified by films of Jean-Luc Godard and Alain Resnais in 1960's. **2.** (music) post-punk rock, involving bizarre clothing; popular in U.S. during 1980's.

New Year The first day of the year; in the Gregorian calendar, January 1. Also **New Year's Day.** Compare CALENDAR.

New Year's Eve
The evening of December 31.

New York 1 A State of the NE United States on the Atlantic; 49,576 square miles; capital, Albany; entered the Union July 26, 1788; one of the thirteen original States; nickname, *Empire State*: abbr. NY **2** A port at the mouth of the Hudson River in SE New York, divided into the five boroughs of the Bronx, Brooklyn, Manhattan, Queens, and Richmond, comprising the largest city of the United States; 365 square miles: also *Greater New York.*

NEW YORK HARBOR

New York Bay An inlet of the Atlantic Ocean at the mouth of the Hudson River, forming **New York Harbor** and divided by the Narrows into **Upper New York Bay** and **Lower New York Bay.**

New York·er (yôr'kər) An inhabitant of New York; specifically, a native or resident of New York City.

New York State Barge Canal A waterway system of central New York, connecting the Hudson River with Lake Erie and with Lake Champlain; total length, 525 miles.

New Zea·land (zē'lənd) A self-governing member of the Commonwealth of Nations, comprising a group of islands, principally North Island and South Island, in the South Pacific SE of Australia; 103,416 square miles, excluding island territories; capital, Wellington.

New Zea·land·er (zē'lən·dər) *n.* A resident of New Zealand; formerly, a Maori.

next (nekst) *adj.* **1** Being nearest to, in time, space, order, rank, etc.; immediately succeeding or preceding. **2** Almost: *next* to impossible. See synonyms under ADJACENT, IMMEDIATE. —*adv.* In the nearest time, place, or rank; especially, immediately succeeding: when I *next* meet her. —*prep.* Nearest to. [OE *nēahst,* superl. of *nēah nigh*]

next-door (neks'dôr', -dōr') *adj.* In the next house: a *next-door* neighbor.

next door 1 The nearest or adjacent house. **2** In the next house: the lady *next door.*

next friend *Law* A person who, as the nearest friend, appears to prosecute an action in behalf of someone under legal disability, as a minor child, etc.

next of kin 1 *Law* The kindred of a person who would share in his estate according to the statutes of distribution. **2** The person most closely related to one.

nex·us (nek'səs) *n. pl.* **·us·es** or **·us** A bond or tie between the several members of a group or series; link. [< L < *nectere* tie]

Nez Per·cé (nez' pûrs', *Fr.* nā per·sā') One of a tribe of North American Indians of Shahaptian stock, formerly dwelling in Idaho, Oregon, and Washington. [< F, pierced nose]

Ni·ag·a·ra Falls (nī·ag'ər·ə, -rə) **1** A city on the Niagara River, western New York. **2** See under NIAGARA RIVER.

Niagara River A river between Ontario province, Canada, and New York State, flowing 34 miles from Lake Erie to Lake Ontario; in its course occurs **Niagara Falls,** a cataract divided by Goat Island into the American Falls, 167 feet high and 1,000 feet wide, and Horseshoe Falls on the Canadian side, 160 feet high and 2,500 feet wide.

Nia·mey (nyä·mā') A port on the Niger, capital of the Republic of Niger.

nib (nib) *n.* **1** A projecting, pointed part. **2** A beak of a bird; neb. **3** The point of a pen. **4** The point of anything. —*v.t.* **nibbed, nib·bing 1** To furnish with a nib. **2** To sharpen or mend the nib or point of. [Var. of NEB]

nib·ble (nib′əl) v. **·bled, ·bling** v.t. **1** To eat (food) with small, quick bites. **2** To bite gently or cautiously, as bait. —v.i. **3** To bite off or eat little bits. **4** To take gentle or cautious bites: usually with *at.* —n. The act of nibbling; a little bite. [Cf. LG *nibbelen*] —**nib′bler** n.

Ni·be·lung (nē′bə-loong′ən) n. pl. **·lungs** or **·lung·en** (-loong′ən) **1** In Teutonic mythology, one of the children of the mist, a dwarf people who held a magic ring and hoard of gold, which were wrested from them by Siegfried. **2** In the *Nibelungenlied,* one of the Burgundian kings.

Ni·be·lung·en·lied (nē′bə-loong′ən-lēt′) The lay of the Nibelungs, a Middle High German epic poem written by an unknown author during the early 13th century, embodying legends of the Burgundian kings which were based on various compilations: the source of Wagner's operatic cycle, *The Ring of the Nibelung.*

nib·lick (nib′lik) n. A golf club with a slanted iron head for lifting the ball out of bunkers, long grass, etc. See illustration under GOLF CLUB. [Origin uncertain]

Nic·a·ra·gua (nik′ə-rä′gwə) A republic of Central America; 57,143 square miles; capital, Managua.

nic·co·lite (nik′ə-līt) n. A usually massive, brittle, metallic, pale copper-red nickel arsenide, NiAs, crystallizing in the hexagonal system: also called *copper nickel.* [< NL *niccolum* nickel]

nice (nis) adj. **nic·er, nic·est 1** Characterized by discrimination and judgement; acute; discerning. **2** Refined and pure in tastes or habits; refined; hence, overparticular; dainty; modest; fastidious; scrupulous. **3** Requiring careful consideration, discrimination, or treatment; delicate; subtle. **4** Exactly fitted or adjusted; accurate. **5** Delicately constructed; hence, easily disarranged or injured; fragile; tender. **6** Agreeable or pleasant in any way: a wide use. **7** Agreeable socially; respectable: *nice* people. See synonyms under CHOICE, FINE¹, NEAT¹, PRECISE, TASTEFUL. ◆ Homophone: *gneiss.* [< OF, stupid < L *nescius* ignorant < *ne-* not + *scire* know] —**nice′ly** adv. —**nice′ness** n.

Nicene Creed *Eccl.* **1** A Christian confession of faith, adopted against the Arian heresy by the first Council of Nicaea, A.D. 325. **2** A similar creed, later attributed to the Council of Constantinople, A.D. 381, and accepted by the Greek Church: also called *Constantinopolitan* or *Niceno-Constantinopolitan Creed.* **3** A modification of this, containing a clause referring to the Holy Spirit, adopted by the Council of Toledo, A.D. 589.

ni·ce·ty (nī′sə-tē) n. pl. **·ties 1** The quality of being nice. **2** A delicate point or distinction; refinement of criticism; subtlety. **3** A rare or delicious thing; delicacy. **4** Fastidiousness. **5** *Obs.* Coyness; shyness. [< OF *niceté* folly < *nice.* See NICE.]

niche (nich) n. **1** A recessed space or hollow; specifically, a recess in a wall for a statue or the like. **2** Hence, any position specially adapted to its occupant. —v.t. **niched, nich·ing** To put in a niche. [< F < *nicher* nest, ult. < L *nidus* a nest]

nich·er (nikh′ər) See NICKER².

Nich·o·las (nik′ə-ləs) A masculine personal name. Also *Lat.* **Ni·co·la·us** (nik′ō-lā′əs), *Fr.* **Ni·co·las** (nē′kō·lä′), *Ital.* **Nic·co·lò** (nēk′kō-lô′), *Pg.* **Ni·co·lá·o** (nē′kō-lä′oo), *Sp.* **Ni·co·lás** (nē′kō-läs′), *Ger.* **Ni·ko·laus** (nē′kō-lous), *Russian* **Ni·co·lai** (nē′kō-lī′). [< Gk., victory of the people]

—**Nicholas,** Saint Fourth century prelate, bishop of Myra; patron saint of Russia, seamen, and children. In Dutch nursery lore, the Santa Claus who brings presents to children on Christmas Eve. See SANTA CLAUS.

—**Nicholas I,** 1796–1855, czar of Russia 1825–55.

—**Nicholas II,** 1868–1918, czar of Russia 1894–1917; executed.

NICHE

nick (nik) n. **1** A slight cut, chip, or indentation in the surface or edge of anything. **2** A score or tally: from the use of notched sticks for keeping tally. **3** A point of time; critical moment. **4** *Printing* A groove on the shank of a type character to aid in correct alinement. —v.t. **1** To make a nick or nicks in; notch. **2** To record or tally by making nicks. **3** To cut through or into. **4** *Slang* To cheat or trick. **5** To hit or catch at the exact moment; guess or understand exactly. **6** *Brit. Slang* To arrest; catch. [Origin uncertain] —**nick′er** n.

Nick (nik) The devil. Also **Old Nick.** [Nickname of NICHOLAS]

nick·el (nik′əl) n. **1** A hard, malleable, metallic element (symbol Ni, atomic number 28), widely used in metallurgy and the arts. See PERIODIC TABLE. **2** A five-cent coin of the United States, of a nickel-and-copper alloy. —v.t. To plate with nickel. [< Sw. < G *(kupfer)nickel,* lit., copper demon; because its ore looks like copper but contains none]

nick·el·bloom (nik′əl-bloom′) n. Annabergite.

nickel carbonyl *Chem.* A yellow, volatile, highly poisonous liquid, Ni(CO)₄, obtained by passing carbon monoxide over finely divided nickel. Also **nickel tetracarbonyl.**

nick·el·ic (nik′əl-ik) adj. Of, pertaining to, or containing nickel, especially trivalent nickel.

nick·el·if·er·ous (nik′əl·if′ər·əs) adj. Containing nickel, as ore.

nick·el·o·de·on (nik′əl-ō′dē·ən) n. **1** An early type of motion–picture theater charging an admission fee of five cents. **2** An automatic slot machine, such as a cinematograph or a phonograph, which performs when a nickel is inserted. [< NICKEL (def. 2) + *odeon,* var. of ODEUM]

nick·el·ous (nik′əl-əs) adj. Of, pertaining to, or containing nickel, especially bivalent nickel.

nick·el-plate (nik′əl-plāt′) v.t. **-plat·ed, -plat·ing** To cover with nickel by electroplating. —**nick′el-plat′ed** adj.

nickel plate A thin layer of nickel deposited on the surface of objects by electrolysis.

nickel silver German silver.

nick·er¹ (nik′ər) n. A seed of the nickernut tree, used by children in games resembling marbles. Also **nick′er·nut.** [? < Du. *knikker* a marble]

nick·er² (nik′ər) n. & v.i. **1** Neigh. **2** Laugh. Also, *Scot., nicher.* [Imit.]

nick·er·nut tree (nik′ər-nut′) **1** A tropical American climbing shrub (*Caesalpinia crista*) with prickly, oval pods bearing seeds or nuts called *nickernuts* or *bonducnuts.* **2** The Kentucky coffee tree. [? < NICKER¹, from the use of its seeds as marbles]

nick–nack (nik′nak′) See KNICK–KNACK.

nick–name (nik′nām′) n. **1** A familiar name, sometimes a diminutive, as Tom for Thomas. **2** A descriptive or facetious name given to a person, place, or thing in derision, affection, or acclaim, as Longshanks, Honest Abe, Empire State, etc. —v.t. **·named, ·nam·ing 1** To give a nickname to. **2** To misname. [ME *ekename* a surname; later *an ekename* was taken as *a nickname*]

nic·o·tine (nik′ə-tēn, -tin) n. A poisonous, colorless, oily, liquid alkaloid, $C_{10}H_{14}N_2$, with a very acrid taste, contained in the leaves of tobacco. Also **nic′o·tin.** [after Jean *Nicot,* 1530–1604, French courtier, who introduced tobacco into France from Portugal] —**nic·o·tin·ic** (nik′ə-tin′ik) adj.

nicotinic acid The anti–pellagra factor of the vitamin B complex; a colorless, crystalline, water–soluble compound, $C_6H_5NO_2$, present in liver, kidney, muscle meats, fish, milk, and green vegetables, and also made by the oxidation of nicotine: also called *niacin.*

nic·o·tin·ism (nik′ə-tin-iz′əm) n. The morbid effects resulting from the excessive use of tobacco.

nic·ti·tate (nik′tə-tāt) v.i. **·tat·ed, ·tat·ing** To wink. Also **nic′tate.** [< Med. L *nictitatus,* pp. of *nictitare,* freq. of L *nictare* wink]

nictitating membrane The third or lateral eyelid, in birds, crocodiles, etc., springing from the inner and anterior border of the eye.

nic·ti·ta·tion (nik′tə-tā′shən) n. **1** The act of winking. **2** *Pathol.* Rapid and involuntary winking due to nervous derangement. Also

nic·ta′tion.

nide (nīd) n. A nest or brood of young pheasants. —v.i. **nid·ed, nid·ing** *Rare* To nest. [< L *nidus* nest]

ni·dic·o·lous (ni-dik′ə·ləs) adj. Remaining in the nest for some time after hatching: said of birds. [< L *nidus* nest + *colere* inhabit]

nid·i·fy (nid′ə-fī) v.i. **·fied, ·fy·ing** To build a nest. Also **nid′i·fi·cate′.** [< L *nidificare* < *nidus* a nest + *facere* make] —**nid′i·fi·ca′tion** n.

ni·dus (nī′dəs) n. pl. **·di** (-dī) **1** A place for the natural deposit of eggs, especially of insects, spiders, etc. **2** A place in an organism adapted to the development of some germ or parasite; hence, a center of infection. [< L]

niece (nēs) n. The daughter of a brother or sister; also, the daughter of a brother–in–law or sister–in–law. [< OF, ult. < L *neptis* niece, granddaughter]

ni·el·lo (nē-el′ō) n. pl. **·li** (-ī) **1** The art of decorating metal plates by incising designs upon them and then filling in the incised lines with a black alloy. **2** A work produced by this method: also **ni·el′lo–work′.** **3** A black alloy used in this work. [< Ital. < L *nigellus* blackish < *niger* black] —**ni·el′list** n.

Nie·tzsche (nē′chə), **Friedrich Wilhelm,** 1844–1900, German philosopher.

Nie·tzsche·ism (nē′chi-iz′əm) n. The principles propounded in the philosophy of Nietzsche; especially, the doctrine of the development of the superman. Also **Nie′tzsche·an·ism.** —**Nie′tzsche·an** adj. & n.

Nifl·heim (niv′əl·hām) The lowest of the nine worlds of Norse mythology, the world of fog or mist; the northern limit of cold and darkness. Also **Nif′el·heim.** [< ON < *nifl* fog + *heimr* world]

nif·ty (nif′tē) adj. **·ti·er, ·ti·est** *Slang* Stylish; pleasing.

Ni·ger (nī′jər, -gər), **Republic of** An independent republic of the French Community in north central Africa; 458,976 square miles; capital, Niamey: formerly a French overseas territory.

Ni·ge·ri·a (nī-jir′ē·ə) An independent state of the British Commonwealth, in west Africa, including the northern part of the former British Cameroons; 356,093 square miles; capital, Lagos: formerly a British dependency. — **Ni·ge′ri·an** adj. & n.

nig·gard (nig′ərd) n. A parsimonious person. —v.t. & v.i. *Obs.* To act or treat in a niggardly manner. —adj. Niggardly. [Cf. ON *hnöggr* stingy]

nig·gard·ly (nig′ərd-lē) adj. Meanly covetous or avaricious; parsimonious; stingy. —adv. In the manner of a niggard. —**nig′gard·li·ness** n.

nig·ger·head (nig′ər-hed′) n. **1** A stone or boulder, especially one having nodules. **2** The black–eyed Susan. **3** *Naut.* A spool about which a hauling rope is wound; a bollard.

nig·gle (nig′əl) v.i. **·gled, ·gling 1** To occupy oneself with trifles; be too precise. **2** To putter; trifle. [Cf. dial. Norw. *nigla*]

nig·gling (nig′ling) n. **1** Work that is too detailed or meticulous. **2** In art, overelaborate or too detailed a treatment. —adj. **1** Fussy; overelaborate. **2** Mean; petty; trite. **3** Troublesome; annoying. —**nig′gling·ly** adv.

nigh (nī) adj. **nigh·er, nigh·est** or, formerly, **next 1** Being close by; near in time or place. **2** On the left: used of a team. **3** Closely allied in kinship; intimate. **4** Most convenient; direct. See synonyms under ADJACENT. —adv. **1** Not remote in time or place; close by; near. **2** Almost; nearly. —prep. Close to; near. —v.t. & v.i. *Rare* To draw near; approach. [OE *neah, neh*]

night (nīt) n. **1** The period during which the sun is below the horizon from sunset to sunrise. ◆ Collateral adjective: *nocturnal.* **2** The close of day; evening. **3** A condition of darkness or gloom; sorrow; misfortune. **4** Death. ◆ Homophone: *knight.* [OE *niht*]

night·bird (nīt′bûrd′) n. A bird that flies or sings by night.

night blindness Nyctalopia.

night–bloom·ing cereus (nīt′bloo′ming) See CEREUS.

night·cap (nīt′kap′) n. **1** A headcovering to be worn in bed. **2** *Colloq.* A drink of liquor taken just before going to bed. **3** *Colloq.* The final event in a day's program of sports competition; specifically, in baseball, the second

night-clothes (nīt'klōz', -klōthz') *n. pl.* Clothes to be worn in bed.

night club A restaurant open at night, providing entertainment, food, and drink.

night-fall (nīt'fôl') *n.* The close of day.

night-glass (nīt'glas', -gläs') *n.* A spyglass or telescope arranged with concentrating lenses for use at night, especially at sea.

night-gown (nīt'goun') *n.* A long, loose gown worn in bed. Also **night'dress'.**

night-hawk (nīt'hôk') *n.* **1** An American goatsucker (genus *Chordeiles*) of nocturnal habits, related to the whippoorwill. **2** The nightjar. **3** One who works or stays up at night.

night heron A bird (genus *Nycticorax*) of somewhat nocturnal habits, having a comparatively short, stout bill. — **black-crowned night heron** One of two forms of night herons (*N. nycticorax*) found in North America.

night-in-gale (nīt'ən-gāl, nī'ting-) *n.* **1** A small, Old World, migratory bird (genus *Luscinia*), of the thrush family (*Turdidae*), noted for the melodious night song of the male. **2** The bulbul. [OE *nihtegale*, lit., night-singer]

Night-in-gale (nīt'ən-gāl, nī'ting-), **Florence,** 1820–1910, English nurse born in Italy; served in the military hospitals during the Crimean War; regarded as the founder of modern nursing service.

night-jar (nīt'jär') *n.* A goatsucker, especially the common European species (*Caprimulgus europaeus*).

night latch A spring latch operated from the outside by a key and from the inside by a knob or the like. Also **night lock.**

night letter A lettergram sent during the night, usually at a reduced rate.

night-long (nīt'lông', -long') *adj.* Lasting through the night.

night-ly (nīt'lē) *adj.* **1** Pertaining to night or to every night; occurring at night or every night. **2** Dark; having the appearance of night. — *adv.* By night; every night.

night-mare (nīt'mâr') *n.* **1** A sensation of oppression or suffocation during sleep, with terrifying dreams and apparent inability to move or speak. **2** Hence, any oppressive influence. **3** An evil spirit formerly supposed to suffocate people during sleep; an incubus. [< NIGHT + MARE[2]] — **night'mar-ish** *adj.*

night owl 1 An owl especially nocturnal in habits. **2** Nighthawk (def. 3).

night raven 1 The nightjar. **2** The night heron.

night rider In the southern United States, any of a band of masked, mounted men who perform lawless acts of violence at night, generally to punish, intimidate, etc.

nights (nīts) *adv.* At night.

night school A school that holds classes during the evening, especially for those who cannot attend day school.

night-shade (nīt'shād) *n.* **1** Any one of a genus (*Solanum*) of flowering plants; especially the **common** or **black nightshade** (*S. nigrum*), a weedlike plant with white flowers and black berries, reputed poisonous, but used medicinally, and the **climbing** or **woody nightshade** (*S. dulcamara*). **2** The belladonna or **deadly nightshade.** **3** The henbane. — **enchanter's nightshade** A low, inconspicuous herb (genus *Circaea*) growing in damp woods.

BLACK NIGHTSHADE
a. Spray showing blossom (*b*) and fruit (*c*).

night-shirt (nīt'shûrt') *n.* A loose, shirtlike garment worn in bed, usually by men or boys.

night soil The contents of privies, cesspools, etc., usually removed at night.

night spot *U.S. Colloq.* A night club.

night-stick (nīt'stik') *n.* A long, stout club carried by policemen, especially at night.

night sweats *Pathol.* Excessive sweating during sleep, often associated with phthisis.

night table A bedside table or stand.

night terrors *Med.* A disorder of children resembling nightmare, with fits of semiconscious screaming; pavor nocturnus.

night-tide (nīt'tīd') *n.* Nighttime.

night-time (nīt'tīm') *n.* The time from sunset to sunrise, or from dark to dawn.

night-walk-er (nīt'wô'kər) *n.* **1** One who walks in his sleep. **2** One who frequents the streets at night. **3** A large angleworm.

night watch 1 A guard for night duty. **2** A watch period of the night hours.

night watchman A person hired to keep watch and be on guard at night.

night-y (nī'tē) *n. pl.* **night-ies** *Colloq.* A nightgown.

nig-ri-tude (nig'rə-tōōd, -tyōōd) *n.* Blackness; darkness. [<L *nigritudo* < *niger* black]

nig-ro-sine (nig'rə-sēn, -sin) *n. Chem.* Any of a group of deep blue or black dyes obtained from aniline and its homologs. [<L *niger* black + -OS(E)[1] + -INE[2]]

ni-hil (nī'hil, nī'-) *n.* Nothing; nil. [<L]

ni-hil-ism (nī'əl-iz'əm, nī'hil-) *n.* **1** The doctrine that nothing exists or can be known; also, the rejection of religious and moral creeds, known as **ethical nihilism.** **2** A political doctrine holding that the existing structure of society should be destroyed; specifically, a movement in Russia in the 19th century advocating the overthrow of the social order and many revolutionary reforms, resulting in violence and terrorism. **3** Loosely, any revolutionary propaganda involving violence. — **ni'hil-ist** *n.* — **ni'hil-is'tic** *adj.*

ni-hil-i-ty (nī-hil'ə-tē, ni-) *n.* Nothingness.

-nik *suffix* One associated, concerned, or connected with: *peacenik.* [<Russ., noun suffix]

Nile (nīl) The longest river in Africa, rising in Lake Victoria and flowing 3,485 miles north to the Mediterranean: between Lake Victoria and Lake Albert it is known as the **Victoria Nile**; between Lake Albert and the Sudan as the **Albert Nile** (Arabic *Bahr-el-Jebel*); between Lake No and Khartoum as the **White Nile** (Arabic *Bahr-el-Abiad*); at Khartoum it receives the **Blue Nile** (Arabic *Bahr-el-Azraq*), a tributary flowing 850 miles from Ethiopia, and is known as the Nile (Arabic *Bahr-en-Nil*) for the rest of its course. — **Battle of the Nile** A British naval victory over the French, near the mouth of the Nile on August 1, 1798.

Nile green Any of several light-green tints.

nil-gai (nil'gī) *n.* A large, short-maned Indian antelope (*Boselaphus tragocamelus*) with the hind legs much shorter than the fore: often spelled *nylghai, nylghau.* Also **nil'gau** (-gô), **nil'ghai, nil'ghau** (-gô). [<Persian *nīlgāu* < *nīl* blue + *gāu* cow]

Ni-lom-e-ter (nī-lom'ə-tər) *n.* A gage for measuring the height of water in the Nile. [<Gk. *Neilometrion* < *Neilos* Nile + *metron* measure] — **Ni-lo-met-ric** (nī'lō-met'rik) *adj.*

Ni-lot-ic (nī-lot'ik) *adj.* **1** Of, pertaining to, or characteristic of the Nile or the peoples native to the Nile basin. **2** Of or pertaining to a subfamily of Sudanic languages spoken by any of these peoples, including Dinka and Fula.

nim (nim) *v.t.* **nam** or **nimmed, no-men** or **nome, nim-ming** *Obs.* To take; steal. [OE *niman*]

nim-ble (nim'bəl) *adj.* **-bler, -blest 1** Light and quick in motion or action; agile. **2** Intellectually alert or acute; keen; quick-witted. **3** Circulating freely, as money. **4** Indicating a ready mind; clever: a *nimble* answer. [OE *numel* quick at learning] — **nim'ble-ness** *n.* — **nim'bly** *adv.*

Synonyms: active, agile, alert, brisk, bustling,

lively, prompt, quick, speedy, sprightly, swift. *Nimble* refers to lightness, freedom, and quickness of motion within a somewhat narrow range, with readiness to turn suddenly to any point; *swift* applies commonly to sustained motion over greater distances; a pickpocket is *nimble*-fingered, a dancer *nimble*-footed; an arrow, a race horse, or an ocean steamer is *swift*. We speak of *nimble* wit, *swift* destruction. *Alert*, which is a synonym for *ready*, sometimes comes near the meaning of *nimble* or *quick*, from the fact that the ready, wide-awake person is likely to be *lively, quick, speedy.* See ACTIVE, ALERT, SPRIGHTLY. *Antonyms:* clumsy, dilatory, dull, heavy, inactive, inert, slow, sluggish, unready.

nim-bus (nim'bəs) *n. pl.* **-bus-es** or **-bi** (-bī) **1** A dark, heavy, rain-bearing cloud: also **nim-bo-stra-tus** (nim'bō-strā'təs, -strat'əs). See CLOUD. **2** A halo or bright disk encircling the head, as of Jesus, saints, etc., in pictures, on medallions, etc. **3** A cloud of glory or surrounding aura of light in which the gods were supposed by the ancients to be clothed when appearing upon earth; hence, any atmosphere or aura of fame, glamour, etc., surrounding a person. [<L, rain cloud]

ni-mi-e-ty (ni-mī'ə-tē) *n.* Redundancy; excess. [<LL *nimietas, -tatis* < *nimis* too much] — **nim-i-ous** (nim'ē-əs) *adj.*

nim-i-ny-pim-i-ny (nim'ə-nē-pim'ə-nē) *adj.* Affectedly nice or delicate; effeminate. [Imit.]

Ni-ña (nē'nə, *Sp.* nē'nyä) *n.* One of the three ships of Columbus on his maiden voyage to America.

nin-com-poop (nin'kəm-pōōp) *n.* A foolish or silly person; simpleton. [Origin unknown]

nine (nīn) *n.* **1** The cardinal number preceding ten and following eight, or any of the symbols (9, ix, IX) representing this number. **2** Anything containing nine members or units, as a playing card with nine pips; specifically, a baseball team. — **the Nine** The Muses. — *adj.* Being or consisting of one more than eight; thrice three; novenary. [OE *nigon*]

nine-fold (nīn'fōld') *adj. & adv.* Nine times as many or as great; nonuplicate.

nine-men's-mor-ris (nīn'menz-môr'is, -mor'-) *n.* A game played on a diagram marked out on the ground, or on a board. Each player, having five, nine, or twelve (according to the number playing) counters or pieces, endeavors to place three in a row, upon doing which he takes one of his opponent's pieces.

nine-pin (nīn'pin') *n.* One of the pins in the game of ninepins.

nine-pins (nīn'pinz') *n. pl.* (construed as singular) A game similar to tenpins, in which nine large wooden pins are employed.

nine-teen (nīn'tēn') *adj.* Being nine more than ten. — *n.* The sum of ten and nine; also, its symbols (19, xix, XIX). — **nine'teenth'** (-tēnth') *adj. & n.*

nine-ty (nīn'tē) *adj.* Being nine times ten. — *n. pl.* **-ties** The sum of ten and eighty: a cardinal numeral; also, its symbols (90, xc, XC). — **nine'ti-eth** *adj. & n.* — **nine'ty-fold'** *adj. & adv.*

nin-ny (nin'ē) *n. pl.* **-nies** A simpleton; dunce. [? Short for *an innocent*]

ni-non (nē'non) *n.* A kind of firm chiffon used for lingerie, neckwear, dresses, etc.: often called *triple voile.* [<F]

ninth (nīnth) *adj.* **1** Next in order after the eighth: the ordinal of *nine.* **2** Being one of nine equal parts. — *n.* **1** One of nine equal parts; the quotient of a unit divided by nine. **2** *Music* **a** An interval of an octave and a second, or a note separated from another by this interval. **b** The two notes written or sounded together. — *adv.* In the ninth order, place, or rank: also, in formal discourse, **ninth'ly.**

Ni-o-be (nī'ō-bē) In Greek mythology, the daughter of Tantalus and wife of Amphion, whose children were killed by Apollo and Artemis after she had vaunted her superiority to their mother Leto: the weeping Niobe was turned by Zeus into a stone from which tears continued to flow.

NIOBE

ni·o·bous (nī·ō′bəs) *adj. Chem.* Denoting a compound which contains trivalent niobium.

nip[1] (nip) *v.* **nipped, nip·ping** *v.t.* **1** To compress tightly between two surfaces or points; squeeze; bite. **2** To sever or remove by pinching or clipping, as shoots. **3** To check or destroy the growth or development of. **4** To affect painfully or injuriously; benumb: said of cold **5** *Slang* To steal; pilfer. **6** *Slang* To snatch; take. —*v.i.* **7** *Brit. Colloq.* To move nimbly or rapidly: with *off, away, in,* etc. —*n.* **1** The act of compressing sharply. **2** A biting, pinching, or clipping off; also, whatever is pinched off; hence, a pinch. **3** A sudden blight, as by frost. **4** A sharp saying; cutting remark; gibe. [Cf. Du. *nijpen* nip]

nip[2] (nip) *n.* A small dram, especially of strong drink. —*v.t. & v.i.* To drink (liquor) in sips. [< earlier *nipperkin,* measure holding about a half pint]

ni·pa (nī′pə, nē′-) *n.* **1** Any of a genus *(Nipa)* of palms of tropical SE Asia. One species *(N. fruticans)* has feathery leaves, used for weaving, thatching, etc., and bunches of edible fruit. **2** An alcoholic beverage made from this palm. [< NL < Malay *nipah*]

nip and tuck A case of near equality, as between two runners; neck and neck.

niph·a·blep·si·a (nif′ə·blep′sē·ə) *n.* Snow blindness. Also **niph·o·typh·lo·sis** (nif′ə·tif·lō′sis). [< NL < Gk. *nipha* (accusative sing.) snow + *ablepsia* blindness]

nip·per (nip′ər) *n.* **1** One who nips. **2** One of various pincers for nipping. **3** An incisor, as of a horse. **4** A great claw, as of a crab. **5** A heavy, padded, woolen mitten or glove, used by New England fishermen.

nip·ping (nip′ing) *adj.* Pinching; biting; cutting; sarcastic. —**nip′ping·ly** *adv.*

nip·ple (nip′əl) *n.* **1** The pigmented cone-shaped process of the breast containing the milk duct; a pap; teat. **2** A protuberance to receive a percussion cap. **3** A small tubular pipefitting. **4** A tip, usually of rubber, for a nursing bottle. [Earlier *neble,* ? dim. of NEB]

Nip·pon (nip′on, ni·pon′; *Japanese* nēp·pōn) See JAPAN. —**Nip′pon·ese′** (-ēz′, -ēs′) *adj. & n.*

nip·py (nip′ē) *adj.* **·pi·er, ·pi·est 1** Biting; sharp; acid; sarcastic. **2** Active; vigorous; alert. **nip′pi·ly** *adv.*

nir·va·na (nir·vä′nə,nər·van′ə) *n.* **1** In Hinduism, a "blowing out" of the spark of life; hence, spiritual reunion with Brahma; bliss. **2** In Buddhism, the ideal and goal of all religious effort: freedom from passion and delusion, and absorption of the individual into the supreme spirit; complete enlightenment. **3** The attainment of complete freedom from all mental, emotional, and psychic tension. [< Skt. *nirvāna* a blowing out < *nirvā* blow]

ni·si (nī′sī) *conj. Law* Unless: used after the word *order, rule, decree,* etc., signifying that it shall become effective at a certain time, unless before the time named it is modified or avoided. [< L < *ni* not + *si* if]

ni·si pri·us (nī′sī prī′əs) *Law* Literally, unless sooner; hence, a general designation suggestive of the trial of civil causes before a judge and jury.

nit (nit) *n.* **1** The egg of a louse or other insect. **2** The immature insect itself. **3** A small speck. **4** *Scot.* A nut. [OE *hnitu*] —**nit′ty** *adj.*

nite (nīt) *n.* A non-standard variant spelling of NIGHT.

ni·ter (nī′tər) *n.* **1** A crystalline white salt; saltpeter; potassium or sodium nitrate. **2** *Obs.* Natron. Also **ni′tre.** [< F *nitre* < L *nitrum* < Gk. *nitron* natron]

nit·id (nit′id) *adj.* **1** *Bot.* Shining; glossy, as many leaves and seeds. **2** *Obs.* Lustrous; bright, as metal. [< L *nitidus* < *nitere* shine]

nit-pick (nit′pik′) *Colloq. v.t.* **1** To fuss over, especially with the aim of picking out petty faults. —*v.i.* **2** To engage in nit-picking. Also **nit′pick.** [Back formation < NIT-PICKING] —**nit′-pick·er** *n.*

nit-pick·ing (nit′pik·ing) *n. Colloq.* A fussing over trivial details, often with the aim of finding fault.

nitr- Var. of NITRO-.

ni·tra·mine (nī′trə·mēn, -min) *n. Chem.* Any of a class of compounds in which a nitro group is attached directly to a trivalent nitrogen atom: also *nitroamine.*

ni·trate (nī′trāt) *v.t.* **·trat·ed, ·trat·ing** *Chem.* To treat or combine with nitric acid or a compound; to change into a nitro derivative. —*n.* **1** A salt or ester of nitric acid: silver *nitrate.* **2** Sodium or potassium nitrate. [< L *nitratus* mixed with natron < *nitrum* niter] —**ni·tra′tion** *n.*

ni·tric (nī′trik) *adj. Chem.* **1** Of, pertaining to, or obtained from nitrogen. **2** Containing nitrogen in the higher state of valence.

nitric acid *Chem.* A colorless, highly corrosive liquid, HNO_3, sometimes formed in the atmosphere in small quantities, but usually made by decomposing sodium or potassium nitrate with sulfuric acid.

nitric bacteria See NITROBACTERIUM.

nitric oxide *Chem.* A colorless, gaseous compound, NO, liberated when certain metals are dissolved in nitric acid.

ni·tride (nī′trīd, -trid) *n. Chem.* A compound of nitrogen with some more positive element, as boron, phosphorus, and any of the metals. Also **ni′trid** (-trid).

ni·tri·fi·ca·tion (nī′trə·fə·kā′shən) *n. Chem.* **1** The method or act of nitrifying. **2** The conversion of ammonium salts into nitrites and nitrates, especially by soil bacteria.

ni·tri·fi·er (nī′trə·fī′ər) *n. Chem.* A substance containing nitrogen that aids in the process of nitrification.

ni·tri·fy (nī′trə·fī) *v.t.* **·fied, ·fy·ing** *Chem.* **1** To combine with nitrogen. **2** To convert, by oxidation, into nitric or nitrous acid or into nitrates or nitrites. **3** To treat or impregnate (soil, etc.) with nitrates. [< F *nitrifier*] —**ni·tri′fi·a·ble** *adj.*

ni·trile (nī′tril, -trēl, -tril) *n. Chem.* Any of a group of cyanogen compounds, yielding ammonia upon saponification, and corresponding to the formula RCN, in which R is an organic radical. Also **ni′tril** (-tril).

ni·trite (nī′trīt) *n. Chem.* A salt of nitrous acid.

nitro- *combining form* **1** *Chem.* **a** Containing the univalent radical NO_2: *nitrophenol.* **b** Of or containing nitrogen in some other form: *nitroglycerin.* **2** Nitrifying: *nitrobacterium.* Also before vowels, *nitr-.* Also **nitri-.** [< L *nitrum* natron]

ni·tro·am·ine (nī′trō·am′ēn, -in) *n.* Nitramine.

ni·tro·bac·te·ri·um (nī′trō·bak·tir′ē·əm) *n. pl.* **·ri·a** (-ē·ə) Any of various soil bacteria involved in the process of nitrification, especially the nitrous group (genus *Nitrosomonas*), which converts ammonia into nitrites, and the nitric group (genus *Nitrobacter*), which oxidizes nitrites into nitrates. Also **nitric** or **nitrous bacterium.**

ni·tro·cel·lu·lose (nī′trō·sel′yə·lōs) *n.* Cellulose nitrate.

ni·tro·chlo·ro·form (nī′trō·klôr′ə·fôrm, -klō′rə-) *n.* Chloropicrin.

ni·tro·cot·ton (nī′trō·kot′n) *n.* Guncotton.

ni·tro·ga·tion (nī′trō·gā′shən) *n.* A method of increasing soil fertility by the addition to irrigation water of anhydrous ammonia in controlled amounts. [< NITRO- + (IRRI)GATION]

ni·tro·gen (nī′trə·jən) *n.* An odorless, colorless, gaseous element (symbol N, atomic number 7) forming 78 percent of the atmosphere by volume and constituting a key element in the substance of living organisms. See PERIODIC TABLE. [< NITRO- + -GEN]

nitrogen balance *Biochem.* The relation between the nitrogen intake and the nitrogen output of a human body. An excess of intake gives a plus balance, an excess of output a minus balance.

nitrogen cycle *Biol.* The sequence of physical and chemical processes by which atmospheric nitrogen is taken into the soil, utilized by plants and animals, and eventually returned to the atmosphere.

nitrogen equilibrium *Physiol.* That condition of the body in which the nitrogen intake and output are equal.

nitrogen fixation 1 The conversion of atmospheric nitrogen into nitrates by soil bacteria, either free-living or in symbiotic relations with the roots of certain leguminous plants. **2** The production of nitrogen compounds, as for fertilizers and explosives, by various electrochemical processes utilizing free nitrogen. —**ni′tro·gen·fix′ing** *adj.*

nitrogen iodide *Chem.* A chocolate-colored powder, $N_2H_3I_3$, explosive when dry.

ni·trog·en·ize (nī·troj′ən·īz, nī′trə·jən·īz′) *v.t.* **·ized, ·iz·ing** To treat or combine with nitrogen.

nitrogen narcosis *Pathol.* A deranged, sometimes fatal nervous and mental condition resembling that of alcoholic intoxication, caused by the action of nitrogen inhaled by divers at excessive depths below the surface of the water.

ni·trog·e·nous (nī·troj′ə·nəs) *adj.* Pertaining to or containing nitrogen. Also **ni·tro·ge·ne·ous** (nī′trō·jē′nē·əs).

ni·tro·glyc·er·in (nī′trō·glis′ər·in) *n. Chem.* A colorless to pale-yellow, oily liquid, $C_3H_5(ONO_2)_3$, made by nitrating glycerol: an explosive and propellant, commonly combined, as with infusorial earth, to form dynamite and reduce the danger of its explosion by percussion. It is sometimes used in medicine. Also **ni′tro·glyc′er·ine.** [< NITRO- + GLYCERIN]

nitro group *Chem.* The univalent NO_2 radical.

ni·tro·hy·dro·chlo·ric acid (nī′trō·hī′drə·klôr′·ik, -klō′rik) Aqua regia.

ni·tro·jec·tion (nī′trō·jek′shən) *n.* The process of injecting anhydrous ammonia gas directly into the soil as a means of increasing soil fertility. [< NITRO- + (IN)JECTION]

ni·trol·ic (nī·trol′ik) *adj. Chem.* Noting a class of acids derived from nitroparaffin by the action of nitrous acid and having the general formula RCN_2O_3H.

ni·trom·e·ter (nī·trom′ə·tər) *n.* An apparatus or instrument used for the determination of nitrogen in some of its combinations when contained in mixtures. [< NITRO- + -METER]

ni·tro·par·af·fin (nī′trō·par′ə·fin) *n. Chem.* Any derivative of the methane series in which hydrogen has been replaced by a nitro group.

ni·tro·phe·nol (nī′trō·fē′nōl, -nol) *n. Chem.* Any of a group of phenol compounds derived by the replacement of one or more hydrogen atoms by the nitro group: used in the making of dyestuffs.

ni·troph·i·lous (nī·trof′ə·ləs) *adj.* **1** Obtaining nutriment from nitrogenous soil. **2** Growing in a soil rich in nitrates.

ni·tro·phyte (nī′trə·fīt) *n.* A plant growing in a soil rich in nitrogen.

ni·tros·a·mine (nī·tros′ə·mēn, -min) *n. Chem.* Any of a group of organic compounds containing the bivalent radical N·NO. Also **ni·tros′a·min** (-min). [< NITROS(O)· + ·AMINE]

nitroso- *combining form Chem.* Of or containing nitrosyl. Also, before vowels, **nitros-.** [< NL *nitrosus* < L, of natron < *nitrum* natron]

ni·tro·starch (nī′trō·stärch′) *n. Chem.* An explosive compounded of starch and sulfuric and nitric acids.

ni·tro·syl (nī·trō′sil, nī′trə·sēl′, nī′trə·sil) *n. Chem.* The univalent radical NO; known only in its combinations.

ni·trous (nī′trəs) *adj. Chem.* Of, pertaining to, or derived from nitrogen: especially applied to those compounds of nitrogen containing less oxygen than the nitric compounds. [< L *nitrosus* full of natron < *nitrum* natron]

nitrous acid *Chem.* An unstable compound, HNO_2, occurring only in solution.

nitrous oxide Laughing gas.

nit·ty-grit·ty (nit′ē-grit′ē) *U.S. Slang. n.* The basic question or details; the heart of the matter. —*adj.* Down-to-earth; basic.

nit·wit (nit′wit′) *n.* A silly or stupid person.

ni·val (nī′vəl) *adj.* Pertaining to the snow; also, growing under the snow. [< L *nivalis* < *nix, nivis* snow]

niv·e·ous (niv′ē·əs) *adj.* Snowy; like snow.

nix[1] (niks) *n.* In Teutonic mythology, a water spirit appearing in male or female form, and sometimes appearing as part fish. [< G *nix*] —**nix′ie** *n. fem.*

nix[2] (niks) *Slang n.* **1** Nothing. **2** No. —*adv.* No. —*interj.* Stop! Watch out!: an exclamation urging someone to stop saying or doing something. —*v.t.* To forbid or disagree with: He *nixed* our suggestions on the matter. [< G *nichts* nothing]

Nix·on (niks′ən), **Richard Milhous,** born 1913, U.S. statesman; vice president of the United States 1953–61; 37th president of the United States 1969–74; resigned.

no[1] (nō) *adv.* **1** Nay; not so: opposed to *yes.* **2** Not at all; not in any wise: used with comparatives: *no* better than the other. **3** *Scot.* Not. **4** Not: used to express an alternative after *or:* whether or *no.* —*adj.* Not any; not one: *No* seats are left. —*n. pl.* **noes 1** A negative reply; a denial: He will not take *no* for an answer. **2** A negative vote or voter: The *noes* have it. [OE *na* < *ne* not + *a* ever]

no² (nō) *n.* The classical drama of Japan, traditionally tragic or noble in theme, requiring masks and elaborate costumes, stylized gesture, music, and dancing. Compare KABUKI. Also spelled *noh.*

No·ah (nō′ə), *Ger.* nō′ä) A masculine personal name. Also *Du.* **No·ach** (nō′äkh), *Fr.* **No·é** (nō-ā′), *Sw.* **No·a** (nō′ä). [< Hebrew, rest] — **Noah** In the Old Testament, a patriarch who, at the command of God, built an ark to save his family and "two of every sort of living thing" from the Flood. *Gen.* vi 14-22.

no-ball (nō′bôl′) *n.* In cricket, a ball unfairly bowled.

No·bel (nō-bel′), **Alfred Bernhard**, 1833–96, Swedish industrialist and philanthropist; inventor of dynamite; founded by his will the **Nobel Prizes**, awarded annually to those whose work in physics, chemistry, medicine, literature, economics, and furtherance of the world's peace is thought of most benefit to humanity.

no·be·li·um (nō-bē′lē-əm) *n.* A synthetic, radioactive metallic element (symbol No, atomic number 102) of the actinide series, having seven isotopes, the most stable of which has an atomic mass of 255 and a half-life of three minutes. See PERIODIC TABLE.

no·bil·i·ar·y (nō-bil′ē-er′ē, -bil′yə-rē) *adj.* Of or pertaining to the nobility. [< F *nobiliaire* < L *nobilis* noble]

nobiliary particle A preposition used as a prefix to a family name, indicating the noble birth of the person concerned, as *de* or *von.*

no·bil·i·ty (nō-bil′ə-tē) *n. pl.* **·ties** 1 The state of being noble, as in character or rank. 2 A class composed of nobles; in Great Britain, the peerage. 3 High-mindedness; magnanimity. 4 Great moral excellence. 5 Noble lineage. [< OF *nobilité* < L *nobilitas, -tatis* < *nobilis* noble]

no·ble (nō′bəl) *adj.* **·bler, ·blest** 1 Exalted in character or quality; excellent; worthy. 2 Characterized by or indicative of virtue or magnanimity; high-minded. 3 Of or pertaining to an aristocracy; of lofty lineage; aristocratic. 4 Imposing in appearance; magnificent; grand. 5 Precious; pure: said of minerals and metals. 6 Chemically resistant or inert, as helium. 7 In falconry, long-winged, as a true falcon: see IGNOBLE. See synonyms under AWFUL, GENEROUS, HIGH, ILLUSTRIOUS, IMPERIAL. —*n.* 1 A person having hereditary title, rank, and privileges; in England, a peer; a member of the Second Estate, as distinct from the clergy and commoners. 2 An old English gold coin weighing 120 grains (1351). [< F < L *nobilis* noble, well-known. Related to L *noscere* know.] —**no′bly** *adv.*

no·ble·man (nō′bəl-mən) *n. pl.* **·men** (-mən) A man of noble rank; in England, a peer.

noble metal *Chem.* A metal which strongly resists oxidation and the action of acids, especially gold and platinum.

no·ble·ness (nō′bəl-nis) *n.* The quality of being noble; nobility.

no·ble·wom·an (nō′bəl-woom′ən) *n. fem. pl.* **·wom·en** (-wim′in) A woman of noble rank.

no·bod·y (nō′bod′ē, -bəd-ē) *pron.* Not anybody. —*n. pl.* **·bod·ies** A person of no importance or influence.

no·cent (nō′sənt) *adj. Rare* 1 Injurious; hurtful. 2 Guilty. [< L *nocens, -entis,* ppr. of *nocere* harm]

no·ci·as·so·ci·a·tion (nō′sē-ə·sō′sē-ā′shən, -sō′·shē-) *n. Physiol.* The loss of nerve force resulting from overstimulation of nociceptors or from shock or exhaustion. [< L *nocere* harm + ASSOCIATION]

no·ci·cep·tor (nō′sē-sep′tər) *n. Physiol.* A sense organ or receptor which responds to and transmits painful stimuli. Compare BENECEPTOR. [< NL < L *nocere* injure + -*ceptor,* as in *receptor*] —**no′ci·cep′tive** *adj.*

nock (nok) *n.* 1 The notch on the butt end of an arrow. 2 The notch on the horn of a bow for securing the bowstring. —*v.t.* 1 To notch, as an arrow or bow. 2 To fit (an arrow) to the bowstring, as for shooting. [ME *nocke,* prob. < Scand. Cf. dial. Sw. *nocke* notch.]

noc·tam·bu·la·tion (nok·tam′byə·lā′shən) *n.* Somnambulism. Also **noc·tam′bu·lism.** [< L *nox, noctis* night + *ambulare* walk]

noc·tam·bu·list (nok·tam′byə·list) *n.* A somnambulist.

nocti- *combining form* By or at night: *noctiflorous.* Also, before vowels, **noct-.** [< L *nox, noctis* night]

noc·ti·flo·rous (nok′tə·flôr′əs, -flō′rəs) *adj. Bot.* Blooming at night. [< L *nox* night + *florere* flower]

noc·ti·lu·ca (nok′tə·loo′kə) *n.* Any bioluminescent marine flagellate of the genus *Noctiluca,* found in warm seas, where its abundant presence gives the waves a brilliantly colored phosphorescent luminosity. [< NL < L *nox, noctis* night + *lucere* shine]

noc·ti·lu·cent (nok′tə·loo′sənt) *adj. Meteorol.* Luminous by night: said especially of certain high altitude clouds visible at night by reflected sunlight.

noc·ti·pho·bi·a (nok′tə·fō′bē·ə) *n.* Nyctophobia.

noc·tu·id (nok′chōō-id) *n.* Any of a large family (Noctuidae) of medium-sized moths, especially those with stout bodies and shining eyes, as the army worm and the cutworm, whose larvae are very destructive pests. —*adj.* Of or pertaining to the *Noctuidae.* [< NL < L *noctua* night owl] —**noc·tu·id·e·ous** (-id′ē·əs) **noc·tu′id·ous, noc·tu·oid** (nok′chōō-oid) *adj.*

noc·tule (nok′chōōl) *n.* A large bat (*Nyctalus noctula*) of Europe.

noc·tur·nal (nok·tûr′nəl) *adj.* 1 Pertaining to night; occurring or active at night. 2 Seeking food by night, as animals. 3 Having blossoms that open by night. Opposed to *diurnal.* —**noc·tur′nal·ly** *adv.*

noc·turne (nok′tûrn) *n.* 1 In painting, a night scene. 2 *Music* A composition of a romantic, dreamy nature regarded as appropriate to night. [< F < L *nocturnus* nightly]

noc·u·ous (nok′yōō·əs) *adj.* Causing harm; noxious. [< L *nocuus* injurious < *nocere* harm] —**noc′u·ous·ly** *adv.* —**noc′u·ous·ness** *n.*

nod (nod) *n.* A forward and downward motion of the head, more or less quick or jerky; also, a similar motion of the top of anything, as a tree. [< *v.*] —*v.* **nod·ded, nod·ding** *v.i.* 1 To make a brief forward and downward movement of the head, as in agreement, invitation, etc. 2 To let the head fall forward briefly and involuntarily, as when drowsy; be sleepy. 3 To be inattentive or careless; make an error. 4 To incline the top or upper part as if nodding: said of trees, flowers, etc. —*v.t.* 5 To bend (the head) forward and downward briefly. 6 To express or signify by nodding: to *nod* approval. 7 To affect in a specified manner by nodding: He *nodded* me from the room. [Cf. G *notteln* shake] —**nod′der** *n.*

nod·dle (nod′l) *n. Colloq.* The head: a humorous use. [< NOD]

nod·dy (nod′ē) *n. pl.* **·dies** 1 A dunce; a fool. 2 A light, two-wheeled, one-horse vehicle. 3 One of several terns (subfamily *Sterninae*), especially *Anous stolidus* of the Atlantic coast. [< NOD]

node (nōd) *n.* 1 A knot or knob; swelling. 2 *Bot.* The joint or knob on the stem of a plant, from which leaves, buds, or other structures grow. 3 *Math.* A point at which a curve cuts or crosses itself. 4 *Astron.* Either of the two points at which the intersection of the planes of two orbits, especially those of a satellite and its primary, pierces the celestial sphere; specifically, the point where the orbit of a heavenly body intersects the ecliptic. The node encountered by a body in its northward passage is called its **ascending node;** in its southward passage, the **descending** or **setting node.** 5 *Anat.* A firm, flattened tumor on a bone, tendon, or the like. 6 The plot of a story or drama. 7 *Physics* A stationary point, line, or plane in a vibrating body where the amplitude of a wave is virtually zero. [< L *nodus* knot] —**no·dal** (nōd′l) *adj.*

nod·i·cal (nod′i·kəl, nō′di-) *adj. Astron.* Of or pertaining to the nodes.

no·dose (nō′dōs, nō-dōs′) *adj.* Having nodes or knots; knobby. [< L *nodosus* full of knots < *nodus* a knot] —**no·dos·i·ty** (nō-dos′ə·tē) *n.*

nod·u·lar (noj′ə·lər) *adj.* Relating to, shaped like, or containing nodules.

nod·ule (noj′ool) *n.* 1 A little knot, lump, or node. 2 *Bot.* A tubercle. [< L *nodulus,* dim. of *nodus* a knot] —**nod′uled** *adj.*

nod·u·lose (noj′ə·lōs) *adj.* Having nodules.

Also **nod′u·lous** (-ləs).

no·dus (nō′dəs) *n.* 1 A knot. 2 Node (def. 5). 3 A difficulty; complexity; knotty point. [< L]

No·el (nō·el′) A masculine personal name. Also *Fr.* **No·ël** (nō·el′). [< L, Christmas]

no·e·mat·ic (nō′ə·mat′ik) *adj.* Of or pertaining to mental processes. [< Gk. *noema* thought]

no·e·sis (nō·ē′sis) *n.* 1 Comprehension by the intellect alone. 2 Cognition, especially as applied to sources of self-evident knowledge. [< Gk. *noēsis* intelligence < *noeein* think]

no·et·ic (nō·et′ik) *adj.* Pertaining to the mind; intellectual. [< Gk. *noētikos* intelligent]

no-fault (nō′fôlt′) *adj.* 1 Describing or pertaining to a form of motor vehicle insurance that insures the policyholder against his own loss rather than against loss to others he may have caused, and in which the assignment of blame is ordinarily irrelevant. 2 Not based on the assignment of blame: *no-fault* divorce.

nog¹ (nog) *n.* 1 A peg or a square or oblong block of wood. 2 A wooden pin driven through a wall. [? Var. of ME *knag* a peg < LG]

nog² (nog) *n.* 1 A strong ale. 2 Eggnog. Also **nogg.** [< dial. E]

nog·gin (nog′in) *n.* 1 A small mug, or its contents. 2 A liquid measure equal to about a gill. 3 *Slang* A person's head. [Origin uncertain]

nog·ging (nog′ing) *n.* 1 Pieces of wood inserted in a masonry wall, to stiffen it, or upon which to nail finishing material. 2 Brick filling in the interstices of a frame wall. [< NOG¹]

no go An impasse; balk. Also **no-go** (nō′gō′) *n.*

Noh (nō) See No.

no-hit (nō′hit′) *adj.* Pertaining to a baseball game in which a pitcher allows no base hits to the other team.

NOGGING

no-hit-ter (nō′hit′ər) *n.* A no-hit game in baseball.

noil (noil) *n.* 1 Short-staple fibers combed out from long-staple during the combing process in preparing wool or cotton yarns. 2 Waste silk produced in the manufacture of spun silk. [Origin uncertain]

noise (noiz) *n.* 1 A sound of any kind, especially a loud or a disturbing sound. 2 In communications, the confused sound caused by discordant vibrations or undesirable random voltages in a channel. 3 *Obs.* Clamor; discussion; gossip. —*v.* **noised, nois·ing** *v.t.* 1 To spread by rumor or report; often with *about* or *abroad.* —*v.i.* 2 To be noisy; make a noise. 3 To talk in a loud and voluble manner. [< OF *noyse;* ult. origin uncertain] *Synonyms:* blare, clamor, clatter, din, hubbub, jangle, outcry, racket, rattle, roar, tumult, uproar. See SOUND¹, TUMULT. *Antonyms:* calmness, noiselessness, peace, quiet, silence.

noise·less (noiz′lis) *adj.* Causing or making no noise; silent. —**noise′less·ly** *adv.* —**noise′·less·ness** *n.*

noise level In acoustics, that value of noise which may be expressed in decibels with reference to a specified frequency range.

noise·mak·er (noiz′mā′kər) *n.* 1 A horn, bell, or other device for making noise at celebrations. 2 One who or that which makes noise.

noi·some (noi′səm) *adj.* 1 Very offensive, particularly to the sense of smell. 2 Injurious; noxious. [< *noy,* aphetic var. of ANNOY + -SOME] —**noi′some·ly** *adv.* —**noi′some·ness** *n.*

Synonyms: deadly, deleterious, destructive, detrimental, fetid, foul, harmful, hurtful, insalubrious, mischievous, noxious, pernicious, pestiferous, pestilential, poisonous, unhealthful, unwholesome. *Noxious* is a stronger word than *noisome,* as referring to that which is injurious or *destructive. Noisome* denotes that which is disgusting, especially to the sense of smell; as, the *noisome* stench of *noxious* gases. *Antonyms:* beneficial, healthful, invigorating, salubrious, salutary, wholesome.

nois·y (noi′zē) *adj.* **nois·i·er, nois·i·est** 1 Making a loud noise. 2 Characterized by noise. —**nois′i·ly** *adv.* —**nois′i·ness** *n.*

Synonyms: blatant, blustering, boisterous, brawling, clamorous, obstreperous, riotous, tumultuous, turbulent, uproarious, vociferous.

Antonyms: dumb, hushed, inaudible, mute, noiseless, quiet, silent, still.

no-knock (nō′nok′) *adj.* Designating the lawful entry by force, without warning, into a suspect's living quarters by police officers.

no·li-me-tan·ge·re (nō′lī-mē-tan′jə-rē) *n.* **1** A warning not to touch or meddle with. **2** Touch-me-not (def. 1). **3** The squirting cucumber. **4** A picture showing Jesus as he appeared to Mary Magdalene after his resurrection: so called from his words of warning to her. **5** Any person or thing not to be touched or interfered with. **6** *Pathol.* Rodent ulcer. [< L *noli me tangere* touch me not]

nol·le pros·e·qui (nol′ē pros′ə-kwī) *Law* An entry of record in a civil or criminal case, to signify that the plaintiff or prosecutor will not press it. Abbr. *nol. pros.* [< L, be unwilling to prosecute]

no·lo con·ten·de·re (nō′lō kən·ten′də·rē) *Law* A plea by a defendant in a criminal action, which, while not an admission of guilt, has the same legal effect as regards the proceedings on the indictment. Such a plea does not debar a defendant from denying the truth of the charges in any other proceedings arising out of the same matter. [< L, I am unwilling to contend]

nol–pros (nol′pros′) *v.t.* **-prossed, -pros·sing** *Law* To subject to a nolle prosequi. [Short for NOLLE PROSEQUI]

nom– Var. of NOMO–.

no·ma (nō′mə) *n. Pathol.* Gangrenous inflammation of the mouth, especially in young children. [< NL < Gk. *nomé* < *nomein* feed]

no·mad (nō′mad, nom′ad) *adj.* Nomadic. —*n.* A rover; one of an unsettled, wandering people, tribe, or race. [< L *nomas, -adis* < Gk. *nomas* < *nomein* pasture, feed] —**no′mad·ism** *n.*

no·mad·ic (nō·mad′ik) *adj.* **1** Pertaining to nomads; roaming. **2** Unsettled. Also **no·mad′i·cal.** —**no·mad′i·cal·ly** *adv.*

no man's land **1** Waste or unowned land; specifically, a plot of land situated beyond the limits of the north wall of the City of London, where executions took place in the 14th century. **2** In warfare, the land between the opposing armies.

no·men·cla·tor (nō′mən·klā′tər) *n.* **1** One who assigns or announces names. **2** One who gives names; a scientific classifier. [< L < *nomen* name + *calare* call]

no·men·cla·ture (nō′mən·klā′chər, nō·men′klə-) *n.* A system of names, as used in any art or science, or by any recognized group, school, system, or authority. [< L *nomenclatura* list of names]

nom·i·nal (nom′ə·nəl) *adj.* **1** Of or pertaining to a name or names. **2** Existing in name only; not actual: a *nominal* peace. **3** So slight or inconsiderable as to be hardly worth naming; trifling: a *nominal* sum. **4** Consisting of or containing names: a *nominal* roll. **5** Assigned to a person by name, as stocks or shares. **6** *Gram.* **a** Pertaining to or like a noun or nouns. **b** Functioning as a noun or nouns. [< L *nominalis* < *nomen* name]

nom·i·nal·ism (nom′ə·nəl·iz′əm) *n. Philos.* The doctrine that abstract or generic conceptions, or universals, have no basis or representation in reality but are names only, and that only individual objects exist: opposed to *realism.* Compare CONCEPTUALISM. —**nom′i·nal·ist** *adj. & n.* —**nom′i·nal·is′tic** *adj.*

nom·i·nal·ly (nom′ə·nəl·ē) *adv.* In a nominal manner; in name only: opposed to *really, actually.*

nom·i·nate (nom′ə·nāt) *v.t.* **·nat·ed, ·nat·ing 1** To name as a candidate for elective office. **2** To appoint to some office or duty. **3** *Obs.* To name; entitle. —*adj.* **1** Nominated. **2** Having a legal or particular name. [< L *nominatus,* pp. of *nominare* < *nomen, -inis* a name] —**nom′i·na′tor** *n.*

nom·i·na·tion (nom′ə·nā′shən) *n.* **1** The act of nominating; the fact or condition of being nominated. **2** The power of appointment, as of a clergyman to a benefice. —**direct nomination** A method of nominating candidates for office by the direct votes of the people instead of by means of a representative convention.

nom·i·na·tive (nom′ə·nə·tiv, nom′ə·nā′tiv) *adj.* **1** *Gram.* Designating the case of the subject of a finite verb, or of a word agreeing with, or in apposition to the subject; in English grammar, subjective. **2** Appointed by nomination;

nominated. **3** Bearing the name of a person, as an invitation or a share of stock. —*n. Gram.* **1** The nominative case. **2** A word in this case.

nom·i·nee (nom′ə·nē′) *n.* **1** One who receives a nomination. **2** A designated person on whose life another's annuity depends.

no·mism (nō′miz·əm) *n.* Strict adherence to religious or moral law. [< Gk. *nomos* law] —**no·mis·tic** (nō·mis′tik) *adj.*

nomo– *combining form* Law; custom; usage: *nomocracy.* Also, before vowels, *nom–.* [< Gk. *nomos* law]

no·mo·gen·e·sis (nō′mə·jen′ə·sis) *n. Biol.* The doctrine which attributes all evolutionary change in plants and animals to the operation of predetermined and unchanging laws. —**no′mo·ge·net′ic** (-jə·net′ik) *adj.*

no·mo·graph (nō′mə·graf, -gräf) *n.* **1** *Math.* A graph consisting of graduated scales for two or more interrelated variables, so arranged that a straight line joining given values of the two known variables will cut the scale of the third variable at the value sought; an isopleth. Also called **no′mo·gram. 2** Any graphic representation of numerical relations.

no·mog·ra·phy (nō·mog′rə·fē) *n.* **1** The art of drafting laws, or a treatise on that art. **2** *Math.* A method for the graphic representation on a plane surface of the relations between two or more variables; the science and technique of graphic computation. —**no·mo·graph·ic** (nō′mə·graf′ik) or **·i·cal** *adj.*

no·mol·o·gy (nō·mol′ə·jē) *n.* **1** The science that treats of law and lawmaking. **2** The branch of any science that treats of the laws that explain its phenomena, as in biology, psychology, etc. — **no·mo·log·i·cal** (nom′ə·loj′i·kəl) *adj.* — **no·mol′o·gist** *n.*

no more **1** Dead; gone. **2** Nothing more: I'll say *no more.* **3** No longer: It rains *no more.* **4** Never again: She'll sing *no more.* **5** Not to any greater extent: We could *no more* see than the blind. **6** Neither: I did not speak, *no more* did he.

nom·o·thet·ic (nom′ə·thet′ik) *adj.* **1** Giving or enacting laws. **2** Nomistic. **3** Pertaining to a science of universal or general laws. Also **nom′o·thet′i·cal.** [< Gk. *nomothetikos* < *nomos* law + *tithēnai* establish]

-nomy *combining form* The science or systematic study of: *astronomy, economy.* [< Gk. *nomos* law]

non– *prefix* Not. [< L *non* not]

non·age (non′ij, nō′nij) *n.* The period of legal minority; immaturity. [< NON– + AGE]

non·a·ge·nar·i·an (non′ə·jə·nâr′ē·ən, nō′nə-) *adj.* Pertaining to the nineties in age. —*n.* A person between the ages of ninety and a hundred. [< L *nonagenarius* of ninety]

non·a·gon (non′ə·gon) *n.* A nine-sided polygon. [< L *nonus* ninth + Gk. *gōnia* angle]

non·ane (non′ān) *n. Chem.* A liquid hydrocarbon, C_9H_{20}, of the methane series. [< L *nonus* ninth; because ninth in the series]

no·na·no·ic acid (nō′nə·nō′ik) Pelargonic acid.

non·ap·pear·ance (non′ə·pir′əns) *n.* Failure to appear, especially failure to appear in court in answer to a summons.

non·bore·safe (non′bôr′sāf, -bōr′-) *adj. Mil.* Designating a type of fuze that does not have a safety device to prevent explosion of the burster charge of a projectile while it is in the bore of the gun.

nonce (nons) *n.* Present time or occasion. —**for the nonce** For the present time or occasion. [ME *for then ones* for the one (occasion), misread as *for the nones*]

nonce word A word coined for one occasion.

non·cha·lance (non′shə·ləns, non′shə·läns′) *n.* Jaunty indifference or unconcern.

non·cha·lant (non′shə·lənt, non′shə·länt′) *adj.* Without concern; casual; indifferent. [< F, orig. ppr. of *nonchaloir* < L *non calere* not be warm, be indifferent] —**non′cha·lant·ly** *adv.*

non·com (non′kom′) *Colloq. adj.* Non-commissioned. —*n.* A non-commissioned officer.

non·com·bat·ant (non′kəm·bat′ənt, -kom′bə·tənt, -kum′-) *n.* **1** One who is not a combatant; especially, one attached to a military force but whose duties do not require that he fight, as a chaplain or medical officer. **2** Anyone not connected with the military service in time of war; a

civilian.

non·com·mis·sioned (non′kə·mish′ənd) *adj.* Not holding a military commission.

non-commissioned officer See under OFFICER.

non·com·mit·tal (non′kə·mit′l) *adj.* Not committal; not having or expressing a decided opinion. —**non′·com·mit′tal·ly** *adv.*

non·com·pli·ance (non′kəm·plī′əns) *n.* Failure or neglect to comply. —**non′·com·pli′ant** *adj. & n.*

non·con·cur (non′kən·kûr′) *v.t.* **·curred, ·curring** To reject, as a bill or resolution.

non·con·duc·tor (non′kən·duk′tər) *n.* A substance or material that offers resistance to the passage of some form of energy: a *non-conductor* of heat or electricity; an insulator or dielectric. —**non′·con·duct′ing** *adj.*

non·con·form·ist (non′kən·fôr′mist) *n.* One who does not conform to established usage, as in religion; specifically, a person, especially a Protestant clergyman, refusing to conform to the Book of Common Prayer where the Church of England is established by law; a dissenter. —**non′con·form′ing** *adj.* —**non′con·for′mi·ty** (-fôr′mə·tē) *n.*

non·co·op·er·a·tion (non′kō·op′ə·rā′shən) *n.* Refusal to cooperate; specifically, civil resistance to a government through disobedience, boycotting of institutions, etc. —**non′·co·op′er·a·tive** (kō·op′rə·tiv, -ə·rā′tiv) *adj.* —**non′·co·op′er·a′tion·ist** *n.* —**non′·co·op′er·a′tor** *n.*

non·de·script (non′di·skript) *adj.* Not distinctive enough to be described. —*n.* A person or thing of no particular type, kind, or character: often used disparagingly. [< NON– + L *descriptus,* pp. of *describere.* See DESCRIBE.]

non·dis·junc·tion (non′dis·jungk′shən) *n. Biol.* The failure of paired chromosomes to separate during cell mitosis.

non·dis·tinc·tive (non′dis·tingk′tiv) *adj.* **1** Not distinctive. **2** *Ling.* Non-relevant.

non·du·ty (non′dōō′tē, -dyōō′-) *adj. Mil.* Designating the status of an enlisted man or officer who, for any reason, is not available for duty with his unit or command.

none (nun) *pron.* **1** Not one; no one. **2** No or not one specifically named person or thing: A bad book is better than *none.* **3** Not any: That is *none* of her business. **4** (*construed as pl.*) Not any (of the persons or things specified): *None* of them have their drawings finished; *None* of the apples are rotten. —*adv.* In no respect; not at all: *none* the worse for wear. —*adj. Archaic* Not one; no one; no: generally before a vowel: *none* other gods before me. [OE *nān* < *ne* not + *ān* one]

non·ef·fec·tive (non′i·fek′tiv) *adj.* **1** Not effective; inoperative. **2** Unfitted or unavailable for active service or duty in the army or navy: a *non-effective* officer. —*n.* A soldier or sailor unfitted for active service or duty, because of sickness, wounds, or the like.

non·e·go (non·ē′gō, -eg′ō) *n. pl.* **·gos 1** Whatever is not the self, or not of or pertaining to the conscious self; more especially, the object of the conscious ego as opposed to or set over against the ego. **2** The objective or material world.

non·en·ti·ty (non·en′tə·tē) *n. pl.* **·ties 1** A person or thing of no account; a nobody. **2** The negation of being; non-existence. [NON– + ENTITY]

nones (nōnz) *n. pl.* **1** The ninth day before the ides in the Roman calendar. **2** The canonical office, originally recited at 3 p.m., or the ninth hour by ancient Roman reckoning. [< OF < L *nonae* < *nonus* ninth < *novem* nine]

none·such (nun′such′) *n.* **1** A person or thing having no equal; an unexampled thing: also spelled **nonsuch. 2** An annual leguminous herb (*Medicago lupulina*) with numerous yellow flowers and pods that turn black: also called *black medic.*

none·the·less (nun′thə·les′) *adv.* In spite of everything; nevertheless. Also **none the less.**

non-Eu·clid·e·an (non′yōō·klid′ē·ən) *adj. Math.* Designating a geometry dealing with a space in which the axioms and postulates of Euclid do not necessarily hold.

non·ex·pend·a·ble (non′ik·spen′də·bəl) *adj.* Designating articles of public property for which there is responsibility and accountability: said especially of war materials which are not consumed or destroyed by the mere act of use.

non·fea·sance (non·fē'zəns) *n. Law* The non-performance of some act which one is bound by legal or official duty to perform. Compare MALFEASANCE, MISFEASANCE. — **non·fea'sor** *n.*

non·fer·rous (non·fer'əs) *adj.* Pertaining to or designating any metal other than or not containing iron, as copper, tin, platinum, etc.

non·fi·nite (non·fī'nīt) *adj. Gram. & Logic* **1** Indefinite; at any unspecified time. **2** Limitless but finite, as a Möbius surface. **3** Endless: starting from the point specified and continuing indefinitely in one direction. **4** Infinite; without limits as to space or time. Example: *Continuing* and *extending*, as gerunds or verbal nouns, are called *non-finite* forms or infinitives in *-ing* by the older grammarians of English. **5** *Theol.* Eternal. Example: God *is* (now, ever was, and always will be). The word *is* here exhibits the eternal aspect of the *non-finite* verb. **6** Transcendent: where time is merely another dimension in the space-time continuum. Example: In the statement "Mass implies inertia," the verb *implies* exhibits the transcendent aspect of the *non-finite* tense, indicating that the relationship mass-energy is always true in the space-time multiverse.

non·frat·er·ni·za·tion (non·frat'ər·nə·zā'shən, -nī·zā'-) *n.* A policy pursued by the U.S. Army during and after World War II, forbidding the association of occupying military forces with civilians.

non·ha·la·tion film (non'hā·lā'shən) Film that has been opaqued to prevent reflection.

non·hy·gro·scop·ic (non·hī'grə·skop'ik) *adj.* Having little or no tendency to absorb moisture: a *non-hygroscopic* gunpowder.

no·nil·lion (nō·nil'yən) *n.* A cardinal number: in the French and American system of numeration, denoted by 1 followed by thirty ciphers; in the English system, 1 with fifty-four ciphers. [<F <L *nonus* ninth (<*novem* nine) + F *million* a million) — **no·nil'lionth** (-yənth) *adj.*

non·in·duc·tive (non'in·duk'tiv) *adj. Electr.* Not inductive: applied to a resistance that offers no greater opposition to a varying than to an unvarying current.

non·in·ter·course (non·in'tər·kôrs, -kōrs) *n.* No intercourse: commonly applied to a legal or diplomatic prohibition of commercial intercourse.

non·in·ter·ven·tion (non'in·tər·ven'shən) *n.* The state or condition of not interfering; refusal to intervene.

non·in·ter·ven·tion·ist (non'in·tər·ven'shən·ist) *n.* One who advocates a policy of nonintervention.

non·ju·ror (non·jŏŏr'ər) *n.* **1** A clergyman in England who refused to take the oath of allegiance to William and Mary after the revolution of 1688. **2** A Scottish Presbyterian who refused the oath abjuring the Stuart Pretenders. [<NON- + JUROR, in obs. sense "one who takes an oath"]

non·le·thal (non·lē'thəl) *adj.* Not capable of causing death: a *non-lethal* drug or chemical agent; non-toxic.

non·met·al (non·met'l) *n. Chem.* Any element (as oxygen, nitrogen, carbon, sulfur, arsenic, and iodine) which has acid rather than basic properties, and is incapable of forming cations in solution.

non·me·tal·lic (non'mə·tal'ik) *adj.* **1** Not metallic. **2** Pertaining to a non-metal.

non·mor·al (non·môr'əl, -mor'-) *adj.* Having no relation to morals or to ethical conceptions and ideals; not moral or immoral. — **non'-mo·ral·i·ty** (-mô·ral'ə·tē, -mə-) *n.*

non·mo·tile (non·mō'til) *adj.* Incapable of motion of itself.

non·nu·cle·at·ed (non·nōō'klē·ā'tid, -nyōō'-) *adj. Biol.* Not having a nucleus, as a cell.

no·no (nō'nō) *n. pl.* **-nos** *Colloq.* Something forbidden or very undesirable.

non·ob·jec·tive art (non'əb·jek'tiv) Art that does not attempt to represent the recognizable form or effect of objects as they appear in nature.

non·pa·reil (non'pə·rel') *adj.* Of unequaled excellence. — *n.* **1** Something of unequaled excellence. **2** *Printing* **a** A size of type between agate and minion: the former and now

seldom used name for 6-point type. **b** A 6-point slug. **3** One of various birds of brilliant coloring of the southern United States, especially the painted bunting. **4** A variety of russet apple. [<OF <*non* not (<L) + *pareil* equal <LL *pariculus*, dim. of L *par* equal]

non·par·ous (non·par'əs) *adj.* Not having borne children.

non·par·tic·i·pat·ing (non'pär·tis'ə·pā'ting) *adj.* Not participating, nor conveying the right to participate, in the surplus or profits of an insurance company; pertaining to insurance in which the policyholders are not allowed to participate in the profits.

non·par·ti·san (non·pär'tə·zən) *adj.* Not pertaining or adhering to any established party.

non·pay (non'pā') *adj.* Designating the status of an enlisted man or officer whose pay is canceled for periods of unauthorized absence.

non·plus (non·plus', non'plus) *v.t.* **·plused** or **·plussed**, **·plus·ing** or **·plus·sing** To bring to a nonplus; baffle; perplex. — *n.* A mental standstill; perplexity, especially as causing silence or indecision. [<L *non plus* no further < *non* not + *plus* more]

non·pro·duc·tive (non'prə·duk'tiv) *adj.* Not producing: a labor term designating clerical workers, inspectors, etc. — **non'pro·duc'tive·ness** *n.*

non·rel·e·vant (non'rel'ə·vənt) *adj.* **1** Not relevant. **2** *Ling.* Denoting those features of a phoneme which do not function to differentiate it from other phonemes in a language, as aspiration in English.

non·rep·re·sen·ta·tion·al (non'rep're·zen·tā'shən·əl) *adj.* Not representational; specifically, denoting a form of art that does not attempt to represent the recognizable form or effect of objects as they appear in nature.

non·res·i·dent (non·rez'ə·dənt) *adj.* Not resident in a place: a *non-resident* landlord. — *n.* One not permanently residing in, or systematically absent from, a particular place. — **non·res'i·dence**, **non·res'i·den·cy** *n.*

non·re·straint (non'ri·strānt') *n.* Absence of restraint; especially, the treatment of insane persons without using a straitjacket or other physical restraint.

non·rig·id (non·rij'id) *adj. Aeron.* Denoting an airship whose form is maintained by the internal pressure in the gas chambers and ballonets.

non·sense (non'sens, -səns) *n.* **1** That which is without sense, or without good sense; meaningless or ridiculous language; absurd behavior. **2** Things of no importance. — **non·sen'si·cal** *adj.* — **non·sen'si·cal·ly** *adv.* — **non·sen'si·cal·ness** *n.*

non se·qui·tur (non sek'wə·tər) The fallacy of irrelevant conclusion; an inference that does not follow from the premises. [<L, it does not follow]

non·skid (non'skid') *adj.* Having the surface treaded or corrugated to reduce skidding: said of tires.

non·stop (non'stop') *adj.* Making, having made, or scheduled to make no stops: a *nonstop* flight; *nonstop* train.

non·stri·at·ed (non·strī'ā·tid) *adj.* Void of striations; without stripes, as muscle fibers.

non·suit (non'sōōt') *Law v.t.* To order the dismissal of the suit of. — *n.* **1** The abandonment of a suit. **2** A judgment dismissing a suit, when the plaintiff either abandons it or fails to establish a cause of action. [<AF *nonsute*, OF *nonsuite* <*non* not (<L) + *suite*. See SUIT.]

non·sup·port (non'sə·pôrt', -pōrt') *n.* Failure or neglect to provide for the support of dependents.

non·un·ion (non·yōōn'yən) *adj.* **1** Not belonging to a trade union. **2** Not employing or recognizing any trade union or its members. — *n.* Lack of union or joining: said specifically of broken bones that do not knit properly.

non·un·ion·ism (non·yōōn'yən·iz'əm) *n.* Nonadherence or opposition to the establishment or the principles of trade unions. — **non·un'ion·ist** *n.*

non·u·ple (non'yə·pəl) *adj.* Consisting of nine; having nine parts or members; ninefold; also, taken by nines. — *n.* A number or sum nine

times as great as another. [<F <L *nonus* ninth; on analogy with *quadruple, quintuple*, etc.]

non·u·pli·cate (non·yōō'plə·kit) *adj.* **1** Ninefold. **2** Raised to the ninth power. [<L *nonus* ninth; on analogy with *duplicate*]

non·us·er (non·yōō'zər) *n. Law* A continued omission to assert or exercise some right or privilege, whereby the right or privilege is lost.

non·vi·a·ble (non·vī'ə·bəl) *adj.* Having no capacity to survive independently: said especially of a fetus.

non·vi·o·lent (non·vī'ə·lənt) *adj.* **1** Free from violence: a *non-violent* demonstration. **2** Not given to or believing in violence. — **non'-vi'o·lence** *n.* — **non'-vi'o·lent·ly** *adv.*

noo·dle[1] (nōōd'l) *n. Slang* **1** A simpleton: also **noo'dle·head'**. **2** The head. [Origin unknown]

noo·dle[2] (nōōd'l) *n.* A thin strip of dried dough, usually made with egg. [<G *nudel*]

nook (nŏŏk) *n.* A narrow and retired place, as in an angle; a recess, as in a garden. [ME *noke* corner, ? <Scand.]

noon (nōōn) *n.* **1** That time of day when the sun is on the meridian; the middle of the day; in an exact sense, 12 o'clock in the daytime. **2** The highest point of any period or career: the *noon* of life. **3** Originally, the ninth hour after sunrise, or about 3 o'clock p.m; midway between 12 o'clock and sunset; hence, the canonical hour of nones. **4** *pl.* A noontime repast. [OE *non* <L *nona (hora)* ninth (hour)]

noon·day (nōōn'dā') *n.* The middle of the day. — *adj.* Pertaining to midday.

noon·tide (nōōn'tīd') *n.* **1** The time of midday. **2** The period of culmination: the *noontide* of glory. **3** The position of the moon at midnight; midnight. — *adj.* Of, occurring at, or characteristic of noon: *noontide* glory. Also **noon'time'** (-tīm').

noose (nōōs) *n.* **1** A loop furnished with a running knot, as in a hangman's halter or a snare; slipknot. **2** Anything that restricts one's freedom. — *v.t.* **noosed, noos·ing 1** To capture or secure with a noose. **2** To make a noose in or with. [<Provençal *nous* <L *nodus* a knot]

Noot·ka fir (nōōt'kə) *Canadian* The Douglas fir.

no·pal (nō'pəl) *n.* **1** Any one of various cacti (especially genus *Nopalea*), as *N. cochenillifer*, used for rearing the cochineal insect. **2** A prickly pear. [<Sp. <Nahuatl *nopalli*]

nor (nôr) *conj.* And not; likewise not. ◆ *Nor* is used, chiefly, as a correlative of a preceding negative, usually *neither* or *not*. It may be used, as for poetical effect, without a correlative: We sat still, *nor* stirred. In older writing and in poetry, it often appears as an introductory negative instead of *neither*: He heeded *nor* praise *nor* blame. [Contraction of ME *nother* neither]

nor- combining form *Chem.* A normal or a parent compound. [<NORMAL]

Nordhausen acid Fuming sulfuric acid. [from *Nordhausen*, where formerly made]

Nor·dic (nôr'dik) *adj. Anthropol.* Pertaining or belonging to the blond-haired subdivision of the Caucasian ethnic stock, inhabiting Scandinavia, Scotland, and England, and to other Germanic peoples of northwestern Europe. — *n.* A member of this subdivision. [<F *nordique* <*nord* north]

nor·ep·i·neph·rine (nôr'ep'ə·nef'rin, -rēn) *n.* A hormone, $C_6H_3(OH)_2 \cdot CHOH \cdot CH_2 \cdot NH_2$, that as a transmitter of nerve signals and as a vasoconstrictor.

Norfolk jacket A loose-fitting jacket, with side pockets, belt and two box pleats at the back and front, worn in shooting, fishing, etc. Also **Norfolk coat.**

nor·gine (nôr'jēn, -jin) *n.* Algin.

no·ri·a (nō'rē·ə) *n.* An undershot water wheel having buckets on its rim: utilized to raise water in the Levant, Spain, etc.: introduced from ancient Persia, and often called *Persian wheel.* [<Sp. <Arabic *nā'ürah*]

NORIA

norm (nôrm) *n.* **1** A rule or authoritative standard; a model, type, pattern, or value considered as representative of a specified group. **2** *Psychol.* The average or median of performance in a given function or test, regarded as a standard for the group concerned. **3** *Stat.* The mode. **4** *Geol.* The theoretical standard of chemical composition of igneous rocks, expressed in terms of oxides: distinguished from *mode.* [< L *norma* rule]

Nor·ma (nôr′mə) A southern constellation. See CONSTELLATION.

nor·mal (nôr′məl) *adj.* **1** In accordance with an established law or principle; conforming to a type or standard; regular; natural. **2** Constituting a standard; model. **3** *Math.* Of, pertaining to, or constituting a normal; perpendicular. **4** Average; mean. **5** *Chem.* **a** Denoting a molecular structure based on an unbranched chain of carbon atoms. **b** Denoting a salt containing no replaceable hydrogen or hydroxide radical. **c** Denoting an aqueous solution containing one gram equivalent of the active solute in one liter of solution. **6** *Biol.* Designating a condition not exposed to or modified by special experimental treatment. **7** *Psychol.* Well adjusted to the outside world; without undue mental tensions. —*n.* **1** *Math.* **a** A perpendicular; specifically, a perpendicular to a curve or curved surface; a straight line perpendicular to a tangent line or plane at the point of tangency. **b** The intercept, on the normal line, between the curve and either the X-axis or the center of curvature. **2** A common or natural condition. **3** A usual or accepted rule or process. **4** The average or mean value of observed quantities. **5** An abbreviated expression for normal temperature, volume, etc. [< L *normalis* < *norma* rule] —**nor·mal·i·ty** (nôr·mal′ə·tē) *n.* —**nor′mal·ly** *adv.* —**nor′mal·ness** *n.*

Synonyms (adj.): common, natural, ordinary, regular, typical, usual. That which is *natural* is according to nature; that which is *normal* is according to the standard or rule which is observed or claimed to prevail in nature; a deformity may be *natural*, symmetry is *normal*; the *normal* color of the crow is black, while the *normal* color of the sparrow is gray, but one is as *natural* as the other. *Typical* refers to such an assemblage of qualities as makes the specimen, genus, etc., a type of some more comprehensive group, while *normal* is more commonly applied to the parts, qualities, etc, of a single object; the specimen was *typical*; color, size, and other characteristics *normal*. The *regular* is that which is steady and constant, as opposed to that which is fitful and changeable; the *normal* action of the heart is *regular*. That which is *common* or *usual* is shared by a great number of persons or things. See COMMON, GENERAL, NATURAL, USUAL. *Antonyms:* abnormal, exceptional, irregular, monstrous, rare, uncommon, unprecedented, unusual.

normal class *Mineral.* The class of highest symmetry in each crystal system; the holohedral class.

nor·mal·cy (nôr′məl·sē) *n.* The state or quality of being normal; normality. Compare NORMAL *n.* (def. 2).

normal distribution *Stat.* The frequency of occurrence of a given series of data for each change in an independent variable: usually represented by a bell-shaped curve.

NORMAL DISTRIBUTION CURVE

nor·mal·ize (nôr′məl·īz) *v.t.* **·ized, ·iz·ing** **1** To make normal; reduce to a standard or normal state or form. **2** *Metall.* To heat (steel) above its critical range and hold it at a given temperature for a stated time before allowing it to cool in still air. —**nor′mal·i·za′tion** *n.* —**nor′mal·iz′er** *n.*

normal school A school for the training of secondary school graduates to become teachers.

normal spin *Aeron.* A tailspin which is continued voluntarily by the pilot.

normal value The average of values over a long period.

Nor·man (nôr′mən) *adj.* Pertaining to Normandy or to the Normans. —*n.* **1** A native of Normandy. See ANGLO-NORMAN, NORSEMAN, NORTHMAN. **2** Norman French. [< OF *Normans*, plural of *Normant* Northman]

Norman architecture The form assumed by Romanesque architecture in Normandy and as developed in England: characterized by the round arch, barrel vault, and massive construction. Also **Norman style.**

Nor·man·dy (nôr′mən·dē) A region and former province of NW France, comprising Cotentin peninsula and the region to the SE and east.

Norman French The dialect of French spoken by the Norman conquerors in England: also called *Anglo-French, Anglo-Norman.*

nor·ma·tive (nôr′mə·tiv) *adj.* Pertaining to, based upon, or establishing a norm, especially a norm assumed to have the prescriptive value of a standard or rule of usage: *normative grammar.* Distinguished from *empirical.* [< NORM + -ATIVE]

normative science A department of knowledge which studies the phenomena and principles of human conduct with a view to establishing standards of value and norms of procedure, as politics, ethics, and esthetics: distinguished from *descriptive science, exact science.*

nor·nic·o·tine (nôr·nik′ə·tēn, -tin) *n. Chem.* A colorless, liquid alkaloid, $C_9H_{12}N_2$, found in the leaves of certain varieties of tobacco and having about half the toxicity of nicotine. [< NOR- + NICOTINE]

Norse (nôrs) *adj.* **1** Scandinavian. **2** West Scandinavian, i.e., Norwegian, Icelandic, and Faroese. —*n.* **1** The Scandinavians or West Scandinavians collectively: with *the.* **2** The Scandinavian or North Germanic group of the Germanic languages; specifically, the language of Norway. **3** The West Scandinavian languages. —**Old Norse** The ancestor of the North Germanic languages, best represented in the literature of the period (before 1500) by Old Icelandic; Old Scandinavian. Abbr. *ON* [Prob. < Du. *Noorsch* a Norwegian, var. of *Noordsch* < *noord* north + *-sch* -ISH]

Norse·man (nôrs′mən) *n. pl.* **·men** (-mən) A Scandinavian of Viking times.

north (nôrth) *n.* **1** One of the four cardinal points of the compass; the direction on the left side of a person facing the rising sun, and opposite to the *south.* For this and other points of the compass, see illustration under COMPASS CARD. **2** Any region north of a given point. **3** *Poetic* The north wind. —*adj.* **1** Lying toward or in the north; northern; boreal. **2** Issuing from or inhabiting the north. **3** Facing or proceeding toward the north. —*adv.* Toward the north; northward. [OE]

North (nôrth) *n.* **1** That portion of the United States north of Maryland, the Ohio River, and Missouri: the Free States opposed to the Confederacy (the South) in the Civil War. **2** The part of England north of the Humber.

North America The northern continent of the western hemisphere; 8,443,600 square miles. —**North American** *adj. & n.*

North American Indian An Indian of any of the tribes formerly inhabiting North America north of Mexico, now the United States and Canada.

north–bound (nôrth′bound′) *adj.* Going northward. Also **north′bound′.**

north by east One point east of north on the mariner's compass. See COMPASS CARD.

north by west One point west of north on the mariner's compass. See COMPASS CARD.

North Car·o·li·na (kar′ə·lī′nə) A SE State of the United States on the Atlantic; 52,712 square miles; capital, Raleigh; entered the Union Nov. 21, 1789, one of the thirteen original States; nickname, *Tarheel State*: abbr. NC —North Car′o·lin′i·an (-lin′ē·ən)

North Channel A strait between Scotland and NE Ireland connecting the Irish Sea with the Atlantic; 13 miles wide at the narrowest point.

North Da·ko·ta (də·kō′tə) A north central State of the United States bordering on Canada; 70,665 square miles; capital, Bismarck; entered the Union Nov. 2, 1889: nickname, *Flickertail State*: abbr. ND —North Da·ko′-

tan

north·east (nôrth·ēst′, *in nautical usage* nôr·ēst′) *n.* That point on the mariner's compass midway between north and east; any region lying toward that point on the horizon. —*adj.* From the northeast. —*adv.* Toward the northeast. —**north′east′er·ly** *adj. & adv.* —**north′east′ern** *adj.* —**north′east′ward** *adj. & adv.* —**north′east′ward·ly** *adv.* —**north′east′wards** *adv.*

northeast by east One point east of northeast on the mariner's compass. See COMPASS CARD.

northeast by north One point north of northeast on the mariner's compass. See COMPASS CARD.

Northeast Corridor The regional corridor along the eastern coast of the United States from Boston to Washington, D.C., including Philadelphia and New York City.

north·east·er (nôrth·ēs′tər, *in nautical usage* nôr·ēs′tər) *n.* **1** A gale from the northeast. **2** A waterproof hat with sloping brim worn by fishermen and other mariners in stormy weather. Also spelled *nor′easter.*

Northeast Passage A water route from the Atlantic to the Pacific along the northern coast of Europe and Asia.

north·er (nôr′thər) *n.* A cold windstorm from the north; specifically, a wind blowing over Texas to the Gulf of Mexico. —**north′er·ly** *adj. & adv.* —**north′er·li·ness** *n.*

north·ern (nôr′thərn) *adj.* Pertaining to the north or the North. —*n.* **1** A northerner. **2** *Poetic* A north wind. [OE *northerne*] —**north′ern·most** *adj.*

Northern Cross The northern constellation Cygnus, so called from the cross formed by its principal stars.

north·ern·er (nôr′thər·nər) *n.* One born or residing in the north.

North·ern·er (nôr′thər·nər) *n.* One from the North, as distinguished from a Southerner.

northern hemisphere The half of the earth north of the equator.

Northern Ireland See IRELAND.

northern lights The aurora borealis.

Northern Rhodesia See ZAMBIA.

Northern Spy A large, yellow–and–red variety of apple.

North Germanic See under GERMANIC.

Difference of latitude, measured toward the north, between any position and the last one determined. **2** *Astron.* North declination. **3** Deviation toward the north.

North Korea See under KOREA.

north·land (nôrth′lənd) *n.* A land in the north. —*adj.* Of or pertaining to a northern land or lands. [OE] —**north′land·er** *n.*

North·man (nôrth′mən) *n. pl.* **·men** (-mən) A Scandinavian; especially, in history, a Scandinavian of the Viking period. Compare NORMAN, NORSEMAN. [OE]

north–north·east (nôrth′nôrth′ēst′, *in nautical usage* nôr′nôr′ēst′) *adj., adv., & n.* Midway between north and northeast. See COMPASS CARD.

north–north·west (nôrth′nôrth′west′, *in nautical usage* nôr′nôr′west′) *adj., adv., & n.* Midway between north and northwest. See COMPASS CARD.

North Pole The northern extremity of the earth's axis; the 90th degree of north latitude, from which all meridians are south. Its prolongation strikes the celestial sphere at a point a little more than 1 degree from Polaris.

North Sea The arm of the Atlantic Ocean between Great Britain and the continent of Europe; 600 by 350 miles; formerly *German Ocean.*

North Star Polaris, the polestar.

North Vietnam 1 The former Democratic Republic of Vietnam, comprisinf the former French protectorate of Tonkin and the northern part of the former Empire of Annan; now combined with the former South Vietnam into the Republic of Vietnam. **2** Tonkin alone, a former kingdom and French protectorate; 44,670 square miles; capital, Hanoi.

north·ward (nôrth′wərd) *adv.* Toward the north. Also **north′wards.** —*adj.* Directed or lying toward the north. —*n.* The northward direction or point of the compass. —**north′·ward·ly** *adj. & adv.*

north·west (nôrth′west′, *in nautical usage* nôr′-west′) *n.* **1** That point on the mariner's compass lying midway between north and west; any region situated toward that point on the horizon. **2** The NW region of the United

States when its western boundary was the Mississippi. **3** The NW part of the United States. **4** The NW part of Canada. —**Old Northwest** The Northwest Territory. —*adj.* From the northwest. —*adv.* Toward the northwest. —**north′west′er·ly** *adj.* & *adv.* —**north′west′ern** *adj.* —**north′west′ward** *adj.* & *adv.* — **north′west′ward·ly, north′west′wards** *adv.*

northwest by north One point north of northwest on the mariner's compass. See COMPASS CARD.

northwest by west One point west of northwest on the mariner's compass. See COMPASS CARD.

north·west·er (nôrth′wes′tər, *in nautical usage* nôr′wes′tər) *n.* A gale which blows from the northwest.

Northwest Passage A water route from the Atlantic to the Pacific along the northern coast of America.

Northwest Territories A region and administrative unit of northern Canada east of Yukon Territory and north of Hudson Strait, Hudson Bay, and the provinces of Manitoba, Saskatchewan, Alberta, and British Columbia; 1,304,903 square miles including fresh water.

Northwest Territory A region awarded to the United States by Britain in 1783, extending from the Great Lakes to the Ohio River between Pennsylvania and the Mississippi: also *Old Northwest.*

Nor·ton Sound (nôr′tən) An arm of the Bering Sea on the southern shore of Seward Peninsula, western Alaska.

Nor·way (nôr′wā) A kingdom of northern Europe, in the western part of the Scandinavian peninsula; 119,240 square miles; capital, Oslo: Norwegian *Norge.*

Norway maple A tall European maple (*Acer platanoides*), an excellent shade tree.

Norway pine The red pine (*Pinus resinosa*) of the eastern United States.

Norway spruce See under SPRUCE.

Nor·we·gian (nôr·wē′jən) *adj.* Of or pertaining to Norway, its inhabitants, or their language. —*n.* **1** A native of Norway. **2** The North Germanic language of Norway. See LANDSMÅL, RIKSMÅL. Abbr. *Norw.* [< Med. L *Norwegia, Norvegia* Norway < ON *Nôrvegr* < *northr* north + *vegr* way]

Norwegian Sea That part of the Atlantic off the coast of Norway.

nor′·west·er (nôr·wes′tər) *n.* An oilskin coat worn by mariners in stormy weather. [Contraction of NORTHWESTER]

nose (nōz) *n.* **1** That part of the face of an animal containing the nostrils and the organ of smell. ◆ Collateral adjectives: *nasal, rhinal.* **2** The power or sense of smelling; scent. **3** That which resembles a nose; a ship's prow; the frontal tapering end of a torpedo; a spout; nozzle, etc. **4** The working end of a tool; also, the threaded end of a lathe or milling–machine spindle. —**on the nose** *Slang* Exactly; precisely. —*v.* **nosed, nos·ing** *v.t.* **1** To perceive or discover by or as by the sense of smell; scent. **2** To examine or touch with the nose; sniff. **3** To make (one's way) carefully and with the front end forward. —*v.i.* **4** To smell; sniff. **5** To pry; meddle. **6** To move, especially carefully. —**to nose out** To defeat by a small margin. —**to nose over** To turn over on its nose, as an airplane. [OE *nosu,* orig. the two nostrils]

nose·band (nōz′band′) *n.* That part of a bridle passing over the nose of a horse and attached to the cheek pieces.

nose·bleed (nōz′blēd′) *n.* **1** Bleeding from the nose; epistaxis. **2** Any of various plants, as the wakerobin, Indian paintbrush, or milfoil.

nose cone The conical and separable forward section of a missile or rocket, designed to carry a warhead, instruments, etc.

nose·dive (nōz′dīv′) *n.* **1** *Aeron.* A steep downward plunge of an airplane. **2** Any sudden descent or crash. —*v.i.* **·dived, ·div·ing** To plunge downward.

nose·gay (nōz′gā′) *n.* A bouquet. [< NOSE + GAY, in obs. senses "a bright object, a pretty flower"]

nose·piece (nōz′pēs′) *n.* **1** Any protective covering for the nose. **2** An attachment on a microscope to permit the use of several objectives without disturbing the focus. **3**

The narrow band fitting across the nose in a pair of spectacles.

nose wheel *Aeron.* A third landing wheel attached under the nose of some types of airplane.

nos·ing (nō′zing) *n.* **1** That part of a stair tread projecting beyond the riser; also, a shield for the edge of a stair tread. **2** *Archit.* A nose-shaped molding or dripstone. [< NOS(E) + -ING[1]]

noso- *combining form* Disease: *nosogenesis.* [< Gk. *nosos* a disease]

no·so·ge·og·ra·phy (nō′sō·jē·og′rə·fē) *n.* The study of the geographical factors and distribution of diseases. [< NOSO- + GEOGRAPHY] —**no′so·ge′o·graph′ic** (-jē′ə·graf′ik) *adj.*

no·sog·ra·phy (nō·sog′rə·fē) *n.* A description and classification of diseases. —**no·sog′ra·pher** *n.*

no·sol·o·gy (nō·sol′ə·jē) *n.* **1** The branch of medical science that treats of the systematic classification of diseases. **2** A list or classification of this kind. **3** The special characteristics of a particular disease; also, opinions regarding it. [< NL *nosologia* < Gk. *nosos* adisease + -logia -LOGY] —**nos·o·log·i·cal** (nos′·ə·loj′i·kəl) *adj.* —**no·sol′o·gist** *n.*

nos·tal·gi·a (nos·tal′jē·ə, -jə) *n.* **1** Severe or poignant homesickness. **2** Any longing for something far away or long ago. **3** *Psychiatry* Prolonged, often morbid fixation of one's thoughts on home, family, and friends. [< NL < Gk. *nostos* a return home + *algos* a pain] —**nos·tal′gic** *adj.*

nos·toc (nos′tok) *n.* Any of a genus (*Nostoc*) of fresh–water algae having a definite, globose or variously expanded, gelatinous or membranaceous thallus. They form greenish masses in fresh water, in damp places, and on stones. [< NL; coined by Paracelsus]

nos·tol·o·gy (nos·tol′ə·jē) *n.* The doctrines or science relating to the phenomena of extreme old age or second childhood; geriatrics. [< Gk. *nostos* a return home + -LOGY] —**nos·to·log·ic** (nos′tə·loj′ik) *adj.*

nos·to·ma·ni·a (nos′tə·mā′nē·ə, -mān′yə) *n.* *Psychiatry* Intense or excessive nostalgia. [< NL < Gk. *nostos* a return home + *mania* madness]

nos·top·a·thy (nos·top′ə·thē) *n.* *Psychiatry* An acute, often morbid fear of returning to one's home or to familiar scenes: the opposite of *nostalgia.* [< Gk. *nostos* a return home + -PATHY] —**nos·to·path·ic** (nos′tə·path′ik) *adj.*

Nos·tra·da·mus (nos′trə·dā′məs), 1503–66, French physician, astrologer, and prophet: original name *Michel de Notredame.*

nos·tril (nos′trəl) *n.* One of the anterior openings in the nose. [OE *nosthyrl* < *nos(u)* nose + *thyrel* a hole < *thurh* through]

nos·trum (nos′trəm) *n.* **1** A favorite remedy; patent medicine; quack recipe. **2** Anything savoring of quackery: political *nostrums.* [< L *nostrum,* neut. of *noster* our own; because prepared by those selling it]

nos·y (nō′zē) *adj.* *Colloq.* **1** Prying; snooping; inquisitive. **2** Stinking; malodorous.

not (not) *adv.* In no manner, or to no extent or degree: used in negation, prohibition, or refusal. [ME, contraction of NOUGHT]

not- Var. of NOTO–.

no·ta·bil·i·ty (nō′tə·bil′ə·tē) *n. pl.* **·ties** **1** Notableness. **2** A person of distinction.

no·ta·ble (nō′tə·bəl, *also for def.* **2** not′ə·bəl) *adj.* **1** Worthy of note; remarkable; distinguished. **2** Eminently careful, thrifty, or skillful, as in housekeeping. —*n.* One who or that which is worthy of note, distinguished, or eminent. [< OF < L *notabilis* < *notare* note < *nota* a mark] —**no′ta·ble·ness** *n.* —**no′ta·bly** *adv.*

no·ta·rize (nō′tə·rīz) *v.t.* **·rized, ·riz·ing** To attest to or authenticate as a notary. —**no′ta·ri·za′tion** *n.*

no·ta·ry (nō′tə·rē) *n. pl.* **·ries** **1** An officer empowered to authenticate contracts, administer oaths, take depositions, etc.: also **notary public.** **2** Formerly, a scrivener, or one who drew up legal papers. [< AF *notarie,* OF *notaire* < L *notarius* a shorthand writer, a clerk < *notare.* See NOTABLE.] —**no·tar·i·al** (nō·târ′ē·əl) *adj.*

no·ta·tion (nō·tā′shən) *n.* **1** The process of designating by figures, etc. **2** Any system of signs, figures, or abbreviations employed for convenience in any science or art, especially algebraic, arithmetical, or musical characters. [< L *notatio, -onis* < *notare.* See NOTABLE.] —**no·ta′tion·al** *adj.*

notch (noch) *n.* **1** A hollow cut or mark made in anything; a nick; indentation; especially, a mark or nick cut into the handle of a gun or other weapon to record each person killed. **2** A narrow, short defile. **3** *Colloq.* A degree: He is a *notch* above the others. —*v.t.* **1** To make a notch or notches in. **2** To record by means of notches; tally. [Prob. < ME *an oche* a notch < OF *oche, osche* < *oschier* notch] —**notch′er** *n.*

note (nōt) *n.* **1** That by which anything may be known; an outward sign. **2** A mark or character used in writing or printing to indicate or call attention to something: a *note* of interrogation (?) or exclamation (!). **3** A brief comment appended to text. **4** A brief record or summary; a memorandum. **5** A complete record or report: Make a *note* of that statement. **6** An official communication in writing from one government to another. **7** A brief letter; a billet. **8** *Logic* A distinctive mark or character of an object such as its qualities afford. **9** Notice; observation. **10** An account or bill. **11** High importance, estimation, or repute; distinction: something of *note.* **12** *Music* **a** An oval character in musical notation, either solid or formed in outline, used to indicate the length of a tone, and also, as placed on a staff, to point out, in conjunction with the signature, the pitch and relative position in a scale system. **b** Loosely, any musical sound: The first *notes* of the fiddles were

NOTES

a. Whole note.	*d.* Eighth note.
b. Half note.	*e.* Sixteenth note.
c. Quarter note.	*f.* Thirty-second note.
	g. Sixty-fourth note.

heard. **c** A key of the keyboard. **13** *Physics* Tone (def. 2): the preferable word in this sense. **14** A melodious or vocal sound, as of a bird; voice; tone. **15** Manner of speaking. **16** A signed promise by one party to another to pay a certain sum of money at a specified time: a promissory *note*; a bank *note.* **17** The general tone, coloring, or quality of a painting. See synonyms under REMARK, SIGN, SOUND. —*v.t.* **not·ed, not·ing** **1** To take notice or note of; observe; remark. **2** To set down, as in writing; make a note of. **3** To mention specially or separately in the course of writing. **4** To annotate. **5** To set down in musical notation. [< OF < L *nota* a mark, orig. pp. fem. of *noscere* know] —**not′er** *n.*

note·book (nōt′book′) *n.* **1** A book in which to enter memoranda. **2** A book in which notes of hand are registered; billbook.

not·ed (nō′tid) *adj.* Well known by reputation or report. See synonyms under EMINENT, ILLUSTRIOUS. —**not′ed·ly** *adv.*

note·less (nōt′lis) *adj.* **1** Not noted; unobserved; obscure. **2** Unmusical.

note of hand A promissory note.

note paper Paper for writing notes or letters.

note·wor·thy (nōt′wûr′thē) *adj.* Worthy of note; remarkable; significant. —**note′wor′thi·ly** *adv.* —**note′wor′thi·ness** *n.*

noth·ing (nuth′ing) *n.* **1** Not any being or existence; also, not any particular thing, act, or event; no thing: opposed to *thing, anything, something:* He has *nothing.* **2** A state of nonexistence; nothingness; hence, insignificance or unimportance: to rise from *nothing.* **3** A person or thing of slight significance, consideration, or value; any trifle. **4** A cipher; zero; naught. — *adv.* In no degree; to no extent; not at all.

noth·ing·ness (nuth'ing·nis) *n.* **1** A state of non-existence. **2** Worthlessness; utter insignificance. **3** A trifle; nothing. **4** Unconsciousness; also, death.

no·tice (nō'tis) *v.t.* **·ticed, ·tic·ing 1** To pay attention to or take cognizance of; remark or observe. **2** To treat courteously or with favor. **3** To mention; refer to or comment on. **4** To serve with a notice; notify. [< *n.*] — *n.* **1** The act of noticing or observing; attention: to take *notice* of. **2** Announcement; information; warning. **3** Respectful treatment; civility. **4** An order communicated to one; especially, a formal written or printed notification, instruction, or warning, as of the termination or intended termination of an agreement; also, a public communication openly displayed. **5** A short literary advertisement or review: a book *notice.* [< F < L *notitia* celebrity] — **no'tice·a·ble** *adj.* — **no'tice·a·bly** *adv.*

no·ti·fi·ca·tion (nō'tə·fə·kā'shən) *n.* **1** The act of notifying. **2** Notice given. **3** The writing that gives information.

no·ti·fy (nō'tə·fī) *v.t.* **·fied, ·fy·ing 1** To give notice to; inform. **2** *Brit.* To give information of; make known. See synonyms under ANNOUNCE, INFORM[1]. [< OF *notifier* < L *notificare* < *notus* known + *facere* make] — **no'ti·fi'er** *n.*

no·tion (nō'shən) *n.* **1** A mental apprehension; an idea. **2** Loosely, an opinion; a hastily formed theory. **3** Intention; inclination. **4** *pl. U.S.* Miscellaneous, small, useful articles, such as ribbons, thread, pins, needles, hairpins, etc. See synonyms under IDEA, THOUGHT[1]. [< L *notio, -onis* < *noscere* know]

no·tion·al (nō'shən·əl) *adj.* **1** Pertaining to, expressing, or consisting of notions or concepts. **2** Existing in imagination only. **3** *U.S.* Given to entertaining pet ideas or hobbies; overfastidious. — **no'tion·al·ly** *adv.*

noto– *combining form* Back: *notochord.* Also, before vowels, **not–.** [< Gk. *nōton* back]

no·to·chord (nō'tə·kôrd) *n. Biol.* A cartilaginous, flexible rod of cells formed along the median line on the dorsal side of vertebrate embryos, in a situation afterwards occupied by the spinal column. It persists in the adult stage of certain primitive chordates, as lampreys and tunicates.

No·to·gae·a (nō'tə·jē'ə) *n.* A zoogeographical realm including the Australian and Neotropical regions. [< Gk. *notos* south + *gaia* earth] — **No'to·gae'al, No'to·gae'an, No'to·gae'ic** *adj.*

no·to·ri·e·ty (nō'tə·rī'ə·tē) *n. pl.* **·ties 1** The character of being notorious. **2** Common knowledge or talk. **3** One who or that which is notorious. See synonyms under FAME. [< F *notoriété* < Med. L *notorius* making known. See NOTORIOUS.]

no·to·ri·ous (nō·tôr'ē·əs, -tō'rē-) *adj.* Being publicly known and the subject of general unfavorable remark. [< Med. L *notorius* < *notus* known, orig. pp. of *noscere* know] — **no·to'ri·ous·ly** *adv.*

Synonyms: egregious, evident, known, manifest, obvious, open, overt, patent, plain, undeniable, undenied, undisputed, unquestionable, well-known.

no·tor·nis (nō·tôr'nis) *n.* A ratite bird (genus *Notornis*) of New Zealand and neighboring islands, with rudimentary wings. [< NL < Gk. *notos* south + *ornis* bird]

No·tre Dame (nō'trə däm', nō'tər däm'; *Fr.* nô'tr' däm') **1** *French* Our Lady (Mary, mother of Jesus). **2** A famous early Gothic cathedral in Paris, built 1163–1257.

no-trump (nō'trump') *n.* In bridge, a bid or a declaration calling for play without a trump suit. — *adj.* Without a trump suit; denoting a hand suitable for playing without a trump suit. — **no'-trump'er** *n.*

no·tun·gu·late (nō·tung'gyə·lāt) *n. Paleontol.* Any member of an extinct order (*Notungulata* or *Notoungulata*) of herbivorous mammals of the Tertiary, whose principal habitat was South America. — *adj.* Of or pertaining to the *Notungulata.* Also **no'to·un'gu·late** (nō'tō·ung'-gyə·lāt). [< NOTO– + UNGULATE]

not·with·stand·ing (not'with·stan'ding, -with-) *adv.* All the same; nevertheless: Though imprisoned, he escaped *notwithstanding.* — *prep.* In spite of: He left *notwithstanding* your

orders. — *conj.* In spite of the fact that; although.

Synonym (*prep.*): despite. *Notwithstanding* simply states that circumstances shall not be or have not been allowed to withstand; *despite* refers primarily to personal and perhaps spiteful opposition; as, he failed *notwithstanding* his good intentions; or, he persevered *despite* bitter hostility.

Synonyms (*conj.*): although, but, howbeit, however, nevertheless, still, though, yet. *However* simply waives discussion and (like the archaic *howbeit*) says, "be that as it may, this is true"; *nevertheless* concedes the truth of what precedes, but claims that what follows is none the less true; *notwithstanding* marshals the two statements face to face, admits the one and its seeming contradiction to the other, while insisting that it cannot, after all, withstand the other. *Yet* and *still* are weaker than *notwithstanding,* while stronger than *but.* *Though* and *although* make as little as possible of the concession, dropping it, as it were, incidentally; as, "*though* we are guilty, thou art good"; to say "we are guilty, *but* thou art good," would make the concession of guilt more emphatic. See BUT[1].

notwithstanding that Although.

nou·gat (nōō'gət, *Fr.* nōō·gä') *n.* A confection consisting usually of a honey or sugar paste mixed with chopped almonds, pistachios, etc. [< F < Provençal, ult. < L *nux, nucis* a nut]

nought (nôt) See NAUGHT.

nou·me·nal (nōō'mə·nəl, nou'-) *adj.* Of or pertaining to noumena or the noumenon: opposed to *phenomenal.* — **nou'me·nal·ly** *adv.* — **nou'me·nal·ism** *n.* — **nou'me·nal·ist** *n.*

nou·me·non (nōō'mə·non, nou'-) *n. pl.* **·me·na** (-mə·nə) *Philos.* **1** An object of intuition by the reason or understanding, as something transcending perception through the senses, opposed to *phenomenon.* **2** The unknown ground or cause of phenomena, regarded as necessarily assumed by the mind, but the real nature of which is wholly transcendent; the unknowable thing in itself. [< NL < Gk., orig. ppr. passive of *noeein* think]

noun (noun) *Gram. n.* **1** A word used as the name of a thing, quality, or action existing or conceived by the mind; a substantive. A **proper noun** is the name of an individual person, place, or thing, as *Paul, Nicole, Venice, Rover, U.S.S. Nautilus,* etc.; a **common noun** is the name an individual object has in common with others of its class, as *man, city, hill*; a **collective noun** is one expressing a collection or aggregate of individuals, as *assembly, army*; an **abstract noun** is one indicating a quality, as *goodness, beauty.* **2** Anything that can be used as subject, object, or appositive, as a substantive clause. — *adj.* Of or pertaining to a noun or nouns: also **noun'al.** [< AF, OF *nun* < L *nomen* name] — **noun'al·ly** *adv.*

nour·ish (nûr'ish) *v.t.* **1** To furnish material to sustain the life and promote the growth of (a living organism). **2** Hence, to support; maintain. **3** To furnish with knowledge; educate. See synonyms under CHERISH. [< OF *noriss-,* stem of *norir* < L *nutrire* nourish] — **nour'ish·a·ble** *adj.* — **nour'ish·er** *n.* — **nour'-ish·ing** *adj.*

nour·ish·ment (nûr'ish·mənt) *n.* **1** Nutriment. **2** The act of nourishing or the state of being nourished. **3** That which promotes growth in any way. See synonyms under FOOD, NUTRIMENT.

nous (nōōs, nous) *n. Philos.* **1** Mind, as employed in thinking, feeling, or willing. **2** The higher reason; emanation of the divine principle. [< Gk. *nous, noos* mind]

no·va (nō'və) *n. pl.* **·vae** (-vē) or **·vas** *Astron.* A star which suddenly flares up in the heavens and fades away again to its former magnitude after a period of a few weeks or months. [< L *novus* new]

no·vac·u·lite (nō·vak'yə·līt) *n.* An extremely fine-grained sedimentary siliceous rock used for hones; whetstone. [< L *novacula* razor]

No·va Sco·tia (nō'və skō'shə) A maritime province of eastern Canada; 21,068 square miles; capital, Halifax: French *Acadia* (1605–1713). — **No'va Sco'tian** *adj. & n.*

no·va·tion (nō·vā'shən) *n.* **1** *Law* A substitution of a new engagement, indebtedness, obligation, creditor, or debtor for an existing one. **2** A making anew; creation; inception. [< L *novatio* making new < *novare* make new

< *novus* new]

nov·el (nov'əl) *n.* **1** A fictional prose narrative of considerable length, representing characters and events as if in real life by a plot or scheme of action of greater or less complexity. **2** The particular type of literature exemplified by fiction of this character: with the definite article: Dostoevsky is one of the fathers of the modern *novel.* **3** In Roman law, a new constitution or decree supplemental to a decree. **4** *Usually pl.* A novella. See synonyms under FICTION. — *adj.* Of recent origin; new, strange, or unusual. See synonyms under FRESH, MODERN, NEW. [Fusion of Ital. *novella* a novel and OF *novel* new, both < LL *novellus* < L *novus* new] — **nov'el·ly** *adj.*

nov·el·ette (nov'əl·et') *n.* A short novel.

nov·el·ist (nov'əl·ist) *n.* A writer of novels.

nov·el·is·tic (nov'əl·is'tik) *adj.* Of, pertaining to, characteristic of, or found in novels. — **nov'el·is'ti·cal·ly** *adv.*

nov·el·ize (nov'əl·īz) *v.t.* **·ized, ·iz·ing** To put into the form of a novel. — **nov·el·i·za'tion** *n.*

no·vel·la (nō·vel'lä) *n. pl.* **·le** (-lā) *Italian* A short tale or narrative, usually with a moral, often of satirical nature: typified by the stories in Boccaccio's *Decameron.*

nov·el·ty (nov'əl·tē) *n. pl.* **·ties 1** The quality of being novel. **2** Something novel or unusual; especially, a small manufactured article or trinket for personal adornment: usually in the plural. **3** An innovation. See synonyms under CHANGE.

No·vem·ber (nō·vem'bər) The eleventh month of the year, containing 30 days. [< L *November* ninth month < *novem* nine]

no·ve·na (nō·vē'nə) *n.* In the Roman Catholic Church, a devotion consisting of a prayer said on nine successive days, asking for some special blessing. [< LL < L *novem* nine]

nov·e·nar·y (nov'ə·ner'ē) *adj.* Relating to the number nine. [< L *novenarius* < *novem* nine]

no·ven·ni·al (nō·ven'ē·əl) *adj.* Occurring every ninth year. [< L *novennis* < *novem* nine + *annus* year]

no·ver·cal (nō·vûr'kəl) *adj.* Of, pertaining to, or suitable for a stepmother. [< L *noverca* stepmother]

nov·ice (nov'is) *n.* **1** A beginner in any business or occupation; an untried or inexperienced person; tyro. **2** *Eccl.* **a** One who enters a religious house or community on probation. **b** One who has been recently converted. **3** In competitive games, etc., a person or animal entered in a class in which he or it has not already won an award. [< F < L *novicus* new < *novus*] — **nov'ice·hood** (-hōōd) *n.*

no·vi·ti·ate (nō·vish'ē·it, -āt) *n.* **1** The state of being a novice. **2** *Eccl.* **a** The period of probation of a novice in a religious order. **b** The part of a monastic establishment inhabited by novices. Also **nov·ice·ship** (nov'-is·ship). **3** A novice. Also **no·vi'ci·ate.**

No·vo·cain (nō'və·kān) *n.* Proprietary name for a brand of procaine, used as a local anesthetic: less toxic than cocaine. Also **No'vo·caine.**

now (nou) *adv.* **1** At once. **2** At or during the present time. **3** Nowadays. **4** In the immediate past: He said so just *now.* **5** In the immediate future: He is going just *now.* **6** In such circumstances; things being as they are: *Now* we can be sure of getting home. **7** At this point in the proceedings, narrative, etc.: The war was *now* virtually over. See synonyms under IMMEDIATELY, YET. — *conj.* Since; seeing that: *Now* the books have arrived, I must stay here and read them. — *n.* The present time, moment, or occasion. ♦ *Now* is often used as an expletive, as in command, remonstrance, etc.: Come *now,* don't make me insist! [OE *nū*]

now·a·days (nou'ə·dāz') *adv.* In the present time or age.

now and again Occasionally; from time to time. Also **now and then.**

no·way (nō'wā') *adv.* In no way, manner, or degree. Also **no'ways'.**

no·where (nō'hwâr') *adv.* In no place; not anywhere. — *n.* No place. Also *U.S. Dial.* **no'wheres'.**

no·whith·er (nō'hwith'ər) *adv.* Toward no definite place.

no·wise (nō'wīz') *adv.* In no manner or degree.

Nox (noks) In Roman mythology, the goddess of night: identified with the Greek *Nyx.*

nox·ious (nok'shəs) *adj.* Causing, or tending to cause, injury to health or morals; pernicious. See synonyms under BAD, INIMICAL, NOISOME, PER-

NICIOUS. [< L *noxius* < *nocere* hurt] — **nox′ious·ly** *adv.* —**nox′ious·ness** *n.*

noz·zle (noz′əl) *n.* **1** A projecting spout or pipe for discharge, as of a teapot, or the muzzle of a gun barrel, etc.; specifically, a rigid tube or vent, commonly tapering, at the end of a flexible tube, as a hose. **2** An inlet or outlet pipe. Also **noz′le.** [Dim. of NOSE]

nth (enth) *adj.* **1** Representing an ordinal equivalent to *n.* **2** Infinitely or indefinitely large or small: raised to the *nth* degree.

nu·ance (nōō·äns′, nōō′äns, nyōō-; *Fr.* nü·äns′) *n.* A shade of difference in tone or color; hence, a slight degree of difference in anything perceptible to the mind. [< F < *nuer* shade, ult. < L *nubes* a cloud]

nub (nub) *n.* **1** A protuberance; knob. **2** The core of a matter; pith or point: the *nub* of the story. [Earlier *knub.* Related to KNOB.]

nub·bin (nub′in) *n.* *U.S.* An imperfectly developed ear of maize; hence, anything small and stunted. [< NUB]

nu·bi·a (nōō′bē·ə, nyōō-) *n.* A soft, light scarf or covering for the head, worn by women. [< L *nubes* cloud]

nu·bile (nōō′bil, nyōō-) *adj.* Of suitable age to marry; marriageable. [< L *nubilis* < *nubere* wed] —**nu·bil′i·ty** *n.*

nu·bi·lous (nōō′bə·ləs, nyōō-) *adj.* **1** Cloudy; foggy. **2** Obscure; indefinite. Also **nu′bi·lose** (-lōs). [< L *nubilus* < *nubes* cloud]

nu·cel·lus (nōō·sel′əs, nyōō-) *n. pl.* **·li** (-ī) *Bot.* The body or essential part of a plant ovule, within which the embryo and its covering are developed. [< NL < L *nucella,* dim. of *nux, nucis* a nut] —**nu·cel′lar** *adj.*

nu·cha (nōō′kə, nyōō-) *n. pl.* **·chae** (-kē) The nape or back of the neck. [< LL < Arabic *nukhā′* spinal marrow] —**nu′chal** *adj.*

nu·cle·ar (nōō′klē·ər, nyōō-) *adj.* **1** Of, pertaining to, forming, of the nature of, or depending upon a nucleus or nuclei. Also **nu′cle·al. 2** Of or employing the energy of the nucleus of the atom: *nuclear* weapons.

nuclear family A family consisting of parents and child or children considered as a discrete group.

nuclear fission *Physics* See under FISSION.

nuclear fusion *Physics* See under FUSION.

nuclear medicine The use of radioisotopes for diagnostic and therapeutic purposes in medicine.

nuclear physics That branch of physics which investigates the atomic nucleus.

nuclear plate *Biol.* Equatorial plate.

nuclear submarine A submarine driven by steam produced in a reactor using fissionable material as fuel: also called *atomic submarine.* Also **nuclear-powered submarine.**

nu·cle·ase (nōō′klē·ās, nyōō-) *n. Biochem.* An enzyme which hydrolyzes nucleic acids.

nu·cle·ate (nōō′klē·āt, nyōō-) *adj.* Having a nucleus. Also **nu′cle·i′ed.** —*v.t. & v.i.* **·at·ed, ·at·ing** To form or gather into a nucleus. —**nu′·cle·a′tion** *n.*

nu·cle·ic (nōō·klē′ik, nyōō-) *adj. Biochem.* Designating a group of complex, non-crystalline acids present in organic nuclear material, as yeast, chromatin, the thymus gland, etc. They contain carbohydrates combined with phosphoric acids and bases derived from purine or pyrimidine.

nucleic acid *Biochem.* A complex acid derived from nuclein and nucleoproteins: it plays an important role in digestion and metabolism.

nu·cle·in (nōō′klē·in, nyōō-) *n. Biochem.* A colorless, amorphous protein containing nucleic acid, and found as a normal constituent of cell nuclei.

nu·cle·o·late (nōō′klē·ə·lāt′, nyōō-) *adj.* Having nucleoli. Also **nu′cle·o·lat′ed.**

nu·cle·o·lus (nōō·klē′ə·ləs, nyōō-) *n. pl.* **·li** (-lī) *Biol.* A dense body or bodies composed mostly of RNA found within the nucleus of a typical cell; plasmosome. [< LL, dim. of *nucleus.* See NUCLEUS.] —**nu·cle′o·lar** *adj.*

nu·cle·on (nōō′klē·on, nyōō-) *n. Physics* One of the particles composing the nucleus of an atom, the proton, or the neutron, regarded as a single variety of particle existing in either of two states.

nu·cle·on·ics (nōō′klē·on′iks, nyōō-) *n.* The practical applications of nuclear physics in any

---

field of science, engineering, and technology, especially in relation to the development of atomic energy. —**nu′cle·on′ic** *adj.*

nucleon number *Physics* Mass number.

nu·cle·o·plasm (nōō′klē·ə·plaz′əm, nyōō-) *n. Biol.* The more fluid part of the nucleus of a cell; karyoplasm. —**nu′cle·o·plas′mic** *adj.*

nu·cle·o·pro·te·in (nōō′klē·ə·prō′tē·in, -tēn, nyōō-) *n. Biochem.* Any of a class of substances found in the nuclei of plant and animal cells, and containing one or more protein molecules combined with nucleic acid.

nu·cle·us (nōō′klē·əs, nyōō-) *n. pl.* **·cle·i** (-klē·ī) **1** A center of development; central mass; kernel. **2** *Biol.* A complex, spheroidal body surrounded by a thin membrane and embedded in the protoplasm of most plant and animal cells. It contains the chromatin which is essential in the processes of heredity, and is the directive center of all the vital activities of the cell, as assimilation, metabolism, growth, and reproduction. **3** *Physiol.* A group of nerve cells within the nervous system from which the nerve fibers originate. **4** *Zool.* The apex, or earliest formed part of a shell; also, the central part, as of an operculum, around which additional parts are formed. **5** *Astron.* The starlike point seen in the head of a comet, and at the center of a nebula. **6** *Physics* The central core of an atom, believed to contain its effective mass and to have a positive charge balanced by the negative charge of the surrounding electrons. Its principal components are the proton and neutron.[< L, a kernel, dim. of *nux, nucis* a nut]

nu·clide (nōō′klīd, nyōō-) *n. Physics* A particular nuclear species as characterized by the atomic number and the mass number.

nude (nōōd, nyōōd) *adj.* **1** Without clothing or covering; naked; bare. **2** *Law* Naked; lacking an essential legal requisite. —*n.* **1** A nude figure, as in painting or sculpture. **2** The state of being unclad: to appear in the *nude.* **3** Any of several light beige or pinkish-beige tints. [< L *nudus* naked, bare] —**nude′·ly** *adv.* —**nude′ness** *n.*

nudge (nuj) *v.* **nudged, nudg·ing** *v.t.* To touch or push gently, as with the elbow, in order to attract attention, convey a meaning, etc. —*v.i.* To give a nudge. —*n.* The act of nudging; a gentle push, as with the elbow. [? Akin to dial. Norw. *nugga* push]

nudi- *combining form* Naked; bare; without covering: *nudicaudate.* [< L *nudus* naked]

nu·di·branch (nōō′di·brangk, nyōō-) *n.* Any of various brightly colored marine gastropods (suborder Nudibranchia) lacking shells and true gills in the adult stage. Also called *sea slug.* [< NUDI- + Gk. *branchia* gills] —**nu′di·bran′chi·ate** (-brang′kē·it) *adj. & n.*

nu·di·cau·lous (nōō′di·kô′ləs, nyōō-) *adj. Bot.* Having naked or leafless stems.

nud·ism (nōō′diz·əm, nyōō-) *n.* The doctrine or practice of living in the state of nudity for hygienic reasons. —**nud′ist** *n.*

nu·di·ty (nōō′di·tē, nyōō-) *n. pl.* **·ties 1** The state of being nude. **2** A naked part; anything unclad.

nu·ga·to·ry (nōō′gə·tôr′ē, -tō′rē, nyōō-) *adj.* **1** Having no power; inoperative. **2** Having no worth or meaning; insignificant. See synonyms under USELESS. [< L *nugatorius* < *nugae* trifles, nonsense] —**nu′ga·to′ri·ly** *adv.* —**nu′·ga·to′ri·ness** *n.*

nug·get (nug′it) *n.* A lump; specifically, a lump of precious metal, usually gold, found in a free state. [? dim. of dial. E *nug* lump]

nug·get·y (nug′it·ē) *adj.* **1** Found in the form of nuggets. **2** Nugget-shaped.

nui·sance (nōō′səns, nyōō-) *n.* **1** That which annoys, vexes, or harms. **2** *Law* That which by its use or existence works annoyance or damage to another. See synonyms under ABOMINATION. [< F < *nuire* harm < L *nocere*]

null (nul) *adj.* **1** Of no legal force or effect; void: especially in the phrase **null and void. 2** Having no existence. **3** Of no avail; useless; nugatory. **4** Lacking distinction or individuality; negative. **5** Zero. See synonyms under USELESS. —*n.* **1** Something that has no force or no meaning; a cipher.

---

2 *Telecom.* A cone of silence. [< L *nullus* no, none]

nul·li·fi·ca·tion (nul′ə·fə·kā′shən) *n.* The act of nullifying; in U.S. history, the claim of right by a State to refuse obedience to the laws of the United States, as by South Carolina in 1832. — **nul′li·fi·ca′tion·ist, nul′li·fi·ca′tor** *n.*

nul·li·fid·i·an nul′ə·fid′ē·ən) *adj.* Having no religious faith. —*n.* One who has no religious faith. [< L *nullus* + *fides* faith]

nul·li·fy (nul′ə·fī) *v.t.* **·fied, ·fy·ing 1** To bring to nothing; render ineffective or valueless. **2** To deprive of legal force or effect; make void; annul. See synonyms under ABOLISH, ANNUL, CANCEL. [< LL *nullificare* < *nullus* none + *facere* make] —**nul′li·fi′er** *n.*

nul·li·par·a (nu·lip′ər·ə) *n. pl.* **·a·rae** (-ə·rē) A woman who has never given birth to a child. Compara PRIMIPARA, MULTIPARA. [< L *nullus* none + *parere* bring forth] —**nul·li·par′i·ty** (nul′ə·par′ə·tē) *n.* **nul·lip′a·rous** *adj.*

nul·li·pore (nul′ə·pôr, -pōr) *n. Bot.* A red-spored, coral-like, lime-secreting seaweed (family *Rhodophyceae*); a coralline. [< L *nullus* not any + *porus* pore] —**nul′li·po′rous** *adj.*

nul·li·ty (nul′ə·tē) *n. pl.* **·ties 1** The state of being null. **2** A nonentity. **3** *Law* A void act or instrument. [< F *nullité* < L *nullitas, -tatis* < *nullus* none]

numb (num) *adj.* Destitute, wholly or partially, of the power of sensation or of motion; benumbed. —*v.t.* To make numb. [Orig. pp. of NIM; *b* added on analogy with *dumb, lamb*] — **numb′ly** *adv.* —**numb′ness** *n.*

Synonyms (*adj.*): benumbed, deadened, dull, insensible, narcotized, paralyzed, stupefied, torpid. *Antonyms:* feeling, impressionable, sensitive, sentient.

num·ber (num′bər) *n.* **1** One of a series of symbols or words used in classifying or arranging quantities; a numeral: Nine is a *number.* When a definite number is mentioned, the sign meaning number (#) is often used, followed by a numeral: R.F.D. #2: abbr. *no.,* or *No.,* from Latin *numero,* by number. See below for principal kinds of number. **2** A collection of units or individuals, whether large or small; an indefinite aggregation: often in the plural: a *number* of facts; large *numbers* of people. **3** *pl.* The science of numerals; arithmetic. **4** The character or quality of being numerous; Reliance is placed more on spirit than on *number.* **5** One of a numbered series, as of a periodical: the May *number* of "The Atlantic"; one of the parts of a literary, artistic, or musical work issued in parts. **6** One of the divisions or movements of a piece of music or of a musical or dancing program. **7** One of a numbered group. **8** *Often pl.* Poetic measure; rhythm; hence, verse or verses. **9** *Gram.* The form of inflection of a noun, pronoun, adjective, or verb, that indicates whether one thing or more is meant. English has the singular and the plural number. Greek and Sanskrit have in addition a dual number. See DUAL, PLURAL, SINGULAR. **10** *Colloq.* An article of merchandise numbered in a catalog; hence, any article, although unnumbered: This is our most popular *number.* —**by the numbers** *Mil.* A preparatory drill command to indicate that each subsequent movement is to be carried out step by step as its number is ordered. —**to get** (or **have**) **someone's number** *Colloq.* To have insight into a person's motives, character, etc. —*v.t.* **1** To determine the total number of; count; reckon. **2** To assign a number to; designate by a number or numbers. **3** To include as one of a collection or group. **4** To amount to; total: We *number* fifty men. **5** To set or limit the number of: Your days are *numbered.* —*v.i.* **6** To make a count; total. **7** To be included, as in a group. [< F *nombre* < L *numerus*] — **num′ber·er** *n.*

—**abstract number** Any number considered without reference to any particular object: distinguished from *concrete number.*

—**algebraic number** Any number which is the solution of an algebraic equation having integer coefficients.

—**composite number** Any integer exactly divisible by one or more integers other than itself or 1: opposed to *prime number.*

—compound number A number containing more than one unit or denomination, as feet and inches.

—concrete number A number applied to particular objects, as, four men; ten dollars; distinguished from *abstract number.*

—irrational number A number which cannot be expressed as an integer or the quotient of integers, as $\sqrt{2}\ \sqrt{5}$, π, etc.

—mixed number A number, as 3 1/2, 5 3/4, which is the sum of an integer and a fraction.

—ordinal number A number that shows the order of a unit in a given series, as, first, second, third, etc.

—prime number A number divisible without remainder by no whole number except itself and unity: opposed to *composite number.*

—rational number A number which can be expressed as an integer or as a quotient of integers.

—real number Any rational or irrational number that does not contain an even root of a negative number.

—square number A number, as 1, 4, 9, 16, which is the square of some integer.

—transcendental number A number which is not an algebraic number, as π.

num·ber·less (num′bər·lis) *adj.* 1 Very numerous; innumerable; countless. 2 Having no number. See synonyms under INFINITE.

numb·skull (num′skul′) See NUMSKULL.

numbers pool A lottery, in which wagers are laid on the appearance of some particular, unpredictable number, as the last digits in the pari-mutuel racing totals of a given day: also called *policy racket.* Also **numbers game.**

numb·fish (num′fish′) *n. pl.* **·fish** or **·fish·es** An electric ray.

nu·mer·a·ble (nōō′mər·ə·bəl, nyōō′-) *adj.* That can be numbered.

nu·mer·al (nōō′mər·əl, nōō′-) *n.* 1 A symbol, character, or letter, alone or in combination with others, used to express a number. 2 A word that expresses number or is used in numerating or counting. **—Arabic numerals** The symbols, 1, 2, 3, 4, 5, 6, 7, 8, 9, 0, based on the decimal system and in general use since the tenth century. **—Roman numerals** The letters used until the tenth century as symbols in arithmetical notation. The basic letters are I(1), V(5), X(10), L(50), C(100), D(500), and M(1000), and intermediate and higher numbers are formed according to the following rules: Any symbol following another of equal or greater value adds to its value, as II = 2, XI = 11; any symbol preceding one of greater value substracts from its value, as IV = 4, IX = 9, XC = 90; when a symbol stands between two of greater value, it is subtracted from the second and the remainder added to the first, as XIV = 14, LIX = 59. **—adj.** 1 Used in expressing a number. 2 Pertaining to number. [< L *numeralis* < *numerus* number] **—nu′mer·al·ly** *adv.*

nu·mer·ar·y (nōō′mə·rer′ē, nyōō′-) *adj.* Pertaining to numbers.

nu·mer·ate (nōō′mə·rāt, nōō′-) *v.t.* **·at·ed, ·at·ing** 1 To enumerate; count. 2 To read, as a numerical expression, according to some system of numeration. [< L *numeratus*, pp. of *numerare* number < *numerus* a number]

nu·mer·a·tion (nōō′mə·rā′shepn, nyōō′-) *n.* 1 The act or art of reading or naming numbers, or a system of reading or naming them, especially those written decimally and according to the Arabic notation. Compare NOTATION. For numbers above and including 1,000,000,000 there are two systems in use: the French, used commonly in the United States, and the English. In the former, the above number is read *one billion;* in the latter, *one thousand million.* In general, in the former the successive names *billion, trillion,* etc., apply to the results obtained by multiplying 1,000 twice, thrice, etc., by itself; in the latter to those obtained by multiplying 1,000 by itself four times, six times, etc. 2 Enumeration.

nu·mer·a·tor (nōō′mə·rā′tər, nyōō′-) *n.* 1 *Math.* In a common fraction, the term which stands above or to the left of the line and denotes how many of the parts of a unit (expressed by the denominator) are taken. 2 One who or that which numbers.

nu·mer·i·cal (nōō·mer′i·kəl, nyōō′-) *adj.* 1 Pertaining to or denoting number. 2 Numerable. 3 Represented by or consisting of numbers or fig-

ures, as in arithmetic, and not by letters, as in algebra. 4 *Math.* **a** Signifying that numbers have the place of letters: opposed to *literal.* **b** Designating a quantity considered opposed to *algebraic.* [< NL *numericus* < L *numerus* a number] **—nu·mer′i·cal·ly** *adv.*

nu·mer·ol·o·gy (nōō′mə·rol′ə·jē, nyōō′-) *n.* 1 The science of numbers. 2 A system that purports to explain the occult influence of numbers, as those of the day of one's birth, the month in the year, and the year in the calendar, on life. **—nu′mer·o·log′i·cal** *adj.*

nu·mer·os·i·ty (nōō′mə·ros′ə·tē, nyōō′-) *n.* 1 The state or condition of being numerous. 2 In symbolic logic, that property of a set, collection, or class which is defined by a cardinal number: the *numerosity* of a triplet, triad, or trilogy is 3.

nu·mer·ous (nōō′mər·əs, nyōō′-) *adj.* Consisting of a great number of units; being many. See synonyms under FREQUENT, MANY. **—nu′mer·ous·ly** *adv.* **—nu′mer·ous·ness** *n.*

nu·mis·mat·ic (nōō′miz·mat′ik, -mis-, nyōō′-) *adj.* Pertaining to or consisting of coins or medals. Also **nu′mis·mat′i·cal.** [< F *numismatique* < L *numisma, -atis* a coin < Gk. *nomisma* < *nomizein* sanction]

nu·mis·mat·ics (nōō′miz·mat′iks, -mis-, nyōō′-) *n. pl.* (*construed as singular*) The science of coins and medals. Also **nu·mis·ma·tol·o·gy** (nōō·miz′mə·tol′ə·jē, -mis′-, nyōō′-). **—nu·mis′ma·tist, nu·mis·ma·tol′o·gist** *n.*

num·mu·lar (num′yə·lər) *adj.* 1 Of or pertaining to coins or money: also **num·ma·ry** (num′ər·ē). 2 Resembling coins: *nummular* sputa. Also **num′mu·lar·y, num′mu·lat·ed.** [< L *nummulus,* dim. of *nummus* a coin]

num·mu·la·tion (num′yə·lā′shən) *n.* The arrangement of red blood corpuscles in columns like stacked-up coins, as seen under the microscope.

num·mu·lite (num′yə·līt) *n.* *Paleontol.* A large foraminifer of a nearly extinct family characteristic of the older Tertiary: preserved fossil forms show it as having a thin, coinlike shell. [< L *nummulus* small coin] **— num′mu·lit′ic** (-lit′ik) *adj.*

num·skull (num′skul) *n.* A blockhead; a dunce: also spelled *numbskull.*

nun[1] (nŏŏn, nōŏn) *n.* The fourteenth Hebrew letter.

nun[2] (nun) *n.* 1 A woman devoted to a religious life, and living in a convent under vows of poverty, chastity, and obedience. 2 One of various birds, as the nunbird. 3 *Naut.* A conical or cone-shaped buoy made of metal: also **nun buoy.** [OE *nunne* < L *nonna,* fem. of *nonnus* an old man] **— nun′nish** *adj.*

nun·bird (nun′bûrd′) *n.* A South American bird (genus *Monasa*) having black plumage, usually with white about the head: also called *trappist.*

nun·ci·a·ture (nun′shē·ə·chŏŏr) *n.* The office or term of office of a nuncio. [< Ital. *nunziatura* < *nunzio* NUNCIO]

nun·ci·o (nun′shē·ō) *n. pl.* **·ci·os** 1 An ordinary ambassador of the pope to a foreign court or government: distinguished from *legate.* 2 Any messenger. Also **nun′ci·us** (-shē·əs). [< Ital. *nuncio* < L *nuntius* a messenger]

nun·cu·pa·tive (nung′kyə·pā′tiv, nung·kyōō′pə·tiv) *adj.* *Law* Oral as distinguished from written: said especially of a will. Also **nun′cu·pa·to′ry** (-pə·tôr′ē, -tō′rē). [< LL *nuncupativus* < *nuncupare* call by name]

nun·ner·y (nun′ər·ē) *n. pl.* **·ner·ies** A convent for nuns. See synonyms under CLOISTER.

nun's-veil·ing (nunz′vā′ling) *n.* A soft, thin, untwilled woolen fabric, used for veiling and as a dress material.

nup·tial (nup′shəl) *adj.* Pertaining to marriage or the marriage ceremony. See synonyms under MATRIMONIAL. [< L *nuptialis* < *nuptus,* pp. of *nubere* marry] **— nup′tial·ly** *adv.*

nuptial flight *Entomol.* The mating flight of many insects, as ants and gnats, during which conspicuous swarming may occur.

nup·tials (nup′shəlz) *n. pl.* (*construed as singular*) The marriage ceremony or state. See synonyms under MARRIAGE.

nurl (nûrl) *v.t.* To mill or roughen, as the rim of a coin. [Var. of KNURL]

nurse (nûrs) *n.* 1 A female servant who takes care of young children: in the case of one who suckles an infant, called a wet-nurse; otherwise, less frequently, a drynurse. 2 One who suckles a babe. 3 A person who cares for the sick, wounded, or enfeebled, especially one who makes a profession of it. 4 One who or that which fosters, nurses, protects, or promotes. 5 One of various sharks, as the nursehound (genus *Ginglymostoma*). 6 *Entomol.* A sexually incomplete bee or ant, etc., whose duty it is to care for the young. **— v. nursed, nurs·ing** *v.t.* 1 To take care of, as in sickness or infirmity. 2 To feed (an infant) at the breast; suckle. 3 To feed and care for in infancy. 4 To promote the growth and development of; foster; cherish. 5 To use or operate carefully; preserve from injury, damage, or undue strain: to *nurse* a weak wrist. 6 To try to cure, as a cold, by taking care of oneself. 7 To clasp or hold carefully or caressingly; fondle. 8 In billiards, to keep (the balls) in a close group so as to score a series of caroms. **— v.i.** 9 To act or serve as a nurse. 10 To take nourishment from the breast. 11 To suckle an infant. See synonyms under CHERISH. [Earlier *nurice* < OF < LL *nutricia* < L *nutrix* < *nutrire* nourish, foster] **— nurs′er** *n.*

nurs·er·y (nûr′sər·ē) *n. pl.* **·er·ies** 1 A room in a house set apart for the occupation and use of children; also, a playroom. 2 A place where trees, shrubs, etc., are raised for sale or transplanting. 3 The place where anything is fostered, bred, or developed; hence, any condition that promotes growth. 4 *Obs.* The act of nursing; also, that which is nursed.

nursery rime A simple story, riddle, proverb, etc., presented in rimed verse or jingle for children.

nursing bottle A small, graduated bottle fitted with a rubber nipple, for feeding infants.

nursing home A small private hospital.

nurs·ling (nûrs′ling) *n.* An infant; also, anything that is carefully tended or supervised. Also **nurse′ling.**

nur·ture (nûr′chər) *n.* 1 The act of nourishing. 2 That which nourishes or fosters; education. 3 *Biol.* The aggregate of environmental conditions and influences acting on an organism subsequent to birth. Compare NATURE. **— v.t. ·tured, ·tur·ing** 1 To feed or support; nourish; rear; foster. 2 To bring up or train; educate. [< OF *nurture,* var. of *nourriture* < LL *nutritura* < L *nutrire* nourish] **— nur′tur·er** *n.*

Synonyms (noun): breeding, discipline, education, instruction, schooling, teaching, training, tuition. *Breeding* and *nurture* include *teaching* and *training,* especially as directed by and dependent upon home life and personal association; *breeding* having reference largely to manners with such qualities as are deemed distinctively characteristic of high birth; *nurture* (literally *nourishing*) having more direct reference to moral qualities, not overlooking the physical and mental. See EDUCATION, CHERISH, TEACH.

nut (nut) *n.* 1 *Bot.* **a** A fruit consisting of a kernel or seed enclosed in a woody shell, as in the hazelnut, beechnut, or chestnut; also, the kernel of such fruit, especially when edible. **b** A hard, indehiscent, one-seeded pericarp resulting from a compound ovary. 2 *Mech.* A small block of metal having an internal screw thread so that it may be fitted upon a bolt, screw, or the like. 3 A person or matter difficult to deal with; a problem. 4 *Slang*

MECHANICAL NUTS

a. Hexagonal, soft.	*e.* Double-cupped.
b. Lock.	*f.* Joint, untapped.
c. Hexagonal, slotted.	*g.* Castle.
d. Square, plain.	*h.* Thumb.
	i. Square, chamfered.

NUMMULITES

nut·crack·er (nut'krak'ər) n. 1 *Chiefly pl.* A device for cracking nuts. 2 One of certain the axis and pole of the earth around the pole of the ecliptic as a center. 2 *Bot.* A spontaneous rotatory movement, as of young growing parts of plants. 3 The act of nodding the head. [<L *nutatio, -onis* <*nutare* nod] — **nu·ta'tion·al** *adj.*

nu·ta·tion (nōō·tā'shən, nyōō-) n. 1 *Astron.* The periodic inequalities in the motion of The head. 5 *Slang* A crazy or irresponsible person. 6 The ridge at the upper end of the neck of stringed instruments, serving to elevate the strings; also, the adjustable end of a fiddle bow. — *v.i.* **nut·ted, nut·ting** To seek or gather nuts. [OE *hnutu*] — **nut'ter** n.

crowlike birds (genus *Nucifraga*), as the common Old World nutcracker (*N. caryocatactes*), or **Clark's nutcracker** (*N. columbiana*) of the coniferous forests of western North America. 3 A nuthatch.

nut-grass (nut'gras', -gräs') n. A perennial herb (*Cyperus rotundus*) of the sedge family bearing nutlike tubers: also called **cocograss.**

nut·hatch (nut'hach') n. A small, short-tailed bird (family *Sittidae*) related to the titmouse, having a slender bill as long as the head and feeding on nuts and insects.

nut·meg (nut'meg) n. 1 The aromatic kernel of the fruit of various tropical trees (genus *Myristica*), especially of the nutmeg tree (*M. fragrans*) of the Molucca Islands. 2 The tree itself. [ME *notemuge*, partial trans. of OF *nois mugue* <*nois* nut + *mugue* musk <L *muscus*]

nut pick A small sharp–pointed instrument for picking out the kernels of nuts.

nu·tri·a (nōō'trē·ə, nyōō'-) n. 1 The coypu. 2 Its soft, brown fur, often dyed to resemble beaver. [<Sp., an otter <L *lutra*]

nu·tri·ent (nōō'trē·ənt, nyōō'-) *adj.* 1 Giving nourishment. 2 Conveying nutrition. — *n.* 1 Something that nourishes. 2 A drug or other substance which acts upon the nutritive processes of an organism. [<L *nutriens, -entis*, ppr. of *nutrire* nourish]

nutrient solution A solution containing, in correct proportions and strength, the various chemical substances required for plant growth: used in hydroponics.

nu·tri·ment (nōō'trə·mənt, nyōō'-) n. 1 That which nourishes; food. 2 That which promotes development. [<L *nutrimentum* <*nutrire* nourish] — **nu'tri·men'tal** *adj.*

Synonyms: aliment, food, meat, nourishment,

provision, sustenance. *Nourishment* and *sustenance* apply to whatever can be introduced into the system as a means of sustaining life; we say of a convalescent: He is taking *nourishment. Aliment* is similar in meaning, but less frequent in use. *Nutriment* and *nutrition* have more of scientific reference to the vitalizing principles of various *foods*; thus, wheat is said to contain a great amount of *nutriment.* Compare FOOD.

nu·tri·tion (nōō·trish'ən, nyōō-) n. 1 The aggregate of all the processes by which food is assimilated, growth promoted, and waste repaired in living organisms. 2 Nutriment. See synonyms under FOOD. [<L *nutrire*] — **nu·tri'tion·al** *adj.* — **nu·tri'tion·al·ly** *adv.*

nu·tri·tion·ist (nōō·trish'ən·ist, nyōō-) n. One who specializes in the processes and problems of nutrition.

nut·shell (nut'shel') n. The shell of a nut. — **in a nutshell** In brief and concise statement or form.

nut·ter (nut'ər) n. One who gathers nuts.

nut·ty (nut'ē) *adj.* **·ti·er, ·ti·est** 1 Abounding in nuts. 2 Having the flavor of nuts. 3 *Slang* Crazy; also, madly in love; very enthusiastic. — **nut'ti·ly** *adv.* — **nut'ti·ness** n.

nut·wood (nut'wŏod') n. 1 Any tree bearing nuts, as walnut, hazel, hickory, etc. 2 The wood of such a tree.

nuz·zle (nuz'əl) v. **·zled, ·zling** *v.i.* 1 To root or dig with the nose or snout, as a hog does. 2 To nestle or snuggle; lie close. — *v.t.* 3 To rub with the nose; push the nose against. 4 To root up with the nose or snout. [Freq. of NOSE, *v.*]

ny·an·za (nī·an'zə) n. A sheet of water; lake; also, a river feeding a lake. [<Bantu]

nyc·ta·gi·na·ceous (nik'tə·ji·nā'shəs) *adj. Bot.* Of or pertaining to a family of plants (*Nyctaginaceae*) widely distributed in warm and tropical lands, including the bougainvillea; the four-o'-clock family. [<NL <*Nyctago, -inis*, former genus name <Gk. *nyx, nyktos* night]

nyc·ta·lo·pi·a (nik'tə·lō'pē·ə) n. *Pathol.* Night blindness; a physical defect of the eyes in which one sees well by daylight, but poorly in the dark or in dim light: sometimes confused with *day blindness* or *hemeralopia.* Also **nyc'ta·lo'py.** [<NL <Gk. *nyx, nyktos* night + *alaos* blind + *ōps* eye] — **nyc'ta·lop'ic** (-lop'ik) *adj.*

nyc·tan·thous (nik·tan'thəs) *adj. Bot.* Pertaining to or designating flowers which open at

night. Also **nyc·ti·gam·ous** (nik'tə·gam'əs). [<NYCT(o) + Gk. *anthos* flower]

nyc·tit·ro·pism (nik·tit'rə·piz'əm) n. *Bot.* The changing of the position of the leaves of certain plants during the night. Also **nyc'ti·nas'ty** (-ti·nas'tē). — **nyc'ti·trop'ic** (-trop'ik) *adj.*

nycto– *combining form* Night; nocturnal: *nyctophobia.* Also, before vowels, **nyct–.** Also **nycti–.** [<Gk. *nyx, nyktos* night]

nyc·to·pho·bi·a (nik'tə·fō'bē·ə) n. Morbid fear of night or of darkness: also called *noctiphobia, scotophobia.* — **nyc'to·pho'bic** *adj.*

Ny·lon (nī'lon) n. A synthetic thermoplastic polyamide derivable from coal, air, and water, which may be formed into fibers, bristles, sheets, and other forms which, when drawn, are characterized by extreme toughness, elasticity, and strength: a trade name.

ny·lons (nī'lonz) n. pl. Stockings made of Nylon.

nymph (nimf) n. 1 In Greek and Roman mythology, a beautiful maiden belonging to a class of lesser divinities inhabiting groves, forests, fountains, springs, mountains, the ocean, etc. 2 Hence, an attractive girl; a lovely young woman. 3 *Entomol.* **a** The young of an insect which undergoes incomplete metamorphosis, at which stage the wing pads are first evident. **b** One of various nymphalid butterflies, as a fritillary. [<L *nympha* <Gk. *nymphē* nymph, bride] — **nymph'al, nym·phe·an** (nim·fē'ən) *adj.* — **nymph'ic, nymph'i·cal** *adj.*

nym·phae·a·ceous (nim'fē·ā'shəs) *adj.* Pertaining to or designating a family (*Nymphaeaceae*) of aquatic, perennial herbs, the waterlily family, with a thick, horizontal rootstock, mainly peltate, floating or submersed leaves, and large solitary flowers living in fresh water. See LOTUS. [<NL <L *nymphaea* waterlily <Gk. *nymphaia*]

nympho– *combining form* Nymph; bride: *nymphomania.* Also, before vowels, **nymph–.** [<Gk. *nymphē* a nymph]

nym·pho·lep·sy (nim'fə·lep'sē) n. 1 A kind of ecstasy or frenzy, said to have taken possession of one who looked upon a nymph. 2 An emotional state caused by an unrealizable desire. [<Gk. *nympholeptos* frenzied < *nymphē* a nymph + *lambanein* take] — **nym'pho·lept** (-lept) n. — **nym'pho·lep'tic** *adj.*

nym·pho·ma·ni·a (nim'fə·mā'nē·ə, -mān'yə) n. *Psychiatry* A morbid and ungovernable sexual desire in women. — **nym'pho·ma'ni·ac** *adj.* & n.

O

o, O (ō) n. pl. **o's, O's,** or **os, Os,** or **oes** (ōz) 1 The 15th letter of the English alphabet: from Phoenician *ayin,* which was a consonant, through Greek *omicron* and *omega,* and Roman *O.* 2 Any sound of the letter *o.* See ALPHABET. — *symbol* 1 *Math.* Zero or naught: called also *round O.* 2 *Chem.* Oxygen (symbol O). 3 Anything shaped like an O; an oval or circle; a spot or spangle: Giotto's *O.* See appendix (ABBREVIATIONS).

O (ō) *interj.* 1 An exclamation prefixed to an expression of address, as a sign of the vocative, used especially in earnest appeal or exhortation, or in prayer to the Deity, to emphasize the feeling or passion conveyed by the words. A note of exclamation usually follows the vocative word, phrase, or clause: *O Lord! O my countrymen!* 2 An ejaculation expressive of a wish: an elliptical form: *O stay!* The object of desire sometimes follows in an interjectional or elliptical phrase, with *for* if a substantive, or *that* if a clause. 3 See OH. ◆ The forms *O* and *oh* are often used indiscriminately. It is, however, generally conceded that the proper form in the vocative use is *O.* — n. An exclamation or lamentation. Also spelled *oh.*

o' *prep.* Of: one *o'*clock, man-*o'*-war, jack-*o'*-lantern.

O' A descendant of: *O'*Conor: a patronymic prefix commonly used in Irish surnames, equivalent to the English and Scandinavian suffixes *-son, -sen.* Compare MAC, FITZ. [<Irish *ó* grandson, descendant]

oaf (ōf) n. 1 Originally, a misshapen bantling left in place of a pretty child supposed to be stolen by fairies; a changeling. 2 A simpleton; a stupid, lubberly person. [Earlier *auf* <ON *alfr* elf. Akin to ELF.]

oaf·ish (ō'fish) *adj.* Stupid; doltish. — **oaf'ish·ly** *adv.* — **oaf'ish·ness** n.

oak (ōk) n. 1 A hardwood, acorn-bearing tree or shrub (genus *Quercus*) of the beech family, valued for the hardness, strength, and durability of its timber. ◆ Collateral adjective: *quercine.* 2 The wood or timber of the oak. 3 One of various other plants having a resemblance or relation to the oak: Jerusalem *oak.* 4 A stout door: so called because usually made of oak. 5 Any of various shades of finished oak wood. 6 The leaves of the oak, as in a garland: used as a crown: in ancient Rome, the reward of a hero who saved the life of a fellow man. 7 Oaken woodwork or furniture. — **quartered oak** Oaken boards cut by quarter–sawing, and exhibiting a striking grain. — **to sport one's oak** To exclude visitors by closing the outer door of one's apartment:

English university slang. [OE *āc*]

oak·en (ō'kən) *adj.* Made of oak.

oak·um (ō'kəm) n. Hemp fiber obtained by untwisting old rope: used in calking, etc. [OE *acuma,* var. of *acumba* <*a-* off, without + *cemban* comb[1]]

oar (ôr, ōr) n. 1 A wooden implement for propelling or, occasionally, for steering a boat, consisting of a long shaft with a blade at one end. 2 An oarsman. 3 An oarlike appendage in certain worms. — *v.t.* 1 To propel with or as with oars; row. 2 To make (one's way) or traverse (water) with or as with oars. — *v.i.* 3 To proceed by or as by rowing; row. ◆ Homophone: *ore.* [OE *ār*] — **oar'less** *adj.*

oared (ôrd, ōrd) *adj.* 1 Having oars for propulsion. 2 Having oarlike feet or swimming appendages.

oar·fish (ôr'fish', ōr'-) n. pl. **·fish** or **·fish·es** Any of several fishes (genus *Regalecus*) of northern seas, with oarlike dorsal rays and a length of up to twenty feet.

oar·lock (ôr'lok', ōr'-) n. A device on the side of a boat for keeping an oar in place; rowlock. [OE *ārloc* <*ār* oar + *loc* lock, enclosure]

oars·man·ship (ôrz'mən·ship, ōrz'-) n. The art of rowing; skill in rowing.

---

add,āce,câre,pälm; end,ēven; it,īce; odd,ōpen,ôrder; tŏŏk,pōōl; up,bûrn; ə = a in *above,* e in *sicken,* i in *clarity,* o in *melon,* u in *focus*; yōō = u in *fuse,* oi,oil; ou,pout; ch,check; g,go; ng,ring; th,thin; ŧh,this; zh,vision. Foreign sounds à,œ,ü,kh,ṅ; and ◆: see page xx. <from; + plus; ? possibly.

o·a·sis (ō·ā′sis, ō′ə·sis) *n.* *pl.* **·ses** (-sēz) **1** An area in a waste or desert made fertile by ground water or by surface irrigation. **2** Any place providing relief or refreshment; refuge: a small city park that provided an *oasis* of quiet amidst the street noises. [<L <Gk. *Oasis,* a city in the Libyan Desert <Egyptian]

oast (ōst) *n.* A kiln for drying hops or malt. [OE *āst* a kiln]

oat (ōt) *n.* **1** *Usually pl.* A cereal grass (*Avena sativa*) extensively cultivated for its edible grain. **2** A musical pipe made from a stem of the oat; a shepherd's pipe; hence, a pastoral song. **— to feel one's oats 1** To feel lively; have a sense of vitality. **2** To feel important. **— to sow one's wild oats** To indulge in the follies or excesses to which youth is liable. [OE *āte*]

oat·cake (ōt′kāk′) *n.* A cake of oatmeal, usually rolled thin and baked hard. Also **oat cake.**

oat·en (ōt′n) *adj.* **1** Made of oats or oatmeal, or of the straw of oats. **2** Sounded on a pipe made from a stem of oat.

oat·grass (ōt′gras′, -gräs′) *n.* **1** Any uncultivated kind of oats. **2** Any of various oatlike grasses.

oath (ōth) *n.* *pl.* **oaths** (ōthz) **1** A solemn attestation in support of a declaration or a promise, by an appeal to God or to some person or thing regarded as high and holy; also, the declaration or promise so supported. **2** *Law* Such an attestation or affirmation of the truth of a statement as renders liable to punishment for perjury one who wilfully thus asserts what is not true. **3** The form of words in which such attestation is made. **4** A frivolous and blasphemous use of the name of the Deity or of any sacred name or object, as in appeal or ejaculation. **5** An imprecation lightly or humorously used. [OE *āth*]
Synonyms: adjuration, affidavit, anathema, ban, blasphemy, curse, denunciation, execration, imprecation, malediction, profanity, reprobation, swearing, vow. In the highest sense, as in a court of justice, "an *oath* is a reverent appeal to God in corroboration of what one says"; an *affidavit* is a sworn statement made in writing in the presence of a competent officer; an *adjuration* is a solemn appeal to a person in the name of God to speak the truth. An *oath* is made to man in the name of God; a *vow* is usually made to God. In the lower sense, an *oath* may be mere *blasphemy* or profane *swearing. Anathema, curse, execration,* and *imprecation* are modes of invoking vengeance or retribution from a superhuman power upon the person against whom they are uttered. *Anathema* is a solemn ecclesiastical condemnation of a person or of a proposition. *Curse* may be just and authoritative; as, the *curse* of God; or, it may be wanton and powerless. *Execration* expresses most of personal bitterness and hatred; *imprecation* refers to the coming of the desired evil upon the person against whom it is uttered. *Malediction* is a general wish of evil, a less usual but very expressive word. Compare TESTIMONY. *Antonyms:* benediction, benison, blessing.

oat·meal (ōt′mēl′) *n.* **1** The meal of oats. **2** Porridge made of it. Also **oat meal.**

ob- *prefix* **1** Toward; to; facing: *obvert.* **2** Against; in opposition to: *object, obstruct.* **3** Over; upon: *obliterate.* **4** Completely: *obdurate.* **5** Inversely: *obovate:* prefixed to adjectives in scientific Neo-Latin and English terms. Also: *o-* before *m,* as in *omit;* *oc-* before *c,* as in *occur;* *of-* before *f,* as in *offend; op-* before *p,* as in *oppress.* [<L *ob* toward, for, against]

ob·bli·ga·to (ob′lə·gä′tō, *Ital.* ôb′blē·gä′tō) *adj.* **1** That cannot be dispensed with; necessary. **2** *Music* Referring to parts or accompaniments essential to the performance of a composition. *— n. pl.* **·tos** or **·ti** (-tē) *Music* A part or accompaniment, usually written for a single instrument. [<Ital. *obbligato, obligato* <L *obligatus,* pp. of *obligare.* See OBLIGE.]

ob·du·ra·cy (ob′dyə·rə·sē) *n.* Obstinacy; obdurateness.

ob·du·rate (ob′dyə·rit, -rāt) *adj.* **1** Unmoved by feelings of humanity or pity; inexorable. **2** Perversely impenitent. **3** Unyielding; stubborn. See synonyms under HARD, OBSTINATE. [<L *obduratus,* pp. of *obdurare* harden <ob-

against + *durare* harden < *durus* hard] **— ob′·du·rate·ly** *adv.* **— ob′du·rate·ness** *n.*

o·be·di·ence (ō·bē′dē·əns, ə·bē′-) *n.* **1** Submission to command, prohibition, law, or duty. **2** The fact of being obeyed, or having subjects obedient to one. **3** *Eccl.* Sphere of authority, or those acknowledging it. See synonyms under ALLEGIANCE, SUBMISSION.

o·be·di·ent (ō·bē′dē·ənt, ə·bē′-) *adj.* Complying with or submitting to a behest, law, etc.; habitually yielding to authority; submissive; dutiful. See synonyms under DOCILE, OBSEQUIOUS. [<OF *obedient* <L *obediens, -entis,* ppr. of *obedire* OBEY] **— o·be′di·ent·ly** *adv.*

o·bei·sance (ō·bā′səns, ō·bē′-) *n.* An act of courtesy or reverence, consisting of bowing or a bending of the knee; a bow or courtesy; homage; deference. [<OF *obeissance* < *obeissant,* ppr. of *obeir* OBEY] **— o·bei′sant** *adj.*

ob·e·lisk (ob′ə·lisk) *n.* **1** A square shaft with pyramidal top, usually monumental. The Egyptian obelisks are always monolithic and slightly tapering. **2** *Printing* The dagger sign (†) used as a mark of reference; obelus. [<L *obeliscus* <Gk. *obeliskos,* dim. of *obelos* a spit, pointed pillar] **— ob′e·lis′cal, ob′e·lis′koid** *adj.*

ob·e·lize (ob′ə·līz) *v.t.* **·lized, ·liz·ing** To mark with an obelus. [<Gk. *obelizein* mark with an obelus < *obelos* an obelus]

ob·e·lus (ob′ə·ləs) *n.* *pl.* **·li** (-lī) **1** A critical mark, as — or ÷., used in ancient manuscripts to designate a suspected reading or to indicate a spurious passage. **2** *Printing* Obelisk. [<L <Gk. *obelos* a spit, obelisk, critical mark]

OBELISK

o·bese (ō·bēs′) *adj.* Very corpulent. See synonyms under CORPULENT. [<L *obesus* fat, orig. pp. of *obedere* devour < *ob-* completely + *edere* eat] **— o·bese′ly** *adv.*

o·bes·i·ty (ō·bē′sə·tē, ō·bes′ə-) *n. Pathol.* An excessive accumulation of fat in the body; morbid corpulency. Also **o·bese′ness.**

o·bey (ō·bā′, ə·bā′) *v.t.* **1** To do the bidding of; be obedient to. **2** To carry into effect; execute, as a command. **3** To act in accordance with; be guided by: to *obey* the law. *— v.i.* **4** To be obedient. [<OF *obeir* <L *obedire,* var. of *oboedire* give ear, obey < *ob-* in the direction of + *audire* hear] **— o·bey′er** *n.*
Synonyms: comply, defer, keep, observe, submit, yield. See FOLLOW, KEEP, SERVE. *Antonyms:* contemn, defy, disobey, infringe, refuse, resist, violate. See synonyms for GOVERN.

ob·fus·cate (ob·fus′kāt, ob′fəs-) *v.t.* **·cat·ed, ·cat·ing** **1** To confuse or perplex; bewilder. **2** To darken or obscure. [<L *obfuscatus,* pp. of *obfuscare* darken, obscure < *ob-* against + *fuscare* darken < *fuscus* dark] **— ob′fus·ca′·tion** *n.*

o·bit (ō′bit, ob′it) *n.* **1** The death or date of death of a person; also, an obituary. **2** A ceremony or service commemorating a death. [<OF <L *obitus* a going down, a death < *obire* go down, die < *ob-* down + *ire* go]

o·bit·u·ar·y (ō·bich′ōō·er′ē) *adj.* Pertaining to the death of a person. *— n. pl.* **·ar·ies** A published notice of a death; a biographical sketch of one recently deceased. [<Med. L *obituarius* <L *obitus.* See OBIT.]

ob·ject¹ (əb·jekt′) *v.i.* **1** To offer arguments or opposition; dissent. **2** To feel or state disapproval; be averse. *— v.t.* **3** To offer as opposition or criticism; charge. See synonyms under OPPOSE. [<L *objectus,* pp. of *objicere* < *ob-* towards, against + *jacere* throw] **— ob·jec′tor** *n.*

ob·ject² (ob′jikt, -jekt) *n.* **1** Anything that lies within the cognizance of the senses; especially, anything tangible or visible; any material thing. **2** That which is affected or intended to be affected by feeling or action. **3** That on which one sets his mind as an end; purpose; aim. **4** *Gram.* A noun or pronoun to which the action of a transitive verb is directed, or which receives or endures the effect of this action. A **direct object** receives the direct action of the verb, as in the sentence "He ate the pie," *pie* is the direct object of *ate;* an **indirect object** receives the secondary action of the verb, as in "She gave him the pie," *him* is the indirect object of *gave.* **5** *Colloq.* A

person of pitiable or ridiculous aspect; any sight that evokes laughter, disgust, pity, etc. See synonyms under AIM, DESIGN, PURPOSE, REASON. [<Med. L *objectum* something thrown in the way <L *objectus.* See OBJECT¹.]

ob·jec·ti·fy (əb·jek′tə·fī) *v.t.* **·fied, ·fy·ing** To present, as in form or character, from an external viewpoint; make objective. [<OBJECT² + -(I)FY] **— ob·jec′ti·fi·ca′tion** *n.*

ob·jec·tion (əb·jek′shən) *n.* **1** The act of objecting. **2** An impediment raised; a dissenting argument; an adverse fact.

ob·jec·tion·a·ble (əb·jek′shən·ə·bəl) *adj.* Deserving of disapproval; offensive. **— ob·jec′·tion·a·bil′i·ty** *n.* **— ob·jec′tion·a·bly** *adv.*

ob·jec·tive (əb·jek′tiv) *adj.* **1** Of or belonging to an object; having the nature of an object or being that which is thought of or perceived, as opposed to that which thinks or perceives; outside the mind: opposed to *subjective.* **2** Directed to or pertaining to an object or end: an *objective* goal. **3** Having independent existence apart from experience or thought; substantive; self-existent. **4** Directing the mind or activity toward external things without reference to personal sensations; also, resulting from such direction; hence, representing things as they are; unbiased by thoughts, emotions, opinions, etc.: said of an artist, a writer, etc., or of his habits of thought. **5** Made up of objects represented precisely as they are, without idealization; realistic: said of a work of art, as a picture. **6** *Gram.* Denoting the case of the object of a transitive verb or of a preposition; accusative. *— n.* **1** *Gram.* **a** The objective or accusative case. **b** A word in this case. **2** *Optics* An object glass. **3** A result to be achieved or a point to be reached in any military action; the assigned goal of a mission. [<Med. L *objectivus* < *objectum.* See OBJECT².] **— ob·jec′tive·ly** *adv.*

ob·jec·tiv·ism (əb·jek′tə·viz′əm) *n.* **1** The power that enables an author or artist to treat subjects objectively, or apart from his own personality. **2** The tendency to give prominence to the facts of sense perception; the theory that human knowledge is based on the external world rather than within the ego. **— ob·jec′tiv·ist** *n.* **— ob·jec′tiv·is′tic** *adj.*

ob·jec·tiv·i·ty (ob′jek·tiv′ə·tē) *n.* **1** The state or relation of being objective. **2** Material reality. Also **ob·jec′tive·ness.**

ob·ject·less (ob′jikt·lis, -jekt-) *adj.* **1** Without aim; purposeless. **2** Having no corresponding object or concrete representation.

object lesson 1 A lesson in which the object to be known, or a representation of it, is shown to the eye. **2** The exemplification of a principle or moral in a concrete form or striking instance.

ob·jur·gate (ob′jər·gāt, əb·jûr′-) *v.t.* **·gat·ed, ·gat·ing** To rebuke severely; scold sharply; berate. [<L *objurgatus,* pp. of *objurgare* rebuke < *ob-* against + *jurgare* scold] **— ob′·jur·ga′tion** *n.* **— ob′jur·ga′tor** *n.* **— ob·jur′ga·to′ri·ly** *adv.* **— ob·jur′ga·to′ry** *adj.*

ob·la·tion (ob·lā′shən) *n.* **1** The act of offering or anything offered in worship, especially the elements of the Eucharist. **2** Hence, any grateful and solemn offering. **3** In canon law, any property given to a church. [<OF, an offering, sacrifice <Med. L *oblatio, -onis* <L < *oblatus.* See OBLATE².] **— ob·la′tion·al** *adj.* **— ob·la·to·ry** (ob′lə·tôr′ē, -tō′rē) *adj.*

ob·li·gate (ob′lə·gāt) *v.t.* **·gat·ed, ·gat·ing** To bind or compel, as by contract, conscience, promise, etc. *— adj.* (ob′lə·git, -gāt) **1** Bound or restricted. **2** *Biol.* Having only one life condition: distinguished from *facultative.* [<L *obligatus,* pp. of *obligare* OBLIGE]

ob·li·ga·tion (ob′lə·gā′shən) *n.* **1** The act of obligating or state of being obligated; also, the duty, promise, etc., by which one is bound. **2** The constraining power of conscience or law. **3** A requirement imposed by the customs of society or the laws of propriety and expediency; what one owes in return for a service, benefit, kindness, favor, etc. **4** A binding legal agreement, contract, bond, etc., bearing a penalty. **5** The condition of being indebted for an act of kindness, a service received, etc.; also, the kindness or service. See synonyms under DUTY. **— ob′li·ga′tor** *n.*

ob·lig·a·to·ry (ə·blig′ə·tôr′ē, -tō′rē, ob′lə·gə-) *adj.* **1** In civil or moral law, binding. **2** Of the nature of, or constituting a duty or obligation; imperative.

o·blige (ə·blīj′) *v.t.* **o·bliged, o·blig·ing** **1** To obligate; constrain. **2** To place under an obligation, as for a favor or kindness. **3** To do a favor or service for. See synonyms under ACCOMMODATE, BIND, COMPEL. [<OF *obliger, obligier* bind by oath or promise <L *obligare,* orig. tie around < *ob-* towards + *ligare* bind] —**o·blig′er** *n.*

o·blig·ing (ə·blī′jing) *adj.* Disposed to do favors; accommodating; kind. See synonyms under GOOD, PLEASANT, POLITE.—**o·blig′ing·ly** *adv.* —**o·blig′ing·ness** *n.*

ob·lique (ə·blēk′, *in military usage* ə·blīk′) **1** Deviating from the perpendicular or from a right line by any angle except a right angle; neither perpendicular nor horizontal; slanting. **2** Differing from a right angle; either acute or obtuse: said of angles. **3** Evasive; indirect; not straightforward; disingenuous. **4** Not in the direct line of descent; collateral. **5** *Bot.* Unequal-sided, as a leaf. **6** *Gram.* Having to do with cases other than the nominative and vocative. **7** *Anat.* Designating several muscles whose fibers run obliquely: the external *oblique* muscle of the abdomen. —*n.* **1** One of the oblique muscles. **2** An oblique line. **3** A veering to the right or left less than ninety degrees, as in sailing. —*v.i.* **·liqued, ·li·quing 1** To deviate from the perpendicular; slant. **2** *Mil.* To march or advance in an oblique direction. [<L *obliquus* < *ob-* against, completely + *liquis* slanting, awry] —**ob·lique′ly** *adv.* —**ob·lique′ness** *n.*

ob·liq·ui·ty (ə·blik′wə·tē) *n. pl.* **·ties 1** Oblique quality or state. **2** Inclination from a vertical or horizontal line or plane; also, the amount or the angle of such inclination. **3** Deviation from right or moral principles or conduct. —**ob·liq′ui·tous** *adj.*

ob·lit·er·ate (ə·blit′ə·rāt) *v.t.* **·at·ed, ·at·ing 1** To destroy utterly; leave no trace of. **2** To blot or wipe out; erase, as writing. See synonyms under ABOLISH, ANNUL, CANCEL. [<L *obliteratus,* pp. of *obliterare* blot out <*ob-* against, upon + *litera* a letter] —**ob·lit′er·a′tion** *n.* —**ob·lit′er·a′tive** *adj.* —**ob·lit′er·a′tor** *n.*

ob·liv·i·on (ə·bliv′ē·ən) *n.* **1** The state or fact of being utterly forgotten. **2** The act or fact of forgetting completely; forgetfulness. **3** Public remission and pardon of offense; amnesty. [<OF <L *oblivio, -onis* < *oblivisci* forget]

ob·liv·i·ous (ə·bliv′ē·əs) *adj.* **1** Forgetful, or given to forgetfulness. **2** ·Lost in thought; abstracted. **3** Inducing forgetfulness. See synonyms under ABSTRACTED. —**ob·liv′i·ous·ly** *adv.* —**ob·liv′i·ous·ness** *n.*

ob·long (ob′lông, -long) *adj.* **1** Longer in one dimension than in another: applied most commonly to rectangular objects somewhat elongated. **2** Having one principal axis longer than the other or others. **3** *Bot.* Bluntly elliptical, as a leaf. —*n.* A figure having greater length than breadth; a long rectangle. [<L *oblongus* somewhat long < *ob-* towards + *longus* long]

ob·lo·quy (ob′lə·kwē) *n. pl.* **·quies 1** The state of one who is under odium or disgrace or spoken ill of. **2** Vilification; defamation; calumny. **3** *Obs.* A cause of disgrace or reproach. See synonyms under SCANDAL. [<LL *obloquium* a contradiction < *obloqui* < *ob-* against + *loqui* speak]

ob·nox·ious (əb·nok′shəs) *adj.* **1** Of a character to give offense or excite aversion; odious; objectionable. **2** *Law* Liable or answerable; amenable. **3** *Obs.* Subject; exposed: *obnoxious* to punishment. See synonyms under SUBJECT. [<L *obnoxiosus* < *obnoxius* exposed to harm, liable < *ob-* towards + *noxa* an injury] —**ob·nox′ious·ly** *adv.* —**ob·nox′ious·ness** *n.*

o·boe (ō′bō, ō′boi) *n.* A wooden double-reed wind instrument with a high, penetrating, melancholy tone. [<Ital. <F *hautbois* HAUTBOY] —**o′bo·ist** *n.*

ob·o·vate (ob·ō′vāt) *adj. Bot.* Inversely ovate, as certain leaves. [<OB- inversely + OVATE]

ob·o·void (ob·ō′void) *adj. Bot.* Solidly obovate, with the broader end upward or outward. [<OB- inversely + OVOID]

ob·scene (əb·sēn′, ob-) *adj.* **1** Offensive to chastity or decency. **2** Offensive to the senses; foul. See synonyms under FOUL, IMMODEST, VULGAR. [<F *obscène* <L *obscenus, obscaenus* ill-omened, filthy <*obs-,* var. of *ob-* towards + *caenum* filth] —**ob·scene′ly** *adv.*

ob·scen·i·ty (əb·sen′ə·tē, -sē′nə-, ob-) *n. pl.* **·ties** Obscene quality of act, thought, speech, or representation; gross indecency; unchaste action; lewdness. Also **ob·scene′ness.** See synonyms under INDECENCY.

ob·scur·ant (əb·skyoor′ənt) *n.* One who obscures; specifically, one who opposes education, popular enlightenment, and freedom of thought. Also **ob·scur′ant·ist.** [<G *obskurant* <L *obscurans, -antis,* ppr. of *obscurare* darken] —**ob·scur′ant·ism** *n.* —**ob·scu·ra·tion** (ob′skyə·rā′shən) *n.*

ob·scure (əb·skyoor′) *adj.* **·scur·er, ·scur·est 1** Dim; dark; dusky; gloomy. **2** Not clear to the mind; vague; abstruse. **3** Faintly marked; hard to discern; undefined. **4** Remote or apart; hidden from view or notice; hence, little known; lowly: *obscure* birth. —*v.t.* **·scured, ·scur·ing 1** To darken or cloud; dim. **2** To hide from view; conceal. **3** To make unintelligible; confuse: to *obscure* an issue. **4** To make indefinite in sound, as a vowel. —*n.* Indistinctness of outline or color. [<OF *obscur, oscur* <L *obscurus,* lit., covered over] —**ob·scure′ly** *adv.* —**ob·scure′ness** *n.*

Synonyms (adj.): abstruse, ambiguous, complicated, dark, difficult, dim, indistinct, involved, profound, unintelligible. That is *obscure* which the eye or mind cannot clearly see or understand. If the matter is *abstruse,* as if removed from the usual way of thinking, it is *difficult* to comprehend. The matter may be *complicated* by the intertwining of its many parts, or it may be so deep as to be *profound.* The expression of the thought may be *ambiguous,* as if looking in two ways, or *involved* and confused in form, or it may be *unintelligible* to the mind. Sometimes it is *dark, dim,* and *indistinct* by reason of lack of light or want of transparency.

ob·scu·ri·ty (əb·skyoor′ə·tē) *n. pl.* **·ties 1** The state or quality of being obscure. **2** Dimness; darkness. **3** Lack of distinctness or perspicuity. **4** The condition of being unknown to fame. **5** An unknown or obscure person, place, or thing.

ob·se·qui·ous (əb·sē′kwē·əs) *adj.* **1** Sycophantic or adulatory in manner; cringing; ·servile. **2** *Rare* Promptly obedient. [<L *obsequiosus* compliant < *obsequium* compliance < *obsequi* comply with < *ob-* towards + *sequi* follow] —**ob·se′qui·ous·ly** *adv.* —**ob·se′qui·ous·ness** *n.*

Synonyms: attentive, compliant, cringing, deferential, fawning, flattering, obedient, servile, slavish, submissive, sycophantic. See BASE², SUPPLE. *Antonyms:* independent, self-assertive, self-respecting. See synonyms for AUSTERE.

ob·serv·a·ble (əb·zûr′və·bəl) *adj.* **1** That can be observed; manifest. **2** Notable. **3** Customary; demanding observance. —**ob·serv′a·ble·ness** *n.* —**ob·serv′a·bly** *adv.*

ob·ser·vance (əb·zûr′vəns) *n.* **1** The act of observing, as a custom or ceremony; compliance, as with law or duty. **2** Any common custom, form, rite, etc. **3** Heedful attention; observation. **4** *Eccl.* **a** The rule or constitution of a religious order. **b** The order, or the house of such an order. **5** *Archaic* Obsequious compliance. See synonyms under FORM, SACRAMENT. [<OF <L *observantia* attention, reverence, < *observans, -antis,* ppr. of *observare* OBSERVE]

ob·ser·vant (əb·zûr′vənt) *adj.* **1** Carefully attentive; habitually noting. **2** Strict in observing rules; heedful of duties. **3** Obedient; attentive. [<F, orig. ppr. of *observer* OBSERVE] —**ob·ser′vant·ly** *adv.*

ob·ser·va·tion (ob′zər·vā′shən) *n.* **1** The act, faculty, or habit of observing; the fact of being observed. **2** Scientific scrutiny of a natural phenomenon, for experiment, verification, or measurement and calculation; also, the record of such an examination and the data connected with it: an astronomical or meteorological *observation:* in this sense distinguished from *experimentation.* **3** Experience or knowledge acquired by observing. **4** An incidental remark. **5** *Obs.* Observance. See synonyms under REMARK. — **to take (or work out) an observation** *Naut.* To calculate the latitude and longitude from angular measurements of the altitude and position of the sun or other celestial body. — **ob′ser·va′tion·al** *adj.*

observation post Any point, open or concealed, in which an observer may gather information of a specified nature; especially, in wartime, a station for directing gunfire, watching enemy action, etc.

ob·ser·va·to·ry (əb·zûr′və·tôr′ē, -tō′rē) *n. pl.* **·ries 1** A building designed and equipped for the systematic observation of natural phenomena: an astronomical *observatory.* **2** A tower built for obtaining a panoramic view. [<NL *observatorium* <L *observatus,* pp. of *observare* OBSERVE]

OBSERVATORY
Schematic plan.

ob·serve (əb·zûrv′) *v.* **·served, ·serv·ing** *v.t.* **1** To notice by the sense of sight; see. **2** To watch attentively; keep under surveillance: to *observe* enemy troop movements. **3** To make methodical observation of, as for scientific purposes: to *observe* sunspots. **4** To abide by the restrictions or provisions of: to *observe* a fast. **5** To celebrate or solemnize (an occasion), as with appropriate festivities or ceremony. **6** To say as a comment or opinion; mention. —*v.i.* **7** To make a remark; comment: often with *on* or *upon.* **8** To take notice. **9** To act as an observer. See synonyms under CELEBRATE, EXAMINE, FOLLOW, OBEY. [<OF *observer* <L *observare* watch < *ob-* towards + *servare* keep, watch] —**ob·serv′ing** *adj.* —**ob·serv′ing·ly** *adv.*

ob·sess (əb·ses′) *v.t.* To occupy or trouble the mind of to an excessive degree; preoccupy; harass; haunt. [<L *obsessus,* pp. of *obsidere* besiege < *ob-* towards, against + *sedere* sit] —**ob·ses′sive** *adj.* —**ob·ses′sor** *n.*

ob·ses·sion (əb·sesh′ən) *n.* **1** A vexing or haunting, as by an evil spirit or morbidly dominant idea; the fact of being thus haunted; also, that which dominates or afflicts anyone in such manner. **2** *Psychiatry* A compulsive idea or emotion associated with the subconscious and exerting a more or less persistent influence upon conduct and behavior; also, the compulsion itself.

ob·sid·i·an (əb·sid′ē·ən, ob-) *n.* A glassy, volcanic rock, usually black and having the composition of rhyolite but containing few or no individualized crystals. [<L *obsidianus,* alter. of *obsianus,* after *Obsius,* a Roman said by Pliny to be its discoverer]

ob·so·lete (ob′sə·lēt) *adj.* **1** Gone out of use, as a word or phrase, a style, fashion, etc.; of a discarded type or fashion. **2** *Biol.* Imperfectly developed; atrophied; suppressed or lacking: said of markings, parts, organs, etc. [<L *obsoletus* grown old, worn out, pp. of *obsolescere.* See OBSOLESCENT.] —**ob′so·lete′ly** *adv.* —**ob′so·lete′ness** *n.* —**ob′so·let′ism** *n.*

Synonyms: ancient, antiquated archaic, disused, obsolescent, old, out-of-date, rare. Some of the most *ancient* words are not *obsolete.* A word is *obsolete* which has quite gone out of use; a word is *archaic* or *obsolescent* which is falling out of use; *archaic* is also applied to a word which is *obsolete* in general usage but which survives in special texts, as the Bible, hymnals, poetry, etc.; a word is *rare* if there are few present instances of its use. See OLD. *Antonyms:* see synonyms for FRESH, MODERN, NEW.

ob·sta·cle (ob′stə·kəl) *n.* That which stands in the way; a hindrance or obstruction in either a physical or a moral sense. See synonyms under BARRIER, IMPEDIMENT. [<OF <L *obstaculum* < *obstare* stand before, withstand < *ob-* before, against + *stare* stand]

ob·ste·tri·cian (ob′stə·trish′ən) *n.* A medical and surgical specialist in childbirth.

ob·stet·rics (əb·stet′riks) *n.* The branch of medical science relating to pregnancy and childbirth; midwifery. [Orig. pl. of *obstetric, adj.,* <L *obstetricus* < *obstetrix, -icis* a midwife < *obstare.* See OBSTACLE.] — **ob·stet′ri·cal,** or **ob·stet′ric** *adj.* — **ob·stet′ri·cal·ly** *adv.*

ob·sti·na·cy (ob′stə·nə·sē) *n. pl.* **·cies** 1 Persistent and usually unreasonable adherence to one's own opinion or purpose; stubbornness. 2 The quality of being difficult to subdue or remedy: said especially of ailments. 3 Stubborn action.

ob·sti·nate (ob′stə·nit) *adj.* 1 Persistently and unreasonably resolved in a purpose or opinion; stubborn. 2 Hard to control or cure. [<L *obstinatus* stubborn < *obstinare* persist < *obstare.* See OBSTACLE.] — **ob′sti·nate·ly** *adv.* — **ob′sti·nate·ness** *n.*

ob·sti·pant (ob′stə·pənt) *n. Med.* A drug or other substance that induces obstipation.

ob·sti·pa·tion (ob′stə·pā′shən) *n. Med.* Persistent or intractable constipation. [<L *obstipatio, -onis* a stopping up, ult. < *ob-* against + *stipare* press together]

ob·strep·er·ous (əb·strep′ər·əs) *adj.* Making a great disturbance; clamorous; boisterous; unruly. See synonyms under NOISY, TURBULENT. [<L *obstreperus* < *obstrepere* make noise against < *ob-* against + *strepere* roar] — **ob·strep′er·ous·ly** *adv.* — **ob·strep′er·ous·ness** *n.*

ob·struct (əb·strukt′) *v.t.* 1 To stop or impede movement through (a way or passage) by obstacles or impediments; barricade; choke; clog. 2 To block or retard the progress or way of; impede; check. 3 To come or be in front of so as to hide from sight. [<L *obstructus,* pp. of *obstruere* block up < *ob-* against + *struere* pile, build] — **ob·struct′er,** **ob·struc′tor** *n.* — **ob·struc′tive** *adj.* — **ob·struc′tive·ly** *adv.* — **ob·struc′tive·ness** *n.*

Synonyms: arrest, bar, barricade, check, choke, clog, embarrass, hinder, impede, interrupt, oppose, retard, stay, stop. To *obstruct* is literally to build up against: The road is *obstructed* by fallen trees. We may *hinder* one's advance by following and clinging to him; we *obstruct* his course by standing in his way. Anything that makes one's progress slower, whether from within or from without, *impedes, checks, hinders, retards,* or *stays;* an obstruction to one's progress is always from without. To *arrest* is to cause to stop suddenly; *obstructing* the way may have the effect of *arresting* progress. See CHECK, HINDER, OPPOSE. *Antonyms:* accelerate, advance, aid, clear, facilitate, forward, free, further, open, promote.

ob·struc·tion (əb·struk′shən) *n.* 1 A hindrance; obstacle. 2 The act of preventing progress; the state of being obstructed. See synonyms under BARRIER, IMPEDIMENT.

ob·tain (əb·tān′) *v.t.* 1 To gain possession of, especially by effort; acquire; get. 2 *Archaic* To arrive at; reach. — *v.i.* 3 To be customary or prevalent; hold good: Chivalry *obtained* until the Renaissance. 4 *Archaic* To succeed; prevail. [<OF *obtenir* <L *obtinere* < *ob-* against + *tenere* hold, keep] — **ob·tain′a·ble** *adj.* — **ob·tain′er** *n.* — **ob·tain′ment** *n.*

Synonyms: acquire, earn, gain, get, procure, receive, secure, win. When one *gets* the object of his desire, he is said to *obtain* it, whether he has *gained* or *earned* it or not. *Win* denotes contest, with a suggestion of chance or hazard; in popular language, a person is often said to *win* a lawsuit, but in legal phrase he is said to *gain* his suit, case, or cause. One *obtains* a thing commonly by some direct effort of his own, he *procures* it commonly by the intervention of someone else; he *secures* what has seemed uncertain or elusive, when he *gets* it firmly into his possession or under his control. Compare GAIN, GET, PURCHASE.

ob·tect (ob·tekt′) *adj. Entomol.* Covered with a hard chitinous case, as the pupa of most flies. Also **ob·tect′ed.** [<L *obtectus,* pp. of *obtegere* < *ob-* over + *tegere* cover]

ob·test (ob·test′) *v.t.* 1 To beseech; implore. 2 To invoke as a witness. — *v.i.* 3 To protest. [<L *obtestari* call to witness < *ob-* on account of + *testari* bear witness] — **ob·tes·ta·tion** (ob′tes·tā′shən) *n.*

ob·trude (əb·trōōd′) *v.* **ob·trud·ed, ob·trud·ing** *v.t.* 1 To thrust or force (oneself, an opinion, etc.) upon others without request or warrant. 2 To push forward or out; eject. — *v.i.* 3 To

intrude oneself. [<L *obtrudere* < *ob-* towards, against + *trudere* thrust] — **ob·trud′er** *n.*

ob·tru·sion (əb·trōō′zhən) *n.* The act of obtruding or the thing obtruded; an instance of obtruding. [<LL *obtrusio, -onis* < *obtrusus,* pp. of *obtrudere* OBTRUDE]

ob·tru·sive (əb·trōō′siv) *adj.* Tending to obtrude; obtruding; pushing; intruding. See synonyms under MEDDLESOME. — **ob·tru′sive·ly** *adv.* — **ob·tru′sive·ness** *n.*

ob·tund (ob·tund′) *v.t.* To make blunt or dull; deaden, as pain. [<L *obtundere* blunt < *ob-* against + *tundere* beat] — **ob·tund′ent** *adj. & n.*

ob·tu·rate (ob′tyə·rāt, -tə-) *v.t.* **·rat·ed, ·rat·ing** 1 To close or stop up (an opening or hole). 2 In ordnance, to close or seal (a gun breech) to prevent the escape of gas in firing. [<L *obturatus,* pp. of *obturare* stop up] — **ob′tu·ra′tion** *n.* — **ob′tu·ra′tor** *n.*

ob·tuse (əb·tōōs′, -tyōōs′) *adj.* 1 *Bot.* Blunt or rounded at the extremity, as a leaf or petal: opposed to *acute.* 2 Dull intellectually or emotionally; stupid; insensible. 3 Heavy, dull, and indistinct, as a sound. See synonyms under BLUNT. [<L *obtusus* blunt, dulled, orig. pp. of *obtundere.* See OBTUND.] — **ob·tuse′ly** *adv.* — **ob·tuse′ness** *n.*

ob·verse (ob·vûrs′, ob′vûrs) *adj.* 1 Turned toward or facing one: opposed to *reverse.* 2 Inverse; narrower at the base than at the apex: an *obverse* leaf. 3 Corresponding to something else as its counterpart. — *n.* (ob′-vûrs) 1 That side of a coin or medal upon which the face or main device is struck: opposed to *reverse;* that side of any object which is meant to be seen; the front as opposed to the back. 2 *Logic* The counterpart of any truth, fact, or statement. [<L *obversus,* pp. of *obvertere* OBVERT] — **ob·verse′ly** *adv.*

ob·ver·sion (ob·vûr′shən, -zhən) *n.* 1 A turning down or toward. 2 *Logic* A form of immediate inference in which the positive and negative or antecedent and consequent terms of a proposition are reversed in such a way that the converse or transverse forms can be legitimately inferred from the original proposition; conversion.

ob·vert (ob·vûrt′) *v.t.* 1 To turn the front, principal, or a different side of (a thing) toward another. 2 *Logic* To infer the obverse, or contradictory predicate of (a proposition). [<L *obvertere* < *ob-* towards, against, down + *vertere* turn]

ob·vi·ate (ob′vē·āt) *v.t.* **·at·ed, ·at·ing** To meet or provide for, as an objection or difficulty, by effective measures; clear away; prevent. [<L *obviatus,* pp. of *obviare* meet, withstand < *ob-* against + *via* a way] — **ob′vi·a′tion** *n.* — **ob′vi·a′tor** *n.*

ob·vi·ous (ob′vē·əs) *adj.* 1 Immediately evident without further reasoning or investigation; palpably true; manifest. 2 *Obs.* Standing or placed in the way. See synonyms under CLEAR, EVIDENT, MANIFEST, NOTORIOUS. [<L *obvius* in the way, obvious < *ob-* against + *via* a way] — **ob′vi·ous·ly** *adv.* — **ob′vi·ous·ness** *n.*

oc·ca·sion (ə·kā′zhən) *n.* 1 A particular event, or juncture of events, considered simply as exciting notice or interest; especially, an important event or celebration. 2 An event or juncture of affairs that presents some reason, motive, or opportunity for action; an opportunity permitting or a reason requiring action; cause: no *occasion* for haste. 3 A determinative condition, as opposed to the main or principal cause. 4 A need or exigency. 5 *pl. Obs.* Needs. 6 *Obs.* Any matter of business requiring attention. See synonyms under CAUSE, OPPORTUNITY. — **by occasion of** In consequence of; by reason of. — **on occasion** On suitable opportunity; at need; now and then. — **to take occasion** To avail oneself of the opportunity. — *v.t.* To cause or bring about; cause accidentally or incidentally. See synonyms under MAKE, PRODUCE. [<L *occasio, -onis* a falling towards, an opportunity < *occidere* fall down < *ob-* towards, down + *cadere* fall]

oc·ca·sion·al·ly (ə·kā′zhən·əl·ē) *adv.* In an occasional manner; more or less frequently at irregular times or intervals.

oc·ci·dent (ok′sə·dənt) *n.* The west: opposed to *orient.* [<OF <L *occidens, -entis* sunset, the west, orig. ppr. of *occidere* fall. See OCCASION.]

Oc·ci·dent (ok′sə·dənt) *n.* 1 The countries west of Asia; specifically, Europe. 2 The western

hemisphere. Opposed to *Orient.*

oc·cip·i·tal (ok·sip′ə·təl) *adj.* 1 Pertaining to the occiput. 2 Pertaining to the occipital bone. — *n.* The occipital bone. [<Med. L *occipitalis* <L *occiput, -itis* OCCIPUT]

occipito- *combining form Anat.* Occipital; occipital and: *occipitofrontal,* pertaining to the occiput and the forehead. [<L *occiput* back of the head]

oc·ci·put (ok′sə·put, -pət) *n. pl.* **·cip·i·ta** (-sip′-ə·tə) *Anat.* The lower back part of the skull. [<L, back of the head < *ob-* against + *caput* head]

oc·clude (ə·klōōd′) *v.* **·clud·ed, ·clud·ing** *v.t.* 1 To shut up or close, as pores or openings. 2 To shut in, out, or off. 3 *Chem.* To take up, either on the surface or internally, but without change of properties: Palladium *occludes* hydrogen. — *v.i.* 4 *Dent.* To meet so that the corresponding cusps fit closely together: said of the teeth of the upper and lower jaws. [<L *occludere* shut < *ob-* against, upon + *claudere* close] — **oc·clu′dent** *adj.* — **oc·clu·sion** (ə·klōō′zhən) *n.* — **oc·clu′sive** (-siv) *adj.*

oc·cult (ə·kult′, ok′ult) *adj.* 1 Of, pertaining to, or designating those mystic arts involving magic, divination, astrology, alchemy, or the like. 2 Not divulged; secret. 3 Beyond human understanding; mysterious. See synonyms under MYSTERIOUS, SECRET. — *n.* Occult arts or sciences. — *v.t.* 1 To hide or conceal from view. 2 *Astron.* To hide or conceal by occultation. — *v.i.* 3 To become hidden or concealed from view. [<L *occultus,* pp. of *occulere* cover over, hide] — **oc·cult′ly** *adv.* — **oc·cult′ness** *n.*

oc·cul·ta·tion (ok′ul·tā′shən) *n.* 1 The act of occulting, cr the state of being occulted. 2 *Astron.* Concealment of one celestial body by another interposed in the line of vision, as of a star or planet by the moon, or of a satellite by a planet. Compare ECLIPSE. 3 A disappearance from view or notice.

oc·cult·er (ə·kul′tər) *n.* A device used in a telescope to screen a light.

oc·cu·pan·cy (ok′yə·pən·sē) *n.* The act of occupying; a taking possession; also, the time during which anything is occupied. See synonyms under OCCUPATION.

oc·cu·pant (ok′yə·pənt) *n.* 1 One who occupies. 2 A tenant. [<L *occupans, -antis,* ppr. of *occupare.* See OCCUPY.]

oc·cu·pa·tion (ok′yə·pā′shən) *n.* 1 One's regular, principal, or immediate business. 2 The state of being busy. 3 The possession and holding of land by military force; the occupancy and holding of a nation by an army of another. 4 Occupancy. [<OF <L *occupatio, -onis* a seizing < *occupatus,* pp. of *occupare.* See OCCUPY.]

Synonyms: occupancy, possession, tenure, use. See BUSINESS, EXERCISE, WORK. *Antonyms:* dispossession, ejectment, eviction, resignation, vacating.

oc·cu·pa·tion·al (ok′yə·pā′shən·əl) *adj.* Of, pertaining to, or caused by, an occupation: *occupational* statistics; *occupational* diseases. — **oc′cu·pa′tion·al·ly** *adv.*

occupational therapy *Med.* The treatment of nervous, mental, or physical disabilities by means of work adapted to favor recovery and normal readjustment to external conditions.

oc·cu·py (ok′yə·pī) *v.t.* **·pied, ·py·ing** 1 To take and hold possession of, as by conquest. 2 To fill or take up (space or time): The estate *occupies* ten acres. 3 To inhabit; dwell in. 4 To hold; fill, as an office or position. 5 To busy or engage; employ: He *occupies* himself with trifles. [<OF *occuper* <L *occupare* seize, take possession of < *ob-* against + *capere* take] — **oc′cu·pi′er** *n.*

Synonyms: busy, employ, engage, fill, have, hold, keep, possess, preoccupy, use. See ENTERTAIN, HAVE, INTEREST, POSSESS.

oc·cur (ə·kûr′) *v.i.* **·curred, ·cur·ring** 1 To happen; come about. 2 To be found or met with; appear: Trout *occur* in this lake. 3 To present itself; come to mind: The theory just *occurred* to me. See synonyms under HAPPEN. [<L *occurrere* run to or against, befall < *ob-* towards, against + *currere* run]

oc·cur·rence (ə·kûr′əns) *n.* 1 The act or fact of occurring. 2 An event considered as simply presenting itself to notice without obvious cause; a happening. See synonyms under CIRCUMSTANCE, EVENT. — **oc·cur′rent** *Rare adj.*

o·cean (ō′shən) *n.* **1** The great body of salt water that covers about two thirds of the earth's surface. **2** Any one of the greater tracts of water that cover the globe: the Atlantic *Ocean.* **3** Any unbounded expanse or quantity. [< OF < L *oceanus* < Gk. *ōkeanos* the great outer sea as opposed to the Mediterranean), orig. *Ōkeanos (potamos)* (the river of) Oceanus]

o·cean·ad (ō′shən·ad) *n.* An ocean-dwelling plant. [< OCEAN + -AD[1]]

ocean gray A light silvery-gray color used on ships of the U.S. Navy in World War II.

o·ce·an·ic (ō′shē·an′ik) *adj.* Relating to, or living in, the ocean; pelagic.

o·cean–lane route (ō′shən·lān′) See LANE ROUTE.

o·ce·an·og·ra·phy (ō′shē·ən·og′rə·fē, ō′shən-) *n.* The branch of physical geography that treats of oceanic life and phenomena. [< OCEAN + -(O)GRAPHY] — **o′ce·an·og′ra·pher** *n.* — **o′ce·an·o·graph′ic** (-ə·graf′ik) or **·i·cal** *adj.* — **o′ce·an·o·graph′i·cal·ly** *adv.*

o·ce·an·oph·i·lous (ō′shē·ən·of′ə·ləs) *adj.* Biol. Living in the ocean, as a plant or animal. [< OCEAN + -(O)PHILOUS]

oc·el·lat·ed (os′ə·lā′tid) *adj.* **1** Having an ocellus or ocelli (of color), as in the tail of a peacock. **2** Resembling an ocellus. **3** Spotted. Also **oc′el·late.** [< L *ocellatus* small-eyed < *ocellus.* See OCELLUS.] — **oc′el·la′tion** *n.*

o·cel·lus (ō·sel′əs) *n. pl.* **·li** (-ī) **1** Biol. A minute simple eye, as of many invertebrates. **2** A spot of color surrounded by a ring or rings of color as in the tail of a peacock. [< L, dim. of *oculus* eye] — **o·cel′lar** *adj.*

o·ce·lot (ō′sə·lot, os′ə-) *n.* A large Central and South American cat *(Felis pardalis)* of a prevailing yellowish- or reddish-gray, with black-edged blotches. [< F, short for Nahuatl *tlaocelotl* < *tlalli* a field + *ocelotl* a jaguar]

o·cher (ō′kər) *n* **1** A native earth varying from light yellow to deep orange or brown, and consisting of iron trioxide and water with varying proportions of clay in impalpable subdivision, largely used as a pigment. **2** Any metallic oxide occurring in an earthy or finely divided form. **3** A dark-yellow color derived from or compared to ocher. —**red ocher** A red, ferruginous native ocher: also called *Indian red, Venetian red.* Also **o′chre.** [< OF *ocre* < L *ochra* < Gk. *ōchra* yellow ocher < *ōchros* pale yellow] —**o′cher·ous, o·chre·ous** (ō′krē·əs), **o′cher·y, o′chry** *adj.*

och·le·sis (ok·lē′sis) *n. Pathol.* Any disease caused by overcrowding. [< NL < Gk. *ochlēsis* a disturbance < *ochlein* move, disturb < *ochlos* a crowd]

och·loc·ra·cy (ok·lok′rə·sē) *n. pl.* **·cies** Rule of the multitude; government by the populace; mob rule. [< MF *ochlocratie* < Gk. *ochlokratia* mob rule < *ochlos* a crowd + *krateein* rule] — **och′lo·crat** *n.* —**och·lo·crat·ic** (ok′lə·krat′ik) *adj.*

och·lo·pho·bi·a (ok′lə·fō′bē·ə) *n.* Morbid fear of crowds; demophobia. [< Gk. *ochlos* a crowd + -PHOBIA]

ock *suffix of nouns* Small; little: now often without perceptible force: *hillock.* [OE *-oc, -uc*]

o'clock (ə·klok′) Of, according to, or by the clock.

o·co·til·lo (ō′kə·tēl′yō, Sp. ō′kō·tē′yō), *n.* The candlewood tree of California and Mexico. [< Sp., dim. of *ocote* Mexican pine < Nahuatl *ocotl*]

oc·re·a (ok′rē·ə, ō′krē·ə) *n. pl.* **oc·re·ae** (ok′ri·ē, ō′kri·ē) **1** *Bot.* **a** A stipule or combined pair of stipules forming a legging-shaped sheath about the stem of a plant. **b** A thin sheath around the seta of a moss: erroneously written *ochrea.* **2** *Ornithol.* A sheath, as the boot of a bird. [< L, a legging, a greave]

oc·re·ate (ok′rē·it, -āt, ō′krē-) *adj.* **1** Having ocreae. **2** *Ornithol.* Booted: said of the tarsi of certain birds.

oct-, octa- See OCTO-.

oc·ta·chord (ok′tə·kôrd) *n.* **1** A musical instrument with eight strings. **2** A diatonic scale of eight tones. [< LL *octochordos* < Gk. *oktachordos* < *okta-* eight + *chordē* a string]—**oc′ta·chor′dal** *adj.*

oc·tad (ok′tad) *n.* **1** A series of eight. **2** *Chem.* An atom, radical, or element that has a com-

bining power of eight. **3** In ancient notation, a group of eight figures arranged similarly to successive powers of ten. [< L *octas, -adis* < Gk. *oktas, -ados* a group of eight < *oktō* eight]—**oc·tad′ic** *adj.*

oc·ta·gon (ok′tə·gon) *n.* A plane figure with eight sides and eight angles. [< L *octagonos* < Gk. *oktagōnos* < *okta-* eight + *gōnia* an angle]

OCTAGON

oc·tag·o·nal (ok·tag′ə·nəl) *adj.* Eight-sided and eight-angled. —**oc·tag′o·nal·ly** *adv.*

oc·ta·he·dral (ok′tə·hē′drəl) *adj.* Having eight equal plane faces.

oc·ta·he·dron (ok′tə·hē′drən) *n. pl.* **·dra** (-drə) A solid figure bounded by eight plane faces. [< Gk. *oktaedron,* orig. neut of *oktaedros* eight-sided < *okta-* eight + *hedra* a seat]

OCTAHEDRON

oc·tam·er·ous (ok·tam′ər·əs) *adj. Bot.* Having the parts in eights, as a flower with eight-members in each set of organs: frequently written *8-merous.* [< Gk. *oktamerēs* < *okta-* eight + *meros* a part]

oc·tam·e·ter (ok·tam′ə·tər) *adj.* In prosody, having eight measures or metrical feet. —*n.* A verse of eight feet. [< L *octameter* < Gk. *oktametros* < *okta-* eight + *metron* a measure]

oc·tan (ok′tən) *adj.* Recurring on the eighth day: an *octan* fever. [< F *octane, octaine*]

oc·tane (ok′tān) *n.* **1** Any of several isomers in the methane series having the empirical formula C_8H_{18}. **2** The normal isomer of octane, a colorless liquid which is used as a solvent. **3** Octane number. [< OCT- + -ANE[2]]

octane number A measure of the antiknock properties of a motor fuel as determined in a standard internal-combustion engine in comparison with standard fuels consisting of normal heptane containing increasing percentages of isooctane, the antiknock effect increasing with increased isooctane content.

oc·tan·gle (ok′tang·gəl) *n.* An octagon. [< LL *octangulus* < *octo* eight + *angulus* an angle]

oc·tan·gu·lar (ok·tang′gyə·lər) *adj.* Eight-angled and eight-sided; octagonal.

oc·tant (ok′tənt) *n.* **1** An eighth part of a circle; an arc subtending an angle of 45 degrees. **2** *Astron.* The position in the heavens that is one eighth of a circle distant from conjunction or quadrature; one of the four positions of the moon midway between new or full moon and quarters. **3** An instrument resembling a sextant but having an arc of only 45 degrees: used for measuring the angular height of the sun, moon, and other celestial bodies as an aid in navigation. **4** *Geom.* One of the eight trihedral compartments of space formed by three planes with the three axes, *x, y,* and *z,* of a Cartesian coordinate system as edges. [< LL *octans* an eighth part < L *octo* eight]—**oc·tant′al** (-tan′təl) *adj.*

CARTESIAN OCTANT
O. Origin. Coordinates of *A*: $x = 4, y = 7, z = 5$; of *B*: $x = 4, y = 7$.

oc·ta·pla (ok′tə·plə) *n.* **1** A Bible written or printed in eight languages or containing eight versions. **2** Any polyglot book in eight languages. [< Gk. *oktapla,* neut. pl. of *oktaploos* eightfold]

oc·tar·chy (ok′tär·kē) *n. pl.* **·chies** **1** A government headed by eight persons. **2** A country under eight rulers. **3** A group of eight allied governments. [< OCT- + -ARCHY]

oc·tave (ok′tiv, -tāv) *n.* **1** *Music* **a** The interval between any note and that given by twice as many or by half as many vibrations in a second. **b** A note at this interval above or below any other, considered in relation to that other. **c** Two notes at this interval, sounded together; also, the resulting consonance. **d** An organ stop giving tones an octave higher than those normally corresponding to the keys played. **2** The eighth day from a feast day, beginning with the feast day as one; also, the lengthening of a festival so as to include a period of eight days. **3** Any group or series of eight. **4** In prosody, the first eight lines in an Italian sonnet, or a stanza of eight lines. —*adj.* **1** Composed of eight. **2** In prosody, composed of eight lines. **3** *Music* Producing tones an octave higher. Also **oc·ta·val** (ok·tā′vəl, ok′tə-) *adj.* [< OF < L *octava,* fem. of *octavus* eighth < *octo* eight]

oc·ten·ni·al (ok·ten′ē·əl) *adj.* **1** Recurring at intervals of eight years. **2** Occupying periods of eight years. [< L *octennium* a period of eight years < *octo* eight + *annus* a year] — **oc·ten′ni·al·ly** *adv.*

oc·tet (ok·tet′) *n.* **1** A musical composition for eight parts or eight performers. **2** A choir of eight voices, or an orchestra of eight performers. **3** Any group of eight; especially, the first eight lines of an Italian sonnet; octave (def. 4). **4** *Physics* A group of eight electrons in the shell of an atom. Also **oc·tette′.** [< L *octo* eight; on analogy with *duet*]

oc·til·lion (ok·til′yən) *n.* A cardinal number: in the French and American systems, represented by a figure 1 with 27 ciphers annexed; in the English system by a figure 1 with 48 ciphers. [< MF < L *octo* eight; on analogy with *million*] —**oc·til′lionth** (-yənth) *adj. & n.*

octo- *combining form* Eight: *octopus:* also, before vowels, *oct-.* Also *octa-.* [< L *octo* and Gk. *oktō* eight]

Oc·to·ber (ok·tō′bər) **1** The tenth month of the year (the eighth of the Roman year), containing 31 days. **2** Ale or cider made in October. [< L, the eighth (month) < *octo* eight]

October Revolution See RUSSIAN REVOLUTION under REVOLUTION.

oc·to·ge·nar·i·an (ok′tə·jə·nâr′ē·ən) *adj.* Being eighty or from eighty to ninety years of age: also **oc·tog·e·nar·y** (ok·toj′ə·ner′ē). —*n.* A person between eighty and ninety years of age. [< L *octogenarius* < *octogeni* eighty each < *octoginta* eighty]

oc·to·he·dral (ok′tə·hē′drəl) See OCTAHEDRAL.

oc·to·lat·er·al (ok′tə·lat′ər·əl) *adj.* Eight-sided. [< OCTO- + LATERAL]

oc·to·nar·y (ok′tə·ner′ē) *adj.* **1** Of or pertaining to the number eight. **2** Having eight parts or members. —*n. pl.* **·nar·ies** **1** In prosody, an octave. **2** An ogdoad. [< L *octonarius* containing eight < *octoni* eight at a time < *octo* eight]

oc·to·pus (ok′tə·pəs) *n. pl.* **·pus·es** or **·pi** (-pī) or **oc·top·o·des** (ok·top′ə·dēz) **1** Any of the marine cephalopod mollusks of the genus *Octopus,* having no shell, a soft, domed head with large eyes and the mouth on the underside surrounded by eight long, partially webbed tentacles bearing two rows of suckers. Also called *devilfish.* **2** Figuratively, any organized power regarded as of far-reaching capacity for harm; specifically, a powerful business organization; a trust. [< NL < Gk. *oktapous* eight-footed < *okta-* eight + *pous* a foot]

OCTOPUS
(Varies according to species, from a 6-inch to a 32-foot span over-all)

add,āce,câre,pälm; end,ēven; it,īce; odd,ōpen,ôrder; tŏŏk,pool; up,bûrn; ə = a in *above,* e in *sicken,* i in *clarity,* o in *melon,* u in *focus;* yōō = u in *fuse;* oi,oil; ou,pout; ch,check; g,go; ng,ring; th,thin; ṯh,this; zh,vision. Foreign sounds a,œ,ü,kh,ṅ; and ◆: see page xx. < from; + plus; ? possibly.

oc·to·syl·lab·ic (ok'tə·si·lab'ik) *adj.* **1** Composed of eight syllables, as a line of verse. **2** Containing lines of eight syllables. —*n.* An octosyllabic line or verse. [< LL *octosyllabus* < L < Gk. *oktasyllabos* < *okta-* eight + *syllabē* a syllable]

oc·tu·ple (ok'tōō·pəl, -tyōō-, ok·tōō'pəl, -tyōō'-) *adj.* **1** Consisting of eight parts or copies. **2** Multiplied by eight. —*v.t.* **·pled, ·pling** To multiply by eight. —*n.* A number or sum eight times as great as another. [< L *octuplus* eightfold < *octo* eight] —**oc'tu·ply** *adv.*

oc·u·lar (ok'yə·lər) *adj.* Pertaining to, like, derived from, or connected with the eye; visual. —*n.* The lenses forming the eyepiece of an optical instrument. [< L *ocularis* < *oculus* eye] —**oc'u·lar·ly** *adv.*

oc·u·list (ok'yə·list) *n.* One skilled in treating diseases of the eye; an opthalmologist. [< MF *oculiste* < L *oculus* eye]

oculo- *combining form* Eye; of or pertaining to the eye: *oculomotor.* Also, before vowels, **ocul-.** [< L *oculus* the eye]

oc·u·lo·mo·tor (ok'yə·lə·mō'tər) *Anat. adj.* Causing or connected with movement of the eye: the *oculomotor* nerve. —*n.* The oculomotor or third cranial nerve, which supplies most of the muscles that move the eyeball.

OD (ō'dē') *n. pl.* **OD's** A narcotic overdose. *v.i.* **OD'd, OD'ing** To become ill, or die, from a narcotic overdose.

odd (od) *adj.* **1** Not even; leaving a remainder when divided by two. **2** Marked with an odd number. **3** Left over after a division. **4** Additional to any round number; thrown in or mentioned without exact enumeration: *two hundred and odd miles*; extra: an *odd fork.* **5** Occasional; causal: *to work at odd jobs.* **6** Peculiar; singular; queer; eccentric. **7** Single: an *odd slipper.* —*n.* In golf, an advantage of one or more strokes given to a less skilful player over his opponent. [< ON *odda-* odd, third < *oddi* a point of land, triangle, odd number] —**odd'ly** *adv.* —**odd'ness** *n.*

Synonyms (adj.): anomalous, bizarre, comical, droll, eccentric, extraordinary, fantastic, fantastical, grotesque, peculiar, quaint, queer, rare, strange, uncommon, unique, unmatched, unusual, whimsical. See QUEER. RARE[1]. *Antonyms:* common, conventional, customary, even, normal, ordinary, usual.

odd·i·ty (od'ə·tē) *n. pl.* **·ties 1** Singularity. **2** An eccentricity. **3** Something odd or peculiar.

odd·ment (od'mənt) *n.* **1** That which is only an irregular and incidental and not an essential part of some course or system; something left over. **2** *Printing* A constituent part of a book other than the text, as the title page, index, etc. **3** *pl.* Small belongings; odds and ends.

odd-pin·nate (od'pin'āt, -it) *adj. Bot.* Pinnate with a single leaflet at the end, as the locust leaf.

odds (odz) *n. pl. (sometimes construed as singular)* **1** An equalizing allowance based on the apparent chances of success of an opponent or contestant. **2** The amount or proportions by which one's bet differs from that of another: The *odds* are three to two. **3** The balance of probability that something will happen or be found to be the case. **4** In a contest of any sort, a difference to the advantage of one side: the *odds* in one's favor. **5** In a contest, the advantage of one side over the opposing side. —**at odds** At variance; disagreeing. —**to give** (or **lay**) **odds** To offer to bet with someone on terms apparently favorable to him. — **to take odds** To agree to a wager on terms apparently favorable to the other person.

odds and ends Fragments; miscellaneous articles.

odds-on (odz'on') *adj.* Considered as having the best chance of winning.

ode (ōd) *n.* **1** In classical prosody, a lyric poem intended to be sung or chanted, exemplified by the **Pindaric ode**, consisting of three stanzas (strophe, antistrophe, and epode), and the **Horatian ode**, consisting of one stanzaic form throughout. **2** In modern usage, a lyric poem, rimed or unrimed, of lofty tone, treating progressively one dignified theme, often in the form of an address. [< MF < LL *ode, oda* < Gk. *ōidē, aoidē* a song < *aeidein* sing] —**od·ic** (ō'dik) *adj.*

-ode[1] *combining form* Way; path: *anode, cathode.* [< Gk. *hodos* a way]

-ode[2] *suffix* Like; resembling; having the nature of: *phyllode.* [< Gk. *-ōdēs* < *eidos* form]

o·de·um (ō'dē·əm) *n. pl.* **o·de·a** (ō'dē·ə) **1** A theater or music hall. **2** In ancient Greece and Rome, a roofed building for musical performances. Also **o·de·on** (ō'dē·on). [< LL < Gk. *ōideion* < *ōidē.* See ODE.]

o·di·ous (ō'dē·əs) *adj.* **1** Exciting hate, repugnance, or disgust. **2** Regarded with aversion or disgust. See synonyms under FOUL. INFAMOUS. [< AF < L *odiosus* < *odium.* See ODIUM.] —**o'di·ous·ly** *adv.* —**o'di·ous·ness** *n.*

o·di·um (ō'dē·əm) *n.* **1** The state of being odious; offensiveness; opprobrium. **2** A feeling of extreme repugnance, disgust, or hate. See synonyms under SCANDAL. [< L, hatred < *odisse* hate]

o·do·graph (ō'də·graf, -gräf) *n.* **1** A pedometer. **2** An odometer. **3** An automatic, portable mapmaking device designed to work from a moving vehicle. [< Gk. *hodos* a way + -GRAPH]

o·dom·e·ter (ō·dom'ə·tər) *n.* An appliance for measuring distance traveled, as a mechanical registering attachment to the wheel of a vehicle: also spelled *hodometer.* [< Gk. *hodometros* < *hodos* a way, a road + *metron* a measure]

o·dom·e·try (ō·dom'ə·trē) *n.* Measurement by odometer.

o·don·a·tous (ō·don'ə·təs) *adj.* Of or pertaining to an order (Odonata) of slender, long-bodied, generally large, predatory insects with four equal, net-veined wings, including the dragonflies and damsel flies. [< NL < Gk. *odous, odontos* a tooth]

o·don·tal·gi·a (ō'don·tal'jē·ə, -jə) *n. Pathol.* Toothache. [< Gk. < *odous, odontos* a tooth + *algos* a pain] —**o'don·tal'gic** *adj.*

odonto- *combining form* Tooth; of the teeth: *odontology.* Also, before vowels, **odont-.** [< Gk. *odous, odontos* a tooth]

o·don·to·blast (ō·don'tə·blast) *n. Anat.* A tooth cell that produces dentine. —**o·don·to·blas'tic** *adj.*

o·don·to·glos·sum (ō·don'tə·glos'əm) *n.* Any of a large genus (Odontoglossum) of tropical American epiphytic orchids with thick, fleshy leaves and large flowers with free, spreading sepals. [< NL < Gk. *odous, odontos* a tooth + *glossa* a tongue]

o·don·to·graph (ō·don'tə·graf, -gräf) *n.* **1** *Mech.* An instrument for correctly laying out gear teeth. **2** *Dent.* A device for showing irregularities occurring in the surface of tooth enamel.

o·don·toid (ō·don'toid) *adj.* **1** Toothlike. **2** Of or pertaining to the odontoid bone or process.

odontoid process *Anat.* A toothlike or peglike projection from the body of the axis or second vertebra of the neck, upon which the atlas rotates: found in mammals and birds. Also **odontoid peg.**

o·don·tol·o·gy (ō'don·tol'ə·jē) *n.* The body of scientific knowledge that relates to the structure, health, and growth of the teeth. [< ODONTO- + -LOGY] —**o·don·to·log·i·cal** (ō·don'tə·loj'i·kəl) *adj.* —**o·don·to·log'i·cal·ly** *adv.* —**o·don·tol'o·gist** *n.*

o·don·to·phore (ō·don'tə·fôr, -fōr) *n. Zool.* **1** A protrusible, ribbonlike organ covered with teeth for rasping, etc., and connected with the mouth of cephalous mollusks. **2** The radula, tongue, or lingual ribbon. [< Gk. *odontophoros* bearing teeth < *odous, odontos* tooth + *-phoros* bearing < *pherein* bear] —**o·don·toph·o·ral** (ō'don·tof'ər·əl) *adj.* —**o'don·toph'o·rine** (-rin, -rēn) *adj. & n.* —**o'don·toph'o·rous** *adj.*

o·don·to·scope (ō·don'tə·skōp) *n.* A small dental mirror, used by a dentist to examine the teeth. [< ODONTO- + -SCOPE]

o·dor (ō'dər) *n.* **1** That quality of a material substance that renders it perceptible to the sense of smell; scent. **2** Regard or estimation: to be in bad *odor.* **3** A perfume; incense. See synonyms under SAVOR. SMELL. Also *Brit.* **o'dour.** [< AF *odour,* OF *odor* < L *odor, -oris*]

o·dor·if·er·ous (ō'də·rif'ər·əs) *adj.* Diffusing an odor. [< L *odorifer* < *odor, -oris* an odor + *ferre* bear] —**o'dor·if'er·ous·ly** *adv.* —**o'dor·if'er·ous·ness** *n.*

o·dor·less (ō'dər·lis) *adj.* Having no odor. —**o'dor·less·ly** *adv.* —**o'dor·less·ness** *n.*

o·dor·ous (ō'dər·əs) *adj.* Having an odor; fragrant. —**o'dor·ous·ly** *adv.* —**o'dor·ous·ness** *n.*

-odynia *combining form Med.* Pain; chronic pain in a (specified) part of the body: *osteodynia,* chronic pain in a bone. [< Gk. *odynē* pain]

O·dys·seus (ō·dis'yōōs, -ē·əs) In Greek legend, king of Ithaca, one of the Greek leaders in the Trojan War, figuring in the *Iliad* and hero of the *Odyssey*; Ulysses.

Od·ys·sey (od'ə·sē) *n.* **1** An ancient Greek epic poem attributed to Homer, describing the wanderings of Odysseus during the ten years after the fall of Troy. **2** A long, wandering journey: often **od'ys·sey.** — **Od'ys·sey'·an** *adj.*

oe– See also words beginning E–.

oec·u·men·i·cal (ek'yōō·men'i·kəl, *Brit.* ē'kyōō·men'i·kəl) See ECUMENICAL.

Oed·i·pus (ed'ə·pəs, ē'də-) In Greek legend, the son of Laius and Jocasta, who, abandoned by them at birth because of an oracle and raised by the king of Corinth, eventually returned to Thebes. After guessing the riddle of the sphinx and accidentally killing his father, he unwittingly married his mother and became king of Thebes; discovering his relationship to Jocasta, he blinded himself and died in exile. Also **Œd'i·pus.** [< L < Gk. *Oidipous,* lit., swollen-footed]

Oedipus complex *Psychoanal.* A strong, typically unconscious attachment to the parent of opposite sex, with antagonism toward the other: productive of various neurotic disorders when it persists unresolved into adult life. Compare ELECTRA COMPLEX.

oe·no·mel (ē'nə·mel, en'ə-) *n.* **1** A beverage of wine and honey. **2** Hence, anything combining sweetness and strength. Also spelled *oinomel.* [< LL *oenomeli* < Gk. *oinomeli* < *oinos* wine + *meli* honey]

oer·sted (ûr'sted) *n.* The cgs unit of magnetic intensity, equal to a force of 1 dyne exerted on a unit magnetic pole. [after Hans C. *Oersted,* 1777–1851, Danish physicist]

oe·soph·a·gus (i·sof'ə·gəs), etc. See ESOPHAGUS, etc.

oes·trin (es'trin, ēs'-) See ESTROGEN.

oes·trum (es'trəm, ēs'-), **oes·trus** (es'trəs, ēs'-) See ESTRUM, ESTRUS.

of (uv, ov; *unstressed* əv) *prep.* **1** Coming from; originating at or from: Anne *of* Cleves; an actor of noble birth. **2** Associated or connected with; included among: Is he *of* your party? **3** Located at: the Leaning Tower *of* Pisa. **4** Away or at a distance from: within six miles *of* home. **5** Named; specified as: the city *of* Newark; a fall *of* ten feet. **6** Characterized by: a man *of* strength. **7** With reference to; as to: quick *of* wit. **8** About; concerning: Good is said *of* him. **9** Because of: dying *of* pneumonia. **10** Possessing: a man *of* means. **11** Belonging to: the lid *of* a box. **12** Pertaining to: the majesty *of* the law. **13** Composed of: a ship *of* steel. **14** Containing: a glass *of* water. **15** Taken from; from the number or class of: six *of* the seven conspirators. **16** So as to be without: relieved *of* anxiety; despoiled *of* ornaments. **17** Proceeding from; produced by: the plays *of* Shakespeare; the work *of* a vanished hand. **18** Directed toward; exerted upon: the massacre *of* the innocents; a love *of* opera. **19** During or at a specified time or occasion: He came *of* a Sunday; *of* recent years. **20** Set aside for or devoted to: a program *of* Lieder. **21** Before; until: used in telling time: ten minutes *of* ten. **22** *Archaic* By: loved *of* all men. [OE, var. of *af, æf* away from]

of– Assimilated var. of OB–.

of course 1 In the usual order or procedure; naturally; as expected. **2** Doubtless; certainly.

off (ôf, of) *adj.* **1** Farther or more distant; remote: an *off* chance. **2** In a (specified) circumstance or situation: to be well *off.* **3** Not in accordance with the facts; wrong: Your reckoning is *off.* **4** Not in the usual health or condition; not up to standard: an *off* season for roses. **5** Not in existence; no longer considered active or effective: The deal is *off.* **6** Away from work; not on duty: He spent his *off* hours at the rink. **7** In riding or driving, on the right: opposed to *near*: Pass on the *off* side. **8** *Naut.* Seaward; farther from the coast. **9** In cricket, to the left of a bowler: said of the side of the field facing the batsman. — *adv.* **1** To a distance; so as to be away: *My horse ran off.* **2** To or at a (specified) future time: *Your engagement is another week off.* **3** To or at a (specified) distance: *The inn is a mile off.* **4** So as to be no longer in place, connection, etc.: *Take off your hat.* **5** So as to be no longer functioning, continuing, or in operation: *Turn the lights off.* **6** So as to be away from one's work, duties, etc.: *to take the day off.* **7** So as to be completed, exhausted, etc.: *to kill off one's enemies; to drink off a draught.* **8** So as to deviate from or be below what is regarded as standard: *His game was off.* **9** *Naut.* Away from land, a ship, the wind, etc.: *Keep her four points off.* **— off with . . . !** *Take off! Remove!: Off with his head!* **— off with you!** *Go away! Leave!* **— right (or straight) off** Forthwith; immediately. **— to be off 1** To leave; depart. **2** *Colloq.* To be insane. **—** *prep.* **1** So as to be separated, detached, distant, or removed from (a position, source, etc.): *Take your feet off the table; twenty miles off course.* **2** Not engaged in or occupied with; relieved from: *off duty.* **3** Extending away or out from; no longer on: *off Broadway.* **4** So as to deviate from or be below (what is regarded as standard): *to be off one's game.* **5** On or from (the material or substance of): *living off nuts and berries.* **6** *Colloq.* No longer using, engaging in, or advocating: *to be off drinking.* **7** *Naut.* Opposite to and seaward of: *the battle off the eastern cape.* **—** *n.* **1** The state or condition of being off. **2** In cricket, the offside (of the field). [ME, orig. stressed var. of OF]

of·fal (ô′fəl) *n.* **1** Those parts of a butchered animal that are rejected as worthless. **2** Rubbish or refuse of any kind. See synonyms under WASTE. [ME *ofall* <OFF + FALL]

off and on Now and then; intermittently.

off·beat (ôf′bēt′, of′-; *for adj.* 2 *esp.* ôf′bēt′, of′-) *n.* *Music* Any secondary or weak beat in a measure. **—** *adj.* **1** *Music* Having primary accents in 4/4 time on the second and fourth beats. **2** *Slang* Unconventional; out of the ordinary.

off·cast (ôf′kast′, -käst′, of′-) *adj.* Rejected; cast off. **—** *n.* Anything thrown away or rejected.

off chance A bare possibility.

off·col·or (ôf′kul′ər, of′-) *adj.* **1** Unsatisfactory in color, as a gem. **2** Bad, indelicate, or indecent by implication; of doubtful virtue. Also *Brit.* **off′-col′our.**

of·fend (ə·fend′) *v.t.* **1** To give displeasure or offense to; displease; affront; anger. **2** To affect (the taste, eyes, etc.) with displeasure. **3** *Obs.* To transgress or violate. **—** *v.i.* **4** To give displeasure or offense; be offensive. **5** To commit an offense or crime; sin. See synonyms under AFFRONT, PIQUE[1]. [<OF *offendre* strike against <L *offendere* < *ob-* against + *fendere* hit, thrust] **— of·fend′er** *n.*

of·fense (ə·fens′) *n.* **1** The act of offending; any sin, wrong, or fault. **2** That which injures the feelings or causes displeasure; that which provokes. **3** The state of being offended; umbrage; anger. **4** Assault or attack: *a weapon of offense.* **5** A cause of sin or stumbling. Also, *Brit., offence.* [<OF <L *offensa* a striking against, orig. pp. fem. of *offendere.* See OFFEND.]

of·fen·sive (ə·fen′siv) *adj.* **1** Serving, adapted, or intended to give offense; displeasing; annoying. **2** Causing unpleasant sensations; disagreeable. **3** Serving as a means of attack. **4** Injurious. See synonyms under FOUL, ROTTEN, VULGAR. **—** *n.* Aggressive methods, operations, or attitude: *with the definite article.* **— of·fen′sive·ly** *adv.* **— of·fen′sive·ness** *n.*

of·fer (ô′fər, of′ər) *v.t.* **1** To present for acceptance or rejection; tender. **2** To suggest for consideration or action; propose. **3** To present with solemnity or in worship; make an offering. **4** To show readiness to do or attempt; propose or threaten: *to offer battle.* **5** To attempt to do or inflict; hence, to do or inflict: *to offer insult or resistance.* **6** To suggest as payment; bid. **7** To present for sale. **—** *v.i.* **8** To present itself; appear: *No opportunity offered.* **9** To make an offering in worship or sacrifice. **—** *n.* **1** The act of offering; a proffer or proposal. **2** An attempt or endeavor to do something. See synonyms

under PROPOSAL. [OE *offrian* offer a sacrifice <L *offerre* present < *ob-* before + *ferre* bring; infl. in meaning by OF *offrir* offer] **— of′·fer·er, of′fer·or** *n.*

Synonyms (verb): adduce, allege, bid, exhibit, extend, present, proffer, propose, tender, volunteer. What one *offers* he brings before another for acceptance or rejection. *Proffer* is a more formal and deferential word, with a suggestion of contingency; as, to *proffer* one's services; the worshiper *offers*, but does not *proffer* sacrifice. See ALLEGE.

of·fer·ing (ô′fər·ing, of′ər-) *n.* **1** The act of making an offer. **2** That which is offered; sacrifice; any gift. **3** A contribution at a religious service.

of·fer·to·ry (ô′fər·tôr′ē, -tō′rē, of′ər-) *n. pl.* **·ries** *Eccl.* **1** *Usually cap.* A section of the eucharistic liturgy, usually following the saying of the creed, during which the bread and wine to be consecrated are offered, and the alms of the congregation are collected. **2** Any collection taken during a religious service; also, the part of a service when it is taken. **3** An antiphon, hymn, or anthem sung during the offertory. **4** A prayer of oblation said by the celebrant over the bread and wine to be consecrated. [<Med. L *offertorium* an offering <LL *offertus*, pp. of L *offerre.* See OFFER.]

off·hand (ôf′hand′, of′-) *adv.* Without preparation; unceremonious or unceremoniously; extempore. **—** *adj.* Done, said, or made extemporaneously. Also **off′hand′ed.** **— off′hand′·ed·ly** *adv.*

of·fice (ô′fis, of′is) *n.* **1** A particular duty, charge, or trust; an employment undertaken by commission or authority; a post or position held by an official or functionary; specifically, a position of trust or authority under a government: *the office of premier.* **2** That which is performed, assigned, or intended to be done by a particular thing, or that which anything is fitted to perform; function; service. **3** A place, building, or series of rooms in which some particular branch of the public service is conducted: *the Patent Office, Post Office*; also, the persons conducting such business; specifically, the head of the department and his immediate assistants: *The Executive Office serves the president.* In the United States the term is applied to those branches of the government business ranking next to the departments, the chiefs of which are not cabinet members; in Great Britain, to all branches of government business over which a secretary of state presides and to certain other departments having their chiefs in the cabinet: *the War Office, Home Office.* **4** A room or building in which a person transacts his business or carries on his stated occupation: distinguished from *shop, store, studio*, etc.: *the lawyer's office.* **5** *pl. Brit.* The outbuildings devoted to culinary or other domestic purposes. **6** The persons collectively, as an association or corporation, whose headquarters are in an office: *The office has telegraphed me to return.* **7** *Eccl.* A prescribed religious or devotional service, particularly that for the canonical hours, or the service itself: *the divine office*; specifically, the daily service of the breviary, morning and evening prayer, the mass, communion, etc. **8** A ceremony; rite. **9** *pl.* A proffered action of any kind; especially, a service: *reinstated through the good offices of a friend.* See synonyms under DUTY. [<AF <L *officium* a service, prob. < *opus* a work + *facere* do, make]

of·fice-hold·er (ô′fis-hōl′dər, of′-) *n.* One who holds an office under a government.

office hours The number of hours one works in an office; also, the hours an office is open for business.

of·fi·cer (ô′fə·sər, of′ə-) *n.* **1** One elected or appointed to office, as in a company, a society, or an ecclesiastical body, or one filling some other semipublic position, as by appointment. **2** One appointed to a certain military or naval rank and authority, specifically by commission. **3** In the merchant marine, etc., the captain or any of the mates. **4** A member of the constabulary or police force. **5** In corporate bodies and other organizations, one who holds a position entailing certain duties, as secretary or treasurer, as distinguished

from an employee. **— commissioned officer** An officer who receives a commission, ranking, in the U.S. Army, from second lieutenant to general, and in the U.S. Navy from ensign to admiral. **— line officer** An officer of a combat branch of the service; officer of the line. **— non-commissioned officer** An officer appointed from the military ranks by an authorized commanding officer. The non-commissioned grades rank from corporal through master sergeant. **— warrant officer** In the U.S. Army, Navy, Air Force, Marine Corps, and Coast Guard, an officer without a commission, but having authority by virtue of a certificate or warrant. His rank is superior to that of a non-commissioned officer. See table under GRADE. **—** *v.t.* **1** To furnish with officers. **2** To command; direct; manage. [<AF *officer*, OF *officier* <Med. L *officiarius* <L *officium* OFFICE]

of·fi·cial (ə·fish′əl) *adj.* **1** Pertaining to or holding an office or public trust. **2** Derived from the proper office or officer; authoritative. **3** In pharmacy, authorized to be used in medicine. **4** Formal; studied; ceremonious. **—** *n.* One holding an office or performing duties of a public nature. [<OF <L *officialis* <*officium* OFFICE] **— of·fi′cial·dom** *n.* **— of·fi′cial·ly** *adv.* **— of·fi′cial·ness** *n.*

of·fi·cial·ism (ə·fish′əl·iz′əm) *n.* **1** Official state, condition, or system. **2** Rigid adherence to official forms.

of·fi·ci·ant (ə·fish′ē·ənt) *n.* One who conducts or officiates at a religious service, office, or ceremony; celebrant. [<Med. L *officians, -antis*, ppr. of *officiare.* See OFFICIATE.]

of·fi·ci·ar·y (ə·fish′ē·er′ē) *n. pl.* **·ar·ies** A body of officials. **—** *adj.* Pertaining to or holding an office.

of·fi·ci·ate (ə·fish′ē·āt) *v.i.* **·at·ed, ·at·ing** **1** To act or serve as a priest or minister; conduct a service. **2** To perform the duties or functions of an office. **3** In sports, to act as a referee, umpire, etc. [<Med. L *officiatus*, pp. of *officiare* perform divine service <L *officium* OFFICE] **— of·fi′ci·a′tion** *n.* **— of·fi′ci·a′tor** *n.*

of·fic·i·nal (ə·fis′ə·nəl) *adj.* **1** Prepared and on hand, as drugs. **2** Employed in the arts or as a medicine. **—** *n.* Any drug or medicine kept ready for sale. [<Med. L *officinalis* <L *officina* workshop, contraction of *opificina* <*opifex* workman <*opus* work + *facere* do]

of·fi·cious (ə·fish′əs) *adj.* **1** Unduly forward in offering one's services. **2** Obtrusive and interfering; meddling with what is not one's concern. **3** *Obs.* Disposed to serve or oblige; friendly. See synonyms under MEDDLESOME. [<L *officiosus* obliging <*officium* OFFICE] **— of·fi′cious·ly** *adv.* **— of·fi′cious·ness** *n.*

off·ish (ô′fish, of′ish) *adj.* Inclined to be distant in manner; aloof. **— off′ish·ness** *n.*

off-line (ôf′līn′, of′-) *adj.* Associated with, but not directly controlled by, an electronic computer.

off-load (ôf′lōd′, of′-) *v.t. & v.i.* To unload.

off-peak (ôf′pēk′, of′-) *adj.* Below the maximum: *an off-peak load in a power plant.*

off-put·ting (ôf′pŏŏt′ing, of′-) *adj.* Putting one off; causing hostility, indifference, etc.

off-scour·ing (ôf′skour′ing, of′-) *n.* That which is scoured off; something vile or despised.

off·set (ôf′set′, of′-) *n.* **1** Anything regarded or advanced as a counterbalance or equivalent; setoff. **2** *Geol.* A spur or branch from a range of mountains or hills. **3** *Bot.* A short lateral branch of a plant that takes root where it rests on the soil, thus serving for propagation. **4** A line drawn from a curved or irregular main line at right angles to an auxiliary line, to assist in measuring areas or in plotting. **5** A ledge or setoff in a wall; also, a fence spur set at right angles to the main fence. **6** A terrace; especially, a terrace on a hill or mountain side. **7** *Archit.* A comparatively thin place in the length of a wall; also, a recess below the general plane of a wall; a sunk panel. **8** A bend in a pipe bringing one part out of, but parallel with, the line of another part. **9** *Printing* **a** The smut or smear of a freshly printed sheet on the surface of the sheet in contact with it. **b** An impression made by the offset printing method. **10** A descendant; offspring; offshoot. —*adj.* **1** *Printing* Of or pertaining to offset printing. **2** *Archit.* Of or pertaining to a ledge, panel, frame or the like not flush with a surface into which it is set. —*v.* (ôf′set′, of′-) **·set, ·set·ting** *v.t.* **1** To compensate for, as by balancing or opposing with an equivalent; counterbalance. **2** To transfer (an impression) from one surface to another. **3** *Printing* **a** To print by offset printing. **b** To smudge or mark with an offset. **4** *Archit.* To make an offset in. —*v.i.* **5** To make an offset, as in printing. **6** To branch off; project as an offset.

off·shoot (ôf′shōōt′, of′-) *n.* **1** *Bot.* A side shoot or branch from the main stem of a plant. **2** Anything that branches off from the parent stock or is regarded as a side issue.

off·shore (ôf′shôr′, -shōr′, of′-) *adj.* **1** Moving or directed away from the shore. **2** Situated or occurring at some distance from the shore. —*adv.* **1** At a distance from the shore. **2** From or away from the shore.

off·side (ôf′sīd′, of′-) *adv.* **1** At or on the wrong side. **2** In football, out of play: said of a player in certain contingencies when he gets in front of the ball during a scrimmage, or when the ball has been last touched by his own side behind him. **3** In hockey, in the attacking zone ahead of the puck.

off·spring (ôf′spring′, of′-) *n.* **1** That which springs from or is the progeny of any person, animal, or plant. **2** A child or children; issue. [OE *offspring* < *of* of, off + *springan* spring]

off·stage (ôf′stāj′, of′-) *n.* The area behind or to the side of a stage, out of view of the audience. —*adj.* In or from this area: *offstage* dialog. —*adv.* To this area: He went *off-stage*.

oft·en (ôf′ən, of′-) *adv.* On frequent or numerous occasions; repeatedly. —*adj. Obs.* Repeated; frequently occurring. [Var. of ME *ofte,* OE *oft*]

oft·en·times (ôf′ən·tīmz′, of′-) *adv.* Frequently; often. Also *Archaic* **oft·times** (ôf′tīmz′, of′-).

og·do·ad (og′dō·ad) *n.* **1** The number eight. **2** Anything constructed of eight parts, individuals, or members; any group of eight. [< LL *ogdoas, -adis* < Gk. *ogdoas, -ados* < *oktō* eight]

o·gle (ō′gəl) *v.* **o·gled, o·gling** *v.t.* **1** To look at with admiring or impertinent glances. **2** To stare at; look at. —*v.i.* **3** To look or stare in an admiring or impertinent manner. —*n.* An amorous or coquettish look. [Prob. < LG *oegelen, ogelen,* freg. of *oegen* look < *oege* an eye] —**o′gler** *n.*

o·gre (ō′gər) *n.* **1** In fairy tales, a man-eating giant or monster. **2** A person regarded as resembling this. [< F; prob. coined by Perrault] —**o′gre·ish, o′grish** *adj.* —**o′gress** *n. fem.*

oh (ō) *interj.* **1** An exclamation expressing surprise, sudden emotion, etc. **2** See O (*interj.*).

O·hi·o (ō·hī′ō) A north central State of the United States, on Lake Erie; 41,222 square miles; capital, Columbus; entered the Union March 1, 1803; nickname, *Buckeye State:* abbr. OH —**O·hi′o·an** *adj. & n.*

ohm (ōm) *n.* The unit of electrical resistance. The international ohm is the resistance at 0°C. of a uniform column of mercury having a mass of 14.4521 grams. It is equal to 1.000495 absolute ohms. [after G. S. *Ohm*] —**ohm′ic** *adj.*

ohm·age (ō′mij) *n.* Electrical resistance of a conductor, expressed in ohms.

ohm·me·ter (ōm′mē′tər) *n.* A galvanometer having a dial or scale graduated to ohms and fractions of ohms, for measuring the resistance of a conductor.

o·ho (ō·hō′) *interj.* An exclamation expressing astonishment, exultation, etc.

-oid *suffix* Like; resembling; having the form of: *ovoid, hydroid.* [< F *-oïdes* < L *-oides* < Gk. *-oeidēs* < *eidos* form]

-oidea *combining form Zool.* Used to form the names of classes or superfamilies: *Asteroidea, Echinoidea.* [< Gk. *-oeidēs* resembling < *eidos* form]

oil (oil) *n.* **1** A greasy or unctuous, generally combustible liquid, of vegetable, animal, or mineral origin, insoluble in water but sometimes soluble in alcohol, and always in ether: variously used as food, for lubricating, illuminating, and fuel, and in the manufacture of soap, candles, cosmetics, perfumery, etc. **2** Petroleum. **3** An oil paint; also, an oil painting. **4** Anything of an oil consistency

5 Fawning or flattering speech; an apology or excuse. —*v.t.* **1** To smear, lubricate, or supply with oil. **2** To bribe; flatter. [< AF *olie,* OF *oile* < L *oleum* oil]

Oil may appear as a combining form in hyphemes or solidemes, or as the first element in two-word phrases; as in:

oil-bearing	oil-forming
oil box	oil-fueled
oil-bright	oil-gage
oil-burning	oil gas
oilcamp	oil groove
oil-carrying	oil harden
oil-containing	oil-hardened
oil crane	oil-hardening
oil cup	oil-heater
oil derrick	oilhole
oil-dispensing	oil industry
oil distiller	oil-insulated
oil-distributing	oil-laden
oil drill	oil-ladened
oil-driven	oil-land
oil engine	oil-lit
oil-fed	oil-press
oil-filled	oil producer
oil-finding	oil-producing
oil-finished	oilproof
oil-fired	oilproffing
oil-pumping	oil stove
oil-refiner	oil tanker
oil refining	oil tar
oil-regulating	oil-tempered
oil-rich	oil-testing
oil-saving	oil-thickening
oil-secreting	oiltight
oilskinned	oiltightness
oilsmelling	oil tube
oil-soaked	oilway
oil-stained	oil-yielding

oil·bird (oil′bûrd′) *n.* The guacharo.

oil burner **1** A furnace or heating unit that operates on oil fuel. **2** An atomizer for spraying oil into such a furnace.

oil·cake (oil′kāk′) *n.* The mass of compressed seeds of cotton, flax, etc., or coconut pulp from which oil has been expressed.

oil·can (oil′kan′) *n.* A can for holding lubricating or fuel oil.

oil·cloth (oil′klôth′, -kloth′) *n.* A cotton fabric coated on one side with a preparation of vegetable oils and pigments mixed with a clay filler, and sometimes ornamented with printed patterns: used for table, shelf, wall, or floor coverings, for bags, luggage, waterproofing, etc.

oil color A pigment ground in linseed or other oil, used chiefly by artists.

oil·er (oi′lər) *n.* **1** One who or that which oils; specifically, one who oils engines or machinery. **2** Any automatic device for oiling machinery. **3** A coat of oilskin. **4** A vessel for the transportation of oil.

oil field An oil-producing area, especially one under active exploitation.

oil gland **1** *Bot.* An oil-secreting gland, as in some plants. **2** *Ornithol.* The gland at the rump of a bird that secretes oil for the dressing of the plumage; the uropygial gland.

oil of lavender A yellow, fragrant oil distilled from the blossoms of lavender, especially the spike lavender: used in medicine and perfumery. Also **oil of spike.**

oil of turpentine See under TURPENTINE.

oil of vitriol Sulfuric acid.

oil of wintergreen Wintergreen (def. 2).

oil painting **1** The art of painting in oils. **2** A painting done in pigments mixed in oil.

oil·paper (oil′pā′pər) *n.* Paper treated with oil for transparency and resistance against moisture and dryness.

oil pool An accumulation of petroleum in sedimentary rocks, usually associated with characteristic geological features.

oil shale A compact, typically laminated, brown or black sedimentary shale impregnated with petroleum in varying proportions.

oil·skin (oil′skin′) *n.* Cloth made waterproof with drying oil, or a garment of such material.

oil slick A smooth area on the surface of water caused by a film of oil.

oil·stone (oil′stōn′) *n.* A smooth stone, used when moistened with oil for sharpening tools.

oil well A well or boring for petroleum.

oil·y (oi′lē) *adj.* **oil·i·er, oil·i·est** **1** Pertaining to

or containing oil. **2** Smeared, rubbed, soaked, or coated with oil. **3** Smooth or deceitfully affable. —**oil′i·ly** *adv.* —**oil′i·ness** *n.*

oi·nol·o·gy (oi·nol′ə·jē) See ENOLOGY.

oi·no·mel (oi′nə·mel) See OENOMEL.

oint·ment (oint′mənt) *n.* A fatty preparation, with which a medicine has been incorporated; an unguent. [< OF *oignement,* ult. < L *unguentum* an unguent; infl. in form by obs. *oint* anoint < F, pp. of *oindre* < L *unguere*]

O·jib·wa (ō·jib′wā) *n. pl.* ·**wa** or ·**was 1** One of a tribe of North American Indians of Algonquian linguistic stock, formerly inhabiting the regions around Lake Superior; Chippewa. **2** The Algonquian language of this tribe. Also **O·jib′way.** [< Algonquian (Ojibwa) *Ojibway* roast till puckered < *ojib* pucker + *ub-way* roast; with ref. to their puckered moccasin seams]

OK (ō′kā′) *interj., adj., & adv.* All correct; all right: expressing approval, agreement, etc. —*v.t.* (ō·kā′) **OK′d, OK′ing** To sign with an *OK;* endorse; approve. Also **O.K., o′kay′; o′keh′.** [< The Democratic *O.K.* Club, organized in 1840 to support President Martin Van Buren, nicknamed *Old Kinderhook,* from *Kinderhook,* N.Y., his birthplace]

o·ka·pi (ō·kä′pē) *n.* An African ruminant (*Okapia johnstoni*) related to the giraffe, but with a smaller body and a shorter neck. [< native Sudanic name]

O·kee·cho·bee (ō′kē·chō′bē), **Lake** A lake in south central Florida; 730 square miles; 35 miles long, 30 miles wide.

OKAPI

O·kla·ho·ma (ō′klə·hō′mə) A State in the south central United States; 69,919 square miles; capital, Oklahoma City; entered the Union Nov. 16, 1907; nickname *Sooner State:* abbr. OK — **O′kla·ho′man** *adj. & n.*

Oklahoma City The capital of Oklahoma.

o·kra (ō′krə) *n.* **1** A tall annual herb (*Hibiscus esculentus*) of African origin, cultivated for its edible capsules containing many mucilaginous seeds. **2** The fingerlike capsules of this plant or a dish prepared with them. Also called *gumbo.* [< Ashanti]

-ol¹ *suffix Chem.* Denoting an alcohol or phenol: *methanol, glycerol.* [< (ALCOH)OL]

-ol² *suffix Chem.* Var. of -OLE¹, as in *benzol.*

old (ōld) *adj.* **old·er** or **eld·er, old·est** or **eld·est 1** Having lived or existed in a certain state for a long time: said of things liable to decay: an *old* elm; having lived beyond the middle period of life; aged: opposed to *young.* **2** Exhibiting discretion and judgment or deportment like a mature and experienced person. **3** Having some specified age: used after the noun expressing time or age: a child two months *old.* **4** Having been made, used, or known for a long time: opposed to *new, fresh, recent,* or *modern;* belonging to an early or remote period of history or development; ancient; antique: the *old* Greeks, *old* coins; also, belonging to a period long past or just preceding the present; not the latest; previous; former. **5** Belonging to the former of two or the earliest of several things: the *Old* Testament. **6** Long cultivated; not newly tilled: *old* land; not of this year's harvest: *old* corn. **7** Worthless on account of age or repeated use; shabby; worn-out: an *old* coat; also, stale; trite: an *old* joke. **8** Continued or established for a long time; known or used long; familiar: used often as an epithet of kindness or friendship: an *old* comrade. **9** Having had long experience or practice; hence, crafty; cunning: an *old* offender, an *old* hand at farming. **10** A general term of endearment or kindly familiarity: *old* boy. **11** In physical geography, in the later stages of a cycle of development: said of topographic forms, streams, etc. **12** Signifying the primeval character of the devil: the *old* enemy. **13** *Colloq.* More than enough; plentiful; great; wonderful: a great *old* racket. —*n.* **1** Past time; days of old. **2** A long time; long standing: my friend of *old.* [OE *ald*] —**old′ness** *n. Synonyms (adj.):* aged, ancient, antiquated, antique, decrepit, elderly, gray, hoary, immemorial, obsolete, olden, patriarchal, remote, senile, time-honored, time-worn, venerable. That is termed *old* which has existed long, or which existed long ago. *Olden* is a statelier form of *old*, and is applied almost exclusively to time, not to places, buildings, persons, etc. As regards periods of time, the familiar are also the near; thus, the *old* times are not too far away for familiar thought and reference; the *olden* times are more remote, *ancient* times still further removed. *Aged* applies chiefly to long-extended human life. *Decrepit, gray,* and *hoary* refer to the effects of age on the body exclusively; *senile* upon the mind also; as, a *decrepit* frame, *senile* garrulousness. One may be *aged* and neither *decrepit* nor *senile. Elderly* is applied to those who have passed middle life, but scarcely reached *old* age. *Remote* primarily refers to space, but is extended to that which is far-off in time; as, at some *remote* period. See ANCIENT[1], OBSOLETE, PRIMEVAL. Compare ANTIQUE. *Antonyms:* compare synonyms for NEW, YOUTHFUL.

Old Baldy A peak in southern Colorado, in the Sangre de Cristo Mountains; 14,125 feet: also *Baldy.*

Old Colony Plymouth Colony.

old country The native land of any emigrant.

Old Dominion Nickname of VIRGINIA.

old·en (ōl'dən) *adj.* Old; ancient. See synonyms under ANCIENT[1], OLD.

Old English See under ENGLISH.

old-fan·gled (ōld'fang'gəld) *adj.* Having a fondness for what is old-fashioned. [<OLD + FANGLED; on analogy with NEW-FANGLED]

old-fash·ioned (ōld'fash'ənd) *adj.* 1 Having the characteristics or customs of former times; antiquated; old-time. 2 Having the notions or ways of an old person. See synonyms under ANTIQUE.

old fo·gy (fō'gē) A person of extremely conservative or old-fashioned ideas. Also **old fo'gey.**

old-fo·gy·ish (ōld'fō'gē·ish) *adj.* Of, pertaining to, or like an old fogy; extremely conservative or behind the times. Also **old'-fo'·gey·ish.**

Old French See under FRENCH.

Old Glory The flag of the United States.

old guard The conservative element in a community, political party, etc.

Old Guard The imperial guard formed by Napoleon I in 1804, composed of veterans of three campaigns. [Trans. of F *Vieille Garde*; so called in contrast with *Jeune Garde* Young Guard, formed 1810]

Old Hickory Nickname of Andrew Jackson.

Old High German See under GERMAN.

Old Icelandic See under ICELANDIC.

Old Irish See under IRISH.

Old Ironsides The U.S. frigate *Constitution*: in allusion to the hardness of her planking.

old·ish (ōl'dish) *adj.* Somewhat old.

Old Latin See under LATIN.

old-light (ōld'līt') *adj.* Favoring old principles; in Scottish ecclesiastical history denoting a party which favored union between church and state. — *n.* One who maintains old-light principles.

old-line (ōld'līn') *adj.* Traditional; conservative; following a beaten path.

Old Line State Nickname of MARYLAND.

old maid An elderly single woman; a spinster. — **old'-maid'ish** *adj.*

old man *Slang* 1 One's father. 2 One's husband. 3 Any man in a position of authority, as one's employer, the captain of a vessel, etc.; especially, the senior officer on board a ship. 4 Old Mr. —: *Old Man* Brown. 5 A term of address, as to a friend. 6 Among North American Indians, a wise man.

old-man's beard (ōld'manz') 1 Spanish moss. 2 The fringe tree. 3 The black gum.

Old Nick The devil.

Old Norse See under NORSE.

Old Northwest See NORTHWEST TERRITORY.

Old Persian See under PERSIAN.

Old Prussian See under PRUSSIAN.

old rose Any of various shades of grayish or purplish red.

Old Saxon See under SAXON.

Old Scandinavian See OLD NORSE under NORSE.

Old South The South before the Civil War.

old squaw A sea duck (*Clangula hyemalis*) of the northern hemisphere: also called *oldwife.*

old·ster (ōld'stər) *n. Colloq.* A person of advanced years; an old or elderly person.

Old Stone Age The Paleolithic period of human culture.

old·style (ōld'stīl') *n. Printing* A style of type first used in the 18th century, the downstrokes and the cross-strokes being of nearly the same thickness. Compare MODERN.

old·style (ōld'stīl') *adj.* Of a former style.

Old Style See GREGORIAN CALENDAR under CALENDAR.

Old Testament The first of the two main divisions of the Bible, containing the books of the old or Mosaic covenant, and including the historical books, the prophets, and the books of wisdom.

old-time (ōld'tīm') *adj.* Of long standing.

old-tim·er (ōld'tī'mər) *n. Colloq.* 1 One who has been a member, resided in a place, or filled a position for a long time. 2 An old-fashioned person.

old·wife (ōld'wīf') *n.* 1 Any of several fishes found in West Indian waters, as the parrotfish, the spot, alewife, menhaden, etc. 2 The old squaw.

old-wom·an·ish (ōld'woom'ən·ish) *adj.* Characteristic of an old woman; fussy.

old-world (ōld'wûrld') *adj.* 1 Of or pertaining to the Old World or eastern hemisphere; not American. 2 Prehistoric; antique.

Old World The eastern hemisphere.

-ole *suffix Chem.* 1 Denoting a heterocyclic compound having five members in the ring and two hetero atoms: *pyrrole.* 2 Denoting certain aldehydes and ethers. Also spelled *-ol.* [<L *oleum* oil]

-ole[2] *suffix* Small; little: *nucleole, petiole.* [<L *-olus,* a diminutive suffix]

o·le·a·ceous (ō'lē·ā'shəs) *adj.* Designating a family (*Oleaceae*) of shrubs and trees; the olive family. It includes many widely distributed plants, including the lilac, jasmine, and ash. [<NL <L *olea* an olive tree]

o·le·ag·i·nous (ō'lē·aj'ə·nəs) *adj.* Pertaining to oil; oily. [<F *oléagineux* <L *oleaginus* pertaining to the olive < *olea* an olive tree] — **o'le·ag'i·nous·ly** *adv.* — **o'le·ag'i·nous·ness** *n.*

o·le·an·der (ō'lē·an'dər) *n.* An Old World evergreen ornamental shrub (*Nerium oleander*) with leathery leaves yielding a poisonous glycoside with medicinal properties, and clusters of fragrant, rose or white flowers. [<MF *oléandre* <Med. L *oleander* <LL *lorandrum,* ? alter. of L *rhododendron* RHODODENDRON]

o·le·as·ter (ō'lē·as'tər) *n.* An ornamental shrub or small tree (*Elaeagnus angustifolia*) of western Asia and southern Europe, with fragrant, yellow flowers; the Russian wild olive. [<L < *olea* an olive tree]

o·le·ate (ō'lē·āt) *n. Chem.* A salt or ester of oleic acid.

o·lec·ra·non (ō·lek'rə·non, ō'lə·krā'non) *n. Anat.* The curved process of the ulnar bone, marking its juncture with the humerus; the point of the elbow. [<Gk. *ōlekranon,* contraction of *ōlenokranon* head or point of the elbow < *ōlenē* elbow + *kranion* head, skull] — **o·lec'ra·nal** *adj.*

o·le·fi·ant (ō'lə·fī'ənt, ō·lē'fē·ənt) *adj.* Producing oil. [<F (*gaz*) *oléfiant* olefiant (gas), ppr. of *oléfier* make oil <L *oleum* oil + *facere* make]

olefiant gas Ethylene.

o·le·fin (ō'lə·fin) *n.* Alkene. [<OLEF(IANT) + -IN] — **o'le·fin'ic** *adj.*

o·le·ic (ō·lē'ik, ō'lē-) *adj.* Of, pertaining to, or derived from oil. [<L *oleum* oil + -IC]

oleic acid *Chem.* An oily compound, $C_{17}H_{33}$·CO_2H, contained as an ester in most mixed oils and fats, and obtained by saponification with an alkali.

o·le·in (ō'lē·in) *n. Chem.* A colorless liquid glyceride of oleic acid, the chief constituent of fatty oils: also *elain.* Also **o·le·ine** (ō'lē·in, ō'li·ēn). [<F *oléine* <L *oleum* oil]

o·le·o (ō'lē·ō) Short for OLEOMARGARINE.

oleo- *combining form* 1 Oil; of oil: *oleoresin.* 2 Olein; oleic: *oleomargarine.* [<L *oleum* oil]

o·le·o·graph (ō'lē·ə·graf', -gräf') *n.* 1 A chromolithograph imitating an oil painting. 2 The pattern assumed by a drop of oil placed on water. [<OLEO- + -GRAPH] — **o·le·og·ra·pher** (ō'lē·og'rə·fər) *n.* — **o'le·o·graph'ic** *adj.* — **o'le·og'ra·phy** *n.*

o·le·o·mar·ga·rine (ō'lē·ō·mär'jə·rin, -rēn, -gə-) *n.* Margarine. [<OLEO- + MARGARINE]

oleo oil Beef tallow, obtained as a yellow liquid consisting of olein with a small amount of palmitin: used in making margarine, soap, and as a base for some lubricants.

o·le·o·res·in (ō'lē·ō·rez'in) *n.* 1 A native compound of an essential oil and a resin. 2 A pharmaceutical preparation consisting of a fixed or volatile oil containing a resin and sometimes other active matter in solution.

ol·fac·tie (ol·fak'tē) *n. Physiol.* A unit of measurement of olfactory sensation, equal to the lowest perceptible concentration of a given scent. Also **ol·fac'ty.** [Coined by Dr. Zwaardemaker, 19th c. Dutch scientist, inventor of the olfactometer]

ol·fac·tion (ol·fak'shən) *n.* The act, sense, or process of smelling; scent. [<L *olfactus.* See OLFACTORY.]

ol·fac·tom·e·ter (ol'fak·tom'ə·tər) *n.* An instrument for measuring the keenness of the sense of smell. [<OLFACTO(RY) + -METER]

ol·fac·to·ry (ol·fak'tər·ē, -trē) *adj.* Pertaining to the sense of smell. — *n. pl.* **·ries** 1 *Usually pl.* The organ of smell. 2 The capacity to smell. [<L *olfactus,* pp. of *olfacere* smell < *olere* have a smell + *facere* make]

o·lib·a·num (ō·lib'ə·nəm) *n.* A gum resin; Oriental frankincense. [<Med. L <LL *libanum* <Gk. *libanos* <Arabic *al-lubān* the frankincense]

ol·i·garch (ol'ə·gärk) *n.* A ruler in an oligarchy. [<Gk. *oligarchēs* < *oligos* few + *archein* rule]

ol·i·gar·chy (ol'ə·gär'kē) *n. pl.* **·chies** A form of government in which supreme power is restricted to a few. [Prob. <Med. L *oligarchia* <Gk. < *oligarchēs.* See OLIGARCH.] — **ol'i·gar'chic, ol'i·gar'chal, ol'i·gar'chi·cal** *adj.*

oligo- *combining form* Small; few; scanty: *oligocythemia.* Also, before vowels, **olig-.** [<Gk. *oligos* few]

Ol·i·go·cene (ol'ə·gō·sēn') *n. Geol.* The third in order of age of the geological epochs or series comprised in the Lower Tertiary system. — *adj.* Of or pertaining to the Oligocene. [<OLIGO- + Gk. *kainos* new, recent]

ol·i·go·chaete (ol'ə·gō·kēt') *n.* One of a class (*Oligochaeta*) of fresh-water and terrestrial, hermaphroditic annelid worms, including the earthworms, which lack a distinct head. — *adj.* Of or pertaining to the Oligochaeta. Also **ol'i·go·chete'.** [<NL <Gk. *oligos* few + *chaitē* bristle, mane; so called because it has a small number of bristly locomotive organs] — **ol'i·go·chae'tous** (-kē'təs) *adj.*

ol·i·go·clase (ol'ə·gō·klās') *n.* A massive, vitreous, whitish, triclinic soda-lime feldspar. [<OLIGO- + Gk. *klasis* a fracture < *klaein* break]

ol·i·go·chro·me·mi·a (ol'ə·gō·krō·mē'mē·ə) *n. Pathol.* A deficiency of hemoglobin in the blood. [<NL *oligochromaemia* <Gk. *oligos* few + *chrōma* color + *haima* blood]

ol·i·go·cy·the·mi·a (ol'ə·gō·sī·thē'mē·ə) *n. Pathol.* A deficiency or diminution of the red blood corpuscles. Also **ol'i·go·cy·thae'mi·a.** [<NL *oligocythaemia* <Gk. *oligos* few + *kytos* hollow, a cell + *haima* blood]

ol·i·go·gen·ics (ol'ə·gō·jen'iks) *n.* Limitation in the number of children; birth control. [<OLIGO- + (EU)GENICS]

ol·i·go·phre·ni·a (ol'ə·gō·frē'nē·ə) *n.* Arrested mental development. [<NL <Gk. *oligos* little + *phrēn* mind] — **ol'i·go·phren'ic** (-fren'ik) *adj.*

ol·i·gop·o·ly (ol'ə·gop'ə·lē) *n. pl.* **·lies** A form of monopoly in which the effective control of a market is exercised by a limited number of competitive sellers. [<OLIGO- + (MONO)P-OLY]

ol·i·gop·so·ny (ol'ə·gop'sə·nē) *n. pl.* **·nies** A market condition in which the purchase of goods and services is restricted to a few buyers. [<OLIG(O)- + Gk. *opsōneein* buy victuals]

ol·i·go·syn·thet·ic (ol′ə·gō·sin·thet′ik) *adj.* **1** Based upon or derived from a few essential components. **2** *Ling.* Describing a language whose lexicon is composed of relatively few roots.

o·li·o (ō′lē·ō) *n. pl.* **o·li·os 1** A miscellaneous collection, as of musical pieces or numbers; a medley. **2** An olla podrida; a seasoned meat and vegetable stew. [<OLLA]

ol·i·va·ceous (ol′ə·vā′shəs) *adj.* Olive-green. [<NL *olivaceus* <L *oliva* an olive]

ol·i·var·y (ol′ə·ver′ē) *adj.* **1** Like an olive, especially in shape. **2** *Anat.* Relating to the **olivary body**, an olive-shaped eminence containing a nucleus of gray matter, found at either side of the medulla oblongata. [<L *olivarius* belonging to olives <*oliva* an olive]

ol·ive (ol′iv) *n.* **1** An evergreen tree (*Olea europaea*) with leathery leaves, hard yellow wood, and an oily fruit. **2** The fruit of the olive tree. **3** A dull, medium yellowish-green color, like that of the unripe olive: also called **olive green. 4** An olive branch. —*adj.* **1** Pertaining to the olive. **2** Having a dull yellowish-green color. [<OF <L *oliva* an olive]

OLIVE
a. Flowering branch.
b. Floret.
c. Olive (fruit).

olive branch 1 A branch of the olive tree, as an emblem of peace. **2** *pl.* Offspring; children: alluding to *Psalms* cxxviii 3.

olive drab 1 Any of several shades of greenish-brown. **2** A woolen material of this color, used for uniforms by the United States Army. —**ol′ive-drab′** (-drab′) *adj.*

olive oil Oil expressed from olives; used in making salad dressings, soap, etc.

ol·i·vine (ol′ə·vēn, -vin) *n.* **1** Chrysolite. **2** Green garnet: used as a gem. [<L *oliva* an olive + -INE²]

ol·la (ol′ə, *Sp.* ô′lyä, ô′yä) *n.* **1** A wide-mouthed pot or jar, usually of earthenware. **2** An olla podrida. [<Sp. <L *olla* a pot]

ol·la po·dri·da (ol′ə pə·drē′də, *Sp.* ô′lyä pō·thrē′thä, ô′yä) **1** A dish of meat and vegetables, usually highly seasoned, cooked together. **2** Any heterogeneous mixture or miscellany. [<Sp., lit., a putrid pot <*olla* an olla + *podrida* putrid <L *putridus*]

ol·o·gy (ol′ə·jē) *n. pl.* **·gies** *Colloq.* A science or branch of learning: a humorous term. [<-LOGY]

o·ly·koek (ō′lē·kōōk) *n. U.S. Dial.* A Dutch cake made like a cruller. [<Du. *oliekoek* a doughnut]

O·lym·pi·a (ō·lim′pē·ə) **1** An ancient city on a plain near Elis in western Peloponnesus, Greece; scene of the Olympic games. **2** A port on Puget Sound; capital of Washington.

O·lym·pi·ad (ō·lim′pē·ad) *n.* **1** The interval of four years between two successive celebrations of the Olympic games, by which intervals the ancient Greeks reckoned time: sometimes erroneously used to designate the games or their celebration. **2** The modern Olympic games. [<MF *Olympiade* <L *Olympias, -adis* <Gk. *Olympias, -ados* <*Olympios* OLYMPIAN]

O·lym·pi·an (ō·lim′pē·ən) *adj.* **1** Pertaining to the great gods of Olympus or to Mount Olympus itself; hence, of eminent, godlike power, excellence, or manner. **2** Pertaining to Olympia or to the Olympic games. Also **O·lym′pic. 3** Grandly disinterested, and likely to be impractical: an *Olympian* proposal to eliminate crime. —*n.* **1** One of the higher gods of Greek mythology, twelve in number, who dwelt on Mount Olympus. **2** A contestant in the Olympic games. **3** A resident or native of Olympia. [<LL *Olympianus* <L *Olympius* <Gk. *Olympios* <*Olympia* Olympia, the Olympic games]

Olympic games 1 Athletic games and races held at the chief ancient Pan-Hellenic festival, which was celebrated every four years at Olympia in honor of Zeus. See OLYMPIAD. **2** A modern revival of the old contests, held every four years at some city chosen for this event, beginning with Athens in 1896. Also **Olympian games, Olympics.**

O·lym·pus (ō·lim′pəs) *n.* **1** The highest mountain of Greece, between Thessaly and Macedonia on the Aegean, regarded in Greek mythology as the home of the Olympian gods; 9,570 feet. Also **Mount O·lym′pus. 2** Any abode of gods; also, the sky; heaven.

Om (ōm) *n.* **1** In Hinduism, a mystic ejaculation representing the name of the Supreme Being, uttered on solemn occasions of invocation to Brahma. **2** In modern occultism, the spiritual essence. [<Skt.]

-oma *suffix Med.* Tumor; morbid growth: *carcinoma.* [<Gk. *-ōma*]

O·ma·ha (ō′mə·hä, -hô) *n.* One of a Siouan tribe of North American Indians now living in Nebraska. [<Siouan (Omaha), lit., those going upstream]

Omaha Beach A name given to that part of the Normandy coast where units of the United States Army landed on June 6, 1944, during the Allied invasion of France, World War II.

O·man (ō′man, ō·man′, ō·män′) **1** The coastal region of the eastern promontory (**Oman Promontory**) of the Arabian peninsula. **2** Muscat and Oman. See TRUCIAL OMAN.

Oman, Gulf of A NW arm of the Arabian Sea between the Oman section of the Arabian peninsula and Iran.

O·mar Khay·yám (ō′mär kī·äm′, ō′mər), died 1123?, Persian poet and astronomer; author of the *Rubáiyát.*

o·ma·sum (ō·mā′səm) *n. pl.* **·sa** (-sə) The manyplies or third stomach of a ruminant; the psalterium. [<NL <L, bullock's tripe, paunch]

om·ber (om′bər) *n.* A gambling game played with 40 cards, popular in the 18th century; also, the player undertaking to win the pool in this game. Also **om′bre.** [<F *ombre* <Sp. *hombre* a man <L *homo, hominis*]

ombro- *combining form* Rain: *ombrophilous.* Also, before vowels, **ombr-.** [<Gk. *ombros* rain]

om·broph·i·lous (om·brof′ə·ləs) *adj. Bot.* Relating to or characterizing plants able to withstand much rain. [<OMBRO- + -PHILOUS] —**om·bro·phile** (om′brə·fīl, -fil) *n.*

om·buds·man (om·budz′mən) *n. pl.* **·men** (-mən) A government official appointed to receive and report grievances against the government. [<Sw.]

-ome *combining form Bot.* Group; mass; body: *caulome.* [<Gk. *-ōma.* See -OMA.]

om·e·let (om′ə·lit, om′lit) *n.* A dish of eggs, etc., beaten together and cooked in a frying pan. Also **om′e·lette.** [<F *omelette* <OF *amelette* <*alemette,* lit., a thin plate <*alemelle* <*la lemelle, lamelle* <L *lamella.* See LAMELLA.]

o·men (ō′mən) *n.* A phenomenon or incident regarded as a prophetic sign. See synonyms under SIGN. —*v.t.* To foretell as or by an omen; presage; preshadow. [<L]

o·men·tum (ō·men′təm) *n. pl.* **·ta** (-tə) *Anat.* A free fold of the peritoneum passing between certain of the viscera. The **small omentum** passes from the lesser curvature of the stomach to the liver; the **great omentum** from the lower border of the stomach to the transverse colon, lying in front of the intestines like an apron. [<NL <L, a membrane enclosing the bowels] —**o·men′tal** *adj.*

om·i·nous (om′ə·nəs) *adj.* **1** Of the nature of or marked by an omen or by a presentiment of evil; portentous; ill-omened: *ominous* fears. **2** Serving as an omen in general; prognostic. [<L *ominosus* <*omen, ominis* an omen] —**om′i·nous·ly** *adv.* —**om′i·nous·ness** *n.*

o·mis·si·ble (ō·mis′ə·bəl) *adj.* That can be omitted; subject to omission.

o·mis·sion (ō·mish′ən) *n.* **1** The act of omitting or state of being omitted or neglected. **2** Anything omitted or neglected. **3** Neglect or failure to do something that can and should be done; also, an instance of this. See synonyms under ERROR. [<L *omissio, -onis* <*omissus,* pp. of *omittere* OMIT] —**o·mis·sive** (ō·mis′iv) *adj.* —**o·mis′sive·ly** *adv.*

o·mit (ō·mit′) *v.t.* **o·mit·ted, o·mit·ting 1** To leave out; fail to include. **2** To fail to do, make, etc.; neglect or forbear. [<L *omittere* let go <*ob-* down, away + *mittere* send]

om·ma·tid·i·um (om′ə·tid′ē·əm) *n. pl.* **·tid·i·a** (-tid′ē·ə) *Zool.* One of the simple elements of a compound eye, as in arthropods. [<NL, dim. of Gk. *omma, -atos* an eye] —**om′ma·tid′i·al** *adj.*

om·mat·o·phore (ə·mat′ə·fôr, -fōr) *n. Zool.* An eyestalk, as of a snail. [<NL *ommatophorus* <Gk. *omma, -atos* eye + *-phoros* bearing <*pherein* bear] —**om·ma·toph·o·rous** (om′ə·tof′ər·əs) *adj.*

omni- *combining form* All; totally: *omnipotent.* [<L *omnis* all]

om·ni·bus (om′nə·bəs, -bus) *n.* **1** A long passenger vehicle sometimes with two decks; a bus. **2** A printed anthology, either of works by a single author or of short stories, poems, etc., of the same general type: an *omnibus* of Westerns; a Conrad *omnibus.* **3** An omnibus box. —*adj.* Covering a full collection of objects or cases: an *omnibus* bill. [<F <L, for all, dat. pl. of *omnis* all]

omnibus bar A bus bar.

omnibus bill Any legislative bill or act, or section thereof, containing miscellaneous unrelated provisions.

omnibus box A large box or loge on a level with the stage of a theater.

om·ni·di·rec·tion·al (om′ni·di·rek′shən·əl) *adj. Telecom.* Capable of or adapted for operating equally well in all directions, as a radio transmitter or antenna.

om·ni·far·i·ous (om′nə·fâr′ē·əs) *adj.* Of all varieties, forms, or kinds. [<L *omnifarius* <*omnis* all + *fari* speak]

om·nif·er·ous (om·nif′ər·əs) *adj.* Producing all kinds. [<L *omnifer* <*omnis* all + *ferre* bear]

om·nif·ic (om·nif′ik) *adj.* All-creating. [<Med. L *omnificus* <*omnis* all + *facere* make]

om·nip·a·rous (om·nip′ə·rəs) *adj.* Producing or bearing all things. [<LL *omniparus* <*omnis* all + *parere* produce]

om·nip·o·tence (om·nip′ə·təns) *n.* **1** Unlimited and universal power, as a divine attribute; hence, **Omnipotence** God. **2** Unlimited power within a certain sphere, or of a certain kind. Also **om·nip′o·ten·cy.**

om·nip·o·tent (om·nip′ə·tənt) *adj.* Almighty; not limited in authority or power. —**The Omnipotent** God. [<OF <L *omnipotens, -entis* <*omnis* all + *potens, -entis* able, powerful] —**om·nip′o·tent·ly** *adv.*

om·ni·pres·ence (om′nə·prez′əns) *n.* The quality of being everywhere present at the same time; ubiquity. [<Med. L *omnipraesentia* <*omnipraesens, -entis* <L *omnis* all + *praesens, -entis* present] —**om′ni·pres′ent** *adj.*

om·ni·range (om′nə·rānj) *n. Aeron.* A network of very-high-frequency radio beams emitted simultaneously in all directions from a system of ground stations, permitting aircraft pilots to chart their courses and positions anywhere within range of the network. [<L *omnis* all + RANGE]

om·nis·cience (om·nish′əns) *n.* **1** Infinite knowledge: an attribute of God; hence, **Omniscience** God. **2** Loosely, very extensive knowledge. Also **om·nis′cien·cy.**

om·nis·cient (om·nish′ənt) *adj.* Knowing all things; all-knowing. —**The Omniscient** God. [<NL *omnisciens, -entis* <L *omnis* all + *sciens, -entis,* ppr. of *scire* know] —**om·nis′cient·ly** *adv.*

om·ni·um-gath·er·um (om′nē·əm·gath′ər·əm) *n.* A miscellaneous collection; a medley. [<L *omnium,* genitive pl. of *omnis* all + GATHER + L *-um,* neut. suffix]

om·niv·o·rous (om·niv′ər·əs) *adj.* **1** Eating food of all kinds indiscriminately; hence, greedy. **2** Eating both animal and vegetable food: said of bears, crows, etc. [<L *omnivorus* <*omnis* all + *vorare* devour] —**om·niv′o·rous·ly** *adv.* —**om·niv′o·rous·ness** *n.*

o·mo·pha·gi·a (ō′mə·fā′jē·ə) *n.* The eating of raw flesh. Also **o·moph·a·gy** (ō·mof′ə·jē). [<NL <Gk. *ōmophagia* <*ōmos* raw + *phagein* eat] —**o·mo·phag·ic** (ōmə·faj′ik), **o·moph·a·gous** (ō·mof′ə·gəs) *adj.* —**o·moph·a·gist** (ō·mof′ə·jist) *n.*

on (on, ôn) *prep.* **1** In contact with the upper surface of; above and supported by: lying *on* the ground. **2** In contact with any surface or part of: a blow *on* the head. **3** So as to be suspended from: a puppet *on* a string. **4** Directed or moving along the course of: Be *on* your way. **5** Near; adjacent to: the town *on* the river bank; the store *on* your right. **6** Within the duration of: He arrived *on* my birthday. **7** At the moment or point of: *on* the hour; at the time of: He withdrew *on* my speaking thus. **8** In a state or condition of: *on* fire; *on* record. **9** By means of; with the support of: *on* wheels; *on* all fours. **10** Using as a means of sustenance, activity, etc.: living *on* fruit. **11** Accumulated with; in addition to: thousands *on* thousands of them. **12** Sustained or confirmed by; with the authority of: committed *on* purpose; I swear to it *on* my honor. **13** In the interest or favor of: betting *on* a horse. **14** Concerning; about: a work *on* economics. **15** Engaged in; occupied or connected with: *on* a journey; *on* duty all night. **16** As a consequence or result of: making a profit *on* tips. **17** In accordance with or relation to; in terms of: measured *on* the Centigrade scale. **18** Directed, tending, or moving toward or against: making war *on* the enemy. **19** Following after: disease *on* the heels of famine. **20** *Colloq.* With; accompanying, as about one's person: Do you have five dollars *on* you? **21** *Colloq.* At the expense of; paid by: The joke is *on* them; drinks *on* the house. See synonyms under ABOVE, AT. —**to have something on** *U.S. Colloq.* To have knowledge, possess evidence, etc., against (a person). —*adv.* **1** In or into a position or condition of contact, adherence, covering, etc.: He put his hat *on.* **2** In the direction of something: He looked *on* while they played. **3** In advance; ahead, in space or time: a collision head *on* ; later *on.* **4** In continuous course or succession: The music went *on.* **5** In or into operation, performance, or existence: to turn the electricity *on.* —**and so on** And like what has gone before; et cetera. —**on and on** Without interruption; continuously. —**to be on to** To be aware of or informed about (someone, something, etc.); understand. —*adj.* **1** In operation, progress, or application: The play is *on*; The brake is *on.* **2** Near; located nearer. **3** In cricket, indicating or pertaining to the side of the wicket and field where the batsman stands. —*n.* **1** The state or fact of being on. **2** In cricket, the on side of the field or wicket. [OE *on, an*]

on·a·ger (on′ə-jər) *n. pl.* **·gers** or **·gri** (-grī) **1** A wild ass *(Equus onager)* of central Asia. **2** A medieval military engine by which stones were hurled with a slinglike device. [< L, a wild ass < Gk. *onagros* < *onos* an ass.+ *agrios* wild]

on·a·gra·ceous (on′ə-grā′shəs) *adj.* Pertaining to or designating a family *(Onagraceae)* of plants of temperate climates; the evening-primrose family. [< NL < L *onagra*, fem. of *onager* ONAGER]

o·nan·ism (ō′nən-iz′əm) *n.* **1** Withdrawal before orgasm; incomplete coitus. **2** Masturbation. [after *Onan.* See *Gen.* xxxviii 9.] —**o′nan·ist** *n.* —**o·nan·is′tic** *adj.*

once (wuns) *adv.* **1** One time, without repetition. **2** During some past time. **3** At any time; ever; also, at some future time. —*adj.* Former; formerly existing; quondam. —*conj.* As soon as; whenever. —*n.* One time. —**all at once** All of a sudden. —**at once. 1** Simultaneously. **2** Immediately. —**once for all** Finally. —**once in a while** Occasionally. —**this once** On this occasion only. [ME *ones,* OE *anes,* genitive of *an* one]

once-o·ver (wuns′ō′vər) *n. Slang* **1** A quick glance or survey. **2** A brief but comprehensive application of labor or study.

On·cid·i·um (on-sid′ē-əm) *n.* A large, varied genus of tropical American orchids with few leaves, and a loose raceme of striking flowers. They are among the most prized of cultivated orchids, *O. papilio,* the butterfly orchid, being one of the best-known. [< NL < Gk. *onkos* an arrow's barb; so called from the form of the lower petal]

on·co·gen·e·sis (on′kō-jen′ə-sis) *n.* The formation and development of tumors. —**on′co·gen′ic** *adj.* —**on′co·ge·ni′ci·ty** *n.*

on·col·o·gy (on-kol′ə-jē) *n.* The science of tumors. [< Gk. *onkos* bulk, a tumor + -LOGY] —**on·co·log′ic** (on′kə-loj′ik), **·i·cal** *adj.* —**on·col′o·gist** *n.*

on·com·ing (on′kum′ing) *adj.* Approaching. —*n.* An approach.

on·do·gram (on′də-gram) *n.* The record made by an ondograph. [< F *onde* a wave (< L *unda*) + -(O)GRAM]

on·do·graph (on′də-graf, -gräf) *n.* An instrument by which electric wave forms, especially those of alternating currents, are recorded autographically. [< F *onde* a wave (< L *unda*) + -(O)GRAPH]

on·dom·e·ter (on-dom′ə-tər) *n.* A meter for registering the frequency of electromagnetic waves. [< F *onde* a wave (< L *unda*) + -(O)METER]

one (wun) *adj.* **1** Being a single individual or object; being a unit. **2** Being an individual or thing thought of as indefinite. **3** Designating a person, thing, or group as contrasted with another; this; that. **4** Single in kind; the same; closely united or alike. **5** Unitary. —*n.* **1** A single unit; the cardinal number preceding two; also, a symbol (1, i, I) representing this number. **2** A single thing or person. —*pron.* **1** Someone or something; anyone or anything. **2** One of certain persons or things already mentioned. **3** Of the same or of no consequence. —**one another** Each other: said of an action or relation involving two or more persons or things reciprocally: They love *one another.* —**one by one** Singly and in succession. —**one day** Some indefinite day or period in the past or future. [OE *ān*]

-one *suffix Chem.* Denoting an organic compound of the ketone group: *acetone.* [< Gk. *-ōnē,* fem. patronymic]

O·nei·da (ō-nī′də) *n.* A member of a tribe of North American Indians of Iroquoian stock.

o·nei·rism (ō-nī′riz-əm) *n. Psychol.* A psychic condition induced by or resembling dreams but prolonged into the waking period. Compare HYPNOPOMPIC. [< Gk. *oneiros* a dream]

oneiro- *combining form* Dream; of dreams: *oneiromancy*: also *oniro-.* Also, before vowels, **oneir-.** [< Gk. *oneiros* a dream]

o·nei·ro·crit·ic (ō-nī′rə-krit′ik) *adj.* Pertaining to or professing power to interpret dreams: also **o·nei′ro·crit′i·cal.** —*n.* One who interprets dreams. [< Gk. *oneirokritikos* pertaining to the interpretation of dreams < *oneiros* a dream + *kritikos* able to discern < *krinein* judge] —**o·nei′ro·crit′i·cal·ly** *adv.*

one-lin·er (wun′lī′nər) *n. Colloq.* A brief remark, meant to be humorous, clever, critical, etc., often used by a comedian in a performance.

one·ness (wun′nis) *n.* **1** Singleness; unity; sameness. **2** Agreement; concord. **3** Quality of being unique. See synonyms under UNION.

on·er·ous (on′ər-əs) *adj.* **1** Burdensome or oppressive. **2** *Law* Legally liable for an obligation or subject to a burden: opposed to *gratuitous.* See synonyms under ARDUOUS, DIFFICULT. [< OF *onereus* < L *onerosus* < *onus, oneris* a burden] —**on′er·ous·ly** *adv.* —**on′er·ous·ness** *n.*

on·er·y (on′ər-ē) See ORNERY.

one·self (wun′self′, wunz′-) *pron.* One's own self or personality; himself or herself.

one-sid·ed (wun′sī′did) *adj.* **1** Of or pertaining to but one side; hence, partial; unfair; inadequate. **2** Unequal-sided, as elm leaves. **3** Unilateral. —**one′-sid′ed·ly** *adv.* —**one′-sid′ed·ness** *n.*

one-step (wun′step′) *n.* **1** A round dance consisting of a long step in two-four time. **2** The ragtime music for such a dance.

one-time (wun′tīm′) *adj.* Former; quondam.

one-way (wun′wā′) *adj.* **1** Moving in one direction only: *one-way* traffic. **2** Permitting traffic in one direction only.

on·go·ing (on′gō′ing) *adj.* Going on, continuing, or progressing.

on·ion (un′yən) *n.* **1** A field-grown edible bulb of an herb *(Allium cepa)* of the lily family; a succulent vegetable remarkable for its pungent odor and taste. **2** One of various allied plants. [< OF *oignon* < L *unio, -onis* unity, a pearl, an onion. Doublet of UNION.]

on·ion·skin (un′yən-skin′) *n.* A thin, translucent paper.

oniro- See ONEIRO-.

on-line (on′lin′, ôn′-) *adj.* Directly connected to, and controlled by, an electronic computer.

on·look·er (on′look′ər, ôn′-) *n.* One who looks on; a spectator.

on·look·ing (on′look′ing, ôn′-) *adj.* **1** Looking on. **2** Looking forward.

on·ly (ōn′lē) *adv.* **1** Without another or others; singly. **2** In one manner or for one purpose

alone. **3** In full; wholly. **4** Solely; merely; exclusively: limiting a statement to a single defined person, thing, or number. —*adj.* **1** Alone in its class; having no fellow or mate; sole; single; solitary. **2** *an only* child. **2** Standing alone by reason of excellence. See synonyms under SOLITARY. —*conj.* Except that; but. [OE *ānlic* < *ān* one + *-lic* -LY]

on·ly-be·got·ten (ōn′lē-bi-got′n) *adj.* Begotten as the sole issue or undisputed and incontestable heir: the *only-begotten* Son of God.

on·o·mas·tics (on′ə-mas′tiks) *n. pl. (construed as sing.)* The study of the origin and evolution of proper names.

on·o·mat·o·ma·ni·a (on′ə-mat′ə-mā′nē-ə, -mān′yə, ō-nom′ə-tə-) *n.* A morbid dread of some particular word or name, or an irresistible impulse to repeat it. [< NL < Gk. *onoma, -atos* a name + *mania* madness]

on·o·mat·o·poe·ia (on′ə-mat′ə-pē′ə, ō-nom′ə-tə-) *n.* **1** The formation of words in imitation of natural sounds, as *crack, splash,* or *bow-wow.* **2** An imitative word. **3** The selection and use of such words. Also **on′o·mat·o·po·e′sis** (-pō-ē′sis), **on′o·mat′o·py** (-mat′ə-pē). [< L < Gk. *onomatopoiia* the making of words < *onoma, -atos* name + *poieein* make] —**on′o·mat′o·poe′ic** or **·i·cal, on′o·mat′o·po·et′ic** (-pō-et′ik) *adj.* —**on′o·mat′o·po·et′i·cal·ly** *adv.*

On·on·da·ga (on′ən-dô′gə, -dä′-) *n.* **1** One of a tribe of North American Indians of Iroquoian stock formerly living in New York and Ontario. **2** *Geol.* A limestone formation of the lower portion of the Devonian period. [< Iroquoian *ononta′gē,* lit., on top of the hill] —**On′on·da′gan** *adj.*

on·rush (on′rush′, ôn′-) *n.* An onward rush or flow.

on·set (on′set′, ôn′-) *n.* **1** An impetuous attack; assault, as of troops. **2** An attack, as of fever; seizure, as of passion. **3** A setting about; outset. See synonyms under ATTACK.

on·shore (on′shôr′, -shōr′, ôn′-) *adv. & adj.* To, toward, or on the shore.

on·side (on′sīd′, ôn′-) *adv.* Not off-side; in position to legally play.

on·slaught (on′slôt′, ôn′-) *n.* A violent hostile assault. See synonyms under AGGRESSION, ATTACK. [Earlier *anslacht,* prob. < Du. *annslag* a striking at, attempt < *slagen* strike; refashioned after *draught, slaughter,* etc.]

on·to (on′too, ôn′-) *prep.* **1** Upon the top of; to and upon: The cat jumped *onto* the table. **2** *Colloq.* Aware of; informed about: I'm *onto* your tricks. Also written **on to.**

onto- *combining form* Being; existence: *ontogeny.* Also, before vowels, **ont-.** [< Gk. *ōn, ontos,* ppr. of *einai* be]

on·tog·e·ny (on-toj′ə-nē) *n. Biol.* The history of the development of the individual organism: distinguished from *phylogeny.* Also **on·to·gen·e·sis** (on′tō-jen′ə-sis). [< ONTO- + -GENY] —**on·to·ge·net·ic** (on′tō-jə-net′ik), **on′to·gen′ic** (-jen′ik) *adj.* —**on·tog′e·nist** *n.*

on·tol·o·gism (on-tol′ə-jiz′əm) *n.* The doctrine that man has an immediate and certain knowledge of God, and that this knowledge is the foundation and guaranty of all his knowledge: opposed to *psychologism.*

on·tol·o·gy (on-tol′ə-jē) *n.* The science of real being; the philosophical theory of reality; the doctrine of the universal and necessary characteristics of all existence. Compare METAPHYSICS, PHILOSOPHY. [< NL *ontologia* < Gk. *ōn, ontos* being + *-logia* < *logos* word, study] —**on·tol′o·gist** *n.*

o·nus (ō′nəs) *n.* A burden or responsibility; a duty. [< L]

on·ward (on′wərd, ôn′-) *adv.* **1** In the direction of progress; forward; ahead. **2** On in time. Also **on′wards.** —*adj.* Moving or leading forward or ahead.

on·yx (on′iks) *n.* A cryptocrystalline variety of quartz consisting of layers of different colors, usually in even planes; a variety of chalcedony. [< Gk., a nail, onyx]

oo- *combining form* **1** Egg; pertaining to eggs: *oology.* **2** *Biol.* An ovum; *oogenesis.* [< Gk. *ōon* egg]

o·o·cyte (ō′ə-sīt) *n. Biol.* **1** An egg which has not reached full development. **2** An immature female gamete, as in certain protozoans. [<OO- + -CYTE]

o·og·a·my (ō·og′ə·mē) *n. Biol.* The union of two gametes of different size and form, called egg and sperm cells. Compare ISOGAMY. [<OO- + -GAMY] —**o·og′a·mous** *adj.*

o·o·gen·e·sis (ō′ə·jen′ə·sis) *n. Biol.* The origin and development of the ovum. Also **o·og·e·ny** (ō·oj′ə·nē). —**o′o·ge·net′ic** (-jə·net′ik) *adj.*

o·o·go·ni·um (ō′ə·gō′nē·əm) *n. pl.* **·ni·a** (-nē·ə) 1 *Bot.* The female reproductive organ in thallophytic plants, a large spherical cell or sac within which the oospheres, or egg cells, are developed. 2 *Biol.* A cell whose divisions give rise to oocytes. Also **o·o·gone** (ō′ə·gōn). [<NL <Gk. *ōon* an egg + *gonos* offspring]

o·ol·o·gy (ō·ol′ə·jē) *n.* The branch of ornithology that treats of eggs. [<OO- + -LOGY] —**o·o·log·ic** (ō′ə·loj′ik), **o′o·log′i·cal** *adj.* —**o·ol′o·gist** *n.*

oo·long (ōō′lông) *n.* A variety of dark tea that is partly fermented before being dried. [<dial. Chinese <Chinese *wu-lung* <*wu* black + *lung* a dragon]

o·o·pho·ri·tis (ō′ə·fə·rī′tis) *n. Pathol.* Inflammation of an ovary or the ovaries, sometimes with inflammation of the Fallopian tubes. [<OO-PHOR(O)- + -ITIS]

oophoro- *combining form* Ovary; ovarian. Also before vowels, **oor-**. [<Gk. *ōophoros* egg-bearing]

o·o·sperm (ō′ə·spûrm) *n.* 1 A fertilized ovum. 2 Oospore.

o·o·sphere (ō′ə·sfir) *n. Bot.* In algae and fungi, the egg cell prior to fertilization.

o·o·spore (ō′ə·spôr, -spōr) *n. Bot.* The fertilized and fully developed oosphere, produced within an oogonium. [<OO- + SPORE] —**o·o·spor·ic** (ō′ə·spôr′ik, -spor′ik), **o·os·po·rous** (o·os′pər·əs) *adj.*

ooze[1] (ōōz) *v.* **oozed, ooz·ing** *v.i.* 1 To flow or leak out slowly or gradually, as through pores or small holes; seep; percolate. 2 To exude moisture. 3 To escape or disappear: His courage *oozed* away. —*v.t.* 4 To give off or exude. [<*n.*] —*n.* 1 A slow, gradual leak; gentle flow: the *ooze* of a small spring. 2 That which oozes. 3 An infusion or decoction of a tanniferous substance, such as oak bark, used in tanning. —*adj.* 1 Designating calfskin, sheepskin, goatskin, or other hide susceptible of a soft, velvety finish on the flesh side. 2 Denoting this kind of finish, or the process by which it is produced: *ooze* calf; *ooze* leather. [OE *wōs* sap, juice; infl. in meaning by OE *wāse* mire, dirt]

ooze[2] (ōōz) *n.* 1 Slimy mud or moist, spongy soil. 2 A deposit of calcareous matter found on the ocean bottom and largely made up of the remains of foraminifers. 3 The fibers on the surface of unfinished cotton thread. 4 A piece of muddy or marshy ground; bog; fen. 5 Seaweed. [OE *wāse* mire, marsh]

oo·zy[1] (ōō′zē) *adj.* **·zi·er, ·zi·est** Slowly leaking; gently dripping. —**oo′zi·ness** *n.*

oo·zy[2] (ōō′zē) *adj.* **·zi·er, ·zi·est** Containing, composed of, or like mud or ooze; slimy. —**oo′zi·ly** *adv.* —**oo′zi·ness** *n.*

o·pac·i·fy (ō·pas′ə·fī) *v.* **·fied, ·fy·ing** *v.t.* 1 To cause to become opaque. —*v.i.* 2 To become opaque; lose transparency, as the lens of the eye. —**o·pac′i·fi·ca·tion** (ō·pas′ə·fə·kā′shən) *n.*

o·pah (ō′pə) *n.* A large fish (genus *Lampris*) of warm seas, noted for the brilliancy of its colors. [<Ibo *úbà*]

o·pal (ō′pəl) *n.* An amorphous, variously colored, hydrous silica, softer and less dense than quartz. The **precious** (or **noble**) **opal** presents a peculiar play of delicate colors, and is valued as a gemstone. The **fire** (or **flame**) **opal** shows its colors disposed in streaks: often called *girasol.* [<L *opalus* <Gk. *opallios* <Skt. *upala* a precious stone]

o·pal·es·cence (ō′pəl·es′əns) *n.* An iridescent play of pearly or milky colors, as in an opal. —**o′pal·es′cent, o′pal·ine** (-ēn, -in) *adj.*

o·paque (ō·pāk′) *adj.* 1 Impervious to light; not translucent. 2 Loosely, imperfectly transparent. 3 Imervious to reason; unintelligent. 4 Impervious to radiant heat, electric radiation, etc. 5 Having no luster; dull. 6 Unintelligible; obscure: an *opaque* style. 7 *Obs.* Dark; lying in shadow. See synonyms under DARK. —*n.* 1 Opacity; that which is opaque. 2 An opaque substance used to block out portions of a photographic negative or positive. —*v.t.* **o·paqued, o·paqu·ing** 1 To make

opaque. 2 To block out parts of with opaque, as a photographic negative or positive. [<L *opacus* shaded, darkened; after F *opaque*] —**o·paque′ly** *adv.* —**o·paque′ness** *n.*

op art (op) A style of art of the 1960's characterized by complex geometric patterns designed to create optical distortions, illusions, and the like. [<*optical art*]

o·pen (ō′pən) *adj.* 1 Affording approach, view, passage, or access because of the absence or removal of barriers, restrictions, etc.; unobstructed: The new road is *open* for traffic; *open* country. 2 Public; unbounded; accessible to all: the *open* market; in *open* competition; the *open* sea. 3 Unconcealed; overt; not secret or hidden: *open* hostility. 4 Expanded; unfolded: an *open* flower. 5 Exposed; not enclosed or covered over; unprotected: an *open* car. 6 Ready for business, appointment, etc.: an *open* day in the schedule. 7 Not settled or decided; pending: an *open* account; an *open* question. 8 Ready and free for engagement, employment, etc.; available: The job is still *open.* 9 Ready to consider proof or argument; unbiased; receptive: often with *to*: an *open* mind; *open* to conviction. 10 Generous; liberal: He gives with an *open* hand. 11 *Phonet.* a Pronounced with a wide opening above the tongue; low: said of vowels, as the *a* in *father*: opposed to *close.* b Ending in a vowel or diphthong: said of a syllable. 12 Frank; ingenuous; not deceptive: *open* and aboveboard. 13 Eager or willing to receive: with *open* arms. 14 In hunting or fishing, without prohibition: *open* season. 15 Liable to attack, robbery, temptation, etc. 16 Having openings, holes, or perforations, as woven goods or needlework; porous. 17 Mild; free from fog, mist, or ice: an *open* winter; *open* weather; *open* water in northern seas. 18 *Printing* a Widely spaced, as a line on a page. b Widely leaded or containing many breaks; fat: said of composed or printed matter. 19 *Music* Not stopped by the finger, as a string, or having the top uncovered, as an organ pipe; also, produced by an open string or pipe: said of a note, tone, etc. 20 Unrestricted by union regulations in the employment of labor: an *open* shop. 21 *U.S. Colloq.* Not under control in the sale of intoxicants, gambling, or vice: an *open* town. 22 Out of doors. 23 *U.S.* Of or designating a policy of admitting students for matriculation to a college or university without regard to their academic preparedness, thus providing an opportunity for members of disadvantaged groups to obtain university degrees: *open* admissions. 24 In the elementary grades, of or characterized by an educational environment designed to encourage self-motivated learning by giving children freedom to move from one small group to another within and sometimes beyond the limits of the classroom: *open* classrooms. See synonyms under BLUFF[2], CANDID, EVIDENT, MANIFEST, NOTORIOUS, OVERT. —*v.t.* 1 To set open or ajar, as a door; unclose; unfasten. 2 To make passable; free from obstacles. 3 To make or force (a hole, passage, etc.). 4 To remove the covering, lid, etc., of: to *open* a package. 5 To expand, as for viewing; unroll; unfold, as a map. 6 To make an opening or openings into: to *open* an abscess. 7 To make or declare ready for commerce, use, etc.: to *open* a store. 8 To make or declare public or free of access, as a park; make available for settlement. 9 To make less compact; expand: to *open* ranks. 10 To make more receptive to ideas or sentiments; enlighten: to *open* the mind. 11 To bare the secrets of; divulge; reveal: to *open* one's heart. 12 To begin; commence, as negotiations. 13 *Law* To undo or recall (a judgment or order) so as to permit its validity to be questioned. —*v.i.* 14 To become open. 15 To come apart or break open; rupture: The wound *opened* again. 16 To come into view; spread out; unroll. 17 To afford access or view: The door *opened* on a courtyard. 18 To become receptive or enlightened. 19 To begin; be started: The season *opened* with a ball. 20 In the theater, to begin a season or tour. —*n.* Any wide space not enclosed, obstructed, or covered, as by woods, rocks, etc.; open land or water: usually with the definite article: in the *open.* [OE. Akin to UP.] —**o′pen·ly** *adv.* —**o′pen·ness** *n.*

o·pen-air (ō′pən-âr′) *adj.* 1 Out of doors; taking place in an open field or street: an *open-air* service. 2 Relating to the plein-air school of painters.

o·pen-and-shut (ō′pən-ənd-shut′) *adj.* Simple; obvious; easily determinable.

o·pen-cut (ō′pən-kut′) *adj.* Open-pit.

open door 1 The policy of giving to all nations the same commercial privileges in a dependency, or recently conquered territory, as those exercised by the dominant country: used attributively in such phrases as **open-door policy, open-door principle**, etc. 2 Opportunity for free trade. 3 Admission to all without charge.

o·pen·er (ō′pən·ər) *n.* 1 An instrument for opening anything firmly closed: usually in combination: a can-*opener.* 2 A person who opens or is employed to open: usually in combination: a pew-*opener.* 3 In poker and similar games: **a** The player who opens the jackpot. **b** *pl.* Cards of sufficient value, as a pair of jacks, to enable the player to open a pot.

o·pen-eyed (ō′pən-īd′) *adj.* Having the eyes open; wary; watchful; also, amazed: in *open-eyed* wonder.

o·pen-faced (ō′pən-fāst′) *adj.* 1 Possessing a countenance suggestive of frankness, simplicity, and honesty. 2 Having a face uncovered by a casing, as a watch.

o·pen-hand·ed (ō′pən-han′did) *adj.* Giving freely; liberal. See synonyms under GENEROUS. —**o′pen-hand′ed·ly** *adv.* —**o′pen-hand′ed·ness** *n.*

o·pen-heart·ed (ō′pən-här′tid) *adj.* Disclosing the thoughts and intentions plainly; frank; candid. —**o′pen-heart′ed·ly** *adv.* —**o′pen-heart′ed·ness** *n.*

o·pen·ing (ō′pən·ing) *n.* 1 The act of becoming open or of causing to be open. 2 Something that is open; a vacant or unobstructed space, as within barriers or boundaries; a hole, passage, or gap; a space. 3 A tract in a forest where trees are lacking or thinly scattered. 4 An aperture in a wall; especially, one for the admission of light or air. 5 The first part or stage, as of a period, act, or process; a beginning; prelude. 6 In chess, checkers, etc., a specific mode of beginning the game; the series of opening moves. 7 An opportunity for action, especially in business. See synonyms under BEGINNING, BREACH, ENTRANCE[1], HOLE, OPPORTUNITY.

o·pen-mind·ed (ō′pən-mīn′did) *adj.* Free from prejudiced conclusions; amenable to reason; receptive. —**o′pen-mind′ed·ly** *adv.*

o·pen-pit (ō′pən-pit′) *adj.* Designating a mine dug directly into the surface, with the pit open to the air.

open range An unfenced area of grazing country.

open shop An establishment in which union labor and non-union labor are employed: opposed to *closed shop.*

open stove A stove having the firebox open to the room; a Franklin stove.

open timber A forest having no undergrowth.

o·pen-work (ō′pən-wûrk′) *n.* Any product of art or handicraft with many small openings.

op·er·a (op′ər·ə, op′rə) *n.* 1 A form of drama in which music is a dominant factor, made up of arias, recitatives, choruses, etc., with orchestral accompaniment, scenery, acting, and sometimes dance: the principal types are **comic opera**, in which there is spoken dialog and the story ends happily; **grand opera**, a dramatic composition generally with a serious or tragic theme, of which the plot is elaborated as in a play and the dialog is set to music throughout; **light opera**, in which the plot has humorous situations, a happy ending, and some spoken dialog. 2 A particular musical drama or its music or libretto; also, its representation. 3 The theater in which operas are given. 4 Plural of OPUS. [<Ital. <L, a work, labor <*opus, operis* work] —**op·er·at·ic** (op′ər·at′ik) *adj.* —**op′er·at′i·cal·ly** *adv.*

op·er·a·ble (op′ər·ə·bəl) *adj.* Capable of treatment by surgical operation. —**op′er·a·bil′i·ty** *n.*

opera glass A binocular telescope of small size, suitable for use at the theater. Also **opera glasses.**

opera house A theater specially adapted for performance of operas; loosely, any theater.

op·er·ant (op′ər·ənt) *adj.* 1 Producing a specified effect. 2 *Psychol.* Designating conditioning by which desired behavior is elicited by rewards that reinforce appropriate responses. — **op′er·ant·ly** adv.

op·er·ate (op′ə·rāt) v. **·at·ed, ·at·ing** v.i. **1** To act or function, especially with force or influence; work. **2** To bring about or produce the proper or intended effect. **3** To perform a surgical operation. **4** To deal in securities, stocks, etc., especially speculatively. **5** To carry on a military or naval operation: usually with *against.* — v.t. **6** To control the working or function of, as a machine. **7** To manage or conduct the affairs of: to *operate* a railroad. **8** To bring about or cause. [<L *operatus,* pp. of *operari* to work, have an effect < *opus, operis* a work] — **op′er·at′a·ble** adj.

op·er·a·tion (op′ə·rā′shən) n. **1** The act or process of operating; the exertion or action of any form of power or energy. **2** A method of exercising or applying force; a mode of action. **3** A single specific act or transaction, especially in the stock market. **4** A course or series of acts to effect a certain purpose; process. **5** The state of being in action: The machinery is in *operation.* **6** Surg. Any systematic manipulation upon the body, performed either with or without instruments, to restore disunited or deficient parts, to remove diseased or injured parts, or to extract foreign matter. **7** Math. **a** The act of making a change in the value or form of a quantity. **b** The change itself as indicated by symbols or rules: distinguished from the process by which such change is accomplished. **8** Some special kind of activity; manner of action; a vital or natural process of activity. **9** A military or naval campaign.

Synonyms: action, agency, effect, execution, force, influence, performance, procedure, result. *Operation* is *action* resulting in change, whether produced by the *agency* or *action* of an intelligent agent or of a material substance or *force;* as, military *operations;* the *operation* of a medicine. *Performance* and *execution* denote intelligent *action,* considered with reference to the actor or to that which he accomplishes; *performance* accomplishing the will of the actor, *execution* often the will of another. Compare ACT, EXERCISE. *Antonyms:* failure, inaction, ineffectiveness, inefficiency, inutility, powerlessness.

op·er·a·tion·al (op′ə·rā′shən·əl) adj. **1** Pertaining to an operation. **2** Organized or prepared to carry out assigned tasks, especially of a military character. **3** Fit or ready for some specified use. **4** In actual service, as a machine, aircraft, etc.

op·er·a·tive (op′ər·ə·tiv, -ə·rā′tiv) adj. **1** Exerting force or influence. **2** Moving or working efficiently; effective. **3** Connected with operations: *operative* surgery. **4** Concerned with practical work, mechanical or manual. **5** Engaged in practical activity, as a workman or mechanic. — n. **1** A person employed as a skilled worker, as in a mill or factory, etc.; artisan. **2** Colloq. A detective; one who works secretly. See synonyms under ARTIST. — **op′er·a·tive·ly** adv.

op·er·a·tor (op′ə·rā′tər) n. **1** One who operates; any skilled worker; specifically, one who works a telephone switchboard, one who receives or sends messages on a telegraph, or one who works a typesetting machine. **2** A broker who acts for others in trading in speculative securities. **3** The owner and director of a coal mine, oil field, or other large industrial organization. **4** Math. A symbol that briefly indicates a mathematical process. See synonyms under AGENT.

o·per·cu·lum (ō·pûr′kyo̅o̅·ləm) n. pl. **·la** (-lə) Biol. **1** A lid, cover, or lidlike part or organ, as of the orifice of the capsule in mosses, of certain capsules (as a pyxis) in flowering plants, of the hair follicles, etc. **2** A horny or shelly plate in many gastropods, serving to close the aperture when the animal is retracted. **3** In fishes, the gill cover; specifically, the hindmost and uppermost bone of the gill cover. **4** In the king crab, the plate that covers the abdominal limbs. **5** The labrum of certain dipterous insects. **6** A part of the cerebral cortex. Also **o·per·cele** (ō·pûr′sēl), **o·per′cule** (-kyo̅o̅l). [<L, a covering, lid < *operire* cover] — **o·per′cu·lar** adj. — **o·per′cu·late,** o-

per′cu·lat·ed adj.

op·e·ret·ta (op′ə·ret′ə) n. A short, humorous opera with dialog. [<Ital., dim. of *opera*]

op·er·ose (op′ə·rōs) adj. Laborious; also, industrious. [<L *operosus*] — **op′er·ose′ly** adv

oph·i·cleide (of′ə·klīd) n. A brass wind instrument resembling a cornet: now replaced in orchestras by the tuba. [<F *ophicléide* <Gk. *ophis* serpent + *kleis, kleidos* key]

o·phid·i·an (ō·fid′ē·ən) n. One of a suborder of limbless reptiles (*Ophidia*), with mandibular rami connected only by an elastic ligament, and having no pectoral arch; a serpent; snake. — adj. Of or pertaining to the Ophidia, or to snakes; snakelike. [<NL <Gk. *ophis* a snake]

oph·i·dism (of′ə·diz′əm) n. Poisoning by the venom of a snake. Also **oph·i·di·a·sis** (of′ə·dī′ə·sis).

ophio- combining form Serpent; of or pertaining to serpents: *ophiolatry.* Also, before vowels, **ophi-.** [<Gk. *ophis* a serpent]

oph·i·ol·a·try (of′ē·ol′ə·trē) n. Serpent worship. [<OPHIO- + -LATRY] — **oph′i·ol′a·trous** adj.

oph·i·ol·o·gy (of′ē·ol′ə·jē) n. The branch of zoology that treats of serpents; herpetology. [<OPHIO- + -LOGY] — **oph′i·o·log′i·cal** (-ə·loj′i·kəl) adj. — **oph′i·ol′o·gist** n.

oph·thal·mi·a (of·thal′mē·ə) n. Pathol. Inflammation of the eye, its membranes, or its lids. Also **oph·thal′my.** [<LL <Gk. < *ophthalmos* an eye]

ophthalmo- combining form Eye; pertaining to the eyes: *ophthalmology.* Also, before vowels, **ophthalm-.** [<Gk. *ophthalmos* the eye]

oph·thal·mol·o·gy (of′thal·mol′ə·jē) n. The science dealing with the structure, functions, and diseases of the eye. — **oph·thal′mo·log′ic** (-mə·loj′ik) or **·i·cal** adj. — **oph·thal′mol′o·gist** n.

oph·thal·mo·scope (of·thal′mə·skōp) n. An optical instrument having a concave mirror with a hole in its center, for illuminating and viewing the center of the eye. — **oph·thal′mo·scop′ic** (-skop′ik) or **·i·cal** adj. — **oph·thal·mos·co·py** (of·thal·mos′kə·pē) n.

OPTHAL-
MOSCOPE

-opia combining form Med. A (specified) defect of the eye, or condition of sight: *myopia.* Also spelled *-opy.* [<Gk. *-ōpia* <*ōps, ōpos* the eye]

o·pi·ate (ō′pē·it, -āt) n. **1** Medicine containing opium; a narcotic. **2** Something inducing sleep. — adj. Consisting of opium; tending to induce sleep. — v.t. (-āt) **·at·ed, ·at·ing 1** To treat with opium or an opiate. **2** To deaden; dull. [<Med. L *opiatus,* pp. of *opiare* treat with opium <L *opium* OPIUM]

o·pin·ion (ə·pin′yən) n. **1** A conclusion or judgment held with confidence, but falling short of positive knowledge. **2** Often pl. A settled judgment or conviction on some subject, as religion or politics. **3** Favorable judgment or estimation; reputation. **4** Specifically, an estimate of the excellence or value of a person or a thing; also, a common or prevailing sentiment; public opinion. **5** Law The formal announcement of the conclusions of a court in a case before it; also, the conclusion of an attorney touching the merits of a submitted case: to take the *opinion* of counsel. [<OF <L *opinio, -onis* < *opinari* think]

op·is·thog·na·thous (op′is·thog′nə·thəs) adj. Having receding jaws: opposed to *prognathous.* [<Gk. *opisthen* behind + *gnathos* jaw] — **op′is·thog′na·thism** (-nə·thiz′əm) n.

op·is·thot·o·nos (op′is·thot′ə·nəs) n. Pathol. A rigid muscular spasm of the neck and back, arching the body backward, as in tetanus. [<Gk. < *opisthen* behind + *tonos* tension < *teinein* stretch]

o·pi·um (ō′pē·əm) n. A milky exudation from the unripe capsules of the **opium poppy** (*Papaver somniferum*), containing a mixture of about 20 alkaloids, the most important of which is morphine. It is a powerful narcotic, with a sticky, gumlike body, bitter taste, and heavy odor. [<L <Gk. *opion* opium, dim. of

opos vegetable juice]

opium den A room or place, usually illegal, for opium-smoking.

o·pos·sum (ə·pos′əm, pos′əm) n. An American marsupial (genus *Didelphis*) of largely arboreal and nocturnal habits, having a prehensile tail and feet adapted for grasping: popularly called *possum.* The **common** (or **Virginia**) **opossum** (*D. virginiana*), which ranges from the central United States to Brazil, has a soft, whitish–gray pelage, with black ears and feet, and is esteemed as food. It is noted for its trick of feigning death, or *playing possum,* when threatened with danger. [<Algonquian (Virginian) *apasum,* lit., a white beast]

opossum shrimp A crustacean (family *Mysidae*) which carries its eggs in a pouch beneath the thorax.

op·pi·late (op′ə·lāt) v.t. **·lat·ed, ·lat·ing** Med. To block or obstruct; constipate. [<L *oppilatus,* pp. of *oppilare* stop up < *ob-* against + *pilare* ram down < *pilus* a pestle] — **op′pi·lant** adj. — **op′pi·la′tion** n.

op·po·nent (ə·pō′nənt) n. One who opposes another, as in battle or debate; antagonist. See synonyms under ENEMY. — adj. **1** Acting against something or someone; opposing. **2** Anat. Bringing one part, as of a muscle, into opposition to another. **3** Standing in front; opposite. [<L *opponens, -entis,* ppr. of *opponere* set against < *ob-* against + *ponere* place] — **op·po′nen·cy** n.

op·por·tune (op′ər·to̅o̅n′, -tyo̅o̅n′) adj. Meeting some requirement; especially seasonable or timely. See synonyms under AUSPICIOUS, CONVENIENT. [<MF, fem. of *opportun* seasonable, exposed <L *opportunus* suitable, lit., at the port < *ob-* before + *portus* a harbor] — **op′·por·tune′ly** adv. — **op′por·tune′ness** n.

op·por·tu·nist (op′ər·to̅o̅′nist, -tyo̅o̅′-) n. One who governs his course by opportunities or circumstances rather than by fixed principles or by regard for consistency or consequences. — **op′por·tu·nis′tic** (-to̅o̅·nis′tik, -tyo̅o̅-) adj. — **op′por·tu′nism** n.

op·por·tu·ni·ty (op′ər·to̅o̅′nə·tē, -tyo̅o̅′-) n. pl. **·ties 1** A fit or convenient time; favorable occasion. **2** Obs. Opportuneness. **3** Obs. Importunity: an erroneous use.

Synonyms: convenience, occasion, opening, season. *Occasion* in the popular sense is a conjunction of circumstances which seems to require or inclines to or is fit for certain action; an *opportunity* is a conjunction of circumstances which makes certain action possible, with probability of success, advantage or gratification; as, I had *occasion* to interfere; I found an *opportunity* for a good investment.

op·pos·a·ble (ə·pō′zə·bəl) adj. **1** Capable of being placed opposite: said especially of the thumb. **2** That can be opposed. — **op·pos′a·bil′i·ty** n.

op·pose (ə·pōz′) v. **·posed, ·pos·ing** v.t. **1** To act or be in opposition to; resist; combat; fight. **2** To set in opposition or contrast: to *oppose* love to hatred. **3** To place before or in front. — v.i. **4** To act or be in opposition. [<OF *opposer, oposer* <L *ob-* against + OF *poser* to POSE¹.] — **op·pos′er** n.

Synonyms: check, combat, confront, contradict, contravene, defy, face, object, obstruct, oppugn, resist, withstand. See CONTEND, CONTRAST, DISPUTE, HINDER¹, OBSTRUCT, REPEL. *Antonyms:* see synonyms for AID.

op·pose·less (ə·pōz′lis) adj. Not to be opposed with effect; irresistible.

op·po·site (op′ə·zit) adj. **1** Situated or placed on the other side, or on each side, of an intervening space or thing; contrary in position: *opposite* ends of the room. **2** Facing or moving the other way; contrary: *opposite* directions. **3** Contrary in tendency or character; diametrically different: *opposite* opinions; the *opposite* sex. **4** Bot. **a** Arranged (as similar parts or organs) in pairs, so that the whole diameter of some intervening body separates them, as leaves on a stem. **b** Having one part or organ immediately before, or vertically over, another, as a stamen before a petal. See synonyms under CONTRARY. — n. **1** Something or someone that is opposite, opposed, or contrary. **2** An antonym. **3** Obs. An antagonist. —*adv.* In an opposite or complementary direction or position. —*prep.* 1 Across from; facing. 2 Complementary to, as in theatrical roles: He played *opposite* her. [<OF <L *oppositus*, pp. of *opponere*. See OPPONENT.] —**op'po·site·ly** *adv.* —**op'po·site·ness** *n.*

op·po·si·tion (op'ə·zish'ən) *n.* 1 The act of opposing or resisting; antagonism. 2 The state of being opposite or opposed; antithesis; also, a position confronting another or a placing in contrast. 3 That which is or furnishes an obstacle to some result: The stream flows without *opposition.* 4 *Often cap.* The political party opposed to the ministry or administration in power. 5 *Astron.* **a** The relative position of two heavenly bodies 180° apart in geometric longitude. **b** The position of a body opposite to the sun designated by the symbol ♂; as, ♂ ♂ ☉, *opposition* of Mars to the sun. 6 *Ling.* A state of contrast between any one phoneme and all the other phonemes in a language, as, /p/ is said to be in *bilateral opposition* to /b/ on the basis of the distinctive feature of voice, and in *multilateral opposition* to /d/ on the basis of the distinctive features of voice and place of articulation. 7 *Logic* The relation between two propositions which have the same subject and predicate but differ in quantity or quality or in both. See synonyms under AMBITION, ANTIPATHY, COLLISION, COMPETITION, EMULATION. — **in opposition** In the position of being opposed or hostile to a political party or measure: The Democratic party is *in opposition.* [<OF <L *oppositio, -onis* <*oppositus.* See OPPOSITE.] —**op'po·si'tion·al** *adj.* —**op'po·si'tion·ist** *n.* — **op'po·si'tion·less** *adj.*

op·pos·i·tive (ə·poz'ə·tiv) *adj.* Placed or capable of being placed in contrast. —**op·pos'i·tive·ly** *adv.* —**op·pos'i·tive·ness** *n.*

op·press (ə·pres') *v.t.* 1 To burden or keep in subjugation by harsh and unjust use of force or authority; tyrannize. 2 To lie heavy upon physically or mentally; weigh down; depress; dispirit. 3 *Obs.* To crush or trample; overwhelm. See synonyms under ABUSE, LOAD, PERSECUTE. [<OF *oppresser, opresser* <Med. L *oppressare*, freq. of L *opprimere* crush <*ob-* against + *premere* press] —**op·pres'sor** *n.*

op·pres·sion (ə·presh'ən) *n.* 1 The act of oppressing. 2 Subjection to unjust hardships; tyranny. 3 Mental depression; languor; dulness of spirits. 4 A sense of weight or of constriction. 5 That which oppresses or is hard to bear; privation; hardship; cruelty.

op·pro·bri·ous (ə·prō'brē·əs) *adj.* 1 Consisting of contemptuous abuse; imputing disgrace. 2 Shameful; disgraceful; odious; held in dishonor. [<OF *opprobrieus* <LL *opprobriosus* <L *opprobrium* OPPROBRIUM] —**op·pro'bri·ous·ly** *adv.* —**op·pro'bri·ous·ness** *n.*

op·pro·bri·um (ə·prō'brē·əm) *n.* 1 The state of being scornfully reproached; ignominy. 2 Reproach mingled with disdain. 3 A cause of disgrace or reproach. [<L, a disgrace <*opprobrare* reproach <*ob-* against + *probum* an infamy]

op·pugn (ə·pyōōn') *v.t.* To assail or oppose with argument; call in question; controvert. See synonyms under OPPOSE. [<L *oppugnare* <*ob-* against + *pugnare* fight <*pugna* a fight] —**op·pugn'er** *n.*

-opsia *combining form Med.* A (specified) type or condition of sight: *macropsia.* Also spelled *-opsy.* [<NL <Gk. *opsis* sight]

op·so·ma·ni·a (op'sə·mā'nē·ə, -mān'yə) *n.* A morbid craving for rich foods and delicate fare. [<NL <Gk. <*opson* cooked meat, dainties + *mania* madness]

op·son·i·fy (op·son'ə·fī) *v.t.* ·fied, ·fy·ing To render (bacteria) susceptible to phagocytosis by the action of opsonins. [<OPSON(IN) + -(I)FY] —**op·son'i·fi·ca'tion** *n.*

op·so·nin (op'sə·nin) *n. Bacteriol.* A component of blood serum which acts upon invading cells or bacteria, so as to assist in their absorption by the phagocytes. [<Gk. *opson* cooked meat + -IN]

op·son·ize (op'sən·īz) *v.t.* ·ized, ·iz·ing To opsonify.

opt (opt) *v.i.* To choose; decide. [<F *opter* <L *optare* choose, wish]

op·ta·tive (op'tə·tiv) *adj.* 1 Expressing or indicative of desire or choice. 2 *Gram.* Denoting that mood in Greek and certain other languages which expresses wish or desire. —*n. Gram.* 1 The optative mood. 2 A word or construction in this mood. [<MF, fem. of *optatif* <LL *optativus* <L *optare* wish] —**op'ta·tive·ly** *adv.*

op·tic (op'tik) *adj.* 1 Pertaining to the eye or to vision. 2 Optical. —*n. Colloq.* An eye. [<MF *optique* <Med. L *opticus* <Gk. *optikos* <*optos* seen <*ops-*, fut. stem of *horaein* see, behold]

op·ti·cal (op'ti·kəl) *adj.* 1 Pertaining to optics. 2 Of or pertaining to eyesight. 3 Designed to assist or improve vision. —**op'ti·cal·ly** *adv.*

optical activity The capacity to rotate the plane of polarization of light.

optical art Op art (which see).

optical fibers Fibers of clear plastic, often in bundles, that transmit light and sharp images along any desired path.

optical glass See under GLASS.

optical maser *Physics* A type of maser that can enormously amplify light. Also called *laser.*

op·ti·cian (op·tish'ən) *n.* One who makes or deals in optical goods. [<F *opticien* <Med. L *optica* OPTICS]

optic nerve *Anat.* The special nerve of vision, connecting the retina with the cerebral centers. See illustration under EYE.

op·tics (op'tiks) *n.* The science that treats of the phenomena of light, vision, and sight. [<OPTIC; trans. of Med. L *optica* <Gk. *ta optika* optical matters]

op·ti·mal (op'tə·məl) *adj.* Of, pertaining to, indicating, or characterized by an optimum.

op·ti·mism (op'tə·miz'əm) *n.* 1 The doctrine that everything is ordered for the best; also, the doctrine that the universe is constantly tending toward a better state. 2 Disposition to look on the bright side of things: opposed to *pessimism.* [<F *optimisme* <L *optimus* best] —**op'ti·mist** *n.* —**op'ti·mis'tic** or ·ti·cal *adj.* —**op'ti·mis'ti·cal·ly** *adv.*

op·ti·mize (op'tə·mīz) *v.* ·mized, ·miz·ing *v.t.* 1 *Technol.* To plan or prepare plans for (industrial production) in order to secure maximum efficiency. 2 To make the most of. —*v.i.* 3 To be optimistic. 4 To work toward obtaining an optimum.

op·ti·mum (op'tə·məm) *n. pl.* ·ma (-mə) or ·mums 1 The condition or degree producing the best result. 2 The combination of conditions, as of food, etc., that produces the best average result in the growth and development of organisms. 3 The most favorable degree, conditions, etc. —*adj.* Producing or conducive to the best results. [<L, neut. of *optimus* best]

op·tion (op'shən) *n.* 1 The right, power, or liberty of choosing; discretion; the exercise of such right, power, or liberty. 2 The purchased privilege of either buying or selling something at a specified price within a specified time. 3 A thing that is or can be chosen. See synonyms under ALTERNATIVE. [<MF <L *optio, -onis* <*optare* choose]

op·tom·e·trist (op·tom'ə·trist) *n.* One who is skilled in optometry.

op·tom·e·try (op·tom'ə·trē) *n.* The profession or occupation of measuring vision and prescribing corrective lenses to compensate for visual defects.

op·u·lent (op'yə·lənt) *adj.* 1 Possessing great wealth. 2 Exuberant; profuse. [<L *opulentus* <*opulens, -entis* <*ops, opis* power, wealth] —**op'u·lent·ly** *adv.*

o·pun·ti·a (ō·pun'shē·ə) *n.* One of a large genus (*Opuntia*) of mainly tropical American cacti, the prickly pears, having a usually flattened, much-branched stem and tubular yellow, red, or purple flowers. [<NL <L *Opuntia* (*herba*) (a plant) native to Opus <*Opus, Opuntis*, a city in ancient Locris <Gk. *Opous*]

o·pus (ō'pəs) *n. pl.* **op·er·a** (op'ər·ə, ōp'rə) A literary or musical work or composition. [<L, a work]

o·pus·cule (ō·pus'kyōōl) *n.* A small or unimportant work. [<OF <L *opusculum*, dim. of *opus* a work]

-opy See -OPIA.

OPUNTIA

or (ôr, *unstressed* ər) *conj.* 1 Introducing an alternative: stop *or* go; red *or* white. 2 Offering a choice of a series: Will you take milk *or* coffee *or* chocolate? 3 Introducing an equivalent: the culinary art *or* art of cookery. 4 Indicating uncertainty: He lives in Chicago *or* thereabouts. 5 Introducing the second alternative of a choice limited to two: with *either* or *whether*: It must be either black *or* white; I don't care whether he goes *or* not. 6 *Poetic* Either; whether: *or* in the heart *or* in the head. [ME, contraction of *other, auther* either, OE *æther*; infl. in meaning by OE *oththe* or]

-or¹ *suffix* The person or thing performing the action expressed in the root verb: *competitor.* See note under -ER¹. [<AF *-our*, OF *-or* <L *-or, -ator*]

-or² *suffix* The quality, state, or condition of: *favor.* [<OF <L]

or·ach (ôr'əch, or'-) *n.* Any of various plants (genus *Atriplex*), especially the **garden orach** or mountain spinach (*A. hortensis*), a tall, hardy annual, formerly common in England as a pot herb. Also **or'ache.** [<AF *arasche*, OF *arroche* <L *atriplex, -plicis* <Gk. *atraphaxys, -yos*]

or·a·cle (ôr'ə·kəl, or'-) *n.* 1 The seat of the worship of some ancient divinity, as of Apollo at Delphi, where prophecies were given out by the priests in answer to inquiries. 2 A prophecy thus given. 3 The deity whose prophecies were given. 4 A person of unquestioned wisdom or knowledge, or something regarded as of infallible authority. [<OF <L *oraculum* <*orare* speak, pray <*os, oris* mouth]

o·rac·u·lar (ô·rak'yə·lər, ō-) *adj.* 1 Pertaining to an oracle. 2 Obscure; enigmatical. 3 Prophetic. —**o·rac'u·lar'i·ty** *n.* —**o·rac'u·lar·ly** *adv.* —**o·rac'u·lar·ness** *n.*

o·ral (ô'rəl, ō'rəl) *adj.* 1 Uttered through the mouth; consisting of spoken words. 2 Pertaining to or situated at or near the mouth. 3 *Psychoanal.* **a** Of or relating to the earliest stage of psychosexual development of the child in which interest in and gratification from feeding, sucking, and biting are dominant. **b** Of, pertaining to, or characterized by qualities in the adult, as aggressiveness or gregariousness, regarded as typifying this stage of development. Compare ANAL, GENITAL. 4 *Zool.* Designating the side of the body on which the mouth is placed. 5 Of, pertaining to, or using speech. 6 Taken or administered by mouth. 7 *Phonet.* Pronounced through the mouth with the nasal passage closed; nonnasal: opposed to *nasal.* See synonyms under VERBAL. —*n.* An oral examination, as in a college. [<L *os, oris* mouth] —**o'ral·ly** *adv.*

or·ange (ôr'inj, or'-) *n.* 1 A large, round, juicy fruit (technically a berry) of a low, much-branched, evergreen tree (genus *Citrus*), with a reddish-yellow rind enclosing membranous divisions and a refreshing, sweetish or subacid pulp. 2 Any of the trees yielding this fruit, as the Spanish sour orange (*C. aurantium*), the sweet orange (*C. sinensis*). 3 Any of many related species, such as the trifoliate orange (*Poncirus trifoliata*). 4 The kumquat. 5 The osage orange. 6 A reddish-yellow color; also, a pigment of this color. — **mandarin orange** A mandarin (def. 2). —*adj.* 1 Reddish-yellow. 2 Pertaining to an orange. [<OF <Provençal *auranja* (infl. by *aur* gold), earlier (*n*)*aranja* <Sp. *naranja* <Arabic *nāranj* <Persian *nārang*]

or·ange·ade (ôr'inj·ād') *n.* A beverage made of orange juice, sugar, and water. [<F]

orange blossom The white blossom of the orange tree: much worn by brides: State flower of Florida.

or·ange·ry (ôr'inj·rē, or'-) *n. pl.* ·ries A place for cultivating orange trees; an orange grove or greenhouse.

or·ange·wood (ôr'inj·wŏŏd', or'-) *n.* The fine-grained, yellowish wood of the orange tree: used in lathe work and in dentistry.

o·rang-u·tan (ô·rang'ə·tan, -ŏŏ·tan) *n. pl.* ·tans or ·tan A large, anthropoid ape (genus *Pongo* or *Simia*) of Borneo and Sumatra, about 4 1/2 feet in height, having brownish-red hair, brown skin, small ears, doglike teeth, narrow lips, and long arms reaching to the ankles: also called *orang.* Also **o·rang'-ou-tang** (-ə·tang, -ŏŏ·tang). [<Malay *orañ utan* <*orañ* a man + *utan* a forest]

o·rate (ô·rāt', ō·rāt', ō'rāt, ō·rāt') *v.i.* **o·rat·ed,**

o·rat·ing To deliver an oration; speechify: chiefly humorous. [<L *oratus*, pp. of *orare*. See ORATION.]

o·ra·tion (ô·rā′shən, ō·rā′-) *n.* **1** An elaborate public speech. **2** A graduation speech. See synonyms under SPEECH. [<L *oratio, -onis* < *oratus*, pp. of *orare* pray, speak < *os, oris* mouth. Doublet of ORISON.]

or·a·tor (ôr′ə·tər, or′-) *n.* **1** One who delivers an oration; an eloquent public speaker. **2** A high school or college student chosen to make a speech. **3** *Law* The complainant in a chancery proceeding; a petitioner in chancery. [<AF *oratour* <L *orator* < *orare*. See ORATION.] — **or′a·tor·ship′** *n.*

or·a·tor·i·cal (ôr′ə·tôr′ə·kəl, -tō′rə-, or′-) *adj.* Of, like, or characteristic of oratory or an orator. — **or′a·tor′i·cal·ly** *adv.*

or·a·to·ri·o (ôr′ə·tôr′ē·ō, -tō′rē·ō, or′-) *n. pl.* **·os** A musical composition, usually on a sacred theme, for solo voices, chorus, and orchestra, dramatic in that it tells a connected story, though without scenery or acting. [<Ital., lit., lit., a small chapel <L *oratorium*. See ORATORY².]

or·a·to·ry¹ (ôr′ə·tôr′ē, -tō′rē, or′-) *n. pl.* **·ries** **1** The art of public speaking; eloquence. **2** Eloquent language. See synonyms under SPEECH. [<L *oratoria (ars)* the oratorical (art), orig. fem. of *oratorius* < *orator* ORATOR]

or·a·to·ry² (ôr′ə·tôr′ē, -tō′rē, or′-) *n. pl.* **·ries** **1** A place for prayer; a private chapel. **2** One of various congregations of priests in the Roman Catholic Church, who live together without vows, primarily for the purpose of teaching. [<LL *oratorium (templum)* (a temple) for prayer, orig. neut. of *oratorius* of prayer < *orator* one who prays < *oratus*. See ORATION.]

orb (ôrb) *n.* **1** A rounded mass; a sphere or globe. **2** A circle or orbit; anything circular. **3** A sphere topped by a cross: symbolic of royal power. **4** *Obs.* The plane of the orbit or the orbit of a planet. — *v.t.* **1** To shape into a sphere or circle. **2** *Poetic* To enclose; encircle. [<L *orbis* a circle]

or·bic·u·lar (ôr·bik′yə·lər) *adj.* **1** Having the form of an orb or orbit. **2** Well-rounded. **3** *Bot.* Circular, as a leaf or petal. [<L *orbicularis* < *orbiculus*, dim. of *orbis* a circle] — **or·bic′u·lar′i·ty** (-lar′ə·tē) *n.*

or·bic·u·late (ôr·bik′yə·lit, -lāt) *adj.* Made into or taking the form of an orb or orbit; orbicular. Also **or·bic′u·lat′ed.** — **or·bic′u·late·ly** *adv.*
    Synonyms: circular, globular, spherical, spheroidal.

or·bit (ôr′bit) *n.* **1** *Astron.* The path in space along which a celestial body moves about its center of attraction. **2** *Anat.* One of the two cavities of the skull containing the eyes. **3** *Ornithol.* The eyelid and skin surrounding the eye of a bird. **4** *Physics* The assumed path of an electron around the atomic nucleus. **5** A range of influence or action: the *orbit* of imperialism. — *v.t.* To cause to move in an orbit, as an artificial satellite. — *v.i.* To move in an orbit. [<L *orbita* track of a wheel, an orbit < *orbis* a wheel, a circle] — **or′bi·tal** *adj.*

orbital cavity *Anat.* The bony socket enclosing and protecting the eyeball in the skull of vertebrates.

orbital decay The progressive spiraling change from elliptical to circular in the orbit of an artificial satellite whose velocity is gradually diminished by the residual air resistance encountered at perigee.

ore (ôrk) *n.* A grampus or some other cetacean: also spelled **ork.** [ME *orgue* <L *orca*, a kind of whale]

or·chard (ôr′chərd) *n.* A plantation of trees grown for their products, as fruit, nuts, oils, etc.; also, the enclosure or ground containing them. [OE *orceard* < *ort-geard* a garden < *ort* (? <Med. L *ortus* a garden <L *hortus*) + *geard* a yard, enclosure]

or·chard·ist (ôr′chərd·ist) *n.* One who cultivates trees in orchards for their products. Also **or′chard·man** (-mən).

orchard oriole A common oriole (*Icterus spurius*) of eastern North America, smaller and having less brilliant plumage than the Baltimore oriole.

or·ches·tra (ôr′kis·trə) *n.* **1** A band of musicians playing together, especially a sym-

---

phony orchestra; also, the instruments on which they play. **2** In theaters, the place immediately before the stage, occupied by the musicians; by extension, the main floor. **3** In the ancient Greek and Roman theaters, the approximately semicircular space from which the tiers of seats rose, in the Greek theater reserved for the chorus, and in the Roman theater reserved for the seats of the senators and other distinguished men. [<L <Gk. *orchēstra*, lit., a dancing space < *orcheesthai* dance] — **or·ches·tral** (ôr·kes′trəl) *adj.* — **or·ches′tral·ly** *adv.*

or·ches·trate (ôr′kis·trāt) *v.t. & v.i.* **·trat·ed, ·trat·ing** **1** To compose or arrange (music) for an orchestra. **2** To arrange or bring about, as by manipulation or careful planning: to *orchestrate* economic growth. **3** To bring into harmony: to *orchestrate* wilderness areas with urban centers.

or·ches·tra·tion (ôr′kis·trā′shən) *n.* **1** The arrangement of music for performance by an orchestra. **2** The act of orchestrating, or the state of being orchestrated; planned or harmonious arrangement.

or·chid (ôr′kid) *n.* **1** Any of a widely distributed family (*Orchidaceae*) of terrestrial or epiphytic monocotyledonous plants having thickened, bulbous roots and often very showy and distinctive flowers. **2** Any of various delicate, rosy-purple colors. [<NL <L *orchis*, an orchid <Gk., orig. a testicle; so called because of the shape of its tubers]

ORCHID FLOWER

or·chid·ol·o·gy (ôr′ki·dol′ə·jē) *n.* The study and cultivation of orchids. — **or′chid·ol′o·gist** *n.*

or·chil (ôr′kil) *n.* **1** A purple or blue dye obtained from archil. **2** Archil. [<OF *orcheil, orchel* ARCHIL]

orchio- *combining form* Testicle; pertaining to the testicles. Also before vowels, **orchi-.** [<Gk. *orchis* a testicle]

or·chis (ôr′kis) *n.* Any plant of the genus *Orchis* having dense spikes of small flowers, frequently of striking shape and structure. [<NL <L, ORCHID]

or·chi·tis (ôr·kī′tis) *n. Pathol.* Inflammation of the testicle. Also **or·chei′tis, or·chi·di·tis** (ôr′ki·dī′tis). — **or·chit′ic** (-kit′ik) *adj.*

or·dain (ôr·dān′)ʹ *v.t.* **1** To order or decree; enact; establish. **2** To predestine; destine: said of God, fate, etc. **3** To invest with ministerial or priestly functions. See synonyms under INSTALL, INSTITUTE. [<OF *ordener* <L *ordinare* order < *ordo, -inis* an order] — **or·dain′er** *n.*

or·deal (ôr·dēl′, -dē′əl, ôr′dēl) *n.* **1** A severe test of character or endurance; a trying course of experience. **2** A medieval form of judicial trial in which the accused was subjected to physical tests, as carrying or walking over burning objects or immersing the hand in scalding water, the result being considered a divine judgment of guilt or innocence. See synonyms under PROOF. [OE *ordāl, ordēl* a judgment < *or-* out + *dǣl* a deal; infl. in meaning by L *ordela* an ordeal <Gmc.]

ordeal bean Calabar bean.

or·der (ôr′dər) *n.* **1** Methodical and harmonious arrangement, as of successive things or as of military units in a formation. **2** Proper or working condition; available state. **3** A command or authoritative regulation. **4** *Law* Any direction of a court made to be entered of record in a cause, and not included in the final judgment. **5** A written commission or instruction to supply, purchase, or sell something. **6** Established use or customary procedure. **7** Established or existing state of things. **8** A class or body of persons united by some common bond, as for mutual insurance, protection, aid, social culture, etc. the *Order* of Odd Fellows; a monastic or religious body: an *order* of mendicant friars. **9** A group of persons upon whom a government or sovereign has conferred an honor or dignity, and who are thus entitled to affix to their names designated initials and to wear specific insignia; also, the insignia worn as a sign of

---

membership in such a group. **10** Social rank. **11** A class or kind of a common degree of excellence. **12** *Usually pl. Eccl.* **a** Any of the various grades or degrees of the Christian ministry: also **holy orders, sacred orders.** In the Anglican Church, there are three orders: bishops, priests, and deacons. The Greek Church recognizes in addition subdeacons and readers. In the Roman Catholic Church, there are seven orders: priests (including bishops), deacons, subdeacons (the **major orders**), acolytes, exorcists, readers, and doorkeepers (the **minor orders**). **b** The rank or position of an ordained clergyman. **c** The rite or sacrament of ordination. **d** A liturgical form for a service or the performance of a rite: the *order* of confirmation. **13** *Archit.* **a** The general character of a column and its parts as distinguishing a style of architecture; a style of architecture. Usually there are considered to be five orders of classical architecture — Doric, Ionic, Corinthian, Tuscan, and Composite. **b** A column with its entablature. **14** *Biol.* A taxonomic category ranking next below the class, and above the family. **15** *Math.* A number expressing the degree of complexity of an algebraic expression. **16** *Gram.* The sequence of words in a sentence or construction. **17** The position of the rifle as a result of the command *order arms.* **18** Any one of the ancient nine grades of angels. **19** *Obs.* Suitable care; preparation: usually in the phrase *to take order.* — **in order** **1** In accordance with rule; hence, apt; appropriate. **2** Neat; tidy. — **in order that** So that; to the end that. — **in order to** For the purpose of; to the end that. — **in short order** Quickly; without delay. — **on order** Ordered but not yet delivered. — **on the order of** Similar to. — **out of order** **1** Not in proper sequence or arrangement. **2** Not in good working condition. **3** Not in accord with established rule or procedure: a senator ruled *out of order.* **4** Uncalled-for; improper: The insinuation was *out of order.* — **to order** According to the buyer's specifications: a shirt made *to order.* — *v.t.* **1** To give a command or direction to. **2** To command to go, come, etc.: They *ordered* him out of the city. **3** To give an order that (something) be done; prescribe. **4** To give an order for: to *order* a new suit. **5** To put in orderly or systematic arrangment; regulate. **6** To ordain: He was *ordered* deacon. — *v.i.* **7** To give an order or orders. — **to order arms** *Mil.* To bring a rifle perpendicularly against the right side, with the butt on the ground. See synonyms under DICTATE, REGULATE. [<OF *ordre* <L *ordo, -inis* a row, series, an order] — **or′der·er** *n.* — **or′der·less** *adj.*

    Synonyms (noun): command, direction, directive, injunction, instruction, prohibition, requirement. *Instruction* implies more superiority of knowledge, *direction* more of authority; a teacher gives *instructions* to his pupils, an employer gives *directions* to his workmen; but the *instructions* of a superior regarding action are viewed as specific *commands.* A *directive* conveys all three of these — *instructions* for action, *directions* for procedure, and *command* for performance. *Order* is more absolute still; soldiers and railroad employees have simply to obey the *orders* of their superiors. *Command* is a loftier word less frequent in common life: the *commands* of God. A *requirement* is imperative, but not always formal; it may be in the nature of things; as, the *requirements* of the position. *Prohibition* is a *command* not to do; *injunction* is now oftenest so used, especially as the *requirement* by legal authority that certain action be temporarily suspended or refrained from.

or·der·ing (ôr′dər·ing) *n.* **1** The act of directing, commanding, or disposing. **2** The act or process of arrangement, or the state of being arranged. **3** Right administration. **4** The act of ordination. **5** The act of arranging for procurement, purchase, or delivery of something.

or·der·ly (ôr′dər·lē) *adj.* **1** Having regard for arrangement; methodical; systematic. **2** Peaceful. **3** Characterized by order. **4** Pertaining to orders. See synonyms under NEAT. — *n. pl.* **·lies** **1** A soldier or non-commissioned officer detailed to carry orders for su-

---

add, āce, câre, pälm; end, ēven; it, īce; odd, ōpen, ôrder; tŏŏk, pōōl; up, bûrn; ə = a in *above,* e in *sicken,* i in *clarity,* o in *melon,* u in *focus;* yōō = u in *fuse,* oi, oil; ou, pout; ch, check; g, go; ng, ring; th, thin; th, this; zh, vision. Foreign sounds á, œ, ü, kh, ṅ; and ◆: see page xx. <*from;* + *plus;* ? *possibly.*

perior officers. 2 A hospital attendant. — *adv.* According to the rules of order; methodically; regularly; properly. —**or'der·li·ness** *n.*

or·di·nal (ôr'də·nəl) *adj.* 1 Denoting position in an order or succession. 2 Pertaining to an order, as of plants, animals, etc. —*n.* An ordinal number. See under NUMBER. [< LL *ordinalis* < L *ordo, -inis* an order]

or·di·nance (ôr'də·nəns) *n.* 1 An authoritative rule; an order, decree, or law of a municipal body. 2 A religious rite or ceremony. 3 *Archit.* A system of arrangement. 4 A law or command of God, or a decree of fate. 5 *Obs.* Order, as arrangement, disposition, rank, position, array, provision, or preparation. 6 *Obs.* The act of devising, arranging, or contriving plans; a design or device. See synonyms under LAW[1], SACRAMENT. [< OF *ordenance* < Med. L *ordinantia* < L *ordinans, -antis,* ppr. of *ordinare* ORDAIN]

or·di·nand (ôr'də·nənd) *n.* A candidate for ordination. [< L *ordinandus,* gerundive of *ordinare* ORDAIN]

or·di·nant (ôr'də·nənt) *adj.* Exercising authority; ruling.

or·di·nar·y (ôr'də·ner'ē) *adj.* 1 Of common or everyday occurrence; customary; usual. 2 According to an established order; regular; normal. 3 Common in rank or degree; of average merit or consequence; commonplace. 4 Having immediate or ex-officio jurisdiction, as a judge. See synonyms under COMMON, GENERAL, HABITUAL, NORMAL, USUAL. —*n. pl.* **·nar·ies** 1 That which is usual or common. 2 *Brit.* A meal provided regularly at a fixed price. 3 *Brit.* An eating house where such meals are served. 4 *Law* One who exercises jurisdiction in his own right, and not by delegation. 5 *U.S.* In some States, a judge exercising probate jurisdiction. 6 *Eccl.* **a** A rule or book prescribing the form for saying mass. **b** The practically unchangeable part of the mass: opposed to the *proper.* 7 An early type of bicycle with a large front wheel and a small rear wheel. 8 *Her.* A charge of the simplest kind, usually bounded between simple lines, as a chief, pale, fess, chevron, bend, cross, saltire, or quarter. —**in ordinary** 1 In actual and constant service. 2 *Naut.* Out of commission; laid up: said of a ship. [< L *ordinarius* regular, usual < *ordo, -inis* an order] —**or'di·nar·i·ness** *n.*

or·di·nate (ôr'də·nit) *adj.* 1 Characterized by order; regular. 2 *Biol.* Arranged in a regular row or rows, as spots on an insect's body or wings. —*n. Math.* 1 The distance of any point from the axis of abscissas, measured on a line parallel to the axis of ordinates in a co-ordinate system. 2 The line or number indicating such distance. [< L *ordinatus,* pp. of *ordinare* ORDAIN]

or·di·na·tion (ôr'də·nā'shən) *n.* 1 *Eccl.* The rite of consecration to the ministry. 2 The state of being ordained, regulated, or settled. 3 Arrangement of things in order; array. 4 Natural or proper order.

or·don·nance (ôr'də·nəns, *Fr.* ôr·dō·näns') *n.* 1 A right arranging of parts, as in a picture, so as to produce the best effect. 2 A law or ordinance; specifically, in French law, a code of laws on any subject. [< F < OF *ordenance* ORDINANCE]

or·dure (ôr'jər, -dyoor) *n.* Excrement; feces. [< OF < *ord* foul, nasty < L *horridus* HORRID]

ore (ôr, ōr) *n.* 1 A natural substance containing an economically valuable metal, and sometimes forming part of a rock. 2 Loosely, a natural substance containing a non-metallic mineral: sulfur *ore.* ◆Homophone: *oar.* [OE *ar, ær* brass, copper; infl. in meaning by OE *ora* unwrought metal]

o·rec·tic (o·rek'tik) *adj. Philos.* Of or pertaining to the appetites or desires; appetent; motive. Also **o·rec'tive.** [< Gk. *orektikos* appetitive < *orektos* stretched out, longed for < *oregein* stretch out, desire]

ore dressing *Metall.* The mechanical separation of valuable metals and minerals from the ores in which they occur.

o·reg·a·no (o·reg'ə·no) *n.* Origan. [< Sp. *orégano* < L *origanum* ORIGAN]

Or·e·gon (ôr'ə·gon, -gən, or'-, ôr'e·gən) A State of the western United States on the Pacific; 96,981 square miles; capital, Salem; entered the Union Feb. 14, 1859; nickname,

Beaver State: abbr. OR —**Or·e·go'ni·an** (gō'ne·ən) *adj. & n.*

Oregon fir The Douglas fir. Also **Oregon pine.**

Oregon Trail A former route extending from the Missouri River about 2,000 miles NW to the Columbia River in Oregon: used by pioneers, 1804–1846.

ore house A building in which mined ore is stored. Also **ore shed.**

o·re·ide (o're·id) See OROIDE.

ore shoot That portion of an ore deposit which is exceptionally rich in metal content.

o·rex·is (o·rek'sis) *n.* Appetite; craving. [< Gk., a desire < *oregein.* See ORECTIC.]

or·fray (ôr'frā) See ORPHREY.

or·gan (ôr'gən) *n.* 1 A musical wind instrument consisting of a collection of pipes made to sound by means of compressed air from bellows and played upon by means of keys: also **pipe organ.** 2 An electronic musical instrument not employing pipes or wind, designed to give the sounds and timbres of a pipe organ. 3 A musical instrument resembling or having some mechanism resembling the pipe organ: a reed *organ;* a barrel *organ.* 4 Any part of an organism, plant, or animal performing some definite function: the digestive *organs.* 5 An instrument or agency for communication of the views of a person or party; especially, a newspaper or periodical published in the interest of some political party or religious denomination. [Fusion of OE *organa* and OF *organe,* both < L *organum* an instrument, engine, organ < Gk. *organon* a tool, a musical instrument]

or·gan·dy (ôr'gən·de) *n. pl.* **·dies** A very thin, crisp, transparent, cotton muslin, plain or figured, used for dresses, collars, cuffs, etc. Also **or'gan·die.** [< F *organdi;* ult. origin uncertain]

or·gan–grind·er (ôr'gən·grin'dər) *n.* The player of a hand organ; specifically, a street musician playing a hand organ.

or·gan·ic (ôr·gan'ik) *adj.* 1 Of, pertaining to, or of the nature of animals and plants. 2 Affecting an organ or organs of an animal or plant: *organic* diseases. 3 Serving the purpose of an organ. 4 *Chem.* Of or pertaining to compounds containing carbon as an essential ingredient. 5 Inherent in or pertaining to the organization or fundamental structure; structural; constitutional. 6 Of or characterized by systematic coordination of parts; organized; systematized. 7 *Law* Designating that system of laws or principles forming the foundation of a government. 8 *Agric.* Pertaining to the use of compost, manure, peat moss, and other natural fertilizers in the cultivation of farms and gardens. Also **or·gan'i·cal.** See synonyms under RADICAL. —**or·gan'i·cal·ly** *adv.*

organic chemistry The branch of chemistry that relates to carbon compounds.

organic disease *Pathol.* A disease that affects some particular organ in its structure, as distinguished from its function.

or·gan·i·cism (ôr·gan'ə·siz'əm) *n.* 1 *Med.* The doctrine that all diseases are caused by specific lesions of one or more organs. 2 *Biol.* The theory of living processes as the result of the activity of all the organs considered as an autonomous, integrated system. 3 *Sociol.* The concept of society as an organism, of which beliefs, ideas, customs, etc., are component parts. —**or·gan'i·cist** *n.*

organic law 1 The law by which a government outlines and establishes its own political structure. 2 An act of Congress providing a form of government for a territory.

or·gan·ism (ôr'gən·iz'əm) *n.* 1 An animal or plant internally organized to maintain vital activities. 2 Anything that is analogous in structure and function to a living thing: the social *organism.* —**or'gan·is'mal** *adj.*

or·gan·ist (ôr'gən·ist) *n.* 1 One who plays the organ. 2 In the Middle Ages, a singer who accompanied the plain song with another part. See ORGANUM (def. 2).

or·gan·i·za·tion (ôr'gən·ə·zā'shən, -ī·zā'-) *n.* 1 The act of organizing, or the state of being organized; also, that which is organized. 2 An animal or vegetable organism. 3 A number of individuals systematically united for some end or work: a military *organization.* 4 The officials, committeemen, etc., who control a political party: also called *machine.* 5 Any combination of parts. Also *Brit.* **or'gan·i·sa'tion.**

or·gan·ize (ôr'gən·īz) *v.* **·ized, ·iz·ing** *v.t.* 1 To bring together or form as a whole or combination, as for a common objective. 2 To arrange systematically; order. 3 To furnish with organic structure. 4 **a** To enlist (workers) in a trade union. **b** To unionize the workers of (a factory, etc.). —*v.i.* 5 To form or join an organization. Also *Brit.* **or'gan·ise.** See synonyms under INSTITUTE. [< Med. L *organizare* < L *organum* ORGAN] —**or'gan·iz'a·ble** *adj.* —**or'gan·iz'er** *n.*

organ of Corti A complex structure in the human ear directly involved with the perception of sound: discovered by Alfonso Corti.

or·ga·no·gen·e·sis (ôr'gə·nō·jen'ə·sis) *n. Biol.* The development of organs in animals and plants. —**or·ga·no·ge·net'ic** (-jə·net'ik) *adj.*

or·ga·nog·ra·phy (ôr'gə·nog'rə·fē) *n.* Scientific description of organs; descriptive organology. —**or'ga·no·graph'ic** (-nō·graf'ik) or **·i·cal** *adj.*

or·ga·nol·o·gy (ôr'gə·nol'ə·jē) *n.* The branch of biology that treats of organs of the body. —**or'ga·no·log'ic** (-nō·loj'ik) or **·i·cal** *adj.* —**or'ga·nol'o·gist** *n.*

or·ga·non (ôr'gə·non) *n. pl.* **·na** (-nə) or **·nons** A system of rules and principles considered as an instrument of guidance, as of knowledge or thought. Also *organum.* [< Gk., organ]

or·ga·no·sil·i·con (ôr'gə·nō·sil'ə·kon) *n. Chem.* Any of an important class of compounds or polymers containing silicon and carbon; a ilicone.

or·ga·no·ther·a·py (ôr'gə·nō·ther'ə·pē) *n. Med.* The treatment of disease by remedies derived from animal organs. Also **or'ga·no·ther'a·peu'tics** (-ther'ə·pyōo'tiks).

organ pipe One of the long tubes of a pipe organ, in which a column of air is made to vibrate so as to produce a tone of definite pitch.

or·ga·num (ôr'gə·nəm) *n. pl.* **·na** (-nə) or **·nums** 1 An organon. 2 In medieval music, a part sung as an accompaniment to the melody or plain song at an interval of a fourth or a fifth above or below it; also, this method of part singing. [< L, ORGAN]

or·gan·za (ôr·gan'zə) *n.* A sheer, crisp fabric used for evening dresses, trimming, etc. [Origin uncertain]

or·gan·zine (ôr'gən·zēn) *n.* 1 A silk thread made of several single threads twisted together; thrown silk. 2 A fabric made of organzine. [< F *organsin* < Ital. *organzine;* ult. origin unknown]

or·gasm (ôr'gaz·əm) *n.* 1 Immoderate or extreme excitement or behavior. 2 *Physiol.* The acme of excitement at the culmination of the sexual act, followed by detumescence. [< F *orgasme* < Gk. *orgasmos* a swelling < *orgaein* swell, be excited] —**or·gas'mic** (ôr·gaz'mik), **or·gas·tic** (ôr·gas'tik) *adj.*

or·geat (ôr'zhat, *Fr.* ôr·zhá') *n.* A sirup made from barley water and sugar flavored with almonds, orange flowers, etc. [< MF < Provençal *orjat* < *ordi, orge* barley < L *hordeum*]

or·gi·as·tic (ôr'jē·as'tik) *adj.* Pertaining to or resembling the Greek orgies; hence, marked by wild revelries. Also **or'gi·ac, or'gic.** [< Gk. *orgiastikos* < *orgiastēs* a celebrator of an orgy < *orgiazein* celebrate orgies]

or·gone (ôr'gōn) *n.* In the psychobiology of Wilhelm Reich, biological energy, accumulated from the environment and discharged gradually in all activity but suddenly in the orgasm: identified with the libido, as defined by Freud and, tentatively, with the ether of older physical theories.

or·gy (ôr'jē) *n. pl.* **·gies.** 1 Wild or wanton revelry; a drunken carousal; debauch. 2 Any immoderate or excessive indulgence in something; an *orgy* of reading. 3 *pl.* The secret rites in honor of certain ancient Greek and Roman deities, as Dionysus, marked by ecstatic or frenzied songs and dances. [Earlier *orgies,* pl. < MF < L *orgia* < Gk., secret rites]

o·ri·bi (ôr'ə·bē, or'-) *n. pl.* **·bis** or **·bi** A small, dun-colored African antelope (genus *Ourebia*), about two feet high at the shoulder: also spelled *ourebi.* [< Afrikaans < Hottentot *arab*]

o·ri·el (ôr'ē·əl, ō'rē-) *n. Archit.* A bay window; especially, one built out from a wall and resting on a bracket or similar support. [< OF *oriol* a porch, gallery, ? < Med. L *oriolum;* ult. origin unknown]

o·ri·ent (ôr'ē·ənt, ō'rē-) *n.* 1 The east; opposed to *occident.* 2 The eastern sky; also, dawn; sunrise. 3 The iridescent luster of a pearl. —*v.t.* 1 To cause to face or turn to the east. **2** To place or adjust, as a map, in exact relation to the points of the compass. **3** To adjust according to first principles or recognized facts or truths; adapt (oneself) mentally to a situation. **4** To adjust in relation to something else: His experience *oriented* his ideas toward science. —*adj.* **1** Resembling sunrise; bright. **2** Ascending. [< OF < L *oriens, -entis* rising sun, east, orig. ppr. of *oriri* rise]

O·ri·ent (ôr′ē·ənt, ō′rē-) The East; Asia, especially eastern Asia: opposed to *Occident*.

o·ri·en·tal (ôr′ē·en′təl, ō′rē-) *adj.* **1** *Astron.* Eastern; appearing or being in the eastern sky: said of stars and planets. **2** Specially bright, clear, and pure: said of gems. **3** Noting a variety of precious corundum, especially sapphire, marked by colors suggestive of other gems: an *oriental* amethyst, *oriental* aquamarine, *oriental* emerald, *oriental* topaz. —**o′ri·en′tal·ly** *adv.*

O·ri·en·tal (ôr′ē·en′təl, ō′rē-) *adj.* **1** Of or pertaining to the Orient; eastern. **2** Magnificent; gorgeous; sumptuous: *Oriental* luxury. **3** Designating a zoogeographical realm or region which includes India, southern Asia, the East Indies, and the Philippine Islands. —*n.* An inhabitant of Asia; an Asian. Opposed to *Occidental.* Also **o′ri·en′tal.**

Oriental rug A rug or carpet hand-woven in one piece in the Orient.

oriental topaz A yellow form of corundum used as a gemstone.

o·ri·en·tate (ôr′ē·en·tāt′, ō′rē-) *v.* **·tat·ed, ·tat·ing** *v.t.* To orient —*v.i.* To face or turn eastward or in some specified direction; be oriented. [< F *orienter* < OF *orient* ORIENT]

o·ri·en·ta·tion (ôr′ē·en·tā′shən, ō′rē-) *n.* **1** The act of orienting, or the state of being oriented. **2** Position, or the determining of position, with relation to the points of the compass. **3** The determination or adjustment of one's position with reference to circumstances, ideals, etc. **4** *Psychol.* Awareness of one's own temporal, spatial, and personal relationships. **5** *Archit.* The construction of a church upon an east-west axis, so as to have the altar in the eastern end. **6** The homing instinct, as in pigeons. **7** *Chem.* The particular disposition of the constituent atoms in a compound, especially as determined by electrical forces.

o·ri·en·ted (ôr′ē·en·tid, ō′rē-, -ən·tid) *adj.* **1** Directed toward; interested in: *oriented* to the arts. **2** Directed ·or centered: used in combination: *child-oriented.*

or·i·fice (ôr′ə·fis, or′-) *n.* A small opening into a cavity; an aperture. See HOLE. [< MF < LL *orificium* < L *os, oris* mouth + *facere* make]

or·i·ga·mi (ôr′i·gä′mē) *n.* The ancient Japanese art of folding single sheets of paper into animal and other forms, usually without the aid of scissors or paste. [< Japanese]

or·i·gan (ôr′ə·gən, or′-) *n.* The wild marjoram *(Origanum vulgare),* an important source of carvacrol: its fragrant leaves are esteemed as a seasoning. Also spelled *oregano.* [< OF < L *origanum* < Gk. *origanon,* an herb like marjoram < *oros, oreos* a mountain + *ganos* brightness, joy]

or·i·gin (ôr′ə·jin, or′-) *n.* **1** The commencement of the existence of anything. **2** A primary source; cause. **3** Parentage; ancestry. **4** *Anat.* The relatively fixed point of attachment of a muscle. Compare INSERTION. **5** *Math.* **a** The point at which the axes of a Cartesian coordinate system intersect; the point where the ordinate and abscissa equal zero. **b** The point in a polar coordinate system where the radius vector equals zero. See illustration under QUADRANT, OCTANT. See synonyms under BEGINNING. [Appar. < OF *origine* < L *origo, -inis* a rise, beginning]

o·rig·i·nal (ə·rij′ə·nəl) *adj.* **1** Of or belonging to the beginning, origin, or first stage of existence of a thing. **2** Immediately produced by one's own mind and thought; not copied or produced by imitation. **3** Able to produce works requiring thought, without copying or imitating those of others; creative; inventive. See synonyms under AUTHENTIC, FIRST, NATIVE, PRIMEVAL, RADI-

CAL, TRANSCENDENTAL. —*n.* **1** The first form of anything. **2** The language in which a book is first written. **3** A person of unique character or genius; also, an eccentric. **4** Originator; also, origin. See synonyms under IDEAL, MODEL.

o·rig·i·nal·i·ty (ə·rij′ə·nal′ə·tē) *n. pl.* **·ties 1** The power of originating inventiveness. **2** The quality of being original or novel.

o·rig·i·nal·ly (ə·rij′ə·nəl·ē) *adv.* **1** At the beginning. **2** In a new and striking manner.

original sin *Theol.* The natural corruption and depravity inherent in mankind because of Adam's first sinful disobedience.

o·rig·i·nate (ə·rij′ə·nāt) *v.* **·nat·ed, ·nat·ing** *v.t.* To bring into existence; create, initiate. —*v.i.* To come into existence; have origin; arise. See synonyms under INSTITUTE, PRODUCE, PROPAGATE. —**o·rig′i·na′tion** *n.* —**o·rig′i·na′tive** *adj.* —**o·rig′i·na′tive·ly** *adv.* —**o·rig′i·na′tor** *n.*

o·ri·na·sal (ôr′ə·nā′zəl, or′-) *adj.* **1** *Anat.* Of or pertaining to the mouth and nose: the *orinasal* duct. **2** *Phonet.* Pronounced with the nasal and oral passages both open, as the French nasal vowels. —*n. Phonet.* An orinasal vowel. [< L *os, oris* mouth + NASAL]

o·ri·ole (ôr′ē·ōl, ō′rē-) *n.* **1** Any of a family *(Oriolidae)* of black-and-yellow passerine birds of the Old World, related to the crows; the common **European** (or **golden**) **oriole** *(Oriolus oriolus)* is bright yellow with sharply contrasting black wings and tail, and builds a hanging nest. **2** One of various black-and-yellow American songbirds (family *Icteridae)* building a hanging nest; especially, the Baltimore oriole and the orchard oriole. [< OF *oriol* < Med. L *oriolus* < L *aureolus,* dim. of *aureus* golden < *aurum* gold]

or·i·son (ôr′i·zən, or′-) *n. Usually pl.* A devotional prayer. See synonyms under PRAYER. [< OF *oreisun, orison* < L *oratio, -onis* a prayer. Doublet of ORATION.]

ork (ôrk) See ORC.

orle (ôrl) *n. Her.* A subordinary bearing consisting of a band, half the width of a bordure, extending round the shield near the edge. [< F < OF *urle, ourle,* dim. < L *ora* a border]

Or·lé·ans (ôr·lā·än′) Name of a cadet branch of the Valois and Bourbon houses of France, many members of which have been prominent in French history from the 14th century. — **Louis Philippe Joseph d′,** 1747–93, revolutionary and egalitarian; guillotined: known as *Philippe Égalité.*

Or·lon (ôr′lon) *n.* A synthetic fiber woven from an acrylic resin: it has high resistance to heat, light, and chemicals and is widely used as a textile material: a trade name.

or·lop (ôr′lop) *n. Naut.* The lowest deck of a ship, especially of a warship. [< Du. *overloop,* orig. a covering < *over* over + *loopen* run; so called because it covers the hold]

or·mer (ôr′mər) *n.* **1** An ear shell; especially, *Haliotis tuberculata,* an edible univalve mollusk of the Channel Islands. **2** An abalone. [< dial. F (Channel Islands) *ormier,* contraction of *oreille de mer,* lit., ear of the sea; so called with ref. to its shape]

or·mo·lu (ôr′mə·lōō) *n.* Gilt or bronzed metallic ware, or lustrous bronze, used in decorating furniture, etc. [< F *or moulu,* lit., ground gold < *or* gold (< L *aurum*) + *moulu,* pp. of *moudre* grind < L *molere*]

or·na·ment (ôr′nə·mənt) *n.* **1** A part or an addition that contributes to the beauty or elegance of a thing. **2** Ornamentation in the abstract, or ornaments collectively. **3** Any thing or person considered as a source of honor or credit. **4** A mark of distinction; decoration. **5** *Music* A decorative note or notes not necessary to the melody; an appoggiatura. —*v.t.* (ôr′nə·ment) To adorn with ornaments; embellish. See synonyms under ADORN, GARNISH. [< OF *ornement* < L *ornamentum* equipment, ornament < *ornare* adorn] —**or′na·ment′er** *n.*

or·na·men·tal (ôr′nə·men′təl) *adj.* Serving to adorn. —*n.* An ornamental object, especially a plant meant for decorative purposes. —**or′na·men′tal·ly** *adv.*

or·na·men·ta·tion (ôr′nə·men·tā′shən) *n.* **1** The act of adorning, or the state of being adorned. **2** Ornamental things collectively;

that with which something is ornamented.

or·nate (ôr·nāt′) *adj.* **1** Ornamented to a marked degree; artistically elaborate, as a literary style. **2** Ornamented; decorated. [< L *ornatus,* pp. of *ornare* adorn] —**or·nate′ly** *adv.* —**or·nate′ness** *n.*

or·ner·y (ôr′nər·ē, ôrn′rē) *adj. U. S. Dial.* **1** Mean; low; also, unruly; stubborn. **2** Common; ordinary. [Alter. of ORDINARY] —**or′ner·i·ness** *n.*

or·nis (ôr′nis) *n.* Avifauna. [< G < Gk., a bird]

or·nith·ic (ôr·nith′ik) *adj.* Of or pertaining to birds. [< Gk. *ornithikos* birdlike < *ornis,* *ornithos* a bird]

or·ni·thine (ôr′nə·thēn, -thin) *n. Biochem.* An amino acid, $C_5H_{12}O_2N_2$, found in the urine of birds; a product of arginine. [< Gk. *ornis, ornithos* a bird + -INE²]

ornitho- *combining form* Bird; of or related to birds: *ornithology.* Also, before vowels, **ornith-.** [< Gk. *ornis, ornithos* a bird]

or·ni·thoid (ôr′nə·thoid) *adj.* Resembling a bird or birds.

or·ni·thol·o·gy (ôr′nə·thol′ə·jē) *n.* The branch of zoology that treats of birds. [< ORNITHO- + -LOGY] —**or′ni·tho·log′ic** (-thə·loj′ik) or **·i·cal** *adj.* —**or′ni·tho·log′i·cal·ly** *adv.* —**or′ni·thol′o·gist** *n.*

or·ni·thoph·i·lous (ôr′nə·thof′ə·ləs) *adj. Bot.* Bird-loving: said of flowers that are adapted for or depend upon birds (usually hummingbirds) to transfer the pollen from the stamens to the stigma; bird-pollinated. [< ORNITHO- + -PHILOUS]

or·ni·tho·pod (ôr′nə·thō·pod, ôr·ni′-) *Paleontol. n.* One of an extinct order *(Ornithischia)* of bipedal dinosaurians of herbivorous habits. — *adj.* Of or pertaining to this order. [< NL *Ornithopoda* < Gk. *ornis, ornithos* a bird + *pous, podos* a foot]

or·ni·thop·ter (ôr′nə·thop′tər) *n.* A theoretical type of aircraft sustained and propelled by an upward and downward movement of the wings, as in the flight of a bird: also called *orthopter.* [< ORNITHO- + Gk. *pteron* a wing]

or·ni·tho·rhyn·chus (ôr′nə·thō·ring′kəs) *n. pl.* **·chi** (-kī) An egg-laying mammal with a duck-like bill; a duckbill. [< NL < Gk. *ornis, ornithos* a bird + *rhynchos* a beak] —**or′ni·tho·rhyn′chous** *adj.*

or·ni·tho·sis (ôr′nə·thō′sis) *n.* An infectious virus disease of turkeys, chickens, and other birds not of the parrot family: it resembles psittacosis and is transmissible to man.

oro-¹ *combining form* Mouth; oral: *oropharynx.* [< L *os, oris* the mouth]

oro-² *combining form Geol.* Mountain; of mountains: *orography.* [< Gk. *oros* a mountain]

or·o·ban·cha·ceous (ôr′ō·bang·kā′shəs, or′-) *adj.* Designating a genus *(Orobanche)* typical of a family *(Orobanchaceae)* of low, leafless, parasitic, yellowish or brownish herbs lacking chlorophyll; the broomrapes. [< NL < L, broomrape < Gk. *orobanchē* < *orobos* a kind of vetch + *anchein* throttle]

o·rog·e·ny (ô·roj′ə·nē, ō-) *n. Geol.* The process of mountain formation. [< ORO-² + -GENY] —**or·o·gen·ic** (ôr′ə·jen′ik, or′-) *adj.*

o·rog·ra·phy (ô·rog′rə·fē, ō-) *n.* The branch of physiography that treats of the development and relations of highlands and mountain ranges. [< ORO-² + -GRAPHY] —**or·o·graph·ic** (ôr′ə·graf′ik, or′-) or **·i·cal** *adj.*

o·ro·ide (ôr′ō·īd, ō′rō-) *n.* An alloy of copper, zinc, tin, and other metals, having a golden luster: also spelled *oreide.* [< F *or* gold (< L *aurum*) + Gk. *eidos* form]

o·rol·o·gy (ô·rol′ə·jē, ō-) *n.* The study of mountains. [< ORO-² + -LOGY] —**or·o·log·i·cal** (ôr′ə·loj′ə·kəl, or′-) *adj.* —**o·rol′o·gist** *n.*

o·rom·e·ter (ô·rom′ə·tər, ō-) *n.* An aneroid barometer having, in addition to the usual scale, a second system of graduations giving elevations above sea level corresponding to barometric pressure; a mountain barometer. [< ORO-² + -METER] —**or·o·met·ric** (ôr′ə·met′rik, or′-) *adj.*

o·ro·phar·ynx (ôr′ō·far′ingks, ō′rō-) *n. pl.* **·pha·ryn·ges** (-fə·rin′jēz) or **·phar·ynx·es** *Anat.* That part of the pharynx behind the mouth: the pharynx proper. [< ORO-¹ + PHARYNX]

o·ro·tund (ôr′ə·tund, ō′rə-) *adj.* **1** Full, clear,

rounded, and resonant: said of the voice or utterance. **2** Pompous; inflated, as a manner of speech. — *n.* An orotund quality of voice: also **o'ro·tun'di·ty.** [< L *ore rotundo* with well-turned speech, lit., with a round mouth < *os, oris* mouth + *rotundus* round]

or·phan (ôr'fən) *n.* A child whose parents are dead. — *adj.* **1** Having lost one or (more commonly) both parents: said of a child. **2** Pertaining to a child so bereaved. — *v.t.* To bereave of parents or of a parent; make an orphan of. [< LL *orphanus* < Gk. *orphanos,* lit., bereaved] — **or'phan·hood** (-hŏŏd) *n.*

or·phan·age (ôr'fən·ij) *n.* **1** The state of being an orphan. **2** An institution for orphans.

Or·phe·us (ôr'fē·əs) In Greek mythology, a musician who could charm beasts and even rocks and trees by his singing to the lyre. When his wife Eurydice died he was permitted to lead her back to earth from Hades provided he would not look at her: he failed in the test and was later killed by the Thracian women who were enraged at his mourning for Eurydice. — **Or'phe·an** *adj.*

or·phrey (ôr'frē) *n.* **1** Gold embroidery, or any costly embroidery. **2** A band of gold embroidery or other rich material put on certain ecclesiastical vestments. Also spelled *orfray.* [< OF *orfreis* < Med. L *aurifrisium* < L *auriphrygium* < *aurum* gold + *Phrygius* Phrygian]

or·pi·ment (ôr'pə·mənt) *n.* An easily cut, pearly, lemon-yellow, native arsenic trisulfide, As_2S_3, used as a pigment and as a dyestuff. [< OF < L *auripigmentum* gold pigment]

or·pine (ôr'pin) *n.* **1** An Old World species of stonecrop (*Sedum telephium*) with tuberous root, stout erect stem, ovate leaves, and white or purple flowers in dense tufts: naturalized in the United States. **2** A Mediterranean herb (*Telephium imperati*) of the pink family, with prostrate stems and white flowers in terminal clusters. Also **or'pin.** [< OF *orpin* < *orpiment* ORPIMENT]

or·re·ry (ôr'ə·rē, or'-) *n. pl.* **·ries** A mechanical apparatus for exhibiting the relative motions and positions of the members of the solar system; a cosmoscope. [after the fourth Earl of *Orrery,* Charles Boyle, 1676–1731, English statesman for whom an early copy of the machine was made]

or·rhol·o·gy (ô·rol'ə·jē, ō-) *n.* Serology. [< Gk. *orrhos* serum + -LOGY]

or·ris (ôr'is, or'-) *n.* Any of the several species of *Iris* having a scented root, especially *I. florentina,* of which the dried rootstock is used in medicine, perfumery, etc. Also **or'rice.** [Prob. alter. of Ital. *ireos* < L *iris* IRIS]

or·seille (ôr·sāl') *n.* Archil. [< F < OF *orchel* ARCHIL]

ort (ôrt) *n.* *Usually pl.* A worthless leaving, as of food after a meal. [< Prob. < Du. *ooraete* remains of food]

or·tet (ôr'tet) *n. Bot.* The plant from which a clon is derived. [< L *ortus* an origin, a rising < *oriri* rise]

or·thi·con (ôr'thə·kon) *n.* A sensitive television camera tube which uses low-velocity electrons in scanning and can pick up scenes under all lighting conditions or by infrared radiations. Also **image orthicon.** [< ORTH(O)- + ICON(OSCOPE)]

ortho- *combining form* **1** Straight; upright; in line: *orthotropic.* **2** At right angles; perpendicular: *orthorhombic.* **3** Correct; proper; right: *orthography.* **4** *Med.* The correction of irregularities or deformities of: *orthodontia.* **5** *Chem.* **a** A compound, usually an acid, containing the greatest possible number of hydroxyl groups: distinguished from *meta-.* **b** A benzene derivative in which the substituted atoms or radicals occupy the positions 1, 2: abbr. *o-.* Compare META-, PARA-. See BENZENE RING. Also, before vowels, **orth-.** [< Gk. < *orthos* straight]

or·tho axis (ôr'thō) *Mineral.* That axis in a crystal of the monoclinic system which is perpendicular to the other two axes.

or·tho·bi·o·sis (ôr'thō·bī·ō'sis) *n.* Sound and correct living; living in accordance with proper hygienic principles.

or·tho·cen·ter (ôr'thō·sen'tər) *n. Geom.* The point at which the three altitudes of a triangle intersect.

or·tho·ce·phal·ic (ôr'thō·sə·fal'ik) *adj.* Having a head in which the ratio between the vertical and transverse diameters is from 70 to 75. Also

or·tho·ceph'a·lous (-sef'ə·ləs). — **or'tho·ceph'a·ly** *n.*

or·tho·chro·mat·ic (ôr'thō·krō·mat'ik) *adj. Phot.* Maintaining natural relations of light and shade, especially by the use of films or plates treated to give correct values to the greens and yellows: also called *isochromatic.* — **or'tho·chro'ma·tism** (-krō'mə·tiz'əm) *n.*

or·tho·clase (ôr'thō·klās, -klāz) *n.* A brittle, colorless to flesh-colored or gray mineral consisting mainly of potassium feldspar, $KAlSi_3O_8$, crystallized in the monoclinic system. [< ORTHO- + Gk. *klasis* a fracture < *klaein* break]

or·tho·clas·tic (ô'thō·klas'tik) *adj.* Having right-angled cleavages, as orthoclase.

or·tho·cy·mene (ôr'thō·sī'mēn) *n. Chem.* One of the three isomeric forms of cymene.

or·tho·dome (ôr'thə·dōm) *n.* A domelike surface parallel to one of the axes in a monoclinic crystal. — **or'tho·dom'ic** (-dom'ik) *adj.*

or·tho·don·tia (ôr'thə·don'shə, -shē·ə) *n.* The branch of dentistry which is concerned with the prevention and correction of irregularities and faulty positions of the teeth. [< NL < Gk. *orthos* right, straight + *odous, odontos* a tooth] — **or'tho·don'tic** (-don'tik) *adj.* — **or'tho·don'tist** *n.*

or·tho·dox (ôr'thə·doks) *adj.* **1** Correct or sound in doctrine; holding the commonly accepted faith, established doctrines, etc.: opposed to *heterodox.* **2** Conforming to the Christian faith as formulated in the early ecumenical creeds. **3** Approved; accepted. [< MF *orthodoxe* < LL *orthodoxus* < Gk. *orthodoxos* having right opinion < *orthos* right + *doxa* opinion < *dokeein* think] — **or'tho·dox'ly** *adv.*

Orthodox Church The Greek Church.

Orthodox Judaism Judaism as practiced by those who hold that both the Scriptures and the oral laws are divinely authoritative and that traditional rituals are to be faithfully observed. Compare CONSERVATIVE JUDAISM, REFORM JUDAISM.

or·tho·dox·y (ôr'thə·dok'sē) *n. pl.* **·dox·ies 1** Belief in estblished doctrine. **2** Agreement with accepted standards, established doctrines, ideas, etc. — **or'tho·dox'i·cal** *adj.*

or·tho·e·pist (ôr·thō'ə·pist, ôr'thō·ə·pist) *n.* An authority on pronunciation. — **or'tho·e·pis'tic** (ôr'thō·ə·pis'tik) *adj.*

or·tho·e·py (ôr·thō'ə·pē, ôr'thō·ep'ē) *n.* **1** The art of correct pronunciation. **2** Pronunciation in general. [< Gk. *orthoepeia* correctness of diction < *orthos* right + *epos* a word] — **or·tho·ep·ic** (ôr'thō·ep'ik) or **-i·cal** *adj.*

or·thog·a·my (ôr·thog'ə·mē) *n.* **1** *Bot.* Immediate or direct self-fertilization of the ovary, as by the stamens of the same flower; autogamy. **2** Normal bisexual union. — **or·tho·gam·ic** (ôr'thō·gam'ik), **or·thog'a·mous** *adj.*

or·tho·gen·e·sis (ôr'thō·jen'ə·sis) *n. Biol.* The doctrine that the phylogenetic evolution of organisms takes place systematically in a definite direction and not accidentally in many directions; variation predetermined by the germ plasm. — **or·tho·ge·net·ic** (-jə·net'ik) *adj.*

or·thog·na·thous (ôr·thog'nə·thəs) *adj.* Having the lower jaw in line with the upper; having straight jaws. Also **or·thog·nath·ic** (ôr'·thog·nath'ik). [< ORTHO- + -GNATHOUS] — **or·thog'na·thism, or·thog'na·thy** *n.*

or·thog·o·nal (ôr·thog'ə·nəl) *adj.* Having or determined by right angles; perpendicular. [< F *orthogonale* < *orthogone* a right triangle < LL *orthogonium* < Gk. *orthogōnios* < *orthos* right + *gōnia* an angle] — **or·thog'o·nal·ly** *adv.*

or·tho·graph·ic (ôr'thō·graf'ik) *adj.* **1** Relating to orthography; also, correctly spelled. **2** Pertaining to right lines or angles. Also **or'tho·graph'i·cal.** — **or'tho·graph'i·cal·ly** *adv.*

orthographic projection A map projection in which the lines lie at right angles to the plane of projection.

or·thog·ra·phy (ôr·thog'rə·fē) *n. pl.* **·phies 1** A mode or system of spelling, especially of spelling correctly or according to usage. **2** The science that treats of letters and spelling. **3** The art or act of drawing in correct architectural projection. — **or·thog'ra·pher, or·thog'ra·phist** *n.*

or·tho·hy·dro·gen (ôr'thō·hī'drə·jən) *n. Chem.* An unstable form of hydrogen in which the molecules consist of two hydrogen atoms spinning in the same direction, giving improperly alined poles. Compare PARAHYDROGEN. [< ORTHO- in line + HYDROGEN]

or·tho·ki·net·ic (ôr'thō·ki·net'ik) *adj.* Pertaining

to or having movement in one direction, as molecules or particles.

or·tho·pe·dics (ôr'thə·pē'diks) *n.* The branch of surgery which is concerned with the correction of skeletal and spinal deformities, especially in children. Also **or'tho·pae'dics.** [< F *orthopédique* < *orthopédie* orthopedics < Gk. *orthos* right + *paideia* training of children < *pais, paidos* child] — **or'tho·pe'dic** *adj.*

or·tho·pe·dist (ôr'thə·pē'dist) *n.* A physician specializing in orthopedics.

or·thoph·o·ny (ôr·thof'ə·nē) *n.* The art of speaking correctly. [< ORTHO- + -PHONY] — **or·tho·phon·ic** (ôr'thə·fon'ik) *adj.*

or·tho·pod (ôr'thə·pod) *n.* An orthopedist.

or·thop·ter (ôr·thop'tər) See ORNITHOPTER.

or·thop·ter·an (ô·thop'tər·ən) *n.* Any of an order (Orthoptera) of insects with membranous hind wings and coriaceous, usually straight fore wings, including locusts, crickets, grasshoppers, cockroaches, etc. — *adj.* Of or pertaining to the *Orthoptera.* Also **or·thop'ter·on.** [< NL < Gk. *orthos* straight + *pteron* a wing] — **or·thop'ter·al, or·thop'ter·ous** *adj.*

or·thop·tic (ôr·thop'tik) *adj.* **1** Of, pertaining to, or characterized by normal binocular vision. **2** Designating a method of correcting defective vision by muscular exercise of the eyes. [< ORTH(O)- + OPTIC]

or·thop·tics (ôr·thop'tiks) *n. pl. (construed as singular)* The treatment of defects in binocular vision and of poor visual habits, especially by training in eye movements.

or·tho·rhom·bic (ôr'thə·rom'bik) *adj.* Pertaining to a crystal system assumed to contain three unequal axes at right angles.

or·tho·scop·ic (ôr'thə·skop'ik) *adj.* **1** Having correct vision. **2** Constructed so as to correct optical distortion: an *orthoscopic* eyepiece of a telescope.

or·tho·stat·ic (ôr'thə·stat'ik) *adj.* Of or relating to an upright standing position.

or·thos·ti·chy (ôr·thos'tə·kē) *n. pl.* **·chies** *Bot.* A vertical row or rank: applied to an arrangement of organs on an axis, as leaves or flowers. [< ORTHO- + Gk. *stichos* a row] — **o·thos'ti·chous** *adj.*

or·tho·trop·ic (ôr'thə·trop'ik) *adj. Bot.* Growing vertically: said of developing plant organs that grow nearly vertically, either upward or downward. — **or·thot·ro·pism** (ôr·thot'rə·piz'əm) *n.*

or·thot·ro·pous (ôr·thot'rə·pəs) *adj. Bot.* Growing straight: said of an ovule in which the nucellus is straight. Also **or·thot'ro·pal.** [< NL *orthotropus* < Gk. *orthos* straight + *trepein* turn] — **or·thot'ro·py** *n.*

or·to·lan (ôr'tə·lən) *n.* **1** An Old World bunting (*Emberiza hortulana*) reddish-green above with blackish spots, and with a greenish-gray head: highly esteemed as a table delicacy. **2** Any of several other birds, as the reedbird or bobolink of the United States. [< F < Provençal < Ital. *ortolano* a gardener < L *hortulanus* < *hortulus,* dim. of *hortus* a garden; so called because it frequents gardens]

-ory[1] *suffix of nouns* A place or instrument for (performing the action of the main element): *dormitory, lavatory.* [< OF -*oire,* -*orie* < L -*orium;* or directly < L]

-ory[2] *suffix of adjectives* Related to; like; resembling: *amatory, laudatory.* [< OF -*oire* < L -*orius;* or directly < L]

o·ryx (ôr'iks, or'-, ō'riks) *n.* A long-horned African antelope (genus *Oryx*), as the gemsbok. [< NL < L < Gk., a pickax, a kind of antelope; so called from its pointed horns]

os[1] (os) *n. pl.* **o·ra** (ôr'ə, ō'rə) *Anat.* A mouth or opening into the interior of an organ. [< L]

os[2] (os) *n. pl.* **os·sa** (os'ə) *Anat.* A bone. ob < L]

os[3] (ōs) *n. pl.* **o·sar** (ō'sär) *Geol.* A sinuous ridge of glacial sand and gravel, deposited by a stream flowing beneath; an esker: also spelled *ose.* [< Sw. *ås* a ridge, a chain of hills]

O·sage (ō'sāj) *n.* One of a tribe of North American Indians of southern Siouan stock, formerly inhabiting the region between the Missouri and Arkansas rivers: now living in Oklahoma. [< Siouan (Osage) *Wazhazhe* war people]

Osage orange A showy, spreading, moraceous tree *(Maclura pomifera)* native to Arkansas and adjacent regions, having alternate, entire, glossy leaves and a large inedible aggregate fruit somewhat like an orange in size and color; also, the fruit of this tree.

Os·car (os′kər) *n.* One of the small gold statuettes awarded annually (since 1928) by the Academy of Motion Picture Arts and Sciences for outstanding performances, productions, photography, etc., in motion pictures. [Said to be from the remark of an Academy secretary that the statuette resembled her uncle *Oscar*]

os·cil·late (os′ə·lāt) *v.i.* **·lat·ed, ·lat·ing 1** To swing back and forth; vibrate, as a pendulum. **2** To vary undecidedly; waver; fluctuate. **3** *Physics* To produce oscillations. See synonyms under FLUCTUATE, SHAKE. [< L *oscillatus,* pp. of *oscillare* swing < *oscillum* a swing]

os·cil·la·tion (os′ə·lā′shən) *n.* **1** The act or state of oscillating. **2** *Physics* **a** A single swing of an oscillating body between two extremes. **b** A continual fluctuation between extreme values of quantity or force, as in a high-frequency electric current, the maximum value of which constantly diminishes with a speed dependent upon the damping effect present. **—os′cil·la·to·ry** (-lə·tôr′ē, -tō′rē) *adj.*

os·cil·la·tor (os′ə·lā′tər) *n.* **1** One who or that which oscillates. **2** Any oscillating machine. **3** *Electronics* A device for producing electromagnetic oscillations of a specified frequency.

os·cil·lo·gram (ə·sil′ə·gram) *n.* A record made by an oscillograph. [< *oscillo-* < L *oscillare* oscillate + -GRAM]

os·cil·lo·graph (ə·sil′ə·graf, -gräf) *n.* A device for making a visible representation of the oscillations of an alternating current, transmitted in the form of reflected light rays to a screen for observation, or to a moving photographic film for purposes of record.

os·cil·lo·scope (ə·sil′ə·skōp) *n.* A cathode-ray oscillograph of low voltage for recording wave forms on a fluorescent screen: used in radio and in sound-ranging devices.

os·cine[1] (os′in -īn) *n.* Any passerine bird of the suborder *Oscines,* having the most highly developed vocal ability among birds, as thrushes, sparrows, etc.: commonly called *singing birds.* —*adj.* Of or pertaining to the *Oscines.* [< NL < L *oscen, oscinis* a singing bird < *ob-* towards + *canere* sing]

os·cine[2] (os′ēn, -in) *n.* *Chem.* A decomposition product of scopolamine. [< G *oscin,* short for *hyoscin* hyoscine]

os·ci·tan·cy (os′ə·tən·sē) *n.* **1** The act of yawning or gaping. **2** Unusual drowsiness; dulness. Also **os′ci·tance.** [< L *oscitans, -antis,* ppr. of *oscitare* gape, yawn < *os* a mouth + *citare* move] —**os′ci·tant** *adj.*

os·cu·lant (os′kyə·lənt) *adj.* *Biol.* **1** Intermediate in character between two groups of organisms; intergrading: an *osculant* genus or family. **2** Closely adherent. [< L *osculans, -antis,* ppr. of *osculari.* See OSCULATE.]

os·cu·lar (os′kyə·lər) *adj.* **1** Of or pertaining to the mouth. **2** *Zool.* Of or pertaining to an osculum. [< L *osculum.* See OSCULATE.]

os·cu·late (os′kyə·lāt) *v.t. & v.i.* **·lat·ed, ·lat·ing 1** To kiss. **2** To bring or come into close contact or union. **3** *Geom.* To touch so as to have three or more points in common, as two curves. **4** *Biol.* To have (characteristics) in common, as two genera or families. [< L *osculatus,* pp. of *osculari* kiss < *osculum* a little mouth, a kiss, dim. of *os* mouth]

os·cu·la·tion (os′kyə·lā′shən) *n.* **1** The act of kissing; also, a kiss. **2** *Math.* A point on a curve where two branches have a common tangent but do not reverse direction. **—os′cu·la·to·ry** (-lə·tôr′ē, -tō′rē) *adj.*

os·cu·lum (os′kyə·ləm) *n. pl.* **·la** (-lə) *Zool.* One of the comparatively large apertures in a sponge by which water with waste products is expelled. Also **os′cule** (-kyōōl). [< L, dim. of *os* a mouth]

ose (ōs) See OS[3].

-ose[1] *suffix of adjectives* **1** Full of or abounding in (what is indicated by the main element): *verbose.* **2** Like; resembling (the main element): *grandiose.* Compare -OUS. [< L *-osus*]

-ose[2] *suffix Chem.* **1** A carbohydrate: *glucose, cellulose.* **2** A derivative of a protein: *proteose.* [< (GLUC)OSE]

o·sier (ō′zhər) *n.* **1** Any various species of willow (genus *Salix*), producing long, flexible shoots used in wickerwork, especially the European **velvet osier** *(Salix viminalis).* **2** One of the shoots of an osier. **3** A similar plant of some other genus or family, or its osierlike shoots, as the squawbush. —*adj.* Consisting of twigs of willow, etc. [< OF, prob. < Med. L *ausaria, osaria* a bed of willows]

-osis *suffix of nouns* **1** The condition, process, or state of: *metamorphosis.* **2** *Med.* **a** A diseased or abnormal condition of: *melanosis.* **b** A formation of: *sclerosis.* [< L < Gk. *-ōsis*]

-osity *suffix of nouns* Forming nouns corresponding to adjectives in *-ose: verbosity, grandiosity.* [< F *-osité* < L *-ositas;* or directly < L]

Os·lo (os′lō, oz′-; *Norw.* ōōs′lōō) The capital of Norway, on **Oslo Fiord,** an arm of the Skagerrak extending 80 miles inland: formerly *Christiania.*

os·mes·the·sia (os′məs·thē′zhə, -zhē·ə) *n.* *Physiol.* A high susceptibility to odors. [< NL < Gk. *osmē* scent + *aisthēsis* perception]

os·mic (oz′mik, os′-) *adj.* *Chem.* Of, pertaining to, or containing osmium, especially in its higher valence.

os·mi·dro·sis (os′mə·drō′sis, oz′-) *n.* *Pathol.* A condition in which the perspiration has an abnormally strong odor. [< Gk. *osmē* an odor + *drosos* dew, moisture]

os·mi·ous (oz′mē·əs, os′-) *adj.* *Chem.* Of, pertaining to, or containing osmium, especially in its lower valence.

os·mi·rid·i·um (os′mə·rid′ē·əm, oz′-) *n.* A varying isomorphous mixture of iridium and osmium, found native in flattened, metallic, tin-white, malleable grains, and used for pointing gold pens: also called *iridosmium.*

os·mi·um (oz′mē·əm, os′-) *n.* A hard, brittle, extremely dense metallic element (symbol Os, atomic number 76) often found associated with platinum. See PERIODIC TABLE. [< Gk. *osmē* odor, from the sharp odor of one of its oxides]

os·mo·pho·bi·a (os′mə·fō′bē·ə, oz′-) *n.* *Psychiatry* A morbid fear of odors. [< Gk. *osmē* an odor + -PHOBIA]

os·mose (oz′mōs, os′-) *v.t. & v.i.* **·mosed, ·mos·ing** To subject to or to undergo the process of osmosis. [< *osmose, n.,* var. of OSMOSIS]

os·mo·sis (oz·mō′sis, os-) *n.* **1** The diffusion of two miscible solutions through a semipermeable membrane in such a manner as to equalize their concentration: it is one of the essential processes of living matter, especially in its cellular forms: also called *diosmosis.* Also *os′mose.* Compare ENDOSMOSIS, EXOSMOSIS. **2** *Colloq.* A process resembling diffusion and marked especially by the absence of directed effort: Living in Paris, he learned French by osmosis. [Earlier *osmose* < *-osmose* (as in *endosmose, exosmose*) < Gk. *ōsmos* a thrust, push] —**os·mot·ic** (oz·mot′ik, os-) *adj.* —**os·mot′i·cal·ly** *adv.*

os·mund (os′mənd, oz′-) *n.* Any of a genus *(Osmunda)* of showy ferns having pinnate fronds growing upright from a large crown, especially the royal fern *(O. regalis).* [< AF *osmunde* < Med. L *osmunda;* ult. origin unknown]

os·na·burg (oz′nə·bûrg) *n.* A tough, unbleached cotton cloth, often part waste, used for upholstery, for grain and cement sacks, and as a material for camouflage. [from *Osnaburg,* var. of OSNABRÜCK]

os·phre·sis (os·frē′sis) *n.* *Physiol.* The sense of smell. Also **os·phre′sia** (-frē′zhə). [< NL < Gk. *osphrēsis* < *osphrainesthai* smell] —**os·phret′ic** (-fret′ik) *adj.*

os·prey (os′prē) *n.* A fish-eating hawk *(Pandion haliaëtus),* brown above and white below, that preys upon fish. [Appar. < L *ossifraga* < *os, ossis* a bone + *frangere* break]

OSPREY

os·sa·ture (os′ə·chər) *n.* *Anat.* The disposition and arrangement of the bones of the body. Compare MUSCULATURE. [< F, skeleton < L *os, ossis* a bone]

os·se·in (os′ē·in) *n.* *Biochem.* The soft protein substance of the bone that remains after the removal of mineral matter: also *ostein.* [< L *osse(us)* bony + -IN]

os·se·ous (os′ē·əs) *adj.* Pertaining to, of the nature of, or containing bones. [< L *osseus* bony < *os, ossis* a bone] —**os′se·ous·ly** *adv.*

os·si·cle (os′i·kəl) *n.* *Anat.* **1** A small bone. **2** One of a chain of three small bones in the tympanic cavity of the ear. **3** One of various small, hard, nodular structures. [< L *ossiculum,* dim. of *os, ossis* a bone] —**os·sic·u·lar** (o·sik′yə·lər) *adj.*

os·sif·er·ous (o·sif′ər·əs) *adj.* Yielding or containing bones. [< L *os, ossis* bone + -FEROUS]

os·si·frage (os′ə·frij) *n.* **1** The osprey. **2** The lammergeier. [< L *ossifraga.* See OSPREY.]

os·si·fy (os′ə·fī) *v.t. & v.i.* **·fied, ·fy·ing 1** To convert or be converted into bones. **2** To make or become set, conventional, etc. [< L *os, ossis* a bone + -FY] —**os·sif·ic** (o·sif′ik) *adj.* —**os·′si·fi·ca′tion** *n.*

os·su·ar·y (os′ōō·er′ē, osh′-) *n. pl.* **·ar·ies** A place for holding the bones of the dead; charnel house; grave mound. [< LL *ossuarium* < L *ossuarius* of, for bones < *os, ossis* a bone]

os·te·al (os′tē·əl) *adj.* Of, pertaining to, or like bone; bony. [< Gk. *osteon* a bone]

os·te·i·tis (os′tē·ī′tis) *n.* *Pathol.* Inflammation of a bone. [< OSTE(O)- + -ITIS]

os·ten·si·ble (os·ten′sə·bəl) *adj.* Offered as real or having the character represented; seeming; professed or pretended. [< F < L *ostensus,* pp. of *ostendere* show < *ob-* against + *tendere* stretch] —**os·ten′si·bly** *adv.*

Synonyms: apparent, assigned, avowed, colorable, displayed, exhibited, expressed, plausible, professed, shown, specious. A man's *apparent* purpose or motive is what appears on the surface, with or without his own intent; his *ostensible* motive or purpose is that which is *assigned, avowed, displayed* by him; the word often implying that the *ostensible* may be only the pretended, a *specious* cover for a purpose or motive of a different sort. Compare synonyms for APPARENT. *Antonyms:* actual, genuine, real, true, veritable.

os·ten·sive (os·ten′siv) *adj.* Exhibiting; showing. —**os·ten′sive·ly** *adv.*

os·ten·so·ri·um (os′tən·sôr′ē·əm, -sō′rē-) *n. pl.* **·ri·a** (-rē·ə) A monstrance. Also **os·ten·so·ry** (os·ten′sər·ē). [< Med. L < L *ostensus.* See OSTENSIBLE.]

os·ten·ta·tion (os′tən·tā′shən) *n.* **1** The act of making elaborate or pretentious display to attract attention or elicit admiration or wonder. **2** *Archaic* Public display. [< OF *ostentacion* < L *ostentatio, -onis* < *ostentatus,* pp. of *ostentare,* freq. of *ostendere* show]

Synonyms: boast, boasting, display, flourish, pageant, pageantry, parade, pomp, pomposity, pompousness, show, vaunt, vaunting. *Ostentation* is an ambitious showing forth of whatever is thought adapted to win admiration or praise; *ostentation* may be without words; as, the *ostentation* of wealth in luxuriously equipped cars; when in words, *ostentation* is rather in manner than in direct statement; as, the *ostentation* of learning. *Boasting* is in direct statement, and is louder and more vulgar than *ostentation.* There may be great *display* or *show* with little substance; *ostentation* suggests something substantial to be shown. *Pomp* is some material demonstration of wealth and power, as in grand and stately ceremonial, etc., considered as worthy of the person or occasion in whose behalf it is manifested; *pomp* is the noble side of that which as *ostentation* is considered arrogant and vain. *Pageant* and *pageantry* are inferior to *pomp,* denoting spectacular *display* designed to impress the public mind. See PRIDE. *Antonyms:* diffidence, modesty, quietness, reserve, retirement, shrinking, timidity.

os·ten·ta·tious (os′tən·tā′shəs) *adj.* Elaborate or showy in order to attract attention; purposefully conspicuous. —**os·ten·ta′tious·ly** *adv.* **os′ten·ta′tious·ness** *n.*

os·te·oc·la·sis (os′tē·ok′lə·sis) *n.* **1** *Surg.* The operation of breaking a bone to correct a deformity or of rebreaking to remedy a bad setting. **2** The gradual absorption of bony tissue by osteoclasts. [< NL < Gk. *osteon* a bone + *klasis* a fracture < *klaein* break]

os·te·o·clast (os'tē·ə·klast') *n.* **1** *Surg.* An instrument for effecting osteoclasis. **2** *Anat.* A large multinucleate cell found in the marrow of bones and concerned in the absorption of bony tissue during the formation of canals, cavities, etc. [< G *osteoklast* < Gk. *osteon* a bone + *klastos* broken < *klaein* break] —**os'te·o·clas'tic** *adj.*

os·te·oid (os'tē·oid) *adj.* Resembling bone; bony.

os·te·ol·o·gy (os'tē·ol'ə·jē) *n.* The science that treats of the bones of the skeleton and of the properties of osseous tissue. —**os'te·o·log'i·cal** (-ə·loj'i·kəl) *adj.* —**os'te·o·log'i·cal·ly** *adv.* —**os'te·ol'o·gist** *n.*

os·te·o·ma·la·ci·a (os'tē·ō'mə·lā'shē·ə) *n. Pathol.* Softening of the bones, with progressive osseous deformity and exhaustion: caused by calcium deficiency. [< NL < Gk. *osteon* a bone + *malakia* softness]

os·te·o·my·e·li·tis (os'tē·ō·mī'ə·lī'tis) *n. Pathol.* Inflammation of the bone marrow. [< OSTEO- + MYEL(O)- + -ITIS]

os·te·op·a·thy (os'tē·op'ə·thē) *n.* A system of healing based on a theory that most diseases are caused by structural abnormalities of the body that may best be corrected by manipulation of the affected parts. [< OSTEO- + -PATHY] —**os'te·o·path'**, **os·te·op'a·thist** *n.* —**os'te·o·path'ic** (-ə·path'ik) *adj.*

os·te·o·phyte (os'tē·ə·fīt') *n. Pathol.* A bony excrescence. —**os'te·o·phyt'ic** (-fit'ik) *adj.*

os·te·o·plas·ty (os'tē·ə·plas'tē) *n. Surg.* **1** An operation to remedy loss of bone. **2** The restoration to its place of a bone temporarily removed. —**os'te·o·plas'tic** *adj.*

os·te·o·po·ro·sis (os'tē·ō·pə·rō'sis) *n. Pathol.* A disease marked by loss of calcium from the bones, causing them to weaken.

os·te·o·scle·ro·sis (os'tē·ō·sklə·rō'sis) *n. Pathol.* A morbid condition marked by a hardening and increased density of bone. —**os'te·o·scle·rot'ic** (-sklə·rot'ik) *adj.*

os·te·o·sis (os'tē·ō'sis) *n. Pathol.* The abnormal formation of bony tissue. [< OSTE(O)- + -OSIS]

os·te·ot·o·my (os'tē·ot'ə·mē) *n. Surg.* The operation of dividing a bone, especially beneath the integuments, as to remedy deformity. —**os'te·ot'o·mist** *n.*

os·ti·ar·y (os'tē·er'ē) *n. pl.* **·ar·ies 1** In the Roman Catholic Church, a cleric belonging to the lowest of the minor orders. **2** A doorkeeper. Also **os'ti·ar'i·us** (-âr'ē·əs). [< L *ostiarius* doorkeeper < *ostium* a door]

os·ti·ole (os'tē·ōl) *n.* **1** A small opening. **2** *Zool.* Any one of the small inhalant orifices of a sponge. [< L *ostiolum*, dim. of *ostium* a door] —**os'ti·o·lar** *adj.*

ost·mark (ôst'märk') See MARK² (def. 1).

os·to·my (os'tə·mē) *n. pl.* **·mies** A surgical operation, as a colostomy or an ileostomy, which involves the creation of an artificial opening in the abdominal wall for the discharge of waste matter. [See -STOMY]

os·tra·cism (os'trə·siz'əm) *n.* **1** Exclusion, as from society or common privileges, by general consent. **2** In ancient Greece, banishment by popular vote. [< Gk. *ostrakismos* < *ostrakizein* OSTRACIZE]

os·tra·cize (os'trə·sīz) *v.t.* **·cized**, **·ciz·ing 1** To shut out or exclude by ostracism. **2** In ancient Greece, to exile by ostracism. Also *Brit.* **os'tra·cise.** See synonyms under BANISH. [< Gk. *ostrakizein* < *ostrakon* a potsherd, shell, voting tablet]

os·trich (ôs'trich, os'-) *n.* **1** A large, two-toed bird (genus *Struthio*) of Africa and Arabia, with aborted wings. Its long, powerful legs give it great speed. The plumage of the male is black, with white plumes at the ends of the wings and tail, much esteemed for ornamental purposes. **2** A rhea. [< OF *obstruce*, *ostruche* < LL *avistruthius* < L *avis* a bird + LL *struthio* an ostrich < Gk. *strouthiōn* < *strouthos* a sparrow, an ostrich]

OSTRICH

Oswego tea *n.* A species of mint (*Monarda didyma*) with a showy head of bright-red flowers, growing in wet places in the eastern, United States: also called *bee balm.*

o·tal·gi·a (ō·tal'jē·ə) *n. Pathol.* Neuralgia of the ear; earache. Also **o·tal'gy.** [< NL < Gk. *ītalgia* < *ous, ītos* an ear + *algos* a pain] —**o·tal'gic** *adj.*

o·ta·ry (ō'tər·ē) *n. pl.* **·ries** or **·ry** An eared seal. [< NL *Otaria*, genus name < Gk. *ītaros* large-eared < *ous, ītos* an ear] —**o·tar·i·an** (ō·târ'ē·ən) *adj.*

oth·er (uth'ər) *adj.* **1** Different from the one specified; not the same. **2** Being over and above; additional. **3** Second: noting the remaining one of two persons or things. **4** Opposite; contrary: the *other* side. **5** Alternate: every *other* day. —**the other day (night**, etc.**)** A day (night, etc.) not long ago; recently. —*pron.* **1** A different person or thing. **2** The second of two; the opposite one. —*adv.* Otherwise: with *than*. [OE *īther*] —**oth'er·ness** *n.*

oth·er·wise (uth'ər·wīz') *adv.* **1** In a different manner or by other means. **2** In other circumstances or conditions. **3** In all other respects: an *otherwise* sensible writer. —*adj.* Different: How could such notions be *otherwise* than useless?

other world The unseen world; the life after death; the future state.

oth·er·world·ly (uth'ər·wûrld'lē) *adj.* **1** Of or characteristic of an ideal world, especially heaven. **2** Concerned with the hereafter to the neglect of the present. —**oth'er·world'li·ness** *n.*

o·tic (ō'tik, ot'ik) *adj.* Pertaining to or situated near the ear. [< Gk. *ōtikos* < *ous, ōtos* ear] **-otic** *suffix of adjectives* **1** *Med.* Of, related to, or affected by: corresponding to nouns in *-osis*: *psychotic*, *sclerotic*. **2** Causing or producing: *narcotic*. [< Gk. *-ōtikos*, suffix of adjectives]

o·ti·ose (ō'shē·ōs, -tē-) *adj.* **1** Being at rest or ease; having nothing to do. **2** Characterized by indolence or easy negligence. **3** Futile; useless. [< L *otiosus* < *otium* leisure] —**o'ti·ose'ly** *adv.* —**o'ti·os'i·ty** (-os'ə·tē) *n.*

o·ti·tis (ō·tī'tis) *n. Pathol.* Inflammation of the mucous membrane of the ear. [< OT(O)- + -ITIS]

oto- *combining form* Ear; pertaining to the ear: *otoscope.* Also, before vowels, *ot-.* [< Gk. *ous, ōtos* the ear]

o·to·cyst (ō'tə·sist) *n. Anat.* **1** An auditory vesicle, as in many invertebrates. **2** The similar vesicle contained in the embryo of a vertebrate.

O·toe (ō'tō) *n.* One of a Siouan tribe of North American Indians living in southeastern Nebraska.

o·to·lar·yn·gol·o·gy (ō'tō·lar'ing·gol'ə·jē) *n.* The branch of medicine which treats of the ear and throat. —**o'to·lar'yn·gol'o·gist** *n.*

o·to·lith (ō'tə·lith) *n. Anat.* **1** One of the concretions of calcium carbonate and calcium phosphate found in the internal ear of vertebrates and in the auditory organ of many invertebrates. **2** An ear bone. [< OTO- + -LITH]

o·tol·o·gy (ō·tol'ə·jē) *n.* The science of the ear and its diseases. —**o·to·log·i·cal** (ō'tə·loj'i·kəl) *adj.* —**o·tol'o·gist** *n.*

o·to·rhi·no·lar·yn·gol·o·gy (ō'tō·rī'nō·lar'ing·gol'ə·jē) *n.* The branch of medicine dealing with the ear, nose, and larynx in health and disease. [< OTO- + RHINO- + LARYNGO- + -LOGY] —**o'to·rhi'no·lar'yn·gol'o·gist** *n.*

o·to·scope (ō'tə·skōp) *n. Med.* An instrument for viewing or examining the interior of the ear; especially, an ear speculum.

Ot·ta·wa (ot'ə·wə) *n.* One of a tribe of North American Indians of Algonquian stock, originally inhabiting the region around Georgian Bay, Lake Huron, Ontario, later migrating to the region around Lake Superior and Lake Michigan. [< dial. F *otaua, otawa* < Algonquian (Cree) *ataweu* a trader]

Ot·ta·wa (ot'ə·wə) The capital of Canada in SE Ontario on the **Ottawa River,** which flows 696 miles SE through Ontario and Quebec to the St. Lawrence.

ot·ter (ot'ər) *n.* **1** A weasel-like, web-footed carnivore (genus *Lutra*) inhabiting streams and lakes, and feeding upon fish. The common otter (*L. ca-*

OTTER

nadensis) is about two feet long, exclusive of the flattened, oarlike tail, and furnishes a valuable, dark-brown fur. **2** The sea otter. [OE *oter.* Akin to WATER.]

otter hound A breed of hound used in England for hunting otters: strongly built, with a close black-and tan coat, a large broad head, and floppy ears.

otter shrew An insectivorous, aquatic animal (family *Potamogalidae*) of central and western Africa.

ot·to·man (ot'ə·mən) *n.* **1** An upholstered, backless and armless seat or sofa. **2** An upholstered footrest. **3** A heavy corded silk or rayon fabric used for coats and trimmings. [< F *ottomane*, orig. fem. of *Ottoman* OTTOMAN]

Ottoman Empire A former empire (1300–1919) of the Turks in Asia Minor, NE Africa, and SE Europe; capital, Constantinople: also *Turkish Empire.*

OTTOMAN EMPIRE 1683–1913

oua·ba·in (wä·bä'in) *n. Chem.* A white, lustrous, extremely poisonous, crystalline glycoside, $C_{29}H_{44}O_{12}$, derived from two South African trees (*Strophanthus glaber* and *A cokanthera ouabaio*): used in medicine as a cardiac stimulant. It is a constituent of Zulu arrow poison. [< F *ouabaio*, a South African tree (< Somali native name) + -IN]

oua·na·niche (wä'nə·nēsh', *Fr.* wà·nà·nēsh') *n.* A small Canadian salmon (*Salmo salar ouananiche*), identified with the Atlantic salmon of Maine. [< dial. F (Canadian) < Algonquian (Cree) *wananish*]

ou·bli·ette (ōō'blē·et') *n.* A secret dungeon with an entrance only through the top. [< OF < *oublier* forget]

ouch¹ (ouch) *interj.* An exclamation indicating sudden pain.

ouch² (ouch) *n.* **1** The setting of a jewel. **2** An ornament, as a clasp or brooch, of gold. —*v.t.* To ornament with or as with ouches. [< AF *nouche* < LL *nusca* < OHG *nuscka, nuscha* a buckle, clasp, appar. ult. < Celtic; in ME *a nouche* became *an ouche*]

ought¹ (ôt) *v.* A defective verb now used only as an auxiliary followed by the infinitive with *to*, or elliptically with the infinitive understood, to express: **1** Obligation or moral duty: He *ought* to keep his promises. **2** Advisability or expedience: You *ought* to be careful. **3** Probability or expectation: He *ought* to be here tomorrow. ♦ A past is formed by placing the following verb in the perfect infinitive, as in *He ought to have been there.* ♦ Homophone: *aught.* [OE *āhte*, past tense of *āgan* owe, possess]

Synonym: should. *Ought* is the stronger word, holding most closely to the sense of moral obligation, or sometimes of imperative logical necessity; *should* may have the sense of moral obligation or may apply merely to propriety or expediency, as in the proverb, "The liar *should* have a good memory"; that is, he will need it. *Ought* is sometimes used as indicating what the mind deems to be logical in view of all the conditions; as, These goods *ought* to go into that space; *should* in such connections would be correct, but less emphatic. Compare DUTY.

ought² (ôt) *n.* Aught; anything. [Var. of AUGHT]

Oui·ja (wē'jə) *n.* A device consisting of a board inscribed with the alphabet and other characters and a planchette, the pointer of which is thought to spell out mediumistic communications: a trade name. Also **oui'ja.**

oui·sti·ti (wis'ti·tē) n. The common marmoset (genus *Callithrix* or *Hapale*) of South America, with tufted ears and a long, banded tail. [<F; name coined by Buffon, imit. of the animal's cry]

ounce¹ (ouns) n. **1** A unit of weight; one sixteenth of a pound avoirdupois, or 28.349 grams; one twelfth of a pound troy, or 31.1 grams. Abbr. *oz.* **2** A fluid ounce. **3** A small quantity. — **fluid ounce 1** *U.S.* One sixteenth of a pint; 29.5737 cubic centimeters; 480 minims. **2** *Brit.* 28.413 cubic centimeters; 480 minims. [<OF *unce* <L *uncia* twelfth part (of a pound or foot), orig. a unit. Doublet of INCH.]

ounce² (ouns) n. **1** A feline carnivorous mammal (*Panthera uncia*) of central Asia, about the size of a leopard, having long fur and a long, thick tail; the snow leopard. **2** Some similar American cat, as the jaguar. [<OF *l'once,* var. of *lonce* the lynx <L *lyncea* <*lynx, lyncis* LYNX]

ounce metal An alloy of copper with five percent each of tin, zinc, and lead: formerly made by adding one ounce of each minor metal to one pound of copper.

our (our) *pronominal adj.* Belonging or pertaining to us: the possessive case of the pronoun *we* employed attributively. [OE *ūre,* earlier *ūser,* genitive of US]

-our See -OR.

ou·rang (ōō·rang') n. The orang-utan. [Var. of ORANG]

ou·ra·nog·ra·phy (ōōr'ə·nog'rə·fē) See URANOGRAPHY.

Ou·ra·nos (ōōr'ə·nəs) See URANUS (def. 1).

ou·ra·ri (ōō·rä'rē) n. Curare. [Var. of WOORALI <Tupian]

ou·re·bi (ōō'rə·bē) See ORIBI.

Our Lady The Virgin Mary.

ouro- See URO-.

ours (ourz) *pron.* **1** Belonging or pertaining to us: That dog is *ours:* the possessive case of *we* used predicatively. **2** The things or persons belonging or pertaining to us: their country and *ours.* — **of ours** Belonging or relating to us; our: the double possessive. [ME *ures* <*ure* OUR]

our·self (our·self') *pron.* Myself: only in formal or regal style.

our·selves (our·selvz') *pron. pl.* We or us.

-ous *suffix of adjectives* **1** Full of; having: *studious, glorious.* **2** *Chem.* Having a lower valence than that indicated by the suffix *-ic: nitrous.* [<OF <L *-osus*]

ou·sel (ōō'zəl) See OUZEL.

oust (oust) *v.t.* To force from possession or occupancy; turn out; eject. See BANISH. [<AF *ouster* take away, ? <L *obstare* obstruct <*ob-* against + *stare* stand]

oust·er (ous'tər) n. *Law* The act of putting one out of possession or occupancy; dispossession.

out (out) *adv.* **1** Away from the inside or center: to go *out;* to branch *out.* **2** Away from a specified or usual place: to set *out* from Paris. **3** From a receptacle or source: to pour *out* wine. **4** So as to free of undesired parts or refuse: to thresh *out* grain; to sweep *out* a room. **5** From among others: to pick *out* a dress. **6** Into the charge or care of another or others: to hire *out* laborers; to deal *out* cards. **7** So as to project or be extended: to stretch *out.* **8** Into extinction or inactivity: The flame went *out;* The excitement died *out.* **9** To a result or conclusion: to fight it *out;* to find *out.* **10** Completely; fully: tired *out.* **11** Into existence or outward manifestation: An epidemic broke *out;* The sun came *out.* **12** Into blossom or leaf. **13** Into public notice or circulation: to bring *out* a new edition. **14** Aloud: to call *out.* **15** On strike. **16** Into disagreement; at odds: to be put *out* over trifles. **17** *Colloq.* Into unconsciousness: to pass *out.* **18** In baseball, cricket, etc., so as to be retired from active or leading play: to strike *out.* — *adj.* **1** External; exterior; outer. **2** Away from one's home, place of work, or other place regarded as a base: to be *out* on maneuvers. **3** Away at a distance: to be *out* in California. **4** Exposed or bare, as by rents in the clothing: *out* at the knees. **5** Visible; manifest: The stars are *out.* **6** Made public; disclosed: The truth is *out.* **7** In blos-

som or leaf. **8** Removed; displaced: The stain is *out.* **9** Mistaken; in error: *out* in one's calculations. **10** Extinguished; exhausted: The fire is *out.* **11** Finished; at an end: before the week is *out.* **12** At odds; in disagreement. **13** At a financial loss; in default: to be *out* five dollars. **14** Not in effective operation: The machine is *out.* **15** *Colloq.* Unconscious: He's *out.* **16** In baseball, cricket, etc., no longer in active or leading play. — *prep.* **1** From within; forth from: *out* the door. **2** Outside; on the outside of: the view *out* this window. — *n.* **1** Something that is out. **2** An escape; a way to dodge responsibility or involvement: He had an *out.* **3** A person not in office or position of power; specifically, in the plural, the party not in power. **4** In baseball, retirement of a batter or base runner. **5** In tennis, a return of the ball, which, untouched by the opponent, falls outside the court. **6** *Printing* Matter in the copy omitted from the composed type. — *v.t.* To drive out; expel. — *v.i.* To come or go out; be revealed: Murder will *out.* — *interj.* Go out! away! begone! [OE *ūt*]

out- *combining form* **1** Living or situated outside; external; away from the center; detached: *outlying, outpatient.* **2** Going forth; issuing; outward: *outbound, outstretch.* **3** Used to denote the time, place, or result of the action expressed by the root verb: *outcome, outcry.* **4** Excessive; surpassing; more; beyond. Dissyllabic nouns with this prefix are pronounced with an almost even stress on each syllable, the first slightly more emphatic. In dissyllabic verbs the stress is usually strongly upon the second element; but when their participles are used as adjectives or nouns, the stress becomes even or, for emphasis, shifts to the first syllable.

out-and-out (out'ənd·out') *adj.* Thoroughgoing; unqualified; genuine. — *adv.* Unqualifiedly; genuinely.

out·back (out'bak') n. *Austral.* Unsettled inland country; the bush.

out·bid (out·bid') *v.t.* **·bid, ·bid·den** or **·bid, ·bid·ding** To bid more than; offer a higher price than.

out·board (out'bōrd', -bôrd') *Naut. adj.* Situated on the outside of a vessel, as a motor for temporary attachment to the stern of a small boat. — *adv.* Away from the center.

OUTBOARD MOTOR
Showing method of attachment.

out·bound (out'bound') *adj.* Outward bound.

out·brave (out·brāv') *v.t.* **·braved, ·brav·ing 1** To surpass in bravery. **2** To stand in defiance of. **3** To excel or surpass in splendor.

out·break (out'brāk') n. A sudden and violent breaking forth: said of passion or of disease affecting large numbers of people at once. See synonyms under TUMULT. — *v.i.* (out'· brāk') **·broke, ·brok·en, ·break·ing** To burst out; break forth.

out·breed (out'brēd') *v.t.* **·bred, ·breed·ing** *Biol.* To breed or mate (individuals) belonging to stocks or families not closely related: opposed to *inbreed.* — **out'breed'ing** n.

out·build·ing (out'bil'ding) n. A smaller building appurtenant to a main building and generally separate from it; specifically, a chicken house, woodshed, smokehouse, etc.

out·burst (out'bûrst') n. A bursting out; a violent manifestation, especially of passion.

out·cast (out'kast', -käst') n. **1** One who is cast out from home or country; one rejected and despised. **2** *Scot.* A quarrel; disagreement. — *adj.* Rejected as unworthy or useless; cast out; forlorn.

out·caste (out'kast', -käst') n. In India, a person who has forfeited his caste; a pariah.

out·class (out·klas', -kläs') *v.t.* To exceed decisively in skill, quality, or powers.

out·come (out'kum') n. The consequence or visible result. See synonyms under CONSEQUENCE, END, EVENT, PRODUCT.

out·crop (out'krop') n. *Geol.* **1** The exposure at or above the surface of the ground of any stratum, vein, etc. **2** The rock so exposed. — *v.i.* (out·krop') **·cropped, ·crop·ping 1** To crop up or out. **2** To appear above the ground, as rocks.

out·cross (out·krôs', -kros') *Biol. v.t.* To mate (individuals) of the same breed but of different strains. — *n.* The act of so mating, or its result. — **out'cross'ing** n.

out·cry (out'krī') n. *pl.* **·cries 1** A vehement or loud cry, as of distress, alarm, or opposition. **2** A public auction. See synonyms under NOISE. — *v.t.* (out·krī') **·cried, ·cry·ing** To surpass in noise or crying; cry down.

out·curve (out'kûrv') n. **1** In baseball, a pitched ball that curves away from the batter: opposed to *incurve.* **2** A small projection in a coastline.

out·date (out·dāt') *v.t.* **·dat·ed, ·dat·ing** To make obsolete or out of date.

out·dat·ed (out·dā'tid) *adj.* Made obsolete; antiquated; old-fashioned.

out·dis·tance (out·dis'təns) *v.t.* **·tanced, ·tanc·ing 1** To outrun; outstrip. **2** To surpass completely; outdo.

out·do (out·dōō') *v.t.* **·did, ·done, ·do·ing** To exceed in performance; surpass; excel. See synonyms under SURPASS. — **out·do'er** n.

out·done (out·dun') *adj. U. S. Colloq.* Tired; exasperated; also, puzzled.

out·door (out'dōr', -dôr') *adj.* Being or done in the open air; belonging or occurring outside the house: *outdoor* sports. Also *out-of-door.*

out·doors (out·dōrz', -dôrz') *adv.* Outside of the house; out of the house; in the open air. — *n.* The world beyond the house; the open air. Also *out-of-doors.* — **all outdoors** *Colloq.* The whole world.

out·en (out'n) *prep. Dial.* Out of.

out·er (ou'tər) *adj.* **1** Being on the exterior side; external. **2** Farther from a center or from something regarded as the inside. — *n.* **1** In rifle practice, the part of a target outside the rings. **2** A shot that strikes this part. Compare INNER. — **out'er·most** *adj. & adv.*

Outer Hebrides See HEBRIDES.

Outer Mongolia See MONGOLIA.

outer space The space beyond the extreme limits of the earth's atmosphere; interplanetary and interstellar space.

out·face (out·fās') *v.t.* **·faced, ·fac·ing 1** To face or stare down. **2** To defy or confront fearlessly or impudently.

out·fall (out'fôl') n. **1** The place where a river, culvert, or conduit discharges; mouth. **2** The discharged matter.

out·field (out'fēld') n. **1** In baseball, cricket, etc., the players who take their positions in the outer part of the field, or the field occupied by them; specifically, in baseball, right, left, and center field, or all the field beyond the bases. **2** *Scot.* Arable land continually cropped without being manured. **3** A field not situated near a house. **4** A bordering region or domain. — **out'field'er** n.

out·fit (out'fit') n. **1** A fitting out or equipment. **2** The expenses occasioned by and incidental to a journey. **3** All the garments and incidentals of a person's costume. **4** The tools or equipment for any particular occupation, calling, or trade; a kit: a painter's *outfit.* **5** Mental acquirements suitable to any intellectual purpose. **6** Any expedition or party, with its proper equipment; hence, any industry, or any group of persons unified in a common undertaking; specifically, the cowboys, horses, wagons, etc., working on a certain ranch. — *v.t. & v.i.* **·fit·ted, ·fit·ting** To provide with or acquire an outfit. — **out'fit'ter** n.

out·flank (out·flangk') *v.t.* To get around and in back of the flank of (an opposing force or army); turn the flank of; flank.

out·flow (out'flō') n. **1** That which flows out, or the process of flowing out. **2** An outlet.

out·foot (out·fōōt') *v.t.* **1** To exceed or surpass, as in running or dancing. **2** *Naut.* To sail faster than; outsail.

out·gen·er·al (out·jen'ər·əl) *v.t.* **·aled** or **·alled, ·al·ing** or **·al·ling** To surpass in generalship; out-maneuver.

out·go (out·gō') *v.t.* **·went, ·gone, ·go·ing** To go farther than; exceed or outstrip. — *n.* (out'· gō') *pl.* **·goes 1** That which goes out; cost or outlay: opposed to *income*. 2 An outgoing. 3 An exit. See synonyms under EXPENSE. —**out′go′er** *n*.

out·go·ing (out′gō′ing) *adj*. 1 Going out; leaving. 2 Friendly; sympathetic. — *n*. 1 The act of going out; departure. 2 That which goes out. 3 *Usually pl*. An expenditure; outlay.

out·grow (out·grō′) *v.t.* **·grew, ·grown, ·grow·ing** 1 To surpass in growth. 2 To grow too large for. 3 To lose or get rid of in the course of time or growth: to *outgrow* a habit.

out·growth (out′grōth′) *n*. That which grows out of something else; an excrescence. See synonyms under CONSEQUENCE.

out·guard (out′gärd′) *n*. An outlying guard or post; an advanced picket.

out·gush (out′gush′) *n*. A gushing out.

out·haul (out′hôl′) *n. Naut*. A rope for extending a sail along a spar.

out·house (out′hous′) *n*. An outbuilding; specifically, a privy.

out·ing (ou′ting) *n*. 1 The act of going out; a holiday excursion; short pleasure trip; airing. 2 The distance out at sea: the farthest *outing*. — *adj*. Of, pertaining to, or suitable for an outing, as various garments and fabrics.

outing flannel A soft, lightweight cotton fabric, usually napped on both sides: used chiefly for sleeping garments.

out·land (out′land′) *n*. Land lying beyond the limits of occupation or cultivation. [OE *ūtland*] — **out′land′er** *n*.

out·land·ish (out·lan′dish) *adj*. 1 Of strange or barbarous aspect or action. 2 Situated in an unfamiliar spot; remote. 3 Not native. Also **out′land**. See synonyms under RUSTIC. [OE *ūtlandisc*] — **out·land′ish·ly** *adv*. — **out·land′ish·ness** *n*.

out·last (out·last′, -läst′) *v.t.* To last longer than.

out·law (out′lô′) *n*. 1 A person deprived of the benefit of the law, as for having committed a crime. 2 One who habitually breaks or defies the law; a freebooter; a person having a price on his head. 3 A vicious horse. — *v.t.* 1 To declare an outlaw; proscribe. 2 To prohibit; ban. 3 To deprive of legal force or protection, as contracts or debts. [OE *ūtlaga* <ON *ūtlagi*]

out·law·ry (out′lô′rē) *n. pl*. **·ries** The state, fact, or process of outlawing or being outlawed.

out·lay (out·lā′) *v.t.* **·laid, ·lay·ing** To expend (money). — *n*. (out′lā′) A laying out or disbursing; hence, that which is disbursed; expenditure. See synonyms under EXPENSE, PRICE.

out·let (out′let) *n*. 1 A passage or vent for escape or discharge; an egress; specifically, in commerce, a market for the sale of any commodity. 2 The act of letting out. 3 *Electr*. That point in a wiring system at which the current is taken to supply fixtures, lamps, motors, etc.

out·li·er (out′lī′ər) *n*. 1 One whose residence is not in the same place as his office or business. 2 One who or that which is beyond or excluded from the main body. 3 A person who camps or lies out in the forest, prairie, or other deserted place. 4 *Geol*. An exposed mass of rock surrounded by older rock strata which have been worn away: opposed to *inlier*.

out·line (out′līn′) *n*. 1 *Often pl*. A preliminary sketch showing the principal features of a thing; general plan. 2 The bordering line that serves to define a figure; hence, a sketch made of such lines without shading; also, the art of making such sketches. See synonyms under SKETCH. — *v.t.* **·lined, ·lin·ing** 1 To draw the outline of; sketch. 2 To describe in general terms; give the main points of.

out·live (out·liv′) *v.t.* **·lived, ·liv·ing** 1 To live longer than (another). 2 To live through; survive.

out·look (out′lŏŏk′) *n*. 1 The expanse in view; hence, the condition or prospect of a thing. 2 Distance of view; hence, foresight. 3 Vigilance. 4 A place where watch is kept. 5 The watch; sentinel.

out·ly·ing (out′lī′ing) *adj*. 1 Situated apart from the main body. 2 Outside the boundary.

out–man (out–man′) *v.t.* **–manned, –man·ning** 1 To surpass in number of men. 2 To excel in manliness.

out·mo·ded (out·mō′did) *adj*. Out of fashion; not in current style.

out·most (out′mōst′) *adj*. Outermost.

out of 1 From or beyond the inside of; from among. 2 Beyond the limits, reach, scope, or proper position of; not in or included in: *out of* sight. 3 Without: *out of* breath. 4 Influenced, inspired, or caused by: *out of* pity; *out of* respect for him.

out-of-bounds (out′əv·boundz′) *adv*. Outside the playing area of a ball field. — *adj*. 1 Being out–of–bounds. 2 Beyond normal or proper limits, as of taste or behavior; uncalled-for.

out of commission Completely out of order; not working; laid aside.

out-of-date (out′əv·dāt′) *adj*. Old-fashioned.

out of sorts 1 Indisposed or unwell. 2 Dissatisfied or unhappy.

out-of-the-way (out′əv·thə·wā′) *adj*. 1 Remotely situated; difficult to reach; secluded. 2 Different from what is common; out of the common range; unusual; singular; eccentric.

out of the woods Clear of doubts and difficulties; safe after peril or hazard.

out part An outer or remote part.

out·pa·tient (out′pā′shənt) *n*. A patient, not an inmate, treated at a hospital or dispensary.

out·play (out·plā′) *v.t.* To play better than; defeat.

out·point (out·point′) *v.t.* 1 To score more points than. 2 *Naut*. To sail closer to the wind than.

out·post (out′pōst′) *n*. 1 A detachment of troops stationed at a distance from the main body as a guard against surprise. 2 The station occupied by them.

out·pour (out·pôr′, -pōr′) *v.t. & v.i.* To pour out. — *n*. (out′pôr′, -pōr′) A free outflow; outpouring. — **out′pour′er** *n*. — **out′pour′ing** *n*.

out·pull (out·pŏŏl′) *v.t.* To pull more strongly than.

out·put (out′pŏŏt′) *n*. 1 The quantity put out or produced in a specified time; amount or rate of production, collective or individual, as from a mine or mines, or from a furnace or a country. 2 That which is excreted from the body by the lungs, skin, or kidneys. 3 The electric power of a dynamo; also, the energy or power given by a machine. See synonyms under PRODUCT.

out·rage (out′rāj′) *n*. 1 An act of shocking violence or cruelty; a gross infringement of morality or decency; a gross insult. 2 Something that violates the feelings or the proprieties. 3 *Obs*. Violent rage; a dangerous display of passion. — *v.t.* **·raged, ·rag·ing** 1 To commit outrage upon; wrong or abuse grossly; violate; offend. 2 To rape. See synonyms for VIOLATE. [<OF *ultrage*, ult. <L *ultra* beyond; infl. in meaning by RAGE]
   Synonyms (noun): abuse, affront, indecency, indignity, injury, insult, offense, violence. An *outrage* combines *insult* and *injury*. See INJURY, OFFENSE, VIOLENCE. Compare synonyms for AFFRONT.

out·ra·geous (out·rā′jəs) *adj*. 1 Of the nature of an outrage; heinous; atrocious. 2 Heedless of authority or decency. 3 Exceeding bounds. See synonyms under FLAGRANT, INFAMOUS, VIOLENT. — **out·ra′geous·ly** *adv*. — **out·ra′geous·ness** *n*.

out·range (out·rānj′) *v.t.* **·ranged, ·rang·ing** 1 To surpass in range; have a greater range than. 2 To go beyond the range of.

out·reach (out·rēch′) *v.t.* 1 To reach or go beyond; surpass. 2 To reach out; extend. — *v.i.* 3 To reach out. — *n*. (out′rēch′) The act of reaching out.

out·ride (out·rīd′) *v.t.* **·rode, ·rid·den, ·rid·ing** To ride faster, farther, or better than.

out·rid·er (out′rī′dər) *n*. 1 A mounted servant who rides in advance of a carriage. 2 One who rides along the edge of a herd of cattle to prevent stampeding or straying. 3 One who rides out or forth.

out·rig·ger (out′rig′ər) *n*. 1 A part built or arranged to project beyond a natural outline, as of a vessel or machine. 2 A projecting contrivance terminating in a boatlike float, braced to the side of a canoe to prevent capsizing. 3 *Naut*. **a** A spar for extending a sail or rope farther than the beam of the vessel would otherwise permit. **b** A boom swung out from a vessel, to which to secure boats. 4 A bracket projecting from the side of a narrow rowboat or shell, and provided with a rowlock for an oar or scull. 5 A boat or shell equipped with such a bracket. 6 *Aeron*. A projecting contrivance to support various components of an airplane: also called *tail boom*.

out·right (out′rīt′) *adj*. 1 Free from reserve or restraint; positive; downright. 2 Complete; entire. 3 Going straight on. — *adv*. (out′rīt′) 1 Without reservation or limitation; entirely; utterly; openly. 2 Without delay.

out·root (out·rŏŏt′, -rōōt′) *v.t.* To root out; eradicate.

out·run·ner (out′run′ər) *n*. 1 An attendant who runs before or beside a carriage. 2 The leading dog in a dog team.

out·sell (out·sel′) *v.t.* **·sold, ·sell·ing** 1 To sell more readily or for a higher price than. 2 To sell more goods than.

out·sen·try (out′sen′trē) *n. pl*. **·tries** An outer sentry.

out·set (out′set′) *n*. A first entrance on any business, journey, or the like; a setting out; beginning; start; opening. Also **out′set′ting**. See synonyms under BEGINNING.

out·shine (out·shīn′) *v*. **·shone, ·shin·ing** *v.t.* 1 To shine brighter than. 2 To surpass, as in wit or finery. — *v.i.* 3 To shine forth. — **out·shin′er** *n*.

out·shoot (out·shōōt′) *v*. **·shot, ·shoot·ing** *v.t.* 1 To excel in shooting. 2 To shoot out or beyond; project. — *v.i.* 3 To shoot out; project. — *n*. (out′shōōt′) 1 A projection; branch; bud, as of a plant. 2 A rushing forth, as of water. 3 In baseball, an outcurve.

out·side (out′sīd′) *n*. 1 The external part of a thing; the side or part that forms or adjoins the surface. 2 The part or side that is seen; hence, superficial appearance. 3 The space beyond a bounding line or surface; outer region: opposed to *inside*. — **at the outside** At the farthest, longest, or most, as in an estimate. — *adj*. 1 Pertaining to, located on, or restricted to the outside; exterior. 2 Originating or situated beyond designated limits; foreign. 3 Reaching the limit; extreme: an *outside* estimate. 4 Slight; inconsequential: There is only an *outside* possibility. — *adv*. 1 On or to the outside; externally. 2 Beyond the outside limits of. 3 In the open air; outdoors. — *prep*. (out′sīd′) 1 On or to the exterior of: *outside* the park; *outside* the box. 2 Beyond the limit of: Don't tell it *outside* the club. 3 *Colloq*. Except: No one knows *outside* yourself.

out·sid·er (out′sī′dər) *n*. 1 One who is outside; an intruder. 2 A race horse whose chance of winning is slight.

out sister A member of a cloistered order of nuns who attends to the business of the order, or convent, with the outside world.

out·size (out′sīz′) *n*. A size, as of clothing, footwear, etc., that is larger than the regular sizes.

out·skirt (out′skûrt′) *n. Often pl*. A place on the skirts or border; outer verge.

out·sole (out′sōl′) *n*. The outside or lower sole of a boot or shoe: distinguished from *insole*. See illustration under SHOE.

out·speak (out·spēk′) *v*. **·spoke, ·spo·ken, ·speak·ing** *v.t.* 1 To outdo in speaking. 2 To say openly or boldly. — *v.i.* 3 To speak out. — **out·speak′er** *n*.

out·spent (out·spent′) *adj*. Completely spent or wearied; tired out.

out·spo·ken (out′spō′kən) *adj*. 1 Bold or free of speech; frank. 2 Spoken boldly or frankly. — **out′spo′ken·ly** *adv*. — **out′spo′ken·ness** *n*.

out·stand·ing (out·stan′ding) *adj*. 1 Standing prominently forth; salient; conspicuous; preeminent. 2 Still standing, as a debt unpaid or not due.

out·stretch (out·strech′) *v.t.* 1 To stretch out; expand; extend. 2 To extend beyond. — **out·stretched′** *adj*.

out·strip (out·strip′) *v.t.* **stripped, ·strip·ping** 1 To leave behind; outrun, as in a race. 2 To excel; surpass. See synonyms under LEAD[1], SURPASS.

out·stroke (out′strōk′) *n*. An outward stroke, as the thrust of an engine's piston toward the crankshaft. Compare INSTROKE.

out·turn (out′tûrn′) *n*. 1 Output; product. 2 In commerce, the quantity, condition, or quality of goods actually turned out and delivered.

out·ward (out′wərd) *adj*. 1 Of or pertaining to the exterior of an object; outer; external; outside: *outward* show. 2 Tending to the outside; directed outward: an *outward* course. 3 Derived or added from without; not inherent; extraneous; extrinsic: *outward* grace. 4 Relating to the physical or bodily as opposed to the mental aspect; external: His *outward* attitude belies his inward feeling. **5** Of or pertaining to the world or the outer man; not spiritual; carnal; corporeal. —*adv.* **1** To or in the direction of the outside; away from an inner place. **2** On the surface; superficially. **3** Away from port or home. Also **out′wards.** —*n.* External form; outside appearance. [OE *ūtweard*] —**out′ward·ly** *adv.* —**out′ward·ness** *n.*

out·wash (out′wäsh′, -wôsh′) *n.* Detritus and waste materials carried away by the water of melting glaciers.

out·wear (out·wâr′) *v.t.* **·wore, ·worn, ·wear·ing 1** To wear or stand use better than; outlast. **2** To wear out, as by constant use. **3** To exhaust; use up. **4** To outlive; outgrow.

out·weigh (out·wā′) *v.t.* **1** To weigh more than. **2** To exceed in importance, value, etc.

out·wit (out·wit′) *v.t.* **·wit·ted, ·wit·ting** To defeat by superior ingenuity or cunning; overreach. See synonyms under BAFFLE, DECEIVE.

out·worn (out·wôrn′) Past participle of OUTWEAR.

ou·zel (ōō′zəl) *n.* **1** One of various European thrushes, as the blackbird (*Turdus merula*), the **ring ouzel** (*T. torquatus*). **2** The related dipper or **water ouzel** (*Cinclus aquaticus*). Also spelled *ousel.* [OE *ōsle*]

o·val (ō′vəl) *adj.* **1** Having the figure of the plane longitudinal section of an egg, usually rounded at one end and tapering at the other. **2** Ellipsoidal. —*n.* A figure or body of such form or outline. [<NL *ovalis* <L *ovum* egg] —**o′val·ly** *adv.* —**o′val·ness** *n.*

o·va·ri·ot·o·my (ō·vâr′ē·ot′ə·mē) *n. Surg.* The excision of either or both ovaries, or of an ovarian tumor: also called *oophorectomy.* [OVARY + -TOMY]

o·va·ry (ō′və·rē) *n. pl.* **·ries 1** *Biol.* The genital gland of female animals in which are produced the essential reproductive elements or ova. In the higher vertebrates there are two. **2** *Bot.* In angiospermous plants, that portion of the pistil or gynoecium in which the ovules are contained. [<NL *ovarium* <L *ovum* an egg] —**o·var′i·an, o·var′i·al** *adj.*

o·vate (ō′vāt) *adj. Bot.* Egg-shaped: said of leaves. [<L *ovatus* <*ovum* egg] —**o′vate·ly** *adv.*

o·va·tion (ō·vā′shən) *n.* **1** A spontaneous acclamation of popularity; enthusiastic reception of a popular personage. **2** In ancient Rome, a secondary triumphal honor. [<L *ovatio, -onis* a rejoicing <*ovare* rejoice, exult] —**o·va′tion·al** *adj.*

ov·en (uv′ən) *n.* **1** An enclosed chamber in which substances are heated or cooked: used also for baking, annealing, etc., as in a kiln or assaying furnace. **2** A furnace. [OE *ofen*]

o·ver (ō′vər) *prep.* **1** In or to a place or position above; higher than: the sky *over* our heads. **2** So as to pass or extend across; from one end or side of to the other: the plane flying *over* the lake; walking *over* the bridge. **3** On the other side of: lying *over* the ocean. **4** Upon the surface or exterior of: Oil was smeared *over* the axle. **5** Here and there upon or within; throughout all parts of: traveling *over* land and sea. **6** So as to rise above, cover, or submerge: The mud is now *over* my boots. **7** So as to close or cover: a cloth tied *over* the mouth of the jar. **8** During the continuance of; through: a diary kept *over* the years. **9** Up to the end of and beyond: Stay with us *over* Christmas. **10** More

than; in excess of, as in amount, degree, number, extent, etc.: *over* a million dollars in assets. **11** In preference to: chosen *over* all other contenders. **12** In higher rank, authority, power, etc., than: They want a strong man *over* them. **13** Upon, as an effect: His influence *over* her is profound. **14** Concerning; with regard to: time wasted *over* trifles. **15** While engaged in or partaking of: falling asleep *over* Shakespeare; a bargain made *over* a bottle of wine. —**over all** From one end or aspect to the other. —**over and above** In addition to; besides. —*adv.* **1** Above; on high. **2** So as to close, cover, or be covered: The pond froze *over.* **3** To pass above from one of two sides or places to the other; across an intervening space, brim, or edge. **4** At or on the other side; at a distance in a specified direction or place: *over* in Europe; They're playing music *over* there. **5** From one side, opinion, or purpose to another: to be won *over* to a point of view. **6** From one person, condition, or custody to another: to make property *over* to someone. **7** From beginning to end; all through; completely: I'll think the matter *over.* **8** With the upper surface downwards; from an upright position, especially so as to invert, reverse, or transpose: to turn one's hand *over*; to topple *over.* **9** With repetition; again: He added his figures *over.* **10** So as to overflow: The cup ran *over.* **11** So as to constitute a surplus; in excess; beyond: enough to have some left *over.* **12** Beyond a stated time; until later: Plan to stay *over.* —**all over with** Finished. —**over again** Once more; afresh. —**over against** Opposite to; as contrasted with; in front of. —**over and over** Repeatedly. —**over there** *Colloq.* In Europe: a phrase popularized in the United States during World War I. —*adj.* **1** Finished; complete. **2** On the other side; having got across. **3** Outer; superior; upper. **4** In excess or addition; extra. —*n.* **1** Something remaining or in addition. **2** In cricket: **a** The succession of four to six balls bowled during a turn at one end of the wicket. **b** The part of the game in which this occurs. **3** *Mil.* A shot hitting or exploding beyond the target. —*v.t.* & *v.i.* To go or pass over. [OE *ofer*]

over- *combining form* **1** Above; on top of; superior: *overlord.* **2** Passing above; going beyond the top or limit of: *overarch, overflow.* **3** Moving or causing to move downward, as from above: *overthrow, overturn.* **4** Excessively; excessive; too much.

Over- is widely used in def. 4 to form compounds, as in the list beginning at the foot of the page.

o·ver·act (ō′vər·akt′) *v.t.* & *v.i.* To act with exaggeration.

o·ver·all (ō′vər·ôl′) *adj.* **1** From one extremity to the other: said of dimensions measured. **2** Including or covering everything.

o·ver·alls (ō′vər·ôlz′) *n. pl.* **1** Loose, coarse trousers, often with suspenders and a piece extending over the breast, worn over the clothing as protection from soiling. **2** *Brit.* Waterproof leggings.

o·ver·arch (ō′vər·ärch′) *v.t.* & *v.i.* To form an arch over (something).

o·ver·awe (ō′vər·ô′) *v.t.* **·awed, ·aw·ing** To subdue or restrain by awe. See synonyms under ABASH.

o·ver·bear (ō′vər·bâr′) *v.* **·bore, ·borne, ·bear·ing** *v.t.* **1** To crush or bear down by physical weight or force. **2** To prevail over; domineer.

—*v.i.* **3** To bear too much fruit; be too fruitful. See synonyms under SUBDUE.

o·ver·bear·ing (ō′vər·bâr′ing) *adj.* **1** Arrogant; dictatorial. **2** Overwhelming; crushing. See synonyms under ARBITRARY, DOGMATIC, IMPERIOUS. —**o′ver·bear′ing·ly** *adv.* —**o′ver·bear′ing·ness** *n.*

o·ver·bid (ō′vər·bid′) *v.t.* & *v.i.* **·bid, ·bid·den** or **·bid, ·bid·ding 1** To outbid (someone). **2** To bid more than the fair value of (something).

o·ver·blow (ō′vər·blō′) *v.t.* **·blew, ·blown, ·blow·ing 1** To blow down, over, or away. **2** To cover by blowing, as with snow or sand.

o·ver·blown (ō′vər·blōn′) *adj.* Too productive of flowers; also, past flowering; past full bloom.

o·ver·board (ō′vər·bôrd′, -bōrd′) *adv.* Over the side of or out of a boat or ship.

o·ver·build (ō′vər·bild′) *v.t.* **·built, ·build·ing 1** To build over: to *overbuild* a ravine. **2** To erect more buildings within (an area) than are needed. **3** To build, as a house, on too elaborate a scale.

o·ver·bur·den (ō′vər·bûr′dən) *v.t.* To load with too much weight.

o·ver·cast (ō′vər·kast′, -käst′, ō′vər·kast′, -käst′) *v.* **·cast, ·cast·ing** *v.t.* **1** To overcloud; darken. **2** To sew, as the edge of a fabric, with long wrapping stitches so as to prevent raveling. —*adj.* **1** Clouded, as the sky. **2** Sewn with a blanket stitch. —*n. Meteorol.* A cloud or clouds covering more than nine tenths of the sky.

o·ver·charge (ō′vər·chärj′) *v.t.* **·charged, ·charg·ing 1** To charge (someone) too high a price. **2** To load or fill to excess; overburden. **3** To exaggerate. —*n.* An excessive charge.

o·ver·check (ō′vər·chek′) *n.* A checkrein passing over a horse's head between the ears to draw the bit upward.

o·ver·coat (ō′vər·kōt′) *n.* An extra outdoor coat worn over a suit; a greatcoat; topcoat.

o·ver·come (ō′vər·kum′) *v.t.* **1** To get the better of in any conflict or struggle; defeat; conquer. **2** To prevail over or surmount, as difficulties, obstacles, etc. **3** To affect violently so as to render helpless, as by emotion, sickness, etc. —*v.i.* **4** To gain mastery; win. See synonyms under BEAT, CONQUER, REPRESS, SUBDUE. [OE *ofercuman*] —**o′ver·com′er** *n.*

o·ver·com·pen·sa·tion (ō′vər·kom′pən·sā′shən) *n.* **1** *Psychol.* More than the necessary or normal adjustments in a given situation. **2** *Psychoanal.* The cultivation of attitudes and forms of behavior designed to compensate in an exaggerated manner for the fact or feeling of inferiority. —**o′ver·com·pen′sa·to·ry** (-kəm·pen′sə·tôr′ē, -tō′rē) *adj.*

o·ver·de·vel·op (ō′vər·di·vel′əp) *v.t.* **1** To develop excessively. **2** *Phot.* To develop (a plate or film) to too great a degree. —**o′ver·de·vel′op·ment** *n.*

o·ver·do (ō′vər·dōō′) *v.* **·did, ·done, ·do·ing 1** To do excessively; carry too far; exaggerate. **2** To overtax the strength of; exhaust: usually used passively or reflexively. **3** To cook too much, as meat. **4** *Poetic* To surpass; outdo. —*v.i.* **5** To do too much. [OE *oferdōn*]

o·ver·dose (ō′vər·dōs′) *v.t.* **·dosed, ·dos·ing** To dose to excess. —*n.* (ō′vər·dōs′) An excessive dose.

o·ver·draft (ō′vər·draft′, -dräft′) *n.* **1** The act of overdrawing an account, as at a bank.

overabound	overargue	overbig	overbrown	overcaution	overcold	overconscious
overabstemious	overassert	overbitter	overbrush	overcautious	overcolor	overconsciousness
overabundance	overassertion	overblame	overbrutal	overcautiously	overcommend	overconservatism
overabundant	overassertive	overblithe	overbulky	overcentralization	overcompetitive	overconservative
overaccentuate	overassess	overboastful	overburdensome	overcharitable	overcomplacency	overconsiderate
overaccumulation	overassessment	overbold	overbusy	overcheap	overcomplacent	overconsideration
overactive	overassumption	overbookish	overbuy	overcherish	overcomplete	overconsume
overactivity	overattached	overborrow	overcapacity	overchildish	overcomplex	overconsumption
overadvance	overattentive	overbravely	overcaptious	overchill	overcompliant	overcontented
overambitious	overbake	overbred	overcaptiousness	overcivil	overconcentration	overcontribute
overanalyze	overbanked	overbreed	overcareful	overcivilized	overconcern	overcook
overanxiety	overbarren	overbright	overcareless	overclean	overcondense	overcool
overanxious	overbashful	overbrilliant	overcaring	overclever	overconfidence	overcoolly
overapprehensive	overbelief	overbroaden	overcarry	overclose	overconfident	overcopious
overapt	overbet	overbroil	overcasual	overcloseness	overconscientious	overcorrect

2 The amount by which a check or draft exceeds the sum against which it is drawn. **3** A current of air passing over, not through, the ignited fuel in a furnace. Also **o'ver·draught'** (-draft', -dräft').

o·ver·draw (ō'vər·drô') v.t. ·drew, ·drawn, ·draw·ing **1** To draw against (an account) beyond one's credit. **2** To draw or strain excessively, as a bow. **3** To exaggerate a representation of. — n. (ō'vər·drô') The act of overdrawing; an overdraft.

o·ver·drive (ō'vər·drīv') v.t. ·drove, ·driv·en, ·driv·ing **1** To push too hard or too far; overwork. **2** To drive too hard. — n. (ō'vər·drīv') Mech. A gearing device which turns a drive shaft at a speed greater than that of the engine, thus decreasing power output: opposed to *underdrive*.

o·ver·ex·pose (ō'vər·ik·spōz') v.t. ·posed, ·pos·ing **1** To expose excessively. **2** Phot. To expose (a film or plate) too long. — **o'ver·ex·po'sure** (-spō'zhər) n.

o·ver·fall (ō'vər·fôl') n. **1** A rapid sea current formed by the peculiarities of the bottom, or by winds, tide, etc.; a race. **2** A sudden drop in the bottom of the sea. **3** A catch basin for overflow, as from a canal.

o·ver·flow (ō'vər·flō') v. ·flowed, ·flown, ·flow·ing v.i. **1** To flow or run over the brim or bank, as water, rivers, etc. **2** To be filled beyond capacity; spill over. **3** To superabound. — v.t. **4** To flow over the brim or bank of. **5** To flow or spread over; cover. **6** To fill beyond capacity; cause to overflow. See synonyms under INUNDATE. — n. (ō'vər·flō') **1** The act of overflowing. **2** That which flows over. **3** A flood. **4** A surplus. **5** A passage or outlet for liquid. [OE *oferflōwan*]

o·ver·gar·ment (ō'vər·gär'mənt) n. An outer garment.

o·ver·glaze (ō'vər·glāz') v.t. ·glazed, ·glaz·ing To glaze over; apply an overglaze to. — n. A decoration or second glaze applied to pottery.

o·ver·grow (ō'vər·grō') v. ·grew, ·grown, ·grow·ing v.t. **1** To grow over; cover with growth. **2** To grow too big for; outgrow. — v.i. **3** To grow or increase excessively; grow too large. — **o'ver·grown'** adj.

o·ver·growth (ō'vər·grōth') n. **1** Luxuriant or excessive growth. **2** A growth upon or over something.

o·ver·hand (ō'vər·hand') adj. **1** In baseball, delivering the ball, or delivered, as the ball, with the hand well above the level of the elbow or shoulder. **2** Made by carrying the thread over and over, as a seam. **3** With the hand above the object which it holds, seizes, or throws. **4** Striking downward. — adv. In an overhand manner. — v.t. In sewing, to overcast. — n. **1** An overhand stroke or delivery in baseball or tennis; also, a ball so served or delivered. **2** The act or method of such delivery or stroke. **3** A kind of knot. See illustration under KNOT.

o·ver·hang (ō'vər·hang') v. ·hung, ·hang·ing v.t. **1** To hang or project over (something); jut over. **2** To impend over; threaten. **3** To adorn with hangings. — v.i. **4** To hang or jut over something. — n. **1** An overhanging portion of a structure, as of a roof, the bow of a ship, etc.; also, the amount or degree of such projection. **2** Aeron. **a** One half the distance in span of any two main supporting surfaces of an airplane: when the upper surface is the greater, it is called positive overhang. **b** The distance from the outer strut attachment to the edge of a wing.

o·ver·haul (ō'vər·hôl') v.t. **1** To examine carefully, as for needed repairs; turn over or take

apart for this purpose. **2** To catch up with; gain on. **3** Naut. **a** To slacken (a rope) by hauling in the opposite direction. **b** To prepare (a tackle) for use by separating the blocks. See synonyms under EXAMINE. — n. (ō'vər·hôl') **1** A thorough inspection or examination. **2** Examination and complete repair. Also **o'ver·haul'ing.**

o·ver·head (ō'vər·hed') adj. **1** Placed or working above or aloft: an *overhead* railway; working from above; working downward: an *overhead* valve. **2** Chosen by random sampling; average: an *overhead* sample. **3** Situated or working overhead; also, passing over the head. **4** Denoting such general expenditure in a financial or industrial enterprise as cannot be attributed to any one department or product, excluding cost of materials, labor, and selling; fixed charges; in transportation, bond interest and other expenses previous to operating expenses, taxes, etc. — n. **1** General expenditure applicable to all departments of a business, as light, heat, taxes, etc. **2** Naut. Ceiling of a cabin or hold. — adv. (ō'vər·hed') **1** Above one's head; aloft. **2** So as to be submerged; over one's head.

o·ver·hear (ō'vər·hir') v.t. ·heard, ·hear·ing To hear (something said or someone speaking) without the knowledge or intention of the speaker. — **o'ver·hear'er** n.

o·ver·hours (ō'vər·ourz') n. pl. **1** Time outside and in addition to the assigned or usual number of hours; overtime. **2** Unduly long hours of employment.

o·ver·is·sue (ō'vər·ish'ōō, -yōō) v.t. ·sued, ·su·ing To issue in excess of a legal or authorized amount, or in excess of ability to meet the demands thus created: to *overissue* stock, notes, or bonds. — n. (ō'vər·ish'ōō, -yōō) An excessive or unauthorized issue.

o·ver·joy (ō'vər·joi') v.t. To delight or please greatly. See synonyms under RAVISH.

o·ver·kill (ō'vər·kil') n. **1** The surplus of nuclear weapons beyond the number considered necessary to demolish all key enemy targets. **2** Colloq. Any action regarded as being more extreme than the circumstances warrant: *Slashing the budget in half was a clear case of overkill.*

o·ver·lade (ō'vər·lād') v.t. ·lad·ed, ·lad·ed or ·lad·en, ·lad·ing To overload: now used chiefly in the past participle.

o·ver·land (ō'vər·land') adj. Journeying or accomplished by or principally by land. — adv. Across, over, or via land. — n. An overland stage or train.

o·ver·lap (ō'vər·lap') v.t. & v.i. ·lapped, ·lap·ping To lie or extend partly over or upon (another or one another); lap over. — n. (ō'vər·lap') **1** The state, condition, or extent of overlapping; also, the part that overlaps. **2** Geol. The extension of younger rock strata beyond the limits of the older underlying strata.

o·ver·lay (ō'vər·lā') n. **1** Printing A piece of paper placed on the tympan of a press to make the impression heavier at the corresponding part of the form, or to compensate for a depression in the form. **2** Anything that overlies, covers, or partly covers something. **3** Ornamental work overlaid on wood, as with veneers, etc. **4** A sheet of transparent material carrying information of a special or confidential nature to supplement the details of the map on which it is laid. **5** Scot. A cravat. — v.t. (ō'vər·lā') ·laid, ·lay·ing **1** To spread something over, as with a decorative pattern or layer. **2** To lay or place over or upon something else. **3** Printing To put an overlay upon. **4** To overburden; weigh down.

o·ver·leaf (ō'vər·lēf') adv. & adj. On the reverse side of a leaf (of paper).

o·ver·leap (ō'vər·lēp') v.t. **1** To leap over or across. **2** To omit; overlook. **3** To leap farther than; outleap. — **to overleap oneself** To miss one's purpose by going too far. [OE *oferhlēapan*]

o·ver·live (ō'vər·liv') v. ·lived, ·liv·ing v.t. To live longer than; survive. — v.i. To survive; live too long. [OE *oferlibban*]

o·ver·look (ō'vər·lŏŏk') v.t. **1** To fail to see or notice; miss. **2** To disregard purposely or indulgently; ignore. **3** To look over or see from a higher place. **4** To afford a view of: *The castle overlooks the harbor.* **5** To supervise; oversee. **6** To examine or inspect. **7** To look upon or bewitch with the evil eye. See synonyms under PARDON. — n. (ō'vər·lŏŏk') **1** The act of looking over, as from a height; an inspection; survey. **2** Oversight; neglect. **3** The jack bean: so called because believed by West Indian Negroes to serve as a watchman.

o·ver·ly (ō'vər·lē) adv. To an excessive degree; too much; too.

o·ver·mas·ter (ō'vər·mas'tər, -mäs'-) v.t. To overcome; overpower. — **o'ver·mas'ter·ing** n. & adj.

o·ver·match (ō'vər·mach') v.t. To be more than a match for; surpass. — n. (ō'vər·mach') **1** One who or that which is superior in strength, skill, etc. **2** A contest in which one party overmatches the other.

o·ver·ma·ture (ō'vər·mə·chŏŏr') adj. Denoting the state of a forest in which, as a result of age, the growth of the trees has almost entirely ceased and degeneration has started.

o·ver·much (ō'vər·much') adj. Exceeding what is necessary or proper; too much. — adv. In too great a degree. — n. An excess; too much.

o·ver·pass (ō'vər·pas', -päs') v.t. **1** To pass across, over, or through; cross. **2** To surpass or exceed. **3** To overlook; disregard. **4** To transgress. — n. (ō'vər·pas', -päs') An elevated section of highway crossing other lines of travel.

o·ver·per·suade (ō'vər·pər·swād') v.t. ·suad·ed, ·suad·ing To persuade (someone) to an action or view, especially against his judgment or inclination. — **o'ver·per·sua'sion** n.

o·ver·play (ō'vər·plā') v.t. **1** To play or act (a part or role) to excess; overdo; exaggerate. **2** To outplay; surpass. **3** In golf, to send (the ball) beyond the putting green.

o·ver·plus (ō'vər·plus') n. That which remains after a certain part has been used or set aside; surplus; excess. See synonyms under EXCESS. [Partial trans. of OF *surplus* < *sur*- over + *plus* more]

o·ver·pow·er (ō'vər·pou'ər) v.t. **1** To gain supremacy over; subdue. **2** To render wholly helpless or ineffective; overcome. **3** To supply with more power than necessary. See synonyms under CONQUER, REPRESS, SUBDUE. — **o'ver·pow'er·ing** adj. — **o'ver·pow'er·ing·ly** adv.

o·ver·prize (ō'vər·prīz') v.t. ·prized, ·priz·ing To value too highly.

o·ver·pro·duce (ō'vər·prə·dōōs', -dyōōs') v.t. ·duced, ·duc·ing To produce too much of or so as to exceed demand.

o·ver·proof (ō'vər·prōōf') adj. Containing a larger proportion of alcohol than proof spirit; said of alcoholic liquors.

o·ver·rate (ō'vər·rāt') v.t. ·rat·ed, ·rat·ing To rate or value too highly; overestimate.

o·ver·reach (ō'vər·rēch') v.t. **1** To reach over or beyond. **2** To spread over; cover. **3** To defeat (oneself), as by trying too hard or being too clever. **4** To miss by stretching or

overcorrupt	overcured	overdelicate	overdilute	overeasy	overenthusiastic	overexpenditure
overcostly	overcurious	overdelicately	overdiscipline	overeat	overesteem	overexpress
overcount	overcuriousness	overdemand	overdiscourage	overeducate	overestimate	overexuberant
overcourteous	overdaintiness	overdemocratic	overdistant	overelaborate	overestimation	overfacile
overcovetous	overdainty	overdepress	overdiversification	overelaboration	overexcelling	overfaithful
overcoy	overdance	overdepressive	overdiversify	overelate	overexcitable	overfamiliar
overcram	overdare	overdesirous	overdogmatic	overelegant	overexcite	overfanciful
overcredit	overdazzle	overdestructive	overdominate	overembellish	overexcitement	overfast
overcredulous	overdear	overdestructiveness	overdoubt	overemotional	overexercise	overfastidious
overcriticize	overdecorate	overdevoted	overdramatic	overemphasis	overexert	overfastidiousness
overcull	overdecorative	overdevotion	overdrink	overemphasize	overexertion	overfasting
overcultivate	overdeepen	overdiffuse	overdry	overemphatic	overexpand	overfat
overcultivation	overdeeply	overdignified	overeager	overenjoy	overexpansion	overfatigue
overcunning	overdeliberate	overdiligence	overearnest	overenrich	overexpect	overfatten
overcunningly	overdeliberation	overdiligent	overeasily	overenter	overexpectant	overfavor

reaching too far. **5** To get the advantage of; outwit; cheat. — *v.i.* **6** To reach too far. **7** To cheat. **8** To hit a toe of the hind foot against the heel of the forefoot: said of horses, etc. See synonyms under DECEIVE. — **o′ver-reach′er** *n.* — **o′ver-reach′ing** *n.*

o-ver-re-act (ō′vər-rē-akt′) *v.i.* To react to a person, situation, etc., in an excessively emotional or uncontrolled manner. — **o′ver-re-ac′tion** *n.*

o-ver-ride (ō′vər-rīd′) *v.t.* **-rode, -rid-den, -rid-ing 1** To ride over or across. **2** To trample down; suppress. **3** To disregard summarily, as if trampling down; supersede; prevail over. **4** To ride (a horse) to exhaustion. **5** *Surg.* To slide over (the corresponding fragment), as one end of a fractured bone. — *n.* A commission paid a sales manager based on the sales of his staff. [OE *oferridan*]

o-ver-rule (ō′vər-rōōl′) *v.t.* **-ruled, -rul-ing 1** To decide against or nullify by superior authority; set aside; invalidate. **2** To disallow the arguments of (someone). **3** To have control over; rule. **4** To influence, as to another opinion or course of action; prevail over.

o-ver-run (ō′vər-run′) *v.* **-ran, -run, -run-ning** *v.t.* **1** To spread or swarm over, especially harmfully, as vermin or invaders do; ravage; invade; infest. **2** To run or flow over; overflow. **3** To spread rapidly across or throughout: said of fads, ideas, etc. **4** To run beyond; pass the limit of. **5** *Printing* **a** To shift (words, lines of type, etc.) from one line, page, or column to another. **b** To rearrange (matter) in this way. **6** *Archaic* To run faster than; outrun. — *v.i.* **7** To run over; overflow. **8** To pass the usual or desired limit. —*n.* (ō′vər-run′) An instance of overrunning; the amount or extent of overrunning.

o-ver-seas (ō′vər-sēz′) *adv.* Beyond the sea; abroad. — *adj.* Coming from or for use beyond the sea; foreign. Also **o′ver-sea′.**

o-ver-see (ō′vər-sē′) *v.t.* **-saw, -seen, -see-ing 1** To direct as supervisor; superintend. **2** To survey; watch. **3** To examine; peruse. [OE *ofersēon*]

o-ver-se-er (ō′vər-sē′ər) *n.* **1** A person who oversees; especially, one who superintends laborers at their work. **2** A parish officer who administrates relief funds: also **overseer of the poor.** See synonyms under MASTER, SUPERINTENDENT.

o-ver-sell (ō′vər-sel′) *v.t.* **-sold, -sell-ing 1** To sell to excess. **2** To sell more of (a stock, etc.) than one can deliver or provide a margin for.

o-ver-set (ō′vər-set′) *v.* **-set, -set-ting** *v.t.* **1** To overcome or disorder mentally or physically; disconcert. **2** *Printing* **a** To set too much (type or copy) in a given space. **b** To set too much type in. **3** *Rare* To cause to overturn; capsize. — *v.i.* **4** To overturn; fall over; spill. — *n.* (ō′vər-set′) **1** A turning over; upset. **2** *Printing* Excess of composed type.

o-ver-shad-ow (ō′vər-shad′ō) *v.t.* **1** To render unimportant or insignificant by comparison; loom above; dominate. **2** To throw a shadow over; dim; obscure. [OE *ofersceadwian*]

o-ver-shine (ō′vər-shīn′) *v.t.* **-shone, -shin-ing 1** To shine over or upon; illumine. **2** To excel in some respect. [OE *oferscīnan*]

o-ver-shoe (ō′vər-shōō′) *n.* A shoe, usually of rubber, worn for protection over another.

o-ver-shoot (ō′vər-shōōt′) *v.* **-shot, -shoot-ing** *v.t.* **1** To shoot or go over or beyond. **2** To go beyond; exceed, as a limit. **3** To drive or force (something) beyond the proper limit.

— *v.i.* **4** To shoot or go over or beyond the mark. **5** To go too far.

o-ver-shot (ō′vər-shot′) *adj.* **1** Surpassed in any way. **2** Projecting, as the upper jaw beyond the lower jaw. **3** Driven by water flowing over from above: an *overshot* wheel.

overshot wheel A water wheel with buckets that are filled by water from a race over the top, the weight and impetus of the water turning the wheel.

OVERSHOT WHEEL

o-ver-sight (ō′vər-sīt′) *n.* **1** An error due to inattention; an inadvertent mistake or omission. **2** Watchful supervision; superintendence.

Synonyms: care, charge, command, control, direction, inspection, management, superintendence, supervision, surveillance, watch, watchfulness. *Oversight* strictly implies constant personal presence; *superintendence* requires only so much of presence or communication as to know that the superintendent's wishes are carried out; the superintendent of a railroad will personally oversee very few of its operations; the railroad company has supreme *direction* of all its affairs without *superintendence* or *oversight*. But a person may look over a matter in order to survey it carefully in its entirety, or he may look over it with no attention to the thing itself because his gaze and thought are concentrated on something beyond; *oversight* has thus two contrasted senses, in the latter sense denoting inadvertent error or omission, and in the former denoting watchful *supervision*. *Control* is chiefly used with reference to restraint or the power of restraint. *Surveillance* signifies watching with something of suspicion. See CARE, ERROR, NEGLECT.

o-ver-signed (ō′vər-sīnd′) *n.* The person whose name appears at the head of an article, document, report, etc.: distinguished from *undersigned*.

o-ver-sleep (ō′vər-slēp′) *v.* **-slept, -sleep-ing** *v.i.* To sleep too long. — *v.t.* To sleep beyond (a specified time).

o-ver-soul (ō′vər-sōl′) *n.* The spiritual being or element of the universe individualized in or uniting together and influencing human souls; the absolute unity, in which subject and object, knower and known, are one: a concept in Emerson's transcendentalist philosophy.

o-ver-spread (ō′vər-spred′) *v.t.* **spread, -spread-ing** To spread or extend over; cover completely. [OE *ofersprædan*]

o-ver-state (ō′vər-stāt′) *v.t.* **-stat-ed, -stat-ing** To state in too strong terms; exaggerate. — **o′ver-state′ment** *n.*

o-ver-step (ō′vər-step′) *v.t.* **-stepped, -step-ping** To step over or go beyond; exceed (some limit or restriction). [OE *ofersteppan*]

o-ver-stuffed (ō′vər-stuft′) *adj.* Excessively stuffed; expecially, as furniture, completely covered with deep upholstery; heavily upholstered.

o-vert (ō′vûrt, ō-vûrt′) *adj.* **1** Open to view; outwardly manifest. **2** *Law* Done with criminal intent. [<OF, pp. of *ovrir* open] — **o′vert-ly** *adv.*

Synonyms: see EVIDENT, MANIFEST, NOTORIOUS, OPEN. *Antonyms:* contemplated, hidden, intended, meditated, secret.

o-ver-take (ō′vər-tāk′) *v.t.* **-took, -tak-en, -tak-ing 1** To catch up with. **2** To come upon suddenly. See synonyms under CATCH.

o-ver-throw (ō′vər-thrō′) *v.t.* **-threw, -thrown, -throw-ing 1** To throw over or down; upset. **2** To bring down or remove from power by force; defeat; ruin. See synonyms under ABOLISH, CONQUER, DEMOLISH, EXTERMINATE, RUIN, SUBVERT. — *n.* (ō′vər-thrō′) **1** The act of overthrowing; destruction; demolition. **2** A throwing of a ball over and beyond the player at whom it is aimed.

o-ver-time (ō′vər-tīm′) *v.t.* **-timed, -tim-ing** *Phot.* To expose too long, as a plate or film. — *n.* (ō′vər-tīm′) Time used in working beyond the specified hours. — *adj.* During or for extra working time: *overtime* pay. — *adv.* Beyond the stipulated time.

o-ver-tone (ō′vər-tōn′) *n.* **1** *Music* A harmonic: so called because it is heard with and above the fundamental tone produced by a musical instrument. **2** The color of the light reflected by a painted surface. **3** The associations, connotations, implications, etc., of language, thoughts, etc. [<G *oberton*]

o-ver-top (ō′vər-top′) *v.t.* **-topped, -top-ping 1** To rise above the top of; tower over. **2** To surpass; excel.

o-ver-topped (ō′vər-topt′) *adj.* Having the crown shaded from above by other contiguous trees: said of a tree.

o-ver-ture (ō′vər-chər) *n.* **1** *Music* **a** An instrumental prelude, as to an opera or other large work. **b** An orchestral piece of varying form, usually illustrating a dramatic or graphic theme. **2** A proposal intended to lead to further negotiations by expressing willingness to make terms; also, the proposal submitted. See synonyms under PROPOSAL. — *v.t.* **-tured, -tur-ing 1** To offer as an overture or proposal. **2** To introduce with or as an overture. [<OF < *ouvert.* See OVERT.]

o-ver-turn (ō′vər-tûrn′) *v.t.* **1** To turn or throw over; capsize; upset. **2** To destroy the power of; overthrow; defeat; ruin. — *v.i.* **3** To turn over; capsize; upset. See synonyms under DEMOLISH, SUBVERT. — *n.* (ō′vər-tûrn′) **1** The act of overturning or the state of being overturned; an upset; overthrow. **2** A subversion or destruction. **3** Turnover (def. 5).

o-ver-view (ō′vər-vyōō′) *n.* A broad survey or review of a subject, activity, etc.

o-ver-watch (ō′vər-woch′, -wôch′) *v.t.* **1** To watch over. **2** To weary with watching.

o-ver-wear (ō′vər-wâr′) *v.t.* **-wore, -worn, -wear-ing 1** To wear out. **2** To outgrow.

o-ver-wea-ry (ō′vər-wir′ē) *adj.* Overtired; exhausted. — *v.t.* **-ried, -ry-ing** To tire to excess.

o-ver-ween-ing (ō′vər-wē′ning) *adj.* Characterized by presumptuous pride or conceit; arrogant; excessive; exaggerated. — *n.* Overconfidence; presumption. [OE *oferwenan* < *ofer-* over + *wēnan* think] — **o′ver-ween′ing-ly** *adv.*

o-ver-weight (ō′vər-wāt′) *n.* **1** Excess of weight, as beyond the legal or customary amount: to give *overweight.* **2** Greater weight; preponderance; also, more than normal weight. — *adj.* Being more than the usual or permitted weight. — *v.t.* (ō′vər-wāt′) To weigh down; overburden.

o-ver-whelm (ō′vər-hwelm′) *v.t.* **1** To bury or

add,āce,câre,pälm; end,ēven; it,īce; odd,ōpen,ôrder; tŏŏk,pōōl; up,bûrn; ə = a in *above,* e in *sicken,* i in *clarity,* o in *melon,* u in *focus;* yōō = u in *fuse;* oi,oil; ou,pout; ch,check; g,go; ng,ring; th,thin; ŧħ,this; zh,vision. Foreign sounds à,œ,ü,kh,ṅ; and ◆: see page xx. < from; + plus; ? possibly.

submerge completely, as with a wave or flood. **2** To overcome or defeat by or as by irresistible force or numbers; crush; render helpless. **3** *Obs.* To overthrow. See synonyms under BURY[1], HIDE[1], INUNDATE, INVOLVE, SUBDUE.

o·ver·wind (ō'vər·wīnd') *v.t.* **·wound, ·wind·ing** **1** To wind too far or too tightly, as a watch. **2** *Electr.* To wind (the magnet of a motor) in order to produce a maximum magnetism with a smaller current than is normally required.

o·ver·work (ō'vər·wûrk') *v.* **·worked** or **·wrought, ·work·ing** *v.t.* **1** To cause to work too hard; exhaust with work or use. **2** To work on or elaborate excessively: to *overwork* an argument. **3** To work up or excite excessively. — *v.i.* **4** To work too hard; do too much work. — *n.* (ō'vər·wûrk') **1** Work done in overtime, or in excess of the stipulated amount. **2** Excessive work.

o·ver·wrought (ō'vər·rôt') *adj.* **1** Worked up or excited excessively; overstrained: *overwrought* feelings. **2** Worked all over, as with embroidery. **3** Worked too hard. **4** Too elaborate; overdone. [< OVERWORK]

o·vi·duct (ō'vi·dukt) *n. Anat.* The passage by which the ova are conveyed from the ovary to the uterus, as the Fallopian tube.

o·vif·er·ous (ō·vif'ər·əs) *adj.* Bearing or holding eggs. [< OVI- + -FEROUS]

o·vine (ō'vīn, ō'vin) *adj.* Of or pertaining to a sheep; sheeplike. — *n.* An ovine animal. [< L *ovinus* < *ovis* sheep]

o·vip·a·ra (ō·vip'ər·ə) *n. pl.* Animals that lay eggs. [< NL < L *oviparus* laying eggs < *ovum* egg + *-parus* < *parere* bring forth]

o·vi·pos·it (ō'vi·poz'it) *v.i.* **1** *Biol.* To lay eggs. **2** *Entomol.* To deposit eggs by means of an ovipositor. [< OVI- + L *positus*, pp. of *ponere* place] — **o·vi·po·si·tion** (ō'vi·pə·zish'ən) *n.*

o·vi·pos·i·tor (ō'vi·poz'ə·tər) *n. Entomol.* The tubular organ at the extremity of the abdomen in many insects, by which the eggs are deposited: sometimes modified as a sting, as in bees and wasps.

o·void (ō'void) *adj.* Egg-shaped: also **o·voi'dal.** — *n.* An egg-shaped body.

o·vu·late (ō'vyə·lāt) *v.i.* **·lat·ed, ·lat·ing** To produce ova; discharge ova from an ovary. [< NL *ovulum*, dim. of L *ovum* an egg]

o·vu·la·tion (ō'vyə·lā'shən) *n. Biol.* The formation and discharge of ova; the period when this occurs.

o·vule (ō'vyōōl) *n.* **1** *Bot.* The rudimentary seed of a plant; the body within the ovary which, upon fertilization, becomes the seed. **2** A small ovum. [< F, dim. of L *ovum* an egg] — **o'vu·lar, o·vu·lar·y** (ō'vyə·ler'ē) *adj.*

o·vum (ō'vəm) *n. pl.* **o·va** (ō'və) **1** *Biol.* **a** A cell formed in the ovary; an egg. **b** An ovule. **2** *Archit.* An egg-shaped ornament. [< L]

owe (ō) *v.* **owed** (*Obs.* **ought**), **ow·ing** *v.t.* **1** To be indebted to the amount of; be obligated to pay or repay. **2** To be obligated to render or offer: to *owe* an apology. **3** To have or possess by virtue of gift, labor, etc.: with *to:* He *owes* his success to his own efforts. **4** To cherish (a certain feeling) toward another: to *owe* a grudge. **5** *Obs.* To own; have. — *v.i.* **6** To be in debt. [OE *āgan*]

ow·ing (ō'ing) *adj.* Due; yet to be paid: six dollars *owing.*

owing to Attributable to; on account of; in consequence of.

owl (oul) *n.* **1** A predatory nocturnal bird of

the order *Strigiformes,* having large eyes and head, short, sharply hooked bill, long powerful claws, and a circular facial disk of radiating feathers. Of the North American owls, prominent species are the circumpolar **snowy owl** (genus *Nyctea*), the **great horned owl,** the **barred owl** (*Syrnium varium*), the **great gray owl** (genus *Scotiaptex*), **screech owl** (genus *Otus*), and the **long–eared** and **short–eared owls** (genus *Asio*). **2** One of a breed of domestic pigeons having an owl–like head and a prominent frill. **3** A person with nocturnal habits. **4** A person of solemn appearance, etc. [OE *ūle*]

owl·ish (ou'lish) *adj.* **1** Like an owl; grave. **2** Nocturnally active. **3** *Brit. Dial.* Stupid. — **owl'ish·ly** *adv.* — **owl'ish·ness** *n.*

own (ōn) *adj.* **1** Belonging to oneself; peculiar; particular; individual: following the possessive (usually a possessive pronoun) as an intensive to express ownership, interest, or individual peculiarity with emphasis, or to indicate the exclusion of others: my *own* horse; his *own* idea; It is my *own:* in this sense often with ellipsis of the noun. **2** Being of the nearest degree: *own* cousin. — **to come into one's own** **1** To obtain possession of one's property. **2** To receive one's reward; come into one's rightful position. — **to hold one's own** **1** To maintain one's place or position. **2** To keep up with one's work, or remain undefeated. — **on one's own** Entirely dependent on one's self for support or success. — *v.t.* **1** To have or hold as one's own; have as a belonging; possess. **2** To admit or acknowledge. — *v.i.* **3** To confess. See synonyms under ACKNOWLEDGE, AVOW, CONFESS, HAVE. [OE *āgen,* orig. pp. of *āgan* owe; possess] — **own'a·ble** *adj.*

own·er (ō'nər) *n.* One who has the legal title or right to or has possession of a thing. See synonyms under MASTER. — **own'er·less** *adj.*

own·er·ship (ō'nər·ship) *n.* The state of being an owner; proprietorship; also, legal title. ◆ Collateral adjective: *allodial.* See synonyms under PROPERTY.

ox (oks) *n. pl.* **ox·en** (ok'sən) **1** An adult castrated male of a domestic bovine quadruped. **2** A bovine quadruped, as a buffalo, bison, or yak; specifically, the common domesticated *Bos taurus,* or the zebu or Indian ox (*Bos indicus*). ◆ Collateral adjective: *bovine.* [OE *oxa*]

ox·a·lis (ok'sə·lis) *n.* A plant of a large, widely distributed genus (*Oxalis*) of mostly stemless herbs of the wood–sorrel family, with purple, rose, or white flowers; wood sorrel. [< L < Gk. < *oxys* sharp, acid]

ox·blood (oks'blud') *n.* A monochrome glaze of Chinese porcelain, in various tones of brilliant, deep, warm red; also, any of the tones of this glaze: also called *sang de boeuf.*

ox·bow (oks'bō') *n.* **1** A bent piece of wood in an ox yoke, that forms a collar for the ox. **2** A bend in a river shaped like this.

ox·eye (oks'ī') *n.* **1** Any of several plants of various genera of the composite family, especially any species of *Buphthalmum,* with large yellow heads. **2** The oxeye daisy. **3** One of various birds, as the least sandpiper. **4** An oval dormer window.

ox·eyed (oks'īd') *adj.* Having large, calm eyes like those of an ox.

oxford gray **1** A very dark gray. **2** A woolen fabric of this color.

ox·heart (oks'härt') *n.* A variety of sweet cherry.

ox·i·dase (ok'si·dās) *n. Biochem.* One of many oxidizing ferments found widely distributed in plant and animal tissues. [< OXID(E) + -ASE] — **ox'i·da'sic** *adj.*

ox·i·da·tion (ok'sə·dā'shən) *n. Chem.* **1** The act of uniting or of causing a substance to unite with oxygen. **2** The state of being so united. **3** Any changes in an element or a compound that result in addition to it of a negative radical or a relative decrease of the positive constituent. **4** The process by which the atoms of an element lose electrons: opposed to *reduction.* — **ox'i·da'tive** *adj.*

ox·i·dize (ok'sə·dīz) *v.* **·dized, ·diz·ing** *v.t. Chem.* **1** To unite with oxygen; cause the oxidation of; rust. **2** To add an electronegative element or radical to, or to decrease by an electropositive element or radical. **3** To remove electrons from (an element or compound). **4** To change (an element) to a higher valence: to *oxidize* ferrous iron to ferric iron. — *v.i.* **5** *Chem.* To become oxidized. Also *Brit.* **ox'i·dise.** — **ox'i·diz'a·ble** *adj.*

ox·lip (oks'lip') *n.* **1** A species of primrose (*Primula elatior*), closely resembling the cowslip. **2** A hybrid primrose.

ox·o·ni·um compound (ok·sō'nē·əm) *Chem.* Any of a class of organic compounds containing a basic oxygen atom combined with a mineral acid.

ox·peck·er (oks'pek'ər) *n.* An African bird of the starling family (genus *Buphagus*) that devours the parasites on oxen, etc.

ox·tail (oks'tāl') *n.* The tail of an ox, especially when skinned for use in soup.

ox·tongue (oks'tung') *n.* Any of various plants having rough, tongue-shaped leaves, as the bugloss.

oxy-[1] *combining form* **1** Sharp; pointed; keen: *oxytone.* **2** Acid: *oxygen.* [< Gk. *oxys* sharp]

oxy-[2] *combining form Chem.* **1** Oxygen; of or containing oxygen, or one of its compounds: *oxyphyte.* **2** An oxidation product of: *oxysulfide.* **3** Containing the hydroxyl group: *oxyacid.* [< OXYGEN]

ox·y·a·cet·y·lene (ok'sē·ə·set'ə·lēn) *adj.* Designating or pertaining to a mixture of acetylene and oxygen, used to obtain high temperatures, as in welding and blowpipe analysis.

ox·y·cal·ci·um (ok'si·kal'sē·əm) *adj.* Pertaining to or produced by oxygen and calcium; especially, designating the action of the oxy-hydrogen flame on lime, as in the calcium light.

ox·y·ceph·a·ly (ok'si·sef'ə·lē) *n.* The condition of having the skull conical in the upper frontal region. Also **ox'y·ce·pha'li·a** (-sə·fā'lē·ə). [< OXY-[1] + Gk. *kephalos* head] — **ox'y·ce·phal'ic** (-sə·fal'ik), **ox'y·ceph'a·lous** *adj.* — **ox'y·ceph'a·lism** *n.*

ox·y·gen (ok'sə·jin) *n.* A colorless, tasteless, odorless gaseous element (symbol O, atomic number 8), occurring free in the atmosphere and combined in numerous compounds (of which water is the most familiar), comprising 21 percent by volume of the atmosphere and about 49 percent by weight of the lithosphere, the agent in combustion and an element essential to the formation and functioning of all forms of life. See PERIODIC TABLE. [< F *oxygène* < *oxy-* OXY-[1] + *-gène* -GEN; so called because formerly considered essential to all acids]

ox·y·gen·ate (ok'sə·jən·āt') *v.t.* **·at·ed, ·at·ing** To treat, combine, or impregnate with oxygen; oxidize. — **ox'y·gen·a'tion** *n.*

ox·y·gen·ic (ok'sə·jen'ik) *adj.* Of, pertaining to, resembling, or containing oxygen. Also **ox·pee·nous** (ok·sij'ə·nəs).

overjocular	overlawful	overlogical	overmeasure	overmortgage	overnumerous	overparticular
overjoyful	overlax	overloud	overmeek	overmournful	overobedient	overpassionate
overjoyous	overlaxness	overlove	overmellow	overmultiply	overobese	overpatient
overjudicious	overlearnedness	overloyal	overmelt	overnarrow	overoblige	overpatriotic
overjust	overlet	overluscious	overmerciful	overnear	overobsequious	overpensive
overkeen	overlewd	overlustiness	overmerrily	overneat	overobsequiousness	overpert
overkind	overliberal	overlusty	overmerry	overneglect	overoffensive	overpessimistic
overknowing	overliberality	overluxuriant	overmighty	overnegligence	overofficious	overpiteous
overlabor	overlighted	overluxurious	overmild	overnegligent	overoften	overplain
overlade	overlinger	overmagnify	overminutely	overnervous	overoptimistic	overplausible
overlarge	overliterary	overmany	overminuteness	overnervousness	overornamented	overplease
overlate	overliveliness	overmasterful	overmix	overnew	overpainful	overplentiful
overlaudatory	overlively	overmasterfulness	overmodest	overnimble	overpamper	overplenty
overlaunch	overload	overmature	overmoist	overnotable	overpartial	overplump
overlavish	overlofty	overmeanness	overmoisten	overnourish	overpartiality	overpointed

overpolemical	overproficient	overpunish	overreflective	overrigorous	overscrupulous	overshort
overpolish	overprolific	overpunishment	overrelax	overripe	overseason	overshorten
overponderous	overprominent	overquick	overreliant	overroast	overseasoned	overshrink
overpopular	overprompt	overquiet	overreligious	overrough	oversecure	oversick
overpopulous	overpromptness	overquietness	overrepresent	overrude	oversensible	oversilent
overpositive	overprosperous	overrapturize	overreserved	oversad	oversensitive	oversimple
overpowerful	overprotect	overrash	overresolute	oversalt	oversententious	oversimplicity
overpraise	overprotract	overrational	overrestrain	oversalty	oversentimental	oversimplification
overprecise	overproud	overrationalize	overretention	oversanguine	overserious	oversimplify
overpreciseness	overprovide	overreadiness	overreward	oversaturate	overservile	overskeptical
overpreoccupation	overprovision	overready	overrich	oversaturation	oversettled	overslander
overpress	overprovocation	overrealism	overrife	oversaucy	oversevere	overslow
overpresumptuous	overprovoke	overrealistic	overrighteous	overscare	overseverely	oversmall
overprocrastination	overpublic	overrefinement	overrighteousness	overscented	overseverity	oversmooth
overproductive	overpublicity	overreflection	overrigid	overscrub	oversharp	oversoak

oxygen mask A device worn over the nose and mouth to aid breathing, as at high altitudes, by conveying oxygen from a container to the user.

oxygen point *Physics* The boiling point of liquid oxygen at standard atmospheric pressure, −182.97° C.: one of the fixed points of the international temperature scale.

oxygen tent A tentlike chamber placed over a patient's head and shoulders and supplied with oxygen for the purpose of facilitating his respiration.

ox·y·hy·dro·gen (ok′si·hī′drə·jən) *adj.* Of, pertaining to, or using a mixture of oxygen and hydrogen, especially for the production of very high temperatures. —*n.* A mixture of oxygen and hydrogen.

oxyhydrogen blowpipe A blowpipe in which jets of oxygen and hydrogen are combined in order to obtain very high temperatures: used in welding.

ox·y·mel (ok′sə·mel) *n.* A mixture of honey and vinegar boiled to a sirup. [< L *oxymel* < Gk. *oxymeli* < *oxys* acid + *meli* honey]

ox·y·mo·ron (ok′si·môr′on, -mō′ron) *n. pl.* **·mo·ra** (-môr′ə, -mō′rə) A figure of speech consisting of that form of antithesis in which, for emphasis or in an epigram, contradictory terms are brought sharply together, as in the phrase; "O heavy lightness, serious vanity!" [< Gk. *oxymōron*, neut. of *oxymoros* < *oxys* keen + *mōros* foolish]

ox yoke A yoke consisting of a heavy piece of wood which lies over the necks of the oxen and from which depend two oxbows.

OX YOKE
With 2 oxbows.

ox·y·phyte (ok′si·fīt) *n. Bot.* A plant adapted to soil which lacks oxygen.

ox·y·sul·fide (ok′si·sul′fīd) *n. Chem.* A compound of a sulfide with an oxide in which part of the sulfur has been replaced by oxygen. Also **ox′y·sul′phide.**

ox·y·toc·ic (ok′si·tos′ik, -tō′sik) *adj. Med.* Bringing on or hastening parturition. —*n.* A medicine efficacious in hastening parturition. [< OXY-¹ + Gk. *tokos* birth]

ox·y·to·cin (ok′si·tō′sin) *n.* **1** *Med.* Any drug which stimulates movements of the uterus, as ergotine. **2** *Physiol.* A hormone of the posterior lobe of the pituitary gland, believed to facilitate uterine contractions during childbirth.

ox·y·tone (ok′si·tōn) *adj.* **1** Having the acute accent on the last syllable. **2** Causing a preceding word to take an acute accent. —*n.* A word thus accented. [< Gk. *oxytonos* < *oxys* sharp + *tonos* pitch] —**ox′y·ton′i·cal** (-ton′i·kəl) *adj.*

o·yer (ō′yər, oi′ər) *n. Law* **1** A hearing or trial of causes; an assize; formerly, in pleading, a petition by a party to an action, praying that he might hear read to him a deed held by the opposite party; in modern practice, the production of such a document, or a copy thereof, by the party holding it. **2** Oyer and terminer: a contracted form. [< AF *oyer* < OF *oir, oyr*, ult. < L *audire* hear]

oys·ter (ois′tər) *n.* **1** Any of various marine mollusks of the family Ostreidae having a rough, unequal bivalve shell closed by a single adductor muscle and attached to stones, shells, etc., on the bottom, including species cultivated for food. **2** The morsel of dark meat found in the hollow of the bone on both sides of a fowl. **3** Some delicacy; titbit; prize. **4** *Slang* A very uncommunicative person. —*v.i.* To gather or cultivate oysters. [< OF *oistre* < L *ostrea* < Gk. *ostreon*]

OYSTER
a. Shell.   *f.* Liver.
b. Hinge.   *g.* Heart.
c. Mantle.   *h.* Adductor.
d. Palpi.   *i.* Stomach.
e. Anus.   *j.* Gills.

oyster bed A place where oysters breed or are grown.

oyster catcher A shore bird of the genus *Haematopus;* especially, the American *H. palliatus*, about 20 inches long, having black-and-white plumage and red feet and bill. It feeds mainly upon small mollusks caught between tide marks. as a purified paraffin. [< Gk. *ozein* smell + *keros* wax]

o·zo·na·tion (ō′zō·nā′shən) *n.* The act or process of producing or treating with ozone.

o·zone (ō′zōn) *n.* A blue gas with a pungent odor like that of chlorine, formed variously, as by the passage of electricity through the air, and regarded as an allotropic form of oxygen containing three atoms in the molecule (O_3). It is unstable and is a powerful oxidizing agent, being much more active than ordinary oxygen: employed for bleaching oils, waxes, ivory, flour, and starch, and for sterilizing drinking water. [< F < Gk. *ozein* smell] —**o·zon·ic** (ō·zon′ik, ō·zō′nik), **o·zo·nous** (ō′zə·nəs) *adj.*

ozone paper A filter paper coated with a mixture of starch and potassium iodide, which turns blue when exposed to the action of ozone.

ozonic ether A solution in ether of hydrogen peroxide and alcohol.

o·zo·nide (ō′zō·nīd) *n. Chem.* Any of a group of unstable, sometimes violently explosive, organic compounds containing ozone held in a double bond.

o·zo·nize (ō′zō·nīz) *v.t.* **·nized, ·niz·ing 1** To treat or charge with ozone. **2** To convert (oxygen) into ozone.

o·zo·niz·er (ō′zō·nī′zər) *n.* An apparatus for generating ozone.

o·zon·o·sphere (ō·zon′ə·sfir) *n.* A narrow layer in the stratosphere at a height of about 20 miles and containing an unusual concentration of ozone formed by the action of ultraviolet solar radiation on oxygen. Also called **ozone layer.** [< *ozono-* (< OZONE) + (STRATO)SPHERE]

oyster crab A smooth-bodied crab *(Pinnotheres ostreum)* living symbiotically in the mantle of the oyster.

oyster cracker A small biscuit or hard, salted cracker served with oysters.

oys·ter·ing (ois′tər·ing) *n.* The gathering or farming of oysters.

oys·ter·man (ois′tər·mən) *n. pl.* **·men** (-mən) **1** A man who dredges for, raises, or sells oysters. **2** A vessel engaged in the oyster trade.

oyster plant 1 Salsify. **2** The sea lungwort.

oyster planting The placing of small oysters on submerged artificial beds for propagation.

oy·ster·root (ois′tər·rōōt′, -rŏŏt′) *n.* Salsify.

oyster white Any of several very light gray tints: also called *off-white.*

O·zark Mountains (ō′zärk) The hilly uplands in SW Missouri, NW Arkansas, and NE Oklahoma; highest point, 2,500 feet. Also **Ozark Plateau.**

O·zarks (ō′zärks), **Lake of the** An artificial lake in the Osage River, central Missouri; 130 miles long.

Ozark State Nickname of MISSOURI.

o·ze·na (ō·zē′nə) *n. Pathol.* An evil-smelling ulceration of the nasal cavities. Also **o·zae′na.** [< L *ozaena* < Gk. *ozaina* < *ozein* smell] —**o·ze′nic, o·zae′nic** *adj.*

oversoft	overspeed	overstretch	oversuspiciously	overtenderness	overtrim	overvigorous
oversoftness	overspeedily	overstrict	oversweet	overtense	overtrust	overviolent
oversolemn	oversqueamishness	overstrident	oversystematic	overtension	overtrustful	overwarm
oversolicitous	overstale	overstriving	oversystematize	overthick	overtruthful	overwarmed
oversoon	overstaring	overstrong	overtalkative	overthin	overunionized	overwary
oversoothing	overstately	overstudious	overtalkativeness	overthoughtful	overurbanization	overwealthy
oversophisticated	oversteadfast	overstudiousness	overtame	overthrifty	overurge	overwet
oversophistication	oversteadfastness	oversublime	overtart	overthrong	over-use	overwilling
overspacious	oversteady	oversubtle	overtask	overthrust	overvaluable	overwily
oversparingly	overstiff	oversubtlety	overtaxation	overtight	overvaluation	overwise
overspecialization	overstimulate	oversufficient	overteach	overtimid	overvariety	overworry
overspecialize	overstimulation	oversuperstitious	overtechnical	overtimorous	overvehement	overworship
overspeculate	overstir	oversure	overtedious	overtinseled	overventilate	overyoung
overspeculation	overstout	oversusceptible	overtenacious	overtire	overventuresome	overyouthful
overspeculative	overstress	oversuspicious	overtender	overtrain	overventurous	overzealous

p, P (pē) *n. pl.* **p's, P's,** or **ps, Ps, pees** (pēz) **1** The 16th letter of the English alphabet: from Phoenician *pe,* Greek *pi,* Roman *P.* **2** The sound of the letter *p,* the voiceless bilabial stop. See ALPHABET. —*symbol* **1** *Chem.* Phosphorus (P). **2** *Genetics* The parental generation: followed by a subscript numeral, as P_1, P_2, to indicate the first, second, etc., parental generation. — **to mind one's P's and Q's** To be careful of one's behavior.

pab·u·lum (pab′yə·ləm) *n.* Any substance affording nourishment; aliment. See synonyms under FOOD. [< L *pabulum* fodder < *pascere* feed] —**pab′u·lar** *adj.*

pac (pak) *n.* A leather moccasin having a wide sole that turns up and is sewed to the upper; also, a heavy half-boot or legged moccasin of felt or leather worn by lumbermen in the winter. [< N. Am. Ind.]

pa·ca (pä′kə, pak′ə) *n.* A large seminocturnal rodent (genus *Cuniculus*) of Central and South America, brownish with white spots. [< Pg. or Sp. < Tupian]

pace[1] (pās) *n.* **1** A step in walking; also, the progress made in one such movement. **2** A conventional measure of length approximating the average length of stride in walking: usually 3 feet, but sometimes 3.3 feet, making 5 paces to the rod. The **Roman pace** was measured from the point where the heel of one foot left the ground to the point where it descended in the next stride, and was 5 Roman feet, equal to about 58.1 inches, a thousand such double strides making a mile. Such a double step is now called a **geometrical pace,** reckoned at 5 feet. The U.S. Army **regulation pace** is 30 inches, quick time; 36 inches, double time. **3** The manner or speed of movement in going on the legs; gait; carriage and action, especially of a horse. **4** Rate of speed, as in movement or work: often applied to a fast or ruinous life: the *pace* that kills; also, the speed with which a baseball pitcher delivers the ball. **5** A gait of a horse, etc., in which both feet on the same side are lifted and moved forward at once. —**to put (one) through his paces** To test the abilities, speed, etc., of. —*v.* **paced, pac·ing** *v.t.* **1** To walk back and forth across: to *pace* the floor. **2** To measure by paces. **3** To set or make the pace for. **4** To train to a certain gait or pace. —*v.i.* **5** To walk with slow or regular steps. **6** To move at a pace (def. 5). [< F *pas* < L *passus* step < *pandere* stretch. Doublet of PASS *n.*]

pa·ce[2] (pā′sē) *adv. & prep.* With the permission (of): used to express courteous disagreement. [< L, ablative of *pax, pacis* peace, pardon]

paced (pāst) *adj.* **1** Having a particular pace: used in compounds: slow-*paced.* **2** Measured in paces or by pacing. **3** Done behind or with the help of a pacemaker.

pace·mak·er (pās′mā′kər) *n.* **1** One who makes or sets the pace for another in a race. **2** *Med.* Any of various devices, chiefly electrical, used to regulate the heartbeat and prevent heartblock. —**pace′mak′ing** *n. & adj*

pac·er (pā′sər) *n.* **1** A pacing horse: usually, five-gaited. **2** One who paces, or measures by paces. **3** A pacemaker.

pach·ou·li (pach′ōō·lē, pə·chōō′lē) See PATCHOULI.

pachy- *combining form* Thick; massive: *pachyderm.* [< Gk. *pachys* thick]

pach·y·ceph·a·ly (pak′i·sef′ə·lē) *n.* Exceptional thickness of the skull. Also **path′y·ce·pha′li·a** (-sə·fā′lē·ə). [< PACHY- + Gk. *kephalē* head] — **pach′y·ce·phal′ic** (-sə·fal′ik), **pach′y·ceph′a·lous** *adj.*

pach·y·derm (pak′ə·dûrm) *n.* **1** Any of certain thick-skinned, non-ruminant ungulates; especially, an elephant, hippopotamus, or rhinoceros: formerly included in the obsolete order *Pachydermata,* which embraced also the horse, pig, tapir, etc. **2** A stolid, thick-skinned, insensitive person. [< F *pachyderme* < Gk. *pachydermos* < *pachys* thick + *derma* skin] — **pach′y·der′ma·tous, pach′y·der′mous** *adj.*

pa·cif·ic (pə·sif′ik) *adj.* Pertaining to the making of peace; inclined or leading to peace or conciliation; peaceable; calm. Also **pa·cif′i·cal.** [< F *pacifique* < L *pacificus* peacemaking < *pax, pacis* peace + *facere* make] —**pa·cif′i·cal·ly** *adv.*

Synonyms: calm, conciliating, conciliatory, gentle, meek, mild, peaceable, peaceful, placid, quiet, smooth, still, tranquil, unruffled, waveless. **Antonyms:** belligerent, contentious, controversial, enraged, exasperated, exasperating, fighting, furious, harsh, hateful, hostile, irritated, irritating, provoked, provoking, quarrelsome, tumultuous, turbulent, warlike.

Pa·cif·ic (pə·sif′ik) *adj.* Pertaining to the Pacific Ocean.

Pacific Ocean An ocean between the American continents and Asia and Australia, extending from the Arctic to the Antarctic Ocean; 70,000,000 square miles: divided by the equator into the **North Pacific Ocean** and the **South Pacific Ocean.**

Pacific Standard Time See STANDARD TIME. Abbr. *P.S.T.*

pac·i·fi·er (pas′ə·fī′ər) *n.* **1** One who or that which pacifies; a peacemaker. **2** A rubber nipple attached to a round guard, used to quiet a fretful baby. **3** A rubber ring used to relieve the teething discomfort of a baby.

pac·i·fist (pas′ə·fist) *n.* One who opposes military ideals, war, or military preparedness, and proposes that all international disputes be settled by arbitration. — **pac′i·fism** *n.* — **pac′i·fis′tic** *adj.*

pac·i·fy (pas′ə·fī) *v.t.* **·fied, ·fy·ing 1** To bring peace to; end war or strife in. **2** To allay the anger or agitation of; appease; calm. See synonyms under ALLAY, TEMPER, TRANQUILIZE. [< F *pacifier* < L *pacificare* < *pacificus.* See PACIFIC.]

pack[1] (pak) *n.* **1** A bundle or large package, especially one to be carried on the back of a man or animal; a collection of anything; heap. **2** A full set of like or associated things usually handled collectively, as cards. **3** A number of dogs or wolves that hunt together; hence, any gang or band, especially one existing for criminal purposes. **4** A large area of floating broken ice: also **ice pack. 5** Face pack. **6** A wrapping of sheets or blankets about a patient, used in certain water-cure treatments: a wet *pack,* cold *pack,* etc. **7** *Obs.* A lewd or low person: usually with *naughty.* **8** A parachute, fully assembled and folded for use. **9** The quantity of something, as vegetables or other foods, put in containers for preservation at one time or in a season. See synonyms under FLOCK, LOAD. —*v.t.* **1** To make a pack or bundle of. **2** To place compactly in a trunk, box, etc., for storing or carrying. **3** To fill compactly, as for storing or carrying: to *pack* a suitcase. **4** To put up for preservation or sale: to *pack* fruit. **5** To compress tightly; crowd together. **6** To fill completely or to overflowing; cram. **7** To cover, fill, or surround so as to prevent leakage, damage, etc.: to *pack* a piston rod. **8** To load with a pack; burden. **9** To carry or transport on the back or on pack animals. **10** To carry or wear habitually: to *pack* a gun. **11** To send or dispatch summarily: with *off* or *away.* **12** To treat with a pack (def. 6). **13** *Slang* To be able to inflict: He *packs* a wallop. —*v.i.* **14** To place one's clothes and belongings in trunks, boxes, etc., for storing or carrying. **15** To allow of being stowed or packed. **16** To crowd together; form a pack or packs. **17** To settle in a hard, firm mass. **18** To leave in haste: often with *off* or *away.* See synonyms under JAM. — **to send packing** To send away or dismiss summarily. [ME *pakke,* appar. < LG *pak*]

pack[2] (pak) *v.t.* To arrange, select, or manipulate to one's own advantage: to *pack* a jury. [? Var. of PACT]

pack·age (pak′ij) *n.* **1** The act or process of packing; also, that which is packed, as for transportation; something wrapped up or bound together; a packet or parcel. **2** A box, case, crate, or other receptacle in which goods are packed. **3** A combination of items considered as a unit: a salary increase and fringe benefits all in one *package.* —*v.t.* **·aged, ·ag·ing** To bind or tie into a package or bundle. [< PACK[1] + -AGE]

pack animal An animal, as a horse or mule, used to carry packs or burdens.

pack·er (pak′ər) *n.* **1** One who packs; specifically, one who makes a business of packing goods for transportation or preservation. **2** One who cures and packs wholesale provisions: a pork-*packer.* **3** One who transports goods on pack animals. **4** Any of certain machines or devices for packing commodities.

pack·et (pak′it) *n.* **1** A small package; parcel. **2** A steamship for conveying mails, passengers, and freight at stated times; especially, one plying up and down a coast or on a canal: also **packet boat.** —*v.t.* To make into a packet. [< AF *pacquet,* dim. of PACK[1]]

pack·ing (pak′ing) *n.* **1** The act or operation of filling an empty space, putting up for transportation, etc. **2** The canning or putting up of meat, fish, fruit, etc., for market, home consumption, etc. **3** The substance used in adjusting or protecting the article packed. **4** A greasy or other material for closing a joint. **5** A fibrous or porous substance for holding oil by absorption and assisting in the lubrication of a journal, etc. **6** A device for making a leakproof fit, as between a piston head and its cylinder.

packing plant *U.S.* A factory where meats and meat products are processed and packed. Also *U.S.* **packing house.**

packing press A press used in baling cotton, hay, or the like.

pack rat A common North American rat (genus *Neotoma*) which feeds chiefly on seeds, nuts, fruit, and green vegetation: so called from its habit of carrying off provisions: also called *wood rat* and *mountain rat.*

pack·sack (pak′sak′) *n.* A canvas or leather traveling sack for blankets, etc.: usually carried across the shoulders.

pack·sad·dle (pak′sad′l) *n.* A saddle for a pack animal, to which the packs are fastened so as to balance evenly.

pack·thread (pak′thred′) *n.* Strong thread or twine used for doing up packages.

pact (pakt) *n.* An agreement; compact. [< OF *pact* < L *pactum* agreement < *pactus,* pp. of *paciscere* agree]

pad[1] (pad) *n.* **1** A cushion; also, any stuffed, cushionlike thing serving to protect from jarring, friction, etc. **2** A launching pad. **3** A soft saddle. **4** A number of sheets of paper packed and gummed together at the edge; a tablet. **5** A large floating leaf of an aquatic plant: a lily *pad.* **6** A soft cushionlike enlargement of skin on the under surface of the toes of many animals. **7** The foot of a fox, otter, etc. **8** The footprint of an animal. **9** A pulvillus. **10** *Slang* A room or apartment; lodgings. —*v.t.* **pad·ded, pad·ding 1** To stuff, line, or protect with pads or padding. **2** To lengthen (speech or writing) by inserting unnecessary matter. **3** To expand (an expense account) by recording non-existent expenditures. [Origin unknown]

pad[2] (pad) *v.i.* **pad·ded, pad·ding 1** To travel by walking; tramp; trudge. **2** To move with soft, almost noiseless footsteps. —*n.* A dull, padded sound, as of a footstep. [Related to PAD[3] (path). Cf. LG *padden* tread.]

pad[3] (pad) *n.* **1** An easy-paced road horse: also **pad horse. 2** A footpad; a highwayman. **3** *Brit. Dial.* A path; road. [< LG *pad* path]

pad·ding (pad′ing) *n.* **1** The act of stuffing or forming a pad. **2** That of which a pad is made. **3** Matter used in writing to fill space.

pad·dle (pad′l) *n.* **1** A broad-bladed implement resembling a short oar, used without a rowlock in propelling a canoe or small boat. **2** The distance covered during one trip in a canoe over a given time. **3** A paddle board. **4** A straight iron tool for stirring ore in a furnace. **5** A bat or pallet, as used in tempering clay. **6** A scoop for stirring and mixing, as used in glassmaking. **7** A paddle-shaped implement for inflicting bodily punishment. **8** A limb or appendage of service in swimming; a flipper. **9** The snout of the paddlefish. **10** The act of paddling. **11** A flat instrument with which clothes are beaten while being washed in a stream. — *v.* **·dled, ·dling** *v.i.* **1** To move a canoe, etc., on or through water by means of a paddle; ply a paddle. **2** To row gently or lightly. **3** To swim with short, downward strokes, as ducks do. **4** To play in water with the hands or feet; dabble; wade. — *v.t.* **5** To propel by means of a paddle or paddles. **6** To convey by paddling. **7** To beat with a paddle; spank. **8** To stir. — **to paddle one's own canoe** To be independent; get along without help. [ME *padell* small spade, prob. var. of *patel* shallow pan <L *patella*] — **pad′dler** *n.*

paddle board One of the broad, paddlelike boards set on the circumference of a paddle wheel or water wheel.

paddle boat A boat propelled by paddle wheels.

paddle box The housing or box over a paddle wheel: usually with semicircular upper outline.

paddle wheel A wheel having projecting floats or boards for propelling a vessel.

pad·dling (pad′-ling) *n.* **1** The act of propelling by paddle. **2** A beating or spanking.

pad·dock (pad′ək) *n.* **1** A pasture lot or enclosure for exercising horses, adjoining a stable. **2** A grassed enclosure at a racecourse where horses are walked about and saddled before a race. **3** In Australia, any enclosed piece of land, whether tilled or untilled. — *v.t.* To confine, as horses, in a paddock. [Alter. of dial. E *parrock,* OE *pearruc* enclosure. Akin to PARK.]

PADDLE WHEEL
As seen on a Mississippi River stern–wheeled steamboat.

pad·dy[1] (pad′ē) *n.* *pl.* **·dies** The ruddy duck. Also *paddywhack.* [from PADDY, proper name]

pad·dy[2] (pad′ē) *n.* *pl.* **·dies** Rice in the husk, whether gathered or growing. [<Malay *pādī* rice in the straw]

pad·lock (pad′lok′) *n.* A detachable lock, designed to hang on the object fastened, having a shackle attached at one end, and devised so as to fasten through a staple. — *v.t.* To fasten with or as with a padlock. [ME *padlocke,* ? <*pad* a basket + LOCK[1]]

pa·dre (pä′drā) *n.* **1** Father: a title used in Italy, Spain, and Spanish America in addressing or speaking of priests, and in India for all clergymen. **2** An army or navy chaplain. [<Ital., Sp., and Pg. <L *pater, patris* father]

pa·dro·ne (pä·drō′nā) *n.* *pl.* **·nes** (-nās) or **·ni** (-nē) **1** Master: an appellation of an Italian house proprietor or employer of labor. **2** The master of a small vessel in the Mediterranean trade. [<Ital. <L *patronus* PATRON] — **pa·dro′nism** *n.*

pae·an (pē′ən) *n.* **1** A choral ode; originally, a song of praise honoring Apollo. **2** Hence, any song of joy or exultation. Also spelled *pean.* [<L <Gk. *paian* a hymn addressed to Paian, the god Apollo]

paed-, paedo- See PEDO-.

pae·do·gen·e·sis (pē′dō·jen′ə·sis) *n.* The reproduction of young in the larval stage, as in the axolotl and certain dipterous insects.

pa·el·la (pī·ä′lə, pī·el′ə, *Sp.* pī·ä′yə, pī·ä′lyə) *n.* A Spanish dish of rice flavored with saffron, to which is added shellfish, chicken and other meats, and vegetables. [<Catalan, lit., casserole–like pot]

pa·gan (pā′gən) *n.* **1** One who is neither a Christian, a Jew, nor a Moslem; a heathen. **2** In early Christian use, an idol–worshiper; a non–Christian. **3** An irreligious person. — *adj.* Pertaining to pagans; heathenish; idolatrous. [<LL *paganus* heathen <L, orig., a rural villager <*pagus* the country] — **pa′gan·dom** *n.* — **pa′gan·ish** *adj.* — **pa′gan·ism** *n.*

pa·gan·ize (pā′gən·īz) *v.t.* & *v.i.* **·ized, ·iz·ing** To make or become pagan.

page[1] (pāj) *n.* **1** A male servant or attendant; specifically, in chivalry, a lad or young man in training for knighthood, or a youth of gentle parentage attending a royal or princely personage. **2** A boy whose duty it is to attend upon legislators while in session. **3** A boy in livery, employed in a hotel, club, theater, or private house to perform light duties. — *v.t.* **paged, pag·ing 1** To seek or summon (a person) by calling his name, as a hotel page does. **2** To wait on as a page. [<OF <Ital. *paggio* <Med. L *pagius,* ? <Gk. *paidion,* dim. of *pais, paidos* child]

page[2] (pāj) *n.* **1** One side of a leaf of a book, letter, manuscript, etc.; also, the type for printing on one side: abbreviated p., *pl.* pp. **2** Hence, any source or record of knowledge. — *v.t.* **paged, pag·ing** To mark the pages of with numbers. [<F <L *pagina* leaf of a book, written page <*pag-,* stem of *pangere* fasten] — **pag′ing** *n.*

pag·eant (paj′ənt) *n.* **1** A community outdoor celebration presenting scenes from local history and tradition. **2** An imposing exhibition or spectacular parade devised for a public ceremony or celebration. **3** A theatrical spectacle; hence, unsubstantial display. **4** Hangings having scenic enrichment. **5** Originally, a traveling car or float having a stage for presenting mystery plays; hence, any pompous or showy object or decoration designed for public parades. See synonyms under OSTENTATION, SPECTACLE. [<Med. L *pagina* a framework, ? <L *pegma* <Gk. *pēgma* a framework, scaffold <*pēgnynai* fasten]

pag·i·nal (paj′ə·nəl) *adj.* Consisting of, or pertaining to, the pages of a book; also, page for page. [<LL *paginalis* <L *pagina* leaf of a book, page]

pag·i·nate (paj′ə·nāt) *v.t.* **·nat·ed, ·nat·ing** To number the pages of (a book) consecutively. [<L *pagina* page + -ATE[1]]

pag·i·na·tion (paj′ə·nā′shən) *n.* **1** The numbering of the pages, as of a book. **2** The system of figures and marks used in paging.

pa·go·da (pə·gō′də) *n.* In the countries of the Far East, a sacred tower or temple, usually pyramidal and profusely adorned. Also **pag·od** (pag′əd, pə·god′). [<Pg. *pagode,* prob. <Persian *butkadah* idol–temple <*but* idol + *kadah* house, ? ult. <Skt. *bhagavati* divine]

pa·go·plex·i·a (pā′gō·plek′sē·ə) *n.* *Pathol.* **1** Frostbite. **2** Chilblain. [<NL <Gk. *pagos* frost + *plēxis* stroke <*plēssein* strike]

pah (pä, pa) *interj.* Bah! faugh! an exclamation of contemptuous disgust.

paid (pād) Past tense and past participle of PAY.

pai·deu·tics (pī·dŏŏ′tiks, -dyŏŏ′-) *n.* The theory or the art of instruction; pedagogy. [<Gk. *paideutikos* of teaching <*paideuein* teach <*pais, paidos* a child]

pail (pāl) *n.* **1** A cylindrical vessel for carrying liquids, etc., properly having a bail as a handle. **2** The amount carried in this vessel. ◆ Homophone: *pale.* [OE *paegel* a gill, wine measure; infl. by OF *paelle* frying pan, liquid measure <L *patella* a small pan] — **pail′ful′** *n.*

pail·lasse (pal·yas′, pal′yas) *n.* A mattress of straw, excelsior, or the like: also spelled *palliasse.* [<F <*paille* straw <L *palea* chaff]

pail·lette (pal·yet′) *n.* **1** A bit of metal or colored foil, used in enamel painting. **2** A spangle; one of a hanging bunch of spangles. [<F, dim. of *paille* straw] — **pail·let′ted** *adj.*

pain (pān) *n.* **1** The sensation or feeling resulting from or accompanying some injury, derangement, overstrain, or obstruction of the physical powers; any distressing or afflicting emotion, or such emotions in general; grief: opposite of *pleasure.* **2** *pl.* Care, trouble, effort, or exertion expended on anything: used often as singular: with much *pains.* **3** *pl.* The pangs of childbirth. — **on** (or **upon** or **under**) **pain of** With the penalty of (some specified punishment). — **to take pains** To be careful; to make an effort. — *v.t.* To cause pain to; hurt or grieve; disquiet. — *v.i.* To cause pain. See synonyms under HURT, PIQUE. ◆ Homophone:

pane. [<OF *peine* <L *poena* <Gk. *poinē* a penalty]

Synonyms (*noun*): ache, affliction, agony, anguish, discomfort, distress, misery, pang, paroxysm, suffering, throe, torment, torture, trouble, twinge, uneasiness, woe, wretchedness. *Pain* is the most general term of this group, including all the others; *pain* is a disturbing sensation from which nature revolts, resulting from some injurious external interference (as from a wound, a bruise, a harsh word, etc.), or from some lack of what one needs, craves, or cherishes (as, the *pain* of hunger or bereavement), or from some abnormal action of bodily or mental functions (as, the *pains* of disease, envy, or discontent). *Ache* is lingering *pain,* more or less severe; *pang,* a *pain* short, sharp, intense, and perhaps repeated. We speak of the *pangs* of hunger or of remorse. *Throe* is a violent *pain. Paroxysm* applies to the alternately recurring and receding *pain,* which comes as though in waves; the *paroxysm* is the rising of the wave. *Torment* and *torture* are intense and terrible *sufferings.* Compare ADVERSITY, AFFLICTION, AGONY, INJURY, SUFFERING. *Antonyms:* comfort, delight, ease, enjoyment, peace, rapture, relief, solace.

pained (pānd) *adj.* **1** Hurt (physically or mentally); distressed. **2** Showing pain: a *pained* expression.

pain·ful (pān′fəl) *adj.* **1** Giving or attended with pain; distressing. **2** Requiring labor, effort, or care; arduous. **3** Affected with pain: said of the body or of some part of it. **4** *Archaic* Painstaking; laborious. See synonyms under TROUBLESOME. — **pain′ful·ly** *adv.* — **pain′ful·ness** *n.*

pain-kill·er (pān′kil′ər) *n.* *U.S. Colloq.* A medicine that relieves pain.

pain·less (pān′lis) *adj.* Free from pain; causing no pain. — **pain′less·ly** *adv.* — **pain′less·ness** *n.*

pains·tak·ing (pānz′tā′king) *adj.* Taking pains; careful; assiduous. — *n.* Diligent and careful endeavor. — **pains′tak′ing·ly** *adv.*

paint (pānt) *n.* **1** A color or pigment, either dry or mixed with oil, water, etc. **2** A cosmetic, as rouge. **3** A film, layer, or coat of pigment applied to the surface of an object. — *v.t.* **1 a** To make a representation of in paints or colors. **b** To make, as a picture, by applying paints or colors. **2** To describe or depict vividly, as in words or thoughts. **3** To cover or coat with or as with paint. **4** To decorate with or as with paints: The setting sun *paints* the clouds red. **5** To apply cosmetics to. **6** To apply (medicine, etc.) with or as with a swab. — *v.i.* **7** To cover or coat something with paint. **8** To practice the art of painting; paint pictures. **9** To apply cosmetics to the face, etc. [<OF *peint,* pp. of *peindre* <L *pingere* paint]

paint-brush (pānt′brush′) *n.* The painted cup.

paint brush A brush for applying paint.

paint·ed (pān′tid) *adj.* **1** Covered or coated with paint. **2** Depicted in colors; existing merely in semblance. **3** Marked with bright or varied colors.

painted beauty A brightly colored butterfly (*Vanessa virginiensis*) having dusky orange wings with two eyelike spots on the under side of each.

painted bunting A brilliantly colored finch (*Passerina ciris*) widely distributed in the southern United States. Also called **painted finch.**

painted cup Any of several showy North American flowers (*genus Castilleja*) of the figwort family, especially the Wyoming painted cup (*C. linariaefolia*) with vivid scarlet bracts and calyxes and yellow corollas: the State flower of Wyoming. Also called *Indian paintbrush.*

painted goose The emperor goose.

painted lady The thistle butterfly.

paint·er[1] (pān′tər) *n.* **1** One whose occupation is painting; specifically, one who covers surfaces with a preservative or decorative coat of paint. **2** An artist who portrays scenes or objects in colors.

paint·er[2] (pān′tər) *n.* *Naut.* A rope with which to fasten a boat by its bow. [Prob. <OF *pentoir* a rope for hanging things <L *pendere* hang]

paint horse In the western United States, a pied or spotted horse; a pinto.

paint·ing (pān'ting) *n.* **1** The act, art, or employment of laying on paints with a brush. **2** The art of representing objects on a surface by means of pigments. **3** A picture.

pair (pâr) *v.t.* **1** To bring together or arrange in a pair or pairs; match; couple; mate. — *v.i.* **2** To come together as a couple or pair. **3** To marry or mate. — **to pair off 1** To separate into couples. **2** To arrange by pairs. — *n.* **1** In general, two persons or things of a kind, joined, related, correspondent, or associated; a couple; brace. **2** A single thing having two like or correspondent parts dependent on each other: a *pair* of scissors: in this sense, always linked with a singular verb when one object is counted. **3** A married couple; two animals mated. **4** In legislative bodies, two opposed members who agree to abstain from voting, and so offset each other. **5** A set of like or equal things making a whole: now restricted in use. **6** In some games of cards, two cards of the same denomination: a *pair* of queens. **7** *Mech.* A combination of two elements forming a unit in the mutual production or constraint of motion, as a piston and cylinder, a screw and nut, etc. **8** A racing shell for two oarsmen. ◆ Current usage calls for *pair* in the plural after a numeral of two or more, as, four *pairs* of shoes, though colloquially the singular is often used, as, four *pair* of shoes. ◆ Homophones: *pare, pear.* [<F *paire* <L *paria,* neut. plural of *par* equal]

pair–oar (pâr'ôr', -ōr') *n.* A boat in which two men sitting one behind the other pull one oar each.

pair production *Physics* The instantaneous conversion of a photon into an electron and positron by its passage through a strong electric field.

pais (pā) *n.* The country; the people; especially, the people from whom a jury is selected: also spelled *pays.* [<OF, the country]

Pais·ley (pāz'lē) *adj.* Made of or resembling a certain patterned woolen fabric made in Paisley, a suburb of Glasgow, Scotland. — *n.* **1** The Paisley fabric. **2** A Paisley shawl: designed to imitate a Kashmir shawl.

Pai·ute (pī-yōot') *n.* One of a tribe of North American Indians of Shoshonean stock, living in SW Utah. Also spelled *Piute.*

TYPE OF
PAISLEY DESIGN

pa·ja·mas (pə·jä'məz, -jam'əz) *n. pl.* **1** Loose trousers of silk or cotton, worn by both men and women in the Orient. **2** Similar trousers with coats to match, used as nightwear. Also, *Brit.,* *pyjamas.* [<Hind. *pājāmā* <Persian *pāi* a leg + *jāmah* a garment] — **pajama** *adj.*

Pa·kis·tan (pak'ə·stan, pä'ki·stän') **Islamic Republic of** An independent republic in southern Asia remaining within the Commonwealth of Nations; 311,406 square miles; capital, Islamabad. — **Pa·ki·sta'ni** *adj. & n.*

pal·ace (pal'is) *n.* **1** A royal residence, or the official residence of some high dignitary, as of a bishop. **2** Any splendid residence or stately building. **3** A large building or room used as a place of public entertainment: an oyster *palace.* See synonyms under HOUSE. [<OF *palais* <L *palatium,* orig., the Palatine Hill at Rome, on which stood the palace of the Caesars]

palae–, palaeo– See words beginning PALE–, PALEO–.

pal·an·quin (pal'ən·kēn') *n.* A type of covered litter used as a means of conveyance in the Orient, borne by poles on the shoulders of two or more men. Also spelled **pal'an·keen'.** [<Pg. *palanquim* <Javanese *pělangki* <Skt. *palyanka,* var. of *paryanka* bed]

pal·at·a·ble (pal'it·ə·bəl) *adj.* **1** Agreeable to the taste or palate; savory. **2** Agreeable to the mind; acceptable: a loss of business that was hardly *palatable* but at least bearable. — **pal'·**

at·a·bil'i·ty *n.* — **pal'at·a·ble·ness** *n.* — **pal'at·a·bly** *adv.*

pal·a·tal (pal'ə·təl) *adj.* **1** Pertaining to the palate. **2** *Phonet.* **a** Produced by placing the front (not the tip) of the tongue near or against the hard palate, as *y* in English *yoke, ch* in German *ich.* **b** Produced with the blade of the tongue near the hard palate, as *ch* in *child, j* in *joy.* — *n. Anat.* **1** A bone of the palate. **2** *Phonet.* A palatal sound. [<F <L *palatum* palate]

pal·a·tal·ize (pal'ə·təl·īz') *v.t. & v.i.* **·ized, ·iz·ing** *Phonet.* To change to a palatal sound, as (s) to (sh) in *censure,* (t) to (ch) in *nature.* — **pal'·a·tal·i·za'tion** *n.*

pal·ate (pal'it) *n.* **1** *Anat.* The roof of the mouth. The **hard** (or **bony**) **palate,** or anterior part, has a bony skeleton; the **soft palate,** or posterior division, is composed of muscular tissue and mucous membrane. **2** The sense of taste; relish: so used originally from the false notion that the palate is the organ of taste: a discriminating *palate.* **3** Intellectual taste: mental relish. ◆ Homophones: *palet, palette, pallet, pallette.* [<OF *palat* <L *palatum* palate]

pa·la·tial (pə·lā'shəl) *adj.* Of, like, or befitting a palace; magnificent. [<L *palatium* PALACE + -AL] — **pa·la'tial·ly** *adv.*

pa·lat·i·nate (pə·lat'ə·nāt, -nit) *n.* **1** A political division ruled over by a prince possessing certain prerogatives of royalty within his own domain. **2** The office of a count palatine or of an elector palatine.

pal·a·tine¹ (pal'ə·tīn, -tin) *adj.* Of or pertaining to the palate. — *n. Anat.* Either of the two bones forming the hard palate. [<F *palatin* <L *palatum* palate]

pal·a·tine² (pal'ə·tīn, -tin) *adj.* **1** Pertaining to a royal palace or its officials. **2** Possessing royal prerogatives; exercising or endowed with regal rights within a certain domain: a count or county *palatine.* — *n.* **1** A high judicial functionary in medieval France and Germany; hence, by the delegation of powers, a lord exercising sovereign power over a province; a vassal enjoying the exercise of royal privileges over his territory. See COUNT PALATINE. **2** The ruler of a palatinate or county palatine. **3** A fur tippet worn by women over the shoulders. — **the Palatine** or **the Palatine Hill** The central hill of the seven on which ancient Rome was built. [<F *palatin* <L *palatinus* < *palatium.* See PALACE.]

pa·lav·er (pə·lav'ər) *n.* **1** Empty talk, especially that intended to flatter or deceive. **2** A profuse parley; hence, public discussion or conference: a term originated by the Portuguese explorers of Africa. — *v.t.* To flatter; cajole. — *v.i.* To talk idly and at length. See synonyms under BABBLE. [<Pg. *palavra* word, speech <LL *parabola* a story, word <L, comparison. Doublet of PARABLE, PARABOLA, PAROLE.] — **pa·lav'er·er** *n.* — **pa·lav'er·ing** *adj. & n.*

pa·lay (pä·lī') *n.* A natural rubber extracted by the natives of Madagascar from wild plants of the genus *Cryptostegia:* also spelled *pulay.* [<Tamil]

pale¹ (pāl) *n.* **1** Originally, a pointed stick of wood for driving into the ground; a stake; a paling; a fence picket. **2** A fence enclosing a piece of ground; hence, any boundary or limit. **3** That which is enclosed within bounds, literally or figuratively: the social *pale.* **4** *Her.* An ordinary consisting of a vertical band through the middle of the shield, occupying one third of its width. — **English pale 1** The varying portion of Irish territory which the Anglo–Normans conquered and governed for several centuries after their invasion of Ireland in the 12th century: also **the Pale.** **2** Formerly, the territory of Calais in France. — *v.t.* **paled, pal·ing** To enclose with pales; fence in. ◆ Homophone: *pail.* [<OF *pal* <L *palus* a stake]

pale² (pāl) *adj.* **1** Of a whitish or ashen appearance; pallid; wan. **2** Of a very light shade of any color; lacking in brightness or intensity of color. — *v.t. & v.i.* To make or turn pale; blanch. ◆ Homophone: *pail.* [<OF *palle* <L *pallidus.* Doublet of PALLID.] — **pale'ly** *adv.* — **pale'ness** *n.* — **pal'ish** *adj.*

Synonyms (adj.): ashy, bloodless, cadaverous, colorless, ghastly, marble, pallid, wan, white. See GHASTLY. *Antonyms:* blushing, flaming, florid, flushed, purple, red, roseate, rosy,

rubicund, ruddy.

pa·le·a (pā'lē·ə) *n. pl.* **·le·ae** (-li·ē) *Bot.* **1** A chafflike bract. **2** One of the chaffy inner scales subtending a flower in the grass spikelet. [<NL <L, chaff] — **pa'le·a'ceous** (-ā'shəs) *adj.*

Pa·le·arc·tic (pā'lē·ärk'tik) *adj.* Designating a zoogeographical realm which embraces Europe, North Africa, and Asia north of the tropic of Cancer: also spelled *Palaearctic.*

pa·le·eth·nol·o·gy (pā'lē·eth·nol'ə·jē) *n.* Ethnology dealing with prehistoric man: also spelled *palaeethnology.* — **pa'le·eth'no·log'ic** (-eth'nə·loj'ik) or **·i·cal** *adj.* — **pa'le·eth·nol'o·gist** *n.*

paleo– *combining form* **1** Ancient; old: *paleography.* **2** Primitive: *paleolithic.* Also, before vowels, **pale–.** Also *palaeo–.* [<Gk. *palaios* old, ancient]

pa·le·o·bi·o·chem·is·try (pā'lē·ō·bī'ō·kem'is·trē) *n.* The study of the chemical composition of extinct plant and animal organisms as shown by their fossil remains.

pa·le·o·bot·a·ny (pā'lē·ō·bot'ə·nē) *n.* The study of fossil plants. — **pa'le·o·bo·tan'ic** (-bə·tan'ik) or **·i·cal** *adj.* — **pa'le·o·bot'a·nist** *n.*

Pa·le·o·cene (pā'lē·ə·sēn') *n. Geol.* The oldest epoch of the Cenozoic era, preceding the Eocene.

pa·le·o·e·col·o·gy (pā'lē·ō·ē·kol'ə·jē) *n.* The study of the environment of plant and animal organisms living in past geologic periods. — **pa'le·o·ec'o·log'i·cal** (-ek'ə·loj'i·kəl) *adj.*

pa·le·o·ge·og·ra·phy (pā'lē·ō·jē·og'rə·fē) *n.* The study and description of earth features in past geologic periods. — **pa'le·o·ge'o·graph'ic** (-jē·ə·graf'ik) *adj.*

pa·le·og·ra·phy (pā'lē·og'rə·fē) *n.* **1** An ancient mode of writing; ancient writings collectively. **2** The science of describing or deciphering ancient writings. — **pa·le·o·graph** (pā'lē·ə·graf', -gräf') *n.* — **pa'le·og'ra·pher** *n.* — **pa'le·o·graph'ic** or **·i·cal** *adj.*

pa·le·o·lith (pā'lē·ō·lith') *n.* A chipped stone object or implement of the Paleolithic period of human culture.

Pa·le·o·lith·ic (pā'lē·ō·lith'ik) *adj. Anthropol.* Of, pertaining to, or associated with a period of human culture contemporaneous with the Pleistocene epoch and followed by the Mesolithic period. It is characterized by stone implements of increasing technical refinement; cave paintings, many in vivid color; sculptured forms and bas-reliefs. Also called *Old Stone Age.* The principal stages, reading from the earliest, are as follows:

LOWER PALEOLITHIC:	UPPER PALEOLITHIC:
Abbevillian	Chatelperronian
Clactonian	Aurignacian
Acheulean	Gravettian
Levalloisian	Solutrean
MIDDLE PALEOLITHIC:	Magdalenian
Mousterian	

pa·le·ol·o·gy (pā'lē·ol'ə·jē) *n.* The study of antiquity or antiquities; archeology: also spelled *palaeology.* [<PALEO- + -LOGY] — **pa'le·o·log'i·cal** (-ə·loj'i·kəl) *adj.* — **pa'le·ol'o·gist** *n.*

pa·le·on·tog·ra·phy (pā'lē·on·tog'rə·fē) *n.* The description of fossils; descriptive paleontology: also spelled *palaeontography.* [<PALEO- + Gk. *ōn, ontos* being, ppr. of *einai* be + -GRAPHY] — **pa'le·on'to·graph'ic** (-on'tə·graf'ik) *adj.*

pa·le·on·tol·o·gy (pā'lē·on·tol'ə·jē) *n.* The science that treats of the ancient life of the globe or of fossil organisms, either plants or animals: also spelled *palaeontology.* — **pa'le·on'to·log'ic** (-on'tə·loj'ik) or **·i·cal** *adj.* — **pa'le·on·tol'o·gist** *n.*

pa·le·o·pa·thol·o·gy (pā'lē·ō·pə·thol'ə·jē) *n.* The study of pathological conditions in fossil or extinct organisms.

pa·le·o·pe·dol·o·gy (pā'lē·ō·pə·dol'ə·jē) *n.* The study of ancient or fossil soils.

pa·le·o·pho·bi·a (pā'lē·ō·fō'bē·ə) *n.* An immoderate hostility toward or fear of the past, considered as a trend in contemporary culture and as a possible factor in the origin and development of certain types of mental disorder. — **pa'le·o·pho'bic** *adj.*

pa·le·o·psy·chol·o·gy (pā'lē·ō·sī·kol'ə·jē) *n.* The investigation of mental phenomena traceable to or persisting from an earlier stage in evolution.

pa·le·o·tem·per·a·ture (pā'lē·ō·tem'pər·ə·chər, -prə·chər) *n.* The condition of heat and cold prevailing on the earth and in the oceans in past geologic eras: a determinative factor in the study of extinct forms of life.

Pa·le·o·zo·ic (pā'lē·ō·zō'ik) *adj. Geol.* Of or pertaining to the era following the Pre-Cambrian and below the Mesozoic. —*n.* The Paleozoic era or group. Also spelled *Palaeozoic.* [< PALEO- + Gk. *zōē* life]

pa·le·o·zo·ol·o·gy (pā'lē·ō·zō·ol'ə·jē) *n.* The branch of paleontology that treats of fossil animals. —**pa'le·o·zo'o·log'i·cal** (-zō'ə·loj'i·kəl) *adj.*

Pal·es·tine (pal'is·tīn) **1** In Biblical times, a territory on the eastern coast of the Mediterranean, the country of the Jews: Old Testament *Canaan:* also *Holy Land.* **2** Parts of this territory, not including Syria or Jordan, placed (1920) under British mandate by the League of Nations: 10,434 square miles; capital, Jerusalem: divided (1947) by the United Nations into independent Arab and Jewish states. See IS-RAEL, JORDAN. —**Pal'es·tin'i·an** (-tin'ē·ən), **Pal'es·tin'e·an** *adj. & n.*

pal·et (pal'it) *n.* A palea. ◆ Homophones: *palate, palette, pallet, pallette.* [< L *palea* chaff + -ET]

pal·e·tot (pal'ə·tō, pal'tō) *n.* A loose overcoat or outer garment. [< F < OF *palletoc,* ? < *palle* cloak + *toque* hood, cap]

pal·ette (pal'it) *n.* **1** A thin tablet, with a hole for the thumb, upon which artists lay and mix their colors for painting. **2** An arrangement of colors placed on the tablet. ◆ Homophones: *palate, palet, pallet, pallette.* [< F, dim. of *pale* shovel < L *pala* spade]

palette knife A thin, flat knife with flexible blade, usually offset from the handle, for mixing and applying oil colors.

pal·imp·sest (pal'imp·sest) *n.* A parchment, etc., written upon two or three times, the earlier writing having been wholly or partially erased to make room for the next. —*adj.* Rewritten or superinscribed. [< L *palimpsestus* < Gk. *palimpsēstos,* lit., scraped again < *palin* again + *pseein* rub]

pal·in·drome (pal'in·drōm) *n.* A word or words that read the same forward or backward, as "Madam, I'm Adam," or "radar." [< Gk. *palindromos* a running back again < *palin* again + *dromos* a running]

pal·in·dro·mi·a (pal'in·drō'mē·ə) *n. Pathol.* The recurrence or worsening of a diseased condition; a relapse. [< NL < Gk. *palin* again + *dromos* a running] —**pal'in·drom'ic** (-drom'ik) *adj.*

pal·ing (pā'ling) *n.* **1** One of a series of upright pales forming a fence; also, such pales or pickets collectively. **2** A fence made of pales or pickets; hence, a limit or enclosure. **3** The act of erecting a fence with pales.

pal·in·gen·e·sis (pal'in·jen'ə·sis) *n.* **1** A new or second birth into a higher or better life or being; a regeneration; theory or belief that souls are continually reborn. **2** *Biol.* The development of an individual in which the ethnic or group history of its ancestors is repeated: opposed to *cenogenesis.* **3** *Entomol.* The metamorphosis of an insect. **4** *Obs.* The supposed generation of an animal from an organism on which it is parasitic

or from decaying animal matter. [< NL < Gk. *palin* again + GENESIS] —**pal'in·ge·net'ic** (-jə·net'ik) *adj.*

pal·i·sade (pal'ə·sād') *n.* **1** A fence or fortification made of strong timbers set in the ground. **2** *pl.* An extended cliff or precipice of rock, usually along the bank of a river. —*v.t.* **·sad·ed, ·sad·ing** To enclose or fortify with a palisade. [< MF *palissade* < *palisser* enclose with pales < L *palus* a stake]

pal·ish (pā'lish) *adj.* Somewhat pale; rather pale: a *palish* countenance.

pall¹ (pôl) *n.* **1** A covering, usually of black cloth, thrown over a coffin or over a tomb; figuratively, that which brings deep sorrow or fear; also, metaphorically, a dark, heavy covering: a *pall* of smoke. **2** *Eccl.* **a** A chalice cover, consisting of a square piece of cardboard faced on both sides with lawn or linen. **b** An altar cloth. **c** A prelate's pallium. —**heraldic pall** The Y-shaped bearing resembling a pallium. —*v.t.* To cover with or as with a pall. ◆ Homophone: *pawl.* [OE *paell* a cloak < L *pallium* a pallium]

HERALDIC PALL From the arms of the See of Canterbury.

pall² (pôl) *v.i.* **1** To become insipid or uninteresting. **2** To have a dulling or displeasing effect: with *on.* —*v.t.* **3** To satiate; cloy; disgust. ◆ Homophone: *pawl.* [Appar. aphetic var. of APPAL]

pal·lad·ic (pə·lad'ik) *adj. Chem.* Pertaining to or designating compounds containing tetravalent palladium.

pal·la·di·um¹ (pə·lā'dē·əm) *n. pl.* **·di·a** (-dē·ə) Any object considered essential to the safety of a community or organization; a safeguard. [< PALLADIUM]

pal·la·di·um² (pə·lā'dē·əm) *n.* A rare metallic element (symbol Pd, atomic number 46) resembling platinum and in the spongy state capable of absorbing hydrogen in large quantities. See PERIODIC TABLE. [< NL, after *Pallas,* an asteroid discovered contemporaneously with the element]

pal·la·dous (pə·lā'dəs) *adj. Chem.* Of, pertaining to, or containing palladium, especially in its lower valence.

pal·lah (pä'lə) See IMPALA.

pall·bear·er (pôl'bâr'ər) *n.* One who attends a coffin at a funeral. [< PALL¹ + BEARER]

pal·les·the·sia (pal'is·thē'zhə, -zhē·ə) *n. Physiol.* Sensitiveness to vibration, as of the skin or a bony prominence to a vibrating tuning fork. [< Gk. *pallein* quiver + ESTHESIA] —**pal'les·thet'ic** (-thet'ik) *adj.*

pal·let¹ (pal'it) *n.* **1** *Mech.* A click or pawl used to convert a reciprocating into a rotary motion, or the reverse, as in a feed motion; also, the lip or point of a pawl. **2** A paddle for mixing and shaping clay for crucibles, etc. **3** A tool used in gilding the backs of books or for taking up gold leaf. **4** A movable platform for the storage or transportation of goods. **5** A painter's palette. ◆ Homophones: *palate, palet, palette, pallette.* [< F *palette.* See PALETTE.]

pal·let² (pal'it) *n.* **1** A small, mean bed or mattress, usually of straw. **2** A blanket laid on the floor for a bed. ◆ Homophones: *palate, palet, palette, pallette.* [< OF *paillet* < *paille* straw < L *palea* chaff]

pal·let·ize (pal'it·īz) *v.t.* **·ized, ·iz·ing** To load or store (goods) on pallets. See PALLET¹ (def. 4). [< PALLET¹ (def. 4) + -IZE]

pal·lette (pal'it) *n.* One of the plates in a suit of armor protecting the armpits. ◆ Homophones: *palate, palet, palette, pallet.* [< F *palette.* See PALETTE.]

pal·liasse (pal·yas', pal'yas) See PAILLASSE.

pal·li·ate (pal'ē·āt) *v.t.* **·at·ed, ·at·ing** **1** To cause (a crime, fault, etc.) to appear less serious or offensive; extenuate. **2** To relieve the symptoms or effects of without curing, as a disease; alleviate; mitigate. [< LL *palliatus,* pp. of *palliare* cloak < *pallium* a cloak] —**pal'li·a'tion** *n.* —**pal'li·a'tor** *n.*

Synonyms: cloak, conceal, cover, excuse,

extenuate, hide, mitigate, screen, veil. *Cloak,* from the French, and *palliate,* from the Latin, are the same in original signification, but have diverged in meaning; to *cloak* a sin is to attempt to *hide* it from discovery; to *palliate* it is to attempt to hide some part of its blameworthiness. Either to *palliate* or to *extenuate* is to admit the fault; but *extenuate* seeks especially to lessen the culpability involved; hence we speak of *extenuating* circumstances, since circumstances, while they cannot change the inherent wrong of an act, may yet lessen the blameworthiness of him who does it. In reference to diseases, to *palliate* is to diminish their violence, or partly to relieve the sufferer. See ALLAY, ALLEVIATE, HIDE. *Antonyms:* see synonyms for AGGRAVATE.

pal·li·a·tive (pal'ē·ā'tiv) *adj.* Having a tendency to palliate; feeble in action. —*n.* That which serves to palliate. —**pal'li·a·tive·ly** *adv.*

pal·lid (pal'id) *adj.* Of a pale or wan appearance; feeble in color. See synonyms under PALE². [< L *pallidus* < *pallere* be pale. Doublet of PALE².] —**pal'lid·ly** *adv.* —**pal'lid·ness** *n.*

pal·li·um (pal'ē·əm) *n. pl.* **·li·a** (-ē·ə) **1** A himation, the distinctive ancient Greek mantle, later adopted by the Romans as a Hellenism. **2** A vestment of the pope, archbishops, and metropolitans in the Roman Catholic Church, and of patriarchs in the Eastern Church; a pall. The Roman pallium is a yokelike band of white wool, with pendants on the breast and back, and is adorned with crosses. **3** *Zool.* The mantle of a brachiopod, mollusk, or bird. **4** *Anat.* The brain mantle or cerebral cortex, which is developed from the anterior vesicle, including the central white substance and the cortical gray. [< L]

pall–mall (pel'mel') *n.* **1** A game formerly played in England and France by driving a wooden ball along an alley and through a raised iron ring by means of a mallet. **2** The mallet used in this game. **3** An alley or long space for playing the game. It gave its name to one of the streets of London, **Pall Mall** (pel' mel', pal' mal'), noted for its numerous clubs. [< MF *pallemaille* < Ital. *pallamaglio* < *palla* a ball + *maglio* a mallet < L *malleus* a hammer]

pal·lor (pal'ər) *n.* The state of being pale or pallid; paleness. [< L < *pallere* be pale]

palm¹ (päm) *n.* **1** The hollow inner surface of the hand between the wrist and the base of the fingers. ◆ Collateral adjective: *thenar.* **2** The breadth (3 or 4 inches) or the length (about 8 1/2 inches) of the hand used as a linear measure. **3** That which covers the palm, as part of a glove or mitten. **4** The flattened, palmate portion of an antler, as of a moose. **5** The flat expanding end of any armlike projection; specifically, the blade of an oar. **6** A shield attached to the palm of the hand, used by sailmakers in pushing a needle through heavy canvas. — **to grease the palm** To give a bribe. —*v.t.* **1** To hide (cards, dice, etc.) in or about the hand, as in sleight of hand. **2** To handle or touch with the palm. — **to palm off** To pass off or impose fraudulently. [< F *paume* < OF *paulme* < L *palma* a hand; refashioned after L]

palm² (päm) *n.* **1** Any of a large and varied family (*Palmaceae*) of tropical trees or shrubs usually having an unbranched columnar trunk topped by a crown of large palmate or pinnate leaves. **2** A leaf or branch of the palm, used as a symbol of victory or joy. **3** Hence, supremacy; triumph; the reward or symbol of victory or preeminence. [OE *palm* < L *palma* a palm tree, orig., a hand; so called because its leaves are hand–shaped] —**pal·ma·ceous** (pal·mā'shəs) *adj.*

pal·ma–Chris·ti (päl'mä·kris'tē) *n.* The castor-oil plant.

pal·mar (pal'mər) *adj.* Pertaining to, like, or situated near or in the palm. [< L *palmaris* < *palma* a hand]

pal·mate (pal'māt) *adj.* **1** Resembling an open hand. **2** Broad and flat, with fingerlike projections, as the antlers of the moose, or some corals. **3** *Bot.* Having lobes (usually five) that diverge from the apex of the petiole, as a leaf. **4** *Zool.* Webbed, as a bird's foot. Also **pal'mat·ed.** [< L *palmatus,* pp. of *palmare* mark with the palm of the hand < *palma* a hand] — **pal′mate·ly** *adv.*

pal·ma·tion (pal·mā′shən) *n.* **1** The state or quality of being palmate. **2** Any division of a palmate structure.

Palm Beach cloth A lightweight summer fabric of cotton warp and mohair filling: a trade name.

palm civet A long-tailed arboreal civet (family *Viverridae*) of Asia and Africa, especially the common *Paradoxurus hermaphroditus* of India.

palm·er (pä′mər) *n.* A medieval pilgrim who had visited Palestine and brought back a palm branch. [<AF <Med. L *palmarius* <L *palma* palm tree + *-arius* -ARY]

palm·er·worm (pä′mər·wûrm′) *n.* The caterpillar of a tineid moth, especially the *Dichomeris ligulella* which skeletonizes apple leaves.

pal·mette (pal·met′) *n.* A conventional carved or painted ornament in ancient art, resembling the palm leaf. [<F, dim. of *palme* a palm tree]

pal·met·to (pal·met′ō) *n. pl.* **·tos** or **·toes** Any one of various fan palms, especially the cabbage palm of the southern United States. [<Sp. *palmito,* dim. of *palma* a palm tree <L; ending infl. by Ital. *-etto,* dim. suffix]

Palmetto State Nickname of SOUTH CAROLINA.

palmi– *combining form* Palm. [<L *palma* palm]

pal·mi·ped (pal′mi·ped) *adj.* Web-footed, as a swimming bird. — *n.* A swimming bird. [<L *palmipes, palmipedis* <*palma* palm + *pes, pedis* foot]

palm·ist (pä′mist) *n.* One who practices palmistry.

palm·is·try (pä′mis·trē) *n.* The art of reading the past life or future of a person by the lines and marks in the palm of the hand. [ME *palmestrie* <*palme* palm + *-estrie,* prob. <OF *maistrie* mastery <L *magister* master]

pal·mi·tate (pal′mi·tāt) *n.* A salt or ester of palmitic acid. [<PALMITIC + -ATE³]

pal·mit·ic (pal·mit′ik) *adj.* Of, pertaining to, or derived from the palm, or especially, from palm oil. [<F *palmitique* <L *palma* a palm tree]

palmitic acid *Biochem.* A crystalline fatty acid, $C_{15}H_{31}CO_2H$, contained in numerous animal and vegetable fats and fixed oils, principally as glycerides: used in making candles and soaps.

pal·mi·tin (pal′mə·tin) *n. Chem.* A colorless crystalline compound, glyceryl palmitate, $(C_{15}H_{31}COO)_3C_3H_5$, contained in those natural fats that yield palmitic acid on saponification, and especially in palm oil: also called *tripalmitin.* [<F *palmitine*]

pal·mi·toyl (pal′mə·toil) *n. Chem.* The univalent radical, $CH_3(CH_2)_{14}CO$, from palmitic acid. [<PALMIT(IC ACID) + -(O)YL]

palm oil 1 A yellow or reddish fat or butter obtained from the fruit of several varieties of palm, especially the African oil palm (*Elaeis guineensis*): used in the manufacture of soap, candles, and for coloring and scenting ointments. **2** *Slang* Money given as a bribe or tip.

palm sugar Sugar made from palm sap.

palm·y (pä′mē) *adj.* **palm·i·er, palm·i·est 1** Marked by prosperity; flourishing. **2** Abounding in or resembling palms.

pal·my·ra (pal·mī′rə) *n.* An East Indian palm (*Borassus flabellifer*) with a cylindrical stem 50 to 100 feet in height bearing a crown of large fan-shaped leaves. [<Pg. *palmeira* a palm tree <L *palma*; infl. by Gk. *Palmyra* PALMYRA]

pal·nut (pôl′nut′, pal′-) *n. Mech.* A thin steel nut having a shallow, concave bottom face which by deformation under stress causes the nut to exert a binding grip on the bolt. [Origin unknown]

pal·o·mi·no (pal′ə·mē′nō) *n. pl.* **·nos** A golden-brown or yellow horse. [<Am. Sp., orig. a dove-colored horse <Sp. *palomillo,* dim. of *paloma* a dove <LL *palumbus* <L *palumbes* a ring dove]

palp (palp) *n.* A palpus. [<F *palpe* <L *palpus.* See PALPUS.]

pal·pa·ble (pal′pə·bəl) *adj.* **1** That may be touched or felt. **2** Readily perceived; obvious. **3** That may be perceived by touch, or by any of the other senses. See synonyms under EVIDENT, MANIFEST. [<LL *palpabilis* <L *palpare* touch] — **pal′pa·bil′i·ty, pal′pa·ble·ness** *n.*

n. — **pal′pa·bly** *adv.*

pal·pate (pal′pāt) *v.t.* **·pat·ed, ·pat·ing** To feel or examine by touch, especially for medical diagnosis. — *adj.* Having a palpus or sense organ. [<L *palpatus,* pp. of *palpare* touch]

pal·pa·tion (pal·pā′shən) *n. Med.* The process of examining or exploring the body by means of touch; a digital exploration.

pal·pe·bra (pal′pi·brə) *n. pl.* **·brae** (-brē) An eyelid. [<NL <L, an eyelid] — **pal′pe·bral** *adj.*

pal·pi·tate (pal′pə·tāt) *v.i.* **·tat·ed, ·tat·ing 1** To quiver; tremble. **2** *Med.* To beat more rapidly than normal; flutter: said especially of the heart. [<L *palpitatus,* pp. of *palpitare* tremble, freq. of *palpare* touch]

pal·pi·ta·tion (pal′pə·tā′shən) *n.* Rapid and irregular pulsation.

pal·pus (pal′pəs) *n. pl.* **·pi** (-pī) *Zool.* A feeler; especially, one of the jointed sense organs attached to the mouth parts of arthropods: also called *palp.* [<NL <L *palpus* a feeler <*palpare* touch]

pal·sy (pôl′zē) *n.* **1** Paralysis. **2** Any impairment or loss of sensation or of ability to control movement. — *v.t.* **·sied, ·sy·ing** To paralyze. [<OF *paralisie* <L *paralysis.* Doublet of PARALYSIS.] — **pal′sied** *adj.*

pal·ter (pôl′tər) *v.i.* **1** To speak or act insincerely; equivocate; lie. **2** To treat something lightly; trifle. **3** To haggle or quibble. [Cf. dial. E *palt* a piece of coarse or dirty cloth] — **pal′ter·er** *n.*

pal·try (pôl′trē) *adj.* **·tri·er, ·tri·est** Having little or no worth or value; trifling; trivial; contemptible; petty. See synonyms under BASE, CHILDISH, INSIGNIFICANT, LITTLE, PITIFUL. [<dial. E, rags, rubbish <*palt* a piece of coarse or dirty cloth] — **pal′tri·ly** *adv.* — **pal′tri·ness** *n.*

pa·lu·dal (pə·lōōd′l) *adj.* Pertaining to a marsh; swampy. [<L *palus, paludis* marsh]

pal·u·dism (pal′yə·diz′əm) *n. Pathol.* The morbid condition observed in those who live among marshes; malaria.

pal·y¹ (pā′lē) *adj.* Lacking brilliance; pale; pallid.

pal·y² (pā′lē) *adj. Her.* Divided palewise, the number of such divisions (always even) being specified. [<OF *palé* a row of stakes <*pal* PALE¹]

pal·y·nol·o·gy (pal′ə·nol′ə·jē) *n.* The scientific study of pollen and other spores, their dispersal and application; pollen analysis. [<Gk. *palynein* strew <*pallein* brandish + -LOGY]

pam·pas (pam′pəz, *Sp.* päm′päs) *n. pl.* The great open treeless plains south of the Amazon river, extending from the Atlantic to the Andes. [<Sp. *pampa* <Quechua, plain]

pampas grass (pam′pəs) A tall, ornamental, reedlike grass (*Cortaderia selloana*) native to South America, having very large, thick, silvery panicles.

pam·pe·an (pam′pē·ən, pam·pē′ən) *adj.* Of or pertaining to the pampas or to their native inhabitants. — *n.* An Indian of the. pampas; a pampero.

pam·per (pam′pər) *v.t.* **1** To treat too indulgently; gratify the whims or wishes of; coddle. **2** *Obs.* To feed with rich food; glut. [Appar. freq. of obs. *pamp* cram] — **pam′per·er** *n.*

Synonyms: caress, coddle, glut, indulge, pet, spoil. See CARESS, INDULGE. *Antonyms:* deny, discipline, harden, inure, starve, stint.

pam·pe·ro (päm·pā′rō) *n. pl.* **·ros 1** A strong, cold, dry, southwest wind of the Argentine pampas, generally advancing with a well-marked and very black cloud front. **2** An Indian of the pampas. [<Sp. <Quechua *pampa* plain + Sp. *-ero* -ARY¹]

pam·phlet (pam′flit) *n.* **1** A printed work stitched or pasted, but not permanently bound. **2** A brief treatise or essay, printed and published without a binding, and usually on a subject of current interest. [<OF *Pamphilet,* popular title of a 12th c. Latin love poem, *Pamphilus, seu de Amore*]

pam·phlet·eer (pam′flə·tir′) *n.* One who writes pamphlets: sometimes a term of contempt. — *v.i.* To write and issue pamphlets.

pan¹ (pan) *n.* **1** A wide, shallow vessel, usually metallic or earthen, for domestic use, as in holding liquids or in cooking. **2** A vessel, either open or closed, for boiling and evaporating. **3** A natural or artificial depression in the earth for evaporating brine. **4** A circular sheet-iron dish with sloping sides, in which

gold is separated. **5** The powder cavity of a flintlock. **6** The skull; brainpan. **7** Any natural depression in the earth containing water or mud. **8** Hardpan. **9** Either of the two receptacles on a pair of scales or a balance. — *v.* **panned, pan·ning** *v.t.* **1** To separate (gold) by washing gold-bearing earth in a pan. **2** To wash (earth, gravel, etc.) for this purpose. **3** To cook and serve in a pan. **4** *Colloq.* To criticize severely. **5** *Colloq.* To obtain; secure. — *v.i.* **6** To search for gold by washing earth, gravel, etc., in a pan. **7** To yield gold, as earth. — **to pan out** *U.S.* To result or turn out; transpire. [OE *panne,* ? <LL *panna* <L *patina* a pan or dish <*patere* stand open]

pan² (pan) *n.* **1** The leaf of the climbing pepper (*Piper betle*) used with the nuts of the betel palm as a masticatory in the East Indies. **2** The masticatory obtained from this leaf. [<Hind. *pān* a betel leaf <Skt. *parṇa* a feather, a leaf]

pan³ (pan) *v.t.* **panned, pan·ning** To move (a motion-picture or television camera) across a scene in order to secure a panoramic effect. [<PANORAMA]

Pan (pan) In Greek mythology, a horned, goat-footed god of forests, flocks, and shepherds: identified with the Roman *Faunus.*

pan– *combining form* **1** All; every; the whole: *panchromatic.* **2** Comprising, including, or applying to all: usually capitalized when preceding proper nouns or adjectives, as in:

Pan–African	Pan–Asian	Pan–Slav
Pan–Arab	Pan–Islam	Pan–Slavic
Pan–Arabian	Pan–Islamic	Pan–Slavonic
Pan–Asia	Pan–Russian	Pan–Syrian

pan·a·ce·a (pan′ə·sē′ə) *n.* **1** A remedy for all diseases; a cure-all. **2** An herb credited with remarkable healing virtues; formerly, allheal. [<L <Gk. *panakeia* a universal remedy <*panakēs* all-healing <*pas* all + *akos, akeos* cure] — **pan′a·ce′an** *adj.*

pa·nache (pə·nash′, -näsh′) *n.* A plume or bunch of feathers, especially as an ornament on a helmet. [<F <Ital. *pennacchio* <*penna* a feather <L]

pa·na·da (pə·nä′də, -nā′-) *n.* A dish made of crackers or bread soaked with boiling water, sweetened and eaten with milk, or flavored with wine, etc. [<Sp. <Ital. *pane* bread <L *panis*]

Pan·a·ma (pan′ə·mä, -mô; *Sp.* pä′nä·mä′) **1** A republic on the Isthmus of Panama; 28,575 square miles (excluding Canal Zone). **2** Its capital, near the Pacific terminus of the Panama Canal.

PANACHE

Panama, Isthmus of An isthmus connecting North and South America and separating the Atlantic and Pacific; 30 miles wide at its narrowest point: formerly *Isthmus of Darien.*

Panama Canal A ship canal across the Isthmus of Panama, extending about 40 miles from Colón on the SE Atlantic (Caribbean) to Panama on the Pacific; completed (1914) by the United States on the leased territory of Canal Zone.

Panama Canal Zone See CANAL ZONE.

Panama fever 1 Yellow fever. **2** Malaria.

Panama hat A hat woven from the young leaves of the jipijapa tree of Central and South America.

Pan·a·ma·ni·an (pan′ə·mä′nē·ən, -mä′-) *adj.* Of or pertaining to the Isthmus of Panama or its inhabitants: also **Pa·nam·ic** (pə·nam′ik). — *n.* A native or naturalized inhabitant of Panama. Also **Pan·a·man** (pan′ə·män′).

Pan American Including or pertaining to the whole of America, both North and South, or to all Americans. Also **Pan′-A·mer′i·can.**

pan·a·tel·a (pan′ə·tel′ə) See PANETELA.

pan·at·ro·phy (pan·at′rə·fē) *n. Pathol.* Atrophy involving many or all parts of the body.

pan-broil (pan′broil′) *v.t. & v.i.* To cook (meat) in a heavy frying pan placed over direct heat, using little or no fat.

pan·cake (pan′kāk′) *n.* **1** A thin battercake fried in a pan or baked on a griddle: also **pan cake. 2** *Aeron.* An abrupt or violent landing effected by an airplane which levels off and settles rapidly on a steep flight path. — *v.i.* **·caked, ·cak·ing** To level off and decelerate an airplane so that it drops to the ground with little forward movement.

pan·chro·mat·ic (pan′krō-mat′ik) *adj. Phot.* Sensitive to all the colors of the spectrum in proportion to their respective visual luminosities: said of an emulsion, film, or plate. — **pan·chro′ma·tism** (-krō′mə-tiz′əm) *n.*

pan·cra·ti·um (pan-krā′shē-əm) *n. pl.* **·ti·a** (-shē-ə) An ancient Greek contest of athletes, including both boxing and wrestling. [< L < Gk. *pan,* neut. of *pas* all + *kratos* strength] — **pan·crat′ic** (-krat′ik) *adj.*

pan·cre·as (pan′krē-əs, pang′-) *n. Anat.* A gland connecting with the alimentary canal; in vertebrates, a large racemose gland behind the peritoneum, between the lower part of the stomach and the vertebrae of the loins, and emptying into the duodenum by one or more small ducts; the sweetbread. [< NL < Gk. *pankreas* sweetbread < *pan,* neut. of *pas* all + *kreas* flesh] — **pan′cre·at′ic** (-at′ik) *adj.*

pancreatic juice *Biochem.* A colorless fluid, containing certain enzymes, secreted by the pancreas and forming an important factor in digestion by emulsifying fats.

pan·cre·a·tin (pan′krē-ə-tin, pang′-) *n.* **1** *Biochem.* One of the active ferments of the pancreatic juice, or a mixture of them. **2** A commercial digestant extract of the pancreas of the ox or hog. [< Gk. *pankreas, -atos* pancreas + -IN]

pan·da (pan′də) *n. pl.* **·das** or **·da 1** A small raccoonlike carnivore (*Ailurus fulgens*) of the southeastern Himalayas, with long reddish-brown fur and ringed tail; the red bearcat. **2** The great or giant panda (*Ailuropoda melanoleuca*) found only in Kansu and Szechwan provinces in NW China, a mammal of bearlike appearance, with black-and-white coat and rings around the eyes: also *giant panda.* [Prob. < Nepalese]

GIANT PANDA
(About the size of a large bear)

Pan·da·nus (pan-dā′nəs) *n.* A genus of trees and shrubs of southeastern Asia (family *Pandanaceae*), characterized by stiltlike aerial roots and the spiral arrangement of their long gracefully recurved leaves; a screwpine. [< NL < Malay *pandan* conspicuous] — **pan·da·na·ceous** (pan′də-nā′shəs) *adj.*

Pan·de·an (pan-dē′ən) *adj.* Pertaining to the god Pan.

Pandean pipes A primitive wind instrument made of graduated reeds; a panpipe.

pan·dect (pan′dekt) *n.* **1** An encyclopedic treatise; a complete digest of some department of knowledge. **2** Any complete system of law. [< F *pandecte* < L *pandecta* < Gk. *pandektēs* an all-receiver < *pan,* neut. of *pas* all + *dechesthai* take]

pan·dem·ic (pan-dem′ik) *adj.* **1** Pertaining to or affecting all the people. **2** *Med.* Widely epidemic. — *n.* A pandemic disease. [< Gk. *pandēmos* pertaining to all the people < *pan,* neut. of *pas* all + *dēmos* people]

pan·de·mo·ni·um (pan′də-mō′nē-əm) *n.* **1** The abode of all demons; the infernal regions; as used by Milton, **Pandemonium,** the palace of Satan in Hell. **2** Hence, any place or gathering remarkable for disorder and uproar. **3** A fiendish or riotous uproar. Also **pan′dae·mo′ni·um.** [< NL < Gk. *pan,* neut. of *pas* all + *daimōn* an evil spirit]

pan·der (pan′dər) *n.* **1** A go-between in sexual intrigues; a procurer; - pimp. **2** One who ministers to the passions or base desires of others. Also **pan′der·er.** — *v.i.* To act as a pander. — *v.t.* To act as a pander for. [after *Pandarus,* with ref. to his role in medieval legend] — **pan′der·age, pan′der·ism** *n.* — **pan′·der·ess** *n. fem.*

pan·dore (pan′dôr, -dōr) *n.* A bandore. Also

pan·do·ra, pan·du·ra (pan-dôr′ə, -dyoōr′ə). [< F *pandore* < L *pandura.* See BANDORE.]

pan·dow·dy (pan-dou′dē) *n. pl.* **·dies** A deep-dish pie or pudding made of baked sliced apples. Also **apple pandowdy.** [Cf. obs. dial. E (Somerset) *pandoulde* a custard]

pan·du·rate (pan′dyə-rāt) *adj. Bot.* Fiddle-shaped, as certain leaves. Also **pan·du·ri·form** (pan-dôr′ə-fôrm, -dyoōr′-). [< L *pandura* a lute + -ATE¹]

pane¹ (pān) *n.* **1** A piece or compartment, particularly if flat and rectangular. **2** A piece of window glass filling one opening in a frame. **3** A flat surface, as on an object having several sides: the *pane* of a tower, nut, or brilliant–cut diamond. **4** A panel, or space between timbers; also, a bay. ◆ Homophone: *pain.* [< OF *pan(e)* < L *pannus* a piece of cloth]

pane² (pān) *n.* The peen of a hammer. ◆ Homophone: *pain.* [Cf. F *panne* peen of a hammer]

pan·e·gyr·ic (pan′ə-jir′ik) *n.* A formal public eulogy, either written or spoken; encomium; laudation in general. See synonyms under EULOGY, PRAISE. — *adj.* Elaborately eulogistic or laudatory: also **pan′e·gyr′i·cal.** [< F *panégyrique* < L *panegyricus* < Gk. *panēgyrikos* of an assembly < *pan,* neut. of *pas* all + *agyris* an assembly < *pan,* neut. of *pas* all + *agyris,* Aeolic form of *agora* gathering] — **pan′e·gyr′i·cal·ly** *adv.* — **pan′e·gyr′ist** *n.*

pan·e·gy·rize (pan′ə-jə-rīz′) *v.* **·rized, ·riz·ing** *v.t.* To deliver or write a panegyric upon; eulogize. — *v.i.* To make panegyrics.

pan·el (pan′əl) *n.* **1** A rectangular piece set in or as in a frame, as in a door, or sunken below it, as a window pane; hence, any such piece, even if raised above the general plane. **2** A bordered member to which the effect of framing is given by moldings or by working away material from the solid plane. **3** One or more pieces of a different fabric and color inserted lengthwise in the skirt of a woman's dress. **4** A tablet of wood, used as the surface for an oil painting; also, the picture on such a tablet. **5** A picture very long for its width, in a simple frame, or with no frame at all. **6** A size of photograph longer than it is wide, usually about 8 1/2 × 4 inches. **7** A face on a hewn stone. **8** A section of a book cover having a framed effect; also, a subdivision of the back of a bound book, between two bands. **9** *Law* The official list of persons summoned for jury duty; the body of persons composing a jury. **10** *Aeron.* **a** One of the construction units forming the wing surface of an airplane. **b** The unit of fabric of which the outer covering of a balloon or the canopy of a parachute is made. **11** An upright board of insulating material sustaining the controlling devices of an electric circuit. **12** An array of dials, gages, and instruments for the operation of an aircraft, automobile, or other complex apparatus. **13** A small group of persons assembled for judging, discussion, etc. — *v.t.* **·eled** or **·elled, ·el·ing** or **·el·ling 1** To fit, furnish, or adorn with panels. **2** To divide into panels. **3** *Scot. Law* To indict. [< OF *panel* a piece of cloth < Med. L *panellus,* dim. of L *pannus* a cloth]

panel fence A kind of worm fence made in sections.

pan·el·ing (pan′əl·ing) *n.* **1** Work in panels; panels collectively. **2** The introduction or use of panelwork. Also **pan′el·ling.**

pan·el·ist (pan′əl·ist) *n.* A person serving on a panel of judges or debaters.

panel truck *U.S.* A small, light, enclosed truck, as for delivery of supplies.

pan·el·work (pan′əl·wûrk′) *n.* **1** Wainscoting; any work using or introducing panels. **2** Panelworking.

pan·el·work·ing (pan′əl·wûrk′ing) *n. Mining* A method of working a colliery by dividing it into large rooms separated by very wide masses of coal.

pan·e·tel·a (pan′ə·tel′ə) *n.* A long, slender, cylindrical-shaped cigar: also spelled *panatela.* Also **pan′e·tel′la.** [< Sp.]

pan fish Any little fish that can be fried whole.

pan-fry (pan′frī′) *v.t.* **-fried, -fry·ing** To fry in a frying pan.

pang (pang) *n.* A sudden and poignant pain; keen transient agony; hence, a throe of mental anguish. See synonyms under AGONY, PAIN. [? Alter. of ME *prange* a prong, point]

pan·ga·my (pang′gə·mē) *n. Biol.* Indiscriminate or random mating. — **pan·gam′ic** (pan·gam′ik), **pan′ga·mous** *adj.* — **pan′ga·mous·ly** *adv.*

pan·gen·e·sis (pan·jen′ə·sis) *n. Biol.* The theory, advanced by Charles Darwin, that all the cells of an organism throw off very minute gemmules, **pangens,** which circulate through the body and develop buds or germ cells which have the power of reproduction and contain the units of heredity which they transmit from parent to offspring. — **pan′ge·net′ic** (-jə·net′ik) *adj.*

pan·go·lin (pang·gō′lin) *n.* A heavily armored, typically long–tailed edentate mammal (genus *Manis*) of Asia and Africa; the scaly ant-eater. [< Malay *peng–goling* a roller < *gōling* roll, in ref. to its power of rolling itself up]

pan·han·dle¹ (pan′han′dəl) *v.i.* **·dled, ·dling** *U.S. Colloq.* To beg, especially on the street. [Back formation from PANHANDLER a beggar < PAN¹ (used to receive alms) + HANDLE, *v.*] — **pan′han′dler** *n.*

pan·han·dle² (pan′han′dəl) *n.* **1** A narrow strip of land attached to a larger region: from its resemblance to the handle of a pan. **2** *Usually cap.* A region of this shape in either Texas or West Virginia.

Panhandle State Nickname of WEST VIRGINIA.

pan·ic (pan′ik) *adj.* **1** Of the nature of or resulting from sudden and infectious terror. **2** Of or pertaining to the Greek god Pan as the cause of fear: *panic* flight. — *n.* **1** A sudden, unreasonable, overpowering fear, especially when affecting a large number simultaneously. **2** Sudden and overpowering alarm or distrust in financial or commercial circles, precipitating mercantile and banking failures. See synonyms under ALARM, FEAR, FRIGHT. — *v.* **·icked, ·ick·ing** *v.t.* **1** To affect with panic. **2** *U.S. Slang* To move to great applause or laughter: He *panicked* his audience. — *v.i.* **3** To become affected with panic. [< MF *panique* < Gk. *panikos* of or for the god Pan, who was believed to cause sudden or groundless fear] — **pan′ick·y** *adj.*

pan ice Loose fragments of ice detached from ice floes and drifting along the seacoast.

panic grass A North American grass (*Panicum capillare*) used for forage: also called *witchgrass.* [< L *panicum* a kind of millet < *panis* bread + GRASS]

pan·i·cle (pan′i·kəl) *n. Bot.* A loose compound flower cluster, produced by irregular branching. [< L *paniculata,* dim. of *panus* a swelling, an ear of millet] — **pan′i·cled** *adj.*

pan·ic–strick·en (pan′ik·strik′ən) *adj.* Overcome by panic. Also **pan′ic–struck′.**

pa·nic·u·late (pə·nik′yə·lāt, -lit) *adj.* Arranged or borne in panicles; panicled. Also **pa·nic′u·lat′ed.** — **pa·nic′u·late·ly** *adv.*

pan·jan·drum (pan·jan′drəm) *n.* An imaginary character of exaggerated importance or great pretensions; hence, a pompous personage in a small place. [Coined by Samuel Foote, English dramatist and actor, in 1755]

pan·mix·i·a (pan·mik′sē·ə) *n.* Indiscriminate interbreeding; unrestricted mating in a mixed population. [< NL < Gk. *pan,* neut. of *pas* all + *mixis* a mixture]

panne satin (pan) Silk or rayon satin with an unusually high luster because of a special finish. [< F *panne,* a type of soft cloth + SATIN]

panne velvet Silk or rayon velvet with a flat-tened pile, lustrous and lightweight.

pan·nier (pan′yər) *n.* **1** One of a pair of baskets adapted to be slung on both sides of a beast of burden. **2** A basket for carrying a load on the back. **3** A light framework for extending a woman's dress at the hips; also, a skirt or overskirt extended at the hips. [< MF < L *panarium* bread basket < *panis* bread]

pan·ni·kin (pan′ə·kin) *n.* A small saucepan or tin cup. [Dim. of PAN¹]

pa·no·cha (pə·nō′chə) *n.* **1** A coarse Mexican sugar. **2** A kind of candy made from brown sugar, milk, and usually containing chopped nuts: also spelled *penuche, penuchi.* Also **pa-**

no'che. [< Am. Sp. < L *panucula, panicula.* See PANICLE.]

pan·o·ply (pan'ə·plē) *n. pl.* **·plies 1** The complete equipment of a warrior. **2** Hence, any complete covering that protects or magnificently arrays. [< Gk. *panoplia* full armor < *pan,* neut. of *pas* all + *hopla* arms] —**pan'o·plied** *adj.*

pan·op·tic (pan·op'tik) *adj.* Inclusive of all that is visible in one view. Also **pan·op'ti·cal.**

pan·o·ram·a (pan'ə·ram'ə, -rä'mə) *n.* **1** A series of pictures representing a continuous scene, arranged to unroll and pass before the spectator. **2** A complete view in every direction; also, a complete or comprehensive view of a subject or of constantly passing events. **3** A cyclorama. [< PAN- + Gk. *horama* sight < *horaein* see] —**pan'o·ram'ic** *adj.* —**pan'o·ram'i·cal·ly** *adv.*

panoramic sight A sight constructed on the periscope principle, intended for use by marksmen.

pan·pipes (pan'pīps') *n. pl.* A wind instrument formed of short hollow tubes (originally reeds) fastened together in proper order to produce a scale.

pan·psy·chism (pan·sī'kiz·əm) *n.* The doctrine that the universe as a whole, and every physical part of it also, has a psychic aspect. [< PAN- + Gk. *psychē* soul, breath] —**pan·psy'chic** *adj.* —**pan·psy'chist** *n.*

pan·so·phism (pan'sə·fiz'əm) *n.* Profession of universal wisdom. —**pan'so·phist** *n.*

pan·so·phy (pan'sə·fē) *n.* Complete or comprehensive knowledge; a system embracing all human knowledge. [< PAN- + Gk. *sophia* wisdom] —**pan·soph·ic** (pan·sof'ik), **pan·soph'i·cal** *adj.*

pan·sy (pan'zē) *n. pl.* **·sies 1** A species of garden violet (*Viola tricolor hortensis*) having blossoms of a variety of colors of great beauty. **2** A bright, deep-purple color, the color of some pansies. [< MF *pensée* thought, orig. pp. of *penser* think]

pant (pant) *v.i.* **1** To breathe rapidly or spasmodically; gasp for breath. **2** To emit smoke, steam, etc., in loud puffs. **3** To gasp with desire; yearn: with *for* or *after.* **4** To beat or pulsate rapidly; throb, as the heart. —*v.t.* **5** To breathe out or utter gaspingly. See synonyms under PUFF. —*n.* A short or labored breath; a gasp; also, a quick or violent heaving, as of the breast; a throb, as of the heart. [Appar. < OF *pantoisier* gasp, ult. < L *phantasia* a nightmare] —**pant'er** *n.*

pant– Var. of PANTO–.

pan·ta·lets (pan'tə·lets') *n. pl.* Long ruffled drawers, formerly worn by women and children. Also **pan'ta·lettes'.** [Dim. of PANTALOON]

pan·ta·loon (pan'tə·lōōn') *n.* **1** In pantomimes, an absurd old man on whom the clown plays tricks. **2** *pl.* Trousers; formerly, a tight-fitting garment for the legs. [< F *pantalon* < Ital. *pantalone* a clown < *Pantalone,* nickname for a Venetian, after *Pantaleone,* a popular Venetian saint]

pan·the·ism (pan'thē·iz'əm) *n.* **1** The form of monism that identifies mind and matter, the finite and the infinite, making them manifestations of one universal or absolute being; the doctrine which holds that the self-existent and self-developing universe, conceived as a whole, *is* God. **2** The worship of all gods. —**pan'the·ist** *n.* —**pan'the·is'tic, pan'the·is'ti·cal** *adj.* —**pan'the·is'ti·cal·ly** *adv.*

pan·the·on (pan'thē·on) *n.* **1** All the gods of a people, collectively. **2** A mausoleum or temple resembling the Roman Pantheon, and commemorating the great. [< L *pantheon* < Gk. *pantheion* a temple consecrated to all the gods < *pan,* neut. of *pas* all + *theos* a god]

Pan·the·on (pan'thē·on) A circular temple at Rome, dedicated to all the gods: built by Agrippa, rebuilt by Hadrian: after A.D. 609, a Christian church (Santa Maria della Rotunda).

pan·ther (pan'thər) *n.* **1** A leopard, especially the black leopard of southern Asia. **2** Some other large feline carnivore, as the North American puma or cougar; also, a jaguar. [< OF *pantère* < L *panthera* < Gk. *panthēr*] —**pan'ther·ess** *n. fem.*

pant·ies (pan'tēz) *n. pl.* A woman's or child's underpants. Also **pant'ie.**

pan·tile (pan'tīl') *n.* A tile displaying a curved cross-section, making laps on each side with adjacent tiles of reverse form.

panto– *combining form* All; every: *pantoscope.* Also, before vowels, *pant–.* [< Gk. *pantos,* genitive of *pas* all]

pan·to·base (pan'tə·bās) *adj. Aeron.* Designating an aircraft capable of landing on or taking off from any kind of terrain, as mud, ice, snow, water, etc.

pan·tof·fle (pan'tə·fəl, pan·tof'əl, -tōō'fəl) *n.* A slipper. Also **pan'to·fle.** [< MF *pantoufle* < Ital. *pantufola, pantofola,* ? < Med. Gk. *pantophellos* cork shoe, lit. whole cork < Gk. *pas, pantos* all + *phellos* cork]

pan·to·graph (pan'tə·graf, -gräf) *n.* **1** An instrument for copying a drawing, diagram, or map, either on the same scale or with reduction or enlargement. **2** *Electr.* A trolley whose current-collecting member is borne on a jointed, quadrilateral frame. —**pan'to·graph'ic** or **·i·cal** *adj.* —**pan·tog·ra·phy** (pan·tog'rə·fē) *n.*

PANTOGRAPH (*def.* 1)

pan·tol·o·gy (pan·tol'ə·jē) *n.* A system comprehending all departments of human knowledge. —**pan·tol'o·gist** *n.*

pan·to·mime (pan'tə·mīm) *n.* **1** A series of actions, as gestures and postures, used to express ideas or convey information. **2** Any play in which the actors express their meaning by action without dialog. **3** An ancient, classical play or part of a play in which the actor used gestures or movement only, while the chorus sang. **4** *Brit.* A play relating some popular story accompanied with burlesque, gorgeous scenery, and music: a Christmastide production. —*v.t. & v.i.* **·mimed, ·mim·ing** To act or express in pantomime. [< F < L *pantomimus* a pantomimist < Gk. *pantomimos* an imitator of all < *pan,* neut. of *pas* all + *mimos* an imitator] —**pan'to·mim'ic** (-mim'ik) or **·i·cal** *adj.* —**pan'to·mi'mist** (-mī'mist) *n.*

pan·to·scope (pan'tə·skōp) *n. Phot.* A very wide-angled lens.

pan·to·then·ic (pan'tə·then'ik) *adj. Biochem.* Designating an acid, $C_9H_{17}NO_5$, of the vitamin B complex, widely distributed in many plant and animal tissues. It is obtained as a pale-yellow, viscous oil forming a calcium salt, and is also made synthetically. [< Gk. *pantothen* from every side]

pan·toum (pän·tōōm') *n.* A verse form of Malay origin, consisting of a series of quatrains in which the second and fourth lines of each quatrain recur as the first and third of the next, and in which the second and fourth lines of the final quatrain repeat the first and third lines of the first. Also **pan·tun'** (-tōōn'). [< F < Malay *pantun*]

pan·try (pan'trē) *n. pl.* **·tries** A room or closet in which to keep provisions, dishes, table linen, etc. [< AF *panetrie,* OF *paneterie* bread room < Med. L. *panetaria* < *panetarius* baker < L *panis* bread]

pants (pants) *n. pl.* Trousers; drawers. [Short for PANTALOONS]

pant·suit (pant'sōōt') *n.* A woman's two-piece garment consisting of a jacket and matching pants. Also **pants suit.**

pan·ty·hose (pan'tē·hōz') *n. pl.* A woman's undergarment that combines panties and stockings.

pan·ty·waist (pan'tē·wāst') *n.* A child's waist with buttons on which to fasten short pants.

pa·nung (pä'nung) *n.* A long, broad strip of cloth worn by Siamese men and women as a loincloth or skirt. [< Siamese < *phā* cloth + *niñ* one]

pan·zer (pan'zər, *Ger.* pän'tsər) *adj.* Armored; also, using armored tanks or mechanized troops: a *panzer* attack. [< G]

Panzer division *Mil.* An armored division; especially, a division of tanks.

pap¹ (pap) *n.* **1** A teat; nipple. **2** A hill or other object having a conical shape. [ME *pappe,* appar. < Scand. Cf. dial. Sw. *papp.*]

pap² (pap) *n.* **1** Any soft food for babes. **2** *Slang* The fees, favors, and privileges of public office.

[ME *pappe,* ? < MLG]

pa·pa¹ (pä'pə, pə·pä') *n.* Father. [< F < L < Gk. *papas,* a child's word]

pa·pa² (pä'pä) *n.* **1** The bishop of Rome; the pope. **2** In the Greek Church, the patriarch of Alexandria; also, a parish priest. [< Med. L < Gk. *papas* father. Doublet of POPE.]

pa·pa·cy (pä'pə·sē) *n. pl.* **·cies 1** The dignity, office, or jurisdiction of the pope of Rome. **2** The succession of popes and the administration of affairs in the Roman Catholic Church. **3** The tenure of office of the pope. [< Med. L *papatia* < *papa.* See PAPA².]

Pa·pa·cy (pä'pə·sē) *n.* The Roman Catholic system of church government.

pa·pa·in (pə·pā'in, pä'pə·in) *n. Biochem.* A vegetable enzyme, resembling the trypsin of the pancreatic juice, contained in the milk of the papaya: used in medicine as a digestive.

pa·pal (pä'pəl) *adj.* **1** Pertaining to the papacy or the pope. **2** Assuming supreme authority. **3** Pertaining to the Roman Catholic Church. [< OF < Med. L *papalis* belonging to the pope < *papa.* See PAPA².]

papal delegate A representative of the pope in a country in which a papal nuncio is not in residence: also called *internuncio.*

Pa·pav·er·a·ce·ae (pə·pav'ə·rā'si·ē) *n. pl. Bot.* A family of widely distributed herbs and shrubs with polypetalous, typically showy flowers and a milky juice yielding several important narcotic alkaloids; the poppy family. [< NL < L *papaver* poppy + *-aceus* of the nature of] —**pa·pav'er·a'ceous** (-rā'shəs) *adj.*

pa·pav·er·ous (pə·pav'ər·əs) *adj.* Having the properties of the poppy.

pa·paw (pä·pô', pô'pô) *n.* **1** A small, deciduous, North American tree (*Asimina triloba,* family *Annonaceae*) bearing edible fruit. **2** The fruit. Also spelled **pawpaw.** [< Sp. *papayo* < Cariban]

pa·pa·ya (pä·pä'yä, pə·pä'yə) *n.* **1** The yellow, melonlike fruit of a tropical American evergreen tree (*Carica papaya*), valued for its nutritious and palatable qualities. The fruit may be eaten raw, cooked, or pickled. **2** The tree. [< Sp. < Cariban]

PAPAYA
(The tree from 15 to 25 feet in height)

Pa·pe·e·te (pä'pā·ā'tā, pə·pē'tē) A port on Tahiti, capital of the Society Islands and of French Oceania.

Pa·pen (pä'pən), **Franz von,** 1879–1969, German diplomat.

pa·per (pä'pər) *n.* **1** A substance made from fibrous cellulose material, as rags, wood, or bark, treated with various chemicals and formed into thin sheets or strips for writing, printing, wrapping and a wide variety of other uses in industry and the arts. **2** A sheet or a web of such material. **3** A printed or written instrument or document. **4** A printed journal; newspaper. **5** A written discourse; essay. **6** Written or printed pledges or promises to pay which are negotiable, as bills of exchange, notes, etc.: called **commercial paper. 7** A package containing in a paper wrapping a limited amount or number: a *paper* of pins. **8** Wallpaper, paperhangings. **9** *Slang* A marked playing card. **10** *pl.* Small strips of paper on which the hair is twisted to be curled: also **curl papers. 11** *pl.* A ship's papers, as invoices, etc. See SHIP'S PAPERS. **12** *pl.* Personal documents or identification, etc. **13** Something having a similar appearance to paper, as papyrus or papier-mâché. **14** Collectively, free orders of admission to a place of amusement; also, an audience so admitted. —**first papers** Papers declaring intention of becoming a citizen of the United States: filed by an applicant for naturalization as the first step in the process. —**second papers** Popular name for a certificate of naturalization. —*v.t.* **1** To put paper on; cover with wallpaper. **2** To fold or enclose in paper. **3** To write or describe on paper. **4** To issue free tickets of admission to (a place of amusement): to *paper* the house. —*adj.* **1** Made of paper. **2** Enrolled, described, or stated on paper; existing only on paper. [< AF *papir,* OF *papier* < L *papyrus.* Doublet of PAPYRUS.]

—pa′per·y *adj.*

pa·per·back (pā′pər·bak′) *adj.* Having a paper cover or binding. —*n.* A book so bound.

pa·per·er (pā′pər·ər) *n.* One who applies paper; a paperhanger.

paper gold Special Drawing Rights (which see).

pa·per·hang·ing (pā′pər·hang′ing) *n.* **1** The act or process of covering walls, etc., with paper. **2** *pl.* Wallpaper. —**pa′per·hang′er** *n.*

pa·per·knife (pā′pər·nīf′) *n. pl.* **·knives** (-nīvz′) A blade of bone or other hard substance, for cutting folded leaves, creasing paper, etc.

paper money 1 Currency consisting of paper on which certain fixed values are printed, as banknotes, government notes, etc. **2** Negotiable commercial papers, as promissory notes, bills of exchange, etc.

paper nautilus A pelagic cephalopod mollusk (genus *Argonauta*), related to and resembling the octopus in having eight tentacles but in the female secreting a delicate, papery shell. Also called *argonaut*.

paper profit A potential profit, as in the stock market, that can be realized only by the sale of an appreciated holding.

paper tiger Something that seems mighty or threatening but is actually ineffectual and not to be taken seriously.

paper wasp Any of various wasps, as the hornets, yellow jackets, and certain other social wasps, that build nests of a material resembling paper.

pa·per·weight (pā′pər·wāt′) *n.* A small, heavy object, often ornamental, used to keep loose papers in place by its weight.

pa·per·work (pā′pər·wûrk′) *n.* Work involving the preparation or handling of reports, letters, correction of papers, etc.

pap·e·terie (pap′ə·trē, *Fr.* páp·trē′) *n.* A box or case containing writing materials. [< F < *papetier* a papermaker, ult. < *papier* paper]

pa·pier-mâ·ché (pā′pər·mə·shā′, *Fr.* pá·pyä′ mä·shā′) *n.* A tough plastic material made from paper pulp containing an admixture of size, paste, oil, resin, etc., or from sheets of paper glued and pressed together. [< F *papier* PAPER + *mâché*, pp. of *mâcher* chew < L *masticare*]

pa·pil·i·o·na·ceous (pə·pil′ē·ō·nā′shəs) *adj. Bot.* Butterfly-shaped, as the corolla of the sweet pea and other leguminous plants. [< NL *papilionaceus* < L *papilio, -onis* butterfly]

Pa·pil·i·on·i·dae (pə·pil′ē·on′i·dē) *n. pl.* A family of butterflies, including mostly large species with a tail-like lobe on each hind wing; the swallowtail butterflies. [< NL < L *papilio, -onis* butterfly] —**pa·pil′i·on′id** *adj. & n.*

pa·pil·la (pə·pil′ə) *n. pl.* **·lae** (-ē) **1** *Anat.* **a** The nipple of the mammary glands. **b** Any small nipplelike process of connective tissue, as on the tongue or the epidermal layer of the skin, or at the root of a developing tooth, hair, feather, etc. **2** *Bot.* A small, elongate, nipple-shaped protuberance on a flower or leaf. [< L, dim. of *papula* a swelling, pimple] —**pap·il·lar·y** (pap′ə·ler′ē) *adj.*

pap·il·lo·ma (pap′ə·lō′mə) *n. pl.* **·ma·ta** (-mə·tə) *Pathol.* A morbid growth on the skin, consisting of small tumors composed of and covered by the normal skin, as corns, warts, or mucous tubercles. [< PAPILLA]

pap·il·lon (pap′ə·lon) *n.* A breed of toy spaniel descended from the European 16th century dwarf spaniel, having large fringed ears resembling the wings of a butterfly, a plumy tail, and a thick, solidly colored coat. [< F, butterfly < L *papilio, -onis*]

pap·il·lose (pap′ə·lōs) *adj.* Papillary; also, pimply; warty. Also **pap′il·lous.** [< NL *papillosus* < L *papilla*] —**pap·il·los′i·ty** (-los′ə·tē) *n.*

pa·pist (pā′pist) *n.* An adherent of the papacy; a Roman Catholic: usually an opprobrious use. [< F *papiste* < Med. L *papa.* See PAPA².]

pap·pus (pap′əs) *n. pl.* **pap·pi** (pap′ī) *Bot.* The peculiar limb on the calyx of a floret of the composite family, consisting either of a downy tuft of hairs, as in thistles, or of teeth, scales, bristles, or awns. [< NL < L *pappus* grandfather] —**pap′pose** (-ōs), **pap′pous** (-əs) *adj.*

pap·py¹ (pap′ē) *adj.* **·pi·er, ·pi·est** Resembling pap; pulpy; soft.

pap·py² (pap′ē) *n. pl.* **·pies** Papa; father. [Dim. of PAPA¹]

pa·pri·ka (pa·prē′kə, pap′rə·kə) *n.* A condiment made from the ripe fruit of a mild variety of red pepper (*Capsicum frutescens*). Also **pa·pri′ca.** [< G < Magyar, red pepper < Gk. *peperi* pepper]

Pap smear A method of early detection of cervical cancer, consisting of removal of cervical cell samples, which are stained and examined. Also **Pap test.** [after George *Papanicolaou*, 1883–1962, U.S. scientist]

Papua and New Guinea, Territory of A United Nations Trust Territory administered by Australia and comprising the formerly separate Territory of Papua and Territory of New Guinea; established 1949; 183,600 square miles; capital, Port Moresby.

pap·u·la (pap′yə·lə) *n. pl.* **·lae** (-lē) *Pathol.* An isolated pimple. Also **pap′ule** (-yōōl). [< L, a pimple]

pap·y·ra·ceous (pap′ə·rā′shəs) *adj.* Made of papyrus; papery.

pa·py·rus (pə·pī′rəs) *n. pl.* **·ri** (-rī) **1** The writing paper of the ancient Egyptians, made from the papyrus plant. **2** A manuscript written on this material. **3** A perennial rushlike plant of the sedge family (*Cyperus papyrus*) having stems 6 to 10 feet high. [< L < Gk. *papyros.* Doublet of PAPER.]

par (pär) *n.* **1** Equality of value; equivalence: parity; specifically, equality between nominal and actual value. Shares of stock are said to be **at** (or **up to**) **par** when exchangeable at face value in money, **above par** when the market price is greater, and **below par** when less than the nominal value. **2** An accepted standard with which to compare variations. **3** In golf, the number of strokes allotted to a round or hole on the basis of faultless play. —**mint par** The reduction of the monetary unit of one country to expression in terms of that of another: also **par of exchange.** —**on a par** On a level. [< L, equal]

par- *prefix* Per-: used in a few words from French: *pardoner.* [< F < L *per-* < *per* through]

para-¹ *prefix* **1** Beside; near by; along with: *paradigm.* **2** Beyond; aside from; amiss: *paradox.* **3** *Chem.* **a** An isomeric or polymeric modification of: *paraldehyde.* **b** A modification of or a compound similar to (not necessarily isomeric or polymeric): *paramorphine.* **c** A benzene derivative in which the substituted atoms or radicals occupy the positions 1, 4: *paradichlorobenzene:* abbr. *p-.* Compare META-, ORTHO-. See BENZENE RING. **4** *Med.* **a** A diseased or abnormal condition: *paranoia.* **b** Accessory to: *parasympathetic.* **c** Similar to but not identical with a true condition or form: *paratyphoid.* Also, before vowels and *h,* usually **par-.** [< Gk. < *para* beside]

para-² *combining form* Shelter or protection against: *parasol.* [< Ital. *parare* defend]

par·a·a·mi·no·ben·zo·ic acid (par′ə·ə·mē′ nō·ben·zō′ik, -am′ə·nō-) A yellowish crystalline compound, $C_7H_7O_2N$, forming part of the vitamin B complex and essential for growth in many organisms.

par·a·blast (par′ə·blast) *n. Biol.* The yolk of a meroblastic egg. —**par·a·blas′tic** *adj.*

par·a·ble (par′ə·bəl) *n.* A comparison; simile; specifically, a short narrative making a moral or religious point by comparison with natural or homely things: the New Testament *parables.* See synonyms under ALLEGORY. [< OF *parabole* < LL *parabola* allegory, speech < L, comparison < Gk. *parabolē* a placing side by side, a comparison < *para-* beside + *ballein* throw. Doublet of PALAVER, PARABOLA, PAROLE.]

pa·rab·o·la (pə·rab′ə·lə) *n Math.* The locus of a point moving in a plane so that its distances from a fixed point (focus) and a fixed straight line (directrix) are equal; the curve formed by the edges of a plane when cutting through a right circular cone at an angle parallel to one of its sides. [< Med. L < Gk. *parabolē.* Doublet of PALAVER, PARABLE, PAROLE.]

pa·rab·o·le (pə·rab′ə·lē) *n.* A rhetorical comparison; a formal simile. [< Gk. *parabolē.* See PARABLE.]

par·a·bol·ic (par′ə·bol′ik) *adj.* **1** Pertaining to a parable. **2** Pertaining to or having the form of a parabola. Also **par·a·bol′i·cal.** [< LL *parabolicus* < LGk. *parabolikos* figurative < *parabolē.* See PARABLE.] —**par·a·bol′i·cal·ly** *adv.*

pa·rab·o·lize (pə·rab′ə·līz) *v.t.* **·lized, ·liz·ing 1** To relate in parable form. **2** *Math.* To give the form of a parabola to.

pa·rab·o·loid (pə·rab′ə·loid) *n. Math.* A surface or solid generated by the rotation of a parabola about its axis. —**pa·rab·o·loi′dal** *adj.*

par·a·ca·se·in (par′ə·kā′sē·in, -sēn) *n. Biochem.* A form of casein produced by the action of rennin.

par·a·cen·tric (par′ə·sen′trik) *adj.* Directed to or from the center: said of motion. Also **par′a·cen′tri·cal.**

par·a·chro·ma·tism (par′ə·krō′mə·tiz′əm) *n. Pathol.* Abnormal perception of colors; color blindness. —**par′a·chro·mat′ic** (-krō·mat′ik) *adj.*

par·a·chute (par′ə·shōōt) *n.* **1** A large, expanding, umbrella-shaped apparatus for retarding the speed of a body descending through the air, especially from an airplane. **2** *Zool.* A lateral extension of the skin in flying squirrels, etc., enabling them to glide through the air. —**pilot parachute** *Aeron.* A small parachute whose release serves to open the canopy of the main parachute quickly and with minimum danger of jamming or tearing. —*v.* **·chut·ed, ·chut·ing** *v.t.* To land (troops, materiel, etc.) by means of parachutes. —*v.i.* To descend by parachute. [< F *para* PARA-² + *chute* fall]

parachute fabric A plain-woven, very firm fabric used for making parachutes: made of silk or nylon if for humans, of rayon if for cargo, bombs, etc.

parachute flare A flare attached to a parachute and released from an aircraft to illuminate the terrain.

par·a·chut·ist (par′ə·shōō′tist) *n.* A person, specifically a soldier, trained and equipped to drop by parachute.

par·a·clete (par′ə·klēt) *n.* One called to the aid of another, especially in legal process; an advocate; hence, **Paraclete,** the Holy Spirit as the helper or comforter. [< OF *paraclet* < LL *paracletus* < LGk. *paraklētos* a comforter, advocate < *parakalein* call to one's aid < *para-* to + *kalein* call]

pa·rade (pə·rād′) *n.* **1** A marshaling and maneuvering of troops for display or official inspection; a review. **2** A ceremonious procession. **3** A ground where military reviews are held. **4** A promenade or public walk. **5** A setting forth or arrangement of persons or things for display. **6** Pompous show; ostentation. See synonyms under OSTENTATION, SPECTACLE. —*v.* **·rad·ed, ·rad·ing** *v.t.* **1** To walk or march through or about: to *parade* the streets. **2** To display or show off ostentatiously; flaunt. **3** To cause to assemble for military parade or review. —*v.i.* **4** To march formally or with display. **5** To walk in public for the purpose of showing oneself. **6** To assemble in military order for inspection or review. See synonyms under FLAUNT. [< MF < Sp. *parada* a stopping place, exercise ground < LL *parare* adorn, prepare < L] —**pa·rad′er** *n.*

par·a·digm (par′ə·dim, -dīm) *n.* **1** *Gram.* An ordered list or table of all the inflected forms of a word or class of words, as of a particular declension, conjugation, etc. **2** Any pattern or example. [< LL *paradigma* < Gk. *paradeigma* a pattern < *para-* beside + *deiknynai* show] —**par′a·dig·mat′ic** (-dig·mat′ik) *adj.*

par·a·dise (par′ə·dīs) *n.* **1** The intermediate place or state where the souls of the saved await the resurrection. **2** Heaven, the ultimate abode of righteous souls; also, the abode of the deceased faithful of Islam. **3** Any region or state of surpassing delight. **4** In the Near East, a park or pleasure ground. [< F *paradis* < L *paradisus* < Gk. *paradeisos* park < OPersian *pairidaēza* an enclosure, park < *pairi* around + *daēza* wall]. —**par·a·di·sa′ic** (-di·sā′ik) or **·i·cal, par·a·dis′i·ac** (-dis′ē·ak) or **par·a·di·si·a·cal** (par′ə·di·sī′ə·kəl) *adj.*

Par·a·dise (par′ə·dīs) The garden of Eden.

par·a·dos (par′ə·dos) *n.* An embankment, as behind a trench, for protection against gunfire from the rear. [< F <*para*-PARA.² + *dos* back]

par·a·dox (par′ə-doks) *n.* **1** A statement, doctrine, or expression seemingly absurd or contradictory to common notions or to what would naturally be believed, but in fact really true. **2** A statement essentially absurd and false. See synonyms under RIDDLE². [< F *paradoxe* < L *paradoxum* < Gk. *paradoxos, -on* incredible < *para*-contrary to + *doxa* opinion < *dokeein* think] — **par′a·dox′i·cal** *adj.* —**par′a·dox′i·cal′i·ty** (-kal′ə-tē), **par′a·dox′i·cal·ness** *n.* —**par′a·dox′i·cal·ly** *adv.*

par·a·drop (par′ə-drop) *n.* The dropping of supplies, equipment, and the like by parachute, especially over terrain not adapted to landings by aircraft. [< PARA(CHUTE) + DROP]

par·af·fin (par′ə-fin) *n. Chem.* **1** A translucent, waxy, solid mixture of hydrocarbons, indifferent to most chemical reagents: it is a constituent of peat, soft coal, and shale, but is derived principally from the distillation of petroleum. **2** Any saturated aliphatic hydrocarbon of the methane series having the formula C_nH_{2n+2}. —*v.t.* To treat or impregnate with paraffin. Also **par′af·fine** (-fin, -fēn). [< G < L *parum* too little + *affinis* related to; so named because it has little affinity for other bodies]

paraffin wax Solid paraffin.

par·a·gen·e·sis (par′ə-jen′ə-sis) *n. Mineral.* The formation of minerals in contact in such manner as to affect the development of the individual crystals. Also **par′a·ge·ne′si·a** (-jə-nē′sē-ə). — **par′a·ge·net′ic** (-jə-net′ik) *adj.*

par·a·go·ge (par′ə-gō′jē) *n.* The addition of an inorganic sound or syllable at the end of a word without a change in meaning, as in *amongs-t, whils-t,* etc. [< L < Gk. *paragōgē* < *para*-beyond + *agōgē* a leading < *agein* lead] —**par′·a·gog′ic** (-goj′ik) *adj.*

par·a·gon (par′ə-gon) *n.* **1** A model of excellence. **2** *Printing* A size of type: about 3½ lines to the inch: 20-point. **3** A round pearl of exceptional size. —*v.t.* Archaic or Poetic **1** To match; equal. **2** To compare with. **4** To hold up as a paragon. [< OF < Ital. *paragone* a touchstone, prob. < Gk. *parakonaein* sharpen one thing against another < *para*-beside + *akonē* whetstone]

pa·rag·o·nite (pə-rag′ə-nīt) *n.* A scaly, pearly, variously colored, translucent mica containing sodium instead of potassium, and found massive. [< Gk. *paragōn,* ppr. of *paragein* lead astray + -ITE¹]

par·a·graph (par′ə-graf, -gräf) *n.* **1** A short passage in a written or printed discourse, begun on a new and usually indented line. **2** A short article, complete and unified; especially, in a newspaper, a short article, item, or comment. **3** A mark (¶) used to indicate where a paragraph is to be begun, or as a reference mark. —*v.t.* **1** To arrange in or into paragraphs. **2** To comment on or express in a paragraph. [< OF *paragraphe* < LL *paragraphus* < Gk. *paragraphos,* orig. a short line in a text marking a break in sense < *para*-beside + *graphein* write] —**par′a·graph′er, par′a·graph′ist** *n.* —**par′·a·graph′ic,** *or* **par′a·graph′i·cal** *adj.*

Par·a·guay (par′ə-gwā, -gwī; *Sp.* pä-rä-gwī′) A republic in south central South America; 157,047 square miles; capital, Asunción. — **Par′a·guay′an** *adj. & n.*

par·a·hyp·no·sis (par′ə-hip·nō′sis) *n. Psychiatry* Abnormal sleep, suggesting the effects of but not necessarily due to hypnosis, as in somnambulism. —**par′a·hyp·not′ic** (-not′ik) *adj.*

par·a·in·flu·en·za (par′ə·in·flŏŏ·en′zə) *n.* An influenzalike respiratory disease caused by any of several viruses.

par·a·jour·nal·ism (par′ə·jûr′nə·liz-əm) *n.* A kind of writing for newspapers and other periodicals that departs from the style and standards of ordinary journalism.

par·a·keet (par′ə·kēt) *n.* **1** Any of certain small parrots, having a long, wedge-shaped tail, as the crimson rosella of Australia *(Platycercus elegans).* **2** The Carolina parakeet *(Conuropsis carolinensis)* of the southern United States: now extinct. [< OF *paroquet,* ? < Ital. *parrochetto,* dim. of *parroco* parson]

par·a·ki·ne·sia (par′ə·ki·nē′zhə, -zhē-ə) *n. Pathol.* Clumsy and unnatural movements, caused by impairment of motor functions. Also **par′a·ki·ne′sis** (-nē′sis). [< NL < Gk. *para*-beside + *kinēsis* movement] —**par′a·ki·net′ic** (-net′ik) *adj.*

par·a·le·gal (par′ə-lē′gəl) *adj.* Pertaining to the law at a subprofessional level. —*n.* A legal paraprofessional.

par·a·leip·sis (par′ə-līp′sis) *n.* In rhetoric, a pretended suppression of what is really said; a feigned omission, as in "not to mention his insufferable conceit"; apophasis. Also **par′a·lep′sis** (-lep′sis), **par′a·lip′sis** (-lip′sis). [< Gk., an omission < *paraleipein* < *para*-beside + *leipein* leave]

par·al·lax (par′ə-laks) *n.* **1** Such difference in the apparent position of an object, specifically a star or other heavenly body, as would appear if it were viewed from two points. It is **diurnal** or **geocentric parallax** when due to the change of place of the observer caused by the earth's rotation; **annual** or **heliocentric parallax** when the observer's change of place is due to the earth's motion around the sun. **2** Any apparent displacement of an object due to an observer's position. [< MF *parallaxe* < Gk. *parallaxis* a change < *parallassein* alter < *para*-beside + *allassein* change] —**par′al·lac′tic** (-lak′tik) *or* **·ti·cal** *adj.* —**par′al·lac′ti·cal·ly** *adv.*

par·al·lel (par′ə-lel) *adj.* **1** Not meeting or intersecting, however far extended: said of straight lines or planes. **2** In projective geometry, meeting at infinity. **3** Having lines or surfaces lying in the same or about the same direction. **4** Having a like course; conforming in action. **5** Essentially alike; similar. **6** *Music* Separated by the same interval: *parallel* fifths. **7** Having sides parallel to one another. **8** *Electr.* Connected between like terminals, as a group of cells, condensers, etc. — *n.* **1** A line extending in the same direction and being equidistant at all points from another line. **2** Essential likeness. **3** A comparison tracing similarity, as between persons. **4** A counterpart. **5** Any person or thing ranked as equal to another; a match. **6** A trench dug parallel to the outline of a fortification. **7** A degree of latitude. —*v.t.* **·leled** *or* **·lelled, ·lel·ing** *or* **·lel·ling 1** To place in parallel; make parallel. **2** To be, go, or extend parallel to. **3** To furnish with a parallel or equal; find a parallel to. **4** To be a parallel to; correspond to. **5** To compare; liken. See synonyms under COMPARE. [< MF *parallele* < L *parallelus* < Gk. *parallēlos* < *para*-beside + *allēlos* one another]

parallel bars Two horizontal crossbars, parallel to each other and supported a few feet from the ground by upright posts: used for gymnastic exercises.

par·al·lel·e·pi·ped (par′ə-lel′ə-pī′ped,-pip′id) *n.* A prism with six faces, each of which is a parallelogram. Also **par′al·lel′o·pi′ped, par′al·lel′e·pip′e·don, par′al·lel′o·pip′e·don** (-pip′ə-don, -pī′pə-). [< Gk. *parallēlepipedon* < *parallēlos* parallel + *epipedon* a plane surface < *epi*-upon + *pedon* ground]

par·al·lel·ism (par′ə-lel·iz′əm) *n.* **1** Parallel position. **2** Essential likeness; similarity; analogy. **3** Correspondence or similarity of construction in successive passages or clauses, especially in Hebrew poetry. **4** *Philos.* The opinion that the relation between physical and mental processes is one of concomitant or parallel variation, and not of cause and effect. —**psychophysical parallelism** *Philos.* The theory that related mental and physical events, although occurring simultaneously, are separate and distinct phenomena: opposed to *interactionism.*

par·al·lel·o·gram (par′ə-lel′ə-gram) *n.* **1** *Geom.* A four-sided plane figure whose opposite sides are parallel and equal, including the *square, rectangle, rhombus,* and *rhomboid.* **2** Any area or object having such form. [< F *parallélogramme* < L *parallelogrammum* < Gk. *parallēlogrammon,* orig. adj., bounded by parallel lines < *parallēlos* parallel + *grammē* a line]

PARALLELOGRAMS
a. Square. *b.* Rectangle. *c.* Rhombus. *d.* Rhomboid.

pa·ral·o·gism (pə-ral′ə·jiz′əm) *n.* A fallacy in reasoning. See synonyms under SOPHISTRY. [< F *paralogisme* < LL *paralogismus* < Gk. *paralogismos* < *paralogizesthai* reason falsely, ult. < *para*-beside + *logos* a word, reason] —**par·a·log′ic** (par′ə-loj′ik) *or* **·i·cal** *adj.*

pa·ral·y·sis (pə-ral′ə-sis) *n.* **1** *Pathol* Partial or complete loss of the power of voluntary motion and sometimes of the power of perceiving sensations; palsy. **2** Loss of power in general. [< L < Gk. < *paralyein* disable < *para*-beside + *lyein* loosen, untie. Doublet of PALSY.]

par·a·lyt·ic (par′ə-lit′ik) *adj.* **1** Pertaining to or affected with paralysis. **2** Subject to paralysis. —*n.* A person subject to or suffering from paralysis. [< OF *paralytique* < L *paralyticus* < Gk. *paralytikos.* See PARALYSIS.]

par·a·lyze (par′ə-līz) *v.t.* **·lyzed, ·lyz·ing 1** To bring about paralysis in; make paralytic. **2** To render powerless, ineffective, or inactive. See synonyms under WEAKEN. [Appar. < F *paralyser*] —**par′a·lyz′er** *n.*

Par·a·mar·i·bo (par′ə-mar′i·bō) A port, capital of Surinam.

par·a·mat·ta (par′ə-mat′ə) *n.* A kind of light, twilled, dress goods with cotton warp and filling of combed merino wool: also spelled *parramatta.* [from *Parramatta,* a city in N. So. Wales, Australia]

par·a·me·cin (par′ə-mē′sin) *n.* A powerful protein transmitted by inheritance within certain strains of paramecium and usually lethal to other strains of this organism.

par·a·me·ci·um (par′ə-mē′shē-əm, -sē-əm) *n. pl.* **·ci·a** (-shē-ə, -sē-ə) A ciliate infusorian (genus *Paramecium)* having a flattened elongate body, and feeding by a primitive oral groove, as *P. caudatum,* found in stagnant water. [< NL < Gk. *paramēkēs* oblong, oval]

par·a·med·ic (par′ə-med′ik) *n.* One trained to assist a physician.

par·a·med·i·cal (par′ə-med′ə-kəl) *adj.* Designating or pertaining to medical personnel trained to assist physicians, as by conducting routine tests, or to attend patients. —**par′a·med′i·cal·ly** *adv.*

pa·ram·e·ter (pə-ram′ə-tər) *n.* **1** *Math.* Any given constant or element whose values characterize one or more of the variables entering into a system of expressions, functions, etc.: A road gradient is a *parameter* of the performance of an automobile. **2** A fixed limit or guideline. [< NL *parametrum* < Gk. *para*-beside + *metron* a measure] —**par·a·met·ric** (par′ə-met′rik) *adj.*

par·a·mil·i·tar·y (par′ə-mil′ə-ter′ē) *adj.* Having a military structure although not officially military; capable of becoming, replacing, or supplementing a military force: said of certain political movements, police forces, etc.

par·a·mor·phism (par′ə-môr′fiz-əm) *n. Mineral.* The alteration of one mineral to another having the same chemical composition but other molecular structure and physical properties [< PARA.¹ + Gk. *morphē* a form + -ISM] —**par′a·mor′phic, par·a·mor′phous** *adj.*

par·a·mount (par′ə-mount) *adj.* **1** Having the highest title. **2** Superior to all others; supremely controlling. —*n.* A supreme lord; highest ruler. [< AF *paramont* above < OF *par* by (< L *per)* + *à mont* up, above < L *ad montem* to the hill] —**par′a·mount·ly** *adv.* —**par′a·mount·cy** *n.* — Synonyms (adj.): chief, eminent, foremost, preeminent, principal, superior, supreme.

par·a·mour (par′ə-mŏŏr) *n.* A lover, especially one who unlawfully takes the place of a husband or wife. [< OF *par amour* with love < *par* by, with (< L *per* through) + *amour* love < L *amor*]

pa·rang (pä′räng) *n.* A short, heavy sheath knife with a straight edge, used especially by the Dyaks of Borneo for chopping and as a weapon. [< Malay *pārang*]

par·a·noi·a (par′ə-noi′ə) *n. Psychiatry* A chronic, often progressive, mental disorder or psychosis, characterized by monomania, systematized delusions of persecution, and sometimes hallucinations. Also **par′a·noe′a** (-nē′ə). [< NL < Gk., madness < *paranoos* distraught < *para*-beside + *noos, nous* mind]

par·a·noi·ac (par′ə-noi′ak) *adj.* Relating to or affected by paranoia. —*n.* One affected by paranoia. Also **par′a·no′ic** (-nō′ik), **par′a·noe′ac** (-nē′ak).

par·a·noid (par′ə-noid) *adj.* Resembling or

suggestive of paranoia. —*n.* A person affected by paranoia.

par·a·no·sis (par′ə-nō′sis) *n. Psychoanal.* The primary advantage obtained by a patient from subjective exploitation of his illness. Compare EPINOSIS. [< NL < Gk. *para-* beside + *nosos* sickness] —**par′a·no′sic** *adj.*

par·a·pet (par′ə-pit, -pet) *n.* **1** A low wall about the edge of a roof, terrace, bridge, fortification, etc. **2** A breastwork. See synonyms under BARRIER. [< F < Ital. *parapetto* < *para-* PARA-² + *petto* breast < L *pectus* breast] —**par′a·pet·ed** *adj.*

par·aph (par′əf) *n.* A flourish made with the pen at the end of a signature, often as a protection against forgery; a rubric. —*v.t.* To affix a paraph to; sign, especially with initials; initial. [< OF *paraphe* < Med. L *paraphus,* var. of L *paragraphus.* See PARAGRAPH]

par·a·pher·na·li·a (par′ə-fər-nā′lē-ə, -nāl′yə, -fə) *n. pl.* **1** Trappings or accessories of equipment or adornment; furnishings, especially for ceremonious occasions; the parts of any outfit, apparatus, or equipment. **2** *Law* Formerly, the personal articles reserved to a wife over and above her dower. [< Med. L *paraphernalia* (*bona*) a wife's own (goods) < L *parapherna* < Gk. < *para-* beside + *phernē* dower < *pherein* carry]

par·a·phone (par′ə-fōn) *n.* Near rime. [< PARA-¹ + Gk. *phōnē* sound]

par·a·phrase (par′ə-frāz) *n.* A restatement of meaning of a passage, work, etc. —*v.t. & v.i.* ·**phrased**, ·**phras·ing** To express in or make a paraphrase. [< F < L *paraphrasis* < Gk. < *paraphrazein* tell the same thing in other words < *para-* beside + *phrazein* tell] —**par′a·phras′er, par′a·phrast** (-frast) *n.* —**par′a·phras′tic** *adj.* —**par′a·phras′ti·cal·ly** *adv.*

par·a·ple·gi·a (par′ə-plē′jē-ə) *n. Pathol.* Paralysis of the lower half of the body, due to disease or injury of the spinal cord. Also **par′a·ple′gy** (-plē′jē). [< NL < Gk. *paraplēgia, paraplēxia* a stroke on one side < *paraplēssein* strike at the side < *para-* beside + *plēssein* strike] —**par·a·ple·gic** (par′ə-plē′jik, plej′ik) *adj. & n.*

par·a·prax·is (par′ə-prak′sis) *n. Psychoanal.* Any faulty action, blunder, or lapse, as a slip of the tongue, failure of memory, etc. [< NL < Gk. *paraprassein* < *para-* beside + *prassein* do]

par·a·pro·fes·sion·al (par′ə-prə-fesh′ə-nal) One who assists professionals, as teachers or physicians, by performing tasks not requiring professional skills.

par·a·psy·chol·o·gy (par′ə-sī·kol′ə·jē) *n.* The investigation of extrasensory perception and the sporadic phenomena supposedly associated with it, such as telepathy, clairvoyance, telekinesis, prevision, dreams that prove prophetic, experiences of déjà vu, and poltergeist activity; metapsychics.

par·a·quat (par′ə-kwot) *n.* A toxic organic compound used as a herbicide. [< PARA-¹ + QUAT(ERNARY), part of the formula]

Pa·rá rubber (pä·rä′) Rubber obtained from the tropical American rubber tree (*Hevea brasiliensis*). [< Pará, Brazil]

par·a·sceve (par′ə-sēv, par′ə-sē′vē) *n.* **1** The day before the Jewish Sabbath, on which preparation is made for the Sabbath; also, what is then prepared. **2** In the Roman Catholic Church, Good Friday. [< L, day of preparation, day before the Sabbath < Gk. *paraskeuē* preparation < *para-* beside, against + *skeuē* equipment]

par·a·se·le·ne (par′ə-si·lē′nē) *n. pl.* ·**nae** (-nē) *Meteorol.* A luminous spot appearing on a lunar halo; a mock moon. [< NL < Gk. *para-* beside, subsidiary + *selēnē* moon]

par·a·site (par′ə-sīt) *n.* **1** *Biol.* An animal or a plant that lives on or in another organism at whose expense it obtains nourishment and shelter. **2** An obsequious sycophant who lives at another's expense. **3** In ancient Greece and Rome, one who secured a welcome at the tables of the rich by means of fawning and flattery. [< L *parasitus* < Gk. *parasitos,* lit., one who eats at another's table < *para-* beside + *sitos* food] —**par′a·sit′ic** (-sit′ik) or ·**i·cal** *adj.* —**par′a·sit′i·cal·ly** *adv.*

parasite drag *Aeron.* That portion of the drag of an aircraft exclusive of the drag of the wings: also called *head resistance.*

par·a·sit·i·cide (par′ə-sit′ə-sīd) *n.* Any agent that destroys parasites. —*adj.* Efficacious for destroying parasites: also **par′a·sit′i·ci′dal.**

par·a·sit·ism (par′ə-sī′tiz-əm) *n.* **1** The condition or conduct of a fawner or sycophant. **2** The state or condition of being parasitic. **3** *Biol.* Destructive symbiosis. **4** *Med.* Disease, especially of the skin, caused by parasites.

par·a·si·tol·o·gy (par′ə-si·tol′ə·jə) *n.* The scientific study of parasites and parasitism. —**par′a·si·to·log′i·cal** (-sī′tə·loj′i·kəl) *adj.* —**par′a·si·tol′o·gist** *n.*

par·a·sol (par′ə-sôl, -sol) *n.* A small, light sunshade carried by women. [< MF < Ital. *parasole* < *para-* PARA-² + *sole* sun]

par·a·sym·pa·thet·ic (par′ə-sim′pə·thet′ik) *adj. Anat.* Designating that part of the autonomic nervous system originating in the cranial and sacral regions of the spinal cord. Its functions include constriction of the pupil, dilation of the blood vessels and salivary glands, slowing of the heart, and stimulation of the digestive and genitourinary systems: also called *cranio-sacral.*

par·a·syn·the·sis (par′ə-sin′thə·sis) *n. Gram.* The principle or process of forming words by both combination and derivation; especially, the creation of a derivative word by compounding with a particle, as in *downfallen.* —**par′a·syn·thet′ic** (-sin·thet′ik) *adj.*

par·a·syph·i·lis (par′ə-sif′ə·lis) *n. Pathol.* A morbid sequela of syphilis, but not itself syphilitic. —**par′a·syph′i·lit′ic** (-sif′ə·lit′ik) *adj.*

par·a·tax·is (par′ə-tak′sis) *n. Gram.* Independent arrangement of clauses, phrases, etc., without connectives, as in "I die, I faint, I fail." Opposed to *hypotaxis.* [< Gk., lit., a placing side by side < *paratassein* place side by side < *para-* beside + *tassein* arrange] —**par′·a·tac′tic** (-tak′tik) or ·**ti·cal** *adj.* —**par′·a·tac′ti·cal·ly** *adv.*

par·a·thi·on (par′ə-thī′on, -ən) *n.* An extremely poisonous synthetic organic compound, used as an agricultural insecticide. [< PARA-¹ + Gk. *theion* sulfur]

par·a·thy·roid (par′ə-thī′roid) *adj. Anat.* **1** Lying near the thyroid gland. **2** Pertaining to or designating one of several (usually four) small, bean-shaped glands found typically in pairs on the inner side near the back of each lobe of the thyroid.

par·a·troop (par′ə-trōop) *n.* A military offensive force, with equipment, trained to land in hostile territory from an airplane by parachutes: also called *parachute troop.* [< PARA(CHUTE) + TROOP] —**par′a·troop′er** *n.*

par·a·ty·phoid (par′ə-tī′foid) *Pathol. adj.* Resembling typhoid fever but not responding to the tests for that disease. —*n.* Paratyphoid fever.

par·a·vane (par′ə-vān) *n.* **1** A torpedo-shaped underwater device equipped with sharp projecting teeth for cutting the moorings of sunken mines. **2** A similar device loaded with high explosives for use against submarines. [< *para-¹* + VANE]

par·boil (pär′boil′) *v.t.* **1** To boil partially. **2** To make uncomfortable with heat. [< OF *parboillir* < LL *parabullire* boil thoroughly < *per-* through + *bullire* bubble]

par·buck·le (pär′buk′əl) *n.* **1** A purchase made by looping a rope in the middle to aid in rolling casks, etc., up or down an incline, or in furling a sail by rolling the yards. **2** A sling made by passing both ends of a rope through its bight. —*v.t.* ·**led,** ·**ling** To hoist or lower by means of a parbuckle. [Earlier *parbunkle*; origin unknown]

par·cel (pär′səl) *n.* **1** Anything wrapped up; a package; bundle. **2** An integral part. **3** A group or lot composed of an indefinite number or quantity (of people or animals). **4** A distinct portion of land. **5** A separated part of anything; an indefinite number. —*v.t.* ·**celed** or ·**celled,** ·**cel·ing** or ·**cel·ling** **1** To divide or distribute in parts or shares: usually with *out.* **2** To make up into a parcel or parcels. **3** *Naut.* To wrap or cover with canvas strips, as a rope. —*adj. & adv.* Half or part; partly; partially. [< F *parcelle* < L *particula,* dim. of *pars, partis* part]

parch (pärch) *v.t.* **1** To make extremely dry; shrivel with heat. **2** To dry (corn, peas, etc.) by exposing to great heat; roast slightly. **3** To dry up or shrivel with cold. —*v.i.* **4** To become extremely dry; shrivel with heat. [ME *parchen, perchen,*? ult. < L *persiccare* < *per-* thoroughly + *siccare* dry]

parch·ment (pärch′mənt) *n.* **1** The skin of sheep, goats, and other animals prepared and polished with pumice stone for writing. **2** An imitation parchment made by treating paper with sulfuric acid and water: also called **vegetable parchment.** **3** A formal writing on parchment. **4** A college graduation diploma. **5** A light-tan or cream color, the color of parchment. [< OF *parchemin* < LL *Pergamena* (*charta*) (paper) of Pergamum < Gk. *Pergamon* the city of Pergamum; because it was used there instead of papyrus]

par·don (pär′dən) *v.t.* **1** To remit the penalty of (a crime, insult, etc.). **2** To release from punishment; forgive for an offense. **3** To grant courteous allowance for or to: *Pardon* my French. —*n.* **1** The act of pardoning; remission of penalty incurred. **2** A waiving, by sovereign prerogative, of the execution of the penal sanctions of the violated law: distinguished from *justification.* **3** Courteous forbearance; acquittal of blame: used in making polite excuses. **4** *Law* Remission of guilt; also, an official warrant declaring the act of pardon. **5** An indulgence. [< OF *pardun* < *pardonner* < LL *perdonare* grant < *per-* through + *donare* give] —**par′don·a·ble** *adj.* —**par′don·a·bly** *adv.*

Synonyms (verb): absolve, acquit, condone, exculpate, excuse, forgive, overlook, release, remit. *Forgive* has reference to feelings, *pardon* to consequences; hence, the executive may *pardon,* but has nothing to do officially with *forgiving.* To *pardon* is the act of a superior, implying the right to punish; to *forgive* is the privilege of the humblest person who has been wronged or offended. In law, to *remit* the whole penalty is equivalent to *pardoning* the offender; but a part of a penalty may be *remitted* and the remainder inflicted, as where the penalty includes both fine and imprisonment. To *condone* is to put aside a recognized offense by some act which restores the offender to forfeited right or privilege, and is the act of a private individual, without legal formalities. To *excuse* is to *overlook* some slight offense, error, or breach of etiquette; *pardon* is often used by courtesy in nearly the same sense. Compare ABSOLVE, MERCY. *Antonyms:* castigate, chasten, chastise, condemn, convict, correct, doom, punish, recompense, scourge, sentence, visit.

Synonyms (noun): absolution, acquittal, amnesty, forbearance, forgiveness, mercy, oblivion, remission. *Acquittal* is a release from a charge, after trial, as not guilty. *Pardon* is a removal of penalty from one who has been adjudged guilty. *Acquittal* is the adjudging one to be not guilty, as by the decision of a court, commonly of a jury; *pardon* is the act of the executive. An innocent man may demand *acquittal,* and need not plead for *pardon. Oblivion* signifies overlooking and virtually forgetting an offense, so that the offender stands before the law in all respects as if it had never been committed. *Amnesty* conveys the same idea. *Pardon* affects individuals; *amnesty* and *oblivion* are said of great numbers. *Pardon* is oftenest applied to the ordinary administration of law; *amnesty* or *oblivion,* to national and military affairs. An *amnesty* is issued after war, insurrection, or rebellion. *Absolution* is a religious word (compare synonyms for ABSOLVE). *Remission* is a discharge from penalty; as, the *remission* of a fine. *Antonyms:* penalty, punishment, retaliation, retribution, vengeance.

par·don·er (pär′dən·ər) *n.* **1** One who pardons. **2** In the Middle Ages, a layman commissioned to collect offerings for which indulgences were promised.

pare (pâr) *v.t.* **pared, par·ing 1** To cut off the covering layer or part of. **2** To cut off or trim away (a covering layer or part): often with *off* or *away.* **3** To reduce or diminish, especially gradually or little by little. ◆ Homophone: **pair, pear.** [< F *parer* prepare, trim < L *parare*] —**par′er** *n.* —**par′ing** *adj. & n.*

pa·re·cious (pə·rē′shəs), etc. See PAROECIOUS, etc.

par·e·gor·ic (par′ə·gôr′ik, -gor′ik) n. 1 A medicine that assuages pain. 2 A camphorated tincture of opium. [< LL *paregoricus* < Gk. *parēgorikos, parēgoros* soothing < *para-* beside + *-agoros* speaking < *agora* assembly, market place]

par·ent (pâr′ənt) n. 1 A father or a mother. 2 Any organism that generates another; a producer. 3 Cause; occasion. [< OF < L *parens, -entis* parent, ancestor, orig. ppr. of *parere* beget]

par·ent·age (pâr′ən·tij) n. 1 The relation of parent to child, of producer to the produced. 2 Relation of cause to effect. 3 Descent or derivation from parents; extraction; lineage; origin. 4 Derivation from any source. 5 Parenthood.

pa·ren·tal (pə·ren′təl) adj. 1 Pertaining to or characteristic of a parent. 2 *Genetics* Pertaining to or designating that generation from whose crossbreeding hybrids are produced. —**pa·ren′tal·ly** adv.

par·en·ter·al (par·en′tər·əl) adj. Med. Pertaining to or designating a mode of assimilation other than through the alimentary canal, as intravenous or subcutaneous. [< Gk. *para-* beside + *enteron* intestine]

pa·ren·the·sis (pə·ren′thə·sis) n. pl. **·ses** (-sēz) 1 *Gram.* A word, phrase, or clause inserted in a sentence that is grammatically complete without it, separated usually by commas, dashes, or upright curves. 2 Either or both of the upright curves ( ) so used. 3 Hence, any intervening episode or incident; interval. [< Med. L < Gk. < *parentithenai* put in beside < *para-* beside + *en-* in + *tithenai* place]

pa·ren·the·size (pə·ren′thə·sīz) v.t. **·sized, ·siz·ing** 1 To insert as a parenthesis. 2 To insert parentheses in. 3 To place within parentheses (def. 2).

par·en·thet·i·cal (par′ən·thet′i·kəl) adj. 1 Pertaining to a parenthesis. 2 Abounding in parentheses. 3 Thrown in; episodical. Also **par′en·thet′ic.** —**par′en·thet′i·cal·ly** adv.

par·ent·hood (pâr′ənt·hood) n. The condition or relation of a parent.

par·ent·ing (pâr′ən·ting) n. The act or process of functioning as parents; the act or process of raising children.

pa·re·sis (pə·rē′sis, par′ə·sis) n. *Pathol.* Partial paralysis affecting muscular motion but not sensation. —**general paresis** General paralysis accompanied by dementia, caused by syphilitic degeneration of the brain. [< NL < Gk., a letting go < *parienai* let go < *para-* beside + *hienai* let go]

par·es·the·sia (par′is·thē′zhə, -zhē-ə) n. *Pathol.* Abnormal or perverted sense of touch; a sensation of itching, tingling, or prickling of the skin: also spelled *paraesthesia.* Also **par′es·the′sis.** —**par′es·thet′ic** (-thet′ik) adj.

pa·ret·ic (pə·ret′ik, -rē′tik) adj. Pertaining to or afflicted with paresis. —n. One who suffers from paresis. —**pa·ret′i·cal·ly** adv.

pa·re·ve (pär′ə·və) adj. Not made with milk or meat. [< Yiddish]

par ex·cel·lence (pär ek′sə·läns, *Fr.* pär ek·se·läns′) Of the highest excellence; beyond comparison; preeminently. [< F, by way of excellence]

par·fait (pär·fā′) n. A frozen dessert or confection made with eggs, sugar, whipped cream, and fruit or other flavoring. [< F, lit., perfect < L *perfectus.* See PERFECT.]

par·fleche (pär·flesh′) n. 1 Rawhide, usually of buffalo skin, which has been freed of hair and dried on a stretcher. 2 An article, as a shield, made from such a hide. Also **par·flesh′.** [< dial. F (Canadian) < F *par-* PARA-² + *flèche* an arrow]

par·get (pär′jit) n. 1 Gypsum. 2 Plaster suitable for lining chimneys. 3 Pargeting. —v.t. **·get·ed** or **·get·ted, ·get·ing** or **·get·ting** To cover or adorn with parget or pargeting. [Appar. < OF *pargeter, parjeter* throw over a surface < *par-* all over + *jeter* throw < L *per-* thoroughly + *jactare,* freq. of *jacere* throw]

par·get·ing (pär′jit·ing) n. 1 Plastering; specifically, ornamental stuccowork or plasterwork in relief. 2 Parget (def. 2).

par·he·lic circle (pär·hē′lik, -hel′ik) A band of light or halo, passing through the sun and parallel to the horizon: it is an effect of solar reflection from the vertical faces of ice crystals in the

atmosphere. Also **parhelic ring.**

par·he·li·on (pär·hē′lē·ən) n. pl. **·li·a** (-lē·ə) One of two bright solar images appearing on the parhelic circle on either side of the sun; a mock sun or sundog. Also **par·he′li·um.** [< L *parelion* < Gk. *parēlion* < *para-* beside + *hēlios* sun] —**par·he′lic, par·he·li·a·cal** (pär′hi·lī′ə·kəl) adj.

pari- *combining form* Equal: *parisyllabic.* [< L *par, paris* equal]

pa·ri·ah (pə·rī′ə, par′ē·ə) n. 1 One of low caste (but not lowest or outcast) people of southern India and Burma, employed as servants. 2 A person of low caste or no caste. 3 A social outcast. [< Tamil *paṛaiyar,* pl. of *paṛaiyon,* lit., (hereditary) drummer < *paṛai* a large festival drum]

pa·ri·es (pâr′i·ēz) n. pl. **pa·ri·e·tes** (pə·rī′ə·tēz) *Usually pl. Biol.* The wall of any cavity in the body, as of any organ. [< L, a wall]

pa·ri·e·tal (pə·rī′ə·təl) adj. 1 *Biol.* Of, pertaining to, or forming the walls of any cavity in the body. 2 Of or pertaining to a wall. 3 Pertaining to the care of or residence within walls or precincts, as of a college. 4 *Bot.* Pertaining to or borne on a wall: said especially of the placentae or ovules borne on the wall of the ovary of a plant. —n. 1 A parietal bone. 2 pl. *U.S.* the rules that govern dormitory visitation for members of the opposite sex.

pa·ril·lin (pə·ril′in) n. *Biochem.* A white crystalline saponin of variable composition, contained in sarsaparilla root, and to which the drug owes its medicinal qualities: often called *smilacin.* Also **pa·ril′lic acid** (pə·ril′ik). [< Sp. *parrilla,* dim. of *parra* a vine + -IN]

par·i·mu·tu·el (par′i·myōō′chōō·əl) n. 1 A system of betting at races in which those who have bet on the winners share in the total amount wagered: also **parimutuel.** 2 A machine for recording bets under this system; a totalisator. [< F, a stake or mutual wager]

par·ing (pâr′ing) n. 1 The act of cutting off the surface or edge of. 2 The part pared off.

par·is (par′is) n. The herb–Paris. [< L *pars, paris* equal; infl. by PARIS]

Par·is (par′is, *Fr.* pȧ·rē′) A port on the Seine, 111 miles from its mouth, and capital of France; ancient *Lutetia.*

Paris blue Prussian blue.

Paris green A poisonous compound prepared from copper acetate and arsenic trioxide, used largely as an insecticide and pigment.

par·ish (par′ish) n. 1 *Eccl.* In the Anglican, Roman Catholic, and some other churches, a district, usually part of a diocese, with its own church, and in charge of a priest or other clergyman. 2 *U.S.* a A religious congregation, comprising all those who worship at the same church. b The district in which they live. 3 *Brit.* A political subdivision of a county, often corresponding to an ecclesiastical parish. 4 In Louisiana, a civil district corresponding to a county. 5 The people of a parish, in any of the above senses. ◆ Collateral adjective: *parochial.* [< OF *paroche, paroisse* < LL *parochia* < Gk. *paroikia,* orig. a neighborhood, later a diocese < *para-* beside + *oikeein* dwell] —**pa·rish′ion·al** adj.

pa·rish·ion·er (pə·rish′ən·ər) n. A member of a parish.

Pa·ri·sian (pə·rizh′ən, -riz′ē·ən) adj. Of or pertaining to the city of Paris. —n. A native or resident of Paris.

par·i·syl·lab·ic (par′i·si·lab′ik) adj. Having the same number of syllables. Also **par′i·syl·lab′i·cal.**

par·i·ty¹ (par′ə·tē) n. 1 Equality, as of condition or rank; like state or degree; equivalent position; equal value. 2 The equivalence in legal weight and quality of the legal tender of one class of money to another. 3 Par (def. 1). 4 Equality between the currency or prices of commodities of two countries or cities. 5 Perfect analogy; close resemblance. 6 *U.S.* A level for farm prices which gives to the farmer the same purchasing power that he averaged during each year of a chosen base period, originally the five years of farm prosperity prior to World War I. 7 *Physics* That property of a wave whereby its function is symmetrically unchanged by inversion in a coordinate system (**even parity**), or changed only in sign (**odd parity**). See synonyms un-

der ANALOGY, SYMMETRY. [< L *paritas* equality < *pars* equal]

par·i·ty² (par′ə·tē) n. *Med.* Fitness or ability to bear offspring. [< L *parere* bear + -ITY]

par·i·vin·cu·lar (par′ə·ving′kyə·lər) adj. *Zool.* Designating a bivalve that has an elongated semicylindrical ligament. [< PARI- + VINCULUM]

park (pärk) n. 1 In English law, a tract of enclosed land stocked with wild beasts of the chase, and held through royal grant or by immemorial prescription. 2 A tract of land for public use in or near a city, usually laid out with walks, drives, and recreation grounds. 3 An open square or plaza in a city, usually containing shade trees and seats. 4 A large area of country containing natural curiosities reserved by the government for public enjoyment: a national *park.* 5 A plateaulike valley between mountain ranges: used most frequently in Colorado and Wyoming. 6 *Mil.* An enclosure where guns, trucks, wagons, animals, etc., are placed for safety; also, the objects thus enclosed: an artillery *park;* also, a complete train of cannon, including equipment, ammunition, gunners, etc., for an army in the field. —v.t. 1 To place or leave (an automobile, etc.) standing for a time, as on the street. 2 *U.S. Colloq.* To place; set: *Park* your hat on the table. 3 To assemble or mass together: to *park* artillery. 4 To enclose in or as in a park. —v.i. 5 To park an automobile, etc. [< OF *parc* a game preserve, ult. < Gmc. Akin to PADDOCK.]

par·ka (pär′kə) n. 1 An outer garment of undressed skins worn by Eskimos. 2 A similar woolen garment, sometimes fur-lined, with attached hood: worn for skiing and other winter sports. Also **par′kee** (-ke). [< Aleut]

HOODED PARKA

park·ing (pär′king) n. 1 Parks collectively, or ground resembling a park, as a strip of sward in a street. 2 The act of leaving a vehicle in a public place.

Par·kin·son's disease (pär′kin·sənz) *Pathol.* A chronic, progressive nervous disease characterized by muscle tremor when at rest, stiffness, and a rigid facial expression. Also **par′kin·son·ism** (-iz′əm). [after James *Parkinson,* 1755–1824, Eng. physician]

park·land (pärk′land′) n. *Often pl.* 1 Land used or designated for use as a park: federal *parklands;* urban *parkland.* 2 Grassland with trees, suitable for use as a park.

park·way (pärk′wā′) n. A wide thoroughfare adorned with turf and trees.

par·lance (pär′ləns) n. 1 Manner of speech; language; phrase: common *parlance,* legal *parlance.* 2 *Archaic* Talk; conversation. [< OF < *parler* speak < LL *parabolare* < *parabola.* See PARABLE.]

par·lan·do (pär·län′dō) adj. & adv. *Music* Declamatory in style; in recitative. Also **par·lan′te** (-ta). [< Ital. ppr. of *parlare* speak < LL *parabolare* < *parabola.* See PARABLE.]

par·lay (pär·lā′, pär′lē) v.t. & v.i. To place (an original bet and its winnings) on a later race, contest, etc. —n. Such a bet. [Alter. of earlier *paroli* < F < Ital., a grand cast at dice < *paro* equal < L *par*]

par·ley (pär′lē) n. 1 An oral conference, as with an enemy; a discussion of terms. 2 Mutual discourse. See synonyms under CONVERSATION. —v.i. To hold a conference, especially with an enemy. Also Obs. **parle** (pärl). [< F *parlée,* fem. pp. of *parler* speak < LL *parabolare* < *parabola.* See PARABLE.]

par·lia·ment (pär′lə·mənt) n. A meeting or assembly for consultation and deliberation; a legislative body; a national legislature, especially when composed of various estates. Also Obs. **par′le·ment.** [< OF *parlement* speaking < *parler* speak < LL *parabolare* < *parabola.* See PARABLE.]

Par·lia·ment (pär′lə·mənt) n. 1 The supreme legislature of Great Britain and Northern Ireland, composed of the three estates of the realm—the Lords Spiritual, the Lords Temporal, and the Commons—together with, in a strict legal sense, the sovereign. 2 The legislature in any of Great Britain's self-governing colonies or dominions. 3 In France, before the French Revolution, one of several tribunals of justice. **4** The legislative assembly of Scotland until 1707, or that of Ireland until 1800. — **Long Parliament** The British Parliament which first assembled in 1640 and finally dissolved by its own consent in 1660: after the enforced expulsion *(Pride's Purge)* of some of its members in 1648, it was known as the **Rump Parliament.**

par·lia·men·tar·i·an·ism (pär′lə·men·târ′e·ən·iz′əm) *n.* The system of government, developed in England, in which the tenure of the cabinet is dependent on the will of the majority in the lower house: also called **parliamentary system.**

par·lia·men·ta·ry (pär′lə·men′tər·e) *adj.* **1** Pertaining to, characterized by, or enacted by a parliament. **2** According to the rules of Parliament; admissible in a deliberative assembly. — **par′lia·men·tar′i·an** *adj. & n.*

par·lor (pär′lər) *n.* **1** A room for reception of callers or entertainment of guests; drawing-room. **2** A room in an inn, hotel, etc., for private conversation, appointments, etc. **3** *U.S.* Formerly, a smartly furnished room for the performance of personal or professional services: a tonsorial *parlor*: a genteelism. Also *Brit.* **par′lour.** [< AF *parlur*, OF *parleor* < Med. L *parlatorium* < *parlare* < LL *parabolare* speak < *parabola.* See PARABLE.]

Parmesan cheese A hard, dry cheese, originally made in Parma: usually grated and served on soups, spaghetti, etc.

par·mi·gia·na (pär′mə·jä′nə) *adj.* Cooked with Parmesan cheese.

pa·ro·chi·al (pə·rō′ke·əl) *adj.* **1** Pertaining to, supported by, or confined to a parish. **2** Hence, narrow; provincial; restricted in scope: *parochial* ideas. [< OF < LL *parochialis* < *parochia.* See PARISH.]

pa·ro·chi·al·ism (pə·rō′ke·əl·iz′əm) *n.* **1** Government or control by a vestry or parochial board. **2** Narrow of view; provincialism.

parochial school See under SCHOOL.

par·o·dy (par′ə·de) *n. pl.* **·dies 1** A literary composition imitating and ridiculing some serious work; a comical imitation, especially of a poem; a travesty. **2** Any burlesque imitation of something serious. **3** A poor imitation. See synonyms under CARICATURE. — *v.t.* **·died, ·dy·ing** To make a parody of; travesty. [< Gk. *parōidia* a burlesque poem or song < *para-* beside + *oide* a song, poem] — **pa·rod·ic** (pə·rod′ik) or **·i·cal** *adj.* — **par′o·dist** *n.*

pa·roe·cious (pə·re′shəs) *adj. Bot.* Having the male and female sexual organs of plants developed side by side or in the same inflorescence, as in many bryophytes: also spelled *parecious.* Also **pa·roi′cous.** [< Gk. *paroikos* dwelling side by side < *paroikeein* < *para-* beside + *oikeein* dwell] — **pa·roe′cious·ly** *adv.* — **pa·roe′cious·ness** *n.* — **pa·roe′cism** (-siz·əm) *n.*

pa·rol (pə·rōl′) *Law n.* **1** Something spoken or said; specifically, in the legal phrase **by parol,** by word of mouth. **2** The pleadings filed in an action. — *adj.* **1** Given or expressed by word of mouth; oral. **2** Written but not under seal. Also **pa·role′.** [< AF, var. of OF *parole* < L *parabola* word. See PARABLE.]

pa·role (pə·rōl′) *n.* **1** A pledge of honor by a prisoner of war that he will not seek to escape or will not serve against his captors until exchanged; also, the condition of being under parole. **2** The release of a prisoner from jail prior to the expiration of his term on his own recognizance. **3** The watchword used only by officers of the guard and of the day: distinguished from *countersign.* **4** *Law* Parol. **5** Word of honor. — *v.t.* **·roled, ·rol·ing** To release (a prisoner) on parole. [< F *parole (d'honneur)* word (of honor) < OF < L *parabola.* Doublet of PALAVER, PARABLE, PARABOLA.]

par·o·no·ma·si·a (par′ə·nō·mā′zhē·ə, -zē·ə) *n.* Any use for effect of words similar in sound, but differing in meaning; a play on words, especially one in which the similarity of sound is the prominent characteristic. Compare PUN. [< L < Gk. *paronomazein* alter slightly in meaning < *para-* beside + *onoma* name] — **par′o·no·ma′si·al, par′o·no·mas′tic** (-mas′tik) or **·ti·cal** *adj.* — **par′o·no·mas′ti·cal·ly** *adv.*

par·o·nym (par′ə·nim) *n.* A word having the same root as another; a cognate word. [< Gk. *parōnymon,* orig. neut. of *paronymos* derivative < *para-* beside < *onyma,* Aeolic var. of *onoma* name] — **pa·ron·y·mous** (pə·ron′ə·məs), **par′o·nym′ic** (-nim′ik) *adj.*

par·o·quet (par′ə·ket) See PARAKEET.

par·o·ral (par·ôr′əl, -ō′rəl) *adj.* Adjacent to the mouth or oral region.

pa·rot·ic (pə·rot′ik, -rō′tik) *adj.* Situated near the ear: the *parotic* region. [< NL *paroticus* < Gk. *para-* beside + *otikos* of the ear < *ous, ōtos* ear]

pa·rot·id (pə·rot′id) *Anat. adj.* **1** Situated near the ear. **2** Designating one of the paired salivary glands in front of and below the external ear in mammals. — *n.* A salivary gland below the ear. [< F *parotide* < L *parotis, -idis* < Gk. *parōtis, -idos* a tumor near the ear < *para-* beside + *ous, ōtos* ear]

par·o·ti·tis (par′ə·tī′tis) *n. Pathol.* Inflammation and swelling of the parotid gland; mumps. Also **par′o·ti·di′tis** (-ti·dī′tis). — **par′o·tit′ic** (-tit′ik) *adj.*

pa·ro·toid (pə·rō′toid) *Biol. adj.* **1** Resembling a parotid gland. **2** Designating a cutaneous gland situated behind the eye and above the tympanum in anurous amphibians. — *n.* A parotoid gland.

-parous *suffix* Giving birth to; bearing; producing: *oviparous.* [< L *-parus* < *parere* beget]

par·ox·ysm (par′ək·siz′əm) *n.* **1** *Pathol.* A periodic attack of disease; a fit. **2** Sudden and violent excitement or emotion, as of anger. **3** A convulsion of any kind. See synonyms under AGONY, PAIN. [< MF *paroxysme* < Med. L *paroxysmus* irritation < Gk. *paroxysmos* < *paroxynein* goad < *para-* beside, beyond + *oxynein* goad < *oxys* sharp]

par·ox·ys·mal (par′ək·siz′məl) *adj.* **1** Relating to, of the nature of, accompanied or characterized by a paroxysm. **2** Resulting from convulsive action of natural forces, as a volcanic eruption, flood, etc. Also **par′ox·ys′mic.** — **par′ox·ys′mal·ly** *adv.*

par·quet (pär·kā′, -ket′) *n.* **1** The main-floor space behind the orchestra of a theater; sometimes, the whole lower floor. **2** Parquetry. — *v.t.* **·queted** (-kād′, -ket′id), **·quet·ing** (-kā′ing, -ket′ing) To make of or ornament with parquetry. Also **par·quette** (pär·ket′). [< F < OF *parchet* a small compartment, dim. of *parc.* See PARK.]

par·quet·ry (pär′kit·rē) *n.* Wooden mosaic, used especially for floor surfaces. [< F *parqueterie*]

parr (pär) *n.* A young salmon before its first migration seaward. [? < dial. E (Scottish)]

par·ra·keet (par′ə·kēt), **par·ra·kee·to** (-tō) See PARAKEET.

par·rel (par′əl) *n.* **1** A chimneypiece or the ornaments of a chimneypiece collectively. **2** *Naut.* A sliding hoop, rope, or chain by which a yard is attached to a mast. Also **par′·ral.** [ME *parail,* aphetic var. of *aparail* equipment. See APPAREL.]

par·ri·cide (par′ə·sīd) *n.* **1** The murder of a parent, or of an ancestor. **2** One who has committed such a crime. [< F < L *paricidium* a killing of a relative, and *paricida* a killer of a relative] — **par′ri·ci′dal** *adj.* — **par′ri·ci′dal·ly** *adv.*

par·ro·quet (par′ə·ket) See PARAKEET.

par·rot (par′ət) *n.* **1** Any of certain birds of warm regions of the order *Psittaciformes,* having a hooked bill, paired toes, and usually brilliant plumage, including the macaws, parakeets, cockatoos, lories, and related genera. Some parrots are noted for their ability to simulate human laughter and speech. ◆ Collateral adjective: *psittacine.* **2** A person who repeats or imitates without understanding. — *v.t.* To repeat or imitate by rote or without understanding. [? < F *perrot,* var. of *Pierrot,* dim. of *Pierre* Peter, a personal name] — **par′rot·er** *n.*

parrot fish 1 Any of many small fishes of the family *Scaridae,* inhabiting warm seas: so called from their vivid coloring and beaklike jaws. **2** A labroid fish of the genus *Labrichthys,* especially the parrot perch (*L. psittacula*) of Australasia.

par·ry (par′ē) *v.* **·ried, ·ry·ing** *v.t.* **1** To ward off, as a thrust in fencing. **2** To avoid or evade. — *v.i.* **3** To make a parry. — *n. pl.* **·ries 1** A defensive movement, as in fencing. **2** An evasion or diversion in a contest of wits. [Prob. < F *parez,* imperative of *parer* ward off < Ital. *parare* defend < L, prepare]

parse (pärs) *v.t.* **parsed, pars·ing 1** To describe (a sentence) grammatically by giving the form, function, etc., of each of its components. **2** To describe (a word) as to its part of speech, form, and relation to the other elements in a sentence. [Prob. < L *pars, partis* part] — **pars′er** *n.*

par·sec (pär′sek) *n. Astron.* A unit of length used in expressing the distance of stars. One parsec is almost exactly 206,265 times the mean distance of the earth from the sun, or 19.2 trillion miles, or 3.26 light years. A star is at a distance of one parsec from the earth if its annual parallax amounts to one second of arc (1″). [< PAR(ALLAX) + SEC(OND) (def. 2)]

par·si·mo·ni·ous (pär′sə·mō′ne·əs) *adj.* Niggardly; penurious. See synonyms under AVARICIOUS, SCANTY. — **par′si·mo′ni·ous·ly** *adv.* — **par′si·mo·ni·ous·ness** *n.*

par·si·mo·ny (pär′sə·mō′ne) *n.* Undue sparingness in the expenditure of money; stinginess. See synonyms under FRUGALITY. [< L *parsimonia* < *parcere* spare]

pars·ley (pärs′lē) *n.* A common umbelliferous herb (*Petroselinum latifolium* or *crispum*) with aromatic, finely divided leaves and greenish-yellow flowers, used as a garnish and for flavoring soups. [Fusion of OF *peresil* and OE *petersilige,* both < LL *petrosilium,* alter. of L *petroselinum* < Gk. *petroselinon* < *petra* rock + *selinon* parsley]

pars·nip (pärs′nip) *n.* A European herb (*Pastinaca sativa*) of the parsley family, with a large, sweetish, edible root, widely cultivated as a vegetable and as fodder. The root of the wild plant is acrid and poisonous. [Alter. of ME *passenep,* ? < OF *pasnaie* < L *pastinaca* < *pastinare* dig up; infl. in form by OE *næp* turnip < L *napus*]

par·son (pär′sən) *n.* **1** The clergyman of a parish or congregation; a minister. **2** Specifically, a beneficed clergyman of the Anglican Church, having full charge of a parish; a rector. [< OF *persone* < Med. L *persona* a rector. Doublet of PERSON.] — **par·son·i·cal** (pär·son′i·kəl), **par·son′ic** *adj.*

par·son·age (pär′sən·ij) *n.* **1** A clergyman's dwelling, especially a free official residence provided for a pastor; in England, a rectory. **2** *Scot.* A tax paid for the maintenance of a parson. **3** The benefice of a parson.

par·son's-nose (pär′sənz-nōz′) *n. Colloq.* The rump of a fowl: also called *pope's-nose.*

part (pärt) *n.* **1** A certain portion or amount of anything; a piece; segment; fraction. **2** *Math.* One of certain fractional portions or components of a thing; an aliquot division; a submultiple: a fifth *part.* **3** An essential portion of a body or an organism; a member. **4** *Usually pl.* A portion of territory; region; quarter: in foreign *parts.* **5** So much as is allotted or belongs to one; an individual share, as of duty, business, or performance: If he'll do his *part,* we'll win. **6** The role or lines assigned to an actor in a play; occasionally, a role played in actual life. **7** A side, cause, or party opposed to another. **8** *Usually pl.* A component or quality of mind or character; talent; intellectual gift or faculty: That man is a person of *parts.* **9** The melody intended for a single voice or instrument in a concerted piece; also, the written or printed copy for the performer's use. **10** A section of a book, poem, or play; also, a portion of a literary work issued at intervals, at a fixed price. **11** A parting or division of the hair. — **for my part** As far as I am concerned. — **in good** (or **ill**) **part** With a good (or a bad) grace. — **in part** Partly. — **part and parcel** An essential part: an emphatic phrase. — **principal part** One of the inflected forms of a verb from which all other inflected forms may be derived. In English, the principal parts of a verb are the infinitive (*go, walk*), the past tense (*went, walked*), and the past participle (*gone, walked*). In this dictionary, the past, past participle, and present participle are shown (*gave, given, giving*); in cases where the past tense and past participle are identical, only the one is shown (*behaved, behaving*). — **to take part** To participate; share or cooperate: usually with *in*. — **to take someone's part** To support someone in a contest or disagreement; side with someone. — *v.t.* **1** To divide or break (something) into parts. **2** To sever or discontinue (a relationship or connection): to *part* company. **3** To separate by being or coming between; keep or move apart: The referee *parted* the two men. **4** To comb (the hair) so as to leave a dividing line on the sides or elsewhere on the scalp. **5** To separate (mingled substances) chemically or mechanically: to *part* gold and silver. **6** *Archaic* To divide into shares or portions. **7** *Obs.* To depart from; leave. — *v.i.* **8** To become divided or broken into parts; come apart; divide. **9** To go away from each other; cease associating; separate. **10** To depart; leave. — **to part from** To separate from; leave. — **to part with 1** To give up; relinquish. **2** To part from. — *adv.* In some degree; to some extent; partly. [<OF <L *pars, partis* part] — *Synonyms (noun)*: atom, component, constituent, division, element, fraction, fragment, ingredient, member, particle, piece, portion, section, segment, share, subdivision. *Part* is the general word, including all the others. A *fragment* is the result of breaking, rending, or disruption of some kind, while a *piece* may be smoothly or evenly separated and have completeness in itself. *Division* and *fraction* are always regarded as in connection with the total; *divisions* may be equal or unequal; a *fraction* is one of several equal *parts* into which the whole is supposed to be divided. A *portion* is a *part* viewed with reference to some one who is to receive it or some special purpose to which it is to be applied; a *share* is a *part* to which one has or may acquire a right in connection with others; a *particle* is an exceedingly small *part*. A *component, constituent, ingredient*, or *element* is a *part* of some compound or mixture; an *element* is necessary to the existence, as a *component* or *constituent* is necessary to the completeness of that which it helps to compose; an *ingredient* may be foreign or accidental. A *subdivision* is a *division* of a *division*. We speak of a *segment* of a circle. Compare BRANCH, PARTICLE, PIECE, PORTION. *Antonyms*: see synonyms for AGGREGATE.

par·take (pär·tāk′) *v.* **·took, ·tak·en, ·tak·ing** *v.i.* **1** To take part or have a share; participate: with *in*. **2** To receive or take a portion or share: with *of*. **3** To have something of the quality or character; bear a trace: with *of*: replies *partaking* of insolence. — *v.t.* **4** To take or have a part in; share. [Back formation < *partaker*, var. of *part–taker*, trans. of L *participes* < *pars, partis* a part + *capere* take] — **par·tak′er** *n.*

part·ed (pär′tid) *adj.* **1** Situated or placed apart; separated; cloven. **2** *Bot.* Cut almost but not quite to the base, as certain leaves. **3** Having or divided into parts. **4** *Archaic* Departed; dead.

Par·the·non (pär′thə·non) The Doric temple of Athena Parthenos on the Acropolis at Athens, now largely in ruins; built under the supervision of Phidias during the administration of Pericles, and dedicated 438 B.C.

THE PARTHENON
Temple of Athena, on the Acropolis at Athens, representative of classical Greek architectural style.

par·tial (pär′shəl) *adj.* **1** Pertaining to, constituting, or involving a part only. **2** Favoring one side; prejudiced; biased. **3** Having a special liking: usually with *to*. [<OF *parcial*

<LL *partialis* <L *pars, partis* a part] — **par′tial·ly** *adv.*

partial fraction See under FRACTION.

par·ti·al·i·ty (pär′shē·al′ə·tē) *n.* **1** The state of being partial. **2** Unfairness; bias. **3** A particular fondness; predilection. Also **par′tial·ness** (-shəl·nis). See synonyms under RELISH.

partial tone *Music* A harmonic. — **upper partial tone** An overtone or harmonic; one of the accessory tones generated by the fundamental.

par·tic·i·pate (pär·tis′ə·pāt) *v.* **·pat·ed, ·pat·ing** *v.i.* **1** To take part or have a share in common with others; partake: with *in*. — *v.t.* **2** *Rare* To partake of. [<L *participatus*, pp. of *participare* < *particeps, -cipis* a partaker < *pars, partis* a part + *capere* take] — **par·tic′i·pa′tion** *n.* — **par·tic′i·pa′tor** *n.*

par·tic·i·pa·to·ry (pär·tis′ə·pə·tôr′ē, -tō′rē) *adj.* Based on or involving participation, especially active, voluntary participation in a political system.

par·ti·ci·ple (pär′tə·sip′əl) *n. Gram.* A verbal derivative that may function as both a verb and an adjective. The **present participle** ends in *-ing* and the **past participle** commonly in *-d, -ed, -en, -n,* or *-t.* — **dangling participle** A participle that modifies the wrong substantive, as in "*Opening* the door, the *room* looked large" instead of "*Opening* the door, *I* saw that the room looked large." [<OF, var. of *participe* <L *participium* a sharing, partaking < *participare.* See PARTICIPATE.]

par·ti·cle (pär′ti·kəl) *n.* **1** A minute part, piece, or portion of matter. **2** Any very small amount or slight degree: without a *particle* of truth. **3** *Physics* One of the elementary components of an atom, as an electron, proton, neutron, meson, etc. **4** *Gram.* **a** A short, uninflected part of speech, as a preposition, an interjection, an article, and especially a conjunction. **b** A prefix or suffix. **c** A small part of a sentence or composition, as a clause. **5** In the Roman Catholic Church, the small Host used for lay communicants; also, a fragment of a consecrated Host. [<L *particula*, dim. of *pars, partis* a part] — *Synonyms*: atom, element, grain, iota, jot, mite, moleculé, scintilla, scrap, shred, tittle, whit. A *particle* is a very small part of any material substance; as, a *particle* of sand or dust; it is a general term, not accurately determinate in meaning. *Atom* etymologically signifies that which cannot be cut or divided, and was formerly considered the smallest conceivable *particle* of matter, regarded as absolutely homogeneous and as having but one set of properties. A *molecule* is made up of *atoms*, and is regarded as separable into its constituent parts. *Element* in chemistry denotes, without reference to quantity, a substance regarded as simple, that is, one incapable of being resolved into simpler substances without losing its specific physico-chemical properties; the *element* gold may be represented by an ingot or by a *particle* of gold dust. In popular language, an *element* is any essential constituent; the ancients believed that the universe was made up of the four *elements*, earth, air, fire, and water; a storm is spoken of as a manifestation of the fury of the *elements*. Compare synonyms for PART. *Antonyms*: aggregate, entirety, mass, quantity, sum, total, whole.

par·tic·u·lar (pər·tik′yə·lər) *adj.* **1** Specifying or comprising a part; separate: a *particular* act. **2** Peculiar or pertaining to a specified person, thing, time, or place; not common or general; private; specific: my *particular* hobby. **3** Specially noteworthy: of *particular* importance. **4** Comprising all details or circumstances; circumstantial: a *particular* description. **5** Marked by, requiring, or giving minute attention; exact in performance or requirement; precise; also, nice in taste; fastidious: *particular* in dress. **6** *Law* Separate or separable; being apart from others; special; limited; part. **7** *Logic* Including some, not all, of a class: opposed to *subalternant* or *universal*: "Some trees are oaks" is a *particular* proposition. — *n.* **1** A separate matter or item, as of a class or number. **2** An individual instance; a single or separate case; a given fact that may be brought under or be the ground of a generalization. [<OF *particulier* <L *particularis* concerning a part

< *particula.* See PARTICLE.] — *Synonyms (adj.)*: accurate, appropriate, characteristic, circumstantial, definite, detailed, distinct, distinctive, especial, exact, individual, peculiar, separate, single, special. See MINUTE[2], PRECISE, SQUEAMISH.

par·tic·u·lar·ism (pər·tik′yə·lə·riz′əm) *n.* **1** Exclusive attachment to the interests of one's particular state, party, people, or religion. **2** Care or regard for particulars; attention to details. **3** The theological doctrine of the election of particular individuals to grace and salvation; particular election. — **par·tic′u·lar·ist** *n.* — **par·tic′u·lar·is′tic** *adj.*

par·tic·u·lar·i·ty (pər·tik′yə·lar′ə·tē) *n. pl.* **·ties 1** The state, character, or quality of being particular; exactitude in description; circumstantiality; strict or careful attention to detail; fastidiousness. **2** Something that is particular; a circumstance or detail; also, a characteristic; peculiarity.

par·tic·u·lar·ize (pər·tik′yə·lə·rīz′) *v.* **·ized, ·iz·ing** *v.t.* To speak of or treat individually or in detail. — *v.i.* To give particulars; be specific. — **par·tic′u·lar·i·za′tion** *n.* — **par·tic′u·lar·iz′er** *n.*

par·tic·u·lar·ly (pər·tik′yə·lər·lē) *adv.* **1** With specific reference; distinctly: a fact *particularly* mentioned. **2** In an unusually great degree; in an especial manner: *particularly* difficult. **3** Part by part; in detail. **4** Severally; personally.

part·ing (pär′ting) *adj.* **1** Of or pertaining to a parting or going away, often in death. **2** Departing; declining. **3** Capable of being parted. **4** Separating; severing; dividing. — *n.* **1** The act of separating, or the state of being separated; division. **2** A leave–taking; a departure; especially, a final separation. **3** *Metall.* The separation of metals in an alloy; specifically, the separation of gold and silver by acid in assaying. **4** A place, line, or surface of separation or division. **5** Something that parts or separates.

parting strip A strip or piece of thin wood or metal separating contiguous parts.

par·ti·san (pär′tə·zən) *adj.* **1** Relating to or unreasonably devoted to a party or faction. **2** Pertaining to or carried on by partisans or irregular troops. — *n.* **1** An adherent and upholder of an individual or of a party or cause; especially, a blind or fanatical adherent or devotee. **2** A member of a body of detached or irregular troops; a guerilla. See synonyms under ADHERENT. Also **par′ti·zan.** [<F <Ital. *partigiano, partisano* < *parte* a part <L *pars, partis*] — **par′ti·san·ship** *n.*

par·tite (pär′tīt) *adj.* **1** Divided into or composed of parts: used in composition: *bipartite, tripartite.* **2** *Bot.* Cleft nearly to the base, as a leaf. [<L *partitus*, pp. of *partire* divide]

par·ti·tion (pär·tish′ən) *n.* **1** Division; separation. **2** A dividing line or boundary. **3** A wall or other barrier dividing one part or apartment from another. **4** An internal wall separating cells or cavities. **5** *Law* The division of property, especially of lands, among co–owners, either by agreement or by judicial decree; also, the dividing of lands held by tenants in common into separate parcels, so that they may be held in severalty. **6** *Math.* The representation of a positive whole number as the sum of whole numbers in all possible ways; also, any one of such ways. **7** *Logic* **a** The form of analysis that systematically unfolds the properties or attributes of a concept. **b** The process of explanation that exhibits the theme by means of its attributes. **8** A compartment; apartment; department; division. — *v.t.* **1** To divide into parts, segments, etc. **2** To separate by a partition: with *off*. **3** To divide, as property, into shares or portions; apportion. [<OF *particion* <L *partitio, -onis* < *partire* divide] — **par·ti′tion·er** *n.*

par·ti·tion·ment (pär·tish′ən·mənt) *n.* **1** The act of partitioning, as property. **2** A compartment; partition.

par·ti·tive (pär′tə·tiv) *adj.* **1** Separating into integral parts or into distinct divisions. **2** *Gram.* Denoting a part as distinct from the whole. Example: *Of* them is the *partitive* genitive in the sentences "Many of them were there" and "They couldn't do it for the life of them." — *n. Gram.* A partitive word or case. [<F *partitif* <L *partitivus* < *partitus*, pp. of *partire* divide] — **par'ti·tive·ly** *adv.*

part·let (pärt'lit) *n.* A garment, frequently ruffled, covering the throat and bust, worn, especially by women, in the 16th century. [Var. of obs. *patlet* <OF *patelette* band of stuff, dim. of *pat* paw, flap]

part·ly (pärt'lē) *adv.* In some part; in some degree; partially.

part music Music with two or more melodies written in harmony and sung or played by two or more performers: said especially of vocal music.

part·ner (pärt'nər) *n.* **1** One who takes part or is associated with another or others; a sharer. **2** One of two or more persons associated by contract for the carrying on of a commercial, manufacturing, or other undertaking with their joint capital, labor, or skill. **3** One of two persons united in some enterprise, as marriage, a dance, or a game. **4** *pl. Naut.* Framing pieces surrounding a mast to strengthen and relieve the deck from strain. See synonyms under ACCESSORY, ASSOCIATE. — **secret** or **sleeping partner** One who is inactive and unknown in the business. — **silent partner** Strictly, one who is inactive, though he may be known to be a partner. The terms *silent partner* and *dormant partner* are often interchanged. — *v.t.* **1** To make a partner or partners. **2** To be or act as the partner of. [Var. of PARCENER; infl. by PART]

part·ner·ship (pärt'nər·ship) *n.* **1** The state of being a partner or partners; joint interests or ownership; also, the group of persons so associated. **2** *Law* An association founded on a contract between two or more persons to combine their money, effects, labor, or skill, or any or all of them, in lawful commerce or business, and to share the profit and bear the loss in certain proportions; a co–partnership. **3** Fellowship (def. 6). See synonyms under ALLIANCE, ASSOCIATION.

part of speech One of the eight traditional classes of words in English; namely: noun, pronoun, verb, adjective, adverb, conjunction, preposition, and interjection.

par·took (pär·took') Past tense of PARTAKE.

par·tridge (pär'trij) *n.* **1** Any of certain small, plump-bodied, Old World, gallinaceous game birds of genera *Perdix, Alectoris* (synonym *Caccabis*), etc. **2** Any of certain other similar birds, often so called, as the ruffed grouse of the northern United States and the bobwhite of the South. Compare QUAIL[1]. **3** A tinamou of the South American pampas. [<OF *perdriz*, var. of *perdiz* <L *perdix, -icis* <Gk. *perdix, -ikos* a partridge]

PARTRIDGE
(The ruffed grouse;
16 to 18 inches in length)

partridge hawk The goshawk: also called *dove hawk.*

part song A song composed of three or more parts; specifically, a secular choral piece without accompaniment.

par·tu·ri·ent (pär·tyoor'ē·ənt, -toor'-) *adj.* Bringing forth or about to bring forth young; pertaining to childbirth: used also figuratively of plans, ideas, etc. [<L *parturiens, -entis,* ppr. of *parturire* be in labor, desiderative of *parere* bring forth] — **par·tu'ri·en·cy** *n.*

par·tu·ri·fa·cient (pär·tyoor'ə·fā'shənt, -toor'-) *Med. adj.* Promoting parturition. — *n.* A medicine promotive of parturition. [<L *parturire* be in labor + -FACIENT]

par·tu·ri·tion (pär'tyoo·rish'ən, -choo-) *n.* The act of bringing forth young; delivery; childbirth. [<L *parturitio, -onis* <*parturire* be in labor]

par·ty (pär'tē) *n. pl.* **·ties** **1** A body of persons united for some common purpose, as political ascendency; a political organization; also, partisanship. **2** A social company or gathering: a tea *party.* **3** *Mil.* A small company or detachment of soldiers: a firing *party.* **4** *Law*

One of the persons named on the record in an action either as plaintiff or defendant; a person interested, as in a contract, deed, suit, etc.: a *party* to a suit. **5** One concerned in or privy to a matter: He was a *party* to the affair. **6** *Colloq.* A person. **7** *Obs.* A cause or interest; side. See synonyms under SECT. — *adj.* **1** Of or pertaining to a political party: *party* platforms. **2** Divided into or consisting of parts, or of different parties; composite. **3** *Her.* Divided; parted: said of a shield. [<OF *partie*, orig., fem. pp. of *partir* divide <L *partire* <*pars, partis* a part]

par·ty–col·ored (pär'tē·kul'ərd) See PARTI-COLORED.

party line **1** A telephone line or circuit serving two or more subscribers: also **party wire.** **2** A boundary line between the properties of two or more owners. **3** A belief or principle of a political party regarded as an essential conviction of every loyal member.

par·ve·nu (pär'və·noo, -nyoo) *n.* One who has suddenly attained wealth or position beyond his birth or worth, as by accident of fortune; an upstart. — *adj.* **1** Being a parvenu. **2** Like or characteristic of a parvenu. [<F, orig., pp. of *parvenir* arrive <L *pervenire*]

par·vis (pär'vis) *n.* **1** An enclosed or raised area in front of a church. **2** A portico or colonnade before a church. [<F <L *paradisum* paradise; later, the court in front of St. Peter's, Rome]

pas (pä) *n.* **1** A step. **2** A dance. **3** Right of going before; precedence. [<F, a step]

pas·chal (pas'kəl) *adj.* Pertaining to the Jewish Passover or to Easter: *paschal* sacrifice. — *n.* **1** A paschal candle or candlestick. **2** The celebration of the Passover; also, the paschal lamb; the paschal supper. [<OF *pascal* <LL *paschalis* <L *pascha* PASCH]

paschal flower The pasqueflower.

paschal lamb The lamb eaten at the feast of the Passover.

Paschal Lamb Jesus Christ.

pas de deux (pä də dœ') *French* A dance or ballet figure for two persons.

pa·sha (pə·shä', pash'ə, pä'shə) *n.* A Turkish honorary title placed after the name, formerly given to generals, governors of provinces, etc.: also spelled *pacha.* [<Turkish *pāshā* <*bāsh* head]

pa·sha·lik (pə·shä'lik) *n.* The province or jurisdiction of a pasha: also spelled *pachalic.* Also **pa·sha'lic.** [<Turkish *pāshālik*]

pasque·flow·er (pask'flou'ər) *n.* Any of several plants (genus *Anemone*) with showy white, red, or purple flowers, blooming about Easter; especially, the daneflower or campana (*A. pulsatilla*) of the Old World, or *A. ludoviciana,* the State flower of South Dakota. Also **pasch'flow'er.** [Earlier *passeflower* <F *passefleur* <*passer* excel + *fleur* flower; infl. in form by F *pasque* Easter]

pas·quin (pas'kwin) *n.* **1** A pasquinade. **2** A pasquinader. [<Ital. *pasquino*, orig., a disinterred statue at Rome on which satirical verses were pasted]

pas·quin·ade (pas'kwin·ād') *n.* An abusive or coarse personal satire posted in a public place; a malicious squib. — *v.t.* **·ad·ed, ·ad·ing** To attack or ridicule in pasquinades; lampoon. — **pas'quin·ad'er** *n.*

pass (pas, päs) *v.* **passed** (*Rare* past), **passed** or **past, pass·ing** *v.t.* **1** To go by or move past and leave behind. **2** To go across, around, over, or through. **3** To permit to go unnoticed or unmentioned. **4** To undergo; experience: to *pass* a bad night. **5** To undergo successfully, as a test; meet the requirements of. **6** To go beyond or exceed; surpass: It *passes* comprehension. **7** To cause to go or move: to *pass* one's eyes over a book; to *pass* a rope through a pulley. **8** To cause to go or move past: to *pass* troops in review. **9** To cause or allow to advance or proceed: They *passed* him through their ranks. **10** To cause or allow to elapse; spend: to *pass* the night at an inn. **11** To give approval to; sanction; allow. **12** To enact, as a law. **13** To be approved by: The bill *passed* the senate. **14** To omit paying (a dividend). **15** To cause to go from person to person; put in circulation; transmit: *Pass* the word.

16 To utter or pronounce, especially judicially, as judgment or sentence. **17** To excrete (waste). **18** To pledge, as one's word. **19** To perform a pass (*n.* def. 5) on or over. **20** In sports, to transfer (the ball, etc.) to another player on the same side. **21** *Law* To transfer or assign ownership of to another by will, deed, etc. — *v.i.* **22** To go or proceed; move. **23** To have course or direction; extend: The road *passed* under a bridge. **24** To go away; depart. **25** To come to an end; disappear. **26** To elapse or go by; be spent: The day *passed* slowly. **27** To die. **28** To go by; move past in or-as in review. **29** To go from person to person; obtain currency; circulate. **30** To be mutually given and received, as greetings or recriminations. **31** To go or change from one condition, circumstance, etc., to another; alter: to *pass* from hot to cold. **32** To take place; happen; occur. **33** To be allowed or tolerated; go unheeded or unpunished. **34** To undergo a test, examination, etc., successfully; meet the requirements. **35** To be approved, ratified, enacted, etc. **36** To obtain or force passage; make a way: They shall not *pass!* **37** To be excreted or voided. **38** *Law* **a** To give or pronounce judgment, sentence, etc.: with *on* or *upon.* **b** To sit in inquest: with *on* or *upon.* **c** To adjudicate: with *between.* **d** To be transferred or assigned to another by will, deed, etc. **39** In sports, to transfer the ball, etc., to another player on the same side. **40** In fencing, to make a pass or thrust; lunge. **41** In card games, to decline to make a play, bid, etc. — **to pass away** **1** To come to an end; disappear. **2** To die. **3** To allow (time) to elapse. — **to pass for** To be accepted as, usually incorrectly. — **to pass off** **1** To come to an end; disappear. **2** To give out or circulate as genuine; palm off. **3** To be emitted, as a vapor. — **to pass out** **1** To distribute. **2** *Colloq.* To faint. — **to pass over** To fail to notice or consider. — **to pass up** *Colloq.* To reject or fail to take advantage of, as an offer or opportunity. — *n.* **1** A way or opening that affords a passage; a place through which one can pass; a gap in a mountain range through which a road may be or has been made; a defile; waterway. **2** Permission or a permit to pass; a ticket; passport: a *pass* through an army's lines. **3** A state of affairs; crisis. **4** The successful undergoing of an examination, test, or inspection; in a university, a degree gained without honors. **5** A movement of a hand, wand, or the like, as in mesmeric manipulation; transference of objects in sleight–of–hand tricks, magic, etc. **6** A movement made in attempting to stab or strike; a thrust; lunge; also, figuratively, a verbal thrust; a witty sally. **7** In football, hockey, lacrosse, etc., the action of passing the ball between players, in the course of the game. **8** In court tennis, a ball so served that it strikes the penthouse or the floor of the court between the main wall and the pass line. **9** In baseball, a base on balls. **10** *Mil.* Authority in writing given a soldier to be absent from duty or station for a specified period. — **forward pass** In football, the throwing or passing of the ball toward the opponent's goal. — **lateral pass** In football, a pass which does not travel towards either goal. — **to bring to pass** To cause to be fulfilled, accomplished, or realized. — **to come to pass** To happen; come about; be realized. — **to make a pass at** **1** To attempt to hit. **2** *Slang* To attempt to caress. [<OF *passer* <L *passus* a step; *n.,* doublet of PACE]

pass·a·ble (pas'ə·bəl, päs'-) *adj.* **1** Capable of being passed in any sense; capable of being penetrated or traversed. **2** Fairly good or acceptable; not open to great objection; moderate; mediocre; tolerable. **3** Fit for general circulation. — **pass'a·bly** *adv.*

pas·sage (pas'ij) *n.* **1** The act of passing; a passing by, through, or over; transition from one state or condition to another. **2** A journey by conveyance, as by a vessel; a voyage: a stormy *passage.* **3** Hence, conveyance on a journey; right of transportation, especially on a ship; also, money paid for conveyance. **4** A way or channel by which a person or thing may pass; a way through or over.

5 Any corridor, hall, or gallery affording communication between apartments in a building: also called *passageway*. **6** Liberty or power of passing; free entrance, exit, or transit. **7** A separate portion of a discourse, treatise, or writing; a clause, verse, paragraph, or similar division. **8** The course of a legislative measure through the various stages of debate and action; especially, its enactment by the final vote or approval by the supreme authority. **9** A part of a train of events; a series of incidents; episode. **10** A navigable route; especially, a channel connecting large bodies of water. **11** A personal encounter; a fight or a dispute: a *passage* with swords. **12** Migration, especially of birds; a migratory flight. **13** An evacuation of the bowels. **14** *Music* **a** A portion of a musical composition. **b** A run or series of short notes. **15** *Obs.* Departure; hence, death. See synonyms under CAREER, MOTION, ROAD, WAY. —*v.i.* **·saged, ·sag·ing 1** To make a journey. **2** To fence physically or verbally. [< OF < *passer*. See PASS.]

pas·sage² (pas′ij) *v.* **·saged, ·sag·ing** *v.t.* In equitation, to cause (a horse) to sidle or walk sidewise. —*v.i.* In equitation: **a** To move sidewise; sidle. **b** To cause a horse to move sidewise. —*n.* A sidewise movement made by a horse in which diagonal pairs of feet are raised alternately. [< F *passager*, alter. of *passéger* < Ital. *passeggiare* walk < L *passus* a step]

pass·book (pas′bŏŏk′, päs′-) *n.* **1** A bankbook. **2** A book given by a merchant to a customer, showing all items bought on credit.

passed ball In baseball, a pitched ball that the batsman fails to hit, which passes by the catcher and enables a runner to advance a base.

pas·sen·ger (pas′ən·jər) *n.* **1** A person who travels in a conveyance. **2** *Rare* A traveler; passer-by: a foot *passenger*. [< OF *passager* (with intrusive *-n*), orig. passing < *passage*. See PASSAGE.]

passenger pigeon The wild pigeon of North America (*Ectopistes migratorius*): now extinct.

pas·ser-by (pas′ər·bī′, päs′-) *n. pl.* **pas·sers-by** A person who passes by.

Pas·ser·i·for·mes (pas′ər·i·fôr′mēz) *n. pl.* An order of birds, including all singing birds, and more than half of the living birds of various sizes ranging from crows and jays to sparrows and titmice. [< NL < L *passer, -eris* a sparrow + *forma* form]

pas·ser·ine (pas′ər·ēn, -in) *adj.* **1** Pertaining to the *Passeriformes*. **2** Resembling or characteristic of a sparrow. —*n.* One of the *Passeriformes*. [< L *passer* sparrow + -INE¹]

pas·si·ble (pas′ə·bəl) *adj.* Capable of feeling or of suffering. [< F < LL *passibilis* < L *passus*, pp. of *patiri* suffer] — **pas′si·bil′i·ty, pas′si·ble·ness** *n.*

pass·ing (pas′ing, päs′-) *adj.* **1** Going by or away. **2** Transitory; fleeting. **3** Happening or occurring; current. **4** Done, said, found, used, or given in or as in passing; cursory. **5** Indicating fulfilment of requirements for advancement: satisfactory: a *passing* grade. **6** *Obs.* Surpassing. See synonyms under TRANSIENT. —*n.* **1** A going by or away; hence, dying. **2** An act of passing or passage. **3** A means of passing, as a ford. — **in passing** Incidentally; in the course of discussion. —*adv.* In a surpassing degree or manner; exceedingly.

passing bell A bell tolled to announce a person's death.

passing note A note or tone foreign to the harmony: used in passing from one chord to another.

pas·sion (pash′ən) *n.* **1** Intense or overpowering emotion. **2** An eager outreaching of mind toward some special object, as art, travel, etc.; fervid devotion. **3** Ardent affection for one of the opposite sex; love; also, the object of such feeling. **4** A fit of intense and furious anger; rage. **5** Any transport of excited feeling; violent agitation. **6** A strong impulse tending to physical indulgence. **7** *pl.* Inordinate appetites; sexual desires. **8** The state or condition of being acted upon; subjecting to external force, as opposed to acting or doing: the philosophical sense. **9** The endurance of some painful infliction; suffering. **10** *Obs.* Some painful disease. See synonyms under ANGER, APPETITE, ENTHUSIASM, FEELING, LOVE, VIOLENCE, WARMTH. [< OF *passiun* < L

passio, -onis suffering < *passus*, pp. of *patiri* suffer]

Pas·sion (pash′ən) *n.* **1** The sufferings of Christ, especially in the agony of the garden and on the cross; also, their representation in art. **2** That part of the Gospels which relates the Passion and death of Christ.

pas·sion·al (pash′ən·əl) *adj.* Of, pertaining to, or characterized by passion, especially amorous: *passional* poetry. — *n.* A book descriptive of the sufferings of saints and martyrs.

pas·sion·ate (pash′ən·it) *adj.* **1** Capable of or inclined to strong passion; susceptible of vehement emotion; excitable. **2** Easily moved to anger; quick-tempered. **3** Expressing or displaying some passion; characterized by passion; intense; ardent. **4** Of a strong, ardent quality or excessive degree: said of feeling. See synonyms under ARDENT, HOT, IMPETUOUS, VIOLENT. [< Med. L *passionatus*, ult. < L *passio, -onis*. See PASSION.] — **pas′sion·ate·ly** *adv.* — **pas′sion·ate·ness** *n.*

Passion play A mystery or drama representing the Passion of Christ.

Passion Sunday *Eccl.* The second Sunday before Easter.

Passion Week *Eccl.* **1** The week that begins with Passion Sunday. **2** Formerly, Holy Week.

pas·sive (pas′iv) *adj.* **1** Acted upon or receiving impressions from external agents or causes; being the object rather than the subject of action; moved by or as by external force or influence. **2** In a state of rest or quiescence; not vitally or mentally active; unresponsive. **3** Unresisting; submissive; *passive* obedience. **4** *Chem.* Characterized by a disinclination to enter into combination; inactive; inert. **5** *Gram.* Designating a voice of the verb which indicates that the subject is being acted upon, as, *was killed* is in the passive voice in *Caesar was killed by Brutus*: opposed to *active*. **6** Not bearing interest: said of bonds which yield the holder a profit or benefit, while no rate percent is named; having reference to a debt which, by agreement, is non-interest-bearing; of the nature of a liability. **7** *Med.* Designating certain abnormal conditions marked by relaxation of blood vessels and tissues, indicating impaired vitality and reaction. **8** Not provided with, or not making use of, motive power. —*n. Gram.* **1** The passive voice. **2** A verb or construction in this voice. [< L *passivus* < *passus*, pp. of *pati* suffer] —**pas′sive·ly** *adv.* —**pas′sive·ness** *n.*

passive euthanasia Euthanasia (def. 3).

passive immunity Resistance to a disease acquired by a susceptible subject through the transfer of exogenous antibodies contained in the serum of an animal with active immunity.

passive resistance Opposition to constituted authority that does not offer open violence, but resorts instead to voluntary fasting, refusal to obey laws, etc.

pas·siv·i·ty (pa·siv′ə·tē) *n.* **1** Passiveness. **2** The suspension or abeyance of the rational functions and the reduction of the physical functions to the lowest possible degree. **3** Resistance to oxidation and chemical reagents, as iron which has been immersed in strong nitric acid.

Pass·o·ver (pas′ō′vər, päs′-) *n.* **1** A Jewish feast commemorating the night when the Lord, smiting the first-born of the Egyptians, "passed over" the houses of the children of Israel. *Ex.* xii. **2** By extension, the entire festival of seven days following the paschal supper; the feast of unleavened bread.

pass·port (pas′pôrt′, -pōrt′, päs′-) *n.* **1** An official warrant certifying the citizenship of the bearer and affording protection to him when traveling abroad; a safe conduct. **2** A permit to travel or convey goods through a foreign country. **3** A documentary permission for a ship to proceed on a voyage. **4** A means or authority to pass; that which empowers one to arrive at anything: a *passport* to success. **5** That which gives the privilege or right to enter into some sphere of action. See NAVICERT. [< F *passeport* < *passer* pass + *port* harbor]

pas·sus (pas′əs) *n. pl.* **·sus** or **·sus·es** A part or canto, as of a poem. [< Med. L < L, a stop < *pandere* stretch]

past (past, päst) *adj.* **1** Belonging to time gone by; hence, accomplished or ended. **2** In the usage of some societies, having completed a full term

and been succeeded by another person: a *Past Master* in Masonry. **3** *Gram.* Denoting a tense or construction which refers to time or action belonging to the past. —*n.* **1** Time gone by; an antecedent period; former days collectively. **2** One's antecedents or record, especially if disreputable or kept secret. **3** *Gram.* **a** The past tense. **b** A verb or construction in this tense. —*adv.* In such manner as to go by and beyond. —*prep.* **1** Beyond in time; at a later period than; after: It is now *past* noon. **2** Beyond in place or position; farther than: walking *past* the house. **3** Beyond the reach, scope, power, or influence of: The matter is *past* hope. **4** Beyond in amount or degree: He couldn't count *past* ten. [Orig. pp. of PASS.]

pas·ta (päs′tə) *n.* Any of several noodlelike pastes or doughs containing semolina, as spaghetti, macaroni, etc. [< Ital. < LL, dough]

paste (pāst) *n.* **1** An adhesive mixture, usually of flour and water: used for joining or affixing paper articles and the like, and in bookbinding, etc. **2** A mixture of flour and water, often with other materials, for culinary purposes; dough. **3** Any doughy or moist plastic substance; anything of the consistency of paste, as for consumption or application: usually with a qualifying word: fish *paste*; almond *paste*. **4** A vitreous composition for making imitation gems. **5** A confection made of fruit juices, sugar, gum, etc. **6** A mixture of clay for making stoneware or porcelain. —*v.t.* **past·ed, past·ing 1** To stick or fasten with paste or the like. **2** To cover by applying pasted material. —*adj.* Made of paste; artificial. [< OF < LL *pasta* < Gk. *pastē* barley porridge]

paste·board (pāst′bôrd′, -bōrd′) *n.* **1** Paper pulp compressed, or paper pasted together and rolled into a stiff sheet. **2** A board on which dough for pastry is rolled. **3** *Colloq.* A visiting card; also, a playing card; playing cards generally. —*adj.* Made of or resembling pasteboard; hence, thin and flimsy.

pas·tel (pas·tel′, pas′tel) *n.* **1** A picture drawn with colored crayons. **2** The art of drawing such pictures. **3** A hard crayon made of pipe clay and a pigment, mixed with gum water. **4** A sketchy poetic study in prose. —*adj.* **1** Of or pertaining to a pastel. **2** Having a delicate, soft, or grayish tint. [< MF < Ital. *pastello* PASTEL²] —**pas′tel·ist** or **pas′tel·list** *n.*

pas·tern (pas′tərn) *n.* **1** That part of a horse's foot that is between the fetlock and the coffin joint. **2** A hobble for a horse's foot. [< OF *pasturon* < *pasture* a tether for a grazing animal]

Pas·teur (päs·tœr′), **Louis,** 1822–95, French chemist and bacteriologist.

pas·teur·ism (pas′tə·riz′əm) *n. Med.* A method of progressive inoculation developed by Pasteur for the prevention or cure of certain diseases, as hydrophobia.

pas·teur·i·za·tion (pas′tər·ə·zā′shən, -chər-) *n.* A process of arresting or preventing fermentation in liquids, as beer, milk, wine, etc., by heating to a temperature of 60° to 70° C., so as to destroy the vitality of the ferment. Also *Brit.* **pas′teur·i·sa′tion.**

pas·teur·ize (pas′tə·rīz, -chə·rīz) *v.t.* **·ized, ·iz·ing 1** To treat (milk, beer, etc.) by pasteurization. **2** To treat by pasteurism. Also *Brit.* **pas′teur·ise.**

pas·tic·cio (päs·tē′chō) *n.* A work of art, music, or literature made up of fragments from various sources, as from other works, connected so as to form a complete work; medley. [< Ital., a paste < Med. L *pasticium* < LL *pasta*. See PASTE¹.]

pas·tiche (pas·tēsh′, päs-) *n.* A pasticcio, especially one imitating or satirizing the style of other works of art or artists. [< F < Ital. *pasticcio* PASTICCIO]

pas·tille (pas·tēl′, -til′) *n.* **1** A compound of aromatic substances with niter for fumigating. **2** A troche; lozenge. **3** A flavored confection. **4** A small paper disk coated with a chemical that changes color on exposure to X-rays: used to determine X-ray dosages. **5** Pastel¹ (def. 3). Also **pas·til** (pas′til). [< MF < L *pastillus* a little loaf, a lozenge, ? dim. of *pasta* PASTE¹]

pas·time (pas′tīm′, päs′-) *n.* Something that serves to make time pass agreeably; recreation; sport. See synonyms under ENTERTAINMENT, SPORT. [< PASS, *v.* + TIME; trans. of F *passetemps*]

past master 1 One who has held the office of master in certain social and benevolent organizations. **2** One who has thorough experience in something; an adept.

pas·tor (pas′tər, -päs′-) *n.* **1** A Christian minister who has a church or congregation under his official charge. **2** *Obs.* A shepherd. [< AF *pastour*, OF *pastur* < L *pastor, -oris* a shepherd, lit., a feeder < *pascere* feed]

pas·tor·al (pas′tər·əl, päs′-) *adj.* **1** Pertaining to the life of shepherds and rustics; rural in spirit or sentiments: a *pastoral* poem. **2** Pertaining to a pastor and his work. See synonyms under RUSTIC. —*n.* **1** A poem dealing with rural matters; a bucolic; an idyl. **2** A picture illustrating rural scenes. **3** *Eccl.* A letter from a pastor to his flock. **4** A simple melody in 6/8 time in a rustic style; also, a complete symphony portraying a series of pastoral scenes. **5** A book or treatise on the cure of souls. **6** *pl.* The pastoral epistles. **7** A crozier or pastoral staff. [< L *pastoralis* < *pastor.* See PASTOR.] —**pas′tor·al·ism** *n.*

pas·to·ra·le (pas′tə·rä′lē, päs′-, pas′tə·ral′) *n.* A cantata or operetta on a rustic theme; also, a piece of instrumental music simple and idyllic in character.

pastoral epistles In the New Testament, the three epistles addressed to Timothy and Titus, and ascribed to St. Paul: so called because they deal with Christian pastorship.

pas·tor·ate (pas′tər·it, päs′-) *n.* **1** The office or jurisdiction of a pastor. **2** The duration of a pastoral charge. **3** Pastors collectively.

past participle See under PARTICIPLE.

past perfect *Gram.* The verb tense indicating an action completed prior to the occurrence of some other past action or before some specified past time. Example: *He had finished* before the bell rang, or, *He had finished* by last Friday. Also called *pluperfect.*

pas·tra·mi (pə·strä′mē) *n.* Smoked beef, heavily seasoned and usually cut from the shoulder. [< Yiddish < Magyar]

pas·try (pās′trē) *n. pl.* **·tries** Articles of food made with a crust of shortened dough, as pies. [Appar. < PAST(E)[1] + -RY]

pas·tur·age (pas′chər·ij, päs′-) *n.* **1** Grass and herbage for cattle. **2** Ground used or suitable for grazing. **3** The business or right of grazing cattle. [< OF < *pasturer* feed < *pasture.* See PASTURE.]

pas·ture (pas′chər, päs′-) *n.* **1** Ground for the grazing of domestic animals. **2** Grass or herbage that cattle or other grazing domestic animals eat. —*v.t.* **·tured, ·tur·ing 1** To lead to or put in a pasture to graze. **2** To graze on (grass, land, etc.). **3** To provide pasturage for (cattle, etc.): said of land. [< OF < L *pastura,* lit., feeding < *pastus,* pp. of *pascere* feed] —**pas′tur·a·ble** *adj.* —**pas′tur·er** *n.*

pat (pat) *v.* **pat·ted, pat·ting** *v.t.* **1** To touch or tap lightly with something flat, especially with the hand in caressing, soothing, etc. **2** To shape or mold by a pat or pats. **3** To strike or tap with lightly sounding steps, as in running. —*v.i.* **4** To tap or strike gently. **5** To run or walk with light steps. —*n.* **1** A light, caressing stroke; a gentle tap. **2** The sound of patting or pattering. **3** A small, molded mass, as of butter. —*adj.* **1** Exactly suitable in time or place; fitting; apt. **2** Formulated in a customary way without much thought; too neat; facile: a *pat* response to a complex question. **3** Satisfactory; needing no change: a *pat* hand in a card game. —*adv.* **1** Firm; steadfast: to stand *pat.* **2** In a fit or convenient manner; aptly; also, perfectly; unforgettably: to know one's lesson *pat.* [ME *patte;* prob. imit.] —**pat′ness** *n.* —**pat′ter** *n.*

patch (pach) *n.* **1** A small piece of material, especially of cloth, used to repair a garment, etc. **2** Something resembling a patch, as a piece of courtplaster or the like, applied to the skin to hide a blemish or to set off the complexion; a beauty spot. **3** A small piece of ground; also, the plants growing on it: a *patch* of corn; a small area in a larger expanse. **4** A piece of cloth or other material worn over an injured eye. **5** Any small part of a surface not agreeing with the general character or appearance of the whole. **6** A shred or scrap. —*v.t.* **1** To put a patch or

patches on. **2** To repair, make whole, or put together, especially hurriedly or crudely: often with *up* or *together.* **3** To make of patches, as a quilt. [ME *pacehe;* origin uncertain] —**patch′a·ble** *adj.* —**patch′er** *n.*

patch·head (pach′hed′) *n.* The surf scoter. Also **patchhead coot.**

patch·ou·li (pach′ŏŏ·lē, pə·chōō′lē) *n.* **1** An East Indian herb (*Pogostemon heyneamus* or *patchouly*) of the mint family. **2** A perfume obtained from it. Also spelled **pachouli.** Also **patch′ou·ly.** [< F < Tamil *paccilai* < *paccu* green + *ilai* a leaf]

patch test *Med.* A test for allergy in which an area of unbroken skin is covered by a small patch of linen or blotting paper impregnated with the suspected substance: upon removal of the patch the skin reaction is noted.

patch·work (pach′wûrk′) *n.* **1** A fabric made of patches of cloth, as for quilts, etc. **2** Work made up of heterogeneous materials; work done hastily or carelessly; a jumble.

patch·y (pach′ē) *adj.* **patch·i·er, patch·i·est 1** Abounding in patches; resembling patchwork; hence, lacking in proper effect; incongruous: a *patchy* architectural design. **2** Peevish; irritable. —**patch′i·ly** *adv.* —**patch′i·ness** *n.*

pate (pāt) *n.* The top of the head, especially a human head; often, the head in reference to brains; intellect: usually derogatory. [ME; origin uncertain]

pâ·té (pä·tā′) *n.* A little pie or pasty; a patty. [< F < *pasté* < LL *pasta.* See PASTE[1].]

pâté de foie gras (də fwä grä′) *French* A paste of fat goose liver.

pa·tel·la (pə·tel′ə) *n. pl.* **·lae** (-ē) **1** *Anat.* The flat, movable, oval bone in front of the knee joint; kneecap. **2** A small pan or dish. [< L, dim. of *patina* a pan, dish < *patere* lie open] —**pa·tel′lar** *adj.* —**pa·tel·late** (pə·tel′āt, -it) *adj.*

pa·tel·li·form (pə·tel′i·fôrm) *adj.* **1** Having the form of a patella or kneepan, or of a flattened cone. **2** Having the shape of a limpet shell. [< NL *patelliformis* < L *patella* a patella + *forma* form]

PATELLA
a. Femur.
b. Patella.
c. Tibia.
d. Fibula.

pat·en (pat′n) *n.* **1** A plate; especially, a plate for the eucharistic bread, or one held beneath the chin of the person receiving it. **2** A thin, metallic plate. [< OF *patène* < L *patena, patina* a pan < *patere* lie open]

pa·ten·cy (pāt′n·sē) *n.* **1** The condition of being patent or evident. **2** The state of being open, spread, enlarged, or without obstruction.

pat·ent (pat′nt) *n.* **1** A government protection to an inventor, securing to him for a specific time the exclusive right of manufacturing, exploiting, using, and selling an invention; the right granted. **2** Hence, any official document securing a right. **3** A government grant or franchise of land; also, land so granted; the official certificate of such a grant. **4** That which is protected by a patent or its distinctive marks or features. —*v.t.* **1** To obtain a patent on (an invention). **2** *Rare* To grant a patent for or to.

—**pa·tent** (pāt′nt *for defs. 1, 4, 5;* pat′nt *for defs. 2, 3, 6) adj.* **1** Manifest or apparent to everybody. **2** Protected or conferred by letters patent. **3** Open for general inspection or use: letters *patent.* **4** Expanded; spreading widely, as leaves from the stem of a plant. **5** Open; unobstructed, as an intestine. **6** Designating grades of flour, usually those of superior quality. See synonyms under EVIDENT, MANIFEST, NOTORIOUS, OPEN. ◆ In British English, pāt′nt is the usual pronunciation, except in *Patent Office* and *letters patent.* [< F < L *patens, -entis,* ppr. of *patere* lie open] —**pat′ent·a·bil′i·ty** *n.* —**pat′ent·a·ble** *adj.*

patent leather (pat′nt) Leather finished with a glossy, black, varnishlike coat; lacquered leather.

pa·tent·ly (pāt′nt·lē, pat′nt-) *adv.* Manifestly.

Patent Office A bureau of the U. S. Department of Commerce where applications for patents are examined and patents are issued.

pat·en·tor (pat′n·tər) *n.* One who grants a patent, as of land: correlative of *patentee.*

patent right 1 An exclusive right conferred

by a government grant. **2** The exclusive privilege, for a limited time, to the use and control of an invention and its manufacture.

pa·ter (pā′tər) *n.* Father. [< L]

pa·ter·fa·mil·i·as (pā′tər·fə·mil′ē·əs) *n.* **1** The father of a family or master of a house. **2** In Roman law, an independent person; the head of a family. [< L < *pater* father + *familias,* archaic genitive of *familia* family, household]

pa·ter·nal (pə·tûr′nəl) *adj.* **1** Pertaining to a father; fatherly. **2** Derived from, related through, or connected with one's father; hereditary. [< LL *paternalis* < L *paternus* fatherly < *pater* a father] —**pa·ter′nal·ly** *adv.*

pa·ter·nal·ism (pə·tûr′nəl·iz′əm) *n.* The care or control of a country, community, group of employees, etc., in a manner suggestive of a father looking after his children. —**pater′nal·is′tic** *adj.* —**pa·ter′nal·is′ti·cal·ly** *adv.*

pa·ter·ni·ty (pə·tûr′nə·tē) *n.* **1** The condition of being a father. **2** Parentage on the male side; descent from a father. **3** Origin in general; authorship. [< OF *paternité* < L *paternitas, -tatis* < *paternus.* See PATERNAL.]

pa·ter·nos·ter (pā′tər·nos′tər) *n.* **1** The Lord's Prayer: the prayer taught to his disciples by Jesus. *Matt.* vi 9–13. Also **Pater Noster.** **2** A recitation of this prayer. **3** A bead of the rosary, indicating that a paternoster is to be recited. **4** Any formula repeated in a low voice. [< L *pater noster* our father, the opening words of the prayer in Latin]

path (path, päth) *n. pl.* **paths** (pathz, päthz, paths, päths) **1** A walk or way, as one beaten by the foot, used by men or animals. **2** Any road, track, or course. **3** Hence, course or way of life or action. See synonyms under ROAD, WAY. [OE *pæth*]

pa·thet·ic (pə·thet′ik) *adj.* Of the nature of or expressing sadness, pity, tenderness, etc.; arousing compassion. Also **pa·thet′i·cal.** See synonyms under PITIFUL. [< LL *patheticus* < Gk. *pathetikos* sensitive < *path-,* stem of *paschein* suffer] —**pa·thet′i·cal·ly** *adv.* —**pa·thet′i·cal·ness** *n.*

path·find·er (path′fīn′dər, päth′-) *n.* **1** One skilled in leading or finding a way; especially, one who opens new trails into unknown regions; an explorer; also, one who opens new fields, as in science, philosophy, art. **2** An aircraft carrying flares to light targets in enemy territory for raiding bombers.

-pathia See -PATHY.

patho- *combining form* Suffering; disease: *pathogenesis.* Also, before vowels, **path-.** [< Gk. *pathos* suffering]

path·o·gen (path′ə·jən) *n.* Any disease-producing bacterium or micro-organism. Also **path′o·gene** (-jēn).

path·o·gen·e·sis (path′ə·jen′ə·sis) *n. Med.* The production or development of any morbid or diseased condition: also called *nosogenesis.* Also **pa·thog·e·ny** (pə·thoj′ə·nē).

path·o·gen·ic (path′ə·jen′ik) *adj. Med.* Productive of or pertaining to the production of disease. Also **path′o·ge·net′ic** (-jə·net′ik).

path·o·log·i·cal (path′ə·loj′i·kəl) *adj.* **1** Pertaining to pathology. **2** Related to, involving, concerned with, or caused by disease. Also **path′o·log′ic.** —**path′o·log′i·cal·ly** *adv.*

pa·thol·o·gist (pə·thol′ə·jist) *n.* One skilled in pathology.

pa·thol·o·gy (pə·thol′ə·jē) *n. pl.* **·gies 1** The branch of medical science that treats of morbid conditions, their causes, nature. etc. **2** The sum of the morbid conditions, processes, and results in the course of a disease. [< PATHO- + -LOGY]

path·o·mi·me·sis (path′ō·mi·mē′sis, -mī·mē′-) *n. Psychiatry* The simulation of a disease or of its symptoms, found in hysteria. Also **path′o·mim′i·cry** (-mim′i·krē). —**path′o·mi·met′ic** (-mi·met′ik, -mī·met′-) *adj.*

path·o·mor·phism (path′ō·môr′fiz·əm) *n. Pathol.* Any abnormality of bodily structure and appearance: said of extreme physical types. [< PATHO- + -MORPH(O)- + -ISM] —**path′o·mor′phic** *adj.*

path·o·pho·bi·a (path′ə·fō′bē·ə) *n.* A morbid fear of disease or of being sick. —**path′o·pho′bic** *adj.*

pa·thos (pā′thos) *n.* **1** The quality, attribute, or element, in events, speech, or art, that rouses emotion or passion, especially the tender emotions, as compassion or sympathy; also, tender or sorrowful feeling. **2** In art, the quality of the contingent and evanescent phenomena of life, as the facts of personality, individuality, human passion, or emotion, that the artist's conception embodies or concretely expresses: opposed to the quality of the ideal or *ethos*. **3** *Obs.* Suffering. See synonyms under FEELING. [<Gk., suffering < *path-*, stem of *paschein* suffer]

-pathy *combining form* **1** Suffering; affection: *sympathy*. **2** *Med.* Disease, or the treatment of disease: *psychopathy*. Also spelled *-pathia*. [<Gk. *-patheia* < *pathos* suffering]

pa·tience (pā′shəns) *n.* **1** The quality or habit of enduring without complaint. **2** The exercise of sustained endurance and perseverance. **3** Forbearance toward the faults or infirmities of others. **4** Tranquil waiting or expectation. **5** Ability to await events without perturbation. **6** Any solitaire card game. **7** *Obs.* Permission or sufferance. [< OF *pacience* <L *patientia* < *patiens.* See PATIENT.]

Synonyms: calmness, composure, endurance, forbearance, fortitude, leniency, long-suffering, resignation, submission, sufferance. *Endurance* hardens itself against suffering, and may be merely stubborn; by modifiers it may be made to have a passive force, as when we speak of "passive *endurance*"; *fortitude* is *endurance* animated by courage; *patience* is not so hard as *endurance* nor so self-effacing as *submission*. *Submission* is ordinarily and *resignation* always applied to matters of great moment, while *patience* may apply to slight worries and annoyances. *Patience* may also have an active force denoting uncomplaining steadiness in doing, as in tilling the soil. Compare INDUSTRY, SUBMISSION. *Antonyms:* see synonyms for ANGER, IMPATIENCE.

pa·tient (pā′shənt) *adj.* **1** Possessing quiet, uncomplaining endurance under distress or annoyance; long-suffering. **2** Tolerant, tender, and forbearing. **3** Capable of tranquilly awaiting events. **4** Capable of bearing: with *of*: *patient* of hunger. **5** Persevering. — *n.* **1** A person undergoing treatment for disease or injury. **2** Anything passively affected; the object of external impressions or actions: opposed to *agent*. See synonyms under CHARITABLE, PASSIVE. [<OF *pacient* <L *patiens, -entis,* ppr. of *patiri* suffer] — **pa′tient·ly** *adv.*

pat·i·na¹ (pat′ə-nə) *n. pl.* **·nae** (-nē) An earthenware or metal bowl or basin used as a domestic utensil by the Romans; a patella. [< L < *patere* lie open]

pat·i·na² (pat′ə-nə) *n.* **1** A green rust or aerugo that covers ancient bronzes, copper coins, medals, etc. **2** An aspect of the surface of stone implements, giving evidence of antiquity. **3** Any surface of antique appearance. Also **pa·tine** (pə-tēn′). [< Ital. <F *patine,* prob. <L *patina* a plate; with ref. to the tarnish on a copper dish]

pa·ti·o (pä′tē-ō, pat′ē-ō; *Sp.* pä′tyō) *n. pl.* **·ti·os 1** The open inner court of a Spanish or Spanish-American dwelling. **2** *U.S.* The enclosed outdoor terrace of a ranch-type dwelling. [<Sp., prob. <L *patere* lie open]

pa·to·la (pə-tō′lə) *n.* An East Indian silk fabric, used especially for native wedding garments. [<Skt. *paṭola*]

patri– *combining form* Father: *patricide.* [<L *pater, -tris* father]

pa·tri·arch (pā′trē-ärk) *n.* **1** The leader of a family or tribe who rules by paternal right. **2** One of the earliest fathers of the human race, from Adam to Noah: in full: **antediluvian patriarch. 3** One of the fathers of the Hebrew race, Abraham, Isaac, or Jacob. **4** One of the twelve sons of Jacob considered as the progenitors of the tribes of Israel. **5** A venerable man; especially the founder of a religion, order, etc. **6** In later Jewish history, the title of the president of the Sanhedrin in Syria and Babylon. **7** *Eccl.* **a** In the primitive Christian church, any of the bishops of Antioch, Alexandria, Rome, Constantinople, or Jerusalem. **b** In the Roman Catholic Church, a prelate inferior only to the pope and the cardinals, appointed as head of one of the ancient eastern patriarchates or of some modern Uniat churches. **c** In the Greek Orthodox Church, any of the bishops of Constantinople, Alexandria, Antioch, or Jerusalem, sometimes also a prelate of other cities. The bishop of Con-

stantinople, the highest ranking dignitary in the Greek Church, is titled the **ecumenical patriarch. d** The title of the heads of other Eastern churches, as the Coptic, Armenian, Jacobite, or Nestorian churches. **8** In the Mormon Church, one of the superior order of priests, with special authority and jurisdiction in bestowing blessings. [<OF *patriarche* <L *patriarcha* <Gk. *patriarchēs* head of a family < *patria* family, clan + *archein* rule]

pa·tri·ar·chal (pā′trē-är′kəl) *adj.* **1** Of or pertaining to a patriarch; governed by a patriarch: a *patriarchal* see. **2** Of the nature of a patriarchy. **3** Of or belonging to the patriarchs. **4** Having the nature or character of a patriarch; venerable. — **pa′tri·ar′chal·ly** *adv.*

pa·tri·ar·chate (pā′trē-är′kit) *n.* **1** The office, dominion, or residence of a patriarch. **2** A patriarchal system of government.

pa·tri·ar·chy (pā′trē-är′kē) *n. pl.* **·chies 1** A patriarchate. **2** A system of government in which the father or the male heir of his choice rules.

pa·tri·cian (pə-trish′ən) *adj.* **1** Pertaining to the aristocracy. **2** Noble or aristocratic. **3** Of or pertaining to the Roman aristocracy; also, relating to patricians of the Italian republics, German free cities, etc. — *n.* **1** An aristocrat; specifically, a member of the hereditary aristocracy that, for the first four centuries of her history, monopolized the government and priesthood of Rome. **2** Any one of the upper classes. **3** An honorary title bestowed by the later Roman emperors. **4** In medieval history, one of the upper class in the Italian republics, German free cities, etc. [<OF *patricien* <L *patricius* belonging to the senatorial class < *pater, -tris* a senator, lit., a father] — **pa·tri′cian·ly** *adv.*

pa·tri·ci·ate (pə-trish′ē-it, -āt) *n.* **1** The patricians as a class; the nobility. **2** The rank, dignity, or term of office of a patrician.

pat·ri·cide (pat′rə-sīd) *n.* **1** The killing of a father. **2** One who slays a father; a parricide. — **pat′ri·ci′dal** *adj.*

— **Patrick, Saint,** 389?–461?, apostle to and patron saint of Ireland.

pat·ri·cli·nous (pat′rə-klī′nəs) *adj.* Showing hereditary characteristics inclining toward the paternal side: opposed to *matriclinous.* Also **pat′ro·cli′nous.** [<PATRI- + Gk. *klinein* lean]

pat·ri·lin·e·al (pat′rə-lin′ē-əl) *adj.* Derived from or descending through the male line. Compare MATRILINEAL.

pat·ri·lo·cal (pat′rə-lō′kəl) *adj. Anthropol.* Describing that form of residence in clan societies in which a married couple lives in the husband's community. Compare MATRILOCAL. [<PATRI- + L *locus* a place]

pat·ri·mo·ny (pat′rə-mō′nē) *n. pl.* **·nies 1** An inheritance from a father or an ancestor; also, any inheritance. **2** An endowment, as of a church. [<OF *patrimoine* <L *patrimonium* < *pater, -tris* a father] — **pat′ri·mo′ni·al** *adj.* — **pat′ri·mo′ni·al·ly** *adv.*

pa·tri·ot (pā′trē-ət, -ot) *n.* One who loves his country and zealously guards its welfare; especially, a defender of popular liberty. [<F *patriote* <LL *patriota* a fellow countryman <Gk. *patriotēs,* < *patris* fatherland]

pa·tri·ot·ic (pā′trē-ot′ik) *adj.* Characterized by patriotism; intended for the public good. — **pa′tri·ot′i·cal·ly** *adv.*

pa·tri·ot·ism (pā′trē-ə-tiz′əm) *n.* Devotion to one's country.

pa·tris·tic (pə-tris′tik) *adj.* Of or pertaining to the fathers of the Christian church or to their writings. Also **pa·tris′ti·cal.** [<L *pater, -tris* father + -IST + -IC] — **pa·tris′ti·cal·ly** *adv.*

Pa·tro·clus (pə-trō′kləs) In the *Iliad,* a Greek soldier and friend of Achilles in the Trojan War: wearing Achilles' armor, he was mistaken for him and killed by Hector.

pa·trol (pə-trōl′) *v.t. & v.i.* **·trolled, ·trol·ling** To walk or go through or around (an area, town, etc.) for the purpose of guarding or inspecting. — *n.* **1** One or more soldiers, policemen, etc., patrolling a district. **2** A reconnaissance or safety group sent out from a security detachment or by the main body in air, ground, or naval warfare. **3** The act of patrolling. **4** A division of a troop of Boy Scouts. [<MF *patrouille* a night watch < *patrouiller,* alter. of *patouiller,* orig. paddle in mud, ? ult. < *patte* a paw, foot] — **pa·trol′.**

ler *n.*

pa·trol·man (pə-trōl′mən) *n. pl.* **·men** (-mən) One who patrols; specifically, a policeman assigned to a beat.

patrol wagon A police wagon or truck for the conveyance of prisoners, etc.

pa·tron (pā′trən) *n.* **1** One who protects, fosters, countenances, or supports some person or thing; a protector or benefactor. **2** A regular customer. **3** A saint regarded as the peculiar protector of some special person, country, cause, etc.; a tutelary saint; also, the canonized founder of a religious order. **4** In Greek and Roman religion, a tutelary deity; protector of some city, cause, occupation, etc. **5** One in the position of father, guardian, or helper, as one who sponsors a concert or charitable entertainment, one who champions a cause. **6** In ancient Rome, a master who freed his slave and sustained toward him a legal relation analogous to that of father. [<OF *patrun* <L *patronus* protector < *pater, -tris* father] — **pa′tron·al** *adj.*

pa·tron·age (pā′trən·ij, pat′rən-) *n.* **1** Special countenance; guardianship. **2** An uncalled-for distribution of favors, or an overly condescending manner. **3** The right to control the distribution of offices, etc., in the public service; also, the offices, etc., so distributed. **4** The financial support given by customers to commercial enterprises; the customers themselves, as a group.

pa·tron·ess (pā′trən·is, pat′rən-) *n.* A female patron; a matron who promotes and assists in the management of a social event.

pa·tron·ize (pā′trən·īz, pat′rən-) *v.t.* **·ized, ·iz·ing 1** To act as a patron toward; give support or protection to. **2** To treat in a condescending manner. **3** To trade with as a regular customer; frequent. — **pa′tron·iz′er** *n.* — **pa′·tron·iz′ing·ly** *adv.*

pat·ro·nym·ic (pat′rə-nim′ik) *adj.* Formed after one's father's name. — *n.* **1** A name derived from an ancestor; a family name. **2** A name formed by the addition of a prefix or suffix to a proper name: Fitzhugh, son of Hugh; Johnson, son of John. Also **pat′ro·nym** *n.* [<Gk. *patronymos* (< *patēr, -tros* father + *onyma, onoma* name) + -IC] — **pat′·ro·nym′i·cal·ly** *adv.*

pat·te·mar (pat′ə·mär) See PATAMAR.

pat·ten (pat′n) *n.* A shoe having a thick, wooden sole; a clog. [<OF *patin,* prob. < *patte* a paw, foot]

pat·ter¹ (pat′ər) *v.i.* **1** To make a succession of light, sharp sounds. **2** To move with light, quick steps. — *v.t.* **3** To cause to patter. — *n.* Pattering, or the sound of pattering. [Freq. of PAT¹]

pat·ter² (pat′ər) *v.t. & v.i.* To speak or say glibly or rapidly; mumble or recite (prayers, etc.) mechanically or indistinctly. — *n.* **1** Glib and rapid talk, as used by comedians, etc. **2** Patois or dialect; any professional jargon. **3** Rapid speech set to music. [Short for PATERNOSTER; from the rapid repetition of the prayer] — **pat′ter·er** *n.*

pat·tern (pat′ərn) *n.* **1** An original or model proposed for or worthy of imitation: Ancient Athens was a *pattern* of democracy. **2** Anything shaped or designed to serve as a model or guide in making something else: a *pattern* for a coat. **3** Any decorative design or figure, or such design worked on something: a vase with a geometrical *pattern.* **4** Arrangement of natural or accidental markings: the *pattern* of a butterfly's wings. **5** The stylistic composition or design of a work of art: the *pattern* of Hardy's novels. **6** A complex of integrated parts functioning as a whole: the behavior *pattern* of a five-year-old; *patterns* of American culture. **7** In gunnery, the distribution of shot or shots about a target. **8** A representative example; sample or instance: a book of *patterns.* **9** *U.S.* Material in sufficient quantity to make a garment, especially a dress. **10** *Obs.* Something made after a model or prototype; a copy. See synonyms under EXAMPLE, IDEA, IDEAL, MODEL, SIGN. — *v.t.* **1** To make after a model or pattern: with *on, upon,* or *after.* **2** To decorate or furnish with a pattern. [Alter. of PATRON]

Pat·ton (pat′n), **George Smith,** 1885–1945, U.S. Army officer in World War II.

pat·tu (put′ōō) *n.* An East Indian homespun wool or tweed, used for shawls, etc. [<Hind.

pattu]
pat·ty (pat'ē) n. pl. **·ties** A small pie. [Alter. of F *pâté*. See PÂTÉ.]

patty shell A small puff–paste shell in which to serve creamed meat, fish, vegetables, or fruit.

pat·u·lous (pach'ŏŏ·ləs) adj. 1 Spreading; gaping. 2 Bot. Spreading slightly, as a calyx. 3 Having a wide aperture. [< L *patulus* standing open < *patere* lie open] — **pat'u·lous·ly** adv. — **pat'u·lous·ness** n.

pau·ci·ty (pô'sə·tē) n. Smallness of number or quantity; fewness; also, scarcity; insufficiency. [< L *paucitas, -tatis* < *paucus* few]

— **Paul** The apostle to the Gentiles, a Hebrew who, before his conversion, was called *Saul of Tarsus*; author of various New Testament books; died about A.D. 67. Also *Paul the Apostle, Saint Paul.*

— **Paul 1,** 1754–1801, emperor of Russia 1798–1801; assassinated.

— **Paul I,** born 1901, king of Greece 1947–.

— **Paul III,** 1468–1549, pope 1534–49; real name Alessandro Farnese; excommunicated Henry VIII; approved Jesuit order.

— **Paul VI,** born 1897, pope 1963–; real name Giovanni Battista Montini.

Paul Bunyan The famous hero lumberjack of American folklore, of superhuman size and strength and credited with amazing feats.

paul·dron (pôl'drən) n. A detachable piece of plate armor to protect the shoulder. [Aphetic var. of OF *espauleron* < *espaule* shoulder; with intrusive -d]

pau·lin (pô'lin) n. A sheet of heavy canvas, usually waterproof. [Short for TARPAULIN]

Paul·ine (pô'lēn, -līn) adj. 1 Relating to the apostle Paul, his teachings, or writings. 2 Characterized by the assumed trend of Paul in his theological thinking. — **Paul'in·ism** n. — **Paul'in·ist** n.

Pau·ling (pô'ling), **Linus Carl,** born 1901, U.S. chemist.

Pau·li·nus (pô·lī'nəs), **Saint,** died 644, a Roman missionary to England in 601; archbishop of York.

Paul·ist (pô'list) n. A member of the Congregation of the Missionary Priests of St. Paul the Apostle, founded in New York in 1858.

paunch (pônch) n. 1 The abdomen; the belly; also, a potbelly. 2 The first stomach of a ruminant. [< AF *panche* < L *pantex, -ticis* belly, bowels] — **paunch'i·ness** n.

pau·per (pô'pər) n. One dependent on charity; a destitute person who receives, or is entitled to receive, public charity; any very poor person. [< Med. L *(in forma) pauperis* (in the character) of a poor man < *pauper* poor; orig. a legal phrase. Doublet of POOR.]

pau·per·ism (pô'pə·riz'əm) n. 1 Poverty. 2 Paupers collectively. See synonyms under POVERTY.

pau·per·ize (pô'pər·īz) v.t. **·ized, ·iz·ing** To make a pauper of.

pauper's oath An oath that one is destitute and incapable of supporting oneself: sometimes required when making a plea for public assistance.

pau·ro·me·tab·o·lous (pô'rō·mə·tab'ə·ləs) adj. Entomol. Having a gradual or incomplete metamorphosis, as in the grasshopper and certain other insects. Also **pau'ro·met'a·bol'ic** (-met'ə·bol'ik). [< Gk. *pauros* small + *metabolos* changing]

pause (pôz) v.i. **paused, paus·ing** 1 To cease action or utterance temporarily; stop; hesitate; delay. 2 To dwell or linger: with *on* or *upon*: to *pause* on a word. See synonyms under CEASE, STAND. [< n.] — n. 1 A ceasing of action; an intermission; rest; stop. 2 A holding back because of doubt or irresolution; suspense; hesitation. 3 A momentary cessation in speaking or music for the sake of meaning or expression. 4 A character or sign indicating such cessation, as most marks of punctuation, a break, or a paragraph, or, in music, a hold or a rest. 5 A calculated interval of silence in a meter, or the place at which the voice naturally pauses in reading a verse. See CAESURA. See synonyms under RESPITE, REST¹. [< MF < L *pausa* a stop < Gk. *pausis* < *pauein* stop] — **paus'er** n.

pav·an (pav'ən) n. 1 A slow, stately dance of the 16th and 17th centuries. 2 The music for this dance. Also **pav·ane** (pav'ən, Fr. pà·vàn'). [< MF *pavane* < Sp. *pavana*, prob. < *pavo* a peacock < L *pavo, -onis*]

pave (pāv) v.t. **paved, pav·ing** To cover or surface with asphalt, gravel, concrete, macadam, etc., as a road. — **to pave the way (for)** To make preparation (for); lead up to. [< F *paver* < L *pavire* ram down]

pa·vé (pä·vā') n. 1 A street pavement. 2 The close setting of jewels in which no metal shows. [< F, orig. pp. of *paver*. See PAVE.]

pave·ment (pāv'mənt) n. 1 A hard, solid, surface covering or flooring for a road or footway, usually resting immediately on the ground. 2 A paved road or footway. 3 The material with which a surface is paved. [< OF < L *pavimentum* a rammed floor < *pavire* ram down]

pa·vil·ion (pə·vil'yən) n. 1 A movable or open structure for temporary shelter or dwelling; a large tent; summerhouse. 2 A related or connected part of a principal building, especially such a structure appropriated to amusement: the dancing *pavilion*. 3 A canopy. 4 The external ear. 5 The sloping surface of a brilliant–cut gem between the girdle and the culet. 6 A detached building for patients, as at a hospital. — v.t. 1 To provide with a pavilion or pavilions. 2 To shelter by a pavilion. [< OF *pavillon* < L *papilio, -onis* a butterfly, tent]

Pav·lov (päv'lôf), **Ivan Petrovich** (päv'lôf), 1849–1936, Russian physiologist.

Pav·lo·va (päv·lō'və), **Anna,** 1885–1931, Russian ballet dancer.

Pa·vo (pā'vō) A southern constellation, the Peacock; its principal star, also called Peacock, is used by navigators. See CONSTELLATION. [< L, a peacock]

pav·o·nine (pav'ə·nīn, -nin) adj. 1 Resembling or characteristic of the peacock. 2 Iridescent like the tail of a peacock. [< L *pavoninus* like a peacock < *pavo, -onis* a peacock]

paw (pô) n. 1 The foot of an animal having nails or claws. 2 A clumsy human hand. — v.t. & v.i. 1 To strike or scrape with the feet or paws: to *paw* the air; to *paw* at the ground. 2 Colloq. To handle rudely or clumsily; maul. [< OF *powe*, prob. < Gmc.] — **paw'er** n.

pawl (pôl) n. Mech. A hinged or pivoted member shaped to engage with ratchet teeth, either to drive a ratchet wheel or to stop its reverse motion; a click or detent. ◆ Homophone: pall. [? < Welsh, a pole, prob. ult. < L *palus* a stake]

PAWLS

A. Types of pawls: a. Hook; b. Straight gravity; c. Spring.
B. Double pawl.
C. Reversible double pawl.

pawn¹ (pôn) n 1 A chessman of lowest rank, that moves on file but captures diagonally. 2 Hence, any insignificant person used at another's will. [< AF *poun*, OF *paon*, var. of *peon, pedon* a foot soldier < LL *pedo, -onis* < L *pes, pedis* a foot. Doublet of PEON.]

pawn² (pôn) n. 1 Something pledged as security for a loan; especially, personal property pledged to secure a loan. 2 The condition of being held as a pledge for money loaned. 3 The act of pawning. — v.t. 1 To give (personal property) as security for a loan. 2 To risk or stake; pledge: to *pawn* one's life. [< OF *pan*, prob. < L *pannus* a cloth; infl. in meaning by MDu. *pand* a pledge < Gmc.] — **pawn'a·ble** adj. — **pawn'age** n.

pawn·brok·er (pôn'brō'kər) n. One engaged in the business of lending money on pledged personal property. — **pawn'brok·ing** n.

Paw·nee (pô·nē') n. A member of one of four tribes of North American Indians of Caddoan linguistic stock, formerly inhabiting the region between the Arkansas River and the Platte River, Nebraska: now living in Oklahoma.

Pax (paks) In Roman mythology, the goddess of peace: identified with the Greek *Irene.*

pax·wax (paks'waks) n. A strong fibrous band extending from the dorsal vertebrae to the occiput, and supporting the head in many mammals, as horses: also spelled *packwax*. [Alter. of dial. *fax-wax* < OE *feax* hair + *weaxan* grow]

pay¹ (pā) v. **paid, pay·ing** v.t. 1 To give to (someone) what is due for a debt, purchase, etc.; recompense; remunerate. 2 To give (money, etc.) for a purchase, service rendered, etc. 3 To provide or hand over the amount of; discharge, as a debt, bill, etc. 4 To yield as return or recompense. 5 To afford profit or benefit to: It wouldn't *pay* me to do it. 6 To defray, as expenses. 7 To requite, as for an insult. 8 To render or give, as a compliment, attention, etc. 9 To make, as a call or visit. — v.i. 10 To make recompense or payment. 11 To afford compensation or profit; be worthwhile: It *pays* to be honest. — **to pay back** To repay. — **to pay off** 1 To pay the entire amount of (a debt, mortgage, etc.). 2 to pay the wages of and discharge. 3 To gain revenge upon or for. 4 Colloq. To afford full return; be fully effective. 5 Naut. To turn or cause to turn to leeward. — **to pay out** 1 To disburse or expend. 2 Naut. To let out by slackening, as a rope or cable. — **to pay up** To make full payment of. — n. 1 That which is given as a recompense or to discharge a debt; compensation; wages. 2 The act of paying or the state of being paid. 3 Whatever compensates for labor or loss; an equivalent. 4 Requital; reward; also, punishment; retaliation. 5 A person considered from the point of view of his ability to pay or his promptness or slowness in paying. 6 A worthwhile yield of metal in a vein or ore. 7 Retribution. See synonyms under SALARY. — adj. 1 Of or pertaining to payments, persons who pay, or services paid for: *pay* day, *pay* students, a *pay* library, etc. 2 Yielding enough metal to be worth mining: *pay* dirt, *pay* quartz, etc. [< OF *payer* pay, appease < L *pacare* appease < *pax, pacis* peace] — **pay'er** n.

pay² (pā) v.t. **paid** or **payed, pay·ing** To coat with pitch or other waterproof composition, as the seams of a vessel, etc. [< AF *peier* < L *picare* < *pix, picis* pitch]

pay·a·ble (pā'ə·bəl) adj. 1 Due and unpaid. 2 Capable of being discharged by payment; that can or will be paid. 3 Likely to be profitable; specifically, likely to yield a surplus, as a mine. — **pay'a·bly** adv.

pay dirt Soil containing enough metal, especially gold, to be profitable to mine.

pay·ee (pā·ē') n. A person to whom money has been or is to be paid.

pay·load (pā'lōd') n. 1 That part of a cargo producing revenue. 2 The explosive material in the warhead of a guided missile. 3 The persons, instruments, etc., carried in a spacecraft that are directly related to the objective of the flight rather than to the operation of the craft.

pay·mas·ter (pā'mas'tər, -mäs'-) n. One who has charge of the paying of employees.

pay·ment (pā'mənt) n. 1 The act of paying. 2 Pay; requital; recompense. 3 Punishment. See synonyms under SALARY.

pay·off (pā'ôf', -of') n. 1 Payment; specifically, the time or act of payment of wages to employees; also, the time or act of paying an employee in full and discharging him. 2 Colloq. Any settlement; the end; reward or punishment. 3 Colloq. The climax of an incident or narrative. 4 U.S. Slang A bribe.

pay·o·la (pā·ō'lə) n. U.S. Slang A secret payment for favors, as for publicizing a commercial product.

pay·roll (pā'rōl') n. A list of those entitled to receive pay, with the amounts due them; also, the total sum of money needed to make the payments. Also **pay roll.**

pea (pē) n. pl. **peas** or **pease** 1 A climbing annual leguminous herb (*Pisum sativum*) having pinnate leaves. 2 Its edible seed. 3 The seed of any one of various other plants of the same family, as the chickpea or cowpea. [< PEASE, incorrectly taken as a plural]

peace (pēs) *n.* **1** A state of quiet or tranquillity; freedom from disturbance or agitation; calm; repose. **2** Specifically, absence or cessation of war. **3** General order and tranquillity; freedom from riot or violence. **4** A state of reconciliation after strife or enmity; peaceable or friendly relations; agreement; concord. **5** Freedom from mental agitation or anxiety. **6** Spiritual content. See synonyms under REST. —**to hold** (or **keep**) **one's peace** To be silent. —*v.i. Obs. except as an imperative.* To be or become quiet or silent. ◆ Homophone: *piece.* [< OF *pais* < L *pax, pacis*]

peace·a·ble (pē'sə·bəl) *adj.* **1** Inclined to peace. **2** Peaceful; tranquil. —**peace'a·ble·ness** *n.* —**peace'a·bly** *adv.*

Peace Corps A U.S. government organization, established in 1961, that trains and sends volunteers to live in and aid underdeveloped countries by teaching farming, building, etc.

peace·ful (pēs'fəl) *adj.* **1** Exempt from war, riot, or commotion; undisturbed. **2** Averse to strife. **3** Inclined to or used in peace. See synonyms under CALM, PACIFIC. —**peace'ful·ly** *adv.* —**peace'ful·ness** *n.*

peace officer Any conservator of the peace, especially a justice of the peace, sheriff, constable, or policeman.

peach (pēch) *n.* **1** The fruit of the peach tree (*Prunus persica*), a fleshy, juicy, edible drupe. **2** The tree, widely cultivated in many varieties. **3** The orange-yellow color of the fruit. **4** *Slang* Any person or thing particularly beautiful, pleasing, or excellent. [< OF *peche, pesche* < LL *persica* < L *Persicum (malum)* Persian (apple) < Gk. *persikos*]

peach·bloom (pēch'blōōm') *n.* **1** A monochrome glaze in Chinese porcelain in various tones of pinkish-red: also **peach'blow'** (-blō'). **2** A kind of ware thus glazed or tinted. **3** A delicate pink color.

peach·y (pē'chē) *adj.* **peach·i·er, peach·i·est 1** Resembling a peach, especially in color or downiness. **2** *Slang* Delightfully pleasant. —**peach'i·ness** *n.*

pea·coat (pē'kōt') *n.* A peajacket. [< PEA(JACKET) + COAT]

pea·cock (pē'kok) *n.* The male of a gallinaceous crested bird (genus *Pavo*), which has the tail coverts enormously elongated, erectile, and marked with ocelli or eyelike spots, and the neck and breast of an iridescent greenish-blue. ◆ Collateral adjective: *pavonine.* —*v.i.* To strut vainly; make a display. [OE *pēa, pāwa* a peacock (< L *pavo*) + COCK[1]]

PEACOCK
(Body length about 30 to 36 inches; tail up to 6 feet)

peacock blue A vivid greenish blue, the color of the blue in a peacock's feathers.

peacock copper Bornite.

pea·cock·ish (pē'kok·ish) *adj.* Vain; pretentious. Also **pea'cock·y.**

peacock moth A large moth (*Saturnia pyri*) of southern Europe and western Asia.

pea·fowl (pē'foul) *n.* A peacock or peahen. [< obs. *pea*, OE *pēa* a peacock + FOWL]

pea green Any of several shades of light yellowish green.

pea·hen (pē'hen) *n.* A female peafowl. [OE *pēa* a peacock + *henne* a hen]

pea·jack·et (pē'jak·it) *n.* A short coat of thick woolen cloth, worn by seamen. [Prob. < obs. *pee* a coat of coarse wool < MDu. *pie* + JACKET]

peak[1] (pēk) *n.* **1** A projecting point or edge; an end terminating in a point; summit: the *peak* of a roof. **2** A mountain with pointed summit; a conspicuous or precipitous mountain. **3** The highest point in a pattern of change or development: at the *peak* of his career. **4** *Naut.* **a** The after upper corner of a fore-and-aft sail. **b** The upper end of a gaff. **c** The sharply narrowed part of the hull or hold of a vessel at the bow or stern, called respectively the *forepeak* and *afterpeak*. **5** A

point formed on the forehead by the growth or cut of the hair: a widow's *peak*. See synonyms under SUMMIT. —*v.i.* **1** To reach a peak; climax: His campaign *peaked* two weeks before the election. —*v.t.* **2** *Naut.* To raise to or almost to a vertical position, as a gaff. ◆ Homophones: *peek, pique.* [OE *pīc*; def. 2 infl. by Sp. *pico* a beak, peak; *v.* infl. by *peak* vertically, aphetic var. of *apeak* < F *à pic* to a peak]

peak[2] (pēk) *v.i.* To become sickly, weak, or dispirited. ◆ Homophones: *peek, pique.* [Origin unknown]

peak·ed (pē'kid, pēkt) *adj.* Having a thin or sickly appearance. [< PEAK[2]]

peak load *Electr.* The maximum power load consumed or produced by a generating unit or group of units during a specified time.

peal (pēl) *n.* **1** A prolonged, sonorous sound, as of a bell, trumpet, or thunder. **2** A set of large bells attuned to the major scale. **3** The change rung on a chime, usually a scale or part of a scale. —*v.t. & v.i.* To sound with a peal or peals; ring out; resound. See synonyms under ROAR. ◆ Homophone: *peel.* [ME *pele*, aphetic var. of *apele* < OF *apeler*. See APPEAL.]

Peale (pēl) Name of a family of American artists, especially, **Charles Willson,** 1741–1827, who painted many portraits of George Washington; his brother **James,** 1749–1831, and his son **Rembrandt,** 1778–1860.

pea·nut (pē'nut') *n.* **1** The nutlike seed or seed pod of an annual herbaceous vine (*Arachis hypogaea*) of the pea family, ripening underground from the pistillate flowers, which bury themselves after fertilization. **2** The plant. **3** A small or insignificant person.

peanut brittle A hard candy containing roasted peanuts.

pear (pâr) *n.* **1** The juicy, edible, fleshy fruit of a tree (*Pyrus communis*) of the rose family, cultivated in many varieties. **2** The tree. ◆ Homophones: *pair, pare.* [OE *pere* < LL *pera, pira* < L *pira,* orig. pl. of *pirum* a pear]

pearl (pûrl) *n.* **1** A lustrous, calcareous concretion deposited in layers around a central nucleus in the shells of various mollusks, and largely used as a gem. **2** Something like or likened to such a jewel in form, luster, value, etc. **3** Nacre or mother-of-pearl; also, the color of nacre, or **pearl blue. 4** The color of a pearl, a delicate gray: also **pearl gray. 5** *Printing* A size of type, smaller than agate, 5 points. —*adj.* **1** Pertaining to, consisting of, set with, or made of pearl or mother-of-pearl: a *pearl* button; a *pearl* ring. **2** Shaped like a pearl: *pearl* barley. —*v.i.* **1** To seek or fish for pearls. **2** To form beads like pearls. —*v.t.* **3** To adorn or set with or as with pearls. **4** To color or shape like pearls. **5** To make into small round grains, as barley. ◆ Homophone: *purl.* [< OF *perle* < Med. L *perla*; ult. origin unknown]

pearl ash Crude potassium carbonate.

pearl barley Barley reduced to a round shotlike form by pearling: used in soups. Also **pearled barley.**

pearl·es·cent (pûr·les'ənt) *adj.* Having a pearly luster, as certain facial cosmetics; iridescent. [< PEARL + -ESCENT]

Pearl Harbor An inlet on the southern coast of Oahu, near Honolulu, Hawaii; site of a U.S. naval base, attacked by Japanese, December 7, 1941.

pearl·ing (pûr'ling) *n.* **1** The process of removing the outer coat of grain, as in making pearl barley. **2** The business of fishing for pearls.

pearl·ite (pûr'līt) *n.* Perlite.

pearl millet The East Indian millet, a tall cereal grass (*Pennisetum glaucum*) having edible seeds: used as a forage grass.

pearl·y (pûr'lē) *adj.* **pearl·i·er, pearl·i·est** Adorned with, yielding, or resembling pearls; margaric.

pear·main (pâr'mān) *n.* A variety of apple. [< OF *permain, parmain,* lit., of Parma, Italy]

Pea·ry (pir'ē), **Robert Edwin,** 1856–1920, U.S. Arctic explorer; first to reach the North Pole, April 6, 1909.

Peary Land A region of northern Greenland along the Arctic Ocean, the world's northernmost land region.

peas·ant (pez'ənt) *n.* **1** In Europe, a small farmer; a farm laborer; any rustic workman.

2 *Obs.* A rascal; base character; scamp. [< AF *paisant* < OF *païs* country < L *pagensis (ager)* (territory) of a canton < *pagus* a district]

peas·ant·ry (pez'ən·trē) *n.* **1** The peasant class; a body of peasants. **2** Rusticity.

peas·cod (pēz'kod) *n.* A pea pod. Also **pease'·cod.** [< PEAS(E) + COD[2]]

pease (pēz) *n. pl.* Peas collectively. [OE *pise* < LL *pisa* < L, orig. pl. of *pisum* < Gk. *pison* < *pisos* pulse, pease]

peat[1] (pēt) *n.* **1** A substance consisting of partially carbonized vegetable matter, chiefly mosses, found usually in bogs. **2** A block of this substance, pressed and dried for fuel. [< Med. L *peta* a piece of peat, ? < *petia* a fragment]

peat·man (pēt'mən) See PETEMAN.

peat moss 1 A moss that enters largely into the composition of peat. **2** *Brit.* A peat bog.

peat·y (pē'tē) *adj.* **peat·i·er, peat·i·est** Resembling or containing peat.

pea·vy (pē'vē) *n. pl.* **·vies** An iron-pointed lever fitted with a movable hook and used for handling logs. Also **pea'vey.** [after Joseph Peavey, its inventor]

peb·ble (peb'əl) *n.* **1** A small, rounded fragment of rock, its form being due to attrition of water, ice, etc. **2** Quartz crystal; also, a lens made of it. **3** Leather that has been pebbled. **4** Pebbleware. —*v.t.* **·bled, ·bling 1** To impart a rough grain to (leather). **2** To pave, cover, or pelt with pebbles. [OE *pabol(stān)* a pebble(stone)] —**peb'bly** *adj.*

peb·ble·stone (peb'əl·stōn') *n.* **1** A pebble. **2** A material consisting of a mass of pebbles. [See PEBBLE]

peb·ble·ware (peb'əl·wâr') *n.* A ware having different-colored clays in the paste.

pe·can (pi·kan', -kän', pē'kan) *n.* **1** A large hickory (*Carya illinoensis*) of the central and southern United States, with olive-shaped, thin-shelled nuts. **2** The nut borne by this tree, containing a sweet, oily kernel. [Earlier *paccan* < Algonquian (Cree) *pakan*]

pec·ca·ble (pek'ə·bəl) *adj.* Capable of sinning. [< OF < Med. L *peccabilis* < L *peccare* sin] —**pec'ca·bil'i·ty** *n.*

pec·ca·dil·lo (pek'ə·dil'ō) *n. pl.* **·los** or **·loes** A slight or trifling sin; a fault. See synonyms under FOIBLE. [< Sp. *pecadillo,* dim. of *pecado* a sin < L *peccatum,* orig. pp. of *peccare* sin]

pec·cant (pek'ənt) *adj.* **1** Guilty of sin; sinful; offending. **2** Corrupt and offensive; diseased. **3** Violating some rule or principle. [< L *peccans, -antis,* ppr. of *peccare* sin] —**pec'can·cy** *n.* —**pec'cant·ly** *adv.*

pec·ca·ry (pek'ər·ē) *n. pl.* **·ries** Either of two pugnacious hoglike ungulates of Central and South America, secreting an oily, musky substance, the **collared peccary** (*Pecari angulatus*), or the **white-lipped peccary** (*Tayassu pecari*). [< Sp. *pecari* < Cariban *pakira*]

PECCARY
(From 1 1/4 to 1 1/2 feet high at the shoulder)

peck[1] (pek) *v.t.* **1** To strike with the beak, as a bird does, or with something pointed. **2** To make by striking thus: to *peck* a hole in a wall. **3** To pick up, as food, with the beak. —*v.i.* **4** To make strokes with the beak or with something pointed. —*n.* **1** A quick, sharp blow, as with a beak or something pointed. **2** A mark, dent, or hole made by such a blow. [Var. of PICK] —**peck'er** *n.*

peck[2] (pek) *n.* **1** A measure of capacity: the fourth of a bushel, 8 quarts, or 8.8 liters. See DRY MEASURE. **2** A vessel for measuring a peck. **3** *Slang* A great quantity. [< OF *pek,* a measure of oats for horses]

peck-or·der (pek'ôr'dər) *n.* A hierarchy of social privilege and status among the members of a flock of chickens, established by the enforced right of the more aggressive hens or cocks to peck at, harass, and dominate all those lower in the scale.

Pe·cos Bill (pā'kōs) A legendary cowboy of the American West, who was raised by coyotes and performed many fantastic feats, such as digging the Rio Grande.

pec·tase (pek'tās) *n. Biochem.* An enzyme obtained from fruits which combines with pectin to yield pectic acid. [< PECT(IN) +

(DIAST)ASE]

pec·tate (pek′tāt) *n. Chem.* A salt or ester of pectic acid. [<PECT(IC) + -ATE³]

pec·ten (pek′tən) *n. pl.* **·ti·nes** (-tə-nēz) *Zool.* **1** A comb, or comblike part or process; specifically, in birds and reptiles, a vascular pigmented membrane of the eyeball. **2** A scallop. **3** *Anat.* The pubic bone. [<L, a comb, a scallop < *pectere* comb, dress the hair] — **pec′ti·nate, pec′ti·nat′ed** *adj.* — **pec′ti·na′tion** *n.*

pec·tin (pek′tin) *n. Biochem.* Any of a class of compounds of high molecular weight contained in the cell walls of various fruits and vegetables, as apples, lemons, or carrots: it is the basis of fruit jellies. [<PECT(IC) + -IN]

pec·tize (pek′tīz) *v.t. & v.i.* **·tized, ·tiz·ing** To coagulate. [<Gk. *pēktos* congealed + -IZE]

pec·to·ral (pek′tər·əl) *adj.* **1** Of or pertaining to the breast or thorax. **2** As if proceeding from the breast or inner consciousness; more especially, of an emotional character: *pectoral theology.* **3** Adapted to, efficacious in, or designed for relieving or curing diseases of the lungs or chest. — *n.* **1** An ornament worn on the breast; especially, the **pectoral cross** worn on the breast by bishops, abbots, etc. **2** A pectoral organ, fin, or muscle. **3** Any medicine for ailments of the chest. [<L *pectoralis* < *pectus, -oris* the breast]

pectoral arch or **girdle** *Anat.* **1** The arch formed by the collar bone and shoulder blade in man. **2** That part of the skeleton with which the forelimbs of a vertebrate animal are articulated.

pectoral fin *Zool.* One of the anterior paired fins of fishes, homologous with the anterior limb of higher vertebrates.

pec·u·late (pek′yə·lāt) *v.t. & v.i.* **·lat·ed, ·lat·ing** To steal or appropriate wrongfully (funds, especially public funds) entrusted to one's care; embezzle. [<L *peculatus,* pp. of *peculari* embezzle < *peculium.* See PECULIUM.] — **pec′u·la′tion** *n.* — **pec′u·la′tor** *n.*

pe·cul·iar (pi·kyōōl′yər) *adj.* **1** Having a character exclusively its own; unlike anything else or anything of the same class or kind; specific; particular. **2** Singular; odd; strange. **3** Select or special; separate; distinguished. **4** Belonging particularly or exclusively to one. — *n.* **1** A person or thing that is peculiar; formerly, any private possession. **2** A member of the sect known as the Peculiar People. See synonyms under EXTRAORDINARY, ODD, PARTICULAR, QUEER, RARE¹. [<MF *peculier* < L *peculiaris* < *peculium.* See PECULIUM.] — **pe·cul′iar·ly** *adv.*

pe·cu·li·ar·i·ty (pi·kyōō′lē·ar′ə·tē) *n. pl.* **·ties** **1** A characteristic. **2** The quality of being peculiar. See synonyms under CHARACTERISTIC.

Peculiar People 1 A denomination of Christians, founded in England in 1838, who hold that sinless perfection is immediately obtainable by those willing to seek and accept it. **2** In the Scripture, the Jews, as being God's chosen people and separated from the rest of mankind. *Deut.* xxvi 18.

pe·cu·ni·ar·y (pi·kyōō′nē·er′ē) *adj.* **1** Consisting of or relating to money; monetary. **2** Having a monetary penalty; entailing a fine. See synonyms under FINANCIAL. [<L *pecuniarius* < *pecunia* money < *pecus* cattle]

ped-¹ Var. of PEDI-.

ped-² Var. of PEDO-.

-pede Var. of -PEDE.

ped·a·gog (ped′ə·gog, -gôg) *n.* **1** A schoolmaster; especially, a pedantic, narrow-minded teacher. **2** In ancient Greece and Rome, a slave who attended children to school. Also **ped′a·gogue.** [<OF *pedagoge* < L *paedagogus* < Gk. *paidagōgos* < *pais, paidos* a child + *agōgos* a leader < *agein* lead]

ped·a·gog·ic (ped′ə·goj′ik, -gō′jik) *adj.* **1** Pertaining to the science or art of teaching. **2** Of or belonging to a pedagog; affected with a conceit of learning. Also **ped′a·gog′i·cal.** — **ped′a·gog′i·cal·ly** *adv.*

ped·a·gog·ics (ped′ə·goj′iks) *n. pl.* (*construed as singular*) The science and art of teaching; pedagogy.

ped·a·go·gy (ped′ə·gō′jē, -goj′ē) *n.* The science or profession of teaching; also, the theory or the teaching of how to teach.

ped·al (ped′l) *adj.* **1** Of or pertaining to a foot, feet, or a footlike part. **2** Of or pertaining to a pedal. — *n. Mech.* A lever operated by the foot, differing from a treadle in that it is usually applied only to musical instruments, cycles, sewing machines, and light machinery. — *v.t. & v.i.* **·aled** or **·alled, ·al·ing** or **·al·ling** To move or operate by working pedals; use the pedals (of). ◆ Homophone: *peddle.* [<L *pedalis* < *pes, pedis* the foot]

ped·a·lier (ped′ə·lir′) *n.* A pedal keyboard for a pianoforte. [<F *pédalier* < *pédale* <L *pedalis.* See PEDAL.]

pedal point *Music* A tonic or dominant note sustained (usually in the bass) while the other parts proceed with varying harmonies. Also **pedal note.**

ped·ant (ped′ənt) *n.* **1** A scholar who makes needless and inopportune display of his learning, or who insists upon the importance of trifling points of scholarship. **2** *Obs.* A schoolmaster; teacher. [<F *pédant* <Ital. *pedante,* prob. <Med. L *paedagogans, -antis,* ppr. of *paedagogare* teach <L *paedagogus.* See PEDAGOG.] — **pe·dan·tic** (pi·dan′tik) *adj.* — **pe·dan′ti·cal·ly** *adv.*

ped·ant·ry (ped′ən·trē) *n. pl.* **·ries 1** Ostentatious display of knowledge. **2** Undue and slavish adherence to forms or rules.

ped·ate (ped′āt) *adj.* **1** Resembling or having the functions of a foot; having feet. **2** *Bot.* Palmately divided or parted, the lateral divisions being subdivided: said especially of leaves. [<L *pedatus* having feet < *pes, pedis* a foot] — **ped′ate·ly** *adv.*

ped·dle (ped′l) *v.* **·dled, ·dling** *v.i.* **1** To travel about selling small wares. **2** To occupy oneself with trifles; piddle. — *v.t.* **3** To carry about and sell in small quantities. **4** To sell or dispense in small quantities. ◆ Homophone: *pedal.* [Appar. back formation <ME *ped-(d)ler(e)* a peddler; infl. by PIDDLE]

ped·dler (ped′lər) *n.* One who peddles; a hawker: also spelled *pedlar, pedler.* [ME *pedlere,* ? alter. of *pedder* a peddler < *ped* a basket] — **ped′dler·y** *n.*

ped·dling (ped′ling) *adj.* Small; trifling; piddling.

-pede *combining form* Footed: *centipede.* Also spelled *-ped,* as in *quadruped.* [<L *pes, pedis* foot]

ped·er·ast (ped′ə·rast, pē′də-) *n.* One addicted to pederasty: also spelled *paederast.*

ped·er·as·ty (ped′ə·ras′tē, pē′də-) *n.* Sodomy, especially as practiced between men and boys. [<NL *paederastia* <Gk. *paiderastia* < *paiderastēs* a lover of boys < *pais, paidos* a boy + *erastēs* a lover < *eraein* love] — **ped′er·as′tic** *adj.* — **ped′er·as′ti·cal·ly** *adv.*

ped·es·tal (ped′is·təl) *n.* **1** A base or support for a column, statue, or vase. **2** Hence, any foundation, base, or support, either material or immaterial. — **to put on a pedestal** To hold in high estimation; to put in the position of an idol or hero. [<MF *pédesta;* <Ital. *piedestallo* < *pie di stallo* < *piè, pied* foot (<L *pes, pedis*) + *di* of (<L *de*) + *stallo* a stall, standing place <OHG *stal*]

pe·des·tri·an (pə·des′trē·ən) *adj.* **1** Moving on foot; walking; pertaining to walking. **2** Pertaining to common people; plebeian. **3** Hence, commonplace, prosaic, or dull, as prose or mechanical verse. — *n.* One who journeys or moves from place to place on foot; a walker. [<L *pedester, -tris* on foot < *pes, pedis* a foot] — **pe·des′tri·an·ism** *n.*

pedi-¹ *combining form* Foot; related to the foot or feet: *pedicure.* Also, before vowels, *ped-.* [<L *pes, pedis* foot]

pedi-² *combining form* Pedo-. [<Gk. *pais, paidos* a child]

pe·di·a·tri·cian (pē′dē·ə·trish′ən, ped′ē-) *n.* A physician specializing in pediatrics. Also **pe′di·at′rist.**

pe·di·at·rics (pē′dē·at′riks, ped′ē-) *n.* That branch of medicine dealing with the diseases and hygienic care of children: also spelled *paediatrics.* [<Gk. *pais, paidos* a child + -IATRICS] — **pe′di·at′ric** *adj.*

ped·i·cab (ped′i·kab′) *n.* A three-wheeled vehicle operated by pedaling and having an attached seat for a passenger, available for public hire in some Asian countries. [<

PEDI-¹ + CAB¹]

pe·dic·u·lar (pə·dik′yə·lər) *adj.* Of, pertaining to, or infested with lice. [<L *pedicularis* < *pediculus,* dim. of *pedis* a louse]

ped·i·cure (ped′i·kyōōr) *n.* **1** The care of the feet; the surgical treatment of corns, bunions, etc. **2** A chiropodist. **3** The cosmetic treatment of the feet and toenails. — *v.t.* **·cured, ·cur·ing** To treat (the feet) for corns, bunions, etc. [<L *pes, pedis* a foot + *cura* care] — **ped′i·cur′ist** *n.*

ped·i·gree (ped′ə·grē) *n.* **1** A line of ancestors; lineage. **2** A list or table of descent and relationship; a genealogical register, especially of an animal of pure breed. [<MF *pié de grue* a crane's foot; from a three line mark denoting succession in pedigrees]

ped·i·greed (ped′ə·grēd) *adj.* Having a pedigree; of notable ancestry.

PEDIMENT
Pediment of the U. S. Supreme Court, Washington, D.C.

ped·i·ment (ped′ə·mənt) *n. Archit.* **1** A broad triangular part above a portico or door. **2** Any similar piece with a long base surmounting a door, screen, bookcase, etc. [Earlier *periment,* prob. alter. of PYRAMID; infl. in form by *pes, pedis* a foot] — **ped′i·men′tal** (-men′təl) *adj.*

ped·i·palp (ped′i·palp) *n. Zool.* **1** One of the second pair of appendages at the sides of the mouth in arachnids, terminally pincerlike, as in scorpions; long and leglike, as in solpugids; or leglike with the terminal joint serving to convey the semen in copulation, as in male spiders. **2** One of the *Pedipalpi.* — **ped′i·pal′pous** *adj.*

Ped·i·pal·pi (ped′i·pal′pī) *n. pl.* An order of arachnids with segmented abdomen; whip scorpions. [<NL <L *pes, pedis* foot + *palpus* feeler]

pedo- *combining form* Child; children; offspring: also, before vowels, *ped-,* as in *pedagogy.* Also spelled *paedo-.* [<Gk. *pais, paidos* a child]

ped·o·cal (ped′ō·kal) *n.* A type of soil characterized by an accumulation of carbonates of calcium or of calcium and magnesium. Compare PEDALFER. [<Gk. *pedon* ground + CAL(CIUM)]

pe·do·gen·e·sis (pē′dō·jen′ə·sis) *n. Entomol.* Reproduction in the sexually immature or larval stage, as in certain insects.

pe·dol·o·gy¹ (pi·dol′ə·jē) *n.* The scientific study of the development and behavior of children. [<PEDO- + -LOGY] — **ped·o·log·i·cal** (ped′ə·loj′i·kəl) *adj.* — **ped′o·log′i·cal·ly** *adv.* — **pe·dol′o·gist** *n.*

pe·dol·o·gy² (pi·dol′ə·jē) *n.* The science that treats of the origin, nature, and properties of soils, especially in their more fundamental aspects. [<Gk. *pedon* ground + -LOGY] — **pe·dol′o·gist** *n.*

ped·om·e·ter (pi·dom′ə·tər) *n.* An instrument that measures distance traveled by recording the number of steps taken by the person who carries it. [<F *pédomètre* <L *pes, pedis* foot + Gk. *metron* measure]

ped·o·sphere (ped′ə·sfir) *n.* The soil-bearing layer of the earth's surface. [<Gk. *pedon* ground + -SPHERE]

ped·re·gal (ped′ə·gäl′) *n.* In Mexico and SW United States, a rough, rocky tract of land, especially in a volcanic region; a lava field. [<Sp. < *piedra* a stone]

ped·ule (pej′ōōl) *n.* A leg covering of flexible leather, flannel, or other material, worn in ancient and medieval times. [<L, neut. of *pedulis* of or for the feet < *pes, pedis* a foot]

pe·dun·cle (pi·dung′kəl) *n.* **1** *Bot.* The general stalk or support of an inflorescence. **2** *Anat.* A stalk or stem, as for the attachment of an organ or organism: the *peduncles* of the brain. [<NL *pedunculus* a footstalk, dim. of *pes, pedis* a foot] — **pe·dun′cled, pe·dun′cu·lar** *adj.*

pee·been (pē′bēn) *n.* A large hardwood evergreen tree (*Syncarpia hilli*) of the myrtle family, native to Australia: also called *turpentine tree.*

peek (pēk) *v.i.* To look furtively, slyly, or quickly; peep. — *n.* A peep, glance. ◆ Homophones: *peak, pique.* [ME *piken,* ? var. of *kiken* peer; infl. by PEEP²]

peek-a-boo (pē′kə-bōō′) *n.* A children's game in which one hides (one's face) and calls out "peek-a-boo!" or "Bo-peep!"

peel (pēl) *n.* The natural coating of certain kinds of fruit, as oranges and lemons; skin; rind. — *v.t.* 1 To strip off the bark, skin, etc., of. 2 To strip off; remove. — *v.i.* 3 To lose bark, skin, etc. 4 To come off: said of bark, skin, etc. 5 *Slang* To undress. — **to keep one's eye peeled** *Colloq.* To keep watch; be alert. — **to peel off** *Aeron.* To veer off from a flight formation so as to dive or prepare for a landing. ◆ Homophone: *peal.* [Var. of earlier *pill* a skin, covering; infl. by F *peler* strip of skin]

peel² (pēl) *n.* 1 A broad, thin, long-handled, shovel-like implement used by bakers in moving bread, etc., about an oven. 2 The blade or broad part of an oar. ◆ Homophone: *peal.* [<OF *pele* <L *pala* a spade]

peel³ (pēl) *n.* 1 A square stronghold or tower of the 16th century, especially on the borders of Scotland and England: also **peel'-house'** (-hous′). 2 *Obs.* A stake; stockade; palisade. ◆ Homophone: *peal.* [<AF *pel* <L *palus* a stake]

Peel (pēl) A port and resort on the west coast of the Isle of Man; site of an ancient castle.

PEEL
Vaulted lower story often used as a stable; living quarters above.

peen (pēn) *n.* The end of a hammer head opposite the face: usually shaped for indenting, riveting, chipping, etc., as when straight, pointed, conical, hemispherical, or wedge-shaped: ball-*peen,* cross-*peen,* etc. See illustration under HAMMER. — *v.t.* To beat, bend, or shape with the peen. Also spelled *pane, pean, pein.* [Appar. var. of PANE², ? infl. by Scand. Cf. Norw. *paenn* the sharp end of a hammer.]

peep¹ (pēp) *v.i.* 1 To utter the small, sharp cry of a young bird or chick; chirp; cheep. 2 To speak in a weak, small voice. — *n.* 1 The cry of a chick or small bird, or of a young frog; chirp. 2 A small sandpiper; especially, the least sandpiper; sandpeep. [ME *pepen,* var. of *pipen* PIPE]

peep² (pēp) *v.i.* 1 To look through a small hole, from concealment, etc.; look furtively or quickly; peek. 2 To begin to appear; be just visible. — *v.t.* 3 *Rare* To cause to stick out slightly. — *n.* 1 A furtive look; a glimpse or glance. 2 An aperture or crevice through which one may look; peephole. 3 The earliest appearance: the *peep* of day. [ME *pepen.* ? Akin to ME *piken* PEEK.]

peep·er¹ (pē′pər) *n.* An animal that peeps or makes a chirping sound, especially a very young chick or any of several tree frogs.

peep·er² (pē′pər) *n.* 1 One who peeps or peeks; a spying person. 2 *Slang* An eye.

peep·hole (pēp′hōl′) *n.* An aperture, as a hole or crack, through which one may peep; also, a small window in a door.

peep·ing-tom (pē′ping-tom′) *n.* An overly inquisitive or pruriently prying person, especially one who peeps in at windows.

peep sight *Mil.* An adjustable plate on the breech of a gun or cannon, having in its center a small orifice through which an aim can be taken with great accuracy by centering the front sight therein.

peep·pul (pē′pəl) See PIPAL.

peer¹ (pir) *v.i.* 1 To look narrowly or searchingly, as in an effort to see clearly. 2 To come partially into view. 3 The sun *peers* over the horizon. 3 *Poetic* To appear. ◆ Homophone: *pier.* [Cf. obs. *pear, pere,* aphetic var. of APPEAR]

peer² (pir) *n.* 1 An equal, as in natural gifts or in social rank. 2 An equal before the law.

3 A noble; especially, a member of a hereditary legislative body. In the United Kingdom, a duke, marquis, earl, viscount, or baron; also, an archbishop or a bishop having a seat in the House of Lords. Until 1922 peers were of three classes: **Peers of the United Kingdom,** all of whom sit in the House of Lords, **Peers of Scotland,** and **Peers of Ireland.** 4 *Obs.* A companion; mate; associate; also, rival. See synonyms under ASSOCIATE. — **House of Peers** *Brit.* The House of Lords. ◆ Homophone: *pier.* [<OF *per* <L *par* equal]

peer·age (pir′ij) *n.* 1 In England, the office or rank of a peer of the realm, or nobleman. 2 Peers collectively; the nobility. 3 A book containing a genealogical list of the nobility.

peer·ess (pir′is) *n.* A woman who holds a title of nobility, either in her own right or by marriage with a peer.

peer·less (pir′lis) *adj.* Of unequaled excellence. — **peer′less·ly** *adv.* — **peer′less·ness** *n.*

peer of the blood royal A member of the royal family who is entitled to sit as a member of the House of Lords.

peer of the realm One of the lords of Parliament.

peet·weet (pēt′wēt) *n.* The spotted sandpiper. [Imit.]

peeved (pēvd) *adj.* Vexed; discontented; disagreeable.

pee·vish (pē′vish) *adj.* 1 Irritable or querulous; fretful; cross. 2 Showing or marked by petulant discontent and vexation. See synonyms under FRETFUL. [ME *pevische;* origin unknown] — **pee′vish·ly** *adv.* — **pee′vish·ness** *n.*

pee·wee (pē′wē) *n.* 1 The pewee. 2 *Colloq.* Anything or anyone especially small or diminutive. — *adj.* Tiny; insignificant. [Prob. <Algonquian (Massachuset) *pewe* little]

peg (peg) *n.* 1 A wooden pin used for fastening articles together or for holding fast the end of a string and adjusting its tension in a musical instrument. 2 A projecting wooden pin upon which something may be fastened or hung, or which may serve to mark a boundary. 3 Hence, a reason or excuse for an action: a *peg* to hang an argument upon. 4 A degree or step, as in rank or estimation. 5 *Brit.* A drink of brandy and soda or of whisky and soda. 6 *Colloq.* A leg, often one of wood. — **to take (one) down a peg** To lower the self-esteem of (a person), as by humiliating. — *v.* **pegged, peg·ging** *v.t.* 1 To drive or force a peg into; fasten with pegs. 2 To mark or designate with pegs. 3 To strike or pierce with a peg or sharp instrument. 4 *Colloq.* To throw: to *peg* stones. — *v.i.* 5 To work or strive hard and perseveringly: usually with *away.* 6 In croquet, to hit a peg. 7 In cribbage, etc., to mark the score with pegs. [ME *pegge* <LG; cf. MDu. *pegge*]

Peg·a·sus (peg′ə·səs) 1 In Greek mythology, a winged horse, sprung from the blood of Medusa, a blow of whose hoof caused the fountain of poetic inspiration, Hippocrene, to spring from Mount Helicon; hence, poetic inspiration. See BELLEROPHON. 2 *Astron.* A northern constellation. See CONSTELLATION. [<L <Gk. *Pēgasos,* after *pēgai* the springs of Ocean, where Medusa was killed]

peg·ma·tite (peg′mə·tīt) *n.* A very coarse-grained granitic rock composed chiefly of orthoclase, quartz, and mica (usually muscovite); graphic granite: often occurs in veins or dikes. [<Gk. *pēgma, -atos* a solid mass + -ITE¹] — **peg′ma·tit′ic** (-tit′ik) *adj.*

peg top A child's wooden spinning top, pear-shaped and having a sharp metal peg.

pei·gnoir (pān·wär′, pān′wär) *n.* A loose dressing robe worn by women; a bathrobe; a negligee. [<F <*peigner* comb <L *pectinare* < *pecten* a comb]

pein (pēn) See PEEN.

pei·no·ther·a·py (pī′nō·ther′ə·pē) *n. Med.* The treatment of disease by severe fasting and starvation; the hunger cure. [<Gk. *peina* hunger + THERAPY]

pe·jo·ra·tion (pē′jə·rā′shən, pej′ə-) *n.* 1 A worsening; deterioration. 2 *Ling.* A degeneration or lowering in the meaning of a word, as in *silly* (formerly "blessed"): opposed to *melioration.*

pe·jo·ra·tive (pē′jə·rā′tiv, pej′ə-, pi·jôr′ə·tiv, -jor′-) *adj.* Giving a deteriorating effect or meaning, as to the sense of a word. — *n.* A word expressing depreciation. [<L *pejoratus,*

pp. of *pejorare* make worse < *pejor* worse] — **pe′jo·ra′tive·ly** *adv.*

pek·an (pek′ən) *n.* A North American carnivore; the fisher. [< dial. F (Canadian) <Algonquian *pékané*]

pe·kin (pē′kin′) *n.* A silk fabric, usually figured or striped. [<F *pékin* <*Pékin* Peking, China]

Pe·king (pē′king′, *Chinese* bā′jing′) A city in northern Hopeh province, the capital of the People's Republic of China; from 1928 to 1949 known as *Peiping.*

Pe·king·ese (pē′king·ēz′) *n. pl.* **·ese** 1 A native or inhabitant of Peking. 2 The dialect spoken in Peking. 3 (pē′kə·nēz′) A Pekingese dog. — *adj.* Of or pertaining to Peking. Also **Pe′kin·ese′.**

Pekingese dog A variety of the Chinese (or Pekingese) pug, with long silky hair, especially upon the ears, diminutive snub nose, and short legs.

PEKINGESE DOG
(From 7 to 10 inches high at the shoulder)

Peking lacquer Chinese carved lacquer.

Peking man *Paleontol.* Sinanthropus.

pe·koe (pē′kō, *Brit.* pek′ō) *n.* A superior kind of black tea, made from the downy tips of the young buds of the tea plant. [< dial. Chinese (Amoy) *pek-ho* < *pek* white + *ho* down]

pel·age (pel′ij) *n.* The coat or covering of a mammal, as of fur, wool, etc. [<MF <OF *peil, pel* hair <L *pilus*]

pe·la·gi·an (pə·lā′jē·ən) *adj.* Pelagic. — *n.* A deep-sea animal. [<L *pelagius* of the sea <Gk. *pelagios* < *pelagos* the sea]

Pe·la·gi·an·ism (pə·lā′jē·ən·iz′əm) *n. Theol.* The body of doctrines held by the followers of Pelagius, who denied original sin, confined grace to forgiveness, and affirmed that man's unaided will is capable of spiritual good. — **Pe·la′gi·an** *n. & adj.*

pe·lag·ic (pə·laj′ik) *adj.* 1 Of, pertaining to, or inhabiting the sea far from land; oceanic. 2 Living on or near the surface of the ocean. 3 Conducted or operating on the open sea: *pelagic* sealing or sealers. [<L *pelagicus* <Gk. *pelagikos* < *pelagos* the sea]

pelargonic acid *Chem.* A colorless compound, $CH_3(CH_2)_7 \cdot COOH$, liquid at ordinary temperatures, obtained as an ester from oil of pelargonium: also called *nonanoic acid.*

pel·ar·go·ni·um (pel′är·gō′nē·əm) *n.* Any of a large genus (*Pelargonium*) of strong-scented, ornamental evergreen herbs or shrubs, generally known in cultivation as *geraniums,* having entire lobed or dissected leaves, and handsome, variously colored flowers. [<NL <Gk. *pelargos* a stork < *pelos* blackish + *argos* shining] — **pel′ar·gon′ic** (-gon′ik) *adj.*

Pe·las·gi (pə·laz′jī) *n. pl.* A primitive, seafaring people who inhabited the coasts of Greece, Asia Minor, Crete, Thrace, etc.: mentioned by ancient Greek writers as the pre-Greek inhabitants of the eastern Mediterranean region. Also **Pe·las′gi·ans.** — **Pe·las′gi·an** *adj. & n.* — **Pe·las′gic** *adj.*

Pe·le (pā′lā) In Polynesian mythology, the goddess of volcanoes.

pel·er·ine (pel′ə·rēn′) *n.* A waist-length cape worn by women. [<F *pèlerine,* fem. of *pèlerin.* See PILGRIM.]

Pe·le's hair (pā′lāz) Volcanic glass drawn out into long, fine threads by ejected driblets of fused lava; capillary volcanic glass. [after PELE]

Pe·leus (pēl′yōōs, pē′lē·əs) In Greek legend, a king of the Myrmidons and father of Achilles.

pe·lisse (pə·lēs′) *n.* A long outer garment or cloak: originally one of fur or lined with fur. [<F <Med. L *pellicia* <L, a garment of skins or fur < *pellis* skin]

pe·lite (pē′līt) *n.* A sedimentary rock composed of clay, quartz particles, or rock flour: also called *argillite.* [<Gk. *pēlos* clay + -ITE¹] — **pe·lit·ic** (pi·lit′ik) *adj.*

Pel·la (pel′ə) A city of ancient Greece; birthplace of Alexander the Great and capital of Macedonia.

pel·la·gra (pə·lā′grə, -lag′rə) *n. Pathol.* A disease characterized by gastric disturbance, skin eruptions, and nervous derangement: endemic in many parts of the world, and known to be caused by nutritional deficiencies. [<NL prob. <Ital. *pelle agra* rough skin; ? infl. by Gk. *-agra* <*agra* a seizure, as in *podagra* gout, lit., a seizure in the feet] — **pel·la′grous** *adj.*

pel·la·grin (pə·lā′grin, -lag′rin) *n.* A sufferer from pellagra.

pelf (pelf) *n.* Money; wealth: often implying ill-gotten gains. See synonyms under WEALTH. [<AF *peufe*, OF *pelfre* spoil; ult. origin uncertain]

Pe·li·as (pē′lē·əs, pel′ē·əs) In Greek mythology, a son of Poseidon and king of Iolcus; who sent his nephew Jason to get the Golden Fleece: after Jason's return, Medea caused Pelias' death by persuading his daughters to cut their father into little pieces and stew him as a means of restoring his youth.

pel·i·can (pel′i·kən) *n.* A large, gregarious, fish-eating, web-footed bird (genus *Pelecanus*) of warm regions, having a distensible membranous pouch on the lower jaw for the temporary storage of fish. [OE *pellican* <LL *pelicanus, pelecanus* <Gk. *pelekan*, ? <*pelekys* an ax; in ref. to its bill]

WHITE PELICAN

pel·let (pel′it) *n.* 1 A small round ball or imitation projectile, as of wax, paper, bread, etc. 2 A small shot. 3 A very small pill. 4 A slingstone; also, a bullet; cannonball. — *v.t.* 1 To make into pellets. 2 To strike with pellets. [<OF *pelote* a ball <Med. L *pelota, pilota* <L *pila*]

pel·le·tier·ine (pel′ə·tir′in, -ēn) *n. Chem.* A sirupy liquid alkaloid, $C_8H_{15}ON$, from the roots of the pomegranate tree: its salts are powerful anthelminthics. [after Bertrand *Pelletier*, 1761–1797, French chemist]

pel·li·cle (pel′i·kəl) *n.* A thin skin, film, or layer. [<L *pellicula*, dim. of *pellis* skin] — **pel·lic·u·lar** (pə·lik′yə·lər) *adj.*

pel·li·to·ry (pel′ə·tôr′ē, -tō′rē) *n. pl.* **·ries** Any of various diffuse or tufted weedlike herbs of the nettle family (genus *Parietaria*); especially, the European **wall pellitory** (*P. officinalis*), which grows on old walls. [Alter. of earlier *paretarie* <AF *paritarie* <L (*herba*) *parietaria* wall (plant) <*parietarius* of a wall <*paries, -etis* a wall]

pell–mell (pel′mel′) *adv.* 1 In a confused or promiscuous way or manner; indiscriminately; higgledy-piggledy. 2 With a headlong rush. — *adj.* Devoid of order or method. — *n.* A confused crowd or mixture; a medley; disorder. Also **pell′mell′**. [<F *pêle-mêle* <OF *pesle-mesle*, varied reduplication <*mesler* mix]

pel·lu·cid (pə·lōō′sid) *adj.* 1 Permitting to a certain extent the passage of light; translucent; limpid. 2 Transparent; clear; understandable: a *pellucid* style. See synonyms under CLEAR, TRANSPARENT. [<L *pellucidus* <*perlucere* <*per-* through + *lucere* shine] — **pel·lu′cid·ly** *adv.* — **pel·lu′cid·ness, pel·lu·cid·i·ty** (pel′ōō·sid′ə·tē) *n.*

pe·lon (pə·lōn′) *adj.* Hairless: said of animals. [<Am. Sp. <Sp. *pelón* bald]

pelon dog The Mexican hairless dog.

pe·lo·ri·a (pə·lôr′ē·ə, -lō′rē·ə) *n. Bot.* Reversion of an irregular flower form, by abnormal development of complementary irregularities or by the loss of the irregular parts. Also **pel·o·rism** (pel′ə·riz′əm). [<NL <Gk. *peloros* monstrous <*pelōr* a monster] — **pe·lo′ri·ate, pe·lor·ic** (pə·lôr′ik, -lor′-) *adj.*

pe·lo·rus (pə·lôr′əs, -lō′rəs) *n.* 1 *Aeron.* A circular plate having its movable rim graduated in degrees: used to determine the actual or relative bearings of objects. 2 *Nav.* An instrument for correcting errors in the compass by stellar observations. [after *Pelorus*, said to have been Hannibal's pilot]

pelt¹ (pelt) *n.* 1 An undressed fur skin; raw hide; also, a garment made of skin. 2 *Slang* The human skin. [Prob. back formation <AF *pelterie.* See PELTRY.]

pelt² (pelt) *v.t.* 1 To strike repeatedly with or as with missiles or blows. 2 To throw or hurl (missiles). 3 To assail with words. — *v.i.* 4

To beat or descend with violence. 5 To move rapidly; hurry. — *n.* 1 A blow, as one given by something thrown. 2 A steady or swift pace: especially in the expression **full pelt.** [ME *pelten*, ? var. of *pulten* thrust <L *pultare*, freq. of *pellere* beat, drive] — **pelt′er** *n.*

pel·tate (pel′tāt) *adj.* 1 Shield-shaped. 2 *Bot.* Attached to the stalk at or near the center of the lower surface, as a leaf. Also **pel′tat·ed.** See SCUTATE. [<L *peltatus* armed with a shield <Gk. *peltē* a shield] — **pel′tate·ly** *adv.*

pelt·ry (pel′trē) *n. pl.* **·ries** 1 Pelts collectively. 2 A pelt. 3 A place for keeping or storing pelts. [<AF *pelterie* <OF *peletier* a furrier <*pel* a skin <L *pellis*]

pel·vic (pel′vik) *adj.* Of or pertaining to the pelvis.

pelvic arch *Anat.* That part of the skeleton in vertebrates to which the hind limbs (in man, the lower limbs) are attached. Also **pelvic girdle.**

pel·vim·e·try (pel·vim′ə·trē) *n. Med.* The measurement of the size and capacity of the pelvis, especially by X-rays prior to childbirth. — **pel·vi·met·ric** (pel′vi·met′rik) *adj.*

pel·vis (pel′vis) *n. pl.* **·ves** (-vēz) 1 A basin or basinlike structure. 2 *Anat.* **a** The part of the skeleton that forms a bony girdle joining the lower or hind limbs to the body: composed, in man, of two hip bones and the sacrum. **b** The hollow interior portion of the kidney, into which the uriniferous tubules empty; formed by the expanded part of the ureter. [<NL <L, a basin]

HUMAN PELVIS
a. Crest of ilium.
b. Ilium.
c. Coccyx.
d. Socket of thigh bone.
e. Ischium.
f. Pubic symphysis.
g. Head of femur.
h. Sacrum.
i. Lumbar vertebrae.

pem·mi·can (pem′ə·kən) *n.* 1 Lean venison cut into strips, dried, pounded into paste with fat and a few berries, and pressed into cakes. 2 A similar concentrated and nutritious food made from beef and dried fruits: used by Arctic explorers, etc. Also **pem′i·can.** [<Algonquian (Cree) *pimekan* <*pime* fat]

pen¹ (pen) *n.* 1 An instrument for writing with a fluid ink: formerly made of a quill, now usually of metal and fitted to a holder; by extension, pen and holder together. 2 Quality of penmanship or of composition. 3 A writer; also, the profession of writing. 4 *Bot.* The midrib of a leaf. 5 *Zool.* The internal shell of a cuttlefish. 6 *Ornithol.* A feather; quill; also, in the plural, wings. — *v.t.* **penned, pen·ning** To write with a pen; indite. [<OF *penne* a pen, a feather <LL *penna* <L, a feather] — **pen′ner** *n.*

pen² (pen) *n.* 1 A small enclosure, as for pigs; also, the animals contained in a pen collectively. 2 Any small place of confinement, as in a police court. 3 *Slang* A penitentiary. — *v.t.* **penned** or **pent, pen·ning** To enclose in or as in a pen; confine. [OE *penn*]

pen³ (pen) *n.* A female swan. [Origin unknown]

pe·nal (pē′nəl) *adj.* 1 Pertaining to punishment or its means or place. 2 Liable, or rendering liable, to punishment. 3 Enacting or prescribing punishment. [<OF *penal* <L *penalis, poenalis* <*poena* a penalty <Gk. *poinē* a fine]

pe·nal·ize (pē′nəl·īz, pen′əl-) *v.t.* **·ized, ·iz·ing** 1 To subject to a penalty, as for a violation. 2 To declare, as an action, subject to a penalty. Also *Brit.* **pe′nal·ise.** — **pe′nal·i·za′tion** *n.*

pen·al·ty (pen′əl·tē) *n. pl.* **·ties** 1 The consequences, as suffering, detriment, etc., that follow the transgression of laws. 2 Judicial punishment for crime or violation of the law. 3 *Law* **a** A sum of money fixed by a statute as a fine or mulct for a violation of its provisions. **b** A sum of money paid and stipulated to be forfeited in case of the non-performance of the conditions of a contract. 4 A handicap

imposed for a violation of rules or regulations of a game. [<Med. L *poenalitas, -tatis* <L *poenalis* PENAL]

pen·ance (pen′əns) *n.* 1 *Eccl.* A sacramental rite involving contrition, confession to a priest, the acceptance of penalties, and absolution. 2 A feeling of sorrow for sin or fault, evinced by some outward act; repentance. 3 A penalty, suffering, mortification, or act of piety, imposed or voluntarily undertaken as an atonement or outward sign of repentance for sin. 4 The performance of a penitential act or acts. — **to do penance** To perform an act or acts of penance; to repent of one's sins. — *v.t.* **pen·anced, pen·anc·ing** To impose a penance upon. [<OF <L *paenitentia.* Doublet of PENITENCE.]

pe·nang (pē·nang′) *n.* A heavy cotton fabric resembling percale. [? from *Penang*]

pen·cel (pen′səl) *n.* A small pennon or streamer; a pennoncel: also spelled *pensil, pensile.* ♦ Homophone: *pencil.* [<AF, alter. of *penoncel.* See PENNONCEL.]

pen·chant (pen′chənt, *Fr.* päṅ·shäṅ′) *n.* A strong leaning or inclination in favor of something. [<F, orig. ppr. of *pencher* incline, ult. <L *pendere* hang]

pen·cil (pen′səl) *n.* 1 A long, pointed strip of graphite, colored chalk, slate, etc., often encased in wood: used for writing or drawing. 2 A small, finely pointed paint brush: also **hair pencil.** 3 A set of rays diverging from or converging upon a given point. 4 Skill, as in drawing or painting; the painter's art. 5 A small stick of any substance having caustic or styptic properties. 6 An eyebrow pencil. — *v.t.* **·ciled** or **·cilled, ·cil·ing** or **·cil·ling** To mark, write, or draw with or as with a pencil. ♦ Homophone: *pencel.* [<OF *pincel* <L *penicillum* a paint brush, double dim. of *penis* a tail; infl. by *pen¹*] — **pen′cil·er** or **pen′cil·ler** *n.*

pen·ciled (pen′səld) *adj.* 1 Marked with fine lines, with or as if with a finely pointed pencil. 2 Having pencils, or lines or rays. Also **pen′cilled.**

pend (pend) *v.i.* 1 To await or be in process of adjustment or settlement. 2 *Dial.* To hang; depend. [<MF *pendre* hang <L *pendere*]

pen·dant (pen′dənt) *n.* 1 Anything that hangs or depends from something else, either for ornament or for use. 2 Something attached to another thing as an ending; an appendix. 3 A parallel; one of a pair. 4 *Archit.* A hanging ornament, as a long boss or knot, particularly in late Perpendicular work, on ceilings, roofs, etc. 5 The stem of a watchcase and the ring by which it is attached to a chain. 6 A suspended chandelier; also, an electrical fitting hanging from a ceiling, lamp, chandelier, etc., by which to switch on and off a light. Also spelled *pendent.* — *adj.* Pendent. [<OF, orig. ppr. of *pendre* hang. See PEND.]

pen·dent (pen′dənt) *adj.* 1 Hanging loosely; drooping downward; suspended. 2 Projecting or overhanging. 3 Undetermined; pending; incomplete. Also spelled *pendant.* — *n.* Pendant. [Var. of PENDANT, refashioned after L] — **pen′dent·ly** *adv.*

pend·ing (pen′ding) *adj.* 1 Remaining unfinished or undecided. 2 Imminent; impending. — *prep.* 1 During the continuance of. 2 Awaiting; until: The court adjourned *pending* the jury's verdict.

pen·du·lous (pen′jŏŏ·ləs) *adj.* Hanging, especially so as to swing. [<L *pendulus* hanging <*pendere* hang] — **pen′du·lous·ly** *adv.* — **pen′du·lous·ness** *n.*

pen·du·lum (pen′jŏŏ·ləm, -də-) *n.* 1 A body suspended from a fixed point, and free to swing to and fro. 2 Such a device, consisting of rod and bob, and serving, by oscillation under the forces of gravity plus momentum, to regulate the rate of running of a clock. [<NL <L, neut. of *pendulus.* See PENDULOUS.]

Pe·nel·o·pe (pə·nel′ə·pē) A feminine personal name. Also *Fr.* Pé·né·lope (pā·nā·lōp′). [<Gk., a weaver]

PENDULUM

pen·e·tra·li·a (pen'ə·trā'lē·ə) *n. pl.* 1 The inmost parts of anything, but especially of a house or temple; a sanctuary; shrine. 2 Secret things. [<L, orig. neut. pl. of *penetralis* innermost < *penetrare*. See PENETRATE.]

pen·e·trance (pen'ə·trəns) *n. Genetics* A measure of the frequency with which a given gene will show its effects, expressed as a percentage of the total number of cases observed. [<L *penetrans, -antis*, ppr. of *penetrare*. See PENETRATE.]

pen·e·trate (pen'ə·trāt) *v.* **·trat·ed, ·trat·ing** *v.t.* 1 To force a way into or through; pierce; enter. 2 To spread or diffuse itself throughout; permeate. 3 To perceive the meaning of; understand. 4 To affect or move profoundly. — *v.i.* 5 To enter or pass through something. 6 To have effect on the mind or emotions. See synonyms under PIERCE. [<L *penetratus* < *penetrare* put within < *penitus* inside] — **pen'e·tra·ble** (-trə·bəl) *adj.* — **pen'e·tra·bil'i·ty** *n.* — **pen'e·trant** *adj. & n.*

pen·e·trat·ing (pen'ə·trā'ting) *adj.* Tending or having power to penetrate; acute; discerning. See synonyms under ACUTE, ASTUTE, KNOWING, SHARP. — **pen'e·trat'ing·ly** *adv.* — **pen'e·trat'ing·ness** *n.*

pen·e·tra·tion (pen'ə·trā'shən) *n.* 1 The act or power of penetrating physically. 2 Ability to penetrate mentally; acuteness; sagacity. 3 The depth to which a bullet or other projectile sinks in a target. See synonyms under ENTRANCE[1].

pen·e·tra·tive (pen'ə·trā'tiv) *adj.* Tending or having power to penetrate, physically or mentally; insinuating and pervasive; pungent: a *penetrative* odor; acute; discerning: *penetrative* wisdom. See synonyms under ASTUTE. — **pen'·e·tra'tive·ly** *adv.* — **pen'e·tra'tive·ness** *n.*

pen·e·trom·e·ter (pen'ə·trom'ə·tər) *n.* 1 An instrument for indicating the quality and measuring the strength of X-rays. 2 A device for testing the hardness of relatively plastic substances under given conditions. [<L *penetrare* PENETRATE + -METER]

pen·guin (pen'gwin, peng'-) *n.* 1 A web-footed, flightless, aquatic bird (genus *Spheniscus*) of the southern hemisphere, with flipperlike wings, short legs, and plantigrade feet. 2 Originally, the great auk. 3 *Aeron.* An airplane with an engine of low motive power, so as to be incapable of flight: used in the early training of aviators. [Cf. F *pingouin, penguyn* the great auk]

EMPEROR
PENGUIN

pen·i·cil·late (pen'ə·sil'it, -āt) *adj.* 1 Pencil shaped. 2 *Biol.* Bordered or tufted with fine hairs resembling a hair pencil. Also **pen'i·cil'·li·form.** [<L *penicillus* a pencil + -ATE[1]] — **pen'i·cil'late·ly** *adv.* — **pen'i·cil·la'tion** (-si·lā'shən) *n.*

pen·i·cil·lin (pen'ə·sil'in) *n.* A powerful antibacterial substance found in the mold fungus *Penicillium;* prepared in several forms for the treatment of a wide variety of infective conditions. [<PENICILL(IUM) + -IN]

pen·i·cil·li·um (pen'ə·sil'ē·əm) *n. pl.* **·li·a** (-ē·ə) Any member of a genus (*Penicillium*) of ascomycetous fungi characterized by feltlike masses of tubular hyphae, and growing on decaying fruits, ripening cheese, etc. *P. notatum* is the principal source of penicillin. [<NL <L *penicillus* a pencil: so called because of resemblance of its tufts to small paint brushes]

pe·nin·su·la (pə·nin'sə·lə, -syə-) *n.* A piece of land almost surrounded by water, and connected with the mainland by an isthmus. [<L *paeninsula* < *paene* almost + *insula* an island] — **pe·nin'su·lar** *adj.*

pe·nis (pē'nis) *n. pl.* **·nes** (-nēz) The male copulatory organ. [<L, orig. a tail] — **pe'ni·al** (-nē·əl), **pe'nile** (-nil, -nīl) *adj.*

pen·i·tence (pen'ə·təns) *n.* The state of being penitent; sorrow for sin, with desire to amend and atone; contrition. See synonyms under CONTRITION. [<OF *penitence* <L *paenitentia* < *paenitens,* ppr. of *paenitare* repent. Doublet of PENANCE.]

pen·i·tent (pen'ə·tənt) *adj.* Affected by a sense of one's own guilt, and resolved on amendment; repentant; contrite. — *n.* 1 One who is

penitent. 2 One who confesses his sins to a priest and submits himself to the penance prescribed. — **pen'i·tent·ly** *adv.*

pen·i·ten·tial (pen'ə·ten'shəl) *adj.* 1 Pertaining to or expressing penitence. 2 Pertaining to penance or punishment. — *n.* 1 *Eccl.* A book of rules relating to penance and the reconciliation of penitents. 2 A penitent. — **pen'i·ten'tial·ly** *adv.*

pen·i·ten·tia·ry (pen'ə·ten'shər·ē) *n. pl.* **·ries** 1 A prison, especially one operated by a state or government as a place of confinement and correction for those convicted of serious crimes. 2 One who prescribes or superintends penances; also, something that has to do with penances; specifically, in the Roman Catholic Church, an office, having at its head a cardinal (called the **Grand Penitentiary**), for deciding questions of conscience, absolution, special dispensation, etc. — *adj.* 1 Pertaining to penance. 2 Relating to or used for the punishment and discipline of criminals. 3 Rendering the offender liable to imprisonment in a penitentiary. [<Med. L *poenitentiarius* <L *poenitentia* PENITENCE]

pen·knife (pen'nīf') *n. pl.* **·knives** (-nivz') A small pocket knife: formerly used for making or sharpening quill pens.

pen·man (pen'mən) *n. pl.* **·men** (-mən) 1 A person considered with regard to his handwriting; also, a teacher of penmanship, or one skilled in penmanship. 2 A writer.

pen·man·ship (pen'mən·ship) *n.* 1 The art of writing. 2 Handwriting; calligraphy.

Penn (pen), **William,** 1644–1718, English Quaker; founder of Pennsylvania.

pen·na (pen'ə) *n. pl.* **·nae** (-ē) *Ornithol.* A feather; plume; especially, a quill feather of wing or tail. [<NL <L, a feather] — **pen·na·ceous** (pə·nā'shəs) *adj.*

pen name An author's assumed name; pseudonym; nom de plume.

pen·nant (pen'ənt) *n.* 1 A long, narrow flag displayed on a commissioned naval vessel; also, a triangular flag flown as a signal. 2 A small flag peculiar in shape, color or design, flown during a public function. 3 A flag awarded to the winners in some sports leagues; also, the championship thus symbolized. 4 *Music* The hook distinguishing notes shorter than quarter notes. [<PENNON; infl. by PENDANT]

pen·nate (pen'āt) *adj.* Having wings or feathers: usually in composition: *longipennate*. Also **pen'nat·ed.** [<L *pennatus* winged < *penna* a feather]

pen·ni·less (pen'i·lis) *adj.* Being without even a penny; poverty-stricken.

pen·non (pen'ən) *n.* 1 A small, pointed or swallow-tailed flag, borne by medieval knights on their lances and displaying a personal device. 1 A wing. 3 A banner or flag of any sort. [<OF *penon* a streamer, feather of an arrow <L *penna* a feather]

Penn·syl·va·ni·a (pen'səl·vā'nē·ə, -vān'yə) An eastern State of the United States: 45,333 square miles; capital, Harrisburg; entered the Union Dec. 12, 1787; one of the thirteen original States; nickname, *Keystone State* or *Quaker State;* abbr. PA Official name: *Commonwealth of Pennsylvania.*

Pennsylvania Avenue A principal street of Washington, D.C., which runs in part from the Capitol to the White House.

Penn·syl·va·ni·a-Dutch (pen'səl·vā'nē·ə·duch', -vān'yə-) *adj.* 1 Pertaining to the Pennsylvania Dutch. 2 Denoting a style of furniture, pottery, etc., made by these people, characterized by carved or gaily colored decorations of flowers, fruits, etc.

Pennsylvania Dutch 1 Descendants of immigrants from the Palatinate, SW Germany, and Switzerland who settled in Pennsylvania in the 17th and 18th centuries. 2 The language spoken by these people: a High German dialect with an admixture of English. Also **Pennsylvania German.**

pen·ny (pen'ē) *n. pl.* **pen·nies** or *Brit.* **pence** (pens) 1 In the United States and Canada, a cent. 2 A coin of Great Britain, Ireland, and various members of the Commonwealth of Nations, equivalent to 1/12 shilling. 3 In the United Kingdom, a coin equal in value to 1/100 pound: also *new penny.* 4 Money in general. [OE *penning, penig, pending*]

-penny *combining form* Costing (a specified number of) pennies: formerly designating the

cost of nails per hundred, but now denoting their length, beginning at 1 inch for twopenny nails and increasing by quarter-inches up to tenpenny, thereafter irregularly. [<PENNY]

pen·ny-a-line (pen'ē·ə·līn') *adj.* Cheap; inferior: said of writing.

pen·ny-a-lin·er (pen'ē·ə·lī'nər) *n.* A literary drudge; a hack writer.

penny ante A poker game in which the ante is limited to one cent.

pen·ny·roy·al (pen'ē·roi'əl) *n.* 1 A low, erect, branching, strong-scented American herb (*Hedeoma pulegioides*) of the mint family, yielding the oil of pennyroyal used in medicine. 2 A species of European mint (*Mentha pulegium*) resembling the American pennyroyal in taste, odor, and uses. [Alter. of earlier *pulyole ryale* <AF *puliol real* <L *pulegium* fleabane + *regale* royal]

pen·ny·weight (pen'ē·wāt') *n.* The twentieth part of an ounce in troy weight, or 1.55 grams.

pen·ny-wise (pen'ē·wīz') *adj.* Unduly economical in small matters: usually in the phrase **penny-wise and pound-foolish,** economical in small matters, but wasteful in large ones. — **pen'ny-wis'dom** (-wiz'dəm) *n.*

pen·ny·wort (pen'ē·wûrt') *n.* Anyone of various plants with round or peltate leaves, as the several species of *Hydrocotyle,* of the parsley family, the navelwort, and the American gentian (*Obolaria virginica*), with funnel-shaped, white, pink, or purple flowers.

pen·ny·worth (pen'ē·wûrth') *n.* 1 As much as can be bought for a penny. 2 The amount given or received for money paid; a bargain. 3 A small amount; trifle.

Pe·nob·scot (pə·nob'skot) *n.* One of a tribe of North American Indians of the Algonquian confederacy of 1749.

pe·nol·o·gy (pē·nol'ə·je) *n.* The science that treats of the punishment and prevention of crime and of the management of prisons and reformatories: also spelled *poenology.* [<L *poena* a penalty + -LOGY] — **pe·no·log'i·cal** (pē'nə·loj'i·kəl) *adj.* — **pe·nol'o·gist** *n.*

Pen·sa·co·la (pen'sə·kō'lə) A port on **Pensacola Bay,** an arm of the Gulf of Mexico in NW Florida; site of a U.S. naval and air base.

pen·se·mon (pen·sē'mən) See PENSTEMON.

pen·sil (pen'sil), **pen·sile** (pen'sil) See PENCEL.

pen·sile (pen'sil) *adj.* 1 Pendent and swaying; pendulous; suspended. 2 Hanging loosely: a *pensile* nest. 3 Constructing pensile nests: said of birds. [<L *pensilis* hanging down < *pensus,* pp. of *pendere* hang] — **pen'·sile·ness, pen·sil'i·ty** *n.*

pen·sion[1] (pen'shən) *n.* 1 A periodical allowance to an individual or his representative on account of some meritorious work or service; especially, an allowance made by a government to a veteran soldier or to his widow or children. 2 *Obs.* payment; specifically, a payment made to one not a servant to retain his good will, or to a man of science or letters to enable him to carry on his work. See synonyms under SUBSIDY. — *v.t.* 1 To grant a pension to. 2 To dismiss with a pension: with *off.* [<OF <L *pensio, -onis* payment < *pensus,* pp. of *pendere* weigh, pay] — **pen'sion·a·ble** *adj.*

pen·sion[2] (pen'shən, *Fr.* päɴ·syôɴ') *n. French* A boarding school; also, a boarding house.

pen·sion·ar·y (pen'shən·er·ē) *adj.* 1 Living by means of a pension; pensioned. 2 Consisting of a pension: a *pensionary* provision. — *n. pl.* **·ar·ies** 1 A pensioner. 2 A hireling: often used in a contemptuous sense.

pen·sion·er (pen'shən·ər) *n.* 1 One who receives a pension; hence, one who is dependent on the bounty of another. 2 In Cambridge University, England, and Dublin University, Ireland, a student who pays his own expenses: at Oxford University, England, called *commoner.* 3 A boarder, as in a convent or school.

pen·sive (pen'siv) *adj.* 1 Engaged in or addicted to serious or quiet reflection; thoughtful with a touch of sadness. 2 Expressive of, suggesting, or causing sad thoughtfulness. [<OF *pensif, pensive* < *penser* think] — **pen'sive·ly** *adv.* — **pen'sive·ness** *n.*

pen·stock (pen'stok') *n.* 1 A conduit from a millrace to a water-wheel gate. 2 A sluice or floodgate, controlling the discharge of water, as from a pond, or of sewage. 3 A fire hydrant. 4 A penholder.

pent (pent) *adj.* Penned up or in; closely confined. [Pp. of *pend,* obs. var. of PEN², *v.*]

penta– *combining form* Five: *pentahedron.* Also, before vowels, **pent–.** [<Gk. *pente* five]

pen·ta·cle (pen'tə·kəl) *n.* **1** A figure composed of five straight lines, making a star that includes a pentagon. **2** In magic, a circle containing certain mystical figures and symbols; a pentagram: also spelled *penticle.* Also **pen·tal·pha** (pen·tal'fə). [<Med. L *pentaculum,* ult. <Gk. *pente* five]

PENTACLE

pen·tad (pen'tad) *n.* **1** The number five; a group of five things. **2** A period of five years. **3** *Chem.* An atom, radical, or element with a combining power of five. — *adj.* Having a combining power of five. [<Gk. *pentas, -ados* a group of five < *pente* five]

pen·ta·dac·tyl (pen'tə·dak'til) *n.* An animal having five fingers or toes. — *adj.* Having five fingers or toes. [<L *pentadactylus* <Gk. *pentadactylos* < *pente* five + *dactylos* a finger] — **pen'ta·dac'ty·lous** *adj.*

pen·ta·gon (pen'tə·gon) *n.* A figure with five angles and five sides. [<L *pentagonum* <Gk. *pentagōnon* < *pente* five + *gonia* an angle] — **pen·tag·o·nal** (pen·tag'ə·nəl) *adj.* — **pen·tag'o·nal·ly** *adv.*

Pentagon, the, A five-sided building in Arlington, Virginia, housing the Department of Defense and other military and naval installations and government offices.

pen·ta·gram (pen'tə·gram) *n.* A figure having five points or lobes; specifically, a pentacle. [<Gk. *pentagrammon,* neut. of *pentagrammos* having five lines < *pente* five + *grammē* a line]

pen·ta·he·dron (pen'tə·hē'drən) *n.* *pl.* **·dra** (-drə) A solid bounded by five plane faces. — **pen'ta·he'dral** *adj.*

pen·tam·er·ous (pen·tam'ər·əs) *adj.* **1** Composed of or having five similar parts. **2** *Bot.* Five-parted, as a corolla. Also **pen·tam'er·al.**

pen·tam·e·ter (pen·tam'ə·tər) *n.* **1** A line of verse of five metrical feet; especially, English iambic pentameter. **2** Verse comprised of pentameters; heroic verse. **3** In classical prosody, the second line of an elegiac distich: a hexameter with third and sixth feet lacking one long syllable. [<L <Gk. *pentametros* (a verse) of five measures < *pente* five + *metron* a measure]

pen·tar·chy (pen'tär·kē) *n. pl.* **·chies 1** A government administered by five joint rulers; also, a group of five such rulers. **2** An association of five kingdoms, each ruled separately. [<Gk. *pentarchia* < *pente* five + *archein* rule] — **pen·tar'chi·cal** *adj.*

pen·ta·stich (pen'tə·stik) *n.* A stanza of five lines, or a poem containing five lines. [<NL *pentastichus* <Gk. *pentastichos* of five lines < *pente* five + *stichos* a row, line]

Pen·ta·teuch (pen'tə·tōōk, -tyōōk) *n.* The first five books of the Bible taken collectively. [<LL *pentateuchus* <Gk. *pentateuchos* (*biblos*) (the book) of five books < *pente* five + *teuchos* a book, orig. an implement, vessel] — **Pen'ta·teuch'al** *adj.*

pen·tath·lon (pen·tath'lən) *n.* **1** In ancient Greece, an athletic contest of five events — leaping, running, wrestling, throwing the discus, and hurling the spear (earlier, boxing) — that occurred all on the same day between the same contestants. **2** In the modern Olympic games, a contest comprising a 200-meter running race, a 1,500-meter running race, throwing the discus, throwing the javelin, and a running broad jump. [<Gk. < *pente* five + *athlon* a contest] — **pen·tath'lete** (-lēt) *n.* — **pen·tath'lic** *adj.*

Pen·te·cost (pen'tə·kôst, -kost) *n.* **1** A Jewish festival occurring fifty days after the Passover; Shabuoth. **2** The feast of Whitsunday, commemorating the descent of the Holy Ghost upon the apostles on the Jewish Pentecost. *Acts* ii. [<LL *pentecoste* <Gk. *pentēkostē* (*hēmera*) the fiftieth (day) < *pentēkonta* fifty] — **pen'te·cos'tal** *adj.*

pent·house (pent'hous') *n.* **1** An apartment or dwelling on the roof of a building. **2** A shed or roof with a single slope affixed to the wall of another building. **3** A small building, generally one-storied, adjoined to the wall of another building; an annex. **4** A canopy or awning projecting above a doorway or window. [Alter. of *pentice,* aphetic form of OF *apentis, apendis* <LL *appendicium,* lit., an appendage <L *appendere* APPEND]

pen·ti·cle (pen'ti·kəl) See PENTACLE (def. 2).

pen·tom·ic (pen·tom'ik) *adj.* Referring to a U. S. Army division designed primarily for use in nuclear warfare, having as its basic elements five self-contained battle groups of high mobility, supported by atomic weapons. [<Gk. *pente* five + (AT)OMIC]

pent·ste·mon (pent·stē'mən) See PENSTEMON.

pent–up (pent'up') *adj.* Confined; repressed: *pent–up* emotions.

pe·nu·che (pə·nōō'chē), **pe·nu·chi** See PANOCHA.

pe·nuch·le (pē'nuk·əl), **pe·nuck·le** See PINOCHLE.

pe·nult (pē'nult, pi·nult') *n.* The syllable next to the last in a word. Also **pe·nul·ti·ma** (pi·nul'tə·mə). [Short for *penultima* <L *paenultima* (*syllaba*) next to the last (syllable) < *paene* almost + *ultimus* last]

pe·nul·ti·mate (pi·nul'tə·mit) *adj.* **1** Being the last but one. **2** Of or belonging to the last syllable but one. — *n.* A syllable or member of a series that is last but one. [<L *paene* almost + ULTIMATE, on analogy with L *paenultimus* next to the last]

pe·num·bra (pi·num'brə) *n. pl.* **·brae** (-brē) or **·bras 1** A margin of a shadow within which the rays of light from an illuminating body are partly but not wholly intercepted. **2** *Astron.* **a** The partial shadow between the umbra, or region of total eclipse, and the region of unobstructed light. **b** The dark fringe around the central part of a sunspot. **3** In painting, the blending point, or line between light and shade. [<NL <L *paene* almost + *umbra* a shadow] — **pe·num'bral, pe·num'brous** (-brəs) *adj.*

pe·nu·ri·ous (pə·nōōr'ē·əs, -nyōōr'-) *adj.* **1** Excessively sparing or saving in the use of money; parsimonious. **2** Affording or yielding little; scanty. See synonyms under AVARICIOUS. — **pe·nu'ri·ous·ly** *adv.* — **pe·nu'ri·ous·ness** *n.*

pen·u·ry (pen'yə·rē) *n.* Extreme poverty or want. See synonyms under POVERTY. [<OF *penurie* <L *penuria, paenuria* want]

pe·on (pē'ən) *n.* **1** In Latin America: **a** A laborer; servant. **b** Formerly, a debtor kept in virtual servitude until he had worked out his debt. **2** In India: **a** A foot soldier. **b** A messenger, attendant, or orderly. **c** A native police officer or constable. [<Sp. *peón* <LL *pedo, -onis* a foot soldier. Doublet of PAWN¹.]

pe·on·age (pē'ən·ij) *n.* The condition of a peon, or the system of employing this form of labor. Also **pe'on·ism.**

pe·o·ny (pē'ə·nē) *n. pl.* **·nies 1** A plant of the crowfoot family (genus *Paeonia*) having large, handsome, crimson, rose, or white flowers. **2** Its flower. [Fusion of OE *peonie* and AF *pione,* both from L *paeonia* <Gk. *paiōnia* <*Paion* Paeon, the physician of the gods]

peo·ple (pē'pəl) *n. pl.* **·ple** or (*for def.* 1) **·ples 1** The aggregate of human beings living under the same government, speaking the same language, or being of the same blood: a general term, used when the technical terms *race, tribe, nation,* or *language* would be misleading: the *people* of England. **2** Ethnologically, a body of human beings belonging to the same linguistic stock and having the same culture. **3** The whole body of persons composing a state or nation, or that part of the population invested with political rights; the enfranchised: the *people* of the state. **4** Persons collectively: taking a verb in the plural: *people* say; also, bodies of persons classified according to their collective occupation or interest: literary *people.* **5** The commonalty, as distinguished from the titled, the rich, or the learned; the populace: with *the.* **6** Those who are connected with one as subjects, attendants, kinfolk, etc.; formerly, all the Negro slaves belonging to one family. **7** Animals collectively: the ant *people.* **8** Human beings; also, a collection of company. — **chosen peo-**

ple The Israelites. — **good people** In Ireland, fairies: also **little people.** — *v.t.* **·pled, ·pling** To fill with inhabitants; populate. [<AF *people, poeple* <L *populus* the populace] — **peo'pler** *n.*

Synonyms (*noun*): commonwealth, community, folk, nation, population, race, state, tribe. A *community* is the aggregate of persons inhabiting any territory in common and having common interests; a *commonwealth* is such a body of persons having a common government, especially a republican government; as, the *commonwealth* of Massachusetts. A *community* may be very small; a *commonwealth* is ordinarily of considerable extent. A *people* is the aggregate of any public *community,* either in distinction from their rulers or as including them; a *race* is a division of mankind in the line of origin and ancestry; the *people* of the United States includes members of almost every *race.* The term *people* is used ethnologically to mean *folk* having the same linguistic and cultural origins, the same customs, traditions, and beliefs, and usually the same geographic distribution: as distinguished from political affiliations or physical origins. The *population* of a country is simply the aggregate of persons residing within its borders, without reference to *race,* organization, or allegiance; unnaturalized residents form part of the *population,* but not of the *nation,* possessing none of the rights and being subject to none of the duties of citizens. In American usage *state* signifies one *commonwealth* of the federal union known as the United *States. Tribe* is now almost wholly applied to primitive *peoples* with primitive political organization; as, the Indian *tribes;* nomadic *tribes.* Compare MOB, STATE.

People's party A political organization formed in the United States in 1891, its platform being increase in currency, free coinage of silver, public control of railways, an income tax, and limitation of ownership of land: also called *Populist party.*

pep (pep) *Slang n.* Vim; energy; sprightliness; activity; punch; snap; vigor; ginger. — *v.t.* **pepped, pep·ping** To inspire with energy or pep: usually with *up.* [Short for PEPPER] — **pep'pi·ness** *n.* — **pep'py** *adj.*

pep·lum (pep'ləm) *n. pl.* **·la** (-lə) **1** A short over-skirt, ruffle, or flounce attached to a blouse or coat at the waist, and extending down over the hips. **2** A peplos. [<L <Gk. *peplos* a peplos]

pe·po (pē'pō) *n. pl.* **·pos** The fleshy fruit of the gourd family, with hardened rind and numerous enclosed seeds, as the squash, cucumber, pumpkin, melon, etc. Also **pe·pon·i·da** (pi·pon'ə·də), **pe·po·ni·um** (pi·pō'nē·əm). [<L, a pumpkin <Gk. *pepōn* (*sikyos*) a ripe (gourd)]

pep·per (pep'ər) *n.* **1** A pungent aromatic condiment consisting of the dried immature berries of the pepper plant, entire or powdered. It is usually black, but when the outer coating of the seeds is removed, the product is **white pepper. 2** Any plant yielding pepper; especially, a tropical climbing shrub (*Piper nigrum*) of the pepper family (*Piperaceae*), native to India, now widely distributed. **3** Any plant of the genus *Capsicum,* its product, entire or powdered: red *pepper* or Cayenne *pepper.* **4** *Colloq.* Spiciness; pungency; raciness. — *v.t.* **1** To sprinkle or season with pepper. **2** To sprinkle like pepper. **3** To shower, as with missiles; spatter; pelt. — *v.i.* **4** To discharge missiles at something. [OE *pipor,* ult. <L *piper* <Gk. *peperi* < an Oriental source. Cf. Skt. *pippali* a peppercorn.]

pep·per–and–salt (pep'ər·ən·sôlt') *adj.* Mixed white and black, so closely intermingled as to present a finely speckled grayish appearance: said of cloth. — *n.* A pepper–and–salt cloth.

pep·per·corn (pep'ər·kôrn') *n.* **1** A berry of the pepper plant. **2** Anything trifling.

pep·per·mint (pep'ər·mint') *n.* **1** A pungent aromatic herb (*Mentha piperita*), used in medicine and confectionery. **2** An oil or other preparation from peppermint. **3** A confection, usually disk-shaped, flavored with peppermint.

pep·per·pot (pep'ər-pot') *n.* **1** A pepperbox. **2** A West Indian stew of meat or fish with okra, chilis, and other vegetables, flavored with cassareep, Cayenne pepper, and the like. **3** In Pennsylvania, a soup of tripe and dough balls highly seasoned with pepper.

pepper tree 1 A Tasmanian and Australian shrub (*Drimys aromatica*) with small, greenish-yellow flowers and globular berries sometimes used as a substitute for pepper. **2** The Peruvian mastic (*Schinus molle*), whose seeds are used as a spice known as mollé and whose fruit yields an intoxicating beverage.

pep·per·wort (pep'ər-wûrt') *n.* **1** Any plant of the pepper family. **2** Peppergrass.

pep·per·y (pep'ər-ē) *adj.* **1** Pertaining to or like pepper; pungent. **2** Quick-tempered; hasty; stinging. See synonyms under HOT.

pep pill *Slang* Any of various pills or tablets acting to stimulate the central nervous system.

pep·sin (pep'sin) *n.* **1** *Biochem.* A proteolytic enzyme secreted by the gastric juices of the stomach. **2** A medicinal preparation obtained from the stomachs of various animals, as the pig and the calf, used to aid digestion. **3** A similar enzyme found in the cells of certain plants. Also **pep'sine.** [<G <Gk. *pepsis* digestion < *peptein* digest]

pep·sin·o·gen (pep·sin'ə·jən) *n. Biochem.* The inactive form of pepsin, found in the stomach mucosa and converted into pepsin in a slightly acid solution.

pep talk *Colloq.* A brief talk meant to inspire confidence, spark enthusiasm, etc.

pep·tic (pep'tik) *adj.* **1** Of, pertaining to, or promotive of digestion. **2** Of, pertaining to, or producing pepsin. **3** Able to digest: opposed to *dyspeptic.* — *n.* An agent that promotes digestion. [<Gk. *peptikos* able to digest < *peptein* digest]

pep·tone (pep'tōn) *n. Biochem.* Any of the soluble protein compounds into which the albuminous substances contained in food are converted when acted upon by pepsin, by acids and alkalis, by putrefaction, etc. [<G *pepton* <Gk., neut. of *peptos* digested, cooked < *peptein* digest] — **pep·ton·ic** (pep·ton'ik) *adj.*

Pep·ys (pēps, peps, pep'is), **Samuel,** 1633–1703, English diarist. — **Pep·ys'i·an** *adj.*

Pe·quot (pē'kwot) *n.* One of a tribe of North American Indians of Algonquian stock, formerly inhabiting southern New England. Also **Pe'quod** (-kwod).

per (pûr) *prep.* **1** By; by means of; through: used in commercial and business English: *per* bearer. **2** To or for each: ten cents *per* yard. **3** By the; every: especially in Latin phrases: *per diem.* [<L, through, by]

per- *prefix* **1** Through; throughout: *pervade, perennial.* **2** Thoroughly; completely: *perturb.* **3** Away: *pervert, peremptory.* **4** Very: *perfervid.* **5** *Chem.* **a** Denoting the higher degree of valence in two similar compounds: *barium peroxide* as distinguished from *barium monoxide.* **b** Indicating a relatively large amount of the compound or radical named: *perchloric acid,* contrasted with *chloric acid.* ◆ The prefix occurs in other forms in *pardon, paramour, pellucid,* etc. [<L *per* through, by means of; in some words <OF or F]

per·a·cid·i·ty (pûr'ə·sid'ə·tē) *n.* Excessive acidity, as of the stomach.

per·ad·ven·ture (pûr'əd·ven'chər) *adv.* Perchance; it may be; perhaps; not improbably: often preceded by *if* or *unless.* — *n.* Possibility of failure, miscarriage, or error; doubt; question. [<OF *par aventure* by chance; infl. in form by L *adventura* chance]

per·am·bu·late (pə·ram'byə·lāt) *v.* ·lat·ed, ·lat·ing *v.t.* **1** To walk through or over; traverse. **2** To walk through or around so as to inspect, survey, etc. — *v.i.* **3** To walk about; stroll. [<L *perambulatus,* pp. of *perambulare* < *per-* through + *ambulare* walk]

per·am·bu·la·tor (pə·ram'byə·lā'tər) *n.* **1** One who perambulates. **2** A rolling chair. **3** A baby carriage. **4** A surveyor's measuring wheel, constructed on the principle of the odometer. — **per·am'bu·la·to·ry** *adj.*

per an·num (pûr an'əm) *Latin* By the year.

per·cale (pər·kāl', -kal') *n.* A closely woven cotton fabric without gloss, in solid colors or prints. [<F, prob. <Persian *pergālah* a rag]

per·ca·line (pûr'kə·lēn') *n.* A glossy cotton cloth, usually dyed in a solid color: used chiefly as lining. [<F, dim. of *percale* PERCALE]

per cap·i·ta (pûr kap'ə·tə) *Latin* For each person; literally, by heads.

per·ceive (pər·sēv') *v.t. & v.i.* ·ceived, ·ceiv·ing **1** To become aware of (something) through the senses; see, hear, feel, taste, or smell. **2** To come to understand; apprehend with the mind. [<AF *perceivre,* OF *perçoivre* <L *percipere* seize, perceive < *per-* thoroughly + *capere* take] — **per·ceiv'a·ble** *adj.* — **per·ceiv'a·bly** *adv.* — **per·ceiv'er** *n.*

Synonyms: apprehend, comprehend, conceive, know, understand. We *perceive,* primarily, what is presented through the senses. We *apprehend* what is presented to the mind, whether through the senses or by any other means. That which we *apprehend* we catch, as with the hand; that which we *conceive* we are able to analyze and recompose in our mind; that which we *comprehend* we, as it were, grasp around, take together, seize, embrace wholly within the mind. Compare APPREHEND, KNOW, KNOWLEDGE, LEARN. *Antonyms:* ignore, lose, misapprehend, misconceive, miss, overlook.

per·cent (pər·sent') *n.* **1** Number of parts in or to every hundred, often specified: fifty *percent* of the people. **2** Amount or quantity commensurate with the number of units in proportion to one hundred: ten *percent* of fifty is five: (symbol, %). **3** *pl.* Securities bearing a certain percentage of interest. Also **per cent., per cent** [Short for L *per centum* by the hundred]

per·cent·age (pər·sen'tij) *n.* **1** Rate per hundred, or proportion in a hundred parts. **2** A proportion of what is under consideration; a part considered in its quantitative relation to the whole. **3** In commerce, the allowance, commission, duty, or interest on a hundred. **4** *Colloq.* Advantage; profit.

per·cen·tile (pər·sen'tīl, -til) *n. Stat.* Any of 100 points measured within the range of a plotted variable, each of which denotes that percentage of the total cases lying below it in value: thus, 1, 2, 3, etc., percent of the cases are in the first, second, third, etc., percentile.

per·cept (pûr'sept) *n. Psychol.* **1** The object of knowledge as mentally presented in sense perception. **2** Immediate knowledge derived from perceiving. [<L *perceptum* (a thing) perceived, orig. neut. pp. of *percipere* PERCEIVE, on analogy with *concept*]

per·cep·ti·ble (pər·sep'tə·bəl) *adj.* That may be seen or apprehended; perceivable; cognizable; evident. See synonyms under EVIDENT. — **per·cep'ti·bil'i·ty, per·cep'ti·ble·ness** *n.* — **per·cep'ti·bly** *adv.*

per·cep·tion (pər·sep'shən) *n.* **1** The act, power, process, or product of perceiving; knowledge through the senses of the existence and properties of matter and the external world. **2** Cognition of fact or truth in general by the activity of thinking: moral *perception;* apprehension; knowledge. **3** *Psychol.* **a** The faculty or power of acquiring immediate and fundamental knowledge through the senses: often called *sense perception.* **b** The process of acquiring such knowledge. **c** The mental product so obtained, often called the *percept.* **4** Any insight or intuitive judgment that implies unusual discernment of fact or truth. **5** *Law* The taking into possession, as of crops or profits. See synonyms under KNOWLEDGE, SENSATION, UNDERSTANDING. [<OF <L *perceptio, -onis* a receiving < *percipere* PERCEIVE] — **per·cep'tion·al** *adj.*

per·cep·tive (pər·sep'tiv) *adj.* **1** Perceiving, or having the power of perception. **2** Pertaining to perception; perceptional. — **per·cep'tive·ly** *adv.* — **per·cep·tiv·i·ty** (pûr'sep·tiv'ə·tē), **per·cep'tive·ness** *n.*

per·cep·tu·al (pər·sep'chōō·əl) *adj.* Pertaining to or involving the power or act of perceiving. — **per·cep'tu·al·ly** *adv.*

Per·ce·val (pûr'sə·vəl) A knight of Arthur's Round Table, type of high chivalry and purity, who together with Galahad achieved the Grail. Also spelled *Percival, Percivale.*

perch¹ (pûrch) *n.* **1** A staff, pole, or slat, variously used, especially as a roost for poultry, etc.; any place on which birds alight or rest; hence, any elevated seat or situation. **2** A measure: one rod (16.5 feet); or, in surveying, a square rod; also, in stonework, a variable measure, usually about 25 cubic feet. **3** A bracket or corbel; a console. **4** A frame on which cloth is examined for imperfections. **5** A pole set to mark a shallow place in navigable water. **6** A pole connecting the fore gear and hind gear of a spring carriage; a reach. — *v.i.* **1** To alight or sit on or as on a perch; roost. — *v.t.* **2** To set on or as on a perch. **3** To examine (cloth) on a perch. [<OF *perche* <L *pertica* a pole]

perch² (pûrch) *n.* **1** A small, spiny-finned, predaceous, fresh-water fish (genus *Perca*); especially, the common **European perch** (*P. fluviatilis*), and the American **yellow perch** (*P. flavescens*). **2** One of various other similar or related fishes, including many marine forms. [<OF *perche* <L *perca* <Gk. *perkē,* ? <*perknos* dark-colored]

per·chance (pər·chans', -chäns') *adv.* **1** In a possible case; peradventure; perhaps. **2** *Obs.* By chance. [<AF *par chance* by chance < *par* (<L *per* through) + *chance* CHANCE]

Per·che·ron (pûr'chə·ron, -shə-) *adj.* Belonging or originating in Perche: said of a breed of large, usually dapple-gray or black draft horses. The name *Norman* or *Percheron–Norman* is erroneously applied to this breed. — *n.* A horse of the Percheron breed. [<F, from Perche]

PERCHERON

per·cip·i·ent (pər·sip'ē·ənt) *adj.* **1** Having the power of perception. **2** Perceiving rapidly or keenly. — *n.* One who or that which perceives. [<L *percipiens, -entis,* ppr. of *percipere* PERCEIVE] — **per·cip'i·ence** or **·en·cy** *n.*

Per·ci·val, Per·ci·vale (pûr'sə·vəl) See PERCEVAL.

per·coid (pûr'koid) *adj.* Of or pertaining to an order (*Percomorphi*) of spiny-finned teleost fishes, including the fresh-water perches, the sunfishes, mackerels, tunas, blennies, and many others; perchlike. — *n.* One of the *Percomorphi.* Also **per·coi'de·an.** [<L *perca* PERCH² + -OID]

per·co·late (pûr'kə·lāt) *v.t. & v.i.* ·lat·ed, ·lat·ing To pass or cause to pass through fine interstices; filter; strain; permeate. — *n.* **1** That which has percolated; a filtered liquid. **2** A liquid containing the soluble portion of a drug through which it has passed. [<L *percolatus,* pp. of *percolare* < *per-* through + *colare* strain < *colum* a strainer] — **per'co·la'tion** *n.*

per·co·la·tor (pûr'kə·lā'tər) *n.* **1** One who or that which percolates, as a filter. **2** A filtering coffee pot.

per·cuss (pər·kus') *v.t.* **1** To strike or tap quickly or forcibly. **2** *Med.* To test or treat by percussion. [<L *percussus,* pp. of *percutere* strike < *per-* through + *quatere* shake] — **per·cus'sor** *n.*

per·cus·sion (pər·kush'ən) *n.* **1** The sharp striking of one body against another; sudden collision, especially such as causes a shock or sound. **2** The act of striking the percussion cap in a firearm. **3** The shock or vibration produced by collision; the impression of sound upon the ear. **4** *Med.* A light, quick tapping of the finger tips upon the back, chest, or abdomen, for determining, by the resonance, the condition of the organ beneath. **5** Those musical instruments, collectively, whose tone is produced by striking or hitting, as the timpani, glockenspiel, piano, etc. — *adj.* Pertaining to or operating by percussion; percussive: *percussion* cap, *percussion* lock. — **per·cus'sive** (-kus'iv) *adj.* — **per·cus'sive·ly** *adv.* — **per·cus'sive·ness** *n.*

percussion cap A percussion primer.

percussion fuze A fuze within a projectile or bomb that causes explosion by impact.

percussion lock The hammer of a firearm.

percussion primer A small cap of thin metal, containing mercury fulminate, or other detonator, used in ammunition to explode the propelling charge.

per·die, per·dy (pər·dē') See PARDI.

per di·em (pər dē'əm, dī'əm) **1** By the day. **2** An allowance (of money) for expenses each day. [<L]

per·di·tion (pər·dish′ən) *n.* **1** *Theol.* Future misery or eternal death as the condition of the wicked; hell. **2** *Obs.* Utter destruction or ruin. **3** *Obs.* Lessening; diminution. See synonyms under RUIN. [<OF *perdiciun* <L *perditio, -onis* < *perdere* destroy, lose < *per-* through, away + *dare* give]

per·du (pər·dōō′) *adj.* Hidden; concealed. — *n. Obs.* A soldier on a perilous assignment. Also **per·due′.** [<F *perdue,* orig. pp. fem. of *perdre* lose <L *perdere.* See PERDITION.]

per·du·ra·ble (pər·dŏŏr′ə·bəl, -dyŏŏr′-) *adj.* Very durable; lasting. [<OF <LL *perdurabilis* <L *perdurare* < *per-* through + *durare* endure < *durus* hard] — **per·du·ra·bil·i·ty** (pûr′dŏŏr·ə·bil′ə·tē, -dyŏŏr′-) *n.* — **per·du′ra·bly** *adv.*

per·e·gri·nate (per′ə·gri·nāt′) *v.* **·nat·ed, ·nat·ing** *v.i.* To travel from place to place. — *v.t.* To travel through or along. — *adj. Obs.* Of foreign birth or manners; traveled; foreign. [<L *peregrinatus,* pp. of *peregrinari* travel abroad < *peregrinus.* See PEREGRINE.] — **per′·e·gri·na′tion** *n.* — **per′e·gri·na′tor** *n.*

per·e·grine (per′ə·grin) *adj.* **1** Coming from foreign regions. **2** Foreign. **3** Upon a pilgrimage; on one's travels. — *n.* The peregrine falcon. Also **per′e·grin.** [<L *peregrinus* foreign < *pereger* traveling < *per-* through + *ager, agri* a field, land]

peregrine falcon A widely distributed falcon (*Falco peregrinus*) generally blackish-blue above and whitish below, streaked with black in the typical form, and with black cheek patches; formerly much used in falconry on account of its courage and speed; the duck hawk. See FALCON.

per·emp·to·ry (pə·remp′tər·ē, per′əmp·tôr′ē, -tō′rē) *adj.* **1** Not admitting of debate or appeal; decisive; absolute. **2** Positive in judgment or opinion; dogmatic. **3** Intolerant of opposition; dictatorial. **4** *Law* Precluding or putting an end to debate or discussion; final; positively fixed: a *peremptory* challenge. See synonyms under ARBITRARY. [<AF *peremptorie* <L *peremptorius* destructive < *peremptor* a destroyer < *perimere* destroy < *per-* entirely + *emere* buy, take] — **per·emp′to·ri·ly** *adv.* — **per·emp′to·ri·ness** *n.*

per·en·ni·al (pə·ren′ē·əl) *adj.* **1** Continuing or enduring through the year or through many years. **2** Hence, unfailing; unceasing: *perennial* courage. **3** Growing continually; surviving more than one year. **4** *Bot.* Lasting more than two years. See synonyms under ETERNAL, PERPETUAL. — *n.* A plant that grows for three or more years, usually blossoming and fructifying annually. [<L *perennis* < *per-* through + *annus* a year] — **per·en′ni·al·ly** *adv.*

per·fect (pûr′fikt) *adj.* **1** Having all the qualities, excellences, or elements that are requisite to its nature or kind; without defect or lack; consummated; supremely excellent; complete. **2** Thoroughly versed or informed; completely skilled: a *perfect* soldier. **3** Closely correspondent; accurately reproducing: a *perfect* replica. **4** Thoroughly effectual; meeting the requirements of the occasion: a *perfect* antidote; a *perfect* answer. **5** *Colloq.* Excessive in degree; very great: She has a *perfect* horror of spiders. **6** *Bot.* Having the essential organs, stamens, and pistils: said of flowers. **7** *Gram.* Denoting the tense of the verb expressing completed action in the past. Some grammarians note in English a *present perfect, past perfect* (or *pluperfect*), and a *future perfect* tense, a *conditional perfect,* and a *perfect infinitive* and *participle.* **8** *Music* **a** Of a character not altered by inversion: said of interval: a *perfect* fifth or octave. **b** Complete: a *perfect* cadence. **9** *Obs.* Assured; positive. — *n. Gram.* The perfect tense, or a verb in this tense. — *v.t.* (pər·fekt′) **1** To bring to perfection; complete; finish. **2** To make thoroughly skilled or accomplished: to *perfect* oneself in an art. [<OF *parfit* <L *perfectus,* pp. of *perficere* accomplish < *per-* thoroughly + *facere* do, make] — **per·fect′er** *n.* — **per·fect′i·bil′i·ty** *n.* — **per·fect′i·ble** *adj.* — **per′fect·ly** *adv.*

Synonyms (adj.): absolute, accurate, blameless, complete, completed, consummate, correct, entire, faultless, finished, holy, ideal, immaculate, infallible, sinless, spotless, stainless, unblemished, undefiled. That is *perfect* to

which nothing can be added and from which nothing can be taken without impairing its excellence, symmetry, or worth; as, a *perfect* flower; a copy of a document is *perfect* when it is *accurate* in every particular; a vase may be called *perfect* when *entire* and *unblemished,* even if not artistically *faultless;* the best judges never pronounce a work of art *perfect,* because they see always ideal possibilities not yet attained; even the *ideal* is not *perfect,* by reason of the imperfection of the human mind; a human character faultlessly *holy* would be morally *perfect* but finite. That which is *absolute* is free from admixture (as *absolute* alcohol) and from imperfection or limitation. See CORRECT, IMPLICIT, INNOCENT, PURE, RADICAL, RIPE. *Antonyms:* bad, blemished, corrupt, corrupted, defaced, defective, deficient, deformed, fallible, faulty, imperfect, incomplete, inferior, insufficient, marred, meager, perverted, poor, ruined, short, spoiled, worthless.

per·fec·tion (pər·fek′shən) *n.* **1** The state or condition of being perfect; supreme excellence; also, an embodiment of this: also **per′fect·ness. 2** A particular quality that is supreme. **3** The highest degree of a thing: the *perfection* of rudeness. **4** The act or process of perfecting; the fact of having been perfected.

per·fec·tion·ism (pər·fek′shən·iz′əm) *n. Philos.* The theory that moral perfection may be attained, or has been attained, by men: variously held and taught by different sects and schools. Also **per·fect′ism.**

per·fec·tion·ist (pər·fek′shən·ist) *n.* **1** One who demands an exceedingly high degree of excellence in the performance, behavior, etc., of himself or in that of others. **2** One who adheres to the theory of perfectionism.

per·fec·tive (pər·fek′tiv) *adj.* **1** Tending to make perfect. **2** *Gram.* Denoting an aspect of the verb expressing the completion of an action: opposed to *imperfective.* — **per·fec′tive·ly** *adv.* — **per·fec′tive·ness** *n.*

per·fer·vid (pər·fûr′vid) *adj.* Very or excessively fervid; glowing; intensely zealous. [<NL *perfervidus* <L *per-* thoroughly + *fervidus* FERVID]

per·fid·i·ous (pər·fid′ē·əs) *adj.* **1** Characterized by or guilty of perfidy; treacherous. **2** Involving a breach of faith; contrary to loyalty and truth. [<L *perfidiosus* < *perfidia* PERFIDY] — **per·fid′i·ous·ly** *adv.* — **per·fid′i·ous·ness** *n.*

Synonyms: deceitful, disloyal, double-faced, faithless, false, forsworn, perjured, traitorous, treacherous, two-faced, unfaithful, untrue, untrustworthy. *Antonyms:* faithful, honest, incorruptible, staunch, steadfast, true, trustworthy, trusty.

per·fi·dy (pûr′fə·dē) *n. pl.* **·dies** The act of violating faith or allegiance; treachery; faithlessness. [<MF *perfidie* <L *perfidia* treachery < *per-* through, away + *fides* faith]

per·fo·rate (pûr′fə·rāt) *v.t.* **·rat·ed, ·rat·ing 1** To make a hole or holes through, by or as by stamping or drilling. **2** To pierce with holes in rows or patterns, as sheets of stamps, etc. See synonyms under PIERCE. — *adj.* (-rit) Perforated. [<L *perforatus,* pp. of *perforare* < *per-* through + *forare* bore] — **per′fo·ra·ble** *adj.* — **per′fo·ra·tive, per′fo·ra·to′ry** *adj.* — **per′fo·ra′tor** *n.*

per·fo·rat·ed (pûr′fə·rā′tid) *adj.* Pierced with a hole or holes, especially in lines or patterns, as sheets of stamps to facilitate tearing.

per·fo·ra·tion (pûr′fə·rā′shən) *n.* **1** A perforating or state of being perforated. **2** A hole or series of holes drilled in or stamped through something, especially in lines or patterns.

per·force (pər·fôrs′, -fōrs′) *adv.* By force; by or of necessity; necessarily. [<OF *par force* < *par* through, by <L *per-*) + *force* FORCE]

per·form (pər·fôrm′) *v.t.* **1** To carry out in action; execute; do: to *perform* an operation. **2** To act in accord with the requirements or obligations of; fulfil; discharge, as a duty or command. **3** To act (a part) or give a performance of (a play, piece of music, etc.). — *v.i.* **4** To carry through to completion an action, undertaking, etc. **5** To give an exhibition or performance, as of a role in a play, singing, etc.: The actress will *perform* tomorrow. See synonyms under ACCOMPLISH, EFFECT,

EXECUTE, MAKE, TRANSACT. [<AF *parfourmer,* OF *parfournir* accomplish entirely < *par-* thoroughly (<L *per-*) + *fournir* accomplish; infl. in form by OF *former* form] — **per·form′a·ble** *adj.*

per·form·ance (pər·fôr′məns) *n.* **1** The act of performing; also, the thing done; execution; completion; action; achievement. **2** A representation before spectators; an exhibition of feats; any entertainment: two *performances* daily. See synonyms under ACT, EXERCISE, OPERATION, PRODUCTION, WORK.

per·form·er (pər·fôr′mər) *n.* **1** One who performs or acts; one who carries a part upon the stage or in any performance, as an actor, musician, or acrobat. **2** One who carries out his promise or does his duty. See synonyms under AGENT.

per·frig·er·a·tion (pər·frij′ə·rā′shən) *n.* Frostbite. [<L *perfrigeratus,* pp. of *perfrigerare* < *per-* thoroughly + *frigerare* cool < *frigus* cold]

per·fume (pûr′fyōōm, pər·fyōōm′) *n.* **1** A pleasant odor, as from flowers; fragrance. **2** A fragrant substance, usually a volatile liquid, prepared to emit a pleasant odor; scent. See synonyms under SMELL. — *v.t.* (pər·fyōōm′) **·fumed, ·fum·ing** To fill or impregnate with a fragrant odor; scent. [<F *parfum* <Ital. *perfumare,* lit., impregnate with smoke < *per-* through (<L) + *fumare* smoke < *fumus* smoke]

per·fum·er (pər·fyōō′mər) *n.* **1** One who makes or deals in perfumes. **2** One who or that which perfumes.

per·fum·er·y (pər·fyōō′mər·ē) *n. pl.* **·er·ies 1** Perfumes in general, or a specific perfume. **2** A place where perfumes are manufactured.

per·func·to·ry (pər·fungk′tər·ē) *adj.* Done merely for the sake of getting through; mechanical and without interest; half-hearted; negligent; superficial; careless. [<LL *perfunctorius* negligent < *perfunctor* one who performs an act < *perfungi* get through with < *per-* through + *fungi* perform] — **per·func′to·ri·ly** *adv.* — **per·func′to·ri·ness** *n.*

per·fuse (pər·fyōōz′) *v.t.* **·fused, ·fus·ing 1** To overspread, suffuse, or sprinkle with a liquid, color, etc.; permeate. **2** To spread, as a liquid, over or through something; diffuse. [<L *perfusus,* pp. of *perfundere* < *per-* through, all over + *fundere* pour out] — **per·fu′sion** (-zhən) *n.* — **per·fu′sive** (-siv) *adj.*

per·go·la (pûr′gə·lə) *n.* An arbor; specifically, an arbor or trelliswork of a structural nature, covered with vegetation or flowers; a covered walk. [< Ital., an arbor <L *pergula* a projecting roof, arbor < *pergere* go forward <L *per-* through + *regere* keep straight]

PERGOLA

per·haps (pər·haps′) *adv.* It may be; possibly. [<PER + *happes, haps,* pl. of HAP[1]]

peri- *prefix* **1** Around; encircling; all about: *periphery.* **2** Situated near; close; adjoining: *perihelion.* [<Gk. < *peri* around]

per·i·blep·sis (per′ə·blep′sis) *n.* The wild, intense, staring expression of a delirious or insane person. [<NL <Gk. *peri-* around + *blepsis* an act of sight < *blepein* look]

per·i·car·di·al (per′ə·kär′dē·əl) *adj.* Of or pertaining to the pericardium. Also **per′i·car′di·ac** or **·di·an.**

per·i·car·di·um (per′ə·kär′dē·əm) *n. pl.* **·di·a** (-dē·ə) *Anat.* A membranous bag that surrounds and protects the heart. [<NL <Gk. *pericardion* (the membrane) around the heart < *peri-* around + *kardia* heart]

per·i·chon·dri·um (per′ə·kon′drē·əm) *n. pl.* **·dri·a** (-drē·ə) *Anat.* The vascular membrane that envelops the surface of a cartilage between the joints. [<NL <Gk. *peri-* around + *chondros* a cartilage] — **per′i·chon′dri·al** *adj.*

Per·i·cles (per′ə·klēz), died 429 B.C., Athenian statesman and general.

per·i·cline (per′ə·klīn) *n.* One of the varieties of albite found in the Swiss Alps in the form of white twinned crystals. [<Gk. *periklinēs* sloping all around < *peri-* around + *klinein* lean; with ref. to the large inclination between the terminal and lateral faces of the crystals]

per·i·den·tal (per'ə-den'təl) *adj.* Periodontal.

per·i·dot (per'ə-dot) *n.* A yellowish–green gem variety of olivine. [<F *péridot* <OF *peritot*; ult. origin uncertain] — **per'i·dot'ic** *adj.*

per·i·do·tite (per'ə-dō'tīt) *n.* A granular igneous rock composed essentially of olivine or chrysolite. [<PERIDOT + -ITE[1]]

per·i·gee (per'ə-jē) *n. Astron.* The point in the orbit of the moon or of an artificial satellite where it is nearest the earth; opposed to *apogee.* [<MF *périgée* <Med. L *perigaeum* <Gk. *perigeion,* orig. neut. of *perigeios* close around the earth < *peri-* around + *gē* earth] — **per'i·ge'al, per'i·ge'an** *adj.*

per·i·gon (per'ə-gon) *n. Geom.* An angle equal to two straight angles or 360 degrees.

per·i·go·ni·um (per'ə-gō'nē·əm) *n. pl.* **·ni·a** (-nē·ə) The perianth. [<NL <Gk. *peri-* around + *gonos* offspring, a seed]

per·i·he·li·on (per'ə-hē'lē·ən) *n. pl.* **·li·a** (-lē·ə) *Astron.* The point in the orbit of a planet or comet where it is nearest the sun: opposed to *aphelion.* [<NL *perihelium* <Gk. *peri-* close about + *hēlios* the sun; refashioned after Greek]

per·il (per'əl) *n.* Exposure to the chance of injury, loss, or destruction; danger; jeopardy; risk. See synonyms under DANGER, HAZARD. — *v.t.* **·iled** or **·illed, ·il·ing** or **·il·ling** To expose to danger; imperil. [<OF *péril* <L *periculum* trial, danger]

per·il·ous (per'əl·əs) *adj.* Full of, involving, or attended with peril; hazardous. See synonyms under PRECARIOUS. — **per'il·ous·ly** *adv.* — **per'·il·ous·ness** *n.*

pe·rim·e·ter (pə·rim'ə·tər) *n.* **1** The bounding line of any figure of two dimensions. **2** The sum of the sides of a plane figure. **3** An instrument for testing the scope of the field of vision. [<L *perimetros* <Gk. *peri-* around + *metron* a measure] — **per'i·met·ric** (per'ə·met'rik) or **·ri·cal** *adj.* — **per'i·met'ri·cal·ly** *adv.*

pe·rim·e·try (pə·rim'ə·trē) *n.* Measurement of the scope of vision by use of a perimeter.

per·i·morph (per'ə·môrf) *n.* A mineral that encloses another. Compare ENDOMORPH. [< PERI- + Gk. *morphē* a form] — **per'i·mor'phic** or **·phous** *adj.* — **per'i·mor'phism** *n.*

per·i·ne·um (per'ə·nē'əm) *n. pl.* **·ne·a** (-nē'ə) *Anat.* **1** The region of the body at the lower end of the trunk, between the genital organs and the rectum. **2** The entire region at the outlet of the pelvis, comprising the anus and the internal genitals. Also **per'i·nae'um.** [<LL <Gk. *perinaion, perineos*] — **per'i·ne'al** *adj.*

per·i·neu·ri·tis (per'ə·nŏŏ·rī'tis, -nyŏŏ-) *n. Pathol.* Inflammation of the perineurium.

per·i·neu·ri·um (per'ə·nŏŏr'ē·əm, -nyŏŏr'-) *n. pl.* **·ri·a** (-ē·ə) *Anat.* The connective tissue investing one of the bundles of fibers composing a nerve. [<NL <Gk. *peri-* around + *neuron* a nerve] — **per'i·neu'ri·al** *adj.*

pe·ri·od (pir'ē·əd) *n.* **1** A definite portion of time marked and defined by some recurring event or phenomenon. **2** A lapse of time; a series of years; an age; era; also, a stage of life. **3** The concluding limit of any sequence of years, events, acts, or phenomena; termination. **4** The present day or time: with *the.* **5** *Astron.* The time of revolution of a heavenly body about its primary. **6** *Med.* A special phase or epoch distinguishable in the course of a disease: the *period* of augmentation; also, the menses. **7** A dot (.) placed on the line: used as a mark of rhetorical punctuation after every complete declarative sentence, after most abbreviations, as LL.D., pp., after titles, headings, and sideheads, and often after Roman numerals. The same mark serves also as a decimal point. **8** A sentence in which completion of the sense is suspended till the close. **9** *Geol.* One of the divisions of geologic time, intermediate between the shorter *epoch* and the longer *era:* the Cretaceous *period.* **10** *Music* A group of measures arranged in two or more phrases and comprising a complete musical statement. **11** *Math.* **a** The interval between the equal recurring values of a dependent variable. **b** Any one of similar groups into which a number is divided, as when a root is to be extracted: in numeration or in recurring decimals. **c** The length of the smallest subinterval in the graph of the func-

tion of a real variable. **12** *Physics* The time that elapses between two successive similar phases of a vibration. **13** The completion or end of a cycle, event, or series of events. **14** *Obs.* A particular occasion or moment. See synonyms under END, TIME. [<OF *periode* <L *periodus* <Gk. *periodos* a going around, a rounded surface < *peri-* around + *hodos* a way]

pe·ri·od·ic (pir'ē·od'ik) *adj.* **1** Pertaining to or of the nature of a period; characterized by periods; recurring after a definite interval; cyclic. **2** *Gram.* Belonging to a sentence that is grammatically complete. **3** In rhetoric, pertaining to or expressed in complete sentences: pertaining especially to a style in which several clauses hang upon one principal statement or sentence; hence, rhetorically elaborate. See also PERIODIC SENTENCE. **4** *Math.* **a** Of or pertaining to curves with ordinates repeated at equal distances along the abscissa. **b** Of or pertaining to the function of a real variable such that a graph of the function is identical within each subinterval.

pe·ri·od·i·cal (pir'ē·od'i·kəl) *adj.* **1** Pertaining to publications, as magazines, etc., that appear at fixed intervals of more than one day; also, published at regular intervals. **2** Periodic (def. 1). — *n.* A publication, usually a weekly, monthly, or quarterly magazine, appearing at regular intervals. — **pe·ri·od'i·cal·ly** *adv.*

pe·ri·o·dic·i·ty (pir'ē·ə·dis'ə·tē) *n.* The quality of being periodic or of recurring at definite intervals of time, as in sunspots, an electric current, or the symptoms of a disease.

periodic law *Chem.* The statement that the physicochemical properties of the elements are functionally related to their atomic numbers and recur periodically when the elements are arranged in the order of these numbers.

periodic sentence A sentence that is not grammatically complete until the end; specifically, one of several rhetorical clauses so constructed as to suspend completion of both sense and structure until the close.

periodic spiral *Chem.* A complex graphic diagram of the elements arranged in a series of curves so as to illustrate the various relationships of properties, chemical behavior, etc., as expressed in the periodic law.

periodic system *Chem.* A classification of the elements in accordance with the relationships formulated by the periodic law.

periodic table *Chem.* A table in which the elements are arranged in physicochemical groups as determined, formerly by their atomic weights, now by atomic numbers.

per·i·o·don·tal (per'ē·ə·don'təl) *adj. Anat.* Occurring or situated around a tooth: the *periodontal* membrane lining the cement of a tooth: also called *peridental.* [<PERI- + -ODONT(O)- + -AL]

per·i·o·ma·ni·a (per'ē·ə·mā'nē·ə, -mān'yə) *n.* Dromomania. [<Gk. *peraioein* carry across, pass over + MANIA]

per·i·os·te·um (per'ē·os'tē·əm) *n. Anat.* A tough, fibrous, two–layered vascular membrane that surrounds and nourishes the bones. [<NL <L *periosteon* <Gk., neut. of *periosteos* around the bones < *peri-* around + *osteon* a bone] — **per'i·os'te·al, per'i·os'te·ous** *adj.*

per·i·os·ti·tis (per'ē·os·tī'tis) *n. Pathol.* Inflammation of the periosteum. [<PERIOST(EUM) + -ITIS] — **per'i·os·tit'ic** (-tit'ik) *adj.*

per·i·ot·ic (per'ē·ō'tik, -ot'ik) *Anat. adj.* Surrounding the inner ear; specifically, relating to the bony structure or capsule enclosing the labyrinth. — *n.* A periotic bone.

per·i·pa·tet·ic (per'i·pə·tet'ik) *adj.* **1** Walking about; moving from place to place. **2** Rambling, as of speech. — *n.* One given to walking about. [<OF *peripatetique* <L *peripateticus* <Gk. *peripatētikos* given to walking about < *peripatētēs* one who walks about < *peri-* around + *pateein* walk]

Per·i·pa·tet·ic (per'i·pə·tet'ik) *adj.* Pertaining to the philosophy of Aristotle, who lectured to his disciples while walking in the Lyceum at Athens. — *n.* A disciple of Aristotle; an adherent of his teachings.

pe·riph·er·al (pə·rif'ər·əl) *adj.* **1** Of or pertaining to a periphery. **2** Distant from the center; hence, distal; external. Also **per'i·pher'ic** or **·i·cal** (per'ə·fer'i·kəl). — **pe·riph'·**

er·al·ly *adv.*

pe·riph·er·y (pə·rif'ər·ē) *n. pl.* **·er·ies 1** The outer surface. **2** The surface of the body. **3** Circumference. **4** *Geom.* The sum of the sides of any polygon. **5** A surrounding region, country, or area. [<OF *periferie* <LL *peripheria* <Gk. *periphereia* circumference < *peripherēs* moving around < *peri-* around + *pherein* carry]

per·i·phrase (per'i·frāz') *n.* Periphrasis.

pe·riph·ra·sis (pə·rif'rə·sis) *n. pl.* **·ses** (-sēz) Circumlocution, or an instance of it. See synonyms under CIRCUMLOCUTION. [<L <Gk. < *periphrazein* < *peri-* around + *phrazein* speak]

per·i·phras·tic (per'ə·fras'tik) *adj.* **1** Of the nature of or involving periphrasis; employing indirect words; circumlocutory. **2** *Gram.* Denoting a construction in which a phrase is substituted for an inflected form of similar function, as, *the hat of John* for *John's hat.* Also **per'i·phras'ti·cal.** — **per'i·phras'ti·cal·ly** *adv.*

periphrastic conjugation A conjugation formed by simple verbs with the aid of auxiliaries, instead of by inflection of the verb itself, as, *he did run* for *he ran.*

periphrastic genitive A genitive case formed not by inflection, but by a preposition, as in English by *of.*

pe·rip·ter·al (pə·rip'tər·əl) *Archit. adj.* Having a detached row of columns extending around the cella: said especially of a temple. — *n.* A peripteral temple; peristyle: also **per'ip'ter, pe·rip'ter·os** (-tər·os). [<MF *périptère* <Med. L *peripteron* <Gk., neut. of *peripteros* winged about < *peri-* around + *pteron* a wing]

pe·rique (pə·rēk') *n.* A dark, strongly flavored tobacco grown in Louisiana. [<Creole, prob. alter. of slang E *prick* a phallus; so called when made into a carotte]

per·i·scope (per'ə·skōp) *n.* **1** An instrument consisting of a revolving prism capable of reflecting light rays down a vertical tube: used to guide submarine boats or to watch an enemy from a trench. **2** A special variety of photographic objective; a periscopic or wide–angled lens. — **per'i·scop'ic** or **·i·cal** (-skop'i·kəl) *adj.*

per·ish (per'ish) *v.i.* **1** To suffer a violent or untimely death. **2** To be destroyed; pass from existence. See synonyms under DIE. [<OF *periss-,* stem of *perir* <L *perire* < *per-* away + *ire* go]

PERISCOPE
Showing the principle of reflection.

per·ish·a·ble (per'ish·ə·bəl) *adj.* Liable to perish; mortal; liable to speedy decay, as fruit in transportation. — **per'ish·a·ble·ness, per'ish·a·bil'i·ty** *n.* — **per'·ish·a·bly** *adv.*

per·ish·a·bles (per'ish·ə·bəlz) *n. pl.* Goods liable to speedy decay: used chiefly of foods in transit.

per·i·sphere (per'ə·sfir) *n. Physics* That portion of space within which the magnetic, electrical, or gravitational fields of an object produce observable effects.

pe·ris·so·dac·tyl (pə·ris'ō·dak'til) *adj.* **1** Odd–toed. **2** Of or pertaining to an order of ungulates (*Perissodactyla*) with an odd number of digits and an enlarged cecum, including horses, tapirs, rhinoceroses, etc. — *n.* An ungulate mammal belonging to this order. Also **pe·ris'so·dac'tyle.** [<NL <Gk. *perissos* odd, uneven + *dactylos* finger, toe] — **pe·ris'so·dac·tyl'ic, ·dac'ty·lous** *adj.* — **pe·ris'so·dac'ty·lism** *n.*

per·i·stal·sis (per'ə·stôl'sis, -stal'-) *n. pl.* **·ses** (-sēz) *Physiol.* A contractile muscular movement of any hollow organ of the body, as of the alimentary canal and intestines, whereby the contents are gradually propelled toward the point of expulsion. Compare SYSTALTIC. [<NL <Gk. *peristaltikos* < *peristellein* wrap round < *peri-* around + *stellein* place] — **per'i·stal'tic** *adj.*

per·i·ta·sis (pə·ris'tə·sis) *n. Biol.* The total environment of an individual organism, including all its vital processes. [<NL <Gk., an environment < *peri-* around + *stasis* a standing < *histanai* stand]

per·i·style (per′ə·stīl) n. Archit. 1 A system of columns about a building or an internal court. 2 An area or space so enclosed. [<MF péristyle <L peristylum <Gk. peristylon, neut. of peristylos surrounded by a colonnade <peri- around + stylos a pillar] — **per′i·sty′lar** adj.

per·i·to·ne·um (per′ə·tə·nē′əm) n. pl. **·ne·a** (-nē′ə) Anat. A serous membrane that lines the abdominal cavity in mammals and is reflected as a more or less complete investment over the viscera. In the higher vertebrates the peritoneum forms a completely closed sac, except in females, where the Fallopian tubes open into the cavity. Also **per′i·to·nae′um**. [<LL peritonaeum <Gk. peritonaion <peritonos stretched round <peri- around + teinein stretch] — **per′i·to·ne′al** or **·nae′al** adj.

per·i·to·ni·tis (per′ə·tə·nī′tis) n. Pathol. Acute inflammation of the peritoneum. [<periton-(<PERITONEUM) + -ITIS]

pe·rit·ri·cha (pə·rit′rə·kə) n. pl. Bacteria having flagella all around the body. [<NL <Gk. peri- around + thrix, trichos hair] — **pe·rit′ri·chous** adj.

per·i·wig (per′ə·wig) n. A wig; peruke. [Earlier perwyke, alter. of perruck <MF perruque PERUKE]

per·i·win·kle[1] (per′ə·wing′kəl) n. 1 A small marine snail of the genus Littorina, especially the edible **European periwinkle** (L. littorea), now common on the east coast of the United States, or the **American periwinkle** (L. palliata). 2 Any of various other small univalves. [OE pinewinclan, winewinclan, pl., ? <L pinna a mussel (<Gk.) + OE wincla a shellfish; ? infl. in form by PERIWINKLE[2]]

per·i·win·kle[2] (per′ə·wing′kəl) n. A plant of the genus Vinca (family Apocynaceae); especially, either of two European trailing shrubs, V. minor and V. major, with shining, evergreen, opposite leaves, and blue, or sometimes white, flowers. They are commonly called myrtle or creeping myrtle in the United States. [OE peruince <L pervinca <vinca pervinca, prob. <pervincire <per- thoroughly + vincire bind]

periwinkle blue A medium mauve blue, the color of a periwinkle flower.

per·jure (pûr′jər) v.t. **·jured**, **·jur·ing** 1 To make (oneself) guilty of perjury. 2 To find guilty of or involved in perjury: usually in the passive: if they are perjured. [<OF parjurer <L perjurare <per- through, badly + jurare swear] — **per′jur·er** n.

per·jured (pûr′jərd) adj. Guilty of perjury; having sworn falsely; forsworn: a perjured witness. — **per′jured·ly** adv.

per·ju·ry (pûr′jə·rē) n. pl. **·ries** Law The wilful and voluntary giving of false testimony or the withholding of material facts or evidence, in regard to a matter or thing material to the issue or point of inquiry in a legal document or while under oath lawfully administered in a judicial proceeding.

perk (pûrk) v.i. 1 To recover one's spirits or vigor: with up. 2 To carry oneself or lift one's head jauntily. — v.t. 3 To raise quickly or smartly, as the ears: often with up. 4 To make (oneself) trim and smart in appearance: often with up or out. — adj. Holding up the head smartly or jauntily; pert: also perk′y. [ME perken, ? <AF perquer pérch, roost] — **perk′i·ly** adv. — **perk′i·ness** n.

per·lite (pûr′līt) n. An acid, igneous, glassy rock of the composition of obsidian, but divided into small spherical bodies by the stress developed by its contraction on cooling: also spelled pearlite. [<F <perle a pearl] — **per·lit′ic** (-lit′ik) adj.

per·ma·frost (pûr′mə·frôst, -frost) n. That part of the earth's surface in arctic regions which is permanently frozen. [<PERMA(NENT) + FROST]

Perm·al·loy (pûr′mə·loi) n. Any of a group of iron and nickel alloys with small quantities of other metals, characterized by high magnetic permeability: a trade name. [<PERM(EABLE) + ALLOY]

per·ma·nence (pûr′mə·nəns) n. The state of being permanent; durability; fixity. [<Med. L permanentia <L permanens. See PERMANENT.]

per·ma·nent (pûr′mə·nənt) adj. Continuing in the same state or without essential change; durable; fixed; stable: opposed to temporary.

— n. A permanent wave. [<L permanens, -entis <permanere stay to the end <per- through + manere remain] — **per′ma·nent·ly** adv.

Synonyms (adj.): abiding, changeless, constant, durable, enduring, fixed, immutable, invariable, lasting, perpetual, persistent, stable, steadfast, unchangeable, unchanging. Durable is said almost wholly of material substances that resist wear; lasting is said of either material or immaterial things. Permanent is a word of wider meaning; a thing is permanent which is not liable to change; as, a permanent color. Buildings upon a farm are called permanent improvements. Enduring is applied to that which resists both time and change; as, enduring fame. See PERPETUAL. Antonyms: see synonyms for TRANSIENT.

Permanent Court of Arbitration See under COURT.

Permanent Court of International Justice See under COURT.

permanent set Physics A deformation of a rigid body or material that persists after the stress has been removed.

permanent wave An artificial wave mechanically or chemically produced on growing hair and lasting several months.

per·man·ga·nate (pər·mang′gə·nāt) n. Chem. A dark-purple salt of permanganic acid.

per·man·gan·ic (pûr′man·gan′ik) adj. Chem. Of, pertaining to, or designating an acid, $HMnO_4$, which is a powerful oxidizing agent in aqueous solutions.

per·me·a·bil·i·ty (pûr′mē·ə·bil′ə·tē) n. 1 The quality or condition of being permeable. 2 Physics The property of being easily traversed by magnetic lines of force; susceptibility to magnetization. 3 Aeron. The measure of the rate of diffusion of a gas per unit area of a balloon fabric under standard conditions: generally given in liters per square meter per 24 hours.

per·me·a·ble (pûr′mē·ə·bəl) adj. 1 Allowing passage, especially of fluids. 2 Designating a type of protective clothing treated to resist penetration by vapors and gases, but not by liquids. [<L permeabilis <permeare PERMEATE] — **per′me·a·bly** adv.

per·me·ate (pûr′mē·āt) v. **·at·ed**, **·at·ing** v.t. 1 To spread thoroughly through; pervade. 2 To pass through the pores or interstices of. — v.i. 3 To spread itself. [<L permeatus, pp. of permeare <per- through + meare pass] — **per′me·ant** adj. — **per′me·a′tion** n. — **per′me·a′tive** adj.

per mill (pûr mil′) In, into, or by the thousand. Also **per mil**. [<L per by + mille thousand]

per·mil·lage (pər·mil′ij) n. Proportion or rate per thousand; the number of thousandth parts.

per·mis·si·ble (pər·mis′ə·bəl) adj. That can be permitted; allowable. — **per·mis′si·bil′i·ty** n. — **per·mis′si·bly** adv.

per·mis·sion (pər·mish′ən) n. The act of permitting or allowing; license granted; formal authorization; consent. [<L permissio, -onis <permissus, pp. of permittere PERMIT]

Synonyms: allowance, authority, authorization, consent, leave, liberty, license, permit. Authority is rightful power conferred and limited by law; in a more general sense, authority is applied to any conceded power of control. Permission justifies another in acting without interference or censure, and usually implies some degree of approval. A permit is a special authorization, generally given in writing. A license is permission granted rather than authority conferred; the sheriff has authority (not permission or license) to make an arrest. Consent is permission by the concurrence of wills in two or more persons, a mutual approval or acceptance of something proposed. Compare synonyms for ALLOW. Antonyms: denial, hindrance, objection, opposition, prevention, prohibition, refusal, resistance.

per·mis·sive (pər·mis′iv) adj. 1 That permits; granting permission. 2 Permitted; optional. 3 Tolerant; lenient; indulgent: permissive parents. — **per·mis′sive·ly** adv. — **per·mis′sive·ness** n.

per·mis·so·ry (pər·mis′ər·ē) adj. 1 Pertaining to or of the nature of permission. 2 Law

Arising from or founded on permission; authorized; licensed.

per·mit (pər·mit′) v. **·mit·ted**, **·mit·ting** v.t. 1 To allow the doing of; consent to. 2 To give (someone) leave or consent; authorize. 3 To afford opportunity for: His answer permits no misinterpretation. — v.i. 4 To afford possibility or opportunity. — n. (pûr′mit) Permission or warrant; especially, a written authorization to do something. [<L permittere <per- through <mittere send, let go] — **per·mit′ter** n.

Synonyms (verb): allow, authorize, empower, let, license, suffer, tolerate. See ALLOW, ENDURE. Compare synonyms for PERMISSION. Antonyms: disallow, forbid, prohibit, refuse.

per·mut·a·ble (pər·myōō′tə·bəl) adj. Capable of being changed or of undergoing change or interchange.

per·mu·ta·tion (pûr′myōō·tā′shən) n. 1 The act of permuting; change; transformation. 2 Math. a Change in the order of sequence of elements or objects in a series; especially, the making of all possible changes of sequence, as abc, acb, bac, bca, etc. b Any one of the arrangements thus made: distinguished from combination. [<OF permutacion <L permutatio, -onis <permutatus, pp. of permutare. See PERMUTE.]

per·mute (pər·myōōt′) v.t. **·mut·ed**, **·mut·ing** To subject to permutation, especially, to change the order of. [<L permutare <per- thoroughly + mutare change]

per·ni·cious (pər·nish′əs) adj. 1 Having the power of destroying or injuring; tending to kill or hurt; very injurious; deadly. 2 Malicious; wicked. [<OF pernicieux <L perniciosus <pernicies destruction <per- thoroughly + nex, necis death] — **per·ni′cious·ly** adv. — **per·ni′cious·ness** n.

Synonyms: bad, baneful, deadly, destructive, evil, harmful, hurtful, injurious, mischievous, noxious, perverting, ruinous. Pernicious is stronger than injurious; that which is injurious is capable of doing harm; that which is pernicious is likely to be destructive. See BAD, INIMICAL, NOISOME. Antonyms: advantageous, beneficial, favorable, good, healthful, helpful, profitable, salutary, serviceable, wholesome.

per·nick·e·ty (pər·nik′ə·tē) See PERSNICKETY.

Pe·rón (pā·rōn′), **Juan Domingo**, 1895–1974, Argentine president 1946–55; 1973–74.

per·o·rate (per′ə·rāt) v.i. **·rat·ed**, **·rat·ing** 1 To speak at length; harangue. 2 To sum up or conclude a speech.

per·o·ra·tion (per′ə·rā′shən) n. The concluding portion of an oration; the recapitulation and summing up of an argument. [<L peroratio, -onis <peroratus, pp. of perorare speak to the end <per- through + orare speak]

per·ox·ide (pə·rok′sīd) n. Chem. 1 An oxide having a larger proportion of oxygen than any other oxide of the same series: distinguished from protoxide. 2 Hydrogen peroxide. Also **per·ox′id** (-sid). — v.t. **·id·ed**, **·id·ing** To treat with peroxide; bleach, as hair, with peroxide.

per·pend[1] (pər·pend′) v.t. & v.i. Obs. To ponder; consider. [<L perpendere <per- thoroughly + pendere weigh]

per·pend[2] (pûr′pənd) n. In masonry, a stone header extending through a wall so that one end appears on each side of it. Also **perpend stone**, **per′pent** (-pənt). [Var. of parpen <OF parpain, ? <par- through (<L per-) + pan (de mur) a side (of a wall); infl. in form by PEND]

PERPEND

per·pen·dic·u·lar (pûr′pən·dik′yə·lər) adj. 1 Being at right angles to the plane of the horizon; upright or vertical. 2 Math. Meeting a given line or plane at right angles. See synonyms under RIGHT. — n. 1 A perpendicular line. 2 An appliance or instrument used to indicate the vertical line from any point; a plumb rule. 3 A line at right angles to another line or to a plane. 4 A vertical line or vertical face; loosely, any steep incline or face. **5** Perpendicular position. **6** Moral uprightness. [<OF *perpendiculer* <L *perpendicularis* < *perpendiculum* a plumb line < *per-* thoroughly + *pendere* hang] — **per'·pen·dic·u·lar'i·ty** (-lar'ə·tē) *n.* — **per'·pen·dic'u·lar·ly** *adv.*

per·pe·trate (pûr'pə·trāt) *v.t.* **·trat·ed**, **·trat·ing** To do, perform, or commit (a crime, etc.). [<L *perpetratus*, pp. of *perpetrare* carry through < *per-* through + *patrare* effect] — **per'pe·tra'tion** *n.* — **per'pe·tra'tor** *n.*

per·pet·u·al (pər·pech'oo·əl) *adj.* **1** Continuing unlimited in time. **2** Incessant; ceaseless. **3** *Bot.* Being in bloom during all or nearly all the year, as certain hybrid flowers. — *n.* Any perennial plant; also, any of certain perpetual hybrid roses. [<OF *perpetuel* <L *perpetualis* < *perpetuus* < *per-* through + *petere* seek] — **per·pet'u·al·ly** *adv.* — **per·pet'u·al·ness** *n.*

Synonyms (*adj.*): ceaseless, constant, continual, continuous, endless, enduring, eternal, incessant, interminable, lasting, perennial, permanent, sempiternal, unceasing, unending, unfailing, unintermitted, uninterrupted. See CONTINUAL, ETERNAL, PERMANENT. *Antonyms*: see synonyms for TRANSIENT.

perpetual calendar See under CALENDAR.

perpetual motion ·See under MOTION.

per·pet·u·ate (pər·pech'oo·āt) *v.t.* **·at·ed**, **·at·ing** To make perpetual or enduring. [<L *perpetuatus*, pp. of *perpetuare* perpetuate < *perpetuus* PERPETUAL] — **per·pet'u·a'tion** *n.* — **per·pet'u·a'tor** *n.*

per·pe·tu·i·ty (pûr'pə·tōo'ə·tē, -tyōo'-) *n.* *pl.* **·ties 1** The quality or state of being perpetual. **2** Something that has perpetual existence or worth. **3** Unending or unlimited time. **4** *Law* A limitation rendering property inalienable; also, the property so limited. **5** In annuities, a perpetual annuity, or the number of years' purchase to be given for it; the number of years in which the simple interest of a sum becomes equal to the principal. [<OF *perpetuité* <L *perpetuitas* < *perpetuus* PERPETUAL]

per·plex (pər·pleks') *v.t.* **1** To cause to hesitate, as from doubt; confuse, as with difficult problems; puzzle. **2** To make complicated, intricate, or confusing. [Back formation from PERPLEXED]

Synonyms: bewilder, bother, complicate, confound, confuse, distract, embarrass, entangle, harass, involve, mystify, pose, puzzle, trouble. *Antonyms*: clarify, disentangle, elucidate, explain, simplify.

per·plexed (pər·plekst') *adj.* **1** Confused; embarrassed. **2** Of a complicated character; involved. [Appar. alter. of obs. *perplex*, adj., intricate <L *perplexus* involved < *per-* thoroughly + *plexus*, pp. of *plectere* plait] — **per·plex'ed·ly** *adv.* — **per·plex'ed·ness** (-plek'sid·nis) *n.*

per·plex·ing (pər·plek'sing) *adj.* Confusing; puzzling; embarrassing; intricate. — **per·plex'ing·ly** *adv.*

per·plex·i·ty (pər·plek'sə·tē) *n.* *pl.* **·ties 1** Mental difficulty owing to doubt, confusion, etc. **2** That which perplexes; also, an instance of bewilderment. **3** The quality of being intricate or complicated; entanglement.

Synonyms: amazement, astonishment, bewilderment, confusion, distraction, disturbance, doubt, embarrassment. *Perplexity* is the drawing of the thoughts or faculties by turns in different directions or toward contrasted or contradictory conclusions; *confusion* is a state in which the mental faculties are thrown into chaos, so that the clear and distinct action of perception, memory, reason, and will, is lost; *bewilderment* is akin to *confusion*, but is less overwhelming, and more readily recovered from. *Perplexity* has not the unsettling of the faculties implied in *confusion*, nor the overwhelming of the faculties implied in *amazement* or *astonishment*. With an excitable person, *bewilderment* may deepen into *confusion* that will make him unable to think clearly or even to see or hear distinctly. *Amazement* results from the sudden and unimagined occurrence of great good or evil or the sudden awakening of the mind to unthought-of truth. *Astonishment* often produces *bewilderment*, which the word was formerly understood to imply. See AMAZEMENT, ANXIETY, CARE, DOUBT.

per·qui·site (pûr'kwə·zit) *n.* Any incidental profit from service beyond salary or wages;

hence, any privilege or benefit claimed as due. [<Med. L *perquisitum* an acquisition <L, a thing diligently sought, orig. pp. neut. of *perquirere* < *per-* thoroughly + *quaerere* seek]

per·ry (per'ē) *n.* A fermented drink made from the expressed juice of pears. [<OF *peré* <LL *pera*. See PEAR.]

perse (pûrs) *adj.* Grayish-blue. — *n.* A grayish blue. [<OF *pers* <LL *persus*]

per se (pûr sē', sā') *Latin* By itself, himself, or herself; intrinsically; in or of its own nature, without reference to its relations.

per·se·cute (pûr'sə·kyōot) *v.t.* **·cut·ed**, **·cut·ing 1** To harass with cruel or oppressive treatment, especially because of race, religion, or opinions. **2** To annoy or harass persistently. [<OF *persecuter* <L *persecutus*, pp. of *persequi* pursue < *per-* thoroughly + *sequi* follow] — **per'se·cu'tive** *adj.* — **per'se·cu'tor** *n.*

Synonyms: afflict, distress, harass, harry, molest, oppress, torment, worry. See ABUSE. *Antonyms*: advance, advocate, aid, assist, befriend, cherish, countenance, encourage, favor, help, indulge, support, sustain, tolerate.

per·se·cu·tion (pûr'sə·kyōo'shən) *n.* **1** The act or process of persecuting; cruel oppression. **2** Any period characterized by systematic oppression, infliction of torture, death, or the like, on account of religious belief. — **per'se·cu'tion·al**, **per·se·cu·to·ry** (pûr'sə·kyōo'tər·ē) *adj.*

Per·seph·o·ne (pər·sef'ə·nē) In Greek mythology, the daughter of Zeus and Demeter, abducted by Pluto and made queen of the kingdom of the dead, but allowed to return to the earth for a third of each year: identified with the Roman *Proserpine*.

Per·seus (pûr'syōōs, -sē·əs) **1** In Greek mythology, the son of Zeus and Danae, slayer of Medusa and savior and husband of Andromeda. **2** In the Apocrypha, the last king of Macedonia; died about 164 B.C. I *Mac.* viii 5. **3** A northern constellation. See CONSTELLATION. [<L <Gk.]

per·se·ver·ance (pûr'sə·vir'əns) *n.* **1** The act or habit of persevering; persistence. **2** *Theol.* In Calvinism, the continuance in grace and certain salvation of those whom God effectually calls, accepts in Christ, and sanctifies by his spirit. [<OF *perseverance* <L *perseverantia* steadfastness < *perseverans*, *-antis*, pp. of *perseverare* PERSEVERE]

Synonyms: constancy, indefatigableness, persistence, persistency, resolution, steadiness, steadfastness, tenacity. See INDUSTRY. *Antonyms*: caprice, fickleness, fitfulness, inconstancy, irresolution, levity, unsteadiness, vacillation, volatility.

per·se·vere (pûr'sə·vir') *v.i.* **·vered**, **·ver·ing** To persist in any purpose or enterprise; continue striving in spite of difficulties, etc. [<OF *perseverer* <L *perseverare* < *perseverus*, very strict <*per-* thoroughly + *severus* strict]

Synonyms: continue, endure, persist. *Persevere* is almost uniformly employed in the good and high sense of holding to a worthy course against all difficulty, danger, hindrance, or opposition; *persist* is often used of an annoying or perverse adherence to a demand or purpose that might well be abandoned. See INSIST, PERSIST. Compare OBSTINATE. *Antonyms*: see synonyms for CEASE.

Per·sia (pûr'zhə, -shə) The former name for IRAN. See PERSIAN EMPIRE.

Per·sian (pûr'zhən, -shən) *adj.* Of or pertaining to ancient Persia or modern Iran, its people, its language, or its architecture. — *n.* **1** A native or inhabitant of Persia or Iran. **2** The Iranian language of the Persians: historically divided into **Old Persian**, recorded in the cuneiform inscriptions of Darius I and his successors, and closely related to the language of the Avesta; **Middle Persian**, chiefly represented by Pahlavi, a literary language written in a Semitic alphabet, used in the sacred writings of the Zoroastrian religion from the third to the seventh century; and **Modern Persian**, containing many Arabic loan words and written in Arabic script. **3** A fine silk used formerly for linings. **4** *pl.* Persian blinds. [<OF *persien*, ult. <L *Persia* Persia <Gk. *Persis* <OPersian *Pārsa*]

Persian blinds Outside window shutters of thin, movable slats fastened in a frame.

Persian carpet A hand-woven Oriental carpet with connected design, the warp and filling

of silk, wool, or cotton, and the pile of wool.

Persian Gulf An arm of the Arabian Sea between Iran and Arabia; 90,000 square miles.

Persian lamb The young of certain sheep of central Asia, especially of the karakul; also, its skin, used as a fur; astrakan. See KARAKUL.

per·si·enne (pûr'zē·en', *Fr.* per·syen') *n.* **1** An Oriental cambric or muslin with colored printed pattern. **2** *pl.* Persian blinds. [<F, fem. of *persien* PERSIAN]

per·si·flage (pûr'sə·fläzh') *n.* A light, flippant style of conversation or writing. [<F <*persifler* ·banter <L *per-* through + F *siffler* whistle <L *sifilare*]

per·sim·mon (pər·sim'ən) *n.* **1** The orange-red or yellow, plumlike fruit of an American tree of the ebony family (genus *Diospyros*), very astringent in taste until exposed to frost. **2** The tree, its hard blackish wood, or its tonic and astringent bark. [<Algonquian. Cf. Cree *pasiminan* dried fruit.]

per·sist (pər·sist', -zist') *v.i.* **1** To continue firmly in some course, state, etc., especially despite opposition or difficulties. **2** To be insistent, as in repeating a statement. **3** To continue to exist; endure. [<L *persistere* < *per-* thoroughly + *sistere* stand]

Synonyms: continue, endure, insist, last, persevere, remain, stay. As applied to duration, *last* is applied chiefly to things, *endure* to either persons or things. That *remains* or *stays* which is simply let alone; that which *endures* or *persists* does so against opposing forces. A man *insists* upon his demand, *persists* in his refusal. See under INSIST, PERSEVERE. *Antonyms*: see synonyms for CEASE.

per·sis·tence (pər·sis'təns, -zis'-) *n.* **1** The act of persisting in any course or enterprise; the quality of being persistent; perseverance; fixed adherence to a resolve, course of conduct, etc. **2** The continuance of an effect longer than the cause that first produced it. Also **per·sis'ten·cy**. See synonyms under INDUSTRY, PERSEVERANCE.

per·sis·tent (pər·sis'tənt, -zis'-) *adj.* **1** Firm and persevering in a course or resolve. **2** Enduring; permanent; continuous. **3** *Bot.* Not falling away; remaining for a long time or after the neighboring parts have reached maturity, as the calyx or petals in certain flowers. **4** *Zool.* Retained throughout life, as the gills of fishes and some amphibians. Compare DECIDUOUS. See synonyms under INDEFATIGABLE, INFLEXIBLE, OBSTINATE, PERMANENT. [<L *persistens*, *-entis*, pp. of *persistere*. See PERSIST.] — **per·sis'tent·ly** *adv.*

per·snick·e·ty (pər·snik'ə·tē) *adj. Colloq.* **1** Unduly fastidious; fussy; overprecise. **2** Demanding minute care or pains. Also **per·nickety**. [<dial. E, ? alter. of PARTICULAR] — **per·snick'e·ti·ness** *n.*

per·son (pûr'sən) *n.* **1** A human being as including body and mind; an individual. **2** The body of a human being or its characteristic appearance and condition. **3** *Law* Any human being, corporation, or body politic having legal rights and duties. **4** *Theol.* One of the three individualities in the triune God; hypostasis. **5** *Gram.* **a** A modification of the pronoun and verb that distinguishes the speaker (**first person**), the person or thing spoken to (**second person**), and the person or thing spoken of (**third person**). **b** Any of the forms or inflections indicating this, as *I* or *we*, *you*, *he*, *she*, *it*. **6** An individual. **7** Superciliously, a common individual. **8** A part acted on the stage. — **in person** Present in the flesh; present and acting for oneself. [<F *personne* <L *persona* mask for actors. Doublet of PARSON.]

per·so·na (pər·sō'nə) *n.* *pl.* **·nae** (-nē) **1** Literally, person; specifically, a character in a drama, novel, etc.: dramatis *personae*. **2** In Jung's analytic psychology, the conscious artificial or masked personality complex developed by an individual, in contrast to his innate personality characteristics, for purposes of concealment, defense, deception, or adaptation to his environment. [<L, a person, orig. a mask]

per·son·a·ble (pûr'sən·ə·bəl) *adj.* Attractive in person; of good appearance. — **per'son·a·bly** *adv.*

per·son·age (pûr'sən·ij) *n.* **1** A man or woman of importance or rank. **2** An assumed character; an impersonation. **3** A character in fiction, history, etc.; a character in a play. [<OF <L *persona* a person]

per·son·al (pûr′sən·əl) *adj.* **1** Pertaining to or characteristic of a particular person; not general or public: a purely *personal* matter. **2** Belonging or relating to or constituting a person or persons, as distinguished from things; characteristic of human beings or free agents. **3** Performed by or done to the person directly concerned; done in person: a *personal* service. **4** Affecting or relating to one individually: *personal* habits. **5** Of or pertaining to the body or appearance: *personal* beauty. **6** Directly characterizing an individual; hence, concerning one's character or conduct, often in the sense of disparaging. **7** *Law* Appertaining to the person; movable: *personal* effects. **8** *Gram.* Denoting or indicating the person: *personal* pronouns. — *n.* **1** *Law* A movable article of property; chattel. **2** A paragraph or advertisement of personal reference or application. [<OF <LL *personalis* <L *persona* a person]

per·son·al·i·ty (pûr′sən·al′ə·tē) *n. pl.* **·ties 1** That which constitutes a person; also, that which distinguishes and characterizes a person; personal existence. **2** Anything said of a person, especially if disparaging: usually in the plural: offensive *personalities.* **3** A person, especially one of exceptional qualities. — **double** or **multiple personality** *Psychiatry* A condition in which two or more relatively distinct sets of experiences and behavior patterns reveal themselves alternately in the same individual. See synonyms under CHARACTER. [<OF *personalité* <Med. L *personalitas, -tatis* <LL *personalis* of a person]

per·son·al·ize (pûr′sən·əl·īz′) *v.t.* **·ized, ·iz·ing 1** To make personal. **2** To personify.

per·son·al·ly (pûr′sən·əl·ē) *adv.* **1** In proper person; not through an agent. **2** With reference to one's own personality. **3** In a personal manner.

personal pronoun See under PRONOUN.

per·son·al·ty (pûr′sən·əl·tē) *n. pl.* **·ties** Personal property. [<AF *personaltie* <Med. L *personalitas.* See PERSONALITY.]

per·son·i·fi·ca·tion (pər·son′ə·fə·kā′shən) *n.* **1** The figurative endowment of inanimate objects or qualities with personality or human attributes. **2** Striking or typical exemplification of a quality or attribute in one's person; embodiment: She was the *personification* of joy. **3** The emblematic representation of an abstract quality or idea by a human figure. **4** Impersonation.

per·son·i·fy (pər·son′ə·fī) *v.t.* **·fied, ·fy·ing 1** To think of or represent as having life or human qualities. **2** To represent (an abstraction or inanimate object) as a person; symbolize. **3** To be the embodiment of; typify: He *personifies* honor. [<F *personnifier* <L *persona* a mask, person + *facere* make] — **per·son′i·fi′er** *n.*

per·son·nel (pûr′sə·nel′) *n.* **1** Persons collectively. **2** The persons employed in a business or in military service. **3** The collective characteristics of such a body of persons. — *adj.* Of or pertaining to personnel; directing personnel. [<F <OF *personal* PERSONAL]

per·spec·tive (pər·spek′tiv) *n.* **1** The art or theory of representing, by a drawing made on a flat or curved surface, solid objects or surfaces conceived of as not lying in that surface; delineation of objects as they appear to the eye. **2** The art of conveying the impression of depth and distance; representation of scenes as they appear to the eye, by means of correct drawing, shading, etc. **3** The effect of distance upon the appearance of objects, by means of which the eye judges spatial relations. **4** The relative importance of facts or matters from any special point of

PERSPECTIVE
ab. Horizon.
c. Vanishing point (point of sight).
dc. Line of sight.
ef. Ground line.

view; also, their presentation with just regard to their proportional importance. **5** A distant view; vista; prospect: also figuratively. **6** A picture giving the illusion of a scene of nature. — **aerial perspective** The art of indicating the relative distances of objects by gradations of tone and color. — **linear perspective** The art or method of producing an appearance of distance by means of converging lines. — *adj.* Pertaining to the art of perspective; also, drawn in perspective. [<Med. L *perspectiva (ars)* optical (art) <LL *perspectivus* optical <L *perspectus,* pp. of *perspicere* <*per-* through + *specere* look] — **per·spec′tive·ly** *adv.*

per·spi·ca·cious (pûr′spə·kā′shəs) *adj.* **1** Keenly discerning or understanding. **2** Quick–eyed; sharp–sighted. See synonyms under ACUTE, ASTUTE, SAGACIOUS. [<L *perspicax, -acis* sharp–sighted <*perspicere.* See PERSPECTIVE.] — **per′spi·ca′cious·ly** *adv.* — **per′spi·ca′cious·ness** *n.*

per·spi·cac·i·ty (pûr′spə·kas′ə·tē) *n.* Keenness in mental penetration or discernment. See synonyms under ACUMEN.

per·spi·cu·i·ty (pûr′spə·kyōō′ə·tē) *n.* Clearness of expression or style; lucidity.
Synonyms: clearness, distinctness, explicitness, intelligibility, lucidity, plainness. *Antonyms:* ambiguity, cloudiness, confusion, incomprehensibility, indistinctness, intricacy, obscurity, unintelligibility, vagueness.

per·spi·ra·tion (pûr′spə·rā′shən) *n.* **1** The exuding of the saline fluid secreted by the sweat glands of the skin. **2** The saline fluid excreted; sweat. — **per·spir·a·to·ry** (pər·spīr′ə·tôr′ē, -tō′rē) *adj.*

per·spire (pər·spīr′) *v.* **·spired, ·spir·ing** *v.i.* To give off perspiration through the pores of the skin; sweat. — *v.t.* To give off through pores; exude. [<L *perspirare* breathe, blow constantly <*per-* through + *spirare* breathe] — **per·spir′a·ble** *adj.*

per·suade (pər·swād′) *v.t.* **·suad·ed, ·suad·ing 1** To move (a person, etc.) to do something by arguments, inducements, pleas, etc. **2** To induce to a belief; convince. [<L *persuadere* <*per-* thoroughly + *suadere* advise] — **per·suad′a·ble** *adj.* — **per·suad′er** *n.*
Synonyms: allure, coax, convince, dispose, entice, impel, incite, incline, induce, influence, lead, move, urge, win. Of these words *convince* alone has no direct reference to moving the will, denoting an effect upon the understanding only; one may be *convinced* of truth that has no manifest connection with duty or action, as of a mathematical proposition. To *persuade* is to bring the will of another to a desired decision by some influence exerted upon it short of compulsion; one may be *convinced* that the earth is round; he may be *persuaded* to travel around it; but persuasion is so largely dependent upon conviction that it is commonly held to be the orator's work first to *convince* in order that he may *persuade.* *Coax* is a slighter word than *persuade,* seeking the same end by shallower methods, largely by appeal to personal feeling, with or without success; as, a child *coaxes* a parent to buy him a toy. One may be *induced* by means not properly included in persuasion, as by bribery or intimidation; he is *won* over chiefly by personal influence. See ACTUATE, BEND, CONVINCE, INFLUENCE. *Antonyms:* deter, discourage, dissuade, hinder, repel, restrain.

per·sua·sion (pər·swā′zhən) *n.* **1** The act of persuading or of using persuasive methods. **2** The state of being persuaded; settled opinion; conviction. **3** A settled belief; accepted creed; hence, a party, sect, or denomination. **4** *Colloq.* Sort; kind: the male *persuasion.* See synonyms under COUNSEL. [<L *persuasio, -onis* <*persuasus,* pp. of *persuadere* PERSUADE]

per·sua·sive (pər·swā′siv) *adj.* Having power or tendency to persuade. — *n.* That which persuades or tends to persuade. — **per·sua′sive·ly** *adv.* — **per·sua′sive·ness** *n.*

pert (pûrt) *adj.* **1** Disrespectfully forward or free; saucy. **2** *Dial.* Of fine appearance; comely; sprightly. See synonyms under IMPUDENT. [Aphetic var. of APERT] — **pert′ly** *adv.* — **pert′ness** *n.*

per·tain (pər·tān′) *v.i.* **1** To have reference; relate. **2** To belong as an adjunct, function,

quality, etc.: the house and lands that *pertain* thereto. **3** To be fitting or appropriate: the joys that *pertain* to youth. [<OF *partenir* <L *pertinere* extend <*per-* through + *tenere* hold]
Synonyms: appertain, belong, concern, regard, relate.

per·ti·na·cious (pûr′tə·nā′shəs) *adj.* **1** Tenacious of purpose; stubbornly adhering to a pursuit or opinion; also, perversely or doggedly persistent. **2** Continuing without abatement; incessant. See synonyms under INFLEXIBLE, OBSTINATE, URGENT. [<L *pertinax, -acis* <*per-* thoroughly, very + *tenax, -acis* tenacious] — **per′ti·na′cious·ly** *adv.*

per·ti·nent (pûr′tə·nənt) *adj.* Related to or properly bearing upon the matter in hand; relevant. See synonyms under APPROPRIATE. [<OF *partenant,* ppr. of *partenir* PERTAIN; refashioned after L *pertinens, -entis*] — **per′ti·nence, per′ti·nen·cy** *n.* — **per′ti·nent·ly** *adv.*

per·turb (pər·tûrb′) *v.t.* To disquiet or disturb greatly; alarm; agitate. [<OF *perturber* <L *perturbare* <*per-* thoroughly + *turbare* disturb <*turba* turmoil] — **per·turb′a·ble** *adj.*

per·tur·ba·tion (pûr′tər·bā′shən) *n.* **1** The state of being perturbed, or the act of perturbing. **2** *Astron.* Deviation in the motion of a heavenly body, caused by the attraction of some other body than that round which it moves. **3** A cause of disquiet or disturbance. Also **per·turb·ance** (pər·tûr′bəns). [<OF *perturbacion* <L *perturbatio, -onis* <*perturbare* PERTURB]

per·tus·sis (pər·tus′is) *n.* **1** *Pathol.* Whooping cough. **2** Any violent convulsive or spasmodic cough. [<NL <L *per-* thoroughly, very great + *tussis* a cough] — **per·tus′sal** *adj.*

Pe·ru (pə·rōō′, *Sp.* pā·rōō′) A republic in western South America on the Pacific; 533,916 square miles; capital, Lima.

per·ul·ti·mate (pər·ul′tə·mit) *adj.* Designating a magnitude or condition that cannot be exceeded: a *perultimate* yield of crops. [<PER- (def. 2) + ULTIMATE]

pe·ruse (pə·rōōz′) *v.t.* **·rused, ·rus·ing 1** To read carefully or attentively. **2** To read. **3** To examine; scrutinize. [<PER- + USE, *v.*] — **pe·rus′a·ble** *adj.* — **pe·ru′sal** *n.* — **pe·rus′er** *n.*

per·vade (pər·vād′) *v.t.* **·vad·ed, ·vad·ing** To pass or spread through every part of; be diffused throughout; permeate. [<L *pervadere* <*per-* through + *vadere* go] — **per·va′sion** (-zhən) *n.*

per·va·sive (pər·vā′siv) *adj.* Thoroughly penetrating or permeating. [<L *pervasus,* pp. of *pervadere* PERVADE] — **per·va′sive·ly** *adv.* — **per·va′sive·ness** *n.*

per·verse (pər·vûrs′) *adj.* **1** Wrong or erring; different or varying from the correct or normal; also, unreasonable. **2** Thwarting or refractory. **3** Disposed to vex; petulant. [<OF *pervers* <L *perversus* turned the wrong way, orig. pp. of *pervertere.* See PERVERT.] — **per·verse′ly** *adv.* — **per·verse′ness** *n.* — **per·ver′sive** *adj.*
Synonyms: contrary, factious, fractious, froward, intractable, obstinate, petulant, stubborn, ungovernable, untoward, wayward, wilful. *Perverse* signifies wilfully wrong or erring, unreasonably set against right, reason, or authority. The *stubborn* or *obstinate* person will not do what another desires or requires; the *perverse* person will do anything contrary to what is desired or required of him. The *petulant* person frets, but may comply; the *perverse* individual may be smooth or silent, but is wilfully *intractable.* *Wayward* refers to a *perverse* disregard of morality and duty; *froward* is now almost obsolete; *untoward* is rarely heard except in certain phrases; as, *untoward* circumstances. Compare OBSTINATE. *Antonyms:* accommodating, amenable, complaisant, compliant, genial, governable, kind, obliging.

per·ver·sion (pər·vûr′zhən, -shən) *n.* **1** The act of perverting, or the state of being perverted. **2** *Pathol.* A deviation from the normal in structure or function. **3** *Psychiatry* Deviation from the normal in sexual desires or activities.

per·ver·si·ty (pər·vûr′sə·tē) *n. pl.* **·ties 1** The state or quality of being perverse. **2** Perverse nature or behavior. **3** An instance of perverseness.

per·vert (pər·vûrt') v.t. 1 To turn to an improper use or purpose; misapply. 2 To distort the meaning of; misconstrue. 3 To turn from approved opinions or conduct; lead astray; corrupt. —n. (pûr'vûrt) 1 An apostate; renegade: opposed to convert. 2 Psychiatry One affected with or addicted to sexual perversion. [< F pervertir < L pervertere turn around, over < per- away + vertere turn] —per·vert'er n. —per·vert'i·bil'i·ty n. —per·vert'i·ble adj. —per·vert'i·bly adv.

Synonyms (verb): corrupt, distort, falsify, garble, misquote, misrepresent, misstate, stretch, twist. See ABUSE. Antonyms: correct, quote, rectify, restore.

per·vert·ed (pər·vûr'tid) adj. 1 Turned from the right purpose; misused. 2 Wilfully sinful; wicked; vicious. —per·vert'ed·ly adv.

per·vi·ous (pûr'vē·əs) adj. Capable of being penetrated; permeable. [< L pervius having a way through < per- through + via way] —per'vi·ous·ly adv. —per'vi·ous·ness n.

Pe·sach (pä'säkh) n. The feast of the Passover. Also Pe'sah. See JEWISH HOLIDAYS. [< Hebrew pesakh, lit., a passing over < pāsakh pass over]

pe·sade (pə·säd', -zäd', -zäd') n. The act or position of a saddle horse in rearing. [< F, alter. of posade < Ital. posata a pause < posare pause < L pausare halt < pausa a stop]

Pe·shi·to (pə·shē'tō) n. The oldest Syriac version of the Bible. Also Pe·shi'to, Pe·shit'ta (-shē'tä), Pe·shit·to. [< Syriac p'shi(t)to, lit. plain, simple]

pes·ky (pes'kē) adj. ·ki·er, ·ki·est Colloq. 1 Annoying; troublesome; plaguy. 2 Darned; damned: a euphemism. [< dial. E, prob. alter. of pesty < PEST] —pes'ki·ly adv.

pe·so (pā'sō) n. pl. ·sos 1 A monetary unit of Cuba, the Philippines, Mexico, and certain other Latin-American countries, equal to 100 centavos. 2 An old Spanish coin equal to 8 reales; the Spanish dollar or piece-of-eight. [< Sp., orig. a weight < L pensum, orig. pp. neut. of pendere weigh]

pes·si·mism (pes'ə·miz'əm) n. 1 A disposition to take a gloomy view of affairs: opposed to optimism. 2 Cynicism. 3 A theory of cosmology that regards the cosmos, or the world and life, or some main constituent thereof, as essentially evil, or (in its extreme form) as the worst possible world. [< L pessimus worst + -ISM, on analogy with optimism] —pes'si·mist n. —pes'si·mis'tic or ·ti·cal adj. —pes'si·mis'ti·cal·ly adv.

pest (pest) n. 1 A pernicious or vexatious person or thing, especially a destructive or injurious insect. 2 A virulent epidemic; pestilence. [< MF peste < L pestis a plague]

pes·ter (pes'tər) v.t. To harass with petty and persistent annoyances; bother; plague. [Aphetic var. of obs. impester entangle < OF empestrer, empasturer, orig. hobble a grazing horse < em- (< L in- in) + LL pastorium foot shackles < L pastus, pp. of pascere feed] —pes'ter·er n.

pest·hole (pest'hōl') n. A breeding place for pestilence.

pest·house (pest'hous') n. A public hospital where patients suffering from infectious or pestilential diseases are treated and kept isolated.

pes·ti·cide (pes'tə·sīd) n. A chemical or other substance effective in the destruction of such plant and animal pests as fungi, bacteria, insects, and the like. —pes'ti·ci'dal adj.

pes·tif·er·ous (pes·tif'ər·əs) adj. 1 Carrying pestilence. 2 Threatening or bringing danger or evil. 3 Colloq. Annoying; disagreeable. See synonyms under NOISOME. [< L pestiferus bringing plague < pestis a plague + ferre bear] —pes·tif'er·ous·ly adv. —pes·tif'er·ous·ness n.

pes·ti·lence (pes'tə·ləns) n. 1 Any wide-spread and fatal infectious or contagious malady. 2 Figuratively, a noxious or malign doctrine, influence, etc.

pes·ti·lent (pes'tə·lənt) adj. 1 Tending to produce malignant zymotic disease; pestilential. 2 Having a malign influence or effect. 3 Making trouble; causing irritation; vexatious. [< L pestilens, -entis < pestis a plague] —pes'ti·lent·ly adv.

pes·ti·len·tial (pes'tə·len'shəl) adj. 1 Having the nature of or breeding pestilence. 2 Morally harmful or pernicious; baneful. See

synonyms under NOISOME.

pes·tle (pes'əl) n. 1 An implement used for braying, bruising, or mixing substances, as in a mortar. 2 A vertical moving bar employed in pounding, as in a stamp mill, etc. —v.t. & v.i. ·tled, ·tling To pound, grind, or mix with or as with a pestle. [< OF pestel < L pistillum < pistus, pp. of pinsere pound]

PESTLE
a. Pestle.
b. Mortar.

pet¹ (pet) n. 1 A tame, fondled animal. 2 Any loved and cherished creature; also, a favorite: teacher's pet. —adj. 1 Being a pet; indulged and fondled: a pet cat. 2 Regarded as a favorite; cherished: my pet hobby. —v. pet·ted, pet·ting —v.t. 1 Rare To treat as a pet; indulge. 2 To stroke or caress. —v.i. 3 U.S. Slang To make love by kissing and caressing. See synonyms under PAMPER, CARESS. [< dial. E (Scottish), ? back formation < PETTY, in affectionate use]

pet² (pet) n. A fit of pique or ill temper; peevish mood. [< obs. to take the pet take offence, sulk; origin uncertain]

pet·al (pet'l) n. Bot. One of the leaves or subordinate parts of a corolla. [< NL petalum < L, a metal plate < Gk. petalon a thin plate, leaf, orig. neut. of petalos outspread < petannynai expand] —pet'aled or pet'alled adj. -petal combining form Seeking: centripetal.

pet·al·ism (pet'l·iz'əm) n. A form of ostracism in use among the Greeks of ancient Syracuse, who wrote on olive leaves their votes to banish for five years a citizen obnoxious to his fellow citizens. [< Gk. petalismos < petalon a leaf]

pe·tard (pi·tärd') n. 1 An explosive device formerly used for making breaches, etc., as in walls. 2 A small paper bomb used in pyrotechnics to imitate the sound of musketry. [< MF pétard < péter break wind < OF pet a fart < L peditum, orig. pp. neut. of pedere break wind]

PETARD

pet·a·sus (pet'ə·səs) n. 1 A hat, typically with broad brim and low crown, worn by heralds and travelers of ancient Greece. 2 The winged hat of the god Mercury. Also pet'a·sos. [< L < Gk. petasos < petannynai spread out]

pe·ter (pē'tər) v.i. Colloq. To diminish gradually and then cease or disappear; become exhausted: with out. [Orig. U.S. mining slang; origin unknown]

— **Peter, Saint** A Galilean fisherman, one of the Twelve Apostles, reputed author of two epistles of the New Testament; also called "Simon Peter."

— **Peter I,** 1672–1725, czar of Russia 1682–1725, known as **Peter the Great.**

— **Peter II,** 1923–1970, king of Yugoslavia 1934–45.

— **Peter the Hermit,** 1050?–1115?, French monk; preacher of the First Crusade.

Peter Pan 1 In J. M. Barrie's play, Peter Pan (1904), the little boy "who never grew up." 2 A statue, in Kensington Gardens, London, symbolizing perpetual youth; hence, any fully grown person of youthful or childish enthusiasm.

pe·ter·sham (pē'tər·shəm) n. 1 A heavy, rough, tufted woolen cloth. 2 Formerly, a heavy greatcoat of such cloth. [after Viscount Petersham, who introduced it]

Peter's pence 1 Voluntary contributions raised by Roman Catholics for the pope since 1860. 2 The tax of a penny for every house, once paid by the English to support the English hospice in Rome; also, a like tribute paid by them and other peoples to aid the pope: so called because collected on St. Peter's Day: also called hearth money. Also **Peter pence.**

pet·it (pet'ē) adj. Small; lesser; minor; trivial: used in legal phrases: petit larceny: also spelled petty. [< OF, small, ? < Celtic pit something

pointed, thin]

pe·tite (pə·tēt') adj. fem. Diminutive; little. [< F, fem. of petit. See PETIT.]

pe·ti·tion (pə·tish'ən) n. 1 A request, supplication, or prayer; a solemn or formal supplication. 2 A formal request, written or printed, addressed to a person in authority and asking for some grant or benefit, the redress of a grievance, etc. 3 Law A formal application in writing made to a court, requesting judicial action concerning some matter therein set forth. 4 That which is requested or supplicated. —v.t. 1 To make a petition to; entreat. 2 To ask for. —v.i. 3 To make a petition. See synonyms under ASK, PRAY. [< OF peticiun < L petitio, -onis < petere seek; refashioned after L] —pe·ti'tion·ar'y adj. —pe·ti'tion·er n.

Synonyms (noun): appeal, application, craving, entreaty, pleading, prayer, request, supplication. See PRAYER. Antonyms: command, demand, denial, exaction, refusal, requirement.

petit jury See under JURY.

petit larceny The theft of property of less than such amount as may be fixed by statute: the distinction between petit and grand larceny has been almost wholly abolished: also spelled petty larceny.

pe·tit mal (pə·tē' mäl') Pathol. A form of epileptic seizure characterized by a momentary loss of memory or consciousness and a brief interval of helplessness. See GRAND MAL.

pet·i·to·ry (pet'ə·tôr'ē, -tō'rē) adj. Soliciting or solicited by petition. [< LL petitorius < L petitor a candidate < petere seek]

pet·it point (pet'ē) A fine needle-tapestry stitch: also called tent stitch.

pet·its fours (pet'ē fôrz', fōrz'; Fr. pə·tē' foor') Small cakes, often elaborately iced. [< F, lit., little ovens]

pet·rel (pet'rəl) n. A long-winged, black-and-white sea bird (order Procelariiformes); Mother Carey's chicken. [Earlier pitteral, ? a dim. of PETER; from its seeming to walk on the water like St. Peter. Matt. xiv 29]

PETREL
(Body from 7 to 16 inches long; the storm petrel.

pe·tres·cent (pə·tres'ənt) adj. Petrifying or tending to petrify. [< L petra a rock + -ESCENT]

pet·ri·fac·tion (pet'rə·fak'shən) n. 1 Partial or entire replacement of the material of an organism by mineral matter: also pe·tres'cence, pe·tres'cen·cy. 2 Anything petrified. Also pet'ri·fi·ca'tion. [< PETRIFY, on analogy with satisfaction, stupefaction, etc.] —pet'ri·fac'tive adj.

pet·ri·fy (pet'rə·fī) v. ·fied, ·fy·ing v.t. 1 To convert (organic material) into a substance of stony character. 2 To make fixed and unyielding; deaden; harden. 3 To daze or paralyze with fear, surprise, etc. —v.i. 4 To become stone or a stony substance. [< MF pétrifier < L petra a rock + facere make] —pe·trif·ic (pə·trif'ik) adj.

petro- combining form Rock; stone: petroglyph. Also, before vowels, petr-. [< Gk. petra a rock and petros a stone]

pet·ro·chem·is·try (pet'rō·kem'is·trē) n. The chemistry of petroleum and its derivatives, especially the natural and synthetic hydrocarbons. —pet'ro·chem'i·cal adj. & n.

pet·ro·dol·lars (pet'rō·dol'ərz) n. pl. Surplus dollars accumulated by oil-producing countries from oil sales, and usually invested in industrial countries.

pet·ro·glyph (pet'rə·glif) n. A primitive figure or legend cut in rock. [< F pétroglyphe < Gk. petra a rock + glyphē. See GLYPH.] —pet'ro·glyph'ic adj.

pet·ro·graph (pet'rə·graf, -gräf) n. A prehistoric carving or inscription on a rock.

pe·trog·ra·phy (pə·trog'rə·fē) n. The systematic description and classification of rocks. —pe·trog'ra·pher n. —pet·ro·graph·ic (pet'rə·graf'ik) or ·i·cal adj. —pet'ro·graph'i·cal·ly adv.

PETROGRAPH

pet·ro·la·tum (pet′rə·lā′təm) *n.* A fatty semisolid mixture of the paraffin hydrocarbons, obtained from petroleum, used in preparing ointments, and internally: often called *mineral jelly.* [< NL < PETROLEUM]

pe·tro·le·um (pə·trō′lē·əm) *n.* An oily, liquid mixture of numerous hydrocarbons, chiefly of the paraffin series, found in many widely scattered subterranean deposits, and extensively used for heat and light. A number of very important substances are obtained by the fractional distillation of petroleum, such as petroleum ether, gasoline, naphtha, benzine, kerosene, paraffin, etc. [< Med. L < L *petra* a rock (< Gk.) + *oleum* oil]

pe·trol·o·gy (pə·trol′ə·jē) *n.* The science of the origin, structure, constitution, and characteristics of rocks: a branch of geology. —**pet·ro·log·ic** (pet′rə·loj′ik) or **·i·cal** *adj.* —**pet′ro·log′cal·ly** *adv.* —**pe·trol′o·gist** *n.*

pet·rous (pet′rəs, pē′trəs) *adj.* 1 Hard, like stone. 2 *Anat.* Pertaining to or situated near the hard portion of the temporal bone. Also **pe·tro·sal** (pə·trō′səl) [< L *petrosus* rocky < L *petra* rock < Gk.]

pet·ti·coat (pet′ē·kōt) *n.* 1 A skirt or loose garment depending from the waist; especially, a woman's underskirt. 2 One who wears a petticoat; hence, a woman. 3 An electric insulator shaped like an inverted cup, for use on high-tension wires. —*adj.* Of, pertaining to, or influenced by, women: *petticoat* politics. [Earlier *petty coat* < PETTY + COAT]

pet·ti·fog·ger (pet′i·fog′ər, -fôg′ər) *n.* An inferior lawyer, especially one chiefly employed on mean or petty cases, or resorting to small or tricky methods. [Earlier *petty fogger* < PETTY + obs. *fogger* a trickster for gain, prob. < FUGGER] —**pet′ti·fog′ger·y** *n.*

pet·tish (pet′ish) *adj.* Capriciously ill-tempered; testy. See synonyms under FRETFUL. [Prob. < PET² + -ISH] —**pet′tish·ly** *adv.*

pet·ti·toes (pet′ē·tōz′) *n. pl.* The aborted toes at the back of a pig's foot. [Earlier sense "giblets" < F *petit oie* goose giblets, lit., a little goose; later mistakenly understood as *petty toes*]

pet·to (pet′ō) *n.* The breast. —**cardinal in petto** A cardinal appointed, but not yet formally announced. —**in petto** Within one's own breast; to oneself. [< Ital., the breast < L *pectus*]

pet·ty (pet′ē) *adj.* **·ti·er, ·ti·est** 1 Having little worth, importance, position, or rank; trifling; inferior: also spelled *petit.* 2 Having little scope or generosity; narrow-minded. 3 Mean; spiteful. See synonyms under CHILDISH, INSIGNIFICANT, LITTLE, SMALL. —*n.* A small amount of money advanced from a week's wages. [< F *petit* small. See PETIT.] —**pet′ti·ly** *adv.* —**pet′ti·ness** *n.*

petty jury, petty larceny, etc. See PETIT JURY, etc.

petty officer In the navies of the United States and Great Britain, an enlisted man comparable in rank with a non-commissioned officer of the army.

pet·u·lance (pech′ōō·ləns) *n.* 1 Fretfulness; peevishness; temporary ill-humor. 2 *Obs.* Insolence; pertness. Also **pet′u·lan·cy.** See synonyms under IMPATIENCE.

pet·u·lant (pech′ōō·lənt) *adj.* 1 Displaying or characterized by capricious fretfulness; peevish. 2 *Obs.* Saucily rude; insolent; wanton; pert. See synonyms under FRETFUL, PERVERSE. [< OF *petulant* < L *petulans, -antis* forward, ult. < *petere* seek, assail] —**pet′u·lant·ly** *adv.*

pe·tu·ni·a (pə·tōō′nē·ə, -tyōō′-) *n.* A plant of a tropical American genus (*Petunia*) of herbs of the nightshade family with funnel-shaped, fragrant flowers, in various shades of red, purple, and white. [< NL < obs. E *petun* tobacco < F < Guarani *petüñ*; so called because of its close relation to tobacco]

pew (pyōō) *n.* A bench for seating people in church, frequently with a kneeling rack attached; formerly, a boxlike quadrangle, usually raised to a low platform, with seats on three sides for a family. [ME *puwe,* appar. < OF *puye* a parapet < L *podia,* pl. of *podium* a height, a balcony < Gk. *podion* a base, dim. of *pous, podos* a foot]

pew·age (pyōō′ij) *n.* Rent paid for a pew or pews, or income derived from the rental of pews.

pew·ter (pyōō′tər) *n.* 1 An alloy, usually of tin and lead, formerly much used for tableware. 2 Pewter vessels collectively. —*adj.* Made of pewter. [< OF *peutre, pialtre,* prob. < Ital. *peltro*; ult. origin unknown]

pe·yo·te (pā·ō′tē, Sp. pā·yō′tā) *n.* A powerful intoxicant and narcotic drug obtained from the dried upper part of the mescal cactus found in Mexico and Texas. Also **pe·yo′tl** (-yōt′l). [< Am. Sp., the mescal cactus < Nahuatl *peyotl,* lit., a caterpillar; so called because of the down at its center]

pfen·nig (pfen′ikh) *n. pl.* **·nigs** or **pfen·ni·ge** (pfen′i·ge) A small bronze coin of Germany, equivalent to 1/100 of a mark: formerly called *reichspfennig.* [< G, a penny]

Phae·dra (fē′drə) In Greek mythology, a daughter of Minos and Pasiphaë, and wife of Theseus: she fell in love with her stepson Hippolytus and killed herself because he spurned her, indirectly causing his death. Also **Phæ′dra.**

phae·no·gam (fē′nə·gam) *n.* A phanerogam. [< NL *Phaenogama (Vegetabilia)* flowering (plants) < Gk. *phainein* show + *gamos* marriage]

phae·o·phy·ce·an (fē′ə·fī′sē·ən, -fish′ən) *n.* One of a family (*Phaeophyceae*) of brown algae. —*adj.* Of or pertaining to the *Phaeophyceae.* [< NL < Gk. *phaios* dusky + *phykos* seaweed]

Pha·e·thon (fā′ə·thon) In Greek mythology, the son of Helios, who borrowed his father's chariot of the sun, and would have set heaven and earth on fire by his careless driving if Zeus had not slain him with a thunderbolt.

pha·e·ton (fā′ə·tən, *esp. Brit.* fā′tən) *n.* 1 A light four-wheeled boxless carriage, having one or two seats, open at the sides, and sometimes having a top. 2 An open two-seated automobile. [< F < *phaéton* < L *Phaethon* Phaethon]

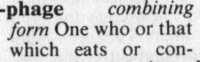

AMERICAN TWO–SPRING PHAETON (def. 1)

-phage *combining form* One who or that which eats or consumes: *bacteriophage.* [< Gk. *phagein* eat]

phago- *combining form* Eating: *phagocyte.* Also, before vowels, **phag-.** [< Gk. *phagein* eat]

phag·o·cyte (fag′ə·sīt) *n.* A leucocyte that engulfs and digests bacteria and other foreign material in the blood and tissues of the body. —**phag′o·cyt′ic** (-sit′ik) *adj.*

phag·o·cy·to·sis (fag′ə·sī·tō′sis) *n.* The destruction and absorption of bacteria of micro-organisms by phagocytes.

pha·gol·y·sis (fə·gol′ə·sis) *n.* The dissolution or destruction of phagocytes. Also **phag·o·cy·tol·y·sis** (fag′ə·sī·tol′ə·sis). —**phag′o·lyt′ic** (-lit′ik) *adj.*

phag·o·ma·ni·a (fag′ə·mā′nē·ə, -mān′yə) *n.* A morbid or uncontrollable desire to eat.

-phagous *combining form* Consuming; tending to eat: *anthropophagous.* [< Gk. *phagein* eat]

-phagy *combining form* The consumption or eating of: *geophagy.* Also **-phagia.** [< Gk. *-phagia* < *phagein* eat]

phal·ange (fal′ənj, fə·lanj′) *n.* A phalanx of the fingers or toes. See illustration under FOOT. [< F < L *phalanx, phalangis* a line of battle]

pha·lan·ge·al (fə·lan′jē·əl) *adj.* Of, pertaining to, or resembling the phalanges. Also **pha·lan′gal** (-gəl), **pha·lan′ge·an.**

pha·lan·ger (fə·lan′jər) *n.* Any one of a family (*Phalangeridae*) of small marsupials of Australia and New Guinea, having long tails, often prehensile: also called *possum.* [< NL < *phalanges,* pl. of *phalanx* phalanx (def. 3); in ref. to the peculiarly constructed phalanges of its hind feet]

pha·lan·ges (fə·lan′jēz) Plural of PHALANX.

phal·an·ster·y (fal′ən·ster′ē) *n. pl.* **·ster·ies** 1 The building inhabited by a community of Fourierites; also, such a community. 2 Any group or community of individuals. [< F *phalanstère* < *phalan(x)* a phalanx + *(mona)stère* < LL *monasterium* a monastery] —**phal′an·ste′ri·an** (-stir′ē·ən) *adj. & n.*

phal·anx (fā′langks, *esp. Brit.* fal′angks) *n. pl.* **pha·lan·ges** (fə·lan′jēz) or **pha·lanx·es** 1 In ancient Greece, a marching order of heavy infantry, with close ranks and files, joined shields, and spears overlapping. 2 Any massed or compact body or corps, such as a group of Fourierites. 3 *Anat.* One of the bones articulating with the joints of the fingers or toes. See synonyms under ARMY. [< L *phalanx, phalangis* < Gk. *phalanx, phalangos* a line of battle]

phal·lin (fal′in) *n.* The characteristic hemolytic poison of the deathcup fungus. [< NL *phall(oides),* species name of the deathcup (< L *phallus* a phallus) + -IN]

phal·lism (fal′iz·əm) *n.* Worship of the generative power in nature as symbolized by the phallus; phallic worship, as in the Dionysiac festivals of ancient Greece. Also **phal′li·cism.** [< PHALL(US) + -ISM] —**phal′list, phal′li·cist** *n.*

phal·lus (fal′əs) *n. pl.* **·li** (-ī) 1 A figure of the male generative organ, used in many systems of religion, especially in the Orient, as a symbol of the generative power of nature. 2 The generative organ of the male or the clitoris of the female. 3 *Psychoanal.* The sexually immature penis. [< L < Gk. *phallos* penis] —**phal′lic** or **phal′li·cal** *adj.*

-phane *combining form* That which resembles or is similar to (a specified substance or material): *cellophane.* [< Gk. *-phanēs* < *phainein* appear]

phanero- *combining form* Visible: *phanerophyte.* Also, before vowels, **phaner-.** [< Gk. *phaneros* visible < *phainein* appear]

Phan·er·o·ga·mi·a (fan′ər·ə·gā′mē·ə) *n. pl.* One of the two primary divisions into which Linnaeus divided all plants, embracing those with flowers having stamens and pistils; flowering plants: distinguished from *Cryptogamia,* or flowerless plants. [< NL < Gk. *phaneros* visible + *gamos* marriage]

phan·tasm (fan′taz·əm), etc. See FANTASM, etc.

phan·tas·ma·go·ri·a (fan·taz′mə·gôr′ē·ə, -gō′rē·ə) See FANTASMAGORIA.

phan·tom (fan′təm) *n.* 1 Something that exists only in appearance. 2 An apparition; specter; illusion. 3 The visible representative of an abstract state or incorporeal person. —*adj.* Illusive; ghostlike: a *phantom* ship. Also spelled *fantom.* [< OF *fantosme* < L *phantasma* < Gk., an appearance < *phantazein* make visible < *phantos* visible < *phainein* show. Doublet of FANTASM.]

phantom section In mechanical drawing, cross-hatching superimposed on an external view of an object, assembly, or structure to show interior construction and details, often eliminating the need for an additional drawing or view.

phantom word A spurious word that exists only through the error of a lexicographer, writer, or printer, as one resulting from a false etymology or wrong attribution of meaning. Also called *ghost word.*

-phany *combining form* Appearance; manifestation: *epiphany, theophany.* [< Gk. *-phaneia* < *phainein* appear]

Phar·aoh (fâr′ō, fā′rō, fâr′ē·ō) *n.* Any one of the monarchs of ancient Egypt. [OE *Pharaon* < LL *Pharao, -onis* < Gk. *Pharaō* < Hebrew *Par′ōh* < Egyptian *pr-′ōh* the great house] —**Phar·a·on′ic** (-ē·on′ik) or **·i·cal** *adj.*

Pharaoh's serpent A stick or pellet of mercuric thiocyanate which, when ignited, glows and swells up, developing a long strip of ash which curls out like a serpent.

phar·i·sa·ic (far′ə·sā′ik) *adj.* 1 Pertaining to the Pharisees. 2 Observing the form, but neglecting the spirit, of religion; self-righteous; hypocritical. Also **phar′i·sa′i·cal.** [< LL *pharisaicus* < Gk. *pharisaïkos* < *pharisaios* PHARISEE] —**phar′i·sa′i·cal·ly** *adv.* —**phar′i·sa′i·cal·ness** *n.*

phar·i·sa·ism (far′ə·sā·iz′əm) *n.* The principles and practices of the Pharisees; hence, formality, self-righteousness, censoriousness, or hypocrisy. Also **phar′i·see·ism** (-sē·iz′əm).

Phar·i·see (far′ə·sē) *n.* 1 One of an ancient, exclusive Jewish sect that paid excessive regard to tradition and ceremonies, and in so doing led its members, by their sense of superior sanctity, to separate themselves from the other Jews. 2 Hence, a formal, sanctimonious, hypocritical person. [OE *fariseus*, infl. by OF *pharise*, both < L *pharisaeus* < Gk. *pharisaios* < Aramaic *perishayā*, pl. of *perish* < Hebrew *pārūsh* separated < *parash* cleave]

phar·ma·ceu·tic (fär'mə-sōō'tik) *adj.* Pertaining to, using, or relating to pharmacy or the pharmacopoeia: also **phar·ma·cal** (fär'mə-kəl). —*n.* A drug. Also **phar'ma·ceu'ti·cal.** [< L *pharmaceuticus* < Gk. *pharmakeutikos* of drugs < *pharmakeutēs* druggist < *pharmakeuein* give drugs < *pharmakon* a drug] —**phar'ma·ceu'ti·cal·ly** *adv.* —**phar'ma·ceu'tist** *n.*

phar·ma·ceu·tics (fär'mə-sōō'tiks) *n.* The science of pharmacy.

phar·ma·cist (fär'mə-sist) *n.* A qualified druggist; pharmaceutist.

pharmaco- *combining form* A drug; of or pertaining to drugs: *pharmacology.* Also, before vowels, **pharmac-.** [< Gk. *pharmakon* a drug]

phar·ma·co·dy·nam·ics (fär'mə-kō-dī-nam'iks) *n.* The experimental science of the action and effects of drugs.

phar·ma·cog·no·sy (fär'mə-kog'nə-sē) *n.* The knowledge of drugs, especially their origin, structure, and chemical constitution. [< NL *pharmacognosia* < Gk. *pharmakon* a drug + *gnōsis* a knowing, knowledge]—**phar'ma·cog'· no·sist** *n.*

phar·ma·col·o·gy (fär'mə-kol'ə-jē) *n.* The science of the action of medicines, their nature, preparation, administration, and effects: includes materia medica and therapeutics.— **phar'ma·co·log'ic** (-kə-loj'ik) or **·i·cal** *adj.* —**phar'ma·co·log'i·cal·ly** *adv.* —**phar'ma·col'o· gist** *n.*

phar·ma·co·ma·ni·a (fär'mə-kō-mā'nē-ə,-mān'yə) *n.* A morbid craving for drugs.

phar·ma·co·poe·ia (fär'mə-kə-pē'ə) *n.* **1** A book, usually published by authority, containing standard formulas and methods for the preparation of medicines, drugs, and other remedial substances. **2** A collection of drugs. [< NL < Gk. *pharmakopoiïa* art of making drugs < *pharmakon* a drug + *poieein* make] —**phar'ma·co·poe'ial** *adj.* —**phar'ma·co·poe'ist** *n.*

phar·ma·cy (fär'mə-sē) *n. pl.* **·cies 1** The art or business of compounding, preserving, and identifying drugs, and of compounding and dispensing medicines. **2** A drugstore. [< OF *farmacie* < LL *pharmacia* < Gk. *pharmakeia* < *pharmakeus* a druggist < *pharmakon* a drug]

pha·ros (fâr'os, fā'rôs, fä'-) *n.* A lighthouse; beacon. [< L < Gk. < *Pharos* Pharos]

pha·ryn·ge·al (fə-rin'jē-əl, far'in-jē'əl) *adj.* Of or pertaining to the pharynx. Also **pha·ryn'gal** (-gəl). [< NL *pharyngeus* < *pharynx, -yngis* PHARYNX]

pharyngo- *combining form* The throat; related to the throat: *pharyngoscope.* Also, before vowels, **pharyng-.** [< Gk. *pharynx* throat]

phar·yn·gol·o·gy (far'ing-gol'ə-jē) *n.* The science of the pharynx and its diseases.

pha·ryn·go·scope (fə-ring'gə-skōp) *n.* An apparatus for examining the pharynx. —**phar· yn·gos·co·py** (far'ing-gos'kə-pē) *n.*

phase (fāz) *n.* **1** The view that anything presents to the eye; any one of varying distinctive manifestations of an object. **2** *Astron.* One of the appearances or forms presented periodically by the moon and planets. **3** *Physics* **a** In an oscillatory motion, the position and character of a wave at any instant: often measured as an angle, the whole period being regarded as a circle, or 360°. **b** The instant when the maximum, zero, or other relative value is attained by any cyclical system, as sound or light waves, an alternating electric current, etc. **c** Any of the homogeneous forms of a given substance that may occur alone, or exist independently as a component of a larger heterogeneous system, as ice in water, water vapor in fog, etc. **4** *Biol.* **a** One of the distinct stages in the reduction or division process of a cell. **b** Any characteristic or decisive stage in the growth, development, or life pattern of an organism. —**to phase out** To terminate work on, production of, etc., step by step and according to plan. Also **pha·sis** (fā'sis). ◆ Homophone: *faze.* [< NL *phasis* < Gk., an appearance < *phainein* make appear] —**pha·sic** (fā'zik) *adj.*

phase meter An instrument for measuring the difference in phase between two alternating oscillations of the same frequency.

-phasia *combining form Med.* Defect or malfunction of speech: *dysphasia.* Also **-phasy.** [< Gk. - *phasia* < *phanai* speak]

pheas·ant (fez'ənt) *n.*
1 A long-tailed gallinaceous bird of *Phasianus* or related genus, noted for the gorgeous plumage of the male: native to Asia, but long semidomesticated elsewhere and bred in game preserves. **2** One of various other birds, as the ruffed grouse. [< AF *fesant* < L *Phasianus* < Gk. *Phasianos (ornis)* the Phasian (bird) < *Phasis* the Phasis, a river in the Caucasus, where it was first found]

RING–NECKED PHEASANT
(From 31 to 36 inches long over-all)

phen·ic acid (fen'ik) See PHENOL.

Phe·ni·cia (fə-nē'shə, -nish'ə), **Phe·ni·cian**, etc. See PHOENICIA, etc.

pheno- *combining form Chem.* Related to benzene; a derivative of benzene: *phenobarbital.* Also, before vowels, **phen-.** [< PHENYL]

phe·no·bar·bi·tal (fē'nō-bär'bə-tal, -tôl) *n.* A barbiturate, $C_{12}H_{12}N_2O_3$, having a long-lasting effect as a sedative, anticonvulsant, and hypnotic. Also **phe'no·bar'bi·tone** (-tōn). [< PHENO- + BARBITAL]

phe·nol·o·gy (fi-nol'ə-jē) *n.* The study of the periodic phenomena of plant life and animal behavior in relation to seasonal changes, climatic and other ecological factors. [Contraction of PHENOMENOLOGY, with a restricted application] — **phe·no·log·ic** (fē'nə-loj'ik) or **·i·cal** *adj.* — **phe'no·log'i·cal·ly** *adv.* —**phe·nol'o·gist** *n.*

phe·nom·e·na (fi-nom'ə-nə) Plural of PHENOMENON: erroneously used as a singular.

phe·nom·e·nal (fi-nom'ə-nəl) *adj.* **1** Pertaining to phenomena. **2** Extraordinary or marvelous. — **phe·nom'e·nal·ly** *adv.*

phe·nom·e·nal·ism (fi-nom'ə-nəl-iz'əm) *n.* The metaphysical opinion that no realities of which the human mind can have knowledge underlie phenomena. Compare POSITIVISM. —**phe· nom'e·nal·ist** *n.* —**phe·nom'e·nal·is'tic** *adj.* — phe·nom'e·nal·is'ti·cal·ly *adv.*

phe·nom·e·nol·o·gy (fi-nom'ə-nol'ə-jē) *n.* **1** The scientific investigation or description of phenomena. **2** *Philos.* The general doctrine of phenomena, as distinguished from ontology. [< PHENOMENO(N) + -LOGY] —**phe·nom'e· no·log'i·cal** (-nə-loj'i-kəl) *adj.* —**phe·nom'e·no· log'i·cal·ly** *adv.*

phe·nom·e·non (fi-nom'ə-non) *n. pl.* **·na** (-nə) **1** Something visible or directly observable, as an appearance, action, change, or occurrence of any kind, as distinguished from the force by which, or the law in accordance with which, it may be produced. **2** Any unusual occurrence; an inexplicable fact; marvel; prodigy. **3** Any fact, appearance, or occurrence in consciousness; that which is apprehended by the senses, in contrast with or in opposition to that which really exists, or to things in themselves: contrasted with *noumenon.* **4** A symptom of disease. [< LL *phaenomenon* < Gk. *phainomenon* an appearance, orig. ppr. passive neut. of *phainein* show]

phe·no·type (fē'nə-tīp) *n. Biol.* A type or strain of organisms distinguishable from others by some visibly manifested group of characters, as contrasted with genetic constitution. Compare GENOTYPE. [< F *phéno-* (< Gk. *phaino-* < *phainein* show, appear) + -TYPE] —**phe'no·typ'ic** (-tip'ik) or **·i·cal** *adj.* —**phe'no·typ'i·cal·ly** *adv.*

phew (fyōō, fōō) *interj.* An exclamation of disgust or surprise.

phi (fī, fē) *n. Greek* The twenty–first letter in the Greek alphabet (Φ, φ): corresponding to English *ph* and *f.* As a numeral it denotes 500.

phi·al (fī'əl) See VIAL.

Phi Be·ta Kap·pa (fī bā'tə kap'ə, bē'tə) An American honorary society founded in 1776 with membership based on conditions of high academic standing.

Phi·dip·pi·des (fī-dip'ə-dēz) See PHEIDIPPIDES.

phil- Var. of PHILO-.

-phil Var. of -PHILE.

phil·a·beg, phil·i·beg (fil'ə-beg) See FILIBEG.

Phil·a·del·phi·a (fil'ə-del'fē-ə) **1** A city on the Delaware River in SE Pennsylvania. **2** An ancient city of Lydia, Asia Minor. — **Phil·a· del'phi·an** *adj. & n.*

Philadelphia Chippendale Fine, usually richly carved mahogany furniture in the Chippendale style, made in Philadelphia in the 18th century.

Philadelphia lawyer An unusually sharp lawyer, especially one adept in phrasing legal technicalities: originally a tribute to the high caliber of the Philadelphia bar, now implying over–shrewd trickery.

phi·lan·der (fi-lan'dər) *v.i.* To make love without serious intentions: said of a man. [< n.] —*n.* A male flirt or suitor: also **phi·lan'der·er.** [< Gk. *philandros* < *phileein* love + *anēr, andros* man; from its use as a proper name for a lover in drama] —**phi·lan'der·ing** *n.*

phi·lan·thro·pize (fi-lan'thrə-pīz) *v.* **·pized, ·piz· ing** *v.t.* To deal with philanthropically. —*v.i.* To act as a philanthropist.

phi·lan·thro·py (fi-lan'thrə-pē) *n. pl.* **·pies** Disposition or effort to promote the happiness or social elevation of mankind; desire, effort, or beneficence, as by making donations, intended to mitigate social evils and increase social comfort; comprehensive benevolence, but often specific in its objects; literally, love of man. See synonyms under BENEVOLENCE. [< LL *philanthropia* < Gk. *philanthrōpia* < *phileein* love + *anthropos* man] —**phil·an· throp·ic** (fil'ən-throp'ik) or **·i·cal** *adj.* —**phil'· an·throp'i·cal·ly** *adv.* —**phi·lan'thro·pist** *n.*

phi·lat·e·ly (fi-lat'ə-lē) *n.* The study and collection of postage stamps, stamped envelopes, wrappers, etc.; stamp collecting. [< F *phila· télie* < Gk. *philos* loving + *ateleia* exemption from tax; with ref. to prepaid postage] —**phil· a·tel·ic** (fil'ə-tel'ik) or **·i·cal** *adj.* —**phil'a·tel'· i·cal·ly** *adv.* —**phi·lat'e·list** *n.*

-phile *combining form* One who supports or is fond of; one devoted to: *bibliophile.* [< Gk. *-philos* loving < *phileein* love]

— **Philemon** In Greek mythology, the husband of Baucis.

— **Philemon** A Greek of Colossae, converted to Christianity by Paul; also, the epistle addressed by Paul to him, forming one of the books of the New Testament.

phil·har·mon·ic (fil'här-mon'ik, -ər-mon'-) *adj.* Fond of harmony or music; often, **Philharmonic**, used in the names of musical societies. [< F *philharmonique* < Ital. *filarmonico* < Gk. *philos* loving + *harmonikos* HARMONIC]

Phil·hel·lene (fil-hel'ēn) *n.* **1** One who loves Greece or the Greeks. **2** A sympathizer with the modern Greeks in their effort (1821–29) to throw off the Turkish yoke and revive the Greek nation. Also **Phil·hel'le·nist.** [< Gk. *philellēn* loving Greeks < *phileein* love + *Hellēn* a Greek] —**Phil·hel·len·ic** (fil'he-len'ik) *adj.* —**Phil·hel'le·nism** *n.*

-philia *combining form* **1** A tendency toward: *hemophilia.* **2** A morbid affection or fondness for: *necrophilia.* Also spelled *-phily.* [< Gk. *-philia* < *phileein* love]

phi·lip·pic (fi-lip'ik) *n.* An impassioned speech characterized by invective: from the **Philippics**, a series of twelve speeches in which Demosthenes denounced Philip of Macedon. [< L *Philippicus* < Gk. *Philippikos* of Philip]

Phil·ip·pine Islands (fil'ə-pēn) An archipelago of 7,083 islands SE of China and NE of Borneo; 114,830 square miles; ceded by Spain to the United States, 1898, for $20,000,- 000; a commonwealth since 1935; seized by Japan, 1942–44, in World War II; since 1946 the **Republic of the Philippines**; capital, Quezon City. Also **Phil'ip·pines.** A native of the Philippines is known as a *Filipino.* — **Phil'ip· pine** *adj.*

Phi·lis·tine (fi-lis'tin, -tēn, -tīn, fil'əs-) *n.* **1** One of a warlike race of ancient Philistia. 1 *Sam.* xvii 23. **2** An ignorant, narrow-minded person, devoid of culture and indifferent to art. [< F *Philistin* < LL *Philistinus*, pl. *Philistini* < Gk. *Philistinoi, Palaistinoi* < Hebrew *p'lishtim*]

Phi·lis·tin·ism (fi-lis'tin-iz'əm) *n.* Blind conventionalism; lack of culture, taste, etc.

Phil·lips screw (fil'ips) A screw having a head (called a **Phillips head**) with crossing grooves for use with a special screwdriver. [after *Phillips* Screws, a trademark]

philo- *combining form* Loving; fond of: *philomath.* Also, before vowels, **phil-.** [< Gk. *philos* loving < *phileein* love]

phil·o·den·dron (fil'ə-den'drən) *n.* Any of a genus (*Philodendron*) of tropical American climbing plants, with thick, glossy, evergreen leaves: cultivated as an ornamental house plant. [<NL <Gk., neut. of *philodendros* fond of trees < *philos* fond + *dendron* a tree]

phi·log·y·ny (fi·loj'ə·nē) *n.* Fondness for or devotion to women: opposed to *misogyny*. [<Gk. *philogynia* < *philos* fond + *gynē* a woman] — **phi·log'y·nist** *n.* — **phi·log'y·nous** *adj.*

phi·lol·o·gy (fi·lol'ə·jē) *n.* 1 The scientific study of written records (chiefly literary works of art), in order to set up accurate texts and determine their meaning, often in terms of linguistic and cultural history. 2 Linguistics. 3 In popular use, etymology. 4 Formerly, literary scholarship, especially classical scholarship. [<F *philologie* <L *philologia* <Gk. < *philologos* fond of argument, words < *philos* fond + *logos* a word] — **phil·o·log·ic** (fil'ə·loj'ik) or **·i·cal** *adj.* — **phil'o·log'i·cal·ly** *adv.* — **phi·lol'o·gist**, **phi·lol'o·ger**, **phil'o·log** or **·logue** (-lôg, -log) *n.*

phil·o·math (fil'ə·math) *n.* One who loves learning; a scholar. [<Gk. *philomathēs* fond of learning < *philos* fond + *math-*, root of *manthanein* learn] — **phil'o·math'ic** or **·i·cal** *adj.* — **phi·lom·a·thy** (fi·lom'ə·thē) *n.*

phil·o·mel (fil'ə·mel) *n.* In poetic usage, the nightingale. Also **phil'o·me'la**. [<F *philomèle* <L *philomela* <Gk. *philomēla*, ? < *philos* fond of + *melos* a song]

Phil·o·me·la (fil'ə·mē'lə) In Greek mythology, a princess of Athens who was raped by her brother-in-law Tereus, who then tore out her tongue; when, in revenge, she and her sister Procne killed his son Itys, the gods changed Tereus into a hoopoe, Procne into a swallow, and Philomela into a nightingale.

phi·lom·e·try (fi·lom'ə·trē) *n.* The study and collecting of postal meter impressions on mail matter: a branch of philately. [<PHILO- + (*postal*) *meter*, on analogy with PHILATELY] — **phi·lom'e·trist** *n.* — **phil·o·met·ric** (fil'ə·met'rik) *adj.*

phil·o·pe·na (fil'ə·pē'nə) *n.* 1 A game in which anyone finding a nut with twin kernels shares it with another person. The one who first says *philopena* when next they meet receives a forfeit from the other. 2 The twin kernels shared. 3 The gift made as a forfeit. Often spelled *fillipeen*. Also **phil'lip·pine**, **phil'li·peen'er**. [Appar. <Du. *phillipine*, alter. of G *vielliebchen* very dear < *viel* much + *liebchen*, dim. of *liebe* love]

phil·o·pro·gen·i·tive (fil'ə·prō·jen'ə·tiv) *adj.* 1 Fond of offspring or of children in general. 2 Prolific. [<PHILO- + L *progenitus*, pp. of *progignere* beget] — **phil'o·pro·gen'i·tive·ly** *adv.* — **phil'o·pro·gen'i·tive·ness** *n.*

phi·los·o·pher (fi·los'ə·fər) *n.* 1 A student of or specialist in philosophy. 2 The creator of a system of philosophy. 3 A man of practical wisdom; one who schools himself to calmness and patience under all circumstances, as originally enjoined by the Stoic philosophy. [<AF *philosophre*, var. of OF *filosofe* <L *philosophus* <Gk. *philosophos* a lover of wisdom < *philos* loving + *sophos* wise]

philosopher's stone An imaginary stone or substance having the property of transmuting the baser metals into gold: sought by the alchemists.

phil·o·soph·i·cal (fil'ə·sof'i·kəl) *adj.* 1 Pertaining to or founded on the principles of philosophy. 2 Proper to or characteristic of a philosopher. 3 Self-restrained and serene; rational; thoughtful; calm. 4 *Archaic* Pertaining to or used in the study of natural philosophy or physics. Also **phil'o·soph'ic**. — **phil'o·soph'i·cal·ly** *adv.*

phi·los·o·phism (fi·los'ə·fiz'əm) *n.* Unsound or pretended philosophy; sophistry.

phi·los·o·phist (fi·los'ə·fist) *n.* One who affects philosophy; a would-be philosopher.

phi·los·o·phize (fi·los'ə·fīz) *v.i.* **·phized**, **·phiz·ing** To speculate like a philosopher; seek ultimate causes and principles; moralize. — **phi·los'o·phiz'er** *n.*

phi·los·o·phy (fi·los'ə·fē) *n.* *pl.* **·phies** 1 The love of wisdom as leading to the search for it; hence, knowledge of general principles—

elements, powers, or causes and laws—as explaining facts and existences. 2 The general laws that furnish the rational explanation of anything: the *philosophy* of banking. 3 The calm judgment and equable temper resulting from study of causes and laws; practical wisdom; fortitude, as in enduring reverses and suffering. 4 Reasoned science; a scientific system; as (formerly), natural *philosophy*, now natural science. 5 A philosophical system or treatise. 6 The sciences as formerly studied in the universities. [<OF *filosofie*, *philosophie* <L *philosophia* <Gk. < *philosophos*. See PHILOSOPHER.]

phlebo- *combining form* Venous: *phlebotomy*. Also, before vowels, **phleb-**. [<Gk. *phleps*, *phlebos* a vein]

phle·bot·o·my (fli·bot'ə·mē) *n.* *Surg.* The practice of opening a vein for letting blood as a remedial measure; bloodletting. [<OF *flebothomie* <L *phlebotomia* <Gk., the opening of a vein < *phleps, phlebos* a vein + *temnein* cut] — **phleb·o·tom·ic** (fleb'ə·tom'ik) or **·i·cal** *adj.* — **phle·bot'o·mist** *n.*

Phleg·e·thon (fleg'ə·thon, flej'-) In Greek mythology, the river of fire, one of the five rivers surrounding Hades. [<Gk., lit., blazing]

phlegm (flem) *n.* 1 *Physiol.* A viscid, stringy mucus secreted in the air passages or in the stomach, especially when produced as a morbid discharge. 2 Apathy; indifference; cold, undemonstrative temper; self-possession. 3 *Obs.* One of the four natural humors (the cold and moist) in ancient physiology. See synonyms under APATHY. [<OF *fleume*, *flemme* <L *phlegma* the clammy humor of the body <Gk., inflammation < *phlegein* blaze; refashioned after Gk.]

phleg·mat·ic (fleg·mat'ik) *adj.* Sluggish; indifferent; not easily moved or excited. Also **phleg·mat'i·cal**. [<OF *fleumatique* <L *phlegmaticus* <Gk. *phlegmatikos* < *phlegma, -matos*. See PHLEGM.] — **phleg·mat'i·cal·ly** *adv.*

phlo·gis·tic (flō·jis'tik) *adj.* 1 Pertaining to phlogiston or to the theory of its existence. 2 Inflammatory; inflamed. [<Gk. *phlogistos* inflammable. See PHLOGISTON.]

phlo·gis·ton (flō·jis'tən) *n.* The fiery principle formerly assumed to be a necessary constituent of all combustible bodies, and to be given up by them in burning. [<NL <Gk., neut. of *phlogistos* inflammable < *phlogizein* set on fire < *phlox, phlogos* a flame < *phlegein* burn]

phlog·o·pite (flog'ə·pīt) *n.* A yellowish-brown to brownish-red monoclinic magnesium mica. [<G *phlogopit* <Gk. *phlogōpos* fiery; so called from its appearance]

phlox (floks) *n.* Any plant or flower of a North American genus (*Phlox*) of herbs of the *Polemoniaceae* family, with opposite leaves and clusters of showy flowers in various shades of red, purple, white, or variegated. [<NL <L, a kind of flower <Gk. *phlox* a wallflower, lit., a flame < *phlegein* burn]

phlyc·te·na (flik·tē'nə) *n. pl.* **·nae** (-nē) *Pathol.* A small blister containing watery or serous fluid. Also **phlyc·tae'na**. [<NL <Gk. *phlyktaina* a blister < *phlyein* swell]

Phnôm-penh (pə·nôm'pen') See PNOM-PENH.

-phobe *combining form* One who fears or has an aversion to: *Anglophobe*. [<Gk. *-phobos* fearing < *phobeesthai* fear]

pho·bi·a (fō'bē·ə) *n.* 1 A morbid, compulsive, and persistent fear of any specified type of object, stimulus, or situation. 2 Any strong aversion or dislike. [<L <Gk. < *phobos* fear] — **pho'bic** (-bik) *adj.*

-phobia *combining form* Psychiatry Aversion to; morbid fear or dislike of. [<Gk. *phobos* fear]

In the following list each entry denotes a morbid fear or dislike of the thing or situation indicated by the translation of the first part of the word:

acrophobia	heights
agoraphobia	open spaces
ailurophobia	cats
algophobia	pain
androphobia	men
astraphobia	thunder and lightning
autophobia	being alone; self
bathophobia	depth
claustrophobia	closed space
cynophobia	dogs (rabies)
demophobia	crowds
dromophobia	crossing streets
genophobia	sex
gynophobia	women
haptephobia	being touched
hemophobia	blood
hydrophobia	water
hypnophobia	falling asleep
musophobia	mice
mysophobia	contamination
neophobia	the new
nyctophobia	night, darkness
ophidiophobia	snakes
photophobia	light
sitophobia	eating; food
taphephobia	being buried alive
thanatophobia	death
toxicophobia	poison
xenophobia	strangers, foreigners
zoophobia	animals

pho·ca (fō'kə) *n. pl.* **·cae** (-sē) One of a genus (*Phoca*) of seals (family *Phocidae*), including the typical earless seals of temperate waters. [<NL <L <Gk. *phōkē* a seal] — **pho'cine** (-sīn, -sin) *adj.* — **pho'coid** (-koid) *adj. & n.*

phoe·be (fē'bē) *n.* An American flycatcher (*Sayornis phoebe*) with grayish-brown plumage and slightly crested head: common throughout the eastern United States. Also **phoebe bird**. [Imit. of its cry; infl. in form by PHOEBE]

Phoe·be (fē'bē) 1 A feminine personal name. 2 In Greek mythology, a Titaness, mother of Leto. 3 A name for Artemis as goddess of the moon. 4 *Poetic* The moon. 5 Saturn's ninth satellite. Also spelled *Phebe*. Also **Phœ'be**. [<Gk., bright]

Phoe·bus (fē'bəs) 1 In Greek mythology, Apollo as god of the sun. 2 *Poetic* The sun. Also **Phœ'bus**.

phoe·nix (fē'niks) *n.* 1 In Egyptian mythology, a legendary bird of great beauty, unique of its kind, which was supposed to live for 500 or 600 years in the Arabian Desert and then consume itself by fire, rising again from its ashes young and beautiful to live through another cycle: a symbol of immortality. 2 A person of matchless beauty or excellence; a paragon. Also spelled *phenix*. [OE *fenix* <Med. L *phenix* <L *phoenix* <Gk. *phoinix* the phoenix]

PHOENIX
Described by Herodotus as golden-winged with eagle-like red body.

Phoe·nix (fē'niks) *Astron.* A southern constellation. See CONSTELLATION.

Phoe·nix (fē'niks) The capital of Arizona.

phon (fon) *n.* *Physics* The unit of loudness level of a sound, numerically equal to the sound-pressure level in decibels, relative to a pressure of 0.0002 microbar, of a simple tone of 1,000 cycles per second which is judged by the listener as equal in loudness. [<Gk. *phōnē* a voice]

phon- Var. of PHONO-.

pho·nate (fō'nāt) *v.t.* **·nat·ed**, **·nat·ing** To make articulate sounds. [<Gk. *phōnē* + -ATE[1]] — **pho·na'tion** *n.*

pho·nau·to·graph (fō·nô'tə·graf, -gräf) *n.* 1 An apparatus designed to record the vibrations of sounds. It was the forerunner of Edison's phonograph. 2 A writing or tracing produced by the mechanical use of sound vibrations. Also **pho·nau'to·gram**. [<Gk. *phōnē* sound + *autos* self + -GRAPH] — **pho·nau'to·graph'ic** or **·i·cal** *adj.* — **pho·nau'to·graph'i·cal·ly** *adv.*

phone[1] (fōn) *n. & v.* *Colloq.* Telephone. [Short for TELEPHONE]

phone² (fōn) *n.* A sound used in human speech. [<Gk. *phōnē* a sound]

-phone *combining form* Voice; sound: used in names of musical instruments and other sound-transmitting devices: *saxophone, microphone.* [<Gk. *phōnē* voice]

pho·neme (fō′nēm) *n.* A class of acoustically similar sounds in a language, usually written with the same phonetic symbol, which differ non-relevantly as conditioned by environment; the smallest unit in the sound system of a language, functioning to distinguish one morpheme from another. The contrasting phonemes /t/ and /p/ distinguish the words *tin* and *pin*, whereas the varying pronunciations of *t* in *tip, stop* and *pit* are not recognized by speakers of English and are considered members of the one phoneme /t/. See ALLOPHONE. [<F *phonème* a sound <Gk. *phōnēma* < *phōnē* a voice, sound]

pho·ne·mic (fə·nē′mik) *adj.* 1 Of or referring to phonemes: the *phonemic* pattern of a language. 2 Involving distinctive speech sounds: a *phonemic* difference. — **pho·ne′mi·cal·ly** *adv.*

pho·ne·mics (fə·nē′miks) *n.* The study of the phonemic system of a language.

pho·nen·do·scope (fə·nen′də·skōp) *n. Med.* An amplifying stethoscope. [<PHON- + END(O)- + -SCOPE]

pho·net·ic (fə·net′ik) *adj.* 1 Of or pertaining to phonetics, or to speech sounds and their production. 2 Representing articulate sounds or speech; specifically, designating the representation of each speech sound by a distinct character, or by a distinctive spelling or mark: *phonetic* alphabet, *phonetic* spelling. Also **pho·net′i·cal.** [<Gk. *phōnētikos* < *phōnē* sound] — **pho·net′i·cal·ly** *adv.*

pho·ne·ti·cian (fō′nə·tish′ən) *n.* An authority on phonetics. Also **pho·net·i·cist** (fə·net′ə·sist), **pho′ne·tist.**

phonetic law A description of a pattern of sound-changes occurring under given conditions in a language or group of languages, as Grimm's law.

pho·net·ics (fə·net′iks) *n.* 1 The branch of linguistics which deals with the analysis, description, and classification of the sounds of speech, including **articulatory phonetics,** the study of the physiological processes involved in speech production, by means of which the sounds of a language are recorded and described, and **acoustic phonetics,** the study of the physical attributes of speech sounds by the use of laboratory instruments. 2 The system of sounds of a language: the *phonetics* of American English.

pho·ney (fō′nē) See PHONY.

-phonia See -PHONY.

phon·ic (fon′ik, fō′nik) *adj.* 1 Pertaining to or of the nature of sound. 2 Caused or accompanied by sound-articulation.

phon·ics (fon′iks, fō′niks) *n. pl.* (construed as singular) 1 The phonetic rudiments used in teaching reading and pronunciation. 2 Acoustics.

phono– *combining form* Sound; speech; voice: *phonograph.* Also, before vowels, **phon–.** [<Gk. *phōnē* a voice]

pho·no·chem·is·try (fō′nō·kem′is·trē) *n.* The study of chemical reactions as induced or affected by sound waves. — **pho′no·chem′i·cal** *adj.*

pho·no·deik (fō′nə·dēk) *n.* An instrument for making sound waves visible by converting them into light waves reflected from a vibrating mirror. [<PHONO- + Gk. *deiknynai* show]

pho·no·gram (fō′nə·gram) *n.* 1 The tracing produced by a phonograph, from which articulate sounds are reproduced; a phonograph record. 2 A graphic character symbolizing an articulate sound, word, syllable, etc. 3 A telephone message taken down on paper and delivered, like a telegram. — **pho′no·gram′ic** or **-gram′mic** *adj.* — **pho′no·gram′i·cal·ly** or **-gram′mi·cal·ly** *adv.*

pho·no·graph (fō′nə·graf, -gräf) *n.* An apparatus for recording and reproducing sounds, as speech, music, etc.

pho·nog·ra·phy (fə·nog′rə·fē) *n.* 1 The art or science of writing by sound; especially, the art of representing words according to a system of sound elements that reduces their graphic reproduction to the simplest form: a style of shorthand which owes its principal development to Isaac Pitman, of Bath, England, upon whose alphabet the majority of

the existing stenographic systems are based. 2 The art of representing articulate sounds by marks or letters. 3 The art of making or using phonographs; the mechanical recording and reproduction of sounds or speech. — **pho·nog′ra·pher, pho·nog′ra·phist** *n.*

pho·no·lite (fō′nə·līt) *n.* A grayish-green compact igneous rock composed essentially of orthoclase, nephelite, and augite; clinkstone. — **pho′no·lit′ic** (-lit′ik) *adj.*

pho·nol·o·gy (fə·nol′ə·jē) *n.* 1 The study of the sound system of a language. 2 The historical study of the sound-changes that have taken place in a language. 3 The phonetic or phonemic pattern of a language. — **pho·no·log·ic** (fō′nə·loj′ik) or **·i·cal** *adj.* — **pho′no·log′i·cal·ly** *adv.* — **pho·nol′o·gist** *n.*

pho·no·ma·ni·a (fō′nə·mā′nē·ə, -mān′yə) *n.* Homicidal mania. [<Gk. *phonos* murder + -MANIA]

pho·nom·e·ter (fə·nom′ə·tər) *n.* An instrument for measuring the intensity of sounds or the frequency of sound vibrations. — **pho·nom′e·try** *n.*

pho·no·scope (fō′nə·skōp) *n.* An instrument for observing, testing, or exhibiting the properties of musical strings or other sounding bodies.

pho·no·type (fō′nə·tīp) *n.* 1 A writing or printing alphabet having a distinct character for each simple sound of speech. 2 A production written or printed in such characters. — **pho′no·typ′ic** (-tip′ik) or **·i·cal** *adj.* — **pho′·no·typ′i·cal·ly** *adv.*

pho·no·typ·y (fō′nə·tī′pē) *n.* The art or practice of representing every elementary sound of articulate speech by a mark or letter of its own; phonetic transcription. — **pho′no·typ′·ist** *n.*

pho·ny (fō′nē) *U.S. Slang adj.* **·ni·er, ·ni·est** Fake; false; spurious; counterfeit. — *n.* 1 Something fake or not genuine. 2 One who impersonates another; an impostor. Also spelled *phoney.* [< slang E *fawney* a gilt brass ring used in a fraud <Irish *fain(n)e* a ring]

-phony *combining form* A (specified) type of sound or sounds: *cacophony.* Also **-phonia,** as in *aphonia.* [<Gk. *phōnē* sound, voice]

-phore *combining form* A bearer or producer of: *semaphore.* [<Gk. *-phoros* < *pherein* bear]

-phorous *combining form* Bearing or producing: found in adjectives corresponding to nouns in *-phore.* [See -PHORE]

phos·phate (fos′fāt) *n.* 1 *Chem.* A salt or ester of phosphoric acid. Phosphates, especially those of calcium, are necessary to the growth of plants, which absorb them in the form of soluble salts. 2 *Agric.* Any fertilizer valued for its phosphoric acid. 3 A beverage of carbonated water, variously flavored, containing small amounts of phosphoric acid. [<F]

phos·pha·tide (fos′fə·tīd, -tid) *n.* A phospholipid. [<PHOSPHAT(E) + -IDE]

phos·pha·tize (fos′fə·tīz) *v.t.* **·tized, ·tiz·ing** 1 To treat with phosphates. 2 To reduce to a phosphate. — **phos′pha·ti·za′tion** *n.*

phos·phite (fos′fīt) *n.* A salt of phosphorous acid.

phospho– *combining form* Phosphorus; of or containing phosphorus, or any of its compounds: *phospholipid.* Also, before vowels, **phosph–.** [<PHOSPHORUS]

Phos·phor (fos′fər) *n.* The morning star, especially Venus, as the harbinger of day. Also **Phos′phore.** [<L *Phosphorus* the morning star <Gk. *phōsphoros.* See PHOSPHORUS.]

phosphor bronze An alloy of copper and tin containing small amounts of phosphorus, noted for its toughness, durability, and high tensile strength.

phos·phor·esce (fos′fə·res′) *v.i.* **·esced, ·esc·ing** To glow with a faint light unaccompanied by sensible heat. [? Back formation <PHOSPHORESCENT]

phos·phor·es·cence (fos′fə·res′əns) *n.* 1 The emission of light without sensible heat, or the light so emitted. 2 The property of continuing to shine in the dark after exposure to light, shown by many mineral substances: distinguished from *fluorescence.* 3 *Biol.* The property of producing a faint light, shown by infusorians, fireflies, etc.

phos·phor·es·cent (fos′fə·res′ənt) *adj.* Exhibiting phosphorescence. [<PHOSPHORUS + -ESCENT]

phos·phor·ite (fos′fə·rīt) *n.* 1 A massive fibrous variety of apatite. 2 Phosphate rock in general.

phos·phor·o·scope (fos′fər·ə·skōp′) *n.* An apparatus for measuring the duration of phosphorescent light after the source is withdrawn.

phos·pho·rus (fos′fər·əs) *n.* 1 A widely distributed nonmetallic element (symbol P, atomic number 15) existing in several allotropic forms, including red phosphorus and the more common white phosphorus, a yellowish, waxy, exceedingly poisonous solid that ignites spontaneously in air. See PERIODIC TABLE. 2 Any phosphorescent substance. [<NL <L *Phosphorus* the morning star <Gk. *phōsphoros (astēr),* lit., light-bringing <*phōs* a light + *phoros* bearing <*pherein* bear]

phot (fot, fōt) *n.* The cgs unit of illumination, equal to one lumen per square centimeter. [<Gk. *phōs, photos* a light]

pho·tic (fō′tik) *adj.* 1 Relating to light and the production of light. 2 Designating those underwater regions which are penetrated by sunlight: the *photic* zone.

pho·to (fō′tō) *n. pl.* **·tos** *Colloq.* A photograph. [Short for PHOTOGRAPH]

photo– *combining form* 1 Light; of, pertaining to, or produced by light: *photometer.* 2 Photograph; photographic: *photoengrave.* [<Gk. *phōs, photos* light]

pho·to·ac·tin·ic (fō′tō·ak·tin′ik) *adj.* Capable of emitting actinic radiation.

pho·to·ar·chive (fō′tō·är′kīv) *n.* A collection of photographs assembled and classified for purposes of study and research.

pho·to·bi·ot·ic (fō′tō·bī·ot′ik) *adj.* 1 Living in the light. 2 Requiring light for life or development.

pho·to·cell (fō′tō·sel′) *n.* A photoelectric cell.

pho·to·chem·is·try (fō′tō·kem′is·trē) *n.* The branch of chemistry dealing with chemical reactions produced or influenced by light. — **pho′to·chem′i·cal** *adj.*

pho·to·chro·mog·ra·phy (fō′tō·krō·mog′rə·fē) *n.* The art of reproducing on a printing press photographic images in several colors.

pho·to·chro·my (fō′tə·krō′mē) *n.* Color photography. [<PHOTO- (def. 2) + CHROM- + -Y¹]

pho·to·chron·o·graph (fō′tō·kron′ə·graf, -gräf) *n.* 1 An instrument for taking pictures at minute, regular, timed intervals, of a body in motion. 2 A picture so taken. 3 A chronograph adapted for use in photographing a moving body, as a star in transit. — **pho′to·chro·nog′ra·phy** (-krə·nog′rə·fē) *n.*

pho·to·com·pos·er (fō′tō·kəm·pō′zər) *n.* Any machine or apparatus which composes printed matter by photographic means.

pho·to·cop·y (fō′tō·kop′ē) *n. pl.* **·cop·ies** A photographic reproduction of printed or other graphic material. — *v.* **·cop·ied, ·cop·y·ing** *v.t.* 1 To make a photocopy of. — *v.i.* 2 To make a photocopy. — **pho′to·cop′i·er** *n.*

pho·to·cur·rent (fō′tō·kûr′ənt) *n.* An electric current produced by the action of light or by the photoelectric effect.

pho·to·dra·ma (fō′tə·drä′mə, -dram′ə) *n.* A motion picture or photoplay. — **pho′to·dra·mat′ic** (-drə·mat′ik) *adj.*

pho·to·dy·nam·ic (fō′tō·dī·nam′ik, -di·nam′-) *adj.* Of, pertaining to, or operating by the energy of light.

pho·to·dy·nam·ics (fō′tō·dī·nam′iks, -di·nam′-) *n.* The study of the action and influence of light on plants and animals.

pho·to·e·lec·tric (fō′tō·i·lek′trik) *adj.* Of or pertaining to the electrical effects due to the action of light, as in the emission of electrons from gaseous, liquid, or solid bodies when subjected to radiation of suitable wavelength. Also **pho′to·e·lec′tri·cal.**

photoelectric cell A vacuum tube, one of whose electrodes gives off electrons under the action of light: incorporated in electrical circuits as a controlling, testing, and counting device: also called *phototube, electric eye,* or *photocell.*

pho·to·e·lec·tron (fō′tō·i·lek′tron) *n.* An electron emitted from a metal surface when exposed to suitable radiation.

pho·to·e·lec·tro·type (fō′tō·i·lek′trə·tīp) *n.* 1 An electrotype produced by a photomechanical process. 2 A picture printed from such a block.

pho·to·en·grav·ing (fō′tō·in·grā′ving) *n.* 1 The act or process of producing by the aid of photography a relief block or plate for printing. **2** A plate or picture so produced.

photo finish The finish of a game or race, as in horse-racing, in which the two leads are so close as they cross the finish line that only a photograph can determine the winner.

pho·to·flash bulb (fō′tō-flash′) An electric bulb containing aluminum or magnesium which, on the passage of a current, ignites and gives an incandescent light of brief duration: used in photography.

pho·to·gel·a·tin (fō′tō-jel′ə-tin) adj. Characterized by the use of gelatin: said of a photographic process.

pho·to·gene (fō′tō-jēn) n. An afterimage.

pho·to·gen·ic (fō′tō-jen′ik) adj. **1** Of or pertaining to the action of light; generating or producing light. **2** Producing phosphorescence; phosphorescent, as fireflies. **3** Having certain characteristics and qualities, as coloration, form, etc., suitable for being photographed. [< PHOTO- + -GENIC; def. 3 coined from PHOTO(GRAPH), on analogy with *pathogenic, eugenic,* etc.] — **pho′to·gen′i·cal·ly** adv.

pho·to·go·ni·om·e·ter (fō′tō-gō′nē·om′ə·tər) n. A device for studying the phenomena of crystal X-ray diffraction and X-ray spectra.

pho·to·gram·me·try (fō′tō-gram′ə·trē) n. The art and technique of making surveys or maps by means of photographs. [< *photogram,* var. of PHOTOGRAPH + -METRY]

pho·to·graph (fō′tə-graf, -gräf) n. A picture taken by photography. —v.t. **1** To take a photograph of. —v.i. **2** To practice photography. **3** To undergo photography. See synonyms under PICTURE.

pho·tog·ra·pher (fə·tog′rə·fər) n. One who makes a business of or is expert in photography.

pho·to·graph·ic (fō′tə-graf′ik) adj. **1** Pertaining to, used in, or produced by photography. **2** Like a photograph; vividly depicted. Also **pho′to·graph′i·cal.** —**pho′to·graph′i·cal·ly** adv.

pho·tog·ra·phy (fə·tog′rə·fē) n. **1** The process of forming and fixing an image of an object or objects by the chemical action of light and other forms of radiant energy on photosensitive surfaces. **2** The art or business of producing and printing photographs.

pho·to·gra·vure (fō′tō·grə·vyŏŏr′, -grāv′yər) n. **1** The process of producing an intaglio plate for printing in which there are no sharp incised lines, but minute depressions, the deep parts producing the shadows, and the high parts showing white. **2** A picture produced from such a plate. [< F]

pho·to·he·li·o·graph (fō′tō·hē′lē·ə·graf′, -gräf′) n. A telescopic photographic instrument, variously constructed, for taking pictures of the sun, as during an eclipse.

pho·to·jour·nal·ism (fō′tō·jûr′nəl·iz′əm) n. A form of journalism in which a story or news item is recounted largely or entirely by means of photographs. —**pho′to·jour′nal·ist** n.

pho·to·lith·o·graph (fō′tō·lith′ə·graf, -gräf) v.t. To reproduce by photolithography. —n. A picture produced by photolithography.

pho·to·li·thog·ra·phy (fō′tō·li·thog′rə·fē) n. The art or operation of producing on stone, largely by photographic means, a printing surface from which impressions may be taken by a lithographic process. —**pho′to·lith′o·graph′ic** (-lith′ə·graf′ik) adj.

pho·tol·y·sis (fō·tol′ə·sis) n. Chemical or biological decomposition due to the action of light. [< NL < Gk. *phōs, phōtos* a light + *lysis* a loosening < *lyein* loosen] —**pho·to·lyt·ic** (fō′tə·lit′ik) adj.

pho·to·map (fō′tə·map′) n. A map composed of one or more aerial photographs, laid off into a grid, contour lines, etc.

pho·to·me·chan·i·cal (fō′tō·mi·kan′i·kəl) adj. Pertaining to a process, illustration, plate, etc., produced by any one of a variety of methods, by which photography is brought to the aid of the etcher or engraver. —**pho′to·me·chan′i·cal·ly** adv.

pho·tom·e·ter (fō·tom′ə·tər) n. **1** Any instrument for measuring the intensity of light or comparing the intensity of two lights. **2** A device for

determining the proper duration of exposure in photography.

pho·tom·e·try (fō·tom′ə·trē) n. **1** The art of measuring the intensity of light, especially by means of the photometer. **2** The branch of optics that treats of such measurement. —**pho·to·met·ric** (fō′tə·met′rik) adj. —**pho·tom′e·trist** n.

pho·to·mi·cro·graph (fō′tō·mī′krə·graf, -gräf) n. A photograph of a microscopic object taken through a microscope. Compare MICROPHOTOGRAPH.

pho·to·mi·crog·ra·phy (fō′tō·mī·krog′rə·fē) n. The art or process of making photographs of minute objects, as by a camera attached to a microscope.

pho·to·mon·tage (fō′tō·mon·täzh′, -môn-) n. The process of montage with photographs; also, a picture produced by this process.

Pho·ton (fō′ton) n. A keyboard-operated machine assembly for the composition of printed matter by means of high-speed photography and photoelectric action geared to a matrix disk bearing the required characters in a series of concentric fonts, thus eliminating the use of metal type: a trade name.

pho·to·off·set (fō′tō·ôf′set, -of′-) n. Offset printing from a metal surface on which the text or design has been imprinted by photography.

pho·to·pe·ri·od (fō′tō·pir′ē·əd) n. The relative duration of illumination in a cycle of darkness and light; whether occurring naturally as night and day or imposed artificially. **pho·to·pe·ri·od·ic** (-pir′ē·od′ik), **·i·cal** adj.

pho·to·pe·ri·od·ism (fō′tō·pir′ē·ə·diz·əm) n. The response of an organism to variations in the duration of day and night or other cyclic illumination. Also **pho·to·pe·ri·od·ic·i·ty** (pir′ē·ə·dis′ə·tē).

pho·to·pho·bi·a (fō′tə·fō′bē·ə) n. **1** Aversion to or intolerance of light. **2** *Pathol.* Morbid sensitivity of the eye to light.

pho·to·pia (fō·tō′pē·ə) n. Vision under lighting conditions which permit color discrimination; daylight vision. [< NL < Gk. *phōs, phōtos* a light + *ōps, ōpos* an eye] —**pho·top·ic** (fō·top′ik) adj.

pho·to·play (fō′tō·plā′) n. **1** The representation of a play in motion pictures. **2** A play arranged for a motion-picture performance.

pho·to·sen·si·tive (fō′tō·sen′sə·tiv) adj. Sensitive to light. —**pho′to·sen′si·tiv′i·ty** n.

pho·to·shock (fō′tō·shok′) n. *Psychiatry* A method of treating certain forms of mental disorder by the application of controlled flashes of light used in connection with appropriate drugs.

pho·to·spec·tro·scope (fō′tō·spek′trə·skōp) n. A spectrograph.

pho·to·sphere (fō′tə·sfir) n. *Astron.* The visible shining surface of the sun, or, more rarely, of a fixed star. —**pho′to·spher′ic** (-sfer′ik) adj.

pho·to·sta·ble (fō′tō·stā′bəl) adj. Unaffected by or resistant to the influence of light.

pho·to·stat (fō′tə·stat) v.t. & v.i. **·stat·ed** or **·stat·ted, ·stat·ing** or **·stat·ting** To make a reproduction (of) with a Photostat. —n. A reproduction so produced. —**pho′to·stat′ic** adj.

Pho·to·stat (fō′tə·stat) n. A camera designed to reproduce documents, drawings, etc., directly, prints being made from the primary negative: a trade name.

pho·to·syn·the·sis (fō′tō·sin′thə·sis) n. *Biol.* **1** The synthesis of chemical compounds by means of light and other forms of radiant energy. **2** The process by which plants form carbohydrates from carbon dioxide and water through the agency of sunlight acting upon chlorophyll. — **pho′to·syn·thet′ic** (-sin·thet′ik) adj. — **pho′to·syn·thet′i·cal·ly** adv.

pho·to·tax·is (fō′tō·tak′sis) n. *Biol.* The assumption by an organism of a definite position with reference to the direction of the incident ray of light, called **negative phototaxis** when the movement is away from the light, and **positive phototaxis** when the movement is toward the light. Also **pho′to·tax′y.** [< NL < Gk. *phōs, phōtos* a light + *taxis* an arrangement] —**pho′to·tac′tic** (-tak′tik) adj. —**pho′to·tac′ti·cal·ly** adv.

pho·to·te·leg·ra·phy (fō′tō·tə·leg′rə·fē) n. **1** The

electrical transmission of messages, photographs, etc., by facsimile. **2** Telephotography. — **pho′to·tel′e·graph′ic** (-tel′ə·graf′ik) adj. — **pho′to·tel′e·graph′i·cal·ly** adv.

pho·to·tel·e·scope (fō′tō·tel′ə·skōp) n. A telescope provided with a photographic apparatus, photographing the heavenly bodies. — **pho′to·tel·e·scop′ic** (-tel′ə·skop′ik) adj.

pho·to·ther·a·py (fō′tō·ther′ə·pē) n. Treatment of diseases, especially diseases of the skin, by the application of light. Also **pho′to·ther′a·peu′tics** (-ther′ə·pyōō′tiks). — **pho′to·ther′a·peu′tic, pho′to·the·rap′ic** (-thə·rap′ik) adj.

pho·to·ther·mic (fō′tō·thûr′mik) adj. Denoting the thermic activity of the light rays.

pho·to·to·pog·ra·phy (fō′tō·tə·pog′rə·fē) n. The art and technique of preparing topographic maps with the aid of photographs, as in the multiplex system or by data provided by aerial photographs. —**pho′to·top′o·graph′ic** (-top′ə·graf′ik) adj.

pho·to·tran·sis·tor (fō′tō·tran·zis′tər) n. A very small disk of germanium which produces a multiplied photocurrent by transistor action.

pho·to·trop·ic (fō′tə·trop′ik) adj. *Biol.* Turning toward the light; heliotropic. —**pho′to·trop′i·cal·ly** adv.

pho·tot·ro·py (fō·tot′rə·pē) n. **1** Phototropism. **2** The color alteration observed in some substances after exposure to light.

pho·to·tube (fō′tō·tōōb′, -tyōōb′) n. A photoelectric cell.

pho·to·type (fō′tə·tīp′) n. **1** A relief plate made for printing by photography. **2** The process by which it is produced. **3** A picture printed from such a plate. —**pho′to·typ′ic** (-tip′ik) adj.

pho·to·ty·pog·ra·phy (fō′tō·tī·pog′rə·fē) n. Any photomechanical process of engraving in relief that may be reproduced in connection with type on a printing press. —**pho′to·ty′po·graph′ic** (-tī′pə·graf′ik) adj.

pho·to·vol·ta·ic (fō′tō·vol·tā′ik) adj. Capable of producing an electromotive force under the action of light; photoelectric.

pho·to·zin·cog·ra·phy (fō′tō·zing·kog′rə·fē) n. Photoengraving which uses a sensitized zinc plate.

phrase (frāz) n. **1** An expression, consisting usually of but a few words, denoting a single idea or forming a separate part of a sentence; specifically, a group of two or more associated words, not containing a subject and predicate: distinguished from *clause.* See synonym below. **2** A concise, sententious expression. **3** Characteristic mode of expression; peculiar habit of language; phraseology. **4** *Music* A fragment of a melody having well-determined motion and repose, but incomplete sense. —v.t. & v.i. **phrased, phras·ing** **1** To express or be expressed in words or phrases. **2** *Music* To execute or divide (notes) into phrases by accentuation. [< LL *phrasis* diction < Gk., speech < *phrazein* point out, tell] — **phras′al** adj.

— *Synonym (noun):* clause. A *clause* is a short sentence forming a distinct part of a composition, or in more extended use a distinct and separable statement forming part of a legal or state document, as of a will, an indictment, etc.; a *phrase* is a group of words conveying a single idea, and forming a distinct part of a sentence. In grammar, a *clause* is a simple sentence which is combined with some other sentence or sentences, so as to form a complex or compound sentence. A simple sentence standing alone is not, in grammatical use, called a *clause,* but every *clause* of a complex or compound sentence is a simple sentence. Thus, the *clause* always contains a subject and predicate. A *phrase* does not contain a subject and predicate, but it may include as many words as a *clause.* See DICTION, TERM.

phra·se·o·gram (frā′zē·ə·gram′) n. A symbol or combination of stenographic signs standing for a phrase. [< PHRASE + -(O)GRAM; on analogy with PHRASEOLOGY]

phra·se·o·graph (frā′zē·ə·graf′, -gräf′) n. A phrase having a symbol or phraseogram. — **phra′se·o·graph′ic** adj.

phra·se·ol·o·gist (frā′zē·ol′ə·jist) n. **1** One who pays much attention to phraseology; a maker of phrases. **2** One who collects phrases.

phra·se·ol·o·gy (frā'zē·ol'ə·jē) *n.* **1** The choice and arrangement of words and phrases in expressing ideas; diction; style. **2** A compilation or handbook of phrases. See synonyms under DICTION. [< NL *phraseologia,* irregularly formed < Gk. *phrasis, -eōs* speech + *logos* a word] —**phra'se·o·log'i·cal** (-ə·loj'i·kəl) *adj.*

phras·ing (frā'zing) *n.* **1** The rendering of phrases. **2** *Music* Grouping and accentuation of the sounds in a melody. **3** Manner or form of verbal expression.

phra·try (frā'trē) *n. pl.* **·tries 1** In ancient Athens, a clan or subdivision of a phyle. **2** Any similar tribal unit among primitive peoples, as a tribe composed of several totemic clans among North American Indians. [< Gk. *phratria* < *phratēr* clansman, brother] —**phra'tric** *adj.*

phre·at·ic (frē·at'ik) *adj.* Of or pertaining to underground waters, especially those at or below the water table and accessible through wells. [< Gk. *phrear, phreatos* well]

phre·net·ic (frə·net'ik) *adj.* **1** Of, pertaining to, or suffering from brain fever. **2** Excessively excited; frantic. Also **phre·net'i·cal.** —*n.* A madman. Also spelled *frenetic.* [< OF *frenetike* < L *phreneticus* < Gk. *phrenētikos,* var. of Gk. *phrenetikos* afflicted with delirium < *phrenitis* PHRENITIS] —**phre·net'i·cal·ly** *adv.*

phren·ic (fren'ik) *adj.* **1** Of or pertaining to the mind. **2** *Anat.* Of or pertaining to the diaphragm; diaphragmatic: the *phrenic* nerve. [< NL *phrenicus* < Gk. *phrēn, phrenos* diaphragm, mind]

phreno- *combining form* **1** Mind; brain: *phrenotropic.* **2** Diaphragm; of or related to the diaphragm. Also, before vowels, **phren-.** [< Gk. *phrēn, phrenos* the diaphragm (thought to be the seat of intellect)]

phre·nol·o·gy (fri·nol'ə·jē) *n.* The doctrine that the conformation of the human skull, its shape and protuberances, indicate the position and degree of development of separate parts of the brain which control the various mental faculties and characteristics; loosely, character analysis by interpreting cranial formations. [< Gk. *phrēn, phrenos* mind + -LOGY] —**phren·o·log·ic** (fren'ə·loj'ik) or **·i·cal** *adj.* —**phren'o·log'i·cal·ly** *adv.* —**phre·nol'o·gist** *n.*

phthi·ri·a·sis (thi·rī'ə·sis, fthi-) *n.* Pediculosis; lousiness. [< L < Gk. *phtheiriasis* < *phtheiriaein* be lousy < *phtheir* a louse]

phthis·i·cal (tiz'i·kəl) *adj.* **1** Relative to or having disease of the lungs; consumptive. **2** Asthmatic; wheezy. Also **phthis'ick·y.**

-phyceae *combining form Bot.* Seaweed: used in the names of various classes of algae: *Rhodophyceae.* [< Gk. *phykos* seaweed]

phyco- *combining form* Seaweed; of or related to seaweed. [< Gk. *phykos* seaweed]

phy·col·o·gy (fī·kol'ə·jē) *n.* The branch of botany dealing with seaweeds or algae.

Phy·co·my·ce·tes (fī'kō·mi·sē'tēz) *n. pl.* A class of fungi, both saprophytic and parasitic, resembling algae, but destitute of chlorophyll, including the water molds and downy mildews. [< NL < Gk. *phykos* seaweed + *mykēs, -ētos* a mushroom] —**phy'co·my·ce'tous** *adj.*

phy·co·phae·in (fī'kō·fē'in) *n.* Fucoxanthin. [< PHYCO- + Gk. *phaios* dusky + -IN]

Phyfe (fīf), **Duncan,** 1768?–1854, American cabinetmaker, noted for the excellence and beauty of his furniture; born in Scotland.

phy·lac·ter·y (fi·lak'tər·ē) *n. pl.* **·ter·ies 1** A charm or amulet worn on the person; specifically, among the Jews, a strip or strips of cowhide parchment inscribed with passages of Scripture (*Ex.* xiii 8–10, 11–16; *Deut.* vi 4–9, xi 13–22) and enclosed in a black calfskin case, having thongs for binding it on the forehead or around the left arm in memory of the early Israelitish history and of the duty to observe the law, or sometimes to serve as an amulet: also **phyl·ac·te·ri·um** (fil'ak·tir'ē·əm). **2** An inscribed scroll represented in medieval art as held in the hands, or issuing from the mouths, of angels. **3** A reminder. [< LL *phylacterium* < Gk. *phylaktērion* a safeguard < *phylaktēr* a guard < *phylassein* guard]

phy·let·ic (fī·let'ik) *adj.* **1** Pertaining to a phyle or clan. **2** Of or pertaining to a phylum. Also **phy·lic** (fī'lik). [< Gk. *phyletikos* < *phyletēs* a tribesman < *phylē* a tribe] —**phy·let'i·cal·ly** *adv.*

phyl·lite (fil'īt) *n.* A lustrous schistose rock containing small particles of mica. [< Gk. *phyllon* a leaf + -ITE[1]]

phyl·li·um (fil'ē·əm) *n.* Any of a genus (*Phyllium*) of green, flattened, leaflike insects (family *Phasmatidae*); a leaf insect. [< NL < Gk. *phyllion,* dim. of *phyllon* a leaf]

phyllo- *combining form* Leaf; pertaining to a leaf: *phyllotaxis.* Also, before vowels, **phyll-.** [< Gk. *phyllon* a leaf]

phyl·lo·dy (fil'ə·dē) *n.* Frondescence.

phyl·loid (fil'oid) *adj.* Resembling a leaf; foliaceous. [< NL *phylloides* < Gk. *phyllon* a leaf + *eidos* form]

phyl·lo·pod (fil'ə·pod) *adj.* **1** Having leaflike feet. **2** Of or pertaining to the *Phyllopoda.* —*n.* One of the *Phyllopoda.*

Phyl·lop·o·da (fi·lop'ə·də) *n. pl.* A division of crustaceans (subclass *Entomostraca*), with the body elongated, a shell or bivalve carapace, and at least four pairs of flattened, leaflike swimming feet which also function as gills, as the freshwater fairy shrimp. [< NL < Gk. *phyllon* a leaf + *pous, podos* a foot] —**phyl·lop'o·dan** *n. & adj.*

phyl·lo·qui·none (fil'ə·kwī'nōn) *n.* Vitamin K₁.

phyl·lo·tax·is (fil'ə·tak'sis) *n. Bot.* **1** The arrangement of leaves upon a stem. **2** The laws governing this arrangement. Also **phyl'lo·tax'y.** [< NL < Gk. *phyllon* a leaf + *taxis* arrangement < *tassein* arrange] —**phyl'lo·tac'tic** (-tak'tik) *adj.*

-phyllous *combining form* Having (a specified kind or number of) leaves: *monophyllous.* [< Gk. *phyllon* a leaf]

phyl·lox·e·ra (fil'ək·sir'ə, fi·lok'sər·ə) *n.* A minute aphis or plant louse (family *Phylloxeridae*), especially the grape phylloxera (*Dactylosphaera vitifoliae*), which is very destructive to grape vines. For illustration see INSECTS (injurious). [< NL < Gk. *phyllon* a leaf + *xēros* dry]

phylo- *combining form* Tribe; race; species: *phylogeny.* Also, before vowels, **phyl-.** [< Gk. *phylē, phylon* a tribe]

phy·log·e·ny (fī·loj'ə·nē) *n. Biol.* The history of the evolution of a species or group; tribal or racial history. Compare ONTOGENY. Also **phy·lo·gen·e·sis** (fī'lə·jen'ə·sis). [< G *phylogenie* < Gk. *phylon* a race + *-geneia* birth, origin < *gen-,* root of *gignesthai* be born] —**phy'lo·ge·net'ic** (-jə·net'ik), **phy'lo·gen'ic** *adj.* —**phy'lo·ge·net'i·cal·ly** *adv.*

phy·lum (fī'ləm) *n. pl.* **·la** (-lə) *Biol.* A great division of animals or plants ranking next below a kingdom and above a class, of which the members are believed to have a common evolutionary ancestor. [< NL < Gk. *phylon* a race < *phyein* produce]

-phyre *combining form Geol.* In petrography, a porphyritic rock: *granophyre.* [< F *porphyre* porphyry]

physi- Var. of PHYSIO-.

phys·ic (fiz'ik) *n.* **1** Medicine in general. **2** A cathartic; a purge. **3** *Archaic* The art or practice of medicine; the medical profession. **4** *Obs.* Physics. —*v.t* **phys·icked, phys·ick·ing 1** To treat with medicine or, especially, a cathartic; purge. **2** To cure or relieve. [< OF *fisique* < L *physica* < Gk. *physikē (epistēmē)* (the knowledge) of nature < *physis* nature < *phyein* produce]

phys·i·cal (fiz'i·kəl) *adj.* **1** Relating to the material universe or to the physical sciences. **2** Pertaining to material things, as opposed to *mental, moral,* or *spiritual;* especially, relating to the human body apart from the mind or spirit; material; corporeal. **3** Of or pertaining to the phenomena treated of in physics. **4** Accessible to the senses; external: *physical* characteristics of a mineral; *physical* changes. [< Med. L *physicalis* < L *physica.* See PHYSIC.] —**phys'i·cal·ly** *adv.*

Synonyms: bodily, corporal, corporeal, material, natural, sensible, tangible, visible. Whatever is composed of or pertains to matter may be termed *material: physical* applies to *material* things considered as parts of a system or organic whole; hence, we speak of *material* substances, *physical* forces. *Bodily, corporal,* and *corporeal* apply primarily to the human body; *bodily* and *corporal* both denote pertaining or relating to the body; *corporeal* signifies of the nature of or like the body; *corporal* is now almost wholly restricted to signify applied to or inflicted upon the

body; we speak of *bodily* sufferings, *bodily* presence, *corporal* punishment, the *corporeal* frame. See NATURAL (def. 8). *Antonyms:* hyperphysical, immaterial, intangible, intellectual, invisible, mental, moral, spiritual, unreal, unsubstantial.

physical anthropology 1 The study of the physical characteristics of man during the course of his evolution from the primate stock, and of the genetic relations between ethnic groups. **2** Anthropometry.

physical chemistry The branch of chemistry that deals with the physical properties of substances, especially in their quantitative relations to energy transformations and chemical change.

physical education Training and development of the human body by means of athletics and other exercises; also, education in hygiene.

physical geography Geography dealing with the natural features of the earth, as vegetation, land forms, drainage, ocean currents, climate, etc.

physical sciences The sciences that treat of the structure, properties, and energy relations of matter apart from the phenomena of life, as physics, astronomy, chemistry, geology, mineralogy, meteorology, etc.

physical therapy The science of treating disability, injury, and disease by external physical means, such as electricity, heat, light, massage, exercise, etc.: also called *physiotherapy.*

phy·si·cian (fi·zish'ən) *n.* **1** One legally authorized to practice medicine; a doctor. **2** One engaged in the general practice of medicine as distinguished from a surgeon. **3** Any healer.

phys·i·cist (fiz'ə·sist) *n.* A student of or specialist in physics.

phys·i·co·chem·i·cal (fiz'i·kō·kem'i·kəl) *adj.* **1** Of or pertaining to the physical and chemical properties of matter. **2** Pertaining to physical chemistry. [< *physico-* (< PHYSICAL) + CHEMICAL]

phys·ics (fiz'iks) *n.* The science that treats of matter and energy and of the laws governing their reciprocal interplay under conditions susceptible to precise observation, experimental control, and exact measurement. Physics generally includes the subjects of mechanics, heat, light and sound, electricity and magnetism, and radiation, but not the phenomena peculiar to living matter or to chemical change.

physio- *combining form* Nature; related to natural functions or phenomena: *physiology.* Also, before vowels, **physi-.** [< Gk. *physis* nature]

phys·i·oc·ra·cy (fiz'ē·ok'rə·sē) *n.* The doctrine of François Quesnay, who taught that society should be governed by a natural order inherent in itself, that land and its unmanufactured products are the only true wealth, the precious metals being a false standard, that the proper source of state revenue is direct taxation of land; and maintained the right of freedom of trade, person, opinion, and property. [< F *physiocratie*] —**phys'i·o·crat'** (-ə·krat') *n.* —**phys'i·o·crat'ic** *adj.*

phys·i·og·no·my (fiz'ē·og'nə·mē, *esp. Brit.* fiz'ē·on'ə·mē) *n. pl.* **·mies 1** The face or features as revealing character or disposition. **2** The outward look of a thing. **3** The art of reading character by the lineaments of the face or form of the body. [< OF *fiznomie* < Med. L *phisnomia* < Gk. *physiognōmonia* the judging of a man's nature (by his features) < *physis* nature + *gnōmōn, -onos* a judge] —**phys'i·og·nom'ic** (-og·nom'ik) or **·i·cal** *adj.* —**phys'i·og·nom'i·cal·ly** *adv.* —**phys'i·og'no·mist** *n.*

phys·i·og·ra·phy (fiz'ē·og'rə·fē) *n.* **1** A description of nature. **2** The study of the development of the features of the earth's surface; physical geography. [< PHYSIO- + -GRAPHY] —**phys'i·og'ra·pher** *n.* —**phys'i·o·graph'ic** (-ə·graf'ik) or **·i·cal** *adj.* —**phys'i·o·graph'i·cal·ly** *adv.*

phys·i·o·log·i·cal (fiz'ē·ə·loj'i·kəl) *adj.* Pertaining to the functions of living organisms. Also **phys'i·o·log'ic.** —**phys'i·o·log'i·cal·ly** *adv.*

phys·i·ol·o·gy (fiz'ē·ol'ə·jē) *n.* **1** The branch of biology that treats of the vital phenomena manifested by animals or plants; the science of organic functions, as distinguished from *anatomy* and *morphology.* **2** The aggregate of organic processes: the *physiology* of the frog. [<F *physiologie* <L *physiologia* <Gk., natural philosophy < *physiologos* a speaker on nature < *physis* nature + *logos* a word] —**phys′i·ol′o·gist** *n.*

phys·i·o·ther·a·py (fiz′ē·ō·ther′ə·pē) See PHYSI-CAL THERAPY.

phy·sique (fi·zēk′) *n.* The physical structure, organization, or appearance of a person. [<F, orig. adj., physical <L *physicus* <Gk. *physikos* natural < *physis.* See PHYSIC.]

-phyte *combining form* A (specified) kind of plant; a plant having a (specified) habitat: *thallophyte, hydrophyte.* [<Gk. *phyton* a plant]

phyto– *combining form* Plant; of or related to vegetation: *phytogenesis.* Also, before vowels, **phyt-.** [<Gk. *phyton* a plant]

phy·to·gen·e·sis (fī′tō·jen′ə·sis) *n.* The science of the generation, origin, and development of plants. Also **phy·tog·e·ny** (fī·toj′ə·nē). — **phy′to·ge·net′ic** (-jə·net′ik) or **·i·cal** *adj.* — **phy′to·ge·net′i·cal·ly** *adv.*

phy·to·gen·ic (fī′tō·jen′ik) *adj.* **1** Phytogenetic. **2** Of plant origin, as coal and some other biogenic formations. Also **phy·tog·e·nous** (fī·toj′ə·nəs).

phy·to·ge·og·ra·phy (fī′tō·jē·og′rə·fē) *n.* That department of geography which deals with the distribution of plants; plant geography: also called *geobotany.*

phy·tog·ra·phy (fī·tog′rə·fē) *n.* Descriptive botany. [<NL *phytographia* <Gk. *phyton* a plant + *graphein* write]

phy·toid (fī′toid) *adj.* Plantlike.

phy·tol·o·gy (fī·tol′ə·jē) *n.* Botany. [<NL *phytologia* <Gk. *phyton* a plant + *logos* a word, study] —**phy·to·log·ic** (fī′tə·loj′ik) or **·i·cal** *adj.*

phy·to·pa·thol·o·gy (fī′tō·pə·thol′ə·jē) *n.* **1** The study of the diseases of plants and their control. **2** The pathology of diseases which are caused by fungi, bacteria, and other plant organisms.

phy·to·plank·ton (fī′tō·plangk′tən) *n.* Free-floating aquatic plants.

phy·to·tron (fī′tə·tron) *n.* A large-scale field laboratory for the study of plant growth under artificially produced climatic conditions ranging from the tropical to the arctic. [<PHYTO- + Gk. *-tron,* instrumental suffix]

pi¹ (pī) *n.* **1** The sixteenth letter in the Greek alphabet (Π, π) corresponding to English *p.* As a numeral it denotes 80. **2** This letter used to designate the ratio of the circumference of a circle to its diameter, 3.14159 +; also, this ratio. [Def. 2 <Gk. *p(eriphereia)* periphery]

pi² (pī) *n. Printing* Type that has been thrown into disorder; hence, any jumble or disorder. —*v.t.* **pied, pie·ing** To jumble or disorder, as type. Also spelled *pie.* [Var. of PIE¹]

pi·ac·u·lar (pī·ak′yə·lər) *adj.* **1** Expiatory; having power to atone. **2** Requiring expiation: criminal. [<L *piacularis* < *piaculum* an expiation < *piare* appease]

piaffe (pyaf) *v.i.* **piaffed, piaf·fing** To perform or move by performing the piaffer. [<F *piaffer* paw the ground, lit., strut; ult. origin uncertain]

piaf·fer (pyaf′ər) *n.* In equitation, a movement in which the horse lifts one forefoot and the opposite hind foot in unison and slowly places them forward, backward, or to the side. [<F *piaffer.* See PIAFFE.]

pi·an·ism (pē·an′iz·əm, pē′ə·niz′əm) *n.* **1** Arrangement of music for the pianoforte. **2** Performance on the piano; the technique of piano playing.

pi·a·nis·si·mo (pē′ə·nis′i·mō, *Ital.* pyä·nēs′sē·mō) *adj. & adv. Music* Very soft or softly; a musical direction: abbr. *pp.* or *ppp.* [<Ital. <L *planissimus,* superl. of *planus.* See PIANO².]

pi·an·ist (pē·an′ist, pē′ə·nist) *n.* One who plays on the piano; specifically, an expert or a professional performer.

pi·an·o¹ (pē·an′ō) *n. pl.* **·an·os** A stringed musical instrument having felt-covered hammers, operated from a manual keyboard, which strike upon steel wires to produce the tones; a pianoforte. — **concert grand piano** The largest size of grand piano, used for

concert performances. — **grand piano** A horizontal, harp–shaped piano, having three or more strings to each note, and action without springs. — **square piano** A piano having a horizontal rectangular case and horizontally strung wires. — **upright piano** A piano in which the case is upright, with the strings vertical and overstrung to save space. [< Ital., short for *pianoforte* PIANOFORTE]

pi·a·no² (pē·ä′nō, *Ital.* pyä′nō) *adv.* With slight force; softly: a direction to a singer or player of a musical instrument: abbr. *p.* — *adj.* Performed or to be performed with slight force; soft: a *piano* passage. —*n.* A passage of music rendered softly and lightly. [<Ital. <L *planus* flat, soft (of sound)]

pi·an·o·for·te (pē·an′ə·fôr′te, -fôr′-, -fôrt′, -fôrt′) *n.* A piano. [<Ital. < *piano e forte* soft and strong]

Pi·a·no·la (pē′ə·nō′lə) *n.* A small, portable, cabinetlike, piano-playing mechanism: a trade name.

Pi·a·rist (pī′ə·rist) *n.* One of a Roman Catholic monastic order the members of which are known as Regular Clerks of the Scuole Pie, an institute of instruction, founded in Rome about 1600. [<NL (*patres scholarum*) *piarum* (fathers of the) religious (schools) <L *pius* dutiful, pious]

pi·as·sa·va (pē′ə·sä′və) *n.* **1** A coarse, stiff fiber obtained from the leafstalks of two Brazilian palms, *Attalea funifera* and *Leopoldinia piassaba:* used for making ropes, brooms, brushes, etc. **2** Either of these palms. Also **pi′a·sa′ba** (-bə), **pi′as·sa′ba, pi′a·sa′va.** [<Pg. *piassava, piassaba* <Tupian *piaçába*]

pi·as·ter (pē·as′tər) *n.* **1** A Turkish and Egyptian coin and monetary unit. **2** The Spanish peso or dollar. Also **pi·as′tre.** [<F *piastre* <Ital. *piastra,* lit., a plate of metal, short for *piastra d'argento* a plate of silver, ult. <L *emplastrum* PLASTER]

pi·az·za (pē·az′ə, *Ital.* pē·at′tsä) *n.* **1** A veranda or porch. **2** In Europe, especially in Italy, a plaza. **3** A covered outer walk or gallery. [<Ital., a square, market place, ult. <L *platea* a broad street <Gk. *plateia* (*hodos*). Doublet of PLACE, PLAZA.]

pi·broch (pē′brokh) *n.* A martial air played on the bagpipe. [<dial. E (Scottish) <Scottish Gaelic *piobaireachd* playing the bagpipe < *piobair* a piper < *piob* a pipe <PIPE]

pi·ca¹ (pī′kə) *n.* A size of type; 12–point; 1/6 inch; also, a standard unit of measurement, as for leads or pages. See POINT SYSTEM.— **small pica** A size of type; about six and a half lines to the inch; 11–point. — **two–line** or **double pica** Type having a depth of body of two lines of pica; 24–point. — Homophone: *pika.* [<Med. L, a pie⁴; ? because used in printing pies]

pi·ca² (pī′kə) *n. Pathol.* A morbid appetite for unusual or unfit food, as clay, chalk, ashes, etc., showing itself especially in hysteria, pregnancy, and chlorosis. — Homophone: *pika.* [<L *pica* a magpie, ? trans. of Gk. *kissa, kitta* a magpie, a craving for strange food; with ref. to the bird's omnivorousness] — **pi′cal** *adj.*

pi·ca·cho (pē·kä′chō) *n. pl.* **·chos** *SW U.S.* An isolated peak of a hill or butte. [<Am. Sp. <Sp. *pico* a peak]

pic·a·dor (pik′ə·dôr, *Sp.* pē′kä·thôr′) *n.* **1** In bullfighting, a horseman armed with a lance, whose function is to enrage the bull. **2** A clever debater; one with ready wit. [<Sp., lit., a pricker < *picar* prick, pierce < *prica.* Akin to PIKE¹.]

pic·a·resque (pik′ə·resk′) *adj.* Pertaining to picaroons or rogues: specifically applied to the **picaresque novel,** a form having a slight plot consisting of episodes loosely connected by the hero, a rogue; originated in Spain in the 17th century, popular in France and England in the 18th century, and still used occasionally. [<Sp. *picaresco* roguish < *pícaro* a rogue; ult. origin uncertain]

pic·a·roon¹ (pik′ə·rōōn′) *n.* **1** One who lives by cheating or robbery: a wrecker or pirate; rogue; adventurer. **2** A pirate vessel. [<Sp. *picaron,* aug. of *pícaro* a rogue]

pic·a·roon² (pik′ə·rōōn′) *n.* A piked pole used by log drivers: also spelled *pickaroon.* [? <MF

piqueron a spur, dim. of *pique* a pike¹]

Pi·cas·so (pē·kä′sō), **Pablo,** 1881–1973, Spanish painter and sculptor active in France.

pic·a·yune (pik′i·yōōn′) *adj. U.S.* Little; worthless; mean. — *n.* **1** A former small Spanish-American coin; a half-real. **2** *U.S.* A person or thing of trifling value. [<F *picaillon* an old Piedmontese coin, a farthing <Provençal *picaioun, picalhoun,* dim. of *picalo* money] — **pic′a·yun′ish** *adj.*

pic·ca·lil·li (pik′ə·lil′ē) *n.* A highly seasoned relish of chopped vegetables. [? <PICKLE¹]

pic·co·lo (pik′ə·lō) *n. pl.* **·los** **1** A small flute with tones an octave higher than those of the ordinary flute. **2** An organ stop of similar tone. [<Ital., small] — **pic′co·lo·ist** *n.*

pice (pīs) *n.* A copper coin of British India; 1/4 anna. [<Hind. *paisā,* ? < *pāi, paī* a quarter <Skt. *pad, padi*]

pic·e·ous (pis′ē·əs, pī′sē-) *adj.* **1** Relating to or resembling pitch; inflammable. **2** Pitch-black. [<L *piceus* < *pix, picis* pitch]

pich·i·ci·a·go (pich′ə·sē·ä′gō, -ā′gō) *n. pl.* **·gos** A small burrowing armadillo (*Chlamydophorus truncatus*) of South America. [<Am. Sp. *pichiciego* <Guarani *pichey* the little armadillo + Sp. *ciego* blind <L *caecus*]

pich·u·rim (pich′ə·rim) *n.* One of the aromatic cotyledons of the seed of a South American tree (genus *Ocotea* or *Nectandra*) of the laurel family, resembling in taste and smell both sassafras and nutmeg: used medicinally and for flavoring. Also **pichurim bean.** [<Tupian]

pick¹ (pik) *v.t.* **1** To choose; select; cull, as from a group or number. **2** To detach; pluck, as with the fingers or beak: to *pick* a flower. **3** To gather or harvest: to *pick* cotton. **4** To prepare by removing the feathers, hulls, leaves, etc.: to *pick* a chicken. **5** To remove extraneous matter from (the teeth, etc.) with the fingers, a pointed instrument, etc. **6** To pull apart, as rags. **7** To break up, penetrate, or indent with or as with a pointed instrument. **8** To form or make in this manner: to *pick* a hole. **9** To seek or point out too critically: to *pick* flaws. **10** To seek or bring on purposely; provoke: to *pick* a quarrel. **11** To remove the contents of by stealth: to *pick* a pocket or purse. **12** To open (a lock) by means other than the key, as by a piece of wire or metal. **13 a** To pluck (the strings) of a musical instrument. **b** To play: to *pick* a banjo. — *v.i.* **14** To work with a pick. **15** To eat daintily or without appetite; nibble. **16** To make careful selection: to *pick* and choose. **17** To pilfer: to *pick* and steal. See synonyms under CHOOSE. — **to pick at 1** To touch or toy with. **2** To eat without appetite. **3** *U.S. Colloq.* To nag at. — **to pick off 1** To remove by picking. **2** To shoot with careful and deliberate aim. — **to pick on** *Colloq.* To single out for attention, duty, etc.; tease; annoy. — **to pick one's way** (or **steps**) To advance by careful selection of one's course or actions. — **to pick out 1** To choose or select. **2** To distinguish (something) from its surroundings. **3** To produce the notes of (a tune) singly or slowly, as by ear. — **to pick over** To examine carefully or one by one. — **to pick to pieces 1** To pull apart. **2** To destroy the arguments or claims of by critical or carping analysis. — **to pick up 1** To take up, as with the hand. **2** To take up or receive into a group, vehicle, etc.: We *picked up* more passengers in Hoboken. **3** To get or acquire casually or by chance. **4** To gain speed; accelerate. **5** To recover spirits, health, etc.; improve. **6** To be able to perceive or receive, as a distant radio station. **7** *Colloq.* To make

TYPES OF PICKS
a. Pickax. *c.* Guitar thumb pick.
b. Mandolin pick. *d.* Ice pick.
e. Quill toothpick.

the acquaintance of, casually or informally. — n. 1 Right of selection; choice; hence, the best. 2 The quantity of certain crops that are picked by hand. 3 A blow, as with a spear. 4 The act of picking. See synonyms under ALTERNATIVE. [ME *piken, pikken,* OE *pican, pician* (assumed), infinitive of OE *picung* pricking, infl. by OF *piquer* pierce. Akin to PIKE¹.]

pick² (pik) *n.* 1 A double-headed, pointed metal tool mounted on a strong wooden handle, as a pickax: used for breaking ground, etc. 2 Any of various implements for picking, as an ice pick, toothpick, or a picklock. 3 A plectrum, as for a stringed instrument. [Appar. var. of PIKE¹]

pick³ (pik) *n.* 1 In weaving, the blow that drives a loom shuttle. 2 A thread: the number of picks to the inch determines the relative value of cotton cloth or muslin. [< dial. E *pick, v.,* var. of PITCH² throw]

pick-a-back (pik′ə-bak′) *adv.* On the back or shoulders: also spelled *piggy-back.* [Earlier *a pickback, a pickpack.* Cf. dial. E *pick* throw, toss.]

pick-a-roon (pik′ə-rōōn′) See PICAROON.

pick-ax (pik′aks′) *n.* A pick or mattock with one arm of the head edged like a chisel and the other pointed; also, one with both arms pointed. Also **pick′axe′**. [Alter. of ME *pikoys* < OF *picois,* ? < *pic* a pike¹; infl. in form by *ax*]

pick-ed¹ (pik′id, pikt) *adj.* 1 Having spines or prickles. 2 Sharp-pointed, as a stick. [< PICK², *n.*]

picked² (pikt) *adj.* 1 Carefully selected; chosen for a purpose. 2 Cleaned by picking out refuse, stalks, etc., as cotton. 3 Caused intentionally or sought out, as a quarrel. See synonyms under CHOICE. [Orig. pp. of PICK⁴, *v.*]

picked-o-ver (pikt′ō′vər) *adj.* 1 Handled; left after the best have been removed. 2 Left after the undesirable ones have been removed, as berries.

pick-er¹ (pik′ər) *n.* 1 One who or that which picks. 2 A machine for loosening up fibrous material. 3 A tool like a graver used by electrotypers. [< PICK¹]

pick-er² (pik′ər) *n.* In a loom, the part that strikes the shuttle. [< dial. E *pick, v.* See PICK³.]

pick-er-el (pik′ər-əl) *n.* 1 A North American fresh-water fish (family *Esocidae*); a pike; especially, one of the smaller species. *Esox reticulatus* is the common pond pickerel of the eastern United States. 2 A young pike. [Dim. of PIKE¹, ? <AF]

pickerel frog A frog (*Rana palustris*) of the eastern United States: also called *marsh frog.*

pick-et (pik′it) *n.* 1 A pointed stick, tent peg, bar, fence paling, or stake. 2 *Mil.* A soldier or detachment of soldiers posted to guard a camp, army, etc. 3 A person stationed by a labor organization outside a place affected by a strike. — *v.t.* 1 To fence or fortify with pickets or pointed stakes. 2 *Mil.* **a** To guard by means of a picket. **b** To post as a picket. 3 To station pickets outside of. 4 To tie to a picket, as a horse. — *v.i.* 5 To act as a picket (def. 3). [< F *piquet* a pointed stake < *piquer* pierce] — **pick′et-er** *n.*

picket pin A long iron pin or wooden stake driven into the ground and having a swivel loop at the upper end: used for tethering horses.

Pick-ford (pik′fərd), **Mary,** born 1893, U.S. motion-picture actress born in Canada: real name *Gladys Smith.*

pick glass A magnifying glass for determining the thread count of fabrics.

pick-ing (pik′ing) *n.* 1 The act of picking; also, that which is or may be picked. 2 *pl.* That which is left to be picked up or gleaned: scanty *pickings.* 3 Pilfering, or that which is pilfered. 4 *Usually pl.* That which is taken by questionable means; spoils.

pick-le (pik′əl) *n.* 1 A preserving, flavoring liquid, as brine or vinegar, sometimes spiced, for meat, fish, vegetables, etc. 2 One of certain objects preserved or flavored in pickle, as a cucumber or onion. 3 Diluted acid used in cleaning metal castings, etc. 4 *Colloq.* An embarrassing condition or position. 5 *Colloq.* A mischievous child. — *v.t.* **led, ·ling** 1 To preserve with brine or vinegar. 2 To im-

merse in diluted acid, as castings, for cleansing. [Appar. <MDu. *pekel, peeckel;* ult. origin uncertain]

pickled finish A finish having the effect of a cloudy white patina over light-toned wood: originally produced on old painted furniture by removing the plaster base of the paint with vinegar, or exposing a surface which had been bleached with lime.

pick-lock (pik′lok′) *n.* 1 A special implement, as a bent wire, for opening a lock; a false key. 2 A burglar.

pick-me-up (pik′mē′up′) *n. Colloq.* A drink, especially an alcoholic drink, taken to renew one's energy or spirits.

pick-pock-et (pik′pok′it) *n.* One who steals from pockets.

pick-up (pik′up′) *n.* 1 Acceleration, as in the speed of an automobile, engine, etc. 2 The electromagnetic vibrating device holding the needle in a phonograph or similar sound-reproducing apparatus. 3 *Telecom.* **a** In radio, the location of microphones in relation to program elements. **b** The system for broadcasting material gathered outside the studio. **c** In television, the scanning of an image by the electron beam. **d** The scanning apparatus. 4 *Colloq.* Gain; improvement; renewal of prosperity, etc. 5 *Slang* A stranger with whom a casual acquaintance is made, usually in a public place and for the purposes of lovemaking. 6 A small, usually open, truck for light loads.

pic-nic (pik′nik) *n.* 1 An outdoor party, usually held in the countryside, during which a meal is eaten. 2 *Slang* An easy or pleasant time or experience. — *v.i.* **·nicked, ·nick-ing** To have or attend a picnic. Also **pick′nick**. [<F *pique-nique,* ? reduplication of *piquer* pick, peck] — **pic′nick-er** *n.*

pi-cot (pē′kō) *n.* A small thread loop on ornamental edging, sometimes having knots or stitches added. — *v.t. & v.i.* To sew with this edging. [<F, dim. of OF *pic* a point]

picot stitch A loop stitch.

pic-quet (pi-kā′, -ket′) See PIQUET.

pic-ric (pik′rik) *adj.* Of, pertaining to, or having an exceedingly bitter taste. [<Gk. *pikros* bitter]

pic-rite (pik′rīt) *n.* An olivine–augite peridotite containing some magnetite or ilmenite, biotite, and brown hornblende. [<Gk. *pikros* bitter + -ITE¹]

picro- *combining form* Bitter: *picrol.* Also, before vowels, **picr-**. [<Gk. *pikros* bitter]

Pict (pikt) *n.* One of an ancient people of uncertain origin who inhabited Britain and the Scottish Highlands, and waged war on the Romans: conquered in 846 by the Scots. [<LL *Picti,* ? <L *pictus,* pp. of *pingere* paint; with ref. to their being painted or tattooed]

Pict-ish (pik′tish) *n.* The language of the Picts, of undetermined relationship. — *adj.* Of or pertaining to the Picts.

pic-to-graph (pik′tə-graf, -gräf) *n.* A picture representing an idea: the earliest form of record. [< *picto-* pictorial (<L *pictus,* pp. of *pingere* paint) + -GRAPH] — **pic′to-graph′ic** *adj.* — **pic′to-graph′i-cal-ly** *adv.* — **pic-tog-ra-phy** (pik-tog′rə-fē) *n.*

pic-to-ri-al (pik-tôr′ē-əl, -tō′rē-) *adj.* 1 Pertaining to or concerned with pictures. 2 Representing in or as if in pictures; graphic. 3 Containing or illustrated by pictures. — *n.* An illustrated publication. See synonyms under GRAPHIC. [<LL *pictorius* <L *pictor.* See PICTOR.] — **pic-to′ri-al-ly** *adv.*

pic-ture (pik′chər) *n.* 1 A surface representation of an object or scene, as by a painting, drawing, engraving, or photograph; also, a mental image. 2 A vivid or graphic verbal delineation. 3 A striking resemblance to another person, object, or general idea: She is the *picture* of her mother; the very *picture* of despair. 4 A tableau vivant: also called **living picture**. 5 A visual image or scene produced by the working of physical laws or their use, as in the lens. 6 A motion picture. — **to be in the picture** To belong to the group or the occasion; also, to be successful. — *v.t.* **·tured, ·tur-ing** 1 To give visible representation to; draw, paint, etc. 2 To describe graphically; depict verbally. 3 To form a mental image of. [<L *pictura* <*pictus,* pp. of *pingere* paint]

Synonyms (noun): cartoon, copy, delineation, drawing, engraving, image, likeness, miniature, painting, photograph, print, representation, resemblance, semblance, similitude, sketch. See IMAGE, SKETCH.

picture hat A woman's hat with a very wide brim which frames the face: often trimmed with plumes, as hats seen in certain famous paintings, especially those of Gainsborough.

Pic-ture-phone (pik′chər-fōn′) *n.* A telephone equipped with a television screen: a trade name.

picture ratio In television, the ratio of the length of the received image to the width.

pic-tur-esque (pik′chə-resk′) *adj.* 1 Having pictorial quality; like or suitable for a picture; especially, having a striking, irregular beauty, quaintness, or charm. 2 Abounding in striking or original expression or imagery; figurative; richly graphic. See synonyms under BEAUTIFUL, GRAPHIC, ROMANTIC. [<F *pittoresque* <Ital. *pittoresco* < *pittore* a painter <L *pictor.* See PICTOR.] — **pic′tur-esque′ly** *adv.* — **pic′tur-esque′ness** *n.*

picture window A large window, usually in a living room, designed to give a wide view of the outside.

pic-tur-ize (pik′chə-rīz) *v.t.* **·ized, ·iz-ing** To make a picture or motion picture of; present pictorially. — **pic′tur-i-za′tion** *n.*

pid-dle (pid′l) *v.* **·dled, ·ding** *v.t.* 1 To trifle; dawdle: usually with *away.* — *v.i.* 2 To trifle; dawdle. 3 To urinate. [Origin unknown]

pid-dling (pid′ling) *adj.* Unimportant; trivial.

pid-dock (pid′ək) *n.* A bivalve mollusk (genus *Pholas*) with an elongated shell, which burrows in clay and sand. [Cf. OE *puduc* wart]

pidg-in (pij′ən) *n.* A mixed language, such as bêche-de-mer, combining the vocabulary and grammar of dissimilar languages and providing a simplified, mutually intelligible form of communication for use in commerce: distinguished from a *creolized language* in that it is used only as an additional, auxiliary language. [<Pidgin English, alter. of BUSINESS]

Pidgin English A jargon composed of English and local native elements, used as the language of commerce between natives and foreigners in areas of China, Melanesia, Northern Australia, and West Africa.

pie¹ (pī) *n.* 1 A baked food consisting of one or two layers or crusts of pastry with a filling of fruit, vegetables, or meat. 2 Pi². 3 *Slang* Anything very good or very easy. 4 *Slang* Political graft. — **to have** (or **put**) **one's finger in the pie** To have a share in an activity or project; hence, to meddle. [ME *pie, pye,* ? <PIE²; with ref. to the variety of objects collected by magpies and of foods baked in pies]

pie² (pī) *n.* A magpie, or a related bird. [<OF <L *pica* a magpie]

pie³ (pī) *n.* A former coin of India of smallest value, worth a third of a pice. [<Hind. *pā′ī* <Skt. *pad, padi* a fourth]

pie⁴ (pī) *n.* 1 In the pre-Reformation English church, a book of rules and directions for services on days when two or more feasts concur. 2 An index; a register. Also spelled *pye.* [<LL *pica* <L, a magpie; ? because its pages resembled the bird's black-and-white plumage]

pie-bald (pī′bôld′) *adj.* Having spots, especially of white and black. — *n.* A spotted or mottled animal, especially a horse. [<PIE² + BALD; because like a magpie's plumage]

piece (pēs) *n.* 1 A small portion considered as forming or having formed a distinct part of a whole. 2 A portion or quantity existing as an individual entity or mass: a *piece* of paper; a *piece* of music. 3 An object considered as forming one of a class or group: a *piece* of furniture, luggage, etc. 4 A definite quantity or length in which an article is manufactured or sold. 5 An instance; specimen; example: a *piece* of luck. 6 A firearm. 7 A coin: a fifty-cent *piece.* 8 A literary composition. 9 A drama; play. 10 A picture. 11 A musical composition. 12 *Dial.* A short time, space, or distance: to walk a *piece.* 13 *Archaic* or *Dial.* A person; individual. 14 Any of the figures used in the game of chess; technically, any man but the pawns. 15 One of the disks or counters used in checkers, backgammon, etc. — **a piece of one's mind** Criticism or censure frankly expressed. — **in one piece** Unharmed; intact. — **of a piece** 1 Of the same kind, sort, or class.

2 Of one piece; undivided. **— to go to pieces 1** To fall apart. **2** To lose moral or emotional self-control. **— to speak one's piece** To voice one's opinions. **—** *adj.* Of, made of, or by the piece. **—** *v.t.* **pieced, piec·ing 1** To add or attach a piece or pieces to, as for enlargement. **2** To unite or reunite the pieces of, as in mending. **3** To unite (parts or fragments) into a whole. **4** To find meaning or coherence in by linking elements: often with *together:* to *piece* together a sequence of events from the testimony of eyewitnesses. ◆ Homophone: *peace.* [<OF *pece* <LL *pettia* (assumed), prob. ult. <Celtic. Cf. Welsh *peth* little.]

pièce de résistance (pyes də rā·zē·stäns′) *pl.* **pièces de résistance** (pyes) *French* The principal or most important work in a collection, as of art, poems, etc.; also, the most substantial dish of a dinner.

piece goods Dry-goods; fabrics, usually sold by the piece, as shirtings and sheetings.

piece·meal (pēs′mēl′) *adj.* Made up of pieces. **—** *adv.* **1** Piece by piece; gradually. **2** In pieces. [ME *pece-mele* < *pece* PIECE + *-mele,* OE *-maelum* < *mael* a measure; partial trans. of OE *styccemaelum* in pieces]

piece·work (pēs′wûrk′) *n.* Work done, or paid for, by the piece or quantity. **— piece′work·er** *n.*

piec·ing (pē′sing) *n.* Pieces of cloth, especially those collected and saved to be sewed together, as for a quilt.

pied (pīd) *adj.* Spotted; piebald; mottled. [<PIE²]

pied·mont (pēd′mont) *adj.* At the foot of a mountain or mountain range: a *piedmont* plain. [<*Piedmont,* Italy <L *Pedimontium* < *pes, pedis* a foot + *mons, montis* a mountain]

Pied Piper of Ham·elin In medieval legend, a piper who rid the town of Hamelin of its rats by leading them with his music into the river: when not rewarded as promised, he led the town's children to a hill into which they disappeared.

pie-eyed (pī′īd′) *adj. Slang* Drunk.

pie plant The garden rhubarb.

PIER
Steamship pier and dock.

pier (pir) *n.* **1** A plain, detached mass of masonry, usually serving as a support: the *pier* of a bridge. **2** An upright projecting portion of a wall. **3** A mole or jetty, or projecting wharf. **4** A solid portion of a wall between window openings, etc. ◆ Homophone: *peer.* [ME *per* <Med. L *pera,* ? ult. <Gk. *petra* rock]

pierce (pirs) *v.* **pierced, pierc·ing** *v.t.* **1** To pass into or through; penetrate, in the manner of a pointed object, weapon, etc.; puncture; stab. **2** To make an opening or hole in, into, or through: Many windows *pierced* the old walls. **3** To make or cut (an opening or hole) in or through something. **4** To force a way into or through: to *pierce* the wilderness. **5** To affect sharply or deeply, as with emotion, pain, etc. **6** To penetrate as if stabbing: Lightning *pierced* the night sky. **7** To penetrate as if seeing; perceive or understand: to *pierce* a mystery. **—** *v.i.* **8** To enter; penetrate. [<OF *percer, percier,* ? <*pertuisier* <L *pertusus,* pp. of *pertundere* perforate < *per-* through + *tundere* beat] **— pierc′er** *n.* Synonyms: bore, drill, enter, penetrate, perforate, puncture, stab, transfix.

Pierce (pirs), **Franklin,** 1804–69, president of the United States 1853–57.

pierc·ing (pir′sing) *adj.* Penetrating by or as if by a sharp-pointed instrument; cutting; keen; poignant; shrill, as a look or cry. See synonyms under ACUTE, BLEAK, SHARP. **—** *n.* Penetration. **— pierc′ing·ly** *adv.* **— pierc′ing·ness** *n.*

pier glass A large, high mirror intended to stand against a pier and thus fill the space between two openings in the wall.

pi·er·i·dine (pī·er′ə·dīn, -din) *adj.* Of or per-

taining to a family (*Pieridae*) of butterflies, including species of predominantly white or yellow color. [<NL *Pierdinae,* subfamily name <*Pieris,* genus name <Gk., a Muse]

Piers Plow·man (pirz plou′mən) The chief character in the 14th century allegorical poem, *Vision of Piers Plowman,* ascribed to William Langland.

pier table A low table occupying the space between two wall openings, usually combined with a pier glass.

Pie·tà (pyā·tä′) *n.* In painting, sculpture, etc., a representation of Mary mourning over the body of Christ in her lap. [<Ital., lit., piety <L *pietas, -tatis* PIETY]

pi·e·tism (pī′ə·tiz′əm) *n.* **1** Piety or godliness; devotion, as distinguished from insistence on religious creeds or forms. **2** Affected or exaggerated piety. **— pi′e·tist** *n.* **— pi·e·tis′tic** *adj.*

Pi·e·tism (pī′ə·tiz′əm) *n.* A movement in the Lutheran Church in Germany during the later 17th century, advocating a revival of the devotional ideal. **— Pi′e·tist** *n.* **— Pi·e·tis′tic** *adj.*

pi·e·ty (pī′ə·tē) *n.* **1** Reverence toward God or the gods; religious devoutness. **2** Religiousness in general. **3** Filial honor and obedience as due to parents, superiors, or country. See synonyms under RELIGION. [<OF *piete* <L *pietas, -tatis* dutifulness < *pius* dutiful. Doublet of PITY.]

piezo– *combining form* Pressure; related to or produced by pressure: *piezometer.* [<Gk. *piezein* press]

pi·e·zo·chem·is·try (pī·ē′zō·kem′is·trē) *n.* The study of chemical reactions under the influence of high pressures.

pi·e·zo·e·lec·tric·i·ty (pī·ē′zō·i·lek′tris′ə·tē, -ē′lek-) *n.* Electricity or electric phenomena resulting from pressure upon certain bodies, especially crystals. **— pi·e′zo·e·lec′tric** or **·tri·cal** *adj.*

pi·e·zom·e·ter (pī′ə·zom′ə·tər) *n.* **1** An instrument for determining pressure; specifically, an apparatus for measuring the compressibility of liquids. **2** An attachment for a sounding line that denotes by the compression of air in a tube the depth of water to which the appliance descends. **3** A similar instrument used in ascertaining the sensitiveness of the skin to pressure. **— pi′e·zo·met′ric** (-zō·met′rik) or **·ri·cal** *adj.* **— pi′e·zom′e·try** *n.*

pif·fle (pif′əl) *Colloq. v.i.* **·fled, ·fling** To talk nonsensically; babble. **—** *n.* Nonsense. [? OE *pyffan* puff + -LE]

pig (pig) *n.* **1** A hog or hoglike animal, especially when small or young; also, its flesh (pork). ◆ Collateral adjective: *porcine.* **2** An oblong mass of metal, especially iron or lead, just run from the smelter and cast in a rough mold, usually in sand; also, the mold or trough. **3** Pig iron or iron pigs in general. **4** *Colloq.* A person regarded as like a pig, especially one who is filthy, gluttonous, or grasping. **5** *Scot.* An earthen article or vessel. **6** *Colloq.* A railroad locomotive: also called *hog.* **—** *v.i.* **pigged, pig·ging 1** To bring forth pigs. **2** To act or live like pigs: with *it.* [ME *pigge,* ? OE *picga,* as in *pic(g)bred* food for hogs]

pig bed The bed of sand into which iron is run in casting pigs.

pig·eon (pij′ən) *n.* **1** Any of a widely distributed family (*Columbidae*) of birds, of arboreal and terrestrial habit, as the rock pigeon (*Columba livia*); a dove. **2** *Slang* One easily swindled. [<OF *pijon* <LL *pipio, -onis* a young chirping bird <L *pipire* chirp]

pigeon hawk The American merlin.

pig·eon-heart·ed (pij′ən-här′tid) *adj.* Timid; fearful.

pig·eon·hole (pij′ən·hōl′) *n.* **1** A hole for pigeons to nest in, especially in a compartmented pigeon house. **2** A small compartment, as in a desk, for filing papers. **—** *v.t.* **·holed, ·hol·ing 1** To place in a pigeonhole; file. **2** To file away and ignore. **3** To place in categories; classify mentally.

pig·eon-liv·ered (pij′ən-liv′ərd) *adj.* Very mild or weak-spirited; meek.

pig·eon-toed (pij′ən·tōd′) *adj.* Having the toes turned inward; toeing in.

pig·eon-wing (pij′ən-wing′) *n.* **1** A fancy dance step. **2** A figure in skating, outlining the shape of a pigeon's spread wing.

pig·fish (pig′fish′) *n. pl.* **·fish** or **·fish·es 1** A salt-water fish that makes a grunting noise; especially, a grunt, as the sailor's-choice (*Orthopristis chrysopterus*), common off the South Atlantic coast of the United States. **2** A sculpin. **3** A sea robin.

pig·gin (pig′in) *n.* A small wooden vessel having one stave projecting above the rim for a handle; also, a pitcher. [? Dim. of dial. E *pig* a crock]

pig·gish (pig′ish) *adj.* Like a pig; greedy; dirty; selfish. **— pig′gish·ly** *adv.* **— pig′gish·ness** *n.*

pig·gy (pig′ē) *n.* A little pig. Also **pig′gie.**

pig·gy-back (pig′ē·bak′) *adv.* Pick-a-back.

pig·gy-back·ing (pig′ē·bak′ing) *n. U.S.* Transshipment of loaded truck bodies on railway flat cars.

pig-head·ed (pig′hed′id) *adj.* Stupidly obstinate. **— pig′-head′ed·ly** *adv.* **— pig′-head′ed·ness** *n.*

pig iron Crude iron poured from a blast furnace into variously shaped molds or pigs of sand or the like.

pig·ment (pig′mənt) *n.* **1** Any of a class of finely powdered, insoluble coloring matters suitable for making paints, enamels, oil colors, etc. **2** Any substance that imparts color to animal or vegetable tissues, as chlorophyll. **3** Any substance used for coloring. [<L *pigmentum* < *pingere* paint. Doublet of PIMENTO.]

pig·men·tar·y (pig′mən·ter′ē) *adj.* Producing, secreting, or containing pigment, as a cell.

pig·men·ta·tion (pig′mən·tā′shən) *n.* **1** Coloration. **2** *Biol.* Deposition of pigment by cells.

pig·my (pig′mē) *adj.* Diminutive; dwarfish: also **pig·me′an.** **—** *n. pl.* **·mies** A dwarf. Also spelled **pygmy.** [<L *pygmaeus* <Gk. *pygmaios* dwarfish, a dwarf < *pygmē,* the length from elbow to knuckles]

Pig·my (pig′mē) See PYGMY.

pig·nut (pig′nut′) *n.* **1** The fruit of a species of hickory (*Carya glabra*) common in the United States. **2** The tree. **3** St. Anthony's nut. **4** The Old World earthnut.

pig·skin (pig′skin′) *n.* **1** The skin of a pig. **2** Something made of this skin, as a saddle or football.

pig-stick·ing (pig′stik′ing) *n.* The hunting of wild boars with spears.

pig·sty (pig′stī′) *n. pl.* **·sties** A sty or pen for pigs.

pig·tail (pig′tāl′) *n.* **1** The tail of a pig. **2** *Colloq.* A cue or plait of hair; also, one who wears a cue. **3** A twist of tobacco. **— pig′tailed′** *adj.*

pi·ka (pī′kə) *n.* A small mammal (family *Ochotonidae*) mostly of North America and Asia; a tailless hare. *Ochotona princeps* is the little chief hare or cony of the Rocky Mountains. ◆ Homophone: *pica.* [<Tungusic *peeka*]

pike¹ (pīk) *n.* A long pole having a metal spearhead, used by foot soldiers in medieval warfare. **—** *v.t.* **piked, pik·ing** To run through or kill with a pike. [<MF *pique* < *piquer* pierce <OF *pic* PIKE⁵]

pike² (pīk) *n.* **1** A slender, long-snouted, voracious, spiny-finned food fish (family *Esocidae*), widely distributed in fresh waters of Europe, Asia, and America. **2** Some other fish resembling it, as the garpike. [Appar. short for *pikefish* <PIKE⁵ + FISH; with ref. to its pointed snout]

PIKE HEADS

pike³ (pīk) *n.* **1** A turnpike road. **2** A tollbar. **—** *v.i. Slang* **piked, pik·ing** To go in haste. [Short for TURNPIKE]

pike⁴ (pīk) *n.* A mountain peak or pointed hill. [? <ON *pik* a pointed mountain. Akin to OE *pīc* PIKE⁵.]

pike⁵ (pīk) *n.* A spike or sharp point, as the central spike in a buckler. [OE *piic, pic,* prob. <OF, ? <L *picus* a woodpecker]

pike·man (pīk′mən) *n. pl.* **·men** (-mən) One of a body of soldiers armed with pikes, as in the

16th and 17th centuries. [<PIKE¹ + MAN]

pike perch A pikelike percoid fish, as the walleyed pike or sauger.

Pike's Peak A mountain in central Colorado; 14,110 feet.

pike·staff (pīk'staf', -stäf') *n.* *pl.* **·staves** (-stāvz') **1** A piked staff, formerly carried by pilgrims, travelers, etc. **2** The wooden handle of a pike. [<PIKE⁵ + STAFF¹]

pi·lar (pī'lər) *adj.* Of, pertaining to, or covered with hair. [<NL *pilaris* <L *pilus* hair]

pi·las·ter (pi·las'tər) *n.* *Archit.* A rectangular column, with capital and base, engaged in a wall. [<F *pilastre* <Ital. *pilastro* <L *pila* a column]

Pi·late (pī'lət), **Pontius** A Roman official; procurator of Judea A.D. 26–36?; delivered Jesus to be crucified.

Pi·la·tus (pē·lä'tŏŏs), **Mount** A peak 7 miles SW of the Lake of Lucerne, Switzerland; 6,998 feet.

pi·lau (pi·lou', -lô') *n.* An Oriental dish of boiled rice, raisins, spice, and some kind of meat or fowl. Also **pi·laf** (pi·läf'), **pi·laff', pi·law** (pi·lô'). [<Turkish *pilâw* <Persian *pilāw*]

PILASTER

pil·chard (pil'chərd) *n.* **1** A herringlike food fish (*Sardinia pilchardus*) of European Atlantic and Mediterranean waters, the sardine. **2** The California sardine. Also *Obs.* **pil'cher, pil'cherd.** [Earlier *pilcher,* ? <Scand. Cf. Norw. *pilk* an artificial bait.]

pile¹ (pīl) *n.* **1** A quantity of anything gathered or thrown together in one place; a heap. **2** *Electr.* Any of various devices for generating an electric current by means of superimposed plates of different metals in contact with a suitable liquid: a galvanic *pile,* voltaic *pile.* **3** A funeral pyre. **4** A large accumulation or number of something. **5** A massive building or group of buildings. **6** A pyramid. **7** A great quantity, especially of money; a fortune. **8** *Physics* A reactor. — **to make one's pile** To amass a fortune. — *v.* **piled, pil·ing** *v.t.* **1** To make a heap or pile of: often with *up.* **2** To cover or burden with a pile or piles: to *pile* a plate with food. — *v.i.* **3** To form a heap or pile. **4** To proceed or go in a confused mass: with *in, on, off, out,* etc. See synonyms under HEAP. — **to pile up** **1** To accumulate. **2** *Colloq.* To reduce or become reduced to a pile or wreck. [<OF <L *pila* a pillar, pier]

pile² (pīl) *n.* **1** A heavy timber pointed at one end, forced into the earth to form a foundation; a spile. **2** An arrowhead. **3** Formerly, a pointed stake. **4** *Obs.* A javelin. — *v.t.* **piled, pil·ing** **1** To drive piles into, as for a foundation. **2** To furnish or strengthen with piles. [OE *pil* a dart, pointed stake <L *pilum* a dart, javelin]

pile³ (pīl) *n.* **1** Hair collectively; fur. **2** The manner in which hair is laid or set. **3** A fiber, as of cotton. **4** The cut or uncut loops which make the surface of certain fabrics, as velvets, plushes, corduroys, etc. [<L *pilus* hair] — **piled** *adj.*

CROSS-SECTION OF PILE WEAVE

pi·le·ous (pī'lē·əs) See PILOSE.

piles (pīlz) *n.pl.* Hemorrhoids. [<LL *pilae,* pl. of *pila* a ball]

pile·wort (pīl'wûrt') *n.* **1** An Old World crowfoot (*Ranunculus ficaria*), producing tuberous roots and yellow flowers. **2** An American species of fireweed (*Erechtites hieracifolia*). **3** The princess feather. [Trans. of Med. L *ficaria* <L *ficus* a fig, piles; with ref. to the reputed ability to cure hemorrhoids]

pil·fer (pil'fər) *v.t.* & *v.i.* To steal in small quantities. See synonyms under STEAL. [<OF *pelfrer* rob <*pelfre* plunder] — **pil'fer·er** *n.*

pil·fer·age (pil'fər·ij) *n.* **1** The act of pilfering, or such acts collectively. **2** Goods lost through pilfering.

pil·fer·ing (pil'fər·ing) *n.* Petty thieving.

pil·grim (pil'grim) *n.* **1** One who journeys to some sacred place from religious motives. **2** Any wanderer or wayfarer. [ME *pelegrim* <OF *pelegrin* (assumed) <L *peregrinus.* See PEREGRINE.]

Pil·grim (pil'grim) *n.* One of the English Puritans who founded Plymouth Colony in 1620.

pil·grim·age (pil'grə·mij) *n.* **1** A long journey, especially one made to a shrine or sacred place. **2** Man's life as a journey through the world. See synonyms under JOURNEY. [<OF *pelrimage, pelerinage* <*peleriner* go as a pilgrim <*pelerin,* var. of *pelegrin* PILGRIM]

Pilgrim Fathers The founders of Plymouth Colony, Massachusetts, in 1620.

Pilgrim's Progress A religious allegory in two parts (1678 and 1684) by John Bunyan, depicting the life journey of Christian from the City of Destruction to the Celestial City.

pili– *combining form* Hair; related to the hair. [<L *pilus* a hair]

pil·ing (pī'ling) *n.* **1** Piles collectively. **2** A structure formed of piles. **3** The act or process of driving piles. [<PILE²]

pill¹ (pil) *n.* **1** A medicinal substance put up in a pellet, convenient for swallowing whole. **2** Hence, a disagreeable necessity. **3** *Slang* A person difficult to bear with; a bore. **4** *Colloq.* A baseball or a golf ball. — **the pill** or **the Pill** Any of various oral contraceptive drugs in tablet form, taken by women. — *v.t.* **1** To form into pills. **2** To dose with pills. **3** *Slang* To blackball. [Prob. <MDu. *pille* <L *pilula,* dim. of *pila* a ball]

pill² (pil) *v.t.* & *v.i. Obs.* **1** To pillage. **2** To peel off; scale. **3** To make or become bald. [OE *pylian,* prob. <L *pilare* make hairless, plunder; infl. by OF *piller* plunder and OF *peler* peel]

pil·lage (pil'ij) *n.* **1** The act of pillaging; open robbery, as in war. **2** Spoil; booty. See synonyms under PLUNDER. — *v.* **·laged, ·lag·ing** *v.t.* **1** To strip of money or property by open violence, especially in war; loot. **2** To take as loot. — *v.i.* **3** To take plunder. See synonyms under STEAL. [<OF <*piller* plunder <LL *pillare,* var. of L *pilare* plunder] — **pil'-lag·er** *n.*

pil·lar (pil'ər) *n.* **1** A firm, upright, separate support; column or shaft. **2** Something resembling a column in form or use. **3** One who or that which strongly supports a work or cause. — **from pillar to post** From one thing to another; from one predicament to another; hither and thither. — *v.t.* To adorn or support with or as with pillars. [<OF *piler* <LL *pilare* <L *pila* a pillar]

pill·box (pil'boks') *n.* **1** A small box for pills. **2** A small, round, concrete emplacement for a machine-gun, antitank gun, etc.

pill bug A small isopod crustacean (family *Armadillidiidae*), found under logs, etc.: so called because they roll into tiny pills when disturbed.

pil·lion (pil'yən) *n.* A pad on a horse's back, behind the saddle, on which a second person may ride: formerly used by women. [Appar. <Scottish Gaelic *pillean,* dim. of *pell* a cushion <L *pellis* a skin]

pil·li·winks (pil'ē·wingks) *n.* An old instrument of torture; thumbscrew: also called *pinnywinkle.* [ME *pyrwykes*; origin unknown]

pil·lo·ry (pil'ər·ē) *n.* *pl.* **·ries** Formerly, a framework in which an offender was fastened by the neck and wrists and exposed to public scorn. — *v.t.* **·ried, ·ry·ing** **1** To set in the pillory. **2** To hold up to public scorn or ridicule. [<OF *pellori, pilori,* appar. <dial. OF (Gascon) *espilori* <Provençal *espitlori,* ? <Catalan *espitlera* a little window, peephole]

pil·low (pil'ō) *n.* **1** A case of cloth stuffed with some yielding material, or inflated with air, used as a support for the head, as in sleeping. **2** Any body rest. **3** One of various supporting blocks or devices, as a journal bearing. — *v.t.* **1** To rest on or as on a pillow. **2** To act as a pillow for. — *v.i.* **3** To recline as on a pillow. [OE *pyle, pylu,* ult. <L *pulvinus* a cushion] — **pil'-low·y** *adj.*

PILLORY

pillow block *Mech.* A block or other device resting on firm foundations and designed to support a journal or shaft; a bearing.

pillow case A covering drawn over a pillow. Also **pillow slip.**

pillow lace Bobbin lace.

pillow sham A decorative covering or spread to be laid over a bed pillow.

pi·lose (pī'lōs) *adj.* Covered with hair, especially with fine and soft hair: also spelled *pileous, pilous.* [<L *pilosus* <*pilus* hair] — **pi·los·i·ty** (pī·los'ə·tē) *n.*

pi·lot (pī'lət) *n.* **1** A helmsman; specifically, one duly qualified by training and licensed by law to conduct vessels in and out of port. **2** Any guide. **3** One who controls the operation of an airplane, dirigible, or other aircraft. **4** The cowcatcher of a locomotive. — *v.t.* **1** To act as the pilot of; steer. **2** To guide or conduct through difficulties, intricate dealings, etc. **3** To serve as pilot on, over, or upon. [<MF *pillotte, pilot* <Ital. *pilota,* ? <*pedota,* ult. <Gk. *pēda* a rudder, orig. pl. of *pēdon* an oar]

pi·lot·age (pī'lət·ij) *n.* **1** The act of piloting a vessel or aircraft. **2** The fee for such service.

pilot balloon A small balloon sent up before dispatching a large one, to show the direction and velocity of the wind.

pilot bread Ship biscuit. Also **pilot biscuit.**

pilot cell A selected cell of a storage battery whose voltage, temperature, etc., are considered to indicate the condition of the whole battery.

pilot engine A locomotive preceding and piloting a train.

pilot fish **1** An oceanic fish (*Naucrates ductor*), often seen in warm latitudes in company with sharks; the banded pilot. **2** A whitefish of North American waters (*Prosopium quadrilaterale*).

pilot house An enclosed structure, usually in the forward part of a vessel, containing the steering wheel and compass.

pi·lot·ing (pī'lət·ing) *n.* **1** The occupation of a pilot. **2** The branch of navigation that has to do with steering vessels in and out of ports or along coasts, or finding a ship's position by knowledge of landmarks, buoys, etc.

pilot lamp A small electric light used to indicate whether the power in a given circuit, motor, control unit, etc., is on or off.

pilot light A minute jet of gas kept burning beside an ordinary burner, for igniting the latter as soon as the gas is turned on. Also **pilot burner.**

pilot parachute See under PARACHUTE.

pilot plant An experimental assembly of various units of machinery and other equipment for the purpose of testing the value of new production methods.

pilot snake **1** The copperhead. **2** A black snake (*Elaphe obsoleta*) of the eastern United States.

pilot whale The blackfish.

pi·lous (pī'ləs) See PILOSE.

Piltdown man Eoanthropus.

pil·ule (pil'yŏŏl) *n.* A little pill; pellet. [<L *pilula* <PILL¹.] — **pil'u·lar** *adj.*

pi·men·to (pi·men'tō) *n.* *pl.* **·tos** **1** The dried, unripe, aromatic berries of the West Indian allspice; also, the spice made from these berries, or the tree producing them. **2** The Spanish paprika or the sweet pepper from which it is made; pimiento. [<Sp. *pimienta* pepper <Med. L *pigmentum* a spiced drink, spice <L, a paint, juice of plants. Doublet of PIGMENT.]

pimento cheese Cheese made from processed Neufchâtel curds, cream cheese, or cheddar with pimientos added.

pi·mien·to (pi·myen'tō) *n.* *pl.* **·tos** The sweet pepper, of which the fruit is used as a relish and for stuffing olives. [<Sp. <*pimienta.* See PIMENTO.]

pim·o·la (pi·mō'lə) *n.* An olive which has been stuffed with a sweet red pepper. [<PIM(IENTO) + OL(IVE) + -a]

pimp (pimp) *n.* A pander. — *v.i.* To act as a pimp. [Prob. <F *pimpant* seductive, ppr. of *pimper* dress elegantly; ult. origin uncertain]

pim·per·nel (pim'pər·nel) *n.* A plant of the primrose family (genus *Anagallis*) usually with red flowers, as the common **scarlet pimpernel** (*A. arvensis*). [<OF *pimprenele, piprenelle* <Med. L *pipinella,* ? <a dim. of L *bipennis* two-winged <*bi-* two + *penna* a feather]

pim·ple (pim'pəl) *n.* **1** A minute swelling or small elevation of the skin, with an inflamed base. **2** Any small protuberance. [ME *pimplis* pimples. Cf. OE *pipligende* afflicted with herpes.] — **pim'pled, pim'ply** *adj.*

pin (pin) *n.* **1** A short stiff piece of wire, with a sharp point and a round, usually flattened head, used in fastening together parts of clothing, sheets of paper, etc. **2** An ornamental device mounted on a pin or having a pin as a clasp: often serving to fasten parts of the dress in addition to its use as a decoration: frequently a badge. **3** A peg or bar of metal or

PINS OF VARIOUS TYPES

a. Greek.   *f.* Safety pin.
b. Roman.   *g.* Hairpins.
c. Early French.   *h.* Round–headed.
d. Russian.   *i.* Hatpin.
e. Scandinavian.

wood used for a fastening or support, as the thole of a boat, the bolt of a door, a peg serving to stop a hole or to fasten two beams together, or to keep a wheel from slipping from an axle, or one of the pegs to which the strings of a musical instrument are fastened. **4** Anything like a pin, as a hairpin or clothespin. **5** *Usually pl.* A wooden club turned in long, oval, or cylindrical shape, set up as a mark or target in various bowling or ball–throwing games; a skittle. **6** *pl. Colloq.* Legs. **7** A belaying–pin; a rolling pin; a thole pin. **8** The merest trifle. **9** The cylindrical part of a key forward of the stem that enters the lock. **10** *Obs.* A peg showing the center of a target. — *v.t.* **pinned, pin·ning 1** To fasten with a pin or pins. **2** To transfix with a pin, spear, etc. **3** To seize and hold firmly: to *pin* an opponent against a wall. **4** To force (someone) to make a definite statement, abide by a promise, etc.: usually with *down.* [OE *pinn* a peg, ? ult. <L *pinna* a point, pinnacle]

pi·ña (pē′nyä) *n.* **1** The pineapple. **2** A sweet drink prepared from the pineapple. Also **pi′na** (-nä). [<Sp., a pineapple, orig., a pine cone <L *pinea.* See PINEAL.]

Pi·na·ce·ae (pī·nā′si·ē) *n. pl.* A family of widely distributed coniferous trees and shrubs having needlelike leaves and bearing hard, woody cones, as the pine, cedar, redwood, larch, hemlock, etc.; the pine family. [<NL <L *pinus* a pine] — **pi·na′ceous** (-shəs) *adj.*

PINACEAE

a. White pine. *b.* Red spruce. *c.* Hemlock.

piña cloth A material for scarfs, handkerchiefs, etc., made from the fibers of the pineapple leaf. It is soft, transparent, and pale yellow.

pin·a·fore (pin′ə·fôr, -fōr) *n.* A sleeveless apron, especially for protecting the front of a child's dress. [<PIN + AFORE]

pi·nang (pi·nang′) *n.* The betel palm, or its fruit. [<Malay, an areca, a betel nut]

pin·ball (pin′bôl′) *n.* A game in which a ball, spring–propelled to the top of an inclined board, contacts in its descent any of various numbered pins, holes, etc., the contacts so made comprising the player's score.

pince–nez (pans′nā′, pins′-, *Fr.* paṅs·nā′) *n.* Eyeglasses held upon the nose by a spring. [<F, lit., pinch–nose <*pincer* pinch + *nez* nose]

pin·cers (pin′sərz) *n. pl. (sometimes construed as singular)* **1** An instrument having two handles and a pair of jaws working on a pivot, used for holding objects. **2** *Zool.* A nipperlike organ, as the chela of a lobster. Also spelled *pinchers.* [ME *pinsours,* appar. <AF *pincer,* OF *pincier* pinch]

pinch (pinch) *v.t.* **1** To squeeze between two hard edges, or surfaces, a finger and thumb, etc. **2** To bind or compress painfully: This collar *pinches* my neck. **3** To affect with pain or distress: The cold *pinched* his fingers. **4** To contract or make thin, as from cold or hunger. **5** To reduce in means; distress, as for lack of money; straiten. **6** To move by means of a pinchbar. **7** *Slang* To capture or arrest. **8** *Slang* To steal. **9** *Naut.* To sail (a vessel) close–hauled. — *v.i.* **10** To squeeze; hurt. **11** To be careful with money; be stingy. **12** *Mining* Of veins, to become narrow; also, to disappear: with *out.* **— to pinch pennies** To be economical or stingy. — *n.* **1** The act of pinching. **2** Painful pressure of any kind. **3** A case of emergency. **4** So much of a loose substance as can be taken between the finger and thumb. **5** A narrow or tapering section on a vein of rock or fissure of earth. **6** A pinchbar. **7** *Slang* A theft. **8** *Slang* An arrest or raid. [<AF *pincher,* OF *pincier,* prob. <Gmc.] — **pinch′er** *n.*

pinch·bar (pinch′bär′) *n.* A crowbar with a short projection and a heel or fulcrum at the end so that it may be used to pry forward heavy objects.

pinch·beck (pinch′bek) *n.* **1** An alloy of copper, zinc, and tin, forming a cheap imitation of gold. **2** Anything spurious or pretentious. — *adj.* Made of pinchbeck; spurious. [after Christopher *Pinchbeck,* 1670?–1732, English inventor]

pinch·bug (pinch′bug′) *n.* A stag beetle.

pinch·ers (pin′chərz) See PINCERS.

pinch–hit (pinch′hit′) *v.i.* **–hit, –hit·ting 1** In baseball, to go to bat in place of a regular player, as when a hit is needed. **2** *Colloq.* To substitute for another in an emergency. [<PINCH an emergency + HIT]

pine[1] (pīn) *n.* **1** A cone–bearing tree (genus *Pinus*) having needle–shaped evergreen leaves growing in clusters; especially, the American **white pine** (*P. strobus*), the long–leaved southern **Georgia** or **yellow pine** (*P. palustris*), the **loblolly** or **oldfield pine** (*P. taeda*), the **red pine** (*P. resinosa*) of the eastern United States, and a **nut pine** (*P. cembroides*) of the Pacific States. **2** The wood of any pine tree. **3** *Colloq.* The pineapple. [Fusion of OE *pīn* and OF *pin,* both <L *pinus* a pine tree]

pine[2] (pīn) *v.* **pined, pin·ing** *v.i.* **1** To grow thin or weak with longing, grief, etc. **2** To have great desire or longing: with *for.* — *v.t.* **3** *Archaic* To grieve for. [OE *pīnian* torment, ult. <L *poena* a punishment]

pin·e·al (pin′ē·əl) *adj.* **1** Shaped like a pine cone: the *pineal* body. **2** Pertaining to the pineal body. [<F *pinéal* <L *pinea* a pine cone <*pinus* a pine tree]

pineal body *Anat.* A small, reddish–gray, vascular, conical body of rudimentary glandular structure found behind the third ventricle of the brain, embraced by its two peduncles, but not a part of the brain, and having no known function. Also **pineal gland.**

pineal eye *Biol.* The pineal body which in certain reptiles emerges as an eyelike structure.

pine·ap·ple (pīn′ap′əl) *n.* **1** A tropical American plant (*Ananas comosus*) having spiny, recurved leaves and a cone–shaped fruit consisting of the inflorescence clustering densely around a fleshy axis tipped with a rosette of spiked leaves. **2** The edible fruit of this plant. **3** *Slang* A bomb. **4** In dec-

PINEAPPLE
Fruit in crown of plant.

oration, an ornament frequently in the form of a finial resembling either a pineapple or a pine cone: used especially on furniture. [OE *pīnæppel* a pine cone <*pīn* a pine + *æppel* an apple; so called because the fruit resembles a pine cone]

pine needle The needle–shaped leaf of the pine tree.

pin·er·y (pī′nər·ē) *n. pl.* **·er·ies 1** A hothouse for growing pineapples. **2** A pine forest, especially one where lumbering is carried on. **3** A large collection of pine trees.

pine·sap (pīn′sap′) *n.* A low, fragrant plant (*Hypopitys latisquama*), whitish or reddish, parasitic on roots or living on dead vegetable material: native of the north temperate zone. [<PINE[1] + SAP[2]]

pin feather *Ornithol.* **1** A rudimentary feather. **2** A feather just beginning to grow through the skin.

pin·fish (pin′fish′) *n. pl.* **·fish** or **·fish·es** A sparoid fish (*Lagodon rhomboides*) common on the Atlantic coast of the southern United States.

pin·fold (pin′fōld′) *n.* A pound for stray animals; especially, a cattle pound. — *v.t.* To shut in a pinfold; confine. [OE *pundfald.* See POUND[2], FOLD[2]; infl. in form by *pyndan* enclose.]

ping (ping) *n.* **1** The sound made by a bullet striking an object. **2** The sound made by a bullet as it cuts the air. — *v.i.* To make this sound. [Imit.]

Ping–pong (ping′pong′, -pông′) *n.* The game of table tennis: a trade name.

pin·grass (pin′gras′, -gräs′) *n.* Alfileria.

pin·guid (ping′gwid) *adj.* Containing or resembling oil or fat; unctuous. [<L *pinguis* fat] — **pin·guid′i·ty** *n.*

pin·head (pin′hed′) *n.* **1** A small minnow. **2** *Slang* A brainless or stupid person; a fool.

pin head 1 The head of a pin. **2** Any small object. — **pin–head·ed** (pin′hed′id) *adj.*

pinhole camera A camera of simple design and construction, usually home–made, consisting of a box having a small aperture functioning as a lens at one end, the image being projected on the film at the other end.

pin·ion (pin′yən) *n.* **1** The wing of a bird. **2** A feather; a quill. **3** The outer segment of a bird's wing, bearing the flight feathers. **4** The anterior border of the wing of an insect. — *v.t.* **1** To cut off one pinion or bind the wings of (a bird) so as to prevent flight. **2** To cut or bind (the wings) of a bird. **3** To bind or hold the arms of (someone) so as to render helpless. **4** To shackle; confine. [<OF *pignon* a streamer, a feather <L *penna, pinna* a feather] — **pin′ioned** *adj.*

pink[1] (pingk) *n.* **1** A pale hue of crimson. **2** A flower of any one of several garden plants (genus *Dianthus*) with narrow grasslike leaves and fragrant flowers, as the common pink (*D. plumarius*). **3** The plant itself. **4** A flower or plant of some other genus, including the **moss pink. 5** A type of excellence or perfection: the *pink* of politeness. **6** A red-colored coat; especially, a scarlet hunting coat; also, one who wears such a coat. **7** *Often cap.* A person who holds somewhat radical economic and political opinions. **— in the pink** *Colloq.* In the best possible condition or degree. — *adj.* **1** Having the color called pink; pale rose. **2** Fashionably dainty. [? Short for obs. *pink eye* a small eye (< obs. *pink* small + EYE), trans. of F *oeillet* a pink (flower), orig. dim. of *oeil* an eye]

pink[2] (pingk) *v.t.* **1** To prick or stab with a pointed weapon. **2** To decorate, as cloth or leather, with a pattern of holes. **3** To cut or finish the edges of (cloth) with a notched pattern, as to prevent raveling or for decoration. **4** *Brit.* To adorn; deck. [ME *pynken,* prob. a nasalized form of *pikken* PICK[1]]

PINKED SEAM
(*v.t.* def. 3)

pink³ (pingk) *n. Naut.* **1** A sailing vessel with a narrow stern, originally flat-bottomed with bulging sides. **2** A small sailing vessel with a narrow stern, used for fishing and coasting: also called *pink-stern:* also **pink′ie, pink′y.** [< MDu. *pincke* a small sea-going ship; ult. origin unknown]

pink-eye (pingk′ī) *n.* **1** A febrile contagious keratitis of sheep, with inflammation of the mucous membrane lining the eyelids. **2** *Pathol.* An acute, contagious conjunctivitis in man, marked by redness of the eyeball. **3** A variety of white potato having pink eyes or buds.

pink-ie (pingk′ē) *n. U.S.* The little finger. Also **pink′y.** [Dim. of obs. *pink* small]

pink-ing (pingk′ing) *n.* **1** The act or process of pinking fabrics. **2** The act of stabbing, as with a rapier. [Orig. ppr. of PINK²]

pinking shears Shears with serrated blades for scalloping the edges of fabrics.

pink knot See CAT-EYE.

pink rhododendron The California rosebay (*Rhododendron macrophyllum*) common on the Pacific coast: State flower of Washington.

pink-root (pingk′rōōt′, -rŏŏt′) *n.* **1** The root of any of several perennial herbs (genus *Spigelia*), especially the **Carolina pinkroot** with bright red flowers (*S. marilandica*), a well-known anthelminthic: also called *wormroot.* **2** A plant yielding this root.

pinkster flower An American shrub (*Azalea nudiflora* or *Rhododendron nudiflorum*) with showy, flesh-colored to dark-red flowers, blooming at Whitsuntide: also spelled *pinxter flower.* Also called *wild honeysuckle.*

pink-y (pingk′ē) *adj.* Small and blinking: said of eyes. [Prob. < obs. *pink* small]

pin money An allowance for incidentals; formerly, an allowance made by a husband to his wife for her personal expenses.

pin-nace (pin′is) *n. Naut.* **1** A six- or eight-oared boat, carried by men-of-war; any ship's boat. **2** Formerly, a small schooner-rigged vessel used as a tender, scout, etc. [< OF *pinasse* < Ital. *pinaccia*, prob. < L *pinus* a pine]

pin-na-cle (pin′ə-kəl) *n.* **1** A small turret or tall ornament, as on a parapet. **2** Anything resembling a pinnacle; a high or topmost point, as a mountain peak; summit. — *v.t.* **·cled, ·cling** **1** To place on or as on a pinnacle. **2** To furnish with a pinnacle; crown. See synonyms under SUMMIT. [< OF *pinacle* < LL *pinnaculum*, dim. of L *pinna* a wing, a pinnacle]

pin-nate (pin′āt, -it) *adj.* **1** *Bot.* Having the shape or arrangement of a feather: said of compound leaves or leaflets arranged on each side of a common axis: when terminated by a single leaf, *odd-pinnate*; when lacking a terminal leaf, *abruptly pinnate.* **2** Having winglike parts or appendages. Also **pin′nat-ed.** [< L *pinnatus* feathered < *pinna* a feather, wing] — **pin′nate-ly** *adv.* — **pin-na′tion** *n.*

pin-ner (pin′ər) *n.* **1** One who fastens with pins. **2** A pinafore. **3** A headdress with long flaps at each side, worn by women in the 18th century; also, a cloth band for a dress.

pinni- combining form *Zool.* Web; fin: *pinniped.* [< L *pinna* feather]

pin-ni-grade (pin′ə-grād) *adj. Biol.* Moving by means of flippers, as a seal. [< PINNI- + L *gradi* walk]

pin-ni-ped (pin′ə-ped) *adj.* **1** Having finlike locomotive organs. **2** Of or pertaining to a suborder (*Pinnipedia*) of aquatic carnivorous mammals, the seals and walruses. — *n.* A fin-footed carnivorous mammal, as a walrus, seal, etc. [< NL *Pinnipes, -pedis* < L, wing-footed < *pinna* a wing, fin + *pes, pedis* a foot] — **pin′ni-pe′di-an** (-pē′dē-ən) *adj. & n.*

pin-ny-win-kle (pin′ē-wing′kəl) See PILLIWINKS.

pin oak An oak tree (*Quercus palustris*) common in the eastern United States, forming a conical head with long pendulous branches, the leaves of which turn a bright scarlet in autumn.

pi-noch-le (pē′nuk-əl, -nok-) *n.* A card game resembling bezique played with a double pack of 48 cards, ranking as follows: ace, ten, king, queen, jack, and nine: also spelled *penuchle, penuckle.* Also **pi′noc·le.** — **check pinochle** A four-handed, partnership card game, based on bridge and pinochle, with a double-scoring system of points and checks. [Origin unknown]

pi-no-le (pi-nō′lā) *n. SW U.S.* A meal ground from corn, mesquite beans, or other plant seeds, and roasted. [< Am. Sp. < Nahuatl *pinolli*]

pi-ñon (pin′yən, pēn′yon; *Sp.* pē-nyon′) *n.* **1** The edible seed of any of various pines of the Pacific coast of the United States; especially, the New Mexican piñon (*Pinus cembroides*). **2** The tree: also spelled *pinyon.* [< Sp., a pine nut < L *pinea* a pine cone < *pinus* a pine tree]

pin-point (pin′point′) *n.* **1** The point of a pin. **2** Something extremely small. — *v.t.* To locate or define precisely: to *pinpoint* a target, argument, etc.

pins and needles A tingling or prickling sensation in some part of the body, as the fingers or toes; paresthesia. — **on pins and needles** Uneasy; nervous.

pin-scher (pin′shər) *n.* One of a breed of large, short-haired dogs, originally bred in Germany, usually black, brown, or gray-blue, with rust markings: usually called **Doberman pinscher,** after its first breeder. [< G, a terrier]

DOBERMAN PINSCHER

pin-son (pin′sən) *n.* A thin, light shoe or slipper. [? < OF *pinçon* toe-piece of a horseshoe, dim. of *pince* toe of a hoof]

pint (pint) *n.* **1** A dry and liquid measure of capacity equal to half a quart or (liquids only) four gills or 0.832 British pint. **2** *Scot.* A measure equivalent to three English pints. [< OF *pinte,* prob. < MDu.; ult. origin uncertain]

Pin-ta (pin′tə, *Sp.* pēn′tä) *n.* One of the. three ships of Columbus on his initial voyage to America.

pin-tail (pin′tāl′) *n.* **1** A duck (*Dafila acuta*) of the northern hemisphere, the male of which has a long, sharp tail. **2** A sharp-tailed grouse (*Pediaecetes phasianellus*) of northern North America. **3** The ruddy duck.

pin-tle (pin′təl) *n.* A pin upon which anything pivots, as one of the metal braces or hooks upon which a rudder swings, the pin of a hinge of a gunlock, etc. [OE *pintel* penis. Akin to PIN.]

pin-to (pin′tō) *adj. SW U.S.* Piebald; pied, as an animal. — *n. pl.* **·tos** **1** A pied animal: said especially of a horse, or Western pony. **2** A kind of spotted bean (*Phaseolus vulgaris*) of the southwestern United States: also **pinto bean.** [< Am. Sp. < Sp., lit., painted, ult. < L *pingere* paint]

Pintsch gas (pinch) A fuel and illuminating gas made by the destructive distillation of oil. [after Richard *Pintsch,* 1840–1919, German inventor]

pin-up (pin′up′) *U.S. Colloq. n.* That which is affixed to a board or wall for scrutiny or perusal; specifically, a clipping or photograph, usually of an attractive young woman. — *adj.* Designating a photograph, clipping, or drawing used in this manner, or a person who models such a picture: She's my *pin-up* girl.

pin-weed (pin′wēd′) *n.* Any one of various perennial herbs (genus *Lechea*), with very small greenish or purplish flowers.

pin-wheel (pin′hwēl′) *n.* **1** A firework that revolves when ignited, forming a wheel of fire. **2** A wheel with pins set in its face in place of cogs on the periphery. **3** A child's toy resembling a windmill, made of colored paper, revolving on a pin attached to a stick.

pin-worm (pin′wûrm′) *n.* A nematode worm (*Enterobius vermicularis*) parasitic in the lower intestines and rectum of man, especially of children.

pinx-ter flower (pingk′stər) See PINKSTER FLOWER.

Pin-yin (pin′yin′) *n.* The official Chinese system of transliterating Chinese into Roman alphabet characters. [< Chinese]

pin-yon (pin′yən) See PIÑON.

pinyon jay A small, short-tailed, uncrested corvine bird (*Cyanocephalus cyanocephalus*) of the Rocky Mountain region having a dark plumage and a long, sharp bill.

pi-on (pī′on) *n.* A pi-meson. [< PI + (MES)ON]

pi-o-neer (pī′ə-nir′) *n.* **1** One of the first explorers, settlers, or colonists of a new country or region. **2** One of the first investigators or developers in a new field of research, enterprise, etc. **3** *Mil.* An engineer who goes before the main body building roads, bridges, etc. See synonyms under HERALD. — *v.t.* **1** To prepare (a way, etc.). **2** To prepare the way for. **3** To be a pioneer of. — *v.i.* **4** To act as a pioneer. [< F *pionnier* < OF *paonier,* orig. a foot soldier < *peon, pion*]

pi-ous (pī′əs) *adj.* **1** Actuated by reverence for a Supreme Being; religious; godly. **2** Marked by a reverential spirit. **3** Practiced in the name of religion. **4** *Obs.* Exhibiting filial respect and affection; filial. See synonyms under GOOD, MORAL. [< L *pius* dutiful, devout] — **pi′ous-ly** *adv.* — **pi′ous-ness** *n.*

pip¹ (pip) *n.* **1** The seed of an apple, orange, etc. **2** *Slang* An admirable person or thing. [Short for PIPPIN]

pip² (pip) *n.* **1** A spot, as on a playing card, domino, or die. **2** Any of the small buds of the lily-of-the-valley. **3** Any dormant rootstock of several flowering plants, as anemones and peonies. **4** One of the diamond-shaped sections on the rind of a pineapple. **5** A sharp sound or luminous signal produced mechanically or electronically, as in radar. [< earlier *peep;* origin unknown]

pip³ (pip) *v.* **pipped, pip-ping** *v.t.* To break through (the shell), as a chick in the egg. — *v.i.* To peep; chirp. [Prob. var. of PEEP¹]

pip⁴ (pip) *n.* **1** A contagious disease of fowls in which mucus forms in the throat or a scale on the tongue. **2** *Slang* A mild human ailment: used humorously; also, a grouch; an ill temper. [< MDu. *pippe* < LL *pipita* < L *pituita* mucus, the pip]

pip-age (pī′pij) *n.* **1** Pipes collectively; a system of pipes. **2** The carriage of oil, gas, water, etc., through pipes.

pi-pal (pē′pəl) *n.* The sacred fig tree of India (*Ficus religiosa*): also spelled *peepul.* [< Hind. *pipal* < Skt. *pippala*]

pipe (pip) *n.* **1** An apparatus, usually a small bowl with a hollow stem, for smoking tobacco, opium, or other narcotic. **2** Enough tobacco to fill the bowl of a pipe. **3** A long conducting passage of wood, metal, tiling, etc., for conveying a fluid. **4** A single tube or long, hollow case: when part of a line of piping, often called a *piece of pipe.* **5** Any hollow or tubular part in an animal or plant body. **6** *Music* **a** A tubular wind instrument, such as the flageolet. **b** *pl.* The bagpipe. **7** The voice; also, a bird's note or call. **8** A large cask for wine; also, a liquid measure of half a tun. **9** *Metall.* A conical cavity in the head of a steel ingot, made by an escape of gas while the metal was cooling. **10** *Slang* An easy college course. **11** A boatswain's whistle. **12** *Mining* An elongated, usually vertical or highly inclined body of mineral or rich ore: also called a *chimney.* — *v.* **piped, pip-ing** *v.i.* **1** To play on a pipe. **2** To make a shrill sound. **3** *Naut.* To signal the crew by means of a boatswain's pipe. **4** *Metall.* To form conical cavities in hardening, as ingots. — *v.t.* **5** To convey by or as by means of pipes. **6** To provide with pipes. **7** To play, as a tune, on a pipe. **8** To utter shrilly or in a high key. **9** *Naut.* To call to order by means of a boatswain's pipe. **10** To lead, entice, or bring by piping. **11** To trim, as a dress, with piping. — **to pipe down** *Slang* To become silent; stop talking or making noise. — **to pipe up** **1** To start playing or singing: *Pipe up* the band! **2** To speak out, especially in a shrill voice. [OE *pipe,* ult. < L *pipare* cheep. Doublet of FIFE.]

pipe clay A white clay used for pottery, especially pipes, and, formerly, for whitening military accouterments: also called *terra alba.*

pipe dream Any wish, plan, or groundless hope; a daydream.

pipe-fish (pīp′fish′) *n. pl.* **·fish** or **·fish-es** **1** One of a family (*Syngnathidae*) of slender marine and fresh-water fishes having a straight, tubelike snout and bodies enclosed in a series of bony rings. **2** A sea horse.

pipe-fit-ter (pīp′fit′ər) *n.* One who joins pipes together; a plumber.

pipe-line (pīp′lin′) *n.* **1** A line of pipe, as for the transmission of water, oil, etc. **2** A channel for the transmission of information, usually private or secret. — *v.t.* **1** To convey by pipeline. **2** To furnish with a pipeline.

pipe of peace The calumet.

pipe organ An organ having pipes: distinguished from a *reed organ.*

pip·er (pī′pər) *n.* **1** One who lays pipes. **2** One who plays upon a pipe, especially a bagpipe.

pipe stem 1 The stem of a tobacco pipe. **2** *pl.* Thin skinny legs. —**pipe-stem** (pīp′stem′) *adj.*

pipe·stone (pīp′stōn′) *n.* An indurated red clay much valued by the American Indians for making tobacco pipes.

pi·pette (pī·pet′, pi-) *n.* **1** A small tube, often graduated, for removing small portions of a fluid. **2** A funnel-like can used in applying liquid decoration. Also **pi·pet′.** [< F, dim. of *pipe* pipe]

pip·ing (pī′ping) *adj.* **1** Playing on the pipe. **2** Hissing or sizzling: *piping* hot. **3** Having a shrill sound. **4** Characterized by peaceful rather than martial music. —*n.* **1** The act of one who pipes. **2** The music of pipes; hence, a wailing or whistling sound. **3** A system of pipes, as for drainage. **4** A narrow strip of cloth folded on the bias, used for trimming dresses. **5** A cordlike decoration of icing on a cake.

pip·it (pip′it) *n.* **1** One of various lark-like singing birds (genus *Anthus*) widely distributed in North America; especially, the common American pipit (*A. spindetta*); a titlark. **2** The Missouri skylark (*A. spraguei*): also called *Sprague's pipit.* [Prob. imit.]

AMERICAN PIPIT
(About 6 inches long)

pip·kin (pip′kin) *n.* **1** A small earthenware jar. **2** A piggin. [? Dim. of PIPE]

pip·pin (pip′in) *n.* **1** An apple of many varieties. **2** A seed; pip. **3** *Slang* An admirable person or thing. [< OF *pepin* seed of a fruit; origin uncertain]

pip-squeak (pip′skwēk′) *n.* **1** A petty and contemptible person or thing. **2** A small, insignificant person. [Orig. imit. name for a small German high-velocity shell employed in World War I]

pip·y (pī′pē) *adj.* **pip·i·er, pip·i·est 1** Pipelike; tubular; containing pipes. **2** Piping; thin and shrill, or reedlike, in sound.

pi·quant (pē′kənt) *adj.* **1** Having an agreeably pungent or tart taste. **2** Interesting; tart; racy; also, charmingly lively. **3** *Obs.* Stinging; sharp. [< F, orig. ppr. of *piquer* sting] —**pi′quan·cy** *n.* —**pi′quant·ly** *adv.*

pique¹ (pēk) *n.* A feeling of irritation or resentment. —*v.t.* **piqued, pi·quing 1** To excite resentment in. **2** To stimulate or arouse; provoke. **3** To pride (oneself): with *on* or *upon.* ◆ Homophones: *peak, peek.* [< MF < *piquer* sting, prick]

Synonyms (noun): displeasure, grudge, irritation, offense, resentment, umbrage. *Pique* signifies primarily a prick or a sting, as of a nettle; the word denotes a sudden feeling of mingled pain and anger, usually transient, arising from some neglect or *offense*, real or imaginary. *Umbrage* is a deeper and more persistent *displeasure* at being overshadowed or subjected to any treatment that one deems unworthy of oneself. *Resentment* rests on more solid grounds, and is deep and persistent. See ANGER. *Antonyms:* approval, complacency, contentment, delight, gratification, pleasure, satisfaction.

Synonyms (verb): affront, annoy, chafe, displease, fret, goad, irritate, nettle, offend, pain, provoke, rouse, stimulate, sting, stir, urge, vex, wound. See ANGER.

pique² (pēk) *n.* In piquet, the scoring of 30 points in one hand before the other side scores at all. —*v.t.* To win a pique from. ◆ Homophones: *peak, peek.* [< F *pic* a mountain peak]

pi·qué (pē·kā′) *n.* A fabric of cotton, rayon, or silk, with raised cord or welts, called wales, running lengthwise in the fabric. [< F, lit., quilted, orig. pp. of *piquer* prick, backstitch]

pi·ra·cy (pī′rə·sē) *n. pl.* ·**cies 1** Robbery on the high seas. **2** The unauthorized publication, reproduction, or use of another's in-

vention, idea, or literary creation. [< Med. L *piratia* < Gk. *peirateia* < *peiratēs* a pirate]

pi·ra·gua (pi·rä′gwə) *n.* **1** A dug-out canoe. **2** A flat-bottomed boat with two masts: used in the Caribbean Sea. Also called *pirogue.* [< Sp. < Cariban, a dug-out]

pi·ra·nha (pi·rä′nyə) *n.* A caribe. Also **pi·ra′ya** (-rä′yä). [< Pg. (Brazilian) < Tupian, toothed fish < *piro* a fish + *sainha* a tooth]

pi·rate (pī′rit) *n.* **1** A rover and robber on the high seas. **2** A vessel engaged in piracy. **3** A person who appropriates without right the work of another. See synonyms under ROBBER. —*v.t. & v.i.* ·**rat·ed,** ·**rat·ing 1** To practice or commit piracy (upon). **2** To publish or appropriate (the work, ideas, etc., of another) wrongfully or illegally; plagiarize. [< L *peirates* < Gk. *peiratēs* < *peiraein* attack] —**pi·rat′ic** (pī·rat′ik) or ·**i·cal** *adj.* —**pi·rat′i·cal·ly** *adv.*

pirn (pûrn) *n. Scot.* **1** A small spindle. **2** Yarn on a shuttle. **3** A spinning-wheel bobbin. **4** A fishing-rod reel.

pi·rogue (pi·rōg′) *n.* A piragua. [< F < Cariban *piragua*]

pi·rou·ette (pir′ŏŏ·et′) *n.* A rapid whirling upon the toes in dancing. —*v.i.* ·**et·ted,** ·**et·ting** To make a pirouette. [< F, lit., a spinning top, prob. < dial. F *piroue* a top; ult. origin uncertain]

Pi·sa (pē′zə, *Ital.* pē′sä) A city on the Arno river in north central Italy; celebrated for its Leaning Tower. —**Pi′san** *adj. & n.*

pis·ca·ry (pis′kər·ē) *n. pl.* ·**ries 1** *Law* The right of fishing in waters that belong to another: now usually in the phrase **common of piscary.** **2** A fishing place; fishery. [< Med. L *piscaria* fishing rights, orig. neut. pl. of L *piscarius* of fishing < *piscis* a fish]

pis·ca·tol·o·gy (pis′kə·tol′ə·jē) *n.* The science of fishing. [< L *piscatus*, pp. of *piscari* fish + -LOGY]

pis·ca·tor (pis·kā′tər) *n.* An angler; fisherman. [< L]

pis·ca·to·ri·al (pis′kə·tôr′ē·əl, -tō′rē-) *adj.* **1** Pertaining to fishes or fishing. **2** Engaged in fishing. Also **pis′ca·to′ry.** [< L *piscatorius* < *piscator* a fisherman < *piscatus*, pp. of *piscari* fish] —**pis′ca·to′ri·al·ly** *adv.*

Pis·ces (pis′ēz, pī′sēz) *n. pl.* **1** A class of vertebrates: the true fishes. **2** The twelfth sign of the zodiac. See ZODIAC. **3** *Astron.* A zodiacal constellation south of Pegasus and Andromeda; the Fish or Fishes. See CONSTELLATION. [< L, pl. of *piscis* a fish]

pisci- *combining form* Fish; of or related to fish; piscivorous. Also, before vowels, **pisc-.** [< L *piscis* a fish]

pis·ci·cul·ture (pis′i·kul′chər) *n.* The hatching and rearing of fish. —**pis′ci·cul′tur·al** *adj.* —**pis′ci·cul′tur·ist** *n.*

pis·ci·na (pi·sī′nə, -sē′-) *n. pl.* ·**nae** (-nē) *Eccl.* A stone basin with a drain in which the priest washes the chalice after administering communion. [< Med. L < L, lit., a fish pond, basin < *piscis* fish] —**pis·ci·nal** (pis′ə·nəl) *adj.*

pis·cine (pis′īn, -in) *adj.* Of, pertaining to, or resembling a fish or fishes. [< L *piscis* a fish + -INE¹]

pis·civ·o·rous (pi·siv′ər·əs) *adj.* Feeding or subsisting on fish.

Pis·gah (piz′gə), **Mount** A mountain in Jordan, NE of the Dead Sea: in the Old Testament, the peak from which Moses beheld the Promised Land; highest peak, Mount Nebo.

pish (pish) *interj.* An exclamation of contempt. —*v.t. & v.i.* To use this exclamation (to).

pi·si·form (pī′sə·fôrm) *adj.* **1** Shaped like a pea. **2** *Anat.* Pertaining to a pea-shaped bone on the inner or ulnar side of the carpus. [< NL *pisiformis* < L *pisum* a pea + *forma* form]

pis·mire (pis′mīr) *n.* An ant. [ME *pissemyre* < *pisse* urine + *myre, mire* an ant; with ref. to urinous smell of an anthill]

pi·so·lite (pī′sə·līt) *n.* A coarse concretionary limestone, composed of globules with a distinct pisiform structure. [< NL *pisolithus* < Gk. *pisos* a pea + *lithos* a stone] —**pi′so·lit′ic** (-lit′ik) *adj.*

piss (pis) *n.* Urine. [< v.] —*v.i.* To urinate. —*v.t.* To discharge as or with the urine. [< OF *pissier*; prob. orig. imit.]

Pis·sar·ro (pē·sà·rō′), **Camille**, 1831?–1903, French painter.

pis·ta·chi·o (pis·tä′shē·ō, -tash′ē·ō) *n. pl.* ·**chi·os 1** The edible nut of a small tree (genus *Pistacia*) of western Asia and the Levant. **2** The tree. **3** The flavor produced by, or a delicacy flavored with the pistachio nut. **4** A delicate shade of green, the color of the pistachio nut. Also **pis·tache′** (-täsh′). [< Ital. *pistacchio* < L *pistacium* < Gk. *pistakion* < *pistakē* a pistachio tree, prob. < OPersian *pistah* a pistachio nut]

pis·til (pis′til) *n. Bot.* The seed-bearing organ of flowering plants, composed of the ovary, with its contained ovules, and the stigma, usually with a style. [< F < L *pistillum* a pestle]

pis·tol (pis′təl) *n.* A small firearm having a stock to fit the hand, and a short barrel: now either the revolver or automatic type fired from one hand. —*v.t.* ·**toled** or ·**tolled,** ·**tol·ing** or ·**tol·ling** To shoot with a pistol. [< F *pistole* < Ital. *pistola,* prob. ult. < PISTOIA]

pis·to·leer (pis′tə·lir′) *n.* One who fires a pistol; formerly, a soldier carrying a pistol. Also **pis′to·lier′.**

pis·ton (pis′tən) *n.* **1** *Mech.* A disk fitted to slide in a cylinder, as in a steam engine, and connected with a rod for receiving the pressure of or exerting pressure upon a fluid in the cylinder. **2** A valve in a wind instrument for altering the pitch of tones. [< F < Ital. *pistone* a piston, var. of *pestone* a large pestle < *pestare* pound < LL *pistare,* freq. of L *pinsere* pound]

STEAM-ENGINE PISTON
a. Piston. *b.* Cylinder.
c. Piston rod.

piston ring *Mech.* An adjustable ring, usually of cast iron, fitted within a groove on the piston body and designed to prevent leakage of the fluid by expansion against the cylinder wall.

piston rod *Mech.* A rod attached to a piston at one end and to a cross-head or crankpin at the other: used to impart motion.

pit¹ (pit) *n.* **1** A natural or artificial cavity in the ground, especially when relatively wide and deep. **2** A pitfall for snaring animals; snare. **3** An abyss so deep that one cannot return from it, as the grave. **4** Hell. **5** Great distress or trouble. **6** The main floor of the auditorium of a theater, especially, in Great Britain, that portion under the first balcony; also, that part of the audience occupying this portion of the theater. Compare ORCHESTRA, PARQUET. **7** An enclosed space in which animals trained for combat are pitted against each other. **8** Any natural cavity or depression in the body: the *armpit,* the *pit* of the stomach. **9** An indention like that made by a smallpox pustule; any slight depression or excavation. **10** A thin spot in the cell walls of some plants. **11** That part of the floor of an exchange where a special line of trading is done: the wheat *pit.* **12** A mining excavation, or the shaft of a mine. —*v.* **pit·ted, pit·ting** *v.t.* **1** To mark with dents, pits, or hollows. **2** To put, bury, or store in a pit. **3** To match as antagonists; set in opposition. —*v.i.* **4** To become marked with pits. [OE *pytt* < L *puteus* a well]

pit² (pit) *n.* The kernel of certain fruits, as the plum. —*v.t.* **pit·ted, pit·ting** To remove pits from, as fruits. [< Du. < MDu. *pitte* kernel, pith. Akin to PITH.]

pi·ta (pē′tə) *n.* **1** The fiber of the century plant and other allied species of *Agave:* used for making paper, cordage, etc. **2** The plant yielding the fiber. **3** The fiber obtained from several kinds of yucca. [< Sp. < Quechua, a fine thread made from vegetable fiber]

pit-a-pat (pit′ə·pat′) *v.i.* ·**pat·ted,** ·**pat·ting** To move or sound with a succession of light, quick steps or pulsations. —*n.* A tapping or succession of taps, steps, or similar sounds. —*adv.* With a rapid succession of light steps, beats or taps; flutteringly. Also spelled *pitty-pat.* [Imit.]

Pit·cairn Island (pit′kârn) A British colony in

the South Pacific, settled in 1790 by mutineers of the British ship *Bounty*; 2 square miles; with dependencies 18.5 square miles.

pitch[1] (pich) *n.* **1** A thick, viscous, dark substance obtained by boiling down tar from the residues of distilled turpentine, etc. used in coating seams. **2** Any of a class of hydrocarbon residues obtained from the refining of fats, oils, and greases: linseed *pitch*, cottonseed *pitch*, etc. **3** The resinous sap of pines. **4** Bitumen or asphaltum, especially when unrefined. — *v.t.* To smear, cover, or treat with or as with pitch. [OE *pic* < L *pix, picis* pitch]

pitch[2] (pich) *v.t.* **1** To erect or set up (a tent, camp, etc.). **2** To throw or hurl; toss; fling. **3** To set the level, angle, degree, etc., of. **4** To put in a definite place or position. **5** To set in order; arrange: obsolete except in *pitched battle*. **6** In baseball, to deliver (the ball) to the batter. **7** *Music* To set the pitch or key of. **8** In card games, to determine or announce (the trump suit) by leading a card of that suit. — *v.i.* **9** To fall or plunge forward or headlong. **10** To lurch. **11** To rise and fall alternately at the bow and stern, as a ship: to *pitch* and roll. **12** To incline downward; slope. **13** To encamp; settle. **14** To decide, especially at random: with *on* or *upon*. **15** In baseball, to deliver the ball to the batter; act as pitcher. — **to pitch in** *Colloq.* To start vigorously. — **to pitch into** To attack; assail. — *n.* **1** Point or degree of elevation or depression; especially, the extreme top or bottom point; hence, the ultimate reach. **2** The degree of descent of a declivity; also, a descent, slope, or inclination to the horizon. **3** In building, the inclination of a roof. **4** *Aeron.* **a** An angular displacement about an axis parallel to the lateral axis of an aircraft. **b** The distance an aircraft advances along its flight path for one revolution of the propeller. **5** *Mech.* **a** The amount of advance of a screw thread in a single turn. **b** The distance between two corresponding points on the teeth of a gearwheel. **6** *Physics* The dominant frequency of a sound wave perceived by the ear, ranging from a low tone of about 20 cycles per second to a maximum high approaching 30,000 cycles. **7** *Music* The acuteness or gravity of all the tones of a given instrument with reference to some standard. The pitch of an instrument is expressed by the vibrations per second of some one of its notes, generally middle C, treble C, or the A between them. The high pitch, known as **concert pitch**, has about 450 vibrations for middle A. In 1859 a commission of French musicians and scientists determined the pitch of A′ as 435 (true C″ 522, equal temperament C″ 517) which is known as **French, international,** or **low pitch.** The present standard or **philharmonic pitch** has 440 vibrations for middle A. **8** In games, the act of pitching; a throw; specifically, in baseball, the delivery of the ball by the pitcher; also, the place of pitching or the distance pitched. **9** *Geol.* The inclination or dip of a rock stratum or vein of ore. **10** The act of dipping or plunging downward; the pitching of a ship: correlative of *scend*. **11** A game of cards; seven-up. **12** A location or station for a vender, on a sidewalk, etc. **13** A short, steep stretch of a mountain climb. **14** An attempt to sell or persuade: to make a *pitch*. — **auction pitch** A variety of the game of pitch in which the privilege of pitching is sold at auction by the player entitled to it. — **full pitch** In cricket, bowled to hit the wicket before touching the ground. [ME *picchen*; origin uncertain]

pitch–black (pich′blak′) *adj.* Intensely black; as dark as pitch.

pitch·blende (pich′blend′) *n.* A black or brown uranium oxide with a luster resembling that of pitch: the chief source of uranium and radium. See URANINITE. [< G *pechblende* < *pech* pitch[1] + *blende* blende]

pitch–dark (pich′därk′) *adj.* Very dark; as black as pitch.

pitch·er[1] (pich′ər) *n.* One who pitches; specifically, in baseball, the player who delivers the ball to the batter. [< PITCH[2]]

pitch·er[2] (pich′ər) *n.* **1** A vessel with a spout and a handle, used for holding liquids to be poured out. **2** A peculiar form of leaf suggestive of a pitcher. [< OF *pichier, picher* < LL *bicarium* a jug < Gk. *bikos* a wine jar]

pitch·er·plant (pich′ər·plant′, -plänt′) *n.* A plant having leaves arranged in the form of pitchers, urns, or goblets which often function as insect traps; especially, the common American pitcher plant (genus *Sarracenia*).

pitch·fork (pich′fôrk′) *n.* **1** A large fork with which to handle hay, straw, etc. **2** A tuning fork. — *v.t.* To lift and throw with or as with a pitchfork. [< PITCH[2] + FORK]

AMERICAN PITCHERPLANT
(From 6 inches to 4 feet tall according to variety)

pitch·out (pich′out′) *n.* **1** In baseball, a pitch deliberately wide of the strike zone so that the catcher has a better chance to throw out a runner trying to steal a base. **2** In football, a lateral pass, usu. from the quarterback to a running back.

pit·e·ous (pit′ē·əs) *adj.* **1** Exciting pity, sorrow, or sympathy. **2** *Archaic* Affected with or feeling pity. See synonyms under PITIFUL. [< OF *pitos, piteus,* ult. < L *pietas, -tatis.* See PIETY.] — **pit′e·ous·ly** *adv.* — **pit′e·ous·ness** *n.*

pit·fall (pit′fôl′) *n.* A pit contrived for entrapping wild beast or men; hence, any hidden danger. [ME *pitfalle, putfal* < PIT[1] + *falle, fal* < OE *fealle* a trap]

pith (pith) *n.* **1** *Bot.* The cylinder of soft, spongy tissue in the center of the stems and branches of certain plants. **2** *Ornithol.* The spongy substance of the interior of the shaft of a feather. **3** The marrow of bones or of the spinal cord. **4** Concentrated force; vigor; substance; hence, the essential part; quintessence; gist. — *v.t.* **1** To destroy the central nervous system or spinal cord of, as a frog, by passing a wire through the vertebral column. **2** To remove the pith from, as a plant stem. **3** To kill (cattle) by severing the spinal cord. [OE *pitha.* Akin to PIT[2].]

Pith·e·can·thro·pus (pith′ə·kan′thrə·pəs, -kan·thrō′pəs) *n. pl.* **·pi** (-pī) *n. Paleontol.* The type genus of two small–brained Pleistocene primates transitional between ape and man: *P. erectus,* represented by a fossil cranium, femur, and other fragments discovered near Trinil, central Java, in 1891; and *P. robustus,* based upon skeletal remains found in the same area about 1938. Also called *Java man, Trinil man.* [< NL < Gk. *pithēkos* an ape + *anthrōpos* a man] — **pith′e·can′thro·pine** (-pēn, -pin) *adj.*

pith·y (pith′ē) *adj.* **pith·i·er, pith·i·est** **1** Consisting of pith; like pith. **2** Forcible; effective. See synonyms under TERSE. — **pith′i·ness** *n.*

pit·i·a·ble (pit′ē·ə·bəl) *adj.* **1** Arousing or meriting pity or compassion; pathetic. **2** Insignificant; contemptible. See synonyms under PITIFUL. [< OF *piteable* < *piteer, pitier* pity < *pitie* PITY] — **pit′i·a·ble·ness** *n.* — **pit′i·a·bly** *adj.*

pit·i·ful (pit′i·fəl) *adj.* **1** Calling forth pity or compassion; miserable; wretched. **2** Calling forth a feeling of contempt, because of littleness, meanness, or the like; contemptible. **3** *Archaic* Full of pity; compassionate. — **pit′i·ful·ly** *adv.* — **pit′i·ful·ness** *n.*

Synonyms: abject, base, contemptible, despicable, lamentable, miserable, mournful, moving, paltry, pathetic, piteous, pitiable, sorrowful, touching, woeful, wretched. *Pitiful* originally signified full of pity; as, "the Lord is very *pitiful* and of tender mercy"; but this usage is now archaic, and the meaning in question is appropriated by such words as merciful and compassionate. *Pitiful* and *pitiable* now refer to what may be deserving of pity, *pitiful* being used chiefly for that which is merely an object of thought, *pitiable* for that which is brought directly before the senses; as, a *pitiful* story; a *pitiable* condition. Since pity, however, always implies weakness or inferiority in that which is pitied, *pitiful* and *pitiable* are often used, by an easy transition, for what might awaken pity, but does awaken contempt; as, a *pitiful* excuse; He presented a *pitiable* appearance. *Piteous* is now rarely used in its earlier sense of feeling pity,

but in its derived sense applies to what really excites the emotion; as, a *piteous* cry. See MERCIFUL. Compare HUMANE, MERCY, PITY. *Antonyms:* august, beneficent, commanding, dignified, exalted, glorious, grand, great, lofty, mighty, noble, superb.

pit·i·less (pit′i·lis) *adj.* Having no pity or mercy; ruthless. See synonyms under IMPLACABLE. — **pit′i·less·ly** *adv.* — **pit′i·less·ness** *n.*

pi·ton (pi·ton′, *Fr.* pē·tôṅ′) *n.* An iron spike, with an eye or ring in one end, that can be driven into a crack in rock or ice: used in mountaineering as a hold or support for hand or foot, or fork arabiner and rope. See KARABINER. [< F, ? < Sp., a little horn; ult. origin unknown]

PITON WITH KARABINER AND PITON HAMMER

piton hammer A short–handled hammer for driving in pitons.

Pi·tot tube (pē·tō′) **1** A device for measuring the velocity of a fluid flow, consisting of a narrow bent tube with its opening against the current and its upper portion above the surface of the fluid. **2** Any similar device for measuring pressure or pressure differences. [after Henri *Pitot,* 1695–1771, French hydraulic engineer]

pit·tance (pit′əns) *n.* **1** A small allowance of money. **2** Any meager income or remuneration. [< OF *pitance,* orig. a monk's food allotment, pity < Med. L *pietantia* < L *pietas, -tatis.* See PIETY.]

pit·ter-pat·ter (pit′ər·pat′ər) *n.* A rapid series of light sounds or taps. [Varied reduplication of PATTER[1]]

pit·ty-pat (pit′ē·pat′) See PIT–A–PAT.

pi·tu·i·tar·y (pi·tōō′ə·ter′ē, -tyōō′-) *adj.* **1** Secreting mucus; mucous. **2** Of or pertaining to the pituitary gland. — *n. pl.* **·tar·ies** **1** The pituitary gland. **2** Any of various preparations made from extracts of the anterior or posterior lobe of the pituitary gland. [< L *pituitarius* pertaining to mucus < *pituita* phlegm < *sputus,* pp. of *spuere* spit]

pituitary gland *Anat.* A small, rounded body at the base of the brain in vertebrates, consisting of an anterior and a posterior lobe, which secretes hormones having a wide range of effects upon the growth, metabolism, and other functions of the body; the hypophysis cerebri. Also **pituitary body.**

pi·tu·i·tous (pi·tōō′ə·təs, -tyōō′-) *adj.* Containing, due to, resembling, or discharging mucus. [< L *pituitosus* < *pituita* phlegm. See PITUITARY.]

pit viper See under VIPER.

pit·y (pit′ē) *n. pl.* **pit·ies** **1** The feeling of grief or pain awakened by the misfortunes or sorrows of others; compassion. **2** That which arouses compassion; misfortune. — *v.t. & v.i.* **pit·ied, pit·y·ing** To feel compassion or pity (for). [< OF *pitet, pitié* < LL *pietas, -tatis.* Doublet of PIETY.] — **pit′i·er** *n.* — **pit′y·ing·ly** *adv.*

Synonyms (noun): commiseration, compassion, condolence, mercy, sympathy, tenderness. *Pity* is a feeling of grief or pain aroused by the weakness, misfortunes, or distresses of others, joined with a desire to help or relieve. *Sympathy* (feeling or suffering with) implies some degree of equality, kindred, or union; *pity* is for what is weak or unfortunate; hence *pity* is often resented where *sympathy* would be welcomed. We have *sympathy* with one in joy or grief, in pleasure or pain, *pity* only for those in suffering or need. *Pity* may be only in the mind, but *mercy* does something for those who are its objects. *Compassion,* like *pity,* is exercised only with respect to the suffering or unfortunate, but combines with the tenderness of *pity* the dignity of *sympathy* and the active quality of *mercy. Commiseration* is as tender as *compassion,* but more remote and hopeless; we have *commiseration* for sufferers whom we cannot reach or cannot relieve. *Condolence* is the expression of *sympathy.* See MERCY. *Antonyms:* barbarity, brutality, cruelty, ferocity, hard–heartedness, harshness, inhumanity, mercilessness, pitilessness, rigor, ruthlessness, severity, sternness, truculence.

Pi·us (pī′əs) **1** A masculine personal name. **2** Appellation of 12 popes. [< L, dutiful, devout]

—**Pius II**, 1405–64, real name Aeneas Silvius Piccolomini, pope 1458–64; diplomat, humanist, and historian.

—**Pius IV**, 1499–1565, real name Giovanni Angelo Medici, pope 1559–65; issued the *Tridentine Creed.*

—**Pius V**, 1504–72, real name Michele Ghislieri, pope 1566–72; promoted the Counter Reformation.

—**Pius VII**, 1742–1823, real name Luigi Barnaba Chiaramonti, pope 1800–23; crowned Napoleon I as emperor of France, was later imprisoned by him at Fontainebleau.

—**Pius IX**, 1792–1878, real name Giovanni Maria Mastai–Ferretti, pope 1846–78; lost temporal power to Victor Emmanuel, 1870.

—**Pius X**, 1835–1914, real name Giuseppi Melchiore Sarto, pope 1903–14; canonized in 1954.

—**Pius XI**, 1857–1939, real name Achille Ratti, pope 1922–39; signed treaty with Mussolini establishing Vatican City as a sovereign state and regulating the position of the Roman Catholic Church in Italy.

—**Pius XII**, 1876–1958, real name Eugenio Pacelli, pope 1939–58.

Pi·ute (pī·ōōt′) See PAIUTE.

piv·ot (piv′ət) *n.* **1** *Mech.* Something, typically a pin or a short shaft, upon which a related part turns, oscillates, or rotates: often a short cylindrical bearing, fixed on only one end, for

PIVOT
a. Bearing point.

carrying or rotating a swinging part. **2** Something on which an important matter hinges or turns; a turning point. **3** *Mil.* In wheeling troops, the soldier, officer, or point upon which the line turns. — *v.t.* To place on, attach by, or provide with a pivot or pivots. — *v.i.* To turn on a pivot; swing. [< F. Cf. Ital. *pivolo* a peg.] — **piv′ot·al** *adj.* — **piv′ot·al·ly** *adv.*

pix·i·la·ted (pik′sə·lā′tid) *adj.* **1** Affected by the pixies; mentally unbalanced; fey. **2** *Slang* Drunk. [Prob. alter. of dial. E (Cornish) *pixyled* bewitched]

pix·y (pik′sē) *n. pl.* **pix·ies** A fairy or elf: also spelled **pyxie.** Also **pix′ie.** [< dial. E *pixey, pisky* < Scand. Cf. dial. Sw. *pysk, pyske* a small fairy, dwarf.]

Pi·zar·ro (pi·zär′ō, *Sp.* pē·thär′rō), Francisco, 1475?–1541, Spanish conqueror of Peru.

piz·azz (pə·zaz′) *Slang. n.* A quality of irresistible and exciting charm. Also, **piz·zazz.**

piz·za (pēt′sə, *Ital.* pēt′tsä) *n.* An Italian food comprising a doughy crust overlaid with a mixture of cheese, tomatoes, spices, etc., and baked. [< Ital., ? < dial. Ital. *picca* a pie]

piz·ze·ri·a (pēt′sə·rē′ə) *n.* A place where pizzas are prepared, sold, and eaten. [< Ital. < *pizza* a pizza]

pla·ca·ble (plā′kə·bəl, plak′ə-) *adj.* Appeasable; yielding; forgiving. [< OF < L *placabilis* < *placare* appease] — **pla′ca·bil′i·ty, pla′ca·ble·ness** *n.* — **pla′ca·bly** *adv.*

plac·ard (plak′ärd) *n.* **1** A printed or written paper publicly displayed, as a proclamation or poster. **2** A tag or plate bearing the owner's name.

—**pla·card** (plə·kärd′, plak′ärd) *v.t.* **1** To announce by means of placards. **2** To post placards on or in. **3** To display as a placard. [< OF *plackart* < *plaquier* plaster, lay flat < M Flemish *placken* bedaub, plaster]

pla·cate (plā′kāt, plak′āt) *v.t.* **·cat·ed, ·cat·ing** To appease the anger of; pacify. [< L *placatus,* pp. of *placare* appease] — **pla′cat·er** *n.*

pla·ca·to·ry (plā′kə·tôr′ē, -tō′rē, plak′ə-) *adj.* Tending or intended to placate or appease. Also **pla′ca·tive.**

place (plās) *n.* **1** A particular point or portion of space, especially that part of space occupied by or belonging to a thing under consideration; a definite locality or location. **2** An occupied situation or building; space regarded as abode or quarters; an estate, town, military post, etc. **3** An open space or square in a city; also, a court or street. **4** Position in relative order; hence, station in life; degree; rank. **5** An office, appointment, or employment; also, rank, position, or station. **6** Room for

occupation; hence, reception; welcome; lodgment; seat. **7** Room; stead; hence, precedence: One thing gives *place* to another. **8** A particular passage, as in a book; a text; a topic. **9** The second position among the first three competitors in a horse race. **10** The position of a figure in relation to the other figures of a given arithmetical series or group. —**in place 1** In its natural position; also, in a suitable place, situation, job, etc. **2** In situ. —**in place of** In substitution or exchange for; instead of. —**out of place** Removed from or not situated in the natural or appropriate place, order, or relation; unsuitable; inappropriate; ill-timed. —**to go places** *Slang* To rise to success. —**to take place** To happen; occur. — *v.* **placed, plac·ing** *v.t.* **1** To put in a particular place or position. **2** To put or arrange in a particular relation or sequence. **3** To find a place, situation, home, etc., for. **4** To appoint to a post or office. **5** To identify; classify: Historians *place* him in the time of Nero. **6** To arrange for the satisfaction, handling, or disposition of: to *place* an order for a garbage truck. **7** To bestow or entrust: I *place* my life in your hands. **8** To invest, as funds. **9** To emphasize or resonate tones of (the voice) consciously, as in singing or speaking. — *v.i.* **10** In racing, to finish among the first three contestants; especially, to finish second. See synonyms under PUT, SET. ◆ Homophone: *plaice.* [< OF, *ult.* < L *platea* a wide street < Gk. *plateia (hodos)* < *platys* wide. Doublet of PIAZZA, PLAZA.]

Synonyms (noun): locality, location, part, position, post, room, site, situation, space, spot, station. See SCENE.

pla·ce·bo (plə·sē′bō) *n. pl.* **·bos** or **·boes 1** In the Roman Catholic Church, the opening antiphon of the vespers for the dead. **2** *Med.* Any harmless substance given to humor a patient or as a test in controlled experiments on the effects of drugs. **3** Anything said to flatter or please. [< L *placebo* I shall please < *placere* please]

place·ment (plās′mənt) *n.* **1** The act of placing or the state of being placed. **2** In football, the putting of the ball in position for a place kick from the field; also, the kick itself.

pla·cen·ta (plə·sen′tə) *n. pl.* **·tas** or **·tae** (-tē) **1** *Anat.* In higher mammals, the vascular, spongy organ of interlocking fetal and maternal tissue by which the fetus is nourished in the uterus. **2** *Bot.* The part of the ovary that supports the ovules. [< NL *placenta (uterina)* (uterine) cake < L, a cake < Gk. *plakoeis, -oentos* a flat cake < *plax, plakos* a flat plate] — **pla·cen′tal, plac·en·tar·y** (plas′ən·ter′ē, plə·sen′tər·ē) *adj.*

placer digging The act of obtaining minerals from deposits by washing.

plac·id (plas′id) *adj.* Having a smooth, unruffled surface, as a sheet of still water; unruffled; calm. See synonyms under CALM, PACIFIC. [< L *placidus* pleasing < *placere* please] — **pla·cid·i·ty** (plə·sid′ə·tē), **plac′id·ness** *n.* — **plac′id·ly** *adv.*

plack·et (plak′it) *n.* **1** The opening or slit in the upper part of a petticoat or skirt: also **placket hole. 2** A pocket in a woman's skirt. [? Var. of *placat,* var. of *placard,* in obs. sense of "a breastplate, top of a skirt"]

plac·oid (plak′oid) *adj.* Platelike, as the hard, spiny scales resembling teeth found on sharks and rays. — *n.* A fish having platelike scales; an elasmobranch. [< Gk. *plax, plakos* a flat plate + -OID]

pla·fond (plà·fôn′) *n. Archit.* **1** A flat or arched ceiling, decorated with painting or carving. **2** The under side of a projecting member (cornice, soffit, balcony, etc.); the under face of an architrave between columns, or of a staircase. **3** A painting on a ceiling. [< F < MF *platfond* < *plat* flat + *fond* bottom < L *fundus*]

pla·gia·rism (plā′jə·riz′əm, -jē·ə-) *n.* The act of plagiarizing, or something plagiarized. — **pla′gia·rist** *n.* — **pla′gia·ris′tic** *adj.*

pla·gia·rize (plā′jə·rīz, -jē·ə-) *v.* **·rized, ·riz·ing** *v.t.* **1** To appropriate and pass off as one's own (the writings, ideas, etc., of another). **2** To appropriate and use passages, ideas,

etc., from. — *v.i.* **3** To commit plagiarism. Also *Brit.* **pla′gia·rise.** — **pla′gia·riz′er** *n.*

pla·gia·ry (plā′jər·ē, -jē·ər·ē) *n.* **1** Plagiarism, the act or its result. **2** A plagiarist. [< L *plagiarius* a kidnapper, a plagiarist < L *plagium* a kidnapping < Gk. *plagios* oblique, treacherous]

plagio- *combining form* Oblique; slanting: *plagiotropism.* Also, before vowels, **plagi-.** [< Gk. *plagios* slanting]

plague (plāg) *n.* **1** Anything troublesome or harassing, producing mental distress; affliction. **2** A pestilence or epidemic disease of man or animals, occurring in many forms and usually intensely malignant and contagious: bubonic *plague,* pulmonary *plague.* **3** Any great natural evil or calamity. **4** *Colloq.* Nuisance; bother. See synonyms under ABOMINATION. — *v.t.* **plagued, pla·guing 1** To harass or torment; vex; annoy. **2** To afflict with plague or disaster. [< OF *plage, plague* < LL *plaga* a pestilence < L, a stroke, prob. < dial. Gk. (Doric) *plaga* a stroke < *plag-,* root of *plēssein* strike]

plaid (plad) *adj.* Having a tartan pattern; checkered. — *n.* An oblong woolen scarf of tartan or checkered pattern, worn in the Scottish Highlands as a cloak fastened over one shoulder; also, any fabric of this pattern. [< Scottish Gaelic *plaide* a blanket < *peallaid* a sheepskin < *peall* < L *pellis* a skin] — **plaid′ed** *adj.*

Argyle   Blanket   Tartan   Tattersall

PLAIDS

plain (plān) *adj.* **1** Having no noticeable elevation or depression; flat; smooth. **2** Presenting few difficulties; easy. **3** Clear; understandable; *plain* English; also, straightforward; guileless. **4** Lowly in condition or station; unlearned. **5** Having no conspicuous ornamentation; unadorned; unvariegated; in the case of cloths, not figured or twilled. **6** Homely. **7** Not rich, as food. — *n.* An expanse of level, treeless land; a prairie. ◆ Homophone: *plane.* [< OF < L *planus* flat; *n.,* doublet of PLAN] — **plain′ly** *adv.* — **plain′ness** *n.*

Synonyms (adj.): clear, distinct, explicit, intelligible, perspicuous, straightforward, transparent, unadorned, unambiguous, unequivocal. That is *clear* which offers no impediment to vision—is not dim, dark, or obscure. *Transparent* refers to the medium through which a substance is seen, *clear* to the substance itself, without reference to anything to be seen through it; we speak of a stream as *clear* when we think of the water itself; we speak of it as *transparent* with reference to the ease with which we see objects at the bottom. *Plain* is level to the thought, so that one goes straight on without difficulty or hindrance; as, *plain* language; a *plain* statement; a *clear* explanation. *Perspicuous* is often equivalent to *plain,* but *plain* never wholly loses the meaning of *unadorned,* so that we can say the style is *perspicuous* even if highly ornate, when we could not call it at once ornate and *plain.* See APPARENT, BLANK, CLEAR, EVIDENT, EXPLICIT, HORIZONTAL, LEVEL, MANIFEST, NOTORIOUS, RUSTIC, SMOOTH. *Antonyms:* see synonyms for EQUIVOCAL, OBSCURE.

plain-clothes man (plān′klōz′, -klōthz′) A member of a police force not in uniform; specifically, a detective.

plain-dress (plān′dres′) *n.* A radiotelegraph message carrying the address either in plain text or in a cipher different from that used for the message. Compare CODRESS. [< PLAIN + (AD)DRESS]

plain-laid (plān′lād′) *adj.* Consisting of strands twisted together in the ordinary way: a *plain-laid* rope.

Plains Indian A member of any of the tribes of American Indians formerly inhabiting the Great Plains of North America, belonging variously to the Algonquian, Athapascan, Caddoan, Kiowan, Siouan, and Uto–Aztecan linguistic stocks, but having in common the nomadic culture of the plains and dependence on the buffalo: also called *Buffalo Indian.*

Plains of Abraham See ABRAHAM, PLAINS OF.

plain people *U.S.* The Amish, Mennonites, and Dunkers: so called from their plain dress.

plaint (plānt) *n.* **1** Audible utterance of sorrow or grief; lamentation; a complaint. **2** In English law, a writ setting forth a grievance and asking redress. [<OF *plainte* <Med. L *plancta* <L, pp. fem. of *plangere* lament]

plain text In cryptography, the original text of a message to be converted into or reconverted from a code or cipher cryptogram: also called *clear text.*

plain-tiff (plān'tif) *n.* The party that begins an action at law; the complaining party in an action. [<OF *plaintif, plaintive* plaintive <L *planctus.* See PLAINT.]

plain-tive (plān'tiv) *adj.* Expressing a subdued sadness; mournful. [<OF, fem. of *plaintif*] — **plain'tive-ly** *adv.* — **plain'tive-ness** *n.*

plait (plāt, *Brit.* plat) *v.t.* **1** To braid. **2** To pleat. **3** To make by pleating or braiding. — *n.* **1** A braid, especially of hair. **2** A pleat. [<OF *pleit* <L *plicitum* a folded thing, orig. pp. neut. of *plicare* fold]

plan (plan) *n.* **1** An arrangement of means or steps for the attainment of some object; a scheme; method; design. **2** A drawing showing the proportion and relation of parts, as of a building; any outline sketch; draft. **3** A mode of action. **4** One of a number of hypothetical planes perpendicular to the line of vision in which the size of the pictured object is increased or diminished proportionately to the distance from the eye at which they are interposed. See PERSPECTIVE. See synonyms under DESIGN, IDEA, PROJECT, PURPOSE, SKETCH. — *v.* **planned, plan-ning** *v.t.* **1** To form a scheme or method for doing, achieving, etc. **2** To make a plan of, as a building; design. **3** To have as an intention or purpose. — *v.i.* **4** To make plans. [<OF, a plane (surface), a ground plan <Ital. *plano* <L *planus* flat. Doublet of PLAIN[1], *n.*] — **plan'ner** *n.*

Synonyms (verb): concoct, contrive, design, devise, invent, plot, project, propose, purpose, scheme, sketch. Compare BREW, PROPOSE.

pla-nar (plā'nər) *adj.* Of or pertaining to a plane; lying in one plane; flat. [<L *planaris* <*planum* a plane <*planus* flat]

planch (planch, plänch) *n.* A plank; board. Also **planche.** [<OF *planche* <LL *planca*]

planch-et (plan'chit) *n.* A piece of metal ready to receive an impression. [Dim. of PLANCH, in sense "a flat plate of metal"]

plan-chette (plan-chet', -shet') *n.* **1** A small board, usually resting on a vertical pencil and two casters; believed by some to spell out messages, as on a ouija board, when the fingers are rested lightly upon it, independently of the volition of the persons touching it: used in the investigation of psychic phenomena. [<F, dim. of *planche* a plank]

Planck (plängk), **Max,** 1858–1947, German physicist; developed the quantum theory.

plane[1] (plān) *n.* **1** *Geom.* A surface such that a straight line joining any two of its points lies wholly within the surface. **2** Hence, any flat or uncurved surface. **3** A grade of development; stage; level, as of thought, knowledge, rank, etc. **4** *Aeron.* A supporting surface of an airplane: often used in combination: *monoplane.* **5** An airplane. — *adj.* **1** Lying in a plane; level; flat. **2** Having a flat surface; dealing only with flat surfaces: *plane* geometry. See synonyms under HORIZONTAL, LEVEL, SMOOTH. ◆ Homophone: *plain.* [Var. of PLAIN[2], *n.*; refashioned after L *planus* flat]

plane[2] (plān) *n.* **1** A tool used for smoothing boards or other surfaces of wood. **2** A trowel–like tool for striking off clay that projects above the mold. — *v.* **planed, plan-ing** *v.t.* **1** To make smooth or even with or as with a plane. **2** To remove with or as with a plane. — *v.i.* **3** To use a plane. **4** To do the work of a plane. ◆ Homophone: *plain.* [<MF *plane* <OF *plain* <LL *plana* a plane <*planare* plane <L *planus* flat]

plane[3] (plān) *n.* A plane tree. ◆ Homophone: *plain.* [<OF *plane* <*plasne* <L *platanus* <Gk. *platanos* <*platys* broad; because of its broad leaves]

plane[4] (plān) *v.i.* **planed, plan-ing** **1** To rise partly out of the water, as a power boat when driven at high speed. **2** To glide; soar. **3** To travel by airplane. ◆ Homophone: *plain.* [<F *planer* <*plan* a plane <L *planus* flat]

plan-er (plā'nər) *n.* **1** A machine for planing wood or metal. **2** A smooth wooden block used for leveling a form of type, etc. **3** One who or that which planes. [<PLANE[2]]

plane–sheer (plān'shir') See PLANK–SHEER.

plan-et (plan'it) *n.* **1** *Astron.* One of the non-self-luminous bodies of the solar system revolving around the sun as their center of motion. Those within the Earth's orbit, Mercury and Venus, are called **inferior planets;** those beyond it, the **superior planets,** are Mars, the asteroids or planetoids (known collectively as **minor planets),** Jupiter, Saturn, Uranus, Neptune, and Pluto. **2** In ancient astronomy, one of the seven heavenly bodies (the Sun, Moon, Mercury, Venus, Mars, Jupiter, and Saturn) that have an apparent motion among the fixed stars. **3** One of these bodies considered in relation to its supposed influence on human beings and their affairs. [<OF *planete* <LL *planeta* <Gk. *(asteres) planētai* wandering (stars) <*planaesthai* wander]

plan-et–struck (plan'it-struk') *adj.* Affected by the influence of planets; blasted; moon-struck. Also **plan'et-strick'en** (-strik'ən).

plan-gor-ous (plang'gər-əs) *adj.* Wailing; moaning; lamenting.

pla-ni-cop-ter (pla'ni-kop'tər) *n.* A convertiplane.

pla-ni-form (plā'nə-fôrm, plan'ə-) *adj.* Having the surfaces nearly flat.

plan-i-gale (plan'i-gāl) *n.* A tiny insectivorous marsupial (*Planigali ingrami*) of Australia, the smallest of the marsupials.

pla-nim-e-ter (plə-nim'ə-tər) *n.* An instrument for measuring the area of any plane surface, however irregular, by moving a pointer around its boundary and reading the indications of a scale. [<F *planimètre*] — **pla-ni-met-ric** (plā'nə-met'rik, plan'ə-) or **-ri-cal** *adj.* — **pla-nim'e-try** *n.*

PLANIMETER

plan-ish (plan'ish) *v.t.* To condense, smooth, toughen, or polish, as metal, by hammering,

TABLE OF MAJOR PLANETS

NAME	Symbol	Distance from sun: millions of miles	Mean diameter: miles	Period of side-real revolu-tion	Period of rota-tion	No. of satellites	Mass: Earth con-sidered as 1.	Escape velocity: in miles per second.
Mercury	☿	36	3,000	88 days	88 days?	0	0.0543	2
Venus	♀	67	7,600	225 "	20–30 d.	0	0.8136	6.3
Earth	⊕	93	7,918	365.25 d.	23 h. 56 m.	1	1.0000	6.95
Mars	♂	142	4,200	687 days	24 h. 37 m.	2	0.1069	3.1
Jupiter	♃	483	87,000	12 years	9 h. 50 m.	12	318.35	37.
Saturn	♄	886	72,000	29.5 "	10 h. 14 m	9	95.3	22.
Uranus	♅	1780	29,600	84 "	10 h. 45 m.	5	14.58	13.
Neptune	♆	2790	27,700	165 "	15 h. 48 m.	2	17.26	15.
Pluto	♇	3670	4,000	248 "	?	0	.1?	?

plane-ta-ble (plān'tā'bəl) *n.* A surveying instrument used in mapping in the field. [<PLANE[1] + TABLE]

plan-e-tar-i-um (plan'ə-târ'ē-əm) *n.* *pl.* **-tar-i-ums** or **-tar-i-a** **1** An apparatus for exhibiting the features of the heavens as they exist at any time and for any place on earth, consisting of a suitably mounted projector installed in a room having a circular dome. **2** An apparatus or model representing the planetary system. [<NL <LL *planetarius* PLANETARY]

plan-e-tar-y (plan'ə-ter'ē) *adj.* **1** Of or pertaining to a planet or the planets: the *planetary* bodies. **2** Mundane; terrestrial. **3** Having the character anciently ascribed to the planets; wandering; erratic: a *planetary* career. **4** *Mech.* Pertaining to or noting a type of gearing in which one or more small

PLANETARY GEARING

wheels mesh with the toothed circumference of a larger wheel, around which they revolve, at the same time rotating axially. **5** In astrology, under the influence or domination of some of the planets. [<LL *planetarius* an astrologer <*planeta* PLANET]

plan-et-fall (plan'it-fôl') *n.* The descent of a rocket or artificial satellite to the surface of a planet.

plan-e-toid (plan'ə-toid) *n.* An asteroid. **plan'e-toi'dal** *adj.*

plan-e-tol-o-gy (plan'ə-tol'ə-jē) *n.* The science that treats of the history, composition, and structure of the planets and other natural bodies, as comets, asteroids, etc., in orbit around the sun.

rolling, etc. [<MF *planiss-,* stem of *planir* flatten <*plan* flat <L *planus* flat]

plan-i-sphere (plan'ə-sfir) *n.* A plane projection of the sphere; especially, a polar projection of the heavens on a chart, which shows the stars visible at a given place and time. [<OF *planisphère* <Med. L *planisphaerium* <L *planus* flat + *sphaera* a sphere]

plank (plangk) *n.* **1** A broad piece of sawed timber, thicker than a board. **2** Timber when sawed into planks. **3** Anything that sustains or upholds; a support. **4** One of the principles of a political platform. — **to walk the plank** To walk off a plank projecting from the side of a ship: a method once used by pirates for executing prisoners. — *v.t.* **1** To cover, furnish, or lay with planks. **2** To broil or bake and serve on a plank, as fish. **3** *Colloq.* To put down emphatically or forcibly. **4** *Colloq.* To pay: with *out, down,* etc. [<AF *planke* <LL *planca* a board, slab, prob. <Gk. *plax, plakos* flat]

plank-ton (plangk'tən) *n.* *Biol.* The floating, weakly swimming or drifting plant or animal organic life of the sea, as distinguished from the coastal or the bottom forms: used also of analogous life forms in fresh–water lakes. Compare BENTHOS. [<G <Gk., neut. of *planktos* drifting, wandering <*plazesthai* wander] — **plank-ton-ic** (plangk-ton'ik) *adj.*

plano-[1] *combining form* Roaming; wandering: *planoblast.* Also, before vowels, **plan-.** [<Gk. *planos* wandering]

plano-[2] *combining form* Flat; level; plane: *plano–convex;* also, before vowels, **plan-.** Also **plani-.** [<L *planus* flat]

pla-no-con-cave (plā'nō-kon'kāv) *adj.* Flat or plane on one side and concave on the other. See illustration under LENS. [<PLANO-[2] + CONCAVE]

pla-no-con-vex (plā'nō-kon'veks) *adj.* Flat or plane on one side and convex on the other. See illustration under LENS. [<PLANO-[2] + CONVEX]

plant (plant, plänt) *n.* **1** A living organism belonging to the vegetable, as distinguished from the animal kingdom, having typically rigid cell walls, promoting an indefinite growth of tissue, and characterized by growth from the synthesis of simple, usually inorganic food materials from soil, water, and air or, in some cases, from other organisms. **2** Loosely, one of the smaller forms of vegetable life, in distinction from shrubs and trees. **3** A set of machines, tools, apparatus, etc., necessary to conduct a manufacturing enterprise or other business: a chemical *plant*: often including the buildings and grounds, or, in case of a railroad, the rolling stock, but not including the material or product; hence, the permanent appliances needed for any institution, as a post office, a college, etc. **4** A sapling; a slip or cutting from a tree or bush. **5** *Slang* A trick; dodge; imposition; swindle. **6** A person placed in a theater audience to encourage applause, speak lines, or contribute to the action of a play. **7** An apparently trivial passage early in a story or play that later becomes important in shaping the outcome of the action. — *v.t.* **1** To set in the ground for growing. **2** To furnish with plants or seed: to *plant* a field. **3** To set or place firmly; put in position. **4** To found; establish. **5** To introduce into the mind; implant, as an idea or principle. **6** To introduce into a country, as a breed of animal. **7** To deposit (fish or spawn) in a body of water. **8** To stock, as a river. **9** To bed (oysters). **10** *Slang* To deliver, as a blow. **11** *Slang* To place or station for purposes of deception, observation, etc.: to *plant* evidence. **12** *Slang* To hide; bury. [OE *plante* < L *planta* a sprout, something planted] **Synonyms** (verb): seed, set, sow. We *set* or *set out* slips, cuttings, young trees, etc., but we may also be said to *plant* them; we *plant* corn, potatoes, etc., which we put in definite places, as in hills; we *sow* wheat or other small grains and seeds which are scattered in the process. Land is *seeded* to grass. See SET. *Antonyms*: eradicate, extirpate, uproot.

Plan·tag·e·net (plan·taj′i·net) A patronymic of the English sovereigns from Henry II (1154) to the accession of the House of Tudor (1485): from the sprig of broom (in Medieval Latin, *planta genista*) worn by Geoffrey of Anjou, founder of the line. See table under ENGLAND.

plan·tain[1] (plan′tin) *n.* An annual or perennial herb (genus *Plantago*) widely distributed in temperate regions; especially, the **common** or **greater plantain** (*P. major*) with large, ovate, or oval, ribbed leaves. [< OF < L *plantago, -ginis* < *planta* sole of the foot; with ref. to its broad, flat leaves]

plan·tain[2] (plan′tin) *n.* A tropical perennial herb (*Musa paradisiaca*); also, its edible, bananalike fruit [Earlier *plantan* < Sp. *plátano, plántano* < Cariban *balatanna*; infl. in form by PLANTAIN[1]]

plan·tar (plan′tər) *adj.* Pertaining to the sole of the foot. See illustration under FOOT. [< L *plantaris* < *planta* sole of the foot]

plan·ta·tion (plan·tā′shən) *n.* **1** Any place that is planted; especially, a farm or estate of many acres in the southern United States planted in cotton, tobacco, rice, or sugarcane, and formerly worked by slave labor. **2** A colony. **3** An oyster bed or oyster farm. **4** A grove cultivated to provide a certain product. **5** The act of planting. [< L *plantatio, -onis* a planting < *plantare* plant]

plant·er (plan′tər) *n.* **1** One who plants. **2** An early settler or colonizer. **3** An owner of a plantation. **4** An agricultural implement for dropping seed in soil. **5** A decorative container in which shrubs and flowers are planted, especially outdoors.

plan·ti·grade (plan′tə·grād) *adj.* Walking on the whole sole of the foot, as men, bears, etc. —*n.* A plantigrade animal. Compare DIGITIGRADE. [< F < NL *plantigradus* < L *planta* the sole of the foot + *gradi* walk]

plant louse 1 A small insect (family *Aphididae*) which infests plants and sucks the juices from leaves and stalks; an aphid. See illustration under INSECTS (injurious). **2** A similar leaping insect (family *Psyllidae*).

plaque (plak) *n.* **1** A plate, disk, or slab of metal, porcelain, ivory, etc., artistically ornamented, as for wall decoration. **2** A brooch. **3** A deposit of bacteria-bearing mucus on teeth, often leading to decay. [< F < MDu. *placke* flat disk, tablet. Doublet of PLACK.]

plash[1] (plash) *n.* A slight splash. —*v.t.* & *v.i.* To splash lightly, as water. [Prob. imit.] —**plash′y** *adj.*

plash[2] (plash) *n.* A small pool. [OE *plæsc* a pool]

plash[3] (plash) *v.t.* **1** To bend down and interweave, as twigs or branches, so as to form a hedge or arbor. **2** To form or trim (a hedge) in this manner. [< OF *plaissier* < L *plectere* weave] —**plash′er** *n.*

-plasia combining form Growth; development; formative action: *heteroplasia*: also spelled **-plasy.** Also **-plasis.** [< Gk. *plasis* a molding < *plassein* make, form]

-plasm combining form *Biol.* The viscous material of an animal or vegetable cell: *protoplasm.* [< Gk. *plasma* figure, form < *plassein* mold, make]

plas·ma (plaz′mə) *n.* **1** The liquid portion of nutritive animal fluids, as blood, lymph, or intercellular fluid. **2** The clear, fluid portion of blood, freed from blood cells and used for transfusions. **3** The viscous material of a cell; protoplasm. **4** A green, translucent variety of chalcedony, used among the Romans as a gem. **5** *Physics* That region in a gas-discharge tube which is rendered nearly neutral by the presence of approximately equal numbers of positive ions and electrons. [< LL, a molded thing < Gk. *plasma* < *plassein* mold, form] —**plas·mat·ic** (plaz·mat′ik), **plas′mic** *adj.*

plasmo- combining form Plasma; of or pertaining to plasma: *plasmolysis.* Also, before vowels, **plasm-.** [See -PLASM]

plas·mo·di·um (plaz·mō′dē·əm) *n.* *pl.* **·di·a** (-dē·ə) **1** A mobile, naked, slimy mass of protoplasm resulting from the fusion of ameboid organisms, typical of the slime molds. **2** A malaria parasite. [< NL < Gk. *plasma* + *eidos* form]

Plas·mo·di·um (plaz·mō′dē·əm) *n.* A genus of protozoan blood parasites (class *Sporozoa*) which includes the causative agents of malaria in man and animals, especially *P. vivax, P. malariae,* and *P. falciparum.*

-plast combining form An organized living particle or cell: *protoplast.* [< Gk. *plastos* formed < *plassein* form]

plas·ter (plas′tər, pläs′-) *n.* **1** A composition of lime, sand, and water for coating walls and partitions. **2** Calcined gypsum for making sculptor's casts, etc.; plaster of Paris. **3** A viscid substance spread on linen, silk, etc., and applied to some part of the body: used for healing purposes. — *v.t.* **1** To cover or overlay with or as with plaster. **2** To apply a plaster to, as a boil or part of the body. **3** To apply like plaster or a plaster: to *plaster* posters on a fence. **4** To cause to adhere or lay flat like plaster. **5** *Slang* To strike with great force or effect. [OE < LL *plastrum* < L *emplastrum* < Gk. *emplastron, emplaston* < *en-* on + *plassein* daub, mold; defs. 1, 2, and 4 reborrowed in ME from cognate OF *plastre*] —**plas′ter·er** *n.* —**plas′ter·ing** *n.*

plas·ter·board (plas′tər·bôrd′, pläs′-, -bōrd′) *n.* A board made of a slab of gypsum mixed with fibers or of plaster between sheets of fibrous paper, used as wallboard or as backing for a plaster finish on walls.

plaster cast 1 A cast or model of a person or object made by molding plaster of Paris. **2** *Surg.* An application of gauze stiffened with plaster of Paris, applied to an injured or broken part of the body to prevent movement, allow knitting of bones, etc.

plaster of Paris Calcined gypsum: mixed with water it sets readily and is useful in making molds, casts, bandages, etc.

plas·tic (plas′tik) *adj.* **1** Giving form or fashion to matter. **2** Capable of being molded; pliable. **3** Pertaining to modeling or molding; sculptural. **4** Made of plastic. **5** *Surg.* Efficacious or instrumental in recreating or remodeling injured or destroyed protoplasm; also, capable of being thus renewed. **6** *Slang* Not genuine; sham: *plastic moral values.* —*n.* **1** Anything moldable; specifically, any material, natural or synthetic, which

may be fabricated into a variety of shapes, usually by the application of heat and pressure. **2** *Chem.* One of a class of organic compounds synthesized from hydrocarbons, proteins, cellulose, or resins, capable of being molded, extruded, cast, or otherwise fabricated into various shapes: usually in the plural, **plas′tics.** [< L *plasticus* < Gk. *plastikos* moldable < *plastos* formed < *plassein* form, mold] —**plas′ti·cal·ly** *adv.*

-plastic combining form Growing; developing; forming: *cytoplastic.* [< Gk. *plastikos* plastic]

plas·tic·i·ty (plas·tis′ə·tē) *n.* **1** Plastic quality. **2** *Physics* The ability of certain bodies to exhibit a continous change of shape under suitable distorting forces. **3** Capacity for mental or spiritual molding.

plas·ti·cize (plas′tə·sīz) *v.t.* & *v.i.* **·cized, ·ciz·ing** To make or become plastic.

plastic surgery Surgery that deals with the restoration or healing of lost, wounded, or deformed parts of the body; anaplasty.

plas·ti·sol (plas′tə·sôl, -sol) *n.* A suspension of finely divided resin particles in a plasticizer: useful in the application of plastic coatings to surfaces. [< PLASTI(C) + SOL[4]]

plas·tom·e·ter (plas·tom′ə·tər) *n.* An instrument for measuring the plasticity of a substance. [< *plasto-* (< PLASTICITY) + -METER]

plas·tron (plas′trən) *n.* **1** An ornamental addition to the front of a woman's dress, reaching from the throat to the waist. **2** A leather shield worn on the breast by fencers. **3** *Zool.* The under or ventral part of the shell or armor of a turtle or tortoise: also **plas′trum.** **4** The starched bosom of a man's shirt. **5** An iron breastplate worn under a coat of mail. [< F, orig. a breastplate < Ital. *piastrone,* aug. of *piastra* a breastplate] —**plas′tral** *adj.*

-plasty combining form *Med.* An operation in plastic surgery involving: **a** A (specified) part of the body: *osteoplasty.* **b** Tissue from a (specified) source: *zooplasty.* **c** A (specified) process or formation: *neoplasty.* [< Gk. *-plastia* formation < *plastos.* See -PLAST.]

-plasy See -PLASIA.

plat[1] (plat) *v.t.* **plat·ted, plat·ting** To plait or braid. —*n.* A plait. [ME *platten,* var. of *playten* < OF *pleit* PLAIT]

plat[2] (plat) *n.* **1** A small piece of ground; a plot. **2** A plotted map, chart, or plan. —*v.t.* To make a plot or plan of. [Var. of PLOT; infl. in form by obs. *plat* a flat thing or area < OF. See PLATE.]

plat- Var. of PLATY-.

plat·an (plat′ən) *n.* The plane tree. Also **plat′ane.** [< L *platanus* PLANE[3]]

plate (plāt) *n.* **1** A flat, extended, rigid body of metal or any material of slight but even thickness. **2** Metal in sheets. **3** A shallow vessel, formerly often of wood or pewter, now usually of crockery, in which food is served or from which it is eaten at table. **4** Articles of household service, as goblets, tea sets, etc., made originally of precious metals, but now largely of base metal coated with precious metals. **5** A portion of food served at table; a dish; a plateful; also, a whole course served on one plate. **6** A cup or other article of silver or gold offered as a prize in a race or other contest. **7** A piece of flat metal bearing a design or inscription, either for use in that form, as in a door plate or coffin plate, or intended for reproduction by stamping, printing, or otherwise, as in a bookplate; also, an impression from a plate of the latter kind. **8** An electrotype or stereotype. **9** A horizontal timber laid on a wall to receive a framework. **10** *Dent.* A piece of metal, vulcanite, or plastic, fitted to the mouth and holding one or more artificial teeth. **11** Plate armor. **12** A thin part of the brisket of beef. **13** *Phot.* A sensitized sheet of glass, metal, or the like, for taking photographs. **14** In baseball, the home base, a flat, pentagonal figure, 12 inches in diameter and usually of hard white rubber level with the surface of the diamond. **15**

Biol. A lamina; a lamella. **16** *Geol.* One of the vast discrete sections into which the earth's crust is divided, that float on the underlying magma. **17** A dish like a table plate used in taking up collections, as in churches; also, a collection. **18** A hinge. See illustration under HINGE. **19** The principal anode in a vacuum tube. **20** *Obs.* A piece of silver money. — *v.t.* **plat·ed, plat·ing 1** To coat with a thin layer of gold, silver, etc. **2** To cover or sheathe with metal plates for protection. **3** In papermaking, to give a high gloss to (paper) by pressure between metal plates. **4** *Printing* To make an electrotype or stereotype from. [< OF, a plate of metal, orig. fem. of *plat* flat < LL *plattus*, prob. < Gk. *platys* broad, flat]

plate armor *Mil.* **1** Defensive armor of strong metallic plates for protecting ships or fortifications against artillery. **2** Formerly, defensive armor for the person made of overlapping plates, in distinction from chain or mail. See ARMOR.

pla·teau (pla·tō′, *esp. Brit.* plat′ō) *n. pl.* ·teaus or ·teaux (-tōz′) **1** An extensive stretch of elevated and comparatively level land; tableland; mesa. **2** A broad, low stand for table decorations; also, a decorative plaque. **3** *Psychol.* A relatively level portion in the curve indicating a subject's rate of learning; also, the condition it typifies. **4** *Mil.* A device for making a rough preliminary setting on certain gun sights. [< F < OF *platel* a flat piece of metal or wood, orig. dim. of *plat.* See PLATE.]

plat·ed (plā′tid) *adj.* **1** Provided with plates of metal, as for defense. **2** Coated with a layer of silver, tin, etc. **3** Having one kind of yarn on the face and another on the back: said of certain fabrics.

plate glass See under GLASS.

plate hinge A hinge with one long, narrow plate as the movable unit. See illustration under HINGE.

plate·let (plāt′lit) *n.* **1** A small, platelike object. **2** *Physiol.* One of the small, disk-shaped bodies found in blood and thought to aid in the process of clotting. [Dim. of PLATE]

plat·er (plā′tər) *n.* **1** One who plates articles with a layer of gold, silver, etc. **2** One who makes or works upon metallic plates. **3** An inferior race horse.

plate rail A shelflike molding around a room, for holding ornamental plates or bric-a-brac.

plat·form (plat′fôrm) *n.* **1** Any floor or flat surface raised above the adjacent level, as a stage for public speaking, a raised walk upon which passengers alight from railroad cars. **2** A projecting stage at the end of a car or similar vehicle. **3** A formal scheme of principles put forth by a religious, political, or other body; also, the document stating the principles of a political party. **4** The business of public speaking. [< MF *plateforme* < *plate* flat + *forme* form]

platform car A flat car.

platform scale A scale for weighing heavy objects, having a platform on which the load may stand.

pla·til·la (plə·til′ə) *n.* A kind of white linen fabric, originally of Silesian manufacture. [< Sp., appar. orig. dim. of *plata* silver]

pla·ti·na (plat′ə·nə, plə·tē′nə) *n.* **1** Platinum. **2** A white, brittle alloy of zinc and copper. [< NL < Sp., platinum, orig. dim. of *plata* silver]

plat·ing (plā′ting) *n.* **1** A layer of metal of varying thickness: silver *plating.* **2** A sheathing of metal plates, or plate armor for protection. **3** The act or process of sheathing or coating something with plates or metal.

plat·i·nize (plat′ə·nīz) *v.t.* ·nized, ·niz·ing To coat or combine with platinum, especially by electroplating.

platino- *combining form* Platinum; of, related to, or containing platinum: *platinocyanic.* Also, before vowels, **platin-.** [< PLATINUM]

plat·i·noid (plat′ə·noid) *adj.* Like platinum. — *n.* **1** An alloy of German silver and 1 or 2 percent of tungsten, used in the manufacture of resistance coils and other electrical appliances. **2** A platinum metal.

plat·i·no·type (plat′ə·nō·tīp′) *n. Phot.* **1** A process in which the positive is obtained by a deposit of finely precipitated platinum in combination with iron salts. **2** A positive print obtained by the foregoing process.

plat·i·num (plat′ə·nəm) *n.* **1** A whitish, steel-gray, malleable and ductile metallic element (symbol Pt), usually found native, and also in combination. It is very infusible and resistant to most acids, has a high electrical resistance, and is widely used as a catalyst, for jewelry, and in dental work. See ELEMENT. **2** A color resembling that of platinum, but having a slightly bluish tone. [< NL, alter. of Sp. *platina* PLATINA]

platinum blond A very light, almost white, blond.

plat·i·tude (plat′ə·tood, -tyood) *n.* **1** A flat, dull, or common place statement; an obvious truism. **2** Dulness; triteness. [< F, flatness < *plat* flat]

plat·i·tu·di·nize (plat′ə·too′də·nīz, -tyoo′-) *v.i.* ·nized, ·niz·ing To utter platitudes.

Pla·to (plā′tō), 427?–347? B.C., Greek philosopher.

Platonic love Love which is purely spiritual, or devoid of sensual feeling.

Platonic year See PRECESSION OF THE NOXES.

Pla·to·nism (plā′tə·niz′əm) *n.* **1** The philosophy of Plato; specifically, the doctrine that objects are copies or images of eternal ideas, that these ideas are the ultimate metaphysical realities and therefore the object of true knowledge. **2** A tenet or maxim of the Platonic philosophy. **3** The doctrine or practice of Platonic love. — **Pla′to·nist** *n.*

pla·toon (plə·tōon′) *n.* **1** A subdivision of a company, troop, or other military unit, commanded by a lieutenant. **2** A company of people; set. **3** In football, a group of players assigned to play either defense or offense and put into or taken from the game as a unit. [< F *peloton* ball, group of men, dim. of *pelote* a ball]

plat·ter (plat′ər) *n.* **1** An oblong shallow dish for serving meat or fish. **2** *Colloq.* A phonograph record. [< AF *plater* < *plat* dish]

plat·ting (plat′ing) *n.* **1** The process of weaving by hand. **2** Any fabric made by coarse weaving, as a straw hat.

platy- *combining form* Flat: *platyrrhine.* Also, before vowels, **plat-.** [< Gk. *platys* flat]

plat·y·pus (plat′ə·pəs) *n. pl.* ·pus·es A burrowing egg-laying and aquatic monotrematous mammal (*Ornithorhynchus anatinus*) of Australia, with a ducklike bill and webbed forepaws; duckbill. [< PLATY- + Gk. *pous* foot]

PLATYPUS
(Body about 18 inches in length)

plat·yr·rhine (plat′ə·rīn, -rin) *adj.* **1** Having a broad nose, with widely separated nostrils. **2** *Zool.* Designating a group of monkeys (the *Platyrrhini*) inhabiting the New World. — *n.* A broad-nosed person or monkey. Also **plat′yr·rhin′i·an** (-rin′ē·ən). [< PLATY- + Gk. *rhis, rhinos* nose]

plau·dit (plô′dit) *n.* An expression of applause, praise bestowed. See synonyms under APPLAUSE. [Short for L *plaudite*, 2nd pl. imperative of *plaudere* applaud]

plau·si·ble (plô′zə·bəl) *adj.* **1** Seeming likely to be true, but open to doubt; specious. **2** Superficially trustworthy; endeavoring or calculated to gain trust or confidence: a *plausible* speaker. **3** *Colloq.* Apparently believable; credible. See synonyms under OSTENSIBLE. [< L *plausibilis* deserving applause] — **plau′si·bil′i·ty, plau′si·ble·ness** *n.* — **plau′si·bly** *adv.*

plau·sive (plô′siv) *adj.* **1** Manifesting praise; applauding. **2** *Obs.* Plausible.

play (plā) *v.i.* **1** To engage in sport or diversion; amuse oneself; frolic; gambol. **2** To take part in a game of skill or chance; gamble. **3** To act in a way which is not to be taken seriously. **4** To act or behave in a specified manner: to *play* false. **5** To deal carelessly; behave lightly or insincerely: with *with.* **6** To make love sportively. **7** To move quickly or irregularly as if frolicking: lights *playing* along a wall. **8** To discharge or be discharged freely or continuously: a fountain *playing* in the square. **9** To perform on a musical instrument. **10** To give forth musical sounds; sound: The bugles are *playing.* **11** To be performed or exhibited: *Hamlet* is *playing* to-

night. **12** To act on or as on a stage; perform. **13** To move freely or loosely, especially within limits, as part of a mechanism. — *v.t.* **14** To engage in (a game, etc.). **15** To pretend to be; imitate in play: to *play* cowboys and Indians. **16** To perform sportively or wantonly: to *play* a trick. **17** To oppose in a game or contest. **18** To move or employ (a piece, card, etc.) in a game. **19** To employ (someone) in a game as a player. **20** To cause; bring about: to *play* hob. **21** To perform upon (a musical instrument). **22** To perform or produce, as a piece of music, a play, etc. **23** To act the part of on or as on the stage; assume the character of: to *play* the fool. **24** To perform or act in: to *play* Chicago. **25** To cause to move quickly or irregularly: to *play* lights over a surface. **26** To put into or maintain in action; wield; ply. **27** In angling, to let (a hooked fish) tire itself by maintaining pressure on the line. **28 a** To bet. **b** To bet on. — **to play at 1** To take part in. **2** To pretend to be doing; do half-heartedly. — **to play down** To treat as being of little importance; minimize. — **to play into the hands of** To act to the advantage of (a rival or opponent). — **to play it cool** *Slang* To act unconcerned or nonchalant. — **to play off 1** To oppose against one another. **2** To decide (a tie) by playing one more game. — **to play on 1** To take unscrupulous advantage of (another's hopes, emotions, etc.) for one's own advantage. **2** To continue: The band *played on.* — **to play out 1** To come to an end; be exhausted. **2** To continue to the end; finish. — **to play the game** To behave in a fair manner. — **to play up** *Colloq.* To emphasize. — **to play up to** *Colloq.* To try to win the favor of by flattery, etc. — *n.* **1** Action without special aim or for amusement: opposed to *work.* **2** Exercise or action for recreation or diversion; sport; jest; fun; competitive trial of skill for amusement. **3** Gambling. **4** Manner of contending in a game; also, a move in a game: rough *play*, a fine *play*, sword *play.* **5** A dramatic composition; also, a dramatic representation; especially, a public theatrical exhibition. **6** Action without specified or special hindrance; freedom of movement. **7** Manner of acting toward others; dealing. **8** Active operation. **9** Light, quick, fitful movement. **10** Length of stroke, as of a piston. — **to make a play for** *Colloq.* To attempt to ingratiate oneself with. [OE *plegan*] — **play′a·ble** *adj.*

pla·ya (plä′yä) *n.* A plain with a hard clayey surface intermittently covered by a shallow lake. [< Sp.]

play·bill (plā′bil′) *n.* A bill or program advertising or giving the cast of a play.

play·boy (plā′boi′) *n.* **1** *Colloq.* An irresponsible pleasure-seeker. **2** One who assumes a role for his own advantage or glory; a pretender: from the central character in J. M. Synge's *The Playboy of the Western World.*

played out 1 Performed until finished. **2** Used up; exhausted: originally employed by gamblers.

play·er (plā′ər) *n.* **1** One who takes part in a game; also, one who specializes in a game: a tennis *player.* **2** One who performs on the dramatic stage; an actor. **3** A performer on a musical instrument. **4** One who works without a purpose or makes idle pretensions; also, an idler; a trifler. **5** A gambler. **6** An automatic device for playing a musical instrument; specifically, a mechanical device for playing a piano: also **player piano.**

play·ful (plā′fəl) *adj.* Frolicsome; merry; jocose. See synonyms under WANTON. — **play′ful·ly** *adv.* — **play′ful·ness** *n.*

play·ground (plā′ground′) *n.* A ground used for playing games; space set aside for recreation.

play·house (plā′hous′) *n.* **1** A theater. **2** A small house for children to play in.

playing card One of a pack of cards used in playing various games, the pack usually consisting of 52 cards divided into four suits (spades, hearts, diamonds, clubs) of 13 cards each.

play·mate (plā′māt′) *n.* A companion in sports, games, or recreation; especially, a child's companion in play.

play·off (plā′ôf′, -of′) *n.* In sports, a decisive game or contest, especially after a tie.

play upon words Words used with double

play·wright (plā'rīt') *n.* A writer of plays.

pla·za (plä'zə, plaz'ə; *Sp.* plä'thä) *n.* An open square or market place, especially in a Spanish or Spanish–American town. [<Sp. <L *platea.* Doublet of PIAZZA, PLACE.]

plea (plē) *n.* **1** An act of pleading, or that which is pleaded; an appeal; entreaty; prayer: a *plea* for aid. **2** An excuse; pretext or justification: necessity, the tyrant's *plea.* **3** *Law* **a** An allegation made by either party in a cause; a pleading. **b** In common-law practice, a defendant's answer of fact to the plaintiff's declaration, known in the United States as the *answer.* **c** In equity, a special answer, showing a reason why the writ should be dismissed, delayed, or barred. **d** A suit or action: usually in the plural. See synonyms under APOLOGY. — **Common Pleas** The Court of Common Pleas. See under COURT. — **special plea** A plea to prevent action which, while admitting the plaintiff's allegations, avoids them by setting up new matter. [<OF *plait* <L *placitum* opinion, orig. pp. of *placere* seem right, please]

plea–bar·gain·ing (plē'bär'gən·ing) *n.* A process in which a defendant in a law case arranges, as with a district attorney, to plead guilty to a lesser charge in order to avoid standing trial for a more serious one and the risk of severer punishment.

pleach (plēch) *v.t.* To plait (vines or twigs) together, as in forming a hedge or arbor; interweave. [<AF *plechier,* OF *plaissier* <L *plectere* weave]

plead (plēd) *v.* **plead·ed** (*Colloq.* or *Dial.* **pled**), **plead·ing** *v.i.* **1** To make earnest entreaty; implore; beg. **2** *Law* **a** To advocate a case in court. **b** To file a pleading. — *v.t.* **3** To allege as an excuse or defense: to *plead* insanity. **4** *Law* To discuss or maintain (a case) by argument. [<OF *plaider* <*plait.* See PLEA.] — **plead'a·ble** *adj.* — **plead'er** *n.*

Synonyms: advocate, argue, ask, beg, beseech, entreat, implore, press, solicit, urge. To *plead* for one is to employ argument or persuasion, or both, in his behalf, with earnestness or importunity. One *argues* a case solely on rational grounds with fair consideration of both sides; he *advocates* one side for the purpose of carrying it, and under the influence of motives that may range all the way from cold self-interest to the highest and noblest impulses; he *pleads* a cause, or *pleads for* a person, with still more intense feeling. *Beseech, entreat,* and *implore* imply impassioned earnestness, with direct and tender appeal to personal considerations. *Press* and *urge* imply determined or perhaps authoritative insistence. *Solicit* is a weak word denoting merely an attempt to secure one's consent or cooperation.

plead·ing (plē'ding) *n.* **1** The act of making a plea or argument in behalf of someone or something; specifically, the oral advocacy of a cause in court. **2** *Law* The art, science, or system of preparing the formal written statements of the parties to an action, leading to the joinder of issue; also, any one of such statements: collectively called the *pleadings* in a case. See synonyms under PETITION. — **plead'ing·ly** *adv.*

pleas·ant (plez'ənt) *adj.* **1** Giving or promoting pleasure; pleasing; agreeable. **2** Conducive to merriment; gay. [<F *plaisant* <L *placens,* ppr. of *placere* please] — **pleas'ant·ly** *adv.* — **pleas'ant·ness** *n.*

Synonyms: agreeable, attractive, good-natured, kind, kindly, obliging, pleasing, pleasurable. That is *pleasing* from which pleasure is received, or may readily be received, without reference to any action or intent in that which confers it; as, a *pleasing* picture; a *pleasing* landscape. Whatever has active qualities adapted to give pleasure is *pleasant;* as, a *pleasant* breeze; a *pleasant* (not a *pleasing*) day. As applied to persons, *pleasant* always refers to a disposition ready and desirous to please, and in this sense is near akin to *kind,* but *kind* refers to act or intent, while *pleasant* stops with the disposition. *Pleasant* keeps always something of the sense of actually giving pleasure, and thus surpasses the meaning of *good–natured;* there are *good–natured* people who by reason of rudeness

and ill-breeding are not *pleasant* companions. A *pleasing* face has good features, complexion, expression, etc.; a *pleasant* face indicates a *kind* heart and an *obliging* disposition, as well as *kindly* feelings in actual exercise. See AGREEABLE, AMIABLE, ATTRACTIVE, COMFORTABLE, DELIGHTFUL, GOOD, VIVACIOUS. *Antonyms:* arrogant, austere, crabbed, disagreeable, displeasing, dreary, forbidding, gloomy, glum, grim, harsh, hateful, ill-humored, ill-natured, offensive, repellent, repulsive, unkind, unpleasant.

pleas·an·try (plez'ən·trē) *n. pl.* **·tries** **1** The spirit of playful and jocose companionship; playfulness. **2** A playful, amusing, or good-natured remark, jest, or trick. See synonyms under SPORT, WIT[1].

please (plēz) *v.* **pleased, pleas·ing** *v.t.* **1** To give pleasure to; be agreeable to; gratify. **2** To be the wish or will of: May it *please* you. — *v.i.* **3** To give satisfaction or pleasure. **4** To have the will or preference; wish: Go when you *please.* See synonyms under ENTERTAIN, INDULGE, REJOICE. [<OF *plaisir* <L *placere* please]

pleas·ing (plē'zing) *adj.* Affording pleasure or satisfaction. See synonyms under AGREEABLE, AMIABLE, LOVELY, PLEASANT. — **pleas'ing·ly** *adv.* — **pleas'ing·ness** *n.*

pleas·ur·a·ble (plezh'ər·ə·bəl) *adj.* Affording gratification; pleasant. See synonyms under DELIGHTFUL, PLEASANT. — **pleas'ur·a·ble·ness** *n.* — **pleas'ur·a·bly** *adv.*

pleas·ure (plezh'ər) *n.* **1** An agreeable sensation or emotion; gratification; enjoyment. **2** Sensual or mental gratification. **3** Amusement in general; diversion. **4** One's preference; choice. See synonyms under COMFORT, ENTERTAINMENT, HAPPINESS, SPORT. — *v.* **·ured, ·ur·ing** *v.t.* To give or afford pleasure to; please; gratify. — *v.i.* To take pleasure; delight. [<OF *plaisir.* See PLEASE.]

pleat (plēt) *n.* A fold of cloth doubled on itself and pressed or sewn in place. — *v.t.* To make a pleat or pleats in. Also *plait.* [Var. of PLAIT]

plebe (plēb) *n.* **1** *U.S.* A member of the lowest class in the academies at West Point and Annapolis. **2** *Obs.* Plebs. [Short for PLEBEIAN]

ple·be·ian (pli·bē'ən) *adj.* Pertaining to the common people, originally to the common people of ancient Rome; hence, common. — *n.* One of the common people. [<L *plebeius* <*plebs* the common people] — **ple·be'ian·ism** *n.* — **ple·be'ian·ly** *adv.* — **ple·be'ian·ness** *n.*

pleb·i·scite (pleb'ə·sīt, -sit) *n.* An expression of the popular will by means of a vote by the whole people, usually resorted to in important changes, as those dealing with the constitution, sovereignty, [<F *plébiscite* <L *plebiscitum* <*plebs* people + *scitum* decree < *scire* know] — **ple·bis·ci·tar·y** (plə·bis'ə·ter'ē) *adj.*

plebs (plebz) *n.* **1** The lower order of the ancient Roman people. **2** The populace. [<L, common people]

ple·cop·ter·an (plə·kop'tər·ən) *n.* Any of an order (*Plecoptera*) of soft–bodied, flattened insects of which the nymphs are aquatic: the adults usually have a pair of long caudal appendages, and two pairs of wings folding flat over the abdomen; a stone fly. [<Gk. *plekein* twine + *pteron* wing]

plec·tog·nath (plek'tog·nath) *n.* Any of an order of suborder (*Plectognathi*) of teleost fishes having spiny bodies, generally inedible and often poisonous flesh, and including a large number of odd forms, as the triggerfishes, swellfishes, globefishes, etc., — *adj.* Of or pertaining to the *Plectognathi.* [<Gk. *plektos* twisted + *gnathos* jaw]

plec·trum (plek'trəm) *n. pl.* **·tra** (-trə) A small implement with which the player on a lyre, zither, etc., picks or strikes the strings to set them in vibration. Also **plec'tron** (-tron). [<L <Gk. *plēktron* spur <*plēssein* strike]

pledge (plej) *v.t.* **pledged, pledg·ing** **1** To give or deposit as security for a loan, etc.; pawn. **2** To bind by or as by a pledge. **3** To promise solemnly, as assistance. **4** To offer (one's word, life, etc.) as a guaranty or forfeit. **5** To drink a toast to. **6** To promise to join (a fra-

ternity). **7** To accept (someone) as a pledge (def. 5). [<*n.*] — *n.* **1** A guaranty for the performance of an act, contract, or duty. **2** A formal promise to do or not to do something; especially, a vow to abstain from intoxicating liquors. **3** The drinking of a health or to good cheer. **4** A pawn of personal property; also, the property delivered. **5** One who has promised to join a fraternity but who has not yet been formally inducted. [<OF *plege* security, prob. <Gmc.]

pledg·ee (plej·ə') *n.* The person to whom anything is pledged.

pledg·et (plej'it) *n.* **1** A little plug. **2** A compressed wad of lint, cotton, etc., as for a wound. **3** An oakum string used in calking. [Origin unknown]

–plegia *combining form Med.* A (specified) kind of paralysis, or paralytic condition: *hemiplegia.* Also **–plegy.** [<Gk. <*plēgē* a stroke]

Plei·a·des (plē'ə·dēz, plī'-) **1** In Greek mythology, the seven daughters of Atlas (Maia, Electra, Taygeta, Alcyone, Celaeno, Sterope, and Merope), who were set by Zeus among the stars: also called *Atlantides.* **2** *Astron.* A loose cluster of many hundred stars in the constellation Taurus, six of which are visible to ordinary sight and represent the daughters of Atlas, of whom the seventh, Merope, is known as the **Lost Pleiad.**

plein–air (plän'âr') *adj.* Characterizing the work of a school of French impressionist painters concerned with the representation of objects seen under brilliant sunlight, and other outdoor effects. [<F, open–air] — **plein–air·ism** (plän'âr'iz·əm) *n.* — **plein–air'ist** *n.*

Plei·o·cene (plī'ə·sēn) See PLIOCENE.

plei·o·syl·lab·ic (plī'ə·si·lab'ik) *adj.* Having more than one syllable; especially, having two or three syllables. See POLYSYLLABLE. [<Gk. *pleiōn* more + *syllabē* syllable]

ple·na·ry (plē'nə·rē, plen'ə-) *adj.* **1** Full in all respects or requisites; entire; absolute; also, complete, as embracing all the parts or members: *plenary* authority. **2** Having full powers: *plenary* jurisdiction. **3** Fully or completely attended; consisting of the full number of members: said of an assembly. [<L *plenus* full] — **ple'na·ri·ly** *adv.* — **ple'na·ri·ness** *n.*

ple·nip·o·tent (plə·nip'ə·tənt) *adj.* Possessing full power or authority.

plen·i·po·ten·ti·ar·y (plen'i·pə·ten'shē·er'ē, -shə·rē) *adj.* Possessing or conferring full powers. — *n. pl.* **·ar·ies** **1** A person fully empowered, especially an ambassador, minister, or envoy, invested with full powers by a government. **2** Specifically, a diplomatic representative of the second class ranking next below an ambassador, accredited by the sovereign or head of one state to that of another: full title *envoy extraordinary and minister plenipotentiary.* [<L *plenus* full + *potens* powerful]

plen·i·tude (plen'ə·tōōd, -tyōōd) *n.* The state of being full, complete, or abounding; also, that which fills to repletion. [<L *plenitudo* < *plenus* full]

plen·te·ous (plen'tē·əs) *adj.* **1** Characterized by plenty; amply sufficient. **2** Yielding an abundance. See synonyms under AMPLE, PLENTIFUL. [<OF *plentieus, plentivous* <*plenté* PLENTY] — **plen'te·ous·ly** *adv.* — **plen'te·ous·ness** *n.*

plen·ti·ful (plen'ti·fəl) *adj.* **1** Existing in great quantity; abundant. **2** Yielding or containing plenty; affording ample supply. — **plen'ti·ful·ly** *adv.* — **plen'ti·ful·ness** *n.*

Synonyms: abounding, abundant, adequate, affluent, ample, bounteous, bountiful, complete, copious, enough, exuberant, full, generous, large, lavish, liberal, luxuriant, overflowing, plenteous, profuse, replete, rich, sufficient, teeming. *Plentiful* is used of supplies, as of food, water, etc. We may say a *copious* rain; but *copious* can also be applied to thought, language, etc., where *plentiful* cannot well be used. *Affluent* and *liberal* both apply to riches, resources; *liberal,* with especial reference to giving or expending. *Affluent,* referring especially to riches, may be used of thought, feeling, etc. Neither *affluent, copious,* nor *plentiful* can be used of time or space; a field is sometimes called *plentiful,* with reference to its productiveness. *Complete* expresses not excess or overplus, and yet not mere sufficiency, but harmony, proportion, fitness to a design, or ideal. *Ample* and *abundant* may be applied to any subject and mean more than *enough*. *Lavish* and *profuse* imply a decided excess. We rejoice in *abundant* resources, and honor *generous* hospitality; *lavish* or *profuse* expenditure suggests extravagance and wastefulness. *Luxuriant* is used especially of that which is *abundant* in growth; as, a *luxuriant* crop. Compare ADEQUATE, AMPLE, ENOUGH. *Antonyms*: deficient, drained, exhausted, impoverished, inadequate, insufficient, mean, miserly, narrow, niggardly, poor, scanty, scarce, scrimped, short, small, sparing, stingy, straitened.

plen·ty (plen′tē) *n.* **1** The state of being abundantly sufficient, or of having an abundance, particularly of necessaries and comforts: to live in peace and *plenty*. **2** As much as can be required; an abundance or sufficiency: now generally without the article: *plenty* of water; I have *plenty*. See synonyms under COMFORT, WEALTH. —*adj.* Existing in abundance; plentiful. —*adj. Colloq.* In a sufficient degree: The house is *plenty* large enough. [<OF *plenté* < L *plenitas, -tatis* <*plenus* full]

ple·num (plē′nəm) *n. pl.* **·nums** or **·na** (-nə) **1** Fullness of matter in space; that state of things in which space is considered as fully occupied by matter, especially by absolutely continuous matter. **2** Space so considered: opposed to *vacuum*. **3** Any condition of fullness or plethora, or that which produces it. **4** An enclosed body of gas under greater than normal pressure. **5** A completely attended meeting, as of an association or legislative body. **6** Fullness. —*adj.* Pertaining to or utilizing fullness (of air, etc.) [<L <*plenus* full]

ple·o·nasm (plē′ə·naz′əm) *n.* **1** The use of needless words; redundancy; tautology or any instance of it; a redundant word or phrase. **2** A superabundance of parts, as in an organism. [<Gk. *pleonasmos* <*pleōn* more] —**ple′·o·nas′tic** (-nas′tik) *adj.* —**ple′o·nas′ti·cal·ly** *adv.*

ple·si·o·saur (plē′sē·ə·sôr) *n. Paleontol.* Any of an extinct genus (*Plesiosaurus*) of fish–eating marine reptiles which flourished in the Jurassic period, having a small head, long neck, and limbs modified into swimming paddles. Also **ple′si·o·sau′rus**. [<Gk. *plēsios* near + *sauros* lizard]

PLESIOSAUR
(Up to 50 feet in length)

ples·sor (ples′ər) *n.* Plexor.

pleth·o·ra (pleth′ər·ə) *n.* **1** A state of excessive fullness; superabundance; excess. **2** *Bot.* An excess of juices. **3** *Pathol.* Superabundance of blood in the whole system or in an organ or part. [<Med. L <Gk. *plēthōrē* fullness <*plēthein* be full]

ple·thor·ic (ple·thôr′ik, -thor′-, pleth′ə·rik) *adj.* **1** Affected or characterized by plethora. **2** Excessively full; overloaded; turgid; inflated. See synonyms under CORPULENT. —**ple·thor′i·cal·ly** *adv.*

ple·thys·mo·graph (ple·thiz′mə·graf, -gräf, -this′-) *n.* An instrument for recording variations in size of parts of the body, especially as caused by the circulation of the blood. [<Gk. *plēthysmos* enlargement (<*plēthein* increase) + -GRAPH]

pleurisy root **1** Butterfly weed. **2** Its root, formerly used in treating pleurisy.

pleuro- *combining form* **1** Of or pertaining to the side: *pleurodont*. **2** *Med.* Of, related to, or affecting the pleura: *pleurotomy*. Also, before vowels, **pleur-**. [<Gk. *pleura* side and *pleuron* rib]

plex·i·form (plek′sə·fôrm) *adj.* Having the form of a plexus; complicated.

Plex·i·glas (plek′si·glas, gläs) *n.* A thermoplastic acrylic resin used in the fabrication of

---

transparent objects, as windows for airplane gun turrets, gages, etc.: a trade name.

plex·im·e·ter (plek·sim′ə·tər) *n.* A plate to be placed against the body to receive the blows in percussion. [<Gk. *plēxis* a stroke + -METER] —**plex·i·met·ric** (plek′si·met′rik) *adj.* —**plex·im′e·try** *n.*

plex·us (plek′səs) *n. pl.* **·us·es** or **·us** **1** A network or interlacement; a complication of structures, such as nerves. [<L, braid]

pli·a·ble (plī′ə·bəl) *adj.* **1** Easily bent or twisted; flexible. **2** Easily persuaded or controlled. See synonyms under DOCILE, SUPPLE. —**pli′a·bil′i·ty, pli′a·ble·ness** *n.* —**pli′a·bly** *adv.*

pli·an·cy (plī′ən·sē) *n.* The state or quality of being pliant; pliability: opposite of *rigidity*.

pli·ant (plī′ənt) *adj.* **1** Capable of being bent or twisted with ease; supple; lithe. **2** Easily yielding to influence; tractable. [<OF, ppr. of *plier*. See PLY.] —**pli′ant·ly** *adv.*

pil·ca (plī′kə) *n. pl.* **·cae** (-sē) **1** A fold of membrane, skin, or the like, as between the fingers. **2** *Zool.* A ridge, as on the outer wall of the body whorl in a shell, or on the wing covers of some beetles. **3** *Pathol.* A disease affecting the hair, causing it to become matted and agglutinated. [<Med. <L *plicare* fold]

pli·cate (plī′kāt) *adj.* Plaited; folded in plaits like a fan, as a leaf. Also **pli′cat·ed.** —**pli′cate·ness** *n.* —**pli′cate·ly** *adv.*

pli·ca·tion (plī·kā′shən) *n.* A folding, or that which is folded; a fold. Also **plic·a·ture** (plik′ə·choor).

pli·er (plī′ər) *n.* **1** One who or that which plies. **2** *pl.* Small pincers for bending, holding, or cutting.

plight[1] (plīt) *n.* A condition, state, or case: usually distressed or complicated. [<OF *ploit*, var. of *pleit*. See PLAIT.]

plight[2] (plīt) *n.* A solemn engagement; betrothal; a pledge subject to forfeiture. —*v.t.* **1** To pledge (one's word, faith, etc.). **2** To promise, as in marriage; betroth: She is *plighted* to a judge. —**to plight one's troth** **1** To pledge one's solemn word. **2** To promise oneself in marriage. [OE *pliht* peril] —**plight′er** *n.*

plinth (plinth) *n. Archit.* **1** The slab, block, or stone on which a column, pedestal, or statue rests. **2** A thin course, as of slabs, usually projecting: also **plinth course.** [<L *plinthus* < Gk. *plinthos* a brick]

Pli·o·cene (plī′ə·sēn) *Geol. adj.* Of or pertaining to the latest epoch of the Tertiary period, following the Miocene and succeeded by the Pleistocene. —*n.* The Pliocene epoch or rock series. Also **Pleiocene.** [<Gk. *pleiōn* more + *kainos* new] —**Pli′o·cen′ic** (-sen′ik) *adj.*

Pli·o·film (plī′ə·film) *n.* A flexible, transparent rubber sheeting, used for raincoats, umbrellas, etc.: a trade name.

plod (plod) *v.* **plod·ded, plod·ding** *v.t.* **1** To walk heavily or laboriously; trudge. **2** To work in a steady, laborious manner; drudge. —*v.t.* **3** To walk along heavily or laboriously. —*n.* **1** A tiring walk; tramp; act or duration of plodding. **2** The sound of a heavy step, as of a horse. [Imit.] —**plod′ding** *adj.* —**plod′ding·ly** *adv.*

plod·der (plod′ər) *n.* One who plods; a drudge; also, a slow but perservering person.

–ploid *combining form Biol.* In cytology and genetics, having a (specified) number of chromosomes: *diploid*. Corresponding nouns end in **–ploidy.** [<Gk. *-ploos,* as in *diploos* twofold]

plop (plop) *v.t. & v.i.* **plopped, plop·ping** To drop with a sound like that of a pebble striking the water without making a splash. —*n.* The act or sound of plopping. —*adv.* Suddenly with the sound of plop: They fell *plop* into the river. [Imit.]

---

plot (plot) *n.* **1** A piece or patch of ground set apart; also called *plat.* **2** A chart or diagram, as of a building, for showing certain data; also, a surveyor's map. **3** A secret plan to accomplish some questionable purpose; conspiracy. **4** The series of incidents forming the plan of action of a story, play, or poem. —*v.* **plot·ted, plot·ting** *v.t.* **1** To make a map, chart, or plan of, as a ship's course, a building, etc. **2** To plan for secretly: to *plot* an enemy's ruin. **3** To arrange the plot of (a novel, etc.) **4** *Math.* **a** To represent graphically the position of (a measured value) by a point located with reference to its coordinates on plotting paper. **b** To draw (a curve) through a series of such points. —*v.i.* **5** To form a plot; conspire. [OE]

plotting paper Paper which has been ruled into small squares for plotting curves, and making diagrams.

plov·er (pluv′ər, plō′vər) *n.* **1** A shore bird (family *Charadriidae*), especially of *Charadrius* or related genus, with long, pointed wings and a short tail, especially the **American golden plover** (*Pluvialis dominica*). **2** Any of certain related shore birds, as the ruddy turnstone and the **upland plover** (*Bartramia longicauda*). [<AF, ult. <L *pluvia* rain]

plow (plou) *n.* **1** An implement (usually drawn by horses, or oxen, or by mechanical power) for cutting, turning over, stirring, or breaking up the soil. **2** Any implement that operates like a plow: often in combination: a *snowplow;* also, any one of various furrowing or grooving tools. **3** Figuratively, agriculture. —*v.t.* **1** To turn up the surface of (land) with a plow. **2** To make or form (a furrow, ridge, etc.) by means of a plow. **3** To furrow or score the surface of: Shot *plowed* the field. **4** To dig out or remove with a plow: with *up* or *out.* **5** To move out or cut through (water): to *plow* the waves. **6** To pluck (def. 7). —*v.i.* **7** To turn up soil with a plow. **8** To undergo plowing in a specified way, as land. **9** To move or proceed as a plow does: usually with *through* or *into.* **10** To advance laboriously; plod. —**to plow under** *U.S.* To put from sight by or as by plowing in such a way as to cover with soil; obliterate. Also spelled **plough.** [OE *ploh*] —**plow′a·ble** *adj.* —**plow′er** *n.*

Plow The group of seven stars commonly called *Charles's Wain* or *the Dipper,* sometimes also *Ursa Major.* Also **Plough.**

plow beam The horizontal projecting part of a plow frame, whose front end is attached to the swingletree. See illustration under SWINGLETREE.

plow·share (plou′shâr′) *n.* The blade of a plow. Also **plough′share′.**

plow·staff (plou′staf′, -stäf′) *n.* The handle of a plow. Also **plough′staff′.**

ploy (ploi) *v.i. Mil.* To diminish front; maneuver from line into column: opposite of *deploy.* [<DEPLOY] —**poly′ment** *n.*

pluck (pluk) *v.t.* **1** To pull out or off; pick: to *pluck* a flower. **2** To pull with force; snatch or drag: with *off, away,* etc. **3** To pull out the feathers, hair, etc., of: to *pluck* a chicken. **4** To give a twitch or pull to, as a sleeve. **5** To cause the strings of (a musical instrument) to sound by such action. **6** To rob; swindle. **7** *Brit. Slang* To reject (a candidate) for failure to pass an examination. —*v.i.* **8** To give a sudden pull; tug: with *at.* —**to pluck up** To rouse or summon (one's courage). —*n.* **1** Confidence and spirit in the face of difficulty or danger; courage. **2** The heart, liver, windpipe, and lungs of an animal. **3** A sudden pull; twitch. **4** The act of plucking or state of being plucked; also, the person plucked. See synonyms under COURAGE. [OE *pluccian*] —**pluck′er** *n.*

pluck·y (pluk′ē) *adj.* **pluck·i·er, pluck·i·est** Brave and spirited; courageous. —**pluck′i·ly** *adv.* —**pluck′i·ness** *n.*

plug (plug) *n.* **1** Anything, as a piece of wood or a cork, used to stop a hole; a wedge or peg driven into anything. **2** A spark plug. **3** *Electr.* A device containing conducting material, as projecting prongs, for inserting in an outlet, etc., so as to complete a circuit or make contact. **4** A flat cake of pressed or twisted tobacco. **5** Any worn–out or useless thing, particularly a horse past its prime: often with *old.* **6** *U.S. Slang* A man's high silk hat; also **plug hat.** **7** *Slang* Mention of a product, song, etc., as on a radio or television program, to give it publicity; an advertisement. **8** *Geol.* The hard core of igneous rock which fills the neck of a volcano. **9** The discharge outlet from a water main: also called *hydrant.* **10** *Mech.* The cylindrical part of a cylinder lock which contains the keyhole and is turned by the key. **11** In angling, a type of lure, usually cylindrical and with several hooks attached, similar to a spoon. — *v.* **plugged, plug·ging** *v.t.* **1** To stop or close, as a hole, by inserting a plug: often with *up.* **2** To insert as a plug. **3** *Slang* To shoot a bullet into. **4** *U.S. Slang* To advertise frequently or insistently; publicize. — *v.i.* **5** *Colloq.* To work doggedly; persevere. — **to plug in** To insert the plug of (a lamp, etc.) in an electrical outlet. [< MDu. *plugge*] — **plug′ger** *n.*

plum (plum) *n.* **1** The edible drupaceous fruit of any one of various trees of the genus *Prunus,* especially *P. domestica,* the **European** or **garden plum. 2** The tree. **3** The plumlike fruit of any one of various other trees having an edible drupe; also, the tree bearing such fruit. **4** A raisin, especially as used in cooking: *plum* pudding. **5** The best part of anything; a choice piece or portion; a desirable post or appointment. **6** *Brit. Slang* A sum of £100,000 sterling; a handsome fortune, or the possessor of it. **7** Any of various shades of dull reddish purple or purplish red. **8** A sugarplum; anything resembling a plum, as in shape or flavor. ◆ Homophone: *plumb.* [OE *plume* < LL *pruna.* Doublet of PRUNE¹.]

plum·age (plōō′mij) *n.* **1** The feathers that cover a bird, collectively. **2** Gaudy costume; adornment. [< F < *plume* plume]

plu·mate (plōō′māt) *adj.* Resembling plumage or feathers. [< L *plumatus* feathered]

plumb (plum) *n.* **1** A lead weight on the end of a line used by masons, carpenters, etc., to find the exact perpendicular; a plumb bob; a plummet. **2** A plummet or nautical sounding lead; a sinker on a fishing line, etc. — **off** (or **out of**) **plumb** Not exactly vertical; not in alinement. — *adj.* **1** True, accurate, and upright; vertical or perpendicular; hence, figuratively, upright in principle. **2** *Colloq.* Sheer; complete: also **plum.** — *adv.* **1** In a line perpendicular to the plane of the horizon; vertically. **2** *Colloq.* With exactness; correctly; exactly; completely; entirely: also **plum.** — *v.t.* **1** To test the perpendicularity of with a plumb. **2** To make vertical; straighten: usually with *up.* **3** To test the depth of; sound. **4** To reach the lowest level or extent of; fathom: to *plumb* the depths of despair. **5** To seal with lead. ◆ Homophone: *plum.* [< F *plomb* < L *plumbum* lead]

plumb– Var. of PLUMBO–.

plum·ba·go (plum·bā′gō) *n. pl.* **·gos 1** Graphite: used for pencils, crucibles, lubricating, and in electroplating to coat non-conducting surfaces, as gutta-percha. **2** A drawing made with a lead-pointed instrument. **3** Any of a genus (*Plumbago*) of hardy, shrubby plants cultivated for their showy blue, white, or purplish flowers: also called *leadwort.* [< L *plumbum* lead] — **plum·bag′i·nous** (-baj′ə-nəs) *adj.*

plum·bif·er·ous (plum·bif′ər-əs) *adj.* Containing or yielding lead.

plumb·ing (plum′ing) *n.* **1** The art or trade of putting into buildings the tanks, pipes, etc., for water, gas, and sewage. **2** The pipe system of a building. **3** The act of sounding for depth, etc., with a plumb line.

plumb line 1 A cord by which a weight is suspended to test the perpendicularity or depth of something. **2** A plumb bob and its cord together. **3** A sounding line.

plumbo– *combining form* Lead; of or containing lead. Also, before vowels, *plumb–,* as in *plumbiferous.* [< L *plumbum* lead]

plumb rule A narrow rule furnished with a plumb line or a cross level, with which masons and carpenters test the verticality of their work.

plum·bum (plum′bəm) *n.* Lead: so called in pharmacy and old chemistry. [< L]

plum duff A suet and flour pudding with raisins, currants, etc., boiled in a cloth bag.

plume (plōōm) *n.* **1** A feather, especially when long and ornamental. **2** A large feather or tuft of feathers worn as an ornament, especially on a helmet; a panache. **3** *Her.* Three feathers, unless more are specified. **4** A featherlike form or part; the plumose appendage of a seed. **5** Plumage. **6** A decoration of honor; a prize. — *v.t.* **plumed, plum·ing 1** To adorn, dress, or furnish with or as with plumes. **2** To smooth or dress (itself or its feathers); preen. **3** To congratulate or pride (oneself): with *on* or *upon.* [< F < L *pluma* small soft feather]

plu·mi·ped (plōō′mə·ped) *adj.* Having feathered feet. — *n.* A plumiped bird, as an owl. Also **plu′mi·pede** (-pēd). [< L *pluma* feather + -PED]

plum·met (plum′it) *n.* **1** A piece of lead or heavy substance, attachable to a line for making soundings, adjusting walls to the vertical, etc.; a plumb bob; hence, a standard of truth or rectitude. **2** A plumb rule. **3** A weight; especially an oppressive weight. — *v.i.* To drop straight down; plunge. [< OF *plommet,* dim. of *plom* lead]

plu·mose (plōō′mōs) *adj.* **1** Bearing feathers or plumes. **2** Having fine processes on opposite sides, like the vane of a feather. **3** Resembling plumes. [< L *plumosus* < *pluma* feather] — **plu′mose·ly** *adv.* — **plu·mos·i·ty** (plōō·mos′ə·tē) *n.*

plump¹ (plump) *adj.* Swelled out or enlarged to the full; somewhat fat. See synonyms under ROUND¹. — *v.t. & v.i.* To make or become plump: often with *up* or *out.* — *n. Archaic* A closely united group; a cluster or clump. [< MDu. *plomp*] — **plump′ly** *adv.* — **plump′·ness** *n.*

plump² (plump) *v.i.* **1** To fall suddenly or heavily; drop with full impact. **2** To give one's complete support: with *for.* — *v.t.* **3** To drop or throw down heavily or all at once. **4** To utter bluntly or abruptly: often with *out.* — *n.* The act of plumping or falling; the sound made by the impact of a falling object. — *adj.* Containing no reservation or qualification; blunt; downright. — *adv.* **1** With a sudden impact or fall into or as into water; in a sudden or forcible manner; also, unexpectedly. **2** Directly; without hesitation, circumlocution, or qualification; bluntly. [< MDu. *plompen*] — **plump′ly** *adv.*

plump·er¹ (plum′pər) *n.* **1** A heavy fall or drop. **2** Votes cast all for one candidate instead of for several; also, a person so voting. **3** *Brit. Slang* An unqualified lie.

plump·er² (plum′pər) *n.* A disk or padding placed in the mouth, as by persons who have lost their teeth, to distend the cheek and give it an appearance of plumpness.

plum pudding A boiled pudding made with flour, raisins, suet, currants, spices, etc.

plun·der (plun′dər) *v.t.* **1** To rob of goods or property by open violence, as in war; pillage; loot. **2** To despoil by robbery or fraud. **3** To take as plunder. — *v.i.* **4** To take plunder; steal. See synonyms under STEAL. — *n.* **1** That which is taken by plundering; booty. **2** The act of plundering or robbing. **3** *U.S. Colloq.* Personal belongings or goods, etc. **4** Political booty. [< G *plündern*] — **plun′der·er** *n.*
Synonyms (noun): booty, pillage, prey, rapine, robbery, spoil.

plun·der·age (plun′dər·ij) *n.* Pillage.

plunge (plunj) *v.* **plunged, plung·ing** *v.t.* **1** To thrust or force suddenly into a fluid, penetrable substance, hole, etc. **2** To force into some condition or state: to *plunge* a nation into debt. — *v.i.* **3** To dive, jump, or fall into a fluid, chasm, etc. **4** To move suddenly or with a rush: to *plunge* through a door. **5** To move violently forward and downward, as a horse or ship. **6** To descend abruptly or steeply, as a road or cliff. **7** *Colloq.* To gamble or speculate heavily and recklessly. See synonyms under IMMERSE. — *n.* **1** The act of plunging; a leap; dive. **2** A sudden and violent motion, as of a breaking wave. **3** A place, tank, or pool for diving or swimming.

PLUME (def. 3)
Prince of Wales.

4 An extravagant or reckless bet or speculation. [< OF *plunjer,* ult. < L *plumbum* lead]

plung·er (plun′jər) *n.* **1** One who or that which plunges; a heavy or reckless speculator. **2** *Mech.* Any appliance having or adapted for a plunging motion, as the piston of a pump. **3** A cuplike device made of rubber and attached to a stick, used to clean out clogged drains, etc.: also called *plumber's friend.*

plunk (plungk) *Colloq. v.t.* **1** To pluck, as a banjo or its strings; strum. **2** To place or throw heavily and suddenly: with *down.* — *v.i.* **3** To emit a twanging sound. **4** To fall heavily or suddenly; plump. — *n.* **1** A heavy blow, or its sound. **2** *Slang* A dollar. [Imit.]

plu·per·fect (plōō·pûr′fikt) See PAST PERFECT.

plu·ral (plŏŏr′əl) *adj.* **1** Containing, consisting of or designating more than one. **2** *Gram.* Denoting more than one (in languages that have dual number, such as Sanskrit and Greek, more than two): opposed to *singular.* — *n. Gram.* The plural number, or a word in this number. [< L *pluralis* < *plus* more] — **plu′·ral·ly** *adv.*

◆ English nouns regularly form their plurals by adding *s* or *es* to the singular; most nouns ending in *f* change the *f* to *v* and add *es;* as wol*f,* wol*ves;* hal*f,* hal*ves.* Nouns ending in *y* change it to *ies* if it is preceded by a consonant: bod*y,* bod*ies;* or merely add an *s* if it is preceded by a vowel; as donke*y,* donke*ys.* Some nouns of Old English origin have an irregular plural in *en,* as, child, child*ren;* or by a vowel change; as, mouse, *mice;* goose, *geese;* man, *men;* tooth, *teeth.* A few nouns retain the singular form unchanged in the plural; as, *deer, hose, moose, series, sheep, species, vermin.* Some such nouns, especially the names of animals, have also an alternative plural regularly formed: as, fish, *fish* or *fishes. Fish* is the usual collective plural; *fishes* is used to indicate more than one genus, variety, species, etc. Many words of foreign derivation retain the plural form peculiar to the languages from which they are severally derived; as, addendum, *addenda;* antithesis, *antitheses;* crisis, *crises;* datum, *data,* etc. Many nouns of this class have also a plural of the regular English form; as, appendix, *appendixes* or *appendices;* beau, *beaus* or *beaux;* cherub, *cherubs* or *cherubim;* focus, *focuses* or *foci;* index, *indexes* or *indices,* etc. Compounds commonly form the plural regularly by adding *s* or *es* to the complete word; as, armful, *armfuls;* cut-throat, *cut-throats;* football, *footballs;* teaspoonful, *teaspoonfuls.* If the last element of the compound forms its plural irregularly, the same form usually appears in the plural of the compound; as, footman, *footmen.* Nouns that end in *-man,* but are not compounds, form the plural regularly by adding *s,* as Mussulman, *Mussulmans.* Hyphenated compounds in which the principal word forms the first element change that element to form the plural; as, father-in-law, *fathers-in-law.*

plu·ral·ism (plŏŏr′əl·iz′əm) *n.* **1** The condition of being plural. **2** *Eccl.* The holding of more than one office, or, in the Anglican church, of more than one ecclesiastical living, at one time. **3** *Philos.* The doctrine that there is a plurality of ultimate substances, as spirit and matter: opposed to *monism.* **4** The existence within a society of diverse groups, as in religion, race, or ethnic origin, which contribute to the cultural matrix of the society while retaining their distinctive characters; also, a doctrine advocating this. — **plu′ral·is′tic** *adj.*

plu·ral·ist (plŏŏr′əl·ist) *n.* **1** One who holds more than one ecclesiastical benefice at the same time. **2** Anyone who holds a plurality of offices. **3** One who believes in or advocates pluralism.

plu·ral·i·ty (plŏŏ·ral′ə·tē) *n. pl.* **·ties 1** The state of being plural. **2** The larger portion or greater number; majority. **3** In U.S. politics, the greatest of more than two numbers, whether it is or is not a majority of the whole; also, the excess of the highest number of votes cast for any one candidate over the next highest number. **4** *Eccl.* Pluralism; also, one of the livings held by a pluralist. **5** Polygamy.

plu·ral·ize (plŏŏr′əl·īz) *v.t.* **·ized, ·iz·ing 1** To make plural. **2** To express in the plural.

pluri- *combining form* More; many; several: *pluriaxial.* [< L *plus, pluris* more]

plus (plus) *prep.* **1** Added to or to be added to: Three *plus* two equals five: opposed to *minus.* **2** Increased by: salary *plus* commission. —*adj.* **1** Being or indicating more than nothing; above zero; positive. **2** Electrified positively. **3** *Colloq.* Possessing (something) in addition: used predicatively: He was *plus* a new hat. **4** Extra; supplemental: *plus* value. **5** *Colloq.* Denoting a value higher than ordinary in a specified grade: B *plus.* **6** *Bot.* Designating a form of sexual differentiation in certain plants: the *plus* strain of heterothallic fungi. —*n. pl.* **plus·es 1** The plus sign. **2** An addition; an extra quantity. **3** A positive quantity. **4** *Colloq.* Something considered advantageous or desirable: a definite *plus* for the business. —*adv. Electr.* Positively. [< L, more]

plush (plush) *n.* A pile fabric of silk, rayon, or mohair having a deeper pile than velvet. —*adj.* **1** Of or made of plush. **2** *Slang* Luxurious. [< F *pluche, peluche* < L *pilus* hair] —**plush′y** *adj.*

plus sign The symbol (+) signifying addition or a positive quantity: opposed to *minus sign.*

plu·tar·chy (ploo′tär·kē) *n. pl.* **·chies** Government by the rich. [< Gk. *ploutos* wealth + *archein* rule]

Plu·to (ploo′tō) **1** In Greek and Roman mythology, the god of the infernal regions and spouse of Persephone: identified with the Greek *Hades* and the Roman *Dis.* **2** *Astron.* The ninth planet of the solar system in order of distance from the sun, invisible to the naked eye: discovered 1930. See PLANET. [< L < Gk. *Ploutōn*]

plu·toc·ra·cy (ploo·tok′rə·sē) *n. pl.* **·cies 1** A class in a community that controls the government by its wealth; the wealthy classes. **2** Plutarchy. [< Gk. *ploutokratia* < *ploutos* wealth + *kratein* rule]

plu·to·crat (ploo′tə·krat) *n.* One who has or exercises power by virtue of his wealth; one of a plutocracy. —**plu′to·crat′ic** or **·i·cal** *adj.* —**plu′to·crat′i·cal·ly** *adv.*

plu·to·ma·ni·a (ploo′tə·mā′nē·ə, -mān′yə) *n.* An excessive desire for great wealth. [< Gk. *ploutos* wealth + -MANIA]

plu·to·ni·um (ploo·tō′nē·əm) *n.* A toxic, radioactive metallic element (symbol Pu, atomic number 94) occurring in minute traces in uranium ores and produced in quantity in nuclear reactors by irradiation of uranium. See PERIODIC TABLE. [< NL < *Pluto* (the planet)]

plu·vi·al (ploo′vē·əl) *adj.* **1** Pertaining to rain; rainy. **2** Arising from the action of rain. [< L *pluvialis* < *pluvia* rain]

pluvio- *combining form* Rain; pertaining to rain: *pluviometer.* Also, before vowels, **pluvi-.** [< L *pluvia* rain]

plu·vi·om·e·ter (ploo′vē·om′ə·tər) *n.* An instrument for measuring the depth of rainfall. [< PLUVIO- + -METER] —**plu′vi·o·met′ric** (-ə·met′rik) or **·ri·cal** *adj.* —**plu′vi·o·met′ri·cal·ly** *adv.* —**plu′vi·om′e·try** *n.*

plu·vi·ous (ploo′vē·əs) *adj.* Pertaining to rain; rainy. Also **plu′vi·ose** (-ōs). [< L *pluviosus*]

ply[1] (plī) *v.* **plied, ply·ing** *v.t.* To bend; mold; shape. —*v.i. Obs.* To bend or yield. —*n. pl.* **plies 1** A web, layer, fold, or thickness, as in a carpet, cloth, etc. **2** A strand, turn, or twist of rope, yarn, thread, etc.: used in combination to mean (a certain) number of folds, twists, or strands: three-*ply* yarn. **3** A bent or bias; inclination to one side, as of the mind. [< F *plier* < L *plicare*]

ply[2] (plī) *v.* **plied, ply·ing** *v.t.* **1** To use in working, fighting, etc.; wield; employ. **2** To work at; be engaged in: He *plies* the trade of shoemaker. **3** To subject to repeated action, as by offering unwanted gifts, asking questions insistently, etc.: to *ply* a person with drink; to *ply* one with requests. **4** To strike or assail persistently: He *plied* the donkey with a whip. **5** To traverse regularly: ferryboats that *ply* the river. —*v.i.* **6** To make regular trips; sail: usually with *between.* **7** To work steadily; do one's or its work. **8** *Poetic* To proceed; steer. **9** *Naut.* To beat; tack. [Aphetic var. of APPLY]

ply·er (plī′ər) *n.* **1** A plier. **2** *pl.* A balance of crossed timbers used in raising and lowering a drawbridge.

Plym·outh (plim′əth) **1** A city of eastern Massachusetts; first settlement *(Plymouth Colony)* in New England; site of Plymouth Rock. **2** A port on **Plymouth Sound,** an inlet of the English Channel between Cornwall and Devon in SW England.

Plymouth Colony The colony on the shore of Massachusetts Bay founded by the Pilgrim Fathers who sailed from Plymouth, England, in 1620.

Plymouth Rock 1 The rock at Plymouth, Massachusetts, on which the Pilgrim Fathers are said to have stepped when landing from the *Mayflower* in 1620. **2** One of a breed of domestic fowls of large size, with small single comb and buff, white, black, or gray barred plumage.

ply·wood (plī′wood′) *n.* Laminated wood consisting of an odd number of sheets or plies tightly glued together, the grains of adjoining layers usually being at right angles to each other: widely used as a structural and building material.

pneu·ma (noo′mə, nyoo′-) *n.* The breath of life; the soul or spirit. [< Gk.]

pneu·mat·ic (noo·mat′ik, nyoo-) *adj.* **1** Pertaining to the science of pneumatics. **2** Describing machines or devices that make use of compressed air: a *pneumatic* engine. **3** Pertaining to or containing air or gas, especially compressed air: a *pneumatic* tire. Also **pneu·mat′i·cal.** —*n.* A pneumatic tire. [< L *pneumaticus* < Gk. *pneumatikos* < *pneuma* breath < *pneein* breathe] —**pneu·mat′i·cal·ly** *adv.*

pneu·mat·ics (noo·mat′iks, nyoo-) *n.* The branch of physics that treats of the mechanical properties of air and other gases, such as their pressure, elasticity, and density, and also of pneumatic mechanisms.

pneumato- *combining form* **1** Air: *pneumatophore.* **2** Breath; breathing: *pneumatometer.* **3** Spirit; spirits: *pneumatology.* Also, before vowels, **pneumat-.** [< Gk. *pneuma, pneumatos* air, spirit, breath]

pneu·ma·tog·ra·phy (noo′mə·tog′rə·fē, nyoo′-) *n.* Spirit writing. [< PNEUMATO- + -GRAPHY]

pneu·ma·tol·o·gy (noo′mə·tol′ə·jē, nyoo′-) *n.* **1** The doctrine of the nature and operation of spirit, or a treatise on that science; the science of spiritual beings or existence. **2** The science of the beliefs of men touching a world of spirits. **3** The science dealing with the physiology of air or gases. **4** *Obs.* Pneumatics. —**pneu′ma·to·log′ic** (-tə·loj′ik) or **·i·cal** *adj.* —**pneu′ma·tol′o·gist** *n.*

pneu·ma·tom·e·ter (noo′mə·tom′ə·tər, nyoo′-) *n.* An instrument for measuring the volume of air exhaled or inhaled at one breath; a spirometer. —**pneu′ma·tom′e·try** *n.*

pneumo- *combining form* Lung; related to the lungs; respiratory: *pneumobacillus:* also *pneumono-.* Also, before vowels, **pneum-.** [< Gk. *pneumon, pneumonos* a lung]

pneu·mo·ba·cil·lus (noo′mō·bə·sil′əs, nyoo′-) *n. pl.* **·cil·li** (-sil′ī) A bacillus *(Klebsiella pneumoniae)* found in infections of the respiratory tract.

pneu·mo·coc·cus (noo′mō·kok′əs, nyoo′-) *n. pl.* **·coc·ci** (-kok′sī) Any of a group of bacteria that cause a common type of pneumonia and some other diseases. —**pneu′mo·coc′cal, pneu′mo·coc′cous, pneu′mo·coc′cic** (kok′sik) *adj.*

pneu·mo·dy·nam·ics (noo′mō·dī·nam′iks, nyoo′-) *n.* The dynamics of gases; pneumatics.

pneu·mo·gas·tric (noo′mō·gas′trik, nyoo′-) *adj.* **1** Of or pertaining to the lungs and the stomach. **2** Of or pertaining to the vagus. —*n.* The vagus.

pneu·mo·graph (noo′mə·graf, -gräf, nyoo′-) *n.* An instrument which records movements of the chest in breathing.

pneu·mo·ni·a (noo·mōn′yə, nyoo-) *n. Pathol.* An infectious disease characterized by inflammation of the lung tissue. The two principal types are *bronchopneumonia,* involving the bronchi and parenchyma of the lungs; and *lobar* or *croupous pneumonia,* affecting one or more lobes of the lungs. [< NL < Gk. *pneumonia* < *pneumōn* lung < *pneein* breathe]

pneu·mon·ic (noo·mon′ik, nyoo-) *adj.* **1** Affected with pneumonia; pertaining to pneumonia. **2** Pulmonary. [< NL *pneumonicus* < Gk. *pneumonikos*]

pneumono- *combining form* Pneumo-.

pneu·mo·tho·rax (noo′mō·thôr′aks, -thō′raks, nyoo′-) *n.* An accumulation of air or gas within the pleural cavity: sometimes artificially induced to collapse the lung in tuberculosis.

Pnom-Penh (nom′pen′, pnoom-pen′y′) A city on the Mekong, capital of Cambodia; also *Phnompenh.* Also **Pnom Penh.**

poach[1] (pōch) *v.t.* To cook (eggs without their shells, fish, etc.) in boiling water, milk, or other liquid until coated. [< OF *pochier* put in a pocket < *poche* pocket; from the "pocketed" position of the egg yolk]

poach[2] (pōch) *v.i.* **1** To trespass on another's property, etc., especially for the purpose of taking game or fish. **2** To take game or fish unlawfully. **3** To become soft and muddy by being trampled: said of land. **4** To sink into mud or soft earth while walking. —*v.t.* **5** To trespass on, as for taking game or fish. **6** To take (game or fish) unlawfully. **7** To make muddy or tear up (land, etc.) by trampling. **8** To reduce to a uniform consistency by mixing with water, as clay. [< OF *pochier* thrust one's fingers into < LG *poken* poke] —**poach′er** *n.*

poach·y (pō′chē) *adj.* Easily trodden into holes by cattle; soft and miry. [< POACH[2] (def. 3)] —**poach′i·ness** *n.*

Po·ca·hon·tas (pō′kə·hon′təs), 1595?–1617, American Indian princess; daughter of Powhatan, a Virginian chief; she reputedly saved the life of Captain John Smith.

po·chard (pō′chərd, -kərd) *n.* A sea duck (genus *Aythya*) having the head and neck reddish, found in America, Europe, and South Africa. *A. ferina* is the **common pochard** of the Old World; *A. americana,* the **American pochard** or redhead. [Origin uncertain]

pock (pok) *n.* **1** A pustule in an eruptive disease, as in smallpox; a pockmark. **2** *Obs.* Smallpox. [OE *poc*]

pock·et (pok′it) *n.* **1** A small bag or pouch; especially, a pouch attached to a garment, as for carrying money. **2** Hence, money; pecuniary means or interests. **3** A cavity, opening, or receptacle. **4** *Mining* A cavity containing gold or other ore; also, an accumulation of alluvial gold in one spot. **5** One of the pouches in a billiard or pool table, into which the balls are driven. **6** A bin for holding grain, coal, etc., for storage. **7** A glen among mountains. **8** In horse-racing, a position in which a horse is behind the leading horse or horses, and is kept from going past by others at the side. **9** An air pocket. —**in one's pocket 1** On terms of intimacy as close to one as one's pocket. **2** Under one's influence or control. —*adj.* **1** Diminutive, as if pocketable. **2** Pertaining to, for, or carried in a pocket: *pocket* lining, *pocket* knife. —*v.t.* **1** To put into or confine in a pocket. **2** To appropriate as one's own, especially dishonestly, as profits or funds. **3** To enclose as if in a pocket. **4** To accept or endure without open resentment or reply, as an insult. **5** To conceal or suppress: *Pocket* your pride. **6** To retain without signing. See POCKET VETO. **7** In billiards, etc., to drive (a ball) into a pocket. [< AF *pokette, poquette,* dim. of OF *poque, poche* bag, pouch] —**pock′et·a·ble** *adj.* —**pock′et·er** *n.*

pock·et·book (pok′it·book′) *n.* **1** A small book or case for carrying money and papers in the pocket; wallet. **2** A woman's purse or handbag. **3** A notebook or other book for the pocket. **4** Money or pecuniary resources.

pock·mark (pok′märk′) *n.* A pit or scar left on the skin by smallpox or similar diseases. —**pock′marked′** *adj.*

pock·y (pok′ē) *adj.* **pock·i·er, pock·i·est 1** Pertaining to, resembling, or affected with smallpox; pockmarked. **2** Syphilitic.

po·co (pō′kō) *adv. Music* Slightly; a little. [< Ital.]

po·co a po·co (pō′kō ä pō′kō) *Music* Little by little; gradually. [< Ital.]

pod[1] (pod) *n.* **1** A seed vessel or capsule of a plant; a legume. **2** Any dry and many-seeded dehiscent fruit. —*v.i.* **pod·ded, pod·ding 1** To fill out like a pod. **2** To produce pods. [Origin uncertain]

pod[2] (pod) *n.* A flock or collection of animals, especially of seals, whales, or walruses. [Origin unknown]

pod[3] (pod) *n. Mech.* **1** The lengthwise groove in certain augers, bits, and gimlets. **2** An auger so grooved. [Origin unknown]

-pod *combining form* **1** One who or that which has (a specified number or kind of) feet: *arthropod.* **2** A (specified kind of) foot: *pleopod.* Also **-pode.** [< Gk. *pous, podos* a foot]

-poda *combining form Zool.* Plural of -POD: used in names of phyla, orders, classes, etc.: *Arthro-*

poda. [<NL <Gk. *pous, podos* a foot]

podg·y (poj′ē) *adj.* **podg·i·er, podg·i·est** Dumpy and fat. [Var. of PUDGY] —**podg′i·ness** *n.*

po·di·a·try (pə·dī′ə·trē, pō-) *n.* The study and treatment of diseases of the feet. [<Gk. *pous, podos* foot + -IATRY] —**po·di′a·trist** *n.*

po·di·um (pō′dē·əm) *n. pl.* **·di·a** (-dē·ə) **1** *Archit.* **a** A solid basement or pedestal supporting a structure, as a Roman temple. **b** The parapet surrounding the arena of an ancient amphitheater or circus, and hence also the platform or path behind or above it. **2** A dais, platform, or stage; especially, the platform for the conductor of an orchestra. **3** *Zool.* A foot, or any footlike structure. [<L <Gk. *podion,* dim. of *pous, podos* foot]

-podium *combining form* A footlike part: *pseudopodium.*

-podous *combining form* -footed: used in adjectives corresponding to nouns in -pod and -poda: *arthropodous.* [<-POD + -OUS]

Po·dunk (pō′dungk) *n.* One of a tribe of North American Indians of Algonquian stock, formerly inhabiting parts of Connecticut and Massachusetts.

Po·dunk (pō′dungk) *n.* Any small town regarded as typically dull and non-progressive. [? from *Podunk,* Massachusetts <N. Am. Ind.]

po·du·rid (pō·dŏŏr′id, -dyŏŏr′-) *n.* Any of a widely distributed family (*Poduridae*) of primitive insects which includes the springtails. [<NL *Podura* <Gk. *pous, podos* foot + *oura* tail; from their ability to leap by sudden extensions of their infolded tails]

pod·zol (pod′zol) *adj.* Of, pertaining to, or designating a major soil type of northern regions developed principally under forest conditions and characterized by a strongly acid, infertile humus underlying a thin mat of leaves and decayed vegetation. Also **pod·zol′ic.** —*n.* Podzol soil. Also **pod′sol** (-sol). [<Russian, ashlike, salty <*sol′* salt]

Poe (pō), **Edgar Allan,** 1809–49, U.S. poet, critic, and short story writer.

po·em (pō′əm) *n.* **1** A composition in verse, either in meter or in free verse, characterized by the imaginative treatment of experience and a heightened use of language more intensive than ordinary speech. **2** Any composition in verse. **3** Any composition characterized by intensity and beauty of language or thought: a prose *poem.* **4** Any experience which produces an effect upon the mind similar or likened to that of a poem: a *poem* in stone. See synonyms under POETRY, SONG. [<F *poème* <L *poema* <Gk. *poiēma,* lit., anything made <*poiein* make]

poe·nol·o·gy (pē·nol′ə·jē) See PENOLOGY.

po·e·sy (pō′ə·sē, -zē) *n. pl.* **·sies 1** *Poetic* Poetry taken collectively. **2** *Poetic* The art or faculty of writing poetry. **3** *Obs.* A poem. **4** *Obs.* A motto or conceit, as one engraved on jewelry. See synonyms under POETRY, SONG. [<OF *poesie* <L *poesia* <Gk. *poiēsis* <*poiein*]

po·et (pō′it) *n.* **1** One who writes poems. **2** One especially endowed with imagination, the power of rhythmical expression, and the creative faculty or power of artistic construction. [<OF *poete* <L *poeta* <Gk. *poiētēs* <*poiein* make]. —**po′et·ess** *n. fem.*

po·et·as·ter (pō′it·as′tər) *n.* An inferior poet; a mere rimer or writer of mediocre verse. [<NL]

po·et·ic (pō·et′ik) *adj.* **1** Pertaining to poetry; having the nature or quality of or expressed in poetry: a *poetic* theme. **2** Pertaining to, befitting, or characteristic of a poet: *poetic* fire. **3** Fit to be described in poetry; of a nature to evoke poetic expression: a *poetic* incident or scene. **4** Having or showing the sensibility, feelings, faculty, etc., of a poet. **5** Celebrated or recounted in poetry or verse. Also **po·et′i·cal.** —*n.* Poetics. [<F *poétique* <L *poeticus* <Gk. *poiētikos*]

poetic justice The distribution of rewards to the good and punishment to the evil as often represented in literature; ideal justice.

poetic license The departure from the rules of diction, pronunciation, or from what is generally

regarded as fact, for the sake of rime, meter, or an over-all enhancement of effect.

po·et·ics (pō·et′iks) *n. pl.* (construed as singular) **1** The principles and nature of poetry or, by extension, of any art: the *poetics* of music. **2** A treatise on poetry. Also *poetic.*

po·et·ize (pō′it·īz) *v.* **·ized, ·iz·ing** *v.i.* **1** To write poetry. —*v.t.* **2** To turn into or describe by means of poetry; express in poetic form. **3** To make poetic. —**po′et·iz′er** *n.*

poet laureate *pl.* **poets laureate 1** The poet officially invested with the title of laureate by the crown of England, an officer of the royal household receiving a salary and formerly expected to write for public occasions. **2** In former times, a poet publicly crowned with laurel in recognition of his merits, usually by a sovereign. **3** A poet acclaimed as the most eminent in a locality.

po·et·ry (pō′it·rē) *n.* **1** The writing of poems; the art by which the poet projects feeling and experience onto an imaginative plane, in rhythmical words, to stir the imagination and the emotions. **2** The quality or effect of a poem manifested in any work of literature. **3** That which resembles poetry: Dancing is the *poetry* of motion. **4** A work or works metrically composed; verse or poems collectively; also, metrical composition in general: a book of *poetry.* [<OF *poetrie* <LL *poetria* <L *poeta* poet]

Synonyms: meter, numbers, poem, poesy, rime, song, verse. In ordinary usage, *poetry* is both imaginative and metrical. *Poetry* often exists without *rime*; it may exist without regular *meter,* as in free verse; substitution may be made for *meter,* as in the Hebrew parallelism; *poetry* may be expressed in a way beautiful, lyrically comic, or sharply satiric, but it must involve, besides the artistic form, the exercise of the fancy or imagination to heighten, intensify, and integrate feeling or experience. Failing this, there may be *verse, rime,* and *meter,* but not *poetry.* In a very wide sense *poetry* may be anything rhythmical; as, the *poetry* of motion. There is much in literature that is beautiful and sublime in thought and artistic in construction, which is yet not *poetry,* in the strict sense, because quite devoid of the rhythmical element, and the patterned arrangement and economy of words; the dividing line between poetry and "the other music of prose" is hard to draw. Compare METER², SONG. *Antonym:* prose.

po·go stick (pō′gō) A stiltlike toy, with a spring at the base and fitted with two projections for the feet, on which a person may stand and propel himself in a series of hops.

po·gy (pō′gē, pog′ē) *n. pl.* **·gies** or **·gy** The menhaden. [<N. Am. Ind. *pauhagen*]

poh (pō) *interj.* Pshaw! bah! an expletive signifying disgust or contempt. [Imit.]

Po·hai (bō′hī′), **Strait of** See CHIHLI, STRAIT OF.

poi (poi, pō′ē) *n.* A native Hawaiian food made from the ground root of the taro. [<Hawaiian]

-poietic *combining form* Making; producing; creating: *hemapoietic.* [<Gk. *poiētikos* forming <*poiein* make]

poign·ant (poin′yənt, poi′nənt) *adj.* **1** Severely painful or acute to the spirit; keenly piercing; bitter; severe: *poignant* grief; a *poignant* retort. **2** Sharp or stimulating to the taste; pungent; biting. See synonyms under VIOLENT. [<OF, ppr. of *poindre* prick <L *pungere*] —**poign′· an·cy** = **poign′ant·ly** *adv.*

poin·set·ti·a (poin·set′ē·ə) *n.* Any of a genus (*Euphorbia*) of American plants of the spurge family, with large showy bracts and inconspicuous flowers, especially an ornamental evergreen hothouse shrub (*E. pulcherrima*) from Mexico, with richly colored, red, leaflike bracts. [after J. R. *Poinsett,* 1779–1851, U.S. statesman]

POINSETTIA Flower in bracts.

point (point) *n.* **1** The sharp end of a thing, particularly

of anything that tapers so as to be very small and keen at the extremity: the *point* of a needle or a thorn. **2** *pl.* The extremities of a horse. **3** An object, as a tool or instrument, having a sharp or tapering end, as a needle, etching tool, etc. **4** A tapering tract of land extending into water; a promontory; cape: *Point* Judith. **5** A prominent feature or peculiarity; typical attribute; salient quality; essential physical characteristic: the *points* of a thoroughbred horse. **6** That to which effort is directed, on which attention is fixed, or to which especial importance is attached; the precise subject of discussion; aim; gist; purport: the *point* of a story. **7** A particular place, location, or position. **8** A position considered as one of a series; a unit of fluctuation, as of count in a game: to gain a *point.* **9** A precise grade, limit, or degree attained or determined, especially in temperature. **10** A particular juncture in the course of events. **11** Any single item or particular; detail. **12** A vital step or division of an argument or discourse; a proposition; head: to note every *point*; to contest *point* by *point.* **13** In schools and colleges, a unit of credit equal to a certain number of hours of academic work. **14** An indivisible portion of time; a particular moment. **15** The moment when something is about or likely to be done or to take place; verge: on the *point* of starting; at the *point* of death. **16** Point lace. **17** A cord or strap by which a thing is fastened, as a rope for reefing sails. **18** In 16th and 17th century costume, a ribbon or string with an aglet on one end, used to fasten together two pieces of clothing. **19** A mark made by or as by the end of a pointed instrument or tool; a prick; puncture; dot. **20** Any mark of punctuation; especially, among printers, a period; stop; end. **21** *Ling.* A vowel point as used in Hebrew. **22** *Music* A dot or other mark to designate time, or formerly tone; also, a short tune or strain; also, such tune when played on an instrument as a signal. **23** A decimal point. **24** Point system (def. 5). **25** The attitude of a pointer or setter when it finds game: The dog came to a *point.* **26** In fencing, a thrust; also, in dancing, the act of pointing the foot downward. **27** A trifle; punctilio: a mere *point.* **28** In cricket, a fielder stationed the nearest to the right of the wicket and slightly in advance of it; also, the position thus occupied. **29** *pl.* In baseball, the positions occupied by the pitcher and catcher. **30** The leading group of an advanced guard. **31** One of the 32 divisions of the compass. See POINT OF THE COMPASS. **32** That which is conceived to have position, but not parts or dimensions, as the extremity of a line. **33** A unit of variation in price of shares, stocks, etc., in the stock market; also, a rumor on which speculation is made; a tip. **34** A fixed place from which position and distance are reckoned. **35** A spot or place which is regarded as having position only, without extent, as a locality. **36** The tail of an animal: used in the phrase *heads and points.* **37** *Electr.* Any of a set of contacts determining the direction of current flow in a circuit. See synonyms under CIRCUMSTANCE, END, TOPIC. — **at** (or **on, upon**) **the point of** On the verge of. — **beside the point** Irrelevant. — **in point** Pertinent. — **in point of** In the matter of; as regards. — **to make a point of** To treat as vital or essential. — **to see the point** To understand the purpose of a course of action; get the important meaning of a story, joke, etc. — **to stretch a point** To make an exception. — **to the point** Relevant. —*v.t.* **1** To direct or aim, as a finger or weapon. **2** To indicate; direct attention to: often with *out:* to *point* the way; to *point* out errors. **3** To give force or point to, as a meaning or remark: often with *up.* **4** To shape or sharpen to a point. **5** To punctuate, as writing. **6** To mark or separate with points, as decimal fractions: with *off.* **7** In hunting, to indicate the presence or location of (game) by standing rigid and directing the muzzle toward it: said of dogs. **8** In masonry, to fill and finish the joints of (brickwork) with mortar. **9** *Ling.* To mark with a vowel point. —*v.i.* **10** To call attention or indicate direction by or as by extending the finger: usually with *at* or *to*. **11** To direct the mind: Everything *points* to your being wrong. **12** To be directed; have a specified direction; tend; face: with *to* or *toward*. **13** To point game: said of hunting dogs. **14** *Med.* To come to a head, as an abscess. **15** *Naut.* To sail close to the wind. See synonyms under ALLUDE. [Fusion of OF *pointe* a sharp point (<Med. L *puncta* <L *punctus*) + OF *point* prick, dot, moment <L *punctum*, neut. of *punctus*, pp. of *pungere* prick]

point alphabet The alphabet of the point system for the blind.

Point Bar·row (bar'ō) See BARROW, POINT.

point·blank (point'blangk') *adj.* **1** Aimed directly at the mark; in gunnery, fired horizontally without allowing for dropping. **2** Hence, direct; plain: a *pointblank* question. — *n.* A shot with direct aim. — *adv.* In a horizontal line; hence, directly; without circumlocution.

point–de·vice (point'di·vīs') *adj.* Scrupulously neat; precise; finical. — *adv.* Precisely; exactly. Also **point'–de·vise'**. [ME *(at point) devis*, i.e., (at an) exact (point) <OF *devis* exact]

point·ed (poin'tid) *adj.* **1** Having a point. **2** Piquant; pungent; epigrammatic; to the point. **3** Aimed at a particular person; emphasized; conspicuous. See synonyms under ACUTE, SHARP. — **point'ed·ly** *adv.* — **point'ed·ness** *n.*

point·er (poin'tər) *n.* **1** One who or that which points. **2** A hand or index finger, as on a clock or scale. **3** A long tapering rod used in class rooms to point out things on wall maps, charts, diagrams, etc. **4** One of a breed of dogs trained to scent and point out game. **5** A useful bit of information; hint. **6** *Nav.* One whose business is to bring the gun or turret to its proper elevation. Compare TRAINER. **7** The cowboy who rides at the head of the herd in a cattle drive.

pointes (points) *n. pl.* In ballet, dancing on tiptoe. [<F]

poin·til·lism (pwan'tə·liz'əm) *n.* A French neo-impressionist method of producing effects of light by placing small spots of varying hues on a surface in close proximity, the eye blending them together. [<F *pointillisme* <*pointiller* mark with dots] — **point'til·list** *n.*

point·ing (poin'ting) *n.* **1** The act of sharpening or bringing to a point. **2** Punctuation. See under PUNCTUATION. **3** In sculpture, the making of a plaster or clay model with points or marks at intervals and the transferring of these points to the surface of a stone block as an aid in reproducing the model accurately. **4** *Archit.* **a** The process of treating joints in masonry, slating, or tiling, by filling interstices, smoothing out, etc., to finish or repair and to weatherproof. **b** The removal of the thin top layer of mortar between courses of brick and masonry, to replace it with a more moisture-resistant compound. **5** In milling, the rubbing off of the points of grain.

point lace Needlepoint (def. 2). — **point–laced** (point'lāst') *adj.*

point·less (point'lis) *adj.* Without a point; dull; also, having no significance: a *pointless* remark. See synonyms under BLUNT, FLAT[1]. — **point'less·ly** *adv.* — **point'less·ness** *n.*

point of order In parliamentary language, a question of procedure under the rules.

point of the compass One of the 32 equidistant directions or division points marked on the card of the mariners' compass, or a corresponding point in the horizon, or a vertical plane passing through the horizon and one of such points. See COMPASS CARD.

point of view The relative position from which one sees an object, a proposition, or the like. Compare STANDPOINT.

point system 1 *Printing* A standard system of sizes for type bodies, 996 points of which are equal to 35 centimeters, one point being .0138 inch (or approximately 1/72 inch), as adopted by the Typefounders' Association of the United States. **2** Any system of raised letters for the blind, as braille, in which the alphabet is formed of groups of raised dots or points. **3** An academic system of allowing students to progress according to points or credits earned in individual subjects. **4** Any method of rating based on the accumulation of points.

point target A particular structure, object, or installation selected for direct gunfire or bombing. Compare AREA TARGET.

poise[·] (poiz) *v.* **poised, pois·ing** *v.t.* **1** To bring into or hold in balance; maintain in equilibrium. **2** To hold; support, as in readiness. **3** *Rare* To weigh. — *v.i.* **4** To be balanced or suspended; hover. — *n.* **1** The state or quality of being balanced; equilibrium; equipoise; also, indecision; suspense. **2** Equanimity; repose; dignity, as in bearing or carriage. **3** A balance weight or counterpoise. **4** Any position that indicates suspended motion. [<OF *il poise, peise*, 3rd person sing. of *peser* <L *pensare*, intens. of *pendere* weigh] — **pois'er** *n.*

poi·son (poi'zən) *n.* **1** Any substance which, introduced into an organism in relatively small amounts, acts chemically upon the tissues to produce serious injury or death. **2** *Physics* Any substance or material which, by absorbing neutrons, prevents fission in an atomic reactor. **3** Anything that tends to taint or destroy character or to mislead, corrupt, or pervert. — *v.t.* **1** To administer poison–to; kill or injure with poison. **2** To put poison into or on. **3** To affect wrongfully; corrupt; pervert: to *poison* one's mind. — *adj.* Killing; venomous; corrupting. [<OF <L *potio, -onis* a drink, poisonous draft. Doublet of POTION.] — **poi'son·er** *n.*

poison dogwood, poison elder Poison sumac.

poison gas Any of a class of toxic chemical agents, usually a liquid under high vapor pressure, employed in warfare for the purpose of disabling or killing enemy personnel.

poison hemlock See under HEMLOCK.

poison ivy A climbing shrub (*Toxicodendron radicans* or *Rhus toxicodendron*), a species of sumac with three broadly ovate, variously notched, sinuate or cut–lobed leaflets and whitish berries: poisonous to many persons by touch.

poison oak 1 A species of poison sumac, especially *Toxicodendron quercifolium*. **2** A species of poison ivy (*T. rydlergii*) common in the western United States.

poi·son·ous (poi'zən·əs) *adj.* **1** Containing or being a poison. **2** Having the effect of a poison; toxic; vitiating. See synonyms under NOISOME. — **poi'son·ous·ly** *adv.* — **poi'son·ous·ness** *n.*

poison sumac 1 A handsome shrub or small tree (*Toxicodendron vernix* or *Rhus vernix*), growing in swamps in the United States and Canada. It has smooth, entire leaflets, and loose panicles of smooth greenish–yellow drupes. The whole plant is poisonous to taste or touch. **2** Poison ivy.

poi·trel (poi'trəl) *n.* The armor formerly used to protect the breast of a war horse. [<OF *poitral* <L *pectorale* breastplate <*pectus* breast]

poke[1] (pōk) *v.* **poked, pok·ing** *v.t.* **1** To push or prod, as with the elbow; jab: to *poke* a person in the ribs. **2** To make by or as by thrusting: to *poke* a hole. **3** To thrust or push in, out, through, from, etc.: to *poke* one's head from a window. **4** To stir (a fire, etc.) by prodding: often with *up.* — *v.i.* **5** To make thrusts, as with a stick or weapon: often with *at.* **6** To intrude or meddle. **7** To go or look curiously; pry. **8** To appear or show: logs *poking* above the surface. **9** To proceed slowly; dawdle; putter. — **to poke one's nose into** To meddle in. — **to poke fun at** To ridicule, especially slily. — *n.* **1** A push; prod. **2** A yokelike collar with long projections to prevent animals from passing through fences. **3** One who moves sluggishly; a dawdler. **4** *Colloq.* A punch. [ME *poken.* Cf. LG, Du. *poken* push.]

poke[2] (pōk) *n.* A pocket, or small bag. See POCK[2]. [<OF <Gmc. Cf. ON *poki* and MDu. *poke.*]

pok·er[1] (pō'kər) *n.* **1** One who or that which pokes. **2** An iron rod for poking a fire.

pok·er[2] (pō'kər) *n.* Any of several games of cards in which the players bet on the value of the cards, usually five, dealt to them, and he whose hand contains the group of highest value wins the entire sum wagered, provided he has not dropped out of the betting. The groups usually recognized, in the ascending order of value, are the *pair, two pairs, three of a kind, straight, flush, full hand* or *house, four of a kind, straight flush.* [Origin uncer-

tain. Cf. G *pochspiel*, lit., bragging game < *pochen* brag.]

pok·er·face (pō'kər·fās') *n.* A face that reveals nothing: so called from the controlled and inscrutable faces of professional poker–players.

pok·er·ish (pō'kər·ish) *adj.* **1** Stiff or unbending, as a poker. **2** Ghastly; unearthly. — **pok'er·ish·ly** *adv.*

pok·ing (pō'king) *adj.* **1** Drudging; servile; mean. **2** Projecting.

pok·y (pō'kē) *adj.* **pok·i·er, pok·i·est** **1** Lacking life or spirit; dull; slow. **2** Shabby. **3** Cramped; stuffy. Also **poke'y.**

po·lac·ca (pō·lak'ə) *n.* A two- or three–masted Mediterranean vessel. Also **po·la·cre** (pō·lä'kər). [<Ital.]

Po·land (pō'lənd) A republic of north central Europe; 120,359 square miles; capital, Warsaw: Polish *Polska.*

po·lar (pō'lər) *adj.* **1** Pertaining to the poles of a sphere, as of the earth. **2** Coming from or found near the North or South Pole. **3** Pertaining to the poles of a magnet or other center of attraction or repulsion. **4** Exhibiting ionization. **5** Having or proceeding from a point of radiation. **6** Attracting; guiding. **7** *Math.* **a** Of or pertaining to a coordinate system of representing equations graphically whereby a point is located by its linear distance from the pole and by the angle subtended by a line from the point to the pole and the polar axis. **b** Of or pertaining to a curve or an equation traced or traceable by means of such coordinates. [<Med. L *polaris* <*polus* pole]

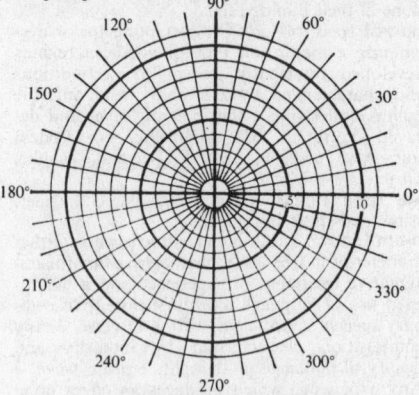

POLAR COORDINATE SYSTEM
The polar axis is the horizontal axis.

polar axis *Math.* A fixed line directed from the pole in the polar coordinate system from which angles are measured in a counterclockwise direction.

polar bear A large, amphibious, white bear of arctic regions (*Thalarctus maritimus*).

polar circles The Arctic and Antarctic circles.

polar distance Codeclination.

po·lar·im·e·ter (pō'lə·rim'ə·tər) *n.* **1** An instrument for measuring the rotation of the plane of polarization or the proportion of polarized light in a beam. **2** A form of polariscope. [<L *polaris* polar + -METER]

Po·lar·is (pō·lar'is) **1** The polestar or North Star: Alpha in the constellation Ursa Minor. See under STAR. **2** An intermediate range ballistic missile of the U.S. Navy designed to be launched from a submerged submarine. [<L]

po·lar·i·scope (pō·lar'ə·skōp) *n.* An optical instrument for exhibiting or measuring the polarization of light. [<L *polaris* polar + -SCOPE]

po·lar·i·ty (pō·lar'ə·tē) *n.* **1** The quality of having opposite poles. **2** *Physics* That quality of a body by which it exhibits certain properties related to a line of direction through its mass, the properties at one end of this line being of opposite or contrasting nature to the properties at the other end, as in a magnet. **3** The quality of being attracted to one pole and repelled from the other.

po·lar·i·za·tion (pō'lər·ə·zā'shən, -ī·zā'-) *n.* **1** The act of polarizing, or state of being polarized; bestowal or gaining of polarity. **2** *Physics* A condition of radiant energy, most noticeable in light, in which its vibrations assume a definite form or direction when subjected to special influences. Light may be polarized by reflection, at an angle which differs for different substances, or by transmission, as through most crystals or solutions. If light thus treated be examined by subjecting it to such reflection or transmission a second time, it is found that in certain positions of the reflector or crystal it will pass most easily, while in the positions at right angles to these it will be totally quenched, and in intermediate positions it will pass partially. The plane of polarization is altered or rotated by the passage of light through suitable media; this is called **rotary polarization,** which takes two directions, right–handed and left–handed. 3 *Electr.* A change in the potential of the electrode of a cell due to the accumulation upon it of dissociation products liberated by the current. **— angle of polarization** or **polarizing angle** That angle of reflection from a plane surface at which light is polarized. **— plane of polarization** The plane in which the light vibrations occur when polarized.

POLARIZATION
Of the light emitted at *a,* only the part whose electric oscillations are parallel to the axis of polarizing medium *b* can pass through it. This is blocked at polarizing medium *c,* whose axis is at right angles to that of *b.*

po·lar·ize (pō′lə·rīz) *v.t.* **·ized, ·iz·ing 1** To develop polarization in; give polarity to. **2** To give a special meaning or direction to. Also *Brit.* **po′lar·ise. — po′lar·iz′a·ble** *adj.* **— po′lar·iz′er** *n.*
polar lights The aurora borealis or the aurora australis.
Po·lar·oid (pō′lə·roid) *n.* A material composed of a sheet of specially prepared plastic between layers of glass and having the property of polarizing and thus reducing the intensity of the light passing through it: a trade name.
Polar Regions The areas within the Arctic and Antarctic circles.

NORTH POLAR REGIONS

pol·der (pōl′dər) *n.* A tract of marshy land, lower than the sea, which has been diked and reclaimed to cultivation. Also **pol′der·land′.** [<Du.]

pole¹ (pōl) *n.* **1** Either of the extremities of an axis or sphere. **2** One of two points where the axis of rotation, as of the earth, meets the surface. **3** Either of the Polar Regions of the earth; also, either of the two extremities of the earth's axis, called the North *Pole* and the South *Pole.* See CELESTIAL POLE. **4** *Physics* One of the two points at which opposite physical qualities are concentrated; especially, a point (usually one of two) of maximum intensity of electric or magnetic force. **5** The

polestar. **6** *Biol.* The differentiated extremities of an ovum or other cell. **7** *Physiol.* The point of a nerve cell where a process has its origin. **8** *Math.* In polar coordinate and spherical coordinate systems, that point where all radius vectors equal zero. ◆ Homophone: *poll.* [<L *polus* <Gk. *polos* pivot, pole <*pelein* be in motion]
pole² (pōl) *n.* **1** A long slender piece of wood or metal, commonly tapering and more or less rounded; a Maypole, beanpole, the mast of a vessel, etc. **2** The tongue of a vehicle. **3** In linear and surface measure, a perch or rod. **4** A fishing rod. — *v.* **poled, pol·ing** *v.t.* **1** To propel, push, or strike with a pole. **2** To support on poles, as growing beans. — *v.i.* **3** To push a boat, raft, etc., with a pole. ◆ Homophone: *poll.* [OE *pal* <L *palus* stake]
pole·cat (pōl′kat′) *n.* **1** One of certain European carnivores (genus *Mustela*) of the weasel family, noted for a fetid odor when irritated or alarmed. **2** *U.S.* A skunk. [<F *poule* pullet + CAT; from its predacity]
po·lem·ic (pō·lem′ik) *adj.* Pertaining to controversy; disputatious. Also **po·lem′i·cal.** — *n.* **1** A controversy; also, the speeches, papers, etc., comprising this. **2** One who engages in controversy. [<Gk. *polemikos* warlike < *polemos* war]
po·lem·ics (pō·lem′iks) *n.* The art or practice of disputation; especially, the use of aggressive argument to refute errors of doctrine.
pol·er (pō′lər) *n.* **1** The draft animal harnessed nearest the pole of a cart or wagon; a wheeler. **2** One who poles a boat.
pole·star (pōl′stär′) *n.* **1** *Astron.* The North Star; Polaris; Alpha in Ursa Minor. **2** That which governs, guides, or directs; an attracting or controlling principle.
pole vault A vault or jump with a long pole, usually over a light horizontal bar: an athletic field event.
po·lice (pə·lēs′) *n.* **1** A body of civil officers, especially in a city, organized under authority to maintain order and enforce law; constabulary. **2** The whole system of internal regulation of a state, or the local government of a city or town; that department of government that maintains and enforces law and order, and prevents, detects, or deals with crime. **3** The cleansing or keeping clean of a camp or garrison; also, the soldiers detailed for the duties of policing in camp. — *v.t.* **·liced, ·lic·ing 1** To protect, regulate, or maintain order in (a city, country, etc.) with or as

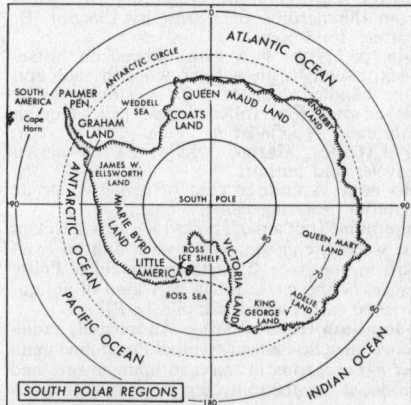

SOUTH POLAR REGIONS

with police. **2** *U.S.* To make clean or orderly, as a military camp. [<F <LL *politia* governmental administration <Gk. *politeia* polity < *politēs* citizen <*polis* city]
police court A municipal court where minor criminal cases are tried. Its jurisdiction corresponds with that of a justice of the peace.
police power The broad authority of a state to limit private rights to the extent necessary to promote the peace, good order, morals, health, and safety of the general community.
police state A country whose citizens are rigidly supervised by a national police, often working secretly.
pol·i·clin·ic (pol′i·klin′ik) *n.* The dispensary

of a hospital, or that part of it in which out-patients are treated. Compare POLYCLINIC. [<G *poliklinik* <Gk. *polis* city + G *klinik* clinic]
pol·i·cy¹ (pol′ə·sē) *n. pl.* **·cies 1** Prudence or sagacity in the conduct of affairs. **2** A course or plan of action, especially of administrative action. **3** Any system of management based on self–interest as opposed to equity; finesse in general; artifice. **4** *Obs.* Political science; government. See synonyms under POLITY. [<OF *policie* <L *politia* <Gk. *politeia.* See POLICE.]
pol·i·cy² (pol′ə·sē) *n. pl.* **·cies 1** A written contract of insurance. **2** A gambling game in which certain numbers (12 or 13) are drawn from a possible 78, bets being made as to what combinations will appear; also, any variation of this game. [<F *police* < Ital. *polizza,* aphetic alter. of Med.L *apodixa, apodissa* receipt <Gk. *apodeixis* proof < *apodeiknynai* make known]
policy racket Numbers pool.
po·li·o (pō′lē·ō) *n. Colloq.* Poliomyelitis.
po·li·o·my·e·li·tis (pol′ē·ō·mī′ə·li′tis, pō′lē-) *n. Pathol.* An acute, communicable disease caused by infection with a virus, occurring especially in children, and characterized by inflammation of the gray matter of the spinal cord, followed by paralysis and atrophy of various muscle groups: also called *infantile paralysis.* [<NL <POLIO- + Gk. *myelos* marrow + -ITIS]
pol·ish (pol′ish) *n.* **1** Smoothness or glossiness of surface; finish. **2** A substance used to produce a bright, smooth, or glossy surface; a varnish. **3** Refinement of manner or style. **4** The process of polishing. — *v.t.* **1** To make smooth or lustrous, as by rubbing. **2** To make complete; finish; perfect. **3** To free from crudeness; make refined or elegant: to *polish* the mind. — *v.i.* **4** To take a gloss; shine. **5** To become elegant or refined. **— to polish off 1** To do or finish completely or quickly. **2** To dispose of; overwhelm. **— to polish up** To make better; improve. [<OF *poliss-,* stem of *polir* <L *polire* make smooth] **— pol′ish·er** *n.*
Po·lish (pō′lish) *adj.* Pertaining to Poland, its inhabitants, or their language. — *n.* The West Slavic language of the Poles.
pol·ished (pol′isht) *adj.* **1** Made smooth by polishing. **2** Naturally smooth and glossy. **3** Refined and polite. See synonyms under FINE¹, POLITE, SMOOTH.
po·lite (pə·līt′) *adj.* **1** Exhibiting in manner or speech a considerate regard for others; courteous; also, cultivated: *polite* society. **2** Finished and elegant in style. [<L *politus,* pp. of *polire* polish] **— po·lite′ly** *adv.* **— po·lite′ness** *n.*
Synonyms: accomplished, civil, complaisant, courteous, courtly, cultivated, cultured, elegant, genteel, gracious, obliging, polished, urbane, well–behaved, well–bred, well–mannered. A man may be *civil* with no consideration for others, simply because self–respect forbids him to be rude; but one who is *polite* has at least some care for the opinions of others, and if *polite* in the highest and truest sense, he cares for the comfort and happiness of others in the smallest matters. *Civil* is a colder and more distant word than *polite; courteous* is fuller and richer, dealing often with greater matters, and is used only in the good sense. *Courtly* suggests that which befits a royal court, and is used of external grace and stateliness without reference to the prompting feeling. *Genteel* refers to an external elegance, which may be showy and superficial, and the word is thus inferior to *polite* or *courteous. Urbane* refers to a politeness that is genial and successful in giving others a sense of ease and cheer. *Polished* refers to external elegancies of speech and manner without reference to spirit or purpose; as, a *polished* gentleman or a *polished* scoundrel; *cultured* refers to a real and high development of mind and soul, of which the external manifestation is the smallest part. *Complaisant* denotes a disposition to please or favor. *Antonyms:* awkward, bluff, blunt, boorish, brusk, clownish, coarse, discourteous, ill–behaved, ill–bred, ill–mannered, im-

pertinent, impolite, impudent, insolent, insulting, raw, rude, rustic, uncivil, uncouth, unpolished, untaught, untutored.

pol·i·tic (pol'ə·tik) *adj.* **1** Sagacious and wary in planning; artful; crafty; shrewd, especially in statesmanship. **2** Wisely adapted to an end; specious. **3** *Rare* Pertaining to public polity, or to the state or its government; political. See BODY POLITIC. [<OF *politique* <L *politicus* <Gk. *politikos* civic < *politēs* citizen] — **pol'i·tic·ly** *adv.*
Synonyms: artful, crafty, cunning, diplomatic, discreet, judicious, prudent, sagacious, shrewd, wary, wily, wise.
po·lit·i·cal (pə·lit'i·kəl) *adj.* **1** Pertaining to public policy; concerned in the administration of government: a *political* system: distinguished from *civil*. **2** Belonging to the science of government; treating of polity or politics: *political* principles. **3** Having an organized system of government; administering a polity. **4** Pertaining to or connected with a party or parties controlling or seeking to control government in a state: *political* methods. [<L *politicus*] — **po·lit'i·cal·ly** *adv.*
political science The science of the form and principles of civil government, and the extent and manner of its intervention in public and private affairs; politics.
pol·i·ti·cian (pol'ə·tish'ən) *n.* **1** One engaged in politics, especially professionally. **2** *U.S.* One who engages in politics for personal or partisan aims rather than for reasons of principle; also, a political schemer or opportunist. **3** *Brit.* One skilled in the science of government or politics; a statesman. **4** The white-eyed vireo: so called because it feathers its nest with bits of newspaper or whatever comes easily. [<F *politicien*]
po·lit·i·cize (pə·lit'ə·sīz) *v.t.* **·cized, ·ciz·ing 1** To make politically active or aware. **2** To make into a political issue. Also **po·lit'i·cal·ize'** (-kəl·īz'). — **po·lit'i·ci·za'tion** *n.*
pol·i·tick·ing (pol'ə·tik·ing) *n.* Involvement in politics. — **pol'i·tick·er** *n.*
po·lit·i·co (pə·lit'i·kō) *n. pl.* **·cos** A politician. [<Sp. *político*]
pol·i·tics (pol'ə·tiks) *n.* **1** The science of civil government. **2** Political affairs in a party sense; party intrigues, etc. **3** One's political sentiments: construed as plural. — **to play politics** To speak or act for political reasons; hence, to scheme for an advantage.
pol·i·ty (pol'ə·tē) *n. pl.* **·ties 1** The form or method of government of a nation, state, church, etc. **2** Any community living under some definite form of government. [<OF *politie*, var. of *policie*. See POLICY[1].]
Synonym: policy. *Polity* is the permanent system of government of a state, a church, or a society; *policy* is the method of management with reference to the attainment of certain ends; the national `polity of the United States is republican; each administration has a *policy* of its own. *Policy* is often used as equivalent to expediency; as, Many think honesty to be good *policy*. *Polity* in ecclesiastical use serves a valuable purpose in distinguishing that which relates to administration and government from that which relates to faith and doctrine. See LEGISLATION.
Polk (pōk), **James Knox,** 1795–1849, president of the United States 1845–49.
pol·ka (pōl'kə, pō'-) *n.* **1** A round dance of Bohemian origin in common time, with three steps to every second measure. **2** Music for such a dance: a lively Bohemian or Polish tune in 2/4 time. — *v.i.* **·kaed, ·ka·ing** To dance the polka. [<F <Czech *pulka* half (step)]
polka dot 1 One of a series of spots of various sizes and spacing on a textile fabric. **2** A pattern made up of such spots.
poll (pōl) *n.* **1** The head; hence, a person; also, the top or back of the head; crown. **2** A list of persons. **3** The voting at an election; the votes thus registered or voted; also, the place where they are registered or voted: used in the United States in the plural. **4** A poll tax. **5** The blunt or round end of a hammer or ax. **6** A survey of public opinion on a given subject, usually obtained from a sample group. — *v.t.* **1** To receive (a specified number of votes). **2** To enrol, as for taxation or voting; register. **3** To cast at the polls. **4** To canvass in a poll (def. 6). **5** To

cut off or trim, as hair, horns, etc.; clip; shear. **6** To cut off or trim the hair, horns, top, etc., of: to *poll* cattle; to *poll* a tree. — *v.i.* **7** To vote at the polls; cast one's vote. ◆ Homophone: *pole*. [<MDu. *polle* top of the head] — **poll'er** *n.*
polled (pōld) *adj.* **1** Shorn of the head or top. **2** Shorn of the hair; bald.
pol·len (pol'ən) *n.* The fine yellowish powder formed within the anther of the flowering plant; the fecundating element in seed plants. [<L, fine flour]
pollen count A measure of the relative concentration of pollen grains in the atmosphere at a given locality and date: usually expressed in the number of grains of a specified variety of pollen per cubic yard.
pol·lex (pol'eks) *n. pl.* **pol·li·ces** (pol'ə·sēz) The first or radial digit of the hand or forelimb of a vertebrate; the thumb. [<L] — **pol'li·cal** *adj.*
pol·li·nate (pol'ə·nāt) *v.t.* **·nat·ed, ·nat·ing** To supply or convey pollen to. Also **pol'len·ate.**
pol·li·na·tion (pol'ə·nā'shən) *n.* The transfer of pollen from anthers to stigmas. Also **pol'len·a'tion.**
pol·lin·i·um (pə·lin'ē·əm) *n. pl.* **·i·a** (-ē·ə) A mass or body of pollen grains more or less coherent; a pollen mass. [<NL <L *pollen, pollinis* fine flour]
pol·li·wog (pol'ē·wog) *n.* A tadpole. Also **pol'ly·wog.** [ME *polwygle.* Cf. POLL[1], WIGGLE.]
poll·ster (pōl'stər) *n.* One who takes public opinion polls. Also **poll'ist.**
poll tax A tax on a person, as distinguished from that on property, especially as a prerequisite for voting.
pol·lut·ant (pə·lōō'tənt) *n.* **1** That which pollutes. **2** Any of various noxious chemicals and refuse materials which impair the purity of water, soil, or the atmosphere.
pol·lute (pə·lōōt') *v.t.* **·lut·ed, ·lut·ing** To make unclean or impure; dirty; corrupt; profane. [<L *pollutus,* pp. of *polluere* make unclean] — **pol·lut'ed** *adj.* — **pol·lut'ed·ly** *adv.* — **pol·lut'ed·ness** *n.* — **pol·lut'er** *n.* — **pol·lu'tion** *n.*
Synonyms: abuse, contaminate, corrupt, debauch, defile, degrade, deprave, dishonor, infect, ravish, soil, stain, taint, violate, vitiate. See CORRUPT, DEFILE[1], VIOLATE. *Antonyms:* clarify, clean, cleanse, clear, filter, fine, purge, purify, redeem, refine, renew, restore.
Pol·lux (pol'əks) See CASTOR AND POLLUX.
Pol·ly·an·na (pol'ē·an'ə) *n.* A person who always finds good in everything: so called from the heroine of stories by Eleanor H. Porter, 1868–1920.
po·lo (pō'lō) *n.* **1** A game played on horseback, usually with a light wooden ball and long-handled mallets. **2** A similar game played on ice or roller skates. [Cf. Tibetan *pulu* ball] — **po'lo·ist** *n.*
Po·lo (pō'lō), **Marco,** 1254?–1324?, Venetian traveler and author.
polo coat A tailored coat of camel's hair or material imitating camel's hair.
pol·o·naise (pol'ə·nāz', pō'lə-) *n.* **1** A garment for women, consisting of a waist and an overskirt in one piece. **2** A stately marchlike Polish dance, or the music for it. **3** A kind of antique Oriental carpet with a silk pile. [<F]
po·lo·ni·um (pə·lō'nē·əm) *n.* An intensely radioactive metallic element (symbol Po, atomic number 84) occurring in traces in uranium ores and produced synthetically by neutron bombardment of bismuth and other metals. See PERIODIC TABLE. [<NL <Med. L *Polonia,* Poland]
pol·ter·geist (pōl'tər·gīst) *n.* A ghost or spirit reputed to make its presence known by any kind of clatter, as knockings and the noises of moving objects. [<G <*poltern* make a noise + *geist* spirit]
pol·troon (pol·trōōn') *n.* **1** A mean-spirited coward; dastard. **2** A lazy idler; sluggard. — *adj.* Cowardly; contemptible. [<F *poltron* <Ital. *poltrone* cowardly, sluggish <*poltro* bed] — **pol·troon'er·y** *n.*
poly- *combining form* **1** Many; several; much: *polygamy, polygon.* **2** Excessive; abnormal: *polydactylism.* [<Gk. *polys* much, many]
pol·y·an·dry (pol'ē·an'drē) *n.* **1** The civil condition of having more than one husband. **2** A social order than includes a plurality of husbands.

3 *Bot.* Having 20 or more stamens. [<POLY- + Gk. *anēr, andros* a man] — **pol'y·an'drous** *adj.*
pol·y·ar·chy (pol'ē·är'kē) *n. pl.* **·chies** Government by several persons of whatever class. — **pol'y·ar'chic** or **·chi·cal** *adj.*
pol·y·cen·trism (pol'i·sen'triz·əm) *n.* The existence of several centers of power within an organization or political system, especially in the Communist world. — **pol'y·cen'trist** *n. & adj.*
pol·y·chrome (pol'i·krōm) *adj.* Done in several or many colors. — *n.* An association of several colors, as in decoration.
pol·y·chro·mic (pol'i·krō'mik) *adj.* Exhibiting many colors or changes of color. Also **pol'y·chro·mat·ic** (-krō·mat'ik) **pol'y·chro'mous.**
pol·y·chro·my (pol'i·krō'mē) *n.* The art of decorating or executing in several or many colors, as in ancient statuary and architecture.
pol·y·clin·ic (pol'i·klin'ik) *n.* **1** An institution furnishing clinical instruction in all kinds of diseases. **2** A general hospital in which many diseases are treated. Compare POLICLINIC.
pol·y·con·ic (pol'i·kon'ik) *adj.* Of, relating to, or based on many cones.
polyconic projection A type of map projection in which the parallels of latitude are arcs of circles which are not concentric and the meridians, except the central one, are curved lines.

POLYCONIC PROJECTION

Po·lyc·ra·tes (pə·lik'rə·tēz), died 522 B.C., tyrant of Samos; crucified.
pol·y·cy·the·mi·a (pol'ē·sī·thē'mē·ə) *n.* The presence of an abnormally large number of erythrocytes in the bloodstream. [<POLY- + CYT- + -EMIA]
pol·y·dac·tyl (pol'i·dak'til) *adj.* Having an abnormally large number of fingers or toes; many-fingered or many-toed: also **pol'y·dac'ty·lous.** — *n.* A polydactyl animal. — **pol'y·dac'tyl·ism** *n.*
Pol·y·deu·ces (pol'i·dōō'sēz, -dyōō'-) Pollux. See CASTOR and POLLUX.
pol·y·er·gic (pol'ē·ûr'jik) *adj.* Capable of accomplishing many tasks; energetically versatile. [<POLY- + Gk. *ergon* work]
pol·y·es·ter fiber (pol'ē·es'tər) *Chem.* A synthetic fiber of high tensile strength made by the esterification of ethylene glycol and other organic compounds.
pol·y·ga·la (pə·lig'ə·lə) *n.* **1** Any of a large genus (*Polygala*) of herbs and shrubs, natives of temperate and subtropical regions, and distinguished by simple, entire leaves, sometimes dotted, and showy magenta, purple, or white flowers; especially, the North American fringed polygala (*P. paucifolia*). **2** The milkwort. [<POLY- + Gk. *gala* milk]
pol·y·ga·mous (pə·lig'ə·məs) *adj.* **1** Of, pertaining to, or characterized by polygamy. **2** Mating with more than one of the opposite sex. **3** *Bot.* Bearing male, female, and bisexual or hermaphrodite flowers on the same plant. [<POLY- + -GAMOUS] — **po·lyg'a·mous·ly** *adv.*
po·lyg·a·my (pə·lig'ə·mē) *n.* **1** The condition of having more than one wife or husband at the same time. **2** The state of having more than one mate. Compare MONOGAMY. — **po·lyg'a·mist** *n.*
pol·y·glot (pol'i·glot) *adj.* **1** Expressed in several tongues. **2** Speaking several languages. — *n.* **1** A book giving versions of the same text, as of the Scriptures, in several languages. **2** One who speaks or writes several languages. [<Gk. *polyglōttos*]
pol·y·gon (pol'i·gon) *n. Geom.* A closed, usually plane, figure bounded by straight lines or arcs, especially more than four; a figure having many sides and angles. [<LL *polygonum* <Gk. *polygōnon*]

polygonal number See under NUMBER.
po·lyg·o·num (pə·lig'ə·nəm) *n.* Any of a large and widely distributed genus (*Polygonum*) of annual or perennial herbs. The common smartweed, the prince's-feather, and the bistort are among the best-known species. Also **po·lyg'o·ny.** [<NL <L *polygonos* <Gk. *polygonon* knotgrass <*poly-* many + *gony* knee; from its many joints]
pol·y·graph (pol'i·graf, -gräf) *n.* **1** A device for

reproducing a drawing or writing many times; a copy pad. **2** A mechanism for multiplying a drawing or writing. **3** A versatile or prolific author. **4** A collection of different treatises or books. **5** *Med.* A device for recording variations in the heartbeat and in respiratory movements: used as a lie detector. Compare PSYCHOGALVANOMETER. [< Gk. *polygraphos*] —**pol′y·graph′ic** or **·i·cal** *adj.*

po·lyg·ra·phy (pə·lig′rə·fē) *n.* **1** The use of a polygraph. **2** The art of writing in or of interpreting various ciphers.

po·lyg·y·nous (pə·lij′ə·nəs) *adj.* **1** Of, pertaining to, or practicing polygyny. **2** *Bot.* Having many styles.

po·lyg·y·ny (pə·lij′ə·nē) *n.* The marriage, mating, or cohabitation of one male with more than one female. [< POLY- + Gk. *gynē* woman]

pol·y·he·dral (pol′i·hē′drəl) *adj.* Of or pertaining to a polyhedron.

polyhedral angle *Geom.* The angle formed by three or more planes passing through a point; an angle at a vertex of a solid.

POLYHEDRAL ANGLE
Lateral angles *bac, bad*, etc., form angle at vertex *a*.

pol·y·he·dron (pol′i·hē′drən) *n. pl.* **·dra** (-drə) or **·drons** *Geom.* A solid bounded by plane faces, especially by more than four. [< NL < Gk. *polyedros* many-sided < *polys* many + *hedra* side]

pol·y·math (pol′ə·math) *n.* One who is learned in many different fields or disciplines. [< POLY- + Gk. *mathanein* learn] —**pol′y·math′ic** *adj.*

pol·y·morph (pol′i·môrf) *n.* A substance or organism that exhibits polymorphism. [< Gk. *polymorphos* < *poly*- many + *morphē* form]

pol·y·mor·phism (pol′i·môr′fiz·əm) *n.* **1** *Zool.* The property of assuming or passing through several forms, as an animal exhibiting seasonal changes in coloration. **2** *Mineral.* The occurrence in a mineral of two or more distinct crystal forms of identical chemical composition.

pol·y·mor·phous–per·verse (pol′i·môr′fəs·pər·vûrs′) *adj. Psychoanal.* Designating the generalized sexual potentialities of an individual, especially of a young child.

Pol·y·ne·sia (pol′i·nē′zhə, -shə) The islands of Oceania in the central and SE Pacific, extending east of Melanesia and Micronesia from the Hawaiian Islands to New Zealand; total, about 10,000 square miles.

Pol·y·ne·sian (pol′i·nē′zhən, -shən) *n.* **1** One of the native brown–skinned people of Polynesia: believed to be either of Malay stock originally stemming from a Caucasian strain of Asia, or of mixed Melanesian, Malay, and Caucasian stock. **2** A subfamily of the Austronesian family of languages spoken by these people. —*adj.* Of or pertaining to Polynesia, its people, or their languages.

Pol·y·ni·ces (pol′i·nī′sēz) In Greek legend, a son of Oedipus and Jocasta. See SEVEN AGAINST THEBES.

pol·y·no·mi·al (pol′i·nō′mē·əl) *adj.* Of, pertaining to, or consisting of many names or terms. —*n.* **1** *Math.* An expression, as in algebra, containing two or more terms. **2** *Biol.* A scientific name consisting of more than two terms. [< POLY- + (BI)NOMIAL]

pol·y·ose (pol′ē·ōs) *n.* Polysaccharide. [< POLY- + -OSE²]

pol·yp (pol′ip) *n.* **1** *Zool.* **a** A many–tentacled, sessile aquatic coelenterate having a radially symmetrical body typically cylindrical or cup–shaped, as a sea anemone or coral. **b** A single unit of a colonial organism. **2** *Pathol.* A polypus. [< MF *polype* < L *polypus* a cuttlefish, a polypus < Gk. *polypous* < *poly*- many + *pous* a foot]

pol·y·pha·gi·a (pol′i·fā′jē·ə) *n.* **1** Excessive craving for food; voracity. **2** *Zool.* The practice of eating many kinds of food. [< NL < Gk. < *polyphagos* eating to excess < *poly*- much + *phagein* eat] —**pol′y·pha′gi·an** *n.* & *adj.*

pol·y·phag·ic (pol′i·faj′ik) *adj.* Eating many things; subsisting on various kinds of food. Also **po·lyph·a·gous** (pə·lif′ə·gəs).

pol·y·phe·mus (pol′i·fē′məs) *n.* **1** An animal,

or sometimes a person, having but one eye. **2** A large American silkworm moth (*Telea polyphemus*) having a conspicuous ocellus on each hind wing. [< NL < L, POLYPHEMUS]

Pol·y·phe·mus (pol′i·fē′məs) In Homer's *Odyssey*, the Cyclops who imprisoned Odysseus and his companions in a cave, from which they escaped after blinding him in his sleep. [< L < Gk. *Polyphēmos*, a Cyclops, lit., many–voiced < *poly*- many + *phēmē* a voice]

pol·y·phon·ic (pol′i·fon′ik) *adj.* **1** *Phonet.* Representing more than one sound or combination of sounds, as some written characters. **2** Consisting of many sounds or voices. **3** *Music* **a** Designating or involving the simultaneous and harmonious combination of two or more independent parts or melodies. **b** Denoting an instrument, as a piano, by which two or more sounds may be produced simultaneously. Also **po·lyph·o·nous** (pə·lif′ə·nəs). [< Gk. *polyphōnos* having many tones < *poly*- many + *phōnē* a voice, sound]

polyphonic prose A poem set down on the page as prose: closer to the rhythms of prose than to those of verse and employing such devices as rime, assonance, and alliteration to produce poetic effects.

po·lyph·o·ny (pə·lif′ə·nē, pol′i·fō′nē) *n.* **1** Multiplicity of sounds, as in an echo. **2** *Phonet.* The representation by one written character or sign of more than one sound. **3** Counterpoint. [< Gk. *polyphōnia* a variety of tones or speech < *polyphōnos*. See POLYPHONIC.]

po·lyp·i·dom (pə·lip′ə·dəm) *n.* A polypary. [< L *polypus* a polypus + *domus* house < Gk. *domos*]

pol·y·ploid (pol′i·ploid) *adj. Genetics* Having more than two basic chromosome sets in the body cells. —*n.* A polyploid cell. [< POLY- + -PLOID]

pol·y·pod (pol′i·pod) *adj.* **1** Having many feet. **2** *Zool.* Pertaining to many–footed organisms. —*n.* A myriapod. [< POLY- + -POD]

pol·y·pous (pol′i·pəs) *adj.* **1** Having many feet or roots. **2** Pertaining to or resembling a polyp. **3** *Pathol.* Pertaining to, afflicted with, or resembling polypi.

pol·yp·tych (pol′ip·tik) *n.* An altarpiece or panel having more than three folds or leaves. [< Gk. *polyptychos* having many folds < *poly*- many + *ptyx, ptychos* a fold]

pol·y·pus (pol′i·pəs) *n. pl.* **·pi** (-pī) *Pathol.* **1** A smooth growth of hypertrophied mucus found in mucous membrane, as in the nasal passages, bladder, rectum, etc. **2** A tumor. [< NL < L, a polypus]

POLYPTYCH

pol·y·sac·cha·rid (pol′i·sak′ə·rīd, -rid) *n. Chem.* Any of a class of carbohydrates of high molecular weight, formed by the union of three or more monosaccharide molecules: they include starch, dextrin, inulin, cellulose, mucilage, and glycogen. Also **pol′y·sac′cha·rose** (-rōs).

pol·y·sty·rene (pol′i·stī′rēn) *n. Chem.* A thermoplastic polymer of styrene, C_8H_8; a clear, colorless, water–resistant resin: much used in the making of plastics, housewares, light fixtures, electrical components, surface coatings, etc. [< POLY(MER) + STYRENE]

pol·y·syl·la·ble (pol′i·sil′ə·bəl) *n.* A word of several syllables, especially of more than three. [< Med. L (*vox*) *polysyllaba* (a) many–syllabled (word), fem. of *polysyllabus* polysyllabic < Gk. *polysyllabos* < *poly*- many + *syllabē* a syllable] —**pol′y·syl·lab′ic** (-si·lab′ik) or **·i·cal** *adj.* —**pol′y·syl′la·bism** *n.*

pol·y·syn·de·ton (pol′i·sin′də·ton) *n.* Repetition of connectives or conjunctions for rhetorical effect, as, "east and west and south and north": distinguished from *asyndeton*. [< NL < Gk. *poly*- much + *syndetos* bound together < *syndein* < *syn*- together + *deein* bind]

pol·y·syn·thet·ic (pol′i·sin·thet′ik) *adj. Ling.*

Describing a language, such as Eskimo, or certain of the American Indian languages, in which the subject, object, verb, etc., of a sentence are combined into a single word and have no existence as separate elements. [< Gk. *polysynthetos* much compounded < *poly*- much + *syntithenai* < *syn*- together + *tithenai* put]

pol·y·tech·nic (pol′i·tek′nik) *adj.* Embracing many arts: also **pol′y·tech′ni·cal.** —*n.* A school of applied science and the industrial arts. [< F *polytechnique* < Gk. *polytechnos* skilled in many arts < *poly*- many + *technē* an art]

pol·y·the·ism (pol′i·thē·iz′əm) *n.* The belief in and worship of more gods than one. [< F *polythéisme* < Gk. *polytheos* of many gods < *poly*- many + *theos* a god] —**pol′y·the′ist** *n.* —**pol′y·the·is′tic** or **·is′ti·cal** *adj.*

pol·y·troph·ic (pol′i·trof′ik, -trō′fik) *adj.* Obtaining nourishment from several sources, as certain pathogenic bacteria. [< Gk. *polytrophos* highly nourished < *poly*- much + *trephein* feed]

pol·y·typ·ic (pol′i·tip′ik) *adj.* Existing in many types or forms. Also **pol′y·typ′i·cal.** [< POLY- + Gk. *typikos* < *typos* a type]

pol·y·un·sat·u·rat·ed (pol′ē·un′sach′ə·rā′tid) *adj. Chem.* Pertaining to or designating an aliphatic compound having many pairs of adjacent carbon atoms linked by two or more pairs of shared valence electrons: used especially of edible oils and fats.

pol·y·u·re·thane (pol′ē·yŏŏr′ə·thān′) *n. Chem.* Any of a group of synthetic, nitrogen–containing polymers with diverse properties, widely used in the manufacture of rigid or flexible solid foams for insulation and upholstery, resins for waterproofing, etc.

pom·ace (pum′is) *n.* **1** The substance of apples or like fruit crushed by grinding. **2** Fish scrap. **3** The cake left after the expression of oil from castor beans. [< Med. L *pomacium* cider < L *pomum* an apple]

pomace fly A fruit fly.

po·ma·ceous (pō·mā′shəs) *adj.* **1** Relating to or made of apples. **2** Of or pertaining to a pome, or to trees of the rose family that produce pomes. [< NL *pomaceus* < L *pomum* an apple]

po·made (pō·mād′, -mäd′) *n.* A perfumed dressing for the hair or an ointment for the scalp. —*v.t.* **·mad·ed, ·mad·ing** To anoint with pomade. [< MF *pommade* < Ital. *pomata* < *pomo* an apple, fruit < L *pomum*]

po·man·der (pō′man·dər, pō·man′dər) *n.* A perfume ball, or perfumed powder, formerly worn as an amulet; also, a box for carrying such perfume. [Earlier *pomamber* < OF *pomme d'ambre* apple of amber < *pomme* an apple (< L *pomum*) + *ambre* amber]

pome (pōm) *n. Bot.* A fleshy, many–celled fruit with a core, as an apple, quince, pear, or the like. [< OF, an apple < L *pomum*, orig. a fruit]

pome·gran·ate (pom′gran·it, pum′-, pəm·gran′it) *n.* **1** The fruit of a tropical Asian and African tree (*Punica granatum*), about the size of an orange and having a hard rind and subacid red pulp with many seeds. **2** The tree. [< OF *pome grenate* < *pome* an apple (< L *pomum*) + *grenate* < LL *granata* < L *granatum*, orig. neut. of *granatus* very seedy < *granum* a grain, a seed]

pom·e·lo (pom′ə·lō) *n. pl.* **·los** A small variety of the shaddock; grapefruit. [Prob. < POME; infl. in form by Du. *pompelmoes* a pompelmous]

Pom·e·ra·ni·an (pom′ə·rā′nē·ən) *adj.* Relating to Pomerania or its inhabitants. —*n.* **1** A native or inhabitant of Pomerania. **2** A small dog with pointed ears and muzzle, a bushy tail turned over the back, and long, straight, silky coat varying in color: believed to have originated in Pomerania.

POMERANIAN
(From 7 to 10 inches high; weight, 3 to 7 pounds)

po·mi·cul·ture (pō′mi·kul′chər) *n.* Fruit culture. [< *pomi-* (<L *pomum* an apple, fruit) + CULTURE]

po·mif·er·ous (pō·mif′ər·əs) *adj.* Pome-bearing. [<L *pomifer* < *pomum* an apple, fruit + *ferre* bear]

pom·mel (pum′əl, pom′-) *v.t.* **·meled** or **·melled**, **·mel·ing** or **·mel·ling** To beat with or as if with the pommel of a sword or with the fists. See synonyms under BEAT. —*n.* **1** A knob at the front of a saddle or on the hilt of a sword. **2** The butt of a firearm. Also spelled *pummel.* [<OF *pomel* a rounded knob, dim. of *pome.* See POME.]

po·mol·o·gy (pō·mol′ə·jē) *n.* The science of fruits and the art of fruit culture. [<NL *pomologia* <L *pomum* an apple, fruit + *-logia* -LOGY] — **po·mo·log·i·cal** (pō′mə·loj′i·kəl) *adj.* — **po′mo·log′i·cal·ly** *adv.* —• **po·mol′o·gist** *n.*

Po·mo·na (pə·mō′nə) In Roman mythology, the goddess of fruit and fruit trees.

pomp (pomp) *n.* **1** Magnificent or ostentatious display, especially in costume, equipage, etc. **2** *Obs.* A grand procession; pageant. See synonyms under OSTENTATION. [<OF *pompe* <L *pompa* <Gk. *pompē* a sending, pomp < *pempein* send]

pom·pa·dour (pom′pə·dôr, -dŏŏr, -dŏŏr) *n.* **1** A style of arranging the hair by brushing it up from the forehead in a manner reminiscent of an 18th century style. **2** A style of bodice with low, square neck. —*adj.* Characterizing anything made fashionable by the Marquise de Pompadour: *pompadour* silk. [after Marquise de *Pompadour*]

Pom·pa·dour (pôṅ′pȧ·dŏŏr′), **Marquise de,** 1721–64, Jeanne Antoinette Poisson, mistress of Louis XV of France.

pom·pa·no (pom′pə·nō) *n. pl.* **·nos 1** A highly prized carangoid food fish (genus *Trachinotus*) of warm seas, especially *T. carolinus,* found off the coasts of the South Atlantic States. **2** A food fish of the American Pacific coast (*Rhombus simillimus*). [<Sp. *pámpano*]

Pom·pe·ii (pom·pā′ē) An ancient city of southern Italy SE of Naples; destroyed by an eruption of Vesuvius, A.D. 79. — **Pom·pe·ian** (pom·pā′ən, -pē′ən) *adj. & n.*

pom·pel·mous (pom′pel·mŏŏs) *n.* An East Indian variety of shaddock. [<Du. *pompelmoes,* ? <Du. *pompoen* a pumpkin + older Malay *limoes* a shaddock <Pg., pl. of *limão* a lemon, citron]

Pom·pey (pom′pē) Anglicized name of Gnaeus Pompeius Magnus, 106–48 B.C., Roman general, statesman, and triumvir; rival of Julius Caesar: known as *Pompey the Great.*

pom·pho·ly·he·mi·a (pom′fə·li·hē′mē·ə) *n. Pathol.* An abnormal accumulation of gas bubbles in the blood, as in caisson disease. [<NL <Gk. *pompholyx* a bubble (< *pomphos* a blister) + *haima* blood]

pom–pom (pom′pom′) *n.* A rapid-fire, automatic cannon used especially as an anti-aircraft weapon. [From the sound made by the charge when fired]

pom·pon (pom′pon, Fr. pôṅ·pôṅ′) *n.* **1** In millinery, a tuft or ball, as of feathers or ribbon. **2** The colored ball of wool on the front of a shako, or on top of a sailor's cap. **3** A variety of chrysanthemum or dahlia having a small, compact, globe-shaped flower head. [<F <MF *pomper* exhibit pomp <OF *pompe* pomp]

pom·pous (pom′pəs) *adj.* **1** Marked by assumed stateliness; overbearing; ostentatious. **2** Magnificent; marked by ceremonious or impressive display. — **pom·pos·i·ty** (pom·pos′ə·tē), **pom′pous·ness** *n.* — **pom′pous·ly** *adv.*

Po·na·pe (pō′nä·pā) One of the most important of the eastern Caroline Islands; 129 square miles; formerly *Ascension.*

Ponce de Le·ón (pons′ də lē′ən, Sp. pôn′·thā thā lā·ôn′), **Juan,** 1460–1521, Spanish discoverer of Florida.

pon·cho (pon′chō) *n. pl.* **·chos 1** A South American cloak like a blanket with a hole in the middle for the head. **2** A similar garment, waterproofed or rubberized, and used as a raincoat. [<Sp. <Araucan *poncho, pontho*]

pond (pond) *n.* A body of still water, smaller than a lake. [ME *ponde,* var. of POUND²]

pon·der (pon′dər) *v.t.* To weigh in the mind; consider carefully. —*v.i.* To meditate; reflect. See synonyms under CONSIDER, DELIBERATE, EXAMINE, MUSE. [<OF *ponderer* <L *ponderare* < *pondus, ponderis* a weight] — **pon′der·a·ble**

adj. — **pon′der·a·bil′i·ty** *n.* — **pon′der·er** *n.*

pon·der·ous (pon′dər·əs) *adj.* **1** Having great weight; also, huge; bulky. **2** Heavy to the extent of dulness; lumbering; labored. See synonyms under HEAVY. [<OF *pondereux* <L *ponderosus* < *pondus, ponderis* a weight] — **pon′der·os′i·ty** (-dә·ros′ə·tē), **pon′der·ous·ness** *n.* — **pon′der·ous·ly** *adv.*

pond·lil·y (pond′lil′ē) *n. pl.* **·lil·ies** The water-lily.

pond scum Any of a group of free-floating, fresh-water, green algae (*Spirogyra* and related genera).

pond·weed (pond′wēd′) *n.* Any of various submersed or partially floating perennial aquatic plants (genus *Potamogeton*) common in the Old and the New World.

pone¹ (pōn) *n.* **1** Bread made of cornmeal, sometimes with milk and eggs: also *corn pone.* **2** A small cake or patty of cornbread. [< Algonquian (Virginian), bread < *ápân* something baked]

pone² (pōn) *n.* In card games, the player at the dealer's right. [<L, imperative sing. of *ponere* place]

po·nent (pō′nənt) *adj.* Affirmative; constructive; positing: term used in logic. [<L *ponens, -entis,* ppr. of *ponere* place]

pon·gee (pon·jē′) *n.* A thin, natural, unbleached silk with a knotty, rough weave, originally made in China from the product of wild silkworms. [? Alter. of dial. Chinese *pen chi* home loom <Chinese *pun ki*]

Pon·ti·ac (pon′tē·ak), died 1769, Ottawa Indian chief who made war on the British.

Pon·ti·ac (pon′tē·ak) An industrial city in SE Michigan, 24 miles NW of Detroit.

pon·ti·a·nak (pon′tē·ä′näk) *n.* **1** A grayish-white gum resin obtained from the jelutong tree of Borneo: used as a friction compound on belting, etc. **2** A variety of copal from various species of dammar pine (genus *Agathis*): used in varnishes. [after *Pontianak*]

pon·ti·fex (pon′tə·feks) *n. pl.* **pon·tif·i·ces** (pon·tif′ə·sēz) A member of the highest priestly college of ancient Rome, the Pontifical College, which had supreme jurisdiction in religious matters. [<L *pontifex, -ficis* <Osco-Umbrian *puntis* a sacrificial offering + L *facere* make; infl. in form by L *pons, pontis* a bridge]

pon·tiff (pon′tif) *n.* **1** The pope; also, any bishop. **2** A pontifex of ancient Rome. [<F *pontife* <L *pontifex* a pontifex] — **pon·tif′ic** *adj.*

pon·tif·i·cal (pon·tif′i·kəl) *adj.* **1** Of, pertaining to or appropriate for a pontiff. **2** Having the pomp or dogmatism sometimes ascribed to a pontiff; hence, haughty; pompous; dogmatic. [<L *pontificalis* < *pontifex* a pontifex]

pon·tif·i·cate (pon·tif′ə·kit, -kāt) *n.* **1** The office of a pontiff. **2** A pope's term of office. —*v.i.* (-kāt) **·cat·ed, ·cat·ing 1** To perform the offices of a pontiff. **2** To act or speak pompously or dogmatically.

pon·til (pon′til) *n.* An iron rod used in glass-making to shape hot glass; a punty. [<F, appar. <Ital. *pontello, puntello,* dim. of *punto* a point <L *punctus*]

pontil mark The slight excrescence or scar left on a finished glass article after detaching it from the pontil: also spelled *punty mark.*

pon·tine (pon′tīn) *adj.* Of or pertaining to a bridge or bridges. [<L *pons, pontis* a bridge + -INE¹]

Pon·tius (pon′shəs, -tē·əs) See PILATE.

pon·ton (pon′tən) *n.* A pontoon. [<OF. See PONTOON.]

pon·to·nier (pon′tə·nir′) *n.* **1** A soldier in charge of pontoons. **2** A builder of pontoon bridges. [<OF *pontonnier* <Med. L *pontonarius* <L, *ponto, -onis* a pontoon]

pon·toon (pon·tōn′) *n.* **1** A flat-bottomed boat, an airtight cylinder, or the like, used in the construction of floating bridges, to support the roadway. **2** A bridge so supported: in the United States Army, usually *ponton.* **3** A float or a raft to ferry goods across water. **4** A float

PONTOON BRIDGE
a. Pontoons.
b. Locking bridge sections.
c. Shore.

on the landing gear of a hydroplane. [<OF *ponton* <L *ponto, pontonis* < *pons, pontis* a bridge]

pontoon bridge A bridge supported on pontoons: distinguished from *fixed bridge.* Also **ponton bridge.**

po·ny (pō′nē) *n. pl.* **·nies 1** A very small horse, especially one of a small breed; specifically, an Indian pony. **2** Anything small of its kind; specifically, a pony engine. **3** *U.S. Slang* A translation used in the preparation of foreign language lessons; a crib; trot. **4** In British racing slang, the sum of 25 pounds. **5** *Colloq.* A very small glass, for spirits, beer, etc. —*v.t. & v.i.* **·nied, ·ny·ing** *U.S. Slang* **1** To translate (lessons) with the aid of a pony or trot. **2** To pay (money) that is due: with *up.* [Var. of dial. E (Scottish) *powney,* prob. <OF *poulenet,* dim. of *poulain* a foal, colt <LL *pullanus* <L *pullus* a young animal]

pony engine *U.S.* A small locomotive for use in railroad yards.

pony express In 1860–61, a postal system by which mail was relayed from Missouri to California by riders mounted on swift ponies; also, the rider. See HORSE-POST.

po·ny·tail (pō′nē·tāl′) *n.* **1** A style of arranging long hair by gathering it tightly at the back of the head and letting it hang down like a pony's tail. **2** Hair so worn.

pooch (pŏŏch) *n. Slang* A dog, especially a small mongrel. [? < dial. E and obs. *pooch,* var. of POUCH; ? with ref. to appetite]

poo·dle (pŏŏd′l) *n.* One of a breed of dogs of high intelligence, with long, curly, usually white or black hair. [<G *pudel* <LG, short for *pudelhund* < *pudeln* splash in water; with ref. to its being a water dog]

pooh (pŏŏ) *interj.* Bah! foh!: an exclamation of disdain: also spelled *poh.*

pooh–pooh (pŏŏ′pŏŏ′) *v.t.* To reject or speak of disdainfully. — **pooh′–pooh′er** *n.*

pool¹ (pŏŏl) *n.* **1** A small body, usually of fresh water, as a spring. **2** A deep place in a stream. **3** Any small, isolated body of liquid: a *pool* of blood; a puddle. [OE *pōl*]

pool² (pŏŏl) *n.* **1** A collective stake in a gambling game. **2** A combination, generally formed to overcome the effects of excessive competition, whereby companies or corporations agree to fix rates or prices and divide the collective profits pro rata; also, any combination formed for a speculative operation, as in stocks or the like, or the common fund raised for that purpose. **3** Any of various games played on a six-pocket billiard table, in which the object is to drive balls numbered from 1 to 15 into the pockets. **4** A combining of efforts or resources, as for a purpose or the benefit of the contributors. —*v.t.* To combine in a mutual fund or pool, as to satisfy a mutual need, finance an enterprise, etc. —*v.i.* To form a pool. [<F *poule* a stake, orig. a hen <L *pulla*; infl. in form by POOL¹]

pool·room (pŏŏl′rŏŏm′, -rŏŏm′) *n.* A place equipped for playing pool, billiards, etc.

poop¹ (pŏŏp) *Naut. n.* **1** A short deck built over the after part of the spar deck of a vessel of war; hence, generally, the stern of a vessel: also **poop deck.** **2** A cabin covered by the poop deck: also **poop cabin.** —*v.t.* **1** To break over the stern or poop of: said of a wave. **2** To take (a wave) over the stern. [<OF *pupe, pope* <Ital. *poppa* <L *puppis*]

poop² (pŏŏp) *U.S. Slang v.t.* To bring to exhaustion; weary: usually used passively: He was *pooped* by the long climb. —*v.i.* To stop; cease or withdraw. [Origin uncertain]

poor (pŏŏr) *adj.* **1** Lacking means of comfortable subsistence; indigent; needy. **2** Lacking in good qualities, or the qualities that render a thing valuable; specifically, lacking in abundance or quality; scanty: a *poor* crop; of inferior workmanship or quality: a *poor* watch; deficient in vigor; feeble: *poor* health; lean; thin; feeble from ill feeding: That animal is *poor;* lacking in fertility; sterile: *poor* soil. **3** Wanting in strength or spirit; cowardly. **4** Devoid of elegance or refinements; uncomfortable: *poor* surroundings. **5** Deserving of pity; unhappy; wretched: the *poor* dog. **6** Devoid of merit; unsatisfactory: a very *poor* speaker. See synonyms under BAD¹, BASE², HUMBLE, MEAGER, SCANTY. [<OF *povre* <L *pauper.* Doublet of PAUPER.] — **poor′ness** *n.*

Poor Clare A member of a religious order

founded in 1212 by St. Clare of Assisi and following a rule prescribed by St. Francis of Assisi; a Franciscan nun.

poor·house (pŏŏr′hous′) *n.* A public establishment maintained as a dwelling for paupers.

poor·ly (pŏŏr′lē) *adv.* 1 With poor results. 2 Imperfectly; badly. 3 In the manner of the poor. 4 In a spiritless manner. — *adj. Colloq.* Poor in health; somewhat ailing.

Poor Richard Richard Saunders, the imaginary author of wise precepts in almanacs issued by Benjamin Franklin from 1732 to 1757.

poor–spir·it·ed (pŏŏr′spir′it·id) *adj.* Having little spirit or courage; cowardly. See synonyms under BASE². — **poor′–spir′it·ed·ness** *n.*

pop¹ (pop) *v.* **popped, pop·ping** *v.i.* 1 To make a sharp, explosive sound. 2 To burst open or explode with such a sound. 3 To move or go suddenly or quickly: with *in, out,* etc. 4 To protrude; bulge: His eyes *popped.* 5 In baseball, to bat the ball into the air so that an opposing player can catch it, thus retiring the batter: with *up* or *out.* — *v.t.* 6 To cause to burst or explode, as corn by heating. 7 To thrust or put suddenly: with *in, out,* etc.: He *popped* his head out of the window. 8 To fire (a gun, etc.). 9 To shoot; also, to hit. 10 In baseball, to bat (the ball) into the air. 11 *Slang* To take (habit–forming or harmful drugs) by mouth or injection: to *pop* pills. — **to pop the question** *Colloq.* To make a proposal of marriage. — *n.* 1 A sharp explosive noise; a small report: the *pop* of a pistol. 2 The shot of a firearm. 3 A flavored soft drink containing carbon dioxide. 4 A shot, as in basketball. — *adv.* Like, or with the sound of, a pop; suddenly. [Imit.]

pop² (pop) *n. Slang* Papa. [Short for *poppa,* var. of PAPA]

pop³ (pop) *adj. Colloq.* 1 Of or pertaining to a pervasive mass culture, especially that of young people. 2 Of or characteristic of the music favored by this group. 3 Of or suggesting pop art. [Short for POPULAR]

pop art *U.S.* A style of painting the subjects and manner of which resemble those of comic strips and advertising posters.

pop·corn (pop′kôrn′) *n.* A variety of maize, the kernels of which explode when heated, forming large white balls; also, the corn after popping.

pope (pōp) *n.* 1 *Often cap.* The bishop of Rome, the visible head of the Roman Catholic Church, accounted by that church the vicar of Christ and successor of St. Peter. He is elected by the college of cardinals, usually from their own number. 2 Any person having, or thought to have, similar great authority. 3 In the Greek Church, a parish priest. [OE *papa* <LL <LGk. *papas* a bishop, father <Gk. *pappas* father]

Pope (pōp), **Alexander,** 1688–1744, English poet and satirist. — **John,** 1822–92, U.S. general in the Civil War.

pope·dom (pōp′dəm) *n.* The office or dominion of a pope; papacy.

pop·er·y (pō′pər·ē) *n.* The religion of the Roman Catholic Church with all its doctrines and practices: an opprobrious term.

pope's–nose (pōps′nōz′) See PARSON'S-NOSE.

pop–eyed (pop′īd′) *adj.* Having bulging or protruding eyes; hence, amazed.

pop·gun (pop′gun′) *n.* A tube with a piston that expels a pellet with a pop.

pop·in·jay (pop′in·jā) *n.* 1 A coxcomb. 2 The figure of a bird, formerly used as a mark in archery, and later for firearms. 3 *Archaic* A parrot. [<OF *papegai* <Med. Gk. *papagas* a parrot <Arabic *babhagā*; infl. in form by AF *gai,* OF *geai* a jay]

pop·ish (pō′pish) *adj.* Pertaining to popes or popery: used opprobriously. — **pop′ish·ly** *adv.* — **pop′ish·ness** *n.*

pop·lar (pop′lər) *n.* 1 Any of a genus (*Populus*) of dioecious trees and bushes of the willow family, widely distributed in the northern hemisphere; especially, the **white** or **silver poplar** (*P. alba*) or the **Lombardy poplar** (*P. nigra*). 2 The wood of any of these trees. 3 Any one of several trees in some way resembling a poplar: the **Queensland poplar** (*Homalanthus populifolius*) of tropical Australia, and the **western, white,** or **yellow poplar** of the

United States, more properly called *tuliptree.* [<OF *poplier* <L *populus*]

pop·lin (pop′lin) *n.* A durable plain–weave silk, cotton, rayon, or wool fabric, having cross ribs made of warp threads finer than the woof or filling threads: used for dresses, upholstery, etc. [<F *popeline, papeline* <Ital. *papalina* papal; with ref. to Avignon, a papal residence where the fabric was originally made]

pop·o·ver (pop′ō′vər) *n.* A very light egg muffin: so named from its rising over the dish in which it is baked.

pop·pet (pop′it) *n.* 1 *Mech.* A poppet head or a poppet valve. 2 A dainty little person; darling: a pet name. 3 One of several small bits of wood on a boat's gunwale to support the rowlocks. [Earlier form of PUPPET]

poppet head A pulley frame over a mine shaft, bearing the hoisting gear.

pop·ple (pop′əl) *v.i.* **·pled, ·pling** To have a heaving motion; ripple; bubble, as agitated water. — *n.* Rippling or bubbling water; bubbling, or its sound. [Prob. imit.]

pop·py (pop′ē) *n. pl.* **·pies** 1 Any plant of the genus *Papaver,* typical of a widely distributed family (*Papaveraceae*) having lobed or toothed leaves and vivid red, violet, orange, or white flowers; especially, the **opium poppy** (*P. somniferum*), the **oriental poppy** (*P. orientale*), the **Iceland poppy** (*P. nudicaule*), the **mission poppy** (*P. californicum*), etc. ◆ Collateral adjective: *papaverous.* 2 The medicinal extract from such a plant. 3 The bright scarlet color of certain poppy blossoms: also **poppy red.** See CALIFORNIA POPPY. [OE *popæg, papoeg* <L *papaver*]

pop·py·cock (pop′ē·kok) *n. Colloq.* Pretentious talk; humbug; nonsense. [<colloq. Du. *pappekak,* lit., soft dung]

pop·py·head (pop′ē·hed′) *n.* A small, carved wooden finial, particularly at the end of a church pew.

Pop·si·cle (pop′sik·əl) *n.* A slab of frozen colored and flavored water at the end of two flat sticks: a trade name. Also **pop′si·cle.**

pop·u·lace (pop′yə·lis) *n.* The body of the common people; the masses. See synonyms under MOB¹. [<MF <Ital. *popolaccio, popolazzo* <L *populus*]

pop·u·lar (pop′yə·lər) *adj.* 1 Pertaining to the people at large: *popular* demonstrations or government. 2 Widely approved or admired: a *popular* officer. 3 Suitable for the common people; easily comprehended: *popular* lectures. 4 Prevalent among the people: *popular* errors. 5 Suited to the means of the people: *popular* prices. 6 Of folk origin: the *popular* ballad. 7 Used by the people; current; colloquial: said also of many words on the borderline between slang and reputable usage. 8 Plebeian; vulgar; common. See synonyms under COMMON, GENERAL. [L *popularis* <*populus* the people] — **pop′u·lar·ly** *adv.*

popular etymology A folk etymology.

pop·u·lar·i·ty (pop′yə·lar′ə·tē) *n.* The condition of being popular, especially of possessing the confidence and favor of the people or of a set of people.

pop·u·lar·ize (pop′yə·lə·rīz′) *v.t.* **·ized, ·iz·ing** To make popular. Also *Brit.* **pop′u·lar·ise′.** — **pop′u·lar·i·za′tion** *n.* — **pop′u·lar·iz′er** *n.*

pop·u·late (pop′yə·lāt) *v.t.* **·lat·ed, ·lat·ing** 1 To furnish with inhabitants; people. 2 To inhabit. [<Med. L *populatus,* pp. of *populare* <L *populus* the people]

pop·u·la·tion (pop′yə·lā′shən) *n.* 1 The whole number of people in a place or given area; also, any specific portion of that number: the foreign *population* of New York. 2 The act or process of populating or furnishing with inhabitants; the multiplying of inhabitants. 3 *Biol.* The total number of individual organisms being studied by statistical or biometric methods. See synonyms under PEOPLE. [<LL *populatio, -onis* <L *populus* the people]

Pop·u·list (pop′yə·list) *adj.* Of or pertaining to the Populist or People's party. — *n.* A member of the People's party. [<L *populus* the people] — **Pop′u·lism** *n.* — **Pop′u·lis′tic** *adj.*

Populist party See PEOPLE'S PARTY.

pop·u·lous (pop′yə·ləs) *adj.* Containing many inhabitants; thickly settled. [<L *populosus*

<*populus* the people] — **pop′u·lous·ly** *adv.* — **pop′u·lous·ness** *n.*

por·bea·gle (pôr′bē·gəl) *n.* A large voracious shark (*Lamna nasus*) of northern waters, sometimes 10 feet long. [<dial. E (Cornish); ult. origin unknown]

porce·lain (pôrs′lin, pôrs′-, pôr′sə-, pôr′-) *n.* A white, hard, translucent ceramic ware, usually glazed, existing in many varieties, according to its composition and method of manufacture; china; chinaware. It is made from pure clay to which a little of the more fusible feldspar is added. [<OF *porcelaine* <Ital. *porcellana,* orig. a cowry] — **por·ce·la·ne·ous** (pôr′sə·lā′nē·əs, pôr′-) or **por′cel·la′ne·ous** *adj.*

porch (pôrch, pōrch) *n.* 1 A covered structure forming an entrance to a building, outside and with a separate roof, or as a recess in the interior as a kind of vestibule; a veranda. 2 An ancient covered walk or portico. Compare LOGGIA. — **the Porch** The Stoic school of philosophy in ancient Athens, named from the Stoa Poecile, or Painted Porch. See STOIC. [<OF *porche* <L *porticus* a colonnade <*porta* a gate. Doublet of PORTICO.]

por·cine (pôr′sin, -sin) *adj.* Pertaining to, like, or characteristic of swine. [<F, fem. of *porcin* <L *porcinus* <*porcus* a hog]

por·cu·pine (pôr′kyə·pīn) *n.* A large, hystricomorphic rodent, having coarse hair thickly interspersed with erectile quill–like spines used for defense. *Hystrix cristata* is the common porcupine of the Mediterranean region; *Erethizon dorsatum* is the common Canada porcupine of eastern North America: also called *hedgehog.* [<OF *porc espin,* lit., a spiny hog <*porc* a hog (<L *porcus*) + *espin* a thorn <L *spina*]

CANADA PORCUPINE
(From 30 to 35 inches long in body length)

porcupine ant–eater An echidna.

porcupine fish A globefish.

pore¹ (pôr, pōr) *v.i.* **pored, por·ing** 1 To gaze steadily or intently. 2 To study or read with care and application: with *over*: to *pore* over one's accounts. 3 To meditate; ponder. [ME *pouren;* origin unknown]

pore² (pôr, pōr) *n.* 1 A small orifice or opening, especially a minute perforation in a membrane or tissue, as in the skin. 2 A minute interstice between the molecules of a body. 3 Any inlet or means of absorption or communication. [<OF *pore, porre* <L *porus* < Gk. *poros*]

po·rif·er·ous (pô·rif′ər·əs, pō-) *adj.* 1 Bearing or having pores. 2 Of or pertaining to a phylum (*Porifera*) of primitive, aquatic, chiefly marine animals, having bodies perforated by pores which lead to an internal cavity, and living attached to rocks, shells, and other supports; the sponges. [<NL *porifer* <L *porus* a pore + *ferre* bear]

pork (pôrk, pōrk) *n.* 1 The flesh of swine used as food. 2 A swine or swine collectively. 3 *U.S. Slang* Government money, distinctions, favors, etc., obtained by a representative for his constituency: a form of political patronage. [<OF *porc* <L *porcus* a hog]

pork barrel 1 A barrel in which pork is pickled and kept. 2 *U.S. Slang* A Federal appropriation for some local enterprise that will favorably impress a representative's constituents.

pork·er (pôr′kər, pōr′-) *n.* A pig or hog, especially regarded as a source of pork.

pork–pie (pôrk′pī, pōrk′-) *n.* 1 A thick-crusted pie with pork filling. 2 A man's hat with a low, flat crown.

pork·y (pôr′kē, pōr′-) *adj.* **pork·i·er, pork·i·est** 1 Of or like pork. 2 Obese; fat.

porn (pôrn) *Slang adj.* Pornographic. — *n.* Pornography. Also **por·no** (pôr′nō).

por·nog·ra·phy (pôr·nog′rə·fē) *n.* 1 Depictions of sexual acts or behavior, as in writing, photographs, motion pictures, etc., to stimulate erotic feelings. 2 The material containing such descriptions. [<Gk. *pornographos* writing of harlots < *pornē* a harlot + *graphein* write] — **por·nog′ra·pher** *n.*

po·ros·co·py (pô·ros′kə·pē, pō-) *n.* The study of the character and arrangement of the sweat pores, especially as shown on fingerprints: used in identification. [< *poro-* (<Gk. *poros* a pore) + -SCOPY] — **po·ro·scop·ic** (pôr′ə·skop′ik, pō′rə-) or **-i·cal** *adj.*

po·ros·i·ty (pô·ros′ə·tē, pō-) *n.* **1** The property of being porous; porousness. **2** A porous part or structure. [<Med. L *porositas, -tatis* <*porosus* <L *porus* a pore]

po·rous (pôr′əs, pō′rəs) *adj.* Having pores. — **po′rous·ly** *adv.* — **po′rous·ness** *n.*

por·phy·rit·ic (pôr′fə·rit′ik) *adj.* **1** Pertaining or relating to porphyry. **2** *Mineral.* Containing well-defined, relatively large crystals in a fine-grained, glassy base or groundmass. Also **por′phy·rit′i·cal.** [<Med. L *porphyriticus* <L *porphyrites* porphyry <Gk. *porphyrítēs* (*lithos*), lit., (a) purplelike (stone) <*porphyros* purple]

por·phy·ry (pôr′fə·rē) *n. pl.* **·ries** An igneous rock that has a groundmass enclosing crystals of feldspar or quartz. [<OF *porfire* <Med. L *porphyreus* <Gk. *porphyros* purple < *porphyra* the purple whelk and its dye]

por·poise (pôr′pəs) *n. pl.* **·poises** or **·poise** **1** A gregarious cetacean, of the genus *Phocaena,* without a distinct beak; especially, *P. phocaena* of the North Atlantic and Pacific, from 5 to

COMMON PORPOISE
(Smaller than the 7 to 8 foot common dolphin)

6 feet long, blackish above and white below. **2** Any small cetacean; popularly, the common dolphin or the bottlenose. [<OF *porpeis, porpois,* lit., hog fish <L *porcus* a hog + *piscis* a fish]

por·ridge (pôr′ij, por′-) *n.* **1** A soft food made by boiling meal or flour in water or milk until it becomes thick. **2** A broth or stew of vegetables, sometimes containing meat. [Alter. of POTTAGE; infl. in form by OF *poree* vegetable soup]

por·rin·ger (pôr′in·jər, por′-) *n.* A small, shallow dish, having straight sides and sometimes ears. [Earlier *pottanger* <MF *potager* a soup bowl; infl. in form by PORRIDGE]

port[1] (pôrt, pōrt) *n.* **1** A harbor or haven; hence, a place of customary entry and exit for vessels, as for commerce. **2** *Law* Any place designated as a point at which persons or merchandise may enter or pass out of a country, under specified supervision: also *port of entry.* [Fusion of OE and OF, both <L *portus* a harbor]

port[2] (pôrt, pōrt) *n.* **1** An opening in the side of a ship, as for a gun, light and air, or for the passage of cargo. **2** A gate, portal, door, or other entrance. **3** An orifice for the passage of a motive fluid, as air, gas, etc.: a steam *port;* exhaust *port.* [Prob. fusion of OE and OF, both <L *porta* a gate, door]

port[3] (pôrt, pōrt) *n.* **1** The way in which one bears or carries himself; mien; external manner: a majestic *port.* **2** The position of a rifle when ported. See synonyms under AIR[1]. — **high port** *Mil.* The position in which a soldier carries his rifle, diagonally across his body, while running or jumping. — *v.t.* **1** *Mil.* To carry, as a rifle, saber, or other weapon, diagonally across the body and sloping to the left shoulder. **2** To carry. [<OF *porte* < *porter* carry <L *portare*]

port[4] (pôrt, pōrt) *Naut. n.* The left side of a vessel as one looks from stern to bow: formerly called *larboard:* opposed to *starboard.* — *v.t.* To put or turn to the port or larboard side: to *port* the helm. — *adj.* Left; larboard: *port* side. [Prob. <PORT[1]]

port[5] (pôrt, pōrt) *n.* A sweet variety of wine, usually of a dark-red color. [Short for *Oporto wine,* from *Oporto,* Portugal; so called because orig. shipped from there]

port·a·ble (pôr′tə·bəl, pōr′-) *adj.* **1** That can be readily carried or moved. **2** *Obs.* Endurable; supportable. [<LL *portabilis* <L *portare* carry] — **port′a·ble·ness, port·a·bil′i·ty** *n.* — **port′a·bly** *adv.*

port·age (pôr′tij, pōr′-) *n.* **1** The act of transporting, especially canoes, boats, and goods, from one navigable water to another. **2** The

route over which such transportation is made, or that which is transported. **3** The charge for transportation. [<F <OF <Med. L *portaticum* <L *portare* carry]

por·tal (pôr′təl, pōr′-) *n.* **1** A passage for gaining entrance; door; gate; especially, one that is grand and imposing. **2** The architectural composition that includes the entrances and porches of a large church or similar building. **3** Any opening or entrance resembling or suggesting the portal of an edifice: often in the plural. See synonyms under ENTRANCE[1]. — *adj.* **1** Pertaining to or entering at a port or gate: **2** *Anat.* Pertaining to or arranged like the **portal vein,** which conveys blood from the intestines and other abdominal viscera to the liver, there subdividing into capillaries. [<OF, a gate <Med. L *portale* a city gate, a porch, orig. neut. of *portalis* <L *porta* a gate]

por·tal-to-por·tal pay (pôr′təl·tə·pôr′təl, pōr′-) A wage computed on the full time spent on mine or factory property from arrival to departure, not on actual working time.

port arms *Mil.* **1** A command to carry a rifle, saber, or other weapon at the port. **2** The position of the weapon when so carried. [< PORT[3], *v.* + ARMS]

por·ta·tive (pôr′tə·tiv, pōr′-) *adj.* **1** Of or pertaining to carrying; capable of carrying. **2** Portable. [<OF, fem. of *portatif,* lit., portable <L *portatus,* pp. of *portare* carry]

Port-au-Prince (pôr′ō·prins′, pōr′-; *Fr.* pôr·tō·praNs′) A port, capital of Haiti.

port authority Any official body having charge of the coordination of all rail and water traffic of a port.

Port Blair The capital of the Andaman and Nicobar Islands, a port on SE South Andaman Island.

port·cul·lis (pôrt·kul′is, pōrt-) *n.* A grating made of strong bars of wood or iron that can be let down suddenly to close the portal of a fortified place. [<OF *porte coleïce* < *porte* a gate <L *porta*) + fem. of *coleis* sliding <L *colare* strain, filter]

MEDIEVAL PORTCULLIS

por·tée (pôr·tē′, -tā′, pōr-) *adj.* Towed, carried, or transported by vehicles: said of artillery, cavalry units, etc. Also **por·té′** (-tē′, -tā′). [<F, pp. fem. of *porter* carry <L *portare*]

por·tend (pôr·tend′, pōr-) *v.t.* **1** To warn of as an omen; presage; forebode. **2** *Obs.* To mean; signify. See synonyms under AUGUR. [<OF *portendre* stretch forth <L *portendere,* var. of *protendere* <*pro-* forth + *tendere* stretch]

por·tent (pôr′tent, pōr-) *n.* **1** Anything that portends what is to happen, especially a momentous or calamitous event. **2** The quality of portending; ominous significance. **3** A prodigy; marvel. [<L *portentum* < *portendere.* See PORTEND.]

por·ten·tous (pôr·ten′təs, pōr-) *adj.* **1** Full of portents of ill; ominous. **2** Of strange and ill-boding character, as if supernatural; monstrous; prodigious. See synonyms under AWFUL, FRIGHTFUL. — **por·ten′tous·ly** *adv.* — **por·ten′tous·ness** *n.*

por·ter[1] (pôr′tər, pōr′-) *n.* **1** One who carries things; especially, a man who carries travelers' luggage, etc., for hire, as in a hotel or at a railroad station. **2** *U.S.* An attendant in a Pullman car. [<OF *porteour* <L *portator* <*portatus,* pp. of *portare* carry]

por·ter[2] (pôr′tər, pōr′-) *n.* **1** A keeper of a door or gate. **2** One who waits at a door to carry messages. [<AF, OF *portier* <LL *portarius* <L *porta* a gate, a door]

por·ter[3] (pôr′tər, pōr′-) *n.* A dark-brown, heavy, English malt liquor resembling ale. [Short for *porter's beer* <PORTER[1]; so called because formerly drunk chiefly by porters]

Por·ter (pôr′tər, pōr′-), **Cole,** born 1893, U.S. composer and lyricist. — **David,** 1780–1843, U.S. commodore. — **David Dixon,** 1813–91, U.S. admiral; son of David Porter. — **Jane,** 1776–1850, English novelist. — **Noah,** 1811–1892, U.S. educator and editor. — **William**

Sydney See O. HENRY.

por·ter·age (pôr′tər·ij, pōr′-) *n.* **1** The business of a porter. **2** The cost of carriage by a porter.

por·ter·house (pôr′tər·hous′, pōr′-) *n.* **1** A place where porter, ale, etc., are retailed. **2** A restaurant; chophouse. **3** A choice cut of beefsteak including a part of the tenderloin, usually next to the sirloin: also **porterhouse steak.** [<PORTER[3] + HOUSE]

port·fo·li·o (pôrt·fō′lē·ō, pōrt-) *n. pl.* **·li·os** **1** A portable case for holding drawings, writing materials, documents, etc. **2** The position or office of a minister of state or member of a government. **3** A list of investments. [Earlier *porto folio* <Ital. *portafoglio* < *portare* carry (<L) + *foglio* a leaf <L *folium*]

port·hole (pôrt′hōl′, pōrt′-) *n.* **1** A small opening in a ship's side. **2** Hence, an embrasure; loophole for shooting through. **3** The entrance to a port in an engine. See PORT[2].

por·ti·co (pôr′ti·kō, pōr′-) *n. pl.* **·coes** or **·cos** An open space or ambulatory with roof upheld by columns; a porch. [<Ital. <L *porticus.* Doublet of PORCH.] — **por′ti·coed** *adj.*

por·tion (pôr′shən, pōr′-) *n.* **1** A part of a whole, whether separated from it or not. **2** An allotment; share; especially, the quantity of any kind of food usually served to one person. **3** The part of an estate coming to an heir. **4** A dowry (def. 1). **5** One's fortune or destiny. — *v.t.* **1** To divide into shares for distribution; parcel: often with *out.* **2** To give a dowry to; dower. **3** To assign; allot. [<OF *porcion* <L *portio, -onis*] — **por′tion·a·ble** *adj.* — **por′tion·less** *adj.*

Synonyms (noun): part, proportion. When any whole is divided into *parts,* any *part* that is allotted to some person, subject, or purpose is called a *portion,* whether or not the division may be by some fixed rule or relation. But when we speak of a *part* as a *proportion,* we think of the whole as divided according to some rule or scale, so that the different *parts* bear a contemplated and intended relation or ratio to one another; thus, the *portion* allotted to a child by will may not be a fair *proportion* of the estate. See PART.

por·tion·er (pôr′shən·ər, pōr′-) *n.* One who divides in shares or holds a share or shares.

Port Lou·is (loo′is, loo′ē) A port, capital of Mauritius.

port·ly (pôrt′lē, pōrt′-) *adj.* **·li·er, ·li·est** **1** Somewhat corpulent; stout. **2** Of a stately appearance and carriage; impressive, especially on account of size. See synonyms under CORPULENT. [<PORT[3] + -LY] — **port′li·ness** *n.*

port·man·teau (pôrt·man′tō, pōrt-) *n. pl.* **·teaus** or **·teaux** (-tōz) **1** Originally, a case for carrying clothing, etc., behind a saddle. **2** An oblong leather suitcase, hinged at the back, and fitted with catches, straps, and a lock, and with handles by which it can be carried. [<MF < *porter* carry (<L *portare*) + *manteau* a coat <OF *mantel* a mantle]

portmanteau word A word arbitrarily formed of two distinct words, as *chortle,* from *chuckle* and *snort; cyclotron,* from *cycle* and *electron;* a telescope word; a blend. [Coined by Lewis Carroll]

port of call A port where vessels put in for supplies, repairs, discharge or taking on of cargo, etc.

port of entry A place, whether on the coast or inland, designated as a point at which persons or merchandise may enter or pass out of a country under the supervision of customs and other proper authorities.

Port-of-Spain (pôrt′əv·spān′, pōrt′-) A port of NW Trinidad, capital of Trinidad and Tobago colony. Also **Port of Spain.**

Por·to-No·vo (pôr′tō·nō′vō, pōr′-) A port in western Africa, capital of Benin.

Por·to Ri·co (rē′kō) The former official name of PUERTO RICO.

por·trait (pôr′trit, pōr′-, -trāt) *n.* **1** A likeness of an individual, especially of the face, produced by an artist in oils, water color, etc., or by photography. **2** Hence, a vivid description of something or someone having existence. [<MF, orig. pp. of *portraire* <OF *pourtraire* PORTRAY]

por·trait·ist (pôr′trā·tist, pōr′-) *n.* One who makes portraits; a portrait painter or photographer.

por·trai·ture (pôr′tri·chər, pōr′-) *n.* **1** A representation of an object. **2** The act or art of portraying; especially, the art or practice of making portraits. **3** Portraits or pictures collectively. [<OF <*pourtrait*, pp. of *pourtraire* PORTRAY]

por·tray (pôr·trā′, pōr-) *v.t.* **1** To represent by drawing, painting, etc.; delineate. **2** To describe in words; depict verbally. **3** To represent, as in a play; act. See synonyms under IMITATE. [<OF *pourtraire* <Med. L *protrahere* <L, draw forth <*pro-* forth + *trahere* draw] — **por·tray′a·ble** *adj.* — **por·tray′er** *n.*

por·tray·al (pôr·trā′əl, pōr-) *n.* **1** The act of portraying by any method of depiction or delineation: the *portrayal* of a character on the stage. **2** The making of a likeness of persons, places, or things; picturing. **3** A portrait.

por·tress (pôr′tris, pōr′-) *n.* A woman porter or doorkeeper. Also **por′ter·ess.**

Port–Roy·al (pôr′roi′əl, pōr′-; *Fr.* pôr·rwȧ·yȧl′) A Cistercian abbey SW of Paris, France; noted as a Jansenist center in the 17th century; suppressed, 1709. Also **Port–Royal–des–Champs** (-dā·shäṅ′).

Por·tu·gal (pôr′chə·gəl, pōr′-; *Pg.* pôr′tŏŏ·gäl′) A republic of SW Europe in the western Iberian Peninsula; 34,222 square miles; including the Azores and Madeira islands, 35,419 square miles; capital Lisbon: ancient *Lusitania.*

Por·tu·guese (pôr′chə·gēz′, -gēs′, pōr′-) *adj.* Pertaining to Portugal, its inhabitants, or their language. — *n.* **1** A native or inhabitant of Portugal. **2** The people of Portugal collectively: with *the.* **3** The Romance language of Portugal and Brazil. [<Pg. *Portuguez* <*Portugal* <*Portucal* <Med. L *Portus Cale* Oporto]

Portuguese Guin·ea (gin′ē) A Portuguese overseas province on the coast of western Africa; 13,944 square miles; capital, Bissau.

Portuguese West Africa See ANGOLA.

Portuguese man–of–war A pelagic siphonophore (genus *Physalia*) of warm seas, having long, stinging tentacles hanging down from a bladderlike float: also *man–of–war.*

pose¹ (pōz) *n.* **1** The position of the whole or part of the body, especially such a position assumed for or represented by an artist, photographer, etc.: the *pose* of the head. **2** Hence, a mental attitude; attitudinizing for effect. See synonyms under ATTITUDE. — *v.* **posed, pos·ing** *v.i.* **1** To assume or hold an attitude or position, as for a portrait. **2** To affect poses; attitudinize. **3** To represent oneself: to *pose* as an expert. — *v.t.* **4** To cause to assume an attitude or position, as an artist's model. **5** To state or propound; put forward, as a theory or problem. [<F <*poser* put down, rest; fusion of L *pausare* lie down and *pos-,* stem of *ponere* lay down, put]

pose² (pōz) *v.t.* **posed, pos·ing** **1** To puzzle or confuse by asking a difficult question. **2** *Obs.* To question closely. [Aphetic var. of obs. *appose,* var. of OPPOSE]

Po·sei·don (pō·sī′dən) In Greek mythology, brother of Zeus and husband of Amphitrite, god of the sea and of horses: identified with the Roman *Neptune.* — **Po′sei·do′ni·an** (-dō′nē·ən) *adj.*

pos·er¹ (pō′zər) *n.* One who poses; one who strikes affected attitudes. [<POSE¹, *v.*]

pos·er² (pō′zər) *n.* A question or problem that baffles. [<POSE², *v.*]

po·seur (pō·zœr′) *n.* One who assumes or affects a particular attitude to make an impression on others. [<F <*poser* POSE¹, *v.*]

posh (posh) *adj. Slang* Very luxurious or elegant. [Origin unknown] — **posh′ly** *adv.* — **posh′ness** *n.*

pos·it (poz′it) *v.t.* To lay down or assume as a fact; affirm; postulate. Compare INFER. — *n.* That which is posited. [<L *positus,* pp. of *ponere* place]

po·si·tion (pə·zish′ən) *n.* **1** The manner in which a thing is placed; also, the place of its location. **2** Disposition of the parts of the body, especially with reference to therapeutic, surgical, or obstetric procedures; posture. **3** Relative social standing; high rank: Wealth commands *position.* **4** Employment or job: He lost his *position.* **5** The act of positing a principle or proposition, or the proposition posited; also, ground of argument; hence, the attitude assumed with reference to a subject; point of view: my *position* on the labor question. **6** *Music* The arrangement of the notes of a chord, as in voice parts. **7** In ancient prosody, the situation of a short vowel before two consonants or their equivalent, causing prolonged utterance: In "texunt," the vowels are long by *position.* See synonyms under ATTITUDE, CIRCUMSTANCE, PLACE. — *v.t.* To place in a particular or appropriate position. [<OF <L *positio, -onis* <*positus,* pp. of *ponere* place] — **po·si′tion·al** *adj.*

position paper A report from a person or group setting forth a set of principles, a description of policy, or recommendations for action on a specific issue.

pos·i·tive (poz′ə·tiv) *adj.* **1** That is or may be directly affirmed; real; actual; existing: opposed to *negative.* **2** Inherent in a thing by and of itself, regardless of its relations to other things; absolute: opposed to *relative.* **3** Openly and plainly expressed; explicit; express; emphatic: opposed to *implied* or *inferred:* a *positive* denial. **4** Imperative: opposed to *discretionary.* **5** Dependent on authority, agreement, or convention: opposed to *natural:* *positive* law. **6** Not admitting of doubt or denial; incontestable: *positive* proof. **7** Free from doubt or hesitation; confident; certain; also, overconfident; dictatorial. **8** *Philos.* Pertaining to positivism (def. 2). **9** Noting one of two opposite directions, qualities, properties, etc., which is taken as primary, or as indicating increase or progression. **10** *Math.* Greater than zero; plus: said of quantities. **11** *Electr.* Having a relatively high potential: the *positive* electrode of a cell; specifically, designating the kind of electricity exhibited by a glass object when rubbed with silk. **12** *Physics* Having a deficiency of electrons: said of atoms which yield electrons. **13** *Biol.* Noting the response of an organism toward a stimulus: a *positive* tropism. **14** *Bacteriol.* Noting the presence of a specified condition or organism: a *positive* bacterial culture. **15** *Mech.* Operated by mechanical power, not by springs or gravity; operated or communicating power through intermediate inelastic parts that are under exact control. **16** Noting the north-seeking pole of a magnet and the corresponding (south) pole of the earth. **17** *Phot.* Having the lights and shades in their natural relation, as in a photograph. **18** *Gram.* Denoting the simple, uncompared degree of the adjective or adverb. See synonyms under DOGMATIC, RADICAL, SURE. — *n.* **1** That which is capable of being directly and certainly affirmed. **2** *Philos.* In positivism, that which is cognizable by the senses. **3** *Phot.* A picture giving the lights and shades as in nature; a print from a negative. **4** *Gram.* The positive degree of an adjective or adverb; also, a word in this degree, as *good, glad.* **5** *Electr.* A positive plate, pole, etc. See synonyms under CERTAINTY. [<OF, fem. of *positif* <L *positivus* <*positus.* See POSITION.] — **pos′i·tive·ly** *adv.* — **pos′i·tive·ness** *n.*

pos·i·tiv·ism (poz′ə·tiv·iz′əm) *n.* **1** A way of thinking that regards nothing as ascertained or ascertainable beyond the facts of physical science or of sense. **2** A system of philosophy elaborated by Auguste Comte, holding that man can have no knowledge of anything but actual phenomena and facts and their interrelations, rejecting all speculation concerning ultimate origins or causes. Compare HUMANITARIANISM. **3** Certitude, or the claim of certitude, in knowledge. — **pos′i·tiv·ist** *n.* — **pos′i·tiv·is′tic** *adj.*

po·sol·o·gy (pō·sol′ə·jē) *n.* The branch of medicine that treats of the dosages of drugs. [<F *posologie* <Gk. *posos* how much + *logos* word, study] — **pos·o·log·ic** (pos′ə·loj′ik) or **·i·cal** *adj.*

pos·se (pos′ē) *n.* **1** A posse comitatus. **2** A force of men; squad. **3** *Law* Possibility: chiefly in the phrase *in posse* (capable of being): distinguished from *in esse.* [<Med. L, power, armed force <L, be able]

pos·se com·i·ta·tus (pos′ē kom′ə·tā′təs) The body of men that a sheriff or other peace officer calls or may call to his assistance in the discharge of his official duty, as to quell a riot or make an arrest. [<Med. L, power of the county <*posse* a posse + *comitatus* a county <*comes, -itis* a count]

pos·sess (pə·zes′) *v.t.* **1** To have as property; own. **2** To have as a quality, attribute, etc.: to *possess* a conscience. **3** To enter and exert control over; dominate: often used passively: He was *possessed* by a devil; The idea *possessed* him. **4** To maintain control over (oneself, one's mind, etc.): *Possess* yourself in patience. **5** To put in possession, as of property, news, etc.: with *of.* **6** To have knowledge of, as a language. **7** To imbue or impress, as with an idea: with *with.* **8** *Obs.* To seize; gain. See synonyms under HAVE, OCCUPY. [<OF *possessier* <L *possessus,* pp. of *possidere* possess] — **pos·ses′sor** *n.*

pos·sessed (pə·zest′) *adj.* **1** Having; owning: *possessed* of a ready tongue. **2** Calm; cool: to be *possessed* in time of danger. **3** Controlled by or as if by evil spirits; beyond self-control; frenzied. — **like all possessed** *U.S. Colloq.* As if driven by the devil; frenziedly.

pos·ses·sion (pə·zesh′ən) *n.* **1** The act or state of possessing. **2** A thing possessed or owned. **3** *pl.* Property; wealth. **4** The state of being possessed, as by evil spirits. **5** Self-possession. See synonyms under OCCUPATION, PROPERTY, WEALTH. Compare POSSESS.

pos·ses·sive (pə·zes′iv) *adj.* **1** Pertaining to or expressive of possession. **2** *Gram.* Designating a case of the noun or pronoun that denotes possession, origin, or the like. In English, this is formed in nouns by adding 's to the singular and to irregular plurals: *John's* book; *men's* souls; the *boss's* office; and a simple apostrophe to the regular plural and sometimes to singulars and proper names ending in a sibilant: *boys'* shoes; *Dickens'* (or *Dickens's*) writings; *James'* (or *James's*) brother. See also –'s¹. Pronouns in the possessive case have special forms, as *my, mine, his, her, hers, its, our, ours, your, yours, their, theirs, whose.* By some grammarians possessive nouns and pronouns are called *possessive adjectives.* — *n. Gram.* **1** The possessive case. **2** A possessive form or construction. — **double possessive** A redundant possessive. Example: a book *of Mike's.*

pos·ses·sive·ness (pə·zes′iv·nis) *n.* Strong or excessive concern with one's own possessions.

pos·set (pos′it) *n.* A drink of hot milk curdled with liquor, sweetened and spiced. [ME *poshote, possot;* origin unknown]

pos·si·bil·i·ty (pos′ə·bil′ə·tē) *n. pl.* **·ties** **1** The fact or state of being possible. **2** A possible thing. See synonyms under ACCIDENT, EVENT.

pos·si·ble (pos′ə·bəl) *adj.* **1** That may be or may become true: opposed to *actual:* said of a thing, an event, or a statement. **2** That may be true in some contingency; imaginably true: sometimes used to denote extreme improbability: opposed to *certain, necessary, impossible.* [<OF <L *possibilis* <*posse* be able <*potis* able + *esse* be] — **pos′si·bly** *adv.*

pos·sum (pos′əm) *n.* **1** *Colloq.* An opossum. **2** *Austral.* A phalanger. — **to play possum** To pretend; deceive; feign ignorance or inattention; dissemble: from the fact that the opossum feigns death when threatened. [Short for OPOSSUM]

possum glider *Austral.* A flying phalanger.

post¹ (pōst) *n.* **1** An upright piece of timber or other material used as a support, a point of attachment, etc., as in a building. **2** A central projection in a lock for receiving the tube of a key. **3** A line or post serving to mark the starting or finishing point of a racecourse. — *v.t.* **1** To put up (a poster, etc.) in some public place. **2** To fasten posters upon; placard. **3** To announce by or as by a poster: to *post* a reward. **4** To denounce thus: to *post* one as a coward. **5** To publish the name of on a list. **6** To publish the name of (a ship) as lost or overdue. See synonyms under SET. [OE <L *postis* a door post]

post² (pōst) *n.* **1** Any fixed place or station, occupied or for occupation; especially, a place occupied by a detachment of troops; also, the garrison of such a station; the limits of a sentry's beat; the beat or position to which a policeman is assigned. **2** *U.S.* A local unit of a veterans' organization. **3** An office or employment; a position, as of trust or emolument; situation; especially, a public office. **4** A trading post or settlement. **5** *Brit.* One of the two bugle calls known respectively as **first post** and **last post.** The latter corresponds to *taps* in the army of the United States. See synonyms under PLACE. — *v.t.* **1** To assign to a particular position or post; station, as a sentry. **2** To appoint to a military or naval command. [<MF *poste* a post, a station < Ital. *posto* <LL *postum,* contraction of L *positum,* pp. neut. of *ponere* place]

post³ (pōst) *n.* **1 a** A rider or courier who travels over a fixed route or between stations on such a route carrying letters, dispatches, etc. **b** Any of the series of stations furnishing relays of men and horses on such a route. **2** An established system, especially a government system, for transporting the mails; also, the aggregate of mail matter transported from one place to another at one time; the mail; by extension, a post office: *Has the post* come in? Put your letter in the *post.* **3** A size of writing paper, 16 by 20 inches: so called because it bore a postman's horn for watermark. — *v.t.* **1** *Brit.* To place in a mailbox or post office; mail. **2** To inform: He *posted* us on the latest news. **3** In bookkeeping: **a** To transfer (items or accounts) to the ledger. **b** To make the proper entries in (a ledger). — *v.i.* **4** To travel with post horses. **5** To travel with speed; hasten. **6** In horseback riding, to rise from the saddle in rhythm with a horse's gait when trotting. — *adv.* By post horses; hence, rapidly. [<MF *poste* <Ital. *posta,* orig. a station <LL, contraction of L *posita,* pp. fem. of *ponere* place]

post– *prefix* **1** After in time or order; following: *postdate, postwar.* **2** Chiefly in scientific terms, after in position; behind: *postorbital.* [<L *post–* < *post* behind, after]

post·age (pōs′tij) *n.* **1** The charge levied on mail matter. **2** The act of going by post. [< POST³ (def. 2) + -AGE]

postage stamp A small, printed label issued and sold by a government to be affixed to letters, parcels, etc., in payment of postage.

pos·tal (pōs′təl) *adj.* Pertaining to the mails or to mail service. — *n.* A postal card.

postal currency An emergency stamp money, used during the Civil War in the United States (1862–65). Also **postage currency.**

Postal Union An aggregation of countries, organized in 1874, agreeing to deliver foreign mail: officially designated *Universal Postal Union.*

post–bel·lum (pōst′bel′əm) *adj.* Coming or occurring after the war, especially the Civil War. [<L, after the war < *post* after + *bellum* a war]

post box A mailbox.

post·date (pōst′dāt′) *v.t.* **·dat·ed, ·dat·ing 1** To assign or affix a date later than the actual date to (a check, document, etc.). **2** To follow in time.

post·di·lu·vi·al (pōst′di·lōō′vē·əl) *adj.* Coming after the deluge.

post·di·lu·vi·an (pōst′di·lōō′vē·ən) *n.* One living after the deluge. — *adj.* Postdiluvial.

post·ed (pōs′tid) *adj.* Possessed of the latest information or news: Keep me *posted.* [< POST³, *v.* (def. 2)]

pos·teen (pos·tēn′) *n.* An Indian garment made of sheepskin with the fleece left on: also *postin.* [<Persian *pōstīn* of leather < *pōst* a skin]

post·er (pōs′tər) *n.* **1** A placard or bill used for advertising, public information, etc., to be posted on a wall or other surface. **2** A billposter. [< POST¹, *v.*]

pos·te·ri·or (pos·tir′ē·ər) *adj.* **1** Situated behind or toward the hinder part: opposed to *anterior.* **2** Coming after another in a series; especially, subsequent in point of time; later: in this sense opposed to *prior.* **3** *Bot.* Situated or growing on the side next the parent axis: the *posterior* side of an axillary flower. **4** *Zool.* In the direction of the tail; caudal. **5** *Anat.* Dorsal. — *n.* Often *pl.* The buttocks. [<L *posterior,* comp. of *posterus* following < *post* after]

pos·te·ri·or·i·ty *(pos·tir′ē·ôr′ə·tē, -or′ə-)* *n.*

The state of being posterior or later in point of time: opposed to *priority.*

pos·te·ri·or·ly (pos·tir′ē·ər·lē) *adv.* **1** Subsequently. **2** Behind.

pos·ter·i·ty (pos·ter′ə·tē) *n.* **1** The stock that proceeds from a progenitor; a person's descendants; also, succeeding generations, taken collectively: the *posterity* of Adam. **2** Posteriority. [<OF *posterite* <L *posteritas* < *posterus.* See POSTERIOR.]

pos·tern (pōs′tərn, pos′-) *n.* **1** A back gate or door; a private entrance, especially a small gate beside a large one in a fortified place. **2** A covered passage closed by a gate and leading from a bastion to the ditch. — *adj.* Situated at the back; private: a *postern* gate. [<OF *posterne, posterle* <L *posterus.* See POSTERIOR.]

Post Exchange An establishment for the sale of merchandise and services to military personnel: abbr. *PX.*

post·fix (pōst′fiks′) *v.t.* To add at the end of a word, as a letter, syllable, etc.: opposed to *prefix.* — *n.* (pōst′fiks′) That which is so added; a suffix. [<POST- + (AF)FIX]

post·grad·u·ate (pōst′graj′ōō·it, -āt) *adj.* Of or pertaining to studies pursued after receiving a first degree; graduate. — *n.* One who pursues or has completed a postgraduate course.

post·haste (pōst′hāst′) *adj.* Done with speed; instant. — *n.* Great haste or speed like that of the post. — *adv.* With utmost speed; hurriedly. [Appar. < *Haste, post, haste,* an old direction written on letters]

post·hu·mous (pos′chŏŏ·məs) *adj.* **1** Born after the father's death: said of a child. **2** Published after the author's death, as a book. **3** Arising or continuing after a person's death: a *posthumous* reputation. [<LL *posthumus* <L *postumus* latest, last, superl. of *posterus.* See POSTERIOR.] — **post′hu·mous·ly** *adv.*

pos·tiche (pôs·tēsh′) *adj.* **1** Added after the completion of the work: said especially of a superadded and inappropriate architectural ornament. **2** Spurious; artificial. — *n.* **1** Pretense; sham. **2** An imitation; artificial substitute. Also **pos·tique′** (-tēk′). [<F <Ital. *posticcio* counterfeit <LL *appositicius* < *appositus.* See APPOSITE.]

pos·til (pos′til) *n.* A marginal note; especially, one written on the margin of the Scriptures; also, a series of Scriptural comments. [<OF *postille* <Med. L *postilla* a gloss on the gospel, ? <L *post illa (verba textus)* after those (words of the text) < *post* after + *illa* those]

pos·til·ion (pōs·til′yən, pos-) *n.* A rider of one of the near horses of a team drawing a vehicle, with or without a coachman. Also **pos·til′lion.** [<MF *postillon* <Ital. *postiglione* < *posta* a post, station]

post·im·pres·sion·ism (pōst′im·presh′ən·iz′əm) *n.* The methods, theories, or practice of a group of painters of the late 19th century who emphasized the subjective prerogatives of the artist as opposed to the literal or idealistic representation of academic painting and the supposed objectivity of impressionism. Cézanne, Van Gogh, and Gauguin are considered its chief exponents. —**post′im·pres′sion·ist** *n.* & *adj.* —**post′im·pres·sion·is′tic** *adj.*

pos·tin (pos·tēn′, -tin′) See POSTEEN.

post·li·min·i·um (pōst′li·min′ē·əm) *n.* In international law, a right (*Latin* jus *postliminii*), derived from Roman law, whereby persons or things taken in war by the enemy are restored to their former civil condition or previous ownership upon their coming again under the power of the nation to which they belonged. Also **post·lim·i·ny** (pōst′lim′ə·nē). [<L < *post* after, behind + *limen, liminis* a threshold]

post·lude (pōst′lōōd) *n.* An organ voluntary concluding a church service. See PRELUDE. [< POST- + (PRE)LUDE]

post·man (pōst′mən) *n. pl.* **·men** (-mən) A letter-carrier; mail-carrier; formerly, a courier. **post′wo·man** *n. fem.*

post·mark (pōst′märk′) *n.* The stamp of a post office on mail matter handled there, sometimes also serving to cancel stamps, and giving the name of the office and the day (in large cities also the hour) of mailing or arrival. — *v.t.* To stamp with a postmark.

post·mas·ter (pōst′mas′tər, -mäs′-) *n.* **1** An official having charge of a post office. **2** One who provides horses for posting. —**post′mis′tress**

(-mis′tris) *n. fem.*

postmaster general *pl.* **postmasters general** The executive head of the postal service of a government.

post·me·rid·i·an (pōst′mə·rid′ē·ən) *adj.* Pertaining to the afternoon. Also **post′me·rid′i·o·nal.** [<L *postmeridianus* < *post-* after + *meridianus* MERIDIAN.]

post me·rid·i·em (pōst mə·rid′ē·əm) After midday: abbr. *p.m.* or *P.M.* [<L]

post–mor·tem (pōst′môr′təm) *n.* Expert examination of a human body after death for pathological or judicial purposes; an autopsy. [<L, after death < *post* after + *mors, mortis* death]

post note A promissory note issued by a bank and payable at a fixed time after its date.

post–o·bit (pōst–ō′bit) *adj.* Made or done after death; taking effect after death: also **post′o·bit′u·ar′y** (-ō·bich′ōō·er′ē). — *n.* A bond given to secure payment by the obligor of a sum of money on the death of a designated person, generally one from whose estate he has expectations: also **post–obit bond.** [Contraction of POST OBITUM]

post office 1 That branch of the civil service of a government charged with carrying and delivering the mails. **2** An office for the receipt, transmission, and delivery of mails, and for the transaction of business connected with the same. **3** Any town or place having a post office. **4** A kissing game. —**post–of·fice** (pōst′ôf′is, -of′-) *adj.*

post–paid (pōst′pād′) *adj.* Having postage prepaid.

post–par·tum (pōst′pär′təm) *adj. Med.* After childbirth; a *postpartum* fever. [< POST- + L *partus* childbirth < *parere* bear]

post·pone (pōst·pōn′) *v.t.* **·poned, ·pon·ing 1** To put off to a future time; defer; delay. **2** To subordinate. [<L *postponere* < *post-* after + *ponere* put] —**post·pon′a·ble** *adj.* —**post·pone′ment** *n.* —**post·pon′er** *n.*

Synonyms: adjourn, defer, delay, procrastinate. *Adjourn* signifies literally to put off to another day, and, hence, to any future time. A deliberative assembly may *adjourn* to another day or to another hour of the same day, and resume business, where it left off, as if there had been no interval; or it may *adjourn* to a definite later date or, when no day can be fixed, to meet at the call of the president or other officer. In common usage, to *adjourn* a matter is to hold it in abeyance until it may be more conveniently or suitably attended to; in such use *defer* and *postpone* are close synonyms of *adjourn; defer* is simply to lay or put aside temporarily; to *postpone* is strictly to lay or put aside until after something else occurs, or is done, known, obtained, or the like; but *postpone* is often used without such limitation. *Adjourn, defer,* and *postpone* all imply definite expectation of later consideration or action; *delay* is much less definite, while *procrastinate* is hopelessly vague. One who *procrastinates* gives no assurance that he will ever act. Compare HINDER, PROCRASTINATE. *Antonyms:* act, complete, consummate, dispatch, do, expedite, hasten, hurry, quicken.

post·po·si·tion (pōst′pə·zish′ən) *n.* **1** The act of placing after or state of being placed behind. **2** *Gram.* A word placed after another word, as an enclitic; especially, a suffixed element which functions as a preposition, as *-de* in Greek *oikade* homeward. [<L *postpositus,* pp. of *postponere.* See POSTPONE.]

post position The place, in relation to the inner rail, occupied by a horse at the start of a race.

post·pos·i·tive (pōst′poz′ə·tiv) *Gram. adj.* Appended to something; suffixed; enclitic. — *n.* An appended word; a postposition. [< L *postpositus.* See POSTPOSITION.]

post·pran·di·al (pōst·pran′dē·əl) *adj.* After-dinner.

post·script (pōst′skript′) *n.* **1** A supplemental addition to a written or printed document. **2** Something added to a letter after the writer's signature: abbr. *P.S.* [< L *postscriptum,* pp. of *postscribere* write after]

post terminal A point or port of destination to which goods are transshipped after being delivered by an oceanic carrier: usually applied to additional rates for extra haulage.

pos·tu·lant (pos′chə·lənt) *n.* **1** One who or that which presents a request. **2** *Eccl.* An applicant for admission into a religious order or the sacred ministry. Compare NOVICE. [< F < L *postulans, -antis,* ppr. of *postulare* demand] —**pos′tu-lant-ship** *n.*

pos-tu-late (pos′chə-lit) *n.* **1** A position claimed or basis of argument laid down as well known or too plain to require proof; a self-evident truth. **2** *Geom.* A self-evident statement regarding the possibility of a geometrical construction: distinguished from *axiom.* **3** A condition precedent that must be assumed to explain or account for a thing: Peace is a *postulate* of prosperity. **4** A hypothesis; an unproved assumption. —*v.t.* (pos′chə-lāt) **-lat-ed, -lat-ing 1** To claim; demand; require. **2** To set forth as self-evident or already known: to *postulate* the existence of matter. **3** To assume the truth or reality of, especially as a basis for discussion: His theory *postulates* the validity of an older theory. See synonyms under ASSUME. [< L *postulatus,* pp. of *postulare* demand] —**pos′tu-la′tor** *n.*

pos-tu-la-tion (pos′chə-lā′shən) *n.* **1** The act of postulating or supposing something as not needing proof; the assumption of a thing as a fact or truth. **2** *Eccl.* The election or presentation of a person to an office notwithstanding some disqualification.

pos-tu-la-tum (pos′chə-lā′təm) *n. pl.* **-ta** (-tə) A postulate. [< L]

pos-ture (pos′chər) *n.* **1** The visible disposition, either natural or assumed, of the several parts of a material thing, and especially of a living thing, with reference to each other; attitude; pose; in art, the position of a figure with regard to its members. **2** Situation as connected with or resulting from a relation of parts; state: the *posture* of national affairs. **3** Mental or spiritual attitude or condition. See synonyms under ATTITUDE. —*v.t. & v.i.* **-tured, -tur-ing** To place in or assume a posture; pose. [< F < L *positura* < *positus,* pp. of *ponere* place] —**pos′tur-al** *adj.* —**pos′tur-er, pos′tur-ist** *n.*

pos-tur-ize (pos′chə-rīz) *v.t. & v.i.* **-ized, -iz-ing** To posture.

po-sy (pō′zē) *n. pl.* **-sies 1** A bunch of flowers, or a single flower; a bouquet; nosegay. **2** Generally, a brief inscription or motto, originally one in verse; especially, one inscribed on a ring or other trinket. [Contraction of POESY]

pot (pot) *n.* **1** A round earthen, metal, or glass vessel for culinary and other domestic purposes. **2** A metal drinking cup; mug. **3** The contents of a pot; hence, liquor; drink. **4** The amount of stakes wagered or played for; the pool, as in poker. **5** *Colloq.* A large sum of money. **6** A chimney pot. **7** *Scot.* A deep pit. **8** In fishing, the circular part of a net; also, a basketlike trap for catching lobsters, eels, fish, etc. **9** *Colloq.* A pot shot. **10** *Slang* A potbelly. **11** *Slang* Marihuana. —*v.* **pot-ted, pot-ting** *v.t.* **1** To put into a pot. **2** To preserve, as meat, in pots or jars. **3** To cook in a pot; stew. **4** To shoot (game) for food rather than for sport. **5** To shoot with a pot shot. **6** *Colloq.* To secure, capture, or win; bag. —*v.i.* **7** To take a pot shot. [OE *pott*]

po-ta-ble (pō′tə-bəl) *adj.* Suitable for drinking: said of water. —*n.* Something drinkable; a drink. [< F < L *potabilis* < *potare* drink]

pot-ash (pot′ash′) *n.* **1** Potassium hydroxide: also called *caustic potash* or *potassa.* **2** The crude potassium carbonate obtained by leaching the ashes of plants: when purified it is called *pearl ash.* **3** The oxide of potassium, K_2O. **4** Potash water. Also, in pharmaceutical use, **po-tass** (pə-tas′). [Earlier *potashes,* pl., after Du. *potasschen;* from being prepared in iron pots]

po-tas-sa (pə-tas′ə) *n.* Potassium hydroxide.

po-tas-si-um (pə-tas′ē-əm) *n.* A soft, silvery, very light element (symbol K, atomic number 19) of the alkali group, an essential element in living systems and in nature containing traces of a long-lived radioactive isotope. See PERIODIC TABLE. [< NL < POTASSA] —**po-tas′sic** *adj.*

po-ta-tion (pō-tā′shən) *n.* **1** The act of drinking; a drink. **2** A drinking bout. [< OF < L *potatio, -onis* < *potatus,* pp. of *potare* drink]

po-ta-to (pə-tā′tō) *n. pl.* **-toes 1** One of the edible, farinaceous tubers of a plant *(Solanum tuberosum)* of the nightshade family. **2** The plant. **3** The sweet potato. [< Sp. *patata* < Arawakan (Taino) *batata* sweet potato]

potato beetle 1 The Colorado beetle *(Leptinotarsa decemlineata),* yellowish, with ten longitudinal black stripes on the wing covers. Both the adult and the larva feed on the leaves of the potato, tomato, and similar plants, and are among the world's greatest agricultural pests: also **potato bug.** For illustration see also INSECTS (injurious). **2** Any of several beetles feeding on the foliage of the potato, especially *Lema trilineata,* with three longitudinal black stripes on the wing covers.

POTATO BEETLE
First described in 1824; widespread by 1874. (About 3/8 inch long; 1/4 inch wide)

potato chip A very thin slice of potato fried crisp and salted.

potato rot A disease of the potato caused by a mildew (genus *Phytophthora*).

po-ta-to-ry (pō′tə-tôr′ē, -tō′rē) *adj.* Pertaining to potation; given or addicted to drinking: a *potatory* club. [< L *potatorius* < *potator* drinker < *potare* drink]

potato stone A quartz geode resembling a potato.

Pot-a-wat-o-mi (pot′ə-wot′ə-mē) *n.* One of a tribe of North American Indians of Algonquian stock, formerly inhabiting the western shores of Lake Michigan.

pot-bel-ly (pot′bel′ē) *n. pl.* **-lies** A protuberant belly. —**pot′bel′lied** *adj.*

pot-boil-er (pot′boi′lər) *n. Colloq.* A literary or artistic work produced simply to obtain the means of subsistence. —**pot′boil′ing** *n.*

pot cheese Cottage cheese.

pot companion A boon companion; fellow toper.

po-teen (pō-tēn′) *n.* In Ireland, illicitly manufactured whisky: also spelled *potheen, potteen.* [< Irish *poitín,* dim. of *poite* pot]

po-ten-cy (pōt′n-sē) *n. pl.* **-cies 1** The quality of being potent; inherent ability; mental, moral, or physical power. **2** The power of effecting particular results: the *potency* of a drug or liquor. **3** In homeopathy, the efficacy of a drug as increased by dilution or attenuation; also, the degree to which such attenuation has been carried. **4** Power arising from external circumstances; authority: the *potency* of the prime minister; hence, power to move or influence. **5** Capacity to respond to certain influences; latent power. Also **po′tence.** [< L *potentia*]

po-tent (pōt′nt) *adj.* **1** Physically powerful; able to accomplish material results; efficacious: a *potent* drug. **2** Morally powerful; of a character to influence; convincing: a *potent* argument. **3** Having great authority: a *potent* prince. **4** Sexually competent; able to procreate. See synonyms under POWERFUL. [< L *potens, -entis,* ppr. of *posse* be able, have power < *potis* able + *esse* be] —**po′tent-ly** *adv.* —**po′tent-ness** *n.*

po-ten-tate (pōt′n-tāt) *n.* One having great power or sway; a sovereign. [< LL *potentatus*]

po-ten-tial (pə-ten′shəl) *adj.* **1** Possible but not actual. **2** Having capacity for existence, but not yet existing. **3** *Physics* Existing by virtue of position: said of energy: distinguished from *kinetic.* **4** *Gram.* Indicating possibility or power. See POTENTIAL MOOD. **5** Having force or power. —*n.* **1** Anything that may be possible; a possible development. **2** *Gram.* The potential mood. **3** *Physics* A condition at a point in space, due to local attraction or repulsion, such that a mass, electric charge, etc., at that point becomes capable of doing work. **4** *Electr.* The ratio of the potential energy possessed by an electrically charged body because of its position in an electric field to the charge carried by the body. [< LL *potentialis*] —**po-ten′tial-ly** *adv.*

potential energy Energy stored in any of numerous forms, as chemical energy in coal, mechanical energy in a coiled spring, etc.

po-ten-ti-al-i-ty (pə-ten′shē-al′ə-tē) *n. pl.* **-ties 1** Inherent capacity for development or accomplishment; capability; power; efficiency.

2 Potential quality or being; possibility. [< Med. L *potentialitas, -tatis*]

potential mood *Gram.* The verb phrase made up by means of the auxiliaries *may, can, could, must, should,* or *would,* with an infinitive, and expressing power, liberty, or possibility: I *could* go; it *may* be.

po-ten-ti-om-e-ter (pə-ten′shē-om′ə-tər) *n.* An apparatus for measuring electromotive force or difference of potential. [< L *potenti(a)* potency + -METER]

po-tent-ize (pōt′n-tīz) *v.t.* **-ized, -iz-ing** In homeopathy, to render potent, as drugs, by attenuation. —**po′tent-iz′er** *n.*

pot-head (pot′hed′) *n. U.S. Slang* A person who habitually smokes marihuana.

po-theen (pō-thēn′) See POTEEN.

poth-er (poth′ər) *n.* Excitement mingled with confusion; bustle; fuss. —*v.t. & v.i.* To worry; bother. [Origin uncertain]

pot herb Any plant, especially greens, cooked by boiling, or used to flavor boiled foods.

pot-hole (pot′hōl′) *n.* **1** A pot-shaped cavity in a rock, as that worn by loose stone gyrated in an eddy. **2** A deep hole, as in a road.

pot-hook (pot′hook′) *n.* **1** A curved or hooked piece of iron for lifting or hanging pots. **2** A curved mark or elementary stroke used in teaching penmanship; also, a scrawl, or, popularly, any curved stroke in stenography.

pot-house (pot′hous′) *n.* An alehouse; saloon.

pot-hunt-er (pot′hun′tər) *n.* **1** One who kills game for food rather than for sport: usually a contemptuous use. **2** One who engages in a competition simply to win the prizes offered. —**pot′hunt′ing** *adj. & n.*

po-tiche (pō-tēsh′) *n.* A vase having an elongated round body, a cylindrical neck, and a detached cover. [< F]

po-tion (pō′shən) *n.* A draft, as a large dose of liquid medicine: often used of a magic or poisonous draft. [< F < L *potio, -onis* < *potare* drink. Doublet of POISON.]

pot-latch (pot′lach) *n.* **1** Among American Indians of the northern Pacific coast: **a** A gift. **b** *Often cap.* A winter festival. **2** A ceremonial feast in which gifts are exchanged and property destroyed in a competitive show of wealth. Also **pot′lach, pot′lache.** [< Chinook *patshatl* gift]

pot-lead (pot′led′) *n.* Graphite, especially as used on the bottoms of racing vessels to reduce friction.

pot liquor The liquid left in a pot after cooking greens and meat (usually pork or bacon) together.

pot luck Whatever may chance to be in the pot; hence, a meal or food not prepared for guests: usually in the phrase **to take pot luck.**

pot marigold The calendula.

pot metal 1 Cast iron suitable for making pots. **2** A copper-and-lead alloy formerly used for large pots. **3** A kind of glass colored throughout while still in a molten state.

po-to-ma-ni-a (pō′tə-mā′nē-ə, -mān′yə) *n.* Delirium tremens; dipsomania. [< Gk. *potos* drunk + -MANIA]

po-tom-e-ter (pō-tom′ə-tər) *n.* An instrument for measuring the amount of moisture absorbed by a plant, as determined by the amount lost in transpiration. [< Gk. *poton* drink + -METER]

pot-pie (pot′pī′) *n.* A pie, baked in a deep dish, containing meat and vegetables and having only a top crust; also, meat stewed with dumplings.

pot-pour-ri (pot-poor′ē, *Fr.* pō-poo-rē′) *n.* **1** A ragout of meats and vegetables; a stew. **2** A mixture of dried sweet-smelling flower petals used to perfume a room; also, a small covered jar for containing such a mixture. **3** A collection of various things; miscellany. [< F, lit., rotten pot. See OLLA PODRIDA.]

pot roast Meat braised and cooked in a pot until tender, often with vegetables.

pot-sherd (pot′shûrd′) *n.* A bit of broken crockery. Also **pot′shard** (-shärd). [< POT + SHARD]

pot shot 1 A shot fired to kill, without regard to the rules of sports. **2** A shot fired, as from ambush, at a person or animal within easy range. **3** A random shot.

pot-stone (pot′stōn′) *n.* Steatite.

pott (pot) *n.* A size of paper, varying in size according to use, but generally about 15 1/2 × 12 1/2 inches. [Var. of POT; so named from having once borne the watermark of a pot]

pot·tage (pot′ij) *n.* **1** A thick broth or stew. **2** A porridge. [<F *potage* <*pot* pot]

pot·ted (pot′id) *adj.* **1** Placed or kept in a pot. **2** Cooked or preserved in a pot. **3** *Slang* Drunk.

pot·teen (po·tēn′) See POTEEN.

pot·ter (pot′ər) *n.* **1** One who makes earthenware or porcelain. **2** One who pots meats, vegetables, etc. [OE *potere*]

potter's field A piece of ground appropriated as a burial ground for the destitute and the unknown. *Matt.* xxvii 7.

potter's flint Finely pulverized quartz mixed with porcelain to impart strength and rigidity and to reduce shrinkage: used also in enamel mixtures.

potter's wheel A horizontal rotating disk used by potters for holding and manipulating prepared clay.

POTTER'S WHEEL
a. Molding clay.
b. Rotating wheel.
c. Shaft.
d. Treadle.

potter wasp A digger wasp (genus *Eumenes*) which constructs vaselike cells of mud as a nest, especially the North American potter wasp, *E. fraterna.* For illustration see INSECTS (beneficial).

pot·ter·y (pot′ər·ē) *n. pl.* **·ter·ies 1** A factory where potters' ware is made. **2** The manufacture of earthenware or porcelain. **3** Clay ware molded and hardened. ◆ Collateral adjective: *fictile.* [<F *poterie* <*potier* a potter <*pot* a pot]

pot·ting (pot′ing) *n.* **1** The preserving of articles of food in pots for future use. **2** The placing of buds, bulbs, or plants in pots.

pot·tle (pot′l) *n.* **1** A drinking vessel, pot, or tankard holding about half a gallon. **2** An old liquid measure of half a gallon. **3** A small vessel or basket for holding fruit. [<OF *potel,* dim. of *pot* pot]

pot·to (pot′ō) *n. pl.* **·tos** A small, nocturnal, arboreal primate (*Perodicticus potto*) of African forests, having a stumpy tail and feet and hands adapted for grasping. See KINKAJOU. [<West African native name]

pot·ty (pot′ē) *adj. Brit. Colloq.* **1** Insignificant. **2** Slightly drunk; hence, a little silly. [Prob. <POT, in the phrase *go to pot* deteriorate]

pot·val·iant (pot′val′yənt) *adj.* Courageous from drink. —**pot′·val′ian·cy, pot′·val′ian·try, pot′·val′or** (-val′ər) *n.*

pouch (pouch) *n.* **1** A small bag or sack, or something serving a similar purpose, as a pocket or a purse. **2** *Zool.* A saclike part for temporarily containing food, as in gophers and pelicans; also, a marsupium. **3** *Bot.* Any pouchlike cavity, as the silique of the mustard plant. **4** A leather receptacle for carrying small-arms ammunition; also, a wooden cartridge box. **5** An inner mailbag. —*v.t.* **1** To put in or as in a pouch; pocket. **2** To fashion or arrange in pouchlike form. **3** To swallow. —*v.i.* **4** To take on a pouchlike shape; form a pouchlike cavity. [<OF *poche,* var. of *poke, poque* bag] —**pouch′y** *adj.*

pouched rat 1 A rodent with cheek pouches; especially, a pocket gopher. **2** A kangaroo rat. **3** Any of certain ratlike rodents of Africa having large cheek pouches (genera *Cricetomys* and *Saccostomus*).

pouf (poof) *n.* **1** A hair arrangement in high rolled puffs, popular in the 18th century. **2** Any puffed part of a dress. **3** An upholstered tabouret for one or more persons. [<F, a puff]

pou·lard (poo·lärd′) *n.* A pullet having the ovaries removed to produce abnormal growth and fattening and superior quality; hence, a fat pullet. Compare CAPON. [<F *poularde* <*poule* pullet]

pou·lard (poo·lärd′) *n.* A variety of spring or winter wheat closely related to durum, having broad leaves, thick culms, and hard, starchy kernels. Also **poulard wheat.** [<POULARD[1]; so named because suitable only for stock feed]

poult (pōlt) *n.* A young turkey, chicken, etc. [Contraction of ME *pulet* pullet]

poul·ter·er (pōl′tər·ər) *n.* A dealer in poultry. [<POULTER + -ER[2]]

poulter's measure A verse form consisting of alternating lines of twelve and fourteen syllables: so called from the poulterer's custom of sometimes giving fourteen eggs to the dozen.

poul·tice (pōl′tis) *n.* A mollifying remedy of a moist, heated nature, applied to inflamed surfaces. —*v.t.* **·ticed, ·tic·ing** To cover or treat with a poultice. [<L *pultes,* pl. of *puls* porridge]

poul·try (pōl′trē) *n.* Domestic fowls, generally or collectively, as hens, ducks, etc. [<OF *pouleterie* <*poulet* fowl]

pounce[1] (pouns) *v.i.* **pounced, pounc·ing** To swoop or spring in or as in seizing prey: with *on, upon,* or *at.* —*n.* **1** A talon or claw. **2** The act of pouncing; a sudden leap, swoop, spring, or seizure. [Origin uncertain] —**pounc′er** *n.*

pounce[2] (pouns) *v.t.* **1** To perforate with holes in decorative patterns; scallop; pink. **2** To emboss (metalwork) with a design hammered on the reverse side. [<OF *poinçonnier, ponchonner* <*poinçon, poinchon* a punchon]

pounce[3] (pouns) *n.* **1** A powder formerly used to absorb excess of ink, as on a manuscript. **2** A finely pulverized substance used in transferring designs. —*v.t.* **pounced, pounc·ing** To sprinkle, smooth, or rub with pounce. [<F *ponce* <L *pumex, pumicis* pumice]

pounce box 1 A box with perforated lid formerly used for dusting out pounce as a perfume; a perfume box. **2** A box formerly used for dusting powder or sand on freshly written paper. Also **poun·cet** (poun′sit) **box.**

pound[1] (pound) *n.* **1** A variable unit of weight (symbol lb.): the avoirdupois pound is 16 ounces, 7,000 grains, or 453.59 grams; the troy pound, 12 ounces, 5,760 grains, or 373.24 grams. **2** An English money of account, equal to 20 shillings; specifically, a pound sterling (symbol £). See SOVEREIGN. [OE *pūnd* <L *pondus* weight]

pound[2] (pound) *n.* **1** A place, enclosed by authority, in which stray or trespassing cattle and distrained cattle or goods are left till redeemed; also, a similar enclosure for stray dogs. **2** An enclosed shelter for cattle or sheep. **3** A trap for wild animals. **4** An area or place in which to catch or stow fish; a poundnet. —*v.t.* To confine in or as in a pound; impound; restrain. [OE *pund(fald)* pinfold] —**pound′keep′er** (-kē′pər) *n.*

pound[3] (pound) *v.t.* **1** To strike heavily and repeatedly, as with a hammer; beat. **2** To reduce to a pulp or powder by beating; pulverize; triturate. **3** To teach or impress by constant repetition: to *pound* facts into someone's head. **4** To walk tediously or heavily: to *pound* a beat. —*v.i.* **5** To strike heavy, repeated blows: with *on, at,* etc. **6** To move or proceed heavily or vigorously. **7** To rise and fall heavily, as a ship in rough water. **8** To throb heavily or resoundingly: Her heart was *pounding* from fear and excitement. —*n.* **1** A heavy blow; thump; thud. **2** The act of pounding. See synonyms under BEAT. [OE *punian*] —**pound′er** *n.*

pound·age[1] (poun′dij) *n.* **1** A rate on the pound sterling. **2** Formerly, in England, a subsidy to the crown on each pound of merchandise exported or imported.

pound·age[2] (poun′dij) *n.* **1** The charges for the redemption of impounded cattle. **2** The act of impounding cattle.

pound cake A rich cake having ingredients equal in weight, as a pound each of flour, butter, and sugar, with eggs added.

pound·er (poun′dər) *n.* **1** Anything weighing a pound: The trout's a *pounder.* **2** A person or thing weighing, having, or having a certain relation to, a given number of pounds: used only in compounds: The baby is an eight-*pounder.*

pound-fool·ish (pound′foo′lish) *adj.* **1** Extravagant with large sums, but watching small sums closely: penny-wise and *pound-foolish.* **2** Having little capacity for business.

pound-net (pound′net′) *n.* A weir or arrangement of nets supported upon stakes to form a trap for fish.

pour (pôr, pōr) *v.t.* **1** To cause to flow in a continuous stream, as water, sand, etc. **2** To send

forth, emit, or utter profusely or continuously: The radio *poured* forth music. —*v.i.* **3** To flow in a continuous stream; gush. **4** To rain heavily. **5** To move in great numbers; swarm: The northern hordes *poured* over Italy. **6** To serve as a hostess at a social tea. —*n.* A pouring, flow, or downfall. [Origin unknown] —**pour′er** *n.*

pous·sette (poo·set′) *n.* A dance figure in which a couple or couples swing round and round while holding hands. —*v.i.* **·set·ted, ·set·ting** To perform a poussette. [<F, dim. of *pousse* a push <*pousser* push]

pou sto (poo′ stō′, pou′) A place to stand on; hence, a foundation for operations in any line of endeavor. [<Gk. *pou stō* where I may stand: from the alleged saying of Archimedes on his discovery of the lever, "Give me a place where I may stand and I will move the earth."]

pout[1] (pout) *v.i.* **1** To thrust out the lips, especially in ill humor. **2** To be sullen; sulk. **3** To swell out; protrude. —*v.t.* **4** To thrust out (the lips, etc.). **5** To utter with a pout. —*n.* A pushing out of the lips as in pouting; hence, a fit of ill humor. [Cf. Sw. *puta* be swollen]

pout[2] (pout) *n.* **1** One of various fresh-water catfishes having a pouting appearance. **2** The eelpout. [OE *(æle)pūte* eelpout]

pout·er (pou′tər) *n.* **1** One who or that which pouts. **2** A breed of pigeon having the habit of puffing out the crop.

pov·er·ty (pov′ər·tē) *n.* **1** The state of being poor or without competent subsistence; need; penury. **2** The condition that relates to the absence or scarcity of requisite substance or elements. **3** A lack or meagerness of supply; dearth. [<OF *po·vreté* <L *paupertas* <*pauper* poor]

Synonyms: beggary, destitution, distress, indigence, mendicancy, need, pauperism, penury, privation, want. *Poverty* denotes a condition below that of easy, comfortable living; *privation* denotes a condition of painful lack of what is useful or desirable; *indigence* is lack of ordinary means of subsistence; *destitution* is lack of the comforts, and even of the necessaries of life; *penury* is cramping *poverty; pauperism* is such *destitution* as throws one upon public charity for support; *beggary* and *mendicancy* denote *poverty* that appeals for indiscriminate private charity.

pow·der (pou′dər) *n.* **1** A finely ground or comminuted mass of free particles formed from a solid substance in the dry state; dust. **2** A pulverized cosmetic preparation for toilet use. **3** A medicine in the form of powder. **4** An explosive dry powder, as gunpowder. —*v.t.* **1** To reduce to powder; pulverize. **2** To sprinkle or cover with or as with powder. **3** To sprinkle with small objects or ornaments. —*v.i.* **4** To be reduced to powder. **5** To use powder as a cosmetic. [<OF *poudre* <L *pulvis, pulveris* dust] —**pow′der·er** *n.*

powder blue 1 Pulverized smalt having a deep-blue color: used as laundry bluing. **2** Its deep-blue color. **3** A valuable porcelain glaze. **4** The color of this glaze, a soft medium blue.

powder room 1 A women's rest-room. **2** A small room or bathroom decorated daintily for use as a woman's dressing-room.

pow·der·y (pou′dər·ē) *adj.* **1** Consisting of or like fine powder or dust. **2** Covered with or as with powder; mealy; dusty. **3** Capable of being easily powdered or crumbled; friable.

pow·er (pou′ər) *n.* **1** Ability to act; potency; specifically, the property of a substance or being that is manifested in effort or action, and by virtue of which that substance or being produces change, moral or physical. **2** Potential capacity. **3** Strength or force actually put forth. **4** The right, ability, or capacity to exercise control; legal authority, capacity, or competency, particularly, authority to do some act in relation to lands, as to create estates therein or charges thereon; also, a legal instrument or document conferring it. See POWER OF APPOINTMENT. **5** Any agent that exercises power, as in control or dominion; a military or naval force; an important and influential sovereign nation. **6** Great or telling force or effect. **7** *Colloq.* A great number or quantity. **8** Religious frenzy, especially as exemplified in exhortation: believed to be by possession of the Holy Spirit. **9** Any form of energy available for doing work; specifically, energy developed by mechanical or electrical means. **10** *Physics* The time rate at which energy is transferred, or converted into work. **11** *Math.* **a** The product of a number multiplied by itself a given number of times. **b** An exponent. **12** *Optics* Magnifying capacity, as of a lens. **13** *pl.* The sixth of the nine grades or orders of angels. —*v.t.* **1** To provide with means of propulsion. **2** *Colloq.* To force or push in the act of overcoming resistance: *powered* his way through for a touchdown. —*v.i.* **3** *Colloq.* To move forcefully: to *power* through mud. [< OF *poeir,* ult. < L *posse* be able]

Synonyms: ability, capacity, efficacy, efficiency, energy, force, might, potency, puissance, strength. *Power* is the most general term of this group of words, including every quality, property, or faculty by which any change, effect, or result is, or may be, produced, as, the *power* of the legislature to enact laws; the *power* of the executive to enforce them; the *power* of an acid to corrode a metal; the *power* of a polished surface to reflect light. *Ability* is nearly coextensive with *power,* but does not reach its positiveness and vigor, *ability* often implying latent, as distinguished from active, *power. Power* and *ability* include *capacity,* which is *power* to receive; but *ability* is often distinguished from *capacity,* as *power* that may be manifested in doing, as *capacity* is in receiving. *Efficacy* is *power* to produce effects; *efficiency* is effectual agency, competent *power. Energy* is *power* both actual and potential; *force* is *power* enough to overcome resistance. *Puissance* is a poetic or literary synonym. See ABILITY, CAUSE, GENIUS, WEIGHT.

power- *combining form* Powered by a motor or by electricity: *power drill, power mower.*

pow·er·ful (pou′ər·fəl) *adj.* **1** Possessing great force; very efficient; strong. **2** Having great intensity or energy. **3** Exercising great authority, or manifesting high qualities; mighty. **4** Having great effect on the mind; convincing. —*adv. Colloq.* Very; exceedingly. —**pow′er·ful·ly** *adv.*

Synonyms (adj.): able, cogent, commanding, controlling, effective, effectual, efficacious, efficient, forceful, influential, mighty, potent, puissant, robust, strong, sturdy, vigorous.

pow·er·house (pou′ər·hous′) *n.* **1** *Electr.* A station where electricity is generated. **2** *Slang* A person or thing of great might or force.

pow·er·less (pou′ər·lis) *adj.* **1** Destitute of power; unable to accomplish an effect; impotent. **2** Without authority. —**pow′er·less·ly** *adv.* —**pow′er·less·ness** *n.*

power of appointment *Law* Authority conferred, as by power of attorney, deed, or will, to appoint or designate a person or persons to make disposition of an estate or interest in the property of another.

power of attorney *Law* **1** The authority or power to act conferred upon an agent. **2** The instrument or document by which that power or authority is conferred or guaranteed. See under ATTORNEY.

pow·wow (pou′wou′) *U.S. n.* **1** A North American Indian medicine man, priest, or magician. **2** The ceremony of a medicine man involving a dance, feast, or other demonstration, to cure the sick or effect success in hunting, war, etc. **3** Hence, magic; witchcraft. **4** An Indian council. **5** *Colloq.* Any meeting for conference. —*v.i.* To hold a deliberative council. [< Algonquian (Massachuset) *pauwaw,* lit., he dreams]

pox (poks) *n.* **1** Any disease characterized by eruptions of a purulent nature: chicken *pox.* **2** Syphilis [Var. of *pocks,* pl. of POCK]

prac·ti·ca·ble (prak′tə·kə·bəl) *adj.* **1** That can be put into practice; feasible. **2** That can be used for an intended purpose; usable. —**prac′ti·ca·bil′i·ty,** **prac′ti·ca·ble·ness** *n.* —**prac′ti·ca·bly** *adv.*

prac·ti·cal (prak′ti·kəl) *adj.* **1** Pertaining to or governed by actual use and experience or action, as contrasted with ideals and speculations. **2** Trained by or derived from practice or experience. **3** Having reference to useful ends to be attained; applicable to use. **4** Manifested in practice. **5** Being such to all intents and purposes; virtual. [< obs. *practic* < obs. F *practique* < LL *practicus* < Gk. *praktikos* fit for doing < *prassein* do] —**prac′ti·cal′i·ty** (-kal′ə·tē), **prac′ti·cal·ness** *n.*

practical joke A joke involving action instead of wit or words; a prank or trick.

prac·ti·cal·ly (prak′tik·lē) *adv.* **1** In a practical

manner. **2** To all intents and purposes; in fact or effect; virtually.

practical nurse A nurse with practical experience in the care of the sick, but who is not a registered nurse.

prac·tice (prak′tis) *v.* **·ticed, ·tic·ing** *v.t.* **1** To make use of habitually or often: to *practice* economy. **2** To apply in action; make a practice of: *Practice* what you preach. **3** To work at or pursue as a profession: to *practice* law. **4** To do or perform repeatedly in order to acquire skill or training; rehearse. **5** To instruct, as pupils, by repeated exercise or lessons. —*v.i.* **6** To repeat or rehearse something in order to acquire skill or proficiency: to *practice* for a concert. **7** To work at or pursue a profession: He *practiced* for twenty years. **8** *Rare* To conspire; scheme. —*n.* **1** Any customary action or proceeding regarded as individual; habit. **2** An established custom or usage. **3** The act or process of executing or accomplishing; doing or performance: distinguished from *theory.* **4** The regular prosecution of a business pursuit requiring education; professional business. **5** Frequent and repeated exercise in any matter. **6** *pl.* Stratagems or schemes for bad purposes; tricks. **7** A rule or method in arithmetic to facilitate multiplying quantities in different denominations. **8** The rules governing legal proceedings. Also **prac′tise.** [< OF *practiser* < *practiquer* < Med. L *practicare* < LL *practicus.* See PRACTICAL.] —**prac′tic·er** *n.*

♦ In Britain, *practice* is almost invariably the spelling used for the noun, *practise* for the verb. In the U.S., the noun form is more commonly *practice,* although *practise* is also used; both spellings are widely used as verbs.

Synonyms (noun): drill, exercise. *Exercise* is action with a view to employing, maintaining, or increasing power, or merely for enjoyment; *practice* is systematic *exercise* with a view to the acquirement of facility and skill; a person takes a walk for *exercise,* or takes time for *practice* on the piano. *Practice* is also used of putting into action and effect what one has learned or holds as a theory; as, the *practice* of law or medicine. Educationally, *practice* is the voluntary and persistent attempt to make skill a *habit;* as, *practice* in penmanship. *Drill* is systematic, rigorous, and commonly enforced *practice* under a teacher or commander. See CUSTOM, EXERCISE, HABIT, MANNER.

prac·ticed (prak′tist) *adj.* **1** Expert by practice; skilled by use or habit; experienced. **2** Acquired by practice. Also **prac′tised.**

prac·ti·tion·er (prak·tish′ən·ər) *n.* **1** One who practices an art or profession. **2** A Christian Science healer. [< earlier *practician* < OF *practicien,* ult. < L *practica* practice]

prae- See PRE-.

prae·ci·pe (pres′i·pē, prē′si-) See PRECIPE.

prae·di·al (prē′dē·əl), **prae·fect** (prē′fekt), etc. See PREDIAL, PREFECT, etc.

praeter- See PRETER-.

prae·tex·ta (prē·teks′tə) *n. pl.* **·tae** (-tē) An ordinary white toga with a purple border or stripe, worn by free-born Roman boys until they assumed the toga virilis at 14–16 years, and by girls until they were married. It was also the distinctive mark of the Roman curule magistrates, censors, state priests (when performing their functions), and emperors. [< L, lit., woven before, fringed, fem. of *praetextus,* pp. of *praetexere*]

prae·tor (prē′tər), **prae·to·ri·al** (prē·tôr′ē·əl, -tō′rē-), **prae·to·ri·an** (prē·tôr′ē·ən, -tō′rē-), etc. See PRETOR.

prag·mat·ic (prag·mat′ik) *adj.* **1** Pertaining to the accomplishment of duty or of business; specifically, relating to the civil affairs of a sovereign state. **2** Pertaining to or occupied with the scientific evolution of causes and effects; philosophical: said especially of history: the *pragmatic* method. **3** Pragmatical; practical. **4** Of or pertaining to the philosophy of pragmatism. [< L *pragmaticus* active or skilled in practical affairs < Gk. *pragmatikos* < *pragma, pragmatos* a thing

done, an affair < *prassein* do, perform]

prag·mat·i·cal (prag·mat′i·kəl) *adj.* **1** Inclined to be officious or meddlesome; self-important; busy. **2** Relating to or engrossed with everyday business; practical; hence, commonplace. —**prag·mat′i·cal·ly** *adv.* —**prag·mat′i·cal·ness** *n.*

pragmatic sanction An imperial or royal edict or decree operating as a fundamental law. The most famous of these edicts was that of Charles VI of Austria in 1724, which admitted heirs in the female line to the Austrian succession.

prag·ma·tism (prag′mə·tiz′əm) *n. Philos.* The doctrine that thought or ideas have value only in terms of their practical consequences, and that results are the sole test of the validity or truth of one's beliefs. —**prag′ma·tist** *n.*

Prague (präg) The capital of Czechoslovakia, on the Vltava, in central Bohemia. *German* **Prag** (präkh), *Czech* **Pra·ha** (prä′hä).

prai·rie (prâr′ē) *n.* A level or rolling tract of treeless land covered with coarse grass and generally of rich soil, especially as in parts of the western United States. [< F, a large meadow < Med. L *prataria* < L *pratum* meadow]

prairie chicken See under GROUSE. Also **prairie hen.**

PRAIRIE DOG
(Body from 12 to 15
inches long; tail, 3 to
4 inches)

prairie dog A burrowing rodent (genus *Cynomys*) of the plains of North America; specifically, *C. ludovicianus,* which lives in large communities and is very destructive to vegetation. Also **prairie squirrel.**

prairie owl 1 The burrowing owl. **2** The short-eared owl.

prairie schooner A covered wagon.

prairie state One of the States of the prairie regions of the Western and Middle Western United States.

Prairie State Nickname of ILLINOIS.

prairie wolf A coyote: distinguished from *timber wolf.*

praise (prāz) *v.t.* **praised, prais·ing 1** To express approval and commendation of; applaud; eulogize. **2** To express adoration of; glorify (God, etc.). —*n.* **1** Commendation expressed, as of a person for his virtues, or concerning meritorious actions; utterance of approval; honor given; also, applause. **2** Thanksgiving for blessings conferred; laudation to God; worship expressed in song. **3** The object, ground, reason, or subject of praise. ♦ Homophone: *prase.* [< OF *preisier* < LL *pretiare* prize < L *pretium* price. See PRICE.] —**prais′er** *n.*

Synonyms (verb): adore, applaud, approve, bless, celebrate, commend, eulogize, extol, flatter, glorify, honor, laud, magnify, worship. See PUFF. *Antonyms:* see synonyms for ASPERSE. BLAME.

Synonyms (noun): acclaim, acclamation, adulation, applause, approbation, approval, commendation, compliment, encomium, eulogy, flattery, laudation, panegyric, plaudit, sycophancy. *Praise* is the hearty approval of an individual, or of a multitude considered individually, and is expressed by spoken or written words; *applause,* the spontaneous outburst of many at once. *Applause* is expressed by stamping of feet, clapping of hands, waving of handkerchiefs, etc., as well as by the voice; *acclamation* is the spontaneous and hearty approval of many at once, and strictly by the voice alone. One is chosen moderator by *acclamation* when he receives a practically unanimous viva voce vote; he could not be nominated by *applause. Acclaim* is the more poetic term for *acclamation;* as, a nation's *acclaim. Plaudit* is a shout of *applause,* and is commonly used in the plural; as, the *plaudits* of a throng. *Applause* is also used in the general sense of *praise. Approbation* is a milder and more qualified word than *praise; praise* is always uttered, *approbation* may be silent. The industry and intelligence of a clerk win his employer's *approbation;* his decision in a special instance receives his *approval. Praise* is always understood as genuine and sincere, unless the contrary is expressly stated; *compliment* is a light form of *praise* that may or may not be sincere; *flattery* is often insincere. Compare APPLAUSE, EULOGY. *Antonyms*: abuse, animadversion, blame, censure, condemnation, contempt, denunciation, disapprobation, disapproval, disparagement, obloquy, reproach, reproof, repudiation, scorn, slander, vilification, vituperation.

pra·line (prä'lĕn, prä'-) *n.* A crisp confection made of pecans or other nuts browned in boiling sugar. [<F, after Marshal Duplessis-*Praslin*, 1598–1675, whose cook invented it]

pram (pram) *n. Brit. Colloq.* A baby carriage. [Short for PERAMBULATOR]

prance (prans, präns) *v.* pranced, pranc·ing *v.i.* 1 To move proudly with high steps, as a spirited horse; spring from the hind legs. 2 To ride gaily, proudly, or insolently, as on a prancing horse. 3 To move in an arrogant or elated manner; swagger. 4 To gambol; caper. —*v.i.* 5 To cause to prance. —*n.* The act of prancing; a high step; a caper. [ME *prauncen*, ? <Scand. Cf. dial. Dan. *pranse* walk proudly.] —**pranc'er** *n.*

pran·di·al (pran'dē·əl) *adj.* Of or pertaining to a meal, especially a dinner. [<L *prandium* breakfast or lunch]

prank[1] (prangk) *v.t.* To decorate gaudily; deck with showy ornaments. —*v.i.* To make an ostentatious show. [Cf. Du. *pronken*, G *prunken* make a show of]

prank[2] (prangk) *n.* A mischievous or frolicsome act. See synonyms under FROLIC, SPORT. —*v.i.* To play pranks or tricks. [Origin uncertain] —**prank'ish** *adj.*

pranked (prangkt) *adj.* Decorated; dressed up: often with *out* or *up*.

pra·se·o·dym·i·um (prā'zē·ō·dim'ē·əm, prā'sē-) *n.* A soft, silvery, ductile metallic element (symbol Pr, atomic number 59) of the lanthanide series. See PERIODIC TABLE. [<NL <Gk. *prasios* light green + (DI)DYMIUM]

prate (prāt) *v.* prat·ed, prat·ing *v.i.* To talk idly and at length; chatter. —*v.t.* To utter idly or emptily. See synonyms under BABBLE. —*n.* Idle talk; prattle. [Cf. MDu. & MLG *praten* chatter, ON *prata* talk] —**prat'er** *n.* —**prat'ing·ly** *adv.*

prat·fall (prat'fôl') *n. Slang* A fall on the buttocks.

prat·tle (prat'l) *v.* ·tled, ·tling *v.i.* To talk foolishly or like a child; prate. —*v.t.* To utter in a foolish or childish way: to *prattle* secrets. See synonyms under BABBLE. —*n.* 1 Childish speech; babble. 2 Idle or foolish talk. [Freq. of PRATE] —**prat'tler** *n.*

prawn (prôn) *n.* An edible shrimplike decapod (suborder *Natantia*) occurring in a variety of genera and species, especially numerous in tropical and temperate waters, principally marine. [ME *prane*; origin unknown]

PRAWN
(Up to 6 inches
in length)

prax·is (prak'sis) *n.* Exercise or discipline for a specific purpose; practical application of rules as distinguished from theory. [<NL <Gk. <*prassein* accomplish, do]

pray (prā) *v.i.* 1 To address prayers to a deity, idol, etc.; say prayers. 2 To make entreaty; beg. —*v.t.* 3 To address by means of prayers; say prayers to. 4 To ask (someone) earnestly; entreat. 5 To ask for by prayers or entreaty. 6 To effect by prayer. ◆Homophone: *prey*. [<OF *preier* <LL *precare* <L *precari* ask, pray <*prex*, *precis* prayer]

Synonyms: ask, beg, beseech, bid, conjure, entreat, implore, importune, invoke, petition, request, supplicate. See ASK.

prayer (prâr) *n.* 1 The act of offering reverent petitions, especially to God. 2 The act of beseeching earnestly; entreaty. 3 *Often pl.* A religious service of which prayer is the most prominent part: evening *prayers*. 4 Communion with God and recognition of His presence, as in praise, thanksgiving, intercession, etc. 5 A form of words appropriate to prayer. 6 A memorial or petition. 7 *Law* The request in a bill in equity for the specific relief sought

by the complainant; also, the part of the bill in which the request is made. — **common prayer** The prescribed form of public worship of the Anglican Church as contained in the *Book of Common Prayer*. [<OF *preiere* < Med. L *precaria* <L *precarius* obtained by prayer < *precari*. See PRAY.]

Synonyms: adoration, devotion, invocation, litany, orison, petition, request, suit, supplication. See PETITION.

prayer wheel A wheel, cylinder, or vertical drum containing written prayers, which is revolved to make the prayers efficacious: used by the Buddhists of Tibet. Also **praying wheel.**

praying mantis The mantis.

pre- *prefix* 1 Before in time or order; prior to; preceding; as in:

preaccusation	preconfiguration
preacquaint	preconfirm
preacquaintance	preconnection
preacquire	preconnubial
preact	preconsent
preaction	preconsideration
preadapt	preconsign
preadaptation	preconstitute
preadjust	preconstruction
preadjustment	preconsult
preadministration	preconsultation
preadmit	preconsume
preadmonish	precontract
preadmonition	precontrive
preadvertise	preconviction
preadvertiser	pre–cool
preadvise	precorrupt
preadviser	precounsel
preaestival	pre–Darwinian
preallege	predecision
preannounce	prededication
preannouncement	predeliberation
preannouncer	predemand
preantiquity	predescribe
preapperception	predesign
preappoint	predeterminable
preappointment	predevised
preapproval	predirect
prearm	prediscipline
prearrange	prediscovery
prearrangement	preelect
pre–Aryan	preelection
preassemble	preembodiment
preassigned	preembody
preassume	preemploy
preassurance	preenact
preassure	preengage
preattachment	preengagement
preattune	pre–epic
preavowal	preestablish
prebaptize	preestablishment
prebasal	preexamination
prebasilar	preexamine
preboding	preexist
preboil	preexistence
prebranchial	preexistent
pre–British	preexpose
prebronchial	preform
prebuccal	preglacial
precalculable	preheat
precalculate	preheater
precalculation	preinhabitation
precancerous	preinstruct
pre–Carboniferous	preintimation
pre–Centennial	preknowledge
precerebellar	prepaid
pre–Christian	pre–Paleozoic
pre–Christianize	pre–Reformation
precited	pre–Renaissance
preclassical	prerequire
precogitate	prerevolutionary
precogitation	pre–Roman
precognition	preselect
precognizable	preshadow
precognizant	pre–Shakespearian
precollection	preshow
pre–Columbian	presuccess
precompose	pre–Tertiary
precomputation	pretribal
precompute	pretypify
preconception	preunite
preconclusion	pre–Victorian
precondemn	prewarm
precondemnation	prewarn

2 Before in position; anterior: chiefly in scientific terms; as in:

preabdomen	precardiac	prerectal
preanal	precerebral	prerenal

preaortic	precostal	preretinal
preauricular	prepatellar	prevertebral

3 Preliminary to; preparing for; as in:

precollege	prelegal	premedical
preflight	prelexical	pre–military

[<L *prae-* <*prae* before]

preach (prēch) *v.i.* 1 To deliver a sermon, as on a religious topic or a text of Scripture. 2 To give advice or instruction, especially persistently and intrusively. —*v.t.* 3 To advocate or recommend urgently: to *preach* temperance. 4 To proclaim; expound upon: to *preach* the gospel. 5 To deliver (a sermon, etc.). [<OF *prechier* <L *praedicare* proclaim <*prae-* before + *dicare* make known]

preach·ing (prē'ching) *n.* 1 The act or practice of delivering sermons. 2 The style of a preacher. 3 The doctrine preached.

preach·ment (prēch'mənt) *n.* A preaching or moral lecture; especially, a wearisome exhortation. [<OF *prechement*]

preach·y (prē'chē) *adj.* preach·i·er, preach·i·est Given to or resembling preachments; marked by sanctimony or cant: not a complimentary term.

pre·ag·o·nal (prē·ag'ə·nəl) *adj.* Immediately preceding the death agony. [<PRE- + AGON(Y) + -AL[1]]

pre·am·ble (prē'am·bəl) *n.* 1 A statement introductory to and explanatory of what follows; the introductory portion of a writing or speech: used chiefly of formal resolutions. 2 *Law* An introductory clause in a constitution, contract, or other instrument. [<F *préamble* <Med. L *praeambulum*, orig. neut. of L *praeambulus* walking before <L *praeambulare* precede <*prae-* before + *ambulare* walk] — **pre·am'bu·lar'y** *adj.*

preb·en·dar·y (preb'ən·der'ē) *n. pl.* ·dar·ies A person, as a canon, who receives a stated income from the revenues of a cathedral. [<Med. L *prebendarius*]

pre·car·i·ous (pri·kâr'ē·əs) *adj.* 1 Subject to continued risk; that may be taken away at another's pleasure or by accident; uncertain. 2 Subject or leading to danger; hazardous. 3 Not firmly established; untrustworthy; without foundation. [<L *precarius*. See PRAYER.] — **pre·car'i·ous·ly** *adv.* — **pre·car'i·ous·ness** *n.*

Synonyms: doubtful, dubious, equivocal, hazardous, insecure, perilous, risky, unassured, uncertain, unsettled, unstable, unsteady. *Uncertain* is applied to things that human knowledge cannot certainly determine or that human power cannot certainly control; *precarious* originally meant dependent on the will or pleasure of another; now it also means dependent on chance or hazard; one holds office by a *precarious* tenure, or land by a *precarious* title; the strong man's hold on life is *uncertain*, the invalid's is *precarious*. *Antonyms*: assured, certain, firm, immutable, incontestable, settled, stable, steady, strong, sure, undoubted, unquestionable.

pre·cast (prē'kast', -käst') *adj.* Receiving a finished shape before being put to final use: *pre-cast* concrete blocks.

prec·a·tive (prek'ə·tiv) *adj.* Expressing entreaty; supplicatory. Also **prec'a·to'ry.** [<L *precativus*]

pre·cau·tion (pri·kô'shən) *n.* 1 Prudent forethought, as against danger, etc. 2 A provision made for some emergency. See synonyms under CARE. [<F *précaution* <LL *praecautio, -onis* <L *praecautus*, pp. of *praecavere* guard against beforehand <*prae-* before + *cavere* take care]

pre·cede (pri·sēd') *v.* ·ced·ed, ·ced·ing *v.t.* 1 To go before in order, place, rank, time, etc. 2 To preface; introduce. —*v.i.* 3 To have or take precedence. [<F *précéder* <L *praecedere* go before <*prae-* before + *cedere* go]

Synonyms: head, herald, lead. See LEAD[1]. *Antonyms*: see synonyms for FOLLOW.

pre·ce·dence (pri·sēd'ns, pres'ə·dəns) *n.* The act or right of preceding, or the state of being precedent; priority in place, time, or rank. Also **pre·ce'den·cy.**

Synonyms: antecedence, ascendency, lead, leadership, preeminence, preference, priority, superiority, supremacy. *Antonyms*: inferiority, subjection, subjugation, subordination.

prec·e·dent (pres'ə·dənt) *n.* 1 Previous usage

or established mode of precedure. **2** An antecedent. **3** A judicial decision taken as furnishing a rule for subsequent decisions. — **pre·ce·dent** (pri·sēd′nt) *adj.* Former; previous; preceding. [<F *précédent* <L *praecedens, -entis,* ppr. of *praecedere.* See PRECEDE.]

Synonyms (noun): antecedent, case, example, instance, pattern, warrant. A *precedent* is an authoritative *case, example,* or *instance. Cases* decided by irregular or unauthorized tribunals are not *precedents* for the regular administration of law. See ANTECEDENT, CAUSE, EXAMPLE.

pre·ced·ing (pri·sē′ding) *adj.* Going before, as in time, place, or rank; earlier; foregoing; immediately antecedent: *The citation was on the preceding page.*

pre·cept (prē′sept) *n.* **1** A prescribed rule of conduct or action; instruction or direction regarding a given course or action; especially, a maxim in morals: distinguished from *counsel.* **2** *Law* A judicial command in writing; writ; process. See synonyms under ADAGE. [<OF <L *praeceptum,* pp. of *praecipere* give rules, instruct < *prae-* before + *capere* receive, take]

pre·cep·tor (pri·sep′tər) *n.* A teacher; instructor: specifically, the principal of a school. [<L *praeceptor*] — **pre·cep·to·ri·al** (prē′sep·tôr′ē·əl, -tō′rē-) *adj.*

pre·cep·to·ry (pri·sep′tər·ē) *adj.* Preceptive; mandatory. — *n. pl.* **·ries** A place of instruction; specifically, a religious house of the Knights Templars. [<Med. L *praeceptoria*]

pre·ces·sion (pri·sesh′ən) *n.* The act of preceding or coming in advance of time or of other persons or things. [<LL *praecessio, -onis* < *praecessus,* pp. of *praecedere.* See PRECEDE.]

pre·cinct (prē′singkt) *n.* **1** A place definitely marked off by fixed lines; also, the boundary of a designated place. **2** A minor territorial or jurisdictional district. **3** An election district of a town, township, county, etc. **4** A police subdivision of a city or town, or its police station. **5** *Brit.* The immediate neighborhood of a church or temple. **6** *pl.* Neighborhood; environs. [<LL *praecinctum* boundary, orig. neut. of *praecinctus,* pp. of *praecingere* gird about < *prae-* before + *cingere* gird]

pre·ci·os·i·ty (presh′ē·os′ə·tē) *n.* Extreme fastidiousness or affected refinement, as in speech, style, or taste. [<OF *preciosité* <L *pretiositas* < *pretiosus.* See PRECIOUS.]

pre·cious (presh′əs) *adj.* **1** Highly priced or prized, as for rarity, or for intrinsic, exchangeable, or other value; valuable. **2** Beloved; dear. **3** Good-for-nothing; undeserving: used ironically. **4** *Colloq.* Very considerable; surpassing: *a precious scoundrel.* **5** Overnice; fastidious: *a precious writer.* See synonyms under CHOICE, EXCELLENT, GOOD, RARE[1]. [<OF *precios* <L *pretiosus* < *pretium* price] — **pre′cious·ly** *adv.* — **pre′cious·ness** *n.*

prec·i·pice (pres′i·pis) *n.* **1** A high, steep place; the brink of a cliff. **2** A perilous situation. [<F *précipice* <L *praecipitium* < *praeceps* heading < *prae-* before + *caput* head]

pre·cip·i·ta·ble (pri·sip′ə·tə·bəl) *adj.* Capable or susceptible of being precipitated: *a precipitable salt.*

pre·cip·i·tant (pri·sip′ə·tənt) *adj.* **1** Rushing or falling headlong; moving onward quickly and heedlessly: *precipitant speed.* **2** Rash in thought or action; overhasty; impulsive; precipitate; sudden; abrupt. — *n. Chem.* Any substance, as a reagent, that when added or applied to a solution results in the formation of a precipitate. [<L *praecipitans, -antis,* ppr. of *praecipitare.* See PRECIPITATE.] — **pre·cip′i·tant·ly** *adv.*

pre·cip·i·tate (pri·sip′ə·tāt, -tit) *adj.* **1** Rushing down headlong; moving or moved speedily or hurriedly. **2** Wanting due deliberation; hasty; rash. **3** Done prematurely; hurried; undeliberated. **4** Sudden and brief, as a disease. See synonyms under IMPETUOUS. — *v.* (pri·sip′ə·tāt) **·tat·ed, ·tat·ing** *v.t.* **1** To bring about before expected or needed; hasten the occurrence of: *to precipitate a quarrel.* **2** To throw headlong; hurl from or as from a height. **3** *Meteorol.* To cause (vapor, etc.) to

condense and fall as dew, rain, etc. **4** *Chem.* To separate (a constituent) in solid form, as from a solution. — *v.i.* **5** *Meteorol.* To fall as condensed vapor. **6** *Chem.* To separate and settle, as a substance held in solution. **7** To fall headlong; rush. — *n.* (pri·sip′ə·tāt, -tit) *Physics* A deposit of solid matter formed in a solution by the action of chemical reagents or by certain physical forces, as low temperature. [<L *praecipitatus,* pp. of *praecipitare* < *praeceps.* See PRECIPICE.] — **pre·cip′i·tate·ly** *adv.* — **pre·cip′i·tate·ness** *n.* — **pre·cip′i·ta·tive** *adj.* — **pre·cip′i·ta·tor** *n.*

pre·cip·i·ta·tion (pri·sip′ə·tā′shən) *n.* **1** The act of casting down; the state of being thrown downward. **2** Headlong or rash haste or hurry; precipitancy; hastening; acceleration. **3** A falling, flowing, or rushing down with violence or rapidity. **4** *Chem.* The process of rendering insoluble and so separating any of the constituents of a solution, as by reagents; also, the precipitate. **5** *Meteorol.* The deposition of moisture from the atmosphere upon the general surface of the earth. **6** Materialization, as of spirits. [<F *précipitation*]

pre·cip·i·tous (pri·sip′ə·təs) *adj.* **1** As steep as or consisting of a precipice; very steep. **2** Headlong and downward in motion. **3** Headlong in disposition; precipitate; hasty. See synonyms under STEEP[1]. [<MF *précipiteux*] — **pre·cip′i·tous·ly** *adv.* — **pre·cip′i·tous·ness** *n.*

pré·cis (prā·sē′, prā′sē) *n. pl.* **·cis** (-sēz′, -sēz) A concise, brief summary of the ideas and point of view of a book, article, or document. [<F]

pre·cise (pri·sīs′) *adj.* **1** Sharply or clearly determined; strictly accurate; exact. **2** No more and no less than. **3** Noting or confined to a certain thing; particular; identical. **4** Scrupulously observant of rule; punctilious. [<F *précis* <L *praecisus,* pp. of *praecidere* cut off short < *prae-* before + *caedere* cut] — **pre·cise′ly** *adv.* — **pre·cise′ness** *n.*

Synonyms: accurate, careful, correct, definite, distinct, exact, explicit, faultless, flawless, minute, nice, particular, perfect, rigid, right, scrupulous, strict. *Accurate, correct, definite, exact, precise, nice,* all denote absolute conformity to some standard or truth. *Accurate* indicates conformity secured by *scrupulous* care. An *accurate* measurement or account can be verified and found true in all particulars. *Careful* carries less sharp certainty. *Exact* indicates that which is worked out to the utmost limit of requirement in every respect; *precise* refers to a like conformity or to an excessive *exactness. Exact* and *precise* are often interchangeable; but *precise* has often an invidious meaning, denoting excessive care of petty details; we speak of the martinet as insufferably *precise,* not insufferably *exact. Correct* applies to a required or enforced correspondence with a standard. This is especially seen in the use of the verb; the printer *corrects* the proof. That is *correct* which is free from fault or mistake. *Nice* denotes a very fine and discriminating exactness, and refers to intellectual distinctions oftener than to material measurements. Compare CORRECT, MINUTE[2]. *Antonyms:* careless, doubtful, erroneous, false, faulty, inaccurate, inexact, loose, mistaken, misty, nebulous, untrue, vague, wrong.

pre·ci·sian (pri·sizh′ən) *n.* One who adheres punctiliously to rules and forms: a term especially applied in a religious sense to the Puritans.

pre·ci·sion (pri·sizh′ən) *n.* The quality of being precise; accuracy of limitation, definition, or adjustment. [<F *précision* <L *praecisio, -onis*] — **pre·ci′sion·ist** *n.*

pre·clude (pri·klōōd′) *v.t.* **·clud·ed, ·clud·ing** **1** To render impossible or ineffectual by antecedent action; prevent. **2** To shut out; exclude. [<L *praecludere* < *prae-* before + *cludere* shut] — **pre·clu′sion** (-klōō′zhən) *n.* — **pre·clu′sive** (-klōō′siv) *adj.* — **pre·clu′sive·ly** *adv.*

Synonyms: obviate, prevent. To *obviate* is to *prevent* by interception and making unnecessary; to *preclude,* to close or shut in advance, is to *prevent* by anticipation or by logical necessity; walls and bars *precluded* the possibility of escape; a supposition is *precluded;*

a necessity or difficulty is *obviated.* Compare PROHIBIT, SHUT.

pre·co·cious (pri·kō′shəs) *adj.* **1** Developing before the natural season. **2** Unusually forward or advanced, especially mentally. **3** *Bot.* Flowering or ripening early, as certain plants. [<OF *precoce* <L *praecox, praecocis* < *praecoquere* cook or ripen beforehand < *prae-* before + *coquere* cook] — **pre·co′cious·ly** *adv.* — **pre·co′cious·ness, pre·coc′i·ty** (-kos′ə·tē) *n.*

pre·con·cep·tion (prē′kən·sep′shən) *n.* **1** An idea or opinion formed or conceived in advance. **2** A prejudice or misconception; bias. — **pre′con·cep′tion·al** *adj.*

pre·con·cert (prē′kən·sûrt′) *v.t.* To arrange in advance, as by agreement. — *n.* (prē′kon′sûrt) Previous arrangement.

pre·co·nize (prē′kə·nīz) *v.t.* **·nized, ·niz·ing** **1** To announce the appointment of (a new bishop) in public consistory: said of the pope. **2** To proclaim or extol publicly. [<LL *praeconizare* proclaim <L *praeco, praeconis* crier, herald]

pre·cur·sive (pri·kûr′siv) *adj.* Going before as a precursor or harbinger; premonitory; preliminary. Also **pre·cur′so·ry** (-sər·ē).

pre·cur·sor (pri·kûr′sər) *n.* One who or that which precedes and gives intimation of a coming event. See synonyms under HERALD. [<L *praecursor* < *praecursus,* pp. of *praecurrere* run before < *prae-* before + *currere* run]

pre·da·cious (pri·dā′shəs) *adj.* Predatory. Also **pre·da′ceous.** [<L *praeda* prey] — **pre·da′cious·ness, pre·dac′i·ty** (-das′ə·tē) *n.*

pred·a·to·ry (pred′ə·tôr′ē, -tō′rē) *adj.* **1** Characterized by or undertaken for plundering. **2** Addicted to pillaging. **3** Constituted for living by preying upon others, as a beast or bird; raptorial. [<L *predatorius* < *praeda* prey] — **pred′a·to′ri·ly** *adv.* — **pred′a·to′ri·ness** *n.*

pred·e·ces·sor (pred′ə·ses′ər) *n.* **1** One who goes or has gone before another in point of time, as an early settler, a previous incumbent of an office, etc. **2** An ancestor. [<OF *predecesseur* <LL *praedecessor* < *prae-* before + *decessor* retiring official < *decessus* pp. of *decedere* go away. See DECEASE.]

pre·des·ti·nar·i·an (prē·des′tə·nâr′ē·ən) *adj.* **1** Pertaining to predestination. — *n.* A believer in theological predestination; also, a fatalist. — **pre·des′ti·nar′i·an·ism** *n.*

pre·des·ti·nate (prē·des′tə·nit, -nāt) *adj.* **1** Designed for some special fate. **2** Foreordained by divine decree, as to salvation. — *n.* One who is predestined, as to salvation. — *v.t.* (-nāt) **·nat·ed, ·nat·ing** **1** To destine or decree beforehand; foreordain. **2** *Theol.* To foreordain by divine decree or purpose. [<L *praedestinatus,* pp. of *praedestinare* < *prae-* before + *destinare* destine]

pre·des·ti·na·tion (prē·des′tə·nā′shən) *n.* **1** The act of predestinating, or the state of being predestinated; destiny; fate. **2** *Theol.* The foreordinace of all things by God, including the future bliss or sorrow of men. See CALVINISM. [<LL *praedestinatio, -onis*]

pre·de·ter·mi·nate (prē′di·tûr′mə·nit, -nāt) *adj.* Decided or decreed beforehand.

pre·de·ter·mine (prē′di·tûr′min) *v.t.* **·mined, ·min·ing** **1** To determine beforehand; decide in advance. **2** To foreordain. **3** To imbue with an antecedent tendency. — **pre′de·ter′mi·na′tion** *n.*

pre·di·al (prē′dē·əl) *adj.* Of, pertaining to, or attached to the land. Also spelled *praedial.* [<OF <Med. L *praedialis* <L *praedium*]

pred·i·ca·ble (pred′i·kə·bəl) *adj.* That may be predicated or affirmed. — *n.* **1** Anything ascribable. **2** *Logic* A property or attribute affirmable of a class. [<F *prédicable* <L *praedicabilis* < *praedicare.* See PREACH.] — **pred′i·ca·bil′i·ty, pred′i·ca·ble·ness** *n.*

pre·dic·a·ment (pri·dik′ə·mənt) *n.* **1** A trying, embarrassing, puzzling, or amusing situation or plight. **2** A specific state, position, or situation. **3** *Logic* A class or kind distinguished by definite marks; a category. [<LL *praedicamentum* that which is predicated < *praedicare.* See PREACH.]

pred·i·cate (pred′i·kāt) *v.* **·cat·ed, ·cat·ing** *v.t.* **1** To declare; affirm; proclaim. **2** To state

or affirm concerning the subject of a proposition. **3** To affirm as a quality or attribute of something. **4** To imply or connote. **5** *U.S.* To found or base (an argument, proposition, etc.): with *on* or *upon*. — *v.i.* **6** To make a statement or affirmation. See synonyms under AFFIRM. — *adj.* (-kit) **1** Predicated. **2** *Gram.* Belonging, relating to, or of the nature of a predicate: a *predicate* adjective. — *n.* (-kit) **1** *Gram.* The word or words in a sentence that express what is affirmed or denied of a subject, as, in the sentence, "Life is short," "is short" is the *predicate.* **2** A quality or property inherent in or asserted to belong to a thing. **3** *Logic* In a proposition, that which is stated about a subject. [< L *praedicatus*, pp. of *praedicare* make known] — **pred′i·ca′tive** *adj.* — **pred′i·ca′tive·ly** *adv.*
predicate adjective *Gram.* An adjective which describes the subject of a copulative verb, as, He is *sad*; The water turned *green*, etc.
predicate noun *Gram.* A noun which designates or identifies the subject of a copulative verb, as, He was *king*; The water became *ice.*
pred·i·ca·tion (pred′i·kā′shən) *n.* **1** The act of publicly setting forth or proclaiming. **2** The act of predicating or asserting. **3** *Logic* The assertion of something of or concerning a subject; assertion. **4** Something predicated; a predicate. [< L *praedicatio, -onis*] — **pred′i·ca′tion·al** *adj.*
pred·i·ca·to·ry (pred′i·kə·tôr′ē, -tō′rē) *adj.* **1** Of or pertaining to a preacher or preaching. **2** Proclaimed. [< LL *praedicatorius*]
pre·dict (pri·dikt′) *v.t.* **1** To make known beforehand; prophesy; foretell. **2** To assert on the basis of theory, data, or experience but in advance of proof: Einstein *predicted* that space was curved; The computer *predicted* the winning candidate based on a sample poll of voters. — *v.i.* **3** To make a prediction. See synonyms under AUGUR, PROPHESY. [< L *praedictus*, pp. of *praedicere* speak beforehand < *prae-* before + *dicere* say] — **pre·dict′a·ble** *adj.* — **pre·dict′a·bly** *adv.*
pre·dic·tion (pri·dik′shən) *n.* **1** The act of predicting. **2** The thing predicted; forecast: an accurate *prediction.* [< L *praedictio, -onis*] — **pre·dic′tive** *adj.* — **pre·dic′tive·ly** *adv.*
pre·di·gest (prē′di·jest′, -dī-) *v.t.* To treat (food) by a process of partial digestion before introduction into the stomach; peptonize. — **pre′di·ges′tion** *n.*
pre·di·lec·tion (prē′də·lek′shən, pred′ə-) *n.* A favorable prepossession or predisposition; partiality; preference: with *for.* See synonyms under FANCY, INCLINATION, RELISH. [< F *prédilection* < Med. L *praedilectio, -onis* < *prae-dilectus,* pp. of *praedilegere* prefer < L *prae-* before + *diligere* love, choose]
pre·dis·pose (prē′dis·pōz′) *v.t.* **·posed, ·pos·ing** **1** To give a tendency or inclination to; make susceptible or liable: Exhaustion *predisposes* one to sickness. **2** To dispose beforehand. **3** To dispose of beforehand; bequeath. — **pre·dis·po·si·tion** (prē′dis·pə·zish′ən) *n.*
pre·dom·i·nant (pri·dom′ə·nənt) *adj.* Superior in power, influence, effectiveness, number, or degree; prevailing over others. [< F *prédominant*] — **pre·dom′i·nant·ly** *adv.*
Synonyms: ascendent, chief, commanding, controlling, dominant, prevailing, prevalent, regnant, sovereign, superior, supreme. *Antonyms:* accessory, complementary, contributory, inferior, subordinate, subsidiary, unimportant.
pre·dom·i·nate (pri·dom′ə·nāt) *v.i.* **·nat·ed, ·nat·ing** **1** To have governing influence or control; be in control: often with *over.* **2** To be superior to all others, as in power, height, number, etc.; prevail; preponderate. [< Med. L *praedominatus*] — **pre·dom′i·nat′ing·ly** *adv.* — **pre·dom′i·na′tion** *n.*
pre·em·i·nent (prē·em′ə·nənt) *adj.* **1** Supremely eminent; distinguished above all others; transcendent; supreme. **2** Extraordinary in degree; outstanding; conspicuous; superlative. See synonyms under PARAMOUNT. [< L *praeëminens, -entis,* ppr. of *praeëminere* be prominent < *prae-* before + *eminere* stand out, project] — **pre·em′i·nent·ly** *adv.* — **pre·em′i·nence** *n.*
pre·empt (prē·empt′) *v.t.* **1** To acquire or appropriate beforehand. **2** To secure by preemption; occupy (public land) so as to acquire by preemption. [Back formation <

PREEMPTION] — **pre·emp′tor** *n.* — **pre·emp′to·ry** (-tər-ē) *adj.*
pre·emp·tion (prē·emp′shən) *n.* **1** The right or act of purchasing before others. **2** Public land obtained by exercising this right. [< Med. L *praeëmptio, -onis* < L *prae-* before + *emptus,* pp. of *emere* buy]
preen (prēn) *v.t.* **1** To trim and dress with the beak, as birds their feathers. **2** To dress or adorn (oneself) carefully; primp; prink. — *v.i.* **3** To primp; prink. [Prob. var. of PRUNE³]
pre·fab·ri·cate (prē·fab′rə·kāt) *v.t.* **·cat·ed, ·cat·ing** **1** To fabricate or build beforehand. **2** To manufacture in standard sections that can be rapidly assembled. — **pre·fab′ri·ca′tion** *n.*
pref·ace (pref′is) *n.* **1** A brief explanation or address to the reader at the beginning of a book or other publication. **2** Any introductory speech, writing, etc. — *v.t.* **·aced, ·ac·ing** **1** To introduce or furnish with a preface. **2** To serve as a preface for. [< OF < L *praefatio* < *praefatus,* pp. of *praefari* utter beforehand, premise < *prae-* before + *fari* speak]
pre·fect (prē′fekt) *n.* **1** In ancient Rome, any of various civil and military officials, as certain magistrates, governors, and commanders. **2** Any magistrate, chief official, etc.; specifically, in France, the chief administrator of a department, or the head of the Paris police. **3** In Roman Catholic schools, the dean. **4** *Brit.* A senior pupil charged with maintaining order and discipline among other pupils. Also spelled *praefect.* [< OF < L *praefectus,* orig. pp. of *praeficere* set over < *prae-* before + *facere* make, do]
pre·fec·ture (prē′fek·chər) *n.* **1** The office, jurisdiction, or province of a prefect. **2** The official building for his use. [< L *praefectura*] — **pre·fec′tur·al** *adj.*
pre·fer (pri·fûr′) *v.t.* **·ferred, ·fer·ring** **1** To hold in higher regard or esteem; like better. **2** To give priority to, as one creditor or form of securities over others. **3** To advance or promote, as in status or rank. **4** To offer, as a suit or charge, for consideration or decision. See synonyms under CHOOSE, PROMOTE. [< F *préferer* < L *praeferre* carry, set in front < *prae-* before + *ferre* bear] — **pre·fer′rer** *n.*
pref·er·a·ble (pref′ər·ə·bəl) *adj.* To be preferred; more desirable; worthy of choice. — **pref′er·a·ble·ness, pref′er·a·bil′i·ty** *n.* — **pref′er·a·bly** *adv.*
pref·er·ence (pref′ər·əns) *n.* **1** The act of preferring; estimation or choice of one thing or person over another; also, the privilege of making such choice. **2** The state of being preferred. **3** That which is preferred; an object of favor or choice. **4** A priority of payment given by an insolvent debtor to one or to a certain class of his creditors over others; also, priority of payment by operation of law. **5** Promotion; preferment. **6** The granting of special advantage over others to one country or group of countries in international trade. See synonyms under ALTERNATIVE, PRECEDENCE. [< F *préférence* < L *praeferentia,* orig. neut. pl. of *praeferens, -entis,* ppr. of *praeferre.* See PREFER.]
pref·er·en·tial (pref′ə·ren′shəl) *adj.* **1** Indicating or arising from preference or partiality. **2** Possessing or giving priority or preference, as in tariffs or railroad charges. — **pref′er·en′tial·ism** *n.* — **pref′er·en′tial·ly** *adv.*
pre·fer·ment (pri·fûr′mənt) *n.* **1** The act of preferring. **2** The state of being preferred. **3** The act of promoting or appointing to higher office; advancement; promotion. **4** A superior post or dignity: said especially of ecclesiastical rank.
pre·ferred (pri·fûrd′) *adj.* **1** Having the first claim: *preferred* bonds or stock. **2** Having gained promotion. **3** Chosen by preference.
pre·fig·ure (prē·fig′yər) *v.t.* **·ured, ·ur·ing** **1** To represent in advance; serve as an indication or suggestion of; foreshadow. **2** To imagine or picture to oneself beforehand. [< LL *praefigurare*]
pre·fix (prē′fiks) *n.* **1** *Gram.* A non-separable syllable, or syllables, affixed to the beginning of a word to modify or alter the meaning, as *pre-* in prefix, *be-* in behead, *dis-* in disagree, *re-* in renew, *post-* in postwar, *un-* in

unhorse, etc. **2** Something placed before, as a title before a noun. Compare SUFFIX. — *v.t.* (prē·fiks′) **1** To put or attach before or at the beginning; add as a prefix: opposed to *postfix.* **2** *Obs.* To arrange or settle beforehand. [< OF *prefixer* < L *praefixus,* pp. of *praefigere* < *prae-* before + *figere* fix] — **pre′fix·al** *adj.* — **pre′fix·al·ly** *adv.* — **pre·fix·ion** (prē·fik′shən) *n.*
preg·na·ble (preg′nə·bəl) *adj.* Weak enough to be conquered; likely to yield when attacked, as a fort. [< OF *prenable* < *prendre* take < L *prehendere* seize] — **preg′na·bil′i·ty** *n.*
preg·nan·cy (preg′nən·sē) *n.* **1** The state of being with young or with child. **2** *Obs.* Quickness of intelligence.
preg·nant (preg′nənt) *adj.* **1** Carrying a growing fetus in the uterus; with child; impregnated; gestating. **2** Carrying great weight or significance; full of meaning or contents; leading to important results. **3** Fruitful; prolific; teeming with ideas; imaginative; inventive. **4** In rhetoric and logic, implying more than is expressed. [< L *praegnans, -antis,* ult. < *prae-* before + *gnasci* be born] — **preg′nant·ly** *adv.*
pre·hen·si·ble (pri·hen′sə·bəl) *adj.* Capable of being apprehended or grasped. [< L *prehensus,* pp. of *prehendere* seize]
pre·hen·sile (pri·hen′sil) *adj.* Adapted for grasping or holding; formed to grasp or coil around and cling to objects, as the tail of a monkey. [< F *préhensile*] — **pre·hen·sil·i·ty** (prē′hen·sil′ə·tē) *n.*
pre·hen·sion (pri·hen′shən) *n.* The act of grasping, physically or mentally. [< L *prehensio, -onis*]
pre·his·tor·ic (prē′his·tôr′ik, -tor′-) *adj.* Of or belonging to a period before that covered by written history. Also **pre′his·tor′i·cal.** — **pre′·his·tor′i·cal·ly** *adv.*
pre·his·to·ry (prē·his′tə·rē) *n.* The history of the development of mankind based on archeological and ethnological findings; the period of history preceding written records.
pre·judge (prē·juj′) *v.t.* **·judged, ·judg·ing** To judge before or without proper inquiry; pass judgment on hastily or beforehand. [< F *préjuger* < *praejudicare* < *prae-* before + *judicare* judge] — **pre·judg′er** *n.* — **pre·judg′ment, Brit. pre·judge′ment** *n.*
prej·u·dice (prej′oo·dis) *n.* **1** A judgment or opinion, favorable or unfavorable, formed beforehand or without due examination; a mental decision based on other grounds than reason or justice; especially, a premature or adversely biased opinion. **2** Detriment arising from a hasty and unfair judgment; injury; harm. — **in** (or **to**) **the prejudice of** To the injury or detriment of. — **without prejudice** *Law* Without detriment to any right that previously existed: usually applied to the dismissal of a bill in equity without consideration of the merits; or to the reservation, express or implied, of all rights in favor of one who offers to compromise a claim or litigation, in case his offer is rejected. — *v.t.* **·diced, ·dic·ing** **1** To affect or influence with a prejudice; bias. **2** To affect injuriously or detrimentally; damage; impair. [< OF < L *praejudicium* < *prae-* before + *judicium* judgment]
Synonyms (noun): bias, preconception, predilection, prepossession, unfairness. A *prejudice* or *prepossession* is grounded often on feeling, fancy, associations, etc. A *prepossession* is always favorable, a *prejudice* usually unfavorable, unless the contrary is expressly stated. See INJURY. *Antonyms:* certainty, conclusion, conviction, demonstration, evidence, reason, reasoning.
prej·u·di·cial (prej′oo·dish′əl) *adj.* Having power or tendency to prejudice or injure; injurious; detrimental. — **prej′u·di′cial·ly** *adv.*
prel·a·cy (prel′ə·sē) *n.* *pl.* **·cies** **1** The system of church government by prelates: often a hostile term for episcopacy. **2** The dignity or function of a prelate. **3** Prelates collectively. [< AF *prelacie* < Med. L *praelatia* < *praelatus.* See PRELATE.]
prel·ate (prel′it) *n.* One of a higher order of clergy, as a bishop or abbot. [< OF *prelat* < L *praelatus,* pp. to *praeferre* set over. See PREFER.] — **prel′ate·ship** *n.* — **pre·lat·ic** (pri·lat′ik) or **·i·cal** *adj.*
pre·lect (pri·lekt′) *v.i.* To lecture; discourse. [< L *praelectus,* pp. of *praelegere* read before < *prae-* before + *legere* read] — **pre·lec′tion** *n.*

— **pre·lec′tor** n.

pre·li·ba·tion (prē′lī·bā′shən) n. 1 A preliminary offering. 2 A tasting beforehand or by anticipation; anticipation. [<LL *praelibatio, -onis* < *prae-* before + *libatio* a libation]

pre·lim·i·nar·y (pri·lim′ə·ner′ē) adj. Antecedent or introductory to the main discourse, proceedings, or business; prefatory; preparatory. —n. pl. **·ries** 1 An initiatory step; a preparatory act. 2 A preliminary examination. See synonyms under ANTECEDENT. [<PRE- + L *liminaris* pertaining to a threshold < *limen, liminis* threshold] — **pre·lim′i·nar′i·ly** adv.

pre·lit·er·ate (prē·lit′ər·it) adj. Without written records; prehistoric: said especially of the earliest human cultures.

prel·ude (prel′yŏŏd, prē′lŏŏd) n. 1 Music a An independent instrumental composition of moderate length, in a free style suggesting improvisation. b An opening piece at the start of a church service; a voluntary. c The overture of an opera. d An opening strain or movement at the beginning of a musical composition, usually introducing the theme of the whole work. 2 Any introductory or opening performance or event, or that which foreshadows a coming event. —v. **·ud·ed, ·ud·ing** v.t. 1 To introduce with a prelude. 2 To serve as a prelude to. —v.i. 3 To serve as a prelude. 4 To provide or play a prelude. [<F *prélude* <Med. L *praeludium* <L *praeludere* play before < *prae-* before + *ludere* play] — **pre·lud·er** (pri·lŏŏ′dər, prel′yə·dər) n. — **pre·lu·di·al** (pri·lŏŏ′dē·əl) adj.

pre·ma·ture (prē′mə·chŏŏr′, -tŏŏr′, -tyŏŏr′) adj. Existing, happening, matured or developed before the natural period; done before the proper time; untimely. [<L *praematurus* < *prae-* before + *maturus* ripe, seasonable] — **pre′ma·ture′ly** adv. — **pre′ma·tu′ri·ty, pre′·ma·ture′ness** n.

pre·med·i·tate (prē·med′ə·tāt) v.t. & v.i. **·tat·ed, ·tat·ing** To plan or consider beforehand. [<L *praemeditatus,* pp. of *praemeditari* think over < *prae-* before + *meditari.* See MEDITATE.] — **pre·med′i·tat′ed·ly** adv. — **pre·med′i·ta′tive** adj. — **pre·med′i·ta′tor** n.

pre·med·i·ta·tion (prē·med′ə·tā′shən) n. The considering and planning of a subsequent act; deliberate intention and plan to do a certain thing, especially to commit a crime.

pre·mi·er (prē′mē·ər, esp. Brit. prem′yər) adj. 1 First in rank or position; principal: the *premier* place, *premier* officer. 2 First in order of occurrence; earliest; specifically, first in order of creation; senior: the *premier* duke of England. —n. (prē′mē·ər, pri·mir′; Brit. prem′yər) The head of government; the prime minister of England, France, etc. [<F <L *primarius* <L *primus* first] — **pre′mi·er·ship′** n.

pre·mière (pri·mir′, Fr. prə·myâr′) adj. First. —n. 1 The leading lady in a theatrical company. 2 The first public presentation of a play, etc. [<F]

prem·ise (prem′is) n. 1 A proposition laid down, proved, supposed, or assumed, that serves as a ground for argument or for a conclusion; a judgment leading to another judgment as a conclusion. 2 Logic Either of the two propositions in a syllogism from which, their truth being granted, the conclusion necessarily follows. 3 pl. Law a Foregoing statements; facts previously stated. b That part in a deed that sets forth the date, names of parties, the land or thing conveyed or granted, the consideration, and all other matters down to the phrase "to have and to hold." 4 pl. A distinct portion of real estate; land or lands; land with its appurtenances, as buildings: He lingered about the *premises.* Also **prem′iss.** — **major premise** Logic The premise in which the predicate of the conclusion of a syllogism, called the **major term,** is contained; the first proposition of a syllogism. — **minor premise** Logic The premise in which the subject of the conclusion of a syllogism, called the **minor term,** is contained; the second proposition of a syllogism. — **pre·mise** (pri·mīz′, prem′is) v. **·mised, ·mis·ing** v.t. 1 To stay or state beforehand, as by way of introduction or explanation.

2 To state or assume as a premise or basis of argument. 3 Obs. To send in advance. —v.i. 4 To make a premise. [<OF *premisse* <Med. L *praemissa,* orig. fem. of L *praemissus,* pp. of *praemittere* send before < *prae-* before + *mittere* send]

pre·mi·um (prē′mē·əm) n. 1 A reward or prize for a superior performance or production in competition. 2 A price paid for a loan; a sum offered or given to secure a loan, either a sum in addition to interest, a bonus, or the interest itself. 3 The rate or price at which stocks, shares, or money are valued in excess of their nominal or par value: bank shares at a *premium* of five percent. 4 The amount paid for insurance, as admission fees, annual dues, periodical payments, etc., according to the kind of insurance secured. 5 Any object offered free to those who purchase goods to a certain value, as a set of books given free as an inducement to subscribe to a magazine. 6 A fee for instruction in a trade or a profession. See synonyms under SUBSIDY. — **at a premium** Above par; hence, valuable and in demand. [<L *praemium,* ult. < *prae-* before + *emere* buy]

pre·mon·ish (pri·mon′ish) v.t. To admonish in advance; forewarn. [<PRE- + MONISH]

pre·mo·ni·tion (prē′mə·nish′ən, prem′ə-) n. 1 An actual warning of something yet to occur. 2 A presentiment not based on information received; an instinctive foreboding. [<OF *premonicion* <LL *praemonitio, -onis* < *praemonitus,* pp. of *praemonere* premonish < *prae-* before + *monere* warn] — **pre·mon·i·to·ry** (pri·mon′ə·tôr′ē, -tō′rē) adj. — **pre·mon′i·to′·ri·ly** adv.

pre·name (prē′nām′) n. A forename; Christian name. [Trans. of L *praenomen*]

pre·na·tal (prē·nāt′l) adj. Before birth: *prenatal* care or health. — **pre·na′tal·ly** adv.

pre·no·men (prē·nō′mən) See PRAENOMEN.

pre·oc·cu·pa·tion (prē·ok′yə·pā′shən) n. 1 The act of occupying before others, or the state of being or having a prior occupant: also **pre·oc′cu·pan·cy.** 2 The state of being preoccupied, as in mind, attention, or inclination; prepossession. 3 Something that preoccupies. [<L *praeoccupatio, -onis*] — **pre·oc′cu·pant** n.

pre·oc·cu·pied (prē·ok′yə·pīd) adj. 1 Engrossed in thought or business; abstracted. 2 Previously occupied. 3 Already in use, as a scientific name. See synonyms under ABSTRACTED.

pre·oc·cu·py (prē·ok′yə·pī) v.t. **·pied, ·py·ing** 1 To engage fully; engross, as the mind. 2 To occupy or take possession of in advance of another or others. See synonyms under OCCUPY. [<L *praeoccupare*]

prep·a·ra·tion (prep′ə·rā′shən) n. 1 The act, process, or operation of preparing. 2 An act or proceeding designed to bring about some event; a precaution; provision: *preparations* for war or for a journey. 3 The fact or state of being prepared; readiness. 4 Something made or prepared, as a compound, composition, etc.: medicinal or chemical *preparations.* 5 Preliminary study; training, as for college or business. 6 Music The previous introduction, as an integral part of a chord, of a note which is then continued into a following dissonance; also, the note so treated. 7 Eccl. Devotional exercises introducing an office, as that of the Eucharist. [<OF <L *praeparatio, -onis*]

pre·par·a·tive (pri·par′ə·tiv) adj. Serving or tending to prepare. —n. 1 That which is preparatory. 2 An act of preparation. — **pre·par′a·tive·ly** adv.

pre·par·a·to·ry (pri·par′ə·tôr′ē, -tō′rē) adj. 1 Serving as a preparation. 2 Occupied in preparation: a *preparatory* scholar. —adv. As a preparation: *Preparatory* to writing, I will consider this: also **pre·par′a·to·ri·ly.**

preparatory school A school in which students are prepared for admission to a college or university.

pre·pare (pri·pâr′) v. **·pared, ·par·ing** v.t. 1 To make ready, fit, or qualified; put in readiness. 2 To provide with what is needed; outfit; equip: to *prepare* an expedition. 3 To bring to a state of completeness, as a meal, lesson, or prescription. 4 Music To introduce by a preliminary note or

notes. —v.i. 5 To make preparations; get ready. [<F *préparer* <L *praeparare* < *prae-* before + *parare* make ready] — **pre·par·ed·ly** (pri·pâr′id·lē) adv. — **pre·par′er** n.

pre·par·ed·ness (pri·pâr′id·nis, -pârd′-) n. Readiness; especially, a condition of military readiness for war.

pre·pense (pri·pens′) adj. Premeditated; considered beforehand: chiefly in the phrase *malice prepense.* [<OF *purpensé,* pp. of *purpenser* < *pur-* (<L *pro-*) ahead + *penser* think <L *pensare*] — **pre·pense′ly** adv.

pre·pon·der·ance (pri·pon′dər·əns) n. Superiority in weight, influence, force, quantity, etc. Also **pre·pon′der·an·cy.**

pre·pon·der·ant (pri·pon′dər·ənt) adj. Having such superior force, weight, importance, efficacy, quantity, or number as to overbalance something else or all other things of a class; predominant. — **pre·pon′der·ant·ly** adv.

pre·pon·der·ate (pri·pon′də·rāt) v.i. **·at·ed, ·at·ing** 1 To be of greater weight. 2 To incline downward or descend, as the scale of a balance. 3 To be of greater power, importance, quantity, etc.; predominate; prevail. [<L *praeponderatus,* pp. of *praeponderare* < *prae-*before + *ponderare* weigh < *pondus, ponderis* weight] — **pre·pon′der·a′tion** n.

prep·o·si·tion (prep′ə·zish′ən) n. Gram. 1 In some languages, a word functioning to indicate the relation of a substantive (the object of the preposition) to another substantive, a verb, or an adjective: one of the eight traditional parts of speech. Some English prepositions are *by, for, from, in, to, with.* A preposition is usually placed before its object (whence its name), and together they constitute a prepositional phrase which serves as an adjectival or an adverbial modifier: He sat *beside* the fire; sick *at* heart; a man *of* honor. There is a close relationship between certain prepositions and adverbs, and the same word may have either function, depending on the context: We saw it *through* (adverb); It sailed out *through* the window (preposition). 2 Any word or construction that functions in a similar manner: He telephoned *in reference to* (equals *about*) your letter. — **inseparable preposition** A preposition so closely connected with a verb as to have all the force of a compound: to *laugh at.* — **participial preposition** A participle used without direct connection with a subject, so that it has the force of a preposition: They spoke to him *concerning* that affair. — **postpositive preposition** A preposition in postposition; also, a suffix added to a noun and serving as a preposition: Hope soars heaven*ward.* [<L *praepositio, -onis* < *praepositus,* pp. of *praeponere* place before < *prae-* before + *ponere* place]

prep·o·si·tion·al (prep′ə·zish′ən·əl) adj. Pertaining to, formed with, or having the character or force of prepositions. — **prep′o·si′tion·al·ly** adv.

pre·pos·i·tive (prē·poz′ə·tiv) adj. 1 Prefixed. 2 Gram. Placed before the word governed or qualified. —n. Gram. A prepositive word or particle. [<L *praepositivus* < *praepositus.* See PREPOSITION.]

pre·pos·sess (prē′pə·zes′) v.t. 1 To preoccupy to the exclusion of other ideas, beliefs, etc.; prejudice; bias. 2 To impress or influence beforehand or at once, especially favorably. 3 Rare To take possession of in advance of others, as land.

pre·pos·sess·ing (prē′pə·zes′ing) adj. Inspiring a favorable opinion from the beginning. — **pre′·pos·sess′ing·ly** adv.

pre·pos·ter·ous (pri·pos′tər·əs) adj. Contrary to nature, reason, or common sense; strikingly or utterly absurd or impracticable. See synonyms under ABSURD, EXTRAORDINARY, RIDICULOUS. [<L *praeposterus* the last first, inverted < *prae-* before + *posterus* last] — **pre·pos′ter·ous·ly** adv. — **pre·pos′ter·ous·ness** n.

pre·po·ten·cy (pri·pō′tən·sē) n. 1 The quality of superior potency; preponderance of influence or efficiency. 2 Biol. The pronounced capacity of one parent, strain, or breed to transmit its own characteristics to the offspring. Also **pre·po′tence.** [<PREPOTENT]

pre·po·tent (pri·pō′tənt) adj. 1 Endowed with prevailing potency; predominant. 2 Having potential power or efficacy; possessing power to shape or influence what comes after. **3** Pertaining to or exhibiting prepotency. Also **pre·po·ten·tial** (prē'pə·ten'shəl). [< L *praepotens, -entis* very powerful] —**pre·po'tent·ly** *adv.*

pre·req·ui·site (prē·rek'wə·zit) *adj.* Required as an antecedent condition; necessary to something that follows. —*n.* A necessary antecedent condition.

pre·rog·a·tive (pri·rog'ə·tiv) *n.* **1** An indefeasible and unquestionable right belonging to a person or body of persons by virtue of position or relation, and exercised without control or accountability; specifically, a hereditary or official right: the royal *prerogative.* **2** Hence, any characteristic and generally recognized privilege peculiar to a person or class: It is a woman's *prerogative* to change her mind. **3** Precedence; preeminence. See synonyms under RIGHT. — *adj.* Of or pertaining to a prerogative; possessing or held by prerogative. [< OF < L *praerogativa* right of voting first < *praerogatus*, pp. of *praerogare* ask before another < *prae-* before + *rogare* ask]

pres·age (pres'ij) *n.* **1** An indication of something to come; prophetic token; portent; omen. **2** A prophetic impression; presentiment; foreboding. **3** Prophetic meaning or import; prediction; foresight. See synonyms under SIGN.
— **pre·sage** (pri·sāj') *v.* **·saged, ·sag·ing** *v.t.* **1** To give presage or portent of; betoken; foreshadow. **2** To have a presentiment of. **3** To predict; foretell. —*v.i.* **4** To make a prediction; prophesy. See synonyms under AUGUR. [< F *présage* < L *praesagium* omen < *praesagire* perceive beforehand < *prae-* before + *sagire* be aware of. Akin to SAGACIOUS] —**pre·sage'ment** *n.* —**pre·sag'er** *n.*

pres·by·ter (prez'bə·tər, pres'-) *n.* **1** In the early church, one of the elders of a church. **2** *Eccl.* **a** In hierarchical churches, a priest. **b** In Presbyterian churches, an ordained clergyman (a **teaching elder**); also, a layman who is a member of the governing body of a congregation (a **ruling elder**). [< LL < Gk. *presbyteros* an elder. Doublet of PRIEST.]

pres·byt·er·ate (prez·bit'ər·it, -ə·rāt, pres-) *n.* **1** The office or dignity of a presbyter or elder. **2** The order or the body of presbyters.

Pres·by·te·ri·an (prez'bə·tir'ē·ən, pres'-) *n.* **1** One who believes in the government of the church by presbyters. **2** A member of any of various Protestant churches, mostly Calvinist in doctrine, and holding to the government of the church by presbyters. —*adj.* Of or pertaining to the Presbyterian Church, its form of government, or its doctrines. [< LL *presbyterium* presbytery +-IAN] —**Pres·by·te'ri·an·ism** *n.*

pre·school (prē·skōōl') *adj.* For or designating a child past infancy but under school age.

pre·sci·ence (prē'shē·əns, presh'ē-) *n.* Knowledge of events before they take place. See synonyms under WISDOM. [< OF < L *praescientia,* orig. neut. pl. of *praesciens, -entis,* ppr. of *praescire* know beforehand < *prae-* before + *scire* know]

pre·sci·ent (prē'shē·ənt, presh'ē-) *adj.* Having prescience; foreknowing; also, far-seeing. [< F < L *presciens, -entis.* See PRESCIENCE.] —**pre'sci·ent·ly** *adv.*

pre·scind (pri·sind') *v.t.* **1** To set apart in thought; consider separately. **2** To cut off; remove. —*v.i.* **3** To withdraw the attention: with *from.* [< L *praescindere* cut off in front < *prae-* before + *scindere* cut]

pre·scribe (pri·skrib') *v.* **·scribed, ·scrib·ing** *v.t.* **1** To set down as a direction or rule to be followed; ordain; enjoin. **2** *Med.* To order the use of (a medicine, treatment, etc.) as a remedy. **3** *Law* To render invalid by lapse of time. —*v.i.* **4** To lay down laws or rules; give directions. **5** *Law* **a** To assert a title to something on the basis of prescription: with *for* or *to.* **b** To become invalid or unenforceable by lapse of time. See synonyms under DICTATE, SET. [< L *praescribere* write beforehand < *prae-* before + *scribere* write] —**pre·scrib'er** *n.*

pre·script (prē'skript) *n.* A prescription or direction, as a rule of conduct. —*adj.* (pri·skript', prē'skript) Prescribed as a rule or model; laid down. [< L *praescriptus,* pp. of *praescribere.* See PRESCRIBE.]

pre·scrip·tion (pri·skrip'shən) *n.* **1** The act of

prescribing, directing, or dictating. **2** That which is prescribed or appointed, as a rule or precept; a prescript. **3** *Med.* **a** A physician's formula for compounding and administering a medicine. **b** The remedy so prescribed. **c** A formula issued by a licensed oculist or optometrist giving directions for the grinding of eyeglass lenses. **4** *Law* A title to property, or a mode of acquiring title to property, founded on uninterrupted possession; a mode of losing a right or title by failure to assert it within a given time; the period after which a neglected right or title cannot be asserted; also, the period, if any, after which prosecution for a crime is barred. **5** Old or continued custom, particularly when considered authoritative. **6** A claim based on long usage. [< L *praescriptio, -onis*]

pre·scrip·tive (pri·skrip'tiv) *adj.* **1** Making strict requirements or rules: *prescriptive* grammar. **2** Sanctioned by custom or long use: a *prescriptive* right to grumble. **3** *Law* Acquired by immemorial use; based on prescription: a *prescriptive* title. [< LL *praescriptivus*] —**pre·scrip'tive·ly** *adv.*

pres·ence (prez'əns) *n.* **1** The state or fact of being present; opposed to *absence.* **2** Situation face to face; close approach or vicinity within view or access. **3** Something invisible but near and sensible, as a spiritual being. **4** Personal appearance; bearing. **5** Personal qualities collectively; self; personality: used also absolutely of a sovereign. **6** *Obs.* A distinguished assembly, as before a prince or exalted personage. **7** Formerly, the room or apartment in which a high dignitary or ruler received assemblies: also **presence chamber.** [< OF < L *praesentia,* orig. neut. pl of *praesens, -entis,* ppr. of *praeesse.* See PRESENT.]

presence of mind Full command of one's faculties; coolness, alertness, and readiness of resource in a situation of sudden danger, embarrassment, etc.

pres·ent[1] (prez'ənt) *adj.* **1** Being in a place or company referred to or contemplated; being at hand: opposed to *absent.* **2** Now going on; current; not past or future. **3** Actually in mind. **4** Immediately impending or actually coming on; not delayed; instant. **5** *Gram.* Relating to or signifying what is going on at the time being: the *present* tense, *present* participle. **6** Ready at hand; prompt in emergency: a *present* wit, a *present* aid. See synonyms under IMMEDIATE. —*n.* **1** Present time; now; the time being. **2** *Gram.* The present tense; also, a verbal form denoting it. **3** A present matter or affair; a question under consideration. **4** *pl. Law* Present writings: term for the document in which the word occurs: Know all men by these *presents.* —**at present** Now. —**for the present** For the time being. [< OF < L *praesens, -entis* being in front of or at hand, ppr. of *praeesse* < *prae-* before + *esse* be]

pre·sent[2] (pri·zent') *v.t.* **1** To bring into the presence or acquaintance of another; introduce, especially to a superior: The ambassador was *presented* to the king. **2** To exhibit to view or notice; display. **3** To suggest to the mind: This *presents* a problem. **4** To put forward for consideration or action; submit, as a petition. **5** To make a gift or presentation of or to, usually formally. **6** *Archaic* To represent on the stage; act. **7** *Law* **a** To offer, as a charge, for judicial action or inquiry. **b** To bring a charge or indictment against.
—**pres·ent** (prez'ənt) *n.* That which is presented or given; a gift; donation. [< OF *presenter* < L *praesentare* set before < *praesens, -entis* present. See PRESENT[1].] —**pre·sent'er** *n.*

pre·sent·a·ble (pri·zen'tə·bəl) *adj.* **1** Fit to be presented; in suitable condition or attire for company. **2** Capable of being offered, exhibited, or bestowed. —**pre·sent·a·bil'i·ty, pre·sent'a·ble·ness** *n.* —**pre·sent'a·bly** *adv.*

present arms A command requiring a soldier to salute by holding his gun or other weapon vertically, in front of and close to his body. Correct position for the gun is muzzle up and trigger facing forward.

pres·en·ta·tion (prez'ən·tā'shən, prē'zən-) *n.* **1** The act of presenting or proffering for acceptance, approval, etc.; especially, the formal offering of a complimentary gift. **2** *Rare* That which is bestowed; a present. **3** The act of introducing or bringing to notice; formal introduction, especially to a superior: *presentation* at court. **4** *Eccl.*

The nomination of a clergyman to a living; also, the right of such nomination. **5** The manner of bringing into view, as a play, thought, or case; way of putting; exhibition; representation; also, that which is represented. **6** The fact or process of being present in consciousness; also, the object of consciousness, without added reference. **7** *Med.* The position of the fetus at birth: designated by the part that is first presented to the touch at the mouth of the womb: breech *presentation,* etc. **8** The condition of being placed in a certain position or direction, with regard to something else, or to an observer. **9** Presentment; the offering of a negotiable instrument for payment. [< OF *presentacion* < L *praesentatio, -onis*]

pres·en·tee (prez'ən·tē') *n.* **1** One who is presented, as to a benefice or at court. **2** The recipient of a gift.

pre·sen·ti·ment (pri·zen'tə·mənt) *n.* A prophetic sense of something to come; a foreboding. See synonyms under ANTICIPATION. [< MF < L *praesentire* perceive beforehand < *prae-* before + *sentire* feel]

pre·sen·tive (pri·zen'tiv) *adj.* Conveying or embodying (as nouns, adjectives, and most verbs) a distinct and complete conception, whether of an object, act, or quality: distinguished from *symbolic.* —*n.* A presentive word. —**pre·sen'tive·ly** *adv.* —**pre·sen'tive·ness** *n.*

pre·sent·ment (pri·zent'mənt) *n.* **1** The act of presenting; also, the state or manner of being presented; presentation. **2** That which is represented or exhibited; a representation or picture; semblance. **3** *Law* A report made by a grand jury, concerning some wrongdoing, and presented to the court; also, the finding and setting forth of charges in an indictment by a grand jury; an indictment. **4** The presentation of a negotiable instrument for payment. **5** *Philos.* The mental images of a perception or idea.

present participle See under PARTICIPLE.

present perfect *Gram.* The verb tense expressing an action completed by the present time: By now he *has finished* the task.

present tense The tense marking present time: I *go, do go, am going.*

pre·ser·va·tive (pri·zûr'və·tiv) *adj.* Serving or tending to preserve. —*n.* That which serves or tends to preserve; a substance that preserves; a safeguard. [< F *préservatif, -ive* < Med. L *praeservativus*]

pre·serve (pri·zûrv') *v.* **·served, ·serv·ing** *v.t.* **1** To keep in safety; protect from destruction, loss, death, or detriment; guard: May the gods *preserve* you. **2** To keep intact or unimpaired; maintain: to *preserve* appearances. **3** To prepare (food) for future consumption, as by boiling with sugar or salting. **4** To keep from decomposition or change, as by chemical treatment: to *preserve* a specimen in alcohol. **5** To keep for one's private hunting or fishing: to *preserve* foxes; to *preserve* a wood. —*v.i.* **6** To make preserves, as of fruit. **7** To maintain a game preserve. —*n.* **1** *Usually pl.* Fruit which has been cooked, usually with sugar, to prevent its fermenting. **2** Something preserved or which preserves. **3** A place set apart for one's own private use, or in which game or fish are protected for purposes of sport. [< OF *preserver* < LL *praeservare* < L *prae-* before + *servare* keep] —**pre·serv·a·bil'i·ty** *n.* —**pre·serv'a·ble** *adj.* —**pres·er·va·tion** (prez'ər·vā'shən) *n.* —**pre·serv'er** *n.*

Synonyms (verb): conserve, defend, guard, keep, maintain, protect, save, secure, sustain, uphold. See KEEP, RETAIN. *Antonyms:* abandon, lavish, lose, neglect, scatter, spend, spoil, waste.

pre·side (pri·zid') *v.i.* **·sid·ed, ·sid·ing** **1** To sit in authority, as over a meeting; be in charge of an assembly, government, etc.; act as chairman or president. **2** To exercise direction or control. [< F *présider* < L *praesidere* sit in front of, protect, guard < *prae-* before + *sedere* sit] —**pre·sid'er** *n.*

pres·i·dent (prez'ə·dənt) *n.* **1** One who is chosen to preside over an organized body; specifically, the chief executive of a republic. **2** The chairman of the meetings and chief executive officer of a department of the government, a corporation, society, etc. **3** The chief officer of a college or university. **4** The chairman of a meeting conducted under parliamentary rules. [< F *président*

< L *praesidens, -entis,* ppr. of *praesidere.* See PRE-SIDE.] —**pres·i·den·tial** (prez′ə·den′shəl) *adj.*

pre·sid·i·al (pri·sid′ē·əl) *adj.* Of or having a garrison or a garrisoned post. [< F *présidial* < LL *praesidium* a garrison, fort]

pre·sid·i·o (pri·sid′ē·ō) *n. pl.* **·sid·i·os** 1 A garrisoned post; fort; fortified settlement. 2 A Spanish penal settlement in a foreign country. —**the Presidio** A U.S. military reservation in San Francisco. [< Am. Sp.]

press[1] (pres) *v.t.* 1 To act upon by weight or pressure: to *press* a button. 2 To compress so as to extract the juice: to *press* grapes. 3 To extract by pressure, as juice. 4 To exert pressure upon so as to smooth, shape, make compact, etc. 5 To smooth or shape by heat and pressure, as clothes; iron. 6 To embrace closely; hug. 7 To force or impel; drive. 8 To distress or harass; place in difficulty: I am *pressed* for time. 9 To urge persistently; importune; entreat: They *pressed* me for an answer. 10 To advocate persistently; insist on; emphasize. 11 To put forward insistently: to *press* a gift on a friend. 12 To urge onward; hasten. 13 *Obs.* To crowd. —*v.i.* 14 To exert pressure; bear heavily. 15 To advance forcibly or with speed: *Press* on! 16 To press clothes, etc. 17 To crowd; cram. 18 To be urgent or importunate. See synonyms under IMPRESS[1], JAM, PLEAD, PUSH. —*n.* 1 A dense throng. 2 The act of crowding together or of straining forward. 3 Hurry or pressure of affairs; urgency: the *press* of business. 4 A movable upright closet or case in which clothes, books, etc., are kept: a linen *press.* 5 An apparatus or machine by which pressure is applied, as for making wine, compressing bulky substances for packing, etc.; a printing press. 6 Newspapers or periodical literature collectively, or the body of persons collectively, as editors, reporters, etc., engaged upon such publications; also, printed literature in the abstract. 7 The art, process, or business of printing. 8 The place of business in which a printing press is set up and where printing is carried on: the Clarendon *Press;* to go to *press.* 9 Criticism, comments, news, etc., in newspapers and periodicals. See synonyms under THRONG. [< OF *presser* < L *pressare,* freq. of *premere* (pp. *pressus*) press]

press[2] (pres) *v.t.* 1 To force into military or naval service; impress. 2 To put to use in a manner not intended or desired. —*n.* A commission to impress men into the public service; also, the impressment of men. [< obs. *prest* engage for military service by payment of earnest money < OF *prester* lend < L *praestare* guarantee, furnish money for < *prae-* before + *stare* stand; influenced in form and meaning by *press*[1]]

press agent A person employed to advance the interests of his client by advertisements and other notices; a publicity agent for any person or business. —**press-a·gen·try** (pres′ā′jən·trē) *n.*

presser foot A footpiece in a sewing machine to hold the fabric down to the feed plate.

press·gang (pres′gang′) *n.* A detachment of men detailed to press men into naval or military service. Also **press gang.**

press·ing (pres′ing) *adj.* 1 Demanding immediate attention; urgent; important. 2 Importunate. —**press′ing·ly** *adv.*

press·man (pres′mən) *n. pl.* **·men** (-mən) 1 A man who has charge of a press, as a printing press. 2 A man who presses clothes. 3 *Brit.* A member of the press; journalist.

press·mark (pres′märk′) *n.* 1 A mark in a book to point out its particular place in a book press or bookcase of a library. 2 A mark, as a number or letter on the margin of a newspaper, showing on which press it was printed.

press·pahn (pres′pän) *n.* Fullerboard. [< G]

press proof 1 The last proof taken before printing. 2 A proof taken on a press.

press release A bulletin, prepared by a press agent, public relations department, or other official representative, announcing an event, de-

velopment in a business, newsworthy decision, etc.

pres·sure (presh′ər) *n.* 1 The act of pressing, or the state of being pressed. 2 *Physics* Any force which acts against an opposing force; a thrust, stress, or strain between opposed masses, uniformly distributed over the surfaces in contact: steam *pressure;* the *pressure* of gas in a confined space. 3 An impelling or constraining moral force; compulsory motive: bringing *pressure* to bear. 4 Exigent demand on one's time or strength; urgency: the *pressure* of business. 5 The oppressive influence or depressing effect of something hard to bear; weight, as of grief or trouble; onerousness: *pressure* of taxation; *pressure* of calamity. 6 A printed character; stamp; an impression. —**fluid pressure** Pressure of a fluid or resembling that of a fluid, being invariable and uniform in all directions. —*v.t.* **·sured, ·sur·ing** *Colloq.* To compel, as by forceful persuasion or influence: He was *pressured* to accept the job. [< OF < L *pressura* < *pressus,* pp. of *premere* press]

pressure group An organized minority group which seeks, through propaganda and lobbying, to influence legislators and public opinion in behalf of its own special interests, or to defeat restrictive legislation.

pres·sur·ize (presh′ə·rīz) *v.t.* **·ized, ·iz·ing** 1 To subject to high pressure. 2 *Aeron.* To maintain normal atmospheric pressure in (the cabin or cockpit of an airplane) at high altitudes. —**pres′sur·i·za′tion** *n.*

pres·ti·dig·i·ta·tion (pres′tə·dij′ə·tā′shən) *n.* The practice of sleight of hand; jugglery; legerdemain. [< F < *preste* (< Ital. *presto* < LL *praestus*) nimble + L *digitus* finger] —**pres′·ti·dig′i·ta′tor** *n.*

pres·tige (pres·tēzh′, pres′tij) *n.* Authority or importance based on past achievements or reputation; ascendency based on recognition of power; renown. [< F < L *praestigium* illusion, juggler's trick, spell < *praestringere* bind fast < *prae-* before + *stringere* bind]

pres·ti·gious (pres·tij′əs, -tē′jəs) *adj.* Having or bestowing prestige. —**pres·ti′gious·ly** *adv.* —**pres·ti′gious·ness** *n.*

pres·to (pres′tō) *adv. & adj.* 1 *Music* In fast time. 2 At once; speedily. —*n. Music* A movement, passage, or phrase performed in fast tempo. [< Ital. < L *praesto.* See PREST[1].]

pre·sum·a·ble (pri·zoō′mə·bəl) *adj.* That may be assumed or presumed; reasonable. See synonyms under APPARENT, LIKELY, PROBABLE. —**pre·sum′a·bly** *adv.*

pre·sume (pri·zoōm′) *v.* **·sumed, ·sum·ing** *v.t.* 1 To take upon oneself without warrant or permission; dare; venture: usually with the infinitive: Do you *presume* to address me? 2 To take for granted; assume to be true until disproved: I *presume* you are right. 3 To indicate the probability of; seem to prove: The receipt for this month *presumes* preceding payments. —*v.i.* 4 To act or proceed presumptuously or overconfidently. 5 To make excessive demands; rely too heavily: with *on* or *upon:* He *presumes* on my good nature. See synonyms under ASSUME. [< OF *presumer* < L *praesumere* take first < *prae-* before + *sumere* take] —**pre·sum·ed·ly** (pri·zoō′mid·lē) *adv.* —**pre·sum′er** *n.*

pre·sump·tion (pri·zump′shən) *n.* 1 Blind or overweening confidence or self-assertion. 2 A passing beyond the ordinary bounds of good breeding, respect, or reverence; offensively forward or arrogant conduct or expression; effrontery. 3 The act of forming a judgment on probable grounds, awaiting further evidence; also, the judgment so formed, or a ground or reason for it. 4 That which may be logically or legally assumed to be true until disproved: the *presumption* of guilt. 5 *Law* The inference of a fact on proof of circumstances that usually or necessarily attend such a fact. See synonyms under ARROGANCE, ASSURANCE, IMPUDENCE, PROBABILITY, TEMERITY. [< OF *presomption* < L *praesumtio, -onis* < *praesumptus,* pp. of *praesumere.* See PRESUME.]

presumptive heir See HEIR PRESUMPTIVE.

pre·sump·tu·ous (pri·zump′choō·əs) *adj.* 1 Unduly confident or bold; audacious; arro-

gant; insolent. 2 Exhibiting, characterized by, or founded on presumption; presuming unduly, as upon success or the forbearance of others; foolhardy. [< OF *presumptuoux* < LL *praesumptiosus*] —**pre·sump′tu·ous·ly** *adv.* —**pre·sump′tu·ous·ness** *n.*

pre·sup·pose (prē′sə·pōz′) *v.t.* **·posed, ·posing** 1 To imply or involve as a necessary antecedent condition. 2 To take for granted; assume to start with. [< F *présupposer*] —**pre·sup·po·si·tion** (prē′sup·ə·zish′ən) *n.*

pre·tend (pri·tend′) *v.t.* 1 To assume or display a false appearance of; feign: to *pretend* friendship for an enemy. 2 To claim or assert falsely: He *pretended* that there was gold on his property. 3 To feign in play; make believe. —*v.i.* 4 To make believe, as in play or for the purpose of deception: She is only *pretending* when she says that. 5 To put forward a claim: with *to.* [< OF *pretendre* < L *praetendere* spread out before < *prae-* before + *tendere* spread out]

Synonyms: affect, assume, counterfeit, feign, profess, sham, simulate. See ASSUME, MASK[1].

pre·tend·er (pri·ten′dər) *n.* 1 One who advances a claim or title; a claimant; specifically, a claimant of a throne who is an heir of a deposed dynasty. 2 In English history, the son and grandson of James II, the former being known in literature as the **Pretender** or the **Old Pretender,** and the latter as the **Young Pretender.** 3 A hypocrite. See synonyms under HYPOCRITE.

pre·tense (pri·tens′, prē′tens) *n.* 1 That which is pretended; a pretext; a ruse or wile. 2 The act or state of pretending, or of being a pretender or claimant; specifically, a false assumption of a character or condition; hence, affectation; ostentation. 3 Any act of simulation. 4 A right or title asserted. 5 An intention, aim, or effort. Also *Brit.* **pre·tence′.** [< AF *pretensse* < Med. L *praetensus,* alter. of L *praetentus,* pp. of *praetendere.* See PRETEND.]

Synonyms: affectation, air, assumption, cloak, color, disguise, dissimulation, excuse, mask, pretension, pretext, ruse, seeming, semblance, show, simulation. A *pretense,* in the unfavorable and usual sense, is something advanced or displayed for the purpose of concealing the reality. A person makes a *pretense* of something for the credit or advantage to be gained by it; he makes what is allowed or approved a *pretext* for doing what would be opposed or condemned; a tricky schoolboy makes a *pretense* of doing an errand which he does not do, or he makes the actual doing of an errand a *pretext* for playing truant. A *ruse* is something employed to blind or deceive so as to mask an ulterior design, and enable a person to gain some end that he would not be allowed to approach directly. A *pretension* is a claim that is or may be contested; the word is now commonly used in an unfavorable sense. See DISGUISE, HYPOCRISY. *Antonyms:* actuality, candor, fact, guilelessness, honesty, ingenuousness, openness, reality, simplicity, sincerity, truth.

pre·ten·sion (pri·ten′shən) *n.* 1 A claim put forward, whether true or false. 2 Affectation; display. 3 A bold or presumptuous assertion. See synonyms under PRETENSE.

pre·ten·tious (pri·ten′shəs) *adj.* Characterized by pretension; making an ambitious outward show; ostentatious. [< F *prétentieux*] —**pre·ten′tious·ly** *adv.* —**pre·ten′tious·ness** *n.*

preter- *prefix* Beyond; past; more than: *preternatural.* [< L *praeter* beyond < *prae* before]

pret·er·it (pret′ər·it) *adj.* 1 *Gram.* Signifying past time or completed past action. 2 *Rare* Belonging to the past; bygone. —*n. Gram.* The tense that expresses absolute past time; the past tense. Also **pret′er·ite.** [< OF *preterit* < L *praeteritus* past, pp. of *praeterire* go past < *praeter-* beyond + *ire* go]

pret·er·i·tion (pret′ə·rish′ən) *n.* 1 The act of passing over or omitting. 2 The omission or passing by of a natural heir without mention by a testator in his will. 3 In the doctrine of predestination, the passing-by of the non-elect. [< LL *praeteritio, -onis* < L *praeteritus.* See PRETERIT.]

PRESS
Cider, wine, and fruit press.

pre·ter·mit (prē'tər·mit') *v.t.* **·mit·ted**, **·mit·ting** **1** To fail or cease to do; neglect; omit. **2** To let pass without noticing; overlook; disregard. [<L *praetermittere* let go by < *praeter-* beyond + *mittere* send] — **pre·ter·mis'sion** (-mish'ən) *n.*

pre·ter·nat·u·ral (prē'tər·nach'ər·əl) *adj.* Diverging from or exceeding the common order of nature; inexplicable in terms of the known facts and laws of science, but not outside the universal natural order: distinguished from *supernatural.* See synonyms under SUPERNATURAL. — **pre'ter·nat'u·ral·ism** *n.* — **pre'ter·nat'u·ral·ly** *adv.*

pre·text (prē'tekst) *n.* **1** A fictitious reason or motive advanced to conceal a real one. **2** A specious excuse or explanation. See synonyms under PRETENSE. [<F *prétexte* <L *praetextus.* See PRAETEXTA.]

Pre·to·ri·a (pri·tôr'ē·ə, -tō'rē·ə) Capital of Transvaal province and administrative capital of the Republic of South Africa, in south central Transvaal.

pret·ti·fy (prit'i·fī) *v.t.* **·fied**, **·fy·ing** To make pretty; embellish overmuch. [<PRETTY + -FY]

pret·ty (prit'ē) *adj.* **·ti·er**, **·ti·est** **1** Characterized by delicacy, gracefulness, or proportion rather than by striking beauty; pleasing; attractive. **2** Decent; good; sufficient: often used ironically as a term of deprecation: A *pretty* mess you've made of it! **3** *Colloq.* Considerable; rather large in size or degree. **4** Sweet; precious: a diminutive of endearment: *pretty* girl. **5** Characterized by effeminacy; affected; foppish. **6** *Scot.* Bold; vigorous; athletic. **7** *Obs.* Strong; able; cunning. See synonyms under BEAUTIFUL. — *adv.* **1** Moderately; somewhat; to a fair extent: He looked *pretty* well. **2** Very; quite: He's grown *pretty* fast. **3** *Dial.* Prettily; finely. — **sitting pretty** *Colloq.* In good circumstances. — *n.* A pretty thing or person. [OE *prættig* tricky, cunning] — **pret'ti·ly** *adv.* — **pret'ti·ness** *n.*

pret·zel (pret'səl) *n.* A glazed salted biscuit baked in the form of a loose knot. [<G *brezel*]

pre·vail (pri·vāl') *v.i.* **1** To gain mastery; be victorious; triumph: with *over* or *against.* **2** To be effective or efficacious; succeed. **3** To use persuasion or influence successfully: with *on, upon,* or *with.* **4** To be or become a predominant feature or quality; be prevalent. **5** To have general or wide-spread use or acceptance; be in force. See synonyms under SUCCEED. [<OF *prevaloir* <L *prevalere* < *prae-* before + *valere* be strong]

pre·vail·ing (pri·vā'ling) *adj.* **1** Current; prevalent. **2** Having effective power or influence; efficacious. See synonyms under PREDOMINANT, USUAL. — **pre·vail'ing·ly** *adv.* — **pre·vail'ing·ness** *n.*

prev·a·lent (prev'ə·lənt) *adj.* **1** Predominant. **2** Of wide extent or frequent occurrence; common. **3** Efficacious; effective. See synonyms under GENERAL, PREDOMINANT, USUAL. [<L *praevalens, -entis,* ppr. of *praevalere* PREVAIL] — **prev'a·lence** *n.* — **prev'a·lent·ly** *adv.*

pre·var·i·cate (pri·var'ə·kāt) *v.i.* **·cat·ed**, **·cat·ing** To speak or act in a deceptive, ambiguous, or evasive manner; quibble; lie. [<L *praevaricatus,* pp. of *praevaricare,* lit., walk crookedly < *prae-* before + *varicare* straddle < *varicus* straddling < *varus* crooked] — **pre·var'i·ca·tor** *n.*

pre·var·i·ca·tion (pri·var'ə·kā'shən) *n.* **1** The act of prevaricating. **2** Misleading or equivocal statement. **3** A trick. See synonyms under DECEPTION, SOPHISTRY.

pre·ven·ience (pri·vēn'yəns) *n.* The act or state of going before; anticipation.

pre·ven·ient (pri·vēn'yənt) *adj.* **1** Preceding or preventing. **2** Anticipatory; expectant. [<L *praeveniens, -entis,* ppr. of *praevenire.* See PREVENT.]

pre·vent (pri·vent') *v.t.* **1** To keep from happening, as by previous measures or preparations; preclude; thwart. **2** To keep from doing something; forestall; hinder. **3** *Obs.* To anticipate; precede. [<L *praeventus;* pp. of *praevenire* precede, come before, anticipate < *prae-* before + *venire* come] — **pre·vent'a·ble** or **pre·vent'i·ble** *adj.* — **pre·vent'a·bil'i·ty** or **pre·vent'i·bil'i·ty** *n.* — **pre·vent'er** *n.*

Synonyms: anticipate, forestall. The original sense of *prevent,* to go or come before, act in advance of, now practically obsolete, was still in good use when the authorized version of

the Bible was made, as appears in such passages as "Thou *preventest* him with the blessings of goodness" (that is, by sending the blessings before the desire is formulated or expressed), *Ps.* xxi 3. *Anticipate* is now the only single word usable in this sense; to *forestall* is to take or act in advance in one's own behalf and to the prejudice or hindrance of another. But to *anticipate* is very frequently used in the favorable sense; as, his thoughtful kindness *anticipated* my wish (that is, met the wish before it was expressed); or one *anticipates* a payment (by making it before the time). For the present use of *prevent,* see synonyms for HINDER¹, PRECLUDE, PROHIBIT.

pre·ven·tion (pri·ven'shən) *n.* **1** The act of preventing. **2** A hindrance; obstruction. **3** A preventive.

pre·ven·tive (pri·ven'tiv) *adj.* Intended or serving to ward off harm, diseases, etc.: *preventive* medicine. — *n.* That which prevents or hinders, as a medicine to ward off disease; a precautionary measure. Also **pre·vent·a·tive** (pri·ven'tə·tiv). — **pre·ven'tive·ly** *adv.* — **pre·ven'tive·ness** *n.*

pre·verb (prē'vûrb') *n.* A verbal prefix, as *be-* in *behave.*

pre·ver·nal (pri·vûr'nəl) *adj.* **1** Prior to spring. **2** *Bot.* Flowering in the early spring, as certain trees and plants.

pre·view (prē'vyōō') *n.* **1** An advance showing, as of a motion picture, a fashion show, etc., to invited guests before it is presented publicly. **2** In motion pictures, the showing of scenes or parts of scenes to advertise a coming picture.

pre·vi·ous (prē'vē·əs) *adj.* **1** Being or taking place before something else in time or order; antecedent; prior to. **2** *Colloq.* Acting, occurring, or speaking too soon; premature. [<L *praevius* going before < *prae-* before + *via* way, road] — **pre'vi·ous·ly** *adv.* — **pre'vi·ous·ness** *n.*

Synonyms: antecedent, anterior, earlier, foregoing, former, precedent, preceding, preliminary, prior. *Antecedent* may denote simple priority in time, implying no direct connection between that which goes before and that which follows; as, the striking of one clock may be always *antecedent* to the striking of another with no causal connection between them. *Antecedent* and *previous* may refer to that which goes or happens at any distance in advance; *preceding* is limited to that which is immediately next or next before; an *antecedent* event may have happened at any time before; the *preceding* transaction is the one completed just before the one with which it is compared; a *previous* statement or chapter may be in any part of the book that has gone before; the *preceding* statement or chapter comes next before without an interval. *Foregoing* is used only of that which is spoken or written; as, the *foregoing* statements. *Anterior,* while it can be used of time, is coming to be employed chiefly with reference to place; as, the *anterior* lobes of the brain. *Prior* bears exclusive reference to time, and commonly where that which is first in time is first also in right; as, a *prior* demand. *Former* is used of time, or of position in written or printed matter, not of space in general. We say *former* times, a *former* chapter, etc. *Former* has a close relation, or sharp contrast, with something following; the *former* always implies the latter, even when not fully expressed. Compare ANTECEDENT. *Antonyms:* after, concluding, consequent, following, hind, hinder, hindmost, later, latter, posterior, subsequent, succeeding.

pre·vise (prē·vīz') *v.t.* **·vised**, **·vis·ing** **1** To see beforehand; foresee. **2** To notify beforehand; forewarn. [<L *praevisus,* pp. of *praevidere* foresee < *prae-* before + *videre* see]

pre·vi·sion (prē·vizh'ən) *n.* **1** The act or power of foreseeing; prescience; foresight. **2** A prophetic or anticipatory vision. See synonyms under ANTICIPATION. [<F *prévision*]

pre·vue (prē'vyōō') *n.* A preview. [<F *prévue,* fem. pp. of *prévoir* foresee]

prey (prā) *n.* **1** Any animal seized by another for food. **2** Booty; plunder; pillage. **3** Anything made the victim of that which is hostile or evil. **4** The act of preying; depredation; robbery. See synonyms under PLUNDER. — *v.i.* **1** To seek or take prey for food: Cats *prey* on birds. **2** To take booty; plunder. **3** To make a victim of someone, as by cheat-

ing. **4** To exert a wearing or harmful influence: His losses *preyed* on his mind. ◆ Homophone: *pray.* [<OF *preie* <L *praeda* booty] — **prey'er** *n.*

pri·a·pus (prī·ā'pəs) *n.* A phallus. [<PRIAPUS]

price (prīs) *n.* **1** An equivalent given or asked in exchange; valuation; cost (to the buyer). **2** Anything given or done to obtain something: Death is the *price* of glory. **3** The quality of possessing value; worth; especially, high value. **4** A bribe or anything used for a bribe. **5** A reward for the capture or death of. — **beyond price** **1** So valuable that no adequate price can be set; priceless. **2** Unbribable. — **market price** The price that something will bring in the open market. — **to set a price on one's head** To offer a reward for the capture of a person, dead or alive. — *v.t.* **priced, pric·ing** **1** To ask the price of. **2** To set a price on; value; appraise. [<OF *pris* <L *pretium.* Related to PRAISE.]

Synonyms (noun): charge, cost, expenditure, expense, outlay, value, worth. The *cost* of a thing is all that has been expended upon it, whether in discovery, production, refinement, decoration, transportation, or otherwise, to bring it to its present condition in the hands of its present possessor; the *price* of a thing is what the seller asks for it. *Price* always implies that an article is for sale; what a man will not sell he declines to put a *price* on. *Value* is the estimated equivalent for an article, whether the article is for sale or not; the market *value* is what something would bring if it were for sale in the open market; the intrinsic *value* is the inherent *worth* of the article considered by itself alone; the market *value* of an old and rare volume may be very great, while its intrinsic *value* may be practically nothing. *Value* has always more reference to others' estimation (literally, what the thing will avail with others) than *worth,* which regards the thing in and by itself; thus, intrinsic *value* is a weaker expression than intrinsic *worth.* *Charge* has especial reference to services, *expense* to outlays; as, the *charges* of a lawyer or physician; traveling *expenses,* etc.

price-fix·ing (prīs'fik'sing) *n.* **1** The establishment and maintenance of a scale of prices agreed upon within specified groups of producers or distributors. **2** The establishing by government action of maximum or minimum or fixed prices for certain goods and services. **3** The fixing by a manufacturer or producer of the price at which retailers must sell his product. — *adj.* Of or pertaining to price-fixing.

price·less (prīs'lis) *adj.* **1** Beyond price or valuation; invaluable. **2** *Colloq.* Wonderfully amusing or absurd.

prick (prik) *v.t.* **1** To pierce slightly, as with a sharp point; puncture. **2** To affect with sharp mental pain; sting; spur. **3** To mark, outline, or indicate by or as by punctures. **4** *Obs.* To urge on with or as with a spur; goad. **5** In farriery: **a** To drive a nail into the quick of (a horse's hoof), causing lameness. **b** To nick (a horse's tail). **6** To transplant, as young plants, preparatory to later planting. — *v.i.* **7** To have or cause a stinging or piercing sensation. **8** *Archaic* To ride at full speed; go at a gallop. — **to prick up one's (or its) ears** **1** To raise the ears erect. **2** To listen attentively. — *n.* **1** The act of pricking; the state or sensation of being pricked. **2** A mental sting or spur: the *prick* of conscience. **3** That which pricks; a slender, sharp-pointed thing, as a thorn or pointed weapon. **4** A mark made by a sharp, pointed instrument; puncture; dot. **5** The footprint of an animal, as a rabbit or deer. **6** *Archaic* A goad or spur. [OE *prica* sharp point] — **prick'er** *n.*

prick·ing (prik'ing) *n.* **1** The act of puncturing with a sharp point, or the resulting sensation. **2** The laming of a horse by improper shoeing. **3** The nicking of a horse's tail.

pricking wheel A toothed wheel mounted on a handle, used by saddlers to mark equidistant places for stitch holes, or by dressmakers in copying patterns. Also **prick wheel.**

prick·le (prik'əl) *n.* **1** A small, sharp point, as on the bark of a plant. **2** A prickling or stinging sensation. — *v.* **·led, ·ling** *v.t.* **1** To prick; pierce. **2** To cause a prickling or stinging sensation in. — *v.i.* **3** To have a prickling or stinging sensation; tingle. [OE *pricel*]

prick·ly (prik′lē) *adj.* **1** Furnished with prickles. **2** Stinging, as if from a prick or sting: a *prickly* sensation.

prickly heat *Pathol.* A summer rash of bright red pimples, with heat, itching, and pricking as if by needles; miliaria.

pride (prīd) *n.* **1** An undue sense of one's own superiority; inordinate self-esteem; arrogance or superciliousness; conceit. **2** A proper sense of personal dignity and worth; honorable self-respect. **3** That of which one is justly proud; a cause of exultation. **4** The acme of excellence. **5** Consciousness of youth or power; high spirits; mettle. **6** *Obs.* Sexual desire. **7** *Archaic* Ostentatious splendor; display. **8** A group or company: said only of lions. — *v.t.* **prid·ed**, **prid·ing** To take pride in (oneself) for something: with *on* or *upon*. [OE *prýte* < *prút* proud]

Synonyms (noun): conceit, ostentation, self-complacency, self-conceit, self-esteem, self-exaltation, self-respect, vainglory, vanity. *Conceit* and *vanity* are associated with weakness, *pride* with strength. *Conceit* may be founded upon nothing, *pride* is founded upon something that one is, or has, or has done; *vanity*, too, is commonly founded on something real, but far slighter than would afford foundation for *pride*. *Vanity* is eager for admiration and praise and seeks them; *pride* could never solicit admiration or praise. *Conceit* is stronger than *self-conceit*. *Self-conceit* is ridiculous; *conceit* is offensive. *Self-respect* is a thoroughly worthy feeling; *self-esteem* is a more generous estimate of one's own character and abilities than the rest of the world is ready to allow. *Vainglory* is more pompous and boastful than *vanity*. Compare synonyms for ARROGANCE, EGOTISM, OSTENTATION, RESERVE. *Antonyms:* humility, lowliness, meekness, modesty, self-abasement.

prie-dieu (prē-dyœ′) *n.* A small desk arranged to support a book or books and with a footpiece on which to kneel; a praying desk. [<F, pray God]

PRIE–DIEU

pri·er (prī′ər) *n.* One who pries.

priest (prēst) *n.* **1** One especially consecrated to the service of a divinity, and serving as mediator between the divinity and his worshipers in sacrifice, worship, prayer, teaching, etc. **2** In the Anglican, Greek, and Roman Catholic churches, a clergyman in the second order of the ministry, ranking next below a bishop, and having authority to administer the sacraments. **3** Any ordained clergyman or pastor; an official minister of any religious system: distinguished from *layman*. **4** In the early Christian church, an elder or presbyter. **5** One who performs functions or duties similar to those of a priest. — **parish priest** The priest in charge of a parish; specifically, in the Roman Catholic Church, a priest exercising personal jurisdiction in a parish, all members of which are obliged to apply to him for the ministrations of the church: distinguished from *rector* and *curate*. [OE *prēost*, ult. < L *presbyter*. Doublet of PRESBYTER.]

priest·craft (prēst′kraft′, -kräft′) *n.* **1** Priestly arts and wiles: an invidious term. **2** The knowledge and skill of priests.

priest·ess (prēs′tis) *n.* A woman or girl who exercises priestly functions or who performs sacred rites.

priest·hood (prēst′hood) *n.* **1** The priestly office or character. **2** The priestly order; priests collectively.

priest·ly (prēst′lē) *adj.* **1** Of or pertaining to a priest or the priesthood; sacerdotal. **2** Suitable to or befitting a priest. — **priest′li·ness** *n.*

prig (prig) *n.* A formal and narrow-minded person who assumes superior virtue, wisdom, or learning; pedant. [Origin unknown]

prig·gish (prig′ish) *adj.* Like a prig; conceited. — **prig′gish·ly** *adv.* — **prig′gish·ness** *n.*

prill (pril) *n.* **1** A small metal particle formed in assay work. **2** A spherical pellet about the size of buckshot. — *v.t.* To convert into prills for some purpose or use. [? <Cornish]

prim (prim) *adj.* Minutely or affectedly precise and formal; stiffly proper and neat. See synonyms under NEAT¹. — *v.* **primmed**, **prim·ming** *v.i.* To fix the face or mouth in a precise or prim expression; be prim. — *v.t.* To fix in a precise or prim manner. [Prob. <OF *prim* first, prime, fine, delicate <L *primus* first] — **prim′ly** *adv.* — **prim′ness** *n.*

pri·ma·cy (prī′mə·sē) *n. pl.* **·cies** **1** The state of being first, as in rank or excellence. **2** The office or province of a primate; archbishopric: also **pri′mate·ship** (-mit·ship). [<OF *primacie* <Med. L *primatia* <LL *primas, primatis* one of the first. See PRIMATE.]

pri·ma don·na (prē′mə don′ə) **1** A leading female singer, as in an opera company. **2** *Colloq.* A temperamental or vain person. [<Ital., lit., first lady]

prima-facie evidence Evidence which, if unexplained or uncontradicted, would establish the fact alleged.

pri·mal (prī′məl) *adj.* **1** Being at the beginning or foundation; first; original. **2** Most important; chief. See synonyms under PRIMEVAL. [<Med. L *primalis*]

primal cut Any one of the cuts into which a side of beef may be divided for sale at wholesale. These cuts are: hindquarter, trimmed full loin, round sirloin, short loin, flank, flank steak, kidney, hanging tender, forequarter, cross-cut chuck, triangle, arm chuck, rib, short plate, brisket, fore shank, back, regular chuck.

pri·ma·quine (prī′mə·kwīn) *n.* An antimalarial drug synthesized from chemicals derived from corn and coal tar. [<PRIM(E) + A(MINO)-QUIN(OLIN)E]

pri·ma·ri·ly (prī′mer·ə·lē, -mər·ə·lē, *emphatic* prī·mâr′ə·lē) *adv.* In the first place; originally; essentially.

pri·ma·ry (prī′mer·ē, -mər·ē) *adj.* **1** First in time or origin; primitive; original. **2** First in a series or sequence. **3** First in degree, rank, or importance; chief. **4** Constituting the fundamental or original elements of which a whole is comprised; basic; elemental: the *primary* forces of life. **5** Of the first stage of development; elementary; lowest: *primary* school. **6** *Ornithol.* Of or pertaining to the principal flight feathers of a bird's wing. **7** *Geol.* Paleozoic. **8** *Electr.* Of, pertaining to, or noting an inducing current or its circuit: a *primary* coil. **9** *Chem.* **a** Having some characteristic in the first degree, as an initial replacement, substitution, etc. **b** In organic compounds, denoting a radical in which a carbon atom is directly joined to only one other carbon atom. **c** Denoting a compound containing such a radical. — *n. pl.* **·ries** **1** That which is first in rank, dignity, or importance, as a primary planet in distinction from a satellite. **2** A primary meeting or balloting of the voters belonging to one political party in an election district to nominate candidates. **3** *Ornithol.* One of the large flight feathers of the pinion or hand bones of a bird's wings. See synonyms under FIRST, PRIMEVAL. — **direct primary election** A primary election in which candidates for office are nominated directly by the voters and not by a convention or by a body of delegates. [<L *primarius* < *primus* first]

primary colors See under COLOR.

pri·mate (prī′mit, -māt) *n.* **1** The prelate highest in rank in a nation or province. **2** Any of an order (*Primates*) of mammals, including the tarsiers, lemurs, marmosets, monkeys, apes, and man. [<OF *primat* <LL *primas, primatis* of the first <L *primus*] — **pri·ma·tial** (prī·mā′shəl) *adj.*

pri·ma·tol·o·gy (prī′mə·tol′ə·jē) *n.* The branch of zoology which treats of the origin, structure, evolution, and development of primates. — **pri′ma·tol′o·gist** *n.*

prime¹ (prīm) *adj.* **1** First in rank, dignity, or importance; chief. **2** First in value or excellence; of excellent quality; first-rate. **3** First in time or order; original; primitive;

primeval. **4** *Math.* Divisible by no whole number except itself and unity: said of a number. Two or more numbers are said to be *prime* to each other when they have no common factor but unity. **5** Having or pertaining to the strength and vigor of fresh maturity; blooming. **6** Original; not derived; first: opposed to *secondary*. **7** Marked with the sign (′). See synonyms under EXCELLENT, PRIMEVAL. — *n.* **1** The period of fresh, full vigor, beauty, and power succeeding youth and preceding age; formerly, youth. **2** The period of full perfection in anything. **3** The beginning of anything, as of the day; dawn; spring. **4** The best of anything; a prime grade. **5** A prime number. **6** A mark or accent (′) written above and to the right of a letter or figure; also, an inch, a minute, etc., as indicated by that sign, used in indicating and measuring degrees. **7** *Music* The tonic; the interval of unison; also, a note in unison with another. — *v.* **primed**, **prim·ing** *v.t.* **1** To prepare; make ready for some purpose. **2** To put a primer into (a gun, mine, etc.) preparatory to firing. **3** To pour water into (a pump) so as to displace air and promote suction. **4** To cover (a surface) with sizing, a first coat of paint, etc. **5** To supply beforehand with facts, information, etc.: to *prime* a witness. — *v.i.* **6** To carry water along with the steam into the cylinder: said of a steam boiler or engine. **7** To make something ready, as for firing, pumping, etc. [<OF <L *primus*] — **prime′ly** *adv.* — **prime′ness** *n.*

prime² (prīm) *n.* **1** The first canonical hour succeeding lauds; first of the day hours. **2** The office recited at this time. [OE *prim* <LL *prima (hora)* first (hour)]

prime meridian A meridian from which longitude is reckoned: now, generally, the one that passes through Greenwich, England, but formerly that of the local capital, as, in the United States, Washington, D.C.: in France, Paris; etc.

prime minister The chief of the cabinet or ministry; in Great Britain, the principal minister of the sovereign. Compare PREMIER.

prime mover **1** An original or chief force in an undertaking. **2** That which is regarded as an original or natural source of the energy required to perform work or develop power, as muscular force, wind, the motion of water, etc. **3** An object or machine used to convert natural forces to productive power, as a turbine, water wheel, windmill, or the like. **4** In Aristotelian philosophy, the first cause of all movement, which does not itself move.

prime number See under NUMBER.

prim·er¹ (prim′ər) *n.* **1** An elementary textbook; especially, a beginning reading book. **2** Originally, a small prayer book or the like. **3** *Printing* Either of two sizes of type, **great primer** (18-point) and **long primer** (10-point). [<Med. L *primarius*]

prim·er² (prī′mər) *n.* **1** Any device, as a cap, tube, etc., used to detonate the main charge of a gun, mine, etc. **2** One who or that which primes.

pri·me·val (prī·mē′vəl) *adj.* Belonging to the first ages; primitive in time; primary. [<L *primaevus* youthful < *primus* first + *aevum* age] — **pri·me′val·ly** *adv.*

Synonyms: aboriginal, ancient, autochthonic, immemorial, indigenous, native, old, original, primal, primary, prime, primitive, primordial, pristine. *Aboriginal* signifies pertaining to the earliest known inhabitants of a country in the widest sense, including not merely human beings, but animals and plants. *Primeval* signifies strictly belonging to the first ages, earliest in time, but often only the earliest of which man knows or conceives. *Prime* and *primary* may signify either first in time, or first in importance; *primary* has also the sense of elementary or preparatory; we speak of a *prime* minister, a *primary* school. *Primal* is chiefly poetic, in the sense of *prime*; as, the *primal* curse. *Primordial* is first in an order of existence or development; as, a *primordial* leaf. *Primitive* frequently signifies having the original characteristics of that which it represents, as well as standing first in time; as, the *primitive* church, or early characteristics without remoteness in time. *Primeval* simplicity is the simplicity of the earliest ages; *primitive* simplicity may be found in retired villages now. *Pristine* is used almost exclusively in a good sense of that which is *original* and perhaps *ancient*; as, *pristine* purity, innocence, vigor. *Immemorial* refers solely to time, independently of quality, denoting, in legal phrase, that "whereof the memory of man runneth not to the contrary." Compare synonyms for ANCIENT, FIRST, OLD. *Antonyms:* adventitious, exotic, foreign, fresh, late, modern, new, novel, recent.

pri·mi·ge·ni·al (prī′mə·jē′nē·əl) *adj.* Being the first or first–born; primal; primitive; original. [<L *primigenius* first, original]

pri·mip·a·ra (prī·mip′ər·ə) *n. pl.* **·a·rae** (-ər·ē) A woman pregnant for the first time or one who has borne just one child. [<L <*primus* first + *parere* give birth to] — **pri·mi·par·i·ty** (prī′mi·par′ə·tē) *n.* — **pri·mip′a·rous** *adj.*

prim·i·tive (prim′ə·tiv) *adj.* **1** Pertaining to the beginning or origin; first; earliest; primary. **2** Resembling the manners or style of long ago; old–fashioned; simple; plain. **3** *Geol.* Of, belonging to, or characterized by the earliest geological period: said especially of the crystalline, unstratified, and massive rocks, the oldest known. **4** *Anthropol.* Of or pertaining to the beginning or earliest anthropological forms or civilizations: *primitive* man, *primitive* weapons. **5** *Biol.* **a** Being or occurring at an early stage of development or growth; first–formed; rudimentary. **b** Not much changed by evolution: a *primitive* species. **6** *Ling.* Standing in original relation, as a word from which a derivative is made; radical: opposed to *derived.* **7** *Theol.* Adhering to strictly traditional interpretation of doctrine and Scripture: the *primitive* church. — *n.* **1** *Ling.* A primary or radical word; also, a word from which another is derived. **2** *Math.* A form in algebra or geometry from which another is derived. **3** An artist, or a work of art, belonging to a very early period of art, or to the earliest phase of an art development or movement; also, a work of any period resembling or imitating such art, or an artist producing it: often characterized by simplicity or a childlike quality. See synonyms under FIRST, PRIMEVAL, RADICAL. [<L *primitivus* < *primus* first] — **prim′i·tive·ly** *adv.* — **prim′i·tive·ness, prim′i·tiv′i·ty** *n.*

prim·i·tiv·ism (prim′ə·tiv·iz′əm) *n.* Belief in or adherence to primitive forms and customs.

pri·mo·gen·i·tor (prī′mə·jen′ə·tər) *n.* An earliest ancestor; a forefather. [<Med. L <L *primus* first + *genitor* a father]

pri·mo·gen·i·ture (prī′mə·jen′ə·chər) *n.* **1** The state of being the first–born child of the same parents. **2** The right of the eldest son to inherit the property, title, etc., of a parent, to the exclusion of all other children. See ULTIMOGENITURE. [<Med. L *primogenitura* <L *primus* first + *genitura* birth < *genitus,* pp. of *gignere* beget]

pri·mor·di·al (prī·môr′dē·əl) *adj.* **1** First in order or time; original; elemental. **2** *Biol.* First in order of appearance in the growth or development of an organism. — *n.* An elementary principle. See synonyms under FIRST, PRIMEVAL, TRANSCENDENTAL. [<LL *primordialis* < *primordius* original < *primordium* beginning < *primus* first + *ordiri* begin a web] — **pri·mor′di·al·ly** *adv.*

pri·mor·di·al·ism (prī·môr′dē·əl·iz′əm) *n.* The survival or persistence of primitive arts and customs.

primp (primp) *v.t. & v.i.* To prink; dress up, especially with superfluous attention to detail. [Akin to PRIM]

prim·rose (prim′rōz) *n.* **1** An early–blossoming perennial herb (genus *Primula*) with tufted basal leaves and variously colored flowers. **2** The flower. **3** The evening primrose. **4** A pale–yellow color, named for the common English primrose: a term indiscriminately applied to various yellow pigments. — *adj.* **1** Pertaining to a primrose; of primrose color. **2** Flowery; gay. [Alter. of ME *primerole* <OF <Med. L *primula,* fem. dim. of L *primus* first; infl. by *rose*]

PRIMROSE
(def. 1)
(The wild species
from 1 to 18
inches tall)

primrose path The life of worldly or sensual pleasures.

prince (prins) *n.* **1** A non–reigning male member of a royal family. **2** A male monarch or sovereign. **3** *Brit.* The son of a sovereign or of a son of the sovereign. **4** One of a high order of nobility. **5** The ruler of a small state; head of a principality. **6** A chief or leader, or one of the highest rank of the class to which he belongs: a merchant *prince.* See synonyms under MASTER. [<OF <L *princeps* first, principal < *primus* first + stem of *capere* take]

Prince Albert A long, double–breasted frock coat.

prince consort The husband of a reigning female sovereign.

prince·kin (prins′kin) *n.* A little or inferior prince.

prince·ling (prins′ling) *n.* **1** A young prince. **2** A subordinate prince. Also **prince′let** (-lit).

prince·ly (prins′lē) *adj.* **·li·er, ·li·est 1** Like or characteristic of a prince; liberal; generous. **2** Belonging to, ruled by, or suitable for a prince. **3** Having the rank of a prince. See synonyms under KINGLY. — *adv.* In a princely manner. — **prince′li·ness** *n.*

Prince of Darkness Satan.

Prince of Peace Jesus Christ.

Prince of Wales The eldest son or male heir apparent of the British sovereign: he is born Duke of Cornwall, and becomes Prince of Wales only by creation.

Prince of Wales plumes In furniture and decoration, a motif of three ostrich feathers tied with a bowknot.

prin·cess (prin′sis) *n.* **1** A non–reigning female member of a royal family. **2** The consort of a prince. **3** A female sovereign. **4** *Brit.* The daughter of a sovereign or of a son of the sovereign. [<F *princesse*]

prin·cesse (prin·ses′, prin′sis) *adj.* Designating a woman's close–fitting garment cut in a single piece from shoulder to flared hem. Also **prin′cess.** [<F, princess]

princess royal The eldest daughter of a sovereign.

Prince·ton (prins′tən) A borough of central New Jersey; scene of an American victory in the Revolutionary War (1777) and seat of Princeton University, founded 1746.

prin·ci·pal (prin′sə·pəl) *adj.* First in rank, character, or importance; chief. See synonyms under FIRST, PARAMOUNT. — *n.* **1** One who takes a leading part; one concerned directly and not as an auxiliary; one who is a leader or chief in some action. **2** *Law* **a** The actor in a crime, or one present aiding and abetting. **b** The employer of one who acts as an agent. **c** One primarily liable for whom another has become surety. **d** The most important thing, or part of a given property, to which other things or parts are incidental. **e** The capital or body of an estate. **3** One who is at the head of some body; a chief; one in authority; a presiding officer, as of a society. **4** The head teacher or master in a public or private school. **5** The chief executive of some colleges and universities in Great Britain. **6** Property or capital, as opposed to interest or income. **7** A rafter extending to the ridge pole; a principal rafter. **8** *Music* **a** The chief metal organ stop, an octave higher in pitch than the other diapasons. **b** The subject of a fugue: distinguished from *answer.* See synonyms under CHIEF, MASTER. ◆ Homophone: *principle.* [<F <L *principalis* < *princeps* chief] — **prin′ci·pal·ly** *adv.* — **prin′ci·pal·ship′** *n.*

prin·ci·pal·i·ty (prin′sə·pal′ə·tē) *n. pl.* **·ties 1** The territory of a reigning prince, or one that gives to a prince a title of courtesy. **2** *pl.* Powers or powerful influences, as celestial or demoniacal powers; in the celestial hierarchy of Dionysius, the seventh of the nine emanations from the Divine.

prin·cip·i·um (prin·sip′ē·əm) *n. pl.* **·cip·i·a** (-sip′ē·ə) **1** Beginning; origin; first principle. **2** *pl.* Fundamentals. [<L]

prin·ci·ple (prin′sə·pəl) *n.* **1** A general truth or law, basic to other truths: the *principle* of self-government. **2** A settled law or rule of personal conduct: He followed the *principle* of the Golden Rule. **3** That which is inherent in anything, determining its nature; essential character; essence. **4** A source or cause from which a thing proceeds; fundamental cause. **5** An established mode of action or operation in natural phenom-

ena: the *principle* of Archimedes. **6** *Chem.* An essential constituent of a compound or substance that gives character to it. **7** Moral standards collectively. See synonyms under DOCTRINE, LAW¹, REASON. ◆ Homophone: *principal.* [<L *principium* a beginning]

prink (pringk) To dress or (oneself) for show. — *v.i.* To dress oneself showily or fussily. [Prob. alter. of PRANK¹ under infl. of PREEN] — **prink′er** *n.*

print (print) *n.* **1** An impression with ink from type, plates, etc.; printed characters collectively; printed matter. **2** Anything printed from an engraved plate or lithographic stone; a proof; a printed picture or design. **3** A newspaper, pamphlet, or the like. **4** An impression or mark made upon or sunk into a substance by pressure; imprint. **5** A reproduction from such an impression. **6** Any fabric stamped with a design by means of dyes used on engraved rollers, wood blocks, or screens. **7** Any tool or device bearing a pattern or design, or that upon which it is impressed. **8** *Phot.* A positive picture made from a negative. **9** Newsprint. **—in print 1** Printed; also, for sale in printed form: opposed to *out of print.* **2** *Obs.* In an exact or formal manner. **—India print** Muslin printed, specifically hand blocked, with the native patterns and glowing colors of India. **—out of print** No longer on sale, the edition being exhausted. See synonyms under MARK¹, PICTURE. — *v.t.* **1** To mark, as with inked type, a stamp, die, etc. **2** To stamp or impress (a mark, seal, etc.) on or into a surface. **3** To fix as if by impressing: The scene is *printed* on my memory. **4** To produce (a book, newspaper, etc.) by the application of inked type, plates, etc., to paper or similar material. **5** To cause to be put in print; publish: The newspaper *printed* the story. **6** To write in letters similar to those used in print: Please *print* your name and address. **7** *Phot.* To produce (a positive picture) by transmitting light through a negative onto a sensitized surface. — *v.i.* **8** To be a printer. **9** To take or give an impression in printing. **10** To form letters similar to printed ones. **—to print out** To deliver (information) automatically in printed form, as a computer. See synonyms under IMPRESS¹. [<OF *preinte, priente,* fem. of pp. of *preindre* <L *premere* press] — **print′a·ble** *adj.*

print·er (prin′tər) *n.* **1** One engaged in the trade of typographical printing; one who sets type or runs a printing press; specifically, a compositor. **2** One who owns a printing establishment and employs printers. **3** One who prints, stamps, impresses, or transfers copies of anything as a business.

print·ing (prin′ting) *n.* **1** The making and issuing of matter for reading by means of type and the printing press. **2** Presswork. **3** The act of reproducing a design upon a surface by any process. **4** That which is printed.

print·out (print′out′) *n.* Material printed automatically, as by a computer.

pri·or (prī′ər) *adj.* Preceding in time, order, or importance. See synonyms under ANTECEDENT, ANTERIOR. **—prior to** Before: The theater closed *prior to* our arrival. — *n.* **1** A monastic officer next in rank below an abbot. **2** Formerly, an Italian magistrate. [<L, earlier; superior] — **pri′or·ate** (-it), **pri′or·ship** *n.*

pri·or·ess (prī′ər·is) *n.* A woman holding a position corresponding to that of a prior; a nun next in rank below an abbess.

pri·or·i·tize (prī·ôr′ə·tiz) *v.t.* **·tized, ·tiz·ing** *Colloq.* To arrange in order of priority: to *prioritize* one's goals.

pri·or·i·ty (prī·ôr′ə·tē, -or′-) *n. pl.* **·ties 1** Antecedence; precedence: opposed to *posteriority.* **2** A first right established on emergency or need: Defense plants have *priority* on steel in time of war. **3** A certificate giving this right to a manufacturer or contractor; hence, a restriction on the use of a commodity or service.

pri·or·y (prī′ər·ē) *n. pl.* **·or·ies** A monastic house presided over by a prior or prioress. See synonyms under CLOISTER. [<OF *priorie*]

prise (prīz) *n. & v.t.* Prize²; lever.

prism (priz′əm) *n.* **1** *Geom.* A solid whose bases or ends are any similar equal and parallel plane figures, and whose lateral faces are parallelograms. **2** *Optics* An instrument consisting of such a solid, usually having triangular ends and made of glass or other translucent substance, its refracting surfaces making an angle with each other. **3** Any

PRISM

medium that resolves a seemingly simple matter into its elements. **4** The spectrum. **5** *Mineral.* A crystal form consisting of three or more intersecting planes whose intersections are parallel and vertical. —**Nicol prism** A prism of calcite (Iceland spar) so cut that light emerging from it is polarized in a definite plane: used in polarizing microscopes, etc. [<LL *prisma* <Gk., something sawed < *prixein* saw]

pris·mat·ic (priz·mat'ik) *adj.* **1** Refracted or formed by a prism. **2** Resembling the spectrum; exhibiting rainbow tints. **3** Pertaining to or shaped like a prism. **4** Orthorhombic. Also **pris·mat'i·cal.** [<Gk. *prisma, prismatos*] — **pris·mat'i·cal·ly** *adv.*

pris·on (priz'ən) *n.* A place of confinement; specifically, a public building for the safekeeping of persons in legal custody; a penitentiary. —*v.t.* To imprison. [<F *prisoun* <L *praehensio, -onis* seizure < *praehensus,* pp. of *praehendere*]

pris·on-breach (priz'ən-brēch') *n.* The escape of a prisoner, against the will of his custodian, from the place where he is held in lawful custody. Also **pris'on-break'ing** (-brā'king).

pris·on·er (priz'ən·ər, -nər) *n.* **1** One who is confined in a prison or whose liberty is forcibly restrained; one held in custody; a captive; specifically, in law, a person confined in a prison by virtue of an order of arrest or of a legal committal. **2** A person confined to a place or position through some cause over which he has no control: *A sick man is a prisoner to his bed.* [<OF *prisonier*]

prison fever Malignant typhus: so called from its former prevalence in prisons: also called *ship fever.*

pris·sy (pris'ē) *adj.* **·si·er, ·si·est** Effeminate; over precise; prim. —*n.* A person who acts, dresses, or speaks very meticulously. [Blend of PRIM or PRECISE + SISSY]

pris·tine (pris'tēn, -tin; *Brit.* pris'tīn) *adj.* Of or pertaining to the earliest state or time; primitive; untouched. See synonyms under FIRST. [<L *pristinus* primitive]

pri·va·cy (prī'və·sē) *n. pl.* **·cies** **1** The condition of being private; seclusion; retirement. **2** A matter that is or should be private. **3** The state of being secret; avoidance of display or publicity; secrecy. **4** A place of seclusion; retreat. See synonyms under RETIREMENT, SECLUSION, SOLITUDE.

pri·vate (prī'vit) *adj.* **1** Removed from public view; retired; secluded; confidential; secret: a *private* parlor, a *private* agreement. **2** Personal or unofficial, as opposed to public; hence, without rank: a *private* citizen, *private* property, a *private* soldier. **3** Not common or general; special: a *private* interpretation. **4** *Obs.* Privy. See synonyms under SECRET. —*n.* **1** A soldier in the ranks. See table under GRADE. **2** *pl.* The private parts; genitals. **3** Privacy. —**in private** In secret; privately. See synonyms under SECRET. [<L *privatus* apart from the state, orig. pp. of *privare* set apart < *privus* single, one's own. Doublet of PRIVY.] —**pri'vate·ly** *adv.* —**pri'vate·ness** *n.*

private enterprise **1** Business owned and operated by private individuals, as opposed to government-owned operations. **2** An economic system based upon private ownership and operation of business. Also called *free enterprise.*

pri·va·teer (prī'və·tir') *n.* **1** A vessel owned and officered by private persons, but carrying on maritime war under letters of marque. **2** The commander or one of the crew of a

privateer: also **pri'va·teers'man.** —*v.i.* To cruise in or as a privateer. —**pri'va·teer'ing** *n.*

private first class A soldier ranking next above a private and below a corporal. See table under GRADE.

pri·va·tion (prī·vā'shən) *n.* **1** The state of lacking something necessary or desirable; especially, want of the common comforts of life. **2** Deprivation. **3** *Logic* The absence from an object of what ordinarily or naturally belongs to objects of that kind. **4** *Eccl.* Suspension or degradation from office, as of a priest. See synonyms under LOSS, POVERTY, WANT. [<OF <L *privatio, -onis* < *privare.* See PRIVATE.]

priv·a·tive (priv'ə·tiv) *adj.* **1** Causing privation, want, or destitution; depriving. **2** *Gram.* Altering a word so as to express a negative instead of a positive meaning; also, denoting negation: *privative* particles (such prefixes and suffixes as *a-, an-, in-, -less*). **3** *Logic* Noting or denoting negation or privation. —*n.* **1** That which has its only reality in the absence of something; a negative conception. **2** *Gram.* A prefix indicating negation; an adjective indicating the absence of that which is ordinarily or naturally inherent. [<L *privativus*] —**priv'a·tive·ly** *adv.* —**priv'a·tive·ness** *n.*

priv·i·lege (priv'ə·lij) *n.* **1** A special or peculiar benefit, favor, or advantage; a right or immunity enjoyed only under special conditions; a prerogative, franchise, or permission: the *privileges* of the rich. **2** A special right or power conferred on or possessed by one or more individuals, in derogation of the general right; also, the law or grant conferring it. **3** An exemption, by virtue of one's office or station, from burdens or liabilities to which others are subject: the *privilege* of a member of Congress. **4** A fundamental or specially important legal or political right: the *privilege* of voting. **5** A form of contract used by speculators, but not recognized by the exchanges, giving the holder the privilege of putting (tendering to) or calling for, or either (in which latter case the privilege is called a *straddle*), a certain number of shares of a certain stock, or a specified quantity, as of grain or provisions, under specified conditions as to time and price. Compare OPTION. **6** An advantage. See synonyms under RIGHT. —*v.t.* **·leged, ·leg·ing** **1** To grant a privilege to. **2** To exempt or free: with *from.* [<OF <L *privilegium* a piece of special legislation < *privus* one's own + *lex, legis* law]

priv·i·leged (priv'ə·lijd) *adj.* Having or invested with a privilege; enjoying a peculiar right or immunity.

priv·i·ly (priv'ə·lē) *adv.* Privately; secretly.

priv·i·ty (priv'ə·tē) *n. pl.* **·ties** **1** Knowledge shared with another or others regarding a private matter: usually implying consent or concurrence. **2** *Law* **a** A mutual or successive relationship to the same rights of property. **b** A participation in interest. **c** A relation to another founded on common knowledge. **3** *Obs.* Privacy; secrecy; a secret. [<OF *privité* <L *privus* one's own]

priv·y (priv'ē) *adj.* **1** Participating with another or others in the knowledge of a secret transaction: with *to*: *privy* to the plot. **2** *Archaic* Removed from publicity; clandestine; secret: a *privy* meeting. **3** Designed for individual or private use; personal: a *privy* purse, *privy* chamber. —*n. pl.* **priv·ies** **1** One who is concerned with another in a matter affecting the interests of both: *privies* in contract, *privies* in estate. **2** A small room or outhouse for evacuation and disposal of feces. See WATERCLOSET. [<F *privé* <L *privatus.* Doublet of PRIVATE.]

prize¹ (prīz) *n.* **1** That which is offered or won as an honor and reward for superiority or success, as in a contest; an award. **2** Anything to be striven for; a desirable acquisition; also, anything offered or won in a scheme of chance. —*adj.* **1** Offered or awarded as a prize: a *prize* medal. **2** Having drawn a prize; entitled to a prize. **3** Highly valued or esteemed. —*v.t.* **prized, priz·ing** **1** To value highly; regard as very valuable. **2** To estimate the value of; appraise. See synonyms under APPRECIATE, ESTEEM. [Var. of PRICE]

prize² (prīz) *n.* **1** In international law, prop-

erty, as a vessel and cargo, captured by a belligerent at sea in conformity with the laws of war. **2** The act of capturing; also, the person or thing captured. **3** A lever or pry; also, the hold or purchase of a lever: also spelled *prise.* —*v.t.* **prized, priz·ing** **1** To seize as a prize, as a ship. **2** To raise or force with a lever; pry: also spelled *prise.* [<F *prise* something taken, booty, orig. fem. of pp. of *prendre* take <L *praehendere* seize]

prize court A court sitting for the adjudication of prize causes. In the United States the federal courts have exclusive jurisdiction as prize courts.

prize crew A crew put on board a captured vessel by the captor, to navigate and carry her into port.

prize fight A fight between pugilists for a wager or prize, generally limited to a specified number of rounds. —**prize fighter** —**prize fighting**

pro¹ (prō) *n. pl.* **pros** **1** An argument or vote in favor of something: in the phrase *pros and cons.* **2** One who votes for or favors a proposal: usually in the plural. —*adv.* In behalf of; in favor of; for: to argue *pro* and con. [<L *pro* for]

pro² (prō) *n. pl.* **pros** *Colloq.* **1** A professional athlete. **2** An expert in any field.

pro-¹ *prefix* **1** Forward; to or toward the front from a position behind; forth: *produce,* to lead forth; *project,* to throw forth. **2** Forth from its place; away: *profugate,* to flee away. **3** To the front of; forward and down: *prolapse,* to slip forward and down. **4** Forward in time or direction: *proceed,* to go forward. **5** In front of: *prohibit,* to hold in front of. **6** In behalf of: *prolocutor.* **7** In place of; substituted for: *procathedral, proconsul.* **8** In favor of: *pro-Russian.* [<L *pro-* < *pro* before, forward, for]

pro-² *prefix* **1** Prior; occurring earlier in time: *prognosis.* **2** Situated in front; forward; before: *prognathous.* [<Gk. *pro-* < *pro* before, in front]

prob·a·bil·i·ty (prob'ə·bil'ə·tē) *n. pl.* **·ties** **1** The state or quality of being probable; likelihood; also, a probable event or statement. **2** *Stat.* The ratio of the chances favoring an event to the total number of chances for and against it. [<F *probabilité* <L *probabilitas, -tatis* < *probabilis.* See PROBABLE.]
Synonyms: chance, credibility, likelihood, likeliness, presumption, verisimilitude. *Antonyms:* doubt, dubiousness, impossibility, improbability, inconceivability, inconceivableness, unlikelihood.

prob·a·ble (prob'ə·bəl) *adj.* **1** Having more evidence than the contrary, but not proof; likely to be true or to happen, but leaving room for doubt. **2** That renders something worthy of belief, but falls short of demonstration: *probable* evidence. [<OF <L *probabilis* < *probare* prove, test]
Synonyms: credible, likely, presumable, reasonable. See APPARENT, LIKELY. *Antonyms:* doubtful, dubious, improbable, incredible, questionable, unlikely.

probable cause A state of facts to warrant the belief that an accused person committed the crime charged.

prob·a·bly (prob'ə·blē) *adv.* In all probability; so far as the evidence shows; presumably.

pro·bate (prō'bāt) *adj.* **1** Of or pertaining to a probate court. **2** Pertaining to making proof: *probate* proceedings. —*n.* **1** Formal, legal proof, as of a will. **2** The right or jurisdiction of proving wills. Compare PROBATE COURT under COURT. —*v.t.* **·bat·ed, ·bat·ing** To secure probate of, as a will. [<L *probatus,* pp. of *probare* prove]

pro·ba·tion (prō·bā'shən) *n.* **1** A proceeding designed to test character, qualifications, etc., as of candidates for holy orders; examination; trial; novitiate. **2** In criminal administration, a method of allowing a person convicted of a minor offense to go at large under suspension of sentence, but usually under the supervision of a probation officer. **3** The period throughout which a trial or examination extends. **4** The act of proving; also, proof. [<L *probatio, -onis*] —**pro·ba'tion·al, pro·ba'tion·ar'y** *adj.*

pro·ba·tion·er (prō·bā'shən·ər) *n.* **1** One on

probation or trial; a novice. **2** A candidate for membership in a church. **3** A convicted criminal or delinquent allowed to be at large but under the supervision of the convicting court and its probation officer.

probation officer A person delegated by the magistrate of a municipal criminal court to supervise an offender on suspended sentence.

pro·ba·tive (prō′bə·tiv) *adj.* **1** Serving to prove or test. **2** Pertaining to probation; proving. Also **pro·ba·to·ry** (prō′bə·tôr′ē, -tō′·rē). [<L *probativus*]

probe (prōb) *v.* **probed, prob·ing** *v.t.* **1** To explore with a probe. **2** To investigate or examine thoroughly. — *v.i.* **3** To penetrate; search. — *n.* **1** *Med.* An instrument for exploring cavities, the course of wounds, etc. **2** That which proves or tests. **3** *U.S.* An examination; a searching investigation or inquiry, especially into crime. **4** A space probe. [<L *probare* <*probus* good, proper. Doublet of PROVE.] — **prob′er** *n.*

pro·bi·ty (prō′bə·tē, prob′ə-) *n.* Virtue or integrity tested and confirmed; strict honesty. See synonyms under VIRTUE. [<F *probité* <L *probitas* <*probus* good, honest]

prob·lem (prob′ləm) *n.* **1** A perplexing question demanding settlement, especially when difficult or uncertain of solution; also, any puzzling circumstance or person. **2** *Math.* A proposition in which some operation or construction is required, as to bisect an angle; anything proposed to be worked out. See synonyms under RIDDLE². — *adj.* **1** Presenting and dealing with a problem, especially a moral, sociological, or emotional problem: *problem* drama. **2** Being a problem, especially in point of behavior, maladjustment, etc.: a *problem* child. [<L *problema* <Gk. *problēma* something thrown forward (for discussion) <*pro-* forward + *ballein* throw]

prob·lem·at·ic (prob′ləm·at′ik) *adj.* Constituting or involving a problem; questionable; contingent. Also **prob′lem·at′i·cal.** [<Gk. *problēmatikos*] — **prob′lem·at′i·cal·ly** *adv.*

pro·bos·cis (prō·bos′is) *n.* *pl.* **·bos·cis·es** or **·bos·ci·des** (-bos′ə·dēz) **1** *Zool.* A long flexible snout, as in the tapir; specifically, the trunk of an elephant. **2** *Entomol.* One of various tubular structures protruding or capable of being protruded from the front of the head of certain insects, as the combined mouth parts adapted for sucking in bees, or in certain dipterous insects, as the mosquito, the sheath and needlelike organs for piercing. **3** A human nose, especially when unusually large or prominent: a humorous use. [<L <Gk. *proboskis* <*pro-* before + *boskein* feed]

pro·ce·dure (prə·sē′jər) *n.* **1** A manner of proceeding or acting; also, an act or a special course of action. **2** The methods or forms of conducting a business, collectively. **3** *Law* The methods of conducting judicial proceedings as distinguished from the legal definition and recognition of rights. **4** A course of action; a proceeding. **5** The manner of carrying on parliamentary affairs. See synonyms under OPERATION. [<F *procédure*] — **pro·ce′du·ral** *adj.*

pro·ceed (prə·sēd′) *v.i.* **1** To go on or forward, especially after a stop or interruption. **2** To begin and carry on an action or process: He *proceeded* to strike her about the head. **3** To issue or come, as from some cause, source, or origin: with *from.* **4** *Law* To institute and carry on legal proceedings. [<OF *proceder* <L *procedere* go forward <*pro-* forward + *cedere* go] — **pro·ceed′er** *n.*

pro·ceed·ing (prə·sē′ding) *n.* **1** An act or course of action; a transaction or procedure: an outrageous *proceeding.* **2** The action of issuing forth; emanation. **3** *pl.* The records or minutes of the meetings of a society, etc. **4** *Law* **a** Any action instituted in a court: a judicial *proceeding.* **b** Any of the various steps taken in a cause by either party: a *proceeding* by writ of error. See synonyms under ACT, TRANSACTION.

pro·ceeds (prō′sēdz) *n. pl.* The useful or material results of an action or course; also, that which accrues therefrom; the amount derived from the disposal of goods, work, or the use of capital; return; yield. See synonyms under HARVEST, PRODUCT, PROFIT.

pro·ce·leus·mat·ic (pros′ə·lōōs·mat′ik) *adj.* **1** In prosody, composed of four short syl-

lables, or pertaining to feet so composed. **2** Animating or inciting, as a song. — *n.* A metrical foot of four short syllables. [<Gk. *prokeleusmatikos* <*prokeleusma* incitement <*prokeleuein* incite <*pro-* before + *keleuein* rouse]

proc·ess (pros′es, *esp. Brit.* prō′ses) *n.* **1** A course or method of operations in the production of something: a metallurgical *process.* **2** A forward movement; progressive or continuous proceeding; passage; advance; course. **3** Any judicial writ or order issued at the commencement or during the progress of an action, as summons, citation, subpoena, or execution; especially, a writ issued to bring a defendant into court; also, the whole course of proceedings in a cause, civil or criminal, from beginning to end. **4** *Biol.* An accessory outgrowth or prominence of an organism. **5** *Physiol.* The fibrous prolongation from the body of the nerve cell (neuron) that carries the outgoing nervous impulse. **6** In patent law, a means of effecting a result otherwise than by mechanism, as by chemical action. **7** *Phot.* Any of the modern methods of producing relief printing surfaces by photography and mechanical or chemical means. — *adj.* **1** Produced by a special method: *process* butter; *process* cheese. **2** Pertaining to, for, or made by, a mechanical or chemical photographic process: a *process* illustration. — *v.t.* **1** To treat or prepare by a special method. **2** *Law* a To issue or serve a process on. **b** To proceed against. [<L *processus* progress, orig. pp. of *procedere.* See PROCEED.]

processing tax A tax imposed by the government on the processing of various farm products.

pro·ces·sion (prə·sesh′ən) *n.* **1** An array, as of persons or vehicles, arranged in succession and moving in a formal manner; a parade: a funeral *procession*; also, any continuous course: the *procession* of the stars. **2** The act of proceeding or issuing forth: the *procession* of the Holy Ghost from the Father. **3** A litany or hymn sung by persons moving in orderly array; a processional. — *v.i.* To march in procession. [<OF]

Synonyms: cavalcade, column, cortège, train. *Antonyms:* herd, mob, rabble, rout.

pro·ces·sion·al (prə·sesh′ən·əl) *adj.* Of or pertaining to or moving in a procession. — *n.* **1** A book containing the services in a religious procession. **2** A hymn sung during a religious procession. — **pro·ces′sion·al·ly** *adv.*

process printing Color printing from half-tone plates each of which carries one of the primary colors, red, ′yellow, and blue, with sometimes a fourth plate for black.

process server A person, as a deputy sheriff, who serves summonses or processes.

pro·claim (prō·klām′) *v.t.* **1** To announce or make known publicly or officially; declare. **2** To make plain; manifest: His manner *proclaimed* his innocence. **3** To outlaw, prohibit, or restrict by proclamation. See synonyms under ANNOUNCE, AVOW, PUBLISH. [<OF *proclamer* <L *proclamare* <*pro-* before + *clamare* call] — **pro·claim′er** *n.*

proc·la·ma·tion (prok′lə·mā′shən) *n.* **1** The act of proclaiming. **2** That which is proclaimed; a public authoritative announcement. [<OF *proclamacion*]

pro·clit·ic (prō·klit′ik) *adj.* Attached to or dependent on a following word: said of monosyllables attached so closely as to have no separate accent. Compare ENCLITIC, ATONIC. — *n.* A proclitic word. [<NL *procliticus* <Gk. *proklinein* lean forward; formed on analogy of ENCLITIC]

pro·cliv·i·ty (prō·kliv′ə·tē) *n.* *pl.* **·ties** Natural disposition or tendency; propensity: usually with *to*: a *proclivity* to grumble. See synonyms under APPETITE, DESIRE, INCLINATION. [<L *proclivitas* <*proclivus* downward <*pro-* before + *clivus* slope]

pro·cras·ti·nate (prō·kras′tə·nāt) *v.* **·nat·ed, ·nat·ing** *v.i.* To put off taking action until a future time; be dilatory. — *v.t.* To defer or postpone. [<L *procrastinatus*, pp. of *procrastinare* <*pro-* forward + *crastinus* pertaining to the morrow <*cras* tomorrow] — **pro·cras′ti·na′tor** *n.*

Synonyms: adjourn, defer, delay, postpone. See POSTPONE. *Antonyms:* accelerate, dispatch, drive, expedite, hasten, hurry, press, quicken, urge.

pro·cras·ti·na·tion (prō·kras′tə·nā′shən) *n.* The act, tendency, or habit of procrastinating; dilatoriness; delay.

pro·cre·ant (prō′krē·ənt) *adj.* Effecting, conducive to, or connected with procreation or reproduction; generating; fruitful. [<L *procreans, -antis*]

pro·cre·ate (prō′krē·āt) *v.t.* **·at·ed, ·at·ing** **1** To engender or beget (offspring). **2** To originate; produce. See synonyms under PROPAGATE. [<L *procreatus*, pp. of *procreare* <*pro-* before + *creare* create] — **pro′cre·a′tion** *n.* — **pro′cre·a′tor** *n.*

pro·cre·a·tive (prō′krē·ā′tiv) *adj.* Possessed of generative power; reproductive; pertaining to procreation.

Pro·crus·te·an (prō·krus′tē·ən) *adj.* **1** Pertaining to or characteristic of Procrustes. **2** Hence, ruthlessly or violently forcing to conform.

Pro·crus·tes (prō·krus′tēz) In Greek mythology, an Attic giant, killed by Theseus, who tied travelers to an iron bed and amputated or stretched their limbs until they fitted it. [<L <Gk. *Prokroustēs* <*prokrouein* stretch out <*pro-* thoroughly + *krouein* beat]

procto- *combining form Med.* Related to or affecting the rectum or anus: *proctology.* Also, before vowels, **proct-.** [<Gk. *proktos* the anus]

proc·tol·o·gy (prok·tol′ə·jē) *n.* The branch of medicine which treats of the anatomy, physiology, and diseases of the rectum. [<PROCTO- + -LOGY] — **proc·to·log·i·cal** (prok′tə·loj′i·kəl) *adj.* — **proc·tol′o·gist** *n.*

proc·tor (prok′tər) *n.* **1** An agent acting for another; attorney; proxy; specifically, a practitioner in an admiralty, ecclesiastical, or probate court. **2** A university or college official charged with maintaining order, supervising examinations, etc. — *v.t.* & *v.i.* To supervise (an examination). [ME *proketour, procutour,* contraction of L *procurator* PROCURATOR] — **proc·to·ri·al** (prok·tôr′ē·əl, -tō′rē-) *adj.* — **proc′tor·ship** *n.*

proc·to·scope (prok′tə·skōp) *n.* A surgical instrument for examining the interior of the rectum. — **proc·tos·co·py** (prok·tos′kə·pē) *n.*

pro·cum·bent (prō·kum′bənt) *adj.* **1** *Bot.* Lying on the ground; trailing: said of certain vines and trailing plants. **2** Leaning forward or lying down or on the face; prone; prostrate. [<L *procumbens, -entis,* ppr. of *procumbere* lean forward <*pro-* forward + *cubare* lie down]

proc·u·ra·cy (prok′yər·ə·sē) *n. pl.* **·cies** The management of another's affairs; the office or service of a procurator or proctor.

proc·u·ra·tor (prok′yə·rā′tər) *n.* **1** A person authorized and employed to act for and manage the affairs of another. **2** In ancient Rome, one who had charge of the imperial revenues; an imperial collector, especially in a province; a provincial administrator; a viceroy. **3** The public magistrate of some Italian cities. [<L *procurare.* See PROCURE.] — **proc·u·ra·to·ri·al** (-rə·tôr′ē·əl, -tō′rē-) *adj.* — **proc·u·ra′tor·ship** *n.*

pro·cure (prō·kyōōr′) *v.* **·cured, ·cur·ing** *v.t.* **1** To obtain by some effort or means; acquire. **2** To bring about; cause. **3** To obtain (women) for the gratification of the lust of others. — *v.i.* **4** To be a procurer or procuress. See synonyms under GAIN, GET, OBTAIN, PROVIDE, PURCHASE. [<F <L *procurare* look after <*pro-* on behalf of + *curare* attend to <*cura* care]

pro·cur·er (prō·kyōōr′ər) *n.* One who procures for another, as to gratify lust; a pander. [<AF *procurour* <L *procurator*] — **pro·cur′ess** *n. fem.*

prod (prod) *v.t.* **prod·ded, prod·ding 1** To punch or poke with or as with a pointed instrument. **2** To arouse mentally; urge; goad. — *n.* **1** Any pointed instrument used for prodding; a goad. **2** A thrust or punch with or as with a prod; a poke. **3** Hence, a reminder. [Origin unknown] — **prod′der** *n.*

prod·i·gal (prod′ə·gəl) *adj.* **1** Addicted to wasteful expenditure, as of money, time, or strength; extravagant. **2** Yielding in profusion; bountiful. **3** Lavish; profuse. — *n.* One who is wasteful or profligate; a spendthrift. See synonyms under IMPROVIDENT. [<OF <Med. L *prodigalis* <L *prodigus* wasteful <*prodigere* drive forth, get rid of <*pro-* forward + *agere* drive] — **prod′i·gal·ly** *adv.*

prod·i·gal·i·ty (prod'ə·gal'ə·tē) *n. pl.* **·ties** Extravagance; wastefulness; lavishness; also, bounteousness. See synonyms under EXCESS. [< OF *prodigalité*]

pro·dig·ious (prə·dij'əs) *adj.* **1** Enormous or extraordinary in size, quantity, or degree; vast; excessive. **2** Marvelous; amazing. **3** *Obs.* Of the nature of a prodigy. See synonyms under IMMENSE. [< L *prodigiosus*] — **pro·dig'ious·ly** *adv.* —**pro·dig'ous·ness** *n.*

prod·i·gy (prod'ə·jē) *n. pl.* **·gies** **1** Something so extraordinary as to excite wonder and admiration. **2** A person or thing of remarkable qualities or powers: an infant *prodigy*. **3** Something out of the ordinary course of nature; a monstrosity. **4** *Archaic* A portent. [< L *prodigium*]

Synonyms: marvel, monster, miracle, portent, wonder.

pro·duce (prə·dōōs', -dyōōs') *v.* **·duced, ·duc·ing** *v.t.* **1** To bring forth or bear; yield, as young or a natural product. **2** To bring forth by mental effort; compose, write, etc.: to *produce* a book. **3** To bring about; cause to happen or be: His words *produced* a violent reaction. **4** To bring to view; exhibit; show: to *produce* evidence. **5** To manufacture; make. **6** To bring to performance before the public, as a play. **7** To extend or lengthen, as a line. **8** *Econ.* To create (anything with exchangeable value). —*v.i.* **9** To yield or generate an appropriate product or result.

—**prod·uce** (prod'ōōs, -yōōs, prō'dōōs, -dyōōs) *n.* That which is produced; a product; specifically, farm products collectively. See synonyms under HARVEST, PRODUCT, WEALTH. [< L *producere* lead forward < *pro-* forward + *ducere* lead]—**pro·duc'i·ble** *adj.*

Synonyms (verb): bear, breed, cause, create, effect, engender, furnish, generate, make, manufacture, occasion, originate, propagate, yield. See ALLEGE, EFFECT, PROVIDE.

prod·uct (prod'əkt, -ukt) *n.* **1** Anything produced or obtained as a result of some operation or work, as by generation, growth, labor, study, or skill. **2** *Math.* The result obtained by multiplication. **3** *Chem.* Any substance resulting from chemical change. Compare EDUCT. [< L *productus*, pp. of *producere*. See PRODUCE.]

Synonyms: crop, effect, fruit, harvest, outcome, output, proceeds, produce, production, result, return, yield. See HARVEST, WORK.

pro·duc·tile (prə·duk'til) *adj.* Capable of being extended or drawn out. [< PRO·[1] + DUCTILE]

pro·duc·tion (prə·duk'shən) *n.* **1** The act or process of producing. **2** In political economy, a producing for use, involving the creating or increasing of economic wealth: in contradistinction to *consumption* (by use). **3** That which is produced or made; any tangible result of industrial, artistic, or literary labor. [< F < L *productio, -onis* a prolongation]

Synonyms: composition, performance, work. See PRODUCT, WORK.

pro·duc·tive (prə·duk'tiv) *adj.* **1** Producing or tending to produce; fertile; creative, as of artistic things. **2** Producing or tending to produce profits or increase in quantity, quality, or value: *productive* labor. **3** Causing; resulting in: with *of*. See synonyms under FERTILE, PROFITABLE. [< Med. L *productivus* < LL, fit for production] —**pro·duc'tive·ly** *adv.* —**pro·duc·tiv·i·ty** (prō'·duk·tiv'ə·tē), **pro·duc'tive·ness** *n.*

pro·em (prō'əm) *n.* An introductory statement; preface; prelude. [< OF *proeme* < L *prooemium* < Gk. *prooimion* an overture < *pro-* before + *oimē* way of a song, lay] —**pro·e·mi·al** (prō·ē'mē·əl) *adj.*

prof·a·na·tion (prof'ə·nā'shən) *n.* **1** The act of profaning; abuse or dishonoring of sacred things; desecration. **2** Abusive or improper treatment of anything; misuse. [< F < LL *profanatio, -onis*]

pro·fane (prə·fān') *v.t.* **·faned, ·fan·ing 1** To treat (something sacred) with irreverence or abuse; desecrate; pollute. **2** To put to an unworthy or degrading use; debase. See synonyms under VIOLATE. —*adj.* **1** Manifesting irreverence, disrespect, or undue familiarity toward the Deity or sacred things; blasphemous. **2** Secular: opposed to *sacred*. **3** Not initiated into the inner myster-

ies; hence, vulgar; common. [< F *profaner* < L *profanare* < *profanus* before or outside the temple, hence, unsacred < *pro-* before + *fanum* temple] —**pro·fan·a·to·ry** (prə·fan'ə·tôr'ē, -tō'rē) *adj.* —**pro·fane'ly** *adv.* —**pro·fan'er** *n.*

Synonyms (adj.): blasphemous, godless, impious, irreligious, sacrilegious, secular, temporal, unconsecrated, ungodly, unhallowed, unholy, unsanctified, wicked, worldly. *Antonyms*: consecrated, devout, godly, holy, pious, religious, reverent, sacred, piritual.

pro·fan·i·ty (prə·fan'ə·tē) *n. pl.* **·ties 1** The state of being profane. **2** Profane speech or action. Also **pro·fane'ness** (-fān'nis). See synonyms under OATH.

pro·fess (prə·fes') *v.t.* **1** To declare openly; avow; affirm. **2** To assert, usually insincerely; make a pretense of: to *profess* remorse. **3** To declare or affirm faith in: to *profess* Taoism. **4** To claim skill or learning in; have as one's profession: to *profess* the law. **5** To receive into a religious order. —*v.i.* **6** To make open declaration; avow; offer public affirmation. **7** To take the vows of a religious order. See synonyms under ACKNOWLEDGE, AVOW, PRETEND. [< OF *professe*, fem. of *profes* bound by a vow < L *professus*, pp. of *profiteri* avow, confess < *pro-* before + *fateri* confess]

pro·fes·sion (prə·fesh'ən) *n.* **1** An occupation that properly involves a liberal education or its equivalent, and mental rather than manual labor; especially, one of the **three learned professions**, law, medicine, or theology. **2** Hence, any calling or occupation other than commercial, manual, etc., involving special attainments or discipline, as editing, music, teaching, etc.; also, the collective body of those following such vocation. **3** The act of professing or declaring; declaration; avowal: *professions* of good will. **4** That which is avowed or professed; a declaration; a faith; also, a pretense: His *professions* are not trustworthy. See synonyms under BUSINESS. [< F]

pro·fes·sion·al (prə·fesh'ən·əl) *adj.* **1** Connected with, preparing for, engaged in, appropriate, or conforming to a profession: *professional* courtesy, a *professional* soldier, a *professional* job. **2** Of or pertaining to a special occupation, often for gain: opposed to *amateur*: a *professional* ball game or player. —*n.* **1** One who pursues as a business some vocation or occupation. **2** A person who engages for money to compete in sports: opposed to *amateur*. **3** One skilled in a profession. —**pro·fes'sion·al·ly** *adv.*

pro·fes·sion·al·ism (prə·fesh'ən·əl·iz'əm) *n.* **1** The methods, manner, or spirit of a profession; also, its practitioners. **2** The practice of some profession as a business: opposed to *amateurism*.

pro·fes·sor (prə·fes'ər) *n.* **1** A teacher of the highest grade in a university or college, or in an institution where professional or technical studies are pursued; usually, an officer holding a chair in some particular branch of higher instruction. **2** One who professes skill and offers instruction in some sport or art: a *professor* of gymnastics. **3** One who makes open declaration of his opinions or sentiments; specifically, one who avows a religious faith. [< L, a public teacher < *professus*. See PROFESS.]

pro·fes·so·ri·al (prō'fə·sôr'ē·əl, -sō'rē-, prof'ə-) *adj.* Of or pertaining to a professor; pedagogic; academic. —**pro·fes·so·ri·al·ly** *adv.*

prof·fer (prof'ər) *v.t.* To offer for acceptance. —*n.* The act of proffering, or that which is proffered; a tender; offer. [< AF *proffrir*, OF *poroffrir* < *por-* (< L *pro-*) in behalf of + L *offerre*. See OFFER.] —**prof'fer·er** *n.*

pro·fi·cien·cy (prə·fish'ən·sē) *n. pl.* **·cies** An advanced state of attainment in some knowledge, art, or skill; expertise.

pro·fi·cient (prə·fish'ənt) *adj.* Thoroughly versed, as in an art or science; skilled; expert. —*n.* An expert in any branch of skill or knowledge; an adept. See synonyms under SKILFUL. [< L *proficiens, -entis*, ppr. of *proficere* make progress, go forward < *pro-* forward + *facere* do] —**pro·fi'cient·ly** *adv.*

pro·file (prō'fīl, *esp. Brit.* prō'fēl) *n.* **1** An outline, or contour; a drawing in outline. **2** *Archit.* The outline of a perpendicular section of a building, fort, etc., or the con-

tour of an architectural member, as a base or cornice. **3** A drawing showing the outline of a human face or figure as seen from the side. **4** A short biographical sketch vividly presenting the most striking characteristics of a personality. **5** Degree of exposure to public attention; public image: The army generals who seized control maintained a very low *profile*. **6** A vertical section of soil extending from the surface through all its levels to the underlying parent material. —*v.t.* **filed, fil·ing 1** To draw a profile of; outline. **2** To write a profile of. [< Ital. *profilo, proffilo* outline < *proffilare* draw in outline < L *pro-* forward + *filum* thread, line]

PROFILE OF GRAND CANYON AND KAIBAB PLATEAU

prof·it (prof'it) *n.* **1** Any accession of good—physical, mental, or moral—from labor or exertion; benefit; return. **2** Often *pl.* Excess of returns over outlay or expenditure: a business yielding fair *profits*. **3** The return from the employment of capital after deducting the amount paid for raw material and for wages, real or estimated rent, interest, insurance, etc. **4** That part of the amount received for goods which exceeds the sum originally paid for them with or without all secondary expenses involved. **5** The income of invested property without 'counting its increased value by any actual rise in the market. **6** In invested capital, the ratio of the increment to the actual amount of capital for a given year. —**gross profit** The profit apparent on the face of a transaction or business; the excess of receipts from sales over expenditures for purchase: opposed to **net profit**, the surplus remaining after all necessary deductions, as for interest, transportation, bad debts, etc. —*v.i.* **1** To be of advantage or benefit. **2** To derive gain or benefit. —*v.t.* **3** To be of profit or advantage to. ♦ Homophone: *prophet*. [< OF < L *profectus*, pp. of *proficere* go forward. See PROFICIENT.]

Synonyms (noun): advantage, avail, benefit, emolument, expediency, gain, good, improvement, proceeds, receipts, return, returns, service, utility, value. The *returns* or *receipts* include all that is received from any outlay or investment; the *profit* is the excess (if any) of the *receipts* over the outlay; hence, in government, morals, etc., the *profit* is what is really good, helpful, useful, valuable. *Utility* is chiefly used in the sense of some immediate or personal and generally some material *good*. *Advantage* is that which gives one a vantage ground, either for coping with competitors or with difficulties, needs, or demands; as, to have the *advantage* of a good education; it is frequently used of what one has beyond another or secures at the expense of another; as, to have the *advantage* in argument, or to take *advantage* in a bargain. *Gain* is what one secures beyond what he previously possessed. *Benefit* is anything that does one good. *Emolument* is *profit, return*, or *value* accruing through official position. *Expediency* has respect to *profit* or *advantage*, real or supposed, considered apart from or perhaps in opposition to right, in actions having a moral character. See UTILITY. *Antonyms*: damage, detriment, disadvantage, harm, hurt, injury, loss, ruin, waste.

prof·it·a·ble (prof'it·ə·bəl) *adj.* Bringing profit or gain; remunerative; advantageous. —**prof'it·a·ble·ness** *n.* —**prof'it·a·bly** *adv.*

Synonyms: advantageous, beneficial, desirable, expedient, gainful, lucrative, productive, remunerative, useful. See EXPEDIENT, GOOD, USEFUL. Compare synonyms for PROFIT. *Antonyms*: detrimental, disadvantageous, disastrous, fruitless, harmful, hurtful, undesirable, unproductive, unprofitable, worthless.

prof·i·teer (prof′ə·tir′) v.i. To seek or obtain excessive profits. —n. One who is given to making excessive profits, especially to the detriment of others. —**prof′i·teer′ing** n.

prof·it–shar·ing (prof′it–shâr′ing) n. A system of remuneration by which workmen are given a percentage, according to wages, of the net profits of a business. —adj. Of or related to profit–sharing.

prof·li·ga·cy (prof′lə·gə·sē) n. 1 Corruptness of morals; viciousness of character or conduct. 2 Great extravagance; wastefulness; overabundance. Also **prof′li·gate·ness** (-git·nis, -gāt′nis).

prof·li·gate (prof′lə·git, -gāt) adj. 1 Lost or insensible to principle, virtue, or decency; abandoned to vice. 2 Recklessly extravagant; in great profusion. —n. 1 A depraved or dissolute person. 2 A reckless spendthrift. See synonyms under IMMORAL. [<L profligatus, pp. of profligare strike to the ground, destroy <pro- forward + fligere dash] — **prof′li·gate·ly** adv.

prof·lu·ent (prof′lōō·ənt) adj. Fluent. [<L profluens, -entis, ppr. of profluere flow along <pro- before + fluere flow] — **prof′lu·ence** n.

pro·found (prə·found′) adj. 1 Intellectually deep; thorough; exhaustive: profound learning. 2 Reaching to, arising from, or affecting the depth of one's nature or of any matter: profound respect. 3 Situated far below the surface; deep; unfathomable. 4 Bent low: said of a bow. —n. 1 A fathomless depth; an abyss. 2 The ocean; the deep. See synonyms under OBSCURE, WISE. [<OF profond <L profundus <pro- very + fundus deep] — **pro·found′ly** adv. — **pro·found′ness** n.

pro·fuse (prə·fyōōs′) adj. 1 Giving or given forth lavishly; liberal; extravagant; prodigal. 2 Copious; overflowing: profuse vegetation. [<L profusus, pp. of profundere pour forth <pro- forward + fundere pour] — **pro·fuse′ly** adv. — **pro·fuse′ness** n.

pro·fu·sion (prə·fyōō′zhən) n. 1 A lavish supply or condition; plenty: a profusion of ornaments. 2 The act of pouring forth or supplying in great abundance; prodigality: profusion in giving. See synonyms under EXCESS. [<F]

pro·gen·i·tor (prō·jen′ə·tər) n. A forefather or parent. [<L <progenitus, pp. of progignere beget <pro- forth + gignere beget] — **pro·gen′i·tor·ship**′ n.

prog·e·ny (proj′ə·nē) n. pl. ·nies Offspring. [<L progenies <progignere. See PROGENITOR.]

prog·na·thous (prog′nə·thəs, prog·nā′-) adj. Having projecting jaws: opposed to opisthognathous. Also **prog·nath·ic** (prog·nath′ik). [<PRO-² + -GNATHOUS] — **prog·na·thism** (prog′nə·thiz′əm), **prog·na·thy** (prog′nə·thē) n.

prog·no·sis (prog·nō′sis) n. pl. ·ses (-sēz) 1 Med. A prediction or conclusion in regard to the course and termination of a disease. 2 Any prediction or forecast; foreknowledge. [<NL <Gk. prognōsis <pro- before + gignōskein know]

prog·nos·ti·cate (prog·nos′tə·kāt) v.t. ·cat·ed, ·cat·ing 1 To foretell (future events, etc.) by present indications. 2 To indicate beforehand; foreshadow. See synonyms under AUGUR, PROPHESY. [<Med. L prognosticatus, pp. of prognosticare <L prognosticum. See PROGNOSTIC.] — **prog·nos′ti·ca′tor** n.

pro·gram (prō′gram, -grəm) n. 1 A list giving in order the items, turns, selections, etc., making up an entertainment; also, the selections, etc., collectively. 2 Any prearranged plan or course of proceedings; a prospectus. 3 Electronics A sequence of instructions set up on the control panels of an electronic computer as guides in the performance of a desired operation or group of operations. 4 A preface, or prefatory statement. 5 Obs. A public proclamation; official edict or decree. Also Brit. **pro′gramme.** —v.t. ·gramed or ·grammed, ·gram·ing or ·gram·ming 1 To arrange in an appropriate sequence the separate items of (a program, set of instructions, etc.). 2 To schedule (an act, performer, etc.) for a program. 3 To furnish a program for (a computer). 4 To feed (information, instructions, etc.) into a computer. [<F programme <LL programma public announcement <Gk. <prographein write in public < pro- before + graphein write] — **pro′gram·er** or **pro′gram·mer** n. — **pro·gram·mat·ic** (prō′grə·mat′ik) adj.

programed instruction Instruction in which the learner responds to a prearranged series of questions, items, or statements, using various printed texts, audio–visual means, or a teaching machine. Also **programmed instruction.**

prog·ress (prog′res, esp. Brit. prō′gres) n. 1 A moving forward in space; movement forward nearer a goal. 2 Advancement toward maturity or completion; gradual development, as of mankind or civilization; improvement. 3 A journey of state, as of a monarch.
—**pro·gress** (prə·gres′) v.i. 1 To move forward or onward. 2 To advance toward completion or fuller development. [<OF progres <L progressus, pp. of progredi go forward <pro- forward + gradi walk]
Synonyms (noun): advance, advancement, attainment, development, growth, improvement, increase, proficiency, progression. Attainment, development, and proficiency are more absolute than the other words of the group, denoting some point of advantage or of comparative perfection reached by forward or onward movement; we speak of attainments in scholarship, proficiency in music or languages, the development of new powers or organs; proficiency includes the idea of skill. Advance denotes a forward movement or the point gained by forward movement; progress (Latin progredior, walk forward) is steady and constant forward movement, admitting of pause, but not of retreat. Compare ATTAIN. Antonyms: check, decline, delay, retreat, recession, retrogression, stay, stop, stoppage.

pro·gres·sion (prə·gresh′ən) n. 1 The act of progressing; advancement. 2 Math. A sequence of numbers or quantities each of which is derived from the preceding by a constant law. See ARITHMETIC PROGRESSION, GEOMETRIC PROGRESSION, SERIES (def. 2). 3 Music a An advance from one tone or chord to another. b A sequence or succession of tones or chords. 4 Course or lapse of time; passage. See synonyms under PROGRESS. [<L progressio, -onis] — **pro·gres′sion·al** adj. — **pro·gres′sion·ism** n.

pro·gres·sion·ist (prə·gresh′ən·ist) n. 1 One who believes that society is progressing toward perfection. 2 An evolutionist.

pro·gres·sive (prə·gres′iv) adj. 1 Moving forward; advancing; progressive movement; also, moving forward gradually or step by step. 2 Aiming at or characterized by progress. 3 Spreading from one part to others; increasing: said of a disease: progressive paralysis. 4 Striving for or favoring progress or reform, especially social, political, educational or religious: a progressive party, progressive schools. 5 Gram. Designating an aspect of the verb which expresses the action as being in progress at some time in the past, present, or future: formed with any tense of the auxiliary be and the present participle; as, He is speaking; he had been speaking; he was to have been speaking; he will be speaking. See synonyms under GRADUAL. —n. 1 One who believes in progress or progressive methods; especially, one who favors or promotes reforms or changes, as in politics or religion; a radical: opposed to conservative or reactionary. 2 Gram. A progressive verb form. — **pro·gres′sive·ly** adv. — **pro·gres′sive·ness** n. — **pro·gres′siv·ism** n. — **pro·gres′siv·ist** n.

pro·hib·it (prō·hib′it) v.t. 1 To forbid, especially by authority or law; interdict. 2 To prevent or hinder. [<L prohibitus, pp. of prohibere <pro- before + habere have] — **pro·hib′it·er** n.
Synonyms: debar, disallow, forbid, hinder, inhibit, interdict, preclude, prevent. Debar is said of persons; disallow of acts; one is debarred from anything when shut off by authority or necessity; an act is disallowed by the authority that might have allowed it. Forbid is less formal and more personal, prohibit more official and judicial, with the implication of readiness to use force; a parent forbids a child to take part in some game or to associate with certain companions; the opium trade is now prohibited by the leading nations of the world. Many things are prohibited by law which cannot be wholly prevented, as gambling and prostitution; on the other hand, things may be prevented which are not prohibited, as the services of religion, the payment of bets or military conquest. Compare ABOLISH, HINDER, PREVENT, SHUT.

Antonyms: allow, authorize, command, direct, empower, enjoin, let, license, order, permit, require, sanction, suffer, tolerate, vouchsafe, warrant.

pro·hi·bi·tion (prō′ə·bish′ən) n. 1 The act of prohibiting, preventing, or stopping; also, a decree or order forbidding anything; an interdiction. 2 The forbidding of the manufacture, transportation, and sale of alcoholic liquors as beverages: instituted in the United States effective January 16, 1920. See synonyms under BARRIER, ORDER. [<L prohibitio, -onis]

Prohibition Amendment The Eighteenth Amendment to the Constitution of the United States, ratified January 1919, prohibiting the manufacture, sale, or transportation of intoxicating liquors for beverage purposes: repealed in 1933. Compare VOLSTEAD ACT.

Pro·hi·bi·tion·ist (prō′ə·bish′ən·ist) n. 1 One who believes in prohibition. 2 One who favors the prohibition by law of the manufacture and sale of alcoholic liquors as beverages.

pro·hib·i·tive (prō·hib′ə·tiv) adj. Prohibiting or tending to prohibit. Also **pro·hib′i·to·ry** (-tôr′ē, -tō′rē). — **pro·hib′i·tive·ly** adv.

proj·ect (proj′ekt) n. 1 Something proposed or mapped out in the mind, as a course of action; a plan. 2 In schools, a problem involving the theory of the subject matter, given to a student or group of students to be worked out in practice.
—**pro·ject** (prə·jekt′) v.t. 1 To cause to extend forward or out. 2 To throw forth or forward, as missiles. 3 To visualize as an external reality: to project an image of one's destiny. 4 To cause (an image, shadow, etc.) to fall on a surface. 5 To propose or plan. 6 Math. a To make a projection of (a solid, etc.) on a plane. b To reproduce (a figure) by drawing lines from a vertex through every point (of the figure) to the corresponding point of the reproduction. — v.i. 7 To extend forward or out; protrude. See synonyms under PLAN, THROW. [<L projectus, pp. of projicere throw out, cause to protrude <pro- before + jacere throw]
Synonyms (noun): contrivance, design, device, invention, plan, purpose, scheme.

pro·jec·tile (prə·jek′təl) adj. 1 Projecting, or impelling forward. 2 Capable of being or intended to be projected or shot forth. 3 Protrusile. —n. 1 A body projected or thrown forth by force. 2 Mil. A missile for discharge from a gun or cannon. [<F]

ARMOR–PIERCING PROJECTILE
a. Windshield.
b. Armor–piercing cap.
c. Body.
d. Bursting charge.
e. Bourrelet.
f. Copper rotating band.
g. Fuze.
h. Plug.

pro·jec·tion (prə·jek′shən) n. 1 The act of projecting; a jutting, throwing, or shooting out or forth. 2 That which projects; a prominence; projecting part or subject. 3 A scheme; project. 4 A system of lines drawn on a given fixed plane, as in a map, which represents, point for point, a corresponding system of imaginary lines on a given terrestrial or celestial datum surface: when used in delineating part of the earth's surface, called a map projection. 5 Psychol. The process or result of externalizing or objectifying a perception or mental image: compare INTROJECTION. 6 The exhibiting of motion pictures or lantern slides upon a screen. [<F <L projectio, -onis] — **pro·jec′tion·al** adj.

pro·jec·tion·ist (prə·jek′shən·ist) n. 1 One who projects. 2 The operator of motion–picture and sound–reproducing equipment.

pro·jec·tor (prə·jek′tər) n. 1 One who devises projects; a schemer; a promoter. 2 That which projects something. 3 A mirror or combination of lenses for projecting a beam of light. 4 An apparatus for throwing illuminated images or motion pictures upon a screen. 5 A device for throwing grenades, bombs, etc.

pro·late (prō′lāt) adj. 1 Extended lengthwise.

2 Lengthened toward the poles, as a spheroid generated by the revolution of an ellipse around its long axis: opposed to *oblate*. [<L *prolatus*, pp. to *proferre* extend, carry forward < *pro-* forward + *ferre* carry]

pro·leg (prō′leg) *n. Entomol.* One of the abdominal legs of insect larvae, as of caterpillars. [<PRO-¹ + LEG]

pro·le·gom·e·non (prō′lə·gom′ə·non) *n. pl.* **·na** (-nə) *Often pl.* An introductory remark or remarks; a preface. [<Gk., neut. passive ppr. of *prolegein* say beforehand < *pro-* before + *legein* say] —**pro′le·gom′e·nous** *adj.*

pro·lep·sis (prō·lep′sis) *n. pl.* **·ses** (-sēz) **1** Anticipation. **2** A rhetorical figure consisting in the anticipation, and answering or nullifying beforehand, of objections or opposing arguments. **3** The use of an adjective or a noun as an objective predicate in anticipation of the result of the verbal action: to shoot a person *dead*. **4** An error by which a date earlier than the true date is assigned to an event. [<L <Gk. *prolēpsis* anticipation < *prolambanein* take beforehand < *pro-* before + *lambanein* seize, take] —**pro·lep′tic** (-tik) or **·ti·cal** *adj.*

pro·le·tar·i·an (prō′lə·târ′ē·ən) *adj.* **1** Formerly, of or pertaining to the lower classes of society. **2** Of or pertaining to proletarians or the proletariat. —*n.* **1** Formerly, a person of the lowest or poorest class. **2** A laborer; a wageworker. [<L *proletarius* < *proles* offspring; so called because, being propertyless, they served the state only by having children] —**pro′le·tar′i·an·ism** *n.*

pro·le·tar·i·at (prō′lə·târ′ē·ət) *n.* **1** Formerly, the indigent classes collectively of a community; the lower classes. **2** Wageworkers collectively, regarded as the creators of wealth; workingmen. **3** *Bot.* Self-pollinated plants having a small or limited reserve of food materials. [<F *prolétariat.* See PROLETARIAN.]

pro·li·cide (prō′lə·sīd) *n.* The crime of killing one's own child, before or after birth; infanticide. [<L *proles* offspring + -CIDE]

pro·lif·er·ate (prō·lif′ə·rāt) *v.t. & v.i.* **·at·ed, ·at·ing** To produce, reproduce, or grow, especially with rapidity, as cells in tissue formation. [<PROLIFER(OUS) + -ATE¹] —**pro·lif′er·a′tion** *n.* —**pro·lif′er·a′tive** *adj.*

pro·lif·er·ous (prō·lif′ər·əs) *adj.* **1** Producing offspring freely. **2** Producing branchlets; as a coral. **3** *Bot.* Having an excessive development of parts; developing buds, branches, and flowers from unusual places; bearing progeny in the way of offshoots, buds, etc. [<Med. L *prolifer* <L *proles, prolis* offspring + *ferre* bear]

pro·lif·ic (prō·lif′ik) *adj.* **1** Producing abundantly, as offspring or fruit; fertile. **2** Producing results abundantly; creative: a *prolific* writer. See synonyms under FERTILE. [<F *prolifique* <Med. L *prolificus* <L *proles, prolis* offspring + stem of *facere* make] —**pro·lif′i·ca·cy** (-i·kə·sē), **pro·lif′ic·ness** *n.* —**pro·lif′i·cal·ly** *adv.*

pro·lix (prō′liks, prō·liks′) *adj.* **1** Unduly long and verbose, as an address. **2** Indulging in long and wordy discourse; tedious: a *prolix* orator. [<F *prolixe* <L *prolixus* extended < *pro-* before + stem of *liquere* flow] —**pro·lix·i·ty** (prō·lik′sə·tē), **pro′lix·ness** *n.* —**pro′lix·ly** *adv.*

pro·loc·u·tor (prō·lok′yə·tər) *n.* **1** One who speaks for another; a spokesman or advocate. **2** The presiding officer of a convocation; specifically, the speaker or chairman of the lower house of convocation in the Church of England. [<L < *prolocutus,* pp. of *proloqui* declare, speak for < *pro-* in behalf of + *loqui* talk]

pro·log (prō′lôg, -log) *n.* A prefatory statement to a poem, discourse, or performance; specifically, an introduction, often in verse, spoken or sung by an actor before a play or opera; hence, any anticipatory act or event. —*v.t.* To introduce with a prolog or preface. Also **pro′logue.** [<OF *prologue* <L *prologus* <Gk. *prologos* < *pro-* before + *logos* discourse]

pro·long (prə·lông′, -long′) *v.t.* To extend in time or space; continue; lengthen. See synonyms under INCREASE, PROTRACT. Also **pro·lon′gate** (-lông′gāt, -long′-). [<OF *prolonguer* <L *prolongare* < *pro-* forth + *longus* long] —**pro·long′er** *n.* —**pro·long′ment** *n.*

pro·lon·ga·tion (prō′lông·gā′shən, -long-) *n.* **1** The act of prolonging. **2** That by which anything is increased; an extension. [<F]

pro·lu·sion (prō·lōō′zhən) *n.* **1** That which is introductory to the principal effort or performance; a preliminary attempt; a prolog; prelude. **2** An essay written as a test of the writer's powers, or as preliminary to a more elaborate treatise. [<L *prolusio, -onis* prelude < *prolusus,* pp. of *proludere* play beforehand < *pro-* before + *ludere* play]

prom (prom) *n. U.S. Colloq.* A formal college or school dance or ball: short for *promenade*.

prom·e·nade (prom′ə·nād′, -näd′) *n.* **1** A walk for amusement or exercise, or as part of a formal or social entertainment. **2** A ceremonious parade on horseback or in a vehicle. **3** A place for promenading. **4** A concert or ball opened with a formal march; also, the march. —*v.* **·nad·ed, ·nad·ing** *v.i.* **1** To take a promenade. —*v.t.* **2** To take a promenade through or along. **3** To take or exhibit on or as on a promenade; parade. [<F < *promener* take for a walk <L *prominare* drive forward < *pro-* before + *minare* drive (cattle)] —**prom′e·nad′er** *n.*

Pro·me·theus (prə·mē′thē·əs) In Greek mythology, a Titan who stole fire from heaven for mankind and as a punishment was chained to a rock, where an eagle daily devoured his liver, which was made whole again at night: he was released by Hercules.

prom·i·nence (prom′ə·nəns) *n.* **1** The state of being prominent; conspicuousness; fame. **2** That which is prominent; a protuberance.

prom·i·nent (prom′ə·nənt) *adj.* **1** Jutting out; projecting; protuberant. **2** Conspicuous in position, character, or importance. **3** Eminent. See synonyms under EMINENT, IMPORTANT. [<L *prominens, -entis,* ppr. of *prominere* project] —**prom′i·nent·ly** *adv.*

pro·mis·cu·i·ty (prō′mis·kyōō′ə·tē, prom′is-) *n.* **1** Condition or state of being promiscuous; indiscriminate or confused mixture. **2** Promiscuous sexual union.

pro·mis·cu·ous (prə·mis′kyōō·əs) *adj.* **1** Composed of individuals or things confusedly mingled. **2** Unrestricted in distribution or application; exercised or shared without discrimination. **3** Indiscriminate; not fastidious, especially in sexual relations. **4** *Colloq.* Lacking plan or purpose; casual; irregular. [<L *promiscuus* mixed < *pro-* thoroughly + stem of *miscere* mix] —**pro·mis′cu·ous·ly** *adv.* —**pro·mis′cu·ous·ness** *n.*

prom·ise (prom′is) *n.* **1** An assurance given by one person to another that the former will or will not do a specified act. **2** Reasonable ground for hope or expectation, especially of future excellence or satisfaction; a youth of great *promise*. **3** Something promised; the fulfilment or obtainment of that which is promised. See synonyms under CONTRACT. —*v.* **·ised, ·is·ing** *v.t.* **1** To engage or pledge by a promise: used with the infinitive or a clause: He *promised* that he would do it. **2** To make a promise of (something) to someone. **3** To give reason for expecting: The sky *promised* rain. **4** *Colloq.* To assure (someone). —*v.i.* **5** To make a promise. **6** To give reason for expectation: often with *well* or *fair*. [<F *promesse* <L *promissum,* pp. of *promittere* send forward < *pro-* forth + *mittere* send] —**prom′is·er** *n.*

prom·is·ing (prom′is·ing) *adj.* Giving promise of good results or development. See synonyms under AUSPICIOUS. —**prom′is·ing·ly** *adv.*

prom·is·so·ry (prom′ə·sôr′ē, -sō′rē) *adj.* **1** Containing or of the nature of a promise; expressing an engagement to pay: a *promissory* note. **2** Indicating what is to be required or to take place after the signing of an insurance contract. Compare WARRANTY. [<Med. L *promissorius*]

promissory note A written promise by one person to pay another unconditionally a certain sum of money at a specified time: also called *note of hand*.

prom·on·to·ry (prom′ən·tôr′ē, -tō′rē) *n. pl.* **·ries** **1** A high point of land extending into the sea; headland. **2** *Anat.* A rounded projection or part. [<LL *promontorium* <L *promunturium,* ? < *prominere.* See PROMINENT.]

pro·mote (prə·mōt′) *v.t.* **·mot·ed, ·mot·ing** **1** To contribute to the progress, development, or growth of; further; encourage. **2** To advance to a higher position, grade, or honor. **3** To work in behalf of; advocate actively: to *promote* social reforms. **4** In education, to advance (a pupil) to the next higher school grade. [<L *promotus,* pp. of *promovere* move forward < *pro-* forward + *movere* move]
Synonyms: advance, aid, assist, elevate, encourage, exalt, excite, foment, forward, foster, further, help, prefer, raise. We *promote* a person by *advancing, elevating,* or *exalting* him to a higher position or dignity. A person *promotes* a scheme or an enterprise which others have projected or begun, and which he *encourages, forwards, furthers,* especially when he acts as the agent of the prime movers of the enterprise. One who *excites* a quarrel originates it; to *promote* a quarrel is strictly to *foment* it, the one who *promotes* keeping himself in the background. See ABET, ENCOURAGE, QUICKEN, SERVE. *Antonyms:* see synonyms for ABASE, ALLAY.

pro·mot·er (prə·mō′tər) *n.* **1** One who or that which promotes. **2** One who assists (by securing capital, etc.) in promoting a financial or commercial enterprise, or who makes this his regular business. **3** *Chem.* A substance used to increase the action of a catalyst. See synonyms under AGENT, AUXILIARY.

pro·mo·tion (prə·mō′shən) *n.* **1** Advancement or preferment in honor, dignity, rank or grade. **2** Furtherance; encouragement. **3** The act of promoting. **4** The state of being promoted. —**pro·mo′tion·al** *adj.*

prompt (prompt) *v.t.* **1** To incite to action; instigate. **2** To suggest or inspire (an act, thought, etc.). **3** To remind of what has been forgotten or of what comes next; give a cue to. —*v.i.* **4** To give help or suggestions. See synonyms under ACTUATE, ENCOURAGE, INFLUENCE, STIR¹. —*adj.* **1** Acting, or ready to act, at the moment; quick to respond or decide; punctual. **2** Done or rendered with readiness or alacrity; taking place at the appointed time. See synonyms under ACTIVE, ALERT, NIMBLE. —*n.* **1** A term of credit allowed for the payment of a debt as stated in a prompt-note. **2** An act of prompting; also, the information imparted by prompting; a reminder. [<OF <L *promptus* brought forth, hence, at hand, pp. of *promere* < *pro-* forth + *emere* take] —**prompt′ly** *adv.* —**prompt′ness** *n.*

prompt·book (prompt′book′) *n.* An annotated script of a play used by a prompter or director.

prompt·er (promp′tər) **1** In a theater, one who follows the lines and prompts the actors. **2** One who or that which prompts.

promp·ti·tude (promp′tə·tōōd, -tyōōd) *n.* The quality, habit, or fact of being prompt; promptness. [<F]

pro·mul·gate (prō·mul′gāt, prom′əl·gāt) *v.t.* **·gat·ed, ·gat·ing** To make known or announce officially and formally; put into effect by public proclamation, as a law or dogma. See synonyms under ANNOUNCE, PUBLISH, SPREAD. [<L *promulgatus,* pp. of *promulgare* make known, prob. alter. of *provulgare* < *pro-* forth + *vulgus* the people] —**pro·mul·ga·tion** (prō′mul·gā′shən, prom′əl-) *n.* —**pro·mul·ga·tor** (prō·mul′gā·tər, prom′əl-) *n.*

prone (prōn) *adj.* **1** Lying flat, especially with the face, front, or palm downward; prostrate: opposed to *supine*. **2** Leaning forward or downward; also, moving or sloping sharply downward. **3** Mentally inclined or predisposed: with *to*. See synonyms under ADDICTED, SUBJECT. [<L *pronus* prostrate < *pro-* before] —**prone′ly** *adv.* —**prone′ness** *n.*

prong·horn (prông′hôrn′, prong′-) *n. pl.* **·horns** or **·horn** A ruminant (*Antilocapra americana*) of western North America, having deciduous branched horns; the Rocky Mountain antelope: not a true antelope.

PRONGHORN
(About 3 feet high
at the shoulder)

pronominal adjective The possessive case of a personal pronoun used attributively: *my, your, his, her, its, our, their, whose,* and, poetically, *mine* and *thine.*

pro·noun (prō'noun) *n.* A word used as a substitute for a noun, as *he, she, that.* [<OF *pronom* <L *pronomen* < *pro-* in place of + *nomen* name, noun]
— **adjective pronoun** Any pronoun used like an adjective; as, *that* boy, *this* house, *which* man. Any demonstrative pronoun, any indefinite pronoun (except *none*), and any interrogative and relative pronoun (except *who*) may be used as an adjective pronoun.
— **demonstrative pronoun** A pronoun that directly points out its antecedents.

Singular	Plural
this	these
that	those

The same forms are used for all genders, persons, and cases.
— **indefinite pronoun** A pronoun that represents an object indefinitely or generally. The principal indefinite pronouns are *another, any, both, each, either, none, one, other, some, such. None* and *any* are both singular and plural.
— **interrogative pronoun** A pronoun that is used to ask a question.

Singular	Subjective	Possessive	Objective
	who	whose	whom
and	which	whose, of	which
		which	
Plural	what	of what	what

Of what occurs in such sentences as *Of what are you speaking? What are you speaking of?*
— **personal pronoun** A pronoun that shows by its form the person speaking, the person spoken to, or the person or thing spoken of.

Singular	Subjective	Possessive	Objective
1st person	I	my *or* mine	me
2nd person	you	your *or* yours	you
	(thou)	(thy *or* thine)	(thee)
3rd person			
masculine	he	his	him
feminine	she	her *or* hers	her
neuter	it	its	it
Plural:			
1st person	we	our *or* ours	us
2nd person	you (ye)	your *or* yours	you
3rd person	they	their *or* theirs	them

— **reflexive pronoun** A pronoun formed by adding *-self* or *-selves* to the oblique cases of the personal pronoun. They serve as an intensive: I, *myself*, was there; or a reference back to a personal pronoun where the same person is both subject and object: He hit *himself.*

	Singular	Plural
1st person	myself	ourselves
2nd person	yourself	yourselves
3rd person	himself, her-	themselves
	self, itself	

— **relative pronoun** A pronoun that relates to an antecedent and introduces a qualifying clause: We found a boatman *who* ferried us.

Subjective	Possessive	Objective
who	whose	whom
which	of which	which
what	of what	what
that		that

Sometimes *as* and *but* are regarded as relative pronouns: Such men *as* survived the accident; There is not a man *but* remembers that day. ◆ The relative pronouns *who* (with its inflected forms *whose* and *whom*), *which*, and *what*, are identical in form with the interrogative pronouns but they undergo shifts of meaning in interrogative use, often being indefinite and general in reference: *What* (if anything or of all possible things) is he talking about? But: He is talking about *what* (specifically) he knows best. These pronouns, when used to introduce an indirect question, are by nature both relative and interrogative: They asked *what* he wanted; *whom* he preferred as a colleague; *which* party he belonged to. Similarly, *that* is not only a demonstrative but a relative pronoun and it makes a specific and limiting reference in either use.

pro·nounce (prə·nouns') *v.* ·nounced, ·nounc·ing *v.t.* **1** To utter or deliver officially or solemnly; proclaim. **2** To assert; declare, especially as one's judgment: The judge *pronounced* her insane. **3** To give utterance to; articulate (words, etc.). **4** To articulate in a

prescribed manner. **5** To indicate the sound of (a word) by phonetic symbols. — *v.i.* **6** To make a pronouncement or assertion. **7** To articulate words; speak. See synonyms under ASSERT, SPEAK. [<OF *pronuncier* <LL *pronunciare* <L *pronuntiare* proclaim < *pro-* forth + *nuntiare* announce] — **pro·nounce'a·ble** *adj.* — **pro·nounc'er** *n.*

pro·nounced (prə·nounst') *adj.* Of marked character; decided.

pro·nounc·ing (prə·noun'sing) *adj.* Pertaining to or serving as a guide in pronunciation.

pron·to (pron'tō) *adv. U.S. Slang* Quickly; promptly; instantly. [<Sp. <L *promptus.* See PROMPT.]

pro·nun·ci·a·men·to (prə·nun'sē·ə·men'tō, -shē·ə-) *n. pl.* ·**tos** A public announcement; proclamation; manifesto. [<Sp. *pronunciamiento,* lit., a pronouncement <L *pronuntiare.* See PRONOUNCE.]

pro·nun·ci·a·tion (prə·nun'sē·ā'shən) *n.* The act or manner of pronouncing words; articulation. [<L *pronunciatio, -onis* < *pronuntiatus,* pp. of *pronuntiare.* See PRONOUNCE.]

proof (proof) *n.* **1** The act or process of proving, in any sense; specifically, the establishment of a fact by evidence or a truth by other truths. **2** A trial of strength, truth, fact, or excellence, etc.; a test. **3** Evidence and argument sufficient to induce belief. **4** *Law* Anything that serves to convince the mind of the truth or falsity of a fact or proposition, including facts and admissions of parties, which are properly called *evidence,* and presumptions either of fact or of law, and citations of law. **5** The state or quality of having successfully undergone a proof or test; impenetrability; also, impenetrable armor. **6** The standard of strength of alcoholic liquors: see PROOF SPIRIT. **7** *Printing* A printed trial sheet showing the contents or condition of matter in type or of a plate, or the like, either with or without marked corrections. **8** In engraving and etching, a trial impression taken from an engraved plate, stone, or block; also, a perfect impression from such a plate, etc., when finished, and usually before the title or inscription has been added. **9** *Phot.* A trial print from a negative. **10** *Math.* A process to check a computation by using its result; also, a demonstration. **11** Anything proved true; experience. **12** In philately, an experimental printing of a stamp. — *adj.* **1** Employed in or connected with proving or correcting. **2** Capable of resisting successfully; firm; impenetrable: with *against: proof* against bribes. **3** Of standard alcoholic strength, as liquors. [<OF *prueve* <LL *proba* < *probare* PROVE]

Synonyms (noun): attestation, certification, confirmation, demonstration, essay, evidence, fact, ordeal, test, testimony, trial. See CERTAINTY, DEMONSTRATION, TESTIMONY. *Antonyms:* assertion, conjecture, disproof, failure, fallacy, fancy, hypothesis, imagination, likelihood, possibility, presumption, probability, refutation.

-proof *combining form* **1** Impervious to; able to withstand; not damaged by: *waterproof, bombproof.* **2** Protected against: *mothproof, stormproof.* **3** As strong as: *armorproof.* **4** Resisting; showing no effects of: *joyproof, panicproof.* Adjectives formed with *-proof* may also be used as verbs. [<PROOF, *adj.*]

proof·read (proof'rēd') *v.t.* & *v.i.* ·**read** (-red') ·**read·ing** (-rē'ding) To read and correct (printers' proofs).

proof spirit An alcoholic liquor that contains a standard amount of alcohol: in the United States, half its volume of alcohol, with a specific gravity of 0.7939 at 60° F., which is rated *100-proof.*

prop¹ (prop) *v.t.* **propped, prop·ping** **1** To support or keep from falling by or as by means of a prop. **2** To lean or place: usually with *against.* **3** To support; sustain. — *n.* That which sustains an incumbent weight; a buttress; stay. [<MDu. *proppe* a vine prop, a support]
Synonyms: bolster, brace, buttress, shore, stay, support, sustain. See SUPPORT.

prop² (prop) *n. Colloq.* On a theater stage, any adjunct except the scenery or the costumes of the actors; a property. [Short for PROPERTY]

pro·pae·deu·tic (prō'pə·dōō'tik, -dyōō'-) *adj.* Pertaining to or of the nature of preliminary instruction; relating to or introductory to an art or science: also **pro'pae·deu'ti·cal.** — *n.* A preparatory or introductory subject or course. [<Gk. *propaideuein* teach beforehand < *pro-* before + *paideuein* teach < *pais, paidos* a child]

prop·a·ga·ble (prop'ə·gə·bəl) *adj.* That can be propagated; capable of being disseminated or spread abroad, as principles, etc. [<L *propagare* PROPAGATE + -ABLE]

prop·a·gan·da (prop'ə·gan'də) *n.* **1** Any institution or scheme for propagating a doctrine, or system. **2** Effort directed systematically toward the gaining of public support for an opinion or course of action. **3** The tenets, views, etc., put forward by propaganda. [<PROPAGANDA]

prop·a·gan·dize (prop'ə·gan'dīz) *v.* ·dized, ·diz·ing *v.t.* **1** To subject to propaganda. **2** To spread by means of propaganda. — *v.i.* **3** To carry on or spread propaganda.

PROOFREADER'S MARKS

Symbols in the column headed MARGIN are used only in the outer margins of the proof: the symbols used within the body of the text are given in the TEXT column.

MARGIN		TEXT
l.c.	Set in lower-case type	circled or /
Cap.	Set in capitals	underscored
s.c.	Set in small capitals	underscored
C↓s.c.	Set in caps and small caps	
l.f.	Set in lightface type	circled
b.f.	Set in boldface type	underscored
Rom.	Set in roman type	circled
Ital.	Set in italic type	underscored
⊙	Insert period	∧
⁝	Insert colon; semicolon	∧ ∧
⌃	Insert comma	∧
⌄	Insert apostrophe	∧
/?/	Insert interrogation mark	∧
/!/	Insert exclamation mark	∧
/=/	Insert hyphen	∧
⌄⌄	Insert quotation marks	∧
⌄	Insert superior figure or letter	∧
⌂	Insert inferior figure or letter	∧
—	Insert one em-dash	∧
ℰ	Take out (delete matter)	/
wf.	Wrong font	circled or /

MARGIN		TEXT
✕	Broken letter: examine	circled
tr.	Transpose matter marked	⌐⌐
eq. #	Equalize spacing	⌄⌄⌄ ∧∧∧
⌐	Move to left to point marked	⌐
⌐	Move to right to point marked	⌐
⌐⌐	Raise to point marked	⌐⌐
⌐⌐	Lower to point marked	⌐⌐
⌣	Push down space	/
⌒	Close up	⌒
℘	Begin new paragraph	⌐
no ℘	Run matter on, not a paragraph	⌒
═	Aline type	
Stet.	Retain words crossed out	.....
ℐ	Take out and close up	ℐ
‖	Line up matter	‖
Out	Omission here; see copy	∧
⌐	Move this to left	
⌐	Move this to right	
Qu.?	Query: is this right?	∧
Sp.	Spell out	circled
#	Insert space	∧

prop·a·gate (prop'ə-gāt) *v.* **·gat·ed**, **·gat·ing** *v.t.* **1** To cause (animals, plants, etc.) to multiply by natural reproduction; breed. **2** To reproduce (itself). **3** To spread abroad or from person to person; diffuse; disseminate. **4** To transmit through a medium; extend the action of: to *propagate* heat. **5** *Obs.* To increase. — *v.i.* **6** To multiply by natural reproduction; have offspring; breed. [<L *propagatus*, pp. of *propagare* slip or layer a plant, multiply < *propago* a slip for transplanting < *pro-* forth + *pag-*, root of *pangere* fasten] — **prop'a·ga·tive** *adj.* — **prop'a·ga·tor** *n.*
Synonyms: beget, breed, engender, generate, increase, multiply, originate, procreate. See PRODUCE, SPREAD. *Antonyms:* annihilate, destroy, eradicate, exterminate, extirpate.

prop·a·ga·tion (prop'ə·gā'shən) *n.* **1** The act of propagating; reproduction. **2** Dissemination; diffusion.

pro·par·ox·y·tone (prō'pə·rok'sə·tōn) *adj.* Having an acute accent on the antepenult. — *n.* A word with an acute accent on the antepenult. [<Gk. *proparoxytonos* < *pro-* before + *paroxytonos* paroxytone]

pro·pel (prə·pel') *v.t.* **·pelled**, **·pel·ling** To cause to move forward or ahead; drive or urge forward. See synonyms under DRIVE, PUSH, SEND. [<L *propellere* drive before one < *pro-* forward + *pellere* drive]

pro·pel·lant (prə·pel'ənt) *n.* **1** That which propels. **2** *Mil.* An explosive which, upon ignition, propels a projectile from a gun. **3** A solid or liquid fuel which serves to propel a rocket, guided missile, or the like.

pro·pel·ler (prə·pel'ər) *n.* **1** One who or that which propels. **2** Any device for propelling a craft through water or air; especially, one having blades mounted at an angle on a power-driven shaft and producing a thrust by their rotary action on the fluid.

pro·pen·si·ty (prə·pen'sə·tē) *n.* *pl.* **·ties** **1** Natural disposition to or for; tendency. **2** *Obs.* A liking for; partiality. See synonyms under APPETITE, DESIRE, INCLINATION. [<L *propensus*. See PROPENSE.]

prop·er (prop'ər) *adj.* **1** Having special adaptation or fitness; specially suited; applicable; appropriate. **2** Conforming to a standard; becoming; seemly; correct. **3** Naturally belonging to a person or thing; particular; peculiar. **4** Understood in the most correct sense; strictly so called: commonly following the noun modified. **5** *Gram.* Belonging to an individual person, family, place, or the like: a *proper* noun: opposed to *common.* **6** *Archaic* Belonging to or affecting oneself; own. **7** *Her.* Represented in the natural color. **8** *Eccl.* Appointed for special use: the *proper* psalms for Christmas. **9** *Archaic* Of becoming form or appearance. **10** *Archaic* Good; excellent; pleasant. **11** *Obs.* Respectable; worthy; honest. See synonyms under APPROPRIATE, BECOMING, CONVENIENT, CORRECT, GOOD, MODEST. — *n.* A collection of prayers; specifically, that portion of the breviary or missal containing the prayers and collects suitable to special occasions. [<OF *propre* <L *proprius* one's own] — **prop'er·ness** *n.*

prop·er·ly (prop'ər·lē) *adv.* In a proper manner; suitably; rightly.

prop·er·tied (prop'ər·tēd) *adj.* Owning property.

prop·er·ty (prop'ər·tē) *n.* *pl.* **·ties** **1** Any object of value that a person may lawfully acquire and hold; anything that may be owned; stocks, land, etc.; any possession. **2** Ownership or dominion; the legal right to the possession, use, enjoyment, and disposal of a thing; a valuable legal right or interest in or to particular things. **3** Whatever belongs or pertains to any object, as a distinguishing quality or characteristic; a peculiarity. **4** In the theater, any portable article, except scenery, which is not personally owned by the actors, but which is used by them in the performance, as flowers, books, dishes, etc. **5** A characteristic attribute of a body or substance under stated conditions, especially in relation to the senses, as color, odor, hardness, density, etc. **6** Any typical mode of action or behavior observed in natural phenomena: a *property* of radiation. [<OF *proprieté* <L *proprietas*, *-tatis* < *proprius*

one's own. Doublet of PROPRIETY.]
Synonyms: chattels, estate, goods, means, money, ownership, possessions, resources, right, wealth. See ATTRIBUTE, CHARACTERISTIC, MONEY, WEALTH.

proph·e·cy (prof'ə·sē) *n.* *pl.* **·cies** **1** A prediction made under divine influence and direction; loosely, any prediction. **2** Discourse delivered by a prophet under divine inspiration: the common Biblical sense. **3** A book of prophecies. **4** *Obs.* Public interpretation of Scripture; preaching. [<OF *profecie* <LL *prophetia* <Gk. *prophēteia* < *prophētēs*. See PROPHET.]

proph·e·sy (prof'ə·sī) *v.* **·sied**, **·sy·ing** *v.t.* **1** To utter or foretell with or as with divine inspiration. **2** To predict (a future event). **3** To point out beforehand. — *v.i.* **4** To speak by divine influence, or as a medium between God and man. **5** To foretell the future; make predictions. **6** To explain or teach religious subjects; preach. [<OF *prophecier* < *profecie* PROPHECY] — **proph'e·si·er** *n.*
Synonyms: augur, divine, foretell, predict, prognosticate. *Prophesy* differs from *predict* by assuming a claim to supernatural or divine inspiration. To *prognosticate* is to *predict* from observed signs, indications, or conditions. To *prophesy* in the Scriptural sense is to utter religious truth under divine inspiration, not necessarily to *foretell* future events, but to warn, exhort, comfort, etc. See AUGUR. *Antonyms:* chronicle, recall, recite, recollect, record, remember.

proph·et (prof'it) *n.* **1** One who delivers divine messages or interprets the divine will. **2** One who foretells the future; especially, an inspired predictor. **3** A religious leader. **4** An interpreter or spokesman for any cause. **5** A mantis. — **the Prophet** According to Islam, Mohammed. — **the Prophets** The Old Testament books written by the prophets. ♦ Homophone: *profit.* [<Gk. *prophētēs* < *pro-* before + *phanai* speak] — **proph'et·ess** *n. fem.* — **proph'et·hood** (-hood) *n.*

pro·phet·ic (prə·fet'ik) *adj.* **1** Of or pertaining to a prophet or prophecy; vatic. **2** Pertaining to or involving prediction or presentiment; predictive. Also **pro·phet'i·cal.** — **pro·phet'i·cal·ly** *adv.* — **pro·phet'i·cal·ness** *n.*

pro·phy·lac·tic (prō'fə·lak'tik, prof'ə-) *adj.* Operating to ward off something, especially disease; preventive. — *n.* A prophylactic medicine or appliance. [<Gk. *prophylaktikos* < *prophylassein* be on guard < *pro-* before + *phylassein* guard]

pro·phy·lax·is (prō'fə·lak'sis, prof'ə-) *n.* Preventive treatment for disease. [<NL <Gk. *pro-* before + *phylaxis* a guarding]

pro·pin·qui·ty (prō·ping'kwə·tē) *n.* **1** Nearness in place or time. **2** Kinship. See synonyms under APPROXIMATION. [<OF *propinquité* <L *propinquitas*, *-tatis* < *propinquus* near]

pro·pi·theque (prō'pə·thēk') *n.* Sifaka. [<F <NL *Propithecus* <Gk. *pro-* before + *pithēkos* an ape]

pro·pi·ti·ate (prō·pish'ē·āt) *v.t.* **·at·ed**, **·at·ing** To cause to be favorably disposed; appease; conciliate. [<L *propitiatus*, pp. of *propitiare* render favorable, appease < *propitius* PROPITIOUS] — **pro·pi·ti·a·ble** (prō·pish'ē·ə·bəl) *adj.* — **pro·pi'ti·at'ing·ly** *adv.* — **pro·pi'ti·a'tive** *adj.* — **pro·pi'ti·a'tor** *n.*

pro·pi·ti·a·tion (prō·pish'ē·ā'shən) *n.* **1** The act of propitiating. **2** That which propitiates.
Synonyms: atonement, expiation, reconciliation, satisfaction. *Atonement* (at-one-ment), originally denoting *reconciliation*, or the bringing into agreement of those who have been estranged, is now chiefly used, as in theology, in the sense of some offering, sacrifice, or suffering sufficient to win forgiveness or make up for an offense. *Expiation* is the enduring of the full penalty of a wrong or crime. *Propitiation* is an offering, action, or sacrifice that makes the governing power propitious toward the offender. *Satisfaction* denotes the rendering a full legal equivalent for the wrong done. *Propitiation* appeases the lawgiver; *satisfaction* meets the requirements of the law. *Antonyms:* alienation, condemnation, estrangement, offense, penalty, punishment, reprobation.

pro·pi·tious (prō·pish'əs) *adj.* **1** Kindly disposed; gracious. **2** Attended by favorable circumstances; auspicious. [<OF *propicius* <L *propitius* favorable, prob. < *pro-* before, forward + *petere* seek] — **pro·pi'tious·ly** *adv.* — **pro·pi'tious·ness** *n.*
Synonyms: auspicious, benign, benignant, clement, favorable, friendly, gracious, kind, kindly, merciful. That which is *auspicious* is of *favorable* omen; that which is *propitious* is of favoring influence or tendency; as, an *auspicious* morning; a *propitious* breeze. *Propitious* applies to persons, implying *kind* disposition and *favorable* inclinations, especially toward the suppliant; *auspicious* is not used of persons. See AUSPICIOUS. *Antonyms:* adverse, antagonistic, ill-disposed, inauspicious, repellent, unfavorable, unfriendly, unpropitious.

prop·o·lis (prop'ə·lis) *n.* A resinous, adhesive substance elaborated by bees to serve as a cementing material. [<L <Gk. <*pro-* before + *polis* a city]

pro·po·nent (prə·pō'nənt) *n.* **1** One who makes a proposal or puts forward a proposition; one who propounds a thing. **2** *Law* One who presents a will for probate. **3** One who advocates or supports a cause or doctrine. [<L *proponens*, *-entis*, ppr. of *proponere* set forth < *pro-* forth + *ponere* put]

pro·por·tion (prə·pôr'shən, -pōr'-) *n.* **1** Relative magnitude, number, or degree, as existing between parts, a part and a whole, or different things. **2** Fitness and harmony; symmetry. **3** A proportionate or proper share; any share or part. **4** An equality or identity between ratios. **5** *Math.* That rule by which, when three numbers are given, a fourth can be found having the same ratio to the third as the second has to the first: also called *the rule of three,* three of the four terms being always given. **6** *pl.* Size; dimensions: a picture of large *proportions.* See synonyms under ANALOGY, PORTION, SYMMETRY. — *v.t.* **1** To adjust properly as to relative magnitude, amount, or degree: to *proportion* one's expenses to one's means. **2** To form with a harmonious relation of parts. [<OF *proporcion* <L *proportio*, *-onis* < *pro-* before + *portio*, *-onis* a share] — **pro·por'tion·a·ble** *adj.* — **pro·por'tion·a·bly** *adv.* — **pro·por'tion·er** *n.*

pro·por·tion·al (prə·pôr'shən·əl, -pōr'-) *adj.* **1** Of, pertaining to, or being in proportion. **2** *Math.* **a** Constituting the terms of a proportion: said of four quantities: The numbers 2, 3, and 8, 12 are *proportional.* **b** Varying so that corresponding values form a proportion. — *n.* Any quantity or number in proportion to another or others. — **pro·por'tion·al·ly** *adv.* — **pro·por'tion·al'i·ty** (-al'ə·tē) *n.*

pro·por·tion·ment (prə·pôr'shən·mənt, -pōr'-) *n.* The act of placing or putting things in proportion; arrangement; distribution.

pro·po·sal (prə·pō'zəl) *n.* **1** An offer proposing something to be accepted or adopted. **2** An offer of marriage. **3** Something proposed, as a scheme or plan.
Synonyms: bid, offer, overture, proposition. An *offer* or *proposal* puts something before one for acceptance or rejection, *proposal* being the more formal word; a *proposition* sets forth truth (or what is claimed to be truth) in formal statement. The *proposition* is for consideration, the *proposal* for action; as, a *proposition* in geometry, a *proposal* of marriage; but *proposition* is often used nearly in the sense of *proposal* when it is a matter for deliberation; as, a *proposition* for the surrender of a fort. A *bid* is commercial and often verbal; as, a *bid* at an auction. An *overture* opens negotiation or conference, and the word is especially used of some movement toward reconciliation; as, *overtures* of peace. See synonyms under DESIGN. *Antonyms:* acceptance, decision, denial, refusal, rejection, repulse.

pro·pose (prə·pōz') *v.* **·posed**, **·pos·ing** *v.t.* **1** To put forward for acceptance or consideration. **2** To nominate, as for admission or appointment. **3** To intend; purpose. **4** To suggest the drinking of (a toast or health). — *v.i.* **5** To form or announce a plan or design. **6** To make an offer, as of marriage. [<OF *proposer* < *pro-* forth (<L) + *poser.*

See POSE[1].] —**pro·pos'er** n.

Synonym: purpose. In its most frequent use, *propose* differs from *purpose* in that what we *purpose* lies in our own mind as a decisive act of will, a determination; what we *propose* is offered or stated to others. In this use of the word, what we *propose* is open to deliberation, as what we *purpose* is not. In another use of the word one *proposes* something to or by himself which may or may not be stated to others. In this latter sense *propose* is nearly identical with *purpose.* See PLAN, PURPOSE.

prop·o·si·tion (prop'ə·zish'ən) n. **1** A scheme or proposal offered for consideration or acceptance. **2** *U.S. Colloq.* Any matter or person to be dealt with: a tough *proposition.* **3** *Colloq.* An indecent or immodest proposal. **4** A subject or statement presented for discussion. **5** *Logic* A statement in which something (the *subject*) is affirmed or denied in terms of something else (the *predicate*), the two being related usually by a copula. In the propositions, *Grass is green* and *Grass is not red,* grass in each case is the subject and green and red are the predicates respectively. **6** *Math.* A statement of a truth to be demonstrated (a *theorem*) or of an operation to be performed (a *problem*). See synonyms under PROPOSAL. —*v.t. Colloq.* To make an improper suggestion to. [< OF < L *propositio, -onis* a setting forth < *propositus,* pp. of *proponere.* See PROPONENT.] —**prop'o·si'tion·al** adj. — **prop'o·si'tion·al·ly** adv.

pro·pound (prō·pound') v.t. To put forward for consideration, solution, etc. See synonyms under AFFIRM, ANNOUNCE. [Earlier *propone* < L *proponere* set forth. See PROPONENT.] —**pro·pound'er** n.

pro·pri·e·tar·y (prə·prī'ə·ter'ē) adj. **1** Pertaining to a proprietor; subject to exclusive ownership. **2** Designating an article, as a therapeutic device or medicine, protected as to name, composition, or process of manufacture by copyright, patent, secrecy, or other means. —n. pl. **·tar·ies 1** A proprietor or proprietors collectively. **2** Proprietorship. [< LL *proprietarius* < *proprietas* PROPERTY]

pro·pri·e·tor (prə·prī'ə·tər) n. A person having the exclusive title to anything. —**pro·pri'e·tor· ship'** n. —**pro·pri'e·tress** n. *fem.*

pro·pri·e·ty (prə·prī'ə·tē) n. pl. **·ties 1** The character or quality of being proper; especially, accordance with recognized usage, custom, or principles; becomingness; fitness; correctness. **2** *Obs.* An exclusive right of possession; also, a possession or property owned. —**the proprieties** The methods or standards of good society. [< OF *propriété.* Doublet of PROPERTY.]

pro·pul·sion (prə·pul'shən) n. **1** The act or operation of propelling. **2** An impulse given or received. [< F < L *propulsus,* pp. of *propellere* PROPEL] —**pro·pul'sive** (-siv) adj.

prop·y·lae·um (prop'ə·lē'əm) n. pl. **·lae·a** (-lē'ə) *Usually pl.* A structure forming an imposing entrance or gateway before an ancient temple; more widely, a porch or vestibule. [< L < Gk. *propylaion* < *pro-* before + *pylē* a gate]

prop·y·lon (prop'ə·lon) n. pl. **·la** (-lə) A monumental gateway placed before the principal entrance of an important building of ancient Egypt, as a temple. [< L < Gk. < *pro-* before + *pylē* a gate]

pro ra·ta (prō rā'tə, rat'ə, rä'tə) In proportion: The loss was shared *pro rata.* [< L *pro rata* (*parte*) according to the calculated (share)]

pro·rate (prō·rāt', prō'rāt') v.t. & v.i. **·rat·ed, ·rat·ing** To distribute or divide proportionately. [< PRO RATA] —**pro·rat'a·ble** adj. —**pro·ra'tion** n.

pro·ro·ga·tion (prō'rə·gā'shən) n. **1** The act of proroguing, as a session of the British Parliament. **2** The act of prolonging or extending in time; also, continuance; prolongation. [< OF *prorogacion* < L *prorogatio, -onis* < *prorogatus,* pp. of *prorogare* PROROGUE]

pro·rogue (prō·rōg') v.t. **·rogued, ·ro·guing 1** To discontinue a session of (an assembly, especially the British Parliament). **2** *Obs.* To put off or postpone. **3** *Obs.* To protract or prolong. [< MF *proroguer* < L *prorogare* prolong < *pro-* forth + *rogare* ask]

pro·sa·ic (prō·zā'ik) adj. **1** Lacking in those qualities that impart animation or interest; unimaginative; commonplace; dull. **2** Per-

taining to or having the form of prose. Also **pro·sa'i·cal.** [< LL *prosaicus* < L *prosa* prose] —**pro·sa'ic·ness** n.

pro·sce·ni·um (prō·sē'nē·əm) n. pl. **·ni·a** (-nē·ə) **1** In a modern theater or similar building, that part of the stage between the curtain or drop scene and the orchestra, sometimes including the curtain and its arch. **2** In the ancient theater, the wall that formed a background for the actors. [< L < Gk. *proskēnion* < *pro-* before + *skēnē* a stage, orig. a tent]

pro·sciut·to (prō·shoo'tō) n. A spicy, cured ham. [< Ital.]

pro·scribe (prō·skrīb') v.t. **·scribed, ·scrib·ing 1** To denounce or condemn; prohibit; interdict. **2** To outlaw or banish. **3** In ancient Rome, to publish the name of (one condemned or exiled). [< L *proscribere* < *pro-* before + *scribere* write] —**pro·scrib'er** n.

pro·scrip·tion (prō·skrip'shən) n. The act of proscribing, or state of being proscribed; interdiction; ostracism; outlawry. [< L *proscriptio, -onis* < *proscriptus,* pp. of *proscribere* PROSCRIBE] —**pro·scrip'tive** adj. —**pro·scrip'tive·ly** adv. —**pro·scrip'tive·ness** n.

prose (prōz) n. **1** Speech or writing without metrical structure: opposed to *verse* or *poetry.* **2** Common place or tedious discourse. **3** *Eccl.* A hymn of irregular meter sometimes sung in the eucharistic liturgy after the gradual; a sequence. **4** A proser. —adj. Pertaining to prose; not poetic; hence, tedious. —v.t. & v.i. **prosed, pros·ing** To write or speak in prose. [< OF < L *prosa* (*oratio*) straightforward (discourse) < *prorsus* < *pro-* forward + *versus,* pp. of *vertere* turn]

pro·sect (prō·sekt') v.t. To dissect for purposes of anatomical demonstration and instruction. [Back formation < *prosector* an anatomist < LL < L *prosectus,* pp. of *prosecare* cut up < *pro-* before + *secare* cut] —**pro·sec'tion** (-sek'shən) n. — **pro·sec'tor** n.

pros·e·cute (pros'ə·kyoot) v. **·cut·ed, ·cut·ing** v.t. **1** To go on with so as to complete; pursue to the end: to *prosecute* an inquiry. **2** To carry on or engage in, as a trade or profession. **3** *Law* **a** To bring suit against for redress of wrong or punishment of crime. **b** To seek to enforce or obtain, as a claim or right, by legal process. —v.i. **4** To begin and carry on a legal proceeding. See synonyms under PUSH. [< L *prosecutus,* pp. of *prosequi* pursue < *pro-* before + *sequi* follow]

prosecuting attorney The attorney empowered to act in behalf of the government, whether state, county, or national, in prosecuting for penal offenses.

pros·e·cu·tion (pros'ə·kyoo'shən) n. **1** The act or process of prosecuting. **2** *Law* **a** The instituting and carrying forward of a judicial proceeding to obtain some right or to redress and punish some wrong. **b** The institution and continuance of a criminal proceeding. **c** The party instituting and conducting it.

pros·e·lyte (pros'ə·lit) n. One brought over to any opinion, belief, sect, or party, especially from one religious belief to another. See synonyms under CONVERT. —v. **·lyt·ed, ·lyt·ing** v.i. To make proselytes. —v.t. To make a convert of. [< LL *proselytus* < Gk. *prosēlytos* a convert to Judaism, orig. a newcomer < *prosēlyth-,* stem of *proserchesthai* approach]

pros·e·lyt·ism (pros'ə·lit'iz·əm, -li·tiz'əm) n. The making of converts to a religion, sect, or party, or the state of being thus converted. — **pros'e·lyt·ist** n.

pros·e·lyt·ize (pros'ə·lit·iz') v.t. & v.i. **·ized, ·iz·ing** To proselyte. Also *Brit.* **pros'e·lyt·ise'.**

pros·er (prō'zər) n. A dull or tedious writer or talker; a bore.

Pros·er·pine (pros'ər·pin, prō·sûr'pə·nē) In Roman mythology, the daughter of Ceres and wife of Pluto: identified with the Greek *Persephone.* Also **Pro·ser·pi·na** (prō·sûr'pə·nə).

pro·sim·i·an (prō·sim'ē·ən) adj. *Zool.* Designating any member of a suborder or group (*Prosimii*) of widely distributed early primates, as lemurs, indris, lorises, and tarsiers, characterized by small size, primitive brain development, and extensive adaptive radiation. —n. Any primate of this group. [< NL < Gk. *pro-* before + L *simia* an ape]

pro·sit (prō'sit) *Latin* Literally, may it benefit (you): a toast used in drinking health.

pro·slav·er·y (prō·slā'vər·ē, -slāv'rē) adj. In United States history, advocating Negro slavery or the policy of non-interference with it. —n. The advocacy of slavery.

pros·o·dy (pros'ə·dē) n. The science of poetical forms, including quantity and accent of syllables, meter, and versification and metrical composition. [< L *prosodia* the accent of a syllable < Gk. *prosōidia* a song sung to music < *pros-* to + *ōidē* a song] —**pro·sod·ic** (prō·sod'ik) or **·i·cal, pro·so·di·ac** (prō·sō'dē·ak). **pro·so·di·al** (prō·sō'· dē·əl) adj.

pro·so·po·pe·ia (pros'ō·pə·pē'ə) n. **1** A rhetorical figure in which the speaker impersonates another. **2** Personification. Also **pro·so'po·poe'ia.** [< L *prosōpopoiia* < *prosōpon* a face, person + *poieein* make]

pros·pect (pros'pekt) n. **1** A future probability based on present indications. **2** A scene spread out before one's eyes; an extended view. **3** The direction in which anything faces; an exposure; outlook. **4** A prospective buyer. **5** The act of observing; sight; survey. **6** *Mining* **a** An indication of the presence of mineral ore. **b** A place having promising signs of the presence of mineral ore. **c** The sample or specimen of mineral obtained by washing a small portion of ore or dirt. **7** A consideration of the future; foresight. See synonyms under SCENE. —v.t. & v.i. To explore (a region) for gold, oil, etc. [< L *prospectus* a look-out, view < *prospicere* look forward < *pro-* forward + *specere* look]

pro·spec·tive (prə·spek'tiv) adj. **1** Being still in the future; anticipated; expected. **2** Looking toward or concerned with the future; anticipatory. —**pro·spec'tive·ly** adv.

pros·pec·tor (pros'pek·tər) n. One who searches or examines a region for mineral deposits or precious stones.

pro·spec·tus (prə·spek'təs) n. **1** A paper containing information of a proposed literary, commercial, or industrial undertaking. **2** A summary; outline. [< L. See PROSPECT.]

pros·per (pros'pər) v.i. To be prosperous; thrive; flourish. —v.t. To render prosperous: God *prospers* the Republic. [< OF *prosperer* < L *prosperare* cause to succeed or prosper < *prosper, prosperus* prosperous]

pros·per·i·ty (pros·per'ə·tē) n. The state of being prosperous; attainment of the object desired; material well-being; success.

pros·per·ous (pros'pər·əs) adj. **1** Successful; flourishing. **2** Favoring or tending to success; auspicious. **3** Promising; favorable. [< MF *prospereus* < OF *prospere* < L *prosper, prosperus* favorable] —**pros'per·ous·ly** adv. —**pros'· per·ous·ness** n.

pros·ta·glan·din (pros'tə·glan'din) n. Any of a class of hormonelike compounds composed of fatty acids, occurring in tissues throughout the body and affecting circulation, neural activity, female reproduction, and other functions. [< PROSTA(TE) + GLAND + -IN]

pros·tate (pros'tāt) adj. **1** *Anat.* Designating a partly muscular gland at the base of the bladder around the urethra in male mammals. **2** Standing in front. —n. The prostate gland. [< Med. L *prostata* < Gk. *prostatēs* one who stands before < *proïstania* < *pro-* before + *histanai* set] — **pro·stat·ic** (prō·stat'ik) adj.

pros·the·sis (pros'thə·sis) n. **1** The addition of a letter or syllable to a word, especially at the beginning, as *yclept, bewail:* also spelled *prothesis.* **2** *Surg.* The fitting of artificial parts to the body, as a glass eye, a false tooth, etc. **3** Replacement or substitution of parts. [< L < Gk., addition < *prostithenai* add < *pros-* toward, besides + *tithenai* place, put] —**pros·thet·ic** (pros·thet'ik) adj.

pros·thet·ics (pros·thet'iks) n. The branch of surgery or dentistry which specializes in artificial parts and organs. [< Gk. *prosthetikos* additional < *prosthetos* added, put on < *prostithenai.* See PROSTHESIS.] —**pros·the·tist** (pros'thə·tist) n.

pros·ti·tute (pros'tə·toot) n. **1** A woman who practices prostitution; a harlot; whore. **2** Any base hireling; a corrupt person. —v.t. **·tut·ed, ·tut·ing 1** To apply to base or unworthy purposes: to *prostitute* one's talent. **2** To offer (oneself or another) for lewd purposes, especially for hire. See synonyms under ABUSE. —adj. **1** Openly devoted to lewdness or promiscuity, as a woman. **2** Surrendered to base purposes. [< L *prostitutus,* pp. of *prostituere* expose publicly; prostitute < *pro-* before + *statuere* cause to stand] —**pros'ti·tu'tor** n.

pros·ti·tu·tion (pros'tə-tōō'shən, -tyōō'-) n. 1 The act or business of prostituting; the offering, by a woman, of her body for purposes of intercourse with men for hire. 2 The act of hiring or devoting to base purposes, as one's honor, talents, resources, etc.

pros·trate (pros'trāt) adj. 1 Lying prone, or with the face to the ground; hence, figuratively, brought low in mind or spirit. 2 Lying at the mercy of another; defenseless. 3 Bot. Trailing along the ground; procumbent. —v.t. **·trat·ed, ·trat·ing** 1 To bow or cast (oneself) down, as in adoration or pleading. 2 To throw flat; lay on the ground. 3 To overthrow or overcome; reduce to weakness or helplessness. [< L prostratus, pp. of prosternere lay flat < pro- before + sternere stretch out] —**pros'tra·tor** n.

pros·tra·tion (pros-trā'shən) n. 1 The act of prostrating in any sense. 2 Exhaustion of body or mind; great dejection or depression.

pros·y (prō'zē) adj. **pros·i·er, pros·i·est** 1 Like mere prose; prosaic. 2 Dull; tedious; commonplace. —**pros'i·ly** adv. —**pros'i·ness** n.

prot- Var. of PROTO-.

pro·tag·o·nist (prō-tag'ə-nist) n. The actor who played the chief part in a Greek drama; hence, a leader in any enterprise or contest. [< Gk. prōtagōnistēs < prōtos first + agōnistēs a contestant, an actor]

prot·a·sis (prot'ə-sis) n. 1 In a conditional sentence, the clause (usually introductory) that contains the condition or antecedent: distinguished from apodosis. 2 The introductory or subordinate clause in a sentence not conditional. 3 In classical drama, the introductory part of a play. [< LL < Gk., a hypothesis < pro- before + teinein stretch]

pro·te·an (prō'tē-ən, prō-tē'ən) adj. Readily assuming different forms or various aspects; changeable. —n. Biochem. Any of a group of derived proteins which are the first product of protein hydrolysis. [< PROTEUS]

pro·tect (prə-tekt') v.t. 1 To shield or defend from attack, harm, or injury; guard; defend. 2 Econ. To assist (domestic industry) by means of protective tariffs. 3 In commerce, to provide funds to guarantee payment of (a draft, etc.). See synonyms under CHERISH, KEEP, PRESERVE, SHELTER. [< L protectus, pp. of protegere protect < pro- before + tegere cover] —**pro·tect'ing** adj. —**pro·tect'ing·ly** adv.

pro·tec·tant (prə-tek'tənt) n. That which protects or guards against damage, disease, or injury; especially, a germicide, insecticide, fungicide, or the like.

pro·tect·ed (prə-tek'tid) adj. Shielded from harm; cared for; guarded.

pro·tec·tion (prə-tek'shən) n. 1 The act of protecting; a protected condition; that which protects. 2 Specifically, a system aiming to protect the industries of a country by governmental action, as by imposing duties. See PROTECTIVE TARIFF. 3 A safe-conduct; passport. 4 U.S. Slang Security purchased under threat of violence from racketeers; also, the money so paid. See synonyms under DEFENSE, REFUGE, SHELTER.

pro·tec·tion·ism (prə-tek'shən·iz'əm) n. The economic doctrine or system of protection. —**pro·tec'tion·ist** n.

pro·tec·tive (prə-tek'tiv) adj. 1 Affording or suitable for protection; sheltering; defensive; specifically, in political economy, insuring or intended to insure protection to home industries: a protective tariff. 2 Providing or alleging to provide protection: protective custody. —n. Something that protects; specifically, an aseptic covering for a wound. —**pro·tec'tive·ly** adv. —**pro·tec'tive·ness** n.

protective coloration Biol. Any coloration of a plant or animal that makes it almost indistinguishable from its natural or habitual environment, and thus safe from detection by its enemies.

protective tariff Econ. A tariff that is intended to insure protection of domestic industries against foreign competition: opposed to free trade.

pro·tec·tor·ate (prə-tek'tər·it) n. 1 A relation of protection and partial control by a strong nation

over a weaker power. 2 A country or region under the protection of another. 3 The office, or period of office, of a protector of a kingdom. Also **pro·tec'tor·ship.**

pro·tec·to·ry (prə-tek'tər·ē) n. pl. **·to·ries** An institution for the care and education of homeless or destitute children.

pro·té·gé (prō'tə·zhā), Fr. prô·tā·zhā') n. One specially cared for by another who is older or more powerful. [< F pp. of protéger < L protegere PROTECT] —**pro'té·gée** n. fem.

pro·te·in (prō'tē·in, -tēn) n. Biochem. Any of a class of highly complex nitrogenous organic compounds occurring naturally in all living matter, and forming an essential part of animal food requirements. They are composed principally of amino acids in varying combinations, and are usually classified as: simple (hydrolyzed only by enzymes or acids into alpha-amino acids or their derivatives); conjugated (simple proteins combined with non-proteins in a form other than a salt); derived (obtained by the action of heat, enzymes, or reagents upon naturally occurring proteins). Also **pro'te·id** (-id). [< G < Gk. prōteios chief < prōtos first; so called because the chief constituent of living matter]

pro tem·po·re (prō tem'pə·rē) Latin For the time being; temporary: abbr. pro tem.

pro·test (prō'test) n. 1 The act of protesting; a solemn or formal objection or declaration. 2 A public expression of dissent, especially if organized. 3 A formal notarial certificate attesting the fact that a note or bill of exchange has been presented for acceptance or payment and that it has been refused. 4 In maritime law, a written declaration by the master of a vessel stating that an injury to the vessel or the cargo was not owing to the neglect or misconduct of the master. 5 A formal statement in writing made by a person called upon by public authority to pay a sum of money, as an import duty or a tax, in which he declares that he does not concede the legality of the claim. —adj. Of or relating to public protest: protest demonstrations. —v. (prə·test') v.t. 1 To assert earnestly or positively; state formally, especially against opposition or doubt. 2 To make a protest against; object to: I protested his actions. 3 To declare formally that payment of (a promissory note, etc.) has been duly submitted and refused. —v.i. 4 To make solemn affirmation. 5 To make a protest; object. See synonyms under AFFIRM, ASSERT, AVOW. [< OF protester < L protestari < pro- forth + testari affirm, give evidence < testis a witness] —**pro·test'er** n.

prot·es·tant (prot'is·tənt, prə·tes'-) n. One who makes a protest. [< MF < L protestans, -antis, ppr. of protestari PROTEST]

Prot·es·tant (prot'is·tənt) n. 1 A member of one of those bodies of Christians that adhere to Protestantism, as opposed to Roman Catholicism: a use opposed by some Anglicans. 2 In the 17th century, a Lutheran or Anglican. 3 Originally, one of those German princes who, at the second Council of Spires, April 19, 1529, protested against the decree of the majority representing the Roman Catholic states which involved a virtual submission to the authority of the Roman Catholic Church. —adj. Pertaining to Protestants or Protestantism.

Protestant Episcopal Church A religious body in the United States which is descended from the Church of England, but has been organized as a separate and independent body since 1789.

prot·es·ta·tion (prot'is·tā'shən) n. 1 The act of protesting; also, that which is protested. 2 A formal declaration of dissent. 3 Any solemn or urgent avowal.

pro·test·ing·ly (prə·tes'ting·lē) adv. In such a manner as to protest.

Pro·te·us (prō'tē·əs, -tyōōs) In Greek mythology, a sea god who had the power of assuming different forms. —**Pro'te·an** adj.

pro·tha·la·mi·on (prō'thə·lā'mē·on, -ən) n. pl. **·mi·a** (-mē·ə) A song celebrating a marriage; a nuptial song. Also **pro'tha·la'mi·um** (-me·əm). [< NL < Gk. pro- before + thalamos a bridal chamber; coined by Spenser on analogy with epithalamion]

proth·e·sis (proth'ə·sis) n. 1 Prosthesis (def. 1). 2

In the Greek Orthodox Church, a service by which the elements are prepared for consecration in the Eucharist. [< LL < Gk., a placing before, or in public < protithenai set before < pro- before + tithenai place] —**pro·thet·ic** (prō·thet'ik) adj. —**pro·thet'i·cal·ly** adv.

prothonotary warbler A North American warbler (Protonotaria citrea) the male of which is noted for the brilliant yellow to orange coloring of its head and under parts, with bluish-gray wings and tail.

proto- combining form 1 First in rank or time; chief; typical: protomartyr. 2 Primitive; original: prototype. 3 Chem. a Designating the first or lowest member of a series; having the least amount (of an element or radical): protoxide. b Denoting the parent form or source of: protoactinium. Also, before vowels, prot-. [< Gk. prōto- < prōtos first]

pro·to·col (prō'tə·kol) n. 1 The preliminary draft of an official document, as a treaty; specifically, the preliminary draft or report of the negotiations and conclusions arrived at by a diplomatic conference, having the force of a treaty when ratified. 2 The rules of diplomatic and state etiquette and ceremony. —v.i. To write or form protocols. [< OF prothocole < Med. L protocollum < LGk. prōtokollon the first glued sheet of a papyrus roll < prōtos first + kolla glue]

pro·to·derm (prō'tə·dûrm) n. Dermatogen.

pro·to·gene (prō'tə·jēn) n. The hypothetical prototype of the gene, assumed to have been formed from complex carbon compounds at the time when life evolved from inorganic matter.

pro·to·lith·ic (prō'tō·lith'ik) adj. Pertaining to the earliest period of the stone age; eolithic.

pro·to·mar·tyr (prō'tō·mär'tər) n. The first martyr or victim in any cause. [< OF prothomartir < Med. L protomartyr < Gk. prōtomartyr < prōtos first + martyr a witness]

pro·ton (prō'ton) n. Physics 1 The positively charged nucleus of the atom of the light isotope of hydrogen (symbol, H^1), constituting its principal mass. 2 One of the elementary particles in the nucleus of an atom, having a unitary positive charge and a mass of approximately 1.672×10^{-24} gram. The atomic number of an element is equivalent to the number of protons in its nucleus. [< NL < Gk. prōton, neut. of prōtos first]

pro·ton·o·tar·y (prō·ton'ə·ter'ē, prō'tə·nō'tər·ē) See PROTHONOTARY.

pro·to·plasm (prō'tə·plaz'əm) n. Biol. 1 The physicochemical basis of living matter, a viscid, grayish, translucent, colloidal substance of granular structure and complex composition that forms the essential part of plant and animal cells. 2 The cytoplasm of the cell, as distinguished from the nuclear material. [< G protoplasma < Gk. prōtos first + plasma form. See PLASMA.] —**pro'to·plas'mic** or **·plas'mal** or **·plas·mat'ic** adj.

pro·to·plast (prō'tə·plast) n. Biol. 1 That which is first formed; the original or primordial cell. 2 The parent pair or one of the parent pair of the first-formed individuals of a species. 3 The protoplasmic contents of a cell. 4 A plastid. [< F protoplaste < LL protoplastus < Gk. protoplastos formed first < prōtos first + plastos formed < plassein form] —**pro'to·plas'tic** adj.

pro·to·troph·ic (prō'tə·trof'ik, -trō'fik) adj. Biol. Capable of assimilating only simple inorganic substances: said of the earliest forms of life.

pro·to·type (prō'tə·tīp) n. 1 Biol. A primitive or ancestral organism; an archetype: opposed to ectype. 2 A first or original model on which subsequent forms are to be based. 3 An accepted standard to which all others must conform. See synonyms under EXAMPLE, IDEAL, MODEL. [< MF < NL prototypon < Gk. prōtotypon, orig. neut. sing. of prōtotypos original < prōtos first + typos a model] —**pro'to·typ'al** (-tī'pəl), **pro'to·typ'ic** (-tip'ik), **pro'to·typ'i·cal** adj.

pro·to·zo·an (prō'tə·zō'ən) n. Any of a large, diverse, and universal phylum of eucaryotic microorganisms, including free-living unicellular and colonial forms, often having complicated life cycles and parasitizing various animals.

Also **pro'to·zo'on** pl. **·zo'a.** [< NL < Gk. *prōtos* first + *zōia,* pl. of *zōion* an animal] — **pro'to·zo'an, pro'to·zo'ic** adj.

pro·to·zo·ol·o·gy (prō'tō-zō-ol'ə-jē) n. The branch of biology concerned with protozoans. —**pro'to·zo'o·log'i·cal** (-zō'ə-loj'i-kəl) adj. — **pro'to·zo·ol'o·gist** n.

pro·tract (prō-trakt') v.t. 1 To extend in time; prolong. 2 In surveying, to draw or map by means of a scale and protractor; plot. 3 *Zool.* To protrude or extend: opposed to *retract.* [< L *protractus,* pp. of *protrahere* extend < *pro-* forward + *trahere* draw] —**pro·trac'tive** adj.

Synonyms: continue, delay, elongate, extend, lengthen, prolong. To *protract* is to cause to occupy a longer time than is usual, expected, or desirable. We *protract* a negotiation which we are slow to conclude; *delay* may be used either of the beginning or of any stage in the proceedings; we may *delay* a person as well as an action, but *protract* is not used of persons. *Elongate* is used only of material objects or extension in space; *protract* is rarely, except in mathematics, used of concrete objects or extension in space; we *elongate* a line, *protract* a discussion. *Protract* has usually an unfavorable sense; *continue* is neutral, applying equally to the desirable or the undesirable. Compare HINDER. *Antonyms:* abbreviate, abridge, conclude, contract, curtail, hasten, hurry, limit, reduce, shorten.

pro·tract·ed (prō-trak'tid) adj. Unduly or unusually extended or prolonged.

protracted meeting A series of religious, usually revival, meetings, held morning, afternoon, and evening, and sometimes continued for several days.

pro·trac·tile (prō-trak'til) adj. Capable of being protracted or protruded; protrusile.

pro·trac·tion (prō-trak'shən) n. 1 The act of drawing out or lengthening in time; the act of delaying the termination of anything. 2 In prosody, the irregular lengthening of a syllable ordinarily short. 3 The making of a surveyor's plot on paper.

pro·trac·tor (prō-trak'tər) n. 1 An instrument for measuring and laying off angles. 2 A tailor's adjustable pattern. 3 *Anat.* A muscle that extends a limb or moves it forward. 4 *Surg.* An instrument for extracting foreign bodies from a wound.

pro·trude (prō-trood') v.t. & v.i. **·trud·ed, ·trud·ing** To push or thrust out; project outward. [< L *protrudere* < *pro-* forward + *trudere* thrust]

pro·tru·sile (prō-troo'sil) adj. Adapted to being thrust out, often rapidly, as the tongue of an ant-eater. Also **pro·tru'si·ble.** [< L *protrusus,* pp. of *protrudere* PROTRUDE + -ILE]

pro·tru·sion (prō-troo'zhən) n. 1 The act of protruding, or the state of being protruded. 2 The part or object protruded. [< F < L *protrusus.* See PROTRUSILE.]

pro·tru·sive (prō-troo'siv) adj. 1 Tending to protrude; protruding. 2 Pushing or driving forward. —**pro·tru'sive·ly** adv. —**pro·tru'sive·ness** n.

pro·tu·ber·ance (prō-too'bər-əns, -tyoo'-) n. 1 Something that protrudes; a knob; prominence. 2 The state of being protuberant. Also **pro·tu'ber·an·cy, pro·tu'ber·a'tion.**

pro·tu·ber·ant (prō-too'bər-ənt, -tyoo'-) adj. Swelling out beyond the surrounding surface; bulging [LL *protuberans, -antis,* ppr. of *protuberare* bulge out < L *pro-* forth + *tuber* a swelling] —**pro·tu'ber·ant·ly** adv.

pro·tu·ber·ate (prō-too'bər-āt, -tyoo'-) v.i. **·at·ed, ·at·ing** To be protuberant; bulge out. [< LL *protuberatus,* pp. of *protuberare.* See PROTUBERANT.]

pro·tyle (prō'til, -til) n. The hypothetical primitive material of the universe; a substance of which all existing elements have been supposed to be modifications. Also **pro'tyl** (-til). [< Gk. *prōtos* first + *hylē* timber, matter]

proud (proud) adj. 1 Actuated by, possessing, or manifesting pride; arrogant; haughty; also, self-respecting. 2 Sensible of honor and personal elation: generally followed by *of* or by a verb in the infinitive. 3 High-mettled, as a horse; spirited. 4 Proceeding from or inspired by pride. 5 Being a cause of honorable pride, as a distinction or achievement. 6 *Obs.* Bold; fearless; daring. See synonyms under HAUGHTY, HIGH. [OE *prūt, prūd* < OF *prud, prod,* prob. ult. < L *prodesse* be of value] —**proud'ly** adv.

prove (proov) v. **proved, proved** or **prov·en, prov·ing** v.t. 1 To show to be true or genuine, as by evidence or argument. 2 To determine the quality or genuineness of; test: to *prove* a gun. 3 To establish the authenticity or validity of, as a will. 4 *Math.* To verify the accuracy of (a calculation or demonstration) by an independent process. 5 *Printing* To take a proof of or from. 6 *Archaic* To learn by experience; undergo. —v.i. 7 To be shown to be by the result or outcome; turn out to be: His hopes *proved* vain. 8 *Archaic* To make trial. See synonyms under CONFIRM. [OF *prouver* < L *probare* test, try. Doublet of PROBE.] —**prov'a·ble** adj. —**prov'er** n.

prov·en (proo'vən) Alternative past participle of PROVE: the less common form. —adj. Proved; established; verified.

prov·en·der (prov'ən-dər) n. Food for cattle; especially, dry food, as hay; rarely, provisions generally. See synonyms under FOOD. —v.t. To provide with food, as cattle. [< OF *provendre, provende* an allowance of food < L *praebenda.* See PREBEND.]

prov·e·ni·ence (prō-vē'nē-əns, -vēn'yəns) n. The origin or source of a thing: used especially in the fine arts and archeology. [< L *proveniens, -entis,* ppr. of *provenire.* See PROVENANCE.]

prov·erb (prov'ərb) n. 1 A pithy saying, especially one condensing the wisdom of experience; adage; saw; maxim. 2 An enigmatical saying: to speak in a *proverb.* 3 Something proverbial; a typical example; byword. [< OF *proverbe* < L *proverbium* < *pro-* before + *verbum* a word]

Synonyms: adage, aphorism, apothegm, axiom, byword, dictum, maxim, motto, precept, saw, saying, truism. The *proverb* or *adage* gives homely truth in condensed, practical form; the latter especially gains authority by long usage. An *aphorism* is a summary statement of a general truth. An *apothegm* is a sententious statement. A *dictum* is a statement of some person or school, on whom it depends for authority. A *saying* is impersonal, current among the people. A *saw* is a *saying* that is old, but somewhat worn and tiresome. *Precept* is a command or a rule for behavior; a *motto* or *maxim* is a brief statement of cherished truth, the *maxim* being more uniformly and directly practical. A *byword* is a *saying* used reproachfully or contemptuously. Compare ADAGE, AXIOM.

pro·ver·bi·al (prō-vûr'bē-əl) adj. 1 Of the nature of, pertaining to, or like a proverb: *proverbial* brevity. 2 Supplying the subject for a proverb; being the object of general remark, especially as a typical case; well-known; notorious. —**pro·ver'bi·al·ly** adv.

Prov·erbs (prov'ərbz) An Old Testament didactic poetical book of moral sayings and instructions.

pro·vide (prə-vīd') v. **·vid·ed, ·vid·ing** v.t. 1 To supply or furnish. 2 To afford; yield. 3 To prepare, make ready, or procure beforehand. 4 To set down as a condition; stipulate. —v.i. 5 To take measures in advance: with *for* or *against.* 6 To furnish means of subsistence: usually with *for.* 7 To make a stipulation. [< L *providere* foresee < *pro-* before + *videre* see. Doublet of PURVEY.]

Synonyms: arrange, cater, furnish, prepare, procure, produce, supply. *Antonyms:* alienate, divert, lose, misemploy, mismanage, neglect, overlook, scatter, squander, waste.

pro·vid·ed (prə-vī'did) conj. On condition: with *that* expressed or understood: He will get the loan *provided* he offers good security. See synonyms under BUT. [Orig. pp. of PROVIDE]

prov·i·dence (prov'ə-dəns) n. 1 The care exercised by the Supreme Being over the universe. 2 An event or circumstances ascribable to divine interposition. 3 The exercise of foresight and care for the future; prudent economy. See synonyms under FRUGALITY, PRUDENCE. [< OF < L *providentia* < *providens, -entis,* ppr. of *providere.* See PROVIDE.]

Prov·i·dence (prov'ə-dəns) God; the Deity.

Prov·i·dence (prov'ə-dəns) The capital of Rhode Island, a port of entry on Narragansett Bay.

prov·i·dent (prov'ə-dənt) adj. Exercising foresight; economical; anticipating and making ready for future wants or emergencies. See synonyms under THOUGHTFUL. —**prov'i·dent·ly** adv.

prov·i·den·tial (prov'ə-den'shəl) adj. Resulting from or exhibiting the action of God's providence. —**prov'i·den'tial·ly** adv.

prov·id·er (prə-vī'dər) n. One whose income supports a family: He's a good *provider.*

prov·ince (prov'ins) n. 1 A considerable country incorporated with a kingdom or empire and subject to the central administration without having itself any voice in that administration. 2 Any large administrative division of a country with a permanent local government: the *provinces* of the Roman Empire, the *Provinces* of the Dominion of Canada or of the Union of South Africa, the United *Provinces* of Agra and Oudh. The word is often loosely used in the plural to denote those regions that lie at a distance from the capital; specifically, in Great Britain, the whole country except London. 3 A comprehensive department or sphere of knowledge or activity: the *province* of chemistry. 4 A definite sphere of action, especially one authoritatively assigned or properly belonging to a person: The *province* of the judge is to apply the laws. 5 *Ecol.* A zoogeographical area less than a region, having its own special flora, fauna, and types of mankind. [< OF < L *provincia* an official duty or charge, a province]

pro·vin·cial (prə-vin'shəl) adj. 1 Pertaining to or characteristic of a province. 2 Confined to a province; rustic; hence, local, as a word or idiom; also, narrow; uncultured; illiberal: said of people. —n. A native or inhabitant of a province; one who is provincial, in any sense. —**pro·vin'ci·al'i·ty** (-shē·al'ə·tē) n. —**pro·vin'cial·ly** adv.

pro·vi·sion (prə-vizh'ən) n. 1 Measures taken or means made ready in advance; the act of taking such measures. 2 pl. Food or a supply of food; victuals. 3 Something provided or prepared, as against future need. 4 A stipulation or requirement; the part of an agreement, instrument, etc., referring to one specific thing. 5 Appointment to a see or benefice not yet vacant, including designation, institution, and installation; especially, such appointment when made by the pope, before a vacancy, so as to set aside nomination by the ordinary patron. 6 pl. Medieval English statutes by which certain important matters were provided for: the *provisions* of Oxford. See synonyms under NUTRIMENT, STOCK. —v.t. To provide with food or provisions. [< OF < L *provisio, -onis* a foreseeing < *provisus,* pp. of *providere.* See PROVIDE.] —**pro·vi'sion·er** n.

pro·vi·sion·al (prə-vizh'ən-əl) adj. Provided for a present service or temporary necessity: a *provisional* army; adopted tentatively or for lack of something better. —**pro·vi'sion·al·ly** adv.

pro·vi·so (prə-vī'zō) n. pl. **·sos** or **·soes** A conditional stipulation; a clause, as in a contract or statute, limiting, modifying, or rendering conditional its operation. [< Med. L *proviso (quod)* it being provided (that), ablative neut. sing. pp. of L *providere.* See PROVIDE.]

pro·vi·so·ry (prə-vī'zər·ē) adj. 1 Containing or made dependent on a proviso; conditional. 2 Provisional. —**pro·vi'so·ri·ly** adv.

prov·o·ca·tion (prov'ə-kā'shən) n. 1 The act of provoking. 2 An incitement to action; stimulus; something that stirs to anger. [< OF < L *provocatio, -onis* < *provocatus,* pp. of *provocare* PROVOKE]

pro·voc·a·tive (prə-vok'ə-tiv) adj. Serving to provoke; stimulating. —n. That which provokes or tends to provoke. —**pro·voc'a·tive·ly** adv. —**pro·voc'a·tive·ness** n.

pro·voke (prə-vōk') v.t. **·voked, ·vok·ing** 1 To stir to anger or resentment; irritate; vex. 2 To arouse or stimulate to some action. 3 To stir up or bring about: to *provoke* a quarrel. 4 To induce or cause; elicit: to *provoke* a smile. 5 *Obs.* To call forth; summon. [< OF *provoker* < L *provocare* challenge < *pro-* forth + *vocare* call] —**pro·vok'ing** adj. —**pro·vok'ing·ly** adv. —**pro·vok'ing·ness** n.

prov·ost (prov'əst) n. 1 A person having charge or authority over others. 2 The chief magistrate of a Scottish city, corresponding to the English mayor: in Edinburgh, Dundee, Glasgow, and Aberdeen called **Lord Provost.** 3 In some English and American colleges, the head of the faculty. **4** The head of a collegiate chapter or a cathedral; a dean. **5** (prō'vō) Provost marshal. [Fusion of OE *profost, prafost* and AF. OF *provost*, both < LL *propositus* < L *praepositus* a prefect, orig. pp. of *praeponere* < *prae-* before + *ponere* place] — **prov'ost·ship** *n.*

pro·vost court (prō'vō) A summary military court for trying those (especially civilians in a theater of war) charged with minor offenses committed within areas controlled by the army. They are usually guided by the rules of evidence. Their jurisdiction is concurrent with that of courts martial. The military commission is resorted to in like situations for graver offenses such as espionage.

pro·vost sergeant (prō'vō) A non-commissioned officer who supervises the work and duties of the military police.

prow (prou) *n.* **1** The fore part of a vessel's hull or of an airship; the bow. **2** Any pointed projection. **3** *Poetic* A ship. [< MF *prove* < Provençal *proa* < L *prora* < Gk. *prōira*]

prow·ess (prou'is) *n.* **1** Strength, skill, and courage in battle. **2** A daring and valiant deed. [< OF *prouesse, proece* < *prou* PROW²]

Synonyms: bravery, courage, gallantry, heroism, intrepidity, strength, valor. *Bravery, courage, heroism,* and *intrepidity* may be silent, spiritual, or passive; they may be exhibited by a martyr at the stake. *Courage* is a nobler word than *bravery,* involving more of the deep, spiritual, and enduring elements of character; it applies to matters to which *valor* and *prowess* cannot, as submission to a surgical operation, or the facing of censure or detraction for conscience' sake. *Prowess* and *valor* imply both daring and doing. *Valor* meets odds or perils with courageous action, doing its utmost to conquer at any risk or cost; *prowess* has power and ability adapted to the need; dauntless *valor* is often vain against superior *prowess.* Compare synonyms for BRAVE, COURAGE, FORTITUDE. *Antonyms:* cowardice, cowardliness, effeminacy, fear, timidity.

prowl (proul) *v.t.* & *v.i.* To roam about stealthily, as in search of prey or plunder. — *n.* A roaming about for prey. [ME *prollen* search; ult. origin uncertain] — **prowl'er** *n.*

prox·i·mate (prok'sə·mit) *adj.* Being in immediate relation with something else; next. See synonyms under IMMEDIATE. [< LL *proximatus,* pp. of *proximare* come near < L *proximus* nearest, superl. of *prope* near] — **prox'i·mate·ly** *adv.*

prox·im·i·ty (prok·sim'ə·tē) *n.* The state or fact of being near or next; nearness. [< MF *proximité* < L *proximitas, -tatis* < *proximus.* See PROXIMATE.]

prox·i·mo (prok'sə·mō) *adv.* In or of the next or coming month: opposed to *ultimo.* Abbr. *prox.* [< L *proximo* (*mense*) in the next (month), ablative of *proximus.* See PROXIMATE.]

prox·y (prok'sē) *n. pl.* **prox·ies** A person empowered by another to act for him, the office or right so to act, or the instrument conferring it. [Contraction of PROCURACY]

prude (prōōd) *n.* A person who makes an affected display of modesty and propriety, especially in matters relating to sex. [< F, prob. back formation < *prudefemme* an excellent woman < OF *prou, prode* honest, upright + *feme* a woman]

pru·dence (prōōd'ns) *n.* The quality of being prudent; sagacity; economy; discretion.

Synonyms: care, carefulness, caution, circumspection, consideration, discretion, forecast, foresight, forethought, frugality, judgment, judiciousness, providence, wisdom. *Care* may respect only the present; *prudence* and *providence* look far ahead and sacrifice the present to the future, *prudence* watching, saving, guarding, *providence* planning, doing, preparing, and perhaps expending largely to meet the future demand. *Frugality* is in many cases one form of *prudence. Foresight* merely sees the future, and may even lead to the recklessness and desperation to which *prudence* and *providence* are strongly opposed. *Forethought* is thinking of the future, a *consideration* of what might arise. See CARE, FRUGALITY, WISDOM. *Antonyms:*

folly, heedlessness, improvidence, imprudence, indiscretion, rashness, recklessness, thoughtlessness.

pru·dent (prōōd'nt) *adj.* **1** Habitually careful to avoid errors and in following the most politic and profitable course; cautious; worldly-wise. **2** Exercising sound judgment; sagacious; judicious. **3** Characterized by practical wisdom or discretion; not extravagant. **4** Decorously discreet: a *prudent* maiden. [< OF < L *prudens, -entis* knowing, skilled, contraction of *providens.* See PROVIDENCE.] — **pru'dent·ly** *adv.*

Synonyms: careful, cautious, circumspect, considerate, discreet, economical, frugal, judicious, politic, provident, sagacious, thoughtful, thrifty, wary, wise. See POLITIC. Compare synonyms for PRUDENCE. *Antonyms:* audacious, daring, desperate, foolhardy, foolish, imprudent, indiscreet, rash, reckless, spendthrift, thoughtless, unwary.

prud·ish (prōō'dish) *adj.* Showing prudery; prim. — **prud'ish·ly** *adv.* — **prud'ish·ness** *n.*

prune¹ (prōōn) *n.* **1** The dried fruit of any of several varieties of plum. **2** Any of various plums that may be dried without spoiling. **3** *Slang* A stupid or uninteresting person. [< OF < LL *pruna* < L *prunum* < Gk. *proumnon, prounon* a plum. Doublet of PLUM.]

prune² (prōōn) *v.t.* & *v.i.* **pruned, prun·ing** **1** To trim or cut superfluous branches or parts (from) so as to improve growth, appearance, etc. **2** To cut off (superfluous branches or parts). See Synonyms under ABBREVIATE. [< OF *prooignier, proignier, ?* < *provaignier* cut < *provain* a slip < L *propago;* prob. infl. in form by *rooignier* cut off, ult. < L *rotundus* round] — **prun'er** *n.*

pru·nel·la (prōō·nel'ə) *n.* **1** A strong woolen cloth used for the uppers of shoes. **2** A similar twilled heavy dress fabric. **3** *pl.* Shoes made partly of prunella. Also **pru·nel'lo** (-nel'ō). [< F *prunelle* a sloe, dim. of *prune* plum, prune; prob. from its dark color]

pru·nelle (prōō·nel') *n.* **1** A small yellow prune, usually packed with the stone and skin removed. **2** A plum-flavored liqueur. [< F, dim. of *prune.* See PRUNE¹.]

pru·nif·er·ous (prōō·nif'ər·əs) *adj.* Plum-bearing. [< *pruni-* plum (< L *prunum*) + -FEROUS]

pru·ri·ent (prōōr'ē·ənt) *adj.* **1** Impure in thought and desire; lewd. **2** Having lustful cravings or desires. **3** Longing; desirous. [< L *pruriens, -entis* ppr. of *prurire* itch, long for] — **pru'ri·ence, pru'ri·en·cy** *n.* — **pru'ri·ent·ly** *adv.*

pry¹ (prī) *v.i.* **pried, pry·ing** To look or peer carefully, curiously, or slyly; snoop. — *n. pl.* **pries** **1** A sly and searching inspection. **2** One who pries; an inquisitive, prying person. [ME *prien;* ult. origin unknown] **pry'ing** *adj.* & *n.* — **pry'ing·ly** *adv.*

pry² (prī) *v.t.* **pried, pry·ing** **1** To raise, move, or open by means of a lever; prize. **2** To obtain by effort. — *n.* A lever, as a bar, stick, or beam; also, leverage. [Back formation < PRIZE², *v.,* mistaken as a 3rd person sing.]

pry·er (prī'ər) See PRIER.

psalm (säm) *n.* A sacred song or lyric, especially one of those contained in the Old Testament Book of Psalms; a hymn. See synonyms under SONG. — *v.t.* To celebrate or praise in psalms; hymn. [Fusion of OE *sealm, psalm* and OF *salme, psaume,* both < LL *psalmus* < Gk. *psalmos* a song sung to the harp, lit., a twanging < *psallein* twitch]

psalm·ist (säm'ist) *n.* **1** A maker or composer of psalms. **2** In the early Christian church, one of the minor clergy who led the singing; a precentor. — **the Psalmist** King David, as the traditional author of many of the Scriptural psalms.

psalm·o·dy (säm'mə·dē, sal'-) *n. pl.* **-dies** **1** The use of psalms in divine worship; psalm-singing. **2** A collection of psalms. [< LL *psalmodia* < Gk. *psalmōidia* singing to the harp < *psalmōidos* a psalmist < *psalmos* a psalm + *ōidē* a song] — **psalm'o·dist** *n.*

Psalms (sämz) A lyrical book of the Old Testament, containing 150 hymns, many ascribed to David. Also **Book of Psalms.**

psal·ter (sôl'tər) *n.* **1** The psalms appointed to be read or sung at any given service. **2** In the Ro-

man Catholic Church, a rosary of 150 beads, equaling the number of the Psalms. [OE *psaltere, saltere* < L *psalterium* a psaltery] — **psal·te·ri·an** *adj.*

Psal·ter (sôl'tər) *n.* **1** The Book of Psalms; specifically, the version of Psalms in the Book of Common Prayer. **2** The Latin version of Psalms used in the Roman Catholic breviary. Also **Psal'ter·y.**

psal·ter·y (sôl'tər·ē) *n. pl.* **-ter·ies** An ancient stringed musical instrument, similar to a dulcimer but played by plucking with the fingers or a plectrum. [< OF *sautere, psalterie* < L *psalterium* < Gk. *psaltērion* < *psallein* twitch, twang]

PSALTERY
Twelfth century.

psam·mite (sam'īt) *n.* Fine-grained sandstone. [< F < Gk. *psammos* sand + -*ite* -ITE¹]

psel·lism (sel'iz·əm) *n.* Imperfect articulation; stammering. [< Gk. *psellismos* stammering < *psellizein* stammer]

pse·phite (sē'fīt) *n.* A conglomeration of small pebbles; fragmental rock. [< Gk. *psēphos* a pebble + -ITE¹]

pseph·ol·o·gy (sef·ol'ə·jē) *n.* The study and statistical analysis of the elective process and its results. [< Gk. *psēphos* pebble used in voting, the vote itself + -LOGY; coined by R. B. McCallum of Oxford University in 1952] — **pseph·ol'o·gist** *n.*

pseu·dax·is (sōō·dak'sis) *n.* A sympodium. [< PSEUD(O)- + AXIS]

pseu·de·pig·ra·pha (sōō'də·pig'rə·fə) *n. pl.* Spurious writings; especially, spurious religious writings, falsely ascribed to Scriptural characters or times and not considered as canonical by any branch of the Christian church. [< Gk., neut. pl. of *pseudepigraphos* with a false title < *pseudēs* false + *epigraphein.* See EPIGRAPH.] — **pseu·de·pig·raph·ic** (sōō'dep·i·graf'ik) or **-i·cal, pseu·de·pig·ra·phous** *adj.*

pseu·do (sōō'dō) *adj.* Pretended; sham.

pseudo- *combining form* **1** False; pretended: *pseudonym.* **2** Counterfeit; not genuine: *pseudepigrapha.* **3** Closely resembling; serving or functioning as: *pseudopodium.* **4** Illusory; apparent: *pseudoaquatic.* **5** Abnormal; erratic: *pseudocarp.* Also, before vowels, **pseud-.** [< Gk. < *pseudēs* false]

pseu·do·a·quat·ic (sōō'dō·ə·kwat'ik, -kwot'-) *adj.* Not really aquatic, but native to or found — in wet places.

pseu·do·clas·sic (sōō'dō·klas'ik) *adj.* Emulating classic style; pretending to be classic; wrongly classed as classic.

pseu·do·morph (sōō'dō·môrf) *n.* **1** An irregular or false form. **2** *Mineral.* A mineral having the external crystalline form of another mineral. [< PSEUDO- + -MORPH] **pseu'do·mor'phic** *adj.* **pseu'do·mor'phism** *n.* — **pseu'do·mor'phous** *adj.*

pseu·do·nym (sōō'də·nim) *n.* A fictitious name; pen name. [< F < Gk. *pseudonymon,* orig. neut. of *pseudonymos* having a false name < *pseudēs* false + *onoma, onyma* a name] **pseu·don·y·mous** (sōō·don'ə·məs) *adj.* — **pseu·don'y·mous·ly** *adv.* **pseu·don'y·mous·ness, pseu·do·nym'i·ty** *n.*

pseu·do·pod (sōō'də·pod) *n.* **1** A pseudopodium. **2** An organism with pseudopodia; a rhizopod. — **pseu·dop·o·dal** (sōō·dop'ə·dəl) *adj.*

pshaw (shô) *interj.* & *n.* An exclamation of annoyance, disapproval, disgust, or impatience. — *v.t.* & *v.i.* To exclaim *pshaw* at (a person or thing).

psi¹ (sī, psī, psē) *n.* The twenty-third letter in the Greek alphabet (Ψ, ψ): equivalent to English *ps.*

psi² (sī) *n.* Pounds per square inch: a unit of pressure.

psi·lo·cy·bin (sī'lə·sī'bin) *n.* A hallucinogenic drug derived from a Mexican mushroom, used in Indian religious rites. [< *Psilocybe* (*mexicana*), the mushroom from which it is obtained

+-IN]

Psi·lo·ri·ti (psē'lô·rē'tē) See IDA.

Psit·ta·ci·for·mes (sit'ə·si·fôr'mēz) *n. pl.* An order of climbing, arboreal birds, including the parrots, macaws, and cockatoos. [< NL < Gk. *psittakos* a parrot +L *forma* form]

psit·ta·co·sis (sit'ə·kō'sis) *n.* An acute, infectious, wasting disease of parrots and related birds, caused by a filtrable virus: transmitted to man, it causes fever and nausea, with complications resembling influenza and typhoid fever: also called *parrot fever.* [< NL < Gk. *psittakos* a parrot +-*osis*-OSIS]

Pso·cop·ter·a (sō·kop'tər·ə) See CORRODENTIA.

pso·ri·a·sis (sə·rī'ə·sis) *n. Pathol.* A non-contagious, inflammatory skin disease, chronic or acute, characterized by reddish patches and white scales. [< NL < Gk. *psōriasin* have an itch < *psōra* an itch]—**pso·ri·at·ic** (sôr'ē·at'ik, sō'rē-) *adj.*

psych (sīk) *v.t. Slang* **1** To make mentally ready, as by inducing alertness or tension; key up: often with *up.* **2** To cause to lose self-assurance, especially in order to place at a competitive disadvantage; demoralize: often with *out:* to *psych* rivals. **3** To manipulate by the use of psychology; especially, to outwit: often with *out: psyched* him into giving me a loan. **4** To understand: with *out:* couldn't *psych* it out. Also **psyche.**

psych- See PSYCHO-.

psy·che (sī'kē) *n.* **1** The human soul; the mind; the intelligence. **2** *Psychoanal.* The aggregate of all the psychic components constituting a human individual, sometimes considered as an entity functioning apart from or independently of the body. **3** A knot of hair coiled at the back of the head by women in imitation of an ancient Greek style of hairdressing: also **Psyche knot.** [< Gk. *psychē* < *psychein* breathe, blow]

Psy·che (sī'kē) In Greek and Roman mythology, a maiden beloved by Eros, who, after many tribulations caused by the jealousy of Venus, is united with her lover and accorded a place among the gods as a personification of the soul.

psy·che·de·li·a (sī'kə·dē'lē·ə, -dēl'yə) *n.* Psychedelic drugs and accessories, or things associated with them.

psy·che·del·ic (sī'kə·del'ik) *adj.* Causing or having to do with an abnormal stimulation of consciousness or perception: *psychedelic* drugs; a *psychedelic* experience. [< Gk. *psychē* +*del(os)* manifest +-IC]

psy·chi·a·trist (si·kī'ə·trist) *n.* A medical doctor specializing in the practice of psychiatry.

psy·chi·a·try (si·kī'ə·trē) *n.* The branch of medicine that treats disorders of the mind or psyche, especially psychoses, but also neuroses. [< PSYCH- + -IATRY]—**psy·chi·at·ric** (sī'kē·at'rik) or **-ri·cal** *adj.*

psy·chic (sī'kik) *adj.* **1** Pertaining to the mind or soul; mental, as distinguished from physical and physiological. **2** *Psychol.* Pertaining to or designating those mental phenomena which are, or appear to be, independent of normal sensory stimuli and which cannot be fully explained in terms of the known data of experimental science, as clairvoyance, telepathy, and extrasensory perception. Compare PARAPSYCHOLOGY. **3** Caused by, proceeding from, associated with, or attributed to a non-material or occult agency. **4** Sensitive to mental or occult phenomena. Also **psy'chi·cal.** —*n.* **1** A person sensitive to mental or extrasensory phenomena; especially, a spiritualistic medium. **2** The field of extrasensory phenomena: with *the.* [< Gk. *psychikos* < *psychē* soul]—**psy'chi·cal·ly** *adv.*

psy·cho (sī'kō) *n. pl.* **-chos** *Slang* A mentally disturbed person; a neurotic or psychopath. —*adj.* **1** Psychologically disturbed. **2** Psychological or psychiatric. [< PSYCHO(NEUROTIC)]

psycho- *combining form* Mind; soul; spirit: *psychosomatic.* Also, before vowels, *psych-.* [< Gk. *psychē* spirit, soul]

psy·cho·ac·tive (sī'kō·ak'tiv) *adj.* Having a specific effect on mental activities: *psychoactive* drugs.

psy·cho·a·nal·y·sis (sī'kō·ə·nal'ə·sis) *n.* **1** The doctrine that mental life and all forms of behavior may be interpreted in terms of reciprocally acting forces largely governed by the dynamic interplay of conflicting drives and processes origi-

nating in the unconscious. **2** A system of psychotherapy originated and developed by Freud which seeks to alleviate mental and nervous disorders by the technical analysis of controlling factors persistently repressed in, and manifested through, the unconscious. —**psy'cho·an'a·lyt'ic** (-an'ə·lit'ik) or **·i·cal** *adj.* —**psy'cho·an'a·lyt'i·cal·ly** *adv.*

psy·cho·bi·ol·o·gy (sī'kō·bī·ol'ə·jē) *n.* **1** The study of the mind and of mental processes in relation to anatomy, physiology, and the nervous system, with special reference to the influence of the environment. **2** Psychology in its biological aspects. Also called *biopsychology.* —**psy'cho·bi'o·log'i·cal** (-bī'ə·loj'i·kəl) *adj.* —**psy'cho·bi·ol'o·gist** *n.*

psy·cho·dra·ma (sī'kō·drä'mə, -dram'ə) *n.* A form of psychotherapy in which the patient acts out situations involving his problems. —**psy'cho·dra·mat'ic** *adj.*

psy·cho·dy·nam·ics (sī'kō·dī·nam'iks) *n.* The study of mental processes in action. —**psy'cho·dy·nam'ic** *adj.*

psy·cho·gen·e·sis (sī'kō·jen'ə·sis) *n.* **1** The development of the individual soul; the science of the origin of psychic life. **2** Genesis or specific change due to vitality of the organism, as opposed to external influences. Also **psy·chog'·e·ny** (sī·koj'ə·nē). —**psy'cho·ge·net'ic** (-jə·net'ik) *adj.* —**psy'cho·ge·net'i·cal·ly** *adv.*

psy·cho·gen·ic (sī'kō·jen'ik) *adj.* Having mental origin, or being affected by mental actions and states.

psy·chog·no·sis (sī'kog·nō'sis) *n.* The close study and diagnosis of mental states. [< PSYCHO-+-GNOSIS]—**psy'chog·nos'tic** (-nos'·tik) *adj.*

psy·cho·graph (sī'kə·graf, -gräf) *n.* **1** A chart graphically representing the personality traits of an individual: also **psy'cho·gram** (-gram). **2** A description of the personality traits of an individual, especially in literary form. —**psy'cho·graph'ic** *adj.*

psy·chog·ra·phy (sī·kog'rə·fē) *n.* **1** Involuntary or unconscious writing, as by a medium. **2** The making of a psychograph.

psy·cho·his·to·ry (sī'kō·his'tə·rē, -his'trē) *n.* History or a work of history in which major emphasis is given the psychological states or dispositions of important participants as contributing causes of certain actions, decisions, or developments. —**psy'cho·his'tor'i·an** (-his'tôr'ē·ən, -tō'rē-) *n.* —**psy'cho·his·tor'i·cal** *adj.* —**psy'cho·his'tor'i·cal·ly** *adv.*

psy·cho·ki·ne·sis (sī'kō·ki·nē'sis) *n.* The alleged power of controlling the chance behavior of physical objects, as cards, dice, etc., by the direct influence upon them of emotional states, strong desire, or other psychic factors.

psy·cho·log·i·cal (sī'kə·loj'i·kəl) *adj.* **1** Of or pertaining to psychology. **2** Of or in the mind. **3** Suitable for affecting the mind: the *psychological* moment. Also **psy'cho·log'ic.** —**psy'cho·log'i·cal·ly** *adv.*

psy·chol·o·gism (sī·kol'ə·jiz'əm) *n.* Idealistic philosophy as opposed to sensationalism. Compare ONTOLOGISM.

psy·chol·o·gist (sī·kol'ə·jist) *n.* A student of or a specialist in psychology.

psy·chol·o·gy (sī·kol'ə·jē) *n.* **1** The science of the human mind in any of its aspects, operations, powers, or functions. **2** The systematic investigation of mental phenomena, especially those associated with consciousness, behavior, and the problems of adjustment to the environment. **3** The aggregate of the emotions, traits, and behavior patterns regarded as characteristic of an individual or type: the *psychology* of a fanatic. [< NL *psychologia* < Gk. *psychē* soul +-LOGY]

psy·chom·e·try (sī·kom'ə·trē) *n.* **1** The science of the measurement of psychophysical processes, especially of their accuracy or duration in time; mental testing: also **psy·cho·met·rics** (sī·kō·met'riks). **2** Divination by physical contact or proximity of the properties of things touched or approached. —**psy·chom'e·trist** *n.*

psy·cho·path (sī'kō·path) *n.* One subject to or afflicted by mental instability.

psy·cho·pa·thol·o·gy (sī'kō·pə·thol'ə·jē) *n.* The pathology of the mind. —**psy'cho·path'o·log'i·cal** (-path'ə·loj'i·kəl) *adj.* —**psy'cho·pa·thol'o·gist** *n.*

psy·chop·a·thy (sī·kop'ə·thē) *n.* **1** Mental disorder, especially as apart from disease of the brain, and typified by emotional immaturity and instability, moral deficiency, and perversions. **2** Psychotherapy.

psy·cho·phar·ma·col·o·gy (sī'kō·fär'mə·kol'ə·jē) *n.* The branch of pharmacology which investigates the properties and uses of drugs acting primarily on the nervous system and serving to modify human behavior.

psy·cho·phys·ics (sī'kō·fiz'iks) *n.* The science of the relations between mental and physical phenomena. —**psy'cho·phys'i·cal** *adj.* —**psy'cho·phys'i·cist** *n.*

psy·cho·phys·i·ol·o·gy (sī'kō·fiz'ē·ol'ə·jē) *n.* The physiology of mental processes.

psy·cho·sex·u·al (sī'kō·sek'shoo·əl) *adj.* Of or pertaining to the psychological aspects of sexuality or sexual development. —**psy'cho·sex'u·al'i·ty** (-sek'shoo·al'ə·tē) *n.* —**psy'cho·sex'u·al·ly** *adv.*

psy·cho·sis (sī·kō'sis) *n. pl.* **·ses** (-sēz) *Psychiatry* A mental disorder, severe in character, often involving disorganization of the total personality, with or without organic disease. ◆ Homophone: *sycosis.* [< NL < Gk. *psychōsis* a giving of life < *psychoein* animate < *psychē* a soul]

psy·cho·so·mat·ic (sī'kō·sō·mat'ik) *adj.* **1** Of or pertaining to the interrelationships of mind and body, with especial reference to disease. **2** Designating a branch of medicine which investigates the reciprocal influences of body and mind in the cause, prevention, treatment, and cure of disease.

psy·cho·sur·ger·y (sī'kō·sûr'jər·ē) *n.* Brain surgery performed to treat a mental disorder or alter behavior. —**psy'cho·sur'geon** (-sûr'jən) *n.* —**psy'cho·sur'gi·cal** *adj.*

psy·cho·tech·ni·cian (sī'kō·tek·nish'ən) *n.* One skilled in psychotechnics.

psy·cho·tech·nics (sī'kō·tek'niks) *n.* The direct application of psychological principles and methods to practical ends, especially in the management of large industrial and business enterprises. —**psy'cho·tech'ni·cal** *adj.*

psy·cho·ther·a·py (sī'kō·ther'ə·pē) *n.* The treatment of nervous and mental disorders, especially by psychological methods, as hypnosis, re-education, psychoanalysis, etc. Also **psy'cho·ther'a·peu'tics** (-ther'ə·pyoo'tiks). —**psy'chother'a·peu'tic** *adj.* —**psy'cho·ther'a·pist** *n.*

psy·chot·ic (sī·kot'ik) *n.* One suffering from a psychosis. —*adj.* Of or characterized by a psychosis.

psy·chot·o·mi·met·ic (sī·kot'ō·mə·met'ik) *adj.* Pertaining to or productive of psychotic behavior: *psychotomimetic* drugs. —**psy·chot'·o·mi·met'i·cal·ly** *adv.*

psy·cho·trop·ic (sī'kō·trop'ik) *adj.* Acting on or affecting the mind, as certain drugs. —*n.* A psychotropic drug. [< PSYCHO- + -TROPIC]

psychro- *combining form* Cold: *psychrophobia.* [< Gk. *psychros* cold]

psy·chrom·e·ter (sī·krom'ə·tər) *n.* An instrument for measuring the vapor tension and relative humidity of the air, consisting of two thermometers, the bulb of one being kept moist. [< PSYCHRO- + -METER]

psy·chro·ther·a·py (sī'krō·ther'ə·pē) *n.* Medical treatment by the use of cold.

psyl·li·um (sil'ē·əm) *n.* **1** A plantain of Asia Minor (*Plantago psyllium*). **2** Its small, reddish-brown seeds, resembling flaxseed in medicinal properties, used as a mild laxative. [< L < Gk. *psyllion* < *psylla* a flea; so called because supposed to destroy fleas]

Pt *Chem.* Platinum (symbol Pt).

Ptah (ptä, päkh) In ancient Egyptian religion, the chief divinity of ancient Memphis, the creator of gods and men.

ptar·mi·gan (tär'mə·gən) *n. pl.* **·gans** or **·gan** A grouse (genus *Lagopus*) of the northern hemisphere, with the winter plumage chiefly pure white, and with feathered toes. [< Scottish Gaelic *tarmachan;* excrescent *p* prob. due to false analogy with Gk. *pteron* wing]

PT boat A patrol torpedo boat.

pter·i·do·phyte (ter'i·dō·fīt') *n.* Any of a phylum (*Pteridophyta*) of flowerless plants comprising the ferns, clubmosses, and their allies. [< NL < Gk. *pteris, pteridos* a fern + *phyton* a plant]—**pter'i·do·phyt'ic** (-fit'ik), **pter'i·doph'·y·tous** (-dof'ə·təs) *adj.*

ptero- *combining form* Wing; feather; plume; resembling wings: *pterodactyl*. Also, before vowels, **pter-**. [< Gk. *pteron* wing]

pter·o·dac·tyl (ter'ə-dak'til) *n. Paleontol.* **1** Any of a genus (*Pterodactylus*) of extinct flying reptiles which flourished in the Jurassic period, characterized by a large, birdlike skull, long jaws, and flying membrane somewhat like that of a bat. **2** A pterosaurian. [< NL < Gk. *pteron* a wing + *daktylos* a finger]

PTERODACTYL
(American Cretaceous:
wing span about 6 feet)

pter·y·goid (ter'ə-goid) *adj.* **1** Having the form of a wing; winglike. **2** *Anat.* Pertaining to, or situated near the winglike processes of the sphenoid. Also **pter'y·goi'dal, pter·y·goi'de·an.** —*n. Anat.* A pterygoid bone, plate, process, or muscle. [< Gk. *pteryx, pterygos* a wing + -OID]

ptis·an (tiz'ən) *n.* **1** A slightly medicinal decoction or tea of herbs: also spelled *tisane*. **2** The juice of grapes drained off without pressure. **3** A decoction of barley water. [< OF *ptisane, tisane* < L *ptisana* barley groats, a drink made from them < Gk. *ptisanē* peeled barley < *ptissein* peel]

Ptol·e·ma·ic (tol'ə-mā'ik) *adj.* Of or pertaining to Ptolemy, the astronomer, or to the Ptolemies, the Egyptian kings.

Ptolemaic system The ancient astronomical system of Ptolemy, which assumed that the earth was the central body around which the sun, planets, and celestial bodies revolved: this system was accepted till replaced in the 16th century by the Copernican system.

Ptol·e·my (tol'ə-mē) Second century A.D. astronomer, mathematician, and geographer of Alexandria: full name *Claudius Ptolomaeus*.

Ptol·e·my (tol'ə-mē) Name of 14 kings of Egypt, of whom the most noted are:
—**Ptolemy I,** 367?–283? B.C., king 323–285; a general of Alexander the Great; founded the dynasty: called "Soter."
—**Ptolemy II,** 309–246 B.C., king 285–46; patron of literature and the arts: called "Philadelphus."
—**Ptolemy III,** 282?–221 B.C., king 246–21; conquered much of the Seleucid dominions; built many temples: called "Euergetes."

ptomaine poisoning Poisoning due to bacteria or bacterial toxins in food: an inexact term.

pty·a·lism (tī'ə-liz'əm) *n.* Abnormal flow of saliva. [< Gk. *ptyalon* saliva + -ISM]

pub (pub) *n. Brit. Slang* A public house; an inn; tavern. [Short for *public house*]

pu·ber·ty (pyoō'bər·tē) *n.* The period in life at which a person of either sex becomes functionally capable of reproduction: in civil law, usually the age of 14 years in males and 12 in females. [< OF *puberte* < L *pubertas* < *pubes, puberis* an adult]

pu·bes (pyoō'bēz) *n.* **1** *Anat.* The part of the lower central hypogastric region covered with hair in the adult; the pubic region. **2** The hair that appears on the body at puberty; specifically, the hair on the pubic region. **3** *Biol.* Pubescence. [< L, pubic hair, groin]

pu·bes·cence (pyoō·bes'əns) *n.* **1** The state or quality of being pubescent (def. 1). **2** *Biol.* A covering or growth of soft, fine hairs or down, especially that upon certain plants.

pu·bes·cent (pyoō·bes'ənt) *adj.* **1** Arriving or having arrived at puberty. **2** *Biol.* Covered with hairs, especially fine, soft, short hairs; hairy or downy, as leaves etc. [< MF < L *pubescens, -entis,* ppr. of *pubescere* become downy, attain puberty < *pubes.* See PUBES.]

pu·bic (pyoō'bik) *adj.* Of or pertaining to the region in the lower part of the abdomen.

pub·lic (pub'lik) *adj.* **1** Of, pertaining to, or affecting the people at large or the community: distinguished from *private* or *personal*. **2** Open to all; maintained by or for the public: *public* parks; participated in by the people: a *public* demonstration. **3** For the use of the public; specifically, for hire: a *public* cab, hall, etc. **4** Done or made in public or without concealment; well-known; open; notorious: a *public* scandal. **5** Occupying an official or professional position; acting before or for the community: a *public* speaker. See synonyms under COMMON, GENERAL. —*n.* The people collectively; or in general, of a particular locality or nation; also, all those persons who may be grouped together for any given purpose: the church-going *public*. [< OF < L *publicus*, alter. of *poplicus* (through infl. of *pubes* an adult) < *poplus, populus* people]

pub·li·can (pub'lə·kən) *n.* **1** In England, the keeper of a public house. **2** In ancient Rome, one who farmed or collected the public revenues. [< OF *publicain* < L *publicanus* a tax farmer, tax gatherer < *publicum* public revenue, orig. neut. of *publicus* PUBLIC]

pub·li·ca·tion (pub'lə·kā'shən) *n.* **1** The act of publishing or offering to public notice; notification to people at large orally or by writing or print; promulgation; proclamation. **2** In the law of libel and slander, the communication of a defamation to a third person. **3** That which is published; any printed work placed on sale or otherwise distributed or offered for distribution. See PUBLISH. [< OF *publicacion* < L *publicatio, -onis* < *publicatus,* pp. of *publicare* PUBLISH]

public debt The national debt.

public domain Lands owned by a state or national government; public lands. —**in the public domain** Available for unrestricted use: said of material on which copyright or patent right has expired.

public enemy 1 Any government with which a nation is at open war. **2** A person, especially a criminal, regarded as a menace to the public.

Public Health Service *U.S.* A Federal agency under the Surgeon General, which, as a constituent organization of the Department of Health, Education, and Welfare, is responsible for protecting and improving the health of the nation.

public house 1 An inn, tavern, or hotel. **2** In England, a place licensed to sell intoxicating liquors; a saloon.

pub·li·cist (pub'lə·sist) *n.* **1** A writer on international law or on topics of public interest. **2** A public-relations man or publicity agent. [< F *publiciste*]

pub·lic·i·ty (pub·lis'ə·tē) *n.* **1** The state of being public, or the act or fact of making or becoming public; exposure; notoriety: opposed to *secrecy*. **2** Advertising; advance information, or personal news intended to promote the interests of individuals, institutions, causes, etc., especially that appearing in print. **3** The attention or interest of the public gained by any method.

pub·li·cize (pub'lə·sīz) *v.t.* **·cized, ·ciz·ing** To give publicity to; advertise.

pub·lic·ly (pub'lik·lē) *adv.* **1** In an open or public manner; openly. **2** In the name or with the consent and concurrence of the public.

public relations 1 The activities and techniques utilized by public and private organizations and enterprises to establish favorable attitudes and responses in their behalf on the part of the general public or of special groups: included are analysis of attitudes, appraisal of procedures and policies, recommendations for internal change, and effective presentation of the organization's purposes and objectives. **2** The public conduct of the affairs of an organization with regard to its reputation and standing and to public opinion. **3** The relationship between the general public and an institution of any kind.

public servant A government official.

public service 1 Official employment under the government, especially in the civil departments. **2** The radio or television broadcasting of announcements of civic interest.

pub·lic-ser·vice corporation (pub'lik-sûr'vis) Any corporation operating a public utility, as a railroad, gas, electric, or water company.

public utility A business organization or industry which performs some public service, as the supplying of water or electric power, and is subject to particular governmental regulations; a public-service corporation.

public works Permanent architectural or engineering works or improvements built with public money, as post offices, museums, canals, harbors, parks, playgrounds, roads, bridges, etc.

pub·lish (pub'lish) *v.t.* **1** To make known or announce publicly; promulgate; proclaim. **2** To print and issue (a book, magazine, map, etc.) to the public. **3** *Law* To communicate (a defamation) to a third person. **4** To print and issue the work of: to *publish* Hemingway. —*v.i.* **5** To engage in the business of publishing books, magazines, newspapers, etc. **6** To have one's work printed and issued. [< OF *publier, puplier* < L *publicare* make public < *publicus* PUBLIC] —**pub'lish·a·ble** *adj.*

Synonyms: advertise, announce, blazon, bruit, communicate, declare, disclose, divulge, impart, proclaim, promulgate, reveal, spread, tell. See ANNOUNCE, SPREAD. *Antonyms:* conceal, cover, hide, hush, suppress, withhold.

pub·lish·er (pub'lish·ər) *n.* One who publishes; especially, one who makes a business of publishing books or periodicals.

Puc·ci·ni (poot·chē'nē), **Giacomo,** 1858–1924, Italian operatic composer.

puce (pyoōs) *adj.* Of a dark-brown or purplish-brown. [< F, flea color, a flea < L *pulex, -icis* a flea]

puck[1] (puk) *n.* **1** An evil sprite or hobgoblin. **2** In English folklore, **Puck,** a mischievous elf or goblin: also called *Robin Goodfellow*; specifically, in Shakespeare's *A Midsummer Night's Dream*, a mischievous fairy servant of Oberon. [OE *pūca* a goblin] —**puck'ish** *adj.* —**puck'ish·ly** *adv.*

puck[2] (puk) *n.* The hard rubber disk used in playing hockey. [< dial. E, strike. Akin to POKE[1].]

puck·er (puk'ər) *v.t. & v.i.* To gather or draw up into small folds or wrinkles. —*n.* **1** A wrinkle, or group of wrinkles. **2** *Colloq.* Agitation; perplexity; confusion. [Appar. freq. of POKE[2].] —**puck'er·y** *adj.*

pud·ding (poōd'ing) *n.* **1** A sweetened and flavored dessert of soft food, usually farinaceous. **2** A skin or gut filled with seasoned minced meat, blood, or the like, and usually boiled or broiled. [ME *poding,* orig. sausage, black pudding, prob. < OF *bodin, boudin*]

pud·dle (pud'l) *n.* **1** A small pool of dirty water. **2** Puddling (def. 2). —*v.t.* **·dled, ·dling 1** *Metall.* To convert (molten pig iron) into wrought iron by melting and stirring in the presence of oxidizing substances. **2** To mix (clay, etc.) with water so as to obtain a watertight paste. **3** To line, as canal banks, with such a mixture. **4** To make muddy; stir up. [ME *podel,* appar. dim. of OE *pudd* a ditch] —**pud'dly** *adj.*

pu·den·cy (pyoō'dən·sē) *n.* Shame; modesty; also, prudishness. [< LL *pudentia* < L *pudens, -entis,* ppr. of *pudere* be ashamed]

pu·den·dum (pyoō·den'dəm) *n. pl.* **·da** (-də) **1** The vulva. **2** *pl.* The external genitals of either sex. [< L, neut. of *pudendus* (something) to be ashamed of, gerundive of *pudere* be ashamed] —**pu'dic, pu·den'dal** *adj.*

pudg·y (puj'ē) *adj.* **pudg·i·er, pudg·i·est** Short and thick; fat. [? < dial. E (Scottish) < *pud* belly] —**pudg'i·ly** *adv.* —**pudg'i·ness** *n.*

pueb·lo (pweb'lō *for def. 1,* pwā'blō *for defs. 2 and 3) n. pl.* **·los 1** A communal adobe or stone building or group of buildings of the Indians of the SW United States. **2** A town or village of Indians or Spanish Americans, as in Mexico. **3** In the Philippines, a municipality: originally the civilian quarter of a Spanish community. [< Sp., a town, people < L *populus*]

HOPI INDIAN PUEBLO

Pueb·lo (pweb'lō) *n.* A member of one of the Indian tribes of Mexico and the SW United States, representing several linguistic stocks, as Zuñi, Uto-Aztecan, ect., but having in common the pueblo culture.

pu·er·ile (pyoō'ər·il, *Brit.* pyoō'ə·rīl) *adj.* Pertaining to or characteristic of childhood; juvenile;

hence, immature; weak; silly: a *puerile* suggestion. See synonyms under CHILDISH, YOUTHFUL. [< MF *puéril* < L *puerilis* < *puer, pueri* a boy] — **pu'er·ile·ly** *adv.* —**pu'er·ile·ness** *n.*

pu·er·il·ism (pyōō'ər·il·iz'əm) *n.* Childishness, especially as indicative of mental disorder.

Puerto Ri·co (rē'kō) The easternmost island of the Greater Antilles, ceded to the United States by Spain in 1898; since 1952 a commonwealth; 3,423 square miles; capital, San Juan: former official name, *Porto Rico.* Abbr. PR —**Puer'to·Ri'can** *adj. & n.*

puff (puf) *n.* **1** A breath emitted suddenly and with force; a sudden emission, as of air, smoke, or steam; a whiff. **2** A light, air-filled piece of pastry: a cream *puff.* **3** A light ball, tuft, wad, or pad for dusting powder on the hair or skin; a powder puff. **4** A loose roll of hair in a coiffure, or a light cushion over which it is rolled. **5** A quilted bed coverlet, usually filled with cotton, wool, or down; a comforter. **6** In dressmaking, a part of a fabric so gathered as to produce a loose, fluffy distention. **7** A public expression of fulsome praise, as in a newspaper or advertisement. **8** A puffball. —*v.i.* **1** To blow in puffs, as the wind. **2** To breathe hard, as after violent exertion. **3** To emit smoke, steam, etc., in puffs. **4** To smoke a cigar, etc., with puffs. **5** To move, act, or exert oneself while emitting puffs: with *away, up,* etc. **6** To swell as with air or pride; dilate: often with *up* or *out.* —*v.t.* **7** To send forth or emit with short puffs or breaths. **8** To move, impel, or stir up with or in puffs. **9** To smoke, as a pipe or cigar, with puffs. **10** To swell or distend: He *puffed* his cheeks with pride. **11** To praise fulsomely; advertise in a puff (def. 7). **12** To arrange (the hair) in a puff. [ME *puf* < *puffen, pyffan*]
Synonyms (verb): blow, compliment, flatter, inflate, pant, praise, swell. Compare SWELL. *Antonyms:* belittle, contract, disparage, shrink, shrivel.

puff adder 1 A large, sluggish, venomous African viper (*Bitis arietans*), with variously colored chevron-and-crescent markings and a habit of violently puffing out its breath. **2** The American hognose snake.

puff·er (puf'ər) *n.* **1** One who puffs. **2** A plectognath fish that inflates its body with air; a globefish. **3** The little harbor porpoise (*Phocaena phocaena*) of the North Atlantic and Pacific oceans.

puff·er·y (puf'ər·ē) *n.* **·er·ies 1** The act or practice of puffing. **2** Fulsome public praise or commendation.

puf·fin (puf'in) *n.* **1** A sea bird allied to the auk and murre (family *Alcidae*), with deep compressed bill and thick naked skin at the corner of the mouth; especially, the common puffin (*Fratercula arctica*) of the North Atlantic; the Labrador auk. **2** The Pacific coast sea parrot (*Lunda cirrhata*). [Prob. < PUFF: with ref. to its puffed-out beak or the plumpness of its young]

PUFFIN
(Body from 12 to 15 inches long)

puff paste A short flaky paste for fine pastry.

puff·y (puf'ē) *adj.* **puff·i·er, puff·i·est 1** Swollen with air or any soft matter; soft; bloated. **2** Inflated in manner; bombastic. **3** Blowing in puffs. —**puff'i·ly** *adv.* —**puff'i·ness** *n.*

pug[1] (pug) *n.* **1** Clay ground and worked with water, for molding pottery or bricks. **2** A machine in which clay is ground and mixed or tempered: also **pug mill.** —*v.t.* **pugged, pug·ging 1** To knead or work (clay) with water, as in brickmaking. **2** To fill in with clay, etc. **3** To fill in or cover with mortar, felt, etc., to deaden sound. [< dial. E, ? < *pug* punch]

pug[2] (pug) *n.* **1** A breed of dog characterized by a

short, square body, upturned nose, curled tail, and short, smooth coat. **2** A pug nose. [Prob. alter. of PUCK]

pugh (pyōō, pōō) *interj.* An exclamation of contempt or disgust.

pu·gi·lism (pyōō'jə·liz'əm) *n.* The art or practice of boxing or fighting with the fists, as in the prize ring. [< L *pugil* a boxer]

pu·gi·list (pyōō'jə·list) *n.* One who fights with his fists; a boxer; specifically, a prize fighter. —**pu'gi·lis'tic** *adj.*

pug·na·cious (pug·nā'shəs) *adj.* Disposed or inclined to fight; quarrelsome. [< L *pugnax, -acis* < *pugnare* fight < *pugnus* a fist] —**pug·na'cious·ly** *adv.*

pug·nac·i·ty (pug·nas'ə·tē) *n.* The quality of being pugnacious; quarrelsome disposition; combativeness. Also **pug·na'cious·ness** (-nā'shəs·nis).

pug nose A thick, short nose, tilted upward at the end. [< PUG² + NOSE] —**pug–nosed** (pug'nōzd') *adj.*

pu·is·sance (pyōō'ə·səns, pyōō·is'əns, pwis'əns) *n.* The power to accomplish or achieve, especially against resistance; potency. [< OF]

pu·is·sant (pyōō'ə·sənt, pyōō·is'ənt, pwis'ənt) *adj.* Powerful; mighty. See synonyms under POWERFUL. [< OF < L *posse* be able] —**pu'is·sant·ly** *adv.*

puke (pyōōk) *v.t. & v.i.* **puked, puk·ing** To vomit or cause to vomit. —*n.* Vomit, or the act of vomiting. [Cf. LG *spucken* spew, spit < L *spuere*]

puk·ka (puk'ə) See PUCKA.

pu·lay (pə·lī') See PALAY.

pul·chri·tude (pul'krə·tood, -tyood) *n.* Beauty; grace; physical charm. [< L *pulchritudo, -inis* < *pulcher* beautiful]

pul·chri·tu·di·nous (pul'krə·tood'ə·nəs, -tyoo'-) *adj.* Beautiful; lovely; especially, having physical beauty.

pule (pyōōl) *v.i.* **puled, pul·ing** To cry plaintively, as a child; whimper; whine. [Cf. F *piauler* < MF *pioler* chirp] —**pul'er** *n.*

pu·li·cene (pyōō'lə·sēn) *adj.* Of, pertaining to, or abounding with fleas. [< L *pulex, -icis* a flea]

pul·ing (pyōō'ling) *n.* A plaintive cry; whining. —*adj.* Whimpering; whining. —**pul'ing·ly** *adv.*

Pu·litz·er (pyōō'lit·sər, pool'it-), **Joseph,** 1847–1911, U.S. journalist and publisher, born in Hungary.

Pulitzer Prize One of several annual awards for outstanding work in American journalism and literature: established by Joseph Pulitzer.

pull (pool) *v.t.* **1** To apply force to so as to cause motion toward or after the person or thing exerting force; drag; tug. **2** To draw or remove from a natural or fixed place: to *pull* a tooth or plug. **3** To give a pull or tug to. **4** To pluck, as a fowl. **5** To draw asunder; tear; rend: with *to pieces, apart,* etc. **6** To strain so as to cause injury: to *pull* a ligament. **7** In sports, to strike (the ball) so as to cause it to curve obliquely from the direction in which the striker faces. **8** *Slang* To put into effect; carry out: often with *off:* to *pull* off a prank. **9** *Slang* To make a raid on; arrest. **10** *Slang* To draw out so as to use: to *pull* a knife. **11** *Printing* To make or obtain by impression from type: to *pull* a proof. **12** In boxing, to deliver (a punch, etc.) with less than one's full strength. **13** In horse-racing, to rein in or otherwise restrain (a horse) so as to prevent its winning. **14** In rowing: **a** To operate (an oar) by drawing toward one. **b** To propel or transport by rowing. **c** To be propelled by: The gig *pulls* four oars. —*v.i.* **15** To use force in hauling, dragging, moving, etc. **16** To move: with *out, in, away, ahead,* etc. **17** To drink deeply: to *pull* at a bottle. **18** To inhale deeply: to *pull* at a cigar. **19** To row. See synonyms under DRAW. —**to pull for** To strive in behalf of. **2** *Colloq.* To declare one's allegiance to. —**to pull oneself together** To regain one's composure. —**to pull out** *Aeron.* To return to level flight after a dive, as an airplane. —**to pull through 1** Succeed. **2** To survive. —**to pull up To** come to a halt. **2** To advance to a position even with. —*n.* **1** The act of pulling; the exertion of force to draw something toward one. **2** Something that is pulled; specifically, the handle of a doorbell, drawer, cabinet, or the like. **3** An impression made

by pulling the lever of a hand press. **4** A long swallow, or a deep puff, as on a pipe or cigar. **5** Exercise in rowing: a *pull* on the river. **6** The exertion expended in climbing a mountain; hence, any steady, continuous effort. **7** *Slang* A means of influencing those in power: political *pull;* influence to one's advantage. **8** Attraction: These ads have *pull.* **9** The action of restraining a horse by pulling on the reins; specifically, in horse–racing, the dishonest checking of a horse so that he may be defeated. **10** In sports, the act of pulling the ball. [OE *pullian* pluck] —**pull'er** *n.*

pull-doo (pool'doo) *n.* The coot. [< F *poule d'eau* a water hen]

pul·let (pool'it) *n.* A young hen, or one not fully grown. [< OF *polete, poulet,* dim. of *poule* a hen < L *pullus* a chicken, young animal]

pul·ley (pool'ē) *n.* **1** A wheel grooved to receive a rope, and usually mounted in a block, used to increase the mechanical advantage of an applied force and to transmit or change the direction of power by means of a flexible belt or rope; a sheave. **2** A block with its pulleys or tackle. **3** *Mech.* A flat or flanged wheel driving, carrying, or being driven by a flat belt, used in a system for transmitting power. [< OF *polie* < Med. L *poleia,* prob. ult < Gk. *polos* a pivot, axis]

PULLEYS
a. Single fixed.   *c.* Fixed and runner.
b. Single runner.   *d.* First system.
e. Second system.

Pull·man (pool'mən) *n.* A sleeping–car or chair car on a passenger train: a trade name. Also **Pullman car.** [after George M. *Pullman,* 1831–97, U.S. inventor]

pull–o·ver (pool'ō'vər) *adj.* Donned by being drawn over the head. —*n.* A garment so donned, as a sweater or shirt.

pul·lu·late (pul'yə·lāt) *v.i.* **·lat·ed, ·lat·ing 1** To germinate; bud. **2** To breed in abundance; swarm; teem. [< L *pullulatus,* pp. of *pullulare* sprout < *pullulus,* dim. of *pullus* a young animal] —**pul'lu·la'tion** *n.* —**pul'lu·la'tive** *adj.* —**pul'lu·la'tive·ly** *adv.*

pul·mom·e·ter (pul·mom'ə·tər) *n.* An instrument for determining lung capacity by measuring the quantity of air in a single respiration; a spirometer. [< L *pulma* lung + -METER] —**pul·mom'e·try** *n.*

pul·mo·nar·y (pul'mə·ner'ē) *adj.* **1** Pertaining to or affecting the lungs. **2** Having lunglike organs. [< L *pulmonarius* < *pulmo, -onis* lung]

pul·mo·nate (pul'mə·nāt, -nit) *adj.* **1** Having lunglike organs. **2** Of or pertaining to an order of gastropods (*Pulmonata*), including most land snails, slugs, and fresh–water snails, which have lunglike organs. —*n.* One of the *Pulmonata.* [< NL *pulmonatus* < L *pulmo, -onis* lung]

pul·mon·ic (pul·mon'ik) *adj.* **1** Pertaining to or affecting the lungs; pulmonary. **2** Pertaining to pneumonia. —*n.* **1** A medicine for lung disease. **2** One affected by lung disease. [< MF *pulmonique* < L *pulmo, -onis* lung]

pulp (pulp) *n.* **1** A moist, soft, slightly cohering mass of matter, usually organic, as chyme, or the soft, succulent part of fruit. **2** A mixture of wood fibers or rags, reduced to a pulpy consistency, and forming the basis from which paper is made. **3** *pl.* Magazines printed on rough, unglazed, wood–pulp paper, and usually having contents of a cheap, sensational nature: distinguished from *slicks.* **4** Powdered ore mixed with water; slime. **5** A pulplike organ or part. **6** *Dent.* The soft tissue of vessels and nerves that fills the central cavity of a tooth. —*v.t.* **1** To reduce to pulp. **2** To remove the pulp or envelope from. — *v.i.* **3** To be or become of a pulpy consistency. [< MF *pulpe* < L *pulpa* flesh, pulp of fruit, pith] — **pulp'less** *adj.*

pulp·ous (pul'pəs) *adj.* Resembling pulp; pulpy.

pul·pit (pool'pit) *n.* **1** An elevated stand or desk for a preacher in a church. **2** The office or work of preaching; hence, the clergy as a class. **3** An elevated platform usually boxed in and variously used: the harpooner's *pulpit* on a whaling vessel. — *adj.* Of or pertaining to the pulpit: *pulpit* oratory. [< L *pulpitum* a scaffold, stage, platform]

pulp·wood (pulp'wŏŏd') *n.* The soft wood of certain trees, as the spruce, used in the manufacture of paper.

pulp·y (pul'pē) *adj.* **pulp·i·er, pulp·i·est** **1** Consisting of or resembling pulp. **2** Of a soft, juicy consistency; succulent. — **pulp'i·ly** *adv.* — **pulp'i·ness** *n.*

pul·sar (pul'sär) *n.* An astronomical object that emits radio waves in pulses whose repetition rate is extremely uniform. [< *puls(ating)* + *(st)ar*]

pul·sate (pul'sāt) *v.i.* **·sat·ed, ·sat·ing** **1** To move or throb with rhythmical impulses, as the pulse or heart. **2** To vibrate; quiver. [< L *pulsatus*, pp. of *pulsare*, freq. of *pellere* (pp. *pulsus*) beat]

pul·sa·tile (pul'sə-til) *adj.* **1** Pulsatory. **2** That must be struck in order to produce sound; specifically, in music, percussive.

pul·sa·tion (pul·sā'shən) *n.* **1** A throbbing or vibrating. **2** A single throb or heartbeat.

pul·sa·tive (pul'sə-tiv) *adj.* Pulsating; throbbing; pulsatile. — **pul'sa·tive·ly** *adv.*

pul·sa·tor (pul·sā'tər) *n.* A machine which operates by pulsation, as a pneumatic rock drill operated by puffs of air.

pul·sa·to·ry (pul'sə·tôr'ē, -tō'rē) *adj.* Of or pertaining to pulsation; having rhythmical movement; throbbing; beating; pulsatile.

pulse (puls) *n.* **1** *Physiol.* The rhythmic beating of the arteries due to the successive contractions of the heart, especially as felt in pressing upon the radial artery at the wrist. ◆ Collateral adjectives: *sphygmic, sphygmoid.* **2** Any throbbing characterized by a short, quick, regular stroke or motion; pulsation. **3** *Telecom.* A brief surge of electrical or electromagnetic energy, usually transmitted as a signal in communication. **4** Any movement, drift, or tendency indicative of general opinion, feeling, or sentiment. — *v.i.* **pulsed, pulsing** To manifest a pulse; pulsate; throb. [< OF *pous* < L *pulsus (venarum)* the beating (of the veins), orig. pp. of *pellere* beat] — **pulse'less** *adj.*

pul·sim·e·ter (pul·sim'ə·tər) *n.* An instrument for indicating and registering the frequency, force, and variations of the pulse; a sphygmograph. [< *pulsi-* (< PULSE[1]) + -METER]

pul·som·e·ter (pul·som'ə·tər) *n.* **1** A device for pumping liquids by steam pressure, operating without pistons and consisting of two pear-shaped chambers connected by valves; a vacuum pump. **2** A pulsimeter.

pul·ver·a·ble (pul'vər·ə·bəl) *adj.* Pulverizable.

pul·ver·a·ceous (pul'və·rā'shəs) *adj.* Having a powdery surface; pulverulent. [< L *pulvis, pulveris* a powder + -ACEOUS]

pul·ver·ize (pul'və·rīz) *v.* **·ized, ·iz·ing** *v.t.* **1** To reduce to powder or dust, as by grinding or crushing. **2** To demolish; annihilate. — *v.i.* **3** To become reduced to powder or dust. Also *Brit.* **pul'ver·ise**. [< MF *pulveriser* < LL *pulverizare* < L *pulvis, pulveris* a powder, dust] — **pul'ver·iz'a·ble** *adj.* — **pul'ver·i·za'tion** *n.* — **pul'ver·iz'er** *n.*

pu·ma (pyŏŏ'mə) *n.* An American carnivore (*Felis couguar*) ranging from Canada to Patagonia, of a reddish-tawny color, about 4 feet in length, exclusive of the tail; the cougar: also called *mountain lion*. [< Sp. < Quechua]

PUMA
(From 2 to 2 1/2 feet
at the shoulder)

pum·ice (pum'is) *n.* Spongy or cellular volcanic lava, used as an abrasive and polishing ma-

terial, especially when powdered: also **pumice stone**. — *v.t.* **·iced, ·ic·ing** To smooth, polish, or clean with pumice. [< OF *pomis, pumis* < L *pumex, pumicis*] — **pu·mi·ceous** (pyŏŏ·mish'əs) *adj.*

pum·mel (pum'əl) See POMMEL.

pump[1] (pump) *n.* A mechanical device for raising, circulating, exhausting, or compressing a liquid or gas by drawing or pressing it through apertures and pipes. — *v.t.* **1** To raise with a pump, as water or other liquid. **2** To remove the water, etc., from. **3** To inflate with air by means of a pump. **4** To propel, discharge, force, etc., from or as if from a pump: The heart *pumps* blood. **5** To cause to operate in the manner of a pump or pump handle. **6** To question or obtain information from persistently or subtly: to *pump* a witness. **7** To obtain (information) in such a manner. — *v.i.* **8** To work a pump; raise water or other liquid with a pump. **9** To move up and down like a pump or pump handle. [< MDu. *pompe*, prob. < Sp. *bomba*; prob. ult. imit.] — **pump'er** *n.*

pump[2] (pump) *n.* A low-cut slipper without a fastening, having either a high or a low heel. [? < F *pompe* pomp]

pum·per·nick·el (pum'pər·nik'əl) *n.* A coarse, dark, sour bread made from unsifted rye. [< G, Westphalian rye bread, orig. a lout, a peasant]

pump·kin (pump'kin, pung'-) *n.* **1** A large trailing vine (*Cucurbita pepo*) with heart-shaped leaves. **2** Its large, round, edible, yellow fruit. **3** In Europe, the winter squash (*C. maxima*) or any of its varieties. [Earlier *pompion* < MF *pompon, popon* < L *pepo, peponis* < Gk. *pepon* a melon, lit., ripe, cooked by the sun]

pun (pun) *n.* The witty use of two words having the same or similar sounds but different meanings, or of two different, more or less incongruous meanings of the same word. — *v.* **punned, pun·ning** *v.i.* **1** To make a pun or puns. — *v.t.* **2** To treat as a pun. **3** To affect in a specified manner by puns. [? < Ital. *puntiglio* a fine point, a verbal quibble. See PUNCTILIO.] — **pun'ning·ly** *adv.*

pu·na[1] (pŏŏ'nä) See POON.

pu·na[2] (pŏŏ'nä) *n.* **1** A cold, arid region at high altitudes, as in the Andes. **2** Mountain sickness; illness caused by rarefaction of the air; soroche. [< Sp. < Quechua]

punch[1] (punch) *n.* **1** A tool for perforating or indenting, or for driving out or in an object inserted in a hole: frequently tapered at one end. The working end may have a cutting edge enclosing an area or a pattern: often used in connection with a die or counter having a hole in which the punch fits with slight clearance. **2** A machine for impressing a design or stamping a die. — *v.t.* To perforate, shape, indent, etc., with a punch. [Short for ME *punchon* a puncheon[1]]

PUNCHES
a. Blacksmith's square.   *d.* Ticket.
b. Center.   *e, g.* Stamping.
c. Revolving belt.   *f, h, i.* Cutting.

punch[2] (punch) *v.t.* **1** To strike sharply, especially with the fist. **2** To poke with a stick; prod. **3** *Western U.S.* To drive (cattle). — *n.* **1** A swift blow with the fist; also, a thrust or nudge. **2** *Slang* Hence, vitality; effectiveness; force; directness: an editorial with *punch*. [Prob. var. of POUNCE[2]]

punch[3] (punch) *n.* A beverage having wine or spirits, milk, tea, or fruit juices as a basic ingredient, sweetened, sometimes spiced, and diluted with water. [< Hind. *pānch* < Skt. *pañchan* five; from the five original ingredients: arrack, tea, sugar, water, and lemon]

Punch (punch) The quarrelsome, grotesque hero of a comic puppet show, **Punch and Judy.** — **pleased as Punch** Extremely pleased; highly gratified. [Short for PUNCHINELLO]

punch card In data processing, a card having a well-defined arrangement of positions by means of which information can be stored by the presence or absence of punched holes. Also **punched card** (puncht).

punch-drunk (punch'drungk') *adj.* **1** Suffering from the effects of repeated blows so as to be groggy, slow in movement, etc.: said usually of prize fighters. **2** Confused; dazed. Also *Slang* **punch·y** (punch'ē).

pun·cheon[1] (pun'chən) *n.* **1** An upright supporting timber. **2** A punch or perforating tool, especially one for chipping stone or for stamping figures. **3** A broad, heavy piece of roughly dressed timber, having one flat, hewed side. [< OF *poinçon, poinchon* a punch, ult. < L *punctus*, pp. of *pungere* prick]

pun·cheon[2] (pun'chən) *n.* **1** A liquor cask of variable capacity, from 72 to 120 gallons. **2** A liquor measure of varying amount: mostly of wine, 84 gallons. [< OF *ponçon, poinchon*; ult. same as PUNCHEON[1]]

punch press A machine equipped with dies for cutting or forming metal.

punc·tate (pungk'tāt) *adj.* **1** Covered or studded with dots, points, or minute depressions. **2** Pointed. Also **punc'tat·ed.** [< NL *punctatus* < L *punctum* a point] — **punc·ta'tion** *n.*

punc·til·i·o (pungk·til'ē·ō) *n. pl.* **·til·i·os** **1** A nice point of etiquette. **2** Preciseness in the observance of etiquette or ceremony. [< Sp. *puntillo* < Ital. *puntiglio*, dim. of *punto* a point < L *punctum*]

punc·til·i·ous (pungk·til'ē·əs) *adj.* **1** Very nice or exact in the observance of forms of etiquette, etc. **2** Of or pertaining to precise etiquette. [< F *pointelleux* < *pointille* < Ital. *puntiglio* small point] — **punc·til'i·ous·ly** *adv.* — **punc·til'i·ous·ness** *n.*

punc·tu·al (pungk'chŏŏ·əl) *adj.* **1** Exact as to appointed time; acting or arriving promptly; prompt. **2** Done or made precisely at an appointed time. **3** Punctilious; exact. **4** Consisting of or confined to a point as related to space. [< Med. L *punctualis* < L *punctus* a pricking, a point] — **punc'tu·al·ly** *adv.*

punc·tu·al·i·ty (pungk'chŏŏ·al'ə·tē) *n. pl.* **·ties** The quality, characteristic, or habit of being punctual, in any sense.

punc·tu·ate (pungk'chŏŏ·āt) *v.* **·at·ed, ·at·ing** *v.t.* **1** To divide or mark with punctuation. **2** To interrupt at intervals. **3** To emphasize. — *v.i.* **4** To use punctuation. [< Med. L *punctuatus*, pp. of *punctuare* < L *punctus* a point] — **punc'tu·a'tor** *n.*

punc·tu·a·tion (pungk'chŏŏ·ā'shən) *n.* The use of points or marks in written or printed matter, to indicate the separation of the words into sentences, clauses, and phrases, and to aid in the better comprehension of the meaning and grammatical relation of the words; also, the marks so used. See also under PRINTING. — **punc'tu·a'tive** *adj.* The chief punctuation points are:

period	parentheses ( )
colon :	brackets [ ]
semicolon ;	dash (em–dash) —
comma ,	(en–dash) –
interrogation point ?	hyphen -
(question mark)	quotation marks " "
exclamation point !	virgule (virgil) /

punc·ture (pungk'chər) *v.* **·tured, ·tur·ing** *v.t.* **1** To pierce with a sharp point. **2** To make by pricking, as a hole. **3** To cause to collapse: to *puncture* a reputation. — *v.i.* **4** To be pierced or punctured. See synonyms under PIERCE. — *n.* **1** A small hole, as in a pneumatic tire, made by piercing with something sharp-pointed. **2** A minute depression; pit. **3** The act of puncturing. [< LL *punctura* a prick, puncture < L *punctus*, pp. of *pungere* prick] — **punc'tur·a·ble** *adj.*

pun·dit (pun'dit) *n.* A learned Brahman, especially one versed in Sanskrit lore and in the science, laws, and religion of the Hindus; hence, any learned man. [< Hind. *pandit* < Skt. *pandita*, lit., learned, skilled]

pun·gent (pun'jənt) *adj.* **1** Having or causing sharp pricking, stinging, piercing, or acrid effects upon the senses. **2** Affecting the mind or feelings, as by sharp points, so as to cause pain; piercing; sharp. **3** Caustic; keen; racy: *pungent* sarcasm. **4** Terminating in a hard sharp point, as a pine needle. See synonyms under BITTER, HOT, RACY. [<L *pungens, -entis*, ppr. of *pungere* prick] — **pun′gence** or **pun′gen·cy** n. — **pun′gent·ly** adv.

pun·ish (pun′ish) v.t. **1** To subject (a person) to pain, confinement, or other penalty for a crime or fault. **2** To subject the perpetrator of (an offense) to a penalty: to *punish* forgery. **3** To use roughly; injure; hurt. **4** To make heavy inroads upon; deplete, as a stock of food. See synonyms under AVENGE, CHASTEN, REQUITE. [<OF *puniss-*, stem of *punir* <L *punire* <*poenire* <*poena* a punishment, penalty, fine] — **pun′ish·er** n.

pun·ish·a·ble (pun′ish·ə·bəl) adj. Deserving of or liable to punishment: said of offenders or offenses. — **pun′ish·a·bil′i·ty** n.

pun·ish·ment (pun′ish·mənt) n. **1** Penalty imposed, as for transgression of law. ◆ Collateral adjective: *penal.* **2** Any ill suffered in consequence of wrongdoing. **3** The act of punishing. **4** *Colloq.* Rough handling, as in a pugilistic encounter, a naval engagement, etc.

pu·ni·tive (pyōo′nə·tiv) adj. **1** Pertaining to or inflicting punishment. **2** *Law* Of a character to punish or vindicate. Also **pu′ni·to·ry** (-tôr′ē, -tō′rē). [<Med. L *punitivus* <L *punitus*, pp. of *punire* PUNISH] — **pu′ni·tive·ly** adv. — **pu′ni·tive·ness** n.

punk[1] (pungk) n. **1** Wood decayed through the action of some fungus, and useful as tinder; touchwood. **2** An artificial preparation that will smolder without flame. [<Algonquian (Lenape) *punk, ponk* fine ashes]

punk[2] (pungk) n. **1** *U.S. Slang* Rubbish; nonsense; anything worthless. **2** *U.S. Slang* A petty hoodlum. **3** *Obs.* A prostitute. — adj. *U.S. Slang* Worthless; useless. [Origin uncertain]

pun·ka (pung′kə) n. A fan; especially, a rectangular strip of cloth, etc., swung from the ceiling and moved by a servant or by machinery. Also **pun′kah.** [<Hind. *pankhā* a fan <Skt. *pakshaka* <*paksha* a wing]

pun·kie (pung′kē) n. [<Du. *punki* <Algonquian (Lenape) *punk, ponk,* orig. fine ashes]

pun·ster (pun′stər) n. One who puns; one addicted to punning. Also **pun′ner.**

punt[1]   (punt)   n. A flat-bottomed, square-ended boat, usually with a seat in the middle and a well or seat at one or each end, for use in shallow waters, and propelled with

PUNT

a pole. — v.t. **1** To propel (a boat) by pushing with a pole against the bottom of a shallow stream, lake, etc. **2** To convey in a punt. — v.i. **3** To go or hunt in a punt. [OE <L *ponto, -onis* a punt, a pontoon <*pons, pontis* a bridge] — **punt′er** n.

punt[2] (punt) v.i. To gamble or bet, especially against a bank, as at faro, roulette, or baccarat. [<F *ponter* <*ponte* a point <L *punctum*] — **punt′er** n.

punt[3] (punt) n. In football, a kick made by dropping the ball from the hands and kicking it before it strikes the ground. — v.t. In football, to propel (the ball) with a punt. — v.i. In football, to make a punt. [Prob. var. of BUNT] — **punt′er** n.

pup (pup) n. **1** A puppy (def. 1). **2** A young seal. — v.i. **pupped, pup·ping** To bring forth pups. [Short for PUPPY]

pu·pa (pyōo′pə) n. pl. **·pae** (-pē) **1** *Entomol.*

PUPAE illustration

PUPAE
a. Three pupal stages of a bumblebee.
b. Aquatic pupa of a gnat.
c. Suspended pupa of a butterfly.
d. Girdled pupa of a butterfly.

The quiescent stage in the development of an insect that undergoes a complete metamorphosis, following the larval and preceding the adult stage; also, an insect in such a stage. **2** *Zool.* A similar developmental state in some echinoderms, as holothurians. [<NL <L, a girl, doll, puppet] — **pu′pal** adj.

pu·pate (pyōo′pāt) v.i. **·pat·ed, ·pat·ing** To enter upon or undergo the pupal condition. — **pu·pa′tion** n.

pu·pil[1] (pyōo′pəl) n. **1** A person of either sex or of any age under the care of a teacher; scholar; learner. **2** In civil law, a minor who is under the age of puberty and has a guardian. See synonyms under SCHOLAR.[< OF *pupille,* orig. an orphan, ward <L *pupillus,* dim. of *pupus* a boy and *pupilla,* dim. of *pupa* a girl]

pu·pil[2] (pyōo′pəl) n. *Anat.* The contractile opening in the iris of the eye, through which light reaches the retina. [<L *pupilla* a figure reflected in the eye, the pupil of the eye, dim. of *pupa.* See PUPA.]

pu·pip·a·rous (pyōo·pip′ər·əs) adj. Of or pertaining to a division (*Pupipara*) of dipterous insects in which the young are born ready to pupate, as bat ticks, sheep ticks, etc. [<NL <PUPA + L *parere* bring forth]

pup·pet (pup′it) n. **1** A small figure of a human being, that by means of strings or wires is made to perform mock drama; a marionette. **2** A person slavishly subject to the will of another; a tool. **3** A doll. — adj. **1** Of or pertaining to puppets or mummery. **2** Performing the will of an unseen power; not autonomous: a *puppet* state or government. [<OF *poupette* <L *pupa* a girl, doll, puppet]

pup·pet·eer (pup′i·tir′) n. A person who manipulates puppets.

puppet show A mock drama, with puppets for the actors.

pup·py (pup′ē) n. pl. **·pies** **1** The young of a canine mammal, as of a dog; a pup. **2** A conceited and forward young man; a silly fop. [<OF *poupee, popee* <L *pupa* a girl, doll] — **pup′py·ish** adj.

puppy love Adolescent love; sentimental, temporary infatuation.

pup tent A shelter tent.

pur (pûr) See PURR.

Pu·ra·na (pŏŏ·rä′nə) n. Any of a number of Hindu scriptures in the form of verse dialogs, coming next in order after the Vedas, dealing mainly with theogony and cosmogony, especially with the god Vishnu and his incarnations. There are 18 Puranas and 18 Upa Puranas or subordinate works. [<Skt. *purāna,* lit., ancient <*purā* of old]

pur·blind (pûr′blīnd′) adj. **1** Afflicted with dimness of vision; near-sighted. **2** Having little or no insight or understanding. **3** *Obs.* Totally blind. [ME *pur blind* <*pur* (<OF, plain) + *blind* blind] — **pur′blind′ly** adv. — **pur′blind′ness** n.

pur·chas·a·ble (pûr′chəs·ə·bəl) adj. That can be purchased; hence, venal; corrupt. — **pur′chas·a·bil′i·ty** n.

pur·chase (pûr′chəs) v.t. **·chased, ·chas·ing** **1** To acquire by paying money or its equivalent; buy. **2** To obtain by exertion, sacrifice, flattery, etc. **3** *Law* To acquire (property) by means other than descent or inheritance. **4** To move, hoist, or hold by a mechanical purchase. — n. **1** The act of purchasing; acquisition by giving an equivalent in money or other exchange, or by exertion, risk, etc. **2** That which is purchased; especially, that which is bought with money. **3** A mechanical hold or grip. **4** A device that gives a mechanical advantage, as a tackle or lever. **5** Leverage. **6** Any means of increasing influence or advantage. **7** *Law* The act of acquiring property by payment of a price or value; hence, any lawful mode of acquiring property other than by inheritance or descent or by the mere operation of law. **8** Value; worth, especially as measured by the annual income, expressed in terms of years to indicate the period at the end of which the income received from a property will have covered the price paid for it: to buy at ten years' *purchase.* **9** A small territorial division in New Hampshire, originally made when the land was sold in lots to individuals by the State. **10** *Obs.* A seeking; also, attempt; endeavor. [<AF *purchacer,* OF *porchacier* seek for <*pur-, por-* for (<L *pro-*) + *chacier* CHASE] — **pur′chas·er** n.

Synonyms (verb): acquire, buy, get, obtain, procure, secure. *Buy* and *purchase* are close synonyms, in numerous cases freely interchangeable, but with the difference usually found between words of Anglo-Saxon and French or Latin origin. The Anglo-Saxon *buy* is used for all the concerns of common life, the French *purchase* is often restricted to transactions of more dignity; yet *buy* is commonly more emphatic, and also appeals more strongly to the feelings. One may either *buy* or *purchase* fame, favor, honor, pleasure, etc., but we speak of victory or freedom as dearly *bought.* Antonyms: barter, exchange, sell.

pure (pyŏŏr) adj. **1** Free from mixture or contact with that which weakens, impairs, or pollutes; containing no foreign or vitiating material. **2** Free from adulteration; clear; clean; hence, genuine; stainless: *pure* food, *pure* motives. **3** Free from moral defilement; innocent; chaste; unsullied; also, free from coarseness; refined: a *pure* life, *pure* language. **4** Free from foreign or imported elements: said especially of language and works of art. **5** *Music* Mathematically correct as to intervals; free from harsh quality in tone; also, correct in form or style; finished. **6** *Philos.* Considered apart from its attributes or from concrete experience; abstract; also, a priori. **7** *Phonet.* Having a single, unvarying tone or sound: said of vowels. **8** Theoretical; concerned with fundamental research, as distinguished from practical application: said of sciences. **9** *Genetics* Breeding true with respect to one or more characters; homozygous. **10** Nothing but; real; sheer: *pure* mischief, *pure* luck. [<OF *pur* <L *purus* clean, pure] — **pure′ness** n.

Synonyms: absolute, chaste, classic, classical, clean, clear, continent, fair, genuine, guileless, guiltless, holy, immaculate, incorrupt, innocent, mere, perfect, real, sheer, simple, spotless, stainless, true, unadulterated, unblemished, uncorrupted, undefiled, unmingled, unmixed, unpolluted, unspotted, unstained, unsullied, untainted, untarnished, upright, virtuous. Material substances are called *pure* in the strict sense when free from foreign admixture of any kind; as, *pure* oxygen; the word is often used to signify free from any defiling or objectionable admixture (the original sense); we speak of water as *pure* when it is bright, clear, and refreshing, even if it contains mineral salts in solution; in the medical and chemical sense, only distilled water (*aqua distillata*) is *pure.* In moral and religious use *pure* denotes positive excellence of a high order; one is *innocent* who knows nothing of evil and has experienced no touch of temptation; one is *pure* who, with knowledge of evil and exposure to temptation, keeps heart and soul *unstained. Virtuous* refers primarily to right action, *pure* to right feeling; as, "Blessed are the *pure* in heart: for they shall see God." *Matt.* v 8. See FINE[1], INNOCENT, MODEST, VIRTUOUS. Antonyms: adulterated, defiled, dirty, filthy, gross, impure, indecent, indelicate, lewd, mixed, obscene, polluted, stained, sullied, tainted, tarnished, unchaste, unclean; see also synonyms for FOUL, IMMODEST.

pure·bred (pyŏŏr′bred′) adj. Bred from stock having had no admixture for many generations: said of livestock. — n. (pyŏŏr′bred′) A purebred animal.

pu·rée (pyŏŏ·rā′, pyŏŏr′ā; *Fr.* pü·rā′) n. A thick pulp, usually of vegetables, boiled and strained. — v.t. **·réed, ·rée·ing** To put (cooked or soft food) through a sieve, blender, etc.: to *purée* vegetables. [<F <OF, pp. fem. of *purer* strain <L *purare* purify <*purus* pure]

pure·ly (pyŏŏr′lē) adv. **1** So as to be free from admixture, taint, or any harmful substance. **2** Chastely; innocently. **3** Merely.

pur·fle (pûr′fəl) v.t. **·fled, ·fling** To decorate, as with a wrought or flowered border; border. — n. A richly ornamented border: also **pur′fling.** [<OF *porfiler, pourfiler* <*por-, pour-* for (<L *pro-*) + *fil* a thread <L *filum*]

pur·ga·tive (pûr′gə·tiv) adj. Efficacious in purging; cathartic. — n. A cathartic.

pur·ga·to·ry (pûr′gə·tôr′ē, -tō′rē) n. pl. **·ries** **1** In Roman Catholic theology, a state or place where the souls of those who have died penitent are made fit for paradise by expiating venial sins and undergoing any punishment remaining for previously forgiven sins. **2** Any place or state of temporary banishment, suffering, or punishment. [<AF *purgatorie,* OF *purgatoire* <Med. L *purgatorium* <L *purgatorius* cleansing <*purgare* PURGE] — **pur′ga·to′ri·al** adj.

purge (pûrj) v. **purged, purg·ing** v.t. **1** To cleanse of what is impure or extraneous; purify. **2** To remove (impurities, etc.) in cleansing: with *away, off,* or *out.* **3** To rid (a group, nation, etc.) of elements regarded as undesirable or inimical, especially by killing. **4** To remove or kill (a person or persons) in such a manner. **5** To cleanse or rid of sin, fault, or defilement. **6** *Med.* **a** To cause evacuation of (the bowels, etc.). **b** To induce evacuation of the bowels of. **7** *Law* To clear of accusation, suspicion, or guilt. — v.i. **8** To become clean or pure. **9** *Med.* To have or induce evacuation. — n. **1** The act or operation of purging, in any sense. **2** That which purges; specifically, a medicine causing active evacuation of the bowels; a cathartic; also, its administration or operation. [< OF *purgier* < L *purgare* cleanse < *purigare* < *purus* pure] — **purg′er** n. — **purg′ing** n.

pu·ri·fi·ca·tion (pyōō′rə·fə·kā′shən) n. **1** The act or operation of purifying: said of things physical or spiritual. **2** The act or observance of formal cleansing from ceremonial defilement. ◆ Collateral adjective: *lustral.*

pu·ri·fy (pyōō′rə·fī) v. **·fied, ·fy·ing** v.t. **1** To make pure or clean; rid of extraneous or noxious matter. **2** To free from sin or defilement. **3** To free of foreign or debasing elements, as a language. — v.i. **4** To become pure or clean. [< OF *purifier* < L *purificare* < *purus* pure + *facere* make] — **pu·ri·fi·ca·to·ry** (pyōō·rif′ə·kə·tôr′ē, -tō′rē-) adj. — **pu′·ri·fi′er** n.

Synonyms: clarify, clean, cleanse, filter, refine, wash. See AMEND, CHASTEN, CLEANSE. *Antonyms:* contaminate, corrupt, debase, defile, deprave, infect, poison, taint, vitiate.

pur·ism (pyōō′riz·əm) n. Extreme strictness in regard to the use of words, or an instance of it. — **pur′ist** n. — **pu·ris′tic** adj.

Pu·ri·tan (pyōō′rə·tən) n. **1** One of a group or party of English Protestants (1599) who advocated simpler forms of creed and ritual in the established church, freedom of conscience and worship, and condemned all laxity of morals. Many of them emigrated to the American colonies in the 17th century, especially to the Massachusetts Bay colony. **2** One who is scrupulously strict, or censorious and exacting in his religious life: often not capitalized. — adj. Of or pertaining to the Puritans or their beliefs or customs. [< LL *puritas* purity < L *purus* pure + -AN; orig. used by opponents to suggest a resemblance to the *Cathari* (lit., purists)] — **Pu′ri·tan′ic** adj.

pu·ri·tan·i·cal (pyōō′rə·tan′i·kəl) adj. Governed by the Puritan code; rigidly scrupulous in religious observance and morals; strict. — **pu′ri·tan′i·cal·ly** adv. — **pu′ri·tan′i·cal·ness** n.

pu·ri·ty (pyōō′rə·tē) n. **1** The character or state of being pure, in any sense; as freedom from dirt or foreign or adulterating matter; cleanness; moral cleanness; innocence; freedom from sinister or improper design; absence of admixture. **2** Saturation: said of a color. **3** The use of no foreign words, phrases, or idioms; use of words with only the precise form, connection, and meaning assigned to them by good usage. See synonyms under INNOCENCE, VIRTUE.

purl¹ (pûrl) v.i. **1** To whirl; turn. **2** To flow with a bubbling sound; ripple. **3** To move in eddies. — n. **1** A circling movement of water; an eddy. **2** A gentle, continued murmur, as of a rippling stream. ◆ Homophone: *pearl.* [Cf. Norw. *purla* gush out, bubble up]

purl² (pûrl) v.t. **1** To purfle. **2** In knitting, to make (a stitch) backward. **3** To edge with lace, embroidery, etc. — v.i. **4** To do edging with lace, etc. [< n.] — n. **1** An edge of lace, embroidery, etc.; in lacework, a spiral of gold or silver wire. **2** In knitting, the inversion of the knit stitch giving a horizontal rib effect. ◆ Homophone: *pearl.* [Earlier *pyrle,* orig. twisted gold or silver thread < *pyrl* twist; ult. origin unknown]

pur·lieu (pûr′lōō) n. **1** *pl.* The outlying districts or outskirts of any place. **2** A place in which one is free to come and go; a haunt. **3** Formerly, ground unlawfully taken from a royal forest, but afterward disafforested and restored to its rightful owners. [< AF *puralee* < OF < *puraler* go through < *pur-* through (< L *per-*) + *aler* go; infl. in form by MF *lieu* a place]

pur·loin (pûr·loin′) v.t. & v.i. To steal; filch. See synonyms under ABSTRACT, STEAL. [< AF *purloignier,* OF *porloignier* remove, put far off < *pur-, por-* for (< L *pro-*) + *loing, loin* far < L *longe*] — **pur·loin′er** n.

pur·ple (pûr′pəl) n. **1** A color of mingled red and blue, between crimson and violet; in ancient times, the color obtained from the murex, properly a crimson. **2** Cloth or a garment of this color, worn formerly by sovereigns, especially the emperors of Rome; hence, royal power or dignity; preeminence in rank or wealth. **3** The office of a cardinal: from the official red hat and robes; also, the episcopal dignity: from its purple insignia. — v.t. & v.i. **·pled, ·pling** To make or become purple. — adj. **1** Of the color of purple. **2** Hence, imperial; regal. **3** Conspicuously brilliant or ornate; exalted of language. [Alter. of ME *purpre,* OE *purpure,* the color purple < L *purpura,* orig. the shellfish yielding Tyrian purple dye, the dye, or cloth dyed with it < Gk. *porphyra*]

Purple Heart A decoration of honor of the **Order of the Purple Heart** in the form of a purple enameled heart surrounded by a gold-colored border and bearing the head of George Washington in gold-colored relief: established by George Washington in 1782, revived 1932: awarded to members of the armed forces or to citizens of the United States honorably wounded in action, or as a result of enemy action.

PURPLE HEART

purple medic or **medick** Alfalfa.

purple of Cassius A rich and powerful pigment obtained from a mixture of stannic, stannous, and gold chlorides: used chiefly in miniature painting and enamel painting.

pur·plish (pûr′plish) adj. Somewhat purple.

pur·port (pər·pôrt′, -pōrt′, pûr′pôrt, -pōrt) v.t. **1** To have or bear as its meaning; signify; imply. **2** To claim or profess (to be), especially falsely. See synonyms under IMPORT. — n. (pûr′pôrt, -pōrt) **1** That which is conveyed or suggested to the mind as the meaning or intention; import; significance. **2** The substance of a statement, etc., given in other than the exact words. See synonyms under PURPOSE. [< AF, OF *purporter* extend < *pur-* forth (< L *pro-*) + *porter* carry < L *portare*] — **pur·port′ed·ly** adv.

pur·pose (pûr′pəs) v.t. & v.i. **·posed, ·pos·ing** To have the intention of doing or accomplishing (something); intend; aim; design. — n. **1** The idea or ideal kept before the mind as an end of effort or action; plan; design; aim. **2** The particular thing to be effected or attained; practical advantage or result; consequence; use: words to little *purpose.* **3** Settled resolution; determination; constancy. **4** Purport; intent, as of spoken or written language. **5** A proposition; proposal; question or issue. — **on purpose** With previous design; intentionally. [< OF *porposer,* var of *proposer.* See PROPOSE.]

Synonyms (noun): aim, design, determination, drift, end, intent, intention, meaning, motive, object, plan, project, purport, resolution, resolve, view. Compare AIM, CAUSE, DESIGN, END, IDEA, PLAN, PROJECT, REASON, SERVICE. *Antonyms:* See synonyms for ACT.

Synonyms (verb): design, determine, intend, mean, propose, resolve. See PROPOSE.

pur·pose·ful (pûr′pəs·fəl) adj. Having, or marked by, purpose; intentional; important; significant. — **pur′pose·ful·ly** adv. — **pur′pose·ful·ness** n.

pur·pose·less (pûr′pəs·lis) adj. Having no definite design or use; aimless. See synonyms under FAINT. — **pur′pose·less·ly** adv.

pur·pose·ly (pûr′pəs·lē) adv. For a purpose; intentionally; deliberately; on purpose.

pur·po·sive (pûr′pə·siv) adj. **1** Pertaining to, having, or indicating purpose. **2** Functional. —

pur·po·sive·ly adv. — **pur′po·sive·ness** n.

pur·pure (pûr′pyoor) n. Purple: one of the colors or tinctures used in heraldic description. [OE]

pur·pu·ric (pûr·pyoor′ik) adj. **1** Of or pertaining to a purple tint. **2** Relating to or resembling purpura.

purr (pûr) n. An intermittent murmuring sound, such as a cat makes when pleased. — v.i. To make such a sound. — v.t. To express by or as by purring. Also spelled *pur.* [Imit.]

purse (pûrs) n. **1** A small bag or pouch of leather or the like, often having the mouth drawn together with a drawstring; especially, one for carrying money; hence, anything for carrying money on the person. **2** Available resources or means; a treasury: the public *purse.* **3** A sum of money offered as a prize or tendered as a gift, as for a contest or charitable collection. — v.t. **pursed, purs·ing 1** To contract into wrinkles or folds like the mouth of a purse; pucker: to *purse* the lips. **2** *Rare* To place in a purse. [OE *purs* < LL *bursa* < Gk. *byrsa* a skin, a hide]

purse-pride (pûrs′prīd′) n. Arrogance due to the possession of wealth. — **purse′proud′.** (-proud′) adj.

purs·er (pûr′sər) n. An officer having charge of the accounts, etc., of a vessel; formerly, a naval paymaster. — **purs′er·ship** n.

pur·su·ance (pər·sōō′əns) n. The act of pursuing; a following after or following out; prosecution: usually in the phrase *in pursuance of.*

pur·su·ant (pər·sōō′ənt) adj. Done in accordance with or by reason of something; conformable. — adv. In accordance; conformably: usually with *to:* also **pur·su′ant·ly.**

pur·sue (pər·sōō′) v. **·sued, ·su·ing** v.t. **1** To follow in an attempt to overtake or capture; chase. **2** To seek or attain or gain: to *pursue* fame. **3** To advance along the course of; keep to the direction or provisions of, as a path, plan, or system. **4** To apply one's energies to or have as one's profession or chief interest: to *pursue* one's studies. **5** To follow persistently; harass; worry. — v.i. **6** To follow. **7** To continue. See synonyms under FOLLOW. [< AF *pursuer,* OF *persievre* < LL *prosequere* < L *prosequi* < *pro-* forth + *sequi* follow] — **pur·su′a·ble** adj. — **pur·su′er** n.

pur·suit (pər·sōōt′) n. **1** The act of pursuing; a chase. **2** That which is followed as a continued employment; a business; vocation. See synonyms under HUNT. [< AF *purseute,* OF *porsieute, poursuite* < *porsievre* PURSUE]

pur·sui·vant (pûr′swi·vənt) n. **1** An attendant upon a herald; an officer of the third and lowest rank in the College of Heralds, performing similar duties to a herald. **2** *Obs.* A follower; especially, a military attendant of the king. [< OF *porsivant,* ppr. of *porsievre* pursue]

purs·y (pûr′sē) adj. **purs·i·er, purs·i·est** Short-breathed; asthmatic; hence, fat. See synonyms under CORPULENT. [Earlier *pursive* < AF *pursif,* OF *polsif* < *polser* pant, gasp] — **purs′i·ness** n.

pu·ru·lent (pyoor′ə·lənt, -yə·lənt) adj. Consisting of or secreting pus; suppurating. [< L *purulentus* < *pus, puris* pus] — **pu′ru·lence** or **·len·cy** n. — **pu′ru·lent·ly** adv.

pur·vey (pər·vā′) v.t. & v.i. To furnish or provide (provisions, etc.). [< AF *purveier,* OF *porveier* < L *providere.* Doublet of PROVIDE.]

pur·vey·ance (pər·vā′əns) n. **1** The act of purveying. **2** That which is purveyed or supplied; provisions. **3** A former prerogative of royalty, abolished in 1660, enabling a monarch to buy goods at an appraised value, and also to enforce personal service.

pur·vey·or (pər·vā′ər) n. **1** One who furnishes supplies for living, especially for the table; a caterer. **2** Formerly, an officer who, by exaction or otherwise, made provision for the king's household.

pur·view (pûr′vyoo) n. **1** Extent, sphere, or scope of anything, as of official authority. **2** Range of view, experience, or understanding; outlook. **3** *Law* The body or the scope or limit of a statute. [< AF *purveu* provided, OF *porveu,* pp. of *porveier* PURVEY; orig. in AF legal phrases *purveu est* it is provided and *purveu que* provided that]

pus (pus) n. *Med.* A secretion from inflamed tissues, as in healing wounds, usually viscid or creamy, and consisting of modified leucocytes and other cells in a liquid plasma: the result of suppuration. [< L. Akin to PUTRID.]

push (poŏsh) *v.t.* **1** To exert force upon or against (an object) for the purpose of moving. **2** To force (one's way), as through a crowd, jungle, etc. **3** To press forward, prosecute, or develop with vigor and persistence: to *push* trade with South America. **4** To urge, advocate, or promote vigorously and persistently: to *push* a new product. **5** To bear hard upon; distress; harass: I am *pushed* for time. **6** *Slang* To sell (narcotic drugs) illegally. —*v.i.* **7** To exert steady pressure against something so as to move it. **8** To move or advance vigorously or persistently. **9** To exert great effort. **10** To project; extend; reach: The island *pushed* out far into the sea. —*n.* **1** A propelling or thrusting pressure; repulsion as opposed to attraction or pull; a shove. **2** *Colloq.* An extremity; exigency: at a *push* for money. **3** Determined activity; energy. **4** Anything pushed to cause action; a pushbutton. **5** *Slang* The crowd; a number of friends or associates: He fooled the whole *push;* also, an influential clique. **6** *Austral. Slang* A body of larrikins. [< OF *pousser, polser* < L *pulsare.* See PULSATE.]

push·er (poŏsh′ər) *n.* **1** One who or that which pushes; especially, an active, energetic person. **2** *Aeron.* An airplane with the propeller in the rear of the wings. **3** *U.S. Slang* One who sells illegally, especially one who sells narcotics to addicts.

push·ing (poŏsh′ing) *adj.* **1** Possessing business enterprise and energy. **2** Possessing aggressiveness; impertinent. —**push′ing·ly** *adv.*

push·o·ver (poŏsh′ō′vər) *v. Slang* A susceptible person; an easy mark; also, anything done or that can be done with little or no effort.

Push·tu (push′toō) *n.* The Iranian language of the dominant peoples of Afghanistan; Afghan: also spelled *Pashto.* Also **Push′to** (-tō).

pu·sil·la·nim·i·ty (pyoō′səl·ə·nim′ə·tē) *n.* Faintheartedness; indecision; cowardice. Also **pu′sil·lan′i·mous·ness.**

pu·sil·lan·i·mous (pyoō′sə·lan′ə·məs) *adj.* **1** Lacking strength of mind, courage, or spirit; mean-spirited; cowardly. **2** Characterized by weakness of purpose or lack of courage. [< LL *pusillanimis* < L *pusillus* very little + *animus* mind] —**pu′sil·lan′i·mous·ly** *adv.*
Synonyms: cowardly, dastardly, faint-hearted, feeble, mean-spirited, recreant, spiritless, timid, timorous, weak. *Antonyms:* see synonyms for BRAVE.

puss (poŏs) *n.* **1** A cat. **2** A child or young woman: a term of affection. [Cf. Du. *poes*, LG *puus*, a name for a cat]

pus·sy¹ (poŏs′ē) *n. pl.* **·sies 1** Puss; a cat: a diminutive. **2** A fuzzy catkin, as of a willow, a birch, etc. [Dim. of PUSS¹]

pus·sy² (pus′ē) *adj.* Full of pus.

pus·sy·foot (poŏs′ē·foŏt′) *v.i.* **1** To move softly and stealthily, as a cat does. **2** To act or proceed without committing oneself or revealing one's intentions.

pus·sy willow (poŏs′ē) **1** A small American willow (*Salix discolor*) with silky catkins in early spring: also called *glaucous willow.* **2** One of various other willows bearing catkins in early spring.

pus·tu·lant (pus′choō·lənt) *adj.* Causing pustules. —*n.* A medicine that causes pustules.

PUSSY WILLOW

pus·tu·lar (pus′choō·lər) *adj.* **1** Proceeding from or marked by pustules: a *pustular* eruption. **2** Pustulate.

pus·tu·late (pus′choō·lāt) *v.t. & v.i.* **·lat·ed, ·lat·ing** To form into or become pustules. —*adj.* (-lāt, -lit) Covered with pustules or pustule-like elevations. [< L *pustulatus*, pp. of *pustulare* blister < *pustula* a pustule]

pus·tule (pus′choōl) *n.* **1** *Pathol.* A small, circumscribed elevation of the skin with an inflamed base containing pus. **2** Any elevation resembling a pimple or a blister. [< L *pustula*]

put (poŏt) *v.* **put, put·ting** *v.t.* **1** To bring into

or set in a specified or implied place or position; lay: *Put* the book on the table. **2** To bring into a specified state, condition, or relation: to *put* a prisoner to death. **3** To apply; bring to bear: *Put* your back into it! **4** To impose: to *put* a tariff on bicycles. **5** To ascribe or attribute, as the wrong interpretation on a remark. **6** To place according to one's estimation: I *put* the time at five o'clock. **7** To throw with a pushing motion of the arm: to *put* the shot. **8** To incite; prompt. Who *put* him up to it? **9** To bring forward for debate, answer, consideration, etc.: to *put* a question. **10** To subject: Let's *put* it to a vote. **11** To express in words; state: That's *putting* it mildly. **12** To risk; bet: I'll *put* six dollars on that horse. —*v.i.* **13** To go; proceed: to *put* to sea. —**to put about** *Naut.* To change to the opposite tack; change direction. —**to put aside (or away or by) 1** To place in reserve; save. **2** To thrust aside; discard. —**to put down 1** To repress; crush. **2** To degrade; demote. **3** To write. —**to put forth 1** To extend, as the arm or hand. **2** To grow, as shoots or buds. **3** To exert. **4** To set out; leave port. —**to put forward** To advance; urge, as a claim. —**to put in 1** *Naut.* To enter a harbor or place of shelter. **2** To interpolate; interpose. **3** *Colloq.* To devote; expend, as time. **4** To advance (a claim, etc.). **5** To submit, as an application. —**to put off 1** To delay; postpone. **2** To discard. **3** To make uneasy or uncomfortable; disconcert. —**to put on 1** To don. **2** To bring into action; turn on. **3** To simulate; pretend. **4** To give a representation of; stage. —**to put out 1** To extinguish. **2** To expel; eject. **3** To disconcert; embarrass. **4** To inconvenience. **5** To put forth. **6** In baseball, to retire (a batter or base runner). —**to put over 1** To place in command or charge. **2** *Colloq.* To accomplish successfully. —**to put one (or something) over on** *Colloq.* To deceive or dupe. —**to put through 1** To bring to successful completion. **2** To cause to perform. —**to put up 1** To erect; build. **2** To preserve or can. **3** To wager. **4** To provide (money, capital, etc.). **5** To sheathe, as a weapon. —**to put upon** To deceive; cheat. —**to put up with** To endure; tolerate. —*n.* **1** The act of putting, as a cast or throw. **2** A contract by which one person, in consideration of money paid to another, acquires the privilege of selling or delivering to the latter within a certain time some article named, as wheat or cotton, or shares at a stipulated price: opposed to *call.* —*adj. Colloq.* Fixed; settled as fixed: My hat won't stay put. [Fusion of OE *putian* place, *potian* thrust, and *pȳtan* push, prob. all <Scand. Cf. Dan. *putte.*]
Synonyms (verb): deposit, lay, place, set. *Put* is the most general term for bringing an object to some point or within some space, however exactly or loosely; we may *put* a horse in a pasture, or *put* a bullet in a rifle or into an enemy. *Place* denotes more careful movement and more exact location; as, to *place* a crown on one's head, or a garrison in a city. To *lay* is to *place* in a horizontal or recumbent position; to *set* is to *place* or adjust in a certain place or position; we *lay* a cloth, and *set* a dish upon a table. To *deposit* is to *put* in a place of security for future use; as, to *deposit* money in a bank; the original sense, to *lay* down is also common; as, the stream *deposits* sediment; insects *deposit* eggs. Compare SET.

pu·ta·tive (pyoō′tə·tiv) *adj.* Supposed; reported; reputed. [<MF *putatif* <LL *putativus* <L *putatus*, pp. of *putare* think] —**pu′ta·tive·ly** *adv.*

put·log (poŏt′lôg, -log, put′-) *n.* A crosspiece in a scaffolding, its inner end resting in a hole in the wall and its outer on a ledger. [Earlier *putlock* <*put*, pp. of PUT¹]

pu·tre·fac·tion (pyoō′trə·fak′shən) *n.* **1** The progressive chemical decomposition of organic matter, as by the agency of anaerobic bacteria, with the production of evil-smelling compounds. **2** The state of being putrefied. **3** Putrescent or putrefied matter. [<OF <L *putrefactio, -onis* < *putrefacere* PUTREFY]

pu·tre·fy (pyoō′trə·fī) *v.t. & v.i.* **·fied, ·fy·ing 1** To decay or cause to decay with fetid odor; rot; decompose. **2** To make or become gangrenous. [<L *putrefacere* <*putrere* decay (< *puter* rotten) + *facere* make] —**pu′tre·fi′er** *n.*

Synonyms: corrupt, decay, decompose, rot. See CORRUPT, DECAY. *Antonyms:* disinfect, embalm, freshen, preserve, purify, vitalize.

pu·tres·cence (pyoō·tres′əns) *n.* **1** The state of undergoing putrefaction. **2** Something that is putrescent.

pu·tres·cent (pyoō·tres′ənt) *adj.* **1** Becoming putrid; undergoing putrefaction. **2** Pertaining to putrefaction. [<L *putrescens, -entis*, ppr. of *putrescere* grow rotten, inceptive of *putrere.* See PUTREFY.]

pu·tres·ci·ble (pyoō·tres′ə·bəl) *adj.* Liable to putrefy. —*n.* A substance that decomposes at a certain temperature in contact with air and moisture: generally containing nitrogen. —**pu·tres′ci·bil′i·ty** *n.*

pu·trid (pyoō′trid) *adj.* **1** Being in a state of putrefaction; decomposed or decomposing; rotten: *putrid* meat. **2** Indicating or produced by putrefaction: a *putrid* smell. **3** Rotten; corrupt. See synonyms under BAD¹, ROTTEN. [<L *putridus* <*putrere.* See PUTREFY.] —**pu·trid′i·ty** *n.* —**pu′trid·ness** *n.*

Putsch (poŏch) *n.* An outbreak or rebellion; an attempted coup d'état. [<G <dial. G (Swiss), lit., a push, blow]

putt (put) *n.* In golf, a light stroke made on a putting green to place the ball in or near the hole. [< *v.*] —*v.t. & v.i.* To strike (the ball) with such a stroke. [Var. of PUT¹]

put·tee (put′ē, pu·tē′) *n.* A strip of cloth wound spirally about the leg from knee to ankle, as used by soldiers, sportsmen, etc.; also, a leather gaiter strapped around the leg. Also **put′ty.** [<Hind. *paṭṭī* a bandage <Skt. *paṭṭa* a strip of cloth]

put·ter¹ (put′ər) *n.* **1** One who putts: He is a poor *putter.* **2** An upright, stiff-shafted golf club used on the putting green. [<PUTT]

put·ter² (put′ər) *v.i.* To act, work, or proceed in a dawdling or ineffective manner; trifle. —*v.t.* To waste or spend (time, etc.) in dawdling or puttering. [Var. of POTTER¹]

put·ti·er (put′ē·ər) *n.* One who putties; a glazier. [<PUTTY]

putting green (put′ing) In golf, the smooth ground within twenty yards of the hole; also, a place set aside for putting practice. [<PUTT]

put·ty (put′ē) *n.* **1** Whiting mixed with linseed oil to the consistency of dough: used for filling holes or cracks in wood surfaces, securing panes of glass in the sash, making relief ornaments, etc. **2** Fine lime mortar for filling cracks, finishing, etc. —**iron putty** Ferric oxide mixed with boiled linseed oil: used in making pipe-joint connections. —**red-lead putty** Red and white lead mixed with boiled linseed oil, used mainly for cementing pipe joints. —*v.t.* **·tied, ·ty·ing** To fill, stop, fasten, etc., with putty. [<OF *potee* calcined tin, lit., a potful < *pot* a pot]

Pu-yi (poō′yē′), **Henry**, 1906–1967, last Manchu emperor of China 1908–12; abdicated; puppet emperor of Manchukuo 1934–45, under name *Kang Te;* abdicated.

puz·zle (puz′əl) *v.* **·zled, ·zling** *v.t.* **1** To confuse or perplex; mystify. **2** To solve by investigation and study, as something perplexing: with *out.* —*v.i.* **3** To be perplexed or confused. See synonyms under PERPLEX. —**to puzzle over** To attempt to understand or solve. —*n.* **1** A thing difficult to understand or explain; perplexing problem; an enigma or problem. **2** Something, as a toy, purposely arranged so as to require time, patience, and ingenuity to solve its intricacies. **3** The state of being puzzled; a quandary; perplexity. See synonyms under RIDDLE². —**crossword puzzle** A pattern of white and black spaces, of which the white spaces are to be filled with letters that form words, vertically, horizontally, or diagonally, to agree with accompanying definitions. [Related to ME *poselet* confused; ult. origin unknown]

puz·zle·ment (puz′əl·mənt) *n.* State of being nonplused; perplexity.

puz·zler (puz′lər) *n.* One who or that which puzzles; a knotty question.

PX A military post exchange or general store. [<P(OST) (E)X(CHANGE)]

py- Var. of PYO-.

pyc·nom·e·ter (pik·nom′ə·tər) *n.* A specific-gravity bottle or flask. [<Gk. *pyknos* dense, thick + -METER]

pye (pī) See PIE⁴.

py·e·lo·gram (pī′ə·lō·gram′) *n.* A picture

taken by pyelography. [<*pyelo-* <Gk. *pyelos* a trough,] pelvis + -GRAM]

py·e·log·ra·phy (pī′ə·log′rə·fē) *n.* The technique of making X-rays of the ureter and the kidney by the use of a radiopaque dye. [<*pyelo-* <Gk. *pyelos* a trough, pelvis + -GRAPHY] — **py′e·lo·graph′ic** (-lō·graf′ik) *adj.*

Pyg·ma·li·on (pig·mā′lē·ən, -māl′yən) In Greek mythology, a sculptor of Cyprus, who fell in love with his statue, Galatea, which Aphrodite later brought to life.

pyg·my (pig′mē) See PIGMY.

Pyg·my (pig′mē) *n. pl.* **·mies** 1 A member of a Negroid people of equatorial Africa, ranging in height from four to five feet. 2 Any of the Negrito peoples of the Philippines, Andaman Islands, and Malaya. 3 In the *Iliad*, one of a race of dwarfs. [<L *pygmaeus.* See PIGMY.]

py·ic (pī′ik) *adj.* Of or pertaining to pus; purulent. [<PY- + -IC]

py·ja·mas (pə·jä′məz, -jam′əz) See PAJAMAS.

pyk·nic (pik′nik) *adj.* Characterized by plump contours and a broad, stocky build; fat; squat. — *n.* A person of this physical type. [<Gk. *pyknos* thick, compact]

py·lon (pī′lon) *n.* 1 *Archit.* A monumental structure constituting an entrance to an Egyptian temple or other large edifice, consisting of a central gateway, flanked on each side by a truncated pyramidal tower. 2 A stake marking the course in an airdrome or turning point in an aerial race. 3 One of the tall, mastlike metal structures from whose summits high-tension wires are carried across open country. 4 *Surg.* An artificial leg, usually temporary. [<Gk. *pylōn* a gateway <*pylē* a gate]

py·lo·rus (pī·lôr′əs, -lō′rəs, pi-) *n. pl.* **·ri** (-rī) *Anat.* The opening between the stomach and the duodenum, surrounded by circular muscle fibers; also, the adjoining portion of the stomach. [<LL <Gk. *pylōros* a gatekeeper <*pylē* a gate + *ouros* a watcher] — **py·lor′ic** (-lôr′ik, -lor′ik) *adj.*

pyo- *combining form* Pus; of or related to pus: *pyorrhea.* Also, before vowels, *py-.* [<Gk. *pyon* pus]

py·oid (pī′oid) *adj.* Resembling pus; purulent. [<PY- + -OID]

Pyong·yang (pyông·yäng) A city in northern Korea, capital of the Democratic People's Republic of Korea: Japanese **Hei·jo** (hā·jō).

py·o·sis (pī·ō′sis) *n.* Suppuration. [<NL <Gk. *pyōsis* <*pys, pyos* pus]

pyr- Var. of PYRO-.

py·ra·can·tha (pī′rə·kan′thə, pir′ə-) *n.* The firethorn. [<L <Gk. *pyrakantha* <*pyr, pyros* fire + *akantha, -ēs* a thorn]

py·ral·i·did (pi·ral′ə·did) *adj.* Of or pertaining to a family (*Pyralididae*) of small or medium-sized moths of slender build and broad hind wings, including many groups sometimes classified as separate families. — *n.* A moth belonging to this family. Also **pyr·a·lid** (pir′ə·lid). [<NL <L *pyralis, -idis* a winged insect supposed to live in fire <Gk. <*pyr, pyros* a fire] — **py·ral′i·dan** *adj. & n.*

pyr·a·mid (pir′ə·mid) *n.* 1 *Archit.* A solid structure of masonry with a square base and triangular sides meeting in an apex. Such structures were used as tombs or temples. The pyramids of Egypt, raised over the sepulchral chambers of kings, are the best examples. The most interesting group is at Giza, near Cairo. The pyramids of Mexico

THE PYRAMIDS AT GIZA

served as temples. The largest is the pyramid near Cholula on the Pueblo plateau, in central Mexico. 2 Something in pyramidal form. 3 *Geom.* A solid consisting of a polygonal

base and triangular sides, the apices of the triangles coming together at the vertex. 4 *Mineral.* A crystal form consisting of three or more similar planes having a common point of intersection. 5 *Physiol.* One of various pyramidal or conical structures found in animal organisms. 6 *Anat.* A small bony projection in the cavity of the tympanum. 7 Any tree trained in pyramidal form. 8 The operations involved in pyramiding. — *v.t. & v.i.* 1 To arrange or form in the shape of a pyramid. 2 To buy or sell (stock) with paper profits shown by the change in price of stock already purchased or sold, without any additional deposit of money being made, and to continue so buying or selling on each movement in price. [<F *pyramide* <L *pyramis, -idis* <Gk. *pyramis, -idos*, prob. <Egyptian *pi-mar* a pyramid]

py·ram·i·dal (pi·ram′ə·dəl) *adj.* Of or shaped like a pyramid. Also **pyr·a·mid·ic** (pir′ə·mid′ik), **pyr′a·mid′i·cal.** — **py·ram′i·dal·ly** *adv.*

Pyr·a·mus and This·be (pir′ə·məs, thiz′bē) In classical legend, two Babylonian lovers: believing Thisbe slain by a lion, Pyramus killed himself, and Thisbe, finding his body, took her own life.

py·ra·nom·e·ter (pī′rə·nom′ə·tər) *n.* An instrument for measuring sky radiation or radiation from the earth, especially at night. [<PYR- + ANO- + -METER]

py·rar·gy·rite (pī·rär′jə·rīt) *n.* A metallic, black sulfide of antimony and silver, Ag_3SbS_3, crystallizing in the rhombohedral system. [<PYR- + Gk. *argyros* silver + -ITE[1]]

pyre (pīr) *n.* 1 A heap of combustibles arranged for burning a dead body. 2 Any pile or heap of combustible material. [<L *pyra* a hearth, funeral pile <Gk. <*pyr* a fire]

Py·rene (pī′rēn) *n.* Carbon tetrachloride, prepared for use as a chemical fire extinguisher: a trade name.

Pyr·e·nees (pir′ə·nēz) A mountain chain between France and Spain, extending about 270 miles from the Bay of Biscay to the Mediterranean; highest point, Pico de Aneto, 11,168 feet. — **Pyr′e·ne′an** *adj.*

py·re·noid (pī·rē′noid) *adj.* Having the form of a fruit stone. — *n.* 1 *Bot.* A small, colorless mass of protein substance of a crystalline form, appearing in the chloroplasts of green algae. 2 *Zool.* A transparent body in the chromatophores of certain protozoa. [<Gk. *pyrēnoeidēs* <*pyrēn* a fruit stone + *eidos* a form, shape] — **py·re·no·de·an** (pī′ri·nō′dē·ən) *adj.*

Py·re·no·my·ce·tes (pī·rē′nō·mī·sē′tēz) *n. pl.* A large class of fungi characterized by the forcible expulsion of ascospores from the perithecium, including many parasitic species, as ergot. [<NL <Gk. *pyrēn* a fruit stone + *mykēs, mykētis* a mushroom]

py·reth·rum (pī·reth′rəm, -rē′thrəm) *n.* 1 The dried and powdered roots of the pellitory used in medicine as a sialogog and rubefacient. 2 The powdered flowers of a chrysanthemum (*Chrysanthemum cinerariaefolium*), used medically as an ointment, and as an insecticide. [<L, feverfew <Gk. *pyrethron* <*pyr* fire]

py·ret·ic (pī·ret′ik) *adj.* 1 Affected with or relating to fever; febrile. 2 Remedial in fevers. — *n.* A febrifuge. [<NL *pyreticus* <Gk. *pyretos* a fever <*pyr* fire]

pyr·e·tol·o·gy (pir′ə·tol′ə·jē, pī′rə-) *n.* The department of medical science that treats of fevers. [<Gk. *pyretos* a fever + -LOGY] — **pyr′e·tol′o·gist** *n.*

pyr·e·to·ther·a·py (pir′ə·tō·ther′ə·pē, pī′rə-) *n.* Medical treatment by the artificial induction of fever by electricity, bacterial infection, etc.; fever therapy. [<Gk. *pyretos* (a fever) + THERAPY]

Py·rex (pī′reks) *n.* A type of heat-resisting glass having a high silica content, with additions of soda, aluminum, and boron: a trade name.

pyr·i·form (pir′ə·fôrm) *adj.* Pear-shaped. [<NL *pyriformis* <Med. L *pyrum* a pear (<L *pirum*) + L *forma* form]

py·rite (pī′rīt) *n. pl.* **py·ri·tes** (pī·rī′tēz) A metallic, pale brass-yellow, opaque, isometric iron disulfide, FeS_2; fool's gold; iron pyrites.

[<L *pyrites* <Gk. *pyritēs* flint <*pyritēs (lithos)* fire (stone) <*pyr* fire] — **py·rit′ic** (-rit′ik) or **-i·cal** *adj.*

py·ri·tes (pī·rī′tēz) *n. pl.* The common name for various metallic sulfides: copper *pyrites.* Compare CHALCOPYRITE, PYRITE.

py·ro (pī′rō) *n.* Pyrogallol: so called in photography. [Short for PYROGALLOL]

pyro- *combining form* 1 Fire; heat: *pyromania.* 2 *Chem.* Denoting actual or hypothetical derivation by the action of heat; specifically, in certain inorganic acids, indicating derivation from two molecules of an ordinary acid by the elimination of one molecule of water: $2H_3AsO_4$ (arsenic acid) — H_2O = $H_4As_2O_7$ (pyroarsenic acid). 3 *Geol.* Resulting from the action of fire or heat: *pyrolusite.* Also, before vowels, *pyr-.* [<Gk. *pyr, pyros* fire]

py·ro·cel·lu·lose (pī′rō·sel′yə·lōs) *n.* A form of guncotton used as a propellant in smokeless powder. Also **py′ro·cot′ton** (-kot′n).

Py·ro·ce·ram (pī′rō·sə·ram′) *n.* A strongly heat-resistant, crystalline ceramic material formed from glass and characterized by extreme hardness, great tensile strength, and high dielectric properties: a trade name.

py·ro·chem·i·cal (pī′rə·kem′i·kəl) *adj.* Pertaining to chemical changes induced or effected by high temperature.

py·ro·con·duc·tiv·i·ty (pī′rə·kon′duk·tiv′ə·tē) *n.* Conductivity of an electric current dependent upon or improved by the application of heat. — **py′ro·con·duc′tive** (-kən·duk′tiv) *adj.*

py·ro·crys·tal·line (pī′rə·kris′tə·lin, -līn, pir′ə-) *adj.* Crystallized from materials in a state of fusion: *pyrocrystalline* masses.

py·ro·e·lec·tric (pī′rō·i·lek′trik, pir′ō-) *adj.* 1 Of or pertaining to pyroelectricity. 2 Manifesting pyroelectricity; developing poles when heated. — *n.* A substance that becomes polar when heated.

py·ro·e·lec·tric·i·ty (pī′rō·i·lek′tris′ə·tē, -ē′lek-, pir′ō-) *n.* 1 Electrification or electric polarity developed in certain minerals by a change in temperature. 2 The branch of science treating of this phenomenon.

py·ro·gal·late (pī′rə·gal′āt, pir′ə-) *n.* A salt of pyrogallol.

py·ro·gen·ic (pī′rə·jen′ik, pir′ə-) *adj.* 1 Causing or produced by heat. 2 Caused by or inducing fever. 3 Igneous. Also **py·rog·e·nous** (pī·roj′ə·nəs, pir′ə-).

py·rog·nos·tics (pī′rog·nos′tiks, pir′əg-) *n. pl.* The characteristics of a mineral as shown by heat of varying intensity produced with a blowpipe. [<PYRO- + Gk. *gnostikos* knowing]

py·rog·ra·phy (pī·rog′rə·fē, pi-) *n.* The art or process of producing a design, as on wood or leather, by a red-hot point or fine flame. — **py·ro·graph** (pī′rə·graf, -gräf, pir′ə-) *n.* — **py·rog′ra·pher** *n.* — **py′ro·graph′ic** *adj.*

py·ro·gra·vure (pī′rō·grə·vyŏŏr′, pir′ō-) *n.* 1 The art or process of producing a design on wood by pyrography. 2 A picture thus made.

py·ro·lig·ne·ous (pī′rə·lig′nē·əs, pir′ə-) *adj.* Pertaining to that which is derived from wood by heat, specifically by dry distillation. [<PYRO- + LIGNEOUS]

pyroligneous acid Crude acetic acid as derived from wood by distillation; wood vinegar.

py·rol·o·gy (pī·rol′ə·jē, pi-) *n.* 1 The scientific examination of materials by heat; blowpipe analysis. 2 The branch of physics that treats of heat. [<PYRO- + -LOGY] — **py·ro·log·i·cal** (pī′rə·loj′i·kəl, pir′ə·loj′i·kəl) *adj.*

py·ro·lu·site (pī′rə·lōō′sīt, pī·rol′yə·sīt) *n.* A soft, metallic, iron-black or steel-gray manganese dioxide, MnO_2, of great value in the arts, and used in the manufacture of oxygen, chlorine, etc. [<G *pyrolusit* <Gk. *pyr, pyros* a fire + *lousis* a washing (<*louein* wash) + G -*it* -ITE[1]]

py·ro·mag·net·ic (pī′rō·mag·net′ik, pir′ō-) *adj.* Of, pertaining to, or produced by the changes in magnetic intensity caused by change of temperature.

py·ro·man·cy (pī′rə·man′sē, pir′ə-) *n.* Divination by fire. [<PYRO- + -MANCY]

py·ro·ma·ni·a (pī′rə·mā′nē·ə, -mān′yə, pir′ə-) *n.* A morbid propensity to set things on fire. — **py′ro·ma′ni·ac** (-ak) *adj. & n.* — **py·ro·ma·ni·a·cal** (pī′rō·mə·nī′ə·kəl, pir′ō-) *adj.*

py·ro·man·tic (pī′rə·man′tik, pir′ə-) *adj.* Of or

pertaining to pyromancy. — *n.* One who professes to divine by means of fire.

py·rom·e·ter (pī·rom′ə·tər) *n.* An instrument for measuring high degrees of heat, as caused by electrical resistance, degree of incandescence, expansion, radiation, etc. — **py·ro·met·ric** (pī′rə·met′rik, pir′ə-) or **·ri·cal** *adj.* — **py·rom′e·try** *n.*

py·ro·mor·phite (pī′rə·môr′fīt, pir′ə-) *n.* A resinous, variously colored phosphate and chloride of lead, found in masses or crystals; green lead ore. [<G *pyromorphit* <Gk. *pyr, pyros* a fire + *morphos* form]

py·rope (pī′rōp) *n.* A variety of deep-red garnet: also called *precious garnet.* [<OF *pirope* <L *pyropus* gold-bronze <Gk. *pyrōpos,* lit., fiery-eyed < *pyr, pyros* a fire < *ōps, ōpos* eye, face]

py·ro·phor·ic (pī′rə·fôr′ik, -for′ik) *adj.* **1** Fire-bearing; spontaneously combustible. **2** Designating materials which are easily and quickly inflammable, as finely divided metals on exposure to air. [<Gk. *pyrophoros* < *pyr, pyros* a fire + *pherein* carry] — **py′ro·phore** (-fôr, -fōr) *n.*

py·ro·phos·phate (pī′rə·fos′fāt, pir′ə-) *n.* A salt of pyrophosphoric acid.

py·ro·pho·tom·e·ter (pī′rō·fō·tom′ə·tər, pir′ō-) *n.* A pyrometer used to determine high temperatures by means of the luminosity of a substance.

py·ro·phyl·lite (pī′rə·fil′īt, pir′ə-) *n.* A compact, soft, variously colored, hydrous aluminum silicate, HAlSi₂O₆, used in making slate pencils. [<PYRO- + PHYLL(O)- + -ITE¹]

py·ro·stat (pī′rə·stat, pir′ə-) *n.* A thermostat; specifically, one for the higher temperatures. [<PYRO- + -STAT]

py·ro·sul·fate (pī′rə·sul′fāt, pir′ə-) *n.* A salt of pyrosulfuric acid; a disulfate.

py·ro·tech·nic (pī′rə·tek′nik, pir′ə-) *adj.* Pertaining to fireworks or their manufacture. Also **py′ro·tech′ni·cal.**

py·ro·tech·nics (pī′rə·tek′niks, pir′ə-) *n.* **1** The art of making or using fireworks: also **py′ro·tech′ny. 2** A display of fireworks. **3** An ostentatious display, as of oratory. [Earlier *pyrotechny* <F *pyrotechnie* <Gk. *pyr, pyros* fire + *technē* an art; infl. in form by *pyrotechnic*] — **py′ro·tech′nist** *n.*

py·rot·ic (pī·rot′ik, pi-) *adj.* Caustic. — *n.* A caustic substance or remedy. [<NL *pyroticus* <Gk. *pyrōtikos* < *pyroein* burn < *pyr* fire]

py·ro·tox·in (pī′rə·tok′sin, pir′ə-) *n. Biochem.* Any one of a number of toxic substances found in the body as a result of bacterial action and inducing a rise of bodily temperature, or symptoms of fever.

py·rox·ene (pī′rok·sēn) *n.* **1** A monoclinic mineral, usually in short, prismatic crystals, composed principally of calcium and magnesium: next to feldspar, the most frequent component of igneous rocks. **2** Any member of the pyroxene group, as diopside and augite: they are essentially metasilicates. [<F *pyroxène* <Gk. *pyr, pyros* fire + *xenos* a stranger; because at first considered alien to igneous rocks] — **py·rox·en·ic** (pī′rok·sen′ik) *adj.*

py·rox·e·nite (pī·rok′sə·nīt) *n.* A granitoid igneous rock composed mostly of pyroxene, but without olivine. [<PYROXENE + -ITE¹]

pyr·rhic¹ (pir′ik) *n.* A foot in ancient prosody composed of two short syllables. — *adj.* Of, pertaining to, or composed of pyrrhics. [<L (*pes*) *pyrrhicius* a pyrrhic (foot) <Gk. (*pous*) *pyrrichios* warlike, martial]

pyr·rhic² (pir′ik) *adj.* In Greek antiquity, pertaining to a martial dance in which the movements necessary to assail and avoid an enemy were imitated. — *n.* The pyrrhic dance. [<L *pyrrhicius* <Gk. *pyrrhichios* < *pyrrhichē* a war-dance <*Pyrrhichos* Pyrrhichus, a Greek said to have invented it]

Pyrrhic victory A victory gained at a ruinous loss, such as that of Pyrrhus over the Romans at Heracles Asculum, 279 B.C. [after *Pyrrhus*]

pyr·rho·tite (pir′ə·tīt) *n.* A metallic, bronze-colored, magnetic iron sulfide, FeS; magnetic pyrites. Also **pyr′rho·lite** (-līt), **pyr′rho·tine** (-tīn). [<Gk. *pyrrhotēs* redness (< *pyrrhos* flame-colored < *pyr* a fire) + -ITE¹]

Py·thag·o·ras (pi·thag′ər·əs) Greek philosopher of the sixth century B.C. — **Py·thag′o·re′an** *adj. & n.*

Py·thag·o·re·an·ism (pi·thag′ə·rē′ən·iz′əm) *n.* The mystical philosophy taught by Pythagoras, its central idea being that number is the essence of all things and the metaphysical principle of rational order in the universe. The leading theological doctrine was metempsychosis. [<L *Pythagoreus* <Gk. *Pythagoreios* <*Pythagoras* Pythagoras]

Pythagorean numbers See under NUMBER.

PYTHAGOREAN THEOREM

Sum of squares ABDE and BCGF equals square ACHK (a² + b² = c²)

Pythagorean theorem *Math.* The theorem that the sum of the squares of the legs of a right triangle is equal to the square of the hypotenuse.

Pyth·i·a (pith′ē·ə) In ancient Greece, the priestess of the Pythian Apollo at Delphi, who was believed to be inspired by the god when seated on a tripod over the rock sacred to him, and to utter his oracles. — **Pyth′ic** *adj.*

Pythian games Games held every four years in ancient Greece, of which musical contests were a feature.

Pyth·i·as (pith′e·əs) See DAMON AND PYTHIAS. Also *Phintias.*

py·tho·gen·e·sis (pī′thō·jen′ə·sis, pith′ō-) *n.* Generation from or because of filth. [< Gk. *pythein* rot + GENESIS] — **py·tho·gen·ic, py′tho·ge·net′ic** (-jə·net′ik) *adj.*

pythogenic fever *Pathol.* **1** Typhoid fever. **2** Any fever due to filth. Also **pythogenetic fever.**

py·thon (pī′thon, -thən) *n.* **1** A large, non-venomous serpent (genus *Python*) that crushes its prey in its folds. **2** Any non-venomous serpent related to the boas. **3** A soothsayer or soothsaying spirit: from the tradition that the Python delivered oracles at Delphi; also, a ventriloquist. [<L < Gk. *Pythōn* Python < *Pytho.* See PYTHIAN.]

Py·thon (pī′thon, -thən) In Greek mythology, a monstrous serpent which haunted the caves of Parnassus and was killed by Apollo near Delphi.

py·thon·ic (pīthon′ik, pi-) *adj.* **1** Of, pertaining to, or resembling pythons or a python. **2** Inspired; prophetic.

py·u·ri·a (pī·yŏŏr′ē·ə) *n. Pathol.* The presence of pus in the urine. [< NL < Gk. *pyon* pus + *ouron* urine]

pyx (piks) *n.* **1** A vessel or casket, usually of precious metal, in which the Host is preserved. **2** A receptacle for coins selected for trial at the British mint: short for **pyx chest.** [<L *pyxis* a box < Gk. < *pyxos* a box tree. Doublet of BOX.]

pyx·is (pik′sis) *n. pl.* **pyx·i·des** (pik′sə·dēz) **1** A box or pyx; especially, an ancient form of ornamental jewel case or toilet box. **2** An emollient ointment. **3** *Bot.* A capsule or seed vessel with transverse dehiscence, the upper portion separating as a lid, as in the common purslane: also **pyx·id·i·um** (pik·sid′ē·əm). [< L. See PYX.]

PYTHON
(From 3 to 32 feet in length)

Q

q, Q (kyōō) *n. pl.* **q's Q's** or **qs, Qs, ques** (kyōōz) **1** The 17th letter of the English alphabet, from Phoenician *Q'oph* and Greek *koppa,* which was present in five eastern Greek alphabets, obsolete in the late alphabets of Elis and Athens, but survived in the Chalcidian and Boeotian, whence it passed into the Italian, to Roman *Q.* **2** The sound of the letter *q.* In English *q* is always followed by *u* and is pronounced *kw,* as in quack, queen, quest, quote, conquest, equal, etc. In some words borrowed from French, however, it retains its French pronunciation of *k,* as in appliqué, conquer, coquette, pique, piquant, toque. Final *-que* is always pronounced as *k,* as in antique, oblique, physique, unique, etc. See ALPHABET.

Qa·tar (kä′tär) An independent Arab sheikdom, containing the whole **Qatar Peninsula** on the Persian Gulf coast of the Arabian Peninsula; about 8,000 miles; capital, Doha.

Qat·ta·ra Depression (kä·tä′rä) A desert basin in the Libyan Desert of northern Egypt; 7,500 square miles. Also **Qat·ta′rah.**

Q-boat (kyōō′bōt′) *n.* A merchant vessel having masked guns: used in World War I as a decoy for submarines. Also **Q′-ship′.**

qua (kwā, kwä) *adv.* In the capacity of; by virtue of being; in so far as. [< L, ablative sing. fem. of *qui* who]

Quaa·lude (kwā′lüd′) *n.* Methaqualone: a trade name.

quack¹ (kwak) *v.i.* To utter a harsh, croaking cry, as a duck. — *n.* The sound made by a duck, or a similar croaking noise. [Imit.]

quack² (kwak) *n.* **1** A pretender to medical knowledge or skill. **2** A charlatan. — *adj.* Of or pertaining to quacks or quackery; ignorantly or falsely pretending to cure. — *v.i.* To play the quack. [Short for QUACKSALVER] — **quack′ish** *adj.* — **quack′ish·ly** *adv.*

Synonyms (noun): charlatan, empiric, humbug, impostor, mountebank. *Antonyms:* adept, expert, master.

quack·er·y (kwak′ər·ē) *n. pl.* **·er·ies** Ignorant or fraudulent practice.

[<MDu. < *quacken* quack¹ + *salf* a salve]

quad¹ (kwod) *n. Colloq.* A quadrangle of a college or prison. [Short for QUADRANGLE]

quad² (kwod) *n. Printing* A quadrat. [Short for QUADRAT]

quad³ (kwod) See QUOD.

quad⁴ (kwod) *adj.* Quadraphonic.

quad·ra·ge·nar·i·an (kwod′rə·jə·nâr′ē·ən) *adj.* Forty years old or relating to this age. — *n.* A person forty years old. [<L *quadragenarius* < *quadrageni* forty each < *quadraginta* forty]

quad·ra·ges·i·mal (kwod′rə·jes′ə·məl) *adj.* **1** Of or pertaining to the number forty, especially the forty days of Lent. **2** Used during or appropriate to Lent; Lenten.

quad·ran·gle (kwod′rang·gəl) *n.* **1** *Geom.* A plane figure having four sides and four angles. **2** A court, square, or oblong, as within a public building. **3** A tract of land as represented by the United States Geological Survey on one of its atlas sheets. [< L *quadrangulum* < *quattuor* four + *angulus* angle] — **quad·ran′gu·lar** *adj.*

quad·rant (kwod′rənt) *n.* **1** The quarter of a circle, or of its circumference. **2** An instrument having a graduated arc of 90°, with a movable radius for measuring angles on it; especially, a nautical instrument for measuring the altitude of the sun. **3** *Geom.* In a Cartesian coordinate system, any of the four sections formed by the intersection of the axes: beginning with the upper right-hand quadrant where the ordinate and abscissa are positive, they are called the **first, second, third,** and **fourth quadrants,** in counter-clockwise order. See illustration on page 1030. **4** A device or machine-part having the shape of, or suggesting the quadrant of a circle. [< L *quadrans, -antis* a fourth part < *quattuor* four] —**quad·ran·tal** (kwod·ran′təl) *adj.*

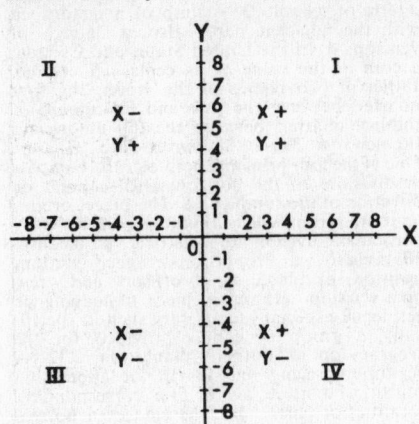

CARTESIAN QUADRANT

quad·ra·phon·ic (kwod′rə·fon′ik) *adj.* Of, pertaining to, or employing a system of sound reproduction that uses four transmission channels and loudspeakers.

quad·rate (kwod′rāt, -rit) *n.* **1** *Zool.* A bone of cartilaginous element suspending the lower jaw in certain vertebrates below the mammals. **2** In astrology, an aspect of two heavenly bodies in which they are distant from each other 90°. **3** A cubical or square object, or an object resembling a cube. —*adj.* **1** Square; four-sided, as a muscle. **2** Distant from each other 90°: said of two heavenly bodies. **3** Of or pertaining to the quadrate bone or cartilage. —*v.* (-rāt) -**rat·ed,** -**rat·ing** *v.i.* To correspond or agree: with *with.* —*v.t.* To cause to conform; bring in accordance with. [< L *quadratus,* pp. of *quadrare* square < *quatuor* four]

quad·rat·ic (kwod·rat′ik) *adj.* **1** Pertaining to or resembling a square. **2** Relating to a quadratic equation. —*n. Math.* **1** An equation of the second degree. It is a **pure, simple,** or **incomplete quadratic** when it contains only the second power of the variable, as $ax^2 + c = 0$; a **complete** or **adfected quadratic** when it contains also the first power, as $ax^2 + bx + c = 0$. **2** A formula, $x = \dfrac{-b \pm \sqrt{b^2 - 4ac}}{2a}$, for computing the roots of the standard quadratic equation, $ax^2 + bx + c = 0$. **3** *pl.* The part of algebra that treats of quadratic equations.

quad·ra·ture (kwod′rə·chər) *n.* **1** The act or process of squaring. **2** The finding in square measure of the area of any surface, especially one bounded by a curve. **3** *Astron.* **a** The relative position of two heavenly bodies that are 90° apart as viewed from the center of a third body. **b** Either intersection of an orbit with a line whose ends terminate in the curve drawn perpendicular to the major axis through the focus.

quad·ren·ni·al (kwod·ren′ē·əl) *adj.* **1** Occurring once in four years. **2** Comprising four years. — **quad·ren′ni·al·ly** *adv.*

quad·ren·ni·um (kwod·ren′ē·əm) *n. pl.* -**ren·ni·a** (-ren′ē·ə) A space or period of four years. Also **quad·ri·en·ni·um** (kwod′rē·en′ē·əm). [< L]

quadri- *combining form* Four: *quadrinomial.* Also, before vowels, **quadr-:** also *quadru-.* [< L *quattuor* four]

quad·ri·cen·ten·ni·al (kwod′ri·sen·ten′ē·əl) *n.* A four-hundredth anniversary. —*adj.* Of or pertaining to such an anniversary.

quad·ri·lat·er·al (kwod′rə·lat′ər·əl) *adj.* Formed or bounded by four lines; four-sided. —*n.* **1** *Geom.* **a** A figure bounded by four straight lines terminated at four angles. **b** A figure formed of four infinite straight lines, having six intersections. **2** A space or area defended by four enclosing fortresses. [< L *quadri-laterus* < *quattuor* four + *latus, lateris* side]

QUADRILATERAL
abdc. Quadrilateral.
ad., bc. Diagonals.
ebfc. Quadrilateral.
a., b., c., d., f. Vertices.
ai., bh., ei. Diagonals.
g., hh.., i. Centers.

quad·ri·lin·gual (kwod′rə·ling′gwəl) *adj.* **1** Consisting of, or knowing, four languages. **2** Written in four languages.

qua·drille (kwə·dril′) *n.* **1** A square dance for four couples and having five figures. **2** Music for such a dance. [< F < Sp. *cuadrilla* little square < L *quadrum* < *quattuor* four]

quadrille paper See GRAPH PAPER.

quad·ril·lion (kwod·ril′yən) *n.* **1** In the French and United States system of numeration, a thousand trillions, or 1 followed by 15 ciphers. **2** In the English system, a million trillions, or 1 followed by 24 ciphers. [< F < *quatre* four + *(m)illion*]

quad·ri·par·tite (kwod′rə·pär′tīt) *adj.* **1** Consisting of or embracing four parts. **2** Having four parties, as an agreement or contract. [< L *quadripartitus* < *quattuor* four + *partitus* divided] — **quad·ri·par·ti′tion** (-tish′ən) *n.*

quad·ri·ple·gi·a (kwod′rə·plē′jē·ə) *n. Pathol.* Paralysis of the arms and legs. —**quad·ri·ple·gic** (kwod′rə·plē′jik, -plej′ik) *n.*

quad·riv·i·al (kwod·riv′ē·əl) *adj.* **1** Having four radiating ways. **2** Leading to or going in four directions: *quadrivial* streets. [< L *quadrivius* < *quattuor* four + *via* way]

quad·riv·i·um (kwod·riv′ē·əm) *n. pl.* -**i·a** (-ē·ə) In the Pythagorean system, the four sciences, geometry, astronomy, arithmetic, and music, making up with the trivium the seven liberal arts. Compare TRIVIUM. [< L, a place where four roads meet]

quad·ro·min·i·um (kwod′rə·min′ē·əm) *n.* A multiple residence containing four condominiums.

quad·roon (kwod·rōōn′) *n.* A person having one-fourth Negro and three-fourths white blood. [< Sp. *cuarteron* < *cuarto* fourth]

quadru- Var. of QUADRI-.

quad·ru·ma·nous (kwod·rōō′mə·nəs) *adj.* **1** Four-handed; having four feet resembling hands. **2** Of or pertaining to a former order (*Quadrumana*) of mammals now classed with man under the primates. [< QUADRU- + L *manus* hand]

quad·ru·ped (kwod′rŏŏ·ped) *n.* An animal having four feet; especially, a four-footed mammal. —*adj.* Having four feet. [< L *quadrupes, -pedis* < *quattuor* four + *pes* foot] —**quad·ru·pe·dal** (kwod·rŏŏ′pə·dəl, kwod′rŏŏ·ped′l) *adj.*

quad·ru·ple (kwod·rōō′pəl, kwod·rŏŏ′pəl) *adj.* Consisting of four; having four parts or members; fourfold; also, taken by fours. —*n.* A number or sum four times as great as another. —*v.t. & v.i.* -**pled,** -**pling** To multiply by four; make or become four times larger. —*adv.* Fourfold. [< L *quadruplus*]

quad·ru·plet (kwod·rōō′plit, kwod·rŏŏ′-) *n.* **1** A compound or combination of four things or objects. **2** One of four offspring born of the same mother at one birth.

quad·ru·plex (kwod′rŏŏ·pleks, kwod·rŏŏ′-) *adj.* **1** Fourfold. **2** Pertaining to or designating a telegraph system such that four messages, two in each direction, may be sent simultaneously over one wire. —*n.* A sending instrument used in quadruplex telegraphy. [< L < *quattuor* four + stem of *plicare* fold]

quad·ru·pli·cate (kwod·rōō′plə·kit, -kāt) *adj.* **1** Fourfold. **2** Raised to the fourth power. —*v.t.* (-kāt) -**cat·ed, -cat·ing** To multiply by four; quad-

ruple. —*n.* One of four like things. — **quad·ru′pli·ca′tion** *n.* —**quad·ru′pli·cate·ly** *adv.*

quae·re (kwē′rē) *n.* Literally, seek; inquire: an annotation inserted, as in law reports. [< L. See QUERY.]

quaff (kwaf, kwof, kwôf) *v.t. & v.i.* To drink, especially copiously or with relish. —*n.* A drink; swallow. [< earlier *quaft,* ? blend of QUENCH and DRAUGHT] —**quaff′er** *n.*

quag·ga (kwag′ə) *n.* **1** A South African equine mammal (*Equus quagga*) intermediate between the ass and the zebra and resembling the latter: now extinct. **2** A zebra: an erroneous use. [< native Hottentot name]

quag·gy (kwag′ē, kwog′ē) *adj.* Yielding to or quaking under the foot, as soft, wet earth; boggy.

QUAGGA
(About 11 hands high at the withers)

quag·mire (kwag′mīr′, kwog′-) *n.* **1** Marshy ground that gives way under the foot; bog. **2** A difficult situation. [< QUAG + MIRE] — **quag′mired′, quag′mir′y** *adj.*

quail[1] (kwāl) *n.* **1** An Old World migratory game bird (*Coturnix coturnix*) similar to the partridge, having a very short tail. **2** Any of various small American game birds related to the partridge (family *Perdicidae*), especially the bobwhite and the California quail (*Lophortyx californica*). See BOBWHITE. **3** *Obs.* A prostitute. [< OF *quaille,* prob. < Gmc.]

quail[2] (kwāl) *v.i.* To shrink with fear; lose heart or courage. [ME *quailen;* origin uncertain]

quaint (kwānt) *adj.* **1** Combining an antique appearance with a pleasing oddity, fancifulness, or whimsicalness. **2** Hence, pleasingly odd or old-fashioned; fanciful. **3** *Obs.* Curiously wrought; hence, ornamental. **4** *Obs.* Crafty. See synonyms under ANTIQUE. ODD, QUEER. [< OF *cointe* < L *cognitus* known] —**quaint′ly** *adv.* —**quaint′ness** *n.*

quake (kwāk) *v.i.* **quaked, quak·ing** **1** To shake, as with violent emotion or cold; quiver. **2** To shake or tremble, as earth during an earthquake. —*n.* A shaking, tremulous motion, quickly repeated; a shaking or shuddering. [OE *cwacian* shake]

Synonyms (verb): quaver, quiver, shake, shiver, shudder, tremble, vibrate, waver. See SHAKE.

Quak·er (kwā′kər) *n.* A member of the Society of Friends: originally a term of derision, and still not used within the society. See SOCIETY OF FRIENDS. [< QUAKE, *v.;* with ref. to their founder's admonition to them to tremble at the word of the Lord] — **Quak′er·ess** *n. fem.* — **Quak′er·ish** *adj.* — **Quak′er·ish·ly** *adv.*

Quaker gun A dummy gun, as one made of wood: from the Friends' doctrine of non-resistance.

Quaker meeting **1** Any meeting of the Society of Friends for worship, in which, following their usage, they remain silent until the Spirit moves some member to speak or pray aloud. **2** Any silent gathering.

Quaker State Nickname of PENNSYLVANIA.

quak·y (kwā′kē) *adj.* **quak·i·er, quak·i·est** Shaky; tremulous. — **quak′i·ly** *adv.* — **quak′i·ness** *n.*

qual·i·fi·ca·tion (kwol′ə·fə·kā′shən) *n.* **1** The act of qualifying, or the state of being qualified. **2** That which fits a person or thing for something. **3** A restriction; mitigation. See synonyms under ABILITY.

qual·i·fied (kwol′ə·fīd) *adj.* **1** Competent or fit, as for public office. **2** Restricted or modified in some way. See synonyms under COMPETENT. — **qual′i·fied′ly** *adv.*

qual·i·fy (kwol′ə·fī) *v.* -**fied, -fy·ing** *v.t.* **1** To make fit or capable, as for an office, occupation, or privilege. **2** To make legally capable, as by the administration of an oath. **3** To limit or restrict, as by conditions or exceptions. **4** To attribute a quality to; describe; characterize or name. **5** To make less strong or extreme; soften; moderate. **6** To change the strength or flavor of. **7** *Gram.* To modify. —*v.i.* **8** To be or become qualified or fit;

meet the requirements, as for entering a race. See synonyms under CHANGE. [<MF *qualifier* <Med. L *qualificare* <L *qualis* of such a kind + *facere* make] — **qual′i·fi′a·ble** *adj.* — **qual′i·fi′er** *n.*

qual·i·ta·tive (kwol′ə·tā′tiv) *adj.* Of or pertaining to quality: distinguished from *quantitative.* [<LL *qualitativus* <L *qualitas* quality] — **qual′i·ta′tive·ly** *adv.*

qualitative analysis *Chem.* The process of finding how many and what elements or ingredients are present in a substance or compound.

qual·i·ty (kwol′ə·tē) *n. pl.* ·ties **1** That which makes a being or thing such as it is; a distinguishing element or characteristic. **2** The characteristics of anything regarded as determining its value, place, worth, rank, position, etc., or the condition of a thing as so determined; character; kind; when unqualified, peculiar excellence. **3** A moral trait or characteristic. **4** Degree of excellence; relative goodness; grade: high *quality* of fabric. **5** Capability of producing specific effects. **6** Particular character or part; capacity; function. **7** *Archaic* Social rank; persons of rank, collectively. **8** *Music* That which distinguishes sounds of the same pitch and intensity from different sources, as from different instruments; timbre. **9** *Logic* The character of a proposition or judgment as asserting or denying. **10** *Philos.* An essential property or attribute. **11** *Phonet.* The character of a vowel sound as determined by the resonance of the oral cavity. See synonyms under ATTRIBUTE, CHARACTERISTIC. — *adj.* Characterized by high quality: a *quality* product. [<L *qualitas, -tatis* <*qualis* of such a kind]

qualm (kwäm, kwôm) *n.* **1** A feeling of sickness. **2** A twinge of conscience; moral scruple. **3** A sensation of fear or misgiving. [OE *cwealm* death]

quam·ash (kwom′ash, kwə·mash′) *n.* Camas.

quan·da·ry (kwon′dər·ē, -drē) *n. pl.* ·da·ries A state of hesitation or perplexity; predicament. [Origin uncertain]

quan·ta (kwon′tə) Plural of QUANTUM.

quan·ti·fy (kwon′tə·fī) *v.t.* ·fied, ·fy·ing **1** To determine the quantity of. **2** *Logic* To express the quantity of explicitly, as by using *all, some,* or *none.* [<Med. L *quantificare* <L *quantus* how great + *facere* make] — **quan′ti·fi·ca′tion** *n.* — **quan′ti·fi′er** *n.*

quan·ti·ta·tive (kwon′tə·tā′tiv) *adj.* **1** Of or pertaining to quantity. **2** Having to do with quantities only: distinguished from *qualitative.* [<LL *quantitativus* <L *quantitas* quantity] — **quan′ti·ta′tive·ly** *adv.* — **quan′ti·ta′tive·ness** *n.*

quantitative analysis *Chem.* The process of finding the amount or percentage of each element or ingredient present, as in a compound.

quan·ti·ty (kwon′tə·tē) *n. pl.* ·ties **1** The condition of being much. **2** That property of a thing which admits of exact measurement and numerical statement. **3** An object regarded as possessing a certain determinable magnitude, as of length, size, mass, volume, or number. **4** *Electr.* The strength of a current, as opposed to intensity or potential. **5** In prosody, the relative period of time, regarded as short or long, required to pronounce a syllable. **6** *Music* The duration of a musical note. **7** A specified, or indefinite, number of persons or things. **8** *Logic* The extent of a general term or proposition as applying to the whole or to a part of a class. Considered with reference to quantity, propositions are *universal,* as "all men are mortal," and *particular,* as "some men are honest," while with reference to conceptions quantity relates either to their extension, or to their intension or comprehension. **9** Considerable bulk or amount. [<OF *quantité* <L *quantitas, -tatis* <*quantus* how much, how large]

quan·tum (kwon′təm) *n. pl.* ·ta (-tə) **1** An object that has quantity or is concrete. **2** A certain amount; also, a prescribed or a sufficient quantity. **3** *Physics* A fundamental unit of energy or action as provided for in the quantum theory. [<L, neuter of *quantus* how much]

quantum state Energy level.

quantum theory *Physics* The theory that energy is not a smoothly flowing continuum but is manifested by the emission from radiat-

ing bodies of discrete particles or *quanta,* the values of which are expressed as the product of Planck's constant, *h,* and the frequency, *v,* of the given radiation.

Qua·paw (kwä′pô) *n.* One of a tribe of North American Indians of Siouan stock, formerly living in Arkansas, now in Oklahoma: also called *Arkansas.*

quar·an·tine (kwor′ən·tēn, kwor′-) *n.* **1** The enforced isolation for a fixed period of persons, ships, or goods arriving from places infected with contagious disease, or of any persons who have been exposed to such infection. **2** A place designated for the enforcement of such interdiction. **3** The enforced isolation of any person or place infected with contagious disease; loosely, any enforced isolation. **4** A period of forty days. — *v.t.* ·tined, ·tin·ing To subject to or retain in quarantine; isolate by or as by quarantine. [<Ital. *quarantina* <L *quadraginta* forty]

quark (kwärk) *n. Physics* Any of a group of three types of hypothetical fundamental particles proposed as the entities of which all other strongly interacting particles are composed. [Coined by Murray Gell-Mann, born 1929, U.S. physicist, appar. after use by James Joyce in *Finnegans Wake*]

quar·rel[1] (kwôr′əl, kwor′-) *n.* **1** An unfriendly, angry, or violent dispute. **2** A falling out or contention; breach of amity; a lover's *quarrel.* **3** The cause for dispute. — *v.i.* ·reled or ·relled, ·rel·ing or ·rel·ling **1** To engage in a quarrel; dispute; contend; fight: to *quarrel* about money. **2** To break off a mutual friendship; fall out; disagree. **3** To find fault; cavil. [<F *querelle* <L *querela* complaint] — **quar′rel·er** or **quar′rel·ler** *n.*

Synonyms (noun): affray, altercation, bickering, brawl, breach, broil, contention, contest, controversy, disagreement, discussion, dispute, dissension, feud, fracas, fray, fuss, jangle, jar, misunderstanding, quarreling, rupture, scene, squabble, strife, wrangle. A *quarrel* is in word or act, or both, and is often slight and transient, as we speak of childish *quarrels;* but *quarrel* may denote the cause or ground of *contention* or *strife,* and so be deep and enduring. *Contention* and *strife* may be in word or deed; *contest* ordinarily involves some form of action. *Controversy* is commonly in words; *strife* extends from verbal controversy to the contests of armies. See ALTERCATION, FEUD[1]. *Antonyms:* accord, amity, acquiescence, concord, harmony, peace, reconciliation.

quar·rel[2] (kwôr′əl, kwor′-) *n.* **1** A dart or arrow with a four-edged head, formerly used with a crossbow. **2** A graver, stonemason's chisel, glazier's diamond, or other tool having a several-edged point. [<OF <LL *quadrellus,* dim. of L *quadrum* a square <*quattuor* four]

quar·rel·some (kwôr′əl·səm, kwor′-) *adj.* Inclined to quarrel; contentious. — **quar′rel·some·ly** *adv.* — **quar′rel·some·ness** *n.*

quar·ri·er (kwôr′ē·ər, kwor′-) *n.* A workman in a stone quarry.

quar·ry[1] (kwôr′ē, kwor′ē) *n. pl.* ·ries **1** A beast or bird hunted, seized, or killed, as in the chase; game; prey: now chiefly poetical. **2** Anything hunted, slaughtered, or eagerly pursued. **3** *Obs.* A heap of slaughtered game. [<OF *cuirée* <L *corium* hide]

quar·ry[2] (kwôr′ē, kwor′ē) *n. pl.* ·ries An excavation from which stone is taken by cutting, blasting, or the like. — *v.t.* ·ried, ·ry·ing **1** To cut, dig, or take from or as from a quarry. **2** To establish a quarry in. [<Med. L *quareia, quareria* <LL *quadraria* place for squaring stone <*quadrare.* See QUADRATE.]

quar·ry[3] (kwôr′ē, kwor′ē) *n. pl.* ·ries **1** A square or lozenge. **2** A small square or lozenge-shaped pane of glass, tile, etc. **3** In archery, a quarrel. [<OF *quarré* <L *quadratus.* See QUADRATE.]

quart (kwôrt) *n.* **1** A measure of capacity; the fourth part of a gallon, or two pints. In the United States, the dry quart is equal to 1.10 liters and the liquid quart is equal to 0.946 liter. **2** A vessel of such capacity. [<F *quarte* <L *quartus* fourth]

quar·tan (kwôr′tən) *adj.* Pertaining to the fourth in a series; especially, occurring every fourth day. — *n. Pathol.* A malarial fever caused by the parasite *Plasmodium malariae,* in which the paroxysms recur every fourth

day, or 72 hours, reckoning inclusively. [<F *quartaine* <L *quartanus* <*quartus* fourth]

quar·ter (kwôr′tər) *n.* **1** One of four equal parts into which anything is or may be divided; a fourth part; specifically, the fourth of a hundredweight; eight bushels; a fourth of a ton (of grain); the fourth of a yard, or a span; a fourth of a pound; a fourth of a mile; fifteen minutes or the fourth of an hour, or the moment with which it begins or ends. **2** A fourth of a year or three months; hence, a term of school. **3** A limb of a quadruped with the adjacent parts; also, a haunch of venison. **4** In the United States and Canada, a coin of the value of 25 cents. **5** *Astron.* Either of two phases of the moon: the first quarter, between the new and full moon; or the last quarter, between the full moon and the new. **6** *Music* A quarter note. **7** *Nav.* One of the four principal points of the compass or divisions of the horizon; also, a point or direction of the compass. **8** The place, origin, or source from which anything comes. **9** A particular division or district; a locality. **10** *Usually pl.* Proper or assigned station, position, or place, as of officers and crew on a warship. **11** *pl.* A place of lodging or residence, especially temporary shelter; specifically, a group of cabins provided for the Negroes on a Southern plantation. **12** A region embracing one fourth, or about one fourth, of a space; one of four corresponding localities or parts. **13** The side of a horse's hoof, just in front of the heel; also that part of a boot or shoe from the middle of the heel to the line of the ankle bone. **14** *Naut.* **a** The upper part of a vessel's side from the after part of the main chains to the stern. **b** That part of a yard outside the slings. **15** *Her.* Any of four equal divisions into which a shield is divided, or an ordinary occupying such a division. **16** Mercy shown to a vanquished foeman by sparing his life; clemency. **17** One of the four periods into which a game, as football, is divided. — **at close quarters** Close by; at close range. — *adj.* **1** Being one of four equal parts. **2** Having one fourth of a standard value. — *v.t.* **1** To divide into four equal parts. **2** To divide into a number of parts or pieces. **3** To cut the body of (an executed person) into four parts: He was hanged, drawn, and *quartered.* **4** To range from one side to the other of (a field, etc.) while advancing: The dogs *quartered* the field. **5** To furnish with quarters or shelter; lodge, station, or billet. **6** *Her.* **a** To divide (a shield) into quarters by vertical and horizontal lines. **b** To bear or arrange (different coats of arms) quarterly upon a shield or escutcheon. **7** *Mech.* To mark or place at intervals of a quarter, especially of a quarter of a circle. — *v.i.* **8** To be stationed or lodged. **9** To range from side to side of an area, as dogs in hunting. **10** *Naut.* To blow on a ship's quarter: said of the wind. [<OF <L *quartarius* <*quartus* fourth]

quar·ter·age (kwôr′tər·ij) *n.* **1** A quarterly allowance or payment. **2** Board and lodging; quarters, especially for troops, a work gang, etc.; also, the cost of lodging or shelter.

quar·ter·back (kwôr′tər·bak′) *n.* In American football, one of the backfield, who often calls the signals.

quar·ter–day (kwôr′tər·dā′) *n.* One fourth of a day.

quarter day Any of the days of the year when quarterly payments are due. Quarter days for the U.S. government are the first days of January, April, July, and October; for England, Lady Day (March 25), Midsummer Day (June 24), Michaelmas (September 29), and Christmas (December 25).

quar·ter–deck (kwôr′tər·dek′) *n. Naut.* The rear part of a ship's upper deck, reserved for officers.

quar·tered (kwôr′tərd) *adj.* **1** Divided into four quarters. **2** *Her.* Divided into quarterings. **3** Quarter-sawed: *quartered* oak. **4** Lodged; stationed; also, having quarters.

quar·ter·fi·nal (kwôr′tər·fī′nəl) *n.* A competition immediately preceding the semifinal in sporting events; also, one of four competitions in a tournament, the winners of which play in the two semifinals. — *adj.* Next to the semifinal. — **quar′ter·fi′nal·ist** *n.*

quar·ter·foil (kwôr′tər·foil′) See QUATREFOIL.

Quarter horse A breed of horse descendent from the thoroughbred stallion *Janus* imported from England in 1756: first known as a racing breed, now widely popular as a ranch horse and cow pony. [From the quarter-of-a-mile path over which it was raced by the early settlers of Virginia]

quar·ter·ing (kwôr′tər·ing) *adj.* **1** *Naut.* **a** Blowing against or being on the quarter. **b** Blowing from any point between beam and stern: a *quartering* wind. **c** Sailing so as to have the wind on the quarter. **2** Set or being at right angles. — *n.* **1** A dividing or marking off into quarters. **2** *Her.* **a** The grouping of two or more coats of arms in compartments on one shield, to indicate family alliances, etc. **b** Any of the coats which are quartered on the shield, or the quarter containing it. **3** Quarters, or the assigning of quarters, as for soldiers.

QUARTERING

quar·ter·ly (kwôr′tər·lē) *adj.* **1** Containing or being a fourth part. **2** Occurring at intervals of three months. — *n. pl.* **·lies** A publication issued once every three months. — *adv.* **1** Once in a quarter of a year. **2** In or by quarters.

Quartermaster Corps A branch of the U.S. Army which is responsible for the supply of food, fuel, clothing, and other equipment.

quar·tern (kwôr′tərn) *n.* **1** A fourth part of certain measures or weights, as of a peck or pound; a gill. **2** A four-pound loaf of bread. [< OF *quarteron* < *quarte* a fourth part < L *quartus* fourth]

quarter note *Music* A note having one fourth the value of a semibreve. See illustration under NOTE.

quar·ter·sec·tion (kwôr′tər·sek′shən) *n.* A tract of land half a mile square, containing one fourth of a square mile; 160 acres.

quar·ter·tone (kwôr′tər·tōn′) *n.* **1** In photoengraving, a coarse zinc halftone plate having 65 lines or less to the inch. **2** *Music* Half of a semitone: **quarter tone.**

quar·tet (kwôr·tet′) *n.* **1** A composition for four voices or instruments. **2** The set of four persons who render such compositions. **3** A stanza of four lines. **4** Any group or set of four things of a kind. Also **quar·tette′.** [< Ital. *quartetto* < *quarto* fourth]

quar·tile (kwôr′tīl, -til) *n.* **1** In astrology, a quadrate. **2** *Stat.* That portion of a frequency distribution which comprises an exact fourth of the total observed cases. — *adj.* Of or pertaining to a quartile. [< LL *quartilis* < L *quartus* fourth]

quar·to (kwôr′tō) *adj.* Having four leaves or eight pages to the sheet: a *quarto* book. — *n. pl.* **·tos** A book or pamphlet whose pages are of the size of the fourth of a sheet: often written 4to or 4°. [< L (*in*) *quarto* (in) fourth]

quartz (kwôrts) *n.* Silicon dioxide, SiO_2, a hard, vitreous, widely distributed mineral occurring in many varieties, sometimes massive, as jasper and chalcedony: sometimes in colorless and transparent or diversely colored forms crystallizing in the hexagonal system. [< G *quarz*]

quartz crystal A thin section of pure quartz, accurately ground so as to vibrate at the required frequency in radio transmission; a piezoelectric oscillator. Also **quartz plate.**

quartz lamp A mercury-vapor lamp enclosed in a quartz tube, which transmits ultraviolet wavelengths.

qua·sar (kwā′zär, -sär) *n. Astron.* Any of a class of very distant, celestial objects that are strong radio sources, have unusual light spectra, show large red shifts, and have a vast, unexplained energy output. [< QUAS(I) + (STELL)AR]

quash¹ (kwosh) *v.t. Law* To make void or set

---

aside, as an indictment; annul. See synonyms under ANNUL, CANCEL. [< OF *quasser* < LL *cassare* < *cassus* empty]

quash² (kwosh) *v.t.* To put down or suppress forcibly or summarily. [< OF *quasser* < L *quassare*, freq. of *quatere* shake]

quasi- *prefix* **1** (With nouns) Resembling; not genuine, as in:

quasi-accident	quasi-injury
quasi-adult	quasi-insight
quasi-approval	quasi-integrity
quasi-artist	quasi-invasion
quasi-attack	quasi-kindred
quasi-authority	quasi-lament
quasi-bargain	quasi-luxury
quasi-blunder	quasi-market
quasi-certificate	quasi-method
quasi-characteristic	quasi-miracle
quasi-comprehension	quasi-neutrality

2 (With adjectives) Nearly; almost, as in:

quasi-absolute	quasi-grateful
quasi-amiable	quasi-hereditary
quasi-beneficial	quasi-human
quasi-classic	quasi-humorous
quasi-colloquial	quasi-important
quasi-comic	quasi-infinite
quasi-complex	quasi-internal
quasi-tangible	quasi-valid
quasi-theatrical	quasi-vital
quasi-typical	quasi-willing

3 *Law* Superficially resembling but intrinsically different, as in:

quasi-corporation	quasi-entail
quasi-delict	quasi-legislative
quasi-deposit	quasi-partner

[< L, as if]

qua·si-con·tract (kwā′sī·kon′trakt, -zī-, kwā′sē-) *n.* An obligation to do something, enforceable by a contract remedy, but imposed by operation of law regardless of the consent of the defendant.

qua·si-ju·di·cial (kwā′sī·jōō·dish′əl, -zī-, kwā′sē-) *adj.* Exercising functions of a judicial nature as a guide for official action, as a committee investigating facts and drawing conclusions from them.

quas·qui·cen·ten·ni·al (kwäs′kwi·sen·ten′ē·əl) *adj.* Of or pertaining to a century and a quarter. — *n.* A 125th anniversary, or its celebration. [coined < L *quadrans que* plus a fourth + CENTENNIAL, for Delavan, Illinois (1962).]

qua·ter·na·ry (kwə·tûr′nə·rē) *adj.* **1** Consisting of four things. **2** Fourth in order. — *n. pl.* **·ries** **1** The number four; a group of four things. **2** *Math.* A quantic function having four variables. [< L *quaternarius* < *quaterni* by fours]

qua·ter·ni·on (kwə·tûr′nē·ən) *n.* **1** A set, system, or file of four. **2** *Math.* **a** An operator or factor that changes one vector into another: so called because expressible as the sum of four quantities. **b** The form of the calculus of vectors based on and making use of the quaternion operator. [< LL *quaternio, -onis* < *quattuor* four]

quat·rain (kwot′rān) *n.* A stanza of four lines. [< F < *quatre* four]

quat·re·foil (kat′ər·foil′, kat′rə-) *n.* **1** *Bot.* A leaf or flower with four leaflets or petals. **2** *Archit.* An ornament with four foils or lobes. Sometimes spelled *quarterfoil.* [< OF *quatre* four + *foil* leaf]

quat·tro·cen·to (kwät′trō·chen′tō) *n.* The 15th century as connected with the revival of art and literature (especially in Italy). — *adj.* Of or pertaining to the quattrocento. [< Ital., four hundred < *quattro* four + *cento* hundred]

qua·ver (kwā′vər) *v.i.* **1** To tremble or shake: said usually of the voice. **2** To produce trills or quavers in singing or in playing a musical instrument. — *v.t.* **3** To utter or sing in a tremulous voice. See synonyms under QUAKE, SHAKE. — *n.* **1** A quiver-

QUATREFOILS

---

ing or tremulous motion. **2** A shake or trill, as in singing. **3** An eighth note. [Freq. of obs. *quave*, ME *cwafian* tremble] — **qua′ver·y** *adj.*

quay (kē) *n.* A wharf or artificial landing place where vessels unload. ◆ Homophone: **key.** [< F]

quay·age (kē′ij) *n.* **1** Wharfage; quay dues. **2** Space for quays; quays collectively.

quean (kwēn) *n.* **1** A brazen or ill-behaved woman; harlot; prostitute. **2** *Scot.* A young or unmarried woman; a girl. [OE *cwene* prostitute]

quea·sy (kwē′zē) *adj.* **·si·er, ·si·est** **1** Sick at the stomach. **2** Nauseating; also, caused by nausea. **3** Easily nauseated; hence, fastidious; squeamish. **4** Requiring to be carefully treated; delicate; ticklish. **5** Uncertain; hazardous. [Cf. Norw. *kveis* nausea] — **quea′si·ly** *adv.* — **quea′si·ness** *n.*

Que·bec (kwi·bek′) **1** A province in eastern Canada; 523,860 square miles: formerly *Lower Canada*: abbr. *Que.* or *P.Q.* **2** Its capital, a port on the St. Lawrence River; captured from the French under Montcalm by Wolfe, Sept. 13, 1759.

Quech·ua (kech′wä) *n.* **1** One of a tribe of South American Indians which dominated the Inca empire prior to the Spanish conquest. **2** The language of the Quechuas, still spoken as a mother tongue in parts of Peru and Ecuador: also called *Incan.* Also spelled *Kechua.*

queen (kwēn) *n.* **1** The wife of a king. **2** A female sovereign or monarch. **3** A woman preeminent in a given sphere. **4** The most powerful piece in chess, capable of moving any number of squares in a straight line. **5** A playing card bearing a conventional picture of a queen in her robes. **6** *Entomol.* The single fully developed female in a colony of social insects, as bees, ants, etc.: distinguished from workers, soldiers, and unproductive females. — *v.t.* **1** To make a queen of. **2** In chess, to make a queen of (a pawn) by moving it to the eighth row. — *v.i.* **3** To reign as or play the part of a queen: usually with *it.* [OE *cwēn* woman, queen]

Queen Anne's lace The wild carrot (*Daucus carota*), having filmy white flowers in umbels.

Queen Anne style 1 *Archit.* A style prevalent in England in the early 18th century, or a style similar to it used in the United States in the latter part of the 19th century, characterized by the use of red brickwork on which relief ornaments are carved, and by plain, unpretentious design. **2** A type of furniture characterized by much upholstery and marquetry.

queen consort The wife of a reigning king, who does not share his sovereignty.

queen dowager The widow of a king who has reigned in his own right.

queen·ly (kwēn′lē) *adj. & adv.* Like a queen; stately; reginal. See synonyms under IMPERIAL. — **queen′li·ness** *n.*

queen mother A queen dowager who is mother of a reigning sovereign.

queen olive A large variety of Spanish olive.

queen-post (kwēn′pōst′) *n.* One of two upright suspending or sustaining posts or compression members in a truss.

queen regent 1 A queen who rules in behalf of another. **2** A queen who rules in her own right: also **queen regnant.**

Queens (kwēnz) The easternmost borough of New York City, located on Long Island; 108 square miles.

Queens·land (kwēnz′lənd) The second largest state of the Commonwealth of Australia, in the NE part; 670,500 square miles; capital, Brisbane.

queen's metal An alloy of tin, antimony, bismuth, and lead, used for ornamental purposes.

queen snake A water snake (*Natrix lebris*) of the central and eastern United States.

queen's ware Fine, glazed, cream-colored English earthenware; specifically, cream-colored Wedgwood: named for Queen Charlotte by Josiah Wedgwood, 1761.

queer (kwir) *adj.* **1** Being out of the usual course of events in minor respects; singular; odd. **2** Of questionable character; open to

---

suspicion; mysterious. **3** *Slang* Counterfeit. — *n. Slang* **1** Counterfeit money. **2** A homosexual, especially a male homosexual: a contemptuous term. — *v.t. U.S. Slang* To jeopardize or spoil. [<G *quer* oblique] — **queer′ly** *adv.* — **queer′ness** *n.*

Synonyms (adj.): anomalous, bizarre, crotchety, curious, droll, eccentric, erratic, fantastic, funny, grotesque, laughable, ludicrous, mysterious, odd, peculiar, quaint, ridiculous, singular, strange, unique, unusual, whimsical. *Odd* is unmated, as an *odd* shoe, and so uneven, as an *odd* number. *Singular* is alone of its kind; as, the *singular* number. What is *singular* is *odd*, but what is *odd* may not be *singular*, as, a drawerful of *odd* gloves. A *strange* thing is something either unnatural or extraordinary. A *singular* coincidence is one the happening of which is unusual; a *strange* coincidence is one the cause of which is hard to explain. That which is *peculiar* belongs especially to a person as his own; in its ordinary use there is the implication that the thing *peculiar* to one is not common to the majority. *Eccentric* is off center, and so off or aside from the ordinary and normal course; as, genius is commonly *eccentric*. *Eccentric* is a higher and more respectful word than *odd* or *queer. Erratic* signifies wandering, a stronger and more censorious term than *eccentric. Queer* is aside from the common in a way that is comical or perhaps slightly *ridiculous* or *mysterious. Quaint* denotes that which is pleasingly *odd* and fanciful, often with something of the antique; as, the *quaint* architecture of medieval towns. That which is *funny* is calculated to provoke laughter; that which is *droll* is more quietly amusing. That which is *grotesque* in the material sense is irregular or misshapen in form or outline or ill-proportioned so as to be somewhat *ridiculous*; the French *bizarre* is practically equivalent to *grotesque.* See ODD. *Antonyms:* common, customary, familiar, natural, normal, ordinary, regular, usual.

quell (kwel) *v.t.* **1** To put down or suppress by force; extinguish. **2** To quiet; allay, as pain. [OE *cwellan* kill] — **quell′er** *n.*

quench (kwench) *v.t.* **1** To put out or extinguish, as a fire. **2** To put an end to; cause to cease. **3** To slake or satisfy (thirst). **4** To suppress or repress, as emotions. **5** To cool, as heated iron or steel, by thrusting into water or other liquid. [ME *cwenken*] — **quench′a·ble** *adj.* — **quench′er** *n.*

quer·cit·ron (kwûr′sit·ron) *n.* **1** The crushed and powdered inner bark of the American black oak (*Quercus velutina*), used in dyeing and tanning. **2** The yellow dye made therefrom. **3** The dyer's oak (*Q. coccinea*). [<L *quercus* oak + CITRON]

que·rist (kwir′ist) *n.* An inquirer; questioner.

querl (kwûrl) *v.t.* & *n. U.S. Dial.* Curl; twist: also spelled *quirl.* [? <G]

quern (kwûrn) *n.* **1** An old form of hand mill for grinding grain. **2** A small hand mill for grinding spices. [OE *cweorn*]

quer·u·lous (kwer′ə·ləs, -yə·ləs) *adj.* **1** Disposed to complain or be fretful; faultfinding. **2** Indicating or expressing a complaining or whining disposition. **3** Quarrelsome. [<LL *querulosus* <L *querulus* <*queri* complain] — **quer′u·lous·ly** *adv.* — **quer′u·lous·ness** *n.*

que·ry (kwir′ē) *v.* **·ried, ·ry·ing** *v.t.* **1** To inquire into; ask about. **2** To ask questions of; interrogate. **3** To express doubt concerning the correctness or truth of, especially, as in printing, by marking with a query. — *v.i.* **4** To have or express doubt; question. See synonyms under INQUIRE, QUESTION. — *n. pl.* **·ries 1** An inquiry, or a memorandum of an inquiry, to be answered; a question. **2** A doubt; interrogation: often indicated, as in printing, by the interrogation point (?). See synonyms under INQUIRY, QUESTION. [<L *quaere*, imperative sing. of *quaerere* ask]

quest (kwest) *n.* **1** The act of seeking; a looking for something; a search, as an adventure or expedition in medieval romance; also, the person or persons making the search. **2** *Rare* An inquest. — *v.i.* **1** To go on a quest. **2** To make a search. **3** To search for game; also, to bay on the trail of game: said of hunting dogs. — *v.t.* **4** To search for; seek. [<OF *queste* <L *quaesitus*, pp. of *quaerere* ask, seek] — **quest′er** *n.*

ques·tion (kwes′chən) *n.* **1** An interrogative sentence calling for an answer; an inquiry. **2** A subject of inquiry or debate; a matter to be decided; a point at issue; problem. **3** A subject of dispute; a controversy; difference: A *question* rose about it. **4** A proposition under discussion in a deliberative assembly. **5** Objection raised or entertained; doubt: a statement accepted without *question.* **6** Interrogation: the act of asking or inquiring. — *v.t.* **1** To put a question or questions to; interrogate. **2** To be uncertain of; doubt. **3** To make objection to; challenge; dispute. — *v.i.* **4** To ask a question or questions. [< AF *questiun* <L *quaestio, -onis* <*quaerere* ask] — **ques′tion·er** *n.*

Synonyms (noun): doubt, inquiry, inquisition, interrogation, interrogatory, investigation, query. An *inquiry* seeks information for the benefit of the inquirer; a *question* may do the same, or may have the intent to perplex, confuse, or entrap the one of whom it is asked; one makes *inquiry* as to his way; we speak of idle or frivolous *questions* rather than of idle or frivolous *inquiries.* A *query* is a *question* more or less vaguely formulated and indefinite in purpose, often amounting to no more than a suspense of judgment. An *interrogation* or *interrogatory* is a formal *inquiry. Interrogatory* has a special legal use, denoting an *inquiry* in writing by order of a court, to be answered under oath. An *investigation* is an elaborate search for truth or fact, not only by *questions*, but by every other means of procuring information; an *inquisition* is an *investigation* which is either unwarranted, unduly minute, or in some other way offensive. See DOUBT, INQUIRY, TOPIC.

Synonyms (verb): ask, challenge, dispute, doubt, inquire, interrogate, investigate, query, quiz. To *ask* is to seek information, favor, or aid; *inquire, question, interrogate,* respect only the obtaining of information. To *interrogate* is to *examine* formally or officially, commonly by a series of questions. One may *inquire* casually and indifferently; he *questions* intently and resolutely. *Question* also has nearly the meaning of *challenge;* as, "I *question* that statement." See INQUIRE.

ques·tion·a·ble (kwes′chən·ə·bəl) *adj.* **1** Liable to be called in question; debatable; open to question or to suspicions; dubious; suspicious: *questionable* motives. **2** Of doubtful meaning; difficult to decide. **3** *Obs.* Capable of being questioned or inquired of. See synonyms under EQUIVOCAL. — **ques′tion·a·ble·ness, ques′tion·a·bil′i·ty** *n.* — **ques′tion·a·bly** *adv.*

ques·tion·ar·y (kwes′chən·er′ē) *adj.* Of the nature of an examination; interrogatory. — *n. pl.* **·ar·ies** A questionnaire.

ques·tion·less (kwes′chən·lis) *adj.* Unquestionable; indubitable; also, unquestioning. — **ques′tion·less·ly** *adv.*

question mark 1 An interrogation point (?). **2** Something open to question; an unknown.

ques·tion·naire (kwes′chə·nâr′) *n.* A written or printed form comprising a series of questions submitted to a number of persons in order to obtain data for a survey or report. [<F]

ques·tor (kwes′tər) See QUAESTOR.

quet·zal (ket·säl′) *n. pl.* **·zal·es** (-sä′läs) **1** A trogon (*Pharomacrus mocinno*) of brilliant plumage, the national symbol of Guatemala, and anciently regarded as a deity by the Mayas, whose chiefs alone were permitted to wear its plumes. **2** A silver coin, the monetary unit of Guatemala. Also **que·zal** (kā·säl′). [<Sp. <Nahuatl]

Quet·zal·co·a·tl (ket·säl′kō·at′l) A traditional god and heroic figure of the Aztecs.

queue (kyōō) *n.* **1** A pendent braid of hair on the back of the head; a pigtail. **2** A line of persons or vehicles waiting in the order of their arrival. — *v.i.* **queued, queu·ing** *Brit.* To form such a line: usually with *up.* Also spelled *cue.* [<F <OF *coe, coue* <L *cauda* a tail]

QUETZAL

Que·zon City (kā′sôn, -thôn) The capital (since 1948) of the Philippines, in southern Luzon, NE of Manila.

quib·ble (kwib′əl) *n.* **1** An evasion of a point or question; an equivocation. **2** *Rare* A pun. — *v.i.* **·bled, ·bling** To use quibbles; evade the truth or the point in question. [<obs. *quib* <L *quibus,* ablative pl. of *qui* who, which; with ref. to its use in legal documents] — **quib′bler** *n.*

quiche (kēsh) *n.* Any of various non–dessert, custardlike pies, having meat, cheese, vegetables, etc., as principal ingredients. [<F]

Qui·ché (kē·chā′) *n.* **1** An Indian of a tribe of Mayan linguistic stock inhabiting Guatemala. **2** The Mayan language of this tribe.

quick (kwik) *adj.* **1** Done or occurring in a short time; expeditious; brisk; rapid; swift; speedy. **2** Characterized by rapidity or readiness of movement or action; nimble; prompt. **3** Sharp; steep, as a curve. **4** Alert; sensitive; perceptive: a *quick* ear; *quick* wit. **5** Responding readily to impressions; excitable; hasty. **6** Having life; living: opposed to *dead:* an archaic use. **7** Pregnant; with child. **8** Burning briskly; fiery. **9** Shifting; moving: said of soil or sand. **10** Refreshing; bracing. See synonyms under ACTIVE, ALIVE, CLEVER, IMPETUOUS, NIMBLE, SWIFT[1], VIVID. — *n.* **1** That which has life; those who are alive: chiefly in the phrase **the quick and the dead. 2** The living flesh; any vital or tender part; especially, the tender flesh under a nail; hence, the feelings: cut to the *quick.* **3** A hedge plant; quickset. — *adv.* Quickly; rapidly. [OE *cwic* alive]

quick·en (kwik′ən) *v.t.* **1** To cause to move more rapidly; hasten or accelerate. **2** To make alive or quick; give or restore life to. **3** To excite or arouse; stimulate: to *quicken* the appetite. — *v.i.* **4** To move or act more quickly; become more rapid. **5** To come or return to life; revive. **6** To reach the stage of pregnancy at which the motions of the fetus first become perceptible: said of the mother. **7** To begin to manifest signs of life: said of the fetus. — **quick′en·er** *n.*

Synonyms: accelerate, advance, dispatch, drive, expedite, facilitate, further, hasten, hurry, promote, speed, urge. To *quicken* is to increase speed, move or cause to move more rapidly, as through more space or with a greater number of motions in the same time. To *accelerate* is to increase the speed of action or of motion. A motion whose speed increases upon itself is said to be *accelerated*, as the motion of a falling body, which becomes swifter with every second of time. To *accelerate* any work is to *hasten* it toward a finish. To *dispatch* is to do and be done with, to get a thing off one's hands. To *dispatch* an enemy is to kill him outright and quickly; to *dispatch* a messenger is to send him in haste; to *dispatch* a business is to bring it quickly to an end. To *promote* a cause is in any way to bring it forward, *advance* it in power, prominence, etc. To *speed* is really to secure swiftness; to *hasten* is to attempt it, whether successfully or unsuccessfully. *Hurry* always indicates something of confusion. To *facilitate* is to *quicken* by making easy; to *expedite* is to *quicken* by removing hindrances. *Antonyms:* check, clog, delay, drag, hinder, impede, obstruct, retard.

quick fire The firing of quick successive shots: faster than *rapid fire,* and used chiefly against moving or bobbing targets. — **quick–fire** (kwik′fīr′) *adj.*

quick–freeze (kwik′frēz′) *v.t.* **–froze, –fro·zen, –freez·ing** To subject (food) to rapid refrigeration for storing at or below freezing temperatures. — **quick′–fro′zen** *adj.*

quick·ie (kwik′ē) *n. U.S. Slang* Anything done hastily, as by short cuts or makeshift methods.

quick·lime (kwik′līm′) *n.* Unslaked lime. See LIME[1].

quick·ly (kwik′lē) *adv.* In a quick manner; rapidly; soon.

quick march A march in quick time; quickstep.

quick·match (kwik′mach′) *n.* A cord impregnated with black powder and used as a fast-burning fuse for flares, fireworks, etc.

quick·ness (kwik′nis) *n.* **1** The state or quality of being quick; speed; celerity; liveliness; readiness. **2** Acuteness of perception or sensibility; sharpness; keenness.

quick·sand (kwik'sand') n. A bed of sand so water–soaked as readily to engulf any person or animal that attempts to move or rest upon it.

quick·set (kwik'set') n. 1 A hedge plant, especially hawthorn. 2 A hedge made of it. — adj. Composed of quickset.

quick·sil·ver (kwik'sil'vər) n. 1 Metallic mercury: widely used in metallurgy, industry, and the arts. All of its compounds are poisonous. 2 An amalgam of tin, used for the backs of mirrors. [Trans. of L argentum vivum]

quick·step (kwik'step') n. A march or dance written in a rapid tempo; also, a quick march.

quick time A marching step of 120 paces a minute, each pace of 30 inches: used in military drills and ceremonies.

quick·wa·ter (kwik'wô'tər, -wot'ər) n. A stream or that part of a stream having a decided current.

quick–wit·ted (kwik'wit'id) adj. Having a ready wit or quick discernment; keen; alert. See synonyms under CLEVER, SAGACIOUS. — **quick'–wit'ted·ly** adv. — **quick'–wit'ted·ness** n.

quid[1] (kwid) n. 1 A small portion of chewing tobacco. 2 A cud, as of a cow. [Var. of CUD]

quid[2] (kwid) n. Brit. Slang In England, a pound sterling, or a sovereign. [Origin uncertain]

quid·di·ty (kwid'ə·tē) n. pl. ·ties 1 The essence of a thing. 2 A subtle or trifling distinction or objection; cavil. [<LL quidditas, -tatis <L quid which, what]

quid·nunc (kwid'nungk') n. One who seeks or affects to know all that is going on; an inquisitive busybody. [<L quid nunc what now]

qui·es·cent (kwī·es'ənt, kwē-) adj. 1 Being in a state of repose or inaction; quiet; still. 2 Resting free from anxiety, emotion, or agitation. 3 Phonet. In Semitic languages, having no sound; silent. See synonyms under PASSIVE. [<L quiescens, -entis, ppr. of quiescere be quiet] — **qui·es'cence** n. — **qui·es'cent·ly** adv.

qui·et (kwī'ət) adj. 1 Being in a state of repose; still; calm; motionless. 2 Free from turmoil, strife, or alarm; tranquil; peaceful. 3 Silent. 4 Gentle or mild of disposition. 5 Undisturbed by din or bustle; retired; secluded: a quiet nook. 6 Restful to the eye; soft in hue; hence, not showy or obtrusive; as dress. See synonyms under CALM, PACIFIC, SEDATE, SOBER. — n. The condition or quality of being free from motion, disturbance, noise, etc.; peace; calm. See synonyms under REST[1]. — v.t. & v.i. To make or become quiet: often with down. See synonyms under ALLAY, REPRESS, SETTLE, TRANQUILIZE. — adv. In a quiet or peaceful manner. [<OF quiete <L quietus <quies rest, repose. Doublet of COY.] — **qui'et·ly** adv. — **qui'et·ness** n.

qui·e·tude (kwī'ə·tōōd, -tyōōd) n. A state or condition of calm or tranquillity; repose; rest.

qui·e·tus (kwī·ē'təs) n. 1 A silencing or suppressing; death; repose. 2 A final discharge or quittance; a settlement. 3 A killing blow. [<L quietus est he is quiet]

quill[1] (kwil) n. 1 Ornithol. One of the large, strong flight feathers or tail feathers of a bird. 2 A pen made from a feather; hence, any pen. 3 The hollow, horny stem of a feather; a calamus. 4 Such a stem used for a receptacle or measure, as for a drug, or as a plectrum for playing a stringed instrument. 5 Zool. One of the large, sharp spines of a porcupine or hedgehog. 6 A piece of cane or reed used as a musical pipe. 7 A slow–burning fuse made formerly of the quill of a feather filled with powder. 8 A piece of bark rolled into cylindrical form: a cinnamon quill. 9 A quill toothpick. 10 Mech. A hollow shaft, with or without openings, designed to revolve on a solid shaft when the clutches are engaged. 11 In weaving, a spindle or bobbin; pirn. 12 A fluted, rounded ridge, or cylindrical fold, as in a ruff or ruffle. — v.t. 1 To make or iron (a garment or fabric) with rounded plaits or ridges. 2 To wind (thread or yarn) on a quill or quills. — v.i. 3 To wind thread or yarn on a quill or quills. [Cf. LG quiele a quill of a feather]

quill·back (kwil'bak') n. A carplike fish (Carpiodes velifer) common in the Mississippi Valley.

quilt (kwilt) n. 1 A bedcover made by stitching together firmly two layers of cloth or patchwork with some soft and warm substance (as wool or cotton) between them. 2 Any bedcover, especially if thick. 3 A quilted skirt or other quilted article. 4 Obs. A mattress. — v.t. 1 To stitch together (two pieces of material) with a soft substance between. 2 To stitch in ornamental patterns or crossing lines. 3 To sew up or secure between two layers. 4 To pad or line with something soft. — v.i. 5 To make a quilt or quilted work. [<OF cuilte <L culcita]

quilt·ing (kwil'ting) n. 1 The act or process of making a quilt, or of stitching as in making a quilt. 2 Material for quiltwork. 3 A quilting bee or party.

quilting bee A social gathering of the women of a community for working on a quilt or quilts. Also **quilting frolic, quilting party.**

quin·a·crine (kwin'ə·krēn) n. Atabrine.

qui·na·ry (kwī'nər·ē) adj. Consisting of or containing five parts or elements; arranged by fives, or in sets or groups of five. — n. pl. ·ries A number, body, group, or system of five; something composed of five like parts. [<L quinarius <quini five each]

qui·nate (kwī'nāt, kwin'āt) adj. 1 Arranged in five. 2 Bot. Having five similar parts together, as the five leaflets of the Virginia creeper. [<L quini five each <quinque five]

quince (kwins) n. 1 The hard, acid, applelike, yellowish fruit, used for preserves, of a small deciduous Asian tree (Cydonia oblonga) of the rose family. 2 The tree. [Orig. pl. of obs. coyn <OF cooin <L cotoneum, var. of (malum) cydonium (apple) of Cydonia <Gk. Kydōnia, a town in Crete]

quin·cun·cial (kwin·kun'shəl) adj. 1 Arranged in the form of a quincunx. 2 Bot. Arranged in a set of five, as leaves. Also **quin·cunx'ial** (-kungk'shəl). — **quin·cun'cial·ly** adv.

quin·cunx (kwin'kungks) n. 1 An arrangement of five things, as trees, in a square having one in each corner and one in the center. 2 A disposition of such squares repeated indefinitely. 3 A quincuncial arrangement, as of flower parts. [<L quincunx five twelfths <quinque five + uncia twelfth part]

quin·de·cen·ni·al (kwin'di·sen'ē·əl) n. A fifteenth anniversary. — adj. Of or pertaining to the fifteenth anniversary. [<L quindecim fifteen + annus year]

quin·dec·i·mal (kwin·des'ə·məl) adj. Fifteen. [<L quindecim fifteen]

quin·ic (kwin'ik) adj. Of, pertaining to, or derived from quinine.

qui·nine (kwī'nīn, esp. Brit. kwi·nēn') n. Chem. A white, amorphous or slightly crystalline, very bitter alkaloid, $C_{20}H_{24}N_2O_2$, contained in cinchona barks. Its salts, as the hydrochlorate, sulfate, and others, are largely used in medicine on account of their tonic and antipyretic qualities, especially in malarial affections of all kinds. Also **quin·in** (kwin'in). [< earlier quina (<Sp. <Quechua kina bark) + -INE[2]]

quin·qua·ge·nar·i·an (kwin'kwə·jə·nâr'ē·ən) adj. Being fifty years old; relating to this age. — n. A person fifty years old.

quin·qua·gen·a·ry (kwin'kwə·jen'ər·ē) adj. 1 Consisting of or containing fifty. 2 Denoting a group or set of fifty. [<L quinquagenarius <quinquageni fifty each]

quin·qua·ges·i·ma (kwin'kwə·jes'ə·mə) adj. Fiftieth. — n. A period of fifty days. [<L quinquagesima (dies) fiftieth (day)]

quinque– combining form Five: quinquefoliate. Also, before vowels, **quinqu–.** [<L quinque five]

quin·quen·ni·al (kwin·kwen'ē·əl) adj. Occurring every five years, or once in five years; also, lasting five years. — n. 1 A fifth anniversary or its celebration. 2 A quinquennium. [<L quinque five + annus year]

quin·quen·ni·um (kwin·kwen'ē·əm) n. A period of five years. [<L]

quint (kwint) n. 1 A fifth. 2 A set of five. 3 The E string of a violin. 4 Colloq. A quintuplet. 5 In piquet, a sequence of five of the same suit: if of the five highest cards, called a **quint major.** 6 An organ stop giving tones a fifth above those of the keys that are pressed. [<L quintus <quinque five]

quin·tal (kwin'təl) n. A measure of weight, a hundredweight; in the metric system, 100 kilograms: also called metric centner. See METRIC SYSTEM. [<OF <Arabic qintar]

quin·tan (kwin'tən) adj. Recurring on every fifth day, reckoning inclusively: a quintan fever. — n. A quintan fever. [<L quintanus <quintus fifth]

quin·tes·sence (kwin·tes'əns) n. 1 An extract from anything, containing in concentrated form its most essential principle. 2 The purest and most essential part, manifestation, or embodiment of anything. 3 Philos. In the doctrine of the Pythagoreans, the fifth or celestial essence, ether, above the four elements of earth, air, fire, and water. [<F <L quinta essentia fifth essence] — **quin·tes·sen'tial** adj.

quin·tet (kwin·tet') n. 1 A musical composition arranged for five voices or instruments; also, the five persons performing it. 2 Any group of five; anything arranged for a set of five performers, as in a game. Also **quin·tette'.** [<Ital. quintetto <quinto fifth]

quin·tile (kwin'til) n. 1 In astrology, the aspect of planets separated by 72°, or the fifth part of the zodiac. 2 Stat. a That part of a frequency distribution containing one fifth of the total observations or cases. b The point marking such a part. [<L quintus fifth, on analogy with quartile]

quin·til·lion (kwin·til'yən) n. In the French system of numeration, almost universally followed in the United States, 1 followed by 18 ciphers; in the English system, 1 followed by 30 ciphers. [<L quintus fifth + MILLION] — **quin·til'lionth** (-yənth) adj. & n.

quin·tu·ple (kwin'tōō·pəl, -tyōō-, kwin·tōō'pəl, -tyōō'-) v.t. & v.i. ·pled, ·pling To multiply by five; make or become five times as large. [< adj.] — adj. 1 Consisting of five united or of five parts. 2 Multiplied by five. — n. A number or a sum five times as great as another. [<F <L quintuplex <quintus fifth + plic-, stem of plicare fold]

quin·tu·plet (kwin'tōō·plit, -tyōō-, kwin·tōō'plit, -tyōō'-) n. 1 Five things of a kind used or occurring together. 2 One of five born of the same mother at one birth.

quin·tu·pli·cate (kwin·tōō'plə·kit, -tyōō'-) adj. 1 Fivefold. 2 Raised to the fifth power. — v.t. & v.i. (-kāt) ·cat·ed, ·cat·ing To multiply by five; quintuple. — n. (-kit) One of five identical things. [<L quintuplex, -icis + -ATE[1]] — **quin·tu'pli·cate·ly** adv. — **quin·tu'pli·ca'tion** n.

quip (kwip) n. 1 A sarcastic or sharp jest, remark, or retort; gibe; also, a clever or witty sally without sarcasm. 2 A quibble. 3 An odd, fantastic action or object. — v.i. **quipped, quip·ping** To make a witty remark; jest. [Earlier quippy <L quippe indeed] — **quip'pish** adj.

quip·ster (kwip'stər) n. One who makes quips.

qui·pu (kē'pōō, kwip'ōō) n. An aboriginal Peruvian device for recording and conveying information, consisting of a series of varicolored and knotted strings tied at one end to a thicker cord. The order, color, and knots of the strings were used like elements of a written language. Also **quip'pu.** [<Quechua quipu knot]

PERUVIAN QUIPU

quire[1] (kwīr) n. 1 The twentieth part of a ream of paper; 24 (or 25) sheets. 2 A set of all the sheets necessary to make a book; hence, a book. — v.t. **quired, quir·ing** To fold or separate into quires. ◆ Homophone: choir. [<OF quaire <L quaterni by fours]

quire[2] (kwīr) See CHOIR.

quirk (kwûrk) n. 1 A short or sharp turn; twist. 2 A quaint turn of the fancy; bright retort; hence, a personal peculiarity; caprice. 3 An artful turn for evasion or subterfuge; quibble. 4 A sudden curve or flourish, especially in drawing or writing. 5 *Archit.* **a** A small groove in, beside, or between moldings or beads. **b** A molding or bead having a groove on one or both edges. See synonyms under WHIM. [Origin uncertain]

quirk·y (kwûrk'ē) *adj.* **quirk·i·er**, **quirk·i·est** Peculiar, unpredictable, and idiosyncratic: a *quirky* individual. — **quirk'i·ly** *adv.* — **quirk'·i·ness** *n.*

quis·ling (kwiz'ling) *n.* One who betrays his country to the enemy and is then given political power by the conquerors. [after Vidkun *Quisling,* 1887–1945, Norwegian Nazi party leader and traitor] — **quis'ling·ism** *n.*

quit (kwit) *v.* **quit** or **quit·ted**, **quit·ting** *v.t.* **1** To cease or desist from; discontinue. **2** To give up; renounce; relinquish. **3** To go away from; leave. **4** To let go of (something held). **5** *Archaic* To acquit (oneself). —*v.i.* **6** To stop; cease; discontinue. **7** To leave; depart. **8** *Colloq.* To resign from a position, etc. See synonyms under ABANDON, CEASE, END, RE-QUITE. — *adj.* Released, relieved, or absolved from something, as a duty, obligation, encumbrance, or debt; clear; free; rid. — *n.* The act of quitting. — **to be quits** To be even (with another). — **to cry quits** To declare to be even, or that neither has the advantage; declare (oneself) willing to stop competing. [<OF *quiter* <LL *quietare* set free <L *quies* rest, repose]

quite (kwīt) *adv.* **1** To the fullest extent; without limitation or reservation; fully; totally: *quite* dead. **2** *Colloq.* To a great or considerable extent; noticeably; very: *quite* ill. [ME; var. of QUIT, *adj.*]

Qui·to (kē'tō) The capital of Ecuador; 9,343 feet above sea level in the Andes of north central Ecuador.

quit·tance (kwit'ns) *n.* **1** Discharge or release, as from a debt or obligation; acquittance. **2** Something given or tendered by way of requital; repayment. [<F *quiter* QUIT]

quit·ter[1] (kwit'ər) *n.* One who quits needlessly; a shirker; slacker; coward.

quit·ter[2] (kwit'ər) *n.* **1** A fistulous sore on the hoof of a horse or any solid-hoofed animal: also **quit'ter·bone** (-bōn'), **quit'tor. 2** Purulent matter. [? <OF *quiture* a cooking]

quiv·er[1] (kwiv'ər) *v.i.* To shake with a slight, tremulous motion; vibrate; tremble. See synonyms under QUAKE, SHAKE. — *n.* The act or fact of quivering; a trembling or shaking. [Prob. related to QUAVER]

quiv·er[2] (kwiv'ər) *n.* A portable case or sheath for arrows; also, its contents. [<AF *quiver,* OF *coivre* <Gmc.]

quix·ot·ic (kwik·sot'ik) *adj.* Pertaining to or like Don Quixote, the hero of a Spanish romance ridiculing knight-errantry; hence, ridiculously chivalrous or romantic; having high but impractical sentiments, aims, etc.; extravagant; visionary. See synonyms under IMAGINARY. — **quix·ot'i·cal·ly** *adv.* — **quix·ot·ism** (kwik'sə·tiz'əm) *n.*

quiz (kwiz) *n. pl.* **quiz·zes 1** The act of questioning; specifically, an oral or written examination of a class or individual. **2** Something or someone odd or ridiculous; an eccentric. **3** A hoax; practical joke. — *v.t.* **quizzed, quiz·zing 1** To examine by asking questions; question. **2** *Brit.* To make fun of; ridicule. See synonyms under QUESTION. [Origin unknown] — **quiz'zer** *n.*

quod·li·bet (kwod'li·bet) *n.* **1** A debatable or nice point; subtlety; especially, a scholarly dissertation on such a subject. **2** *Music* A fantasia or medley, usually humorous. [<L, anything at all] — **quod·li·bet·ic** (kwod'li·bet'ik) or **·i·cal** *adj.*

quo·hog (kwô'hôg, -hog, kwə·hôg', -hog') *n.* A quahaug.

quoin (koin, kwoin) *n.* **1** A large square ashlar or stone at the angle of a wall. **2** An external angle of a building. **3** A vertical, angular, ornamental projection from a wall face. **4** A wedge-shaped stone of an arch. **5** A block cut obliquely at the bottom to support a vertical column or pilaster on an inclined plane. **6** An internal angle, as of a room; a corner. **7** A wedge, or wedgelike piece. **8** *Printing* A wedge, or pair of wedges, by which to lock up type in a chase or galley. —*v.t.* To fasten or provide with a quoin or quoins. [Var. of COIN]

QUOINS
A. Printer's metal quoins.
   a. Single quoin.
   b. Pair of quoins ready for locking with key.
B. Quoins of dressed stone.

quon·dam (kwon'dəm) *adj.* Having been formerly; former. [<L]

Quon·set hut (kwon'sit) A portable structure resembling the Nissen hut, designed for use by the U.S. armed services: a trade name. [from *Quonset,* a town in Rhode Island where first made]

QUONSET HUT

quo·rum (kwôr'əm, kwō'rəm) *n.* **1** Such a number of members of any deliberative or corporate body as is necessary for the legal transaction of business: commonly, a majority. **2** Formerly, in England, certain designated justices of the peace without the presence of some one of whom the others could not act: now applied loosely to all justices. **3** A select or chosen body. [<L, of whom <*qui* who]

quo·ta (kwō'tə) *n.* A proportional part or share required for making up a certain number or quantity; proportionate contribution. [<Med. L *quota (pars)* how great (a part) <L *quotus* how great]

quo·ta·tion (kwō·tā'shən) *n.* **1** The act of quoting. **2** The words quoted or cited; a passage from a book or writing, cited or adduced. **3** A price quoted or current, as of securities, etc. [<Med. L *quotatio, -onis* <*quotare.* See QUOTE.] — **quo·ta'tion·al** *adj.* —**quo·ta'tion·al·ly** *adv.* — **quo·ta'tion·ist** *n.*

quotation mark One of the marks placed at the beginning and end of a quoted word or passage. In English usage, one or two inverted commas (',") mark the beginning of a quotation, and, correspondingly, one or two apostrophes (',") the close, the single marks usually being used to set off a quotation within a quotation.

quote (kwōt) *v.* **quot·ed, quot·ing** *v.t.* **1** To repeat or reproduce the words of. **2** To repeat or cite (a rule, author, etc.), as for authority or illustration. **3** In commerce: **a** To state (a price). **b** To give the current or market price of. **4** *Printing* To enclose within quotation marks. —*v.i.* **5** To make a quotation, as from a book. —*n.* A quotation; also, a quotation mark. [<Med. L *quotare* distinguish by number <L *quot* how many] —**quot'a·ble** *adj.* —**quot'er** *n.* —**quote'·wor·thy** (-wûr'thē) *adj.* —**quot'ing·ly** *adv.*

Synonyms (verb): cite, excerpt, extract, paraphrase, plagiarize, recite, repeat. To *quote* is to give an author's words, either exactly, as in direct quotation, or in substance, as in indirect quotation; to *cite* is, etymologically, to call up a passage, as a witness is summoned. In *citing* a passage its exact location by chapter, page, or otherwise must be given, so that it can be promptly called into evidence; in *quoting,* the location may or may not be given, but the words or substance of the passage must be given. To *paraphrase* is to state an author's thought more freely than in indirect quotation, keeping the substance of his thought and his order of statement, but changing the language and style, and perhaps expanding by explanation, inference, etc. To *plagiarize* is to *quote* without credit, appropriating another's words or thought as one's own. To *recite* or *repeat* is usually to *quote* orally, but *recite* is applied in legal phrase to a particular statement of facts which is not a quotation.

quoth (kwōth) *v.t.* Said or spoke; uttered: the imperfect tense of the obsolete verb *queth,* used only in the first and third persons, the nominative always following the verb, as *quoth* he. [OE *cwœth,* pt. of *cwethan* say]

quo·tid·i·an (kwō·tid'ē·ən) *adj.* Recurring or occurring every day. — *n.* A fever whose paroxysms return every day. [<L *quotidianus* daily]

quo·tient (kwō'shənt) *n. Math.* The result obtained by division; a number indicating how many times one number or quantity is contained in another. [<L *quotiens* how often <*quot* how many]

R

r, R (är) *n. pl.* **r's, R's** or **rs, Rs, ars** (ärz) **1** The 18th letter of the English alphabet: from Phoenician *resh,* Greek *rho,* Roman *R.* **2** The sound of the letter *r.* See ALPHABET. —*symbol* **1** *Chem.* An organic radical. **2** *Math.* Ratio. **3** *Electr.* Resistance. —**the three R's** Reading, writing, and arithmetic (regarded humorously as spelled *reading, 'riting,* and *'rithmetic*); hence, the essential elements of a primary education.

Ra (rä) The supreme Egyptian deity, the sun-god, usually represented as a hawk-headed man crowned with the solar disk and uraeus: also spelled *Re.* [<Egyptian *Rā* the sun]

RA

rab·bet (rab'it) *n.* **1** A recess or groove in or near the edge of one piece of wood or other material to receive the edge of another piece. **2** A joint so made. **3** A rabbet plane. —*v.* **·bet·ed, ·bet·ing** *v.t.* **1** To cut a rectangular groove in. **2** To unite in a rabbet. —*v.i.* **3** To be jointed by a rabbet. Also spelled *rebate.* ◆ Homophone: *rabbit.* [<OF *rabat* <*rabattre* beat down. See REBATE.]

RABBET JOINTS

rabbet plane A plane for cutting a rectangular groove, as in or near the edge of a plank.

rab·bi (rab'ī) *n. pl.* **·bis** (-bīz) Master, teacher: a Jewish title for those distinguished for learning, authoritative teachers of the Law, and appointed spiritual heads of a community. Also **rab'bin** (-in). [OE <L <Gk. *rhabbi* <Hebrew *rabbī* my master <*rab* great, master + *-i* my (pronominal suffix)]

rab·bin·ate (rab'in·āt) *n.* **1** The office or term of office of a rabbi. **2** Rabbis collectively. [<Med. L *rabbinus* rabbi]

Rab·bin·ic (rə·bin'ik) *n.* The language or dialect of the rabbis; especially, the Hebrew language as used in Biblical and Talmudic exegesis by Jewish scholars of the late ancient and early medieval periods.

rab·bin·ist (rab'in·ist) *n.* One among the Jews who adhered to the Talmud and the traditions of the rabbis, in opposition to those who rejected the traditions. Also **rab'bin·ite** (-īt). [<Med. L *rabbinus*] — **rab'bin·is'tic, rab'bin·is'ti·cal, rab'bin·it'ic** (-it'ik) *adj.* — **rab'bin·is'ti·cal·ly** *adv.*

rab·bit (rab'it) *n.* **1** Any of various small burrowing rodents (family *Leporidae*), resembling but smaller than the hare, as the common American cottontail (*Sylvilagus* *floridanus*). **2** A hare. **3** The pelt of a rabbit or hare. **4** Welsh rabbit. —*v.i.* To hunt rabbits. ◆ Homophone: *rabbet.* [ME *rabette.* Akin to Walloon *robbett,* Flemish *robbe.*] — **rab′bit·er** *n.*

rab·bit-foot (rab′it-fŏŏt′) *n.* **1** A common clover (*Trifolium arvense*) having soft, hairy flower heads supposed to resemble rabbits' paws: also **rabbit's-foot clover. 2** The left hind foot of a rabbit carried as a good-luck charm.

rab·ble (rab′əl) *n.* A rude crowd; mob. — **the rabble** The populace; hoi polloi: used contemptuously. —*adj.* Of or pertaining to, suited to, or characteristic of a rabble; noisy; disorderly. —*v.t.* **·bled, ·bling** To mob. [? <RABBLE³]

rab·ble·ment (rab′əl-mənt) *n.* **1** An uproar; disturbance. **2** A rabble; crowd.

rab·ble-rous·er (rab′əl-rou′zər) *n.* One who tries to incite mobs by arousing prejudices and passions; a demagog.

rab·id (rab′id) *adj.* **1** Affected with, arising from, or pertaining to rabies; mad. **2** Unreasonably zealous; fanatical; violent. **3** Furious; raging. Also **rab′ic.** [<L *rabidus* < *rabere* be mad. Akin to RAGE.] — **rab′id·ly** *adv.* — **rab′id·ness** *n.*

ra·bies (rā′bēz, -bi·ēz) *n.* An acute infectious disease of animals, especially of dogs, caused by a virus and affecting the central nervous system; hydrophobia: readily transmissible to man by the bite of an affected animal. [<L < *rabere* rave] — **ra′bi·et′ic** (-et′ik) *adj.*

ra·ca (rā′kə, rə·kä′) *adj.* Worthless; contemptible. *Matt.* v 22. [<LL <Gk. *rhakē* <Aramaic *rēqā*]

rac·coon (ra·kōōn′) *n.* **1** An American nocturnal plantigrade carnivore (genus *Procyon*): the common North American raccoon (*P. lotor*) is grayish-brown, with a black cheek patch, and black-and-white-ringed bushy tail. **2** The fur of this animal. Also spelled *racoon.* [Alter. of Algonquian *arakunem* hand-scratcher]

RACCOON
(Body from 20 to 30 inches long; tail, 10 to 12 inches)

race¹ (rās) *n.* **1** One of the major subdivisions of mankind, regarded as having a common origin and exhibiting a relatively constant set of physical traits. On the basis of the more commonly used criteria such as stature, the cephalic index, the nasal index, prognathism, skull capacity, texture of the hair, degree of pilosity, color of the skin, and hair and eye color, mankind has been divided into primary stocks or races, each of which is regarded as including a varying number of ethnic groups. According to some, the primary stocks are: the Caucasoid, the Mongoloid, and the Negroid. A number of races, such as the Australian and Polynesian, are of doubtful classification. **2** Any group of people or any grouping of peoples having, or assumed to have, common characteristics. **3** A nation: the German *race.* **4** A genealogical or family stock; clan: the *race* of MacGregor. **5** Pedigree; lineage: a noble *race.* **6** Any class of beings having characteristics uniting them, or differentiating them from others: the *race* of lawyers. **7** *Biol.* A group of plants or animals, having characteristics clearly differentiating it from other groups within the same species, which breeds true except for minor variations; a variety: a *race* of wheat. **8** A stock, breed, or strain of domestic animals or plants. **9** A quality or aggregate of qualities by which origin is determined; especially, the characteristic flavor or taste of wine. See synonyms under AFFINITY, KIN, PEOPLE, SORT. [<F <Ital. *razza* <L (*gene*)*ratio* lineage, breed]

race² (rās) *n.* **1** A contest to determine the relative speed of the contestants. **2** Any contest. **3** Movement or progression; swift movement. **4** Duration of life; course; career. **5** A swift current of water or its channel. **6** A swift current or heavy sea resulting from the meeting of two tides: the Portland *Race.*

7 A sluice or channel by which to conduct water to or from a waterwheel or around a dam. See HEADRACE, MILLRACE, TAILRACE. **8** Any groove or channel along which some part of a machine slides or is guided. **9** Slipstream. —*v.* **raced, rac·ing** *v.i.* **1** To take part in a contest of speed. **2** To move at great or top speed. **3** To move at an accelerated or too great speed, usually because of decreased resistance: said of machinery. —*v.t.* **4** To contend against in a race. **5** To cause to take part in a race. **6** To cause to move at an accelerated or too great speed: to *race* an engine. [<ON *rās.* Akin to OE *rǣs* a rushing.]

race³ (rās) *n.* A root; specifically, a root of ginger. [<OF *rais* <L *radix* root]

race knife A tool having a very narrow U-shaped blade, used for tracing or outlining on metal or glass or for scribing on wood.

rac·e·mize (ras′ə·mīz, rā·sē′mīz) *v.t.* **·mized, ·miz·ing** *Chem.* To change (an optically active compound) into an optically inactive compound. — **rac′e·mi·za′tion** *n.*

race psychology A division of psychology which investigates human traits and behavior in relation to racial factors, actual or assumed.

rac·er (rā′sər) *n.* **1** One who races, or one who contends in a race. **2** Anything having unusually rapid speed, as a race horse, steamer, or yacht; also, an automobile designed for racing. **3** A turntable on which a heavy gun is turned to left or right. **4** One of various colubrine snakes, as the blacksnake.

race suicide The slow reduction in numbers of a people through voluntary failure on the part of individuals to maintain the birth rate at or above the level of the death rate.

race·track (rās′trak′) *n.* A racecourse.

race·way (rās′wā′) *n.* **1** A channel for conducting water. **2** A tube for protecting wires, as in a subway. **3** *U.S.* A racecourse for trotting horses.

ra·chis (rā′kis) *n.* *pl.* **ra·chi·des** (rā′kə·dēz) or **·chis·es 1** *Bot.* The axis of an inflorescence; a raceme. **2** *Ornithol.* The shaft of a feather, especially the part filled with pith, which bears the barbs. **3** *Anat.* The spinal column. Sometimes spelled *rhachis.* [<NL <Gk. *rhachis* spine] — **ra·chi·al** (rā′kē·əl) *adj.*

Rach·ma·ni·nov (räkh·mä′ni·nôf), **Sergei Vassilievich,** 1873–1943, Russian pianist and composer. Also **Rach·ma′ni·noff.**

ra·cial (rā′shəl) *adj.* Pertaining to or characteristic of a race, races, or descent. — **ra′cial·ly** *adv.*

ra·cial·ism (rā′shəl·iz′əm) *n.* **1** The doctrine of the preponderant influence of actual or assumed racial factors in the origin, development, and rank of various human societies; race prejudice. **2** Racism. — **ra′cial·ist** *n.*

Ra·ci·bórz (rä·chē′bōōsh) See RATIBOR.

ra·cism (rā′siz·əm) *n.* An excessive and irrational belief in or advocacy of the superiority of a given group, people, or nation, on racial grounds alone; race hatred. — **ra′cist** *n.*

rack¹ (rak) *n.* **1** An open grating, framework, or the like, in or on which articles may be placed, as a frame to hold dishes, a tier or row of pigeonholes, or a framework to hold fodder for horses, cattle, or sheep. **2** A triangular frame for arranging the balls on a billiard table. **3** A device in an airplane for carrying bombs: also **bomb rack. 4** *Mech.* A bar or the like having teeth that engage with those of a gearwheel, pinion, or worm gear. **5** A machine for stretching or making tense; especially, an intrument of torture which stretches the limbs of victims. **6** Torture or punishment as by the rack; hence, intense mental or physical suffering. **7** A wrenching or straining, as from a storm. —*v.t.* **1** To place or arrange in or on a rack. **2** To torture on the rack. **3** To cause suffering to; torment. **4** To strain, as with the effort of thinking: to *rack* one's brains. **5** To raise (rents) excessively: see RACK-RENT. ◆ Homophone: *wrack.* [ME *rekke,* prob. <MDu. *rec, recke* <*recken* stretch] — **rack′er** *n.*

rack² (rak) *n.* The single-foot. —*v.i.* To proceed or move with this gait. ◆ Homophone: *wrack.* [? Var. of ROCK²]

rack³ (rak) *n.* **1** Thin, flying, or broken

clouds. **2** Any floating vapor. —*v.i.* To move rapidly; send, as clouds before the wind. Also spelled *wrack.* [<Scand. Cf. ON *rek* drifting wreckage, *reka* drive, drift.]

rack⁴ (rak) *n.* Wrack; wreck; demolition: obsolete except in the phrase "to go to rack and ruin." [Var. of WRACK²]

rack⁵ *v.t.* To draw off from the lees, as liquor. ◆ Homophone: *wrack.* [<Provençal *arracar* <*raca* refuse of grapes]

rack and pinion *Mech.* A machine movement in which a toothed rack and a pinion mesh together for converting rotary motion into reciprocating motion or vice versa.

RACK AND PINION

rack·et¹ (rak′it) *n.* **1** An implement for striking a ball, as in the game of tennis. It is a nearly elliptical hoop of bent wood, usually strung with catgut, and has a handle. **2** A large wooden sole or shoe to support the weight of a man or horse on swampy ground. **3** A snowshoe. **4** A ratchet: a misnomer. **5** An organ stop. **6** *sing. & pl.* A game resembling court tennis, played in a court with four walls. Often spelled *racquet.* [<F *raquette* < Arabic *rāha* palm of the hand]

TYPES OF RACKETS

a. Tennis.	*c, d.* Squash.
b. Badminton.	*e.* Table tennis.

rack·et² (rak′it) *n.* **1** A clattering, vociferous, or confused noise; fuss; commotion. **2** *Colloq.* **a** A scheme for getting money or other benefits by fraud, intimidation, or other illegitimate means. **b** Any business or occupation: the retailing *racket.* **3** Social activity or excitement. —*v.i.* **1** To make a loud, clattering noise. **2** To indulge in noisy sport or diversion; carouse. [? Metathetic var. of dial. *rattick* make a din, clatter]

rack·et·eer (rak′ə·tir′) *n.* **1** One who extorts money from, or seeks to gain control over, a person or organization by intimidation, fraud, violence, or other criminal means; one engaged in a racket. **2** Formerly, a bootlegger or rum-runner. — **rack′et·eer′ing** *n.*

rack·et·y (rak′it·ē) *adj.* Making a racket; noisy.

rack-rent (rak′rent′) *n.* An exorbitant rent (equal or nearly equal to the full annual value of the property). —*v.t.* To exact rack-rent from or for. [<RACK¹ (stretch) +RENT¹]

ra·con (rā′kon) *n.* A device for the immediate identification of friendly or hostile aircraft by means of radar signals automatically transmitted in code: adapted also as an aid in navigation. [<RA(DAR) (BEA)CON]

ra·coon (ra·kōōn′) See RACCOON.

rac·quet (rak′it) See RACKET¹.

rac·quet·ball (rak′it·bôl′) *n.* **1** An indoor walled-court game played with a hollow rubber ball and a short-handled racquet. **2** The ball used in this game, somewhat larger and softer than a handball.

rac·y (rā′sē) *adj.* **rac·i·er, rac·i·est 1** Having a spirited or pungent interest; spicy; piquant: a *racy* style. **2** Having a characteristic flavor assumed to be indicative of origin, as wine; rich, fresh, or fragrant. **3** Suggestive; slightly immodest: a *racy* story. [<RACE¹] — **rac′i·ly** *adv.* — **rac′i·ness** *n.*

Synonyms: flavorous, forcible, high-flavored, lively, piquant, pungent, rich, spicy, spirited. *Racy* applies (def. 2) to the pleasing flavor characteristic of certain wines. *Pungent* denotes something sharply stimulating to the organs of taste or smell, as vinegar, ammonia; *piquant* denotes a quality similar in kind to *pungent* but less in degree, alluring and agreeable; *pungent* spices may be deftly compounded in a *piquant* sauce. *Antonyms:* dull, flat, flavorless, insipid, tasteless, vapid.

ra·dar (rā′där) *n. Electronics* A locating device which instantaneously detects the presence and indicates the position of aircraft, ships, etc., by measuring the interval between the emission and return of high–frequency radio waves effective under varied conditions. [< RA(DIO) D(ETECTING) A(ND) R(ANGING)]

rad·dle[1] (rad′l) See REDDLE, RUDDLE.

rad·dle[2] (rad′l) *v.t.* **·dled**, **·dling** To intertwine or weave together. [< obs. raddle a wattle < AF *reidele*, OF *reddale* stout stick]

ra·di·al (rā′dē·əl) *adj.* **1** Pertaining to, consisting of, or resembling a ray or radius. **2** Extending from a center in the manner of rays. **3** Of or pertaining to the radius or a radiating part. **4** Developing uniformly on all sides. —*n.* **1** A radiating part. **2** A radial tire. —**ra′di·al·ly** *adv.*

radial tire A pneumatic tire constructed with plies of fabric that are laid at right angles to the circumference of the tread and extend to the beads, sometimes reinforced with other plies, as of steel, laid at right angles to the radial plies under the tread. Also **ra·di·al–ply tire** (rā′dē·əl·plī′).

ra·di·ance (rā′dē·əns) *n.* The quality or state of being radiant; brilliant or sparkling luster; lightness; effulgence. Also **ra′di·an·cy**, **ra′di·ant·ness**.

ra·di·ant (rā′dē·ənt) *adj.* **1** Emitting rays of light or heat. **2** Beaming with light or brightness, kindness, or love: a *radiant* smile. **3** Resembling rays; consisting of or transmitted by radiations: *radiant* heat. See synonyms under BRIGHT. —*n.* **1** A straight line proceeding from and conceived as revolving around a given point. **2** *Astron.* That point in the heavens from the direction of which, during a meteoric shower, the meteors seem to shoot. **3** The luminous point from which light proceeds or is made to radiate. **4** That which radiates. [< L *radians, -antis,* ppr. of *radiare* emit rays < *radius* ray] —**ra′di·ant·ly** *adv.*

ra·di·ate (rā′dē·āt) *v.* **·at·ed**, **·at·ing** *v.i.* **1** To emit rays or radiation; be diant. **2** To issue forth in rays, as light from the sun. **3** To spread out from a center, as the spokes of a wheel. —*v.t.* **4** To send out or emit in rays. **5** To cause to spread as if from a center; diffuse; disseminate. —*adj.* (-dē·it) **1** Divided or separated into rays; having rays; radiating. **2** *Bot.* Bearing rays or ray flowers. **3** *Zool.* Characterized by radial symmetry, as echinoderms and coelenterates. **4** Adorned with rays, as a head on a coin; radiated. —*n.* (-dē·it) **1** An organism having radial symmetry. **2** A ray or raylike projection. [< L *radiatus,* pp. of *radiare* emit rays. See RADIANT.] —**ra′di·a′tive** *adj.*

ra·di·a·tion (rā′dē·ā′shən) *n.* **1** The act of radiating or the state of being radiated. **2** *Physics* **a** The emission and propagation of radiant energy or of alpha or beta rays. **b** The energy so propagated. **c** The stages of emission, absorption, and transmission involved in such propagation: distinguished from *conduction.* **3** *Biol.* Adaptive radiation.

radiation sickness *Pathol.* A morbid condition due to the body's absorption of excess radiation and marked by fatigue, nausea, vomiting, internal hemorrhage, and progressive tissue breakdown.

ra·di·a·tor (rā′dē·ā′tər) *n.* **1** That which radiates. **2** A chamber, coil, or flat hollow vessel, through which is passed steam or hot water for warming a building or apartment. **3** In engines, a nest of tubes for cooling water flowing through them. —**ra′di·a·to′ry** (-ə·tôr′ē, -tō′rē) *adj.*

rad·i·cal (rad′i·kəl) *adj.* **1** Of, proceeding from, or pertaining to the root or foundation; essential; fundamental; inherent; basic. **2** Thoroughgoing; unsparing; extreme: a *radical* operation; *radical* measures. **3** *Math.* Pertaining to the root or roots of a number. **4** In philology, belonging or referring to a root or a root syllable; underived. **5** *Bot.* Springing

from or belonging or relating to the root: *radical* leaves. **6** *Chem.* Pertaining to a radical. **7** Of or pertaining to political radicals. —*n.* **1** One who carries his theories or convictions to their furthest application; an extremist. **2** In politics, one who advocates wide–spread governmental changes and reforms at the earliest opportunity. **3** The primitive or underived part of a word; a primitive word or syllable; a root; radicle. **4** *Math.* **a** A quantity of which the root is to be extracted or used in calculation; a radical expression. **b** The radical sign. **5** *Chem.* A fundamental constituent or part of a compound; specifically, a group of atoms which acts as a unit in a compound and may either pass unchanged through a series of reactions or be replaced as though it were a single atom. ◆ Homophone: *radicle.* [< LL *radicalis* having roots < L *radix, radicis* root] —**rad′i·cal·ness** *n.*

Synonyms (adj.): basic, complete, constitutional, entire, essential, extreme, fundamental, ingrained, inherent, innate, native, natural, organic, original, perfect, positive, primary, primitive, thorough, thoroughgoing, total. The widely divergent senses in which the word *radical* is used, by which it can be at sometime interchanged with any word in the above list, are all formed upon the one primary sense of that which is connected with the root (Latin *radix*). A *radical* difference is one that springs from the root, and is thus *constitutional, essential, fundamental, organic, original;* a *radical* change is one that does not stop at the surface, but reaches down to the very root, and is *entire, thorough, total;* since the majority find superficial treatment of any matter the easiest and most comfortable, *radical* measures, which strike at the root of evil or need, are apt to be looked upon as *extreme.* See NATURAL. *Antonyms:* compromising, conciliatory, conservative, half–way, inadequate, incomplete, moderate, palliative, partial, superficial.

rad·i·cal·ism (rad′i·kəl·iz′əm) *n.* **1** The state of being radical. **2** Advocacy of thoroughgoing or extreme measures.

rad·i·cal·ize (rad′i·kə·līz′) *v.t.* **·ized**, **·iz·ing** To make radical, especially in politics. —**rad·i·cal·i·za·tion** (rad′i·kə·lə·zā′shən), **rad′i·cal·iz′er** *n.*

rad·i·cal·ly (rad′ik·lē) *adv.* **1** Completely; thoroughly; fundamentally. **2** With reference to root or origin; originally; primitively.

rad·i·cel (rad′i·sel) *n.* A rootlet. [< NL *radicella,* dim. of L *radix, radicis* root]

rad·i·cle (rad′i·kəl) *n.* **1** *Bot.* **a** The embryonic root below the cotyledon of a plant. **b** A diminutive root or rootlet. **2** *Anat.* A rootlike part, as the stem of an embryo, the initial fiber of a nerve, the beginning of a vein, etc. **3** *Chem.* A radical. ◆ Homophone: *radical.* [< L *radicula,* dim. of *radix, radicis* root]

ra·di·i (rā′dē·ī) Plural of RADIUS.

ra·di·o (rā′dē·ō) *n. pl.* **·os** **1** The science, art, and process of communicating by means of radiant energy transmitted directly through space in waves. **2** The wireless transmission of radio waves within assigned frequencies and their reception by devices adapted for reconverting the frequencies into their corresponding original signals. **3** A radio program or broadcast; also, the combined operations for its production. **4** A radio receiving set and its accessories. **5** A radio message or radiogram. **6** The exploitation and development of radio as a commercial enterprise; the radio business and industry. —*adj.* **1** Of, pertaining to, designating, employing, or produced by radiant energy, especially in the form of electromagnetic waves: a *radio* beam. **2** Wireless. —*v.t. & v.i.* To transmit (a message, etc.) or communicate with (someone) by radiotelegraphy or radiotelephony. [< RADIO(TELEGRAPHY)]

ra·di·o·ac·tive (rā′dē·ō·ak′tiv) *adj.* Pertaining to, exhibiting, caused by, or characteristic of radioactivity: a *radioactive* isotope.

ra·di·o·ac·tiv·i·ty (rā′dē·ō·ak·tiv′ə·tē) *n. Physics* **1** The propagation of radiant energy. **2** The spontaneous nuclear disintegration of certain elements and isotopes, with the emission of alpha particles, electrons, positrons, or electromagnetic radiation. **3** A particular form of such disintegration: gamma *radioactivity.*

radio astronomy That branch of astronomy and astrophysics which studies celestial phe-

nomena by the interception and analysis of radio waves emitted by stars and other objects in interstellar space.

ra·di·o·au·tog·ra·phy (rā′dē·ō·ô·tog′rə·fē) *n.* Autoradiography. [< RADIO- + AUTOGRAPH + -Y]

ra·di·o·au·to·gram (rā′dē·ō·ô′tə·gram) *n.* Autoradiograph. Also **ra′di·o·au′to·graph** (-graf, -gräf).

radio beam **1** A steady flow of radio signals concentrated along a given course or direction. **2** The narrow zone marked out for the guidance of aircraft by the overlapping of recurrent signals transmitted from ground radio stations on either side of an assigned flight course.

ra·di·o·car·bon (rā′dē·ō·kär′bən) *n. Physics* The radioactive isotope of carbon of mass 14, with a half–life of about 5,700 years: it is much used in the dating of fossils, artifacts, and certain kinds of geological formations. Also called *carbon 14.*

ra·di·o·car·di·o·gram (rā′dē·ō·kär′dē·ə·gram) *n.* The record made in radiocardiography.

ra·di·o·chem·is·try (rā′dē·ō·kem′is·trē) *n.* That branch of chemistry dealing with the properties and reactions of radioactive substances, as radium and thorium.

radio circuit A radio system consisting of two stations in direct communication with each other.

radio conductor Any material or apparatus that indicates, by some alteration of its conductivity, the presence and strength of electric waves, such as the coherer of a wireless telegraph.

ra·di·ode (rā′dē·ōd) *n.* **1** A radium container, built to prevent any dangerous leakage of radioactivity. **2** *Med.* An apparatus used in some forms of radiotherapy. [< RADIO- + -ODE[1]]

ra·di·o·dust (rā′dē·ō·dust′) *n.* Radioactive dust particles precipitated from the atmosphere, especially in the fall–out from an atomic or thermonuclear bomb.

radio fix The position of an aircraft, ship, or radio transmitter, as determined with reference to radio signals from two or more stations, or by similar means.

radio frequency Any wave frequency, or set of frequencies, adapted for the transmission of radio signals. The range is roughly from the upper limit of normal audibility to the lower limit of heat and light waves, or upwards from about 10 kilocycles per second.

ra·di·o·ge·net·ics (rā′dē·ō·jə·net′iks) *n.* The study of genetics in relation to the effects of radioactivity upon the processes of inheritance and the nature of hereditary changes. —**ra′di·o·ge·net′ic** *adj.*

ra·di·o·gen·ic (rā′dē·ō·jē′nik, -jen′ik) *adj.* Resulting from or developed by radioactivity.

ra·di·o·gram (rā′dē·ō·gram′) *n.* **1** A message sent by wireless telegraphy. **2** A radiographic negative or print.

ra·di·o·graph (rā′dē·ō·graf, -gräf′) *n.* A negative or picture made by means of radioactivity; an X–ray photograph. —*v.t.* To make a radiograph of. —**ra′di·og′ra·pher** (-og′rə·fər) *n.* —**ra′di·o·graph′ic** or **·ic** *adj.* —**ra′di·og′ra·phy** *n.*

ra·di·o·im·mu·no·as·say (rā′dē·ō·im′yə·nō·ə·sā′, -im·yoo′-) *n.* A method of assaying the amount or other characteristics of a substance by labeling it with a radioactive chemical and combining it with an antibody to induce an immunological reaction.

ra·di·o·i·so·tope (rā′dē·ō·ī′sə·tōp) *n. Physics* A radioactive isotope, usually one produced artificially from a normally stable element: extensively used in biological and physical research and used in medicine for diagnostic and therapeutic purposes.

ra·di·o·lo·ca·tion (rā′dē·ō·lō·kā′shən) *n.* Radar.

ra·di·ol·o·gy (rā′dē·ol′ə·jē) *n.* That branch of science that relates to radiant energy and its applications, especially in the diagnosis and treatment of disease. [< RADIO- + -LOGY] —**ra·di·o·log·i·cal** (rā′dē·ə·loj′i·kəl) or **ra′di·o·log′ic** *adj.* —**ra′di·ol′o·gist** *n.*

ra·di·o·lu·cent (rā′dē·ō·loo′sənt) *adj.* Permeable to X–rays and other forms of electromagnetic radiation. See RADIOPAQUE.

ra·di·o·lu·mi·nes·cence (rā′dē·ō·loo′mə·nes′·əns) *n.* Luminescence produced by, or resulting from, any form of radiant energy, as X–rays, radioactivity, etc. —**ra′di·o·lu′mi·nes′·cent** *adj.*

ra·di·o·ma·te·ri·al (rā′dē-ō-mə·tir′ē-əl) *n.* Any material that is, or has been made, radioactive.

ra·di·om·e·ter (rā′dē·om′ə·tər) *n.* An instrument for detecting and measuring radiant energy by converting it into mechanical energy, as by the rotation of blackened disks suspended in a vacuum and exposed to sunlight. [< RADIO- + METER¹] —**ra′di·o·met′ric** (-ō·met′rik) *adj.* —**ra′di·om′e·try** *n.*

ra·di·o·mi·crom·e·ter (rā′dē·ō·mī·krom′ə·tər) *n.* An instrument, consisting primarily of an extremely sensitive thermoelectric couple suspended in a magnetic field, for measuring minute variations of heat.

RADIOMETER

ra·di·o·paque (rā′dē·ō·pāk′) *adj.* Impermeable to X–rays or other forms of electromagnetic radiation. [<RADIO + OPAQUE]

ra·di·o·phone (rā′dē·ō·fōn′) *n.* **1** Any device for the production or transmission of sound by radiant energy. **2** A radiotelephone. —**ra·di·o·phon′ic** (-fon′ik) *adj.* —**ra′di·oph′o·ny** (-of′ə·nē) *n.*

ra·di·o·pho·tog·ra·phy (rā′dē·ō·fə·tog′rə·fē) *n.* The transmission of a photograph by radio in such a way that each spot on the picture is reproduced by an electric impulse. —**ra′di·o·pho′to·graph** (-fō′tə·graf, -gräf) *n.*

ra·di·o·prax·is (rā′dē·ō·prak′sis) *n.* Radiotherapy.

ra·di·o·scope (rā′dē·ō·skōp′) *n.* An apparatus for detecting radioactivity or X–rays.

ra·di·os·co·py (rā′dē·os′kə·pē) *n.* Examination of opaque bodies with the aid of X–rays or some other form of radiant energy. [<RADIO- + -SCOPY] —**ra·di·o·scop′ic** (-skop′ik) or **·i·cal** *adj.*

ra·di·o·sen·si·tive (rā′dē·ō·sen′sə·tiv) *adj.* **1** Sensitive to X–rays and ultraviolet rays. **2** *Med.* Reducible or destructible by X–rays. as certain tumors.

ra·di·o·sonde (rā′dē·ō·sond′) *n. Meteorol.* A device, attached to a small balloon sent aloft, which measures the pressure, temperature, and humidity of the upper air and radios the data to the ground. Also **ra′di·o·me′te·or·o·graph′** (-mē′tē·ər·ə·graf′, -gräf′). [<RADIO- + F *sonde* sounding]

radio spectrum The full range of frequencies pertaining to and associated with radiant energy; specifically, those frequencies employed in radio and television.

RADIOSONDE
a. Instrument box.

radio star Any of a large number of stars which may be identified and studied by means of the characteristic electromagnetic impulses which they emit.

radio station An installation of all the equipment and apparatus necessary for effective radio communication.

ra·di·o·stron·tium (rā′dē·ō·stron′shəm, -tē·əm) *n.* Any of the synthetic radioactive isotopes of strontium, especially the most stable of them, strontium 90.

ra·di·o·tel·e·gram (rā′dē·ō·tel′ə·gram) *n.* A message sent by radiotelegraphy.

ra·di·o·te·leg·ra·phy (rā′dē·ō·tə·leg′rə·fē) *n.* Telegraphic communication by means of radio waves. —**ra′di·o·tel′e·graph′ic** (-tel′ə·graf′ik) *adj.* —**ra′di·o·tel′e·graph** (-graf, -gräf) *n.*

ra·di·o·tel·e·phone (rā′dē·ō·tel′ə·fōn) *n.* A telephone set that, without the agency of connecting wires, transmits a verbal message to a similar set by means of radio waves. —**ra′di·o·tel′e·phon′ic** (-tel′ə·fon′ik) *adj.* —**ra′di·o·te·leph′o·ny** (-tə·lef′ə·nē) *n.*

radio telescope A sensitive astronomical instrument designed on the principle of a radio receiver, but adapted to intercept and amplify electromagnetic waves in the megacycle range

emanating from interstellar space.

ra·di·o·ther·a·py (rā′dē-ō·ther′ə·pe) *n.* The treatment of disease with electromagnetic radiation or with radioactive substances. Also called *actinotherapy.*

ra·di·o·tho·ri·um (rā′dē·ō·thôr′ē·əm, -thō′rē·əm) *n.* A radioactive product of the thorium series, with a half-life of 1.9 years.

radio transcription An electrically recorded radio program, speech, musical selection, or the like, intended for subsequent broadcasting.

radio tube A vacuum tube for radio.

radio wave Any of a class of electromagnetic waves propagated at frequencies intermediate between those of audible sound and infrared.

rad·ish (rad′ish) *n.* **1** A tall, branching herb (*Raphanus sativus*) of the mustard family. **2** Its pungent, edible root, commonly eaten raw. [<F *radis* < Ital. *radice* < L *radix, radicis* root. Doublet of RADIX.]

ra·di·um (rā′dē·əm) *n.* A luminescent, intensely radioactive metallic element (symbol Ra, atomic number 88) chemically related to barium, occurring in small amounts in uranium ores, emitting alpha and beta particles and gamma rays, and having 16 known isotopes, the most abundant of which has a half-life of 1620 years. See PERIODIC TABLE. [< NL < L *radius* ray]

radium therapy The treatment of skin diseases and of cancer by means of radium.

ra·di·us (rā′dē·əs) *n. pl.* **·di·i** (-dē-ī) **1** A straight line from the center of a circle or sphere to its periphery. **2** *Anat.* The thicker and shorter bone of the forearm, on the same side as the thumb. **3** *Bot.* A ray floret of a composite flower; also, a branch of an umbel. **4** *Zool.* **a** In radiolarians and similar organisms, the imaginary line or plane dividing the body into two theoretically equal parts. **b** A ray or radiating part, as, the barb of a feather. **c** A lateral part of a cirriped shell when overlapping others. **5** *Entomol.* One of the main longitudinal veins of an insect's wings. **6** In a sextant, quadrant, etc., a pivoted arm, mounted so as to move radially, as on a graduated arc or circle. **7** *Mech.* A wheel spoke; a rod or bar which with others extends from a common point. **8** A circular area or boundary measured by the length of its radius. **9** Sphere, scope, or limit, as of activity. **10** A fixed limit of travel beyond which higher fares are charged. [< L, orig., rod, spoke of a wheel, hence radius, ray of light. Doublet of RAY]

ra·dix (rā′diks) *n. pl.* **rad·i·ces** (rad′ə·sēz, rā′də-) or **ra·dix·es 1** *Rare* The origin or source. **2** *Math.* A number or symbol used as the basis of a scale of enumeration: 10 is the *radix* of the common system of logarithms. **3** *Bot.* The root of a plant. **4** An original word from which others are derived; radical; root; etymon. [< L, root. Doublet of RADISH.]

ra·don (rā′don) *n.* A heavy, radioactive, chemically inert gaseous element (symbol Rn, atomic number 86) having isotopes which are decay products in the several natural radioactive series. See PERIODIC TABLE. [< RAD(IUM) + -ON, as in *neon*]

rad·waste (rad′wāst′) *n.* Radioactive waste.

raff (raf) *n.* **1** The rabble; riff-raff. **2** *Scot. & Brit. Dial.* A disorderly collection. [< RIFF-RAFF]

raf·fi·a (raf′ē-ə) *n.* **1** A cultivated palm (*Raphia pedunculata*) of Madagascar, the leafstalks of which furnish fiber for making hats, mats, baskets, etc. **2** Its fiber. Also spelled *raphia.* [< Malagasy *rafia*]

raff·ish (raf′ish) *adj.* **1** Tawdry; gaudy; flashy. **2** Disreputable. [< RAFF + -ISH¹]

raf·fle¹ (raf′əl) *n.* A form of lottery in which a number of people buy chances on an object. — *v.* **·fled, ·fling** *v.t.* To dispose of by a raffle: often with *off.* — *v.i.* To take part in a raffle. [< OF *rafle* a clean sweep at dice < *rafler* snatch, prob. < Gmc.] —**raf′fler** *n.*

raf·fle² (raf′əl) *n.* A jumble of rubbish; tangle: a nautical term. [Prob. < RAFF]

raft¹ (raft, räft) *n.* A float of logs, planks, etc., fastened together for transportation by water. — *v.t.* **1** To transport on a raft. **2** To form into a raft. — *v.i.* **3** To travel by, be employed on, or manage a raft. [< ON *raptr* log]

raft² (raft, räft) *n. Colloq.* A large number or an

indiscriminate collection of any kind. [< RAFF]

raft·er (raf′tər, räf′-) *n.* A timber or beam giving form, slope, and support to a roof. [OE *ræfter*]

rag¹ (rag) *v.t.* **ragged, rag·ging** *Slang* **1** To tease or irritate. **2** To scold. **3** *Brit.* To play a practical joke on. **4** *Brit.* To wreck; make a mess of. — *n. Brit.* A ragging. [? < ON *ragna* curse, swear]

rag² (rag) *n.* **1** A torn piece of cloth; a fragment or semblance of anything. **2** *pl.* Cotton or linen textile remnants used in the making of rag paper. **3** *pl.* Tattered or shabby clothing; hence, any clothing: a jocular use. **4** A cloth of any kind, or something resembling one or characterized as such: used humorously or in disparagement. **5** In citrus fruits, the axis and carpellary walls. —**glad rags** *Slang* One's best clothes. —**to chew the rag** *Slang* To talk or argue at great length. [< ON *rögg* tuft or strip of fur]

rag³ (rag) *n.* **1** A roofing slate rough on one side, and measuring 2 × 3 feet. **2** *Brit.* Any hard rock of cellular or coarsely granular texture. [Origin uncertain]

rag⁴ (rag) *v.t.* **ragged, rag·ging** To compose or play in ragtime. — *n.* Ragtime.

rag·a·muf·fin (rag′ə·muf′in) *n.* Anyone, especially a boy, wearing very ragged clothes; a vagabond. [after *Ragamoffyn*, demon in a 15th century mystery play < RAG² + fanciful ending]

rage (rāj) *n.* **1** Violent anger; wrath; fury. **2** Any great violence or intensity, as of a fever or a storm. **3** Extreme eagerness or emotion; ardent desire; great enthusiasm. **4** Any object eagerly sought after; a fad; fashion: Crossword puzzles are all the *rage.* See synonyms under ANGER, VIOLENCE. — *v.i.* **raged, rag·ing 1** To speak, act, or move with unrestrained anger; feel or show violent anger. **2** To act or proceed with great violence: The storm *raged* for three days. **3** To spread or prevail uncontrolled, as an epidemic. [< OF < LL *rabia* < L *rabies* madness] —**rag′ing·ly** *adv.* —**rag′ing·ly** *adv.*

rag·ged (rag′id) *adj.* **1** Rent or worn into rags; frayed: a *ragged* coat. **2** Wearing worn, frayed, or shabby garments; ill-dressed. **3** Of rough, broken or uneven character or aspect; harsh; dissonant: *ragged* rocks, *ragged* sounds. **4** Naturally of a rough or shaggy appearance (the original meaning): a *ragged* horse or sheep. See synonyms under ROUGH. —**rag′ged·ly** *adv.* —**rag′ged·ness** *n.*

ragged edge *Colloq.* The extreme or precarious edge; the verge: the *ragged edge* of starvation; *ragged edge* of insanity. —**on the ragged edge** Dangerously near to losing one's self-control, sanity, etc.

rag·lan (rag′lən) *n.* An overcoat or topcoat, the sleeves of which extend in one piece up to the collar. — *adj.* Denoting a garment with such sleeves. [after Lord Fitzroy Raglan]

Rag·na·rök (räg′nä·rœk) In Norse mythology, the twilight of the gods, and the doomsday of the world, preceding its regeneration. Also **Rag′na·rok** (-rok). [< ON < *ragna* of the gods (genitive pl. of *regin*) + *rök* judgment]

ra·gout (ra·gōō′) *n.* A highly seasoned dish of meat and vegetables stewed; hence, something spicy or piquant. — *v.t.* **ra·gouted** (-gōōd′), **ra·gout·ing** (-gōō′ing) To make into a ragout. [< F < *ragouter* revive the appetite < *re-* anew + *-à* (< L *ad*) to + *goût* (< L *gustus*) taste]

rag·stone (rag′stōn′) *n.* **1** Rag; a rough, sandy, fossiliferous limestone: also **ragg. 2** Stone quaried in thin slabs, as for pavements. Also **ragg′stone.′**

rag-tag (rag′tag′) *n.* Ragged people; the rabble. Also **rag-tag and bobtail.**

rag·time (rag′tīm′) *n.* **1** A kind of American dance music, developed from about 1890 to 1920, achieving its effects by highly syncopated rhythm in fast time. **2** The rhythm of this dance. [< *ragged time*]

Ra·gu·el (rə·gyōō′el) One of the seven archangels of Hebrew and Christian legend.

rag·weed (rag′wēd′) *n.* **1** A coarse, very common, annual or perennial herb (genus *Ambrosia*), especially the common ragweed (*A. artemisifolia*), which induces hay fever, and the **great ragweed** (*A. trifida*), a tall species with stout hairy stem 5 to 15 feet high: also called *hogweed.* **2** *Brit.* The ragwort.

---

add,āce,câre,pälm; end,ēven; it,īce; odd,ōpen,ôrder; tŏŏk,pōōl; up,bûrn; ə = a in *above*, e in *sicken*, i in *clarity*, o in *melon*, u in *focus* ; yōō = u in *fuse*, oi,oil; ou,pout; ch,check; g,go; ng,ring; th,thin; ŧh,this; zh,vision. Foreign sounds á,œ,ü,kh,ṅ; and ◆: see page xx. < from; + plus; ? possibly.

rah (rä) *interj.* Hurrah! a cheer used chiefly in college yells. [<HURRAH]

Ra·hab (rā'hab) In the Old Testament, a symbolical name for Egypt. Isaiah li 9.

ra·ia (rä'yə, rī'ə) See RAYAH.

raid (rād) *n.* **1** A hostile or predatory incursion by a rapidly moving body of troops or an armed vessel; a foray. **2** An attack by military aircraft; an air raid. **3** Any sudden invasion, capture, or irruption, as by the police. **4** An attempt to lower stock prices. See synonyms under INVASION — *v.t.* To make a raid on. — *v.i.* To participate in a raid. [Scottish var. of ROAD] — **raid'er** *n.*

rail¹ (rāl) *n.* **1** A bar, usually of wood or iron, resting on supports, as in a fence, at the side of a stairway, or capping the bulwarks of a ship; a horizontal wooden piece between panels, joining the stiles; also, a railing. **2** One of a series of parallel bars, of iron or steel, resting upon cross–ties, forming a support and guide for wheels, as of a railway. **3** A railway track considered as a means of transportation: to ship by *rail.* —**to go by rail** To travel by train. —**to ride (someone) on a rail** To put (a person) astride a rail and carry around or beyond the limits of a community, as a punishment. — *v.t.* To furnish or shut in with rails; fence. [<OF *reille* <L *regula.* Doublet of RULE.]

RAIL FENCE

rail² (rāl) *n.* **1** Any of numerous marsh-haunting, wading birds (family *Rallidae,* subfamily *Rallinae*) having very short wings, moderately long legs and toes, a short turned-up tail, long compressed bill, and soft, dun-colored plumage; specifically, in North America, the **king rail** (*Rallus elegans*), the **clapper rail** or mud hen (*R. longirostris*), and the **sora** or **Carolina rail.** They are esteemed as game birds. ◆ Collateral adjective: **ralline.** **2** Any of various other birds of northern Europe, as the **corn crake.** Also **rail'bird'.** [<OF *raale, ralle,* prob. ult. <L *radere* scratch]

rail³ (rāl) *v.i.* To use scornful, insolent, or abusive language: with *at* or *against.* — *v.t.* To drive or force by railing. [<F *railler* <Pg. *ralhar* chatter, prob. <L *ragere* shriek. Doublet of RALLY².] — **rail'er** *n.*

rail·head (rāl'hed') *n.* **1** On an incompleted railroad, the farthest point to which rails have been laid. **2** That point on a railroad from which a military unit draws its supplies, ammunition, etc.

rail·ing (rā'ling) *n.* **1** A series of rails; a balustrade. **2** Rails, or material from which rails are made.

rail·ler·y (rā'lər·ē) *n. pl.* **·ler·ies** Merry jesting or teasing; a merry jest or bantering speech. [<F *raillerie* jesting]

rail·road (rāl'rōd') *n.* **1** A graded road, having metal rails supported by ties or sleepers, for the passage of rolling stock drawn by locomotives. **2** The system of tracks, stations, rolling stock, etc., used in transportation by rail. **3** The corporation or persons owning or operating such a system. — *v.t.* **1** To transport by railroad. **2** *U.S. Colloq.* To rush or force with great speed or without deliberation: to *railroad* a bill through Congress. **3** *U.S. Slang* To cause to be imprisoned on false charges or without fair trial. — *v.i.* **4** To work on a railroad.

rail·road·ing (rāl'rō'ding) *n.* The construction, operation, or business of a railroad.

rail·way (rāl'wā') *n.* **1** A railroad: the common British term. **2** A trackway or set of rails, as in a warehouse or factory, for convenience in handling heavy articles, etc.: a parcel *railway* in a store.

rain (rān) *n.* **1** The condensed vapor of the atmosphere falling in drops. ◆ Collateral adjective: *hyetal.* **2** The fall of such drops. **3** A fall or shower of anything in the manner of rain, or the substance poured down: a *rain* of bombs. **4** A rainstorm; shower; in the plural, the rainy season in a tropical country; also, a rainy region of the Atlantic Ocean. — *v.i.* **1** To fall from the clouds in drops of water: usually with *it* as the subject. **2** To fall like

rain, as tears. **3** To send or pour down rain: said of clouds, God, etc. — *v.t.* **4** To send down like rain; shower. ◆ Homophones: *reign, rein.* [OE *regn*]

rain·bow (rān'bō') *n.* **1** An arch of light formed opposite the sun during or after the close of a shower, exhibiting the colors of the spectrum, and caused by refraction, reflection, and dispersion of light in drops of water falling through the air. **2** Hence, any brilliant display of color. [OE *regnboga*]

rain·bow–chas·er (rān'bō'chā'sər) *n.* One who seeks the legendary pot of gold at the foot of the rainbow; a visionary.

rainbow trout See under TROUT.

rain check The stub of a ticket to an outdoor event, as a baseball game, entitling the holder to free admission at a future date if for any reason the event is called off: used figuratively of any postponed invitation.

rain crow The yellow–billed or the black–billed cuckoo (genus *Coccyzus*), so called from the belief among farmers that its cry is a sign of rain.

rain·drop (rān'drop') *n.* A drop of rain.

rain·fall (rān'fôl') *n.* **1** A fall of rain. **2** *Meteorol.* The amount of water precipitated in a given region over a stated time, as rain, hail, snow, or the like: measured in inches.

rain gage An instrument for measuring rainfall at a given place or during a given time; a pluviometer. Also **rain gauge.**

rain·mak·er (rān'mā'kər) *n.* One reputedly able to cause rain; specifically, among certain American Indians, one who brings rain by incantation.

rain·out (rān'out') *n.* **1** *Physics* Precipitation of radioactive water droplets from cloud masses resulting from an underwater nuclear explosion. **2** A baseball game postponed because of rain. **3** Postponement of an outdoor event, esp. a baseball game.

rain·proof (rān'proof') *adj.* Impervious to or shedding rain: said of garments. — *n. Brit.* A raincoat.

rain·spout (rān'spout') *n.* A waterspout (def. 2).

rain·y (rā'nē) *adj.* **rain·i·er, rain·i·est** Characterized by, abounding in, or bringing rain. — **rain'i·ly** *adv.* — **rain'i·ness** *n.*

rainy day A time of need; hard times.

raise (rāz) *v.* **raised, rais·ing** *v.t.* **1** To cause to move upward or to a higher level; lift; elevate. **2** To place erect; set up. **3** To construct or build; erect. **4** To make greater in amount, size, or value: to *raise* the price of corn. **5** To advance or elevate in rank, estimation, etc. **6** To increase the strength, intensity, or degree of. **7** To breed; grow: to *raise* chickens or tomatoes. **8** *U.S.* To rear (children, a family, etc.). **9** To give utterance to; cause to be heard: to *raise* a hue and cry. **10** To cause; occasion, as a smile or laugh. **11** To stir to action or emotion; arouse. **12** To waken; animate or reanimate: to *raise* the dead. **13** To gather together; obtain or collect, as an army, capital, etc. **14** To bring up for consideration, as a question. **15** To cause to swell or become lighter; leaven. **16** To put an end to, as a siege. **17** In poker, to bet more than. **18** *Naut.* To cause to appear above the horizon, as land or a ship, by approaching nearer. **19** *Scot.* To madden; enrage. — *v.i.* **20** *Colloq.* To cough up phlegm. **21** *Dial.* To rise or arise. **22** In poker, to make a raise. —**to raise Cain** (or **the devil, the dickens, a rumpus,** etc.) *Colloq.* To make a great disturbance; stir up confusion. —**to raise steam** To get or produce steam, as in a boiler, for the purpose of starting up a steam engine. — *n.* **1** The act of raising, in any sense; specifically, an increase, as of wages or a bet. **2** *Brit. Dial.* Something raised; an ascent; mound. ◆ Homophone: *raze.* [<ON *reisa* lift, set up. Akin to OE *ræran* rear.] ◆ In British usage, *rise* is used for an increase in wages. —**rais'er** *n.*

Synonyms (verb): aggrandize, elevate, erect, exalt, lift, rear, uplift. See HEIGHTEN, INCREASE, PROMOTE. *Antonyms:* degrade, depress, humble, lower, reduce, sink.

raised (rāzd) *adj.* **1** Elevated in low relief. **2** Made with yeast or leaven.

rai·sin (rā'zən) *n.* A grape of a special sort dried in the sun or in an oven, and used for a dessert or in cookery. [<OF <L *racemus* bunch of grapes]

rais·ing (rā'zing) *n.* **1** The act or process of causing to rise, in any sense. **2** A gathering of persons for the purpose of erecting the frame of a building: also **raising bee.**

raj (räj) *n.* In India, sovereignty; rule. [<Hind. *raj*]

ra·ja (rä'jə) *n.* A Hindu prince or chief of a tribal state in India; also, a Malay or Javanese ruler: often a mere title of distinction. Also **ra'jah.** [<Hind. *rāja* <Skt. *rājan* king]

Raj·ab (ruj'ab) See under CALENDAR (Mohammedan). [<Arabic]

Raj·put (räj'poot) *n.* One of a powerful and warlike Hinducaste, said to be a branch of the Kshatriyas, which gives its name to Rajputana. Also **Raj'poot.** [<Hind. *rajpūt* prince <Skt. *rājaputra* <*rajan* a king, ruler + *putra* son]

rake¹ (rāk) *n.* A toothed implement for drawing together loose material, or making a surface loose. — *v.* **raked, rak·ing** *v.t.* **1** To scrape or gather together with or as with a rake. **2** To smooth, clean, or prepare with a rake: to *rake* a lawn. **3** To gather by diligent effort; scrape together. **4** To search or examine carefully. **5** To direct heavy gunfire along the length of, as a ship or column of troops; enfilade. — *v.i.* **6** To use a rake. **7** To scrape or pass roughly or violently: with *across, over,* etc. **8** To make a search. —**to rake in** *Colloq.* To earn or acquire (money, etc.) in large quantities. [OE *raca*] —**rak'er** *n.*

TYPES OF RAKES
a. Refuse. *b.* Clam. *c.* Garden. *d* Steel lawn *e* Broom lawn

rake² (rāk) *v.* **raked, rak·ing** *v.i.* To lean from the perpendicular, as a ship's masts. — *v.t.* To cause to lean; incline. — *n.* Inclination from the perpendicular or horizontal, as of the sustaining surfaces of an airplane, or the edge of a cutting tool. [Origin uncertain. Cf. G *ragen* project.] —**raked** *adj.*

rake³ (rāk) *n.* A dissolute, lewd person; debauchee. — *v.i.* **raked, rak·ing** To play the rake; live a lewd, dissolute life: with *it.* [Short for RAKEHELL.]

rake⁴ (rāk) *v.i.* **raked, rak·ing 1** To hunt with the nose to the ground, thus following by track rather than by wind: said of hunting dogs. **2** To fly after game: said of hawks; also, to fly wide of the game. [OE *racian* go forward, proceed]

rake–off (rāk'ôf', -of') *n. U.S. Slang* A share, as of profits; commission; rebate, usually illegitimate.

rak·i (rak'ē, rä'kē) *n. Turkish* An aromatic liquor flavored with mastic; mastic brandy; also, a coarse liquor made from grain spirit. Compare ARRACK. Also **rak'ee.** [<Turkish *raqi* <Arabic *'araq.* Akin to ARRACK.]

rak·ish (rā'kish) *adj.* **1** *Naut.* Having the masts unusually inclined: usually connoting a suggestion of speed. **2** Dashing; jaunty. [<RAKE²; def. 2 infl. by *rakish²*] —**rak'ish·ly** *adv.* —**rak'ish·ness** *n.*

rak·ish² (rā'kish) *adj.* Like or behaving like a rake; dissolute; profligate. —**rak'ish·ly** *adv.* —**rak'ish·ness** *n.*

Ra·leigh (rô'lē) The capital of North Carolina.

Ra·leigh (rô'lē), **Sir Walter,** 1552–1618. English courtier, colonizer of Roanoke, soldier, and author; beheaded. Also spelled **Ra'legh.**

ral·li·form (ral'ə·fôrm) *adj.* Pertaining to or like the rails. See RAIL². [<NL *rallus* (<OF *ralle* rail²) + -FORM]

ral·line (ral'in, -in) *adj.* Of, pertaining to, or belonging to the rail subfamily of birds (*Rallinae*). [<NL *rallus* rail²]

ral·ly¹ (ral'ē) *n. pl.* **·lies 1** An assembling or reassembling, as of scattered troops. **2** A rapid recovery of a normal condition after exhaustion or depression: a *rally* from sickness.

a *rally* in stocks. **3** A mass meeting to arouse enthusiasm. **4** In tennis, the interchange of several strokes before one side wins the point. —*v.* **·lied, ·ly·ing** *v.t.* **1** To bring together and restore to effective discipline: to *rally* fleeing troops. **2** To summon up or revive: to *rally* one's spirits. **3** To bring together for common action. —*v.i.* **4** To return to effective discipline or action: The enemy *rallied*. **5** To unite for common action. **6** To make a partial or complete return to a normal condition. **7** In tennis, to engage in a rally. See synonyms under ENCOURAGE. [<F *rallier* <*re-* again + *allier* join. See ALLY.] —**ral'li·er** *n.*

ral·ly² (ral'ē) *v.t. & v.i.* To attack with raillery; joke; tease; banter. See synonyms under RIDICULE. [<F *railler* rail. Doublet of RAIL³.] —**ral'li·er** *n.*

ram (ram) *n.* **1** A male sheep. **2** An instrument or device for driving, forcing, or crushing by heavy blows or thrusts; specifically, a battering-ram, the striking weight of a pile driver or steamhammer, or the plunger of a force pump. **3** Formerly, a projection or beak on the bow of a warship, for crushing or cutting into an opposing vessel; also, a warship constructed with such a beak. **4** An instrument for raising water by pressure of condensed air; a hydraulic ram. —*v.t.* **rammed, ram·ming 1** To strike with or as with a ram; dash against. **2** To drive or force down or into something. **3** To cram; stuff. [OE] —**ram'mer** *n.*

Ram (ram) *Astron.* The zodiacal constellation Aries.

Ra·ma (rä'mə) In Hindu mythology, the name of three heroes, especially that of Ramachandra.

Ram·a·dan (ram'ə·dän') *n.* The Mohammedan ninth month, the time of the annual fast of thirty days; also, the fast. See under CALENDAR. Also **Ram'a·dhan', Ram'a·zan'** (-zän'). [<Arabic *ramaḍan*, lit., the hot month]

Ra·ma·pi·the·cus (rä'mə·pith'ə·kəs) *n.* a manlike primate, originally discovered in the Siwalik Range of NW India. [<RAMA + Gk *pithēkos* ape]

Ra·ma·ya·na (rä·mä'yə·nə) A Hindu epic poem in seven books, of about 400 B.C. Compare MAHABHARATA. [<Skt. *Rāmāyana* < *Rāma* Rama + *-ayana* relating to]

ram·ble (ram'bəl) *v.i.* **·bled, ·bling 1** To walk about freely and aimlessly; roam. **2** To write or talk aimlessly or without sequence of ideas. **3** To proceed with turns and twists; meander. —*n.* **1** The act of rambling; an aimless movement with change of direction; a leisurely stroll. **2** A meandering path; maze. [Origin unknown]
Synonyms (verb): range, roam, rove, stray, stroll, wander. See WANDER.

ram·bler (ram'blər) *n.* **1** One who or that which rambles. **2** Any of several varieties of roses, as the crimson rambler (*Rosa barbierana*), with climbing stems and huge clusters of small or medium-sized flowers.

ram·bling (ram'bling) *adj.* Showing absence of plan or system; aimless; wandering. —**ram'bling·ly** *adv.*

Ram·bouil·let (ram'boo-lā, *Fr.* rän·boo·ye') *n.* A variety of merino sheep bred in France for meat and wool. [from *Rambouillet*, a town in northern France]

ram·bunc·tious (ram·bungk'shəs) *adj. U.S. Colloq.* Rude and boisterous; rough and uncontrollable. [Prob. <RAM + alter. of BUMPTIOUS]

ram·bu·tan (ram·boo'tən) *n.* **1** The spiny, bright-red, pleasantly acid fruit of an East Indian and Malaysian tree (*Nephelium lappaceum*). **2** The tree that bears it. [< Malay <*rambut* hair]

ram·e·kin (ram'ə·kin) *n.* **1** A seasoned dish of bread crumbs baked with eggs and cheese. **2** A dish in which ramekins are baked. **3** Any dish used both for baking and serving. Also **ram'e·quin.** [<F *ramequin*]

ra·men·tum (rə·men'təm) *n. pl.* **·ta** (-tə) **1** A part of something scraped off; a minute part. **2** *Bot.* A thin, membranous, chaffy scale, formed on the surface of leaves, the stems of

ferns, etc.: an outgrowth from the epidermis. [<L, scraping <*radere* scrape] —**ram·en·ta·ceous** (ram'ən·tā'shəs) *adj.*

Ram·e·ses (ram'ə·sēz) Name of 12 Egyptian monarchs: also spelled *Ramses.*
—**Rameses II,** 1292–25 B.C., built many temples; sometimes said to be the pharaoh who oppressed the Israelites.

ram·ie (ram'ē) *n.* **1** A shrubby Chinese and East Indian perennial (*Boehmeria nivea*) of the nettle family, with numerous rodlike stems and large heart-shaped leaves. **2** The fine, glossy bast fiber yielded by its stem, used for cordage and certain coarse textile fabrics. Also **ram'ee.** [<Malay *rami*]

ram·i·fi·ca·tion (ram'ə·fə·kā'shən) *n.* **1** The act or process of ramifying. **2** *Bot.* The arrangement of branches or parts, as on a plant; also, one of the parts. **3** An offshoot or subdivision.

ram·i·form (ram'ə·fôrm) *adj.* **1** Branch-shaped. **2** Branched. [<L *ramus* branch + -FORM]

ram·i·fy (ram'ə·fī) *v.t. & v.i.* **·fied, ·fy·ing** To divide or spread out into or as to branches; branch out. [<F *ramifier* <Med. L *ramificare* <L *ramus* branch + *facere* make]

ram·mish (ram'ish) *adj.* **1** Like a ram; strong-scented. **2** Lustful. Also **ram'my.** —**ram'mish·ness** *n.*

ram·jet (ram'jet') *n.* A type of jet engine which provides continuous jet propulsion on the principle of the athodyd.

ra·mose (rä'mōs, rə·mōs') *adj.* **1** Branching. **2** Consisting of or having branches. [<L *ramosus* <*ramus* branch]

ramp (ramp) *n.* **1** An inclined passageway or roadway, as between floors or different levels of a building. **2** In building, a concave part at the top or cap of a railing, wall, or coping. [<F *rampe* <*ramper* climb]

ramp² (ramp) *v.i.* **1** To rear up on the hind legs and stretch out the forepaws. **2** *Her.* To be in a rampant or threatening position. **3** To act in a violent or threatening manner; storm; rampage. —*n.* The act of ramping. [<OF *ramper* climb]

ram·page (ram'pāj) *n.* Boisterous agitation or excitement; a dashing about with anger or violence. —*v.i.* (ram·pāj') **·paged, ·pag·ing 1** To rush or act violently. **2** To storm; rage. [Prob. <RAMP²] —**ram·pag'er** *n.*

ram·pa·geous (ram·pā'jəs) *adj.* Violent; boisterous. —**ram·pa'geous·ly** *adv.* —**ram·pa'geous·ness** *n.*

ram·pan·cy (ram'pən·sē) *n.* The condition or quality of being rampant.

ram·pant (ram'pənt) *adj.* **1** Exceeding all bounds; unrestrained; wild. **2** Widespread; unchecked, as an erroneous belief or superstition. **3** Standing on the hind legs; rearing; leaping: said of a quadruped. **4** *Her.* Standing on the sinister hind leg, with both forelegs elevated, the dexter above the sinister, and the head in profile: said of a beast of prey. **5** *Archit.* Springing from points on an inclined plane. [<OF, ppr. of *ramper* climb] —**ram'pant·ly** *adv.*

RAMPANT

ram·part (ram'pärt, -pərt) *n.* **1** The embankment surrounding a fort, on which the parapet is raised: sometimes including the parapet. **2** A bulwark or defense. —*v.t.* To supply with or as with ramparts; fortify. [<F *rempart* <*remparer* fortify <*re-* again + *emparer* prepare <L *ante* before + *parare* prepare]
Synonyms (noun): barbican, barricade, barrier, breastwork, bulwark, defense, embankment, fence, fortification, guard, mole, mound, outwork, security, wall.

ram·rod (ram'rod') *n.* **1** A rod used to drive home the charge of a muzzleloading gun or pistol. **2** A similar rod used for cleaning the barrel of a rifle, etc.

Ram·ses (ram'sēz) See RAMESES.

ram·shack·le (ram'shak'əl) *adj.* About to go to pieces from age and neglect; shaky; unsteady. [Origin uncertain]

ra·mus (rā'məs) *n. pl.* **·mi** (-mī) **1** A branch. **2** *Biol.* One division of a forked structure, as the branch of a nerve, etc. [<L, branch]

ran (ran) Past tense of RUN.

ra·nar·i·um (rə·nâr'ē·əm) *n. pl.* **·nar·i·a** (-nâr'ē·ə) A place where frogs are raised or kept. [<L *rana* frog]

rance (rans) *n.* A fine hard stone, dull red in color, with blue and white markings; Belgian marble. [<F]

ranch (ranch) *n.* **1** An establishment for rearing or grazing cattle, sheep, horses, etc., in large herds. **2** The buildings, personnel, and lands connected with it. **3** A large farm: a fruit *ranch.* Also **ranche.** —*v.i.* To manage or work on a ranch. [<Sp. *rancho* mess]

ranch·er (ran'chər) *n.* **1** The owner of a ranch. **2** One who works on a ranch; a cowboy.

ranch·ing (ran'ching) *n.* **1** The operation of a ranch. **2** Work on a ranch.

ran·cho (ran'chō, rän'-) *n. pl.* **·chos** *SW U.S.* **1** A hut or group of huts, in which ranchmen lodge. **2** A stock farm; ranch. [<Sp.]

ran·cid (ran'sid) *adj.* Having the peculiar tainted smell of oily substances that have begun to spoil owing to oxidation or hydrolysis; rank; sour. Compare SWEET. [<L *rancidus* <*rancere* be rancid]

ran·cid·i·ty (ran·sid'ə·tē) *n.* **1** The quality or state of being rancid. **2** A rancid smell or taste. Also **ran'cid·ness.**

ran·cor (rang'kər) *n.* Bitter and vindictive enmity; malice; spitefulness. Also *Brit.* **ran'cour.** See synonyms under ENMITY, HATRED. [<OF <L <*rancere* be rank] —**ran'cor·ous** *adj.* —**ran'cor·ous·ly** *adv.* —**ran'cor·ous·ness** *n.*

rand¹ (rand) *n.* **1** In shoe manufacturing, a strip of leather at the heel of a shoe to which the lifts are attached. **2** *Brit. Dial. & Scot.* A river border overgrown with reeds, or the unplowed border round a field; margin; strip. [OE, border, edge]

rand² (rand, ränd) *n.* The standard monetary unit of South Africa, worth in 1964 about $1.40. [< THE RAND]

ran·dan (ran'dan, ran·dan') *n.* **1** A boat rowed by three persons, the one amidships having two oars and the others one each. **2** This style of rowing. [Origin uncertain]

ran·dem (ran'dəm) *adv.* With three horses harnessed one in front of the other. —*n.* A team or vehicle driven random. Also **ran'dem-tan'dem.** [<RANDOM, on analogy with *tandem*]

RANDEM

ran·dom (ran'dəm) *n.* **1** Want of definite aim or intention. **2** Something done, made, or chosen without method or purpose. **3** *Printing* A sloping board for holding galleys of type matter intended for making up forms. —**at random** Without definite purpose or aim; haphazardly. —*adj.* **1** Done or chosen without definite aim or deliberate purpose; chance; casual. **2** In statistics, erratic. [<OF *randon* force, violence <*randonner, rander* move rapidly, gallop] —**ran'dom·ly** *adv.*

random sample *Stat.* A limited group of individuals, cases, or observations, so assembled from the total array as to be truly representative of its characteristics, properties, trends, and the like. Also **random selection.**

ran·dy (ran'dē) *Scot. adj.* **1** Disorderly; riotous; also, coarse. **2** Lewd; lustful. —*n.* **1** An impudent beggar. **2** A boisterous, coarse, or loose woman; also, a virago.

ra·nee (rä'nē) See RANI.

rang (rang) Past tense of RING².

range (rānj) *n.* **1** The area over which anything moves, operates, or is distributed. **2** *U.S.* An extensive tract of land over which cattle, sheep, etc., roam and graze. **3** *U.S.* Pasturage; grazing ground. **4** *Bot. & Zool.* The geographical area throughout which a specific plant or animal exists. **5** The extent or scope of something: the whole *range* of politics. **6** The extent to which any power can be made effective: *range* of vision; *range* of influence. **7** The extent of variation of anything: the temperature *range.* **8** The extent of possible variation in pitch: said of musical instruments or the voice. **9** A line, row, or series, as of mountains. **10** *U.S.* A row of townships, each six miles square, numbered east or west from a base meridian. **11** *Rare* Rank; order. **12** The horizontal distance between a gun and its target. **13** The horizontal distance covered by a projectile. **14** A place for shooting at a mark: a rifle *range*. **15** In archery, the number of ends shot at each given distance: compare ROUND. **16** A large cooking stove for conducting several cooking operations at one time. **17** *Stat.* The inclusive difference between the extreme values in any series of variable data: a *range* of 20 from a value of 0 to a value of 19. — *adj.* Of or pertaining to a range. — *v.* **ranged, rang·ing** *v.t.* **1** To place or arrange in definite order, as in rows or lines. **2** To assign to a class, division, or category; classify; rank. **3** To move about or over (a region, etc.), as in exploration. **4** To put (cattle) to graze on a range. **5** *Mil.* To obtain the range of (a target) by firing alternately above and below it. **6** To place in position; adjust or train, as a telescope or gun. **7** *Naut.* To lay out (the anchor cable) on deck so that the anchor may descend without hindrance. — *v.i.* **8** To move over an area in a thorough, systematic manner, as a dog hunting game. **9** To rove; roam. **10** To occur; extend; be found: said of plants and animals. **11** To extend or proceed: The shot *ranged* to the right. **12** To exhibit variation within specified limits: weights *ranging* from 20 to 50 pounds. **13** To lie in the same direction, line, etc. **14** *Mil.* To be capable of achieving a specified range (def. 12): That old cannon *ranged* about one mile. See synonyms under RAMBLE, WANDER. [<OF < *ranger, rengier* arrange < *renc* row <Gmc. Doublet of RANK[1].]

range finder An instrument with which to determine the distance of an object or target from a given point, as from a gun.

rang·er (rān′jər) *n.* **1** One who or that which ranges; a rover. **2** One of an armed band, usually mounted, designed to protect large tracts of country. **3** One of a herd of cattle that feeds on a range. **4** *Brit.* A government official in charge of a royal forest or park: formerly a gamekeeper. **5** *U.S.* A warden employed in patrolling forest tracts. — **rang′er·ship** *n.*

Rang·er (rān′jər) *n.* One of a select group of U. S. soldiers who were trained for raiding action on enemy territory: the equivalent of the English *Commando*.

range rake A T-shaped instrument for obtaining quick angular measurements in correcting deviations in the range of a gun.

Ran·goon The capital of Myanmar, a port city, on the Yangoon by the junction of two inland rivers, flowing 25 miiles SE to the Andaman Sea. Also Yangon.

rang·y (rān′jē) *adj.* **rang·i·er, rang·i·est** **1** Disposed to roam, or adapted for roving, as cattle. **2** Having long legs adapted to a long, limber gait. **3** Having long thin arms and legs: said of a person. **4** Affording wide range; roomy. **5** Resembling a mountain range.

ra·ni (rä′nē) *n.* **1** The wife of a raja or prince. **2** A reigning Hindu queen or princess. Also spelled *ranee*. [<Hind.]

Ran·jit Singh (run′jēt siṅ′hə), 1780–1839, maharajah of the Punjab; founded Sikh empire. Also *Runjeet Singh.*

rank[1] (rangk) *n.* **1** A series of objects ranged in a line or row; a range. **2** Degree of official standing, especially in the army and navy. See table under GRADE. **3** A line of soldiers drawn up side by side in close order: distinguished from *file*. **4** *pl.* An army; also, the mass of soldiery; the order of private soldiers: The colonel rose from the *ranks*. **5** A row of eight squares on a chessboard extending from the left of the player to the right. **6** Relative position in a scale of dignity or of life; degree; grade: the *rank* of baronet; the *rank* of a plant or animal organism. **7** High degree or position; especially, the state of being a member of a titled nobility: a lady of *rank*. **8** Degree of worth or excellence; relative status. See synonyms under CLASS, SORT. — *v.t.* **1** To place or arrange in a rank or ranks. **2** To place in a class, order, etc.; assign to a position or classification. **3** To take precedence of; outrank: Sergeants

rank corporals. — *v.i.* **4** To hold a specified place or rank: His poetry *ranks* with the best. **5** To have the highest rank or grade. [<OF *ranc, renc* <Gmc. Doublet of RANGE.]

rank[2] (rangk) *adj.* **1** Very vigorous and flourishing in growth as from fertilization or moisture. **2** Strong and disagreeable to the taste or smell. **3** Excessive or immoderate, in unfavorable sense: *rank* injustice. **4** Producing a luxuriant growth; fertile. **5** *Law* Inequitable; excessive. **6** Strong or deep: said of a cut or the adjustment of the tool making a cut. **7** *Obs.* In heat; lustful. [OE *ranc* strong] — **rank′ly** *adv.* — **rank′ness** *n.*

rank and file **1** The common soldiers of an army, including all from the corporals downward. **2** Those who form the bulk of any organization, as distinct from officers or leaders.

rank·er (rangk′ər) *n.* **1** One who has served in the ranks. **2** A commissioned officer who has risen from the ranks.

rank·ing (rangk′ing) *adj.* Superior in rank; taking precedence (over others in the grade): a *ranking* senator, officer, etc.

ran·kle (rang′kəl) *v.* **·kled, ·kling** *v.i.* **1** To cause continued resentment, sense of injury, etc.: The defeat *rankles* in his breast. **2** To become irritated or inflamed; fester. — *v.t.* **3** To irritate; embitter. [<OF *rancler,* alter. of *draoncler* fester <Med. L *dracunculus,* dim. of *draco* dragon]

ran·pike (ran′pīk′) *n.* A rampike.

ran·sack (ran′sak) *v.t.* **1** To search through every part of. **2** To search throughout for plunder; pillage. See synonyms under EXAMINE. [<ON *rannsaka* search a house < *rann* house + *sækja* seek] — **ran′sack·er** *n.*

ran·som (ran′səm) *v.t.* **1** To secure the release of (a person, property, etc.) for a required price, as from captivity or detention. **2** To set free on payment of ransom. **3** To redeem from sin or its consequences. See synonyms under DELIVER. — *n.* **1** The consideration paid for the release of a person or property captured or detained. **2** Release purchased, as from captivity. [<OF *rançon, raençon* <L *redemptio, -onis* redemption < *redimere* redeem. Doublet of REDEMPTION.] — **ran′som·er** *n.* — **ran′som·less** *adj.*

rant (rant) *v.i.* **1** To speak in loud, violent, or extravagant language; declaim vehemently; rave. **2** *Scot. & Brit. Dial.* To frolic noisily; be uproariously jolly. — *v.t.* **3** To exclaim or utter in a ranting manner. — *n.* **1** Declamatory and bombastic talk. **2** *Scot. & Brit. Dial.* Wild gaiety; a boisterous revel. [<MDu. *ranten* rave] — **rant′ing** *adj.* — **rant′ing·ly** *adv.*

rant·er (ran′tər) *n.* One who rants; a noisy, boisterous speaker or declaimer: applied opprobriously to various religious speakers.

rap[1] (rap) *v.* **rapped, rap·ping** *v.t.* **1** To strike sharply and quickly; hit. **2** To utter in a sharp manner; with *out*: to *rap* out an oath. **3** *Slang* To criticize severely. — *v.i.* **4** To strike sharp, quick blows. **5** *Slang* To have a frank discussion; talk. — *n.* **1** A sharp blow. **2** A sound caused by or as by knocking; specifically, such a sound ascribed to the agency of spirits. **3** *Slang* A reprimand; blame; also, consequences: to take the *rap*. **4** *Slang* A prison sentence. **5** *Slang* A severe criticism. **6** *Slang* A talk; discussion. See synonyms under BLOW[2]. **7** *Slang* Marked by frank discussion: a *rap* session. [Imit. Cf. Dan. *rap,* Sw. *rapp.*] — **rap′per** *n.*

ra·pa·cious (rə·pā′shəs) *adj.* **1** Given to plunder or rapine. **2** Extortionate; grasping. **3** Predaceous; subsisting on prey seized alive: said of hawks, etc. [<L *rapax, -acis* < *rapere* seize] — **ra·pa′cious·ly** *adv.*

ra·pac·i·ty (rə·pas′ə·tē) *n.* The quality or character of being rapacious. Also **ra·pa′cious·ness.** [<L *rapacitas, -tatis*]

Ra·pa Nu·i (rä′pä nōō′ē) The native name for EASTER ISLAND.

rape[1] (rāp) *v.* **raped, rap·ing** *v.t.* **1** To commit rape upon; ravish. **2** To plunder or sack (a city, etc.). **3** *Archaic* To carry off by force. — *v.i.* **4** To commit rape. See synonyms under VIOLATE. — *n.* **1** The act of a man who has sexual intercourse with a woman against her will or (called **statutory rape**) with a girl below the age of consent. **2** Any unlawful sexual intercourse or sexual connection by force or threat: homosexual *rape* in prison. **3** The plundering or sacking of a city, etc. **4**

Any gross violation, assault, or abuse: the *rape* of our natural resources. [<AF <L *rapere* seize]

rape[2] (rāp) *n.* **1** *pl.* In winemaking, refuse stalks and skins of grapes. **2** A filter used in vinegarmaking. [<F *râpe* <Med. L *raspa* < *raspare* grate <Gmc. Cf. OHG *raspon.*]

rape oil A yellowish to brown oil obtained from rapeseed: used as a lubricant and in the manufacture of rubber substitutes, soft soaps, etc. Also called *colza oil.*

ra·phe (rā′fē) *n.* *pl.* **·phae** (-fē) **1** *Anat.* A seamlike appearance often seen in organs, especially at the median line of the body. **2** *Bot.* The fibrovascular cord that connects the hilum of plant ovules with the chalaza. **3** A line or rib connecting the nodules on a diatom valve. Also spelled *rhaphe.* [<NL <Gk. *rhaphē* seam < *rhaptein* stitch together]

ra·phi·a (rā′fē·ə) See RAFFIA.

rap·id (rap′id) *adj.* **1** Having great speed. **2** Bearing the marks of or characterized by rapidity. **3** Done or completed in a short time; advancing speedily to a termination: *rapid* growth. See synonyms under SWIFT[1]. — *n.* *Usually pl.* A descent in a river less abrupt than a waterfall. [<L *rapidus* < *rapere* seize, rush] — **rap′id·ly** *adv.* — **rap′id·ness** *n.*

rap·id–fire (rap′id·fīr′) *adj.* **1** Firing shots rapidly. **2** Characterized by speed: *rapid–fire* repartee. Also **rap′id–fir′ing.**

rapid fire A rate of gunfire lower than that of quick fire.

ra·pid·i·ty (rə·pid′ə·te) *n.* The quality or state of being rapid; swiftness.

rapid transit The local transportation of passengers by means faster than surface vehicles; specifically, elevated or subway passenger transportation.

ra·pi·er (rā′pē·ər, rāp′yər) *n.* **1** In the 16th and 17th centuries, a long, straight, two-edged sword with a large cup hilt, used in dueling, chiefly for thrusting. **2** The French small sword of the 18th century, a shorter straight sword without cutting edge and therefore used for thrusting only. [<F *rapière,* prob. < *raspière* poker, rasper; appar. first used derisively]

rap·ine (rap′in) *n.* The taking of property by force, as in war; spoliation; pillage. See synonyms under PLUNDER. [<F <L *rapina* < *rapere* seize. Doublet of RAVEN[2], *n.,* RAVINE.]

rap·ist (rā′pist) *n.* One who commits rape.

rap·loch (rap′ləkh) *Scot. & Brit. Dial. adj.* Unkempt; coarse. — *n.* Coarse homespun cloth made of inferior undyed wool.

RAPIER

Rap·pa·han·nock (rap′ə·han′ək) A river in northern Virginia, flowing 212 miles SE to Chesapeake Bay.

rap·pa·ree (rap′ə·rē′) *n.* **1** An Irish guerrilla of the 17th century. **2** A freebooter or bandit. [<Irish *rapaire* short pike]

rap·pee (ra·pē′) *n.* A dark, coarse, strong-flavored snuff. [<F (*tabac*) *râpé* grated (tobacco), pp. of *râper* scrape]

rap·pel (ra·pel′) *v.i.* **·pelled, ·pel·ling** In mountaineering, to descend from a precipitous height by letting oneself down on a rope. — *n.* Descent by means of a rope. [<F]

rap·per (rap′ər) *n.* **1** One who raps. **2** A spiritualist medium. **3** A knocker, as on a door or at the mouth of a mining shaft.

rap·port (ra·pôrt′, -pôrt′; *Fr.* rå·pôr′) *n.* Harmony of relation; accordance; sympathetic relation: commonly with *in.* — **en rapport** *French* In close accord. [<F < *rapporter* refer, bring back < *re-* again + *apporter* bring <L *apportare* < *ad-* to + *portare* bring]

rap·scal·lion (rap·skal′yən) *n.* A rogue; scamp; rascal. [< earlier *rascallion* <RASCAL + fanciful ending]

rapt (rapt) *adj.* **1** Carried away with lofty emotion; enraptured; transported. **2** Engrossed; intent; deeply engaged. Sometimes erroneously spelled *wrapt.* [<L *raptus,* pp. of *rapere* seize]

rap·to·ri·al (rap·tôr′ē·əl, -tō′rē-) *adj.* **1** Seizing and devouring living prey; predatory. **2** *Ornithol.* Having talons adapted for seizing and holding prey: said especially of hawks, vultures, eagles, owls, and other carnivorous birds. [<L *raptor* snatcher <*raptus,* pp. of *rapere* seize]

rap·ture (rap′chər) *n.* **1** The state of being rapt or transported; ecstatic joy; ecstasy. **2** The act of transferring a person from one place to another: Elijah's *rapture* to heaven. **3** An act or expression of excessive delight. **4** *Obs.* A snatching away; violent seizure. — *v.t.* **·tured, ·tur·ing** To enrapture. [<RAPT]
Synonyms (noun): bliss, delight, ecstasy, exultation, happiness, joy, rejoicing, transport, triumph. *Rejoicing* is *happiness* or *joy* that finds utterance in word, song, festivity, etc. *Delight* is vivid, overflowing *happiness* of a somewhat transient kind; *ecstasy* is a state of extreme or extravagant *delight; rapture* is closely allied to *ecstasy,* but is more serene, exalted, and enduring. *Transport* is the condition of one carried away out of himself by some powerful passion or emotion, whether joyous or the reverse. *Triumph* is such *joy* as results from victory, success, achievement. See ENTHUSIASM, HAPPINESS. *Antonyms:* agony, apathy, dejection, despair, distress, ennui, horror, misery, pain, tedium, torture, woe, wretchedness.

rap·tur·ous (rap′chər·əs) *adj.* Being in a state of, exhibiting, or characterized by rapture. See synonyms under HAPPY. — **rap′tur·ous·ly** *adv.* — **rap′tur·ous·ness** *n.*

rare[1] (râr) *adj.* **1** Of infrequent occurrence. **2** Highly esteemed because of infrequency or uncommonness; valuable; choice. **3** Rarefied: now chiefly of the atmosphere. **4** *Obs.* Dispersed. [<F <L *rarus* rare]
Synonyms: curious, extraordinary, incomparable, infrequent, odd, peculiar, precious, remarkable, scarce, singular, strange, uncommon, unique, unusual. *Extraordinary,* signifying greatly beyond the ordinary, is a neutral word, capable of a high and good sense or of an invidious, opprobrious, or contemptuous signification. *Unique* is alone of its kind; *rare* is *infrequent* of its kind; great poems are *rare.* To say of a thing that it is *rare* is simply to affirm that it is now seldom found, whether previously common or not; as, a *rare* old book; a *rare* word; to call a thing *scarce* implies that it was at some time more plentiful, as when we say money is *scarce.* A particular coin may be *rare; scarce* applies to demand and use, and almost always to concrete things; to speak of virtue, genius, or heroism as *scarce* would be somewhat ludicrous. See CHOICE, EXTRAORDINARY, OBSOLETE, ODD. *Antonyms:* see synonyms for COMMON.

rare[2] (râr) *adj.* Not thoroughly cooked: applied to roasted or broiled meat retaining its redness and juices: in England commonly termed *underdone.* [OE *hrēre* lightly boiled]

rare·bit (râr′bit) *n.* Welsh rabbit. [Alter. of (WELSH) RABBIT]

rare–earth elements (râr′ûrth′) *Chem.* A group of metallic elements comprising the lanthanide series. Also **rare–earth metals.**

rar·ee show (râr′ē) **1** A show carried or contained in a box; a peepshow. **2** A cheap street show or any street show or spectacle. [Alter. of *rare show;* after the mispronunciation characteristic of the Savoyard promoters of these shows]

rar·e·fac·tion (râr·ə·fak′shən) *n.* The process or act of making rare or less dense. Also **rar′e·fi·ca′tion.** [<L *rarefactus,* pp. of *rarefacere*] — **rar′e·fac′tive** *adj.*

rar·e·fy (râr′ə·fī) *v.* **·fied, ·fy·ing** *v.t.* **1** To make rare, thin, less solid, or less dense; expand by dispersion of the particles. **2** To refine or purify. — *v.i.* **3** To become rare, thin, or less solid. **4** To become more pure. [<F *raréfier* <L *rarefacere* <*rarus* rare + *facere* make] — **rar′e·fi′a·ble** *adj.*

rare·ly (râr′lē) *adv.* **1** Not often; infrequently. **2** With unusual excellence or effect; finely: The breeze blows *rarely.* **3** Exceptionally; extremely; in an unusual degree: She dressed in raiment *rarely* rich.

rare·ripe (râr′rīp′) *adj.* Ripening early. — *n.* A fruit that ripens early: applied especially to many varieties of peaches, and to a variety of onion. [OE *hrathe* early, soon + RIPE]

rar·i·ty (râr′ə·tē) *n. pl.* **·ties 1** The quality or state of being rare, uncommon, or infrequent; infrequency. **2** That which is exceptionally valued from scarceness. **3** The state of being rare, thin, or tenuous; tenuity: opposed to *density.* [<L *raritas, -tatis*]

Ra·ro·ton·ga (rä′rō·tông′gə) The largest and southwesternmost of the Cook Islands, capital of the group; 26 square miles.

ras·cal (ras′kəl) *n.* **1** An unprincipled fellow; a rogue; knave: sometimes used playfully. **2** *Obs.* One of the common herd; a man of low birth or station. — *adj.* Pertaining to the rabble; contemptible; base; mean. [<OF *rascaille* <*rasque* filth, shavings, ult. <L *radere* shave, scrape]

ras·cal·i·ty (ras·kal′ə·tē) *n. pl.* **·ties 1** The quality of being rascally. **2** A rascally act.

ras·cal·ly (ras′kəl·ē) *adj.* Worthy of a rascal; knavish; base. See synonyms under BAD[1]. — *adv.* After the manner of a rascal.

rase (rāz) *v.t.* **rased, ras·ing** To raze. [Var. of RAZE]

rash[1] (rash) *adj.* **1** Acting without due caution or regard of consequences; reckless; precipitate. **2** Exhibiting recklessness or precipitancy. **3** *Obs.* Quick; speedy. See synonyms under IMPETUOUS, IMPRUDENT. [ME *rasch.* Akin to Du. & G *rasch* quick.] — **rash′ly** *adv.* — **rash′ness** *n.*

rash[2] (rash) *n.* A superficial eruption of the skin, often localized. [? <F *rache* <OF *rasque.* See RASCAL.]

rash·er (rash′ər) *n.* A thin slice of meat: used especially of bacon. [Prob. <obs. *rash* cut, slash]

ra·so·ri·al (rə·sôr′ē·əl, -sō′rē-) *adj.* In the habit of scratching the ground for food, as domestic fowl and other gallinaceous birds. [<NL *Rasores,* lit., scratchers <L *rasum,* pp. of *radere* scrape]

rasp (rasp, räsp) *n.* **1** A filelike tool having coarse pyramidal projections for abrasion. **2** A machine containing a large cylindrical grater. **3** The act or sound of rasping. — *v.t.* **1** To scrape with or as with a rasp. **2** To scrape or rub roughly. **3** To affect unpleasantly; irritate. **4** To utter in a rough voice. — *v.i.* **5** To grate; scrape [<OF *raspe* < *rasper* scrape, prob. <Gmc.] — **rasp′er** *n.*

rasp·ber·ry (raz′ber′ē, -bər·ē, räz′-) *n. pl.* **·ries 1** The round fruit of certain brambles (genus *Rubus*) of the rose family, composed of drupes clustered around a fleshy receptacle. **2** The plant yielding this fruit. **3** *Slang* A vulgar sound indicating contempt and produced by vibrating the tongue between the lips [< earlier *rasp raspberry* (? <OF *(vin) raspé* thin wine < *râpe* RAPE[3]) + BERRY]

rasped (raspt, räspt) *adj.* Rough or roughened, with or as with a coarse file: said of uncut book edges.

rasp·ing (ras′ping, räs′-) *adj.* Making a harsh sound; hence, irritating.

Ras·pu·tin (ras·pyōō′tin, *Russian* räs·pōō′tin), **Grigori,** 1871–1916, Russian monk, favorite of Czar Nicholas II and his wife; assassinated: real name Novikh.

rasp·y (ras′pē, räs′-) *adj.* **rasp·i·er, rasp·i·est 1** Inclined to rasp; rough; grating. **2** Irritable.

ra·sure (rā′zhər) *n.* Erasure.

rat (rat) *n.* **1** A destructive and injurious rodent (family *Muridae*) of world-wide distribution, larger and more aggressive than the mouse: especially the **Norway rat** (*Rattus norvegicus*) and the smaller **roof** or **black rat** (*R. rattus*): both are carriers of the plague bacillus transmitted by the rat flea. **2** Some other mammal like or likened to the rat. **3** *Slang* A cowardly or selfish person who deserts or betrays his associates. **4** A slender cushion of curled hair or the like, worn by women, with the natural hair rolled over it. — *v.i.* **rat·ted, rat·ting 1** To hunt rats. **2** *Slang* To desert one's party, companions, etc., especially for one's own safety or advantage. **3** *Slang* To inform; act the betrayer. [OE *ræt*]

rat·a·fi·a (rat′ə·fē′ə) *n.* **1** A cordial flavored with fruits. **2** A flavoring essence based on the essential oil of bitter almonds. **3** A sweet biscuit. Also **rat′a·fee′** (-fē′). [<F]

ra·tal (rāt′l) *n.* An amount on which rates are assessed. [<RATE + -AL[1]]

ra·tan (ra·tan′) See RATTAN.
rat·a·ny (rat′ə·nē) See RHATANY.
rat·a·plan (rat′ə·plan′) *n.* A rapidly repeated sound, as of the beating of a drum. — *v.t. & v.i.* **·planned, ·plan·ning** To sound a rataplan (on). [<F; imit. of drumming]

rat·a·tat·tat (rat′ə·tat′tat′) *n.* A quick, sharp rapping sound, as a knock at a door. [Imit.]

ratch·et (rach′it) *n.* **1** A mechanism consisting of a notched wheel, the teeth of which engage with a pawl, permitting motion of the wheel in one direction only. **2** The pawl or the wheel thus used. Also **ratchet wheel.** [<F *rochet* spool <Ital. *rochetto* bobbin, dim. of *rocca* distaff <Gmc. Cf. OHG *roccho* spindle.]

rate[1] (rāt) *n.* **1** The measure of a thing by its relation to a standard; proportional or comparative amount or degree: a high *rate* of interest. **2** Degree of value; price: railway *rates;* also, the unit cost of a commodity or service: the *rate* for electricity, gas, water, and the like. **3** Comparative rank or class; condition. **4** The amount of variation of a timepiece; gain or loss in seconds. **5** A ratio for the assessment of property taxes: a *rate* of 40 mills per thousand dollars. **6** *Brit.* A local tax on property. **7** The proportion which a given fact or event bears to the total of relevant cases involved: a death *rate,* marriage *rate.* **8** A fixed allowance or amount. **9** *Obs.* Degree; estimation. See synonyms under TAX. — **at any rate** In any case; under any circumstances; anyhow. — **differential rate** The lower of two rates given usually by two competing railroad lines to one of two places in the same territory in order to make profits even: in England called **preferential rate.** — *v.* **rat·ed, rat·ing** *v.t.* **1** To estimate the value or worth of; appraise. **2** To place in a certain rank or grade. **3** To fix the amount of tax or liability on. **4** To consider; regard: He is *rated* as a great statesman. **5** To fix the rate for the transportation of (goods), as by rail, water, or air. — *v.i.* **6** To have rank, rating, or value. See synonyms under CALCULATE. [<OF <L *rata (pars)* reckoned (part), fem. of *ratus,* pp. of *reri* reckon]

rate[2] (rāt) *v.t. & v.i.* **rat·ed, rat·ing** To reprove with vehemence; rail at; scold. [Origin uncertain. Cf. OF *rater* scold and Sw. *rata* find fault.]

ra·tel (rā′təl, rä′-) *n.* A nocturnal carnivore (genus *Mellivora*) resembling the badger, ashy-gray above and black below, of South and West Africa and India. [<Afrikaans *rateldas* <Du. *raat* honeycomb + *das* badger]

rat·er[1] (rā′tər) *n.* One who or that which rates or estimates.

rat·er[2] (rā′tər) *n.* One who scolds or berates.

rat–foot dots In Chinese painting, a method of representing pine boughs or branches by brush strokes that resemble the print of a rat's foot: four or five slightly curved strokes radiating from a white center dot.

rath·er (rath′ər, rä′thər) *adv.* **1** With preference for one of two things or courses; more willingly. **2** With more reason; more wisely; more strictly or accurately. **3** Somewhat; in a greater or less degree; to a certain extent. **4** Very much; exceedingly. **5** *Obs.* Sooner; earlier; more quickly. [OE *hrathor* sooner, compar. of *hrathe* soon, quick]

rat·i·fi·ca·tion (rat′ə·fə·kā′shən) *n.* The act of ratifying, or the state of being ratified.

rat·i·fy (rat′ə·fī) *v.t.* **·fied, ·fy·ing** To give sanction to, especially official or authoritative sanction; make valid by approving, especially the work of an agent or representative; confirm. [<F *ratifier* <Med. L *ratificare* <L *ratus* fixed, reckoned + *facere* make] — **rat′i·fi′er** *n.*
Synonyms: accept, approve, confirm, corroborate, endorse, establish, justify, sanction, seal, settle, substantiate, validate. See ASSENT, CONFIRM, JUSTIFY. *Antonyms:* abolish, abrogate, annul, cancel, deny, disavow, disown, extinguish, nullify, repeal, rescind, revoke.

rat·ing (rā′ting) *n.* **1** Classification according to a standard; grade; rank. **2** The classification of a vessel. **3** An evaluation of the financial standing of a business firm or an individual. **4** The designation of the operating capacity of a piece of machinery, as expressed in horsepower, kilowatts, etc. **5** Any specialist grade held by an enlisted man or officer: the *rating* of a pilot, gunner, parachutist, etc., in the U.S. Army, or of boatswain's mate in the Navy. **6** *Brit.* An enlisted man in the Royal Navy. See synonyms under TAX.

rat·ing² (rā′ting) *n.* A harsh rebuke; scolding. [<RATE²]

ra·tio (rā′shō, -shē·ō) *n. pl.* **·tios 1** Relation of degree, number, etc.; relative amount; proportion; rate: There has always been a *ratio* between demand and supply. **2** The relation between two numbers or two magnitudes of the same kind; especially, the quotient of one magnitude divided by the other, or the factor that, multiplied into one, will produce the other. **3** Formerly, the relation expressed by subtracting one quantity from the other; the difference. **4** *Obs.* A portion; ration. [<L. Doublet of RATION, REASON.]

ra·ti·oc·i·nant (rash′ē·os′ə·nant) *adj.* Reasoning, as contrasted with *ratiocinate.* [See RATIOCINATE]

ra·ti·oc·i·nate (rash′ē·os′ə·nāt) *v.i.* **·nat·ed, ·nat·ing** To make a deduction from premises; reason. —*adj.* Reasoned about. [<L *ratiocinatus,* pp. of *ratiocinari* calculate, deliberate < *ratio* reckoning. See REASON.] —**ra·ti·oc′i·na′tor** *n.*

ra·ti·oc·i·na·tion (rash′ē·os′ə·nā′shən) *n.* The deduction of conclusions from premises; reasoning. See synonyms under REASONING. [<L *ratiocinatio, -onis*]

ra·ti·oc·i·na·tive (rash′ē·os′ə·nā′tiv) *adj.* **1** Of or pertaining to the act or process of reasoning. **2** Given to ratiocination; argumentative. [<L *ratiocinativus*]

ra·tion (rash′ən, rā′shən) *n.* **1** A portion; share. **2** A fixed allowance or portion of food, etc., allotted in time of scarcity. — **emergency ration** Portions of canned beef, hardtack, milk chocolate, etc., for use in the field by soldiers. —*v.t.* **1** To provide with rations; issue rations to, as an army. **2** To give out or allot in rations, as gasoline, rubber, butter, etc. [<F <L *ratio, -onis.* Doublet of RATIO, REASON.] —**ra′tion·ing** *n.*

ra·tion·al (rash′ən·əl) *adj.* **1** Possessing the faculty of reasoning. **2** Conformable to reason; judicious; sensible. **3** Pertaining to reason; attained by reasoning. **4** Pertaining to rationalism. **5** *Math.* **a** Pertaining to a rational number. **b** Denoting an algebraic expression containing variables within radicals, as $\sqrt{x^2 - y^2}$, $\sqrt{4x} - 1$. Compare IRRATIONAL. **6** In Greek and Latin prosody, denoting the measurement of metrical units; capable of being measured in metrical units. —*n.* That which is rational. [<L *rationalis* < *ratio, -onis*] —**ra′tion·al·ly** *adv.* —**ra′tion·al·ness** *n.*
Synonym (adj.): reasonable. A *rational* mind is one that is capable of the ordinary and normal processes of thought; a *reasonable* mood is one at the time susceptible to the influence of reasons. A *rational* man is capable of using his reasoning powers; a *reasonable* man has them habitually in exercise. *Rational* is opposed to *insane, reasonable* to *fanatical, misguided, obstinate, unreasonable, visionary.* See SAGACIOUS, SANE¹, WISE¹.

ra·tion·ale (rash′ən·al′, -ä′lē, -ā′lē) *n.* **1** A rational exposition of principles. **2** The logical basis of a fact; the reason or reasons collectively. [<L, neut. of *rationalis*]

ra·tion·al·ism (rash′ən·əl·iz′əm) *n.* **1** The formation of opinions by relying upon reason alone, independently of authority or of revelation: opposed to *supernaturalism.* **2** *Philos.* **a** The theory of a priori ideas, that truth and knowledge are attainable through reason rather than through experience: opposed to *empiricism.* **b** The theory that reason itself is a source of knowledge independent of sense perception: opposed to *sensationalism.* —**ra′tion·al·ist** *n.* —**ra′tion·al·is′tic** or **·ti·cal** *adj.* —**ra′tion·al·is′ti·cal·ly** *adv.*

ra·tion·al·i·ty (rash′ən·al′ə·tē) *n. pl.* **·ties 1** Sanity; reasonableness; naturalness. **2** The cause or reason; rationale. [<LL *rationalitas*]

ra·tion·al·i·za·tion (rash′ən·əl·ə·zā′shən, -ī·zā′shən) *n.* **1** The act or process of rationalizing. **2** *Psychol.* The act or process of devising acceptable reasons for desires, emotions, acts, beliefs, or opinions which cannot be credit-

ably justified to oneself or to others in terms of their actual motives. **3** *Brit.* The act of bringing an industry into accord with up-to-date methods of organization and operation.

ra·tion·al·ize (rash′ən·əl·īz′) *v.* **·ized, ·iz·ing** *v.t.* **1** *Psychol.* To explain (one's behavior) on grounds ostensibly rational but not in accord with the actual or unconscious motives. **2** To explain or treat from a rationalistic point of view. **3** To make rational or reasonable; render conformable to reason. **4** *Math.* To remove the radicals containing variables from (an expression or equation); also, to alter the radicals so as to change (the expression) into more workable form: thus, if $\sqrt{x^2 + 2x}$ = 3, then, by squaring, $x^2 + 2x = 9$, and $x^2 + 2x - 9 = 0$. —*v.i.* **5** To think in a rational or rationalistic manner. **6** *Psychol.* To rationalize one's behavior. —**ra′tion·al·iz′er** *n.*

rat·ite (rat′īt) *adj.* Designating a division of flightless birds (*Ratitae*), including ostriches, cassowaries, kiwis, emus, etc., which have aborted wings and a breastbone without a keel. —*n.* One of the *Ratitae.* [<L *ratis* raft]

rat kangaroo Any of several tiny kangaroos, as the **rufous rat kangaroo** (*Aepyprymnus rufescens*).

rat·line (rat′lin) *n. Naut.* **1** One of the small ropes fastened across the shrouds of a ship, used as the rounds of a ladder for going aloft or descending. **2** The material so used. See SHROUD². Also **rat′lin** (-lin), **rat′·ling** (-ling). [Origin unknown]

ra·toon (ra·tōōn′) *n.* **1** A new shoot from the root of a cropped plant, as from a sugarcane. **2** One of the heart leaves in a tobacco plant. —*v.i.* To sprout from a root planted the previous year. [<Sp. *retoño* <Hind. *ratun*]

RATLINES

rat race *Slang* A frantic, usually fruitless, struggle; a wearisome hustle or strife.

rats·bane (rats′bān′) *n.* Rat poison.

rat·tan (ra·tan′) *n.* **1** The long, tough, flexible stem of a palm (genera *Calamus* and *Daemonorops*) growing in East India, Africa, and Australia. **2** The palm itself. **3** A cane or switch of rattan. Also spelled *ratan.* [<Malay *rotan*]

rat·ter (rat′ər) *n.* **1** A dog or cat that catches rats. **2** *Slang* A deserter or traitor.

rat·tish (rat′ish) *adj.* Belonging to or resembling a rat.

rat·tle¹ (rat′l) *v.* **·tled, ·tling** *v.i.* **1** To make a series of sharp noises in rapid succession, as by striking together: dead limbs *rattling* in the wind. **2** To move or act with such noises. **3** To talk rapidly and foolishly; chatter. —*v.t.* **4** To cause to rattle: to *rattle* pennies in a tin cup. **5** To utter or perform rapidly or noisily. **6** *Colloq.* To confuse; disconcert: Her reaction *rattled* me. See synonyms under SHAKE. —*n.* **1** A series of short, sharp sounds in rapid succession, as from the collision of small, hard objects. **2** A plaything, implement, etc., adapted to produce a rattling noise: a watchman's *rattle.* **3** The series of jointed horny rings in the tail of a rattlesnake, or one of these; also, the noise produced by the vibration of this organ. **4** Rapid and noisy talk; chatter. **5** One who talks fast and foolishly. **6** A râle; the death rattle, caused by the passage of air through mucus. See synonyms under NOISE. [Imit.]

rat·tle² (rat′l) *v.t.* **·tled, ·tling** *Naut.* To fit with ratlines: used in the phrase **to rattle down the rigging.** [<RATLINE]

rat·tle·brain (rat′l·brān′) *n.* A talkative, flighty person; foolish chatterer. Also **rat′tle·head′** (-hed′), **rat′tle·pate′** (-pāt′). —**rat′tle·brained′** *adj.*

RATTLESNAKE
(From 2 to 8 feet in length)

rat·tle·snake (rat′l·snāk′) *n.* Any of various venomous, thick-bodied American snakes (genera *Crotalus* and *Sistrurus,* family *Viperidae*) with a tail ending in a series of horny, loosely connected, modified joints, which clash together with a rattling noise when the tail is vibrated.

rattlesnake flag One of the early flags of the American Revolution, bearing a rattlesnake and the motto "Don't Tread On Me."

rattlesnake root 1 Any of several erect perennial herbs (genus *Prenanthes*) considered to be a cure for the bite of a rattlesnake. **2** The root or tuber of such plants. **3** Senega.

rat·tle·trap (rat′l·trap′) *n.* **1** Any rickety, clattering, or worn-out vehicle or article. **2** *Slang* A loquacious or gossipy person. —*adj.* Shaky; dilapidated.

rat·tling (rat′ling) *adj.* **1** Making a clatter. **2** Garrulous; sprightly. **3** *Colloq.* Very; extraordinary; good. —*adv. Colloq.* Extraordinarily; very: a *rattling* good time.

rat·tly (rat′lē) *adj.* **1** Inclined to rattle. **2** Clattering.

rat·trap (rat′trap′) *n.* **1** A trap for catching rats. **2** A situation from which escape is impossible; any hopeless or fatal predicament.

rat·ty (rat′ē) *adj.* **·ti·er, ·ti·est 1** Ratlike, or abounding in rats. **2** *Slang* Disreputable; shabby.

rau·cous (rô′kəs) *adj.* Rough in sound; hoarse; harsh. [<L *raucus*] —**rau′ci·ty** (-sə·tē), **rau′cous·ness** *n.* —**rau′cous·ly** *adv.*

raunch·y (rôn′chē, rän′-) *adj. Slang* **raunch·i·er, raunch·i·est 1** Sloppy; inept; slovenly. **2** Sexually vulgar; lewd; a *raunchy* joke. **3** Lustful. [? Alter. of Scot. *randy* disorderly, lewd; ult. origin unknown] —**raunch′i·ly** *adv.* —**rauch′i·ness** *n.*

rav·age (rav′ij) *v.* **·aged, ·ag·ing** *v.t* To lay waste, as by pillaging or burning; despoil; ruin. —*v.i.* To wreak havoc; be destructive. —*n.* Violent and destructive action, or its result; ruin; desolation. [<F <*ravir.* See RAVISH.] —**rav′ag·er** *n.*

rave¹ (rāv) *v.* **raved, rav·ing** *v.i.* **1** To speak wildly or incoherently. **2** To speak with extravagant enthusiasm. **3** To make a wild, roaring sound; rage: The wind *raved* through the trees. —*v.t.* **4** To utter wildly or incoherently. —*n.* **1** The act or state of raving; a frenzy. **2** *Colloq.* A highly favorable critical comment: The play drew *raves.* —*adj. Colloq.* Extravagantly enthusiastic: *rave* reviews. [<OF *raver, rever* <L *rabere* rage]

rave² (rāv) *n.* **1** A vertical sidepiece in a wagon body, or in a hand car or sleigh. **2** The wooden or iron piece that fastens the beam to the runners of a logging sled. [Origin unknown]

rav·el (rav′əl) *v.* **·eled or ·elled, ·el·ing or ·el·ling** *v.t.* **1** To separate the threads or fibers of; unravel. **2** To make clear or plain; explain: often with *out.* **3** *Archaic* To tangle; confuse. —*v.i.* **4** To become separated thread from thread or fiber from fiber; unravel; fray. **5** *Archaic* To become tangled or confused. —*n.* **1** A broken or rejected thread. **2** A raveling. [? <MDu. *ravelen* tangle] —**rav′el·er** or **rav′el·ler** *n.*

rav·el·ing (rav′əl·ing) *n.* **1** A thread or threads raveled from a fabric. **2** The act of raveling. **3** The process of being raveled. Also **rav′el·ling.**

rav·el·ment (rav′əl·mənt) *n.* A ravel, or the act of raveling; confusion.

ra·ven¹ (rā′vən) *n.* A large, omnivorous, crowlike bird (*Corvus corax*) of North America, Europe, and Asia, having lustrous black plumage, with the feathers of the throat elongated and lanceolate. —*adj.* Black and shining, like the plumage of a raven. [OE *hræfn*]

rav·en[2] (rav′ən) v.t. **1** To devour hungrily or greedily. **2** To take by force; ravage. —v.i. **3** To search for or take prey or plunder. **4** To eat voraciously; be ravenous. —n. The act of plundering; spoliation; pillage. [< OF *raviner* < *ravine* rapine < L *rapina; n.* doublet of RAPINE, RAVINE] —**rav′en·er** n.

rav·en·ing (rav′ən·ing) adj. **1** Seeking eagerly for prey; rapacious. **2** Mad; rabid. —n. **1** Propensity for prey or booty; rapacity. **2** The prey seized. [ppr. of RAVEN[2]] —**rav′en·ing·ly** adv.

rav·en·ous (rav′ən·əs) adj. **1** Violently voracious or hungry. **2** Extremely eager for gratification. See synonyms under GREEDY. [< OF *ravinos.* See RAVEN[2].] —**rav′en·ous·ly** adv. —**rav′en·ous·ness** n.

rav·in (rav′in) n. **1** The act of plundering or ravaging. **2** That which is obtained by violence or robbery. —v.t. & v.i. To raven. [< OF *ravine.* See RAPINE.]

ra·vine (rə·vēn′) n. **1** A deep gorge or gully, especially one worn by a stream or flow of water. **2** A long, narrow cleft between heights. See synonyms under VALLEY. [< F. Doublet of RAVEN[2], n., RAPINE.]

rav·ing (rā′ving) adj. **1** Furious; delirious; frenzied. **2** *Colloq.* Excessive; extraordinary: a *raving* beauty. —n. Furious, incoherent, or irrational utterance. See synonyms under FRENZY. Compare INSANITY.

ra·vio·li (rä·vyō′lē, rä′vē·ō′lē, rav′ē-) n. pl. Balls of forcemeat, encased in little envelopes of dough and boiled in broth or water: commonly construed in the singular. [< Ital., dim. pl. of dial. *rava* < L *rapa* turnip, beet]

rav·ish (rav′ish) v.t. **1** To fill with strong emotion, especially delight; enrapture. **2** To commit a rape upon. **3** To carry off (a woman) by force. **4** To seize and carry off by violence. [< OF *raviss-*, stem of *ravir* carry off < L *rapere* seize. Related to RAPE, RAPTURE.] —**rav′ish·er** n. —**rav′ish·ing·ly** adv.

Synonyms: capitivate, charm, delight, enchant, enrapture, entrance, overjoy, transport. See ABUSE, CHARM[1], POLLUTE, REJOICE.

rav·ish·ing (rav′ish·ing) adj. Filling with transports of delight; enchanting.

rav·ish·ment (rav′ish·mənt) n. The act of ravishing or the state of being ravished; especially, ecstasy; delight. [< OF *ravissement*]

raw (rô) adj. **1** Not changed or prepared by cooking; in its natural state; uncooked. **2** Not covered with whole skin; abraded. **3** Bleak; chilling: a *raw* wind. **4** In a natural state; crude; unprepared, as wool, drugs, etc.; also, untempered or without tone, as colors; unrefined; unfinished. **5** Newly done; fresh: *raw* paint, *raw* work. **6** Inexperienced; undisciplined: a *raw* recruit. **7** Unrefined; crude; off-color: a *raw* joke. **8** Unexposed: said of photographic film. —n. **1** A sore or abraded spot; a sensitive point. **2** The state of being raw, untamed, or unspoiled: nature in the *raw.* [OE *hrēaw*] —**raw′ly** adv. —**raw′ness** n.

raw-boned (rô′bōnd′) adj. Having large bones and little flesh; bony; gaunt.

Raw·bones (rô′bōnz′) Death.

raw deal *Slang* Harsh or unfair treatment in a transaction.

raw fibers Textile fibers in their natural state, as silk in the gum or cotton as it comes from the bale.

raw·hide (rô′hīd′) n. **1** A hide dressed without tanning. **2** A whip made of such hide.

raw·ish (rô′ish) adj. Somewhat raw.

raw material Unprocessed material (animal, vegetable, or mineral) needed and used in manufacturing, as contrasted with finished products.

raw milk Unpasteurized milk.

ray (rā) n. **1** A narrow beam of light or other line of propagation of any form of radiant energy; line of radiating force; radiation. **2** A manifestation of intellectual light. **3** One of several lines radiating from an object. **4** *Geom.* A straight line emerging from a center and unlimited in one direction only. **5** A streak or line; a straight row. **6** *Zool.* **a** One of the rods supporting the membrane of a fish's fin. **b** One of the radiating parts of a radiate animal, as a starfish. **7** *Bot.* **a** A ray-like flower. **b** One of the pedicels or flower stalks of an umbel. **8** *Physics* A stream of particles spontaneously emitted by a radioactive substance. **9** A trace or minute particle: Not a *ray* of life was present. —v.i. **1** To emit rays; shine. **2** To issue forth as rays; radiate. —v.t. **3** To send forth as rays. **4** To mark with rays or radiating lines. **5** To irradiate. **6** To treat with or expose to X-rays, etc. [< OF *rai* < L *radius.* Doublet of RADIUS.]

ra·yah (rä′yə, rī′ə) n. A non-Moslem inhabitant of Turkey: sometimes spelled *raia.* Also **ra′ya.** [< Arabic *ra′iyah* flock, herd]

ray·on (rā′on) n. A lustrous synthetic fiber variously made by chemical means from cellulose or with cellulose as a base, the viscous material being forced through fine spinnerets to produce filaments suitable for textiles and fabrics. [< F, ray; from its sheen]

raze (rāz) v.t. **razed, raz·ing 1** To level to the ground; tear down; demolish. **2** *Rare* To scrape or shave off. **3** *Obs.* To wound slightly; graze. See synonyms under DEMOLISH. Also spelled *rase.* ◆ Homophone: *raise.* [< F *raser* < L *rasum,* pp. of *radere* scrape]

ra·zee (rä·zē′) v.t. To make lower by cutting down, as a ship of war by removing the upper deck or decks; reduce; abridge. —n. A vessel that has been reduced by cutting away the upper deck or decks. [< F *rasé,* pp. of *raser* shave, raze]

ra·zor (rā′zər) n. A sharp cutting implement used for shaving off the beard or hair. —**safety razor** A razor provided with a guard or guards or the blade to prevent accidental gashing of the skin. [< OF *rasor* < *raser* scrape]

ra·zor·back (rā′zər·bak′) n. **1** A rorqual. **2** A lean-bodied, half-wild hog with long legs, common in the southeastern United States. **3** A hill with a sharp narrow ridge. —**ra′zor·backed′**adj.

ra·zor·billed **auk** (rā′zər·bild′) A small auk (*Alca torda*) of the North Atlantic, having a compressed and deeply furrowed bill. Also **ra′zor·bill′.**

razor clam A clam (genus *Ensis*) having a long, narrow, slightly curved shell resembling a razor. Also **ra′zor·shell′.clam.**

RAZOR-BILLED AUK

razor strop A strip, of specially prepared leather, canvas, or other material, upon which the blade of a razor is stroked to give it a fine edge.

razz (raz) n. *Slang* Raspberry (def. 3). —v.t. To heckle; deride. [< RASPBERRY]

raz·zi·a (raz′ē·ə) n. A foray or armed expedition, as for plunder or conquest. [< F < Arabic *ghāzīah* < *ghasw* war, battle]

raz·zle-daz·zle (raz′əl·daz′əl) n. *U.S. Slang* Anything bewildering and exciting; dazzling activity or performance [Varied reduplication of DAZZLE]

razz·ma·tazz (raz′mə·taz′) n. *U.S. Slang* **1** Razzle-dazzle. **2** Skill.

re[1] (rā) n. *Music* The second note of any major scale in solmization. [< L *re(sonare)* resound. See GAMUT.]

re[2] (rē) prep. Concerning; about; in the matter of: used in business letters: *re* your letter of the 6th instant. [< L, ablative of *res* thing]

Re (rā) See RA.

re- prefix **1** Back: *reduce* to lead back, *remit* to send back. **2** Again; anew; again and again: *regenerate. Re-* in this second sense is freely used in Modern English, as in the list of words below. It is hyphenated, in certain cases, to prevent confusion with a similarly spelled word having a different meaning (*re-treat* to treat again, *retreat* to go back), to prevent mispronunciation (*re-argue, re-urge*), and also in the coining of new words. Also, before vowels, sometimes *red-,* as

in *redeem.* [< L *re-, red-* back, again]

reach (rēch) v.t. **1** To stretch out or forth, as the hand or foot. **2** To present by means of or as by means of the outstretched hand; deliver; hand over. **3** To extend as far as; touch or grasp, as with the hand: Can you *reach* the top shelf? **4** To arrive at or come to by motion or progress; attain: When do we *reach* Miami? **5** To achieve communication with; gain access to. **6** To amount to; total. **7** To strike or hit, as with a blow or missile. —v.i. **8** To stretch the hand, foot, etc., out or forth. **9** To attempt to touch or grasp something: He *reached* for his wallet. **10** To have extent in space, time, amount, or influence: The ladder *reached* to the ceiling. **11** *Naut.* To sail on a tack with the wind on or forward of the beam. —n. **1** The act or power of reaching; also, the distance one is able to reach, as with the hand, an instrument, or missile, or by thought, influence, etc.; scope; range. **2** A point, position, or result attained or attainable. **3** An unbroken stretch, as of a stream; a vista or expanse. **4** A pole or bar connecting the rear axle, truck, or runners of a vehicle with some part at the forward end. **5** *Naut.* The sailing, or the distance sailed, by a vessel on one tack. [OE *ræcan.* Akin to G *reichen* reach]

Synonyms (verb): attain, gain, hit, land, make, strike, touch. To *reach,* in the sense here considered, is to come to by motion or progress. *Attain* is now oftenest used of abstract relations; as, to *attain* success. To *gain* is to *reach* or *attain* a thing eagerly sought; the wearied swimmer *reaches* or *gains* the shore. See ARRIVE, GET, MAKE[1], STRETCH.

reach·less (rēch′lis) adj. That cannot be reached; unattainable; lofty.

re·act (rē·akt′) v.i. **1** To act in response, as to a stimulus. **2** To act in a manner contrary to some preceding act; come into or tend toward a former state or an opposite state. **3** *Physics* To exert an opposite and equal force on an acting or impinging body: said of the body acted upon. **4** *Chem.* To exert mutual action, as substances undergoing chemical change. Compare RE-ACT.

re-act (rē·akt′) v.t. To act again.

re·ac·tion (rē·ak′shən) n. **1** Reverse or return action; tendency toward a former or reversed state of things; especially, a trend toward an earlier social, political, or economic policy or condition. **2** *Physiol.* Contrary action or reversed effects following a stimulus; a reflex action. **3** *Psychol.* The partial or total response made to any kind or degree of stimulation. **4** *Physics* In the second law of motion, the equal and opposite force exerted on an agent by the body acted upon. **5** *Chem.* The mutual action of substances subjected to chemical change, or some distinctive result of such action. **6** *Biol.* The effect upon any organism or any of its parts made by the introduction of any foreign substance for diagnostic or therapeutic purposes, or for testing, immunizing, etc. —**re·ac′tive**adj.

re·ac·tion·ar·y (rē·ak′shən·er′ē) adj. Of, relating to, favoring, or characterized by reaction. —n. pl. **·ar·ies** One who favors political or social reaction; a conservative. Also **re·ac′tion·ist.**

reaction engine An engine which obtains thrust by the expulsion of the hot gases of combustion to the rear; a jet engine.

reaction time *Physiol.* **1** The time required for a response to a sensory stimulus. **2** The time required for an electric current to act on a muscle.

re·ac·ti·vate (rē·ak′tə·vāt) v.t. **·vat·ed, ·vat·ing** To make active or effective again. —**re·ac′ti·va′tion** n.

re·ac·tive (rē·ak′tiv) adj. **1** Reacting, tending to react, or resulting from reaction. **2** Responsive to a stimulus.

re·ac·tor (rē·ak′tər) n. **1** One who or that which reacts. **2** *Electr.* A device for introducing reactance into a circuit, as for starting motors, controlling current, and the like. **3** *Biol.* An animal or person giving a positive reaction to a specified bacteriological or medical test. **4** *Physics* Any of variously designed assemblies for the initiation and control of nuclear fission, consisting essentially of reserves of fissionable material used as fuel, moderators to check the rate of nuclear reactions, reflectors, and auxiliary structures, equipment, shielding, etc.: also called *pile*.

read (rēd) *v.* **read** (red), **read·ing** (rē′ding) *v.t.* **1** To apprehend the meaning of (a book, writing, etc.) by perceiving the form and relation of the printed or written characters. **2** To utter aloud (something printed or written). **3** To understand the significance of as if by reading: to *read* the sky. **4** To apprehend the meaning of something printed or written in (a foreign language). **5** To make a study of; also, to obtain knowledge of: to *read* law. **6** To discover the true nature of (a person, character, etc.) by observation or scrutiny. **7** To interpret (something read) in a specified manner. **8** To take as the meaning of something read. **9** To have or exhibit as the wording: The passage *reads* "principal," not "principle." **10** To indicate or register: The meter *reads* zero. **11** To bring in to a specified condition by reading: I *read* myself to sleep. —*v.i.* **12** To apprehend the characters of a book, musical score, etc. **13** To utter aloud the words or contents of a book, etc. **14** To gain information by reading: with *of* or *about*. **15** To learn by means of books; study. **16** To have a specified wording: The contract *reads* as follows. **17** To admit of being read in a specified manner. **18** To give a public reading or recital. —**to read between the lines** To perceive or infer what is not expressed or obvious, as a hidden or true meaning, implication, or motive. —**to read into** To discern (implicit meanings or implications) in a statement or position: Don't *read* anything *into* my decision not to run for office. —**to read out** To expel from a religious body, political party, etc., by proclamation or concerted action. —**to read up** (or **up on**) To learn by reading. —*adj.* (red) Informed by books or reading; acquainted with books or literature: well *read*. —*n.* (rēd) *Colloq.* A reading; a period spent in reading. [OE *rædan* advise, read]

read·a·ble (rē′də·bəl) *adj.* **1** Legible. **2** Easy and pleasant to read. —**read′a·bil′i·ty, read′a·ble·ness** *n.* —**read′a·bly** *adv.*

read·er (rē′dər) *n.* **1** One who reads; specifically, a professional reciter or elocutionist. **2** One who reads and criticizes manuscripts offered to publishers. **3** A proofreader. **4** A layman authorized to read the lesson in church services. **5** A textbook containing matter for exercises in reading. **6** *Brit.* A university or college lecturer.

read·er·ship (rē′dər·ship) *n.* The estimated number of people who read a particular author, publication, or kind of reading material.

read·i·ly (red′ə·lē) *adv.* **1** In a ready manner; promptly; easily. **2** Willingly.

read·i·ness (red′i·nis) *n.* **1** The quality or state of being ready. **2** The quality of being quick or prompt; facility; aptitude. **3** A disposition for prompt compliance; willingness.

read·ing (rē′ding) *n.* **1** The act, practice or art of reading, in any sense of the verb; a public recital; the act of reading formally to a legislative body a bill, etc., proposed for adoption. **2** Literary research; study; scholarship. **3** Matter which is read or is designed to be read. **4** The indication of a graduated instrument, as a thermometer. **5** The form in which any passage or word appears in any copy of a work. **6** An interpretation, as of a riddle, or of any latent and hidden meaning; delineation; rendering. See synonyms under EDUCATION. —*adj.* Pertaining to or suitable for reading.

reading desk A desk adapted to hold books, manuscripts, etc., for a speaker or reader, as in church services.

reading room A room provided with periodicals, books, etc., in which the public, or certain classes of readers, may read.

read·just (rē′ə·just′) *v.t.* & *v.i.* To adjust again or anew; rearrange. —**read′just′er** *n.*

READING DESK

read·just·ment (rē′ə·just′mənt) *n.* **1** The act or process of readjusting, or the state of being readjusted. **2** The reorganization of a com-

pany or corporation, usually voluntary.

re·ad·mit (rē′əd·mit′) *v.t.* **·nit·ted, ·mit·ting** To admit again; allow to enter again. —**re′ad·mis′sion, re′ad·mit′tance** *n.*

read·out (rēd′out′) *n.* The information displayed from computer memory in readable form, or transcribed therefrom.

read·y (red′ē) *adj.* **read·i·er, read·i·est 1** Prepared for use or action. **2** Prepared in mind; willing. **3** Likely or liable: with *to*: *ready* to sink. **4** Quick to act, follow, occur, or appear; prompt. **5** At hand; immediately available; convenient; handy. **6** Designating the standard position in which a rifle is held just before aiming. **7** Quick to understand; alert; quick; facile: a *ready* wit. **8** *Obs.* Here; present: used in answering a roll call. See synonyms under ACTIVE, ALERT, GOOD, RIPE[1]. —*n.* **1** In the manual of arms, the position in which a rifle is held before aiming, the left hand at the balance, the right hand at the small of the stock. **2** *Slang* Cash: with *the*. —*v.t.* **read·ied, read·y·ing** To make ready; prepare. [OE *ræde, geræde*]

read·y-made (red′ē·mād′) *adj.* **1** Not made to order; prepared or kept on hand for general demand: said especially of clothing. **2** Prepared beforehand; not impromptu. **3** Prepared by someone else. **4** Borrowed; lacking in originality; inferior.

ready money Money in hand; cash.

read·y-wit·ted (red′ē·wit′id) *adj.* Quick to apprehend or learn; alert.

Rea·gan (rā′gən), **Ronald,** 1911–, 40th president of the United States 1981–

re·a·gent (rē·ā′jənt) *n.* **1** One who or that which reacts; a source of reflex action. **2** *Chem.* Any substance used to ascertain the nature or composition of another by means of their mutual chemical action. **3** *Psychol.* The subject of an experiment; particularly, one who or that which reacts to a stimulus. [< RE- + AGENT]

re·al[1] (rē′əl, rēl) *adj.* **1** Having existence or actuality as a thing or state; not imaginary: a *real* event. **2** Being in accordance with appearance or claim; genuine; not artificial or counterfeit. **3** Representing the true or actual, as opposed to the apparent or ostensible: the *real* reason. **4** Unaffected; unpretentious: a *real* person. **5** *Philos.* Having actual existence, and not merely possible, apparent, or imaginary. **6** *Law* Of, pertaining to, or consisting of land and tenements: *real* property, as contrasted with personal property. **b** Pertaining to things, as distinguished from persons. —*n.* That which is real; a real thing. —*adv. Colloq.* Very; extremely: to be *real* glad. [< OF < Med. L *realis* < L *res* thing] —**re′al·ness** *n.*

re·al[2] (rē′əl, *Sp.* rä·äl′) *n.* **1** *pl.* **re·als** or **re·a·les** (rä·ä′lās) A small silver coin of several Spanish countries, including Mexico, and formerly current in the United States, where it was called a *bit*, and had the value of 12½ cents. **2** *pl.* **reis** (rās) A former Portuguese and Brazilian coin; one thousandth of a milreis. [< Sp., lit., royal < L *regalis*]

real estate Land, including whatever is made part of or attached to it by man or nature, as trees, houses, etc. Also **real property.**

re·al·i·a (rē·ā′lē·ə) *n. pl.* Real or actual objects used in teaching.

real image See under IMAGE.

re·al·ism (rē′əl·iz′əm) *n.* **1** In literature and art, the principle of depicting persons and scenes as they exist, without any attempt at idealization. **2** The tendency to be concerned solely with reality, as opposed to ideals; specifically, the tendency to think and act in the light of actuality, disregarding idealistic motives. **3** *Philos.* **a** The doctrine that universals (abstract concepts) have objective existence and are more real than things: opposed to *nominalism*. Compare CONCEPTUALISM. **b** The doctrine that things have reality apart from the conscious perception of them: opposed to *idealism*. —**re′al·is′tic** *adj.* —**re′al·is′ti·cal·ly** *adv.*

re·al·ist (rē′əl·ist) *n.* **1** An adherent of the doctrine of realism in any of its forms, as applied in literature, art, or philosophy. **2** One who is devoted to what is real rather than imaginary or ideal.

re·al·i·ty (rē·al′ə·tē) *n. pl.* **·ties 1** The fact, state, condition, or quality of being real or genuine. **2** That which is real; an actual person, thing, situation, or event; in the aggregate, the sum of real things; also, the substance that lies back of form and external appearances. **3** That which exists, as contrasted with what is fictitious; that which

is objective, not merely an idea. **4** *Philos.* The absolute; that which is self-existent; the ultimate, as contrasted with phenomena or the apparent. See synonyms under VERACITY. [< Med. L *realitas, -tatis* < *realis* real]

re·al·i·za·tion (rē′əl·i·zā′shən) *n.* **1** The act of realizing. **2** The state of being realized. **3** A product or instance of realizing. **4** The conversion into fact or action (of plans, ambitions, fears, etc.).

re·al·ize (rē′əl·īz) *v.* **·ized, ·iz·ing** *v.t.* **1** To understand or appreciate fully. **2** To make real or concrete. **3** To cause to appear real. **4** To obtain as a profit or return. **5** To obtain money in return for: He *realized* his holdings for a profit. **6** To bring as a profit or return: said of property. —*v.i.* **7** To sell property for cash. See synonyms under ACCOMPLISH, EFFECT, GAIN[1], KNOW. —**re′al·iz′a·ble** *adj.* —**re′al·iz′er** *n.*

re·al·iz·ing (rē′əl·ī′zing) *adj.* **1** Conceiving of as real; comprehending. **2** Able to visualize vividly. **3** Converting (hopes, plans, etc.) into fact, or (assets) into money.

re·al·ly (rē′ə·lē, rē′lē) *adv.* In reality; in point of fact; as a matter of fact; actually; indeed: also used without precise meaning, for emphasis.

realm (relm) *n.* **1** A kingdom. **2** The domain or jurisdiction of any power or influence: the *realm* of imagination. **3** A primary division of the globe with reference to its fauna; a zoogeographical area larger than a region; also, as used by some authors, a division equivalent to a region. [< OF *realme* < L *regalis* royal. See REGAL.]

Re·al·tor (rē′əl·tər, -tôr) *n.* A person engaged in the real estate business, as a broker, appraiser, manager, etc., who is a member of the National Association of Realtors: a trade name.

re·al·ty (rē′əl·tē) *n. pl.* **·ties** *Law* Real estate or real property in any form. [< REAL[1] (def. 6) + -TY[1]]

real wages Wages evaluated in terms of purchasing power, as contrasted with *nominal wages*, evaluated in money.

ream[1] (rēm) *n.* **1** Twenty quires of paper; properly, 480 sheets (a **short ream**), but often 500 sheets (a **long ream**) or, in a **printer's** or **perfect ream**, 516 sheets. **2** *pl. Colloq.* A prodigious amount of printed, written, or spoken material: *reams* of footnotes. [< OF *reyme* < Sp. *resma* < Arabic *rizmah* packet < *raxama* pack together]

ream[2] (rēm) *v.t.* **1** To increase the size of (a hole). **2** To enlarge or taper (a hole) with a rotating cutter or reamer. **3** To turn or roll over the edge of: to *ream* a cartridge shell. **4** To get rid of (a defect) by reaming. [OE *rēman* enlarge, make room. Akin to ROOM.]

ream·er (rē′mər) *n.* **1** one who or that which reams. **2** A finishing tool with a rotating cutting edge for reaming: sometimes spelled *rimmer*. **3** A device with a ridged cone for extracting juice from citrus fruits.

re·an·i·mate (rē·an′ə·māt) *v.t.* **·mat·ed, ·mat·ing 1** To bring back to life; resuscitate. **2** To revive; encourage. —**re′an·i·ma′tion** *n.*

REAMERS
a. Adjustable.
b. Square.
c. Center.
d. Rose-shell.
e. Roughening taper.
f. Root reamer.

reap (rēp) *v.t.* **1** To cut or gather (grain); harvest or gather (a fruit or product) with a scythe, reaper, or the like. **2** To cut the growth from or gather the fruit of, as a field. **3** To obtain as the result of action or effort; receive as a return or result. —*v.i.* **4** To harvest grain, etc. **5** To receive a return or result. See synonyms under GAIN[1] [OE *repan*] —**reap′a·ble** *adj.* —**reap′ing** *n.*

reap·er (rē′pər) *n.* **1** One who reaps. **2** A machine for harvesting standing grain; a reaping machine.

reaping machine A machine for harvesting standing grain. It usually consists of a reciprocating cutter resembling that of a mowing machine, a platform or table on which the cut grain falls, and a dropper which is dropped to deposit the bundles of grain. In addition, it often has a reel for bending the grain toward the cutter, or a raking mechanism for pressing the grain down on the table and sweeping it off in bundles, and a binding mechanism. Also called *harvester*.

rear[1] (rir) *n.* **1** The hinder or hindmost part. **2** A place or position at the back of or behind any person or thing. **3** That division of a military force which is last or farthest from the front: opposed to *van*. —*adj.* Being in the rear; last; hindmost. [Aphetic form of ARREAR]

rear[2] (rir) *v.t.* **1** To lift upright; raise; elevate. **2** To build; erect. **3** To care for and bring to maturity. **4** To breed or grow. —*v.i.* **5** To rise upon its hind legs, as a horse. **6** To rise high; tower: The mountain *rears* above the forest. See synonyms under RAISE. [OE *rǣran* set upright, causative of *risan* rise. Akin to ON *reisa* raise.] — **rear′er** *n.*

rear admiral See under ADMIRAL.

rear-end (rir′end′) *n.* In automobiles, the after part of the drive train, consisting of the differential gears and rear axles with their housings and the driving wheels. — *adj.* Of or pertaining to the rear-end of an automobile.

rear guard A body of troops to protect the rear of an army. [<AF *reregard*, OF *rereguarde*. Doublet of REARWARD[2].]

rear-horse (rir′hôrs′) *n.* A mantis. [From its habit of rearing when touched]

re-arm (rē·ärm′) *v.t. & v.i.* **1** To arm again. **2** To arm with more modern weapons. — **re·ar′ma·ment** *n.*

rear-most (rir′mōst′) *adj.* Coming or stationed last.

rear-mouse (rir′mous′) See REREMOUSE.

rear sight The sight of a gun which is nearest the breech.

rear-view mirror (rir′vyōō′) In motor vehicles, a mirror so placed in front of the driver that he can see the reflection of the road and vehicles behind. Also **rear′-vi′sion mirror.**

rear-ward (rir′wərd) *adj.* Coming last or toward the rear; hindward. — *adv.* Toward or at the rear; backward. Also **rear′wards.** — *n.* Hindward position; the rear; end.

rea-son (rē′zən) *n.* **1** That which is thought or alleged as the basis or ground for any opinion, determination, or action; something adduced or adapted to influence the mind in determining or acting; proof; argument; motive; principle. **2** That which explains or accounts for any fact, act, proceeding, or event; loosely, an efficient or final cause, or a condition. **3** The entire mental or rational nature of man, as distinguished from the intelligence of the brute; the mind; in a more limited sense, the purely intellectual faculties. **4** Specifically, the normal exercise of the rational faculties. **5** That which is in conformity to general opinion; common sense: The anarchist was brought to *reason*. **6** A logical ground for thinking; an antecedent; also, the premise or premises of an argument, generally the minor premise. **7** That which is right or befitting; just procedure; a reasonable act or proposition. **8** Intuition. — *v.i.* **1** To think logically; obtain inferences or conclusions from known or presumed facts. **2** To talk or argue logically. — *v.t.* **3** To think out carefully and logically; analyze: with *out*. **4** To influence by means of reason; persuade or dissuade. **5** To argue; debate. See synonyms under ARGUE, DISPUTE. [<OF *raison* <L *ratio, -onis* <*ratus*, pp. of *reri* reckon. Doublet of RATION, RATIO.]

Synonyms (noun): account, aim, argument, cause, consideration, design, end, ground, motive, object, principle, purpose. While the *cause* of any event, act, or fact, as commonly understood, is the power that makes it to be, the *reason* of or for it is the explanation given by the human mind; but *reason* is often used as equivalent to *cause*, especially in the sense of *final cause*. In the statement of any reasoning, the *argument* may be an entire syllogism, or the premises considered together apart from the conclusion, or in logical strictness the middle term only by which the particular conclusion is connected with the general statement. But when the reasoning is not in strict logical form, the middle term following the conclusion is called the *reason*; thus in the statement "All tyrants deserve death; Caesar was a tyrant; therefore Caesar deserved death," "Caesar was a tyrant" would in the strictest sense be called the *argument*; but if

we say "Caesar deserved death because he was a tyrant," the latter clause would be termed the *reason*. See CAUSE, INTELLECT, MIND, REASONING, UNDERSTANDING, WISDOM. Compare BECAUSE.

rea-son-a-ble (rē′zən·ə·bəl) *adj.* **1** Conformable to reason; sensible. **2** Having the faculty of reason; rational. **3** Governed by reason in acting or thinking. **4** Moderate, as in price; fair. See synonyms under JUST, LIKELY, PROBABLE, RATIONAL, WISE[1]. [<OF *raisonable*; after L *rationabilis*] — **rea′son·a·bil′i·ty, rea′son·a·ble·ness** *n.* — **rea′son·a·bly** *adv.*

rea-soned (rē′zənd) *adj.* Founded upon or characterized by reason; premeditated or studied.

rea-son-ing (rē′zən·ing) *n.* The act or process of the mind by which from propositions known or assumed new propositions are reached; argumentation; also, the reasons, proofs, or arguments employed in such process.

Synonyms: argument, argumentation, debate, ratiocination. *Argumentation* and *debate* always suppose two parties alleging reasons for and against a proposition. *Reasoning* may be the act of one alone, as it is simply the orderly setting forth of reasons, whether for the instruction of inquirers, the confuting of opponents, or the clear establishment of truth for oneself. *Reasoning* may be either deductive or inductive. *Argument* or *argumentation* was formerly used of deductive *reasoning* only. With the rise of the inductive philosophy these words have come to be applied to inductive processes also; but while *reasoning* may be informal or even unconscious, *argument* and *argumentation* strictly imply logical form. Compare INTELLECT, REASON.

re-as-sur-ance (rē′ə·shŏŏr′əns) *n.* **1** The act of reassuring; repeated assurance. **2** Restored confidence. **3** Reinsurance.

re-as-sure (rē′ə·shŏŏr′) *v.t.* **-sured, -sur-ing** **1** To restore to courage or confidence. **2** To assure again. **3** To reinsure. See synonyms under ENCOURAGE. — **re′as·sur′ing** *adj.* — **re′as·sur′ing·ly** *adv.*

re-bate[1] (rē′bāt, ri·bāt′) *v.t.* **-bat-ed, -bat-ing** **1** To allow as a deduction. **2** To make a deduction from. **3** *Obs.* To blunt, as a sharp edge. — *n.* A deduction from a gross amount; discount: also **re·bate′ment.** [<OF *rabattre* beat down <*re-* again + *abattre*. See ABATE.] — **re′bat·er** *n.*

re-bate[2] (rē′bāt, rab′it) See RABBET.

re-ba-to (re·bä′tō) *n. pl.* **-tos** A collar turned down and falling over the shoulders: worn by both sexes in the 15th and 16th centuries. Also spelled *rabato*. [<MF *rabat* <*rabattre* beat down. See REBATE.]

re-bec (rē′bek) *n.* The earliest form of the violin. Also **re′beck.** [<F alter. of OF *rebebe* <Arabic *rabāb*]

MEDIEVAL THREE-STRING REBEC

re-bel (ri·bel′) *v.i.* **-belled, -bel-ling** **1** To rise in armed resistance against the established government or ruler of one's land. **2** To resist any authority or established usage. **3** To react with violent aversion: usually with *at*. — **reb·el** (reb′əl) *n.* One who rebels; specifically, one who espoused the American Revolution, or the cause of the South during the Civil War. — *adj.* Rebellious; refractory. [<OF *rebeller* <L *rebellare* make war again <*re-* again + *bellare* make war <*bellum* war. Doublet of REVEL.]

reb-el-dom (reb′əl·dəm) *n.* **1** The domain of rebels; specifically, the Confederate States during the Civil War; also, rebels collectively. **2** Rebellious behavior.

re-bel-lion (ri·bel′yən) *n.* **1** The act of rebelling. **2** Organized resistance to a government or to any lawful authority. See synonyms under REVOLUTION. — **the Rebellion** The American Civil War. [<OF <L *rebellio, -onis*]

re-bel-lious (ri·bel′yəs) *adj.* **1** Being in a state

of rebellion; insubordinate. **2** Of or pertaining to a rebel or rebellion. **3** Resisting control; refractory: *rebellious* curls. — **re·bel′lious·ly** *adv.* — **re·bel′lious·ness** *n.*

Synonyms: contumacious, disobedient, insubordinate, intractable, mutinous, refractory, seditious, uncontrollable, ungovernable, unmanageable. *Ungovernable* applies to that which successfully defies authority and power; *unmanageable* to that which resists the utmost exercise of skill or of skill and power combined; *rebellious* to that which is defiant of authority, whether successfully or unsuccessfully; *seditious* to that which partakes of or tends to excite a *rebellious* spirit, *seditious* suggesting more of covert plan, scheming, or conspiracy, *rebellious* more of overt act or open violence. While the *unmanageable* or *ungovernable* defies control, the *rebellious* or *seditious* may be forced to submission. *Insubordinate* applies to the disposition to resist and resent control as such; *mutinous*, to open defiance of authority, especially in the army, navy, or merchant marine. A *contumacious* act or spirit is contemptuous as well as defiant. See RESTIVE, TURBULENT. Compare OBSTINATE, REVOLUTION. *Antonyms*: compliant, controllable, deferential, docile, dutiful, manageable, obedient, submissive, subservient, tractable, yielding.

re-birth (rē·bûrth′, rē′bûrth′) *n.* **1** A new birth. **2** A revival or renaissance.

re-bo-ant (reb′ō·ənt) *adj.* Bellowing back; resounding loudly. [<L *reboans, -antis*, ppr. of *reboare* resound <*re-* again + *boare* bellow. Ult. imit.]

re-born (rē·bôrn′) *adj.* Born again; having undergone emotional or mental regeneration; renascent.

re-bound (ri·bound′) *v.i.* To bound back; recoil. — *v.t.* To cause to rebound. — *n.* (rē′bound′, ri·bound′) **1** Recoil; elasticity. **2** Something which rebounds or resounds; an echo. **3** Reaction of feeling or emotion after a disappointment: to fall in love on the *rebound*. [<F *rebondir* <*re-* back + *bondir* bound]

re-broad-cast (rē·brôd′kast′, -käst′) *v.t.* **-cast** or **-cast-ed, -cast-ing** **1** To broadcast (the same program) more than once from the same station. **2** To broadcast (a program received from another station). — *n.* A program so transmitted.

re-buff (ri·buf′) *v.t.* **1** To reject or refuse abruptly or rudely. **2** To drive or beat back; repel; repulse. — *n.* **1** A sudden repulse; curt denial. **2** A sudden check; defeat. **3** A beating back. [<MF *rebuffer* <Ital. *ributtare*, metathetic alter. of *baruffare* <OHG *biroufan* scuffle]

re-buke (ri·byōōk′) *v.t.* **-buked, -buk-ing** **1** To reprove sharply; reprimand. **2** *Obs.* To check or restrain by a command. See synonyms under ADMONISH, BLAME, REPROVE. — *n.* A strong and authoritative expression of disapproval. See synonyms under ANIMADVERSION, REPROOF. [<AF *rebuker*, OF *rebuchier* <*re-* back + *bucher* beat] — **re·buk′a·ble** *adj.*

re-bus (rē′bəs) *n.* A puzzle representing a word, phrase, or sentence by letters, numerals, pictures, etc., often with pictures of objects whose names have the same sounds as the words represented. [<L, ablative pl. of *res* thing]

re-but (ri·but′) *v.t.* **-but-ted, -but-ting** **1** *Law* To overthrow by contrary evidence; contradict by countervailing proof; disprove; refute. **2** *Obs.* To push or drive back. [<OF *rebouter* push back <*re-* back + *bouter, boter*. See BUTT[1].]

re-but-tal (ri·but′l) *n.* The act of rebutting; refutation.

re-cal-ci-trant (ri·kal′sə·trənt) *adj.* Not complying; obstinate; rebellious; refractory. — *n.* One who is recalcitrant. [<L *recalcitrans, -antis*, ppr. of *recalcitrare* kick back <*re-* back + *calcitrare* kick <*calx, calcis* heel] — **re·cal′ci·trance, re·cal′ci·tran·cy** *n.*

re-cal-ci-trate (ri·kal′sə·trāt) *v.i.* **-trat-ed, -trat-ing** To refuse compliance or submission; be recalcitrant. [<L *recalcitratus*, pp. of *recalcitrare*. See RECALCITRANT.] — **re·cal′ci·tra′tion** *n.*

re-ca-lesce (rē′kə·les′) *v.i.* **-lesced, -lesc-ing** To grow hot again; specifically, in physics, to exhibit recalescence. [<L *recalescere* <*re-* again + *calescere* grow warm, inceptive of *calere* be warm]

re·ca·les·cence (rē'kə·les'əns) n. 1 A glowing again. 2 *Physics* A phenomenon peculiar to heated iron or steel of glowing more brightly when certain temperatures are reached in the process of gradual cooling from a state of high incandescence. [< L *recalescens*, ppr. of *recalescere*. See RECALESCE.] — **re'ca·les'cent** adj.

re·call (ri·kôl') v.t. 1 To call back; order or summon to return. 2 To summon back in awareness or attention. 3 To recollect; remember. 4 To take back; revoke; countermand. 5 *Poetic* To revive; restore. See synonyms under REMEMBER, RENOUNCE. — n. (ri·kôl', rē'kôl') 1 A calling back or to mind. 2 A signal to call back soldiers, etc., as by a bugle call, the display of a flag, etc. 3 Revocation, as of an order. 4 In certain States, a system whereby public officials may be removed from office by popular vote.

re·cant (ri·kant') v.t. To withdraw formally one's belief in (something previously believed or maintained). — v.i. To disavow an opinion or belief previously held. [< L *recantare* < *re-* again + *cantare* sing, freq. of *canere* sing] — **re·can·ta·tion** (rē'kan·tā'shən) n. — **re·cant'er** n.

Synonyms: abandon, abjure, deny, disavow, discard, disclaim, disown, forswear, recall, renounce, repudiate, retract, revoke. To *recant* is to *deny* formally and publicly some opinion or statement, especially in religion, that one has held or advocated. *Abjure* is etymologically the exact equivalent of the Saxon *forswear*, signifying to put away formally and under oath, as an error, heresy, or evil practice, or a condemned and detested person. A man *recants* his belief, *abjures* or *renounces* his allegiance, *repudiates* another's claim, *renounces* his own, *retracts* a false statement. A person may *deny, disavow, disclaim, disown* what has been truly or falsely imputed to him or supposed to be his. He may *deny* his signature, *disavow* the act of his agent, *disown* his child; he may *repudiate* either a just claim or a base suggestion. Compare ABANDON, RENOUNCE.

re·cap (rē'kap', rē·kap') v.t. **·capped, ·cap·ping** To reprocess (an automobile tire) by vulcanizing new rubber onto the surface which comes into contact with the road. — n. (rē'kap') A tire which has been so treated. Also *retread*. [RE- + CAP]

re·cap·i·tal·ize (rē·kap'ə·təl·īz') v.t. **·ized, ·iz·ing** To capitalize again or differently. — **re·cap'i·tal·i·za'tion** n.

re·ca·pit·u·late (rē'kə·pich'ŏŏ·lāt') v.t. & v.i. **·lat·ed, ·lat·ing** To review briefly; sum up. [< LL *recapitulare* < *re-* again + *capitulare*. See CAPITULATE.]

re·ca·pit·u·la·to·ry (rē'kə·pich'ŏŏ·lə·tôr'ē, -tō'rē) adj. Containing or of the nature of recapitulation. Also **re'ca·pit'u·la'tive** (-lā'tiv).

re·cap·ture (rē·kap'chər) v.t. **·tured, ·tur·ing** 1 To capture again; obtain by recapture. 2 To recall; remember. — n. 1 The act of retaking; especially, in war, the forcible recovery of booty or goods. 2 A prize retaken; anything recaptured. 3 The taking by the public of the earnings of a public service corporation over and above a stated profit.

re·cast (rē·kast', -käst') v.t. **·cast, ·cast·ing** 1 To form anew; cast again. 2 To fashion anew by changing style, arrangement, etc., as a discourse. 3 To calculate anew. — n. (rē'kast', -käst') Something which has been recast.

re·cede (ri·sēd') v.i. **·ced·ed, ·ced·ing** 1 To move back; withdraw, as flood waters. 2 To withdraw, as from an assertion, position, agreement, etc. 3 To slope backward: a *receding* forehead. 4 To become more distant; incline away. [< L *recedere* < *re-* back + *cedere* go]

re–cede (rē·sēd') v.t. **·ced·ed, ·ced·ing** To cede back; grant or yield to a former owner. [< RE- + CEDE]

re·ceipt (ri·sēt') n. 1 The act or state of receiving anything: to be in *receipt* of good news. 2 That which is received: usually in the plural: cash *receipts*. 3 A written acknowledgment of the payment of money, of the delivery of goods, etc. 4 A recipe. — v.t. 1 To give a receipt for the payment of. 2 To write acknowledgment of payment on, as a bill. — v.i. 3 To give a receipt, as for money paid. [< OF *recete* < L *recepta*, fem. of *receptus*, pp. of *recipere* RECEIVE; refashioned after Latin]

re·ceiv·a·ble (ri·sē'və·bəl) adj. 1 Capable of being received; fit to be received, as legal tender. 2 Maturing for payment: said of a

bill.

re·ceiv·a·bles (ri·sē'və·bəlz) n. pl. Outstanding accounts listed among the assets of a business.

re·ceive (ri·sēv') v. **·ceived, ·ceiv·ing** v.t. 1 To take into one's hand or possession (something given, offered, delivered, etc.); acquire; accept. 2 To gain knowledge or information of: He *received* the news at breakfast. 3 To take from another by hearing or listening: The king *received* his oath of fealty. 4 To bear; support: These columns *receive* the weight of the building. 5 To experience; meet with: to *receive* abuse. 6 To undergo; suffer: He *received* a wound in his arm. 7 To intercept or encounter the force of (a blow, etc.). 8 To contain; hold. 9 To allow entrance to; admit to one's presence; greet. 10 To perceive mentally; understand. 11 To accept as true, proven, authoritative, etc. — v.i. 12 To be a recipient; get, obtain, or acquire something from some other person or source. 13 To welcome visitors or callers. 14 To partake of the Eucharist. 15 *Telecom.* To convert incoming radio waves into intelligible sounds or shapes, as a radio or television receiving set. See synonyms under ACCOMMODATE, GET, OBTAIN. [< OF *receivre* < L *recipere* < *re-* back + *capere* take]

Received Standard The form of educated English identified with that spoken at the English public schools and the universities of Oxford and Cambridge.

re·ceiv·er (ri·sē'vər) n. 1 One who receives; a recipient. 2 An official assigned to receive money due. 3 *Law* A person appointed by a court to take into his custody, control, and management the property or funds of another pending judicial action concerning them. 4 One who buys or receives stolen or embezzled goods, knowing them to be stolen. 5 Something which receives; a receptacle. 6 A vessel considered as a receptacle for a gas or fluid, as a jar for receiving and condensing a fluid that has been distilled. 7 A bolthead. 8 *Telecom.* An instrument in an electric circuit serving to receive and reproduce signals transmitted from another part of the circuit: a telephone *receiver*. 9 A radio or television receiving set.

re·ceiv·er·ship (ri·sē'vər·ship) n. 1 The office and functions pertaining to a receiver under appointment of a court. 2 *Law* The state of being in the hands of a receiver.

receiving set An apparatus for the reception of radio or television signals.

re·cen·sion (ri·sen'shən) n. 1 A critical revision of the text of a book; also, the edition so revised. 2 A review; critique. [< L *recensio, -onis* enumeration < *recensere* examine, survey < *re-* thoroughly + *censere* estimate, value]

re·cent (rē'sənt) adj. Pertaining to, or formed, developed, or created in time not long past; modern; fresh; new. See synonyms under FRESH, MODERN, NEW. [< OF < L *recens, -entis*] — **re'cent·ly** adv. — **re'cen·cy, re'cent·ness** n.

re·cep·ta·cle (ri·sep'tə·kəl) n. 1 Anything that serves to contain or hold other things. 2 *Bot.* The base to which the parts of the flower, fruit, or seeds are fixed. 3 An outlet (def. 3). [< OF < L *receptaculum* < *receptare*, freq. of *recipere* RECEIVE]

re·cep·tion (ri·sep'shən) n. 1 The act of receiving, or the state of being received; receipt. 2 A formal social entertainment of guests: a wedding *reception*; also, the manner of receiving a person or persons: a warm *reception*. 3 Mental acceptance, as of a proposition. 4 In radio and television, the act or process of receiving or, especially, the quality of reproduction achieved: This radio gives very poor *reception*. [< OF < L *receptio, -onis* < *receptus*, pp. of *recipere* RECEIVE]

re·cep·tion·ist (ri·sep'shən·ist) n. A person employed to receive callers, provide information, and the like, at the entrance to an office.

reception room 1 A room for callers in a private house. 2 A waiting room in a hospital, or adjoining a doctor's, dentist's, or lawyer's office. 3 A large room for a formal reception.

re·cep·tive (ri·sep'tiv) adj. Able or inclined to receive, as truths or impressions; able to take in or hold. [< OF *receptif* < Med. L *receptivus* < L *recipere* RECEIVE] — **re·cep'tive·ly** adv. — **re·cep·tiv·i·ty** (rē'sep·tiv'ə·tē), **re·cep'tive·ness** n.

re·cess (ri·ses', rē'ses; *for def. 2, usually* rē'ses) n. 1 A depression or indentation in any otherwise continuous line, especially in a wall; niche; alcove. 2 A time of cessation from employment or occupation: The school took a *recess*. 3 *Usually pl.* A quiet and secluded spot; withdrawn or inner place: the *recesses* of the mind. 4 *Anat. & Bot.* A depression or cavity. — v. (ri·ses') v.t. 1 To place in or as in a recess. 2 To make a recess in, as a wall. 3 To interrupt for a recess: to *recess* a court. — v.i. 4 To take a recess. [< L *recessus*, pp. of *recedere*. See RECEDE[1].]

re·ces·sion (ri·sesh'ən) n. 1 The act of receding; a withdrawal. 2 The procession of the clergy, choir, etc., as they leave the chancel after a church service. 3 An economic setback in commercial and industrial activity; especially, one occurring as a downward turn during a period of generally rising prosperity; a slight depression. [< L *recessio, -onis* < *recedere*. See RECEDE[1].]

re·ces·sion (rē·sesh'ən) n. The act of ceding again; a giving back.

re·ces·sion·al (ri·sesh'ən·əl) adj. Of or pertaining to recession. — n. A hymn sung as the choir or clergy leave the chancel after service: also **recessional hymn**.

re·ces·sive (ri·ses'iv) adj. 1 Having a tendency to recede or go back; receding. 2 Failing to come into expression. 3 *Genetics* Designating that one of a pair of contrasted allelomorphic characters which is suppressed in a hybrid offspring when both are present: opposed to *dominant*. — n. *Genetics* 1 A hybrid which carries and transmits a character suppressed by the corresponding dominant character. 2 The suppressed character. — **re·ces'sive·ly** adv.

re·cid·i·vist (rə·sid'ə·vist) n. 1 Anyone who relapses into a former state or condition. 2 A confirmed criminal; in the United States, one committed to prison for a second term. [< F *récidiviste* < L *recidivus* relapsing < *cidere* < *re-* back + *cadere* fall] — **re·cid'i·vism, rec·i·div·i·ty** (res'ə·div'ə·tē) n. — **re·cid'i·vis'tic** adj.

re·cid·i·vous (rə·sid'ə·vəs) adj. Liable to backslide.

rec·i·pe (res'ə·pē) n. 1 A formula or list of ingredients of a mixture, giving the exact proportions together with proper directions for compounding, cooking, etc. 2 A medical prescription: so called from its opening word: usually abbreviated to ℞. 3 A method prescribed for attaining a desired result. [< L, take, imperative of *recipere*. See RECEIVE.]

re·cip·i·ence (ri·sip'ē·əns) n. 1 The process or act of receiving. 2 Receptivity. Also **re·cip'i·en·cy**.

re·cip·i·ent (ri·sip'ē·ənt) adj. Receiving or ready to receive; receptive. — n. One who or that which receives; one who accepts a gift or favor. [< L *recipiens, -entis*, ppr. of *recipere* RECEIVE]

re·cip·ro·cal (ri·sip'rə·kəl) adj. 1 Done or given by each of two to the other; mutual. 2 Mutually interchangeable. 3 Alternating; moving to and fro. 4 So related, as two concepts, that if the first determines the second, then the second determines the first. 5 Expressive of mutual relationship or action: used in connection with certain pronouns and verbs or their meaning. 6 *Math.* Of or pertaining to a fraction the numerator and denominator of which have been reversed. — n. 1 That which is reciprocal. 2 *Math.* The quotient obtained by dividing unity by a number or expression, as $\frac{1}{x}$ is the reciprocal of x. In a fraction, this reverses the numerator and denominator, as $\frac{3}{2}$ is the reciprocal of $\frac{2}{3}$. See synonyms under MUTUAL. [< L *reciprocus*] — **re·cip·ro·cal·i·ty** (-kal'ə·tē), **re·cip'ro·cal·ness** n. — **re·cip'ro·cal·ly** adv.

reciprocal pronouns *Gram.* Pronouns or pronominal phrases denoting reciprocal action or relation, as *each other, one another*.

re·cip·ro·cate (ri·sip'rə·kāt) v. **·cat·ed, ·cat·ing** v.t. 1 To cause to move backward and forward alternately. 2 To give and receive mutually, as favors or gifts; interchange. 3 To give, feel, do, etc., in return; requite, as an emotion. — v.i. 4 To move backward and forward. 5 To make a return in kind. 6 To give and receive favors, gifts, etc., mutually. 7 To correspond; be equivalent. See synonyms under REQUITE. [< L *reciprocatus*, pp. of *reciprocare* move to and fro < *reciprocus* returning] — **re·cip'ro·ca·tive** *adj.* — **re·cip'ro·ca'tor** *n.*

reciprocating engine An engine having a piston or pistons which move to and fro: distinguished from *rotary engine.*

re·cip·ro·ca·tion (ri·sip'rə·kā'shən) *n.* The act of reciprocating; a mutual giving and returning; alternation; alternate motion. See synonyms under INTERCOURSE. [<L *reciprocatio, -onis* < *reciprocus* returning]

re·cip·ro·ca·to·ry (ri·sip'rə·kə·tôr'ē, -tō'rē) *adj.* Alternating in direction or movement; reciprocating: opposed to *rotary.*

rec·i·proc·i·ty (res'ə·pros'ə·tē) *n.* **1** Reciprocal obligation, action, or relation. **2** That trade relation or policy between two countries by which each makes concessions favoring the importation of the products of the other. See synonyms under INTERCOURSE. [<F *réciprocité*]

re·ci·sion (ri·sizh'ən) *n.* **1** The act of rescinding. **2** The act of pruning. [<OF <L *recisio, -onis* < *recisum,* pp. of *recidere* cut off < *re-* back + *caedere* cut]

re·cit·al (ri·sīt'l) *n.* **1** A telling over in detail, or that which is thus told; a narration. **2** A public delivery of something previously memorized. **3** A musical program performed by one person, or consisting of works by one person. **4** A detailed statement. See synonyms under HISTORY, REPORT, STORY[1].

rec·i·ta·tion (res'ə·tā'shən) *n.* **1** The act of repeating from memory; the reciting of a lesson, or the meeting of a class for that purpose. **2** That which is allotted for recital or actually recited. [<L *recitatio, -onis* < *recitare.* See RECITE.]

rec·i·ta·tive[1] (res'ə·tā'tiv, ri·sī'tə·tiv) *adj.* Of the nature of a recital as of facts or details; narrative.

rec·i·ta·tive[2] (res'ə·tə·tēv', rə·sit'ə·tiv) *n. Music* Language uttered as in ordinary speech, but in musical tones; that style of singing or a vocal passage so rendered. Also *Italian* **re·ci·ta·ti·vo** (rä'chē·tä·tē'vō). — *adj.* Having the character of a recitative. [<Ital. *recitativo,* ult. <L *recitare*]

re·cite (ri·sīt') *v.* **·cit·ed, ·cit·ing** *v.t.* **1** To declaim or say from memory, especially formally, as a lesson in class. **2** To tell in particular detail; relate. **3** To enumerate. — *v.i.* **4** To declaim or speak something from memory. **5** To repeat or be examined in a lesson or part of a lesson in class. See synonyms under RELATE. [<F *réciter* <L *recitare* < *re-* again + *citare.* See CITE.] — **re·cit'er** *n.*

reck·less (rek'lis) *adj.* **1** Foolishly heedless of danger; rash. **2** Indifferent; neglectful. See synonyms under IMPROVIDENT, IMPRUDENT, WANTON. [OE *recceléas*] — **reck'less·ly** *adv.* — **reck'less·ness** *n.*

reck·on (rek'ən) *v.t.* **1** To count; compute; calculate. **2** To look upon as being; regard: They *reckon* him a fool. **3** *Dial.* To suppose or guess; expect. — *v.i.* **4** To make computation; count up. **5** To rely or depend: with *on* or *upon:* to *reckon* on help. See synonyms under CALCULATE. — **to reckon for** To pay for; receive the penalty of. — **to reckon with 1** To settle accounts with. **2** To take into consideration; bear in mind; consider. — **to reckon without one's host** To reckon a bill without consulting the landlord; hence, to neglect important facts in reaching a conclusion. [OE *recenian* explain. Akin to G *rechnen* count.]

reck·on·er (rek'ən·ər) *n.* **1** One who reckons. **2** A book or device for aiding one to compute: often called **ready reckoner.**

reck·on·ing (rek'ən·ing) *n.* **1** The act of counting; computation; a settlement of accounts. **2** Account; score; bill, as at a hotel. **3** *Naut.* The calculation of a ship's position, especially when made only by log and compass; dead reckoning. **4** An accounting to God.

re·claim (ri·klām') *v.t.* **1** To bring (swamp, desert, etc.) into a condition to support cultivation or life, as by draining or irrigating. **2** To obtain (a substance) from used or waste products: to *reclaim* rubber. **3** To cause to return from wrong or sinful ways of life; reform. **4** *Obs.* To tame, as a hawk. — *n.* **1** The act of reclaiming or state of being reclaimed; also, that which is reclaimed. **2** A fresh claim. [<OF *reclamer* call back <L *reclamare*

< *re-* against + *clamare* cry out] — **re·claim'a·ble** *adj.* — **re·claim'er, re·claim'ant** *n.*

Synonyms (verb): amend, convert, correct, recover, redeem, reform, renew, rescue, restore, subdue, tame. *Antonyms:* corrupt, degrade, deprave, destroy, seduce, vitiate.

rec·la·ma·tion (rek'lə·mā'shən) *n.* **1** The act or process of reclaiming, in any sense. **2** Restoration, as to ownership, cultivation, usefulness, or a moral life. — **Bureau of Reclamation** A branch of the U. S. Department of the Interior which constructs and operates Federal waterpower plants and irrigation projects. [<F *réclamation* <L *reclamatio, -onis* a cry of disapproval < *reclamare.* See RECLAIM.]

re·cline (ri·klīn') *v.* **·clined, ·clin·ing** *v.i.* To assume a recumbent position; lie down or back. — *v.t.* To cause to assume a recumbent position; lay down or back. See synonyms under LEAN[1], REST[1]. [<L *reclinare* < *re-* back + *clinare* lean] — **rec·li·na·tion** (rek'lə·nā'shən) *n.* — **re·clin'er** *n.*

rec·luse (rek'lōōs, ri·klōōs') *n.* **1** One who lives in retirement or seclusion. **2** One who retires from intercourse with the world, as a religious devotee; specifically, one who lives shut up in a cell and practices exceptional austerities. — **re·cluse** (ri·klōōs') *adj.* Secluded or retired from the world; solitary. [<OF *reclus* <LL *reclusus,* pp. of L *recludere* shut off < *re-* again + *claudere* close] — **re·clu'sive** *adj.*

re·clu·sion (ri·klōō'zhən) *n.* **1** The state of being a recluse; retirement from the world. **2** Rigorous immurement as practiced by certain ascetics in the Middle Ages. **3** Imprisonment; especially, solitary confinement.

re·clu·sive (ri·klōō'siv) *adj.* Affording or living in seclusion; recluse.

rec·og·ni·tion (rek'əg·nish'ən) *n.* **1** The act of recognizing; the process of memory that identifies an object, person, etc., as already known or experienced. **2** Acknowledgment of a fact or claim. **3** Friendly notice; salutation; attention: *recognition* of a speaker by the chair. **4** Acknowledgment and acceptance on the part of one government of the independence and validity of another. See synonyms under KNOWLEDGE. [<L *recognitio, -onis* < *recognitus,* pp. of *recognoscere.* See RECOGNIZANCE.] — **re·cog·ni·to·ry** (ri·kog'nə·tôr'ē, -tō'rē), **re·cog'ni·tive** *adj.*

rec·og·nize (rek'əg·nīz) *v.t.* **·nized, ·niz·ing 1** To know again; perceive as identical with someone or something previously known. **2** To identify or know, as by previous experience or knowledge: I *recognize* poor poetry when I see it. **3** To perceive as true; realize: to *recognize* the facts in a case. **4** To acknowledge the independence and validity of, as a newly constituted government. **5** To indicate appreciation or approval of: to *recognize* merit. **6** To approve formally; regard as valid or genuine: to *recognize* a claim. **7** To give (someone) permission to speak, as in a legislative body. **8** To admit the acquaintance of; greet. **9** *Law* To bind by a recognizance. See synonyms under ACKNOWLEDGE, CONFESS, DISCERN. [Back formation <RECOGNIZANCE] — **rec'og·niz'a·ble** *adj.* — **rec'og·niz'a·bly** *adv.* — **rec'og·niz'er** *n.*

re·coil (ri·koil') *v.i.* **1** To start back, as in fear or loathing; shrink: He *recoiled* at the sight. **2** To spring back, as from force of discharge or force of impact. **3** To return to the source; react: with *on* or *upon:* Crime *recoils* upon its perpetrator. **4** To move or draw back; retreat. — *n.* (rē'koil') **1** A backward movement or impulse, as of a gun at the moment of firing; rebound; also, a shrinking. **2** The condition existing as the result of a recoil. [<OF *reculer* <L *re-* again + *culus* buttocks] — **re·coil'er** *n.*

re·coil-op·er·at·ed (rē'koil·op'ə·rā'tid) *adj.* Operated or working by the energy generated in recoil, as certain automatic weapons.

rec·ol·lect (rek'ə·lekt') *v.t.* To call back to the mind; revive in the memory; remember. — *v.i.* To have a recollection of something. See synonyms under REMEMBER. [<L *recollectus,* pp. of *recolligere* gather together again < *re-* again + *colligere.* See COLLECT.]

re-col·lect (rē'kə·lekt') *v.t.* **1** to collect again, as things scattered. **2** To collect or compose (one's thoughts or nerves); compose or recover (oneself). [<RE- + COLLECT]

rec·ol·lect·ed (rek'ə·lek'tid) *adj.* Recalled to mind; remembered.

re-col·lect·ed (rē'kə·lek'tid) *adj.* Calm; composed; collected.

rec·ol·lec·tion (rek'ə·lek'shən) *n.* **1** The act or power of recollecting or remembering; remembrance. **2** Something remembered; a reminiscence; a memory. See synonyms under MEMORY. — **rec'ol·lec'tive** *adj.* — **rec'ol·lec'tive·ly** *adv.*

re-col·lec·tion (rē'kə·lek'shən) *n.* The act of re-collecting, or the state of being re-collected.

rec·om·mend (rek'ə·mend') *v.t.* **1** To commend with favorable representations; praise as desirable, worthy, etc. **2** To make attractive or acceptable: His sagacity *recommends* him. **3** To advise; urge. **4** To give in charge; commend. [<Med. L *recommendare* < *re-* again + *commendare.* See COMMEND.] — **rec'om·mend'er** *n.*

rec·om·men·da·tion (rek'ə·men·dā'shən) *n.* **1** The act of recommending, or that which recommends. **2** A note commending a person to confidence or favor. See synonyms under COUNSEL.

rec·om·mend·a·to·ry (rek'ə·men'də·tôr'ē, -tō'rē) *adj.* **1** Serving to recommend. **2** Advisory but not imperative, as applied to certain official appointments.

rec·om·pense (rek'əm·pens) *v.t.* **·pensed, ·pens·ing 1** To give compensation to; pay or repay; reward; requite. **2** To give compensation for; make up for, as a loss. See synonyms under PAY[1], REQUITE. — *n.* An equivalent for anything given, done, or suffered; payment or repayment; compensation; reward. [<OF *recompenser* <LL *recompensare* <L *re-* again + *compensare.* See COMPENSATE.]

Synonyms (noun): amends, compensation, indemnification, indemnity, remuneration, repayment, requital, retribution, reward, satisfaction. See RESTITUTION, SALARY.

re·com·pose (rē'kəm·pōz') *v.t.* **·posed, ·pos·ing 1** To restore the composure of; tranquilize. **2** To compose or form anew; rearrange; reconstitute; recombine. — **re·com·po·si·tion** (rē'kom·pə·zish'ən) *n.*

rec·on·cil·a·ble (rek'ən·sī'lə·bəl) *adj.* **1** Capable of being reconciled or of renewing friendship. **2** Capable of being adjusted or harmonized. — **rec'on·cil'a·bil'i·ty, rec'on·cil'a·ble·ness** *n.* — **rec'on·cil'a·bly** *adv.*

rec·on·cile (rek'ən·sīl) *v.t.* **·ciled, ·cil·ing 1** To bring back to friendship after estrangement; also, to make friendly; win the good will of. **2** To settle or adjust, as a quarrel. **3** To bring to acquiescence, content, or submission: to *reconcile* one to his lot. **4** To make or show to be consistent or congruous; harmonize: often with *to* or *with:* Can he *reconcile* his statement with his conduct? See synonyms under ACCOMMODATE. [<OF *reconciler* <L *reconciliare* < *re-* again + *conciliare* unite. See CONCILIATE.] — **rec'on·cile'ment** *n.* — **rec'on·cil'er** *n.*

rec·on·cil·i·a·tion (rek'ən·sil'ē·ā'shən) *n.* **1** The act of reconciling, or the state of being reconciled; atonement. **2** The effecting or showing of agreement between things; explanation of differences. See synonyms under PROPITIATION. — **rec·on·cil'i·a·to·ry** (-sil'ē·ə·tôr'ē, -tō'rē) *adj.*

rec·on·dite (rek'ən·dīt, ri·kon'dīt) *adj.* **1** Remote from ordinary or easy perception; abstruse; secret. **2** Dealing in abstruse matters; profound. **3** Hidden; not readily observed. See synonyms under MYSTERIOUS, SECRET. [<L *reconditus,* pp. of *recondere* put away, hide < *re-* back + *condere* construct, hide] — **rec'on·dite'ly** *adv.* — **rec'on·dite'ness** *n.*

re·con·di·tion (rē'kən·di'shən) *v.t.* To put into good or working condition, as by making repairs; overhaul.

re·con·nais·sance (ri·kon'ə·səns, -säns) *n.* **1** A reconnoitering; a preliminary examination or survey, as of the territory and resources of a country. **2** The act of obtaining information of military value, especially regarding the position, strength, and movement of enemy forces. Also **re·con'nois·sance.** [<F]

re·con·noi·ter (rē'kə·noi'tər, rek'ə-) *v.t.* To examine by the eye; survey, as for military, engineering, or geological purposes. — *v.i.* To make a reconnaissance. Also **re'con·noi'tre.** [<OF *reconoistre.* See RECOGNIZANCE.] — **re'con·noi'ter·er, re'con·noi'trer** *n.*

re·con·sid·er (rē'kən·sid'ər) *v.t.* **1** To consider again, especially with a view to a reversal of previous action. **2** In parliamentary usage, to bring before the house for renewed action (a matter previously decided). — *v.i.* **3** To reconsider a matter or decision. — **re′con·sid′er·a′tion** *n.*

re·con·sign (rē′kən·sīn′) *v.t.* To consign again; specifically, to consign (goods) to a different place or person while still in transit. — **re′·con·sign′ment** *n.*

re·con·sti·tute (rē·kon′stə·tōōt, -tyōōt) *v.t.* **·tut·ed, ·tut·ing** To constitute again; make over: to *reconstitute* dehydrated fruits by adding water. — **re·con′sti·tu′tion** *n.*

re·con·struct·ed (rē′kən·struk′tid) *adj.* Rebuilt or made anew: said especially of gems artificially made: a *reconstructed* ruby.

re·con·struc·tion (rē′kən·struk′shən) *n.* **1** The act of reconstructing, or the state of being reconstructed; specifically, the restoration of the seceded States as members of the Union under the **Reconstruction Acts** of March 2 and 23, 1867. **2** The repair of mutilated limbs, as of soldiers, by means of mechanical appliances. — **re′con·struc′tive** *adj.*

Reconstruction Finance Corporation A former (1932–54) branch of the Federal Loan Agency of the U.S. Department of the Interior, authorized to extend financial assistance to agriculture, industry, and commerce.

Reconstruction period *U.S.* The period following the Civil War during which the seceded Southern States were reorganized in accordance with the Congressional program.

re·con·vey (rē′kən·vā′) *v.t.* To convey back to an original owner or place. — **re′con·vey′·ance** *n.*

rec·ord (rek′ərd) *n.* **1** An account in written or other permanent form serving as a memorial or authentic evidence of a fact or event. **2** Something on which such an account is made, as a document or monument. **3** Information on facts or events, preserved and handed down: the heaviest rainfall on *record*. **4** The known career or performance of a person, animal, organization, etc., regarded as a series of things done or achieved: a good *record* in politics. **5** The best listed achievement, as in a competitive sport: to beat the world *record*. **6** *Law* **a** A written account of an act, statement, or transaction made by an officer acting under authority of law, and intended as permanent evidence thereon. **b** An official written account of a judicial or legislative proceeding, including the judgments or enactments and an official copy of all related documents. **7** A cylinder, disk, roll, or other article perforated, indented, or otherwise prepared so as to reproduce sounds. — **off the record 1** Unofficial or unofficially. **2** Not for quotation or publication, or not from a source to be identified. — *adj.* Surpassing any previously recorded achievement or performance of its kind: a *record* vote. — **re·cord** (ri·kôrd′) *v.t.* **1** To write down or otherwise inscribe, as for preserving an authentic account, evidence, etc. **2** To indicate; register, especially in permanent form, as a cardiograph does. **3** To make a phonograph record of. — *v.i.* **4** To record something. [< OF < *recorder* < L *recordari* call to mind < *re-* again + *cor, cordis* heart, mind]

Synonyms (*noun*): account, archives, catalog, chronicle, document, enrolment, entry, enumeration, history, inscription, instrument, inventory, memorandum, memorial, muniment, register, roll, scroll. *Record* is a word of wide signification, applying to any writing, mark, or trace that serves as a *memorial* giving enduring attestation of an event or fact; an extended *account, chronicle,* or *history* is a *record*; so, too, may be a brief *inventory* or *memorandum.* A *memorial* is any object, whether a writing, a monument, or other permanent thing that is designed or adapted to keep something in remembrance. A *register* is a formal or official written *record*, especially a series of entries made for preservation or reference; as, a *register* of births and deaths. *Archives*, in the sense here considered, are *documents* or *records*, often legal *records*, preserved in a public or official depository; the word *archives* is also applied to the place where such *documents* are regularly deposited and preserved. *Muniments* are *records* that enable one to defend his title. See CHARACTER, HISTORY, REPORT, STORY[1].

re·cord·er (ri·kôr′dər) *n.* **1** One who records. **2** A magistrate having criminal jurisdiction in a city or borough. **3** A registering apparatus. **4** A fipple flute, having eight holes and any one of four ranges: treble, alto, tenor, or bass. **5** A tape recorder or wire recorder. — **re·cord′er·ship** *n.*

re·count (ri·kount′) *v.t.* **1** To relate the particulars of; narrate in detail. **2** To enumerate; recite. See synonyms under RELATE. [< AF, OF *reconter* relate]

re-count (rē·kount′) *v.t.* To count again. — *n.* (rē′kount′, rē·kount′) A repetition of a count; specifically, a second count of votes cast.

re·count·al (ri·koun′təl) *n.* A thing told, or the act of telling; a detailed narration. Also **re·count′ment.**

re·coup (ri·kōōp′) *v.t.* **1** To recover or obtain an equivalent for; make up, as a loss. **2** To reimburse for a loss; indemnify. **3** *Law* To keep back (something due) in order to make good a counterclaim. — *n.* The act or process of recouping. [< F *recouper* < *re-* again + *couper* cut. See COUP.] — **re·coup′a·ble** *adj.* — **re·coup′ment** *n.*

re·course (rē′kôrs, -kōrs, ri·kôrs′, -kōrs′) *n.* **1** Resort to or application for help or security in trouble. **2** *Law* The right to exact payment from a party secondarily liable, where the first party liable has failed to pay. **3** A source of help or supply; the person or thing resorted to. **4** *Obs.* Admission; entrance. — **without recourse** A restricted or qualified endorsement of a promissory note or transfer thereof, which signifies that the endorser merely transfers the title to the instrument, but disclaims liability for non-payment. — **to have recourse to** To go to for advice or help. [< OF *recours* < L *recursus* a running back < *recurrere*. See RECUR.]

re·cov·er (ri·kuv′ər) *v.t.* **1** To obtain again after losing; regain, as property, self-control, health, etc. **2** To make up for; retrieve, as a loss. **3** To restore (oneself) to natural balance, health, etc. **4** In sports, to regain (one's normal position of guard, balance, etc.). **5** To reclaim, as land, **6** *Law* To gain in judicial proceedings: to *recover* judgment. **b** To gain or regain by legal process. — *v.i.* **7** To regain health, composure, etc. **8** *Law* To succeed in a lawsuit. **9** In sports, to regain one's balance or position of guard. [< OF *recovrer* < L *recuperare*. See RECUPERATE.] — **re·cov′er·a·ble** *adj.* — **re·cov′er·er** *n.*

Synonyms: cure, heal, reanimate, recruit, recuperate, regain, repossess, restore, resume, retrieve. See RECLAIM. *Antonyms:* die, fail, lapse, sink.

re·cov·er·y (ri·kuv′ər·ē) *n. pl.* **·er·ies 1** The act of recovering. **2** The state of being or having recovered. **3** Restoration from sickness or from any undesirable or abnormal condition. **4** In boating, the forward movement of an oarsman, after having finished one stroke, to take the next. **5** In fencing and sparring, the act of regaining a defensive position after attack. **6** The extraction of valuable substances and materials from original sources, by-products, waste, etc. **7** The retrieval of a flying object, as a balloon, space vehicle, meteorite, etc., after it has fallen to earth. [< AF *recoverie*]

rec·re·ant (rek′rē·ənt) *adj.* **1** Unfaithful to a cause or pledge; apostate; false. **2** Crying for mercy, as in the old trial by combat; hence, craven; cowardly. See synonyms under PUSILLANIMOUS. — *n.* A cowardly or faithless person; also, a deserter; an apostate. [< OF, ppr. of *recreire* surrender allegiance < Med. L *recredere* < L *re-* back + *credere* believe] — **rec′re·an·cy, rec′re·ance** *n.* — **rec′re·ant·ly** *adv.*

rec·re·ate (rek′rē·āt) *v.* **·at·ed, ·at·ing** *v.t.* To impart fresh vigor to; refresh, especially after toil, by some form of relaxation or entertainment. — *v.i.* To take recreation. See synonyms under ENTERTAIN, RELAX. [< L *recreatus,* pp. of *recreare* create anew < *re-* again + *creare* create] — **rec′re·a′tive** *adj.*

TREBLE RECORDER

rec·re·a·tion (rek′rē·ā′shən) *n.* **1** Refreshment of body or mind, but generally of both; diversion; amusement. **2** Any pleasurable exercise or occupation. See synonyms under ENTERTAINMENT, REST[1], SPORT. — **rec′re·a′tion·al** *adj.*

re·crim·i·nate (ri·krim′ə·nāt) *v.* **·nat·ed, ·nat·ing** *v.t.* To accuse in return. — *v.i.* To repel one accusation by making another in return. [< Med. L *recriminatus,* pp. of *recriminare* < L *re-* again + *criminare.* See CRIMINATE.] — **re·crim′i·na′tive, re·crim′i·na·to·ry** (ri·krim′ə·nə·tôr′ē, -tō′rē) *adj.* — **re·crim′i·na′tor** *n.*

re·crim·i·na·tion (ri·krim′ə·nā′shən) *n.* **1** The act of recriminating. **2** An accusation made in return; a countercharge.

re·cru·desce (rē′krōō·des′) *v.i.* **·desced, ·desc·ing** To break out or become active again. [< L *recrudescere* < *re-* again + *crudescere* become harsh, break out < *crudus* raw, harsh]

re·cru·des·cence (rē′krōō·des′əns) *n.* **1** A breaking out afresh, as of a disease or wound. **2** A reappearance; return. [< L *recrudescens, -entis* ppr. of *recrudescere.* See RECRUDESCE.] — **re′cru·des′cent** *adj.*

re·cruit (ri·krōōt′) *v.t.* **1** To enlist (men) for military or naval service. **2** To muster; raise, as an army, by enlistment. **3** To supply with recruits. **4** To regain or revive (lost health, strength, etc.). **5** *Rare* To replenish. — *v.i.* **6** To enlist new men for military or naval service. **7** To regain lost health or strength. **8** To gain or raise new supplies of anything lost or needed. — *n.* **1** A newly enlisted soldier, sailor, or marine; loosely, any new adherent of a cause, organization, or the like. **2** *Obs.* A new supply of something necessary or useful. [< F *recruter* < *recrute* a recruit < *recrû* grown again, pp. of *recroître* < L *re-* again + *crescere* grow, increase] — **re·cruit′er** *n.* — **re·cruit′ment** *n.*

Synonyms (*verb*): enlist, reinforce, repair, replenish. See RECOVER. *Antonyms:* decimate, disperse, lose, reduce, scatter.

rec·tal (rek′təl) *adj. Anat.* Relating to, involving, or in the region of the rectum.

rec·tan·gle (rek′tang′gəl) *n.* A right-angled parallelogram. [< F < LL *rectiangulum* < L *rectus* straight + *angulus* angle]

rec·tan·gu·lar (rek·tang′gyə·lər) *adj.* **1** Having one or more right angles. **2** Resembling a rectangle in shape or appearance. — **rec·tan′gu·lar′i·ty** (-lar′ə·tē) *n.* — **rec·tan′gu·lar·ly** *adv.*

recti- *combining form* Straight: *rectilinear.* Also, before vowels, **rect-.** [< L *rectus* right]

rec·ti·fi·ca·tion (rek′tə·fə·kā′shən) *n.* **1** The act or process of rectifying. **2** A setting right of what is wrong. **3** Refining by fractional or renewed distillation. [< F]

rec·ti·fy (rek′tə·fī) *v.t.* **·fied, ·fy·ing 1** To make right; correct; amend. **2** *Chem.* To refine, as a liquid, by repeated distillations until a desired degree of purity is obtained. **3** *Electr.* To change (an alternating current) into a direct current by reversing the direction of alternate impulses. **4** *Math.* To determine the length of (a curve or arc). **5** To allow for errors or inaccuracies in, as a compass reading. **6** To adjust for accurate calculations: to *rectify* a globe. See synonyms under AMEND. [< OF *rectifier* < LL *rectificare* < L *rectus* right + *facere* make] — **rec′ti·fi′a·ble** *adj.*

rec·ti·lin·e·ar (rek′tə·lin′ē·ər) *adj.* Pertaining to, consisting of, moving in, or bounded by a right line or lines; straight. Also **rec′ti·lin′e·al.** — **rec′ti·lin′e·ar·ly** *adv.*

rec·ti·tude (rek′tə·tōōd, -tyōōd) *n.* **1** Upright in principles and conduct. **2** Freedom from error; correctness of judgment, method, or application; accuracy. **3** *Obs.* Straightness. See synonyms under JUSTICE, VIRTUE. [< F < LL *rectitudo* < L *rectus* right]

rec·to (rek′tō) *n. pl.* **·tos** A right-hand page, as of a book: opposed to *verso* (or *reverso*). [< L *recto (folio)* on the right (page)]

recto- *combining form* Rectal; pertaining to the rectum: *rectocele,* hernia of the rectum. Also, before vowels, **rect-.** [See RECTUM]

rec·tor (rek′tər) *n.* **1** In the Church of England, a priest who has full charge of a parish, and receives the parochial tithes: distinguished from *vicar.* **2** In the Protestant Episcopal Church, a priest in charge of a parish. **3** In the Roman Catholic Church: **a** A priest in charge of a congregation or church, especially one not having parochial status: distinguished from *parish priest.* **b** The head of a seminary or religious house. 4 In certain universities, colleges, and schools, the head or chief officer. [<L *rectus*, pp. of *regere* rule] —**rec′tor·ate** (-it) *n.* —**rec·to·ri·al** (rek·tôr′ē·əl, -tō′rē-) *adj.*

rec·to·ry (rek′tər·ē) *n. pl.* **·ries** 1 A rector's dwelling. 2 In England, a parish domain with its buildings, revenue, etc.

rec·tum (rek′təm) *n. pl.* **·ta** (-tə) *Anat.* The terminal portion of the large intestine, extending from the sigmoid bend of the colon to the anus. [<NL *rectum (intestinum)* straight (intestine)]

rec·tus (rek′təs) *n. pl.* **·ti** (-tī) *Anat.* A straight muscle, as of the eye, the abdomen, the femur, etc. [<NL <L, straight]

re·cum·ben·cy (ri·kum′bən·sē) *n. pl.* **·cies** 1 The state of being recumbent. 2 The act of reclining. 3 A recumbent attitude. Also **re·cum′bence.**

re·cum·bent (ri·kum′bənt) *adj.* 1 Lying down, wholly or partly; reclining; leaning. 2 *Biol.* Tending to rest upon a surface from which they extend: said of certain structures. [<L *recumbens, -entis,* ppr. of *recumbere* <*re-* back + *cumbere* lie, nasalized var. of *cubare* lie down] —**re·cum′bent·ly** *adv.*

re·cu·per·ate (ri·kōō′pə·rāt, -kyōō′-) *v.* **·at·ed, ·at·ing** *v.i.* 1 To regain health or strength. 2 To recover from loss, as of money. —*v.t.* 3 To obtain again after loss; recover. 4 To restore to vigor and health. See synonyms under RECOVER. [<L *recuperatus,* pp. of *recuperare*]

re·cu·per·a·tion (ri·kōō′pə·rā′shən, -kyōō′-) *n.* The recovery of lost power or excellence, especially of health or strength.

re·cu·per·a·tive (ri·kōō′pə·rā′tiv, -pər·ə·tiv, -kyōō′-) *adj.* Tending, assisting, or pertaining to recovery; restorative. Also **re·cu′per·a·to′ry** (-pər·ə·tôr′ē, -tō′rē).

re·cu·per·a·tor (ri·kōō′pə·rā′tər, -kyōō′-) *n.* 1 One who or that which recuperates. 2 A mechanism, operated by springs or compressed air, for restoring a gun to firing position after the recoil. 3 *Chem.* An apparatus for the recovery of heat from hot gases.

re·cur (ri·kûr′) *v.i.* **·curred, ·cur·ring** 1 To happen again or repeatedly, especially at regular intervals: a paroxysm that *recurs.* 2 To come back or return; especially, to return to the mind or in recollection. 3 *Rare* To turn for aid; have recourse. [<L *recurrere* <*re-* back + *currere* run]

re·cur·rence (ri·kûr′əns) *n.* The act or fact of recurring; recourse. Also **re·cur′ren·cy.**

re·cur·rent (ri·kûr′ənt) *adj.* 1 Happening or appearing again or repeatedly; recurring. 2 Running back: said of arteries and nerves. See synonyms under FREQUENT. [<L *recurrens, -entis,* ppr. of *recurrere.* See RECUR.] —**re·cur′rent·ly** *adv.*

recurrent fever Relapsing fever.

recurring decimal A circulating decimal.

re·cur·vant (ri·kûr′vənt) *adj. Her.* Coiled with the head raised to strike: said of a serpent. [<L *recurvans, -antis,* ppr. of *recurvare* bend back]

re·cur·vate (ri·kûr′vit, -vāt) *adj.* Bent back. [<L *recurvatus,* pp. of *recurvare.* See RE-CURVE.] —**re·cur′va·ture** (-və·chər) *n.*

re·curve (ri·kûrv′) *v.t. & v.i.* **curved, ·curv·ing** To curve or bend back or down. [<L *recurvare* <*re-* back + *curvus* curved] —**re·cur·va·tion** (rē′kûr·vā′shən) *n.*

rec·u·sant (rek′yə·zənt, ri·kyōō′zənt) *adj.* Persistently refusing to conform; specifically, in English history, refusing to attend services of the Anglican Church. —*n.* One of a recusant character, position, or party; a non-comformist. [<L *recusans, -antis,* ppr. of *recusare.* See RECUSE.] —**rec′u·san·cy** *n.*

re·cy·cle (rē·sī′kəl) *v.t.* **·cy·cled, ·cy·cling** To reclaim (waste materials, as newsprint, bottles, etc.) by using in the manufacture of new products. —**re·cy′cla·ble** *adj.*

red¹ (red) *adj.* **red·der, red·dest** 1 Of a bright color resembling blood; of the same hue as that color of the spectrum farthest from the violet; also, of a hue approximating red: *red* gold. 2 Ultra-radical in politics; especially, communistic. 3 Pertaining to the pole of a magnet which points to the north. Compare BLUE. —*n.* 1 One of the primary colors,

occurring at the opposite end of the spectrum from violet; the color of fresh human blood. 2 Any pigment or dye having or giving this color. 3 An ultra-radical in political views, especially a communist. 4 A red object considered with special reference to its color: the *red* (color) in roulette, the *red* (ball) in billiards. —**in the red** *Colloq.* Operating at a loss; owing money: from the practice of making entries in the debit column of an account book in red ink. —**to see red** To be very angry. [OE *rēad*] —**red′ly** *adv.* —**red′ness** *n.*

red² (red) See REDD.

Red (red) *n.* 1 A member of the Communist party of Russia; hence, often, any Russian. 2 A member of the Communist party of any country. 3 Any person who supports or approves of the aims of the Communist party. 4 An ultra-radical; anarchist. [<RED; from the color of their flags and banners]

re·dact (ri·dakt′) *v.t.* 1 To prepare, as for publication; edit; revise. 2 To draw up or frame, as a message or edict. [<L *redactus,* pp. of *redigere* reduce to order <*re-* back + *agere* drive] —**re·dac′tor** *n.*

re·dac·tion (ri·dak′shən) *n.* 1 The act of reducing or shaping, as literary matter, into proper form and condition for publication; editing. 2 Literary matter so edited or revised. [<F *rédaction* <LL *redactio, -onis* <*redactus.* See REDACT.]

red algae See RHODOPHYCEAE.

re·dan (ri·dan′) *n.* A fortification with two parapets meeting at a salient angle. See also illustration under BASTION. [<F *redan* <OF *redent* <*re-* back + *dent* tooth; from its appearance]

Red Army The army of the U.S.S.R.: now officially the Soviet Army.

red-blood·ed (red′blud′id) *adj.* Having vitality and vigor; hence, manly.

red·cap (red′kap′) *n.* 1 *U.S.* A railroad porter: so called from his red-colored cap. 2 The European goldfinch.

red cent A United States copper one-cent piece. —**not worth a red cent** *U.S. Colloq.* Worthless.

red·coat (red′kōt′) *n.* 1 A person wearing a red coat. 2 A British soldier of the period when a red coat was part of the uniform worn by the British Army, during the American Revolution and the War of 1812.

red corpuscle An erythrocyte.

red cross 1 The cross of St. George, the emblem of the English. 2 A Greek cross, red on a white ground.

Red Cross Convention See GENEVA CONVENTION.

Red Cross Society A society for the succor of the sick and wounded in war, formed in accordance with the international convention signed at Geneva in 1864, the members wearing a red Geneva cross as a badge of neutrality. These societies are now national organizations, as the **American Red Cross,** and continue their beneficent activities in times of peace, as in fighting disease, etc.

red deer 1 The common European and Asian stag *(Cervus elaphus).* 2 The common Virginia white-tailed deer in its rufous summer coat.

red·den (red′n) *v.t.* To make red. —*v.i.* To grow red; flush.

red·dish (red′ish) *adj.* Mixed with or somewhat red. —**red′dish·ness** *n.*

red·dle (red′l) *n.* Red ocher or red chalk, used for marking sheep. —*v.t.* **·dled, ·dling** To mark or stain with reddle. Also spelled *raddle.* [Var. of RUDDLE]

red·dle·man (red′l·mən) *n. pl.* **·men** (-mən) One who deals in reddle.

re·deem (ri·dēm′) *v.t.* 1 To regain possession of by paying a price; specifically, to recover, as mortgaged property. 2 To pay off; receive back and satisfy, as a promissory note. 3 To set free; rescue; ransom. 4 *Theol.* To rescue from sin and its penalties. 5 To fulfil, as an oath or promise. 6 To make amends for; compensate for: The play was *redeemed* by its acting. See synonyms under DELIVER, RECLAIM. [<F *rédimer* <L *redimere* <*re-* back + *emere* buy] —**re·deem′a·ble** *adj.*

re·deem·er (ri·dē′mər) *n.* One who redeems. —**The Redeemer** Jesus Christ.

re·de·fec·tor (rē′di·fek′tər) *n.* One who returns to his native country after having previously fled because of real or imagined injustice.

re·de·liv·er (rē′di·liv′ər) *v.t.* 1 To deliver again, as a message or a speech. 2 To give back; return; restore. —**re′de·liv′er·ance, re′de·liv′er·y** *n.*

re·demp·ti·ble (ri·demp′tə·bəl) *adj.* Redeemable. [<L *redemptus* + -IBLE]

re·demp·tion (ri·demp′shən) *n.* 1 The act of redeeming, or the state of being redeemed. 2 The recovery of what is mortgaged or pledged. 3 The payment of a debt or obligation; specifically, the paying of the value of its notes, warrants, etc., by a government. 4 *Theol.* Salvation from sin through the atonement of Christ. [<OF <L *redemptio, -onis* <*redemptus,* pp. of *redimere* redeem. Doublet of RANSOM.]

re·demp·tion·er (ri·demp′shən·ər) *n.* One who redeems himself, as an emigrant by service in payment of passage money.

re·demp·tive (ri·demp′tiv) *adj.* Serving to redeem, or connected with redemption. Also **re·demp′to·ry** (-tər·ē). [<L *redemptus,* pp. of *redimere.* See REDEEM.]

Re·demp·tor·ist (ri·demp′tər·ist) *n.* A member of a religious order, the Congregation of the Most Holy Redeemer, founded in 1732 by St. Alphonso de Liguori.

re·de·vel·op (rē′di·vel′əp) *v.t.* 1 To develop again. 2 *Phot.* To intensify with chemicals and put through a second developing process. —*v.i.* 3 To develop again. —**re′de·vel′op·er** *n.* —**re′de·vel′op·ment** *n.*

red-eyed vireo (red′īd′) See under VIREO.

red-fig·ured (red′fig′yərd) *adj.* Having red figures or markings; specifically, denoting an ancient Greek ceramic ware in which a black glaze was painted over the surface so as to leave the design in the red of the body: a style developed early in the fifth century B.C.

red fir 1 Any of several varieties of fir, as the **California red fir** *(Abies magnifica),* the largest of the genus. 2 The wood of any of these trees. 3 Douglas fir.

red fire A mixture of easily combustible ingredients, especially strontium salts, that burns with a red light.

red fox The common American fox. See under FOX.

red-hand·ed (red′han′did) *adj.* 1 Having hands red with blood, as a murderer caught in the act; hence, having just committed any crime. 2 Caught in the act of doing some particular thing: not always in a bad sense. —**red′-hand′ed·ly** *adv.* —**red′-hand′ed·ness** *n.*

red·head (red′hed′) *n.* 1 A person with red hair. 2 An American duck *(Aythya americana);* the pochard. 3 The red-headed woodpecker.

red-head·ed woodpecker (red′hed′id) See under WOODPECKER.

red heat 1 The state of being red-hot. 2 The temperature at which a metal is red-hot.

red herring 1 Herring dried and smoked to a reddish brown color. 2 An irrelevant topic introduced in order to divert attention from the main point under discussion: from the use of a red herring to distract a hunting dog from the scent being followed (used to train hounds to ignore such distractions).

red-hot (red′hot′) *adj.* 1 Heated to redness. 2 New, as if just from the fire. 3 Heated; excited: *red-hot* argument. 4 Extreme.

red·in·gote (red′ing·gōt) *n.* An outer coat with long full skirts. [<F *redingote,* alter. of E *riding coat*]

red·in·te·grate (ri·din′tə·grāt) *v.t.* **·grat·ed, ·grat·ing** To restore to a perfect state; make complete; renew. —*adj.* Restored to a whole or perfect state; renewed. [<L *redintegratus,* pp. of *redintegrare* <*red-,* var. of *re-* again + *integrare.* See INTEGRATE.]

re·din·te·gra·tion (ri·din′tə·grā′shən) *n.* 1 The act or process of restoration to a whole or sound state. 2 *Psychol.* The act or tendency of the mind to complete again a complex mental state previously experienced, upon the renewal of any part of it.

re·dis·count (rē·dis′kount) *n.* 1 A second (or any subsequent) discount on a sum. 2 *Usually pl.* Commercial paper which has been rediscounted. —*v.t.* To discount again.

---

add,āce,câre,pälm; end,ēven; it,īce; odd,ōpen,ôrder; tōōk,pōōl; up,bûrn; ə = a in *above,* e in *sicken,* i in *clarity,* o in *melon,* u in *focus;* yōō = u in *fuse;* oi,oil; ou,pout; ch,check; g,go; ng,ring; th,thin; ŧh,this; zh,vision. Foreign sounds à,œ,ü,kh,ň; and ◆ : see page xx. <from; + plus; ? possibly.

re·dis·trict (rē-dis′trikt) *v.t.* To district again; especially, to redraw the boundaries of the election districts of.

red·i·vi·vus (red′ə-vī′vəs) *adj.* Come or brought into existence again; revived; restored. [< LL < *redivivus* renewed]

Red Jacket, 1751–1830, a chief of the Senecas, ally of the United States in the War of 1812: real name *Sagoyewatha*.

red lead (led) A lead preparation having a fine red color, used chiefly as a pigment; minium.

red–lead ore (red′led′) Crocoite.

red–let·ter (red′let′ər) *adj.* Happy, fortunate, or memorable: from the use on calendars of red letters to indicate holidays.

red light 1 A traffic signal light meaning stop: opposed to *green light.* 2 Any similar light used to warn of danger or an emergency.

red–light district (red′līt′) That part of a city or town in which brothels, sometimes marked by a red light, are numerous.

red·line (red′līn′) *v.t.* ·lined, ·lin·ing. *U.S.* 1 To cross out with, or as with, a red line; cancel. 2 To discriminate against economically, esp. by refusing to grant mortgages or by charging unreasonably high mortgage.

red lobelia The cardinal flower.

red maple The swamp maple.

red·neck (red′nek′) *n. U.S.* In the rural South, a poor, uneducated, white person, especially one having violently anti–Negro sentiments: a disparaging term. Also **red′-neck′.**

red·o·lent (red′ə-lənt) *adj.* Full of or diffusing a pleasant fragrance; odorous: often figuratively: *redolent* of the past. [< OF < L *redolens, -entis,* ppr. of *redolere* emit a smell < *red-* thoroughly + *olere* smell] —**red′o·lence, red′o·len·cy** *n.* —**red′o·lent·ly** *adv.*

re·dou·ble (rē-dub′əl) *v.t. & v.i.* ·led, ·ling 1 To make or become double. 2 To increase greatly. 3 To echo or re-echo. 4 To fold or turn back. 5 In bridge, to double (an opponent's double).

re·doubt (ri-dout′) *n.* 1 An enclosed fortification, especially a temporary one of any form, employed to defend a pass, a hilltop, etc. 2 An earthwork or simple fortification placed within the main rampart line of a permanent fortification. [< F *redoute* < Ital. *ridotto* < Med. L *reductus,* lit., a refuge, orig. pp. of *reducere* lead back]

re·doubt·a·ble (ri-dou′tə-bəl) *adj.* 1 Inspiring fear; formidable. 2 Deserving respect or deference. Also **re·doubt′ed.** See synonyms under FORMIDABLE. [< F *redoubtable* < *redouter* fear, dread < L *re-* thoroughly + *dubitare* doubt] —**re·doubt′a·ble·ness** *n.* —**re·doubt′a·bly** *adv.*

re·dound (ri-dound′) *v.i.* 1 To have an effect, as by reaction, to the credit, discredit, advantage, etc., of the original agent; return; react; accrue. 2 *Obs.* To surge or flow back. 3 *Obs.* To overflow. —*n.* A return by way of consequence; result; requital. [< F *redonder* < L *redundare* overflow < *red-* back + *undare* surge < *unda* wave]

red·o·wa (red′ə-wa, -və) *n.* Either of two Bohemian dances, one in ³/₄ time, resembling a mazurka, the other in ²/₄ time. [< F < Czech *rejdovák* < *rejdovati* steer, whirl, carouse]

re·draft (rē′draft′, -dräft′) *n.* 1 A second draft or copy. 2 A bill of exchange drawn by the holder of a protested bill on the drawer or endorsers for the reimbursement of the amount of the original bill with costs and charges.

re·dress (ri-dres′) *v.t.* 1 To set right, as a wrong, by compensation or by punishment of the wrongdoer; make reparation for. 2 To make reparation to; compensate: to *redress* the victims of injustice. 3 To remedy; correct. 4 To adjust, as balances. —*n.* (rē′dres, ri-dres′) 1 Satisfaction for wrong done; reparation; amends. 2 A restoration; reformation; correction. [< F *redresser* straighten < *re-* again (< L) + *dresser.* See DRESS.] —**re·dress′er** or **re·dres′sor** *n.*

Red Sea An elongated sea between Egypt and Arabia; 1,450 miles long; 170,000 square miles; joined to the Mediterranean by the Suez Canal and connected with the Indian Ocean by the Gulf of Aden.

red·shank (red′shangk′) *n.* 1 A Scottish Highlander: so called in allusion to the national costume of Scotland, which leaves the legs bare. 2 A common Old World shore bird (*Totanus totanus*); a tattler.

red·shirt (red′shûrt′) *n.* A member of Garibaldi's brigade in the struggle for Italian independence.

red squirrel The chickaree.

red–tailed buzzard (red′tāld′) See under BUZZARD.

red tape Rigid official procedure involving delay or inaction: from the tying of public documents with red tape. —**red-tape** (red′·tāp′) *adj.* —**red′-tap′ism** *n.*

red tide The episodic appearance of a reddish discoloration in coastal waters due to the proliferation of certain minute, toxic protozoans.

re·duce (ri-dōōs′, -dyōōs′) *v.* ·duced, ·duc·ing *v.t.* 1 To make less in size, amount, number, intensity, etc.; diminish. 2 To bring from a higher to a lower condition; lower; degrade. 3 To bring to submission; subdue; conquer. 4 To bring to a specified condition or state: with *to*: to *reduce* rock to powder; to *reduce* a person to desperation. 5 To thin (paint, etc.) with oil or turpentine. 6 *Math.* To change (an expression) to a more elementary form. 7 *Surg.* To restore (displaced parts) to normal position. 8 *Chem.* **a** To decrease the positive valence of (an element) by the addition of electrons. **b** To deprive wholly or partially of oxygen; deoxidize. 9 *Phot.* To diminish the density of (a photographic negative). —*v.i.* 10 To become less in any way. 11 To decrease one's weight, as by dieting. [< L *reducere* < *re-* back + *ducere* lead] —**re·duc′i·ble** *adj.* —**re·duc′i·bly** *adv.*

Synonyms: compress, concentrate, condense, consolidate, contract, diminish, solidify, thicken. See ABASE, ABATE, ABBREVIATE, ALLAY, ALLEVIATE, CONQUER, IMPAIR, RELAX, RETRENCH, SCRIMP, SUBDUE, WEAKEN.

reducing agent *Chem.* A substance used to effect a chemical reduction; more specifically, any element which gives up a valence electron to another.

reducing glass A concave lens of considerable diameter used to produce a minified view of drawings, to see how they will appear when they are reduced in size.

reducing valve A valve for maintaining uniform reduced pressure of a fluid, as steam or gas, above or below the valve.

re·duc·tion (ri-duk′shən) *n.* 1 The act or process of reducing, or its results. 2 *Biol.* The halving of the total number of chromosomes during meiotic cell division. 3 *Chem.* **a** The process of depriving a compound of oxygen. **b** The process of decreasing the positive valence of an element by the addition of electrons: distinguished from *oxidation.* 4 *Math.* **a** One of those formulas by means of which trigonometric functions of angles greater than 90° can be reduced to functions of angles less than 90°. **b** The process of expressing a fraction in decimal terms. See synonyms under ABBREVIATION. [< F *réduction* < L *reductio, -onis* < *reductus,* pp. of *reducere.* See REDUCE.] —**re·duc′tion·al** *adj.* —**re·duc′tive** *adj.*

re·dun·dance (ri-dun′dəns) *n.* 1 The condition or quality of being redundant. 2 That which is redundant. 3 Excess; surplus. See synonyms under CIRCUMLOCUTION, EXCESS.

re·dun·dan·cy (ri-dun′dən-sē) *n. pl.* ·cies 1 Redundance. 2 In information theory, deliberate repetition in a message, in whatever medium expressed, in order to lessen the possibility of error.

re·dun·dant (ri-dun′dənt) *adj.* 1 Being more than is required; constituting an excess. 2 Unnecessarily verbose; tautological. [< L *redundans, -antis,* ppr. of *redundare.* See REDOUND.] —**re·dun′dant·ly** *adv.*

re·du·pli·cate (ri-dōō′plə-kāt, -dyōō′-) *v.* ·cat·ed, ·cat·ing *v.t.* 1 To repeat again and again; redouble; iterate. 2 *Ling.* To affix a reduplication to. —*v.i.* 3 To undergo reduplication. —*adj.* (-kit) 1 Repeated again and again; duplicated; doubled. 2 *Bot.* Valvate with the margins reflexed. [< L *reduplicatus,* pp. of *reduplicare* < *re-* again + *duplicare.* See DUPLICATE.]

re·du·pli·ca·tion (ri-dōō′plə-kā′shən, -dyōō′-) *n.* 1 The act of reduplicating, or the state of being reduplicated; a redoubling. 2 A rhetorical figure in which the ending of a sentence, line, or clause is repeated and emphasized at the beginning of the next. 3 *Ling.* **a** The repetition of an initial element or elements in a word; especially, in the verbs of some Indo-European languages, repetition of some part of the root, usually with vowel modification, serving as a mark of the perfect, as in Greek *bebeka* I have walked, Latin *dedidi* I

have given. **b** The doubling of all or part of a word, often with vowel or consonant change, as in *fiddle-faddle, razzle-dazzle.* **c** The sound or syllable thus repeated.

re·du·pli·ca·tive (ri-dōō′plə-kā′tiv, -dyōō′-) *adj.* 1 Tending to reduplicate. 2 Of or formed by reduplication. 3 *Bot.* Reduplicate.

red·wood (red′wŏŏd′) *n.* 1 An immense California tree (*Sequoia sempervirens,* family *Taxodiaceae*). See SEQUOIA. 2 Its durable reddish wood. 3 Any one of various other trees yielding a reddish wood, or the wood itself, which yields a red dye.

red–yel·low (red′yel′ō) *n.* One of the range of colors situated between the red and yellow portions of the visible spectrum, sharing the hue of each but identical with neither.

REDWOOD

ree (rē) See REEVE³.

reed (rēd) *n.* 1 The slender, frequently jointed stem of certain tall grasses growing in wet places, or the grasses themselves. 2 A thin, elastic plate of reed, wood, or metal nearly closing an opening, as in a pipe: used in reed organs, the reed pipes of pipe organs, and instruments of the bassoon and clarinet order, to produce a musical tone either by itself or when reinforced by the vibration of air in a pipe. 3 A musical pipe made of the hollow stem of a plant; a shepherd's pipe. 4 *Archit.* A semicylindrical ornamental molding or bead. 5 That part of a loom that drives the filling against the woven fabric, consisting of two horizontal parallel bars near together and connected by numerous thin parallel slips. See illustration under LOOM. 6 An arrow. 7 An ancient Hebrew measure of length; six cubits. —*v.t.* 1 To fashion into or decorate with reeds. 2 To thatch with reeds. [OE *hrēod*]

reed·buck (rēd′buk′) *n.* An antelope (*Redunca arundineum*) of southern Africa that frequents reedy places; the reitbok.

reed·ing (rē′ding) *n.* 1 Beading or semicylindrical moldings collectively. 2 Ornamentation by such moldings. 3 A molding of this kind: the reverse of *fluting.* 4 The knurling on the edge of a coin, as distinguished from *milling.*

reed·ling (rēd′ling) *n.* The European bearded titmouse (*Panurus biarmicus*), common in reedy places. The male has a black tuft of feathers on each side of the chin.

reed organ A keyboard musical instrument sounding by means of free reeds.

reed pipe An organ pipe having a reed whose vibrations set in motion the air column: distinguished from *flue pipe.*

reed-stop (rēd′stop′) *n.* An organ stop controlling a set of reed pipes.

reed·y (rē′dē) *adj.* reed·i·er, reed·i·est 1 Full of reeds. 2 Like a reed. 3 Having a thin, sharp tone, like a reed instrument. —**reed′i·ness** *n.*

reef¹ (rēf) *n.* 1 A ridge of sand or rocks, or especially of coral, at or near the surface of the water. 2 A lode, vein, or ledge. 3 A shoal. [< ON *rif* rib, reef] —**reef′y** *adj.*

reef² (rēf) *Naut. n.* 1 The part of a sail that is folded and secured or untied and let out in regulating its size on the mast. 2 The tuck taken in a sail when reefed. —*v.t.* 1 To reduce (a sail) by folding a part and tying it round, and usually fastening it to, a yard or boom. 2 To shorten or lower, as a topmast by taking part of it in. [ME *riff,* prob. < ON *rif* rib]

reef·er¹ (rē′fər) *n.* 1 One who reefs. 2 A short double-breasted coat or jacket of heavy material.

reef·er² (rē′fər) *n. U.S. Slang* A marihuana cigarette. [? from its resemblance to the reef of a sail]

reef knot A square knot. See illustration under KNOT.

reek (rēk) *v.i.* 1 To give off smoke, vapor, etc. 2 To give off a strong, offensive smell. 3 To be pervaded with anything offensive. —*v.t.* 4 To expose to smoke or its action. 5 To give off; emit. —*n. Scot.* Smoke; vapor; steam. ◆Homophone: *wreak.* [OE *rēc*] —**reek′er** *n.*

reek·y (rē′kē) *adj.* reek·i·er, reek·i·est Having been smoked; smoky; soiled by or emitting smoke. Also **reek′ie.**

reel¹ (rēl) *n.* 1 A rotatory device or frame for winding rope, cord, photographic film, or other flexible substance. 2 In cinematography, the film wound on one reel: used as a unit of length, usually from 1,000 to 2,000 feet. 3 A wooden spool for wire, thread, etc. 4 Material, such as thread, paper, and the like, when wound on a reel. —*v.t.* 1 To wind on a reel or bobbin, as a line. 2 To draw in by reeling a line: with *in*: to *reel* a fish in. 3 To say, do, etc., easily and fluently: with *off*. [OE *hrēol*] —**reel′a·ble** *adj.* —**reel′er** *n.*

reel² (rēl) *v.i.* 1 To stagger, sway, or lurch, as when giddy or drunk. 2 To whirl round and round. 3 To have a sensation of giddiness or whirling: My head *reels*. 4 To waver or fall back, as attacking troops. —*v.t.* 5 To cause to reel. See synonyms under SHAKE. —*n.* 1 A staggering motion; giddiness. 2 A lively Scottish dance, or its music; also, the Virginia reel. [<REEL¹] —**reel′er** *n.*

re·en·force (rē′en·fôrs′, -fōrs′), **re·en·force·ment** (rē′en·fôrs′mənt, -fōrs′-), etc. See RE-INFORCE, etc.

reentering angle An angle which is turned inward, as in a figure or structure.

re·en·trant (rē·en′trənt) *adj.* Reentering; extending inward. —*n.* 1 One who or that which reenters. 2 A reentering angle, as in a fortification wall.

re·en·try (rē·en′trē) *n.* 1 The act of entering again. 2 *Law* The act of resuming possession of lands or tenements. 3 In whist and bridge, a card by which a player gains or can gain the lead. 4 *Aerospace* The return into the atmosphere of an object launched into space from the earth.

re·ex·change (rē′iks·chānj′) *v.t.* **·changed, ·chang·ing** To exchange again. —*n.* 1 A second or renewed exchange. 2 The sum that the holder of a bill of exchange may demand of the drawer or indorser as indemnity for the loss incurred by its dishonor in a foreign country, where it was payable.

re·fec·tion (ri·fek′shən) *n.* 1 Refreshment by food; a light meal. 2 In civil law, repair of property. 3 *Med.* Spontaneous recovery, as from an ailment or the effects of a vitamin deficiency. [<OF <L *refectio, -onis* < *refectus,* pp. of *reficere* remake, refresh < *re-* again + *facere* make] —**re·fec′tion·er** *n.* —**re·fec′tive** *adj.*

re·fec·to·ry (ri·fek′tər·ē) *n.* *pl.* **·ries** A room for eating; usually, in a religious house or college, a hall set apart for meals. [<Med. L *refectorium* <L *refectus.* See REFECTION.]

re·fer (ri·fûr′) *v.* **·ferred, ·fer·ring** *v.t.* 1 To direct or send for information or other purpose: I *refer* you to another department. 2 To hand over or submit for consideration, settlement, etc.: They *referred* the bill to a special committee. 3 To attribute the cause or source of; assign; relate: He *refers* his success to unceasing application. 4 To assign or attribute to a group, class, period, etc. —*v.i.* 5 To make reference; allude. 6 To turn, as for information, help, or authority; have recourse: to *refer* to the dictionary. See synonyms under ALLUDE, ATTRIBUTE. [<OF *referer* <L *referre* < *re-* back + *ferre* bear, carry] —**refer·a·ble** (ref′ər·ə·bəl), **re·fer′ra·ble** or **re·fer′ri·ble** *adj.*

ref·e·ree (ref′ə·rē′) *n.* 1 A person to whom a thing is referred. 2 In certain games, as football, an official who has general control of the game. 3 *Law* A person to whom a case is sent by order of court for investigation and report; an arbitrator. See synonyms under JUDGE. —*v.t.* & *v.i.* To judge as a referee.

ref·er·ence (ref′ər·əns, ref′rəns) *n.* 1 The act of referring. 2 An incidental allusion or direction of the attention: *reference* to a recent event. 3 A note or other indication in a book, referring to some other book or passage: compare CROSS-REFERENCE. 4 One who or that which is or may be referred to. 5 The state of being referred or related: used in the phrases *with* or *in reference to.* 6 *Law* The act or process of submitting a matter to a referee; also, the proceedings of and before a referee. 7 The person or persons to whom one seeking employment may refer for recommendation; also, a written statement or testimonial, as of character or dependability. —**ref′er·enc·er** *n.*

ref·er·end (ref′ə·rend) *n.* The instrument, vehicle, or means by which an act of reference is made. [<REFERENDUM]

ref·er·en·dum (ref′ə·ren′dəm) *n.* *pl.* **·dums** or **·da** (-də) 1 The submission, by a diplomatic representative to his government, of a proposition not covered by his original instructions. 2 The submission of a proposed public measure or law, which has been passed upon by a legislature or convention, to a vote of the people for ratification or rejection. [<L, gerund of *referre.* See REFER.]

ref·er·ent (ref′ər·ənt) *n.* The particular object, concept, class, event, or the like to which reference is made in any verbal statement or its symbolic equivalent. [<L *referens, -entis,* ppr. of *referre.* See REFER.]

re·fer·ral (ri·fûr′əl) *n.* 1 The act of referring, or the condition of being referred. 2 One who has been referred.

re·fill (rē·fil′) *v.t.* To fill again. —*n.* (rē′fil′) Any commodity packaged to fit and fill a container originally containing that commodity: a *refill* for a lipstick case.

re·fine (ri·fīn′) *v.* **·fined, ·fin·ing** *v.t.* 1 To make fine or pure; free from impurities or extraneous matter. 2 To make polished or cultured; free from coarseness or vulgarity. —*v.i.* 3 To become fine or pure. 4 To become more polished or cultured. 5 To make fine distinctions; use subtlety. See synonyms under CHASTEN, PURIFY. —**re·fin′er** *n.*

re·fined (ri·fīnd′) *adj.* 1 Characterized by refinement or polish. 2 Free from impurity; purified; clarified. 3 Exceedingly precise or exact; subtle: *refined* tortures. See synonyms under FINE.

re·fine·ment (ri·fīn′mənt) *n.* 1 Fineness of thought, taste, language, etc.; freedom from coarseness or vulgarity; delicacy; culture. 2 The act, effect, or process of refining; purification. 3 A nice distinction; subtlety; also, fastidiousness. [<REFINE]

Synonyms: civilization, cultivation, culture. *Civilization* applies to nations, denoting the sum of those civil, social, economic, and political attainments by which a community is removed from barbarism; a people may be civilized while still far from *refinement* or *culture,* but *civilization* is susceptible of various degrees and of continued progress. *Refinement* applies either to nations or individuals, denoting the removal of what is coarse and rude, and a corresponding attainment of what is delicate, elegant, and beautiful. *Culture,* in the fullest sense, as distinct from *cultivation,* denotes that degree of *refinement* and development which results from continued *cultivation* through successive generations; a man's faculties may be brought to a high degree of *cultivation* in some specialty, while he himself remains uncultured even to the extent of coarseness and rudeness. See HUMANITY. *Antonyms:* barbarism, boorishness, brutality, clownishness, coarseness, grossness, rudeness, rusticity, vulgarity.

re·fin·er·y (ri·fī′nər·ē) *n.* *pl.* **·er·ies** A place where some crude material, as sugar or petroleum, is purified.

re·fit (rē·fit′) *v.t.* & *v.i.* **·fit·ted, ·fit·ting** To make or be made fit or ready again; return to serviceable condition, as by making repairs, replacing equipment, etc. —*n.* The repair of damages or wear, as of a ship.

re·flect (ri·flekt′) *v.t.* 1 To turn or throw back, as rays of light, heat, or sound. 2 To give back an image of; mirror. 3 To cause to rebound or return; cast: He *reflects* credit on his teacher. 4 *Obs.* To bend or fold back. —*v.i.* 5 To send back rays, as of light or heat. 6 To return in rays: The light *reflects* into my eyes. 7 To give back an image; also, to be mirrored. 8 To think carefully; ponder. 9 To bring blame, discredit, etc.: with *on* or *upon.* See synonyms under CONSIDER, DELIBERATE, MUSE. [<OF *reflecter* <L *reflectere* < *re-* back + *flectere* bend]

reflecting telescope See under TELESCOPE.

re·flec·tion (ri·flek′shən) *n.* 1 The act of reflecting, or the state of being reflected. 2 *Physics* The throwing off or back (from a surface) of impinging light, heat, sound, or any form of radiant energy. 3 The result of reflecting; reflected rays or an image thrown by reflection. 4 Consideration of or meditation upon past knowledge or experience; thought: *Reflection* increases wisdom; also, its result: a wise *reflection.* 5 The casting of blame; censure. 6 *Anat.* The folding of a part upon itself; a fold, as in a membrane. 7 Reflex action, as of the nerves. Also spelled reflexion. [<OF *reflexion* <L *reflexio, -onis*] —**re·flec′tion·al** or **re·flex′ion·al** *adj.*

Synonyms: cogitation, consideration, contemplation, deliberation, meditation, musing, rumination, study, thinking, thought. See ANIMADVERSION, THOUGHT¹. *Antonyms:* carelessness, heedlessness, imprudence, inconsiderateness, negligence, thoughtlessness.

re·flec·tive (ri·flek′tiv) *adj.* 1 Given to reflection or thought; meditative: a *reflective* person. 2 Used in or capable of consideration or reflection. 3 Having the quality of throwing back light, heat, sound, etc. —**re·flec′tive·ly** *adv.* —**re·flec′tive·ness** *n.*

re·flec·tor (ri·flek′tər) *n.* 1 That which reflects. 2 A polished surface, of glass or metal (usually concave), for reflecting light, heat, or sound, and also pictures or slides in a particular direction. 3 A telescope which transmits an image from a reflecting surface to the eyepiece. 4 *Physics* A substance placed around the core of a nuclear reactor for the purpose of reducing neutron leakage and maintaining the level of the chain reaction: sometimes called a *tamper.* 5 *Telecom.* The rear portion of an antenna, serving to increase its directional characteristics.

re·flet (rə·fle′) *n.* 1 Iridescence of surface; especially, the metallic glaze on pottery. 2 Pottery having metallic or iridescent luster. [<F, reflection]

re·flex (rē′fleks) *adj.* 1 Turned or thrown backward; reflected, as light. 2 *Physiol.* Of, pertaining to, or produced by a reflex. 3 Turned back upon itself or in the direction whence it came: *reflex* motion. 4 Bent back; reflexed. 5 *Telecom.* Designating a radio receiving circuit in which a single vacuum tube serves for the simultaneous amplification of two different frequencies. —*n.* 1 Reflection, or an image produced by reflection, as from a mirror or like surface. 2 An image or copy; also, an adaptation from another language or dialect, as of a word. 3 Light reflected from an illuminated surface to a shady one. 4 *Physiol.* An involuntary movement or action produced by the transmission of an afferent impulse to a nerve center and its reflection thence as an efferent impulse, as in winking when the eye is threatened: also reflex action. —*v.t.* (ri·fleks′) To bend back; turn back or reflect. [<L *reflexus* reflected, pp. of *reflectere.* See REFLECT.]

re·flex·ive (ri·flek′siv) *adj.* 1 Reflex. 2 *Gram.* Reflected upon or referring to itself or its subject: in the sentence "He dresses himself," "dresses" is a *reflexive* verb, "himself" is a *reflexive* pronoun. —*n.* A reflexive verb or pronoun. —**re·flex′ive·ly** *adv.* —**re·flex′ive·ness, re·flex·iv·i·ty** (rē′flek·siv′ə·tē) *n.*

ref·lu·ent (ref′lōō·ənt) *adj.* Flowing back; ebbing, as the tide. [<L *refluens, -entis,* ppr. of *refluere* flow back < *re-* back + *fluere* flow] —**ref′lu·ence, ref′lu·en·cy** *n.*

re·flux (rē′fluks′) *n.* A flowing back; ebb; return: the flux and *reflux* of fortune. [<L *refluxus,* pp. of *refluere.* See REFLUENT.]

re·form (ri·fôrm′) *v.t.* 1 To make better by removing abuses, altering, etc.; restore to a better condition: to *reform* a corrupt city government; to *reform* inefficient business procedures. 2 To make better morally; persuade or educate from a sinful to a moral life: to *reform* a prostitute. 3 To put an end to; stop (an abuse, malpractice, etc.). —*v.i.* 4 To give up sin or error; become better. See synonyms under AMEND, RECLAIM. —*n.* An act or result of reformation; change for the better, especially in administration; correction of evils or abuses; abandonment of vicious habits. [<OF *reformer* <L *reformare* < *re-* again + *formare* form] —**re·form′a·tive** *adj.* —**re·form′er, re·form′ist** *n.*

Reform Judaism Judaism as practiced by those who emphasize the historical continuity of the Jewish community and the ethical and prophetic content of the Scriptures and the oral laws, and reject or modify much of the traditional ritual. Compare CONSERVATIVE JUDAISM, ORTHODOX JUDAISM.

ref·or·ma·tion (ref'ər·mā'shən) n. 1 The act of reforming. 2 The state of being reformed. 3 Moral or religious restoration or revival.

Ref·or·ma·tion (ref'ər·mā'shən) n. The religious revolution of the 16th century in Europe which began as a movement to reform Catholicism and ended with the establishment of Protestantism in many parts of northern and western Europe.

re·for·ma·to·ry (ri·fôr'mə·tôr'ē, -tō'rē) adj. Having a tendency or aiming to produce reformation. — n. pl. ·ries An institution for the reformation and instruction of juvenile offenders.

Re·formed (ri·fôrmd') adj. Designating those Protestant churches which separated from the Lutherans in the 16th century on questions of doctrine; specifically, those churches which follow the teachings of Calvin and Zwingli. See CALVINISM, ZWINGLIAN.

reform school A reformatory.

re·fract (ri·frakt') v.t. 1 To deflect (a ray) by refraction. 2 Optics To determine the degree of refraction of (an eye or lens). [<L refractus, pp. of refringere turn aside < re- back + frangere break]

refracting telescope See under TELESCOPE.

re·frac·tion (ri·frak'shən) n. Physics The change of direction of a ray, as of light or heat, in oblique passage from one medium to another of different density, or in traversing a medium whose density is not uniform.

LIGHT REFRACTION

— **double refraction** The property possessed by certain types of crystals of breaking up a beam of light into two differently refracted and polarized rays. — **re·frac'tive** adj. — **re·frac'tive·ness, re·frac·tiv·i·ty** (rē'frak·tiv'ə·tē) n. — **re·frac'tor** n.

re·frac·tom·e·ter (rē'frak·tom'ə·tər) n. Any instrument for measuring indices of refraction. [<REFRACT + -(O)METER]

re·frac·to·ry (ri·frak'tər·ē) adj. 1 Not amenable to control; disobedient; unmanageable; obstinate. 2 Resisting ordinary methods of reduction: said of an ore. See synonyms under OBSTINATE, REBELLIOUS, RESTIVE, TURBULENT. — n. pl. ·ries 1 A refractory or obstinate person or thing. 2 Any of various materials highly resistant to the action of great heat, as fireclay, graphite, magnesite, etc. [<L refractarius] — **re·frac'to·ri·ly** adv. — **re·frac'to·ri·ness** n.

re·fra·ga·ble (ref'rə·gə·bəl) adj. Capable of being refuted. [<Med. L refragabilis <L refragari oppose]

re·frain¹ (ri·frān') v.i. To keep oneself back; abstain from action; forbear. — v.t. To restrain; curb. [<OF refrener <L refrenare curb <re- back + frenum a bridle] — **re·frain'er** n. Synonyms: abstain, forbear, restrain. See CEASE, KEEP. Antonyms: begin, continue, persevere, persist.

re·frain² (ri·frān') n. 1 A phrase or strain repeated at intervals, generally regular, in a poem or a song; the burden. It generally recurs at the end of a stanza or strophe, and is common in old ballads and in Provençal poetry. 2 Any saying that is repeated over and over. [<OF <refraindre check, repeat <L refringere break off. See REFRACT.]

re·fran·gi·ble (ri·fran'jə·bəl) adj. Capable of being refracted, as light. [<RE- + L frangere break + -IBLE] — **re·fran'gi·bil'i·ty, re·fran'gi·ble·ness** n.

re·fresh (ri·fresh') v.t. 1 To make (a person) fresh or vigorous again, as by food or rest; reinvigorate; revive. 2 To make fresh, clean, cool, etc. 3 To stimulate, as the memory. 4 To renew or replenish with or as with new supplies. — v.i. 5 To become fresh again; revive. 6 To take refreshment. 7 To lay in provisions. [<OF refreschier <re- again (<L) + fres fresh. See FRESH.]

re·fresh·er (ri·fresh'ər) n. 1 One who or that which refreshes. 2 A refresher course. — adj. Designating something that reacquaints one with the material of subjects previously

studied and forgotten: a refresher course.

re·fresh·ing (ri·fresh'ing) adj. Serving to refresh: often used sarcastically: refreshing impudence. See synonyms under DELIGHTFUL. — **re·fresh'ing·ly** adv.

re·fresh·ment (ri·fresh'mənt) n. 1 The act of refreshing, or the state of being refreshed; restoration of vigor or liveliness. 2 That which refreshes, as food or drink. 3 pl. Food, or food and drink, served as a light meal.

re·frig·er·ant (ri·frij'ər·ənt) adj. Cooling or freezing; allaying heat or fever. — n. 1 Any medicine or material, as ice, which reduces abnormal heat of the body. 2 A substance used for obtaining and maintaining a low temperature, as carbon dioxide, ammonia, or methyl chloride; a freezing mixture; a freezing agent. [<L refrigerans, -antis, ppr. of refrigerare. See REFRIGERATE.]

re·frig·er·ate (ri·frij'ə·rāt) v.t. ·at·ed, ·at·ing 1 To keep or cause to become cold; cool. 2 To freeze or chill (foodstuffs) for preservative purposes. [<L refrigeratus, pp. of refrigerare <re- thoroughly + frigerare cool < frigus, frigoris cold] — **re·frig'er·a'tion** n. — **re·frig'er·a'tive** adj. & n.

re·frig·er·a·tor (ri·frij'ə·rā'tər) n. 1 That which makes or keeps cold. 2 A box, cabinet, room, railroad car, etc., equipped with apparatus for preserving the freshness of perishable foods, etc., by means of ice or other refrigerant.

reft (reft) Past tense and past participle of REAVE.

ref·uge (ref'yōōj) n. 1 Shelter or protection, as from danger or distress. 2 One who or that which shelters or protects. 3 A safe place; asylum. 4 Brit. A raised or enclosed safety area for the use of pedestrians at busy street crossings. — v.t. & v.i. Obs. To give or take refuge. [<OF <L refugium < refugere retreat <re- back + fugere flee] Synonyms (noun): asylum, cover, covert, harbor, hiding-place, protection, retreat, sanctuary, stronghold. See SHELTER.

ref·u·gee (ref'yōō·jē') n. 1 One who flees to a refuge. 2 One who flees from invasion, persecution, or political danger. [<F réfugié, pp. of réfugier <L refugere. See REFUGE.]

re·ful·gence (ri·ful'jəns) n. Splendor; brilliant radiance. Also **re·ful'gen·cy.**

re·ful·gent (ri·ful'jənt) adj. Shining with a bright light; brilliant; splendid. See synonyms under BRIGHT. [<L refulgens, -entis, ppr. of refulgere reflect light <re- back + fulgere shine] — **re·ful'gent·ly** adv.

re·fund (ri·fund') v.t. 1 To give or pay back (money, etc.). 2 Obs. To pour back. — v.i. 3 To make repayment. — n. (rē'fund) A repayment; refunding; also, the amount repaid. [<L refundere pour back <re- back + fundere pour out, discharge] — **re·fund'er** n. — **re·fund'ment** n.

re·fus·al (ri·fyōō'zəl) n. 1 The act of refusing; denial of what is asked. 2 The privilege of accepting or rejecting; an option.

re·fuse¹ (ri·fyōōz') v. ·fused, ·fus·ing v.t. 1 To decline to do, permit, take, or yield. 2 Mil. To turn back (the wing of a line of troops), so that it stands at an angle with the main body. 3 To decline to jump over: said of a horse at a ditch, hedge, etc. 4 Obs. To disown; renounce; resign. — v.i. 5 To decline to do, permit, take, or yield something. [<OF refuser <L refusus, pp. of refundere. See REFUND.] — **re·fus'er** n.

ref·use² (ref'yōōs) adj. Rejected as worthless. — n. Anything worthless; rubbish. See synonyms under WASTE. [<OF refus, pp. of refuser. See REFUSE¹.]

ref·u·ta·tion (ref'yōō·tā'shən) n. The act of refuting or proving the falsity or error in a statement, proposition, or argument; evidence applied to overthrow an erroneous statement or position. Also **re·fu·tal** (ri·fyōōt'l). [<L refutatio, -onis <refutare stop, repel]

re·fute (ri·fyōōt') v.t. ·fut·ed, ·fut·ing 1 To prove the incorrectness or falsity of (a statement). 2 To prove (a person) to be in error; confute. [<L refutare] — **re·fut'a·bil'i·ty** n. — **re·fut'a·ble** adj. — **re·fut'a·bly** adv. — **re·fut'er** n. Synonyms: confound, confute, disprove. To refute and to confute are to answer so as to admit of no reply. Refute applies either to arguments and opinions or to accusations; confute is not applied to accusations and

charges, but to overwhelming arguments or opinions that confound; a person is confuted when his arguments are refuted.

re·gain (ri·gān') v.t. 1 To get possession of again, as something lost; gain anew. 2 To reach again; get back to: He regained the street. See synonyms under RECOVER. [<MF regaigner] — **re·gain'er** n.

re·gal (rē'gəl) adj. Belonging to or fit for a king; royal; also, stately. See synonyms under IMPERIAL, KINGLY. [<OF <L regalis <rex, regis king. Doublet of ROYAL.] — **re'gal·ly** adv.

re·gale (ri·gāl') v. ·galed, ·gal·ing v.t. 1 To give unusual pleasure to; delight: He regaled us with stories. 2 To entertain royally or sumptuously; feast. — v.i. 3 To feast. — n. Obs. 1 A sumptuous feast. 2 Refreshment. 3 A choice dish. [<F régaler; ult. origin uncertain] — **re·gale'ment** n.

re·ga·li·a (ri·gā'lē·ə, -gāl'yə) n. pl. 1 The insignia and emblems of royalty, as the crown, scepter, verge, vestments, etc. 2 The distinctive symbols, insignia, etc., of any society, order, or rank; hence, fine clothes; fancy trappings. 3 In old English law, royal rights; the six prerogatives of sovereignty: the powers of judicature, life and death, war and peace, taxation, minting money, and taking masterless goods, as waifs, strays, etc. [<L, neut. pl. of regalis kingly <rex, regis king]

re·gal·i·ty (ri·gal'ə·tē) n. pl. ·ties 1 Sovereign jurisdiction; royalty. 2 A territorial jurisdiction conferred by the crown on a subject. 3 A country subject to royal authority; a kingdom. [<OF regalité]

re·gard (ri·gärd') v.t. 1 To look at or observe closely or attentively. 2 To look on or think of in a certain or specified manner; consider: I regard him as a friend. 3 To take into account; consider. 4 To have relation or pertinence to; concern. 5 Obs. To care for. — v.i. 6 To pay attention. 7 To gaze or look. See synonyms under ESTEEM, LOOK, PERTAIN. — n. 1 Observant attention or notice; heed; consideration. 2 Common estimation or repute, especially good repute: a man of regard. 3 Reference; relation. 4 A look or aspect; view. 5 Usually pl. Respect; affection: My kindest regards to your family. 6 Motive. [<OF regarder look at <re- again + garder guard, heed. Doublet of REWARD.] Synonyms (noun): esteem, favor, respect. Regard is more personal and less distant than esteem, and adds a special kindliness; respect is a more distant word than esteem. Respect may be wholly on one side, while regard is more often mutual; respect in the fullest sense is given to what is lofty, worthy, and honorable, or to a person of such qualities; we may pay an external respect to one of lofty station, regardless of personal qualities, showing respect for the office. See ATTACHMENT, ESTEEM, FAVOR, FRIENDSHIP, LOVE. Antonyms: abhorrence, antipathy, aversion, contempt, dislike, hatred, loathing, repugnance.

re·gard·ful (ri·gärd'fəl) adj. 1 Having or showing regard; heedful. 2 Respectful. — **re·gard'ful·ly** adv. — **re·gard'ful·ness** n.

re·gard·ing (ri·gär'ding) prep. In reference to; with regard to.

re·gard·less (ri·gärd'lis) adj. Having no regard or consideration; heedless; negligent. See synonyms under INATTENTIVE. — adv. Colloq. In spite of everything.

re·gat·ta (ri·gat'ə, -gä'tə) n. A boat race, or a series of such races. [<Ital. <regatar strive]

re·ge·la·tion (rē'jə·lā'shən) n. The refreezing of melting ice by reducing the pressure to which it is subjected, thus raising the freezing point.

re·gen·er·ate (ri·jen'ə·rāt) v. ·at·ed, ·at·ing v.t. 1 To cause complete moral and spiritual reformation or regeneration in. 2 To produce or form anew; re-create; reproduce. 3 To make use (of heat or other energy that might otherwise be wasted) by means of various devices. 4 Biol. To grow or form by regeneration. 5 Electronics To raise the amplification of (a vacuum tube) by transferring to the input circuit some of the power of the output circuit. — v.i. 6 To form anew; be reproduced. 7 To become spiritually regenerate. 8 To effect regeneration. — adj. (ri·jen'ər·it) 1 Having new life; restored. 2 Spiritually renewed; regenerated. [<L regeneratus, pp. of regenerare generate again <re- again +generare. See

GENERATE.]

re·gen·er·a·tion (ri·jen'ə·rā'shən) *n.* **1** The act of regenerating, or the state of being regenerated. **2** The impartation of spiritual life by divine grace. **3** *Biol.* **a** The reproduction of a lost part or organ, as in lizards. **b** The renewal or reproduction of cells, tissues, etc., in the ordinary vital processes: the *regeneration* of the ectodermic layers. **4** The process by which, in various devices, heat or other forms of energy are saved and re-utilized. **5** *Electronics* The amplification of radiosignal strength by returning part of the output of a vacuum tube to the grid: an effect of feedback. [<OF] **—re·gen·er·a·tive** (ri·jen'ə·rā'tiv, -ər·ə·tiv) *adj.* **—re·gen'er·a'tive·ly** *adv.*

re·gent (rē'jənt) *n.* **1** One who rules in the name and place of the sovereign. **2** Any ruler or governor; one who governs. **3** resident master who takes part in the government of a university or college. **4** One of various officers having charge of the higher education, as of a state. *—adj.* **1** Exercising authority in another's place. **2** Governing; ruling. [<OF <L *regens, -entis,* ppr. of *regere* rule]

reg·gae (reg'ā) *n.* A simple, lively, rhythmic kind of rock 'n' roll music, of West Indian origin. [< a native West Indian name]

reg·i·cide (rej'ə·sīd) *n.* **1** The killing of a king or sovereign. **2** The killer of a king or sovereign. [<L *rex, regis* king + -CIDE] **—reg'i·ci'dal** *adj.*

re·gime (ri·zhēm') *n.* **1** System of government or administration. **2** Prevalent mode in social matters; social system. **3** Regimen (def. 1). Also **ré·gime** (rā·zhēm'). [<F *régime* <L *regimen.* Doublet of REGIMEN.]

reg·i·men (rej'ə·mən) *n.* **1** A systematized course of living, as to food, clothing, etc. **2** Government; control. **3** *Gram.* The influence of one word in determining the form of another connected with it; grammatical government. See synonyms under FOOD. [<L *regimen* <*regere* rule. Doublet of REGIME.]

reg·i·ment (rej'ə·mənt) *n.* **1** A body of soldiers constituting the unit of infantry, cavalry, artillery, etc., commanded by a colonel. **2** *Obs.* Government over a people or country. *—v.t.* **1** To form into a regiment or regiments; organize. **2** To assign to a regiment. **3** To form into well-defined or specific units or groups; systematize. **4** To make uniform at the expense of individual differences: Certain types of education *regiment* children. [<OF <LL *regimentum* <L *regere* rule] **—reg'i·men'tal** *adj.*

reg·i·men·tals (rej'ə·men'təlz) *n. pl.* Military uniform; the uniform worn by the men and officers of a regiment.

reg·i·men·ta·tion (rej'ə·men·tā'shən)*n.* **1** The act of regimenting; formation into or as into a regiment. **2** Organization into disciplined, uniform groups.

re·gi·nal (ri·jī'nəl) *adj.* Pertaining to a queen; queenly; also, supporting or favoring a queen. [<Med. L *reginalis*]

re·gion (rē'jən) *n.* **1** A portion of territory or space; a country or district; also, realm; specifically, one of the strata into which the air or the sea is divided by imaginary boundaries. **2** A zoogeographical division of the earth's surface: the Australian *region.* **3** A portion of the body, arbitrarily circumscribed for anatomical and medical purposes: the abdominal *region.* See synonyms under LAND. [<AF *regiun,* OF *regium* <L *regio, -onis* <*regere* rule]

re·gion·al (rē'jən·əl) *adj.* **1** Of or pertaining to a particular region; sectional; local: *regional* planning. **2** Of or pertaining to an entire region or section, especially a geographic one: *regional* features. **—re'gion·al·ly** *adv.*

re·gion·al·ism (rē'jə·nə·liz'əm) *n.* **1** An emotional loyalty or strong feeling for a particular region. **2** An emphasis on regional flavor in art and literature. **3** A specific habit, custom, or way of speaking of a certain region.

reg·is·ter (rej'is·tər) *n.* **1** An official record, the book containing it, or an entry therein; roll; list; schedule; a registry. **2** A registrar. **3** That which registers; a registering apparatus, as for recording velocity, pressure, etc. **4** A

device for regulating the admission of heated air to a room. **5** A machine or apparatus which automatically records cash intake; a cash register. **6** *Music* **a** The range or compass of a voice or musical instrument. **b** A class or series of tones of a particular quality or belonging to a particular portion of the compass of a voice or of some instruments. The normal and natural register of the voice is the chest, or thick, register; a middle and an upper register are also recognized, the latter being also termed a head, or thin, register. **7** *Phot.* Relation of position between the sensitive plate or film and the focusing screen. **8** *Printing* **a** Exact correspondence of the lines and margins on the opposite sides of a printed sheet. **b** Correct relation of the colors in color printing. See synonyms under HISTORY, RECORD. *—v.t.* **1** To enter in or as in a register; enrol; specifically, to record formally, as a document, securities, etc. **2** To indicate on a scale. **3** To express or indicate: His face *registered* his disapproval. **4** To effect the exact correspondence of (parts), as the two sides of a printed sheet, the separate plates or films of a color print, etc. **5** To cause (mail) to be recorded, on payment of a fee, when deposited with the postal system, so as to insure delivery. *—v.i.* **6** To enter one's name in a register, poll, etc. **7** To have effect; make an impression. **8** *Printing* To be in register. See synonyms under ENROL. [<OF *registre* <Med. L *registrum* <L *regesta* records, neut. pl of *regestus,* pp. of *regerere* record <*re-* back + *gerere* carry] **—reg·is·tra·ble** (rej'is·trə·bəl) *adj.*

reg·is·tered (rej'is·tərd) *adj.* **1** Recorded, as a birth, a voter, an animal's pedigree, etc. **2** Having a required or official certificate, as a nurse.

registered mail First-class mail, specially entered and recorded at a higher fee, to insure safe delivery.

registered nurse A graduate nurse licensed to practice by the appropriate State authority and entitled to add R.N. after her name.

reg·is·trant (rej'is·trənt) *n.* One who registers, as a voter; especially, one who registers a trademark or patent. [<F]

reg·is·trar (rej'is·trär, rej'is·trär') *n.* The authorized keeper of a register or of records; especially, a college or university officer who records the enrolment of students, their grades, etc. [<Med. L *registrarius*]

reg·is·tra·tion (rej'is·trā'shən) *n.* **1** The act of entering in a registry; also, an entry in a registry. **2** The registering of voters; also, the number of voters registered. **3** Enrolment in a school, college, or university. **4** The combination of stops used in playing a composition on the organ. [<Med. L *registratio, -onis*]

reg·nal (reg'nəl) *adj.* Of or pertaining to a reign, a king, or a kingdom. [<LL *regnalis* <L *regnum* reign]

re·gorge (ri·gôrj') *v.* **gorged,** **·gorg·ing** *v.t.* To vomit up; disgorge. *—v.i.* To gush or flow back. [<F *regorger* <*re-* again + *gorger* gorge <*gorge* throat <L *gurges* whirlpool. Related to REGURGITATE.]

re·grate (ri·grāt') *v.t.* **·grat·ed,** **·grat·ing** **1** To buy up, as provisions, for the purpose of selling at a higher price in or near the same market. **2** To retail, as provisions. [<OF *regrater;* ult. origin uncertain]

re·gress (rē'gres) *n.* **1** Passage back; return; also, the power or right of passing back or returning. **2** Retrogression. *—v.i.* (ri·gres') **1** To go back; move backward; return. **2** *Astron.* To move in a direction opposite to that of the general motion of the heavenly bodies, as the moon's nodes. **3** *Stat.* To return to the mean value of a series of observations. [<L *regressus,* pp. of *regredi* go back <*re-* back + *gradi* walk] **—re·gres'sor** *n.*

re·gres·sion (ri·gresh'ən) *n.* **1** The act of moving back or returning. **2** *Astron.* Motion in a direction opposite to that of the general motion of the heavenly bodies. **3** *Psychoanal.* A retreat of the libido to earlier levels of development or to infantile tendencies belonging to a period preceding the obstacles which prevented their normal fulfilment.

4 *Stat.* The return to a mean or average value. **5** *Med.* The subsidence of a disease or of its symptoms.

re·gres·sive (ri·gres'iv) *adj.* **1** Passing back; returning. **2** Retroactive. **3** Retrogressive. **—re·gres'sive·ly** *adv.*

re·gret (ri·gret') *v.t.* **·gret·ted,** **·gret·ting 1** To look back upon with a feeling of distress or loss. **2** To feel sorrow or grief concerning. See synonyms under MOURN. *— n.* **1** Distress of mind in recalling some past event; a wish that something had or had not happened. **2** Remorseful sorrow; compunction. **3** An expression of sorrow or disappointment. **4** *pl.* A polite declination in response to an invitation. See synonyms under GRIEF, REPENTANCE. [<OF *regreter;* ult. origin uncertain] **re·gret'ter** *n.*

re·gret·ful (ri·gret'fəl) *adj.* Feeling, expressive of, or full of regret. **—re·gret'ful·ly** *adv.* **— re·gret'ful·ness** *n.*

re·gret·ta·ble (ri·gret'ə·bəl) *adj.* Causing or demanding regret; unfortunate; deplorable. **— re·gret'ta·bly** *adv.*

reg·u·lar (reg'yə·lər) *adj.* **1** Made according to rule; symmetrical; normal. **2** Acting according to rule; recurring without fail; methodical; orderly: *regular* habits. **3** Constituted, appointed, or conducted in the proper manner; duly authorized: a *regular* meeting, a *regular* practitioner. **4** *Gram.* Undergoing the inflection that is normal or most common to the class of words to which it belongs; following the rule; not exceptional. **5** *Bot.* Having all the parts or organs of the same kind uniform in structure or shape and size: said mainly of flowers. **6** *Zool.* Conforming to an established type; exhibiting radial or bilateral symmetry. **7** *Music* Following strict and classical rules of composition: a *regular* movement. **8** *Eccl.* Bound by a religious rule; pertaining or belonging to a religious order: the *regular* clergy. **9** *Mil.* Belonging to the standing army; permanent. **10** In politics, adhering loyally to a party organization or platform; also, nominated by the official party organization: said of a candidate. **11** *Geom.* Having equal sides and angles. **12** Controlled or governed by one law or operation throughout: a *regular* equation. **13** *Colloq.* Thorough; unmitigated; absolute. **14** *Slang* Fine; good: a *regular* guy. **15** *U.S.* Designating that component of a branch of the armed services which consists of persons in continuous service on active duty in both peace and war: the **Regular Army, Regular Navy, Regular Air Force.** See synonyms under CONTINUAL, GRADUAL, HABITUAL, NORMAL, SOBER, USUAL. *— n.* **1** A soldier belonging to a standing army as opposed to a volunteer, draftee, or member of a reserve unit. **2** *Colloq.* One regularly employed or engaged; also, a habitual customer. **3** *Eccl.* A member of a religious or monastic order. **4** A person loyal to a certain political party. [<L *regularis* <*regula* rule] **—reg'u·lar·ness** *n.*

reg·u·lar·i·ty (reg'yə·lar'ə·tē) *n. pl.* **·ties** The state, quality, or character of being regular: *regularity* of form or in occurrence. See synonyms under SYMMETRY, SYSTEM.

reg·u·lar·ize (reg'yə·lə·rīz') *v.t.* **·ized,** **·iz·ing** To make regular. **— reg'u·lar·i·za'tion** *n.*

reg·u·lar·ly (reg'yə·lər·lē) *adv.* In a regular manner; according to the usual method or order.

reg·u·late (reg'yə·lāt) *v.t.* **·lat·ed,** **·lat·ing 1** To direct, manage, or control according to certain rules, principles, etc. **2** To adjust according to a standard, degree, etc.: to *regulate* currency. **3** To adjust to accurate operation: to *regulate* a watch. **4** To put in order; set right. [<LL *regulatus,* pp. of *regulare* rule <L *regula* a rule <*regere* rule, lead straight] **— reg'u·la'tive** *adj.*

Synonyms: adjust, arrange, conduct, direct, dispose, govern, guide, manage, methodize, order, rule, systematize. See SET, SETTLE. *Antonyms:* confuse, derange, disorder, displace, distract, disturb, unsettle.

reg·u·la·tion (reg'yə·lā'shən) *n.* **1** The act of regulating, or the state of being regulated. **2** A rule prescribed for conduct: army *regulations:* also used adjectively. See synonyms under LAW[1], RULE.

reg·u·la·tor (reg′yə·lā′tər) *n.* **1** One who or that which regulates. **2** A clock used as a standard; also, an index arm for regulating the rate of a watch. **3** *Mech.* A contrivance for governing or equalizing motion or flow; the governor of a steam engine; a damper or other device for regulating a draft; a throttle valve. **4** A register (def. 4). **5** A thermostat. **6** *Electr.* A device for keeping at constant strength the current produced by a dynamo. — **reg′u·la·tor·ship** *n.*

reg·u·la·to·ry (reg′yə·lə·tôr′ē, -tō′rē) *adj.* Tending or serving to regulate: *regulatory* measures. Also **reg′u·la·tive.**

re·gur·gi·tate (ri·gûr′jə·tāt) *v.* **·tat·ed, ·tat·ing** *v.i.* To rush, pour, or surge back; vomit. — *v.t.* To cause to surge back, as partially digested food; vomit. [<LL *regurgitatus,* pp. of *regurgitare* < *re-* back + *gurgitare* flood, engulf < L *gurges, gurgites* whirlpool] — **re·gur′gi·tant** *adj.*

re·gur·gi·ta·tion (ri·gûr′jə·tā′shən) *n.* **1** The act of rushing back or reswallowing. **2** *Physiol.* The backward rush of blood into the heart, due to defective valves.

re·ha·bil·i·tate (rē′hə·bil′ə·tāt) *v.t.* **·tat·ed, ·tat·ing** **1** To restore to a former state, capacity, privilege, rank, etc.; reinstate. **2** To make one capable of becoming a useful member of society again: to *rehabilitate* a crippled soldier. [<Med. L *rehabilitatus,* pp. of *rehabilitare* < *re-* back + *habilitare.* See HABILITATE.] — **re′ha·bil′i·ta′tion** *n.*

re·hash (rē·hash′) *v.t.* To work into a new form; go over again. — *n.* (rē′hash′) Something hashed over, or made or served up from something used before, as old matter issued under a new name.

re·hears·al (ri·hûr′səl) *n.* **1** The act of rehearsing, as a play. **2** The act of reciting or telling over again.

re·hearse (ri·hûrs′) *v.* **·hearsed, ·hears·ing** *v.t.* **1** To perform privately in preparation for public performance, as a play or song. **2** To cause to perform or recite by way of preparation; instruct by rehearsal. **3** To say over again; repeat aloud; recite. **4** To give an account of; relate. **5** To enumerate. — *v.i.* **6** To rehearse a play, song, dance, etc. See synonyms under RELATE. [<OF *reherser* harrow over, repeat < *re-* again + *herser* harrow < *herse.* See HEARSE.] — **re·hears′er** *n.*

Reich (rīkh) Germany or its government. — **First Reich** The Holy Roman Empire from its establishment in the ninth century to its collapse in 1806. — **Second Reich** The German Empire, 1871–1919, or the Weimar Republic, 1919–1933, or both German governments in the period 1871–1933. — **Third Reich** The Nazi state under Adolf Hitler, 1933–45. [<G, realm]

re·i·fy (rē′ə·fī) *v.t.* **·fied, ·fy·ing** To make real or concrete; materialize: to *reify* an idea. [<L *res, rei* thing + -FY] — **re′i·fi·ca′tion** *n.* — **re′i·fi′er** *n.*

reign (rān) *n.* **1** The possession or exercise of supreme political power; sovereignty; dominion. **2** The time or duration of a sovereign's rule. — *v.i.* **1** To hold and exercise sovereign power; be the head of a monarchy. **2** To hold sway; be predominant; prevail: Winter *reigns.* See synonyms under GOVERN. ◆ Homophones: *rain, rein.* [<F *règne* < L *regnum* rule]

Reign of Terror The period of the French Revolution from May, 1793, to August, 1794, during which Louis XVI, Marie Antoinette, and thousands of other persons were guillotined, and confiscation, violence, and terror reigned under the revolutionary leaders.

re·im·burse (rē′im·bûrs′) *v.t.* **·bursed, ·burs·ing** **1** To pay back (a person) an equivalent for what has been spent or lost; recompense; indemnify. **2** To pay back; refund. [< RE- + obs. *imburse* <LL *imbursare* <L *in-* in + *bursa* purse] — **re′im·burse′ment** *n.* — **re′im·burs′er** *n.*

re·im·pres·sion (rē′im·presh′ən) *n.* **1** A new or second impression of anything. **2** A reprint of a book without editorial change.

rein (rān) *n.* **1** Usually *pl.* A strap attached to the bit to control a horse or other draft animal. **2** Any means of restraint or control; government. — *v.t.* **1** To guide, check, or halt with or as with reins. **2** To furnish with reins. — *v.i.* **3** To check or halt a horse by

means of reins: with *in* or *up.* **4** To obey the reins. See synonyms under REPRESS. ◆ Homophones: *rain, reign.* [<AF *redne,* OF *resne* <L *retinere.* See RETAIN.]

re·in·car·nate (rē′in·kär′nāt) *v.t.* **·nat·ed, ·nat·ing** To cause to undergo reincarnation.

re·in·car·na·tion (rē′in·kär·nā′shən) *n.* A rebirth of the soul in successive bodies; specifically, in Vedic religions, the becoming of an avatar again: one of the series in the transmigrations of souls. — **re′in·car·na′tion·ist** *n.*

re·in·force (rē′in·fôrs′, -fōrs′) *v.t.* **·forced, ·forc·ing** **1** To give new force or strength to. **2** To increase the military or naval strength of by providing with more troops or ships. **3** To add some strengthening part or material to; thicken; strengthen. Support. See synonyms under RECRUIT. — *n.* That which strengthens or reinforces, as the part of a cannon near the breech that is cast thicker than the rest. Also spelled *reenforce.* [<RE- + *inforce,* var. of ENFORCE]

re·in·force·ment (rē′in·fôrs′mənt, -fōrs′-) *n.* **1** The act of reinforcing. **2** Increase of force; a fresh body of troops or additional vessels: often in the plural. See synonyms under INCREASE. Also spelled *reenforcement.*

re·in·state (rē′in·stāt′) *v.t.* **·stat·ed, ·stat·ing** To restore to a former state, position, etc. — **re′in·state′ment** *n.*

re·in·sure (rē′in·shoor′) *v.t.* **·sured, ·sur·ing** **1** To protect (the risk on a policy already issued) by obtaining insurance from a second insurer: said of a first insurer. **2** To insure anew. — **re′in·sur′ance** *n.* — **re′in·sur′er** *n.*

re·is·sue (rē·ish′ōō) *n.* **1** A second or subsequent issue, as of a publication changed only in form or price. **2** A second printing of postage stamps from the same plates. — *v.t.* **·sued, ·su·ing** To issue again.

re·it·er·ate (rē·it′ə·rāt) *v.t.* **·at·ed, ·at·ing** To say or do again and again; repeat. [<L *reiteratus,* pp. of *reiterare* < *re-* again + *iterare.* See ITERATE.] — **re·it′er·a′tion** *n.*

re·it·er·a·tive (rē·it′ə·rā′tiv) *adj.* Characterized by reiteration. — *n.* **1** A word or syllable repeated, usually with some slight change, so as to make a reduplicated word; also, the word so formed, as *tittle-tattle.* **2** A word expressing repeated action. — **re·it′er·a′tive·ly** *adv.*

re·ject (ri·jekt′) *v.t.* **1** To refuse to accept, recognize, believe, etc. **2** To refuse to grant; deny, as a petition. **3** To refuse (a person) recognition, acceptance, etc. **4** To expel, as from the mouth; vomit. **5** To cast away as worthless; discard. — *n.* (rē′jekt) A person or thing that has been discarded or rejected. [<L *rejectus,* pp. of *reicere* fling back < *re-* back + *jacere* throw] — **re·ject′er** or **re·jec′tor** *n.*

re·jec·ta·men·ta (ri·jek′tə·men′tə) *n. pl.* Things thrown away; especially, things rejected from a living organism; excrement. [<NL <L *rejectare,* freq. of *reicere* fling back]

re·jec·tion (ri·jek′shən) *n.* **1** The act of rejecting. **2** That which is rejected.

re·joice (ri·jois′) *v.* **·joiced, ·joic·ing** *v.i.* To feel joyful; be glad. — *v.t.* To fill with joy; gladden. [<OF *rejoiss-, resjoiss-,* stem of *resjoir* enjoy < *re-* again (<L) + *esjoir* <L *ex-* thoroughly + *gaudere* be joyous < *gaudium* joy] — **re·joic′er** *n.*

Synonyms: cheer, delight, enjoy, enrapture, exhilarate, exult, gladden, gratify, joy, please, ravish, triumph. Compare HAPPINESS, HAPPY. **Antonyms:** afflict, agonize, bewail, grieve, lament, mourn, pain, regret, sadden, sorrow.

re·joic·ing (ri·jois′ing) *adj.* Pertaining to or characterized by rejoicing. See synonyms under HAPPY. — *n.* The feeling or expression of joy. See synonyms under HAPPINESS, LAUGHTER, RAPTURE.

re·join[1] (ri·join′) *v.t.* **1** To say in reply; answer. — *v.i.* **2** To answer. **3** *Law* To make answer to the plaintiff's replication. [<F *rejoindre* < *re-* again (<L) + *joindre.* See JOIN.]

re·join[2] (rē·join′) *v.t.* **1** To come again into company with. **2** To join together again; reunite. — *v.i.* **3** To come together again. [<RE- + JOIN]

re·join·der (ri·join′dər) *n.* **1** An answer to a reply; also, any reply or retort. **2** *Law* The answer filed by a defendant to a plaintiff's replication. See synonyms under ANSWER. [< F *rejoindre* answer, reply]

re·ju·ve·nate (ri·jōō′və·nāt) *v.t.* **·nat·ed, ·nat·**

ing **1** To make young; give new vigor or youthfulness to. **2** *Geog.* To restore (a mature or old river) to its youthful condition by the development of lakes, as by obstruction through mountain growth or elevation. Also **re·ju′ve·nize.** [<RE- again + L *juvenis* young + -ATE[1]] — **re·ju′ve·na′tion** *n.*

re·ju·ve·nes·cence (ri·jōō′və·nes′əns) *n.* **1** A renewal of youth; the state of being or growing young again. **2** *Biol.* The transformation of the entire protoplasm of a vegetative cell into a primordial cell, which subsequently invests itself with a new cell wall, and forms the starting point of the life of a new individual. [<L *rejuvenescens,* ppr. of *rejuvenescere* renew youth < *re-* again + *juvenescere* grow young < *juvenis* young] — **re·ju′ve·nes′cent** *adj.*

re·lapse (ri·laps′) *v.i.* **·lapsed, ·laps·ing** **1** To lapse back, as into disease after partial recovery. **2** To return to bad habits or sin; backslide. — *n.* (also rē′laps) A relapsing; lapse into a former evil state. [<L *relapsus,* pp. of *relabi* slide back < *re-* back + *labi* slide] — **re·laps′er** *n.*

re·late (ri·lāt′) *v.* **·lat·ed, ·lat·ing** *v.t.* **1** To tell the events or the particulars of; narrate. **2** To bring into connection or relation. — *v.i.* **3** To have relation: with *to.* **4** To have reference: with *to.* [<F *relater* <L *relatus,* pp. to *referre.* See REFER.] — **re·lat′er** *n.*

Synonyms: describe, detail, narrate, recite, recount, rehearse, report, state, tell. See PERTAIN. **Antonyms:** deny, hide, suppress, withhold.

re·lat·ed (ri·lā′tid) *adj.* **1** Standing in relation; connected. **2** Of common ancestry; connected by blood or marriage; akin. **3** Narrated. **4** Belonging to the same harmonic or melodic series. — **re·lat′ed·ness** *n.*

re·la·tion (ri·lā′shən) *n.* **1** The fact or condition of being related or connected, or that by which things are connected, either objectively or in the mind; interdependence; connection. **2** The act of relating or narrating; also, that which is related or told. **3** Connection by blood or marriage; kinship. **4** A person connected by blood or marriage; a kinsman: now mostly supplanted by *relative.* **5** *Law* **a** The statement of the grounds of a complaint or grievance by a relator. **b** The reaching back and taking effect of an act or judicial decree at a date anterior to its actual occurrence: Assignment in bankruptcy operates by *relation* back to the date of filing the petition. **6** Reference; regard; allusion: chiefly in the phrase, **in relation to.** **7** The position of one person with respect to another: the *relation* of ruler to subject. **8** *pl.* Conditions in general which bring an individual in touch with his fellows; also, the various ways in which one country may come into contact with another politically and commercially. See synonyms under ANALOGY, KINDRED, KINSMAN, REPORT, STORY[1]. [<L *relatio, -onis* < *relatus,* pp. to *referre.* See REFER.]

re·la·tion·al (ri·lā′shən·əl) *adj.* **1** Pertaining to or expressing relation: said especially of certain parts of speech. **2** Having relation or kinship.

re·la·tion·ship (ri·lā′shən·ship) *n.* The state of being related; connection. See synonyms under AFFINITY, KIN.

rel·a·tive (rel′ə·tiv) *adj.* **1** Having connection; pertinent: an inquiry *relative* to one's health. **2** Resulting from or depending upon relation; comparative: a *relative* truth. **3** Intelligible only in relation to each other: the *relative* terms "father" and "son." **4** Referring to, relating to, or qualifying an antecedent term: a *relative* pronoun. **5** Having the same key signature, as major and minor keys and scales. — *n.* **1** One who is related; a kinsman. **2** A relative word or term; especially, a relative pronoun. See synonyms under KINDRED, KINSMAN. [<F *relatif* <LL *relativus* <L *relatus*] — **rel′a·tive·ly** *adv.* — **rel′a·tive·ness** *n.*

relative pronoun See under PRONOUN.

rel·a·tiv·i·ty (rel′ə·tiv′ə·tē) *n.* **1** The quality or condition of being relative; relativeness. **2** *Philos.* Existence only as an object of, or in relation to, a thinking mind; phenomenality: sometimes called the doctrine of the relativity of existence. **3** A condition of dependence or of close relation, as of the solar system on the sun. **4** *Physics* The principle of the interdependence of matter, energy, space, and time, as mathematically formulated by A. Einstein. The **special theory of relativity** states that the velocity of light is independent of the motion of its source and that motion itself is a meaningless concept except as between two physical systems or material bodies moving relatively to each other. The **general theory of relativity** extends these principles to the law of gravitation and the motions of the heavenly bodies.

re·lax (ri·laks′) *v.t.* **1** To make lax or loose; make less tight or firm. **2** To make less stringent or severe, as discipline. **3** To abate; slacken, as efforts. **4** To relieve from strain or effort: to *relax* the eyes. — *v.i.* **5** To become lax or loose; loosen. **6** To become less stringent or severe. **7** To rest; engage in relaxation. **8** To unbend; become less formal. [< L *relaxare* < *re-* again + *laxare* loosen < *laxus* loose. Doublet of RELEASE.] — **re·lax′·a·ble** *adj.* — **re·lax′er** *n.*
  Synonyms: abate, divert, ease, loose, loosen, mitigate, recreate, reduce, relieve, remit, slacken, unbend. Compare WEAKEN. *Antonyms:* bind, confine, contract, strain, stretch, tighten.

re·lax·a·tion (rē′lak·sā′shən) *n.* **1** The act of relaxing, or the state of being relaxed. **2** Indulgence in diversion, or the diversion indulged in; entertainment. [< L *relaxatio, -onis*] — **re·lax·a·tive** (ri·lak′sə·tiv) *adj. & n.*

re·lay (rē′lā, ri·lā′) *n.* **1** A fresh set, as of men, horses, or dogs, to replace or relieve a tired set. **2** A supply of anything kept in store for anticipated use or need. **3** A relay race, or one of its laps or legs. **4** *Electr.* A device which utilizes variations in the condition or strength of a current in a circuit to effect the operation of similar devices in the same or another circuit: a telegraph *relay*. — *v.t.* **1** To send onward by or as by relays. **2** To provide with relays. **3** *Electr.* To operate or retransmit by means of a relay. [< F *relais* < Ital. *rilascio* < *rilasciare, rilassare* leave behind, release < L *relaxare* loosen again. See RELAX.]

re·lease (ri·lēs′) *v.t.* **·leased, ·leas·ing** **1** To set free; liberate; deliver from worry, pain, obligation, etc. **2** To free from something that holds, binds, etc. **3** To permit the circulation, sale, performance, etc., of, as a motion picture, phonograph record, or news item. — *n.* **1** The act of releasing or setting free, or the state of being released; liberation from restraint of any kind. **2** A deliverance or final relief, as from anything grievous or oppressive. **3** A discharge from responsibility or penalty, as from a debt. **4** *Law* An instrument of conveyance by which one of two persons having a mutual interest in lands surrenders and relinquishes all his interest and estate to the other; quitclaim. **5** A motion picture, phonograph record, news item, or the like ready for distribution or circulation. **6** Exhaust of motive fluid in a steam engine; also, the point at which such exhaust begins. **7** *Mech.* Any catch or device to hold and release a mechanism, weights, etc. [< OF *relaisser* let free < L *relaxare*. Doublet of RELAX.] — **re·leas′er** *n.*
  Synonyms (verb): deliver, discharge, disengage, emancipate, exempt, extricate, free, liberate, loose, unbind, unfasten, unloose, untie. See ABSOLVE.

rel·e·gate (rel′ə·gāt) *v.t.* **·gat·ed, ·gat·ing** **1** To send off or consign, as to an obscure position or place. **2** To assign, as to a particular class or sphere. **3** To refer (a matter) to someone for decision. **4** To banish; exile. See synonyms under COMMIT. [< L *relegatus,* pp. of *relegare* send away < *re-* away, back + *legare* send] — **rel·e·ga′tion** *n.*

re·lent (ri·lent′) *v.i.* To soften in temper; become more gentle or compassionate. — *v.t. Obs.* To cause to relent. [< OF *ralentir* < *relentescere* grow soft < *re-* again + *lentus* soft]

re·lent·less (ri·lent′lis) *adj.* **1** Indifferent to the pain of others; not relenting; pitiless. **2** Unremitting; continuous. See synonyms under AUSTERE, IMPLACABLE. — **re·lent′less·ly** *adv.* — **re·lent′less·ness** *n.*

rel·e·vant (rel′ə·vənt) *adj.* **1** Fitting or suiting given requirements; pertinent; applicable: com-

monly with *to.* **2** *Ling.* Designating those features of a phoneme which function to distinguish it from other phonemes in a language, as place of articulation in English consonants. [< Med. L *relevans, -antis,* ppr. of *relevare* bear upon < L, raise up. See RELIEVE.] — **rel′·e·vance, rel′e·van·cy** *n.* — **rel′e·vant·ly** *adv.*

re·li·a·ble (ri·lī′ə·bəl) *adj.* **1** That may be relied upon; worthy of confidence; trustworthy. **2** *Stat.* Exhibiting a reasonable consistency in results obtained, as in a group of repeated tests: distinguished from *valid.* [< RELY + -ABLE] — **re·li·a·bil′i·ty, re·li′a·ble·ness** *n.* — **re·li′a·bly** *adv.*
  Synonyms: trustworthy, trusty. *Trusty* and *trustworthy* refer to inherent qualities of a high order, *trustworthy* being especially applied to persons, and denoting moral integrity and truthfulness; we speak of a *trusty* sword, a *trustworthy* man. *Reliable* is inferior in meaning, denoting merely the possession of such qualities as are needed for safe reliance; as, a *reliable* pledge, *reliable* information. A man is said to be *reliable* with reference not only to moral qualities, but to judgment, knowledge, skill, habit, or perhaps pecuniary ability. A *reliable* messenger is one who may be depended on to do his errand correctly and promptly; a *trusty* or *trustworthy* messenger is one who may be admitted to knowledge of the views and purposes of those who employ him.

re·li·ance (ri·lī′əns) *n.* **1** The act of relying or the condition of being reliant; confidence; trust; pendence. **2** That upon which one relies; a ground of confidence. See synonyms under BELIEF, FAITH. [< RELY + -ANCE]

rel·ic (rel′ik) *n.* **1** Some remaining portion or fragment of that which has vanished or is destroyed: a *relic* of barbarism. **2** Something cherished in memory of one deceased; an object of sacred reverence or of affection; a keepsake or memento. **3** The body or part of the body of a saint, or an object connected with a saint or his tomb; a sacred memento. **4** *pl. Obs.* A corpse; remains. Also spelled *relique.* [< F *relique* < L *reliquiae* remains, leavings < *relinquere* leave. See RELINQUISH.]

re·lief (ri·lēf′) *n.* **1** The act of relieving, or the state of being relieved; removal in whole or in part of any evil, hardship, or trial; alleviation; comfort. **2** That which relieves. **3** Charitable aid, given in the form of money or food to the needy. **4** The release, as of a sentinel or guard, from his post or duty, and the substitution of some other person or persons; also, the person or persons so substituted. **5** In architecture and sculpture, the projection of a figure, ornament, etc., from a surface; also, any such figure: opposed to *round.* Sculptural relief is of three principal kinds: *alto–relievo, bas–relief,* and *mezzo–relievo.* Extremely low relief is called *stiacciato.* **6** In painting, the apparent projection of forms and masses from the plane or ground of a picture given by the arrangement of the lines, colors, or gradations of color; hence, sharpness of outline caused by contrast. **7** In feudal law, a tribute of a fee paid to the lord by the vassal–heir of a deceased tenant for the right of assuming the lapsed tenancy. **8** *Geog.* **a** The unevenness of land surface, as caused by mountains, hills, etc. **b** The parts of a map which portray the configuration of the district represented; contour lines. **—on relief** Receiving money, food, clothing, etc., from a local or other government because of need. [< OF < *relever.* See RELIEVE.]

re·lieve (ri·lēv′) *v.t.* **·lieved, ·liev·ing** **1** To free wholly or partly from pain, embarrassment, etc. **2** To lessen or alleviate, as pain or anxiety. **3** To give aid or assistance to: to *relieve* a besieged city. **4** To free from obligation, injustice, etc. **5** To release from duty, as a sentinel, by providing or serving as a substitute. **6** To make less monotonous, harsh, or unpleasant; vary. **7** To bring into relief or prominence; display by contrast. See synonyms under ALLAY, ALLEVIATE, RELAX. [< OF *relever* give assistance to, succor < L *relevare* lift up < *re-* again + *levare* lift, raise < *levis* light] — **re·liev′a·ble** *adj.* — **re·liev′er** *n.*

re·lig·ion (ri·lij′ən) *n.* **1** A belief binding the

spiritual nature of man to a supernatural being, as involving a feeling of dependence and responsibility, together with the feelings and practices which naturally flow from such a belief. **2** Any system of faith and worship: the Christian *religion.* **3** An essential part or a practical test of the spiritual life. See *James* i 27. **4** An object of conscientious devotion or scrupulous care: His work is a *religion* to him. **5** *Obs.* Religious practice or belief. [< OF < L *religio, -onis*]
  Synonyms: devotion, faith, godliness, holiness, pietism, piety, worship. *Piety* is primarily filial duty, and hence, in its purest sense, a loving obedience and service to God as the heavenly Father; *pietism* often denotes a mystical, sometimes an affected *piety; religion* is the reverent acknowledgment of a divine being. *Religion* includes *worship* whether it be external and formal, or the reverence of the human spirit for the divine, seeking outward expression. *Devotion,* which in its fullest sense is self–consecration, is often used to denote an act of *worship,* especially prayer or adoration; as, He is engaged his *devotions. Godliness* is a character and spirit like that of God. *Holiness* is the highest sinless perfection of any spirit, whether divine or human, and often used for purity or for consecration. *Faith,* strictly a firm reliance on the truth of religious doctrines, is often used as a comprehensive word for a whole system of *religion* considered as the object of *faith;* as, the Christian *faith,* the Buddhist *faith. Antonyms:* atheism, blasphemy, godlessness, impiety, infidelity, irreligion, profanity, sacrilege, unbelief, ungodliness.

re·lig·ion·ism (ri·lij′ən·iz′əm) *n.* The practice of or adherence to religion: used derogatorily to imply affectation and insincerity. — **re·lig′ion·ist** *n.*

re·lig·ious (ri·lij′əs) *adj.* **1** Feeling and manifesting religion; devout; pious. **2** Of or pertaining to religion; teaching or setting forth religion: a *religious* teacher. **3** Having thorough and genuine fidelity; strict in performance; conscientious: a *religious* loyalty. **4** Belonging to the monastic life; bound by monastic vows; following or devoted to a life of religion and devotion. — *n. pl.* **·ious** A person or people devoted to a life of piety and devotion; a monk or nun. [< OF *religious* < L *religiosus*] — **re·lig′ious·ly** *adv.* — **re·lig′ious·ness** *n.*

re·lin·quish (ri·ling′kwish) *v.t.* **1** To give up; abandon; surrender. **2** To cease to demand; renounce: to *relinquish* a claim. **3** To let go (a hold or something held). See synonyms under ABANDON, SURRENDER. [< OF *relinquiss-,* stem of *relinquir* < L *relinquere* < *re-* back, from + *linquere* leave] — **re·lin′quish·er** *n.* — **re·lin′quish·ment** *n.*

rel·i·quar·y (rel′ə·kwer′ē) *n. pl.* **·quar·ies** A casket, coffer, shrine, or other repository for relics. [< F *reliquaire* < L *reliquiae* remains. See RELIC.]

rel·ique (rel′ik, ri·lēk′) See RELIC.

rel·ish (rel′ish) *n.* **1** Appetite; appreciation; liking: a *relish* for excitement. **2** The flavor, especially when agreeable, in food and drink; figuratively, the quality in anything that lends spice or zest: Danger gives *relish* to adventure. **3** A slight savory dish served to stimulate appetite; also, something taken with food to lend it flavor or zest; a condiment. **4** An admixture or a small but important characteristic; flavoring: no *relish* of nature in his poetry. — *v.t.* **1** To like the taste or savor of; enjoy: to *relish* a dinner or a joke. **2** To give pleasant flavor to. — *v.i.* **3** To have an agreeable flavor; afford gratification. See synonyms under LIKE. [ME *reles* < OF *reles,* var. of *relais* remainder < *relaisser* leave behind. See RELEASE.] — **rel′ish·a·ble** *adj.*
  Synonyms (noun): appetite, appreciation, fondness, gusto, inclination, partiality, predilection, taste, zest. See APPETITE, SAVOR. *Antonyms:* antipathy, aversion, disgust, dislike, distaste, loathing, repugnance.

re·lu·cent (ri·lōō′sənt) *adj.* Shining back; reflecting light; gleaming. [< L *relucens, -entis,* ppr. of *relucere* < *re-* back + *lucere* shine. See LUCENT.]

re·luct (ri·lukt′) *v.i.* **1** To show reluctance;

hesitate. 2 To rebel; make opposition. [<L *reluctari*. See RELUCTANT.]

re·luc·tance (ri·luk′təns) *n.* 1 The state of being reluctant; unwillingness. 2 *Electr.* Capacity for opposing magnetic induction: the reciprocal of *permeance.* 3 *Obs.* Resistance; opposition. Also **re·luc′tan·cy.** [<RELUCTANT]

re·luc·tant (ri·luk′tənt) *adj.* 1 Disinclined to yield to some requirement; unwilling. 2 Marked by unwillingness or rendered unwillingly. 3 *Obs.* Struggling; offering opposition. [<L *reluctans, -antis,* ppr. of *reluctari* fight back <*re-* back + *luctari* fight] — **re·luc′tant·ly** *adv.*

Synonyms: averse, backward, disinclined, indisposed, loath, opposed, slow, unwilling. *Reluctant* signifies struggling against what one is urged or impelled to do, or is actually doing; *averse* signifies turned away as with dislike or repugnance; *loath* signifies having a repugnance, disgust, or loathing for, but the adjective *loath* is not so strong as the verb *loathe.* A man may be *slow* or *backward* in entering upon that to which he is by no means *averse.* A man is *loath* to believe evil of his friend, *reluctant* to speak of it, absolutely *unwilling* to use it to his injury. A legislator may be *opposed* to a certain measure, while not *averse* to what it aims to accomplish. Compare ANTIPATHY. *Antonyms:* desirous, disposed, eager, favorable, inclined, willing.

re·lume (ri·lōōm′) *v.t.* ·lumed, ·lum·ing 1 To light again; rekindle. 2 To illuminate again. Also **re·lu·mine** (ri·lōō′min). [<RE- + (IL)LUME]

re·ly (ri·lī′) *v.i.* ·lied, ·ly·ing To place trust or confidence: with *on* or *upon.* See synonyms under LEAN¹. [<OF *relier* bind (together), adhere to <L *religare* <*re-* again + *ligare* bind]

REM (rem) *n.* See REM SLEEP. [Acronym formed from *rapid eye movement*]

re·main (ri·mān′) *v.i.* 1 To stay or be left behind after the removal, departure, or destruction of other persons or things. 2 To continue in one place, condition, or character: He *remained* in office. 3 To be left as something to be done, dealt with, etc.: It *remains* to be proved. 4 To endure or last; abide. See synonyms under ABIDE, PERSIST, STAND. [<OF *remaindre* <L *remanere* <*re-* back + *manere* stay, remain]

re·main·der (ri·mān′dər) *n.* 1 That which remains; something left after a subtraction, expenditure, or passing over of a part; a residue; remnant. 2 *Math.* a That which is left after the subtraction of one quantity from another. b In division, the excess of the dividend over the product of the divisor by the integral part of the quotient. 3 *Law* An estate in expectancy, but not in actual possession and enjoyment; that remnant or residue of interest which, on the creation of a particular prior estate, is by the same instrument limited to another to be enjoyed on the termination of that estate. 4 In philately, an obsolete issue of stamps, demonetized by the government and sold at a large discount, generally to dealers. 5 A copy or part of an edition of a book remaining with a publisher after sales have ceased. — *adj.* Left over; remaining. — *v.t.* To sell as a remainder (def. 5). [<AF <OF *remaindre* REMAIN]

re·mains (ri·mānz′) *n. pl.* 1 That which is left after a part has been removed or destroyed; remnants. 2 The body of a deceased person; a corpse. 3 Writings of an author published after his death. 4 Survivals of the past, as fossils, monuments, etc.: the *remains* of ancient Troy. See synonyms under BODY.

re·mand (ri·mand′, -mänd′) *v.t.* 1 To order or send back: to *remand* a soldier to his post. 2 *Law* a To recommit to custody, as an accused person after a preliminary examination. b To send back to a lower court, as a case improperly brought before the court so ordering. — *n.* 1 Recommittal, as of an accused person to custody; also, the recommitted person. 2 A judicial order of recommittal. [< OF *remander* <LL *remandare* <L *re-* back + *mandare* order] — **re·mand′ment** *n.*

rem·a·nence (rem′ə·nəns) *n.* 1 The state or quality of remaining; permanence; also, the remainder. 2 *Electr.* That part of magnetic induction remaining in a material after the removal of an applied magnetomotive force. [<L *remanens, -entis,* ppr. of *remanere* remain] — **rem′a·nent** *adj.*

re·mark (ri·märk′) *n.* 1 A comment or saying,

oral or written; a casual observation; also, conversational speech in general: I enjoyed his *remarks.* 2 The act of observing or noticing; observation; notice. 3 Remarque. — *v.t.* 1 To say or write by way of comment. 2 To take particular notice of. 3 *Obs.* To mark; distinguish. — *v.i.* 4 To make remarks: with *on* or *upon.* [<F *remarque* observation <*remarquer* notice <*re-* again + *marquer* mark. See MARK.] — **re·mark′er** *n.*

Synonyms (noun): annotation, comment, note, observation, utterance. A *comment* is an explanatory or critical *remark,* as upon some passage in a literary work or some act or speech in common life. A *note* is something to call attention, hence a brief written statement; in correspondence, a *note* is briefer than a letter. *Annotations* are especially brief *notes,* commonly marginal, and closely following the text. *Comments, observations,* or *remarks* may be oral or written, *comments* being oftenest written, and *remarks* oftenest oral. An *observation* is properly the result of fixed attention and reflection; a *remark* may be the suggestion of the instant.

re·mark·a·ble (ri·mär′kə·bəl) *adj.* Worthy of special notice; hence, extraordinary; unusual; conspicuous; distinguished. See synonyms under EMINENT, RARE, EXTRAORDINARY. — **re·mark′a·ble·ness** *n.* — **re·mark′a·bly** *adv.*

Rem·brandt (rem′brant, *Du.* rem′bränt), 1606–1669, Dutch painter and etcher: full name *Rembrandt Harmenszoon van Rijn* or *van Ryn.*

re·me·di·a·ble (ri·mē′dē·ə·bəl) *adj.* Capable of being cured or remedied. [<F *remédiable*] — **re·me′di·a·bly** *adv.*

re·me·di·al (ri·mē′dē·əl) *adj.* Of the nature of or adapted to be used as a remedy. [<L *remedialis*] — **re·me′di·al·ly** *adv.*

rem·e·dy (rem′ə·dē) *v.t.* ·died, ·dy·ing 1 To cure or heal, as by medicinal treatment. 2 To make right; repair; correct. 3 To overcome or remove (an evil or defect). — *n. pl.* ·dies 1 That which cures or affords relief to bodily disease or ailment; a medicine; also, remedial treatment. 2 A means of counteracting or removing evil; relief. 3 *Law* A legal mode for enforcing a right or redressing or preventing a wrong. 4 Tolerance (def. 5). [<AF <L *remedium* <*re-* thoroughly + *mederi* heal, restore]

re·mem·ber (ri·mem′bər) *v.t.* 1 To bring back or present again to the mind or memory; recall; recollect. 2 To keep in mind carefully, as for a purpose. 3 To bear in mind with affection, respect, awe, etc. 4 To bear in mind as worthy of a reward, gift, etc.: She *remembered* me in her will. 5 To reward; tip: *Remember* the steward. 6 *Obs.* To remind. — *v.i.* 7 To have or use one's memory. — **to remember (one) to** To inform a person of the regard of: *Remember* me *to* your wife. [<OF *remembrer* <LL *rememorari* <L *re-* again + *memorare* bring to mind <*memor* mindful] — **re·mem′ber·er** *n.*

Synonyms: recall, recollect, retain. Compare synonyms for MEMORY. Antonyms: forget, overlook.

re·mem·brance (ri·mem′brəns) *n.* 1 The act or power of remembering; the state of being remembered; memory. 2 The period within which one can remember. 3 That which is remembered; a reminiscence. 4 A memento; keepsake; also, a token or message of friendship: often in the plural. 5 Mindful regard. See synonyms under MEMORY.

re·mind (ri·mīnd′) *v.t.* To bring to (someone's) mind; cause to remember. See synonyms under ADMONISH. [<RE- + MIND] — **re·mind′er** *n.*

rem·i·nisce (rem′ə·nis′) *v.i.* ·nisced, ·nisc·ing To recall incidents or events of the past; indulge in reminiscences. [Back formation < REMINISCENT]

rem·i·nis·cence (rem′ə·nis′əns) *n.* 1 The recalling to mind of past incidents and events; also, the narration of past experiences. 2 The act or power of reproducing past cognitions in consciousness. 3 An expression, fact, or feature serving as a reminder of something else. See synonyms under MEMORY. [<F]

rem·i·nis·cent (rem′ə·nis′ənt) *adj.* 1 Of the nature of or possessing reminiscence; also, recalling or dwelling upon the past; remembering. 2 Inducing a reminiscence of a person or thing; suggestive. [<L *reminiscens, -entis,* ppr. of *reminisci* recollect <*re-* again + *memini* remember] — **rem′i·nis′cent·ly** *adv.*

re·mise (ri·mīz′) *Law v.t.* ·mised, ·mis·ing To give; surrender; release; relinquish: used in conveyancing. — *n.* The act of remising. [<F, fem. of *remis,* pp. of *remettre* <L *remittere* send back. See REMIT.]

re·miss (ri·mis′) *adj.* Slack or careless in matters requiring attention; dilatory; negligent; hence, lacking in earnestness or energy. See synonyms under INATTENTIVE. [<L *remissus,* pp. of *remittere* send back, slacken. See REMIT.] — **re·miss′ness** *n.*

re·mis·si·ble (ri·mis′ə·bəl) *adj.* Capable of being remitted or pardoned, as sins. [<F *rémissible*] — **re·mis′si·bil′i·ty** *n.*

re·mis·sion (ri·mish′ən) *n.* 1 The act of remitting, or the state of being remitted; specifically, discharge from penalty; pardon; deliverance, as from a debt or obligation. 2 Abatement, as of a fine erroneously imposed. 3 Relaxation, as from work or study. 4 Temporary abatement of a disease or of pain. 5 The act of sending a remittance. [<OF <L *remissio, -onis*]

re·mit (ri·mit′) *v.* ·mit·ted, ·mit·ting *v.t.* 1 To send, as money in payment for goods; transmit. 2 To refrain from exacting or inflicting, as a penalty. 3 To pardon; forgive, as a sin or crime. 4 To abate; relax, as vigilance. 5 To restore; replace. 6 To put off; postpone. 7 To refer or submit for judgment, settlement, etc., as to one in authority. 8 *Law* To refer (a legal proceeding) to a lower court for further consideration. 9 *Rare* To send back, as to prison. 10 *Obs.* To resign; renounce. 11 *Obs.* To free; release. — *v.i.* 12 To send money, as in payment. 13 To diminish; abate. — *n.* The act of remitting; specifically, the sending of a legal cause from one tribunal to another. [<L *remittere* send back <*re-* back + *mittere* send] — **re·mit′ta·ble** *adj.* — **re·mit′ter** or **re·mit′tor** *n.*

re·mit·tal (ri·mit′l) *n.* Remission.

re·mit·tance (ri·mit′ns) *n.* The act of transmitting money or credit; also, that which is remitted, as money.

re·mit·tent (ri·mit′nt) *adj.* 1 Having remissions. 2 Having partial, irregular, or temporary diminutions of energy or action: a *remittent* fever or geyser. — *n.* A remittent fever. [<L *remittens, -entis,* ppr. of *remittere.* See REMIT.]

rem·nant (rem′nənt) *n.* 1 That which remains of anything; specifically, the piece of cloth, silk, etc., left over after the last cutting. 2 A remaining trace or survival of anything, suggestive of former condition, use, or belief. 3 A small piece or quantity. 4 A small remaining number of people. See synonyms under TRACE¹. — *adj.* Remaining. [<OF *remenant,* ppr. of *remaindre.* See REMAIN.]

re·mon·e·tize (ri·mon′ə·tīz) *v.t.* ·tized, ·tiz·ing To reinstate, especially silver, as lawful money. [<RE- again + L *moneta* money + -IZE] — **re·mon′e·ti·za′tion** *n.*

re·mon·strance (ri·mon′strəns) *n.* 1 The act of remonstrating; protest; expostulation. 2 Expostulatory counsel or reproof. [<OF]

re·mon·strant (ri·mon′strənt) *adj.* Having the character or tendency of a remonstrance; expostulatory. — *n.* One who presents or signs a remonstrance. [<Med. L *remonstrans, -antis,* ppr. of *remonstrare.* See REMONSTRATE.]

re·mon·strate (ri·mon′strāt) *v.* ·strat·ed, ·strat·ing *v.t.* 1 To say or plead in protest or opposition. 2 *Obs.* To point out; demonstrate. — *v.i.* 3 To urge strong reasons against any course or action; protest; object. [<Med. L *remonstratus,* pp. of *remonstrare* demonstrate <L *re-* again + *monstrare* show] — **re·mon·stra′tion** (rē′mon·strā′shən, rem′ən-) *n.* — **re·mon′stra·tive** (-strā·tiv) *adj.* — **re·mon′stra·tor** (strā·tər) *n.*

rem·o·ra (rem′ər·ə) *n.* 1 Any of a genus (*Remora*) of fish (family *Echeneididae*) having on its head an oval suctorial disk by means of which it attaches itself to sharks, other fishes, or floating objects, being thus carried great distances. 2 Any delay or impediment. [<L, hindrance <*re-* back + *mora* delay]

re·morse (ri·môrs′) *n.* 1 The keen or hopeless anguish caused by a sense of guilt; compunction; distressing self-reproach. 2 *Obs.* Compassion; pity. See synonyms under REPENTANCE. [<OF *remors* <LL *remorsus* a biting back <L *remordere* keep biting <*re-* again + *mordere* bite] — **re·morse′ful** *adj.* — **re-**

morse'ful·ly *adv.* — **re·morse'ful·ness** *n.*

re·morse·less (ri·môrs'lis) *adj.* Having no compassion; pitiless; cruel. — **re·morse'less·ly** *adv.* — **re·morse'less·ness** *n.*

re·mote (ri·mōt') *adj.* **1** Located far from a specified place or some place regarded as a point of reference: *remote* regions. **2** Removed far from present time; distant in time: the *remote* future. **3** Having slight relation or connection; separated; foreign; distant in relation: a *remote* cause, *remote* kinship. **4** Not obvious; inconsiderable; slight: a *remote* likeness or analogy. **5** Abstracted; absent-minded; hence, aloof. — *n.* A television or radio broadcast made from a mobile camera or microphone operated at a distance from the station, and sent to the transmitter by cable or through relay towers. See synonyms under ALIEN. [< L *remotus,* pp. of *removere* remove < *re-* again + *movere* move] — **re·mote'ly** *adv.* — **re·mote'ness** *n.*

re·mo·tion (ri·mō'shən) *n.* **1** The act of removing; removal. **2** *Obs.* Departure. [< OF]

re·mount (rē·mount') *v.t. & v.i.* To mount again or anew. — *n.* (rē'mount') **1** A new setting or framing. **2** A fresh riding horse. [< OF *remonter*]

re·mov·a·ble (ri·mōō'və·bəl) *adj.* Capable of being removed; movable; also, capable of being displaced, dismissed, or obliterated: *removable* walls, officials, or stains. — **re·mov'a·bil'i·ty** *n.* — **re·mov'a·bly** *adv.*

re·mov·al (ri·mōō'vəl) *n.* **1** The act of removing or the state of being removed. **2** Dismissal, as from office. **3** Changing of place, especially of habitation.

re·move (ri·mōōv') *v.* **·moved, ·mov·ing** *v.t.* **1** To take or move away or from one place to another. **2** To take off; doff, as a hat. **3** To get rid of; do away with: to *remove* abuses. **4** To kill; assassinate. **5** To displace or dismiss, as from office. **6** To take out; extract: with *from.* — *v.i.* **7** To change one's place of residence or business; move. **8** *Poetic* To go away; depart. See synonyms under ABOLISH, ABSTRACT, ALLEVIATE, CANCEL, CARRY, CONVEY, DISPLACE, EXTERMINATE, SEPARATE. — *n.* **1** A removal; a move; the act of removing, as one's business or belongings. **2** The space moved over in changing an object from one position to another; hence, a degree of difference; step; interval: He is only one *remove* from a fool. **3** *Brit.* A dish or course at dinner removed to give place to another. **4** *Obs.* A period of absence. [< OF *remouvoir* < L *removere* < *re-* again + *movere* move] — **re·mov'er** *n.*

re·moved (ri·mōōvd') *adj.* **1** Separated, as by intervening space, time, or relationship, or by difference in kind: a cousin twice *removed.* **2** Taken away; transferred.

REM sleep A recurrent stage of normal sleep characterized by distinctive patterns of brain waves, rapid movement of the eyes under closed lids, and dreaming: also called *paradoxical sleep.*

re·mu·ner·ate (ri·myōō'nə·rāt) *v.t.* **·at·ed, ·at·ing** To make just or adequate return to or for; compensate; pay or pay for; reward. See synonyms under PAY, REQUITE. [< L *remuneratus,* pp. of *remunerari* < *re-* again + *munus, muneris* gift] — **re·mu'ner·a·bil'i·ty** *n.* — **re·mu'ner·a·ble** *adj.*

re·mu·ner·a·tion (ri·myōō'nə·rā'shən) *n.* **1** The act or fact of remunerating. **2** That which remunerates; pay; compensation; recompense. See synonyms under RECOMPENSE, RESTITUTION, SALARY.

re·mu·ner·a·tive (ri·myōō'nə·rā'tiv, -nər·ə·tiv) *adj.* **1** Profitable; lucrative. **2** Serving to pay or remunerate: *remunerative* justice. — **re·mu'ner·a'tive·ly** *adv.* — **re·mu'ner·a'tive·ness** *n.*

Re·mus (rē'məs) In Roman mythology, the twin brother of Romulus, by whom he was killed.

ren·ais·sance (ren'ə·säns', -zäns', ri·nā'səns; *Fr.* rə·ne·säns') *n.* A new birth; resurrection; renascence. [< F < *renaître* to be reborn < *re-* again + L *natus,* pp. of *nasci* be born]

Ren·ais·sance (ren'ə·säns', -zäns', ri·nā'səns; *Fr.* rə·ne·säns') *n.* **1** The revival of letters and art in Europe, marking the transition from medieval to modern history: it began in Italy

in the 14th century and gradually spread to other countries. **2** The period of this revival, from the 14th to the 16th century; also, the style of art, literature, etc., marked by a classical influence, that was developed in and characteristic of this period. Also *Renascence.* — *adj.* Of or characteristic of the Renaissance.

Renaissance architecture A style of building and decoration that followed the medieval, originating in Italy in the 15th century, and based on the classic Roman style.

re·nal (rē'nəl) *adj.* *Med.* Of, pertaining to, affecting, or situated near the kidneys. [< F *rénal* < L *renalis* < *renes* kidneys]

renal capsule or **gland** The suprarenal gland.

Re·nan (rə·nän'), **Joseph Ernest,** 1823–1892, French historian, philologist, and critic.

RENAISSANCE
ARCHITECTURE

re·nas·cence (ri·nas'əns) *n.* Rebirth; new birth or life; a renaissance; a revival.

[< L *renascens, -entis,* ppr. of *renasci* < *re-* again + *nasci* be born] — **re·nas'cent** *adj.*

rend (rend) *v.* **rent** or **rend·ed, rend·ing** *v.t.* **1** To tear apart forcibly; split; break. **2** To pull or remove forcibly: with *away, from, off,* etc. **3** To pass through (the air) violently and noisily. **4** To distress (the heart, etc.), as with grief or despair. — *v.i.* **5** To split; part. [OE *rendan* tear, cut down] — **rend'er** *n.*
Synonyms: break, burst, cleave, lacerate, mangle, rip, rive, rupture, sever, slit, sunder, tear. *Rend* and *tear* are applied usually to the sundering of textile substances, *tear* being the milder, *rend* the stronger word. To *rip,* as applied to articles made by sewing or stitching, is to divide along the line of a seam by cutting or breaking the stitches. *Rive* is a woodworkers' word for parting wood in the way of the grain without a clean cut, as by splitting. To *lacerate* is to *tear* roughly the flesh or animal tissue, as by the teeth of a wild beast. *Mangle* is a stronger word than *lacerate; lacerate* is more superficial, *mangle* more complete. To *burst* or *rupture* is to tear or rend by force from within, *burst* denoting the greater violence; as, to *burst* a gun; to *rupture* a blood vessel. Compare BREAK. *Antonyms:* heal, join, mend, reunite, secure, stitch, unite, weld.

ren·der (ren'dər) *v.t.* **1** To give, present, or submit for action, approval, payment, etc. **2** To provide or furnish; give: to *render* aid to the poor. **3** To give as due: to *render* obedience. **4** To perform; do: to *render* great service. **5** To give or state formally: to *render* judgment. **6** To give by way of requital or retribution: to *render* double for one's sins. **7** To represent or depict, as in music or painting. **8** To cause to be or become: to *render* a ship seaworthy. **9** To express in another language; translate. **10** To melt and clarify, as lard. **11** To give back; return: often with *back.* **12** To surrender; give up: to *render* a fortress. See synonyms under INTERPRET. — *n.* **1** A payment, specifically of rent, made to a superior. **2** A coat of plaster applied without intervening lathing. [< F *rendre* < L *reddere* give back < *re-* back + *dare* give] — **ren'der·a·ble** *adj.* — **ren'der·er** *n.*

ren·dez·vous (rän'dā·vōō, -də-; *Fr.* rän·de·vōō') *n. pl.* **·vous** (-vōōz, *Fr.* -vōō') **1** An appointed place of meeting. **2** A meeting or an appointment to meet. **3** A base for naval ships or for military units. **4** *Obs.* A resort; refuge. — *v.t. & v.i.* **·voused** (-vōōd), **·vous·ing** (-vōō'ing) To assemble or cause to assemble at a certain place or time. [< F *rendez-vous,* lit., betake yourself < *se rendre* betake oneself]

ren·di·tion (ren·dish'ən) *n.* **1** A translation; the interpretation of a text. **2** Artistic, dramatic, or musical interpretation; also, the

performance or execution of a dramatic or musical composition. **3** A surrendering, especially of a person. **4** The act of rendering, or the amount rendered. [< obs. F < *rendre* render]

ren·e·gade (ren'ə·gād) *n.* **1** An apostate. **2** A traitor; deserter. Also **ren'e·ga'do** (-gä'dō). — *adj.* Traitorous. [< Sp. *renegado,* pp. of *renegar* deny < Med. L *renegare* < L *re-* again and again + *negare* deny]

re·nege (ri·nig', -neg', -nēg') *v.i.* **·neged, ·neg·ing 1** In card games, to fail to follow suit when able to do so. See REVOKE. **2** *Colloq.* To fail to fulfil a promise. **3** *Obs.* To renounce; deny. Also **re·nig'.** [< Med. L *renegare.* See RENEGADE.] — **re·neg'er** *n.*

re·new (ri·nōō', -nyōō') *v.t.* **1** To make new or as if new again; restore to a former or sound condition. **2** To begin again; resume: to *renew* an argument. **3** To repeat: to *renew* an oath of loyalty. **4** To acquire again; regain (vigor, strength, etc.). **5** To cause to continue in effect; extend: to *renew* a subscription. **6** To revive; reestablish. **7** To replenish or replace, as provisions. — *v.i.* **8** To become new again. **9** To begin or commence again. See synonyms under RECLAIM. [< RE- again + NEW] — **re·new'a·ble** *adj.*

re·new·al (ri·nōō'əl -nyōō'-) *n.* The act of renewing, or the state of being renewed.

re·newed (ri·nōōd', -nyōōd') *adj.* Made new; restored; revived; repeated. See synonyms under FRESH. — **re·new·ed·ly** (ri·nōō'id·lē, -nyōō'-) *adv.*

reni- *combining form* Kidney; of or related to the kidneys: *reniform:* also, before vowels, *ren-.* Also *reno-.* [< L *ren, renis* a kidney]

ren·i·form (ren'ə·fôrm, rē'nə-) *adj.* Kidney-shaped. [< RENI- + -FORM]

re·ni·tent (ri·nī'tənt, ren'ə·tənt) *adj.* Offering resistance to any influence or force; continuously reluctant; recalcitrant; specifically, presenting elastic resistance to pressure. [< L *renitens, -entis,* ppr. of *reniti* resist < *re-* back + *niti* struggle] — **re·ni'tence, re·ni'ten·cy** *n.*

ren·net (ren'it) *n.* **1** The dried stomach of certain young hoofed animals, especially the mucous membrane lining the fourth stomach of a suckling calf or sheep, which is capable of curdling milk. **2** Anything used to curdle milk. **3** An aqueous or vinous infusion of animal rennet. **4** Rennin. [Alter. of ME *rennels* < OE *rinnan* run together, coagulate]

Re·noir (rə·nwàr'), **Pierre Auguste,** 1841–1919, French Impressionist painter.

re·nounce (ri·nouns') *v.* **·nounced, ·nounc·ing** *v.t.* **1** To give up, especially by formal statement. **2** To disown; repudiate. **3** In card games, to indicate inability to follow (a suit led) by playing a card of another suit. — *v.i.* **4** In card games, to renounce the suit led. [< F *renoncer* < L *renuntiare* protest against, announce < *re-* back, against + *nuntiare* report < *nuntius* messenger] — **re·nounce'ment** *n.* — **re·nounc'er** *n.*
Synonyms: abandon, abjure, deny, disavow, discard, disclaim, disown, forswear, recall, recant, refuse, reject, repudiate, retract, revoke. *Abjure, discard, forswear, recall, recant, renounce, retract,* and *revoke,* like *abandon,* imply some previous connection. *Renounce* is to declare against and give up formally and definitively; as, to *renounce* the pomps and vanities of the world. *Retract* is to take back something that one has said as not true or as what one is not ready to maintain; as, to *retract* a charge or accusation; one *recants* his own opinions or beliefs. *Repudiate* is to put away with emphatic and determined repulsion; as, to *repudiate* a debt. To *deny* is to affirm to be not true or not binding; as, to *deny* a statement or relationship; or to refuse to grant, as a request or petition. To *discard* is to cast away as useless or worthless; thus, one *discards* a worn garment. *Revoke,* etymologically the equivalent of the English *recall,* is to take back something given or granted; as, to *revoke* a command, a will, or a grant; *recall* may be used in the exact sense of *revoke,* but is often applied to persons, as *revoke* is not; we *recall* a messenger and *revoke* an order. Compare ABANDON, ABDICATE, ABJURE, RECANT. *Antonyms:* acknowl-

edge, advocate, assert, avow, cherish, claim, defend, hold, maintain, own, proclaim, retain, uphold, vindicate.

ren·o·vate (ren′ə·vāt) *v.t.* **·vat·ed, ·vat·ing 1** To make as good as new; repair. **2** To renew; refresh; reinvigorate. — *adj.* Renovated. [<L *renovatus*, pp. of *renovare* < *re-* again + *novare* make new < *novus* new] — **ren′o·va′·tion** *n.* — **ren′o·va′tor** *n.*

re·nown (ri·noun′) *n.* **1** Exalted reputation; celebrity; the state of being widely known for great achievements or merits; fame. **2** *Obs.* Rumor; report. See synonyms under FAME. — *v.t. Obs.* To spread the fame of; render famous. [<OF *renon* < *renomer* name again, make famous <L *re-* again + *nominare* name < *nomen* a name]

re·nowned (ri·nound′) *adj.* Having renown; famous. See synonyms under ILLUSTRIOUS.

rent[1] (rent) *n.* **1** Compensation made in any form by a tenant to a landlord or owner for the use of land, buildings, etc.; especially, such compensation paid in money at regular or specified intervals. **2** Similar payment for the use of any property, movable or fixed. **3** *Econ.* **a** Income derived by the owner from the use of his land or property. **b** The return afforded by cultivated land in excess of the costs, as of labor or materials. **c** That which is yielded by land in excess of the yield of the poorest land cultivated under equal conditions: also called **economic rent. d** Hence, a return derived from a similar advantage, as in a monopoly of natural resources. **4** *Obs.* **a** Landed or other property affording revenue. **b** Income or revenue. — **for rent** Available for use or occupancy by the paying of rent. — *v.t.* **1** To obtain the temporary possession and use of for a compensation, usually made at fixed intervals. **2** To grant the temporary possession and use of for a rent. — *v.i.* **3** To be let for rent. [<OF *rente* <LL *rendita*, L *reddita* what is given back or paid, fem. of pp. of *reddere*. See RENDER.] — **rent′a·ble** *adj.*

rent[2] (rent) Alternative past tense and past participle of REND. — *n.* **1** A hole or slit made by rending or tearing; tear; rip; fissure. **2** A schism; violent separation; split. See synonyms under BREACH, HOLE. [<REND]

rent·al (ren′təl) *n.* **1** The revenue derived from rented property. **2** A schedule of rents. — *adj.* Of or pertaining to rent. [<AF]

re·nun·ci·a·tion (ri·nun′sē·ā′shən, -shē-) *n.* **1** The act of renouncing or disclaiming; repudiation. **2** A declaration, statement, or formula in which something is renounced. [<L *renunciatio, -onis* a proclamation] — **re·nun′ci·a′tive** *adj.* — **re·nun·ci·a·to·ry** (ri·nun′sē·ə·tôr′ē, -tō′rē, -shē-) *adj.*

rep (rep) *n.* A silk, cotton, rayon, or wool fabric having a distinctive crosswise rib: also spelled *repp*. [<F *reps* <E *ribs*]

re·pair[1] (ri·pâr′) *v.t.* **1** To restore to sound or good condition after damage, injury, decay, etc.; mend. **2** To make amends for (an injury); remedy. **3** To make up, as a loss; compensate for. See synonyms under AMEND, RECRUIT. — *n.* **1** Restoration, as after decay, waste, injury, etc.; reparation. **2** Condition after use or after repairing: in good *repair*. [<OF *reparer* <L *reparare* < *re-* again + *parare* prepare, make ready] — **re·pair′er** *n.*

re·pair[2] (ri·pâr′) *v.i.* **1** To betake oneself; go: to *repair* to the garden. **2** To return. — *n.* **1** The act of repairing, or the place to which one repairs; a haunt. **2** *Scot.* A concourse of people to a certain spot. [<OF *repairer* <LL *repatriare* < *re-* again + *patria* native land]

rep·a·ra·ble (rep′ər·ə·bəl) *adj.* Capable of repair or reparation. Also **re·pair·a·ble** (ri·pâr′-ə·bəl). [<F *réparable* <L *reparabilis*] — **rep′·a·ra·bil′i·ty** *n.* — **rep′a·ra·bly** *adv.*

rep·a·ra·tion (rep′ə·rā′shən) *n.* **1** The act of making amends; atonement; amends; indemnity; also, that which is done by way of amends or satisfaction. **2** The act of repairing or the state of being repaired. **3** *pl.* Repairs; specifically, indemnities paid by defeated countries for acts of war. See synonyms under RESTITUTION. [<L *reparatio, -onis* a renewal] — **re·par·a·tive** (ri·par′ə·tiv) *adj.*

rep·ar·tee (rep′är·tē′, -ər-) *n.* **1** Conversation marked by quick and witty replies. **2** Skill or quickness in such conversation. **3** A witty or quick reply; a sharp rejoinder. See synonyms under ANSWER. [<F *repartie*, pp. of *repartir*

depart again, reply < *re-* again + *partir* depart]

re·par·ti·tion (rē′pär·tish′ən) *n.* **1** Distribution; allotment. **2** Redistribution.

re·past (ri·past′, -päst′) *n.* **1** Food taken at a meal; hence, a meal. **2** Food in general; also, mealtime. [<OF *repas* <Med.L *repastum*, orig. pp. of LL *repascere* feed again <L *re-* again + *pascere* feed]

re·pa·ten·cy (ri·pāt′n·sē, -pat′n-) *n.* The reopening of a part or vessel that had been closed. [<RE- + L *patentia*, neut. pl. of *patens, patentis*, ppr. of *patere* be open]

re·pa·tri·ate (rē·pā′trē·āt) *v.t. & v.i.* **·at·ed, ·at·ing** To send back or return to his own country, as a soldier interned in a neutral territory; restore to citizenship. — *n.* (rē·pā′trē·it) A person who has been repatriated. [<LL *repatriatus*, pp. of *repatriare* <L *re-* again + *patria* native land] — **re·pa′tri·a′tion** *n.*

re·pay (ri·pā′) *v.* **·paid, ·pay·ing** *v.t.* **1** To pay back; refund. **2** To pay back or refund something to. **3** To make compensation or retaliation for; give a reward or inflict a penalty for. — *v.i.* **4** To make repayment or requital. See synonyms under REQUITE. [<OF *repaier*] — **re·pay′a·ble** *adj.* — **re·pay′ment** *n.*

re·peal (ri·pēl′) *v.t.* **1** To rescind, as a law; revoke. **2** *Obs.* To summon back, as from exile. See synonyms under ABOLISH, ANNUL, CANCEL. — *n.* **1** The act of repealing; revocation; rescission. **2** *Obs.* Recall, as from exile. [<OF *rapeler* recall < *re-* again + *appeler*. See APPEAL.] — **re·peal′a·ble** *adj.* — **re·peal′·er** *n.*

re·peat (ri·pēt′) *v.t.* **1** To say again; reiterate: to *repeat* a question. **2** To recite from memory. **3** To say (what another has just said). **4** To tell, as a secret, to another. **5** To do, make, or experience again. — *v.i.* **6** *U.S.* To vote more than once at the same election: an offense punishable by law. — *n.* **1** The act of repeating; a repetition. **2** *Music* **a** A sign consisting of dots placed in the spaces at the left hand of a bar, to indicate that the preceding passage is to be repeated. **b** A repeated passage, song, refrain, etc. **3** Anything repeated, as a new supply of goods, or a renewed order for such supply. [<OF *repeter* <L *repetere* do or say again < *re-* again + *petere* seek]

re·peat·ed (ri·pē′tid) *adj.* Occurring or spoken again and again; reiterated. See synonyms under FREQUENT. — **re·peat′ed·ly** *adv.*

re·peat·er (ri·pē′tər) *n.* **1** One who or that which repeats. **2** A timepiece, especially a watch, which will strike again the hour last struck when a spring is pressed. **3** A repeating firearm. **4** An instrument for automatically retransmitting electromagnetic signals: a telegraph *repeater*. **5** *U.S.* One who votes, or attempts to vote, more than once at the same election. **6** One who has been repeatedly imprisoned for criminal offenses.

re·pel (ri·pel′) *v.* **·pelled, ·pel·ling** *v.t.* **1** To force or drive back; repulse. **2** To reject; refuse, as a suggestion. **3** To cause to feel distaste or aversion: His manner *repels* me. **4** To refuse to mix with or adhere to: Mercury *repels* iron. **5** To push or keep away, especially with invisible force: Like magnetic poles *repel* each other: opposed to *attract*. — *v.i.* **6** To act so as to drive something back or away. **7** To cause distaste or aversion. [<L *repellere* < *re-* back + *pellere* drive] — **re·pel′ler** *n.*

Synonyms: check, oppose, repulse, resist. *Repulse* is stronger and more conclusive than *repel*; one may be *repelled* by the very aspect of the person whose favor he seeks, but is not *repulsed* except by a direct refusal of his suit. See DRIVE. *Antonyms:* accept, admit, encourage, entertain, favor, grant, welcome.

re·pel·lent (ri·pel′ənt) *adj.* **1** Serving, tending, or having power to repel. **2** Waterproof. **3** Repugnant. — *n.* **1** A waterproof cloth. **2** A remedial application that tends to repel fluids from a swollen part. **3** A chemical compound intended to be distasteful to insects and other vermin and to keep them at a distance. — **re·pel′len·cy, re·pel′lence** *n.*

re·pent (ri·pent′) *v.i.* **1** To feel remorse or regret, as for something done or undone; be contrite. **2** To change one's mind concerning past action because of disappointment, failure, etc.: with *of*: He *repented* of his generosity to the old man. **3** *Theol.* To feel such sorrow for one's sins as to reform. — *v.t.* **4** To feel

remorse or regret for (an action, sin, etc.). **5** To change one's mind concerning (a past action): He *repented* his decision. [<OF *repentir* <L *re-* again + *poenitere* cause to repent < *poena* punishment] — **re·pent′er** *n.*

re·pen·tance (ri·pen′təns) *n.* A turning with sorrow from a past course or action; loosely, regret or contrition; also, the condition of being penitent.

Synonyms: compunction, contrition, penitence, regret, remorse, sorrow. *Regret* is *sorrow* for any painful or annoying matter. One is moved with *penitence* for wrongdoing. To speak of *regret* for a fault of our own marks it as slighter than one for which we should express *penitence*. *Repentance* is *sorrow* for sin with self-condemnation, and complete turning from the sin. *Compunction* is a momentary sting of conscience, in view either of a past or of a contemplated act. *Contrition* is a subduing *sorrow* for sin, as against the divine holiness and love. *Remorse* is, as its derivation indicates, a biting or gnawing back of guilt upon the heart. *Antonyms:* approval, comfort, complacency, content, hardness, impenitence, obduracy, obstinacy, recusancy, stubbornness.

re·per·cus·sion (rē′pər·kush′ən) *n.* **1** The act of driving or throwing back, or the state of being driven back; repulse; also, echo; reverberation. **2** A stroke or blow given in return; recoil after impact; hence, the indirect result of something; aftereffect: the *repercussions* of the peace treaty. **3** *Med.* The motion produced on a fetus by the process of ballottement. [<L *repercussio, -onis* < *repercussus*, pp. of *repercutere* rebound < *re-* again + *percutere* strike. See PERCUSS.]

rep·er·toire (rep′ər·twär, -twôr) *n.* A list of songs, plays, operas, or the like, that a person or company is prepared to perform; also, such pieces collectively. [<F <LL *repertorium*. See REPERTORY.]

rep·er·to·ry (rep′ər·tôr′ē, -tō′rē) *n.* *pl.* **·ries 1** A place where things are gathered together, or the things so gathered; a repository; collection. **2** Repertoire. [<LL *repertorium* inventory <L < *repertus*, pp. of *reperire* find, discover < *re-* again + *parire* produce]

repertory company A theatrical group having a repertoire of productions, each typically running for a few weeks, and usually having some acting personnel continuing from one production to the next. Also **repertory theater.**

rep·e·ti·tion (rep′ə·tish′ən) *n.* **1** The act of repeating; the doing, making, or saying of something again; recital from memory. **2** *Music* The singing or playing of the same note, chord, or passage over again. **3** That which is repeated; a copy. [<F *répétition*]

re·pet·i·tive (ri·pet′ə·tiv) *adj.* Marked by repetition; recurrent. — **re·pet′i·tive·ly** *adv.*

re·pine (ri·pīn′) *v.i.* **·pined, ·pin·ing** To be discontented or fretful; complain; murmur. See synonyms under COMPLAIN. [<RE- + PINE[2]] — **re·pin′er** *n.* — **re·pin′ing** *n.*

re·place (ri·plās′) *v.t.* **·placed, ·plac·ing 1** To put back in place. **2** To take or fill the place of; supersede. **3** To refund; repay. — **re·place′a·ble** *adj.* — **re·plac′er** *n.*

re·place·ment (ri·plās′mənt) *n.* **1** The act of replacing; also, that which takes the place of anything discarded or worn out. **2** *Mineral.* The formation of a new crystal face which obliterates an edge or angle. **3** A soldier available for assignment to fill a vacancy or a quota. **4** The act of putting a thing back in place. **5** *Chem.* A substitution. **6** A substitute.

re·play (rē·plā′) *v.t.* **1** To play again. **2** To show a replay of. — *n.* (rē′plā′) **1** The act of playing again. **2** The playing of a television tape, often in slow motion and usually immediately following the live occurrence of the action shown. **3** The action shown in such a replay.

re·plen·ish (ri·plen′ish) *v.t.* **1** To fill again, as something that has been wholly or partially emptied. **2** To bring back to fullness or completeness, as diminished supplies. **3** To repeople. [<OF *repleniss-*, stem of *replenir* < *re-* again + L *plenus* full] — **re·plen′ish·er** *n.* — **re·plen′ish·ment** *n.*

re·plete (ri·plēt′) *adj.* **1** Full to the uttermost. **2** Gorged with food or drink; sated. **3** Abundantly supplied or stocked; abounding. [<OF

replet <L *repletus*, pp. of *replere* fill again <*re-* again + *plere* fill] — **re·ple′tion** *n.*

rep·li·ca (rep′lə·kə) *n.* 1 A duplicate, as of a picture, executed by the original artist. 2 Any close copy or reproduction. See synonyms under DUPLICATE, MODEL. [<Ital. <L *replicare* reply, answer to. See REPLY.]

rep·li·cate (rep′lə·kit) *adj.* Folded backward, as the upper part of a leaf on the lower, or the wing of an insect. Also **rep′li·cat′ed** (-kā′tid). — *v.t.* (-kāt) **·cat·ed, ·cat·ing** 1 To fold over. 2 To make a replica of. 3 To answer; reply. [<L *replicatus*, pp. of *replicare* answer. See REPLY.]

re·ply (ri·plī′) *v.* **·plied, ·ply·ing** *v.i.* 1 To give an answer, orally or in writing. 2 To respond by some act, gesture, etc.: He *replied* with a blow. 3 To echo. 4 *Law* To file a pleading in answer to the statement of the defense. — *v.t.* 5 To say in answer: often with a clause as object: She *replied* that she would do it. — *n.* *pl.* **·plies** Something said, written, or done by way of answer; a response; rejoinder. See synonyms under ANSWER. [<OF *replier* bend back <L *replicare* fold back, answer to, make a reply < *re-* back + *plicare* fold] — **re·pli′er** *n.*

re·port (ri·pôrt′, -pōrt′) *v.t.* 1 To make or give an account of, especially formally: to *report* the minutes of a meeting, or an event for a newspaper. 2 To relate, as information obtained by investigation: Please *report* your findings. 3 To bear back or repeat to another, as an answer. 4 To complain about, especially to a superior: I'll *report* you to the manager. 5 To state the result of consideration concerning: The committee *reported* the bill. — *v.i.* 6 To make a report. 7 To act as a reporter. 8 To present oneself, as for duty. See synonyms under ANNOUNCE. — *n.* 1 That which is reported; an announcement, statement, or account; the formal statement of the result of an investigation: a medical *report*. 2 Common talk; rumor; hence, fame, reputation, or character: good *report*; *reports* grossly untrue. 3 A record with more or less detail of the transactions of a deliberative body. 4 An account of any occurrence prepared for publication through the press. 5 *Law Usually pl.* A published narration (usually official) of a case or series of cases judicially considered: the Supreme Court *reports.* 6 An explosive sound: the *report* of a gun. [<OF *reporter* carry back <L *reportare* < *re-* back + *portare* carry] — **re·port′a·ble** *adj.*

Synonyms (noun): account, description, narration, narrative, recital, record, rehearsal, relation, rumor, statement, story, tale. *Account,* primarily a commercial summary, carries a similar meaning in the derived sense; an *account* of an occurrence is circumstantial, adequate, complete, and unembellished; we speak of a clear, a full, or a partial *account;* a glowing *account* is still supposed to be circumstantial as well as substantially correct. A *statement* is definite, confined to essentials and properly to matters within the personal knowledge of the one who states them. A *narrative* is a somewhat extended and embellished *account* of events in order of time, ordinarily with a view to please or entertain. A *description* gives especial scope to the pictorial element. A *report* is supposed or intended to bring back the past, and may be concise and formal or highly descriptive and dramatic. Compare ALLEGORY, ANECDOTE, HISTORY, NEWS, RECORD.

re·port·ed·ly (ri·pôr′tid·lē, -pōr′-) *adv.* According to report.

re·port·er (ri·pôr′tər, -pōr′-) *n.* 1 A bearer of news; specifically, one employed by a newspaper to gather and report news for publication. 2 One who edits reports of important cases in court for official publication. [<OF *reporteur*] — **rep·or·to·ri·al** (rep′ər·tôr′ē·əl, -tōr′ē-) *adj.*

re·pose¹ (ri·pōz′) *n.* 1 The act of taking rest, or the state of being at rest; especially, rest in a recumbent posture. 2 Freedom from excitement or anxiety; composure; hence, ease of manner; graceful and dignified calmness. 3 That which conduces to rest or calm. See synonyms under REST. — *v.* **·posed, ·pos·ing** *v.t.* 1 To lay or place in a position of rest: to *repose* oneself on a bed. —

v.i. 2 To lie at rest. 3 To rely; depend: with *on, upon,* or *in.* See synonyms under REST. [<F *reposer* <LL *repausare* < *re-* again + *pausare* pause] — **re·pos′al** *n.* — **re·pos′er** *n.*

re·pose² (ri·pōz′) *v.t.* **·posed, ·pos·ing** 1 To place, as confidence or hope: with *in.* 2 *Rare* To deposit. [<L *repositus,* pp. of *reponere* put back, on analogy with *depose, oppose,* etc.] — **re·pos′al** *n.*

re·pos·it (ri·poz′it) *v.t.* To put in some secure and proper place; deposit. [<L *repositus.* See REPOSE.] — **re·po·si·tion** (rē′pə·zish′ən, rep′ə-) *n.*

re·pos·i·to·ry (ri·poz′ə·tôr′ē, -tō′rē) *n. pl.* **·ries** 1 A place in which goods are or may be stored; a depository. 2 A person to whom a secret is entrusted. 3 A building used as a place of exhibition and sale. 4 A burial vault. 5 A sepulcher (def. 2). [<L *repositorium* < *repositus.* See REPOSE.]

re·pos·sess (rē′pə·zes′) *v.t.* 1 To have possession of again; regain possession of. 2 To give back possession or ownership to. 3 *Scot.* To reinstate: with *in.* See synonyms under RECOVER. — **re′pos·ses′sion** (-zesh′ən) *n.*

repp (rep) See REP¹.

rep·re·hend (rep′ri·hend′) *v.t.* To criticize sharply; find fault with; blame. See synonyms under BLAME, REPROVE. [<L *reprehendere* < *re-* back + *prehendere* hold]

rep·re·hen·si·ble (rep′ri·hen′sə·bəl) *adj.* Deserving blame or censure. — **rep′re·hen′si·bil′i·ty, rep′re·hen′si·ble·ness** *n.* — **rep′re·hen′si·bly** *adv.*

rep·re·sent (rep′ri·zent′) *v.t.* 1 To serve as the symbol, expression, or designation of; symbolize: The letters of the alphabet *represent* the sounds of speech. 2 To express or symbolize in this manner: to *represent* royal power with a scepter. 3 To set forth a likeness or image of; depict; portray, as in painting or sculpture. 4 **a** To produce on the stage, as an opera. **b** To act the part of; impersonate, as a character in a play. 5 To serve as or be the delegate, agent, etc., of: He *represents* the State of Maine. 6 To describe as being of a specified character or condition: They *represented* him as a genius. 7 To set forth in words; state; explain: He *represented* the circumstances of his case. 8 To bring before the mind; present clearly. 9 To serve as an example, specimen, type, etc., of; typify: His use of words *represents* an outmoded school of writing. See synonyms under IMITATE. [<OF *representer* <L *repraesentare* < *re-* again + *praesentare.* See PRESENT².] — **rep′re·sent′a·ble** *adj.* — **rep′re·sent′a·bil′i·ty** *n.*

rep·re·sen·ta·tion (rep′ri·zen·tā′shən) *n.* 1 The act of representing, or the state of being represented. 2 That which represents a likeness; model; picture; statue; statement; description; also, a dramatic performance. 3 The right of acting authoritatively for others, especially in a legislative body; also, the system of electing delegates to act for a constituency. 4 Representatives collectively. 5 The stage or process of mental conservation that consists in the presenting to itself by the mind of objects previously known. 6 *Law* The authorized acting for or in the stead of another in regard to that other's affairs. 7 A setting forth by statement or account; specifically, an argument against some object or proposal. See synonyms under IMAGE, MODEL, PICTURE. [<OF]

rep·re·sen·ta·tive (rep′ri·zen′tə·tiv) *adj.* 1 Typifying or typical of a group or class. 2 Acting, having the power or authority to act, or qualified to act, as an agent. 3 Made up of representatives. 4 Based on or pertaining to the political principle of representation. 5 Presenting, portraying, or representing, or capable of so doing. 6 Having to do with cognition of a memory image: distinguished from *presentative.* — *n.* 1 One who or that which is fit to stand as a type; a typical instance. 2 One who is a qualified agent of any kind. 3 A member of a deliberative or legislative body chosen by vote of the people; specifically, in the United States, a member of the lower house of Congress or of a State legislature. See synonyms under DELEGATE. — **rep′re·sen′ta·tive·ly** *adv.* — **rep′re·sen′ta·tive·ness** *n.*

re·press (ri·pres′) *v.t.* 1 To keep under restraint or

control; curb. 2 To put down; quell, as a rebellion. 3 *Psychoanal.* To effect the repression of, as fears, impulses, etc. [<L *repressus,* pp. of *reprimere* < *re-* back + *premere* press] — **re·press′er** or **re·pres′sor** *n.* — **re·press′i·ble** *adj.*

Synonyms: bridle, chasten, check, crush, curb, overcome, overpower, quiet, rein, restrain, stay, still, subdue, suppress. See LIMIT, RESTRAIN, SUBDUE. *Antonyms:* agitate, animate, arouse, awaken, encourage, excite, incite, inspirit, instigate, kindle, provoke, rouse, stimulate.

re·prieve (ri·prēv′) *v.t.* **·prieved, ·priev·ing** 1 To suspend temporarily the execution of a sentence upon. 2 To relieve for a time from suffering, danger, or trouble. 3 To postpone or delay, as a danger. — *n.* 1 The temporary suspension of a sentence, or the instrument officially ordering such a suspension. 2 Temporary relief or cessation of pain or ill; respite. See synonyms under RESPITE. [<earlier *repry* <F *repris,* pp. of *reprendre* take back; infl. in form by ME *repreven* <OF *reprover* reprove]

rep·ri·mand (rep′rə·mand, -mänd) *v.t.* To reprove sharply or formally. See synonyms under ADMONISH, REPROVE. — *n.* Severe reproof or formal censure, public or private. See synonyms under REPROOF. [<F *réprimande* reproof <L *reprimenda,* fem. of *reprimendus* to be repressed, gerundive of *reprimere.* See REPRESS.]

re·print (rē′print′) *n.* An edition of a printed work that is a verbatim copy of the original; specifically, a copy of matter already printed, as in another country. — *v.t.* (rē·print′) To print a new edition or copy of; print anew or again. — **re·print′er** *n.*

re·pri·sal (ri·prī′zəl) *n.* 1 Forcible seizure of anything from an enemy by way of retaliation or indemnity. 2 Anything taken from an enemy as indemnification or in retaliation; also, any act or infliction by way of retaliation; specifically, the infliction of suffering or death on a prisoner of war in retaliation for acts of inhumanity inflicted by him. 3 Any act of retaliation. 4 *Obs.* A prize seized or gained. [<OF *reprisaille* <re-pris,* pp. of *reprendre* take back <L *reprehendere.* See REPREHEND.]

re·proach (ri·prōch′) *v.t.* 1 To charge with or blame for something wrong; rebuke; censure; upbraid. 2 To bring discredit and disgrace upon; to disgrace. See synonyms under ABUSE, BLAME, REPROVE, REVILE. — *n.* 1 The act of reproaching, or the words of one who reproaches; censure; reproof; rebuke. 2 A cause of blame or disgrace; hence, disgrace or discredit. See synonyms under BLEMISH, REPROOF, SCANDAL. [<F *reprocher.* Origin uncertain.] — **re·proach′a·ble** *adj.* — **re·proach′a·ble·ness** *n.* — **re·proach′a·bly** *adv.* — **re·proach′er** *n.*

rep·ro·bate (rep′rə·bāt) *adj.* 1 Abandoned in sin; lost to all sense of duty; utterly depraved; profligate. 2 Abandoned to punishment; condemned. 3 *Obs.* Not enduring proof or trial; inferior or base. — *n.* One lost to all sense of duty or decency; one abandoned to depravity or doom. — *v.t.* **·bat·ed, ·bat·ing** 1 To disapprove of heartily; condemn. 2 *Theol.* To abandon, condemn, or foreordain to damnation. See synonyms under BLAME, CONDEMN. [<LL *reprobatus,* pp. of *reprobare.* See REPROVE.]

re·pro·duce (rē′prə·dōōs′, -dyōōs′) *v.* **·duced, ·duc·ing** *v.t.* 1 To make a copy, image, or reproduction of. 2 *Biol.* **a** To give rise to (offspring) by sexual or asexual generation. **b** To replace (a lost part or organ) by regeneration. 3 To cause the reproduction of (plant life, etc.). 4 To produce again; bring forward or exhibit anew. 5 To bring into existence again; recreate; revive. 6 To recall to the mind; visualize again; re-create mentally. — *v.i.* 7 To produce offspring. 8 To undergo copying, reproduction, etc. — **re′pro·duc′i·ble** *adj.*

re·pro·duc·tion (rē′prə·duk′shən) *n.* 1 The act or power of reproducing. 2 *Biol.* The process by which an animal or plant gives rise to another of its kind; generation. 3 *Psychol.* The process of the memory by which objects that have previously been known are brought back into consciousness. 4 That which is reproduced, as a revival in drama or a copy in art. See synonyms under DUPLICATE.

re·prog·ra·phy (rē-prog′rɔ-fē) *n.* The reproduction of graphic material, esp. by electronic devices. [< REPRO(DUCTION) + -GRAPHY]

re·proof (ri-proof′) *n.* **1** The act of reproving; rebuke; blame; censure. **2** *Obs.* Ignominy; reproach. Also **re·prov·al** (ri-proo′vɔl). [< OF *prove* < *reprover.* See REPROVE.]

Synonyms: admonition, animadversion, blame, censure, check, chiding, comment, condemnation, criticism, denunciation, disapproval, objurgation, rebuke, reflection, reprehension, reprimand, reproach, reproval, upbraiding. *Blame, censure,* and *disapproval* may either be felt or uttered; *comment, criticism, rebuke, reflection, reprehension,* and *reproof* are always expressed. The same is true of *admonition* and *animadversion. Comment* and *criticism* may be favorable as well as censorious; they imply no superiority or authority on the part of him who utters them; nor do *reflection* or *reprehension,* which are simply turning the mind back upon what is disapproved. *Reprehension* is supposed to be calm and just, and with good intent; *reflection* is often from mere ill feeling, and is likely to be more personal and less impartial than *reprehension. Rebuke,* literally a stopping of the mouth, is administered to a forward or hasty person; *reproof* is administered to one intentionally or deliberately wrong; both words imply authority in the reprover, and direct expression of *disapproval* to the face of the person *rebuked* or *reproved. Reprimand* is official *censure* formally administered by a superior to one under his command. *Rebuke* may be given at the outset, or in the midst of an action; *reflection, reprehension, reproof,* always follow the act; *admonition* is anticipatory, and meant to be preventive. *Check* is allied to *rebuke,* and given before or during action; *chiding* is nearer to *reproof,* but with more personal bitterness and less authority. Compare CONDEMN, REPROVE. *Antonyms:* applause, approbation, approval, commendation, encomium, eulogy, panegyric, praise.

re·prove (ri-proov′) *v.t.* **·proved, ·prov·ing 1** To censure, as for a fault; rebuke. **2** To express disapproval of (an act). **3** *Obs.* To convince; convict. [< OF *reprover* < LL *reprobare* < *re-* again + *probare* test < *probus* upright] —**re·prov′a·ble** *adj.* —**re·prov′er** *n.* —**re·prov′ing·ly** *adv.*

Synonyms: admonish, blame, censure, chasten, check, chide, condemn, rebuke, reprehend, reprimand, reproach, upbraid. To *censure* is to pronounce an adverse judgment that may or may not be expressed to the person *censured;* to *rebuke* is to *reprove* sharply, and often abruptly; to *blame* is a familiar word signifying to pass *censure* upon, make answerable, as for a fault. To *reproach* is to *censure* openly and vehemently, and with intense personal feeling as of grief or anger; as, to *reproach* one for ingratitude; *reproach* knows no distinction of rank or character; a subject may *reproach* a king or a criminal a judge. Compare REPROOF. See ADMONISH, BLAME, CONDEMN. *Antonyms:* see synonyms for PRAISE.

rep·tile (rep′til, -til) *n.* **1** A cold-blooded, air-breathing vertebrate, especially one with scales, as a lizard, snake, or crocodile; a reptilian; any member of the class *Reptilia.* **2** A groveling, abject person; one morally base or odious. —*adj.* **1** Crawling on the belly; creeping; reptant. **2** Groveling morally; sly and base; treacherous; venomous. **3** Of, pertaining to, or resembling a reptile. [< LL, neut. sing. of *reptilis* crawling < *reptus,* pp. of *repere* creep]

rep·til·i·an (rep-til′ē-ɔn) *adj.* **1** Of or pertaining to a class (*Reptilia*) of cold-blooded, air-breathing vertebrates, the reptiles, having fully ossified skeletons and bodies usually covered with horny plates or scales. In addition to the limbless snakes, the class includes crocodiles, alligators, lizards, and turtles. **2** Malicious; base; mean. —*n.* One of the *Reptilia;* any reptile.

re·pub·lic (ri-pub′lik) *n.* **1** A state in which the sovereignty resides in the people or a certain portion of the people, and the legislative and administrative powers are lodged in officers elected by and representing the people; a representative democracy: applied to almost every form of government except kingdoms, empires, and dictatorships. **2** A community of persons working freely in or devoted to the same cause; the *republic* of letters. —**The Republic 1** The United States. **2** Plato's dialog on government. [< F *république* < L *respublica* commonwealth < *res* thing +

publica, fem. of *publicus* public]

re·pub·li·can (ri-pub′li-kɔn) *adj.* Pertaining to, of the nature of, or suitable for a republic; agreeable to the nature of a republic; also, of or pertaining to any party supporting republican government. —*n.* One who advocates or upholds a republican form of government or belongs to a party upholding republican government; one who believes in equality and liberty.

Re·pub·li·can (ri-pub′li-kɔn) *adj.* Pertaining to or belonging to the Republican party of the United States, or to any political group which calls itself by this name: the *Republican* parties of Spain or France. —*n.* A member of the Republican party. —**black Republican** Formerly, a member of the Republican party: derisively so called in allusion to their opposition to Negro slavery.

Republican party 1 One of the two major political parties of the United States, founded in 1854 in opposition to the extension of slavery. **2** The political party founded by Thomas Jefferson in 1792; full name, *Democratic-Republican party.* One of its several factions became, in 1828, the present Democratic party. **3** One of various political parties of foreign countries, devoted to the overthrow of monarchy or the establishment or extension of democratic ideals.

re·pu·di·ate (ri-pyoo′dē-āt) *v.t.* **·at·ed, ·at·ing 1** To refuse to accept as valid, true, or authorized; reject; condemn. **2** To refuse to acknowledge or pay. **3** To cast off; disown, as a son. **4** *Obs.* To divorce; put away (a wife). See synonyms under ABANDON, RECANT, RENOUNCE. [< L *repudiatus,* pp. of *repudiare* divorce < *repudium* divorce, separation, ? < *re-* back + *pudere* feel shame] —**re·pu′di·a′tive** *adj.* —**re·pu′di·a′tor** *n.*

re·pu·di·a·tion (ri-pyoo′dē-ā′shɔn) *n.* **1** The act of repudiating. **2** The state of being repudiated. **3** The rejection of the whole or a part of a contract, debt, or obligation, as by a government.

re·pug·nance (ri-pug′nɔns) *n.* **1** A feeling of aversion and resistance. **2** *Logic* The relation of contradictories; inconsistency. **3** *Obs.* Opposition. Also **re·pug′nan·cy.** See synonyms under ANTIPATHY, HATRED.

re·pug·nant (ri-pug′nɔnt) *adj.* **1** Offensive to taste or feeling; exciting aversion or repulsion. **2** Being inconsistent or opposed; antagonistic. **3** *Law* Contrary to or in conflict with something else in the same or in another document or statute. **4** Hostile; rebellious; resisting. See synonyms under INCONGRUOUS, INIMICAL. [< OF < L *repugnans, -antis,* ppr. of *repugnare.* See REPUGN.]

re·pulse (ri-puls′) *v.t.* **·pulsed, ·puls·ing 1** To drive back; repel, as an attacking force. **2** To repel by coldness, discourtesy, etc.; reject; rebuff. See synonyms under DRIVE, REPEL. —*n.* **1** The act of repulsing, or the state of being repulsed. **2** Rejection; refusal. [< L *repulsus,* pp. of *repellere.* See REPEL.] —**re·puls′er** *n.*

re·pul·sion (ri-pul′shɔn) *n.* **1** The act of repelling or repulsing, or the state of being repelled or repulsed. **2** Aversion; repugnance. **3** *Physics* The mutual action of two bodies which tends to drive them apart: opposed to *attraction.*

re·pul·sive (ri-pul′siv) *adj.* **1** Exciting such feelings, as of dislike, disgust, or horror, that one is repelled; grossly offensive; causing aversion. **2** Such as to forbid approach or familiarity; forbidding. **3** Acting by repulsion: *repulsive* forces. —**re·pul′sive·ly** *adv.* —**re·pul′sive·ness** *n.*

rep·u·ta·ble (rep′yɔ-tɔ-bɔl) *adj.* **1** Having a good reputation; estimable; honorable. **2** Consistent with honorable standing; complying with the usage of the best writers and speakers. —**rep·u·ta·bil′i·ty** *n.* —**rep′u·ta·bly** *adv.*

rep·u·ta·tion (rep′yɔ-tā′shɔn) *n.* **1** The general estimation in which a person or thing is held by others, especially by a community; repute, either good or bad. **2** The state of being in high regard or esteem; good repute: to ruin one's *reputation.* **3** A particular credit or character ascribed to a person or thing: usually with *for:* a *reputation* for honesty. See synonyms under CHARACTER,

FAME. [< L *reputatio, -onis* < *reputatus,* pp. of *reputare* be reputed. See REPUTE.]

re·pute (ri-pyoot′) *v.t.* **·put·ed, ·put·ing** To regard or consider to be as specified; esteem: usually in the passive: They are *reputed* to be an intelligent people. —*n.* **1** Reputation, good or bad. **2** Public opinion; general report. [< L *reputare* reckon, be reputed < *re-* again + *putare* think, count]

re·put·ed (ri-pyoo′tid) *adj.* Generally thought or supposed; having a specified reputation. —**re·put′ed·ly** *adv.*

re·quest (ri-kwest′) *v.t.* **1** To express a desire for, especially politely; ask for; solicit. **2** To address a request to; ask: to *request* a person to do one a favor. See synonyms under ASK, DEMAND, PRAY. —*n.* **1** The act of requesting; entreaty; petition. **2** That which is asked for. **3** The state of being so esteemed as to be in demand; demand: in *request.* See synonyms under PETITION, PRAYER. —*adj.* Having been asked for; in response to a request: a *request* program. [< OF *requeste* < Med. L *requisita,* orig. fem. of L *requisitus,* pp. of *requirere* seek, again. See REQUIRE.]

re·qui·em (rē′kwē-ɔm, rek′wē-) *n.* **1** Any musical hymn, composition, or service for the dead. **2** *Often cap. Eccl.* In the Roman Catholic Church, a solemn mass sung for the repose of the souls of the dead, the **Requiem mass. 3** *Often cap.* A musical setting for such a mass; also a similar piece of music using different words. [< L *Requiem* (*aeternam dona eis, Domine*) rest (eternal give unto them, O Lord), the opening words of the introit of this mass]

req·ui·es·cat (rek′wē-es′kat) *n.* A prayer for the repose of a departed soul: the first word of the Latin petition **requiescat in pa·ce** (in pā′sē), may he rest in peace. Abbr. *R.I.P.* [< L]

re·quire (ri-kwīr′) *v.* **·quired, ·quir·ing** *v.t.* **1** To have need of; find necessary. **2** To demand authoritatively; insist upon: to *require* absolute silence. **3** To command; order: He *requires* us to be punctual. —*v.i.* **4** To make demand or request. See synonyms under ASK, DEMAND, DICTATE, MAKE. [< L *requirere* seek again, be in want of < *re-* again + *quaerere* ask, seek] —**re·quir′a·ble** *adj.* —**re·quir′er** *n.*

re·quire·ment (ri-kwīr′mɔnt) *n.* **1** That which is required; a requisite. **2** The act of requiring, or that which requires; a demand. See synonyms under NECESSITY, ORDER.

req·ui·site (rek′wɔ-zit) *adj.* Required by the nature of things or by circumstances; indispensable. See synonyms under NECESSARY. —*n.* That which cannot be dispensed with; a necessity; requirement. See synonyms under NECESSITY. [< L *requisitus,* pp. of *requirere.* See REQUEST.] —**req′ui·site·ly** *adv.* —**req′ui·site·ness** *n.*

req·ui·si·tion (rek′wɔ-zish′ɔn) *n.* **1** A formal request, summons, or demand, as by a government. **2** A necessity or requirement. **3** The state of being required. **4** A demand for the surrender of a fugitive from justice made by the governing official of one state or country upon another. —*v.t.* To make a requisition for or upon; demand or take upon requisition. [< L *requisitio, -onis* < *requisitus,* pp. of *requirere.* See REQUIRE.]

re·qui·tal (ri-kwīt′l) *n.* **1** The act of requiting. **2** That which requites; adequate return for good or ill; in the favorable sense, reward or compensation; in the unfavorable sense, retaliation. See synonyms under RECOMPENSE, REVENGE. [< REQUITE]

re·quite (ri-kwīt′) *v.t.* **·quit·ed, ·quit·ing 1** To make equivalent return for, as kindness, service, or injury; make up for. **2** To make return to; compensate or repay in kind: Does she *requite* me for my love? **3** To give or do in return. [< RE- + *quite,* obs. var. of QUIT] —**re·quit′a·ble** *adj.* —**re·quit′er** *n.*

Synonyms: avenge, compensate, pay, punish, quit, reciprocate, recompense, remunerate, repay, retaliate, return, revenge, reward, satisfy. *Requite* is often used in the more general sense of *recompense* or *repay,* but always with the suggestion, at least, of the original idea of full equivalent. To *repay* or to *retaliate,* to *punish* or to *reward,* may be to make some return very inadequate to the benefit or injury received or the right or wrong done; but to *requite* is to make such return as to *quit* oneself of all obligation of favor or hostility, of punishment or reward. See PAY. *Antonyms*: absolve, acquit, excuse, forget, forgive, neglect, overlook, pardon, slight.

re·run (rē′run′) *n.* **1** A running over again or a second time. **2** The presenting of a motion picture after its original presentation. — *v.t.* (rē·run′) **·ran, ·run·ning** To run again.

re·scind (ri·sind′) *v.t.* To make void, as an act; abrogate; repeal: to *rescind* a resolution. See synonyms under ANNUL, CANCEL. [< L *rescindere* < *re-* back + *scindere* cut] — **re·scind′a·ble** *adj.* — **re·scind′er** *n.*

re·scis·si·ble (ri·sis′ə·bəl) *adj.* Capable of being rescinded.

res·cue (res′kyōō) *v.t.* **·cued, ·cu·ing** **1** To save or free from danger, captivity, evil, etc.; deliver. **2** *Law* To take or remove forcibly from the custody of the law. See synonyms under DELIVER, RECLAIM. — *n.* The act of rescuing; deliverance. [< OF *rescourre* < Med. L *rescutere* < L *re-* again + *excutere* shake off < *ex-* off, out + *quatere* shake. Related to QUASH.] — **res′cu·a·ble** *adj.* — **res′cu·er** *n.*

re·search (ri·sûrch′, rē′sûrch) *n.* **1** Diligent, protracted investigation; studious inquiry. **2** A systematic investigation of some phenomenon or series of phenomena by the experimental method. See synonyms under INQUIRY. — *v.i.* To make research; investigate. [< F *recherche*] — **re·search′er** *n.*

re·sect (ri·sekt′) *v.t. Surg.* To cut or pare off: distinguished from *excise*. [< L *resectus*, pp. of *resecare* < *re-* back + *secare* cut, amputate]

re·sec·tion (ri·sek′shən) *n.* **1** A cutting or paring off. **2** *Surg.* The operation of cutting out part of a bone, organ, etc. **3** The determination of a position with reference to points of known location, whether on the ground or on a map or chart. [< L *resectio, -onis*]

re·sem·blance (ri·zem′bləns) *n.* **1** The quality of similarity in nature, form, etc.; relative identity; likeness. **2** That which resembles; a semblance or likeness of a person or thing. **3** *Obs.* A characteristic quality or attribute. **4** *Obs.* Probability or likelihood. See synonyms under ANALOGY, APPROXIMATION, PICTURE. [< AF]

re·sem·ble (ri·zem′bəl) *v.t.* **·bled, ·bling** **1** To be similar to in appearance, quality, or character. **2** *Obs.* To compare; liken. See synonyms under IMITATE. [< OF *resembler* < *re-* again and again + *sembler* seem < L *simulare*. See SIMULATE.] — **re·sem′bler** *n.*

re·sent (ri·zent′) *v.t.* To feel or show resentment at; be indignant at, as an injury or insult. [< F *ressentir* feel the effects < *re-* again + *sentir* feel < L *sentire*]

re·sent·ful (ri·zent′fəl) *adj.* Disposed to resent; full of or characterized by resentment. See synonyms under MALICIOUS. — **re·sent′ful·ly** *adv.* — **re·sent′ful·ness** *n.*

re·sent·ment (ri·zent′mənt) *n.* Anger and ill will in view of real or fancied wrong or injury. See synonyms under ANGER, HATRED, OFFENSE, PIQUE.

res·er·va·tion (rez′ər·vā′shən) *n.* **1** The act of reserving. **2** That which is reserved, kept back, or withheld. **3** The unexpressed qualification of a statement, promise, etc., that would, if uttered, so affect or alter its meaning for the person addressed as to vitiate its truth: also **mental reservation. 4** Hence, any limitation. **5** A tract of government land reserved for the use and occupancy of an Indian tribe or for some other special purpose, as the preservation of forests, wild birds, etc. See synonyms under RESERVE. [< OF < LL *reservatio, -onis*]

re·serve (ri·zûrv′) *v.t.* **·served, ·serv·ing** **1** To hold back or set aside for special or future use; store up. **2** To keep as one's own; retain: He *reserves* that privilege for himself. **3** To arrange for ahead of time; have set aside for one's use: I *reserved* two tickets on the train. **4** To set aside (a portion of the consecrated elements of the Eucharist) for communion of the sick. See synonyms under RETAIN. — *n.*

1 That which is reserved; something stored up for future use, as in a reservoir; something set apart for a particular purpose; specifically, a reservation of land. **2** In banking, the amount of funds reserved from investment, in order promptly to meet regular or emergent demands. **3** The act of reserving; reservation. **4** The state of being reserved; silence as to one's feelings, opinions, or affairs; reticence; also, absence of exaggeration. **5** A fighting force held back from action to meet possible emergencies or demands. **6** That component of the armed forces of a nation composed of civilians trained for military service or assignment and subject to call to active duty in emergencies or under particular circumstances; specifically, *U.S.*, the **Army Reserve, Air Force Reserve, Naval Reserve, Marine Corps Reserve,** and **Coast Guard Reserve.** — *adj.* Held in reserve; constituting a reserve: a *reserve* supply of money. [< OF *reserver* < L *reservare* keep back < *re-* back + *servare* keep] — **re·serv′a·ble** *adj.* — **re·serv′er** *n.*

Synonyms (noun): backwardness, coldness, constraint, coyness, haughtiness, limitation, modesty, pride, reservation, reservedness, restraint, reticence, shyness, taciturnity. *Reserve* is the holding oneself aloof from others, or holding back one's feelings from expression, or one's affairs from communication to others; it may spring from *coldness* or *pride*, but is not identical with either and may arise from timidity or policy. See MODESTY.

reserve bank A member of the Federal Reserve System.

reserve clause In professional sports, the stipulation in a contract that commits a player to work for a particular team until released or traded by the employer or until retirement.

re·served (ri·zûrvd′) *adj.* **1** Showing or characterized by reserve of manner; distant; undemonstrative. **2** Retained; kept back. See synonyms under HAUGHTY, TACITURN. — **re·serv·ed·ly** (ri·zûr′vid·lē) *adv.* — **re·serv′ed·ness** *n.*

re·serv·ist (ri·zûr′vist) *n.* A member of the military reserve.

res·er·voir (rez′ər·vwôr, -vwär, -vôr) *n.* **1** A receptacle where some material, especially of a liquid or gas, may be kept in store. **2** A basin, either natural or artificial, for collecting and containing a supply of water, as for use in a city or for water power. **3** An attachment to a stove, machine, or instrument, for containing a fluid to be used in its operation: the *reservoir* of a lamp. **4** An extra supply; a store of anything. [< F *réservoir*]

re·ship (rē·ship′) *v.* **·shipped, ·ship·ping** *v.t.* **1** To ship again. **2** To transfer (oneself) to another vessel. — *v.i.* **3** To go on a vessel again. **4** To sign for another voyage as a crew member or a passenger.

re·ship·ment (rē·ship′mənt) *n.* **1** The act of reshipping. **2** The thing reshipped.

re·side (ri·zīd′) *v.i.* **·sid·ed, ·sid·ing** **1** To dwell for a considerable time; make one's home; live. **2** To exist as an attribute or quality: with *in*. **3** To be vested: with *in*. See synonyms under ABIDE. [< F *résider* < L *residere* sit back, abide < *re-* back + *sedere* sit] — **re·sid′er** *n.*

res·i·dence (rez′ə·dəns) *n.* **1** The place or the house where one resides. **2** The act of residing. **3** Inherence in a thing, as of an attribute in a subject. **4** The fact of being officially present; the statutory presence of an incumbent in a benefice, as a bishop in his diocese: especially in the phrase **in residence:** the canon *in residence.* **5** The seat or place of power or government. **6** The length of time one resides in a place. See synonyms under HOME, HOUSE. [< OF < LL *residentia*]

res·i·dent (rez′ə·dənt) *n.* **1** One who resides or dwells in a place. **2** A diplomatic representative residing at a foreign court or seat of government; specifically, a **minister resident,** a diplomatic agent of the third rank, accredited by the sovereign or head of one country to the sovereign or head of another country; also, an agent in a protectorate. — *adj.* **1** Having a residence; residing. **2**

Abiding in a place in connection with one's official work: a *resident* physician. **3** Inherent: Pungency is *resident* in pepper. **4** Not migratory: said of certain birds. [< OF]

res·i·den·tial (rez′ə·den′shəl) *adj.* **1** Pertaining to, fitted for, or resulting from residence; having residence. **2** Used by residents.

re·sid·u·al (ri·zij′ōō·əl) *adj.* **1** Pertaining to or having the nature of a residue or remainder. **2** Left over as a residue. — *n.* **1** That which is left over from a total mass, magnitude, or quantity which has been acted upon in any specified way; a remainder or remnant. **2** *Stat.* **a** The difference between observed results and those obtained by computation according to formula. **b** The difference between the value of a given observation and the mean of a series to which it belongs. **3** *Often pl.* A payment made to a performer for each rerun of taped or filmed television material in which he or she has appeared. — **re·sid′u·al·ly** *adv.*

res·i·due (rez′ə·dōō, -dyōō) *n.* **1** A remainder or surplus after a part has been separated or otherwise treated. **2** *Chem.* **a** Insoluble matter left after filtration or separation from a liquid. **b** An atom or radical separated from a molecule of a substance. **c** A residuum. **3** *Law* That portion of an estate which remains after all charges, debts, and particular bequests have been satisfied. [< OF *residu* < L *residuum*, neut. of *residuus* remaining < *residere*. See RESIDE.]

re·sid·u·um (ri·zij′ōō·əm) *n.* *pl.* **·u·a** (-ōō·ə) **1** That which remains after any process of subtraction; a residue. **2** *Chem.* A residual product: the *residuum* from the distillation of coal tar. **3** Residue (def. 3). [< L]

re·sign (ri·zīn′) *v.t.* **1** To give up, as a position, office, or trust. **2** To relinquish (a privilege, claim, etc.). **3** To give over (oneself, one's mind, etc.), as to fate or domination. — *v.i.* **4** To resign a position, etc. See synonyms under ABANDON. [< OF *resigner* < L *resignare* sign back, transfer, cancel < *re-* back + *signare* sign] — **re·sign′er** *n.*

res·ig·na·tion (rez′ig·nā′shən) *n.* **1** The act of resigning, as a position, office, or trust, or the formal document declaring such act. **2** The quality of being submissive; unresisting acquiescence. See synonyms under PATIENCE, SUBMISSION. [< F *résignation*]

re·signed (ri·zīnd′) *adj.* Characterized by resignation; submissive. — **re·sign·ed·ly** (ri·zī′nid·lē) *adv.* — **re·sign′ed·ness** *n.*

re·sile (ri·zīl′) *v.i.* **·siled, ·sil·ing** **1** To spring back; recoil. **2** To resume original shape or position after being stretched or compressed. [< MF *resiler* < L *resilire* rebound < *re-* back + *salire* leap]

re·sil·ience (ri·zil′yəns) *n.* **1** The act or power of springing back to a former position or shape; elasticity. **2** *Physics* The quantity of work given back by a body that is compressed to a certain limit and then allowed freely to recover its former size or shape. Also **re·sil′i·en·cy.**

re·sil·ient (ri·zil′yənt) *adj.* **1** Springing back to a former shape or position. **2** Capable of recoiling from pressure or shock unchanged or undamaged. **3** Elastic; buoyant. [< L *resiliens, -entis*, ppr. of *resilire*. See RESILE.] — **re·sil′ient·ly** *adv.*

res·in (rez′in) *n.* **1** An amorphous organic substance exuded from plants, especially from fir or pine trees, yellowish or dark in color and usually translucent or transparent: it is soluble in alcohol and ether, and is a nonconductor of electricity. **2** Any of various substances made by chemical synthesis, especially those used in the making of plastics. **3** The resinous precipitate obtained from a vegetable tincture by treatment with water: used in pharmacy. **4** Rosin. — *v.t.* To apply resin to. [< OF *resine* < L *resina* < Gk. *rhētinē*] — **res·i·na·ceous** (rez′ə·nā′shəs) *adj.*

re·sist (ri·zist′) *v.t.* **1** To strive against; act counter to for the purpose of stopping, preventing, defeating, etc. **2** To be proof against; withstand; defeat. **3** To refrain from: I can't *resist* teasing him. — *v.i.* **4** To offer opposition. See synonyms under DRIVE, HINDER, OPPOSE, REPEL. — *n.* Any substance used to prevent the action of another substance, as a coating applied to a surface to protect it from an acid. [<OF *resister* <L *resistere* cause to stand back < *re-* back + *sistere,* causative of *stare* stand] — **re·sist'er** *n.*

re·sis·tance (ri·zis'təns) *n.* **1** The act of resisting. **2** Any force tending to hinder motion. **3** *Electr.* **a** The opposition offered by a body to the passage through it of an electric current: expressed in ohms: the reciprocal of *conductance.* **b** Impedance. **4** *Psychol.* The force tending to prevent the return to consciousness of unpleasant incidents and experiences. **5** The underground and guerrilla movement opposing an occupying power. See synonyms under DEFENSE. [<F *résistance*]

re·sis·tant (ri·zis'tənt) *adj.* Offering or tending to produce resistance; resisting. — *n.* One who or that which resists. [<F *résistant*]

re·sist·i·ble (ri·zis'tə·bəl) *adj.* Capable of being resisted. — **re·sist'i·bil'i·ty** *n.* — **re·sist'i·bly** *adv.*

re·sis·tive (ri·zis'tiv) *adj.* Having or exercising the power of resistance. — **re·sis'tive·ly** *adv.*

re·sist·less (ri·zist'lis) *adj.* **1** Irresistible. **2** Offering no resistance; powerless. — **re·sist'less·ly** *adv.* — **re·sist'less·ness** *n.*

res·o·lu·ble (rez'ə·lōō·bəl, ri·zol'yə·bəl) *adj.* Capable of being resolved; soluble. [<LL *resolubilis*] — **res'o·lu·bil'i·ty, res'o·lu·ble·ness** *n.*

res·o·lute (rez'ə·lōōt) *adj.* Having a fixed purpose; determined; constant; steady; also, bold; unflinching. See synonyms under FIRM, INFLEXIBLE, OBSTINATE. [<L *resolutus,* pp. of *resolvere.* See RESOLVE.] — **res'o·lute·ly** *adv.* — **res'o·lute·ness** *n.*

res·o·lu·tion (rez'ə·lōō'shən) *n.* **1** The act of resolving or of reducing to a simpler form. **2** The state of being resolute; active fortitude; resoluteness. **3** The making of a resolve; also, the purpose or course resolved upon; a resolve; determination. **4** Chemical, mechanical, or mental analysis; separation of anything into component parts. **5** A proposition offered to or adopted by an assembly. **6** *Law* A judgment or decision of a court. **7** *Med.* The termination of an abnormal condition. **8** *Music* **a** The replacement of a dissonant tone or chord by a higher or lower one so that a consonance, or, sometimes, another dissonance occurs. **b** The tone or chord replacing the original dissonant tone or chord. See synonyms under COURAGE, DETERMINATION, FORTITUDE, PURPOSE, PERSEVERANCE, WILL. — **concurrent resolution** A resolution adopted by both of the houses of Congress and having the force of law without the signature of the President. — **joint resolution** A resolution which, when passed by both houses of Congress and approved by the President, has the force of law. [<L *resolutio, -onis* < *resolutus.* See RESOLUTE.] — **res'o·lu'tion·er, res'o·lu'tion·ist** *n.*

re·solv·a·ble (ri·zol'və·bəl) *adj.* Capable of being resolved, analyzed, or solved. — **re·solv'a·bil'i·ty, re·solv'a·ble·ness** *n.*

re·solve (ri·zolv') *v.* **·solved, ·solv·ing** *v.t.* **1** To decide; determine (to do something). **2** To cause to decide or determine. **3** To separate or break down into constituent parts; analyze. **4** To make clear; explain or solve, as a problem. **5** To explain away; remove (doubts, etc.). **6** To state or decide by vote, as in a legislative assembly. **7** To transform; convert: He *resolves* his anger into pride. **8** *Music* To change, as a chord, from dissonance to consonance; cause to undergo resolution. **9** *Chem.* To separate (a racemic compound) into its optically active components. **10** *Optics* To make distinguishable the structure or parts of. **11** *Med.* To cause to disperse or be absorbed without the formation of pus. **12** *Obs.* To melt; dissolve. **13** *Obs.* To inform. — *v.i.* **14** To make up one's mind; arrive at a decision: with *on* or *upon.* **15** To become separated into constituent parts. **16** *Music* To undergo resolution. — *n.* **1** Fixity of purpose; resolution. **2** A fixed determination; a resolution. **3** The action of a deliberative body expressing formally its intention or purpose. See synonyms under DETERMINATION, PURPOSE. [<L *resolvere* loosen again, relax < *re-* again + *solvere* loosen] — **re·solv'er** *n.*

re·solved (ri·zolvd') *adj.* Fixed or set in purpose; determined; also, having formed a resolve. See synonyms under OBSTINATE. — **re·solv·ed·ly** (ri·zol'vid·lē) *adv.*

re·solv·ent (ri·zol'vənt) *adj.* Having the power to cause the dissolution or resolution of a thing into its elements; solvent. — *n.* **1** That which has the power of resolving or dissolving; a solvent. **2** *Med.* A preparation which has the property of reducing or dispersing a swelling. [<L *resolvens, -entis,* ppr. of *resolvere.* See RESOLVE.]

res·o·nant (rez'ə·nənt) *adj.* **1** Sending back or having the quality of sending back or prolonging sound. **2** Resounding; specifically, having resonance. [<L *resonans, -antis,* ppr. of *resonare* resound, echo < *re-* back, again + *sonare* sound] — **res'o·nant·ly** *adv.*

res·o·nate (rez'ə·nāt) *v.i.* **·nat·ed, ·nat·ing** **1** To have or produce resonance. **2** To manifest sympathetic vibration, as a resonator. [<L *resonatus,* pp. of *resonare.* See RESONANT.]

re·sorb (ri·sôrb') *v.t.* To reabsorb. [<L *resorbere* drink in again, suck back < *re-* back, again + *sorbere* drink in, suck up] — **re·sorp·tion** (ri·sôrp'shən) *n.*

re·sort (ri·zôrt') *v.i.* **1** To go frequently or habitually; repair. **2** To have recourse; apply or betake oneself for relief or aid: with *to.* — *n.* **1** The act of frequenting a place. **2** A place resorted to or frequented to regain health, or for amusement or entertainment. **3** The use of something as a means; a recourse; refuge. [<OF *resortir* < *re-* again + *sortir* go out] — **re·sort'er** *n.*

re·sound (ri·zound') *v.i.* **1** To be filled with sound; echo; reverberate. **2** To make a loud, prolonged, or echoing sound. **3** To ring; echo: said of sounds. **4** *Poetic* To be famed or extolled. — *v.t.* **5** To give back (a sound, etc.); re-echo. **6** *Poetic* To celebrate; extol. **7** *Rare* To utter or repeat loudly. See synonyms under ROAR. [<OF *resoner* <L *resonare.* See RESONANT.]

re·source (ri·sôrs', -sōrs', rē'sôrs, -sōrs) *n.* **1** That which is resorted to for aid or support; resort. **2** *pl.* Available means or property; a supply that can be drawn on; any natural advantages or products: natural *resources.* **3** Capacity for finding or adapting means; power of achievement. **4** Fertility in expedients; resourcefulness; skill or ingenuity in meeting any situation. See synonyms under ALTERNATIVE, PROPERTY. [<OF *ressource* < *resourdre* rise again < *re-* (<L *re-*) back + *sourdre* <L *surgere* rise, surge]

re·spect (ri·spekt') *v.t.* **1** To have deferential regard for; esteem. **2** To treat with propriety or consideration. **3** To regard as inviolable; avoid intruding upon. **4** To have relation or reference to; concern. See synonyms under ADMIRE, DEFER, VENERATE. — *n.* **1** A just regard for and appreciation of worth; honor and esteem: I have great *respect* for the man. **2** Demeanor or deportment indicating deference; courteous regard: to have *respect* for one's elders. **3** *pl.* Expressions of consideration or esteem; compliments: to pay one's *respects.* **4** Conformity to duty or obligation; compliance or observance: *respect* for the law. **5** The condition of being honored or respected: He is held in *respect* by his colleagues. **6** A specific aspect or feature; detail: In what *respect* is he wanting? **7** Reference or relation: usually with *to:* with *respect* to profits. **8** Undue inclination or bias of mind: to have *respect* of persons. **9** *Obs.* Consideration. [<L *respectare* < *respectus,* pp. of *respicere* look back, consider < *re-* again + *specere* look]

re·spect·a·bil·i·ty (ri·spek'tə·bil'ə·tē) *n.* *pl.* **·ties** **1** The characteristic or quality of being respectable; fair social standing; good repute. **2** The respectable people of a community, collectively. **3** *pl.* Certain conventions and other features of conduct presumed to be signs of gentility, social position, morality, etc. Also **re·spect'a·ble·ness.**

re·spect·a·ble (ri·spek'tə·bəl) *adj.* **1** Deserving of respect; being of good name or repute; also, respected. **2** Being of moderate excellence; fairly good; considerable in number, quantity, size, quality, etc.; average. **3** Having a good appearance; presentable. **4** Conventionally correct or socially acceptable in conduct; of decent character. — **re·spect'a·bly** *adv.*

re·spect·ful (ri·spekt'fəl) *adj.* Marked by or manifesting respect; deferential. — **re·spect'-**

ful·ly *adv.* — **re·spect'ful·ness** *n.*

re·spect·ing (ri·spek'ting) *prep.* In relation to; regarding.

re·spec·tive (ri·spek'tiv) *adj.* **1** Pertaining or relating severally to each of those under consideration; several; particular. **2** *Obs.* Characterized by partiality. **3** *Obs.* Attentive.

re·spec·tive·ly (ri·spek'tiv·lē) *adv.* As singly or severally considered; singly in the order designated: The first, second, and third seats belong to John, James, and William *respectively.*

re·spir·a·ble (ri·spīr'ə·bəl, res'pər·ə·bəl) *adj.* **1** Capable of being respired or breathed; fit for respiration. **2** Able to breathe or respire. [<F]

res·pi·ra·tion (res'pə·rā'shən) *n.* **1** The act of inhaling air into the lungs and expelling it; breathing. **2** The process by which a plant or animal takes in oxygen from the air and gives off carbon dioxide and other products of oxidation in the tissues. [<L *respiratio, -onis*]

res·pi·ra·tor (res'pə·rā'tər) *n.* **1** A screen, as of fine gauze, worn over the mouth or nose, as a protection against dust, etc. **2** A device worn over the nose and mouth for the inhalation of medicated vapors, or to warm or sift the air for lung patients. **3** A gas mask. **4** An apparatus for artificial respiration, as a Pulmotor. [<L *respiratus,* pp. of *respirare.* See RESPIRE.]

re·spire (ri·spīr') *v.* **·spired, ·spir·ing** *v.i.* **1** To inhale and exhale air; breathe. **2** To breathe again; recover vitality, hope, ambition, courage, etc. — *v.t.* **3** To inhale and exhale; breathe. **4** *Rare* To breathe or give forth; exhale. [<F *respirer* <L *respirare* < *re-* again + *spirare* breathe]

res·pite (res'pit) *n.* **1** Postponement; delay. **2** Temporary intermission of labor or effort; an interval of rest. **3** *Law* Temporary suspension of the execution of a sentence for a capital offense; reprieve. — *v.t.* **·pit·ed, ·pit·ing** **1** To relieve by a pause or rest. **2** To grant delay in the execution of (a penalty, sentence, etc.). **3** To put off or postpone. [<OF *respit* <Med. L *respectus* delay <L, consideration, regard < *respicere.* See RESPECT.]

Synonyms (noun): delay, forbearance, interval, pause, postponement, reprieve, rest, stay. *Antonyms:* accomplishment, completion, consummation, effect, execution, operation, performance.

re·splen·dence (ri·splen'dəns) *n.* The state or quality of being resplendent; brilliant luster; splendor. Also **re·splen'den·cy.**

re·splen·dent (ri·splen'dənt) *adj.* Shining with brilliant luster; vividly bright; splendid; gorgeous. See synonyms under BRIGHT. [<L *resplendens, -entis,* ppr. of *resplendere* glitter < *re-* again and again + *splendere* shine] — **re·splen'dent·ly** *adv.*

re·spond (ri·spond') *v.i.* **1** To give an answer; reply. **2** To act in reply or return. **3** *Law* To be liable or answerable. — *v.t.* **4** To say in answer; reply. — *n.* *Archit.* A pilaster, semi·column, or similar feature placed against a wall, to receive an arch. [<L *respondere* give back in return < *re-* back + *spondere* pledge, promise] — **re·spond'er** *n.*

re·spon·dence (ri·spon'dəns) *n.* **1** The character or condition of being respondent. **2** The act of responding. **3** Agreement. Also **re·spon'den·cy.**

re·spon·dent (ri·spon'dənt) *adj.* **1** Giving response, or given as a response; answering; responsive. **2** *Law* Occupying the position of defendant. **3** *Obs.* Correspondent. — *n.* **1** One who responds or answers. **2** *Law* The party called upon to answer an appeal or petition; a defendant; especially, the defendant in a suit in equity, admiralty, or divorce. [<L *respondens, -entis,* ppr. of *respondere.* See RESPOND.]

re·sponse (ri·spons') *n.* **1** The act of responding, or that which is responded; words or acts evoked by the words or acts of another or others; an answer; reply. **2** *Eccl.* A portion of a liturgy or church service said or sung by the congregation or choir in reply to the officiating priest; also, an anthem sung or said during or after a reading. **3** *Biol.* The action of an organism or a part, or the cessation of action, resulting from a stimulus or influence; a reaction. [<OF <L *responsum,*

neut. of pp. of *respondere.* See RESPOND.]

Synonyms: answer, rejoinder, repartee, reply, retort. A *rejoinder* is strictly an *answer* to a *reply,* while often used in the general sense of *answer,* but always with the implication of something more or less controversial or opposed, yet lacking the conclusiveness implied in *answer.* A *response* is accordant or harmonious, designed or adapted to carry on the thought of the words that called it forth, or to meet the wish of him who seeks it; as, The appeal for aid met a prompt and hearty *response. Repartee* is a prompt, witty, and commonly good-natured *answer* to some argument or attack; a *retort* may also be witty, but is severe and may be even savage in its intensity. See ANSWER.

re·spon·si·bil·i·ty (ri-spon′sə-bil′ə-tē) *n.* *pl.* **·ties 1** The state of being responsible or accountable. **2** That for which one is answerable; a duty or trust. **3** Ability to meet obligations or to act without superior authority or guidance. See synonyms under DUTY. Also **re·spon′si·ble·ness.**

re·spon·si·ble (ri-spon′sə-bəl) *adj.*˙ **1** Answerable legally or morally for the discharge of a duty, trust, or debt. **2** Having capacity to perceive the distinctions of right and wrong; having ethical discrimination. **3** Able to meet legitimate claims; having sufficient property or means for the payment of debts. **4** Involving accountability or obligation. **5** Denoting the status of a cabinet or ministry with respect to the legislative body to which it is answerable. [<obs. F *responsible* <L *responsus,* pp. of *respondere.* See RESPOND.] — **re·spon′si·bly** *adv.*

re·spon·sive (ri-spon′siv) *adj.* **1** Inclined or ready to respond; being or reacting in accord, sympathy, or harmony; responding. **2** Constituting, or of the nature of, response or reply. **3** Characterized by or containing responses. **4** *Obs.* Correspondent. — **re·spon′sive·ly** *adv.* — **re·spon′sive·ness** *n.*

rest¹ (rest) *v.i.* **1** To cease working, exerting oneself, etc., so as to refresh oneself. **2** To cease from effort or activity for a time. **3** To seek or obtain ease or refreshment by lying down, sleeping, etc. **4** To sleep. **5** To be at peace; be tranquil. **6** To lie in death; be dead. **7** To remain unchanged: And there the matter *rests.* **8** To be supported; stand, lean, lie, or sit: with *against, on,* or *upon.* **9** To be founded or based: with *on* or *upon.* **10** To rely; depend: with *on* or *upon:* Our hopes *rest* on you. **11** To be placed as a burden or responsibility: with *on* or *upon.* **12** To be or lie in a specified place: The blame *rests* with me. **13** To be directed; remain on something, as the gaze or eyes. **14** *Law* To cease presenting evidence in a case. **15** *Agric.* To lie fallow. — *v.t.* **16** To give rest to; refresh by rest. **17** To put, lay, lean, etc., as for support or rest. **18** To found; base. **19** To direct (the gaze, eyes, etc.). **20** *Law* To cease presenting evidence in (a case). — *n.* **1** The act or state of resting; cessation from labor, exertion, action, or motion of any kind; repose; quiet. **2** Freedom from disturbance or disquiet; peace; tranquillity. **3** Sleep; also, death. **4** That on which anything rests; a support; base; basis; foundation; specifically, in billiards and pool, a support for a cue; a bridge. **5** A place of repose or quiet; a stopping place; abode. **6** *Music* **a** A pause, or an interval of silence. **b** A character indicating such pause: an eighth *rest.* **7** In prosody, a pause in a verse; a caesura. **8** *Obs.* Restored or renewed strength. **9** *Mil.* A command given troops, allowing them to relax. ◆ Homophone: *wrest.* [OE *restan*] — **rest′er** *n.*

Synonyms: (*verb*): abide, acquiesce, cease, desist, halt, hold, lean, lie, pause, recline, repose, sleep, slumber, stand, stay, stop, unbend. See ABIDE, LEAN¹. *Antonyms:* contend, fight, labor, strive, struggle, toil, wake, watch, work.

Synonyms (*noun*): calm, calmness, cessation, ease, pause, peace, peacefulness, quiescence, quiet, quietness, quietude, recreation, repose, sleep, slumber, stay, stillness, stop, tranquillity. *Ease* denotes freedom from cause of disturbance, whether external or internal. *Quiet*

denotes freedom from agitation, or especially from annoying sounds. *Rest* is a *cessation* of activity, especially of wearying or painful activity. *Recreation* is some pleasing activity of certain organs or faculties that affords *rest* to other parts of our nature that have become weary. *Repose* is a laying down, primarily of the body, and figuratively, a relaxing freedom from toil or strain of mind. *Sleep* is the perfection of *repose,* the most complete *rest; slumber* is a light and ordinarily pleasant form of *sleep.* See REMAINDER, RESPITE. *Antonyms:* agitation, commotion, disquiet, disturbance, excitement, motion, movement, restlessness, stir, strain, toil, tumult, unrest, work.

rest² (rest) *n.* **1** That which remains or is left over; a remainder. **2** Those remaining or not enumerated; the others: in this sense a collective noun taking a plural verb. **3** A balance, as of resources. — *v.i.* **1** To be and remain; continue; stay: *Rest* content. **2** *Obs.* To be left: Nothing *rests* but hope. — *v.t.* **3** *Obs.* To cause to remain: God *rest* you well. ◆ Homophone: *wrest.* [<OF *reste* <*rester* remain <L *restare* stop, stand <*re-* again + *stare* stand]

res·tau·rant (res′tər-ənt, -tə-ränt) *n.* A place where refreshments or meals are provided; a public dining-room. [<F, lit., restoring, ppr. of *restaurer* <OF *restorer.* See RESTORE.]

res·tau·ra·teur (res′tər-ə-tûr′, *Fr.* res-tō-rá-tœr′) *n.* The proprietor or keeper of a restaurant. [<F]

rest·ful (rest′fəl) *adj.* **1** Full of or giving rest; affording freedom from disturbance, work, or trouble. **2** Being at rest or in repose; quiet. — **rest′ful·ly** *adv.* — **rest′ful·ness** *n.*

rest·ing (res′ting) *adj.* **1** At rest; reposing; also, dead. **2** Dormant.

res·ti·tu·tion (res′tə-tōō′shən, -tyōō′-) *n.* **1** The act of restoring something that has been taken away or lost. **2** The act of making good or rendering an equivalent for injury or loss; indemnification. **3** Restoration to, return to, or recovery of a former position or condition. **4** *Physics* The property of elastic bodies by which they tend to recover their shape after compression. **5** Establishment of the true nature or position of objects distorted in an aerial photograph. [<OF <L *restitutio, -onis* <*restitutus,* pp. of *restituere* restore, set up again <*re-* again + *statuere* set up]

Synonyms: amends, compensation, indemnification, indemnity, recompense, remuneration, reparation, repayment, restoration, return. *Antonyms:* cheat, cheating, defrauding, embezzlement, extortion, fraud, plunder, robbery, stealing, theft.

res·tive (res′tiv) *adj.* **1** Impatient of control; unruly. **2** Restless; fidgety; also, stubborn; balky. [<F *restif* <*rester* remain, balk <L *restare.* See REST².] — **res′tive·ly** *adv.* — **res′tive·ness** *n.*

Synonyms: fidgety, fractious, fretful, frisky, impatient, intractable, mutinous, rebellious, refractory, restless, skittish, unruly, vicious. The disposition to offer active resistance to control by any means whatever is what is commonly indicated by *restive.* A horse may be made *restless* by flies or by martial music, but with no refractoriness; the *restive* animal impatiently resists or struggles to break from control, as by bolting, flinging his rider, or otherwise. With this the metaphorical use of the word agrees, which is always in the sense of such terms as *impatient, intractable, rebellious,* and the like; a people *restive* under despotism are not disposed to "rest" under it, but to resist it and fling it off. *Antonyms:* docile, gentle, manageable, obedient, peaceable, quiet, submissive, tractable, yielding.

rest·less (rest′lis) *adj.* **1** Having no rest; never quiet; unresting: the *restless* waves. **2** Unable or disinclined to rest. **3** Uneasy; constantly seeking change. **4** Discontented. **5** Devoid of or destructive to rest or repose; obtaining no rest or sleep; sleepless. See synonyms under ACTIVE. — **rest′less·ly** *adv.* — **rest′less·ness** *n.*

res·to·ra·tion (res′tə-rā′shən) *n.* **1** The act of restoring a person or thing to a former place or condition. **2** The state of being restored; rehabilitation; renewal. **3** The bringing back of a building or work of art as nearly as may

be to its original state; also, the restored building or object. **4** *Paleontol.* The reconstruction of the skeleton of a fossil animal. **5** *Theol.* The doctrine that all men will eventually be restored to a sinless state and divine favor. See UNIVERSALISM. — **the Restoration 1** The return of Charles II to the English throne in 1660, after the overthrow of the Cromwellian Protectorate; also, the following period until 1685. **2** The return of the Bourbons to power in 1814 under Louis XVIII; also, the period following the return. **3** The return of the Jews to Palestine after the Babylonian captivity. [<OF *restauration* <LL *restauratio, -onis* <L *restauratus,* pp. of *restaurare.* See RESTORE.]

re·sto·ra·tive (ri-stôr′ə-tiv, -stō′rə-) *adj.* **1** Tending or able to restore. **2** Pertaining to restoration. — *n.* That which restores; specifically, something to restore consciousness after a fainting fit.

re·store (ri-stôr′, -stōr′) *v.t.* **·stored, ·stor·ing 1** To bring into existence or effect again: to *restore* peace. **2** To bring back to a former or original condition, appearance, etc.: to *restore* a great painting. **3** To put back in a former place or position; reinstate, as a deposed monarch. **4** To bring back to health and vigor. **5** To give back (something lost or taken away); return. See synonyms under RECLAIM, RECOVER. [<OF *restorer* <L *restaurare* <*re-* again + *-staurare* make firm, as in *instaurare* repair] — **re·stor′er** *n.*

re·strain (ri-strān′) *v.t.* **1** To hold back from acting, proceeding, or advancing; keep in check; repress. **2** To deprive of freedom or liberty, as by placing in a prison or asylum. **3** To restrict or limit. [<OF *restraindre, restreindre* <L *restringere* <*re-* back + *stringere* draw tight] — **re·strain′a·ble** *adj.* — **re·strain′ed·ly** *adv.*

Synonyms: abridge, bridle, check, circumscribe, confine, constrain, curb, hinder, hold, keep, repress, restrict, suppress. *Constrain* is positive; *restrain* is negative; one is *constrained* to an action; he is *restrained* from an action. *Constrain* refers almost exclusively to moral force, *restrain* frequently to physical force, as when we speak of putting one under restraint. To *restrain* an action is to hold it partially or wholly in check, thus controlling it even in performance; to *restrict* an action is to fix a limit or boundary which it may not pass, but within which it is free. To *repress,* literally to press back, is to hold in check, and perhaps only temporarily, that which is still very active; it is a feebler word than *restrain;* to *suppress* is finally and effectually to put down; *suppress* is a much stronger word than *restrain;* as, to *suppress* a rebellion. See ARREST, BIND, GOVERN, KEEP, LIMIT, REFRAIN, REPRESS, TEMPER. *Antonyms:* aid, animate, arouse, emancipate, encourage, excite, free, impel, incite, release.

re·straint (ri-strānt′) *n.* **1** The act of restraining. **2** The state of being restrained; abridgment of liberty; confinement. **3** That which restrains; a restriction. **4** Self-repression; constraint. See synonyms under BARRIER, RESERVE. [<OF *restrainte,* noun use of pp. of *restraindre.* See RESTRAIN.]

re·strict (ri-strikt′) *v.t.* To hold or keep within limits or bounds; confine. See synonyms under BIND, CIRCUMSCRIBE, LIMIT, RESTRAIN. [<L *restrictus,* pp. of *restringere.* See RESTRAIN.]

re·strict·ed (ri-strik′tid) *adj.* **1** Limited; confined. **2** Not for general consumption, use, or service: *restricted* traffic or supplies. **3** Denoting specified defense information the unauthorized publication or dissemination of which is prohibited by law. — **re·strict′ed·ly** *adv.*

re·stric·tion (ri-strik′shən) *n.* **1** The act of restricting, or the state of being restricted; limitation. **2** That which restricts; a restraint. **3** Reservation; self-repression. See synonyms under BARRIER.

re·sult (ri-zult′) *n.* **1** The outcome of an action, course, process, or agency; consequence; effect; conclusion. **2** *Math.* A quantity or value ascertained by calculation. **3** The final determination of a deliberative assembly. See synonyms under CONSEQUENCE, END, EVENT, HARVEST, OPERATION, PRODUCT. — *v.i.* **1** To be a result or outcome; be a physical or logical consequent; follow: with *from*. **2** To have an issue; terminate; end: with *in*. [< Med. L *resultare* < L, spring back, freq. of *resilire* rebound. See RESILE.]

re·sul·tant (ri·zul′tənt) *adj.* Arising or following as a result. — *n.* **1** That which results; a consequence. **2** *Physics* A force, velocity, etc., resulting from the action of two or more quantities of the same kind. [< L *resultans, -antis,* ppr. of *resultare.* See RESULT.]

re·sume (ri·zoom′) *v.* **·sumed, ·sum·ing** *v.t.* **1** To begin again; take up again after cessation or interruption. **2** To take or occupy again: *Resume* your places. **3** To take for oneself again: to *resume* a title. — *v.i.* **4** To continue after cessation or interruption. See synonyms under RECOVER. [< F *résumer* < L *resumere* take up again, take back < *re-* again + *sumere* take, seize] — **re·sum′a·ble** *adj.* — **re·sum′er** *n.*

res·u·mé (rez′oo·mā′, rez′oo·mā) *n.* A summary, as of one's employment record. [< F]

re·su·pine (rē′soo·pīn′) *adj.* Lying on the back; supine. [< L *resupinus* < *re-* again + *supinus* on the back]

re·surge (ri·sûrj′) *v.i.* **·surged, ·surg·ing** **1** To rise again; be resurrected. **2** To surge or sweep back again, as the tide. [< L *resurgere* < *re-* again + *surgere* rise]

re·sur·gence (ri·sûr′jəns) *n.* A rising again.

re·sur·gent (ri·sûr′jənt) *adj.* **1** Rising again, as from the grave. **2** Surging back or again. [< L *resurgens, -entis,* ppr. of *resurgere*]

res·ur·rect (rez′ə·rekt′) *v.t.* **1** To bring back to life; raise from the dead. **2** To bring back into use or to notice. — *v.i.* **3** To rise again from the dead. [Back formation < RESURRECTION]

res·ur·rec·tion (rez′ə·rek′shən) *n.* **1** A rising again from the dead. **2** The state of those who have risen from the dead. **3** Any revival or renewal, as of a practice or custom, after disuse, decay, etc.; restoration; rebirth. **4** In Christian Science, spiritualization of thought; a new and higher idea of immortality, or spiritual existence; material belief yielding to spiritual understanding. — **the Resurrection** *Theol.* **1** The rising of Christ from the dead. **2** The rising again of all the dead at the day of final judgment. [< L *resurrectio, -onis* < *resurrectus,* pp. of *resurgere.* See RESURGE.] — **res′ur·rec′tion·al** *adj.*

res·ur·rec·tion·ist (rez′ə·rek′shən·ist) *n.* **1** One who steals bodies from the grave; a body-snatcher. **2** One who brings to light anything buried in obscurity. **3** A believer in the rising again of the dead. — **res′ur·rec′tion·ism** *n.*

re·sus·ci·tate (ri·sus′ə·tāt) *v.t.* & *v.i.* **·tat·ed, ·tat·ing** To bring or come back to life; revive from unconsciousness or apparent death. [< L *resuscitatus,* pp. of *resuscitare* < *re-* again + *suscitare* revive < *sub-* under + *citare* call, rouse. See CITE.] — **re·sus′ci·ta′tive** *adj.* — **re·sus′ci·ta′tor** *n.*

re·sus·ci·ta·tion (ri·sus′ə·tā′shən) *n.* The act of resuscitating, or the state of being resuscitated; revivification; reanimation.

re·ta·ble (ri·tā′bəl) *n.* **1** A shelf or ledge raised above the back of an altar to support ornaments, lights, etc. **2** A panel containing a picture or bas-relief of subjects from sacred history. [< F < OF *rere-table* < Med. L *retro-tabulum* < L *retro-* behind + *tabula* plank]

re·tail (rē′tāl) *n.* The selling of goods in small quantities: opposed to *wholesale.* — *adj.* Of, pertaining to, or concerned in the sale of goods in small quantities or parcels. — *v.t.* **1** To sell in small quantities; sell directly to the ultimate consumer. **2** (ri·tāl′) To repeat, as gossip. — *v.i.* **3** To be sold at retail. [< OF, cutting < *retailler* cut up < *re-* again + *tailler* cut < LL *taliare* split]

re·tail·er (rē′tā·lər) *n.* One who sells in small quantities to the consumer.

re·tain (ri·tān′) *v.t.* **1** To keep or continue to keep in one's possession; hold. **2** To maintain in use, practice, etc.: to *retain* one's standards. **3** To keep in a fixed condition or place. **4** To keep in mind; remember. **5** To hire, as a servant; also, to engage (an attorney or other representative) by paying a retainer. [< OF *retenir* < L *retinere* < *re-* back + *tenere* hold] *Synonyms:* detain, employ, engage, hire, hold, keep, maintain, preserve, reserve, secure, withhold. See KEEP, REMEMBER. *Antonyms:* abandon, cede, discard, discharge, dismiss,

eject, relinquish, renounce, resign, surrender.

re·tain·er¹ (ri·tā′nər) *n.* **1** One retained in the service of a person of rank or position. **2** One who retains or keeps. **3** *Mech.* A device for holding the parts of ball or roller bearings in place.

re·tain·er² (ri·tā′nər) *n.* **1** The fee paid, or the agreement made, to employ an attorney to serve in a suit; a retaining fee. **2** A similar fee paid to anyone to retain his services. [< OF *retenir* hold back, in a noun use]

re·take (rē·tāk′) *v.t.* **·took, ·tak·en, ·tak·ing** **1** To take back; receive again. **2** To recapture. **3** To photograph again. — *n.* (rē′tāk′) A motion-picture scene or sequence photographed again.

re·tal·i·ate (ri·tal′ē·āt) *v.* **·at·ed, ·at·ing** *v.i.* To return like for like; especially, to repay evil with evil. — *v.t.* To repay (an injury, wrong, etc.) in kind; revenge. See synonyms under AVENGE. [< L *retaliatus,* pp. of *retaliare* < *re-* back + *talio* punishment in kind < *talis* such] — **re·tal′i·a′tive** *adj.*

re·tal·i·a·tion (ri·tal′ē·ā′shən) *n.* The act of retaliating; reprisal; requital. See synonyms under REVENGE.

re·tard (ri·tärd′) *v.t.* To cause to move or proceed slowly; hinder the advance or course of; impede; delay. — *v.i.* To be delayed. See synonyms under HINDER, OBSTRUCT. — *n.* Delay; retardation. [< F *retarder* < L *retardare* < *re-* back + *tardare* make slow < *tardus* slow] — **re·tard′a·tive** *adj.* — **re·tard′er** *n.*

re·tard·ant (ri·tär′dənt) *n.* Something that retards. — *adj.* Tending to hinder.

re·tard·ate (ri·tär′dāt) *n.* A mentally retarded person.

re·tar·da·tion (rē′tär·dā′shən) *n.* **1** The act of retarding. **2** The state of being retarded. **3** A lessening of velocity, gain, or progress; a delaying. **4** The amount of delay or hindrance effected. **5** That which retards; a hindrance. **6** Slowness. **7** *Music* A gradual slackening of the time. [< L *retardatio, -onis*]

re·tard·ed (ri·tärd′id) *adj.* Abnormally slow in development, especially mentally.

retch (rech) *v.i.* To make an effort to vomit; strain; heave. ♦ **Homophone:** *wretch.* [OE *hræcan* bring up (blood or phlegm)]

re·tent (ri·tent′) *n.* That which is retained. [< L *rententus,* pp. of *retinere.* See RETAIN.]

re·ten·tion (ri·ten′shən) *n.* **1** The act of retaining. **2** The ability to remember; memory. **3** The keeping up or maintenance, as of a custom, practice, opinion, or intention. **4** *Med.* A holding within the body of materials normally excreted, as urine, etc. [< OF < L *retentio, -onis*]

re·ten·tive (ri·ten′tiv) *adj.* Having the power or tendency to retain; retaining: a *retentive* memory.

re·ten·tive·ness (ri·ten′tiv·nis) *n.* **1** The capacity of holding or retaining. **2** *Psychol.* The preservative function of memory.

ret·i·cence (ret′ə·səns) *n.* The quality, act, or an instance of being reserved in speech; reserve; taciturnity. Also **ret′i·cen·cy.** See synonyms under RESERVE. [< L *reticentia,* orig. neut. pl. of *reticens.* See RETICENT.]

ret·i·cent (ret′ə·sənt) *adj.* Habitually silent or reserved in utterance. See synonyms under TACITURN. [< L *reticens, -entis,* ppr. of *reticere* remain silent < *re-* again + *tacere* be silent] — **ret′i·cent·ly** *adv.*

re·tic·u·lar (ri·tik′yə·lər) *adj.* **1** Like a network; reticulate; intricate. **2** *Anat.* Of or pertaining to a reticulum. Also **re·tic′u·lar′y.** [< NL *reticularis* < L *reticulum.* See RETICULUM.]

re·tic·u·late (ri·tik′yə·lāt) *v.* **·lat·ed, ·lat·ing** *v.t.* **1** To make a network of. **2** To cover with or as with lines of network. — *v.i.* **3** To form a network. — *adj.* (-lit, -lāt) Having the form or appearance of a network; having lines or veins crossing, as in leaves: also **re·tic′u·lat′ed.** [< L *reticulatus* < *reticulum.* See RETICULUM.]

ret·i·cule (ret′ə·kyool) *n.* **1** A small bag formerly used by women for carrying personal articles, sewing materials, etc. **2** *Optics* A reticle. [< F *réticule*]

re·ti·form (rē′tə·fôrm, ret′ə-) *adj.* Arranged like a network; reticulate. [< F *rétiforme* < L *rete* net + *forma* shape]

ret·i·na (ret′ə·nə, ret′nə) *n. pl.* **·nas** or **·nae** (-nē) *Anat.* The inner membrane at the back

of the eyeball, containing the light-sensitive rods and cones which receive the optical image. See illustration under EYE. [< LL < L *rete* net] — **ret′i·nal** *adj.*

ret·i·ni·tis (ret′ə·nī′tis) *n. Pathol.* Inflammation of the retina.

ret·i·nue (ret′ə·noo, -nyoo) *n.* The body of retainers attending a person of rank; an escort; cortège. [< F *retenue,* fem. of *retenu,* pp. of *retenir.* See RETAIN.]

re·tire (ri·tīr′) *v.* **·tired, ·tir·ing** *v.i.* **1** To go away or withdraw, as for privacy, shelter, or rest. **2** To go to bed. **3** To withdraw oneself from business, public life, or active service. **4** To fall back; retreat, as troops under attack. **5** To move back; recede or appear to recede. — *v.t.* **6** To remove from active service, as an officer of the army or navy. **7** To pay off and withdraw from circulation: to *retire* bonds. **8** To withdraw (troops, etc.) from action. **9** In baseball, etc., to keep (a batter or runner) from reaching base or scoring by putting him out, or to remove (a side) from an opportunity of scoring. [< F *retirer* < *re-* back + *tirer* draw]

re·tired (ri·tīrd′) *adj.* **1** Withdrawn from public view; existing or passed in seclusion; solitary; secluded: a *retired* life. **2** Withdrawn from active service, business, office, or public life: a *retired* sea captain. **3** Due or received by a person withdrawn from active service: *retired* pay. See synonyms under SECRET.

re·tir·ee (ri·tīr′ē) *n.* A person who is retired.

re·tire·ment (ri·tīr′mənt) *n.* **1** The act of retiring, or the state of being retired; withdrawal; seclusion. **2** A secluded place.

Synonyms: loneliness, privacy, seclusion, solitude. In *retirement* one withdraws from association he has had with others; in *seclusion* one shuts himself off from the society of all except intimate friends or attendants; in *solitude* no other person is present. As private denotes what concerns ourselves individually, *privacy* denotes freedom from the presence or observation of those not concerned or whom we do not wish to have concerned in our affairs; *privacy* is more temporary than *seclusion;* we speak of a moment's *privacy.* There may be *loneliness* without *solitude,* as amid an unsympathizing crowd, and *solitude* without *loneliness,* as when one is glad to be alone. See SECLUSION, SOLITUDE. *Antonyms:* association, companionship, company, fellowship, society.

re·tir·ing (ri·tīr′ing) *adj.* **1** Shy; modest; reserved; unobtrusive. **2** Pertaining to retirement: a *retiring* pension. See synonyms under MODEST.

re·tort¹ (ri·tôrt′) *v.t.* **1** To direct (a word or deed) back upon the originator. **2** To reply to, as an accusation or argument, by a similar one. — *v.i.* **3** To make answer, especially sharply. — *n.* A retaliatory speech; a turning back of an accusation or insult upon the one who makes it; a keen rejoinder or caustic riposte; also, the act of making such reply: to be quick at *retort.* See synonyms under ANSWER. [< L *retortus,* pp. of *retorquere* < *re-* back + *torquere* twist] — **re·tort′er** *n.*

RETORTS
a. Retort with receiver.
b. Common retort.

re·tort² (ri·tôrt′) *n.* **1** *Chem.* A vessel with a bent tube, for the heating of substances, or for distillation. **2** *Metall.* A vessel in which ore may be heated for the removal of its metal content. [< L *retortus* bent back. See RETORT¹.]

re·tor·tion (ri·tôr′shən) *n.* **1** The act of retorting. **2** A bending, turning, or twisting back. **3** Retaliation; in international law, the infliction by one nation upon the subjects of another of the same ill treatment that its own citizens have received from the latter government. Also **re·tor′sion.** [< Med. L *retortio, -onis*]

re·touch (rē·tuch′) *v.t.* **1** To add new touches to; modify; revise. **2** *Phot.* To change, or improve, as a print, by a hand process in which a hard, sharp pencil or fine brush is used. — *n.* (also rē′tuch′) An additional touch, as to a picture, model, or other work of art, previously regarded as finished. [< F *retoucher*] — **re·touch′er** *n.*

re·trace (ri·trās′) *v.t.* **·traced, ·trac·ing** **1** To go back over; follow backward, as a path. **2** To trace the whole story of, from the beginning. **3**

To go back over with the eyes or mind. [< F *re-tracer*] —**re·trace′a·ble** *adj.*

re·tract (ri·trakt′) *v.t. & v.i.* **1** To take back (an assertion, accusation, admission, etc.); make a disavowal (of); recant. **2** To draw back or in, as the claws of a cat. See synonyms under RECANT, RENOUNCE. [< F *rétracter* < L *retractare* draw back < *re-* back + *tractare* draw violently, freq. of *trahere* draw] —**re·tract′a·ble** or **-i·ble** *adj.* — **re·trac·ta·tion** (rē′trak·tā′shən) *n.*

re·trac·tion (ri·trak′shən) *n.* **1** The act of retracting or drawing something back or in. **2** The state of being retracted. **3** The act of withdrawing or recalling something said or avowed; recantation; revocation.

re·tral (rē′trəl) *adj.* Situated at the back; posterior. [< L *retro* backward + -AL¹]

re·tread (rē′tred′) *n.* A new outer covering of a pneumatic tire, to replace a worn or damaged one. —*v.t.* (rē·tred′) **·tread·ed, ·tread·ing** To fit or furnish (an automobile tire) with a new tread. Also *recap.*

re·treat (ri·trēt′) *v.i.* **1** To go back or backward; withdraw; retire. **2** To curve or slope backward. —*v.t.* **3** In chess, to move (a piece) back. —*n.* **1** The act of retreating, as from contest or danger. **2** The retirement of a naval or land force from a position of danger or from an enemy; also, a signal for retreating, made by trumpet or drum. **3** In the army or navy, a signal, as by bugle, for the lowering of the flag at sunset. **4** Retirement; seclusion; solitude. **5** A place of retirement, quiet, or security; a refuge; shelter; haunt. **6** Religious retirement; also, the time spent in religious retirement. **7** An establishment for the mentally ill, for alcoholics, etc. See synonyms under REFUGE, SECLUSION, SHELTER. Compare RETIREMENT. [< F *retraite*, orig. fem. of pp. of *retaire* draw back < L *retrahere* < *re-* again + *trahere* draw]

re·trench (ri·trench′) *v.t.* **1** To cut down or reduce; curtail (expenditures). **2** To cut off or away; remove; omit. —*v.i.* **3** To make retrenchments; economize. [< MF *retrencher* < *re-* back + *trencher* cut. See TRENCH.]
Synonyms: abridge, clip, curtail, cut, decrease, diminish, economize, lessen, reduce. *Antonyms:* elongate, expand, extend, lavish, lengthen, prolong, protract, squander, waste.

re·trench·ment (ri·trench′mənt) *n.* **1** The act of retrenching. **2** Reduction, as of expenses, for the sake of economy. **3** An interior breastwork or rampart from which the enemy can be resisted should the outer line be taken.

ret·ri·bu·tion (ret′rə·byoo′shən) *n.* **1** The act of requiting; impartial infliction of punishment. **2** That which is done or given in requital. **3** A reward or (especially) a punishment. See synonyms under RECOMPENSE, REVENGE. [< OF < L *retribu-tio, -onis* < *retributus*, pp. of *retribuere* pay back < *re-* back + *tribuere* pay]

re·trib·u·tive (ri·trib′yə·tiv) *adj.* Tending to reward or punish. Also **re·trib′u·to·ry** (-tôr′ē, -tō′rē).

re·triev·al (ri·trē′vəl) *n.* **1** The act of retrieving. **2** Restoration from loss, damage, or failure.

re·trieve (ri·trēv′) *v.* **·trieved, ·triev·ing** *v.t.* **1** To get back; regain. **2** To restore; revive, as flagging spirits. **3** To make up for; remedy the consequences of. **4** To call to mind; remember. **5** To find and bring in (wounded or dead game): said of dogs. —*v.i.* **6** To retrieve game. See synonyms under RECOVER. —*n.* The act of retrieving; retrieval; recovery. [ME *retreve* < OF *retroev-*, stressed stem of *retrouver* find again < *re-* again + *trouver* find] —**re·triev′a·bil′i·ty** *n.* — **re·triev′a·ble** *adj.* —**re·triev′a·bly** *adv.*

retro- *prefix* **1** Back; backward: *retroflex, retrograde.* **2** Chiefly in scientific terms, behind: *retrolental.* [< L *retro-* < *retro* back, backward]

ret·ro·act (ret′rō·akt′, rē′trō-) *v.i.* **1** To act reciprocally or in return; react. **2** *Law* To affect past acts, obligations, or penalties. [Back formation < RETROACTIVE] —**ret′ro·ac′tion** *n.*

ret·ro·ac·tive (ret′rō·ak′tiv, rē′trō-) *adj.* Having or designed to have a retrospective effect or reversed action; in effect also during a specified

prior period. —**ret′ro·ac′tive·ly** *adv.* — **ret′ro·ac·tiv′i·ty** *n.*

ret·ro·cede (ret′rō·sēd′) *v.* **·ced·ed, ·ced·ing** *v.t.* To cede, grant, or give back. —*v.i.* To go back; recede. [< L *retrocedere* < *retro-* back + *cedere* go]

ret·ro·ces·sion (ret′rō·sesh′ən) *n.* **1** The act of retroceding or giving back. **2** *Law* The conveyance of an estate to a former owner. [< LL *retrocessio, -onis*]

ret·ro·fit (ret′rō·fit′) *v.t.* **·fit·ted, ·fit·ting** To furnish (something previously manufactured) with new parts, equipment, or materials.

ret·ro·flex (ret′rə·fleks) *adj.* **1** Bent or turned backward; reflexed. **2** *Phonet.* Cacuminal. Also **ret′ro·flexed.** [< LL *retroflexus*, pp. of *retroflectere* < L *retro-* back + *flectere* bend]

ret·ro·grade (ret′rə·grād) *v.* **·grad·ed, ·grad·ing** *v.i.* **1** To move or appear to move backward; recede. **2** To grow worse; decline; degenerate. **3** *Astron.* To have a retrograde motion. —*v.t.* **4** To cause to move backward; reverse. —*adj.* **1** Going, moving, or tending backward; contrary; reversed. **2** Declining to or toward a worse state or character. **3** *Astron.* Apparently moving from east to west relatively to the fixed stars. **4** Reversed; inverted. **5** *Obs.* Opposed; contrary. —*n.* A retrograde movement; decline. [< L *retrogra-dus*] —**ret′ro·gra·da′tion** (-grā·dā′shən) *n.*

ret·ro·gress (ret′rə·gres) *v.i.* To go back to an earlier or worse condition. [< L *retrogressus*, pp. of *retrogradi* < *retro-* backward + *gradi* walk]

ret·ro·gres·sion (ret′rə·gresh′ən) *n.* **1** A retreat; degeneration; motion in a reverse direction. **2** A moving toward a lower plane. **3** *Biol.* Descent to or toward a less complex or less perfect structure.

re·trorse (ri·trôrs′) *adj.* Turned, bent, or directed backward. [< L *retrorsus*, contraction of *retroversus* < *retro-* backward + *versus*, pp. of *vertere* turn] —**re·trorse′ly** *adv.*

ret·ro·spect (ret′rə·spekt) *v.i.* *Rare* **1** To think about the past. **2** To look or refer back. —*v.t.* **3** *Rare* To consider or think about in retrospect. —*n.* A looking back on things past; view or contemplation of something past. See synonyms under MEMORY. [< L *retrospectus*, pp. of *retros-picere* reexamine, look back < *retro-* back + *spe-cere* look]

ret·ro·spec·tion (ret′rə·spek′shən) *n.* A calling to remembrance; a looking back upon or recollection of the past.

ret·ro·spec·tive (ret′rə·spek′tiv) *adj.* **1** Looking back on the past; of, pertaining to, or referring to the past. **2** Retroactive: said of some legislation. **3** Characterized by retrospection. —**ret′ro·spec′tive·ly** *adv.*

ret·ro·ver·sion (ret′rə·vûr′zhən, -shən) *n.* **1** A tipping or bending backward. **2** The state of being turned backward. **3** The act of looking or turning back.

ret·ro·vert (ret′rə·vûrt′) *v.t.* To turn back. [< LL *retrovertere* < L *retro-* back + *vertere* turn]

ret·ro·vi·rus (ret′rō·vī′rəs; ret′rō·vī′rəs) *n.* Any of a family of viruses that contain RNA genetic material, and are responsible for AIDS, leukemia, etc.

re·turn (ri·tûrn′) *v.i.* **1** To come or go back, as to or toward a former place or condition. **2** To come back or revert in thought or speech. **3** To revert to a former owner. **4** To answer; respond. —*v.t.* **5** To bring, carry, send, or put back; restore; replace. **6** To give in return for something: to *return* ingratitude for kindness. **7** To repay or requite, especially with an equivalent: to *return* a compliment. **8** To yield or produce, as a profit or interest. **9** To send back; reflect, as light or sound. **10** To render (a verdict, etc.) **11** To submit, as a report or writ, to one in authority. **12** To report or announce officially. **13** To replace (a weapon, etc.) in its holder. **14** In card games, to lead (a suit previously led by one's partner). —*n.* **1** The act, process, state, or result of coming back or returning; also, that which is re-

turned; resumption; restoration or replacement; repayment or requital; response; answer; retort; reappearance or recurrence. **2** That which accrues, as from investments, labor, or use; profit. **3** A coming back, reappearance, or recurrence, as of a periodical event or season. **4** A report, list, etc.; especially, a formal or official report, or, in the plural, a set of tabulated statistics: election *returns.* **5** *Archit.* A continuation of a dripstone, hood molding, etc., to form a termination having a different direction from the main part. **b** A part or face of a building at an angle with the main part of the façade. **6** The sending back by a sheriff of a writ to the court from which it was issued; also, a sheriff's report on such writ. **7** *Law* A brief statement, usually endorsed on a writ by the officer to whom it was issued, of what has been done under it; also, the filing of the writ thus endorsed in the office of the clerk or the tribunal whence it was issued. **8** In card games, a returned lead. **9** Any volley, stroke, or thrust received from an opponent; specifically, in a game, the sending of an object, as a tennis ball, from one player to another from whom he has received it. See synonyms under HARVEST, INCREASE, PRODUCT, PROFIT, RESTITUTION. —*adj.* Of or pertaining to a return; given, taken, or done in return; returning: a *return* visit; a *return* ticket. [< OF *returner*] — **re·turn′er** *n.*

re·turn·a·ble (ri·tûr′nə·bəl) *adj.* **1** Capable of being or suitable to be returned. **2** Due and required: said of a judicial writ in reference to the time when and the place where it is to be returned by the officer to whom it is directed.

re·un·ion (rē·yoon′yən) *n.* **1** The act of reuniting; renewed harmony. **2** A social gathering of persons who have been separated: a family *reunion.*

re·u·nite (rē′yoo·nīt′) *v.t. & v.i.* **·nit·ed, ·nit·ing** To unite, cohere, or combine again after separation. —**re′u·nit′er** *n.*

rev (rev) *n.* A revolution, as of a motor or machine part. —*v.t. & v.i.* **revved, rev·ving** To alter the speed of (a motor): with *up* or *down.*

re·vamp (rē·vamp′) *v.t.* **1** To vamp (a boot or shoe) anew. **2** To patch up; make over. —*n.* A thing which is revamped. [< RE- + VAMP]

re·veal (ri·vēl′) *v.t.* **1** To make known; disclose; divulge. **2** To make visible; expose to view; exhibit; show. See synonyms under ANNOUNCE, INFORM, PUBLISH. —*n. Archit.* The vertical side of an aperture or opening in a wall; especially, the portion of the side of a door or window between the line where the window frame or door frame stops and the outer edge of the opening. [< OF *reveler* < L *revelare* unveil < *re-* back + *velum* veil] —**re·veal′a·ble** —**re·veal′er** *n.*

re·veal·ment (ri·vēl′mənt) *n.* A revelation; act of revealing; disclosure.

re·veil·le (rev′i·lē) *n.* **1** A morning signal by drum or bugle, notifying soldiers or sailors to rise. **2** The hour at which this signal is sounded. [< F *reveillez-vous*, imperative of *se reveiller* wake up < *re-* (< L *re-*) again +L *vigilare* watch. See VIGIL.]

rev·el (rev′əl) *v.i.* **·eled** or **·elled, ·el·ing** or **·el·ling** **1** To take delight; indulge freely: with *in*: He *revels* in his freedom. **2** To make merry; engage in boisterous festivities. —*n.* **1** Merrymaking; carousing; noisy festivity. **2** An occasion of boisterous festivity; a celebration. [< OF *reveler* make an uproar < L *rebellare.* Doublet of REBEL.] —**rev′el·er** or **rev′el·ler** *n.*
Synonyms (noun): carnival, carousal, carouse, feast, festivity, jollification, merrymaking, revelry, rout.

rev·e·la·tion (rev′ə·lā′shən) *n.* **1** The act or process of revealing, or the state of being revealed. **2** That which is or has been revealed. **3** *Theol.* **a** The act of revealing or communicating divine truth, especially by divine agency or supernatural means. **b** That which has been so revealed, as concerning God in his relations to man. **c** That which is revealed in the Bible itself. [< OF < LL *revelatio, -onis* < L *revelatus*, pp. of *revelare.* See REVEAL.]

rev·e·la·tor (rev′ə·lā′tər) *n.* A revealer. [< LL]

rev·el·ry (rev′əl·rē) *n. pl.* **·ries** Noisy or boisterous merriment.

rev·e·nant (rev′ə·nənt) n. 1 One who or that which returns. 2 A ghost; an apparition. [< F, ppr. of *revenir* come back < *re-* back + *venir* come]

re·venge (ri·venj′) v. **·venged, ·veng·ing** v.t. 1 To inflict punishment, injury, or loss in return for; to take vengeance for; avenge. 2 To take or seek vengeance in behalf of. — v.i. 3 *Obs.* To take vengeance. — n. 1 The act of returning injury for injury; the infliction of injury or punishment in the spirit of personal vindictiveness; retaliation. 2 A mode or means of avenging oneself or others. 3 The desire for vengeance. [< OF *revenger* < *re-* (< L *re-*) again + *venger* take vengeance < L *vindicare*. See VINDICATE.] — **re·veng′er** n.

Synonyms (noun): avenging, requital, retaliation, retribution, vengeance. *Retaliation* and *revenge* are personal and often bitter. *Retaliation* may be partial; *revenge* is meant to be complete and may be excessive. *Vengeance*, which once meant an indignant vindication of justice, now signifies the most furious and unsparing *revenge*. *Revenge* emphasizes more the personal injury in return for which it is inflicted. A *requital* is an even return, such as to quit one of obligation for what has been received, and may be good or bad. *Avenging* and *retribution* give a solemn sense of exact justice, *avenging* being more personal in its infliction, and *retribution* the impersonal visitation of the doom of righteous law. See HATRED. Antonyms: compassion, excuse, forgiveness, grace, mercy, pardon, pity.

re·venge·ful (ri·venj′fəl) adj. Vindictive; disposed to, or full of, revenge. — **re·venge′ful·ly** adv. — **re·venge′ful·ness** n.

rev·e·nue (rev′ə·nyoo, -noo) n. 1 Total current income of a government, except duties on imports: also **internal revenue.** 2 Income from any form of property. 3 The department of government or civil service which collects the national funds: in the United States, the **Internal Revenue Service** of the Department of the Treasury. 4 A source of an item of income. [< F, fem. of *revenu*, pp. of *revenir* return]

revenue sharing *U.S.* The distribution among state and municipal governments, based on their population, of a part of the revenue from Federal taxes.

re·ver·ber·ant (ri·vûr′bər·ənt) adj. Resounding. [< L *reverberans, -antis,* ppr. of *reverberare.* See REVERBERATE.]

re·ver·ber·ate (ri·vûr′bə·rāt) v. **·at·ed, ·at·ing** v.i. 1 To resound or re-echo. 2 To be reflected or repelled. 3 To bend back, as flames in a reverberatory furnace. 4 To rebound or recoil. — v.t. 5 To echo back (a sound); re-echo. 6 To reflect. 7 To cause to bend back, as flames in a reverberatory furnace; deflect. 8 To expose to heat in a reverberatory furnace. See synonyms under ROAR. [< L *reverberatus,* pp. of *reverberare* strike back, cause to rebound < *re-* back + *verberare* beat]

re·ver·ber·a·tion (ri·vûr′bə·rā′shən) n. 1 The act or process of reverberating. 2 That which constitutes reverberating. 3 The rebound or reflection or light, heat, or sound waves. — **re·ver′ber·a′tive** adj.

reverberatory furnace A furnace having a vaulted ceiling that deflects the flame and heat toward the hearth or the upper surface of the substance to be treated.

re·vere (ri·vir′) v.t. **·vered, ·ver·ing** To regard with veneration; reverence; venerate. See synonyms under ADMIRE, DEFER, VENERATE, WORSHIP. [< L *revereri* feel awe of < *re-* again and again + *vereri* fear] — **re·ver′er** n.

Re·vere (ri·vir′), **Paul,** 1735–1818, American silversmith, famous for his midnight ride from Charlestown to Lexington, Mass., the night of April 17–18, 1775, to warn the colonists of the approach of British troops.

rev·er·ence (rev′ər·əns) n. 1 A feeling of profound respect often mingled with awe and affection; veneration. 2 An act of respect; an obeisance. 3 The quality or character that commands respect. 4 A reverend person: used as a respectful appellation or title, especially applied to a clergyman. — v.t. **·enced, ·enc·ing** To regard with reverence. See synonyms under VENERATE. [< OF < L *reverentia*]

Synonyms (noun): adoration, awe, homage, honor, veneration, worship. See VENERATION. *Antonyms:* contumely, derision, dishonor, insult, irreverence, mockery, outrage, ridicule, scoff, scoffing.

rev·er·end (rev′ər·ənd) adj. 1 Worthy of reverence. 2 Being a clergyman; of or pertaining to the clergy or the clerical office. — n. *Colloq.* A clergyman; minister. [< L *reverendus,* gerundive of *revereri.* See REVERE.]

rev·er·ent (rev′ər·ənt) adj. 1 Impressed with or feeling reverence. 2 Expressing reverence. [< L *reverens, -entis*] — **rev′er·ent·ly** adv.

rev·er·ie (rev′ər·ē) n. pl. **·er·ies** 1 Abstracted musing; dreaming. 2 A product of such musing in written or musical composition. Also **rev′er·y.** See synonyms under DREAM, THOUGHT. [< F *rêverie* < *rêver* dream, rave, ? < L *rabere* rage]

re·ver·sal (ri·vûr′səl) n. 1 The act of reversing. 2 *Physics* The change of a dark to a bright spectral line, or vice versa. 3 *Law* An annulling or setting aside: the *reversal* of a decree.

re·verse (ri·vûrs′) adj. 1 Turned backward; contrary or opposite in direction, character, order, etc. 2 On the other side; backward; inverted. 3 Causing backward motion: the *reverse* gear of an automobile. — n. 1 That which is directly opposite or contrary: The *reverse* of what you say is true. 2 The back, rear, or secondary side or surface, as distinguished from the front or principal side. 3 A reversing; change to an opposite position, direction, or state; reversal: a *reverse* of a gun or gun carriage. 4 A change or alteration for the worse; a check or partial defeat; misfortune. 5 *Mech.* A reversing gear or movement. See synonyms under MISFORTUNE. — v. **·versed, ·vers·ing** v.t. 1 To turn upside down or inside out; invert or overturn. 2 To turn in an opposite direction. 3 To transpose; exchange. 4 To change into something different or opposite; alter: to *reverse* policy. 5 To set aside; annul: to *reverse* a decree. 6 *Mech.* To cause to have an opposite motion or effect: *Reverse* engines! — v.i. 7 To move or turn in the opposite direction, as in dancing. 8 To reverse its action: said of engines, etc. See synonyms under ABOLISH. [< OF *revers* < L *reversus,* pp. of *revertere.* See REVERT.] — **re·vers′er** n.

re·vers·i·ble (ri·vûr′sə·bəl) adj. 1 Capable of being reversed in direction or position. 2 Capable of going either forward or backward, as a chemical reaction or physiological process. 3 Capable of being used or worn inside out or backward: a *reversible* coat. 4 Having the finish on both sides, as a fabric. — n. A reversible coat. — **re·vers′i·bil′i·ty, re·vers′i·ble·ness** n. — **re·vers′i·bly** adv.

re·ver·sion (ri·vûr′zhən, -shən) n. 1 A return to or toward some former state or condition. 2 The act of reversing or the state of being reversed. 3 A return, as to a former practice or belief. 4 *Biol.* a The recurrence or reappearance in an individual of characteristics which had not been evident for two or more generations; atavism. b An example of such recurrence. 5 *Law* a The return of an estate to the grantor or his heirs after the expiration of the grant. b The estate so returning. c The right of succession to an estate. 6 *Obs.* Remainder. [< OF < L *reversio, -onis.* See REVERT.]

re·ver·so (ri·vûr′sō) n. pl. **·sos** A left-hand page: opposed to *recto.* [< Ital. *riverso* reverse]

re·vert (ri·vûrt′) v.i. 1 To go or turn back to a former place, condition, attitude, topic, etc. 2 *Biol.* To return to or show characteristics of an earlier, primitive type. 3 *Law* To return to the former owner or to his heirs. — n. 1 One who is reconverted to a former faith. 2 That which reverts. [< OF *revertir* < L *revertere* turn back < *re-* back + *vertere* turn] — **re·vert′i·ble** adj. — **re·ver′tive** adj.

re·vest (rē·vest′) v.t. 1 To vest again, as with rank, authority, or ownership; reinvest. 2 To vest again, as office or powers. — v.i. 3 To take effect again, as a title reverting to a former owner. [< OF *revestir* < LL *revestire* reclothe < L *re-* again + *vestire* clothe < *vestis* a garment]

re·vet (ri·vet′) v.t. **·vet·ted, ·vet·ting** To face, as an embankment, with masonry. [< F *revêtir*

clothe < L *revestire.* See REVEST.]

re·view (ri·vyoo′) v.t. 1 To go over or examine again; look at or study again. 2 To look back upon, as in memory; think of retrospectively. 3 To go over, as a manuscript, so as to correct defects. 4 To make an inspection of, especially formally. 5 To write or make a critical review of, as a new book. 6 *Law* To examine (something done or adjudged by a lower court) so as to determine its legality or correctness. — v.i. 7 To write a review or reviews, as for a magazine. [< RE- + VIEW; modeled on F *revoir* look at again] — n. 1 A second, repeated, or new view, examination, consideration, or study of something; a retrospective survey. 2 A lesson studied or recited again. 3 Critical study or examination. 4 An article or essay containing a critical examination, discussion, or notice of some work; a criticism; critique. 5 A periodical devoted to essays in criticism and on general subjects. 6 A formal or official inspection or view, as of troops. 7 *Law* A judicial revision by a superior court of the order or decree of a subordinate court. 8 A revision, as of a work by its author; examination with a view to correction or improvement. [< MF *reveue* < pp. of *revoir* < L *revidere* < *re-* again + *videre* see]

re·vile (ri·vīl′) v. **·viled, ·vil·ing** v.t. To assail with abusive or contemptuous language; vilify; abuse. — v.i. To use abusive or contemptuous language. [< OF *reviler* treat as vile < *re-* + *vil* vile] — **re·vile′ment** n. — **re·vil′er** n. — **re·vil′ing·ly** adv.

Synonyms: abuse, asperse, calumniate, defame, malign, reproach, slander, traduce, upbraid, vilify. See ABUSE, ASPERSE. *Antonyms:* see synonyms for PRAISE.

re·vise (ri·vīz′) v.t. **·vised, ·vis·ing** 1 To read or read over so as to correct errors, suggest or make changes, etc.: to *revise* a manuscript or the proofs of a book. 2 To change; alter: He has *revised* his opinions. — n. 1 The act or result of revising or reviewing; a revision. 2 A corrected proof after revision. [< F *reviser* < L *revisere* look back, see again < *re-* again + *visum,* pp. of *videre* see] — **re·vis′er** or **re·vi′sor** n.

re·vi·sion (ri·vizh′ən) n. The act or result of revising; a revised version or edition. — **re·vi′sion·al, re·vi′sion·ar′y** adj.

re·vi·tal·ize (rē·vī′tal·īz) v.t. **·ized, ·iz·ing** To restore vitality to; bring back to life; revive. — **re·vi′tal·i·za′tion** n.

re·viv·al (ri·vī′vəl) n. 1 The act of reviving, or the state of being revived; specifically, a recovery, as from depression. 2 A restoration or resuscitation after neglect, oblivion, or obscurity: the *revival* of letters. 3 A renewal of special interest in and attention to religious services and duties and the subject of personal salvation; a religious awakening. 4 A series of emotional and sensational evangelical meetings.

re·viv·al·ism (ri·vī′vəl·iz′əm) n. 1 The spirit and methods of religious revivals or revivalists, or that promote revivals. 2 A tendency to restore former conditions or principles.

re·viv·al·ist (ri·vī′vəl·ist) n. A preacher or leader in a religious revival movement.

revival of learning or **literature** See RENAISSANCE.

re·vive (ri·vīv′) v. **·vived, ·viv·ing** v.t. 1 To bring to life again after real or apparent death; restore to consciousness. 2 To give new vigor, health, etc., to. 3 To bring back into use or currency. 4 To make effective or operative again. 5 To renew in the mind or memory; refresh; reawaken. 6 To produce again, as an old play. — v.i. 7 To come back to life again; return to consciousness. 8 To assume new vigor, health, etc. 9 To come back into use or currency. 10 To become effective or operative again. [< F *revivre* < L *revivere* < *re-* again + *vivere* live] — **re·viv′er** n.

re·viv·i·fy (rē·viv′ə·fī) v.t. **·fied, ·fy·ing** To give new life or spirit to; revive. [< F *revivifier* < LL *revivificare* < *re-* again + *vivificare* vivify < *vivus* alive + *facere* make] — **re·viv′i·fi·ca′tion** n.

re·vi·vis·cence (rev′ə·vis′əns) n. A renewal of life or of vital activities and vigor; a return to life; restoration; revival. Also **rev′i·vis′cen·cy.** [< L *reviviscens, -entis,* ppr. of *reviviscere* < *re-* again + *viviscere* come to life, freq. of *vivere* live] — **rev′i·vis′cent** adj.

REVERBERATORY FURNACE
A. Flames and gases.
B. Bed of molten iron.

rev·o·ca·ble (rev′ə·kə·bəl) *adj.* Capable of being revoked. [< F *révocable*] — **rev′o·ca·bil′i·ty** *n.* — **rev′o·ca·bly** *adv.*

rev·o·ca·tion (rev′ə·kā′shən) *n.* **1** The act of revoking, or the state of being revoked; repeal; reversal. **2** *Law* The annulment or cancellation of an instrument, act, or promise by or in behalf of the party who made it. **3** *Obs.* A summoning back or recalling. [< OF *revocacion*] — **rev·o·ca·to·ry** (rev′ə·kə·tôr′ē, -tō′rē) *adj.*

re·voice (rē·vois′) *v.t.* **·voiced, ·voic·ing 1** To restore or give the proper quality of tone to: to *revoice* an organ pipe. **2** To voice again or in return; echo.

re·voke (ri·vōk′) *v.* **·voked, ·vok·ing** *v.t.* **1** To annul or make void by recalling; cancel; rescind. **2** *Obs.* To call or summon back; recall. — *v.i.* **3** In card games, to fail to follow suit when possible and when required by the rules. See synonyms under ABOLISH, ANNUL, CANCEL, RECANT, RENOUNCE. — *n.* **1** An annulling or cancellation. **2** In card games, neglect to follow suit; a renege. [< OF *revoquer* < L *revocare* < *re-* back + *vocare* call] — **re·vok′er** *n.*

re·volt (ri·vōlt′) *n.* **1** A throwing off of allegiance and subjection; an uprising against authority; a rebellion or mutiny; insurrection. **2** An act of protest, refusal, revulsion, or disgust. See synonyms under REVOLUTION. — *v.i.* **1** To rise in rebellion against constituted authority; renounce allegiance; mutiny; rebel. **2** To turn away in disgust or abhorrence; be shocked or repelled: with *against, at,* or *from.* — *v.t.* **3** To cause to feel disgust or revulsion; repel. [< F *révolte* < *révolter* < Ital. *rivoltare* < L *revolutus,* pp. of *revolvere.* See REVOLVE.] — **re·volt′er** *n.*

re·volt·ing (ri·vōl′ting) *adj.* Abhorrent; loathsome; nauseating. — **re·volt′ing·ly** *adv.*

rev·o·lu·tion (rev′ə·lōō′shən) *n.* **1** The act or state of revolving. **2** A motion in a closed curve around a center, or a complete or apparent circuit made by a body in such a course: used generally in this sense in distinction from *rotation.* **3** Rotation about an axis; especially, a complete rotation so that every part of the moving body returns to the position from which it started. **4** *Mech.* Any winding or turning about an axis, as in a spiral or other bend, so as to come to a point corresponding to the starting point. **5** A group, round, or cycle of successive events or changes; a cycle; also, the period of space or time occupied by a cycle or by the accomplishment of a circuit. **6** The overthrow and replacement of a government or political system by those governed. **7** An extensive or drastic change in a condition, method, idea, etc.: a *revolution* in industry. [< OF *revolucion* < LL *revolutio, -onis* < L *revolutus,* pp. of *revolvere.* See REVOLVE.]

Synonyms: anarchy, confusion, disintegration, disorder, insubordination, insurrection, lawlessness, mutiny, rebellion, revolt, riot, sedition, tumult. The essential idea of *revolution,* in definition 6, is a change in the form of government or constitution, or a change of rulers, otherwise than as provided by existing laws of succession, election, etc.; while such change is apt to involve armed hostilities, these make no necessary part of a *revolution,* which may be accomplished without a battle. *Anarchy* refers to the condition of a state when government is superseded or destroyed by factions. A *revolt* is an uprising against existing authority without the comprehensive views of change in the form or administration of government that are involved in *revolution.* See CHANGE. Compare ANARCHY, REBELLION, REVOLT. *Antonyms*: authority, command, control, domination, dominion, empire, government, law, loyalty, obedience, order, rule, sovereignty, submission, supremacy.

—American Revolution The war for independence carried on by the thirteen American colonies against Great Britain, 1775–83. Also *Revolutionary War.* See table under WAR.

—Chinese Revolution The events in China during the years 1911–12, inspired by Sun Yat-sen, which overthrew the authority of the Dowager Empress and the Manchu Empire, and resulted in the establishment of a republic. **—English Revolution** The course of events in England in

1642–89 that brought about the execution of Charles I, the rise of the Commonwealth, the dethronement of James II, and the establishment of a constitutional government under William III and Mary: called in England **The Revolution,** sometimes with reference to the events of 1688.

—French Revolution The revolution which began in 1789, overthrew the French monarchy, and culminated in the Empire of Napoleon I.

—Russian Revolution The conflict (1917–22), beginning in a Petrograd uprising on March 12, 1917, that resulted in a provisional moderate government and the abdication of Nicholas II. On November 6 (October 24, Old Style), the Bolsheviks under Lenin overthrew this government (the *October Revolution*), and after resisting counter-revolution and libertarian revolution until December, 1922, united the soviet states in the Union of Soviet Socialist Republics under Communist (Bolshevik) control.

rev·o·lu·tion·ar·y (rev′ə·lōō′shən·er′ē) *adj.* **1** Pertaining to or of the nature of revolution, especially political; causing or tending to produce revolution. **2** Rotating; revolving. — *n. pl.* **·ar·ies** A revolutionist.

rev·o·lu·tion·ist (rev′ə·lōō′shən·ist) *n.* One who takes part in a revolution.

rev·o·lu·tion·ize (rev′ə·lōō′shən·īz) *v.t.* **·ized, ·iz·ing** To effect a radical or entire change in the character, government, or affairs of: to *revolutionize* a country.

re·volve (ri·volv′) *v.* **·volved, ·volv·ing** *v.i.* **1** To move in an orbit about a center; move in a circle. **2** To rotate. **3** To move in cycles; recur periodically. — *v.t.* **4** To cause to move in a circle or orbit. **5** To cause to rotate. **6** To turn over mentally; consider; ponder. [< L *revolvere* < *re-* back + *volvere* roll, turn] — **re·volv′a·ble** *adj.* — **re·volv′ing** *adj.*

Synonyms: roll, rotate, turn. Any round body *rolls* which continuously touches with successive portions of its surface successive portions of another surface; a wagon wheel *rolls* along the ground. To *rotate* is said of a body that has a circular motion about its own center or axis; to *revolve* is said of a body that moves about a center outside of itself. A *revolving* body may also either *rotate* or *roll* at the same time; the earth *revolves* around the sun, and *rotates* on its own axis. Any object that is in contact with or connected with a *rolling* body is often said to *roll*; as, The car *rolls* smoothly along the track. Objects whose motion approximates or suggests a rotary motion along a supporting surface are also said to *roll*; as, Ocean waves *roll* in upon the shore. *Antonyms*: bind, chafe, grind, slide, slip, stick.

re·volv·er (ri·vol′vər) *n.* **1** One who or that which revolves. **2** A type of pistol with a revolving cylinder in the breech chambered to hold several cartridges so that it may be fired in succession without reloading.

NOMENCLATURE OF THE REVOLVER

a. Stock.	*f.* Hammer.	*l.* Rifling.
b. Frame.	*g.* Extractor.	*m.* Cylinder stop.
c. Trigger	*h.* Cylinder.	*n.* Trigger
spring.	*i.* Barrel pin.	guard.
d. Sear.	*j.* Barrel.	*o.* Trigger.
e. Bolt.	*k.* Front sight.	*p.* Mainspring.

revolving door A door rotating like a turnstile about a central post and consisting of three or four adjustable leaves so encased in a doorway as to exclude drafts of air.

re·vue (ri·vyōō′) *n.* A kind of musical comedy, without plot or dramatic sequence, characterized by songs and dances, and by a series of skits which lampoon or burlesque contemporary peo-

ple and events. [< F. See REVIEW.]

re·vul·sion (ri·vul′shən) *n.* **1** A sudden change of feeling, conduct, or conditions; a strong reaction of any kind. **2** The drawing back or away from something; violent withdrawal or recoil. **3** *Med.* A turning or diverting of any disease from one part of the body to another, as by counterirritation. [< OF < L *revulsio, -onis,* < *revulsus,* pp. of *revellere* pluck away < *re-* back + *vellere* pluck, pull] — **re·vul′sive** *adj.*

re·ward (ri·wôrd′) *n.* **1** Something given or done in return; especially, a gift, prize, or recompense for merit, service, or achievement; also, punishment or retribution for evil. **2** Money offered for information, for the return of lost goods, the apprehension of criminals, etc. **3** Merited results; just deserts: He has gone to his *reward.* See synonyms under RECOMPENSE, SUBSIDY. — *v.t.* To give a reward to or for; requite; be a reward for; recompense. See synonyms under PAY, REQUITE. [< AF *rewarder,* OF *regarder* look at. Doublet of REGARD.] — **re·ward′er** *n.*

re·ward·ing (ri·wôrd′ing) *adj.* Yielding intangible rewards; worthwhile; satisfying.

re·write (rē·rīt′) *v.t.* **·wrote, ·writ·ten, ·writ·ing 1** To write over again. **2** In American journalism, to put into publishable form (a story submitted by a reporter). — *n.* (rē′rīt′) A news item sent in by a reporter and rewritten for publication.

Rey·kja·vik (rā′kyä·vēk′) The capital of Iceland, a port on the SW coast.

rhab·do·man·cy (rab′də·man′sē) *n.* Divination; the discovery of springs, precious metals, etc., by means of a divining rod: also spelled *rabdomancy.* [< LL *rhabdomantia* < Gk. *rhabdomanteia* < *rhabdos* a rod + *manteia* divination] — **rhab′do·man′tist** *n.*

rha·chis (rā′kis) See RACHIS.

Rhae·to·Ro·man·ic (rē′tō·rō·man′ik) *adj.* Of or pertaining to the peoples of SE Switzerland, northern Italy, and Tirol, or to their Romance dialects known as Ladin, Romansch, and Friulian. — *n.* These dialects as a group.

-rhage, -rhagia, -rhagy See -RRHAGIA.

rha·phe (rā′fē) See RAPHE.

-raphy See -RRHAPHY.

rhap·so·dist (rap′sə·dist) *n.* **1** Among the ancient Greeks, a wandering minstrel who recited epic poems, either his own or another's; especially, one who declaimed the Homeric poems. **2** One who expresses himself with exaggeration of sentiment in speech or writing.

rhap·so·dize (rap′sə·dīz) *v.t. & v.i.* **·dized, ·diz·ing** To express or recite rhapsodically.

rhap·so·dy (rap′sə·dē) *n. pl.* **·dies 1** A series of disconnected and often extravagant sentences, extracts, or utterances, gathered or composed under excitement; rapt or rapturous utterance. **2** In ancient Greece, an epic poem, or a part of such a poem, especially from the *Odyssey* or *Iliad,* recited by a rhapsodist; also, the recitation itself. **3** *Music* An instrumental composition of irregular form, often suggesting the qualities of improvisation. **4** A miscellaneous collection; a medley. [< F *rapsodie* < L *rhapsodia* < Gk. *rhapsōidia* < *rhapsōidos* rhapsodist < *rhaptein* stitch together + *ōidē* song] — **rhap·sod·ic** (rap·sod′ik) or **·i·cal** *adj.* — **rhap·sod′i·cal·ly** *adv.*

rhe·a (rē′ə) *n.* A ratite bird (genus *Rhea*) of the plains of South America, smaller than true ostriches, and having three toes: also called *ostrich.* [< NL]

Rhe·a (rē′ə) In Greek mythology, the daughter of Uranus and Gaea, wife of her brother Kronos, and mother of Zeus, Poseidon, Hades, Hera, Demeter, and Hestia: identified with the Phrygian *Cybele* and the Roman *Ops*: also called *Mother of the Gods.* See KRONOS.

-rhea See -RRHEA.

rheo- *combining form* Current or flow, as of water or electricity: *rheostat.* [< Gk. *rheos* a current]

rhe·ol·o·gy (rē·ol′ə·jē) *n.* The study of the properties and behavior of flowing substances; the science of flow. [< RHEO- + -LOGY] — **rhe·ol′o·gist** *n.*

rhe·om·e·ter (rē·om′ə·tər) *n.* A device for indicating the force or velocity of blood circulation. [< RHEO- + -METER]

rhe·o·scope (rē′ə-skōp) *n.* A galvanoscope. —**rhe′o·scop′ic** (-skŏp′ĭk) *adj.*

rhe·o·stat (rē′ə-stat) *n. Electr.* A device for regulating current-strength of electricity, as by resistance coils. [< RHEO- + Gk. *statos* standing] —**rhe′o·stat′ic** *adj.*

rhe·o·tax·is (rē′ə-tăk′sĭs) *n. Biol.* The response of an organism to the influence of a current, especially of water. —**rhe′o·tac′·tic** (-tăk′tĭk) *adj.*

rhe·ot·ro·pism (rē-ŏt′rə-pĭz′əm) *n. Biol.* A tendency in plant or animal organisms, when exposed to the influence of a current of water, to arrange themselves with their long axes either in the direction of or against the current. —**rhe·o·trop·ic** (rē′ə-trŏp′ĭk) *adj.*

rhe·sus (rē′səs) *n.* A macaque *(Macaca mulatta)* with a moderate tail, common throughout India. [< NL < Gk. *Rhēsos* Rhesus; arbitrarily assigned]

Rhe·sus factor (rē′səs) See RH FACTOR.

rhe·tor (rē′tər) *n.* **1** Formerly, one who taught rhetoric. **2** An orator. [< L < Gk. *rhētōr*]

rhet·o·ric (rĕt′ə-rĭk) *n.* **1** The art of discourse; skill in the use of language. **2** The power of pleasing or persuading. **3** A textbook treating of discourse; especially, written discourse. **4** Affected and exaggerated display in the use of language. **5** Prose, as opposed to verse. [< F *rhétorique* < L *rhetorica* < Gk. *rhētorikē (technē)* rhetorical (art)]

rhe·tor·i·cal (rĭ-tôr′ĭ-kəl, -tŏr′-) *adj.* **1** Pertaining to rhetoric; oratorical; declamatory. **2** Designed for showy oratorical effect. —**rhe·tor′i·cal·ly** *adv.* —**rhe·tor′i·cal·ness** *n.*

rhetorical question A question put only for oratorical or literary effect, the answer being implied in the question.

rhetorical stress The emphasis required by the meaning of a line or the lines in a poem: opposed to *metrical stress.*

rhet·o·ri·cian (rĕt′ə-rĭsh′ən) *n.* **1** A master or teacher of rhetoric. **2** An orator; one who writes or speaks eloquently. [< F *rhétoricien*]

rheum (rōōm) *n.* **1** *Pathol.* Catarrhal discharge from the nose and eyes; hence, a cold. **2** *Med.* Any thin watery flux, as tears or saliva. [< OF *reume* < L *rheuma* < Gk. *rheuma* a flow < *rheein* flow] —**rheum′y** *adj.*

rheu·mat·ic (rōō-măt′ĭk) *adj.* Pertaining to, causing, or affected with rheumatism. —*n.* **1** One affected with or liable to rheumatism. **2** *pl. Colloq.* Rheumatic pains. [< OF *reumatique* < L *rheumaticus* < Gk. *rheumatikos* < *rheuma.* See RHEUM.]

rheumatic fever *Pathol.* A severe, probably infectious disease chiefly affecting children and young adults, characterized by painful inflammation around the joints, typically intermittent fever, and inflammation of the pericardium and valves of the heart.

rheu·ma·tism (rōō′mə-tĭz′əm) *n. Pathol.* **1** A variable, shifting, painful inflammation and stiffness of the muscles, joints, or other structures. **2** Rheumatic fever. **3** Rheumatoid arthritis. [< L *rheumatismus* rheum < Gk. *rheumatismos* < *rheuma* rheum]

rheu·ma·toid (rōō′mə-toid) *adj. Pathol.* **1** Resembling rheumatism or rheumatic symptoms: *rheumatoid* arthritis. **2** Afflicted with rheumatism. Also **rheu′ma·toi′dal** (-toid′l). —**rheu′·ma·toi′dal·ly** *adv.*

rheumatoid arthritis *Pathol.* A persisting inflammatory disease of the joints, marked by atrophy, rarefaction of the bones, and deformities.

Rh factor *Biochem.* Any of a group of genetically transmitted agglutinogens present in the blood of most individuals (Rh positive) and which may cause hemolytic reactions under certain conditions, as during pregnancy or following transfusions with blood lacking this factor (Rh negative). Also called *Rhesus factor.*

rhin- Var. of RHINO-.

rhi·nal (rī′nəl) *adj.* Of or pertaining to the nose; nasal. [< RHIN- + -AL]

Rhine (rīn) The principal river of west central Europe, flowing 810 miles north from SE Switzerland, through Germany and Netherlands, to the North Sea, forming part of the SW boundary of Germany, and dividing, in the Netherlands, into the *Waal,* the *Lek,* the *Oude Rijn,* and the *Ijssel:* ancient *Rhenus,* German *Rhein,* Dutch *Rijn.* French *Rhin* (răṅ).

rhi·nen·ceph·a·lon (rī′nen-sef′ə-lon) *n. pl.* **·la** (-lə) *Anat.* That portion of the brain which forms the olfactory lobe, consisting of the olfactory tubercle, tract, and bulb, which give origin to the sense of smell. [< RHIN- + ENCEPHALON] —**rhi·nen·ce·phal·ic** (rī′nen-sə-fal′ĭk) *adj.*

rhine·stone (rīn′stōn′) *n.* A highly refractive, colorless glass or paste, used as an imitation gemstone. [Trans. of F *caillou du Rhin*; orig. made at Strasbourg]

rhi·ni·tis (rī-nī′tĭs) *n. Pathol.* Inflammation of the mucous membranes of the nose; nasal catarrh. [< RHIN- + -ITIS]

rhi·no (rī′nō) *n. pl.* **·nos** A rhinoceros.

rhino- *combining form* Nose; nasal: *rhinoplasty.* Also, before vowels, *rhin-.* [< Gk. *rhis, rhinos* nose]

rhi·noc·e·ros (rī-nŏs′ər-əs) *n. pl.* **·ros·es** or **·ros** A large, herbivorous, odd-toed mammal (family *Rhinocerotidae*) of Africa and Asia, with one or two keratin-fiber horns on the snout, a very thick hide, and the upper lip protruded and prehensile. [< LL < Gk. *rhinokerōs* < *rhis, rhinos* nose + *keras* horn]

RHINOCEROS
a. African: About 5 feet at the shoulder; to 3000 pounds.
b. Indian: About 5 1/2 feet at the shoulder; to 4000 pounds.

rhi·nol·o·gy (rī-nŏl′ə-jē) *n.* The branch of medicine that relates to the nose and its diseases. [< RHINO- + -LOGY] —**rhi·nol′o·gist** *n.*

rhi·no·plas·ty (rī′nō-plas′tē) *n.* Plastic surgery of the nose. —**rhi′no·plas′tic** *adj.*

rhi·no·scope (rī′nə-skōp) *n.* An instrument for inspecting the nasal cavities.

rhizo- *combining form* Root; pertaining to a root or to roots: *rhizogenic.* Also, before vowels, **rhiz-.** [< Gk. *rhiza* a root]

rhi·zoid (rī′zoid) *adj.* Rootlike; similar to or resembling a root. —*n. Bot.* A delicate filiform or hairlike organ developed on all kinds of thalli, moss stems, etc.: the analog of the roots of flowering plants, serving for absorption and attachment. —**rhi·zoi·dal** (rī-zoid′l) *adj.*

rhi·zome (rī′zōm) *n. Bot.* A procumbent or subterranean rootlike stem, producing roots from its lower surface and leaves or shoots from its upper surface; a rootstock. Also **rhi·zo·ma** (rī-zō′mə). [< NL *rhizoma* < Gk. *rhizōma* mass of roots, ult. < *rhiza* root] —**rhi·zom·a·tous** (rī-zom′ə-təs, -zō′mə-) *adj.*

RHIZOME

rhi·zoph·a·gous (rī-zof′ə-gəs) *adj.* Feeding on roots. [< RHIZO- + -PHAGOUS]

rhi·zo·pod (rī′zə-pod) *n.* Any member of a subclass (*Rhizopoda*) of protozoans with pseudopodia for locomotion and the ingestion of food. —**rhi·zop·o·dan** (rī-zop′ə-dən) *adj. & n.* —**rhi·zop′o·dous** *adj.*

rho (rō) *n.* The seventeenth letter and twelfth consonant in the Greek alphabet (P, ρ): equivalent to the English *r* aspirated. As a numeral it denotes 100. [< Gk. *rhō*]

Rhode Island (rōd) A southern New England State of the United States; 1,214 square miles; capital, Providence; entered the Union May 29, 1790, one of the original thirteen States: officially **The State of Rhode Island and Providence Plantations;** the smallest State in the Union; nickname *Little Rhody:* abbr. **RI** —**Rhode Islander**

Rhode Island Red An American breed of domestic fowls, reddish and black in color, having smooth yellow legs and a small single comb.

Rhodes (rōdz) **1** The largest island of the Dodecanese group; 545 square miles. **2** Its chief city, capital of the Dodecanese Islands. Italian *Rodi.* Greek **Ró·dhos** (rô′thôs). See COLOSSUS OF RHODES.

Rhodes, Knights of See HOSPITALER.

Rho·de·sia (rō-dē′zhə, -zhē·ə) **1** Formerly, a region of south central Africa divided by the Zambezi river into **Northern Rhodesia,** a British Protectorate, and **Southern Rhodesia,** a British Colony. See ZAMBIA. **2** A British Colony in south central Africa consisting of the former Southern Rhodesia; unilaterally declared its independence in 1965; 150,333 sq. mi.; capital, Salisbury. —**Rho·de′sian** *adj. & n.*

Rho·de·sian man (rō-dē′zhən) An African forerunner (*Homo rhodesiensis*) of Neanderthal man, represented by the massive upper jaw and cranium of a skull discovered in 1921 at Broken Hill, Rhodesia.

Rhodes scholarship Any of a number of scholarships, tenable at Oxford University, established by the will of Cecil John Rhodes and providing for the support of selected students from the British colonies, Germany, and the States and Territories of the United States.

rho·di·um (rō′dē-əm) *n.* A silvery-white metallic element (symbol Rh, atomic number 45) sometimes occurring native and in ores associated with platinum, used in alloys. See PERIODIC TABLE. [< NL < Gk. *rhodon* rose; from the color of its salts]

rho·do·chro·site (rō′də-krō′sīt) *n.* A vitreous rose-red or variously colored rhombohedral manganese carbonate, $MnCO_3$. [< G *rhodochrosit* < Gk. *rhodochrōs* rose-colored < *rhodon* rose + *chrōs* color]

rho·do·den·dron (rō′də-den′drən) *n.* Any of a genus (*Rhododendron*) of showy evergreen shrubs or small trees of the heath family, with profuse clusters of beautiful flowers, found growing wild in mountainous regions; especially, the **great rhododendron** (*R. macrophyllum*), the State flower of Washington, and the **rosebay rhododendron** (*R. maximum*), the State flower of West Virginia. [< L < Gk. < *rhodon* rose + *dendron* tree]

rho·do·lite (rō′də-līt) *n.* A pale rose-colored garnet, used as a gem. [< Gk. *rhodon* rose + -LITE]

rho·do·nite (rō′də-nīt) *n.* A vitreous, red or pink manganese silicate, $MnSiO_3$, crystallizing in the triclinic system, and often used as an ornamental stone. [< Gk. *rhodon* rose]

rho·do·ra (rō-dôr′ə, -dō′rə) *n.* A handsome shrub (*Rhododendron canadense*), from 1 to 3 feet high, with terminal clusters of pale-purple flowers preceding the leaves. It is found in cool bogs, from Pennsylvania to Canada. [< L *rhodora* meadowsweet]

-rhoea See -RRHEA.

rhomb (rom, romb) *n.* A rhombus. [< F *rhombe.* See RHOMBUS.]

rhom·bic (rom′bĭk) *adj.* **1** Pertaining to or having the shape of a rhombus. **2** Orthorhombic. Also **rhom′bi·cal.**

rhombohedral system In the classification of some authors, the trigonal division of the hexagonal crystal system.

rhom·bo·he·dron (rom′bə-hē′drən) *n. pl.* **·drons** or **·dra** (-drə) *Geom.* A prismatic form included within six equal rhombic faces.

RHOMBOHEDRONS
a. Acute. *b.* Obtuse.

rhom·boid (rom′boid) *n. Geom.* **1** A parallelogram having opposite sides and opposite angles equal but no right angle. **2** A solid bounded by such parallelograms. —*adj.* **1** Having the character or shape of a rhomboid. **2** Having a shape approaching that of a rhombus, as one of two muscles attached to the shoulder blades. [< F *rhomboïde*] —**rhom·boi·dal** (rom·boid′l) *adj.*

rhom·bus (rom′bəs) *n. pl.* **·bus·es** or **·bi** (-bī) *Geom.* **1** An equilateral parallelogram having the angles usually, but not necessarily, oblique: A square may be considered as a special case of the *rhombus*. **2** A rhombohedron. [< L < Gk. *rhombos* spinning top, rhomb]

rhu·barb (rōō′bärb) *n.* **1** A stout, coarse, perennial herb (genus *Rheum*) of the buckwheat family, having large leaves and small clusters of flowers on tall fleshy stalks; especially, the common rhubarb or pie plant (*R. rhaponticum*), whose acid leaf stalks are used in cooking. **2** The dried roots of the medicinal rhubarb (*R. officinale* and *R. palmatum*), used as a cathartic and bitter tonic. **2** *U.S. Slang* A heated argument; scuffle or quarrel. [< OF *reubarbe* < LL *rhabarbarum* < Gk. *Rha* Volga river, Volga plant, rhubarb + *barbaron* foreign; so called because orig. imported from Russia]

rhum·ba (rum′bə) See RUMBA.

rhumb line A line or course along the surface of a sphere crossing successive meridians at the same angle; a loxodromic curve.

Rhus (rus) *n.* A large genus of trees or shrubs of the cashew family, including the true sumacs. Poison ivy and poison oak, also often included, are now placed in the genus *Toxicodendron.* [< NL < L < Gk. *rhous* sumac]

rhyme (rīm), **rhym·er** (rī′mər), **rhyme·ster** (rīm′stər), etc. See RIME, etc.

rhyn·cho·ce·pha·li·an (ring′kō-sə-fā′lē-ən) *adj.* Pertaining to or designating a nearly extinct order of lizardlike reptiles (*Rhynchocephalia*), represented by only one genus (*Sphenodon*), the tuatara of New Zealand. —*n.* One of the *Rhynchocephalia.* [< NL *Rhynchocephalia*, name of the order < Gk. *rhynchos* snout + *kephalē* head]

rhy·o·lite (rī′ə·līt) *n.* A highly acidic, variously colored volcanic rock. [< Gk. *rhyax* stream + -LITE]

rhythm (rith′əm) *n.* **1** Movement characterized by regular measured or harmonious recurrence of stress, beat, sound, accent, or motion: the *rhythm* of the pulse, the *rhythm* of moving oars. **2** The musical property dependent on the regular succession of accents or tone-impulses; accent-movement or accent-structure; also, a system or kind of accentuation as determined by the make-up of the accentual divisions. **3** In poetry, the cadenced flow of sound as determined by the succession of long and short syllables (**classical rhythm**), or accented and unaccented syllables (**modern rhythm**). When definitely measured by feet or bars or periods, which make lines or verses, it becomes **meter. 4** A metrical foot or measure. **5** Verse or rime. See synonyms under METER. [< F *rhythme* < Gk. *rhythmos* < *rheein* flow]

CHARACTERISTIC DANCE RHYTHMS
a. Cracovienne. *b.* Polka. *c.* Mazurka.

rhythm and blues Rock-and-roll music with blues elements added.

rhythm method A method of birth control that involves not having intercourse during the female's period of ovulation.

rhyth·mic (rith′mik) *adj.* Relating to or characterized by rhythm: contrasted with *harmonic.* Also **rhyth′mi·cal.** —**rhyth′mi·cal·ly** *adv.*

rhyth·mics (rith′miks) *n.* The science of rhythm.

rhyth·mist (rith′mist) *n.* A master of rhythmical composition; also, one versed in rhythmics.

ri·al (rī′əl) *n.* The monetary unit of Iran; a silver coin, twenty of which equal one pahlavi. [< OF *rial, real* royal]

ri·al·to (rē·al′tō) *n. pl.* **·tos** A market or place of exchange. [from *Rialto* < *Rivo Alto* ancient name of the island on which Venice was founded about 800 < Ital. *rivo* channel (< L *rivus* brook) + *alto* deep < L *altus*]

ri·ant (rī′ənt) *adj.* Laughing. [< F, laughing, ppr. of *rire* laugh] —**ri′ant·ly** *adv.*

ri·a·ta (rē·ä′tə) *n.* A lasso; lariat. [< Sp. *reata* < *reatar* tie again < L *re-* again + *aptare* fit]

rib (rib) *n.* **1** *Anat.* One of the series of bony rods attached to the spine of most vertebrates, and nearly encircling the thoracic cavity. In man there are twelve ribs on each side, forming the walls of the thorax, of which the first seven (**true** or **sternal ribs**) are attached to the sternum, the last five (**false** or **asternal ribs**) being either attached by their edges to the rib above, as in the upper three, or free distally (**floating ribs**), as in the lower two. ◆ Collateral adjective: *costal.* **2** Something likened to the rib of animal; a ridge, strip, or band. **3** A curved side timber bending away from the keel in a boat or ship, or a curved timber or support in a vault. **4** A raised wale or stripe in cloth or knit goods, as stockings. **5** *Aeron.* An element in the construction of an airplane wing, usually extending fore and aft and crossing the wing spars, to hold the fabric of the wing in shape. **6** *Bot.* A vein or nerve of a leaf, especially the middle one; any ridge on a plant. **7** Cut of meat including one or more ribs. **8** A wife: in jocular allusion to *Gen.* ii 22. **9** *Slang* A practical joke. —*v.t.* **ribbed, rib·bing 1** To make with ridges: to *rib* a piece of knitting. **2** To strengthen or protect by or enclose within ribs. **3** *Slang* To make fun of; tease. [OE *ribb*]

rib·ald (rib′əld) *adj.* Pertaining to or indulging in coarse or offensive language or vulgar jokes; coarsely jocular. —*n.* One who uses coarse or abusive language. [< OF *ribauld* < Gmc. Cf. MHG *riben* copulate, MDu. *ribe* whore.]

rib·ald·ry (rib′əl·drē) *n.* Coarse or ribald language. [< OF *ribauderie*]

rib·bing (rib′ing) *n.* An arrangement or collection of ribs, as in ribbed cloth, etc.

rib·bon (rib′ən) *n.* **1** A narrow strip of fine fabric, usually silk or satin, having two selvages, and commonly less than eight inches wide, made in a variety of weaves: used as trimming. **2** Something shaped like or suggesting a ribbon, as a watch spring, or a painted stripe on the side of a vessel. **3** A narrow strip; a shred: torn to *ribbons.* **4** An ink-bearing strip of cloth in a typewriter. **5** A ribband. **6** *pl. Colloq.* Driving reins. **7 a** A colored strip of cloth worn to signify membership in an order, the award of a prize, etc. **b** A similar strip of cloth worn on the left breast of a military or naval uniform to indicate campaigns served in, medals won, etc. **8** A ticker tape. —*v.t.* To ornament with ribbons; also, to form or tear into ribbons. —*adj.* **1** Made of or like ribbon. **2** Having parallel bands or streaks, as certain minerals: *ribbon* jasper. **3** Of a standard to receive a prize in a competitive show: a *ribbon* hog. [< OF *riban*; origin unknown]

ri·bo·fla·vin (rī′bō·flā′vin) *n. Biochem.* A member of the vitamin B complex, vitamin B₂, an orange-yellow, crystalline compound, $C_{17}H_{20}N_4O_6$, found in milk, green leafy vegetables, egg yolk, and meats, and also made synthetically: formerly called *lactoflavin, vitamin G.* [< RIBO(SE) + FLAVIN]

-ric *combining form* Realm or jurisdiction of: *bishopric.* [OE *rice* kingdom, realm]

rice (rīs) *n.* **1** An annual cereal grass (*Oryza sativa*), widely cultivated on wet land in warm climates. **2** The edible grain or seeds of this plant. [< F *riz* < L *oryza* < Gk. *oryza*]

rice·braid (rīs′brād′) *n.* Braid made to resemble rice grains strung together lengthwise.

rice paper 1 Paper made from rice straw. **2** A delicate vegetable paper made from the pith of a Chinese shrub, the **rice-paper plant** (*Tetrapanax papyriferus*), pared into thin rolls and flattened into sheets.

ric·er (rī′sər) *n.* A kitchen utensil consisting of a perforated container through which potatoes and other vegetables are pressed, emerging in small particles resembling grains of rice.

rich (rich) *adj.* **1** Having large possessions, as of money, goods, or lands; wealthy; opulent. **2** Composed of rare or precious materials; valuable; costly: *rich* fabrics. **3** Having in a high degree qualities pleasing to the senses; luscious to the taste: often implying an unwholesome excess of butter, fats, flavoring, etc. **4** Full, satisfying, and pleasing, as a tone, voice, color, or perfume. **5** Luxuriant; abundant: *rich* hair; *rich* crops. **6** Yielding abundant returns; fruitful. **7** Abundantly supplied: often with *in* or *with.* **8** Abounding in desirable qualities; of full strength, as blood. **9** *Colloq.* Exceedingly humorous; amusing or ridiculous: a *rich* joke. See synonyms under FERTILE, RACY. [OE *rīce*; infl. in form by OF *riche* < Gmc.] —**rich′ly** *adv.* —**rich′ness** *n.*

—**Richard I,** 1157–99, king of England 1189–1199; went on Third Crusade: called "Coeur de Lion" or "the Lion-Hearted."

—**Richard II,** 1367–1400, king of England 1377–99, deposed by Henry IV.

—**Richard III,** 1452–85, king of England 1483–85; usurped throne; killed at Bosworth.

Richard Roe See JOHN DOE.

rich·es (rich′iz) *n. pl.* [In Middle English, this was a singular noun and spelled *richess* or *richesse*; now, from its form, used in the plural] **1** Abundant possessions; wealth. **2** Hence, abundance of whatever is precious. See synonyms under WEALTH. [< F *richesse* < *riche* < Gmc.]

Rich·ter scale (rik′tər) A logarithmic measure of the estimated energy released by earthquakes according to which 1 represents an imperceptible tremor and 10 a theoretical maximum about one thousand times greater than any recorded earthquake. [after Charles R. *Richter*, born 1900, U.S. seismologist]

ric·in·o·le·ic (ris′in·ō·lē′ik) *adj.* Of, pertaining to, or derived from the castor bean.

rick (rik) *n.* **1** A stack, as of hay, having the top rounded and thatched to protect the interior from rain. **2** A haycock in the field. —*v.t.* To pile in ricks. [OE *hrēac*]

rick·ets (rik′its) *n. Pathol.* A disease of early childhood, chiefly due to a deficiency of calcium salts as provided by vitamin D, characterized by softening of the bones and consequent deformity; rachitis. [Origin uncertain]

rick·et·y (rik′it·ē) *adj.* **1** Ready to fall; tottering. **2** Affected with rickets. —**rick′et·i·ly** *adv.* —**rick′et·i·ness** *n.*

rick·ey (rik′ē) *n.* A cooling drink of which spirits, lime juice, and carbonated water are the chief ingredients. [Origin uncertain]

rick·rack (rik′rak′) *n.* Flat braid in zigzag form, made of cotton, rayon, silk, or wool; also, the openwork trimming made with this serpentine braid. [Reduplication of RACK²]

rick·shaw (rik′shô) *n.* A jinriksha. Also **rick′sha.** [Short for JINRIKSHA]

ric·o·chet (rik′ə·shā′, -shet′) *v.i.* **·cheted** (-shād′) or **·chet·ted** (-shet′id), **·chet·ing** (-shā′ing) or **·chet·ting** (-shet′ing) To glance from a surface, as a projectile over the water; make a series of skips or bounds. —*n.* **1** A bounding, as of a projectile over a surface. **2** The method of firing by which a projectile is made to rebound. **3** A projectile so rebounding. [< OF]

ri·cot·ta (ri·kot′ə; *Ital.* rē·kôt′tä) *n.* An unripened cheese, Italian in origin and similar to cottage cheese but smoother. [< Ital. < *recoquere* to cook again]

ric·tus (rik′təs) *n.* **1** The expanse of the open mouth; a gaping. **2** A fissure or cleft. [< L, open, gaping mouth < *ringi* open the mouth wide] —**ric′tal** *adj.*

rid¹ (rid) *v.t.* **rid** or **rid·ded, rid·ding 1** To free, as from a burden or annoyance; clear: usually with *of:* to *rid* a house of vermin. **2** *Obs.* To rescue; deliver. **3** *Obs.* To drive away; expel; banish. —*adj.* Free; clear; quit: with *of: We* are well *rid* of him. [Fusion of OE *geryddan* clear (land) + ON *rythja* clear (land) of trees]

rid² (rid) Obsolete past tense and past participle of RIDE.

rid·a·ble (rī′də·bəl) *adj.* That may be ridden on, through, or over, as an animal or a road.

rid·dance (rid′ns) *n.* A ridding of something undesirable, or the state of being rid.

rid·den (rid′n) Past participle of RIDE.

rid·dle[1] (rid′l) *v.t.* **·dled, ·dling** 1 To perforate in numerous places, as with shot. 2 To sift through a coarse sieve. 3 To damage, injure, refute, etc., as if by perforating: to *riddle* a theory. [< *n.*] —*n.* 1 A coarse sieve, such as one used in a foundry or in washing for gold. 2 A board set with pins, used for straightening wire. [OE *hriddel* sieve] —**rid′·dler** *n.*

rid·dle[2] (rid′l) *n.* 1 A puzzling question or conundrum; anything ambiguous or puzzling. 2 Any mysterious object or person. —*v.* **·dled, ·dling** *v.t.* To solve; explain. —*v.i.* To utter or solve riddles; speak in riddles. [OE *rædels* < stem of *rædan* interpret, solve]

Synonyms (noun): conundrum, enigma, paradox, problem, puzzle. *Conundrum* signifies some question or statement in which some hidden and fanciful resemblance is involved, the answer often depending upon a pun; an *enigma* is a dark saying; a *paradox* is a true statement or fact that appears absurd or contradictory. The *riddle* is not so petty as the *conundrum*; it is an ambiguous or paradoxical statement with a hidden meaning to be guessed by the mental acuteness of the one to whom it is proposed; a *problem* may require simply study and scholarship, as a *problem* in mathematics; a *puzzle* may be in something other than a verbal statement, as a dissected map or any perplexing mechanical contrivance. Both *enigma* and *puzzle* may be applied to any matter difficult of answer or solution, *enigma* conveying an idea of greater dignity, *puzzle* applying to something more commonplace and mechanical. *Antonyms:* answer, axiom, explanation, proposition, solution.

ride (rīd) *v.* **rode** (*Obs.* **rid**), **rid·den** (*Obs.* **rid**), **rid·ing** *v.i.* 1 To sit on and be borne along by a horse or other animal, especially while guiding or controlling its motion. 2 To be borne along as if on horseback. 3 To travel or be carried on or in a vehicle or other conveyance. 4 To be supported in moving: The wheel *rides* on the shaft. 5 To move; be borne; float: The ship *rides* on the waves. 6 To support and carry a rider in a specified manner: This car *rides* easily. 7 To seem to float in space, as a star. 8 *Naut.* To lie at anchor, as a ship. 9 To overlap or overlie, as broken bones. 10 To work or move upward out of place: with *up*: His sleeve has *ridden* up. 11 *Slang* To continue unchanged: Let it *ride.* —*v.t.* 12 To sit on and control the motion of (a horse, bicycle, etc.). 13 To move or be borne or supported upon: The glider *rides* air currents. 14 To overlap or overlie. 15 To travel or traverse (an area, etc.) on horseback, in an automobile, etc. 16 To control imperiously or oppressively: usually in the past participle: a king-*ridden* people. 17 To accomplish by riding: to *ride* a race. 18 To cause to ride. 19 To place (someone) astride something and carry him, especially as a punishment: They *rode* him out of town on a rail. 20 *Naut.* To keep at anchor. 21 *Colloq.* To tease or harass by ridicule or petty criticisms; tyrannize. See synonyms under DRIVE. —**to ride out** To survive; endure successfully. —*n.* 1 An excursion by any means of conveyance, as on horseback, by car, etc. 2 A road intended for riding. —**to take for a ride** *Slang* 1 To remove (a person) to a place with the intent to murder. 2 To cheat; swindle. [OE *rīdan*]

rid·er (rī′dər) *n.* 1 One who or that which rides; a horseman; a bicyclist; specifically, one who breaks in horses. 2 Any device that rides upon or weighs down something else, actually or figuratively. 3 A separate piece of writing or print added to a document, record, or the like. 4 An addition or proposed addition to a legislative bill, adding to or modifying its original purport. 5 A metallic weight for use astride the graduated beam of a delicate balance. 6 The top rail of a rail fence.

ridge (rij) *n.* 1 An elevation or protuberance long in proportion to its width and height and generally having sloping sides; a raised strip; especially, a lengthened elevation of land; a long hill, or range of hills. 2 That part of a roof where the rafters meet the ridge pole. 3 A slight elevation of earth in a garden or field thrown up by the plow, hoe, or other implement. 4 The back or backbone of an animal, especially of a whale. 5 *Meteorol.* A relatively narrow band of high pressure between two cyclone areas, as shown on a weather map. —*v.* **ridged, ridg·ing** *v.t.* 1 To mark with ridges. 2 To form into ridges. —*v.i.* 3 To form ridges. [OE *hrycg* spine, ridge]

ridge pole A horizontal timber at the ridge of a roof, to which the upper ends of the rafters are nailed. Also **ridge beam, ridge piece, ridge plate.**

ridg·y (rij′ē) *adj.* Having ridges; raised in a ridge; ridged.

rid·i·cule (rid′ə·kyōōl) *n.* 1 Language calculated to make a person or thing the object of contemptuous humorous disparagement; also, looks or acts expressing amused contempt; derision; mockery. 2 An object of mocking merriment; butt. 3 *Obs.* Ridiculousness. —*v.t.* **·culed, ·cul·ing** To make fun of; hold up as a laughingstock; deride. [< OF < L *ridiculum* a jest, joke, orig. neut. of *ridiculus* comical < *ridere* laugh] —**rid′i·cul′er** *n.*

Synonym (noun): derision. *Ridicule* may be merely sportive or thoughtless; *derision* is always hostile or malicious. See BANTER.

Synonyms (verb): banter, chaff, deride, flout, jeer, lampoon, mock, quiz, rally, satirize, scoff, scout, taunt. *Antonyms:* applaud, celebrate, compliment, eulogize, extol, honor, praise.

ri·dic·u·lous (ri-dik′yə·ləs) *adj.* Exciting or calculated to excite ridicule; absurdly comical; unworthy of consideration. [< L *ridiculus*] —**ri·dic′u·lous·ly** *adv.* —**ri·dic′u·lous·ness** *n.*

Synonyms: absurd, comical, droll, farcical, funny, grotesque, laughable, ludicrous, preposterous, risible, silly, trifling, trivial. See ABSURD, QUEER. *Antonyms:* clever, commendable, grave, imposing, judicious, majestic, sensible, venerable, wise.

rid·ing (rī′ding) *n.* The act of one who rides; a ride. —*adj.* 1 To be ridden on or in; suitable for riding: a *riding* horse. 2 To be used while riding: *riding* boots. 3 For use while at anchor: a *riding* light.

riding habit Apparel worn by horseback riders, especially that designed for women, consisting usually of a jacket and breeches or jodhpurs.

rife (rīf) *adj.* 1 Great in number or quantity; plentiful; abundant; prevalent; current. 2 Containing in abundance: followed by *with*. [OE *rīfe* abundant]

riff (rif) *n.* In jazz music, a melodic phrase or motif, played repeatedly as background or used as the main theme. [Prob. back formation of RIFFLE]

rif·fle (rif′əl) *n.* 1 *U.S.* A shoal or rocky obstruction lying beneath the surface of a river or other stream. 2 A stretch of shallow, choppy water caused by such a shoal; a rapid. 3 A way of shuffling cards. —*v.t.* & *v.i.* **·fled, ·fling** 1 To cause or form a rapid. 2 To shuffle (cards) by bending up adjacent corners of two halves of the pack, and permitting the cards to slip together as they are released. 3 To thumb through (the pages of a book). [? Blend of RIPPLE and RUFFLE]

rif·fler (rif′lər) *n.* 1 A file with curved working surfaces at one or both ends and a smooth center serving as a handle: used in sculpture, woodcarving, diemaking, etc. 2 A workman in any of these fields who handles such a tool. [< RIFFLE[2]]

riff-raff (rif′raf′) *n.* 1 The populace; rabble. 2 Miscellaneous rubbish. [< OF *rif et raf* every bit]

ri·fle[1] (rī′fəl) *n.* 1 A firearm, of any size, having grooves, now always spiral, on the surface of the bore for imparting rotation to the projectile and increasing the accuracy of the weapon. 2 One of these grooves. 3 Such a weapon fired from the shoulder, as distinguished from pistols, a carbine, or artillery, and provided with a device for attaching a bayonet. 4 *pl.* A body of soldiers equipped with rifles. 5 An emery-coated stick for whetting scythes. —**magazine rifle** A rifle with a chamber containing extra cartridges which are brought one by one into position for firing; a semi-automatic or repeating rifle. —*v.t.* **·fled, ·fling** To cut a spirally grooved bore in (a firearm, etc.). [Cf. G *reifeln* flute, LG *rifeln* furrow, F *rifler* scratch; *n.*, short for *rifled gun*]

ri·fle[2] (rī′fəl) *v.t.* **·fled, ·fling** 1 To search through and rob, as a safe. 2 To search and rob (a person). 3 To seize and take away by force. [< OF *rifler* scratch, plunder < Gmc.]

rifle salute A salute in the position of right shoulder arms or order arms, with the left hand carried smartly to the rifle, palm down and fingers together.

ri·fling (rī′fling) *n.* 1 The operation of forming the grooves in a rifle. 2 The grooves of a rifle collectively: shallow or deep *rifling*. [< RIFLE[1]]

rift[1] (rift) *n.* An opening made by riving or splitting; a cleft; fissure. —*v.t.* & *v.i.* To rive; burst open; split. [< Scand. Cf. Dan. *rift* cleft, ON *ript* < *ripta* break. Akin to RIVE.]

rift[2] (rift) *n.* 1 A shallow place in a stream; fording place. 2 The wash up the beach after a wave has broken. [? Alter. of *riff*, obs. var. of REEF[1]]

rig[1] (rig) *v.t.* **rigged, rig·ging** 1 To fit out; equip. 2 *Naut.* **a** To fit, as a ship, with rigging. **b** To fit (sails, stays, etc.) to masts, yards, etc. 3 *Colloq.* To dress; clothe, especially in finery. 4 To make or construct hurriedly or by makeshifts: often with *up*: to *rig* up a door from old boards. —*n.* 1 *Naut.* The arrangement of sails, rigging, spars, etc., on a vessel. 2 *Colloq.* A style of dress; costume. 3 *U.S. Colloq.* A turnout for driving; a horse or horses and vehicle. 4 Gear, machinery, or equipment: an oil-well *rig*. 5 Fishing tackle. [< Scand. Cf. ON *rigga* wrap around, Norw. *rigga* bind.]

rig[2] (rig) *v.t.* **rigged, rig·ging** To control fraudulently; manipulate: to *rig* an election. —**to rig the market** To manipulate the exchange market by raising or lowering prices without regard to the value of the security or commodity traded in, in order to derive a profit. —*n.* 1 A practical joke; a trick; jest. 2 A tumult; frolic. [Origin uncertain]

Ri·ga (rē′gə) The capital of Latvia, a port on the Gulf of Riga, an arm of the Baltic Sea between Estonia and Latvia.

rig·ging (rig′ing) *n.* 1 *Naut.* The entire cordage system of a vessel. 2 Tackle used in logging.

right (rīt) *adj.* 1 Done in accordance with or conformable to moral law or to some standard of rightness; equitable; just; righteous. 2 Conformable to truth or fact; correct; true; accurate; not mistaken. 3 Conformable to a standard of propriety or to the conditions of the case; proper; fit; suitable. 4 Most desirable or preferable; also, fortunate. 5 Pertaining to that side of the body which is toward the south when one faces the sunrise: opposed to *left*. 6 Holding one direction, as a line; straight; direct. 7 Properly placed, disposed, or adjusted; well-regulated; orderly; correctly done. 8 Sound in mind or body; healthy; well. 9 *Geom.* Formed with reference to a line or plane perpendicular to another line or plane: a *right* angle. See ANGLE. 10 Designed to be worn outward or placed toward an observer in use: the *right* side of cloth. 11 *Law* Rightful; legal. 12 *Obs.* Real or genuine in character; not spurious. —*adv.* 1 In accordance with justice or moral principle. 2 According to the fact or truth; correctly. 3 In a straight line; directly. 4 Very: used dialectically or in some titles: a *right* good time, *Right* Reverend. 5 Suitably;

AMERICAN RIFLES
A. Springfield—Civil War.
B. Garand—World War II.
C. M–14, Automatic—1958.

properly. **6** Precisely; just; also, immediately. **7** Without delay or evasion. **8** Toward the right. **9** Completely or quite: The house burned *right* to the ground. — *n.* **1** That which is right; moral rightness: opposed to *wrong*; also, justice. **2** A just and proper claim or title to anything, or that which may be claimed on just, moral, legal, or customary grounds: often in the plural. **3** *Law* A claim or title to, or interest in, anything whatsoever that is enforceable by law. **4** The right hand, side, or direction. **5** Anything adapted for right–hand use or position. **6** *Often cap.* In politics, a conservative or reactionary position, or a party or group advocating such a position, so designated because of the views of the party occupying seats on the right side of the presiding officer in certain European legislative bodies: used with *the.* Compare LEFT. **7** The outside or front side of a thing: opposed to *reverse.* **8** In boxing, a blow delivered with the right hand. **9** A stockholder's privilege to purchase new stock in a corporation at a special price, usually at par. — **natural rights** Rights with which mankind is supposedly endowed by nature, such as the right to life, liberty, security, and the pursuit of happiness. — *v.t.* **1** To restore to an upright or normal position. **2** To put in order; set right. **3** To make correct or in accord with facts. **4** To make reparation for; redress or avenge: to *right* a wrong. **5** To make reparation to (a person); do justice to. — *v.i.* **6** To regain an upright or normal position. — *interj.* I agree! I understand! — **right on** *Colloq.* An interjectory phrase expressing enthusiastic agreement or encouragement: also used adjectivally. ◆ Homophones: *rite, wright, write.* [OE *riht*] — **right′er** *n.*
  Synonyms (adj.): correct, direct, equitable, fair, good, honest, just, lawful, perpendicular, rightful, straight, true, unswerving, upright. See CORRECT, INNOCENT, JUST, MORAL, PRECISE, VIRTUOUS. *Antonyms:* bad, evil, false, improper, incorrect, iniquitous, unjust, wrong.
  Synonyms (noun): advantage, claim, exemption, franchise, immunity, liberty, license, prerogative, privilege. In the sense of that which one may rightly claim, a *right* may be either general or special, natural or artificial. "Life, liberty, and the pursuit of happiness" are the natural and inalienable *rights* of all men; *rights* of property, inheritance, etc., are individual and special, and often artificial, as the *right* of inheritance by primogeniture. A *privilege* is always special, exceptional, and artificial. It is something peculiar to one or some, as distinguished from others. A *privilege* may be of doing or avoiding; in the latter case it is an *exemption* or *immunity*; as, a *privilege* of hunting or fishing; *exemption* from military service; *immunity* from arrest. A *franchise* is a specific *right* or *privilege* granted by the government or established as such by governmental authority; as, the elective *franchise*, a railroad *franchise*. A *prerogative* is an official *right* or *privilege*, especially one inherent in the royal or sovereign power; in a wider sense it is an exclusive and peculiar *privilege* which one possesses by reason of being what he is; as reason is the *prerogative* of man; kings and nobles have often claimed *prerogatives* and *privileges* opposed to the inherent *rights* of the people. See DUTY, JUSTICE, PROPERTY.
right–a·bout (rīt′ə·bout′) *n.* **1** The opposite direction. **2** A turning in or to the opposite direction, physically or mentally.
right away At once; immediately.
right·eous (rī′chəs) *adj.* Conforming in disposition and conduct to a standard of right and justice; upright; virtuous; blameless; morally right; equitable; right–thinking. See synonyms under GOOD, INNOCENT, JUST, MORAL, VIRTUOUS. [OE *rihtwīs* < *riht* right + *wīs* wise] — **right′eous·ly** *adv.*
right·eous·ness (rī′chəs·nis) *n.* **1** The quality or character of being righteous; uprightness; rectitude. **2** A righteous act or quality. **3** Rightfulness; justice. See synonyms under DUTY, JUSTICE, VIRTUE.
right·ful (rīt′fəl) *adj.* **1** Characterized by or conformed to a right or just claim according to established laws or usage; also, owned or held by just claim: *rightful* heritage. **2** Conso-

nant with moral right or with justice and truth. **3** Proper. **4** Upright; just. See synonyms under JUST, RIGHT. [OE *rihtful*] — **right′ful·ly** *adv.* — **right′ful·ness** *n.*
right–hand (rīt′hand′) *adj.* **1** Of, pertaining to, or situated on the right side; dextral. **2** Chiefly depended on: my *right–hand* man.
right·ism (rī′tiz·əm) *n.* The advocacy of conservative or reactionary policies. — **right′ist** *n. & adj.*
right·ly (rīt′ē) *adv.* **1** Correctly. **2** Honestly; uprightly. **3** Properly; aptly.
right–mind·ed (rīt′mīn′did) *adj.* Having approved feelings or opinions.
right·ness (rīt′nis) *n.* **1** The quality or condition of being right. **2** Moral rectitude. **3** Correctness. **4** Straightness. See synonyms under VIRTUE.
right off Right away.
right of search In international law, the right of a belligerent vessel in time of war to verify the nationality of a vessel and to ascertain, if neutral, whether it carries contraband goods. Also **right of visit and search.**
right of way **1** *Law* The right, general or special, of a person to pass over the land of another; also, the path or piece of land over which passage is made. **2** The strip of land, acquired by easement, condemnation, or purchase, over which a railroad lays its tracks, or that land on which a public highway is built; also, the strip of land above which a high–tension power line is built. **3** The legal or customary precedence which allows one vehicle or vessel to cross in front of another.
right on *Informal* An interjectional phrase expressing enthusiastic agreement or encouragement; also used adjectivally: He was *right on* in that speech.
right–to–work law *U.S.* Any law that guarantees a worker's right to a job, whether or not he or she joins a union.
right whale A whale, especially *Balaena mysticetus* of circumpolar seas, having a large head with long, narrow, highly elastic whalebone plates in its mouth, for straining food: it yields more oil than any other species. [Prob. orig. so called because advantageous to pursue]

ATLANTIC, OR SOUTHERN, RIGHT WHALE
(From 50 to 60 feet in length;
the pigmy right whale to 20 feet)

right wing **1** A political party or group advocating moderate or conservative policies. **2** That part of any group advocating conservative policies. Also **Right Wing.** — **right′–wing′** *adj.* — **right′–wing′er** *n.*
rig·id (rij′id) *adj.* **1** Resisting change of form; stiff. **2** Rigorous; severe. **3** Strict; exact, as reasoning. **4** *Aeron.* Designating a type of airship whose gas compartments are enclosed within a rigid structure. See synonyms under AUSTERE, HARD, INFLEXIBLE, PRECISE, SEVERE. [< L *rigidus* < *rigere* be stiff] — **rig′id·ly** *adv.* — **rig′id·ness** *n.*
ri·gid·i·ty (ri·jid′ə·tē) *n.* **1** The character of being rigid; inflexibility. **2** The property of bodies by which they resist a change in shape: opposed to *ductility.*
rig·ma·role (rig′mə·rōl) *n.* A succession of confused or nonsensical statements; incoherent talk or writing; nonsense. [Alter. of *ragman (roll)* document (with pendant seals), catalog, ME *rageman* document; origin unknown]
rig·or (rig′ər) *n.* **1** The condition of being stiff or rigid. **2** Stiffness of opinion or temper; harshness. **3** Exactness without allowance or indulgence; inflexibility; strictness; severity. **4** Inclemency, as of the weather; hardship. **5** A severe, harsh, or cruel act. **6** *Med.* **a** A violent chill from cold or nervous shock. **b** The trembling observed in the chill preceding a fever. **7** *Biol.* A rig-

id state in an organism or in any of its parts, caused by adverse or unfavorable conditions. Also *Brit.* **rig′our.** [< L < *rigere* be stiff]
rig·or mor·tis (rig′ər môr′tis, rī′gər) The rigidity that affects the body of an animal a few hours after death due to coagulation of the muscle protein myosin. [< L, stiffness of death]
rig·or·ous (rig′ər·əs) *adj.* **1** Marked by or acting with rigor; uncompromising; severe. **2** Logically accurate; exact; strict. **3** Inclement; severe; bitter; causing hardship: a *rigorous* climate. See synonyms under AUSTERE, SEVERE. [< OF *rigoureux*] — **rig′or·ous·ly** *adv.* — **rig′or·ous·ness** *n.*
Rig–Ve·da (rig·vā′də, ·vē′–) The oldest collection of hymns and verses in Hindu sacred literature; supposed date, 2000 B.C. See VEDA. [< Skt. *Rigveda* < *ric* praise, hymn + *veda* knowledge]
rile (rīl) *v.t. Colloq.* or *Dial.* **1** To vex; irritate. **2** To roil; make muddy. [Var. of ROIL]
ril·ey (rī′lē) *adj.* **1** Roiled; muddy. **2** Ill-tempered; also, irritated.
rill (ril) *n.* **1** A small stream; rivulet. **2** A long, narrow, and generally straight valley on the face of the moon: also **rille.** See synonyms under STREAM. [Cf. Du. *dil,* G *rille*]
ril·let (ril′it) *n.* A little rill (def. 1).
rim (rim) *n.* **1** The edge of an object, usually of a circular object; a margin; border. **2** The peripheral part of a wheel, connected to the hub by spokes. **3** On an automobile wheel, the detachable band over which the tire is fitted. **4** The frame of a pair of spectacles surrounding the lenses. See synonyms under BANK. — *v.t.* **rimmed, rim·ming** **1** To provide with a rim; border. **2** In sports, to roll around the edge of (the basket, cup, etc.) without falling in: The ball *rimmed* the cup. [OE *rima*]
rime¹ (rīm) *n.* [The spelling *rhyme*, introduced in the 17th century through association with *rhythm*, is etymologically unjustified.] **1** A correspondence of sounds in two or more words, especially at the ends of lines of poetry. See also NEAR RIME, INTERNAL RIME, TERMINAL RIME. **2** A verse, line, etc., corresponding in terminal sound with another. **3** A word corresponding in sound with another. **4** Poetry; verse; also, a tale in verse. See synonyms under POETRY. — *v.* **rimed, rim·ing** *v.i.* **1** To make rimes or verses; compose poetry. **2** To correspond in sound or in terminal sounds. — *v.t.* **3** To put or write in rime or verse. **4** To use as a rime. **5** To cause to correspond in sound. Also spelled *rhyme.* [Prob. fusion of OF *rime* < Gmc. + OE *rīm* a number] — **rime′less** *adj.*
rime² (rīm) *n.* **1** Hoarfrost. **2** *Meteorol.* A rough or feathery coating of ice deposited by fog on terrestrial objects. — *v.t. & v.i.* **rimed, rim·ing** To cover with or congeal into rime. [OE *hrīm* frost]
rim·er (rī′mər) *n.* One who makes riming verse, especially inferior verse: also spelled *rhymer.*
rime royal A stanza of seven lines in iambic pentameter, rimed *ababbcc:* first used in Chaucer's *Complaint unto Pity.*
rime scheme The pattern of rimes in a stanza or poem, usually represented by letters: A standard *rime scheme* is abab.
rime·ster (rīm′stər) *n.* One who makes rimes; a mere versifier; a maker of inferior verses: also spelled *rhymester.*
ri·mose (rī′mōs, rī·mōs′) *adj.* Full of fissures or cracks; chinky. Also **ri′mous.** [< L *rimosus* < *rima* chink] — **ri′mose·ly** *adv.* — **ri·mos·i·ty** (rī·mos′ə·tē) *n.*
rim·ple (rim′pəl) *n.* A fold or wrinkle. — *v.t. & v.i.* **·pled, ·pling** To wrinkle; rumple. [OE *hrympel*]
rim·y (rī′mē) *adj.* **1** White with rime. **2** Cold; frosty.
rind¹ (rīnd) *n.* The skin or outer coat that may be peeled or taken off, as of flesh, fruit, or trees. [OE *rind* bark, crust]
rind² (rind, rīnd) See RYND.
rin·der·pest (rin′dər·pest) *n.* An infectious disease of cattle and sometimes of sheep, characterized by inflammation of the mucous membranes of the intestines; cattle plague: formerly known as *murrain.* [< G < *rinder* cattle + *pest* plague]
ring¹ (ring) *n.* **1** Any circular object having an

opening of nearly its own diameter. 2 A circular band of precious metal, worn on a finger. 3 Any metal or wooden band used for holding or carrying something: a napkin *ring;* also, a hoop. 4 A group of persons or things in a circle. 5 A combination of persons, often for corrupt or mercenary cooperation, as in business or politics; a clique. 6 A place where the bark has been cut away around a branch or tree trunk. 7 One of a series of concentric layers of wood in an exogenous stem, formed by annual growth: also **annual ring.** 8 An area or arena, as that in which boxers fight; hence prize fighting in general; a circular racecourse or track, as of a circus or horse show. 9 The field of competition or rivalry: *He tossed his hat into the ring.* 10 Thearea set apart for bookmakers and other betters at a racetrack. 11 *Chem.* An arrangement of atoms in a closed chain: the benzene *ring.* 12 The space between two concentric circles. —*v.* **ringed, ring·ing** *v.t.* 1 To surround with a ring; encircle. 2 To form into a ring or rings. 3 To provide or decorate with a ring or rings. 4 To cut a ring of bark from (a branch or tree); girdle. 5 To put a ring in the nose of (a pig, bull, etc.). 6 To hem in (cattle, etc.) by riding in a circle around them. 7 In certain games, to cast a ring over (a peg or pin). —*v.i.* 8 To form a ring or rings. 9 To move or fly in rings or spirals; circle. ◆ Homophone: *wring.* [OE *hring*]

ring² (ring) *v.* **rang, rung, ring·ing** *v.i.* 1 To give forth a resonant, sonorous sound, as a bell when struck. 2 To sound loudly or be filled with sound or resonance; reverberate; resound. 3 To cause a bell or bells to sound, as in summoning a servant. 4 To have or suggest a sound expressive of a specified quality: *His story rings true.* 5 To have a continued sensation of ringing or buzzing: *My ears ring.* —*v.t.* 6 To cause to ring, as a bell. 7 To produce, as a sound, by or as by ringing. 8 To announce or proclaim by ringing: to *ring the hour.* 9 To summon, escort, usher, etc., in this manner: with *in* or *out:* to *ring out* the old year. 10 To strike (coins, etc.) on something so as to test their quality by the sound produced. 11 To call on the telephone: often with *up.* — **to ring the changes** See under CHANGE. —*n.* 1 The sound produced by a bell or other vibrating, sonorous body; the act of sounding a bell; also, a telephone call. 2 Any reverberating sound, as of acclamation. 3 A sound that is characteristic or indicative: *His words have the ring of truth.* 4 A set, chime, or peal of bells. ◆ Homophone: *wring.* [OE *hringan*]

ring–billed (ring'bild') *adj.* Having a ring of color around the beak: said of certain birds.

ring–billed gull The common gull (*Larus delawarensis*) having a black ring around the bill.

ring bolt A bolt having a ring through an eye in its head.

ring·bone (ring'bōn') *n.* A bony enlargement or excrescence on the pastern bones of a horse, usually causing lameness.

ring dove 1 The cushat: also called *wood pigeon.* 2 One of several other pigeons related to the turtle dove (*Streptopelia risoria*) of southeastern Europe.

ringed (ringd) *adj.* 1 Having a wedding ring; hence, lawfully married. 2 Encircled by raised or depressed lines or bands, as the stems or roots of some plants. 3 Encircled by a ring or rings of color; composed of rings.

ring·er¹ (ring'ər) *n.* 1 One who or that which rings (a bell or chime). 2 *Slang* An athlete who illegally enters a contest by concealing facts which would disqualify him. 3 *Slang* A person who bears a marked resemblance to another: *You are a ringer for Jones.*

ring·er² (ring'ər) *n.* 1 One who or that which rings or encircles. 2 A quoit or ho seshoe that falls around one of the pɪ sɪs.

ring finger The third finger of the left hand, on which the marriage ring is worn.

ring·hals (ring'hals) *n.* The spitting snake. [<G, lit., ring–neck]

ring·head (ring'hed') *n.* An instrument for stretching woolen cloth.

ring·lead·er (ring'lē'dər) *n.* A leader or organizer of any undertaking, especially of an unlawful undertaking like a riot.

ring·let (ring'lit) *n.* 1 A long, spiral lock of hair; a curl. 2 A small ring.

ring·mas·ter (ring'mas'tər, -mäs'-) *n.* One who has charge of a circus ring and of the performances in it.

ring·neck (ring'nek') *n.* 1 The ring snake. 2 The ring plover. 3 The ring–necked duck.

ring–necked (ring'nekt') *adj.* Having a ring of color around the neck: said of certain birds and animals.

ring–necked duck A North American duck (*Aythya collaris*), blackish with a chestnut collar about the neck: also called *marsh bluebill.* Also spelled *ringneck.*

ring plover Any of certain small plovers (genus *Charadrius*) marked with a black breast-encircling band; especially *C. semipalmatus* and the smaller piping plover (*C. melodus*) of eastern North America; also, a European plover (*C. niaticula*); also *ringneck.*

ring·shake (ring'shāk') *n.* A cupshake.

ring·side (ring'sīd') *n.* The space or seats immediately surrounding a ring, as at a prize fight.

ring snake 1 A small, harmless, grayish–green snake of North America (*Diadophis punctatus*) having a bright yellow ring around the neck: also *ringneck.* 2 The hoop snake.

ring·ster (ring'stər) *n. U.S. Colloq.* A member of a political ring.

ring–streaked (ring'strēkt') *adj.* Streaked with encircling rings, as an animal. Also *Archaic* **ring'straked'** (-strākt').

ring·worm (ring'wûrm') *n. Pathol.* One of several contagious skin diseases affecting both man and domestic animals, caused by certain fungi, and marked by the localized appearance of discolored, scaly patches on the skin and by disorders of the scalp.

rink (ringk) *n.* 1 A smooth, artificial surface of ice, usually covered, used for ice-skating. 2 A smooth floor, similarly enclosed, used for roller-skating. 3 A building containing a surface smoothed and prepared for ice-skating or roller-skating. 4 An area on a field of ice marked off for the game of curling. 5 The part of a bowling green occupied by one side. 6 In bowling, quoits, and curling, the players on one side. [< dial. E (Scottish), prob. <OF *renc* row, rank]

rinse (rins) *v.t.* **rinsed, rins·ing** 1 To remove soap from by putting through clear water. 2 To wash lightly, as by dipping in water or by running water over or into. 3 To remove (dirt, etc.) by this process. See synonyms under CLEANSE. —*n.* The act of rinsing. [<OF *rincer, reincer,* ? ult. <L *recens* recent, fresh] —**rins'er** *n.*

rins·ing (rin'sing) *n.* 1 A rinse. 2 The liquid in which anything is rinsed. 3 That which is removed by rinsing.

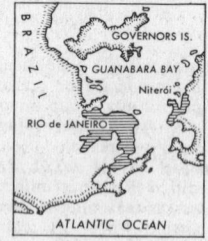

Ri·o de Ja·nei·ro (rē'ō də jə·nâr'ō, zhə·nâr'ō; *Pg.* rē'ōō the zhə·nā'rōō) The capital of Brazil (until the transfer of the federal capital, in April, 1960, to the new city of **Bra·si·li·a** (brə·zē'lē·ə), located in a federal district, on the central plateau of Goiás state, about 120 miles NE of Goiânia, the state capital), a port on Guanabara Bay or **Rio de Janeiro Bay:** also **Rio.** An inhabitant of the city is known as a *Carioca.* 2 A state in SE Brazil; 16,439 square miles; capital, Niterói.

Ri·o Grande (rē'ō grand') 1 A river flowing 1,800 miles from the Rocky Mountains in SW Colorado to the Gulf of Mexico and forming the boundary between Texas and Mexico: Mexican *Río Bravo.* 2 See RIO GRANDE DO SUL (def. 2).

ri·ot (rī'ət) *n.* 1 A disturbance consisting of wild and turbulent conduct of a large number of persons, as a mob; uproar; tumult. 2 *Law* Specifically, a tumultuous disturbance of the public peace by three or more assembled persons who, in the execution of some private object, do an act, lawful or unlawful, in a manner calculated to terrorize the people. 3 A state of confusion; a jumble: *The garden was a riot of color.* 4 Boisterous festivity; revelry. 5 *U.S. Slang* An uproariously amusing person, thing, or performance. See synonyms under REVOLUTION, TUMULT. — **to run riot** 1 To act or move wildly and without restraint. 2 To grow rankly, as vines. —*v.i.* 1 To take part in a riot or public disorder. 2 To live a life of unrestrained feasting, drinking, etc.; revel. —*v.t.* 3 To spend (time, money, etc.) in riot or revelry. [<OF *riote* < *rioter,* prob. dim. of *ruir* make an uproar <L *rugire* roar] — **ri'ot·er** *n.*

riot act Any forceful or vigorous warning or reprimand. — **to read the riot act to** To reprimand bluntly and severely.

riot gun A short–barreled shotgun for use on guard duty or against rioters.

ri·ot·ous (rī'ət·əs) *adj.* 1 Pertaining to riot; engaged in riot or tumultuous disorder; tumultuous. 2 Indulging in revelry; also, profligate: more *riotous* spending. See synonyms under NOISY, TURBULENT. — **ri'ot·ous·ly** *adv.* — **ri'ot·ous·ness** *n.*

rip¹ (rip) *v.* **ripped, rip·ping** *v.t.* 1 To tear or cut apart roughly or violently; slash. 2 To tear or cut from something else in a rough or violent manner: with *off, away, out,* etc. 3 To saw or split (wood) in the direction of the grain. —*v.i.* 4 To be torn or cut apart; split. 5 *Colloq.* To utter with vehemence: with *out.* 6 *Colloq.* To rush headlong. — **to rip into** *Colloq.* To attack violently, as with blows or words. — **to rip off** *Slang* 1 To steal or steal from. 2 To copy, imitate, or reproduce illegally or dishonestly. 3 To swindle; dupe; cheat. — **to rip out** To utter with vehemence. See synonyms under REND. —*n.* 1 A place torn or ripped open, especially along a seam; a tear. 2 A ripsaw. [ME *rippen,* prob. <LG. Cf. Frisian *rippe,* Flemish *rippen.*]

rip² (rip) *n.* 1 A ripple; a rapid in a river. 2 A riptide. [? <RIP¹]

rip³ (rip) *n. Colloq.* 1 A dissipated or worthless person. 2 A worn–out, worthless animal or object. [? Var. of *rep,* short for REPROBATE]

ri·par·i·an (ri·pâr'ē·ən, rī-) *adj.* 1 Pertaining to the bank of a river: *riparian* rights. 2 Growing naturally in the sides or banks of watercourses, ponds, etc. [<L *riparius* < *ripa* bank of a river]

ri·par·i·ous (ri·pâr'ē·əs, rī-) *adj.* Growing or living along the banks of streams, as an animal or a plant.

rip·cord (rip'kôrd') *n. Aeron.* 1 The cord, together with the handle and fastening pins, which, when pulled, releases the canopy of a parachute from its pack. 2 A cord attached to the rip panel of a balloon, which, when pulled, frees the panel from the envelope.

ripe (rīp) *adj.* 1 Grown to maturity and fit for food, as fruit or grain. 2 Brought by keeping and care to a condition for use, as wine. 3 Fully developed; matured. 4 In full readiness to do or try; prepared; ready: *The men are ripe for mutiny.* 5 Fit; opportune: *The times are ripe for war.* 6 Resembling ripe fruit; rosy; luscious. 7 *Surg.* Ready for an operation of removal or opening, as an appendix or an abscess. [OE *rīpe* ready for reaping] — **ripe'ly** *adv.* — **ripe'ness** *n.*

Synonyms: complete, consummate, finished, fit, mature, matured, mellow, perfect, perfected, ready, seasoned. *Antonyms:* budding, callow, crude, green, immature, imperfect, sour, undeveloped.

rip·en (rī'pən) *v.t. & v.i.* To make or become ripe; mature. — **rip'en·er** *n.*

rip–off (rip'of', -ôf') *n. Slang* 1 The act of ripping off; an act of stealing or cheating. 2 Anything dishonest, illegal, or exploitative.

ri·poste (ri·pōst') *n.* 1 A return thrust, as in fencing. 2 A quick, clever reply. —*v.i.* 1 To make a riposte. 2 To reply quickly. Also **ri·post'.** [<F *riposte* <Ital. *risposta,* properly fem. of pp. of *rispondere* <L *respondere.* See RESPOND.]

rip·per (rip'ər) *n.* 1 One who or that which rips. 2 A tool for ripping, as a ripsaw. 3 A double–ripper. 4 *Brit. Slang* A thoroughgoing or efficient person or thing; something or someone very good.

rip·ple¹ (rip'əl) *v.* **·pled, ·pling** *v.i.* 1 To become slightly agitated on the surface, as water running over a rough, pebbly surface or blown on by a light breeze; form small waves or undulations. 2 To flow with small waves or undulations on the surface. 3 To make a sound like water flowing in small waves. —*v.t.*

4 To cause to form ripples. —*n.* **1** One of the wavelets on the surface of water; a ruffle, or slight curling wave. **2** Any sound like that made by rippling. **3** Any appearance like a wavelet. [Origin uncertain] — **rip′pler** *n.* — **rip′pling** *adj.* — **rip′pling·ly** *adv.*

rip·ple² (rip′əl) *n.* A toothed tool, especially a comblike instrument for cleaning flax fiber or broomcorn. —*v.t.* **·pled, ·pling** To cleanse, as flax or hemp, by removing the seeds and capsules from the stalk. [<Gmc. Cf. Frisian *ripelje.*]

rip·plet (rip′lit) *n.* A small ripple.

rip·ply (rip′lē) *adj.* Marked by or sounding like ripples.

rip–rap (rip′rap′) *n.* **1** Broken stones loosely thrown together for a foundation, as in deep water or on a soft bottom, or for a sustaining wall, as along a river bank; also, the stones used, or the foundation so made. **2** *pl.* Artificial islands in Chesapeake Bay. —*v.t.* **–rapped, –rap·ping** To make a rip–rap in or upon; strengthen with rip–raps.

rip–roaring (rip′rôr′ing, -rōr′-) *adj. U.S. Slang* **1** Excellent; superior; exciting: a *rip–roaring* time. **2** Lively; full of vigor.

rip–saw (rip′sô′) *n.* A coarse–toothed saw used for cutting wood in the direction of the grain.

rip·snort·er (rip′snôr′tər) *n.* **1** Any person or thing exciting excessively noisy, violent, or striking. **2** A violent windstorm.

rip·tide (rip′tīd′) *n.* Water agitated and made dangerous for swimmers by conflicting tides or currents. Also called *rip, tiderip.*

rise (rīz) *v.* **rose, ris·en, ris·ing** *v.i.* **1** To move upward; go from a lower to a higher position. **2** To slope gradually upward: The ground *rises* here. **3** To have height or elevation; extend upward: The city *rises* above the plain. **4** To gain elevation in rank, status, fortune, or reputation. **5** To swell up: Dough *rises.* **6** To become greater in force, intensity, height, etc. **7** To become greater in amount, value, etc. **8** To become erect after lying down, sitting, etc.; stand up. **9** To get out of bed. **10** To return to life. **11** To revolt; rebel: The people *rose* against the tyrant. **12** To adjourn: The House passed the bill before *rising.* **13** To appear above the horizon: said of heavenly bodies. **14** To come to the surface, as a fish after a lure. **15** To have origin; begin: The river *rises* in the mountains. **16** To become perceptible to the mind or senses: The scene *rose* in his mind. **17** To occur; happen. **18** To be able to cope with an emergency, danger, etc.: Will he *rise* to the occasion? —*v.t.* **19** To cause to rise. **20** *Naut.* To cause, as a ship, to appear above the horizon by drawing nearer to it. —**to rise above** To prove superior to; show oneself indifferent to. —*n.* **1** The act of rising; ascent. **2** Degree of ascent; elevation; also, an ascending course. **3** The act of beginning to be or appear, as from a source: the *rise* of a stream. **4** An elevated place; rising ground; a small hill. **5** The act of appearing above the horizon. **6** Increase or advance, as in price. **7** Advance, as in rank, prosperity, or importance; also, elevation morally, mentally, or spiritually. **8** The spring or height of an arch above the impost level. **9** The height of a stair step. **10** Ascent in the diatonic scale; also, increase in volume of tone; a swell. **11** The ascent of a fish to food or bait; also, the flying up of a game bird. **12** *Colloq.* An emotional reaction; a response or retort. **13** *Brit.* An increase in salary. See synonyms under BEGINNING. [OE *rīsan*]

Synonyms (verb): arise, ascend, flow, spring.

ris·en (riz′ən) Past participle of RISE.

ris·er (rī′zər) *n.* **1** One who rises or gets up, as from bed: He is an early *riser.* **2** The vertical part of a step or stair.

ris·i·bil·i·ty (riz′ə·bil′ə·tē) *n. pl.* **·ties** **1** A tendency to laughter. **2** *pl.* Impulses to laughter; appreciation of what seems ridiculous: also **ris′i·bles.**

ris·i·ble (riz′ə·bəl) *adj.* **1** Having the power of laughing. **2** Of a nature to excite laughter. **3** Pertaining to laughter. See synonyms under RIDICULOUS. [<F <LL *risibilis* <L *risus,* pp. of *ridere* laugh] — **ris′i·bly** *adv.*

ris·ing (rī′zing) *adj.* **1** Increasing in wealth, power, or distinction. **2** Ascending: the *rising* moon; also, sloping upward: a *rising* hill. **3** Advancing to adult years or to a state of vigor and activity; growing: the *rising* generation. —*n.* **1** The act of one who or that which rises. **2** That which rises above the surrounding surface; specifically, a tumor; wen. **3** An insurrection or revolt; an uprising. **4** Yeast or leaven used to make dough rise; also, the quantity of dough prepared at once. —*prep. Dial.* **1** Approaching; going on: He's six years old, *rising* seven. **2** More than; upwards of: a crop *rising* 5,000 bushels.

risk (risk) *n.* **1** A chance of encountering harm or loss; hazard; danger. **2** In insurance, hazard of loss, as of a ship or cargo, or of goods or other property; also, degree of exposure to loss or injury. **3** An obligation or contract of insurance on the part of the insurer: to take a *risk* on a cargo. **4** An applicant for an insurance policy considered with regard to the advisability of placing insurance upon him. See synonyms under DANGER, HAZARD. —*v.t.* **1** To expose to a chance of injury or loss; hazard. **2** To incur the risk of. [<F *risque* <Ital. *rischio* <*risicare* dare, ult. <Gk. *rhiza* cliff, root] — **risk′er** *n.*

risk·y (ris′kē) *adj.* **risk·i·er, risk·i·est** Attended with risk; hazardous; dangerous. See synonyms under PRECARIOUS.

ri·sot·to (rē·sôt′tō) *n.* Rice cooked in broth and served with meat, cheese, and various condiments. [<Ital. <*riso* rice]

ris·qué (ris·kā′, *Fr.* rēs·kā′) *adj.* Bordering on or suggestive of impropriety; bold; daring; off-color: a *risqué* story or play. [<F]

ris·sole (ris′ōl, *Fr.* rē·sôl′) *n.* In cookery, a sausagelike roll consisting of minced meat or fish, enclosed in a thin puff paste and fried. [<F, <OF *ruissolle, rousole* <LL *russeola,* fem. of L *russeolus* reddish <*russus* red]

ri·sus (rī′səs) *n.* A grin or laugh, especially the **risus sar·do·ni·cus** (sär·don′i·kəs), the twisted, grinning expression caused by spasm of the facial muscles, as in tetanus. [<L, a grimace <*ridere* laugh]

rite (rīt) *n.* **1** A solemn or religious ceremony performed in an established or prescribed manner, or the words or acts constituting or accompanying it. **2** Any formal practice or custom. See synonyms under FORM, SACRAMENT. ◆ *Homophones: right, wright, write.* [<L *ritus*]

rite de pas·sage (rēt də pa·sàzh′) *pl.* **rites de pas·sage** (rēt) *Sociol.* A ritual event signifying a change in status in the course of life of an individual, as one marking puberty, marriage, the achievement of adult responsibility, or death. Also **rite of passage.** [<F]

rit·u·al (rich′ōō·əl) *n.* A prescribed form or method for the performance of a religious or solemn ceremony; any body of rites or ceremonies; also, a book setting forth such a system of rites or observances. See synonyms under FORM. —*adj.* Of, pertaining to, or consisting of a rite or rites. [<OF <L *ritualis* <*ritus* rite] — **rit′u·al·ly** *adv.*

rit·u·al·ism (rich′ōō·əl·iz′əm) *n.* **1** A system of conducting public worship according to prescribed or established forms. **2** Strenuous insistence upon ritual.

rit·u·al·ist (rich′ōō·əl·ist) *n.* One who practices or advocates ritualism. —*adj.* Ritualistic.

rit·u·al·is·tic (rich′ōō·əl·is′tik) *adj.* **1** Of or pertaining to ritual or ritualism. **2** Advocating ritualism. — **rit′u·al·is′ti·cal·ly** *adv.*

ritz·y (rit′sē) *adj. U.S. Slang* Smart; elegant; classy. [after César *Ritz,* 1850–1918, Swiss hotelier who founded hotels bearing his name in London, Paris, and New York]

ri·val (rī′vəl) *n.* **1** One who strives to equal or excel another, or is in pursuit of the same object as another; a competitor. **2** One equaling or nearly equaling another, in any respect. **3** *Obs.* An associate, or companion in office. See synonyms under ENEMY. —*v.* **·valed** or **·valled, ·val·ing** or **·val·ling** *v.t.* **1** To strive to equal or excel; compete with. **2** To be the equal of or a match for. —*v.i.* **3** *Archaic* To be a competitor. —*adj.* Standing in competition or emulation; having opposing claims to the same object; competing. [<F <L *rivalis*]

ri·val·ry (rī′vəl·rē) *n. pl.* **·ries** **1** The act of rival-ing. **2** The state of being a rival or rivals; competition. See synonyms under AMBITION, COMPETITION, EMULATION.

rive (rīv) *v.* **rived, rived** or **riv·en, riv·ing** *v.t.* **1** To split asunder by force; cleave. **2** To break (the heart, etc.). —*v.i.* **3** To become split. See synonyms under BREAK, REND. [<ON *rifa* tear, rend] — **riv·er** (rī′vər) *n.*

rived (rīvd) Alternative past participle of RIVE. —*adj.* Split instead of sawed.

riv·en (riv′ən) Alternative past participle of RIVE. —*adj.* Rent, burst, or torn asunder; split; cleaved.

riv·er (riv′ər) *n.* **1** A large, natural stream of water, usually fed by converging tributaries along its course and discharging into a larger body of water, as into the ocean, a lake, or another stream. ◆ Collateral adjective: *fluvial.* **2** A large stream of any kind; copious flow. See synonyms under STREAM. —**to sell down the river 1** Formerly, to sell (a Negro slave) into unsparing and rigorous servitude: from the severe conditions on the lower Mississippi cane and cotton plantations. **2** Hence, to betray the trust of; deceive. —**to send up the river** To send to the penitentiary: from the fact that Sing Sing is up the Hudson from New York. [<OF *rivière* <LL *riparia* <L *riparius.* See RIPARIAN.]

river basin *Geog.* An extensive area of land drained by a river and its branches.

river bottom Low-lying alluvial land along a river.

riv·er·ine (riv′ə·rīn, -ər·in) *adj.* Pertaining to or like a river; riparian.

riv·et (riv′it) *n.* A short, soft metal bolt, having a head on one end, used to join objects, as metal plates, by passing the shank throughholes and forming a new head by flattening out the headless end. —*v.t.* **1** To fasten with or as with a rivet. **2** To batter the headless end of (a bolt, etc.) so as to make fast. **3** To fasten firmly. **4** To engross or attract (the eyes, attention, etc.). [<OF <*river* clench] — **riv′et·er** *n.*

riv·u·let (riv′yə·lit) *n.* A small stream or brook; streamlet. See synonyms under STREAM. [<Ital. *rivoletto,* dim. of *rivolo* <L *rivulus,* dim. of *rivus* brook]

rix–dol·lar (riks′dol′ər) *n.* **1** Any one of several small silver coins formerly current in the Scandinavian countries and the Netherlands: also called *rigsdaler, rijksdaalder.* **2** A former British silver coin of Ceylon, Cape Colony, etc. [<Du. *rijksdaler* dollar of the realm]

Ri·yadh (rē·yäd′) The capital of Nejd and (with Mecca) of Saudi Arabia. Also **Ri·yad′.**

Ri·za Shah Pah·la·vi (ri·zä′ shä′ pä′lə·vē), 1877–1944, shah of Iran 1925–41; abdicated.

ro (rō) *n. Archit.* In Japanese houses, a firepan set into the floor and used in connection with formal tea ceremonies.

Ro (rō) *n.* An artificial, international language based on the classification of ideas and dispensing with existing words and roots. [Coined by Rev. E. P. Foster of Ohio, who devised it in 1906]

roach¹ (rōch) *n.* **1** A European fresh-water fish (*Rutilus rutilus*) of the carp family, with a green-ish back. **2** One of certain other related cyprinoid fishes, as the American fresh-water sunfish. [<OF *roche*]

roach² (rōch) *n.* A cockroach. [See COCKROACH]

roach³ (rōch) *v.t.* To clip or trim, as the mane of an animal. [Origin unknown]

road (rōd) *n.* **1** An open way for public passage, especially from one city, town, or village to another; a highway: distinguished from a *street.* **2** Any way of advancing or progressing; any course followed in a journey; a path. **3** A roadstead: commonly in the plural: Hampton *Roads.* **4** *U.S.* A railroad. —**on the road. 1** On tour: said of circuses, theatrical companies, etc. **2** Traveling, as a canvasser or salesman. **3** Living the life of a tramp or hobo. [OE *rād* a ride, a riding <*ridan* ride. Related to RIDE.]

Synonyms: course, highway, lane, passage, path, pathway, route, street, thoroughfare, track, turnpike, way. See WAY

road–a·gent (rōd′ā′jənt) *n.* A highway robber;

highwayman, especially on stage routes of the western United States.

road·bed (rōd′bed′) *n.* **1** The graded foundation of gravel, etc., on which the ties, rails, etc., of a railroad are laid. **2** The graded foundation or surface of a road.

road·block (rōd′blok′) *n.* **1** An obstruction in a road. **2** Any arrangement of men and materials for blocking passage, as of enemy troops along a course of advance or retreat.

road hog An automobilist or other driver who keeps his vehicle in or near the middle of a road, making it difficult for other drivers to pass.

road·house (rōd′hous′) *n.* A restaurant, dance hall, or similar establishment located at the side of the road in a rural area.

road metal Broken stone or the like, used for making or repairing roads.

road·run·ner (rōd′run′ər) *n.* A long-tailed ground cuckoo (genus *Geococcyx*), especially *G. californianus*, inhabiting open regions of southwestern North America, and running with great swiftness: also called *chaparral cock* or *hen*.

ROADRUNNER

road·ster (rōd′stər) *n.* **1** A light, open automobile, usually single-seated and having a luggage compartment or a rumble seat in the rear. **2** A horse adapted for use on the road, as in light driving; also, a buggy or light carriage. **3** One who journeys a great deal on roads.

road test 1 A test of a person's ability to operate a motor vehicle, esp. as part of an official driving-licence examination. **2** A test of a motor vehicle in actual driving situations on a road or highway.

road·way (rōd′wā′) *n.* A road; specifically, that part over which vehicles pass.

roam (rōm) *v.i.* To move about purposelessly from place to place; wander; rove. —*v.t.* To wander over; range: to *roam* the fields. See synonyms under RAMBLE, WANDER. —*n.* The act of roaming; a ramble. [ME *romen;* origin unknown] —**roam′er** *n.*

roan (rōn) *adj.* **1** Of a color consisting of bay, sorrel, or chestnut, thickly interspersed with gray or white, as a horse. **2** Made of roan leather. —*n.* **1** A roan color. **2** An animal of a roan color. **3** A soft sheepskin leather, tanned to a roan color and used in bookbinding: also **roan leather.** [< OF < Sp. *roano,* ? ult. < L < *ravus* grayish-yellow]

roar (rôr, rōr) *v.i.* **1** To utter a deep, prolonged cry, as of rage or distress. **2** To make a loud noise or din, as the sea or a cannon. **3** To laugh loudly. **4** To move, proceed, or act noisily. **5** To make a labored, rasping sound in breathing, as a horse. —*v.t.* **6** To utter or express by roaring: The crowd *roared* its disapproval. —*n.* **1** A full, deep, resonant cry, as of a beast; a similar cry of a human being, as in pain, grief, or anger. **2** Any loud, prolonged sound, as of wind or waves, or a confused mingling of sounds suggesting the cry of wild beasts. See synonyms under NOISE. [OE *rārian*]

Synonyms (verb): bawl, bellow, boom, bray, shout, shriek, yell. See CALL.

roar·ing (rôr′ing, rōr′ing) *adj.* **1** Emitting or uttering roars; bellowing. **2** *Archaic* Characterized by riotous merriment; boisterous. **3** *Colloq.* Very prosperous or brisk: a *roaring* business. —*n.* **1** A loud, deep, continued sound, as of some animals, or of the waves. **2** A disease among horses, characterized by labored, rasping breathing.

roast (rōst) *v.t.* **1** To cook by subjecting to the action of heat, as in an oven. **2** Originally, to cook before an open fire, or by placing in hot ashes, embers, etc. **3** To heat excessively, or to an extreme degree. **4** To dry and parch under the action of heat: to *roast* coffee. **5** *Metall.* To heat (ores) with access of air, but without fusing, for the purpose of driving off or volatilizing impurities, or for oxidizing them. **6** *Colloq.* To banter or ridicule severely. —*v.i.* **7** To roast food in an oven, etc. **8** To be cooked or prepared by this method. **9** To be uncomfortably hot. —*n.* **1** Something roasted; a piece of meat that is adapted or prepared for roasting, or that

is roasted. **2** The act of roasting. —*adj.* Roasted. [< OF *rostir* < OHG *rosten* < *rost* a gridiron, a roast]

roast·er (rōs′tər) *n.* **1** A person who roasts. **2** A pan for roasting. **3** Something suitable for roasting, especially a pig.

rob (rob) *v.* **robbed, rob·bing** *v.t.* **1** To seize and carry off the property of by unlawful violence or threat of violence; commit robbery upon. **2** To deprive (a person) of something belonging or due; defraud. **3** To plunder; rifle, as a house. **4** To steal. —*v.i.* **5** To commit robbery. See synonyms under STEAL. [< OF *rober* < OHG *roubon.* Akin to REAVE, ROBE.]

rob·ber (rob′ər) *n.* A plunderer, as a burglar or highwayman.

Synonyms: bandit, brigand, buccaneer, burglar, depredator, footpad, freebooter, highwayman, marauder, pillager, pirate, plunderer, thief. A *robber* seeks to obtain the property of others by force or intimidation; a *thief* by stealth and secrecy.

robber fly The assassin fly.

rob·ber·y (rob′ər·ē) *n. pl.* **·ber·ies** The act of robbing; the taking away of the property of another unlawfully, by force or fear. See synonyms under PLUNDER.

robe (rōb) *n.* **1** A long, loose, flowing garment, worn over other dress; a gown. **2** *pl.* Such a garment worn as a badge of office or rank. **3** Any kind of costume; dress; figuratively, anything that covers in the manner of a robe. **4** A blanket or covering, as for use in a carriage or automobile: lap *robe.* **5** The dressed skin of an animal, formerly especially of the American bison, used as a garment or blanket. —*v.* **robed, rob·ing** *v.t.* To put a robe upon; clothe; dress. —*v.i.* To put on robes. [< OF, orig. booty < OHG *roub* spoils, robbery. Akin to ROB.]

Robes·pierre (rōbz′pir, *Fr.* rô·bəs·pyâr′), **Maximilien François Marie Isidore de,** 1758–1794, French revolutionist; guillotined.

rob·in (rob′in) *n.* **1** A large North American thrush (*Turdus migratorius*) with black head and tail, grayish wings and sides, and reddish-brown breast and underparts. **2** A small European bird (*Erithacus rubecula*) of the thrush family, especially common in Great Britain, with the forehead, cheeks, and breast yellowish-red. [< OF *Robin,* dim. of ROBERT]

Rob·in Good·fel·low (rob′in good′fel′ō) **1** In English folklore, a merry and mischievous sprite: originally identified with Puck, but later believed to work his mischief around houses. Compare PUCK. **2** Any fairy or elf.

Robin Hood A legendary medieval hero of England, bold, chivalrous, courteous, and generous, an outlaw of great skill in archery, who robbed the rich to relieve the poor, especially in Sherwood Forest in Nottinghamshire, England. Compare ALLAN–A–DALE, FRIAR TUCK.

robin redbreast The European or American robin.

Rob·in·son Cru·soe (rob′in·sən krōō′sō) In Defoe's *Robinson Crusoe* (1719), the hero, a sailor shipwrecked on a tropical island, where, by ingenious devices, he maintained himself until rescued. See FRIDAY; SELKIRK, ALEXANDER.

rob·o·rant (rob′ər·ənt) *adj.* Restoring strength; strengthening. —*n.* Any strengthening medicine; a tonic. [< L *roborans, -antis,* ppr. of *roborare* strengthen < *robur, -oris.* See ROBUST.]

ro·bot (rō′bət, rob′ət) *n.* **1** An automaton; a manufactured, mechanical person that performs all hard work. **2** One who works mechanically and heartlessly. [after a creation introduced by Karel Čapek, Bohemian playwright, in his *Rossom's Universal Robots (R. U. R.)* in 1921; ult. < Czech *robota* work, compulsory service < *robotiti* drudge]

robot bomb See under BOMB.

robot pilot An automatic pilot.

ro·bust (rō·bust′, rō′bust) *adj.* **1** Possessing or characterized by great strength or endurance; rugged; healthy. **2** Requiring strength. **3** Violent; rude. **4** Rich, as in flavor: a *robust* soup. See synonyms under FIRM, POWERFUL, STRONG. [< L *robustus* < *robur, roboris,* a hard variety of oak, strength] —**ro·bust′ly** *adv.* —**ro·bust′ness** *n.*

roc (rok) *n.* In Arabian and Persian legend, an enormous and powerful bird of prey. [< Arabic *rokh, rukhkh* < Persian *rukh*]

roches mou·ton·nées (rosh′ mōō·tô·nā′, rôsh′) Rounded knobs of rock ground down and smoothed by glacial action: so called because smooth and rounded like a sheep's back: also called *sheepbacks*. [< F, sheep–shaped rocks]

roch·et (roch′it) *n.* A ceremonial garment similar to a surplice, but with closer sleeves or without sleeves: worn by bishops and other high churchmen. [< ΟF, dim. of *roc* a cloak < Gmc. Cf. G *rock* coat.]

rock[1] (rok) *n.* **1** Any large mass of stone or stony matter; a boulder; also, a stone small enough to throw; stony fragments; a cliff. **2** A firm or immovable support; refuge; defense. **3** That on which one may be wrecked, as a reef; some source of ruin or injury. **4** *Geol.* The consolidated material forming the crust of the earth; any mass of mineral matter forming an essential part of the earth's crust. **5** The rockfish, or striped bass. **6** The rock dove. **7** A hard confection, of varied flavors. **8** Any of several very hard objects, as ice, rock candy, rock salt, etc.; also, a kind of cooky. **9** *U.S. Slang* A dollar; in the plural, money. —**on the rocks** *U.S. Slang* **1** Ruined; also, destitute; bankrupt. **2** Served with ice cubes but without soda or water: said of whisky or other spirituous beverage. —*adj.* Made or composed of rock; hard; stony: a *rock* wall. [< OF *roque, roke;* ult. origin uncertain]

rock[2] (rok) *v.i.* **1** To move backward and forward or from side to side; sway. **2** To sway, reel, or stagger, as from a blow; shake. **3** *Mining* To be washed in a cradle, as ores. —*v.t.* **4** To move backward and forward or from side to side, especially so as to soothe or put to sleep. **5** To cause to sway or reel: The earthquake *rocked* the houses. **6** *Mining* To wash (ores) in a cradle. **7** In mezzotint engraving, to prepare (a plate) by roughing its surface with a rocker (def. 8). See synonyms under SHAKE. —*n.* The act of rocking; a rocking motion. [OE *roccian*]

Rock, the Gibraltar.

rock·a·by (rok′ə·bī) *interj.* Go to sleep: from a nursery song intended to lull a child to slumber. —*n.* A lullaby. Also **rock′a·bye, rock′–a·bye.**

rock·a·hom·i·ny (rok·ə·hom′ə·nē) *n.* Indian corn parched and pounded; hominy. [< N. Am. Ind. (Algonquian) < *roc* corn + *oham* grind + termination *-min*]

rock·air (rok′âr) *n.* A rocket launched from an aircraft, usually equipped with instruments for the investigation and recording of conditions in the upper atmosphere. Compare ROCKOON.

rock–and–roll (rok′ən·rōl′) *adj.* Describing a form of popular music, derived from hillbilly styles, achieving its effect by repetition of simple melodic elements, strongly marked rhythms, and exaggerated vocal mannerisms. —*n.* Rock–and–roll music. Also **rock 'n' roll.**

rock·a·way (rok′ə·wā) *n.* A four–wheeled, two–seated pleasure carriage with standing top. [from *Rockaway,* town in New Jersey]

rock bottom 1 The very bottom; the lowest possible level: Prices have hit *rock bottom.* **2** The basis or foundation of any issue. —**rock′–bot′tom** *adj.*

rock–bound (rok′bound′) *adj.* Encircled by or bordered with rocks.

rock candy Sugar candied in hard, clear crystals.

rock cork A variety of asbestos. Also called *rock leather.*

rock crystal Colorless transparent quartz.

rock dove The European wild pigeon (*Columba livia*), the parent of domestic varieties.

Rock·e·fel·ler (rok′ə·fel′ər) Name of a family of American capitalists and philanthropists, including **John Davison,** 1839–1937; his son, **John Davison, Jr.,** 1874–1960; and the latter's sons, **John Davison, III,** 1906–1978; **Nelson Aldrich,** 1908–1979, vice president of the United States (1974–77); **Laurance S.,** born 1910; **Winthrop,** born 1912, and **David,** born 1915.

rock·er (rok′ər) *n.* **1** One who or that which rocks, in any sense. **2** One of the curved pieces on which a rocking chair or a cradle rocks. **3** A rocking chair. **4** A rock shaft. **5** A rocking–horse. **6** *Mining* A cradle. **7** An ice skate having a curved runner. **8** A small steel plate with a serrated edge for preparing a copper plate for a mezzotint.

rock·er·y (rok′ər-ē) *n. pl.* **·er·ies** 1 Rockwork. 2 A rock garden.

rock·et[1] (rok′it) *n.* 1 A firework, projectile, missile, or other device, usually cylindrical in form, that is propelled by the reaction of escaping gases produced during flight. 2 A vehicle operated by rocket propulsion and designed for space travel. — *v.i.* 1 To move like a rocket. 2 To fly straight up into the air, as a bird when alarmed. — *v.t.* 3 To propel by means of a rocket. [< Ital. *rocchetta* spool, dim. of *rocca* distaff <OHG *roccho*; from its resemblance to a distaff]

rock·et[2] (rok′it) *n.* 1 Any of several ornamental Old World herbs (genus *Hesperis*), especially the common garden **dame rocket** (*H. matronalis*), or damewort. 2 An annual (*Eruca sativa*) used in southern Europe as a salad. [< F *roquette*, ult. < L *eruca* colewort]

rocket bomb See under BOMB.

rock·et·eer (rok′ə·tir′) *n.* One who designs or launches rockets.

rocket gun A gun having the barrel open at both ends and used for the discharge of rocket projectiles. Compare BAZOOKA.

rocket projector A device for aiming and discharging rockets.

rock·et·ry (rok′it-rē) *n.* The science, art, and technology of rocket flight, including all aspects from fundamental research to design, engineering, construction, and operation.

ROCKET
a. Head.
b. Bursting-charge.
c. Composition.
d. Clay choke.
e. Fuse.
f. Gas exhaust.
g. Stick.

Rock fever Undulant fever. [from ROCK (OF GIBRALTAR)]

rock flour Finely pulverized rock produced by the grinding action of glacier ice: also called *glacier meal*.

rock garden A garden with flowers and plants growing in rocky ground or among rocks arranged to imitate this.

rocking chair A chair having the legs set on rockers.

rock·ing-horse (rok′ing-hôrs′) *n.* A toy horse mounted on rockers, large enough to be ridden by a child.

rock·oon (rok-ōōn′) *n.* A small rocket equipped with various meteorological recording devices and attached to a balloon from which it is released at altitudes determined chiefly by its weight. Compare ROCKAIR. [< ROCK(ET) + (BALL)OON]

rock rabbit A hyrax.

rock salt Halite.

rock shaft A shaft made to rock on its bearings; particularly, such a shaft for operating a slide valve in an engine: also called *rocker, rocker shaft*.

rock wool Mineral wool.

rock·work (rok′wûrk′) *n.* 1 A mound or wall of stones set with mortar and arranged to imitate a rocky surface. 2 An artificial grotto.

rock·y[1] (rok′ē) *adj.* **rock·i·er, rock·i·est** 1 Consisting of, abounding in, or resembling rocks. 2 Tough; unfeeling; hard; also, disreputable.

rock·y[2] (rok′ē) *adj.* **rock·i·er, rock·i·est** *Colloq.* Shaky or dizzy, as if rocking; unsteady in the head, as from past intoxication. — **rock′i·ness** *n.*

Rocky Mountain goat A conspicuous, typically white antelope (*Oreamnos americanus*) found in the mountains of NW North America.

Rocky Mountain National Park A mountainous region in northern Colorado; 395.5 square miles; established, 1915.

ROCKY MOUNTAIN GOAT
(About 40 inches high at the shoulder)

Rocky Mountains The major mountain system of western North America, extending from the Arctic to Mexico; highest peak, Mount Elbert, 14,431 feet. Also **Rock′ies.**

Rocky Mountain sheep The bighorn.

Rocky Mountain spotted fever *Pathol.* An acute infectious rickettsial disease caused by a micro-organism (*Rickettsia rickettsii*) transmitted by the bite of certain ticks (genus *Dermacentor*): it is marked by fever, chills, headache, and diffuse pains, and is endemic in Rocky Mountain and Pacific coast States.

ro·co·co (rə·kō′kō) *n.* 1 A style of decoration and architecture, developed from the baroque and distinguished by profuse, elaborate, and often delicately executed ornament in imitation of rockwork, shells, foliage, and scrolls massed together: prevalent during the 17th and 18th centuries. 2 Anything regarded as florid, fantastic, or odd in literature. — *adj.* 1 Having, or built in, the style of rococo. 2 Overelaborate; florid. [< F, fanciful alter. of *rocaille* shellwork < *roc* rock]

rod (rod) *n.* 1 A shoot or twig of any woody plant; a straight, slim piece of wood or other material, used as an instrument of punishment, a badge of office, etc.; hence, with the definite article, discipline; correction. 2 A scepter; hence, dominion; power. 3 A bar, commonly of metal, forming part of a machine; a connecting rod. 4 A light pole used to suspend and manipulate a fishing line. 5 A measure of length, equal to 5.5 yards or 16.5 feet, or 5.02 meters; also, in England, a **cubic rod**, a unit of volume equal to 1,000 cubic feet. 6 A measuring rule. 7 One of the rodlike bodies of the retina sensitive to faint light. 8 A particular line of family descent. 9 *U.S. Slang* A pistol. 10 A lightning rod. 11 The drawbar of a freight train. — **to ride the rods** *U.S. Slang* To steal a ride by getting on the metal framework underneath a freight train. See synonyms under STICK. [OE *rod*. Related to ROOD.]

rode (rōd) Past tense of RIDE.

ro·dent (rōd′nt) *n.* A gnawing mammal (order *Rodentia*) having in each jaw two (rarely four) incisors, growing continually from persistent pulps, and no canine teeth, as a squirrel, beaver, or rat. — *adj.* 1 Gnawing. 2 Pertaining to the rodents. [< L *rodens, -entis,* ppr. of *rodere* gnaw] — **ro·den·tial** (rō·den′shəl) *adj.*

ro·de·o (rō′dē·ō, rō·dā′ō) *n. pl.* **·de·os** 1 The driving of cattle together to be branded, counted, inspected, etc.; a roundup. 2 An enclosure in a stock farm, in which cattle are collected to be counted and branded. 3 A public spectacle in which the more exciting features of a roundup are presented, as the riding of broncos, branding, lariat-throwing, etc. [< Sp. < *rodear* go around < *rueda* wheel < L *rota*]

rod·man (rod′mən) *n. pl.* **·men** (-mən) One who uses or carries a surveyor's leveling rod. Also **rods′man.**

rod·o·mon·tade (rod′ə·mon·tād′, -täd′) *n.* Vainglorious boasting; bluster. — *adj.* Bragging. — *v.i.* **·tad·ed, ·tad·ing** To boast; bluster; brag. [< F < Ital. *rodomontata* < *Rodomonte,* name of a boastful Saracen king in Ariosto's *Orlando Furioso*]

roe[1] (rō) *n.* 1 The spawn or eggs of female fish. 2 The milt of male fish. 3 The eggs of crustaceans. ◆ Homophone: *row.* [Var. of dial. *roan,* appar. <ON *hrogn*]

roe[2] (rō) *n.* 1 A small, graceful deer (genus *Capreolus*) of Europe and western Asia, with slender antlers rising vertically from the head. Also **roe deer.** 2 Improperly, the doe of the red deer. ◆ Homophone: *row.* [OE *rā*]

roe·buck (rō′buk′) *n.* A roe, especially the male.

roent·gen (rent′gən, runt′-; *Ger.* rœnt′gən) *n.* The international unit of X-ray intensity; the quantity of radiation which, with full use of secondary electrons and without loss to the walls of the chamber, produces in 1 cubic centimeter of air at normal temperature and pressure 1 electrostatic unit of electricity of either sign: also spelled *röntgen.* [after Wilhelm Konrad *Roentgen*]

Roent·gen (rent′gən, runt′-; *Ger.* rœnt′gən),

Wilhelm Konrad, 1845-1923, German physicist; discoverer of Roentgen rays, better known as X-rays.

roentgen equivalent man See REM.

roentgen equivalent physical See REP.

roent·gen·ize (rent′gən·iz, runt′-) *v.t.* **·ized, ·iz·ing** To subject or expose to the action of X-rays. — **roent′gen·i·za′tion** *n.*

roentgeno- *combining form* X-rays; using, produced by, or producing X-rays: *roentgenogram.* Also, before vowels, **roentgen-.** [<ROENTGEN]

roent·gen·o·gram (rent′gən·ə·gram′, runt′-) *n.* An X-ray photograph, especially one taken for medical or therapeutic purposes; a skiagraph.

roent·gen·ol·o·gy (rent′gən·ol′ə·jē, runt′-) *n.* The science which treats of the properties, action, and effects of X-rays. — **roent′gen·ol′o·gist** *n.*

roent·gen·o·paque (rent′gən·ō·pāk′, runt′-) *adj.* Impervious to X-rays.

Roentgen rays X-rays.

ro·ga·tion (rō·gā′shən) *n.* 1 In ancient Rome, the submission of a proposed law by the executive (consul or tribune) to the people, requesting its adoption; also, a law submitted in this manner and accepted. 2 Litany; supplication. [< L *rogatio, -onis* < *rogatus,* pp. of *rogare* ask]

Rogation days *Eccl.* The three days immediately preceding Ascension Day, observed as days of special supplication by litanies, processions, etc.

ro·ga·to·ry (rō′gə·tôr′ē, -tō′rē) *adj.* 1 Commissioned to gather information. 2 Officially requesting another court to ascertain and report certain facts: letters *rogatory.*

Rog·er (roj′ər) *interj.* 1 Message received: a code signal used in radiotelephone communication. 2 *U.S. Colloq.* All right; O.K. [from *Roger,* personal name]

rogue (rōg) *n.* 1 A dishonest and unprincipled person; trickster; rascal. 2 One who is innocently mischievous or playful: sometimes said familiarly and endearingly. 3 An idle, sturdy beggar; a roving vagrant. 4 *Biol.* A variation from a standard. 5 A fierce and dangerous elephant separated from the herd: in this sense also used adjectively: a *rogue* elephant. — *v.* **rogued, ro·guing** *v.t.* 1 To practice roguery upon; defraud. 2 To eliminate (inferior individuals) from a plot of plants undergoing selection. — *v.i.* 3 To live or act like a rogue. [Origin uncertain]

ro·guer·y (rō′gər·ē) *n. pl.* **·guer·ies** 1 Knavery, cheating, or dishonesty; or an instance of it. 2 Playful mischievousness.

rogues' gallery A collection of photographs of criminals taken to aid the police in their future identification.

rogues' march Music played in derision of a person when he is expelled or driven away in disgrace, as from a military body or community.

ro·guish (rō′gish) *adj.* 1 Playfully mischievous. 2 Knavish; dishonest. — **ro′guish·ly** *adv.* — **ro′guish·ness** *n.*

roil (roil) *v.t.* 1 To make muddy, as a liquid, by stirring up sediment. 2 To irritate or anger. Also spelled *rile.* [< F *rouiller* rust, make muddy <OF *rouil* mud, rust]

roil·y (roi′lē) *adj.* 1 Full of sediment; stirred up; turbid. 2 Irritated; vexed.

roist·er (rois′tər) *v.i.* 1 To act in a blustery manner; swagger. 2 To engage in revelry; riot. [< earlier *roister* loud bully <OF *ruistre* <L *rusticus.* See RUSTIC.] — **roist′er·er** *n.* — **roist′er·ing** *adj.*

rok·e·lay (rok′ə·lā) See ROQUELAURE.

role (rōl) *n.* A part or character taken by an actor; any assumed character or function. Also **rôle.** ◆ Homophone: *roll.* [< F]

roll (rōl) *v.i.* 1 To move forward upon a surface by turning round and round, as the wheel of a vehicle. 2 To move or be moved on wheels: The cart *rolled* down the hill. 3 To rotate wholly or partially: Her eyes *rolled* with pleasure. 4 To assume the shape of a ball or cylinder by turning over and over upon itself. 5 To move or appear to move in undulations or swells, as waves or plains. 6 To sway or move from side to side, as a ship:

to pitch and *roll*. **7** To walk with a swaying motion; swagger; also, to stagger. **8** To make a sound as of heavy, rolling wheels; rumble: Thunder *rolled* across the sky. **9** To become spread or flat because of pressure applied by a roller, etc.. The metal *rolls* easily. **10** To perform a periodic revolution, as the sun. **11** To move ahead; progress. — *v.t.* **12** To cause to move along a surface by turning round and round, as a ball, log, etc. **13** To move, push forward, etc., on wheels or rollers. **14** To impel or cause to move onward with a steady, surging motion: The ocean *rolls* its waves upon the shore. **15** To rotate, as the eyes. **16** To impart a swaying motion to. **17** To spread or make flat by means of a roller. **18** To wrap round and round upon itself. **19** To cause to assume the shape of a ball or cylinder by means of rotation and pressure: to *roll* a cigarette. **20** To wrap or envelop in or as in a covering. **21** To utter with a trilling sound: to *roll* one's r's. **22** To emit in a full and swelling manner, as musical sounds. **23** To beat a roll upon, as a drum. **24** To cast (dice) in the game of craps. **25** *Printing* To apply ink to (a form) by means of a roller or rollers. See synonyms under REVOLVE. **— to roll back** To cause (prices or wages) to return to a previous, lower level, as by government order. **— to roll in 1** To arrive. **2** To gather. **3** *Colloq.* To luxuriate; wallow. **— to roll out 1** To unroll. **2** *Colloq.* To leave. **3** To flatten by means of rollers. **— to roll up 1** To assume or cause to assume the shape of a ball or cylinder by turning over and over upon itself. **2** To accumulate; amass: to *roll up* large profits. — *n.* **1** Anything rolled up in cylindrical form: a *roll* of parchment. **2** Hence, an official writing, especially a list of names or a register. **3** *U.S. Slang* A wad of paper money; also, money in general. **4** A long strip, as of ribbon or carpet, rolled upon itself or upon a core: sometimes of an agreed length used as a measure of quantity. **5** Any food rolled up in preparation for use, as bread by rolling up pieces of dough, meat for roasting, or a pudding or cake formed in a similar way: a jelly *roll*. **6** A roller; particularly, a cylinder in fixed bearings used as a roller. **7** A reverberation, as of thunder. **8** A trill. **9** The rapid beating of a drum to make its sound continuous. **10** A rolling gait or movement; also, motion from side to side, as of a ship in a seaway. **11** *Aeron.* A single turn of an airplane about its long axis without change in the direction of flight: also called **barrel roll**; when performed quickly, called a **snap roll**. **12** A strip of leather or other material fitted with pockets to hold tools or toilet articles, etc., around which it is rolled and fastened. See synonyms under RECORD. ◆ Homophone: role. [<OF *roller* <L *rotula* < *rota* wheel]

roll call 1 The act of calling over a roll or list of the names of a number of persons, as soldiers or workmen, to ascertain which are present. **2** The time of or signal for calling the roll.

roll·er (rō′lər) *n.* **1** One who or that which rolls anything. **2** Any cylindrical device that rolls. **3** The wheel of a caster or roller skate. **4** A rod for carrying a curtain, towel, map, or the like. **5** A heavy cylinder for rolling, smoothing, or crushing something: a steam *roller*. **6** *Printing* A cylindrical device, often of hard rubber, to spread the ink on a form before impressing on paper. **7** *Surg.* A long rolled bandage to be wrapped around a limb or the like. **8** One of a series of long, swelling waves which break on a coast, especially after a storm. **9** *Ornithol.* **a** An Old World bird of crowlike form with gaudy colors, remarkable for its irregular rolling or tumbling flight, especially the common roller (*Coracias garrula*) found in Europe. **b** A tumbler pigeon.

roller bearing A bearing employing steel rollers to lessen friction between the parts of a mechanism.

roller coaster A circular switchback railway with many steep inclines, over which small cars are run: common at amusement parks.

ROLLER BEARING

roller derby *U.S.* A race between two teams on roller skates: a player scores points for his team by

overtaking opposing players after skating completely around the track within a given time limit.

roller hockey *(sports)* hockey played on roller skates.

roller skate A skate having rollers or wheels instead of a runner.

rol·lick (rol′ik) *v.i.* To move in a careless, frolicsome manner; act carelessly and jovially. [Blend of ROMP and FROLIC]

rol·lick·ing (rol′ik·ing) *adj.* **1** Moving in a careless or swaggering manner; jovial. **2** Expressive of a careless, frolicsome spirit: *rollicking* behavior. Also **rol·lick·some** (-səm), **rol′lick·y.**

roll·ing (rō′ling) *adj.* **1** Having a succession of sloping elevations and depressions; undulating: *rolling* prairies. **2** Turned back or down as if over a roll: a *rolling* collar. **3** Of or pertaining to rolling; used in rolling. **4** Moving on or as if on wheels; rotating. **5** Surging in puffs or billows, as smoke, clouds, etc. **6** Recurring; elapsing: said of time. **7** Swaying from side to side: a *rolling* gait. — *n.* The act of a person or thing that rolls, or of one who uses a rolling tool.

rolling hitch A hitch with one or more intermediate turns between the first and last hitch. See illustration under HITCH.

rolling mill An establishment in which metal is rolled into sheets, bars, etc.

rolling pin A roller, usually of wood, with a handle at each end, for rolling out dough, etc.

rolling stock The wheeled transportation equipment of a railroad.

rolling stone 1 A stone worn smooth by friction and wear. **2** A person of restless, unsettled habits and occupation.

roll–top (rōl′top′) *adj.* Having a cover which slides back out of the way: a *roll–top* desk.

roll·way (rōl′wā′) *n.* An inclined way, natural or artificial, down which logs may be rolled or shot; chute.

ro·ly–po·ly (rō′lē·pō′lē) *adj.* Short and fat; pudgy; dumpy. — *n.* **1** *Brit.* A pudding made of a sheet of pastry dough spread with fruit, preserves, etc., rolled up and cooked. **2** A pudgy person. [Reduplication of ROLL]

Ro·ma·ic (rō·mā′ik) *adj.* Pertaining to or characteristic of the language or people of modern Greece. — *n.* Modern Greek, especially the popular spoken form. [<LL *Romaicus* <Gk. *Rhômaikos* Roman <*Rhômê* Rome]

ro·maine (rō·mān′) *n.* A variety of lettuce (*Lactuca sativa longifolia*) characterized by long, crisp leaves. [<F, fem. of *romain* Roman]

ro·man (rō′mən) *adj. Printing* Designating or pertaining to a common style of type or letter, characterized chiefly by serifs, perpendicularity, and the greater thickness of its upright strokes than of its horizontal strokes: This line is set in roman: distinguished from *italic*. — *n.* Roman type. Also **Ro′man.**

Ro·man (rō′mən) *adj.* **1** Of, pertaining to, or characteristic of Rome or its people. **2** Belonging to or connected with the Church of Rome or its head; Roman Catholic. **3** Somewhat aquiline: a *Roman* nose. — *n.* **1** A native, resident, or citizen of modern Rome or a citizen of ancient Rome. **2** A Roman Catholic. **3** *pl.* The Epistle to the Romans. **— Epistle to the Romans** One of the books of the New Testament; a letter from the apostle Paul to the Christians at Rome. [<OF *romain* <L *Romanus* < *Roma* Rome]

Roman alphabet The Latin alphabet.

Roman architecture A style of architecture

ROMAN ARCHITECTURE
Pantheon, Rome, A.D. 123

which is characterized by the size, massive-

ness, and boldness of its round arches and vaults, by the somewhat lavish adoption of Greek embellishments, and by excellent stonemasonry and brickmasonry of every kind.

Roman candle A firework consisting of a tube filled with a composition which discharges colored balls and sparks of fire.

Roman Catholic Church The church in communion with the pope, whom it recognizes as its supreme head on earth: an official designation. Also called the *Catholic Church*.

ro·mance (rō·mans′, rō′mans) *n.* **1** Adventurous, heroic, or picturesque character or nature; strange and fascinating appeal: the *romance* of faraway places. **2** A disposition to delight in the mysterious or adventurous: a child of *romance*. **3** A love affair. **4** A long narrative from medieval legend, presenting chivalrous ideals and aristocratic society and usually involving heroes in strange adventures and affairs of love. **5** Any long fictitious narrative embodying scenes and events remote from common life and filled with extravagant adventures and often long digressions. **6** The class of literature consisting of romances (defs. 4 and 5). **7** An extravagant or fanciful falsehood. **8** *Music* A simple rhythmic melody, often sentimental, suggestive of a love song. See synonyms under DREAM, FICTION. — *v.* (rō·mans′) **·manced, ·manc·ing** *v.i.* **1** To tell romances. **2** To think or act in a romantic manner. **3** *Colloq.* To make love. — *v.t.* **4** *Colloq.* To make love to; woo. [<OF *romans* a story written in French <L *Romanice* in Roman style <*Romanicus* Roman]

Ro·mance (rō·mans′) *adj.* Pertaining or belonging to one or more, or all, of the languages which have developed from the vulgar Latin speech, and which exist now as French, Italian, Spanish, Portuguese, Catalan, Provençal, Rhaeto–Romanic, and Rumanian. — *n.* One, or all collectively, of the Romance languages.

ro·manc·er (rō·man′sər) *n.* **1** A writer of romances. **2** One who indulges in extravagant fictions or fancies.

Ro·man de la Rose (rō·män′ də là rôz′) An allegorical Old French verse romance, begun by Guillaume de Lorris about the middle of the 13th century, and completed in satirical tone by Jean de Meung toward the end of the century: source of Chaucer's *Romaunt of the Rose*.

ROMAN EMPIRE
At Its Greatest Extent A.D. 117

Roman Empire The empire of ancient Rome, established by Augustus in 27 B.C. and continuing until the reign of Theodosius in A.D. 395, when it was divided into the Eastern Roman Empire and the Western Roman Empire.

ro·man·esque (rō′mən·esk′) *adj.* Romantic; fabulous; fanciful. [<F <Ital. *romanesco* <Med. L *romaniscus* <L *romanus* Roman]

Ro·man·esque (rō′mən·esk′) *adj.* **1** Pertaining to or designating the Romanesque style of architecture. **2** Pertaining to or characterized by the Romance languages, especially Provençal. — *n.* **1** Romanesque architecture. **2** The vernacular of Languedoc and other provinces in southern France.

Romanesque architecture The prevailing style, developed from Roman principles, of Western architecture from the 5th to the 12th centuries, embracing the Saxon, Norman, Lombard, etc., characterized by the round arch and general massiveness. It reached its

ROMANESQUE ARCHITECTURE
Notre Dame la Grande, Poitiers, France,
A.D. 11th Century.

best form in France in the 11th and 12th centuries.

Roman holiday 1 A day of gladiatorial and other contests in ancient Rome. 2 Enjoyment or profit whereby others suffer.

Roman mile See MILE.

ro·man·tic (rō-man′tik) *adj.* 1 Characterized or influenced by romance or the extravagantly ideal; imaginative; marvelous; fanciful: a *romantic* tale. 2 Given to feelings or thoughts of romance; dreamy: a *romantic* girl. 3 Characterized by or conducive to love or amorousness. 4 Visionary; fantastic; impractical: a *romantic* scheme. 5 Strangely wild or picturesque: *romantic* scenery. 6 Of, pertaining to, or characteristic of a style of art and literature tending toward free expression of subjective feeling, impressive picturesqueness, imagination, sensuousness, etc.: opposed to *classic* or *classical*. 7 Of or pertaining to romanticism in art and literature in the 19th century. — *n.* 1 An adherent of romanticism; a romanticist. 2 A romantic person. 3 A romantic trait, idea, etc. [<F *romantique* < *romant, roman* romance, novel] — **ro·man′ti·cal·ly** *adv.*
Synonyms (adj.): airy, chimerical, dreamy, extravagant, fanciful, fantastic, fictitious, ideal, imaginative, picturesque, poetic, sentimental, visionary, wild. *Antonyms:* exact, historical, literal, precise, truthful, unadorned, unimaginative, unvarnished.

ro·man·ti·cism (rō-man′tə-siz′əm) *n.* 1 The quality or characteristic of being romantic. 2 In art, music, and literature, a romantic style as opposed to the classical. 3 In the late 18th century and the 19th, a social and esthetic movement, beginning as a reaction to neo-classicism, that sought to free the individual from unpleasant realities by appealing to his aspirations for wonder and mystery. It emphasized a love for strange beauty, for the past and the far-away, and for the wild, irregular, or grotesque in nature, and found creative expression in spontaneity, lyricism, reverie, sentimentalism, mysticism, and individualism. — **ro·man′ti·cist** *n.*

ro·man·ti·cize (rō-man′tə-sīz) *v.t.* **·cized, ·ciz·ing** To regard or interpret in a romantic manner.

Romantic Movement See ROMANTICISM (def. 3).

Rom·a·ny (rom′ə-nē) *adj.* Of or pertaining to the Gipsies or their language. — *n.* 1 A Gipsy. 2 The Indic language of the Gipsies, containing elements of the language of each country in which they live: also called *Gipsy.* Also **Rom′ma·ny.** [<Romany *romani* < *rom* man]

ro·maunt (rō·mänt′, -mônt′) *n.* A romance, usually in verse. [<OF *romant*, var. of *romans.* See ROMANCE.]

Rome (rōm) 1 A city on the Tiber river, capital of Italy and the site of Vatican City, center of the Roman Catholic Church; formerly the capital of the Roman republic, the Roman Empire, and the States of the Church. *Italian* and *Latin* **Ro·ma** (rō′mä). 2 The Roman Catholic Church. 3 Roman Catholicism. 4 A city in central New York.

Ro·me·o (rō′mē·ō) In Shakespeare's tragedy *Romeo and Juliet,* the hero of the play, son of Montague, in love with Juliet, daughter of Capulet who is the enemy of the house of the Montagues.

romp (romp) *v.i.* 1 To play boisterously. 2 To win easily. — *n.* 1 One, especially a girl, who romps. 2 Noisy, exciting frolic or play. [Var. of RAMP²]

romp·er (rom′pər) *n.* 1 One who romps. 2 *pl.* A combination of waist and bloomers, as worn by young children at play.

romp·ing (rom′ping) *n.* Boisterous playing. — **romp′ing·ly** *adv.*

romp·ish (rom′pish) *adj.* Inclined toward boisterousness in play. — **romp′ish·ly** *adv.* — **romp′ish·ness** *n.*

Rom·u·lus (rom′yə·ləs) In Roman mythology, a son of Mars and founder of Rome, later deified as *Quirinus:* abandoned in the Tiber with his twin brother Remus, the infant Romulus was reared by a she-wolf, later killing his brother to become the first ruler of Rome.

ron·deau (ron′dō, ron·dō′) *n.* A poem of French origin, consisting of thirteen lines with only two rimes: the opening words of the first line are added, as an unrimed refrain, after the eighth and thirteenth lines. [<F < *rondel* < *rond* round]

ron·del (ron′dəl, -del) *n.* A form of French verse consisting of 13 or 14 lines, in two stanzas of four and one of five or six lines, the first two lines being repeated, as a refrain, in the seventh and eighth lines, and again in the thirteenth and fourteenth. The names *rondeau* and *rondel* are often used interchangeably in English. [<F. See RONDEAU.]

ron·de·let (ron′də·let) *n.* A brief French verse form with a refrain, which generally consists of two or more words of the first line. [<OF, dim. of *rondel.* See RONDEAU.]

ron·do (ron′dō, ron·dō′) *n.* 1 *Music* A composition or movement having a main theme and several contrasting episodes, the former being repeated in its original key after each subordinate theme. 2 The musical setting of a rondeau. [<Ital., round]

ron·dure (ron′jər) *n.* Anything circular or spherical; a curve or swell. [<F *rondeur* roundness]

rood (rood) *n.* 1 A cross or crucifix; specifically, a crucifix or a representation of the Crucifixion over the altar screen of a church. 2 A square land measure, **square rood,** equivalent to one fourth of a statute acre, or 40 square rods. 3 A linear measure varying locally between six and eight yards. ◆ Homophone: *rude.* [OE *rōd* rod, measure of land, cross. Related to ROD.]

rood beam A beam over the entrance to a choir for supporting a cross or crucifix.

rood screen An enriched screen, usually surmounted by a rood, separating the choir presbytery from the nave.

roof (roof, roof) *n.* 1 The exterior upper covering of a building. 2 Any top covering, as of a car or oven. 3 A house; home. 4 The most elevated part of anything; top; summit. — *v.t.* To cover with or as with a roof. [OE *hrōf*]

ROOF CONSTRUCTION—KINGPOST TYPE
a. Common rafters.   *e.* Principal rafters.
b. Purlin.   *f.* Struts.
c. Kingpost.   *g.* Pole plate.
d. Ridge pole.   *h.* Tie beams.

roof·age (roo′fij, roof′ij) *n.* The material forming a roof; roofing.

roof·ing (roo′fing, roof′ing) *n.* 1 Roofs collectively. 2 Material for roofs. 3 Shelter.

4 The act of covering with a roof.

roof·less (roof′lis, roof′-) *adj.* 1 Having no roof. 2 Destitute of shelter; homeless.

roof of the mouth The hard palate.

roof·tree (roof′trē′, roof′-) *n.* 1 The ridge pole of a roof. 2 The roof. 3 A home or dwelling.

rook¹ (rook) *n.* 1 An Old World corvine bird with the feathers of the face lost in the adult state; especially, the common *Corvus frugilegus,* noted for its gregariousness. 2 A sharper; cheat; trickster. — *v.t.* & *v.i.* To cheat; defraud. [OE *hrōc*]

rook² (rook) *n.* One of a pair of castle-shaped chessmen which can move any number of unoccupied squares parallel to the sides of the board; a castle. [<OF *roc* <Persian *rukh*; orig. meaning unknown]

rook·er·y (rook′ər·ē) *n. pl.* **·er·ies** 1 A colony or breeding place of rooks. 2 A breeding place of sea birds, seals, etc. 3 A rambling building; an old tenement densely populated.

rook·ie (rook′ē) *n. Slang* 1 A raw recruit in the army, police, or any other service. 2 A novice in professional baseball. [Prob. alter. of RECRUIT]

rook·y (rook′ē) *adj.* 1 Pertaining to rooks and their habits. 2 Gregarious. 3 Abounding in rooks.

room (room, room) *n.* 1 Extent of space considered with regard to its sufficiency for some implied or specified purpose; free or open space. 2 A space for occupancy or use enclosed on all sides, as in a building; an apartment; chamber. 3 Suitable or warrantable occasion; opportunity: *room* for doubt. See synonyms under PLACE. — *v.i.* To occupy a room; lodge. [OE *rūm* space]

room·er (room′ər, room′ər) *n.* A lodger; especially, one who rents a room and eats elsewhere.

room·ette (room·et′, room·et′) *n.* A compartment with a single bed in some railroad sleeping-cars.

room·ful (room′fool′, room′-) *n.* 1 As many or as much as a room will hold. 2 A number of persons present in a room considered collectively.

rooming house A house for roomers; lodging house.

room·mate (room′māt′, room′-) *n.* One who occupies a room with another or others.

room·y (roo′mē, room′ē) *adj.* **room·i·er, room·i·est** Having abundant room; spacious. — **room′i·ly** *adv.* — **room′i·ness** *n.*

roor·back (roor′bak) *n. U.S.* A fictitious report circulated for political purposes. [after *Roorback,* purported author of a (non-existent) book of travel, which was cited as authority for certain defamatory charges made against President Polk in the 1844 campaign]

Roo·se·velt (rō′zə·velt, rōz′velt, -vəlt), **(Anna) Eleanor,** 1884–1962, *née* Roosevelt, U.S. lecturer, writer, and diplomat; wife of F. D. Roosevelt. — **Franklin Delano,** 1882–1945, president of the United States 1933–45; re-elected to fourth consecutive term 1944. — **Theodore,** 1858–1919, president of the United States 1901–09.

roost (roost) *n.* 1 A perch upon which fowls rest at night; also, any place where birds resort to spend the night. 2 Any temporary resting place. — *v.i.* 1 To sit or perch upon a roost. 2 To come to rest; settle. [OE *hrōst*]

roost·er (roos′tər) *n.* The male of the chicken; cock. [<ROOST + -ER¹]

root¹ (root, root) *n.* 1 The underground portion or descending axis of a plant, which absorbs moisture, obtains or stores nourishment, and provides support. It differs from the stem in that it branches irregularly and lacks joints or leaves. 2 Loosely, any underground growth, as a tuber or bulb. 3 One of certain other growths serving for attachment, support, etc., as in the ivy or mistletoe. 4 That from which anything derives origin, growth, or life and vigor: Money is the *root* of evil; Industry is the *root* of prosperity. 5 An antecedent; ancestor. 6 Some rootlike part of an organ or structure: the *root* of a tooth or nerve. 7 *Ling.* A morpheme serving as the common center or basic constituent element of a related group of words, as *know* in *unknown, knowledge, knowable,* and *knowingly.* A root to which affixes or other morphemes may be added directly is equivalent to a stem. **8** *Math.* A quantity that, taken a specified number of times as a factor, will give another quantity called its *power:* 2 is the fourth *root* of 16. The number of times the root is thus taken as a factor is called its *index,* and roots are named from the indices, the words **square root** and **cube root** being often used for *second* and *third root.* **9** A tone on which a chord is built up. —*v.i.* **1** To put forth roots and begin to grow; take root. **2** To be or become firmly fixed or established. —*v.t.* **3** To fix or implant by or as by roots. **4** To pull, dig, or tear up by or as by the roots; extirpate; eradicate: with *up* or *out.* [OE *rōt* <ON *rōt*]

root² (rŏot, rŏot) *v.t.* **1** To turn up or dig with the snout or nose, as swine. —*v.i.* **2** To turn up the earth with the snout. **3** To search for something; rummage. **4** To work hard; toil. [OE *wrōtan* root up < *wrōt* snout]

root³ (rŏot, rŏot) *v.i. U.S. Colloq.* To cheer for or encourage a contestant: with *for: He rooted* for Harvard. [Prob. var. of ROOT³]

root beer A beverage made with yeast and the extracts of several roots.

root climber Any plant that climbs by means of adventitious roots developed from stems.

root·er (rŏo′tər, rŏot′ər) *n.* One who or that which roots, as a swine, or tears up as by rooting; a destroyer; eradicator.

root·stock (rŏot′stok′, rŏot′-) *n.* **1** A rhizome. **2** Original source; origin.

root·y (rŏo′tē, rŏot′ē) *adj.* **root·i·er, root·i·est 1** Full of or consisting of roots. **2** Resembling roots. —**root′i·ness** *n.*

rope (rōp) *n.* **1** A construction of twisted fibers, as of hemp, cotton, flax, etc., so intertwined in several strands as to form a thick cord. **2** A collection of things plaited or united in a line. **3** A slimy or glutinous filament or thread. **4** A cord or halter used in hanging; hence, execution or death by strangling or hanging. **5** A lasso. —**to give (one) plenty of rope** To allow (a person) to pursue unchecked a course that will end in disaster. —**to know the ropes** To be familiar with all the conditions in any sphere of activity; hence, to be sophisticated in the ways of the world. —*v.* **roped, rop·ing** *v.t.* **1** To tie or fasten with or as with rope. **2** To enclose, border, or divide with a rope: usually with *off: He roped* off the arena. **3** To catch with a lasso. **4** *Colloq.* To deceive; take in: with *in.* —*v.i.* **5** To become drawn out or extended into a filament or thread. [OE *rāp*]

rope band Roband.

rope-dancer (rōp′dan′sər, -dän′-) *n.* One who performs on the tightrope. —**rope′-danc′ing** *n.*

rope ferry A set of ropes overhanging a stream or defile, over which supplies and equipment may be pulled by a towline.

rop·er·y (rō′pər·ē) *n.* **1** A ropewalk. **2** *Archaic* Roguery.

rope's end 1 A short piece of rope used for flogging. **2** A hangman's noose.

rope-walk (rōp′wôk′) *n.* A long alley formerly used for the spinning of rope yarn: now in general superseded by some structure using improved machinery.

rop·y (rō′pē) *adj.* **rop·i·er, rop·i·est 1** That may be drawn into threads, as a glutinous substance; stringy. **2** Resembling ropes or cordage. — **rop′i·ly** *adv.* —**rop′i·ness** *n.*

roque (rōk) *n.* A form of croquet requiring more skill than the ordinary game. [Aphetic alter. of CROQUET]

Roque·fort (rōk′fərt, *Fr.* rôk-fôr′) A village in south central France. Also **Roquefort-sur-Soul·zon** (-sür-sōōl-zôn′).

Roquefort cheese A strong cheese with a blue mold *(Penicillium roqueforti)* made from ewe's and goat's milk at Roquefort, France.

roqu·e·laure (rok′ə·lôr, rok′lôr, -lōr) *n.* A form of short cloak worn by men in the 18th century: also spelled **rokelay.** [after Duc de *Roquelaure,* 1656–1738, French nobleman]

ro·quet (rō·kā′) *v.t. & v.i.* **·queted** (-kād′) **·quet·ing** (-kā′ing) In croquet, to strike (another player's ball). —*n.* The act of roqueting. [See ROQUE]

Ro·rai·ma (rō·rī′mä), **Mount** A peak at the junction of the Brazil-Venezuela-Guyana boundaries; 9,219 feet.

ror·qual (rôr′kwəl) *n.* Any of a genus *(Balaenoptera)* of whales of the Atlantic and Pacific oceans; especially, *B. physalis* of the North Atlantic: also called *finback, finback whale.* [<F <Norw. *röyrkval*]

RORQUAL
(About 60 feet in length)

Ror·schach test (rôr′shäk, -shäkh, rôr′-) *Psychol.* A test in which personality characteristics are made accessible to analysis by the subject's interpretation of the nature and meaning of a series of standard inkblot patterns. [after Hermann *Rorschach,* 1884–1922, Swiss psychiatrist]

ro·sa·ceous (rō·zā′shəs) *adj.* **1** *Bot.* Of or belonging to a large family (Rosaceae) of trees, shrubs, and herbs widely distributed in northern temperate regions and including many important ornamental and fruit-yielding plants such as roses, apples, cherries, strawberries, and plums. **2** Resembling a rose; rosy. [<L *rosaceus*]

ro·sa·ry (rō′zə·rē) *n. pl.* **·ries 1** *Eccl.* **a** A series of prayers, consisting in its common form (**Dominican rosary**) of fifteen decades, each containing ten Aves preceded by a paternoster and followed by the Gloria Patri, and each related to a mystery or event in the life of Christ or the Virgin Mary which is contemplated during its recitation. **b** A string of beads for keeping count of the prayers thus recited. **2** A garden or bed of roses. **3** A chaplet or garland, as of roses. **4** A collection of literary selections. [<LL *rosarium* a rose garden <L *rosa* a rose]

rose¹ (rōz) *n.* **1** A hardy, erect or climbing shrub (genus *Rosa*) grown in many varieties, with rodlike, prickly stems. In cultivation the stamens are transformed into petals and the flowers become double. It is the national flower of England and the State flower of New York, North Dakota, and Iowa. **2** The flower, having 5, or rarely 4, sepals. **3** Any one of various other plants or flowers having some real or fancied likeness to the true rose. **4** A light pinkish red, like the color of many roses. **5** An ornamental knot, as of ribbon or lace; a rosette. **6** A perforated cap, plate, or nozzle at the end of a pipe, for throwing water in a fine spray. **7** A compass rose. **8** A form in which gems, especially diamonds, are often cut, characterized by a flat base with a hemispherical upper surface covered with small facets; also, a diamond so cut. **9** Erysipelas. —**golden rose** A rose of wrought gold, blessed by the pope and presented, usually to a Roman Catholic sovereign, as a distinguished honor. —**under the rose** In secret. See SUB ROSA. —*v.t.* **rosed, ros·ing** To cause to blush; redden; flush. [OE <L *rosa* <Gk. *rhodon*]

rose² (rōz) Past tense of RISE.

ro·se·ate (rō′zē·it, -āt) *adj.* **1** Of a rose color. **2** Rosy; rose-colored; hence, optimistic. [<L *roseus*] —**ro′se·ate·ly** *adv.*

roseate spoonbill A tropical American wading bird *(Ajaia ajaja)* having a bare head and throat and pink plumage.

rose beetle 1 The goldsmith beetle. **2** The rose chafer.

rose·bud (rōz′bud′) *n.* **1** The bud of a rose. **2** A young girl; a debutante.

rose chafer A hairy, fawn-colored beetle *(Macrodactylus subspinosus)* injurious to roses: also called *rose beetle.* Also **rose bug.** For illustration see INSECTS (injurious).

rose cold *Pathol.* A variety of hay fever, assumed to be caused by rose pollen. Also **rose fever.**

rose-col·ored (rōz′kul′ərd) *adj.* Pink or crimson, as a rose. —**to see through rose-colored glasses** To see things in an unduly favorable light; to look too much or only on the bright side. Compare COULEUR DE ROSE.

rose-cross (rōz′krôs′, -kros′) *n.* The symbol of the Rosicrucians, a rose and cross combined in some form.

rose·mar·y (rōz′mâr′ē) *n. pl.* **·mar·ies** An evergreen, fragrant shrub *(Rosmarinus officinalis)* of the mint family of southern Europe and western Asia, with usually blue flowers: cultivated for its

stimulating and refreshing perfume, for an oil obtained from it, and for use in cookery. [Alter. of L *rosmarinus* <*ros* dew + *marinus* marine; infl. by *rose, Mary*]

rose of Jericho A small annual *(Anastatica hierochuntica)* growing in desert places from Syria to Algeria, which rolls up when dry and expands again when moist: also called *resurrection plant, Jericho rose.*

rose of Sharon 1 In the Bible (Song of Sol. 2:1), an unknown flower, perhaps the autumn crocus or the narcissus. **2** A tall, hardy deciduous shrub or small tree *(Hibiscus syriacus)* of Asian origin, having large, usually roseate flowers. Also called *althea, hibiscus.* **3** A species *(Hypericum calycinum)* of shrubby plants having evergreen leaves and large yellow flowers.

ro·se·o·la (rō·zē′ə·lə) *n. Pathol.* A rose-colored rash appearing on the skin. Also **rose rash.** [<NL, dim. of L *roseus* rosy]

rose quartz A translucent to semitransparent variety of quartz, pink or rose in color and often asteriated: used for ornament, as a gemstone, etc.

Ro·set·ta stone (rō·zet′ə) A tablet of basalt containing an inscription in two forms of Egyptian hieroglyphics (demotic and hieratic) and in Greek, found near Rosetta, Egypt, in 1799. It supplied Champollion with the key to the ancient inscriptions of Egypt.

ro·sette (rō·zet′) *n.* **1** An ornament or badge having some resemblance to a rose; specifically, a painted or sculptured architectural ornament with parts circularly arranged. **2** A ribbon badge worn in the lapel buttonhole of civilian clothes to indicate possession of a certain military decoration. **3** A ribbon decoration shaped like a full-blown or double rose and made of gathered or pleated silk, lace, etc. **4** A flowerlike cluster or combination of leaves, organs, parts, or markings, arranged in circles, as in certain plants. [<F, little rose]

ROSETTE

rose-wa·ter (rōz′wô′tər, -wot′ər) *n.* A fragrant toilet and pharmaceutical water made variously by the distillation of rose petals or rose oil with water. —*adj.* **1** Made with or resembling rosewater. **2** Extremely or affectedly delicate or sentimental: *rosewater* philosophy.

rose window A circular window filled with tracery, called, when this takes the form of spokes, a *wheel window.*

Rosh Ha·sha·na (rosh hə·shä′nə, rösh) The Jewish New Year, celebrated on Tisri 1st and 2nd (September–early October). Also **Rosh Ha·sho′nah** (-shō′-). [<Hebrew *rōsh* head of + *hash-shānāh* the year]

Ro·si·cru·cian (rō′zə·krōō′shən, roz′ə-) *n.* One who is a member of an international fraternity, said to have originated in Egypt, and devoted to the practical application of an occult philosophy to human relationship. See ILLUMINATI. —*adj.* Of or pertaining to this society, its members, or its doctrines. [<L *rosae crucis* roses of the cross; said to be the trans. of the name of Christian *Rosenkranz,* 1387–1484, a German to whom the founding of this order has been attributed] —**Ro′si·cru′cian·ism** *n.*

ros·in (roz′in) *n.* **1** Resin. **2** The hard, amber-colored resin forming the residue after the distillation of oil of turpentine from crude turpentine; colophony. —*v.t.* To apply rosin to. [Var. of RESIN] —**ros′in·y** *adj.*

rosin oil Retinol.

ro·so·lio (rō·zō′lyō) *n.* A cordial made from raisins and brandy in the Mediterranean countries. [<Ital. <Med. L *ros solis* (<L *ros* dew + *solis* of the sun) sundew, from which it was once extracted]

ros·tel·late (ros′tə·lāt, -lit) *adj.* Having a small beak or rostellum. [<NL *rostellatus*]

ros·tel·lum (ros·tel′əm) *n. pl.* **·tel·la** (-tel′ə) **1** *Bot.* A small, beaklike structure developed from the stigma of an orchid. **2** *Zool.* The hooked scolex of a tapeworm. [<L, dim. of *rostrum* beak]

ros·ter (ros'tər) *n.* 1 A list of officers and men enrolled for duty; also, a list of active military organizations. 2 Any list of names. [<Du. *rooster* list]

ros·tral (ros'trəl) *adj.* 1 Of or pertaining to a rostrum. 2 Having a rostrum, or beaklike process; beaked: often used in combination, as in *curvirostral,* having a crossed or curved-down beak. Also **ros'trate** (-trāt). [<LL *rostralis*]

ros·trum (ros'trəm) *n. pl.* **·trums** or **·tra** (-trə) 1 A pulpit or platform. 2 *pl.* **ros·tra** The orators' platform in the Roman forum: embellished with the beaks of the Latin ships captured 338 B.C. 3 A beak or snout; a beaklike process or part. 4 One of various beaklike parts, as the beak or prow of an ancient war galley. [<L *rostrum* beak]

ROSTRUM *(def. 4)*

ros·y (rō'zē) *adj.* **ros·i·er, ros·i·est** 1 Like a rose; rose-red; blooming; blushing. 2 Figuratively, bright, pleasing, or flattering. 3 Made of or ornamented with roses. 4 Auguring success; favorable: *rosy* predictions. 5 Optimistic. **—ros'i·ly** *adv.* **—ros'i·ness** *n.*

rot (rot) *v.* **rot·ted, rot·ting** *v.i.* 1 To undergo decomposition; decompose; decay. 2 To fall or pass by decaying: with *away, off,* etc. 3 To become morally rotten. —*v.t.* 4 To cause to decompose; decay. 5 To ret. See synonyms under DECAY, PUTREFY. —*n.* 1 That which is rotten, or the process of rotting. 2 A wasting disease, as of the lungs. 3 A parasitic disease affecting sheep and other domestic animals. 4 A form of decay in plants, caused by fungi and bacteria. 5 *Colloq.* Trashy and nonsensical opinions or expressions; twaddle; bosh. —*interj.* Nonsense; bosh. [OE *rotian*]

ro·ta (rō'tə) *n.* 1 A roll of names, giving order of duty; a roster. 2 A routine. 3 A wheel. [<L, wheel]

Ro·ta (rō'tə) *n.* In the Roman Catholic Church, an ecclesiastical court composed of ten prelates or auditors, subject only to papal authority, and serving as a court of final appeal: also known as *Sacra Romana Rota.*

Ro·tar·i·an (rō-târ'ē-ən) *n.* A member of a Rotary Club. —*adj.* Of or pertaining to the organization of Rotary Clubs or to their members. **—Ro·tar'i·an·ism** *n.*

ro·ta·ry (rō'tər-ē) *adj.* 1 Turning around its axis, like a wheel, or so constructed as to turn thus. 2 Having some part that so turns: a *rotary* press. [<LL *rotarius* < *rota* wheel]

Rotary Club A club belonging to an international association of clubs, **Rotary International,** whose aim is to improve civic service, and whose motto is "Service."

rotary engine 1 An engine in which rotary motion is directly produced without reciprocating parts, as in a steam turbine: distinguished from *reciprocating engine.* 2 In internal-combustion engines, a radial engine revolving about a fixed crankshaft.

rotary press A printing press using curved type plates which revolve against the paper.

ro·tate (rō'tāt) *v.t.* & *v.i.* **·tat·ed, ·tat·ing** 1 To turn or cause to turn on or as on its axis. 2 To alternate in a definite order or succession. See synonyms under REVOLVE. —*adj.* 1 Wheel-shaped; circular, as the corollas of certain flowers. 2 Forming a circle around a part, as spines or hairs. [<L *rotatus,* pp. of *rotare* turn < *rota*] **—ro'tat·a·ble** *adj.*

ro·ta·tion (rō-tā'shən) *n.* 1 The act or state of rotating; rotary motion. 2 Change by alternation; order of succession, variation, or sequence: *rotation* of crops or office. 3 The period represented by the age of a forest, or a part of a forest, at the time when it is cut, or intended to be cut. **—ro·ta'tion·al** *adj.*

ro·ta·tive (rō'tə-tiv) *adj.* Pertaining to or causing rotation; turning.

ro·ta·tor (rō'tā·tər) *n.* 1 One who or that

which rotates or causes rotation. 2 *pl.* **ro·ta·to·res** (rō'tə-tôr'ēz, -tō'rēz) *Anat.* A muscle that rolls or rotates a part upon its axis. [<L]

Ro·ta·to·ri·a (rō'tə-tôr'ē·ə, -tō'rē·ə) See RO·TIFER.

ro·ta·to·ry (rō'tə-tôr'ē, -tō'rē) *adj.* 1 Having, pertaining to, or producing rotation. 2 Following in succession. 3 Alternating or recurring.

rote (rōt) *n.* 1 Mechanical routine. 2 Repetition of words as a means of learning them, with slight attention to the sense. **— by rote** Mechanically; without intelligent attention: to learn *by rote.* [Var. of ROUTE]

Roth·schild (rôth'child, *Ger.* rōt'shilt) A family of European bankers, of whom the first, **Meyer Amschel,** 1743–1812, established a bank in Frankfort on the Main. His sons opened branches: **James,** 1792–1868, at Paris; **Karl,** 1788–1855, at Naples; **Nathan Meyer,** 1777–1836, at London; **Salomon,** 1774–1855, at Vienna.

ro·ti·form (rō'tə-fôrm) *adj.* Shaped like a wheel; rotate. [<L *rota* wheel + -FORM]

ro·tis·se·rie (rō-tis'ə-rē') *n.* 1 A restaurant where patrons select uncooked food and have it roasted and served. 2 A shop where food is roasted and sold. 3 A rotating device for roasting meat, etc. [<F < *rôtir* roast]

rotl (rot'l) *n. pl.* **ar·tal** (är'təl) A weight used in Moslem countries, varying in different localities between one and five pounds. [< Arabic *ratl*]

ro·to·graph (rō'tə-graf, -gräf) *n.* One of a series of photographs printed from a developed roll of sensitized paper that bears the images. [< L *rota* wheel + -GRAPH]

ro·to·gra·vure (rō'tə-grə-vyoor', -grāv'yər) *n.* 1 A picture engraved on a cylindrical printing surface and run through a rotary press that prints both sides of the paper at the same time. 2 The process of making such pictures. [< L *rota* wheel + GRAVURE]

ro·tor (rō'tər) *n.* 1 *Electr.* The portion of an alternating-current motor which revolves. 2 A revolving part of a machine, as the wheel or wheels of a turbine. Compare STATOR. 3 *Aeron.* The horizontally rotating unit of a helicopter. [Contraction of ROTATOR]

ro·tor·craft (rō'tər·kraft') *n.* An aircraft, esp. a helicopter, supported while airborne by rotors.

rot·ten (rot'n) *adj.* 1 Decomposed by natural process; putrid. 2 Unsound; liable to break. 3 Untrustworthy; treacherous; also, venal; corrupt. 4 Afflicted with the rot, as sheep. 5 *Colloq.* Worthless. [< ON *rotinn*] **—rot'ten·ly** *adv.* **—rot'ten·ness** *n.*

Synonyms: carious, corrupt, decayed, deceitful, decomposed, defective, fetid, offensive, putrefied, putrescent, putrid, tainted, treacherous, unsound. See BAD. *Antonyms:* complete, fresh, healthful, healthy, perfect, pure, sound, sweet, untainted, wholesome.

Rot·ter·dam (rot'ər·dam) The largest port of the Netherlands, in the western part.

rot·wei·ler (rot'wī'lər, -vī'-) *n.* A breed of strong, shorthaired, black or black and tan dogs.

ro·tund (rō·tund') *adj.* 1 Rounded out; spherical; plump. 2 Full-toned, as a voice or utterance; in style, using sonorous words. 3 Complete; entire. 4 Circular, or nearly so; orbicular. See synonyms under ROUND. [< L *rotundus* < *rota* wheel. Doublet of ROUND.] **—ro·tund'ly** *adv.* **—ro·tund'ness** *n.*

ro·tun·da (rō·tun'də) *n.* A circular building or an interior hall, surmounted with a dome. [< Ital. *rotonda* < L *rotunda,* fem. of *rotundus.* See RO·TUND.]

ro·tun·di·ty (rō·tun'də·tē) *n.* 1 The condition of being rotund; sphericity. 2 A protuberance.

rou·ble (rōō'bəl) See RUBLE.

rouche (rōōsh) See RUCHE.

rou·é (rōō·ā') *n.* A sensualist; debauchee. [< F, jaded, orig. pp. of *rouer* break on the wheel, beat severely < *roue* wheel < L *rota;* from the appearance of a debauchee]

rouge (rōōzh) *n.* 1 Any cosmetic used for coloring the cheeks or lips pink or red. 2 A ferric oxide used in polishing metals and glass. —*v.* **rouged, roug·ing** *v.t.* To color, as the face, with rouge. —*v.i.* To apply rouge. [< F, red < L *ru·*

beus ruby]

rough (ruf) *adj.* 1 Having an uneven surface; having small inequalities on the surface; not smooth or polished: *rough* stone. 2 Coarse in texture; shaggy; also, disordered or ragged; shabby: said of dress or appearance: a *rough* suit, a *rough* shock of hair. 3 Having the surface broken; uneven: a *rough* country. 4 Characterized by rude or violent action: *rough* sports. 5 *Naut.* Boisterous or tempestuous; stormy: a *rough* passage. 6 Characterized by harshness of spirit; brutal. 7 Lacking the finish and polish bestowed by art or culture; unpolished; crude. 8 Done or made hastily and without attention to details; approximate. 9 *Phonet.* Uttered with an aspiration; aspirated: a *rough* breathing. 10 Harsh to the ear; grating; inharmonious: *rough* sounds. —*n.* 1 A low, rude, and violent fellow; a ruffian; a rowdy. 2 A crude, incomplete, or unpolished object, material, or condition. 3 Any part of a golf course on which tall grass, bushes, etc., grow. 4 A spike for insertion in a horseshoe, to prevent slipping. —*v.t.* 1 To make rough; roughen. 2 To treat roughly; specifically, in football, to treat (a player) with needless and intentional violence. 3 To make, cut, or sketch roughly: with *in* or *out:* to *rough* in the details of a plan. —*v.i.* 4 To become rough. 5 To behave roughly. **—to rough it** To live under rough, hard, or impoverished conditions; also, to camp out or travel in a rough manner; rusticate. —*adv.* In a rude manner; roughly. ◆Homophone: *ruff.* [OE *rūh*] **—rough'ly** *adv.* **—rough'ness** *n.*

Synonyms (adj.) coarse, craggy, harsh, jagged, ragged, rude, rugged, shaggy, uneven, unfinished, unhewn, unpolished. See AWKWARD, BLUFF. *Antonyms:* bland, even, glossy, level, plain, polished, sleek, smooth.

rough·age (ruf'ij) *n.* 1 Any coarse or tough substance. 2 Food material containing a high percentage of indigestible constituents, as cellulose.

rough-and-ready (ruf'ən-red'ē) *adj.* 1 Characterized by or acting with rude but effective promptness. 2 Unpolished but good enough.

rough-and-tum·ble (ruf'ən-tum'bəl) *adj.* 1 Disregarding all rules: said of a certain kind of fighting. 2 Scrambling; disorderly. —*n.* 1 A fight disregarding procedure according to rule, or in which anything goes; also, a scuffle. 2 Rough or adventurous existence.

rough-cast (ruf'kast', -käst') *v.t.* **-cast, -cast·ing** 1 To shape or prepare in a preliminary or incomplete form. 2 To roughen the surface of (pottery) before firing. 3 To coat, as a wall, with coarse plaster, and cover with thin mortar by dashing it on. —*n.* 1 Very coarse plaster for the outside of buildings. 2 A rude model; the form of a thing in its first rough stage. **—rough'-cast'er** *n.*

rough-draft (ruf'draft', -dräft') *v.t.* To make a rough or unfinished draft of; design or sketch hastily, as a plan or discourse.

rough·en (ruf'ən) *v.t.* & *v.i.* To make or become rough.

rough·er (ruf'ər) *n.* One who makes things in the rough.

rough-hew (ruf'hyōō') *v.t.* **-hewed, -hewed** or **-hewn, -hew·ing** 1 To hew or shape roughly or irregularly or without smoothing. 2 To make crudely; rough-cast.

rough-house (ruf'hous') *Slang n.* A noisy, boisterous or violent game or disturbance; rough play, especially within a room or house. —*v.* **-housed, -hous·ing** *v.i.* To make a disturbance; engage in horseplay or violence. —*v.t.* To handle or treat roughly but without hostile intent.

rough-rid·er (ruf'rī'dər) *n. U.S.* 1 One skilled in breaking broncos or performing dangerous feats in horsemanship. 2 A western cowboy.

Rough Riders The 1st U.S. Volunteer Cavalry in the Spanish-American War of 1898, mainly organized and subsequently commanded by Theodore Roosevelt.

rough-shod (ruf'shod') *adj.* Shod with rough shoes to prevent slipping, as a horse. **—to ride rough-shod (over)** To act overbearingly; domineer without consideration.

rou·lade (rōō·läd') *n.* 1 In singing, a run of short

notes on one syllable; also, a roll or flourish, as on a drum. 2 A slice of meat rolled around a filling and cooked. [< F < rouler roll]

rou·leau (rōō-lō′) n. pl. **·leaux** (-lōz) or **·leaus** 1 A roll of coins in paper. 2 Usually pl. In millinery, a roll or fold of ribbon used for piping. [< F, dim. of rôle roll]

rou·lette (rōō-let′) n. 1 A game played at a table divided into spaces numbered and colored red and black, and having in the center a rotating disk on which a ball is rolled until it drops into one of 37 correspondingly numbered and colored spaces, a player winning if he has staked his money on that space or its color or on a combination including it. 2 An engraver's disk of tempered steel, as for tracing points on a copperplate; also, a draftsman's wheel for making dotted lines. 3 In philately, a series of incisions, made in any of several shapes, without removal of paper. Compare PERFORATION. —v.t. **·let·ted**, **·let·ting** To use or produce a roulette upon. [< F, dim. of rouelle, dim. of roue wheel < L rota]

round (round) adj. 1 Having such a contour that a section in some direction will be circular or approximately so; circular, spherical, or cylindrical. 2 Having a curved contour or surface; not angular or flat; convex or concave. 3 Liberal; ample; large: a good round fee. 4 Easy and free, as in motion; brisk: a round pace. 5 Of full cadence; well-balanced; full-toned: a round sentence or tone. 6 Made without reserve; bold; outspoken: a round assertion. 7 Open; just; honorable. 8 Formed or moving in rotation or a circle: a round dance. 9 Returning to the point of departure, usually by the same means of transportation: a round trip. 10 Passing through the same or a like series of mutations: the round year. 11 Free from fractions; also, not exact in the small denominations; especially, evenly divisible by 10: round numbers. 12 Semicircular: a round arch; also, characterized by the round arch: the round style. 13 Phonet. Labialized; rounded. —n. 1 Something round, as a globe, ring, or cylinder, a rung of a ladder, a crossbar connecting the legs of a chair, a portion of the thigh of a beef, etc. 2 A circular course or range; circuit; beat: often in the plural; also, revolving motion or one revolution. 3 A series of recurrent movements; a routine; a completed succession or order: the daily round of life. 4 One of a series of concerted actions performed in succession by a number of persons: a round of toasts or applause. 5 One of the divisions of a boxing match; a bout. 6 In archery, the total number of arrows shot; the sum of all arrows in two or three ranges. 7 A short melody taken up at intervals by several voices; a rondo, roundel, or roundelay. 8 A firing by a company or squad in which each soldier fires once; volley. 9 A single charge of ammunition. 10 A round dance. 11 The state of being carved out on all sides: opposed to relief. 12 The state or condition of being circular; roundness. 13 A thick slice from a haunch: a round of beef. — **to go the rounds 1** To take the usual walk of inspection. 2 To pass from mouth to mouth or person to person of a certain group. —v.t. 1 To make round. 2 To bring to completion; perfect: usually with off or out. 3 To free of angularity; fill out to fullness of form. 4 Phonet. To utter (a vowel) with the lips in a rounded position; labialize. 5 To travel or go around; make a circuit of. 6 Archaic To encircle; surround. —v.i. 7 To become round. 8 To come to completeness or perfection. 9 To fill out; become plump. 10 To make a circuit; travel a circular course. 11 To turn around. — **to round off** Math. To reduce the number of decimal places to which a number is carried in a calculation: usually, a final figure less than 5 is eliminated and a final figure of 5 or greater increases the preceding figure to its next highest value, as, 2.1414, rounded off, becomes 2.141; 3.14159 becomes 3.1416. — **to round up 1** To collect (cattle, etc.) in a herd, as for driving to market. 2 Colloq. To gather together; assemble. —adv. 1 On all sides; in such a manner as to encircle: A crowd gathered round. 2 With a circular or rotating motion: The wheel turns round. 3 Through a circle or circuit; more or less completely from person to person or point to point: provisions enough to go round. 4 In circumference: a

log 3 feet round. 5 From one view or position to another; hither and yon; to and fro. 6 In the vicinity; to hang round. See AROUND. — prep. 1 Enclosing; encircling: a belt round his waist. 2 On every side of, or from every side toward; surrounding. 3 Toward every side from; about: He peered round him. [< OF roonde, form of roond < L rotundus. Doublet of ROTUND.] — **round′ness** n.

Synonyms (adj.): circular, curved, curvilinear, cylindrical, globose, globular, orbed, orbicular, plump, rotund, spherical, spheroidal. See BLUNT. Antonyms: angular, conical, cubical, flat, polygonal, quadrangular, quadrilateral, rectangular, square, triangular.

round–a·bout (round′ə-bout′) adj. 1 Circuitous; indirect. 2 Covering the whole field; ample. 3 Encircling. — n. 1 An outer garment reaching to the waist; a jacket. 2 Brit. A merry-go-round.

round–about chair A corner chair.

round clam A quahaug.

round dance 1 A country dance in which the dancers form a circle. 2 A dance with a revolving motion, as a waltz or polka, performed by two persons.

round·ed (roun′did) adj. 1 Round or spherical. 2 Phonet. Labialized.

roun·del (roun′dəl) n. 1 A roundelay. 2 In prosody, a modification of the rondeau, introduced by Swinburne, written in three stanzas of three lines each, with a refrain after the first and third. Compare RONDEL. 3 Archit. A semicircular recess, small round window, etc. [< OF rondel a roundelay]

roun·de·lay (roun′də-lā) n. 1 A simple melody. 2 A musical setting of a poem with a recurrent refrain. 3 A dance performed in a circle. [< OF rondelet, dim. of rondel < rond round]

round–hand (round′hand′) n. A style of handwriting in which the tendency is to make all letters round, full, and distinct.

Round–head (round′hed′) n. A member of the Parliamentary party in England in the civil war of 1642–49: so called in contempt by the Royalists, from their close-cropped hair.

round·house (round′hous′) n. 1 A cabin on the after part of the quarter-deck of a vessel. 2 A round building with a turntable in the center for housing and switching locomotives. 3 Obs. A lockup. 4 A round trip in pinochle.

round·ing (roun′ding) adj. 1 Pertaining to or denoting something, as a tool, used in or for rounding. 2 Becoming round; also, somewhat round.

round·ish (roun′dish) adj. Somewhat round. — **round′ish·ness** n.

round·let (round′lit) n. A little circle. [< F rondelet]

round·ly (round′lē) adv. 1 In a round manner or form; circularly; spherically. 2 Severely; vigorously: to be roundly denounced. 3 Frankly; bluntly. 4 Thoroughly; completely.

round–nose (round′nōz′) adj. Designating a kind of pliers whose gripping surfaces meet in a round, tapering point. See illustration under PLIERS.

round ringing A method of change-ringing a set of chimes in sequence from the bell of the highest note to that of the lowest, and then repeating this sequence while the earlier overtones are still vibrating, thus producing an effect like a round.

round robin 1 A number of signatures, as to a petition, written in a circle so as to avoid giving prominence to any single name; also, a paper so signed. 2 The cigar fish. 3 A tournament, as in tennis or chess, in which each player meets every other player.

rounds (roundz) n. pl. The position of a set of chiming bells when struck in a descending scale from highest to lowest.

round–shoul·dered (round′shōl′dərd) adj. Having the back rounded or the shoulders stooping.

rounds·man (roundz′mən) n. pl. **·men** (-mən) A police officer having charge of a group of patrolmen.

round table Any meeting place for conference or discussion; also, any discussion group. — **round–ta·ble** (round′tā′bəl) adj.

Round Table The table of King Arthur, made exactly circular so as to avoid any question of precedence among his knights; also, collectively, King Arthur and the body of knights

having places there.

round tower 1 Any cylindrical tower; especially, a slender, tapering tower of circular plan, with a conical cap. 2 In Ireland, a detached campanile built as a watchtower to guard church treasures, etc., against viking raids.

round trip 1 A trip to a place and back again; a return trip. 2 In pinochle, a meld of four kings and four queens: also called roundhouse. — **round′–trip′** adj.

round·up (round′up′) n. 1 The bringing together of cattle scattered over a range for inspection, branding, or selection for sale. 2 The cowboys, horses, etc., employed in this work. 3 U.S. Colloq. A bringing together of several persons: a roundup of pickpockets by the police.

round·worm (round′wûrm′) n. A nematode worm, especially one parasitic in the human intestines.

rouse (rouz) v. roused, rous·ing v.t. 1 To cause to awaken from slumber, repose, unconsciousness, etc. 2 To excite to vigorous thought or action; stir up. 3 To startle or drive (game) from cover. — v.i. 4 To awaken from sleep or unconsciousness. 5 To become active. 6 To start from cover: said of game. See synonyms under PIQUE, SPUR, STIR. — n. 1 The act of rousing; an awakening to or signal for action. 2 Brit. Reveille. [Origin unknown] — **rous′er** n.

rouse·ment (rouz′mənt) n. A stirring up of interest or enthusiasm; especially, a widespread religious awakening or excitement.

rous·ing (rou′zing) adj. 1 Able to rouse or excite: a rousing speech. 2 Lively; active; vigorous: a rousing trade.

roust (roust) v.t. & v.i. Colloq. To arouse and drive (a person or thing); stir up: usually with out. [Blend of ROUSE and ROUT]

roust·a·bout (roust′ə-bout′) n. 1 A laborer on river craft or on the waterfront; a deck hand. 2 One employed for casual work, especially, a transient laborer. 3 A man of all work on a cattle ranch or in a cow camp.

rout¹ (rout) n. 1 A disorderly and overwhelming defeat or flight. 2 A boisterous and disorderly assemblage; the rabble. 3 An entourage; a retinue. 4 Law A disturbance of the peace by three or more persons with riotous intent. 5 Archaic A large and festive evening social gathering. 6 Archaic Any assembly; a throng. See synonyms under REVEL.— v.t. To defeat disastrously; put to flight. See synonyms under CONQUER. [< OF route < L rupta, fem. of ruptus, pp. of rumpere break]

rout² (rout) v.i. 1 To root, as swine. 2 To search; rummage. — v.t. 3 To dig or turn up with the snout. 4 To disclose to view; turn up as if with the snout: with out. 5 To hollow, gouge, or scrape, as with a scoop. 6 To drive or force out. [Var. of ROOT²]

route (rōōt, rout) n. 1 A course, road, or way taken in passing from one point to another by any person or moving object. 2 The specific course over which mail is sent; also, the territory covered by a newsboy. See synonyms under ROAD, WAY. — v.t. rout·ed, rout·ing To dispatch or send by a certain way, as passengers, goods, etc. [< OF < L rupta (via) broken (road), fem. of ruptus, pp. of rumpere break] — **rout′er** n.

route march Close marching order for troops.

route formation An open formation of military aircraft prior or subsequent to action.

route march A troop march with discipline reduced to permit singing, talking, etc. Also **route step.**

route of march In a military march order, the designation of the way to be taken and the location of headquarters for each evening.

rout·er (rou′tər) n. 1 One who scoops or routs. 2 A tool for routing. 3 A plane devised for working a molding around a circular sash. [< ROUT²]

rou·tine (rōō-tēn′) n. 1 A detailed method of procedure, regularly followed; prescribed course of action: an official routine. 2 Habitual methods of action induced by circumstances. See synonyms under HABIT. — adj. Customary; habitual; everyday. [< F < route way, road]

rou·tin·ism (rōō-tē′niz-əm) n. Adherence to routine or routine methods in general. — **rou·tin′ist** n.

rove[1] (rōv) v. **roved**, **rov·ing** v.i. To wander from place to place; go or move without any definite destination. —v.t. To roam over, through, or about. See synonyms under RAMBLE, WANDER. —n. The act of roving or roaming; a ramble. [< Du. *rooven* rob]

rove[2] (rōv) v.t. **roved**, **rov·ing** 1 To join and elongate, as a number of slivers from a carding machine, by passing between one or more pairs of rollers. 2 To pass through an eye. 3 To draw into thread; ravel out. 4 To reduce the diameter of with a hooked, flat tool: to *rove* a grindstone. —n. 1 A slightly twisted wool, cotton, flax, jute, or silk sliver. 2 A metal ring or washer for use in clinching a nail in boatbuilding. [Origin uncertain]

rove[3] (rōv) Past participle of REEVE[1].

rov·er[1] (rō′vər) n. 1 One who roves; a wanderer. 2 A pirate, or pirate vessel. 3 A croquet ball that has been sent through all the arches and has only to strike the final stake to go out. [< MDu., a robber. Akin to ROBBER.]

rov·er[2] (rō′vər) n. In archery, any object, usually distant, chosen as a mark. Also **roving mark.** [Origin unknown]

row[1] (rō) n. An arrangement or series of persons or things in a continued line; a rank; file; specifically, a line of houses on a street, or the street: Park *Row*; also, a line of plants, trees, etc., in a field or garden. —a long row to hoe A hard task or undertaking. —at the end of one's row Exhausted; also, having used up one's resources. —v.t. To arrange in a row: with *up.* ◆ Homophone: *roe.* [OE *rāw, ræw* line]

row[2] (rō) v.i. 1 To use oars, sweeps, etc., in propelling a boat. —v.t. 2 To propel across the surface of the water with oars, as a boat. 3 To transport by rowing. 4 To be propelled by (a specific number of oars): said of boats. 5 To make use of (oars or rowers), especially in a race. 6 To row against in a race. —n. A trip in a rowboat; also, a turn at the oars, or the distance covered. ◆ Homophone: *roe.* [OE *rōwan*]

row[3] (rou) n. A noisy disturbance or quarrel; dispute; brawl; hence, any disturbance. —v.t. & v.i. To engage in a row or brawl. [Prob. back formation < ROUSE[2] (taken as a pl.)]

row·dy (rou′dē) n. pl. **·dies** One inclined to create disturbances or engage in rows; a rough, quarrelsome person. —adj. **·di·er**, **·di·est** Rough and loud; disorderly. [Origin uncertain] —**row′dy·ish** adj. —**row′dy·ism**, **row′di·ness** n.

row·el (rou′əl) n. 1 A spiked or toothed wheel, as on a spur. 2 The spur so furnished. 3 A hair or silk thread passed through a horse's skin, to facilitate the discharge of pus. —v.t. **·eled** or **·elled**, **·el·ing** or **·el·ling** 1 To prick with a rowel; spur. 2 To attach or apply a rowel to. [< OF *roele* < LL *rotella* little wheel < L *rota* wheel]

ROWEL ON SPUR

row·lock (rō′lok′) n. Brit. A device in which an oar plays and which serves as a point for applying its power to a boat: also called *oarlock.* [Alter. of OARLOCK; infl. by *row*[2]]

ROWLOCK

Rox·an·a (rok·san′ə) A feminine personal name. Also **Rox·y** (rok′sē), Fr. **Rox·ane** (rôk·sàn′). [< Persian, dawn of day]
—**Roxane** In Rostand's *Cyrano de Bergerac*, the heroine.

roy·al (roi′əl) adj. 1 Pertaining to a monarch; kingly. 2 Under the patronage or authority of a king, or connected with a monarchical form of government: the *Royal* Society; a *royal* governor. 3 Like a king; princely; regal. 4 Of superior quality or size: *royal* octavo. 5 Surpassingly pleasant or fine: We had a *royal* time. See synonyms under IMPERIAL, KINGLY. —n. 1 A size of paper, 19 × 24 for writing, 20 × 25 for printing. 2 *Naut.* A sail next above the topgallant, used in a

light breeze. [< F < L *regalis* kingly < *rex* king. Doublet of REGAL.] —**roy′al·ly** adv.

royal blue 1 Originally, the color of smalt, or cobalt blue; also, Prussian blue. 2 A more modern, brilliant blue; a reddish blue.

royal flush See under FLUSH.

roy·al·ism (roi′əl·iz′əm) n. Adherence to the principles or cause of royalty.

roy·al·ist (roi′əl·ist) n. A supporter of a royal dynasty. —adj. Supporting a royal house; pertaining to royalists: also **roy′al·is′tic.**

Roy·al·ist (roi′əl·ist) n. 1 In English history, a Cavalier or adherent of King Charles I, as against the Parliament, in the middle of the 17th century. 2 In French history, a supporter of the Bourbon or Orléans claims to the throne since 1793. 3 In the American Revolution, a supporter of the king; Loyalist; Tory.

royal purple 1 A very deep violet color verging toward blue. 2 Originally, a rich crimson.

royal tine The tine of an antler projecting away from or above the bez tine: also called *trez tine.* For illustration see ANTLER.

royal touch The touch of a reigning monarch once believed to cure scrofula (king's evil).

roy·al·ty (roi′əl·tē) n. pl. **·ties** 1 Royal rank, birth, or lineage; kingly nature or quality; kingliness; regal authority; sovereignty. 2 A royal personage; royal persons collectively. 3 A share of proceeds paid to a proprietor, author, or inventor, by those doing business under some right belonging to him. 4 A tax or seigniorage paid to the crown on the produce of royal mines, or on gold and silver coinage. 5 A royal possession or domain; hence, domain or province in general. [< OF *roialté*]

-rrhagia combining form Pathol. A morbid or violent discharge or flow; an eruption: *metrorrhagia*: also spelled **-rhagia.** Also **-rrhage, rrhagy.** Corresponding adjectives are formed in -**rrhagic.** [< Gk. < *rrhag-*, root of *rrhēgnynai* burst]

-rrhaphy combining form A sewing together; a suture: *neurorrhaphy*, the suturing of a nerve. Also spelled **-rhaphy.** [< Gk. *rrhaphē* a seam]

-rrhea combining form Pathol. An abnormal or excessive flow or discharge: *diarrhea*: also spelled **-rhea, -rhoea.** Also **-rrhoea.** [< Gk. *-rrhoia* < *rhein* flow]

rub (rub) v. **rubbed**, **rub·bing** v.t. 1 To move or pass over the surface of with pressure and friction. 2 To cause (something) to move or pass with friction; scrape; grate. 3 To cause to become frayed, worn, or sore from friction: This collar *rubs* my neck. 4 To clean, shine, burnish, etc., by means of pressure and friction, or by means of a substance applied thus. 5 To apply or spread with pressure and friction: to *rub* polish on a table. 6 To force by rubbing: with *in* or *into*: to *rub* oil into wood. 7 To remove or erase by friction: with *off* or *out.* —v.i. 8 To move along a surface with friction; scrape. 9 To exert pressure and friction. 10 To become frayed, worn, or sore from friction; chafe. 11 To undergo rubbing or removal by rubbing: with *off, out,* etc. —to rub it in *Slang* To harp on someone's errors, faults, etc. —to rub out *Slang* To kill. —to rub the wrong way *Slang* To irritate; annoy. See synonyms under WEAR. Compare FRICTION. —n. 1 A subjection to frictional pressure; rubbing: Give it a *rub.* 2 That which renders progress difficult; a hindrance or a doubt: There's the *rub.* 3 Something that rubs or is rough to the feelings; a sarcasm: a *rub* in debate. 4 A roughness or unevenness of surface, quality, or character. [ME *rubben*, prob. < LG. Cf. G *reiben.*]

rub-a-dub (rub′ə-dub′) n. The sound of a drum when beaten; hence, any clatter. [Imit.]

ru·bái·yát (rōō′bī·yät′, -bē-) n. pl. 1 In Persian poetry, four-lined stanzas; quatrains. 2 Hence, **Rubáiyát**, a poem by Omar Khayyám and an English translation of it by Edward FitzGerald. [< Arabic *rubā′iyāt*, pl. of *rubā′iyah* quatrain, fem. of *rubā′i* fourfold < *rubā* four]

ru·basse (rōō·bas′, -bäs′) n. A crystalline variety of quartz stained a ruby red by spangles of hematite. Also **ru·bace′.** [< F *rubace* < *rubi.* See RUBY.]

ru·ba·to (rōō·bä′tō) adj. Music Literally, robbed; noting the lengthening of one note at the expense of another. —n. pl. **·tos** A rubato modification. [< Ital.]

rub·ber[1] (rub′ər) n. 1 A tenacious, elastic material obtained by coagulating the milky latex of certain tropical plants, especially the tree *Hevea brasiliensis.* When purified, the crude rubber or caoutchouc is a white polymerized isoprene; it is insoluble in water or alcohol, and for commercial use is mixed with various vulcanizing agents, fillers, and pigments, then heated and molded into the desired form. 2 Anything used for rubbing, erasing, polishing, etc. 3 One who or that which rubs. 4 An article made of rubber, as an elastic band or an overshoe. —adj. Made of rubber. [< RUB] —**rub′ber·y** adj.

rub·ber[2] (rub′ər) n. In bridge, whist, and other card games, a series of two or three games played by the same partners against the same adversaries, terminated when one side has won two games; also, the odd game which breaks a tie between the players.

rub·ber·ize (rub′ər·īz) v.t. **·ized**, **·iz·ing** To coat, impregnate, or cover, as silk, with a preparation of rubber.

rub·ber·neck (rub′ər·nek′) n. U.S. Slang One who cranes his neck in order to see something; a sightseer; tourist. —v.i. To stretch or crane one's neck; gape.

rubber plant 1 Any of several plants yielding rubber. 2 An East Indian tree of the mulberry family (*Ficus elastica*) having large, glossy, leathery leaves: much cultivated as an ornamental house plant.

rub·ber-stamp (rub′ər·stamp′) v.t. 1 To endorse, initial, or approve with the mark made by a rubber stamping device. 2 Colloq. To pass or approve as a matter of course or routine.

rub·bish (rub′ish) n. Waste refuse, or broken matter; trash. [Origin unknown]

rub·bish·y (rub′ish·ē) adj. Worthless; without value.

rub·ble (rub′əl) n. 1 Rough, irregular pieces of broken stone. 2 The debris to which buildings of brick, stone, etc., have been reduced by a violent action, such as earthquake or bombing. 3 (also rōō′bəl) a In quarrying, the weathered or friable surface layer of rock. b Rough pieces of stone for use in construction, especially in residences. 4 Water-worn stones. 5 Rubblework. [Origin uncertain. Prob. related to RUBBISH.]

rub·ble·work (rub′əl·wûrk′) n. Masonry composed of irregular or broken stone, or fragments of stone mingled with cement or clay.

rub-down (rub′doun′) n. A massage.

rube (rōōb) n. Slang A countryman; farmer; rustic. [Abbreviation of REUBEN]

ru·be·fa·cient (rōō′bə·fā′shənt) adj. Causing redness, as of the skin. —n. A medicament for producing irritation of the skin. [< L *rubefaciens, -entis* < *rubefacere* redden < *rubeus* red + *facere* make] —**ru′be·fa′cience** n. —**ru′be·fac′tion** (-fak′shən) n.

ru·bel·la (rōō·bel′ə) n. Pathol. A contagious eruptive fever intermediate between scarlatina and measles: also called *German measles.* [< NL, neut. pl. of L *rubellus* reddish, dim. of *ruber* red]

ru·bel·lite (rōō′bə·līt) n. A red, usually transparent, tourmaline: used as a gem. [< L *rubellus.* See RUBELLA.]

ru·be·o·la (rōō·bē′ə·lə) n. Pathol. 1 Measles. 2 Rubella. [< NL, neut. pl. dim. of L *rubeus* red] —**ru·be′o·lar** adj.

ru·bes·cent (rōō·bes′ənt) adj. Becoming red; reddening. [< L *rubescens, -entis*, ppr. of *rubescere* grow red, inceptive of *rubere* < *rubeus* red] —**ru·bes′cence** n.

ru·bi·cund (rōō′bə·kənd) adj. Red, or inclined to redness; rosy. [< L *rubicundus* red] —**ru′bi·cun′di·ty** n.

ru·big·i·nous (rōō·bij′ə·nəs) adj. Having a rusty or brownish-red color: *rubiginous* plants. Also **ru·big′i·nose** (-nōs). [< LL *rubiginosus* < L *rubigo, rubiginis* rust]

ru·bi·go (rōō·bī′gō, -bē′-) n. Red iron oxide, used as a polishing powder and pigment. [< L, rust]

ru·bi·ous (rōō′bē-əs) *adj.* Red; ruby-colored. [< RUBY]

ru·ble (rōō′bəl) *n.* The Russian monetary unit containing 100 kopecks, and equivalent to one tenth of a chervonets: also spelled *rouble.* [< Russian *rubl*]

ru·bric (rōō′brik) *n.* **1** That exceptional part of an early manuscript or a book that appears in red, or in some distinctive type: once used to indicate initial letters, caption words, headings, etc. **2** The heading or title of a statute or of a section in a code of law, formerly written in red. **3** *Eccl.* A direction or rule printed in devotional or liturgical office, as in a prayer book, missal, or breviary; also, such rules collectively. **4** A division, group, or category. **5** The color red. **6** *Obs.* Red ochre or chalk; reddle. **7** Any direction or rule of conduct. **8** A distinguishing flourish or mark after a person's signature. —*adj.* **1** Red or reddish. **2** Written or printed in red. —*v.t.* ·**bricked,** ·**brick·ing** *Rare* To rubricate. [< OF *rubrique* < L *rubrica* red earth < *ruber* red] —**ru′bri·cal** *adj.* —**ru′bri·cal·ly** *adv.*

ru·bri·cate (rōō′brə·kāt) *v.t.* ·**cat·ed,** ·**cat·ing 1** To mark or tint with red; illuminate with red, as a book. **2** To furnish with a rubric or rubrics; arrange in permanent form. —*adj.* Marked, written, or printed in red. [< L *rubricatus,* pp. of *rubricare* redden < *rubrica.* See RUBRIC.] —**ru·bri·ca′tion** *n.* —**ru′bri·ca′tor** *n.*

ru·bri·cian (rōō·brish′ən) *n.* One versed in the knowledge of, or punctiliously adhering to, rubric or rubrics.

ru·by (rōō′bē) *n. pl.* ·**bies 1** A red variety of corundum including specimens of great value as gemstones. **2** An ornament or a watchmaker's jewel fashioned of ruby. **3** A rich red color like that of a ruby. **4** Something like a ruby in color, as red wine or a carbuncle. **5** In England, a size of type (5½ points): equivalent to the American *agate.* —*adj.* Pertaining to or like a ruby; being of a rich crimson: *ruby* lips. —*v.t.* ·**bied,** ·**by·ing** To redden; tint with the color of a ruby. [< OF *rubi* < L *rubeus* red]

ru·by-crowned kinglet (rōō′bē·kround′) See under KINGLET.

ruche (rōōsh) *n.* A quilted or ruffled strip of fine fabric, worn about the neck or wrists of a woman's costume: also spelled *rouche.* [< F, beehive < Med. L *rusca* tree bark, ? < Celtic]

ruch·ing (rōō′shing) *n.* Material for ruches; ruches collectively.

ruck¹ (ruk) *n.* The common herd or run; a crowd; also, trash; rubbish. [< Scand. Cf. Norw. *ruka* heap, crowd.]

ruck² (ruk) *v.t. & v.i.* **1** To wrinkle, rumple, crease, etc. **2** To annoy; ruffle: usually with *up.* —*n.* A wrinkle, crease, or ridge, as in cloth or paper; a wrinkled place. [< ON *hrukka* wrinkle]

ruck·sack (ruk′sak′, rŏŏk′-) *n.* A canvas knapsack. [< G, lit., back sack]

ruck·us (ruk′əs) *n. U.S. Slang* An uproar; commotion; rumpus. [Prob. blend of RUMPUS and RUCTION]

rud·der (rud′ər) *n.* **1** *Naut.* A broad, flat device hinged vertically at the stern of a vessel to direct its course. **2** Anything that guides or directs a course. **3** *Aeron.* A hinged or pivoted surface, used to control the position of an aircraft about its vertical axis. [OE *rōthor* oar, scull] —**rud′der·less** *adj.*

RUDDER
A. Sailboat *B.* Motorboat.
r. Rudder
s. Screw.

rudder fish Any of various fishes that follow vessels, as the pilot fish, etc.

rudder stock The vertical shaft to which the rudder of a ship or boat is attached, having at its upper portion a yoke (the **rudder cross-head**) or tiller by which it may be turned. Also **rudder post.**

rud·dle (rud′l) *n.* A variety of red ocherous iron ore; reddle. —*v.t.* ·**dled,** ·**dling** To color or stain with red ocher. Also spelled *raddle.* [OE *rudu* red color]

rud·dle·man (rud′l·mən) *n. pl.* ·**men** (-mən) A reddleman.

rud·dock (rud′ək) *n.* The European robin. [OE *rudduc* robin < *rudu* red color]

rud·dy (rud′ə) *adj.* ·**di·er,** ·**di·est 1** Tinged with red. **2** Having a healthy glow; rosy: a *ruddy* complexion. See synonyms under FRESH. [OE *rudig*] —**rud′di·ly** *adv.* —**rud′di·ness** *n.*

ruddy duck A small North American duck (*Erismatura jamaicensis rubida*) having the tail feathers stiffened with narrow webs. The adult male is bright chestnut-reddish above. Also called *paddywhack.*

rude (rōōd) *adj.* **rud·er, rud·est 1** Rough or abrupt; severe or tempestuous; offensively blunt or uncivil; impudent. **2** Characterized by lack of polish or refinement; uncultivated; uncouth. **3** Unskilfully made or done; lacking in skill or training; crude; rough: *rude* workmanship. **4** Characterized by robust vigor; strong: *rude* health. **5** Barbarous; savage. **6** Humble; lowly; rustic. See synonyms under BARBAROUS, BLUFF, IMPUDENT, ROUGH, RUSTIC, VULGAR. ◆ Homophone: *rood.* [< OF < L *rudis* rough] —**rude′ly** *adv.*

rude·ness (rōōd′nis) *n.* **1** The state or quality of being rude. **2** A rude action. See synonyms under IMPUDENCE.

ru·di·ment (rōō′də·mənt) *n.* **1** A first principle, step, stage, or condition. **2** That which is as yet undeveloped or only partially developed. **3** *Biol.* **a** Something in a first, embryonic, incomplete, or early stage that may develop by growth; a germ. **b** A part, organ, or other structure that has become aborted or stunted and will always be undeveloped; a vestige; vestigial part. [< L *rudiment* first attempt < *rudis* rough]

ru·di·men·ta·ry (rōō′də·men′tər·ē) *adj.* **1** Pertaining to or of the nature of a rudiment: *rudimentary* knowledge. **2** Being or remaining in an imperfectly developed state; germinal; undeveloped; abortive. Also **ru′di·men′tal.** —**ru′di·men′ta·ri·ly** *adv.* —**ru′di·men′ta·ri·ness** *n.*

—**Rudolf I,** 1218–91, Holy Roman Emperor 1273–91; founded the Hapsburg dynasty.

—**Rudolf II,** 1552–1612, Holy Roman Emperor 1576–1612; persecuted Protestants.

—**Rudolf of Hapsburg,** 1858–89, crown prince of Austria; son of Francis Joseph; committed suicide.

rue (rōō) *v.* **rued, ru·ing** *v.t.* To feel sorrow or remorse for; regret extremely. —*v.i.* To feel sorrow or remorse; be regretful. See synonyms under MOURN. —*n.* **1** Sorrowful remembrance; regret. **2** *Scot.* Repentance. [OE *hrēowan* be sorry] —**ru′er** *n.*

rue·ful (rōō′fəl) *adj.* **1** Feeling or causing sorrow, regret, or pity; deplorable; sorrowful. **2** Expressing sorrow or pity. —**rue′ful·ly** *adv.* —**rue′ful·ness** *n.*

ru·fes·cent (rōō·fes′ənt) *adj.* Inclining to reddishness; somewhat reddish or rufous. [< L *rufescens, -entis,* ppr. of *rufescere* redden < *rufus* red] —**ru·fes′cence** *n.*

ruff¹ (ruf) *n.* **1** A pleated, round, heavily starched collar popular in the 16th century. **2** Ruffle¹ (def. 1). **3** A natural collar of projecting feathers or hair around the neck of a bird or mammal. **4** An Old World sandpiper (*Philomachus pugnax*) of which the male in the breeding season has an erectile frill of elongated feathers about the neck. The female is called a *reeve.* —*v.i.* To become ruffled; stand out like a ruff. ◆ Homophone: *rough.* [Short for RUFFLE¹]

RUFF
17th century.

ruff² (ruf) *n.* **1** The playing of a trump upon another suit when one has no cards of that suit. **2** An old game, the predecessor of whist. —*v.t. & v.i.* To trump when unable to follow suit. ◆ Homophone: *rough.* [< OF *roffle, rouffle, ronfle,* aphetic alter. of *triomphe* triumph. Cf. Ital. *ronfa* a game at cards < *trionfo* triumph. Related to TRUMP¹.]

ruffed (ruft) *adj.* Having a ruff, ruffle, or frill; ruffled.

ruf·fi·an (ruf′ē·ən, ruf′yən) *n.* A lawless, brutal, cruel fellow; a rough; one ready for or given to riotous, cruel, or murderous deeds. —*adj.* Lawlessly or recklessly brutal or cruel. [< F *rufian* < Ital. *rufiano* pimp, ? < OHG *ruf* dirty] —**ruf′fi·an·ism** *n.* —**ruf′fi·an·ly** *adj.*

ruf·fle¹ (ruf′əl) *n.* **1** A pleated strip; frill, as for trim or ornament; also, anything resembling this: also **ruff. 2** A temporary discomposure. **3** A ripple. —*v.* ·**fled,** ·**fling** *v.t.* **1** To disturb or destroy the smoothness or regularity of: The wind *ruffles* the lake. **2** To draw into folds or ruffles; gather. **3** To furnish with ruffles. **4** To erect (the feathers) in a ruff, as a bird when frightened. **5** To disturb or irritate; upset. **6 a** To riffle (the pages of a book). **b** To shuffle (cards). —*v.i.* **7** To be or become rumpled or disordered. **8** To become disturbed or irritated. [ME *ruffelen.* Cf. LG *ruffelen* rumple, ON *hrufla* scratch.]

ruf·fle² (ruf′əl) *n.* A low, continuous beat of a drum, not as loud as a roll: also **ruff.** —*v.t.* ·**fled,** ·**fling** To beat a ruffle upon, as a drum. [< earlier *ruff;* imit.]

ruf·fle³ (ruf′əl) *v.t.* ·**fled,** ·**fling** To act in a rough or turbulent manner; swagger; bluster. [? Special use of RUFFLE²] —**ruf′fler** *n.*

ru·fous (rōō′fəs) *adj.* Dull-red; rust-colored. [< L *rufus* red]

rug (rug) *n.* **1** A heavy textile fabric, made in one piece, to cover a portion of a floor. **2** A covering made from the skins of animals dressed with the hair or wool on. **3** A heavy coverlet or lap robe. [< Scand. Cf. Norw. *rugga* coarse coverlet, *skinrugga* skin rug, ON *rögg* long, rough fleece.]

ru·ga (rōō′gə) *n. pl.* ·**gae** (-jē) A fold, wrinkle, or crease. [< L]

ru·gate (rōō′gāt, -git) *adj.* Covered with or having rugae; corrugated; wrinkled. [< L *rugatus,* pp. of *rugare* wrinkle < *ruga* a wrinkle]

Rugby football A form of football played between two teams of fifteen men each, in which the ball is propelled toward the opponents' goal by kicking or carrying, but in which no player of the side in possession of the ball may be ahead of the ball while it is in play.

rug·ged (rug′id) *adj.* **1** Having a surface full of abrupt inequalities; broken into irregular points or crags; steep and rocky; rough; uneven. **2** Shaggy; unkempt; disordered; ragged. **3** Rough in temper, character, or action; harsh; stern. **4** Having strongly marked features; wrinkled; frowning; furrowed. **5** Lacking culture or refinement; rude. **6** Rough to the ear; grating. **7** Robust; sturdy. **8** Tempestuous; stormy. See synonyms under FIRM, ROUGH. [< Scand. Cf. Sw. *rugga* roughen. Prob. related to RUG¹.] —**rug′ged·ly** *adv.* —**rug′ged·ness** *n.*

ru·gose (rōō′gōs) *adj.* **1** Covered with or full of rugae or wrinkles; corrugate; rugate. **2** *Bot.* Having a rough or wrinkled surface, as some strongly veined leaves. Also **ru′gous.** [< L *rugosus* < *ruga* wrinkle] —**ru·gos·i·ty** (rōō·gos′ə·tē) *n.*

ru·in (rōō′in) *n.* **1** Total destruction of value or usefulness; in morals, the loss of character, chastity, or honor; seduction; corruption. **2** That which remains of something demolished, destroyed, or decayed: often in the plural. **3** A condition of desolation or degradation. **4** That which causes destruction, downfall, decay, or injury: Gambling was his *ruin.* **5** The act of falling down; collapse. —*v.t.* **1** To bring to ruin; destroy; demolish. **2** To bring to bankruptcy or poverty. **3** To deprive of chastity; seduce. —*v.i.* **4** To fall into ruin. See synonyms under ABUSE, DEMOLISH. [< OF *ruine* < L *ruina* < *ruere* fall] —**ru′in·a·ble** *adj.* —**ru′in·er** *n.*

Synonyms (noun): collapse, decay, defeat, desolation, destruction, discomfiture, downfall, fall, overthrow, perdition, subversion, undoing, wreck. See ADVERSITY, MISFORTUNE. *Antonyms:* conservation, preservation, prosperity, recovery, regeneration, reparation, success.

ru·in·a·tion (rōō′in·ā′shən) *n.* **1** The act of ruining. **2** The state of being ruined. **3** Something that ruins.

ru·ined (rōō′ind) *adj.* **1** Destroyed; ravaged; in ruins. **2** Bankrupt.

ru·in·ous (rōō′in·əs) *adj.* **1** Causing or tending to ruin. **2** Falling to ruin; decayed; dilapidated; ruined. See synonyms under PERNICIOUS. [< OF *ruineux* < L *ruinosus*] —**ru′in-**

ous·ly *adv.* — **ru′in·ous·ness** *n.*

rule (rŏŏl) *n.* **1** Controlling power, or its possession and exercise; government; dominion; authority. **2** A method or principle of action; common or regular course of procedure, or customary standard or form: I make early rising my *rule.* **3** An authoritative direction or enactment; a concise direction respecting the doing or method of doing something, as one of the regulations of a legislative or deliberative body for the government of its own proceedings, or a regulation to be observed in playing a given game. **4** A regulation for the conduct of religious services or for the government of life; specifically, the body of directions laid down by or for a religious order: the *rule* of St. Francis. **5** A prescribed form, method, or set of instructions for solving a given class of mathematical problems. **6** An established usage or law, fixing the form or use of words or the construction of sentences: a *rule* for forming the plural. **7** What belongs to the ordinary course of events or condition of things: In some communities illiteracy is the *rule.* **8** Regular or proper method; propriety, as of conduct; regularity. **9** *Law* A formal regulation prescribed by authority touching a certain matter: a *rule* of court; also, a judicial decision on some motion or special application: a *rule* to show cause. A **rule of court** is an order made by a court, and is either *general,* as for regulating the practice of the court, or *special,* as an order sending a case before a referee. **10** A straight-edged instrument for use in measuring, or as a guide in drawing lines; a ruler, usually marked in inches, feet, etc. **11** *Printing* A strip of type-high metal for handling type or for printing a rule or line. **12** A ruled line. — **as a rule** Ordinarily; usually. — *v.* **ruled, rul·ing** *v.t.* **1** To have authority or control over; govern. **2** To influence greatly; dominate: Greed has *ruled* his life. **3** To decide or determine judicially or authoritatively. **4** To restrain; keep in check: *Rule* your temper. **5** To mark with straight, parallel lines. **6** To make (such a line) with or as with a ruler. — *v.i.* **7** To have authority or control; be in command. **8** To maintain a standard of rates: Prices *ruled* high. **9** To form and express a decision: The judge *ruled* on that point. — **to rule out 1** To dismiss from consideration: They *ruled* out a strike. **2** To preclude; prevent. See synonyms under GOVERN, REGULATE. [< OF *reule* < L *regula* ruler, rule < *regere* lead straight, direct. Doublet of RAIL¹.] — **rul′a·ble** *adj.*
   Synonyms (noun): canon, formula, guide, maxim, method, order, regulation, standard. See HABIT, LAW, STICK, SYSTEM.

rule of thumb 1 Measurement by the thumb. **2** Roughly practical rather than scientifically accurate measure.

rul·er (rŏŏ′lər) *n.* **1** One who rules or governs, as a sovereign. **2** A straight-edged strip for guiding a marking implement; a rule; a ruling machine. **3** One who rules lines, as with a ruling machine. See synonyms under CHIEF.

rul·ing (rŏŏ′ling) *adj.* Exercising dominion; controlling; predominant. — *n.* **1** The act of one who rules or governs. **2** A decision, as of a judge or presiding officer. **3** The act of making ruled lines, or the lines so made.

rum (rum) *n.* **1** An alcoholic liquor distilled from fermented molasses or cane juice. **2** Any alcoholic liquor. [Short for obs. *rumbullion* rum, alter. of *Rambouillet,* town in France]

Ru·ma·ni·a (rŏŏ·mā′nē·ə, -mān′yə), **People's Republic of** A state in SE Europe; 91,671 square miles; capital, Bucharest: also *Romania, Roumania:* Rumanian *România.*

rum·ba (rum′bə, *Sp.* rŏŏm′bä) *n.* **1** A frenzied dance formerly performed by Cuban Negroes. **2** A modern dance based on this. Also spelled *rhumba.* [< Sp.]

rum·ble (rum′bəl) *v.* **bled, ·bling** *v.i.* **1** To make a low, heavy, rolling sound, as thunder. **2** To move or proceed with such a sound. — *v.t.* **3** To cause to make a low, heavy, rolling sound. **4** To utter with such a sound. **5** To subject to the action of a tumbling box. — *n.* **1** A continuous low, heavy, rolling sound; a muffled roar. **2** A tumbling box:

also **rum′bler. 3** A seat or baggage compartment in the rear of a carriage. **4** A folding seat in the back of a coupé or roadster: in full, **rumble seat. 5** *U.S. Slang* A fight involving a group, usually deliberately provoked. [ME *romblen* < MDu. *rommelen*] — **rum′bler** *n.* — **rum′bling·ly** *adv.*

ru·men (rŏŏ′men) *n. pl.* **ru·mi·na** (rŏŏ′mə·nə) **1** The first stomach of a ruminant. **2** The cud of a ruminant. [< L, throat]

ru·mi·nant (rŏŏ′mə·nənt) *n.* One of a division (*Ruminantia*) of even-toed ungulates, as a deer, antelope, sheep, goat, or cow, that has a stomach with four complete cavities: the rumen, the reticulum, the manyplies (omasum, psalterium), and the reed or abomasum, the food entering the first being returned to the mouth, rechewed and swallowed, and digested in the other compartments. — *adj.* **1** Chewing the cud. **2** Of or pertaining to the *Ruminantia.* **3** Meditative or contemplative; thoughtful; drowsily quiet. [< L *ruminans, -antis,* ppr. of *ruminare* ruminate < *rumen* gullet]

ru·mi·nate (rŏŏ′mə·nāt) *v.t. & v.i.* **·nat·ed, ·nat·ing 1** To chew (food previously swallowed and regurgitated) over again; chew (the cud). **2** To meditate or reflect (upon); ponder. See synonyms under MUSE. — *adj.* Perforated or mottled, as the albumen of a betelnut or nutmeg: also **ru′mi·nat′ed.** [< L *ruminatus,* pp. of *ruminare.* See RUMINANT.] — **ru′mi·nat′ing·ly** *adv.* — **ru′mi·na′tive** *adj.* — **ru′mi·na′tive·ly** *adv.* — **ru′mi·na′tor** *n.*

ru·mi·na·tion (rŏŏ′mə·nā′shən) *n.* **1** The act, process, or characteristic of chewing the cud. **2** The act of ruminating mentally. **3** The regurgitation of imperfectly digested food. See synonyms under REFLECTION.

rum·mage (rum′ij) *v.* **·maged, ·mag·ing** *v.t.* **1** To search through (a place, box, etc.) by turning over and disarranging the contents; ransack. **2** To find or bring out by searching: with *out* or *up.* — *v.i.* **3** To make a thorough search. — *n.* **1** Any act of rummaging; especially, disarranging things by searching thoroughly. **2** An upheaval or stirring up; bustle. **3** *Obs.* Room in a ship for stowing cargo; also, the arrangement or stowing of the cargo. **4** A rummage sale. [< obs. F *arrumage* place or act of stowage < *arrumer* stow away, ? < *rum* ship's hold < OE *rūm* room] — **rum′mag·er** *n.*

rummage sale 1 A sale of all sorts of second-hand objects gathered up from benevolent givers, to obtain money for some charitable object. **2** A sale of unclaimed articles, or a clearing-out sale prior to restocking.

rum·my (rum′ē) *n.* A card game in which each player in turn draws a card from the talon or the discard pile beside it, and discards another card, the object being to get rid of one's hand in sequences of three cards or more of the same suit. [Origin unknown]

ru·mor (rŏŏ′mər) *n.* **1** Popular report; common gossip; also, reputation. **2** A story circulating without known foundation or authority; an unverified report passing from person to person. **3** *Obs.* A confused sound; confusion; murmur. — *v.t.* To tell or spread as a rumor; report abroad. Also *Brit.* **ru′mour.** [< OF < L, noise]

rump (rump) *n.* **1** The hinder parts or buttocks. **2** The fag-end of anything; an inferior remnant. **3** A legislative group having only a remnant of its former membership and therefore lacking authority because unrepresentative. **4** The piece of beef between aitchbone and loin. [< Scand. Cf. Dan. *rumpl,* ON *rumpr.*]

rum·ple (rum′pəl) *v.t. & v.i.* **·pled, ·pling** To form into creases or folds; wrinkle; ruffle. — *n.* **1** An irregular fold; a rumpled fabric. **2** The condition of being rumpled. [< MDu. *rumpelen*]

rum·pus (rum′pəs) *n. Colloq.* A row; wrangle; to-do. [Origin uncertain]

rumpus room A room for games, informal gatherings, etc.

run (run) *v.* **ran, run, run·ning** *v.i.* **1** To move by rapid steps, faster than walking, in such a manner that both feet are off the ground for a portion of each step. **2** To move rapidly; go

swiftly. **3** To flee; take flight. **4** To make a brief or rapid journey: We *ran* over to Staten Island last night. **5** To make regular trips; ply: This steamer *runs* between New York and Liverpool. **6 a** To take part in a race. **b** To be a candidate or contestant: to *run* for dog-catcher. **7** To finish a race in a specified position: I *ran* a poor last. **8** To move or pass easily: The rope *runs* through the block. **9** To pass continuously and rapidly; elapse: The hours *run* by. **10** To proceed in direction or extent: This road *runs* north. **11** To move in or as in a stream; flow. **12** To become liquid and flow, as wax; also, to spread or mingle confusedly, as colors when wet. **13** To move or pass inadvertently: The ship *ran* aground. **14** To pass into a specified condition: to *run* to seed. **15** To come undone; unravel, as a fabric. **16** To give forth a discharge or flow; suppurate. **17** To leak. **18** To continue or proceed without restraint: The conversation *ran* on and on. **19** To be in operation; be operative; work: Will the engine *run*? **20** To continue in existence or effect; extend in time: Genius *runs* in her family. **21** To be reported or expressed: The story *runs* as follows. **22** To migrate, as salmon from the sea to spawn. **23** To occur or return to the mind: An idea *ran* through his head. **24** To occur with specified variation of size, quality, etc.: The corn is *running* small this year. **25** To be performed or repeated in continuous succession: The play *ran* for forty nights. **26** To make a rapid succession of demands for payment, as on a bank. **27** To continue unexpired or unpaid; as a debt; become payable. — *v.t.* **28** To run or proceed along, as a route or path. **29** To make one's way over, through, or past: to *run* rapids. **30** To perform or accomplish by or as by running: to *run* a race or an errand. **31** To compete against in or as in a race. **32** To enter (a horse) for a race. **33** To present and support as a candidate. **34** To hunt or chase, as game. **35** To bring to a specified condition by or as by running: to *run* oneself out of breath. **36** To drive or force: with *out of, off, into, through,* etc. **37** To cause (a vessel) to move rapidly or freely: They *ran* the ship into port. **38** To move (the eye, hand, etc.) quickly or lightly: He *ran* his hand over the table. **39** To cause to move, slide, etc., as into a specified position: to *run* up a flag. **40** To cause to go or ply: to *run* a train between New York and Washington. **41** To transport or convey in a vessel or vehicle. **42** To smuggle. **43** To cause to flow: to *run* water into a pot. **44** To give forth a flow of; emit: Her eyes *ran* tears. **45** To mold, as from melted metal; found. **46** To sew (cloth) in a continuous line, usually by taking a number of stitches with the needle at a time. **47** To maintain or control the motion or operation of. **48** To direct or control; manage; oversee. **49** To allow to continue or mount up, as a bill. **50** In games, to make (a number of points, strokes, etc.) successively. **51** To publish in a magazine or newspaper: to *run* an ad. **52** To mark, set down, or trace, as a boundary line. **53** To suffer from (a fever, etc.). — **to run across** To meet by chance. — **to run down 1** To pursue and overtake, as a fugitive. **2** To strike down while moving. **3** To exhaust, damage, lessen in worth, vigor, etc., as by abuse or overwork. **4** To speak of disparagingly; decry. — **to run in 1** To insert; include. **2** *Printing* To print without a paragraph or break. **3** *Slang* To arrest and place in confinement. — **to run into 1** To meet by chance. **2** To collide with. — **to run off 1** To produce on a typewriter, printing press, etc. **2** To decide (a tied race, game, etc.) by the outcome of another, subsequent race, game, etc. **3** To flee or escape; elope. — **to run out 1** To come to an end; be exhausted, as supplies. — **to run out of** To exhaust one's supply of. — **to run over 1** To ride or drive over; run down. **2** To overflow. **3** To go over or examine hastily or quickly; rehearse. — **to run through 1** To spend wastefully; squander. **2** To stab or pierce. **3** To run over (def. 3). — **to run up** To produce; make hurriedly, as on a sewing machine. — *n.* **1** The act, or an act of running or going rapidly. **2** A running pace: to break into a *run*. **3** Flow; movement; sweep: the *run* of the tide. **4** A distance covered by running. **5** A journey or passage, especially between two points, made by a vessel, train, etc.: the *run* from New York to Albany. **6** A rapid journey or excursion, marked by a brief stay at the destination: to take a *run* into town. **7** A swift stream or brook. **8** A migration of fish, especially to up-river spawning grounds. **9** A grazing or feeding ground for animals or fowl; a range: a sheep *run*. **10** The regular trail or path of certain animals: an elephant *run*. **11** The bower of a bowerbird. **12** The privilege of free use or access: to have the *run* of the place. **13** A runway. **14** *Music* A rapid succession of tones; a roulade. **15** A series or succession. **16** A sequence of three or more playing cards in consecutive order. **17** A trend or tendency: the general *run* of the market. **18** The direction or course (of something): the *run* of the grain of wood. **19** A continuous length (of something): a *run* of pipe. **20** A continuous spell (of some condition): a *run* of luck. **21** A surge of demands made upon a bank or treasury to meet its obligations. **22** Any great sustained demand. **23** A period of continuous performance, occurrence, popularity, etc.: a play with a long *run*. **24** Class or type: the general *run* of readers. **25** A period of operation of a machine or device: an experimental *run*. **26** The output during such a period. **27** A period during which a liquid is allowed to run. **28** The amount of liquid allowed to flow at one time. **29** A measure of yarn (about 1,600 yards). **30** A narrow, lengthwise ravel, as in a sheer stocking. **31** An approach to a target made by a bombing plane. **32** In baseball, a complete circuit of the bases from home plate and back before three outs are made, thus scoring a point. **33** In cricket, an act in which both batsmen successfully run to opposite popping creases, thereby scoring a point. **34** A hunt, especially on horseback; a chase. **35** *Naut.* The after part of a ship's bottom where it narrows off from the floor timbers to the sternpost. **36** *Mining* A vein. **37** *Austral.* A sheep or cattle station. — **dry run** Any practice test; specifically, an approach to a target made by a bombing plane, without dropping bombs. — **in the long run** As the ultimate outcome of any train of circumstances. — **on the run 1** Almost without pausing while doing something else; hastily: to eat *on the run*. **2** In full retreat. **3** While running. — *adj.* **1** Made liquid; melted. **2** Made by a process of melting and casting or molding: *run* metal; *run* butter. **3** Extracted or drained: *run* honey. **4** Smuggled; contraband: *run* liquor. [OE *rinnan* flow]

run·a·bout (run′ə·bout′) *n.* **1** A light, handy, open automobile for ready service. **2** A light, open wagon. **3** A small motorboat.

run·a·round (run′ə·round′) *n.* **1** *Slang* Artful deception; evasion. **2** Run-round. **3** *Printing* Type set narrower than the body of the text, as around illustrations.

run·a·way (run′ə·wā′) *adj.* **1** Escaping or escaped from restraint or control; fugitive. **2** Brought about by running away: a *runaway* marriage. **3** Easily won: said of a horse race; hence, decisive; one-sided. — *n.* **1** One who or that which runs away or flees; a fugitive or deserter; also, a horse of which the driver has lost control. **2** An act of running away: said especially of a horse.

run·dle (run′dəl) *n.* **1** A rung, as of a ladder. **2** Something that rotates about an axis, as the drum of a capstan. [Var. of ROUNDEL]

rund·let[1] (rund′lit) *n.* A small barrel, or the wine it contains, about 18 wine gallons. Also *runlet*. [< OF *rondelet*. See ROUNDELAY.]

rund·let[2] (rund′lit) See RUNLET[1].

run·down (run′doun′) *adj.* **1** Debilitated; physically weak; tired out. **2** Dilapidated; shabby. **3** Stopped because not wound: said of a timepiece. — *n.* (run′doun′). **1** A summary; resumé. **2** In baseball, a play in which a base runner is put out when trapped between two bases.

rune (rōōn) *n.* **1** A character of the primitive runic alphabet. **2** A Finnish poem or one of its cantos. **3** *pl.* Old Norse lore expressed, or considered as if expressed, in runes; hence, early rimes or poetry in general. **4** Any obscure or mystic song, poem, verse, or saying; a mystery. [< ON

rūn mystery, rune] —**ru′nic** *adj.*

RUNES
Tomb inscription, Sweden, eleventh century.

rung[1] (rung) *n.* **1** A round crosspiece of a ladder or chair; a round; also, a spoke of a wheel. **2** *Naut.* **a** One of the handles on the rim of a ship's tiller. **b** A floor timber of a ship. **3** *Scot. & Brit. Dial.* A heavy club or staff; cudgel. [OE *hrung* crossbar]

rung[2] (rung) Past participle of RING[2].

ru·nic alphabet (rōō′nik) An old Germanic alphabet, probably originating in both the Latin and Greek, consisting originally of 24 characters, or runes, later reduced to 16 in Scandinavian writings. The earliest inscriptions in this alphabet are of the second or third century A.D. In England it was still in occasional use at the end of the Old English period, and was finally completely replaced by the Roman alphabet through the spread of Christian writings. Also called *futhark*.

runic staff A clog almanac.

run·in (run′in′) *n.* **1** A quarrel; bicker. **2** *Printing* Inserted or added matter. — *adj.* (run′in′) *Printing* That is inserted or added.

run·let (run′lit) *n.* A little stream; rivulet; a runnel. Also *rundlet*. See synonyms under STREAM.

run·nel (run′əl) *n.* A streamlet; brooklet; rivulet. [OE *rynel* < *rinnan* run]

run·ner (run′ər) *n.* **1** One who or that which runs; especially, one who runs a race; also, a fugitive or deserter. **2** One who operates or manages anything; especially, the driver of a locomotive. **3** One who runs errands or goes about on any kind of business; a messenger, as for a bank; specifically, one who drums up or solicits patronage or business, as for a hotel. **4** That part on which an object runs or slides: the *runner* of a skate. **5** *Mech.* A device to assist sliding motion. **6** A slender fish (*Elegatis bipinnulatus*) of warm seas with single dorsal and anal pinnules; also, the jurel of the Atlantic coast of America. **7** A cursorial bird; the water rail. **8** *Bot.* **a** A slender, procumbent stem disposed to root at the end and nodes, as in strawberry; also, sometimes, the plant itself. **b** Any of various twining plants: the scarlet *runner*. **9** A smuggler. **10** A blacksnake. **11** A long, narrow rug or carpeting, used in hallways, etc. **12** A narrow strip of cloth, usually of fine quality, used on tables, dressers, etc.

run·ner-up (run′ər·up′) *n.* A contestant or team finishing in second place.

run·ning (run′ing) *adj.* **1** Such as runs: said specifically of horses inclined or trained to a running gait rather than to pacing or trotting. **2** Following one another without intermission; successive: used with words expressing periods of time: He talked for three hours *running*. **3** Continuous; repeated: said of a design: a *running* ornament, a *running* molding, etc. **4** Kept up continuously; also, passing; cursory: *running* comments, a *running* glance. **5** Characterized by easy flowing curves; cursive: a *running* hand. **6** Discharging, as pus from a sore. — *n.* **1** The act or movement of one who or that which runs: a horse trained for fast *running*. **2** That which runs or flows; the amount or quantity that runs. **3** A discharge, as from a sore. **4** Ability or power to run. **5** Competition; race; rivalry: He's out of the *running*. **6** Climbing; sending out runners, as certain plants.

running board A footboard on the side of a locomotive, street car, automobile, etc.

running expenses Daily expenses.

running fits Fright disease.

running hand Writing done with a continuous easy motion without lifting the pen from the paper and usually having the letters slanted forward.

running knot A knot made so as to slip along a noose and tighten when pulled upon.

running lights The sidelights of a vessel.

running mate 1 A horse that is teammate for another; also, a horse entered to set the pace for another entered to run in a horse race. **2** The candidate for the lesser of two offices closely

linked by constitutional provisions, as the vice-presidency with the presidency.

run-off (run′ôf′, -of′) *n.* **1** That part of the rainfall in a particular area which is not absorbed directly by the soil but is drained off in rills or streams. **2** A special contest held to break a tie.

run-of-the-mill (run′əv·thə·mil′) See MILL-RUN.

run-on line Enjambement.

runt (runt) *n.* **1** An unusually small, weak, or stunted animal; also, the smallest and weakest of a litter. **2** A dwarf. **3** *Scot.* An old ox or cow; a withered old man or hag. **4** *Scot. & Brit. Dial.* A stump of a tree or shrub; also, the stem or stalk of a plant. [Origin uncertain] —**runt′i·ness** *n.* —**runt′y** *adj.*

run·way (run′wā′) *n.* **1** A way or path over which something runs. **2** The channel or bed of a stream, or the path over which animals pass to and from their places of feeding or watering. **3** In lumbering, an incline down which logs are slid; a chute. **4** Any track specially laid for wheeled vehicles. Also *run.* **5** *Aeron.* An artificial landing strip for airplanes.

ru·pee (rōō·pē′) *n.* The standard monetary unit of British India: it contains 16 annas. [< Hind. *rupiya* < Skt. *rūpya* silver]

ru·pi·ah (rōō·pē′ä) *n.* The principal Indonesian currency unit.

rup·ture (rup′chər) *n.* **1** The act of breaking apart or the state of being broken apart. **2** Hernia. **3** Breach of peace and concord between individuals or nations. —*v.t. & v.i.* **·tured, ·tur·ing** **1** To break apart; separate into parts. **2** To affect with or suffer a rupture. See synonyms under BREAK, REND. [< F < L *ruptus*, pp. of *rumpere* break] —**rup′tur·a·ble** *adj.*

    Synonyms (noun): blast, breach, break, burst, disruption, fracture. See BREACH, QUARREL[1].

ru·ral (rōōr′əl) *adj.* **1** Pertaining to the country as distinguished from the city or the town; rustic. **2** Pertaining to farming or agriculture. See synonyms under RUSTIC. [< F < L *ruralis* < *rus, ruris* country] —**ru′ral·ism** *n.* —**ru′ral·ist** *n.* —**ru′ral·ly** *adv.* —**ru′ral·ness** *n.*

rural dean Dean (def. 2).

rural free delivery A government service of house-to-house free mail delivery by carrier in rural districts, as distinguished from the general delivery service: in addresses abbreviated *R.F.D.* Often shortened to *R.D.*

ru·ral·i·ty (rōō·ral′ə·tē) *n.* **1** Ruralness. **2** A rural peculiarity. **3** A place in the country.

ru·ral·ize (rōōr′əl·īz) *v.* **·ized, ·iz·ing** *v.t.* To make rural. —*v.i.* To go into or live in the country; rusticate. —**ru′ral·i·za′tion** *n.*

ruse (rōōz) *n.* An action intended to mislead or deceive; a stratagem; trick. See synonyms under ARTIFICE, PRETENSE. [< F < *ruser* dodge, detour, drive back. Related to RUSH[1].]

rush (rush) *v.i.* **1** To move or go swiftly or with violence. **2** To make an attack; charge: with *on* or *upon.* **3** To proceed recklessly or rashly; plunge: with *in* or *into.* —*v.t.* **4** To drive or push with haste or violence; hurry. **5** To do or perform hastily or hurriedly: to *rush* one's work. **6 a** To make a sudden assault upon. **b** To capture by such an assault. **7** *Slang* To seek the favor of with assiduous attentions. **8** In football, to move (the ball) toward the goal of the other team. See synonyms under HUSTLE. —*n.* **1** The act of rushing; a sudden turbulent movement, drive, or onset. **2** A sudden pressing demand; a run: a *rush* on foreign bonds. **3** A sudden exigency; urgent pressure: a *rush* of business. **4** A sudden flocking of people to a new region, especially to an area rumored to be rich in a precious mineral: a gold *rush.* **5** *U.S.* A general contest or scrimmage between students from different classes, as between sophomores and freshmen. **6** In football: **a** An attempt to take the ball through the opposing linemen and toward the goal. **b** Formerly, a player in the rush line: a center *rush.* **7** In motion pictures, the first film prints of a scene or series of scenes, before editing or selection. See synonyms under CAREER. — *adj.* **1** Requiring urgency or haste: a *rush* order. **2**

Characterized by much traffic, business, etc.: the *rush* hours. **3** Denoting a time or function set aside for fraternity or sorority members to meet new students to consider them for membership: *rush* week; a *rush* smoker. [<AF *russher* push, var. of *russer*, OF *ruser*, *reuser* push back, dodge <LL *recusare* push back. See RECUSANT.]

rush–hold·er (rush′hōl′dər) *n.* A candlestick with a clip for supporting a rushlight.

rush hour A time when traffic or business is at its height. — **rush–hour** (rush′our′) *adj.*

rush·ing (rush′ing) *n.* *U.S.* The series of activities in which fraternity and sorority members meet and evaluate new college students wishing to be pledged.

Rush·more (rush′môr), **Mount** A mountain in the Black Hills of western South Dakota, on the side of which are carved gigantic faces of Presidents Washington, Jefferson, Lincoln, Theodore Roosevelt; in **Mount Rushmore National Memorial**; 1,220 acres; established, 1929.

rusine antler An antler having a simple brow tine and a simple fork at the tip of the beam.

rusk (rusk) *n.* **1** A light, sweetened bread or biscuit. **2** Bread or cake that has been crisped and browned in an oven, then often pounded fine to be eaten with milk. [<Sp. *rosca*, twisted loaf of bread]

rus·set (rus′it) *n.* **1** A color formed by combining orange and purple; popularly, any reddish– or yellowish–brown. **2** Russet cloth, clothing, etc.; hence, any coarse homespun cloth or garment; a country dress. **3** Russet leather. **4** A winter apple of greenish color, mottled with brown. — *adj.* **1** Of a reddish– or yellowish–brown color. **2** Made of russet cloth; hence, coarse; homespun; rustic. **3** Finished, but not blacked: said of leather: *russet* shoes. [<OF *rousset*, dim. of *rous* <L *russus* reddish] — **rus′set·y** *adj.*

Rus·sia The largest country in Asia; capital, Moscow; pop. 150,000,000; 6,592,800 square miles. Unified in the 9th century. Russia dissolved into independent dukedoms by 1240; its borders fluctuated through the centuries until the formation of the U.S.S.R. in 1922. In 1991, the Soviet Union dissolved into independent nations to form the Commonwealth of Independent States.

Rus·sian *adj.* Pertaining to Russia, its people, or their language. - *n.* **1** An inhabitant of Russia; especially, one of any of the ethnic Slavic peoples, including the **Great Russians** of the central and northwestern region, the Ukrainians (or **Little Russians**) of the Ukraine and eastern Poland, which group includes also hte Cossacks and Ruthenians, and the **White Russians** of the west, all speaking Indo-European Balto-Slavic languages, such as Russian, Polish, Lithuanian, and Lettish; also, one of any of the peoples of Russia speaking any of the Uralic languages, especially the Finno-Ugric branch; also, one of any of the native peoples of the Caucasus speaking languages unrelated to these others, as Cirassian, Geargian, and the Lesghian group. **2** The language of Russia, belonging to the East Slavic branch of the Balto-Slavic languages, having a separate alphabet including several characters not found in other alphabets.

Russian Soviet Federated Socialist Republic The former constituant republic of the U.S.S.R., occupying 76 per cent of the U.S.S.R. and extending across northern Asia and eastern Europe; abbr. R.S.F.S.R.

Russian dressing Mayonnaise dressing to which chili sauce, pimientos, and chopped pickles have been added.

Russian leather A smooth, well-tanned, high-grade leather of calfskin or light cattle hide, dressed with birch oil and having a characteristic odor.

Russian Revolution See under REVOLUTION.

Russian wolfhound The borzoi.

Rus·so·phile (rus′ə-fīl, -fil) *n.* One who favors Russia, or its principles, policy, or methods.

Rus·so·pho·bi·a (rus′ə-fō′bē-ə) *n.* Fear of the policy or influence of Russia. — **Rus′so·phobe** *n.*

rust (rust) *n.* **1** The reddish or yellow coating

caused on iron and steel by oxidation, as by the action of air and moisture, consisting of ferric hydroxide, $Fe(OH)_3$, and ferric oxide, Fe_2O_3. **2** A film of oxide formed on any metal by corrosion. **3** Any of the parasitic fungi of the order *Uredinales*, living on the tissues of higher plants. **4** The diseases caused by such fungi; incorrectly, any one of several diseases not caused by these fungi. **5** Any coating or accretion formed by a corrosive or degenerative process: *rust* on salted meat. **6** A condition, affection, or tendency that destroys or weakens energy or active qualities: the *rust* of idleness. **7** Any of several shades of reddish–brown, somewhat like the color of rust, but containing more orange. — *v.t.* & *v.i.* **1** To become or cause to become rusty; undergo or cause to undergo oxidation. **2** To contract or cause to contract rust. **3** To become or cause to become weakened or impaired because of inactivity or disuse: to allow one's powers to *rust*. **4** To make or become rust–colored. [OE]

rus·tic (rus′tik) *adj.* **1** Rural; hence, plain; homely: *rustic* garments. **2** Uncultured; rude; awkward: *rustic* manners. **3** Unaffected; artless: *rustic* simplicity. **4** Pertaining to any irregular style of work or decoration appropriate to the country or to work in natural, unpolished wood. — *n.* **1** One who lives in the country; a country person of simple manners or character; also, a coarse or clownish person. **2** Rusticwork. **3** Country dialect. [<F *rustique* <L *rusticus* <*rus* country] — **rus′ti·cal·ly** *adv.*

Synonyms (*adj.*): agricultural, artless, awkward, boorish, bucolic, clownish, coarse, countrified, country, hoydenish, inelegant, outlandish, pastoral, plain, rude, rural, sylvan, uncouth, unpolished, unsophisticated, untaught, verdant. *Rural* refers especially to scenes or objects in the country, considered as the work of nature; *rustic* refers to their effect upon man or to their condition as affected by human agency; as, a *rural* scene; a *rustic* party; a *rustic* lass. We speak, however, of the *rural* population, *rural* simplicity, etc. *Rural* has always a favorable sense; *rustic* often an unfavorable one, as denoting lack of culture and refinement; thus, *rustic* politeness expresses that which is well-meant, but awkward. *Rustic* is, however, often used of a studied simplicity, an artistic rudeness, which is pleasing and perhaps beautiful; as, a *rustic* cottage. *Pastoral* refers to the care of flocks and to the shepherd's life with the pleasing associations suggested by the old poetic ideal of that life; as, *pastoral* poetry. *Bucolic* is kindred to *pastoral*, but is a less elevated term, and sometimes slightly contemptuous. *Antonyms*: accomplished, cultured, elegant, polished, polite, refined, urban, urbane.

rus·tic·i·ty (rus-tis′ə-tē) *n.* *pl.* **·ties** **1** Rustic condition, characters, or manners; simplicity; homeliness; awkwardness. **2** A rustic trait or peculiarity. [<L *rusticitas, -tatis*]

rus·tic·work (rus′tik·wûrk′) *n.* **1** Ashlar masonry, or a method of making it, with rough surfaces, and often with deeply sunk grooves at the joints, to make them conspicuous. **2** Woodwork made of the natural limbs and roots of trees, fancifully arranged.

rus·tle¹ (rus′əl) *v.t.* & *v.i.* **·tled**, **·tling** To fall, move, or cause to move with a quick succession of small, light, rubbing sounds, as dry leaves or sheets of paper. — *n.* A rustling sound. [OE *hruxlan* make a noise. Cf. OE *gehyrstan* murmur.] — **rus′tler** *n.* — **rus′tling** *adj.* — **rus′tling·ly** *adv.*

rus·tle² (rus′əl) *v.t.* & *v.i.* **·tled**, **·tling** **1** *Colloq.* To act with or obtain by energetic or vigorous action. **2** *U.S. Colloq.* To steal (cattle, etc.). [Blend of RUSH and HUSTLE]

rus·tler (rus′lər) *n.* *U.S.* **1** *Slang* Any person who is active, pushing, and bustling in any enterprise. Compare HUSTLER. **2** *Colloq.* **a** A cowboy or ranchman. **b** A cook on a ranch. **c** A cattle or horse thief.

rust·y (rus′tē) *adj.* **rust·i·er**, **rust·i·est** **1** Covered or affected with rust. **2** Consisting of or produced by rust. **3** Having the appearance of rust; having a reddish or yellowish discoloration, as from decomposition: said especially of salted fish or meat that has

become rancid. **4** Impaired by inaction or want of exercise; also, lacking nimbleness; stiff. **5 a** Weakened through neglect of use: My Latin is *rusty*. **b** Having lost skill for want of practice: *rusty* in math. **6** *Biol.* Appearing as if covered with rust; brownish-red. See synonyms under TRITE. [OE *rustig* < *rust* rust] — **rust′i·ly** *adv.* — **rust′i·ness** *n.*

rut¹ (rut) *n.* **1** A sunken track worn by a wheel, as in a road; hence, a groove forming a path for anything. **2** A settled habit or course of procedure; routine. — *v.t.* **rut·ted**, **rut·ting** To wear or make a rut or ruts in. [? Var. of ROUTE]

rut² (rut) *n.* **1** The sexual excitement of various animals, especially deer; estrus; also, the period during which it lasts. **2** A roaring or uproar; especially, the noise made by a rutting stag. — *v.* **rut·ted**, **rut·ting** *v.i.* To be in rut. — *v.t. Rare* To unite with in copulation; cover. [<F <L *rugitus* a roaring, tumult < *rugire* roar] — **rut′ting** *adj.*

ru·ta·ba·ga (roō′tə-bā′gə) *n.* **1** A cultivated plant (*Brassica napobrassica*) allied to the common turnip. **2** Its edible, yellowish root. Also *Swedish turnip*. [<dial. Sw. *rotabagge*]

ruth (roōth) *n.* Sorrow; compassion; pity; also, grief; misery; repentance; regret. [ME *reuthe*, *reowthe* <OE *hrēow* sad]

Ruth A woman of Moab, daughter-in-law of the Israelite Naomi; she left her own people and went to Bethlehem, where she married Boaz, thus becoming an ancestress of David. Her story is told in the Old Testament book of this name.

ru·the·ni·um (roō-thē′nē-əm) *n.* A hard, brittle, gray metallic element (symbol Ru, atomic number 44) found in platinum ores and used as a catalyst and alloying element. See PERIODIC TABLE. [<NL, after *Ruthenia*]

ruth·er·ford (ruth′ər-fərd) *n.* A unit of radioactivity larger than the curie: equal to that quantity of a radioisotope which decays at the rate of a million disintegrations per second. [after Sir Ernest *Rutherford*]

ruth·less (roōth′lis) *adj.* Having no compassion; unrestrained by pity; merciless. — **ruth′less·ly** *adv.* — **ruth′less·ness** *n.*

ru·ti·lant (roō′tə-lənt) *adj.* Of a shining red color; glittering. [<L *rutilans, -antis*, ppr. of *rutilare* glow red < *rutilus*. See RUTILE.]

ru·ti·lat·ed (roō′tə-lā′tid) *adj.* Enclosing rutile needles: *rutilated* quartz.

ru·tile (roō′til, -tēl, -til) *n.* An adamantine, reddish-brown, transparent to opaque titanium dioxide, TiO_2, usually containing a small quantity of iron. [<F, shining <L *rutilus* red]

Rut·ledge (rut′lij), **Ann**, 1816–35, fiancée of Abraham Lincoln. — **Edward**, 1749–1800, American jurist; signer for South Carolina of Declaration of Independence. — **John**, 1739–1800, jurist; a framer of the U.S. Constitution; brother of the preceding.

rut·tish (rut′ish) *adj.* Disposed to rut; lustful; libidinous.

rut·ty (rut′ē) *adj.* Full of ruts. — **rut′ti·ness** *n.*

Ru·wen·zo·ri (roō′wən-zôr′ē, -zō′rē) A mountain group in east central Africa between Albert and Edward lakes, on the boundary between the Belgian Congo and Uganda: identified with the *Mountains of the Moon* of ancient writers; highest peak, 16,795 feet.

Rwan·da (rwän′də) A republic in central Africa, part of the former UN Trust Territory of Ruanda-Urundi; 10,169 square miles; pop. about 2,500,000; capital Kigali.

-ry Var. of -ERY.

Ry·binsk (ri′binsk) See SHCHERBAKOV.

rye¹ (rī) *n.* **1** The grain or seeds of a hardy cereal grass (*Secale cereale*) closely allied to wheat. **2** The plant. **3** Whisky distilled from rye. ◆ Homophone: wry. [OE *ryge* rye]

rye² (rī) *n.* In Gipsy dialect, a gentleman. ◆ Homophone: wry. [<Romany *rei, rae*, prob. <Skt. *rājan* a king]

rye-grass (rī′gras′, -gräs′) *n.* Common darnel: sometimes called *raygrass*.

Ryu·kyu Islands (ryōō-kyōō′) An archipelago between Kyushu and Taiwan; 1,803 square miles; chief island, Okinawa; Japanese possessions, administered by the U.S. after 1945; formally returned to Japan, May 15, 1972. Also *Nansei Islands*.

---

add,āce,câre,pälm; end,ēven; it,īce; odd,ōpen,ôrder; toŏk,pool; up,bûrn; ə = a in *above*, e in *sicken*, i in *clarity*, o in *melon*, u in *focus*; yoō = u in *fuse*; oi,oil; ou,pout; ch,check; g,go; ng,ring; th,thin; th,this; zh,vision. Foreign sounds á,œ,ü,kh,ṅ; and ◆: see page xx. < from; + plus; ? possibly.

S

s, S (es) *n. pl.* **s's, S's** or **ess·es** (es'·iz) **1** The nineteenth letter of the English alphabet, from Phoenician *shin,* through Hebrew *shin,* Greek *sigma,* Roman S. **2** The sound of the letter *s,* usually a voiceless sibilant. See ALPHABET. — *symbol* **1** *Chem.* Sulfur (symbol S). **2** Anything shaped like an S.

-s[1] A variant of *-es*[1], inflectional ending of the plurals of nouns, attached to nouns not ending in a sibilant or an affricate: *books, words, cars.* It is pronounced (s) after a voiceless consonant, and (z) after a voiced consonant or a vowel.

-s[2] An inflectional ending used to form the third person singular present indicative of verbs not ending in a sibilant, affricate, or vowel: *reads, walks, sings.* Compare -ES[2].

-s[3] *suffix* On; of a; at: often used in adverbs without appreciable force: *nights, Mondays, always, towards.* [OE *-es,* genitive ending]

-'s[1] An inflectional ending used to form the possessive of singular nouns and of plural nouns not ending in *-s:* a *man's* world, *women's* fashions. In plurals ending in *-s* (or *-es*) a simple apostrophe is used as a sign of the possessive: a *girls'* school, the *churches'* steeples, the *Joneses'* claim to the inheritance.

-'s[2] Contraction of: **1** Is: *He's* here. **2** Has: *She's* left. **3** Us: *Let's* go.

sa·ba (sä·bä') *n.* A fine Philippine fabric made from fibers of a plant resembling the banana. [< Tagalog]

sab·a·dil·la (sab'ə·dil'ə) *n.* **1** The acrid seeds of a Mexican and Central American bulbous plant *(Schoenocaulon officinale),* used as a source of veratrine, and formerly as an anthelmintic. **2** The plant. Also spelled *cebadilla, cevadilla.* [< Sp. *cebadilla,* dim. of *cebada* barley]

Sa·bah (sä'bä) A state of Malaysia in northern Borneo; 29,387 square miles; capital, Jesselton. Formerly *North Borneo.*

Sa·ba·ism (sä'bə·iz'əm) *n.* Star worship. [< Hebrew *tsābhā* (heavenly) host, army + -ISM] — **Sa'ba·ist** *n.*

Sab·a·oth (sab'ē·oth, sə·bā'oth) *n. pl.* Armies; hosts: chiefly in the phrase *the Lord of Sabaoth. Rom.* ix 29, *James* v 4. [< LL < Gk. *Sabaōth* < Hebrew *tsebāōth,* pl. of *tsābhā* host, army]

sab·bat (sab'ət) *n.* The witches' Sabbath. Also **Sab'bat.** [< OF. See SABBATH.]

sab·ba·tar·i·an (sab'ə·târ'ē·ən) *adj.* Pertaining to the Sabbath or its strict observance. — *n.* **1** A Christian who observes Sunday with strict propriety. **2** A Christian who observes the seventh day as the Sabbath: opposed to *dominical.* [< L *sabbatarius* < *sabbatum* SABBATH] — **Sab'ba·tar'i·an·ism** *n.*

Sab·bath (sab'əth) *n.* **1** The seventh day of the week, appointed in the decalog as a day of rest to be observed by the Jews; now, Saturday. **2** The first day of the week as observed by Christians; Sunday. **3** The institution or observance of a day or time of rest. **4** The sabbatical year of the Jews. *Lev.* xxv 4. [Fusion of OE *sabat* and OF *sabbat, sabat,* both < L *sabbatum* < Gk. *sabbaton* < Hebrew *shabbāth* < *shābath* rest] — **Sab·bat'ic** or **·i·cal** *adj.* — **Sab·bat'i·cal·ly** *adv.*

Synonym: Sunday. *Sabbath* carries a suggestion of rest not in *Sunday,* the first day of the week. See FIRST DAY.

sab·bat·i·cal (sə·bat'i·kəl) *adj.* Of the nature of the Sabbath as a day of rest; offering rest at regular intervals. Also **sab·bat'ic.** — *n.* A sabbatical year. [< *sabbatic* < F *sabbatique* < Gk. *sabbatikos* < *sabbaton* SABBATH]

sabbatical year 1 In the ancient Jewish economy, every seventh year, in which the people were required to refrain from tillage. **2** A year's vacation awarded to teachers in some American educational institutions every seven years.

sa·be (sä'bē) *SW U.S. v.i.* To understand; know. — *n.* Understanding; knowledge. [< Sp. *saber* know]

sa·ber (sä'bər) *n.* A heavy one-edged cavalry sword, with a thick-backed blade, often curved. — *v.t.* **·bered** or **·bred, ·ber·ing** or

·bring To strike, wound, kill, or arm with a saber. Also spelled *sabre.* [< F *sabre, sable* < MHG *sabel,* prob. < Slavic]

sa·ber-toothed (sä'bər·tōōtht') *adj.* Having very long, curved, upper canine teeth, likened to sabers.

saber-toothed tiger *Paleontol.* A large, ferocious, extinct carnivore (subfamily *Machaerodontinae),* characterized by very large, trenchant, upper canine teeth; especially, *Smilodon californicus,* common in the western hemisphere until its extinction in the Pleistocene.

SABER–TOOTHED TIGER

sa·bin (sä'bin) *n. Physics* A unit of sound absorption, equivalent to one square foot of a completely absorbing substance. [after W. C. W. *Sabine,* 1868–1919, U. S. physicist]

sa·ble (sä'bəl) *n.* **1** A carnivore *(Martes zibellina),* of northern Asia and Europe, related to the marten. ◆ Collateral adjective: *zibeline.* **2** The dressed fur of a sable, specifically, of the Asian sable. **3** *pl.* Garments made wholly or partly of this fur. **4** The color black; hence, mourning or a mourning garment. **5** *Her.* Black: represented, when uncolored, by a network of lines crossing each other at right angles. — **Alaska sable** A trade name for natural or dyed skunk. — *adj.* **1** Black, especially as the color of mourning. **2** Made of or having the color of sable fur; dark-brown. See synonyms under DARK. [< OF *sable, saible* < Med. L *sabelum* < Slavic]

sable antelope A large, black, African antelope *(Hippotragus niger)* having annular curved horns.

sa·ble-fish (sä'bəl·fish') *n. pl.* **·fish** or **·fish·es** The coalfish (def. 2).

sa·bot (sab'ō, *Fr.* sȧ·bō') *n.* **1** A wooden shoe, as of a French peasant. **2** A shoe having a wooden sole but flexible shank. See GETA. **3** A disk formerly attached to a projectile to cause it to maintain its position in the bore of a firearm or to take the rifling of the gun. [< F < OF *sabot,* alter. of *savate* an old shoe, ult. < Arabic *sabbāt* a sandal; infl. in form by *bot* a boot]

sab·o·tage (sab'ə·täzh, *Fr.* sȧ·bô·tȧzh') *n.* An act of malicious damage; deliberately poor workmanship intended to cause damage, obstruction of plans, aims, etc., as in secret resistance to an enemy: sometimes resorted to by workmen to secure compliance with demands. — *v.t. & v.i.* **·taged, ·tag·ing** To engage in, damage, or destroy by sabotage. [< F < *saboter* work badly, damage < *sabot* a sabot; with ref. to damage done to machinery with sabots]

sab·o·teur (sab'ə·tûr', *Fr.* sȧ·bô·tœr') *n.* One who engages in sabotage. [< F]

sa·bra (sä'brə) *n. Often cap.* An Israeli born in Israel. [< Heb.]

sa·bre·tache (sä'bər·tash, sab'ər-) *n.* A leather pocket hung from the sword belt of a mounted man. [< F < G *säbeltasche* < *säbel* a saber + *tasche* a pocket]

sab·u·lous (sab'yə·ləs) *adj.* Gritty, like sand. Also **sab'u·lose** (-lōs). [< L *sabulosus* < *sabulum* sand] — **sab·u·los'i·ty** (-los'ə·tē) *n.*

sac (sak) *n. Biol.* A membranous pouch; a cavity or receptacle: the ink *sac* of a squid. [< F < L *saccus.* Doublet of SACK.]

sac·a·ton (sak'ə·tōn') *n.* A coarse perennial grass *(Sporobolus wrightii)* of the United States and Mexico, yielding hay. [< Sp. *zacatón* < *zacate, sacate* < Nahuatl *çacatl* a kind of grass]

sac·cate (sak'it, -āt) *adj.* **1** Sac-shaped. **2** Having a sac, bag, or pouch. [< Med. L *saccatus* < L *saccus* a sack]

sac·cha·ride (sak'ə·rīd, -rid) *n. Chem.* Any of a class of carbohydrates containing sugar, as a *monosaccharide, polysaccharide,* etc.

sac·cha·rin (sak'ər·in) *n. Chem.* A white crystalline compound, $C_7H_5O_3NS$, derived from toluene. It is 300 to 500 times sweeter than cane sugar, and is used as a sweetening agent, especially by diabetics. Also spelled *saccharine.* [< Med. L *saccharum* sugar (< L *saccharon* < Gk. *sakchari, sakcharon,* ult. < Skt. *sharkarā* grit, gravel, sugar) + -IN]

sac·cha·rine (sak'ər·in, -ə·rīn) *adj.* **1** Of, pertaining to, or of the nature of sugar; sweet. **2** Ingratiatingly or cloyingly sweet. — *n.* Saccharin. [< SACCHAR(O)- + -INE[1]] — **sac'cha·rine·ly** *adv.* — **sac'cha·rin'i·ty** *n.*

saccharo- *combining form* Sugar; of or pertaining to sugar: *saccharometer.* Also, before vowels, **sacchar-.** [< Gk. *sakcharon* sugar]

sac·cha·roid (sak'ə·roid) *adj.* **1** Resembling sugar. **2** *Geol.* Having crystalline granular structure: *saccharoid* marble. Also **sac'cha·roi'dal** (-roid'l).

sac·cha·rom·e·ter (sak'ə·rom'ə·tər) *n.* A hydrometer for determining the concentration of sugar in saccharine solutions.

sac·cha·ro·my·ce·tous (sak'ə·rō·mī·sē'təs, -mī'sə-) *adj.* Of or pertaining to a genus *(Saccharomyces)* of fungi, the yeast family, commonly unicellular, but sometimes developing a septate mycelium. Several produce endogenous spores, while most of them cause alcoholic fermentation with evolution of carbon dioxide. [< NL < Gk. *sakcharon* sugar + *mykēs, -ētos* a mushroom, fungus]

sac·cha·rose (sak'ə·rōs) *adj.* Sucrose.

sac·cu·late (sak'yə·lāt) *adj.* Formed into a series of saclike expansions; dilated and constricted alternately. Also **sac'cu·lat'ed.**

sac·cule (sak'yōōl) *n.* **1** A little sac. **2** *Anat.* Part of the membranous labyrinth of the ear. [< L *sacculus* a sacculus]

sac·er·do·tal (sas'ər·dōt'l) *adj.* **1** Pertaining to a priest or priesthood; priestly. **2** Believing in the divine authority of the priesthood. [< OF < L *sacerdotalis* < *sacerdos, -dotis* a priest < *sacer* holy + *do-,* stem of *dare* give] — **sac'er·do'tal·ly** *adv.*

sa·chem (sā'chəm) *n.* **1** A North American Indian hereditary chief. **2** Any chief; the head of a political party; specifically, one of the leaders of the Tammany Society in New York. See synonyms under CHIEF. [< Algonquian (Narraganset). Akin to SAGAMORE.]

sa·chet (sa·shā', *esp. Brit.* sash'ā) *n.* A small ornamental bag for perfumed powder. [< OF, dim. of *sac* < L *saccus* a sack]

sack[1] (sak) *n.* **1** A bag for holding bulky articles. **2** A measure or weight of varying amount. **3** A loosely hanging dress without a waistline, often worn without a belt: also spelled *sacque:* also **sack dress. 4** *Slang* Dismissal: especially in the phrases **to get the sack, to give (someone) the sack. 5** In baseball slang, a base. **6** *Slang* A bed; mattress. — **to be left holding the sack** *Slang* To be left to take the consequences of a bad situation. — *v.t.* **1** To put into a sack or sacks. **2** To dismiss, as a servant. [OE *sacc* < L *saccus* < Gk. *sakkos* < Hebrew *saq* sackcloth, a grain sack. Doublet of SAC.]

sack[2] (sak) *v.t.* To plunder or pillage (a town or city) after capturing. — *n.* **1** The pillaging of a captured town or city. **2** Loot; booty obtained by pillage. [< MF *sac* < Ital. *sacco,* orig. plunder < Med. L *saccare* pillage < L *saccus* a sack; from the use of sacks in carrying off plunder] — **sack'er** *n.*

sack[3] (sak) *n.* Light-colored Spanish dry wine; also, any strong white wine from southern Europe. [Earlier *(wyne)seck* < F *(vin) sec* a dry (wine) < L *siccus* dry]

sack·but (sak'but) *n.* **1** A primitive instrument resembling the trombone. **2** In the Bible, a stringed instrument. [< MF *saquebute,* orig. a hooked lance for horseback fighting < OF *saquer* pull + *bouter* push]

sack·cloth (sak'klôth', -kloth') *n.* **1** A coarse cloth used for making sacks. **2** Coarse cloth or haircloth worn in penance.

sack·ful (sak'fool') *n. pl.* **·fuls** Enough to fill a sack.

sack·ing (sak'ing) *n.* A coarse cloth made of hemp or flax and used for sacks; bagging.

sack race A race in which each contestant has a sack tied over both feet.

sa·cral[1] (sā′krəl) *adj.* Of, pertaining to, or situated near the sacrum. — *n.* A sacral vertebra or nerve. [<NL *sacralis* < *sacrum* SACRUM]

sa·cral[2] (sā′krəl) *adj.* Pertaining to sacred rites. [<L *sacrum* a rite, orig. neut. sing. of *sacer* holy]

sac·ra·ment (sak′rə·mənt) *n.* **1** *Eccl.* A rite ordained by Christ or by the church as an outward and visible sign of an inward and spiritual grace: in the Greek Church, also called *mystery*. Traditionally they are seven in number (baptism, the Eucharist, confirmation, matrimony, orders, penance, and unction) in the Greek, Roman Catholic, and some other churches; since the Reformation only two of these (baptism and the Eucharist) are recognized by most Protestant churches. **2** *Often cap. Eccl.* **a** The Eucharist; the Lord's Supper. **b** The consecrated bread and wine of the Eucharist; often with *the*. See BLESSED SACRAMENT. **3** Any sign or token of a solemn covenant or pledge. **4** Any thing considered to have a secret or mysterious meaning. [<OF *sacrement* <LL *sacramentum* a mystery <L, an oath, pledge < *sacrare*. See SACRED.]

Synonyms: ceremony, communion, Eucharist, observance, ordinance, rite, service, solemnity. A *ceremony* is a form expressing reverence, or respect; as, religious *ceremonies*, the *ceremonies* of a coronation or of a wedding. An *observance* has more than a formal obligation, approaching a religious sacredness; a religious *observance* viewed as established by authority is called an *ordinance*; viewed as an established custom, it is a *rite*. Any religious act, especially a public act, viewed as a means of serving God is called a *service*. *Sacrament* and *ordinance* in the religious sense are often used interchangeably; the *ordinance* derives its sacredness from the authority that ordained it, while the *sacrament* possesses a sacredness due to something in itself, even when viewed simply as a memorial. The Lord's Supper is the Scriptural name for the *observance* commemorating the death of Christ; the word *communion* is once applied to it (I *Cor.* x 16). *Eucharist*, called *The Sacrament*, describes the Lord's Supper as a thanksgiving *service*.

Sac·ra·men·to (sak′rə·men′tō) The capital of California, on the **Sacramento River,** the largest river in the State, flowing 382 miles south from Central Valley to Suisun Bay.

sa·cred (sā′krid) *adj.* **1** Set apart or dedicated to religious use; hallowed: a *sacred* edifice. **2** Pertaining or related to deity, religion, or hallowed places or things. **3** Consecrated by love or reverence; dedicated to a person or purpose. **4** Entitled to reverence or respect; not to be profaned; inviolable. **5** *Rare* Set apart for evil; accursed. See synonyms under HOLY. [Orig. pp. of obs. *sacre* consecrate <OF *sacrer* <L *sacrare* < *sacer* holy] — **sa′cred·ly** *adv.* — **sa′cred·ness** *n.*

sac·ri·fice (sak′rə·fīs) *n.* **1** The act of making an offering to a deity, in worship or atonement. **2** That which is sacrificed; a victim. **3** A giving up of some cherished or desired object. **4** Loss incurred or suffered without return; destruction, as of life. **5** A reduction of price that ·leaves little or no profit or involves loss. **6** In baseball, a sacrifice hit. — *v.* **·ficed, ·fic·ing** *v.t.* **1** To make an offering or sacrifice of, as to a god or deity in propitiation, supplication, etc. **2** To give up, yield, permit injury to, or relinquish (something valued) for the sake of something else, as a person, thing, or idea. **3** To sell at a reduced price; part with at a loss. **4** In baseball, to advance (one or more runners) by means of a sacrifice hit. — *v.i.* **5** To make a sacrifice. **6** To make a sacrifice hit. See synonyms under SURRENDER. [<OF <L *sacrificium* < *sacra* rites, orig. neut. pl. of *sacer* holy + *facere* make] — **sac′ri·fic′er** *n.* — **sac′·ri·fic′ing·ly** *adv.*

sacrifice hit In baseball, a hit by which the batter is retired but by which a base runner is advanced another base, the batter not being charged with a time at bat: when batted into the air also called **sacrifice fly.**

sac·ri·lege (sak′rə·lij) *n.* The act of violating or profaning anything sacred, including sacramental vows. [<OF <L *sacrilegium* < *sacrilegus* a temple robber < *sacer* holy + *legere* gather] — **sac′ri·le′gist** (-lē′jist) *n.*

sac·ri·le·gious (sak′rə·lij′əs, -lē′jəs) *adj.* **1** Having committed, or being ready to commit, sacrilege; impious. **2** Of the nature of sacrilege. See synonyms under PROFANE. — **sac′ri·le′gious·ly** *adv.* — **sac′ri·le′gious·ness** *n.*

sa·cring bell (sā′kring) A small bell rung at the elevation during mass; the tolling of the church bell at this time; the Sanctus bell. [< *sacring,* ppr. of obs. *sacre* consecrate + BELL]

sac·ris·tan (sak′ris·tən) *n.* An officer having charge of the sacristy of a church or religious house and its contents, and of the proper arrangement of all objects needed for divine service. The sacristan of a cathedral is commonly in orders. Compare SEXTON. [<Med. L *sacristanus* <L *sacrista.* Doublet of SEXTON.]

sac·ris·ty (sak′ris·tē) *n. pl.* **·ties** A room in a religious house for the sacred vessels and vestments; a vestry. [<F *sacristie* <Med. L *sacristia* <L *sacrista* a sacrist]

sacro– *combining form Med.* Near, or related to the sacrum: *sacrosciatic.* [<L *(os) sacrum* the sacral (bone)]

sac·ro·il·i·ac (sak′rō·il′ē·ak) *adj. Anat.* Pertaining to the sacrum and the ilium and to the joints or ligaments connecting them. [< SACRO- + ILIAC]

sac·ro·sanct (sak′rō·sangkt) *adj.* Peculiarly and exceedingly sacred; inviolable; preeminent for sanctity: sometimes used ironically. [<L *sacrosanctus* < *sacro,* ablative of *sacrum* a rite (< *sacer* holy) + *sanctus,* pp. of *sancire* make holy, inviolable] — **sac′ro·sanc′ti·ty** *n.*

sa·crum (sā′krəm) *n. pl.* **·cra** (-krə) *Anat.* A composite bone formed by the union of the five vertebrae between the lumbar and caudal regions, constituting the dorsal part of the pelvis. [<NL <L *(os) sacrum* sacred (bone); from its being offered in sacrifices]

sad (sad) *adj.* **sad·der, sad·dest** **1** Sorrowful or depressed in spirits; expressing, or having the external appearance of grief or sorrow; unhappy; mournful; gloomy. **2** Causing sorrow or pity; distressing; unfortunate. **3** *Dial.* Heavy; soggy: said of food. **4** *Colloq.* Vexatious, mischievous, or bad: often humorously or as a mild intensive: That boy is a *sad* tease. **5** Dark–hued; somber. [OE *sæd,* orig. sated] — **sad′ly** *adv.* — **sad′ness** *n.*

Synonyms: afflicted, dejected, depressed, desolate, despondent, disconsolate, dismal, distressed, doleful, downcast, dreary, dull, gloomy, grave, heavy, lugubrious, melancholy, miserable, mournful, sober, somber, sorrowful, sorry, unhappy, woebegone, woeful. *Sad, melancholy, unhappy,* and many similar words may be used either of the personal experience of grief, sorrow, mental depression, etc., or of that which causes grief or pain; a person is *sad* on account of a *sad* event. See synonyms under BAD. *Antonyms:* see synonyms for HAPPY.

sad·den (sad′n) *v.t. & v.i.* To make or become sad or unhappy.

sad·dle (sad′l) *n.* **1** A seat or pad for a rider, as on the back of a horse or on a bicycle. **2** A padded cushion for a horse's back, as part of a harness or to support a pack, etc. For illustration see HARNESS. **3** The two hind-

quarters of a carcass, as of mutton, veal, or venison; also, the undivided loins of such a carcass. **4** Some part like or likened to a saddle, as the lower part of the back of a fowl. See illustration under FOWL. **5** *Geog.* A depression across the summit of a ridge; a pass. **6** *Meteorol.* A low-pressure area between two anticyclones; a col. **7** Something resembling a saddle in form or position, as a bearing for a car axle. — **in the saddle** In control. — *v.* **·dled, ·dling** *v.t.* **1** To put a saddle on: to *saddle* a horse. **2** To load, as with a burden. **3** To place as a burden or responsibility: with *upon.* — *v.i.* **4** To get into a saddle. [OE *sadol*]

saddle bags A pair of pouches connected by a strap or band and slung over an animal's back or attached to a saddle.

under and attached to a saddle, or one under the saddle of a harness.

saddle horse A horse used with or trained for the saddle.

sad·dler (sad′lər) *n.* **1** A maker of saddles, harness, etc. **2** A saddle horse.

saddle roof A roof consisting of two gables and one ridge.

sad·dler·y (sad′lər·ē) *n. pl.* **·dler·ies** **1** Saddles, harness, and fittings, collectively. **2** A saddler's shop. **3** The business of a saddler.

saddle shoe A white sport shoe with a dark band of leather across the instep.

saddle soap A softening and preserving soap for leather, containing pure white soap, usually Castile, and neat's-foot oil.

sad·dle·tree (sad′l·trē) *n.* **1** The frame of a saddle. **2** The tulip tree: so called from its saddle-shaped leaf.

sa·de (sä·dä′) *n.* The eighteenth Hebrew letter: also spelled *tsade.* Also **sa·dhe′.** See ALPHABET.

sad·i·ron (sad′ī′ərn) *n.* A flat iron for smoothing clothes: distinguished from a *box-iron.* [<SAD, obs. sense "heavy" + IRON]

sad·ism (sā′diz·əm, sad′iz·əm) *n. Psychiatry* **1** Sexual gratification obtained through the infliction of pain upon others. **2** A morbid delight in being cruel. [after Comte Donatien de *Sade;* with reference to the various sexual aberrations described in his writings] — **sad·ist** (sā′dist, sad′ist) *n. & adj.* — **sa·dis·tic** (sə·dis′tik, sā-) *adj.* — **sa·dis′ti·cal·ly** *adv.*

sa·do·mas·och·ism (sā′dō·mas′ə·kiz·əm, ·maz′·) *n. Psychiatry.* A condition in which sadism and masochism are combined in one person. — **sa′do·mas′o·chist** *n.* — **sa′do·mas′o·chis′tic** *adj.*

sa·fa·ri (sə·fä′rē) *n.* **1** An expedition or journey, often on foot, as for hunting. **2** The caravan and animals employed in this; also, a day's march: also spelled *suffari.* [<Swahili <Arabic *safara* travel]

safe (sāf) *adj.* **1** Free or freed from danger or evil. **2** Having escaped injury or damage; unharmed. **3** Not hazardous; not involving risk or loss; also, conferring safety; of persons, trusty; prudent. **4** Not likely to disappoint; free from doubt or error: It is *safe* to promise. **5** Not likely to cause or do harm or injury. **6** In politics, adhering to party principles; to be depended on to support certain interests: said of a candidate; also, sure to vote for a certain candidate: said of a district. **7** In baseball, having reached base without being retired: He was ruled *safe* at second. See synonyms under SECURE. — *n.* **1** A strong iron-and-steel receptacle, usually fireproof, for protecting valuables, as money or jewels. **2** Any place of safe storage, as a room, tank, refrigerator, or box, for preserving perishable articles, as meat or fish. [<OF *sauf* <L *salvus* whole, healthy] — **safe′ly** *adv.* — **safe′ness** *n.*

safe-con·duct (sāf′kon′dukt) *n. Law* **1** An official document assuring protection on a journey or voyage, as in time of war; a passport. **2** The act of conducting in safety. — *v.t.* (sāf′kən·dukt′) **1** To convoy in safety. **2** To provide with a safe-conduct.

safe-crack·er (sāf′krak′ər) *n.* One who breaks into safes to rob them.

safe-cracking (sāf′krak′ing) *n.* The breaking open of safes for robbery.

safe-de·pos·it box (sāf′di·poz′it) A box, safe, drawer, or other fireproof receptacle for valuable jewelry, papers, etc., generally in a bank.

safe·guard (sāf′gärd′) *n.* **1** One who or that

NOMENCLATURE–
AMERICAN
STOCK SADDLE

a. Pommel or horn.
b. Cantle.
c. Saddle.
d. Saddle strings.
e. Back cinch.
f. Front cinch.
g. Stirrup strap or leather.
h. Stirrup.
i. Tapadera or stirrup hood.

which guards or keeps in safety, as an escort, guard, or safe-conduct. 2 A mechanical device designed to prevent accident or injury. See synonyms under DEFENSE. —v.t. To defend; protect; guard.

safe-hand (sāf'hand') n. 1 A safe method of transmitting official secret papers. 2 A trustworthy courier.

safe hit In baseball, a fair hit by which the batter reaches first base.

safe house A house or apartment used by a spy where he or she may presume to be safe from capture or discovery.

safe·keep·ing (sāf'kē'ping) n. The act or state of keeping or being kept in safety; protection.

safe·light (sāf'līt') n. A bulb for darkroom use providing light that will not adversely affect photosensitive film or paper.

safe·ty (sāf'tē) n. pl. **·ties** 1 The state or condition of freedom from danger or risk. 2 Freedom from injury. 3 A device or catch designed as a safeguard, as in a firearm. 4 In football, the act or play of touching the ball to the ground behind the player's own goal line when the impetus which sent the ball over the goal line was given to it by one of his own side: also **safe'ty·touch'down'** (-tuch'doun') 5 In baseball, a safe hit.

safety belt 1 An extensible strap encircling the user and a permanently fixed object so that the user may move freely but be safe from falling or slipping: used by linemen, window cleaners, etc. 2 Aeron. A strap fixed to the seat of an aircraft by which the passenger is secured against sudden shocks or turning movements. 3 A life belt.

safety glass See under GLASS.

safety lamp 1 A miner's lamp having the flame surrounded by fine wire gauze, which prevents the ignition of explosive gases: called a *davy* from its inventor, Sir Humphry Davy. 2 A specially protected incandescent electric lamp.

safety lever Mech. 1 A device for controlling the movement of machine parts. 2 A similar contrivance for preventing the accidental discharge of a grenade, automatic pistol, etc.: also **safety catch.**

safety match A match that will ignite only when struck upon a chemically prepared surface.

safety pin 1 A pin whose point springs into place within a protecting sheath. 2 A pin which prevents the premature detonation of a hand grenade.

safety razor See under RAZOR.

safety valve 1 Mech. A valve in a steam boiler, etc., for automatically relieving excessive pressure. 2 Any outlet for pent-up energy or emotion.

saf·flow·er (saf'lou'ər) n. 1 A thistlelike herb (*Carthamus tinctorius*) about 2 feet high, with spiny heads of orange-red flowers. 2 The dried flower heads of this plant pressed into small cakes for export: also **safflower cake.** 3 The reddish dyestuff obtained from the dried flowers. [< Du. *saffloer* < OF *saffleur, safour* < Ital. *saffiore*; infl. in form by SAFFRON and FLOWER]

saf·fron (saf'rən) n. 1 An autumn-flowering species of crocus (*Crocus sativus*). 2 The dried orange-colored stigmas of this plant used for coloring confectionery, varnishes, etc., and in parts of the Old World as a flavoring and coloring ingredient in cookery. 3 A deep yellow orange: also **saffron yellow.** —adj. Of the orange color of saffron. [< OF *safran* < Sp. *azafran* < Arabic *az-za'farān* the saffron]

sag (sag) v. **sagged, sag·ging** v.i. 1 To bend or sink downward from weight or pressure, especially in the middle. 2 To hang unevenly. 3 To lose firmness or determination; weaken, as from exhaustion, age, etc. 4 To decline, as in price or value. 5 Naut. To drift. —v.t. 6 To cause to sag. —n. 1 A sagging, or its extent or degree; a sagging place or part, as of a roof. 2 Naut. A sidewise drift, as of a vessel. 3 A depressed or sunken place in flat land; a marsh. [ME *saggen*, ? < MDu. *zakken* subside, ? < dial. ON (nautical) *sakka* plummet]

sa·ga (sä'gə) n. 1 A medieval Scandinavian (specifically, Icelandic) prose narrative of conventionalized form dealing with legendary or historical exploits, usually of a single hero or a single family. 2 A story, sometimes poetic, having the saga form or manner, often chronicling the history of a family, as Galsworthy's *Forsyte Saga.* [< ON, history, narrative]

sa·ga·cious (sə-gā'shəs) adj. 1 Ready and apt to apprehend and to decide on a course. 2 Characterized by discernment, shrewdness, and wisdom. 3 Quick of scent, as a hound. [< L *sagax, sagacis* wise, foreseeing] —**sa·ga'cious·ly** adv. —**sa·ga'cious·ness** n.

Synonyms: able, acute, apt, clear-sighted, discerning, intelligent, judicious, keen, keen-sighted, keen-witted, perspicacious, quick-witted, rational, sage, sensible, sharp, sharp-witted, shrewd, wise. *Sagacious* refers to a power of tracing the hidden or recondite by slight indications, as by instinct or intuition; with reference to inferior animals it is often applied to special keenness of sense-perception as of a hound in following a trail. In human affairs *sagacious* refers to a power of ready, far-reaching, an accurate inference from observed facts, perhaps in themselves very slight, that seems like a special sense; or to a similar readiness to foresee the results of any action, a kind of prophetic common sense, especially upon human motives or conduct. *Sagacious* is a broader word than *shrewd,* and not capable of the invidious sense which the latter often bears; on the other hand, *sagacious* is less lofty than *wise* in its full sense, and more limited to practical matters. See ACUTE, ASTUTE, KNOWING, POLITIC, WISE[1]. *Antonyms:* absurd, dull, foolish, futile, ignorant, irrational, obtuse, senseless, silly, simple, sottish, stupid, unintelligent.

sage[1] (sāj) n. A venerable man of recognized experience, prudence, and foresight; a profoundly wise counselor or philosopher. —adj. 1 Characterized by or proceeding from calm, far-seeing wisdom and prudence. 2 Befitting a sage; profound; learned; also, grave; serious; shrewd. See synonyms under SAGACIOUS, WISE[1]. [< OF *saige, savie,* ult. < L *sapiens, -entis* wise, ppr. of *sapere* be wise. Doublet of SAPIENT.] —**sage'ly** adv. —**sage'ness** n.

sage[2] (sāj) n. 1 A plant of the mint family (genus *Salvia*), especially the common garden sage (*S. officinalis*), a stiff, shrubby perennial with gray-green leaves and purple, blue, or white flowers: used for flavoring meats, etc. 2 A light, greenish-gray color, like the color of sage leaves. 3 Any other plant of the genus *Salvia,* as the scarlet sage (*S. splendens*). 4 The Jerusalem sage (genus *Phlomis*), also of the mint family. 5 The sagebrush. [< OF *sauge* < L *salvia,* ? < *salvus* safe; with ref. to its reputed healing powers]

sage·brush (sāj'brush') n. An aromatic, bitter, typically perennial herb or small shrub (genus *Artemisia*) of the composite family, widely distributed on the alkali plains of the western United States; especially, *A. tridentata,* the State flower of Nevada. The Old World species are called *wormwood.*

sage sparrow A small, pale-gray, fringilline bird of the western United States (*Amphispiza nevadensis*).

sag·gar (sag'ər) n. 1 A vessel of baked fireproof clay in which are fired delicate pieces of pottery that would be injured by direct exposure to the heat. 2 Clay used for making saggars. Also spelled *seggar.* Also **sag'gard** (-ərd). —v.t. To place or treat in a saggar, as pottery. Also **sag'ger.** [Contraction of SAFEGUARD]

sag·it·tal (saj'ə-təl) adj. 1 Pertaining to or resembling an arrow or arrowhead. 2 Anat. A Straight: the *sagittal* suture between the two parietal bones of the skull. b Of or pertaining to the longitudinal plane dividing an animal into right and left halves. [< L *sagitta* an arrow] —**sag'it·tal·ly** adv.

Sag·it·ta·ri·us (saj'ə-târ'ē-əs) 1 A zodiacal constellation, pictured as a centaur shooting an arrow; the Archer. See CONSTELLATION. 2 The ninth sign of the zodiac, with the symbol ♐ [< L, lit., an archer < *sagitta* an arrow]

sag·it·tate (saj'ə-tāt) adj. Bot. Shaped like an arrowhead, as certain leaves. Also **sag'it·tat'ed, sa·git·ti·form** (sə-jit'ə-fôrm). [< L *sagitta* an arrow]

sa·go (sā'gō) n. 1 Any of several varieties of East Indian palm (genus *Metroxylon*). 2 The dried, powdered pith of this palm used as a thickening agent in puddings, etc. [< Malay *sāgū*]

sa·gua·ro (sä-gwä'rō, -wä'-) n. pl. **·ros** The giant cactus of the SW United States (*Cereus giganteus*): its blossom is the State flower of Arizona. Also **sa·hua'ro** (-wä'-). [< Sp. < Pi-

man]

sa·gum (sā'gəm) n. pl. **·ga** (-gə) The ancient Roman soldiers' military cloak: a symbol of war, as the toga was of peace. [< L, ? ult. < Celtic]

sag·y (sā'jē) adj. Flavored or seasoned with or like sage.

Sa·har·a (sə-har'ə, -hâr'ə, -hä'rə) The world's largest desert area, extending from the Atlantic to the Red Sea in northern Africa; about 3,000,000 square miles. Also **Sahara Desert.**

Sa·hib (sä'ib) n. Master; lord; Mr.; sir: used in India by natives in speaking of or addressing Europeans, also by Hindus and Moslems for people of rank: Raja Sahib. Also **Sa'heb.** [< Urdu *sāhib* < Arabic *ṣāḥib,* lit., a friend]

sai·ga (sī'gə) n. An antelope (*Saiga tatarica*) of the Siberian steppes, resembling a sheep. [< Russian *saiga*]

Sai·gon (sī·gon', Fr. sá·ē·gôn') Former name of Ho Chi Minh City.

sail (sāl) n. 1 Naut. A piece of canvas, etc., attached to the mast of a vessel, to secure its propulsion by the wind: variously shaped and rigged: fore-and-aft or square *sails.* 2 Sails collectively: full *sail.* 3 A sailing vessel or craft: plural same as singular: 30 *sail* in sight. 4 A trip or passage in a sailing vessel, or in any watercraft. 5 Anything resembling a sail in form or use, as the broad part of the arm of a windmill or a bird's wing. 6 A structure rising from the deck of a submarine that houses detection gear. —**to make sail** 1 To

SAILS OF A
CLUB TOPSAIL SCHOONER

a. Jib topsail.   *e.* Foresail.
b. Flying jib.   *f.* Maintopmast staysail.
c. Jib.   *g.* Main club topsail.
d. Fore club topsail.   *h.* Mainsail.

unfurl a sail or sails. 2 To set out on a voyage. —**to set sail** To begin a voyage; get under way. —**under sail** Sailing; with sails spread and driven by the wind. —v.i. 1 To move across the surface of water by the action of wind or, by extension, steam. 2 To travel over water in a ship or boat. 3 To begin a voyage; set sail. 4 To manage a sailing craft: Can you *sail?* 5 To move, glide, or float in the air; soar. 6 To move along in a stately or dignified manner: She *sailed* by haughtily. 7 Colloq. To pass rapidly. 8 Colloq. To proceed boldly into action: with *in.* —v.t. 9 To move or travel across the surface of (a body of water) in a ship or boat. 10 To navigate (a ship, etc.). —**to sail into** 1 To begin with energy. 2 To attack violently. ◆ Homophone: *sale.* [OE *segl*] —**sail'a·ble** adj.

sail·boat (sāl'bōt') n. A small boat propelled by a sail pr sails.

sail·cloth (sāl'klôth', -kloth') n. A very strong, firmly woven, cotton canvas suitable for sails: also called *duck.*

sail·fish (sāl'fish') n. pl. **·fish** or **·fish·es** 1 Any of a genus (*Istiophorus*) of marine fishes allied to the swordfish, having a large or conspicuous dorsal fin likened to a sail. 2 The basking shark.

SAILFISH
(Up to 6 feet in length)

sail·ing (sā'ling) n. 1 The setting forth on or prosecution of a voyage: the *sailing* of a vessel. 2 The art and method of determining the direction and distance sailed by a ship at sea, the point reached, and the course to be taken; navigation; seamanship.

sailing orders Instructions given to a ship's captain, covering all details of a voyage.

sail·loft (sāl′lôft′, -loft′) n. A room where sails are cut out and sewed.

sail·or (sā′lər) n. 1 A seaman; mariner. 2 A sailor hat. —**sail′or·ly** adj.

Synonyms: mariner, seafarer, seaman. In nautical language *sailors* and *seamen* are exclusive of officers, but in literary use all whose vocation is navigation are figuratively termed *sailors* or *seamen*. *Mariner* is one who navigates or assists in navigating a ship; in the United States statutes *mariner* denotes any person, from captain to cook, who serves in any capacity on a ship. *Antonym:* landsman.

sail·plane (sāl′plān′) n. *Aeron.* A light, highly maneuverable glider requiring a relatively low speed for flight, used for soaring. — *v.i.* **·planed, ·plan·ing** To fly a sailplane.

sain·foin (sān′foin) n. An Old World perennial, cloverlike herb (*Onobrychis viciaefolia*) of the bean family, with variegated flowers, cultivated for forage: also called *esparcet.* Also **saint′· foin.** [< F < *sain* wholesome (< L *sanus* healthy) + *foin* hay]

saint (sānt) n. 1 A holy, godly, or sanctified person; in the New Testament, any Christian believer. *Eph.* i 1. 2 Such a person who has died and been canonized by certain churches, as the Roman Catholic. 3 Any one of the blessed in heaven. 4 An angel. 5 A very patient, unselfish person. — *v.t.* To canonize; venerate as a saint. — *adj.* Holy; canonized: as a title, often abbreviated to *St.* [< OF *seint, saint* < L *sanctus,* orig. holy, consecrated, pp. of *sancire* make sacred]

Saint Bernard A working dog of great size and strength, originally bred in Switzerland, characterized by a massive head, and a thick, white coat combined with red or brindle: used to rescue travelers by the hospice at Great St. Bernard Pass in the Swiss Alps.

SAINT BERNARD

Saint·paul·i·a (sānt·pô′lē·ə) n. The African violet, much cultivated as an ornamental house plant. [< NL, after Baron Walter von *Saint Paul,* German botanist, its discoverer]

Saint–Si·mon·ism (sānt–sī′mən·iz′əm) n. The socialistic principles of the Comte de Saint-Simon, advocating the state ownership of all property and the distribution of earnings based on the amount and quality of the work done by each laborer: also called *Simonianism.*

Sai·pan (sī·pän′, -pan′, sī′pan) The largest island of the Marianas group; 47 square miles; capital, Garapan; captured from Japan by United States forces in World War II, 1944; after 1947, a district of the Trust Territory of the Pacific Islands, administered by the U.S. under the United Nations.

sake¹ (sāk) n. 1 Purpose of obtaining or accomplishing: preceded by *for* and followed by *of:* to open the window for the *sake* of air. 2 Interest, regard, or affectionate or reverent consideration, felt for any person or thing; account; well-being; advantage: commonly with *for* and a possessive: for your *sake,* for the *sake* of your children. [OE *saccu* a (legal) case]

sa·ke² (sä′kē) n. A fermented liquor made from rice; by extension, in Japan, any spirituous liquor. Also **sa′ki.** [< Japanese]

Sak·ka·ra (sə·kä′rə) A village of Upper Egypt; site of excavations of many ancient ruins: also *Saqqara.*

sal (sal) n. Salt. [< L]

sa·laam (sə·läm′) n. An oriental salutation or obeisance resembling prostration, the palm of the right hand being held to the forehead; also, a respectful or ceremonious verbal greeting. — *v.t. & v.i.* To greet with or make a salaam. [< Arabic *salām,* orig. peace, in *(as)salām (′alaikum)* peace (be upon you),

a salutation]

sal·a·ble (sā′lə·bəl) adj. Such as can be sold; marketable: also spelled *saleable.* See synonyms under VENAL¹. — **sal′a·bil′i·ty, sal′a·ble·ness** n. — **sal′a·bly** adv.

sa·la·cious (sə·lā′shəs) adj. Lustful; lecherous. [< L *salax, salacis* < *salire* leap] — **sa·la′· cious·ly** adv. — **sa·la′cious·ness, sa·lac′i·ty** (-las′ə·te) n.

sal·ad (sal′əd) n. 1 A dish of green herbs or vegetables, usually uncooked and served with a dressing, sometimes mixed with chopped cold meat, fish, etc. 2 The course consisting of such a dish. [< OF *salade* < Provençal *salada* < L *salata,* pp. of *salare* salt < *sal* salt]

sa·la·dang (sä·lä′däng) n. The East Indian ox (*Bos gaurus*): also called *gaur.* Also spelled *seladang.* [Var. of *seladang* < Malay *sĕladaṅ*]

salad days Days of youth, freshness, and inexperience.

salad dressing A savory sauce used on salads, as mayonnaise, or a mixture of salt, oil, and vinegar, etc.

Sal·a·din (sal′ə·din), 1137?–93, sultan of Egypt and Syria, 1174–93; defended Acre against Crusaders.

sal·a·man·der (sal′ə·man′dər) n. 1 Any of an order (*Caudata*) of tailed, lizardlike amphibians having a smooth, moist, scaleless skin and usually two pairs of limbs, as the American **tiger**

SPOTTED SALAMANDER
(From 6 to 7 inches
long over-all)

salamander (*Ambystoma tigrinum*): once popularly believed able to live in fire. 2 One of the genii fabled to live in fire; an elemental fire spirit in Paracelsus' theory of elementals; hence, a creature fabled to live in fire. 3 Any person or thing that can stand great heat. 4 A large poker or other implement used around or in fire, or when red-hot. 5 A mass of hardened metal or slag remaining in the hearth of a furnace after the fires are drawn: also called *shadrach.* [< OF *salamandre* < L *salamandra* < Gk.] — **sal′a·man′· drine** (-drin) adj.

sa·la·mi (sə·lä′mē) n. A salted, spiced sausage, originally Italian. [< Ital., pl., preserved meat, salt pork, ult. < L *salare* salt < *sal* salt]

sal ammoniac A white, soluble ammonium chloride. [< L *sal Ammoniacum,* lit., salt of Ammon; so called because orig. made from camel's dung near the shrine of Jupiter Ammon in Libya]

sal·a·ried (sal′ər·ēd) adj. 1 In receipt of a salary. 2 Yielding a salary.

sal·a·ry (sal′ər·ē) n. pl. **·ries** A periodic allowance as compensation for official or professional services. — *v.t.* **·ried, ·ry·ing** To pay or allot a salary to. [< AF *salarie* < L *salarium* money paid Roman soldiers for their salt, orig. neut. of *salarius* of salt < *sal* salt]

Synonyms (noun): allowance, compensation, earnings, fee, hire, honorarium, pay, payment, recompense, remuneration, requital, stipend, wages. An *allowance* is a stipulated amount furnished at regular intervals, as of food or of money. *Compensation* signifies a return for a service done. *Remuneration* is applied to matters of great amount or importance. *Recompense* has a still wider meaning; there are services for which affection and gratitude are the sole and sufficient *recompense; earnings, fees, hire, pay, salary,* and *wages* are forms of *compensation* and may be included in *compensation, remuneration,* or *recompense.* *Pay* is commercial, and signifies an exact pecuniary equivalent for a thing or service, except when the contrary is expressly stated, as when we speak of high *pay* or poor *pay.* A *wage* is what a worker receives, and is usually estimated on an hourly or daily rate. *Earnings* is often equivalent to *wages,* but may be used with reference to the real value of work done or service rendered, and even applied to inanimate things; as, the *earnings* of capital. *Hire* is distinctly mercenary or menial. *Salary* is for professional, literary, executive, or clerical work, and is usually estimated on a weekly, monthly, or annual rate. A *fee* is given for a single service or

privilege, and is sometimes a gratuity. Compare REQUITE.

sale (sāl) n. 1 The act of selling; the exchange or transfer of property for money or its equivalent. 2 An auction or selling-off at bargain prices. 3 Opportunity of selling; demand by purchasers; market: Stocks find no *sale.* — **for sale** (or **on sale**) Offered or ready for sale. ◆ Homophone: *sail.* [OE *sala,* prob. <ON]

Synonyms: bargain, barter, change, deal, exchange, trade. A *bargain* is strictly an agreement or contract to buy and sell; (see CONTRACT) but the word is often used to denote the entire transaction and also the thing sold or purchased. *Change* and *exchange* are words of wider signification, applying only incidentally to the transfer of property or value; a *change* secures something different in any way or by any means; an *exchange* secures something as an equivalent or return, but not necessarily as payment for what is given. *Barter* is the *exchange* of one commodity, generally a portable one, for another. *Trade* in the broad sense may apply to vast businesses (as the book *trade*), but as denoting a single transaction is used chiefly in regard to things of moderate value, when it becomes nearly synonymous with *barter. Sale* is commonly limited to the transfer of property for money, or for something estimated at a money value or considered as equivalent to so much money. A *deal* in the political sense is a *bargain,* substitution,′ or transfer for the benefit of certain persons or parties against all others; as, The nomination was the result of a *deal;* in business it may have a similar meaning, but it frequently signifies simply a *sale* or *exchange,* a dealing.

sale·a·ble (sā′lə·bəl) See SALABLE.

sal·ep (sal′ep) n. A farinaceous meal obtained from the dry tubers of various orchids, used as food and formerly as medicine. [< F < Turkish *sâlep* < Arabic *tha′leb, sa′leb,* prob. contraction of *khasyu′th–tha′lab* orchis, lit., fox's testicles]

sal·e·ra·tus (sal′ə·rā′təs) n. Sodium (or formerly potassium) bicarbonate, for use in cookery; baking soda. [< NL *sal aëratus* aerated salt < L *sal* salt + *aër* air, gas; so called because it produces carbon dioxide]

sales·clerk (sālz′klûrk′) n. A clerk who sells goods in a store.

sales·girl (sālz′gûrl′) n. A woman or girl hired to sell merchandise, especially in a store.

sales·la·dy (sālz′lā′dē) n. pl. **·dies** *Colloq.* A woman or girl hired to sell merchandise, especially in a store.

sales·man (sālz′mən) n. pl. **·men** (-mən) A man hired to sell goods, stock, etc., in a store or by canvassing.

sales·man·ship (sālz′mən·ship) n. 1 The work or profession of a salesman. 2 Ability or skill in selling.

sales·per·son (sālz′pûr′sən) n. A person hired to sell merchandise, especially in a store.

sales resistance An attitude or state of mind in an individual or in the buying public that resists buying certain goods because of something antipathetic in the salesman, the advertising, or in the product.

sales·room (sālz′room′, -room′) n. A room where merchandise is displayed for sale.

sales tax A tax on money received from sales of goods.

sales·wom·an (sālz′wŏŏm′ən) n. pl. **·wom·en** (-wim′in) A woman or girl hired to sell merchandise, especially in a store.

sal·ic (sal′ik) adj. *Geol.* Belonging to a group of igneous rocks composed chiefly of silica and alumina, as the feldspars, quartz, etc. [<S(ILICA) + AL(UMINUM) + -IC]

sal·i·ca·ceous (sal′ə·kā′shəs) adj. *Bot.* Of or pertaining to a family (*Salicaceae*) of shrubs and trees forming the order *Salicales,* having alternate undivided leaves and dioecious flowers; the willow family. It includes the willows and the poplars. [< NL *salicaceus* < *salix, -icis* a willow]

salicylic acid *Chem.* A white crystalline compound, $C_7H_6O_3$, occurring naturally in many plants and also made synthetically from phenol. It is an antiseptic and is used sparingly in preserving foods, and, in the form of its salts, for treating rheumatism.

sa·li·ence (sā′lē·əns) *n.* 1 The condition of being salient or, figuratively, noteworthy. 2 A protruding feature or detail. 3 That which arrests attention because of its importance. Also **sa′li·en·cy.**

sa·li·ent (sā′lē·ənt) *adj.* 1 Standing out prominently; striking; conspicuous: a *salient* feature. 2 Extending beyond the general line; projecting. 3 Leaping; springing. — *n.* An angle pointing outwards, as of a fortification (see illustration under BASTION); projecting line or lines of trenches; a sharp curve in a military line protruding toward the enemy. [< L *saliens, -entis*, ppr. of *salire* leap] — **sa′li·ent·ly** *adv.* — **sa′li·ent·ness** *n.*

sa·li·en·ti·an (sā′lē·en′shē·ən) *n.* Any of an order (*Salientia*) of amphibians characterized by broad, stocky bodies and the absence of tails, and having hind legs adapted for leaping, including the frogs and toads. — *adj.* Belonging or pertaining to the *Salientia*. [< NL < *Salientia*. See SALIENT.]

sa·lif·er·ous (sə·lif′ər·əs) *adj.* Containing a considerable proportion of salt in beds or as brine: *saliferous* strata. [< L *sal, salis* salt + -FEROUS]

sa·li·fy (sal′ə·fī) *v.t.* **·fied, ·fy·ing** 1 To combine or impregnate with a salt. 2 To form into a salt, as with an acid. [< F *salifier* < NL *salificare* < L *sal, salis* salt + *facere* make] — **sal′i·fi′a·ble** *adj.* — **sal′i·fi·ca′tion** *n.*

sa·lim·e·ter (sə·lim′ə·tər) *n.* A salinometer. [< L *sal, salis* salt + -METER]

sa·li·na (sə·lī′nə) *n.* 1 A pool, pond, or marsh containing salt water diked in from the sea; also, a salt spring; a saltlick. 2 A saltworks or salt mine. [< Sp. < L *salinae (fodinae)* salt (pits) < *sal,* salt]

sa·line (sā′līn) *adj.* Constituting, consisting of, or characteristic of salt; containing salt; salty. — *n.* 1 A metallic salt, especially a salt of one of the alkalis or of magnesium. 2 A salt solution used in the investigation of biological and physiological processes, and also in medicine, as for an injection. 3 A natural deposit of common or other soluble salt; salina. [< F *salin* < LL (assumed) *salinus* < L *sal, salis* salt]

sa·lin·i·ty (sə·lin′ə·tē) *n.* 1 The state or degree of being salt or saline. 2 The quantity of solid material dissolved in one kilogram of water: expressed in parts per thousand. Compare CHLORINITY.

sa·lin·i·za·tion (sā′lin·ə·zā′shən, -ī·zā′-) *n.* 1 The accumulation of salt. 2 The process by which a soil acquires various kinds of salts, as sodium chloride, calcium sulfate, or the like.

sa·li·nom·e·ter (sal′ə·nom′ə·tər) *n.* A hydrometer graduated to show the percentage of salt in a solution and to measure the density of sea water. [< *salino-* (< SALINE) + -METER] — **sal′i·nom′e·try** *n.*

sa·li·va (sə·lī′və) *n. Physiol.* The slightly alkaline fluid secreted by the glands of the mouth; spittle. It contains a specific amylase called ptyalin, which converts starch into maltose and is therefore considered a promoter of digestion. [< L] — **sal·i·var·y** (sal′ə·ver′ē) *adj.*

sal·i·vate (sal′ə·vāt) *v.* **·vat·ed, ·vat·ing** *v.i.* To secrete saliva. — *v.t.* To produce salivation in. [< L *salivatus*, pp. of L *salivare* < *saliva* saliva]

sal·i·va·tion (sal′ə·vā′shən) *n.* An abnormally increased flow of saliva, especially when due to the effect of drugs, as mercury.

sal·len·ders (sal′ən·dərz) *n. pl.* An eczematic inflammation about the hock joint of a horse. Compare MALANDERS. [< F *solandre*; ult. origin uncertain]

sal·let (sal′it) *n.* A hemispherical helmet of the 15th century. [< OF *salade* < Ital. *celata* < L *caelata (cassis)* an engraved (helmet), orig. pp. fem. of *caelare* engrave]

sal·low[1] (sal′ō) *adj.* Of an unhealthy yellowish color: said chiefly of the human skin. [OE *salo*] — **sal′low·ish** *adj.* — **sal′low·ly** *adv.* — **sal′low·ness** *n.*

sal·low[2] (sal′ō) *n.* 1 A European willow with less flexible shoots than the osiers, especially the goat willow (*Salix caprea*), sometimes called the **great sallow**, and the **gray sallow**

SALLET
Of Italian archer, 15th century.

(*S. caprea cinerea*). 2 An osier; a willow shoot. [OE *sealh*]

sal·ly (sal′ē) *v.i.* **·lied, ·ly·ing** 1 To rush out suddenly. 2 To set out energetically. 3 To go out, as from a room or building. — *n. pl.* **·lies** 1 A rushing forth, as of besieged troops against besiegers; sortie. 2 A going forth, as on a walk or excursion. 3 A sudden overflow of spirits; a witticism or bantering remark. [< OF *saillie*, orig. pp. fem. of *saillir* < L *salire* leap]

sally lunn (lun) A raised and sweetened tea-cake resembling a muffin. [after *Sally Lunn*, pastry cook, of Bath, England, in the 18th century]

sal·ma·gun·di (sal′mə·gun′dē) *n.* 1 A dish of chopped meat, anchovies, eggs, onions, etc., mixed and seasoned. 2 Hence, any medley or miscellany; a potpourri. [< F *salmigondis*, prob. < Ital. *salami conditi* pickled meats < *salame* preserved meat, sausage + *conditi*, pp. of *condire* flavor < L, preserve, pickle]

sal·mi (sal′mē) *n.* A spiced dish of birds or game roasted, minced, and stewed in wine; a ragout. Also **sal·mis** (sal′mē, *Fr.* sál·mē′). [< F, prob. contraction of *salmigondis* SALMAGUNDI]

salm·on (sam′ən) *n.* 1 A clupeid fish (family *Salmonidae*, genus *Salmo*), especially *S. salar* of the North Atlantic, brownish above, silvery on the sides, with black spots. The salmon ascends to the headwaters of rivers to spawn, and surmounts obstructions, as waterfalls of considerable height. It is a highly prized game and food fish, and has delicate reddish-orange flesh. 2 One of other salmonoid fishes, especially the quinnat, ascending rivers flowing to the North Pacific. 3 A color of a reddish- or pinkish-orange tint: also **salm′on-pink′.** — *adj.* Having the color salmon. [< AF *samoun, saumoun, salmun* < L *salmo, -onis*]

salm·on·ber·ry (sam′ən·ber′ē) *n. pl.* **·ries** 1 A hardy raspberry (*Rubus spectabilis*) of the Pacific coast. 2 The cloudberry. 3 A raspberry (*R. parviflorus*) of the United States, having a white blossom.

Sal·mo·nel·la (sal′mō·nel′ə) *n.* A genus of aerobic, rodlike, preponderantly motile bacteria capable of fermenting certain carbohydrates with the formation of acid and gas; especially, *S. paratyphi*, which causes a form of paratyphoid in man. [< NL, after Daniel Elmer *Salmon*, U.S. pathologist, 1850–1914]

sal·mo·nel·lo·sis (sal′mə·ne·lō′səs) *n.* A disease caused by Salmonella bacteria, esp. paratyphoid.

sal·mo·noid (sal′mə·noid) *adj.* Resembling a salmon; belonging to the salmon family. — *n.* A salmonoid.

salmon trout 1 The European sea trout (*Salmo trutta*). 2 Certain other salmonoid fish, as the namaycush or the steelhead. See TROUT.

Sa·lo·me (sə·lō′mē) The daughter of Herodias, who asked from Herod the head of John the Baptist on a silver charger in return for her dancing. *Matt.* xiv 8.

sa·lon (sə·lon′, *Fr.* sá·lôn′) *n.* 1 A room in which guests are received; a drawing-room. 2 The periodic gathering or reception of noted persons, under the auspices of some distinguished woman, especially in Paris in the 17th and 18th centuries. 3 A hall or gallery used for exhibiting works of art. 4 An exhibition of works of art. 5 An establishment devoted to some specific purpose: a beauty *salon*. [< F < Ital. *salone*, aug. of *sala* a room, hall < OHG *sal*]

sa·loon (sə·lōōn′) *n.* 1 *U.S.* A place where alcoholic drinks are sold; a bar. 2 *Brit.* In a public house, a section of the bar set aside for patrons of a higher social status than those in the public bar. 3 A large apartment or room for assemblies, public entertainment, exhibitions, etc. 4 The main cabin of a passenger ship, used by the passengers in general. 5 A salon (def. 1). 6 *Brit.* A sedan (def. 1). [< F *salon* a salon]

sa·loon-keep·er (sə·lōōn′kē′pər) *n.* One who keeps a saloon; a liquor dealer.

sa·loop (sə·lōōp′) *n. Brit.* An infusion of sassafras chips, salep, or similiar aromatic herbs, formerly used largely as a beverage, as a cure for rheumatism, etc.; sassafras tea. [Var. of SALEP]

salp (salp) *n.* Any of a class (Thaliacea) of small, free-swimming, cylindrical tunicates, often having transparent bodies ringed with bands of

muscle. Also **sal·pa** (sal′pə) *pl.* **·pae** or **·pas.** [< NL < L < Gk. *salpē* a kind of sea fish] — **sal′pi·form** *adj.*

Sal·pi·glos·sis (sal′pə·glos′is) *n.* A small genus of South American solanaceous, downy herbs having entire leaves and handsome variegated flowers. [< NL < Gk. *salpinx, -ingos* a trumpet + *glōssa* tongue]

sal·pin·gec·to·my (sal′pin·jek′tə·mē) *n. Surg.* The excision of a Fallopian tube; sterilization of women. [< NL *salpinx, salpingos* a Fallopian tube (< Gk., a trumpet) + -ECTOMY]

sal·pinx (sal′pingks) *n. pl.* **sal·pin·ges** (sal·pin′jēz) *Anat.* A tube in man and other mammals, especially the Eustachian or Fallopian tube. [< NL < Gk., a trumpet]

sal·si·fy (sal′sə·fē) *n.* An Old World plant (*Tragopogon porrifolius*) of the composite family, with a white, edible root: from its flavor called *oyster plant, vegetable oyster*. [< F *salsifis*, prob. < Ital. *sassefrica*; ult. origin unknown]

sal·sil·la (sal·sil′ə) *n.* Any of several tropical American plants of the amaryllis family (genus *Bomarea*), yielding edible tubers resembling those of the Jerusalem artichoke. [< Sp., dim. of *salsa* a sauce]

sal soda Sodium carbonate; washing soda. See SODA.

salt (sôlt) *n.* 1 Sodium chloride, NaCl, a widely distributed compound, used by men from time immemorial as a seasoning preservative: a necessary ingredient of food for most mammals. It is obtained by evaporation or freezing of the water of the ocean, of saline lakes and springs or wells, and by mining in beds of rock salt. ◆ Collateral adjective: *saline*. 2 *Chem.* Any compound produced when all or part of the hydrogen of an acid is replaced by an electropositive radical or a metal. Salts are usually formed by treating a metal with an acid or by the interaction of a base and an acid. Usually the salts derived from acids whose names end in *-ic* take the suffix *-ate*, and those ending in *-ous* take *-ite*. 3 *pl.* A salt used as a laxative or cathartic; also, smelling salts. 4 Piquant humor; dry wit; repartee: from the phrase *Attic salt*. 5 That which preserves, corrects, or purifies: the *salt* of criticism; seasoning. 6 A sailor: an old *salt*. 7 A saltcellar. — **below the salt** In inferior, subordinate, or servile position. — **to take with a grain of salt** To allow for exaggeration; have doubts about. — *adj.* 1 Flavored with salt; salty; briny: opposed to *sweet*. 2 Cured or preserved with salt. 3 Containing, or growing or living in or near, salt water. 4 *Obs.* Salacious; licentious; gross. — *v.t.* 1 To season with salt. 2 To preserve or cure with salt. 3 To furnish with salt: to *salt* cattle. 4 To season as if with salt; add zest or piquancy to. 5 To add something to so as fraudulently to increase the value: to *salt* a mine with gold. — **to salt away** 1 To pack in salt for preserving. 2 *Colloq.* To store up; save. — **to salt out** To separate (coal-tar colors) by adding salt to solutions containing them. [OE *sealt*. Akin to SAL.] **salt′ish** *adj.* — **salt′ness** *n.*

sal·tant (sal′tənt) *adj.* Leaping; jumping; saltatory. [< L *saltans, -antis*, ppr. of *saltare* dance, freq. of *salire* leap]

sal·ta·rel·lo (sal′tə·rel′ō, *Ital.* säl′tä·rel′lō) *n. pl.* **·rel·li** (-rel′ē, *Ital.* -rel′lē) 1 A quick Italian dance, diversified by skips. 2 Music for such a dance. [< Ital., lit., a firecracker < *saltare* dance, leap < L. See SALTANT.]

sal·ta·tion (sal·tā′shən) *n.* 1 A leaping or leap, as in a dance. 2 A throbbing or palpitation, as of a blood vessel. 3 a Mutation. b In evolutionary theory, the abrupt development of new species by a major mutational change. [< L *saltatio, -onis* < *saltatus*, pp. of saltare. See SALTANT.]

sal·ta·to·ri·al (sal′tə·tôr′ē·əl, -tō′rē-) *adj.* 1 Built or adapted for leaping. 2 *Zool.* Adapted for or characterized by leaping. [< SALTATORY]

sal·ta·to·ry (sal′tə·tôr′ē, -tō′rē) *adj.* 1 Of or pertaining to leaping or dancing. 2 Moving by leaps; fitted for leaping; specifically, moving the feet synchronously, as certain birds. [< L *saltatorius* < *saltator* a leaper < *saltare*. See SALTANT.]

salt cake Crude sodium sulfate, especially as obtained by the action of sulfuric acid on sodium chloride.

salt·cel·lar (sôlt′sel′ər) *n.* A small receptacle for salt; a saltshaker.

salt·ed (sôl′tid) *adj.* 1 Treated with or as with salt for any purpose; hence, preserved. 2 Immune from infectious disease by reason of previous attack: a term used in South Africa. 3 *Colloq.* Experienced or expert.

salt·ern (sôl′tərn) *n.* A place or building where salt is manufactured. [OE *sealtœrn*]

salt grass Any of certain grasses found growing on salt marshes or on alkaline western plains, as *Distichlis spicata* or some species of *Spartina*.

salt hay Hay made from salt grass.

salt-horse (sôlt′hôrs′) *n.* Salted beef; corned beef: a sailor's term. Also **salt′-junk′** (-jungk′).

sal·ti·grade (sal′tə·grād) *adj.* Adapted for leaping; said of certain insects, as grasshoppers. [< NL *Saltigradae*, group name of saltigrade spiders < L *saltus* a leap + *gradi* step]

sal·tine (sôl·tēn′) *n.* A crisp, salty cracker.

salt-lick (sôlt′lik′) *n.* A place to which animals resort to lick salt from superficial deposits; a salt spring or dried salt pond.

salt marsh Low coastal land frequently overflowed by the tide, usually covered with coarse grass. Also **salt meadow.**

salt-pan (sôlt′pan′) *n.* 1 A vessel in which salt is made by evaporating saline water. 2 A pond or basin from which salt is obtained by natural evaporation.

salt-pe·ter (sôlt′pē′tər) *n.* Niter: so called colloquially and in commerce. —**Chile saltpeter** Mineral sodium nitrate occurring in beds in a desert region near the boundary of Chile and Peru, but chiefly in Chile. Also **salt′pe′tre.** [< OF *saltpetre* < Med. L *sal petrae*, lit., salt of rock < L *sal* salt + *petra* a rock < Gk.]

salt rheum *Pathol.* One of various skin eruptions, as eczema.

salt-ris·ing (sôlt′rī′zing) *n.* Salted batter used as leaven, or bread made from it.

salt-shak·er (sôlt′shā′kər) *n.* A container with small apertures for sprinkling table salt.

salt spring A flow of salt water from the earth.

salt-wa·ter (sôlt′wô′tər, -wot′ər) *adj.* Of, composed of, or living in salt water.

salt well A well from which brine is obtained.

salt-works (sôlt′wûrks′) *n. pl.* **·works** An establishment where salt is made on a commercial scale: in England the form **saltwork** is preferred in describing a single factory.

salt-wort (sôlt′wûrt′) *n.* 1 Any of various maritime plants (genus *Salsola*), especially the common saltwort *(S. kali)*, used in making soda ash. 2 Any of various glassworts, as the dwarf glasswort *(Salicornia bigelovi)* of the New England coast. [Prob. trans. of Du. *zoutkruid*]

salt·y (sôl′tē) *adj.* **salt·i·er, salt·i·est** 1 Tasting somewhat like salt; of or containing salt. 2 Reminiscent of the sea; smelling of the sea. 3 Piquant; sharp; pungent, as literature, speech, etc. — **salt′i·ly** *adv.* —**salt′i·ness** *n.*

sa·lu·bri·ous (sə·lōō′brē·əs) *adj.* Conducive to health; healthful; wholesome. See synonyms under HEALTHY. [< L *salubris* < *salus* health] — **sa·lu′bri·ous·ly** *adv.* —**sa·lu′bri·ty, sa·lu′bri·ous·ness** *n.*

sa·lu·ki (sə·lōō′kē) *n.* A very old breed of hound, having feathered ears, tail, and legs, and a greyhoundlike body; the "dog" of the Bible, known as the Royal Dog of Egypt: introduced into England in 1840. [< Arabic *salūqi* < *Salūq* an ancient Arabian city]

SALUKI

sal·u·tar·y (sal′yə·ter′ē) *adj.* 1 Calculated to bring about a sound condition by correcting evil or promoting good; corrective; beneficial. 2 Salubrious; wholesome; healthful. See synonyms under HEALTHY, USEFUL. [< F *salutaire* < L *salutaris* < *salus, salutis* health] —**sal′u·tar·i·ly** *adv.* —**sal′u·tar′i·ness** *n.*

sal·u·ta·tion (sal′yə·tā′shən) *n.* 1 The act of saluting. 2 Any form of greeting. 3 The opening words of a letter, as *Dear Sir.* [< OF *salutacion* < L *salutatio, -onis* < *salutatus,* pp. of *salutare* SALUTE]

sa·lu·ta·to·ri·an (sə·lōō′tə·tôr′ē·ən, -tō′rē-) *n.* U.S. In colleges and schools, the graduating student, usually the second (sometimes the first) honor man, who delivers the salutatory at commencement. [< SALUTATORY]

sa·lu·ta·to·ry (sə·lōō′tə·tôr′ē, -tō′rē) *n. pl.* **·ries** An opening oration, as at a college commencement. —*adj.* Pertaining to or consisting in greeting or welcome; specifically, relating to a salutatory address. [< L *salutatorius* pertaining to salutation < *salutare* SALUTE]

sa·lute (sə·lōōt′) *n.* 1 A greeting by display of military, naval, or other official honors, as by presenting arms, firing cannon, etc. 2 The act of or attitude assumed in giving a military salute. 3 A gesture of greeting, compliment, respect, or the like, as a bow, kiss, etc. —*v.* **·lut·ed, ·lut·ing** *v.t.* 1 To greet with an expression or sign of welcome, respect, etc.; welcome. 2 To honor in some prescribed way, as by raising the hand to the cap, presenting arms, firing cannon, etc. —*v.i.* 3 To make a salute. See synonyms under ADDRESS. [< L *salutare* < *salus, salutis* health] —**sa·lut′er** *n.*

sal·va·ble (sal′və·bəl) *adj.* Capable of being saved or salvaged. [< LL *salvare* SAVE] — **sal′va·bil′i·ty** *n.*

sal·vage (sal′vij) *v.t.* **·vaged, ·vag·ing** To save, as a ship or its cargo, from wreck, capture, etc.; salve. —*n.* 1 The saving of a ship, cargo, etc., from loss; hence, any act of saving property. 2 The compensation allowed to persons by whose voluntary exertions a vessel, her cargo, or the lives of those belonging to her are saved from danger or loss: termed legally **civil salvage**, as distinguished from **military salvage**, which consists in the liberation of property from the enemy in time of war. 3 That which is saved from a wrecked or abandoned vessel or from or after a fire; hence, anything saved from destruction. [< OF < *salver* SAVE] —**sal′vag·er** *n.*

sal·va·tion (sal·vā′shən) *n.* 1 The process or state of being saved; preservation from impending evil. 2 *Theol.* Deliverance from sin and penalty, realized in a future state; redemption. 3 Any means of deliverance from danger, evil, or ruin. [< OF *sauvacion* < LL *salvatio, -onis* < *salvatus,* pp. of *salvare* SAVE]

Salvation Army A religious and charitable organization on semimilitary lines, founded by William Booth in England in 1865 as the Christian Mission, which took the title of Salvation Army in 1878.

salve[1] (sav, säv) *n.* 1 A thick, adhesive ointment for local ailments. 2 Anything that heals, soothes, or mollifies; hence, praise or flattery. — *v.t.* **salved, salv·ing** 1 To dress with salve or ointment. 2 To soothe; appease, as conscience, pride, etc. [OE *sealf*]

salve[2] (salv) *v.t.* **salved, salv·ing** To save from loss; salvage. [Back formation < SALVAGE]

sal·ver (sal′vər) *n.* A tray, as of silver. [< OF *salve* < Sp. *salva*, orig. the foretasting of food, as for a king < *salvar* taste, save < LL *salvare* SAVE]

sal·vi·a (sal′vē·ə) *n.* Any of a genus *(Salvia)* of ornamental plants of the mint family; the sage. [< NL < L, SAGE[2]]

sal·vo[1] (sal′vō) *n. pl.* **·vos** or **·voes** 1 A simultaneous discharge of artillery, or of two or more bombs from an aircraft. 2 A salute given by firing all the guns, as at the funeral of an officer; hence, any salute or simultaneous discharge: *salvos* of applause, a *salvo* of rockets. 3 The concentrated fire of many pieces, as in a naval engagement. 4 A successive and specified number of discharges of guns, from right to left, or left to right, at prescribed intervals. [Orig. *salva* < Ital., a salute < L *salve* SALVE[3]]

sal·vo[2] (sal′vō) *n. pl.* **·vos** 1 A saving clause; proviso. 2 An evasion, reservation, or bad excuse. 3 An expedient. [< L *salvo (jure)* (right) being reserved, ablative of *salvus* uninjured, safe]

sal·vor (sal′vər) *n.* One who or a ship which saves or helps to save vessels or property from loss at sea; a salvager. Also **salv′er.** [< SALVE[2] + -OR]

Salz·burg (zälts′bŏŏrkh) A city in west central Austria; the birthplace of Mozart.

sam·a·ra (sam′ər·ə, sə·mâr′ə) *n. Bot.* A one-seeded indehiscent fruit, as of the elm, ash, or maple, provided with a membrane or wing; a key or key fruit. [< NL < L, elm seed]

Sa·mar·i·a (sə·mâr′ē·ə) 1 In the Bible, a city of Palestine, capital of the northern kingdom of Israel, or the hill on which it was built, on the site of modern Sebastye in western Jordan. 2 In the Bible, the territory occupied by the kingdom of Israel, or, later, a restricted portion of central Palestine west of the Jordan occupied by the Samaritans.

Sa·mar·i·tan (sə·mar′ə·tən) *n.* 1 One of the people of Samaria, a mixed population. II *Kings* xvii. 2 The Northwest Semitic language of this people. —**Good Samaritan** A humane, compassionate person who helps one in trouble: from the parable in *Luke* x 30–37. —*adj.* Of or pertaining to Samaria. [< LL *Samaritanus* < Gk. *Samareitēs* < *Samareia* Samaria]

sa·mar·i·um (sə·mâr′ē·əm) *n.* A hard, brittle, metallic element (symbol Sm, atomic number 62) of the lanthanide series, three of whose seven naturally occurring isotopes are weakly radioactive. See PERIODIC TABLE. [< NL < SAMAR(SKITE); so called because first found in the spectrum of samarskite]

sa·mar·skite (sə·mär′skīt) *n.* An orthorhombic, vitreous, black mineral, source of several elements, as samarium, etc. [< G *samarskit,* after Col. Samarski, 19th c. Russian mine officer]

sam·ba (sam′bə, säm′bä) *n.* A dance of Brazilian origin in two-four time. —*v.i.* To dance the samba. [< Pg. < a native African name]

sam·bu·ca (sam·byōō′kə) *n.* In ancient music, a sharp-toned, triangular, stringed instrument resembling a harp: of Asian origin. Also **sam·buke** (sam′byōōk). [< L < Gk. *sambykē,* prob. < Aramaic *sabbĕkhā*]

sam·bur (sam′bər, säm′-) *n.* A rusine deer, especially *Cervus aristotelis,* of hilly districts in India, Burma, and China. Also **sam′bar.** [< Hind. *sābar* < Skt. *shambara*]

same (sām) *adj.* 1 Having individual or specific identity or quality; identical; equal: with *the.* 2 Similar in kind or quality. 3 Aforesaid; identical: said of a person or thing just mentioned or held in mind. 4 Equal in degree of preference; indifferent. 5 Unchanged; monotonous. See synonyms under IDENTICAL, SYNONYMOUS. —**all the same** 1 Nevertheless. 2 Equally significant; equally acceptable or unacceptable. —**just the same** 1 Nevertheless. 2 Exactly identical or corresponding; unchanged. —*pron.* The identical person, thing, event, etc. —*adv.* In like manner; equally: with *the.* [ME < ON *samr, sami.* Akin to OE *same* equally.]

sa·mek (sä′mek) *n.* The fifteenth Hebrew letter. Also **sa′mech, sa′mekh.** See ALPHABET.

same·ness (sām′nis) *n.* 1 Lack of change or variety; dull monotony. 2 Close similarity. 3 Identity.

sam·i·sen (sam′i·sen) *n.* A Japanese guitarlike instrument with three strings, played with a plectrum. [< Japanese < Chinese *san hsien* three strings]

SAMISEN

sa·mite (sā′mīt, sam′īt) *n.* A rich medieval fabric of silk, often interwoven with gold or silver. [< OF *samit* < Med. L *samitum,* var. of *examitum* < Med. Gk. *hexamiton* < *hexamitos,* woven with six threads < Gk. *hex* six + *mitos* a thread]

sam·iz·dat (säm′iz·dät′) *n.* 1 In the Soviet Union, the secret publication and distribution of officially banned literature. 2 The literature that is so published and distributed. [< Russian < *sam* self + *izdat* publishing]

sam·let (sam′lit) *n.* A young salmon; a parr. [Contracted dim. of SALMON; infl. by earlier SALMONET]

Sa·mo·a (sə·mō′ə) An island group in the SW Pacific; 1,209 square miles; formerly *Navigators' Islands;* divided by the 171st meridian into: (1) **American** (or **Eastern**) **Samoa**, an unincorporated territory of the United States, comprising Tutuila, Rose, Swains, and Manua; 76 square miles; capital, Pago Pago, on Tutuila. (2) **Western Samoa**, a former trusteeship administered by New Zealand, independent 1962, and comprising Savaii, Upolu, and several smaller islands; 1,133 square miles; capital, Apia, on Upolu.

sam·o·var (sam′ə-vär, sam′ə-vär′) *n.* A metal urn containing a tube for charcoal for heating water, as for making tea. [<Russian, lit., self-boiler <*samo*- self + *varit* boil]

Sam·o·yed (sam′ə-yed′) *n.* **1** One of a Mongoloid people inhabiting the Arctic coasts of Siberia. **2** A large dog characterized by a thick white coat of long hair, originally bred by the Samoyeds as a sled dog and for herding reindeer. —*adj.* Samoyedic. Also **Sam′·o·yede′** (-yed′). [<Russian, lit., self-eater, i.e., a cannibal]

samp (samp) *n.* Coarse, hulled Indian corn; also, a porridge made of it. [<Algonquian (Narraganset) *nasaump* softened with water]

sam·pan (sam′pan) *n.* A small flat-bottomed boat or skiff used along rivers and coasts of China and Japan. [<Chinese *san-pan* <*san* three + *pan* board]

SAMPAN
Shown with typical lateen rig

sam·phire (sam′fir) *n.* **1** A European herb (*Crithmum maritimum*) of the parsley family, having fleshy leaves (formerly used in pickles). **2** A species (*Salicornia europaea*) of glasswort. [Earlier *sampere* <F (*l'herbe de*) *Saint Pierre* (the herb of) Saint Peter; ? infl. in form by CAMPHIRE]

sam·ple (sam′pəl) *n.* A portion, part, or piece taken or shown as a representative of the whole. —*v.t.* **·pled**, **·pling** To test or examine by means of a portion or sample. [ME, aphetic var. of *asample* <OF *essample* EXAMPLE]

Synonyms (noun): case, example, exemplification, illustration, instance, specimen, A *sample* is a portion taken at random out of a quantity supposed to be homogeneous, so that the qualities found in the *sample* may reasonably be expected to be found in the whole; as, a *sample* of sugar, a *sample* of cloth. A *specimen* is one unit of a series, or a fragment of a mass, all of which is supposed to possess the same essential qualities; as, a *specimen* of coinage, or of quartz. No other unit or portion may be exactly like the *specimen*, while all the rest is supposed to be exactly like the *sample*. An *instance* is a *sample* or *specimen* of action. See EXAMPLE.

sam·pler (sam′plər) *n.* A piece of needlework, as a sample, designed to show a beginner's skill. [Aphetic var. of OF *essamplair* <LL *examplarium* <L *exemplum* EXAMPLE]

sam·pling (sam′pling) *n.* **1** A small part of something or a number of items from a group selected for examination or analysis in order to estimate the quality or nature of the whole. **2** The act or process of making this selection.

sam·sa·ra (sən·sä′rə) *n.* **1** In Buddhism, the course of mundane existence; the endless cycle of birth, death and rebirth; the wheel of causation. **2** Transmigration; metempsychosis. [<Skt. *samsāra*, lit., a passage through a succession of states]

Sam·u·rai (sam′ŏŏ·rī) *n. pl.* **·rai** *Japanese* Under the Japanese feudal system, a member of the soldier class of the lower nobility, acting as a military retainer of the daimios; also, the class itself.

San An·to·ni·o (san an·tō′nē·ō) A city in south central Texas, the third largest in the State; a port of entry with a free port zone on the **San Antonio River**, which, rising here, flows 195 miles SE to join the Guadalupe River near its mouth on San Antonio Bay.

san·a·tive (san′ə·tiv) *adj.* Healing; sanatory; health–giving. [<OF, fem. of *sanatif* <Med. L *sanativus* <L *sanatus*, pp. of *sanare* heal]

san·a·to·ri·um (san′ə·tôr′ē·əm, -tō′rē-) *n. pl.*

·to·ri·ums or **·to·ri·a** (-tôr′ē·ə, -tō′rē·ə) **1** A health retreat, especially one in the mountains. **2** An institution for treatment of disease by curative waters or climate, or for the care of invalids. [<NL <LL *sanatorius* SANATORY]

san·a·to·ry (san′ə·tôrē, -tō′rē) *adj.* Promotive of health; curative [<LL *sanatorius* <L *sanatus*, pp. of *sanare* heal]

san·be·ni·to (san′bə·nē′tō) *n. pl.* **·tos** A black garment worn by a condemned heretic or a yellow cloak worn by a penitent under the Inquisition. [<Sp. *sambenito* <*San Benito* Saint Benedict; so called from its resemblance to a Benedictine's cloak.]

San Blas (sän bläs′), **Gulf of** An inlet of the Caribbean on the north coast of Panama, east of the Panama Canal.

San·cho Pan·za (san′chō pan′zə, *Sp.* sän′chō pän′thä) In Cervantes' *Don Quixote*, a credulous peasant who acts as squire to the Don.

San Cris·to·bal (san kris·tō′bəl) One of the British Solomon Islands; 80 miles long, 25 miles wide. Also **San Cris·to′val** (-tō′vəl).

San Cris·tó·bal Island (san kris·tō′bəl) The chief island of the Galápagos group; 195 square miles; also *Chatham Island*.

sanc·ti·fied (sangk′tə·fīd) *adj.* Made holy; freed from sin; consecrated; also, sanctimonious.

sanc·ti·fy (sangk′tə·fī) *v.t.* **·fied**, **·fy·ing 1** To set apart as holy or for holy purposes; consecrate. **2** To free of sin; purify or make holy. **3** To give religious sanction to; render sacred or inviolable, as a vow. **4** To render productive of or conductive to holiness or spiritual blessing. [<OF *saintifier*, *sanctifier* <LL *sanctificare* <L *sanctus* holy + *facere* make] —**sanc′ti·fi·ca′tion** *n.* —**sanc′ti·fi′er** *n.*

sanc·ti·mo·ni·ous (sangk′tə·mō′nē·əs) *adj.* **1** Making an ostentatious display or a hypocritical pretense of sanctity. **2** *Obs.* Saintly. —**sanc′ti·mo′ni·ous·ly** *adv.* —**sanc′ti·mo′ni·ous·ness** *n.*

sanc·ti·mo·ny (sangk′tə·mō′nē) *n.* Assumed or outward sanctity; a show of holiness or devoutness; exaggerated gravity or solemnity. See synonyms under HYPOCRISY, SANCTITY. [<OF *sanctimonie* <L *sanctimonia* holiness < *sanctus* holy]

sanc·tion (sangk′shən) *v.t.* **1** To approve authoritatively; confirm; ratify. **2** To countenance; allow. See synonyms under ABET, ALLOW, CONFIRM, RATIFY. —*n.* **1** Final and authoritative confirmation; justification or ratification. **2** A formal decree. **3** A provision for securing conformity to law, as by the enactment of rewards or penalties or both; a reward or penalty. **4** *pl.* In international law, a coercive measure adopted, usually by several nations at the same time, to force a nation which is violating international law to desist or yield to adjudication, by withholding loans, limiting trade relations, or by military force and blockade. **5** In ethics, that which makes virtue morally obligatory, or which furnishes a motive for man to seek it. [<MF <L *sanctio, -onis* ordaining something inviolable, a decree < *sanctus*, pp. of *sancire* make, sacred, decree]

sanc·ti·ty (sangk′tə·tē) *n. pl.* **·ties 1** The state of being sanctified; holiness. **2** Sacredness; solemnity. [<OF *sainteté* <L *sanctitas, -tatis* <*sanctus* holy]

Synonyms: holiness, sanctimoniousness, sanctimony. As referring to character, *sanctity* is *holiness*, while *sanctimoniousness*, or *sanctimony* is the pretense or affectation of *holiness*. Compare synonyms for HOLY.

sanc·tu·ar·y (sangk′chōō·er′ē) *n. pl.* **·ar·ies 1** A holy or sacred place; especially, a building or space, as a church, mosque, temple, or structure devoted to the worship of any deity. **2** The most sacred part of a place in a sacred structure; especially, the part of a church where the principal altar is situated; in Scripture, the holy of holies of the Jewish tabernacle and temple; also, the adytum of an ancient Greek or Roman temple. **3** A place of refuge; asylum; hence, immunity. See synonyms under REFUGE, SHELTER. [<OF *sainctuarie* < LL *sanctuarium* <L *sanctus* holy]

sanc·tum (sangk′təm) *n. pl.* **·tums** or **·ta** (-tə) **1** A sacred place. **2** A private room where one is not to be disturbed. [<L, neut. of *sanctus* holy]

sanc·tum sanc·to·rum (sangk′təm sangk·tôr′əm, -tō′rəm) **1** The holy of holies. **2** A place

of great privacy: often used humorously. [<L <*sanctum*, neut. nominative sing. + *sanctorum*, neut. genitive pl. of *sanctus* holy]

Sanc·tus (sangk′təs) *n. Eccl.* **1** An ascription of praise to God, occurring at the end of the Preface in many eucharistic liturgies. **2** A musical setting for this. [<L *sanctus* holy, its thrice repeated opening word]

Sanctus bell *Eccl.* In the celebration of the Eucharist, a bell rung at the singing of the Sanctus, the elevation of the Host, etc.: also called *mass bell, sacring bell.*

San·cy (sän·sē′), **Puy de** The highest peak of the Massif Central, France; 6,817 feet.

sand (sand) *n.* **1** A hard, granular, comminuted rock material finer than gravel and coarser than dust. **2** *pl.* Sandy wastes; stretches of sandy beach. **3** *pl.* Sandy grains or particles, as those of the hourglass; hence, moments of time or life. **4** *Slang* Strength of character; endurance; grit; courage. **5** A reddish–yellow color. —*v.t.* **1** To sprinkle or cover with sand. **2** To smooth or abrade with sand or sandpaper. **3** To mix sand with: to *sand* sugar. **4** To fill with sand, as a harbor by the action of currents. [OE]

Sand (sand, *Fr.* sänd), **George** Pseudonym of Amandine Aurore Lucie Dudevant, 1803–76, *née* Dupin, French novelist.

San·da·kan (sän·dä′kän) A port of Sabah, chief town and once capital of the former North Borneo colony.

san·dal¹ (san′dəl) *n.* **1** A foot covering, consisting usually of a sole only, held to the foot by thongs. **2** A light slipper. **3** An overshoe of rubber, cut very low. **4** A strap or latchet for fastening a low shoe on the foot. **5** Sendal. [<L *sandalium* < Gk. *sandalion*, dim. of *sambalon*, *sandalon*] —**san′daled** *adj.*

SANDALS
a. Japanese. c. Greek.
b. Roman. d. Egyptian.

san·dal² (san′dəl) *n.* Sandalwood.

sandal tree A Burmese evergreen tree (*Sandoricum koetjape*), extensively cultivated in the tropics. Its fruit is an applelike edible berry.

san·dal·wood (san′dəl·wŏŏd′) *n.* **1** The fine-grained, dense, fragrant wood of any of several East Indian trees (genus *Santalum*). **2** The similar wood of other trees, as the East Indian **red sandalwood** (*Pterocarpus santalinus*): also called *sanderswood*. [<obs. *sandal* sandalwood (<Med. L *sandalum*, ult. <Skt. *śandana*) + WOOD]

Sandalwood Island A former name for SUMBA.

san·da·rac (san′də·rak) *n.* A pale–yellow aromatic gum resin that exudes in drops from the sandarac tree: used as a lacquer and as an incense. See GUM¹. Also **san′da·rach**. [<L *sandaraca* <Gk. *sandarakē* <an Oriental source]

sandarac tree A medium–sized North African tree (*Tetraclinis articulata*), yielding sandarac gum and a hard, dark–colored, fragrant wood susceptible of a high polish and used in ornamental work. Also **sandarach tree.**

sand·bag (sand′bag′) *n.* **1** A bag filled with or intended for holding sand: used for building fortifications, for ballast, etc. **2** A long, narrow bag filled with sand and used as a club or weapon. —*v.t.* **·bagged**, **·bag·ging 1** To fill or surround with sandbags. **2** To strike or attack with or as with a sandbag. **3** To coerce in some forceful way. —**sand′bag′ger** *n.*

sand·bar (sand′bär′) *n.* A ridge of silt or sand in rivers, along beaches, etc., formed by the action of currents or tides.

sand bird Any of various birds frequenting the seashore, as a snipe or sandpiper.

sand·blast (sand′blast′, -bläst′) *n.* **1** An apparatus for propelling a jet of sand, as for engraving patterns on glass. **2** The jet of sand. **3** A sandstorm. —*v.t.* To clean or engrave by means of a sandblast.

sand·blind (sand′blind′) *adj.* Partially blind; having the vision affected by appearance of moving specks, etc. —**sand′blind′ness** *n.*

sand·box (sand′boks′) *n.* **1** A box with a perforated top, formerly used for sanding freshly written paper to avoid blotting. **2** A reservoir on a locomotive filled with sand to be poured on the rail treads in front of the forward drivers to prevent slipping. **3** A box of sand for children to play in. **4** The sandbox tree.

sandbox tree A tropical American tree (*Hura crepitans*), often cultivated for its curious woody capsules which burst with a loud report when ripe.

sand·bur (sand′bûr′) *n.* **1** A pernicious weed (*Solanum rostratum*) of the great plains of the western United States, having prickly foliage. **2** An ambrosiaceous weed (*Franseria acanthicarpa*) common in western North America. Also **sand′burr′**.

Sand·burg (sand′bûrg, san′-), **Carl**, 1878–1967, U.S. poet.

sand·crack (sand′krak′) *n.* A crack running down from the coronet of a horse's hoof and apt to cause lameness if neglected. See QUARTER-CRACK.

sand dab See under DAB[1].

sand dollar Any small, flat sea urchin (genus *Echinarachnius*) having a circular shell, found on sandy bottoms from New Jersey to Labrador and on the Pacific coast.

sand·ed (san′did) *adj.* **1** Filled, covered, or clogged with sand. **2** Of a sandy color; minutely speckled.

sand eel One of a family (*Ammodytidae*) of fishes with elongate bodies. Also **sand lance** or **sand launce**.

sand·er (san′dər) *n.* **1** One who or that which sands, as a locomotive sandbox. **2** A sandpapering machine.

san·der·ling (san′dər·ling) *n.* A small sandpiper (*Crocethia alba*) of arctic breeding habits, the adult gray and white in winter but having a rusty breast in summer. [<SAND + OE *yrthling* a kind of small bird, a ploughman]

san·ders·wood (san′dərz·wŏŏd′) *n.* Sandalwood (def. 2). Also **san′ders.**

sand flea 1 The chigoe. **2** A beach flea.

sand fly Any of various minute hairy flies (family *Psychodidae*) found near the seashore and in damp places: some of the genus *Phlebotomus* are carriers of the tropical disease leishmaniasis.

sand grouse An Old World bird (family *Pteroclidae*) of pigeonlike form, with long pointed wings and short feathered legs, inhabiting sandy tracts.

san·dhi (san′dē, sän′-) *n. Ling.* **1** A phonetic environment in which a word undergoes assimilative change from its absolute form under the influence of neighboring words: "Did you" becomes dij′ŏŏ) in *sandhi.* **2** The assimilative changes occurring in combined sounds in consecutive speech: "Has" becomes (s) by *sandhi* in the sentence "Jack's done that." [<Skt. *saṁdhi* a placing together]

sand–hill·er (sand′hil′ər) *n.* A poor white inhabitant of the sand–hill districts of Georgia and South Carolina; a cracker.

sand·hog (sand′hôg′, -hog′) *n.* One who works under air pressure, as in caisson-sinking, tunnel-building, etc.: also called *ground hog.*

sand hopper A flea (def. 2).

Sand·hurst (sand′hûrst) A village in Berkshire, England; seat of the Royal Military College.

San Di·e·go (san dē·ā′gō) A port and U.S. naval base in SW California, on **San Diego Bay**, a landlocked natural harbor separated from the Pacific Ocean by overlapping peninsulas.

sand lily A low–growing herb (*Leucocrinum montanum*) of the lily family, with fragrant white flowers, native in western and Pacific States: also *star lily.*

sand–lot (sand′lot′) *adj.* Of or in a vacant lot in or near an urban area: applied to games played in such lots: *sand–lot* baseball.

sand·man (sand′man′) *n.* In nursery lore, a mythical person supposed to make children sleepy by casting sand in their eyes.

sand martin The bank swallow.

sand painting An indigenous Amerindian art form practiced especially by the Navaho. Pigments of finely ground sand in five colors are trickled on a ground base of neutral–colored sand to give highly symbolic representations (usually the gods, a rainbow, lightning, etc.). Each painting, whether three or twenty feet

in diameter, has to be started at dawn and finished by sunset.

sand·pa·per (sand′pā′pər) *n.* Stout paper coated with sand for smoothing or polishing. — *v.t.* To rub or polish with sandpaper.

sand pine The smooth–barked pine (*Pinus clausa*) of sandy areas of the southern United States, especially common to the Gulf coast of Florida.

sand·pi·per (sand′pī′pər) *n.* Any of certain small wading birds (family *Scolopacidae*), mostly frequenting seashores in flocks. The two best known are the **common sandpiper** (*Actitis hypoleuca*) of Europe, and the **spotted sandpiper** (*A. macularia*) of North America. —**least sandpiper** A tiny, common, American marsh and shore bird (*Enolia minutilla*): also **sand′peep′** (-pēp′).

SANDPIPER
(From 7 to 9
inches long)

San·dring·ham (san′dring·əm) A royal estate and parish of NW Norfolk, England.

San·dro·cot·tus (san′drō·kot′əs) See CHANDRAGUPTA I.

sand·stone (sand′stōn′) *n.* A rock consisting chiefly of quartz sand cemented with silica.

sand·storm (sand′stôrm′) *n.* A high wind by which sand or dust is carried along.

San·dus·ky (san·dus′kē) A port of entry on Lake Erie in northern Ohio.

sand verbena A trailing annual or perennial plant (genus *Abronia*) with vivid red, yellow, or white flowers, native in deserts of the western United States.

sand viper 1 The hog–nosed snake. **2** The horned viper.

sand·wich (sand′wich, san′-) *n.* Two thin slices of bread, having between them meat, cheese, etc.; hence, any combination of alternating dissimilar things pressed together. — *v.t.* To place between two layers or objects; insert between dissimilar things. [after John Montagu, fourth Earl of *Sandwich*, 1718–92, who is said to have originated it in order to eat without leaving the gaming table]

Sand·wich (sand′wich) A municipal borough in Kent, England, near Dover; the most ancient of the Cinque Ports.

Sandwich Islands A former name for the HAWAIIAN ISLANDS.

sand·wich–man (sand′wich·man′, -mən, san′-) *n. pl.* **–men** (-men′, -mən) A man carrying advertising boards slung in front and behind.

sand·y (san′dē) *adj.* **sand·i·er, sand·i·est 1** Consisting of or characterized by sand; containing, covered with, or full of sand. **2** Yellowish–red: a *sandy* beard. —**sand′i·ness** *n.*

Sandy Hook A peninsula, 6 miles long, extending north from eastern New Jersey, at the entrance to New York Bay.

sane[1] (sān) *adj.* **1** Mentally sound; not deranged. **2** Proceeding from a sound mind. [<L *sanus* whole, healthy] —**sane′ly** *adv.* —**sane′ness** *n.*

Synonyms: healthy, lucid, rational, sober, sound, underanged, unperverted. See SOBER.

sane[2] (sān) See SAIN.

San·ford (san′fərd), **Mount** The highest peak of the Wrangell Mountains in southern Alaska; 16,208 feet.

San·for·ize (san′fə·rīz) *v.t.* **·ized, ·iz·ing** To treat (cloth) by a special mechanical process so as to prevent more than slight shrinkage: a trade name. [after *Sanford* L. Cluett, inventor of the process, 1874–1968] —**San′for·ized** *adj.* —**San′for·iz·ing** *adj. & n.*

San Fran·cis·co (san′ frən·sis′kō) The second largest city of California, a port on **San Francisco Bay**, a landlocked inlet of the Pacific Ocean in

western California. Colloquially shortened to *Frisco.* —**San′ Fran·cis′can** *n. & adj.*

san·ga·ree (sang′gə·rē′) *n.* A tropical drink of wine or brandy and water, spiced and sweetened. [<Sp. *sangria*, lit., bleeding <*sangre* blood <L *sanguis*]

sang–froid (sän·frwä′) *n.* Calmness amid trying circumstances; coolness; composure. [<F, lit., cold blood]

san·gri·a (sang·grē′ə) *n.* An alcoholic drink made from red wine and fruit juice. [<Sp. *sangria* <*sangre* blood]

san·guic·o·lous (sang·gwik′ə·ləs) *adj.* Inhabiting the blood, as a parasite. [<L *sanguis* blood + *colere* inhabit]

san·guif·er·ous (sang·gwif′ər·əs) *adj.* Conducting blood, as the organs of circulation. [<L *sanguis* blood + -FEROUS]

san·gui·nar·i·a (sang·gwə·nâr′ē·ə) *n.* The bloodroot, or its medicinal preparation which is emetic. [<NL <L (*herba*) *sanguinaria*, fem. of *sanguinarius* SANGUINARY]

san·gui·nar·y (sang′gwə·ner′ē) *adj.* **1** Attended with bloodshed. **2** Prone to shed blood; bloodthirsty. **3** Consisting of blood. [<L *sanguinarius* <*sanguis*, -*inis* blood] —**san′gui·nar′i·ly** *adv.* —**san′gui·nar′i·ness** *n.*

Synonyms: blood thirsty, bloody, cruel, inhuman, murderous, sanguine, savage. *Sanguinary* applies either to the act of shedding blood or to the spirit that delights in bloodshed; *bloody* applies more directly to the actual staining with blood; we may say either a *sanguinary* or a *bloody* battle, but a *bloody* (not a *sanguinary*) field. *Sanguine* is sometimes used in poetic or elevated style in the sense of *bloody*; as, a *sanguine* stain. See BLOODY.

san·guine (sang′gwin) *adj.* **1** Of buoyant disposition; hopeful; confident; originally, having a temperament supposed to be due to active blood. **2** Having the color of blood; of, like, or full of blood. **3** *Obs.* Bloodthirsty; sanguinary. [<OF *sanguin* <L *sanguineus* < *sanguis, sanguinis* blood] —**san′guine·ly** *adv.* —**san′guine·ness** *n.*

Synonyms: animated, ardent, buoyant, confident, enthusiastic, hopeful. *Sanguine*, from the same root as *sanguinary*, came to denote full-blooded or plethoric, hence, *ardent, confident, hopeful*, because these qualities were supposed to be associated with fullness of blood. For the rare use of *sanguine* in direct literal sense, see synonyms under SANGUINARY.

san·guin·e·ous (sang·gwin′ē·əs) *adj.* **1** Pertaining to, consisting of, or forming blood. **2** Full-blooded; sanguine; hence, hopeful. **3** Of the color of blood. [<L *sanguineus* SANGUINE]

San·he·drin (san′hi·drin, san′i-) *n.* **1** In ancient times, the supreme council and highest court of the Jewish nation: also **Great Sanhedrin. 2** Figuratively, any council or assembly. Also spelled *Synedrion*, *Synedrium*. Also **San′he·drim** (-drim). [<Hebrew *sanhedrin* <Gk. *synedrion*, lit., a sitting together <*syn-* together + *hedra* a seat]

san·i·cle (san′i·kəl) *n.* Any of a genus (*Sanicula*) of smooth perennial herbs of the carrot family, reputed to have medicinal roots. [<OF <Med. L *sanicula*, prob. dim. <L *sanus* healthy; with ref. to its reputed healing powers]

sa·ni·es (sā′ni·ēz) *n. Pathol.* A serous, greenish, blood-tinged fluid discharged from ulcers. [<NL <L]

sa·ni·ous (sā′nē·əs) *adj.* **1** Of or like sanies; watery and blood-tinged. **2** Producing or discharging sanies.

san·i·tar·i·an (san′ə·târ′ē·ən) *n.* A person skilled in matters relating to sanitation and public health.

san·i·tar·i·um (san′ə·târ′ē·əm) *n. pl.* **·tar·i·ums** or **·tar·i·a** (-târ′ē·ə) A sanatorium. [<NL <L *sanitas* health]

san·i·tar·y (san′ə·ter′ē) *adj.* **1** Relating to the preservation of health. **2** Cleanly; disease-preventing. See synonyms under HEALTHY. —*n. pl.* **·tar·ies** A public watercloset or urinal. [<F *sanitaire* <L *sanitas* health <*sanus* healthy] —**san′i·tar′i·ly** *adv.*

sanitary napkin An absorbent pad used by women during menstruation.

san·i·ta·tion (san′ə·tā′shən) *n.* The practical application of sanitary science; the removal or

san·i·tize (san′ə·tīz) *v.t.* **·tized, ·tiz·ing 1** To make sanitary, as by scrubbing, washing, or sterilizing. **2** To make acceptable or unobjectionable, as by deleting offensive parts: *a sanitized version of the fairy tale.*

san·i·ty (san′ə·tē) *n.* **1** The state of being sane or sound; soundness of mind; mental health. **2** Moderation; reasonableness. [< MF *sanité* < L *sanitas* health < *sanus* healthy]

San Jo·sé (sän hō·zā′) **1** The capital of Costa Rica. **2** (san′hō·zā′) A city on San Francisco Bay in western California.

San Juan (sän hwän′) **1** A port, capital of Puerto Rico. **2** A province of west central Argentina; 33,249 square miles; capital, San Juan.

San·khya (säng′kyə) *n.* The oldest system of Indian philosophy, professing unqualified dualism: founded by Kapila, fabled son of Brahma. [< Skt. *Sāmkhya* < *samkhyā* enumeration; with ref. to its enumeration of twenty–four material principles *(tattva)* and one independent immaterial principle]

San Ma·ri·no (mä·rē′nō) An independent republic in eastern Italy near the coast of the Adriatic Sea; 23 square miles; capital, San Marino.

San Mar·tín (mär·tēn′), **José de,** 1778–1850, South American general and statesman.

san·nup (san′up) *n.* A married male American Indian; the husband of a squaw. Also **san′. nop.** [< Algonquian (Narraganset) *sannop*]

sans (sanz, *Fr.* sän) *prep.* Without. [< OF *sens, sanz,* alter. of L *absentia* absence, infl. by *sine* without]

San Sal·va·dor (san′ sal′və·dôr, *Sp.* sän säl′vä·thōr′) The capital of El Salvador.

San Salvador Island An island in the central Bahamas, the first landing place of Columbus in the New World, 1492: also called *Watling Island.*

sans·cu·lotte (sanz′kyōō·lot′, *Fr.* sän·kü·lôt′) *n.* **1** A revolutionary: first applied by the aristocrats as a term of contempt for those who started the revolution of 1789; later it became a popular name for one of a revolutionary mob; a Jacobin. **2** Any revolutionary republican or radical. **3** Any ragged or strangely dressed person. [< F, lit., without knee breeches] — **sans′cu·lot′tic** *adj.* — **sans′·cu·lot′. tism** *n.*

San·sei (sän·sā) *n. pl.* **·sei** An American citizen of Japanese descent whose grandparents settled in the United States; a third–generation Japanese American. [< Japanese, third generation]

san·se·vi·e·ri·a (san′sə·vi·ir′ē·ə) *n.* Any of a genus *(Sansevieria)* of erect perennial herbs of the lily family, native in Africa but sometimes grown as an ornamental plant. [< NL, after the Prince of *Sanseviero,* 1710–71, a Neapolitan savant]

San·skrit (san′skrit) *n.* The ancient and classical language of the Hindus of India, belonging to the Indic branch of the Indo–Iranian subfamily of Indo–European languages. It includes specifically **Vedic Sanskrit,** the language of the Vedas, and the later **classical Sanskrit** of India's great religious, philosophical, and poetic literature, still used for sacred or learned writings, and distinguished from the vernacular Prakrit. Also **San′scrit.** *Abbr.* Skt. [< Skt. *samskrita* well-formed < *sam–* together + *kr* make, do] — **San′skrit·ist** *n.*

sans ser·if (sanz ser′if) *Printing* A style of type without serifs.

San·ta Claus (san′tə klōz′) In nursery folklore, a friend of children who brings presents at Christmas time: usually represented as a fat, jolly old man. The patron saint of children, figuring in the nursery lore of many countries and identified with *St. Nicholas.* [< dial. Du. *Sante Klaus* Saint Nicholas]

San·ta Fe (san′tə fā′) **1** The capital of New Mexico, in the northern part of the State. **2** (sän′tä fā′) A province of NE central Argentina; 51,341 square miles; capital, Santa Fe.

Santa Fe trail The trade route, important from 1821 to 1880, between Independence, Missouri, or a nearby terminus, and Santa Fe, New Mexico.

san·ta·la·ceous (san′tə·lā′shəs) *adj. Bot.* Of or pertaining to a family *(Santalaceae)* of apetalous shrubs, herbs, and some trees; the sandal-

wood family. [< NL < *Santalum,* genus name < Med. L, sandalwood]

san·tal·ic (san·tal′ik) *adj.* Of, pertaining to, or derived from sandalwood, as **santalic acid,** a red crystalline coloring matter, $C_{15}H_{14}O_5$. [< NL *santal(um)* sandalwood (< Med. L) + -IC]

San·ta·ya·na (sän·tä·yä′nä), **George,** 1863–1952, U.S. philosopher and author born in Spain.

San·ti·a·go (sän′tē·ä′gō) **1** The capital of Chile. Also **Santiago de Chi·le** (thä chē′lä). **2** Santiago de Compostela. **3** Santiago de los Caballeros.

Santiago de Cu·ba (thä kōō′bä) **1** The second largest city of Cuba and capital of Oriente province, on the southern coast. **2** The former name for ORIENTE province, Cuba.

San·to Do·min·go (sän′tō dō·ming′gō) The capital of the Dominican Republic, a port on the south coast; the oldest continuously occupied European settlement in the Western Hemisphere: formerly *Ciudad Trujillo.*

san·ton·i·ca (san·ton′i·kə) *n.* **1** An Old World plant of the composite family, especially the European wormwood *(Artemisia maritima).* **2** The unexpanded flower heads of this plant, used as a vermifuge. [< NL < L *(herba) Santonica* a kind of wormwood, fem. sing. of *Santonicus* of the Santoni < *Santoni* the Santoni, a people of Aquitania]

São To·mé e Prín·ci·pe (souñ tô·me′ e preñ′sē·pə) A Portuguese province in the Bight of Biafra, comprising the islands of **São Tomé** (also **São Thomé,** English *St. Thomas);* 320 square miles; and **Principe** (English *Prince Island);* 52 square miles.

sap[1] (sap) *n.* **1** The aqueous juices of plants, which contain and transport the materials necessary to vegetable growth. **2** Any vital fluid; vitality. **3** Sapwood. **4** *Slang* A foolish, stupid, or ineffectual person. [OE *sæp*]

sap[2] (sap) *v.* **sapped, sap·ping** *v.t.* **1** To weaken or destroy gradually and insidiously; enervate; exhaust. **2** To approach or undermine (an enemy fortification) by digging a sap or saps. — *v.i.* **3** To dig a sap or saps; undermine an enemy fortification. See synonyms under WEAKEN. — *n.* A deep, narrow trench or tunnel dug so as to approach or undermine a fortification. [< MF *saper, sapper < sappe* a spade < Ital. *zappe < zappa* a goat; with ref. to resemblance of the handle to a goat's horns]

sap·a·jou (sap′ə·jōō, *Fr.* sá·pá·zhōō′) *n.* A South American monkey, the capuchin: often seen in captivity. Also called *sajou.* [< F < Tupian]

sa·pan·wood (sə·pan′wŏŏd′) *n.* **1** The brownish–red dyewood obtained from a medium–sized East Indian tree *(Caesalpinia sappan)* of the bean family. **2** The tree. Also spelled *sappanwood:* also called *brazil.* [Trans. of Du. *sapanhout* < Malay *sapang* sapanwood + Du. *hout* wood]

SAPAJOU
(Head and body about 1 1/2 feet long)

sa·phe·na (sə·fē′nə) *n. pl.* **·nae** (-nē) *Anat.* One of the two large superficial veins of the leg. [< Med. L, a vein in the leg < Arabic *sāfin*] — **sa·phe′nous** *adj.*

sap·id (sap′id) *adj.* Affecting the sense of taste; savory; agreeable. [< L *sapidus < sapere* taste] — **sa·pid′i·ty, sap′id·ness** *n.*

sa·pi·ence (sā′pē·əns) *n.* Wisdom; learning: often ironical. Also **sa′pi·en·cy.** [< OF < L *sapientia* wisdom < *sapiens, -entis* SAPIENT]

sa·pi·ent (sā′pē·ənt) *adj.* Wise; sagacious: often ironical. See synonyms under WISE[1]. [< L *sapiens, -entis,* ppr. of *sapere* know, taste] — **sa′pi·ent·ly** *adv.*

sa·pi·en·tial (sā′pē·en′shəl) *adj.* Of, marked by, or expounding wisdom; especially, the *sapiential* books of the Bible, as Proverbs. — **sa′pi·en′tial·ly** *adv.*

sap·in·da·ceous (sap′in·dā′shəs) *adj. Bot.* Of or pertaining to a family *(Sapindaceae)* of mostly tropical trees, shrubs, and vines, the soapberry family, including some genera with edible fruit, as the litchi tree. [< NL < *Sapindus,* genus name < L *sapo* soap + *Indicus*

Indian]

sap·less (sap′lis) *adj.* **1** Destitute of sap; withered. **2** Wanting vitality, spirit, or vivacity; insipid; dull.

sap·ling (sap′ling) *n.* **1** A young tree. **2** A youth. [Dim. of SAP[1]]

sap·o·dil·la (sap′ə·dil′ə) *n.* **1** A large evergreen tree *(Achras zapota)* of the West Indies and Central America. **2** Its luscious apple–shaped fruit, the **sapodilla plum,** for which it is cultivated. Often called *mamey, marmalade tree.* Also **sa·po·ta** (sə·pō′tə), **sap′a·dil′lo, sap′o·dil′lo.** [< Sp. *zapotille,* dim of *zapota* < Nahuatl *zapotl, sapotl*]

sap·o·na·ceous (sap′ə·nā′shəs) *adj.* Of the nature of soap; soapy. [< NL *saponaceus < L sapo, saponis* soap]

sa·pon·i·fi·ca·tion (sə·pon′ə·fə·kā′shən) *n.* **1** The process or result of making soap. **2** *Chem.* **a** A decomposition in which an ester is changed into an acid and an alcohol. **b** The conversion of certain acid derivatives, as nitrates, acid amides, etc., into the corresponding acids.

sa·pon·i·fy (sə·pon′ə·fī) *v.t.* **·fied, ·fy·ing** To convert (a fat or oil) into soap by the action of an alkali. [< F *saponifier* < NL *saponificare* < L *sapo, saponis* soap + *facere* make] — **sa·pon′i·fi′a·ble** *adj.* — **sa·pon′i·fi′er** *n.*

sap·o·nin (sap′ə·nin) *n. Biochem.* One of several nearly white amorphous glycosides contained in various plants and characterized by their ability to form emulsions and soapy lathers. Also **sap′o·nine** (-nēn, -nin). [< F *saponine* < L *sapo, saponis* soap + F -ine -INE[2]]

sap·o·nite (sap′ə·nīt) *n.* A soft, hydrous silicate of magnesium and aluminum, found as an amorphous soaplike mass in nodules, or filling cavities in rock. [< L *sapo, saponis* soap + -ITE[1]]

sa·por (sā′pər, -pôr) *n.* That quality of a substance affecting the sense of taste; flavor; taste. Also *Brit.* **sa′pour.** [< L, taste < *sapere* taste, know] — **sap·o·rif·ic** (sap′ə·rif′ik), **sap′o·rous** *adj.*

sap·o·ta·ceous (sap′ə·tā′shəs) *adj. Bot.* Of or pertaining to a family *(Sapotaceae)* of trees and shrubs yielding a milky juice of considerable economic importance, and also some edible fruits, as the sapodilla family. [< NL < *sapota* < Sp. *zapote* SAPODILLA]

sap·per (sap′ər) *n.* **1** One who or that which saps. **2** A soldier employed in making trenches, tunnels, and underground fortifications. [< SAP[2] + -ER]

Sap·phic (saf′ik) *adj.* **1** Pertaining to or in the manner of Sappho. **2** Denoting a meter or verse form used by Sappho, especially a stanza of three Sapphics followed by an Adonic. — *n.* A line of trochaic pentameter with a dactyl in the third foot: much used by Sappho, Alcaeus, Horace, and other classical poets. [< F *sapphique, saphique* < L *Sapphicus* < Gk. *Sapphikos* < *Sapphō* Sappho]

sap·phire (saf′īr) *n.* **1** Any of various gemstones consisting of corundum of a color other than red but especially blue. **2** A jewel fashioned of sapphire. **3** Deep pure blue. [< OF *sapir* < L *sapphirus, sapp(h)ir* < Gk. *sappheiros,* a gemstone < Semitic, ? ult. < Skt. *sanipriya* dear to the planet Saturn]

Sap·pho (saf′ō) Greek poetess of Lesbos; lived about 600 B.C.

Sap·po·ro (säp·pō·rō) The capital of Hokkaido island, Japan.

sap·py (sap′ē) *adj.* **·pi·er, ·pi·est 1** Full of sap; juicy. **2** *Slang* Immature; silly. **3** Vital; pithy. — **sap′pi·ly** *adv.* — **sap′pi·ness** *n.*

sa·pre·mi·a (sə·prē′mē·ə) *n. Pathol.* Blood poisoning by the products of putrefaction. Also **sa·prae′mi·a.** [< NL < Gk. *sapros* putrid + *haima* blood] — **sa·pre′mic** *adj.*

sapro– *combining form* **1** Decomposition or putrefaction: *saprogenic.* **2** Saprophytic: *saproplankton.* [< Gk. *sapros* rotten]

sap·ro·gen·ic (sap′rə·jen′ik) *adj.* **1** Productive of putrefaction. **2** Developing in or living upon putrefying matter. Also **sa·prog·e·nous** (sə·proj′ə·nəs).

sap·ro·lite (sap′rə·līt) *n. Geol.* Thoroughly decomposed, earthy rock, lying in its original place. [< SAPRO– + -LITE] — **sap′ro·lit′ic** (-lit′ik) *adj.*

sa·proph·a·gous (sə·prof′ə·gəs) *adj.* Feeding on decaying substances. [< SAPRO– + -PHAGOUS]

sap·ro·phyte (sap′rə·fīt) *n.* An organism that lives on dead or decaying organic matter, as certain fungous or other plants, various bacteria, etc. [<SAPRO- + -PHYTE] —**sap′ro·phyt′ic** (-fit′ik) adj.

sap·ro·plank·ton (sap′rə-plangk′tən) n. Plankton found on the surface of stagnant water. [<SAPRO- + PLANKTON]

sap·sa·go (sap′sə-gō) n. A hard green Swiss cheese flavored with melilot, used chiefly in cooking. [Alter. of G schabzieger <schaben shave, scrape + zieger whey]

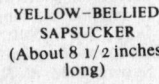

YELLOW–BELLIED
SAPSUCKER
(About 8 1/2 inches
long)

sap·suck·er (sap′suk′ər) n. Any small black-and-white woodpecker (genus Sphyrapicus), especially the **yellow-bellied sapsucker** (S. varius), which damages orchard trees by exposing and devouring the sapwood.

sap·wood (sap′wo͝od′) n. The layer of newly formed and functional xylem cells between the cambium and the heartwood of a woody stem. Also called alburnum.

Saq·qa·ra (sə-kä′rə) See SAKKARA.

sar·a·band (sar′ə-band) n. A stately Spanish dance in triple time, of the 17th and 18th centuries; also, the music for or in the rhythm of this dance, often used as one of the movements of the classical suite. Also **sar′a·bande.** [<F sarabande <Sp. zarabanda, ult. <Persian sarband a kind of dance and song]

Sar·a·cen (sar′ə-sən) n. 1 Originally, a nomad Arab of the Syrian-Arabian desert, who harassed the frontiers of the Roman Empire. 2 A Moslem enemy of the Crusaders. 3 Any Arab. 4 Obs. A heathen; pagan. [Fusion of OE Sarracene and OF Sarazin, Saracin, both <LL Saracenus <LGk. Sarakēnos, ? <Arabic] —**Sar′a·cen′ic** (-sen′ik) or **-i·cal** adj.

Sa·ra·je·vo (sä′rä-yä′vō) A city in central Yugoslavia; the former capital of Bosnia where Archduke Francis Ferdinand was assassinated, June 28, 1914: also Serajevo.

sa·ran (sə-ran′) n. Any of a class of synthetic fibers and textile materials obtained by the chemical treatment of petroleum and natural brines. [Coined by Dow Chemical Co.]

Saratoga Springs A resort city in eastern New York, noted for horse-racing and mineral waters.

Sa·ra·wak (sə-rä′wäk) A State of Malaysia in NW Borneo; 47,071 square miles; capital, Kuching. —**Sa·ra·wak·ese** (sə-rä′wäk-ēz′, -ēs′) adj. & n.

sar·casm (sär′kaz-əm) n. 1 A keenly ironical or scornful utterance; contemptuous and taunting language. 2 The use of biting gibes or cutting rebukes. See synonyms under BANTER. [<LL sarcasmus <Gk. sarkasmos <sarkazein tear flesh, speak bitterly <sarx, sarkos flesh]

sar·cas·tic (sär-kas′tik) adj. 1 Characterized by or of the nature of sarcasm. 2 Taunting. Also **sar·cas′ti·cal.** —**sar·cas′ti·cal·ly** adv.

Sar·ci·na (sär′sī′nə) n. A genus of parasitic, usually Gram-positive bacteria, which divide to form clusters of individuals: many are saprophytic. See illustration under BACTERIA. [<NL <L, a bundle <sarcire patch, mend]

sarco- combining form Flesh; of or related to flesh: sarcogenic. Also, before vowels, **sarc-.** [<Gk. sarx, sarkos flesh]

Sar·co·di·na (sär′kō-dī′nə) n. pl. A class of marine and fresh-water protozoa which move by means of pseudopodia, including both naked forms, as the Amoebae, and those with protective shell covering, as the Foraminifera. [<NL <Gk. sarkōdēs fleshy <sarx, sarkos flesh]

sar·co·gen·ic (sär′kō-jen′ik) adj. Flesh-producing. Also **sar·cog·e·nous** (sär-koj′ə-nəs).

sar·co·ma (sär-kō′mə) n. pl. **-ma·ta** (-mə-tə) Pathol. A tumor, or group of tumors, often malignant, composed of embryonal lymphoid or connective tissue in which the cell elements predominate. [<NL <Gk. sarkōma <sarkaein become fleshy <sarx, sarkos flesh] —**sar·co′ma·toid, sar·co′ma·tous** (-kō′mə-təs, -kom′ə-) adj.

sar·co·ma·to·sis (sär-kō′mə-tō′sis) n. Pathol. The formation of sarcomatous growths in the body. [<NL <Gk. sarkōma, -ōmatos SARCOMA + -ōsis -OSIS]

sar·coph·a·gus (sär-kof′ə-gəs) n. pl. **-gi** (-jī) 1 A stone coffin or tomb; hence, a large ornamental coffin of marble or stone placed in a crypt or exposed to view. 2 A kind of limestone, used by the Greeks for coffins and said to reduce flesh to dust. [<L <Gk. sarkophagos, orig. adj., flesh-eating <sarx, sarkos flesh + phagein eat]

sar·co·plasm (sär′kō-plaz′əm) n. Anat. The substance resembling hyaloplasm that lies between the columns of a striated muscle fiber.

sar·cous (sär′kəs) adj. Of, pertaining to, or composed of flesh or muscle. [<Gk. sarx, sarkos flesh]

sard (särd) n. The deep brownish-red variety of chalcedony, translucently blood-red: used as a gem. Also called sardine, sardius. [<OF sarde <L sarda <Gk. sardios. See SARDIUS.]

sar·dine (sär-dēn′) n. 1 A small fish preserved in oil as a delicacy, especially the California pilchard (Sardinia coerulea). 2 The young of the herring or some like fish similarly prepared. [<OF <Ital. sardina <L <Gk. sardēnē <sarda a kind of fish, prob. <Sardō Sardinia]

Sar·din·i·a (sär-din′ē-ə) 1 An Italian island in the Mediterranean, west of Italy; 9,196 square miles; forming, with its neighboring islands, an autonomous region of Italy; 9,298 square miles; capital, Cagliari. Italian **Sar·de·gna** (sär-dā′nyä). 2 A former kingdom (1720–1860) of northern Italy, including the island of Sardinia with Savoy and Piedmont. —**Sar·din′i·an** adj. & n.

sar·di·us (sär′dē-əs) n. 1 A sard. 2 A stone in the breastplate of the Hebrew high priest. Ex. xxviii 17. [<LL <Gk. sardios, sardion <Sardeis Sardis]

sar·don·ic (sär-don′ik) adj. Scornful or derisive; sneering; mocking; cynical. [<F sardonique <L sardonius <Gk. sardonios <sardanios bitter, scornful; infl. in form by Sardō Sardinia, because thought to be <sardanē, a bitter plant of Sardinia causing fatal, laughterlike convulsions] —**sar·don′i·cal·ly** adv. —**sar·don′i·cism** n.

sar·do·nyx (sär′dō-niks) n. A variety of onyx, consisting of alternate layers of light-colored chalcedony and reddish carnelian. [<L <Gk., appar. <sardios sardius + onyx onyx]

sar·gas·so (sär-gas′ō) n. Gulfweed. [<Pg. sargaço <sarga, a kind of grape]

sa·ri (sär′ē) n. A long piece of cotton or silk cloth, constituting the principal garment of Hindu women: worn round the waist, one end falling to the feet, and the other crossed over the bosom, shoulder, and sometimes over the head. Also **sa′ree.** [<Hind. sarī, sarhī <Skt. śāṭī]

sar·men·tose (sär-men′tōs) adj. Bot. Having or producing sarmenta; having runners. Also **sar·men·ta·ceous** (sär′mən-tā′shəs), **sar·men′tous.** [<L sarmentosus full of twigs <sarmentum. See SARMENTUM.]

sar·men·tum (sär-men′təm) n. pl. **-ta**(-tə) Bot. The slender runner of a plant, as in a vine. Also **sar′ment.** [<NL <L, a twig lopped off <sarpere prune (trees)]

sa·rod (sə-rōd′) n. A lutelike Indian stringed instrument. [<Hindi sarod]

sa·rong (sə-rong′) n. 1 A skirtlike garment of colored silk or cloth worn by both sexes in the Malay Archipelago, etc. 2 The material used for this garment. [<Malay sārung, prob. <Skt. sāranga variegated]

sar·ra·ce·ni·a (sar′ə-sē′nē-ə) n. Any of a genus of plants, having trumpetlike or pitcher-shaped leaves by which insects are entrapped and then digested by the plants; a pitcherplant. [<NL, orig. Sarracena, after Dr. D. Sarrazin, 17th–18th c. physician of Quebec who sent a specimen to the botanist Tournefort in 1700] —**sar′ra·ce′ni·a·ceous** (-sē′nē-ā′shəs) adj.

sar·rus·o·phone (sa-rus′ə-fōn) n. A musical instrument resembling a bassoon but with a metal tube. [after Sarrus, 19th c. French bandmaster, its inventor + -(O)PHONE]

sar·sa·pa·ril·la (sas′pə-ril′ə, sär′sə-pə-ril′ə) n. 1 The dried roots of certain tropical American climbing plants (genus Smilax). 2 A medicinal preparation or a beverage made from them. 3 Any one of various plants, so called

from some resemblance to true sarsaparilla, as the wild sarsaparilla (Aralia nudicaulis). [< Sp. zarzaparilla <zarza a bramble +parilla, dim. of parra a vine]

sar·sar (sär′sər) n. A cold, whistling wind of Moslem lands: also spelled sansar. [<Arabic ṣarṣar a cold wind]

sarse·net (särs′nit) n. A fine, thin silk, used for linings: also spelled sarcenet. [<AF sarzinet, dim. of ME sarzin a Saracen; prob. infl. by OF drap sarrasinois, lit., Saracen cloth <Med. L pannus saracenicus]

Sar·to (sär′tō), **Andrea del,** 1487–1531, Florentine painter.

sar·tor (sär′tər) n. A tailor: a humorous or literary term. [<L, a patcher, mender <sartus, pp. of sarcire mend]

sar·to·ri·al (sär-tôr′ē-əl, -tō′rē-) adj. 1 Pertaining to a tailor or his work; also, pertaining to men's clothes: sartorial perfections. 2 Anat. Relating to the sartorius. —**sar·to′ri·al·ly** adv.

sar·to·ri·us (sär-tôr′ē-əs, -tō′rē-) n. Anat. A long, narrow muscle of the thigh that aids in flexing the knee; the longest muscle in the human body: so called from its use in crossing the legs, as in the manner in which tailors traditionally sat down to work. [<NL <L <sartor a or]

Sar·tre (sär′tr′), **Jean Paul,** born 1905, French philosopher, novelist, and dramatist.

sash[1] (sash) n. An ornamental band or scarf, worn as a girdle, or around the waist or over the shoulder, often as part of a uniform or as a badge of distinction. [Orig. shash <Arabic shāsh muslin, turban]

sash[2] (sash) n. A frame, as of a window, in which glass is set. —v.t. To furnish with a sash. [Alter. of CHASSIS, taken as a pl.]

sa·shi·mi (sä′shē-mē) n. In Japan, raw fish slices.

sa·sin (sä′sin) n. The common black buck. [< Nepalese]

Sas·katch·e·wan (sas-kach′ə-won) A province of west central Canada; 251,700 square miles; capital, Regina: abbr. Sask.

sas·ka·toon (sas′kə-tōōn′) n. A small tree (Amelanchier alnifolia) of the rose family, with thick leaves and a globular purple fruit; a shadbush. [<Algonquian (Cree) misāskwatomin <misāskwat the shadbush + min a fruit, a berry]

Sas·quatch (sas′kwach, -kwôch) n. A hairy, bigfooted creature supposed to live in the forests of the Pacific Northwest.

sass (sas) Colloq. n. Impudence; back talk. —v.t. To talk to impudently or disrespectfully. [Dial. alter. of SAUCE.]

sas·sa·by (sas′ə-bē) n. pl. **-bies** A large dark-red South African antelope (genus Damaliscus), with almost black back and face. [<Bantu tsessébe, tsessábi]

sas·sa·fras (sas′ə-fras) n. 1 A tree (genus Sassafras) of the laurel family. 2 The bark of the roots, yielding an aromatic stimulant and an essential oil used in cosmetics. [<Sp. sasafrás, prob. <N. Am. Ind. name; infl. in form by Sp. sassifragia <L saxifraga saxifrage]

sas·sy[1] (sas′ē) adj. **-si·er, -si·est** U.S. Dial. Saucy; impertinent.

sas·sy[2] (sas′ē) n. A West African tree (Erythrophleum guineense) with poisonous bark and juice. Also **sas′sy·wood** (-wo͝od). [<native W. African name, ? <E saucy]

Sa·tan (sā′tən) In the Bible, the great adversary of God and tempter of mankind; the Devil: identified with Lucifer who, in Semitic mythology, led a revolt against God, was defeated by the archangel Michael, and cast into hell as punishment for his pride. Luke iv 5–8; Rev. xii 7–9. [<Hebrew sātān an enemy <sātan oppose, plot against]

sa·tang (sä-tang′) n. pl. **sa·tang** A bronze coin and money of account in Thailand; one one-hundredth of a baht. [<Siamese satāṅ]

sa·tan·ic (sā-tan′ik) adj. Devilish; infernal; wicked. Also **sa·tan′i·cal.** See synonyms under INFERNAL —**sa·tan′i·cal·ly** adv.

Sa·tan·ism (sā′tən-iz′əm) n. Satan-worship; specifically, a cult addicted to profane mockeries of the holy rites of Christian worship. —**Sa′tan·ist** n.

sat·a·ra (sat′ər-ə, sə-tä′rə) n. A lustrous ribbed woolen fabric. [from Satara, a town about 100 miles from Bombay, India]

satch·el (sach′əl) n. A small handbag. [<OF

add, āce, câre, pälm; end, ēven; it, īce; odd, ōpen, ôrder; tōōk, pōōl; up, bûrn; ə = a in above, e in sicken, i in clarity, o in melon, u in focus; yōō = u in fuse; oi, oil; ou, pout; ch, check; g, go; ng, ring; th, thin; t͟h, this; zh, vision. Foreign sounds á, œ, ü, kh, ṅ; and ◆: see page xx. <from; + plus; ? possibly.

sachel <L *sacellus,* dim. of *saccus* a sack]

sate (sāt) *v.t.* **sat·ed, sat·ing** To satisfy the appetite of; satiate. See synonyms under SATISFY. [Appar. alter. of obs. *sade* sate, OE *sadian*; refashioned after L *sat, satis* enough]

sa·teen (sa·tēn′) *n.* A cotton fabric woven so as to give it a satin surface: usually mercerized cotton. [Alter. of SATIN; infl. inform by VELVETEEN]

sat·el·lite (sat′ə·līt) *n.* **1** *Astron.* A smaller body attending upon and revolving round a larger one; a moon. **2** One who attends upon a person in power. **3** Any obsequious attendant. **4** A small nation politically, economically, or militarily dependent on a great power. **5** A town or community whose activities are largely determined by those of a neighboring metropolis. **6** An airfield, base, or installation dependent upon a larger one. **7** A man–made object launched from and revolving around the earth: compare SPUTNIK. [<F <L *satelles, satellitis* an attendant, a guard]

TYPE OF AMERICAN SATELLITE
A. Satellite. *B.* Rocket, which carries satellite into orbit, in position for launching.

sa·ti·a·ble (sā′shē·ə·bəl, -shə·bəl) *adj.* Capable of being satiated. —**sa′ti·a·bil′i·ty, sa′ti·a·ble·ness** *n.* —**sa′ti·a·bly** *adv.*

sa·ti·ate (sā′shē·āt) *v.t.* **·at·ed, ·at·ing 1** To satisfy the appetite or desire of; gratify. **2** To fill or gratify beyond natural desire; glut; surfeit. See synonyms under SATISFY. —*adj.* Filled to satiety; satiated. [<L *satiatus,* pp. of *satiare* fill <*satis* enough] —**sa′ti·a′tion** *n.*

sa·ti·e·ty (sə·tī′ə·tē) *n. pl.* **·ties** Repletion; surfeit. [<F *satieté* <L *satietas, -tatis* <*satis* enough]

sat·in (sat′ən) *n.* A silk, cotton, rayon, or acetate fabric of thick texture, with glossy face and dull back. —*adj.* Of or similar to satin; glossy; smooth. [<OF <Med. L *satinus, setinus,* ult. <L *seta* silk]

sat·i·net (sat′ə·net′) *n.* **1** A strong fabric with cotton warp and woolen filling. **2** A thin satin. Also **sat′i·nette′.** [<F, dim. of *satin* satin]

sat·in·flow·er (sat′ən·flou′ər) *n.* The garden flower honesty: so called from the satiny luster of its silvery silicles. Also **sat′in·pod′** (-pod′).

satin spar A silky fibrous mineral, a variety either of calcite, aragonite, orgypsum.

sat·in·wood (sat′ən·wŏŏd′) *n.* **1** The satinlike wood of an East Indian tree (*Chloroxylon swietenia*) of the mahogany family. **2** The tree. **3** A West Indian tree (*Zanthoxylum flavum*) of the rue family, having a fine-textured, golden–yellow wood much used in fine cabinet work.

sat·in·y (sat′ən·ē) *adj.* Resembling or characteristic of satin; glossy.

sat·ire (sat′īr) *n.* **1** The use of sarcasm, irony, or keen wit in denouncing abuses or follies; ridicule. **2** A written composition in which vice, folly, or incapacity is held up to ridicule. See synonyms under BANTER. [< MF <L *satira, satura* a satire, earlier, a discursive verse composition on a number of subjects, orig. a medley <(*lanx*) *satura* a fruit salad, lit., a full (dish), fem. of *satur* full]

sa·tir·i·cal (sə·tir′i·kəl) *adj.* **1** Given to or characterized by satire: a *satirical* writer. **2** Severely sarcastic; biting; caustic: a *satirical* laugh. **3** Satiric. —**sa·tir′i·cal·ly** *adv.* —**sa·tir′i·cal·ness** *n.*

sat·is·fac·tion (sat′is·fak′shən) *n.* **1** The act of satisfying, or the state of being satisfied; complete gratification. **2** The making of amends, reparation, or payment; extinguishment of a claim or obligation by payment, performance, restitution, or the rendering of an equivalent. **3** That which satisfies; atonement; compensation. [<OF *satisfactiun* <L *satisfactio, -onis* <*satisfactus,* pp. of *satisfacere* SATISFY]

Synonyms: comfort, complacence, content, contentment, enjoyment, gratification. See COMFORT, HAPPINESS, PROPITIATION, RECOMPENSE. *Antonyms:* annoyance, discontent, dislike, displeasure, dissatisfaction, disturbance, pain, sorrow, trouble, vexation.

sat·is·fac·tion–piece (sat′is·fak′shən·pēs′) *n.* A formal acknowledgment given by one who has received satisfaction of a mortgage or judgment, to authorize the entry of such satisfaction on the record.

sat·is·fac·to·ry (sat′is·fak′tər·ē) *adj.* **1** Giving satisfaction; answering fully all desires, expectations, or requirements; sufficient. **2** Making satisfaction; atoning or expiatory. See synonyms under ADEQUATE, COMFORTABLE. —**sat′is·fac′to·ri·ly** *adv.* —**sat′is·fac′to·ri·ness** *n.*

sat·is·fy (sat′is·fī) *v.* **·fied, ·fy·ing** *v.t.* **1** To supply fully with what is desired, expected, or needed; cause to have enough; gratify; content. **2** To free from doubt or anxiety; assure; convince. **3** To give what is due to. **4** To pay or discharge (a debt, obligation, etc.). **5** To answer sufficiently or convincingly, as a question or objection. **6** To fulfil the conditions or requirements of, as an equation. **7** To make reparation for; expiate. —*v.i.* **8** To give satisfaction. [<OF *satisfier* <L *satisfacere* <*satis* enough + *facere* do] —**sat′is·fi′er** *n.* —**sat′is·fy′ing** *adj.* —**sat′is·fy′ing·ly** *adv.*

Synonyms: cloy, content, fill, glut, sate, satiate, suffice, surfeit. To *satisfy* is to furnish enough to meet physical, mental, or spiritual desire. To *sate* or *satiate* is to gratify desire so fully as to extinguish it for a time. To *cloy* or *surfeit* is to gratify to the point of revulsion or disgust. *Glut* is a strong word applied to the utmost satisfaction of vehement appetites and passions; as, to *glut* a vengeful spirit with slaughter; we speak of *glutting* the market with a supply so excessive as to extinguish the demand. Much less than is needed to *satisfy* may *suffice* a frugal or abstemious person; less than a sufficiency may *content* one of a patient and submissive spirit. See INDULGE, PAY[1], REQUITE. *Antonyms:* check, deny, disappoint, refuse, restrain, restrict, starve, stint, tantalize.

sa·to·ri (sä·tō·rē) *n.* In Japanese Buddhism, enlightenment; especially, the abrupt or "sudden" enlightenment of Zen Buddhism. [<Japanese, lit., comprehension, perception]

sa·trap (sā′trap, sat′rap) *n.* **1** A governor of a province in ancient Persia. **2** Any petty ruler under a despot. **3** A subordinate ruler or governor. [<L *satrapes* <Gk. *satrapēs* <O Persian *shathraparan,* lit., a protector of a province]

sa·trap·y (sā′trə·pē, sat′rə·pē) *n. pl.* **·trap·ies** The territory or the jurisdiction of a satrap. Also **sa·trap·ate** (sā′trə·pit, sat′rə-).

sat·u·rant (sach′ə·ənt) *adj.* Saturating. —*n.* A substance that fully neutralizes another.

sat·u·rate (sach′ə·rāt) *v.t.* **·rat·ed, ·rat·ing 1** To soak or imbue thoroughly; fill or impregnate to the utmost capacity for absorbing or retaining. **2** *Chem.* To utilize fully the combining powers of the atoms in (a molecule). —*adj.* **1** Filled to repletion; saturated. **2** Very intense; deep: said of colors. [<L *saturatus,* pp. of *saturare* fill up <*satur* full] —**sat·u·ra·ble** (sach′ər·ə·bəl) *adj.* —**sat′u·ra′tor** or **sat′u·rat′er** *n.*

sat·u·ra·tion (sach′ə·rā′shən) *n.* **1** The act of saturating, or the state of being saturated; full impregnation. **2** The impregnation of one substance with another till no more can be received. Saturation may be by solution or by chemical combination. **3** *Meteorol.* The filling of the atmosphere with any vapor to the point of condensation. **4** The maximum magnetization of which a body is capable. **5** The degree of vividness or purity of chromatic color, as indicated by its freedom from admixture with white. **6** A massive concentration, in any given area, as of advertising, military force, etc., for a specific purpose: often used attributively: *saturation* bombing.

Sat·ur·day (sat′ər·dē, -dā) *n.* The seventh or last day of the week; the day of the Jewish Sabbath. [OE *Sæterdæg, Sæternesdæg,* trans. of L *Saturni dies* Saturn's day]

Saturday night special *U.S.* A kind of cheap, easily obtainable pistol.

Sat·urn (sat′ərn) **1** The planet next beyond Jupiter and next to Jupiter in size, remarkable for its 9 satellites and its flat, luminous, encircling rings. In astrology it was regarded as a melancholy planet. See PLANET. **2** In Roman mythology, the god of agriculture: identified with the Greek *Kronos* [OE *Sætern, Saturnus* <L *Saturnus*]

sat·ur·na·li·a (sat′ər·nā′lē·ə) *n.* Any season or period of general license or revelry: generally construed as singular: a *saturnalia* of crime. [<L. See SATURNALIA.]

Sat·ur·na·li·a (sat′ər·nā′lē·ə) *n. pl.* The feast of Saturn held at Rome in mid–December, celebrating the winter solstice, and marked by wild reveling and licentious abandon. [<L, orig. neut. pl. of *Saturnalis* of Saturn < *Saturnus* Saturn] —**Sat′ur·na′li·an** *adj.*

sa·tur·ni·id (sə·tûr′nē·id) *n.* Any of a family (*Saturniidae*) of large, hairy, brightly–colored moths widely distributed in most temperate regions. Many of them produce cocoons useful in the production of silk. —*adj.* Of or pertaining to the *Saturniidae.* [<NL <*Saturnia,* genus name <L *Saturnius* of Saturn < *Saturnus* Saturn]

sat·ur·nine (sat′ər·nīn) *adj.* **1** Having a grave, gloomy, or morose disposition or character; heavy; dull. **2** In old chemistry, pertaining to lead. **3** *Pathol.* Pertaining to or produced by lead. [<OF *saturnin* of Saturn, of lead, heavy <Med. L *Saturnus* lead, Saturn <L, Saturn]

sat·urn·ism (sat′ərn·iz′əm) *n.* Lead poisoning. [<Med. L *Saturnus.* See SATURNINE.]

Sat·ya·gra·ha (sut′yə·gru′hə) *n.* **1** A movement characterized by non–violent resistance and non–cooperation, adopted in India, 1919, by the followers of M. K. Gandhi in protest against certain civil and religious abuses. **2** The non–violent force characterizing this movement, defined as an active love for one's opponents and a radical insistence on truth. [<Hind., truth–force, lit., a grasping for truth <Skt. *satya* truth + *graha* a grasping]

sat·yr (sat′ər, sā′tər) *n.* **1** In Greek mythology, a woodland deity in human form, having pointed ears, pug nose, short tail and budding horns, and of wanton nature. **2** A very lascivious man. **3** Any butterfly of the family *Agapetidae,* commonly brown and gray with eyelike spots. [<L *satyrus* <Gk. *satyros*] —**sa·tyr·ic** (sə·tir′ik) or **·i·cal** *adj.*

SATYR

sat·y·ri·a·sis (sat′ə·rī′ə·sis) *n. Psychiatry* A morbid lasciviousness in males. [<NL <Gk. *satyriaein* suffer from satyriasis <*satyros* a satyr]

sauce (sôs) *n.* **1** An appetizing dressing or liquid relish for food; loosely, any appetizing garnish of a meal; formerly, any condiment, as salt, pepper. **2** A dish of fruit pulp stewed and sweetened: cranberry *sauce.* **3** *Colloq.* Table vegetables, as roots or greens: also **garden sauce. 4** *Colloq.* Pert or impudent language. —*v.t.* **sauced, sauc·ing 1** To flavor with sauce; season. **2** To give zest or piquancy to. **3** *Colloq.* To be saucy to. [<OF < LL *salsa,* orig. fem. of L *salsus* salted, pp. of *salire* salt <*sal* salt]

sauce·pan (sôs′pan′) *n.* A metal or enamel pan with projecting handle, for cooking food.

sau·cer (sô′sər) *n.* **1** A small dish for holding a cup. **2** Any small, round, shallow vessel of similar shape. [<OF *saussier* <*sauce* sauce]

sau·cy (sô′sē) *adj.* **·ci·er, ·ci·est 1** Disrespectful to superiors; impudent. **2** Piquant; sprightly; amusing. See synonyms under IMPUDENT. —**sau′ci·ly** *adv.* —**sau′ci·ness** *n.*

Sa·u·di Arabia (sä·ōō′dē) A kingdom (1932) in the northern and central part of Arabia; 927,000 square miles; dual capitals, Mecca and Riyadh.

sauer·bra·ten (sour′brät′n, *Ger.* zou′ər·brä′tən) *n.* Beef marinated in vinegar before being braised. [<G <*sauer* sour + *braten* roast]

sauer·kraut (sour′krout′) *n.* Shredded and salted cabbage fermented in its own juice: also spelled *sourcrout*. [<G <*sauer* sour + *kraut* cabbage, vegetable, a plant]

sau·ger (sô′gər) *n.* A percoid fish, the smaller American pike perch (*Cynoperca canadensis*), resembling the walleye. [<N. Am. Ind.]

sau·na (sou′nə, sô′-) *n.* 1 A Finnish steam bath in which the steam is produced by running water over heated stones. 2 A bath in which the bather is exposed to very hot, dry air. 3 A room or enclosure for a sauna. [< Finnish]

saun·ter (sôn′tər) *v.i.* To walk in a leisurely or lounging way; stroll. See synonyms under LINGER. — *n.* 1 A slow, aimless manner of walking. 2 An idle stroll. [ME *santren* muse, meditate; ult. origin unknown]

sau·rel (sôr′əl) *n.* A horse mackerel (genus *Trachurus*), especially *T. trachurus* and *T. symmetricus* of America and Europe. [<F <Gk. *sauros* a horse mackerel]

sau·rian (sôr′ē·ən) *n.* One of a suborder (*Sauria*) of reptiles, the lizards: formerly including also crocodiles, dinosaurians, pterodactyls, and other fossil forms. — *adj.* Pertaining to the *Sauria*. [<NL <Gk. *sauros* a lizard]

sau·ris·chi·an (sô·ris′kē·ən) *adj. Paleontol.* Of, pertaining to, or belonging to an order (*Saurischia*) of reptilelike dinosaurs that flourished through most of the Mesozoic era. — *n.* A member of this order. [<NL <Gk. *sauros* a lizard + *ischion* a hip]

sauro- *combining form* Lizard: *sauropod.* Also, before vowels, *saur-.* [<Gk. *sauros* a lizard]

sau·ro·pod (sôr′ə·pod) *n. Paleontol.* One of a suborder (*Sauropoda*) of amphibious four-footed dinosaurs of the Triassic, Jurassic, and Cretaceous periods. — *adj.* Of or pertaining to the *Sauropoda.* [<NL <Gk. *sauros* a lizard + *pous, podos* a foot] — **sau·rop·o·dous** (sô·rop′ə·dəs) *adj.*

-saurus *combining form Zool.* Lizard: used to form genus names: *Brontosaurus, Plesiosaurus.* Corresponding class names end in –*sauria,* family names in –*sauridae,* and individual names in –*saur* or –*saurid.* [<Gk. *sauros* a lizard]

sau·ry (sôr′ē) *n. pl.* ·ries An edible fish (*Scomberesox saurus*) of the Atlantic, having the jaws developed into a slim beak. It travels in predatory shoals. Also **saury pike.** [<NL *saurus* <Gk. *sauros* a lizard]

sau·sage (sô′sij) *n.* 1 Finely chopped and highly seasoned meat, commonly stuffed into the cleaned and prepared entrails of some animal or artificial casings. 2 *Aeron.* A type of airship or captive observation balloon, shaped like a sausage. [<AF *saussiche* <LL *salsicia,* ult. <L *salsus.* See SAUCE.]

saus·su·rite (sô·sŏor′īt, sôs′yə·rīt) *n.* A tough, compact, impure form of labradorite. [after Prof. H. B. de *Saussure,* 1740–99, Swiss geologist] — **saus·su·rit·ic** (sôs′yə·rit′ik) *adj.*

sau·té (sō·tā′, sō-) *adj.* Fried quickly with little grease. — *v.t.* ·téed, ·té·ing To fry quickly in a little fat. [<F, pp. of *sauter* leap]

sau·terne (sō·tûrn′, sō-; *Fr.* sō·tern′) *n.* A sweet, white French wine; often, in America, any white wine, dry or sweet. Also **sau·ternes.** [from *Sauternes,* district in SW France]

sav·age (sav′ij) *adj.* 1 Of a wild and untamed nature; not domesticated; hence, ferocious; fierce. 2 Living in or belonging to the most primitive and rude condition of human life and society; uncivilized; uncultivated: *savage* tribes. 3 Enraged; cruel; furious: said of man or beast. 4 *Obs.* Remote from human abode; belonging to the wilderness: a *savage* trail. See synonyms under BARBAROUS, BITTER, FIERCE, GRIM, SANGUINARY. — *n.* 1 A primitive or uncivilized human being. 2 A brutal, fierce, and cruel person; a barbarian. [<OF *salvage, sauvage* <L *silvaticus, salvaticus* < *silva* a wood] — **sav′age·ly** *adv.*

sav·age·ry (sav′ij·rē) *n. pl.* ·ries 1 The state of being savage: also **sav′age·ness.** 2 Cruelty in disposition or action; a cruel or savage act. 3 Savages collectively: also **sav′age·dom.** Also **sav′ag·ism.**

sa·van·na (sə·van′ə) *n.* 1 A tract of level land covered with low vegetation; a treeless plain. 2 Any large area of tropical or subtropical grassland, covered in part with trees and spiny shrubs. Also **sa·van′nah.** [Earlier *zavana* <Sp. <Cariban]

Sa·van·nah (sə·van′ə) A port in eastern Georgia, at the mouth of the **Savannah River,** which flows 314 miles SE to the Atlantic and forms the boundary between Georgia and South Carolina.

sa·vant (sə·vänt′, sav′ənt; *Fr.* sȧ·vän′) *n.* A man of exceptional learning. See synonyms under SCHOLAR. [<F, orig. ppr. of *savoir* know <L *sapere* be wise]

save[1] (sāv) *v.* **saved, sav·ing** *v.t.* 1 To preserve or rescue from danger, harm, etc. 2 To keep from being spent, expended, or lost; avoid the loss or waste of. 3 To set aside for future use; accumulate: often with *up.* 4 To treat carefully so as to avoid fatigue, harm, etc.: to *save* one's eyes. 5 To avoid the need or trouble of; prevent by timely action: A stitch in time *saves* nine. 6 *Theol.* To deliver from spiritual death or the consequences of sin; redeem. — *v.i.* 7 To avoid waste; be economical. 8 To preserve something from danger, harm, etc. 9 To admit of preservation, as food. See synonyms under DELIVER, PRESERVE, SCRIMP. [<OF *salver, sauver* <LL *salvare* save <L *salvus* safe] — **sav′a·ble** or **save′a·ble** *adj.* — **sav′a·ble·ness** *n.* — **sav′er** *n.*

save[2] (sāv) *prep.* Except; but. — *conj.* 1 Except; but. 2 *Archaic* Unless. See synonyms under BUT[1]. [<OF *sauf* being excepted, orig. safe <L *salvus*]

save–all (sāv′ôl′) *n.* 1 A contrivance for preventing waste; anything that saves fragments. 2 A child's savings bank. 3 An overall or pinafore.

saved (sāvd) *adj.* 1 Delivered from punishment after death. 2 Converted to religion. 3 Not spent or lost; amassed.

sav·e·loy (sav′ə·loi) *n.* A kind of highly seasoned, dried sausage made of salted pork. [Alter. of F *cervelas* <Ital. *cervellata* < *cervello* the brain <L *cerebellum.* See CEREBELLUM.]

Savile Row A street in London famous for fashionable men's tailor shops; hence, sartorially magnificent.

sav·in (sav′in) *n.* 1 A bushy shrub or small tree (*Juniperus sabina*) of the cypress family. 2 The young shoots of this plant, yielding an acrid volatile oil used in medicine. 3 The red cedar (*Juniperus virginiana*). Also called **sabine.** [OE *safine* <OF *savine* <L (*herba*) *Sabina* the Sabine (herb), fem. of *Sabinus*]

sav·ing (sā′ving) *adj.* 1 That saves; preserving, as from destruction. 2 Redeeming; delivering. 3 Avoiding needless waste or expense; economical; frugal. 4 Incurring no loss, if not gainful: a *saving* investment. 5 Holding in reserve; making an exception; qualifying: a *saving* clause. — *n.* 1 Preservation from loss or danger. 2 Avoidance of waste; economy. 3 The result of this; reduction in cost: a *saving* of 16 percent. 4 That which is saved; especially, in the plural, sums of money not expended. 5 *Law* Reservation; exception. See synonyms under FRUGALITY. — *prep.* 1 With the exception of; save. 2 With due respect for: *saving* your presence. — *conj.* Save. — **sav′ing·ly** *adv.* — **sav′ing·ness** *n.*

savings account An account drawing interest at a savings bank.

savings bank 1 An institution for receiving and investing savings and paying interest on deposits. 2 A container with a slot for coins.

sav·ior (sāv′yər) *n.* One who saves. Also *Brit.* **sav′iour.** [<OF *saveour* <LL *salvator, -oris* <L *salvare* SAVE]

Sav·iour (sāv′yər) *n.* He who saves men from death and sin: a title sometimes applied directly to God, but chiefly to Jesus Christ, as the Redeemer: usually with *the.* Also **Sav′ior.**

sa·voir faire (sȧ·vwȧr fâr′) *French* Ability to see and to do the right thing; readiness in proper and gracious actions and speech; tact; literally, to know how to act.

sa·voir vi·vre (sȧ·vwȧr vē′vr′) *French* Good breeding; good social manners; literally, to know how to live.

Sav·o·na·ro·la (sav′ə·nə·rō′lə, *Ital.* sä′vō·nä·rō′lä), **Girolamo,** 1452–98, Italian monk; reformer; burned at the stake for heresy.

sa·vor (sā′vər) *n.* 1 That quality of a thing that affects the taste and smell, or both; flavor; odor. 2 Specific or characteristic quality or approach to a quality; flavor. 3 Relish; zest: The conversation had *savor.* 4 *Archaic* Character; reputation. — *v.i.* 1 To have savor; taste or smell: with *of.* 2 To have a specified savor or character: with *of.* — *v.t.* 3 To give flavor to; season. 4 To taste or enjoy with pleasure; relish. 5 To have the savor or character of. Also *Brit.* **sa′vour.** [<OF *savour* <L *sapor* taste < *sapere* taste, know] — **sa′vor·er** *n.* — **sa′vor·ous** *adj.*

Synonyms (noun): flavor, fragrance, odor, relish, scent, smell, taste. See SMELL.

sa·vor·less (sā′vər·lis) *adj.* Tasteless; insipid.

sa·vor·y[1] (sā′vər·ē) *adj.* 1 Of an agreeable taste and odor; appetizing. 2 Piquant to the taste. 3 In good repute. See synonyms under DELICIOUS. — *n. Brit.* A small, hot serving of food eaten at the end or beginning of a dinner. Also *Brit.* **sa′vour·y.** [<OF *savouré,* pp. of OF *savourer* taste <*savour* SAVOR] — **sa′vor·i·ly** *adv.* — **sa′vor·i·ness** *n.*

sa·vor·y[2] (sā′vər·ē) *n.* A hardy, annual, aromatic culinary herb of the mint family (*Satureia hortensis*) used for seasoning. Also **summer savory.** [<OF *savoreie,* alter. of L *satureia;* infl. in form by OF *savour* savor]

sa·voy (sə·voi′) *n.* A variety of cabbage with wrinkled leaves and a compact head. [<F (*chou de*) *Savoie* (cabbage of) Savoy]

sav·vy (sav′ē) *Slang v.i.* ·vied, ·vy·ing To understand; comprehend. — *n.* Understanding; good sense. [Alter. of Sp. ¿ *Sabe* (*usted*)? Do (you) know? < *saber* know <L *sapere* know, taste]

saw[1] (sô) *n.* 1 A cutting instrument with pointed teeth arranged continuously along the edge of the blade: used to cut or divide wood, bone, metal, etc. See illustrations under BUCKSAW, FRET SAW, HACKSAW. 2 A machine for operating a saw or gang of saws. 3 Any tool or instrument without teeth used like a saw, as a steel disk for cutting armor plate, etc. — **circular saw** A disk having saw teeth in or on its periphery, and mounted on an arbor, with which it is rotated, usually at high speed. — *v.* **sawed, sawed** or **sawn, saw·ing** *v.t.* 1 To cut or divide with a saw. 2 To shape or fashion with a saw. 3 To cut or slice (the air, etc.) as if using a saw: The speaker *saws* the air. 4 To cause to move with a to-and-fro motion like that of a saw. — *v.i.* 5 To use a saw. 6 To cut: said of a saw. 7 To be cut with a saw: This wood *saws* easily. [OE *sagu, saga*] — **saw′er** *n.*

saw[2] (sô) *n.* A proverbial or familiar saying; old maxim. See synonyms under ADAGE. [OE *sagu.* Akin to SAGA.]

saw·bill (sô′bil′) *n.* A motmot.

saw·bones (sô′bōnz′) *n. Slang* A surgeon.

saw·buck (sô′buk′) *n.* 1 A rack or frame consisting of two X-shaped ends joined by a connecting bar or bars, for holding sticks of wood while they are being sawed. Compare SAW-HORSE. 2 *U.S. Slang* A ten-dollar bill: so called from the resemblance of X, Roman numeral ten, to the ends of a sawbuck. [Trans. of Du. *zaagbok*]

SAWBUCK AND SAWHORSE
a. Sawbuck. *b.* Bucksaw. *c.* Sawhorse.

saw·dust (sô′dust′) *n.* Small particles of wood cut or torn out by sawing.

sawed–off (sôd′ôf′, -of′) 1 *adj.* Having one end sawed off. 2 Short; not of average height or length: a *sawed-off* shotgun.

saw·fish (sô′fish′) *n. pl.* ·fish or ·fish·es Any of a family (Pristidae) of large, viviparous rays found chiefly in tropical estuaries and having a long body and a snout prolonged into a flat blade with toothlike projections on each side.

saw·fly (sô'flī') *n. pl.* **·flies** A hymenopterous insect (family *Tenthredinidae*) having in the female a sawlike ovipositor for piercing plants, soft wood, etc., in which to lay eggs.

saw-grass (sô'gras', -gräs') *n.* A sedge (genus *Mariscus*) with saw-toothed leaves, growing in marshes along the Atlantic coast from North Carolina to Florida and westward.

saw-horse (sô'hôrs') *n.* **1** A frame consisting of a long wooden bar or plank supported by four extended legs: used by carpenters. Compare SAWBUCK. **2** A packsaddle.

saw log A log of suitable size for sawing.

saw·mill (sô'mil') *n.* **1** An establishment for sawing logs with power-driven machinery. **2** A large sawing machine.

saw palmetto Either of two palmettos (*Serenoa repens* and *Paurotis wrighti*) of the southern United States and the West Indies.

saw·pit (sô'pit') *n.* A pit over which a timber is laid to be sawed by two sawyers, one of whom stands in the pit and the other above.

saw set An instrument to give set to, or bend slightly outward, the teeth of a saw.

saw-toothed (sô'tōōtht') *adj.* Serrate; having teeth or toothlike processes similar to those of a saw.

saw·yer (sô'yər) *n.* **1** One who saws logs; specifically, a lumberman who fells trees by sawing, or one who works in a sawmill: also spelled *sawer.* **2** Any beetle of the genus *Monochamus* having wood-boring larvae. [Alter. of SAWER]

sax¹ (saks) *n.* **1** A chopping tool for trimming edges of roofing slates: also called *slate ax.* **2** A long knife. **3** A short, broad sword. [OE *seax* a knife]

sax² (saks) *n. Colloq.* A saxophone. [Short for SAXOPHONE]

sax·a·tile (sak'sə·til) *adj.* **1** Pertaining to rocks. **2** Saxicoline. [< L *saxatilis* < *saxum* a rock]

sax·horn (saks'hôrn') *n.* A brass wind instrument having a long winding tube and cup-shaped mouthpiece, used in military bands. [after Antoine Joseph *Sax*, (called *Adolphe*), 1814–94, Belgian instrument maker + HORN]

sax·ic·o·line (sak·sik'ə·lēn, -lin) *adj. Ecol.* Living or growing among rocks. Also **sax·ic'o·lous.** [< NL *saxicola* < L *saxum* rock + *colere* inhabit]

sax·i·fra·ga·ceous (sak'sə·frə·gā'shəs) *adj. Bot.* Of or pertaining to a widely distributed family (*Saxifragaceae*) of herbs, shrubs, and trees, including gooseberries and witch hazel. [< NL < L *saxifraga*. See SAXIFRAGE.]

sax·i·frage (sak'sə·frij) *n.* **1** Any plant of the genus *Saxifraga,* growing in rocky places. **2** Any of various related plants. Also called *stonebreak.* [< OF < L (*herba*) *saxifraga,* lit., stone-breaking (herb)]

Sax·o·ny (sak'sə·nē) *n. pl.* **·nies 1** A fabric made from wool raised in Saxony, central Germany. **2** A variety of fine yarn. **3** A glossy woolen cloth.

sax·o·phone (sak'sə·fōn) *n.* A brass wind instrument with about 20 finger keys, tonally like, but more powerful than, a clarinet. [after Antoine Joseph *Sax* (called Adolphe), 1814–94, Belgian instrument maker, who invented it about 1840 + -PHONE] —**sax'o·phon'ist** *n.*

sax·tu·ba (saks'tōō'bə, -tyōō'-) *n.* A large saxhorn. [< SAX(HORN) + TUBA]

say¹ (sā) *v.* **said, say·ing** *v.t.* **1** To pronounce or utter; speak. **2** To declare or express in words; tell; state. **3** To state positively or as an opinion: *Say* which you prefer. **4** To recite; repeat: to *say* one's prayers. **5** To report; allege. **6** To assume as possibly true or as a hypothesis: He is worth, *say,* a million. —*v.i.* **7** To make a statement; speak. —**that is to say** In other words. —*n.* **1** What one has said or has to say; testimony; word: Let him have his *say.* **2** *Colloq.* Right or turn to speak or choose: Now it is my *say.* **3** Authority: to have the *say.* —*interj. U.S. Colloq.* A hail or an introductory exclamation to command attention: also *Brit.* **I say!** Compare LISTEN. [OE *secgan*] —**say'er** *n.*

Synonyms (verb): allege, assert, speak.

say² (sā) *n.* A fine, thin serge used in the 16th century, sometimes partly of silk, later entirely of wool. [< OF *saie* < L *saga,* pl. of *sagum* a military cloak]

say·id (sī'id, sä'yid) *n.* Lord: a title applied to men who claimed to be descendants of Mohammed through his elder grandson, Husain: also spelled *said, saiyid.* Also **say'yid.** [< Arabic *sayyid*]

say·ing (sā'ing) *n.* An utterance; also, a maxim. See synonyms under ADAGE.

sa·yo·na·ra (sä'yō·nä'rä) *n. Japanese* goodby.

say-so (sā'sō') *n. Colloq.* **1** An unsupported assertion or decision. **2** Right or power to make decisions: He has the *say-so.*

Sb *Chem.* Antimony (symbol Sb). [< L *stibium*]

S-brack·et (es'brak'it) *n.* In mechanical construction, a bracket or other piece in the shape of the letter S: also called *S-piece.*

Sc *Chem.* Scandium (symbol Sc).

scab (skab) *n.* **1** A crust formed on the surface of a wound or sore. **2** A contagious disease among sheep, resembling mange; scabies. **3** Any of certain plant diseases of bacterial or fungous origin, in which there is a roughened or warty exterior. **4** *Slang* A mean, paltry fellow. **5** A workman who does not belong to or will not join or act with a labor union; one who takes the place of a striker; a strikebreaker. —*v.i.* **scabbed, scab·bing 1** To form or become covered with a scab. **2** To take the place of a striker; act as a scab. [Fusion of ON *skabbr* (assumed) and OE *sceabb;* infl. in meaning by L *scabies.* See SCABIES.] —**scabbed** *adj.* —**scab'bi·ly** *adv.* —**scab'bi·ness** *n.* —**scab'by** *adj.*

scab·bard (skab'ərd) *n.* A sheath for a weapon, as for a bayonet or a sword. —*v.t.* To sheathe in or furnish with a scabbard. [< OF *escalberc,* prob. < OHG *scara* a sword + *bergan* hide, protect]

scabbard fish 1 The cutlas fish (*Trichiurus lepturus*) having a long, eel-like body, found in the warm coastal waters of the United States and West Indies. **2** Any long, slender, silvery fish of the genus *Lepidopus* of European coasts.

scab·ble (skab'əl) *v.t.* **·bled, ·bling** In stoneworking, to dress or shape roughly. [Earlier *scapple* < OF *escapeler* dress timber]

scab·bling (skab'ling) *n.* A stone chip or fragment.

sca·bi·es (skā'bi·ēz, -bēz) *n.* The itch; especially, a contagious skin disease of sheep caused by any of certain itch mites, as *Psoroptes communis.* [< L, roughness, an itch < *scabere* scratch, scrape. Akin to SHAVE.]

sca·bi·ous² (skā'bē·əs) *adj.* **1** Pertaining to scabies. **2** Having scabs. [< L *scabiosus* < *scabies.* See SCABIES.]

sca·bi·ous¹ (skā'bē·əs) *n.* Any of a genus (*Scabiosa*) of herbs of the teasel family, with involucrate heads of variously colored flowers, as the sweet scabious (*S. atropurpurea*). Also **sca·bi·o'sa** (-ō'sə). [< NL < Med. L (*herba*) *scabiosa* fem. sing. of *scabiosus* SCABIOUS¹]

sca·brous (skā'brəs) *adj.* **1** Roughened with minute points; rugged; scurfy. **2** Knotty; difficult to handle tactfully. [< LL *scabrosus* < *scabere* scratch] —**sca'brous·ly** *adv.* —**sca'brous·ness** *n.*

scac·cog·ra·phy (ska·kog'rə·fē) *n.* The literature pertaining to the science and art of chess. [< Ital. *scacchi* chess, pl. of *scacco* a square on a chessboard + -(O)GRAPHY] —**scac·chic** (ska-k'ik) *adj.* —**scac·cog'ra·pher** *n.*

scad (skad) *n.* A saurel. [? Var. of SHAD]

scads (skadz) *n. pl. Colloq.* A large amount or quantity. [? Var. of dial. E *scald* a large amount, great number]

scaf·fold (skaf'əld, -ōld) *n.* **1** A temporary elevated structure for the support of workmen, materials, etc., as in building. **2** A raised wooden framework used for drying hay, tobacco, fish, etc. **3** A platform for the execution of criminals. **4** A stage, as for exhibition purposes. **5** A raised wooden frame formerly used by certain North American Indians for the disposal of their dead. —*v.t.* **1** To furnish or support with a scaffold: to *scaffold* a building in order to repaint the exterior. **2** To place on a scaffold. [< OF (*e*)*schaffaut, escadafaut.* Related to CATAFALQUE.]

scag (skag) *n. Slang* Heroin. [Origin unknown]

scagl·ia (skal'yə) *n.* An Italian calcareous

rock, corresponding to the chalk of England. [< Ital., a scale, a chip of marble < Med. L *scalia* < Gmc.]

scagl·io·la (skal·yō'lə) *n.* Hard, polished plasterwork imitating marble, granite, or other stone: made of powdered gypsum and glue, colored in various ways. [< Ital. *scagliuola,* dim. of *scaglia* SCAGLIA]

scal·age (skā'lij) *n.* **1** A percentage by which something is scaled down to allow for shrinkage. **2** The amount of lumber estimated to be in a log or logs being scaled. [< SCALE² + -AGE]

sca·lar (skā'lər) *adj.* Completely definable by a single number or by a point on a scale: said of a quantity having magnitude but no direction, as a volume or mass: distinguished from *vector.* —*n. Math.* A pure number, especially one representing only a magnitude. [< L *scalaris* of a ladder < *scala* a ladder. See SCALE².]

sca·la·re (skə·lā'rē, -lä'rä) *n.* **1** A deep-bodied cichlid fish of South American rivers (genus *Pterophyllum*), noted for its striking coloration and popular as an aquarium fish: also called *angelfish.* **2** A related fish of the Amazon, the **blue scalare** (*Symphysodon discus*), with a brownish-green, disk-shaped body. [< NL < L *scalaris* of a ladder; so called because marked with dark crossbars]

sca·lar·i·form (skə·lar'ə·fôrm) *adj. Biol.* Ladderlike: said of cells or vessels. [< NL *scalariformis* < L *scalaris* of a ladder + *forma* form]

scal·a·wag (skal'ə·wag) *n.* **1** *Colloq.* A worthless fellow; scamp. **2** *U.S.* A native Southern white who became or remained a Republican during the Reconstruction period: a contemptuous term used by Southern Democrats. Compare CARPETBAGGER. Also spelled *scallawag, scallywag.* [Origin uncertain]

scald¹ (skôld) *v.t.* **1** To burn with or as with hot liquid or steam. **2** To cleanse or treat with boiling water. **3** To heat (a liquid) to a point just short of boiling. **4** To cook in a liquid which is just short of the boiling point. —*v.i.* **5** To be or become scalded. —*n.* **1** A burn or injury to the skin by a hot fluid, as steam or water. **2** An act of scalding. **3** A destructive parasitic disease of cranberries. **4** A discoloration of plant tissue due to improper conditions of growth, bad storage, etc. [< AF *escalder* < LL *excaldare* wash with hot water < *ex-* very + *calidus* hot]

scald² (skôld, skäld) *n.* An ancient Scandinavian bard, minstrel, or reciter of eulogies: also spelled *skald.* [< ON *skald*] —**scal·dic** (skôl'dik, skäl'-) *adj.*

scale¹ (skāl) *n.* **1** One of the thin, flat, horny, membranous or bony outgrowths of the skin of various vertebrates, as most fishes, usually overlapping and forming a nearly complete investment. **2** A scab. **3** A scale insect. **4** *Bot.* A rudimentary or metamorphosed leaf, as of a pine cone. **5** *Metall.* The coating of oxide that forms on heated iron, etc.: also, an incrustation, as on the inside of boilers. **6** Any hard, thin, scalelike formation, as a flake, husk, shell, peel, or exfoliation. —*v.* **scaled, scal·ing** *v.t.* **1** To strip or clear of scale or scales. **2** To form scales on; cover with scales. **3** To take off in layers or scales; pare off. **4** To throw (a thin, flat object) so that its edge cuts the air or so that it skips along the surface of water. —*v.i.* **5** To come off in layers or scales; peel. **6** To shed scales. **7** To become incrusted with scales. [< OF *escale* a husk < Gmc.; infl. in meaning by OF *escaille* a fish's scale, an oyster's shell < Med. L *scalia* < Gmc.] —**scal'er** *n.*

scale² (skāl) *n.* **1** A piece of metal, wood, or glass bearing accurately spaced lines or graduations for use in measurement, or the series of marks so used. **2** Any system of designating units of measurement or in which a fixed proportion is used in determining quantities:

SCALE
a. Ascending. *b.* Descending.

a *scale* of 1 inch to the mile. **3** *Math.* A system of notation in which the successive places determine the value of figures, as the decimal system. **4** Any progressive or graded series; a graduation: the social *scale*. **5** *Music* All the tones or notes of a key in regular ascending or descending order, in an octave or more. **6** *Phot.* The range of light values which may be reproduced by a photographic paper. **7** An escalade. **8** A succession of steps; ladder; stairs: the original meaning. — **major scale** *Music* A scale having semitones between the 3–4 and 7–8 notes. — **minor scale** *Music* A scale having semitones between 2–3, 5–6, 7–8 notes (the harmonic form); or between 2–3, 7–8 ascending, 6–5, 3–2 descending (the melodic form). — *v.* **scaled, scal·ing** *v.t.* **1** To climb to the top of; go up by or as by means of a ladder. **2** To make according to a scale. **3** To regulate or adjust according to a scale or ratio: with *up, down,* etc. **4** To measure (logs) or estimate the amount of lumber in (standing timber). — *v.i.* **5** To climb; ascend. **6** To rise, as in steps or stages: Mountains *scaling* to the skies. [< Ital. *scala* a ladder < L < *scandere* climb] — **scal′a·ble** *adj.* — **scal′er** *n.*

scale³ (skāl) *n.* **1** The bowl, scoop, or platform of a weighing instrument or balance. **2** The balance itself; hence, figuratively, the *scale* or *scales* of Justice. **3** *Usually pl.* Any form of weighing machine. — **to turn the scales** To determine; decide. — *v.* **scaled, scal·ing** *v.t.* **1** To weigh in scales. **2** To amount to in weight. — *v.i.* **3** To be weighed in scales. [< ON *skāl* a bowl, in pl. a weighing balance. Akin to SHALE, SHELL.]

scale insect One of numerous small, hemipterous, plant-feeding insects (family *Coccidae*) which as adults are degenerate, sedentary, and covered with a scalelike, waxy protective shield.

scale moss Any plant belonging to the class *Hepaticae*; any of the liverworts: so called because of their scalelike leaves.

sca·lene (skā′lēn, skā·lēn′) *adj.* **1** *Geom.* **a** Having no two sides equal: said of a triangle. **b** Having the axis inclined to the base: said of a cone or cylinder. **2** *Anat.* Designating one of several deeply placed muscles attached to the cervical vertebrae and first and second ribs and acting to flex or bend the neck. Also **sca·le·nous** (skā·lē′nəs). [< LL *scalenus* < Gk. *skalēnos* uneven]

Scales (skālz) A sign of the zodiac, called also *Libra* or *The Balance.*

scall (skôl) *n. Pathol.* **1** A cutaneous eruption of small pustular vesicles containing a purulent fluid: often epidemic among children. **2** Any scabby or scaly eruption. Also called *scald.* [< ON *skalle* a bald head]

scal·la·wag (skal′ə·wag), **scal·ly·wag** (skal′ē·wag) See SCALAWAG.

scal·lion (skal′yən) *n.* **1** A young, tender onion with a small, underdeveloped white bulb. **2** A shallot or leek. [< AF *scalun,* OF *eschalogne,* ult. < L *(caepa) Ascalonia* (onion) of Ashkelon, a Palestinian seaport]

scal·lop (skal′əp, skol′-) *n.* **1** A bivalve (genus *Pecten*) having a nearly circular shell with radiating ribs and wavy edge. **2** Its adductor muscle, which as a rule is edible and very succulent. **3** Its shell, formerly worn as a pilgrim's badge. **4** A dish or pan (originally a scallop shell) in which oysters are cooked or served. **5** One of a series of semicircular curves along an edge, as for ornament. — *v.t.* **1** To shape the edge of with scallops; ornament with scallops. **2** To bake (food) in a casserole with a liquid or sauce, often topped with bread crumbs. Also spelled *escallop, scollop.* [ME *scalop* < MF *escalope* shell < Gmc. Akin to SCALE¹.] — **scal′lop·er** *n.*

SCALLOP
SHELL

scalp (skalp) *n.* **1** The skin of the top and back of the human skull, usually covered with hair; also, a portion of this, cut or torn away as a war trophy among certain North American Indians, particularly of the St. Lawrence region. **2** A similar piece taken from the

head of a wild animal as an evidence that it has been killed for the collection of a bounty. **3** A political victory or defeat. **4** A denuded or bare summit, as of a hill or cliff. **5** On the stock exchange, a small profit taken by a speculator. — *v.t.* **1** To cut or tear the scalp from. **2** *Colloq.* To buy (tickets) and sell again at prices exceeding the established rate. **3** *Colloq.* To buy and sell again quickly in order to make a small profit. — *v.i.* **4** *Colloq.* To scalp bonds, tickets, etc. [ME, prob. < Scand. Cf. ON *skālpr* a sheath.] — **scalp′er** *n.*

scalp dance A ceremonial victory dance of certain North American Indians, in which the women of the tribe display the trophies and perform the dances, accompanied by the singing of the warriors.

scal·pel (skal′pəl) *n.* A small pointed knife with a very sharp, thin blade, used in dissections and in surgery. [< L *scalpellum,* dim. of *scalprum* a knife < *scalpere* cut]

scalp lock A long lock of hair left on the crown of the head by certain North American Indians, often braided and interwoven with feathers or fur: a challenge to an enemy.

scal·y (skā′lē) *adj.* **scal·i·er, scal·i·est** **1** Having a covering of scales; hence, also, exfoliated; scurfy. **2** Of the nature of a scale; squamous. **3** Incrusted, as a boiler. **4** *Slang* Mean; dishonorable. [< SCALE¹ + -Y¹] — **scal′i·ness** *n.*

scaly ant-eater A pangolin.

scam (skam) *n. U.S. Slang* **1** A fraudulent bankruptcy planned as a swindle. **2** Any fraudulent scheme; swindle. [? Alter. of *scheme*]

scam·mo·ny (skam′ə·nē) *n.* **1** A climbing plant (*Convolvulus scammonia*) of the morning-glory family, native in Asia Minor, with tuberous roots containing a milky juice. **2** The dried resin of scammony roots, used as a strong cathartic. [< L *scammonia* < Gk. *skammōnia*]

scamp¹ (skamp) *n.* A confirmed rogue; good-for-nothing fellow; rascal. [< obs. *scamp, v.,* roam, contraction of SCAMPER] — **scamp′ish, scamp′y** *adj.*

scamp² (skamp) *v.t.* To perform (work) carelessly or dishonestly. [Orig. dial. E, ? < ON *skemma* shorten < *skammr* short. Akin to SCANT, SKIMP.] — **scamp′er** *n.*

scam·per (skam′pər) *v.i.* To run quickly or hastily, as from danger; hurry away. — *n.* A hurried flight. [? < obs. Du. *schampen* run away < AF *escamper,* OF *eschamper* decamp, run off hurriedly, escape, ult. < L *ex* out from + *campus* a plain, battlefield] — **scam′per·er** *n.*

scam·pi (skam′pē) *n.pl.* Large shrimp, usually served in a garlic sauce. [< Ital.]

scan (skan) *v.* **scanned, scan·ning** *v.t.* **1** To examine in detail; scrutinize closely. **2** To pass the eyes over quickly; glance at, as a page of manuscript. **3** To separate (verse) into metrical feet; ascertain the rhythm of. **4** To read (verse) aloud so as to ascertain the metrical structure. **5** In television, to pass a beam of light or electrons rapidly over every point of (a surface) so as to reproduce an image being televised. — *v.i.* **6** To scan verse. **7** To conform to metrical rules: said of verse. **8** In television, to scan a surface. See synonyms under LOOK. [< LL *scandere* scan verses < L, climb] — **scan′na·ble** *adj.* — **scan′ner** *n.*

scan·dal (skan′dəl) *n.* **1** The heedless or malicious repetition of evil reports; aspersion of character. **2** Reproach caused by outrageous or improper conduct. **3** A discreditable circumstance, event, or action; cause of reproach. **4** Injury to reputation, or general comment causing it. **5** *Law* Malicious defamation by word of mouth. **6** One whose conduct disgraces. [< AF *escandle* < L *scandalum* a cause of stumbling < Gk. *skandalon* a snare; refashioned after MF *scandale* < L *scandalum.* Doublet of SLANDER.]

Synonyms: aspersion, backbiting, calumny, defamation, detraction, obloquy, odium, reproach, slander. *Scandal* may be odious truth; *slander* is certain falsehood. *Antonyms:* applause, celebrity, credit, eulogy, fame, glory, honor, renown, reputation, repute.

scan·dal·ize (skan′dəl·īz) *v.t.* **·ized, ·iz·ing** To shock the moral feelings of, as by improper, frivolous, or offensive conduct; outrage. — **scan′dal·iz′er** *n.*

scan·dal·ous (skan′dəl·əs) *adj.* **1** Causing, or tending to cause, scandal; being a scandal; opprobrious; disgraceful; shocking to the sense of truth, decency, or propriety. **2** Consisting of evil or malicious reports; tending to injure reputation. **3** *Law* Libelous; irrelevant. See synonyms under FLAGRANT, INFAMOUS. — **scan′dal·ous·ly** *adv.* — **scan′dal·ous·ness** *n.*

scan·dent (skan′dənt) *adj.* Climbing, or aiding to climb, as a plant. [< L *scandens, -entis,* ppr. of *scandere* climb]

Scan·di·na·vi·a (skan′də·nā′vē·ə) The region of NW Europe occupied by Sweden, Norway, and Denmark; 315,156 square miles; Finland, Iceland, and the Faeroe Islands are often included: total area, 485,539 square miles.

scan·di·um (skan′dē·əm) *n.* A soft, silvery-white metallic element (symbol Sc, atomic number 21) widely distributed in small amounts in many minerals. See PERIODIC TABLE. [< NL < L *Scandia* Scandinavia]

scan·ning (skan′ing) *n.* **1** Scansion. **2** The process by which the electron beam of a television transmitting unit passes rapidly over every point of the image on the photosensitive screen.

scan·sion (skan′shən) *n.* The act or art of scanning verse to show its metrical parts. Compare METER² (def. 2). [< FF < LL *scansio, -onis* < *scandere* to scan. See SCAN.]

scan·so·ri·al (skan·sôr′ē·əl, -sō′rē-) *adj. Zool.* Pertaining to or adapted for climbing. Also **scan·so′ri·ous.** [< L *scansorius* < *scansus,* pp. of *scandere* climb]

scant (skant) *adj.* **1** Scarcely enough; meager in measure or quantity. **2** Being just short of the measure specified; of limited extent: often with the indefinite article even with a plural noun: a *scant* half-hour, a *scant* five yards. **3** Insufficiently supplied with something: with *of:* We were *scant* of breath. See synonyms under SCANTY. — *v.t.* **1** To restrict or limit in supply; stint. **2** To treat briefly or inadequately. See synonyms under SCRIMP. — *adv. Dial.* Scarcely; barely; not quite. [< ON *skamt,* neut. of *skammr* short] — **scant′ly** *adv.* — **scant′ness** *n.*

scant·ling (skant′ling) *n.* **1** A timber of moderate cross-section, used for studding, etc. **2** Such timbers collectively. **3** The dimensions of a timber in breadth and depth, but not in length; also, the dimensions of a stone in length, breadth, and thickness. **4** A small quantity or part; a sample. [Alter. of obs. *scantillon* < OF *eschantillon* specimen, corner-piece, chip; ? infl. in meaning by SCANT]

scant·y (skan′tē) *adj.* **scant·i·er, scant·i·est** **1** Limited in extent; small; close; cramped. **2** Restricted in quantity or number; scarcely sufficient. **3** Sparing. [< SCANT] — **scant′i·ly** *adv.* — **scant′i·ness** *n.*

Synonyms: deficient, insufficient, limited, narrow, niggardly, parsimonious, poor, scant, scarce, scrimped, scrimping, short, sparing, sparse. *Antonyms:* see synonyms under AMPLE.

scape¹ (skāp) *n.* **1** *Bot.* A long, naked peduncle rising from a depressed stem, as in the dandelion. **2** *Biol.* A stemlike part, as of an insect antenna, or the shaft of a feather. **3** *Archit.* The shaft of a column, or the apophyge of a shaft. [< L *scapus* < dial. Gk. (Doric) *scapos.* Akin to SCEPTER.]

scape² (skāp) *n.* A scene, as of land, sea, clouds, or the like. [Back formation < LANDSCAPE]

scape·goat (skāp′gōt′) *n.* **1** The goat upon whose head Aaron symbolically laid the sins of the people on the day of atonement, after which it was led away into the wilderness. *Lev.* xvi. **2** Any animal or person on whom the bad luck or sins of an individual or group are symbolically placed, and which is then turned loose: a world-wide folk custom of great antiquity. **3** Any person bearing blame for others. [< SCAPE³, *n.* + GOAT]

scape·grace (skāp′grās′) *n.* A mischievous or incorrigible person. [< SCAPE³ + GRACE (def. 4)]

scaph·oid (skaf′oid) *adj.* Boat-shaped. — *n. Anat.* A proximal bone of the wrist on the radial side; the navicular; also, a bone of the tarsus. [< NL *scaphoides* < Gk. *skaphoeidēs* < *skaphē* a boat + *eidos* form]

scapi- *combining form* A stalk or stem; a shaft: *scapiform,* resembling a scape. Also, before vowels, **scap-**. [< L *scapus* a stalk]

scap·u·la (skap'yə·lə) *n. pl.* **·lae** (-lē) *Anat.* The shoulder blade; the superior or proximal element of the pectoral girdle in the skeleton of vertebrates. [< LL, shoulder < L *scapulae* shoulder blades]

scap·u·lar (skap'yə·lər) *n.* **1** An outer garment worn by members of certain religious orders and consisting of two strips of cloth hanging down front and back and joined across the shoulders; formerly, a monastic working dress. **2** Two small rectangular pieces of woolen cloth connected by strings: worn as a badge of membership by certain religious orders. **3** *Surg.* A bandage passing over the shoulder blade. **4** *Ornithol.* The shoulder feathers of a bird lying along the sides of the back. —*adj.* Of or pertaining to the scapula or scapulars. Also **scap'u·lar·y** (-ler'ē). [< Med. L *scapulare* < LL *scapula.* See SCAPULA.]

scar¹ (skär) *n.* **1** The mark left on the skin after the healing of a wound or sore; a cicatrix. **2** Any mark resulting from past injury: often applied figuratively to the effects on a character of crimes or sorrows. **3** The mark left on or made by an organ, as by leaves after separation from a stem or branch. **4** An indentation or mark made by use, motion, or contact. —*v.t. & v.i.* **scarred, scar·ring** To mark or become marked with a scar. [< OF *escare* < LL *eschara* a scab < Gk.] —**scar'less** *adj.*

scar² (skär) *n.* **1** A bare rock standing alone. **2** A cliff or rocky place on the side of a hill or mountain. Also, *Scot., scaur.* [< ON *sker*]

scar·ab (skar'əb) *n.* **1** A scarabaeid beetle, especially the large, black, dung beetle (*Scarabaeus sacer*), held sacred by the ancient Egyptians as the symbol of resurrection and fertility. **2** A gem representing this beetle and inscribed with symbols, used in ancient Egypt as an amulet. Also **scar·a·bee** (skar'ə·bē). [< MF *scarabée* < L *scarabaeus*]

SCARAB

scar·a·bae·id (skar'ə·bē'id) *adj.* Pertaining to a large family (*Scarabaeidae*) of beetles, including cockchafers, etc. —*n.* A member of this family of beetles. Also **scar'a·bae·an, scar'a·bae'oid.** [< NL < L *scarabaeus* scarab]

scar·a·mouch (skar'ə·mouch, -mōōsh) *n.* A boastful, cowardly character; a swaggering buffoon: so called from a character in old Italian comedy. [< F *Scaramouche* < Ital. *Scaramuccia,* lit., a skirmish < Gmc.]

scarce (skârs) *adj.* **1** Rarely met with; infrequent. **2** Not plentiful, scant; insufficient. **3** Characterized or attended by insufficiency or want. See synonyms under RARE¹, SCANTY. —**to make oneself scarce** *Colloq.* To go away, or stay away. [< AF *scars, escars,* OF *eschars* scanty, insufficient, ult. < L *excerptus.* See EXCERPT.] —**scarce'ness** *n.*

scarce·ly (skârs'lē) *adv.* **1** Only just; barely. **2** Not quite; hardly.

scar·ci·ty (skâr'sə·tē) *n. pl.* **·ties** Scantiness; insufficiency; lack of necessities; dearth. See synonyms under WANT.

scare (skâr) *v.* **scared, scar·ing** *v.t.* **1** To strike with sudden fear; frighten. **2** To drive or force by frightening: with *off* or *away:* to *scare* away an intruder. —*v.i.* **3** To take fright; become scared. See synonyms under FRIGHTEN. —**to scare up** *Colloq.* To get together hurriedly; discover; produce: to *scare up* votes, food, a group of people, etc. —*n.* **1** Sudden fright, especially from slight or imaginary cause; terror. **2** A panic (def. 2). —*adj. Colloq.* Intended or likely to scare, or to provoke alarm or concern: *scare* tactics. [< ON *skirra* frighten < *skiarr* shy] —**scar'er** *n.* —**scar'ing·ly** *adv.*

scare·crow (skâr'krō') *n.* **1** Any effigy set up to scare crows and other birds from growing crops. **2** A cause of false alarm. **3** A wretched-looking person.

Synonyms: bogy, bugbear, fright, goblin, hobgoblin.

scare·head (skâr'hed') *n.* An exceptionally large newspaper headline in very bold type

for news of sensational interest.

scare·mon·ger (skâr'mung'gər, -mong'-) *n.* One who spreads an alarming rumor; an alarmist.

scarf¹ (skärf) *n. pl.* **scarfs** **1** In carpentry, a lapped joint made as by notching two timbers at the ends, and bolting them together so as to form one continuous piece without increased thickness: also **scarf joint.** **2** The notched end of either of the timbers so cut. **3** A cut or incision in the blubber of a whale. —*v.t.* **1** To unite with a scarf joint. **2** To cut a scarf in. [? < ON *skarfr* a notch in a timber]

TYPES OF SCARF JOINTS

scarf² (skärf) *n. pl.* **scarfs** or **scarves** (skärvz) **1** A long and wide band, especially when worn about the head and neck; also, any sash. **2** A necktie or cravat. **3** A runner for a bureau or dresser. **4** An official sash, denoting rank. **5** A tippet or neckpiece. —*v.t.* **1** To cover or decorate as with a scarf. **2** To use as a scarf; wrap loosely around one. [< AF *escarpe,* OF *escharpe,* ? < *escreppe* a scrip²]

scarf·pin (skärf'pin') *n.* An ornamental pin worn on a tie or scarf.

scar·i·fy (skar'ə·fī) *v.t.* **·fied, ·fy·ing** **1** To scratch or make slight incisions in, as the skin in surgery. **2** To criticize severely; make cutting comments on. **3** *Agric.* To stir the surface of, as soil. **4** To prune. [< MF *scarifier* < LL *scarificare* < L *scarifare* < Gk. *skariphasthai* scratch an outline, sketch < *skariphos* a stylus] —**scar'i·fi·ca'tion** *n.*

scar·i·ous (skâr'ē·əs) *adj.* **1** *Bot.* Thin, dry, membranaceous, and not green: said of plants. **2** Scaly. Also **scar'i·ose** (-ōs). [< F *scarieux* < NL *scariosus* < L *scaria* a thorny shrub]

scar·let (skär'lit) *n.* **1** A brilliant red, inclining to orange. **2** A bright-red dye formerly obtained from the kermes or cochineal insect. **3** Any one of several coal-tar colors, varying from yellow to brown and used for dyeing. **4** Cloth or clothing of a scarlet color. —*adj.* **1** Brilliant-red, inclining to orange. **2** Clothed in scarlet. [< OF *escarlate* < Med. L *scarlatum,* prob. < Arabic *siqillāt* < Persian *saqalāt* a rich, scarlet cloth]

scarlet fever *Pathol.* An acute infectious fever caused by certain strains of hemolytic streptococci and characterized by a diffused scarlet rash followed by scaling off of the skin. Also *scarlatina.*

scarlet letter A scarlet "A," a badge of shame, which women convicted of adultery were once compelled to wear.

scarlet runner A tall climbing bean (*Phaseolus coccineus*) of tropical America, with vivid red flowers and long seed pods, now widely cultivated as a vegetable; a string bean.

scarp (skärp) *n.* Any steep slope; an abrupt declivity; an escarpment. Compare illustration under BASTION. —*v.t.* To cut to a steep slope. [< AF *escarpe* < Ital. *scarpa*]

scar·pet·ti (skär·pet'ē) *n. pl.* Rope-soled shoes used by mountain climbers. [< Ital. *scarpetto* a light shoe, dim. of *scarpa* a shoe]

scar·y (skâr'ē) *adj.* **scar·i·er, scar·i·est** *Colloq.* **1** Easily scared. **2** Somewhat frightened; anxious; timid. **3** Giving cause for alarm.

scat¹ (skat) *v.i.* **scat·ted, scat·ting** *Colloq.* To go away; depart: usually in the imperative. [? < *ss,* imit. of a hiss + CAT]

scat² (skat) *n. Slang* A type of jazz singing in which meaningless syllables are improvised on the melodic line. [Prob. < SCAT¹]

scathe (skāth) *v.t.* **scathed, scath·ing** **1** To criticize severely. **2** To injure severely; harm; blast. —*n.* **1** Severe injury; harm; loss. Also **scath** (skath). Also, *Scot., skaith.* [< ON *skatha < skathi* harm] —**scathe'ful** *adj.*

scath·ing (skā'thing) *adj.* Damaging by scorching or blasting; withering: now usually figuratively: a *scathing* rebuke. —*n.* Harm; injury. —**scath'ing·ly** *adv.*

scato- *combining form* Dung; excrement: *scatology.* Also, before vowels, **scat-**. [< Gk. *skōr, skatos* dung]

sca·tol·o·gy (skə·tol'ə·jē) *n.* **1** The study of

excrement, considered as a branch of paleontology, medicine, and psychiatry. **2** Preoccupation with filth or obscenity, as in literature. Also **scat·o·lo·gi·a** (skat'ə·lō'jē·ə). [< SCATO- + -LOGY] —**sca·tol'o·gist** *n.*

scat·o·man·cy (skat'ō·man'sē) *n.* In folklore, divination, or determination of disease, by means of feces.

scat·ter (skat'ər) *v.t.* **1** To throw about in various places; sprinkle; strew, as seed. **2** To separate and drive away in different directions; rout. **3** *Physics* To reflect (heat or light) irregularly. —*v.i.* **4** To separate and go in different directions; disperse; dissipate. See synonyms under SPREAD, SQUANDER. [ME *scateren* squander. ? Akin to SHATTER.] —**scat'ter·er** *n.*

scat·ter·brain (skat'ər·brān') *n.* A person without concentration of mind; a heedless person. —**scat'ter·brained'** *adj.*

scat·ter·good (skat'ər·good') *n.* **1** One who wastes that which is good; a spendthrift. **2** One who or that which distributes charities.

scat·ter·ing (skat'ər·ing) *n.* **1** Dispersion. **2** *Physics* The deflection of a beam of particles or waves into a variety of directions upon collision with any obstacle preventing continuous propagation in the original direction. **3** The dispersion, over an area, of votes for candidates. —*adj.* Placed at intervals or at a distance. —**scat'ter·ing·ly** *adv.*

scat·ter·ling (skat'ər·ling) *n.* A person without a home; a vagrant. [< SCATTER + -LING¹]

scaup (skôp) *n.* A sea duck (genus *Aythya*) of northern regions, related to the canvasback, having the head and neck black in the male; especially, the common American bay duck (*A. marila*). Also **scaup duck.** [Short for *scaup duck* < SCAUP² + DUCK]

scav·enge (skav'inj) *v.* **·enged, ·eng·ing** *v.t.* **1** To remove filth, rubbish, and refuse from, as streets. **2** To remove exhaust gases from (the cylinder of an internal-combustion engine). **3** *Metall.* To remove impurities from (a metal or alloy). —*v.i.* **4** To act as a scavenger. **5** To search for food. [Back formation < SCAVENGER]

scav·en·ger (skav'in·jər) *n.* **1** A street-cleaner. **2** An animal that feeds on carrion, as the buzzard. [ME *scavager* < AF *scawager* < *scawage* inspection < *escauwer* inspect < Flemish *scauwen* see]

sce·nar·i·o (si·nâr'ē·ō, -nä'rē·ō) *n. pl.* **·nar·i·os** **1** The plot of a dramatic work, or a skeleton libretto. **2** The written plot and arrangement of incidents of a motion picture. **3** An outline or plan of a projected series of actions or events. [< Ital. < LL *scenarius* of stage scenes < L *scena.* See SCENE.]

sce·nar·ist (si·nâr'ist, -nä'rist) *n.* One who writes scenarios.

scene (sēn) *n.* **1** A locality and all connected with it, as presented to view; a landscape. **2** The place in which the action of a drama is supposed to occur; setting or locality. **3** The place and surroundings of any event, real or imagined, as in literature or art. **4** A division of an act of a play; one comprehensive event in a play. **5** Any incident or episode that may serve as the subject of a description. **6** The painted canvas screen or screens for the background for a play. **7** Any striking exhibition or display; especially, a display of passion or excited feeling. **8** *Slang* A place or realm of a currently popular activity: the pop music *scene.* —**behind the scenes** **1** Out of sight of a theater audience; backstage. **2** Privately; in secret. [< OF < L *scena, scaena* < Gk. *skēnē* tent, stage] *Synonyms:* action, display, event, exhibition, incident, landscape, place, prospect, situation.

scen·er·y (sē'nər·ē) *n. pl.* **·er·ies** Natural or theatrical scenes collectively. [< Ital. *scenario.* See SCENARIO.]

sce·nic (sē'nik, sen'ik) *adj.* **1** Artistic in grouping and effect. **2** Picturesque. **3** Relating to stage scenery.

sce·nog·ra·phy (sē·nog'rə·fē) *n.* The art of making drawings in perspective. [< F *scénographie* < L *scaenographia* < Gk. *skēnographia* < *skēnē* a scene, tent + *graphein* write] —**scen·o·graph·ic** (sen'ə·graf'ik, sē'nə-) *adj.*

scent (sent) *n.* **1** An odor, pleasant or unpleasant. **2** The effluvium by which an animal can be tracked. **3** A clue aiding investigation. **4** Scraps of paper, in the game of hare and hounds, dropped by the hares in their flight to enable the hounds to follow them. **5** A fluid essence containing extracts from flowers or other fragrant bodies; perfume. **6** The sense of smell. — *v.t.* **1** To perceive by the sense of smell. **2** To form a suspicion of. **3** To cause to be fragrant; perfume. — *v.i.* **4** To hunt by the sense of smell: said of hounds. ◆ Homophone: *cent.* [< OF *sentir* discern by the senses, feel < L *sentire*] — **scent′less** *adj.*

Synonyms (noun): savor, smell.

scep·ter (sep′tər) *n.* **1** A staff or wand carried as the badge of command or sovereignty. **2** Hence, kingly office or power. — *v.t.* **1** To confer the scepter on; invest with royal power. **2** To furnish with or as with a scepter or scepters. Also **scep′tre** (-tər), *sceptre* < L *sceptrum* < Gk. *skēptron* a staff < *skēptesthai* prop oneself, lean on] **scep·tic** (skep′tik), **scep·ti·cal, scep·ti·cism,** etc. See SKEPTIC, etc.

Schac·a·bac (shak′ə·bak) In the *Arabian Nights,* the beggar invited to the Barmecide feast.

SCEPTER

schanz (shäns) *n.* A breastwork of earth and stones. — *v.t.* To protect with a schanz. [< Du. *schans*]

schap·pe (shä′pə) *n.* A fabric woven from spun silk. — *v.t.* **schapped, schap·ping** To ferment (silk) so as to remove its gum coating. [< dial. G (Swiss), a waste, impurity]

schat·chen (shät′khən) *n.* One who arranges marriages for a fee; a marriage-broker: chiefly among Russian Jews. Also **schad′chan.** [< Yiddish, a marriage broker < Hebrew *shadhkhān*]

sched·ule (skej′ool, *Brit.* shed′yool) *n.* **1** A written or printed statement, usually in tabular form, specifying the details of some matter, and often annexed to statutes, petitions, and other documents. **2** A list; catalog; an inventory. **3** A timetable; also, a detailed and timed plan for any procedure. **4** A program. — *v.t.* **·uled, ·ul·ing 1** To place in or on a schedule. **2** To make a schedule of. **3** *Colloq.* To appoint or plan for a specified time or date: He *scheduled* his appearance for five o'clock. [Alter. of ME *sedule* < OF *cedule* < LL *scedula,* dim. of L *scida, scheda* a leaf of paper < Gk. *schidē* a wood splinter < *schizein* split; infl. in form by Med. L *schedula*]

schee·lite (shē′līt) *n.* A vitreous, variously colored, tetragonal calcium tungstate. [after K. W. *Scheele,* who discovered tungstic acid]

schef·fer·ite (shef′ə·rīt) *n.* A brown manganese pyroxene often containing iron. [after H. T. *Scheffer,* 1710–59, Swedish chemist]

Sche·her·e·za·de (shə·her′ə·zä′də, -zäd′) In the *Arabian Nights,* the bride of a sultan who had sworn to kill each of his wives after her wedding night. Scheherezade tricked the sultan into sparing her life by telling him an exciting story each night, not revealing the ending until the following day. Also **Sche·her′a·za′de.**

scheik (shēk) See SHEIK.

sche·ma (skē′mə) *n. pl.* **sche·ma·ta** (skē′mə·tə) **1** A scheme, synopsis, or summary. **2** A diagrammatic representation of certain relations in some system of knowledge. **3** Any figure drawn in outline; formerly, a geometric diagram. [< L. See SCHEME.]

sche·ma·tism (skē′mə·tiz′əm) *n.* **1** A particular form or disposition of anything. **2** Orderly arrangement of parts, as in a philosophic system; the classification of knowledge, etc.; design.

sche·ma·tize (skē′mə·tīz) *v.t.* **·tized, ·tiz·ing** To form into or arrange according to a scheme or schema. [< Gk. *schēmatizein* < *schēma, -atos* a form] **—sche′ma·ti·za′tion** *n.*

scheme (skēm) *n.* **1** A plan of something to be done; a plot or device for the accomplishment of an object. **2** A combination of various things according to a general plan or design; systematic arrangement. **3** A formal plan or

arrangement, or a statement of such a plan; also, a table or schedule. **4** An outline drawing or sketch; diagram. **5** In astrology, a plan representing the aspects of the heavenly bodies at any given time. See synonyms under DESIGN, HYPOTHESIS, PLAN, PROJECT. — *v.* **schemed, schem·ing** *v.t.* **1** To make a scheme for; devise; plan. **2** To plan or plot in an underhand manner. — *v.i.* **3** To make schemes; plan or plot; connive. [< L *schema* a shape, figure of speech < Gk. *schēma, -atos* a form, plan] **—sche·mat·ic** (skē·mat′ik) or **-i·cal** *adj.* **—sche·mat′i·cal·ly** *adv.* **—schem′er** *n.* **—schem′ing** *adj.*

schenk beer (shengk) Beer fermented in 4 to 6 weeks and brewed for immediate use in the winter. [< G *schenkbier* < *schenken* pour out + *bier* beer; so called with ref. to its being put on schenk (draft) as soon as it is made, to keep it from turning sour]

scher·zan·do (sker·tsän′dō) *adv. Music* In a sportive or playful manner. [< Ital., ppr. of *scherzare* play < *scherzo.* See SCHERZO.]

scher·zo (sker′tsō) *n. pl.* **·zos** or **·zi** (-tsē) *Music* A sportive or lightsome movement, usually following a slow movement, especially in a symphony or sonata. [< Ital., a jest < G *scherz*]

Schick test A test to determine the susceptibility of a person to diphtheria by injecting a diluted diphtheria toxin: a positive reaction gives a reddening of the skin. [after Dr. Béla *Schick,* who devised it]

schil·ler (shil′ər) *n. Mineral.* A bronzelike luster or iridescence due to the reflection of particles dispersed in certain minerals. [< G, a play of colors < *schillern* change color]

schil·ler·ize (shil′ə·rīz) *v.t.* **·ized, ·iz·ing** To impart schiller to. **—schil′ler·i·za′tion** *n.*

schil·ling (shil′ing) *n.* The monetary unit of Austria since 1924; a former North German silver coin. [< G]

schip·per·ke (skip′ər·kē) *n.* A Belgian breed of dog used as a watchdog and sometimes for hunting. It is usually tailless, has a thick-set body, foxlike head, and a rather thick, short, black coat. Formerly called *Spits* or *Spitske.* [< dial. Du., a little boatman, dim. of Du. *schipper;* so called because orig. used as watchdogs on boats]

schism (siz′əm) *n.* **1** A division of a church into factions. **2** The offense of causing division in a church or a religious community. **3** An ecclesiastical body separated from a larger or older body, as from an established church. **4** The act of dividing, or the state of being divided; division. See synonyms under SECT. [< OF *cisme, scisme* < LL *schisma* < Gk., a split < *schizein* split]

schis·mat·ic (siz·mat′ik) *adj.* Relating to, having the character of, implying, or promoting schism: also **schis·mat′i·cal.** —*n.* One who makes or participates in an ecclesiastical schism: a term of opprobrium. [< OF *cismatique, scismatique* < LL *schismaticus* < L Gk. *schismatikos* < Gk. *schisma, -atos.* See SCHISM.] **—schis·mat′i·cal·ly** *adv.* **—schis·mat′i·cal·ness** *n.*

schist (shist) *n. Geol.* Any rock that readily splits or cleaves; specifically, a rock that has had a parallel or foliated structure secondarily developed in it: also spelled *shist.* [< F *schiste* < L *schistos* readily split < Gk. < *schizein* split] **—schist′ous, schist·ose** (shis′tōs) *adj.*

schis·ta·ceous (shis·tā′shəs) *adj.* Bluish-gray; of a light slaty color. [< SCHIST + -ACEOUS]

schisto- *combining form* Schistose. Also, before vowels, **schist-.** [< Gk. *schistos* split]

schis·to·some (shis′tə·sōm) *n.* Any of a genus (*Schistosoma*) of trematode worms, including certain species parasitic in the blood of man, as the blood fluke (*S. haematobium*) common in Africa. [< NL < Gk. *schistos* split (< *schizein* split) + *sōma* a body]

schis·to·so·mi·a·sis (shis′tə·sō·mī′ə·sis) *n. Pathol.* A wasting disease caused by infestation with worms of the genus *Schistosoma,* endemic in Egypt and other parts of Africa: also called *bilharziasis.* [< NL < *Schistosoma* a schistosome]

schizo- *combining form* Split; divided: *schizophrenia.* Also, before vowels, **schiz-.** [< Gk. *schizein* split]

schiz·o·carp (skiz′ə·kärp) *n. Bot.* A split fruit;

a pericarp splitting at maturity into two or more one-seeded indehiscent portions. Compare illustration under FRUIT. **—schiz′o·car′pous, schiz′o·car′pic** *adj.*

schiz·o·gen·e·sis (skiz′ō·jen′ə·sis) *n. Biol.* Reproduction by fission.

schi·zog·o·ny (ski·zog′ə·nē) *n. Biol.* Reproduction by multiple fission, as in certain protozoa. [< NL *schizogonia* < Gk. *schizein* split + *genesthai* become]

schiz·oid (skiz′oid) *adj.* Resembling schizophrenia. —*n.* One having characteristics suggestive of schizophrenia. [< SCHIZ(OPHRENIA) + -OID]

schiz·o·my·cete (skiz′ō·mī·sēt′) *n.* One of the *Schizomycetes;* a bacterium. [< NL < Gk. *schizein* split + *mykēs, -ētos* a mushroom] **—schiz′o·my·ce′tous** *adj.*

Schiz·o·my·ce·tes (skiz′ō·mī·sē′tēz) *n. pl.* A class of widely distributed, minute, unicellular plants reproducing by fission and allied to the fungi: it comprises the bacteria and, in the Bergey classification, includes the following orders:

Eubacteriales	Simple undifferentiated forms
Actinomycetales	Moldlike bacteria
Chlamydobacteriales	Algalike iron bacteria
Caulobacteriales	Aquatic, gum-secreting bacteria
Thiobacteriales	Sulfur bacteria
Myxobacteriales	Slime-mold bacteria
Spirochaetales	Protozoanlike bacteria

schiz·o·my·co·sis (skiz′ō·mī·kō′sis) *n. Pathol.* A morbid condition or disease due to the presence of schizomycetes. [< NL]

schiz·ont (skiz′ont, skī′zont) *n.* The mature trophozoite of a sporozoan, as the malaria parasite, from which new cells, or merozoites, are liberated into the blood by schizogony. [< Gk. *schizōn, -ontos,* ppr. of *schizein* split]

schiz·o·phre·ni·a (skiz′ō·frē′nē·ə) *n.* A group of mental disorders beginning in early adulthood and characterized by disturbances of affect, behavior, and intellection and often by delusions and hallucinations. Formerly called *dementia praecox.* [< NL < Gk. *schizein* split + *phrēn* mind] **—schiz′o·phren′ic** (-fren′ik) *adj. & n.*

schiz·o·phyte (skiz′ə·fīt) *n.* One of a division or phylum (*Schizophyta*) of unicellular or simple multicellular plants which reproduce by fission or by asexual spores: it includes the bacteria and the blue-green algae. —*adj.* Of or pertaining to the Schizophyta: also **schiz′o·phyt′ic** (-fit′ik). [< NL < Gk. *schizein* split + *phyton* a plant]

schiz·o·pod (skiz′ə·pod) *n.* Any of a former order (*Schizopoda*) of crustaceans having a soft carapace and resembling the shrimp: now included in the subclass *Malacostraca.* [< NL < Gk. *schizopous, -podos* having parted toes < *schizein* split + *pous, podos* a foot]

schiz·o·thy·mi·a (skiz′ō·thī′mē·ə) *n. Psychiatry* A schizophrenic condition marked by introversion and a withdrawing from the world, but milder than schizophrenia. [< NL < Gk. *schizein* split + *thymos* spirit] **—schiz′o·thyme** *n.* **—schiz′o·thy′mic** *adj.*

schle·miel (shlə·mēl′) *n. Slang* An inept, easily duped person; a bungler; dolt. Also **schle·mihl′.** [< Yiddish, an unlucky person < Hebrew *Shelumiēl,* a personal name]

schlep (shlep) *Slang v.* **schlepped, schlep·ping** *v.t.* **1** To drag awkwardly; lug. — *v.i.* **2** To drag something awkwardly. **3** To proceed wearily or heavily: to *schlep* uptown. —*n.* **1** A difficult journey. **2** A stupid, awkward person. Also **schlepp.** [< Yiddish *shleppen* to drag] **—schlep′per** *n.*

schlie·re (shlē′rə) *n. pl.* **·ren** (-rən) *Geol.* In an igneous rock, an irregular, commonly not sharply bounded, portion differing in composition or texture from the general mass of the rock. [< G, lit., a streak] **—schlie′ric** *adj.*

schlie·ren (shlē′rən) *n. Physics* Any disturbance in the light path of an interferometer which alters the density of the air and thus changes the interference pattern of the light

waves. [<G, pl. of *schliere*, lit., a streak]
schlock (shlok) *Slang n.* Shoddy, inferior merchandise. —*adj.* Of inferior quality; tawdry. Also spelled *shlock.* [<Yiddish] —**schlock′y** *adj.*

schmaltz (shmälts) *n. Slang* 1 Anything which is overly sentimental, as in music or literature. 2 Extreme sentimentalism. [<Yiddish <G *schmalz*, lit., melted fat] —**schmaltz′y** *adj.*

Schmidt telescope A reflecting telescope that yields undistorted images of a very wide field. [after B. *Schmidt*, died 1935, German optical designer]

schnapps (shnäps, shnaps) *n.* Holland gin; Hollands; loosely, any ardent spirits. Also **schnaps.** [<G, a dram, a nip <Du. *snaps*, lit., a gulp, mouthful]

schnau·zer (shnou′zər) *n.* A small, active terrier originally developed in Germany, having a wiry black or pepper–and–salt coat. —**miniature schnauzer** A toy terrier bred from the standard schnauzer and a pinscher. [<G *Schnauze* snout]

STANDARD SCHNAUZER

schnor·kel (shnôr′kəl) *n.* 1 An apparatus for the ventilation of a submerged submarine, consisting of retractable tubes for the intake of fresh air and the removal of the toxic gases. 2 A snorkel. [<G *schnörkel* spiral]

schnor·rer (shnôr′ər) *n.* A professional or habitual beggar. [<Yiddish <G *schnurrer* < slang *schnorren* go begging, orig. whirr, purr; with ref. to musical instruments of beggars]

schnoz·zle (shnoz′əl) *n. Slang* Nose. [<Yiddish <G *schnauze*. Akin to SNOUT.]

schol·ar (skol′ər) *n.* 1 A person eminent for learning. 2 The holder of a scholarship. 3 One who learns under a teacher; a pupil. —**Rhodes scholar** A male student selected from a college or university of the United States or of any British dominion or colony, to receive one of the scholarships established by Cecil Rhodes for attendance at Oxford University, England. [Prob. fusion of OE *scolere* and OF *escoler*, both <LL *scholaris* <L *schola*. See SCHOOL¹.]
—*Synonyms:* disciple, learner, pupil, savant, student. Historically the primary sense of a *scholar* is one who is being schooled; thence the word passes to designate one who is apt in school work, and finally one who is thoroughly schooled, master of what the schools can teach, an erudite or accomplished person: when used without qualification, the word is generally understood in this sense; as, He is manifestly a *scholar*. *Pupil* signifies one under the close personal supervision or instruction of a teacher or tutor.

schol·arch (skol′ärk) *n.* 1 In Greek antiquity, the head of a school of philosophy in Athens. 2 The head of any school. [<Gk. *scholarchē* < *scholē* a school + *archein* rule]

schol·ar·ly (skol′ər·lē) *adj.* Like a scholar; learned; erudite.

schol·ar·ship (skol′ər·ship) *n.* 1 Learning; erudition. 2 Maintenance or a stipend for a student awarded by an educational institution; also, the position of such a student. See synonyms under KNOWLEDGE, LEARNING.

scho·las·tic (skō·las′tik, skə-) *adj.* 1 Pertaining to or characteristic of scholars, education, or schools. 2 Pertaining to or characteristic of the medieval schoolmen. 3 Precise; pedantic. 4 Pertaining to the theological grade of students of the Jesuit order. Also **scho·las′ti·cal.** —*n.* 1 A student; pupil. 2 *Often cap.* A schoolman; an advocate of scholasticism. 3 A pedant. [<L *scholasticus* <Gk. *scholastikos* < *scholazein* be at leisure, devote leisure to study < *scholē*. See SCHOOL¹.]

scho·las·ti·cate (skō·las′tə·kāt, skə-) *n.* A general house of higher studies for Jesuit scholastics. [<NL *scholasticatus* <L *scholasticus* SCHOLASTIC]

scho·las·ti·cism (skō·las′tə·siz′əm, skə-) *n.* 1 *Often cap.* The systematized Christian logic, philosophy, and theology of medieval scholars from the 10th to the 15th centuries, based on Aristotle's *Logic* and *Metaphysics* and the writings of the early Christian fathers. See HUMANISM. 2 Any system of teaching which

insists on traditional doctrines and forms. 3 A similar teaching of the present day given especially in seminaries of the Roman Catholic Church.

scho·li·ast (skō′lē·ast) *n.* A commentator; especially, an ancient grammarian or annotator of classical texts. See SCHOLIUM. [<L *scholiasta* <Gk. *scholiastēs* < *scholion* a commentary < *scholē* a school] —**scho′li·as·tic** *adj.*

scho·li·um (skō′lē·əm) *n. pl.* **·li·ums** or **·li·a** (-lē·ə) 1 An explanatory marginal note, as on a classical text by an ancient grammarian. 2 An interpolated note accompanying a mathematical proof. [<LL *scholium* <Gk. *scholion*. See SCHOLIAST.]

school¹ (skōol) *n.* 1 An educational institution. 2 The place in which formal instruction is given; also, the instruction itself. 3 A period or session of an educational institution; a course of study at a school: *School* begins tomorrow. 4 The pupils in an educational institution. 5 A subdivision of a university devoted to a special branch of higher education: a *school* of education, medicine, etc. 6 The prescribed drill, duties, instruction, and training of any branch of the army or navy: gunnery *school*, aviation *school*; also, the manual of such instruction. 7 A body of disciples of a teacher or system; a sect, etc.; also, the system, methods, or opinions characteristic of those thus associated: the Scottish *school* of philosophy, a painting of the Flemish *school*. 8 A general style of life, manners, etc. 9 In medieval times, specifically, a seminary of logic, metaphysics, and theology; in the plural, the seats of the scholastic philosophy. 10 Any sphere or means of instruction: the *school* of example. —*v.t.* 1 To instruct in a school; train; educate. 2 To subject to rule or discipline. [OE *scōl* <L *schola* <Gk. *scholē* leisure or that which is done during leisure time, a school]
—**common school** One of the free public elementary schools in the United States.
—**consolidated school** A school, usually rural, consisting of several elementary schools and sometimes a high school, merged into one organization, for pupils from outlying districts.
—**continuation school** Comprehensively, a school for the further education of persons already employed; specifically, a school for employed boys and girls below the legal age for leaving school, attended a few hours a week on the employers' time.
—**dame school** An early form of school kept by a woman who drilled young children in their ABC's and the beginnings of reading.
—**elementary school** A school giving a course of education of from six to nine years, pupils usually entering at about six years of age.
—**finishing school** A school that prepares girls for entrance into society.
—**grammar school** 1 In graded public schools, the grades between primary and high school, grades one to eight inclusive. 2 Popularly, an elementary school. 3 *Brit.* A secondary school, often preparatory for college; originally for the teaching of Latin and Greek, but now offering broader curriculums.
—**high school** The highest division of the common schools, typically comprising grades 9, 10, 11, and 12: often preparatory for college or the vocations. —**junior high school** A school usually consisting of the 7th, 8th, and 9th grades, but sometimes of only 7th and 8th or 8th and 9th grades: also **intermediate school.** —**senior high school** A corresponding division of the public schools, consisting usually of grades 10, 11, and 12.
—**industrial school** 1 An institute for the practical development of manual and industrial skills. 2 A school for the care and training of neglected children.
—**parochial school** A school, usually elementary, supported by the parish of a church, especially by a Roman Catholic church.
—**primary school** A school for the teaching of the youngest pupils; the first grades of common schools beyond kindergarten.
—**private school** A school maintained under private or corporate management, usually for profit: in the United States, contradistinguished from *public school.*
—**public school** 1 A school maintained by public funds for the free education of the

children of the community, usually covering elementary and secondary grades. 2 In England, a private or endowed school not run for profit; specifically, the exclusive endowed schools preparing students for the universities, as Eton, Harrow, etc.: so called because it serves the country at large, and not merely one community.
—**secondary school** A high school or preparatory school intermediate between the grammar school and college.
—**trade school** A vocational school designed to give a knowledge of processes and a skill of hand adequate for work in a specific trade.
—**vocational school** In general, a school training in the practical application of knowledge to business, the professions, or the technical arts and crafts.

school² (skōol) *n.* A large number of fish, whales, etc., swimming together; shoal. —*v.i.* To swim together in a school. [<Du., a crowd, school of fishes. Akin to SHOAL².]

school board A legal board or committee having oversight of public schools.

school·book (skōol′bŏŏk′) *n.* A book for use in school; textbook.

school·house (skōol′hous′) *n.* A building in which a school is conducted.

school·ing (skōo′ling) *n.* 1 Instruction given at school; also, any preparatory training or discipline. 2 Price paid for instructing pupils. 3 The training of horses and riders. See synonyms under EDUCATION, NURTURE.

school·marm (skōol′märm′) *n. Colloq.* A woman schoolteacher, especially one considered to be prudish, spinsterish, or strict. Also **school′ma′am′** (-mam′).

school·mas·ter (skōol′mas′tər, -mäs′-) *n.* 1 A man who teaches school. 2 One who or that which instructs or disciplines in any way: Necessity was his *schoolmaster*. 3 A Caribbean fish (*Neomaenis apoda*) of the snapper family. See synonyms under MASTER.

school·mate (skōol′māt′) *n.* A fellow pupil; a schoolfellow.

school·mis·tress (skōol′mis′tris) *n.* A woman who teaches school.

school·room (skōol′rŏŏm′, -rŏŏm′) *n.* A room in which instruction is given.

school ship A vessel in which boys and young men are trained in seamanship.

school·teach·er (skōol′tē′chər) *n.* One who gives instruction in a school below the college level.

school·yard (skōol′yärd′) *n.* The grounds about a school used for play.

schoon·er (skōo′nər) *n.* 1 A fore-and-aft rigged vessel having originally two masts, but now often three or more. 2 A prairie schooner. 3 A large beer glass, holding usually about a pint or more. [Appar. coined in New England < dial. *scoon* skim on water, prob. <Scand.]

SCHOONER

schoon·er-yacht (skōo′nər-yot′) *n.* A yacht rigged like a schooner.

Scho·pen·hau·er·ism (shō′pən·hou′ə·riz′əm) *n.* The philosophy (pessimistic determinism) of Arthur Schopenhauer, who taught that egoism, manifested in the "will to live," must be overcome; that the world is evil and should not be perpetuated; and that God, free will, and the immortality of the soul are illusions.

schorl (shôrl) *n.* Tourmaline, especially the black variety: also spelled *shorl.* [<G *schörl*]

schot·tische (shot′ish) *n.* A dance in 2/4 time similar to the polka, but somewhat slower; also, the music for such a dance. [<G (*der*) *schottische* (*tanz*) (the) Scottish (dance)]

schtick (shtik) *n.* See SHTICK.

schuss (shŏŏs) *v.i.* To ski down a steep slope at high speed. —*n.* A straight, steep ski course, or the act of skiing this course. [<G, lit., a shot]

Schutz·staf·fel (shŏŏts′shtä′fəl) *n. pl.* **·feln** (-fəln) *German* Hitler's personal bodyguard, known as the Black Shirts; later, the chief section, the Elite Guard, of the Nazi militia, used to maintain order in Germany and occupied countries. Abbr. *SS.*

schwa (shwä, shvä) *n.* 1 *Phonet.* A weak or

obscure, central vowel sound occurring in most of the unstressed syllables in English speech. The sound, regardless of spelling, is that of the *a* in *alone*, the *o* in *lemon*, or the *u* in *circus*: written ə. **2** In Hebrew, the obscure vowel sound: written : and often transliterated by *e*. [<G <Hebrew *shewa*]

Schwei·tzer (shvī′tsər), **Albert**, 1875–1965, Alsatian clergyman, physician, missionary, philosopher, and musicologist.

Schweitzer's reagent *Chem.* An aqueous solution of cupric hydroxide precipitated in ammonium hydroxide: used as a solvent for cellulose, especially in the cuprammonium process. Also called *cuprammonia*. [after Mathias E. *Schweitzer*, 1818–1860, German chemist]

sci·ae·noid (sī-ē′noid) *n.* Any of a family (*Sciaenidae*) of spiny–finned, carnivorous, mostly marine fishes (order *Percomorphi*), as croakers, drums, weakfish, etc. — *adj.* Of or pertaining to the Sciaenidae. Also **sci·ae′nid** (-ē′nid). [<NL <L *sciaena* <Gk. *skiaina*, a kind of fish]

sci·at·ic (sī-at′ik) *adj.* Pertaining to or affecting the hip or its nerves; ischial. — *n.* A sciatic nerve or part. [<MF *sciatique* <Med. L *sciaticus*, alter. of L *ischiadicus* <Gk. *ischiadikos* < *ischion* hip, hip joint]

sci·at·i·ca (sī-at′i-kə) *n. Pathol.* **1** Neuralgia, affecting the sciatic nerve traversing the hip and thigh. **2** Any painful affection of these or adjoining parts. [<Med. L *sciatica (passio)* (the) sciatic (disease), fem. of *sciaticus* SCIATIC]

sci·ence (sī′əns) *n.* **1** Knowledge as of facts, phenomena, laws, and proximate causes, gained and verified by exact observation, organized experiment, and correct thinking; also, the sum of universal knowledge. **2** An exact and systematic statement or classification of knowledge concerning some subject or group of subjects. **3** Any department of knowledge in which the results of investigation have been systematized in the form of hypotheses and general laws subject to verification. **4** Expertness, skill, or proficiency resulting from knowledge. **5** Any one of the seven liberal arts (grammar, rhetoric, logic, arithmetic, music, geometry, astronomy): an ancient use. [<OF <L *scientia* <*sciens, -entis*, ppr. of *scire* know]

Synonyms: knowledge, art, learning, scholarship. *Knowledge* may be a medley of facts which gain real value only when coordinated and systematized by the man of *science. Art* relates to something to be done or produced by skill, *science* to something to be known. Creative *art* seeking beauty for its own sake is closely akin to fundamental *science* seeking *knowledge* for its own sake. See ART¹, KNOWLEDGE.

science fiction *n.* Fiction employing scientific ideas or devices as elements of plot or background. — **sci′ence-fic′tion** *adj.*

sci·en·tif·ic (sī′ən-tif′ik) *adj.* **1** Of, pertaining to, discovered by, derived from, or used in science; of the nature of science. **2** Agreeing with the rules, principles, or methods of science; accurate; systematic; exact. **3** Versed in science or a science; eminently learned or skilful. Also **sci·en·tif′i·cal.** [<F *scientifique* <LL *scientificus* <*scientia* knowledge + *facere* make; orig. trans. of Gk. *epistēmonikos* pertaining to knowledge, science] — **sci′en·tif′i·cal·ly** *adv.*

scientific method A method of inquiry depending upon the reciprocal interplay of observable data and generalizations. It consists typically of the statement of a problem and the accumulation and analysis of relevant data that may lead to the construction of a hypothesis, in turn tested by the reliability and accuracy of deductions from it and by its consistency with other hypotheses and observed data.

sci·en·tism (sī′ən-tiz′əm) *n.* **1** Adherence to or belief in the aims and methods of scientists. **2** Uncritical or unsuitable application of scientific concepts or terms.

sci·en·tist (sī′ən-tist) *n.* One versed in science or devoted to scientific study or investigation.

sci·en·tol·o·gy (sī′ən-tol′ə-jē) *n. Often cap.* A religious and psychotherapeutic cult purporting to solve personal problems, cure mental

and physical disorders, and increase intelligence. [<L *scientia* science + -LOGY] — **sci′en·tol′o·gist** *n.*

sci–fi (sī′fī′) *Colloq. n.* Science fiction. — *adj.* Science–fiction.

scil·i·cet (sil′ə·set) *adv.* Namely; to wit; that is to say: introducing a word to be supplied, or an explanation: generally abbreviated *scil., sc.,* or *ss.* [<L, contraction of *scire licet* it is permitted to know]

scim·i·tar (sim′ə·tər) *n.* **1** An Oriental sword or saber of extreme curve. **2** A billhook of somewhat similar form. Also **scim′e·tar, scim′i·ter:** formerly variously spelled with *si–, ci–,* etc. [<MF *cimeterre*; infl. in form by Ital. *scimitarra*; both ? <Persian *shamshīr*]

scin·coid (sing′koid) *n.* One of a family (*Scincidae*) of lizardlike viviparous reptiles (order *Squamata*) with typically smooth scales; a skink. — *adj.* Of or pertaining to the Scincidae. Also **scin·coi·di·an** (sing·koi′dē·ən). [< NL *scincoides* <L *scincus* skink]

SCIMITAR

scin·til·la (sin·til′ə) *n.* A spark; hence, a trace; iota: usually of something abstract: There was not a *scintilla* of truth in the remark. See synonyms under PARTICLE. [<L]

scin·til·late (sin′tə·lāt) *v.* **·lat·ed, ·lat·ing** *v.i.* **1** To give off sparks. **2** To sparkle; glitter. **3** To twinkle, as a star. — *v.t.* **4** To give off as a spark or sparks. See synonyms under SHINE. [<L *scintillatus*, pp. of *scintillare* scintillate < *scintilla* a spark] — **scin′til·lat′ing** *adj.*

scin·til·la·tion (sin′tə·lā′shən) *n.* **1** The act or state of scintillating; a sparkling, tremulous flashing or twinkling. **2** A spark or sparkle. **3** The twinkling of the stars. See synonyms under LIGHT.

sci·o·lism (sī′ə·liz′əm) *n.* Charlatanism; pretentious superficial knowledge. [<LL *sciolus* a smatterer, dim. of L *scius* knowing <*scire* know]

sci·o·list (sī′ə·list) *n.* One who has a smattering of knowledge, especially a pretender to scientific attainment. — **sci′o·lis′tic, sci′o·lous** *adj.*

sci·on (sī′ən) *n.* **1** *Bot.* A cion. **2** A child or descendant. [<OF *cion*, prob. blend of *scier* saw and L *sectio, -onis* a cutting, both <L *secare* cut]

sci·oph·i·lous (sī·of′ə·ləs) *adj. Ecol.* Shade-loving; able to live in shade; thriving in the shade. [<Gk. *skia* shade + -PHILOUS]

sci·o·phyte (sī′ə·fīt) *n.* A plant growing or adapted to live in shade. [<Gk. *skia* shade + -PHYTE] — **sci′o·phyt′ic** (-fit′ik) *adj.*

sci·os·o·phy (sī·os′ə·fē) *n.* Any system of thought founded on beliefs which are at variance with contemporary scientific knowledge and resistant to the procedures of scientific method. [<Gk. *skia* a shadow + -SOPHY] — **sci·os′o·phist** *n.*

scir·rhus (skir′əs, sir′-) *n. pl.* **scir·rhi** (skir′ī) or **scir·rhus·es** *Pathol.* A hard tumor; specifically, a hard cancerous tumor. [<NL <L *scirros* <Gk. *skirrhos* a tumor <*skiros* hard] — **scir·rhos·i·ty** (ski·ros′ə·tē, si-) *n.* — **scir′rhous, scir′rhoid** *adj.*

scis·sile (sis′il) *adj.* Capable of being cut or split easily and evenly. [<L *scissilis* <*scissus*, pp. of *scindere* cut]

scis·sion (sizh′ən, sish′-) *n.* The act of cutting or splitting, or the state of being cut; hence, any division. [<OF <LL *scissio, -onis* <*scissus*, pp. of *scindere* cut]

scis·sor (siz′ər) *v.t. & v.i.* To cut with scissors.

scis·sors (siz′ərz) *n. pl. & sing.* **1** A cutting implement with handles and a pair of blades pivoted face to face: sometimes a *pair of scissors.* **2** In wrestling, a hold secured by clasping the legs about the body or head of the opponent. **3** Gymnastic feats in which the movement of the legs suggests the opening and closing of scissors. [<OF *cisoires* <LL *cisoria*, pl. of *cisorium* a cutting instrument < *caedere* cut; infl. in form by L *scissor* one who cuts <*scindere* cut]

scissors kick In swimming, a kick performed usually with the side stroke, in which both legs are thrust apart, the upper leg bent at the knee

while the lower is kept straight, then brought sharply together.

scis·sor·tail (siz′ər·tāl′) *n.* A flycatcher (*Muscivora forficata*) of the SW United States and Mexico having a scissorlike tail.

scis·sure (sizh′ər, sish′-) *n.* **1** A lengthwise cut; fissure. **2** Any division, rupture, or schism. [<MF <L *scissura* <*scissus.* See SCISSION.]

sci·u·rine (sī′yōō-rīn, -rin) *adj.* Belonging or pertaining to a family (*Sciuridae*) of rodents, including squirrels, chipmunks, woodchucks, marmots, etc. — *n.* One of the *Sciuridae.* [<L *sciurus* a squirrel <Gk. *skiouros* <*skia* a shadow + *oura* a tail + -INE¹]

sci·u·roid (sī-yōō′roid) *adj.* **1** Of or pertaining to the *Sciuridae.* **2** *Bot.* Resembling a squirrel's tail, as the tufted spikes of certain cereal grasses. [<NL <L *sciurus* a squirrel + Gk. *eidos* a form]

scle·ra (sklir′ə) *n. Anat.* The hard, firm, fibrous outer coat of the eye, continuous with the cornea; the white of the eye. Also **scle·rot′i·ca** (sklə·rot′i·kə). See illustration under EYE. [<NL <Gk. *sklēros* hard]

scle·ren·chy·ma (sklə·reng′kə·mə) *n. Bot.* The tough, stony, thick-walled tissue composing the hard parts of plants. [<NL <Gk. *sklēros* hard + *enchyma* an infusion] — **scle·ren·chym·a·tous** (sklir′eng·kim′ə·təs) *adj.*

scle·ri·a·sis (sklə·rī′ə·sis) *n. Pathol.* Any morbid hardening or induration of parts. [<NL <Gk. *sklēriasis* hardness <*sklēros* hard]

scle·rite (sklir′īt) *n.* **1** *Zool.* **a** One of the definite hard pieces of the integument of an arthropod. **b** A hard element in the integument of a polyp. **2** A spicule. [<Gk. *sklēros* hard + -ITE¹] — **scle·rit·ic** (sklə·rit′ik) *adj.*

scle·ri·tis (sklə·rī′tis) *n. Pathol.* Rheumatic ophthalmia; inflammation of the sclera of the eye. Also **scle·ro·ti·tis** (sklir′ō·tī′tis, skler′-). [<NL <*sclera* the white of the eye] — **scle′ro·tit′ic** (-tit′ik) *adj.*

sclero- *combining form* Hardness; hard: *scleroderma.* Also, before vowels, **scler-.** [<Gk. *sklēros* hard]

scle·ro·der·ma (sklir′ō-dûr′mə, skler′-) *n. Pathol.* Hardening of the skin. [<NL <Gk. *sklēros* hard + *derma* skin]

scle·ro·der·ma·tous (sklir′ō-dûr′mə·təs, skler′-) *adj. Zool.* Provided with a horny or bony covering, as an armadillo. [<Gk. *sklēros* hard + *derma, -atos* skin]

scle·roid (sklir′oid) *adj. Biol.* Hard; sclerous; hard in texture, as the shells of nuts, etc. [<Gk. *sklēroeidēs* <*sklēros* hard + *eidos* form]

scle·ro·ma (sklə·rō′mə) *n. Pathol.* Hardening of the cellular tissue; sclerosis; scleroderma. [<NL <Gk. *sklērōma* <*sklēroein* harden <*sklēros* hard]

scle·rom·e·ter (sklə·rom′ə·tər) *n.* An instrument for determining the degree of hardness of a mineral.

scle·ro·pro·te·in (sklir′ō-prō′tē·in) *n.* Any of a class of animal proteins forming supportive tissues in the body, such as keratin, fibroin, etc. Also called albuminoid. [<SCLERO- + PROTEIN]

scle·rosed (sklə·rōst′) *adj.* Affected with sclerosis; grown abnormally hard. [<SCLEROS(IS) + -ED³]

scle·ro·sis (sklə·rō′sis) *n.* **1** *Pathol.* The morbid thickening and hardening of a tissue; especially, the hardening of the coats of the arteries. **2** *Bot.* The hardening of a plant cell wall by the formation of lignin in it. [<Med. L *sclirosis* <Gk. *sklērōsis* <*sklēroein* harden <*sklēros* hard] — **scle·ro′sal** *adj.*

scle·rot·ic (sklə·rot′ik) *adj.* **1** Dense; hard, as the white of the eye. **2** *Pathol.* Pertaining to or affected with sclerosis. [<NL *scleroticus* <Gk. *sklērotēs* hardness <*sklēroein.* See SCLEROMA.]

scle·rot·o·my (sklə·rot′ə·mē) *n. Surg.* Incision of the sclera. [<SCLER(A) + -(O)TOMY]

scle·rous (sklir′əs) *adj.* Hard or indurated; bony. [<SCLER(O). + -OUS]

scob (skob) *n.* A defect in fabric caused by failure of the warp to interlace in the weaving. [? <Irish and Scottish Gaelic *sgolb* a splinter]

scoff (skôf, skof) *v.i.* To speak with contempt or derision; jeer: often with *at.* — *v.t.* To deride;

mock. —*n.* An expression or an object of contempt or derision. See synonyms under SNEER. [ME *scof*, prob. < Scand. Cf. Dan. *skof* a jest, mockery.] —**scoff'er** *n.*

scoff·law (skôf'lô', skof'-) *n.* One who scoffs at the law; especially, a habitual or deliberate violator of traffic, safety, or public-health regulations.

scold (skōld) *v.t.* To find fault with harshly. —*v.i.* To find fault harshly or continuously. —*n.* One who scolds, especially a virago: also **scold'er.** [Appar. < ON *skáld* a poet, satirist] —**scold'ing** *adj. & n.* —**scold'ing·ly** *adv.*

sco·lex (skō'leks) *n. pl.* **sco·le·ces** (skō-lē'sēz) or **scol·i·ces** (skol'ə-sēz, skōlə-) *Zool.* The knoblike head of a tapeworm, equipped with a circular disk of hooks and a group of two or four suckers. [< NL < Gk. *skōlēx* a worm]

sco·li·o·sis (skō'lē-ō'sis, skol'ē-) *n. Pathol.* A lateral curvature of the spine. Also **sco'li·o'ma.** [< NL < Gk. *skoliōsis* < *skolios* curved] —**sco'li·ot'ic** (-ot'ik) *adj.*

scol·lop (skol'əp) *n.*, etc. See SCALLOP, etc.

scol·o·pen·drid (skol'ə-pen'drid) *n.* One of a family of chilopods (*Scolopendridae*) including the typical centipedes. [< NL < L *scolopendra* < Gk. *skolopendra* a milliped] —**scol'o·pen'drine** (-drīn, -drin) *adj.*

scom·broid (skom'broid) *adj.* Of or pertaining to a family (*Scombridae*) of acanthopterygian fishes, including mackerels, tunnies, and related genera. —*n.* One of the *Scombridae.* [< NL < L *scomber* a mackerel < Gk. *skombros*]

sconce[1] (skons) *n.* **1** A small earthwork or fort. **2** A protective shelter, covering, or screen. [< Du. *schanz* a fortress, wicker basket; infl. in form by SCONCE[2]]

sconce[2] (skons) *n.* An ornamental wall bracket for holding a candle or other light. [< OF *esconse* a dark lantern, hiding place < Med. L *sconsa,* short for L *absconsa,* pp. fem. of *abscondere* hide]

sconce[3] (skons) *n. Colloq.* **1** The head or skull. **2** Brains; wit. [? Special use of SCONCE[1]]

sconced, sconc·ing To fine; mulct. [? < SCONCE[3]]

scone (skōn, skon) *n. Scot.* Originally, a thin oatmeal cake, baked on a griddle; hence, a teacake or soda biscuit.

scoop (skoop) *n.* **1** A shovel-like instrument or large shovel with high sides for scooping. **2** A small shovel-like implement or ladle used by grocers, druggists, etc. **3** An implement for bailing, as water from a boat. **4** A spoon-shaped instrument for using in a cavity: a surgeons' *scoop.* **5** An act of scooping; a movement in a curved line convex downward. **6** The amount scooped at once: a *scoop* of water. **7** *Colloq.* A large gain, especially in speculation: He made a big *scoop* on that deal. **8** A bowl-shaped cavity; hollow excavation. **9** In newspaper slang, a news story obtained and published ahead of rival papers. —*v.t.* **1** To take or dip out with or as with a scoop. **2** To hollow out, as with a scoop; excavate. **3** To empty with a scoop. **4** *Colloq.* To heap up or gather in as if in scoopfuls; amass. **5** In newspaper slang, to obtain and publish a news story before (a rival). [Fusion of MDu. *schope* a vessel for bailing out water, and *schoppe* a shovel] —**scoop'er** *n.* —**scoop'ful** *n.*

scoot (skoot) *v.i. Colloq.* To go quickly; dart off. —*n.* The act of scooting; a darting off hurriedly. [Prob. < Scand.; cf. ON *skióta* shoot. Akin to SHOOT.]

scoot·er (skoo'tər) *n.* **1** A child's vehicle consisting of a board mounted on two tandem wheels and steered by a long handle attached to the front axle: the rider stands with one foot on the board, using the other foot to push. **2** A similar vehicle powered by an internal-combustion motor and provided with a driver's seat: also *motor scooter.* **3** A sailboat so constructed that it may be sailed in water and on ice. **4** A small plow with a single shovel used for opening the soil: also *scooter plow.*

scope (skōp) *n.* **1** A range of view or action; outlook. **2** Room for the exercise of faculties or function; extent; capacity for achievement. **3** End in view; aim; purpose. **4** Length or

sweep, as of a cable. **5** The range of a missile. [< Ital. *scopo* < L *scopus* < Gk. *skopos* a watcher < *skopeein* look at]

-scope *combining form* An instrument for viewing, observing, or indicating: *microscope.* [< Gk. *skopos* a watcher < *skopeein* watch]

sco·pol·a·mine (skō-pol'ə-mēn, -min, skō'pə-lam'ēn, -in) *n. Chem.* An alkaloid, $C_{17}H_{21}O_4N$, extracted from the dried rhizomes of certain solanaceous plants, as *Scopolia carniolica*: its salts are used in medicine as a mydriatic, hypnotic, and sedative: also called *hyoscine.* [< G *scopolamin* < NL *Scopolia,* genus name of plants from which it is obtained, after G. A. Scopoli, 1723–88, Italian naturalist]

sco·po·line (skō'pə-lēn, -lin) *n. Chem.* A crystalline compound, $C_8H_{13}O_2N$, derived from scopolamine: also called *oscine.* [< SCOPOL(AMINE) + -INE[2]]

sco·po·phil·i·a (skō'pə-fil'ē-ə) *n. Psychiatry* Pleasure, especially of a sexual nature, derived from the act of observing, contemplating, or looking at something. Also **scop'to·phil'i·a** (skop'tə-). [< Gk. *skopos* a watcher + -PHILIA]

sco·po·pho·bi·a (skō'pə-fō'bē-ə) *n. Psychiatry* A morbid fear of being looked at. [< Gk. *skopos* a watcher + -PHOBIA]

scop·u·late (skop'yə-lit, -lāt) *adj.* Broomshaped. [< L *scopulae* a little broom, pl. of *scopula* a broom twig, dim. of *scopa* a twig, a broom]

-scopy *combining form* Observation; viewing: microscopy. [< Gk. -*scopia* < *skopeein* watch]

scor·bu·tic (skôr-byoo'tik) *adj.* Relating to, like, or affected with scurvy: also **scor·bu'ti·cal.** —*n.* A person affected with scurvy. [< NL *scorbuticus* < Med. L *scorbutus* SCORBUTUS] —**scor·bu'ti·cal·ly** *adv.*

scor·bu·tus (skôr-byoo'təs) *n. Pathol.* Scurvy. [< NL < Med. L, appar. < MDu. *scheurbot, scheurbuik* < *scheuren* break, lacerate + *bot, buik* belly]

scorch (skôrch) *v.t.* **1** To change the color, taste, etc., of by slight burning; char the surface of. **2** To wither or shrivel by heat. **3** To affect painfully, as if by heat; criticize severely. —*v.i.* **4** To become scorched. **5** *Colloq.* To go at high speed. —*n.* **1** A superficial burn. **2** A mark caused by heat, as a slight burn. [Prob. related to ME *skorken* < ON *skorpna* dry up, shrivel; infl. in form by OF *escorchier* flay < L *excorticare* < *ex-* off + *cortex, -icis* bark] —**scorch'ing** *adj.* —**scorch'ing·ly** *adv.*

scorched–earth policy (skôrcht'ûrth') The policy of destroying all crops, industrial equipment, dwellings, etc., before an advancing enemy so as to leave nothing for his use or aid.

scorch·er (skôr'chər) *n.* **1** Something that scorches or is hot enough to scorch: Today was a *scorcher.* **2** Something severe or caustic, as criticism. **3** One who or that which moves or may move at great speed.

scor·da·to (skôr-dä'tō) *adj. Music* Out of tune; altered in tuning; made discordant. [< Ital., pp. of *scordare* be out of tune, short for *discordare* < L. See DISCORD.]

scor·da·tu·ra (skôr'dä-too'rä) *n. Music* An intentional changing of the normal tuning of a stringed instrument: resorted to for effect. [< Ital. *scordato* SCORDATO]

score (skôr, skōr) *n.* **1 a** A notch, cut, groove, mark, or line. **b** A notch or line used in keeping a tally or score; hence, an account or reckoning kept by notches or marks. **2** Any record, especially of indebtedness; debt; bill: to run up a *score* at a grocery. **3** Something charged or laid up against one; grudge; difference: to pay off old *scores;* an account; a credit; motive. **4** The record of the winning points, counts, or runs in competitions and games; also, the whole number of such points made by a player or side or in the game. **5** *Music* The collective notes in which a composition is written, when placed on two or more connected staffs one above another. **6** The number twenty, originally indicated by a special notch on a tally; twenty units or things: in the plural often indicating indefinitely large numbers. **7** *Psychol.* A quantitative value assigned to an individual or group response to a test or series of tests, as of intelligence or performance. —*v.* **scored, scor·ing** *v.t.* **1** To mark with notches, cuts, or lines. **2** To mark with cuts or lines for the purpose of

keeping a tally or record. **3** To obliterate or cross out by means of a line drawn through: with *out.* **4** To make or gain, as points, runs, etc. **5** To count for a score of, as in games: A touchdown *scores* six points. **6** To rate or grade, as an examination paper; evaluate. **7** *Music* **a** To orchestrate. **b** To arrange or adapt for an instrument. **8** *U.S.* To criticize severely; scourge. **9** In cooking, to make superficial cuts in (meat, etc.). —*v.i.* **10** To make points, runs, etc., as in a game. **11** To keep score. **12** To make notches, cuts, etc. **13** To win an advantage; achieve a success. [OE *scoru* < ON *skor* a notch, tally] —**scor'er** *n.*

score–keep·er (skôr'kē'pər, skōr'-) *n.* One who keeps score.

sco·ri·a (skôr'ē-ə, skō'rē-ə) *n. pl.* **·ri·ae** (-ī-ē) Fragmentary lava; slag; refuse of ores or metals. [< L < Gk. *skōria* refuse < *skōr* dung] —**sco'ri·a'ceous** (-ā'shəs) *adj.*

sco·ri·fy (skôr'ə-fī, skō'rə-) *v.t.* **·fied, ·fy·ing** *Metall.* **1** To separate, as gold or silver, from an ore by smelting with lead, borax, etc. **2** To reduce to scoria or dross. [< SCORI(A) + -FY] —**sco'ri·fi·ca'tion** *n.*

scorn (skôrn) *n.* **1** Disdain; a feeling entertained toward someone or something as so inferior as to be unworthy of attention. **2** The expression of such a feeling; derision. **3** An object of supreme contempt. —*v.t.* **1** To hold in or treat with contempt; despise. **2** To reject with scorn; disdain; spurn. —*v.i.* **3** *Obs.* To mock; jeer. [< OF *escarn* < *escarnir* < Gmc.] —**scorn'er** *n.* —**scorn'ful** *adj.* —**scorn'ful·ly** *adv.* —**scorn'ful·ness** *n.*

Synonyms (noun): contempt, contumely, derision, despite, disdain, dishonor, mockery, scoff, scoffing, sneer, sneering, taunt. *Antonyms:* admiration, approbation, approval, attention, consideration, courtesy, deference, esteem, honor, regard, respect, reverence.

Synonyms (verb): abhor, contemn, despise, detest, disdain, spurn. *Antonyms:* see synonyms for CHERISH.

scor·pae·noid (skôr-pē'noid) *adj.* Belonging to a family (*Scorpaenidae*) of spiny-finned marine fishes. —*n.* A scorpaenoid fish: also **scor·pae'nid** (-nid). [< NL < L *scorpaena* a kind of fish + Gk. *eidos* form]

Scor·pi·o (skôr'pē-ō) *n. Astron.* The Scorpion, a zodiacal constellation between Libra and Sagittarius, containing the brilliant red star Antares. See CONSTELLATION. **2** The eighth sign of the zodiac. Also **Scor'pi·on** (-ən), **Scor'pi·us** (-əs). [< L, a scorpion]

scor·pi·oid (skôr'pē-oid) *adj.* **1** Scorpionlike. **2** Rolled or curled like the tail of a scorpion: specifically said of a terminal unilateral inflorescence, as in the borage family of plants. [< Gk. *skorpioeidēs* < *skorpios* a scorpion + *eidos* form]

scor·pi·on (skôr'pē-ən) *n.* **1** One of an order (*Scorpionida*) of rapacious arachnids with elongated, lobsterlike bodies and segmented tails which bear a poisonous sting: they are chiefly tropical but occur as far north as Canada.

INDIAN SCORPION
s. Stinger.

2 The harmless pine lizard (genus *Sceloporus*) of the southern United States. **3** An instrument of chastisement; a whip or scourge. I *Kings* xii 11. **4** An ancient ballistic engine. [< OF < L *scorpio, -onis* < Gk. *skorpios*]

scorpion fly A mecopterous insect (genus *Panorpa*) living on the banks of shaded streams and in moist woods: in the male, the end of the abdomen is upcurved like a scorpion's sting. See illustration under INSECTS (beneficial).

scot (skot) *n.* An assessment; tax; a contribution, reckoning, or fine. [Fusion of ON *skot,* OF *escot;* ? infl. by OE *sceot, scot* payment]

scotch[1] (skoch) *v.t.* **1** To cut; scratch. **2** To wound so as to maim or cripple. **3** To put down; crush or suppress. **4** To dress, as stone, with a pick. —*n.* **1** A superficial cut; a scratch; a notch. **2** A line traced on the ground, as for hopscotch. [Origin uncertain]

scotch[2] (skoch) *v.t.* To block, as a wheel or log, with a chock or wedge to prevent moving or slipping. —*n.* A block put behind or under something, as a wheel, to prevent rolling or sliding. [Origin unknown]

Scotch (skoch) *n.* **1** The people of Scotland collectively: with *the.* **2** One or all of the dialects spoken by the people of Scotland. **3** Scotch whisky. —*adj.* Of or pertaining to Scotland, its inhabitants, or their language; Scottish; Scots.

◆ **Scotch, Scots, Scottish** Of these three proper adjectives, the form *Scotch* developed in the dialects of the Midland and southern England, and is accepted even in Scotland as applying to *Scotch* plaid, *Scotch* terriers, *Scotch* whisky, etc.; in Scotland and in northern England, however, the forms *Scots* and *Scottish* (earlier *Scottis*) prevailed, and are preferred as applying to the people, culture, and institutions of Scotland: *Scots* or *Scottish* English, the *Scottish* church. This distinction is now widely accepted.

Scotch broom See under BROOM.

Scotch tape A rolled strip of transparent cellulose tape having an adhesive on one side: a trade name.

Scotch whisky Whisky having rather a smoky flavor and made (originally in Scotland) from malted barley.

Scotch woodcock Eggs cooked and served on toast or crackers spread with anchovy paste.

sco·ter (skō′tər) *n.* A sea duck (genera *Oidemia* and *Melanitta*) of northern regions, having the bill gibbous or swollen at the base, especially the **American scoter** (*O. americana*) also called *coot,* or **scoter duck.** [< dial. E *scote,* var. of SCOOT]

scot-free (skot′frē′) *adj.* Free from scot; untaxed; unharmed.

sco·ti·a (skō′shē·ə, -shə) *n. Archit.* A concave molding common in the bases of classical columns. [< L < Gk. *skotia* darkness < *skotos*; so called from the darkness in its concavity]

Scot·land (skot′lənd) A political division and the northern part of Great Britain; a separate kingdom until its legislative union with England, 1707; 30,405 square miles; capital, Edinburgh.

Scotland Yard 1 The former headquarters of the London metropolitan police, situated in Great Scotland Yard, a short street in central London; removed to **New Scotland Yard,** on the Thames Embankment, 1890. **2** The police force at headquarters; specifically, the detective bureau of the London police.

scoto- *combining form* Darkness: *scotophobia.* Also, before vowels, **scot-.** [< Gk. *skotos* darkness]

sco·to·ma (skə·tō′mə) *n. pl.* **·ma·ta** (-mə·tə) *Pathol.* A defect in the field of vision; a blind or dark spot. [< LL < Gk. *skotōma* dizziness < *skotoein* darken < *skotos* darkness]

scot·o·phil·i·a (skot′ə·fil′ē·ə) *n.* A love of darkness. [< SCOTO- + -PHILIA]

scot·o·pho·bi·a (skot′ə·fō′bē·ə) *n.* A morbid fear of darkness: also called *nyctophobia.* [< SCOTO- + -PHOBIA]

sco·to·pi·a (skə·tō′pē·ə) *n. Physiol.* Adaptation of the eye for night vision. [< NL < Gk. *skotos* darkness + *ōps, ōpos* an eye] —**sco·top′ic** (-top′ik) *adj.*

scoun·drel (skoun′drəl) *n.* A mean, thoroughgoing rascal; a rogue; villain. —*adj.* Scoundrelly. [Prob. dim. < AF *escoundre,* OF *escoundre* abscond < L *ex-* off + *condere* hide]

scour¹ (skour) *v.t.* **1** To clean or brighten by thorough washing and rubbing, as with sand or steel wool. **2** To remove dirt, etc., from; clean: to *scour* wool. **3** To remove by or as by rubbing away. **4** To clear by means of a strong current of water; flush. **5** To purge the bowels of. **6** To clean (wheat) before milling. —*v.i.* **7** To rub something vigorously so as to clean or brighten it. **8** To become bright or clean by rubbing. See synonyms under CLEANSE. —*n.* **1** The act of scouring. **2** A place scoured, as by running water. **3** A cleanser used in cleaning wool. **4** *Usually pl.* A watery diarrhea in cattle. [Prob. < MDu. *schuren* < OF *escurer,* ult. < L *ex-* out + *curare* take care of < *cura* care]

scour² (skour) *v.t.* **1** To range over or through, as in making a search. **2** To move or run swiftly over or along. —*v.i.* **3** To range about, as in making a search. **4** To move or run swiftly. [ME

scoure. Cf. ON *skura* rush, run.]

scour·er¹ (skour′ər) *n.* **1** One who or that which cleanses, removes stains, etc. **2** A cathartic. **3** A grain scourer. [< SCOUR¹]

scour·er² (skour′ər) *n.* One who prowls about the streets by night; a vagabond. [< SCOUR²]

scourge (skûrj) *n.* **1** A whip for inflicting suffering or punishment. **2** Any instrumentality or means for causing suffering or death; hence, severe punishment; also, a cause of suffering. —*v.t.* **scourged, scourg·ing 1** To whip severely; lash; flog. **2** To punish severely; chastise; afflict. See synonyms under BEAT. [< AF *escorge* < LL *excoriare* flay < L *ex-* off + *corium* a hide] —**scourg′er** *n.*

scour·ing rush (skour′ing) Any species of horsetail, formerly much used for polishing wood and metal; scrub grass.

scour·ings (skour′ingz) *n. pl.* The residue after scouring: said especially of grain.

scouse (skous) *n.* A sailor's dish of sea biscuit and vegetables with or without meat; a hasty pudding of corn and rye meal. [Short for LOBSCOUSE]

scout¹ (skout) *n.* **1** One who or that which is engaged in scouting; specifically, a person sent out to observe and get information, as of the position or strength of an enemy in war. **2** The act of scouting. **3** At Oxford University, an undergraduate's manservant. **4** In cricket, a fielder: applied chiefly to one who fields at a distance in practice. **5** A boy scout; a girl scout. See synonyms under SPY. —*v.t.* To observe or spy upon for the purpose of gaining information; reconnoiter, as an enemy position. —*v.i.* To go or act as a scout. —**to scout around** To go in search. [< OF *escoute* a listener, listening < *escouter* listen < L *auscultare*] —**scout′er** *n.*

scout² (skout) *v.t. & v.i.* To reject with disdain; mock; jeer. See synonyms under RIDICULE. [< Scand. Cf. ON *skūta* a taunt.]

scout·mas·ter (skout′mas′tər, -mäs′-) *n.* The leader of a troop of Boy Scouts.

scow (skou) *n.* A large boat with a flat bottom and square ends: chiefly used as a lighter. [< Du. *schouw* a boat propelled by a pole < MDu. *schoude*]

scowl (skoul) *n.* **1** A lowering of the brows, as in anger, strong disapproval, or sullenness. **2** Gloomy aspect. —*v.i.* **1** To lower and contract the brows in anger, sullenness, or disapproval. **2** To look threatening; lower. —*v.t.* **3** To affect or express by scowling. [ME *skoul,* prob. < Scand. Cf. Dan. *skule.*] —**scowl′er** *n.* —**scowl′ing·ly** *adv.*

scrab·ble (skrab′əl) *v.* **·bled, ·bling** *v.i.* **1** To scratch, scrape, or paw, as with the hands. **2** To make irregular or meaningless marks; scribble. **3** To struggle or strive. —*v.t.* **4** To make meaningless marks on; scribble on. **5** To gather hurriedly; scrape together. —*n.* **1** The act of scrabbling; a moving on hands and feet or knees. **2** A scrambling effort. **3** A sparse growth: a *scrabble* of underbrush. [< Du. *schrabbelen* scratch]

scrag (skrag) *v.t.* **scragged, scrag·ging** *Colloq.* To use roughly; wring the neck of; specifically, to kill by hanging; garrote. [< *n.*] —*n.* **1** Something thin or lean and rough; a lean or bony piece or end of meat, especially from the neck. **2** *Slang* The neck. **3** A lean, bony person or animal. [Prob. < Scand. Cf. Norw. *skragg* a lean, feeble person.]

scrag·gly (skrag′lē) *adj.* **·gli·er, ·gli·est** Unkempt; shaggy; irregular; jagged. [Prob. < SCRAGG(Y) + -LY]

scrag·gy (skrag′ē) *adj.* **·gi·er, ·gi·est 1** Rough. **2** Lean; scrawny; bony. [< SCRAG + -Y¹] —**scrag′gi·ly** *adv.* —**scrag′gi·ness** *n.*

scram (skram) *v.i.* **scrammed, scram·ming** *U.S. Slang* To go away; leave quickly. [Prob. short for SCRAMBLE]

scram·ble (skram′bəl) *v.* **·bled, ·bling** *v.i.* **1** To move by clambering or crawling on hands and feet. **2** To struggle with others in a disorderly manner; scuffle; also, to strive for something in such a manner. —*v.t.* **3** To mix together haphazardly or confusedly. **4** To gather or collect hurriedly or confusedly. **5** To cook (eggs) with the

yolks and whites stirred together, usually with milk and butter. **6** *Telecom.* To invert or otherwise alter the frequency spectrum of (radio or wireless messages) so as to insure secrecy. —*n.* The act of scrambling; a disorderly performance or struggle. [Prob. nasalized var. of SCRABBLE]

scrambled eggs Eggs prepared by stirring together the whites and yolks while cooking, usually with milk and butter.

scram·bler (skram′blər) *n.* **1** One who or that which scrambles. **2** *Telecom.* A device for altering the frequencies of radio and wireless signals during transmission.

scrap¹ (skrap) *n.* **1** A small piece cut or broken from something; fragment. **2** A brief extract. **3** *pl.* Pieces of crisp fat tissue after the oil has been expressed by cooking. **4** Old or refuse metal. See synonyms under PARTICLE. —*v.t.* **scrapped, scrap·ping 1** To break up into scrap; make scrap of. **2** To discard; throw away. —*adj.* Having the form of scraps; discarded after use: *scrap* metal. [< ON *skrap* scrapings, scraps < *skrappa* scrape. Akin to SCRAPE.]

scrap² (skrap) *v.i.* **scrapped, scrap·ing** To fight; quarrel. —*n.* A scrimmage; slight disagreement; scuffle; squabble. [< SCRAPE, *n.* (def. 2)]

scrap·book (skrap′book′) *n.* **1** A blank book in which to paste pictures, cuttings from periodicals, etc. **2** A personal notebook.

scrape (skrāp) *v.* **scraped, scrap·ing** *v.t.* **1** To rub, as with something rough or sharp, so as to abrade or to remove an outer layer or adherent matter. **2** To remove thus: with *off, away,* etc. **3** To rub (a rough or sharp object) across a surface. **4** To rub roughly across or against (a surface). **5** To dig or form by scratching or scraping. **6** To gather or accumulate with effort or difficulty; usually with *up* or *together.* —*v.i.* **7** To scrape something. **8** To rub with a grating noise. **9** To emit or produce a grating noise. **10** To draw the foot backward along the ground in bowing: to bow and *scrape.* **11** To manage or get along with difficulty. **12** To be very or overly economical. —**to scrape acquaintance** To make acquaintance without an introduction. —*n.* **1** The act or effect of scraping; also, the noise made by scraping. **2** A difficult situation; predicament. **3** A scraping or drawing back of the foot in bowing. [Prob. fusion of OE *scrapian* and ON *skrapa* scrape, erase]

scrap·er (skrā′pər) *n.* **1** Any instrument used for scraping. **2** A horse-drawn or motor-driven apparatus having a large metal scoop or scoops, for scraping up, transporting, and dumping dirt: a road *scraper,* a road leveller. **3** One who or that which scrapes. **4** A miser. **5** An unskilful player on the violin.

scrap·ie (skrā′pē) *n.* A fatal viral disease affecting the central nervous system of sheep and transmitted to other animals by feeding on affected tissue. [< SCRAPE, from the habit of affected animals of scraping against objects as if to relieve itching]

scrap iron Old pieces of iron suitable for reworking.

scrap·ple (skrap′əl) *n.* A mixture of meal or flour boiled with scraps of pork, seasoned, and allowed to set: usually cooked by frying. [Dim. of SCRAP¹]

scrap·py¹ (skrap′ē) *adj.* **·pi·er, ·pi·est** Composed of scraps; disconnected; fragmentary. [< SCRAP¹ + -Y¹] —**scrap′pi·ly** *adv.* —**scrap′pi·ness** *n.*

scrap·py² (skrap′ē) *adj.* **·pi·er, ·pi·est** Pugnacious; given to picking fights. [< SCRAP² + -Y¹] —**scrap′pi·ly** *adv.* —**scrap′pi·ness** *n.*

scratch (skrach) *v.t.* **1** To tear or mark the surface of with something sharp or rough. **2** To scrape or dig with something sharp or rough, as the claws or nails. **3** To scrape lightly with the nails, etc., as to relieve itching. **4** To rub with a grating sound; scrape. **5** To write or draw awkwardly or hurriedly. **6** To erase or cancel by or as by scratches or marks. **7** To erase or cancel the name of (a candidate) from a political ticket, while supporting the rest of the ticket; also, to bolt (a ticket or party) in this way. **8** To withdraw (an entry) from a race, game, etc. —*v.i.* **9** To use the nails or claws, as in fighting or digging. **10** To scrape the skin, etc., lightly, as to relieve itching. **11** To make a grating noise. **12** To manage or get along with difficulty. **13** To withdraw from a game, race, etc. **14** In billiards and pool, to make a scratch. — *n.* **1** A mark or incision made on a surface by scratching; a shallow mark, groove, furrow, or channel. **2** A slight flesh wound or cut. **3** The line from which contestants start, as in racing: to start from *scratch.* **4** The contestant who competes against an allowance: also **scratch-man.** **5** *Slang* Money. **6** A disease of horses, consisting of dry scabs or chaps on the heel: also **scratch-es.** **7** In billiards, a chance shot; also, a fluke; in billiards and pool, a shot resulting in a penalty; specifically, a shot in which the cue ball goes into a pocket, leaves the table, or fails to hit an object ball. — **from scratch** From the beginning; from nothing. — **up to scratch** *Colloq.* Meeting the standard or requirement in courage, stamina, or performance; in proper or fit condition: He was never *up to scratch* in writing. — *adj.* **1** Done by chance; haphazard. **2** In sports, without handicap or allowance. **3** Made as, or used for, a first try: a *scratch* pad. **4** Chosen at random or by chance: a *scratch* team. [Prob. blend of ME *scratte* scratch (prob. <Scand.; cf. Sw. *kratta* rake) and *cracchen* scratch < MDu. *cratsen*] — **scratch'er** *n.*

scratch test *Med.* A test to determine the substances to which a person is allergic by rubbing allergens in small scratches made in his skin.

scratch-y (skrach'ē) *adj.* **scratch-i-er, scratch-i-est 1** Characterized by scratches. **2** Making a scratching noise. **3** Straggling; shaggy; rough. — **scratch'i-ly** *adv.* — **scratch'i-ness** *n.*

scrawl (skrôl) *v.t. & v.i.* To write hastily or illegibly; scribble. — *n.* Irregular or careless writing. [? <dial. E, var. of CRAWL; ? infl. in meaning by *scribble, scroll,* etc.] — **scrawl'er** *n.*

scraw-ny (skrô'nē) *adj.* **-ni-er, -ni-est** Lean and bony; skinny; thin. [<dial. E *scranny,* var. of SCRANNEL] — **scraw'ni-ness** *n.*

screak (skrēk) *v.i.* To creak; screech. — *n.* A screech; also, a creak. [<ON *skrækja;* prob. imit.]

scream (skrēm) *v.i.* **1** To utter a prolonged, piercing cry, as of pain, terror, or surprise. **2** To make a prolonged, piercing sound. **3** To laugh loudly or immoderately. **4** To use heated, hysterical language. **5** To have an effect as of screaming: This color *screams* in contrast to green. — *v.t.* **6** To utter with a scream. — *n.* A loud, shrill, prolonged cry or sound, generally denoting fear or pain. See synonyms under CALL, ROAR. [ME *scraemen,* ? <ON *skraema* scare]

scream-er (skrē'mər) *n.* **1** One who or that which screams. **2** A South American bird, related to the ducks (family *Anhimidae* or *Palamedidae*) including the **horned screamer** (*Anhima* or *Palamedea cornuta*) and the **crested screamers** (genus *Chauna*). **3** *U.S. Slang* Something calculated to call forth screams of admiration, astonishment, or the like; hence, a person of great size, strength, or skill. **4** *U.S. Slang* A sensational headline in a newspaper.

scree (skrē) *n.* Debris of stones and rock fragments at the foot of a cliff or steep, rocky face: usually a sloping mass. See TALUS. [Back formation <*screes,* earlier *screethes* <ON *skridha* a landslide]

screech (skrēch) *n.* A shrill, harsh cry; shriek. — *v.t.* To utter with or as with a screech. — *v.i.* To make a prolonged, harsh, piercing sound; shriek. [Var. of obs. *scritch,* prob. <Scand. Cf. ON *skrækja;* prob. ult. imit.] — **screech'er** *n.* — **screech'y** *adj.*

screech owl 1 Any of various small owls (genus *Otus*) common from Canada to Brazil; especially, the small, gray *O. asio* of the eastern United States. **2** The English barn owl.

screed (skrēd) *n.* **1** A prolonged tirade; harangue. **2** A wooden strip or a strip of mortar laid on a wall at intervals, to gage the thickness of the plastering. **3** A long torn strip or shred; hence, any detached strip or fragment: the original meaning, now chiefly Scottish. **4** *Scot.* A tearing; rent; tear; also, a drinking spree. — *v.t.* **1** To rend or tear into shreds. **2** *Scot.* To repeat glibly. [Var. of SHRED]

screen (skrēn) *n.* **1** That which separates or cuts off, shelters or protects, as a light par-

---

tition. **2** A sieve or riddle, for sifting. **3** A smooth surface, as a canvas or curtain, on which motion pictures, etc., may be shown. **4** A motion picture or motion pictures collectively. **5** A plate of glass bearing very finely ruled lines, placed between the object and the camera in photographing for reproduction by the half-tone process. **6 a** *Mil.* A detachment of troops sent to deceive an enemy as to the movement of the main force. **b** *Nav.* A formation of ships arranged for the protection of heavier vessels from enemy submarines, etc. **7** *Physics* Any of various devices for confining the action of a physical agency or instrument to a definite area: a magnetic *screen.* **8** *Psychoanal.* A person who stands for someone else or others having some common characteristic, as in a dream: a form of concealment. — *v.t.* **1** To shield from observation or annoyance with or as with a screen. **2** To pass through a screen or sieve; sift. **3** To show or exhibit on a screen, as a motion picture. **4** *Psychol.* To separate from a group (those individuals showing indications of, or tendencies toward, mental or physical incapacity for specified activities): often with *out.* See synonyms under HIDE, PALLIATE, SHELTER. [Prob. <OF *escren, escrin,* prob. < OHG *skirm*] — **screen'a-ble** *adj.* — **screen'er** *n.*

screen-ing (skrēn'ing) *n.* **1** A meshlike material, as for a window screen. **2** A showing of a motion picture.

screen-ings (skrē'ningz) *n. pl.* The waste of anything passed through a sieve, as coal or defective grains; siftings.

screw (skrōō) *n.* **1** A device resembling a nail but having a slotted head and a tapering or cylindrical spiral for driving into wood with a screwdriver, or for insertion into a corresponding grooved part: called **male** or **external screw.** **2** A cylindrical socket with a

TYPES OF SCREWS

a. Lagscrew.   *f.* Shoulder screw.
b. Wood screw.   *g, h.* Thumbscrews.
c. Saw screw.   *i.* Collar screw.
d. Fillister screw.   *j.* Slotted screw.
     e. Skein screw.

spiral groove: called **female** or **internal screw.** **3** Anything having the form of a screw. **4** A screw propeller. **5** A turn of or as of a screw. **6** Pressure; force. **7** *Brit. Slang* Salary; pay. **8** *Slang* A prison guard. **9** A haggler over prices; a crafty bargainer. **10** *Brit.* A worthless horse. **11** *Brit.* A small packet of tobacco. **12** *Slang* An act of sexual intercourse: a vulgar term. — **to have a screw loose** *Slang* To be mentally deranged, eccentric, etc. — **to put the screws on** (or to) *Slang* To exert pressure or force upon. — *v.t.* **1** To tighten, fasten, attach, etc., by or as by a screw or screws. **2** To turn or twist. **3** To force as if by the pressure of a screw; urge: to *screw* one's courage to the sticking point. **4** To twist out of shape; contort, as one's features. **5** To practice oppression or extortion on; defraud. **6** To obtain by extortion. **7** *Slang* To have sexual intercourse with: a vulgar term. **8** *Slang* To act maliciously toward; harm. — *v.i.* **9** To turn or admit of being turned as a screw. **10** To be attached or become detached by means of a screw or screws: with *on, off,* etc. **11** To have turns like those of a screw. **12** To practice oppression or extortion. **13** *Slang* To have sexual intercourse with: a vulgar term. — **to screw up** *Slang* To botch; make a mess of: He *screwed up* his career. [Appar. <OF *escroue* a nut, female screw, ? <L *scrofa* sow; infl. in OF by L *scrobis* vulva] — **screw'er** *n.*

---

screw-ball (skrōō'bôl') *n.* **1** In baseball, a pitch thrown with a wrist motion opposite to that used for the out-curve, and breaking sharply and often unpredictably. **2** *U.S. Slang* An unconventional or erratic person.
screw-bean (skrōō'bēn') *n.* **1** The seed of the spirally twisted pod of a species of mesquite (*Strombocarpa odorata*). **2** The tree bearing this seed.
screw-driv-er (skrōō'drī'vər) *n.* A tool for turning screws.
screwed-up (skrōōd'up') *adj. Slang* **1** Disorganized or disorderly. **2** Mentally ill or emotionally distressed.
screw jack 1 A hoisting or lifting jack operated by a screw; jackscrew. **2** A dental implement for regulating the position of the teeth.
screw log A patent log.
screw-pile (skrōō'pīl') *n.* A pile having a strong metal base with a screw thread to ensure firm penetration of hard ground or bedrock. See illustration under LIGHTHOUSE.
screw-pine (skrōō'pīn') *n.* Any of a tropical genus (*Pandanus*) of plants having a screwlike arrangement of the clustered leaves and aerial roots.

SCREW JACK

screw propeller A mechanism consisting of a revolving shaft with radiating blades set at an angle to produce a spiral action: used in propelling ships, etc.
screw thread 1 The projecting spiral ridge of uniform pitch on the outer or inner surface of a cylinder or cone, as of a screw or nut. **2** A complete revolution of any point in this ridge.
screw-y (skrōō'ē) *adj.* **screw-i-er, screw-i-est** *Slang* Extremely irrational; crazy.
scrib-ble (skrib'əl) *v.* **-bled, -bling** *v.t.* **1** To write hastily and carelessly. **2** To cover with careless or illegible writing or marks. — *v.i.* **3** To write in a careless or hasty manner. **4** To make illegible or meaningless marks. — *n.* **1** Hasty, careless writing. **2** Meaningless lines and marks; any scrawl. [<Med. L *scribillare,* freq. of L *scribere* write]
scrib-ler (skrib'lər) *n.* **1** One who scribbles. **2** A writer of no reputation; a petty or inferior author.
scribe (skrīb) *n.* **1** One who writes or copies manuscripts. **2** A clerk, public writer, or amanuensis. **3** An author, penman, or journalist: used humorously. **4** An ancient Jewish teacher, interpreter, or writer of the Mosaic law. **5** A pointed instrument for marking wood, bricks, etc. — *v.* **scribed, scrib-ing** *v.t.* **1** To mark or scratch with a pointed instrument. **2** To write, inscribe, or engrave. **3** In carpentry, to mark and fit closely. — *v.i.* **4** *Rare* To write; work as a scribe. [<L *scriba* <*scribere* write] — **scrib'al** *adj.*
scrib-er (skrī'bər) *n.* **1** One who or that which scribes. **2** Any sharp-pointed tool used in scribing.
scrim (skrim) *n.* **1** A lightweight, open-mesh, coarse cotton fabric, usually white or écru, used for draperies, etc. **2** In the theater, a similar fabric, often painted, used as a transparency, to support artificial foliage, etc. [Origin unknown]
scrim-mage (skrim'ij) *n.* **1** A rough-and-tumble contest; fracas; formerly, a skirmish. **2** In American football, a mass play from the line of scrimmage after the ball has been placed on the ground and snapped back, the play ending when the ball is dead. **3** In Rugby football, a scrummage. — **line of scrimmage** In football, the hypothetic line, parallel to the goal lines, on which the ball rests and along which the opposing linemen take position at the start of play. — *v.t. & v.i.* **-maged, -mag-ing** To engage in a scrimmage. Also spelled *scrummage.* [Alter. of *scrimish,* var. of SKIRMISH]
scrimp (skrimp) *v.i.* **1** To be very or overly economical; be niggardly. — *v.t.* **2** To be overly sparing toward; skimp. **3** To cut too small, narrow, etc. — *adj.* Scanty; short: also **scrimp'y.** See synonyms under SCANTY. — *n.* A miser; niggard. [?. Related to OE *scrimman* shrink, shrivel] — **scrimp'i-ness** *n.*
Synonyms (verb): contract, curtail, econo-

mize, limit, pinch, reduce, save, scant, shorten, straiten. *Antonyms:* dissipate, lavish, squander, waste.

scrim·shaw (skrim'shô) *v.t. & v.i.* To ornament (ivory, whale's teeth, etc.) by cutting or carving: a sailor's term. — *n.* A neat example of mechanical work; especially, a scrimshawed article, ornamented with fanciful carving. [?< the surname *Scrimshaw*]

scrip[1] (skrip) *n.* **1** A scrap of paper, especially one containing writing. **2** A writing; a certificate, schedule, or written list. **3** A piece of paper money less than a dollar formerly issued in the United States: also called *shinplaster.* [<SCRIPT, prob. infl. in form by SCRAP]

scrip[2] (skrip) *n.* A provisional document (or documents collectively) certifying that the holder is entitled to receive something else, as shares of stock or land. [Short for obs. *subscription receipt*]

scrip dividend A distribution of surplus to stockholders in the form of scrip or promises to pay the dividend at a certain time.

script (skript) *n.* **1** Writing of the ordinary cursive form. **2** Type, or printed or engraved matter, in imitation of handwriting. **3** *Law* A writing, especially an original; in English practice, a will; codicil. **4** A piece of writing; a manuscript or typescript; especially, a prepared copy, often containing suggestions, for the use of actors in a theatrical, radio, or television performance. — *v.t. & v.i. U.S. Colloq.* To prepare a script for (a radio, television, or theatrical performance). [<OF *escript* <L *scriptum,* pp. neut. of *scribere* write]

This line is in script.

scrip·to·ri·um (skrip·tôr'ē·əm, -tō'rē-) *n. pl.* **·ri·ums** or **·ri·a** (-ē·ə) The writing-room of a monastery, where records, annals, and manuscripts were written, copied, or illuminated. [<Med. L <L *scriptus,* pp. of *scribere* write]

scrip·tur·al (skrip'chər·əl) *adj.* Relating to writing; written. — **scrip'tur·al·ly** *adv.* — **scrip'tur·al·ness** *n.*

Scrip·tur·al (skrip'chər·əl) *adj.* Pertaining to, contained in, quoted from, or warranted by the Bible; Biblical. — **Scrip'tur·al·ly** *adv.* — **Scrip'tur·al·ness** *n.*

scrip·ture (skrip'chər) *n.* **1** The sacred writings of any people. **2** Originally, anything written, as a document, book, or inscription, or its contents; a writing. [<OF *escripture* <L *scriptura* < *scriptus,* pp. of *scribere* write]

Scrip·ture (skrip'chər) *n.* **1** The books of the Old and New Testaments, including often the Apocrypha; specifically, the Bible: usually plural. **2** A text or passage from the Bible.

script·writ·er (skript'rī'tər) *n.* A writer who prepares copy for the use of a radio or television actor or announcer.

scrive (skrīv) *v.t.* **scrived, scriv·ing** **1** To engrave. **2** *Obs.* To write; scribe. [<OF *escrivre* write <L *scribere*]

scri·vel·lo (skri·vel'ō) *n. pl.* **·loes** or **·los** An elephant's tusk. [<Pg. *escrevelho,* ? var. of *escaravelho* a pin, peg]

scriv·en·er (skriv'ən·ər, skriv'nər) *n.* **1** One who prepares deeds, contracts, and other writings; a clerk or scribe. **2** Formerly, a moneylender. [<obs. *scrivein* <OF *escrivain* <Ital. *scrivano* <L *scribere* write]

scro·bic·u·late (skrō·bik'yə·lit, -lāt) *adj. Biol.* Marked with many small depressions; furrowed or pitted. Also **scro·bic'u·lat'ed** (-lā'tid). [<L *scrobiculus,* dim. of *scrobis* a trench]

scrod (skrod) *n.* A young codfish, especially when split and prepared for broiling. [?<MDu. *schrode* a piece cut off. Akin to SHRED.]

scrof·u·la (skrof'yə·lə) *n. Pathol.* A tuberculous condition of the lymphatic glands, characterized by enlargement, suppurating abscesses, and cheeselike degeneration; the king's evil. [Orig. pl. <LL *scrofulae,* dim. pl. < *scrofa* a breeding sow: so called because sows were supposed to be subject to the disease]

scrof·u·lous (skrof'yə·ləs) *adj.* **1** Pertaining to, affected with, or of the nature of scrofula. **2** Like scrofula; hence, morally diseased. — **scrof'u·lous·ly** *adv.* — **scrof'u·lous·ness** *n.*

scroll (skrōl) *n.* **1** A roll of parchment, paper, or the like, especially one containing or intended for writing; also, the writing on such a roll; specifically, an outline; draft. **2** Anything resembling or suggestive of a parchment roll; specifically, a convoluted ornament or an ornamental space or tablet on sculptured work. **3** The curved head of a violin or similar instrument. **4** *Her.* A ribbon bearing a motto. See synonyms under RECORD. [Earlier *scrowle,* alter. of obs. *scrow* <AF *escrowe* a scroll; prob. infl. in form by ME *rowle* a roll]

scroll saw A narrow-bladed saw, or a sawing machine bearing such a blade, for doing curved or irregular work.

scroll·work (skrōl'wûrk') *n.* Ornamental work of scroll-like pattern; particularly, fanciful designs cut from thin material by means of scroll saws.

Scrooge (skrōōj), **Ebenezer** In Dickens's *Christmas Carol,* a miser whose hard nature is transformed by the revelations of human joy and sorrow given to him by three spirits that visit him on Christmas Eve.

scroop (skrōōp) *v.i.* To give forth a harsh, scraping sound or cry; creak; grate. — *n.* A harsh grating or crunching sound; harsh cry. [Imit.; infl. by SCRAPE]

scroph·u·lar·i·a·ceous (skrof'yə·lâr'ē·ā'shəs) *adj.* Of or pertaining to a family (*Scrophulariaceae*) of herbs, shrubs, and a few trees, the figwort family, including the veronica, snapdragon and digitalis. [<NL <*Scrophularia,* type genus <Med. L *scrophula* SCROFULA; so called from its supposed power to cure scrofula]

scro·tum (skrō'təm) *n. pl.* **·ta** (-tə) *Anat.* The pouch that contains the testes. [<L] — **scro'tal** *adj.*

scrounge (skrounj) *v.t. & v.i.* **scrounged, scroung·ing** *Slang* **1** To hunt about and take (something); pilfer. **2** To mooch; sponge; beg. [?<dial. E *scrunge* steal, var. of SCROUGE] — **scroung'er** *n.*

scroung·y (skroun'jē) *adj.* **scroung·i·er, scroung·i·est** *Slang* **1** Given to scrounging. **2** Unkempt; unclean; grubby.

scrub[1] (skrub) *v.* **scrubbed, scrub·bing** *v.t.* **1** To rub vigorously, as with the hand or a brush, in washing. **2** To remove (dirt, etc.) by such action. **3** To cleanse (a gas). — *v.i.* **4** To rub something vigorously in washing. See synonyms under CLEANSE. — *n.* The act of scrubbing. [?<Scand. Cf. Dan. *skrubbe.*]

scrub[2] (skrub) *n.* **1** A stunted tree. **2** A thicket or tract of stunted trees or shrubs. **3** A domestic animal of inferior or impure breed. **4** A poor, insignificant person. **5** In sports, a player not on the varsity or regular team. **6** A game of baseball contrived hastily by a few players. — *adj.* **1** Undersized or stunted-looking; inferior. **2** Consisting of or participated in by untrained players or scrubs: *scrub* team; *scrub* game. [Dial. var. of SHRUB[1]]

scrub·by (skrub'ē) *adj.* **·bi·er, ·bi·est** **1** Of stunted growth. **2** Covered with or consisting of scrub or underbrush. [<SCRUB[2]] — **scrub'bi·ness** *n.*

scrub grass The scouring rush.

scrub·land (skrub'land') *n.* Land covered with scrub.

scrub oak Any of various dwarf oaks of the United States, as *Quercus ilicifolia* and *Q. prinoides,* common in New England; especially, the turkey oak or *Q. laevis* of the sandy barrens of the South.

scrub pine Any of several American dwarf pines; especially, the common Jersey pine (*Pinus virginiana*) and the shore pine of California, a variety of lodgepole pine (*P. contorta*).

scrub typhus *Pathol.* Tsutsugamushi disease.

scruff (skruf) *n.* The nape or outer back part of the neck. [Earlier *scuff* (<ON *skopt* hair); infl. in form by *scruff,* var. of SCURF]

scrum (skrum) *n. Brit. Colloq.* Scrummage: an abbreviated form.

scrum·mage (skrum'ij) *v.t. & v.i.* **·maged, ·mag·**

ing To scrimmage. — *n.* **1** Scrimmage. **2** In Rugby football, a formation, around the ball, of the opposing sets of forwards, each of which endeavors by superior weight or compactness to dislodge the opponent, secure and break away with the ball, or kick it out. [Var. of SCRIMMAGE] — **scrum'mag·er** *n.*

scrump·tious (skrump'shəs) *adj. Slang* **1** Elegant or stylish; fine; delightful; splendid. **2** Fastidious; overly particular; nice. [<dial. E, mean, stingy, ult. <SCRIMP; prob. infl. in meaning by SUMPTUOUS]

scrunch (skrunch) *v.t. & v.i.* To crush; squeeze; crunch. — *n.* A crunch. [Imit. alter. of CRUNCH]

scru·ple (skrōō'pəl) *n.* **1** Doubt or uncertainty regarding a question of moral right or duty; reluctance arising from conscientious disapproval. **2** An apothecaries' weight of twenty grains, or 1.295 grams (symbol: ℈). **3** A minute quantity. **4** An ancient Roman coin. — *v.t. & v.i.* **·pled, ·pling** To have scruples (about); hesitate (doing) from considerations of right or expediency. [<OF *scrupule* <L *scrupulus,* dim. of *scrupus* a sharp stone]

scru·pu·lous (skrōō'pyə·ləs) *adj.* **1** Cautious in action for fear of doing wrong; nicely conscientious. **2** Resulting from the exercise of scruples; exact; careful. See synonyms under PRECISE, SQUEAMISH. [<L *scrupulosus* < *scrupulus* (a scruple)] — **scru'pu·lous·ly** *adv.* — **scru'pu·lous·ness, scru'pu·los'i·ty** (-los'ə·tē) *n.*

scru·ti·ny (skrōō'tə·nē) *n. pl.* **·nies** **1** The act of scrutinizing; close investigation. **2** A method of electing the pope by secret ballot. **3** An official examination of votes after an election. See synonyms under INQUIRY. [<LL *scrutinium* <L *scrutari* examine, appar. < *scruta* trash, rags; with ref. to a careful search, including even trash and rags]

scu·ba (skōō'bə, skyōō'-) *n.* A device worn by a free-swimming diver to provide a supply of air for breathing. [< s(elf-)c(ontained) u(nderwater) b(reathing) a(pparatus)]

scud (skud) *v.i.* **scud·ded, scud·ding** **1** To move, run, or fly swiftly. **2** *Naut.* To run rapidly before the wind; especially, to run before a gale with little or no sail set. — *n.* **1** The act of scudding or moving swiftly. **2** Light clouds driven rapidly before the wind; a misty rain. **3** *Brit. Slang* A swift runner. **4** *Scot.* A slap with the open hand. **5** *pl. Scot.* Foaming beer or ale. [Prob. <Scand. (cf. Norw. *skudda* push); ?infl. in meaning by *scut,* in earlier sense of "a hare"]

scu·do (skōō'dō) *n. pl.* **scu·di** (skōō'dē) A former Italian and Sicilian silver or gold coin. [<Ital. <L *scutum* a shield]

scuff (skuf) *v.i.* **1** To walk with a dragging movement of the feet; shuffle. — *v.t.* **2** To scrape (the floor, ground, etc.) with the feet. **3** To make the surface of rough by rubbing or scraping. — *n.* The act of scuffing; also, the noise so made. [Prob. <ON *skúfa* shove]

scuf·fle[1] (skuf'əl) *v.i.* **·fled, ·fling** **1** To struggle roughly or confusedly. **2** To drag one's feet; schuffle. — *n.* A disorderly struggle carried on by grappling, pulling, pushing, or the like; confused fracas. [Prob. freq. of SCUFF] — **scuf'fler** *n.*

scuf·fle[2] (skuf'əl) *n.* A form of hoe used by pushing in the manner of a spade. Also **scuffle hoe.** See illustration under HOE. [<Du. *schoffel* a weeding hoe]

scull[1] (skul) *n.* **1** A long oar worked from side to side over the stern of a boat. **2** A light, short-handled spoon oar, used in pairs by one person. **3** A small boat for sculling. — *v.t. & v.i.* To propel (a boat) by a scull or sculls. ♦ Homophone: *skull.* [ME *sculle, skulle;* origin unknown] — **scull'er** *n.*

scull[2] (skul) *n. Scot.* A large, shallow wicker basket. ♦ Homophone: *skull.*

scul·ler·y (skul'ər·ē) *n. pl.* **·ler·ies** A room where kitchen utsensils are kept and cleaned; a back kitchen. [<OF *escuelerie* care of dishes < *escuelle* a dish <L *scutella* a tray]

scul·lion (skul'yən) *n.* **1** A servant who washes and scours dishes, pots, and kettles. **2** A low wretch. [<OF *escouillon* a mop < *escouve* a broom <L *scopae* a bundle of twigs, pl. of *scopa* a twig]

sculp (skulp) *v.t. & v.i. Colloq.* To sculpture. [Short for SCULPTURE]

scul·pin (skul'pin) *n.* 1 One of several broad-mouthed fishes (family *Cottidae*), of inferior food value, with large, spiny head. The **daddy sculpin** (*Acanthocothus scorpius*) is a common North Atlantic species of which the North American form is a variety. 2 A fish (*Scorpaena guttata*) having a large head and spiny fins, found in southern California. 3 *Brit.* A contemptible fellow; mischief-maker. [Prob. alter. of F *escorpene* < L *scorpaena*, a scorpionlike fish < Gk. *skorpaina* < *skorpios* a scorpion]

DADDY SCULPIN
(Rarely over 4 inches long)

sculp·tor (skulp'tər) *n.* One who designs sculpture by carving wood, modeling plastics, or chiseling stone. [< L < *sculpere* sculpture] — **sculp'tress** (-tris) *n. fem.*

sculp·ture (skulp'chər) *n.* 1 The art of fashioning figures of stone, wood, clay, or bronze. 2 Figures or groups carved, cut, hewn, cast, or modeled in wood, stone, clay, or metal. 3 Raised or incised lines, or markings, as upon a shell. — *v.t.* **·tured, ·tur·ing** 1 To fashion, as statuary, by modeling, carving, or casting. 2 To represent or portray in sculpture. 3 To embellish with sculpture. 4 To change, as the face of a valley or canyon, by erosion and deposition. [< L *sculputra* < *sculptus*, pp. of *sculpere* carve in stone < *scalpere* cut] — **sculp'tur·al** *adj.*

sculp·tur·esque (skulp'chə·resk') *adj.* Resembling sculpture; coldly, calmly, or grandly beautiful; statuesque; well-proportioned; majestic. — **sculp'tur·esque'ly** *adv.* — **sculp'tur·es·que'ness** *n.*

scum (skum) *n.* 1 Impure or extraneous matter that rises to the surface of boiling or fermenting liquids. 2 Minute vegetation on stagnant water. 3 Scoria or dross of molten metals; also, foam; froth. 4 Figuratively, vile element; refuse. See synonyms under WASTE. — *v.* **scummed, scum·ming** *v.t.* To take scum from; skim. — *v.i.* To become covered with or form scum. [< MDu. *schuum*] — **scum'mer** *n.* — **scum'my** *adj.*

scum·ble (skum'bəl) *v.t.* **·bled, ·bling** In drawing and painting, to soften the outlines or blend the colors of by rubbing, as with comparatively dry or opaque color. — *n.* 1 The softening or blending of colors so produced. 2 The material used in scumbling. [Freq. of SCUM]

scup (skup) *n.* 1 A valuable sparoid food fish (*Stenotomus chrysops*) of the eastern coast of the United States; the porgy; also **scup·paug** (skup'ôg, skə·pôg'). 2 A related species (*S. aculeatus*) found southward from Cape Hatteras and on the Gulf Coast to Texas. [< Algonquian (Narraganset) *mishcup* < *mishe* large + *cuppi* a scale]

COMMON SCUP
(About 12 inches long)

scup·per·nong (skup'ər·nông, -nong) *n.* 1 A variety of muscadine grape cultivated in the southern United States. 2 A sweet, straw-colored wine made from this grape. [from the *Scuppernong* River in Tyrrell County, N.C.]

scurf (skûrf) *n.* 1 Loose scarfskin thrown off in minute scales, as in dandruff. 2 Any extraneous scaly matter adhering to a surface. 3 Worthless or impure coating or covering. [OE, alter. of *sceorf*; prob. infl. in form by Scand. Cf. Dan. *skurv.*] — **scurf'i·ness** *n.* — **scurf'y** *adj.*

scur·ri·lous (skûr'ə·ləs) *adj.* 1 Grossly offensive or vulgar; opprobrious. 2 Expressed with or given to low buffoonery. Also **scur·rile** (skûr'-

·il), **scur'ril.** [Earlier *scurrile* < L, neut. of *scurri·lis* buffoon-like < *scurra* a buffoon] — **scur'ri·lous·ly** *adv.* — **scur'ri·lous·ness** *n.*

scur·ry (skûr'ē) *v.i.* **·ried, ·ry·ing** To move or go hurriedly; scamper. — *n. pl.* **·ries** 1 The act or sound of scurrying; a precipitate movement. 2 A flurry, as of snow; whirl. 3 A short, fast run or race on horseback. [Short for HURRY-SCURRY; ? infl. by SCOUR]

S-curve (es'kûrv') *n.* A curve shaped like an S.

scur·vy (skûr'vē) *adj.* **·vi·er, ·vi·est** 1 Meanly low or contemptible; base. 2 *Obs.* Afflicted with scurvy; also, scabby. See synonyms under BAD[1], BASE[2]. — *n. Pathol.* A disease characterized by livid spots under the skin, swollen and bleeding gums, and great prostration: caused by lack of vitamin C in the diet. [< SCURF] — **scur'vi·ly** *adv.* — **scur'vi·ness** *n.*

scurvy grass A biennial herb (*Cochlearia officinalis*) highly prized by Arctic explorers as a remedy for scurvy.

scut (skut) *n.* 1 A short or docked tail. 2 *Slang* A contemptible person. — *v.t. Obs.* To dock (an animal's tail). — *adj.* Short. [ME, a tail, a hare, prob. < Scand. Cf. Icelandic *skott* a fox's tail.]

scu·tage (skyōō'tij) *n.* A tax enacted from feudal knights instead of personal military service for their lands. [< Med. L *scutagium* < L *scutum* a shield]

scu·tate (skyōō'tāt) *adj. Biol.* 1 Covered with horny, shieldlike plates or large scales. 2 Shaped like a shield. Also *scutellate.* See PELTATE. [< L *scutatus* provided with a shield < *scutum* a shield]

scutch (skuch) *v.t.* 1 To dress (textile fiber) by beating. 2 To separate the woody parts from the valuable fiber of (flax, etc.) by beating. — *n.* An implement for scutching hemp and flax. [Prob. < OF *escousser* shake, ? < Scand. Cf. Norw. *skoka* a scutch.] — **scutch'er** *n.*

scutch·eon (skuch'ən) *n.* 1 An escutcheon or anything shaped like it. 2 A metal plate or shield; a name plate or the like. [Aphetic var. of ESCUTCHEON]

scute (skyōōt) *n.* 1 *Zool.* A thin plate or scale, as a scale of a reptile, forming the shell on turtles, etc. 2 Scutellum. [< L *scutum* a shield]

scu·tel·late (skyōō·tel'it, skyōō'tə·lāt) *adj. Zool.* 1 Platelike; shield-shaped. 2 Covered with transverse scales; scutate. Also **scu·tel·lat·ed** (-lā'tid). [< NL *scutellatus* < L *scutella* a platter, dim. of *scutra* a tray; infl. in meaning by L *scutum* a shield]

scu·ti·form (skyōō'tə·fôrm) *adj.* Shield-shaped. [< NL *scutiformis* < L *scutum* a shield + *forma* form]

scut·ter (skut'ər) *v.i.* To scurry; scuttle. — *n.* A hasty running. [SCUTT(LE)[3] + -ER[4]]

scut·tle[1] (skut'l) *n.* 1 A small opening or hatchway with movable lid or cover, especially in the roof or wall of a house, or in the deck or side of a ship. 2 The lid closing such an opening. 3 A sea cock in the bottom of a ship. — *v.t.* **·tled, ·tling** To sink (a ship) by making holes in the bottom or by opening the sea cocks. [< MF *escoutille* a hatchway < Sp. *escotilla*, prob. < Gmc.]

scut·tle[2] (skut'l) *n.* 1 A metal vessel or hod for coal. 2 Rarely, a vessel or pail for other purposes. [OE *scutel* a disk, platter < L *scutella*]

scut·tle[3] (skut'l) *v.i.* **·tled, ·tling** To run in haste; scurry. — *n.* A hurried run or departure. [? Var. of *scuddle*, freq. of SCUD; prob. infl. in form by dial. E *scut* a hare, a short tail; with ref. to the rapid movement of the hare]

scut·tle·butt (skut'l·but) *n.* 1 A drinking fountain aboard ship; formerly, a cask containing the day's drinking water. 2 *U.S. Slang* Rumor; gossip. [Orig. *scuttled butt* a lidded cask for drinking water]

scut·tler (skut'lər) *n.* The striped lizard of the southern United States.

scu·tum (skyōō'təm) *n. pl.* **·ta** (-tə) 1 The large oval or rectangular shield of the Roman legionaries. 2 *Zool.* Some platelike piece or part in a turtle, fish, etc.; a large scale. [< L]

scuz·zy (skuz'ē) *adj.* **·zi·er, ·zi·est** *Slang* Foul; nasty; unpleasant; filthy. — **scuz'zi·ness** *n.*

Scyl·la (sil'ə) In Greek mythology, a six-headed sea monster who dwelt in a cave on the Italian coast opposite the whirlpool Charybdis. See SCILLA. — **between Scylla and Charybdis** Be-

tween two dangers, where one cannot be avoided without incurring equally great peril from the other.

scypho- *combining form* Cup; vessel: also, before vowels, **scyph-.** Also **scyphi-**, as in *scyphiform*, cup-shaped. [< L *scyphus* and Gk. *scyphos* a cup]

scy·pho·zo·an (sī'fə·zō'ən) *n.* Any of a class (*Scyphozoa*) of coelenterates including the sea anemones, corals, and jellyfish. — *adj.* Of or resembling the *Scyphozoa.* [< NL < Gk. *skyphos* a cup + *zōon* an animal]

scythe (sith) *n.* 1 A long curved blade for mowing, reaping, etc., fixed at an angle to a long bent handle or snath. 2 The implement so formed. 3 A curved blade attached to the axles or wheels of some ancient war chariots. — *v.t.* **scythed, scyth·ing** To cut or mow as with a scythe. [OE *sithe*]

Se *Chem.* Selenium (symbol Se).

sea (sē) *n.* 1 The great body of salt water covering the larger portion of the earth's surface; the ocean. 2 A large or considerable body of oceanic water partly or almost entirely enclosed by land: the Adriatic *Sea.* 3 A large inland body of water, salt or fresh: the Dead *Sea* or the *Sea* of Galilee. 4 The swell of the ocean; the course, flow, or set of the waves. 5 Anything that resembles or suggests the sea, as something vast, boundless, or wide-spread. — **at sea** 1 On the ocean. 2 At a loss what to do or think; bewildered. — **to follow the sea** To follow the occupation of a sailor. — **the high seas** The unenclosed expanse of the ocean; also, that part of the ocean beyond a country's territorial waters. — **the seven seas** All the oceans of the world: the North and the South Atlantic, the North and the South Pacific, the Indian, the Arctic, and the Antarctic oceans. ◆ Homophone: *see.* [OE *sǣ*]

sea anchor A drag anchor; a heavy float or canvas bag or sail serving to hold a ship's head to the wind in order to ride out a gale or reduce drifting.

sea anemone A soft-bodied marine coelenterate (class *Anthozoa*, order *Actinaria*), that attaches itself to rocks, etc., suggesting a flower by its coloring and outspread tentacles.

SEA ANEMONE
a. Tentacles contracted.
b. Tentacles extended.

sea bag A cylindrical canvas bag, fastened with a drawstring, in which sailors stow their clothes.

sea bass 1 A dusky-brown or black serranoid food fish (*Centropristes striatus*) common from Cape Cod to Florida: also called *blackfish.* 2 A related fish of California waters (*Stereolepis gigas*). Also **black sea bass.** 3 The white sea bass of California (*Cynoscion nobilis*). 4 The related shortfin sea bass (*C. parvipinnis*).

Sea·bee (sē'bē') *n.* A member of the Construction Battalions of the U.S. Navy, which build base facilities, airfields, etc. [< C(onstruction) B(attalion)]

sea bird Any web-footed bird frequenting the oceans or their coasts, as albatrosses, gulls, gannets, petrels, frigate birds, shearwaters, etc.

sea biscuit Hardtack.

sea·board (sē'bôrd', -bōrd') *adj.* Bordering on the sea. — *n.* The seashore or seacoast; also, the land or region bordering the sea. [< SEA + *board* a border, OE *bord*]

sea bread An unsalted hard biscuit used at sea; hardtack.

sea bream Any of several Old World sparoid food fishes; specifically, a common migratory species (*Pagellus centrodontus*).

sea butterfly A pteropod.

sea calf The common harbor seal (*Phoca vitulina*) of the North Atlantic.

sea cock A cock or valve controlling connection with the water through a vessel's hull.

sea coconut The very large and heavy bilobate fruit of a palm (*Lodoicea maldivica*) native to islands of the Indian Ocean, weighing 40 or 50 pounds and containing four nuts 18 inches long: also called *double coconut*.

sea cow 1 Any aquatic herbivorous mammal of the order *Sirenia,* sometimes attaining a length of about 25 feet; especially, the manatee or the dugong. **2** The walrus. **3** The hippopotamus.

sea craft 1 Skill in navigation. **2** Seagoing vessels.

sea cucumber A large holothurian (genera *Cucumaria* and *Thyone*) found on both coasts of the Atlantic: named from the form it commonly assumes.

sea devil 1 A devilfish. **2** An angelfish.

sea dog 1 The harbor seal or the California sea lion. **2** The piked or spiny dogfish. **3** A sailor with long experience at sea. **4** A fog dog.

sea drake 1 The male of the eider duck. **2** A cormorant.

sea drift Anything cast up by the sea; flotsam, especially vegetable or animal matter.

sea duck Any duck that frequents salt water, belonging to the subfamily *Nyrocinae;* especially, the American eider duck *(Somateria mollissima dresseri),* ranging from Labrador to Maine and as far westward as the Great Lakes. See DUCK.

sea eagle 1 An eagle, related to the bald eagle, which lives principally on fish; especially, **Steller's sea eagle** *(Thalassoaëtus pelagicus),* found on the islands off Alaska. **2** The osprey.

sea fan A coral *(Gorgonia flabellum)* of Florida and the West Indies, with fanlike branches.

sea·far·ing (sē′fâr′ing) *adj.* Following the sea as a calling. —*n.* Traveling over the ocean.

sea fire The phosphorescence of sea water.

sea floor The bottom of the sea.

sea flower A sea anemone or related anthozoan.

sea foam 1 Foam of the ocean. **2** Meerschaum. **3** A fluffy candy made of spun sugar.

sea food Edible fish, shellfish, etc.

sea fowl A sea bird or sea birds collectively.

sea front Land that borders on the sea; buildings, etc., that face the sea.

sea gage 1 The depth to which a vessel sinks in the water; the draft of a vessel. **2** A sounding instrument showing the depth of water by the pressure on a column of fissure. Also **sea gauge.**

sea·girt (sē′gûrt′) *adj.* Surrounded by waters of the sea or ocean. [< SEA + GIRT²]

sea·go·ing (sē′gō′ing) *adj.* **1** Adapted for use on the ocean. **2** Skilful in navigation; seafaring.

sea grape A tropical American tree *(Coccolobis uvifera)* of the buckwheat family, with glossy, red-veined leaves, white flowers, and clusters of a purple fruit resembling grapes.

sea green A deep bluish green, like the color of sea water.

sea gull Any gull or large tern.

sea hog A porpoise.

sea holly A European coarse herb *(Eryngium maritimum)* of the carrot family.

sea horse 1 A teleost fish, usually 3 inches long, found in warm seas and allied to the pipefish; especially, *Hippocampus guttatus,* having a head resembling that of a horse. **2** A hippopotamus. **3** A walrus. **4** A fabulous animal, half horse and half fish, driven by Neptune. **5** A large white-crested wave.

Sea Island cotton A valuable long-staple variety of cotton formerly grown on the Sea Islands, now also cultivated elsewhere.

Sea Islands A chain of small islands off the coasts of South Carolina, Georgia, and northern Florida.

sea kale A hardy perennial herb *(Crambe maritima)* of the mustard family, cultivated for its edible young shoots.

sea king 1 A viking as a maritime leader; Norse pirate king of the Middle Ages. **2** Neptune.

seal¹ (sēl) *n.* **1** An instrument or device used for making an impression

SEA HORSE
(From 2 to 12 inches in length)

upon some tenacious substance, as wax or a wafer; also, the impression made. **2** The wax, wafer, or similar token affixed to a document as a proof of authenticity; also, an impression, scroll, ormark on the paper. **3** A substance employed to secure a letter, door, lid, wrapper, joint, etc., firmly. **4** Anything that confirms or ratifies; a pledge; authentication. **5** Any instrumentality that keeps something close, secret, or unknown. **6** The fluid filling thetrap of a drainage pipe and preventing the upward flow of gas. **7** An ornamental stamp for packages, etc. —*v.t.* **1** To affix a seal to, as to prove authenticity or prevent tampering. **2** To stamp or otherwise impress a seal upon in order to attest to weight, fineness, quality, etc. **3** To fasten or close with or as with a seal: to *seal.*a letter; to *seal* a glass jar. **4** To grant or assign under seal. **5** To establish or settle finally; determine. **6** In Mormon usage, to solemnize forever, as a marriage or the adoption of a child. **7** To sign with the cross; also, to baptize or confirm. **8** To secure, set, or fill up, as with plaster. **9** To supply with a device or trap for preventing a return flow of gas or air. ◆ Homophone: *ceil.* [< OF *seel* < L *sigillum* a small picture, seal, dim. of *signum* a sign] —**seal′a·ble** *adj.*

seal² (sēl) *n.* **1** An aquatic carnivorous mammal (order or suborder *Pinnipedia*) mostly of high latitudes, of which some species, as the **fur seal,** yield valuable fur; any member of *Pinnipedia* except the walrus. Seals feed mostly on fish, and frequent seacoast rocks, ice floes, etc. In the breeding season they congregate on seacoasts, wild islands, etc. ◆ Collateral adjective: *phocine.* **2** The fur of a fur seal; sealskin. **3** Leather made from the hide of a seal. **4** Any fur prepared so as to look like sealskin. —*v.i.* To hunt seals. ◆ Homophone: *ceil.* [OE *seolh*]

SEAL
(Species vary from 7 to 12 feet long)

seal·ant (sē′lənt) *n.* Any substance which secures the contents of a container against contamination, evaporation, spoilage, or leakage.

sea lavender Any of a genus *(Limonium)* of mostly Old World maritime herbs bearing lavender-colored flowers.

sea leather The skins of sharks, porpoises, and dogfishes prepared for use as leather.

sealed orders Orders given in a sealed envelope, with instructions to open at a given time or place under specified conditions; specifically, such orders given to the master of a ship before sailing.

sea legs The ability to walk aboard ship without losing one's balance.

seal·er¹ (sē′lər) *n.* **1** A person or thing that seals. **2** An officer who attests and certifies weights, materials, etc. [< SEAL¹]

seal·er² (sē′lər) *n.* A person or ship employed in hunting seals. [< SEAL²]

seal·er·y (sē′lər·ē) *n.* *pl.* **·er·ies** **1** The business of hunting seals. **2** A place where seals are regularly hunted.

sea lettuce A green seaweed (genus *Ulva*) often used for food.

sea level The level continuous with that of the surface of the ocean at mean tide, between high and low water: used in reckoning altitudes.

sea lily A crinoid; a stalked marine invertebrate resembling a flower.

sealing wax A mixture of shellac and resin with turpentine and pigment that is fluid when heated but becomes solid as it cools: used for sealing papers and bottles.

sea lion One of various large, eared seals (family *Otariidae*), especially the California sea lion *(Zalophus californianus).*

seal ring A signet ring; a finger ring containing an engraved stone.

seal·skin (sēl′skin′) *n.* **1** The under fur of the fur seal when prepared for use by removing the long hairs and dyeing dark-brown or black. **2** A coat or other article made of this fur.

sea lungwort An attractive American herb *(Mertensia maritima)* of the borage family, with white, long-stalked flowers, common to northern coasts.

seam¹ (sēm) *n.* **1** A visible line of junction between parts, especially the edges of two pieces of cloth sewn together. **2** A crack; fissure; rent. **3** A ridge made in joining two pieces or left by a mold upon a casting. **4** A scar or cicatrix; also, a wrinkle. **5** A thin layer or stratum of rock. **6** A suture. —*v.t.* **1** To unite by means of a seam. **2** To mark with a cut, furrow, wrinkle, etc. **3** In knitting, to give the appearance of a seam to; purl. —*v.i.* **4** To crack open; become fissured. **5** In knitting, to form seams. ◆ Homophone: *seem.* [OE *sēam*] —**seam′er** *n.*

seam² (sēm) *n.* *Obs.* Any kind of grease; hence, fatness. ◆ Homophone: *seem.* [< OF *saim,* ult. < L *sagina* a fattening]

sea maiden *Poetic* A sea nymph or a mermaid. Also **sea maid.**

sea·man (sē′mən) *n.* *pl.* **·men** (-mən) **1** An enlisted man in the Navy or in the Coast Guard, graded according to his rank. **2** One skilled in the work of a ship and the ways of the sea; mariner; sailor. —**sea′man·like′** (-līk′) *adj.* —**sea′man·ly** *adj.* & *adv.*

sea·man·ship (sē′mən·ship) *n.* The skill and ability of a seaman in the operation and handling of a boat or ship.

sea·mark (sē′märk′) *n.* Any landmark that serves as a guide in navigation; a beacon; lighthouse.

sea mew A gull, especially the European mew *(Larus canus).* [< SEA + MEW³]

sea mile See under MILE.

sea milkwort See under MILKWORT.

seam·less (sēm′lis) *adj.* Having no seam.

sea monster 1 Any huge, terrifying, or strange marine creature, as a devilfish or octopus. **2** A fabulous or mythical man-eating monster of the sea.

sea·mount (sē′mount′) *n.* Any of a widely distributed group of orogenic formations which rise to various heights from the ocean floor and serve as indicators of geologic processes; a submarine mountain.

sea mouse One of a family *(Aphroditidae)* of annelids with iridescent hairlike setae.

seam·ster (sēm′stər) *n.* A person employed in sewing. [OE *seamestre*]

seam·stress (sēm′stris) *n. fem.* A woman skilled in needlework, especially one whose occupation is sewing. Also spelled *sempstress.* [< OE *seamestre* a seamster + -ESS]

seam·y (sē′mē) *adj.* **seam·i·er, seam·i·est 1** Full of seams, as the wrong side of a garment. **2** Showing the worst aspect: the *seamy* side. —**seam′i·ness** *n.*

sé·ance (sā′äns, *Fr.* sā·äns′) *n.* **1** A session or sitting. **2** A meeting of persons seeking spiritualistic manifestations. [< F < OF *seoir* sit < L *sedere*]

sea onion A bulbous herb *(Urginea maritima)* of the Old World, the source of squill.

sea otter A nearly extinct otter *(Enhydra lutris)* of the rocky shores of the North Pacific, about four feet long, and feeding principally on shellfish. The deep, rich fur, silvery-gray brown superficially, liver-brown beneath, is extremely valuable.

sea palm See under KELP.

sea pen A polyp (genus *Pennatula*) having a rodlike base with the polyps borne on lateral pinnae, giving the appearance of a feather.

sea·plane (sē′plān′) *n.* An airplane designed to rise from and descend upon the water.

sea·port (sē′pôrt′, -pōrt′) *n.* **1** A harbor or port on a coast accessible to seagoing ships. **2** A town located on such a harbor.

sea potato A brown alga (genus *Leathesia*) having a rounded, tuberous appearance.

sea power 1 A nation of great naval importance. **2** The naval strength of a nation.

---

sea purse *Zool.* The rectangular capsule enclosing the eggs or embryo of certain sharks, skates, and rays.

SEA PURSE

sea·quake (sē'kwāk') *n.* An agitation of the sea from a submarine earthquake; a seismic disturbance under the sea.

sear[1] (sir) *v.t.* **1** To wither; dry up. **2** To burn the surface of; scorch. **3** To burn or cauterize, as with a hot iron; brand. **4** To make callous; harden. — *v.i.* **5** To become withered; dry up. — *adj.* Dried or blasted; withered. — *n.* A scar or brand. Also spelled *sere.* ◆ Homophones: *cere, sere.* [OE *sēarian* wither < *sear* dry]

sear[2] (sir) *n.* The pawl in a gunlock, which holds the hammer at half or full cock. ◆ Homophones: *cere, sere.* [< OF *serre* a grasp < *serrer* close, press < LL *serrare* bolt, bar < L *serare* bolt, bar < *sera* a lock; infl. in LL by L *serrare* saw]

sea raven 1 A deep-water sculpin. **2** The cormorant.

search (sûrch) *n.* **1** The act of seeking or looking diligently. **2** Investigation; inquiry. **3** A critical examination or scrutiny. **4** *Law* Right of search. — *v.t.* **1** To look through or explore thoroughly in order to find something; go over or through in making a search. **2** To subject (a person) to a search, as for concealed weapons, etc. **3** To examine with close attention; probe. **4** To penetrate or pierce: The wind *searches* my clothes. **5** To learn by examination or investigation: with *out.* — *v.i.* **6** To make a search. See synonyms under EXAMINE, HUNT. [< OF *cercher* < L *circare* go round, explore < *circus* a ring] — **search'a·ble** *adj.* — **search'er** *n.*

search·ing (sûr'ching) *adj.* **1** Investigating minutely. **2** Keenly penetrating. — **search'ing·ly** *adv.* — **search'ing·ness** *n.*

search·light (sûrch'līt') *n.* An apparatus containing a reflector, and so mounted that a beam of intensely brilliant light may be thrown in various directions for search or signaling; the beam of light from this apparatus.

search warrant A warrant directing an officer to search a house or other specified place for things alleged to be unlawfully concealed there.

sea risk Danger or hazard at sea; specifically, in marine insurance, a peril of the sea.

sea robin One of various gurnards, especially the American brown-finned species (*Prionotus strigatus*).

sea room Sufficient offing or space for a vessel to be maneuvered.

sea·scape (sē'skāp') *n.* **1** An ocean view, especially when picturesque. **2** A picture presenting a marine view. [< SEA + (LAND)SCAPE]

sea serpent A snakelike animal, of monstrous size, believed by many to inhabit the ocean in very limited numbers.

sea·shell (sē'shel') *n.* The shell of a marine mollusk.

sea·shore (sē'shôr', -shōr') *n.* Land adjacent to or bordering on the ocean; the ground between high- and low-water marks.

sea·sick·ness (sē'sik'nis) *n.* Nausea, dizziness, and prostration caused by the motion of a vessel.

sea·side (sē'sīd') *n.* The seashore, especially as a place of resort; also, the side abutting or facing the sea.

sea snake 1 A venomous fish-eating snake (subfamily *Hydrophinae*) of tropical seas, especially of the Indian Ocean. **2** A sea serpent.

sea·son (sē'zən) *n.* **1** A division of the year as determined by the earth's position with respect to the sun, and as marked by the temperature, moisture, vegetation, etc. The ancient Greeks had three seasons, spring, summer, and winter (mentioned by Homer and Hesiod); autumn appears first in Alcman: these four seasons are still used. **2** A period of time. **3** Any of the periods into which the Christian year is divided. **4** A period of special activity: usually with the definite article: the opera or hunting *season.* **5** A fit or suitable time. **6** That which imparts relish; seasoning. See synonyms under OPPORTUNITY, TIME. — **in season 1** In condition and obtainable for use: Clams are *in season* during the summer. **2** In good or sufficient time; oppor-

tunely. **3** To be killed or taken by permission of the law. **4** Ready to mate or breed: said of animals. — *v.t.* **1** To increase the flavor or zest of (food), as by adding spices, etc. **2** To add zest or piquancy to. **3** To render more suitable for use, especially by drying or hardening, as timber. **4** To make accustomed or inured; harden: to *season* troops by strict discipline. **5** To mitigate or soften; moderate. — *v.i.* **6** To become seasoned. [< OF *seson* < LL *satio, -onis* sowing time < L, a sowing < *satus,* pp. of *serere* sow] — **sea'son·er** *n.*

sea·son·a·ble (sē'zən·ə·bəl) *adj.* **1** Being in keeping with the season. **2** Done at the proper time. See synonyms under CONVENIENT. — **sea'son·a·ble·ness** *n.* — **sea'son·a·bly** *adv.*

sea·son·al (sē'zən·əl) *adj.* Characteristic of, or occurring at, a certain season. — **sea'son·al·ly** *adv.*

sea·son·ing (sē'zən·ing) *n.* **1** The act or process by which something, as lumber, is rendered fit for use. **2** Something added to food to give relish; especially, a condiment; hence, figuratively, something added to increase enjoyment or to relieve monotony. **3** The gradual process of acclimation to a new country or climate.

season ticket A ticket or pass entitling the holder to daily trips on a train for a certain period or to admission to a series of entertainments.

seat (sēt) *n.* **1** That on which one sits; a chair, bench, or stool. **2** That part of a thing upon which one rests in sitting, or upon which an object or another part rests. **3** That part of the person which sustains the weight of the body in sitting, or the corresponding portion of a garment. **4** The place where anything is situated, settled, or established: the *seat* of pain, the *seat* of a government; a site. **5** A place of abode; an estate or mansion, especially a country estate. **6** The privilege or right of membership in a legislative body, stock exchange, or the like. **7** The manner of sitting, as on horseback. **8** A surface or part upon which the base of anything rests. **9** A position in a legislature or an office. — *v.t.* **1** To place on a seat or seats; cause to sit down. **2** To have seats for; furnish with seats: The theater *seats* only 299 people. **3** To put a seat on or in; renew or repair the seat of. **4** To locate, settle, or center: usually in the passive: The French government is *seated* in Paris. **5** To fix or set firmly or in place. [< ON *sāti.* Akin to SIT.]

sea tangle A large brown seaweed (genus *Laminaria*) of the temperate zones.

seat·ing (sē'ting) *n.* **1** The act of providing with seats. **2** Fabric for upholstering seats. **3** A fitted support or base; a seat.

SEATO (sē'tō) Southeast Asia Treaty Organization.

seat of government 1 Any city (usually the capital) of a state or nation where the administrative offices of the government are located. **2** A town where a county court sits; a county seat.

sea trout 1 A trout that descends to the sea after spawning. **2** A weakfish.

seat·stone (sēt'stōn') *n.* Underclay.

Se·at·tle (sē·at'l) A port on Puget Sound in west central Washington.

sea urchin An echinoderm (class *Echinoidea*) having a soft rounded body covered with a variously shaped shell bearing numerous movable spines.

sea wall 1 A wall or an embankment for preventing the encroachments of the sea or for breaking the force of the waves. **2** A ridge of stones, etc., washed up by the sea. — **sea·walled** (sē'wôld') *adj.*

sea walnut Any of various ctenophores having an ovate body somewhat resembling a walnut, especially of the genus *Pleurobrachia.*

sea·wan (sē'wən) *n.* An oblong bead made from shell; hence, wampum: used by the Algonquian Indians of North America: also spelled *sewan.* Also **sea'want** (-wənt). [< Algonquian (Narraganset) *seawohn* scattered, i.e., unstrung (shell beads)]

sea·ward (sē'wərd) *adj.* **1** Going toward the sea. **2** Blowing, as wind, from the sea. — *adv.* In the direction of the sea: also **sea'wards.**

sea·way (sē'wā') *n.* **1** A way or lane over the sea. **2** An inland waterway that receives ocean shipping. **3** The headway made by a ship. **4** A rough sea: usually in *in a seaway.*

sea·weed (sē'wēd') *n.* Any of a widely distributed class (*Algae*) of plants growing in the sea, including the kelps, rockweeds, dulse, sea lettuce, etc.

sea·wor·thy (sē'wûr'thē) *adj.* In fit condition for a voyage: said of a vessel. See synonyms under STAUNCH. — **sea'wor'thi·ness** *n.*

sea wrack Seaweed, especially a kelp or other large species.

se·ba·ceous (si·bā'shəs) *adj. Physiol.* **1** Pertaining to, appearing like, or secreting fat. **2** Designating the compound, saclike glands in the corium of the skin. [< NL *sebaceus* < L, a tallow candle < *sebum* tallow]

sebi– *combining form* Fat; fatty matter: *sebiferous:* also, before vowels, **seb–.** Also **sebo–.** [< L *sebum* tallow]

seb·or·rhe·a (seb'ə·rē'ə) *n. Pathol.* A morbid increase of secretion from the sebaceous glands: also called *steatorrhea.* Also **seb'or·rhoe'a.** [< L *sebum* tallow + -RRHEA]

se·bum (sē'bəm) *n. Physiol.* A fatty matter secreted by the sebaceous glands. [< L, tallow]

sec (sek) *adj. French* Dry: said of wines. Also *Italian* **sec·co** (sek'kō).

se·cant (sē'kənt, -kant) *adj.* Cutting, especially into two parts; intersecting. — *n.* **1** *Geom.* A straight line intersecting a given curve. **2** *Trig.* **a** A line drawn from the center of a circle through one extremity of an arc to the tangent drawn from the other extremity of the same arc. **b** The ratio of this line to the radius of the circle: the reciprocal of the cosine. [< L *secans, -antis,* ppr. of *secare* cut]

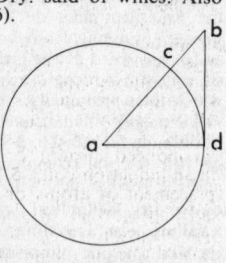

SECANT
Ratio of *ab* to *ad* is the secant of angle *a. ab* is the secant of arc *cd.*

se·cede (si·sēd') *v.i.* **·ced·ed, ·ced·ing** To withdraw formally from a union, fellowship, or association, especially from a political or religious organization. [< L *secedere* withdraw < *se-* apart + *cedere* go] — **se·ced'er** *n.*

se·ces·sion (si·sesh'ən) *n.* **1** The act of seceding; withdrawal from fellowship, especially from political or religious association. **2** *Usually cap. U.S.* The withdrawal of the Southern States from the Union in 1860–61. [< L *secessio, -onis* < *secedere* SECEDE] — **se·ces'sion·al** *adj.*

seck (sek) *adj.* Barren; profitless; unenforceable by distress: said of rent. [< F *sec* < L *siccus* dry]

se·clude (si·klood') *v.t.* **·clud·ed, ·clud·ing 1** To remove and keep apart from company or society of others; isolate. **2** To screen or shut off, as from view: usually in the past participle. [< L *secludere* < *se-* apart + *claudere* shut]

se·clud·ed (si·kloo'did) *adj.* **1** Separated; withdrawn; living apart from others. **2** Protected or screened. — **se·clud'ed·ly** *adv.* — **se·clud'ed·ness** *n.*

se·clu·sion (si·kloo'zhən) *n.* **1** The act of secluding, or the state or condition of being secluded; solitude; retirement. **2** A secluded place. [< Med. L *seclusio, -onis* < L *seclusus,* pp. of *secludere* SECLUDE]

Synonyms: privacy, retirement, retreat, secrecy, separation, solitude. See RETIREMENT, SOLITUDE. *Antonyms:* crowd, multitude, numbers, publicity, society, throng, world.

se·clu·sive (si·kloo'siv) *adj.* Having a tendency to seclusion. — **se·clu'sive·ly** *adv.* — **se·clu'sive·ness** *n.*

sec·ond[1] (sek'ənd) *n.* **1** A unit of time, 1/60 of a minute. **2** *Geom.* A unit of angular measure, 1/60 of a minute of arc. Symbol: ''. **3** In the duodecimal notation, 1/12 of an inch or prime. [< OF *seconde* < Med. L *seconda (minuta),* lit., second (minute), i.e., the result of the second operation of sexagesimal division, fem. of L *secundus* SECOND[2]]

sec·ond[2] (sek'ənd) *adj.* **1** Next in order, authority, responsibility, etc., after the first: the ordinal of *two.* **2** Ranking next to or below the first or best; of inferior quality or value; secondary; subordinate. **3** Identical in character with another or preceding one; another; other. **4** *Music* Lower in pitch, or rendering a lower part than the principal one. — *n.* **1** The one next after the first in position, rank, importance, or quality. **2** An attendant who supports or aids another, as in a duel. **3** *pl.* Articles of merchandise of imperfect manufacture, of second grade, or of inferior quality. **4** *Music* **a** The interval between any note and the next above or below in the diatonic scale. **b** A note separated by this interval from any other. **c** Two notes at this interval written or sounded together. **d** The resulting dissonance. **e** A second or subordinate part, instrument, or voice. **5** In parliamentary law, an utterance whereby a motion is seconded: Do I hear a *second*? — **major second** *Music* A second between whose tones is a difference of pitch of a step. — *v.t.* **1** To act as a supporter or assistant of; promote; stimulate; encourage. **2** In deliberative bodies, to support formally, as a motion, resolution, etc., as a prerequisite to discussion or adoption. See synonyms under AID, HELP. — *adv.* In the second order, place, or rank: also, in formal discourse, **sec'ond·ly.** [<OF <L *secundus* following < *sequi* follow]

sec·on·dar·y (sek'ən·der'ē) *adj.* **1** Of second rank, grade, or influence; subordinate; auxiliary; subsequent; resultant. **2** Depending on what is primary or original. **3** *Ornithol.* Of or pertaining to the secondaries of a bird's wings. **4** *Electr.* Of, pertaining to, or noting an induced current or its circuit, especially in an induction coil. **5** *Chem.* Formed by replacement of atoms or radicals in the molecules of certain organic compounds: a *secondary* alcohol. **6** *Geol.* Subsequent in origin; involving some chemical or physical change of the original mineral: contrasted with *primary.* **7** Pertaining to instruction in a secondary school. — *n.* *pl.* **·dar·ies 1** One who acts in a secondary or subordinate capacity; an assistant; a deputy or delegate. **2** Anything of secondary size, position, or importance. **3** A secondary planet; a satellite. **4** *Ornithol.* One of the feathers that grow on the second joint or forearm of a bird's wing. See illustrations under BIRD, FOWL. **5** One of the hind wings of an insect. — **sec'on·dar'i·ly** *adv.*

secondary education High school or preparatory school education; schooling beyond the elementary or primary, and below the college level.

secondary electron *Physics* An electron emitted from a surface by the direct impact of electrons or ions, as produced by an X-ray machine.

secondary emission *Physics* The emission of secondary electrons from a substance exposed to direct radiation, as by X-rays, etc. Also **secondary radiation.**

second base In baseball, the second base reached by the runner, situated between first and third base. See illustration under BASEBALL.

second childhood A time or condition of foolishness or dotage; senility.

sec·ond-class (sek'ənd·klas', -kläs') *adj.* **1** Ranking next below the first or best; inferior; mediocre. **2** Of, pertaining to, or belonging to a class next below the first: *second-class mail, second-class standing, second-class ticket,* etc. — *adv.* By second-class ticket or by using second-class conveniences: to travel *second-class.*

second class A class of mail including all periodical printed matter.

sec·ond·er (sek'ən·dər) *n.* One who seconds, supports, or approves what is attempted, moved, or proposed by another.

second fiddle 1 The part played by the second violins in an orchestral composition. **2** Any secondary status; a substitute — **to be (or play) second fiddle** To be of secondary importance in an undertaking or in the affections of another.

sec·ond-hand (sek'ənd·hand') *adj.* **1** Having been previously owned, worn, or used by another; not new. **2** Received from another; not direct from the original source: *second-hand* information. **3** Employed in handling or dealing in merchandise that is not new. **4** Of inferior grade; being a poor imitation: a

second-hand statesman. — *n.* That which is second-hand or a poor imitation.

second hand The hand that marks the seconds on a clock or a watch.

sec·on·dine (sek'ən·dīn, -din) See SECUNDINE.

second mortgage A mortgage given next after and subordinate to a first mortgage.

second nature A disposition or character that is acquired and not innate; deep-seated habits that have become fixed.

se·con·do (sā·kôn'dō) *n.* *pl.* **·di** (-dē) *Italian* The second part in concerted music, especially in a pianoforte duet; also, the performer of this part.

sec·ond-rate (sek'ənd-rāt') *adj.* Second in quality, size, rank, importance, etc.; second-class. — *n.* That which is mediocre or of inferior value: also **sec'ond-rat'er.**

second sight 1 The faculty or power of seeing the invisible. **2** The power of prophecy; intuition; clairvoyance. — **sec'ond-sight'ed** *adj.*

second sound *Physics* The peculiar vibratory motion, resembling that of sound waves, associated with the rapid transfer of heat by helium atoms cooled to within two degrees of absolute zero.

Second World War See WORLD WAR II in table under WAR.

se·cre·cy (sē'krə·sē) *n.* *pl.* **·cies 1** The condition or quality of being secret or hidden; concealment. **2** The character of being secretive; secretiveness. **3** Privacy; retirement; solitude. Also **se'cret·ness.** See synonyms under SECLUSION. [Earlier *secretee* < obs. *secre* <OF *secré* secret; refashioned after *primacy, lunacy,* etc.]

se·cret (sē'krit) *adj.* **1** Kept separate or hidden from view or knowledge, or from all persons except the individuals concerned; not immediately apparent; unseen; occult. **2** Affording privacy; secluded. **3** Good at keeping secrets; close-mouthed. **4** Unrevealed or unavowed as such: a *secret* partner. **5** *U.S.* Designating defense information classified second to top-secret material with regard to required security and protection. Compare TOP-SECRET, CONFIDENTIAL (def. 4). — *n.* **1** Something not to be told. **2** A thing undiscovered or unknown. **3** An underlying reason; that which, when known, explains; key. **4** A secret contrivance. **5** Secrecy. — **in secret** In privacy; in a hidden place. [<OF *secré, secret* <L *secretus,* orig. pp. of *secernere* < *se-* apart + *cernere* separate] — **se'cret·ly** *adv.*

Synonyms (adj.): clandestine, concealed, covered, covert, furtive, hid, hidden, latent, mysterious, obscure, occult, private, recondite, retired, unknown, unrevealed, unseen, veiled. See MYSTERIOUS. *Antonyms:* aboveboard, apparent, clear, evident, manifest, obvious, plain, transparent, unconcealed, undisguised.

se·cret·age (sē'krə·tij) *n.* A process of preparing or dressing furs by means of mercury or some of its salts, in order to facilitate felting and matting; carroting. Also **se'cret·ing.** [<F *sécréter* conceal; because it was at first a secret process]

sec·re·tar·i·at (sek'rə·târ'ē·it, -at) *n.* **1** A secretary's position. **2** The place where a secretary transacts his business and preserves his official records. **3** The entire staff of secretaries in an office; especially, the department headed by a governmental secretary. Also **sec're·tar'i·ate.** [<F *secrétariat* <Med. L *secretariatus* the office of secretary < *secretarius* SECRETARY]

Sec·re·tar·i·at (sek'rə·târ'ē·it, -at) *n.* The administrative organ of the former League of Nations and of the present United Nations, consisting of the Secretary General, his officials, and secretaries.

sec·re·tar·y (sek'rə·ter'ē) *n.* *pl.* **·tar·ies 1** A person employed to deal with correspondence, keep records, and handle clerical business for a person, business, committee, or organization. **2** An executive officer presiding over and managing a department of government. **3** A writing desk with a bookcase or cabinet with pigeonholes on top. — **under-secretary** In a government department, the official who ranks next below the secretary. [<Med. L *secretarius* <L *secretum* a secret, neut. of *secretus* SECRET] — **sec're·tar'i·al** (-târ'ē·əl) *adj.*

secretary bird A South African bird (genus *Sagittarius*), having long legs and a crested head: so named from the resemblance of its crest to quill pens stuck behind the ear. It preys on serpents.

SECRETARY BIRD

secretary general *pl.* **secretaries general** A chief secretary; an assistant to a governor general. — **sec're·tar'y-gen'er·al·cy** *n.*

se·crete (si·krēt') *v.t* **·cret·ed, ·cret·ing 1** To remove or keep from observation; conceal; hide. **2** *Biol.* To separate or elaborate from blood or sap. [Alter. of obs. *secret, v.* conceal; refashioned after L *secretus* SECRET] — **se·cre'tor** *n.*

Synonym: conceal. *Secrete* is a stronger word than *conceal,* and is used chiefly of such material objects as may be separated from the person, or from their ordinary surroundings, and put in unlooked-for places; a man *conceals* a scar on his face, but does not *secrete* it; a thief *secretes* stolen goods; an officer may also be said to *secrete* himself to watch the thief. See HIDE.

se·cre·tin (si·krē'tin) *n. Biochem.* A hormone found in the lining of the intestinal wall and stimulating the flow of pancreatic juice. [<SECRET(ION) + -IN]

se·cre·tion (si·krē'shən) *n.* **1** *Biol.* The process by which materials are separated from blood or sap and elaborated into new substances: the *secretion* of milk, gastric juice, or urine. Secretion in animals is generally performed by glandular epithelial cells. Compare EXCRETION. **2** The substance secreted, as saliva or milk. **3** The act of concealing. **4** A deposit of mineral matter in successive coatings, filling cavities, and fissures.

se·cre·tive (si·krē'tiv) *adj.* **1** (*also* sē'krə·tiv) Inclined to secrecy; reticent. **2** Producing or causing secretion. — **se·cre'tive·ly** *adv.* — **se·cre'tive·ness** *n.*

se·cre·to·ry (si·krē'tər·ē) *adj.* Pertaining to secretion. — *n.* *pl.* **·ries** A secreting vessel or gland.

secret service 1 Investigation conducted secretly for a government. **2** The secret or espionage work of various government agencies in time of war.

secret society A society or association that uses secret signs, oaths, rites, or symbols.

sect (sekt) *n.* **1** A body of persons distinguished by peculiarities of faith and practice from other bodies adhering to the same general system; specifically, the adherents collectively of a particular creed or confession; a denomination, or an organized body of dissenters from an established or older form of faith. **2** Adherents of a particular philosophical system or teacher. **3** Any number of persons united in opinion or interest, as in the state or in society; a party or faction; an order. **4** A cutting in horticulture. [<OF *secte* <L *secta* a following, a faction < *sequi* follow. Doublet of SET.]

Synonyms: church, communion, denomination, heresy, heterodoxy, party, schism, school. *Heresy* or *heterodoxy* is a departure from the established doctrine; a *schism* is a division of the *church* either on matters of faith or practice; *schism* is applied also to non-religious organizations. A *sect* or *denomination* is an organized body of believers distinct in doctrine or practice, or in both, from others; *sect* is an opprobrious and *denomination* an honorable term for the same body. Within a *denomination* there may be *schools* differing on minor matters, or *parties* favoring or opposing certain persons or measures, without breach of essential and organic unity. *Church* is often used as synonymous with *denomination;* as, the Presbyterian *Church. Communion* designates those who share a common faith with reference to their spiritual unity.

-sect *combining form* Cut; divided (in a specified manner or number of parts): *vivisect.* Also **-sected,** as in *bisected.* [<L *sectus,* pp. of

secare cut]

sec·tar·i·an (sek·târ′ē·ən) *adj.* Pertaining to a sect; bigoted. — *n.* A member of a sect, especially if bigoted.

sec·tar·i·an·ism (sek·târ′ē·ən·iz′əm) *n.* Sectarian character or tendency; excessive devotion to or zeal for a particular sect.

sec·tar·i·an·ize (sek·târ′ē·ən·īz′) *v.t.* **·ized, ·iz·ing** To make sectarian.

sec·ta·ry (sek′tər·ē) *n. pl.* **·ries** **1** A sectarian: mostly used opprobriously. **2** A dissenter from an established church; a nonconformist. **3** *Obs.* A religious sect. Also **sec′ta·rist.** [< MF *sectaire* <Med. L *sectarius* <L *secta* a sect]

sec·tile (sek′til) *adj.* Admitting of being cut or severed smoothly. [<F <L, neut. of *sectilis* < *sectus,* pp. of *secare* cut] — **sec·til·i·ty** (sek·til′ə·tē) *n.*

sec·tion (sek′shən) *n.* **1** A separate part or division; a portion of a book, treatise, or writing; a subdivision of a chapter; also, a division of law. **2** A distinct part of a country, community, etc. **3** *U.S.* An area of public land one mile square, containing 640 acres and constituting 1/36 of a township. **4** A portion of a railway company's tracks under the care of a particular set of men. **5** In a sleeping-car, a space containing two berths. **6** A tactical unit of the U.S. Army, smaller than a platoon and larger than a squad. **7** A division of an animal group, of indeterminate rank. **8** A representation, picture, or drawing of a building, machine, geological formation, etc., as if cut by an intersecting plane; also, the thing so cut or viewed. **9** A very thin slice of anything, especially for microscopic examination. **10** The character §, indicating a subdivision: used also as a reference mark. **11** The act of cutting; division by cutting, as in surgical operations. **12** The figure formed by the intersection of a plane or other surface with a solid. In mechanical drawing the following sections are distinguished: **lengthwise** or **longitudinal section,** usually representing objects as cut lengthwise through the center; **cross-section** or **transverse section,** cut crosswise; **horizontal section,** cut horizontally, and usually through the center; **oblique section,** cut at various angles. See synonyms under PART. — **frozen section** A cutting, slice, or sliced surface of a frozen part: much employed in anatomy. — *v.t.* **1** To cut or divide into sections. **2** To shade (a drawing) so as to designate a section or sections. [<MF <L *sectio, -onis* < *sectus,* pp. of *secare* cut]

-section *combining form* The act or process of cutting or dividing: *vivisection.* [<L *sectio, -onis* a cutting < *secare* cut]

sec·tion·al (sek′shən·əl) *adj.* **1** Pertaining to a section, as of a country; local; characteristic of the people of a certain section or area: a *sectional* dialect. **2** Dividing or alienating one section from another: *sectional* problems. **3** Made up of sections. — **sec′tion·al·ly** *adv.*

sec·tion·al·ism (sek′shən·əl·iz′əm) *n.* Regard for a particular section of the country rather than the whole; sectional feeling. — **sec′tion·al·ist** *n.*

sec·tor (sek′tər) *n.* **1** *Geom.* A part of a circle bounded by two radii and the arc subtended by them. **2** A mathematical instrument consisting of two arms marked with various scales and hinged together at one end. **3** *Mil.* A part of a front in contact with the enemy. — *v.t.* To divide into sectors. [<LL <L, a cutter < *sectus,* pp. of *secare* cut]

SECTOR
abc is a sector of the circle.

sec·to·ri·al (sek·tôr′ē·əl, -tō′rē-) *adj.* **1** Of or pertaining to a sector. **2** *Zool.* Adapted for cutting; carnassial.

sec·u·lar (sek′yə·lər) *adj.* **1** Of or pertaining to this world or the present life; temporal; worldly: contrasted with *religious* or *spiritual.* **2** Not under the control of the church; civil; not ecclesiastical. **3** Not concerned with religion; not sacred: *secular* art. **4** Not bound

by monastic vows: opposed to *regular:* the *secular* clergy. **5** Occurring or observed but once in an age or century. **6** Lasting for ages. See synonyms under PROFANE. — *n.* **1** One in holy orders who is not bound by monastic vows. **2** A layman. [<OF *seculer* <LL *saecularis* <L, belonging to an age < *saeculum* a generation, an age]

se·cund (sē′kund, sek′und) *adj. Bot.* Having the parts or organs arranged on one side only, as certain flowers; unilateral. [<L *secundus* following. See SECOND².]

sec·un·dine (sek′ən·dīn, -din) *n.* **1** *Bot.* The inner, first-developed coat or integument of an ovule. **2** That which remains in the womb to be expelled after childbirth: usually in the plural. Also spelled *secondine.* [<LL *secundinae,* pl., the afterbirth <L *secundus* following. See SECOND².]

se·cure (si·kyŏŏr′) *adj.* **1** Guarded against or not likely to be exposed to danger; safe. **2** Free from fear, apprehension, etc. **3** Confident; careless. **4** Assured; certain; sure: followed by *of,* sometimes by an infinitive. **5** So strong or well made as to render loss, escape, or failure impossible. — *v.* **·cured, ·cur·ing** *v.t.* **1** To make secure; protect. **2** To make firm, tight, or fast; fasten. **3** To make sure or certain; insure; guarantee. **4** To obtain possession of; get. — *v.i.* **5** To be or become secure; take precautions. See synonyms under ARREST, BIND, CATCH, GET, OBTAIN, PRESERVE, PURCHASE, RETAIN. [<L *securus* < *se-* without + *cura* care. Doublet of SURE.] — **se·cur′a·ble** *adj.* — **se·cure′ly** *adv.* — **se·cure′ment** *n.* — **se·cure′ness** *n.* — **se·cur′er** *n.*

Synonyms (adj.): assured, careless, certain, confident, defended, guarded, impregnable, insured, protected, safe, sure, unassailable, undisturbed, unmolested, unsuspecting, untroubled. See FIRM. *Antonyms:* dangerous, dubious, exposed, hazardous, imperiled, insecure, perilous, risky.

se·cur·i·ty (si·kyŏŏr′ə·tē) *n. pl.* **·ties** **1** The state of being secure; specifically, freedom from danger, risk, care, poverty, or apprehension. **2** One who or that which secures or guarantees; surety. **3** *pl.* Written promises or something deposited or pledged for payment of money, as stocks, bonds, etc. **4** Methods adopted for insuring freedom or secrecy of action, communications, etc., as in wartime; also, the protection afforded by such methods.

Synonyms: bail, collateral, earnest, gage, pledge, surety. The first four words agree in denoting something given or deposited as an assurance of something to be given, paid, or done. An *earnest* is a portion delivered in advance, as when part of the purchase money is paid, "to bind the bargain." A *pledge* or *security* may be wholly different in kind from that to be given or paid; it may greatly exceed it in value, and may be of real or personal property; a *pledge* (as here considered) is always of personal property or chattels. Every pawnshop contains unredeemed *pledges;* land, merchandise, bonds, etc., are frequently offered and accepted as *security. Collateral* is property, as stocks, bonds, etc., actually deposited as *security,* often termed *collateral security.* A person may become *security* or *surety* for another's payment of a debt, appearance in court, etc.; in the latter case, he is said to become *bail* for that person; the person accused gives *bail* for himself. *Gage* survives only as a literary word, chiefly in certain phrases; as, "the *gage* of battle."

se·dan (si·dan′) *n.* **1** A closed automobile having one compartment for passengers and driver. **2** A closed chair, for one passenger, carried by two or more men by means of poles at the sides: also **sedan chair.** [? <Ital. *sedere* sit <L]

se·date (si·dāt′) *adj.* Characterized by habitual composure; staid. [<L *sedatus,* pp. of *sedare* make calm, settle < *sedere* sit] — **se·date′ly** *adv.* — **se·date′ness** *n.*

Synonyms: calm, contemplative, demure, grave, quiet, serene, serious, sober, solemn, staid, still, thoughtful, tranquil, undisturbed, unruffled. See CALM, SERIOUS, THOUGHTFUL. *Antonyms:* agitated, disturbed, excited, flighty, flurried, frolicsome, gay, lively, mad, merry.

se·da·tion (si·dā′shən) *n. Med.* The act of reducing distress, irritation, excitement, etc.,

particularly by administering sedatives.

sed·a·tive (sed′ə·tiv) *adj.* **1** Having a soothing tendency. **2** *Med.* Allaying irritation; assuaging pain. — *n.* Any means, as a medicine, of allaying irritation or pain.

sed·en·tar·y (sed′ən·ter′ē) *adj.* **1** Sitting much of the time; accustomed to sit much or to work in a sitting posture; hence, settled in one place, as certain tribes; sluggish; inactive. **2** Characterized by sitting. **3** Resulting from much or long sitting. **4** *Zool.* Remaining in one place; attached or fixed to an object; sessile. [<L *sedentarius* < *sedens, -entis,* ppr. of *sedere* sit] — **sed′en·tar′i·ly** *adv.* — **sed′en·tar′i·ness** *n.*

Se·der (sā′dər) *n. pl.* **Se·da·rim** (sə·där′im) or **Se·ders** In Judaism, a ceremonial dinner commemorating the Exodus, held on the eve of the first day of Passover, and traditionally on the eve of the second day by Jews outside of Israel.

sedge (sej) *n.* **1** A grasslike cyperaceous herb (genus *Carex*) with flowers densely clustered in spikes: widely distributed in marshy places. **2** Any coarse, rushlike or flaglike herb growing in a wet place. [OE *secg*] — **sedged** *adj.* — **sedg′y** *adj.*

se·dile (si·dī′lē) *n. pl.* **·dil·i·a** (-dil′ē·ə) A seat (usually one of three) near the altar in the chancel of a church, for officiating clergy: usually in the plural. Also **se·dil′i·um.** [<L, a seat < *sedere* sit]

sed·i·ment (sed′ə·mənt) *n.* **1** Matter that settles to the bottom of a liquid; settlings; dregs; lees. **2** *Geol.* Fragmentary material deposited by water or air. See synonyms under WASTE. [<MF *sédiment* <L *sedimentum* a settling < *sedere* sit, settle]

sed·i·men·ta·ry (sed′ə·men′tər·ē) *adj.* **1** Pertaining to or having the character of sediment. **2** *Geol.* Designating rocks, as shale and sandstone, composed of fragments of other rocks deposited after transportation from their sources, and including also rocks formed by precipitation, as gypsum, or by calcareous secretions of animals, as certain limestones. Also **sed′i·men′tal.**

se·di·tion (si·dish′ən) *n.* **1** Language or conduct directed against public order and the tranquillity of the state. **2** The incitement of such disorder, tending toward treason, but lacking an overt act. **3** Dissension; revolt. See synonyms under REVOLUTION. [<OF <L *seditio, -onis* < *sed-* aside + *itio, -onis* a going < *ire* go]

se·di·tious (si·dish′əs) *adj.* **1** Pertaining to, promotive of, or having the character of sedition. **2** Inclined to, taking part in, or guilty of sedition. See synonyms under REBELLIOUS, TURBULENT. [OF *seditieux* <L *seditiosus* < *seditio, -onis* SEDITION] — **se·di′tious·ly** *adv.* — **se·di′tious·ness** *n.*

se·duce (si·dōōs′, -dyōōs′) *v.t.* **·duced, ·duc·ing** **1** To lead astray; entice into wrong, disloyalty, etc.; tempt. **2** To induce, as a woman, to surrender chastity; debauch. See synonyms under ALLURE. [<L *seducere* lead apart < *se-* apart + *ducere* lead] — **se·duc′er** *n.* — **se·duc′i·ble** or **se·duce′a·ble** *adj.*

se·duc·tion (si·duk′shən) *n.* **1** The act of seducing. **2** Something which seduces; an enticement. Also **se·duce′ment.** [<MF *séduction* <L *seductio, -onis* < *seductus,* pp. of *seducere.* See SEDUCE.]

sed·u·lous (sej′ŏŏ·ləs) *adj.* Constant in application or attention; persevering in effort; assiduous. See synonyms under INDUSTRIOUS. [<L *sedulus* careful, appar. < *sedulo* sincerely < *se dolo* without guile] — **sed′u·lous·ly** *adv.* — **sed′u·lous·ness** *n.*

se·dum (sē′dəm) *n.* Any of a large genus (*Sedum*) of chiefly perennial smooth plants, the stonecrops, having very thick leaves and cymose flowers. [<L, house leek]

see¹ (sē) *v.* **saw, seen, see·ing** *v.t.* **1** To perceive with the eyes; gain knowledge or awareness of by means of one's vision. **2** To perceive with the mind; understand; comprehend. **3** To find out or ascertain; inquire about: *See* who is at the

SEDUM

door. **4** To have experience or knowledge of; undergo: We have *seen* more peaceful times. **5** To encounter; chance to meet: I *saw* your husband today. **6** To have a meeting or interview with; visit or receive as a guest, visitor, etc.: The doctor will *see* you now. **7** To attend as a spectator; view. **8** To accompany; escort. **9** To take care; be sure: with a clause as object: *See* that you do it! **10** In poker, to accept (a bet) or equal the bet of (a player) by betting an equal sum. — *v.i.* **11** To have or exercise the power of sight. **12** To find out; inquire: I will go and *see*. **13** To understand; comprehend. **14** To think; consider. **15** To take care; be attentive: *See* to your work. **16** To gain certain knowledge, as by awaiting an outcome: We will *see* if you are right or wrong. — **to see about 1** To inquire into the facts, causes, etc., of. **2** To take care of; attend to. — **to see through 1** To penetrate, as a disguise or deception. **2** To aid or protect, as throughout a period of difficulty or danger. See synonyms under LOOK. ◆ Homophone: *sea*. [OE *séon*]

see² (sē) *n.* **1** The local seat from which a bishop, an archbishop, or the pope exercises jurisdiction; episcopal or papal jurisdiction, authority, or rank; a bishop's or pope's office. **2** *Obs.* A seat, especially of dignity or power. — **Holy See** The pope's jurisdiction, court, or office; erected as an independent state, Feb. 11, 1929: also **See of Rome**. ◆ Homophone: *sea*. [<OF *se, sie, sed* <L *sedes* a seat]

seed (sēd) *n.* **1** The ovule from which a plant may be reproduced; the fertilized ovule containing an embryo. **2** That from which anything springs; source. **3** Offspring; children. **4** The male fertilizing element; semen; milt. **5** Any small seedlike fruit; also, any part of a plant from which it may be propagated, as bulbs, tubers, etc. **6** A young oyster fit for transplanting. **7** Race; generation; birth. **8** The seed-bearing stage; hence, overripeness. **9** *U.S. Dial.* An animal or animals used for breeding. — *v.t.* **1** To sow with seed. **2** To sow (seed). **3** To remove the seeds from: to *seed* raisins. **4** To strew (moisture-bearing clouds) with crystals, as of dry ice, silver iodide, etc., in order to initiate precipitation. **5** In sports: **a** To arrange (the drawing for positions in a tournament, etc.) so that the more skilled competitors meet only in the later events. **b** To rank (a skilled competitor) thus. — *v.i.* **6** To sow seed. **7** To grow to maturity and produce or shed seed. — **to go to seed 1** To develop and shed seed. **2** To become shabby, useless, etc. ◆ Homophone: *cede*. [OE *sǣd*] — **seed′less** *adj.*

seed-bed (sēd′bed′) *n.* **1** A bed of earth planted with seeds, especially for later transplanting. **2** A place of early growth or nurture: the *seedbed* of neurosis.

seed cake 1 A sweet cake containing aromatic seeds, as caraway. **2** Cottonseed-oil cake.

seed-case (sēd′kās′) *n. Bot.* A seed vessel; pericarp.

seed coat *Bot.* The integument of a seed, usually the outer one or testa.

seed leaf *Bot.* A cotyledon.

seed-ling (sēd′ling) *n.* **1** *Bot.* A plant grown from seed, as distinguished from one propagated by grafting. **2** A very small or young tree or plant.

seed money Funds used to experiment or innovate with a new venture to test its workability.

seed pearl A small pearl, especially one used for ornamenting bags, etc., or in embroidery.

seed plant A plant which bears seeds; spermatophyte.

seed-time (sēd′tīm′) *n.* The proper time for sowing seed.

seed vessel *Bot.* The part of a plant that contains the seeds; pericarp.

seed-y (sēd′ē) *adj.* **seed-i-er, seed-i-est 1** Abounding with seeds; going to seed. **2** Poor and ragged; shabby. **3** Feeling or looking wretched. — **seed′i-ly** *adv.* — **seed′i-ness** *n.*

see-ing (sē′ing) *n.* The act of seeing; vision; sight. — *conj.* Taking into consideration; since; in view of the fact.

seek (sēk) *v.* **sought, seek-ing** *v.t.* **1** To go in

search of; look for. **2** To strive for; try to get or obtain: to *seek* glory. **3** To endeavor or try: with an infinitive as object: He *seeks* to mislead me. **4** To ask or inquire for; request: to *seek* information. **5** To go to; betake oneself to: to *seek* a warmer climate. **6** *Obs.* or *Dial.* To search or explore. — *v.i.* **7** To make a search or inquiry. [OE *sēcan*] — **seek′er** *n.*

seem (sēm) *v.i.* **1** To give the impression of being; appear. **2** To appear to oneself: a form of reflexive use: I *seem* to hear strange voices. Compare MESEEMS. **3** To appear to exist: There *seems* no reason for hesitating. **4** To be evident or apparent: It *seems* to be raining. [<ON *sǣma* honor, conform to] — **seem′er** *n.*

seem-ing (sē′ming) *adj.* Having the appearance of reality; apparent; often implying non-reality. See synonyms under APPARENT. — *n.* Appearance; semblance; especially, false show. — **seem′ing-ly** *adv.* — **seem′ing-ness** *n.*

seem-ly (sēm′lē) *adj.* **-li-er, -li-est** Befitting the proprieties; becoming; proper; decorous; suited to the occasion. See synonyms under BECOMING. — *adv.* Becomingly; decently; appropriately. [<ON *sǣmiligr* honorable, becoming < *sǣmr* fitting] — **seem′li-ness** *n.*

seen (sēn) Past participle of SEE.

seep (sēp) *v.i.* To soak through pores or small interstices; percolate; ooze. — *n.* A small spring; a place out of which water, oil, or other liquid oozes. [OE *sipian* soak]

seep-age (sē′pij) *n.* **1** The oozing or percolation of fluid. **2** The fluid or moisture that oozes.

seer (sē′ər *for def. 1;* sir *for defs. 2 and 3*) *n.* **1** One who sees. **2** One who foretells events; a prophet. **3** One believed to have second sight. [<SEE¹ + -ER] — **seer′ess** *n. fem.*

seer-suck-er (sir′suk′ər) *n.* **1** A thin linen or linen and silk fabric, usually striped in colors, with crinkled surface. **2** A similar lightweight cotton or rayon crinkled fabric made by having some of the warp threads slack and others tight. [<Hind. *shirshaker* <Persian *shīr o shakkar,* lit., milk and sugar]

see-saw (sē′sô′) *n.* **1** A sport in which persons sit or stand on opposite ends of a balanced plank and make it move up and down. **2** A plank or board balanced for this sport. **3** Any up-and-down or to-and-fro movement. **4** A crossruff. — *v.t. & v.i.* To move or cause to move on or as if on a see-saw. — *adj.* Moving to and fro; vacillating. [Reduplication of SAW¹ <*See saw sack a downe,* a sawyer's jingle]

seethe (sēth) *v.* **seethed** (*Obs.* **sod**), **seethed** (*Obs.* **sod-den, sod**), **seeth-ing** *v.i.* **1** To boil. **2** To foam or bubble as if boiling. **3** To be agitated or excited, as by rage. — *v.t.* **4** To soak in liquid; steep. **5** *Archaic* To boil. — *n.* The act of seething; turmoil. [OE *sēothan*]

seg-ment (seg′mənt) *n.* **1** A part cut off or divided from the other parts of anything; a section. **2** *Geom.* **a** A part of a figure cut off by a line or plane: especially, the part of a circle included within a chord and its arc. **b** A finite part of a divided line. **3** *Zool.* One of the serial divisions of an animal; somite; metamere; also, the portion of a limb between two joints. See synonyms under PART. — *v.t. & v.i.* To divide into segments. [<L *segmentum* < *secare* cut] — **seg-men-tal** (seg-men′təl) *adj.* — **seg-men′tal-ly** *adv.* — **seg-men-tar-y** (seg′mən-ter′ē) *adj.*

seg-men-ta-tion (seg′mən-tā′shən) *n.* **1** The act of cutting or dividing into segments. **2** The state of being so divided. **3** The cleavage of a cell into parts.

se-gno (sā′nyō) *n. pl.* **-gni** (-nyē) *Music* A sign; specifically, the musical sign :*S:* or *𝄋*, indicating the beginning or end of a repeat. [< Ital. <L *signum*]

se-go (sē′gō) *n. pl.* **-gos 1** A perennial herb (*Calochortus nuttalli*) of the lily family, having white flowers lined with purple: it is the State flower of Utah. **2** Its edible bulb. Also **sego lily**. [<Shoshonean (Ute) *sigo*]

seg-re-gate (seg′rə-gāt) *v.* **-gat-ed, -gat-ing** *v.t.* **1** To place apart from others or the rest; isolate. — *v.i.* **2** To separate from a mass and gather about nuclei or along lines of fracture, as in crystallization or solidification. **3** To undergo segregation. — *adj.* **1** Separated or set apart from others; select. **2** Simple;

solitary; not compound. [<L *segregatus,* pp. of *segregare* separate < *se-* apart + *grex, gregis* a flock] — **seg′re-ga′tive** *adj.* — **seg′re-ga′tor** *n.*

se-gue (sā′gwā, seg′wā) *v.i.* **se-gued, se-gue-ing** *Music* To flow without any break into the next section or theme. [<Ital., (there) follows <*seguire* to follow]

se-gui-dil-la (sā′gē-dē′lyä) *n. Spanish* **1** A lively Spanish dance, in triple time, for two dancers. **2** The music of such a dance, or its movement, based on a stanza of four to seven lines, partly assonant. **3** *pl.* An air to which the dancers sing a group of these stanzas.

seiche (sāsh) *n.* An occasional oscillation of water above and below the mean level of lakes or landlocked seas, lasting from a few minutes to an hour or more. [< dial. F (Swiss), ? ult. <L *siccus* dry]

Seid-litz powder (sed′lits) An aperient powder consisting of two separate parts: tartaric acid and sodium bicarbonate mixed with Rochelle salt: a mild cathartic used by dissolving separately, mixing the solutions, and drinking while effervescing: also called *Rochelle* powder. [from *Seidlitz;* so called because of its aperient property, similar to that of the water from the spring there]

seign-ior (sēn′yər) *n.* **1** A lord; in southern Europe, equivalent to English *sir.* **2** A lord or feudal lord. Also **sei-gneur** (sēn-yûr′). [< AF *segnour,* OF *seignor* <L *senior* older] — **sei-gnio-ri-al** (sēn-yôr′ē-əl, -yō′rē-) *adj.*

seign-ior-age (sēn′yər-ij) *n.* **1** Something charged or claimed as a prerogative. **2** A charge made by a government for coining bullion; also, the difference between the cost of bullion and the face value of coin made from it. **3** A royalty. Compare BRASSAGE.

seine (sān) *n.* Any long fishnet, having floats at the top edge and weights at the bottom, and hauled by its ends to close around a body of fish. — *v.t. & v.i.* **seined, sein-ing** To fish or catch with a seine. [OE *segne* <L *sagena* <Gk. *sagēnē* a fishing net]

seism (sī′zəm, -səm) *n.* An earthquake. [<Gk. *seismos.* See SEISMIC.]

seis-mic (sīz′mik, sīs′-) *adj.* Pertaining to, characteristic of, or produced by earthquakes. Also **seis′mal, seis′mi-cal.** [<Gk. *seismos* an earthquake <*seiein* shake]

seis-mism (sīz′miz-əm, sīs′-) *n.* The process or phenomena involved in earth movements.

seismo- *combining form* Earthquake: *seismograph.* Also, before vowels, **seism-.** [<Gk. *seismos* an earthquake]

seis-mo-gram (sīz′mə-gram, sīs′-) *n.* The record of an earthquake or earth tremor made by a seismograph.

seis-mo-graph (sīz′mə-graf, -gräf, sīs′-) *n.* An instrument for automatically recording the intensity, direction, and duration of an earthquake shock. — **seis′mo-graph′ic** *adj.* — **seis-mog-ra-pher** (sīz-mog′rə-fər, sīs-) *n.*

SEISMOGRAPH
Vertical motion type.

a. Concrete base.
b. Clock.
c. Seismogram.
d. Stylus.
e. Weight.
f. Spring suspension.

seis-mog-ra-phy (sīz-mog′rə-fē, sīs-) *n.* The study or description of earthquakes. [<SEISMO- + -GRAPHY]

seis-mol-o-gy (sīz-mol′ə-jē, sīs-) *n.* The science of earthquake phenomena. [<SEISMO- + -LOGY] — **seis-mo-log-ic** (sīz′mə-loj′ik, sīs′-) — **-i-cal** *adj.* — **seis′mo-log′i-cal-ly** *adv.* — **seis-mol′o-gist** *n.*

seis-mo-scope (sīz′mə-skōp, sīs′-) *n.* A simple form of seismograph; a device for indicating the time and occurrence of earthquake waves without measuring them. — **seis′mo-scop′ic** (-skop′ik) *adj.*

seize (sēz) v. **seized, seiz·ing** v.t. **1** To take hold of suddenly and forcibly; clutch; grasp. **2** To grasp mentally; comprehend; understand. **3** To take possession of by authority or right. **4** To take possession of by or as by force: The usurper *seized* the throne. **5** To take prisoner; capture; arrest. **6** To act upon with sudden and powerful effect; attack; strike: Terror *seized* the attackers and they fled. **7** To take advantage of immediately, as an opportunity. **8** *Law* To put into legal possession: usually spelled *seise*. **9** *Naut.* To fasten or bind by turns of cord, line, or small rope; lash. —v.i. **10** To take a sudden or forcible hold. See synonyms under ARREST, CATCH, GRASP. [< OF *saisir, seisir* < Med. L *(ad propriam) sacire* take (into one's own possession), prob. < Gmc.] —**seiz'a·ble** adj.

sei·zure (sē'zhər) n. **1** The act of seizing. **2** A sudden or violent attack, as of epilepsy or neuralgia; fit; spell.

se·jant (sē'jənt) adj. *Her.* Sitting with the fore limbs erect, as a lion. Also **se'jeant.** [< AF *sejant*, OF *seant*, ppr. of AF *seier*, OF *seoir* sit < L *sedere*]

Sejm (sām) n. *Polish* An assembly or diet having legislative power; specifically, the former Constituent Assembly of the Polish Republic.

Se·la·chi·i (si·lā'kē·ī) n. pl. An order or subclass of elasmobranch fishes, including the sharks, skates, dogfishes, and rays, with their immediately related fossil allies. [< Gk. *selachos* a shark] —**se·la'chi·an** adj. & n. —**sel·a·choid** (sel'ə·koid) adj. & n.

sel·a·gi·nel·la (sel'ə·ji·nel'ə) n. One of a widely distributed genus (*Selaginella*) of flowerless branching herbs with scalelike leaves. [< NL, dim. of L *selago, -inis,* a plant like the savin]

sel·dom (sel'dəm) adv. At widely separated intervals, as of time or space; infrequently. [OE *seldum, seldan,* dative pl. of *seld-* rare, strange]

se·lect (si·lekt') v.t. To take in preference to another or others; pick out; choose. —v.i. To make a choice; choose. See synonyms under ALLOT, CHOOSE. —adj. **1** Chosen in preference to others; taken as being most fit or desirable; choice. **2** Exclusive. **3** Very particular in selecting. See synonyms under CHOICE, EXCELLENT. [< L *selectus,* pp. of *seligere* < *se-* apart + *legere* choose] —**se·lect'ness** n. —**se·lec'tor** n.

se·lec·tee (si·lek'tē') n. One selected; specifically, a person called up for military service under selective service.

se·lec·tion (si·lek'shən) n. **1** The act of selecting; choice. **2** Anything selected; a collection made with care. **3** *Biol.* The process, natural or artificial, by which certain organisms, or any of their characteristics, are favored in the struggle for perpetuation and survival.

se·lec·tive (si·lek'tiv) adj. **1** Pertaining to selection; tending to select. **2** Having or characterized by good selectivity, as a radio receiver. —**se·lec'tive·ly** adv.

selective service Compulsory military service according to specified conditions of age, fitness, etc. —**se·lec'tive-ser'vice** adj.

se·lec·tiv·i·ty (si·lek'tiv'ə·tē) n. **1** The state or condition of being selective. **2** *Telecom.* That characteristic of a radio receiver by which certain frequencies can be received to the exclusion of others.

se·lect·man (si·lekt'mən) n. pl. **·men** (-mən) One of a board of town officers, elected annually in New England, except in Rhode Island, to exercise executive authority in local affairs.

sel·e·nate (sel'ə·nāt) n. *Chem.* A salt of selenic acid. [< SELEN(IC) + -ATE³]

se·len·ic (si·len'ik, -lē'nik) adj. *Chem.* Of, pertaining to, or derived from selenium, especially in its higher valence. [< SELEN(IUM) + -IC]

selenic acid *Chem.* A transparent, colorless liquid, H_2SeO_4, obtained variously, as by decomposing a selenate with hydrogen sulfide.

se·le·ni·ous (si·lē'nē·əs) adj. *Chem.* Of, pertaining to, or derived from selenium, especially in its lower valence, as the colorless, crystalline **selenious acid,** H_2SeO_3.

sel·e·nite¹ (sel'ə·nīt) n. A pearly, usually transparent variety of gypsum. [< L *selenites* < Gk. *selēnitēs (lithos),* lit., moonstone < *selēnē* the moon; so called because it was thought to wax and wane with the moon]

sel·e·nite² (sel'ə·nīt) n. A salt of selenious acid. [< SELEN(IUM) + -ITE²]

se·le·ni·um (si·lē'nē·əm) n. A nonmetallic element (symbol Se, atomic number 34) resembling sulfur chemically and having several allotropic forms, and in the usual gray, crystalline form having the property of varying in electric resistance when exposed to light of varying intensity. See PERIODIC TABLE. [< NL < Gk. *selēnē* the moon]

selenium cell A photoelectric cell in which plates of selenium respond in accordance with the action of light upon them.

seleno- *combining form* Moon; pertaining to the moon; lunar: *selenography.* Also, before vowels, **selen-.** [< Gk. *selēnē* the moon]

sel·e·nog·ra·phy (sel'ə·nog'rə·fē) n. The science or study of the moon's surface. [< SELENO- + -GRAPHY] —**sel'e·nog'ra·pher** or **·phist** n. — **sel'e·no·graph'ic** (-nō-graf'ik) or **·i·cal** adj.

sel·e·nol·o·gy (sel'ə·nol'ə·jē) n. The science that treats of the movements and astronomical relations of the moon. [< SELENO- + -LOGY] — **se·le·no·log·i·cal** (si·lē'nō·loj'i·kəl) adj. —

self (self) adj. **1** Same; identical: obsolete except in the compound *selfsame.* **2** Pure; unmixed: applied especially to colors. —n. pl. **selves 1** An individual known or considered as the subject of his own consciousness; anything considered as having a distinct personality. **2** Personal interest or advantage. **3** Any thing, class, or attribute that, abstractly considered, maintains a distinct and characteristic individuality or identity. [OE]

self-ab·ne·ga·tion (self'ab'ni·gā'shən) n. The complete putting aside of self and claims of self for the sake of some person or object; self-sacrifice.

Synonyms: self-control, self-denial, self-devotion, self-renunciation, self-sacrifice. *Self-control* is holding oneself within due limits in pleasures and duties, as in all things else; *self-denial,* the giving up of pleasures for the sake of duty. *Self-renunciation* surrenders conscious rights; *self-abnegation* forgets that there is anything to surrender. A mother will care for a sick child with complete *self-abnegation,* but without a thought of *self-denial. Self-devotion* is whole-hearted consecration of self to a person or cause with readiness for any needed sacrifice. *Self-sacrifice* is the strongest term of all, and contemplates the gift of self as actually made. *Antonyms:* self-gratification, self-indulgence, self-will.

self-a·buse (self'ə·byoos') n. **1** The disparagement of one's own person or powers. **2** Masturbation.

self-ad·dressed (self'ə·drest') adj. Addressed to and by oneself.

self-as·sured (self'ə·shoord') adj. Confident in one's own abilities; self-reliant. —**self'-as·sur'ance** n.

self-col·ored (self'kul'ərd) adj. **1** Having the natural color. **2** Of but one color or tint. Also *Brit.* **self'-col'oured.**

self-com·mand (self'kə·mand', -mänd') n. The state of having all the faculties and powers fully and effectively at command: more positive and less repressive than *self-control.*

self-com·posed (self'kəm·pōzd') adj. Calm; controlling one's emotions.

self-con·ceit (self'kən·sēt') n. An unduly high opinion of oneself or of one's own abilities, acquirements, etc.; self-esteem; vanity; egotism. See synonyms under EGOTISM, PRIDE. — **self'-con·ceit'ed** adj.

self-con·fi·dence (self'kon'fə·dəns) n. Confidence in oneself or in one's own unaided powers, judgment, etc. See synonyms under ASSURANCE, EGOTISM. — **self'-con'fi·dent** adj. — **self'-con'fi·dent·ly** adv.

self-con·scious (self'kon'shəs) adj. **1** Unduly conscious that one is observed by others, or manifesting such consciousness; embarrassed by inability to forget oneself; ill at ease. **2** Conscious of one's existence. — **self'-con'scious·ly** adv. — **self'-con'scious·ness** n.

self-con·tained (self'kən·tānd') adj. **1** Keeping one's thoughts and feelings to oneself; uncommunicative; impassive. **2** Exercising self-control. **3** Complete and independent; bearing its own motor, as a machine; mounted on its own boiler, as a steam engine.

self-con·tra·dic·tion (self'kon'trə·dik'shən) n. **1** The contradicting of oneself or itself. **2** That which contradicts itself. — **self'-con'·tra·dic'to·ry** adj.

self-con·trol (self'kən·trōl') n. The act, power,

or habit of having one's faculties or energies under control of the will. Compare SELF-COMMAND.

self-de·fense (self'di·fens') n. Defense of oneself, one's property, or one's reputation. Also **self'-de·fence'.** — **self'-de·fen'sive** adj.

self-de·ni·al (self'di·nī'əl) n. The act or power of denying oneself gratification; passive self-sacrifice. See synonyms under ABSTINENCE, SELF-ABNEGATION. — **self'-de·ny'ing** adj. — **self'-de·ny'ing·ly** adv.

self-de·ter·mi·na·tion (self'di·tûr'mə·nā'shən) n. **1** The principle of free will; decision by oneself without extraneous force or influence. **2** Decision by the people of a country or section as to its future political status. — **self'-de·ter'min·ing** adj. & n.

self-de·vo·tion (self'di·vō'shən) n. The devoting of oneself, with one's claims, wishes, or interests, to the service of a person or a cause. See synonyms under SELF-ABNEGATION. — **self'-de·vo'tion·al** adj.

self-ed·u·cat·ed (self'ej'oo·kā'tid) adj. **1** Educated through one's own efforts without the aid of instructors. **2** Educated at one's own expense. — **self'-ed·u·ca'tion** n.

self-es·teem (self'es·tēm') n. A good opinion of oneself; an overestimate of oneself. See synonyms under EGOTISM, PRIDE.

self-ev·i·dent (self'ev'ə·dənt) adj. Carrying its evidence or proof in itself; requiring no proof of its truth. — **self'-ev'i·dence** n. — **self'-ev'i·dent·ly** adv.

self-ex·e·cut·ing (self'ek'sə·kyoo'ting) adj. Containing provisions for securing its own execution independent of legislation: said of a law, etc.

self-ex·ist·ence (self'ig·zis'təns) n. Inherent, underived, independent existence: an attribute of God. — **self'-ex·ist'ent** adj.

self-ex·pres·sion (self'ik·spresh'ən) n. Expression of one's own temperament or emotions, as in art.

self-feed·er (self'fē'dər) n. A machine, boiler, or other mechanical device that feeds itself automatically. — **self'-feed'ing** adj.

self-fer·til·i·za·tion (self'fûr'təl·ə·zā'shən, -ī·zā'shən) n. *Biol.* Fertilization of an ovum by semen from the same animal or of a plant ovule by its own pollen.

self-gov·ern·ment (self'guv'ərn·mənt, -ər·mənt) n. **1** Self-control. **2** Government of a country or region by its own people; especially, government of a colony by the inhabitants rather than by the mother country. — **self'-gov'ern·ing, self'-gov'erned** adj.

self-hard·en·ing (self'här'də·ning) adj. *Metall.* Pertaining to or designating certain steels which will harden properly without the need for quenching.

self-heal (self'hēl') n. **1** A weedy, perennial herb (genus *Prunella*) with violet or purple flowers, formerly reputed to cure disease, especially the common selfheal of North America (*P. vulgaris*). **2** One of various similar plants, as the sanicle.

self-hood (self'hood) n. **1** The state of being an individual, or that which constitutes such a state; personality. **2** Selfishness.

self-i·den·ti·ty (self'ī·den'tə·tē) n. **1** The identity of a thing with itself. **2** *Psychol.* That state of consciousness by or through which the self recognizes itself as one and the same.

self-im·por·tance (self'im·pôr'təns) n. Pompous self-conceit. — **self'-im·por'tant** adj.

self-in·duced (self'in·doost', -dyoost') adj. *Electr.* Characterizing an electromotive force induced in a circuit because of variations of the current in that circuit.

self-in·duc·tion (self'in·duk'shən) n. *Electr.* The production of an induced or extra current in a circuit by the variation of the current in that circuit, especially when it is started or stopped. — **self'-in·duc'tive** adj.

self-in·sur·ance (self'in·shoor'əns) n. That proportion of the insurance risk which the insured assumes himself by the premium payments he makes.

self-in·ter·est (self'in'tər·ist, -in'trist) n. Personal interest or advantage, or the pursuit of it; selfishness. — **self'-in·ter·est·ed** adj.

self·ish (sel'fish) adj. **1** Caring chiefly for self or for one's own interests or comfort; influenced by personal motives to the disregard of the welfare or wishes of others. **2** Proceeding from or characterized by undue love of self. See synonyms under GREEDY.

— self'ish·ly adv.

self·ish·ness (sel'fish-nis) n. The quality of being selfish; undue regard for one's own interest, regardless of others.
Synonym: self-love. *Self-love* is a due care for one's own happiness and well-being, which is perfectly compatible with justice, generosity, or benevolence toward others; *selfishness* is an undue or exclusive care for one's own comfort or pleasure, regardless of the happiness, and often of the rights, of others. *Self-love* is necessary to high endeavor, and even to self-preservation; *selfishness* limits endeavor to a narrow circle of intensely personal aims. *Antonyms*: See synonyms under BENEVOLENCE.

self·less (self'lis) adj. Regardless of self; unselfish.

self·liq·ui·dat·ing (self'lik'wə-dā'ting) adj. Designating a business transaction in which goods in great demand are converted into cash over a short period.

self·load·ing (self'lō'ding) adj. Automatically reloading: said of a gun using the energy of recoil to eject and reload.

self·love (self'luv') n. Love of oneself; the desire or tendency that leads one to seek to promote his own well-being. See synonym under SELFISHNESS.

self·made (self'mād') adj. 1 Having attained honor, wealth, etc., by one's own efforts. 2 Made by oneself.

self·per·cep·tion (self'pər·sep'shən) n. Perception of one's own existence or mental states; introspection.

self·pol·li·na·tion (self'pol'ə·nā'shən) n. Bot. The transfer of pollen from stamens to pistils of the same flower.

self·pos·ses·sion (self'pə·zesh'ən) n. 1 The full possession or control of one's powers or faculties; freedom from perturbation, perplexity, or excitement. 2 Presence of mind; self-command. **— self'·pos·sessed'** adj.

self·pres·er·va·tion (self'prez'ər·vā'shən) n. 1 The protection of oneself from destruction. 2 The urge to protect oneself regarded as an instinct.

self·prof·it (self'prof'it) n. Self-interest.

self·re·li·ance (self'ri·lī'əns) n. Reliance on one's own abilities, resources, or judgment. See synonyms under ASSURANCE. **— self'·re·li'ant** adj.

self·re·nun·ci·a·tion (self'ri·nun'sē·ā'shən) n. Renunciation of one's own rights, privileges, or claims. **— self'·re·nun'ci·a·to'ry** (-sē·ə·tôr'ē, -tō'rē) adj.

self·re·spect (self'ri·spekt') n. Such regard for one's own character as will restrain one from unworthy action; rational self-esteem. See synonyms under PRIDE **— self'·re·spect'ing** adj.

self·re·straint (self'ri·strānt') n. Restraint, as of the passions, by the force of one's own will; self-control.

self·right·eous (self'rī'chəs) adj. Righteous in one's own estimation; pharisaic. **— self'·right'eous·ly** adv. **— self'·right'eous·ness** n.

self·ris·ing (self'rī'zing) adj. 1 That rises of itself. 2 Having the leaven already added by the millers, as some flours.

self·sac·ri·fice (self'sak'rə·fīs) n The sacrifice or subordination of one's self or one's personal welfare or wishes, for the sake of duty or for others' good. See synonyms under SELF-ABNEGATION. **— self'·sac'ri·fic'ing** adj.

self·same (self'sām') adj. Exactly the same; identical. See synonyms under IDENTICAL. **— self'·same'ness** n.

self·sat·is·fac·tion (self'sat'is·fak'shən) n. Satisfaction with one's own actions and characteristics; conceit; self-complacency. **— self'·sat'is·fied** adj. **— self'·sat'is·fy'ing** adj.

self·seek·ing (self'sē'king) adj. Given to the exclusive pursuit of one's own interests or gain. **—** n. Self-aggrandizement; selfishness. **— self'·seek'er** n.

self·ser·vice (self'sûr'vis) n. Designating a particular type of café, restaurant, or store where patrons serve themselves.

self·start·er (self'stär'tər) n. 1 An internal-combustion engine, with automatic or semi-automatic starting mechanism; also, such mechanism. 2 Slang One who requires no outside stimulus to start or accomplish work.

self·styled (self'stīld') adj. Characterized (as such) by oneself: a *self-styled* gentleman.

self·suf·fi·cient (self'sə·fish'ənt) adj. 1 Able to support or maintain oneself without aid or cooperation from others. 2 Having overweening confidence in oneself. Also **self'·suf·fic'ing** (-sə·fī'sing). **— self'·suf·fi'cien·cy** n.

self·will (self'wil') n. Pertinacious adherence to one's own will or wish, especially with disregard of the wishes of others; obstinacy. **— self'·willed'** adj.

self·wind·ing (self'wīn'ding) adj. Having a magnetic, electrical, or other attachment which automatically winds a clock or other mechanism at certain times.

Sel·juk (sel·jook') n. A member of one of several Turkish dynasties which reigned over a large part of central and western Asia from the 11th to the 13th centuries. **—** adj. Pertaining to a Seljuk. Also **Sel·ju·ki·an** (sel·jōō'-kē·ən). [<Turkish *seljûq*, after *Seljûq*, a Turkish chieftain, reputed ancestor of the Seljuk dynasties]

sell (sel) v. **sold, sell·ing** v.t. 1 To transfer (property) to another for a consideration; dispose of by sale. 2 To deal in; offer for sale. 3 To deliver, surrender, or betray for a price or reward: to *sell* one's honor. 4 *Colloq.* To cause to accept or approve something: They *sold* him on the scheme. 5 *Colloq.* To cause the acceptance or approval of. 6 *Slang* To deceive; cheat. **—** v.i. 7 To transfer ownership for a consideration; engage in selling. 8 To be on sale; be sold. See synonyms under CONVEY. **—** n. 1 *Slang* A trick; joke; swindle. 2 On the stock exchange, a stock that ought to be sold. ◆ Homophone: *cell*. [OE *sellan* give]

sell·out (sel'out') n. 1 An act of selling out. 2 *Colloq.* A performance for which all seats have been sold. 3 *Slang* A betrayal through a secret bargain or agreement.

Selt·zer (selt'sər) n. An effervescing mineral water. Also **Seltzer water, Sel·ters** (sel'tərz). [Alter. of G *Selterser*, from *Nieder Selters*, a village in SW Prussia, its place of origin]

sel·vage (sel'vij) n. 1 The edge of a woven fabric so finished that it will not ravel. 2 An edge. 3 The edge plate of a lock having an opening for a bolt. Also **sel'vedge**. [<SELF + EDGE, trans. of MDu. *selfegghe*]

se·man·tics (si·man'tiks) n. pl. *(construed as singular)* 1 *Ling.* The study of the meanings of speech forms, especially of the development and changes in meaning of words and word groups. 2 *Logic* The relation between signs or symbols and what they signify or denote: also called *semasiology, semiotics.* Compare GENERAL SEMANTICS. 3 Loosely, verbal trickery, especially by adulteration or shift of meaning within a word; amphibology.

sem·a·phore (sem'ə-fôr, -fōr) n. An apparatus for making signals, as with movable arms, disks, flags, or lanterns. **—** v.t. To send by semaphore. [<F *sémaphore* <Gk. *sēma* a sign + *pherein* carry] **— sem'·a·phor'ic** (-fôr'ik, -for'ik) or **·i·cal** adj.

Se·ma·rang (sə·mä'räng) A port of northern Java: also *Samarang*.

SEMAPHORE
a. Clear. b. Approach. c. Stop.

se·ma·si·ol·o·gy (si·mā'sē·ol'ə·jē, -zē-) n. Semantics (def. 2). [<Gk. *sēmasia* the signification of a word <*sēma* sign + -LOGY] **— se·ma·si·o·log·i·cal** (si·mā'sē·ə·loj'i·kəl, -zē-) adj.

se·mat·ic (si·mat'ik) adj. Of the nature of a sign; warning: in animal coloration, serving to distinguish as a means of recognition or warning. [<Gk. *sēma, -atos* a sign]

sem·bla·ble (sem'blə-bəl) adj. 1 Resembling; similar. 2 Apparent; not real. **—** n. A thing resembling another thing. Also **sem'bla·tive.** [<OF <*sembler*. See SEMBLANCE.]

sem·blance (sem'bləns) n. 1 A mere show without reality; pretense. 2 Outward appearance; look; aspect. 3 A pictorial representation; likeness; resemblance. See synonyms under PRETENSE. [<OF <*sembler* seem <L *simulare, similare* simulate <*similis* like]

sem·ble (sem'bəl) v.i. **·bled, ·bling** It seems; it would seem: used only in law, and generally in abbreviated form, **sem.** or **semb.** [<F, it seems <*sembler.* See SEMBLANCE.]

se·mé (sə·mā', *Fr.* se·mā') adj. *Her.* Strewn or scattered over with small bearings, as fleurs-de-lis; powdered. [<OF, pp. of *semer* sow <L *seminare* <*semen* a seed]

se·mei·ol·o·gy (sē·mī·ol'ə·jē, sē'mē-), **se·mei·ot·ics** (sē'mī·ot'iks, sē'mē-), etc. See SEMIOLOGY, SEMIOTICS, etc.

Sem·e·le (sem'ə·lē) In Greek mythology, the mother of Dionysus by Zeus: she was destroyed by lightning when she asked to see Zeus as he appeared to the gods.

se·meme (sē'mēm) n. *Ling.* The meaning of a morpheme. [<Gk. *sēma* a sign; on analogy with *phoneme*]

se·men (sē'mən) n. 1 The impregnating fluid of male animals. 2 Seed. [<L <*serere* sow]

se·mes·ter (si·mes'tər) n. A college half-year; hence, a period of instruction, usually lasting 17 or 18 weeks. [<G <L *(cursus) semestris* (a period) of six months <*sex* six + *mensis* a month] **— se·mes'tral** adj.

sem·i (sem'ē) n. pl. **sem·is** *Colloq.* 1 *U.S.* A semitrailer. 2 *Brit.* A semi-detached house. **— the semis** *Colloq.* The semifinal round of competition in a sports competition.

semi- prefix 1 Half; partly; not fully: *semi*-automatic, *semi*civilized. 2 Exactly half: *semi*-circle. 3 Occurring twice (in the period specified): *semi*weekly. [<L]
Semi-, meaning not fully, partially, or partial, is found in solidemes and hyphemes, as in the list beginning at the foot of this page.

sem·i·an·nu·al (sem'ē·an'yōō·əl) adj. Issued or occurring twice a year; half-yearly. **—** n. A publication issued twice a year. **— sem'i·an'·nu·al·ly** adv.

sem·i·a·quat·ic (sem'ē·ə·kwat'ik, -kwot'ik) adj. *Biol.* Adapted for living or growing near water, as certain types of plants and animals.

semi·au·to·mat·ic (sem'ē·ô'tə·mat'ik) adj. Only partly automatic: said especially of guns which are self-loading but not self-firing.

sem·i·breve (sem'ē·brēv') n. *Music* A note equal to half a breve; a whole note.

sem·i·cell (sem'ē·sel') n. *Biol.* Half of a complete cell, usually joined to the other half by an isthmus, as in certain green algae. Compare DESMID.

sem·i·cen·ten·ni·al (sem'ē·sen·ten'ē·əl) adj. Occurring or celebrated at the end of fifty years from some event. **—** n. The fiftieth anniversary of an event, or its celebration.

sem·i·cir·cle (sem'ē·sûr'kəl) n. 1 A half-circle; an arc or a segment of 180°. 2 Anything formed or arranged in a half-circle. **— sem'i·cir'cu·lar** adj.

semicircular canal *Anat.* One of the three tubular structures in the inner ear of most vertebrates, which together serve as the organ of balance. See illustration under EAR.

sem·i·cir·cum·fer·ence (sem'ē·sər·kum'fər·əns, -frəns) n. One half of a circumference.

sem·i·civ·i·lized (sem'ē·siv'ə·līzd) adj. Half or partly civilized.

sem·i·co·lon (sem'ē·kō'lən) n. A mark (;) of punctuation, indicating a greater degree of separation than the comma.

sem·i·con·duc·tor (sem'ē·kon·duk'tər) n. *Physics* 1 One of a class of crystalline solids, as germanium, silicon, and lead sulfide, which are electronic conductors at ordinary temperatures: used in the manufacture of transistors. 2 Any substance or material having an electrical conductivity intermediate between metals and dielectrics.

sem·i·con·scious (sem'ē·kon'shəs) adj. Partly conscious; half-conscious.

sem·i·de·tached (sem'ē·di·tacht') adj. Joined to another on one side only: said of two houses built side by side with one common wall.

sem·i·di·am·e·ter (sem'ē·dī·am'ə·tər) n. A radius; half of a diameter.

sem·i·di·ur·nal (sem'ē·dī·ûr'nəl) adj. 1 Pertaining to or continuing during a half-day; occurring or accomplished in a half-day, or once each half-day. **2** Designating either half of the arc described by a heavenly body during its rising or setting. [<SEMI- + DIURNAL]

sem·i·dome (sem′ē·dōm′) *n. Archit.* A roof structure resembling a portion, approximately half, of a dome divided vertically.

SEMIDOME

sem·i·el·lip·ti·cal (sem′ē·i·lip′ti·kəl) *adj.* Having the form of half of an ellipse that has been divided along either diameter.

sem·i·fi·nal (sem′ē·fī′nəl) *n.* **1** A competition which precedes the final in a list of sporting events. **2** One of two competitions in a tournament, the winners of each meeting in the final. — *adj.* Next before the final. — **sem′i·fi′nal·ist** *n.*

sem·i·flu·id (sem′ē·floo′id) *adj.* Fluid, but thick and viscous. — *n.* A thick, viscous fluid. — **sem′i·flu·id′ic** (-floo·id′ik) *adj.*

sem·i·liq·uid (sem′ē·lik′wid) *adj.* Half liquid. — *n.* A partly liquid substance.

sem·i·lu·nar (sem′ē·loo′nər) *adj.* Resembling or shaped like a half-moon; crescentic. Also **sem′i·lu′nate** (-loo′nāt).

sem·i·mo·bile (sem′ē·mō′bēl) *adj.* Partly mobile: said especially of military units not fully equipped with motor vehicles.

sem·i·month·ly (sem′ē·munth′lē) *adj.* Taking place twice a month. — *n. pl.* **·lies** A publication issued twice a month. — *adv.* At half-monthly intervals.

sem·i·nal (sem′ə·nəl) *adj.* **1** Pertaining to or containing seeds, germs, or primal elements. **2** Having productive power; germinal; propagative. **3** Not developed; embryonic; rudimentary. [<OF <L *seminalis* <*semen, seminis* semen, a seed] — **sem′i·nal·ly** *adv.*

sem·i·nar (sem′ə·när) *n.* **1** A group of advanced students at a college or university, meeting regularly and informally with a professor for discussion of research problems. **2** The course thus conducted. [<G <L *seminarium.* See SEMINARY.]

sem·i·nar·y (sem′ə·ner′ē) *n. pl.* **·nar·ies** **1** A special school, as of theology; also, a school of higher education. **2** A seminar. **3** The place where anything is nurtured. **4** A seminary priest. — *adj.* **1** Seminal. **2** Pertaining to a seminary. [<MF *séminaire* <L *seminarium* a seed plot, orig. neut. of *seminarius* seminal <*semen, seminis* a seed, semen]

sem·i·na·tion (sem′ə·nā′shən) *n.* **1** The act of sowing or spreading; dispersion of seeds. **2** Propagation. [<L *seminatio, -onis* <*semen, seminis* a seed, semen]

sem·i·nif·er·ous (sem′ə·nif′ər·əs) *adj.* **1** Carrying or producing semen. **2** Seed-bearing. [<L *semen, seminis* a seed, semen + *ferre* bear]

sem·i·niv·o·rous (sem′ə·niv′ər·əs) *adj.* Feeding on seeds. [<L *semen, seminis* a seed, semen + -VOROUS]

Sem·i·nole (sem′ə·nōl) *n.* One of a Florida tribe of North American Indians of Muskhogean linguistic stock, an offshoot of the Creeks: now chiefly in Oklahoma, a remnant remaining in Florida. [<Muskhogean (Creek) *Simanóle,* lit., a separatist, a runaway]

sem·i·of·fi·cial (sem′ē·ə·fish′əl) *adj.* Having official authority or sanction; official to a certain extent. — **sem′i·of·fi′cial·ly** *adv.*

se·mi·ol·o·gy (sē′mē·ol′ə·jē, sē′mī-) *n.* **1** The science that relates to sign language. **2** *Med.* Symptomatology. **3** The use of signs in signaling. Also spelled *semeiology.* [<Gk. *sēmeion,* dim. of *sēma* a mark + -LOGY]

se·mi·ot·ic (sē′mē·ot′ik, sē′mī-) *adj.* **1** Of or pertaining to semantics (def. 2). **2** *Med.* Relating to symptomatology. Also spelled *semeiotic.* Also **se′mi·ot′i·cal.** [<Gk. *sēmeiotikos* <*sēmeion.* See SEMIOLOGY.]

se·mi·ot·ics (sē′mē·ot′iks, sē′mī-) *n. pl.* (construed as singular) **1** Semantics (def. 2). **2** *Med.* Symptomatology. Also spelled *semeiotics.* [<Gk. *sēmeiotikos.* See SEMIOTIC.]

sem·i·o·vip·a·rous (sem′ē·ō·vip′ər·əs) *adj.* Giving birth to imperfectly developed offspring, as a marsupial.

sem·i·pal·mate (sem′ē·pal′māt, -mit) *adj. Ornithol.* Having the toes connected by webs

for less than half their length, as many shore birds. Also **sem′i·pal′mat·ed.**

sem·i·par·a·sit·ic (sem′ē·par′ə·sit′ik) *adj. Biol.* Partly parasitic: said especially of certain bacteria and of chlorophyll-bearing plants, as the mistletoe.

sem·i·per·me·a·ble (sem′ē·pûr′mē·ə·bəl) *adj.* Partially permeable: said especially of osmotic membranes that separate a solvent from the dissolved substance.

sem·i·post·al (sem′ē·pōs′təl) *adj.* Designating a postage stamp or series of stamps sold by postal authorities for more than the franking value, the additional proceeds usually going to a philanthropic purpose. — *n.* A semipostal stamp.

sem·i·pre·cious (sem′ē·presh′əs) *adj.* Designating a gem or class of gems that are not as valuable as those classified precious: *semiprecious* stones.

sem·i·qua·ver (sem′ē·kwā′vər) *n. Music* A note one sixteenth the value of a semibreve or whole note.

sem·i·rig·id (sem′ē·rij′id) *adj. Aeron.* Partly rigid, as in an airship in which an exterior stiffener supports the load. — *n.* A semirigid airship.

sem·i·round (sem′ē·round′) *adj.* Having one side round and the other flat. — *n.* A semiround object.

sem·i·skilled (sem′ē·skild′) *adj.* Partly skilled, but not enough to perform highly specialized work.

sem·i·sol·id (sem′ē·sol′id) *adj.* Partly solid; so viscous as to be nearly solid.

Sem·ite (sem′īt, sē′mīt) *n.* **1** A person believed to be or considered as a descendant of Shem. **2** One of a people of Caucasian stock, now represented by the Jews and Arabs, but originally including the ancient Babylonians, Assyrians, Arameans, Phoenicians, etc. Also *Shemite.* [<NL *Semita* <LL *Sem* Shem <Gk. *Sēm* <Hebrew *shēm*]

Se·mit·ic (sə·mit′ik) *adj.* Of or pertaining to the Semites, or to any of their languages. — *n.* A subfamily of the Hamito-Semitic family of languages, divided into three groups — **East Semitic** (Akkadian), **Northwest Semitic** (Phoenician, ancient and modern Hebrew, Aramaic, etc.), and **Southwest Semitic** (Arabic, Ethiopic, Amharic, etc.).

sem·i·tone (sem′ē·tōn′) *n. Music* An interval approximately equal to half a major tone on the scale: the smallest interval in most European music. — **sem·i·ton·ic** (sem′ē·ton′ik) *adj.*

sem·i·trail·er (sem′ē·trāl′ər) *n.* **1** A trailer having wheels only at the rear, the front end being attached to the rear of a truck tractor. **2** A tractor and its attached semitrailer considered as a unit: also called *trailer truck.*

sem·i·trop·i·cal (sem′ē·trop′i·kəl) *adj.* Nearly tropical.

sem·i·vit·ri·fied (sem′ē·vit′rə·fīd) *adj.* Half vitrified; partially made into glass.

sem·i·vow·el (sem′i·vou′əl) *n. Phonet.* A vowel-like sound used as a consonant, as (w), (y), and (r): also called *glide.* — **sem′i·vo′cal** (-vō′kəl) *adj.*

sem·i·week·ly (sem′ē·wēk′lē) *adj.* Issued or occurring twice a week. — *n. pl.* **·lies** A publication issued twice a week. — *adv.* At half-weekly intervals.

sem·o·li·na (sem′ə·lē′nə) *n.* The gritty or grain-like portions of wheat retained in the bolting machine after the fine flour has been passed through. [Alter. of Ital. *semolino,* dim. of *semola* bran <L *simila* fine flour]

sem·per fi·de·lis (sem′pər fi·dē′lis, fi·dā′lis) *Latin* Always faithful: motto of the U.S. Marine Corps.

sem·per pa·ra·tus (sem′pər pə·rā′təs) *Latin* Always prepared: motto of the U.S. Coast Guard.

sem·per·vi·rent (sem′pər·vī′rənt) *adj.* Evergreen. [<L *semper* always + *virens, -entis,* ppr. of *virere* be green]

sem·pi·ter·nal (sem′pə·tûr′nəl) *adj.* Enduring or existing to all eternity; everlasting. See synonyms under IMMORTAL, PERPETUAL. [<OF *sempiternel* <LL *sempiternalis* <L *sempiternus* everlasting < *semper* always] — **sem′·pi·ter′ni·ty** *n.*

sem·pre (sem′prā) *adv. Music* Always; throughout the passage or composition: *sempre legato,* piano, etc. [<Ital. <L *semper*]

sen (sen) *n. Japanese* A Japanese copper or

bronze coin, equal to 1/100 of a yen.

sen′ (sen) *v.t. & v.i., n. Scot.* Send[1].

sen·a·ry (sen′ər·ē) *adj.* Of or pertaining to six; containing six units. [<L *senarius* <*seni* six each < *sex* six]

sen·ate (sen′it) *n.* **1** The governing body of some universities and institutions of learning. **2** An advisory body of members of the faculty and representative students in a school or college. **3** A body of distinguished or venerable men; council; legislative body. [<OF *senat* <L *senatus,* lit., a council of old men < *senex, senis* old]

Sen·ate (sen′it) *n.* **1** The upper branch of national or state legislative bodies of the United States, and of France and other governments; especially, the **United States Senate,** composed of two Senators elected by popular vote from each State. **2** In ancient Rome, the state council, whose originally very extensive powers were curtailed under the empire: limited to 100 patricians under the kings, it consisted, under the republic, of 300 patricians, plebeians, and high officials; under Augustus, there were 600 senators.

sen·a·tor (sen′ə·tər) *n.* A member of a senate. [<OF *senateur* <L *senator* < *senex, senis* an old man, old] — **sen′a·tor·ship** *n.*

sen·a·to·ri·al (sen′ə·tôr′ē·əl, -tō′rē-) *adj.* **1** Pertaining to or befitting a senator or senate. **2** Entitled to elect a senator, as a district. — **sen′a·to′ri·al·ly** *adv.*

send[1] (send) *v.* **sent, send·ing** *v.t.* **1** To cause or direct to go; dispatch, as a messenger. **2** To cause to be conveyed to another place; transmit; forward: to *send* a letter. **3** To cause to issue; emit or discharge, as heat, light, smoke, etc.: with *forth, out,* etc. **4** To throw or drive by force; impel. **5** To cause to come, happen, etc.; grant: God *send* us peace. **6** To bring into a specified state or condition; drive: The decision *sent* him into bankruptcy. **7** To transmit, as a current or electromagnetic impulses. — *v.i.* **8** To dispatch an agent, messenger, or message. — **to send for** To summon by a message or messenger. — **to send in one's papers** To resign. — *n.* A messenger. [OE *sendan*] — **send′er** *n.*

Synonyms (verb): cast, delegate, depute, discharge, dispatch, dismiss, emit, fling, forward, hurl, impel, lance, launch, project, propel, sling, throw, transmit. *Send* in its most common use involves personal efficiency without personal presence; according to the adage, "If you want your business done, go; if not, *send*"; one *sends* a letter or a bullet, a messenger or a message. To *dispatch* is to *send* hastily or very promptly, ordinarily with a destination in view; to *dismiss* is to *send* away from oneself without reference to a destination; as, to *dismiss* a clerk, an application, or an annoying subject. To *discharge* is to *send* away so as to relieve a person or thing of a load; we *discharge* a gun or *discharge* the contents; as applied to persons, *discharge* is a harsher term than *dismiss.* To *emit* is to *send* forth from within, with no reference to a destination; as, The sun *emits* light and heat. *Transmit,* from the Latin, is a dignified term, often less vigorous than the Saxon *send,* but preferable at times in literary or scientific use; as, to *transmit* a charge of electricity. *Transmit* fixes the attention more on the intervening agency, as *send* does upon the points of departure and destination. *Antonyms:* bring, carry, convey, get, give, hand, hold, keep, receive, retain.

send[2] (send) *Naut. n.* **1** The flow or impulse of the waves. **2** Scend. — *v.i.* **1** To move by the force of waves. **2** To scend. [<SEND[1]; prob. infl. in meaning by ASCEND]

sen·dal (sen′dəl) *n.* **1** A light, thin, silken fabric much used for dresses, etc., in the Middle Ages. **2** An article made of it. Also spelled *sandal.* [<OF *cendal, sendal,* ult. <Gk. *sidōn* fine linen]

send-off (send′ôf′, -of′) *n.* **1** The act of sending off; a start. **2** A farewell dinner or other celebration or demonstration at parting. **3** Encouragement, as in starting a career.

send-up (send′up′) *n. Brit. Slang* A parody; take-off.

Sen·e·ca (sen′ə·kə) *n.* One of a tribe of North American Indians of Iroquoian stock formerly inhabiting western New York, the largest tribe of the confederation known as the Five Nations: still numerous in New York and

Ontario. [<Du. *Sennacaas* the Five Nations <Algonquian (Mohegan) *A'sinnika*, trans. of Iroquoian *Oneñiute*, short for *oneñiute' roñ non* Oneida, lit., people of the standing rock]

sen·e·ga (sen'ə-gə) *n.* **1** The dried root of an herb (*Polygala senega*) of the milkwort family, used as a stimulating expectorant, as in treating bronchitis. **2** The plant itself. Also **senega root.** [<NL, alter. of SENECA; so called because thought, by the Seneca Indians, to be good for snakebites]

Sen·e·gal (sen'ə-gôl'), **Republic of** An independent republic of the French Community in west Africa; 76,124 square miles; capital, Dakar: formerly a French overseas territory. — **Sen'e·ga·lese'** (-gə·lēz', -lēs') *adj. & n.*

se·nes·cent (si·nes'ənt) *adj.* **1** Growing old. **2** Characteristic of old age. [<L *senescens, -entis,* ppr. of *senescere* grow old <*senex* old] — **se·nes'cence** *n.*

sen·e·schal (sen'ə-shəl) *n.* **1** An official in the household of a medieval prince or noble who had charge of feasts, etc.; a steward or majordomo. **2** A magistrate or governor. **3** *Brit.* A cathedral official. [<OF <Gmc. Cf. OHG *siniskalk* old servant.]

se·nile (sē'nīl, -nil) *adj.* **1** Pertaining to, proceeding from, or characteristic of old age. **2** Infirm; weak; doting. **3** *Geog.* Almost worn away to base level: a *senile* continent. [<L *senilis*< *senex* old] — **se'nile·ly** *adv.*

senile dementia *Psychiatry* The progressive deterioration of cerebral functions and mental faculties associated with old age. Also **senile psychosis.**

sen·ior (sēn'yər) *adj.* **1** Older in years; elder; especially, after personal names (usually in the abbreviated form *Sr.*), to denote the elder of two related persons of the same name, especially a father and his son. **2** Older in office; more advanced in service; superior in rank or dignity. **3** Pertaining to the closing year of a high school or college course. — *n.* **1** One older in years or office, or more advanced in rank or dignity than another. **2** Hence, any elderly person. **3** A member of a senior class. **4** A graduate or one of the older fellows of an English college. [<L, compar. of *senex, senis* old]

senior citizen An elderly person, especially one of or over the age of retirement.

sen·ior·i·ty (sēn·yôr'ə·tē, -yor'-) *n.* *pl.* **·ties 1** The state of being older in years or in office; priority of age, service, or rank. **2** An assembly of seniors or, in England, senior fellows of a college.

sen·na (sen'ə) *n.* **1** The dried leaflets of any one of several leguminous plants (genus *Cassia*), used medicinally for their purgative properties; especially, the Old World species *C. acutifolia* and *C. angustifolia.* **2** Any one of the plants yielding true senna or a similar product. [<NL *senna, sena* <Arabic *sanā*]

sen·nit (sen'it) *n.* **1** Plaited cordage, of from 3 to 9 strands, used for gaskets on ships. **2** Plaited grass or straw for hatmaking. [Earlier *sinnet,* ? <SEVEN + KNIT]

se·no·pi·a (si·nō'pē·ə) *n.* An apparent restoration of normal vision in formerly myopic people who have become hypermetropic in old age. Also called *gerontopia.* [<NL <L *senex* old + Gk. *ōps, ōpos* an eye]

se·ñor (sā·nyôr') *n.* *pl.* **·ño·res** (-nyō'rās) *Spanish* A Spanish title of courtesy; a gentleman; Mr.; sir: used before a name, like *Mr.,* or alone, like *Sir.*

se·ño·ra (sā·nyō'rä) *n. Spanish* A Spanish lady; Mrs.; madam.

se·ño·ri·ta (sā'nyō·rē'tä) *n. Spanish* A young, unmarried Spanish lady; miss.

sen·sate (sen'sāt) *adj.* Perceived or appreciated by the senses: *sensate* matters: also **sen'sat·ed.** — *v.t.* **·sat·ed, ·sat·ing** To perceive by the senses. [<LL *sensatus* gifted with sense <L *sensus* sense]

sen·sa·tion (sen·sā'shən) *n.* **1** *Physiol.* **a** That aspect of consciousness resulting from the stimulation of a nerve process beginning at any point in the body and passing through the brain, especially by those stimuli affecting any of the sense organs, as hearing, taste, touch, smell, and sight. **b** The capacity to respond to such stimulation. **2** That which

produces interest or excitement; an excited condition: to cause a *sensation.* **3** A condition of mind resulting from inherent feeling; emotion. [<Med. L *sensatio, -onis* <LL *sensatus.* See SENSATE.]

Synonyms: emotion, feeling, perception, sense. *Sensation* is the mind's consciousness due to bodily response to stimuli, as heat or sound; *perception* is the cognition of some external object which causes the *sensation.* While *sensations* are connected with the body, *emotions* add the reactions of the mind. *Feeling* is a term popularly denoting what is felt, whether through the body or by the mind alone, and includes both *sensation* and *emotion.* A *sense* is an organ or faculty of *sensation* or of *perception.* See FEELING.

sen·sa·tion·al·ism (sen·sā'shən·əl·iz'əm) *n.* **1** *Philos.* The theory that all knowledge originates in sensation, or is composed of transformed sense elements, that all consciousness is modified sensation, and all mental phenomena have a sensory basis: a branch of modern empiricism. **2** The use of melodramatic methods in writing or speaking. **3** The theory that feeling is the only criterion of good. — **sen·sa'tion·al·ist** *n.* — **sen·sa'tion·al·is'tic** *adj.*

sense (sens) *n.* **1** The faculty of sensation; sense perception. **2** Any of certain agencies by or through which an individual receives impressions of the external world; popularly, one of the five senses. **3** *Physiol.* Any receptor, or group of receptors, specialized to receive and transmit stimuli, either external, as of sight, taste, smell, etc., or internal, as of hunger, thirst, sex, equilibrium, muscular and visceral movements, etc. **4** Rational perception accompanied by feeling; realization; discriminating cognition: a *sense* of wrong. **5** Normal power of mind or understanding; sound or natural judgment: The fellow has no *sense;* often in the plural: She is coming to her *senses.* **6** Signification; import; meaning. **7** Opinion, view, or judgment of the majority: The *sense* of the meeting was manifest. **8** That which commends itself to the understanding as being in accordance with reason and good judgment: to talk *sense.* **9** Capacity to perceive or appreciate: a *sense* of color. **10** *Geom.* One of two opposite directions in which a magnitude may be described or generated. **11** Direction; trend. See synonyms under FEELING, MIND. — **the five senses** The Aristotelian division of senses into sight, hearing, smell, taste, and touch: now collectively known as the **special senses.** — **sixth sense 1** Capacity for perception beyond the normal range of the senses; extrasensory perception. **2** Intuitive or premonitory knowledge, especially as affecting or affected by the senses. **3** Cenesthesia. — *v.t.* **sensed, sens·ing 1** To become aware of through the senses. **2** *Colloq.* To comprehend; understand. [<MF *sens* <L *sensus* perception <*sentire* feel]

sense·less (sens'lis) *adj.* **1** Deprived of consciousness; unconscious. **2** Incapable of feeling or perception; insensate. **3** Devoid of sense; foolish; stupid. — **sense'less·ly** *adv.* — **sense'less·ness** *n.*

sense organ *Physiol.* A structure specialized to receive sense impressions, as the eye, nose, ear, etc.; a receptor (def. 2).

sen·si·bil·i·ty (sen'sə·bil'ə·tē) *n.* *pl.* **·ties 1** The capability of sensation; power to perceive or feel. **2** The capacity of sensation and rational emotion, as distinguished from intellect and will. **3** Susceptibility or sensitiveness to outside influences or mental impressions; sometimes, abnormal sensitiveness: often in the plural. **4** Appreciation accompanying mental apprehension; discerning judgment. **5** Delicacy or sensitiveness of an instrument. **6** Responsiveness to pathos or to artistic or esthetic values. **7** *Archaic* Sentimentality.

Synonyms: sensitiveness, sensibility, susceptibility. In popular use *sensibility* denotes sometimes capacity of feeling of any kind; as, *sensibility* to heat or cold; sometimes, a peculiar readiness to be the subject of feeling, especially of the higher feelings: as the *sensibility* of the artist or the poet. *Sensitiveness* denotes an especial delicacy of *sensibility,*

ready to be excited by the slightest cause, as displayed, for instance, in the sensitive plant. *Susceptibility* is rather a capacity to receive, to contain feeling, so that a person of great *susceptibility* is capable of being readily and deeply moved; *sensitiveness* is more superficial, *susceptibility* more pervading. In physics, the *sensitiveness* of a magnetic needle is the ease with which it may be deflected, as by another magnet; its *susceptibility* is the degree to which it can be magnetized by a given magnetic force or the amount of magnetism it will hold. A person of great *sensitiveness* is quickly and keenly affected by any external influence, as by music, pathos, or ridicule, while a person of great *susceptibility* is not only touched, but moved to his utmost soul. See FEELING. *Antonyms:* coldness, deadness, hardness, insensibility, numbness, unconsciousness.

sen·si·ble (sen'sə·bəl) *adj.* **1** Possessed of good mental perception; exhibiting sound sense and judgment; discreet; judicious. **2** Capable of physical sensation; sensitive: *sensible* to pain. **3** Perceptible or appreciable through the senses: *sensible* heat. **4** Emotionally or mentally sensitive. **5** Having a perception or cognition; fully aware; persuaded. **6** Great enough to be perceived; appreciable. **7** *Obs.* Sensitive to minute changes. See synonyms under CONSCIOUS, EXPEDIENT, INTELLIGENT, PHYSICAL, SAGACIOUS. — *n.* **1** A substance capable of being felt or observed. **2** A sentient being. **3** *Music* The leading note; the seventh of a scale: also **sensible note** (or **tone**). [<OF <L *sensibilis* <*sensus,* pp. of *sentire* feel, perceive] — **sen'si·ble·ness** *n.* — **sen'si·bly** *adv.*

sen·si·tive (sen'sə·tiv) *adj.* **1** Easily affected by outside operations or influences; excitable or impressible; touchy; easily offended. **2** *Chem. & Phot.* Reacting readily to the proper agents or forces: paper *sensitive* to light. **3** Pertaining to or depending on the senses or sensation: *sensitive* motions. **4** Closing or moving when touched or irritated, as certain plants. **5** Liable to fluctuation. **6** *Obs.* Wise; sensible. **7** Capable of indicating minute changes or differences; delicate. See synonyms under FINE, MOBILE. [<OF *sensitif* <Med. L *sensitivus* <L *sensus.* See SENSIBLE.] — **sen'si·tive·ly** *adv.* — **sen'si·tive·ness** *n.*

sensitive plant A shrubby tropical herb (*Mimosa pudica*), whose leaves close at a touch: often cultivated in hothouses.

sen·si·tiv·i·ty (sen'sə·tiv'ə·tē) *n.* **1** The state or degree of being sensitive; sensitiveness. **2** *Physiol.* The degree of acuteness with which sensations are discriminated; irritability, as of organs: distinguished from *sensibility,* in which the mental side is more prominent. **3** The degree of responsiveness to an electric current or to radio waves. **4** *Phot.* Sensitiveness to light.

sen·si·tize (sen'sə·tīz) *v.t.* **·tized, ·tiz·ing 1** To render sensitive. **2** *Phot.* To make sensitive to light, as a plate or film. **3** *Med.* To make susceptible or hypersensitive to the action of a drug by repeated injections. [<SENSIT(IVE) + -IZE] — **sen'si·ti·za'tion** *n.* — **sen'si·tiz'er** *n.*

sen·si·tom·e·ter (sen'sə·tom'ə·tər) *n.* An apparatus by which the sensitiveness to light of a photographic film or body tissue may be tested or measured. [<SENSIT(IVE) + -(O)METER]

sen·sor (sen'sər) *adj.* Sensory: applied to nerves and nerve organs. [Short for SENSORY]

sen·so·ri·mo·tor (sen'sə·ri·mō'tər) *adj. Physiol.* Of or pertaining to muscular and nervous responses induced by sensory stimuli. Compare IDEOMOTOR. [<SENSORY + MOTOR]

sen·so·ry (sen'sər·ē) *adj.* **1** Pertaining to the sensorium or to sensation. **2** Conveying or producing sense impulses. Also **sen·so·ri·al** (sen·sôr'ē·əl, -sō'rē-). [<LL *sensorium* SENSORIUM]

sen·su·al (sen'shōō·əl) *adj.* **1** Unduly indulgent to the appetites or sexual pleasure; exhibiting a predominance of the animal nature; lewd. **2** Pertaining to the body or the physical senses; also, fleshly; carnal: opposed to *spiritual.* **3** Pertaining to sensualism: usually opprobrious. See synonyms under BRUTISH. [<MF *sensuel* <LL *sensualis* <L *sensus* SENSE] — **sen'su·al·ly** *adv.*

sen·su·al·i·ty (sen'shoo·al'ə·tē) *n.* **1** The state of being sensual, or sensual acts collectively. **2** Sensual or animal indulgence. Also **sen'su·al·ness.**

sen·su·al·ize (sen'shoo·əl·īz') *v.t.* **·ized, ·iz·ing** To make sensual. Also *Brit.* **sen'su·al·ise'.** — **sen'su·al·i·za'tion** *n.*

sen·su·ous (sen'shoo·əs) *adj.* **1** Pertaining or appealing to or derived from the senses: used in a higher and purer sense than *sensual.* **2** Keenly appreciative of and aroused by beauty, refinement, or luxury. **3** Resembling imagery that appeals to the senses: a *sensuous* portrayal. [<L *sensus* SENSE + -OUS] — **sen'su·ous·ly** *adv.* — **sen'su·ous·ness** *n.*

sent (sent) Past tense and past participle of SEND.

sen·tence (sen'təns) *n.* **1** *Gram.* A word or a related group of words expressing a complete thought, whether a statement of fact (declarative), a question (interrogative), a command (imperative), or an exclamation (exclamatory). Declarative and interrogative sentences usually contain a subject (that which is spoken of) and a predicate (what is said about the subject), but either or both of these elements may be missing in an utterance that, nevertheless, conveys full meaning, as in "Where is John?" "At home." or "Look!" — **simple sentence** A sentence consisting of one independent clause, as *The dog barked.* Its subject and predicate may be simple (having one substantive or one verb) or compound (having two or more substantives or verbs), and there may be modifying words and phrases. — **compound sentence** A sentence consisting of more than one independent clause, as *The sun shone and the birds sang.* — **complex sentence.** A sentence consisting of a principal clause and one or more subordinate clauses, as *After I have read it, I shall give the book to you.* **2** *Law* A final judgment; penalty pronounced upon a person convicted. **3** A determination; opinion, especially as expressed formally. **4** An instructive saying; a maxim. **5** *Music* A complete idea or period, usually consisting of several phrases, as the half of a four-line hymn tune or song. — *v.t.* **·tenced, ·tenc·ing** To pass sentence upon; condemn to punishment. See synonyms under CONDEMN. [<OF <L *sententia* an opinion < *sentire* feel, be of opinion] — **sen·ten·tial** (sen·ten'shəl) *adj.*

sen·ten·tious (sen·ten'shəs) *adj.* **1** Abounding in or giving terse expression to thought; axiomatic; sometimes, opprobriously, pompously formal, or moralizing. **2** Habitually using terse, laconic, or aphoristic language. See synonyms under TERSE. [<L *sententiosus* < *sententia* a maxim. See SENTENCE.] — **sen·ten'tious·ly** *adv.* — **sen·ten'tious·ness, sen·ten·ti·os·i·ty** (sen·ten'shē·os'ə·tē) *n.*

sen·ti·ence (sen'shē·əns, -shəns) *n.* **1** The state of being sentient. **2** Capacity for sensation or sense perception. **3** Consciousness. **4** Sensation regarded as immediate experience and so distinguished from thought or perception. Also **sen'ti·en·cy.**

sen·ti·ent (sen'shē·ənt, -shənt) *adj.* Possessing powers of sense or sense perception; having or actually experiencing sensation or feeling; opposed to *inanimate* and *vegetal.* — *n.* One capable of sensation or perception; loosely, the mind, as the seat of consciousness. [<L *sentiens, -entis,* ppr. of *sentire* feel] — **sen'ti·ent·ly** *adv.*

sen·ti·ment (sen'tə·mənt) *n.* **1** Noble, tender, or artistic feeling, or susceptibility to such feeling; sensibility; also, its verbal expression. **2** A mental attitude or response to a person, object, or idea conditioned entirely by feeling instead of reason; loosely, an exaggerated emotional reaction. **3** Idealistic, personal, or esthetic reaction as distinguished from intellectual or practical. **4** An opinion or judgment; thought as distinguished from its expression: often in the plural. **5** An expressive thought or idea dressed in appropriate language, as a toast aptly uttered. See synonyms under FEELING, IDEA. [<OF *sentement* <Med. L *sentimentum* <L *sentire* feel]

sen·ti·men·tal (sen'tə·men'təl) *adj.* **1** Characterized by sentiment or intellectual emotion; involving or exciting tender emotions or aspirations. **2** Experiencing, displaying, or given to sentiment, often in an extravagant or mawkish manner: a *sentimental* person.

See synonyms under ROMANTIC. — **sen'ti·men'tal·ly** *adv.*

sen·ti·nel (sen'tə·nəl) *n.* A sentry; hence, any watcher or guard. — *v.t.* **·neled** or **·nelled, ·nel·ing** or **·nel·ling** **1** To watch over as a sentinel. **2** To protect or furnish with sentinels. **3** To station or appoint as a sentinel. [<OF *sentinelle* <Ital. *sentinella* <LL *sentinare* avoid danger < *sentire* perceive]

sen·try (sen'trē) *n. pl.* **·tries** **1** A soldier placed on guard to see that only authorized persons pass his post and to give warning of approaching danger; a sentinel. **2** The watch or guard kept by a sentry. [? Short for obs. *centrenel,* var. of SENTINEL]

sentry box A small shelter or cabin to protect a sentry from the weather.

Se·oul (sā·ōōl', sōl; *Korean* syœ·ōōl) The capital of the Republic of Korea (South Korea): also *Kyongsong: Japanese Keijo.*

se·pal (sē'pəl) *n. Bot.* One of the individual leaves of a calyx. [<F *sépale* <NL *sepalum* <L *sep(aratus)* separate + *(pet)alum* a petal] — **sep·a·line** (sep'ə·lin, -līn), **sep'a·lous** *adj.*

sep·a·ra·ble (sep'ər·ə·bəl, sep'rə-) *adj.* Capable of being separated or divided. [<L *separabilis* < *separare* separate] — **sep'a·ra·bil'i·ty, sep'a·ra·ble·ness** *n.* — **sep'a·ra·bly** *adv.*

sep·a·rate (sep'ə·rāt) *v.* **·rat·ed, ·rat·ing** *v.t.* **1** To set asunder; disunite or disjoin; sever. **2** To occupy a position between; serve to keep apart: The Hudson River *separates* New York from New Jersey. **3** To divide into components, parts, etc. **4** To isolate or obtain from a compound, mixture, etc.: to *separate* the wheat from the chaff. **5** To consider separately; distinguish between. **6** *Law* To part by separation. — *v.i.* **7** To become divided or disconnected; draw apart. **8** To part company; withdraw from association or combination. — *adj.* (sep'ər·it, sep'rit) **1** Existing or considered apart from others; distinct; individual: *separate* rooms. **2** Disembodied; disunited from the body. **3** Separated; disjoined. — *n.* **1** An offprint. **2** *pl.* Garments to be worn in various combinations, as skirts and blouses. See synonyms under PARTICULAR. [<L *separatus,* pp. of *separare* < *se-* apart + *parare* prepare] — **sep'a·rate·ly** *adv.* — **sep'a·rate·ness** *n.*

Synonyms (verb): alienate, detach, disconnect, disengage, disjoin, dissever, disunite, divide, part, remove, sever, split, sunder, withdraw. *Antonyms:* see synonyms for MIX.

separate school *Canadian* A private school; specifically, a Roman Catholic parochial school.

sep·a·ra·tion (sep'ə·rā'shən) *n.* **1** The act or process of separating; division. **2** The state of being disconnected or apart. **3** A dividing line. **4** *Law* Relinquishment of cohabitation between husband and wife by mutual consent: distinguished from *divorce.* See synonyms under SECLUSION.

sep·a·ra·tist (sep'ər·ə·tist, sep'rə-) *n.* One who advocates or upholds separation; specifically, a seceder; dissenter. Also **sep'a·ra'tion·ist.** — **sep'a·ra·tism** *n.*

sep·a·ra·tor (sep'ə·rā'tər) *n.* **1** Any device, implement, or apparatus for dividing or separating things into their component parts. **2** A machine for separating the chaff from grain. **3** A centrifugal mechanism for separating cream from milk. **4** One who separates.

sep·a·ra·tum (sep'ə·rā'təm) *n. pl.* **·ta** (-tə) A paper published separately from a series to which it belongs; a reprint of an article previously published as a part of a report.

Se·phar·dim (si·fär'dim) *n. pl.* The Spanish and Portuguese Jews or their descendants: distinguished from the *Ashkenazim.* Also **Se·phar'a·dim** (-ə·dim). [<Hebrew *sephārādhīm* <*Sephāradh,* a country mentioned in *Ob.* iii 20, identified by the rabbis with Spain, but prob. orig. in Asia Minor] — **Se·phar'dic, Se·phar'a·dic** *adj.*

se·pi·a (sē'pē·ə) *n.* **1** A reddish-brown pigment prepared from the ink of the cuttlefish; the color of this pigment. **2** A picture done in this pigment. **3** The ink of the cuttlefish. **4** Any of a genus (*Sepia*) of decapod mollusks having an internal shell, especially the common Atlantic cuttlefish (*S. officinalis*). — *adj.* Executed in or colored like sepia; dark-brown with a tinge of red. [<L <Gk. *sēpia* a cuttlefish]

se·pi·o·lite (sē'pē·ə·līt') *n.* Meerschaum. [<G *sepiolith* <NL *sepium* cuttlebone (<Gk. *sēpion,* dim. of *sēpia* a cuttlefish) + Gk. *lithos* a stone]

se·poy (sē'poi) *n.* A native Indian soldier outfitted and trained in European style; especially, one employed in the former British Indian Army. [<Pg. *sipae* <Urdu *sipāhī* a soldier <Persian < *sipāh* an army]

sep·pu·ku (sep'poo·koo, n.) *Japanese* Hara-kiri.

sep·sis (sep'sis) *n. Pathol.* **1** Poisonous putrefaction. **2** Infection of the blood by putrescent material containing pathogenic microorganisms. [<NL <Gk. *sēpsis* < *sēpein* make putrid]

sep·tan·gle (sep'tang'gəl) *n.* A heptagon. [<LL *septangulus* < *septem* seven + *angulus* an angle] — **sep·tan·gu·lar** (sep·tang'gyə·lər) *adj.*

sep·tar·i·um (sep·târ'ē·əm) *n. pl.* **·tar·i·a** (-târ'ē·ə) *Geol.* A rock nodule or concretion, usually several feet in diameter and roughly spherical, having a compact crust and an internal mass broken up by angular radiating or intersecting cracks usually filled with a foreign mineral: also called *turtlestone.* [<NL <L *septum* an enclosure, wall] — **sep·tar'i·an** *adj.*

sep·tate (sep'tāt) *adj.* Divided by or provided with a partition or partitions; having a septum or septa. [<NL *septatus* <LL, surrounded <L *septum* an enclosure, wall]

sep·tec·to·my (sep·tek'tə·mē) *n. Surg.* Excision of a part of the nasal septum. [<SEPT-² + -ECTOMY]

Sep·tem·ber (sep·tem'bər) The ninth month of the year, containing 30 days; the seventh month in the old Roman calendar. — **massacre of September** The massacre in Paris in September, 1792, when 10,000 persons were put to death in prison by order of Danton: also **September massacre** or **massacres.** [<L *septem* seven]

Sep·tem·brist (sep·tem'brist) *n.* A member of the Parisian mob that massacred political prisoners in the massacre of September 2 to 6, 1792; hence, a cruel and bloodthirsty person; a butcher; murderer.

sep·te·nar·y (sep'tə·ner'ē) *adj.* **1** Consisting of, pertaining to, or being seven. **2** Septennial. **3** Septuple. — *n. pl.* **·nar·ies** **1** The number seven; heptad. **2** A group of seven things of any kind; anything that has some definite relation to the number seven. **3** A verse containing seven feet. Also **sep'te·nar'i·us** (sep'tə·nâr'ē·əs). [<L *septenarius* < *septeni* seven each < *septem* seven]

sep·te·nate (sep'tə·nāt) *adj.* Having seven parts, or the parts in sevens. [<L *septeni* seven each (< *septem* seven) + -ATE¹]

sep·ten·ni·al (sep·ten'ē·əl) *adj.* **1** Recurring every seven years. **2** Continuing or capable of lasting seven years. [<L *septennium* a period of seven years < *septem* seven + *annus* a year] — **sep·ten'ni·al·ly** *adv.*

sep·ten·tri·on (sep·ten'trē·on) *adj.* Of, pertaining to, or coming from the north; boreal. — *n.* The north; northern regions. [<L *septentrionalis* < *septentrio* SEPTENTRIO] — **sep·ten'tri·o·nal** (-trē·ə·nəl) *adj.*

sep·tet (sep·tet') *n.* **1** A group of seven singers, players, or other persons, things, or parts. **2** *Music* A composition for seven voices or instruments. Also **sep·tette'.** [<G <L *septem* seven]

septi-¹ *combining form* Seven: *septilateral.* Also, before vowels, *sept-.* [<L *septem* seven]

septi-² *combining form* **1** A partition; fence: *septicidal.* **2** *Med.* The nasal septum: *septectomy.* Also, before vowels, *sept-.* Also *septo-.* [<L *septum* an enclosure, wall]

sep·tic (sep'tik) *adj.* **1** Of, pertaining to, or caused by sepsis. **2** Productive of putrefaction; putrid. Also **sep'ti·cal.** — *n.* Any substance that produces or promotes putrefaction. [<LL *septicus* <Gk. *sēptikos* < *sēpein* putrefy]

sep·ti·ce·mi·a (sep'tə·sē'mē·ə) *n. Pathol.* A morbid condition of the blood due to infection by pathogenic micro-organisms; blood poisoning: also called *septemia.* Also **sep'ti·cae'mi·a.** [<NL <Gk. *sēptikos* putrefactive + *haima* blood] — **sep'ti·ce'mic** (-sē'mik) *adj.*

sep·ti·ci·dal (sep'tə·sīd'l) *adj. Bot.* Dividing at the partitions: said of the dehiscence of a plant capsule that resolves itself at maturity into its component carpels by splitting through the septa. Also **sep′ti·cide**. [< SEPTI-[2] + L *caedere* cut] — **sep′ti·ci′dal·ly** *adv.*

septic tank A tank in which sewage is allowed to remain until purified by the action of anaerobic bacteria.

sep·tif·ra·gal (sep·tif′rə-gəl) *adj. Bot.* Breaking away from the partitions: said of a form of dehiscence in plants. [< SEPTI-[2] + L *frangere* break]

sep·ti·lat·er·al (sep′tə-lat′ər-əl) *adj.* Seven-sided. [< SETPI-[1] + LATERAL]

sep·til·lion (sep·til′yən) *n.* A cardinal number: in the French system and in the United States, 1 followed by 24 ciphers; in the English system, 1 followed by 42 ciphers. — *adj.* Numbering a septillion. [< F *septillion* < *sept(em)* + F *(m)illion* a million] — **sep·til′·lionth** *adj. & n.*

sep·time (sep′tēm) *n.* The seventh position of a swordsman in fencing. [< L *septimus* seventh < *septem* seven]

sep·tu·a·ge·nar·i·an (sep′chōō-ə-jə-nâr′ē-ən, sep′tōō-) *n.* A person 70 years old, or between 70 and 80. [< L *septuagenarius* < *septuaginta* seventy]

Sep·tu·a·ges·i·ma (sep′chōō-ə-jes′ə-mə, sep′tōō-) *n.* A period of 70 days. [< L *septuagesima (dies)* the seventieth (day), fem. of *septuagesimus* seventieth < *septuaginta* seventy] — **sep′tu·a·ges′i·mal** *adj.*

Sep·tu·a·gint (sep′chōō-ə-jint′, sep′tōō-) *n.* An old Greek version of the Old Testament Scriptures, made in Alexandria between 280 and 130 B.C. It is the version used by the Greek Church. [< L *septuaginta* seventy; from a tradition that it was produced for Ptolemy II in 70 days by a group of 72 scholars] — **Sep′·tu·a·gin′tal** *adj.*

sep·tum (sep′təm) *n. pl.* **·ta** (-tə) *Biol.* **1** A dividing wall between two cavities: the nasal *septum.* **2** A partition, as in coral or in a spore. [< L *sepere* enclose < *sepes* a hedge] — **sep′tal** *adj.*

sep·tu·ple (sep′tōō-pəl, -tyōō-, sep·tōō′-, -tyōō′-) *adj.* **1** Consisting of seven; sevenfold. **2** Multiplied by seven; seven times repeated. — *v.t. & v.i.* **·pled, ·pling** To multiply by seven; make or become septuple. — *n.* A number or sum seven times as great as another. [< L *septuplus* < *septem* seven]

sep·ul·cher (sep′əl-kər) *n.* **1** A burial place, especially one found or made in a rock or solidly built of stone; tomb; vault. **2** A receptacle for relics, especially in an altar slab; a box or urn in a chapel to receive the Holy Sacrament: also called the *repository.* — **the Holy Sepulcher** The rock-hewn tomb in which the body of Jesus was buried. — *v.t.* **·chered** or **·chred, ·cher·ing** or **·chring** To place in a grave; entomb; bury. Also **sep′ul·chre** (-kər) [< OF *sepulcre* < L *sepulcrum* a burial place, tomb < *sepultus*, pp. of *sepelire* bury]

se·pul·chral (si·pul′krəl) *adj.* **1** Pertaining to a sepulcher. **2** Suggestive of burial or the grave; dismal in color or aspect, or unnaturally low or hollow in tone; gloomy: a *sepulchral* color, a *sepulchral* voice. — **se·pul′chral·ly** *adv.*

sep·ul·ture (sep′əl-chər) *n.* **1** The act of entombing; burial. **2** A sepulcher. [< OF < L *sepultura* burial < *sepultus*. See SEPULCHER.]

se·qua·cious (si·kwā′shəs) *adj.* **1** Disposed to follow; following; attendant. **2** Logically consecutive. **3** Ductile; pliable. [< L *sequax. -acis* following, pursuing < *sequi* attend, follow] — **se·qua′cious·ly** *adv.* — **se·quac·i·ty** (si·kwas′ə·tē) *r.*

se·quel (sē′kwəl) *n.* **1** Something which follows and serves as a continuation; a development from what went before. **2** A narrative discourse which, though entire in itself, develops from a preceding one. **3** A consequence; upshot; result. [< OF *sequelle* < L *sequela* < *sequi* follow]

se·que·la (si·kwē′lə) *n. pl.* **·lae** (-lē) **1** One who or that which follows. **2** *Pathol.* A morbid condition resulting from a preceding disease. [< L, a sequel]

se·quence (sē′kwəns) *n.* **1** The process or fact of following in space, time, or thought; succession or order: also **se′quen·cy.** **2** Order of succession; arrangement. **3** A number of things following one another, considered collectively; a series. **4** An effect or conse-

quence. **5** *Music* A regular succession of similar melodic phrases at different pitches. **6** *Eccl.* In the Eucharistic liturgy, a prose or hymn sung immediately after the gradual and before the gospel. **7** In card games, a set of three or more cards next each other in value; in poker, a straight. **8** A section of motion-picture film presenting a single episode, without time lapses or interruptions. **9** *Math.* An ordered succession of quantities, as $2x$, $4x^2$, $8x^3$, $16x^4$ . . . $2^n x^n$, a finite sequence, and x_1, x_2, x_3, . . . , x_n, . . . , or x_n, an infinite sequence. See synonyms under TIME. [< MF *séquence* < L *sequentia* < *sequens, -entis*, ppr. of *sequi* follow]

se·quen·tial (si-kwen′shəl) *adj.* **1** Characterized by or forming a sequence, as of parts. **2** Sequent. — **se·quen·ti·al·i·ty** (si-kwen′shē·al′ə·tē) *n.* — **se·quen′tial·ly** *adv.*

se·ques·ter (si-kwes′tər) *v.t.* **1** To place apart; separate; segregate. **2** To seclude; withdraw: often used reflexively. **3** *Law* To take (property) into custody until a controversy, claim, etc., is settled or satisfied. **4** In international law, to confiscate and control (enemy property) by preemption. [< OF *sequestrer* < LL *sequestrare* remove, lay aside < *sequester* a trustee] — **se·ques′tra·ble** *adj.*

se·ques·tered (si-kwes′tərd) *adj.* Retired; secluded.

se·ques·trate (si-kwes′trāt) *v.t.* **·trat·ed, ·trat·ing** **1** To seize, especially for the use of the government; confiscate. **2** To take possession of for a time, with a view to its final settlement of the claims of creditors. **3** To seclude; sequester. [< LL *sequestratus*, pp. of *sequestrare.* See SEQUESTER.] — **se·ques·tra·tion** (sē′kwes·trā′shən, sek′wəs-) *n.* — **se·ques·tra·tor** (sē′kwes·trā′tər, si·kwes′trā·tər) *n.*

se·ques·trum (si-kwes′trəm) *n. pl.* **·tra** (-trə) *Pathol.* A piece of dead bone remaining in its place, but separated from the living bone. [< NL < L, something separated, orig. neut. of *sequester* standing apart]

se·quin (sē′kwin) *n.* **1** An obsolete gold coin of the Venetian republic later introduced into Turkey: also spelled *zecchino.* **2** A spangle or coinlike ornament sewn on clothing. [< F < Ital. *zecchino* < *zecca* the mint < Arabic *sikka* a coining-die]

se·quoi·a (si-kwoi′ə) *n.* One of a genus (*Sequoia*) of gigantic trees (family *Taxodiaceae*) of the western United States, including only two species, the redwood (*S. sempervirens*) and the mammoth or "big" tree (*S. gigantea* or *Sequoiadendron giganteum*), both natives of California. [< NL, after *Sikwayi*, 1770?–1843, a half-breed Cherokee Indian who invented the Cherokee alphabet]

ser– Var. of SERO–.

se·ra (sir′ə) Plural of SERUM.

sé·rac (sā·ràk′) *n. Geol.* One of the largest angular blocks or tower-shaped forms into which glacier ice breaks in passing down steep inclines. [< dial. F (Swiss), a cheese put up in cubic form; from its resemblance to the shape of this cheese]

ser·a·file (ser′ə·fīl) See SERREFILE.

se·ra·glio (si·ral′yō, -räl′-) *n.* **1** A harem. **2** Loosely, a place of debauchery. **3** The old palace of the sultans at Constantinople with its mosques, official buildings, and gardens. **4** Hence, any residence of a sultan. Also **se·rail** (se·rāl′). [< Ital. *serraglio* an enclosure, ult. < LL *serrare*, var. of L *serare* lock up < *sera* lock; used to render Turkish *serai* a palace, lodging, because of similarity of sound]

se·ra·i (se·rä′ē) *n.* **1** In the Orient, an inn or caravansary. **2** A Turkish palace. [< Turkish < Persian *sarāi*]

se·ra·pe (se·rä′pē) *n.* A shawl or blanketlike outer garment worn in Latin America, especially in Mexico: also spelled *zarape.* [< Sp.]

ser·aph (ser′əf) *n. pl.* **ser·aphs** or **ser·a·phim** (ser′ə·fim) A celestial being; an angel of the highest order. *Is.* vi 2–6. [Back formation from *Seraphim*, pl. < LL < Hebrew *serāphim*, ? ult. < *sāraph* burn] — **se·raph·ic** (si·raf′ik) **se·raph′i·cal** *adj.* — **se·raph′i·cal·ly** *adv.*

ser·a·phim (ser′ə·fim) *n.* **1** Plural of SERAPH: also **ser·a·phin** (-fin). **2** *pl.* **·phims** A seraph, as in *Isaiah* vi 2, 6: an erroneous usage.

ser·a·phine (ser′ə·fēn) *n.* A coarse-toned musi-

cal instrument, a kind of harmonium, played with a keyboard. Also **se·ra·phi·na** (ser′ə·fē′nə). [< SERAPH + -INE[1]]

Ser·bi·a A republic founded from Yugolavia; capital, Belgrade; Formerly an independent kingdom. *Serbo-Croatian* **Sr•bi•ja** - *adj. & n.* **Serb, Ser′bi·an.**

ser·dab (sûr′dab, sûr·däb′) *n.* A secret cell within the masonry of an ancient Egyptian tomb, in which images of the deceased were deposited. [< Arabic *serdāb* a cellar < Persian, an icehouse, a grotto]

sere[1] (sir) See SEAR[1].

sere[2] (sir) *n. Ecol.* The series of changes found in a given plant formation from the initial to the ultimate stage. ◆ Homophones: *cere, sear.* [Back formation < SERIES] — **ser′al** *adj.*

se·rein (sə·ran′) *n. Meteorol.* A fine rain that falls sometimes from an apparently clear sky, especially in the tropics after sunset. [< F]

ser·e·nade (ser′ə·nād′) *n.* **1** An evening song, usually that of a lover beneath his lady's window; also, by extension, music performed in honor of some person in front of his residence in the open air at night. **2** The music for such a song. — *v.t. & v.i.* **·nad·ed, ·nad·ing** To entertain with a serenade. [< F *sérénade* < Ital. *serenata* < *sereno* serene, open air < L *serenus* clear, serene; infl. in meaning by L *sera (hora)* the evening (hour), fem. of *serus* late] — **ser′·e·nad′er** *n.*

ser·e·na·ta (ser′ə·nä′tə) *n. Music* **1** A dramatic cantata, often composed as a complimentary offering for a royal personage. **2** A serenade. [< Ital. See SERENADE.]

ser·en·dip·i·ty (ser′ən·dip′ə·tē) *n.* The faculty of happening upon or making fortunate discoveries when not in search of them. [Coined by Horace Walpole (1754), in *The Three Princes of Serendip* (Ceylon), the heroes of which make such discoveries]

se·rene (si·rēn′) *adj.* **1** Clear, or fair and calm; having its brightness undimmed: a *serene* sky. **2** Marked by peaceful repose; tranquil; unruffled; placid: a *serene* spirit. **3** Of exalted rank: chiefly in the titles of certain continental European princes: His *Serene* Highness. See synonyms under SEDATE. — *n. Rare or Poetic* **1** Clearness, or a serene or clear region. **2** Calmness; placidity. [< L *serenus*] — **se·rene′ly** *adv.* — **se·ren·i·ty** (si·ren′ə·tē), **se·rene′ness** *n.*

serf (sûrf) *n.* **1** A person who is attached to the estate on which he lives; loosely, a peasant. **2** Figuratively, one in servile subjection. ◆ Homophone: *surf.* [< OF < L *servus* a slave] — **serf′dom, serf′age, serf′hood** *n.*

serge (sûrj) *n.* **1** A strong twilled fabric made of wool yarns and characterized by a diagonal rib on both sides of the cloth. **2** In the Middle Ages, a coarse woolen cloth. **3** A rayon lining fabric. ◆ Homophone: *surge.* [< OF *sarge, serge* < L *serica (lana)* (wool) of the Seres < *Seres* the Seres, an eastern Asian people]

ser·geant (sär′jənt) *n.* **1** A non-commissioned military officer ranking next above a corporal. See the table under GRADE. **2** In the United States, a police officer of rank next below a captain (sometimes lieutenant); in England, one next below an inspector. **3** *Brit.* Formerly, one who held land of the king by tenure of military service, or a squire or gentleman of less than knightly rank; one of the household officials of a sovereign. **4** *A* sergeant at arms. **5** A sergeant at law. **6** A constable or bailiff. **7** The sergeant fish. Also *serjeant.* — **color sergeant** A sergeant who standard. — **lance sergeant** A corporal acting carries the regimental or national colors or as sergeant. — **mess sergeant** A non-commissioned officer who plans meals, issues rations, and superintends the company mess under the mess officer. [< OF *sergent, serjant* < L *serviens*, ppr. of *servire* serve] — **ser′gean·cy, ser′geant·cy, ser′geant·ship** *n.*

sergeant at arms **1** An executive officer in a legislative body who enforces order; especially, *Brit.*, the attendant on the lord chancellor or on the speaker of the House of Commons. **2** The title of certain court or city officials who have ceremonial duties.

sergeant at law Formerly, a barrister of high order or rank taking social but not professional precedence of king's counsel.

sergeant fish 1 A large, dusky fish (*Rachycentron canadus*) of warm seas, with a broad black band suggesting a chevron on the sides. 2 The robalo.

sergeant major 1 In the U.S. Army, the principal enlisted assistant to the adjutant of a battalion or higher unit. 2 The highest non-commissioned officer in the U.S. Marine Corps.

se·ri·al (sir′ē-əl) *adj.* 1 Of the nature of a series. 2 Published in a series at regular intervals. 3 Successive; arranged in rows or ranks: also **se·ri·ate** (sir′ē·it, -āt). —*n.* 1 A novel or other story regularly presented in successive instalments, as in a magazine, on radio or television, or in motion pictures. 2 *Brit.* A periodical. 3 A subdivision of a military unit organized for transport or for marching. ◆ Homophone: *cereal.* [<NL *serialis* <L *series* a row, order] —**se′ri·al·ly, se′ri·ate·ly** *adv.*

serial comma A comma placed before an *and* which joins the last two in a series of three or more substantives, adjectives, phrasal modifiers, or adverbs. ◆ Opinion is evenly divided as to whether the serial comma is needed. The best argument for its use, which is observed in this dictionary, is that it makes the meaning unmistakable and the relation between the various modifiers unmistakably clear: *The motion was opposed by Lords Arundel, Salisbury, Somerset, and Say and Sele.* If the last comma (the serial comma) were omitted here, there could be confusion as to the name of the last peer, which is *Say and Sele.*

se·ri·al·ize (sir′ē·əl·īz′) *v.t.* **·ized, ·iz·ing** To arrange or publish in serial form. —**se′ri·al·i·za′tion** *n.*

serial number A number assigned to a person, object, item of merchandise, etc., as a means of identification.

serial symmetry 1 The symmetry of serial parts. 2 Metamerism. Also **serial homology.**

se·ri·a·tim (sir′ē·ā′tim, ser′ē-) *adv.* One after another; in connected order; serially. [<Med. L <L *series*, on analogy with *gradatim*]

se·ri·a·tion (sir′ē·ā′shən) *n.* The arrangement of unorganized material or data in an orderly series.

se·ri·ceous (si-rish′əs) *adj.* 1 Lustrous like silk; silky. 2 *Bot.* Having fine, soft, appressed hairs, as the leaves of certain plants. [<L *sericeus* <*sericum* silk, orig. neut. of *sericus* silken, belonging to the Seres. See SERGE.]

ser·i·cin (ser′ə·sin) *n. Biochem.* A viscous substance formed on the surface of raw silk fiber and usually removed by boiling in soapy water. [<L *sericus* silken + -IN]

ser·i·cul·ture (ser′ə·kul′chər) *n.* The raising and care of silkworms for the production of silk. [Contraction of F *sériciculture* <L *sericum* silk + *cultura* a raising, culture] —**ser′i·cul′tur·al** *adj.* —**ser′i·cul′tur·ist** *n.*

ser·i·e·ma (ser′i·ē′mə, -ā′mə) *n.* 1 A long-legged crested bird (*Cariama cristata*) of the plains of Brazil and Paraguay. 2 The smaller species, Burmeister's cariama (*Chunga burmeisteri*) of Argentina. [<NL *seriema, cariama* <Tupian *siriema, sariama* crested]

se·ries (sir′ēz) *n. pl.* **se·ries** 1 An arrangement of one thing after another; a connected succession of persons, books, objects, observations, etc., on the basis of like relationships. 2 *Math.* An ordered, finite or infinite arrangement of expressions, each a function of another, the sum of which is indicated, as

$x_1 + x_2 + x_3 \dots + x_n + \dots$, or $\sum_{i=1}^{\infty} x_i$

for infinite series, and $x_1 + x_2 + x_3 \dots + x_n$, or $\sum_{i=1}^{n} x_n$ for finite series. 3 *Chem.* A group of compounds or elements resembling one another more or less in their chemical characters and crystalline forms, or differing from each other by a constant difference of certain factors. 4 *Electr.* An arrangement of sources or utilizers of electricity, as batteries or lamps, in which the positive electrode of one is connected with the negative electrode of another. 5 *Gram.* A group of successive coordinate elements of a sentence. [<L <*serere* join, weave together]

ser·if (ser′if) *n. Printing* A hairline; a light line or stroke crossing or projecting from the end of a main line or stroke in a letter: also spelled *ceriph.* [<Du. *schreef* a stroke, line <*schrijve* write <L *scribere*]

ser·i·graph (ser′ə·graf, -gräf) *n.* 1 An artist's color print made by serigraphy. 2 A device for testing the tensile strength and elasticity of textile fabrics, paper, leather, rubber, etc., under specified conditions. [<L *sericum* silk + GRAPH]

se·rig·ra·phy (si·rig′rə·fē) *n.* An adaptation of the silk–screen process in which hand–made color prints are made on any desired surface by the use of stencils painted upon or cemented to the screen, one stencil to each color, the finished print being in all details the work of an individual artist in distinction from those commercially reproduced by silk–screen printing. —**se·rig′ra·pher** *n.* —**ser·i·graph·ic** (ser′ə·graf′ik) *adj.*

ser·in (ser′in) *n.* A small greenish finch (*Serinus canarius*), related to and closely resembling the wild canary, but smaller. [<F; ult. origin unknown]

se·rin·ga (si·ring′gə) *n.* Any of several Brazilian trees (genus *Hevea*) yielding rubber. [<Pg. <L *syringa* SYRINGA]

se·ri·o·com·ic (sir′ē·ō·kom′ik) *adj.* Mingling mirth and seriousness, or the comic with an appearance of gravity. Also **se′ri·o·com′i·cal.** [<*serio-* partly serious <SERIOUS) + COMIC]

se·ri·ous (sir′ē·əs) *adj.* 1 Grave and earnest in quality, feeling, or disposition; thoughtful; sober. 2 Said, planned, or done with full practical intent; not jesting or making a false pretense; being or done in earnest. 3 Of grave importance; weighty; attended with considerable danger or loss: a *serious* matter, a *serious* accident. 4 Particularly attentive to religion. [<MF *sérieux* <LL *seriosus* <L *serius*] —**se′ri·ous·ly** *adv.* —**se′ri·ous·ness** *n.*

— *Synonyms:* dangerous, demure, earnest, grave, great, important, momentous, sedate, sober, solemn. A *serious* person is *sedate, sober, solemn*; a *serious* purpose is *earnest*; a *serious* illness is *dangerous*; a *serious* business is *important*, and may be *momentous*. See BAD, GOOD, IMPORTANT, SEDATE. *Antonyms:* careless, gay, insignificant, jocose, jolly, light, slight, thoughtless, trifling, trivial, volatile.

ser·jeant (sär′jənt) See SERGEANT.

ser·mon (sûr′mən) *n.* 1 A discourse based on a passage or text of the Bible, delivered as part of a church service; hence, any discourse intended for the pulpit. 2 Any discourse of a serious kind; an exhortation to duty or a formal reproof. See synonyms under SPEECH. [<AF *sermun*, OF *sermon* <L *sermo, -onis* talk]

ser·mon·et (sûr′mən·et′) *n.* A brief sermon. Also **ser′mon·ette′.** [Dim. of SERMON]

sero– *combining form* Connected with or related to serum: *serology.* Also, before vowels, *ser–.* [<L *serum* whey]

se·rol·o·gy (si·rol′ə·jē) *n.* The science of serums and their actions: also called *orrhology.* [SERO- + -LOGY] —**se·ro·log·i·cal** (sir′ə·loj′i·kəl) *adj.*

se·ros·i·ty (si·ros′ə·tē) *n.* 1 The condition of being serous or watery. 2 A watery or serous secretion. Also **se′rous·ness.** [<F *sérosité* <NL *serositas* <*serosus* SEROUS]

se·ro·ther·a·py (sir′ō·ther′ə·pē) *n. Med.* The treatment of disease by injecting into the veins serum from immunized animals.

se·rot·i·nous (si·rot′ə·nəs) *adj.* Produced, blossoming, or developing relatively late in the season: used also figuratively. Also **se·rot′i·nal, se·ro·tine** (ser′ə·tin, -tīn). [<L *serotinus* <*serus* late]

se·ro·to·nin (ser′ə·tō′nin) *n. Biochem.* A crystalline protein found in the serum of clotted blood and in various animals and plants: it is associated with a wide range of physiological processes, especially in the brain and blood vessels. [<SERO- + TON- + -IN]

se·rous (sir′əs) *adj.* Pertaining to, producing, or resembling serum. [<F *séreux* <L *serosus* <*serum* serum, whey]

serous membrane *Anat.* A tissue of endothelial cells lining the large cavities of the body, as the peritoneum and the pleura.

ser·ow (ser′ō) *n.* Any of a genus (*Capricornis*) of antelopes ranging from the Himalayas to Japan; especially, the large goat antelope (*C. bubalinus*). [<Tibetan]

ser·pent (sûr′pənt) *n.* 1 A scaly, limbless reptile; a snake, especially when of large size. 2 Anything of serpentine form or appearance, as a certain kind of twisting firework. 3 An obsolete musical wind instrument, bent several times in serpentine form. 4 An insinuating and treacherous person. 5 Satan. [<OF <L *serpens, -entis* a serpent, creeping thing, orig. ppr. of *serpere* creep]

ser·pen·tine (sûr′pən·tēn, -tīn) *adj.* 1 Pertaining to or like a serpent; zigzag or sinuous; crawling sinuously. 2 Subtle; cunning. —*n.* A massive or fibrous, often mottled green or yellow, hydrous magnesium silicate, the fibrous varieties of which are important sources of asbestos, the massive as architecturally decorative stones. [<OF *serpentin* <L *serpentinus* < *serpens* SERPENT]

ser·pi·go (sər·pī′gō) *n. Pathol.* An eruption on the skin; spreading ringworm. [<Med. L *serpere* creep] —**ser·pig·i·nous** (sər·pij′ə·nəs) *adj.*

ser·ra·noid (ser′ə·noid) *adj.* Of or pertaining to the *Serranidae*, a family of fishes including the sea bass, striped bass, and their allies. —*n.* A serranoid fish. [<NL <*Serranus*, genus name (<L *serra* a saw) + Gk. *eidos* form]

ser·ra·tion (se·rā′shən) *n.* 1 The state of being edged as with saw teeth. 2 *Biol.* One of the projections of a serrate formation, or a series of such projections. Also **ser·ra·ture** (ser′ə·chər). [<NL *serratio, -onis* <L *serratus*, pp. of *serrare* saw <*serra* a saw]

ser·ried (ser′ēd) *adj.* Compacted in rows or ranks, as soldiers in company formation. [Pp. of obs. *serry* press close together in ranks <MF *serré*, pp. of *serrer.* See SERREFILE.]

ser·ru·late (ser′ə·lit, -lāt, ser′yə-) *adj.* Diminutively serrate; serrate with small, fine teeth. Also **ser′ru·lat′ed** (-lā′tid). [<L *serrula*, dim. of *serra* a saw + -ATE]

ser·tu·lar·i·an (sûr′chōō·lâr′ē·ən) *n. Zool.* One of a genus (*Sertularia*) of branching colonial hydroids common between tide lines. [<NL <L *sertula*, dim. of *serta* a garland]

se·rum (sir′əm) *n. pl.* **se·rums** or **se·ra** (sir′ə) 1 The more fluid constituent of blood, lymph, milk, and similar animal liquids. 2 The serum of the blood of an animal which has been subjected to the process of immunization; any antitoxic blood serum or lymph. 3 Whey; serum of milk. 4 Any similar secretion. [<L, whey, watery fluid]

serum sickness Illness caused by inoculation of serum.

ser·val (sûr′vəl) *n.* An African wildcat (*Felis serval*), yellow with black spots and having a ringed tail and long legs. [<F <Pg. *lobo cerval* <*lobo* a wolf (<L *lupus*) + *cerval* a stag <L *cervus*]

ser·vant (sûr′vənt) *n.* 1 A person employed to work for another; especially, in law, one employed to render service and assistance in some trade or vocation: an employee. 2 A person hired to assist in domestic matters, sometimes living within the employer's house; hired help. 3 A slave or bondman. 4 A government official. [<OF, orig. ppr. of *servir* SERVE]

serve (sûrv) *v.* **served, serv·ing** *v.t.* 1 To work for, especially as a servant; be in the service of. 2 To be of service to; wait on. 3 To promote the interests of; aid; help: to *serve* one's country. 4 To obey and give homage to: to *serve* God. 5 To satisfy the requirements of; suffice for. 6 To perform the duties connected with, as a public office. 7 To go through (a period of enlistment, term of punishment, etc.). 8 To furnish or provide, as with a regular supply. 9 To offer .or bring food or drink to (a guest, etc.); wait on at table. 10 To bring and place on the table or distribute among guests, as food or drink. 11 To operate or handle; tend: to *serve* a cannon. 12 To copulate with: said of male animals. 13 In tennis, etc., to put (the ball) in play by hitting it to one's opponent. 14 *Law* **a** To deliver (a summons or writ) to a person. **b** To deliver a summons or writ to. 15 *Naut.* To wrap (a rope, stay, etc.), as with marlin or spun yarn, so as to strengthen or protect. —*v.i.* 16 To work as or perform the functions of a servant; wait at table. 17 To perform the duties of any employment, office, etc. 18 To go through a term of service, as in the army or navy. 19 To be suitable or usable, as for a purpose; perform a function. **20** To be favorable, as weather. **21** In tennis, etc., to put the ball in play. — *n.* **1** In tennis, etc., the delivering of the ball by striking it toward an opponent. **2** The turn of the server. [<OF *servir* <L *servire* <*servus* a slave]

Synonyms: advance, aid, assist, attend, benefit, help, minister, obey, promote, subserve, succor, suffice. See ACCOMMODATE. *Antonyms:* command, control, desert, disobey, hinder, obstruct, oppose, retard, thwart, withstand.

serv·er (sûr′vər) *n.* **1** One who serves; especially, an attendant aiding a priest at low mass. **2** That which is used in serving, as a tray. **3** The male of any domestic animal used for breeding. **4** The player who serves the ball in games.

ser·vice (sûr′vis) *n.* **1** Assistance or benefit afforded another: to render a *service*; to be of *service*. **2** A useful result or product of labor which is not a tangible commodity: in the plural, often contrasted with *goods*. **3** The manner in which one is waited upon or served: The *service* in this restaurant is only fair. **4** A system of labor and material aids used to accomplish some regular work or accommodation for the public: telephone *service*, train *service*, postal *service*. **5** A division of public employment devoted to a particular function: the diplomatic *service*. **6** Employment as a public servant in government: to enter public *service*. **7** A public duty or function: jury *service*. **8** Any branch of the armed forces: to enter the *service*. **9** Military duty or assignment: to volunteer for foreign *service*. **10** Devotion to God, as demonstrated by obedience and good works. **11** A formal and public exercise of worship: to attend Sunday *services*. **12** A ritual prescribed for a particular ministration or observance: a burial *service*; a marriage *service*. **13** The music for a liturgical office or rite. **14** The state or position of a servant, especially a domestic servant. **15** A set of tableware for a specific purpose: a tea *service*. **16** Installation, maintenance, and repair of an article provided a buyer by a seller. **17** *Law* **a** The legal communication of a writ or process to a designated person. **b** Duty or work rendered by one person for another. **c** A duty rendered by a feudal tenant as recompense to his lord. **18** In tennis and similar games, the act or manner of serving a ball. **19** *Naut.* The protective cordage wrapped around a rope. **20** In animal husbandry, the copulation or covering of a female. — *adj.* **1** Pertaining to or for service. **2** Used by, or for the use of, servants or tradespeople: a *service* entrance. **3** Of, pertaining to, or belonging to a military service: a *service* flag. **4** Worn during active military service: distinguished from *dress*: a *service* cap, hat, or uniform. — *v.t.* ·**viced**, ·**vic·ing** **1** To maintain or repair: to *service* a car or radio. **2** To supply service to. [<OF *servise* <L *servitium* <*servus* a slave]

Synonyms (noun): advantage, avail, benefit, good, purpose, serviceableness, use, utility. See PROFIT, SACRAMENT, UTILITY.

ser·vice·a·ble (sûr′vis·ə·bəl) *adj.* **1** That can be made of service; beneficial; such as serves or can serve a useful purpose. **2** Capable of rendering long service; durable. **3** *Obs.* Obliging; attentive. — See synonyms under GOOD, USEFUL. — **ser′vice·a·ble·ness**, **ser′vice·a·bil′i·ty** *n.* — **ser′vice·a·bly** *adv.*

ser·vice·ber·ry (sûr′vis·ber′ē) *n.* *pl.* ·**ries** The Juneberry; the shadberry. [<*service*, the service tree + BERRY]

ser·vice·man (sûr′vis·man′) *n.* *pl.* ·**men** (-men′) A member of one of the armed forces. — **ser′·vice·wom′an** *n. fem.*

service station **1** A place for supplying automobiles with gasoline, oil, water, etc. **2** A place where adjustments and repairs can be made and parts obtained for electrical or mechanical devices.

service tree **1** An Old World tree (*Sorbus domestica*) with odd–pinnate leaves, panicled cream–colored flowers, and small edible fruit. **2** The American mountain ash (*S. americana*). **3** The Juneberry. [Orig. *serves*, pl. of obs. *serve*, OE *syrfe* <L *sorbus*]

ser·vi·ette (sûr′vē·et′, -vyet′) *n.* A table napkin. [<MF, prob. <*servir* SERVE]

ser·vile (sûr′vil) *adj.* **1** Having the spirit of a slave; slavish; abject: a *servile* flatterer. **2** Pertaining to or appropriate for slaves or servants: a *servile* insurrection, *servile* employment. **3** Being of a subject class; existing in a condition of servitude. **4** Obedient; subject: with *to*: *servile* to applause. **5** *Ling.* Not belonging to the original root; serving only to modify the construction or pronunciation of a word. **6** Designating tenures of land in England subject to conditions distinguished from those of freehold, as labor instead of rent. See synonyms under BASE, OBSEQUIOUS. — *n.* **1** A slave, or one of slavish spirit; menial. **2** *Ling.* A letter, syllable, or sound used only to modify a word, and not part of its radical form. [<L *servilis* <*servus* a slave] — **ser′vile·ly** *adv.* — **ser·vil′i·ty**, **ser′vile·ness** *n.*

serv·ing (sûr′ving) *n.* **1** A portion of food for one person. **2** The act of one who or that which serves. — *adj.* Used for dealing out food.

ser·vi·tude (sûr′və·tōōd, -tyōōd) *n.* **1** The condition of a slave; slavery; bondage; now, especially, enforced service as a punishment for crime: penal *servitude*. **2** A state of subjection to any claim, demand, or control: *servitude* to vice. **3** The condition or duties of a servant; menial service. **4** The subjection of a person to a person or to a thing, or of a thing to a person or thing. **5** *Law* An easement; a right that one man may have to use the land of another for a special purpose. See synonyms under BONDAGE. [<MF <L *servitudo* <*servus* a slave]

servo– *combining form* In technical use, auxiliary: *servomechanism*. [<L *servus* a slave]

ser·vo·mech·a·nism (sûr′vō·mek′ə·niz′əm) *n.* Any of various relay devices which can be actuated by a comparatively weak force in the automatic control of a complex machine, instrument, operation, or process, as artillery fire, the course of an airplane or ship, etc. [<SERVO– + MECHANISM]

ses·a·me (ses′ə·mē) *n.* An East Indian herb (*Sesamum indicum*), containing seeds which are used as food and as a source of the pale yellow **sesame oil**, used as an emollient. — **open sesame** A charm to secure admission, originally to the robbers' cave in the story of Ali Baba and the Forty Thieves in the *Arabian Nights*. [<F *sésame* <L *sesamum, sesama* <Gk. *sēsamon, sēsamē*, prob. <an Oriental source]

ses·a·moid (ses′ə·moid) *adj.* *Anat.* **1** Having the shape of a sesame seed; obovate; nodular: said specifically of certain bones, cartilages, and nodules. **2** Pertaining to a sesamoid. — *n.* A sesamoid bone or cartilage, as the kneecap. [<L *sesamoides* <Gk. *sēsamoeidēs* <*sēsamon* sesame + *eidos* form]

sesqui– *prefix* **1** One and a half; one–half more; one and a half times: *sesquicentennial*. **2** *Chem.* Indicating the presence of three atoms of one element and two of another in a compound, as chromium *sesquioxide*, Cr_2O_3. [<L *sesqui-* one–half more <*semis* half + *que* and]

ses·qui·cen·ten·ni·al (ses′kwi·sen·ten′ē·əl) *adj.* Of or pertaining to a century and a half. — *n.* A 150th anniversary, or its celebration.

ses·qui·pe·da·li·an (ses′kwi·pi·dā′lē·ən) *adj.* **1** Measuring a foot and a half. **2** Long and ponderous, as polysyllabic words. Also **ses·quip·e·dal** (ses·kwip′ə·dəl, ses′kwi·pēd′l). — *n.* A very long word. [<L *sesquipedalis* <*sesqui-* more by a half + *pes, pedis* a foot]

ses·qui·plane (ses′kwi·plān′) *n.* *Aeron.* A type of biplane one wing of which has half or less than half the area of the other.

ses·sile (ses′il) *adj.* **1** *Bot.* Attached by its base, without a stalk, as a leaf. **2** *Zool.* Fixed; sedentary; firmly or permanently attached. [<L *sessilis* sitting down, stunted <*sessus*, pp. of *sedere* sit] — **ses·sil′i·ty** *n.*

ses·sion (sesh′ən) *n.* **1** The sitting together of a legislative assembly, court, etc., for the transaction of business. **2** A single meeting or series of meetings of an assembly, court, or other body, for conducting business. **3** The governing body of a Presbyterian Church congregation. **4** In some educational institutions, a term. **5** *Law* The term for which a court or legislative body sits continuously for the transaction of business. **6** *pl.* The sitting of a certain court: the quarter–*sessions*; and in the United States, the Court of *Sessions*, a court of criminal jurisdiction; any one of certain courts, especially in England: general *sessions*, petty *sessions*. **7** *Obs.* The act of sitting, or the state of one who is seated. ◆ Homophone: *cession*. [<F <L *sessio, -onis* <*sessus*, pp. of *sedere* sit] — **ses′sion·al** *adj.* — **ses′sion·al·ly** *adv.*

ses·tet (ses·tet′) *n.* **1** The last six lines of a sonnet; any six–line stanza. **2** *Music* A sextet. [<Ital. *sestetto* <*sesto* sixth (<L *sextus*) + -*etto*, dim. suffix]

ses·ti·na (ses·tē′nə) *n.* A verse form consisting of six stanzas of six, generally unrimed, lines each and a three–line envoy: the end words of the first stanza are progressively changed in order in the remaining five, and appear medially and terminally in the envoy. Also **ses′tine** (-tin) [<Ital. <*sesto* sixth <L *sextus*]

set¹ (set) *v.* **set, set·ting** *v.t.* **1** To put in a certain place or position; place. **2** To put into a fixed or immovable position, condition, or state: to *set* brick; to *set* one's jaw. **3** To bring to a specified condition or state: *Set* your mind at ease; to *set* a boat adrift. **4** To restore to proper position for healing, as a broken bone. **5** To place in readiness for operation or use: to *set* a trap. **6** To adjust according to a standard: to *set* a clock. **7** To adjust (an instrument, dial, etc.) to a particular calibration or position. **8** To place knives, forks, etc., on (a table) in preparing for a meal. **9** To bend the teeth of (a saw) to either side alternately. **10** To appoint or establish; prescribe: to *set* a time or limit. **11** To fix or establish a time for: We *set* our departure for noon. **12** To assign for performance, completion, etc.; allot: to *set* a task. **13** To assign to some specific duty or function; appoint; station: to *set* a guard. **14** To cause to sit. **15** To present or perform so as to be copied or emulated: to *set* the pace; to *set* a bad example. **16** To give a specified direction to; direct: He *set* his course for the Azores. **17** To put in place so as to catch the wind: to *set* the jib. **18** To place in a mounting or frame, as a gem. **19** To stud or adorn with gems: to *set* a crown with rubies. **20** To place (a hen) on eggs to hatch them. **21** To place (eggs) under a fowl or in an incubator for hatching. **22** To place (a price or value): with *by* or *on*: to *set* a price on an outlaw's head. **23** To point (game): said of hunting dogs. **24** *Printing* **a** To arrange (type) for printing; compose. **b** To put into ·type, as a sentence, manuscript, etc. **25** *Music* To arrange (music) for words or write (words) to accompany music. **26** To describe (a scene) as taking place: to *set* the scene in Monaco. **27** In the theater, to arrange (a stage) so as to depict a scene. **28** In some games, as bridge, to defeat. — *v.i.* **29** To go or pass below the horizon, as the sun. **30** To wane; decline. **31** To sit on eggs, as fowl. **32** To become hard or firm; solidify; congeal. **33** To begin a journey; start: with *forth, out, off,* etc. **34** To have a specified direction; tend. **35** To hang or fit, as clothes. **36** To point game: said of hunting dogs. **37** *Bot.* To begin development or growth, as a rudimentary fruit. — **to set about** To start doing; begin. — **to set against** **1** To balance; compare. **2** To make unfriendly to; prejudice against. — **to set aside** **1** To place apart or to one side. **2** To reject; dismiss. **3** To declare null and void. — **to set back** To reverse; hinder. — **to set down** **1** To place on a surface. **2** To write or print; record. **3** To judge or consider. **4** To attribute; ascribe. — **to set forth** **1** To state or express. **2** To start, as a journey. — **to set in** **1** To begin. **2** To blow or flow toward shore, as wind or tide. — **to set off** **1** To put apart by itself. **2** To serve as a contrast or foil for; enhance. **3** To cause to explode. — **to set on** To incite or instigate; urge. — **to set out** **1** To present to view; display; exhibit. **2** To lay out or plan. **3** To begin a journey. **4** To begin any enterprise. **5** To plant. — **to set to** **1** To start; begin. **2** To start fighting. — **to set up** **1** To place in an upright position. **2** To raise.

3 To place in power, authority, etc. **4 a** To construct or build. **b** To put together; assemble. **c** To found; establish. **5** To provide with the means to start a new business. **6** To cause to be heard: to *set up* a cry. **7** To propose or put forward (a theory, etc.). **8** To cause. **9** *Colloq.* **a** To pay for the drinks, etc., of; treat. **b** To pay for (drinks, etc.). **10** *Colloq.* To encourage; exhilarate. — *adj.* **1** Established by authority or agreement; prescribed; appointed: a *set* time; a *set* method. **2** Customary; conventional: a *set* phrase. **3** Deliberately and systematically conceived; formal: a *set* speech. **4** Fixed and motionless; rigid. **5** Fixed in opinion or disposition; obstinate. **6** Formed; built; made: with a qualifying adverb: deep–*set* eyes; a low–*set* man. **7** Ready; prepared: to get *set*. — *n.* **1** The act or condition of setting. **2** Permanent change of form, as by chemical action, cooling, pressure, strain, etc. **3** The arrangement, tilt, or hang of a garment, hat, sail, etc. **4** Carriage or bearing: the *set* of his shoulders. **5** The sinking of a heavenly body below the horizon. **6** The direction of a current or wind. **7** A young plant ready for setting out; a cutting, slip, or seedling. **8** *Mech.* The spread in opposite directions given to the alternate teeth of certain saws. **9** *Psychol.* A temporary condition assumed by an organism preparing for a particular response or activity. **10** In tennis, a group of games completed when one side wins six games, or in the event of a score tied at five games, the group of games terminated when one side wins two more games consecutively. [OE *settan* cause to sit. Akin to SIT.]
Synonyms (verb): adapt, adjust, appoint, arrange, assign, determine, dispose, establish, fix, locate, place, plant, post, prescribe, put, regulate, settle, station. See ALLOT, PLANT, PREPARE, PUT, RAISE. *Antonyms:* detach, disestablish, disturb, eradicate, loosen, overthrow, remove, transfer, unsettle, uproot.

set² (set) *n.* **1** A number of persons regarded as associated through status, common interests, etc.: a new *set* of customers. **2** A social group having some exclusive character; coterie; clique: the fast *set*. **3** A number of things belonging together and customarily used together: a *set* of instruments; a *set* of teeth; a *set* of dishes. **4** A number of specific things so grouped as to form a whole: a *set* of lyrics; a *set* of motives; a *set* of features. **5** A group of volumes issued together and related by common authorship or subject. **6** The number of couples needed for a square dance or country dance. **7** The group of movements that compose a square dance. **8** In motion pictures, the complete assembly of properties, structures, etc., required in a scene. **9** Radio or television receiving equipment assembled for use. See synonyms under CLASS, FLOCK. [<OF *sette* <L *secta* a sect; infl. by SET¹. Doublet of SECT.]

se·ta·ceous (si-tā′shəs) *adj.* **1** Bristly; more or less covered with bristles. **2** Of the nature or form of setae. Also **se′tal** (sēt′l). [<NL *setaceus* <L *seta* a bristle]

set–back (set′bak′) *n.* **1** A check; forced return to a point already passed; a reverse in fortune or plan. **2** A countercurrent; eddy. **3** *Archit.* In mammoth buildings, the stepping back of sections in such a way that, while the first section is erected on the street line, the remaining sections are erected in step formation, so as to permit of better light and ventilation in the street below.

set–ham·mer (set′ham′ər) *n.* A hammer the head of which may be easily removed from the handle. See illustration under HAMMER.

seti– *combining form* A bristle: *setiferous.* Also, before vowels, **set–**. [<L *seta* a bristle]

set–off (set′ôf′, -of′) *n.* **1** An offset or counterpoise. **2** A decorative contrast or setting. **3** A counterclaim or the discharge of a debt by a counterclaim. **4** *Archit.* A ledge; offset.

se·ton (sē′tən) *n. Surg.* A bristle, or a few threads, passed through a fold of the skin and left there to produce an issue for relief of subjacent parts. [<Med. L *seto, -onis,* appar. <*seta* silk <L, a bristle]

set–screw (set′skrōō′) *n.* A screw used as a clamp; especially, one having a cup instead of a point: used to screw through one part and slightly into another to bind the parts tightly.

set·tee (se·tē′) *n.* **1** A long wooden seat with a high back. **2** A sofa suitable for two or three people. [<SET¹ + -*ee*, dim. suffix; infl. in meaning by SEAT]

set·ter (set′ər) *n.* **1** One who or that which sets. **2** One of a breed of medium–sized, silky–coated, lithe bird dogs of great intelligence, originally trained to indicate the presence of game birds by crouching, now by standing rigid. —

ENGLISH SETTER
(About 25 inches high at the shoulder)

English setter A setter, white, or white marked with black, tan, yellow, or orange, trained since the 16th century to find and point game. The most famous British strains, the Laveracks and the Llewellins, are popular in field trials and bench shows. — **Gordon setter** A setter having a black coat marked with tan, chestnut, or red, probably crossbred with black–and–tan spaniels: named for the original breeder, the Duke of Gordon, and used especially for cover shooting. — **Irish** (or **red**) **setter** A handsome, useful, and companionable golden–chestnut or red setter, probably a setter–spaniel–pointer combination: extensively bred in America and very popular.

set·ting (set′ing) *n.* **1** The act of anything that sets. **2** An insertion. **3** That in which something is set; a frame; environment. **4** The act of indicating game like a setter. **5** A number of eggs placed together for hatching. **6** The music adapted to a song or poem. **7** The scene or background of a play or narrative. **8** The apparent sinking of the sun, etc., below the horizon. **9** The tableware set out for one person.

set·tle (set′l) *v.* **·tled, ·tling** *v.t.* **1** To put in order; set to rights; to *settle* affairs. **2** To put firmly in place; establish or fix permanently or as if permanently: He *settled* himself on the couch. **3** To free of agitation or disturbance; calm; quiet: to *settle* one's nerves. **4** To cause (sediment or dregs) to sink to the bottom. **5** To cause to subside or come to rest; make firm or compact: to *settle* dust or ashes. **6** To make clear or transparent, as by causing sediment or dregs to sink. **7** *Colloq.* To make quiet or orderly: One blow *settled* him. **8** To decide or determine finally, as an argument or difference. **9** To pay, as a debt; satisfy, as a claim. **10** To establish residents or residence in (a country, town, etc.). **11** To establish as residents. **12** To establish in a permanent occupation, home, etc. **13** To decide (a suit at law) by agreement between the litigants. **14** *Law* To make over or assign (property) by legal act: with *on* or *upon*. — *v.i.* **15** To come to rest, as after moving about or flying. **16** To sink gradually; subside. **17** To sink or come to rest, as dust or sediment. **18** To become more firm or compact. **19** To become clear or transparent, as by the sinking of sediment. **20** To take up residence; establish one's abode or home. **21** To come to a decision; determine; resolve: with *on, upon,* or *with*. **22** To pay a bill, etc. — **to settle down** **1** To start living a regular, orderly life, especially after a period of wandering or irresponsibility. **2** To apply steady effort or attention. — *n.* **1** A long seat or bench, generally of wood, with a high back, originally to direct the draft up the chimney and to provide a warm nook: often with arms and sometimes having a chest from seat to floor. **2** A wide step; platform. **3** *Obs.* A ledge. [OE *setlan* <*setl* a seat]
Synonyms (verb): adjust, allay, arrange, calm, compose, decide, determine, establish, finish, fix, pay, quiet, regulate. Compare CONFIRM, PAY¹, RATIFY, REQUITE, SET. *Antonyms:* agitate, confuse, derange, disarrange, discompose, disorder, disturb, fluster, flutter, mix, muss.

set·tle·ment (set′l·mənt) *n.* **1** The act of settling, or state of being settled; specifically, an adjustment of affairs by public authority. **2** Colonization. **3** Subsidence of a structure, or its effect. **4** An area of country newly occupied by those who intend to live and labor there; a colonized region, village, or town. **5** *Brit.* A regular or settled place of living; one's dwelling place. **6** An accounting;

adjustment; liquidation in regard to amounts. **7** The conveyance of property in such form as to provide for some future object, especially the support of members of the settler's family; also, the property so settled. **8** A religious community. **9** *pl.* A collection or series of frontier dwellings and clearings: distinguished from wild, unsettled territory. **10** Formerly, Negro quarters on a southern plantation. **11** A welfare institution established in a congested part of a city, having a resident staff of workers to conduct educational and recreational activities for the community: also **settlement house.**

set·tler (set′lər) *n.* **1** One who settles; especially, one who establishes himself in a colony or new country; a colonist. **2** One who or that which settles or decides something.

set·tling (set′ling) *n.* **1** The act of settling or sinking. **2** *pl.* Dregs; sediment.

set–to (set′tōō′) *n.* A bout at fighting, fencing, arguing, or any other mode of contest. [< *set to*; see under SET]

set–up (set′up′) *n.* **1** Physique; physical build; make–up. **2** Carriage of the body; bearing. **3** *U.S. Slang* A system or scheme of organization or construction; the salient elements of a situation; circumstances. **4** *U.S. Slang* A contest or match arranged to result in an easy victory; a contest in which the strength of the contestants is so unequal that the result is easily foreseen; also, the weaker of two such contestants. **5** *U.S. Colloq.* Ice, soda water, etc., provided to a customer who has brought his own liquor.

sev·en (sev′ən) *adj.* Being one more than six. — *n.* **1** The sum of one and six. **2** The symbols (7, vii, VII) representing that number. **3** A playing card with seven spots. **4** Something composed of seven units. [OE *seofon*]

Seven Deadly Sins Pride, Lust, Envy, Anger, Covetousness, Gluttony, and Sloth as personified in medieval literature: also known as *cardinal sins.*

sev·en·fold (sev′ən·fōld′) *adj.* **1** Seven times as many or as great. **2** Made up of seven; septuple. **3** Folded seven times. — *adv.* In sevenfold manner or degree.

sev·en·teen (sev′ən·tēn′) *adj.* Being seven more than ten. — *n.* The sum of ten and seven, or the symbols (17, xvii, XVII) representing this number. [OE *seofontȳne*]

sev·en·teenth (sev′ən·tēnth′) *adj.* **1** Seventh in order after the tenth. **2** Being one of seventeen equal parts. — *n.* **1** One of seventeen equal parts of anything. **2** A seventeenth object or unit. [OE *seofontēotha* <*seofontȳne* seventeen]

sev·en·teen–year locust (sev′ən·tēn′yir′) A dark–bodied, wedge–shaped cicada (*Magicicada septemdecim*) native to the eastern United States: the northern variety has an underground nymphal stage of 17 years, and the southern variety of 13 years.

sev·enth (sev′ənth) *adj.* **1** Next in order after the sixth. **2** Being one of seven equal parts. — *n.* **1** One of seven equal parts; the quotient of a unit divided by seven. **2** A seventh object or unit. **3** *Music* **a** The interval between any note and the seventh note above it on the diatonic scale, counting the starting point as one. **b** A note separated by this interval from any other, considered with reference to that other; specifically, the seventh above the keynote. **c** Two notes at this interval written or sounded together. **d** The resulting dissonance. See INTERVAL (def. 5). — *adv.* In the seventh order, place, or rank: also, in formal discourse, **sev′enth·ly**. [ME *seventhe* <SEVEN + -TH, replacing OE *seofande* and *seofotha*]

sev·enth–day (sev′ənth·dā′) *adj.* **1** Pertaining to the seventh day of the week. **2** Advocating the observance of the seventh day as the Sabbath: a *Seventh–Day* Adventist.

Seventh–Day Adventist See under ADVENTIST.

seventh heaven **1** The highest abode or condition of happiness. **2** The highest heaven according to various ancient systems of astronomy or in certain theologies.

sev·en·ti·eth (sev′ən·tē·ith) *adj.* **1** Tenth in order after the sixtieth. **2** Being one of seventy equal parts. — *n.* **1** One of seventy equal parts; the quotient of a unit divided by seventy. **2** A seventieth object or unit. [ME *seventithe* <SEVENTY + -TH]

sev·en·ty (sev′ən·tē) *adj.* Being ten more than sixty, or seven times ten. —*n.* *pl.* **·ties** The sum of ten and sixty, or the symbols (70, lxx, LXX) representing this number. [OE *(hund-) seofontig*] —**sev′en·ty·fold′** *adj.* & *adv.*

Seven Wonders of the World The seven works of man considered the most remarkable in the ancient world: generally considered to be the Egyptian pyramids, the hanging gardens of Babylon, the temple of Diana at Ephesus, the statue of Zeus by Phidias at Olympia, the Mausoleum at Halicarnassus, the Colossus of Rhodes, and the Pharos or lighthouse of Alexandria.

sev·er (sev′ər) *v.t.* **1** To put or keep apart; separate. **2** To cut or break into two or more parts. **3** To break off; dissolve, as a relationship or tie. —*v.i.* **4** To come or break apart or into pieces. **5** To go away or apart; separate. See synonyms under BREAK, CUT, REND, SEPARATE. [<AF *severer*, OF *sevrer* <L *separare* SEPARATE]

sev·er·a·ble (sev′ər·ə·bəl) *adj.* **1** Capable of being severed. **2** *Law* That can be severed from something to which it is attached or of which it forms part: said of a contract consisting of several obligations, when non-fulfilment of one obligation does not invalidate the contract.

sev·er·al (sev′ər·əl, sev′rəl) *adj.* **1** Being of an indefinite number, more than two, yet not large; divers. **2** Considered individually; pertaining to an individual; single; separate. **3** *Law* Pertaining individually and separately to each tenant or party to a bond: opposed to *joint*: a joint and *several* note. **4** Individually different; various or diverse. [<AF <Med. L *separalis* <L *separ* separate, distinct]

sev·er·al·ly (sev′ər·əl·ē, sev′rəl·ē) *adv.* **1** Individually; separately. **2** Respectively.

sev·er·ance (sev′ər·əns, sev′rəns) *n.* The act of severing, or the condition of being severed.

severance pay An amount of money paid to an employee at the termination of employment by the employer, based on regular wages or salary and often related to length of service.

se·vere (si·vir′) *adj.* **1** Trying to one's powers or endurance; hard to bear. **2** Rigorous in the treatment of others; unsparing; harsh; merciless. **3** Conforming to rigid rules; marked by pure and simple excellence; accurate. **4** Serious and austere in disposition or manner; grave; sedate; austerely plain. **5** Causing sharp pain or anguish; extreme: a *severe* pain. [<MF *sévère* <L *severus*] —**se·vere′ly** *adv.*

Synonyms: austere, rigid, rigorous, stern, stiff, unrelenting. That is *severe* which is devoid of all softness, mildness, indulgence, or levity, or (in literature and art) devoid of unnecessary ornament, amplification, or embellishment of any kind; as, a *severe* style; as said of anything painful, *severe* signifies such as heavily taxes endurance or power to resist; as, a *severe* pain, fever, or winter. *Rigid* signifies primarily *stiff*, resisting any effort to change its shape, its will, or course of conduct. *Rigorous* is nearly akin to *rigid*, but is a stronger word, having reference to action or active qualities: a *rigid* rule may be *rigorously* enforced. *Strict* signifies bound or stretched tight, tense, strenuously exact. *Stern* unites harshness and authority with strictness or severity; *stern*, as said even of inanimate objects, suggests something authoritative or forbidding. *Austere* signifies severely simple or temperate, *strict* in self-restraint or discipline, and similarly *unrelenting* toward others. See ARDUOUS, AUSTERE, BAD, DIFFICULT, HARD, IMPLACABLE, MOROSE, VIOLENT.

se·ver·i·ty (si·ver′ə·tē) *n.* *pl.* **·ties** **1** The quality of being severe. **2** Harshness or cruelty of disposition or treatment; power of paining or distressing. **3** Extreme strictness in character or rigor in operation; exactness. **4** Seriousness; austerity. **5** Strict conformity to truth or law. See synonyms under ACRIMONY, VIOLENCE.

sew (sō) *v.* **sewed**, **sewed** or **sewn**, **sew·ing** *v.t.* **1** To make, mend, or fasten with needle and thread. **2** To affect by sewing: often with *up*. —*v.i.* **3** To work with needle and thread. [OE *siwan, siowian*]

sew·age (sōō′ij) *n.* **1** The waste matter from domestic, commercial, and industrial establishments carried off in sewers. **2** Loosely, sewerage. [<SEW(ER) + -AGE]

se·wel·lel (si·wel′el) *n.* A brown, burrowing, nocturnal, vegetarian rodent (*Aplodontia rufa*) of the Pacific coast north of California; the mountain beaver. [<Chinook *shewallal* dual, a blanket of two sewellel skins sewn together (mistaken by Lewis and Clark for the animal's name) <*ogwoolal* a sewellel]

sew·er (sōō′ər) *n.* **1** A conduit, usually laid underground, to carry off drainage and excrement. ♦ Collateral adjective: *cloacal*. **2** Any large public drain. [<OF *seuwiere* a channel from a fish pond, ult. <L *ex-* off + *aqua* water]

sew·er·age (sōō′ər·ij) *n.* **1** A system of sewers. **2** Systematic draining by sewers. **3** Sewage.

sew·ing (sō′ing) *n.* **1** The act, business, or occupation of one who sews. **2** That which is sewed; material on which one is at work with needle and thread; needlework.

sewing bee A social gathering of the women and girls of a community to sew for some charitable purpose.

sewing circle **1** A group of women, usually organized within a church or other welfare organization, meeting periodically to sew for some charitable purpose. **2** A meeting of such a group. Also **sewing society.**

sewn (sōn) Alternative past participle of SEW.

sex (seks) *n.* **1** Either of two divisions, male and female, by which organisms are distinguished with reference to the reproductive functions. **2** Males or females collectively. **3** The character of being male or female. **4** The activity or phenomena of life concerned with sexual desire or reproduction. **5** *Colloq.* Sexual gratification. —**the fair sex** Women. [<OF *sexe′* <L *sexus*, prob. orig. division]

sex- *combining form* Six: *sexpartite*. Also spelled *sexi-*. [<L *sex* six]

sex·a·ge·nar·i·an (sek′sə·jə·nâr′ē·ən) *n.* A person between sixty and seventy years of age. —*adj.* **1** Sixty years old, or between sixty and seventy. **2** Of or pertaining to a sexagenarian. [<SEXAGENARY]

sex·ag·e·nar·y (seks·aj′ə·ner′ē) *adj.* **1** Of or pertaining to the number sixty. **2** Sixty years old, or between sixty and seventy. —*n.* *pl.* **·nar·ies** A sexagenarian. [<L *sexagenarius* <*sexageni* sixty each <*sexaginta* sixty]

sex·an·gle (seks′ang′gəl) *n.* A six-angled figure; a hexagon. [<L *sexangulus* <*sex* six + *angulus* angle] —**sex′an′gu·lar** (-ang′gyə-lər), **sex′an′gled** *adj.* —**sex′an′gu·lar·ly** *adv.*

sex appeal **1** A physical quality or charm which attracts sexual interest. **2** *Slang* The capacity to excite interest or attention: Tax reductions have *sex appeal.*

sex cell A gamete; a sperm or ovum.

sex chromosome *Biol.* A chromosome whose presence in the reproductive cells of certain plants and animals is associated with the determination of the sex of offspring. In mammals the ovum carries two X-chromosomes and sperm an X- and a Y-chromosome; females are produced by a paired XX in the fertilized ovum, males by a paired XY. Also called *allosome, heterochromosome.*

sex·fid (seks′fid) *adj. Bot.* Six-cleft, as a calyx. Also **sex′i·fid.** [<SEX- + -FID]

sex gland A gonad; either of the testes or ovaries.

sex hygiene The division of hygiene having to do with sexual conduct as related to the health of the individual and community.

sexi- Var. of SEX-.

sex·ism (seks′iz·əm) *n.* Sexual prejudice against women. [<SEX + -ISM, on analogy with *racism*] —**sex′ist** *n., adj.*

sex·less (seks′lis) *adj.* Having no sex; neuter. —**sex′less·ly** *adv.* —**sex′less·ness** *n.*

sex linkage *Biol.* That type of inheritance which is associated with the transmission of genes attached to the sex chromosomes. —**sex-linked** (seks′lingkt′) *adj.*

sex·ol·o·gy (seks·ol′ə·jē) *n.* The study of human sexual behavior. [<SEX + -(O)LOGY] —**sex·o·log·ic** (sek′sə·loj′ik) or **·i·cal** *adj.* —**sex·ol′o·gist** *n.*

sex·ploi·ta·tion (seks′ploi·tā′shən) *n.* The commercial exploitation of interest in sex, as by means of pornography.

sex·pot (seks′pot′) *n. Slang* A very sexy woman.

sex ratio The ratio of males to females in a given population, usually expressed as the number of males per 100 females.

sext (sekst) *n.* **1** One of the canonical hours; the office for the sixth hour or noon. **2** The sixth book of the decretals. [<LL *sexta* <L *sexta (hora)* the sixth (hour), fem. of *sextus* sixth <*sex* six]

sex·tant (seks′tənt) *n.* **1** An instrument for measuring angular distance between two objects, as between a heavenly body and the horizon, by a double reflection from two mirrors: used especially in determining latitude at sea. **2** The sixth part of a circle; an arc of 60 degrees. [<L *sextans, -antis* the sixth part <*sextus* sixth]

SEXTANT
a. Scale.   *d.* Reading lens.   *g.* Index glass.
b. Clamp screw.   *e.* Glass shades.   *h.* Telescope.
c. Tangent screw.   *f.* Horizon glass.   *i.* Movable arm.
         j. Handle.

sex·tar·i·us (seks·târ′ē·əs) *n. pl.* **·tar·i·i** (-târ′ē·ī) An ancient Roman measure of capacity. See CONGIUS. [<L, a sixth part <*sextus* sixth <*sex* six]

sex·tet (seks·tet′) *n.* **1** A band of six singers or players; also, a musical composition for six parts. **2** Any collection of six persons or things. Also **sex·tette′.** [Alter. of SESTET; refashioned after L *sex* six]

sex·tile (seks′til) *adj.* Indicated or measured by a distance of 60 degrees. —*n.* **1** *Astron.* The aspect of two planets at a distance of 60 degrees from each other. **2** *Stat.* One of the divisions of a frequency distribution containing exactly one sixth of the total number of cases or observations included. [<L *sextilis (mensis)* the sixth (month, i.e., August <*sextus* sixth]

sex·til·lion (seks·til′yən) *n.* A cardinal number: in the French system and in the United States, 1 followed by 21 ciphers; in the English system, 1 followed by 36 ciphers. [<F <L *sex* six + F *(m)illion* a million]

sex·ton (seks′tən) *n.* **1** A janitor of a church having charge also of ringing the bell, overseeing burials, etc.; also, formerly, a gravedigger. **2** Any of certain carrion beetles (genus *Necrophorus*) that bury small dead animals by excavating the ground beneath them: also called *burying beetle.* The larvae feed on the maggots in the rotting flesh. ♦ Homophone: *sextan.* [<AF *segrestaine*, OF *secrestein* <Med. L *sacristanus.* Doublet of SACRISTAN.] —**sex′ton·ship** *n.*

sex·tu·ple (seks′tōō·pəl, -tyōō-, seks·tōō′-, -tyōō′-) *adj.* **1** Sixfold. **2** Multiplied by six; six times repeated. **3** *Music* Having six beats to the measure. —*v.t.* **·pled, ·pling** To make sextuple; multiply by six. —*n.* A number or sum six times as great as another. [<L *sextus* sixth <*sex* six, formed on analogy with *quadruple, quintuple,* etc.]

sex·tu·plet (seks′tōō·plit. -tyōō-, seks·tōō′-, -tyōō′-) *n.* **1** A set of six similar things. **2** One of six offspring produced at a single birth. [<SEXTUPLE on analogy with *triplet*]

sex·u·al (sek′shōō·əl) *adj.* **1** Of, pertaining or peculiar to, characteristic of, or affecting sex, the sexes, or the organs or functions of sex. **2** Characterized by or having sex: opposed to *asexual.* [<LL *sexualis* <L *sexus* sex] —**sex′u·al·ly** *adv.*

sexual intercourse **1** The sexual act, especially between humans, in which the erect penis is introduced into the vagina for the ejaculation of semen and sexual gratification. **2** Any act of sexual connection, especially between humans.

sex·u·al·i·ty (sek′shōō·al′ə·tē) *n.* **1** The state of having, or of being distinguished by, sex. **2** Preoccupation with sex. **3** Possession of sexual power.

sexual selection In the theory of evolution, a phase of natural selection whereby characters, as bright colors, or fine song, considered especially attractive to the opposite sex, have a tendency to become perpetuated or enhanced.

sex·y (sek′sē) *adj.* **sex·i·er, sex·i·est** *Slang* **1** Provocative of sexual desire: a *sexy* dress; a *sexy* woman. **2** Concerned in large or excessive degree with sex: a *sexy* novel.

Sey·chelles (sā·shel′, -shelz′) An island group in the western Indian Ocean, comprising a British colony; 156 square miles; capital, Victoria, on Mahé.

sfer·ics (sfer′iks) *n. Meteorol.* **1** A cathode-ray tube connected with a directional antenna, used for the detection and plotting of electrical discharges in the atmosphere up to distances of several thousand miles. **2** *pl.* Atmospherics. [Short for ATMOSPHERICS]

sfor·zan·do (sfôr·tsän′dō) *adj. Music* Accented more forcibly than the rhythm requires; especially, sounded, as a note or chord, with sudden explosive force: also spelled *forzando.* Also **sfor·za′to** (-tsä′tō). [< Ital., forcing < *sforzare* force]

shab·by (shab′ē) *adj.* **·bi·er, ·bi·est 1** Threadbare; ragged; soiled or defaced, as from hard use. **2** Characterized by worn or defaced garments. **3** Mean; paltry. See synonyms under BAD¹, BASE². [OE *sceabb* a scab + -Y¹] —**shab′bi·ly** *adv.* —**shab′bi·ness** *n.*

shack¹ (shak) *n.* A rude cabin, as of logs. —**shack up** *Slang* **1** To live together and cohabit: said of unmarried persons. **2** To live or stay, usually briefly, at a specific place. [? < dial. Sp. (Mexican) *jacal* a wooden hut < Nahuatl *xacalli,* prob. infl. by RAMSHACKLE]

shack² (shak) *n.* **1** Fallen acorns or nuts of any kind; mast. **2** Any bait picked up at sea, as dead sea birds, refuse fish, etc.: distinguished from bait regularly carried or newly caught: also **shack bait. 3** A catch of miscellaneous, unsorted fish. [< *shack, v.,* dial. var. of SHAKE]

shack·le (shak′əl) *n.*
1 A ring, clasp, or braceletlike fastening for encircling and fettering a limb; fetter; gyve. **2** Impediment or restraint. **3** One of various forms of fastenings, as the bow of a padlock, a clevis, or a link for coupling railway cars. See synonyms under FETTER. —*v.t.* **·led, ·ling 1** To restrain or confine with shackles; fetter. **2** To keep or restrain from free action or speech. **3** To connect or fasten with a shackle. See synonyms under BIND. [OE *sceacul*] —**shack′ler** *n.*

SHACKLES

shackle bolt 1 A bolt having on its end a shackle or clevis, or a bolt that is passed through the eyes of a shackle. **2** The shackle of a padlock, chain, etc. **3** *Her.* Shackle and padlock: used as a bearing.

shack·o (shak′ō) See SHAKO.

shad (shad) *n. pl.* **shad** A deep-bodied food fish (genus *Alosa*) related to the herring, especially the common or American shad (*Alosa sapidissima*) of the Atlantic coast, which is highly esteemed as food. [OE *sceadd*]

shad–bel·lied (shad′bel′ēd) *adj.* **1** Cutaway: said of a coat. **2** Lean and lank: said of persons.

shad·ber·ry (shad′ber′ē) *n. pl.* **·ries** The shadbush, or its fruit.

shad·bush (shad′boosh′) *n.* **1** The Juneberry. **2** Other smaller and shrublike related forms of the same genus, as *Amelanchier alnifolia* of the northern and western United States. Also **shad′blow′** (-blō′). [< SHAD + BUSH¹; so called because it flowers when the shad appear in U.S. rivers]

shad·dock (shad′ək) *n.* **1** The large, pale-yellow fruit of a tropical tree (genus *Citrus*), varying in size from the smaller grapefruit or pomelo of the United States to the pompelmous, which may be 8 inches in diameter. **2** The tree. [after Capt. *Shaddock,* commander of an East India ship, who brought the seed to the West Indies from the East Indies in 1696]

shade (shād) *v.* **shad·ed, shad·ing** *v.t.* **1** To screen from light by intercepting its rays; put in shade. **2** To make dim with or as with shade; darken; overcast. **3** To screen or protect with or as with a shade. **4** To cause to change, pass, blend, or soften, by gradations. **5 a** To represent (degrees of shade, colors,

etc.) by gradations of light or dark lines or shading. **b** To represent varying shades, colors, etc., in (a picture or painting) thus. **6** To make slightly lower, as a price. —*v.i.* **7** To change or vary by degrees. [< *n.*] —*n.* **1** Relative obscurity from interception of the rays of light: distinguished from *shadow;* hence, gloom; darkness; obscurity; the state of being outshone. **2** A shady place; secluded retreat. **3** Something that serves to intercept or screen from light; hence, a screen that shuts off light, heat, air, dust, etc. **4** A gradation of color; also, slight degree; minute difference. **5** The unilluminated part of a picture, drawing, or engraving: opposed to *light.* **6** A disembodied spirit; ghost; something unreal. **7** *pl. Slang* Sunglasses. See synonyms under SPECTER. —**the shades** The abode of departed spirits; Hades. [OE *sceadu*] —**shade′less** *adj.*

shade grass Pachysandra.

shad·fly (shad′flī′) *n. pl.* **·flies** Any of several flies that appear when the shad are running; especially, a mayfly.

shad·ing (shā′ding) *n.* **1** Protection against light or heat. **2** The lines, dots, etc., by which degrees of darkness, color, or depth are represented in a picture or painting. **3** A slight difference or variation.

shad·ow (shad′ō) *n.* **1** A comparative darkness within an illuminated area caused by the interception of light by an opaque body. **2** The dark figure or image thus produced on a surface and representing the approximate shape of the intercepting body: the *shadow* of a man. **3** The shaded or dark portion of a picture. **4** A mirrored image: to see one's *shadow* in a pool. **5** A delusive image or semblance; anything unreal or unsubstantial. **6** A phantom; ghost; shade. **7** A faint representation or indication; a symbol: the *shadow* of things to come. **8** A remnant; vestige: *shadows* of his former glory. **9** An insignificant trace or portion: not a *shadow* of evidence. **10** *Archaic* Shelter; protection. **11** Gloom; a saddening influence. **12** An inseparable companion. **13** One who trails or follows another, as a detective or spy. See synonyms under IMAGE. —*adj.* Of or pertaining to a shadow cabinet. —*v.t.* **1** To cast a shadow upon; overspread with shadow; shade. **2** To darken or cloud; make gloomy. **3** To represent or foreshow dimly or vaguely: with *forth* or *out.* **4** To follow closely or secretly; spy on. **5** To shade in painting, drawing, etc. **6** *Archaic* To screen; shelter. [OE *sceadwe,* genitive and dative of *sceadu* a shade] —**shad′ow·er** *n.*

shad·ow·box (shad′ō·boks′) *v.i.* To spar with an imaginary opponent as a form of exercise. —**shad′ow·box′ing** *n.*

shadow cabinet In the British or other parliamentary government, a group of opposition leaders who would assume specific cabinet positions if the government in power should fall.

shad·ow·graph (shad′ō·graf, -gräf) *n.* **1** A pictorial image formed by casting a shadow, usually of the hands, upon a lighted surface or screen. **2** A drama produced by a series of these images: also **shadow play. 3** A radiograph.

shadow test Skiascopy.

shad·ow·y (shad′ō·ē) *adj.* **1** Full of or affording shadow; dark; shady: a *shadowy* grove. **2** Like shadows in indistinctness; vague; dim. **3** Unsubstantial or illusory; unreal; ghostly. **4** Symbolic. See synonyms under DARK, IMAGINARY, VAIN. —**shad′ow·i·ness** *n.*

shad·y (shā′dē) *adj.* **shad·i·er, shad·i·est 1** Full of shade; casting a shade. **2** Shaded or sheltered. **3** Morally questionable; dubious; suspicious. **4** Quiet; hidden. See synonyms under DARK. —**to keep shady 1** To stay in hiding; keep out of the way. **2** To hide and protect (another). —**on the shady side of** Older than; past the age of. —**shad′i·ly** *adv.* —**shad′i·ness** *n.*

shaft¹ (shaft, shäft) *n.* **1** The long narrow rod of an arrow, spear, lance, harpoon, etc. **2** An arrow. **3** Anything resembling a missile in appearance or effect: *shafts* of ridicule. **4** A beam or streak of light. **5** A long handle, as of a hammer, ax, etc. **6** *Mech.* A long and usually cylindrical bar, especially if rotating and transmitting motive power. **7** *Archit.* **a** The portion of a column between capital and base. **b** A slender column. **8** An obelisk or memorial column. **9** The

vertical part of a cross. **10** The stem of a feather. **11** *Anat.* **a** A long slender portion, as the diaphysis of a bone. **b** The portion of a hair from the root to the end. **12** On a loom, one of the long laths at the ends of the heddles. **13** A thill. **14** *Slang* Malicious or abusive treatment: with *the,* especially in the phrases **to get the shaft, to give (someone) the shaft.** —*v.t. Slang* To act maliciously or abusively toward. [OE *sceaft*]

shaft² (shaft, shäft) *n.* **1** A narrow, vertical or inclined, excavation connected with a mine; also, a passage for light or air. **2** The tunnel of a blast furnace. **3** An opening through the floors of a building, as for an elevator. [< LG *schacht* rod, shaft; infl. by SHAFT¹]

shaft·ing (shaf′ting, shäf′-) *n.* **1** A system of shafts or rods, as in pulleys or gearwheels, for communicating power. **2** Material from which to make shafts.

shag¹ (shag) *n.* **1** A rough coat or mass, as of hair. **2** A wild growth, as of weeds. **3** A long nap on cloth. **4** Cloth having a rough or long nap; formerly, a silk or worsted cloth having a velvet nap. **5** A cormorant. **6** A coarse, strong tobacco: also **shag tobacco.** —*v.* **shagged, shag·ging** *v.t.* **1** To make shaggy or hairy; roughen. **2** In baseball, to catch (flies) in practice. —*v.i.* **3** To become shaggy or rough. —*adj.* Shaggy: also **shag·ged** (shag′id). [OE *sceacga* rough hair, wool]

shag² (shag) *n.* A dance of the late 1930's, consisting of hopping quickly on alternate feet. —*v.i.* **shagged, shag·ging** To dance the shag.

shag·bark (shag′bärk′) *n.* **1** The white hickory (*Carya ovata*), which yields high-grade nuts. **2** Its wood. Also called *shellbark.*

shag·gy (shag′ē) *adj.* **·gi·er, ·gi·est 1** Having, consisting of, or resembling rough hair or wool; rugged; rough. **2** Covered with any rough, tangled growth; fuzzy; scrubby. **3** Unkempt; unpolished: said of manners. See synonyms under ROUGH. —**shag′gi·ly** *adv.* —**shag′gi·ness** *n.*

sha·green (shə·grēn′) *n.* **1** The rough skin of various sharks and rays: used for polishing. **2** A rough-grained Russian or Oriental leather or parchment, usually dyed green, or a pressed leather made in imitation of it. **3** Chagrin. [< F *chagrin* < Turkish *sāghrī* horse's hide]

shah (shä) *n.* An eastern king or ruler, especially of Persia. [< Persian *shāh,* short for *pādshāh.* See PADISHAH.]

shake (shāk) *v.* **shook, shak·en, shak·ing** *v.t.* **1** To cause to move to and fro or up and down with short, rapid movements. **2** To affect in a specified manner by or as by vigorous action: with *off, out, from,* etc.: to *shake* out a sail; to *shake* off a tackler. **3** To cause to tremble or quiver; jolt; vibrate: The blows *shook* the door. **4** To cause to stagger or totter. **5** To weaken or disturb; unsettle: I could not *shake* his determination. **6** To agitate or rouse; stir: often with *up.* **7** *Slang* To get rid of or away from. **8** *Music* To trill. **9** In dice games, to mix (the dice) before casting. —*v.i.* **10** To move to and fro or up and down in short, rapid movements. **11** To be affected in a specified way by vigorous action: with *off, out, from,* etc. **12** To tremble or quiver, as from cold or fear. **13** To become unsteady; totter. **14** *Music* To trill a note, etc. —**to shake down 1** To cause to fall by shaking; bring down. **2** To cause to settle; make compact. **3** *Slang* To extort money from. —**to shake hands** To clasp hands as a form of greeting, agreement, etc. —*n.* **1** A shaking; concussion; agitation; vibration; shock; jolt. **2** The state of being shaken. **3** *pl. Colloq.* The chill or ague of intermittent fever. **4** A rough, unshaved shingle used to cover barns and shanties. **5** A frost or wind crack in timber; also, a tight fissure in rock. **6** An earthquake. **7** *Slang* An instant; a jiffy. **8** *Music* A trill. **9** *Colloq.* A bargain. —**to give (someone) the shake** To get rid of (someone). [OE *scacan*]

Synonyms (verb): agitate, brandish, flap, fluctuate, flutter, jar, joggle, jolt, jounce, oscillate, quake, quaver, quiver, rattle, reel, rock, shiver, shudder, sway, swing, thrill, totter, tremble, vibrate, wave, waver. A thing is *shaken* which is subjected to short and abruptly checked movements as forward and backward, up and down, from side to side, etc. A thing *rocks* that is held up from below;

it *swings* if suspended from above, as a pendulum, or pivoted at the side, as a crane or a bridge draw; to *oscillate* is to *swing* with a smooth and regular returning motion; a *vibrating* motion may be tremulous or *jarring*. The pendulum of a clock may be said to *swing* or *oscillate*; a steel bridge *vibrates* under the passage of a heavy train; the term *vibrate* is also applied to molecular movements. *Jolting* is a lifting from and letting down suddenly upon an unyielding surface; a *jarring* motion is abruptly and very rapidly repeated through an exceedingly limited space; the *jolting* of the carriage *jars* the windows. *Rattling* refers directly to the sound produced by *shaking*. To *joggle* is to *shake* slightly; as, A passing touch *joggles* the desk on which one is writing. To *agitate* in its literal use is nearly the same as to *shake*, but we speak of the sea as *agitated* when we could not say it is *shaken*; in the metaphorical use *agitate* is more transitory and superficial, *shake* more fundamental and enduring; a person's feelings are *agitated* by distressing news; his courage, his faith, his credit, or his testimony is *shaken*. Compare FLUCTUATE, QUAKE, SWAY, TREMBLE.

shake-down (shāk′doun′) *n.* **1** A bed of straw shaken down; hence, any makeshift bed. **2** *U.S. Slang* A swindle; a share of graft; extortion money. **3** A noisy, energetic dance common among Negroes of the southern United States. — *adj.* For the purpose of adjusting mechanical parts or habituating people: also *shake-down cruise*.

shak·er (shā′kər) *n.* **1** One who or that which shakes; a container for shaking something: a *saltshaker*, cocktail *shaker*, etc. **2** One who shivers or shakes; a totterer.

Shak·er (shā′kər) *n.* One of a sect practicing celibacy and communal living, introduced in America in 1774 under the leadership of Mother Ann Lee, at Lebanon, New York: so called from their characteristic bodily movements during religious meetings. Their official name is *The United Society of Believers in Christ's Second Appearing*. — **Shak′er·ism** *n.*

Shake·speare (shāk′spir) *n.* **William**, 1564–1616, English poet and dramatist. Also **Shake′spere, Shak′speare, Shak′spere.**

shake-up (shāk′up′) *n.* A change of personnel or organization, as in a government administration, a business office, etc.

shaking palsy *Pathol.* A chronic disorder of the central nervous system, characterized by alternations of muscular rigidity and tremor and peculiar gait: also called *paralysis agitans.*

shak·o (shak′ō) *n.* *pl.* **·os** A kind of high, stiff military headdress, having a peak and an upright plume: originally of fur: also spelled *shacko*. [<F *schako* <Hungarian *csákó*]

Shak·ti (shuk′tē) *n.* The female energy of the Hindu god, Siva: worshiped under various forms; Devi: also spelled *Sakti*. [<Skt. *śakti* power] — **Shak′tism** *n.*

Sha·kun·ta·la (shə·kŏŏn′tə·lə) See SAKUNTALA. 　　　　　SHAKO

shak·y (shā′kē) *adj.* **shak·i·er, shak·i·est** **1** Habitually shaking or tremulous; tottering; weak; unsound. **2** Of doubtful credit or solvency; embarrassed. — **shak′i·ly** *adv.* — **shak′i·ness** *n.*

shale¹ (shāl) *n.* A fissile argillaceous rock resembling slate, with fragile, uneven laminae. [<G *schale* shale] — **shal′y** *adj.*

shale² (shāl) *n.* Shell or husk. [OE *scealu*] — **shaled** *adj.*

shale oil Petroleum obtained by the distillation of bituminous shales.

shall (shal) A defective verb having a past tense **should**, an archaic present second person singular, (thou) **shalt**, past (thou) **shouldst** or **shouldest**, and no other inflected forms. It is now used only as an auxiliary followed by the infinitive without *to*, or elliptically with the infinitive unexpressed. Its function is to indicate, now chiefly in formal discourse: **1** In the first person, simple futurity, with a matter-of-fact attitude toward the action or state projected: We *shall* take only the usual precautions. (But see usage note below.) **2** In the second and third persons, futurity combined

with a mood or feeling of: **a** Determination: They *shall* not pass. **b** Promise: You *shall* have whatever you need. **c** Threat: You *shall* pay for this. **d** Command: No one *shall* twice be put in jeopardy. **e** Inevitability: When earthly time *shall* end, will life survive? **3** In all persons, indefinite future time in conditional statements: If and when you or we or the divers *shall* locate the treasure, it will (or, in legal use, the mandatory *shall*) be shared out according to the agreement. **4** In all persons, futurity involving ideal certainty, in clauses following expressions of anxiety, demand, or desire: They are anxious, indeed insist, that you or I or both of us *shall* go, rather than any outsider. [OE *sceal* I am obliged, 1st person sing. of *sceolan*]

◆ **shall vs. will** The traditional view on the use of *shall* and *will* is that to indicate simple futurity *shall* is used in the first person, *will* in the second and third; their roles are reversed to express determination, promise, threat, command, inevitability, etc.; while in questions, the choice between them depends on which one is expected in the answer. These statements hold fairly well for legal usage, but they are too arbitrary to describe accurately the facts of current American usage in speech and writing, except at the most stilted formal level. *Shall* and *will* have had a tendency gradually to exchange roles once each century since 1500, and during the present century it has been the turn of *will* to make its way into the lead. In the important task of indicating simple future time in the first person, *will* has largely replaced *shall*, aided in doing so by the leveling effect of the contraction *'ll*: *I'll* (= I will or I shall) be free at ten. *Shall*, thus displaced, takes on one role assigned by traditional formula to *will*, and is used in the first person to express determination plus inevitability, as in General MacArthur's "I shall return" and Winston Churchill's " . . . and win we *shall*." If *will* in the first person is to express determination according to the formula, it must be stressed or qualified in some way: I *will* too go out and play. In questions in the first person, *shall* is still commonly used to express the simple future, but it is also found as the hortatory *shall*, either humorously formal: *Shall* we (= Let's) dance? or politely threatening: *Shall* we (= Let's) do it my way for once. Again, *will* has won out over *shall* when it comes to giving routine or polite, as distinct from peremptory, commands: You *will* proceed to Hill 90 and occupy it. The peremptory *shall* in the second person is now usually replaced, except in legal usage, by *will* with *have to*: You *will* have to (= shall) go whether you want to or not. It is hazardous to try to sum up the present position of these two forms, but with the few exceptions noted, in American usage *will* now usually indicates the simple future in all persons, while *shall* expresses the future complicated by some feeling about it.

shal·loon (sha·lōōn′) *n.* A light, woven woolen fabric used for linings. [<F *chalon*, from *Châlons*-sur-Marne, France]

shal·lop (shal′əp) *n.* An open boat propelled by oars or sails. [<F *chaloupe* <Du. *sloep.* See SLOOP.]

shal·lot (shə·lot′) *n.* **1** An onionlike culinary vegetable (*Allium ascalonicum*) allied to garlic but having milder bulbs which are used in seasoning and for pickles. **2** A small onion. Also spelled *eschalot*. [<OF *eschalotte*, alter. of *eschaloigne*. See SCALLION.]

shal·low (shal′ō) *adj.* **1** Having the bottom not far below the surface or top; lacking depth; shoal. **2** Lacking intellectual depth; not wise or profound; superficial. — *n.* A shallow place in a body of water; shoal. — *v.t. & v.i.* To make or become shallow. [ME *schalowe*. Prob. related to SHOAL¹.] — **shal′low·ly** *adv.* — **shal′low·ness** *n.*

shalt (shalt) Archaic or poetic second person singular, present tense of SHALL: used with *thou.*

shal·war (shul′wär) *n.* Oriental trousers or pajamas. [<Persian *shalwār*]

sham (sham) *v.* **shammed, sham·ming** *v.t.* **1** To assume or present the appearance of:

counterfeit; feign. **2** To represent oneself as; pretend to be. **3** *Obs.* To delude; deceive. — *v.i.* **4** To make false pretenses; feign something. See synonyms under COUNTERFEIT, PRETEND. — *adj.* False; pretended; counterfeit; mock. See synonyms under FACTITIOUS. — *n.* **1** A pretense; imposture; deception. **2** One who affects or simulates a certain character; a pretender: also **sham′mer. 3** A deceptive imitation; simulation; counterfeit. **4** A bordered strip simulating the edge of a sheet on a made-up bed. See synonyms under HYPOCRISY. [Prob. dial. var. of SHAME]

sha·man (shä′mən, shā′-, sham′ən) *n.* **1** A priest of Shamanism; a magician. **2** Among certain northwestern North American Indians, a tribal medicine man or wizard. — *adj.* Of or pertaining to a shaman: also **sha·man·ic** (shə-man′ik). [<Russian <Tungusic *samān* <Skt. *samaṇa* ascetic]

Sha·man·ism (shä′mən·iz′əm, shā′-, sham′ən-) *n.* A primitive religion of NE Asia and Europe holding that gods, demons, ancestral spirits, etc., work for the good or ill of mankind through the sole medium of its priests, the shamans. Certain Indians of the American Northwest have similar beliefs and practices. — **Sha′man·is′tic** *adj. & n.*

sham·ble (sham′bəl) *v.i.* **·bled, ·bling** To walk with shuffling or unsteady gait. — *n.* A shambling walk. [Origin uncertain]

sham·bles (sham′bəlz) *n. pl.* (generally construed as singular) **1** A place where butchers kill animals; slaughterhouse. **2** Any place of carnage or execution: The trench was a *shambles*. **3** A place marked by great destruction or disorder. **4** *Brit. Dial.* A meat market; in the singular, a table or stall in such a market. [OE *scamel* a bench, stool <L *scamellum*, dim. of *scamnum* bench, stool]

shame (shām) *n.* **1** A painful sense of guilt or degradation caused by consciousness of guilt or of anything degrading, unworthy, or immodest. **2** The restraining sense of pride, decency, or modesty. **3** That which brings reproach; a disgrace. **4** A state of ignominy; sensitiveness or susceptibility to humiliation. See synonyms under ABOMINATION, CHAGRIN. — **to put to shame** **1** To disgrace; make ashamed. **2** To surpass or eclipse. — *v.t.* **shamed, sham·ing** **1** To make ashamed; cause to feel shame. **2** To bring shame upon; disgrace. **3** To impel by a sense of shame: with *into* or *out of*. See synonyms under ABASH. [OE *scamu*]

shame·faced (shām′fāst′) *adj.* Easily abashed; showing shame or bashfulness in one's face; modest; bashful. [Alter. of ME *shamefast*, OE *scamfæst* abashed] — **shame·fac·ed·ly** (shām′fā′sid·lē, shām′fāst′lē) *adv.* — **shame′fac′ed·ness** *n.*

shame·ful (shām′fəl) *adj.* **1** Deserving or bringing shame or disgrace; disgraceful; scandalous. **2** Exciting shame; indecent. See synonyms under FLAGRANT. — **shame′ful·ly** *adv.* — **shame′ful·ness** *n.*

shame·less (shām′lis) *adj.* **1** Impudent; brazen; immodest. **2** Done without shame, indicating a want of decency. See synonyms under INFAMOUS, IMMODEST, IMPUDENT. — **shame′less·ly** *adv.* — **shame′less·ness** *n.*

sham·poo (sham·pōō′) *v.t.* **1** To lather, rub, and wash (the hair and scalp) thoroughly. **2** To cleanse by rubbing. — *n.* The act or process of shampooing, or a preparation used for it. [<Hind. *chāmpnā* press] — **shampoo′er** *n.*

sham·rock (sham′rok) *n.* Any one of several trifoliate plants, accepted as the national emblem of Ireland, especially the wood sorrel (*Oxalis acetosella*), the white clover (*Trifolium repens*), and the black medic (*Medicago lupulina*). [<Irish *seamrōg*, dim. of *seamar* trefoil]

SHAMROCK
a. White clover.
b. Wood sorrel.

shan·dy·gaff (shan′dē·gaf) *n.* An alcoholic drink composed of two liquids mixed, at least one being effervescent: usually ale or

beer and ginger beer. [Origin unknown]

shang·hai (shang'hī, shang·hī') *v.t.* **·haied,** **·hai·ing** **1** To drug or render unconscious and kidnap for service aboard a ship. **2** To cause to do something by force or deception. [from *Shanghai*]

Shang·hai (shang·hī', *Chinese* shäng·hī') A port of eastern China, the largest city on the Asian continent.

Shan·gri-la (shang'gri·lä') *n.* **1** Any imaginary hidden utopia or paradise. **2** The reported taking-off place of the United States Army bombers that raided Tokyo April 18, 1942: a term used by Franklin Roosevelt. **3** Any secret base for air force military operations. [From the locale of James Hilton's novel *Lost Horizon*]

shank (shangk) *n.* **1** The leg proper; that part of the lower limb between the knee and the ankle. **2** A cut of meat from the leg of an animal; the shin. **3** The tarsus of a bird. See the illustration under FOWL. **4** Something resembling a leg. **5** The part of a tool connecting the handle with the working part, as the stem of a drill. **6** The projecting piece or loop by which some forms of buttons are attached. **7** The stem of an anchor. **8** The stem of a key between the bow and the bit. **9** The straight part of a hook. **10** The narrow part of a spoon handle. **11** A continuation of the tang of a tool or instrument. **12** *Printing* The body of a type. **13** The narrow part of a shoe sole in front of the heel. See illustration under SHOE. **14** *Bot.* A pedicel. **15** *Colloq.* The remainder or last part of a thing: the *shank* of the evening. — *v.i.* **1** *Bot.* To decay or fall off the stem because of disease. **2** *Scot.* To travel on foot. [OE *sceanca*]

shanks' mare One's own legs as a means of conveyance.

shan·tung (shan'tung, shan·tung') *n.* A silk fabric similar to pongee and having the same rough, nubby surface: originally made in China of wild silk, now often made of rayon combined with cotton. [from SHANTUNG]

shan·ty (shan'tē) *n. pl.* **·ties** A hastily built shack or cabin; a ramshackle or rickety dwelling. See synonyms under HOUSE, HUT. [<F (Canadian) *chantier* lumberer's shack]

shan·ty·town (shan'tē·toun') *n.* **1** That section of a city or town comprised of ramshackle or hastily constructed shacks. **2** The inhabitants collectively of such a section: All *shanty-town* turned out for the parade.

shape (shāp) *n.* **1** Outward form or construction; configuration; contour. **2** A developed expression or definite formulation; realization or application; embodiment; cast: to put an idea into *shape*. **3** A being, image, or appearance considered with reference to its form, generally incorporeal; ghost; phantom. **4** The character or form in which a thing appears; guise; aspect. **5** Something that gives or determines form; a pattern or mold; in millinery, a stiff frame. **6** The lines of a per-

SHARKS
A. Great white shark (to 40 feet). *B.* Blue shark (to 15 feet). *C.* Hammerhead shark (to 15 feet).

son's body; figure. **7** Manner of execution. **8** Condition as regarding fitness. **9** A blancmange, jelly, etc., cooled and shaped in a mold. — **to take shape** To have or assume a definite form. — *v.* **shaped, shaped** (*Rare* **shap·en**), **shap·ing** *v.t.* **1** To give shape to;

mold; form. **2** To adjust or adapt; modify. **3** To devise; prepare. **4** To give direction or character to: to *shape* one's course of action. **5** To put into or express in words. **6** *Obs.* To appoint; ordain. — *v.i.* **7** To take shape; develop; form: often with *up* or *into*. **8** *Rare* To become adapted; conform. **9** *Rare* To happen; come about. See synonyms under MAKE. [OE *gesceap* creation] — **shap'er** *n.*

shaped (shāpt) *adj.* **1** Formed. **2** Resembling in shape: used in compounds, as in leaf-shaped, club-shaped, key-shaped.

shaped charge An explosive charge so placed in a shell or projectile as to deliver most of its force directly through the nose of the shell instead of scattering it at random: developed especially for anti-tank guns.

shape·less (shāp'lis) *adj.* Having no definite shape; lacking symmetry; formless. — **shape'·less·ly** *adv.* — **shape'less·ness** *n.*

shape·ly (shāp'lē) *adj.* **·li·er, ·li·est** Having a pleasing shape; well-formed; graceful. — **shape'li·ness** *n.*

shape-up (shāp'up') *n.* The selection of a work crew by an employer representative, a labor union deputy, or other agent, who chooses from among a number of men assembled for a work shift: a common practice in hiring longshoremen and workers in other industries in which the relationship between an employee and a specific employer is by the day or otherwise casual.

shard (shärd) *n.* **1** A broken piece of a brittle substance, as of an earthen vessel; a potsherd; a fragment: also spelled *sherd*. **2** *Zool.* A hard, thin shell, or a wing cover, of an insect. [OE *sceard.* Related to SHEAR.]

share (shâr) *n.* **1** A portion; allotted or equitable part. **2** Specifically, one of the equal parts into which the capital stock of a company or corporation is divided. **3** An equitable part of something enjoyed or suffered in common. **4** A plowshare: also spelled *shear*. **5** A blade of a cultivator, seeder, etc. See synonyms under PART. — *v.* **shared, shar·ing** *v.t.* **1** To divide and give out in shares or portions; apportion. **2** To enjoy or endure in common; participate in. — *v.i.* **3** To have a part; participate: with *in*. See synonyms under APPORTION. [OE *scearu* < *sceran* shear. Related to SHEAR.] — **shar'er** *n.*

share-crop·per (shâr'krop'ər) *n.* A tenant farmer who pays a share of his crop as rent for his land.

share·hold·er (shâr'hōl'dər) *n.* An owner of a share or shares of a company's stock; a stockholder.

shark[1] (shärk) *n.* One of a group of voracious elasmobranch fishes (order *Selachii*), mostly marine, of medium to large size, having a cartilaginous skeleton, lateral gill slits, and dun-colored bodies covered with placoid scales. Most species do not molest man; the great white shark (*Carcharodon carcharias*) is the man-eater frequenting warm seas. — *v.i.* To fish for sharks. [Origin uncertain]

shark[2] (shärk) *n.* **1** A bold and dishonest person; a rapacious swindler. **2** *Slang* A person of exceptional skill or ability in some special line. Also **shark'er.** — *v.t. Archaic* To obtain by unscrupulous or deceitful means. — *v.i.* To live by trickery or deceit. [Prob. <G *schurke* scoundrel]

shark·skin (shärk'skin') *n.* **1** The skin of a shark. **2** A summer fabric with a smooth, almost shiny surface, made of acetate rayon and used for sports clothes; originally, a weave of woolen yarns of two colors: so called from its resemblance to sharkskin leather.

sharp (shärp) *adj.* **1** Having a keen edge or an acute point; capable of cutting or piercing. **2** Coming to an acute angle; not obtuse; angular; abrupt: a *sharp* peak. **3** Keen of perception or discernment; also, shrewd in bargaining; artful; overreaching: *sharp* practice. **4** Ardent; quick; eager; keen, as the appetite; impetuous or fiery, as a combat or debate; vigilant or attentive. **5** Affecting the mind or senses, as if by cutting or piercing; afflictive; poignant; painful; harsh; censorious; acrimonious; rigorous; stern; sarcastic; bitter. **6** Shrill. **7** Pinching; cutting, as cold. **8** Having an acid or pungent taste. **9** Distinct, as an outline; not blurred or hazy; well-defined. **10** *Music* Being above the proper or indicated pitch; specifically, being a half-step higher than the indicated note; sharped.

11 Hard and rough; gritty, as sand. **12** *Phonet.* Surd; voiceless: opposed to *flat*: said of consonants. — *adv.* **1** In a sharp manner; sharply. **2** Promptly; exactly; on the instant: at 4 o'clock *sharp.* **3** *Music* Above the proper pitch. — *n.* **1** *Music* A character (♯) used on a natural degree of the staff to make it represent a pitch a half-step higher; the tone so indicated; on the pianoforte, the next higher key; one of the black keys: a loose use in the phrase *sharps and flats.* **2** A sewing needle of long, slender shape. **3** A cheating rogue; sharper: a *cardsharp.* **4** *Obs.* A dueling sword; rapier. — *v.t. Music* To raise in pitch, as by a half-step. — *v.i. Music* To sing, play, or sound above the right pitch. [OE *scearp*] — **sharp'ly** *adv.* — **sharp'ness** *n.*

Synonyms (adj.): acute, cutting, keen, penetrating, piercing, pointed. See ACID, ACUTE, ASTUTE, BITTER, CLEVER, FINE, KNOWING, SAGACIOUS, STEEP, VIOLENT. *Antonyms:* blunt, dull, dulled, edgeless, flat, obtuse, pointless, round, rounded.

sharp·en (shär'pən) *v.t. & v.i.* To make or become sharp. — **sharp'en·er** *n.*

sharp·er (shär'pər) *n.* A swindler; cheat.

sharp-eyed (shärp'īd') *adj.* **1** Having acute eyesight. **2** Keenly observant; alert.

sharp·ie (shär'pē) *n.* A long, sharp, flat-bottomed sailboat having a center-board and one or two masts, each having a triangular sail: originally used in the oyster and scallop fisheries. [<SHARP; in allusion to its outline]

SHARPIE

sharp-shinned (shärp'shind') *adj.* Having slender shanks, somewhat angular in front: specifically said of the North American **sharp-shinned hawk** (*Accipiter velox*).

sharp·shoot·er (shärp'shoo'tər) *n.* **1** A skilled marksman, especially in the use of the rifle. **2** The second grade of skill in small-arms shooting, ranking next above *marksman* and below *expert*; also, a soldier having this grade. — **sharp'shoot'ing** *n.*

sharp-sight·ed (shärp'sī'tid) *adj.* Having keen vision. — **sharp'-sight'ed·ness** *n.*

sharp-tongued (shärp'tungd') *adj.* Bitter or caustic in speech.

sharp-wit·ted (shärp'wit'id) *adj.* Acute; intelligent; discerning. See synonyms under INTELLIGENT, SAGACIOUS. — **sharp'-wit'ted·ness** *n.*

Shasta daisy A cultivated variety of a short-lived perennial (*Chrysanthemum maximum*) having large, white-rayed flowers.

shat·ter (shat'ər) *v.t.* **1** To break into pieces suddenly, as by a blow. **2** To break the health or tone of, as the body or mind; disorder; damage. **3** *Obs.* To scatter. — *v.i.* **4** To break into pieces; burst. See synonyms under BREAK. — *n. Obs.* **1** A shattered fragment; a splinter: a tree rent into *shatters*. **2** A shattered or disordered condition: His nerves are in a *shatter*. [ME *schateren.* ? Akin to SCATTER.]

shave (shāv) *v.* **shaved, shaved** or **shav·en, shav·ing** *v.i.* **1** To cut hair or beard close to the skin with a razor. — *v.t.* **2** To remove hair or beard from (the face, head, etc.) with a razor. **3** To cut (hair or beard) close to the skin with a razor: often with *off*. **4** To trim closely as if with a razor: to *shave* a lawn. **5** To cut thin slices from, as in preparing the surface; pare; plane. **6** To cut into thin slices: to *shave* ice. **7** To touch or scrape in passing; graze; come close to. **8** *U.S.* To buy (commercial paper) at a greater reduction than the bank discount. — *n.* **1** The act or operation of cutting off the beard with a razor. **2** A knife or blade, mounted between two handles, as for shaving wood: also **draw shave, spoke shave.** **3** A shaving; thin slice. **4** An extra or exorbitant discount paid for cashing a note or draft, as a premium given for an extension of time. **5** *Colloq.* The act of rushing by or barely grazing something; hence, a narrow escape: a close *shave*. **6** One who drives hard bargains. [OE *scafan* shave]

shave·ling (shāv'ling) *n.* **1** One who is shaven; opprobriously, a monk or priest. **2** A youth.

shav·en (shā'vən) Alternative past participle

of SHAVE. — *adj.* **1** Shaved; also, tonsured. **2** Trimmed closely.

shave·tail (shāv′tāl′) *n.* *U.S. Slang* **1** A second lieutenant, especially one recently commissioned. **2** An untrained or intractable mule. **3** A tenderfoot. [Formerly in allusion to young, unbroken army mules with their tails bobbed]

shav·ing (shā′ving) *n.* **1** The act of one who shaves; that which shaves. **2** A thin paring shaved from anything, as a board.

shawl (shôl) *n.* A wrap, as a square cloth, or large broad scarf, worn over the upper part of the body. [<Persian *shāl*]

shawm (shôm) *n.* An ancient, double-reed instrument; inaccurately, a cornet or horn. [<OF *chalemie* pipe <LL *calamellus*, dim. of L *calamus* reed]

Shaw·nee (shô·nē′) *n.* One of a warlike tribe of North American Indians of Algonquian stock, formerly living in Tennessee and South Carolina: now in Oklahoma. [<Algonquian (Shawnee) *Shawunogi* southerners <*shawun* south]

shay (shā) *n.* A chaise: a back formation due to mistaking *chaise* for a plural.

she (shē) *pron.* **1** The female person or being previously mentioned or understood, in the nominative case. **2** That woman or female; any woman: *She* who listens learns. — *n.* A female person or being: This puppy is a *she*. [OE *sēo, sīo*, fem. of *sē* the, replacing *hēo* she]

she- *combining form* Female; feminine: in hyphenated compounds: a *she*-lion.

shea (shē) *n.* A large tree (*Butyrospermum parkis*) growing only in western tropical Africa and yielding **shea butter,** used for food, illumination, and making soap. [<Mundingo *si, se*]

sheaf (shēf) *n.* *pl.* **sheaves** (shēvz) **1** A quantity of the stalks of cut grain or the like, bound together; a bundle of straw. **2** Any collection of things, as papers, held together by a band or tie. **3** The quiverful of arrows carried by an archer, usually 24. — *v.t.* To bind in a sheaf; sheave. [OE *scēaf*]

shear (shir) *n.* **1** A two-bladed cutting instrument: obsolete except in the plural. See SHEARS. **2** *Physics* A deformation of a solid body, equivalent to a sliding over each other of adjacent laminar elements, with a progressive relative displacement: also **shearing stress.** **3** The act or result of shearing. **4** A plowshare. **5** *Naut.* Sweep; sheer. — *v.* **sheared** (*Archaic* **shore**), **sheared** or **shorn, shear·ing** *v.t.* **1** To cut the hair, fleece, etc., from. **2** To remove by cutting or clipping: to *shear* wool. **3** To deprive; strip, as of power or wealth. **4** To cut or clip with shears or other sharp instrument: to *shear* a cable. **5** *Dial.* To reap, as grain, with a sickle. — *v.i.* **6** To use shears or other sharp instrument. **7** To slide or break from a shear (def. 2). **8** To proceed by or as by cutting a way: with *through.* **9** *Dial.* To reap with a sickle. See synonyms under CUT. ◆ Homophone: *sheer.* [OE *scēara* scissors <*sceran* shear. Akin to SHARD, SHARE.] — **shear′er** *n.*

shear·ling (shir′ling) *n.* **1** The fleece from the second shearing of a sheep. **2** The sheep from which one fleece has been cut.

shears (shirz) *n. pl.* **1** Any large cutting or clipping instrument worked by the crossing of cutting edges. **2** The ways or guides, as of a lathe. **3** An apparatus for hoisting and moving heavy objects, consisting of two or more spars with lower ends spread out and upper ends jointed to receive the tackle: also **shear legs:** sometimes spelled *sheers.* **4** The side frames of a steam fire engine. [See SHEAR]

shear·wa·ter (shir′wô′tər, -wot′ər) *n.* One of several sea birds (genus *Puffinus*) related to the petrels and albatrosses, found in most seas: so called because they skim close to the water.

sheat·fish (shēt′fish′) *n. pl.* **·fish** or **·fish·es** A catfish (*Siluris glanis*) of the fresh waters of central and eastern Europe. It is the largest fresh-water fish in Europe. [OE *scēota* trout + FISH]

sheath (shēth) *n.* **1** An envelope or case, as for a sword; scabbard. **2** *Bot.* A case enclosing a part or an organ, as the lower part of the leaves in grasses. **3** *Zool.* Any covering in animals that resembles a sheath. **4** *Entomol.*

An elytron of a beetle. **5** *Agric.* A bar connecting the beam and sole in a plow [OE *scæth*] — **sheath′less** *adj.*

sheath–bill (shēth′bil′) *n.* Any of a small number of species of sea birds of the family *Chionididae,* natives of the Antarctic islands. They are pure white in plumage and have a horny sheath at the base of the bill.

sheathe (shēth) *v.t.* **sheathed, sheath·ing** **1** To put into a sheath. **2** To plunge (a sword, etc.) into flesh, as if into a sheath. **3** To incase or protect with a covering, as the hull of a ship with metal. **4** To draw in, as claws. [<SHEATH]

sheath·ing (shē′thing) *n.* **1** A casing, as of a building, or the protective covering of a ship's hull; that which sheathes; also, the material used. **2** The act of one who sheathes. **3** *Archit.* The covering or waterproof material on outside walls or roof

sheath knife A large case knife carried in a sheath attached to a belt, worn by sailors and riggers.

sheave¹ (shēv) *v.t.* **sheaved, sheav·ing** To gather into sheaves; collect. [<SHEAF]

sheave² (shēv) *n.* **1** A grooved pulley wheel; also, a pulley wheel and its block. **2** An eccentric, or its disk. **3** *Scot.* A slice or cut. Also spelled *sheaf, sheeve.* [Var. of SHIVE¹]

SHEAVE

sheaves (shēvz) Plural of SHEAF.

She·ba (shē′bə), **Queen of** A queen, called Balkis in the Koran, who visited Solomon to test his wisdom. I Kings x 1–13.

she·bang (shi·bang′) *n.* *U.S. Slang* **1** A building, vehicle, saloon, theater, etc. **2** Any matter of present concern; thing; contrivance; outfit: tired of the whole *shebang.* [Var. of SHEBEEN]

she·been (shi·bēn′) *n.* *Irish & Scot.* A groggery; specifically, a place where liquors are sold without a license; hence, weak ale or beer. [<Irish *sibín* little mug]

shed¹ (shed) *v.* **shed, shed·ding** *v.t.* **1** To pour forth in drops; emit, as tears or blood. **2** To cause to pour forth. **3** To send forth or abroad; diffuse; radiate, as light. **4** To throw off without allowing to penetrate, as rain; repel. **5** To cast off by natural process, as hair, skin, a shell, etc. — *v.i.* **6** To cast off or lose hair, skin, etc., by natural process. **7** To fall or drop, as leaves or seed. — **to shed blood** To kill. — *n.* **1** That which sheds, as a sloping surface or watershed. **2** The act of shedding: *bloodshed.* **3** A separation or division; parting: applied technically to the opening in the warp through which the shuttle is thrown in weaving, and in parts of Great Britain to the parting of the hair. See illustration under LOOM. **4** The slope of a hill. [OE *scēadan* separate, part]

shed² (shed) *n.* **1** A small low building, often with front or sides open; also, a lean-to: a wagon *shed.* **2** *Brit.* A storehouse; barn. **3** A temporary covering; cabin. **4** A hangar. See synonyms under HUT. [Var. of SHADE]

sheen (shēn) *n.* **1** A glistening brightness, as if from reflection. **2** Bright, shining attire. See synonyms under LIGHT. — *adj.* Shining; radiant; beautiful. — *v.i.* To shine; gleam; glisten. [OE *scēne* beautiful; infl. in meaning by SHINE. Akin to G *schön* beautiful.] — **sheen′y** *adj.*

sheep (shēp) *n. pl.* **sheep** **1** A medium-sized,

SHEEP
Nomenclature of anatomical parts.

domesticated ruminant of the genus *Ovis* (family *Bovidae*), highly prized for its flesh, wool, and skin. ◆ Collateral adjective: *ovine.* **2** Leather made from the skin of the sheep, as for bookbinding: also *sheepskin.* **3** Someone with the supposed temperament of a sheep; hence, a meek, bashful, or timid person. [OE *scēap*]

sheep·ber·ry (shēp′ber′ē) *n. pl.* **·ries 1** One of the black, oval, edible drupes of the sweet viburnum (*Viburnum lentago*). **2** The tree itself.

sheep·cote (shēp′kōt′) *n.* A small enclosure for the protection of sheep; a sheepfold. Also **sheep′cot′** (-kot′).

sheep dip Any of several liquid disinfectants which contain creosote, nicotine, cresol, arsenic, etc., used for dipping sheep.

sheep dog 1 A dog trained to guard and control sheep; shepherd's dog: often a collie, but also a rough-coated, heavy, short-tailed dog much used by drovers in England. **2** Figuratively, a chaperon. — **old English sheep dog** A bob-tailed dog of undetermined origin, used as a sporting dog, and, in Great Britain, to herd flocks: characterized by a strong, muscular, thick-set body, covered with a very thick gray, grizzle, or blue-gray shaggy coat.

sheep·fold (shēp′fōld′) *n.* A place where sheep are enclosed at night; a pen for sheep.

sheep·herd·er (shēp′hûr′dər) *n.* A herder of sheep. — **sheep′herd′ing** *n.*

sheep·ish (shē′pish) *adj.* Foolish, as a sheep; awkwardly diffident; abashed. — **sheep′ish·ly** *adv.* — **sheep′ish·ness** *n.*

sheep laurel Lambkill.

sheep ranch A ranch and range where sheep are bred and raised. Also *Brit.* **sheep′walk′,** *Austral.* **sheep run.**

sheep's eyes Bashful, sidelong, or amorous glances.

sheeps·head (shēps′hed′) *n.* **1** A common deep-bodied sparoid food fish (*Archosargus probatocephalus*) of the Atlantic coast of the United States. **2** The Great Lakes drumfish, also found in the Mississippi region. **3** The dollarfish. **4** A foolish or silly person.

sheep·shear·ing (shēp′shir′ing) *n.* **1** The act of shearing sheep. **2** The shearing season; an occasion at which sheep are shorn, and the feast or celebration given at the occasion. — **sheep′shear′er** *n.*

sheep·skin (shēp′skin′) *n.* **1** The skin of a sheep, tanned or untanned, or anything made from it, as parchment. **2** A document written on parchment; hence, a diploma.

sheep sorrel An herb (*Rumex acetosella*) of the buckwheat family, widely distributed in dry places, and having leaves of an acrid taste.

sheer¹ (shir) *v.i.* To swerve from a course; turn aside. — *v.t.* To cause to swerve or deviate. — *n.* **1** *Naut.* **a** The rise, or the amount of rise from a level, of the lengthwise lines of a vessel's hull. **b** A position of a vessel that enables it to swing clear of a single anchor. **2** A swerving or curving course. ◆ Homophone: *shear.* [<SHEAR]

sheer² (shir) *adj.* **1** Having no modifying conditions; unmitigated; absolute; downright; utter: *sheer* folly; *sheer* nonsense. **2** Exceedingly thin and fine: said of fabrics. **3** Perpendicular; steep; ascending vertically: a *sheer* precipice. **4** Pure; pellucid. **5** *Obs.* Bright; shining. See synonyms under PURE, STEEP. — *n.* Any very thin fabric used for clothes. — *adv.* Entirely; perpendicularly: also **sheer′ly.** ◆ Homophone: *shear.* [ME *schere.* Cf. ON *skærr* clear, bright and OE *scīr* bright. shining.] — **sheer′ness** *n.*

sheers (shirz) See SHEARS (def. 3).

sheet (shēt) *n.* **1** A very thin and broad piece of any substance; that which is or can be spread, as upon a surface, or can be laid in broad folds; anything having a considerable expanse with very little thickness. **2** A large rectangular piece of linen or cotton cloth, used in making up a bed. **3** A piece of paper, especially one of a regular size; hence, a newspaper, or a leaf of a book. **4** A piece of metal or other substance hammered, rolled, fused, or cut very thin: a *sheet* of glass. **5** A broad, flat surface; superficial expanse: a *sheet* of water; a *sheet* of flame. **6** *Naut.* **a** A rope or chain from a lower corner of a sail to extend it or move it. **b** *pl.* In an open boat, the space

at the bow and stern not occupied by the thwarts. The former is termed the **fore sheets** and the latter the **stern sheets**. **7** A sail: a literary use. **8** *Geol.* **a** An originally horizontal or moderately inclined layer of igneous rock of small thickness as compared with its lateral extent. **b** Any superficial deposit, as of gravel left by a glacier, or of soil or ice. **9** The large, unseparated block of stamps printed by one impression of a plate. — **three sheets in the wind** *Slang* Tipsy; drunk. — *v.t.* **1** To stretch by hauling on a sheet: used only in the expression **to sheet home**, to stretch the clews of a sail to the extremities of the next lower yard. **2** To cover with or wrap in a sheet. **3** To furnish with sheets. — *v.i.* **4** To extend in a particular direction: said of the sheets of a sail. [OE *scēte* linen cloth]

sheet·ing (shē′ting) *n.* **1** The act of sheeting, in any sense. **2** Cotton, muslin, linen, or cotton percale, for making bleached, unbleached, or colored sheets for beds.

sheet lightning Lightning appearing in sheetlike form as a momentary and broadly diffused radiance in the sky, caused by the reflection of a distant lightning flash.

sheet metal Metal rolled and pressed into sheets.

sheet music Music printed on separate sheets of paper.

sheeve (shēv) See SHEAVE².

sheik (shēk, *Brit.* shāk) *n.* **1** A Moslem high priest, a venerable man; the chief or head of an Arab tribe or family: often used as a title of respect. **2** A man who fascinates women; a lady–killer: from *The Sheik*, a novel (1921) by Edith M. Hull. Also **sheikh.** Also spelled *scheik, shaik, sheyk.* [< Arabic *sheikh, shaykh,* lit., an elder, chief < *shakha* grow old]

sheik·dom (shēk′dəm) *n.* The land ruled by a sheik. Also **sheikh′dom.**

shek·el (shek′əl) *n.* **1** An Assyrian, Babylonian, and, later, Hebrew unit of weight and money; a coin having this weight. **2** *pl. Slang* Money; riches. [< Hebrew *sheqel* < *shāqal* weigh]

shel·drake (shel′drāk) *n.* **1** A large Old World duck of either of the genera *Tadorna* or *Casarca,* as the common sheldrake (*T. tadorna*), or the **ruddy sheldrake** (*C. rutila*) of southeastern Europe and North Africa. **2** A merganser, especially the red–breasted merganser or **salt–water sheldrake** (*Mergus serrator*). **3** The canvasback duck. [< dial. E *sheld* piebald, dappled + DRAKE]

shelf (shelf) *n. pl.* **shelves** (shelvz) **1** A board or slab set horizontally into or against a wall to support articles, as books; one of the boards in a bookcase or closet; the contents of a shelf. **2** Any flat projecting ledge, as of rock. **3** A steep–sided bank or shallow place in a body of water; a reef; shoal. **4** The stratum of bedrock met in sinking a shaft. — **on the shelf** No longer in use; discarded. [< LG *schelf* set of shelves]

shell (shel) *n.* **1** A hard structure incasing an animal, as a mollusk, or an egg or fruit. **2** A mollusk; shellfish: much used in composition. **3** A hollow structure or vessel, generally thin and weak; also, a framework with its interior removed or destroyed, or one to be filled out or built upon. **4** A very light, long, and narrow racing rowboat. **5** A hollow metallic projectile filled with an explosive or chemical; especially, an artillery projectile filled with high explosive: used against materiel and fortifications and distinguished from shrapnel used against personnel. **6** The plates, etc., constituting the framework of a steam boiler or the like. **7** A metallic or paper cartridge case for breechloading small arms (see illustration under CARTRIDGE); also, any paper case used to contain the explosives of fireworks, such as torpedos. **8** *Physics* One of the orbits in which the electrons of an atom revolve. **9** A shape or outline that merely simulates a reality; hollow form; external semblance. **10** The external ear; auricle. **11** The lyre: originally a stringed tortoise shell. **12** A reserved or impersonal attitude: to come out of one's *shell.* — *v.t.* **1** To divest of or remove from a shell; strip from the husk, pod, or shell. **2** To separate from the cob, as Indian corn. **3** To bombard with shells, as a fort. **4** To cover with shells. — *v.i.* **5** To shed or become freed from the shell or pod. **6** To fall

off, as a shell or scale. — **to shell out** *Colloq.* To hand over, as money. [OE *scell* shell] — **shell′er** *n.* — **shell′–less** *adj.* — **shell′y** *adj.*

shel·lac (shə·lak′) *n.* **1** A purified lac obtained as plates or cakes and extensively used in varnish, sealing wax, insulators, etc. **2** A solution, orange or white, of flake shellac dissolved in methylated spirit: used for coating floors, woodwork, etc. — *v.t.* **·lacked, ·lack·ing 1** To cover or varnish with shellac. **2** *Slang* **a** To belabor; beat. **b.** To defeat utterly. Also **shel·lack′.** [< SHELL + LAC¹, trans. of F *laque en écailles* lac in fine sheets]

shel·lack·ing (shə·lak′ing) *n. Slang* **1** A beating; assault. **2** A thorough defeat.

shellac varnish Any of several varnishes containing dissolved shellac and giving a thin, hard, sometimes glossy, coat.

shell·bark (shel′bärk′) *n.* The shagbark or one of its nuts.

shell·fire (shel′fīr′) *n.* The firing of artillery shells.

shell·fish (shel′fish′) *n. pl.* **·fish** or **·fish·es** Any aquatic animal having a shell, as a mollusk.

shell game 1 A swindling game in which the victim bets on the location of a pea covered by one of three nutshells; thimblerig. **2** Any game in which the victim cannot win.

shell·proof (shel′prōōf′) *adj.* Built to resist the destructive effect of projectiles and bombs.

shell shock Combat fatigue. — **shell–shocked** (shel′shokt′) *adj.*

shel·ter (shel′tər) *v.t.* To provide protection or shelter for; shield, as from danger or inclement weather. — *v.i.* To take shelter. — *n.* **1** That which covers or shields from exposure or danger; a place of safety. **2** The state of being sheltered or protected. **3** A cover from the weather, as a box for meteorological instruments, etc. **4** One who protects; a guardian. [Appar. alter. of ME *scheltrum* < OE *sceld–truma,* a body of men armed with shields, phalanx, protection] — **shel′ter·er** *n.* — **shel′ter·less** *adj.*

Synonyms (verb): cover, defend, guard, harbor, protect, screen, shield, ward. To *cover* generally means to extend completely over something; a vessel is *covered* with a lid; the head is *covered* with hair. To *shelter* is to cover so as to *protect* from injury or annoyance; as, the roof *shelters* from the storm. To *defend* implies the actual, *protect* implies the possible use of force or resisting power; *guard* implies sustained vigilance with readiness for conflict. *Protect* is more complete than *guard* or *defend;* an object may be faithfully *guarded* or bravely *defended* in vain, but that which is *protected* is secure. See CHERISH. Compare synonyms for DEFENSE. *Antonyms:* betray, expel, expose, refuse, reject, surrender.

Synonyms (noun): asylum, cover, covert, defense, harbor, haven, protection, refuge, retreat, sanctuary, shield. See DEFENSE. *Antonyms:* assault, attack, danger, exposure, onslaught, peril.

shelve (shelv) *v.* **shelved, shelv·ing** *v.t.* **1** To place on a shelf. **2** To postpone indefinitely; put aside. **3** To retire. **4** To provide or fit with shelves. — *v.i.* **5** To incline gradually; slope. [< SHELF] — **shelv′y** *adj.*

shelves (shelvz) Plural of SHELF.

shelv·ing (shel′ving) *n.* **1** Shelves collectively. **2** Material for the construction of shelves. **3** The act of putting away on shelves; hence, putting aside; dismissing. **4** A slight inclining.

Shen·an·do·ah (shen′ən·dō′ə) A river in Virginia and West Virginia, flowing 55 miles to the Potomac at Harper's Ferry. The **Shenandoah Valley,** part of the Great Appalachian Valley, was the scene of many battles during the Civil War.

she·nan·i·gan (shi·nan′ə·gən) *n. Colloq.* Trickery; foolery; nonsense; also, treacherous action or a treacherous act. [Prob. < Irish *sionnach* fox]

she·ol (shē′ōl) *n.* Hell. [< Hebrew *she′ōl* cave < *shā′al* dig]

shep·herd (shep′ərd) *n.* **1** A keeper or herder of sheep. **2** Figuratively, a pastor, leader, or guide. — *v.t.* To watch and tend as a shepherd; guard; protect. [OE *scēaphyrde*] — **shep′herd·ess** *n. fem.*

shep·herd's–purse (shep′ərdz·pûrs′) *n.* A common herbaceous weed (*Capsella bursa-pastoris*) bearing small white flowers and notched triangular pods (whence its name).

sher·bet (shûr′bit) *n.* **1** A flavored water ice. **2** An Oriental drink, made of fruit juice sweetened and diluted with water and sometimes cooled with snow. [< Turkish *sharbat* < Arabic *sharbah* a drink < *shariba* drink. Doublet of SIRUP.]

sherd (shûrd) *n.* A fragment of pottery: often in composition: *potsherd:* also spelled *shard.* [Var. of SHARD]

she·rif (she·rēf′) *n.* **1** A member of a princely Moslem family which claims descent from Mohammed through his daughter Fatima. **2** The chief magistrate of Mecca: also **grand sherif. 3** An Arab chief. Also **she·reef′.** [< Arabic *sharif* noble]

sher·iff (sher′if) *n.* The chief administrative officer of a county, who executes the mandates of courts, etc. In the United States, the sheriff is elected by the legislature or by direct vote of the citizens and must be of age, a citizen of the country, and reside in the county he represents. [OE *scīr–gerefa* shire reeve] — **sher′iff·dom** *n.*

Sher·lock Holmes (shûr′lok hōmz′) A fictitious English detective, the central character of numerous stories by Arthur Conan Doyle.

sher·ry (sher′ē) *n. pl.* **·ries** The fortified wines of Jerez (formerly Xerez), Spain, or a wine made in imitation of these, as in California. [from *Xerez,* Spain]

Sherwood Forest An ancient forest, chiefly in Nottinghamshire, central England; celebrated as the home of Robin Hood and his men.

Shet·land Islands (shet′lənd) A Scottish island group NE of the Orkney Islands, comprising a county of northern Scotland (**Shetland:** also *Zetland*); 551 square miles; several hundred islands, 24 inhabited; capital, Lerwick, on Mainland, the largest island.

Shetland pony A small, hardy, shaggy breed of pony originally bred on the Shetland Islands.

Shetland wool Thin, very loosely twisted yarn from the wool of Shetland sheep; also, the wool.

shew·bread (shō′bred′) *n.* Unleavened bread formerly displayed in the Jewish temple: also spelled *showbread.*

she–wolf (shē′woolf′) *n. pl.* **–wolves** (-woolvz′) A female wolf.

shib·bo·leth (shib′ə·leth) *n.* A test word or pet phrase of a party; a watchword: from the Hebrew word *shibboleth,* given by Jephthah (*Judges* xii 4–6) as a test to distinguish his own men from the Ephraimites, who used the pronunciation *sibboleth.* [< Hebrew *shibbōleth* ear of corn]

shied (shīd) Past tense and past participle of SHY.

shield (shēld) *n.* **1** A broad piece of defensive armor, commonly carried on the left arm; a large buckler. **2** Something that protects or defends; a defender; shelter. **3** Any device for covering or protecting something. **4** *Mil.* A screen of steel attached to a gun to protect the men who are serving it. **5** *Mining* A framework or screen of wood or iron protecting the workers: pushed forward as the work advances. **6** *Her.* The escutcheon upon which emblems of heraldry are depicted. **7** *Zool.* A platelike protective part, as the carapace of a crustacean. **8** A policeman's badge. See synonyms under DEFENSE, SHELTER. — *v.t.* **1** To protect from danger as with a shield; defend; guard. **2** *Archaic* To avert; forbid. — *v.i.* **3** To act as a shield or safeguard. See synonyms under SHELTER. [OE *sceld*] — **shield′er** *n.* — **shield′-bear′er** (-bâr′ər) *n.* — **shield′–shaped′** (-shāpt′) *adj.*

SHIELDS
a. Anglo-Saxon.
b. Greek.

shield–fern (shēld′fûrn′) *n.* A fern (genus *Dryopteris*), so called from its shield–shaped sporangia.

shi·er (shī′ər), **shi·est** (shī′ist) Comparative and superlative of SHY.

shift (shift) *v.t.* **1** To change or move from one position, place, etc., to another. **2** To change for another or others of the same class. **3** To change (gears) from one arrangement to another. **4** *Ling.* To alter phonetically as part of a systematic change. —*v.i.* **5** To change position, place, etc. **6** To try varied expedients; do the best one can; manage. **7** To evade; equivocate. **8** To shift gears: The car *shifts* automatically. —*n.* **1** The act of shifting. **2** A recourse or contrivance adopted in the absence of direct means: We'll make *shift* to get along; hence, a dodge; artifice; trick; evasion. **3** *Archaic* or *Dial.* An undergarment; chemise. **4** A change of clothes. **5** A change of place, direction, or form: a *shift* in the wind; transfer, as of a burden. **6** A change of the position of the hand when playing on the fingerboard of an instrument of the viol class. **7** A relay of workers; also, the working time of each group. **8** *Physics* Any of various displacements of spectral lines caused by velocity of the light source, gravitational effect, etc. Compare EINSTEIN SHIFT, DOPPLER EFFECT. **9** *Geol.* The relative displacement of areas on opposite sides of a rock fault and outside of the zone of dislocation. **10** *Ling.* **a** A patterned phonetic or phonemic change, as the consonant *shift* described in Grimm's Law. **b** Functional shift. See synonyms under CHANGE, CONVEY. [OE *sciftan* divide] —**shift'er** *n.*

shift·less (shift'lis) *adj.* **1** Unable or unwilling to shift for oneself; inefficient or lazy. **2** Inefficiently done; showing lack of energy or resource. See synonyms under IMPROVIDENT. —**shift'less·ly** *adv.* —**shift'less·ness** *n.*

shift·y (shif'tē) *adj.* **shift·i·er**, **shift·i·est** **1** Full of expedients; alert; capable. **2** Artful; tricky; fickle. —**shift'i·ly** *adv.* —**shift'i·ness** *n.*

Shi·ite (shē'īt) *n.* A Shiah. —**Shi·it'ic** (-it'ik) *adj.*

shill (shil) *n.* *Slang* The assistant of a sidewalk peddler or gambler who makes a purchase or bet to encourage onlookers to buy or bet; a capper. [Origin unknown]

shil·le·lagh (shi·lā'lə, -lē) *n.* In Ireland, a stout cudgel made of oak or blackthorn. See synonyms under STICK. Also **shil·la'lah**, **shil·lea'lah**, **shil·le'lah.** [from *Shillelagh*, a town in Ireland famed for its oaks]

shil·ling (shil'ing) *n.* **1** A current silver coin of Great Britain, first issued in 1504; twelvepence. Compare SOLIDUS (def. 2). **2** A former denomination of money in the United States varying in value from 12 1/2 to 16 2/3 cents. —**King's shilling** An English shilling formerly handed to a recruit on his joining the British military service: considered as binding as the signing of a contract: also **Queen's shilling.** [OE *scilling*]

PINE–TREE SHILLING
Issued by Massachusetts in
1652 (actual size).

shil·ly–shal·ly (shil'ē·shal'ē) *v.i.* **·lied**, **·ly·ing** **1** To act with indecision; be irresolute; vacillate. **2** To trifle. —*adj.* Weak; hesitating. —*n.* Weak or foolish vacillation; irresolution; any trifling. —*adv.* In an irresolute manner. [Dissimilated reduplication of *shall I*?] —**shil'ly–shal'li·er** *n.*

shim (shim) *n.* In machinery, stoneworking, and railroading, a piece of metal or other material used to fill out space, as where joints are worn loose, or between something and its support. —*v.t.* **shimmed**, **shim·ming** To wedge up or fill out to a proper position or level by inserting a shim. [Origin uncertain]

shim·mer (shim'ər) *v.i.* To shine faintly; give off or emit a tremulous light; glimmer. —*n.* A tremulous shining or gleaming; glimmer; gleam. See synonyms under LIGHT. [OE *scimerian*, prob. freq. of *scinan* shine] —**shim'mer·y** *adj.*

shim·my (shim'ē) *n.* *pl.* **·mies** *U.S.* **1** *Colloq.* A chemise. **2** A jazz dance accompanied by

shaking movements: also **shimmy shake.** **3** Unusual vibration, as in automobile wheels. —*v.i.* **·mied**, **·my·ing** **1** To vibrate or wobble. **2** To dance the shimmy. [Alter. of CHEMISE]

shin¹ (shin) *n.* **1** The front part of the leg below the knee; also, the shin bone. **2** The lower foreleg: a *shin* of beef. —*v.t.* & *v.i.* **shinned**, **shin·ning** **1** To climb (a pole) by gripping with the hands or arms and the shins or legs: usually with *up.* **2** To kick (someone) on the shins. [OE *scinu*]

shin² (shēn) *n.* The twenty–first Hebrew letter. See ALPHABET.

shin bone The tibia.

shin·dig (shin'dig) *n.* *U.S. Slang* A dance or noisy party. [? < *a dig on the shin*]

shine (shīn) *v.i.* **shone** or (*esp. for def.* 5) **shined**, **shin·ing** **1** To emit light; beam; glow. **2** To gleam, as by reflected light. **3** To excel or be conspicuous in splendor, beauty, or intellectual brilliance; be preeminent. —*v.t.* **4** To cause to shine. **5** To brighten by rubbing or polishing. —**to shine up to** *Slang* To try to please. —*n.* **1** The state or quality of being bright or shining; radiance; luster; sheen. **2** Fair weather; sunshine. **3** *U.S. Colloq.* A liking or fancy. **4** *U.S. Colloq.* A smart trick or prank. **5** A gloss or polish on shoes. See synonyms under LIGHT. —**to take a shine to** *U.S. Colloq.* To become fond of. [OE *scinan*]

Synonyms (*verb*): beam, coruscate, glare, gleam, glisten, glitter, glow, scintillate, sparkle.

shin·er (shī'nər) *n.* **1** One who or that which shines or causes to shine. **2** A bright or gold coin. **3** One of various silvery cyprinoid freshwater fishes (genus *Notropis*) common in North America. **4** A bristletail. **5** *Slang* A black eye from a blow.

shin·gle (shing'gəl) *n.* **1** A thin, tapering piece of wood or other material, usually about 18 inches long and 4 or more inches wide, used in courses to cover roofs. **2** A small sign board, as a shingle or a brass plate, bearing the name of a doctor, lawyer, etc., and placed outside his office. **3** A short haircut. —*v.t.* **·gled**, **·gling** **1** To cover (a roof, building, etc.) with or as with shingles. **2** To cut (the hair) short all over the head. [Alter. of ME *schindle* <L *scindula*, var. of *scandula* a shingle] —**shin'gler** *n.*

shin·gles (shing'gəlz) *n.* *Pathol.* A skin disease, most commonly due to an infection, but also to nervous trouble, accompanied by neuralgia, with eruptions sometimes extending half round the body like a girdle: also called *herpes zoster.* [Alter. of Med. L *cingulus* <L *cingulum* girdle < *cingere* gird]

shin·ing (shī'ning) *adj.* **1** Emitting or reflecting a continuous light; gleaming; luminous. **2** Of unusual brilliance or excellence; conspicuous. —**shin'ing·ly** *adv.*

shin·leaf (shin'lēf') *n.* A low perennial herb (*Pyrola elliptica*), with rounded evergreen root leaves, common in the woods of the northern United States. [From the use of its leaves for shinplasters]

shin·ny (shin'ē) *v.i.* **·nied**, **·ny·ing** *U.S. Colloq.* To climb using one's shins: usually with *up.*

Shin·to (shin'tō) *n.* The primitive religion of Japan, consisting chiefly in ancestor worship, nature worship, and the worship of many ethnic divinities, from the chief of whom the Emperor is thought to be descended, and thus himself a god: as **State Shinto,** it was the state religion of Japan, 1868–1945, and in that period incorporated many nationalistic and militaristic elements, later minimized. Also **Shin'to·ism.** [<Japanese, way of the gods < Chinese *shin* god + *tao* way or law] —**Shin'·to·ist** *n.*

shin·y (shī'nē) *adj.* **shin·i·er**, **shin·i·est** **1** Glistening; glossy; polished. **2** Bright; clear.

ship (ship) *n.* **1** Any vessel suitable for deepwater navigation: a *steamship,* sailing *ship.* **2** A large seagoing sailing vessel with at least three masts, carrying square–rigged sails on all three. **3** An airship or airplane. **4** Figuratively, fortune: when my *ship* comes in. —**capital ship** Any vessel of war of the first rank, as a battleship, battle cruiser, or aircraft carrier. —*v.* **shipped, ship·ping** *v.t.* **1** To transport by ship or other mode of convey-

ance. **2** To send by any established mode of transportation, as by rail. **3** To hire and receive for service on board a vessel, as sailors. **4** *Naut.* To receive over the side, as in rough weather: to *ship* a wave. **5** *Colloq.* To get rid of. **6** To set or fit in a prepared place on a boat or vessel, as a mast, or a rudder; also, to draw (oars) inside a boat from rowlocks. —*v.i.* **7** To go on board ship; embark. **8** To undergo shipment: Raspberries do not *ship* well. **9** To enlist as a seaman. [OE *scip*]

FULL–RIGGED SHIP
With double topsails and staysails.
a. Flying jib. *b.* Jib. *c.* Foretopmast staysail. *d.* Foresail. *e.* Mainsail. *f.* Crossjacksail. *g.* Spanker. *h.* Maintopmast staysail. *i.* Mizzentopmast staysail. *j.* Lower foretopsail. *k.* Lower maintopsail. *l.* Lower mizzentopsail. *m.* Upper foretopsail. *n.* Upper maintopsail. *o.* Upper mizzentopsail. *p.* Foretopgallant sail. *q.* Maintopgallant sail. *r.* Mizzentopgallant sail. *s.* Fore royal. *t.* Main royal. *u.* Mizzen royal. *v.* Main skysail. *w.* Maintopgallant staysail. *x.* Mizzentopgallant staysail. *y.* Main royal staysail.

–ship *suffix of nouns* **1** The state, condition, or quality of: *friendship.* **2** Office, rank, or dignity of: *kingship.* **3** The art or skill of: *marksmanship.* [OE *-scipe*]

ship·board (ship'bôrd', -bōrd') *n.* The side or deck of a ship; hence, a vessel: only in phrase **on shipboard.**

ship canal A waterway or canal deep enough for seagoing vessels.

ship·load (ship'lōd') *n.* The quantity that a ship carries or can carry; a cargo.

ship·mas·ter (ship'mas'tər, -mäs'-) *n.* The captain or master of a merchant ship.

ship·mate (ship'māt') *n.* A fellow sailor.

ship·ment (ship'mənt) *n.* The act of shipping, or that which is shipped; a consignment.

ship·pa·ble (ship'ə·bəl) *adj.* That can be shipped or transported.

ship·per (ship'ər) *n.* **1** One who or that which ships. **2** Any appliance for shifting some part of a machine, as in a loom. **3** A skipper; mariner.

ship·ping (ship'ing) *n.* **1** Ships collectively; the body of vessels belonging to a country or port; also, tonnage. **2** The act of shipping, in any sense. **3** *Obs.* A voyage.

ship·shape (ship'shāp') *adj.* Well arranged; trim; orderly; neat. —*adv.* In a seamanlike manner; neatly.

ship's papers The documents required by international law to be carried by a ship, as bills of lading, bill of health, invoices, logbook, proofs of ownership; also, certificate of registry, crew–list, clearance, license, and shipping articles. Compare MANIFEST.

ship's time *Naut.* The time as shown by the deck clock: usually local mean time at whatever meridian a vessel happens to be.

ship·way (ship'wā') *n.* **1** The ways on which a ship is built or examined. **2** A ship canal.

ship·worm (ship'wûrm') *n.* One of a family (*Teredinidae*) of marine bivalves, resembling worms, especially *Teredo navalis,* which burrows into the timbers of ships, piers, wharfs, etc.: also called *borer.*

ship·wreck (ship'rek') *n.* **1** The partial or total destruction of a ship at sea. **2** Utter or practical destruction; ruin. **3** Scattered remnants, as of a wrecked ship; wreckage. —*v.t.* **1** To wreck, as a vessel. **2** To bring to disaster; ruin; destroy.

ship·wright (ship'rīt') *n.* A ship carpenter or builder; one who works on the wooden parts of ships.

ship·yard (ship'yärd') *n.* An enclosure where ships are built or repaired.

shire (shīr) *n.* 1 A territorial division of Great Britain; a county. 2 A county in America: used only in compounds and proper names borrowed from England. [OE *scīr*]

shire horse One of a breed of large draft horses originating in the shires or midland counties of England. Also **Shire.**

shire town The capital of a county; county seat; county town.

shirk (shûrk) *v.t.* 1 To avoid the doing of; evade doing (something that should be done). 2 *Obs.* To obtain by trickery. — *v.i.* 3 To avoid work or evade obligation. [< *n.*] — *n.* One who shirks; also **shirk'er.** [Prob. < G *Schurke* rascal. Akin to SHARK².]

shirr (shûr) *v.t.* 1 To gather on parallel gathering threads. 2 To bake with crumbs in a buttered dish, as eggs. — *n.* 1 A fulling or gathering by threads. 2 A rubber thread woven into a fabric to make it elastic. [Origin unknown]

shirt (shûrt) *n.* 1 A loose garment for the upper part of the body, usually having collar and cuffs and a front closing. 2 A closely fitting undergarment for the upper part of the body. 3 The inner lining of a blast furnace. —**to keep one's shirt on** *Slang* To remain calm; keep one's temper. —**to lose one's shirt** *Slang* To lose everything. [OE *scyrte* shirt, short garment. Akin to SKIRT.] —**shirt'less** *adj.*

shirt·ing (shûr'ting) *n.* Closely woven material of cotton, linen, silk, etc., used for making shirts, blouses, dresses, etc.

shirt·waist (shûrt'wāst') *n.* A tailored, sleeved blouse or shirt: usually worn tucked in under skirt or trousers.

shish ke·bab (shish' kə·bäb') Beef or lamb, cut into cubes and cooked on skewers with onions, green peppers, and tomatoes. [< Arm. *shish kabab*]

shist (shist) See SCHIST, etc.

shiv (shiv) *n. Slang* In the criminal underworld, a knife or razor: often spelled *chevy, chiv.* Also **shive, shiv'y.** [< Romany *chiv* goad]

Shi·va (shē'və) See SIVA.

shiv·a·ree (shiv'ə·rē') *n. U.S.* A charivari, especially in the sense of the burlesque serenade of newly-weds. [Alter. of CHARIVARI]

shiv·er¹ (shiv'ər) *v.i.* To tremble, as with cold or fear; shake; vibrate; quiver. — *v.t. Naut.* To cause to flutter in the wind, as a sail. See synonyms under QUAKE. — *n.* The act of shivering; a shaking or quivering from any cause. [? Blend of SHAKE and QUIVER]

shiv·er² (shiv'ər) *v.t. & v.i.* To break suddenly into fragments; shatter. See synonyms under BREAK, SHAKE. — *n.* A splinter; sliver. [ME *schivere*, origin uncertain]

shiv·er·y¹ (shiv'ər·ē) *adj.* Chilly; tremulous.

shiv·er·y² (shiv'ər·ē) *adj.* Easily shivered; brittle.

shlock (shlok) See SCHLOCK.

shoal¹ (shōl) *n.* 1 A shallow place in any body of water. 2 A sandbank or bar, especially one seen at low water. Compare BANK and REEF. — *v.i.* 1 To become shallow. — *v.t.* 2 To make shallow. 3 To sail into a lesser depth of (water), as shown by soundings: The ship *shoaled* her water off Cape Hatteras. — *adj.* Of little depth; shallow. Also, *Scot., shaul.* [OE *sceald* shallow]

shoal² (shōl) *n.* An assemblage or multitude; throng, as of fish. — *v.i.* 1 To throng in shoals or multitudes. 2 To school: said of fish. [OE *scolu* shoal of fish. Akin to SCHOOL².]

shoal duck The American eider duck: so called from Isles of Shoals, off Portsmouth, New Hampshire.

shoat (shōt) *n.* 1 A young hog. 2 A worthless fellow. Also spelled *shote.* [Cf. West Flemish *schote* young pig]

shock¹ (shok) *n.* 1 A violent collision or concussion; impact; blow. 2 A sudden and violent sensation, as if causing one to shake or tremble; a stroke: a *shock* of paralysis. 3 A sudden agitation of the mind; startling emotion. 4 *Pathol.* Prostration of bodily functions, as from sudden injury. 5 The passage of a strong electric current through the body, or the phenomena it produces: characterized by involuntary muscular contractions. See synonyms under BLOW, COLLISION. — *v.t.* 1

To shake by sudden collision; jar; give a shock to. 2 To disturb the emotions or mind of; horrify; disgust. 3 To encounter with hostile intent; meet with sudden encounter. — *v.i.* 4 *Archaic* To come into violent contact; collide. [< F *choc* < *choquer* < Gmc. Cf. MDu. *schokken* collide.]

shock² (shok) *n.* A number of sheaves of grain, stalks of maize, or the like, stacked for drying upright in a field. — *v.t. & v.i.* To gather (grain) into a shock or shocks. [ME *schokke* < Gmc. Cf. MLG *schok.*] —**shock'er** *n.*

shock³ (shok) *adj.* Shaggy; bushy. — *n.* 1 A coarse, tangled mass, as of hair. 2 A dog with a woolly coat. [? Var. of SHAG]

shock absorber *Mech.* 1 A device designed to absorb the energy of sudden impacts or of abrupt changes in velocity, as the springs of an automobile, or an airplane landing gear. 2 A type of damper which absorbs motion, as of a part or mechanism, by hydraulic action, friction, etc.

shock·ing (shok'ing) *adj.* Causing a mental shock; striking as with horror or disgust; repugnant; distressing. See synonyms under AWFUL, FLAGRANT, FRIGHTFUL. — **shock'ing·ly** *adv.* — **shock'ing·ness** *n.*

shock therapy *Med.* The treatment of certain nervous and mental disorders by the subcutaneous injection of drugs, as Metrazol, insulin, camphor, etc., or by electrical shocks.

shock wave *Physics* A wave (of air, sound, etc.) having a pattern of flow which changes abruptly, with corresponding changes in temperature, pressure, and density: characteristic of bodies moving at or above the speed of sound.

shod (shod) Past tense and alternative past participle of SHOE.

shod·dy (shod'ē) *n. pl.* **·dies** 1 Reclaimed wool obtained by shredding discarded woolens or worsteds: longer fiber than mungo and better quality. 2 Fiber or cloth manufactured of inferior material or of shredded woolen rags. 3 Vulgar assumption or display; pretension; sham. 4 Refuse; waste. — *adj.* **·di·er, ·di·est** 1 Made of or containing shoddy. 2 Sham; inferior. [Origin uncertain] — **shod'di·ly** *adv.* — **shod'di·ness** *n.*

shoe (shōō) *n. pl.* **shoes** (*Obs.* **shoon**) 1 An outer covering, usually of leather, for the human foot, usually distinguished from a *boot* by not reaching above the ankle. 2 Something resembling a shoe in position or use. 3 A rim or plate of iron to protect the hoof of an animal from wear or injury. 4 A strip of iron, steel, or other hard material fitted under a sleigh or sledge runner to receive friction. 5 A drag of iron or wood placed under the wheel of a vehicle to retard its motion in going downhill; also, the part of a brake that presses upon the wheel. 6 An iron socket or ferrule for protecting the point of a wooden pile, or the end of a handspike, pole, or staff. 7 The tread or outer covering of a pneumatic tire, as for an automobile. 8 The part of a bridge on which the superstructure rests. 9 The sliding contact plate on an electric car. — *v.t.* **shod, shod** or **shod·den, shoe·ing** 1 To furnish with shoes or the like. 2 To furnish with a guard of metal, wood, etc., for protection, as against wear. [OE *scōh*]

PARTS OF A SHOE
a. Tongue.   *h.* Slipsole.
b. Top.   *i.* Insole.
c. Lacing.   *j.* Shank.
d. Eyelets.   *k.* Heel.
e. Vamp.   *l.* Counter.
f. Toe cap.   *m.* Backstay.
g. Outsole.   *n.* Backstrap.

shoe·bill (shōō'bil') *n.* A heron (*Balaeniceps rex*) of central Africa, with a huge vaulted and hooked bill.

shoe·horn (shōō'hôrn') *n.* A smooth curved implement of horn or other material shaped to aid in putting on a shoe.

shoe·shine (shōō'shīn') *n.* 1 The waxing and polishing of a pair of shoes. 2 The polished appearance thus given to the shoes.

shoe string A lace, cord, or ribbon for tying a shoe. Also **shoe lace.**

shoe·tree (shōō'trē') *n.* A wooden or metal form for inserting in boots and shoes to preserve their shape or to stretch them: also

called *boot–tree.*

sho·far (shō'fär) *n.* A ram's horn used in Jewish ritual, sounded on solemn occasions and in war. It is still blown on the Jewish New Year and on the Day of Atonement: also spelled *shophar.* [< Hebrew *shōphār*]

sho·gun (shō'gun, -gōōn) *n.* The hereditary commander in chief of the Japanese army until 1868: known to foreigners as the *tycoon.* [< Japanese < Chinese *chiang–chün* leader of an army] — **sho'gun·ate** (-it, -āt) *n.*

shone (shōn, shon) Past tense and past participle of SHINE.

shoo (shōō) *interj.* Begone! be off! away!: used in driving away fowls. — *v.t.* To drive away by crying "shoo." — *v.i.* To cry "shoo." [Imit.]

shoo·fly (shōō'flī) *n. U.S.* 1 A shuffling dance; also, the music for it. 2 An enclosed child's rocker with sides representing horses, swans, etc. 3 A kind of pie with a sirupy filling made with molasses and brown sugar: also **shoofly pie.**

shoo–in (shōō'in') *n. Colloq.* One who is virtually certain to win, as an election.

shook¹ (shŏŏk) Past tense of SHAKE.

shook² (shŏŏk) *n.* 1 A collection of barrel staves, shaped, chamfered, and arranged for assembling, conveniently bundled for transportation. 2 A set of boards in order for nailing together into a packing box, and conveniently bundled for transportation. 3 A shock of sheaves. [? Var. of SHOCK²]

shoot (shōōt) *v.* **shot, shoot·ing** *v.t.* 1 To hit, wound, or kill with a missile discharged from a weapon. 2 To discharge (a missile) from a bow, rifle, etc. 3 To discharge (a weapon): often with *off:* to *shoot* a cannon. 4 To take the altitude of with a sextant, etc.: to *shoot* the sun. 5 To send forth as if from a weapon, as questions, glances, etc. 6 To pass over or through swiftly: to *shoot* rapids. 7 To go over (an area) in hunting game. 8 To emit, as rays of light. 9 To photograph; film. 10 To cause to stick out or protrude; extend. 11 To put forth in growth; send forth (buds, leaves, etc.). 12 To push into or out of the fastening, as the bolt of a door. 13 To propel, discharge, or dump, as down a chute or from a container. 14 To variegate, as with streaks of color: usually in the past participle: The morning clouds were *shot* with silver. 15 In games: **a** To score (a goal, point, etc.) by kicking or otherwise forcing the ball, etc., to the objective. **b** To play (golf, craps, pool, etc.). **c** To propel (a marble) from between the thumb and forefinger; play (marbles). **d** To cast (the dice). 16 *Slang* To inject (a drug, especially a narcotic). — *v.i.* 17 To discharge a missile from a bow, firearm, etc.: Don't shoot! 18 To go off; discharge. 19 To move swiftly; dart. 20 To hunt game. 21 To jut out; extend or project. 22 To put forth buds, leaves, etc.; germinate; sprout. 23 To take a photograph. 24 To start the cameras, as in motion pictures. 25 In games, to make a play by propelling the ball, puck, etc., in a certain manner. — **to shoot at** (or **for**) *Colloq.* To strive for; attempt to attain or obtain. — **to shoot down** To bring to earth by shooting. — **to shoot off one's mouth** *Slang* To talk too freely or too much. — **to shoot up** 1 To move or grow upward quickly. 2 To strike with several or many shots. 3 *SW U.S.* To ride through (a town, etc.) shooting recklessly in all directions. — *n.* 1 A young branch or sucker of a plant; offshoot. 2 A narrow passage in a stream; a rapid. 3 An inclined passage down which anything may be shot; a chute. 4 The act of shooting. 5 A shooting match, hunting party, etc. 6 The thrust of an arch. 7 An antler or horn just pushing up. 8 Shooting distance; range. 9 A rapid thrusting movement [OE *scēotan*]

shooting gallery A place where one can go for target practice.

shooting iron *U.S. Slang* A firearm.

shooting star 1 A meteor. 2 Any of certain small perennial herbs (genus *Dodecatheon*); especially, the American cowslip (*D. meadia*) with oblong leaves and clusters of cyclamenlike flowers.

shoot–out (shōōt'out') *n.* A battle involving an exchange of gunfire.

shop (shop) *n.* 1 A place for the sale of goods at retail: in the United States commonly called a *store*. 2 A place for making or repairing any article, or the carrying on of a craft. 3 One's own craft or business as a subject of conversation: to talk *shop.* —*v.i.* **shopped, shop·ping** To visit shops or stores to purchase or look at goods. [OE *sceoppa* booth]

sho·phar (shō'fär) See SHOFAR.

shop·keep·er (shop'kē'pər) *n.* One who keeps a shop or store; a tradesman.

shop·lift·er (shop'lif'tər) *n.* One who steals goods exposed for sale in a shop. —**shop'. lift'ing** *n.*

shopping center A group of retail stores, restaurants, etc., including an ample parking area, usually built as a unit and accessible chiefly by automobile.

shop talk Conversation limited to one's job or profession.

shop·worn (shop'wôrn', -wōrn') *adj.* Soiled or otherwise deteriorated from having been handled or on display in a shop.

sho·ran (shôr'an, shō'ran) *n.* A high-precision electronic navigation system which transmits pulses, usually from an aircraft or ship, to ground stations at distances determined by the elapsed time between emission and return of the pulses. [<SHO(RT) RA(NGE) N(AVIGATION)]

shore[1] (shôr, shōr) *n.* 1 The coast or land adjacent to an ocean, sea, lake, or large river. ◆ Collateral adjective: *littoral.* 2 *Law* The ground between the ordinary high-water mark and low-water mark. See synonyms under BANK[1], LAND, MARGIN. — **in shore** Near or toward the shore. — *v.t.* **shored, shor·ing** 1 To set on shore. 2 To surround as with a shore. [ME *schore*; origin uncertain]

shore[2] (shôr, shōr) *v.t.* **shored, shor·ing** To prop, as a wall, by a vertical or sloping timber: usually with *up.* — *n.* A beam set endwise as a prop, as against the side of a building, a ship on the stocks, etc., especially as a temporary support. See illustration under DRYDOCK. [Cf. Du. *schoor* prop, ON *skordha* stay]

shore bird Any of various birds (suborder *Charadrii*) which frequent beaches and also the shores of inland waters.

shore·line (shôr'līn', shōr'-) *n.* The line or contour of a shore.

shore patrol A detail of the U. S. Navy, Coast Guard, or Marine Corps assigned to police duties ashore.

shore·ward (shôr'wərd, shōr'-) *adj. & adv.* Toward the shore. Also **shore'wards.**

shor·ing (shôr'ing, shō'ring) *n.* 1 The operation of propping, as with shores. 2 Shores, collectively.

shorl (shôrl) See SCHORL.

shorn (shôrn, shōrn) Alternative past participle of SHEAR.

short (shôrt) *adj.* 1 Having little linear extension; not long; of little extent; of no great distance. 2 Being below the average stature; not tall. 3 Having little extension in time; of limited duration; brief. 4 Abrupt in manner or spirit; curt; petulant; cross. 5 Not reaching or attaining a requirement, result, or mark; deficient; inadequate; scant: often with *of.* 6 In finance or commerce, not having in possession when selling, but having to procure in time to deliver as contracted; not being in possession of the seller, as stocks or shares; of or pertaining to short stocks or commodities: *short* sales. 7 Not comprehensive or retentive; at fault; in error; narrow: said of persons or their faculties: *short* memory. 8 Breaking easily; friable; crisp. 9 *Phonet.* **a** Relatively brief in pronunciation: said of vowels. **b** Designating a set of vowel sounds which contrast with the "long" vowels. See LONG[1] (def. 9). 10 In classical prosody, requiring a relatively short time to pronounce: said of syllables containing a short vowel (epsilon, omicron, etc.) not followed by two consonants or a double consonant. 11 In English prosody, unaccented. 12 Less than: with *of.* 13 Concise; compressed. See synonyms under LITTLE, SCANTY, TERSE, TRANSIENT. —*n.* 1 The compressed substance or pith of a matter. 2 Anything that is short; a short syllable or vowel. 3 A deficiency, as in a payment. 4 A short contract or sale; one who has sold short; a bear. 5 *pl.* Bran mixed with coarse meal or flour. 6 *pl.*

Trousers with legs extending part way to the knees: worn by both men and women. 7 *pl.* A man's undergarment covering the loins and often a portion of the legs. 8 In baseball slang, a shortstop. 9 *pl.* Clippings, scraps, etc., left over in the manufacture of different products and used to make an inferior quality of the product. 10 *Electr.* A short circuit. 11 A motion picture of relatively short duration as compared with the feature attraction on a program. —**for short** For brevity: Edward was called Ed *for short.* —**in short** In a word; briefly. —**the short and the long** The whole; the entire sum and substance. —*adv.* In a short manner or method, in any sense of the adjective: to stop *short,* to turn *short,* to sell *short.* —*v.t. & v.i.* To short-circuit. [OE *sceort* short] —**short'ish** *adj.* —**short'ness** *n.*

short·age (shôr'tij) *n.* The amount by which anything is short; deficiency.

short·bread (shôrt'bred') *n.* A rich, dry cake or cooky made with shortening.

short·cake (shôrt'kāk') *n.* 1 A cake made short and crisp with butter or other shortening. 2 Cake or biscuit served with fruit usually between layers: strawberry *shortcake.*

short·change (shôrt'chānj') *v.t.* **·changed, ·chang·ing** To give less change than is due to; hence, to cheat or swindle. —**short'chang'er** *n.*

short circuit *Electr.* 1 A path of low resistance established between any two points in an electric circuit, thus shortening the distance traveled by the current. 2 Any defect in an electric circuit or apparatus which may result in a dangerous or wasteful leakage of current.

short·com·ing (shôrt'kum'ing) *n.* 1 Failure; remissness; delinquency. 2 A falling off; shortage, as of a crop.

short·cut (shôrt'kut') *v.t. & v.i.* To take a short cut (in).

short cut 1 A byway or path between two places shorter than the regular road. 2 A means or method that saves distance or time.

short·en (shôr'tən) *v.t.* 1 To make short or shorter; curtail. 2 To reduce; diminish; lessen. 3 To furl or reef (a sail) so that less canvas is exposed to the wind. 4 To make brittle or crisp, as pastry, by adding shortening. —*v.i.* 5 To become short or shorter. See synonyms under ABBREVIATE, SCRIMP. —**short'en·er** *n.*

short·en·ing (shôr'tən·ing) *n.* 1 A fat, such as lard or butter, used to make pastry crisp. 2 An abbreviation. 3 The act of one who shortens.

short·fall (shôrt'fôl') *n.* A failure to reach a certain amount, or a specific goal: an energy *shortfall.*

short·hand (shôrt'hand') *n.* Any system of rapid writing, as stenography or phonography. —*adj.* 1 Written in shorthand. 2 Using shorthand.

short·hand·ed (shôrt'han'did) *adj.* Not having a sufficient or the usual number of assistants, workmen, or hands.

short·horn (shôrt'hôrn') *n.* One of a breed of cattle with short horns, originally from northern England.

short·lived (shôrt'līvd', -livd') *adj.* Living or lasting but a short time.

short·ly (shôrt'lē) *adv.* 1 At the expiration of a short time; quickly; soon. 2 In few words; briefly. 3 Curtly; abruptly.

short sale A sale for future delivery of goods or stocks not in possession at time of sale.

short shrift 1 A short time in which to confess before dying. 2 Little or no mercy or delay in dealing with a person or disposing of a matter.

short·sight·ed (shôrt'sī'tid) *adj.* 1 Unable to see clearly at a distance; myopic; near-sighted. 2 Lacking foresight. 3 Resulting from or characterized by lack of foresight. See synonyms under IMPRUDENT. —**short'-sight'ed·ly** *adv.* —**short'sight'ed·ness** *n.*

short·stop (shôrt'stop') *n.* In baseball, an infielder stationed between second and third bases.

short story A narrative prose story presenting a central theme or impression, usually subordinated to a single mood or characterization: shorter than a novel or novelette, usually under 10,000 words.

short-tem·pered (shôrt'tem'pərd) *adj.* Easily aroused to anger.

short-term (shôrt'tûrm') *adj.* Payable a short time after issue: said of securities.

short wave A radio wave having a length of about 100 meters or less, corresponding to a frequency ranging upwards from about 3000 kilocycles. —**short'-wave'** *adj.*

short-wind·ed (shôrt'win'did) *adj.* Affected with difficulty of breathing; becoming easily out of breath.

shot[1] (shot) *n.* 1 *pl.* **shot** A solid missile, as a ball of iron, or a bullet or pellet of lead, to be discharged from a firearm; also, such spherules or pellets collectively. See illustration under CARTRIDGE. 2 The act of shooting; any stroke, hit, or blow. 3 One who shoots; a marksman. 4 The distance traversed or that can be traversed by a projectile; reach; range. 5 A blast, as in mining. 6 A stroke, especially in certain games, as in billiards. 7 A conjecture; guess. 8 An attempted performance. 9 A metal sphere which a competitor puts, pushes, or slings, in a distance contest. 10 A hypodermic injection. 11 A drink of liquor. 12 An action or scene recorded on motion-picture film. 13 A picture taken with a camera. 14 *Naut.* A unit of chain length: in the United States, 15 fathoms; in Great Britain, 12½ fathoms. 15 *Obs.* Any projectile. —*v.t.* **shot·ted, shot·ting** To load or weight with shot. —*adj.* 1 Of changeable color, as when warp and weft are of different colors. 2 *Slang* More or less intoxicated. 3 *Colloq.* Completely done for; ruined. [OE *scot*]

shot[2] (shot) Past tense and past participle of SHOOT.

shote (shōt) See SHOAT.

shot glass A small glass for holding or measuring out one shot of liquor.

shot·gun (shot'gun') *n.* A light, smoothbore gun, either single-or double-barreled, adapted for the discharge of shot at short range. —*adj.* 1 Having a clear passageway straight through: a *shotgun* house. 2 Coerced with, or as with, a shotgun: a *shotgun* wedding.

SHOTGUNS
a. Double-barrel hammerless shotgun.
b. Repeating shotgun.

shot-put (shot'pŏot') *n.* 1 An athletic contest in which a shot is thrown, or put, for distance. 2 A single put of the shot. —**shot'-put'ter** *n.*

should (shŏod) Past tense of SHALL, but rarely a true past, rather chiefly used as a modal auxiliary which, while conveying varying shades of present and future time, expresses a wide range of subtly discriminated feelings and attitudes: 1 Obligation or propriety in varying degrees, but milder than *ought*: You *should* write that letter; *Should* we tell him the truth about his condition? His father thought that he *should* go; You *should* really taste that cake! 2 Condition: **a** Simple contingency, but involving less probability than *shall* or the present with future sense: If I *should* die before I wake . . . If I *should* go, he would go too. **b** Assumption: *Should* (= *Assuming that*) the space platform prove practicable, as seems almost certain, a trip to the moon will be easy. 3 Surprise at an unexpected event in the past: When I reached the station, whom *should* I run into but the detective! 4 Expectation: I *should* be at home by noon. ("I said that I *should* be home by noon" implies expectation, whereas "I said that I *would* be home by noon" implies intention.) 5 *U.S. Colloq.* Irony, in positive statement with negative force: He'll be fined heavily, but with all his money he *should* (= *need not*) worry! 6 Hesitation or deprecatory modesty, in the first person: I *should* hardly think so; We *should* like to have you come to dinner, if you are free and have nothing better to do. (Ordinarily, in American usage, but not in British, *would* is used in the first person, as well as in the second and third, before *like, prefer,* etc.: We *would,*

---

add,āce,câre,pälm; end,ēven; it,īce; odd,ōpen,ôrder; tŏŏk,pōōl; up,bûrn; ə = a in *above,* e in *sicken,* i in *clarity,* o in *melon,* u in *focus;* yōō = u in *fuse,* oi,oil; ou,pout; ch,check; g,go; ng,ring; th,thin; th,this; zh,vision. Foreign sounds á,œ,ü,kh,ṅ; and ◆ : see page xx. <from; + plus; ? possibly.

or We'd, like to have you come to visit us.) See usage note under WOULD. [OE *scolde*, pt. of *sculan* owe]

shoul·der (shōl′dər) *n.* **1** The part of the trunk between the neck and the free portion of the arm or forelimb; also, the joint connecting the arm or forelimb with the body. **2** Anything which supports, bears up, or projects like a shoulder. **3** The forequarter of various animals. **4** An enlargement, projection, or offset, as for keeping something in place, or preventing movement past the projection. **5** *Printing* The top of the shank of a type when extending above or below the face of the letter. **6** Either edge of a road or highway. **7** The angle of a bastion included between a face and the adjacent flank: also **shoulder angle. — shoulder to shoulder 1** Side by side and close together. **2** With united effort; in cooperation. **— straight from the shoulder** *Colloq.* Candidly; straightforwardly. **— v.t. 1** To assume as something to be borne; sustain; bear. **2** To push with or as with the shoulder or shoulders. **3** To fashion with a shoulder or abutment; make a shoulder on. **— v.i. 4** To push with the shoulder or shoulders. **— to shoulder arms** To rest a rifle against the shoulder, holding the butt with the hand on the same side, the arm being held bent and close to the side. [OE *sculder* shoulder]

shoulder blade The scapula.

shoulder screw A screw having a shoulder, as for limiting the depth to which it may be sunk. See illustration under SCREW.

shoulder weapon Any small-arm weapon designed to be held against the shoulder in firing, as a rifle, carbine, etc.

shout (shout) *n.* **1** A sudden and loud outcry, such as a call or command, but also expressing emotion, as of joy, exultation, courage, or derision; a loud burst of voice or voices. **2** *Austral. Slang* **a** A free drink or round of drinks. **b** One's turn to buy drinks. **c** One's turn to pay. **— v.t.** To utter with a shout; say or express loudly. **— v.i. 1** To utter a shout; cry out loudly. **2** *Austral. Slang* To buy drinks for another or others. See synonyms under CALL, ROAR. [Origin unknown]

shove (shuv) *v.t. & v.i.* **shoved, shov·ing 1** To push, as along a surface: to *shove* a boat with a pole. **2** To press forcibly (against); jostle. See synonyms under PUSH. **— to shove off 1** To push along or away, as a boat. **2** *Colloq.* To depart. **— n. 1** The act of pushing or shoving; strong push. **2** The woody center of flax. **3** *Can.* A forward movement of ice in a river. [OE *scūfan*] **— shov′er** *n.*

shov·el (shuv′əl) *n.* **1** A flattened scoop with a handle, as for digging, lifting earth, rock, etc. **2** *Colloq.* A shovel hat. **— v. ·eled** or **·elled, ·el·ing** or **·el·ling** *v.t.* **1** To take up and move or gather with a shovel. **2** To toss hastily or in large quantities as if with a shovel. **3** To clear or clean with a shovel, as a path. **— v.i. 4** To work with a shovel. [OE *scofl*]

shov·el·board (shuv′əl·bôrd′, -bōrd′) *n.* Shuffleboard.

shov·el·er (shuv′əl·ər, shuv′lər) *n.* **1** One who or that which shovels. **2** A large river duck (genus *Spatula*) with spatulate bill broadening roundly toward the end; especially, the **common shoveler** (*S. clypeata*) of the northern hemisphere: also **shovelbill.** Also **shov′el·ler.**

shovel hat A hat with broad brim turned up at the sides and projecting in front.

shov·el·head (shuv′əl·hed′) *n.* **1** A shark (*Sphyrna tiburo*) resembling the hammerhead, about 5 feet long. **2** The paddlefish. **3** The shovelnose (def. 1).

shov·el·nose (shuv′əl·nōz′) *n.* **1** A sturgeon (*Scaphirhynchus platyrhynchus*), common in the Mississippi valley, having a broad, depressed, shovel-shaped snout. **2** Any of several varieties of shark with a shovel-like nose; especially, the cow shark (*Hexanchus corinus*), found on the Pacific coast of the United States.

shov·el·nosed (shuv′əl·nōzd′) *adj.* Having a broad, flattened snout or beak.

show (shō) *v.* **showed, shown** or **showed, show·ing** *v.t.* **1** To cause or permit to be seen; present to view; exhibit; manifest; display. **2** To give in a marked or open manner; confer; bestow: to *show* favor. **3** To cause or allow (something) to be understood or known;

explain; reveal; tell. **4** To cause (someone) to understand or see; explain something to; convince; teach. **5** *Law* To advance an allegation; plead: to *show* cause. **6** To make evident by logical process; prove; demonstrate. **7** To guide; lead; introduce, as into a room or building: with *in* or *up*: to *show* a caller in. **8** To indicate: The thermometer *shows* the temperature. **9** To enter in a show or exhibition. **— v.i. 10** To become visible or known; be manifested or displayed. **11** To appear; seem. **12** To make one's or its appearance; be present. **13** *Colloq.* To give a theatrical performance; appear: to *show* in Newark. **14** *Colloq.* In racing, to be the third (horse, dog, etc.) to finish in a race. **— to show off 1** To exhibit proudly or ostentatiously. **2** To make an ostentatious display of oneself, or of one's accomplishments. **— to show up 1** To expose or be exposed, as faults. **2** To be evident or prominent. **3** To attend; arrive; make an appearance. **4** *Colloq.* To be better than. **— n. 1** That which is shown; a public spectacle; a theatrical performance, circus, or motion picture; exhibition. **2** The act of showing; specifically, display; parade. **3** Pretense; semblance. **4** That which shows; an indication; promise; appearance; a sign of precious metal in a mine: a *show* of ore. **5** *Colloq.* An opportunity or chance. **6** *U.S. Colloq.* The third place in a race. **— the whole show** The center of interest or notice. [OE *scēawian*]

show·bill (shō′bil′) *n.* A poster announcing a play or show.

show biz *U.S. Slang* Show business.

show·boat (shō′bōt′) *n.* A boat, such as the old stern-wheelers on the Mississippi, on which a traveling troupe gives a theatrical performance.

show·bread (shō′bred′) See SHEWBREAD.

show business The entertainment arts, especially the theater, motion pictures, television, etc., collectively considered as an industry.

show·case (shō′kās′) *n.* A glass case for exhibiting and protecting articles for sale.

show·down (shō′doun′) *n.* **1** In poker, the play in which the hands are laid on the table face up. **2** Any action or any disclosure of facts, plans, etc., that brings an issue to a head.

show·er (shou′ər) *n.* **1** A fall of rain, hail, or sleet, especially heavy rain of short duration within a local area. **2** A copious fall, as of tears, sparks, or other small objects. **3** A shower bath. **4** A variety of fireworks for simulating a shower of stars. **5** A party for the bestowal of gifts, as to a bride; also, the gifts. **— v.t. 1** To sprinkle or wet with or as with showers. **2** To discharge in a shower; pour out. **3** To bestow with liberality. **— v.i. 4** To fall as in a shower. **5** To take a shower bath. [OE *scūr*] **— show′er·y** *adj.*

show·ing (shō′ing) *n.* **1** Show; display, as of a quality. **2** Presentation; statement, as of a subject.

show-off (shō′ôf′, -of′) *n. Colloq.* One who makes a pretentious display of himself; a swaggerer.

show·piece (shō′pēs′) *n.* **1** A prized object considered worthy of special exhibit. **2** An object on display.

show·y (shō′ē) *adj.* **show·i·er, show·i·est 1** Making a great display; gaudy; gay; splendid. **2** Given to display; ostentatious. **— show′i·ly** *adv.* **— show′i·ness** *n.*

shrap·nel (shrap′nəl) *n. pl.* **·nel** *Mil.* **1** A field artillery projectile for use against personnel, containing a quantity of metal balls and a time fuze and base charge which expel the balls in mid-air. **2** Shell fragments. [after Henry *Shrapnel*, 1761–1842, British artillery officer]

SHRAPNEL SHELL
a. Brass casing.　　*e.* Steel shell body.
b. Percussion primer.　*f.* Shrapnel balls.
c. Smokeless powder.　*g.* Time fuze.
d. Black powder.

shred (shred) *n.* **1** A small irregular strip torn or cut off. **2** A bit; fragment; particle. See synonyms under PARTICLE. **— v.t. shred·ded** or

shred, shred·ding 1 To tear or cut into shreds, as fibrous material. **2** *Brit. Dial.* To lop off; trim. [OE *scrēade* cutting]

shred·der (shred′ər) *n.* **1** One who or that which shreds. **2** A machine for cutting up corn or cane stalks, or for shredding wheat.

shrew (shrōō) *n.* **1** Any of numerous diminutive, mouse-like, insectivorous mammals (family *Soricidae*) having a long pointed snout and soft fur, as the **long-tailed shrew** (*Sorex longicauda*): also **shrew′mouse**.

SHREW
(Species vary from 1 1/2 to 6 inches in body length)

◆ Collateral adjective: *soricine*. **2** A woman of vexatious, scolding, or nagging disposition. **— v.t.** *Obs.* To berate; curse. [OE *scrēawa*]

shrewd (shrōōd) *adj.* **1** Having keen insight; sharp; sagacious. **2** Artful; sly. **3** *Obs.* Keen or sharp; biting. **4** *Obs.* Shrewish; also, vexatious, vicious; dangerous. See synonyms under ACUTE, ASTUTE, INTELLIGENT, KNOWING, POLITIC, SAGACIOUS. [ME *shrewed*, pp. of *schrewen* curse < *shrew* malicious person] **— shrewd′ly** *adv.* **— shrewd′ness** *n.*

shrew·ish (shrōō′ish) *adj.* Like a shrew; ill-tempered. **— shrew′ish·ly** *adv.* **— shrew′ish·ness** *n.*

shriek (shrēk) *n.* A sharp shrill outcry or scream. **— v.i.** To utter a shriek. **— v.t.** To utter with or in a shriek. See synonyms under CALL, ROAR. [<ON *skrækja*] **— shriek′er** *n.*

shrike (shrīk) *n.* Any of numerous birds (family *Laniidae*) with hooked bill, short wings, and long tail; especially, the **loggerhead shrike** (*Lanius ludovicianus*) of the southern Atlantic coast. [OE *scrīc* thrush]

shrill (shril) *adj.* **1** Having a high and piercing quality; sharp and piercing, as a sound. **2** Emitting a sharp, piercing sound. **3** *Poetic* Sharp to other senses than that of hearing; keen. **— v.t.** To cause to utter a shrill sound. **— v.i.** To make a shrill sound. **— adv.** Shrilly. [<Gmc. Cf. LG *schrell* having a sharp tone.] **— shrill′ness** *n.*

shrimp (shrimp) *n. pl.* **shrimp** or **shrimps 1** Any of numerous diminutive, long-tailed, principally marine crustaceans (genus *Crago*), especially the edible shrimp (*C. vulgaris*) of the northern hemisphere. **2** *Slang* A small or insignificant person. [Akin to OE *scrimman* shrink]

SHRIMP
a. Cephalothorax.
b. Abdomen.

shrine (shrīn) *n.* **1** A receptacle for sacred relics. **2** A place, as a tomb or a chapel, sacred to some holy personage, or considered as sanctified by the remains or presence of such. **3** A thing or spot made sacred by historic or other association. **— v.t. shrined, shrin·ing** To enshrine. [OE *scrīn* < L *scrinium* case, chest]

shrink (shringk) *v.* **shrank** or **shrunk, shrunk** or *less commonly* **shrunk·en, shrink·ing** *v.i.* **1** To draw together; contract, as from heat, cold, etc. **2** To diminish; become less or smaller. **3** To draw back, as from disgust, horror, or timidity; withdraw; recoil: with *from*. **4** To flinch; wince. **— v.t. 5** To cause to shrink, contract, or draw together. See synonyms under WITHER. **— n. 1** The act of shrinking; contraction. **2** *Slang* A psychiatrist or psychoanalyst. [OE *scrincan*] **— shrink′a·ble** *adj.* **— shrink′er** *n.*

shrink·age (shringk′ij) *n.* **1** Contraction, as of metal by cooling, or wood by drying. **2** The amount lost by contraction, depreciation, etc. **3** Decrease in value; depreciation.

shrive (shrīv) *v.* **shrove** or **shrived, shriv·en** or **shrived, shriv·ing** *v.t.* **1** To receive the confession of and give absolution to. **2** To obtain absolution for (oneself) by confessing one's sins and doing penance. **— v.i. 3** To make confession. **4** To hear confession. [OE *scrīfan*, ult. < L *scribere* write, prescribe] **— shriv′er** *n.*

shriv·el (shriv′əl) *v.t. & v.i.* **·eled** or **·elled, ·el-**

ing or **·el·ling** **1** To contract into wrinkles; shrink and wrinkle: often with *up.* **2** To make or become impotent; wither. [Origin uncertain. Cf. Sw. *skryvla.*]

shroud[1] (shroud) *n.* **1** A dress or garment for the dead; winding sheet. **2** Something that envelops or conceals like a garment. —*v.t.* **1** To dress for the grave; clothe in a shroud. **2** To envelop, as with a garment. **3** *Archaic* To shelter. —*v.i.* **4** *Obs.* To take shelter; go under cover; also, to gather together, as beasts, for warmth. See synonyms under MASK[1]. [OE *scrūd* a garment] —**shroud'less** *adj.*

shroud[2] (shroud) *n.* **1** *Naut.* **a** One of a set of ropes fitted in pairs and constituting part of the standing rigging of a vessel; specifically, one of the ropes, often of wire, stretched from a masthead to the sides or rims of a top, serving as means of ascent and as a lateral strengthening stays to the masts. **b** One of a pair or set of stay ropes or chains to give lateral support to a topmast, bowsprit, etc. **2** A guy, as a support for a smokestack: usually in the plural. **3** One of the supporting ropes attached to the edges of a parachute canopy. [< SHROUD[1]]

SHROUDS
a. Chain plates.
b. Shrouds.
c. Swifter.
d. Deadeyes.
e. Lanyards.
f. Ratlines.
g. Topmast backstays.

shroud–laid (shroud'lād') *adj.* Made of four strands twisted around a core: said of rope.

shrove (shrōv) Alternative past tense of SHRIVE.

shrub (shrub) *n.* A woody perennial plant of low stature, characterized by persistent stems and branches springing from the base. ◆ In popular language a shrub is a *bush.* [OE *scrybb* brushwood] —**shrub'by** *adj.*

shrub–al·the·a (shrub'al·thē'ə) *n.* A hardy shrub (*Hibiscus syriacus*) of the mallow family: also called *rose of Sharon.*

shrub·ber·y (shrub'ər·ē) *n. pl.* **·ber·ies** **1** Shrubs collectively. **2** A shrubby place; a collection of shrubs, as in a garden.

shrug (shrug) *v.t.* & *v.i.* **shrugged, shrug·ging** To draw up (the shoulders), as in displeasure, doubt, surprise, etc. —*n.* The act of shrugging the shoulders. [Origin uncertain]

shtick (shtik) *n. U.S. Slang* An artificial or contrived device, mannerism, special area of knowledge, etc., intended to make one appear distinctive or unique; gimmick. Also spelled *schtick.* [< Yiddish < G *stück* piece, bit]

shuck (shuk) *n.* **1** A husk, shell, or pod, as of maize or peas; the outer covering of nuts. **2** A shell of an oyster or a clam. **3** *U.S. Colloq.* Something of little or no value: usually plural: *not worth shucks.* —*v.t.* **1** To remove the shucks of or from; remove the husk or shell from (corn, oysters, etc.). **2** *Colloq.* To take off or cast off, as clothes, or any outer covering. [? Metathetic alter. of HUSK] —**shuck'er** *n.*

shud·der (shud'ər) *v.i.* To tremble or shake, as from fright or cold; shiver; quake. —*n.* The act of shuddering; convulsive shiver, as from horror or fear; tremor. See synonyms under QUAKE, SHAKE. [Prob. freq. of OE *scūdan* move, shake] —**shud'der·ing** *adj.* —**shud'der·ing·ly** *adv.*

shuf·fle (shuf'əl) *n.* **1** A mixing or changing of the order of things, as of cards in a pack before each deal. **2** A hesitating, evasive, or tricky course; prevarication; artifice. **3** A scraping of the feet, as in walking; a slow, dragging gait. **4** A dance, or the step used in it, where the dancer pushes his foot along the floor at each step. —*v.* **·fled, ·fling** *v.t.* **1** To shift this way and that; mix; confuse; disorder; especially, to change the order of by mixing, as cards in a pack. **2** To move (the feet) along the ground or floor with a dragging gait. **3** To change from one place to another. **4** To make up or remove fraudulently or hastily; also, to put aside carelessly: with *up, off,* or *out.* —*v.i.* **5** To change position; shift ground. **6** To resort to indirect methods; prevaricate. **7** To dance the shuffle. **8** To scrape the feet along. **9** To scrape or struggle along awkwardly. [Prob. < LG

schuffeln move with dragging feet, mix cards, etc.]

shuf·fle·board (shuf'əl·bôrd', -bōrd') *n.* **1** A game in which wooden or composition disks are slid by means of a pronged cue along a smooth surface toward numbered spaces. **2** The board or surface on which the game is played. Also spelled *shovelboard.*

shul (shōōl) *n.* A synagogue. [< Yiddish]

shun (shun) *v.t.* **shunned, shun·ning** **1** To keep clear of; avoid; refrain from. **2** *Obs.* To escape; evade. **3** *Obs.* To abhor. See synonyms under ABHOR, ESCAPE. [OE *scunian*] —**shun'ner** *n.*

shunt (shunt) *n.* **1** A turning aside; the act of using a switch or shunt. **2** A railroad switch. **3** *Electr.* A conductor joining two points in a circuit and serving to divert part of the current. The proportion of the current diverted is regulated by the resistance of the shunt employed. —*v.t.* **1** To turn aside. **2** In railroading, to switch, as a train or car, from one track to another. **3** *Electr.* To distribute by means of shunts. **4** To evade by turning away from; put off on someone else, as a task. —*v.i.* **5** To move to one side. **6** *Electr.* To be diverted by a shunt: said of current. **7** To shift or transfer one's views or course. [Origin uncertain] —**shunt'er** *n.*

shush (shush) *v.t.* To try to quiet; hush up, especially by making a noise like the sound (sh). [Imit.; infl. in form by HUSH]

shut (shut) *v.* **shut, shut·ting** *v.t.* **1** To bring into such position as to close an opening or aperture; close, as a door, lid, or valve. **2** To close (an opening, aperture, etc.) so as to prevent ingress or egress. **3** To close and fasten securely, as with a latch or lock. **4** To forbid entrance into or exit from. **5** To keep from entering or leaving; confine or exclude; bar: with *in, out, from,* etc. **6** To close, fold, or bring together, as extended, expanded, or unfolded parts: to *shut* an umbrella. **7** To hide from view; obscure. —*v.i.* **8** To be or become closed or in a closed position. —**to shut down** **1** To cease from operating, as a factory or mine; close up; stop work. **2** To lower; come down close: The fog *shut down.* **3** *Colloq.* To suppress: with *on.* —**to shut one's eyes to** To ignore. —**to shut out** In sports, to keep (an opponent) from scoring during the course of a game. —**to shut up** **1** *Colloq.* To stop talking or cause to stop talking. **2** *Colloq.* To become exhausted and stop running, as a horse in a race. **3** To close all the entrances to, as a house. **4** To imprison; confine. —*adj.* **1** Made fast or closed. **2** Not sonorous; dull: said of sound. **3** *Phonet.* **a** Formed by closing the oral and nasal passages completely, preparatory to uttering certain sounds: said of certain consonants, as *t, p, k, b,* and *d.* **b** Cut off sharply by succeeding consonants: said of vowels, as *i* in *pit* and *o* in *top.* **4** *Dial.* Freed, as from something disagreeable; rid: with *of.* —*n.* **1** The act of shutting; also, the time of shutting, closing, or ending: the *shut* of day. **2** The place of shutting or closing together; specifically, the junction between welded pieces of metal. [OE *scyttan*]

Synonyms (verb): bar, beleaguer, block, blockade, close, confine, enclose, exclude, imprison, intercept, preclude, prohibit, seal, stop. *Antonyms:* expand, liberate, open, unbar, unclose, undo, unfasten.

shut·down (shut'doun') *n.* The closing of or ceasing of work in a mine, mill, factory, or other industrial plant.

shut·eye (shut'ī') *n. Slang* Sleep.

shut·in (shut'in') *n.* An invalid who has to stay at home. —*adj.* **1** Obliged to stay at home. **2** Inclined to avoid people.

shut·off (shut'ôf', -of') *n. Mech.* A device for shutting something off.

shut·out (shut'out') *n.* **1** A shutting out; especially, a lock-out. **2** In sports, a game in which one side is prevented from scoring; also, the action or the play that prevents scoring.

shut·ter (shut'ər) *n.* **1** One who or that which shuts. **2** That which shuts out or excludes; specifically, a cover, usually hinged, for closing an opening. **3** A hinged screen or cover for a window. **4** *Phot.* Any of various mechanisms for mo-

mentarily admitting light through a camera lens to the film or plate. —*v.t.* To furnish, close, or divide off with shutters.

shut·ter·bug (shut'ər·bug') *n. Slang.* A photography enthusiast. [< SHUTTER + BUG[1]]

shut·tle (shut'l) *n.* **1** A device used in weaving to carry the weft to and fro between the warp threads. **2** A similar rotating or other device in a sewing machine or the like. **3** A transport system operating between two nearby points. —*v.t.* & *v.i.* **·tled, ·tling** To move to and fro, like a shuttle. —*adj.* Pertaining to or designating any contrivance, action, etc., intended to operate back and forth between two points: *shuttle* bombing. [OE *scytel* missile; so called because shot to and fro in weaving]

SHUTTLE (*def. 1*)

shuttle armature An H-armature.

shut·tle·cock (shut'l·kok') *n.* A rounded piece of cork, with a crown of feathers, used in the game of badminton and of battledore and shuttlecock; the game itself. —*v.t.* To send or knock back and forth like a shuttlecock. [< SHUTTLE + COCK[1]]

shy[1] (shī) *v.i.* **shied, shy·ing** **1** To start suddenly aside, as in fear: said of a horse. **2** To draw back, as from doubt or caution: with *off* or *away.* [< *adj.*] —*adj.* **shy·er, shy·est,** or **shi·er, shi·est** **1** Easily frightened or startled, timorous. **2** Bashful; reserved; coy. **3** Circumspect, as from motives of caution; watchful; wary: with *of.* **4** Not easy to perceive, seize, or secure; elusive: a *shy* expression. **5** Not prolific: said of plants, trees, or, rarely, birds. **6** *Colloq.* Having a less amount of money than is called for or required. **7** Short; lacking: often with *on.* —*n.* A starting aside, as in fear. [OE *scēoh* timid. Akin to ESCHEW.] —**shy'ly** *adv.* —**shy'ness** *n.*

shy[2] (shī) *v.t.* & *v.i.* **shied, shy·ing** To throw with a swift, sidelong motion. —*n. pl.* **shies** **1** A careless throw; fling, hence, a verbal fling; a sneer. **2** A trial; experiment. [Origin unknown]

shy·ster (shīs'tər) *n.* **1** Anyone who conducts his business in an unscrupulous or tricky manner. **2** A lawyer who practices in an unprofessional manner, preys on petty criminals, etc. [? < SHY[1], in slang sense of "disreputable" + -STER]

Si *Chem.* Silicon (symbol Si).

si·al (sī'al) *n. Geol.* A rock formation rich in silica and alumina which underlies sedimentary rock in continental land masses. —**si·al'ic** *adj.* [< SI(LICA) + AL(UMINA)]

si·a·lid (sī'ə·lid) *n.* Any member of a family of insects (*Sialidae*, order *Megaloptera*), with enlarged or enlongated thorax, including the hellgrammite and related genera. —*adj.* Of or pertaining to the *Sialidae*. Also **si·al·i·dan** (sī·al'ə·dən). [< Gk. *sialis*, kind of bird]

sialo- *combining form* Saliva; pertaining to saliva: *sialogog.* Also, before vowels, **sial-**. [< Gk. *sialon* saliva]

si·al·o·gog (sī·al'ə·gog) *n.* Any agent exciting a flow of saliva. Also **si·al'a·gogue, si·al'o·gogue.** [< SIAL(O-) + -AGOG] —**si·a·lo·gog·ic** (sī'ə·lō·goj'ik) *adj.* & *n.*

si·a·loid (sī'ə·loid) *adj.* Like or resembling saliva.

si·a·mang (sē'ə·mang) *n.* A large black gibbon (genus *Symphalangus*) found in Sumatra. [< Malay *siaman* < *iaman* black]

Siamese cat A breed of short-haired cat native in Siam, now extensively bred in the United States, typically fawn-colored or pale cream, with dark-tipped ears, tail, feet, and dark mask, a wedge-shaped head, and bright- or deep-blue, gently slanting eyes.

Siamese twins **1** Originally, the two Chinese males, Eng and Chang, 1811–74, born in Siam, whose bodies were joined by a fleshy band from the navel to the xiphoid cartilage. **2** Any twins joined together at birth.

SIAMESE CAT
(About 11 inches at the shoulder)

sib (sib) *n.* 1 A blood-relation; kinsman. 2 Kinsmen collectively; relatives. —*adj.* 1 Related to blood; akin. 2 Related; similar. Also **sibb.** [OE *sibb*]

Siberian husky A breed of working dog of medium size with a strong, closely knit body, head resembling that of a fox, brush tail, and thick, soft outer coat.

sib·i·lant (sib′ə·lənt) *adj.* 1 Hissing. 2 *Phonet.* Describing those consonants which are uttered with a hissing sound, as (s), (z), (sh), and (zh). —*n. Phonet.* A sibilant consonant. [< L *sibilans, -antis,* ppr. of *sibilare* hiss] —**sib′i·lance, sib′i·lan·cy** *n.* —**sib′i·lant·ly** *adv.*

sib·ling (sib′ling) *n.* A blood-relation; a relative: used in eugenics, psychology, and anthropology to denote brothers and sisters. [OE, a relative]

sib·yl (sib′əl) *n.* 1 In ancient Greece and Rome, any of several women who prophesied under the supposed inspiration of some deity, chiefly of Apollo, and delivered their oracles in a frenzied state. 2 A fortune-teller; sorceress. [< L *sibylla* < Gk.]

sib·yl·line (sib′əl·īn, -ēn, -in) *adj.* 1 Pertaining to or characteristic of the sibyls; uttered or composed by sibyls; hence, prophetic; oracular; occult. 2 Exorbitant; excessive. Also **si·byl·ic** (si·bil′ik), **si·byl′lic.**

sic (sik) *adv.* So; thus: sometimes inserted in brackets after something quoted, to indicate that the quotation is literal, and that, in the opinion of the one making the insertion, what immediately precedes is questionable or incorrect. [< L]

sic·ca·tive (sik′ə·tiv) *adj.* Causing to dry; drying. —*n.* That which has a drying effect; a drying agent or medicine. [< LL *siccativus* < L *siccatus,* pp. of *siccare* dry < *siccus* dry]

Sic·i·ly (sis′ə·lē) The largest island in the Mediterranean, just SW of Italy (9,831 square miles); comprising with some small neighboring islands an autonomous region of Italy; 9,926 square miles; capital, Palermo: ancient *Trinacria.* Italian **Si·ci·lia** (sē·chē′lyä). —**Si·cil′i·an** *adj. & n.*

sick¹ (sik) *adj.* 1 Affected with disease; ill; ailing. 2 Of or used by ill persons: often used in combination: *sickroom.* 3 Affected by nausea; nauseated; desiring to vomit. 4 Expressive or suggestive of nausea; sickly: a *sick* laugh. 5 Impaired or unsound from any cause; weakened; out of condition. 6 Pallid; wan: said of colors. 7 Depressed and longing because of some unattained desire; languishing: *sick* for the sea. 8 Disinclined by reason of satiety or disgust; surfeited: with *of: sick* of music. 9 Exhausted; as soil; unable to produce a profitable yield; also, diseased. —*n.* Sick people collectively: with *the.* [OE *sēoc*]

sick² (sik) *v.t.* 1 To seek or attack: used in the imperative to order a dog to attack. 2 To urge to attack: I'll *sick* the dog on you. Also spelled *sic.* [Var. of SEEK]

sick·bay (sik′bā′) *n.* That part of a ship or of a naval base set aside for the care of the sick, including operating room, dispensary, and hospital.

sick·bed (sik′bed′) *n.* The bed upon which a sick person lies.

sick call *Mil.* 1 The daily period for reporting to the medical officer all non-hospitalized sick or injured military personnel. 2 The call or signal which announces it.

sick·en (sik′ən) *v.t. & v.i.* To make or become sick or disgusted. —**sick′en·er** *n.*

sick·en·ing (sik′ən·ing) *adj.* Disgusting; nauseating. —**sick′en·ing·ly** *adv.*

sick headache Headache accompanied by nausea and stomach disorders; migraine.

sick·ish (sik′ish) *adj.* 1 Somewhat sick. 2 Slightly nauseating: a sweet, *sickish* odor. See synonyms under SQUEAMISH. —**sick′ish·ly** *adv.* —**sick′ish·ness** *n.*

sick·le (sik′əl) *n.* A reaping implement with a long, curved blade mounted on a short handle. —*v.t.* **·led, ·ling** To cut with a sickle, as grass, hay, etc. [OE *sicel* < L *secula* < *secare* cut]

sick·le·bill (sik′əl·bil′) *n.* Any of several birds having a strongly curved bill, as a hummingbird or the long-billed curlew (*Numenius americanus*).

sick·le-cell anemia (sik′əl·sel′) A severe, hereditary anemia occurring among the offspring of parents who both have sickle-cell trait.

sickle-cell trait A tendency in erythrocytes to become deformed into a sickle shape and to clog small blood vessels, occurring chiefly among Negroes and due to the presence of a genetic hemoglobin abnormality inherited from one parent. Also **sickl·e·mi·a** (sik′əl·ē′mē·ə).

sick·ly (sik′lē) *adj.* **·li·er, ·li·est** 1 Habitually indisposed; ailing; unhealthy: a *sickly* child. 2 Marked by the prevalence of sickness: a *sickly* summer. 3 Nauseating; disgusting; also, mawkish; sickening. 4 Pertaining to or characteristic of the sick or sickness: a *sickly* appearance. 5 Weak- or sick-looking; faint: a *sickly* moon. —*adv.* In a sick manner; poorly. —*v.t.* **·lied, ·ly·ing** To make sickly or sickish, as in color or complexion. —**sick′li·ly** *adv.* —**sick′li·ness** *n.*

sick·ness (sik′nis) *n.* 1 Illness; the state of being sick. 2 A particular form of disease. 3 Specifically, nausea. 4 Any disordered and weakened state: the soul's *sickness.* See synonyms under DISEASE, ILLNESS.

side (sīd) *n.* 1 Any one of the bounding lines of a surface or of the bounding surfaces of a solid object: often limited to a particular bounding line or surface, as distinguished from top, or bottom: the *side* of a box, house, or mountain. 2 A lateral part of a surface or object. 3 One of two or more contrasted surfaces, parts, or places: *inside* and *outside.* 4 Any distinct party or body of competitors or partisans; a faction. 5 An opinion, aspect, or point of view considered with respect to its opposite: my *side* of the question. 6 Family connection, especially by descent through one parent: my grandfather on my father's *side.* 7 The lateral half of a slaughtered animal or of a tanned skin or hide. 8 Either half of the human body as divided by the median plane. 9 The space beside someone. 10 A page of written or printed paper. 11 *Naut.* The part of a ship's hull from stem to stern above the waterline. 12 In billiards, a lateral spin given to the cue ball; english. 13 Abounding line of a geometrical figure. 14 *Brit. Slang* Superciliousness of manner; pretentiousness. —**off side** See OFFSIDE. —*adj.* 1 Situated at or on one side; lateral: a *side* window. 2 Being or viewed as if from one side; oblique: a *side* glance; incidental: a *side* issue. —*v.t.* **sid·ed, sid·ing** 1 To provide with sides, as a building. 2 To cut into sides, as a carcass. 3 To thrust aside. —**to side with** To range oneself on the side of; take the part of. [OE]

side arms Weapons worn at the side, as swords, pistols, bayonets, etc.

side·bands (sīd′bandz′) *n. pl. Telecom.* The bands of frequencies on either side of the carrier wave within which fall the frequencies produced by modulation.

side·board (sīd′bôrd′, -bōrd′) *n.* 1 A piece of dining-room furniture for holding tableware. 2 *pl. Brit.* Sideburns.

side·burns (sīd′bûrnz′) *n. pl.* 1 Whiskers grown on the cheeks; burnsides. 2 The hair growing on the sides of a man's face below the hairline: usually worn with the rest of the beard shaved off. [Alter. of BURNSIDES]

side·car (sīd′kär′) *n.* 1 A small, one-wheeled passenger car attached to the side of a motorcycle. 2 A cocktail containing equal parts of lemon juice, brandy, and curaçao or Cointreau. 3 A jaunting car.

side dish A portion of food subordinate to the main dish or dishes of a course; also, the small dish in which it is served.

side effect *Med.* A secondary, often injurious effect resulting from a drug or other form of therapy whose action is not restricted to the condition for which it was administered.

side·kick (sīd′kik′) *n. U.S. Slang* A close friend; buddy.

side·light (sīd′līt′) *n.* 1 A side window. 2 A light coming from the side; hence, incidental illumination or information. 3 *Naut.* One of the colored lights (red on the port side, green on the starboard) displayed on the sides of ships at night; a running-light; also, a nightlight in the gangway of a war vessel.

side·line (sīd′līn′) *n.* 1 An auxiliary line of goods sold by a store or a commercial traveler. 2 Any additional or secondary work differing from one's main job. 3 A track or road, especially of a railroad, branching off from the main line. 4 A line used to hobble a horse by connecting the fore and hind feet

of the same side: also **side′-hob′ble** (-hob′əl). 5 One of the lines bounding the two sides of a football field, tennis court, or the like; also, the area just outside these lines: often in the plural. 6 The point of view of an outsider or non-participant.

side·ling (sīd′ling) *adj.* Having a slanting or oblique position or motion; indirect. —*adv.* Sidewise; obliquely; indirectly.

side·long (sīd′lông, -long) *adj.* Inclining or tending to one side; lateral. —*adv.* 1 In a lateral or oblique direction. 2 Steeply inclined.

side·man (sīd′man′) *n. pl.* **·men** (-men′) One of the supporting musicians, as distinguished from the featured performers, of a band, especially a jazz band.

si·de·re·al (sī·dir′ē·əl) *adj.* 1 Pertaining or relative to stars; constituted of or containing stars. 2 Measured by means of the stars: said of periods of time. [< L *sidereus* < *sidus, sideris* star] —**si·de′re·al·ly** *adv.*

sidereal time See under TIME.

sid·er·ite (sīd′ə·rīt) *n.* 1 A vitreous, native ferrous carbonate, $FeCO_3$; spathic iron ore: also called *chalybite.* 2 An indigo-blue variety of quartz. 3 An iron meteorite. [< L *siderites* < Gk. *sideros* iron < *sideros* iron] —**sid′er·it·ic** (-rit′ik) *adj.*

sidero-¹ *combining form* Iron; of or pertaining to iron: *siderolite.* Also, before vowels, **sider-.** [< Gk. *sideros* iron]

sidero-² *combining form* Star; stellar: *siderostat.* Also, before vowels, **sider-.** [< L *sidus, sideris* a star]

sid·er·o·lite (sīd′ər·ə·līt′) *n.* 1 A spongy meteoric iron containing embedded grains of certain minerals, as chrysolite. 2 A meteorite. [< SIDERO-¹ + -LITE]

sid·er·o·scope (sīd′ər·ə·skōp′) *n.* A magnetic device for detecting the presence of iron or steel particles in the eyes.

sid·er·o·sis (sīd′ə·rō′sis) *n. Pathol.* 1 Abnormal deposit of iron in the tissues of the body, and especially of the lungs. 2 Any lung disease caused by the inhalation of metallic dust; pneumonoconiosis.

sid·er·o·stat (sīd′ər·ə·stat′) *n. Astron.* A mirror turning by clock motion so as to reflect the light of a star in an invariable direction into a fixed telescope or other astronomical instrument. [< SIDERO-² + Gk. *statos* standing] —**sid′er·o·stat′ic** *adj.*

side-sad·dle (sīd′sad′l) *n.* A woman's saddle having but one stirrup and a cushioned horn on the same side, about which the right knee fits.

side show 1 A small show incidental to a larger or more important one; especially, one connected with a circus but charging an extra entrance fee; also, a minor exhibit at a fair. 2 Any subordinate issue or attraction.

side-split·ting (sīd′split′ing) *adj.* Having a tendency as if to split the sides with laughter; mirth-provoking.

side-step (sīd′step′) *v.* **-stepped, -step·ping** *v.i.* To step to one side; avoid responsibility. —*v.t.* To avoid, as an issue, or postpone, as a decision; evade. —*n.* 1 A step or a movement to one side, as of a pugilist. 2 A step on the side of a thing for ascending and descending. —**side′-step′per** *n.*

side·swipe (sīd′swīp′) *n.* A sweeping blow along the side. —*v.t. & v.i.* **·swiped, ·swip·ing** To strike or collide with such a blow.

side·track (sīd′trak′) *v.t. & v.i.* 1 To move to a siding, as a railroad train. 2 To divert or depart from the main issue or subject; distract or be distracted. —*n.* A railroad siding; also, a branch line.

side·walk (sīd′wôk′) *n.* A path or pavement at the side of the street for the use of pedestrians.

side·wall (sīd′wôl′) *n.* The side surface of a rubber tire, between the tread and the rim.

side·ways (sīd′wāz′) *adv.* 1 From one side. 2 So as to incline toward the side, or with the side forward: Hold it *sideways.* 3 Toward one side; askance; obliquely; indirectly. —*adj.* Moving to or from one side: a *sideways* glance. Also **side′way′, side′wise′.**

sid·ing (sī′ding) *n.* 1 A railway track by the side of the main track. 2 The boarding that covers the side of a wooden house or is prepared for that purpose: often in the plural. 3 The act of dressing timbers to correct breadths, as in shipbuilding, or the timbers themselves. 4 The act of taking sides, as in a controversy.

si·dle (sīd'l) *v.i.* ·**dled,** ·**dling** To move sideways, especially in a cautious or stealthy manner. — *n.* A sideways step or movement. [< obs. *sidling* sidelong] — **si'dler** *n.*

siege (sēj) *n.* **1** The besieging of a town or fortified place; beleaguerment. ◆ Collateral adjective: *obsidional.* **2** A steady attempt to win something; also, the protracted period spent in the effort: He laid *siege* to her heart. **3** The time during which one undergoes a protracted illness or difficulty. **4** *Obs.* A seat; chair; throne. **5** *Obs.* Rank, station. — *v.t.* **sieged, sieg·ing** To besiege. [< OF < L *sedes* seat < *sedere* sit; infl. in meaning by L *obsidium* siege]

Sieg·fried (sēg'frēd, *Ger.* zēkh'frēt) The hero of the *Nibelungenlied* and several other Germanic legends. [< G, peace of victory]

Si·en·a (sē·en'ə, *Ital.* syä'nä) A city in Tuscany, central Italy. — **Si·en·ese** (sē'ən·ēz', -ēs') *adj.* & *n.*

si·en·na (sē·en'ə) *n.* **1** A brownish orange-yellow natural clay with oxides of iron and manganese: used as a pigment. **2** Orange-yellow, the color of this pigment. [< Ital. *(terra di) Siena* (earth of) Siena]

sier·o·zem (sir'ə·zem) *n.* A grayish-brown soil that merges gradually into a calcareous or hardpan layer: formed usually in a temperate to cool climate. [< Russian, gray earth]

sier·ra (sē·er'ə) *n.* **1** A mountain range or chain, especially one having a jagged or serrated outline: a term occurring in the names of ranges in Spain and former Spanish colonies. **2** Any of several large mackerel-like fishes, as the cero. [< Sp. < L *serra* saw]

Si·er·ra Le·o·ne (sē·er'rä lā·ō'nä) **1** An independent state on the west coast of Africa; 27,925 square miles, mostly on the **Sierra Leone Peninsula,** extending 25 miles into the Atlantic; capital, Freetown: formerly a British dependency. **2** An estuary in western Sierra Leone, flowing 25 miles past Freetown to the Atlantic.

Si·er·ra Ma·dre (sē·er'rä mä'thrä) A Mexican mountain chain bordering the central plateau on the east and west and divided into the **Sierra Madre del Sur** in the south, the **Sierra Madre Occidental** in the west, and the **Sierra Madre Oriental** in the east; highest point, 18,700 feet.

Si·er·ra Ne·vad·a (sē·er'ə nə·vad'ə, -vä'də; *Sp.* sē·er'rä nā·vä'thä) **1** A mountain range of eastern California, extending 400 miles north and south; highest point, 14,495 feet. **2** A mountain range in southern Spain; highest peak, 11,411 feet.

si·es·ta (sē·es'tə) *n.* A midday or afternoon nap. [< Sp. < L *sexta (hora)* sixth (hour), noon < *sex* six]

sieur (syœr) *n.* Sir; master: a former French title of respect. [< F < L *senior* older]

sieve (siv) *n.* **1** A utensil or apparatus for sifting, consisting of a frame provided with a bottom of mesh wire. **2** A garrulous person. — *v.t.* & *v.i.* **sieved, siev·ing** To sift. [OE *sife* sieve]

sieve cell *Bot.* A thin-walled, elongated cell having perforations, **sieve pores,** and sieve plates that permit communication between contiguous cells, forming sieve tubes.

sieve plate *Bot.* One of the thickened terminal sections of a sieve cell.

sieve tissue *Bot.* Phloem tissue containing or made up of vascular bundles of sieve cells.

sieve tube *Bot.* An arrangement of sieve cells in plants by means of which conduction is accomplished.

si·fak·a (si·fak'ə) *n.* Any of a genus (*Propithecus*) of lemuroid primates characterized by long tails, black skin, short arms, and powerful hind limbs: native in Madagascar: also called *propitheque.* [< Malagasy]

sif·fle (sif'əl) *v.t.* & *v.i.* ·**fled,** ·**fling** To whistle; hiss. — *n.* A sibilant râle. [< F *siffler* < L *sibilare* hiss]

sift (sift) *v.t.* **1** To pass through a sieve in order to separate the fine parts from the coarse. **2** To scatter by or as by a sieve. **3** To examine carefully. **4** To separate as if with a sieve; distinguish: to *sift* fact from fiction. — *v.i.* **5** To use a sieve; sift something. **6** To fall or pass through or as

through a sieve: The light *sifts* through the trees. [OE *siftan* sift] — **sift'er** *n.*

sift·ings (sif'tingz) *n. pl.* Something removed or separated by a sieve.

sigh (sī) *v.i.* **1** To draw in and exhale a deep, audible breath, as in expressing sorrow, weariness, pain, etc. **2** To make a sound suggestive of a sigh, as the wind. **3** To yearn; long. — *v.t.* **4** To express with a sigh. **5** To lament with sighs. — *n.* The act or sound of or as of sighing. [Back formation <ME *sighte,* pt. of *siken* <OE *sican* sigh]

sight (sīt) *n.* **1** The faculty, act, or fact of seeing; vision. **2** That which is seen; a view; spectacle; show; as used absolutely, something remarkable and strange. **3** *pl.* Things worth seeing: the *sights* of the town. **4** The range or scope of vision; limit of eyesight. **5** A point of view; estimation. **6** Insight; opportunity for investigation or study. **7** A device to assist aim, as on a gun, leveling instrument, etc. **8** An aim or observation taken with a telescope or other sighting instrument. **9** A view; glimpse. **10** The part of a drawing or painting within the marginal lines or the frame. **11** *Colloq.* A great quantity or number: a *sight* of people. — **at** (or **on**) **sight 1** As soon as seen: to read or shoot *at sight.* **2** On presentation for payment: said of drafts, bills, and notes. — **battle sight** The position of the rear sight on a rifle in which the leaf is laid down. — **bore sight** An auxiliary sighting device with parts attached to the muzzle and breech of a gun, used to secure alinement of the axis of the bore with the axis of the gun sight. — **leaf sight** A rear sight for small arms, containing a movable peep sight and hinged to permit raising and lowering. — **peep sight** A sight attached to the breech end of a firearm, and provided with a small hole in the center for close aiming. — *v.t.* **1** To perceive with the eyes; see: to *sight* a whale. **2** To take a sight of; observe; look at through a telescope or similar instrument. **3** To furnish with sights, or adjust the sights of, as a gun. **4** To give the proper aim or elevation to, as a gun; take aim with. **5** *Colloq.* To bring to notice; present, as a bill to its drawee. — *v.i.* **6** To take aim. **7** To make an observation or sight. — *adj.* **1** Understood or performed on sight without previous familiarity or preparation. **2** Payable when presented: a *sight* draft. ◆ Homophones: *cite, site.* [OE *gesiht*]

sight–hole (sīt'hōl') *n.* A peephole.

sight·less (sīt'lis) *adj.* **1** Without the power of sight; blind. **2** Invisible. — **sight'less·ly** *adv.* — **sight'less·ness** *n.*

sight·ly (sīt'lē) *adj.* ·**li·er,** ·**li·est 1** Pleasant to the view; comely. **2** Affording a grand view. — **sight'li·ness** *n.*

sight–read (sīt'rēd') *v.t.* & *v.i.* ·**read** (red), ·**read·ing** (rē'ding) To understand or perform (something requiring interpretation or translation) on sight without previous familiarity or preparation: to *sight-read* music or a foreign language. — **sight reader** — **sight reading**

sight·see·ing (sīt'sē'ing) *n.* The visiting of objects of interest. — **sight'se'er** *n.*

sight unseen Without examing: to exchange stamps *sight unseen.*

sig·il (sij'il) *n.* A seal or signature; also, a mark or sign supposed to exercise occult power. [< L *sigillum* seal] — **sig'il·lary** (-ə·ler'ē) *adj.*

sig·ma (sig'mə) *n.* **1** The 18th letter in the Greek alphabet, written Σ (capital), σ (small initial), or ς (small final): corresponding to English *s* in *so.* As a numeral it denotes 200. **2** *Math.* The symbol signifying that the sum is to be taken of a series or sequence following. **3** Something shaped like a sigma. [< Gk. *sigma* the letter *s*]

sig·mate (sig'māt) *adj.* Having the shape or form of S or of sigma.

sig·moid (sig'moid) *adj.* **1** Shaped like the Greek capital letter sigma (Σ), or like the letter S. **2** Pertaining to the sigmoid flexure. Also **sig·moi·dal** (sig·moid'l). [< Gk. *sigmoeidēs*]

sigmoid flexure *Anat.* A fold in the colon just above the rectum.

sign (sīn) *n.* **1** A motion or action indicating thought, desire, or command; a pantomimic

gesture. **2** A board, plate, or representation of any sort, generally bearing an inscription and used to indicate a place of business or resort. **3** An arbitrary mark used to express meaning, rank, condition, value, etc. **4** Any evidence of a recent presence, as tracks, droppings, etc.; a vestige; trace. **5** A mark used in place of a signature by persons unable to write. **6** *Music* Any mark used in musical notation, as a flat or sharp. **7** *Math.* A conventional mark to indicate an operation or relation, as one of the symbols $+, -, \times, \div$, indicating the four fundamental operations of addition, subtraction, multiplication, and division. **8** Any indicative or significant object or event; a symbol; token. **9** In the Bible, a miraculous deed as a proof of divine commission or supernatural power; a miracle. **10** *Astron.* One of the twelve equal divisions of the zodiac, named from the constellations that formerly occupied them. See ZODIAC. **11** In hunting, a trace left by an animal; spoor. **12** *Med.* A symptom of disease that is apparent to someone other than the patient. **13** *Eccl.* The sign of the Cross: used in service books and before signatures of bishops. — *v.t.* **1** To write one's signature or initials on. **2** *Law* To acknowledge an instrument by affixing a mark or seal to. **3** To indicate or represent by a sign; stand for. **4** To mark or consecrate with a sign, especially with a cross. **5** To engage by obtaining the signature of to a contract: to *sign* a baseball player; also, to hire (oneself) out for work: often with *on.* **6** To dispose of by signature: with *off* or *away.* **7** To express or indicate with a sign. — *v.i.* **8** To make signs or signals. **9** To write one's signature or initials. — **to sign off** *Telecom.* To announce the close of a program from a broadcasting station and stop transmission. — **to sign up** To enlist, as in a branch of military service. ◆ Homophone: *sine.* [< OF *signe* < L *signum*] — **sign'er** *n.*

Synonyms (noun): emblem, indication, manifestation, mark, note, omen, pattern, presage, prognostic, signal, symbol, symptom, token, type. A *sign* is any distinctive *mark* by which a thing may be recognized or its presence known, and may be intentional or accidental, natural or artificial, suggestive, descriptive or wholly arbitrary. While a *sign* may be involuntary, and even unconscious, a *signal* is always voluntary; a ship may show *signs* of distress to the casual observer, but *signals* of distress are a distinct appeal for aid. A *symptom* is a vital phenomenon resulting from a diseased condition; in medical language a *sign* is an *indication* of any physical condition, whether morbid or healthy; thus, a hot skin and rapid pulse are *symptoms* of pneumonia, dulness of some portion of the lungs under percussion is one of the physical *signs.* See CHARACTERISTIC, EMBLEM, LETTER, MARK[1], TRACE[1].

sig·nal (sig'nəl) *n.* **1** A sign or means of communication agreed upon or understood, and used to convey information or command, as at a distance. **2** *Telecom.* A radio wave or electric current which transmits intelligence, whether direct or in code. **3** An event that incites to action or movement. **4** In some card games, a lead or play that conveys certain information to one's partner. See synonyms under SIGN. — *adj.* **1** Distinguished by some special sign or characteristic; notable; conspicuous. **2** Used to signal: a *signal* fire. See synonyms under EMINENT, EXTRAORDINARY. — *v.* ·**naled** or ·**nalled,** ·**nal·ing** or ·**nal·ling** *v.t.* **1** To make signals to; inform or notify by signals. **2** To communicate by signals. — *v.i.* **3** To make a signal or signals. [< F < L *signalis* < *signum* sign] — **sig'nal·er** or **sig'nal·ler** *n.*

signal fire A fire used as a signal; a beacon fire.

signal generator An electromagnetic oscillator used to supply currents of known frequencies through a specified range in testing the performance of a radio receiver.

sig·nal·ize (sig'nəl·īz) *v.t.* ·**ized,** ·**iz·ing 1** To render noteworthy. **2** To point out with care.

sig·nal·ly (sig'nəl·ē) *adv.* In a signal manner; eminently.

sig·nal·ment (sig'nəl·mənt) *n.* **1** The act of signaling. **2** Description of a person for identification by peculiar or characteristic marks, as in the case of a criminal. [<F *signalement*]

signal smoke A smoke from a fire used to signal to a distance, by a system either of puffs, spirals, or clouds.

signal tower 1 Any tower from which signals are displayed. **2** A small railroad tower from which semaphore or block-system signals are controlled.

sig·na·to·ry (sig'nə·tôr'ē, -tō'rē) *adj.* Bound by the terms of a signed document; having signed: *signatory* powers. —*n.* One who has signed or is bound by a document; specifically, a nation so bound. [<L *signatorius* <*signatus,* pp. of *signare* sign <*signum* a sign]

sig·na·ture (sig'nə·chər) *n.* **1** The name of a person, or something representing his name, written, stamped, or inscribed by himself or by deputy, as a sign of agreement or acknowledgment. **2** *Printing* **a** A distinguishing mark, letter, or number on the first page of each form or sheet of a book, as a guide to the binder. **b** The form or sheet on which this mark is placed. **c** One of the fractional parts of a book; a folded printed sheet, usually comprising 16 pages. **3** *Music* A symbol or group of symbols at the beginning of a staff, indicating time or key. See KEY SIGNATURE, TIME SIGNATURE. **4** In radio, the musical number or sound effect that introduces or closes a given program. **5** *Zool.* A color mark resembling a letter. **6** *Med.* The part of a physician's or pharmacist's prescription that indicates how the medicine is to be taken: usually preceded by *S.* or *Sig.* [<F <Med. L *signatura* <L *signatus.* See SIGNATORY.]

sign·board (sīn'bôrd', -bōrd') *n.* A board on which a sign, direction, or advertisement is displayed.

sig·net (sig'nit) *n.* **1** A seal; especially, in England, one of the seals of the sovereign, used in sealing his private letters and bills of grants, etc. **2** An impression made by or as if by a seal. —*v.t.* To mark or make official with a signet or seal. ◆ Homophone: *cygnet.* [<F, dim. of *signe* sign <L *signum*]

sig·nif·i·cance (sig·nif'ə·kəns) *n.* **1** The character or state of being significant; expressiveness. **2** That which is signified or intended to be expressed; meaning. **3** Importance; consequence: opposed to *insignificance.* Also **sig·nif'i·can·cy.**

sig·nif·i·cant (sig·nif'ə·kənt) *adj.* **1** Having or expressing a meaning; bearing or embodying a meaning. **2** Betokening or standing as a sign for something; having some covert meaning; significative: His manner was *significant.* **3** Important, as pointing out something weighty; momentous: opposed to *insignificant.* **4** *Math.* Having value or the determining or influential value: the *significant* figures in a number. See synonyms under IMPORTANT. —*n.* Something bearing a meaning; specifically, a token or letter. [<L *significans, -antis,* ppr. of *significare* make a sign, mean <*signum* sign + *facere* do, make] —**sig·nif'i·cant·ly** *adv.*

sig·nif·i·ca·tion (sig'nə·fə·kā'shən) *n.* **1** That which is signified; meaning; sense; import. **2** The act of signifying; communication. [<OF *significaciun* <L *significatio, -onis.* See SIGNIFICANT.]

sig·ni·fy (sig'nə·fī) *v.* **·fied, ·fy·ing** *v.t.* **1** To make known by signs or words; express; communicate; announce; declare. **2** Hence, to betoken in any way; mean; import. **3** To amount to; mean: What does his opinion *signify?* **4** To denote (medical use) by signature or markings. —*v.i.* **5** To have some meaning or importance; matter. See synonyms under ALLUDE, IMPORT. —**sig'ni·fi'er** *n.*

sign language 1 Dactylology. **2** A system of communication by means of signs, largely manual; specifically, the system used by the Plains Indians to communicate with tribes speaking other languages.

sign manual *pl.* **signs manual 1** The personal signature of the British sovereign written at the top of state papers. **2** A sign made with the hand; also, any code consisting of manual signs.

si·gnor (sēn'yôr) *n.* **1** An Anglicized form of the Italian title **signore,** used in respectful address to a gentleman: in society equivalent

to the English *sir* when no name follows, to *Mr.* with a name, and to the French *monsieur.* **2** A lord or gentleman; especially, an Italian of rank, official position, or social distinction. Also **si'gnior.** [<Ital. *signore* <L *senior* senior]

si·gno·ra (sē·nyō'rä) *n. Italian* Madam; Mrs.: a title of respectful address.

si·gno·ri·na (sē'nyō·rē'nä) *n. Italian* The equivalent to *miss:* diminutive of Italian *signora.*

si·gno·ri·no (sē'nyō·rē'nō) *n. Italian* A title of respectful address to a young man: diminutive of Italian *signore,* sir.

si·gno·ry (sēn'yə·rē) See SEIGNIORY.

sign·post (sīn'pōst') *n.* A post bearing a sign; sometimes, a guideboard.

Sikh (sēk) *n.* One of a religious and military sect founded by Guru Nának (1469–1538) in India early in the 16th century. —*adj.* Of or pertaining to the Sikhs. [<Hind., lit., disciple]

Sikh·ism (sēk'iz·əm) *n.* The creed and practices of the Sikhs: it is a monotheistic system, combining the teachings of the Persian Sufis with those of Hinduism, rejecting caste, and enjoining purity of life and toleration.

Sik·kim (sik'im) A protectorate of India in the eastern Himalayas, south central Asia; 2,818 square miles; capital, Gangtok.

si·lage (sī'lij) *n.* Ensilage. [<ENSILAGE]

si·le·na·ceous (sī'lə·nā'shəs) *adj.* Caryophyllaceous. [<NL *Silene,* a genus of plants <L *Silenus* Silenus + -ACEOUS]

si·lence (sī'ləns) *n.* **1** The state or quality of being silent; abstinence from speech or noise; taciturnity. **2** Absence of sound or noise; stillness. **3** Absence of note; failure to mention; oblivion; secrecy. **4** *Music* A rest. —*v.t.* **·lenced, ·lenc·ing 1** To render silent; take away the authority to speak or the power of reply from. **2** To stop the motion or activity of; put to rest; quiet. **3** To force (guns, etc.) to cease firing, as by return fire, bombing, or the like. —*interj.* Be silent. [<F <L *silentium* <*silere* be silent]

si·lenc·er (sī'lən·sər) *n.* **1** A tubular device attached to the muzzle of a firearm rendering the discharge noiseless. **2** A muffler (def. 2). **3** A device to prevent the buzzing of telegraph or telephone wires.

MAXIM SILENCER

a. Socket for attaching to gun.

b. Vortex chamber for gases.

c. Passage groove for bullet.

si·lent (sī'lənt) *adj.* **1** Not making any sound or noise; noiseless; still; also, unspoken; unuttered: *silent* grief. **2** Not speaking, or not given to speech; mute; taciturn. **3** Making no mention or allusion; passing by without notice or record. **4** Free from activity, motion, or disturbance; calm; quiet: a *silent* retreat. **5** Interested financially in a business, but having no authority to act: a *silent* partner. **6** Written, but not pronounced: said of a letter, as the *b* in *debt.* [<F <L *silens, -entis,* ppr. of *silere* be silent] —**si'lent·ly** *adv.* —**si'lent·ness** *n.*

Si·le·nus (sī·lē'nəs) In Greek mythology, the foster father and teacher of Bacchus and leader of the satyrs: traditionally represented as a fat, drunken old man with pointed ears and goat's legs, riding on an ass. [<L <Gk. *Seilēnos* Silenus]

Si·le·sia (si·lē'shə, sī-) A region of east central Europe divided between north central Czechoslovakia and SW Poland; formerly a province of Prussia and a crownland of Austria; total area, about 20,000 square miles: German *Schlesien,* Polish *Śląsk,* Czech *Slezsko.* —**Si·le'sian** *adj.* & *n.*

sil·hou·ette (sil'ŏō·et') *n.* **1** A profile drawing or portrait having its outline filled in with uniform color, commonly black: often cut out, as from cardboard. **2** The figure or likeness cast by a shadow; the outline of a solid figure. —*v.t.* **·et·ted, ·et·ting** To cause to appear in silhouette; outline; make a silhouette profile of. [after Étienne de *Silhouette,* 1709–1767, French minister of finance; in mockery of the petty economies for which he was notorious]

SILHOUETTE
Abraham Lincoln

silic- Var. of SILICO-.

sil·i·ca (sil'i·kə) *n.* A white or colorless, extremely hard, crystalline silicon dioxide, SiO_2, the principal constituent of quartz and sand. [<NL <L *silex, silicis* flint]

silica gel A highly adsorbent colloidal silica, used for deodorizing and cleaning air, purifying blast-furnace gases, etc.

si·li·ceous (si·lish'əs) *adj.* **1** Pertaining to, resembling, or containing silica. **2** Growing or living on siliceous soil. Also **si·li'cious.** [<L *siliceus*]

sil·i·cide (sil'ə·sīd) *n. Chem.* A binary compound of silicon with a metal, such as iron, cobalt, nickel, chromium, copper, or magnesium.

si·lic·i·fied wood (si·lis'ə·fīd) Wood that has been replaced by silica crystallizing out from solution so as to become a mass of quartz of the original form and structure of the wood; petrified wood. See PETRIFIED FOREST.

si·lic·i·fy (si·lis'ə·fī) *v.* **·fied, ·fy·ing** *v.t.* To convert into silica, as wood. —*v.i.* To become silica, or become impregnated with it. [<SILIC- + -(I)FY] —**si·lic'i·fi·ca'tion** *n.*

sil·i·cle (sil'i·kəl) *n.* A very short, flat silique. [<L *silicula,* dim. of *siliqua* pod]

silico- *combining form* Silicon; of, related to, or containing silicon. Also, before vowels, *silic-,* as in *silicosis.* [<L *silex, silicis* flint]

sil·i·con (sil'ə·kən) *n.* A nonmetallic element (symbol Si, atomic number 14), in nature combined chiefly with oxygen in rock and sand and forming almost 26 percent by weight of the lithosphere. See PERIODIC TABLE. [<L *silex, silicis* flint]

sil·i·cone (sil'ə·kōn) *n. Chem.* Any of various organosilicon compounds containing a silicon-carbon bond: their great physical, chemical, and electrical stability adapts them for many industrial uses as lubricants, greases, polishes, insulating resins, waterproofing materials, and for the making of a special type of synthetic rubber. [<SILICON]

sil·i·co·sis (sil'ə·kō'sis) *n. Pathol.* A pulmonary disease caused by the inhalation of finely powdered silica or quartz.

sil·ic·u·lose (si·lik'yə·lōs), **si·lic·u·lous** (-ləs) *adj.* Siliquose. [<SILIQUOSE]

si·lique (si·lēk') (sil'ik) *n. Bot.* A narrow, dry, two-valved pod or fruit characteristic of plants of the mustard family. Also **sil·i·qua** (sil'ə·kwə). [<F <L *siliqua* pod]

sil·i·quose (sil'ə·kwōs) *adj.* Silique-bearing; pertaining to or resembling a silique. Also **sil·i·quous** (-kwəs). [<NL *siliquosus* <L *siliqua* pod]

silk (silk) *n.* **1** The creamy-white or yellowish, very fine natural fiber produced by various insects, especially by the larvae of silkworms, to form their cocoons. **2** A similar thread spun by other insects or arachnids. **3** Cloth, thread, or garments made of silk. **4** Anything resembling or suggestive of silk, as the fine soft styles of an ear of corn. —**to hit the silk** *Slang* To descend from an aircraft by parachute. —*adj.* Consisting of silk; silken; silky. —*v.t.* To clothe or cover with silk: grand ladies plumed and *silked.* —*v.i.* To produce the portion of the flower called silk: said of corn. [OE *seoloc,* ult. <L *sericus* silken, lit., pertaining to the Seres (Chinese), from whom silk was bought. Related to SERGE.]

silk cotton The silky seed covering of various species of a genus (*Bombax*) of tropical American trees, and of the West Indian god tree (*Ceiba pentandra*) or corkwood (*Ochroma pyramidale*). Its principal use is for stuffing cushions, packing, etc.

silk-cot·ton tree (silk'kot'n) Any tree producing silk cotton.

silk·en (sil'kən) *adj.* **1** Made of silk. **2** Like silk; glossy; delicate; smooth. **3** Dressed in silk; hence, luxurious.

silk hat A high cylindrical hat covered with fine silk plush: worn by men and used as a dress hat.

silk paper A granite paper made with occasional silk fibers in the pulp.

silk-screen print (silk'skrēn') A reproduction made by the silk-screen process.

silk-screen process A printing process which forces ink through the meshes of a silk screen on which the desired pattern or design has been impressed.

silk-stock·ing (silk'stok'ing) *adj.* Wearing silk stockings; hence, wealthy; luxurious. —*n.* **1** One who wears silk stockings; a member of the wealthy class. **2** A supporter of a branch of the Whig party in the United States in the early 19th century.

.silk vine A deciduous shrub of the milkweed family (*Periploca graeca*) growing in the neighborhood of the Black Sea: its bark yields periplocin. Also called *wolf's-bane.*

silk·worm (silk′wûrm′) *n.* The larva of a moth that produces a dense silken cocoon, especially the common silkworm (*Bombyx mori*), from whose cocoon commercial silk is made.

silk·y (sil′kē) *adj.* **silk·i·er, silk·i·est 1** Like silk in any way; soft; lustrous. **2** Made of or consisting of silk; silken. **3** Long, fine, and appressed, as hairs, or covered with such hairs, as leaves. **4** Gentle or insinuating in manner; smooth and persuasive: usually in a bad sense, implying insincerity. —**silk′i·ly** *adv.* —**silk′i·ness** *n.*

sill (sil) *n.* **1** A horizontal member forming the foundation, or part of the foundation, of a structure of any kind, as at the bottom of a casing in a building; especially, a door sill or a window sill. **2** A timber in the frame of the floor of a railroad car: end *sill*; side *sill*. **3** *Geol.* A relatively thin stratum of igneous rock intruded between level or gently inclined beds of other rock. [OE *syll*]

sil·la·bub (sil′ə-bub) *n.* **1** A dish made by combining milk or cream with wine or cider, and thus forming a soft curd, which is then flavored. It may be whipped into a froth, or made solid by boiling after adding water and gelatin. **2** Figuratively, something frothy, as flowery language. Also spelled *syllabub.* [Alter. of obs. *sillibouk* < SILLY + OE *búc* belly]

sil·ly (sil′ē) *adj.* **·li·er, ·li·est 1** Destitute of ordinary good sense; simple; foolish; imbecile; fatuous; sometimes, senile. **2** Characterized by or resulting from foolishness or imbecility; stupid: *silly* talk. **3** *Rare* Simple; plain; rustic. **4** *Colloq.* Stunned; dazed, as by a blow. **5** *Obs.* or *Brit. Dial.* Frail; feeble; weak; helpless. **6** *Scot.* Mentally or physically incapable; idiotic; imbecilic. **7** *Obs.* Scanty; meager. See synonyms under CHILDISH, RIDICULOUS. —*n. pl.* **·lies** *Colloq.* A silly person. [OE *gesælig* happy] —**sil′li·ly** *adv.* —**sil′li·ness** *n.*

si·lo (sī′lō) *n. pl.* **·los 1** A structure, usually of wood or concrete, as a cylindrical pit or a tower, in which fodder, grain, or other food is stored green to be fermented and used as feed for cattle, etc. See ENSILAGE. **2** A deep cylindrical structure built underground for the housing and launching of guided missiles. —*v.t.* **·loed, ·lo·ing** To put or preserve in a silo; turn into ensilage. < L *sirus* < Gk. *siros* pit for corn]

SILO

silt (silt) *n.* **1** An earthy sediment consisting of extremely fine particles of rock and soil suspended in and carried by water. **2** A deposit of such sediment, as at the mouth of a river. —*v.i.* **1** To become filled or choked with silt: usually with *up.* **2** To ooze; drift. —*v.t.* **3** To fill or choke with silt or mud: usually with *up.* [ME *sylte.* Cf. Dan. *sylt* salt marsh, Norw. *sylta* coast-land washed by the sea.] —**silt′y** *adj.*

Si·lu·ri·an (si-lŏŏr′ē·ən, sī-) *adj.* **1** *Geol.* Of or pertaining to the period or rock system of the Paleozoic era following the Ordovician and preceding the Devonian, sometimes called the era of invertebrates: so called because first identified in southern Wales, the home of the ancient Silures. **2** Of or pertaining to the Silures. —*n.* **1** The Silurian period or system. **2** Originally, the period between the Cambrian and the Devonian.

si·lu·rid (si-lŏŏr′id, sī-) *n.* Any one of a large family of fishes (*Siluridae*), the catfishes, including many fresh-water food fishes of the United States. —*adj.* Of or pertaining to the *Siluridae.* Also **si·lu′roid.** [< NL *Siluridae,* name of the family < L *silurus* a river fish < Gk. *silouros*]

sil·va (sil′və), **sil·van** (sil′vən), etc. See SYLVA, etc.

sil·ver (sil′vər) *n.* **1** A lustrous, gray, ductile,

malleable metallic element (symbol Ag, atomic number 47) having great thermal and electric conductivity, found native and in various ores, crystallizing in the isometric system, and valued as one of the precious metals. See PERIODIC TABLE. **2** The metal silver regarded as a valuable commodity or as a standard of currency. **3** Silver coin considered as money; hence, ready cash or change; money in general. **4** Articles for domestic use, as tableware, made of silver; silver plate; silverware. **5** A luster of color resembling that of silver; also, the color of silver. **6** *Phot.* Silver nitrate or one of the other salts of silver, used for sensitizing paper. —*adj.* **1** Made of or coated with silver. **2** Resembling silver; having a silvery lustre. **3** Having the soft, clear tones of a silver bell; hence, enticing; persuasive; eloquent. **4** Relating to, connected with, or producing silver. **5** Designating a 25th wedding anniversary. **6** White; hoary: said of the hair or beard. **7** Favoring the use of silver as a monetary standard. —*v.t.* **1** To coat or plate with silver. **2** To coat with some substance having a resemblance to silver; specifically, to coat with amalgam of tin and mercury, as a mirror. **3** To make silverlike; cause to glitter like silver. **4** To coat, as photographic paper, with a film of a silver salt. —*v.i.* **5** To become silver or white, as with age; to become silverlike. [OE *siolfor*] —**sil′ver·er** *n.*

sil·ver·bell (sil′vər·bel′) *n.* A small tree (*Halesia carolina*) of the southern United States, with showy white flowers: sometimes called *snowdrop tree.* Also **silverbell tree.**

sil·ver·ber·ry (sil′vər·ber′ē) *n. pl.* **·ber·ries** A shrub (*Elaeagnus commutata*) of the northwestern United States, with silvery foliage, flowers, and edible fruit.

silver bromide *Chem.* A photosensitive compound, AgBr, of silver salts and a bromide: used in photography.

silver certificate Paper currency issued by the United States treasury and validated by silver currency or bullion.

silver chloride *Chem.* A white, curdy precipitate, AgCl, made by treating silver salts with chloride solutions: used in photography for developing and printing.

sil·ver·fish (sil′vər·fish′) *n. pl.* **·fish** or **·fish·es 1** A silvery-white variety of the goldfish. **2** The tarpon. **3** The silversides. **4** Any of numerous primitive, flat-bodied, wingless insects (genus *Lepisma,* order *Thysanura*) having three bristlelike tails and feeding on flour, cereals, bookbindings, and other starchy matter: often called *bristletail.* **5** Any of several similar insects, as the firebrat.

silver fox 1 The red fox (*Vulpes fulva*) of the United States and Canada, in that color phase when the pelage is black with interspersed silver-tipped hairs. **2** The fur.

sil·ver·ing (sil′vər·ing) *n.* **1** A plating or covering of silver, or an imitation of it, as applied to any surface. **2** The art or process of coating surfaces with or as with silver. **3** Sensitization of photographic paper with a silver salt.

sil·ver·ling (sil′vər·ling) *n.* **1** An old Hebrew or Persian silver coin. **2** A tarpon.

sil·ver·ly (sil′vər·lē) *adv.* In the manner of silver; brightly; with sweet tone.

silver maple White maple.

silver nitrate *Chem.* A white, crystalline, poisonous compound, AgNO₃, obtained by treating silver with nitric acid. It is widely used in industry and photography, and in medicine as an astringent, antiseptic, etc.

silver plate 1 Table utensils made of silver. **2** *U.S.* Plated silverware: a trade term.

silver point 1 A drawing implement consisting of a slender silver rod pointed at one end, or of silver wire held in an etching-needle holder. **2** The process of drawing with such an implement. **3** A drawing made with a silver point on paper coated with a white pigment, as Chinese white, characterized by delicacy of line, and often by a tarnish which is highly esteemed. **4** *Physics* The melting point of silver at normal atmospheric pressure, 960.5° C.: one of the basic points in the international temperature scale.

silver poplar The white poplar.

sil·ver·smith (sil′vər·smith′) *n.* A worker in silver; a maker of silverware.

silver standard A monetary standard or system based on silver.

Silver Star A U.S. military decoration in the form of a bronze star inset with a small raised silver star, awarded for gallantry in action: first issued in 1932, and ranking next in honor to the Distinguished Service Cross.

SILVER STAR

Silver State Nickname of Nevada: so called from its native silver ores.

sil·ver·tongued (sil′vər·tungd′) *adj.* Persuasive; eloquent.

sil·ver·ware (sil′vər·wâr′) *n.* Articles made of silver; silver plate; especially, tableware.

sil·ver·weed (sil′vər·wēd′) *n.* A perennial herb (*Potentilla anserina*) of the rose family, growing on shores and meadows, with pinnate silvery leaves and large yellow flowers.

sil·ver·y (sil′vər·ē) *adj.* **1** Containing or adorned with silver. **2** Resembling silver, as in luster, hue, or sound: a *silvery* laugh. —**sil′ver·i·ness** *n.*

sil·vi·cul·ture (sil′vi·kul′chər) *n.* The art of producing and tending a forest and forest trees. See FORESTRY. [< L *silva* forest + CULTURE] —**sil′vi·cul′tur·al** *adj.* —**sil′vi·cul′tur·al·ly** *adv.* —**sil′vi·cul′tur·ist** *n.*

s'il vous plaît (sēl vōō ple′) *French* If you please; please.

si·ma (sī′mə) *n. Geol.* An igneous rock rich in silica and magnesium underlying sial formations in continental land masses. [< SI(LICA) + MA(GNESIUM)]

si·mar (si·mär′) *n.* A light, flowing robe for women. [< F *simarre* < Ital. *cimarra* < Arabic *sammūr* sable]

sim·a·ru·ba (sim′ə·rōō′bə) *n.* Any of a genus (*Simaruba*) of tropical American trees of the quassia family, having diclinous flowers and drupaceous fruits. *S. amara* yields a bark used in pharmacy. Also **sim′a·rou′ba.** [< NL < native Carib name] —**sim′a·ru·ba′ceous** or **·rou·ba′ceous** *adj.*

sim·i·an (sim′ē·ən) *adj.* Like or pertaining to the apes and monkeys. —*n.* An ape or monkey. [< L *simia* ape]

sim·i·lar (sim′ə·lər) *adj.* **1** Bearing resemblance to one another or to something else; like, but not completely identical. **2** Of like characteristics, nature, or degree; of the same scope, order, or purpose. **3** *Music* Having motion in the same direction; ascending or descending together, as two parts. **4** *Geom.* Shaped alike: said of two figures, each of which may become congruous with the other by altering all its linear dimensions in one and the same ratio, its angles remaining unchanged. See synonyms under ALIKE, SYNONYMOUS. [< F *similaire* < L *similis* like]

similar fraction See under FRACTION.

sim·i·lar·i·ty (sim′ə·lar′ə·tē) *n. pl.* **·ties. 1** The quality or state of being similar. **2** The point in which the objects compared are similar. **3** *pl.* Things that coincide with or resemble each other. See synonyms under ANALOGY, APPROXIMATION.

sim·i·lar·ly (sim′ə·lər·lē) *adv.* Likewise.

sim·i·le (sim′ə·lē) *n.* A rhetorical figure expressing comparison or likeness, by the use of such terms as *like, as, so,* etc.: distinguished from *metaphor* and *comparison* proper. [< L, neut. of *similis* similar]

Synonyms: comparison, figure, illustration, image, imagery, likeness, metaphor, similitude, symbol. The *simile* carries its note of *comparison* on the surface, in the words *as, like, such as,* or similar expressions; the *metaphor* is given directly without any note of *comparison.* "God is *like* a rock" is a *simile*; "God *is* a rock" is a *metaphor.* In order that a *comparison* may become a *simile,* objects of different classes must be compared, bringing in some imaginative element. To say, "The Hudson is like the Rhine" is not *simile,* but direct and literal *comparison*; but to say,

"The Hudson flows like the march of time" is to lift the river out of its class and associate it with a great elemental conception, and thus to transform the *comparison* into a *simile. Similitude* is broader in meaning than *simile* or *metaphor,* and may include direct and literal *comparison.* Compare ALLEGORY. ANALOGY. EMBLEM.

si·mil·i·tude (si·mil′ə·tōōd, -tyōōd) *n.* **1** Similarity. **2** One who or that which is similar. **3** A rhetorical figure involving comparison or likeness; loosely, a metaphor or a simile. **4** *Geom.* The relation of identity between two figures irrespective of magnitude. See synonyms under ANALOGY. IMAGE. PICTURE. SIMILE. [< L *similitudo* < *similis* like]

sim·i·ous (sim′ē·əs) *adj.* Simian. Also **sim′i·oid.** [See SIMIAN]

sim·mer (sim′ər) *v.i.* **1** To boil gently or with a singing sound; be or stay at or just below the boiling point. **2** To be on the point of breaking forth, as with rage. —*v.t.* **3** To keep at or just below the boiling point. —*n.* The state or process of simmering; figuratively, a busy pondering over something, or a state of repressed emotion. [< obs. *simper* boil; origin unknown; prob. imit.]

si·mon–pure (sī′mən·pyōōr′) *adj.* Real; genuine; authentic. [after a character in a 17th c. comedy, who is impersonated by a rival; the rival is discomfited when the real Simon Pure appears]

si·mo·ny (sī′mə·nē, sim′ə-) *n.* Traffic in sacred things; the purchase or sale of ecclesiastical preferment. [< Med. L *simonia* < *Simon* (*Magus*), who offered Peter money for the gift of the Holy Spirit]

si·moom (si·mōōm′, sī-) *n.* A hot, dry, dust-laden, exhausting wind of the desert, as in Africa and Arabia: also spelled *samoun.* Also **si·moon′** (-mōōn′). [< Arabic *samūm* < *samma* poison]

simp (simp) *n.* *U.S. Slang* A simpleton.

sim·per (sim′pər) *v.i.* To smile in a silly, self-conscious manner; smirk. —*v.t.* To say with a simper. —*n.* A silly, self-conscious smile; smirk. [Prob. <Scand. Cf. Sw. and Norw. *semper* affected, coy.] —**sim′per·er** *n.* —**sim′per·ing·ly** *adv.*

sim·ple (sim′pəl) *adj.* **·pler, ·plest** **1** Consisting of one thing; single; uncombined; unmingled. **2** Not complex or complicated; easy. **3** Without embellishment; plain; unadorned. **4** Free from affectation; sincere; artless; unsophisticated; also, of humble rank or condition; lowly. **5** Of weak intellect; silly; feeble–minded. **6** Not worth much consideration; insignificant; trifling; ordinary. **7** Without luxury; frugal. **8** Having nothing added; mere: the *simple* truth. **9** *Chem.* That cannot be or has not been decomposed; elementary; also, unmixed. **10** *Bot.* Not subdivided: a *simple* leaf; entire; not divided. **11** *Music* **a** Single. **b** Without overtones. **c** Not developed or elaborated: *simple* harmony. —*n.* **1** That which is simple; an unartificial, uncomplex, or natural thing; an element. **2** A medicinal plant, or the medicine extracted from it: from the former supposition that each single herb was or provided a specific for some disease. **3** A simpleton; a stupid or ignorant person; also, a person of humble position or birth. **4** *Eccl.* A feast of lowest rank which is merely commemorated at the canonical hours. **5** *pl. Colloq.* Foolishness; insanity: He suffers from the *simples.* [< OF < L *simplex, simplus*] *Synonyms (adj.):* chaste, modest, natural, neat, plain, quiet, unadorned, unaffected, unembellished, unpretentious, unstudied, unvarnished. See CANDID, PURE. *Antonyms:* affected, artful, artificial, complex, complicated, elaborate, intricate, involved, ostentatious, pretentious, showy.

simple fraction See under FRACTION.

simple fruit *Bot.* A fruit consisting of a single enlarged and matured ovary, as the date, cherry, peach, apple, and orange.

sim·ple–heart·ed (sim′pəl·härt′id) *adj.* **1** Tender-hearted. **2** Ingenuous in disposition; open; sincere.

simple honors In bridge, three honors of the trump suit held by a player and his partner.

simple interest Interest computed on the original principal alone.

simple machine **1** Any one of certain elementary mechanical contrivances, as the lever, the wedge, the inclined plane, the screw, the wheel and axle, and the pulley. **2** A hand tool

---

having no parts, as a hammer or chisel, or two parts working in simple combination, as shears.

sim·ple–mind·ed (sim′pəl·mīn′did) *adj.* **1** Artless or unsophisticated in character. **2** Defective in intellect; mentally imbecile. —**sim′ple–mind′ed·ly** *adv.* —**sim′ple–mind′ed·ness** *n.*

sim·pler (sim′plər) *n.* A collector or dispenser of herbs or medicinal remedies extracted from them; herbalist.

simple sentence See under SENTENCE.

simple sugar A monosaccharide.

sim·ple·ton (sim′pəl·tən) *n.* A weak-minded or silly person.

sim·plex (sim′pleks) *adj.* **1** Simple. **2** Noting a form of telegraphy in which only one message is sent over a wire at a time. [< L, simple]

simplici– *combining form* Simple. Also, before vowels, **simplic–.** [< L *simplex, simplicis* simple]

sim·pli·ci·den·tate (sim′plə·si·den′tāt) *adj.* Pertaining or belonging to a suborder of rodents (*Simplicidentata*) with a single pair of upper incisors, which includes mice, squirrels, porcupines, and all others with the exception of hares and pikas.

sim·plic·i·dent (sim·plis′ə·dənt) *adj.* Simplicidentate. —*n.* A simplicidentate rodent.

sim·plic·i·ty (sim·plis′ə·tē) *n. pl.* **·ties 1** The state of being simple; freedom from admixture, ornament, formality, ostentation, subtlety, or difficulty; sincerity; unaffectedness. **2** Deficiency of intelligence or good sense, or an instance of it. See synonyms under INNOCENCE. Also **sim′ple·ness.** [< L *simplicitas, -tatis*]

sim·pli·fy (sim′plə·fī) *v.t.* **·fied, ·fy·ing** To make more simple or less complex. [< F *simplifier* <Med. L *simplificare* < L *simplex* simple + *facere* make] —**sim′pli·fi·ca′tion** *n.* —**sim′pli·fi′er** *n.*

sim·plis·tic (sim·plis′tik) *adj.* Tending to ignore or overlook underlying questions, complications, or details; overly simple: *simplistic* attitudes. —**sim·plis′ti·cal·ly** *adv.*

sim·ply (sim′plē) *adv.* **1** In a simple manner; intelligibly; without ostentation or extravagance; without subtlety or affectation; unassumingly. **2** Merely. **3** Without sense or discretion; foolishly. **4** Really; absolutely: *simply* charming: often used ironically.

sim·u·la·crum (sim′yə·lā′krəm) *n. pl.* **·cra** (-krə) **1** That which is made in the likeness of a being or thing; an image. **2** An imaginary, visionary, or shadowy semblance. **3** A sham. [< L, image < *simulare.* See SIMULATE.]

sim·u·lant (sim′yə·lənt) *adj.* Simulating. —*n.* One who or that which simulates. [< L *simulans, -antis,* ppr. of *simulare.* See SIMULATE.]

sim·u·lar (sim′yə·lər) *n.* One who simulates; a pretender. —*adj.* **1** Given to simulation; pretending. **2** Counterfeit.

sim·u·late (sim′yə·lāt) *v.t.* **·lat·ed, ·lat·ing 1** To assume or have the appearance or form of, without the reality; counterfeit; imitate. **2** To make a pretense of. See synonyms under IMITATE, PRETEND. —*adj.* (-lāt, -lit) Simulated; pretended. [< L *simulatus,* pp. of *simulare* imitate < *similis* like] —**sim′u·la′tor** *n.*

sim·u·la·tion (sim′yə·lā′shən) *n.* The act of simulating; counterfeit; sham. See synonyms under PRETENSE. —**sim′u·la·tive, sim′u·la·to′ry** (-lə·tôr′ē, -tō′rē) *adj.* —**sim′u·la·tive·ly** *adv.*

si·mul·cast (sī′məl·kast′, -käst′) *v.t.* **·cast, ·cast·ing** To broadcast by radio and television simultaneously. —*n.* A broadcast transmitted by radio and television simultaneously. [< SIMUL(TANEOUS) + (BROAD)CAST]

si·mul·ta·ne·ous (sī′məl·tā′nē·əs, sim′əl-) *adj.* Occurring, done, or existing at the same time. [< LL *simultaneus* <L *simul* at the same time] —**si′mul·ta′ne·ous·ly** *adv.* —**si′mul·ta′ne·ous·ness, si′mul·ta·ne′i·ty** (-tə·nē′ə·tē) *n.*

simultaneous equations *Math.* A series of algebraic equations such that each will satisfy the conditions of two or more variables, as, $x + y = 7$ and $2x + 3y = 19$, where $x = 2$, $y = 5$.

si·murg (si·mōōrg′) *n.* In Persian mythology, an immense bird possessing great knowledge, who has witnessed the destruction of the world three times; perhaps, the roc. Also **si·murgh′.** [<Persian *simurgh*]

sin (sin) *n.* **1** A lack of conformity to, or a transgression, especially when deliberate, of a law, precept, or principle regarded as having divine authority. **2** The state or condition of having thus transgressed; wickedness.

---

3 A particular instance of such transgression. **4** Any fault or error; an offense against a standard: a literary *sin.* —*v.* **sinned, sin·ning** *v.i.* **1** To commit sin, transgress, neglect, or disregard the divine law or any requirement of right, duty, or propriety; do wrong. —*v.t.* **2** To commit or do wrongfully: to sin a great sin. **3** To effect, consume, drive, etc., by sin. [OE *synn*]

Synonyms (noun): crime, criminality, delinquency, depravity, evil, guilt, ill-doing, immorality, iniquity, misdeed, offense, transgression, ungodliness, unrighteousness, vice, viciousness, wickedness, wrong, wrong-doing. *Sin,* in religious teaching, is any lack of holiness, any defect of moral purity and truth, whether in heart or life, whether of commission or of omission. *Transgression,* as its etymology indicates, is the stepping over a specific enactment, whether of God or man, ordinarily by overt act, but in the broadest sense in volition or desire. *Sin* may be either act or state; *transgression* is always an act, mental or physical. *Crime* is often used for a flagrant violation of right, but in the technical sense denotes specific violation of human law. *Depravity* denotes no act, but a perverted moral condition from which any act of *sin* may proceed. *Immorality* denotes outward violation of the moral law. Compare OFFENSE. *Antonyms:* decorum, godliness, goodness, holiness, integrity, morality, purity, right, righteousness, sinlessness, uprightness, virtue. Compare synonyms for VIRTUE.

Sin·an·thro·pus (sin·an′thrə·pəs, sī′nan·thrō′pəs) *n. Paleontol.* A large-brained, well-developed hominid primate identified from extensive fossil remains discovered between 1927 and 1939 in the Pleistocene deposits of a cave near Peking, China. Also called *Peking man.* [<NL <Gk. *Sinai* Chinese + *anthropos*]

sin·a·pism (sin′ə·piz′əm) *n.* A mustard plaster. [< L *sinapismus* <Gk. *sinapismos* < *sinapi* mustard]

since (sins) *adv.* **1** From a past time, mentioned or referred to, up to the present. **2** At some time between a certain past time or event and the present: He was willing at first, but has *since* refused. **3** In time before the present; ago; before now. —*prep.* **1** During or within the time after or later than: Things have changed *since* you left. **2** Continuously throughout the time after: He has been working *since* noon. —*conj.* **1** During or within the time after which. **2** Continuously from the time when: She has been ill *since* she arrived. **3** Because of or following upon the fact that; inasmuch as. See synonyms under BECAUSE. [ME *sithens* <OE *siththan* afterwards + *-s* (adverbial termination)]

sin·cere (sin·sir′) *adj.* **1** Being in reality as it is in appearance; real; genuine: *sincere* regret. **2** Intending precisely what one says or what one appears to intend; free from hypocrisy; honest in one's action or profession: a *sincere* friend. **3** *Obs.* Being without admixture; free; pure. **4** *Obs.* Blameless. **5** *Obs.* Sound; whole. See synonyms under CANDID, HONEST. [< L *sincerus* uncorrupted < *sin-* without + stem of *caries* decay] —**sin·cere′ly** *adv.*

sin·cer·i·ty (sin·ser′ə·tē) *n.* The state or quality of being sincere; honesty of purpose or character; freedom from hypocrisy, deceit, or simulation. See synonyms under INNOCENCE. Also **sin·cere′ness.**

sin·ci·put (sin′si·put) *n. Anat.* The top of the head, especially the anterior portion. Compare OCCIPUT. [< L < *semi-* half + *caput* head] —**sin·cip·i·tal** (sin·sip′ə·təl) *adj.*

Sin·clair (sin·klâr′), **Upton,** 1878–1968, U. S. author and socialist.

sind (sind) *Scot. v.t.* To rinse; wash down (food) with drink; quench. —*n.* A slight washing; a drink with or after food.

Sind (sind) A former province of West Pakistan, on the Arabian Sea; incorporated into West Pakistan province, 1955: 47,569 square miles; former capital, Hyderabad; total area of Sind and Khairpur, 56,447 square miles, divided into the Commissioners' Divisions of Hyderabad and Khairpur, 1955.

Sind·bad the Sailor (sind′bad) In the *Arabian Nights,* a traveling merchant of Baghdad, who relates the marvelous adventures that befell him on his seven voyages. Also spelled *Sinbad.*

sine[1] (sīn) *n. Trig.* **1** A function of an angle in a right triangle expressible as the ratio of the side opposite the angle to the hypotenuse. **2** A function of any acute angle expressible, when plotted in Cartesian coordinates, as the ratio of the ordinate to the distance from the point where the ordinate crosses one leg of the angle to the origin. Abbreviated *sin*, as, *sin A. AB.* Arc. *AO.* Radius. *BC.* Perpendicular. $\frac{BC}{AO}$ is sine of the arc *AB.* See TRIGONOMETRIC FUNCTION. — **versed sine** One of the trigonometric functions, equal to one minus the cosine: also *versine.* ◆ Homophone: *sign.* [<L *sinus* bend (trans. of Arabic *jayb* bosom of a garment, sine). Doublet of SINUS.]

sine[2] (sī′nē) *prep. Latin* Without.

si·ne·cure (sī′nə·kyŏor, sin′ə-) *n.* **1** An office having emoluments but few or no duties. **2** A benefice without cure of souls. [<L *sine* without + *cura* care] — **si′ne·cur·ism** *n.* — **si′ne·cur·ist** *n.*

sine curve *Math.* The plane curve of the equation *y = sin x.* The curve has a period of *x = 2π* (radians) along the abscissa and a limit along the ordinate of *y = ± 1.*

si·ne qua non (sī′nē kwā non′) *Latin* That which is indispensable; an essential: literally, without which not.

sin·ew (sin′yōō) *n.* **1** A tendon or other fibrous cord. **2** Strength, or that which supplies strength. **3** *Obs.* A nerve. — *v.t.* To strengthen or knit together, as with sinews; supply with sinews. [OE *sinu, seonu*]

sin·ew·less (sin′yōō·lis) *adj.* **1** Without sinews. **2** Without strength or vigor.

sin·ew·y (sin′yōō·ē) *adj.* **1** Characteristic or consisting of a sinew or nerve. **2** Well braced with sinews; strong; brawny. See synonyms under STRONG.

sin·fo·ni·a (sin·fō′nē·ə, *Ital.* sēn′fō·nē′ä) *n. Italian* **1** A symphony. **2** The overture, in operas of early date.

sin·ful (sin′fəl) *adj.* Consisting in, suggestive of, or tainted with sin. [OE *synfull*] — **sin′ful·ly** *adv.* — **sin′ful·ness** *n.*
Synonyms (adj.): bad, criminal, depraved, evil, faulty, flagitious, immoral, iniquitous, nefarious, unholy, unrighteous, unworthy, vicious, vile, villainous, wicked, wrong. See BAD[1], CRIMINAL, IMMORAL. Compare synonyms for SIN[1]. *Antonyms:* godly, good, holy, immaculate, incorrupt, incorruptible, innocent, just, right, righteous, sinless, spotless, stainless, undefiled, unfallen, unperverted, unstained, unsullied, untainted, upright, virtuous, worthy.

sing (sing) *v.* **sang** or (*now less commonly*) **sung**, **sung**, **sing·ing** *v.i.* **1** To utter words or sounds with musical inflections of the voice. **2** To perform vocal compositions professionally or in a specified manner: She *sings* well. **3** To utter melodious sounds, as a bird. **4** To make a continuous, melodious sound suggestive of singing, as a teakettle, the wind, etc. **5** To buzz or hum; ring: My ears are *singing.* **6** To be suitable for singing. **7** To relate something in verse; hence, to compose poetry. **8** *Slang* To confess the details of a crime, and so implicate others. — *v.t.* **9** To perform (a song, etc.) vocally. **10** To chant; intone. **11** To bring to a specified condition by singing: *Sing* me to sleep. **12** To accompany or escort with songs. **13** To acclaim or relate in or as in song: Generations *sing* his deeds. — *n.* **1** The humming sound made by a bullet in flight. **2** *Colloq.* A social gathering at which songs are sung: a community *sing.* [OE *singan*] — **sing′a·ble** *adj.*
Synonyms (verb): carol, chant, chirp, chirrup, hum, warble. To *sing* is primarily and ordinarily to utter a succession of articulate musical sounds with the human voice. The word has come to include any succession of musical sounds; we say the bird or the rivulet *sings,* or the teakettle or the cricket *sings.* To *chant* is to *sing* in solemn and somewhat uniform cadence; *chant* is ordinarily applied to non-metrical religious compositions. To *carol* is to *sing* joyously, and to *warble* is to *sing* with trills or quavers, usually also with the idea of joy. *Carol* and *warble* are especially applied to the *singing* of birds. To *chirp* is to utter a brief musical sound, perhaps often repeated in the same way, as by certain small birds, insects, etc. To *chirrup* is to utter a somewhat similar sound; the word is often used of a brief sharp sound uttered as a signal to animate or rouse a horse or other animal. To *hum* is to utter murmuring sounds with somewhat monotonous musical cadence, usually with closed lips; we speak also of the *hum* of machinery, etc.

Sin·ga·pore (sing′gə·pôr, -pōr, sing′ə-) **1** An island (224 square miles) off the southern end of the Malay Peninsula, comprising with adjacent islands and Christmas Island the State of Malaysia; a former part of the Straits Settlements, 1826–1946; 286 square miles. **2** Its capital, a port on **Singapore Strait,** a channel between Singapore island and the Malay Peninsula, connecting the South China Sea and the Strait of Malacca; 10 miles wide.

singe (sinj) *v.t.* **singed, singe·ing** **1** To burn slightly or superficially; discolor by burning; scorch: to *singe* the nap of cloth. **2** To remove bristles or feathers from by passing through flame. **3** To burn the ends of (hair, etc.). See synonyms under BURN[1]. — *n.* **1** The act of singeing, especially as performed by a barber. **2** A heat that singes. **3** An injury or risk, as if from or of singeing. [OE *sengan* scorch, hiss, causative of *singan* sing; from the singing sound produced]

sing·er (sing′ər) *n.* **1** One who sings, especially as a profession; also, a poet. See synonyms under POET. **2** That which produces a song-like utterance, as a songbird.

sin·gle (sing′gəl) *adj.* **1** Consisting of one only; separate; individual. **2** Having no companion or assistant; alone. **3** Unmarried; also, pertaining to the unmarried state. **4** Of or pertaining to one alone; hence, uncommon; singular; unique. **5** Consisting of only one part; simple; uncompounded. **6** In good condition; sound; also, upright; sincere. **7** Designed for use by only one person: a *single* bed. **8** Designed for use with one thing of which there might be more: a *single* harness (for one horse). **9** *Bot.* Solitary, as a flower when it is the only one on a stem: opposed to *clustered;* in popular usage, having only one row of petals: opposed to *double.* **10** *Obs.* Of medium strength; mild; not double or strong: said of malt liquors. **11** Simplex. See synonyms under PARTICULAR, SOLITARY. — *n.* **1** That which or one who is single; a unit; individual. **2** In baseball, a hit by which the batter reaches first base. **3** A hotel room for one person. **4** A golf match between two players only: opposed to *foursome.* **5** In cricket, a hit which scores one run. **6** In falconry, a talon. — *v.* **gled, ·gling** *v.t.* **1** To choose or select (one) from others: usually with *out.* — *v.i.* **2** To go with the single-foot gait, as a horse. **3** In baseball, to make a single. [<OF <L *singulus*] — **sin′gle·ness** *n.* — **sin′gly** *adv.*

sin·gle-act·ing (sing′gəl·ak′ting) *adj.* Doing effective work in one direction, as a motor having a reciprocating motion.

sin·gle-ac·tion (sing′gəl·ak′shən) *adj.* Designating a type of firearm of which the trigger must be cocked by one action and released by another.

sin·gle-breast·ed (sing′gəl·bres′tid) *adj.* Having only one thickness of cloth over the breast; fastening in front with a single row of buttons, loops, or like means of engagement: said of a coat, waistcoat, etc.

sin·gle-cross (sing′gəl·krôs′, -kros′) *n. Genetics* The first generation of a cross between two inbred lines.

single entry A method of bookkeeping in which the daybook and ledger are the essential books, transactions being carried to a single account only. — **sin′gle-en′try** *adj.*

single file A line of people, animals, etc., disposed one behind the other, with no two abreast.

sin·gle-foot (sing′gəl·fŏot′) *n.* The gait of a horse in which the footfall sequence is right hind, right fore, left hind, left fore, the support of the body being alternately upon one foot and two feet: sometimes called *amble* or *rack.* — *v.i.* To go at this gait.

sin·gle-hand·ed (sing′gəl·han′did) *adj.* **1** Without assistance; unaided. **2** Having but one hand. **3** Capable of being used with a single hand. **4** Having only one workman. Also **sin′gle-hand′.** — **sin′gle-hand′ed·ly** *adv.*

sin·gle-heart·ed (sing′gəl·här′tid) *adj.* Of sincere and frank disposition. — **sin′gle-heart′ed·ly** *adv.*

sin·gle-mind·ed (sing′gəl·mīn′did) *adj.* **1** Having but one purpose or end in view. **2** Free from duplicity; ingenuous; sincere. — **sin′gle-mind′ed·ly** *adv.* — **sin′gle-mind′ed·ness** *n.*

sin·gle-phase (sing′gəl·fāz′) *adj. Electr.* Applied to the current generated by a two-pole alternating dynamoelectric machine.

sin·gles (sing′gəlz) *n. pl.* In lawn tennis, table tennis, etc., a match with only one person on each side: opposed to *doubles.* — *adj.* Having but one player on a side: a *singles* match.

sin·gle-stick (sing′gəl·stik′) *n.* **1** A cudgel; specifically, a basket-hilted stick used in fencing. **2** The art of fencing with singlesticks; also, a bout with cudgels.

sin·gle-sur·faced (sing′gəl·sûr′fist) *adj.* Surfaced, covered, or finished on one side only.

sin·glet (sing′glit) *n.* **1** A woolen or cotton undershirt or jersey. **2** An unlined waistcoat.

sin·gle·ton (sing′gəl·tən) *n.* **1** A single card of a suit in the hand of a player at the deal. **2** Any single thing, distinct from a pair.

sin·gly (sing′glē) *adv.* **1** Without companions or associates; alone; unaided, as an individual. **2** One by one; one at a time. **3** *Obs.* Uprightly; honestly.

Sing Sing (sing′sing′) **1** A State prison near Ossining, New York. **2** The former name of OSSINING.

sing·song (sing′sông′, -song′) *n.* **1** Monotonous cadence in speaking or reading. **2** Inferior verse; doggerel. — *adj.* **1** Monotonous; droning. **2** Rising and falling in pitch.

sing·spiel (sing′spēl, *Ger.* zing′shpēl) *n.* **1** A dramatic representation in which dialog and song alternate. **2** Opera in which music is subordinated to words, especially in dramatic movement. [<G, lit., sing-play]

sin·gu·lar (sing′gyə·lər) *adj.* **1** Extraordinary; remarkable; uncommon: her *singular* beauty. **2** Odd; unconventional; peculiar; not customary or usual: to be *singular* in one's dress. **3** Representing the only one of its type; unique: a *singular* instance. **4** *Gram.* Of or designating a word form which denotes one person or thing, or a class considered as a unit, as *man, dog, he;* not dual or plural. **5** *Logic* Embodying something specific or individual; not general: a *singular* idea. See synonyms under EXTRAORDINARY, QUEER, RARE[1]. — *n. Gram.* The singular number, or a word form having this number. [<OF *singuler* <L *singularis* <*singuli* single] — **sin′gu·lar·ly** *adv.* — **sin′gu·lar·ness** *n.*

sin·gu·lar·i·ty (sing′gyə·lar′ə·tē) *n. pl.* **·ties** **1** The state or quality of being singular; uncommonness; oddity; eccentricity. **2** A character or quality by which a person or thing is distinguished from all or many others; a peculiarity. **3** Something or someone of uncommon or remarkable character.

sin·gu·lar·ize (sing′gyə·lə·rīz′) *v.t.* **·ized, ·iz·ing** To make singular; convert into the singular number.

sin·is·ter (sin′is·tər) *adj.* **1** Morally wrong; malevolent; evil; bad; perverse: *sinister* purposes; a *sinister* expression on the face. **2** Boding, tending toward, or attended with disaster; unlucky; inauspicious: from a superstition that omens seen on the left boded ill. **3** Situated on the left side or hand: opposed to *right* or *right-hand.* **4** *Her.* Of a shield, left as regards the wearer; hence, right as regards the observer: opposed to *dexter.* Compare illustration under ESCUTCHEON. [<F *sinistre* <L *sinister* left] — **sin′is·ter·ly** *adv.* — **sin′is·ter·ness** *n.*

sin·is·trad (sin′is·trad) *adv.* Toward the left aspect of the body: opposed to *dextrad.* [<L *sinister* left]

sin·is·tral (sin′is·trəl) *adj.* Of, pertaining to, or turned toward the left side or left hand. [<OF] — **sin′is·tral·i·ty** (sin′is·tral′ə·tē) *n.* — **sin′is·tral·ly** *adv.*

sin·is·trorse (sin′is·trôrs, sin′is·trôrs′) *adj.* 1 Sinistral. 2 Twined or twining from right to left, as the hop. Compare DEXTRORSE. [< L *sinistrorsus*, contraction of *sinistroversus* turned toward the left side < *sinister* left + *versum* turned, pp. of *vertere*] —**sin′is·tror′sal** *adj.* —**sin′is·tror′sal·ly** *adv.*

sin·is·trous (sin′is·trəs) *adj.* 1 Of, pertaining to, or directed toward the left; sinistral. 2 Sinister; unpropitious; ill-omened. [< L *sinister* left] —**sin′is·trous·ly** *adv.*

sink (singk) *v.* **sank** or **sunk, sunk** (*Obs.* **sunk·en**), **sink·ing** *v.i.* 1 To go beneath the surface or to the bottom, as of water or snow. 2 To descend to a lower level; go down, especially slowly or by degrees: *The flames are sinking.* 3 To descend toward or below the horizon, as the sun. 4 To incline downward; slope, as land. 5 To pass into a specified state: to *sink* into sleep or a coma. 6 To fail, as from ill-health or lack of strength; approach death: *He's sinking fast.* 7 To become less in force, volume, or degree: *His voice sank to a whisper.* 8 To become less in value, price, etc. 9 To decline in moral level, prestige, wealth, etc.: to *sink* into vice. 10 To penetrate a softer body: *The oil sank into the wood.* 11 To be impressed or fixed, as in the heart or mind: with *in*: I think that lesson will *sink* in. —*v.t.* 12 To cause to go beneath the surface or to the bottom. 13 To cause to fall or drop; lower: *He sank his head upon his breast.* 14 To force or drive into place: to *sink* a fence post. 15 To make (a mine shaft, well, etc.) by digging or excavating. 16 To reduce in force, volume, or degree. 17 To debase or degrade, as one's character or honor. 18 To suppress or hide; also, to omit. 19 To defeat; ruin. 20 To invest. 21 To invest and subsequently lose: I *sank* a million in that deal. —*n.* 1 A box-shaped, basinlike, porcelain or metal receptacle with a drainpipe and usually with a water supply; a cesspool or the like. 2 A place where corruption and vice gather or are rampant. 3 A natural pool, marsh, or basin in which a river terminates by evaporation or percolation. [OE *sincan*] —**sink′a·ble** *adj.*

sink·er (singk′ər) *n.* 1 One who or that which sinks, or causes to sink: a die-*sinker*. 2 A weight for sinking a fishing or sounding line. 3 In baseball, a pitch that curves sharply downward as it approaches home plate.

sink·hole (singk′hōl′) *n.* A natural cavity, especially a drainage cavity, as a hole worn by water through a rock along a joint or fracture.

sinking fund The fund so instituted and invested that its gradual accumulations will wipe out a debt at maturity.

sin·less (sin′lis) *adj.* Having no sin; guiltless; innocent. See synonyms under INNOCENT, PERFECT. —**sin′less·ly** *adv.* —**sin′less·ness** *n.*

sin·ner (sin′ər) *n.* 1 One who has sinned. 2 An irreligious person.

Sinn Fein (shin fān) Literally, we ourselves; an Irish society aiming at both independence and the cultural development of the Irish people. It originated about 1905 and in 1916 became active politically, advocating republicanism and causing a revolt in the spring of that year. —**Sinn Fein′er** —**Sinn Fein′ism**

Sino- *combining form* Chinese; of or pertaining to the Chinese people, language, etc. See CHINO-. [< LL *Sinae* the Chinese]

si·no·a·tri·al (sī′nō·ā′trē·əl) *adj. Anat.* Of or pertaining to an area of the right auricle of the heart where the heartbeat is stimulated.

sin offering An offering made in atonement for sin.

Si·nol·o·gy (sī·nol′ə·jē, si-) *n.* The systematic study or investigation of the Chinese people, language, literature, history, and characteristics. —**Sin·o·log·i·cal** (sin′ə·loj′i·kəl, sī′nə-) *adj.* —**Si·nol′o·gist** *n.*

sin·u·ate (sin′yōō·it, -āt) *adj.* 1 Winding in and out, as a margin; tortuous; sinuous; wavy. 2 *Bot.* Having a sinus, or sinuses: a *sinuate* leaf. Also **sin·u·at·ed.** —*v.i.* (sin′yōō·āt) **·at·ed, ·at·ing** To curve in and out; turn; wind. [< L *sinuatus*, pp. of *sinuare* turn, wind < *sinus* curve] —**sin′u·ate·ly** *adv.* —**sin′u·a′tion** *n.*

sin·u·os·i·ty (sin′yōō·os′ə·tē) *n.* 1 Sinuous quality. 2 A winding; deflection.

sin·u·ous (sin′yōō·əs) *adj.* 1 Characterized by bends or folds; winding; undulating. 2 *Bot.* Sinuate. 3 Devious; erring. [< L *sinuosus* < *sinus*

bend] —**sin′u·ous·ly** *adv.* —**sin′u·ous·ness** *n.*

si·nus (sī′nəs) *n.* 1 A recess formed by a bending or folding; an opening or cavity. 2 *Anat.* **a** An air cavity in one of the cranial bones communicating with the nostrils: the frontal *sinus.* **b** A channel or receptacle for venous blood; also, a dilated part of a blood vessel. 3 *Pathol.* Any narrow opening leading to an abscess. 4 *Bot.* A recess or rounded curve between two projecting lobes or teeth of a leaf. [< L. Doublet of SINE.]

si·nu·si·tis (sī′nə·sī′tis) *n. Pathol.* Inflammation of a sinus. Also **sin·u·i·tis** (sin′yōō·ī′tis). [< SINUS + -ITIS]

si·nu·sot·o·my (sī′nə·sot′ə·mē) *n. Surg.* Incision of a sinus.

si·nus·oid (sī′nə·soid) *n.* 1 *Math.* sine curve. 2 *Anat.* A tiny passageway for blood in the liver. **-sion** Var of -TION.

sip (sip) *v.* **sipped, sip·ping** *v.t.* 1 To imbibe in small quantities. 2 To drink from by sips. 3 To take in; absorb. —*v.i.* 4 To drink in sips. —*n.* 1 A very small draft; a mere taste. 2 The act of sipping. [OE *sypian* drink in]

si·phon (sī′fən) *n.* 1 A tube having a bend used for transferring liquids from a higher to a lower level over an intervening elevation by making use of atmospheric pressure. 2 A siphon bottle. 3 *Zool.* A tubular structure in certain aquatic animals, as the squid, for drawing in or expelling liquids. —*v.t.* To draw off by or cause to pass through or as through a siphon. —*v.i.* To pass through a siphon. Also spelled **syphon.** [< F < L *sipho, -onis* < Gk. *siphōn*] —**si′phon·al** *adj.*

si·phon·age (sī′fən·ij) *n.* The use or action of a siphon.

si·pho·nap·ter·ous (sī′fə·nap′tər·əs) *adj.* Of or pertaining to the order of insects (*Siphonaptera*) including the fleas: small, flattened, wingless, bloodsucking insects with great jumping ability. [< NL *Siphonaptera*, name of the order < SIPHON + A-⁴ -PTEROUS]

SIPHON

siphon bottle A bottle containing aerated or carbonated water, which is expelled through a bent tube in the neck of the bottle by the pressure of the gas.

si·pho·no·phore (sī′fə·nə·fôr′, -fōr′, sī·fon′ə-) *n.* A marine organism (order *Siphonophora*) with free-swimming pelagic colonies arising by budding, as the Portuguese man-of-war. [< NL *Siphonophora*, name of the order < Gk. *siphōnophóros* tube-carrying < *siphōn* tube + *pherein* bear]

sip·pet (sip′it) *n.* 1 A triangular or finger-shaped piece of toasted or fried bread used to garnish a dish of hash or minced meat; a crouton. 2 Any eatable, especially bread, cut into small pieces and soaked in some liquid: frequently used in the plural. 3 Hence, any very small quantity. [Blend of SIP and SOP in a dim. form]

sir (sûr) *n.* 1 The conventional term of respectful address to men: used absolutely, and not followed by a proper name. 2 A title given to persons of rank or to officials: *sir* herald, *sir* clerk. 3 An influential or important person. 4 *Archaic* A title of respect for a priest. [< SIRE]

sir·dar (sər·där′) *n.* 1 In India and Oriental countries, a chief or lord. 2 In Egypt, the commander in chief of the army. 3 In India, a head servant; a leader of palanquin-bearers; also, a body-servant or valet: also **sir·dar′-bear′er.** [< Hind. *sardār* leader < *sar* head + *dār* holding] —**sir·dar′ship** *n.*

sire (sīr) *n.* 1 A father; begetter: used also in composition: grand*sire*. The feminine correlative is **dame.** 2 The male parent of a mammal, the female parent (of lower animals) being usually termed the **dam.** 3 A form of address to a superior: now used only in addressing a king or other sovereign. 4 *Obs.* A master; lord; also, a gentleman. —*v.t.* **sired, sir·ing** To beget; procreate: now used chiefly of domestic animals. [< OF < L *senior* older. See SENIOR.]

si·ren (sī′rən) *n.* 1 One of two or, in later Greek legend, three nymphs, living on an island, who lured sailors to destruction by their sweet singing. They are represented as birds

with women's heads, later as women with birds' feet and wings. Odysseus escaped them by sealing his companions' ears with wax and having himself bound to his ship's mast. 2 Hence, a fascinating, dangerous woman; also, a sweet singer. 3 An eel-like amphibian (genus *Siren*) having well developed gills and lacking hind legs; a mud eel. 4 An apparatus having a device with a perforated rotating disk or disks through which sharp puffs of steam or compressed air are permitted to escape in such rapid succession as to produce a continued musical note or a loud whistle: used in acoustical investigations and as a warning signal. —*adj.* Of or pertaining to a siren; hence, alluring; bewitching; dangerously fascinating. Also spelled **syren.** [< L < Gk. *seirēn*]

si·re·ni·an (sī·rē′nē·ən) *n.* One of an order (*Sirenia*) of aquatic mammals, including the manatee, dugong, etc., of somewhat fishlike form with the lower jaw as in ordinary mammals, and having mostly molariform teeth for a herbivorous diet. —*adj.* Of or pertaining to the *Sirenia.* [< NL *Sirenia*, name of the order < L *siren.* See SIREN.]

si·ri·a·sis (si·rī′ə·sis) *n. Pathol.* Sunstroke or thermic fever. [< Gk. *seiriasis* < *seirios* hot, scorching]

sir·loin (sûr′loin) *n.* A loin of beef, especially the upper portion: also spelled **surloin.** [Alter. (after *Sir*, from a legend that the cut was knighted for its excellence) of obs. *surloyn* < OF *surlonge* < *sur-* over, above + *longe* loin < L *lumbus*]

si·roc·co (si·rok′ō) *n. pl.* **·cos** 1 A hot, dry, and dusty southerly wind blowing from the African coast to Italy, Sicily, and Spain. 2 A warm, sultry wind blowing from a warm region toward a center of low barometric pressure. 3 A southeast wind: the popular Italian name. [< Ital. *scirocco* < Arabic *sharq* the east, the rising sun < *sharaqa* rise]

sir·up (sir′əp) *n.* A thick, sweet liquid, as the boiled juice of fruits, sugarcane, etc.: also spelled **syrup.** [< OF *sirop* < Turkish *sharbat.* Doublet of SHERBET.] —**sir′up·y** *adj.*

sis (sis) *n. Colloq.* Sister.

si·sal (sī′səl, sis′əl, sē′səl) *n.* 1 The strong, tough fiber obtained from the leaves of a West Indian agave (*Agave sisalina*). 2 Henequen. Also **sisal grass, sisal hemp.** [from *Sisal*, town in Yucatán, Mexico]

sis·co·wet (sis′kə·wet) *n.* 1 The namaycush. 2 The cisco. Also **sis′ka·wet, sis′ki·wit.** [< F (Canadian) *ciscoette* < Algonquian (Ojibwa) *pemitewiskawet* oily-fleshed creature]

sis·kin (sis′kin) *n.* A finch (genus *Spinus*) related to the goldfinch, as the **European siskin** (*S. spinus*) olive-green and yellow barred with black, or the North American **pine siskin** (*S. pinus*). [< MDu. *cijsken* < LG *zieske* < Polish *czyżyk*, dim. of *czyż* finch]

siss (sis) *v.i.* To hiss; sizzle. —*n.* A hissing or sizzling sound. [Imit.]

sis·si·fied (sis′i·fīd) *adj. U.S. Colloq.* Like a sissy; effeminate.

sis·sy (sis′ē) *U.S. Colloq. n. pl.* **·sies** An effeminate man or boy; a milksop; a weakling, male or female. —*adj.* Being a sissy; effeminate; sissified. [< SIS] —**sis′sy·ish** *adj.*

sis·ter (sis′tər) *n.* 1 A female person or animal having the same parent or parents as another person or animal. Daughters of the same parents are **full** or **whole sisters,** called in law **sisters german.** Those having only one parent in common are **half-sisters.** 2 A woman or girl allied to another or others by some association: *sisters* in spirit: also used figuratively: Astronomy and astrology are *sisters.* 3 *Eccl.* A member of a sisterhood; a nun. 4 A head nurse in the ward of a hospital; also, popularly, any nurse. —**the three** (or **Fatal**) **Sisters** The Fates. —*adj.* Bearing the relationship of a sister or one suggestive of sisterhood. [< ON *systir*] —**sis′ter·ly** *adj.*

sis·ter·hood (sis′tər·hŏŏd) *n.* 1 A body of sisters united by some bond of fellowship or sympathy. 2 *Eccl.* **a** A community of women bound by monastic vows. **b** An association of women set apart for works of mercy and faith, sometimes bound by a revocable vow. 3 The sisterly relationship.

sis·ter-in-law (sis′tər·in·lô′) *n. pl.* **sis·ters-in-law** A sister by marriage: a sister of one's husband, a sister of one's wife, a brother's wife, or, loosely, a brother-in-law's wife.

Sistine Chapel The principal chapel in the Vatican Palace at Rome, constructed by Sixtus IV, and afterward decorated with frescos by Michelangelo and others.

sis·troid (sis'troid) *adj. Geom.* Included by the convex sides of two intersecting curves: said of an angle and opposed to *cissoid*. [<SISTR(UM) + -OID]

sis·trum (sis'trəm) *n. pl.* **·tra** (-trə) or **·trums** A musical rattle used in the worship of Isis in ancient Egypt. [<L <Gk. *seistron < seiein* shake]

Sis·y·phe·an (sis'ə-fē'ən) *adj.* 1 Of or pertaining to Sisyphus. 2 Difficult and interminable: a *Sisyphean* task.

Sis·y·phus (sis'ə-fəs) In Greek mythology, a crafty, greedy king of Corinth, condemned in Hades forever to roll uphill a huge stone that always rolled down again.

SISTRUM

sit (sit) *v.* **sat** (*Archaic* **sate**), **sat, sit·ting** *v.i.* 1 To rest, as upon a chair, with the body bent at the hips, and the spine nearly vertical; rest upon the haunches; take or occupy a seat. 2 To perch or roost, as a bird; brood; also, to cover eggs so as to give warmth for hatching. 3 To be or remain in a seated or settled position. 4 To remain passive or inactive, or in a position of idleness or rest. 5 To assume an attitude of readiness; take a position for a special purpose; pose, as for a portrait. 6 To meet in assembly for deliberation or business; hold a session. 7 To occupy or be entitled to a seat in a deliberative body. 8 To have or exercise judicial authority. 9 To fit or be adjusted; suit: That dress *sits* well. 10 To be suffered or borne, as a burden. 11 To be situated or located; be in some position or direction: The wind *sits* in the east. — *v.t.* 12 To have or keep a seat or a good seat upon: to *sit* a horse. 13 To seat (oneself): *Sit* yourself down. — **to sit in (on)** To join: to *sit in on* a game of cards, or a business deal. — **to sit on** (or **upon**) 1 To belong to (a jury, commission, etc.) as a member. 2 To hold discussions about and look into carefully, as a case. 3 *Colloq.* To suppress or squelch. — **to sit out** 1 To sit quietly till the end of: to *sit out* an entertainment. 2 To sit aside during: They *sat out* a dance. 3 To stay longer than. — **to sit tight** *Colloq.* To wait quietly for the next move on the part of somebody else: Just *sit tight* until I get back. [OE *sittan*]

si·tar (si-tär') *n.* A stringed instrument used in Hindu music, somewhat resembling the guitar, having a variable number of strings, some of which are plucked, others vibrating sympathetically. [<Hind. *sitār*]

sit·com (sit'kom') *n. Slang* A situation comedy. [Blend of SIT(UATION) + COM(EDY)]

sit-down (sit'doun') *n.* 1 A strike during which strikers refuse to leave the factory or other place of employment until agreement is reached. Also **sit-down strike.** 2 A sit-in (def. 2).

site (sit) *n.* 1 Situation; local position. 2 A plot of ground set apart for some specific use. 3 The degree of inclination from the horizontal of a line joining the target and the muzzle of a gun: also **angle of site.** See synonyms under PLACE. ◆ Homophones: *cite, sight.* [<F <L *situs* position]

sit-in (sit'in') *n.* 1 An organized demonstration in which a protesting group occupies an area prohibited to them, as by taking seats in a restricted restaurant, etc. 2 A form of civil disobedience in which demonstrators obstruct some activity by sitting down and refusing to move: also called *sit-down.* — **sit'-in·ner** *n.*

sito- *combining form* Food; related to food: *sitotropism.* [<Gk. *sitos* food]

si·tol·o·gy (si·tol'ə-jē) *n.* The science of foods, diet, and nutrition. — **si·to·log·ic** (si'tə-loj'ik) or **·i·cal** *adj.*

si·tos·ter·ol (si·tos'tə-rōl, -rol) *n. Biochem.* Any of a group of sterols found in higher plants and related to cholesterol, especially *a-sitosterol,* $C_{30}H_{50}O$, from wheat embryos. [<SITO- + STEROL]

si·to·tox·in (si'tō-tok'sin) *n.* Any poison evolved in vegetable foods, especially in cereals, by the action of micro-organisms.

[<SITO- + TOXIN]

si·to·tro·pism (si'tō·trō'piz·əm) *n.* The automatic response of an organism to the positive or negative influence of food. [<SITO- + TROPISM]

sit·ter (sit'ər) *n.* 1 One who sits. 2 A baby sitter (which see). 3 A person sitting as a model. 4 A setting hen.

sit·ting (sit'ing) *adj.* Being in the position of a sitter; also, used for sitting: a *sitting*-room. — *n.* 1 The act or position of one who sits; hence, a seat; also, the place of or the right to a seat, as in a church. 2 A single period of uninterrupted application, as for the painting of a portrait. 3 A session or term. 4 An incubation; period of hatching; also, the number of eggs on which a bird sits at one incubation.

sitting duck 1 A duck resting on water, and therefore an easy target for a hunter. 2 *Colloq.* Any easy target.

sit·ting-room (sit'ing·rōōm', -rŏŏm') *n.* A parlor; living-room.

sit·u·ate (sich'ŏŏ·āt) *v.t.* **·at·ed, ·at·ing** 1 To fix a site for. 2 To place in a certain position or under certain conditions or circumstances; locate. [<Med. L *situatus,* pp. of *situare* place < *situs* a place]

sit·u·at·ed (sich'ŏŏ·ā'tid) *adj.* 1 Having a fixed place or location; placed. 2 Placed in (usually specified) circumstances or conditions: He is *well* situated.

sit·u·a·tion (sich'ŏŏ·ā'shən) *n.* 1 The place in which something is situated; relative local position; locality. 2 Condition as modified or determined by surroundings; status. 3 A salaried post of employment, usually subordinate. 4 A combination of circumstances; complication; specifically, in the drama, a conjuncture, climax, or crisis. See synonyms under CIRCUMSTANCE, PLACE, SCENE. — **sit'u·a'tion·al** *adj.*

situation comedy A television or radio show typically centered about a few characters involved in comical situations and presented in separate episodes.

si·tus (si'təs) *n.* 1 Site; situation; place. 2 A fitting or natural position, as of a part of a plant. [<L]

sitz bath (zits) 1 A small bathtub in which one bathes in a sitting posture. 2 A bath taken in such a tub. [<G *sitzbad*]

Siv·a·pi·the·cus (siv'ə·pi·thē'kəs) *n. Paleontol.* An extinct ape related to Dryopithecus. [<NL <SIVA + Gk. *pithēkos* ape]

six (siks) *n.* The cardinal number following five and preceding seven, or any of the symbols (6, vi, VI) used to represent it; also, anything made up of six units or members, as a playing card with six pips. — *adj.* Being one more than five; twice three. [OE] — **six'fold'** *adj. & adv.*

six bits Seventy-five cents.

six·pence (siks'pəns) *n.* A British coin of the value of six English pennies.

six·pen·ny (siks'pen'ē, -pən·ē) *adj.* 1 Worth, valued at, or sold for sixpence; hence, paltry; trashy. 2 Denoting a size of nails. See –PENNY.

six·score (siks'skôr', -skōr') *adj.* One hundred and twenty.

six-shoot·er (siks'shŏŏ'tər) *n. Colloq.* A revolver that will fire six shots without reloading. — **six'-shoot'ing** *adj.*

six·teen (siks'tēn') *n.* The cardinal number following fifteen and preceding seventeen, or any of the symbols (16, xvi, XVI) representing it. — *adj.* Being one more than fifteen; four times four. [OE *sixtēne*]

sixteenth note *Music* A note of one sixteenth of the value of a whole note; semiquaver.

sixth (siksth) *adj.* 1 Next in order after the fifth. 2 Being one of six equal parts. — *n.* 1 One of six equal parts. 2 *Music* a The interval between any note and the sixth note above or below it on the diatonic scale. b A note separated by this interval from any other, considered with reference to that other. c The sixth above the keynote. d Two notes at this interval written or sounded together, or the resulting consonance. — **chord of the sixth** *Music* A chord consisting of a tone with its minor third and its sixth: also **sixth chord.** — *adv.* In the sixth order, place, or rank: also,

in formal discourse, **sixth'ly.** [OE *sixta*; refashioned to conform to *fourth*]

sixth sense Intuitive perception supposedly not employing the five senses.

six·ti·eth (siks'tē·ith) *adj.* 1 Tenth in order after fiftieth: the ordinal of *sixty.* 2 Being one of sixty equal parts. — *n.* One of sixty equal parts of anything; the quotient of a unit divided by sixty.

six·ty (siks'tē) *n. pl.* **·ties** The cardinal number following fifty-nine and preceding sixty-one, or any of the symbols (60, lx, LX) representing it. — *adj.* Being one more than fifty-nine; ten times six. [OE *sixtig*]

siz·a·ble (si'zə·bəl) *adj.* Of comparatively large or convenient size. Also **size'a·ble.** — **siz'a·ble·ness** *n.* — **siz'a·bly** *adv.*

size¹ (siz) *n.* 1 Measurement or extent of a thing as compared with some standard; comparative magnitude or bulk: when unqualified, implying relative largeness. 2 One of a series of graded measures, or the magnitude between two such limits, as of hats, shoes, etc. 3 A standard of measurement; specified quantity. 4 At Cambridge University, an allotted quantity of provisions; ration. 5 Mental caliber; importance; character. 6 *Colloq.* State of affairs; true situation: That's the *size* of it. 7 Measure or amount. See synonyms under MAGNITUDE. — *v.t.* **sized, siz·ing** 1 To estimate the size of. 2 To distribute or classify according to size. 3 To cut or otherwise shape (an article) to the required size. — **to size up** *Colloq.* 1 To form an estimate, judgment, or opinion of. 2 To meet specifications. [<F *assise.* See ASSIZE.]

size² (siz) *n.* 1 A solution of gelatinous material, usually glue, casein, wax, or clay, used to finish fabrics. 2 A gelatinous substance used to glaze paper, or applied to walls before papering, etc. 3 A viscous preparation used as in fixing gilding. Also *sizing.* — *v.t.* **sized, siz·ing** 1 To treat with size or any size-like substance. 2 To make plastic, as clay. [<OItal. *sisa* painter's glue, aphetic var. of *assisa,* orig., pp. of *assidere* make sit down <L *assidere.* See ASSIZE.]

sized (sizd) *adj.* 1 Having graded dimensions or a definite size: chiefly in composition: large-*sized.* 2 Arranged according to size.

siz·ing (si'zing) *n.* 1 Size², *n.* 2 The process of adding size to a fabric, yarn, etc., to give it additional strength, stiffness, smoothness, weight, etc.

sizz (siz) *v.i.* To make a hissing sound; sizzle. [Imit.]

siz·zle (siz'əl) *v.i.* **·zled, ·zling** To burn or scorch with or as with a hissing sound; emit a hissing sound under the action of heat. — *n.* A hissing sound as from frying or effervescence. [Freq. of SIZZ]

siz·zling (siz'ling) *adj.* 1 Extremely hot. 2 That sizzles: a *sizzling* steak.

sjam·bok (sham'bok) *n.* A short, heavy whip of rhinoceros hide. [<Afrikaans <Du. <Malay *chamboq* <Persian *chābuq* whip]

skat (skät) *n.* 1 A three-handed game played with 32 cards. Any of several varieties of the game can be chosen by the highest bidder who, alone, must oppose the other players. 2 In the game of skat, two cards dealt face down and taken into his hand by the successful bidder or otherwise treated according to rule. [<G, orig. *skart* <Ital. *scartare* discard]

skate¹ (skāt) *n.* 1 A keel-shaped metal runner attached to a plate or frame, with suitable clamps or straps for fastening it to the sole of a boot or shoe, enabling the wearer to glide rapidly over ice; also, such a runner affixed to a shoe or boot. 2 A similar contrivance with wheels instead of a runner, for use on a floor or other smooth surface; a roller skate. 3 An ice-boat runner. — *v.i.* **skat·ed, skat·ing** To glide or move over ice or some other smooth surface, on or as on skates. [< earlier *skates* <Du. *schaats* <OF *escache* stilt <Gmc.]

skate² (skāt) *n.* Any of several flat-bodied rays (genus *Raia*) with enlarged pectoral fins, ventral gill slits, and a pointed snout; especially, the **barn-door skate** (*R. laevis*) of eastern North America, or the common European **gray skate** (*R. batis*). [<ON *skata*]

ske·dad·dle (ski·dad′l) *Colloq. v.i.* **·dled, ·dling** To flee in haste; run away; scamper. — *n.* The act of running away; hasty flight. [< dial. E. spill, scatter. Cf. Gk. *skedannynai* scatter.]

skeet[1] (skēt) *n.* A variety of trapshooting in which a succession of saucer-shaped targets hurled in such a way as to resemble the flight of quail are fired at from various angles by the shooter. [Origin unknown]

skeet[2] (skēt) *n.* A long-handled scoop or dipper, used for wetting sails and decks. [Origin unknown]

skeet gun A short-barreled shotgun.

skeg (skeg) *n. Naut.* The after part of a vessel's keel, or a projection on or continuation of it, as for supporting the lower end of the rudder of a screw steamer. [<Du. *schegge,* prob. <Scand. Cf. ON *skegg* beard.]

skein (skān) *n.* **1** A fixed quantity of yarn, thread, silk, wool, etc., wound to a certain length and then doubled and knotted. **2** A measure of length, 360 feet, or 109.73 meters. [<OF *escaigne,* prob. <Celtic. Cf. Irish *sgainne.*]

skein screw A screw with a broad shallow thread. See illustration under SCREW.

skel·e·tal (skel′ə·təl) *adj.* Of, pertaining to, forming, or like a skeleton.

skel·e·ton (skel′ə·tən) *n.* **1** The framework of an animal body, composed of bone and cartilage. The skeletal structure either surrounds and shields the vital organs, as the *exoskeleton* of a turtle, or is embedded within the body, as the *endoskeleton* of man and the vertebrates. **2** Any open framework constituting the main supporting parts of a structure: the *skeleton* of a house. **3** A mere sketch or outline of anything, especially of some literary production: the *skeleton* of an address. **4** A person or animal very thin by nature or loss of flesh; also, a band or troop whose numbers have been greatly thinned out. See synonyms under SKETCH. — **skeleton in the closet** A secret source of shame or discredit. See FAMILY SKELETON. — *adj.* Consisting merely of a framework or outline; resembling a skeleton in use or appearance; meager; emaciated. [<NL <Gk. *skeleton (sōma)* dried (body), mummy <*skeletos* dried up]

skeleton construction A construction in which the main support is an internal framework of steel, to which the outer walls are affixed, their weight being carried, story by story, by the framework.

skel·e·ton·ize (skel′ə·tən·īz′) *v.t.* **·ized, ·iz·ing 1** To reduce to a skeleton or framework by removing soft tissues or parts; make a skeleton of. **2** To reduce greatly in size or numbers. **3** To draft in outline.

skeleton key A slender false key designed to avoid the wards of a lock, for use as a master key.

skep (skep) *n.* **1** A beehive, especially one made of straw. **2** A receptacle of wickerwork or wood, especially for grain; a basket. [<ON *skeppa* basket]

skep·tic (skep′tik) *n.* **1** One who questions the fundamental doctrines of religion, especially of the Christian religion. **2** One who refuses concurrence in generally accepted conclusions in science, philosophy, etc. **3** An adherent of any philosophical school of skepticism; especially, an adherent of the **Skeptic school** in ancient Greece, of which the Pyrrhonists, with their doctrine of the relativity of knowledge, were the first systematic exponents. **4** One who doubts any particular statement. — *adj.* Skeptical. Also, *Brit.,* sceptic. [<F *sceptique* <L *scepticus* <Gk. *skeptikos* reflective < *skeptesthai* consider]

Synonyms (noun): agnostic, atheist, deist, disbeliever, freethinker, infidel, unbeliever. The *skeptic* doubts divine revelation; the *disbeliever* and the *unbeliever* reject it, the *disbeliever* with more of intellectual dissent, the *unbeliever* (in the common acceptation) with indifference or with opposition of heart as well as of intellect. *Infidel* is an opprobrious term that is commonly applied to any decided opponent of an accepted religion. The *atheist* denies that there is a God; the *deist* admits the existence of God, but denies that the Christian Scriptures are a revelation from him; the *agnostic* denies either that we do know or that we can know whether there is a God. *Antonyms:* believer, Christian.

skep·ti·cism (skep′tə·siz′əm) *n.* **1** A doubt-

ing or incredulous state of mind. **2** *Philos.* The doctrine that absolute knowledge is unattainable and that judgments must be continually questioned and doubted in order to attain approximate or relative certainty: opposed to *dogmatism.* Also, *Brit.,* scepticism.

sketch (skech) *n.* **1** An incomplete but suggestive delineation or presentation of anything, whether graphic or literary; an outline. **2** An artist's preliminary study, graphic or plastic, of a work of art intended for elaboration. **3** A literary or dramatic composition, short, discursive, and of slight construction. **4** A short scene, play, or musical act, especially in vaudeville. — *v.t.* To make a sketch or sketches of; outline. — *v.i.* To make a sketch or sketches. [<Du. *schets* <Ital. *schizzo* <L *schedium* improvisation <Gk. *schédios*] — **sketch′a·ble** *adj.* — **sketch′er** *n.*

Synonyms (noun): brief, delineation, draft, drawing, outline, picture, plan, skeleton. An *outline* gives only the bounding or determining lines of a figure or a scene; a *sketch* may give lines, shading and color, but is hasty and incomplete. The lines of a *sketch* are seldom so full and continuous as those of an *outline. Draft* and *plan* apply especially to mechanical drawing, of which *outline, sketch,* and *drawing* are also used; a *plan* is strictly a view from above, as of a building or machine, giving the lines of a horizontal section, originally at the level of the ground, now in a wider sense at any height; as, a *plan* of the cellar; a *plan* of the attic. A *design* is such a preliminary *sketch* as indicates the object to be accomplished or the result to be attained, and is understood to be original. One may make a *drawing* of any well-known mechanism, or a *drawing* from another man's *design;* but if he says "The *design* is mine," he claims it as his own invention or composition. In written composition an *outline* gives simply the main divisions, and is often called a *skeleton;* a somewhat fuller suggestion of illustration, treatment, and style is given in a *sketch.* A lawyer's *brief* is a succinct statement of the main facts in a case, and of the main heads of his argument on points of law, with reference to authorities. See PICTURE.

sketch·book (skech′bŏŏk′) *n.* **1** A blank book used for sketching. **2** A printed volume of literary sketches. Also **sketch book.**

sketch·y (skech′ē) *adj.* **sketch·i·er, sketch·i·est** Like or in the form of a sketch; roughly suggested without detail; hence, incomplete; superficial; slight. — **sketch′i·ly** *adv.* — **sketch′i·ness** *n.*

skew (skyōō) *v.i.* **1** To take an oblique direction; move or turn aside; swerve. **2** To look obliquely or askance; squint. — *v.t.* **3** To put askew; give an oblique position or direction to. **4** To shape or form in an oblique manner; distort. — *adj.* **1** Placed or turned obliquely; twisted to one side; askew; hence, perverted in use or meaning. **2** *Stat.* Having some elements on opposite sides of a median line reversed or unbalanced; distorted: a *skew* curve. — *n.* **1** A deviation from symmetry or straightness; distortion. **2** A sidelong glance; squint. **3** A slanting coping, as at the corner of a gable. [<AF *eskiuer,* OF *eschiuver* shun <Gmc. Related to ESCHEW.] — **skew′ly** *adv.*

skew arch *Archit.* An arch whose axis is in a vertical plane making other than right angles with its abutments.

skew·back (skyōō′bak′) *n. Archit.* **1** An abutment with inclined face receiving the thrust of a segmented arch. See also illustration under ARCH. **2** A cap or other casting, on the end of a truss, to receive the pull of a tie rod.

SKEWBACK
a. Skewback *(def.* 1).

skew·bald (skyōō′bôld′) *adj.* Piebald, especially when the spots are white and some other color than black. [ME *skewed* piebald]

skew·er (skyōō′ər) *n.* **1** A long pin of wood or metal, used chiefly for fastening meat to keep it in shape while roasting. **2** Any of various articles of similar shape or use. — *v.t.* To run through or fasten with or as

with a skewer. [Var. of SKIVER]

ski (skē, *Norw.* shē) *n. pl.* **skis** or **ski** One of a pair of wooden runners, about 7 feet long and 3½ inches wide, attached to the feet and used in gliding over snow or ice. — *v.i.* **skied, ski·ing 1** To glide or travel on skis. **2** To engage in the sport of gliding over snow-covered inclines on skis. Also spelled *skee.* [< Norw. <ON *skidh* snowshoe] — **ski′er** *n.*

SKI
Side and top view.

ski·a·scope (skī′ə·skōp) *n.* An instrument for examining the refractive power of the eye by the response of the retina to lights and shadows. [<Gk. *skia* shadow + -SCOPE]

skid (skid) *n.* **1** One of a pair of timbers used to support a heavy tilting or rolling object, as a cask, boat, or cannon; also, a log used as a track in sliding heavy articles about, or forming an inclined plane to ease their descent. **2** In lumbering, one of several logs used to make a track on which other logs are slid or piled; also, one of the cross-logs of a skid road. **3** A shoe or drag on a wagon wheel. **4** *Naut.* A fender hung over a vessel's side to protect it from rubbing and scraping: usually in the plural. **5** *Aeron.* A runner in an airplane's landing gear. **6** The act of skidding; a side-slip. **7** A small frame or platform upon which merchandise is stacked to be moved about or temporarily stored. — **on the skids** *Slang* Rapidly declining in prestige or power. — *v.* **skid·ded, skid·ding** *v.i.* **1** To slide instead of revolving, as a wheel which does not rotate though the vehicle is in motion. **2** To slip sideways through inability to grip the road: said of wheels, and, by extension, of vehicles. **3** *Aeron.* To slide sideways away from the center of curvature when turning, by reason of insufficient banking. — *v.t.* **4** To furnish with skids; put, drag, or haul on skids. **5** To brake or hold back with a skid. [? <ON *skidh* piece of wood]

skid·doo (ski·dōō′) *interj. Slang* Go away; get out. [<SKEDADDLE]

skid road 1 A road or track along which logs are hauled to the skidway. **2** A road made of logs laid transversely and spaced about five feet apart. **3** Skid row.

skid row *Slang* An urban section inhabited by vagrants and derelicts and consisting mainly of cheap bars, flophouses, etc.

skid·way (skid′wā′) *n.* A structure made of two logs or skids, about 10 feet apart and laid alongside a log road, on which logs are piled before loading.

skiff (skif) *n.* A light rowboat; formerly, a small sailing vessel. — **St. Lawrence skiff** A small boat, carrying centerboard and spritsail, light enough to be rowed with ease. [<F *esquif* <Ital. *schifo* <OHG *scif* ship, boat]

ski·ing (skē′ing) *n.* The act or sport of gliding on skis.

ski·jor·ing (skē·jôr′ing, -jō′ring) *n.* The sport of traveling over ice or snow on skis, towed by a horse or motor vehicle. [<Norw. *skikjöring* <*ski* ski + *kjöring* driving]

skil·ful (skil′fəl) *adj.* **1** Having skill; clever; dexterous; able. **2** Showing or requiring skill. Also **skill′ful.** — **skil′ful·ly** *adv.* — **skil′ful·ness** *n.*

Synonyms: adept, adroit, apt, deft, dexterous, expert, handy, happy, proficient, skilled, trained. One is *adept* in that for which he has a natural gift, improved by practice; he is *expert* in that of which training, experience, and study have given him a thorough mastery; he is *dexterous* in that which he can do effectively with or without training, especially in work of the hand or bodily activities. A *skilled* workman is one who has thoroughly learned his trade, but he may be naturally quite dull: a *skilful* workman has some natural brightness, ability, and power of adaptation, in addition to his acquired knowledge and dexterity. See CLEVER, GOOD. *Antonyms:* awkward, bulky, clumsy, helpless, inexpert, maladroit, unskilled, untaught, untrained.

ski lift An arrangement of seats usually

attached to an overhead rope or cable for carrying skiers to the top of a slope.

skill (skil) *n.* **1** The familiar knowledge of any science, art, or handicraft, as shown by dexterity in execution or performance, or in its application to practical purposes; technical ability. **2** A specific art or trade; also, a gift; accomplishment. **3** *Obs.* Intellect; understanding. See synonyms under ABILITY, DEXTERITY, INGENUITY, WISDOM. [<ON *skil* knowledge] —**skill′·less** *adj.*

skilled (skild) *adj.* Possessing or requiring skill; expert; proficient. See synonyms under SKILFUL.

skil·let (skil′it) *n.* **1** A frying pan. **2** A small kettle or stew pan, often with a bail and short legs. [? <OF *escuellete*, dim. of *escuelle* porringer <L *scutella*, dim. of *scutra* dish]

skim (skim) *v.* **skimmed, skim·ming** *v.t.* **1** To remove floating matter from the surface of, as with a ladle: to *skim* milk. **2** To remove thus: to *skim* cream. **3** To cover with a thin film, as of ice. **4** To move lightly and quickly across or over. **5** To cause to pass swiftly and lightly, as a coin across a pond. **6** To read or glance over hastily or superficially. —*v.i.* **7** To move quickly and lightly across or near a surface; glide. **8** To make a hasty and superficial perusal; glance: with *over* or *through.* **9** To become covered with a thin film. —*n.* **1** The act of skimming. **2** That which is skimmed off; scum. **3** Something from which floating matter has been removed, as skim milk. **4** A thin scum of ice. —*adj.* Skimmed: *skim* milk. [Var. of SCUM]

skim·mer (skim′ər) *n.* **1** A flat ladle or other utensil for skimming. **2** One who or that which skims. **3** A ternlike bird (genus *Rhynchops*) having the lower mandible compressed, that skims up the small fishes from near the surface of the water. *R. nigra* is the **black skimmer.**

SKIMMER
(Length 16 to 20 inches; wingspread 42 to 50 inches)

skim·ming (skim′ing) *n.* **1** The act of one who or that which skims. **2** That which is skimmed off: usually in the plural.

skimp (skimp) *v.t. & v.i.* To scrimp or scamp. —*adj.* Scant; meager. [Prob. <ON *skemma* shorten; infl. in meaning by SCRIMP]

skimp·y (skim′pē) *adj.* **skimp·i·er, skimp·i·est** **1** Carelessly done. **2** Scanty. **3** Niggardly. —**skimp′i·ly** *adv.* —**skimp′i·ness** *n.*

skin (skin) *n.* **1** The membranous external investment of an animal; the integument. ◆ Collateral adjective: *dermal.* **2** The pelt of a small animal, removed from its body, whether raw or dressed, as distinguished from the *hide* of a large animal. **3** A vessel for holding liquids, made of the skin of an animal: a wine-*skin.* **4** An outside layer, coat, or covering resembling skin, as the epidermis of a plant, fruit, etc.; rind; of pearls, the outermost layer of nacreous matter. **5** Planking or plating of a vessel. **6** A membrane resembling the integument. **7** *Slang* A mean person; skinflint; also, a sharper; blackleg. **8** One's life or physical existence: to save one's *skin.* —**by the skin of one's teeth** Very closely or narrowly; barely. —**under one's skin** Provoking; beneath the surface of control (of irritation, excitation, emotion, etc.). —*v.* **skinned, skin·ning** *v.t.* **1** To remove the skin of; flay; peel. **2** To cover with or as with skin. **3** To remove as if taking off skin: to *skin* a dollar from a roll of bills. **4** *Slang* To cheat or swindle. —*v.i.* **5** To become covered with skin; cicatrize. **6** *Slang* To make off hastily; run away: usually with *off.* [<ON *skinn*]

skin–bound (skin′bound′) *adj.* Affected with a rigid contraction of the skin and hardening of the connective tissue.

skin–deep (skin′dēp′) *adj.* Superficial. —*adv.* Superficially.

skin diving Underwater exploration in which the swimmer is equipped with a self-contained breathing apparatus, goggles, foot fins, rubber garments, etc. —**skin diver**

skin·flint (skin′flint) *n.* A miser; one who drives a hard bargain.

skin·game (skin′gām′) *n.* **1** A gambling game at cards in which the players have no chance of winning against the house or the bank. **2** Any swindle.

skink (skingk) *n.* One of a group of lizards (family *Scincidae*) with short limbs and a conical tail; especially, the blue–tailed skink (*Eumeces skiltonianus*) of the United States. [<L *scincos* <Gk. *skinkos*, kind of lizard]

SKINK
(Up to 8 inches long)

skin·less (skin′lis) *adj.* Without skin.

skin·ner (skin′ər) *n.* **1** One who skins; a flayer of animals. **2** *U.S. Slang* A cheat; swindler. **3** A dealer in skins. **4** *U.S. Slang* A mule driver.

skin·ny (skin′ē) *adj.* **·ni·er, ·ni·est** **1** Wanting flesh; lean. **2** Consisting of or like skin. See synonyms under MEAGER. —**skin′ni·ly** *adv.* —**skin′ni·ness** *n.*

skin–tight (skin′tīt′) *adj.* Fitting tightly to the skin, as a garment.

skip (skip) *v.* **skipped, skip·ping** *v.i.* **1** To move with light springing steps; caper; leap lightly. **2** To be deflected from a surface; ricochet; skim. **3** To pass from one point to another without noticing what lies between. **4** *Colloq.* To leave or depart hurriedly; flee. **5** To be advanced in school beyond the next grade in order —*v.t.* **6** To leap lightly over. **7** To cause to ricochet. **8** To pass over or by without notice. **9** *Colloq.* To leave (a place) hurriedly. —*n.* **1** A light bound or spring; especially, a hop alternating between steps in walking. **2** A passing over without notice; omission. [Prob. <Scand. Cf. Sw. *skuppa* skip.]

skip distance That area within which signals from a radio transmitter are not received: it is between the farthest point reached by the ground wave and the nearest point at which the reflected sky wave strikes the earth.

skip·jack (skip′jak) *n.* **1** Any of various fishes that skip along the surface of the water, as the bonito. **2** Any snapping or click beetle (family *Elateridae*). **3** A Chesapeake Bay sailing vessel with a centerboard and one mast: used in dredging oysters.

skip·per¹ (skip′ər) *n.* **1** One who or that which skips. **2** The saury. **3** A butterfly of the family *Hesperiidae*: so named from its flight. **4** A cheese maggot.

skip·per² (skip′ər) *n.* The master or captain of a small vessel; hence, one in charge of any craft. [<Du. *schipper* <*schip* ship]

skir·mish (skûr′mish) *v.i.* To fight in a preliminary or desultory way. —*n.* **1** A light engagement, as between small parties; desultory fighting between two armies on a skirmish line. **2** Figuratively, any light movement or operation evasive of the main contention or business. See synonyms under BATTLE. [<OF *eskermiss-*, stem of *eskermir* fence, fight <Gmc. Cf. OHG *skirman* defend <*skirm* shield. Related to SCRIMMAGE.] —**skir′·mish·er** *n.*

skirr (skûr) *v.t.* **1** To scour. **2** To skim over. —*v.i.* **3** To move rapidly. —*n.* A whirring sound. [Imit.]

skirt (skûrt) *n.* **1** That part of a dress, gown, or robe that hangs from the waist downward. **2** A separate garment hanging from the waist and covering the lower portion of the body. **3** A cloth or other material that hangs or covers like a skirt: the *skirt* of a dressing table. **4** *Slang* A girl; woman. **5** The margin, border, or outer edge of anything. **6** *pl.* The border, fringe, or edge of a particular area, path, geographical feature, etc.: on the *skirts* of the town, forest, highway, etc. **7** One of the flaps or loose, hanging parts of a saddle: also **saddle skirt.** **8** *Naut.* The leech of a sail. **9** The diaphragm or midriff of a butchered animal. See synonyms under MARGIN. —*v.t.* **1** To lie along or form the edge of; to border. **2** To surround or border: with *with.* **3** To pass around or about, usually to avoid crossing: to *skirt* the town. —*v.i.* **4** To be or pass along the edge or border: to *skirt* along the coast. [ON *skyrt* shirt. Akin to SHIRT.]

skit (skit) *n.* **1** A short literary article, theatrical sketch, etc., usually humorous or satirical. **2** A bantering jest. [<Scand.; cf. ON *skjota* shoot. Prob. akin to SHOOT.]

skit·ter (skit′ər) *v.i.* **1** To glide or skim along, touching ground or water at intervals. **2** To fish by the method known as skittering. [Freq. of SKIT]

skit·ter·ing (skit′ər·ing) *n.* A style of fishing with a hook twitched along the water.

skit·tish (skit′ish) *adj.* **1** Easily frightened, as a horse; hence, shy; timid. **2** Capricious; uncertain; unreliable. **3** Tricky; deceitful. See synonyms under RESTIVE. [<dial. E *skit* caper (said of horses)] —**skit′tish·ly** *adv.* —**skit′tish·ness** *n.*

skit·tle (skit′l) *n.* **1** *pl.* A game of ninepins, in which a flattened ball or thick rounded disk is thrown to knock down the pins. **2** One of the pins used in this game: also **skittle–pin.** —**beer and skittles** Carefree existence, consisting of drink and play; unruffled enjoyment: usually with a negative: Life is not all *beer and skittles.* [Prob. <Dan. *skyttel* child's earthen ball]

skiv·vies (skiv′ēz) *n. pl. Slang* Men's underwear. [Origin uncertain]

skoal (skōl) *interj.* Hail: a toast or salutation in Scandinavian use. —*n.* The act of saluting or toasting with the word "skoal!" [<Scand. Cf. Dan. *skaal* bowl, toast, ON *skál* bowl.]

sku·a (skyōō′ə) *n.* A gull–like bird; a jaeger. Also **skua gull.** [<Faroese *skúgver* <ON *skúfr*]

skul·dug·ger·y (skul·dug′ər·ē) *n. U.S.* Trickery; underhandedness. [Var. of dial. *sculduddery*; origin uncertain]

skulk (skulk) *v.i.* **1** To move about furtively or slily; lie close or keep hidden; lurk. **2** To shirk; evade work or responsibility. —*n.* **1** One who skulks. **2** A troop of foxes. [<Scand. Cf. Dan. *skulke*.] —**skulk′er** *n.*

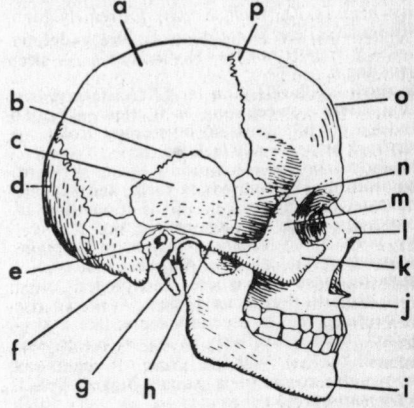

HUMAN SKULL

a.	Parietal bone.	*i.*	Inferior maxillary.
b.	Squamosal suture.	*j.*	Superior maxillary.
c.	Temporal bone.	*k.*	Malar bone.
d.	Occipital bone.	*l.*	Nasal bone.
e.	Opening of ear.	*m.*	Zygomatic bone.
f.	Mastoid process.	*n.*	Sphenoid bone.
g.	Styloid process.	*o.*	Frontal bone.
h.	Zygomatic arch.	*p.*	Coronal suture.

skull (skul) *n.* **1** The bony framework of the head of a vertebrate animal; the cranium. **2** The head considered as the seat of the brain; the mind. ◆ Homophone: *scull.* [<Scand. Cf. dial. Norw. *skul* shell.]

skull and crossbones A representation of the human skull over two crossed thigh bones: used as a symbol of death, as a warning label on poisons, etc., and as an emblem of piracy.

skull·cap (skul′kap′) *n.* **1** The sinciput. **2** Any plant of the genus *Scutellaria*, especially *S. galericulata*, of wet shady places, with large blue flowers.

skull cap **1** A cap closely fitting the skull. **2** A light cap without brim or peak.

skunk (skungk) *n.* **1** A nocturnal, burrowing

carnivore of North America (family *Mustelidae*), usually black with a white stripe running from the nape of the neck to a large, bushy tail: under the tail are perineal glands that secrete a liquid of very offensive odor ejected at will. The common striped skunk (*Mephitis mephitis*) of the United States is about the size of a cat, and there are spotted varieties (genus *Spilogale*). 2 *Colloq.* A low, contemptible person. — *v.t. Slang* To defeat, as in a contest, so thoroughly as to keep from scoring. [<Algonquian *seganku*]

SKUNK
(Up to 16 inches in length; tail: 7 inches)

skunk cabbage 1 A stemless perennial herb (*Symplocarpus foetidus*) of the United States, producing in the early spring a horn-shaped, brownish-purple spathe which encloses the oval spadix and emits a strong odor, especially when crushed or bruised: also called *swamp cabbage.* **2** A somewhat similar plant (*Lysichitum americanum*) of western North America. Also **skunk′weed′** (-wēd′).

sky (skī) *n. pl.* **skies 1** The blue vault, or a part of it, that seems to bend over the earth; the firmament. **2** The upper atmosphere; especially, the region of the clouds. **3** The celestial regions or powers; heaven. **4** Climate; weather. **5** *Obs.* A cloud. — *v.t.* **skied, sky·ing** *Colloq.* In games, to bat or throw (a ball) high into the air. [<ON *skȳ* cloud]

sky·cap (skī′kap′) *n.* A porter employed at an airport.

sky·div·ing (skī′dī′ving) *n.* The sport of jumping from an airplane and performing various maneuvers and assuming various positions before opening the parachute.

Skye (skī), **Isle of** Largest of the Inner Hebrides Islands; 670 square miles.

sky-high (skī′hī′) *adj. & adv.* Extremely high.

sky·jack (skī′jak′) *v.t. Colloq.* To hijack (def. 3). [<SKY + (HI)JACK] — **sky′jack′er** *n.* — **sky′jack′ing** *n.*

sky·lark (skī′lärk′) *n.* A lark (*Alauda arvensis*) that utters a sweet song as it flies. — *v.i.* To indulge in hilarious or boisterous frolic. — **sky′lark′er** *n.* — **sky′lark′ing** *n.*

sky·light (skī′līt′) *n.* A window facing skyward.

sky line 1 The line where earth and sky appear to meet; horizon. **2** The outline of buildings, trees, etc., against the sky.

sky pilot *Slang* A clergyman; also, a chaplain.

sky·rock·et (skī′rok′it) *n.* A rocket that is shot high into the air, where it explodes, often with brilliant pyrotechnic effect. — *v.i.* To rise or cause to rise or ascend steeply, like a skyrocket: used figuratively of wages, prices, etc.

sky·sail (skī′səl, -sāl′) *n. Naut.* A light sail above the royal in a square-rigged vessel.

sky·scrap·er (skī′skrā′pər) *n.* A very high building.

sky·ward (skī′wərd) *adv.* Toward the sky: also **sky′wards.** — *adj.* Moving or directed toward the sky.

sky·writ·ing (skī′rī′ting) *n.* The forming of words in the air by an aviator, by releasing a jet of vapor from the tail of an airplane. — **sky′writ′er** *n.*

slab (slab) *n.* **1** The outside cut made from a log in sawing it into boards, planks, etc., often bearing the bark on one side. **2** A flat plate, piece, mass, or slice, as of metal, stone, chocolate, or the like. **3** *U.S. Slang* In baseball, the pitcher's plate. — *v.t.* **slabbed, slab·bing 1** To saw slabs from, as a log; to square by removing the slabs. **2** To cover with, or form of or into slabs. [ME; origin uncertain]

slack (slak) *adj.* **1** Hanging or extended loosely. **2** Loose or careless in performance; remiss; tardy; slovenly; slow; also, weak; loose: a *slack* mouth. **3** Lacking activity; not brisk or pressing: a *slack* season. **4** Listless; limp: a *slack* grip. **5** Flowing sluggishly, as water between the ebb and flow of the tide; also, blowing slowly, as a wind. **6** Incomplete; underdone; unfinished. See synonyms under SLOW. — *v.t.* **1** To slacken. **2** To slake, as lime. — *v.i.* **3** To be or become slack. — *n.* **1** The part of anything, as a rope, that is slack or loose; also, a slack condition; looseness. **2** A period of inactivity; a slack season. **3** An

extent of water where there is no current. **4** *pl.* Loose-fitting trousers worn by both men and women as part of a casual sports costume; also, cotton or wool trousers in a military uniform. — *adv.* In a slack manner; slackly. [OE *slæc*] — **slack′ly** *adv.* — **slack′ness** *n.*

slack·en (slak′ən) *v.i.* **1** To become slack, as business; diminish; retard. **2** To become less tense or tight; loosen. **3** To become slow or less intense. — *v.t.* **4** To be or become negligent of or remiss in; to avoid, as duty, especially a military duty; shirk. **5** To make slack.

slack·er (slak′ər) *n.* One who shirks his duties or avoids military service in wartime; shirker.

slag (slag) *n.* **1** *Metall.* **a** The fused residue separated in the reduction of ores; metallic dross. **b** A basic iron silicate that floats on the surface of molten iron. **2** Volcanic scoria. — *v.t. & v.i.* **slagged, slag·ging** To form into slag. [<MLG *slagge*] — **slag′gy** *adj.*

slag wool Mineral wool.

slake (slāk) *v.* **slaked, slak·ing** *v.t.* **1** To render inoperative or harmless, especially by satisfying, as an appetite. **2** To lessen the force of in any way; quench; appease; assuage: to *slake* thirst or flames. **3** To mix with water or moist air, so that a chemical combination shall ensue. **4** To disintegrate and hydrate, as lime. **5** To make loose, slow, or less tense. — *v.i.* **6** To become disintegrated and hydrated: said of lime. **7** To slacken; become loose, slow, or less tense. **8** To ease up on one's efforts; slow down. — *n.* The act or period of slackening; an abatement. [OE *slacian* retard < *slæc* SLACK[1]]

sla·lom (slä′ləm, slä′-) *n.* In skiing, a race over a downhill, serpentine course laid out between posts and marked with flags, victory going to the skier who makes the best speed with the best grace and form. — *v.i.* To ski in or as in a slalom. [<Norw.]

slam (slam) *v.* **slammed, slam·ming** *v.t.* **1** To shut with violence and a loud noise; pull or push to loudly: to *slam* a door. **2** To put, dash, throw, or bring with violence and a loud noise; bang: to *slam* a book down. **3** *Slang* To strike with the fist. **4** *Colloq.* To take to task; criticize severely. — *v.i.* **5** To be shut, enter a place, etc., with force and noise. — *n.* **1** A closing or striking with a bang; the act or noise of slamming. **2** *Colloq.* Severe criticism. **3** A card game of the 16th century, resembling ruff. **4** In bridge, the winning of more than eleven tricks: **grand slam** is the winning of all 13 tricks; **little slam** is the winning of 12 tricks. [<Scand. Cf. dial. Norw. *slamra* slam.]

slam-bang (slam′bang′) *adv.* Violently; noisily; also, recklessly. — *v.i.* To move with noise and violence.

slan·der (slan′dər) *n.* A false tale or report, or such tales or reports collectively, uttered with malice and designed or tending to injure the reputation of another; calumny; also, the utterance of such tales or reports; defamation. See synonyms under SCANDAL. — *v.t.* To injure by maliciously uttering a false report; defame; calumniate. — *v.i.* To utter slander. See synonyms under ABUSE, ASPERSE, REVILE. [<AF *esclaundre*, OF *esclandre*, ult. <L *scandalum*. Doublet of SCANDAL.] — **slan′der·er** *n.*

slan·der·ous (slan′dər·əs) *adj.* **1** Uttering slander; guilty of slander. **2** Containing slander; calumnious. — **slan′der·ous·ly** *adv.* — **slan′der·ous·ness** *n.*

slang (slang) *n.* **1** A type of popular language comprised of words and phrases of a vigorous, colorful, or facetious nature, which are invented as needed or derive from the unconventional use of the standard vocabulary. The vocabulary of slang, although usually ephemeral, may achieve wide colloquial currency, and, in the evolution of language, many words originally slang have been adopted by good writers and speakers, and ultimately taken their place as accepted English. **2** The special vocabulary of a certain class, group, or profession: college *slang.* **3** Originally, the argot or jargon of thieves and vagrants. — *v.t.* To abuse or address with slang; also, to scold. — *v.i.* To use slang. [Origin uncertain]
Synonyms: argot, cant, jargon, lingo. The language of the underworld is *argot*, stressing its secrecy; *cant* often signifies the vocabulary of a special occupational group; *jargon* empha-

sizes unintelligibility and cacophonous sound. *Cant*, originally the beggar's whine, then the preacher's drone, acquired, in later usage, the more common meaning of sanctimonious moralizing. *Jargon* has as its commonest sense barbarous-sounding gabble. *Lingo* commonly designates foreign-sounding speech, or a language with which we are unfamiliar.

slant (slant) *v.t.* **1** To give an oblique or sloping direction to; turn from a direct line or level; incline; lean. **2** To write or edit (news or other literary matter) so as to express a special attitude, bias, or opinion. — *v.i.* **3** To have or take an oblique or sloping direction. **4** To have a certain bias or attitude. — *adj.* Lying at an angle; oblique; sloping — *n.* **1** A slanting direction, course, or plane; inclination from a direct line or level; slope; also, a mental or moral bent, opinion, attitude, etc. **2** An oblique reflection; a sarcastic remark. See synonyms under TIP[1]. [<earlier *slent* <Scand. Cf. Norw. *slenta* slope.] — **slant′ing** *adj.* — **slant′ing·ly** *adv.* — **slant′ing·ness** *n.*

slap (slap) *n.* A blow delivered with the open hand or with something flat; also, an insult; slur. — *v.* **slapped, slap·ping** *v.t.* **1** To hit or strike with the open hand or with something flat; also, to rebuff; insult. **2** To put or place violently or carelessly. — *v.i.* **3** To strike or beat as if with slaps: The waves *slapped* against the dock. — *adv.* **1** Suddenly and forcibly; abruptly. **2** *Colloq.* Directly; straight: *slap* into his face. [<LG *slapp*] — **slap′per** *n.*

slap-dash (slap′dash′) *adj.* Done or acting in a dashing or reckless way; impetuous; careless. — *n.* **1** Offhand or careless work, or thoughtless conduct. **2** Rough casting, or rough plastering. — *adv.* In a dashing or heedless manner.

slap-hap·py (slap′hap′ē) *adj. Slang* Giddy and weak-minded because of concussion of the brain; punch-drunk.

slap·jack (slap′jak) *n.* **1** A griddlecake; flapjack. **2** A children's game of cards.

slap·stick (slap′stik′) *n.* **1** A flexible, double paddle formerly used in farces and pantomimes to make a loud report when an actor was struck with it. **2** The use of this apparatus, or the type of rough comedy in which it is used. — *adj.* Using or suggestive of the slapstick: *slapstick* comedy.

slash (slash) *v.t.* **1** To cut by striking violently and without attempt at accuracy; cut with long sweeping strokes; strike violently with or as with an edged instrument; slit; gash. **2** To strike with long sweeping blows of a whip; lash; scourge. **3** To make long gashes, cuts, or slits in; specifically, to slit, as a garment, so as to expose ornamental material or lining in or under the slits. **4** To criticize severely; censure harshly. **5** To cut down wastefully, as timber in a forest. **6** To reduce sharply, as salaries. — *v.i.* **7** To make a long sweeping stroke or several such strokes with or as with something sharp; cut. — *n.* **1** The act or result of slashing; a sweeping, random cut with a cutting weapon or whip; a slit or gash; specifically, an ornamental slit or cut in a garment showing some other material in or through the slit. **2** An opening or gap made in a forest. **3** The loose tops and branches of trees left in a forest after logging or a high wind. **4** A swampy thicket; low-lying boggy land: usually in the plural. **5** *Printing* A virgula. [? <OF *esclachier* break] — **slash′er** *n.*

slat (slat) *n.* **1** One of a number of thin, flat, narrow strips of wood used to support the springs or mattress of a bed. **2** Any thin, narrow strip of wood or metal; a lath. **3** *Aeron.* A movable auxiliary airfoil attached to the leading edge of an airplane wing. — *v.t.* **slat·ted, slat·ting** To provide or make with slats. [<OF *esclat* splinter, chip]

slate (slāt) *n.* **1** Any rock that splits readily into thin and even laminae; specifically, an argillaceous, fine-grained rock that so splits; also, an artificial material made in imitation of it. **2** A piece, slab, or plate of slate used for roofing, writing upon, etc. **3** A record of one's past performance or behavior: a clean *slate.* **4** A list of political candidates made up before their nomination or election; any prearranged list. **5** A dull bluish-gray color resembling that of slate: also **slate gray.** — *adj.* **1** Made of slate: a

slate roof. **2** Slate–colored. —*v.t.* **slat·ed,
slat·ing 1** To roof with slate. **2** To put on a political slate or a list of any sort; hence, to register or designate as if by writing on a slate: He is *slated* for promotion. **3** To remove hair from (hides) with a slater. [<OF *esclate*, fem. of *esclat* a chip, splinter] — **slat′y** *adj.*

slath·er (slath′ər) *Colloq.* or *Dial. v.t.* To daub thickly; spend or use profusely; lavish. —*n.* **1** A thick layer or spread. **2** *pl.* A lot; very much: *slathers* of fun. [Var. of dial. E *slither* slip]

slat·ing (slā′ting) *n.* **1** The act or occupation of laying slates. **2** Slates or slate collectively. **3** A liquid for giving a slatelike surface to blackboards, etc.

slat·tern (slat′ərn) *n.* An untidy or slovenly woman. —*adj.* Untidy; slovenly. [<dial. E *slatter* slop, spill] — **slat′tern·li·ness** *n.* — **slat′tern·ly** *adj. & adv.*

slaugh·ter (slô′tər) *n.* **1** The act of killing; specifically, the butchering of cattle and other animals for market. **2** Wanton or savage killing, especially of human beings; massacre; carnage. **3** *Slang* A sweeping or ruinous reduction in prices. See synonyms under MASSACRE. —*v.t.* **1** To kill for the market; butcher. **2** To kill wantonly or savagely, especially in large numbers. **3** *Slang* To reduce greatly the price of; sell at a low figure. See synonyms under KILL[1]. [<ON *slátr* butcher's meat. Akin to SLAY.] — **slaugh′ter·er** *n.* — **slaugh′ter·ous** *adj.* — **slaugh′ter·ous·ly** *adv.*

slaugh·ter·house (slô′tər·hous′) *n.* A place where animals are butchered; a scene of carnage.

slave (slāv) *n.* **1** One whose person is held as property; a person in slavery; a bondsman; serf. **2** *Law* A person over whose life, liberty, and property someone has absolute control. **3** A person in mental or moral subjection to a habit, vice, or influence: a *slave* of tobacco. **4** One who labors like a drudge. **5** A person of slavish disposition; an abject creature. —*v.* **slaved, slav·ing** *v.i.* To work like a slave; toil; drudge. —*v.t.* *Rare* To enslave. [<F *esclave* <Med. L *slavus, sclavus,* orig. a Slav; because many Slavs were conquered and enslaved]

Slave Coast The coastal region of western Africa extending westward from the mouths of the Niger along the Bight of Benin to Ghana: named for its former trade in slaves.

slave–driv·er (slāv′drī′vər) *n.* **1** A person hired for or charged with the overseeing of slaves at work. **2** Any severe or exacting employer.

slave·hold·er (slāv′hōl′dər) *n.* An owner of slaves. — **slave′hold′ing** *adj. & n.*

slav·er[1] (slav′ər) *v.t.* To dribble saliva over. —*v.i.* To dribble saliva; drool. —*n.* Saliva issuing or dribbling from the mouth. [Prob. <ON *slafra*] — **slav′er·er** *n.*

slav·er[2] (slā′vər) *n.* **1** A person or a vessel engaged in the slave trade. **2** One who procures white slaves.

slav·er·y (slā′vər·ē, slāv′rē) *n.* **1** Involuntary servitude; specifically, the legalized social institution in which humans are held as property or chattels; complete subjection of one person to another. **2** Mental, moral, or spiritual bondage. **3** Slavish toil; drudgery. See synonyms under BONDAGE.

slav·ey (slā′vē, slav′ē) *n. Brit.* A household servant; drudge; usually, a maidservant.

slav·ish (slā′vish) *adj.* **1** Pertaining to or befitting a slave; servile; base. **2** Extremely hard or laborious. **3** Enslaved. See synonyms under BASE[2], OBSEQUIOUS. — **slav′ish·ly** *adv.* — **slav′ish·ness** *n.*

Slavo– *combining form* Slavic; of or pertaining to the Slavs: *Slavophobe.* [<SLAV]

slaw (slô) *n.* Cabbage sliced, shredded, or chopped, and served, usually raw, as a salad. [<Du. *sla,* short for *salade* salad]

slay (slā) *v.t.* **slew, slain, slay·ing 1** To kill, especially by violence; put to death; destroy by, or as by, killing. **2** *Obs.* To smite; strike. See synonyms under KILL[1]. ◆ Homophones: *sleigh, sley.* [OE *slēan*] — **slay′er** *n.*

sleave (slēv) *v.t.* **sleaved, sleav·ing** To separate, as a mass of threads; disentangle. —*n.* Some-

thing tangled, matted, knotted, or unspun, as silk or thread. ◆ Homophone: *sleeve.* [OE *slæfan* divide]

sleave silk Raw untwisted silk; floss.

slea·zy (slē′zē, slā′–) *adj.* **·zi·er, ·zi·est 1** Lacking firmness of texture or substance. **2** Cheap; shoddy; run–down: a *sleazy* bar. [Origin uncertain] — **slea′zi·ly** *adv.* — **slea′zi·ness** *n.*

sled (sled) *n.* **1** A vehicle on runners, designed for carrying people or loads over snow and ice; a sledge. **2** A small, light frame mounted on runners, used especially by children for sliding on snow and ice. —*v.* **sled·ded, sled·ding** *v.t.* To convey on a sled. —*v.i.* To ride on or use a sled. [<MLG *sledde*]

sled·ding (sled′ing) *n.* **1** Condition of roads admitting of the use of sleds: usually with a qualifying word: fine *sledding.* **2** The act of using a sled; use of sleds in hauling, traveling, etc. **3** State or circumstances of progress, work, etc.: We have had hard *sledding.*

SLEDGES
a. Peary North Pole Expedition.
b. Byrd Antarctic Expedition.

sledge[1] (slej) *n.* A vehicle mounted on low runners for moving loads; especially, one designed to be drawn over snow and ice by dogs, horses, or reindeer, or one designed to be drawn on the ground by draft animals; also, a sled. —*v.t. & v.i.* **sledged, sledg·ing** To travel or convey on a sledge. [<MDu. *sledse*]

sledge[2] (slej) *n.* A heavy hammer wielded with one or both hands, for blacksmiths' use, or for breaking stone, coal, etc.: also **sledge′ham′mer** (–ham′ər). —*v.t.* **sledged, sledg·ing** To hammer, break, or strike with a sledge. [OE *slecg*]

sleek (slēk) *adj.* **1** Smooth and glossy; polished. **2** Smooth–spoken; flattering; unctuous; insinuating. See synonyms under SMOOTH. —*v.t.* **1** To make smooth, even, or glossy; polish. **2** To soothe; mollify; also, to make less disagreeable or offensive. Also, *U.S., slick.* [Var. of SLICK] — **sleek′ly** *adv.* — **sleek′ness** *n.* — **sleek′y** *adj.*

sleep (slēp) *n.* **1** A state or period of complete or partial unconsciousness, normal and periodic in man and the higher animals. In animals it is sometimes much prolonged, as in hibernation. **2** A period of slumber. **3** Any condition of inactivity, torpor, or rest; specifically, the rest of the grave; death. **4** Nyctitropism. See synonyms under REST[1]. — **to go to sleep 1** To fall asleep. **2** To become numb, often with a tingling sensation, from retarded circulation. —*v.* **slept, sleep·ing** *v.i.* **1** To be or fall asleep; slumber. **2** To be in a state resembling sleep; to be dormant, inactive or quiet, or to rest in death. **3** To be in a benumbed state from retarded circulation of the blood: My foot *sleeps.* **4** To spin with such velocity as to be without apparent motion, as a top. **5** To undergo nyctitropism. **6** *Bot.* To assume a different position at night, as petals. —*v.t.* **7** To rest or repose in: with a cognate object: to *sleep* the sleep of the dead. **8** To provide with sleeping quarters; lodge: The hotel can *sleep* a hundred guests. See synonyms under REST[1]. — **to sleep away** (or **off** or **out**) To pass or get rid of by or as by sleep: to *sleep off* a hang–over. — **to sleep on** To postpone a decision upon. [OE *slēp*]

sleep·er (slē′pər) *n.* **1** One who sleeps; figuratively, a dead person. **2** A railroad sleeping-car. **3** A hibernating animal. **4** In football, a member of the backfield or an end stationed far out at either side before the ball is put in motion. **5** A heavy beam resting on or in the ground, as a support for a roadway, rails,

etc.; a like support of iron or stone; also, a timber on or near the ground for the lower joists of a building. **6** A deadman. **7** *U.S. Colloq.* A play, motion picture, or book which achieves unexpected and striking success.

sleep·ing–car (slē′ping–kär′) *n.* A passenger railroad car with accommodations for sleeping.

sleeping pill *Med.* A sedative; especially, one of the barbiturates taken to relieve acute or persistent insomnia.

sleeping sickness *Pathol.* **1** The terminal stage of a form of trypanosomiasis prevalent in tropical Africa: it is caused by the presence in the cerebrospinal fluid of certain trypanosomes usually transmitted by the bite of the tsetse fly, and is marked by progressive lethargy, recurrent fever and headaches, terminating in somnolence and death. **2** Epidemic encephalitis lethargica.

sleep·walk·er (slēp′wô′kər) *n.* A somnambulist. — **sleep′walk′ing** *n.*

sleep·y (slē′pē) *adj.* **sleep·i·er, sleep·i·est 1** Inclined to sleep. **2** Drowsy; sluggish; dull; heavy. **3** Conducive to sleep. — **sleep′i·ly** *adv.* — **sleep′i·ness** *n.*

sleet (slēt) *n.* **1** A mixture of snow or hail and rain. **2** A drizzle or shower of partly frozen rain, or rain that freezes as it falls. **3** A thin coating of ice, as on rails, wires, roads, etc. —*v.i.* To pour or shed sleet. [Akin to MLG *slote* hail] — **sleet′y** *adj.*

sleeve (slēv) *n.* **1** The part of a garment that serves especially as a covering for the arm. **2** *Mech.* **a** A tube surrounding something, as a shaft, for protection or to permit motion of itself or or of the shaft. **b** A short pipe receiving the ends of two other pipes or rods; a sleeve coupling or sleeve valve. **3** *Electr.* The cylindrical contacting part of a telephone–circuit plug. —**up one's sleeve** Hidden but at hand. —*v.t.* **sleeved, sleev·ing** To furnish with a sleeve or sleeves. ◆ Homophone: *sleave.* [OE *slēfe*]

sleeve coupling *Mech.* A short tube for connecting shafts or pipes.

sleeve valve *Mech.* A valve consisting of a hollow slotted sleeve in the cylinder of an internal–combustion engine, operating with the piston to allow for intake or exhaust of gases.

sleigh (slā) *n.* A light vehicle with runners for use on snow and ice, adapted especially for pleasure use or travel, as distinguished from hauling. Compare SLED, SLEDGE[1]. —*v.i.* To ride or travel in a sleigh. ◆ Homophones: *slay, sley.* [<Du. *slee,* contraction of *slede* sledge] — **sleigh′er** *n.*

SLEIGH

sleight (slīt) *n.* **1** The quality of being skilful in manipulation; mechanical expertness; skill; dexterity. **2** A juggler's trick so deftly done that the manner of performance escapes observation; feat of legerdemain. **3** Craft; cunning. ◆ Homophone: *slight.* [<ON *slœgdh* slyness]

sleight of hand 1 Skill in performing tricks in juggling. **2** The art or practice, or an instance, of legerdemain.

slen·der (slen′dər) *adj.* **1** Having a small diameter or circumference, in proportion to the length or height; slim; thin. **2** Having little strength or vigor; feeble; frail; delicate. **3** Having slight basis or foundation; of little validity. **4** Small or inadequate; moderate; insignificant: a *slender* income or diet. **5** Meagerly or insufficiently supplied: a *slender* table. **6** Thin in sound or quality; lacking volume. **7** *Phonet.* Denoting vowels which are pronounced with a narrow opening above the tongue, as (ē); close; narrow; opposed to *broad.* See synonyms under FINE[1], LITTLE, MINUTE[2]. [ME *slendre,* prob. <OF *esclendre*] — **slen′der·ly** *adv.* — **slen′der·ness** *n.*

sleuth (slōōth) *n.* **1** *U.S. Colloq.* A detective. **2** A sleuthhound. **3** *Obs.* The track of a man or beast, as followed by the scent. —*v.t.* To follow, as a detective. —*v.i.* To play the detective. [<ON *slōdh* track, trail. Doublet of

SLOT².]

sleuth·hound (slooth′hound′) n. A bloodhound.

slew (sloo) n. U.S. Colloq. A large number, crowd, or amount; a lot: also spelled slue. [Cf. Irish sluagh a large crowd]

slew (sloo) See SLUE¹.

sley (slā) n. 1 The reed guiding the warp threads of a loom. 2 In knitting machines, a groove, slot, or bar for directing the action of a part. —v.t. To separate and arrange the threads of (yarn) in a reed for weaving. ◆ Homophones: slay, sleigh. [OE slege]

slice (slīs) n. 1 A piece; especially, a thin, broad piece cut off from a larger body. 2 One of various tools or devices, used for slicing or resembling a slice in broadness and thinness; specifically, a broad knife used for serving fish, or a broad flat knife used by printers to remove ink; also, a druggist's spatula. 3 In golf, a blow delivered crosswise from right to right, causing the ball to curve to the right. —v. **sliced, slic·ing** v.t. 1 To cut or remove from a larger piece: often with off. 2 To cut into broad, thin pieces; divide; apportion. 3 To sunder, as with a sharp knife; split. 4 To clear out with a slice bar. 5 In golf, to hit (the ball) with a slice. —v.i. 6 In golf, to slice a ball. See synonyms under CUT. [<OF esclice < esclicer <OHG slizan slit] —slic′er n.

slick (slik) adj. 1 Smooth; slippery; sleek. 2 Flattering obsequious; smooth-tongued; plausible. 3 Colloq. Dexterously done; cleverly said; specious; tricky. 4 Smart; clever: said of people. 5 Healthy; plump: said of animals. 6 Smooth; oily, as the surface of water. 7 Glazed, as paper; also, printed on glazed paper: slick magazines. 8 Slang Agreeable; excellent: a slick time. —n. 1 A smooth place on a surface of water, as from oil or the presence of fish; also, a sleek place in the fur or hair of an animal. 2 A broad chisel for paring or slicking: also slick chisel. 3 pl. U.S. Magazines printed on glazed paper: distinguished from pulps. —adv. Slang In a slick or smooth manner; deftly; quickly. —v.t. 1 To make smooth, trim, glossy, or oily. 2 Colloq. To trim up; make presentable: often with up. [ME slike <OE slician make smooth]

slick·er (slik′ər) n. 1 An implement for dressing leather, having a wooden handle. 2 U.S. A waterproof overcoat of oilskin. 3 Colloq. A cheat; clever person.

slide (slīd) v. slid, slid or slid·den, slid·ing v.i. 1 To pass along over a surface with a smooth, slipping movement: to slide on ice. 2 To slip off, as scales in shedding. 3 To move or pass imperceptibly, smoothly, deftly, or easily; pass gradually or imperceptibly: The years slide away swiftly. 4 To move, pass, or proceed by sufferance merely; also, to take care of oneself or itself; go by default or without heed: with let: to let the matter slide. 5 Music To glide from tone to tone without breaking the sound. 6 To make a moral slip; err; sin. 7 To slip; lose one's equilibrium or foothold. 8 In baseball, to throw oneself along the ground toward a base, in order to avoid being tagged by the baseman. —v.t. 9 To cause to slide, as over a surface. 10 To move, put, enter, etc., with quietness or dexterity: with in or into. —n. 1 An act of sliding. 2 The slipping of a mass of earth, snow, etc., from a higher to a lower level; an avalanche. 3 An inclined plane or channel on which persons, goods, logs, etc., slide downward to a lower level. 4 A small plate of glass on which a specimen is mounted and examined through a microscope. 5 A small plate of transparent material bearing a single image for projection on a screen. 6 Phot. In a camera, that part of a plate holder which covers and uncovers the negative. 7 Music a A series of short musical notes leading smoothly to a principal note: a type of ornamentation. b A portamento. c In a trumpet or trombone, a U-shaped portion of the tubing which is pushed in and out to vary the pitch. 8 Mech. a A sliding part. b A groove, rail, etc., on which something slides. [OE slidan]

slide·knot (slīd′not′) n. A slipknot, particularly one made of two half-hitches on a fishing line.

slid·er (slī′dər) n. 1 One who or that which slides. 2 In baseball, a fast pitch that curves slightly at or near the strike zone.

slide rule A device consisting of a rigid ruler with a central sliding piece, both ruler and slide being graduated in a similar logarithmic scale to permit of rapid calculations.

slide valve Mech. 1 A sliding piece in the cylinder of a steam engine, regulated to move back and forth over the ports and connect them alternately with the boiler and the exhaust passage, thus imparting reciprocating motion to the piston. 2 A valve that slides on its seat.

SLIDE VALVE
Arrows show reciprocal action.

sliding scale 1 A schedule affecting imports, prices, or wages, varying under conditions of consumption, demand, or market price of some article. 2 Any graduated scale, as in a clinometer or slide rule, designed to move against a fixed scale in order to facilitate rapid and accurate measurements and computations.

slight (slīt) adj. 1 Of small importance; small in quantity, intensity, or degree; inconsiderable. 2 Slender; frail; delicate; flimsy. 3 Of weak intellect or character. 4 Scot. Smooth; slippery; unscrupulous. See synonyms under FINE¹, FRAGILE, INSIGNIFICANT, LITTLE, SMALL. —v.t. 1 To manifest intentional neglect of or disregard for; snub; omit due courtesy toward or respect for: to slight a friend. 2 To omit due care in the doing or performance of; do imperfectly or thoughtlessly; shirk. 3 To treat as trivial or insignificant. —n. An act or omission involving failure in courtesy or respect toward another; any contemptuous or neglectful action. ◆ Homophone: sleight. [ME. Akin to ON slettr smooth.] —slight′ness n.

Synonyms (noun): disregard, neglect, scorn. *Disregard* is chiefly a matter of intellectual estimate; *slight* is a matter of outward action; *neglect* may be of thought or act. *Disregard* of a thing is setting it aside as not worthy of regard. *Neglect* of a person or thing may be the result of ignorance, thoughtlessness, or preoccupation with other things; a *slight* is an intentional omission of kindness, courtesy, or attention. *Scorn* expresses mingled contempt and bitterness. See NEGLECT. *Antonyms*: esteem, honor, regard, respect, reverence.

slight·ing (slī′ting) adj. Conveying, containing, or characterized by a slight: a slighting remark. —**slight′ing·ly** adv.

slim (slim) adj. slim·mer, slim·mest 1 Small in thickness in proportion to height or length, as a human figure or a tree. 2 Having little logical strength; weak. 3 Constructed unsubstantially; flimsy. 4 Lacking robustness; frail. 5 Insufficient; narrow; meager: a slim attendance; a slim chance. 6 Brit. Dial. Sly; crafty; worthless; bad. —v.t. & v.i. slimmed, **slim·ming** To make or become thin or thinner. [<Du. slim bad] —**slim′ly** adv. —slim′. ness n.

slime (slīm) n. 1 Any soft, sticky or dirty thing; hence, any offensive quality or thing. 2 Soft, moist, adhesive mud or earth; muck. 3 A mucous exudation from the bodies of certain animals, as fishes and snails, and certain plants. 4 Bitumen; asphalt. 5 Usually pl. A mudlike substance formed of ore in an almost impalpable powder, mixed with water. —v. **slimed, slim·ing** v.t. 1 To smear or cover with or as with slime. 2 To remove slime. 2 To remove slime from, as fishes. —v.i. 3 To become covered with or as with slime. [OE slim]

slime mold A fungus belonging to the class *Myxomycetes*. Also **slime fungus.**

sling¹ (sling) n. 1 A strap or pocket with a string attached to each end, for hurling a stone or other missile by centrifugal force. 2 One of various ropes, straps, chains, or the like, for suspending or hoisting something, for holding up an injured limb, lifting and supporting an animal, in case of lameness or other need, carrying a rifle, etc. 3 Naut. A rope or chain by which a lower yard or a gaff is suspended; also, in the plural, the middle portion of a yard. 4 The act of slinging; a sudden throw; cast; fling. [< v.] —v. **slung, sling·ing** v.t. 1 To fling from or as from a sling; hurl. 2 To place or hang up in or as in a sling; move or hoist, as by a rope or tackle. —v.i. 3 To

move at an easy gait. See synonyms under SEND¹. [<ON slyngva hurl] —**sling′er** n.

sling² (sling) n. U.S. A drink of brandy, whisky, or gin, with sugar and nutmeg, lemon juice, and hot or cold water. —v.i. U.S. Colloq. To drink slings; take an alcoholic drink. [Cf. G schlingen swallow]

sling·shot (sling′shot′) n. A weapon or toy consisting of a forked stick with an elastic strap attached to the prongs for catapulting small missiles.

slink (slingk) v. slunk (Obs. slank), slunk, slink·ing v.i. To creep or steal along furtively or stealthily, as in fear. —v.t. To give birth to prematurely; miscarry: said of animals, especially cows. —adj. Produced prematurely, as a calf; too immature to be eaten. —n. An animal, especially a calf, prematurely born; also, its flesh, too immature for proper food. [OE slincan creep] —**slink′ing·ly** adv.

slink·y (slingk′ē) adj. slink·i·er, slink·i·est 1 Sneaking; stealthy. 2 Slang Sinuous or feline in movement or form.

slip¹ (slip) v. slipped or slipt, slip·ping v.t. 1 To cause to move smoothly and easily; cause to glide or slide. 2 To put on or off easily, as a ring or a loose garment. 3 To convey slily or secretly. 4 To free oneself or itself from, as a fetter or bridle. 5 To let loose; unleash, as hounds. 6 To release from its fastening and let run out, as a cable. 7 To give birth to prematurely; slink; cast: said of animals. 8 To dislocate, as a bone. 9 To escape or pass unobserved: It slipped my mind. 10 To overlook; omit negligently: to slip an opportunity. —v.i. 11 To slip so as to cause harm or inconvenience; lose one's footing; become misplaced by failing to hold. 12 To fall into an error or fault; err. 13 To escape, as a ship. 14 To move smoothly and easily; slide; glide. 15 To get free of restraint; be unleashed. 16 To go or come stealthily or unnoticed: often with off, away, or from. — to let slip To say without intending to. —n. 1 An act of slipping; a sudden slide. 2 A lapse or error in speech, writing, or conduct; a slight mistake. 3 U.S. A narrow space between two wharves. 4 An artificial pier sloping down to the water, serving as a landing place. 5 An inclined plane leading down to the water, on which vessels are repaired or constructed. 6 A woman's undergarment. 7 A pillowcase. 8 A leash containing a device which permits quick release of the dog. 9 In cricket, a position on the off side a few yards behind the wicket; also, the player who stands at this position. 10 Naut. a The difference between the speed of a screw propeller and that of the ship. b The velocity of the back current generated by a propeller. 11 Physics The difference between the advance made by a propeller moving in a fluid and the advance it would make if moving in a solid substance. 12 Mech. a The relative motion of two surfaces which are meant to be immovable with respect to each other, as a belt on a pulley. b Allowance made for slipping or play, as between connected members of a mechanism; slippage. 13 Geol. A small dislocation of rock strata. — to give (someone) the slip To elude (someone). [<MLG slippen]

slip² (slip) n. 1 A cutting from a plant for planting or grafting; a cion. 2 A small, slender person, especially a youthful one. 3 A small piece of something, as of paper or cloth, rather long relative to its width; a strip. 4 A small piece of paper for jotting down memoranda, a record, etc. 5 U.S. A narrow pew in a church. —v.t. slipped, slip·ping To cut off for planting; make a slip or slips of. [<MDu. slippe < slippen cut]

slip·cov·er (slip′kuv′ər) n. 1 A fitted cloth cover for a chair, couch, sofa, or other piece of furniture, that can be readily removed. 2 A paper or cloth jacket for a book.

slip·knot (slip′not′) n. 1 A knot so formed, by having part of the material drawn through in a bow, as to be readily untied: also called bowknot. 2 A running knot.

slip·on (slip′on′, -ôn′) n. A garment which can be easily donned or taken off. —adj. Denoting such a garment: a slip-on blouse.

slip·o·ver (slip′ō′vər) adj. Designating a garment easily donned by drawing over the head: a slip-over shirt. —n. A garment of this type.

slip·page (slip′ij) n. 1 The amount by which or distance through which anything slips, as a screw propeller. **2** The difference between actual and calculated speed, due to slipping. **3** The act of slipping; slip.

slip·per (slip′ər) *n.* **1** A low, light shoe, chiefly for indoor wear, into or out of which the foot is easily slipped. **2** One who or that which slips. [<SLIP¹ + -ER²]

slip·per·y (slip′ər·ē) *adj.* **·per·i·er**, **·per·i·est** **1** Having a surface so smooth that bodies slip or slide easily on it. **2** That evades one's grasp; tricky; elusive. **3** Unreliable; undependable; tricky. **4** *Obs.* Wanton. [<SLIPPER² + -Y³] — **slip′per·i·ly** *adv.* — **slip′per·i·ness** *n.*

slippery elm **1** A tree (*Ulmus fulva*) of eastern North America. **2** Its hard wood. **3** Its mucilaginous inner bark, used in medicine as a nutritious demulcent.

slip-ring (slip′ring′) *n. Electr.* One of two or more metal rings of an electric machine serving, through contact with stationary brushes, to deliver or transmit a current.

slip-sheet (slip′shēt′) *Printing n.* A blank piece of paper interleaved between newly printed press sheets to prevent offset. — *v.t.* To insert slip-sheets in.

slip·shod (slip′shod′) *adj.* Wearing shoes or slippers down at the heels; hence, slovenly. [<SLIP¹ + SHOE]

slip·slop (slip′slop′) *n. Colloq.* **1** Sloppy victuals; any weak drink; slop. **2** A blunder, as in speaking.

slip·stream (slip′strēm′) *n. Aeron.* The stream of air driven backwards by the propeller of an aircraft: also called *race*.

slip-up (slip′up′) *n. Colloq.* A mistake; error.

slip·way (slip′wā′) *n.* A slip (def. 5).

slit (slit) *n.* A cut that is relatively straight and long; also, a long, narrow opening. [<*v.*] — *v.t.* **slit, slit·ting** **1** To make a long incision in; slash. **2** To cut lengthwise into strips. See synonyms under REND. [ME *slitten* cut] — **slit′ter** *n.*

slith·er (slith′ər) *v.i.* **1** To slide; slip, as on a loose surface. **2** To glide, as a snake. — *v.t.* **3** To cause to slither. [Var. of dial. E *slidder* <OE *slidrian*, freq. of *slidan* slide] — **slith′er·y** *adj.*

slit trench A narrow, shallow trench, similar to a foxhole.

sliv·er (sliv′ər) *n.* **1** A slender piece, as of wood, cut or torn off lengthwise; a splinter. **2** Corded textile fibers drawn into a fleecy strand. **3** A piece cut longitudinally from the side of a fish: used as bait; also, a filet. — *v.t.* & *v.i.* To cut or split into long thin pieces; splinter. [<dial. E *slive* cleave] — **sliv′er·er** *n.*

Sliv·no (slēv′nō) A city in east central Bulgaria. Also **Sliv·en** (slē′vən).

sli·vo·vitz (slē′vô·vēts) *n.* A white, dry plum brandy drunk especially in central European countries. [<Serbo-Croatian <*sliva* a plum]

Sloan (slōn), **John,** 1871–1951, U.S. painter.

slob (slob) *n.* **1** Mud; mire. **2** Slush; mushy snow. **3** *Slang* A stupid, careless, or unclean person. [<Irish *slab*, prob. <SLAB²]

slob·ber (slob′ər) *v.t.* **1** To wet and foul with liquids oozing from the mouth. **2** To shed or spill, as liquid food, in eating. — *v.i.* **3** To drivel; slaver. **4** To talk or act gushingly. — *n.* **1** Liquid spilled as from the mouth; slaver. **2** Gushing, sentimental talk. [Var. of SLABBER] — **slob′ber·er** *n.* — **slob′ber·y** *adj.*

sloe (slō) *n.* **1** A small, plumlike, astringent fruit. **2** The shrub (*Prunus spinosa*) that bears it; the blackthorn. **3** The blackhaw. **4** The wild yellow plum (*Prunus americana*); also, the Allegheny plum (*P. alleghaniensis*). ◆ Homophone: *slow*. [OE *slā*]

sloe-eyed (slō′īd′) *adj.* Having eyes dark as sloes.

sloe gin A cordial with a gin base, flavored with sloes.

slog (slog) *v.t. & v.i.* **slogged, slog·ging** **1** To slug, as a pugilist. **2** To plod (one's way), as through deep mud. — *n.* A heavy blow. [Var. of SLUG³] — **slog′ger** *n.*

slo·gan (slō′gən) *n.* **1** A battle or rallying cry: originally of the Highland clans. **2** A catchword or motto adopted by a manufacturer, political party, or the like. [<Scottish Gaelic *sluagh* army + *gairm* yell]

sloop (slōōp) *n. Naut.* A single-masted, fore-and-aft rigged sailing vessel with or without a bowsprit and carrying at least one jib: now used principally as a racing vessel. [<Du. *sloep*]

SLOOP

sloop of war In old navies, a vessel rigged either as ship, brig, or schooner, and mounting between 18 and 32 guns; later, any war vessel larger than a gunboat and carrying guns on one deck only.

slop (slop) *v.* **slopped, slop·ping** *v.i.* **1** To splash or spill. **2** To walk or move through slush. — *v.t.* **3** To cause (a liquid) to spill or splash. **4** *U.S.* To feed (a domestic animal) with slops. — **to slop over** **1** To overflow and splash. **2** To do or say more than is necessary, because of excess zeal, sentimentality, etc. — *n.* **1** Slush; watery mud. **2** A dash or puddle of liquid that has been slopped. **3** An unappetizing liquid or watery food. **4** Refuse liquid. **5** *pl.* Waste food or swill, as from a kitchen, used to feed cattle, pigs, etc. **6** *pl.* Distiller's mash which has been deprived of its alcohol. [ME *sloppe*]

slope (slōp) *v.* **sloped, slop·ing** *v.i.* **1** To be inclined from the level or the vertical; slant. **2** To move on an inclined path; go obliquely. **3** *Colloq.* To leave suddenly; run off. — *v.t.* **4** To cause to slope. See synonyms under TIP¹. [<*adj.*] — *n.* **1** Any slanting surface or line; a declivity or acclivity; an inclined plane: the Atlantic *slope* of North America. **2** The degree of inclination of a line or surface from the plane of the horizon. **3** *Math.* **a** The tangent of the positive angle of less than 180° made between the *x*-axis and a tangent to a curve traced in the Cartesian coordinate system; also, the derivative of such a curve at a given point. **b** The tangent of the positive angle of less than 180° made between the *x*-axis and a straight line traced in the Cartesian coordinate system. — *adj.* Slanting; oblique. [Aphetic var. of *aslope*, OE *aslopen*, ppr. of *a-slupan* slip away] — **slop′er** *n.* — **slop′ing** *adj.* — **slop′ing·ly** *adv.* — **slop′ing·ness** *n.*

slop·py (slop′ē) *adj.* **·pi·er, ·pi·est** **1** Slushy; splashy; wet. **2** Watery or pulpy; *sloppy* pudding. **3** Splashed with liquid or slops. **4** *Colloq.* Messy; slovenly; extremely untidy. **5** *Colloq.* Slipshod; careless. **6** *Colloq.* Maudlin; overly sentimental. — **slop′pi·ly** *adv.* — **slop′pi·ness** *n.*

slot¹ (slot) *n.* **1** A long narrow groove or opening; slit. **2** A comparatively long and narrow depression or cavity, particularly one that is rectangular, cut to receive some corresponding part in a mechanism. **3** The opening to receive the coin in a slot machine. **4** *Colloq.* An opening or position, as a job category or place in a sequence. **5** *Aeron.* An opening in an airplane wing to improve the conditions of airflow at high angles of flight. — *v.t.* **slot·ted, slot·ting** **1** To adjust in a slot. **2** To cut a slot in; groove. [<OF *esclot* the hollow between the breasts]

slot² (slot) *n.* The trail of an animal, especially a deer. [<AF *esclot* <ON *slōdh*. Doublet of SLEUTH.]

sloth (slôth, slōth, slōth) *n.* **1** Disinclination to exertion; habitual indolence; laziness. **2** A slow-moving, tree-dwelling edentate mammal (family *Bradypodidae*) of tropical America. The **three-toed sloth** (genus *Bradypus*) has three toes on each foot; the **two-toed sloth** (genus *Choloepus*) has two on the front and

THREE-TOED SLOTH
(Head and body about 21 inches long)

three on the hind feet. **3** A related fossil edentate (family *Megatheriidae*). [<SLOW + -TH¹]

sloth bear A black bear of India and Ceylon (genus *Melursus*), feeding mainly on honey and fruit.

sloth·ful (slôth′fəl, slōth′-, slōth′-) *adj.* Sluggish; lazy; indolent. See synonyms under IDLE. — **sloth′ful·ly** *adv.* — **sloth′ful·ness** *n.*

slot machine A vending machine or gambling machine having a slot in which a coin is dropped to cause operation.

slouch (slouch) *v.i.* **1** To have a downcast or drooping gait, look, or posture. **2** To hang or droop in a careless manner, as a hat. — *n.* **1** A hanging down awkwardly or carelessly; movement or appearance caused by depression or drooping. **2** An awkward or incompetent person. [Origin uncertain] — **slouch′y** *adj.* — **slouch′i·ly** *adv.* — **slouch′i·ness** *n.*

slough¹ (slou *for defs. 1 and 4;* slōō *for defs. 2 and 3*) *n.* **1** A place of deep mud or mire; bog. **2** A depression in a prairie, often dry but sometimes deeply miry, forming part of the natural drainage system. **3** A stagnant swamp, backwater, bayou, inlet, or pond in which water backs up: also spelled *slew, slue*. **4** A state of moral depravity or of despair. [OE *slōh*] — **slough′y** *adj.*

slough² (sluf) *n.* **1** Dead tissue separated and thrown off from the living parts, as in gangrene; also, a scab. **2** The skin of a serpent that has been or is about to be shed; cast. — *v.t.* **1** To cast off, as dead from living tissue; shed. **2** To discard; shed, as a habit or a growth; get rid of as useless or needless. — *v.i.* **3** To be cast off. **4** To cast off a slough or tissue; form a scab. [ME *slouh*] — **slough·y** *adj.*

slov·en (sluv′ən) *n.* One who is careless of dress or of cleanliness; one habitually untidy. [Cf. Flemish *sloef* dirty] — **slov′en·li·ness** *n.* — **slov′en·ly** *adj. & adv.*

slow (slō) *adj.* **1** Having relatively small velocity; not quick in motion, performance, or occurrence; not advancing or growing rapidly. **2** Behind the standard time: said of a timepiece. **3** Taking sufficient time; not precipitate or hasty: *slow* to anger. **4** Dull or tardy in comprehending; mentally sluggish: a *slow* student. **5** Lacking promptness, spirit, or liveliness; also, colloquially, dull or tedious in character. **6** Denoting a condition of a racetrack that retards the horses' speed, but in less degree than a muddy or heavy track: a *slow* track. — *v.t.* **1** To make slow or slower; cause to go at a slower pace; slacken in speed: often with *up* or *down.* **2** To retard; delay. — *v.i.* **3** To go or become slow or slower: often with *up* or *down.* — *adv.* In a slow or cautious manner or speed. ◆ Homophone: *sloe.* [OE *slāw*] — **slow′ly** *adv.* — **slow′ness** *n.*

Synonyms (*adj.*): deliberate, dilatory, drowsy, dull, gradual, inactive, inert, lingering, moderate, slack, sluggish, tardy. *Tardy* is applied to that which is behind the proper or desired time, especially in doing work or arriving at a place; *slow* applies to that which is a relatively long time in passing from one point to another, or in beginning or executing something. A person is *deliberate* who takes a noticeably long time to consider and decide before acting, or who acts or speaks as if he were deliberating at every point; a person is *dilatory* who lays aside, or puts off as long as possible, necessary or required action. *Gradual* signifies advancing by steps, and refers to *slow* but regular and sure progression. *Slack* refers to action that seems to indicate a lack of tension, as of muscle or of will, *sluggish* to action that seems as if reluctant to advance. See GRADUAL, HEAVY, RELUCTANT, TEDIOUS. *Antonyms*: see synonyms for IMPETUOUS, NIMBLE.

slow-down (slō′doun′) *n.* A slackening of pace.

slow-mo·tion (slō′mō′shən) *adj.* Pertaining to or designating a motion picture filmed at greater than standard speed so that the action appears slow in normal projection.

slow-poke (slō′pōk′) *n. Slang* A person who works or moves at an exceedingly slow pace; a laggard.

slow-worm (slō′wûrm′) *n.* A blindworm.

slub (slub) *v.t.* **slubbed, slub·bing** To twist (slivers of wool) slightly in preparation for spinning. —

n. **1** A slightly twisted roll of cotton, wool, or silk. **2** A thick, uneven lump in yarn. [Origin unknown]

sludge (sluj) *n.* **1** Soft, water-soaked mud; mire. **2** A slush of snow or broken or half-formed ice. **3** Muddy or pasty refuse of various kinds, as that produced by the action of a rock drill and in the purification of sewage. **4** The sediment in a water tank or boiler. [< earlier *slutch*. ? Related to SLUSH.] —**sludg′y** *adj.*

slue (slōō) *v.* **slued**, **slu·ing** *v.t.* **1** To cause to move sidewise, as if some portion were pivoted; swing, slide, or skid to the side. **2** To cause to twist or turn in its seat or fastenings: said of a boom or mast. —*v.i.* **3** To move sidewise. —*n.* The act of sluing around sidewise; a skidding or pivoting about; also, the position of a body that has slued. Also spelled *slew.* [Origin unknown]

slug¹ (slug) *n.* **1** A bullet or shot of irregular or oblong shape, especially as used in old muskets. **2** *Printing* **a** A strip of type metal, thicker than a lead and less than type-high, for spacing matter, etc. **b** A metal strip bearing a type-high number, abbreviated title, or the like, used by a compositor's mark. **3** A slugshot; or its metal weight. **4** Any small chunk of metal; especially, one used as a coin in automatic machines, as dial telephones. **5** *Physics* A unit of mass; the mass of a body which, when acted upon by a force of one pound, acquires an acceleration of one foot per second per second: it has the value of about 32.174 pounds or 14.59 kilograms, and is also called *geepound.* —*v.* **slugged**, **slug·ging** *v.i.* To take shape to fit the grooves of a rifle, as a bullet. —*v.t.* To load with slugs. [Origin uncertain. ? Akin to SLAG.]

slug² (slug) *n.* **1** Any of numerous terrestrial gastropod mollusks related to snails but having only a rudimentary shell concealed in the mantle, or none at all. **2** The larva of certain insects, as the sawfly, resembling a slug. **3** A sluggard. [ME *slugge* a sluggard, ? < Scand. Cf. dial. Norw. *slugg* a large, heavy object.]

SLUG

slug³ (slug) *Colloq. n.* **1** A heavy blow, as with the fist or a baseball bat. **2** A drink of undiluted liquor. —*v.t.* **slugged**, **slug·ging** To strike heavily or brutally, or without science, as with the fist or a baseball bat. [Origin uncertain] —**slug′ger** *n.*

slug·a·bed (slug′ə·bed′) *n.* One who lounges late in bed, because of laziness.

slug·gard (slug′ərd) *n.* A person habitually lazy or idle; a drone. —*adj.* Lazy; sluggish. [< SLUG² + -ARD]

slug·gish (slug′ish) *adj.* **1** Having little motion or power of motion; slow; torpid. **2** Habitually idle and lazy. **3** Not active; slow; stagnant: a *sluggish* season. See synonyms under HEAVY, IDLE, SLOW, TEDIOUS. —**slug′gish·ly** *adv.* —**slug′gish·ness** *n.*

sluice (slōōs) *n.* **1** Any artificial channel for conducting water, or the stream so conducted; specifically, a body of water controlled by a floodgate. **2** A floodgate. **3** A flume. **4** *Mining* A board trough having at the bottom baffles holding quicksilver to separate gold from placer dirt carried through the trough by a current of water. **5** That through which anything issues or flows. —*v.* **sluiced**, **sluic·ing** *v.t.* **1** To wet or drench, water or irrigate by or as by means of a sluice. **2** To wash in or by a sluice. **3** To draw out or conduct by or through a sluice. **4** To send (logs) down a sluiceway. —*v.i.* **5** To flow out or issue from a sluice. [< OF *escluse* < L *exclusa*, pp. fem. of *excludere* shut out]

sluice-gate (slōōs′gāt′) *n.* The gate of a sluice; a watergate or floodgate.

slum (slum) *n.* A squalid, dirty, overcrowded street or section of a city, marked by the poverty and poor living conditions of its inhabitants. —*v.i.* **slummed**, **slum·ming** To visit slums, as for reasons of curiosity or philanthropy. [< slang E, a room; ult. origin unknown] —**slum′mer** *n.* —**slum′ming** *n.*

slum·ber (slum′bər) *v.i.* **1** To sleep, especially lightly or quietly. **2** To be inactive; stagnate. —*v.t.* **3** To spend or pass in sleeping. See synonyms under REST. —*n.* Sleep; formerly,

light sleep; more recently, complete, quiet sleep. [OE *slumerian* < *slūma*] —**slum′ber·er** *n.* —**slum′ber·ing·ly** *adv.* —**slum′ber·less** *adj.*

slum·ber·ous (slum′bər·əs) *adj.* Inviting to, being in, suggesting, or resembling slumber; soporific; drowsy; sleepy. Also **slum·brous** (slum′brəs). —**slum′ber·ous·ly** *adv.* —**slum′ber·ous·ness** *n.*

slum·gul·lion (slum·gul′yən) *n.* *Slang* **a** A stew made principally of meat and vegetables. **b** A weak beverage. **2** A servant, especially one who performs menial chores. **3** Refuse drainage from blubber; also, fish offal. **4** A reddish, muddy deposit in mine sluiceways. [< slang E; origin uncertain]

slum·gum (slum′gum′) *n.* The residue of propolis, cocoons, etc., after beeswax is extracted from honeycombs.

slum·lord (slum′lôrd′) *n.* A landlord of a slum dwelling. [< SLUM + (LAND)LORD]

slump (slump) *v.i.* **1** To break through a crust, as of snow or ice, and sink; sink, as a foot, into any soft material. **2** To slide with perceptible motion down a declivity: said of loose earth or rock. **3** To fall or fail suddenly, as in value or quality. **4** To stand, walk, or proceed with a stooping posture; slouch: He *slumps* badly. —*n.* **1** The act of slumping; a collapsing fall. **2** A collapse or failure; also, a sudden fall of prices: a *slump* in stocks. **3** A decline, as of interest, excitement, etc. [Prob. imit.]

slung·shot (slung′shot′) *n.* A weight attached to a thong or cord, used as a weapon.

slunk (slungk) Past tense and past participle of SLINK. —*n.* The body of a stillborn animal, especially of a calf when cut away from the mother's womb. See SLINK.

slur (slûr) *v.t.* **slurred**, **slur·ring** **1** To slight; disparage; depreciate. **2** To pass over lightly or hurriedly; suppress; conceal: to *slur* a fact. **3** To pronounce, as a syllable, hurriedly and indistinctly. **4** *Music* **a** To sing or play as indicated by the slur. **b** To mark with a slur. **5** To smear; soil; contaminate. —*n.* **1** A disparaging remark or insinuation; also, the occasion for it, or the resulting state; a stigma. **2** *Music* **a** A curved line (⁀ or ⌣) indicating that tones so tied are to be sung to the same syllable or performed without a break between them. **b** The legato effect indicated or produced by this mark. **3** A blur. **4** A slurred pronunciation. [< dial. E, orig. fluid mud]

slurp (slûrp) *v.t. & v.i.* *Slang* To sip noisily. [Imit.]

slur·ry (slûr′ē) *n. pl.* **·ries** **1** Any one of several watery mixtures used to make repairs in furnace linings, to neutralize poisonous chemicals, etc. **2** A mixture used in making Portland cement. [See SLUR.]

slush (slush) *n.* **1** Soft, sloppy material, as melting snow or soft mud. **2** Greasy material used for lubrication, etc. **3** The greasy refuse of cooking, especially from a ship's galley: used on shipboard for lubricating the masts. **4** A mixture of lime with white lead or tallow, for coating bright iron or steel parts of machinery to keep them from rusting. **5** Emotional talk or writing; gush; drivel. —*v.t.* **1** To cover or daub with slush, as for lubrication. **2** To fill (spaces in masonry) with mortar: usually with *up*. **3** To wash by throwing water upon, as a deck. [Origin unknown] —**slush′y** *adj.*

slush fund *U.S.* **1** Formerly, on naval vessels, money obtained from the sale of garbage and used to buy small luxuries. **2** Money collected or spent for corrupt purposes, as bribery, lobbying, propaganda, etc.

slut (slut) *n.* **1** A female dog; bitch. **2** A slatternly woman. **3** A drudge. **4** A woman of loose character; hussy. [Origin uncertain]

slut·tish (slut′ish) *adj.* Slatternly; dirty. —**slut′tish·ly** *adv.* —**slut′tish·ness** *n.*

sly (slī) *adj.* **sli·er** or **sly·er**, **sli·est** or **sly·est** **1** Artfully dexterous in doing things secretly; cunning in evading notice or detection. **2** Playfully clever; roguish; mischievous. **3** Meanly or stealthily clever; crafty. **4** Done with or marked by artful secrecy: a *sly* trick. **5** Skilful; possessed of practical ability; wise. See synonyms under INSIDIOUS. —**on the sly** In a stealthy way; with concealment. [< ON *slœgr*] —**sly′ness** *n.*

Sm *Chem.* Samarium (symbol Sm).

smack¹ (smak) *n.* **1** A quick, sharp sound, as of the lips when separated rapidly; a noisy kiss. **2** A sounding blow or slap. **3** The sound of a snap-

ping whip. —*v.t. & v.i.* To give or make a smack, as in tasting, kissing, striking, etc.; slap. [Cf. MDu. *smack* a blow]

smack² (smak) *v.i.* **1** To have a taste or flavor, especially as tested by smacking: usually with *of.* **2** To have, keep, or disclose a slight suggestion: with *of.* —*n.* **1** A suggestive tincture, taste, or flavor. **2** A mere taste; smattering. [OE *smæc* taste]

small (smôl) *adj.* **1** Comparatively less than another or than a standard; diminutive; little. **2** Being of slight moment, weight, or importance. **3** Lacking in moral or mental breadth; narrow; ignoble; mean; paltry. **4** Lacking in the qualities of greatness; not largely gifted. **5** Acting or transacting business in a limited way. **6** Weak in characteristic properties; mildly alcoholic: said of liquors: *small* beer. **7** Having little body or volume; slender; fine; soft, as a voice. **8** Of low degree; obscure. **9** Lacking in power or strength. —**to feel small** To feel humiliated. —*adv.* **1** In a low or faint tone: to sing *small.* **2** Into small pieces. **3** In a small way; trivially; also, timidly; to talk *small.* —*n.* **1** A small or slender part: the *small* of the back. **2** A small thing or quantity. [OE *smæl*] —**small′ness** *n.*

Synonyms (adj.): diminutive, fine, little, mean, microscopic, minute, narrow, petty, puny, tiny. See FINE¹, INSIGNIFICANT, LITTLE.

small·age (smô′lij) *n.* Celery, especially in the wild state. [< SMALL + F *ache* wild celery < L *apium* parsley]

small arms Arms that may be carried on the person, as a rifle, automatic pistol, or revolver.

small beer **1** Insipid or weak beer. **2** *Brit.* An insignificant person or thing.

small capital A capital letter cut slightly larger than the lower-case letters of a specified type size. *Abbr. s.c., s. cap., small cap., sm. cap.*

THIS LINE IS IN CAPITAL LETTERS
THIS LINE IS IN SMALL CAPITAL LETTERS
this line is in lower-case letters

small circle The circumference formed by a plane cutting a sphere but not passing through its center.

small-clothes (smôl′klōthz′, -klōz′) *n. pl.* Close-fitting knee breeches worn by men in the 18th century. Also **smalls.**

small craft **1** Small vessels collectively. **2** Small things or persons generally.

small-fry (smôl′frī′) *n. pl.* **1** Small, young fish. **2** Young children. **3** Small or insignificant people or things.

small hours The early hours of the morning.

small-minded (smôl′mīn′did) *adj.* **1** Having a petty mind; interested in trivialities. **2** Narrow; intolerant; ungenerous.

small-mouth (smôl′mouth′) *n.* An American black bass (*Micropterus dolomieu*).

small potatoes *U.S. Colloq.* Unimportant, insignificant persons or things.

small-pox (smôl′poks′) *n. Pathol.* An acute, infectious, highly contagious disease caused by a filtrable virus and characterized by high inflammatory fever, followed by an eruption of deep-seated pustules; variola.

small stores Small, miscellaneous items, as tobacco, soap, thread, etc., stocked by a ship's store to be sold to the crew.

small talk Unimportant or trivial conversation.

small-time (smôl′tīm′) *adj. U.S. Slang* Petty; unimportant.

smalt (smôlt) *n.* A deep-blue glass colored with cobalt oxide: used when pulverized for painting, etc. [< F < Ital. *smalto* < Gmc.]

smalt·ite (smôl′tīt) *n.* A tin-white to steel-gray cobalt arsenide, crystallizing in the isometric system. Also **smalt·ine** (smôl′tin, -tēn). [< SMALT]

smarm (smärm) *Brit. Colloq. v.t.* To smear or plaster (the hair) with oil. —*v.i.* To behave in a servilely flattering manner; toady. [Var. of dial. E *smalm* smear, plaster]

smarm·y (smär′mē) *adj. Brit. Colloq.* Unctuously flattering; oily; toadying.

smart (smärt) *v.i.* **1** To experience a stinging sensation, generally superficial, either bodily or mental. **2** To cause a stinging sensation. **3** To experience remorse. **4** To have one's feelings hurt. **5** To pay a severe penalty. —*v.t.* **6** To cause to smart. —*adj.* **1** Quick in thought or action; bright; acute; clever. **2** Impertinently witty: often used contemptuously. **3** Vigorous; emphatic; severe; brisk. **4** Causing a smarting sensation; stinging; pungent. **5** Keen or sharp, as a trade; shrewd. **6** In active health; well. **7** *Colloq.* Superior, as in speed, strength, or skill. **8** *Colloq.* Large; considerable: a *smart* crop of wheat. **9** Sprucely dressed; showy. **10** Belonging to the stylish classes; fashionable: a *smart* set. **11** Making a creditable showing: a *smart* regiment. See synonyms under CLEVER. —*n.* **1** An acute stinging sensation, as from a scratch or an irritant. **2** Any distress; poignant mental suffering. **3** *Dial.* A degree, number, or amount: with *right*: a right *smart* of people. [OE *smeortan*] —**smart′ly** *adv.* —**smart′ness** *n.*

smart al·eck (al′ik) *Colloq.* A cocky, offensively conceited person. —**smart-al·eck·y** (smärt′al′ik-ē) *adj.*

smart·en (smär′tən) *v.t.* To improve in appearance; make smart, as oneself or one's habitation: with *up*.

smart set Fashionable society.

smart·weed (smärt′wēd′) *n.* Any of several species of widely distributed herbs (genus *Polygonum*) having jointed stems, long, grasslike leaves, and inconspicuous, greenish flowers, especially the **common smartweed** or water pepper. Also called *knotweed.*

smash (smash) *v.t.* **1** To break in many pieces suddenly, as by a blow, pressure, or collision. **2** To flatten; crush: to *smash* a hat. **3** To dash or fling violently so as to crush or break in pieces. **4** To strike with a sudden blow. **5** To make bankrupt. **6** To destroy, as a theory. **7** In tennis, to strike (the ball) with a hard, swift, overhand stroke. —*v.i.* **8** To go bankrupt; fail, as a business, etc. **9** To move or be moved with force; come into violent contact so as to crush or be crushed; collide; dash: The boats *smashed* together. See synonyms under BREAK. — **to go to smash** *Colloq.* To be ruined; fail. —*n.* **1** An act or instance of smashing, or the state of being smashed: often compounded with *up*: a *smash-up* on a railroad. **2** Any disaster or sudden break-up of any kind: a *smash* in business. **3** A beverage of spirituous liquors, usually brandy, with mint, water, sugar, and ice. **4** In tennis, a strong overhand shot. **5** *Colloq.* Something acclaimed by the public: The film is a box-office *smash.* [Prob. imit.] —**smash′er** *n.*

smash·ing (smash′ing) *adj. Colloq.* Extremely impressive; overwhelmingly good: a *smashing* success.

smat·ter·ing (smat′ər·ing) *n.* **1** A superficial degree or kind of anything, especially of knowledge. **2** A little bit or a few.

smear (smir) *v.t.* **1** To spread, rub, or cover with grease, paint, dirt, etc.; bedaub. **2** To spread or apply in a thick layer or coating: to *smear* grease on an axle. **3** To sully the reputation of; defame; slander. **4** *U.S. Slang* To defeat utterly; overwhelm or stop. **5** To cover with smear (def. 3). **6** *Obs.* To anoint. —*v.i.* **7** To be or become smeared. —*n.* **1** A soiled spot; stain. **2** A small quantity of material, as blood, sputum, etc., placed on a microscope slide or bacterial culture for analysis. **3** A volatile flux for glazing ware. **4** *Obs.* Ointment; grease. **5** A slanderous attack; defamation. **6** *Slang* Anything to spread on bread, as butter, jam, etc. [OE *smerian* < *smeoru* smear]

smear·case (smir′kās′) *n. U.S.* Cottage cheese. [< G *schmierkäse*]

smear·y (smir′ē) *adj.* **smear·i·er, smear·i·est** Greasy, viscous, or staining; also, smeared. —**smear′i·ness** *n.*

smell (smel) *v.* **smelled** or **smelt, smell·ing** *v.t.* **1** To perceive by means of the nose and its olfactory nerves. **2** To perceive the odor or perfume of; scent. **3** To test by odor or smell. **4** To discover, detect, or seek to know, as if by smelling: often with *out.* —*v.i.* **5** To emit an odor or perfume; give off a particular odor: frequently with *of*; also, to give indications of, as if by odor: to *smell* of treason. **6** To be malodorous. **7** To use the sense of smell. **8** To pry; investigate: with *about.* —*n.* **1** That special sense by means of which odors are perceived. **2** The sensation excited through the olfactory nerves. **3** That which

is directly perceived by this sense; an odor; perfume. **4** A faint suggestion; hint; trace. **5** An act of smelling. [ME *smellen*]

Synonyms (*noun*): aroma, bouquet, fragrance, odor, perfume, savor, scent, stench, stink. *Smell* is the generic word including all the rest. *Aroma, fragrance,* and *perfume* are ordinarily pleasing; *odor, savor,* and *scent* may be so. *Odor* is nearly synonymous with *smell,* but is susceptible of more delicate use; as, the *odor* of incense. An *aroma* is a delicate and spicy *odor,* as of fine coffee; *bouquet* is said chiefly of the delicate *odor* of certain wines. We speak of the *fragrance* or *perfume* of flowers, but *fragrance* is more delicate; a *perfume* may be so strong and rich as to be repulsive by excess, There is a tendency to restrict the application of *perfume* to the artificial preparations called collectively "perfumery." *Scent* is chiefly used for the characteristic *odor* of an animal by which it is tracked or avoided by other animals; the word is also applied to any *odor,* natural or artificial, especially when faintly diffused through the air; as, the *scent* of mignonette or of new-mown hay. *Savor* is chiefly said of the appetizing *odor* evolved from articles of food by the processes of cooking. Any *smell* that is at once foul, strong, and pervasive may be called a *stench.* See SAVOR.

smelling salts Pungent or aromatic salts, or mixtures of such, often scented, used as stimulants by smelling; specifically, a preparation of ammonium carbonate.

smell·y (smel′ē) *adj.* **smell·i·er, smell·i·est** Having an unpleasant smell; malodorous.

smelt¹ (smelt) *v.t. Metall.* **1** To reduce (ores) by fusion in a furnace. **2** To obtain (a metal) from the ore by a process including fusion. —*v.i.* **3** To melt or fuse, as a metal. [< MDu. *smelten* melt]

smelt² (smelt) *n.* *pl.* **smelts** or **smelt** Any of certain small silvery food fishes (genus *Osmerus* or a related genus), of the northern Atlantic and Pacific. [OE]

smelt·er (smel′tər) *n.* **1** One engaged in smelting ore. **2** An establishment for smelting: also **smelt′er·y.**

smi·la·ca·ceous (smī′lə·kā′shəs) *adj. Bot.* Of or pertaining to a family (*Smilacaceae*) of herbs or woody-stemmed vines, having dioecious flowers and globular fruits. [< NL < L *smilax.* See SMILAX.]

smi·la·cin (smī′lə·sin) *n.* Parillin.

smi·lax (smī′laks) *n.* **1** Any of a large, widely scattered genus (*Smilax*) of shrubby or herbaceous plants having net-veined leaves, dioecious flowers in umbels, and globular fruit, especially *S. aristolochiifolia,* a source of sarsaparilla: also called *catbrier, greenbrier.* **2** A delicate twining plant (*Asparagus asparagoides*) of the lily family, from South Africa, with greenish flowers: cultivated in greenhouses and extensively used for bouquets, etc. [< L < Gk. *smilax* yew]

SMILAX
Greenbrier.

smile (smīl) *n.* **1** A pleased or amused expression of the face, characterized by lateral upward extension of the lips. **2** A pleasant aspect: the *smile* of spring. **3** Propitious or favorable disposition; favor; blessing: the *smile* of fortune. —*v.* **smiled, smil·ing** *v.i.* **1** To give a smile; wear a cheerful aspect. **2** To show approval or favor: often with *upon.* —*v.t.* **3** To express by means of a smile; effect as by a smile. [ME *smilen,* prob. < LG] —**smil′er** *n.* —**smil′ing** *adj.* —**smil′ing·ly** *adv.* —**smil′ing·ness** *n.*

smirch (smûrch) *v.t.* **1** To soil, as by contact with grime; smear. **2** Figuratively, to defame; degrade: to *smirch* a reputation. —*n.* The act of smirching, or the state of being smirched; a smutch; smear; a moral stain or defect. See synonyms under BLEMISH. [ME *smorchen,* appar. < OF *esmorcher* hurt, torment]

smirk (smûrk) *v.i.* To smile in a silly, self-complacent, or affected manner. —*n.* An affected or artificial smile. Also *Obs.* **smerk.**

[OE *smercian*] —**smirk′ing·ly** *adv.*

smite (smīt) *v.* **smote** (*Obs.* **smit**), **smit·ten** or **smit** or **smote, smit·ing** *v.t.* **1** To strike (something); cause to strike. **3** To cut, sever, or break by a blow: usually with *off* or *out.* **4** To strike with disaster; afflict; destroy by a catastrophe. **5** To affect powerfully with sudden feeling; in the passive, to affect with love. **6** To cause to feel regret or remorse: His conscience *smote* him. **7** To affect as if by a blow; come upon suddenly: The thought *smote* him. **8** To kill by a sudden blow. —*v.i.* **9** To come with sudden force; also, to knock against something: His knees *smote* together. See synonyms under BEAT. [OE *smītan*] — **smit′er** *n.*

smith (smith) *n.* **1** One who shapes metals by hammering: often used in combination: *goldsmith, tinsmith.* **2** A blacksmith. [OE]

smith·er·eens (smith′ə·rēnz′) *n. pl. Colloq.* Fragments produced as by a blow. Also **smith′ers.** [Cf. dial. E (Irish) *smidirin* a fragment]

smith·y (smith′ē, smith′ē) *n.* *pl.* **smith·ies** A blacksmith's shop; a forge.

smit·ten (smit′n) Alternative past participle of SMITE. —*adj.* **1** Struck with sudden force; gravely afflicted. **2** Having the affections suddenly attracted.

smock (smok) *n.* **1** A loose outer garment of light material worn like a coat to protect one's clothes. **2** In colonial times, a woman's undergarment; chemise. —*v.t.* **1** To furnish with or clothe in a smock. **2** To shirr (def. 1). See SMOCKING. [OE *smoc*]

smock·ing (smok′ing) *n.* Shirred work; decorative stitching holding fullness in regular patterns.

smog (smog) *n. Colloq.* A combination of smoke and fog, especially as seen in and about heavy industry and manufacturing areas. [Blend of SM(OKE) + (F)OG]

smok·a·ble (smō′kə·bəl) *adj.* Capable of being smoked. —*n.* Something to be smoked, as a cigarette, cigar, etc.: usually in the plural.

SMOCKING

smoke (smōk) *n.* **1** The volatilized products of the combustion of an organic compound, as coal, wood, etc., charged with fine particles of carbon or soot; less properly, fumes, steam, etc. **2** *Chem.* A colloid system of solid particles in a gas. See COLLOID SYSTEM. **3** Anything transient and unsubstantial; a useless or ephemeral result. **4** The act of smoking a pipe, cigar, etc. **5** A period of time during which one smokes tobacco. **6** *Colloq.* A cigarette, cigar, or pipeful of tobacco. **7** A chemical-warfare agent producing a smoke-like cloud; also, a smudge. **8** A column of smoke, used as a signal by the North American Indians. **9** *U.S. Slang* In baseball, speed in a pitch. **10** A cheap drink, usually of wood alcohol. —*v.* **smoked, smok·ing** *v.i.* **1** To emit or give out smoke: The embers *smoke*; also, to emit smoke excessively or in an undesired direction, as a stove or lamp. **2** To raise dust in rapid riding or driving; hence, to travel rapidly; speed. — *v.t.* **3** To inhale and exhale the smoke of (tobacco, opium, etc.); also, to use, as a pipe, for this purpose. **4** To treat or affect with smoke; treat by the application of smoke; cure; medicate; fumigate; tinge; flavor with smoke. **5** To apply smoke to in order to drive away or expel: to *smoke* bees; hence, to force out of hiding: usually with *out*: to *smoke* out a criminal. **6** To get the scent of; hence, to suspect. **7** To change the color of (glass, etc.) by darkening with smoke. [OE *smoca*]

smoke·house (smōk′hous′) *n.* **1** A building or close room in which meat, fish, hides, etc., are cured by the action of smoke. **2** A building in which anything is disinfected by the use of smoke.

smoke·jump·er (smōk′jum′pər) *n.* A fireman trained and equipped to fight forest fires when parachuted to the affected area by aircraft.

smoke·pot (smōk′pot′) *n.* A small container for generating a dense cloud of smoke.

smoke screen A dense cloud of smoke emitted

to screen an attack or bombardment by land or sea, or to cover a retreat. Also **smoke blanket.**

smoke·stack (smōk'stak') *n.* **1** An upright pipe, usually of sheet or plate iron, through which combustion gases from a boiler furnace are discharged into the air. **2** The funnel of a steamboat or locomotive, or the tall chimney of a factory, etc.

smoke·tree (smōk'trē) *n.* **1** An ornamental Old World shrub or tree *(Cotinus coggygria)* with long feathery stalks resembling smoke or mist. **2** A related American species *(C. americanus).*

smoking jacket A short coat worn instead of a regular suit coat as a lounging jacket.

smok·y (smō'kē) *adj.* **smok·i·er, smok·i·est** **1** Giving forth smoke. **2** Mixed with or containing smoke: *smoky* air. **3** Liable to be filled with smoke, as a house. **4** Emitting smoke improperly and unpleasantly, as from bad draft. **5** Discolored with smoke. **6** Smoke-colored; dark-gray. **7** Covered with mist: said of certain mountains. —**smok'i·ly** *adv.* —**smok'i·ness** *n.*

smol·der (smōl'dər) *v.i.* **1** To burn and smoke in a smothered way, showing little smoke and no flame. **2** Figuratively, to exist in a latent state; to manifest suppressed feeling: His wrath was *smoldering.* —*n.* Smother; smoke. Also spelled *smoulder.* [Dissimilated var. of ME *smorther.* See SMOTHER.]

smolt (smōlt) *n.* A young salmon on its first descent from the river to the sea. [? Related to SMELT[2]]

smooch (smōōch) *n.* A smear; a smutch. —*v.t.* To smear; smudge. —*v.i. Slang* To neck. [Cf. SMUTCH]

smooth (smōōth) *adj.* **1** Having a surface without irregularities; not rough; continuously even. **2** Having no impediments or obstructions; easy; free from shocks or jolts. **3** Calm and unruffled; bland; pleasant; mild. **4** Flowing melodiously: opposed to *rugged:* a *smooth* style. **5** Suave, as in speech; flattering: often implying deceit. **6** *Phonet.* Sounded without the aspirate: opposed to *rough:* a *smooth* breathing. **7** Free from hair; beardless. **8** Having no acidulous or astringent taste or quality: said of liquors. **9** Without lumps; having the elements perfectly blended: a *smooth* mayonnaise. **10** Offering no resistance to a body sliding along its surface; without friction. **11** Having the high points removed by wear, as the surface of a tire. —*adv.* Calmly; evenly. —*v.t.* **1** To make smooth or even on the surface. **2** To make easy or less difficult: to *smooth* one's path. **3** To free from obstructions. **4** To remove (an obstruction): often with *away:* to *smooth* away a mound. **5** To render less harsh or softer and more flowing: to *smooth* one's verses. **6** To soften the worst features of; palliate; extenuate: usually with *over.* **7** To make calm; mollify: to *smooth* one's feelings. **8** To become smooth. Also **smooth'en.** —**to smooth (someone's) ruffled feathers** To mollify. —*n.* **1** The smooth portion or surface of anything: the *smooth* of the neck. **2** The act of smoothing. [OE *smōth*] —**smooth'er** *n.* —**smooth'ly** *adv.* —**smooth'ness** *n.*

Synonyms (adj.): even, flat, glossy, level, plain, plane, polished, sleek, undisturbed, unruffled. An *even* surface is free from any considerable irregularities, as knobs, or splinters, or abrupt changes of direction or curvature; a *smooth* surface is one that the hand may be passed over without friction or in which the eye discerns no noticeable break or flaw. That which is *polished* is brought to a very high degree of smoothness, so as to be not only frictionless to touch but lustrous to the eye. A board is sawed to an *even* surface, planed till it is *smooth,* and sandpapered till it is *polished.* A thing may be *smooth* or *polished* and yet very uneven, as a warped piece of veneering. See BLAND, BLUNT, CALM, FINE[1], LEVEL, PACIFIC. *Antonyms:* see synonyms for ROUGH.

smooth-faced (smōōth'fāst') *adj.* **1** Beardless. **2** Of smooth surface, as a wall, etc. **3** Bland or mild in expression, especially with deceitful intent.

smör·gäs·bord (smôr'gəs·bôrd, Sw. smœr'gös·bôrd) *n.* Scandinavian hors d'oeuvres. Also spelled **smor'gas·bord.** [< Sw.]

smoth·er (smuth'ər) *v.t.* **1** To prevent the respiration of, as by filling or covering the mouth and nostrils; also, to kill by such means; suffocate; stifle. **2** To cover, or cause to smolder, as a

fire. **3** Figuratively, to hide or suppress: to *smother* a scandal. **4** In cooking, to enclose and cook in a covered dish or under a close mass of some other substance. **5** To daub; smear. —*v.i.* **6** To be covered without vent or air, as a fire. **7** To be hidden or suppressed, as wrath. —*n.* **1** That which smothers, as stifling vapor or dust. **2** The state of being smothered; suppression; also, a smoldering fire. **3** A surging of foam or water; a welter. [Earlier *smorther.* Related to OE *smorian* suffocate] —**smoth'er·y** *adj.*

smudge (smuj) *v.* **smudged, smudg·ing** *v.t.* **1** To smear; soil. **2** To protect (from frost, insects, etc.) by a heavy, smoky pall. —*v.i.* **3** To cause a smudge. **4** To be smudged. —*n.* **1** A soiling, as of dry dirt or soot; smear; stain. **2** A smoky fire or its smoke for driving away insects, preventing frost, etc. **3** Paint-pot scrapings and cleanings. [Var. of SMUTCH] —**smudg'i·ly** *adv.* —**smudg'i·ness** *n.* —**smudg'y** *adj.*

smug (smug) *adj.* **smug·ger, smug·gest** **1** Characterized by a smoothly self-satisfied or extremely complacent air. **2** Trim; neat; spruce, especially with suggestions of respectability or self-satisfaction. [Cf. LG *smuk* neat] —**smug'ly** *adv.* —**smug'ness** *n.*

smug-faced (smug'fāst') *adj.* Having a prim, self-satisfied face or expression.

smug·gle (smug'əl) *v.* **·gled, ·gling** *v.t.* **1** To take (merchandise) into or out of a country without payment of lawful duties. **2** To bring in or introduce illicitly or clandestinely. —*v.i.* **3** To engage in or practice smuggling. [< LG *smuggeln*]

smut (smut) *n.* **1** The blackening made by soot, smoke, etc. **2** Obscenity; obscene language. **3** Any of various fungus diseases of plants, in which the affected parts change into a dusty black powder. **4** The parasitic fungus (order *Ustilaginales*) causing such a disease. —*v.* **smut·ted, smut·ting** *v.t.* **1** To blacken or stain, as with soot or smoke. **2** To affect with smut, as growing grain. **3** To remove the smut from (grain). **4** Figuratively, to pollute; defame. —*v.i.* **5** To give off smut. **6** To be or become stained. **7** To be affected with smut, as growing grain. [< LG *schmutt* dirt]

smut·ty (smut'ē) *adj.* **·ti·er, ·ti·est** **1** Soiled with smut; black; stained. **2** Affected by smut: *smutty* corn. **3** Obscene; coarse; indecent. —**smut'ti·ly** *adv.* —**smut'ti·ness** *n.*

Sn *Chem.* Tin (symbol Sn). [< L *stannum*]

snack (snak) *n.* **1** A sip or bite. **2** A slight, hurried meal. **3** A share of something. [Orig. a verb < MDu. *snacken* bite, snap]

sna·fu (sna·fōō') *Slang adj.* In a state of utter confusion; chaotic. —*v.t.* **·fued, ·fu·ing** To put into a confused or chaotic condition. —*n.* Anything which is confused or chaotic. [< S(ituation) n(ormal) a(ll) f(ouled) u(p)]

snag (snag) *n.* **1** A jagged or stumpy knot or protuberance, especially the stumpy base of a branch left in pruning. **2** The root or remnant of a tooth remaining in the jaw; also, a projecting tooth. **3** A branch or point of a deer's antler. **4** The trunk of a tree fixed in the bottom of a river, bayou, etc., by which boats are sometimes pierced. **5** Hence, any unsuspected or hidden obstacle or difficulty. —*v.* **snagged, snag·ging** *v.t.* **1** To injure, destroy, or impede by or as by a snag. **2** To clear of snags. **3** *Colloq.* To block; impede. —*v.i.* **4** To run upon a snag: said especially of river craft. [Prob. < Scand. Cf. dial. Norw. *snag* sharp point, projection.] —**snagged** *adj.*

snag·gle-tooth (snag'əl·tōōth') *n.* A tooth that is broken, projecting, or conspicuously out of alinement with the others. —**snag'gle-toothed'** (-tōōtht', -tōōthd') *adj.*

snail (snāl) *n.* **1** Any of numerous gastropod mollusks of terrestrial or aquatic habit having a spiral shell, a retractile foot, and a distinct head with eyes borne on stalks or tentacles. **2** A slow or lazy person. **3** A cinnamon roll shaped like a snail shell. [OE *snægl*]

snail hawk The small, bluish-gray everglade kite *(Rostrhamus sociabilis plumbeus)* ranging from Florida to Mexico, that feeds on snails.

SNAIL

snake (snāk) *n.* **1** An ophidian reptile (suborder *Serpentes*), having a greatly elongated, scaly body, no limbs, and a specialized swallowing apparatus. The bite of most snakes is non-venomous, but some have much enlarged fangs, connected with venom glands from which a deadly poison flows into the punctures they make. ◆ Collateral adjective: *anguine.* **2** A treacherous or insinuating person. **3** A flexible, resilient wire used to clean clogged drains. etc. —*v.* **snaked, snak·ing** *v.t. Colloq.* To drag by seizing an end or limb and pulling forcibly or quickly; haul along the ground, as a log. —*v.i.* To wind or move like a snake. [OE *snaca*]

Snake (snāk) *n.* A member of any of various Shoshonean tribes of North American Indians, but especially the Walpapi and Yahuskin of eastern Oregon.

SNAKEBIRD

snake·bird (snāk'bûrd') *n.* One of several birds (genus *Anhinga*), with very long slender neck, frequenting southern swamps and feeding upon fish; the water turkey; the darter.

snake·bite (snāk'bīt') *n.* **1** The bite of a snake. **2** Poisoning caused by the venom of a snake.

snake charmer **1** An entertainer who charms venomous snakes by rhythmic motions of his body, and, supposedly, by music. **2** Any entertainer who handles snakes.

snake dance A ceremonial dance of the Hopi Indians of Arizona in which live rattlesnakes are carried in the mouths of the dancers. The Hopis believe the snakes to be influential with the rain gods.

snake hawk The swallow-tailed kite *(Elanoides forficatus)* of North and South America.

snake·mouth (snāk'mouth') *n.* A terrestrial orchid *(Pogonia ophioglossoides)* native in eastern North America, with fragrant rose-pink flowers.

snake·root (snāk'rōōt', -rŏŏt') *n.* **1** One of various plants having roots reputed to be effective against snakebite; especially, the bugbane; the Seneca snakeroot *(Polygala senega),* growing east of the Mississippi; the **Virginia snakeroot** *(Aristolochia serpentaria),* with purplish-brown flowers and fibrous roots; and the **white snakeroot** *(Eupatorium rugosum)* of Europe and the United States. **2** The root of any of these plants.

snak·y (snā'kē) *adj.* **snak·i·er, snak·i·est** **1** Of or like a snake; serpentine; winding. **2** Insinuating; cunning; treacherous. **3** Full of snakes. —**snak'i·ly** *adv.* —**snak'i·ness** *n.*

snap (snap) *v.* **snapped, snap·ping** *v.i.* **1** To make a sharp, quick sound, as of percussion. **2** To break suddenly with a cracking noise; part with a snap. **3** To fly off or give way quickly, as when tension is suddenly relaxed. **4** To make the jaws come suddenly together in an effort to bite: often with *up* or *at.* **5** To seize or snatch suddenly: often with *up* or *at.* **6** To speak sharply, harshly, or irritably: often with *at.* **7** To emit, or seem to emit, a spark or flash of light: said of the eyes. **8** To close, fasten, etc., with a click or snapping sound, as a lock. **9** To move or act with sudden, neat gestures: He *snapped* to attention. —*v.t.* **10** To seize suddenly or eagerly, with or as with the teeth; snatch: often with *up.* **11** To sever with a snapping sound. **12** To utter, address, or interrupt harshly, abruptly, or irritably: often with *out.* **13** To cause to make a sharp, quick sound. **14** To close, fasten, etc., with a snapping sound. **15** To strike, press, etc., with a snap: to *snap* a whip. **16** To cause to move suddenly, neatly, etc. **17** To photograph instantaneously with a camera. **18** In football, to put in play: said of the ball when sent to a back by the center. —**to snap out of it** *Colloq.* **1** To recover. **2** To change one's attitude. —*n.* **1** The act of snapping, or a sharp, quick sound produced by it: the *snap* of a whip. **2** A sudden breaking of anything, or the sound so produced. **3** Any catch, fastener, or other device that closes or springs into place with a snapping sound. **4** A sudden seizing or effort to seize with or as with the teeth; a sharp shutting, as of the jaws or of a trap. **5** A quick blow of the thumb sprung from the finger or of the finger from the thumb. **6** The sudden release of the tension of a spring or elastic cord. **7** A small, thin, crisp cake, usually containing ginger; a gingersnap. **8** Brisk energy; vigor; vim; zip. **9** A brief spell; a sudden turn: said chiefly of cold weather. **10** A hasty meal; snack. **11** Any task or duty easy to perform: often in the phrase **a soft snap**. **12** A bit: It is not worth a *snap*. **13** The instantaneous taking of a photograph; also, the photograph so taken; a snapshot. **14** A stringbean. — *adj.* **1** Made or done suddenly and without consideration; offhand. **2** Contrived to take unawares and at an advantage: a *snap* policy. **3** Fastening with a snap. — *adv.* With a snap; quickly. [< MDu. *snappen* bite at]

snap bean A wax bean.

snap·drag·on (snap′drag′ən) *n.* **1** A plant (genus *Antirrhinum*) of the figwort family, especially the **large-flowered snapdragon** (*A. majus*) having solitary axillary flowers, likened to dragons' heads. **2** Flapdragon.

snap·per (snap′ər) *n.* **1** One who or that which snaps, as a cracker. **2** A large food fish (genus *Lutianus*) of the Gulf coast, as the **red snapper** (*L. blackfordii*). **3** One of various other fishes, as the bluefish, rosefish, etc. **4** A sparoid fish (*Pagrosomus auratus*), reddish with blue bars or spots; one the most important food fishes of Australasia: also called *schnapper*. **5** A snapping turtle.

snapping beetle An elaterid beetle which by a quick, snapping movement of its body is able to right itself when on its back; especially, the eyed elater (*Alaus oculatus*) of eastern North America: also called *click beetle, skipjack*. For illustration see under INSECTS (injurious).

snapping turtle 1 A large voracious turtle of North America, especially *Chelydra serpentina*, much used as food. **2** The alligator turtle (*Macrochelys temminickii*), a related species.

SNAPPING TURTLE
(Up to 2 feet in length; weight to 100 pounds or more)

snap·pish (snap′ish) *adj.* **1** Apt to speak crossly or tartly. **2** Disposed to snap, as a dog. See synonyms under FRETFUL. — **snap′pish·ly** *adv.* — **snap′pish·ness** *n.*

snap·py (snap′ē) *adj.* ·pi·er, ·pi·est **1** *Colloq.* Brisk, vivid, and energetic; vivacious. **2** Smart or stylish in appearance. **3** Snappish. — **snap′pi·ly** *adv.* — **snap′pi·ness** *n.*

snap·shot (snap′shot′) *n.* A photograph taken with a small camera without timing.

snap·weed (snap′wēd′) *n.* Any plant of the genus *Impatiens*; a touch-me-not.

snare (snâr) *n.* **1** A device, as a noose, for catching birds or other animals; a gin; trap. **2** Anything by which one is brought into trouble or caused to sin; an allurement; wile. **3** *Surg.* A loop of wire used to remove tumors and other growths from the body. — *v.t.* **snared, snar·ing 1** To catch with a snare; ensnare; entrap. **2** To capture by trickery; entice; inveigle. [< ON *snara.* Akin to SNARE².] — **snar′er** *n.*

snare drum A small drum to be beaten on one head and having snares or strings of catgut stretched across the other.

snarl¹ (snärl) *n.* A sharp, harsh, angry growl; harsh or quarrelsome utterance. — *v.i.* **1** To growl harshly, as a dog. **2** To speak angrily and resentfully. — *v.t.* **3** To utter or express with a snarl. [Freq. of obs. *snar* growl] — **snarl′er** *n.* — **snarl′ing·ly** *adv.* — **snarl′y** *adj.*

snarl² (snärl) *n.* **1** A tangle, as of hair or yarn. **2** Any complication, perplexity, or entanglement. **3** *Colloq.* A wrangle; quarrel. **4** A knot or gnarl in wood. — *v.i.* **1** To get into a snarl or tangle; become entangled. — *v.t.* **2** To put into a snarl or tangle. **3** To confuse; entangle mentally; embarrass; make entanglements in. **4** To emboss or flute (thin metalware). [< SNARE¹] — **snarl′er** *n.*

snatch (snach) *v.t.* **1** To seize or lay hold of suddenly, hastily, or eagerly. **2** To take or remove suddenly. **3** To take or obtain as the opportunity arises: to *snatch* a few hours of sleep. **4** *Slang* To kidnap. — *v.i.* **5** To attempt to seize swiftly and suddenly: with *at.* **6** To accept with great eagerness: with *at.* — *n.* **1** An act of snatching; a hasty grab or grasp: usually with *at.* **2** A brief period: a *snatch* of rest. **3** A small amount; fragment: *snatches* of a conversation; *snatches* of melody. **4** *Slang.* A kidnaping. [ME *snacchen.* ? Related to SNACK.] — **snatch′er** *n.*

snatch block *Naut.* A single block having an opening in one cheek to receive a rope, and usually having a swivel hook.

sneak (snēk) *v.i.* **1** To move or go in a stealthy manner. **2** To act with covert cowardice or servility. — *v.t.* **3** To put, give, transfer, move, etc., secretly or stealthily. **4** *Colloq.* To pilfer. — *n.* **1** One who sneaks; a mean, cowardly fellow. **2** *pl. Colloq.* Sneakers. **3** A stealthy movement. — *adj.* Stealthy; covert: a *sneak* attack. [Akin to OE *snican* creep]

sneak boat A small, shallow boat used for duck hunting. Also **sneak-box** (snēk′boks′).

sneak·er (snē′kər) *n.* **1** One who sneaks; a sneak. **2** *pl. U.S. Colloq.* Rubber-soled canvas shoes.

sneak·ing (snē′king) *adj.* **1** Cringing; meanly secret and underhand. **2** Secretly entertained or cherished; unavowed: a *sneaking* suspicion. See synonyms under BASE². — **sneak′ing·ly** *adv.*

sneak thief One who steals small miscellaneous articles, without violence, by sneaking in through unfastened doors or windows.

sneak·y (snē′kē) *adj.* **sneak·i·er, sneak·i·est** Like a sneak; sneaking. — **sneak′i·ly** *adv.* — **sneak′i·ness** *n.*

sneer (snir) *n.* **1** A grimace of contempt or derision made by slightly raising the upper lip and nostrils. **2** A mean or contemptuous insinuation; a fling. — *v.i.* **1** To make or show a sneer. **2** To express derision or contempt in speech, writing, etc. — *v.t.* **3** To utter with a sneer or in a sneering manner. See synonyms under SCOFF. [ME *sneren*; ult. origin uncertain] — **sneer′er** *n.* — **sneer′ing** *adj.* — **sneer′ing·ly** *adv.*

Synonyms (noun): fling, gibe, jeer, scoff, taunt. A *sneer* may be simply a contemptuous facial contortion or some brief satirical utterance that throws a contemptuous sidelight on what it attacks without attempting to prove or disprove. The *jeer* and *gibe* are uttered; the *gibe* is bitter, and often sly or covert; the *jeer* is rude and open. A *scoff* may be in act or word, and is commonly directed against that which claims honor, reverence, or worship. A *fling* is careless and commonly pettish; a *taunt* is intentionally insulting and provoking; the *sneer* is supercilious; the *taunt* is defiant. See SCORN.

sneeze (snēz) *v.i.* **sneezed, sneez·ing** *v.i.* To drive air forcibly and audibly out of the mouth and nose by a spasmodic involuntary action. — *v.t.* To utter with or as with a sneeze: often with *out.* — **not to be sneezed at** *Colloq.* Of a character entitling to consideration. — *n.* An act of sneezing: also **sneez′ing**. [Misreading of ME *fnese,* OE *fnēosan* sneeze] — **sneez′er** *n.* — **sneez′y** *adj.*

sneeze·weed (snēz′wēd′) *n.* Any plant of a genus (*Helenium*) of the composite family, especially *H. autumnale*: from the effect of the powdered leaves and flowers when snuffed up: also called *bitterweed.*

sneeze·wort (snēz′wûrt′) *n.* **1** A perennial Eurasian plant (*Achillea ptarmica*) resembling the yarrow. Its powdered dry leaves produce sneezing. **2** Sneezeweed.

snell (snel) *n.* A short line of gut, horsehair, etc., bearing a fish hook, to be attached to a longer line. [Origin unknown]

snick (snik) *n.* **1** A small cut; nick; snip. **2** A knot in thread or the like. **3** In cricket, a glancing hit. — *v.t.* **1** To cut a nick in. **2** To hit (a ball) a glancing blow. — **to snick and snee** To thrust and cut. [Back formation < *snick or snee.* See SNICKERSNEE.]

snick·er (snik′ər) *n.* A half-suppressed or smothered laugh. — *v.i.* To utter a snicker; laugh slyly and foolishly with audible catches

of the voice; giggle. — *v.t.* To utter or express with a snicker. Also *snigger.* [Imit.]

snick·er·snee (snik′ər·snē′) *n.* **1** A fight with knives. **2** A knife suitable for thrusting and cutting. Also **snick and snee, snick′-a-snee, snick or snee.** [Alter. of earlier *snick or snee* thrust or cut, ult. < Du. *steken* thrust + *snijen* cut]

snide (snīd) *adj.* Malicious or derogatory; nasty. — *n.* A snide person. [Origin unknown]

sniff (snif) *v.i.* **1** To breathe through the nose in short, quick, audible inhalations. **2** To express contempt, etc., by sniffing: often with *at.* **3** To inhale a scent in sniffs. — *v.t.* **4** To breathe in through the nose; inhale. **5** To smell or attempt to smell with sniffs: to *sniff* smoke. **6** To perceive as if by sniffs: to *sniff* peril. **7** To express (contempt) by sniffs. — *n.* **1** An act or the sound of sniffing. **2** Perception by or as by sniffing; that which is inhaled by sniffing. [Appar. back formation < SNIVEL]

snif·fle (snif′əl) *v.i.* **·fled, ·fling 1** To snuffle. **2** To snivel or whimper; whine; sniff. — *n.* A snuffle. [Freq. of SNIFF]

snif·ter (snif′tər) *n.* **1** A liquor glass, pear-shaped, with a small opening to concentrate the aroma. **2** *U.S. Slang* A small drink of liquor, usually a dram. [< *snift,* var. of SNIFF]

snig·ger (snig′ər) *n.* A snicker, especially a derisive snicker. — *v.i.* To snicker, especially in derision. [Var. of SNICKER] — **snig′ger·er** *n.*

snip (snip) *v.* **snipped, snip·ping** *v.t.* To clip, remove, or cut with a short, light stroke or strokes of scissors or shears: often with *off.* — *v.i.* To cut with small, quick strokes. — *n.* **1** An act of snipping. **2** A small piece snipped off. **3** *U.S. Colloq.* A small or insignificant person or thing. **4** *pl.* Small shears for cutting metal. [< Du. *snippen*]

snipe (snīp) *n. pl.* **snipe** or **snipes 1** A shore bird (genus *Capella*), allied to the woodcock and much esteemed as a game bird; especially, the common **European** or **whole snipe** (*C. gallinago*), and the common **American** or **Wilson's snipe** (*C. delicata*). **2** One of other snipelike birds, as the **lesser snipe** or **jack snipe** of Europe (*Limnocryptes minimus*). **3** *U.S. Slang* A cigarette or cigar butt. — *v.i.* **sniped, snip·ing 1** To hunt or shoot snipe. **2** To shoot at or pick off individual enemies from cover or ambush. **3** *U.S. Slang* To hunt for cigarette or cigar butts. [< ON *snipa*]

snip·er (snī′pər) *n.* One who shoots an enemy from cover; a sharpshooter.

snip·pet (snip′it) *n.* **1** A small piece snipped off. **2** A small portion or share.

snip·pet·y (snip′it·ē) *adj.* **1** Arrogant; brusk; snippy. **2** Trivial, as if composed of little pieces snipped off; small; trifling.

snip·py (snip′ē) *adj.* **·pi·er, ·pi·est** *Colloq.* **1** Supercilious; pert; impertinent. **2** Fragmentary.

snit (snit) *n. Colloq.* An irritable or angry mood: usually preceded by *in* or *into*: the affront put him in a *snit.* [Origin unknown]

snitch (snich) *Slang v.t.* To grab quickly; steal. — *v.i.* To inform; peach: usually with *on.* [? Var. of SNATCH]

sniv·el (sniv′əl) *v.i.* **·eled** or **·elled, ·el·ing** or **·el·ling** To cry in a snuffling manner; run at the nose; snuffle; make affectedly tearful professions. — *n.* **1** Discharge from the nose. **2** The act of sniveling. [OE (assumed) *snyflan* < *snyflung* mucus from the nose] — **sniv′el·er** *n.* — **sniv′el·ing** *adj. & n.*

snob (snob) *n.* **1** One who makes birth, wealth, or education the sole criterion of worth. **2** One who is cringing to superiors and overbearing with inferiors in position. **3** *Obs. Brit.* A scab; rat: said of a workingman. [Origin uncertain] — **snob′ber·y** *n.*

snood (snōōd) *n.* **1** A small meshlike cap or bag attached to the back of a hat, worn by women to keep the hair in place. **2** *Scot.* A fillet formerly worn about the hair by an unmarried woman in Scotland as an emblem of virginity. — *v.t.* To bind with a snood, as hair. [OE *snōd*]

snook·er (snŏŏk′ər) *n.* A pool game played with fifteen red object balls (one point each) and six variously colored object balls (2 to 7 points). The player pocketing a red ball may try for any varicolored ball. When all red balls have been pocketed, the varicolored balls must be played in order. Also **snooker pool**. [Origin uncertain]

snoop (snoop) *Colloq. v.i.* To look or pry into things with which one has no business; thrust one's nose into things. — *n.* One who snoops: also **snoop′er**. [<Du. *snoepen* eat goodies on the sly] — **snoop′y** *adj.*

snoot (snoot) *n. Colloq.* A person's nose or face; also, a grimace. [Var. of SNOUT]

snoot·y (snoo′tē) *adj.* **snoot·i·er, snoot·i·est** *U.S. Colloq.* Conceited or supercilious.

snooze (snooz) *Colloq. v.i.* **snoozed, snooz·ing** To sleep lightly; doze. — *n.* A short and light sleep. [Origin uncertain]

snore (snôr, snōr) *v.i.* **snored, snor·ing** To breathe in sleep through the nose and open mouth, with a hoarse rough noise and rattling vibrations of the soft palate. — *n.* An act or the noise of snoring. [Imit.] — **snor′er** *n.*

snor·kel (snôr′kəl) *n.* **1** A long ventilating tube capable of extending from a submerged submarine to the surface of the water. **2** A similar device used for underwater breathing. — *v.i.* To swim with a snorkel. [<G *Schnorkel*] — **snor′kel·er** *n.*

snort (snôrt) *v.i.* **1** To force the air violently and noisily through the nostrils, as spirited horses. **2** To express indignation, ridicule, etc., by a snort. **3** *Colloq.* To laugh with a boisterous outburst. — *v.t.* **4** To utter or express by snorting. **5** To expel by or as by a snort. — *n.* **1** The act or sound of snorting. **2** *Slang* A small drink. [ME *snorten.* ? Related to SNORE.] — **snort′er** *n.*

snot (snot) *n.* **1** Mucus from or in the nose: a vulgar usage. **2** *Slang* A low or mean fellow. [OE *gesnot*]

snot·ty (snot′ē) *adj.* **·ti·er, ·ti·est** **1** Dirtied with snot: a vulgar usage. **2** *Slang* Contemptible; mean; paltry. **3** *Slang* Impudent; proudly conceited; saucy.

snout (snout) *n.* **1** The forward projecting part of a beast's head, especially of a swine's; proboscis; muzzle. **2** Some similar anterior prolongation of the head of an animal, as the rostrum of a gastropod or that of a weevil. **3** Something resembling a hog's snout, such as the nozzle of a hose, a pipe, or the like; a blunt projection, as of rock; or, contemptuously, a person's nose. — *v.t.* To provide with a snout or nozzle. [ME *snūte.* Related to OE *snȳtan* blow the nose.]

snow (snō) *n.* **1** Precipitation taking the form of minute ice crystals formed from an aqueous vapor in the air when the temperature is below 32° F., and usually falling in irregular masses or flakes. ◆ Collateral adjective: *nival.* **2** A similar aggregation that resembles snow in being white or composed of flakes: a *snow* of blossoms. **3** A fall of snow; snowstorm. **4** A winter. **5** *Slang* Cocaine. **6** The pattern of snowlike drops appearing on a television screen as a result of weakened signals in a receiver. — *v.i.* **1** To fall as snow: usually used impersonally: It is *snowing.* — *v.t.* **2** To scatter or cause to fall as or like snow. **3** To cover, enclose, or obstruct with snow: with *in, over, under,* or *up.* [OE *snāw*]

SNOW CRYSTALS

snow·ball (snō′bôl′) *n.* **1** A small round mass of snow compressed to be thrown, as in sport. **2** The guelder-rose (*Viburnum opulus*): so called from its ball-shaped clusters of white flowers: also **snowball bush** or **tree**. — *v.i.* **1** To throw snowballs. **2** To gain in size, importance, etc., as a snowball that rolls over snow. — *v.t.* **3** To throw snowballs at.

snow·bell (snō′bel′) *n.* Any of a genus (*Styrax*) of trees and shrubs of warm regions, bearing showy white flowers in racemes; especially, *S. americana* of the SE United States.

snow·ber·ry (snō′ber′ē) *n. pl.* **·ries 1** A bushy American shrub (*Symphoricarpos albus*) having a loose, leafy cluster of snow-white berries. **2** A West Indian shrub (*Chiococca alba*) of the madder family: it produces the cainca root and is often cultivated in greenhouses for

its white berries: also called *milkberry.*

snow·bird (snō′bûrd′) *n.* **1** A small finch (genus *Junco*) of northern North America, commonly seen in flocks during the winter. **2** The snow bunting. **3** *Slang* A cocaine or heroin addict.

snow blindness An impairment of vision, caused by exposure of the eye to the glare of snow. — **snow′-blind′** *adj.*

snow-bound (snō′bound′) *adj.* Hemmed in or forced to remain in a place by heavy snow; snowed in.

snow bridge A natural arch formation of snow bridging a crevasse.

snow bunting A bird (genus *Plectrophenax*), especially *P. nivalis* of northern regions, the male of which in the breeding season is snow-white with black markings. Also called *snowbird, snowflake.*

snow-bush (snō′boosh′) *n.* A California shrub of the genus *Ceanothus,* as *C. cordulatus,* that bears numerous small white flowers.

snow·drift (snō′drift′) *n.* A pile of snow heaped up by the wind.

snow·drop (snō′drop′) *n.* **1** A low, European, early-blooming bulbous plant (*Galanthus nivalis*) bearing a single, white, drooping flower. **2** The common anemone.

snowdrop tree The silverbell.

snow·fall (snō′fôl′) *n.* **1** A fall of snow. **2** The amount of snow that falls in a given period.

snow fence Portable fencing consisting of thin, closely placed pickets, used to prevent the drifting of snow over roads, fields, etc.

snow·flake (snō′flāk′) *n.* **1** One of the small feathery masses in which snow falls. **2** The snow bunting. **3** Any of certain plants (genus *Leucojum*) allied to and resembling the snowdrop; especially, the **spring snowflake** (*L. vernum*), the **summer snowflake** (*L. aestivum*), and the **autumn snowflake** (*L. autumnale*).

snow goose Any of certain North American geese (genus *Chen*) which breed in the Arctic, snow-white with black primary feathers.

snow leopard The ounce.

snow lily An attractive spring-blooming herb (*Erythronium grandiflorum*) of the lily family native in the Rocky Mountains.

snow line 1 The limit of perpetual snow on the sides of mountains, varying in position with the latitude, the season, and the climate. **2** The extreme distance north and south of the equator within which snow never falls. Also **snow limit**.

snow·mo·bile (snō′mō·bēl′) *n.* Any of various motor vehicles, often with caterpillar treads and steerable front runners, used for traveling over snow, ice, etc. [<SNOW + (AUTO)MOBILE]

snow plant A handsome, blood-red saprophytic herb (*Sarcodes sanguinea*) found in the rich humus of mountain forests in southern California, frequently covered with snow in its blooming season.

snow·shed (snō′shed′) *n.* A timber structure, as one built over portions of a railway, as a protection from snow slides.

snow·shoe (snō′shoo′) *n.* A device, usually a network of sinew in a wooden frame, to be fastened on the foot by a strap across the toes, as a support in walking over snow. — *v.i.* **·shoed, ·shoe·ing** To walk on snowshoes.

SNOWSHOES
a. Sioux Indian. *b.* Iroquois Indian.

snow·slide (snō′slīd′) *n.* An avalanche of snow.

snow·suit (snō′soot′) *n.* A heavy outer garment worn by young children in cold weather, consisting either of one piece or of ankle-length, tight-fitting pants and a snug jacket with a hood.

snow tire An automobile tire with a heavy tread designed to provide more traction on snow or ice.

snow·y (snō′ē) *adj.* **snow·i·er, snow·i·est 1**

Abounding in or full of snow. **2** Snow-white; hence, pure; unblemished; spotless: *snowy* linen. — **snow′i·ly** *adv.* — **snow′i·ness** *n.*

snowy heron The common small white egret (*Egretta thula*) of the southern United States and northern South America.

snub (snub) *v.t.* **snubbed, snub·bing 1** To treat with contempt or disdain; slight. **2** To rebuke or check with a sharp or cutting remark. **3** To stop or check, as a rope in running out, by taking a turnabout a post, etc.; also, to make fast (a boat, etc.) thus. **4** *Obs.* To clip; stunt; nip. — *adj.* Short; pug: said of the nose. — *n.* **1** An act of snubbing; a deliberate and intentional slight. **2** A sudden checking, as of a running rope or cable. **3** A snub nose. [<ON *snubba* snub] — **snub′ber** *n.*

snub-nosed (snub′nōzd′) *adj.* Having a pug or snub nose.

snuff[1] (snuf) *v.t.* **1** To draw in (air, etc.) through the nose. **2** To catch the scent of; smell; sniff; also, to examine by smelling. — *v.i.* **3** To snort; sniff. **4** To inhale air in disdain or anger. — *n.* **1** An act of snuffing; sniff; also, perception by smelling. **2** Resentment expressed by sniffing. [<MDu. *snuffen*]

snuff[2] (snuf) *n.* The charred portion of a wick. — *v.t.* **1** To crop the snuff from (a wick). **2** To put out or extinguish: with *out.* [Cf. G *schnuppe* snuff of a candle]

snuff[3] (snuf) *n.* **1** Pulverized tobacco to be inhaled into the nostrils. **2** The quantity of it taken at one time. **3** Any medicinal powder to be drawn into the nostrils. — **up to snuff** *Colloq.* **1** Meeting the usual standard, as in quality, health, etc. **2** Not easily deceived; sharp-witted. — *v.i.* To take or use snuff. [< Du. *snuf,* appar. short for *snuiftabak,* lit., tobacco to be inhaled]

snuff·box (snuf′boks′) *n.* A small box for carrying snuff about the person.

snuf·fle (snuf′əl) *v.* **·fled, ·fling** *v.i.* **1** To breathe through the nose noisily and with difficulty, as when it is obstructed by mucus. **2** To breathe noisily, as a dog following a scent. **3** To talk through the nose; snivel. — *v.t.* **4** To utter in a nasal tone. — *n.* **1** An act of snuffling, or the sound made by it. **2** *pl.* Nasal catarrh. **3** An affected nasal or emotional voice or twang; hence, cant. [Freq. of SNUFF[1]] — **snuf′fler** *n.* — **snuf′fly** *adj.*

snug (snug) *adj.* **snug·ger, snug·gest 1** Closely and comfortably sheltered, covered, or situated. **2** Close or compact; having room enough, but not too much; comfortable; cozy; also, having everything closely secured; trim: said of a ship. **3** Fitting closely but comfortably, as a garment. See synonyms under COMFORTABLE. — *v.* **snugged, snug·ging** *v.t.* To make snug. — *v.i.* To snuggle; move close. — **to snug down** To make a vessel ready for a storm by reducing sail, etc. [Prob. <LG. Cf. Du. *snugger* clean, smooth.] — **snug′ly** *adv.* — **snug′ness** *n.*

snug·ger·y (snug′ər·ē) *n. pl.* **·ger·ies** A cozy and comfortable place or room.

snug·gle (snug′əl) *v.t. & v.i.* **·gled, ·gling** To lie or draw close; nestle; cuddle: often with *up* or *together.* [Freq. of SNUG, *v.*]

so[1] (sō) *adv.* **1** To this or that or such a degree; to this or that extent; in the same degree, quantity, or proportion: either used alone, the degree being implied or understood: Why *so* long; or followed by or preceded by a dependent expression introduced by *as, that,* or *but.* **2** In this, that, or such a manner; in the same or a like or corresponding manner; in the manner mentioned: often following a clause beginning with *as,* or preceding one beginning with *that.* **3** Just as said, directed, suggested, or implied; also, according to fact: referring to a preceding (sometimes following) statement or suggestion. **4** To an extreme degree; extremely; very. **5** The fact being thus: used as an expletive. **6** About as many or as much as stated; thereabouts: I shall stay a day or *so.* **7** At all events; in any case; at all: now only in the compounds *whosoever, whichsoever,* etc. **8** According to the truth of what is sworn to or averred: said in oaths or asseverations: So help me God. **9** Indeed! elliptical for *Is it so?* **10** To such an extent: used elliptically for *so much:* I love him *so!* **11** Too: used in emphatic denial: You can *so!* **12** Indicative of surprise or disapproval: So there you are. **13** So as to follow immediately;

then; therefore. **14** Let it be that way; very well. — *conj.* **1** With the purpose that: often with *that:* They left the hotel early *so* (that) they would not encounter him. **2** In such a way that; as a consequence of which: He consented, *so* they went away. **3** *Obs.* As. — *interj.* **1** Stay still! **2** Is that so! **3** In nautical parlance, steady! [OE *swā*]

so² (sō) *n. Music* The fifth of the syllables used in singing the scale: also *sol.* [See GAMUT]

soak (sōk) *v.t.* **1** To place in liquid till thoroughly saturated; steep. **2** To wet thoroughly; drench: The rain *soaks* the earth. **3** To take in through or as through pores or interstices; suck up; absorb: with *in* or *up.* **4** *Colloq.* To drink, especially to excess. **5** *U.S. Slang* **a** To charge exorbitantly. **b** To pawn. **c** To strike hard; beat. — *v.i.* **6** To remain or be placed in liquid till saturated. **7** To penetrate; pass: with *in* or *into.* **8** *U.S. Slang* To drink to excess. — *n.* **1** The process or act of soaking, or state of being soaked. **2** Liquid in which something is soaked. **3** ◆ *Slang* A hard drinker; a drinking spree. ◆ Homophone: *soke.* [OE *socian.* Akin to SUCK.]

so-and-so (sō'ən·sō') *n.* **1** An unnamed or undetermined person or thing. **2** *Colloq.* A euphemism for many offensive epithets.

soap (sōp) *n.* **1** A cleansing agent consisting of sodium or potassium salts of fatty acids, made by decomposing the glyceryl esters of fats and oils with alkalies; a detergent. *Hard* soaps are made by the use of soda, while the potash soaps are *soft.* **2** A metallic salt of one of the fatty acids. **3** *U.S. Slang* Money used for sinister purposes; hence, any means of obtaining an end. — *v.t.* To rub with soap; treat with soap. [OE *sāpe*]

soap·bark (sōp'bärk') *n.* **1** The bark of the quillai. **2** The bark of a tropical American shrub (genus *Pithecellobium*), used as a substitute for soap. Also **soapbark tree.**

soap·ber·ry (sōp'ber'ē) *n. pl.* **·ries 1** The fruit of any one of several trees or shrubs (genus *Sapindus*) of the family *Sapindaceae.* **2** Any one of the trees producing it, especially *S. saponaria,* of tropical America and southern Florida, the pulp of whose fruit is used in washing textile fabrics.

soap·box (sōp'boks') *n.* **1** A box or crate for soap. **2** Any box or crate used as a platform by street orators. — **soapbox oratory** Impromptu or crude oratory, marked by vigor rather than logic. Also **soap box.**

soap·box·er (sōp'bok'sər) *n. Colloq.* A loud and ranting speaker; a street-corner orator; a tubthumper.

soap bubble 1 An inflated bubble of soapsuds, forming a hollow globule. **2** Anything attractive but unsubstantial.

soap opera A daytime television or radio drama presented serially and usually dealing with domestic themes of a highly emotional character: so called in reference to the soap commercials often presented on such programs.

soap plant Any of several plants whose bulbs are used for soap, especially a lilywort (*Chlorogalum pomeridianum*) of California.

soap·stone (sōp'stōn') *n.* Steatite: so called from its soapy feel.

soap·suds (sōp'sudz') *n. pl.* Soapy water, especially when worked into a foam.

soap·wort (sōp'wûrt') *n.* A perennial herb (*Saponaria officinalis*) of the pink family having clusters of pink or whitish, often double, flowers: so called because its juice forms a lather with water. Also called *bouncing Bet.*

soar (sôr, sōr) *v.i.* **1** To float aloft through the air on wings, as a bird. **2** To sail through the air without perceptibly moving the wings, as a hawk or vulture. **3** To glide without losing altitude, as an airplane. **4** To rise above any usual level: Prices will *soar* if the ceilings are removed. See synonyms under FLY¹. — *n.* An act of soaring; a range of upward flight. [< F *essorer* < L *ex* out + *aura* breeze, air] — **soar'er** *n.*

sob (sob) *n.* A convulsive, audible inhalation of air under the impulse of painful or hysterical emotion, and usually accompanied with tears; the act or the sound of sobbing; also, any similar sound, as of the wind. Also **sob'-**

bing. — *v.* **sobbed, sob·bing** *v.i.* **1** To weep with audible, convulsive catches of the breath. **2** To make a sound like a sob, as the wind. — *v.t.* **3** To utter with sobs. **4** To bring to a specified condition by sobbing: to *sob* oneself to sleep. [Imit.]

so·be·it (sō·bē'it) *n.* An amen. — *conj.* If so; if only; provided: originally **so be it.**

so·ber (sō'bər) *adj.* **1** Possessing properly controlled faculties; even-tempered; well-balanced; temperate in action or thought. **2** Grave; sedate; realizing the importance and seriousness of life. **3** Not under the influence of an intoxicant; not drunk. **4** Moderate in or abstinent from the use of intoxicating drink. **5** Of subdued or modest color. — *v.t. & v.i.* To make or become sober. [< OF *sobre* < L *sobrius*] — **so'ber·ly** *adv.* — **so'ber·ness** *n.* *Synonyms (adj.):* abstemious, abstinent, calm, collected, cool, dispassionate, moderate, quiet, regular, sane, staid, steady, temperate, unimpassioned, unintoxicated. See SAD, SANE¹, SEDATE, SERIOUS. *Antonyms:* agitated, crazy, drunk, drunken, ecstatic, excited, extravagant, extreme, frantic, furious, immoderate, impassioned, intemperate, intoxicated, passionate, unreasonable.

so·bri·e·ty (sō·brī'ə·tē) *n. pl.* **·ties 1** The state of being sober. **2** Moderateness in temper or conduct; sedateness; seriousness; temperance. See synonyms under ABSTINENCE. [< L *sobrietas, -tatis* < *sobrius* sober]

so·bri·quet (sō'bri·kā) *n.* A fanciful or humorous appellation; a nickname: also spelled *soubriquet.* [< F; ult. origin unknown]

sob sister *U.S. Slang* A journalist who writes mawkishly sentimental news stories.

sob story *Slang* A sad personal narrative told to elicit pity or sympathy.

soc·age (sok'ij) *n.* The feudal tenure of land by certain determinate services other than knight-service; hence, later, tenure by any fixed service other than military. [< *soc,* var. of SOKE] — **soc'ag·er** *n.*

so-called (sō'kôld') *adj.* Called as stated; generally styled thus: usually implying a doubtful or improper form.

soc·cer (sok'ər) *n.* A form of football in which the ball is propelled toward the opponents' goal by kicking or by striking with the head or body, other than the shoulders or arms, the goalkeepers being the only players allowed to use their hands and arms in deflecting or carrying the ball: officially called *association football.* [Alter. of ASSOCIATION]

so·cia·ble (sō'shə·bəl) *adj.* **1** Inclined to seek company; social. **2** Agreeable in company; companionable; genial. **3** Characterized by or affording occasion for agreeable conversation and friendliness. See synonyms under AMICABLE, FRIENDLY. — *n.* **1** An informal social gathering: also *social.* **2** A four-wheeled open carriage with facing seats. [< F < L *sociabilis* < *socius* friend] — **so'cia·bly** *adv.*

so·cial (sō'shəl) *adj.* **1** Of or pertaining to society or its organization; relating to persons as living in society or to the public as an aggregate body: *social* life, *social* questions. **2** Disposed to hold friendly intercourse with others; sociable. **3** Constituted to live in society; having developed or fulfilled tendencies to organize in society as a race or people: *social* beings. **4** Of or pertaining to public welfare: *social* insurance. **5** Pertaining to or characteristic of persons of fashion: *social* register. **6** Living in communities: *social* ants or bees; aggregate; compound; colonial. **7** Grouping compactly, as individual plants; partly or wholly covering a large area of land: said of plant species. **8** Venereal: *social* disease: a euphemism. **9** Pertaining to or between allies or confederates, as the wars waged by Rome in 90–89 B.C., and by Athens in 357–355 B.C. against their allies. See synonyms under FRIENDLY, GOOD. — *n.* A sociable. [< L *socialis* < *socius* ally]

social climber A person who attempts to become friendly with prominent or wealthy people.

social contract *Philos.* The supposed original agreement by which individuals were united in political associations for their mutual protection, the surrender of their individual

sovereignty having been made not through force but by mutual consent: a theory of Hobbes, Locke, Rousseau, etc.

so·cial·ism (sō'shəl·iz'əm) *n.* Public collective ownership or control of the basic means of production, distribution, and exchange, with the avowed aim of operating for use rather than for profit, and of assuring to each member of society an equitable share of goods, services, and welfare benefits: as a system of social and economic organization planned, attempted, or achieved through various methods—in **Utopian** or **Christian Socialism,** through cooperative communal groups holding all things in common (approximating the philosophic anarchism of Thoreau, Tolstoy, and Kropotkin, and the communalism and commensalism of the early and undivided church); in **Guild Socialism,** through organization of producer groups and the professions in syndicalist guilds to be represented in a federal legislative body; in **Fabian** or **British Labour Party Socialism,** through parliamentary democracy using gradualist evolutionary processes; in **Marxist–Leninist State Socialism,** through revolution, expropriation, and dictatorship of the so-called proletariat, in short, Communism. Compare MIXED ECONOMY. — **creeping socialism** Anything considered as a gradual or piecemeal encroachment upon the system of private property and free enterprise through state action: used as an epithet.

so·cial·ite (sō'shəl·īt) *n.* A person prominent in fashionable society.

so·cial·ize (sō'shəl·īz) *v.* **·ized, ·iz·ing** *v.t.* **1** To convert from an anti-social to a social attitude; make friendly, cooperative, or sociable. **2** To arouse to an interest in humanity. **3** To convert or adapt to social uses or needs. **4** To put under group control; especially, to regulate according to socialistic principles. — *v.i.* **5** To take part in social activities. Also *Brit.* **so'cial·ise.** — **so'cial·i·za'tion** *n.*

socialized medicine A system proposing to supply the public with medical care at nominal cost, by regulating services and fees, by government subsidies to physicians and medical projects, or by cooperative projects.

social register A directory of persons prominent in fashionable society.

social science 1 The body of knowledge that relates to man as a member of society, or of any component part of society, as the state, family, or any systematized human institution. **2** Any field of knowledge dealing with human society, as economics, history, sociology, education, politics, ethics, etc.

social security 1 Any public system which provides welfare services for members of the community in need. **2** *U.S.* A Federal program of old-age and unemployment insurance, public assistance to the blind, disabled, and dependent, and maternal and child welfare services, administered by the **Social Security Administration.**

social settlement An institution or settlement, usually in the poor quarters of a large city, devoted to the aid and instruction of the poor.

social studies Social science, as a part of the curriculum in elementary and high school.

social work Any clinical, social, or recreational service for improving community welfare, as through health clinics, recreational facilities, aid to the poor and the aged, etc. — **social worker**

so·ci·e·ty (sə·sī'ə·tē) *n. pl.* **·ties 1** The system of community life, in which individuals, ordinarily in a territorial establishment, form a continuous and regulatory association for their mutual benefit and protection. **2** The body of persons composing such a community. **3** A number of persons in a community regarded as forming a class having certain common interests, status, etc.: high *society.* **4** The fashionable or cultured portion of a community, considered as constituting a class. **5** A body of persons associated for a common purpose or object; an association: a medical *society.* **6** *U.S.* In some States, an incorporated religious congregation. **7** A club or fraternity. **8** Association based on friendship or intimacy; companionship; company: to enjoy the *society* of working men. **9** *Ecol.* A group of plants or animals living together under the same physiographic conditions and influences and characterized by a principal species. See synonyms under ACQUAINTANCE, ALLIANCE, ASSOCIATION, CLASS. [< OF *societe* < L *societas, -tatis* < *socius* a friend]

socio- *combining form* **1** Society; social: *sociology*. **2** Sociology; sociological: *sociobiology*. [< F < L *socius* a companion]

so·ci·o·bi·ol·o·gy (sō′sē·ō·bī·ol′ə·jē, sō′shē-) *n.* The study of social behavior in animals and humans, as determined by the biological characteristics. —**so′ci·o·bi·ol′o·gist** *n.*

so·ci·o·ec·o·nom·ic (sō′sē·ō·ek′ə·nom′ik, sō′shē-, -ē′kə-) *adj.* Social and economic: considered as a unit based upon the interrelationship of social and economic factors. —**so′ci·o·ec′o·nom′i·cal·ly** *adv.*

so·ci·o·ge·net·ic (sō′sē·ō·jə·net′, -shē·ō-) *adj.* Of or pertaining to the origin, development, and preservation of human society in any of its aspects.

so·ci·o·lin·guis·tics (sō′sē·ō·ling·gwis′tiks, sō′shē-) *n.* The study of language as a social instrument and in its social context, in which the principles and investigative techniques of both sociology and linguistics are employed. [< SOCIO- + LINGUISTICS] —**so′ci·o·lin·guis′tic** *adj.* —**so′ci·o·lin·guis′ti·cal·ly** *adv.*

so·ci·ol·o·gy (sō′sē·ol′ə·jē, sō′shē-) *n.* The science that treats of the origin and evolution of human society and social phenomena, the progress of civilization, and the laws controlling human institutions and functions. —**so′ci·ol′o·gist** *n.*

so·ci·om·e·try (sō′sē·om′ə·trē, sō′shē-) *n.* The study of the interrelationships of individuals within a community or social group, especially as expressed by attitudes of acceptance or rejection. —**so′ci·o·met′ric** (-ə·met′rik) *adj.*

so·ci·o·path (sō′sē·ə·path, sō′shē-) *n.* One who suffers from a mental disorder that causes a lack of moral restraint or responsibility toward fellow members of society.

sock¹ (sok) *n.* **1** A short stocking. **2** The light shoe worn by comic actors in the Greek and Roman drama; hence, comedy. Compare BUSKIN. [OE *socc* < L *soccus* slipper]

sock² (sok) *Slang v.t.* To strike or hit, especially with the fist; to punch. —*n.* A hard blow. [Origin unknown]

sock·et (sok′it) *n.* **1** *Mech.* A cavity or an opening specially adapted to receive and hold some corresponding piece or fixture: the *socket* for an electric-light bulb. **2** *Anat.* A cavity or hollowed depression for the reception of an organ or part. —*v.t.* To furnish with, hold by, or put into a socket. [< AF *soket,* dim. of OF *soc* a plowshare < Celtic]

sock·eye (sok′ī) *n.* The red salmon of the Pacific coast *(Oncorhynchus nerka),* highly valued as a food fish. [Alter. of Salishan *sukkegh*]

Soc·ra·tes (sok′rə·tēz), 469?–399 B.C., Athenian philosopher; the chief character in the dialogs of Plato: accused of impiety and innovation, he was imprisoned, condemned to death, and forced to drink an infusion of hemlock.

Socratic method The dialectic method of instruction by questions and answers, as adopted by Socrates in his disputations, leading either to a foreseen conclusion or to admissions damaging to an opponent.

sod (sod) *n.* **1** Grassy surface soil held together by the matted roots of grass and weeds; sward; also, a piece of such soil. **2** Grassy ground; lawn; the earth or soil. —**the old Sod** Ireland. —*v.t.* **sod·ded, sod·ding** To cover with sod. [< MDu. *sode* piece of turf]

so·da (sō′də) *n.* **1** Any of several white alkaline compounds widely used in medicine, industry, and the arts, especially sodium bicarbonate (baking soda), sodium carbonate, sodium hydroxide, and sodium oxide. **2** Soda alum. **3** Soda salts. **4** Soda water; also, a soft drink containing carbonated water, flavoring, and, sometimes, ice-cream. **5** In faro, the first card to appear face up in the dealing box before the start of play. [< Med. L < Ital. *soda (cenere)* solid (ash) < L *solidus*]

soda alum *Chem.* A double salt of sodium sulfate and aluminum.

soda ash Crude sodium carbonate.

soda biscuit 1 A biscuit leavened with sodium bicarbonate. **2** A soda cracker.

soda cracker A thin, crisp cracker made with yeast-leavened dough containing soda.

soda fountain 1 An apparatus from which soda water is drawn, usually containing receptacles for sirups, ice, and ice-cream. **2** A counter at which soft drinks and ice-cream are dispensed.

soda jerk *U.S. Slang* A clerk who serves at a soda fountain.

soda lime A mixture made from sodium hydroxide and calcium oxide.

so·da·lite (sō′də·līt) *n.* A vitreous, translucent silicate of sodium and aluminum, with some chlorine. [< SODA + -LITE]

so·dal·i·ty (sō·dal′ə·tē) *n. pl.* **·ties** A brotherhood or fraternity; especially, a brotherhood for devotional or charitable purposes. [< L *sodalitas, -tatis* < *sodalis* companion]

soda water 1 An effervescent drink consisting of water strongly charged under pressure with purified carbon dioxide gas, formerly generated from sodium bicarbonate: often flavored with a fruit sirup. **2** Alkaline water as found in natural reservoirs or springs.

sod·den (sod′n) *adj.* **1** Soaked with moisture: *sodden* ground. **2** Doughy; soggy, as bread, biscuits, etc. **3** Flabby and pale; flaccid, especially from dissipation: said of persons or their features. **4** Dull; dreary: a *sodden* life. —*v.t.* & *v.i.* To make or become sodden. [ME *sothen,* orig. pp. of SEETHE] —**sod′den·ly** *adv.* —**sod′den·ness** *n.*

sod house A dwelling built of sod or turf walls, often having a wooden roof: used by early settlers on the prairies.

so·di·um (sō′dē·əm) *n.* A soft, light, very reactive metallic element (symbol Na, atomic number 11) constituting about 2.6% of the lithosphere, usually in the form of sodium chloride, an essential element in all living systems. See PERIODIC TABLE. [< NL < Med. L. *soda* SODA]

Sodium Am·y·tal (am′i·tôl, -tal) Proprietary name of a white, hygroscopic powder, $C_{11}H_{17}O_2N_2Na$, used in medicine as a sedative and hypnotic.

sodium benzoate *Chem.* A white, odorless, amorphous, granular or crystalline powder, $NaC_7H_5O_2$, used as an antipyretic, antirheumatic, antiseptic, as an food preservative, and to disguise taste, as of poor-quality food.

sodium bicarbonate *Chem.* A white crystalline compound, $NaHCO_3$, of alkaline taste, used in medicine and cookery; baking soda.

sodium carbonate *Chem.* A strongly alkaline compound, Na_2CO_3: in crystalline hydrated form known as washing soda, $Na_2CO_3 \cdot 10H_2O$, used in the manufacture of glass, soap, paper, etc., and in medicine and photography.

sodium chlorate *Chem.* A white crystalline compound, $NaClO_3$, used as a mordant, insecticide, weed-killer, and as an oxidizing agent.

sodium chloride Common salt, NaCl.

sodium hydroxide *Chem.* A white, caustic, fusible compound, NaOH: used in various solutions in chemistry, metallurgy, as a bleaching agent, etc.; caustic soda.

sodium hyposulfite 1 Sodium thiosulfate. **2** A colorless crystalline salt, $Na_2S_2O_4$.

sodium nitrate A white compound, $NaNO_3$, used in the manufacture of nitric acid and as a manure. It occurs abundantly in nature.

sodium peroxide *Chem.* A yellowish solid, Na_2O_2, used in combination with other chemicals as a bleaching agent.

sodium phosphate *Chem.* A sodium salt of phosphoric acid, Na_2HPO_4, crystallizing in the presence of water: the tribasic form is used as a laxative and also as a fixing agent in textile coloring.

sodium propionate *Chem.* A colorless, crystalline, water-soluble compound, $NaC_3H_5O_2$, used in medicine as a fungicide and to retard bacterial and mold growth in foods.

sodium silicate A material used in making artificial stone and in various industrial processes: known also as *soluble glass* or *waterglass.*

sodium sulfide *Chem.* A bleaching and decontaminating agent, Na_2S, especially effective against mustard gas.

Sod·om (sod′əm) In the Bible, a city on the Dead Sea, destroyed with Gomorrah because of the wickedness of its people. *Gen.* xiii 10.

sod·om·y (sod′əm·ē) *n.* Carnal copulation between male persons or with beasts. [< OF *sodomie* < LL *Sodoma* Sodom, to whose people this practice was imputed]

so·ev·er (sō·ev′ər) *adv.* To or in some conceivable degree: used in generalizing and emphasizing what follows: a word often added to *who, which, what, where, when, how,* etc., to form the compounds *whosoever,* etc., giving them specific force. Often used separately: *how* great *soever* he might be.

so·fa (sō′fə) *n.* A wide seat, upholstered and having a back and raised ends. [< F < Arabic *soffah* a part of a floor raised to form a seat]

sofa bed A sofa which may be opened up to form a large bed.

so·far (sō′fär) *n.* A system for locating stranded ships or aircraft by means of underwater sound waves, set up by depth charges released by the survivors and detected by hydrophones operated from ground stations. [< SO(UND) F(IXING) A(ND) R(ANGING)]

sof·fit (sof′it) *n. Archit.* The under side of a staircase, entablature, lintel, archway, or cornice. [< F *soffite* < Ital. *soffita* < L *suffixus.* Doublet of SUFFIX.]

So·fi·a (sō′fē·ə, sō·fē′ə) The capital of Bulgaria, in the western part. *Bulgarian* **So·fi·ya** (sō′fē·yä).

soft (sôft, soft) *adj.* **1** Being or composed of a substance whose shape is changed easily by pressure, without fracture; impressible; pliable, ductile, or malleable; easily worked: *soft* wood: opposed to *hard.* **2** Smooth and delicate to the touch: *soft* skin. **3** Gentle in its effect upon the ear; not loud or harsh. **4** Mild in any mode of physical action; gentle; bland: a *soft* breeze; a *soft* ripple. **5** Of subdued coloring or delicate shading; not glaring or abrupt: *soft* tints; *soft* outline. **6** Gentle; conciliatory; expressing mildness or sympathy; courteous: *soft* words. **7** Giving or enjoying rest; placid: *soft* sleep. **8** Easily or too easily touched in feeling; tender; sympathetic: a *soft* heart. **9** Incapable of bearing hardship; susceptible; tender; delicate: *soft* muscles. **10** Of yielding character; weak; effeminate. **11** *Colloq.* Of weak intellect; also, yielding to emotion; maudlin. **12** Free from mineral salts which prevent the detergent action of water and soap: said of water. **13** Bituminous, as opposed to anthracite: said of coal. **14** Describing *c* and *g* when articulated fricatively as in *cent* and *gibe:* opposed to *hard;* also, voiced and weakly articulated; also, palatalized, as certain consonants in the Slavic languages. **15** *Colloq.* Easy: a *soft* job. **16** *Scot. & Brit. Dial.* Characterized by moisture or thawing: said of the weather. See synonyms under BLAND, SUPPLE. —*n.* **1** That which is soft; softness; a soft part or material. **2** *Colloq.* One who is soft or foolish; a softy. —*adv.* **1** Softly. **2** Quietly; gently. —*interj. Archaic* Proceed softly; be quiet or slow. [OE *sōfte*] —**soft′ly** *adv. & interj.* —**soft′ness** *n.*

soft·ball (sôft′bôl′, soft′-) *n.* A variation of baseball, requiring a smaller diamond, a larger, softer ball, ten players on a team, and seven innings for play.

soft-boiled (sôft′boild′) *adj.* **1** Boiled, as an egg, for only a short while, so that the yolk and albumen are soft or semiliquid. **2** *Colloq.* Mild in disposition: lenient.

soft clam The common long clam *(Mya arenaria)* of the north Atlantic coast.

soft coal Bituminous coal.

soft-cov·er (sôft′kuv′ər, soft′-) *adj.* Designating a book having flexible sides, as of paper: contrasted to *hard-cover.*

soft drink A nonalcoholic beverage, as sweetened soda water, ginger ale, etc.

sof·ten (sôf′ən, sof′-) *v.t.* & *v.i.* To make or become soft or softer. See synonyms under ALLAY, ALLEVIATE, CHASTEN, TEMPER. —**sof′ten·er** *n.*

softening of the brain 1 *Pathol.* Degeneration of the brain tissue, especially as resulting from paresis; encephalomalacia. **2** *Colloq.* Dementia.

soft-finned (sôft′find′, soft′-) *adj. Zool.* Having fins whose membrane is supported on flexible or jointed rays: opposed to *spiny-finned.*

soft focus *Phot.* A slightly blurred effect obtained by an imperfect focusing of the lens upon a scene or object.

soft·head (sôft'hed', soft'-) *n.* A foolish or simple person. — **soft'-head'ed** *adj.*

soft-heart·ed (sôft'här'tid, soft'-) *adj.* Tender-hearted; merciful. — **soft'heart'ed·ly** *adv.* — **soft'heart'ed·ness** *n.*

soft-ped·al (sôft'ped'l, soft'-) *v.t.* **·aled** or **·alled, ·al·ing** or **·al·ling** 1 To mute the tone of by depressing the soft pedal. 2 *Colloq.* To render less emphatic; moderate; tone down.

soft pedal A pedal which mutes the tone, as in a piano.

soft sell *U.S. Colloq.* The use of subtle, non-insistent methods of salesmanship.

soft-shell (sôft'shel', soft'-) *adj.* 1 Having a soft shell, as certain clams, or a crab or lobster after shedding its shell: also **soft'-shelled'.** 2 *U.S. Colloq.* Somewhat moderate in opinion or doctrine; somewhat liberal; not hidebound: a *soft-shell* Baptist. — *n.* A crab which has lately shed its shell: also **soft-shelled crab.**

soft-shelled turtle Any member of a family (*Trionychidae*) of turtles having a long snout and a soft, leathery shell, especially *Trionyx* (or *Amyda*) *spinifera*, common from the Gulf States to the St. Lawrence River.

soft soap 1 Fluid or semifluid soap. 2 *Colloq.* Flattery; blarney.

soft·ware (sôft'wâr', soft'-) *n.* In a digital computer, any of the programs designed to control various aspects of the operation of the machine, such as input and output operations: distinguished from *hardware* (def. 4).

soft·wood (sôft'wŏŏd', soft'-) *n.* 1 A coniferous tree or its wood. 2 Any soft wood, or any tree with soft wood.

soft·y (sôf'tē, sof'-) *n. pl.* **soft·ies** *Colloq.* 1 An extremely sentimental person. 2 A weak or effeminate man or boy; one not inured to hardship; a sissy.

sog·gy (sog'ē) *adj.* **·gi·er, ·gi·est** 1 Saturated with water or moisture; wet and heavy; soaked. 2 Heavy: said of pastry. 3 Soft; boggy: said of land. 4 Dull; logy: said of a person or an animal. Also **sog·ged** (sog'id). [< dial. E *sog* a swamp, bog < Scand. Cf. dial. Norw. *soggjast* get wet.] — **sog'gi·ness** *n.*

soi-di·sant (swä-dē-zän') *adj. French* Self-styled; pretended: usually implying false pretense.

soi·gné (swä-nyā') *adj. French* Cared for; well-groomed.

soil[1] (soil) *n.* 1 Finely divided rock mixed with decayed vegetable or animal matter, constituting that portion of the surface of the earth in which plants grow. 2 The ground in general; native land; country. 3 A mixture of lampblack, glue, and water used in plumbing. See synonyms under LAND. [< OF *soile, sueil* < L *solium* a seat, mistaken for *solum* the ground]

soil[2] (soil) *v.t.* 1 To make dirty; smudge. 2 To disgrace; defile. 3 *Obs.* To manure. — *v.i.* 4 To become dirty. See synonyms under BLEMISH, DEFILE[1], POLLUTE, STAIN. — *n.* 1 That which soils; foul matter; a foul spot; hence, a taint. 2 Manure: confused in use with *soil*[1]. 3 A slough or marshy place in which a hunted boar takes refuge; hence, water or a wet place resorted to by other game. [< OF *soillier,* ult. < L *suculus,* dim. of *sus* a pig]

soil·age (soi'lij) *n.* Green crops for feeding animals.

soil·ure (soi'yər) *n.* Soiling, or the condition of being soiled.

soi·rée (swä-rā', *Fr.* swà·rā') *n.* A party or reception given in the evening. Also **soi·ree'.** [< F < *soir* evening]

so·ja (sō'jə, sō'yə) *n.* The soybean. [< NL < Du. *soya* the soybean]

so·journ (sō'jûrn, sō·jûrn') *v.i.* To stay or dwell temporarily; abide for a time. See synonyms under ABIDE. — *n.* (sō'jûrn) A temporary residence or stay, as of one in a foreign land. [< OF *sojorner, sojourner,* ult. < L *sub-* under + *diurnus* daily] — **so'journ·er** *n.*

soke (sōk) *n.* 1 In feudal law, a franchise, privilege, or liberty; jurisdiction; a privilege to administer justice within a certain territory, as a manor. 2 The district within which such privilege was exercised. ◆ Homo-

phone: *soak.* [< Med. L *soca* < OE *sōcn* jurisdiction]

sol·ace (sol'is) *v.t.* **·aced, ·ac·ing** 1 To comfort or cheer in trouble, grief, or calamity; console. 2 To alleviate, as grief; soothe; assuage; mitigate. — *n.* Comfort in grief, trouble, or calamity; also, that which supplies such comfort or alleviation: also **sol'ace·ment.** [< OF *solacier, solasier* < *solas* comfort < L *solacium*] — **sol'ac·er** *n.*

so·lan (sō'lən) *n.* The gannet, a bird related to the pelicans. Also **so·land** (sō'lənd, -lən), **solan goose.** [< ON *súla* the gannet]

sol·a·na·ceous (sol'ə·nā'shəs) *adj. Bot.* Pertaining or belonging to a widely distributed family (*Solanaceae*) of frequently narcotic poisonous plants, the nightshade family, having colorless juice and alternate simple leaves. The family includes belladonna, tobacco, eggplant, and potato. [< NL < L *solanum* nightshade]

so·lan·der (sə·lan'dər) *n.* A hinged case or box, usually in the form of a book, adapted to hold a variety of objects, as jewelry, cigarettes, writing materials, pamphlets, maps, rare books and the like. [after Daniel C. *Solander,* 1736–82, English inventor born in Sweden]

so·la·no (sō·lä'nō) *n.* A hot, violent, south-easterly wind of the Mediterranean. [< Sp. < L *sol* sun]

so·la·num (sə·lā'nəm) *n.* Any of a genus (*Solanum*) of herbs and shrubs, the nightshades, typifying the family *Solanaceae,* especially *S. tuberosum,* the common potato. [< NL < L, nightshade]

so·lar (sō'lər) *adj.* 1 Pertaining to, proceeding from, or connected with the sun. 2 Affected, determined, or measured by the sun. 3 Operated by the action of the sun's rays: a *solar* engine. [< L *solaris* < *sol* sun]

solar constant The amount of solar energy falling on one square centimeter of the earth's surface at normal incidence, having a mean value of 1.92 small calories per minute.

solar energy Energy radiated by the sun, the primary source of chemical and other forms of energy, but utilized directly in only minor applications.

so·lar·im·e·ter (sō'lə·rim'ə·tər) *n.* An instrument for measuring solar radiation.

so·lar·i·um (sō·lâr'ē·əm) *n. pl.* **·i·a** (-ē·ə) A room or enclosed porch exposed to the sun's rays, as in a sanatorium. [< L]

so·lar·i·za·tion (sō'lər·ə·zā'shən, -ī·zā'-) *n.* 1 Exposure to the sun's rays. 2 *Phot.* Injury to a sensitized film resulting from overexposure to strong light, or from overprinting.

so·lar·ize (sō'lə·rīz) *v.* **·ized, ·iz·ing** *v.t.* 1 To affect or injure by the action of the sun's rays. 2 *Phot.* To overexpose. — *v.i.* 3 *Phot.* To be overexposed.

solar month A twelfth of a solar year; the time during which the sun is passing through one of the signs of the zodiac.

solar myth A primitive etiological story explaining symbolically some natural phenomenon of the sun; also, a folk tale arising among an agricultural people explaining or symbolizing the power or influence of the sun.

solar panel a group of solar cells used as a power source, e.g., in a spacecraft *Cf* SOLAR SAIL.

solar plexus 1 *Anat.* The large network of the sympathetic nervous system, found behind the stomach, and containing important ganglia serving the abdominal viscera. 2 *Colloq.* The pit of the stomach.

solar system The sun and the heavenly bodies that revolve about it.

solar wind The streams of charged particles emanating outward in all directions from the surface of the sun.

sol·der (sod'ər) *n.* 1 A fusible metal or alloy used for joining metallic surfaces or margins: applied in a melted state, either as a **hard solder,** melting only at a red heat, or as a **soft solder,** melting below a red heat. 2 Anything that unites or cements. — *v.t.* 1 To unite or repair with solder. 2 To join together; bind. — *v.i.* 3 To work with solder. 4 To be united by or as by solder. [< OF *soldure < souder* make hard < L *solidare < solidus* firm, hard] — **sol'der·er** *n.*

sol·dier (sōl'jər) *n.* 1 A person serving in an army. 2 A private in an army, as distinguished from a commissioned officer. 3 A brave,

skilful, or experienced warrior. 4 One who serves loyally in any cause. 5 *Colloq.* One who makes a show of working but does little; a shirker; malingerer. 6 *Entomol.* **a** An asexual form (neuter or worker) of a termite or white ant, in which the head and jaws are largely developed, and whose office is to defend the community. **b** A similar neuter of certain true ants. See synonyms under ARMY. — *v.i.* 1 To be a soldier; perform military service. 2 To make a show of working; shirk; malinger. [< OF < *soude* pay, wages < LL *solidus.* See SOL[2].]

sol·dier·ly (sōl'jər·lē) *adj.* Like a true soldier; brave; martial. See synonyms under WARLIKE.

soldier of fortune A military adventurer; a soldier who serves where fortune summons him.

sol·dier·y (sōl'jər·ē) *n. pl.* **·dier·ies** 1 Soldiers collectively. 2 Military service.

sole[1] (sōl) *n.* 1 The bottom surface of the foot. ◆ Collateral adjectives: *plantar, volar*[2]. 2 The bottom surface of a shoe, boot, etc. 3 The lower part of a thing, or the part on which it rests when standing; especially, the bottom part of a plowshare. 4 The bottom part of the head of a golf club. — *v.t.* **soled, sol·ing** 1 To furnish with a sole; resole, as a shoe. 2 In golf, to allow (the clubhead) to rest flat on the ground, just behind the ball. ◆ Homophone: *soul.* [< OF < Med. L *sola,* var. of L *solea* a sandal]

sole[2] (sōl) *n.* 1 Any of several flatfishes allied to the flounders, having a small mouth and small eyes set close together on one side of the head; especially, the common **European sole** (*Solea solea*), highly esteemed as food, and the **American sole** (genus *Achirus*), common on the Atlantic coast of the United States. 2 One of various flounders, as *Psettichthys melanostictus,* a food fish of the Pacific coast of the United States. ◆ Homophone: *soul.* [< OF < L *solea*]

sole[3] (sōl) *adj.* 1 Being alone or the only one; existing or acting without another; only; individual. 2 *Law* **a** Unmarried; single: feme *sole* (an unmarried woman). **b** Having exclusive rights; absolute: opposed to *joint*: a *sole* tenant. 3 *Archaic* Solitary. See synonyms under SOLITARY. ◆ Homophone: *soul.* [< OF *sol* < L *solus* alone]

sol·e·cism (sol'ə·siz'əm) *n.* 1 A violation of grammatical rules or of the approved idiomatic usage of language. 2 Any impropriety or incongruity. [< L *soloecismus* < Gk. *soloikismos* < *soloikos* speaking incorrectly < *Soloi,* a Cilician town whose people spoke a substandard Attic dialect] — **sol'e·cist** *n.* — **sol·e·cis'tic** or **·ti·cal** *adj.*

sole·ly (sōl'lē) *adv.* 1 By oneself or itself alone; singly. 2 Completely; entirely. 3 Without exception; exclusively.

sol·emn (sol'əm) *adj.* 1 Characterized by majesty, mystery, or power; exciting grave or serious thought; impressive; awe-inspiring. 2 Characterized by ceremonial observances; religious; sacred. 3 Marked by gravity; serious; earnest; also, affectedly serious. 4 *Law* Done in due form of law; executed formally: a *solemn* protest. 5 *Obs.* Of great reputation, dignity, or importance. 6 *Obs.* Somber; sober: said of color. See synonyms under AWFUL, SEDATE, SERIOUS. [< OF *solemne* < L *solemnis*] — **sol'em·ness, sol'emn·ness** *n.* — **sol'emn·ly** *adv.*

so·lem·ni·ty (sə·lem'nə·tē) *n. pl.* **·ties** 1 The state or quality of being solemn; solemn feeling; gravity; reverence. 2 A rite expressive of religious reverence; also, any ceremonious observance. 3 A thing of a solemn or serious nature. 4 Mock seriousness; affected gravity. 5 *Law* A formality to be seriously observed and requisite to the validity or legality of an act. See synonyms under SACRAMENT.

sol·em·nize (sol'əm·nīz) *v.t.* **·nized, ·niz·ing** 1 To perform as a ceremony or solemn rite, or according to legal or ritual forms: to *solemnize* a marriage. 2 To dignify as with a ceremony; celebrate. 3 To make solemn, grave, or serious. Also *Brit.* **sol'em·nise.** See synonyms under CELEBRATE. — **sol·em·ni·za'tion** *n.* — **sol'em·niz'er** *n.*

Solemn League and Covenant See under COVENANT.

so·le·noid (sō′lə·noid) *n. Electr.* A conducting wire in the form of a cylindrical coil or helix, capable of setting up a magnetic field by the passage through it of an electric current. [<Gk. *sōlēn* a channel + -OID] — **so′le·noi′·dal** *adj.* — **so′le·noi′dal·ly** *adv.*

SOLENOID

sol·fa·ta·ra (sōl′fä·tä′rä) *n. Geol.* An area or phase of volcanic action characterized by the escape of steam, various gases, and sublimates. [<Ital., a dormant crater near Naples, Italy < *solfo* sulfur] — **sol′fa·ta′ric** *adj.*

sol·feg·gio (sōl·fej′ō) *n. pl.* **·feg·gi** (-fej′ē) or **·feg·gios** *Music* **1** A singing exercise of runs, broken chords, etc., sung either to different syllables or all to the same syllable or vowel. **2** Solmization. [<Ital. < *solfa.* See SOL-FA.]

sol·fe·ri·no (sōl′fe·rē′nō) *n.* **1** A bright purplish red. **2** Fuchsin. [from *Solferino*; named in honor of a battle fought there in 1859]

so·lic·it (sə·lis′it) *v.t.* **1** To ask for earnestly; seek to obtain by persuasion or entreaty. **2** To beg or entreat (a person) persistently. **3** To influence to action; tempt; especially, to entice (one) to an unlawful or immoral act. — *v.i.* **4** To make petition or solicitation. See synonyms under ASK, PLEAD. [<OF *solliciter* <L *sollicitare* agitate]

so·lic·i·tor (sə·lis′ə·tər) *n.* **1** A person who does any kind of soliciting; especially, one who solicits gifts of money or subscriptions to magazines. **2** The legal advisor to certain branches of the public service. **3** In England, a lawyer who may advise clients or who prepares cases for presentation in court, but who may appear as an advocate in the lower courts only. See BARRISTER. Also **so·lic′i·ter.** — **so·lic′i·tor·ship** *n.*

so·lic·i·tous (sə·lis′ə·təs) *adj.* **1** Full of anxiety or concern, as for the attainment of something. **2** Full of eager desire; willing. See synonyms under URGENT. — **so·lic′i·tous·ly** *adv.* — **so·lic′i·tous·ness** *n.*

so·lic·i·tude (sə·lis′ə·tōōd, -tyōōd) *n.* **1** The state of being solicitous; uneasiness of mind. **2** That which makes one solicitous. See synonyms under ANXIETY, CARE.

sol·id (sol′id) *adj.* **1** Having its constituent particles so firmly coherent as to resist stress; compact, firm, and unyielding: opposed to *fluid.* **2** Substantial; firm and stable. **3** Filling the whole of the space occupied by its apparent form; completely filled; not hollow. **4** Having no aperture or crevice; compact. **5** Manifesting strength and firmness; not weak or sickly; sound. **6** Characterized by reality; substantial or satisfactory. **7** Exhibiting united and unbroken characteristics, opinions, etc.; being or acting in unison; unanimous: the *solid* vote; This county is *solid* for the Democratic party; also, blindly or unreasonably partisan. **8** Financially sound or safe. **9** *U.S. Colloq.* Certain and safe in approval and support: They were *solid* with the boss. **10** Having or relating to the three dimensions of length, breadth, and thickness. **11** Written without a hyphen: said of a compound word. See SOLIDEME. **12** Cubic in /shape: a *solid* yard. **13** Unadulterated; unalloyed: *solid* gold. **14** Carrying weight or conviction: a *solid* argument. **15** Serious; reliable; exhibiting sound judgment: a *solid* citizen. **16** Continuous; unbroken: a *solid* hour. **17** *Printing* Having no leads or slugs between the lines; not open. See synonyms under FIRM¹, HARD, IMPENETRABLE. — *n.* **1** A mass of matter of which the shape cannot be changed permanently and greatly without fracture. **2** A magnitude that has length, breadth, and thickness, as a cone, cube, pyramid, prism, or sphere. [<F *solide* <L *solidus*] — **sol′id·ly** *adv.* — **sol′id·ness** *n.*

sol·i·da·go (sol′ə·dā′gō) *n. pl.* **·gos** Any of a large North American genus (*Solidago*) of perennial plants of the composite family; a goldenrod: the State flower of Alabama, Kentucky, and Nebraska. [<NL <L *solidare* strengthen; with ref. to its alleged curative powers]

sol·i·dar·i·ty (sol′ə·dar′ə·tē) *n. pl.* **·ties** Coherence and oneness in nature, relations, or interests, as of a race, class, etc.

sol·i·deme (sol′ə·dēm) *n.* A solid compound word. Compare HYPHEME. [<SOLID + -*eme,* as in *phoneme*]

solid geometry That part of geometry which includes all three dimensions of space in its reasoning.

so·lid·i·fy (sə·lid′ə·fī) *v.t. & v.i.* **·fied, ·fy·ing** **1** To make or become solid, hard, firm, or compact, as water crystallizing into ice. **2** To bring or come together in unity. — **so·lid′i·fi·ca′tion** *n.*

so·lid·i·ty (sə·lid′ə·tē) *n. pl.* **·ties** **1** The quality or state of being solid; the property of occupying space; extension in the three dimensions of space; incompressibility. **2** Mental, moral, or financial soundness; substantial or reliable character or quality; firm standing; stability. **3** *Aeron.* The ratio of the total blade area of a rotor or propeller to the area of the disk swept by the blades. **4** *Geom.* Cubic contents; volume.

solid state physics That branch of physics which deals with the physical properties of solids, especially as exhibited by atoms and molecules when in the solid state. It includes the study of crystal structure, elasticity, and friction, semiconductors and plastics, defects in materials, thermal properties, and a wide range of electrical and magnetic phenomena.

sol·i·dus (sol′ə·dəs) *n. pl.* **·di** (-dī) **1** A gold coin of the Byzantine Empire: first issued under Constantine, it remained the standard unit of currency during the Middle Ages, when it was called a *bezant.* **2** A medieval coin, equal to 12 denarii: often called *shilling.* **3** The sign (/) used to divide shillings from pence: 10/6 (10s. 6d.), being originally the long *f* written for shilling: sometimes also used instead of a horizontal line to express fractions: 3/4. See VIRGULE. [<LL]

sol·i·fid·i·an (sol′ə·fid′ē·ən) *n.* One who maintains that faith alone, without works, is the one requisite to salvation. — *adj.* Maintaining that faith alone is necessary to insure salvation; also, pertaining to such belief. [<L *solus* alone + *fides* faith]

so·lil·o·quy (sə·lil′ə·kwē) *n. pl.* **·quies** A talking to oneself, regardless of the presence or absence of others; a monolog. [<LL *soliloquium* <L *solus* alone + *loqui* talk]

sol·i·on (sol′ī′ən) *n. Physics* A small electrochemical cell so constructed that the movement of ions in solution serves to indicate minute changes in temperature, pressure, sound or light waves, acceleration, and other external conditions: used as an electronic control device. [<*ion*(s *in*) *sol*(*ution*)]

sol·ip·sism (sol′ip·siz′əm) *n.* The theory or belief that only knowledge of the self is possible, and that, for each individual, the self itself is the only thing really existent, and therefore that reality is subjective. [<L *solus* alone + *ipse* self] — **sol′ip·sist** *n.*

sol·i·taire (sol′ə·târ′) *n.* **1** A diamond or other gem set alone. **2** One of many games, especially of cards, played by one person. **3** A bird (*Pezophaps solitarius*) somewhat resembling the dodo but more slender and graceful: formerly a native of Réunion but now extinct. [<F <L *solitarius* solitary]

sol·i·tar·y (sol′ə·ter′ē) *adj.* **1** Living, being, or going alone. **2** Made, done, or passed alone: a *solitary* life. **3** Unfrequented by human beings; secluded; lonely; desolate. **4** Lonesome; lonely. **5** Single; one: Not a *solitary* soul was there. — *n. pl.* **·tar·ies** A hermit; recluse; one who lives alone. [<L *solitarius* < *solus* alone] — **sol′i·tar′i·ly** *adv.* — **sol′i·tar′i·ness** *n.*

Synonyms (adj.): alone, companionless, deserted, lone, lonely, lonesome, only, single, sole, unaccompanied, unattended. *Antonyms:* manifold, many, multiplied, multitudinous, myriad, numerous.

sol·i·ter·ra·ne·ous (sol′ə·tə·rā′nē·əs) *adj.* Pertaining to the joint influence of solar and terrestrial forces, especially in relation to meteorological phenomena. [<L *sol, solis* the sun + *terra* the earth]

sol·i·tude (sol′ə·tōōd, -tyōōd) *n.* **1** Loneliness; seclusion. **2** A deserted or lonely place; hence, a desert. [<OF <L *solitudo* < *solus* alone]

Synonyms: isolation, loneliness, privacy, retirement. See RETIREMENT, SECLUSION.

sol·mi·za·tion (sol′mə·zā′shən) *n. Music* The

use of syllables as names for the notes or tones of the scale. The syllables now commonly used are *do, re, mi, fa, sol, la, ti.* [<SOL + MI]

so·lo (sō′lō) *n. pl.* **·los** or **·li** (-lē) **1** A musical composition or passage for a single voice or instrument, with or without accompaniment. **2** Any of several card games, especially one in which the player who bids to take the highest number of tricks plays alone against the others. **3** Any performance accomplished alone or without assistance. — *adj.* **1** Composed or written for, or executed by, a single voice or instrument; performed as a solo. **2** Done by a single person alone: a *solo* flight. — *v.i.* **·loed, ·lo·ing** To fly an airplane alone, especially for the first time. [<Ital. <L *solus* alone]

So·lo man (sō′lō) *Paleontol.* A species of early man (*Homo soloensis*) identified from a group of skulls found near the Solo river at Ngandong, Java, in 1931: it is thought to be an evolutionary advance over Pithecanthropus. Also called *Ngandong man.*

Sol·o·mon′s–seal (sol′ə·mənz·sēl′) *n.* Any one of several rather large perennial herbs of the lily family (genus *Polygonatum*), having tubular, six-toothed flowers and rootstocks marked at intervals by circular scars.

So·lon (sō′lən), 638?–558? B.C., Athenian lawgiver; hence, **solon,** any wise lawmaker. — **So·lo·ni·an** (sə·lō′nē·ən) *adj.*

so long *Colloq.* Good-by.

sol·pu·gid (sol·pyōō′jid) *n.* A predatory, spiderlike arachnid (order *Solpugida*) of warm climates that hides by day. [<L *solpuga, soli-puga,* a kind of venomous ant or spider]

sol·stice (sol′stis) *n.* **1** *Astron.* The time of year when the sun is at its greatest distance from the celestial equator, either north or south, and seems to pause before returning on its course; either the **summer solstice,** about June 22 in the northern hemisphere, or the **winter solstice,** about December 22. **2** A culminating or high point; epoch; limit. [<F <L *solstitium* < *sol* sun + *sistere* cause to stand] — **sol·sti·tial** (sol·stish′əl) *adj.*

sol·u·ble (sol′yə·bəl) *adj.* **1** Capable of being uniformly dissolved in a liquid: Sugar is *soluble* in water. **2** Susceptible of being solved or explained. [<OF <L *solubilis* < *solvere* solve, dissolve] — **sol′u·bly** *adv.*

soluble cotton Nitrocellulose which is soluble in acetone, amyl acetate, ethanol, and certain other solvents: used in making nail polish and similar lacquers.

soluble glass Sodium silicate.

so·lum (sō′ləm) *n.* That part of a soil profile above the parent material in which the processes of soil formation take place; the soil proper. [<L *solum* ground]

so·lus (sō′ləs) *adj. Latin* Alone: used in stage directions. — **so·la** (sō′lə) *adj. fem.*

sol·ute (sol′yōōt, sōl′ōōt) *n.* The substance dissolved in a solution as distinguished from the solvent.

so·lu·tion (sə·lōō′shən) *n.* **1** A homogeneous mixture formed by dissolving one or more substances, whether solid, liquid, or gaseous, in another substance, usually a liquid but sometimes a solid or a gas. **2** Any homogeneous mixture of which the solute is uniformly dispersed through the solvent, and whose composition may undergo continuous variation within certain limits. **3** The act or process by which such a mixture is made. **4** The act or process of explaining, settling, or disposing, as of a difficulty, problem, or doubt. **5** *Law* Payment or satisfaction of a claim or debt. **6** *Med.* The crisis of a disease; termination of a disease with critical signs. **7** *Math.* The answer to a problem; also, the method of finding the answer. **8** Separation; disruption: the *solution* of continuity. [<OF <L *solutio, -onis* <*solutus,* pp. of *solvere* dissolve]

solution pressure *Chem.* The pressure caused by the tendency of atoms or molecules to dissolve. In the case of metals it produces the current in a primary artery.

sol·u·tive (sol′yə·tiv) *adj.* **1** Loosening; laxative. **2** Soluble.

Sol·vay process (sol′vā) A process of making soda by treating a concentrated solution of common salt with ammonia and carbon dioxide, yielding sodium bicarbonate, which is converted into soda by heat, carbon dioxide and water being expelled. [after Ernst *Solvay,* 1838–1922,

Belgian chemist]

solve (solv) *v.t.* **solved, solv·ing** To arrive at or work out the correct explanation or solution of; find the answer to; resolve. [< L *solvere* solve, loosen] —**solv′er** *n.*
Synonyms: clear, decipher, do, elucidate, explain, guess, interpret, resolve, understand, unfold. *Antonyms:* confound, confuse, perplex.

sol·vent (sol′vənt) *adj.* **1** Having means sufficient to pay all debts; having more assets than liabilities. **2** Having the power of dissolving. —*n.* **1** That which solves. **2** A substance, generally a liquid, capable of dissolving other substances; that in which another substance is dissolved. **3** A medicine used for dissolving morbid concretions or obstructions in or upon some organ. [< L *solvens, -entis,* ppr. of *solvere* solve, loosen]

sol·vol·y·sis (sol·vol′ə·sis) *n. Chem.* Any of various double-decomposition reactions similar to hydrolysis, as the reaction of mercuric chloride with liquid ammonia to form a basic salt. [< L *solvere* loosen + Gk. *lysis* a loosening] — **sol·vo·lyt·ic** (sol′və·lit′ik) *adj.*

so·ma (sō′mə) *n. pl.* **·ma·ta** (-mə·tə) *Biol.* The body of any organism, excluding the germ, or germ plasm. [< Gk. *sōma* body]

So·ma·lia (sō·mä′lyə) An independent republic in eastern Africa comprising the former United Nations Trust Territory of Somalia, administered by Italy, and British Somaliland; about 270,000 square miles; capital, Mogadishu. — **So·ma′li** *adj. & n.*

so·ma·tal·gi·a (sō′mə·tal′jē·ə) *n. Pathol.* Pain due to physical causes: distinguished from *psychalgia.* [< SOMAT(O)- + Gk. *algos* a pain]

so·mat·ic (sō·mat′ik) *adj. Biol.* **1** Of or relating to the body, as opposed to the spirit; physical; corporeal. **2** Of or pertaining to the framework or walls of a body, as distinguished from the viscera; parietal. **3** Pertaining to those elements or processes of an organism which are concerned with the maintenance of the individual as distinguished from the reproduction of the species: *somatic* cells. [< Gk. *sōmatikos* < *sōma* body]

somatic cell *Biol.* A cell that assists with maintenance of the body rather than reproduction of the species: distinguished from *germ cell.*

somato- *combining form* Body; of, pertaining to, or denoting the body: *somatology.* Also, before vowels, **somat-.** [< Gk. *sōma, sōmatos* the body]

so·ma·to·gen·ic (sō′mə·tō·jen′ik) *adj. Biol.* Originating in the soma or body cells of an organism: said of variations due to the direct influence of environment: *somatogenic* or acquired characters. Also **so′ma·to·ge·net′ic** (-jə·net′ik). — **so′ma·to·gen′e·sis** *n.*

so·ma·tol·o·gy (sō′mə·tol′ə·jē) *n.* **1** The science of organic bodies, especially of the human body: embracing anatomy and physiology. **2** The branch of anthropology that treats of the physical nature of man. [< SOMATO- + -LOGY] — **so′ma·to·log′ic** (-tō·loj′ik), **so′ma·to·log′i·cal** *adj.* —**so′ma·to·log′i·cal·ly** *adv.* —**so′ma· tol′o·gist** *n.*

so·ma·to·plasm (sō′mə·tə·plaz′əm) *n. Biol.* The protoplasm making up the somatic cells.

so·ma·to·pleure (sō′mə·tō·ploŏr′) *n. Biol.* In the embryonic development of vertebrates, the outer of the two layers into which the mesoblast divides, together with its investing epiblast. [< SOMATO- + Gk. *pleura* side]

so·ma·to·tro·pin (sō′mə·tō·trō′pin) *n. Biol.* The hormone that regulates bodily growth, produced in the pituitary gland.

som·ber (som′bər) *adj.* **1** Partially deprived of light or brightness; dusky; murky; gloomy. **2** Somewhat melancholy; producing or denoting gloomy feelings; depressing. Also **som′bre,** *Obs.* **som′brous.** See synonyms under DARK, SAD. [< F *sombre;* ult. origin uncertain] —**som′ber·ly** *adv.* —**som′ber·ness** *n.*

som·bre·ro (som·brâr′ō) *n. pl.* **·ros** A broadbrimmed hat, usually of felt, much worn in Spain, Latin America, and the southwestern United States: humorously called a *ten-gallon hat.* [< Sp. < *sombra* shade]

some (sum) *adj.* **1** Of indeterminate quantity, number, or amount. **2** Limited in degree or amount; moderate. **3** Conceived or thought of, but not definitely known: *some* person. **4** *Logic* Part (more than one) but not all of a class. **5** *U.S.*

Slang Of considerable account; worthy of notice; extraordinary: That was *some* birthday party. — *pron.* **1** A certain undetermined quantity or part; a portion. **2** Certain particular ones not definitely known or not specifically designated. — *adv.* **1** *U.S. Colloq.* In an approximate degree; as nearly as may be estimated; about: *Some* eighty people were present. **2** *Slang* Somewhat. ◆ Homophone: **sum.** [OE *sum* some]

-some[1] *suffix of adjectives* Characterized by, or tending to be (what is indicated by the main element): *blithesome, frolicsome, darksome.* [OE *-sum* like, resembling]

-some[2] *suffix of nouns* A body: *chromosome, merosome.* Also spelled **-soma.** [< Gk. *sōma* a body]

-some[3] *suffix of nouns* A group consisting of (a specified number): *twosome, foursome.* [< SOME]

some·bod·y (sum′bod′ē, -bəd·ē) *pron.* A person unknown or unnamed: *Somebody* loves me. —*n. pl.* **·bod·ies** A person of consequence or importance: She thinks herself a *somebody.*

some·day (sum′dā′) *adv.* At some future time.

some·how (sum′hou′) *adv.* In some way or in some manner not explained.

some·one (sum′wun′, -wən) *pron.* Some person; somebody. —*n.* A somebody.

som·er·sault (sum′ər·sôlt′) *n.* A leap in which a person turns heels over head and lights on his feet. —*v.i.* To perform a somersault. Also spelled **summersault, summerset.** Also **som′er·set.** [< OF *sombresault,* alter. of *sobresault,* ult. < L *supra* above + *saltus* a leap]

so·mes·the·sis (sō′məs·thē′sis) *n.* A diffuse, generalized awareness of the body and of bodily sensation. Also **so′mes·the′si·a** (-thē′zhē·ə, -zhə). [< Gk. *sōma* body + *esthesis*] —**so′mes· thet′ic** (-thet′ik) *adj.*

some·thing (sum′thing) *n.* **1** A particular thing indefinitely conceived or stated. **2** Some portion or quantity. **3** A person or thing of importance. —*adv.* Somewhat: archaic except in special phrases, as **something like.**

some·time (sum′tīm′) *adv.* **1** At some future time not precisely stated; eventually. **2** At some indeterminate time or occasion. —*adj.* Former; quondam: a *sometime* student at Oxford.

some·times (sum′tīmz′) *adv.* **1** At times; occasionally. **2** *Obs.* Formerly; once.

some·way (sum′wā′) *adv.* In some way or other; somehow. Also **some way, some′ways′.**

some·what (sum′hwot′, -hwət) *n.* **1** An uncertain quantity or degree; something. **2** An individual or thing of consequence. —*adv.* In some degree.

some·where (sum′hwâr′) *adv.* **1** In, at, or to some place unspecified or unknown. **2** In one place or another. **3** In or to some existent place: opposed to *nowhere.* **4** Approximately. —*n.* An unspecified or unknown place.

some·wise (sum′wīz′) *adv.* In some way or other: obsolete except in the phrase, **in somewise.**

so·mite (sō′mīt) *n. Zool.* A serial segment of the body of an animal, especially of an annelid or arthropod. [< Gk. *sōma* body + -ITE[1]] —**so·mi·tal** (sō′mə·tal), **so·mit·ic** (sō·mit′ik) *adj.*

Somme (sôm) A river in northern France, flowing 150 miles west to the English Channel; scene of battles in World War I (1916, 1918), and in World War II (1940, 1944).

som·me·lier (sô·me·lyā′) *n. French* A wine steward.

som·nam·bu·late (som·nam′byə·lāt) *v.* **·lat·ed, ·lat·ing** *v.i.* To walk or wander about while asleep. —*v.t.* To walk over or through while asleep. [< L *somnus* sleep + AMBULATE]

som·nam·bu·lism (som·nam′byə·liz′əm) *n.* The act or state of walking during sleep. Also **som·nam′bu·la′tion.** —**som·nam′bu·lant** (-lənt) *adj.* —**som·nam′bu·list** *n.* —**som·nam′bu·lis′tic** *adj.*

somni- *combining form* Sleep; of or pertaining to sleep: *somnifacient.* [< L *somnus* sleep]

som·ni·fa·cient (som′nə·fā′shənt) *adj.* Promoting sleep; hypnotic. —*n.* A drug which induces sleep. [< SOMNI- + -FACIENT]

som·nif·er·ous (som·nif′ər·əs) *adj.* Tending to

produce sleep; soporiferous; narcotic. Also **som·nif′ic.** [< SOMNI- + -FEROUS]

som·nil·o·quy (som·nil′ə·kwē) *n.* **1** The act of talking when asleep, especially in mesmeric sleep. **2** The words so spoken. [< SOMNI- + L *loqui* speak] —**som·nil′o·quist** *n.*

som·no·lent (som′nə·lənt) *adj.* **1** Inclined to sleep; drowsy. **2** Tending to induce drowsiness. [< F < L *somnolentus* < *somnus* sleep] — **som′no·lent·ly** *adv.*

son (sun) *n.* **1** A male child considered with reference to either parent or to both parents. **2** Any male descendant. **3** One who occupies the place of a son, as by adoption, marriage, or regard. **4** A person regarded as a native of a particular country or place. **5** A male person who is characterized or influenced by some quality or thing or by a being representing some quality or character: a *son* of liberty; *sons* of Belial. Homophone: **sun.** [OE *sunu*]

so·nance (sō′nəns) *n.* **1** A sound, as of music; also, a tune or air. **2** The state or quality of being sonant.

so·nant (sō′nənt) *adj.* **1** Sounding; resonant. **2** *Phonet.* Voiced: opposed to *surd, voiceless.* —*n. Phonet.* **1** A voiced speech sound. **2** A syllabic sound; in the Indo-European languages, a sonorant. [< L *sonans, -antis,* ppr. of *sonare* resound]

so·nar (sō′när) *n.* **1** A method of using underwater sound waves, at either audible or ultrasonic frequencies, for sounding, navigating, range finding, detection of submerged objects, communication, etc. **2** The equipment for accomplishing the transmission or reception of underwater sound waves. —*adj.* Of, or pertaining to, the equipment, personnel, or methods employed in underwater acoustic signaling. [< SO(UND) NA(VIGATION AND) R(ANGING)]

so·na·ta (sə·nä′tä) *n. Music* A composition for one or two instruments, written in three or four movements, each of which is distinct from the others in tempo and mood but akin to them in style and key. [< Ital. < *sonare* sound]

sonata form *Music* The outline upon which the construction of a movement, specifically the first, of a sonata, quartet, symphony, etc., is based. A movement written in sonata form falls into three sections, called *exposition,* or statement of themes, *development,* and *recapitulation.*

so·na·ti·na (son′ə·tē′nə) *n. pl.* **·ti·ne** (-tē′nä) *Music* A short or easy sonata. [< Ital., dim. of *sonata* SONATA]

son·der (zon′dər) *n. Naut.* A class of small yachts, of which the sum of the water-line length, extreme beam, and extreme draft must not be greater than thirty-two feet. Also **son′der·class′** (-klas′, -kläs′). [Short for G *sonderklasse* < *sonder* particular + *klasse* class]

sone (sōn) *n. Physics* A unit of loudness, equivalent to a simple tone having a frequency of 1,000 cycles per second at 40 decibels above the threshold of hearing. [< L *sonus* sound]

song (sông, song) *n.* **1** The rendering of vocal music; more widely, any melodious utterance, as of a bird. **2** A musical composition for the voice or for several voices. **3** A short poem whether intended to be sung or not; a lyric or ballad. **4** Poetry; verse. **5** A mere trifle: to sell something for a *song.* [OE] —**song′less** *adj.*

song and dance 1 A short theatrical act consisting of a song and dance, often having no connection with the rest of the program; especially, a vaudeville act. **2** *Colloq.* Any highly interesting or entertaining statement of no pertinence to the subject under consideration; a rigmarole.

song·bird (sông′bûrd′, song′-) *n.* A bird that utters a musical call; an oscine bird.

son·ic (son′ik) *adj.* **1** Of, pertaining to, determined or affected by sound: *sonic* vibrations. **2** Having a speed approaching that of sound. [< L *sonicus* < *sonus* sound]

so·nif·er·ous (sō·nif′ər·əs) *adj.* Producing or conducting sound. [< L *sonus* sound + -FEROUS]

son-in-law (sun′in·lô′) *n. pl.* **sons-in-law** The husband of one's daughter.

son·net (son′it) *n.* **1** A poem of fourteen decasyllabic (or rarely) octosyllabic lines, originally composed of an octave and a sestet, properly expressing two successive phases of a single thought or sentiment. In the **Petrarchan,** or **Italian, sonnet** the rime scheme for the octave is *abbaabba,* followed by two or three other rimes in the sestet, with a slight change in thought after the octave. In the **Elizabethan,** or **Shakespearean, sonnet** the rime scheme is *ababcdcdefefgg.* **2** A short poem; an amatory lyric. See synonyms under SONG. —*v.t.* To celebrate in sonnets. —*v.i.* To compose sonnets. [<F <Ital. *sonnetto* <Provençal *sonet,* dim. of *son* a sound <L *sonus*]

son·o·gram (son'ō-gram) *n.* Echogram.

so·no·rant (sə-nôr'ənt, -nō'rənt) *n. Phonet.* A voiced consonant of relatively high resonance, as (l), (r), (m), and (n), capable of constituting a syllable.

so·nor·i·ty (sə-nôr'ə-tē, -nor'-) *n.* Sonorous quality or state; resonance. Also **so·no'rous·ness.**

so·no·rous (sə-nôr'əs, -nō'rəs) *adj.* **1** Productive or capable of sound vibrations; sounding. **2** Loud and full-sounding; resonant. **3** *Phonet.* Sonant. [<L *sonorus* <*sonare* resound] —**so·no'rous·ly** *adv.*

soon (sōn) *adv.* **1** At a future or subsequent time not long distant; shortly. **2** Without delay; in a speedy manner; also, with ease; readily. **3** With willingness or readiness: usually with *would as, had as,* etc. **4** In good season; early. **5** *Obs.* At once; immediately. [OE *sōna* immediately]

soon·er (sōo'nər) *n. U.S. Slang* **1** A person who goes before the appointed time to take up free public land, and thus obtains one of the most desirable sites. **2** One who makes an unfair and premature start.

soot (sōot, sŏot) *n.* A black substance, essentially carbon from the combustion of wood or coal, as deposited on the inside of chimneys and other surfaces in contact with smoke. —*v.t.* To soil or cover with soot. [OE *sōt*]

sooth (sōoth) *Archaic adj.* **1** True; real. **2** Soothing; smooth. —*n.* Truth. Also spelled *soth.* [OE *sōth*] —**sooth'ly** *adv.*

soothe (sōoth) *v.* **soothed, sooth·ing** *v.t.* **1** To restore to a quiet or normal state; calm. **2** To mitigate, soften, or relieve, as pain or grief. **3** *Obs.* To yield assent to; agree with. —*v.i* **4** To afford relief; have a calming or relieving effect. See synonyms under ALLAY, TEMPER, TRANQUILIZE. [OE *sōthian* verify <*sōth* truth] —**sooth'er** *n.*

sooth·ing (sōo'thing) *adj.* Calming; quieting, as a sedative; pacifying. —**sooth'ing·ly** *adv.*

sooth·say (sōoth'sā') *v.i* **·said, ·say·ing** To announce the future, as a soothsayer. —**sooth'·say'ing** *n.*

sooth·say·er (sōoth'sā'ər) *n.* **1** One who claims to have supernatural insight and to be able to foretell events. **2** *Obs.* A truthful person: the original meaning.

soot·y (sōot'ē, sŏot'ē) *adj.* **soot·i·er, soot·i·est 1** Blackened or stained by soot. **2** Producing or consisting of soot. **3** Black like soot. —**soot'i·ly** *adv.* —**soot'i·ness** *n.*

sooty grouse A blue grouse *(Dendrogapus fuliginosus).*

sop (sop) *v.* **sopped, sop·ping** *v.t.* **1** To dip or soak in a liquid. **2** To drench. **3** To take up by absorption: often with *up.* —*v.i.* **4** To be absorbed; soak in. **5** To be or become saturated or drenched. —*n.* **1** Anything softened in liquid, as bread. **2** Anything given to pacify, as a bribe. **3** Any soggy mass. [OE *sopp*] —**sop'py** *adj.*

soph·ism (sof'iz-əm) *n.* **1** A false argument intentionally used to deceive. **2** The doctrine or method of the sophists. See synonyms under SOPHISTRY. [<L *sophisma* <Gk., ult. <*sophos* wise]

soph·ist (sof'ist) *n.* **1** A philosopher; a learned man; a thinker. **2** One who argues cleverly but fallaciously or unnecessarily minutely. —*adj.* Pertaining to the art or method of sophists, or to sophistry. [<L *sophista* <Gk. *sophistēs,* ult. <*sophos* wise]

Soph·ist (sof'ist) *n.* **1** A member of a certain school of early Greek philosophy, preceding the Socratic school. **2** One of the later Greek teachers of philosophy and rhetoric, who acquired great skill in subtle disputation under logical forms.

so·phis·ti·cate (sə-fis'tə-kāt) *v.* **·cat·ed, ·cat·ing** *v.t.* **1** To make less simple or ingenuous in mind

or manner; render worldly-wise or artificial. **2** To mislead or corrupt (a person). **3** To adulterate. **4** To falsify (a text, statement, etc.) by unauthorized or deceptive alterations. —*v.i.* **5** To indulge in sophistry; be sophistic. —*n.* (-kit, -kāt) A sophisticated person. [<Med. L *sophisticatus,* pp. of *sophisticare* <*sophisticus* sophistic] —**so·phis'ti·ca'tor** *n.*

so·phis·ti·cat·ed (sə-fis'tə-kā'tid) *adj.* **1** Worldly-wise; deprived of natural simplicity; disillusioned. **2** Pretentiously wise; possessing superficial information. **3** Of a kind that appeals to the worldly-wise. **4** Very complicated in design, capabilities, etc.: said of mechanical and electronic devices.

soph·is·try (sof'is-trē) *n. pl.* **·tries 1** Subtly fallacious reasoning or disputation. **2** The art or methods of the Greek Sophists.
Synonyms: casuistry, chicanery, evasion, fallacy, hair-splitting, paralogism, prevarication, quibbling, sophism, subterfuge, trickery.

Soph·o·cles (sof'ə-klēz), 495?-406 B.C., Athenian tragic poet. —**Soph·o·cle'an** *adj.*

soph·o·more (sof'ə-môr, -mōr) *n.* In American high schools, colleges, and universities having a four-year course, a second-year student. [Earlier *sophomer* a dialectician <*sophom.* var. of SOPHISM (def.1), because they studied dialectics; later infl. in meaning by Gk. *sophos* wise + *mōros* a fool]

soph·o·mor·ic (sof'ə-môr'ik, -môr'-) *adj.* Of, pertaining to, or like a sophomore; hence, marked by a shallow assumption of learning or by empty grandiloquence; immature; callow. Also **soph'o·mor'i·cal.** —**soph'o·mor'i·cal·ly** *adv.*

-sophy *combining form* Knowledge pertaining to a (specified) field: *theosophy.* [<Gk. *sophia* wisdom]

so·po·rif·ic (sō'pə-rif'ik, sop'ə-) *adj.* **1** Causing or tending to cause sleep. **2** Drowsy; sleepy; characterized by lethargy. —*n.* A medicine that produces sleep.

sop·ping (sop'ing) *adj.* Wet through; drenched; soaking.

so·pran·o (sə-pran'ō, -prä'nō) *n. pl.* **so·pran·os** or **so·pra·ni** (sə-prä'nē) **1** A woman's or boy's voice of the highest range, usually extending from middle C upward about two octaves. **2** The music intended for such a voice; the treble. **3** A person having a treble or high-range voice, or singing such a part. —*adj.* Of or pertaining to a soprano voice or part. [<Ital. <*sopra* above <L *supra.* Related to SOVEREIGN.]

so·ra (sôr'ə, sō'rə) *n.* A small grayish-brown North American rail *(Porzana carolina),* esteemed as food. Also **sora rail.** [? <N. Am. Ind.]

sor·be·fa·cient (sôr'bə-fā'shənt) *adj.* Conducive to absorption; absorptive. —*n.* A medicine that promotes absorption. [<L *sorbere* absorb + -FACIENT]

Sor·bonne (sôr-bôn') **1** A former theological college founded in Paris by Robert de Sorbon in 1255-59. **2** The seat of the faculties of literature and science of the University of Paris.

sor·cer·er (sôr'sər-ər) *n.* A wizard; conjurer; magician. —**sor'cer·ess** *n. fem.*

sor·cer·y (sôr'sər-ē) *n. pl.* **·cer·ies 1** Pretended employment of supernatural agencies; magic; witchcraft. **2** Any remarkable or inexplicable means of accomplishment; witchery. [<OF *sorcerie* <*sorcier* <L *sors* fate] —**sor'cer·ous** *adj.* —**sor'cer·ous·ly** *adv.*
Synonyms: divination, enchantment, incantation, magic, necromancy, spell, voodoo, witchcraft.

sor·did (sôr'did) *adj.* **1** Of, pertaining to, or actuated by a low desire for gain; mercenary. **2** Of degraded character; vile; base; squalid. **3** Of a dull, dirty, or muddy hue. **4** Foul: the old sense. See synonyms under AVARICIOUS, BASE². [<L *sordidus* squalid] —**sor'did·ly** *adv.* —**sor'did·ness** *n.*

sore (sôr, sōr) *n.* **1** A place on an animal body where the skin or flesh is bruised, broken, or inflamed; an ulcer or diseased spot. **2** A painful memory; distressing evil; trouble; grief; controversy. —*adj.* **sor·er, sor·est 1** Morbidly tender; having a sore or sores. **2** Pained or distressed in mind; aggrieved; touchy. **3** Arousing painful feelings; irritating; distressing. **4** Causing extreme distress; severe; also,

very great; extreme: *He was in sore need of money.* **5** *Colloq.* Offended; aggrieved; angry. —*adv. Archaic* Sorely. [OE *sār*] —**sore'ness** *n.*

so·re·di·um (sə-rē'dē-əm) *n. pl.* **·di·a** (-dē·ə) *Bot.* A scalelike structure of algal cells in a lichen, enveloped in a network of hyphae and capable of independent vegetative growth. Also **so·rede** (sō'rēd). [<NL <Gk. *sōros* a heap]

sore·head (sôr'hed', sōr'-) *U.S. Slang n.* A disgruntled or offended person. —*adj.* Dissatisfied; discontented.

sore·ly (sôr'lē, sōr'-) *adv.* **1** Grievously; distressingly. **2** Greatly; in high degree: *His aid was sorely needed.*

sor·ghum (sôr'gəm) *n.* **1** A stout canelike tropical grass (genus *Sorghum*) cultivated for its saccharine juice and as fodder, especially any of the varieties of *Sorghum vulgare.* **2** Molasses prepared from the sweet juices of the plant. [<NL <Ital. *sorgo,* ult. <L *Syricus* of Syria, where originally grown]

so·ri (sôr'ī, sō'rī) Plural of SORUS.

sor·i·cine (sôr'ə-sīn, -sin, sor'-) *adj.* Pertaining or belonging to a subfamily (*Soricinae*) typical of a family (*Soricidae*) of small, mouselike mammals, the shrews, widely distributed in the northern hemisphere; shrewlike. [<NL <L *sorex, soricis* a shrew]

so·ri·tes (sō-rī'tēz, sō-) *n. Logic* A form of compound syllogism made up of successive coordinate members: Bucephalus is a horse; a horse is a quadruped; a quadruped is an animal; therefore Bucephalus is an animal. [<L <Gk. *sōreitēs* <*sōros* a heap] —**so·rit'·i·cal** (-rit'i·kəl) *adj.*

so·ror·ate (sôr'ə-rāt, sō'rə-rāt) *n. Anthropol.* The marriage of a man with the sister or sisters of his wife, or with other close female relatives. Compare LEVIRATE. [<L *soror* a sister]

so·ror·i·cide (sə-rôr'ə-sīd) *n.* **1** The killing of a sister. **2** One who kills a sister. [<LL *sororicidium* <*soror* a sister + *caedere* kill; def. 2 <L *sororicida*]

so·ror·i·ty (sə-rôr'ə-tē, -ror'-) *n. pl.* **·ties** A sisterhood; specifically, a women's national or local association having chapters in a secondary school, college, or university. [<Med. L *sororitas, -tatis,* <L *soror* a sister]

so·ro·sis (sə-rō'sis) *n. Bot.* A type of multiple fruit consisting of a fleshy mass formed by the merging of many flowers, as in the mulberry. [<NL <Gk. *sōros* a heap]

sorp·tion (sôrp'shən) *n.* Any process by which one substance takes up and holds the molecules of another substance, as by absorption or adsorption. [<NL *sorptio, -onis* <L *sorbere*]

sor·rel¹ (sôr'əl, sor'-) *n.* **1** Any of several low perennial herbs (genus *Rumex*) with acid leaves, especially the common sorrel (*R. acetosa*). **2** The wood sorrel (genera *Oxalis* or *Xanthoxalis*). [<F *surele* <*sur* <OHG, sour]

sor·rel² (sôr'əl, sor'-) *n.* **1** A reddish- or yellowish-brown color. **2** An animal of this color. **3** A buck of the third year. Also spelled *sorel.* [<OF *sorel* <*sor,* a hawk with red plumage]

sorrel tree An American tree (*Oxydendrum arboreum*) of the heath family, with drooping clusters of white flowers and sour evergreen leaves.

sor·row (sor'ō, sôr'ō) *n.* **1** Pain or distress of mind because of loss, injury, or misfortune, the commission of sin, or sympathy with suffering; grief. **2** An event that causes pain or distress of mind; affliction; a trial; misfortune; woe. **3** The expression of grief; lamentation; mourning. See synonyms under GRIEF, MISFORTUNE, REPENTANCE. —*v.i.* To feel sorrow; grieve; lament; be sad. See synonyms under MOURN. [OE *sorg* care] —**sor'row·er** *n.*

sor·row·ful (sor'ə-fəl, sôr'-) *adj.* Sad; unhappy; mournful. See synonyms under BAD¹, PITIFUL, SAD. —**sor'row·ful·ly** *adv.* —**sor'row·ful·ness** *n.*

sor·ry (sor'ē, sôr'ē) *adj.* **·ri·er, ·ri·est 1** Grieved or pained; affected by sorrow from any cause. **2** Causing sorrow; melancholy; dismal. **3** Pitiable or worthless; poor; paltry. **4** Painful; grievous. See synonyms under BAD, SAD. [OE *sārig* <*sār* sore] —**sor'ri·ly** *adv.* —**sor'ri·ness** *n.*

sort (sôrt) *n.* **1** Any number or collection of persons or things characterized by the same or similar qualities; a kind; species; class; set.

2 Form of being or acting; character; nature; quality; also, manner; way; style. **3** *Printing* A character or type considered as a portion of a font: usually in the plural. **4** *Obs.* Social rank, especially high rank. **5** *Obs.* A lot; destiny. — **of sorts** Originally, of various or different kinds; now, of a poor or unsatisfactory kind: used disparagingly: an actor *of sorts.* — **sort of** Somewhat. — *v.t.* **1** To arrange or separate into grades, kinds, or sizes; classify; assort. — *v.i.* **2** To agree; be suitable; correspond. **3** To associate; consort. [<OF *sorte* <L *sors, sortis* lot, condition] — **sort′a·ble** *adj.* — **sort′a·bly** *adv.* — **sort′er** *n.* *Synonyms (noun):* character, condition, degree, denomination, description, kind, nature, order, race, rank, style.

sor·tie (sôr′tē) *n. Mil.* **1** A sally of troops from a besieged place to attack the besiegers. **2** A single trip of an aircraft on an assigned military or naval mission. [<F <*sortir* go forth]

sor·ti·lege (sôr′tə·lij) *n.* The act or practice of drawing lots; divination by lot; also, sorcery. [<OF *sortilege* <LL *sortilegus* a diviner <L *sors, sortis* a lot + *legere* pick, choose]

so·rus (sôr′əs, sō′rəs) *n.* *pl.* **so·ri** (sôr′ī, sō′rī) *Bot.* In ferns and fernlike plants, a cluster of spore cases (sporangia); a fruit dot. [<NL <Gk. *sōros* a heap]

S O S The code signal of distress adopted by the Radiotelegraphic Convention in 1912, and used by airplanes, ships, etc.; hence, any call for assistance.

so–so (sō′sō′) *adj.* Passable; neither very good nor very bad; mediocre. — *adv.* Indifferently; tolerably.

sos·te·nu·to (sôs′te·nōō′tō) *Music adj.* Sustained or continuous in tone; prolonged or held. — *n.* A sostenuto passage or movement. Also **sos′ti·nen′to** (-tē·nen′tō), **sos′te·nen′do** (-te·nen′dō). [<Ital.]

sot (sot) *n.* A habitual drunkard. [OE <OF <LL *sottus* a drunkard]

So·thic cycle (sō′thik, soth′ik) A period of about 1,460 years, based on an ordinary year of 365 days; or 1,461 years, based on a Sothic year of the Egyptians. See under YEAR. Also **Sothic period.**

so·tol (sō′tōl) *n.* Any one of a genus (*Dasylirion*) of yuccalike plants found in the SW United States. [<Mexican Sp. <Nahuatl *tzotolli*]

sot·to vo·ce (sot′ō vō′chē, *Ital.* sôt′tō vō′chā) Softly; in an undertone; privately; under the breath. [<Ital., under the (normal) voice]

sou (sōō) *n.* A former French coin of varying value; now, colloquially, something trivial or negligible. [<F <LL *solidus,* a gold coin]

sou·a·ri (sōō·ä′rē) *n.* Any of several tropical American trees (genus *Caryocar*), yielding a durable timber known as **souari wood,** and edible nuts called **souari nuts** or butternuts; especially, *C. nuciferum.* [<F *saouari* <native name]

sou·bise (sōō·bēz′) *n. French* A sauce of onions, butter, and white sauce: also **soubise sauce.**

sou·brette (sōō·bret′) *n.* **1** An actress in light comedy; originally, a pert, intriguing lady's maid. **2** A frivolous or coquettish maidservant. [<F <Provencal *soubreto* <*soubret* shy, coy] — **sou·bret′tish** *adj.*

sou·chong (sōō′chong′, -shong′) *n.* A variety of black tea, made from the youngest leaves of the earliest pickings, or the infusion made from it: also spelled **soochong.** [<F <Chinese *siao* small + *chung* plant]

souf·fle (sōō′fəl) *n.* A low whispering or blowing sound or murmur heard on auscultation: the respiratory *souffle.* [<F <*souffler* blow]

souf·flé (sōō·flā′) *adj.* Made light and frothy, and fixed in that condition by heat: also **souf·fléed′** (-flād′). — *n.* A light, baked dish made fluffy with beaten egg whites combined with the yolks, and often with cheese, mushrooms, or other ingredients. [<F, orig. pp. of *souffler* blow <L *sufflare* <*sub-* under + *flare* blow]

sough (suf, sou) *v.i.* To make a sighing sound, as the wind. — *n.* A deep, murmuring sound, as of wind through trees. — **to keep a calm sough** *Scot.* To be silent. [OE *swōgan* sound, roar, rustle]

soul (sōl) *n.* **1** The rational, emotional, and volitional faculties in man, conceived of as forming an entity distinct from, and often existing independently of, his body. **2** *Theol.* **a** The divine principle of life in man. **b** The moral or spiritual part of man as related to God, considered as surviving death and liable to joy or misery in a future state. **3** The emotional faculty of man as distinguished from his intellect: He puts his *soul* into his acting. **4** Fervor; emotional force; heartiness; vitality; nobleness: His music lacks *soul.* **5** The animating principle of a thing; an essential or vital element: Justice is the *soul* of law. **6** The leading figure or inspirer of a cause, movement, party, etc.: Lee was the *soul* of the Confederacy. **7** A person considered as the embodiment of a quality or attribute: He is the *soul* of generosity. **8** A living person; a human being: Every *soul* trembled at the sight. **9** The disembodied spirit of one who has died; a ghost. **10** In Christian Science, Spirit; Deity. **11** Among U.S. Negroes: **a** The awareness of a black African heritage. **b** A strongly emotional pride and solidarity based on this awareness. **c** The qualities that arouse such feelings, especially in black culture and art. **12** Soul music. **13** Soul food. — *adj.* Of or pertaining to soul (def. 11). ◆ *Homophone: sole.* [OE *sawol*] — **souled** *adj.*

Synonyms: mind, spirit. The *soul* includes the intellect, sensibilities, and will; beyond what is expressed by the word *mind,* the *soul* denotes especially the moral, the immortal nature. *Spirit* is used especially in contradistinction from matter; it may in many cases be substituted for *soul,* but *soul* has commonly a fuller and more determinate meaning. In the figurative sense, *spirit* denotes animation, excitability, perhaps impatience; as, a lad of *spirit. Soul* denotes energy and depth of feeling, as when we speak of *soulful* eyes; or it may denote the very life of anything; as, the *soul* of harmony. Compare MIND.

soul food Any of various Southern foods or dishes popular with American Negroes, as fried chicken, ham hocks, chitterlings, yams, etc.

soul·ful (sōl′fəl) *adj.* Full of that which appeals to or satisfies the higher feelings; emotional; spiritual. — **soul′ful·ly** *adv.* — **soul′ful·ness** *n.*

soul music A type of popular music strongly emotional in character and influenced chiefly by the blues and gospel hymns.

soul–search·ing (sōl′sûrch′ing) *n.* A deep examination of one's motives, desires, etc.

sound¹ (sound) *n.* **1** The sensation of hearing, produced by stimulation of the auditory centers of the brain by vibratory waves propagated through the atmosphere or other elastic medium. **2** The vibrations that produce sound waves, having for the normal human ear frequencies from about 20 to 20,000 cycles per second. **3** Noise of any specified quality: the *sound* of bugles; any tone, voice, or note. **4** Significance; implication: The story has a sinister *sound.* **5** Sounding or hearing distance; earshot: We were within the *sound* of battle. **6** Mere noise without significance: full of *sound* and fury. **7** *Obs.* Rumor. — *v.i.* **1** To give forth a sound or sounds. **2** To give a specified impression; seem: The story *sounds* true. — *v.t.* **3** To cause to give forth sound. **4** To give a signal or order for or announcement of: to *sound* retreat; to *sound* the hour. **5** To utter audibly; pronounce. **6** To make known or celebrated: to *sound* a hero's fame. **7** To test or examine by sound; auscultate. — **to sound in tort** To act as or have the nature of a tort. [<OF *son* <L *sonus*]

Synonyms (noun): noise, note, tone. *Sound* is the most comprehensive word, applying to anything that is audible. *Tone* is sound considered from the point of view of quality or pitch, or as expressive of some feeling; *noise* is *sound* considered without reference to musical quality or as distinctly unmusical or discordant. In music, *tone* may denote a musical *sound* or the interval between two such *sounds,* but in the most careful usage the latter is now distinguished as the "interval." *Note* in music strictly denotes the character representing a *sound,* but in loose popular usage it denotes the *sound* also, and becomes practically equivalent to *tone.*

sound² (sound) *adj.* **1** Having all the organs or faculties complete and in normal action and relation; healthy. **2** Free from injury, flaw, mutilation, defect, or decay: *sound* timber. **3** Founded in truth; right; substantial; valid; legal. **4** Correct in views or processes of thought. **5** Solvent. **6** Profound, as rest; deep; unbroken; also, resting profoundly. **7** Complete and effectual; thorough. **8** Solid; stable; firm; safe; hence, trustworthy. **9** Based on good judgment. See synonyms under HEALTHY, SANE¹, STAUNCH, WISE¹. [OE *gesund*] — **sound′ly** *adv.* — **sound′ness** *n.*

sound³ (sound) *n.* **1** A long and narrow body of water, more extensive than a strait, connecting larger bodies. **2** The air bladder of a fish. [Fusion of OE *sund* sea, a swimming and ON *sund* a strait, swimming]

sound⁴ (sound) *v.t.* **1** To test the depth of (water, etc.), especially by means of a lead weight at the end of a line. **2** To measure (depth) thus. **3** To explore or examine (the bottom of the sea, etc.) by means of a sounding lead adapted for bringing up adhering particles. **4** To discover or try to discover the views and attitudes of (a person) by means of conversation and round-about questions: usually with *out.* **5** To try to ascertain or determine (beliefs, attitudes, etc.) in such a manner. **6** *Surg.* To search or examine, as with a sound. — *v.i.* **7** To measure depth, as with a sounding lead. **8** To dive down suddenly and deeply, as a whale when harpooned. **9** To make investigation; inquire. — *n. Surg.* An instrument for exploring a cavity; a probe. [<OF *sonder,* ? <L *sub-* under + *unda* a wave] — **sound′a·ble** *adj.*

sound·board (sound′bôrd′, -bōrd′) *n.* A thin board, as in a piano or violin, forming the upper plate of a resonant box: also called **belly.**

sound·box (sound′boks′) *n.* That part of a phonograph which by means of a sensitive diaphragm relays to the surrounding air the acoustic vibrations transmitted to it by the stylus in the record groove.

sound effects In motion pictures, radio, etc., the incidental and often mechanically produced sounds, as of rain, hoofbeats, fire, etc., required to heighten the illusion of reality.

sounding board **1** A structure or suspended dome over a pulpit or speaker's platform to amplify and clarify the speaker's voice. **2** Any device that gives force to an opinion or speech.

sounding lead The lead or other weight used on a sounding line; a plummet.

sounding line A weighted line marked at fathom intervals with pieces of leather, cloth, etc., used for determining the depth of water.

sound locator An apparatus for locating the position of aircraft by means of the sound waves which they emit.

sound·proof (sound′prōōf′) *adj.* Resistant to the penetration or spread of sound. — *v.t.* To make soundproof.

sound ranging A method of locating the point of origin of a sound by checking time intervals as recorded from microphones of known position.

sound track That portion along the edge of a motion–picture film which carries the sound record.

sound truck A truck with a mounted loudspeaker.

soup (sōōp) *n.* **1** Liquid food made by boiling meat, vegetables, etc., in water: distinguished from *broth,* which is usually strained. **2** *Phot.* A developer. **3** *U.S. Slang* Nitroglycerin. — **in the soup** *U.S. Slang* In difficulties; in a quandary. — **to soup up** *U.S. Slang* To supercharge or otherwise modify (an automobile) for high speed. [<F *soupe* <Gmc.]

soup·çon (sōōp·sôn′) *n. French* Literally, a suspicion; hence, a minute quantity; a taste.

soup kitchen A place where soup is served to the needy either free or at very low cost.

soup·y (sōō′pē) *adj.* **soup·i·er, soup·i·est** Like soup in appearance or consistency.

sour (sour) *adj.* **1** Sharp to the taste; acid; tart, like vinegar: designating one of the four fundamental taste sensations. **2** Having an acid or rancid taste as the result of fermenta-

add,āce,câre,pälm; end,ēven; it,īce; odd,ōpen,ôrder; tŏŏk,pōōl; up,bûrn; ə = a in *above,* e in *sicken,* i in *clarity,* o in *melon,* u in *focus;* yōō = u in *fuse,* oi,oil; ou,pout; ch,check; g,go; ng,ring; th,thin; ŧh,this; zh,vision. Foreign sounds à,œ,ü,kh,ṅ; and ◆: see page xx. <from; + plus; ? possibly.

tion; also, pertaining to fermentation. **3** Having a rancid, acid smell or vapor; dank. **4** Misanthropic and crabbed; cross; morose: a *sour* person, a *sour* smile. **5** Cold and wet; unpleasant: *sour* weather. **6** Acid; harsh to crops: said of land. **7** Containing sulfur compounds: said of gasoline. — *v.t. & v.i.* To become or make sour. — *n.* **1** Something sour or distasteful. **2** An acid solution used in bleaching or in curing skins. **3** A treatment with such a solution. **4** A sour or acid beverage: a whisky *sour*. [OE *sūr*] — **sour′ly** *adv.* — **sour′ness** *n.*

source (sôrs, sōrs) *n.* **1** That from which any act, movement, or effect proceeds; an originator; creator; origin. **2** A place where something is found or whence it is taken or derived. **3** The spring or fountain from which a stream of water proceeds; a fountainhead; fountain. **4** A person, writing, or agency from which information is obtained. **5** The initiator of a payment, dividend, etc. [<OF, orig. pp. of *sourdre* rise <L *surgere*] *Synonyms:* beginning, fountain, fountainhead, origin, spring. See BEGINNING, CAUSE. *Antonyms:* close, completion, conclusion, end, expiration, result, termination.

sour·dough (sour′dō′) *n.* **1** *Dial.* Fermented dough for use as leaven in making bread. **2** *U.S. & Can. Slang* A pioneer or prospector; especially, an Alaskan or Canadian prospector who carries fermented dough for use in making bread.

sour gourd 1 One of a genus (*Adansonia*) of trees with huge trunk, having a woody gourdlike, capsule; especially, the Australian tree (*A. gregorii*). **2** The acid fruit of this tree. **3** The Madagascar baobab.

sour grapes That which a person affects to despise, because it is beyond his attainment: in allusion to the fable of the fox and the grapes.

sour·gum (sour′gum′) *n.* Any of several species of trees of the genus *Nyssa*, especially the blackgum tree and the tupelo.

sour·puss (sour′poos′) *n. Slang* A person with a sullen, peevish expression or character.

sour·sop (sour′sop′) *n.* **1** A tree (*Annona muricata*) of tropical America. **2** The pulpy, somewhat acid fruit of this tree.

sou·sa·phone (soo′zə·fōn, -sə-) *n.* A large brass wind instrument, resembling a tuba, but circular and with flaring bell frontward: used in military bands. [after John P. *Sousa*]

souse (sous) *v.t. & v.i.* **soused, sous·ing 1** To dip or steep in a liquid. **2** To pickle. **3** *Slang* To make or get drunk. — *n.* **1** Pickled meats; especially, the feet and ears of swine, pickled or soused in brine; formerly, any salt pickle. **2** A plunge in water. **3** Brine. **4** *Slang* A drunkard; sot. [<OF *sous* <OHG *sulza* brine]

sou·tane (soo·tän′) *n.* A Roman Catholic priest's cassock. [<F <Ital. *sottana* <*sotto* under <L *subtus*]

south (south) *n.* **1** That one of the four cardinal points of the compass which is directly opposite to north, and at the right hand of an observer who faces the sunrise. **2** The direction in which the point lies. **3** A region lying in this direction. **4** A south wind. — *adj.* **1** Situated in a southern direction relatively to the observer or to any given place or point. **2** Facing toward the south. **3** Belonging to or proceeding from the south. — *v.i.* **1** To turn southward. **2** *Astron.* To cross the meridian. — *adv.* **1** Toward or at the south. **2** From the south. [OE *sūth*]

South, the 1 The portion of the United States lying south of the Mason–Dixon line, and east and south of the western and northern borders of Missouri. **2** The Confederacy.

South Africa, Republic of An independent republic at the southern end of Africa, consisting of four provinces; 472,359 square miles; seat of government, Pretoria; seat of legislature, Cape Town. Formerly *Union of South Africa.*

South African War See BOER WAR in table under WAR.

South America The southern continent of the western hemisphere; about 6,900,000 square miles. — **South American.**

south–bound (south′bound′) *adj.* Going southward. Also **south′bound′.**

South Carolina A SE State of the United States, on the Atlantic; 31,055 square miles; capital, Columbia; entered the Union May 23,

---

1788; one of the thirteen original States; nickname *Palmetto State*: abbr. SC —**South Carolinian**

South Dakota A State in the north central United States; 77,047 square miles; capital, Pierre; entered the Union Nov. 2, 1889; nickname *Coyote State*: abbr. SD —**South Dakotan**

south·east (south′ēst′, *in nautical usage* sou′·ēst′, *n.* That point on the mariner's compass midway between south and east; any region lying toward that point on the horizon. — *adj.* Of, pertaining to, toward, or from the southeast. — *adv.* Toward or from the southeast. — **south′east′ern** *adj.* — **south′east′ern·most** *adj.* — **south′east′ward** *adj. & adv.* — **south′·east′ward·ly, south′east′wards** *adv.*

south·east·er (south′ēs′tər, *in nautical usage* sou′ēs′tər) *n.* A gale from the southeast.

south·ern (suth′ərn) *adj.* **1** Pertaining to the south or a place relatively in the south. **2** Proceeding from the south, as a wind. [OE *sutherne*] — **south′ern·er** *n.* — **south′ern·ly** *adv.* — **south′ern·most** *adj.*

southern lights The aurora australis.

south·ern·wood (suth′ərn·wood′) *n.* A European plant (*Artemisia abrotanum*) allied to wormwood.

south·ing (sou′thing) *n.* **1** The difference of latitude measured toward the south between any position and the last one determined. **2** *Astron.* **a** The passage across the meridian, in its diurnal motion, of a celestial object that culminates south of the zenith. **b** The attainment of this position, or the time at which it is reached. **3** Deviation or progression toward the south.

south·paw (south′pô′) *Slang n.* **1** In baseball, a left–handed pitcher. **2** Any left–handed person or player. — *adj.* Left–handed.

South Pole The southern extremity of the earth's axis; the 90th degree of south latitude, from which all terrestrial directions are north.

South Sea Islands The islands of the South Pacific Ocean.

south·west (south′west′, *in nautical usage* sou′west′) *n.* That point on the mariner's compass midway between south and west; any region lying toward that point on the horizon. — *adj.* Of, pertaining to, facing, or toward the southwest; blowing from the southwest. — *adv.* Toward or from the southwest. — **south′west′ern, south′west′ern·most** *adj.* — **south′west′ward** *adj. & adv.* — **south′·west′ward·ly, south′west′wards** *adv.*

Southwest, the The SW part of the United States: generally including Oklahoma, Texas, New Mexico, Arizona, and southern California.

south·west·er (south′wes′tər, *in nautical usage* sou′wes′tər) *n.* **1** A wind, gale, or storm from the southwest. **2** A waterproof hat of oilskin, canvas, etc., with a broad brim behind to protect the neck: worn in stormy weather. Also **sou′′west′er.**

sou·ve·nir (soo′və·nir′, soo′və·nir′) *n.* A token of remembrance; memento. [<F, remember <L *subvenire* come to mind]

sov·er·eign (sov′rin, suv′-) *n.* **1** One who possesses supreme authority, especially a person or a determinate body of persons in whom the supreme power of the state is vested; a monarch. **2** An English gold coin equivalent to one pound sterling or twenty shillings, first issued by Henry VII. **3** A former gold coin of Austria. See synonyms under MASTER. — *adj.* **1** Exercising or possessing supreme jurisdiction or power; royal. **2** Free, independent, and in no way limited by external authority or influence: a *sovereign* state. **3** Possessing supreme excellence or greatness; preeminent; paramount. **4** Superior in efficacy; potent: a *sovereign* remedy. See synonyms under IMPERIAL, PREDOMINANT. Also, *Poetic, sovran.* [<OF *soverain*, ult. <L *super* above. Related to SOPRANO.] — **sov′er·eign·ly** *adv.*

sov·er·eign·ty (sov′rin·tē, suv′-) *n. pl.* **·ties 1** The state of being sovereign; supreme authority. **2** The ultimate, supreme power in a state. **3** A sovereign state. **4** The status or dominion of a sovereign. Also, *Poetic, sovranty.* — **popular sovereignty** The theory that the right to legislate and choose a government belongs to the body of the people.

So·vi·et *n.* **1** In the former Soviet Union, any of the legislative bodies existing at various government levels. **2** Any of vari-

---

ous similar legislative bodies. [Russian] sovyet: a council.

so·vi·et·ism (sō′vē·ə·tiz′əm) *n.* The policies and principles of, or goverment by peoples' councils or congresses, especially as practiced in Soviet Russia. — **so′vi·et·ist** *n.*

sow[1] (sō) *v.* **sowed, sown** or **sowed, sow·ing** *v.t.* **1** To scatter (seed) over land for growth. **2** To scatter seed over (land). **3** To spread abroad; disseminate; implant: to *sow* the seeds of distrust. **4** To cover or sprinkle. — *v.i.* **5** To scatter seed. See synonyms under PLANT. [OE *sāwan*] — **sow′er** *n.* — **sow′ing** *n.*

sow[2] (sou) *n.* **1** A female hog. **2** *Metall.* **a** The connection between pieces of pig iron before breaking up. **b** The conduit to the pig bed for molten metal. [OE *sū, sugu*]

sow·bel·ly (sou′bel′ē) *n. U.S. Colloq.* Salt pork.

sow·bread (sou′bred) *n.* The cyclamen.

sow bug A small crustacean (family *Oniscidae*) found under logs and stones; a wood louse.

sow thistle Any of a genus (*Sonchus*) of spiny plants, especially the common sow thistle.

soy (soi) *n.* **1** A small, erect herb (*Glycine soja*) of the bean family, growing in India and China and cultivated for forage. **2** Its edible bean, a source of oil, flour, and other products: also **soy·a** (soi′ə), **soy′bean′.** **3** A sauce prepared in China and Japan from soybeans that have been fermented and steeped in brine: also **soy sauce.** [<Japanese *soy, shoy,* short for *shōyu* soy]

so·zin (sō′zin) *n. Biochem.* Any protein normally contained in the body of an animal and forming a natural protection against germs. Also **so′zine.** [<Gk. *sōzein* save + -IN]

spa (spä) *n.* Any locality frequented for its mineral springs; a mineral spring. [from SPA]

space (spās) *n.* **1** An interval between points or objects; a limited portion of extension; distance; area. **2** The abstract possibility of extension; that which is characterized by illimitable dimension; continuous boundless extension in all directions. **3** An interval of time; period; hence, a little while. **4** An occasion or opportunity. **5** *Printing* A piece of type metal, less than type–high, used for spacing between lines; specifically, one less than one en in width. **6** One of the degrees of a musical staff. **7** One of the intervals during the transmission of a telegraph message when the key is open or not in contact. **8** Reserved accommodations, as on a train or airplane. **9** *Math.* A system of continuous, unlimited, corresponding points in a series; an ordered set of infinite numbers. **10** Outer space. See synonyms under PLACE. — *v.t.* **spaced, spac·ing 1** To separate by spaces. **2** To divide into spaces. [<OF *espace* <L *spatium*] — **space′less** *adj.* — **spac′er** *n.*

space band *Printing* In Linotype operation, an adjustable wedge–shaped metal strip used for spacing.

space–cab·in simulator (spās′kab′in) A chamber built to resemble the cabin of a spaceship, for testing human or animal reactions under physiological conditions simulating those in actual space travel.

space charge *Physics* **1** An electric charge uniformly distributed through a given space. **2** A grouping of electrons around the filament of a vacuum tube, imparting a negative charge which inhibits the free emission of other electrons.

space·craft (spās′kraft′, -kräft′) *n.* **1** Any vehicle, manned or unmanned, designed for flight in outer space. **2** Spacemanship.

spaced–out (spāst′out′) *adj. U.S. Slang* Dazed or drugged, as by the use of narcotics.

space·flight (spās′flīt′) *n.* Flight in outer space by a man–made object or vehicle.

space lattice *Physics* The characteristic arrangement of the atoms or structural units in a crystal, such that corresponding units are separated by constant intervals along any straight line drawn through their centers.

SPACE LATTICE

space·man·ship (spās′mən·ship) *n.* The science and art of space travel, especially as regards the design, construction, fueling, launching, and operation of vehicles and missiles equipped for flight beyond the earth's atmosphere.

space medicine The branch of aviation medicine which deals with the biological, physiological, and psychological aspects of travel in outer space.

space·port (spās'pôrt', -pōrt') *n.* A base for rockets and other spacecraft, including the equipment necessary for their testing, storage, maintenance, launching, etc.

space probe A spacecraft designed and equipped to obtain information of phenomena and conditions in outer space.

space·ship (spās'ship') *n.* Any of various vehicles designed for the transport of men and materials through outer space, especially between and among the planets.

space shuttle A vehicle used for transferring passengers and freight from earth to an orbiting space station.

space station A large, usually manned satellite orbiting the earth, used for observation, experiments, as a relay station, etc.

space time A four-dimensional continuum within which may be precisely located any magnitude having both extension and duration: it consists of three spatial coordinates and one coordinate of time. Also **space–time continuum.**

space travel Travel in regions above the earth's atmosphere or beyond its gravitational field, whether within or outside of the solar system.

spa·cial (spā'shəl) See SPATIAL.

spac·ing (spā'sing) *n.* 1 The arrangement of spaces. 2 A space or spaces, as in a line of print.

spa·cious (spā'shəs) *adj.* 1 Of indefinite or vast extent. 2 Affording ample room; capacious. See synonyms under LARGE. —**spa'cious·ly** *adv.* —**spa'cious·ness** *n.*

spade[1] (spād) *n.* 1 An implement used for digging in the ground, ditching, cutting turf, etc., heavier than a shovel and having a flatter blade. 2 A tool or implement resembling a spade; specifically, a large chisel–like implement for flensing whales. 3 A heavy piece of metal at the end of a gun–carriage trail which helps to keep the carriage in position when the gun recoils. —**to call a spade a spade** To call a thing by its right name; speak the plain, uncompromising truth. —*v.t.* **spad·ed, spad·ing** To dig or cut with a spade. [OE *spadu*] —**spade'ful** *n.* —**spad'er** *n.*

spade[2] (spād) *n.* 1 A figure, resembling a heart with a triangular handle, on a playing card. 2 A card so marked. 3 The suit of cards so marked: usually in the plural. [< Sp. *espada* a sword < L *spatha* < Gk. *spathē*]

spade·fish (spād'fish') *n. pl.* **·fish** or **·fish·es** 1 A spiny–finned food fish (*Chaetodipterus faber*) of the Atlantic coast from Massachusetts to the West Indies. 2 The paddlefish.

spade·work (spād'wûrk') *n.* 1 Work done with a spade. 2 Any preliminary work necessary to get a project under way.

spa·di·ceous (spā·dish'əs) *adj.* 1 Of or like a spadix. 2 Of a clear brown or bay color.

spa·dix (spā'diks) *n. pl.* **spa·di·ces** (spā·di'sēz) *Bot.* A spike or head of flowers with a fleshy axis, usually enclosed within a spathe. [< Gk. *spadix* < *spaein* break]

spa·ghet·ti (spə·get'ē) *n.* 1 A cordlike food paste, in size between macaroni and vermicelli. 2 Insulated cloth tubing through which wire is passed, as in a radio circuit. [< Ital., pl. dim. of *spago* a small cord]

spa·gyr·ic (spə·jir'ik) *adj.* Alchemical. Also **spa·gir'ic, spa·gyr'i·cal.** [< NL *spagyricus*; prob. coined by Paracelsus]

Spain (spān) A nominal monarchy in SW Europe; continental Spain alone, 189,626 square miles; including the Balearic and Canary Islands, 194,368 square miles; capital, Madrid; Spanish *España.*

spall (spôl) *v.t.* To break up; chip; prepare for sorting, as ore. —*v.i.* To chip at the edges, as a stone under pressure. —*n.* A chip, splinter, or flake, as from a stone. [ME *spalle*. ? Related to MLG *spalden* split.]

spal·la·tion (spa·lā'shən) *n.* 1 The act or process of reducing to fragments. 2 *Physics* The

splitting of an atomic nucleus into numerous parts instead of the two or three characteristic of ordinary fission. [< SPALL + -ATION]

spal·peen (spal·pēn', spal'pēn) *n.* A wandering harvester; hence, a good–for–nothing. [< Irish *spailpín* laborer]

span[1] (span) *v.t.* **spanned, span·ning** 1 To measure, especially with the hand with the thumb and little finger extended. 2 To encircle or grasp with the hand, as in measuring. 3 To stretch across; extend over or from side to side of: This road *spans* the continent. 4 To provide with something that stretches across or extends over. [< *n.*] —*n.* 1 The extreme space over which the hand can be expanded: 9 inches, or 22.86 centimeters. 2 Any small interval or distance, in space or in time. 3 *Archit.* The space or distance between the supports of an arch, abutments of a bridge, etc. 4 That which spans. 5 *Aeron.* The maximum lateral distance from tip to tip of airplane wings. [OE *spann*]

span[2] (span) *v.* **spanned, span·ning** *v.t.* To bind; make fast; fetter. —*v.i.* To match in color and size: said of horses. —*n.* 1 A rope or chain used as a fastening on a ship. 2 A pair of matched horses or oxen. 3 In South Africa, a team of oxen or bullocks, of two or more yokes. [< MDu. *spannen* fasten, join, draw together]

span·drel (span'drəl) *n. Archit.* 1 The triangular space between the outer curve of an arch and the rectangular figure formed by the moldings or framework surrounding it. 2 The space between the shoulders of two adjoining arches. See illustration under ARCH. Also **span'dril.** [Dim. of AF *spaundre*, prob. < OF *espandre* expand]

spa·ne·mi·a (spə·nē'mē·ə) *n. Pathol.* Poverty of blood; anemia. Also **spa·nae'mi·a.** [< NL < Gk. *spanos* lacking + *haima* blood] —**spa·ne'mic** (-nē'mik, -nem'ik) *adj.*

spang (spang) *v.t. Brit. Dial.* To throw or bang down. —*v.i. Brit. Dial.* To spring. —*adv. U.S. Colloq.* Abruptly; straight: He ran *spang* into the wall.

span·gle (spang'gəl) *n.* 1 A small bit of brilliant tin or other metal foil, or other substances, used for decoration in dress, as in theatrical costume. 2 Any small sparkling object. —*v.* **·gled, ·gling** *v.t.* To adorn with or as with spangles; cause to glitter. —*v.i.* To sparkle as spangles; glitter. [Dim. of MDu. *spang* a clasp, brooch] —**span'gly** *adj.*

span·iel (span'yəl) *n.* 1 A small or medium–sized dog having large pendulous ears and long silky hair: used especially for hunting small game in the fields, retrieving water birds, etc. 2 One who follows like a dog; an obsequious follower. [< OF *espaignol* Spanish (dog)]

—**Blenheim spaniel** A variety of English toy spaniel having a white coat with rich chestnut or ruby–red markings: originally bred at Blenheim, England, from cocker spaniels sent to the Duke of Marlborough from China: formerly used for woodcock shooting, now usually a pet.

—**Clumber spaniel** A small, stout–bodied, short–legged spaniel having a straight silky coat usually white with lemon markings: named from Clumber, the estate of the second Duke of Newcastle, where they were bred.

—**cocker spaniel** The smallest of the sporting spaniels, of solid or various coloring, characterized by sturdy body and rather short legs: an excellent retriever, especially in thick covers and swamps, and named for its special skill in woodcock hunting.

—**English springer spaniel** A spaniel of moderate size, strongly built, with a long and broad skull, deep chest, and wavy or flat coat; usually liver and white or tan, black and white or tan, etc.: named for its characteristic method of flushing game.

—**field spaniel** A black or varicolored spaniel used for hunting small game, having a long, low body, short legs, and a larger, stronger appearance than the cocker.

—**Irish water spaniel** A sporting dog of a breed developed in Ireland, having a curly, waterproof, liver–colored coat: used especially as a duck retriever.

—**Japanese spaniel** A breed of toy dog, thought to have originated in China, squarely built with small–boned feathered legs, a proportionally large head, and a long, straight coat which may be black and white or red and white.

—**King Charles spaniel** An English toy spaniel, originating in the Far East at an unknown date, having a long, silky, black–and–tan coat, feathery ears and feet, rounded head, and a short, turned–up nose.

—**Sussex spaniel** A field spaniel bred in Sussex county, England, somewhat slow in speed, having a very keen nose, massive muscular body, heavy head, rather large ears, long back, short large–boned legs, and a thick coat of a rich, golden–liver color.

—**Welsh springer spaniel** A dark, rich red–and–white sporting spaniel of uncertain origin, found chiefly in Wales and the west of England: larger than the cocker, and an excellent watchdog.

Spanish America The parts of the western hemisphere in which Spanish is the common language: Mexico, the countries of Central America, except British Honduras, the countries of South America except Brazil and the Guianas, and most of the Caribbean islands: also *Hispanic America.*

Spanish–American War See table under WAR.

Spanish Armada See under ARMADA.

Spanish cedar Cedar (def. 4).

Spanish dagger Any of various species of yucca, with sword–shaped leaves. Also **Spanish bayonet.**

SPANISH DAGGER

Spanishfly A bright–green blister beetle (*Lytta vesicatoria*) of the Mediterranean region, used in the preparation of the drug cantharidin. See illustration under INSECTS (beneficial).

Spanish moss A long, pendent, epiphytic plant (*Tillandsia* or *Dendropogon usneoides*) that grows upon trees of the southern United States near the seacoast: not a true parasite: sometimes called *long moss, Florida moss.* Also **Spanish beard.**

Spanish needles 1 A smooth annual plant (*Bidens bipinnata*) of the composite family, with bipinnate leaves and spiny achenia. 2 The barbed, prickly fruit of this plant.

Spanish onion A large, fleshy variety of onion, usually mild flavored.

Spanish paprika A cultivated variety of paprika, widely used as a condiment.

spank (spangk) *v.t.* To slap or strike, especially on the buttocks with the open hand as a punishment. —*v.i.* To move briskly. —*n.* A smack on the buttocks; a spanking. [Imit.]

spank·er (spangk'ər) *n.* 1 One who or that which spanks. 2 *Naut.* A fore–and–aft sail extended by a boom and a gaff from the mizzenmast of a ship or bark. 3 Any person or thing uncommonly large or fine. 4 One who or that which proceeds rapidly.

spank·ing (spangk'ing) *adj.* 1 Moving or blowing rapidly; swift; dashing; lively; strong. 2 *Brit. Colloq.* Uncommonly large or fine. —*n.* A series of slaps on the buttocks; the act of administering such punishment.

span·less (span'lis) *adj.* That cannot be spanned.

span·ner (span'ər) *n.* 1 One who or that which spans. 2 *Brit.* A hand–tool used to turn nuts, bolts, etc.: a form of wrench. 3 A measuring worm. [def. 2 < G]

spar[1] (spär) *n.* 1 *Naut.* A round timber for extending a sail, as a mast, yard, or boom. 2 A similar heavy, round timber forming part of a derrick, crane, etc., or used for various other purposes. 3 *Aeron.* That part of an airplane wing which carries the ribs. 4 *Naut.* A spar buoy: see under BUOY. —*v.t.* **sparred, spar·ring** 1 To furnish with spars. 2 *Archaic* To fasten, as with a bolt. [< ON *sparri* a beam]

spar² (spär) *v.i.* **sparred, spar·ring 1** To box, especially with care and adroitness. **2** To bandy words; wrangle. **3** To fight, as cocks, by striking with spurs. — *n.* The act or practice of boxing, as by pugilists; a boxing match: also **spar'ring.** [<OF *esparer* <Ital. *sparare* kick <L *parare* prepare]

spar³ (spär) *n.* A vitreous, crystalline, easily cleavable, lustrous mineral. [<MDu. Akin to OE *spær* gypsum.]

spar·a·ble (spar'ə·bəl) *n.* A species of small headless nail used by shoemakers in soling boots. [Alter. of *sparrow bill*; so called from resemblance in shape]

spare (spâr) *v.* **spared, spar·ing** *v.t.* **1** To refrain from injuring, molesting, or killing; treat with mercy or lenience. **2** To free or relieve (someone) from (pain, expense, etc.): *Spare* us the sight. **3** To use frugally; refrain from using or exercising: *Spare* the rod and spoil the child. **4** To dispense or dispense with; do without: Can you *spare* a dime? — *v.i.* **5** To be frugal; live or act economically. **6** To be lenient or forgiving; show mercy. — *adj.* **spar·er, spar·est 1** That can be spared or used at will; disposable; available. **2** Held in reserve; additional; extra; surplus. **3** Having little flesh; thin; lean. **4** Not lavish or abundant; scanty. **5** Economical; chary; stingy; parsimonious. See synonyms under MEAGER. — *n.* **1** That which has been saved or stored away; something unused. **2** A duplicate; an item kept as a substitute in case the original breaks down, as an automobile tire or a mechanical part. **3** In bowling, the act of overturning all the pins with the first two balls; also, the score thus made. [OE *sparian*] — **spare'ly** *adv.* — **spare'ness** *n.* — **spar'er** *n.*

spare·rib (spâr'rib') *n.* A piece of meat, especially pork, consisting of ribs somewhat closely trimmed.

sparge (spärj) *v.t.* & *v.i.* **sparged, sparg·ing** To scatter; sprinkle; shower. — *n.* A sprinkling. [<OF *espargier* <L *spargere* sprinkle]

sparg·er (spär'jər) *n.* **1** A sprinkler or sprinkling apparatus. **2** In brewing, a hot–water sprinkler for use in a mashing tub.

spar·ing (spâr'ing) *adj.* **1** Scanty; slight. **2** Frugal; stingy. **3** Merciful; forbearing. See synonyms under SCANTY. — *n.* The act of one who spares; frugality; parsimony. See synonyms under FRUGALITY. — **spar'ing·ly.** *adv.* — **spar'ing·ness** *n.*

spark¹ (spärk) *n.* **1** An incandescent particle thrown off from a red–hot or burning body or struck from a flint. **2** Any glistening or brilliant point or transient luminous particle. **3** Anything that kindles or animates. **4** *Electr.* **a** The luminous effect of a disruptive electric discharge, or the discharge itself. **b** A small transient arc or an incandescent particle thrown off from such an arc. **5** A small diamond, or bit of diamond used as in cutting glass. **6** A small trace or indication. — *v.i.* **1** To give off sparks; sparkle; scintillate. **2** In an internal–combustion engine, to have the electric ignition operating. — *v.t.* **3** To bring into action or being; activate or cause: The shooting *sparked* a revolution. [OE *spearca*]

spark² (spärk) *n.* **1** A man fond of gallantry. **2** A lover; suitor; gallant. — *v.t.* & *v.i.* To play the spark (to); woo; court. [Special use of SPARK¹]

spark arrester 1 A sievelike device for catching sparks, as on a locomotive. **2** *Electr.* An apparatus to prevent injurious sparking at the opening of a circuit made and broken frequently.

spark coil *Electr.* An induction coil used with an internal–combustion engine, wireless telegraph equipment, etc., to secure sparking.

spark gap *Electr.* **1** An arrangement of two electrodes between which a disruptive electric charge may pass. **2** The space so covered.

spark generator *Electr.* Any device capable of generating a sufficiently high voltage to discharge across a spark gap.

spark·ish (spär'kish) *adj.* **1** Jaunty; sprightly; airy; gay. **2** Showy; fine; well–dressed.

spark killer *Electr.* A device, usually a condenser, or condenser and resistance in series, for reducing harmful sparking at frequently interrupted points in a circuit. Also **spark suppressor.**

spar·kle (spär'kəl) *v.i.* **·kled, ·kling 1** To give

off flashes of light; scintillate; glitter. **2** To emit sparks. **3** To effervesce. **4** To be brilliant or vivacious: His words *sparkle* with wit. See synonyms under SHINE. — *n.* A spark; gleam. See synonyms under LIGHT¹. [Freq. of SPARK¹]

spar·kler (spär'klər) *n.* **1** Something that sparkles. **2** A sparkling gem. **3** A thin, rod-like firework that emits sparks. **4** A person who shines with spirit or vivacity.

spar·kling (spär'kling) *adj.* Giving out sparks or flashes; glittering; figuratively, brilliant; vivacious. — **spar'kling·ly** *adv.* — **spar'kling·ness** *n.*

spark plug A device for igniting the charge in an internal–combustion engine by means of an electric current.

spark transmitter *Telecom.* A radio transmitter which obtains its alternating current from the discharge of a condenser across a spark gap.

spar·ling (spär'ling) *n.* **1** A smelt, parr, or other young fish. **2** A young herring. [<OF *esperlinge* <Gmc.]

spar·oid (spâr'oid, spar'-) *adj.* Of or pertaining to a family (*Sparidae*) of spiny–finned marine fishes allied to the grunts and including the porgy, sheepshead, etc. — *n.* A sparoid fish; the sea bream. [<L *sparus* <Gk. *sparos* gilthead + -OID]

spar·row (spar'ō) *n.* **1** Any of various small, plainly colored, passerine birds (family *Fringillidae*) related to the finches, grosbeaks, and buntings; especially, the European **house sparrow** (*Passer domesticus*), known in the United States as the **English sparrow. 2** Some other singing bird like or likened to the house sparrow, as the song sparrow. [OE *spearwa*]

spar·row–grass (spar'ō–gras', –gräs') *n. Dial.* Asparagus: a corruption. Also **spar'ry–grass'** (spar'ē-).

sparrow hawk 1 A small falconine bird that preys on sparrows, as the kestrel, or the **eastern sparrow hawk** (*Falco sparverius*). **2** A small European hawk (*Accipiter nisus*) that preys on other birds.

spar·ry (spär'ē) *adj.* **·ri·er, ·ri·est** Of, abounding in, or like spar.

sparse (spärs) *adj.* Scattered at considerable distances apart; thinly diffused; not dense. [<L *sparsus*, pp. of *spargere* sprinkle, scatter] — **sparse'ly** *adv.* — **sparse'ness, spar·si·ty** (spär'sə·tē) *n.*

Spar·ta (spär'tə) An ancient city in the Peloponnesus, southern Greece; capital of ancient Laconia: also *Lacedaemon.*

Spar·tan (spär'tən) *adj.* Pertaining to Sparta or the Spartans; heroically brave and enduring. — *n.* A native or citizen of Sparta; hence, one of exceptional valor and fortitude. — **Spar'tan·ism** *n.*

spasm (spaz'əm) *n.* **1** Any sudden or convulsive action or effort, as of the body, mind, or nature, especially such a one as is abnormal or temporary. **2** *Pathol.* Any involuntary convulsive contraction of muscles: when manifested by alternate contractions and relaxations it is a **clonic spasm**; when persistent and steady, it is a **tonic spasm.** [<L *spasma, spasmus* <Gk. *spasmos* <*spaein* draw, pull]

spas·mod·ic (spaz·mod'ik) *adj.* **1** Of the nature of a spasm; convulsive. **2** Violent, or impulsive and transitory. Also **spas·mod'i·cal.** — **spas·mod'i·cal·ly** *adv.*

spas·mol·y·sis (spaz·mol'ə·sis) *n. Med.* The checking or relief of spasms. — **spas·mo·lyt·ic** (spaz'mə·lit'ik) *adj.*

spas·mo·phil·i·a (spaz'mə·fil'ē·ə) *n. Pathol.* A constitutional tendency to spasms and convulsions. — **spas'mo·phil'ic** *adj.*

spas·tic (spas'tik) *adj.* Of, pertaining to, or characterized by spasms; spasmodic; tetanic: *spastic* hemiplegia. — *n.* A person afflicted with spastic seizures. [<L *spasticus* <Gk. *spastikos* <*spaein* draw, pull] — **spas'ti·cal·ly** *adv.*

spat (spat) *n.* **1** Spawn of shellfish; specifically, spawn of the oyster. **2** A young oyster, or young oysters collectively. — *v.i.* **spat·ted, spat·ting** To spawn, as oysters. [? Related to SPIT¹]

spat (spat) *n.* **1** A slight blow; slap. **2** A splash, as of rain; spatter. **3** A petty dispute. — *v.* **spat·ted, spat·ting** *v.i.* **1** To strike with a slight sound; slap. **2** To engage in a petty quarrel. — *v.t.* **3** To slap. [Prob. imit.]

spat (spat) *n.* A short gaiter worn over a shoe and fastened underneath with a strap: usually in the plural. [Short for SPATTERDASH]

spate (spāt) *n.* **1** A freshet; overflow. **2** A sudden, violent rainstorm; also, a waterspout. **3** A sudden or vigorous outpouring, as of words, feeling, etc. Also **spait.** [Origin uncertain]

spa·tha·ceous (spə·thā'shəs) *adj. Bot.* Bearing or of the nature of a spathe. Also **spa·thal** (spā'thəl).

spathe (spāth) *n. Bot.* A large bract or pair of bracts sheathing a flower cluster, as a spadix. [<L *spatha* <Gk. *spathē* broadsword] — **spa·those** (spā'thōs, spath'ōs) *adj.*

spath·ic (spath'ik) *adj. Mineral.* Of, pertaining to, or resembling spar. Also **spath·ose** (spath'ōs). [<G *spath* spar]

spa·tial (spā'shəl) *adj.* Pertaining to space; involving or having the nature of space. Also **spacial.** [<L *spatium* space] — **spa·ti·al·i·ty** (spā'shē·al'ə·tē) *n.* — **spa'tial·ly** *adv.*

spa·ti·o–tem·po·ral (spā'shē·ō·tem'pər·əl) *adj.* Of or pertaining to both space and time.

spat·ter (spat'ər) *v.t.* **1** To scatter in drops or splashes, as mud or paint. **2** To splash with such drops; bespatter. **3** To defame. — *v.i.* **4** To throw off drops or splashes; sputter. **5** To fall in a shower, as raindrops. — *n.* **1** The act of spattering, or the matter spattered; a splash. **2** A pattering noise, as of falling rain. [OE *spat-*, stem of *spatlian* spit out + -ER⁴]

spat·ter·dash (spat'ər·dash') *n.* A legging reaching to the knee, worn as a protection from mud, especially when riding: used chiefly in the plural. — **spat'ter·dashed'** *adj.*

spat·ter·dock (spat'ər·dok') *n.* The yellow pondlily (*Nuphar advena*).

spat·u·la (spach'ŏŏ·lə) *n.* **1** A knifelike instrument with a flat, flexible blade, used to spread plaster, cake icing, etc. **2** *Med.* An instrument used to press the tongue down or aside, as in examinations. [<L, dim. of *spatha*. See SPATHE.] — **spat'u·lar** *adj.*

spat·u·late (spach'ŏŏ·lit, ·lāt) *adj.* **1** Shaped like a spatula. **2** *Bot.* Oblong, with an attenuated base, as many leaves.

spav·in (spav'in) *n.* A disease of the hock joint of horses, occurring either as an infusion of lymph within the joint (**blood spavin** or **bog spavin**) or as a bony deposit stiffening the joint (**bone spavin**). Also *Scot.* **spa·vie** (spā'vē, spav'ē). [<OF *espavain, esparvain*; ult. origin uncertain] — **spav'ined** *adj.*

spawn (spôn) *n.* **1** *Zool.* The eggs of fishes, amphibians, mollusks, etc., especially in masses. **2** Derisively, the offspring of any animal; also, outcome or results; product; yield. **3** The spat of the oyster. **4** Very small fish; fry. **5** *Bot.* The mycelium of mushrooms or other fungi. [<*v.*] — *v.i.* **1** To produce spawn; deposit eggs or roe. **2** To come forth as or like spawn. — *v.t.* **3** To produce (spawn). **4** To give rise to; originate. **5** To bring forth abundantly or in great quantity. **6** To plant with spawn or mycelium. [<AF *espaundre*, OF *espendre* <L *expandere.* Doublet of EXPAND.]

spay (spā) *v.t.* To remove the ovaries from (a female animal). [<AF *espeier*, OF *espeer* cut with a sword <*espee* a sword <L *spatha*]

speak (spēk) *v.* **spoke** (*Archaic* **spake**), **spo·ken** (*Archaic* **spoke**), **speak·ing** *v.i.* **1** To employ the vocal organs in ordinary speech; utter words. **2** To express or convey ideas, opinions, etc., in or as in speech: to *speak* about a matter; Actions *speak* louder than words. **3** To make a speech; deliver an address. **4** To converse. **5** To make a sound; also, to bark, as a dog. — *v.t.* **6** To express or make known in or as in speech. **7** To utter in speech: to *speak* words of love. **8** To use or be capable of using (a language) in conversation. **9** To speak to. **10** *Naut.* To hail and exchange communications with (a vessel) at sea. — **to speak daggers** To express hatred. — **to speak for 1** To speak in behalf of; represent officially. **2** To lay claim to; bespeak; engage. [OE *specan, spreccan*]

Synonyms: announce, articulate, converse, declaim, declare, deliver, dictate, enunciate, express, pronounce, say, talk, tell, utter. See TALK.

speak–eas·y (spēk'ē'zē) *n. pl.* **–eas·ies** A saloon where liquor is sold contrary to law.

speak·er (spē'kər) *n.* **1** One who speaks; an

orator. **2** The presiding officer in any one of various legislative bodies. **3** A volume of oratorical selections, for declamation. **4** A loudspeaker. — **speak′er·ship** *n.*

speak·ing (spē′king) *adj.* **1** Having the power of effective speech; uttering speech. **2** Expressive; vivid; telling; lifelike. — *n.* **1** The act of utterance; vocal expression. **2** Oratory; public declamation. — **speak′ing·ly** *adv.*

spear (spir) *n.* **1** A weapon consisting of a pointed head on a long shaft. **2** A similar instrument, barbed and usually forked, as for spearing fish. **3** A spearman. **4** A leaf or slender stalk, as of grass: sometimes called a *spire.* — *v.t.* **1** To pierce or capture with a spear. — *v.i.* **2** To pierce as a spear does. **3** To send forth spears or spires, as a plant. [OE *spere* spear] — **spear′er** *n.*

spear·fish (spir′fish′) *n. pl.* **·fish** or **·fish·es** A powerful marine fish (genus *Tetrapturus*) with a long snout, related to the swordfish.

spear·head (spir′hed′) *n.* **1** The point of a spear or lance. **2** The military units which lead in a massed attack on enemy positions. — *v.t.* To be in the lead of (an attack, etc.).

spear·mint (spir′mint′) *n.* An aromatic herb (*Mentha spicata*) similar to peppermint.

spear·wort (spir′wûrt′) *n.* Any of several species of crowfoot having lance-shaped or linear leaves, especially, the **lesser spearwort** (*Ranunculus flammula*).

spe·cial (spesh′əl) *adj.* **1** Having some peculiar or distinguishing characteristic or characteristics; out of the ordinary; uncommon; particular. **2** Designed for or assigned to a specific purpose; limited or specific in range, aim, or purpose. **3** Of or pertaining to, constituting, or designating a species; specific; distinguishing; differential. **4** Unique; singular; exceptional. **5** Extra or additional, as a dividend. **6** Intimate; esteemed; beloved: a *special* favorite. See synonyms under PARTICULAR. — *n.* **1** A person or thing made, detailed for, or appropriated to a specific service or occasion, as a train, a newspaper edition, etc. **2** A featured dish or course in a restaurant or cafeteria. **3** A temporary sale. **4** A television show that is not regularly scheduled but is produced for a single presentation. [<OF *especial* <L *specialis* <*species* kind, species] — **spe′cial·ly** *adv.*

special delivery *U.S.* Mail delivery by special courier in advance of regular delivery: a postal service obtained for an additional fee.

spe·cial·ist (spesh′əl·ist) *n.* A person devoted to some one line of study, occupation, or professional work. — **spe′cial·is′tic** *adj.*

spe·ci·al·i·ty (spesh′ē·al′ə·tē) *n. pl.* **·ties** **1** A specific or individual characteristic; peculiarity. **2** Specialty (defs. 3, 4, 5). ◆ In British usage, this form is preferred instead of *specialty.*

spe·cial·ize (spesh′əl·īz) *v.* **·ized, ·iz·ing** *v.i.* **1** To concentrate on one particular activity or subject; engage in a specialty. **2** *Biol.* To take on a special form or forms by specialization or adaptation. — *v.t.* **3** To adapt for some special use or purpose; endow with a particular character. **4** *Biol.* To develop by specialization or adaptation, as an organ or part. **5** To endorse, as a check, to a payee. **6** To mention specifically. Also *Brit.* **spe′cial·ise.**

special pleading **1** *Law* **a** A pleading made with reference to some new or particular matter instead of the general issue. **b** The allegation of new or special matter in reply to the opposing party's averments, rather than an offer of a direct denial. **2** A presentation of the favorable aspects of an argument while avoiding or suppressing the unfavorable.

spe·cial·ty (spesh′əl·tē) *n. pl.* **·ties** **1** The state of being special or of having peculiar characteristics. **2** An individual characteristic; peculiarity; distinguishing mark. **3** An occupation or study limited to one particular line. **4** An article dealt in exclusively or chiefly, or a manufactured product of peculiar character. **5** *Law* A sealed contract; deed. — **specialty of the house** A featured dish or course in a restaurant.

spe·ci·a·tion (spē′shē·ā′shən) *n. Biol.* The formation of a species by the action of evolutionary processes upon plant and animal organisms.

spe·cie (spē′shē) *n.* Coined money; coin. See synonyms under MONEY. — **in specie** **1** In coin. **2** *Law* In kind; in the shape mentioned; in sort. [<L (*in*) *specie* (in) kind]

spe·cies (spē′shēz, -shiz; *Lat.* spē′shi·ēz) *n. pl.* **·cies** **1** *Biol.* A category of animals or plants subordinate to a genus but above a breed, race, strain, or variety. The species name follows immediately after the name of the genus to which it belongs, and with it forms the scientific name of the individual plant or animal, as *Oreamnos americanus,* the Rocky Mountain goat. **2** A group of individuals or objects agreeing in some common attribute or attributes and designated by a common name. **3** A mental image considered as having the likeness of some object in nature. **4** A kind; sort; variety; form. **5** *Eccl.* **a** The visible form of bread or of wine retained by the eucharistic elements after consecration. **b** The consecrated elements of the Eucharist. **6** *Obs.* Specie; coin. [<L, form, kind. Doublet of SPICE.]

spe·cif·ic (spi·sif′ik) *adj.* **1** Distinctly and plainly set forth; definite or determinate; particular; explicit. **2** Of, pertaining to, or distinguishing a species: a *specific* name of an animal. **3** Peculiar; special. **4** Having some distinct medicinal or pathological property; distinguishable or determinate: a *specific* medicine, a *specific* germ. **5** Having or designating a particular property, composition, ratio, or quantity serving to identify a given substance or phenomenon in relation to some arbitrary but constant standard of comparison: *specific* heat, *specific* volume, etc. **6** Denoting a customs duty chargeable upon imported merchandise by quantity, weight, or number, without regard to value: contrasted with ad valorem duty. Also *Rare* **spe·cif′i·cal.** — *n.* Anything specific or adapted to effect a specific result, as a medicine specially indicated to cure or prevent some particular disease. [<L *specificus* <*species* kind, class + *facere* make] — **spec·i·fic·i·ty** (spes′ə·fis′ə·tē) *n.*

spec·i·fi·ca·tion (spes′ə·fə·kā′shən) *n.* **1** The act of specifying. **2** A definite and complete statement, as in a contract; also, one detail in such a statement. **3** In patent law, the detailed statement of an inventor's scheme, setting forth the nature of the invention and the precise method of constructing and applying it. **4** A specific description of certain dimensions, types of material, etc., to be used in a construction or engineering project; also, any item in this description.

specific gravity *Physics* The ratio of the mass of a body to that of an equal volume of some standard substance, water in the case of solids and liquids, and air or hydrogen in the case of gases.

specific heat *Physics* The amount of heat required to raise the temperature of a given quantity of a substance one degree.

spec·i·fy (spes′ə·fī) *v.t.* **·fied, ·fy·ing** **1** To mention specifically; state in full and explicit terms. **2** To embody in a specification. [<OF *specifier* <L *species* kind, species + *facere* make]

spec·i·men (spes′ə·mən) *n.* **1** One of a class of persons or things regarded as representative of the class; an example; sample. **2** *Biol.* A plant or an animal, entire or in part, prepared and kept as an example to illustrate a species or variety. **3** A sample for urinalysis. **4** *Colloq.* A person of pronounced or curious type; a character; a case: What a *specimen!* See synonyms under EXAMPLE, SAMPLE. [<L *specere* look at]

spe·cious (spē′shəs) *adj.* **1** Apparently good or right, but without merit; plausible: *specious* reasoning. **2** Pleasing or attractive in appearance, but deceptive; fair-seeming: a *specious* promise. **3** Beguiling, but lacking in sincerity: a *specious* hypocrite. **4** *Archaic* Showy; pleasing to the view. See synonyms under OSTENSIBLE. [<L *speciosus* fair] — **spe′cious·ly** *adv.* — **spe′cious·ness** *n.*

speck (spek) *n.* **1** A small spot; a little stain or discoloration. **2** Any very small thing; a particle. See synonyms under BLEMISH. — *v.t.* To mark with spots or specks; speckle. [OE *specca*]

speck·le (spek′əl) *v.t.* **·led, ·ling** To mark with specks or speckles. — *n.* A diminutive spot;

speck.

spec·ta·cle (spek′tə·kəl) *n.* **1** That which is exhibited to public view; a grand display; pageant; parade; show. **2** An unwelcome or deplorable exhibition; a painful sight. **3** *pl.* A pair of eyeglasses, with hinged bows to secure them before the eyes: used to correct defects in vision, or to protect the eyes, as from glare. **4** *pl.* A marking on animals resembling a pair of spectacles. — **compound spectacles** *Optics* **1** Spectacles having supplementary colored glasses hinged to them for use when desired. **2** Supplementary lenses of greater power, similarly hinged. **3** Bifocals; trifocals. [<F <L *spectaculum* <*spectare,* freq. of *specere* see]
Synonyms: display, exhibition, pageant, parade, scene, show, sight. See SIGHT.

spec·tac·u·lar (spek·tak′yə·lər) *adj.* Characterized by grand scenic display; exciting wonder by dramatic or unusual display. — *n.* **1** An imposing exhibition. **2** In television, a lavish dramatic or musical production of 90 minutes duration, especially designed for reproduction in color. **3** An elaborate, illuminated sign. — **spec·tac′u·lar·ly** *adv.* — **spec·tac′u·lar′i·ty** (-lar′ə·tē) *n.*

spec·ta·tor (spek′tā·tər, spek·tā′-) *n.* **1** One who beholds; an eyewitness; an onlooker. **2** One who is present at and views a show, game, spectacle, etc. [<L <*spectare* look at]
Synonyms: beholder, bystander, onlooker, observer, witness.

spec·ter (spek′tər) *n.* A phantom of the dead or of a disembodied spirit; especially, one of a grisly or horrible nature; ghost; apparition. Also **spec′tre.** [<F *spectre* <L *spectrum* vision]
Synonyms: apparition, phantom, ghost, shade, spirit.

spectro– *combining form* **1** Radiant energy, as exhibited in the spectrum: *spectroscope.* **2** Spectroscope; spectroscopic: *spectrobolometer.* [<SPECTRUM]

spec·tro·graph (spek′trə·graf, -gräf) *n. Physics* **1** An apparatus for photographing a spectrum or for forming a representation of the spectrum in any way. **2** A photograph of a spectrum. — **sound spectrograph** An electronic instrument designed to record the frequencies of speech sounds as measured in cycles per second, and the amplitude at any given frequency: used in acoustic phonetics.

spec·tro·he·li·o·graph (spek′trō·hē′lē·ə·graf′, -gräf′) *n.* An instrument for photographing the sun with its prominences by means of monochromatic light.

spec·trom·e·ter (spek·trom′ə·tər) *n.* **1** An instrument by means of which the angular deviation of a ray of light produced by a prism or by a refraction grating can be determined, or a wavelength of a ray of light can be accurately measured. **2** A spectroscope provided with such an instrument. — **spec·tro·met·ric** (spek′trō·met′rik) *adj.*

spec·tro·pho·tom·e·ter (spek′trō·fō·tom′ə·tər) *n.* An instrument for determining the relative intensity of two spectra or of the corresponding bands of color in two spectra.

spec·tro·ra·di·om·e·ter (spek′trō·rā′dē·om′ə·tər) *n.* A form of spectrometer for determining the distribution of the intensity of any type of radiation, especially in the infrared region of the spectrum. — **spec′tro·ra′di·om′e·try** *n.*

spec·tro·scope (spek′trə·skōp) *n.* An optical instrument for forming and analyzing spectra emitted by bodies or substances. — **spec′tro·scop′ic** (-skop′ik) or **·i·cal** *adj.* — **spec′tro·scop′i·cal·ly** *adv.*

PRINCIPLE OF SIMPLE SPECTROSCOPE
a. Prism. *b.* Telescope for viewing prism through eyepiece (*e*). *c.* Collimator with slit (*d*).

spec·trum (spek′trəm) *n. pl.* **·tra** (-trə) **1** The continuously varying band of color observed when a beam of white light is passed through a prism which separates each component of the light according to frequencies ranging from low for red to high for violet: also **visible spectrum, chromatic spectrum. 2** An image formed by radiant energy directed through a spectroscope and brought to a focus in which each wavelength corresponds to a specific band or line in a progressive series characteristic of the emitting source. **3** An after–image. [<L, a vision]

spec·u·lar (spek′yə-lər) *adj.* **1** Pertaining to or assisted by a speculum or a mirror; reflecting. **2** *Obs.* Affording a view; aiding vision. [<L *specularis* < *speculum* mirror]

spec·u·late (spek′yə-lāt) *v.i.* **·lat·ed, ·lat·ing 1** To form conjectures regarding anything without experiment; theorize; conjecture. **2** To make an investment involving a risk, but with hope of gain. [<L *speculatus*, pp. of *speculari* look at, examine < *specere* see]

spec·u·la·tion (spek′yə-lā′shən) *n.* **1** The act of theorizing or conjecturing; speculating. **2** A theory or conjecture. **3** A conclusion reached by or based upon conjecture. **4** An investment involving risk with hope of large profit. **5** The act of engaging in risky business transactions that offer a possibility of large profit. **6** *Archaic* Vision; observation; intuition. See synonyms under HYPOTHESIS, THOUGHT¹.

spec·u·la·tive (spek′yə-lā′tiv, -lə-tiv) *adj.* **1** Of, pertaining to, engaged in, or given to speculation: opposed to *experimental.* **2** Strictly theoretical or purely scientific: opposed to *practical.* **3** Engaging in or involving financial speculation. **4** *Archaic* Pertaining to vision or observation; affording a good view. **5** *Archaic* Prying; observing. **— spec′u·la′tive·ly** *adv.* **— spec′u·la′tive·ness** *n.*

spec·u·la·tor (spek′yə-lā′tər) *n.* One who speculates, in any sense. **— spec′u·la·to′ry** (-lə-tôr′ē, -tō′rē) *adj.*

spec·u·lum (spek′yə-ləm) *n.* *pl.* **·la** (-lə) or **·lums 1** A mirror of polished metal or of glass coated with a metal film used for telescope reflectors and other optical instruments. **2** *Med.* An instrument that dilates a passage of the body for examination. **3** *Ornithol.* A specially colored, typically iridescent area on the wings of certain birds, as ducks. [<L, a mirror < *specere* see]

speech (spēch) *n.* **1** The faculty of expressing thought and emotion by spoken words; the power of speaking. **2** The act of speaking, involving the production of meaningful combinations of distinctive speech sounds. **3** That which is spoken; conversation; talk; a saying or remark. **4** A public address; a discourse. **5** A characteristic manner of speaking: *His speech* is loud and unpleasant. **6** A particular language, idiom, or dialect: American *speech.* **7** Any audible or visible method of communication, including cries, gestures, and sign language. **8** The study of oral communication, including the physiology of articulation, the nature of speech sounds, and the techniques of effective expression. [OE *spec, sprec* < *specan, sprecan* speak]

Synonyms: address, discourse, discussion, disquisition, dissertation, eloquence, harangue, oration, oratory, sermon. *Speech* is the general word for utterance of thought in language. A *speech* is the simplest mode of delivering one's sentiments; an *oration* is an elaborate and prepared *speech*; a *harangue* is a vehement appeal to passion, or a *speech* that has something disputatious and combative in it. A *discourse* is a set *speech* on a definite subject intended to convey instruction. See LANGUAGE. *Antonyms:* hush, silence, stillness.

speech clinic A place where speech disorders are corrected by training and re-education.

speech community All the speakers of a given language or dialect in both contiguous and geographically distributed areas.

speech defect The manifestation or end product of a speech disorder.

speech disorder Disorganization or impairment of speech caused either by physical defect or by mental disorder, such as aphasia, stuttering, etc.

speech·i·fy (spē′chə-fī) *v.i.* **·fied, ·fy·ing** To make speeches: often used derisively. **— speech′i·fi′er** *n.*

speech·less (spēch′lis) *adj.* **1** Unable to speak or temporarily deprived of speech because of physical weakness or strong emotion, etc.: *speechless* with rage. **2** Mute; dumb. **3** Silent; reticent. **4** *Archaic* Unspoken in words: the *speechless* message in her eyes. **5** Unaccompanied by speech: *speechless* joy. **6** *Archaic* Inexpressible. **— speech′less·ly** *adv.* **— speech′less·ness** *n.*

speech·mak·er (spēch′mā′kər) *n.* One who delivers a speech or speeches. **— speech′mak′ing** *n.*

speed (spēd) *n.* **1** The act or state of moving or progressing swiftly; rapidity of motion; celerity; swiftness. **2** *Physics* **a** Rate of motion, especially as considered without reference to direction: a scalar quantity distinguished from *velocity.* **b** Rate of performance, as shown by the ratio of work done to time spent. **3** *Mech.* A transmission gear in a motor vehicle. **4** *Phot.* In a camera lens, the minimum time required for an effective exposure under given conditions, expressed as the ratio of focal length to effective aperture. **5** *Slang* One of the amphetamines taken illicitly, especially by injection. **6** *Archaic* Good luck; success; prosperity. **— v. sped** or **speed·ed, speed·ing** *v.i.* **1** To move or go with speed. **2** *Obs.* To prosper. **3** *Obs.* To fare in a specified manner. **— v.t. 4** To promote the forward progress of; cause to move or go with speed. **5** To promote the success of. **6** To wish Godspeed to: *Speed* the parting guest. **— to speed up** To accelerate in speed or action. See synonyms under FLY¹. **— adj.** Having, pertaining to, characterized by, regulating, or indicating speed: used chiefly in compounds:

speed–cone	speed–lathe	speed–test
speed–gage	speed–pulley	speed–trap
speed–gear	speed–recorder	

[OE *spēd* power]

speed·boat (spēd′bōt′) *n.* A motorboat capable of high speed.

speed indicator 1 An instrument showing the rotation speed of a machine or part of a machine. **2** A speedometer.

speed·ing (spē′ding) *adj.* Moving with speed. **— n.** Travel at high speed; especially, by motor vehicles, travel at an unsafe or reckless speed or above a specified speed limit.

speed limit A legally set maximum speed at which vehicles may travel on certain stretches of roads or through specified districts.

speed·om·e·ter (spi-dom′ə-tər) *n.* A device for indicating the speed of a vehicle or the distance traveled.

speed·ster (spēd′stər) *n.* **1** A speeder. **2** An automobile, usually having two seats, designed for speed.

speed–up (spēd′up′) *n.* An acceleration in work, output, movement, etc.

speed·way (spēd′wā′) *n.* A specially reserved or prepared road for vehicles traveling at high speed.

speed·well (spēd′wel) *n.* One of various low herbs (genus *Veronica*) of the figwort family, bearing blue or white flowers, especially the common speedwell (*V. arvensis*) and the germander speedwell (*V. chamaedrys*), with bright-blue flowers: also called birdseye.

speed·y (spē′dē) *adj.* **speed·i·er, speed·i·est 1** Characterized by speed. **2** Without delay. See synonyms under NIMBLE, SWIFT¹. **— speed′i·ly** *adv.* **— speed′i·ness** *n.*

speed·y–cut (spē′dē-kut′) *n.* An injury on the side of the knee or carpus of a horse caused by a blow from the shoe of the foot of the opposite leg when trotting or moving at any other rapid gait.

speiss (spīs) *n.* An impure mixture consisting of the arsenides of certain metals, as copper, iron, and nickel, that concentrate in smelting certain ores. Also Ger. **spei·se** (shpī′zə). [<G *speise* amalgam]

spe·le·an (spi-lē′ən) *adj.* **1** Dwelling in a cave or caves. **2** Of or pertaining to a cave or caverns. Also **spe·lae′an.** [<L *spelaeum* <Gk. *spēlaion* a cave]

spe·le·ol·o·gy (spē′lē-ol′ə-jē) *n.* **1** The scientific study of caves in their physical, geological, and biological aspects. **2** The exploration of caves as a sport or profession. [<L *spelaeum* a cave + -LOGY] **— spe′le·o·log′i·cal** (-ə-loj′i-kəl) *adj.* **— spe′le·ol′o·gist** *n.*

spell¹ (spel) *v.* **spelled** or **spelt, spell·ing** *v.t.* **1** To pronounce or write the letters of (a word); especially, to do so correctly. **2** To form or be the letters of: C-a-t *spells* cat; hence, to compose; make up. **3** To read with difficulty; hence, to puzzle out and learn: sometimes with *over* or *out.* **4** To signify; mean: Extravagance *spells* disaster. **— v.i. 5** To form words out of letters, especially correctly. [<OF *espeler* <Gmc. Akin to SPELL².]

spell² (spel) *n.* A formula used as a charm; incantation; charm; hence, fascination. **— v.t. spelled, spell·ing** To cast a spell upon; fascinate; bewitch. [OE, story, statement. Akin to SPELL¹.]

spell³ (spel) *n.* **1** A period of time, usually of short length. **2** *Colloq.* A continuous period characterized by a certain type of weather. **3** *Colloq.* A short distance. **4** *Colloq.* A fit of illness, debility, etc. **5** A turn of duty in relief of another. **6** A period of work or employment. **7** *Austral.* A period of relaxation; rest. **— v.t. 1** To relieve temporarily from some work or duty. **2** *Austral.* To give a rest to, as a horse. **— v.i. 3** To take a rest. [OE *gespelia* a substitute, one who spells another]

spell·bind (spel′bīnd′) *v.t.* **·bound, ·bind·ing** To bind or enthral, as if by a spell.

spell·bind·er (spel′bīn′dər) *n.* One who casts a spell over others; specifically, a political orator.

spell·bound (spel′bound′) *adj.* Bound as by a spell; fascinated.

spell·er (spel′ər) *n.* **1** One who spells. **2** A spelling book.

spell·ing (spel′ing) *n.* **1** The act of one who spells. **2** The art of correct spelling; orthography. **3** The way in which a word is spelled.

spelling bee A gathering at which contestants engage in spelling words, those who spell wrongly usually being retired until only one remains.

spelling book A book of exercises for training students to spell.

spel·ter (spel′tər) *n.* Zinc: a commercial term. **— brazing spelter** See BRAZING SOLDER. [Var. of PEWTER]

spe·lun·ker (spē-lung′kər) *n.* An enthusiast in the exploration and study of caves; a speleologist. [<L *spelunca* a cave]

spen·cer¹ (spen′sər) *n.* A trysail.

spen·cer² (spen′sər) *n.* **1** A man's short jacket of the early 19th century. **2** A similar outer garment for women, usually tight-fitting and often knitted or fur-trimmed. [after 2nd Earl *Spencer,* 1758–1834, English nobleman]

spend (spend) *v.* **spent, spend·ing** *v.t.* **1** To pay out or disburse (money). **2** To expend by degrees; use up. **3** To apply or devote, as thought or effort, to some activity, purpose, etc. **4** To pass: to *spend* one's life in jail. **5** To lose: now chiefly in the nautical phrase **to spend a mast. 6** To emit, as a milt or spawn. **— v.i. 7** To pay out or disburse money, etc. **8** *Obs.* To be wasted or exhausted. See synonyms under SQUANDER. [OE *aspendan* <L *expendere* EXPEND] **— spend′er** *n.*

spend·thrift (spend′thrift′) *n.* One who is wastefully lavish of money: also **spend′er. — adj.** Excessively lavish; wasteful; prodigal.

spent (spent) Past tense and past participle of SPEND. **— adj. 1** Worn out or exhausted. **2** Deprived of force: a *spent* bullet or cannon ball.

sperm¹ (spûrm) *n.* **1** The male fertilizing fluid; semen. **2** A male reproductive cell; spermatozoon. [<Gk. *sperma* a seed < *speirein* sow]

sperm² (spûrm) *n.* **1** A sperm whale. **2** Spermaceti. **3** Sperm oil. [Short for SPERMACETI]

-sperm *combining form Bot.* A seed of a specified kind): gymnosperm. [<Gk. *sperma, spermatos* a seed]

sper·ma·ce·ti (spûr′mə-sē′tē, -set′ē) *n.* A white, waxy substance separated from the oil contained in the head of the sperm whale: used for making candles, ointments, etc. [<F <L *sperma ceti* seed of a whale]

sper·ma·ry (spûr′mər-ē) *n.* *pl.* **·ries** The sperm-generating gland of the male; testis.

sper·ma·the·ca (spûr′mə-thē′kə) *n.* *pl.* **·cae** (-sē) *Zool.* A receptacle for receiving and retaining spermatozoa in the females of many invertebrates, as insects, worms, and mollusks. [<L *sperma* a seed + THECA] **— sper′·ma·the′cal** (-thē′kəl) *adj.*

sper·mat·ic (spûr-mat′ik) *adj.* Of or pertaining to sperm or a spermary.

spermatic cord *Anat.* The cord, made up of

the spermatic duct and its accompanying vessels and nerves, that passes from the testis through the inguinal canal into the abdominal cavity.

spermatic fluid *Physiol.* Semen.

sper·ma·tid (spûr'mə·tid) *n. Biol.* A cell resulting from the division of the secondary spermatocytes, and developing into a spermatozoon.

sper·ma·ti·um (spûr·mā'shē·əm) *n. pl.* **·ti·a** (-shē·ə) *Bot.* 1 A minute spore in certain lichens and fungi: formerly regarded as a nonmotile male gamete. 2 A non-motile gamete which, in the red algae, unites with the carpogonium. [<NL <Gk. *spermation,* dim. of *sperma* a seed]

spermato- *combining form* 1 Seed; pertaining to seeds: *spermatophyte.* 2 Spermatozoa; of or related to spermatozoa: *spermatophore.* Also spelled *spermo-.* Also, before vowels, **spermat-.** [<Gk. *sperma, spermatos* a seed]

sper·ma·to·cyte (spûr'mə·tə·sīt') *n. Biol.* A primary cell from which spermatozoa are developed through primary and secondary divisions, resulting in the spermatids.

sper·ma·to·phore (spûr'mə·tə·fôr', -fōr') *n. Zool.* A capsule or case containing spermatozoa, as in many mollusks, worms, and other invertebrates. — **sper'ma·toph'o·ral** (-tof'ər·əl) *adj.*

sper·ma·to·phyte (spûr'mə·tə·fīt') *n.* Any plant of a phylum or division (*Spermatophyta*) of the most highly developed plants; a flowering and seed-bearing plant. — **sper'ma·to·phyt'ic** (-fit'ik) *adj.*

sper·ma·tor·rhe·a (spûr'mə·tə·rē'ə) *n. Pathol.* Excessive or frequent seminal discharge without sexual excitement. Also **sper'ma·tor·rhoe'a.**

sper·ma·to·zo·on (spûr'mə·tə·zō'on) *n. pl.* **·zo·a** (-zō'ə) *Biol.* The male fertilizing element of an animal, usually in the form of a nucleated cell with a long flagellate process or tail by which it swims actively about. [< SPERMATO- + Gk. *zōion* an animal] — **sper'ma·to·zo'al, sper'ma·to·zo'ic** *adj.*

sper·mo·go·ni·um (spûr'mə·gō'nē·əm) *n. pl.* **·ni·a** (-nē·ə) *Bot.* In fungi, a cup- or flask-shaped receptacle, bearing a great number of spermatia.

sperm oil Oil obtained from the head and blubber cavities of the sperm whale.

sperm·o·phile (spûr'mə·fīl, -fil) *n.* A squirrel-like burrowing rodent (*Citellus* and related genera), as the striped gopher or the suslik.

SPERM WHALE
(Up to 80 feet in length)

sperm whale A large, toothed whale (*Physeter catodon*) of warm seas, having a huge truncate head containing a reservoir of sperm oil; the cachalot.

spew (spyōō) *v.t. & v.i.* To vomit; throw up. — *n.* That which is spewed; vomit. [OE *spīwan*]

sphac·e·late (sfas'ə·lāt) *v.i.* **·lat·ed, ·lat·ing** *Pathol.* To become gangrenous; decay; die. [<Gk. *sphakelos* gangrene] — **sphac'e·la'tion** *n.*

sphag·num (sfag'nəm) *n.* Any of a genus (*Sphagnum*) of whitish-gray mosses constituting the family *Sphagnaceae,* the bog or peat mosses: used as packing and in surgical dressings. [<Gk. *sphagnos,* kind of moss] — **sphag'nous** *adj.*

sphal·er·ite (sfal'ər·īt) *n.* A resinous to adamantine native zinc sulfide, ZnS, crystallizing in the isometric system; zinc blende. [<Gk. *sphaleros* deceptive + -ITE[1]]

sphe·nic (sfē'nik) *adj.* Wedge-shaped.

spheno- *combining form* 1 Wedge-shaped: *sphenogram.* 2 *Med.* Pertaining to the sphenoid bone. Also, before vowels, **sphen-.** [<Gk. *sphēn, sphēnos* a wedge]

sphe·no·don (sfē'nə·don) *n.* A lizardlike reptile (*Sphenodon punctatum*), the sole surviving representative of the order *Rynchocephalia*; the hatteria or tuatara of New Zealand.

[<NL <Gk. *sphēn, sphēnos* a wedge + *odous, odontos* a tooth]

sphe·no·gram (sfē'nə·gram) *n.* A cuneiform character or symbol.

sphe·noid (sfē'noid) *n.* 1 *Mineral.* In the tetragonal and orthorhombic crystal systems, a hemihedral form enclosed by four faces, each of which cuts all three axes. 2 The sphenoid bone. — *adj.* Wedge-shaped: the **sphenoid** bone. [<SPHEN(O)- + -OID] — **sphe·noi'dal** (sfi·noid'l) *adj.*

sphere (sfir) *n.* 1 The surface described by a semicircle making one complete rotation on its diameter as a fixed axis; a globular figure enclosed by a surface, every point of which is equidistant from a point within called the center. 2 An approximately globular body; a globe; ball; orb. 3 One of the heavenly bodies; a planet, sun, or star. 4 The apparent outer dome of the heavens on which the heavenly bodies appear to lie. 5 In old astronomy, one of the concentric and transparent globes believed to revolve about the earth and carry the various heavenly bodies, their movement supposedly producing mysteriously beautiful music. 6 Compass or field of activity, endeavor, influence, etc.; range; scope; province. 7 Social rank or position. — *v.t.* **sphered, spher·ing** 1 To place in or as in a sphere; encircle; encompass. 2 To set among the celestial spheres. 3 To make spherical. [<OF *espere* <L *sphaera* < Gk. *sphaira* a ball]

-sphere *combining form* 1 Denoting an enveloping spherical mass: *hydrosphere, atmosphere.* 2 A sphere-shaped body: *oosphere.* 3 Denoting a spherical form: *planisphere.* [<Gk. *sphaira* a ball, sphere]

sphere of influence A country or region, usually backward politically or economically undeveloped, in which a state or states claim and are allowed exclusive rights to colonize, exploit natural and economic resources, or eventually annex.

spher·ic (sfer'ik) *adj.* Pertaining to a sphere or spheres; spherical.

spher·i·cal (sfer'i·kəl) *adj.* 1 Shaped like a sphere; globular. 2 Pertaining to a sphere or spheres. 3 Pertaining to the heavenly bodies; celestial. See synonyms under ORBICULATE, ROUND[1] — **spher'i·cal·ly** *adv.* — **spher'i·cal·ness** *n.*

spherical coordinate system *Math.* A three-dimensional system for indicating the shape of a solid by means of a sphere with the pole at the center. A point is located in terms of its distance along its radius vector from the pole, and in terms of two angles—the colatitude, or angle the radius vector forms with the vertical or polar axis of the sphere; and the longitude, or angle the radius vector makes with a fixed, vertical plane or initial meridian axis.

spherical sailing Navigation in which calculations are based upon a consideration of the spherical or spheroidal shape of the earth: distinguished from *plane sailing.*

spherical triangle *Math.* A spherical polygon the three sides of which are arcs of great circles of a sphere.

spherical trigonometry *Math.* The study of spherical triangles.

sphe·ric·i·ty (sfi·ris'ə·tē) *n. pl.* **·ties** The state of being a sphere; spherical form; roundness.

spher·ics (sfer'iks) *n.* 1 The geometry and trigonometry of figures on the surface of a sphere. 2 Atmospherics.

sphe·roid (sfir'oid) *n. Geom.* A body having nearly the form of a sphere; an ellipsoid. — **sphe·roi'dal** (sfi·roid'l), **sphe·roi'dic** or **·di·cal** *adj.* — **sphe·roi'dal·ly** *adv.*

sphe·roi·dic·i·ty (sfir'oi·dis'ə·tē) *n.* The state or character of being a spheroid. Also **sphe·roi·di·ty** (sfi·roi'də·tē).

sphe·rom·e·ter (sfi·rom'ə·tər) *n.* An instrument for measuring curvature or radii of spherical and other curved surfaces. [<SPHERE + -(O)METER]

spher·ule (sfer'ool) *n.* A small or minute sphere; globule. — **spher'u·lar** (sfer'oo·lər) *adj.*

spher·u·lite (sfer'oo·līt) *n.* A radiating spherical group of minute acicular crystals common in acidic glassy rocks. [<SPHERULE + -ITE[1]] — **spher'u·lit'ic** (-lit'ik) *adj.*

sphinc·ter (sfingk'tər) *n. Anat.* A muscle that surrounds an opening or tube and serves to close it. [<LL <Gk. *sphinktēr* < *sphingein* close] — **sphinc'ter·al** *adj.*

sphinx (sfingks) *n. pl.* **sphinx·es** or **sphin·ges** (sfin'jēz) 1 In Egyptian mythology, a wingless monster with a lion's body and the head of a man (*androsphinx,* or simply *sphinx*), or of a ram (*criosphinx*), or of a hawk (*hieracosphinx*); also, any monumental representation of such a creature. 2 In Greek mythology, a winged monster with a woman's head

SPHINX (*def. 2*)

and breasts and a lion's body, that destroyed those unable to guess her riddle. See OEDIPUS. 3 A mysterious or enigmatical person. 4 A large, stout-bodied, swift-flying moth. — **the Sphinx** The colossal androsphinx at Gizeh, having the body of a couchant lion, representing Harmachis, the Egyptian god of the morning, and dating to the IV dynasty. [<L <Gk. *sphinx* < *sphingein* close, strangle]

sphinx moth A hawk moth.

sphra·gis·tics (sfrə·jis'tiks) *n.* The study of signet rings or engraved seals, including their authenticity, age, history, etc. [<Gk. *sphragistikos* of sealing < *sphragis* seal] — **sphra·gis'tic** *adj.*

sphyg·mic (sfig'mik) *adj. Physiol.* Pertaining to the pulse; pulsatory. [<Gk. *sphygmikos* < *sphygmos* pulse]

sphygmo- *combining form* Pulse; of or related to the pulse: *sphygmogram.* Also, before vowels, **sphygm-.** [<Gk. *sphygmos* pulse]

sphyg·mo·gram (sfig'mə·gram) *n.* A series of connected curves traced by a sphygmograph.

sphyg·mo·graph (sfig'mə·graf, -gräf) *n.* An instrument that, when applied over the heart or an artery, notes and records the character of the pulse and its rate, force, and variations: also called *pulsimeter.* — **sphyg'mo·graph'ic** *adj.* — **sphyg·mog·ra·phy** (sfig·mog'rə·fē) *n.*

sphyg·moid (sfig'moid) *adj. Physiol.* Pulselike.

sphyg·mo·ma·nom·e·ter (sfig'mō·mə·nom'ə·tər) *n.* An instrument for measuring the pressure of the blood in the arteries. Also **sphyg·mom'e·ter** (-mom'ə·tər).

sphyg·mus (sfig'məs) *n.* The pulse. [<NL <L <Gk. *sphygmos* pulse]

spi·ca (spī'kə) *n. pl.* **·cae** (-sē) 1 An ear of grain; a spike. 2 *Surg.* A bandage having a reversed spiral form, somewhat resembling an ear of wheat. [<L, spike, ear of grain]

spice (spīs) *n.* 1 An aromatic, pungent vegetable substance, as cinnamon, cloves, etc., used to flavor food and beverages. 2 Such substances collectively. 3 That which gives zest or adds interest. 4 An aromatic odor; an agreeable perfume. 5 *Obs.* Sort; kind; species: the original meaning; also, a specimen. — *v.t.* **spiced, spic·ing** To season with spice; hence, to add zest or piquancy to. [<OF *espice* <L *species.* Doublet of SPECIES.] — **spic'er** *n.*

spice·ber·ry (spīs'ber'ē) *n. pl.* **·ries** 1 A small tree (*Eugenia rhombea*) found in the West Indies and Florida. 2 The black or orange fruit of this tree. 3 The wintergreen or checkerberry.

spice·bush (spīs'boosh') *n.* An aromatic American shrub (*Lindera benzoin*) of the laurel family, the leaves of which have been used for tea, and the drupes, when powdered, for allspice. Also **spice'wood'** (-wood').

spick (spik) *n. U.S. Slang* A Spanish-speaking person: an offensive term. Also **spic, spig** (spig).

spick-and-span (spik'ən·span') *adj.* 1 Neat and clean. 2 Perfectly new, or looking as if new. [Prob. < *spick,* var. of SPIKE[1] + SPAN-NEW]

spic·ule (spik'yool) *n.* 1 A small, slender, sharp-pointed body; a spikelet. 2 *Zool.* One of the small, needlelike, calcareous growths supporting the soft tissues of certain invertebrates, as sponges, radiolarians, etc. Also **spic·u·la** (spik′yə·lə). [<L *spiculum*, dim. of *spicum* point, spike] — **spic′u·lar, spic′u·late** (-lāt, -lit) *adj.*

spic·y (spī′sē) *adj.* **spic·i·er, spic·i·est** **1** Containing, flavored, or fragrant with spices. **2** Producing spices. **3** Highly flavored; pungent; having zest; hence, somewhat improper; risqué. See synonyms under RACY. — **spic′i·ly** *adv.* — **spic′i·ness** *n.*

spi·der (spī′dər) *n.* **1** Any one of a large number of wingless arachnids (order *Araneae*) having an unsegmented abdomen and capable of spinning silk in the construction of webs for the capture of prey such as flies or other insects. **2** A long-handled iron frying pan, often having legs. **3** A portable electric switching apparatus for use in motion–picture studios. **4** A three-legged iron stool for the support of pots and pans over a fire; a trivet. **5** An apparatus for pulverizing the ground during cultivation. **6** *Electr.* The central part of an armature core. **7** *Naut.* **a** An iron hoop around the mast of a ship for the attachment of shrouds. **b** A magnifying glass for a ship's compass. **8** Any of several vehicles of different types having unusually light frames. [OE *spithra* < *spinnan* spin]

SPIDER CRAB
(Up to 10 inches in breadth)

spider crab Any of a genus (*Libinia*) of decapod crustaceans with long legs, retractable eyes, and spiny growths on the carapace, especially *L. emarginata*, common on the Atlantic coast of North America. **spi·der·flow·er** (spī′dər·flou′ər) *n.* A cleome.

spider monkey An arboreal American monkey (genus *Ateles*) of slender form, with very long limbs, thumbs absent or vestigial, and a long prehensile tail: range from Mexico to Paraguay.

spider phaeton A type of carriage of light construction, having a covered seat in front, and a rear seat for a footman or attendant.

spi·der·wort (spī′dər·wûrt′) *n.* **1** Any species of a genus (*Tradescantia*) of plants, especially *T. virginiana*, an American perennial with deep-blue, three-petaled flowers in umbels. **2** Any plant of the same family (*Commelinaceae*).

spi·der·y (spī′dər·ē) *adj.* Spiderlike.

spiel (spēl) *U.S. Slang v.i.* To talk; orate. — *n.* A speech, especially a long speech. [<G, a game, play < *spielen* play]

spiff·y (spif′ē) *adj. Slang* Smartly dressed; spruce. [< dial. E *spiff* a dandy]

spi·ge·li·a (spī·jē′lē·ə) *n.* Pinkroot: used as a vermifuge. [<NL, after Adrian van den *Spiegel*, 1578–1625, Flemish anatomist]

spig·ot (spig′ət) *n.* **1** A plug or faucet for the bunghole of a cask. **2** A turning plug fitting into a faucet, or the faucet itself. [ME *spigote*. Prob. akin to SPIKE¹.]

spike¹ (spīk) *n.* **1** A stout piece of metal, like a large nail, but thicker in proportion. **2** A projecting, pointed piece of metal, or any similar object, as in the soles of shoes to keep the wearer from slipping. **3** A very high heel on a woman's shoe, narrow at the bottom. **4** A steel pin for plugging cannon vents. **5** A straight, unbranched antler, as of a young deer. **6** A young mackerel. — *v.t.* **spiked, spiking 1** To fasten with spikes. **2** To set or provide with spikes. **3** To block the vent of (a cannon) with a spike, rendering it useless. **4** To block; put a stop to. **5** To pierce with or impale on a spike. **6** In baseball, to injure (another player) with the spikes on one's shoes. **7** *Colloq.* To add spirituous liquor to. [ME <Scand. Cf. ON *spikr* a nail.]

spike² (spīk) *n.* **1** An ear of corn, barley, wheat, or other grain. **2** *Bot.* A flower cluster in which there are numerous flowers arranged closely on an elongated common axis. [<L *spica* ear of grain]

spike·nard (spīk′nərd, -närd) *n.* **1** An ancient fragrant and costly ointment prepared mainly from a plant of the same name. **2** A perennial East Indian herb (*Nardostachys jatamansi*) of the valerian family. **3** An American herb

(*Aralia racemosa*) of the ginseng family. [<L *spica* spike + *nardus* nard]

spile (spīl) *n.* **1** A large timber driven into the ground to serve as a foundation; a pile. **2** A wooden pin or plug used as a vent in a cask; a spigot. **3** A spout driven into a sugar-maple tree to lead the sap to a bucket. — *v.t.* **spiled, spil·ing 1** To pierce for and provide with a spigot. **2** To drive spiles into. [<MDu., skewer, splinter]

spill¹ (spil) *v.* **spilled** or **spilt, spill·ing** *v.t.* **1** To allow or cause to fall or run out or over, as a liquid or a powder. **2** To shed, as blood. **3** *Naut.* To empty (a sail) of wind. **4** *Colloq.* To cause to fall, as from a horse. **5** *Colloq.* To divulge; make known, as a secret. — *v.i.* **6** To fall or run out or over: said of liquids, etc. — **to spill the beans** *Colloq.* To divulge, especially a secret. — *n.* **1** *Colloq.* A fall to the ground, as from a horse or vehicle; tumble. **2** *Colloq.* A downpour, as of rain. **3** A crack, seam, or other defect in iron or steel castings, forgings, etc. [OE *spillan* destroy] — **spill′age** *n.* — **spill′er** *n.*

spill² (spil) *n.* **1** A slip of wood, or rolled strip of paper, used for lighting lamps, etc.; a lamplighter. **2** A slender peg, pin, or bar of wood or metal; especially, a slender plug for stopping a hole in a cask; a spile. [Var. of SPILE¹]

spill·way (spil′wā′) *n.* **1** A passageway in or about a dam to release the water in a reservoir. **2** The paved upper surface of a dam over which surplus water escapes.

SPILLWAY

spil·o·site (spil′ə·sīt) *n.* A greenish schistous rock spotted with chlorite, produced by the shearing of a basic amygdaloid. [<Gk. *spilos* spot + -ITE¹]

spilt (spilt) Alternative past tense and past participle of SPILL¹.

spilth (spilth) *n.* That which is spilled or poured out profusely; effusion; excess of supply.

spin (spin) *v.* **spun** (*Archaic* **span**), **spun, spin·ning** *v.t.* **1** To draw out and twist into threads; also, to draw out and twist fiber into (threads, yarn, etc.). **2** To make or produce as if by spinning. **3** To form (a net, etc.) from filaments of a viscous substance extruded from the body: said of spiders, silkworms, etc. **4** To tell, as a story or yarn. **5** To protract; prolong, as a period of time by delays or a story by additional details: with *out*. **6** To cause to whirl rapidly: to *spin* a top. — *v.i.* **7** To make thread or yarn. **8** To extrude filaments of a viscous substance from the body: said of spiders, etc. **9** To whirl rapidly; rotate. **10** To seem to be whirling, as from dizziness: My head is *spinning*. **11** To move rapidly. **12** To fish with a spoon bait or swivel. — *n.* **1** An act or instance of spinning; a rapid whirling. **2** Any rapid movement or action. **3** *Aeron.* The downward spiral motion of an airplane about a vertical axis, with its longitudinal axis steeply inclined. **4** *Physics* The angular momentum of an atomic particle or nuclide, commonly given in units of Planck's constant divided by 2π. [OE *spinnan* spin]

spi·na·ceous (spi·nā′shəs) *adj.* Of, relating to, or resembling spinach or plants allied to it.

spin·ach (spin′ich, -ij) *n.* **1** An edible garden pot herb (*Spinacia oleracea*) of the goosefoot family. **2** Its fleshy, edible leaves. Also **spin′age.** [<OF *espinage* <LL *spinacia* <Arabic *isbānah*; infl. in form by L *spina* a thorn]

spi·nal (spī′nəl) *adj.* **1** Pertaining to the backbone; vertebral. **2** Pertaining to a spine, spines, or spinous processes. **3** Dependent upon or functioning with a spinal cord, as the vertebrates.

spinal column *Anat.* The series of articulated vertebrae which, with their associated structures, enclose the spinal cord and provide dorsal support for the ribs; the backbone or spine.

spinal cord *Anat.* That portion of the central nervous system enclosed by the spinal column. It is composed of an inner region of gray matter and an outer, larger region of white matter, the whole divided into the cervical, thoracic, lumbar, sacral, and coccygeal areas.

spin·dle (spin′dəl) *n.* **1** A rod having a slit or catch in the top and a whorl of wood or metal at its lower end, formerly used in hand spinning, and on which was wound the thread from the distaff. **2** The slender rod in a spinning wheel by the rotation of which the thread is twisted and wound on a spool or bobbin on the same rod; also, a small rod or pin bearing the bobbin of a spinning machine or a shuttle. **3** *Mech.* A rotating rod, pin, axis, arbor, or shaft, especially when small and bearing something that rotates: the *spindle* of a lathe. **4** The pin on which rotates a fusee in a watch, or the fusee itself. **5** The tapering end of a vehicle axle that enters the hub. **6** A small shaft passing through the lock of a door and bearing the knobs or handles. **7** *Biol.* A spindle-shaped structure of elongated achromatic fibers formed during the mitosis of a cell. **8** A measure of length for cotton or linen yarn, varying according to the number of hanks or cuts: generally 18 hanks, or 15,120 yards. **9** *Naut.* An iron pile or pipe, surmounted by a lantern or other conspicuous object, placed on a rock or shoal for the guidance of seamen. **10** A hydrometer. **11** A needlelike rod mounted on a weighted base, for impaling bills, checks, etc. — *v.* **·dled, ·dling** *v.i.* **1** To grow into a long, slender stalk or body; become extremely long and slender. — *v.t.* **2** To form into or as into a spindle. **3** To provide with a spindle. **4** To puncture or impale on a spindle (def. 11), as a bill, memorandum, etc. [OE *spinel* < *spinnan* spin]

spin·dle-leg·ged (spin′dəl-leg′id, -legd′) *adj.* Having long, slender legs. Also **spin′dle-shanked** (-shangkt′).

spindle tree A European shrub or low-spreading tree (*Euonymus europaeus*), so called from the use of its compact wood in making spindles, slender pins, skewers, etc.

spin·dling (spind′ling) *adj.* Long and thin; disproportionately slender. — *n.* A spindling person or plant shoot.

spin·dly (spind′lē) *adj.* Of a slender, lanky growth or form, suggesting weakness.

spin·drift (spin′drift) *n.* Blown spray or scud: also called *spoondrift*. [Alter. of *spoondrift* < *spoon*, var. of SPUME + DRIFT]

spine (spīn) *n.* **1** The spinal column of a vertebrate; backbone. **2** *Zool.* Any of various hard, pointed outgrowths on the bodies of certain animals, as the porcupine and starfish; a spicule; the fin ray of a fish. **3** *Bot.* A stiff, short-pointed woody process on the stems of certain plants, as the honey locust; thorn. **4** The back of a bound book. **5** A projecting eminence or ridge. **6** Any slender, thornlike process, as of a vertebra or nerve. **7** The central ridge on the underside of a horse's hoof. [<OF *espine* <L *spina* spine, thorn]

spi·nel (spi·nel′, spin′əl) *n.* A hard isometric mineral of various colors and composition, some of which are used as gemstones. [<F *spinelle* <Ital. *spinella*, dim. of L *spina* spine]

spine·less (spīn′lis) *adj.* **1** Having no spine or backbone; invertebrate. **2** Lacking spines. **3** Having a very flexible backbone; limp. **4** Figuratively, lacking decision of character or steadfastness. — **spine′less·ness** *n.*

spin·et (spin′it) *n.* **1** A small keyboard musical instrument of the harpsichord class. **2** A small upright piano. [Perhaps after G. *Spinetti*, 16th-century Venetian inventor]

spini- *combining form* A spine; thorn: *spiniferous*. [<L *spina* a thorn]

spin·i·fex (spin′i·feks, spī′ni-) *n.* An Australian grass (genus *Spinifex*) with pointed leaves.

spin·na·ker (spin′ə·kər) *n. Naut.* A large jib-shaped sail sometimes carried on the mainmast of a racing vessel, opposite the mainsail, and used when sailing before the wind. The foot slides on a spar called the **spinnaker boom** [? < *spinx*, a mispronunciation of *Sphinx*, the name of the first vessel to carry this kind of sail]

spin·ner (spin′ər) *n.* **1** One who or that which spins, as a spider or a machine. **2** In angling, a whirling spoon bait. **3** *Aeron.* A streamlined fairing fitted over the boss of an airplane propeller and revolving with it. See illustration under AIRPLANE **4** A play in football wherein the ball carrier spins around to conceal the direction of the play from his opponents.

spin·ner·et (spin′ə·ret) *n.* **1** An organ, as of spiders and silkworms, for spinning silk. **2** A metal plate pierced with holes through which filaments of plastic material are forced, as in the making of rayon fibers.

spin·ney (spin′ē) n. A small wood or thicket. Also **spin′ny.** [< OF espinei < LL spinetum < L spina a thorn]

spin·ning (spin′ing) n. 1 The action of, or activities involved in, converting fibers into thread or yarn. 2 The product of spinning. —adj. 1 That spins, in any sense. 2 Of or used in the process of spinning.

spinning gland A gland that secretes silk or a silky substance, as in silkworms.

spinning jenny A framed mechanism for spinning more than one strand of yarn at a time: also called jenny.

spinning wheel A household implement formerly used for spinning yarn or thread, consisting of a rotating spindle operated by a treadle and flywheel.

spin-off (spin′ôf′, -of′) n. 1 Action of a corporation in divesting itself, tax free, of a segment or division of its operations by transfer to a new, independently owned and managed company, the stockholders of the original corporation receiving

SPINNING WHEEL

the new shares pro rata. 2 A new application or incidental result, especially if beneficial; offshoot or by-product; also, such applications or results considered collectively: commercial spin-off from the government's aerospace program: also **spin′off′.**

spi·nose (spin′nōs) adj. Bearing, armed with, or having many spines. [< L spinosus < spina a thorn] —**spi′nose·ly** adv.

spi·nos·i·ty (spī-nos′ə-tē) n. pl. ·ties 1 The state of being spinous or spinose. 2 A spinous part or thing.

spi·nous (spī′nəs) adj. 1 Spinelike; prickly. 2 Spinose.

spin·ster (spin′stər) n. 1 An unmarried woman, especially when no longer young; an old maid. 2 Law In England, a woman who has never married: a legal title. 3 A woman who spins; a spinner. [ME < SPIN + -STER] —**spin′ster·hood** n. —**spin′ster·ish** adj.

spin·thar·i·scope (spin-thar′ə-skōp) n. A device for showing the radioactivity of a substance by the scintillations of the alpha rays emitted from a minute particle of the substance and thrown against a fluorescent screen. [< Gk. spintharis spark + SCOPE] —**spin·thar′i·scop′ic** (-skop′ik) adj.

spi·nule (spī′nyool, spin′yool) n. A small spine; spicule. Also **spin·u·la** (spin′yə-lə). [< L spinula, dim. of spina spine]

spin·u·les·cent (spin′yə-les′ənt, spī′nyə-) adj. Furnished with or producing spinules; spiny.

spin·u·lose (spin′yə-lōs, spī′nyə-lōs) adj. Having spinules. Also **spin′u·lous** (-ləs).

spin·y (spī′nē) adj. **spin·i·er, spin·i·est** 1 Having spines; thorny. 2 Difficult; perplexing. —**spin′i·ness** n.

spiny ant-eater The echidna.

spin·y-finned (spī′nē-find′) adj. Characterized by fins bearing one or more sharp, unsegmented rays, as the perch, mackerel, and bass. Also **spine′-finned′.**

spiny lobster One of various large-bodied marine crustaceans (genus Palinurus) with spiny shells but lacking claws; especially, the California spiny lobster (P. interruptus), valued as a sea food. Also called crayfish.

spir·a·cle (spir′ə-kəl, spī′rə-) n. 1 Zool. a An aperture or orifice for the passage of air or water in the respiration of terrestrial arthropods, as the grasshopper and locust. b A breathing hole, as the blowhole or nostril of a cetacean. 2 A minute cone formed on a stream of lava by escaping gases. 3 Any opening to admit or expel air; an airhole. [< OF < L spiraculum airhole < spirare

breathe]

spi·rae·a (spī-rē′ə) n. Any of a genus (Spiraea) of ornamental shrubs of the rose family, having alternate simple or pinnate leaves and small, white or pink flowers; especially, an American variety, the meadowsweet. Also **spi·re′a.** [< L, meadowsweet < Gk. speiraia < speira coil]

spi·ral (spī′rəl) adj. 1 Winding about and constantly receding from a center. 2 Winding and advancing; helical. 3 Winding and rising in a spire, as some springs. —n. 1 Geom. Any plane curve formed by a point that moves around a fixed center and continually increases its distance from it. 2 A curve winding like a screw thread. 3 Something wound as a spiral or having a spiral shape, as a spring or a whorled shell. 4 A sharp or disproportionate rise, as in prices. 5 Aeron. A flight of an airplane in a spiral path. 6 In football, the motion of a ball rotating on its long axis. —v. ·raled or ·ralled, ·ral·ing or ·ral·ling v.t. 1 To cause to take a spiral form or course. —v.i. 2 To take a spiral form or course. 3 To rise sharply or disproportionately, as prices, costs, etc. [< Med. L spiralis < L spira SPIRE²] —**spi′ral·ly** adv.

spiral binding A binding consisting of a wire in spiral form looped through holes in the covers on either side.

spiral nebula Astron. An extragalactic system of celestial bodies exhibiting a spiral configuration, known to be composed of aggregates of stars resembling the Milky Way, as the spiral nebula in Andromeda.

spiral of Archimedes Math. The polar curve traced by a point starting at the pole and moving along its radius vector at a constant velocity while the radius vector moves at a constant angular velocity.

spire¹ (spīr) n. 1 The tapering or pyramidal roof of a tower; a pinnacle; also, loosely, a steeple. 2 A slender stalk or blade. 3 The summit or tapering end of anything; a sharp point. —v. **spired, spir·ing** v.t. 1 To furnish with a spire or spires. —v.i. 2 To shoot or point up in or as in a spire. 3 To put forth a spire or spires; sprout. [OE spīr a stalk, stem] —**spired** adj.

SPIRE

spire² (spīr) n. 1 A spiral or a single turn of one; whorl; twist. 2 The portion of a spiral formed by a single revolution about the central point. 3 Zool. The convoluted portion of a spiral shell. [< F < L spira < Gk. speira coil] —**spired** adj.

spi·reme (spī′rēm) n. Biol. 1 The stage in the division of a cell during which the chromatin appears like a skein of filaments. 2 One of these filaments. Also **spi′rem** (-rem). [< Gk. speirēma a coil]

spir·il·lo·sis (spir′ə-lō′sis) n. 1 Pathol. Any disease caused by the presence of spirilla in the body. 2 A disease of domestic fowls caused by a spirochete transmitted by a tick. [< SPIRILLUM + -OSIS]

spi·ril·lum (spī-ril′əm) n. pl. ·ril·la (-ril′ə) Any of a genus (Spirillum) of flagellate bacteria with cells in spirally twisted and rigid filaments. See illustration under BACTERIUM. [< NL, dim. of L spira a coil]

spir·it (spir′it) n. 1 The principle of life and energy in man and animals, at one time regarded as being composed of an especially refined substance, such as breath or warm air, separable from the body, mysterious in nature, and ascribable to a divine origin. 2 An entity conceived of as that part of a human being that is incorporeal and invisible and is characterized by intelligence, personality, self-consciousness, and will; the mind: opposed to body. 3 The substance or universal aspect of reality, regarded as independent of and opposed to matter. 4 In the Bible, the creative, animating power or divine influence of God. Joel ii 28. 5 A rational, supernatural being without a material body, as an angel, demon, elf, fairy, etc.; specifically,

such a being with a certain character or a particular abode or area of activity: an evil spirit. 6 A disembodied soul regarded as manifested to the senses, often as visible or having some kind of immaterial body: a ghost; specter: Hamlet saw his father's spirit. 7 A person regarded with reference to any peculiar activity, characteristic, or temper: a leading spirit in the community. 8 Usually pl. A state of mind; mood; temper: Success raised his spirits. 9 Vivacity or energy; ardor; dash; fire: an attack made with spirit. 10 Ardent loyalty or devotion: school spirit. 11 True intent or meaning as opposed to outward, formal signification: to keep the spirit of the law. Compare LETTER (def. 5). 12 The emotional or affective faculty of man; the heart: Great poetry stirs the spirit. 13 The characteristic temper or disposition of a period or of a movement: the spirit of the Reformation. 14 pl. A strong alcoholic liquor or liquid obtained by distillation. 15 Usually pl. Chem. a The essence or distilled extract of a substance: spirits of turpentine. b Ethanol. 16 Often pl. In pharmacy, a solution of a volatile principle in alcohol; a tincture; essence: spirits of ammonia. 17 In dyeing, a solution of a tin salt in acid. 18 In alchemy, one of four substances, mercury, sal ammoniac, sulfur, and arsenic (or orpiment). 19 In medieval physiology, one of the three degrees of spirit inherent in the human body: natural spirit, located in the liver and underlying the processes of nutrition, growth, and reproduction; vital spirit, located in the heart, which circulated heat and life through the body; animal spirit, located in the brain, which guided reason and conveyed the powers of motion and sensation to and through the nerves. 20 Obs. Breathed air; breeze; wind. 21 Obs. The breath; life. See synonyms under CHARACTER, COURAGE, MIND, SPECTER. —v.t. 1 To carry off secretly or mysteriously, as if by the agency of a spirit: with away, off, etc. 2 To infuse with spirit or animation; inspirit; encourage: often with up. —adj. 1 Of or pertaining to ghosts or the belief in the existence of departed souls; spiritualistic. 2 Operated by the burning of alcohol: a spirit lamp. [< OF espirit < L spiritus breathing < spirare breathe. Doublet of SPRITE.]

spir·it·ed (spir′it·id) adj. Full of spirit; animated: used in various compound adjectives: high–spirited, mean–spirited. See synonyms under RACY. —**spir′it·ed·ly** adv. —**spir′it·ed·ness** n.

spir·it·ing (spir′it·ing) n. Movement as of a spirit; hence, something dexterously done; the work or ministering of a spirit; inspiration; encouragement.

spirit lamp A lamp that burns alcohol: used in laboratory work, etc.

spir·it·less (spir′it·lis) adj. Lacking in enthusiasm, energy, or courage; lacking in the sense of well-being. —**spir′it·less·ly** adv. —**spir′it·less·ness** n.

spirit level An instrument for adjusting any deviation from the horizontal or perpendicular by reference to the position of a bubble of air in a tube of alcohol or other liquid.

spir·it·u·al (spir′i·chŌŌ·əl) adj. 1 Of or pertaining to spirit, as distinguished from matter; having the nature of spirit; consisting of spirit; incorporeal. 2 Pertaining to or affecting the immaterial nature or soul of man. 3 Of or pertaining to God, his Spirit, or his law, or to the soul as acted upon by the Holy Spirit; holy; pure; not carnal. 4 Sacred or religious; not lay or temporal; ecclesiastical: spiritual authorities: contrasted with secular. 5 Marked or characterized by the highest qualities of the human mind; intellectualized. —n. 1 Anything pertaining to spirit or to sacred matters. 2 A religious folk song originating among the Negroes of the southern United States, typified by colorful rhythm and emotion: sometimes in narrative or ballad form; also, any song composed in imitation of a Negro spiritual. — the Spirituals See under FRATICELLI. [< L spiritualis < spiritus spirit] —**spir′i·tu·al·ly** adv. —**spir′i·tu·al·ness** n.

spir·it·u·al·ism (spir′i·chŌŌ·əl·iz′əm) n. 1 The belief that the spirits of the dead in various ways communicate with and manifest their presence to the living, usually through the agency of a person called a medium; also, the doctrines and practices of those so believing. **2** The doctrine that there are beings not cognizable by the senses or characterized by the properties of matter, and that are therefore spiritual, as distinguished from material: opposed to *materialism.* **3** The doctrine that man is an immortal spirit and as such may know, love, or worship God. **4** A non–materialistic philosophy, a form of idealism which identifies ultimate reality as one universal conscious mind. **5** The state or character of being spiritual. — **spir′i·tu·al·ist** *n.* — **spir′i·tu·al·is′tic** *adj.*

spir·i·tu·ous (spir′i·chŏŏ·əs) *adj.* **1** Containing alcohol. **2** Intoxicating; distilled. **3** *Obs.* Spiritlike; ethereal. **4** *Rare* Lively. — **spir′i·tu·ous·ness** *n.*

spiro–[1] *combining form* Breath; respiration: *spirograph.* Also, before vowels, **spir–.** [<L *spirare* breathe]

spiro–[2] *combining form* Spiral; coiled: *spirochete.* Also, before vowels, **spir–.** [<Gk. *speira* a coil]

spi·ro·chete (spī′rə·kēt) *n.* **1** Any of a genus (*Spirochaeta*) of typically saprophytic bacteria commonly found in water and sewage, and characterized by spiral flexible filaments with apparently rotary movements. See illustration under BACTERIUM. **2** Any of various other similar micro–organisms of the order *Spirochaetales,* including those which cause syphilis and relapsing fever. Also **spi′ro·chaete.** [<Gk. *speira* coil + *chaitē* bristle] — **spi′ro·che′tal** *adj.*

spi·ro·che·to·sis (spī′rə·kē·tō′sis) *n.* **1** *Pathol.* Infection by spirochetes. **2** An infectious septicemia in chickens caused by a spirochete (*Borrelia anserina*).

spi·ro·graph (spī′rə·graf, -gräf) *n.* An instrument for recording the breathing movement. [<SPIRO–[1] + -GRAPH] — **spi′ro·graph′ic** *adj.* — **spi·rog·ra·phy** (spī·rog′rə·fē) *n.*

spi·ro·gy·ra (spī′rə·jī′rə) *n.* Any of a genus (*Spirogyra*) of bright–green, fresh–water algae forming dense masses or beds of growth in slow–running or stagnant water, and characterized by having the chlorophyll bands winding spirally to the right. [<SPIRO–[2] + Gk. *gyros* ring, coil]

spi·roid (spī′roid) *adj.* Resembling a spiral.

spi·rom·e·ter (spī·rom′ə·tər) *n.* An instrument for measuring the capacity of the lungs. [<SPIRO–[1] + -METER] — **spi·ro·met·ric** (spī′rə·met′rik) *adj.* — **spi·rom′e·try** *n.*

spir·u·la (spir′yə·lə, spir′ŏŏ–) *n. pl.* **·lae** (-lē) Any of a genus (*Spirula*) of cephalopods with an internal spiral chambered shell having whorls detached and in the same plane. [<NL <Gk. *speira* coil]

spis·sat·ed (spis′ā·tid) *adj.* Thickened. [<L *spissatus,* pp. of *spissare* thicken]

spit[1] (spit) *v.* **spat** or **spit, spit·ting** *v.t.* **1** To eject (saliva, blood, etc.) from the mouth. **2** To throw off, eject, or utter with violence. **3** To light, as a fuse. — *v.i.* **4** To eject saliva from the mouth. **5** To make a noise like that made in ejecting saliva. **6** To fall in scattered drops or flakes, as rain or snow. — *n.* **1** Spittle; saliva. **2** An act of spitting or expectorating. **3** A frothy, spit-like secretion of the spittle insect; also, a spittle insect. **4** A light, scattered fall or short, driving flurry of snow or rain. **5** *Colloq.* Exact image; likeness; counterpart: He's the *spit* of John. [OE *spittan*] — **spit′ter** *n.*

spit[2] (spit) *n.* **1** A pointed rod on which meat is turned and roasted before a fire. **2** A point of low land, or a long, narrow shoal, extending from a shore into the water. — *v.t.* **spit·ted, spit·ting** To transfix or impale with or as with a spit. [OE *spitu* spit]

spit·ball (spit′bôl′) *n.* **1** Paper chewed in the mouth and shaped into a ball for use as a missile. **2** In baseball, a pitched ball wet with saliva, and rotating deceptively in its course: no longer permitted by the rules. — **spit′ball′er** *n.*

spitch·cock (spich′kok′) *v.t.* To split and broil, as a bird or fish. — *n.* An eel split and broiled. [Origin unknown]

spite (spīt) *n.* **1** Malicious bitterness prompting to vexatious acts; mean hatred; grudge. **2** That which is done in spite. **3** *Archaic* Trouble; bad luck: a Shakespearean usage.

See synonyms under ENMITY, HATRED. — **in spite of** (or **spite of**) Formerly, in contempt of; now, notwithstanding. — *v.t.* **spit·ed, spit·ing** **1** To show one's spite toward; vex maliciously; thwart. **2** *Obs.* To fill with spite; offend; vex. [Short for DESPITE]

spit·fire (spit′fīr′) *n.* A quick–tempered person who is given to saying spiteful things.

spit·ting image (spit′ing) *Colloq.* An exact likeness or counterpart. Also **spit and image.**

spitting snake A venomous snake of South Africa (*Sepedon haemachates*) related to the cobras, that is able to eject its poison for some distance; the ringhals.

spit·tle (spit′l) *n.* **1** The fluid secreted by the mouth; saliva; spit. **2** The salivalike matter in which the larvae of spittle insects live. [OE *spätl;* infl. in form by *spit*[1]]

spittle insect A froghopper.

spit·toon (spi·tōōn′) *n.* A receptacle for spit; a cuspidor.

spitz (spits) *n.* One of a breed of small dogs with a tapering muzzle; a Pomeranian. Also **spitz dog.** [<G, short for *spitzhund*]

splake (splāk) *n. Canadian* A hybrid fish, a cross between the speckled trout and the lake trout: also called *mendigo.*

splash (splash) *v.t.* **1** To dash or spatter (a liquid, etc.) about. **2** To spatter, wet, or soil with a liquid dashed about. **3** To make with splashes: to *splash* one's way. **4** To decorate with splashed ornament. — *v.i.* **5** To make a splash or splashes. **6** To move, fall, or strike with a splash or splashes. — *n.* **1** The act or noise of splashing. **2** The result of splashing; a spot made by a liquid or color splashed on. **3** In logging, a head of water released suddenly from a splash dam to drive a body of logs. [Var. of PLASH[1]]

splash·board (splash′bôrd′, -bōrd′) *n.* **1** Any of various devices to protect against splashes, especially a dashboard for a vehicle. **2** A board for closing the spillway or sluice of a dam. Also **splash′wing′** (-wing′).

splash·down (splash′doun′) *n.* The setting down of a spacecraft or a part of it in the seas following its flight.

splash·y (splash′ē) *adj.* **1** Slushy; wet. **2** Marked by or as by splashes; blotchy. **3** *Colloq.* Sensational; showy: They made a *splashy* appearance.

splat·ter (splat′ər) *v.t. & v.i.* To spatter or splash. — *n.* A spatter; splash. [Blend of SPLASH and SPATTER]

splay (splā) *adj.* Spread out; displayed; broad; clumsy; clumsily formed: a *splay* mouth. — *n. Archit.* A slanted surface or beveled edge, as of the sides of a doorway or window, or of a joist. — *v.t.* **1** To make with a splay; bevel or chamfer away a corner or angle of, as a window opening. **2** To open to sight; spread; cut open; display. **3** In farriery, to dislocate. — *v.i.* **4** To spread out; open. **5** To slant; slope. [Aphetic var. of DISPLAY]

splay·foot (splā′fŏŏt′) *n.* **1** Abnormal flatness and turning outward of the feet. **2** A foot so deformed. — **splay′–foot′ed** *adj.*

spleen (splēn) *n. Anat.* **1** A highly vascular, flattened, ductless organ found near the stomach of most vertebrates, which effects certain modifications in the blood. ◆ Collateral adjective: *lienal.* **2** This organ regarded as the seat of various emotions. **3** Ill temper; spitefulness: to vent one's *spleen.* **4** *Archaic* Lowness of spirits; melancholy; hypochondria. **5** *Obs.* Mode or state of mind; also, caprice; a fit of pique. **6** *Obs.* Violent mirth. [<L *splen* <Gk. *splēn*] — **spleen′ish** *adj.* — **spleen′y** *adj.*

spleen·ful (splēn′fəl) *adj.* Affected with spleen; peevish; ill-tempered. — **spleen′ful·ly** *adv.*

spleen·wort (splēn′wûrt′) *n.* Any of a genus (*Asplenium*) of hardy and cultivated ferns with simple or compound fronds: so called from the use formerly made of some species in disorders of the spleen.

splen·dent (splen′dənt) *adj.* **1** Shining; lustrous. **2** Illustrious. [<L *splendens, -entis,* ppr. of *splendere* shine]

splen·did (splen′did) *adj.* **1** Magnificent; imposing. **2** Inspiring to the imagination; glorious; illustrious. **3** Giving out or reflecting brilliant light; shining. **4** *Colloq.* Very good; excellent: a *splendid* offer. See synonyms under FINE[1], BRIGHT. [<L *splendidus* <*splendere* shine] — **splen′did·ly** *adv.* — **splen′did·ness** *n.*

See synonyms under ENMITY, HATRED.

splen·dif·er·ous (splen·dif′ər·əs) *adj. Colloq.* Exhibiting great splendor; very magnificent: a facetious usage. [<SPLEND(OR) + -(I)FEROUS]

splen·dor (splen′dər) *n.* **1** Exceeding brilliance from emitted or reflected light. **2** Magnificence. **3** Conspicuous greatness of achievement; preeminence. Also *Brit.* **splen′dour.** [<L, brightness <*splendere* shine] — **splen′dor·ous, splen′drous** *adj.*

sple·net·ic (spli·net′ik) *adj.* **1** Pertaining to the spleen. **2** Fretfully spiteful; peevish. See synonyms under MOROSE. Also **sple·net′i·cal, splen·i·tive** (splen′ə·tiv). — *n.* **1** One suffering from disease of the spleen. **2** A peevish person. — **sple·net′i·cal·ly** *adv.*

splen·ic (splen′ik, splē′nik) *adj.* Of, in, or pertaining to the spleen.

sple·ni·tis (spli·nī′tis) *n. Pathol.* Inflammation of the spleen.

sple·ni·um (splē′nē·əm) *n. pl.* **·ni·a** (-nē·ə) **1** *Surg.* A compress or bandage. **2** *Anat.* The rounded posterior end of the corpus callosum. [<NL <Gk. *splēnion* a bandage] — **sple′ni·al** *adj.*

sple·ni·us (splē′nē·əs) *n. pl.* **·ni·i** (-nē·ī) *Anat.* A large, thick muscle of the back of the neck, extending in two parts from the skull to the vertebral spines in the cervical and upper thoracic region. [<NL <Gk. *splēnion* a bandage] — **sple′ni·al** *adj.*

spleno– *combining form Anat. & Med.* The spleen; of or related to the spleen. Also, before vowels, **splen–,** as in *splenitis.* [<Gk. *splēn, splēnos* the spleen]

splice (splīs) *v.t.* **spliced, splic·ing 1** To unite, as two ropes or parts of a rope, so as to form one continuous piece, by intertwining the strands. **2** To connect, as timbers, by beveling, scarfing, or overlapping at the ends. **3** *Slang* To join in marriage: usually in the passive. — **to splice the main brace** To serve or take a glass of grog: chiefly jocular. — *n.* **1** A union at the ends of joined parts, especially of ropes, made by intertwining the strands. **2** The place at which two parts are spliced. [<MDu. *splissen*]

SPLICES

a. Cut splice.	*d–f.* Short splices.
b–c. Long splices.	*g–l.* Eye splices.

spline (splīn) *n.* **1** *Mech.* A metal key permanently set into a slot in one of two connected rotating mechanical parts, as a shaft and a pulley, and engaging with a similar slot cut in the other, thus permitting both parts to have relative lengthwise motion, but not to rotate upon each other: also called *feather, feather key.* **2** A long, flexible strip of wood or hard rubber, used by mechanical draftsmen to lay down ship lines, railway curves, or similar work. **3** A thin strip or tongue of wood or metal used in matching grooved planks, making partitions, filling air spaces, etc. — *v.t.* **splined, splin·ing 1** To make a slot or groove in for a spline. **2** To fit with a spline. [? Related to SPLINT] — **splined** *adj.*

splint (splint) *n.* **1** A thin, flat piece split off; a splinter. **2** A thin, flexible strip of split wood used for basket–making, chair bottoms, etc. **3** In plate armor, one of the flexibly adjusted overlapping laminae. **4** *Surg.* An appliance, as of wood or metal, used for keeping a fractured limb or other injured part in a fixed position. **5** A splint bone. **6** An osseous tumor on the splint bone of a horse, due to inflammation of the periosteum; also, a bony callosity resulting from disease of the splint bones. — *v.t.* To confine, support, or brace, as a fractured limb, with or as with splints. [<MDu. *splinte*]

splint armor Armor made of overlapping

metal plates.

splint bone 1 One of the small rudimentary bones of the metacarpus or metatarsus of the horse and related animals. Compare illustration under HORSE. **2** The fibula.

splin·ter (splin'tər) *n.* A thin, sharp piece of wood, glass, metal, etc., split or torn off lengthwise; a sliver. —*v.t. & v.i.* To split into thin sharp pieces or fragments; shatter; shiver. [<MDu.] —**splin'ter·y** *adj.*

splin·ter·proof (splin'tər·prŏof') *adj.* Resistant to the penetration of splinters: said especially of shelters affording protection from machine-gun fire and shell fragments.

split (split) *v.* **split**, **split·ting** *v.t.* **1** To separate into parts by force, especially into two approximately equal parts. **2** To break or divide lengthwise or along the grain; rive; separate into layers. **3** To divide into groups or factions; disrupt, as a political party. **4** To divide and distribute by portions or shares. —*v.i.* **5** To break apart; divide lengthwise or along the grain. **6** To become divided or disunited through disagreement, etc. **7** To share something with others. **8** *Slang* To leave quickly or abruptly. —**to split hairs** To make fine distinctions; be unnecessarily precise or subtle. —**to split off 1** To break off by splitting. **2** To separate by or as by splitting. —**to split the difference** To divide equally a sum in dispute. —**to split up 1** To separate into parts and distribute. **2** To cease association; separate. —*n.* **1** The act or result of splitting; a longitudinal fissure; cleft; rent. **2** Separation of an aggregate body into factions; rupture; schism: a *split* in the church. **3** A sliver; splinter. **4** A share or portion, as of loot or booty. **5** A six-ounce bottle of an alcoholic beverage or of mineral water. **6** A split osier, used in certain phases of basket weaving. **7** A confection made of a sliced banana, ice-cream, sirup, chopped nuts, and whipped cream. **8** A single thickness of a split skin or hide. **9** In bowling, the position of two or more pins left standing on such spots that a spare is nearly impossible. **10** A split ballot: There were 47 *splits* in the ballot box. **11** An acrobatic trick in which the legs are extended upon the floor in a straight line at right angles to the body. **12** *Slang* A quick departure. —*adj.* **1** Divided, especially longitudinally or with the grain; cleft; fissured. **2** Dressed and cured after being cleaned: said of fish. **3** Given in sixteenths, rather than eighths, as a stock quotation: 10¹/16 is a *split* quotation: opposed to *regular.* **4** Divided: a *split* ballot. [<MDu. *splitten*] —**split'ter** *n.*

split decision In boxing, a decision in which only two of three officials agree on the winner.

split infinitive See under INFINITIVE.

split-lev·el (split'lev'əl) *adj.* Designating a type of dwelling in which the floors of adjoining parts are at different levels, connected by short flights of stairs, permitting a compact arrangement of living and service rooms.

split product *Chem.* Any product of a decomposition, as of a protein into amino acids.

split ticket 1 A ballot on which the voter has distributed his vote among candidates of different parties. **2** A ballot containing names of candidates of more than one party or party faction. Compare STRAIGHT TICKET.

split-ting (split'ing) *adj.* Acute or extreme in kind or degree: a *splitting* pain.

splotch (sploch) *n.* A discolored spot, as of ink, etc.; a daub; splash; spot. —*v.t.* To soil or mark with a splotch or splotches. [Cf. OE *splot* spot] —**splotch'y** *adj.*

splurge (splûrj) *Colloq. n.* **1** An ostentatious display. **2** An extravagant expenditure. —*v.i.* **splurged**, **splurg·ing 1** To show off; be ostentatious. **2** To spend money lavishly or wastefully. [Imit.] —**splurg'y** *adj.*

splut·ter (splut'ər) *v.i.* **1** To make a series of slight, explosive sounds, or throw off small particles, as meat frying in fat. **2** To speak hastily, confusedly, or incoherently, as from surprise or indignation. —*v.t.* **3** To utter excitedly or confusedly; sputter. **4** To spatter or bespatter. —*n.* A noise as of spluttering; bustle; confused stir. [Blend of SPLASH and SPUTTER] —**splut'ter·er** *n.*

spode or **Spode** (spōd) *n.* Fine porcelain or china made at the works founded by Josiah Spode (1754–1827) in Staffordshire, England.

spod·u·mene (spoj'oo·mēn) *n.* A vitreous, transparent to translucent lithium–aluminum silicate, belonging to the pyroxene group and crystallizing in the monoclinic system. [<Gk. *spodoumenos*, ppr. of *spodoesthai* be burned to ashes <*spodos* ashes]

spoil (spoil) *v.* **spoiled** or **spoilt**, **spoil·ing** *v.t.* **1** To impair or destroy the value, usefulness, or beauty of; injure: to *spoil* a book. **2** To weaken or impair the character or personality of, especially by overindulgence: Spare the rod and *spoil* the child. **3** *Obs.* To take property from by force; despoil. **4** *Obs.* To seize by force. —*v.i.* **5** To lose normal or useful qualities; specifically, to become tainted or decayed, as food. **6** *Obs.* To plunder; rob. See synonyms under CORRUPT, DECAY, DEFILE¹, INDULGE, PAMPER.—**to be spoiling for** To long for; crave: He is *spoiling for* a fight. —*n.* **1** Plunder seized by violence; booty; loot. **2** *pl.* The emoluments of public office as the objects of political contests and rewards of political service. **3** The act of pillaging; spoliation. **4** An object to be forcibly seized and taken away. **5** *Obs.* Ruin; destruction. **6** Material removed in digging trenches or excavations. **7** *Obs.* Damage; waste. See synonyms under PLUNDER. [<OF *espoillier* < L *spoliare* <*spolium* booty]

spoil-sport (spoil'spôrt', -spōrt') *n.* A person whose actions or attitudes spoil the pleasures of others.

spoils system The theory, or the practice of a political party after a victorious campaign, of making public offices the rewards of partisan services.

spoke (spōk) *n.* **1** One of the members of a wheel which serve to support the rim (or felly) by connecting it to the hub. **2** One of the radial handles of a ship's steering wheel. **3** A stick or bar for insertion in a wheel to prevent it from turning, as in descending a hill. **4** A rung of a ladder. —**to put a spoke in (someone's) wheel** To hinder or prevent (someone's) action. —*v.t.* **spoked**, **spok·ing 1** To provide with spokes. **2** To fasten (a wheel) with a stick or spoke to prevent its turning. [OE *spāca*]

spokes·man (spōks'mən) *n. pl.* **·men** (-mən) One who speaks in the name and behalf of another or others. —**spokes'wom·an** (-wŏom'·ən) *n. fem.*

spo·li·a·tion (spō'lē·ā'shən) *n.* **1** The act of despoiling; specifically, the plundering of neutral commerce by a belligerent. **2** *Law* Destruction; mutilation; alteration; specifically, the erasure, alteration, mutilation, or destruction of a paper to prevent its being used as evidence. **3** In English canon law, the taking of the fruits of a benefice under a pretended but illegal title, or a writ or suit brought on such grounds. **4** *Law* The destruction of a ship's papers so as to conceal its nationality, the character of its trade, cargo, etc. [<L *spoliatio,, -onis* <*spoliare* despoil] —**spo'li·a'tor** *n.*

spo·li·a·tive (spō'lē·ā'tiv) *adj.* Tending to abstract from or lessen; in medicine, resulting in a considerable loss of blood.

spon·da·ic (spon·dā'ik) *adj.* **1** Pertaining to or of the nature of a spondee; composed of spondees. **2** Having a spondee in a position where another kind of metrical foot is usual. Also **spon·da'i·cal.** [<L *spondaicus* <Gk. *spondeiakos* <*spondē.* See SPONDEE.]

spon·dee (spon'dē) *n.* A metrical foot consisting of two long syllables or, in English verse, of two accented syllables. [<F *spondée* <Gk. *spondeios (pous)* libation (meter) <*spondē* a libation; because used in the solemn chants accompanying a libation]

spon·dy·li·tis (spon'də·lī'tis) *n. Pathol.* Pott's disease.

spondylo- *combining form Anat. & Med.* A vertebra; of or pertaining to vertebrae. Also, before vowels, **spondyl-.** [<Gk. *spondylos* a vertebra]

sponge (spunj) *n.* **1** Any of a phylum (*Porifera*) of fixed, usually marine organisms characterized by a highly porous body without specialized internal organs. **2** The skeleton or network of elastic fibers that remains after the removal of the living matter from certain sponges and that readily absorbs liquids: used as an absorbent, for bathing, etc. **3** Some spongelike implement or substance that serves as an absorbent, as a swabbing implement for cleaning a cannon bore after discharge. **4** Leavened dough, or dough in the process of leavening and before kneading. **5** A porous, spongelike form assumed by finely divided metals, as iron and platinum. **6** *Surg.* An absorbent pad, as of sterilized gauze, used in operations, etc., to absorb blood or other fluid matter. **7** One who consumes or absorbs a great deal, as of food or drink. **8** *Colloq.* A person who lives at the expense of another or others; a parasite. —**to throw (or toss) up (or in) the sponge** *Colloq.* To yield; give up; abandon the struggle. —*v.* **sponged**, **spong·ing** *v.t.* **1** To wipe, wet, or clean with a sponge. **2** To wipe out; expunge; erase. **3** To absorb; suck in, as a sponge does. **4** *Colloq.* To get by mean device or at another's expense. —*v.i.* **5** To be absorbent. **6** To gather or fish for sponges. **7** *Colloq.* To live at the expense of others. See synonyms under CLEANSE. [OE <L *spongia*, ult. <Gk. *spongos.* Akin to FUNGUS.]

sponge cake A cake of sugar, eggs, and flour, containing no shortening and beaten very light.

spong·er (spun'jər) *n.* **1** One who or that which sponges in any sense. **2** A person or vessel that gathers sponges. **3** A human parasite.

spon·gi·form (spun'jə·fôrm, spon'-) *adj.* Resembling a sponge in form or structure.

spong·y (spun'jē) *adj.* **1** Having the nature or character of a sponge; elastic, compressible, and porous. **2** Having the quality of imbibing fluids; absorptive. **3** Existing in a condition of fine division and loose coherence. **4** *Obs.* Wet; soaked. Also **spon·gi·ose** (spun'jē·ōs). —**spong'i·ness** *n.*

spon·sal (spon'səl) *adj.* Relating to marriage or to a spouse. [<L *sponsus*, pp. of *spondere* promise]

spon·sion (spon'shən) *n.* **1** The act of becoming surety or sponsor for another. **2** In international law, an undertaking on behalf of his state by a public officer not specifically empowered to enter into it.

spon·son (spon'sən) *n.* **1** A curved projection from the hull of a vessel or seaplane, to give greater stability or increase the surface area. **2** A similar protuberance on a ship or tank, for storage purposes or for the training of a gun. **3** An air tank built into the side of a canoe, to improve stability and prevent sinking. [Appar. alter. of EXPANSION]

spon·sor (spon'sər) *n.* **1** One who makes himself responsible for a statement by, or the debt or duty of, another; a surety. **2** One who makes the required professions and promises for an infant at baptism and becomes responsible for its religious training; a godfather or godmother. **3** A business firm or enterprise that assumes all the costs of a radio or television program which advertises its product or service. —*v.t.* To act as sponsor for; answer or vouch for. —**spon·so·ri·al** (spon·sôr'ē·əl, -sō'rē-) *adj.* —**spon'sor·ship** *n.*

spon·ta·ne·ous (spon·tā'nē·əs) *adj.* **1** Arising from inherent qualities or tendencies without external efficient cause; done or acting from one's own impulse, prompting, or desire. **2** Not having material causation outside itself. **3** Generated or produced without human labor; wild or sporadic; indigenous. **4** *Biol.* Apparently arising independently of external stimulus, influence, or conditions. [<LL *spontaneus* <L *sponte* of free will] —**spon·ta'ne·ous·ly** *adv.* —**spon·ta'ne·ous·ness** *n.*

Synonyms: automatic, instinctive, involuntary, unbidden, voluntary, willing. That is *spontaneous* which is freely done, with no external compulsion and, in human actions, without special premeditation or distinct determination of the will; that is *voluntary* which is freely done with distinct act of will; that is *involuntary* which is independent of the will, and perhaps in opposition to it; a *will-ing* act is not only in accordance with will, but with desire. Thus *voluntary* and *involuntary*, which are antonyms of each other, are both partial synonyms of *spontaneous*. An infant's smile in answer to that of its mother is *spontaneous*; the smile of a pouting child wheedled into good humor is *involuntary*. In physiology the action of the heart and lungs is *involuntary* action; the growth of the hair and nails is *spontaneous*; the action of swallowing is *voluntary* up to a certain point, beyond which it becomes *involuntary* or *automatic*.

spontaneous combustion The oxidation of a substance with such rapidity as to engender heat sufficient to ignite it, as masses of oiled rags, finely powdered ores, coal, and certain metals.

spontaneous generation *Biol.* Abiogenesis.

spoof (spoof) *Colloq. v.t. & v.i.* To deceive or hoax; joke. — *n.* Deception; humbug; hoax. [after a nonsensical game invented by Arthur Roberts, 1852–1933, English comedian]

spook (spook) *Colloq. n.* A ghost; an apparition; specter. — *v.t.* **1** To haunt (a person or place). **2** To frighten, disturb, or annoy. **3** To startle or frighten (an animal) into flight, stampeding, etc. [<Du.] —**spook′ish** *adj.*

spool (spool) *n.* **1** A small cylinder, commonly of wood and with a flange at each end and an axial bore, upon which thread or yarn is or may be wound. **2** The quantity of thread held by a spool; also, the spool and the thread upon it. **3** Anything resembling a spool in shape or purpose. — *v.t.* To wind on a spool. [<MLG *spole*]

spoon (spoon) *n.* **1** A utensil having a shallow, generally ovoid bowl and a handle, used in preparing, serving, or eating food. **2** Something resembling a spoon or its bowl. **3** A metallic lure attached to a fishing line: also **spoon bait, trolling spoon. 4** A concave overhanging extension on a torpedo tube to keep the launched torpedo in a straight course. **5** A wooden golf club with lofted face and comparatively short, stiff shaft, used by some players for approaching. — *v.t.* **1** To lift up or out with a spoon. **2** To hollow out like the bowl of a spoon. **3** In certain games, to play or hit (the ball) with little force up into the air; in croquet, to shove or scoop (the ball) with the mallet. — *v.i.* **4** To fish with a spoon. **5** In certain games, to spoon the ball. **6** *Colloq.* To make love, especially openly and demonstratively. [OE *spōn* sliver, chip]

SPOON BAIT

spoon·bill (spoon′bil′) *n.* **1** A wading bird (genera *Platalea* or *Ajaia*) related to the ibises, having the bill broad and flattened. **2** The shoveler (def. 2). **3** The paddlefish. — **spoon′-billed′** *adj.*

spoon·bread (spoon′bred′) *n.* A quick bread made of cornmeal, eggs, milk, and shortening, baked soft enough to be served with a spoon: also called *batter bread.*

spoon·er·ism (spoon′nə·riz′əm) *n.* The unintentional transposition of sounds or of parts of words in speaking, as in "half-*warmed fish*" for "half-*formed wish*". [after William A. Spooner, 1844–1930, of New College, Oxford, who was renowned for such slips of the tongue]

spoon-feed (spoon′fēd′) *v.t.* –**fed** (fed), –**feed·ing** (fē′ding) **1** To feed with a spoon. **2** To pamper; spoil. **3** To present (information) in such a manner that little or no thought, initiative, etc., is required of the recipient. **4** To instruct or inform (a person) in this manner.

spoon hook A fish hook with a bright, revolving, spoon-shaped piece of metal attached.

spoor (spoor) *n.* **1** A track; trail. **2** Footprint or other trace of a wild animal. — *v.t. & v.i.* To track by or follow a spoor. [<Du.]

spo·rad·ic (spô·rad′ik, spō-) *adj.* **1** Occurring here and there; occasional. **2** Separate; isolated. **3** Not widely diffused; neither epidemic

nor endemic: said of disease. Also **spo·rad′i·cal.** [<Med. L *sporadicus* <Gk. *sporadikos* < *sporas* scattered] — **spo·rad′i·cal·ly** *adv.* — **spo·rad′i·cal·ness** *n.*

spo·ran·gi·um (spô·ran′jē·əm, spō-) *n. pl.* ·**gi·a** (-jē·ə) *Bot.* A sac in which asexual spores are produced endogenously, as in certain algae and fungi. Also called *spore case.* [<SPOR(O)- + Gk. *angeion* a vessel] — **spo·ran′gi·al** *adj.*

spore (spôr, spōr) *n.* **1** *Bot.* The reproductive body in flowerless plants, but containing no embryo. They are free, usually single-celled and highly resistant bodies, produced externally or in some closed sac or cavity, and are capable of developing at once or after a time into an independent organism or individual. **2** A minute body that develops into a new individual; any minute organism; a germ. — *v.i.* **spored, spor·ing** To develop spores: said of plants. [<Gk. *spora* seed, sowing] — **spo·ra·ceous** (spô·rā′shəs, spō-) *adj.*

spore case A sporangium.

spore fruit *Bot.* An ascocarp; any plant structure producing spores.

sporo– *combining form* Seed; spore: *sporophyte.* Also, before vowels, **spor–.** [<Gk. *spora* a seed]

spo·ro·carp (spôr′ə·kärp, spō′rə-) *n. Bot.* **1** A many-celled form of fruit produced from a fertilized archicarp in certain of the lower cryptogams, especially red algae and ascomycetous fungi: also called *cystocarp.* **2** The sporogonium in mosses.

spo·ro·cyst (spôr′ə·sist, spō′rə-) *n. Zool.* **1** An asexual form of a trematode worm that develops directly from the embryo and in which mouth and intestinal tract are wanting. **2** An encysted organism, especially a protozoan, that gives rise to spores.

spo·ro·cyte (spôr′ə·sīt, spō′rə-) *n. Biol.* The mother cell from which spores are produced.

spo·ro·gen·e·sis (spôr′ə·jen′ə·sis, spō′rə-) *n. Biol.* **1** Reproduction by spores. **2** Sporogony. — **spo·rog·e·nous** (spô·roj′ə·nəs, spō-) *adj.*

spo·ro·go·ni·um (spôr′ə·gō′nē·əm, spō′rə-) *n. pl.* ·**ni·a** (-nē·ə) *Bot.* An elongated stalk having upon its summit a capsule in which the asexual spores of liverworts and mosses are produced.

spo·ro·phyll (spôr′ə·fil, spō′rə-) *n. Bot.* The leaf, or modified leaf, which bears the sporangia. Also **spo′ro·phyl.**

spo·ro·phyte (spôr′ə·fīt, spō′rə-) *n. Bot.* The spore-bearing individual or generation in certain plants which reproduce by alternation of generations.

spo·ro·tri·cho·sis (spôr′ə·tri·kō′sis, spō′rə-) *n. Pathol.* A chronic disease caused by a fungus (genus *Sporotrichum*) and marked by the formation of ulcerated lesions in the lymph nodes or subcutaneous tissue. [<NL *Sporotrichum*, genus of fungi + -OSIS]

-sporous *combining form* Having (a specified number or kind of) spores: *homosporous.* [<SPOR(O)- + -OUS]

spo·ro·zo·an (spôr′ə·zō′ən, spō′rə-) *adj.* Designating or belonging to a class (*Sporozoa*) of parasitic protozoans developing by asexual and sexual stages and reproducing by sporulation, as the malaria parasite. — *n.* One of the class *Sporozoa.* [<SPORO- + Gk. *zōion* animal]

spor·ran (spor′ən) *n.* A skin pouch, generally with the fur on, worn in front of the kilt by Highlanders. [<Scottish Gaelic *sporan* <LL *bursa* purse]

sport (spôrt, spōrt) *n.* **1** That which amuses in general; diversion; pastime. **2** A particular game or play pursued for diversion, especially an outdoor or athletic game, as baseball, football, track, tennis, swimming, etc. **3** A spirit of jesting or raillery. **4** That with which one sports; a toy; plaything. **5** Mockery; an object of derision: to make *sport* of someone; also, a laughingstock; butt. **6** *Biol.* An animal or plant, or one of its parts, that exhibits sudden and spontaneous variation from the normal type; a mutation. **7** *Bot.* A bud variation. **8** *Colloq.* One whose interest in sport lies chiefly in gambling; a gamester or gambler. **9** *Colloq.* One who lives a fast, gay, or flashy life. **10** A person characterized by his observance of the rules of fair play, or by his ability to get along with others: a good *sport.* **11** *Archaic* Amorous fondling; wanton dalliance. — *v.i.* **1** To amuse oneself; play; frolic.

2 To participate in games. **3** To make sport or jest; trifle. **4** *Bot.* **a** To vary suddenly or spontaneously from the normal type; mutate. **b** To display bud variation. **5** *Archaic Dial.* To make love in a sportive or trifling manner. — *v.t.* **6** *Colloq.* To display or wear ostentatiously; show off. **7** *Obs.* To amuse; divert. See synonyms under FRISK. — *adj.* Of, pertaining to, or fitted for sports; also, appropriate for informal outdoor wear: a *sport* coat: also **sports.** [Aphetic var. of DISPORT] — **sport′er** *n.* — **sport′ful** *adj.* — **sport′ful·ly** *adv.* — **sport′ful·ness** *n.*

Synonyms (noun) : amusement, diversion, entertainment, frolic, fun, gaiety, gambol, game, jollity, joviality, merriment, merrymaking, mirth, pastime, play, pleasure, prank, recreation. See ENTERTAINMENT, FROLIC.

sport·ing (spôr′ting, spōr′-) *adj.* **1** Pertaining to, engaged in, or used in connection with athletic games or field sports. **2** Characterized by the spirit of sportsmanship; conforming to the codes or standards of sportsmanship. **3** Interested in or associated with sports for gambling or betting: a *sporting* man. — **sport′ing·ly** *adv.*

sporting chance *Colloq.* A chance involving the risk of loss.

spor·tive (spôr′tiv, spōr′-) *adj.* **1** Relating to or fond of sport or play; frolicsome. **2** Interested in, active in, or related to sports. **3** *Obs.* Wanton or amorous. — **spor′tive·ly** *adv.* — **spor′tive·ness** *n.*

sports car A low, rakish automobile, usually seating two persons, and built for high speed and maneuverability.

sports·cast·er (spôrts′kas′tər, -käs′-, spōrts′-) *n. U.S.* One who broadcasts sports events, news, and comment.

sport shirt A shirt for informal wear, often cut square at the bottom so as to be worn inside or outside slacks. Also **sports shirt.**

sports·man·like (spôrts′mən·līk′, spōrts′-) *adj.* Pertaining to sportsmen; honorable; generous; conforming to the rules of sportsmanship. Also **sports′man·ly.**

sports·man·ship (spôrts′mən·ship, spōrts′-) *n.* **1** The art or practice of field sports. **2** Honorable or sportsmanlike conduct.

sports·wear (spôrts′wâr′, spōrts′-) *n.* Clothes made for informal or outdoor activities.

sport·y (spôr′tē, spōr′-) *adj.* **sport·i·er, sport·i·est** *Colloq.* Relating to or characteristic of a sport; hence, gay, loud, or dissipated. — **sport′i·ly** *adv.* — **sport′i·ness** *n.*

spot (spot) *n.* **1** A particular place of small extent; a definite locality. **2** Any small portion of a surface differing as in color from the rest; blot. **3** A stain or blemish on character; a fault; a reproach. **4** A congenital birthmark. **5** A food fish (*Leiostomus xanthurus*) of the Atlantic coast of the United States, marked with a spot above each pectoral fin; the oldwife. **6** One of the figures or pips with which a playing card is marked; also, a card having (a certain number of) such marks: the five *spot* of clubs. **7** *Slang* A currency note having a specified value: a ten *spot.* **8** *Chiefly Brit.* A portion or bit: a *spot* of tea. **9** *Slang* Position or situation: He was in a good *spot.* **10** *U.S. Slang* A spotlight. See synonyms under BLEMISH, PLACE. — **in a spot** *Slang* In a difficult or embarrassing situation; in trouble. — **in spots** Now and then, in some respects: He is bright *in spots.* — **to go to the spot** To satisfy a definite need or craving. — **to hit the spot** *Slang* To gratify an appetite or need. — **on the spot 1** At once; immediately. **2** At the very place. **3** *Slang* **a** In danger of death. **b** Accountable or in danger of being held accountable for some action. — *v.* **spot·ted, spot·ting** *v.t.* **1** To mark or soil with spots. **2** To decorate with spots; dot. **3** To place on a designated spot; locate; station. **4** *Colloq.* To recognize or detect; see. **5** *Colloq.* To yield (an advantage or handicap) to someone: We *spotted* them five points. — *v.i.* **6** To become marked or soiled with spots. **7** To make a stain or discoloration. **8** *Mil.* To observe the effect of gunfire to obtain data for improving its accuracy. See synonyms under STAIN. — *adj.* **1** Being on the place or spot. **2** Paid or prepared for payment on delivery; also, ready for instant delivery following sale. **3** *Telecom.* Designed for presentation between regular programs and usually very brief: a *spot* TV commercial. [< ME < LG. Cf. MDu. *spotte* a spot.] — **spot′ta·ble** *adj.*

spot cash Immediate payment on actual delivery.

spot·light (spot′līt′) *n.* **1** A circle of powerful light thrown on the stage to bring an actor or actors into clearer view. **2** The apparatus that produces such a light. **3** A pivoted automobile lamp. **4** Notoriety; publicity.

spotted adder The house snake.

spotted crake A small European rail *(Porzana porzana)*, allied to the American sora.

spotted cranesbill A North American woodland herb *(Geranium maculatum)* covered more or less densely with long white hairs and having lavender, rose, or sometimes white flowers. Also called *alumroot, wild geranium.*

spotted fever *Pathol.* **1** Meningitis. **2** Typhus. **3** Rocky Mountain spotted fever.

spot·ty (spot′ē) *adj.* **·ti·er, ·ti·est** **1** Having many spots. **2** Occurring in spots; unevenly distributed. — **spot′ti·ly** *adv.* — **spot′ti·ness** *n.*

spouse (spouz, spous) *n.* A partner in marriage; one's husband or wife. — *v.t.* **spoused, spous·ing** *Obs.* To wed; marry; espouse. [< OF *espous, espouse* < L *sponsus,* pp. of *spondere* promise, betroth]

spout (spout) *v.i.* **1** To pour out copiously and forcibly, as a liquid under pressure. **2** To discharge a fluid either continuously or in jets. **3** *Colloq.* To speak or orate pompously; declaim. — *v.t.* **4** To cause to pour or shoot forth. **5** To utter grandiloquently or pompously. **6** *Brit. Slang* To pawn or pledge. — *n.* **1** A tube, trough, etc., for the discharge of a liquid. **2** A continuous stream of fluid. **3** Formerly, the shoot or lift in a pawnbroker's shop. **4** *Brit. Slang* A pawnbroker's shop. [ME *spoute*; origin uncertain] — **spout′er** *n.*

sprag (sprag) *n.* A billet of wood used to prevent a vehicle from slipping backward, or in mining as a prop to support coal when undermined. [Origin uncertain]

sprain (sprān) *n.* **1** A violent straining or twisting of the ligaments surrounding a joint. **2** The condition due to such strain. [< *v.*] — *v.t.* To cause a sprain in; wrench the muscles of (a joint). [< OF *espreindre* squeeze < L *exprimere.* See EXPRESS]

sprat (sprat) *n.* **1** A herringlike fish *(Clupea sprattus)* found in shoals on the Atlantic coast of Europe. **2** The young of the herring. [OE *sprott*]

sprawl (sprôl) *v.i.* **1** To sit or lie with the limbs stretched out ungracefully. **2** To be stretched out ungracefully, as the limbs. **3** To move with awkward motions of the limbs. **4** To spread out in a straggling manner, as handwriting, vines, etc. — *v.t.* **5** To cause to spread or extend awkwardly or irregularly. — *n.* **1** The act or position of sprawling; an awkward recumbent posture or movement. **2** An unplanned or disorderly group, as of houses, spread out over a broad area: urban *sprawl;* a vast *sprawl* of lights. [OE *spreawlian* move convulsively] — **sprawl′er** *n.*

spray¹ (sprā) *n.* **1** Water or other liquid dispersed in fine particles. **2** An instrument for discharging small particles of liquid; an atomizer. [< *v.*] — *v.t.* **1** To disperse (a liquid) in fine particles. **2** To apply spray to, as with an atomizer. — *v.i.* **3** To send forth or scatter spray. **4** To go forth as spray. [Akin to MDu. *sprayen* sprinkle] — **spray′er** *n.*

spray² (sprā) *n.* **1** A small branch bearing dependent branchlets or flowers. **2** Any ornament, pattern, etc., resembling a collection of twigs or flowers. [ME; origin uncertain]

spread (spred) *v.* **spread, spread·ing** *v.t.* **1** To open or unfold to full width, extent, etc., as wings, sail, a map, etc. **2** To distribute over a surface, especially in a thin layer; scatter or smear. **3** To cover with a layer of something: to *spread* toast with marmalade. **4** To force apart or farther apart: The heavy train has *spread* the rails. **5** To extend over a period of time; prolong: He *spread* the payments over a six-month period. **6** To make more widely known, active, etc.; promulgate or diffuse: to *spread* a rumor; to *spread* contagion. **7** To set (a table, etc.), as for a meal. **8** To arrange or place on a table, etc., as a meal or feast. **9** To set forth or record in full. — *v.i.* **10** To be extended or expanded; increase in size, width, etc. **11** To be distributed or dispersed, as

over a surface or area; scatter. **12** To become more widely known, active, etc. **13** To be forced farther apart; separate. — *n.* **1** The act of spreading: the *spread* of the gospel. **2** An open extent or expanse. **3** The limit or extent of expansion of some designated object, as of sail or a bird's wings. **4** *Aeron,.* The maximum distance from tip to tip of an airplane wing. **5** A cloth or covering for a bed, table, or the like. **6** *Colloq.* An informal feast or banquet; also, a table with a meal set out on it. **7** Anything used to spread on bread: a cheese *spread.* **8** Two pages of a magazine or newspaper facing each other and covered by related material; also, print spread across two or more columns or on facing pages for advertising or display. **9** In finance and commerce, a straddle. **10** Diffusion; dispersion. — *adj.* Having a broad surface; expanded; outstretched. [OE *sprædan*]

Synonyms (verb) : circulate, diffuse, disperse, disseminate, distribute, divulge, expand, extend, promulgate, propagate, scatter. See PUBLISH, STRETCH. *Antonyms* : check, confine, condense, contract, restrain.

spread-ea·gle (spred′ē′gəl) *adj.* **1** Having the arms and legs spread wide apart. **2** Extravagant; bombastic: applied especially to patriotic American oratory. — *v.* **-ea·gled, -ea·gling** *v.t.* To lash to the mast or shrouds in spread-eagle position as a punishment: a former practice. — *v.i.* To deliver an oration in bombastic, patriotic style. — **spread′-ea′gle·ism** *n.*

spread·sheet (spred′shēt′) *n.* A kind of computer program that processes numerical data for financial calculations of various kinds.

spree (sprē) *n.* **1** A drinking spell; drunken carousal. **2** A gay frolic. See synonyms under FROLIC. Compare SPORT. [Origin uncertain]

sprig (sprig) *n.* **1** A shoot or sprout of a tree or plant; an ornament in this form. **2** An offshoot from an ancestral stock; a young man. **3** One of various small, pointed implements.

4 A brad without a head. **5** A small, wedge-shaped piece of metal used to hold glass in a window sash. — *v.t.* **sprigged, sprig·ging** **1** To ornament with a design of sprigs. **2** To form (twigs or plants) into sprays. **3** To fasten with sprigs or brads. **4** To pluck sprigs from. [ME *sprigge*; origin uncertain] — **sprig′ger** *n.*

spright·ly (sprīt′lē) *adj.* **·li·er, ·li·est** Full of animation and spirits; vivacious; lively. — *adv.* Spiritedly; briskly; gaily. — **spright′li·ness** *n.*

Synonyms: airy, animated, brisk, bustling, cheerful, lively, nimble, spry, vivacious. The *sprightly* display a cheerful, pleasing lightness and quickness, spiritlike; *lively* has a similar meaning, as abounding in cheerful life. The *brisk* and *bustling* are full of stir, the former generally to some purpose. See ACTIVE, AIRY, CHEERFUL, HAPPY, NIMBLE, VIVACIOUS, VIVID.

spring (spring) *v.* **sprang** or **sprung, sprung, spring·ing** *v.i.* **1** To move or rise suddenly and rapidly; leap; dart: He *sprang* across the creek; The cat *sprang* into the air. **2** To move suddenly as by elastic reaction; snap: The jaws of the heavy trap *sprang* shut. **3** To move as if with a leap: An angry retort *sprang* to his lips. **4** To rise up suddenly, as birds from cover. **5** To work or snap out of place, as a mechanical part. **6** To become warped or bent, as boards. **7** To explode: said of a mine. **8** To rise above surrounding objects. **9** To come into being: New towns have *sprung* up. **10** To originate; proceed, as from a source. **11** To develop; grow, as a plant. **12** To be descended: He *springs* from good stock. **13** *Poetic* To begin to appear, as light or dawn. — *v.t.* **14** To cause to spring or leap. **15** To cause to act, close, open, etc., unexpectedly or suddenly, as by elastic reaction: to *spring* a trap. **16** To cause to happen, become known, or appear suddenly: to *spring* a surprise. **17** To leap over; vault. **18** To start (game) from cover; flush. **19** To explode (a mine). **20** To warp

or bend; split. **21** To cause to snap or work out of place. **22** To force into place, as a beam or bar. **23** To suffer (a leak). **24** *Slang* To obtain the release of (a person) from prison or custody. See synonyms under LEAP, RISE. — *n.* **1** *Mech.* An elastic body or contrivance that yields under stress, and returns to its normal form when the stress is removed. **2** Elastic quality or energy. **3** The act of flying back from a position of tension; recoil. **4** An energy or power; a cause of action; impelling motive. **5** The act of leaping up or forward suddenly; a jump; bound. **6** The season in which vegetation starts anew; in the north temperate zone, the three months of March, April, and May; in the astronomical year, the period from the vernal equinox to the summer solstice. **7** A flow or fountain, as of water; hence, any source or origin of continued supply; a flow of curative water. **8** A crack or break, as of a plank, beam, or spar, or a thing sprung or warped. **9** *Archit.* The commencement of curvature in an arch. **10** A hinge. See illustration under HINGE. **11** *Scot.* A quick, lively tune. See synonyms under BEGINNING, CAUSE, SOURCE. — *adj.* **1** Pertaining to the season of spring. **2** Resilient; acting like or having a spring. **3** Hung on springs. [OE *springan*]

spring balance A weighing device, often used in classroom experiments, consisting essentially of a spring with a hook at one end to which objects to be weighed may be hung.

spring-beau·ty (spring′byōo′tē) *n. pl.* **·ties** One of a genus *(Claytonia)* of perennial wild flowers of the purslane family; especially, *C. virginica* of the eastern United States, with pink-tinged white flowers. See CLAYTONIA.

spring-board (spring′bôrd′, -bōrd′) *n.* **1** An elastic board used to aid in leaping; a springy board secured at one end, used to give impetus to a dive into the water below. Also *diving board.* **2** A short board inserted by one end in a notch in a tree, on which a workman stands when felling large trees.

spring-bok (spring′bok) *n.* A small South African gazelle *(Antidorcas marsupialis)* noted for its ability to leap high in the air. Also **spring′-buck′** (-buk′). [< Afrikaans]

SPRINGBOK
(About 2 feet high at the shoulder)

spring chicken **1** A young chicken, 10 weeks to 10 months old, especially tender for cooking: so called because usually hatched in the spring. **2** *Colloq.* A young, immature, or unsophisticated person.

spring fever The listlessness and restlessness that overtakes a person with the first warm days of spring.

Spring·field (spring′fēld′) **1** The capital of Illinois. **2** A city in southern Massachusetts; site of a U.S. arsenal. **3** A city in SW Missouri. **4** A city in SW Ohio.

spring·head (spring′hed′) *n.* A fountainhead; source.

spring·house (spring′hous′) *n.* A small building constructed over a spring, and used for keeping milk, meats, etc., cool.

spring·tail (spring′tāl′) *n.* Any of certain very small wingless insects (order *Collembola*) having a tail comprised of two united parts, which bends beneath it and enables it to jump.

spring tide **1** A high tide occurring under the combined attraction of sun and new or full moon. **2** Any great wave of feeling, etc.

spring water Water found in or obtained from a spring.

sprin·kle (spring′kəl) *v.* **·kled, ·kling** *v.t.* **1** To scatter in drops or small particles. **2** To besprinkle; specifically, to apply drops of water to, as a form of baptism: opposed to *immerse.* — *v.i.* **3** To fall or rain in scattered drops. — *n.* A falling in drops or particles, or that which so falls; a sprinkling; hence, a small quantity. [ME *sprenkelen.* Akin to LG *sprin-*

keln scatter.]

sprin·kler (spring′klər) *n.* **1** A nozzle or other device for spraying water on lawns, built either as a portable apparatus or as a unit in a stationary network fed by underground

sprint (sprint) *n.* A short race run at top speed. [< *v.*] — *v.i.* To run fast, as in a sprint. [ME *sprenten* <Scand. Cf. ON *spretta* run.] — **sprint′er** *n.*

sprit (sprit) *n. Naut.* **1** A small spar reaching diagonally from a mast to the peak of a fore-and-aft sail. **2** *Brit.* A pole used for propelling a boat. **3** A bowsprit. [OE *sprēot* pole]

sprite (sprīt) *n.* **1** A fairy, elf, or goblin. **2** A disembodied spirit; a ghost. Also spelled *spright.* [< OF *esprit* < L *spiritus.* Doublet of SPIRIT.]

sprit·sail (sprit′səl, sprit′sāl′) *n. Naut.* A sail extended by a sprit.

SPRITSAIL
a. Sprit. *b.* Spritsail.

sprock·et (sprok′it) *n. Mech.* **1** A projection, as on the periphery of a wheel, for engaging with the links of a chain. **2** A wheel bearing such projections: also **sprocket wheel.** [Origin uncertain]

sprout (sprout) *v.i.* **1** To put forth shoots; begin to grow; germinate. **2** To develop or grow rapidly. — *v.t.* **3** To cause to sprout. **4** To remove shoots from. — *n.* **1** A new shoot or bud on a plant; hence, something like or suggestive of a sprout; a scion. **2** *pl.* Brussels sprouts. — **a course of sprouts** A period of training. [OE *sprūtan*]

spruce[1] (sprōōs) *n.* **1** Any of a genus (*Picea*) of evergreen trees of the pine family, having a sharp-pointed pyramidal crown, needle-shaped leaves, and pendulous cones; especially, the ornamental **Norway spruce** (*P. abies*), and the **Engelmann spruce** (*P. engelmanni*) of the Pacific coast. **2** The wood of any of these trees. **3** Any of certain other coniferous trees, as the Douglas fir. [Earlier *pruce* Prussian <*Pruce* Prussia <Med. L *Prussia*; so called because first known as a product of Prussia]

spruce[2] (sprōōs) *adj.* **1** Having a smart, trim appearance. **2** Fastidious. See synonyms under NEAT[1]. — *v.* **spruced, spruc·ing** *v.t.* To make spruce; dress or arrange neatly: often with *up.* — *v.i.* To make oneself spruce: usually with *up.* [Special use of SPRUCE[3]] — **spruce′ly** *adv.* — **spruce′ness** *n.*

sprue[1] (sprōō) *n.* **1** In founding, a channel connecting with the gate through which the melted metal is poured into the mold; also, dross. **2** A pouring hole in a mold; gate. [Origin uncertain]

sprue[2] (sprōō) *n. Pathol.* **1** A disease of tropical regions marked by anemia, emaciation, and gastrointestinal disturbances; psilosis. **2** Thrush. [< Du *spruw*]

sprung rhythm In prosody, a rhythm involving feet of varying number of syllables but of equal time length, the stress usually falling on the first syllable: a term coined by Gerard Manley Hopkins.

spry (sprī) *adj.* **spri·er** or **spry·er, spri·est** or **spry·est** Quick and active; agile. See synonyms under ACTIVE, SPRIGHTLY. [< dial. E *sprey* <Scand. Cf. Sw. *sprygg* active.] — **spry′ly** *adv.* — **spry′ness** *n.*

spud (spud) *n.* **1** A spadelike tool with narrow blade or prongs for removing the roots of weeds by digging or cutting. **2** *Colloq.* A potato. — *v.t.* **spud·ded, spud·ding** To remove, as weeds, with a spud. [ME *spudde* <Scand. Cf. Dan. *spyd* a spear.]

spume (spyōōm) *n.* Froth, as on an agitated or effervescing liquid; foam; scum. — *v.i.* **spumed, spum·ing** To foam; froth. [< F < L *spuma* foam] — **spu′mous** *adj.* — **spum′y** *adj.*

spu·mo·ne (spə·mō′nē, *Ital.* spōō·mō′nā) *n. pl.* **·ni** (-nē) A dessert or mousse of ice-cream or water ice containing fruit, nuts, or other candied products, in a base of whipped cream. [< Ital., aug. of *spuma* froth < L *spuma*]

spunk (spungk) *n.* **1** Dry wood that burns easily; touchwood; also, a kind of tinder made

from a species of fungus; punk. **2** A small fire, spark, or flame; punk; also, a match. **3** *Colloq.* Quick, fiery temper; mettle; pluck; courage. — **to get one's spunk up** To become defiant or angry; also, to take heart; show courage. — *v.i.* To take fire; flare up; kindle. [< Irish *sponnc* tinder <L *spongia* sponge]

spur (spûr) *n.* **1** A pricking or goading instrument worn on a horseman's heel, and bearing a sharp point or a series of points on a rotating wheel. **2** Anything that incites or urges; instigation; incentive. **3** A part or attachment projecting like or suggestive of a spur, as a crag or mountain peak, a steel gaff fastened to a gamecock's leg, the ergot of rye, etc. **4** A stiff, sharp spine, as on the legs of some insects and the wings of some birds; especially, the spine on the tarsus of the domestic cock. See illustration under FOWL. **5** *Archit.* A buttress or other offset from a wall; also, a claw or the like projecting upon the plinth at the four angles of the base of a column. **6** In carpentry, a brace reinforcing a rafter or post; a strut. **7** *Bot.* A tubular expansion of a foliaceous part, usually some part of the flower, as in the columbine and larkspur. **8** A branch of a lode, railroad, etc. — **on the spur of the moment** Hastily; prompted by an impulse. — *v.* **spurred, spur·ring** *v.t.* **1** To prick or urge with or as with spurs. **2** To furnish with spurs. **3** To injure or gash with the spur, as a gamecock. — *v.i.* **4** To spur one's horse. **5** To hasten; hurry. [OE *spura*] — **spur′rer** *n.*

Synonyms (verb): goad, impel, incite, instigate, provoke, rouse, stimulate, sting, stir, urge. *Antonyms:* check, deter, discourage, dissuade, hold, moderate, rein, restrain.

spurge (spûrj) *n.* **1** Any of several shrubs (genus *Euphorbia*) having fertile flowers with 3-lobed ovaries on long pedicels and yielding a milky juice of bitter taste. **2** One of various related plants of the spurge family (*Euphorbiaceae*). [< OF *espurge* < *espurgier* purge <L *expurgare* < *ex-* out + *purgare* cleanse]

spur gearing *Mech.* Gearing composed of spur wheels.

spurge laurel An evergreen shrub of Europe and Asia (*Daphne laureola*), with oblanceolate leaves and yellowish–green flowers.

SPUR GEARING

spu·ri·ous (spyōōr′ē·əs) *adj.* **1** Not proceeding from the source pretended; not genuine; false. **2** Illegitimate. **3** Apparent, but not real; resembling in appearance but not in structure: a *spurious* fruit. See synonyms under COUNTERFEIT, FACTITIOUS. [< L *spurius*] — **spu′ri·ous·ly** *adv.* — **spu′ri·ous·ness** *n.*

spurn (spûrn) *v.t.* **1** To reject with disdain; refuse contemptuously; scorn. **2** To strike with the foot; kick. — *v.i.* **3** To reject something with disdain. — *n.* The act of spurning; also, a kick. [OE *spurnan* kick, reject] — **spurn′er** *n.*

spurt (spûrt) *n.* **1** A sudden gush of liquid. **2** Any sudden outbreak, as of anger. **3** An extraordinary effort of brief duration; a sudden rise in activity or price. **4** A brief period. — *v.i.* **1** To come out in a jet; gush forth. **2** To make a sudden and extreme effort. — *v.t.* **3** To force out in a jet; squirt. Also spelled *spirt.* [Var. of earlier *spirt,* metathetic var. of *sprit* <OE *spryttan* come forth]

spur track A short side track connecting with the main track of a railroad. Also **spur.**

spur wheel A toothed wheel having external radial teeth on the periphery; a spur gear.

sput·nik (spōōt′nik, sput′-) *n.* A Russian artificial earth satellite: the first to be recorded in world history, called Sputnik I, containing various scientific instruments, was launched October 4, 1957, to an initial height of 560 miles, orbiting at a mean velocity of 18,000 miles per hour. [< Russian, a satellite; lit., that which travels with something else]

sput·ter (sput′ər) *v.i.* **1** To throw off solid or fluid particles in a series of slight explosions. **2** To emit particles of saliva from the mouth, as when speaking excitedly. **3** To speak rapidly or confusedly. — *v.t.* **4** To throw off or emit in small particles. **5** To utter in a confused or excited manner. — *n.* **1** The act

or sound of sputtering; especially, excited talk; jabbering. **2** That which is thrown out in sputtering. **3** Trouble; fuss. [Freq. of SPOUT, *v.*] — **sput′ter·er** *n.*

spu·tum (spyōō′təm) *n. pl.* **·ta** (-tə) Saliva; spittle; expectorated matter. [< L < *spuere* spit]

spy (spī) *n. pl.* **spies 1** One who enters an enemy's military lines covertly to get information; a secret agent. **2** One who watches others secretly: often used contemptuously. **3** A peep; glance; hence, an eye. **4** The act of watching secretly. — *v.* **spied, spy·ing** *v.i.* **1** To keep watch closely or secretly; act as a spy. **2** To make careful examination; pry: with *into.* — *v.t.* **3** To observe stealthily and with hostile intent: usually with *out.* **4** To catch sight of; see; espy. **5** To discover by careful or secret investigation: with *out.* **6** To examine or scrutinize carefully. [< OF *espie* < *espier* espy <Gmc.]

Synonyms (noun): emissary, scout. The *scout* and the *spy* are both employed to obtain information of the numbers, movements, etc., of an enemy. The *scout* lurks on the outskirts of the hostile army with such concealment as the case admits of, but without disguise; a *spy* enters in disguise within the enemy's lines. A *scout,* if captured, has the rights of a prisoner of war; a *spy* is held to have forfeited all rights, and is liable, in case of capture, to capital punishment. Soldiers not in disguise or military aviators are not considered *spies,* even while passing through or over hostile territory. An *emissary* is rather political than military, sent to influence opponents secretly rather than to bring information concerning them.

spy·glass (spī′glas′, -gläs′) *n.* A small field glass or telescope.

squab (skwob) *n.* **1** A young pigeon, especially when an unfledged nestling. **2** A fat, short person. **3** A soft, stuffed cushion; sofa; ottoman. — *adj.* **1** Fat and short; low and bulky; squat. **2** Unfledged or but half-fledged; half-grown, as a pigeon, or figuratively, any fowl. [< dial. E <Scand. Cf. dial. Norw. *skvabb* a soft, wet mass.]

squab·ble (skwob′əl) *v.* **·bled, ·bling** *v.i.* To engage in a petty wrangle or scuffle; quarrel. — *v.t. Printing* To twist (composed type) so as to mix the lines. — *n.* The act of squabbling; a petty wrangle. See synonyms under QUARREL[1]. [Cf. dial. Sw. *skvabbel* dispute, argue] — **squab′bler** *n.*

squab·by (skwob′ē) *adj.* **·bi·er, ·bi·est** Short and fat. Also **squab′bish.**

squad (skwod) *n.* **1** A small group of persons organized for the performance of a specific function; a small detachment of troops or police; specifically, the smallest tactical unit in the infantry of the U.S. Army. **2** Hence, a team; a football *squad.* — *v.t.* **squad·ded, squad·ding 1** To form into a squad or squads. **2** To assign to a squad. [< F *escouade* <OF *esquadre* a square <Ital. *squadra* <L *quattuor* four]

squad car An automobile used by police for patrolling, and equipped with radiotelephone for communicating with headquarters.

squad·ron (skwod′rən) *n.* **1** An assemblage of war vessels smaller than a fleet; one of the divisions of a fleet. **2** A division of a cavalry regiment. **3** The basic unit of the United States Air Force, usually consisting of two or more flights operating as a unit. **4** Any regularly arranged or organized body, as of men. — *v.t.* To arrange in a squadron or squadrons. [< Ital. *squadrone,* aug. of *squadra* SQUAD]

squal·id (skwol′id) *adj.* Having a foul, mean, or poverty-stricken appearance; dirty, neglected, and wretched. See synonyms under BASE[2]. [< L *squalidus* < *squalere* be foul] — **squal′id·ly** *adv.* — **squal′id·ness, squa·lid·i·ty** (skwo·lid′ə·tē) *n.*

squall[1] (skwôl) *n.* A loud, screaming outcry. — *v.i.* To cry loudly; scream; bawl. [Cf. ON *skvala* shout, bawl] — **squall′er** *n.*

squall[2] (skwôl) *n.* A sudden, violent burst of wind, often accompanied by rain or snow. — *v.i.* To blow a squall; be squally. [Cf. Sw. *skval-regn* a sudden rainstorm]

squall line *Meteorol.* A cold front characterized along its edge by a sharp change of wind and the occasional formation of line squalls.

squal·or (skwol′ər) *n.* The state of being squalid, or the filth of thriftless poverty. [<L <*squalere* be foul]

squa·lus (skwā′ləs) *n.* Any of a genus (*Squalus*) of cartilaginous fishes (class *Chondrichthyes*), including the spiny dogfish or shark (*S. acanthias*) common in shore waters of the Atlantic. [<L, large marine fish]

squa·ma (skwā′mə) *n. pl.* **·mae** (-mē) A thin, scalelike structure; a scale. [<L] — **squa′· mate** (-māt) *adj.*

Squa·ma·ta (skwə·mā′tə) *n. pl.* An order of reptiles, including lizards, chameleons, and serpents. [<NL <L *squama* a scale]

squa·mous (skwā′məs) *adj.* 1 Covered with scales; scaly; scalelike. 2 *Anat.* Designating the vertical plate of the temporal bone. Also **squa′mose** (-mōs). [<L *squamosus* < *squama* a scale] — **squa′mous·ly** *adv.* — **squa′mous·ness** *n.*

squan·der (skwon′dər) *v.t.* 1 To spend (money, time, etc.) wastefully; lavish profusely; dissipate. 2 *Obs.* To scatter. — *n.* Prodigality; the act of squandering. [Cf. dial. E *squander* scatter] — **squan′der·er** *n.* — **squan′der·ing·ly** *adv.*

Synonyms (verb): dissipate, expend, lavish, scatter, spend, waste. *Antonyms:* economize, hoard, hold, husband, preserve, reserve, save.

squan·tum[1] (skwon′təm) *n.* Among North American Indians, especially the Narragansets, a spirit or god; an evil spirit.

squan·tum[2] (skwon′təm) *n.* In New England, a picnic or shore dinner; a chowder party; hence, any merrymaking or frolic. [from *Squantum*, Mass., after *Tisquantum*, a Massachuset chief]

square (skwâr) *n.* 1 A parallelogram having four equal sides and four right angles. 2 Any object, part, or surface that is square or nearly so, as a pane of glass, or one of the spots on a checkerboard. 3 An instrument by which to measure or lay out right angles, consisting usually of two legs or branches at right angles to each other, in L-shape or T-shape (in the latter case called a *T-square*.) 4 An open area in a city or village, left between streets at their intersection or formed by their expansion. 5 A town or city block; also, the distance between one street and the next. 6 *Math.* The product of a number or quantity multiplied by itself. 7 Formerly, a body of troops formed in a four-sided array. 8 *Obs.* A standard or pattern; rule. 9 *Slang* A person not conversant with developments in the popular arts, especially the latest fashions in jazz, slang, etc. — **on the square** 1 At right angles. 2 On equal terms. 3 *Colloq.* In a fair and honest manner. 4 In Freemasonry, in good standing; said of members. — **out of square** 1 Not at right angles; obliquely. 2 Incorrectly; askew; out of order. — *adj.* 1 Having four equal sides and four right angles; loosely, approaching a square in form. 2 Formed with or characterized by a right angle; rectangular. 3 Adapted to forming squares or computing in squares: a *square* measure. 4 Direct; fair; just; equitable; honest. 5 Having debit and credit balanced; even; settled. 6 Absolute; complete; unequivocal. 7 Having a broad, stocky frame; hence, strong, sturdy. 8 *Colloq.* Solid; full; satisfying: a *square* meal. 9 *Naut.* At right angles to the mast and keel: said of the yards of a square-rigged ship. 10 *Math.* Raised to the second power; squared: 10 *square* equals 100. 11 Steady: said of a horse's gait. 12 *Mech.* Having the cylinder bore equal, or nearly equal to the piston stroke: said of engines. See synonyms under JUST[1]. — *v.* **squared**, **squar·ing** *v.t.* 1 To make square; form with four equal sides and four right angles. 2 To shape or adjust so as to form a right angle, or a right angle with something else. 3 To mark with or divide into squares. 4 To test for the purpose of adjusting to a straight line, right angle, or plane surface. 5 To bring to a position suggestive of a right angle: *Square* your shoul-

SQUARES
a. T-square.
b. Steel square.
c. Try square.

ders. 6 To make satisfactory settlement or adjustment of: to *square* accounts. 7 To make (the score of a game or contest) equal. 8 To cause to conform; adapt; reconcile: to *square* one's opinions to the times. 9 *Math.* a To multiply (a number or quantity) by itself. b To determine the contents of in square measure. c To find the square equivalent of: to *square* a circle. 10 *Slang* To bribe: to *square* a jockey. — *v.i.* 11 To be at right angles. 12 To conform; agree; harmonize. 13 In golf, to make the ·scores equal. 14 *Obs.* To squabble; quarrel. — **to square away** 1 *Naut.* To set (the yards) at right angles to the keel. 2 To square up. — **to square off** To assume a position for attack or defense; prepare to fight. — **to square up** To adjust satisfactorily. — *adv.* 1 So as to be square, or at right angles. 2 Honestly; fairly. 3 Directly; firmly. [<OF *esquire, esquarre,* ult. <L *quattuor* four] — **square·ness** *n.*

square dance Any dance, as a quadrille, in which the couples form sets in squares.

square deal *Colloq.* 1 In card games, an honest deal. 2 Hence, fair or just treatment.

square knot A common knot, formed of two overhand knots: also called *reef knot.* See illustration under KNOT.

square meal *Colloq.* A full and substantial meal.

square measure A unit or system of units for measuring areas, as in the following table of principal customary standards. See also METRIC SYSTEM.

144 square inches (sq. in.; in²)	=	1 square foot (sq. ft.; ft²)
9 square feet	=	1 square yard (sq. yd.; yd²)
30.25 square yards	=	1 square rod (sq. rd.; rd²)
160 square rods	=	1 acre (A.)
640 acres	=	1 square mile (sq. mi.)

square-rigged (skwâr′rigd′) *adj. Naut.* Having the principal sails extended by horizontal yards; ship-rigged: distinguished from *fore-and-aft-rigged.* Compare illustrations under BARK, BRIG, SHIP.

square root *Math.* A number or quantity that, multiplied by itself, produces the given number or quantity: 4 is the *square root* of 16; a second root. See under CUBE[1], ROOT[1].

square sail *Naut.* A quadrilateral sail usually rigged on a yard set at right angles to the mast.

square shooter *Colloq.* An upright person; one who acts honestly and justly.

square-toed (skwâr′tōd′) *adj.* Having the toes square, as the shoes worn by the Puritans; hence, exact; punctilious.

squaring a log Sawing a log so as to give it four equal sides.

squaring the circle Quadrature of the circle.

squar·rose (skwar′· ōs, skwo·rōs′) *adj.* 1 *Biol.* Rough with projecting scalelike processes. 2 *Bot.* Crowded and rigid: *squarrose* leaves. Also **squar·rous** (skwar′əs). [<L *squarrosus* scurfy]

SQUARING A LOG

squash[1] (skwosh) *v.t.* 1 To beat or press into a pulp or soft mass; crush. 2 To quell or suppress. — *v.i.* 3 To be smashed or squashed. 4 To make a splashing or sucking sound. — *n.* 1 A soft or overripe object; also, a crushed mass. 2 The sudden fall of a heavy, soft, or bursting body; also, the sound made by such a fall. 3 The sucking, squelching sound made by walking through ooze or mud. 4 Either of two games played on an indoor court with rackets and a ball. In one (**squash rackets**) a slow rubber ball is used; in the other (**squash tennis**), a livelier, smaller ball. 5 A beverage of which one ingredient is a fruit juice: lemon *squash.* — *adv.* With a squelching, oozy sound. [<OF *esquasser,* ult. <L *ex-* thoroughly +

quassare crush] — **squash′er** *n.*

squash[2] (skwosh) *n.* 1 The edible fruit of various trailing annuals (genus *Cucurbita*) of the gourd family. 2 The plant that bears it. [<Algonquian. Cf. Massachuset *askoot-asquash,* lit., eaten raw.]

squash bug A large, brownish-black, evil-smelling North American hemipterous insect (*Anasa tristis*) which is destructive to squash vines.

squat (skwot) *v.* **squat·ted** or **squat, squat·ting** *v.i.* 1 To sit on the heels or hams, or with the legs near the body. 2 To crouch or cower down, as to avoid being seen. 3 To settle on a piece of land without title or payment. 4 To settle on government land in accordance with certain government regulations that will eventually give title. — *v.t.* 5 To cause (oneself) to squat. — *adj.* 1 Short and thick; squatty. 2 Being in a squatting position. — *n.* A squatting attitude or position. [<OF *esquatir* < *es-* thoroughly (<L *ex-*) + *quatir* press down <L *coactus,* pp. of *cogere* force < *co-* together + *agere* drive]

squat·ter (skwot′ər) *n.* 1 One who or that which squats; specifically, one who settles on land without permission or right, as on public or unimproved land. 2 In the United States and Australia, one who settles on government land subject to regulations with a view to obtaining title.

squaw (skwô) *n.* 1 An American Indian woman or wife. 2 *Colloq.* Any woman or girl. [<Algonquian, woman]

squaw-bush (skwô′bŏŏsh′) *n.* 1 Any shrub of the genus *Cornus;* especially, the red-osier dogwood. 2 The cranberry tree.

squaw·fish (skwô′fish′) *n. pl.* **·fish** or **·fish·es** 1 A cyprinoid fish (genus *Ptychocheilus*) found in the rivers of the northern Pacific coast. 2 A surf fish.

squawk (skwôk) *v.i.* 1 To utter a shrill, harsh cry, as a parrot. 2 *Slang* To utter loud complaints or protests. — *n.* 1 The harsh cry of certain birds; also, the act of squawking. 2 *Slang* A loud protest or complaint. 3 The black-crowned night heron (*Nycticorax nycticorax*). [Prob. imit.] — **squawk′er** *n.*

squaw man 1 Among the American Indians, a man who lives and works among the women. 2 A white man married to an Indian woman and in possession of tribal rights on that account.

squaw·root (skwô′rŏŏt′, -rŏŏt′) *n.* 1 A yellowish-brown leafless North American herb (*Conopholis americana*) parasitic on roots. 2 One of certain other plants, as the blue cohosh.

squeak (skwēk) *n.* 1 A thin, sharp, penetrating sound. 2 *Colloq.* A narrow margin; the least amount; a hairbreadth: in the phrase **a narrow** (or **close**) **squeak.** — *v.i.* 1 To make a squeak. 2 *Colloq.* To let out information; squeal. 3 To succeed or otherwise progress after narrowly averting failure or reversal: He just managed to *squeak* through. — *v.t.* 4 To utter or effect with a squeak. 5 To cause to squeak. [ME *squeke,* prob. <Scand. Cf. Sw. *sqväka* croak.] — **squeak′er** *n.*

squeal (skwēl) *v.i.* 1 To utter a sharp, shrill, somewhat prolonged cry. 2 *Slang* To turn informer; betray an accomplice or a plot. — *v.t.* 3 To utter with a squeal. — *n.* A shrill, prolonged cry, as of a pig. [Imit.] — **squeal′er** *n.*

squeam·ish (skwē′mish) *adj.* 1 Easily disgusted or shocked; unduly scrupulous. 2 Easily nauseated. [<earlier *squeamous* <AF *escoymous;* ult. origin unknown] — **squeam′ish·ly** *adv.* — **squeam′ish·ness** *n.*

Synonyms: affected, dainty, difficult, fastidious, finical, foolish, hypercritical, overnice, oversensitive, particular, prudish, qualmish, scrupulous, sickish.

squee·gee (skwē′jē) *n.* 1 A wooden implement having a stout straight-edged strip of rubber or leather inserted in its blade, used for removing water from wet decks or floors, window panes, etc. 2 *Phot.* A smaller similar implement, made in the same way or in the form of a roller, used for pressing a film closer to its mount, or for squeezing the moisture from a print. — *v.t.* 1 To smooth down, as a photographic film, with a squeegee. 2 To cleanse with a squeegee. Also spelled *squilgee, squillagee.* [< *squeege,* var. of SQUEEZE]

squeeze (skwēz) *v.* **squeezed, squeez·ing** *v.t.* **1** To press hard upon; compress. **2** To extract something from by pressure: to *squeeze* oranges. **3** To draw forth by pressure; express: to *squeeze* juice from apples. **4** To force or push; cram. **5** To oppress, as with burdensome taxes. **6** To exert pressure upon (someone) to act as one desires, as by blackmailing. **7** To take a squeeze (def. 4) of. —*v.i.* **8** To apply pressure. **9** To force one's way; push: with *in, through,* etc. **10** To be pressed; yield to pressure: These lemons *squeeze* well. See synonyms under JAM¹ —**to squeeze out** To force out of business, or ruin financially, by unscrupulous methods. —*n.* **1** The act or process of squeezing; pressure. **2** A firm grasp of someone's hand; a hearty handclasp; also, an embrace; hug. **3** Something, as juice, extracted or expressed. **4** A facsimile, as of a coin or inscription, produced by pressing some soft substance upon it. **5** *Colloq.* A crowded social gathering. **6** *Colloq.* Pressure exerted for the extortion of money or favors; also, financial pressure. [? < OF *es-* thoroughly (< L *ex-*) + ME *queisen,* OE *cwēsan* crush]— **squeez'a·ble** *adj.*

squeeze play In baseball, a play in which the batter bunts the ball so that a man on third base may score by starting while the pitcher is about to deliver the ball.

squelch (skwelch) *v.t.* **1** To crush; squash. **2** *Colloq.* To subdue utterly; silence, as with a crushing reply. —*v.i.* **3** To make a splashing or sucking noise, as when walking in deep mud. **4** To walk with such a sound. —*n.* **1** A noise made when walking in wet boots. **2** A heavy fall or blow. **3** *Colloq.* A squelcher. [Prob. imit.]

squelch·er (skwel'chər) *n.* **1** One who or that which squelches. **2** *Colloq.* A silencing retort; crushing reply.

sque·teague (skwi·tēg') *n.* A weakfish. [< Algonquian (Narraganset) *pesukwiteaug* they make glue]

squib (skwib) *n.* **1** A roll or case filled with gunpowder, to be thrown or rolled swiftly, finally exploding like a rocket. **2** A tubular case filled with gunpowder and connected with an electric circuit, used for firing a charge in a blasthole, igniting a smokepot, or the like. **3** A broken firecracker that burns with a spitting sound. **4** A short speech or writing in a witty or satirical vein; a mild lampoon. **5** An undistinguished or petty person. —*v.* **squibbed, squib·bing** *v.i.* **1** To write or use squibs. **2** To fire a squib. **3** To explode or sound like a squib. **4** To move quickly or restlessly. —*v.t* **5** To attack with squibs; lampoon. **6** To fire or use as a squib. [Origin unknown]

squid (skwid) *n. pl.* **squid** or **squids** Any of various predaceous marine cephalopod mollusks having a long, slender body, ten tentacles, a vestigial internal shell, and an ink sac. Some species are esteemed as food. —*v.i.* **squid·ded, squid·ding** *Aeron.* to assume a narrow, squidlike shape, as a parachute under excess wind or air pressure. [Origin uncertain]

SQUID
a. Arm.   e. Mouth.
b. Body.   f. Siphon.
c. Fluke.   g. Tentacles.
d. Eye.

squig·gle (skwig'əl) *Colloq. n.* A meaningless scrawl. —*v.i.* To wriggle. [Blend of SQUIRM and WRIGGLE]

squil·gee (skwil'jē, skwil·jē') See SQUEEGEE.

squill¹ (skwil) *n.* **1** A bulbous plant (*Urginea maritima*) of the lily family, growing in the Mediterranean region; the sea onion. **2** Its bulb, dried and sliced, the white variety having diuretic and expectorant properties, and the red variety yielding a rat poison. **3** Any plant of the genus *Scilla,* the more common ones usually called by some other name, as the common English bluebell or wild hyacinth. [< L *squilla* < Gk. *skilla* sea onion]

squill² (skwil) *n.* Any of a genus (*Squilla*) of burrowing crustaceans having the form and appearance of a mantis: sometimes called *mantis shrimp.* Also **squil·la** (skwil'ə). [< L *squilla*

shrimp]

squinch (skwinch) *n. Archit.* A small stone arch or series of arches, or of projecting courses, across an interior angle of a square tower, to support an oblique side of an octagonal spire or lantern. [Alter. of obs. *scunch,* abbreviation of *scuncheon* < OF *escoinson*]

SQUINCH
Salisbury Cathedral, England.

squint (skwint) *v.i.* **1** To look with half-closed eyes, as into bright light. **2** To look with a side glance; look askance. **3** To be cross-eyed. **4** To incline or tend: with *toward,* etc. —*v.t.* **5** To hold (the eyes) half shut, as in glaring light. **6** To cause to squint. —*adj.* **1** Having the optic axes not coincident; affected with strabismus: said of the eyes. **2** Looking obliquely or askance; indirect. —*n.* **1** *Pathol.* An affection of the eyes in which their axes are differently directed; strabismus. **2** The act or habit of squinting. **3** Hence, an indirect leaning, tendency, or drift. **4** A hagioscope. [Origin uncertain] —**squint'er** *n.*

squire (skwīr) *n.* **1** A knight's attendant; an armorbearer. **2** A title of dignity, office, or courtesy ranking in England below that of *knight,* and applied in the United States especially to rural or village lawyers and justices of the peace; also, in England, a landed proprietor. **3** A gentleman who acts as the escort of a lady in public; a gallant. —*v.t. & v.i.* **squired, squir·ing** To attend or serve (someone) as a squire or escort. [Aphetic var. of ESQUIRE]

squirm (skwûrm) *v.i.* **1** To bend and twist the body; wriggle; writhe. **2** To show signs of pain or distress. —*n.* A squirming motion; a wriggle. [Origin uncertain] —**squirm'er** *n.* —**squirm'y** *adj.*

squir·rel (skwûr'əl, *Brit.* skwir'əl) *n.* **1** Any of various slender rodents (family *Sciuridae*) with a very long bushy tail, living mainly in trees and feeding chiefly on nuts, but occasionally on eggs and small birds. The red squirrel (*Sciurus hudsonicus*), the gray squirrel (*S. carolinensis*), and the fox squirrel (*S. niger*) are North American types. ◆ Collateral adjective: *sciurine.* **2** One of various sciuroid rodents, as the rock squirrel (*Otospermophilus grammurus*) of the western United States. **3** The fur of a squirrel. [< OF *esquireul* < LL *scurellus,* dim. of L *sciurus* < Gk. *skiouros* < *skia* shadow + *oura* tail]

GRAY SQUIRREL
(Body to 10 inches; tail to 8 inches)

squirrel corn A smooth and delicate plant (*Dicentra canadensis*) of the northern United States, having white or cream-colored flowers with the spurs rounded and yellow tubers resembling grains of corn.

squirrel glider A flying phalanger (*Petaurus norfolcensis*) of Australia.

squirrel monkey A marmoset.

squirt (skwûrt) *v.i.* **1** To come forth in a thin stream or jet; spurt out. **2** To eject water, etc., thus. —*v.t.* **3** To eject (water or other liquid) forcibly and in a jet. **4** To wet or bespatter with a squirt or squirts. —*n.* **1** The act of squirting or spurting; also, a jet of liquid squirted forth. **2** A syringe or squirt gun. **3** *Colloq.* A conceited, brainless fellow. [Cf. LG *swirtjen*] —**squirt'er** *n.*

squirt gun An instrument or toy shaped like a gun and used for squirting.

squirting cucumber The fruit of a procumbent branching herb (*Ecballium elaterium*) of the gourd family, which, when ripe, ejects its seeds and juice.

squish (skwish) *v.t. & v.i. Colloq.* To squash. —*n.* A squashing sound. [Var. of SQUASH¹] — **squish'y** *adj.*

Sr *Chem.* Strontium (symbol Sr).

stab (stab) *v.* **stabbed, stab·bing** *v.t.* **1** To pierce with a pointed weapon; wound, as with a dagger. **2** To thrust (a dagger, etc.), as into a body. **3** To penetrate; pierce. —*v.i.* **4** To thrust or lunge with a knife, sword, etc. **5** To inflict a wound thus.

See synonyms under PIERCE. —*n.* A thrust made with any pointed weapon. [? < Irish *stob* push, thrust, fix a stake < *stob* a stake] —**stab'ber** *n.*

sta·bile (stā'bil, stab'il) *adj.* **1** Not kept in motion. **2** *Med.* **a** Not affected by moderate heat. **b** Denoting a form of electrotherapy in which one of the electrodes is kept stationary on a part. Compare LABILE. —*n.* An amorphous piece of stationary sculpture. Compare MOBILE. [< L *stabilis.* See STABLE¹.]

sta·bil·i·ty (stə·bil'ə·tē) *n. pl.* **·ties** **1** The condition of being stable; steadiness. **2** The quality or character of being steady or constant; steadfastness of purpose or resolution. **3** *Physics* The state of being in stable equilibrium, or the degree of such equilibrium as measured by the force with which a body tends to maintain its condition of rest or steady motion. **4** *Aeron.* The ability of an aircraft to resume equilibrium when disturbed. **5** A vow to continue in the same profession and order, taken by some Benedictine monks. **6** *Obs.* Rigidity: opposed to *fluidity.* [< L *stabilitas, -tatis* < *stabilis.* < *stare* stand. See STABLE¹.]

sta·bi·liz·er (stā'bə·lī'zər) *n.* **1** *Aeron.* An automatic balancing device; especially, one which steadies the flight of an airplane. See illustration under AIRPLANE. **2** *Chem.* A substance which increases the stability of another substance or compound, especially one which reduces the spontaneous combustion of an explosive.

sta·ble¹ (stā'bəl) *adj.* **1** Standing firmly in place; not easily moved, shaken, or overthrown; fixed. **2** Marked by fixity of purpose; steadfast; inflexible. **3** Having durability or permanence; abiding. **4** *Chem.* Not easily decomposed: said of compounds. **5** *Physics* Resisting forces which tend to cause or distort motion. See synonyms under FIRM, PERMANENT. [< F < L *stabilis* < *stare* stand] — **sta'bly** *adv.* — **sta'ble·ness** *n.*

sta·ble² (stā'bəl) *n.* **1** A building set apart for lodging and feeding horses or cattle. **2** Specifically, race horses belonging to a particular stable; also, the owner and personnel of a particular stable collectively. —*v.t. & v.i.* **·bled, ·bling** To put or lodge in a stable. [< OF *estable* < L *stabulum* < *stare* stand]

stac·ca·to (stə·kä'tō) *adj.* **1** *Music* Played, or to be played, in an abrupt, disconnected manner: opposed to *legato.* **2** Marked by abrupt, sharp emphasis: a *staccato* style of speaking. [< Ital., pp. of *staccare* detach]

stack (stak) *n.* **1** A large, orderly pile of unthreshed grain, hay, or straw, usually conical. **2** Any systematic pile or heap, as a pile of poker chips purchased or won by a player. **3** A group of rifles (usually three) set upright and supporting one another. **4** A case composed of several rows of bookshelves one above the other. **5** *pl.* That part of a library where most of the books are shelved. **6** A vertical main smoke flue, especially of a furnace or boiler; a chimney; smokestack; also, a collection of such chimneys or flues. **7** *Brit.* A measure of fuel (coal or wood), equal to 108 cubic feet or 4 cubic yards. **8** *Colloq.* A great amount; plenty. —*v.t.* To gather or place in a pile; pile up in a stack: to *stack* arms; to *stack* firewood. —**to stack the cards** **1** To arrange cards in the pack in a manner favorable to the dealer. **2** To have an unfair advantage secured beforehand. [< ON *stakkr*]

stad·hold·er (stad'hōl·dər) *n.* Formerly, a viceroy or governor of a province or town of the Netherlands as the representative of the sovereign; specifically, the chief magistrate of the Netherlands, a hereditary office in the family of the princes of Orange. Also **stadt'hold·er** (stat'-). [< Du. *stadhouder* lieutenant < *stad* place + *houder* holder]

sta·di·um (stā'dē·əm) *n. pl.* **·di·a** (-dē·ə), *for def. 2* **·di·ums** **1** In ancient Greece, a course for footraces, with banked seats for spectators, as at Olympia and Athens, where games were held. **2** A similar modern structure in which athletic games are played: the *stadium* at Harvard. **3** An ancient Greek measure of length, equaling 606.75 feet. **4** A degree of progress or development. **5** *Med.* A given stage or period in the course of a disease. [< L < Gk. *stadion,* a measure of length]

staff¹ (staf, stäf) *n. pl.* **staves** (stāvz) or **staffs** *for defs. 1-3,* **staffs** *for defs. 4-6.* **1** A stick or piece of wood carried for some special purpose, as an aid in walking or climbing, or as a cudgel or weapon, or as an emblem of authority. **2** A shaft or pole that forms a support or handle: the *staff* of a spear; a *flagstaff*. **3** A stick used in measuring or testing, as a surveyors' leveling rod. **4** *Mil.* **a** A body of officers not having command but attached in an executive or advisory capacity to an army or navy unit as assistants to the officer in command. The central body is known as the **general staff. b** The personnel of a military establishment, as the officers in charge of construction, ordnance, repairs, equipment, provisions, medicine and surgery, the paymasters, and engineers. **5** A body of persons associated in carrying out some special enterprise under the supervision of a manager or chief: the editorial *staff* of a newspaper. **6** *Music* The combined lines and spaces used to represent the pitches of tones. The staff has always five long horizontal lines and the accompanying long spaces, but is enlarged as the occasion may require, by short lines above or below and the short spaces they bring. See synonyms under STICK. — *v.t.* To provide (an office, etc.) with a staff: to *staff* a management group. [OE *stæf* stick]

staff[2] (staf, stäf) *n.* A composition of plaster, fiber, etc., for temporary buildings, statues, etc. [Prob. <G *staffieren* fill, decorate]

stag (stag) *n.* **1** The male of the red deer (*Cervus elaphus*), especially the matured male. **2** The male of other large deer, as the caribou, and of certain other animals. **3** A castrated bull or boar. **4** *Scot.* A colt: also spelled *staig*. **5** *U.S. Slang* A man, especially when not in the company of women. **6** *U.S. Slang* A social gathering for men only. — *adj. U.S. Slang* Of or for men only: a *stag* party. — *v.i.* **stagged, stag·ging** *Slang* **1** *Brit.* To turn informer; squeal. **2** *U.S.* To attend a social affair unaccompanied by a woman. [OE *stagga*]

STAG HEAD
Showing antlers.

stag beetle A large, lamellicorn beetle (family *Lucanidae*), the male of which has the jaws enormously developed and branched like the antlers of a stag; specifically, the European *Lucanus cervus* and the American *L. dama*: also called *pinchbug*. They are injurious to trees.

stage (stāj) *n.* **1** The raised platform, with its scenery and mechanical appliances, on which the performance in a theater or hall takes place. **2** The theater. **3** The drama. **4** The dramatic profession. **5** The field or plan of action of some notable event: to set the *stage* for a counter-offensive. **6** A definite portion of a journey. **7** The distance traveled between two stopping points. **8** One of the regular stopping places on the route of a stagecoach or postrider. **9** A stagecoach. **10** A step in some development, progress, or process. **11** *Med.* A definite period in the course of a disease, characterized by a certain group of symptoms. **12** *Biol.* Any of the periods of growth in animals or plants: the larval *stage* of insects. **13** *Electronics* One of the radio elements in cascade amplification. **14** A water level: The river rose to flood *stage*. **15** A horizontal section or story of a building. **16** An elevated platform or scaffold for the use of workmen. **17** The horizontal shelf on a microscope which supports the slide or object to be examined. **18** Any raised platform or floor. **19** *Geol.* The stratigraphic subdivision next below a series, corresponding to an *age* in the time scale. **20** *Aerospace* One of the separate propulsion units of a rocket vehicle. Each becomes operational after the preceding one reaches burnout and is jettisoned. — *v.t.* **staged, stag·ing 1** To put or exhibit on the stage. **2** To plan, conduct, or carry out: to *stage* a rally. **3** To organize, perform, or carry out so as to appear authentic, legitimate, or spontaneous when actually not so: The en-

tire incident was *staged* for the benefit of press photographers. [<OF *estage*, ult. <L *status*, pp. of *stare* stand]

stage·coach (stāj'kōch') *n.* A large four-wheeled vehicle having a regular route from town to town.

stage·craft (stāj'kraft', -kräft') *n.* Skill in writing or staging plays.

stage·hand (stāj'hand') *n.* A worker in a theater who handles scenery and props, etc.

stage–struck (stāj'struk') *adj.* Possessed of the idea of becoming an actor or an actress; enamored of theatrical life.

stage whisper A loud whisper, as one uttered on the stage for the audience to hear.

stag·fla·tion (stag'flā'shən) *n. Econ.* Inflation combined with abnormally slow economic growth, resulting in high unemployment. [<STAG(NATION) + (IN)FLATION)]

stag·ger (stag'ər) *v.i.* **1** To move unsteadily; totter; reel. **2** To begin to give way; become less confident or resolute; waver; hesitate. — *v.t.* **3** To cause to stagger. **4** To affect strongly; overwhelm, as with surprise or grief. **5** To place in alternating rows or groups. **6** To arrange so as to prevent congestion or confusion, as by distributing: to *stagger* lunch hours. **7** *Aeron.* To adjust (two surfaces, as the wings of a biplane) so that the edge of one extends beyond the other. — *n.* **1** The act of staggering; a reeling motion. See STAGGERS. **2** *Aeron.* The amount of advance of the leading edge of one wing of a biplane over that of the other. [<obs. *stacker* <ON *stakra*] — **stag'ger·er** *n.* — **stag'ger·ing·ly** *adv.*

stag·gers (stag'ərz) *n. pl. (construed as singular)* **1** Any of various diseases of domestic animals, as horses, characterized by vertigo, staggering, and sudden falling, due to disorder of the brain and spinal cord: also called *blind staggers*. **2** A giddy sensation.

stag·hound (stag'hound') *n.* One of a breed of nearly extinct, large hounds, somewhat resembling the foxhound, formerly used for hunting deer, wolves, etc.: also called *buckhound, deerhound*.

stag·ing (stā'jing) *n.* **1** A scaffolding or temporary platform. **2** The act of putting a play upon the stage. **3** The business of driving or running stagecoaches; also, traveling by stagecoach.

stag·nant (stag'nənt) *adj.* **1** Standing still; not flowing: said of water, as in a pool; hence, foul from long standing. **2** Lacking briskness or activity, as life or business; dull; inert; sluggish. [<F <L *stagnans, -antis*, pp. of *stagnare* stagnate <*stagnum* a pool] — **stag'nan·cy** *n.* — **stag'nant·ly** *adv.*

staid (stād) *adj.* Fixed; steady and sober; sedate. See synonyms under SOBER, SEDATE. [Orig. pt. and pp. of STAY[1]] — **staid'ly** *adv.* — **staid'ness** *n.*

stain (stān) *n.* **1** A discoloration from foreign matter; a spot; smirch; blot. **2** The act of discoloring, or the state of being discolored. **3** A dye or thin pigment used in staining. **4** A chemical reagent for coloring microscopic specimens. **5** A moral taint; tarnish. [<v.] — *v.t.* **1** To make a stain upon; discolor; soil. **2** To color by the use of a dye or stain. **3** To bring a moral stain upon; blemish. **4** To impregnate, as a microscopic specimen, with a substance whose reaction colors some part without affecting others, thus rendering form or structure visible. — *v.i.* **5** To take or impart a stain. [Aphetic var. of DISTAIN] — **stain'a·ble** *adj.* — **stain'er** *n.* — **stain'less** *adj.* — **stain'less·ly** *adv.*

Synonyms (*verb*): blot, color, discolor, disgrace, dishonor, dye, soil, spot, sully, tarnish, tinge, tint. To *color* is to impart a color desired or undesired, temporary or permanent, or, in the intransitive use, to assume a color in any way. To *dye* is to impart a color intentionally and with a view to permanence, and especially so as to pervade the substance or fiber of that to which it is applied. To *stain* is primarily to *discolor*, to impart a color undesired and perhaps unintended, and which may or may not be permanent. *Stain* is, however, used of giving an intended and perhaps pleasing color to wood, glass, etc., by an

application of coloring matter which enters the substance a little below the surface, in distinction from painting, in which coloring matter is spread upon the surface; *dyeing* is generally said of wool, yarn, cloth, or similar materials which are dipped into the *coloring* liquid. To *tinge* is to *color* slightly. It may be used of giving a slight flavor, or a slight admixture of one ingredient or quality with another that is more pronounced. See BLEMISH, DEFILE[1], POLLUTE. Compare FOUL.

stained glass See under GLASS.

stainless steel A steel alloy made resistant to corrosion and atmospheric influences by the addition of from 10 to 30 percent chromium, and other ingredients.

stair (stâr) *n.* **1** A step, or one of a series of steps, for mounting or descending from one level to another. **2** A series of steps: usually in the plural. ◆ Homophone: *stare*. [OE *stæger*]

stair·case (stâr'kās') *n.* A flight or set of stairs, usually from one floor to another, complete with the supports, balusters, etc.

stair·head (stâr'hed') *n.* The top of a staircase.

stair·well (stâr'wel') *n.* A vertical shaft enclosing a staircase.

stake (stāk) *n.* **1** A stick or post, as of wood sharpened for driving into the ground: used as a boundary mark, sign of ownership, to support the rails of a fence, etc. **2** A post to which a person is bound to be burned alive; hence, death by burning at the stake. **3** An upright, set in a socket at the edge of the floor of a car or wagon, to confine loose material. **4** Something wagered or risked, as the money bet on a race. **5** A prize in a contest: sometimes in the plural. **6** An interest in an enterprise; contingent gain or loss. **7** An organizational unit of the Mormon Church, consisting of several wards. **8** A grubstake. — **at stake** In hazard or jeopardy; in question: My whole future was *at stake*. — **to pull up stakes** To wind up one's business in a place and move on; move out. — *v.t.* **staked, stak·ing 1** To fasten or support by means of a stake; tether to a stake. **2** To mark the boundaries of with stakes: often with *off* or *out*. **3** *Colloq.* To put at hazard; wager; risk. **4** *Colloq.* To grubstake; also, to supply with working capital; finance. ◆ Homophone: *steak*. [OE *staca*]

sta·lac·tite (stə·lak'tīt) *n.* **1** An elongated, downward-hanging form in which certain minerals, especially calcium carbonate, are sometimes deposited by slow dripping, as in a cave. **2** Any similar formation. **3** A downward-projecting ornament of a vaulted surface. [<NL *stalactites* <Gk. *stalaktitos* dripping <*stalassein* trickle, drip] — **stal·ac·tit·ic** (stal'ək·tit'ik) or **·i·cal** *adj.*

STALACTITE (*a*)
STALAGMITE (*b*)

sta·lag (stal'ag, *Ger.* shtä'läkh) *n.* A German prison camp for captured enlisted men. [<G, contraction of *stammlager* <*stamm* base + *lager* camp]

sta·lag·mite (stə·lag'mīt) *n.* **1** An incrustation, usually cylindrical, or conical, on the floor of a cavern: the counterpart of a stalactite, often fusing with it into the stalactite column. **2** Any similar formation. [<NL *stalagmites* <Gk. *stalagmos* a dripping <*stalassein* drip] — **stal·ag·mit·ic** (stal'əg·mit'ik) or **·i·cal** *adj.*

stale[1] (stāl) *adj.* **1** Having lost freshness; slightly changed or deteriorated by standing, as air, vapid wine or beer, old bread, etc. **2** Lacking in interest from age or familiarity; worn out; trite: a *stale* joke. **3** In poor condition from prolonged activity, as from overstudy or, in athletics, from overtraining: especially in the phrase **gone stale. 4** Inactive; dull: said of a stock market after a period of overactivity. **5** *Law* In courts of equity, impaired in legal force, due to long neglect in pressing or asserting a claim or to a change in the condition or situation of the parties. See synonyms under TRITE. — *v.i.* **staled, stal·ing** To become stale or trite. [Origin uncertain] — **stale'ly** *adv.* — **stale'ness** *n.*

stale² (stāl) *n.* The urine of cattle or horses. — *v.i.* **staled, stal·ing** To urinate: said of horses and cattle. [Prob. <MLG *stal* horse urine]

stale·mate (stāl'māt') *n.* **1** In chess, a position in which a player, not in check, can make no move without putting his king in check. The result is a drawn game. **2** Hence, any tie or deadlock. — *v.t.* **·mat·ed, ·mat·ing** **1** To put into a condition of stalemate. **2** To bring to a standstill. [<AF *estale* a fixed position + MATE²]

Sta·lin (stä'lin, -lēn), **Joseph,** 1879–1953, U.S.S.R. statesman: real name *Iosif Dzhugashvili.*

Sta·lin·ism (stä'lin·iz'əm) *n.* The doctrines or practices of Stalin; especially, communism involving a rigid implementation of government policy, through coercion, intimidation, and ruthless suppression of opposition, and characterized by ardent patriotism focused upon the Soviet Union and its leader. — **Sta'lin·ist** *n.*

stalk¹ (stôk) *n.* **1** The stem or axis of a plant, especially when herbaceous. **2** Any support on which an organ is borne, as a pedicel. **3** A supporting part or stem: the jointed *stalk* of a sea lily, the *stalk* of a quill. **4** Any stem or main axis, as of a goblet. [ME *stalke,* dim. of OE *stæla* stem of a plant] — **stalked** *adj.* — **stalk'less** *adj.*

stalk² (stôk) *v.i.* **1** To approach game, etc., stealthily. **2** To walk in a stiff, dignified manner: also used figuratively: Murder *stalked* through the streets. **3** *Obs.* To go stealthily; creep. — *v.t.* **4** To approach (game, etc.) stealthily. **5** To pace through: Famine *stalked* the countryside. — *n.* **1** The act of stalking game. **2** A stately step or walk. [OE *bestealcian* move stealthily] — **stalk'er** *n.*

stall (stôl) *n.* **1** A compartment in which a horse or bovine animal is confined and fed. **2** A small booth or compartment in a street, market, etc., for the sale or display of small articles. **3** A partially enclosed seat, as in the orchestra of a theater or the choir of a cathedral. **4** A working compartment in a coal mine. **5** A space set aside for the parking of an automobile. **6** A sheath or covering for a finger or thumb; a cot. **7** *Aeron.* The condition of an airplane which has lost the relative speed necessary for control; the act of stalling. **8** *Colloq.* An evasion or argument made to postpone action or decision. — *v.t.* **1** To place or keep in a stall. **2** To keep in a stall for fattening, as cattle. **3** To bring to a standstill; stop the progress or motion of, especially unintentionally. **4** To cause to stick fast in mud, snow, etc. — *v.i.* **5** To come to a standstill; stop, especially unintentionally. **6** To stick fast in mud, snow, etc. **7** *Colloq.* To make delays; be evasive: to *stall* for time. **8** To live or be kept in a stall. **9** *Aeron.* To go into a stall. [OE *steall*]

stal·lion (stal'yən) *n.* An uncastrated male horse. [<OF *estalon* <OHG *stal* stable]

stal·wart (stôl'wərt) *adj.* **1** Strong and brawny; robust. **2** Resolute; determined; unwavering. **3** Brave; courageous. — *n.* **1** An uncompromising partisan, as in politics. **2** *U.S.* A member of a conservative faction of the Republican party (1874–85) which opposed civil service reform and liberal policies toward the South. [Var. of STALWORTH] — **stal'wart·ly** *adv.* — **stal'wart·ness** *n.*

sta·men (stā'mən) *n.* *pl.* **sta·mens, Rare sta·mi·na** (stam'ə·nə) *Bot.* The pollen–bearing floral organ of a flower, standing inside the floral envelopes and consisting of two parts: the *filament,* or support, and the *anther,* or pollen sac. [<L, warp, thread < *stare* stand]

Stam·ford (stam'fərd) **1** A municipal borough in SW Lincolnshire, England; a 14th century center of learning, at that time comparable to Oxford. **2** A city on Long Island Sound in SW Connecticut.

STAMEN (*a, b, c*)
a. Filament.
b. Anther.
c. Pollen.
d. Pistil.

stam·i·na (stam'ə·nə) *n.* **1** Supporting vitality; strength; vigor; physical or moral capacity to endure or withstand hardship or difficulty. **2** The supporting part of a body. [<L, pl. of *stamen* warp, thread. See STAMEN.]

stam·mer (stam'ər) *v.t.* & *v.i.* To speak or utter with a halting articulation, commonly with nervous repetitions or prolongations of a sound or syllable, and involuntary pauses: to *stammer* an apology. — *n.* A halting, defective utterance. [OE *stamerian*] — **stam'mer·er** *n.*

Synonym: stutter. *Stammer* and *stutter* are virtually interchangeable in general use. Frequently, however, *stammer* is associated with nervousness, excitement, or embarrassment, while *stutter* is reserved by the speech therapists for a particular speech disorder of obscure origin.

stamp (stamp) *v.t.* **1** To strike heavily with the sole of the foot. **2** To bring down (the foot) heavily and noisily. **3** To affect in a specified manner by or as by stamping with the foot: to *stamp* a fire out; to *stamp* out opposition. **4** To make marks or figures upon by means of a die, stamp, etc. **5** To imprint or impress with a die, stamp, etc. **6** To fix or imprint permanently: The deed was *stamped* on his memory. **7** To assign a specified quality to; characterize; brand: to *stamp* a story false. **8** To affix an official seal, stamp, etc., to. **9** To crush, break, or pulverize, as ore. — *v.i.* **10** To strike the foot heavily on the ground. **11** To walk with heavy, resounding steps. See synonyms under IMPRESS¹, INSCRIBE. — *n.* **1** A characteristic mark made by stamping; a device or design impressed upon any object, as by a die. **2** An implement or machine for stamping; specifically, a die having a pattern as for coinworking; any instrument for impressing a mark, design, or copy upon any object or surface: a hand *stamp.* **3** The weight or block as in an ore mill, which by its impact crushes the ore; by extension, the stamping mill itself. **4** A cutting tool for making articles of outline corresponding to the cutting edges: operated by pressure or by blows. **5** Any characteristic mark, as a label or imprint; a brand. **6** Hence, figuratively, characteristic quality or form; kind; sort: I dislike men of his *stamp.* **7** The act of stamping. **8** A printed device prepared and sold by a government, for attachment, as to a letter (**postage stamp**), commodity (**revenue stamp**), etc., as proof that the tax or fee has been paid; also, a trading stamp. See synonyms under MARK¹. — **trading stamp** A stamp of fixed value given by a tradesman to a purchaser and exchangeable, in quantities, for goods selected from a premium list. [ME *stampen.* Akin to OE *stempan* pound.]

stam·pede (stam·pēd') *n.* **1** A sudden starting and rushing off through panic: said primarily of a herd of cattle, horses, etc. **2** Any sudden, impulsive, tumultuous running movement of a crowd, as of a mob. **3** A movement or rush of people toward a certain region or object, as a gold rush or for homestead sites. **4** The sudden unplanned movement to support a certain candidate at a political convention, as from common impulse. — *v.* **·ped·ed, ·ped·ing** *v.t.* To cause a stampede or panic in. — *v.i.* To rush or flee in a stampede. [<Am. Sp. *estampida* crash < *estampar* stamp] — **stam·ped'er** *n.*

stamping ground **1** A place where horses or other animals gather in numbers. **2** A favorite resort; a habitual gathering place.

stamp mill A machine for pulverizing rock for the purpose of extracting the ore it contains.

stance (stans) *n.* **1** Mode of standing; posture. **2** In golf, the position of a player's feet, with reference to the ball and to each other, when making a stroke. **3** *Scot.* A position; a station; hence, a site; foundation. [<OF *estance* <L *stans, stantis,* ppr. of *stare* stand]

stanch (stanch, stänch) *v.t.* **1** To stop or check the flow of (blood, etc.). **2** To stop the flow of blood from (a wound). **3** *Obs.* To quench; quell; put an end to. Also spelled *staunch.* — *adj.* & *n.* Staunch. [<OF *estanchier* halt, bring to a stop, make stand, ult. <L *stare* stand] — **stanch'er** *n.*

stan·chion (stan'shən) *n.* **1** An upright bar forming a principal support. **2** A vertical bar or pair of bars used to confine cattle in a stall. — *v.t.* **1** To provide with stanchions. **2** To support or confine with stanchions. [<OF *estanchon* < *estance* situation, position. See STANCE.]

stand (stand) *v.* **stood, stand·ing** *v.i.* **1** To assume or maintain an erect position on the feet: distinguished from *sit, lie, kneel,* etc. **2** To be in a vertical position; be erect. **3** To measure a specified height when standing: He *stands* six feet. **4** To assume a specified position: to *stand* aside. **5** To be situated; have position or location; lie. **6** To have or be in a specified state, condition, or relation: We *stand* ready to fight; He *stood* in fear of his life. **7** To assume an attitude for defense or offense: *Stand* and fight! **8** To be or remain firm or resolute, as in determination. **9** To be consistent; accord; agree. **10** To remain unimpaired, unchanged, or valid: My decision still *stands.* **11** To collect and remain; also, to be stagnant, as water. **12** To be of a specified rank or class: He *stands* third. **13** To stop or pause; halt. **14** To scruple; hesitate. **15** *Naut.* To take a direction; steer: The brig *stood* into the wind. **16** To point, as a hunting dog. **17** *Brit.* To be a candidate, as for election. — *v.t.* **18** To place upright; set in an erect position. **19** To put up with; endure; tolerate. **20** To be subjected to; undergo: He must *stand* trial. **21** To withstand; resist. **22** *Colloq.* To pay for; bear the expense of: to *stand* a treat. — **to stand a chance** (or **show**) To have a chance or likelihood, as of success. — **to stand by 1** To stay near and be ready to help or operate. **2** To help; support. **3** To abide by; make good; adhere to. **4** To remain passive and watch, as when help is needed. **5** *Telecom.* To wait, as for the continuance of an interrupted transmission. — **to stand clear** To remain at a safe distance. — **to stand down** *Law* To leave the witness stand. — **to stand for 1** To represent; symbolize. **2** To put up with; tolerate. — **to stand from under** To move from beneath, as something about to fall. — **to stand in** *Colloq.* To cost. — **to stand in for** To act as a substitute for. — **to stand off** *Colloq.* **1** To keep at a distance. **2** To fail to agree or comply. — **to stand on 1** To be based on or grounded in; rest. **2** To insist on or demand observance of: to *stand on* ceremony. **3** *Naut.* To keep on the same tack or course. — **to stand on one's own (two) feet** (or **legs**) To be independent; manage one's own affairs. — **to stand out 1** To stick out; project or protrude. **2** To be prominent; appear in relief or contrast. **3** To refuse to consent or agree; remain in opposition. — **to stand over 1** To remain near and watch, as a subordinate. **2** To be postponed. — **to stand pat 1** In poker, to play one's hand as dealt, without drawing new cards. **2** To resist change. See STAND-PATTER. — **to stand to reason** To conform to reason. — **to stand up 1** To stand erect. **2** To withstand wear, criticism, analysis, etc. **3** *Slang* To fail, usually intentionally, to keep an appointment with. — **to stand up for** To side with; take the part of. — **to stand up to** To confront courageously; face. — **to stand up with** To be best man or bridesmaid for. — *n.* **1** A structure upon which persons or things may stand, or on which articles may be kept or displayed. **2** A small table on which things may be placed conveniently. **3** A rack or other piece of furniture on which hats may be hung, or canes, umbrellas, etc., supported: a hall *stand.* **4** A stall, counter, or the like, where merchandise is displayed: a *bookstand.* **5** A structure upon which persons may sit or stand, as a platform, or a series of raised seats: a *bandstand,* a *judges' stand;* also, a small platform in court from which a witness testifies. **6** Any place where or in which something stands; position; place; specifically, the place of one's customary occupation; an assigned or chosen location. **7** The act of standing, especially of standing firmly: to make a *stand* against the enemy. **8** Cessation from motion or progress; a standstill. **9** A complete set; outfit: chiefly in the phrase **stand of arms. 10** A growth on the field, as of corn or grass. **11** A tree grown from seed; also, a young tree left when others are cut down. **12** The growing trees in a forest or in part

of a forest. **13** In the theater, a stop made while on tour to give a performance; also, the place: a one-night *stand*. **14** *Obs.* A troop; force. **15** A curved metal bar attached to the base of a force pump and serving as a fulcrum for the brake which moves the piston up and down. **16** In prosody, an epode: so called because it was originally sung while the chorus stood still. [OE *standan*] — **stand′er** *n.*
Synonyms (verb): abide, continue, endure, halt, pause, remain, stay, stop. See REST¹. *Antonyms:* decline, droop, drop, fail, faint, falter, flee, fly, sink, succumb, yield.

stan·dard (stan′dərd) *n.* **1** A flag, ensign, or banner, used as a distinctive emblem of a government, body of men, or special cause: the *standard* of freedom or revolt. **2** A figure or an image adopted as the emblem of a nation. **3** A long, narrow flag carried by mounted and motorized units of the U. S. Army. **4** Any established measure of extent, quantity, quality, or value. **5** Any type, model, or example for comparison; a criterion of excellence; test: a *standard* of conduct or taste. **6** In coinage, the established proportion by weight of fine metal and alloy. **7** An upright timber, post, pole, or beam, especially as a support. **8** *Bot.* **a** Any tree, shrub, bush, or herb not dwarfed by grafting, and growing on a vigorous upright stem without support of a wall or trellis. **b** The vexillum (def. 2). **9** A heavy or stationary article of furniture. See synonyms under EXAMPLE, IDEAL, RULE. — **National Bureau of Standards** A branch of the U. S. Department of Commerce that maintains scientific, technical, and industrial standards, and acts as a research and testing agency for the government. — *adj.* **1** Having the accuracy or authority of a standard; serving as a gage, test, or model; hence, of recognized excellence or authority: a *standard* book or author. **2** Designating or belonging to the form of a language which, through its use in a region of economic and cultural importance, has gained acceptance and social prestige among all the speakers of the language. ◆ In this dictionary, words and meanings not considered to be at the level of the standard language are appropriately labeled colloquial, slang, dialectal, or illiterate. [<OF *estandard* banner <Gmc.]
stan·dard–bear·er (stan′dərd·bâr′ər) *n.* **1** An officer or soldier of a regiment or other military body who carries the flag or ensign. **2** Hence, one who leads, as a candidate; specifically, a presidential nominee.
stan·dard·bred (stan′dərd·bred′) *n.* A breed of horse notable for its trotters and pacers: descendent from the thoroughbred stallion *Messenger,* imported from England in 1788. **stan·dard–bred** (stan′dərd·bred′) *adj.* Bred so as to be of a required strain, quality, or pedigree, as poultry, horses, etc.

standard deviation *Stat.* The square root of the arithmetic average of the squares of all the deviations from the mean value of a series of observations.

standard gage **1** A gage for determining whether tools, etc., are of a recognized standard size. **2** A railroad track width of 56 1/2 inches, considered as standard. **3** A railroad having such a gage, or a locomotive or car made to run on this gage. — **stan′dard–gage′** (-gāj′) *adj.*

stan·dard·ize (stan′dər·dīz) *v.t.* **·ized, ·iz·ing** To make to or regulate by a standard: to *standardize* equipment. — **stan′dard·i·za′tion** *n.* — **stan′dard·iz′er** *n.*

standard lamp **1** Any of several standard lighting units used in photometric determinations. **2** In the United States, the pentane-burning lamp, equal to 10 international candles, or the Hefner lamp, burning amyl acetate, equal to 0.9 international candle.

standard time Civil time as reckoned from a certain meridian officially established as standard over a large area. Reckoning from the meridian of Greenwich, each time zone, comprising a sector of 15 degrees of longitude, is considered to represent a time interval of one hour, although in practice these zones are adjusted to meet various geographic and other regional conditions, as along the International

STANDARD TIME IN PRINCIPAL CITIES

Referred to noon in Washington, D.C. *(Time Zone +5)* and in Greenwich, England *(Time Zone 0)*. Times have been calculated to the even hour, disregarding a few deviations (up to 30 minutes) resulting from local time-zone adjustments. All hours are for the same day except as indicated by (*) when the time is for the *following* day. Compare the table under TIME ZONE for explanation of the plus and minus factor in column 4.

(1) City	(2) When NOON Washington Time	(3) When NOON Greenwich Time	(4) Time Zone Number
Alexandria	7 P.M.	2 P.M.	−2
Amsterdam	5 P.M.	NOON	0
Athens	7 P.M.	2 P.M.	−2
Auckland	*4 A.M.	11 P.M.	−11
Baghdad	8 P.M.	3 P.M.	−3
Bangkok	MIDNIGHT	7 P.M.	−7
Belfast	5 P.M.	NOON	0
Berlin	6 P.M.	1 P.M.	−1
Bogotá	NOON	7 A.M.	+5
Bombay	10 P.M.	5 P.M.	−5
Boston	NOON	7 A.M.	+5
Brussels	5 P.M.	NOON	0
Bucharest	7 P.M.	2 P.M.	−2
Budapest	6 P.M.	1 P.M.	−1
Buenos Aires	1 P.M.	8 A.M.	+4
Cairo	7 P.M.	2 P.M.	−2
Calcutta	11 P.M.	6 P.M.	−6
Cape Town	6 P.M.	1 P.M.	−1
Caracas	1 P.M.	8 A.M.	+4
Chicago	11 A.M.	6 A.M.	+6
Copenhagen	6 P.M.	1 P.M.	−1
Delhi	10 P.M.	5 P.M.	−5
Denver	10 A.M.	5 A.M.	+7
Detroit	11 A.M.	6 A.M.	+6
Dublin	5 P.M.	NOON	0
Geneva	6 P.M.	1 P.M.	−1
Greenwich	5 P.M.	NOON	0
Halifax	1 P.M.	8 A.M.	+4
Havana	1 P.M.	8 A.M.	+4
Hong Kong	*1 A.M.	8 P.M.	−8
Istanbul	7 P.M.	2 P.M.	−2
Jakarta	MIDNIGHT	7 P.M.	−7
Johannesburg	7 P.M.	2 P.M.	−2
LeHavre	5 P.M.	NOON	0
Lima	NOON	7 A.M.	+5
Lisbon	5 P.M.	NOON	0
Liverpool	5 P.M.	NOON	0
London	5 P.M.	NOON	0
Madrid	6 P.M.	1 P.M.	−1
Manila	*1 A.M.	8 P.M.	−8
Melbourne	*3 A.M.	10 P.M.	−10
Mexico City	11 A.M.	6 A.M.	+6
Montreal	NOON	7 A.M.	+5
Moscow	7 P.M.	2 P.M.	−2
New York	NOON	7 A.M.	+5
Oslo	6 P.M.	1 P.M.	−1
Ottawa	NOON	7 A.M.	+5
Paris	5 P.M.	NOON	0
Peking	*1 A.M.	8 P.M.	−8
Philadelphia	NOON	7 A.M.	+5
Quebec	NOON	7 A.M.	+5
Río de Janeiro	2 P.M.	9 A.M.	+3
Rome	6 P.M.	1 P.M.	−1
St. Louis	11 A.M.	6 A.M.	+6
San Francisco	9 A.M.	4 A.M.	+8
Shanghai	*1 A.M.	8 P.M.	−8
Singapore	MIDNIGHT	7 P.M.	−7
Stockholm	6 P.M.	1 P.M.	−1
Sydney	*3 A.M.	10 P.M.	−10
Teheran	8 P.M.	3 P.M.	−3
Tokyo	*2 A.M.	9 P.M.	−9
Toronto	NOON	7 A.M.	+5
Vancouver	9 A.M.	4 A.M.	+8
Vienna	6 P.M.	1 P.M.	−1
Vladivostok	*2 A.M.	9 P.M.	−9
Warsaw	6 P.M.	1 P.M.	−1
Washington	NOON	7 A.M.	+5
Winnipeg	11 A.M.	6 A.M.	+6
Yokohama	*2 A.M.	9 P.M.	−9
Zurich	6 P.M.	1 P.M.	−1

Date Line. See table above. In the conterminous United States the four standard time zones are the Eastern, Central, Mountain, and Pacific, using respectively the mean local time of the 75th, 90th, 105th, and 120th meridians west of Greenwich, and being 5, 6, 7, and 8

hours slower or earlier than Greenwich time. Canada has in addition a fifth zone, the Atlantic (or Provincial), based on the local time of the 60th meridian, which is 4 hours earlier than Greenwich time. See also TIME ZONE.

standard wavelength *Physics* The wavelength of the red cadmium line observed in dry air at 15 degrees Celsius and 760 millimeters of mercury: equal to 6438.4696 angstrom units.
stand–by (stand′bī′) *n.* *pl.* **–bys** Any person or thing that can be relied on in time of stress or emergency.
stand–in (stand′in′) *n.* **1** A position of influence or favor; a pull. **2** A person who relieves a motion-picture player from tedious waiting intervals and substitutes for him in hazardous actions.
stand·ing (stan′ding) *adj.* **1** Remaining erect; not prostrated or cut down, as grain. **2** Continuing for regular or permanent use; remaining the same indefinitely; not special or temporary: a *standing* rule, a *standing* army. **3** Stagnant; not flowing: *standing* water. **4** Begun while standing: distinguished from *running*: a *standing* high jump. **5** Established; permanent: the *standing* church. — *n.* **1** Place; relative position, as in social, commercial, or moral relations; repute; grade; especially, high grade or rank; good reputation: a man of *standing*. **2** A place to stand in; station. **3** Time in which something stands or goes on; continuance; duration: a feud of long *standing*. **4** The act of one who stands; erectness; stance. — *adv.* At or to a sudden stop or standstill, especially in the phrase **to bring up standing**.
standing order **1** A military order always in force and not subject to change or modification. **2** In parliamentary procedure, a general regulation governing the manner in which the business of a body shall be conducted: in force from session to session until rescinded or voided.
standing room Place in which to stand, as in a building, theater, etc., where the seats are all occupied.
stand–off (stand′ôf′, -of′) *n.* **1** A draw or tie, as in a game. **2** A counterbalancing or neutralization. **3** A feeling or state of indifference or coldness; aloofness. **4** A postponement. — **stand′–off′ish** *adj.*
stand–pat (stand′pat′) *adj.* Characterized by or pertaining to the policy of opposition to change; conservative.
stand·pipe (stand′pīp′) *n.* A vertical pipe, as at a reservoir, into which the water is pumped to give it a head; a water tower.
stand·point (stand′point′) *n.* A position from which things are viewed or judged; point of view; basal principle.
St. Andrew's cross The oblique cross; also, a saltire. See under CROSS.
stand·still (stand′stil′) *n.* A pause; cessation of motion or action; halt; rest. — *adj.* In a state of rest or inactivity; standing still.
stand–up (stand′up′) *adj.* **1** Having an erect position: a *stand-up* collar. **2** Done, consumed, etc., while standing.
stan·iel (stan′yəl) *n.* The kestrel. Also **stan·nel** (stan′əl). [OE *stāngella* <*stān* stone + *gellan* scream]
sta·nine (stā′nīn) *n.* *Psychol.* A composite weighted score of aptitudes and performance based on a scale of nine: it is a form of frequency distribution about a median of 5, 1 being lowest and 9 highest: originally developed to test air crews in the U. S. Army Air Forces. [<STA(NDARD SCALE OF) NINE]
stan·nic (stan′ik) *adj.* *Chem.* Of, pertaining to, or containing tin, especially in its higher valence. [<L *stannum* tin]
stannic acid *Chem.* Any of three compounds derived from stannic chloride by the action of alkalis.
St. Anthony's fire *Pathol.* Erysipelas.
St. Anthony's nut An earthnut *(Conopodium denudatum),* fed to pigs: so called because St. Anthony was once a swineherd: also called *pignut, groundnut.*
stan·za (stan′zə) *n.* A certain number of lines of verse grouped in a definite scheme of meter

and sequence; a metrical division of a poem: often incorrectly called a *verse*. [<Ital., room, stanza <L *stans, stantis* standing. See STANCE.]
— **stan·za·ic** (stan·zā'ik) *adj.*

sta·pe·li·a (stə·pē'lē·ə) *n.* Any of a genus (*Stapelia*) of fleshy African plants of the milkweed family, having leafless toothed stems and showy, starlike, ill-smelling, purple or yellowish flowers sometimes a foot in diameter; a carrion flower. [<NL, after J. B. van *Stapel*, died 1636, Dutch botanist]

staphylo– *combining form* **1** *Anat.* The uvula: *staphyloplasty*. **2** *Med.* Staphylococcic. Also, before vowels, **staphyl–**. [<Gk. *staphylē* bunch of grapes]

staph·y·lo·coc·cus (staf'ə·lō·kok'əs) *n.* *pl.* **·coc·ci** (-kok'sī) Any of a genus (*Staphylococcus*) of typically parasitic bacteria occurring singly, in pairs, or in irregular clusters; especially, *S. aureus*, an infective agent in boils, furuncles, and suppurating wounds. See illustration under BACTERIUM. [<NL <Gk. *staphylos* bunch of grapes + *kokkos* a berry] — **staph'y·lo·coc'cic** (-kok'sik) *adj.*

staph·y·lo·plas·ty (staf'ə·lō·plas'tē) *n.* Reparative surgery of the soft palate and uvula. — **staph'y·lo·plas'tic** *adj.*

staph·y·lor·rha·phy (staf'ə·lôr'ə·fē, -lor'-) *n.* *Surg.* The operation of uniting a cleft palate. Also **staph'y·lor'a·phy**. [<STAPHYLO– + –RHAPHY]

sta·ple[1] (stā'pəl) *n.* **1** A principal commodity or production of a country or region; a well-established article of commerce. **2** A chief element or main constituent of something. **3** The carded or combed fiber of cotton, wool, or flax. **4** Raw material. **5** A commercial emporium; mart. **6** Hence, a source of supply; storehouse. — *adj.* **1** Regularly and constantly produced or sold; hence, main; chief. **2** Commercially established; having regular commercial channels. **3** Marketable. — *v.t.* **·pled, ·pling** To sort or classify according to length, as wool fiber. [<OF *estaple* market, support <Gmc.]

sta·ple[2] (stā'pəl) *n.* A U-shaped piece of metal with pointed ends, or a loop of thin wire, driven into wood, fabrics, paper, etc., to serve as a fastening. — *v.t.* **·pled, ·pling** To fix or fasten by a staple or staples. [OE *stapol* post, prop]

sta·pler[1] (stā'plər) *n.* **1** A sorter of wool according to its staple. **2** A merchant who participated in one of the monopolies formerly granted by royal authority.

sta·pler[2] (stā'plər) *n.* A wire-stitching machine that binds pamphlets, books, etc.

star (stär) *n.* **1** *Astron.* One of a class of self-luminous celestial bodies, exclusive of comets, meteors, and nebulae, but including the sun. The stars are classified according to their relative brightness in what are known as magnitudes, the first being the brightest and the sixth the faintest visible to the naked eye. The table below gives the names of the principal navigational stars and their apparent magnitudes, with the constellation in which each may be found. ◆ Collateral adjectives: *astral, sidereal, stellar*. **2** Loosely, any heavenly body; a planet. **3** A conventional figure having five or more radiating points: used as an emblem or device, as on the shoulder strap of a general. **4** An asterisk (*). **5** A white spot on the forehead of a horse or bovine animal. **6** An actor or actress who plays the leading part; hence, anyone who shines prominently in a calling or profession: a literary *star*. **7** A heavenly body considered as influencing one's fate; hence, fortune; destiny. — **binary star** A pair of stars revolving about a common center. Three types have been noted: *eclipsing*, in which the members successively eclipse each other; *spectroscopic*, in which the members are distinguishable only by shifts in their spectral lines; and *visual*, in which the members may be distinguished through the telescope. — **dark star** An invisible star, non-shining or dimly shining: known only through relation to visible stars, as during eclipsing action. — **double star** Two stars so near to each other as to be almost indistinguishable except through a telescope. — **dwarf star** Any of a class of stars which have reached their greatest temperature and are in the phase of contraction, with luminosity passing from bluish to orange. — **giant star** Any of a class of stars of great mass and high

luminosity which are passing through the early stages of their evolution. — **variable star** Any of several groups of stars whose apparent magnitude varies at different times. The cause may be external, as with binary stars, one of which regularly eclipses the other; or internal, as with true variable stars whose periodic fluctuations in light are caused by internal changes. See CEPHEID VARIABLE, NOVA. — *v.* **starred, star·ring** *v.t.* **1** To set or adorn with spangles or stars. **2** To mark with an asterisk. **3** To transform into a star. **4** To present as a star in a play or motion picture. — *v.i.* **5** To shine brightly as a star; be prominent or brilliant. **6** To play the leading part; be the star. — *adj.* **1** Of or pertaining to a star or stars. **2** Prominent; brilliant: a *star* football player. [OE *steorra*]

TABLE OF PRINCIPAL STARS

Star	Constellation	Magnitude
Achernar	Eridanus	0.60
Acrux	Crucis	1.05
Aldebaran	Taurus	1.06
Alpheratz	Andromeda	2.15
Altair	Aquila	0.89
Antares	Scorpio	1.22
Arcturus	Boötes	0.24
Betelgeuse	Orion	1.20
Canopus	Argo	−0.86
Capella	Auriga	0.21
Deneb	Cygnus	1.33
Fomalhaut	Piscis Austrinus	1.29
Peacock	Pavo	2.12
Polaris	Ursa Minor	2.12
Pollux	Gemini	1.21
Procyon	Canis Minor	0.48
Regulus	Leo	1.34
Rigel	Orion	0.34
Rigil Kentaurus	Centaurus	0.06
Sirius	Canis Major	−1.58
Spica	Virgo	1.21
Vega	Lyra	0.14

star apple 1 The edible fruit of a West Indian tree (*Chrysophyllum cainito*), resembling an apple in size and appearance, and having ten cells and as many seeds disposed stellately around its center. **2** The tree itself.

star·board (stär'bərd) *Naut.* *n.* The right-hand side of a vessel as one looks from stern to bow: opposed to *larboard, port*. — *adj.* Of or pertaining to the right of the observer on a vessel when facing the bow. — *adv.* Toward the starboard side. — *v.t.* To put, move, or turn (the helm) to the starboard side. [OE *steorbord* steering side]

star boarder The senior boarder in a boarding house, or one who pays more than the others, considered as entitled to special privileges.

starch (stärch) *n.* **1** *Biochem.* A white, odorless, tasteless, amorphous, powdery carbohydrate ($C_6H_{10}O_5)_n$, insoluble in cold water, alcohol, and other liquids, found in the seeds, pith, or tubers of most plants. Starch is an exceedingly important component of vegetable foods, reacting with certain digestive enzymes to produce maltose and dextrin; it is also used in the commercial production of glucose, for stiffening linen, and for many industrial purposes. **2** Stiffness or formality; a stiff or formal manner. **3** *U.S. Slang* Energy; vigor. — *v.t.* To apply starch to; stiffen with or as with starch. [ME *sterche* <OE *stercan* stiffen < *stearc* stiff. Related to STARK.]

starch gum Dextrin.

starch sugar Dextrose.

starch·y (stär'chē) *adj.* **starch·i·er, starch·i·est 1** Stiffened with starch; stiff; figuratively, prim; formal; precise: also **starched**. **2** Formed of or combined with starch; farinaceous. —**starch'i·ly** *adv.* —**starch'i·ness** *n.*

star cluster *Astron.* Any of numerous groupings of stars associated in the same region of space, as the Pleiades and Coma Berenices: they are classified as open or galactic, and globular.

star-crossed (stär'krôst', -krost') *adj.* Astrologically ill-fated; unfortunate; ill-starred: a *star-crossed* love affair.

star·dom (stär'dəm) *n.* The status of a movie or theatrical star.

star drift *Astron.* A common proper motion of stars in the same region of the heavens: noticed in close groups of stars and in pairs of widely separated stars.

stare (stâr) *v.* **stared, star·ing** *v.i.* **1** To gaze

fixedly, usually with the eyes open wide, as from admiration, fear, or insolence. **2** To be conspicuously or unduly apparent; glare. **3** To stand on end, as hair. — *v.t.* **4** To stare at. **5** To affect in a specified manner by a stare: to *stare* a person into silence. See synonyms under LOOK. — *n.* A steady, fixed gaze with wide-open eyes. ◆ Homophone: *stair*. [OE *starian*] —**star'er** *n.*

star facet One of eight triangular facets adjoining the table in the crown of a brilliant-cut gem. For illustration see DIAMOND.

star·fish (stär'fish') *n.* *pl.* **·fish** or **·fish·es** Any of various radially symmetrical echinoderms (class *Asteroidea*), commonly with a star-shaped body having five or more arms. Starfish feed mainly on mollusks, including oysters.

STARFISH
Ventral side
showing tube feet.

star·flow·er (stär'·flou'ər) *n.* **1** Any of various plants with conventionally star-shaped flowers; especially, a low perennial (*Trientalis borealis*) with one or more white star-shaped flowers. **2** A starwort. **3** A star of Bethlehem.

star·gaz·er (stär'gā'zər) *n.* **1** One who gazes at or studies the stars; especially, an astrologer or astronomer. **2** A marine carnivorous fish with eyes small and near the front of the top of the head, as *Uranoscopus scaber* of the Mediterranean, and *Astroscopus anoplus* of the Atlantic coast of the United States.

star·gaz·ing (stär'gā'zing) *adj.* Given to watching the stars. — *n.* **1** The act or practice of watching or studying the stars. **2** An absent-minded state; abstraction.

star·grass (stär'gras', -gräs') *n.* Any of various grasslike plants (genus *Hypoxis*) of the amaryllis family, with starlike flowers.

stark (stärk) *adj.* **1** Stiff or rigid, as in death. **2** *Obs.* Stubborn; inflexible. **3** Severe; tempestuous, as weather; strict or grim, as a person; also, deserted or barren, as a landscape. **4** *Obs.* Strong and powerful. **5** Without ornamentation; blunt; complete; utter; downright: *stark* misery. **6** Naked: short for *stark naked*. —*adv.* **1** In a stark manner. **2** Completely; utterly: *stark* mad. [OE *stearc* stiff. Related to STARCH.] —**stark'ly** *adv.*

stark naked Entirely without clothing. [Alter. of ME *stert-naked* <OE *steort* tail + *nacod* naked; infl. in form by STARK]

star·less (stär'lis) *adj.* Being without stars or starlight.

star·let (stär'lit) *n.* **1** A small star. **2** *Colloq.* A young movie actress aspiring to stardom.

star·ling[1] (stär'ling) *n.* Any of several Old World passerine birds (genus *Sturnus*). The common starling (*S. vulgaris*) is brown glossed with black, with metallic purple and green reflections and a buff tip to each feather. It is often caged. [OE *stœrling* < *stœr* starling]

star·ling[2] (stär'ling) *n.* **1** An enclosure of close piling, as around a pier of a bridge for protection. **2** One of the piles of such an enclosure. [OE *statholung* foundation]

star·nose (stär'nōz') *n.* A North American mole (*Condylura cristata*) having a radiate arrangement of fleshy processes around the end of the nose. Also **star-nosed mole**.

star of Bethlehem 1 The large star by which the three Magi were guided to the manger in Bethlehem where the child Jesus lay. **2** An Old World plant (*Ornithogalum umbellatum*) of the lily family, having white stellate flowers striped with green on the outside: naturalized in the eastern United States.

star of David The six-pointed star used as a symbol by the Hebrews; the mogen David.

star of Jerusalem Goatsbeard.

starred (stärd) *adj.* **1** Spangled with stars; marked with stars or a star; specifically, marked with an asterisk. **2** Affected by astral influence: chiefly in composition: ill-*starred*. **3** Presented or advertised as the star of a play or motion picture; featured.

STAR OF DAVID

star·ry (stär'ē) *adj.* **·ri·er, ·ri·est 1** Set with stars or starlike spots or points; abounding in stars. **2** Lighted by the stars. **3** Shining as or like the stars. **4** Star-shaped. **5** Of, pertaining to, proceeding from, or connected with stars. **6** Consisting of stars; stellar. **—star·ri·ness** n.

star·ry-eyed (stär′ē·īd′) adj. Given to fanciful wishes or yearnings.

Stars and Stripes The flag of the United States of America, a field of thirteen horizontal stripes, alternate red and white, and blue union with as many white stars as States: with the definite article.

star sapphire A sapphire that reveals a six-pointed star of light reflected from interior crystal faces when specially cut to present a convex surface without facets.

star·shell (stär′shel′) n. An artillery shell that explodes in mid-air with a shower of bright light: used for illuminating objectives, signaling, etc.

star shower A meteoric shower.

star·span·gled (stär′spang′gəld) adj. Spangled with stars or starlike spots or points: said especially of the United States flag.

Star-Spangled Banner, The 1 The flag of the United States. **2** A poem written by Francis Scott Key in 1814 during the bombardment by the British of Fort McHenry, Md., and adopted by Congress in 1931 as the national anthem of the United States. The music to which it is sung is that of an old English drinking song. *To Anacreon in Heaven.*

start (stärt) v.i. **1** To make an involuntary, startled movement, as from fear or surprise. **2** To move suddenly, as with a spring, leap, or bound; jump. **3** To make a beginning or start; set out. **4** To begin; commence: The play *starts* at eight o'clock. **5** To protrude; seem to bulge: His eyes *started* from his head. **6** To be displaced or dislocated; become loose, warped, etc.: The rivets have *started.* —v.t. **7** To set in motion: to *start* an engine; to *start* a rumor. **8** To begin; commence: to *start* a lecture. **9** To set up; establish. **10** To introduce (a subject) or propound (a question). **11** To displace or dislocate; loosen, warp, etc.: The collision *started* the ship's seams. **12** To rouse from cover; cause to take flight; flush, as game. **13** To draw the contents from; tap, as a cask. **14** *Archaic* To startle. See synonyms under INSTITUTE. **—to start in** To begin. **—to start off** To begin a journey; set out. **—to start out 1** To start off. **2** To make a beginning or start. **—to start up 1** To rise or appear suddenly. **2** To begin or cause to begin operation, as an engine. **—to start with** In the first place; to begin with. —n. **1** A quick, startled movement or feeling; a sudden quickening of sense, pulse, or nerve at something unexpected. **2** A setting out or going forth; beginning. **3** A temporary or spasmodic action or attempt; a brief, intermittent effort: by fits and *starts.* **4** *Archaic* A sudden impulse or effusion; burst; sally: *starts* of wit. **5** Advantage or distance in advance at the outset; lead: I had a *start* of five miles in the race. **6** Impetus at the beginning of motion or, figuratively, of a course of action: to get a *start* in business. **7** A loosened place or condition; crack: a *start* in a ship's planking. See synonyms under BEGINNING. [ME *sterten* start, leap, fusion of ON *sterta* overturn and OE *styrtan* start, jump]

star thistle An Old World weed (*Centaurea calcitrapa*) with spiny heads of tubular flowers, naturalized in the United States; also, another species (*C. solstitialis*) with yellow flowers.

star·tle (stär′təl) v. ·tled, ·tling v.t. To arouse or excite suddenly; cause to start involuntarily; alarm. —v.i. To be aroused or excited suddenly; take alarm. —n. A sudden fright or shock; a scare. [OE *steartlian* kick, struggle] **—star′tler** n.

star·tling (stärt′ling) adj. Rousing sudden surprise, alarm, or the like. **—star′tling·ly** adv.

star·va·tion (stär·vā′shən) n. **1** The act of starving. **2** The state of being starved.

starve (stärv) v. starved, starv·ing v.i. **1** To die or perish from lack of food. **2** To suffer from extreme hunger. **3** To suffer from lack or need: to *starve* friendship. **4** *Dial.* To die of cold. **5** *Obs.* To die. —v.t. **6** To cause to die of hunger; de-

prive of food. **7** To bring to a specified condition by starving: to *starve* an enemy into surrender. [OE *steorfan* die] **—starv′er** n.

starve·ling (stärv′ling) n. A person or animal that is starving, starved, or emaciated. —adj. **1** Starving; emaciated; hungry. **2** Failing to meet needs; inadequate: a *starveling* religion. See synonyms under MEAGER.

stase (stās) n. *Ecol.* A deposit of fossil plants which has not moved from its original position, often occurring as a series of layers of related species. [< Gk. *stasis.* See STASIS.]

stash (stash) v.t. *Slang* To hide or conceal (money or valuables), for storage and safekeeping: often with *away.* [? Blend of STORE + CACHE]

sta·sis (stā′sis, stas′is) n. *Pathol.* **1** Stoppage of the blood in its circulation, especially in the small vessels and capillaries: caused by abnormal resistance of the capillary walls, rather than by any lessening of the heart's action. **2** Retarded movement of the intestinal contents due to obstruction or muscular malfunction. [< NL < Gk., a standing < *histanai* stand]

stat- Var. of STATO-.

-stat *combining form* A device which stops or makes constant: *thermostat, rheostat.* [< Gk. *-statēs* causing to stand < *histanai* stand]

state (stāt) n. **1** Mode of existence as determined by circumstances, external or internal; nature; condition; situation. **2** Frame of mind; mood: a *state* of anxiety. **3** Mode or style of living; station; especially, grand and ceremonious style; pomp; formality. **4** A sovereign political community organized under a distinct government recognized and conformed to by the people as supreme, and having jurisdiction over a given territory; a nation. **5** One of a number of political communities or bodies politic united to form one sovereign state; specifically, one of the United States: in this sense usually written **State.** **6** *pl.* The legislative bodies of a nation; estates. **7** Authority of government; the territorial, political, and governmental entity comprising a state or nation. **8** *Obs.* A person of rank; a noble. **9** *Obs.* An estate; order; class of persons. See synonyms under PEOPLE. **— Department of State** An executive department of the U.S. government (established in 1789), headed by the Secretary of State, which supervises the conduct of foreign affairs, directs the activities of all diplomatic and consular representatives, protects national interests abroad, and assists in the formulation of policies in relation to international problems. Also **State Department.** **— to lie in state** To be placed on public view, with ceremony and honors, before burial. —adj. **1** Of or pertaining to the state, nation, or government: *state* papers. **2** Intended for use on occasions of ceremony. —v.t. stat·ed, stat·ing **1** To set forth explicitly in speech or writing; assert; declare. **2** To fix; determine; settle. **3** *Law* To make known specifically; declare as a matter of fact. See synonyms under AFFIRM, ALLEGE, ASSERT, RELATE. [Aphetic var. of OF *estat* <L *status* condition, state < *stare* stand; defs. 4, 5, and 7 directly <L, as in *status rei publicae* the state of the republic. Doublet of STATUS.] **— sta·tal** (stā′təl) adj.

state·craft (stāt′kraft′, -kräft′) n. The art of conducting affairs of state.

stat·ed (stā′tid) adj. Established; regular; fixed. See synonyms under HABITUAL. **— stat′ed·ly** adv.

state·less (stāt′lis) adj. **1** Without nationality: a *stateless* person. **2** Without a state or community of states: a *stateless* society.

state·ly (stāt′lē) adj. ·li·er, ·li·est Dignified; lofty. See synonyms under AWFUL, GRAND, HAUGHTY, SUBLIME. — adv. Loftily: also **state′li·ly.** **— state′li·ness** n.

state·ment (stāt′mənt) n. **1** A summary of facts; narration; the act of stating. **2** That which is stated. **3** *Law* A formal narration of facts filed as the foundation for judicial proceeding; a pleading. **4** A summary of the assets and liabilities of a bank or firm, showing the balance due. **5** A report sent, usually

at monthly intervals, to a debtor of a business firm or to a depositor in a bank. See synonyms under REPORT.

State rights 1 The rights and powers not delegated to the United States by the Constitution, nor prohibited by it to the States: reserved by the Constitution to the respective States, or to the people of the States, under the Tenth Amendment. **2** That construction of the Constitution which makes these rights and powers as large as possible. **3** The doctrine that the States, being sovereign, have the right to judge and nullify an act of the Federal government. See NULLIFICATION. Also **States' rights.**

state·room (stāt′rōōm′, -rōōm′) n. **1** A small private room having sleeping accommodations on a passenger boat. **2** A private sleeping compartment on a railroad car.

state's evidence 1 One who confesses himself guilty of a crime and testifies as a witness against his accomplices. **2** Evidence produced by the State in criminal prosecutions. Also, in Great Britain, Canada, Australia, etc., *king's* or *queen's evidence.*

state·side (stāt′sīd′) adj. Of or in the continental United States. — adv. In or to the continental United States.

states·man (stāts′mən) n. pl. ·men (-mən) One skilled in the science of government; a political leader of distinguished ability; also, one engaged in government matters, or influential in state affairs or policy. **— states′man·like′, states′man·ly** adj. **— states′man·ship** n.

states·wom·an (stāts′wōōm′ən) n. pl. ·wom·en (-wim′in) A woman engaged or skilled in the conduct of government affairs.

stat·ic (stat′ik) adj. **1** Pertaining to bodies at rest or forces in equilibrium: opposed to *dynamic.* **2** *Physics* Acting as weight, but not moving: *static* pressure. **3** *Electr.* Pertaining to electricity at rest, or to stationary electric charges. **4** At rest; quiescent; dormant; not active. **5** Of or pertaining to non-active elements. **6** In art, simply posed; monumental. **7** Treating of fixed or stable conditions rather than of fluctuations of sales: said of capital or goods. Also **stat′i·cal.** — n. *Electr.* A condition in which electromagnetic waves produced by atmospheric disturbances affect a radio receiving set, interfering with normal reception. [< Gk. *statikos* causing to stand < *histanai* stand] **— stat′i·cal·ly** adv.

stat·ics (stat′iks) n. pl. (construed as singular) The science of bodies at rest and of the relations required to produce equilibrium. Compare DYNAMICS.

static tube *Aeron.* A small closed tube with openings around the side, facing into the wind on an airplane and designed to measure the static pressure of the air.

sta·tion (stā′shən) n. **1** A place where a person or thing usually stands or is; an assigned location. **2** The headquarters of some official person or body of men: a police *station.* **3** An established building or place serving as a starting point, stage, stopping place, or post; specifically, a building for the accommodation of passengers or freight, as on a railroad or bus line; terminal; depot. **4** Social condition; rank; standing. **5** *Mil.* A military post; the place to which an individual, unit, or ship is assigned for duty. **6** The administrative offices, studios, and technical installations of a radio broadcasting unit operating on its assigned frequency. **7** *Mining* A recess in a shaft or passage of a mine. **8** *Austral.* A cattle or sheep run with its appertaining buildings and grounds. **9** In surveying, a point around or from which measurements of angles or distances are made; also, the distance adopted for the standard length. **10** *Eccl.* **a** A stopping place, as a church, shrine, etc., for a solemn religious procession, at which certain prayers are said. **b** A Station of the Cross. — v.t. To assign to a station; set in position. [< F <L *statio, -onis* < *status,* pp. of *stare* stand]

Synonym (noun): depot. Properly, a train stops at a *station* to take on and discharge passengers or freight. Freight is kept in a *depot,* which is a storage room or a storehouse. However, the *station* and the *depot* were so often located in one building in the early days of railroads that the word *depot,* which formerly was thought to be more elegant but now has less dignity than *station,* came to be used for both. See PLACE.

sta·tion·ar·y (stā′shən·er′ē) *adj.* **1** Remaining in one place. **2** Fixed: opposed to *portable.* **3** Exhibiting no change of character or condition. — *n. pl.* **·ar·ies** One who or that which is stationary; especially, a member of a stationary military force. ◆ Homophone: *stationery.*

sta·tion·er (stā′shən·ər) *n.* **1** A dealer in stationery and kindred wares. **2** *Obs.* A bookseller; publisher. [<Med. L *stationarius* stationary, having a fixed location (for business)]

sta·tion·er·y (stā′shən·er′ē) *n.* Writing materials in general; paper, pens, pencils, ink, notebooks, etc. — *adj.* Dealing in or pertaining to stationery. ◆ Homophone: *stationary.*

station house A police station.

sta·tion·mas·ter (stā′shən·mas′tər, -mäs′-) *n.* The person having charge of a bus or railroad station.

Stations of the Cross The fourteen images or pictures ranged in a church or on church property, which form in series the representation of the successive scenes of the Passion of Christ, and before which devotions are performed.

station wagon An automotive vehicle with one or more rows of removable or folding seats located behind the front seat and with a hinged tailgate for admitting luggage, or the like.

stat·ism (stā′tiz·əm) *n.* **1** A theory of government which holds that the returns from group or individual enterprise are vested in the state, as in communism. **2** Loosely, adherence to state sovereignty, as in a republic. **3** *Obs.* Statecraft.

stat·ist (stā′tist) *n.* **1** An adherent of statism. **2** A statistician. **3** *Obs.* A statesman; politician.

sta·tis·tic (stə·tis′tik) *adj.* Statistical. — *n.* **1** Any element entering into a statistical statement or array, as the mean, the standard deviation, number of cases, etc. **2** Statistics. [<G *statistik* <Med. L *statisticus* statesman-like, ult. <L *status.* See STATE.]

sta·tis·ti·cian (stat′is·tish′ən) *n.* One skilled in collecting and tabulating statistical data.

sta·tis·tics (stə·tis′tiks) *n.* **1** Quantitative data, collectively, pertaining to any subject or group, especially when systematically gathered and collated; specifically, such data relating to a large body of people: *statistics* of population: construed as plural. **2** The science that deals with the collection, tabulation, and systematic classification of quantitative data, especially with reference to frequency distribution and as a basis for inference and induction respecting probable future trends: construed as singular. — **sta·tis′ti·cal** *adj.* — **sta·tis′ti·cal·ly** *adv.*

stato- *combining form* Position: *statoscope.* Also, before vowels, *stat-.* [<Gk. *statos* standing, fixed <*histanai* stand]

stat·o·blast (stat′ə·blast) *n. Zool.* One of the chitinous internal buds developed in freshwater sponges and on the funiculus of freshwater polyzoans.

stat·o·cyst (stat′ə·sist) *n. Anat.* One of the sacs in the labyrinth of the internal ear, provided with sensitive hairs and otoliths which are believed to aid in maintaining body equilibrium.

stat·o·lith (stat′ə·lith) *n.* **1** *Bot.* A starch grain or other minute particle in a plant cell, believed to influence the response of a plant organ to the action of gravity. **2** *Anat.* An otolith.

sta·tor (stā′tər) *n.* The stationary portion of a dynamo, turbine, or other power generator. Compare ROTOR. [<NL <L, a supporter <*status.* See STATE.]

stat·o·scope (stat′ə·skōp) *n.* **1** *Meteorol.* A very sensitive form of aneroid barometer having a large reservoir of air, for indicating minute fluctuations in pressure. **2** *Aeron.* A device which indicates small variations in air pressure: used to show changes in altitude of an aircraft.

stat·u·ar·y (stach′ōō·er′ē) *n. pl.* **·ar·ies 1** Statues collectively. **2** One who makes statues; a sculptor. **3** The art of making statues. — *adj.* Of or suitable for statues. [<L *statuaria* <*statua* statue. See STATUE.]

stat·ue (stach′ōō) *n.* A representation of a human or animal figure in marble, bronze, etc., especially when nearly life-size or larger, and preserving the proportions in all directions: distinguished from *painting* or *relief.* See synonyms under IMAGE. — *v.t.* **·ued, ·u·ing** To make a statue of. [<F <L *statua* <*status,* pp. of *stare* stand]

stat·u·esque (stach′ōō·esk′) *adj.* Resembling a statue, as in grace, pose, or dignity. [<STATUE + -ESQUE] — **stat′u·esque′ly** *adv.* — **stat′u·esque′ness** *n.*

stat·u·ette (stach′ōō·et′) *n.* A statue not more than half life-size. [<F, dim. of *statue*]

stat·ure (stach′ər) *n.* **1** The natural height of an animal body, especially of a human body. **2** The height of anything, especially of a tree. **3** Development; growth: used figuratively: moral *stature.* [<OF <L *statura* <*status.* See STATE.]

sta·tus (stā′təs, stat′əs) *n.* **1** State, condition, or relation. **2** Relative position or rank. [<L. Doublet of STATE.]

sta·tus quo (stā′təs kwō, stat′əs) The condition or state in which (a person or thing is or has been): often used with the definite article: to maintain the *status quo.* Also **status in quo.** [<L]

stat·u·ta·ble (stach′ōō·tə·bəl) *adj.* Statutory; agreeing or conforming with statute. — **stat′u·ta·bly** *adv.*

stat·ute (stach′ōōt) *n.* **1** *Law* A legislative enactment duly sanctioned and authenticated by constitutional rule; act of Parliament, Congress, etc.; also, any authoritatively declared rule, ordinance, decree, or law. **2** The act of a corporation or its founder, intended as a permanent rule or law: the *statutes* of a university. See synonyms under LAW[1]. — *adj.* Consisting of or regulated by statute. [<F *statut* <LL *statutum,* neut. of L *statutus,* pp. of *statuere* set, found, constitute]

statute law The law as set forth in statutes.

statute mile See under MILE.

statute of limitations A statute which imposes time limits upon the right of action in certain cases, as by obliging a creditor to demand payment of a debt within a specified time.

stat·u·to·ry (stach′ə·tôr′ē, -tō′rē) *adj.* Pertaining to a statute; created by or dependent upon legislative enactment.

staunch (stônch, stänch) *adj.* **1** Firm in principle; constant; faithful; loyal; trustworthy: a *staunch* friend. **2** Stout; sound; tight; seaworthy: a *staunch* ship; having firm constitution or construction; strong and vigorous; hearty. — *v.t.* To stanch. — *n. Brit. Dial.* A floodgate; weir; dam. Also spelled *stanch.* [<OF *estanche* watertight, reliable <*estanchier* make stand. See STANCH.] — **staunch′ly** *adv.* — **staunch′ness** *n.*

Synonyms (adj.): firm, seaworthy, sound, stout, strong, taut, tight, trim, trustworthy, trusty. See FAITHFUL. *Antonyms:* crazy, leaky, rotten, unseaworthy, untrustworthy.

stau·ro·lite (stôr′ə·līt) *n.* A brown to brownish-black native silicate of iron and aluminum, found in prismatic crystals and sometimes used as a gem. [<Gk. *stauros* cross + -LITE; from the crosslike twin crystals] — **stau·ro·lit′ic** (-lit′ik) *adj.*

stau·ro·scope (stôr′ə·skōp) *n. Optics* An instrument used to determine the directions of the planes of vibration of polarized light in crystals. [<Gk. *stauros* cross + -SCOPE] — **stau·ro·scop′ic** (-skop′ik) *adj.*

stave (stāv) *n.* **1** A curved strip of wood, forming a part of the sides of a barrel, tub, or the like; hence, any narrow strip of material used for a like purpose: iron *staves.* **2** A straight board forming part of a curb, as about a well. **3** *Music* A staff. **4** A stanza; verse. **5** A rod, cudgel, or staff. **6** A rung of a rack or ladder. — *v.* **staved** or **stove,** **stav·ing** *v.t.* **1** To break in the staves or strakes of (a cask or a boat); crush the shell or surface of; smash. **2** To make (a hole) by crushing or collision. **3** To furnish with staves. **4** To ward off, as with a staff; keep at a distance: usually with *off:* to *stave* off hunger. — *v.i.* **5** To be broken in, as a vessel's hull. [Back formation <*staves,* pl. of STAFF]

staves·a·cre (stāvz′ā′kər) *n.* **1** A tall larkspur (*Delphinium staphisagria*) of southern Europe. **2** Its seeds, yielding a poisonous alkaloid

formerly used as a purgative and antispasmodic. [<OF *stafisagre* <Med. L *staphis agria* <Gk. *staphis* raisin + *agrios* wild]

stay[1] (stā) *v.i.* **1** To cease motion; stop; halt. **2** To continue in a specified place, condition, or state: to *stay* indoors; to *stay* healthy. **3** To remain temporarily as a guest, resident, etc.: Where are you *staying?* **4** To pause; wait; tarry. **5** *Colloq.* To have endurance; stand up; last. **6** *Colloq.* To keep pace with a competitor, as in a race. **7** In poker, to remain in a hand by meeting an ante, bet, or raise. **8** *Archaic* To cease. **9** *Archaic* To stand firm. — *v.t.* **10** To bring to a stop; halt; check. **11** To hinder; delay. **12** To put off; postpone. **13** To satisfy the demands of temporarily; quiet; appease: to *stay* the pangs of hunger. **14** To remain for the duration of: I will *stay* the night. **15** To remain till or beyond the end of: with *out:* to *stay* out one's welcome. **16** *Archaic* To quell, as strife. **17** *Obs.* To wait for. See synonyms under ABIDE, HINDER[1], OBSTRUCT, PERSIST, REPRESS, REST[1], STAND. — *n.* **1** The act or time of staying; continuance in a place; sojourn; visit. **2** That which checks or stops; specifically, a suspension of judicial proceedings. **3** Staying power; endurance; persistence. **4** A state of rest; standstill. See synonyms under RESPITE, REST. [<AF *estaier,* OF *ester* <L *stare* stand] — **stay′er** *n.*

stay[2] (stā) *v.t.* **1** To be a support to; prop or hold up. **2** To support mentally; comfort; sustain. **3** To cause to depend or rely, as for support: with *on* or *upon.* — *n.* **1** Anything which props or supports; a prop, buttress, or the like. **2** *pl.* A corset. [<OF *estayer*]

stay[3] (stā) *Naut. n.* **1** A large, strong rope, often of wire, used to support, steady, or fasten a mast or spar. **2** Any rope supporting a mast or funnel; a guy rope. — **in stays** In the act of turning about on another tack. — *v.t.* **1** To support with a stay or stays, as a mast. **2** To put (a vessel) on the opposite tack. — *v.i.* **3** To tack: said of vessels. [OE *stæg*]

stay-at-home (stā′at·hōm′) *adj.* Given to remaining at home; not in the habit of traveling. — *n.* A person accustomed to staying home.

staying power The ability to endure.

St. Croix (sānt kroi′) The largest of the Virgin Islands of the United States; 82 square miles; capital, Christiansted: also *Santa Cruz.*

stead (sted) *n.* **1** Place of another person or thing: preceded by *in:* Serfdom came *in* the *stead* of slavery. Compare INSTEAD. **2** Place or attitude of support; use; avail; service: in the phrase **to stand one in stead** or **in good stead.** **3** A steading or farm: used chiefly in compounds: *homestead, Hempstead.* **4** *Archaic* Position; condition; place, in general. — *v.t. Archaic* To be of advantage to; help; benefit; support. [OE *stede* place]

stead·fast (sted′fast′, -fäst′, -fəst) *adj.* **1** Firmly fixed in faith or devotion to duty; constant; unchanging. **2** Directed fixedly at one point or to one end, as the gaze or purpose; steady. Also spelled *stedfast.* See synonyms under FIRM, INFLEXIBLE, PERMANENT. [OE *stedefæst*] — **stead′fast′ly** *adv.* — **stead′fast′ness** *n.*

stead·y (sted′ē) *adj.* **stead·i·er, stead·i·est 1** Stable in position; firmly supported; fixed. **2** Moving or acting with uniform regularity; constant; unfaltering: a *steady* light; hence, not readily disturbed or upset: *steady* nerves. **3** Free from intemperance and dissipation; industrious, sober, and reliable: *steady* habits. **4** Constant in mind or conduct; not wavering; steadfast; also, regular: a *steady* customer. **5** Uninterrupted; continuous: a *steady* flow of conversation. **6** *Naut.* Having the direction of the ship's head unchanged. See synonyms under FIRM, SOBER. — *v.t.* & *v.i.* **stead·ied, stead·y·ing** To make or become steady. — *interj.* **1** *Naut.* Keep her steady: an order to a helmsman to keep the ship's head pointed in the same direction. **2** Not so fast; keep calm: an order enjoining self-control or composure. — *n. Slang* A sweetheart or steady companion. [<STEAD + -Y[3]] — **stead′i·er** *n.* — **stead′i·ly** *adv.* — **stead′i·ness** *n.*

steak (stāk) *n.* **1** A slice of meat, as of beef, usually broiled or fried; specifically, beefsteak. **2** Meat, chopped for cooking like a steak: hamburger *steak.* ◆ Homophone: *stake.*

[<ON *steik*]

steal (stēl) *v.* **stole, sto·len, steal·ing** *v.t.* **1** To take from another without right, authority, or permission, and usually in a secret manner. **2** To take or obtain in a surreptitious, artful, or subtle manner: He has *stolen* the hearts of the people. **3** To move, place, or convey stealthily: with *away, from, in, into,* etc. **4** In baseball, to reach (a base) without the aid of a hit or error. — *v.i.* **5** To commit theft; be a thief. **6** To move secretly or furtively. — *n.* **1** The act of stealing or that which is stolen; a theft. **2** In baseball, the act of stealing a base. **3** Any financial transaction or other deal that benefits no one but the originators. ◆ Homophones: *steel, stele.* [OE *stelan*] — **steal′er** *n.* — **steal′ing** *n.*
Synonyms (*verb*): abstract, embezzle, extort, filch, pilfer, pillage, plunder, purloin, rob, swindle. To *steal* is, in law, to commit simple *larceny*; but the word may be applied to any furtive, covert, or surreptitious taking of anything, whether material or immaterial. To *pilfer* is to *steal* petty articles. *Filch* especially emphasizes the secrecy and slyness of the act, and is ordinarily applied to things of little value, but may apply to the most precious, as in Shakespeare, "he that *filches* from me my good name." To *purloin* is etymologically to carry far away, and is commonly applied to the dishonest removal of articles of value or importance. To *rob* is, in law, to take feloniously from the person by force or fear, as in highway robbery; it is also applied to the felonious taking of articles of value from places as well as persons generally with suggestion of force and violence. To *abstract* is to take secretly and feloniously from among other things belonging to another. To *embezzle* is to appropriate fraudulently to oneself funds received and held in trust. To *swindle* is to cheat grossly, commonly by false pretenses, but is not a recognized legal offense under that name; one form of *swindling,* "obtaining money by false pretenses," is an indictable offense, but much *swindling* may be carried on under the forms of law. To *plunder* is to take property from an enemy in time of war, and is not a crime at law. See ABSTRACT. *Antonyms:* refund, repay, restore, return, surrender.
stealth (stelth) *n.* **1** The quality or habit of acting secretly; a concealed manner of acting; a secret or clandestine act, movement, or proceeding. **2** *Obs.* Theft or the thing stolen. [ME *stelthe, stalthe* <OE *stelan* steal]
stealth·y (stel′thē) *adj.* **stealth·i·er, stealth·i·est** Moving or acting secretly or slily; done or characterized by stealth; furtive. — **stealth′i·ly** *adv.* — **stealth′i·ness** *n.*
steam (stēm) *n.* **1** Water in the form of vapor. **2** The gas or vapor into which water is changed by boiling. **3** The visible mist into which aqueous vapor is condensed by cooling. **4** Any kind of vaporous exhalation. **5** Energy, force, or power derived from water vapor under pressure, as in cooking, heating, etc. **6** *Colloq.* Vigor; force; speed. — **to let off steam** *Colloq.* To give expression to pent-up emotions or opinions. — *v.i.* **1** To give off or emit steam or vapor. **2** To rise or pass off as steam. **3** To become covered with condensed water vapor: often with *up.* **4** To generate steam. **5** To move or travel by the agency of steam. — *v.t.* **6** To treat with steam, as in softening, cooking, cleaning, etc. — *adj.* **1** Of, driven, or operated by steam: a *steam* gage, *steam* shovel. **2** Containing or conveying steam: a *steam* boiler. **3** Treated by steam. [OE *stēam*]
steam·boat (stēm′bōt′) *n.* A boat or vessel propelled by steam.
steam boiler A closed vessel used in generating steam.
steam engine An engine that derives its motive force from the action of steam; usually by pressure against a piston sliding within a closed cylinder.
steam·er (stē′mər) *n.* **1** Something propelled or worked by steam, as a steamship. **2** A vessel in which something is steamed, as for cooking, washing, etc.
steamer trunk A trunk small enough to fit under a berth in a ship's cabin.

steam·fit·ter (stēm′fit′ər) *n.* A man who sets up or repairs steampipes and their fittings. — **steam′fit′ting** *n.*
steam point *Physics* The boiling point of water at standard atmospheric pressure; 100° C.: one of the fixed points of the international temperature scale.
steam roller **1** A road-rolling machine driven by steam. **2** Any force that ruthlessly overcomes opposition. — **steam′roll′er** *adj.*
steam·ship (stēm′ship′) *n.* A large vessel used for ocean traffic and propelled, usually, by one or more screws operated by steam; a steamer.
steam shovel A steam-operated shovel for digging and excavation.
steam table A long table with openings in which containers of food are placed to be kept warm by hot water or steam circulating beneath them.
steam turbine A turbine operated by steam power.
steam·y (stē′mē) *adj.* **steam·i·er, steam·i·est** Consisting of, like, or full of steam; misty. — **steam′i·ly** *adv.* — **steam′i·ness** *n.*
ste·ar·ic (stē·ar′ik, stir′ik) *adj. Chem.* **1** Of, pertaining to, or derived from stearin. **2** Designating a white fatty acid, $C_{17}H_{35}COOH$, contained in the more solid animal fats and in many vegetable oils. [<F *stéarique* <Gk. *stear* suet]
ste·a·rop·tene (stē′ə·rop′tēn) *n. Chem.* A solid crystalline compound that separates from a volatile oil on standing or exposure to cold. Compare ELAEOPTENE. [<STEAR(IC) + (ELAE)-OPTENE]
ste·a·tite (stē′ə·tīt) *n.* Massive talc; soapstone: found in extensive beds and quarried for hearths, sink linings, coarse utensils, etc. See TALC. [<L *steatitis* <Gk. *stear, steatos* suet, tallow] — **ste·a·tit′ic** (-tit′ik) *adj.*
ste·a·tor·rhe·a (stē′ə·tə·rē′ə) *n. Pathol.* **1** Seborrhea. **2** Excess fat in the stools. Also **ste·a·tor·rhoe′a.** [<Gk. *stear, steatos* suet + -RRHEA]
steed (stēd) *n.* A horse; especially, a spirited war horse: now chiefly a literary use. [OE *stēda* studhorse]
steel (stēl) *n.* **1** A tough alloy of iron containing carbon in variable amounts up to about 2.0 percent, malleable under proper conditions, and greatly hardened by sudden cooling. Commercial grades are classified, on the basis of carbon content, as: **mild** or **soft steel,** with up to about 0.30 percent of carbon; **medium steel,** 0.30 to 0.60 percent of carbon, and **high** or **hard steel,** containing more than 0.60 percent of carbon. The addition of other components gives a large range of alloys having special properties, as **chrome steel, nickel steel,** etc. **2** Something made of steel, as an implement or weapon; a sword; a knife sharpener. **3** Hardness of character; steel-like nature or quality. **4** A strip or band of steel, as for stiffening a corset. **5** The quotation for shares in a steel company. — *adj.* Made or composed of steel; also, resembling steel; hence, hard; obdurate; adamant; unyielding. — *v.t.* **1** To cover with steel; plate, edge, point, or face with steel. **2** To make hard or strong like steel; make unfeeling or unyielding; harden: to *steel* one's heart against misery. ◆ Homophones: *steal, stele.* [OE *stēl*]
steel engraving **1** The art and process of engraving on a steel plate. **2** The impression made from such a plate.
steel·head (stēl′hed′) *n.* **1** A species of migratory trout (*Salmo gairdneri*), found from California to Alaska. **2** The black spotted trout (*S. purpuratus*) of the western United States, especially in its adult marine stage.
steel·ing (stē′ling) *n.* **1** The coating of an engraved copper plate with a protective film of iron by electrolysis to increase its durability. **2** Casehardening.
steel·mak·er (stēl′mā′kər) *n.* A maker of steel; especially, the operator or owner of a steel mill.
steel wool Steel fibers matted together for use as an abrasive or in cleaning, polishing, and finishing utensils and the like.
steel·work·er (stēl′wûr′kər) *n.* One who works

in a steel mill.
steel·y (stē′lē) *adj.* **steel·i·er, steel·i·est** Made of, resembling, or containing steel; suggesting steel; figuratively, having a steel-like hardness: a *steely* obduracy; a *steely* gaze. — **steel′i·ness** *n.*
steel·yard (stēl′yärd′, -yərd) *n.* A simple device for weighing, consisting of a scaled beam, counterpoise, and hooks, the article to be weighed being hung at the short end, and the counterpoise weight on the long arm. Also **steel′yards.** [from *Steelyard,* formerly, the London headquarters for Hanseatic traders; a mistranslation of MLG *stalhof* a court where samples of goods are displayed]

STEELYARDS
a. Pompeian. *b.* Modern.

steep¹ (stēp) *adj.* **1** Making a large angle with the plane of the horizon; precipitous. **2** *Colloq.* Exorbitant; excessive; high, as a price. — *n.* A cliff; hill; precipice; a precipitous place. [OE *stēap*] — **steep′ly** *adv.* — **steep′ness** *n.*
Synonyms (*adj.*): abrupt, high, precipitous, sharp, sheer. *High* is used of simple elevation; *steep* is said only of an incline where the vertical measurement is sufficiently great in proportion to the horizontal to make it difficult of ascent. *Steep* is relative; an ascent of 100 feet to the mile on a railway is a *steep* grade; a rise of 500 feet to the mile makes a *steep* wagon road; a roof is *steep* when it makes with the horizontal line an angle of more than 45°. A *sharp* ascent or descent is one that makes a sudden, decided angle with the plane from which it starts; a *sheer* ascent or descent is perpendicular, or nearly so; *precipitous* applies to that which is of the nature of a precipice, and is used especially of a descent; *abrupt* is as if broken sharply off, and applies to either acclivity or declivity. See HIGH. *Antonyms:* easy, gentle, gradual, level, low, slight.
steep² (stēp) *v.t.* **1** To soak in a liquid, as for softening, cleansing, etc. **2** To saturate; imbue thoroughly: *steeped* in crime. — *v.i.* **3** To undergo soaking in a liquid. — *n.* **1** The process of steeping, or the state of being steeped. **2** A liquid or bath in which anything is or is to be steeped; especially, a fertilizing liquid for seeds. [ME *stepen,* ? <Scand. Cf. ON *steypa* pour.] — **steep′er** *n.*
stee·ple (stē′pəl) *n.* A lofty structure rising above the tower of a church; a spire. [OE *stēpel, stȳpel*]
stee·ple·bush (stē′pəl·bŏŏsh′) *n.* An erect shrub (*Spirae tomentosa*) of the rose family, with dense terminal clusters of rose-colored flowers; the hardhack.
stee·ple·chase (stē′pəl·chās′) *n.* **1** A race on horseback across country, in which obstacles are to be leaped: originating from a race to see which of several riders could first reach a distant church steeple. **2** A race over a course artificially prepared, as with hedges, rails, and water jumps. **3** Any cross-country run. — **stee′ple·chas′ing** *n.*
stee·ple·chas·er (stē′pəl·chā′sər) *n.* A person who takes part in a steeplechase; also, a horse used in or trained for steeplechasing.
stee·ple·jack (stē′pəl·jak′) *n.* A man whose occupation is to climb steeples and other tall structures to inspect or make repairs. [<STEEPLE + obs. *jack* workman]
steer¹ (stir) *v.t.* **1** To direct the course of (a

vessel or vehicle) by means of a rudder, steering wheel, or other device. **2** To follow (a course). **3** To direct; guide; control. —*v.i.* **4** To direct the course of a vessel, vehicle, etc. **5** To undergo guiding or steering: The car *steers* easily. **6** To follow a course: to *steer* for land. **— to steer clear of** To avoid; keep away from. —*n. U.S. Slang* A tip; piece of advice. [OE *stēoran*] **— steer′a·ble** *adj.* **— steer′er** *n.*

steer² (stir) *n.* **1** A young male of the ox kind, especially when castrated and from two to four years old. **2** An ox of any age raised for beef. [OE *stēor*]

steer·age (stir′ij) *n.* **1** That part of an ocean passenger vessel, formerly near the stern, but now usually situated in the forward lower decks, allotted to passengers paying the lowest fares. **2** In a war vessel, the portion of the berth deck just forward of the wardroom, appropriated as the quarters of junior officers, clerks, etc. See GUNROOM. **3** The act of steering. **4** The state of being steered; direction; the effect of the helm on a vessel.

steer·age·way (stir′ij·wā′) *n. Naut.* **1** Sufficient movement of a vessel to enable it to answer the helm. **2** The lowest speed at which a vessel can be accurately steered.

steering committee A committee in a legislature or other assemblage that arranges or directs the course of the business that is to be considered.

steering gear *Mech.* Any arrangement of parts for converting action on the steering wheel into corresponding motion of the rudder of a ship, or, on an automotive vehicle, of the steering axle and its connected members.

steering wheel *Mech.*
1 A vertical wheel with handles along the rim, by which motion is communicated to the rudder of a ship by the wheel ropes or other connections. **2** A hand wheel for guiding an automobile or other heavy vehicle.

SHIP'S STEERING WHEEL

steers·man (stirz′mən) *n. pl.* **·men** (-mən) One who steers a boat: a helmsman.

steg·o·my·ia (steg′ə·mī′ə) *n.* Any of a former genus (*Stegomyia*) of mosquitos; especially, the yellow–fever mosquito (*S. fasciata* or *S. calopus*), which is now called *Aëdes aegypti.* [<NL <Gk. *stegos* a roof + *myia* fly]

steg·o·sau·rus (steg′ə·sôr′əs) *n. pl.* **·sau·ri** (-sôr′ī) *Paleontol.* Any of a genus (*Stegosaurus*) of herbivorous armored dinosaurs of great size which flourished in the western United States during the Upper Jurassic and Lower Cretaceous periods. [<NL <Gk. *stegos* roof + -SAURUS]

stein (stīn) *n.* A beer mug, holding usually a pint; also, the quantity of beer it contains. [<G]

Stein (stīn), **Gertrude,** 1874–1946, U.S. writer, resident in France.
Stein·am·ang·er (shtīn′äm·äng′ər) See SZOMBATHELY.
Stein·beck (stīn′bek), **John Ernst,** 1902–1968, U.S. novelist.
stein·bok (stīn′bok) *n.* A small fawn–colored African antelope (*Raphicerus campestris)*: also spelled **steenbok.** Also **stein′buck′** (-buk′). [< Du. *steenbok* < *steen* stone + *bok* buck]

STEINBOK

ste·le¹ (stē′lē) *n. pl.* **·lae** (-lē) or **·les** (-lēz) An upright sculptured slab or tablet of stone, either sepulchral or intended for public use, as for laws, decrees, treaties, milestones, etc. Also **ste·la** (stē′lə). [<L *stela* <Gk. *stēlē*] **— ste′lar, ste′lene** (-lēn) *adj.*
stele² (stēl) *n. Bot.* An axial cylinder of vascular tissue in plants, sometimes more than one. ◆ Homophones: *steal, steel.* [<STELE¹] **— ste′lic** *adj.*

stel·lar (stel′ər) *adj.* **1** Of or pertaining to the stars; astral. **2** Of or pertaining to an actor or actress who plays a principal role, or to other persons prominent in the arts.

[<LL *stellaris* <L *stella* star]
stel·late (stel′it, -āt) *adj.* Star–shaped or starlike; radiating. See illustration under FROST. Also **stel·lat·ed** (stel′ā·tid). [<L *stellatus,* pp. of *stellare* cover with stars < *stella* star] **— stel′late·ly** *adv.*
stel·lif·er·ous (ste·lif′ər·əs) *adj.* Abounding with stars. [<L *stella* star + -(I)FEROUS]
stel·li·form (stel′ə·fôrm) *adj.* Star-shaped. [<NL *stelliformis* <L *stella* star + *forma* form]
stel·lu·lar (stel′yə·lər) *adj.* Bespangled with fine stars; shaped like or resembling little stars. [<LL *stellula* little star]
stem¹ (stem) *n.* **1** The ascending axis or stalk of a plant, as distinguished from the descending axis or *root*; the main body or stalk of a tree, shrub, or other plant, rising above the ground or other rooting place. **2** The relatively slender growth supporting the fruit, flower, or leaf of a plant; a stalk, peduncle, pedicel, or petiole. ◆ Collateral adjective: *cauline.* **3** A bunch of bananas. **4** The main line of descendants from a particular ancestor. **5** An ethnic line; race. **6** The long, slender, usually cylindrical portion of an instrument: a pipe *stem.* **7** The slender upright support of a goblet, wineglass, vase, etc. **8** A shaft, as of a hair or feather. **9** In a watch, the small projecting rod used for winding the mainspring. **10** In some locks, the central circular part about which the key turns. **11** *Printing* The upright stroke of a type face or letter. **12** *Music* The line attached to the head of a written musical note. **13** *Ling.* The element common to all the members of a given inflection or related groups of words. A stem often consists of more than one morpheme, as the Latin stem *luci-* "light" in *lucifer* "light-bearer" is composed of the root *luc-* plus the thematic vowel *-i-.* **14** *Electr.* The air-sealed, tubular glass section at the base of an incandescent lamp, serving to lead the filaments into the evacuated bulb. See illustration under INCANDESCENT. —*v.* **stemmed, stem·ming** *v.t.* **1** To remove the stems of or from. **2** To supply with stems. —*v.i.* **3** To be descended or derived: to *stem* from John Alden. [OE *stemm, stemn, stæfn* stem of a tree, prow of a ship] **— stem′less** *adj.*
stem² (stem) *n. Naut.* **1** A nearly upright timber or metal piece uniting the two sides of a vessel at the fore-end. **2** The bow or prow of a vessel. **— from stem to stern** From end to end; hence, thoroughly. —*v.* **stemmed, stem·ming** *v.t.* **1** To resist or make progress against, as a current: said of a vessel. **2** To stand firm or make progress against (any opposing force): to *stem* the tide of public opinion. **3** To strike with the stem (of a vessel). [<STEM¹, in obs. sense "a tree trunk"]
stem³ (stem) *v.t.* **stemmed, stem·ming 1** To stop, hold back, or dam up, as a current; stanch. **2** To make tight, as a joint; to plug. [<ON *stemma* stop]
stem·mer (stem′ər) *n.* **1** One who stems. **2** In tobacco manufacture, one who takes out the main stem from the tobacco plant in making strips. **3** A device for stemming fruits, as grapes.

stem turn In skiing, a turn made by placing the points of the skis nearly together and the ends wide apart, then placing the weight on the outside ski.
stem·ware (stem′wâr′) *n.* Drinking vessels with stems, as goblets, taken collectively.
stem–wind·er (stem′wīn′dər) *n.* **1** A watch wound by turning the crown of the stem. **2** *U.S. Slang* A very superior person or thing.
stem–wind·ing (stem′wīn′ding) *adj.* Wound by turning a knob on an outside stem connected with inside mechanism.
stench (stench) *n.* A foul or offensive odor; stink. See synonyms under SMELL. [OE *stenc*]
sten·cil (sten′səl) *n.* **1** A thin sheet or plate in which a pattern is cut by means of spaces or dots, through which applied paint or ink penetrates to a surface beneath. **2** A decoration or the like produced by stenciling. —*v.t.* **·ciled** or **·cilled, ·cil·ing** or **·cil·ling** To mark with a stencil. [Prob. ME *stansel* decorate with many colors <OF *estenceler,* ult. <L *scintilla* a spark] **— sten′cil·er** or **sten′cil·ler** *n.*

STENCIL

STENCIL

steno– *combining form* Tight; narrow; contracted: *stenography.* Also, before vowels, **sten–.** [<Gk. *stenos* narrow]
sten·o·graph (sten′ə·graf, -gräf) *n.* **1** A character or writing in shorthand. **2** A keyboard machine for printing in shorthand.
ste·nog·ra·pher (stə·nog′rə·fər) *n.* One who writes stenography or is skilled in shorthand; especially, a writer of phonography. Also **ste·nog′ra·phist.**
ste·nog·ra·phy (stə·nog′rə·fē) *n.* **1** The art of writing by the use of contractions or arbitrary symbols; shorthand. **2** Loosely, phonography. **— sten·o·graph·ic** (sten′ə·graf′ik) or **·i·cal** *adj.* **— sten′o·graph′i·cal·ly** *adv.*
sten·o·morph (sten′ə·môrf) *n. Ecol.* A plant form that is abnormally undersized because of a cramped habitat. **— sten′o·mor′phic** *adj.*
sten·o·phyl·lous (sten′ō·fil′əs) *adj. Bot.* Characterized by narrow leaves, as certain plants.
sten·o·sis (sti·nō′sis) *n. Pathol.* Narrowing of a duct or canal in the body. [<NL <Gk. *stenōsis* < *stenos* narrow]
sten·o·ther·mal (sten′ō·thûr′məl) *adj. Ecol.* Adapted to a limited range of temperature variations: said especially of certain plants. **— sten′o·ther′my** *n.*
sten·o·trop·ic (sten′ə·trop′ik) *adj. Ecol.* Having a narrow range of adaptability to environmental changes: said of plant and animal species.
sten·o·type (sten′ə·tīp) *n.* A letter or combination of letters representing a word or phrase, especially in shorthand.
sten·o·typ·y (sten′ə·tī′pē) *n.* A system of shorthand representing, by ordinary letters or type, shortened forms of words or phrases.
sten·tor (sten′tôr) *n.* **1** One who possesses an uncommonly strong, loud voice. **2** Any of a genus (*Stentor*) of fresh–water protozoans (class *Ciliata*) having contractile trumpet-shaped bodies capable of attachment by their lower ends. [after *Stentor*]
sten·to·ri·an (sten·tôr′ē·ən, -tō′rē-) *adj.* Extremely loud.
step (step) *n.* **1** An act of progressive motion that requires one of the supporting limbs of the body to be thrust in the direction of the movement, and to reassume its function of support; a pace. **2** The distance passed over in making such a motion; in military quick-time marching, 30 inches. **3** Any short distance; a space easily traversed. **4** That upon which the foot rests in ascending or descending, as a stair or ladder rung. **5** A single action or proceeding regarded as leading to something: a *step* toward emancipation. **6** An advance or promotion that forms one of a series, especially in military usage; grade; degree. **7** The manner of stepping; walk; gait; also, the sound of a footfall. **8** A footprint; track. **9** *pl.* Progression by walking; walk. **10** A combination of foot movements in dancing, forming a pattern that may be repeated, varied, or elaborated: the tango *step.* **11** An interval measuring a difference of musical pitch, corresponding to a degree of the scale or staff. **12** A socket, supporting framework, pocket, or the like: the *step* of a mast. **13** A steplike projection or part, as of the bit of a key. **14** *Mech.* The radial distance between the face of one pulley and that of another stepped on the same shaft. **15** A break in the contour of a float or hull, as of a seaplane, designed to lessen resistance and improve control. **16** A stage in cascade amplification. **— in step** In agreement or synchronism when marching, dancing, etc.; walking evenly with another by taking corresponding steps. **— out of step** Not in step. **— to take steps** To adopt measures, as to attain an end. —*v.* **stepped, step·ping** *v.i.* **1** To move forward or backward by taking a step or steps. **2** To go by foot; walk a short distance: to *step* across the street. **3** To move with measured, dignified, or graceful steps. **4** To move or act quickly or briskly: The old man was *stepping* down the road. **5** To pass into a situation, circumstance, etc., as if in a single step: He *stepped* into a fortune. —*v.t.* **6** To take (a pace, stride, etc.). **7** To perform the steps of: to *step* a quadrille. **8** To place or move (the foot) in taking a step. **9** To measure by taking steps: often with *off*: to *step* off five yards. **10** To cut or arrange in steps. **11** *Naut.* To place the lower end of (a mast) in its step. **— to step down 1** To decrease

gradually, or by steps or degrees. **2** To resign from an office or position; abdicate. **— to step in** To begin to take part; intervene. **— to step on** (or **upon**) **1** To put the foot down on; tread upon. **2** To put the foot on so as to activate, as a brake or treadle. **3** *Colloq.* To reprove or subdue. **— to step on it** To hurry; hasten. **— to step out 1** To go outside, especially for a short while. **2** *Colloq.* To go out for fun or entertainment. **3** To step down (def. 2). **4** To walk vigorously and with long strides. **— to step up** To increase; raise. ◆ Homophone: *steppe*. [OE *stæpe*]

step- *combining form* Related through the previous marriage of a parent or spouse, but not by blood: *stepchild.* [OE *stepo-* < stem of *astypan, astepan* bereave, orphan]

step·broth·er (step′bruth′ər) *n.* The son of one's step-parent by a former marriage.

step·child (step′chīld′) *n.* The child of one's husband or wife by a former marriage.

step·daugh·ter (step′dô′tər) *n.* A female stepchild.

step–down (step′doun′) *adj.* **1** That decreases gradually. **2** *Electr.* Converting a small current of high voltage into a large one of low voltage: said of the usual form of transformer: opposed to *step–up.* **3** Designating a ratio-reducing gear.

step·fa·ther (step′fä′thər) *n.* The husband of one's mother other than one's own father.

step–in (step′in′) *n.* **1** An undergarment like short drawers, without actual legs: also **step′ins′.** **2** A pumplike shoe. *— adj.* Put on, as undergarments or shoes, by being stepped into.

step·lad·der (step′lad′ər) *n.* A set of portable steps with, usually, a hinged frame at the back, which may be extended to support the steps in an upright position.

step·moth·er (step′muth′ər) *n.* The wife of one's father, other than one's own mother.

step–par·ent (step′pâr′ənt) *n.* A stepfather or stepmother.

steppe (step) *n.* A vast plain devoid of forest; specifically, one of the extensive plains in Russia and Siberia. ◆ Homophone: *step.* [<Russian *step′*]

step·per (step′ər) *n.* **1** One who or that which steps: *The horse is a high stepper.* **2** *Slang* A dancer.

step·ping–stone (step′ing·stōn′) *n.* **1** A stone affording a footrest, as for crossing a stream, etc. **2** That by which one advances or rises: *steppingstones* to fortune.

step–re·la·tion (step′ri·lā′shən) *n.* A person related through the remarriage of a parent or spouse and not by blood. **— step′re·la′tion·ship** *n.*

step·sis·ter (step′sis′tər) *n.* The daughter of one's step-parent by a former marriage.

step·son (step′sun′) *n.* A male stepchild.

step–up (step′up′) *adj.* **1** Increasing by stages: a *step-up* transformer: opposed to *step-down.* **2** Designating a ratio-increasing gear.

–ster *suffix of nouns* **1** One who makes or is occupied with: often with pejorative force: *songster, prankster.* **2** One who belongs or is related to: *gangster.* **3** One who is: *youngster.* [OE *-estre*, feminine suffix]

stercori– *combining form* Dung; excrement: *stercoricolous:* also, before vowels, **stercor–.** Also **sterco–.** [<L *stercus, stercoris* dung]

ster·cu·li·a·ceous (stûr·kyōō′lē·ā′shəs) *adj. Bot.* Designating or belonging to a family (*Sterculiaceae*) of chiefly tropical herbs, shrubs, and trees, including the cacao and the colanut tree. [<NL <L *Sterculius*, the deity of manuring < *stercus* dung]

ster·e·o (ster′ē·ō, stir′-) *n. pl.* **·e·os 1** A stereophonic record player, record, tape, etc. **2** Stereophonic sound. **3** A stereotype (defs. 1 & 3). **4** A stereoscopic method; also, a stereoscopic photograph. *— adj.* **1** Stereophonic. **2** Stereotyped. **3** Of or pertaining to the stereoscope.

stereo– *combining form* Solid; firm; hard: *stereoscope.* Also, before vowels, **stere–.** [<Gk. *stereos* hard]

ster·e·o·bate (ster′ē·ə·bāt′, stir′-) *n. Archit.* A substructure, continuous base, or solid platform without columns, as distinguished from a *stylobate*, which has them. [<STEREO-

+ Gk. *batēs* that which steps] **— ster′e·o·bat′ic** (-bat′ik) *adj.*

ster·e·o·chem·is·try (ster′ē·ō·kem′is·trē, stir′-) *n.* The branch of chemistry that treats of the spatial arrangement of atoms and molecules.

ster·e·o·chro·my (ster′ē·ō·krō′mē, stir′-) *n.* The art or process of painting with pigments mixed with waterglass. [<STEREO- + Gk. *chrôma* color] **— ster′e·o′chro′mic** *adj.*

ster·e·og·no·sis (ster′ē·og·nō′sis, stir′-) *n.* Perception of shape, solidity, and weight, especially by the sense of touch. [<STEREO- + Gk. *gnôsis* knowing] **— ster′e·og·nos′tic** (-nos′tik) *adj.*

ster·e·o·gram (ster′ē·ə·gram′, stir′-) *n.* **1** A picture or diagram giving the impression of a solid in relief, or two pictures of an object combined so as to produce the effect of a solid, as in a stereoscopic picture. **2** A stereograph.

ster·e·o·graph (ster′ē·ə·graf′, -gräf′, stir′-) *n.* **1** A photograph or pair of photographs representing objects so that they appear solid; a stereoscopic photograph. **2** An instrument for making projections of solid objects.

ster·e·o·i·som·er·ism (ster′ē·ō·ī·som′ə·riz′əm, stir′-) *n. Chem.* An isomerism which depends on the spatial arrangement of the atoms or groups in an organic compound. **— ster′e·o·i′so·mer′ic** (-ī′sō·mer′ik), **ster′e·o·mer′ic** *adj.*

ster·e·ome (ster′ē·ōm, stir′-) *n. Bot.* The solid supporting elements of the fibrovascular tissues of plants. [<Gk. *stereôme* solid body < *stereos* solid]

ster·e·om·e·try (ster′ē·om′ə·trē, stir′-) *n.* The art of measuring the volume and other spatial elements of solids. [<STEREO- + -METRY] **— ster′e·o·met′ric** (-ō·met′rik) or **·ri·cal** *adj.* **— ster′e·o·met′ri·cal·ly** *adv.*

ster·e·o·phone (ster′ē·ə·fōn′, stir′-) *n.* Any sound–transmitting system equipped with stereophonic devices.

ster·e·o·phon·ic (ster′ē·ə·fon′ik, stir′-) *adj.* **1** Pertaining to, designed for, or characterized by the perception of sound by both ears; binaural. **2** Denoting a system of sound transmission in which two or more microphones or loudspeakers are so placed as to give the effect of hearing with both ears simultaneously, as in wide–screen motion pictures and certain types of radio receivers. **— ster′e·o·phon′i·cal·ly** *adv.*

ster·e·o·phon·ics (ster′ē·ə·fon′iks, stir′-) *n. pl.* (*construed as singular*) The branch of acoustics which investigates the stereophonic reproduction of sound and develops its practical applications.

ster·e·op·sis (ster′ē·op′sis, stir′-) *n.* Vision characterized by stereoscopy; stereoscopic vision. [<STERE(O)- + -OPSIS]

ster·e·op·ti·con (ster′ē·op′ti·kon, stir′-) *n.* A double magic lantern arranged to combine two images of the same object or scene, or used to bring one image after another on the screen by the alternate use of the lanterns; a projection lantern. [<STEREO- + Gk. *optikos* of sight]

ster·e·o·scope (ster′ē·ə·skōp, stir′-) *n.* An instrument for blending into one image two pictures of an object from slightly different points of view, so as to produce upon the eye the impression of relief and solidity. [<STEREO- + -SCOPE] **— ster′e·o·scop′ic** (-skop′ik) or **·i·cal** *adj.* **— ster′e·o·scop′i·cal·ly** *adv.*

ster·e·os·co·py (ster′ē·os′kə·pē, stir′-) *n.* **1** The art of making or using stereoscopes and stereoscopic slides. **2** The viewing of objects as in three dimensions. **— ster′e·os′co·pism** *n.* **— ster′e·os′co·pist** *n.*

ster·e·o·ski·ag·ra·phy (ster′ē·ō·skī·ag′rə·fē, stir′-) *n.* Stereoscopic photography by means of X–rays. [<STEREO- + SKIAGRAPHY]

STEREOSCOPE
Line of sight, *Ll* and *Rr*, of the eyes, combines the images of points *l* and *r* at *O.* A card (at dotted line) shuts off two side images otherwise seen along *Rl* at *l* and *Lr* at *r.*

ster·e·ot·ro·pism (ster′ē·ot′rə·piz′əm, stir′-) *n.* Involuntary response of an organism to contact with a foreign body. Also **ster′e·o·tax′is** (-ō·tak′sis) **— ster′e·o·trop′ic** (-trop′ik) *adj.*

ster·e·o·type (ster′ē·ə·tīp′, stir′-) *n.* **1** A plate taken in type metal from a matrix, as of paper, reproducing the surface from which the matrix was made. **2** Stereotypy. **3** Anything made or processed in this way. **4** A conventional or hackneyed expression, custom, or mode of thought. *— v.t.* **·typed, ·typ·ing 1** To make a stereotype of. **2** To fix firmly or unalterably. **— ster′e·o·typed** (ster′ē·ə·tīpt′, stir′-) *adj.* Formalized as if produced from a stereotype; hackneyed; without originality.

ster·e·o·typ·y (ster′ē·ō·tī′pē, stir′-) *n.* The art or act of making stereotypes. Also **ster′e·o·typ′er·y** (-tī′pər·ē).

ster·e·o·vi·sion (ster′ē·ō·vizh′ən, stir′-) *n.* Three–dimensional vision.

ster·ic (ster′ik, stir′-) *adj. Chem.* Denoting relative position in space: said of the component atoms in a molecule. Also **ster′i·cal.** [<Gk. *stereos* solid]

ster·ile (ster′əl) *adj.* **1** Having no reproductive power; barren. **2** *Bot.* Producing no pistil or no spores; incapable of germinating, as certain plants. **3** Lacking productiveness or fertility; hence, useless; being without result: *sterile* soil. **4** Containing no pathogenic bacteria or other micro–organisms; aseptic: a *sterile* fluid. **5** Destitute of attractiveness or suggestiveness: said especially of literary work: *sterile* verse. [<L *sterilis* barren] **— ster′ile·ly** *adv.* **— ste·ril·i·ty** (stə·ril′ə·tē), **ster′ile·ness** *n.*

ster·il·i·za·tion (ster′əl·ə·zā′shən, -ī·zā′-) *n.* **1** The act or process of making sterile. **2** The condition of being sterile. **3** The deliberate procedure of destroying reproductive power by surgical means.

ster·il·ize (ster′əl·īz) *v.t.* **·ized, ·iz·ing 1** To deprive of productive or reproductive power, especially by surgical operation on the Fallopian tubes or on the vas deferens. **2** To destroy bacteria in; free from germs. **3** To make barren; exhaust the productiveness of. **4** To make powerless. **— ster′il·iz′er** *n.*

ster·let (stûr′lit) *n.* A small sturgeon (*Acipenser ruthenus*) found in the Black, Caspian, and Azov seas, and in rivers of Russia, yielding superior caviar and isinglass. [<Russian *sterlyad′*]

ster·ling (stûr′ling) *n.* **1** The official standard of fineness for British coins: for silver (**sterling silver**), 0.925 until 1920, 0.500 since then; for gold, 0.91666 or 11/12. **2** Sterling silver, 0.925 fine, as used in manufacturing articles, as tableware, etc.; also, an article or articles made of it. **3** A former silver penny of England and Scotland, in circulation as early as the 12th century. *— adj.* **1** Made of or payable in sterling: pounds *sterling.* **2** Made of sterling silver. **3** Having accepted worth; genuine; hence, valuable; esteemed: *sterling* qualities. See synonyms under GOOD. [Prob. OE *steorra* star + -LING; because a star was stamped on some of the coins]

stern¹ (stûrn) *adj.* **1** Proceeding from or marked by severity or harshness; unyielding: a *stern* command. **2** Having an austere disposition; strict; severe: a *stern* judge. **3** Inspiring fear; repelling. **4** Resolute; stout: a *stern* resolve. See synonyms under AUSTERE, GRIM, HARD, SEVERE. [OE *styrne*] **— stern′ly** *adv.* **— stern′ness** *n.*

stern² (stûrn) *n.* **1** *Naut.* The aft part of a ship, boat, etc. **2** The buttocks or tail part of an animal: now chiefly humorous. **3** The hindmost part of any object. *— adj.* Situated at or belonging to the stern. [<ON *stjoren* steering, rudder < *styra* steer]

stern·most (stûrn′mōst′, -məst) *adj.* Farthest to the rear or stern.

sterno– *combining form Anat. & Med.* The sternum: *sternotomy*, cutting through the sternum. Also, before vowels, **stern–.** [<L *sternum* breast]

ster·num (stûr′nəm) *n. pl.* **·na** (-nə) or **·nums** **1** *Anat.* The breastbone which forms the ventral support of the ribs in most vertebrates. **2** *Zool.* The ventral portion of a somite in an arthropod, as an insect or crustacean. [<L

<Gk. *sternon* breast]

ster·nu·ta·tor (stûr′nyə·tā′tər) *n.* One of a class of chemical–warfare agents having a strongly irritant effect upon the nasal and respiratory passages, with resulting physical exhaustion; a sneeze gas.

ster·nu·ta·to·ry (stər·nyōō′tə·tôr′ē, -tō′rē, -nōō′-) *adj.* Causing or tending to cause sneezing: also **ster·nu′ta·tive** (-tə·tiv). — *n.* *pl.* **·ries** Any substance tending to cause sneezing, as snuff.

stern·ward (stûrn′wərd) *adj. & adv.* Toward the stern; astern. Also **stern′wards.**

stern–wheel·er (stûrn′hwē′lər) *n.* A steamboat of small draft propelled by one large paddle wheel at the stern.

STERN–WHEELER

ster·oid (ster′oid) *n.* *Biochem.* Any of a sizable group of organic compounds widely distributed in nature, including the sterols, the bile acids, and the sex hormones. [<STER(OL) + -OID]

ster·ol (ster′ōl, -ol) *n.* *Biochem.* Any of a class of complex, chiefly unsaturated, solid alcohols widely distributed in plant and animal tissue, as cholesterol. [Contraction of CHOLESTEROL]

ster·tor (stûr′tər) *n.* A deep snore or snoring. [<NL <L *stertere* snore]

ster·tor·ous (stûr′tər·əs) *adj.* Characterized by snoring; accompanied by a snoring sound: *stertorous* breathing. — **ster′tor·ous·ly** *adv.* — **ster′tor·ous·ness** *n.*

ster·ule (ster′ōōl, -yōōl) *n.* A small glass container holding a sterile solution. Compare AMPOULE. [<STER(ILE) + -ULE]

stet (stet) Let it stand: a direction used in proofreading to indicate that a word, letter, etc., marked for omission or correction is to remain. — *v.t.* **stet·ted, stet·ting** To cancel a former correction or omission of by marking with the word *stet.* Compare DELE. [<L, 3rd person sing. subjunctive of *stare* stand, stay]

stetho– *combining form* The breast or chest; pectoral: *stethoscope.* Also, before vowels, **steth-.** [<Gk. *stēthos* breast]

ste·thom·e·ter (ste·thom′ə·tər) *n.* An instrument to measure the expansion of the chest in breathing. [<STETHO- + -METER]

steth·o·scope (steth′ə·skōp) *n.* *Med.* An apparatus for auscultation, of various forms, sizes, and materials, adapted for conveying the sounds of the body to the examiner's ear or ears. — **steth′o·scop′ic** (-skop′ik), **steth′·o·scop′i·cal** *adj.* — **steth′o·scop′i·cal·ly** *adv.* — **ste·thos·co·py** (ste·thos′kə·pē) *n.*

Stet·son (stet′sən) *n.* A hat; especially, one of felt with high crown and wide brim: a trade name. [after John Batterson *Stetson*, 1830–1906, U.S. hatmaker]

ste·ve·dore (stē′və·dôr, -dōr) *n.* One whose business is stowing or unloading the holds of vessels. — *v.t. & v.i.* **·dored, ·dor·ing** To load or unload (a vessel or vessels). [<Sp. *estivador* <*estivar* stow <L *stipare* compress, stuff]

stew (stōō, styōō) *v.t. & v.i.* **1** To boil slowly and gently; seethe; keep or be at the simmering point. **2** *Colloq.* To worry. — *n.* **1** Stewed food, especially a preparation of meat or fish cooked by stewing. **2** *Colloq.* Mental agitation; worry. **3** *pl.* *Archaic* A brothel. **4** *Obs.* A room heated for bathing or drying purposes. [<OF *estuver,* prob. ult. <L *ex*- out + Gk. *typhos* steam, vapor]

stew·ard (stōō′ərd, styōō′-) *n.* **1** A person entrusted with the management of estates or affairs not his own; an administrator. **2** A person put in charge of the domestic affairs of an establishment. **3** On shipboard, a petty officer in charge of the service of provisions, or a man who waits on table and takes care of passengers' rooms. **4** *Brit.* A fiscal officer in certain ancient guilds. [OE *stiweard* <*stī* hall, sty + *weard* ward, keeper] — **stew′ard·ess** *n. fem.* — **stew′ard·ship** *n.*

stewed (stōōd, styōōd) *adj.* **1** Cooked by stewing. **2** *Slang* Drunk.

stew pan A cooking vessel used for stewing.

sthe·ni·a (sthē′nē·ə, sthi·nī′ə) *n.* Unusual energy or vigor; excited force: opposed to *asthe-*

nia. [<NL <Gk. *sthenos* strength]

sthen·ic (sthen′ik) *adj.* **1** Exhibiting activity or energy, especially in morbid states. **2** Having power to inspire or animate; indicating vigor. [<Gk. *sthenos* strength]

stiac·cia·to (styät·chä′tō) *n.* Sculpture or a piece of sculpture in lower relief than bas–relief, as the very low relief used on coins. — *adj.* Of or pertaining to this kind of sculpture; in very low relief. [<Ital., crushed, flattened, pp. of *stiacciare*]

stib·i·um (stib′ē·əm) *n.* Antimony. [<L <Gk. *stibi*] — **stib′i·al** *adj.*

stib·nite (stib′nīt) *n.* A metallic steel–gray antimony sulfide, Sb_2S_3, crystallizing in the orthorhombic system: the most important ore of antimony. [<STIB(I)N(E)+ -ITE²]

stich (stik) *n.* **1** A line of the Bible. **2** A line of poetry; a verse: used often in composition: *hemistich.* [<Gk. *stichos* row]

stich·ic (stik′ik) *adj.* **1** Relating to or consisting of stichs. **2** Metrically the same throughout: said of verses.

sti·chom·e·try (sti·kom′ə·trē) *n.* **1** The measurement of the text of a manuscript by lines of measured length into which it is divided; also, the appendix stating the number of lines. **2** The practice of writing prose in line lengths corresponding to the sense of the phrasal cadence. [<Gk. *stichos* line + -METRY] — **stich·o·met·ric** (stik′ə·met′rik) or **·ri·cal** *adj.*

sti·chom·y·thy (sti·kom′ə·thē) *n.* The arrangement of a dialog in alternate lines of verse: characteristic of ancient Greek drama, poetry, and disputation: also spelled *stychomythia.* [<Gk. *stichos* line + *mythos* speech] — **stich·o·myth·ic** (stik′ə·mith′ik) *adj.*

-stichous *combining form* Having (a specified number of) rows: *tristichous.* [<Gk. *stichos* a row, line]

stich·wort (stich′wûrt′) See STITCHWORT.

stick (stik) *n.* **1** A piece of wood that is long, compared with its cross–section; a stiff shoot or branch cut from a tree or bush and used as a rod, wand, staff, club, etc.; also, sometimes one much bigger: a *stick* of timber. **2** *Brit.* A cane. **3** Anything resembling a stick in form: a *stick* of candy or dynamite. **4** *Printing* **a** A composing stick. **b** As much type as a composing stick will hold: about two inches in depth. **c** Copy which will fill this space in a newspaper column: also **stick′ful.** **5** A piece of wood of any size, cut for fuel, lumber, or timber. **6** *Aeron.* The control lever of an airplane which operates the elevators and ailerons. **7** A poke, stab, or thrust with a stick or pointed instrument. **8** *Archaic* A difficulty or obstacle; hesitation; stop. **9** The state of being stuck together; adhesion. **10** In sports, a baseball bat, hockey stick, racing hurdle, etc. **11** A timber tree. **12** *Colloq.* A stiff, inert, or dull person. **13** *Slang* Any alcoholic ingredient in an otherwise non–alcoholic drink. **14** A revolver or rifle. **15** *Colloq.* The mast of a ship. **16** *Mil.* A group of bombs released consecutively in a straight line crossing the target area. **17** A stalk, as of asparagus. **18** *Colloq.* A conductor's baton. — **the sticks 1** A timber forest. **2** *Colloq.* The backwoods; an obscure rural district. — *v.* **stuck** or (*for defs.* 15, 16) **sticked, stick·ing** *v.t.* **1** To pierce, stab, or penetrate with a pin, knife, or other pointed object. **2** To kill or wound by piercing; stab. **3** To thrust or force, as a sword or pin, into or through something else. **4** To force the end of (a nail, etc.) into something so as to be fixed in place: to *stick* a nail in a wall. **5** To fasten in place with or as with pins, nails, etc.: to *stick* a ribbon on a dress. **6** To cover with objects piercing the surface: a paper *stuck* with pins. **7** To fix on a pointed object; impale; transfix. **8** To put or thrust: He *stuck* his hand into his pocket. **9** To fasten to a surface by or as by an adhesive substance. **10** To bring to a standstill; obstruct; halt: usually in the passive: We were *stuck* in Rome. **11** *Colloq.* To smear with something sticky. **12** *Colloq.* To baffle; puzzle. **13** *Slang* To impose upon; cheat. **14** *Slang* To force great expense, an unpleasant task, responsibility, etc., upon. **15** To provide with sticks or brush on which to grow, as a vine. **16** *Printing* To set or compose (type). — *v.i.* **17** To be or become fixed in place by being thrust in: The pins are *sticking* in the cushion. **18** To become or remain attached by or as by

adhesion; adhere; cling. **19** To come to a standstill; become blocked or obstructed; stop; halt. **20** To be baffled or disconcerted. **21** To hesitate; scruple: with *at* or *to.* **22** To persist; persevere, as in a task or undertaking: with *at* or *to.* **23** To remain firm or resolute; be faithful, as to an ideal or bargain. **24** To be extended; protrude: with *from, out, through, up,* etc. — **to be stuck on** *Colloq.* To be enamored of. — **to stick around** *Slang* To remain near or near at hand. — **to stick by** To remain faithful to; be loyal to. — **to stick it out** To persevere to the end. — **to stick up** *Slang* To stop and rob. — **to stick up for** *Colloq.* To take the part of; support; defend. [OE *sticca*]

stick·ball (stik′bôl′) *n.* A kind of baseball played on streets or in vacant lots, with a rubber ball and a narrow stick or a broom handle for a bat.

stick·er (stik′ər) *n.* **1** One who holds tenaciously to anything. **2** One who or that which fastens with or as with paste. **3** A paster. **4** *Colloq.* Anything that confuses or silences a person; a puzzle. **5** A prickly stem, thorn, or bur.

sticking plaster An adhesive material for covering slight cuts, etc.; a court plaster.

stick insect An orthopterous insect (family *Phasmidae*), typically wingless and characterized by a long, sticklike body, as the green or pinkish *Timema* of the Pacific coast.

stick–in–the–mud (stik′in·thə·mud′) *n.* *Colloq.* A person too sluggish or lacking in initiative to take any progressive action.

stick·le¹ (stik′əl) *v.i.* **·led, ·ling 1** To contend about trifling matters. **2** To insist or hesitate for petty reasons. [ME *stightlen* set in order, freq. of OE *stihtan* arrange, dispose]

stick·le² (stik′əl) *n.* A prickle; spine: obsolete except in compounds. [OE *sticel* sting]

stick·le·back (stik′əl·bak′) *n.* A small fresh- or salt–water fish (genera *Gasterosteus* and *Eucalia*) of northern regions, having sharp dorsal spines. The male builds nests for the reception of the eggs laid by the female.

stick·ler (stik′lər) *n.* **1** One who contends over trifles. **2** *Obs.* A referee.

stick·pin (stik′pin′) *n.* An ornamental pin for a necktie.

stick·seed (stik′sēd′) *n.* Any of a genus (*Lappula*) of coarse weeds, whose prickly seeds stick in clothing, the wool of sheep, etc.

stick shift A gearshift operated by hand rather than automatically, located either on the floor or on the steering column.

stick·tight (stik′tīt′) *n.* A coarse herb (genus *Bidens*) of the composite family with prickly achenes; a bur marigold.

stick–to–it·ive (stik–tōō′it·iv) *adj. Colloq.* Persevering; dogged; pertinacious. — **stick–to′–it·ive·ly** *adv.* — **stick–to′–it·ive·ness** *n.*

stick–up (stik′up′) *n. Slang* **1** A robbery or hold–up. **2** A robber who intimidates his victims with a weapon, compelling them to hold their hands in the air.

stick·weed (stik′wēd′) *n.* Ragweed.

stick·y (stik′ē) *adj.* **stick·i·er, stick·i·est 1** Adhering to a surface; adhesive. **2** Warm and humid. See synonyms under ADHESIVE. — **stick′i·ly** *adv.* — **stick′i·ness** *n.*

stiff (stif) *adj.* **1** Resisting the action of a bending force; not flaccid, limp, pliant, or flexible; rigid. **2** Not easily moved; acting with difficulty or friction. **3** Not natural, graceful, or easy; constrained and awkward; formal. **4** Not liquid or fluid; thick; viscous. **5** Taut; tightly drawn. **6** Having a strong, steady movement: a *stiff* breeze. **7** Firm in resistance; obstinate; stubborn. **8** Difficult to achieve, understand, or accept; harsh; severe: a *stiff* penalty. **9** High; dear: a *stiff* price. **10** Firm in prices; strong and steady: a *stiff* market. **11** *Naut.* Heeling over but little, while carrying much sail; not crank: a *stiff* ship. **12** *Scot. & Brit. Dial.* Lusty; strong; sturdy. **13** Dense; not porous, as soil. **14** Strong; potent: a *stiff* drink. **15** Difficult; arduous: a *stiff* climb. **16** *Obs.* Formidable; serious: said of news. See synonyms under INFLEXIBLE, SEVERE. — *n. Slang* **1** A corpse. **2** An awkward or unresponsive person; especially, a bore. **3** A man; fellow: *working* stiff; also, a roughneck. **4** A hobo. **5** An accomplice in dishonest dealings; also, a prospective victim. [OE *stīf*] — **stiff′ly** *adv.* — **stiff′ness** *n.*

stiff·en (stif′ən) v.t. & v.i. To make or become stiff or stiffer.

stiff·en·er (stif′ən-ər) n. One who or that which stiffens. — **bow stiffener** Aeron. A rigid structural member to reinforce the bow of a dirigible or other airship: also **nose stiffener.**

stiff-necked (stif′nekt′) adj. Not yielding; stubborn; incorrigible; obstinate.

sti·fle[1] (stī′fəl) v.t. ·fled, ·fling v.t. 1 To kill by stopping respiration; suffocate; choke. 2 To keep back; suppress or repress, as sobs. — v.i. 3 To die of suffocation. 4 To experience difficulty in breathing, as in a stuffy room. [<ON stīfla stop up, choke] — **sti′·fler** n. — **sti′fling** adj. — **sti′fling·ly** adv.

sti·fle[2] (stī′fəl) n. 1 The stifle joint. 2 Any abnormal condition of the stifle joint or stifle bone. [Origin unknown]

stifle bone The patella or kneepan of a horse, situated at the stifle joint, formerly thought of as stopping or damming up the joint.

sti·fled (stī′fəld) adj. Having some disease of the stifle joint; affected with stifle.

stifle joint The joint in the upper leg of a horse or a dog. See illustration under DOG, HORSE.

stig·ma (stig′mə) n. pl. **stig·ma·ta** (stig′mə·tə, stig·mä′tə) or (for defs. 1–3, usually) **stig·mas** 1 A mark of infamy, or token of disgrace; blemish; a blot on one's good name. 2 Formerly, a brand made with a branding iron on slaves and criminals. 3 Bot. That part of a pistil which receives the pollen. 4 Biol. **a** A mark or spot, as on the wings of certain insects. **b** An aperture, as the gill slit of a tunicate. 5 A small mark or scar; a birthmark. 6 Pathol. A small red or bleeding spot on the skin caused by nervous tension or by capillary congestion. 7 pl. The wounds that Christ received during the Passion and Crucifixion; also, marks on the body corresponding to these wounds: said to be miraculously impressed on certain persons as a token of divine favor. 8 One of the characteristic signs or marks of a disease. See synonyms under BLEMISH. [<L, mark, brand <Gk., pointed end, mark <stizein prick, brand]

stig·mat·ic (stig·mat′ik) adj. 1 Of, pertaining to, or marked with a stigma or stigmata. 2 Infamous; ignominious or vicious; hence, deformed. 3 Anastigmatic. Also **stig·mat′i·cal** — n. One marked with or bearing a stigma or stigmata.

stig·ma·tism (stig′mə·tiz′əm) n. 1 The state of being affected with stigmas. 2 Optics The quality or condition of a lens or of the cornea of the eye through which rays of light are accurately focused.

stig·ma·tize (stig′mə·tīz) v.t. ·tized, ·tiz·ing 1 To characterize or brand as ignominious. 2 To mark with a stigma. 3 To cause stigmata to appear on. Also Brit. **stig′ma·tise.** [<Med. L stigmatizare <Gk. stigmatizein mark < stigma pointed end, mark] — **stig′ma·ti·za′tion** n. — **stig′ma·tiz′er** n.

stil·bes·trol (stil′bes·trōl, -trol) n. Chem. A synthetic sex hormone, $C_{18}H_{20}O_2$, similar in action to but more potent than the naturally occurring estrogens. [<STILB(ENE) + ESTR(ONE) + -OL[1]]

stil·bite (stil′bīt) n. A vitreous native hydrous silicate of aluminum, calcium, and sodium crystallizing in the monoclinic system. [<Gk. stilbein glitter + -ITE[1]]

stile[1] (stīl) n. A step, or series of steps, on each side of a fence or wall to aid in surmounting it; loosely, a turnstile. ◆ Homophone: style. [OE stigel < stīgan climb]

stile[2] (stīl) n. One of the vertical side-pieces in a door or a window sash. ◆ Homophone: style. [< Du. stijl doorpost]

STILE
Over wire fence.

sti·let·to (sti·let′ō) n. pl. ·tos or ·toes 1 A small dagger with a slender blade. 2 A small, sharp-pointed instrument, as of bone, for puncturing eyelets. — v.t. To pierce with a stiletto; stab. Also **sti·let′, sti·lette′.** [<Ital., dim. of stilo dagger <L stilus. See STYLE[1].]

still[1] (stil) adj. 1 Being without movement; motionless. 2 Free from disturbance or agitation; peaceful; tranquil. 3 Making no sound; silent. 4 Low in sound; hushed. 5 Subdued; soft. 6 Dead; inanimate. 7 Having no effervescence: opposed to sparkling: said of wines. 8 Phot. Showing no movement. See synonyms under CALM, PACIFIC, SEDATE. — n. 1 Absence of sound or noise; stillness; calm. 2 A still-life picture. 3 Phot. A still photograph; especially, one taken with a still camera on a motion-picture set, for advertising, promotion, etc. 4 A still alarm. — adv. 1 Now as previously; up to this or that time; yet: He is still here. 2 After or in spite of something; all the same; nevertheless. 3 In increasing degree; even more; even yet: still more. 4 Poetic & Dial. Always; constantly. See synonyms under BUT[1], NOTWITHSTANDING, YET. — conj. Nevertheless. — v.t. 1 To cause to be still or calm. 2 To silence or hush. 3 To quiet or allay, as fears. — v.i. 4 To become still. See synonyms under ALLAY, REPRESS, TRANQUILIZE. [OE stille] — **still′ness** n.

still[2] (stil) n. 1 An apparatus in which a substance is vaporized by heat, and the vapor then liquefied in a condenser and collected: used especially for distilling liquors. 2 A distillery: also **still house.** — v.t. & v.i. To distil. [<L stillare drip < stilla a drop]

STILL

still alarm A fire alarm given by telephone or other call without sounding the regular signal apparatus.

still-birth (stil′bûrth′) n. The bringing forth or birth of a dead child.

still-born (stil′bôrn′) adj. Dead at birth.

still-hunt (stil′hunt′) v.t. & v.i. To hunt (game) stealthily; stalk. — n. 1 The hunting of game by stealth. 2 The cautious, guarded pursuit of anything; specifically, secret or underhand methods in politics.

stil·li·form (stil′ə·fôrm) adj. Drop-shaped. [<NL stilliformis <L stilla drop + forma shape]

still-life (stil′līf′) n. 1 In painting, the representation of fruit, flowers, lifeless animals, and inanimate objects. 2 A picture of such a subject.

stilt (stilt) n. 1 One of a pair of slender poles made with a projection to support the foot above the ground in walking. 2 A tall post or pillar used as a support for a dock or building. 3 Any of several long-legged, three-toed birds (genera Himantopus and Cladorhynchus) related to the avocet, inhabiting ponds and fresh- and salt-water marshes. The American stilt (H. mexicanus) is mostly white with back, wings, crown, and nape a greenish black. The Old World stilt (H. candidus) is white except for wings and back. 4 Scot. A crutch. — v.t. To raise on stilts. — v.i. Scot. To hobble on crutches. [ME stilte, ? <LG. Cf. MLG stelte.]

stilt·ed (stil′tid) adj. Artificially elevated in manner; bombastic; inflated. — **stilt′ed·ly** adv. — **stilt′ed·ness** n.

stilted arch Archit. An arch whose curve springs from a level some distance above that of the impost.

Stil·ton cheese (stil′tən) A rich cheese permeated when ripe with a blue-green mold: originally made at Stilton, England. Also **Stil′ton.**

stim·u·lant (stim′yə·lənt) n. 1 Anything that quickens or promotes the activity of some physiological process, as a drug. 2 Popularly, an alcoholic beverage. — adj. Acting as a stimulant; serving to stimulate. [<L stimulans, -antis, ppr. of stimulare. See STIMULATE.]

stim·u·late (stim′yə·lāt) v. ·lat·ed, ·lat·ing v.t. 1 To rouse to activity or to quickened action by some agency or motive; excite. 2 To arouse, or to increase action in, by applying some form of stimulus: to stimulate the skin. 3 To affect by intoxicants. — v.i. 4 To act as a stimulant. See synonyms under ENCOURAGE, PIQUE[1], SPUR, STIR[1]. [<L stimulatus, pp. of stimulare prick, goad <stimulus a goad] — **stim′u·lat′er, stim′u·la′tor** n. — **stim′u·la′tion** n.

stim·u·lus (stim′yə·ləs) n. pl. ·li (-lī) 1 Anything that rouses the mind or spirits; an incentive; a stimulant; a sting; a spur, or goad. 2 Physiol. **a** Any agent or form of excitation which influences the activity of an organism as a whole or in any of its parts. **b** That which initiates an impulse, as in a nerve or muscle, or produces an altered state of consciousness, as by arousing new or stronger sensations. [<L]

sting (sting) v. stung (Obs. stang), stung, sting·ing v.t. 1 To pierce or prick painfully, as with a sharp, poisonous organ: The bee stung me. 2 To cause to suffer sharp, smarting pain from or as from a sting: The blow stung his cheek. 3 To cause to suffer mentally; pain: His heart was stung with remorse. 4 To stimulate or rouse as if with a sting; goad; spur. 5 Slang To impose upon; get the better of; also, to overcharge. — v.i. 6 To have or use a sting, as a bee. 7 To suffer or cause a sharp, smarting pain. 8 To suffer or cause mental distress; pain. See synonyms under INCENSE[1], PIQUE[1], SPUR. — n. 1 Zool. A sharp offensive or defensive organ, as of a bee or wasp, capable of inflicting a painful and especially a poisonous wound. 2 The act of stinging; the wound made by a sting, or the pain caused by it. 3 Any sharp, smarting sensation; stinging quality: the sting of remorse. 4 A keen stimulus; spur; goad. 5 Bot. One of the sharp-pointed hairs of a nettle; a stinging hair. 6 The point of an epigram. 7 Colloq. A confidence game; swindle. [OE stingan] — **sting′ing·ly** adv.

sting·er (sting′ər) n. 1 One who or that which stings. 2 A plant or animal that stings. 3 An insect's sting. 4 A cocktail made of brandy and white crème de menthe.

stinging hair Bot. One of the hairs of a nettle, charged at the base with an irritating fluid which is injected beneath the skin when touched.

sting·ray (sting′rā) n. Any of a family (Dasyatidae) of bottom-dwelling rays having a long, whiplike tail bearing one or more serrated venomous spines. Also called stingaree. [< STING + RAY[2]]

STING RAY
(Body about 20 inches in length; the stinger, 8 to 15 inches)

stin·gy (stin′jē) adj. ·gi·er, ·gi·est 1 Extremely penurious or selfish; miserly. 2 Scanty, as from penurious giving. See synonyms under AVARICIOUS. [< dial. E stinge a sting] — **stin′gi·ly** adv. — **stin′gi·ness** n.

stink (stingk) n. A strong, foul odor; stench. See synonyms under SMELL. — v. **stank** or **stunk, stunk, stink·ing** v.i. 1 To give forth a foul odor. 2 To be extremely offensive or hateful. — v.t. 3 To cause to stink. — **to stink out** To drive from a den, hideaway, etc., by a foul or suffocating odor. [OE stincan smell] — **stink′ing** adj. — **stink′ing·ly** adv.

stink-ball (stingk′bôl′) n. A jar containing a mixture of various compounds, as gunpowder, asafetida, etc., formerly used for throwing from one warship to another when at close quarters: also called *stinkpot.* Also **stink·bomb** (-bom').

stink·bug (stingk'bug') *n.* Any of a family *(Pentatomidae)* of hemipterous insects, including mostly rather large, broad, flattened bugs which emit a sickening, sweetish odor when disturbed.

stink·er (stingk'ər) *n.* **1** One who or that which stinks, as a stinkball. **2** The fulmar or other petrel that feeds on carrion. **3** *Slang* An unpleasant, disgusting, or irritating person.

stink·horn (stingk'hôrn') *n.* Any of an order *(Phallales)* of basidiomycetous, ill-smelling fungi, especially the carrion fungus *(Ithyphallus impudicus).*

stink·weed (stingk'wēd') *n.* The jimsonweed or stramonium.

stint (stint) *v.t.* **1** To limit, as in amount or share; be stingy with: Don't *stint* yourself. **2** *Archaic* To stop. —*v.i.* **3** To be frugal or sparing. **4** *Archaic* To stop. —*n.* **1** A fixed amount, as of work; a task to be performed within a specified time; allowance. **2** A bound; restriction. **3** A small sandpiper. **4** *Obs.* A cessation. See synonyms under TASK, TOIL¹. [ME *stynten* cause to stop < OE *styntan* stupefy < *stunt* stupid] —**stint'er** *n.* —**stint'ing·ly** *adv.*

stipe (stīp) *n.* **1** *Zool.* A stalk or support. **2** *Bot.* **a** A stalklike support of a gynoecium or carpel. **b** The petiole or support of a fern's frond. **c** The stem supporting the cap of a mushroom or similar fungus. See illustration under MUSHROOM. [< F < L *stipes* branch]

sti·pel (stī'pəl) *n. Bot.* A secondary or small stipule standing at the base of a leaflet. [< NL *stipella,* dim. of *stipes* a branch] —**sti·pel·late** (stī-pel'it, stī'pəl-it, -āt) *adj.*

sti·pend (stī'pend) *n.* **1** An allowance or salary; a fixed payment for services, especially a salary that affords a bare livelihood. **2** *Scot.* A clergyman's salary. **3** *Eccl.* In the Roman Catholic Church, an offering given to a priest for saying a mass with a special intention. See synonyms under SALARY. [< L *stipendium* tax, tribute < *stips* coin, payment in coin + *pendere* weigh, pay ut]

sti·pen·di·a·ry (stī-pen'dē-er'ē) *adj.* **1** Receiving a stipend. **2** Paying tribute; owing feudal service; performing services for a fixed payment. —*n. pl.* **·ar·ies** **1** One who receives a stipend, as a clergyman. **2** A person owing feudal service. **3** A province paying a special tribute to a Roman emperor, instead of a tax. [< L *stipendiarius* < *stipendium* STIPEND]

stip·ple (stip'əl) *v.t.* **·pled, ·pling** To draw, paint, or engrave with dots or short touches instead of lines, so as to produce a shaded effect. —*n.* In painting, etching, etc., a method of representing light and shade by employing dots instead of lines, or the effect thus produced: also **stip'pling.** [< Du. *stippelen* < *stippen* speckle < *stip* dot] —**stip'pler** *n.*

stip·u·late¹ (stip'yə-lāt) *v.* **·lat·ed, ·lat·ing** *v.t.* **1** To specify as the terms of an agreement, contract, etc. **2** To specify as a requirement or condition for agreement. **3** To promise; guarantee. —*v.i.* **4** To demand something as a requirement or condition: with *for.* **5** To make an agreement. [< L *stipulatus,* pp. of *stipulari* bargain] —**stip'u·la·tor** *n.*

stip·u·late² (stip'yə-lit, -lāt) *adj.* Furnished with stipules. Also **stip·u·lat·ed** (-lā'tid).

stip·u·la·tion (stip'yə-lā'shən) *n.* **1** The act of stipulating, or the condition of being stipulated. **2** An agreement or contract. See synonyms under CONTRACT. —**stip'u·la·to·ry** (-lə-tôr'ē, -tō'rē) *adj.*

stip·ule (stip'yōōl) *n. Bot.* One of a pair of leaflike appendages at the base of the petiole of certain leaves. [< L *stipula* stalk]

stir¹ (stûr) *v.* **stirred, stir·ring** *v.t.* **1** To agitate so as to alter the relative position of the particles or components of, as soup with a spoon. **2** To cause to move, especially slightly or irregularly; disturb: The tide *stirred* the boat. **3** To move vigorously; bestir: *Stir* yourself! **4** To rouse, as from sleep, indifference, or inactivity; stimulate. **5** To incite; provoke; often with *up.* **6** To affect strongly; move with emotion. —*v.i.* **7** To move, especially slightly: The log wouldn't *stir.* **8** To be active; move about: They heard him *stirring* in his room. **9** To take place; happen. **10** To undergo stirring: This molasses *stirs* easily. —*n.*

1 The act of stirring, or state of being stirred; activity. **2** Public interest; excitement; to-do; commotion. **3** A poke; nudge. [OE *styrian*] —**stir'rer** *n.*

Synonyms (verb): agitate, animate, arouse, awake, awaken, excite, incite, instigate, move, prompt, provoke, rouse, stimulate, wake. See ACTUATE, INFLUENCE, SPUR. *Antonyms:* see synonyms for ALLAY, ALLEVIATE.

stir² (stûr) *n. Slang* A jail; prison. [Origin uncertain]

stir·pi·cul·ture (stûr'pə-kul'chər) *n.* The breeding of special races or strains of animals and plants. [< L *stirps, stirpis* stem, stock + CULTURE] —**stir'pi·cul'tur·al** *adj.* —**stir'pi·cul'tur·ist** *n.*

stirps (stûrps) *n. pl.* **stir·pes** (stûr'pēz) **1** Race; family. **2** A stock as regards lineage: a source of property-descent: Descent per *stirpes* (as a family) is distinguished from descent per capita (as an individual). **3** *Biol.* The number of organic units existing in and determining the development of a fertilized ovum. [< L]

stir·ring (stûr'ing) *adj.* **1** Stimulating; inspiring. **2** Full of activity or stir; lively. See synonyms under VIVID. —**stir'ring·ly** *adv.*

stir·rup (stûr'əp, stir'-) *n.* **1** A loop, as an inverted U-shaped piece of metal or wood with flat footpiece, suspended from a saddle to support the rider's foot in and after mounting. **2** A loop or metal strap, as for supporting a beam. **3** *Naut.* A rope on a ship depending from a yard and having at its end an eye or thimble to carry a footrope. [OE *stigrāp* mounting rope]

stir·rup-cup (stûr'əp-kup', stir'-) *n.* A cup of liquor, as that taken by a mounted horseman on departing; hence, a farewell drink.

stitch· (stich) *n.* **1** A single passage of a threaded needle or other implement through fabric and back again, as in sewing or embroidery, or, in surgery, through skin or flesh. **2** A single turn of thread or yarn around a needle or other implement, as in knitting or crocheting; also, the link or loop resulting from such a turn. **3** Any peculiar or individual arrangement of a thread or threads used in sewing, embroidery, or crocheting: a chain *stitch.* **4** A sharp sudden pain, especially in the back or side. **5** A ridge between two furrows. **6** *Colloq.* A garment: I haven't a *stitch* to wear. —**to be in stitches** *Colloq.* To laugh uproariously; be overcome with laughter. —*v.t.* **1** To join together with stitches. **2** To ornament with stitches. —*v.i.* **3** To make stitches; sew. [OE *stice* prick, stab]

stitch·er (stich'ər) *n.* One who or that which stitches; especially, a machine for that purpose, as in bookbinding.

stitch·wort (stich'wûrt') *n.* Any of various plants (genus *Stellaria*), especially the common chickweed: also called *starwort, stichwort.* [OE *sticwyrt* < *stice* prick + *wyrt* plant]

St. Johns·wort (sānt jonz'wûrt') Any of a genus *(Hypericum)* of herbs and shrubs, mostly of the northern hemisphere, usually having large yellow or purplish flowers, considered to be typical of the family Guttiferae. Also **St.-John's-wort, Saint Johnswort.**

St. Lawrence River A river of SE Canada, the outlet of the Great Lakes system, flowing 744 miles NE from the NE end of Lake Ontario to the **Gulf of St. Lawrence,** an inlet of the North Atlantic between Newfoundland and eastern Canada; together with the Great Lakes and the St. Marys River it forms a waterway about 2,350 miles long, from the western end of Lake Superior to the Atlantic.

St. Lu·ci·a (sānt lōō'shē·ə, lōō·sē'ə, lōō'shə) A British colony in the Windward Islands, a federating unit of The West Indies (federation); 233 square miles; capital, Castries.

sto·a (stō'ə) *n. pl.* **sto·ae** (stō'ē) or **sto·as** In Greek architecture, a covered colonnade, portico, cloister, or promenade. [< Gk., porch]

STOA

stoat (stōt) *n.* The ermine, especially in its summer coat, redbrown above, yellow below. [ME *stote;* origin uncertain]

stoat² (stōt) *v.t.* To sew with an invisible stitch

that passes only half-way through the cloth. [Origin unknown] —**stoat'ing** *n.*

sto·chas·tic (stō·kas'tik) *adj.* **1** Of, pertaining to, characterized by, or skilled in conjecture; conjectural. **2** *Physics* Subject to the laws of probability; not predictable within a given time limit or spatial framework, as the disintegration of a single radioactive element: the *stochastic* phenomena of microphysics. **3** Denoting the process of selecting, from among a group of theoretically possible alternatives, those elements or factors whose combination will most closely approximate a desired result: a *stochastic* model. [< Gk. *stochastikos* < *stochazesthai* guess at < *stochos* mark, aim]

stock (stok) *n.* **1** The trunk or main stem of a tree or other plant, as distinguished from a branch or root. **2** A line of familial descent. **3** The original progenitor of a family line. **4** An ethnic group; race. **5** *Ling.* A family of languages. **6** A related group or family of plants or animals. **7** *Bot.* **a** A rhizome. **b** A stem upon which a graft is made. **8** *Zool.* A zooid which reproduces by generation. **9** Livestock: in Australia, cattle, not livestock in general. **10** A quantity of something acquired or kept for future use: to lay in a *stock* of provisions. **11** The merchandise or goods which a trader or merchant has on hand. **12** In card games and dominoes, the part of the pack or group of dominoes that is left on the table and drawn from. **13** The broth from boiled meat or fish used in preparing soups, etc. **14** Raw material: paper *stock.* **15** *pl.* A timber frame with holes for confining the ankles and often the wrists, formerly used in punishing petty offenders. **16** *pl.* The timber frame on which a vessel rests during construction. **17** *pl.* A frame for confining an animal for shoeing or veterinary treatment. **18** *Naut.* An anchor crossbar. **19** The wooden block suspending a bell. **20** In firearms: **a** The rear wooden portion of a rifle, musket, or shotgun, to which the barrel and mechanisms are secured. **b** The arm on rapid-fire guns connecting the shoulder piece to the slide. **c** The handle of a pistol or similar firearm. **d** That member of a gun carriage which usually bears the prolonge and trails along the ground. **21** The handle of certain instruments, as of a whip or fishing rod. **22** A theatrical stock company. **23** The collection of dramas produced by a theatrical stock company. **24** A broad stiffened band, formerly worn as a cravat. **25** *Geol.* The rounded mass of plutonic rock rising above ground level: also called *boss.* **26** *Mech.* An adjustable wrench used for grasping and turning thread-cutting dies. **27** An ornamental garden plant, as the gilliflower, or common stock *(Mathiola incana).* **28** In finance: **a** The capital or fund raised by a corporation through the sale of shares, which entitle the holder to interest or dividends and to part ownership of the corporation. The stockholder may not claim repayment of the principal, though he may sell his shares to other investors at the current market value. **b** The proportional part of this capital credited to an individual stockholder and represented by the number of shares he owns. **c** A certificate showing ownership of a specific number of shares. —**common stock** The stock of a corporation which entitles the holder to dividends, or a share in the profits, only after all other obligations have been met and dividends have been rendered to the owners of preferred stock. Direction of a corporation is usually vested in the owners of common stock. —**debenture stock** *Brit.* A debenture of a corporation or public body issued in the form of stock, the certificates of which are usually transferable but not redeemable and entitle the holder to a perpetual annuity. —**no-par stock** Stock issued without a face value on the certificate and sold at whatever price it will command on the market. —**preferred stock** The stock of a corporation which gives the holder prior claim to dividends up to a certain amount. —**to take stock 1** To take an inventory. **2** To make a careful estimate or appraisal. —**to take stock in** To have trust or belief in; give credence to. —*v.t.* **1** To furnish with stock; supply with cattle, as a farm, or with merchandise, as a store. **2** To keep for sale: to *stock* black ink. **3** To put aside for future use.

4 To provide with a handle or stock. **5** *Obs.* To put (a person) in the stocks for punishment. — *v.i.* **6** To lay in supplies or stock: often with *up.* **7** To send out new shoots; sprout. — *adj.* **1** Kept continually ready or constantly brought forth, like old goods: a *stock* joke. **2** Kept on hand: a *stock* size. **3** Banal; commonplace: a *stock* phrase. **4** Used for breeding purposes: a *stock* mare. **5** Employed in handling or caring for the stock: a *stock* clerk. — *adv.* Motionlessly; like a stump or block of wood: used in combination: *stockstill.* [OE *stocc*]

  Synonyms (noun): accumulation, capital, fund, hoard, material, provision, store, supply. See STOCK.

stock·ade (sto·kād′) *n.* **1** A line of stout posts, stakes, etc., set upright in the earth to form a fence or barrier; also, the area thus enclosed. **2** Specifically, a strong, high barrier of upright posts, stakes, etc., formerly used by American settlers as a defense against Indians. **3** A breakwater of piling, as for protecting a pier. — *v.t.* **·ad·ed, ·ad·ing** To surround or fortify with a stockade. [< OF *estocade, estacade* < *estaque* a stake < Gmc.]

stock·breed·er (stok′brē′dər) *n.* One who breeds and raises livestock.

stock·breed·ing (stok′brē′ding) *n.* The breeding and raising of livestock.

stock·bro·ker (stok′brō′kər) *n.* One who buys and sells stocks or securities for others. — **stock′bro′ker·age, stock′bro′king** *n.*

stock car 1 An automobile, as one selected at random, typifying the regular factory stock. **2** Such an automobile, usually a sedan, modified for racing.

stock company 1 An incorporated company that issues stock. **2** A more or less permanent dramatic company under one management, which presents a series of theater pieces.

stock exchange 1 A place where securities are bought and sold. **2** An association of stockbrokers who transact business in stocks, bonds, and other shares.

stock fish Cod, haddock, or the like, cured by splitting and drying in the air, unsalted.

stock·hold·er (stok′hōl′dər) *n.* One who holds certificates of ownership in a company or corporation.

Stock·holm (stok′hōm, *Sw.* stôk′hôlm) The capital of Sweden, a port on the east coast, on the Baltic Sea; called "the Venice of the North" because of its waterways.

stock·i·net (stok′i·net′) *n.* **1** An elastic knitted fabric used chiefly for undergarments. **2** A style of knitting in which the rows are alternately knitted and purled: also **stockinet stitch.** Also **stock′i·nette′.** [Alter. of *stockinget* < STOCKING + -ET]

stock·ing (stok′ing) *n.* **1** A close-fitting woven or knitted covering for the foot and lower leg. **2** Something resembling such a covering. [< STOCK, in obs. sense of "a stocking" + -ING] — **stock′ing·less** *adj.*

stock in trade 1 The goods which a storekeeper has for sale. **2** Resources, either material or spiritual.

stock·ish (stok′ish) *adj.* Like a stock or block of wood; stupid.

stock·job·ber (stok′job′ər) *n.* A dealer or speculator in stocks in his own interest; also, a stockbroker. — **stock′job′ber·y, stock′job′bing** *n.*

stock market 1 A stock exchange. **2** The business transacted in such a place: The *stock market* was active. **3** The rise and fall of prices of securities.

stock·pile (stok′pīl′) *n.* A storage pile of materials or supplies. Also **stock pile.** — *v.t. & v.i.* **·piled, ·pil·ing** To accumulate a supply or stockpile (of).

stock·pot (stok′pot′) *n.* A pot for preparing and keeping soup stock.

stock·rais·ing (stok′rā′zing) *n.* Breeding and raising of livestock. — **stock′·rais′er** *n.*

stock·room (stok′rōōm′, -rōōm′) *n.* A room where reserve stocks of goods are stored.

stock·still (stok′stil′) *adj.* Still as a stock or post; motionless.

stock·whip (stok′wip′) *Austral.* A whip used by stockmen, usually of kangaroo hide with a seven- to eight-foot lash and a cord or horsehair cracker.

stock·y (stok′ē) *adj.* **stock·i·er, stock·i·est** Short and stout; thick-set. — **stock′i·ly** *adv.* — **stock′·i·ness** *n.*

stock·yard (stok′yärd′) *n.* A large yard with pens, stables, etc., where cattle are kept ready for shipping, slaughter, etc.

stodg·y (stoj′ē) *adj.* **stodg·i·er, stodg·i·est 1** Distended; crammed full; bulky; lumpy. **2** Stupid; dull; heavy. **3** Indigestible; satiating. **4** Sticky; muddy. **5** Thick-set; clumsy and stiff. — **stodg′i·ly** *adv.* — **stodg′i·ness** *n.*

sto·gy (stō′gē) *n. pl.* **·gies 1** A stout, coarse boot or shoe. **2** A long, slender, inexpensive cigar: also **sto′gie.** [Earlier *stoga* < (CONE)-STOGA (WAGON), because their drivers wore heavy boots and smoked coarse cigars]

sto·ic (stō′ik) *n.* A person apparently unaffected by pleasure or pain. — *adj.* Indifferent to pleasure or pain; impassive; uncomplaining. Also **sto′i·cal.** — **sto′i·cal·ly** *adv.* — **sto′i·cal·ness** *n.*

Sto·ic (stō′ik) *n.* A member of a school of Greek philosophy founded by Zeno about 308 B.C., holding the pantheistic beliefs that the world is a manifestation of a divine mind, that there is no reality but matter, even the human soul being doomed to dissolution, that wisdom lies in being superior to passion, joy, grief, etc., and in submission to the divine will. — *adj.* Of or pertaining to the Stoics or Stoicism. [< L *Stoicus* < Gk. *Stoikos* < *Stoa (Poikilē)* (Painted) Porch, the colonnade at Athens where Zeno taught]

stoi·chi·om·e·try (stoi′kē·om′ə·trē) *n.* The branch of chemistry that treats of the proportions of elements or compounds involved in reactions, and the methods of calculating them. Also **stoe′chi·om′e·try, stoi′chei·om′e·try.** [< Gk. *stoicheion* element + -METRY] — **stoi′chi·o·met′ric** (-ə·met′rik) or **·ri·cal** *adj.*

stoke[1] (stōk) *v.t. & v.i.* **stoked, stok·ing** To supply (a furnace) with fuel; stir up or tend (a fire or furnace). [Back formation < STOKER]

stoke[2] (stōk) *n. Physics* A unit of kinematic viscosity, equivalent to 1 poise in a fluid having a density of 1 gram per cubic centimeter referred to a specified temperature. [after Sir George G. *Stokes*, 1819–1903, English mathematician and physicist]

stoke·hole (stōk′hōl′) *n.* **1** The space about the mouth of a furnace; the fireroom. **2** The mouth of a furnace. **3** A stokehold.

stok·er (stō′kər) *n.* **1** One who or that which supplies fuel to a furnace, especially of a steam boiler, as in a ship or locomotive; a fireman on a locomotive, ship, etc. **2** A device for feeding coal to a furnace. [< Du. < *stoken* stir a fire < *stok* stick]

stole[1] (stōl) *n.* **1** *Eccl.* A long, narrow band, usually of decorated silk or linen, worn about the shoulders by priests and bishops, and over the left shoulder only by deacons, when officiating; loosely, any ecclesiastical vestment. **2** A fur, scarf, or garment resembling a stole, worn by women. **3** In ancient Rome, a long outer garment worn by matrons. [OE < L *stola* a robe < Gk. *stolē* a garment] — **stoled** *adj.*

stol·id (stol′id) *adj.* Having or expressing no power of feeling or perceiving; impassible; dull. See synonyms under BRUTISH, HEAVY. [< L *stolidus* dull] — **sto·lid·i·ty** (stə·lid′ə·tē), **stol′id·ness** *n.* — **stol′id·ly** *adv.*

sto·lon (stō′lon) *n.* **1** *Bot.* **a** A trailing branch that is capable of taking root. **b** A runner or rootstock by which grasses may propagate. **2** *Zool.* A prolongation of the body of various animals, as corals. [< NL < L *stolo, stolonis*]

sto·ma (stō′mə) *n. pl.* **sto·ma·ta** (stō′mə·tə, stom′ə·tə) **1** A minute orifice; pore. **2** *Biol.* An aperture in the walls of blood vessels or in serous membranes, or in the epidermis of leaves, young stems, etc. [< Gk. *stoma* mouth]

–stoma See -STOME.

stom·ach (stum′ək) *n.* **1** The pouchlike, highly vascular dilation of the alimentary canal, situated in most vertebrates between the esophagus and the small intestine, and serving as one of the principal organs of digestion. ◆ Collateral adjective: *gastric.* **2** Any digestive cavity, as of an invertebrate. **3** The abdomen; belly: an anatomically incorrect use. **4** Desire

for food; appetite; hence, any desire or inclination. **5** Temper; spirit. **6** *Obs.* Pride; haughtiness. — *v.t.* **1** To accept without apparent opposition; to put up with; endure. **2** To take into and retain in the stomach; digest. **3** *Obs.* To resent. [< OF *estomac* < L *stomachus* < Gk. *stomachos* gullet, stomach < *stoma* a mouth]

stomach ache Pain in the stomach, as from indigestion or inflammation.

stom·ach·er (stum′ək·ər) *n.* A former ornamental article of dress for the breast and stomach.

stomach tooth *Dent.* A lower canine tooth of the first dentition: so called because its emergence is frequently accompanied by digestive disturbances.

stomach worm Any of various nematode worms which are parasitic in the stomachs of man and animals, especially the sheep stomach worm *(Haemonchus contortus).*

sto·mat·ic (stō·mat′ik) *adj.* **1** Of or pertaining to the mouth. **2** Of, pertaining to, or like a stoma.

sto·ma·tif·er·ous (stō′mə·tif′ər·əs, stom′ə-) *adj.* Bearing stomata. [< STOMAT(O)- + -(I)FEROUS]

sto·ma·ti·tis (stō′mə·tī′tis, stom′ə-) *n. Pathol.* Inflammation of the mouth.

stomato– *combining form* The mouth; of or pertaining to the mouth: *stomatoplasty.* Also, before vowels, **stomat-.** [< Gk. *stoma, stomatos* the mouth]

sto·ma·tol·o·gy (stō′mə·tol′ə·jē, stom′ə-) *n.* The science treating of the mouth and of its diseases.

sto·ma·to·plas·ty (stō′mə·tə·plas′tē, stom′ə-) *n.* Plastic surgery of the mouth.

sto·ma·to·pod (stō′mə·tə·pod′, stom′ə-) *n.* Any of an order *(Stomatopoda)* of crustaceans having abdominal gills and legs near the mouth, including the squills. — **sto′ma·top′o·dous** (-top′ə·dəs) *adj.*

sto·ma·tous (stō′mə·təs, stom′ə-) *adj.* Having a stoma or stomata.

–stome *combining form* Mouth; mouthlike opening: *peristome.* Also spelled *-stoma.* [< Gk. *stoma* the mouth]

sto·mo·de·um (stō′mə·dē′əm, stom′ə-) *n. pl.* **·de·a** (-dē′ə) *Biol.* The invagination of the ectoderm, or outer layer of the embryo, that forms the mouth. Also **sto′mo·dae′um.** [< NL < Gk. *stoma* mouth + *hodaios* on the way < *hodos* way] — **sto′mo·de′al** or **·dae′al** *adj.*

–stomous *combining form* Having a (specified kind of) mouth: *microstomous.* Also **–stomatous.** [< Gk. *stoma, stomatos* the mouth]

stomp (stomp) *Dial. v.t. & v.i.* To stamp; tread heavily (upon). — *n.* A dance involving a heavy and lively step. [Var. of STAMP]

–stomy *combining form Surg.* An operation to form an artificial opening for or into (a specified organ or part): *colostomy, ileostomy.* [< Gk. *stoma* the mouth]

stone (stōn) *n.* **1** A small piece of rock, as a cobble or pebble. **2** Rock, or a piece of rock hewn or shaped; a milestone; a gravestone; hard, concreted mineral or earthy matter. **3** A precious stone; gem. **4** Anything resembling a stone in shape or hardness: a *hailstone.* **5** *Pathol.* A stony concretion in the bladder, or a disease characterized by such concretions. **6** *Bot.* The hard covering of the kernel in a fruit. **7** *(pl.* **stone)** *Brit.* A measure of weight, avoirdupois, usually 14 pounds. **8** A testicle: usually in the plural. **9** *Printing* An imposing table for type, whether made of stone or metal. — *adj.* **1** Made of stone: a *stone* ax. **2** Made of coarse hard earthenware: a *stone* bottle. **3** Characterized by the use of stone implements: the *Stone Age.* — *v.t.* **stoned, ston·ing 1** To hurl stones at; pelt or kill with stones. **2** To remove the stones or pits from. **3** To furnish or line, as a well, with stone. **4** To castrate; geld, as a hog. **5** *Obs.* To make hard or unyielding, as the heart. [OE *stān*] — **ston′er** *n.*

Stone Age The earliest known period of the cultural evolution of mankind, marked by the creation and use of stone implements and weapons, preceding the Bronze Age, and subdivided into the Eolithic, Paleolithic, and Neolithic periods.

stone·boat (stōn′bōt′) *n. U.S.* A runnerless

plank sled used for transporting rocks or similar heavy objects or, when weighted, dragged across a field to break clods of earth, etc.; also, a platform swung under the axles of a wagon.

stone·break (stōn′brāk′) *n.* Saxifrage.

stone–broke (stōn′brōk′) *adj. Colloq.* Without any money; having no funds. Also **ston′y-broke′.**

stone·chat (stōn′chat′) *n.* A small thrushlike European bird (genus *Saxicola*) with upper parts black and breast dark–reddish. [< STONE + CHAT¹ (def. 2); from its cry suggesting the knocking together of pebbles]

stone·crop (stōn′krop′) *n.* A low spreading mosslike herb (*Sedum acre*) with small fleshy leaves and yellow flowers.

stone·cut·ter (stōn′kut′ər) *n.* One who or that which cuts stone; specifically, a machine for facing stone. —**stone′cut′ting** *n.*

stoned (stōnd) *adj.* **1** Having the stones removed: *stoned* peaches. **2** *U.S. Slang* Intoxicated, as by liquor, marihuana, or a narcotic.

stone–deaf (stōn′def′) *adj.* Completely deaf.

stone fly A plecopteran.

stone fruit A fruit having a stone; a drupe.

stone·ma·son (stōn′mā′sən) *n.* One whose occupation or trade is to prepare and lay stones in building. —**stone′ma′son·ry** *n.*

stone parsley An Old World herb of the parsley family, especially a British perennial (*Sison amomum*) with cream–colored flowers and aromatic seeds.

stone roller 1 A cyprinoid fish (*Campostoma anomalum*) of North America. **2** A North American sucker (*Catastomus nigricans*).

stone's throw (stōnz) **1** The distance a stone may be cast by hand. **2** A short distance.

stone·still (stōn′stil′) *adj.* Perfectly motionless.

stone·wall (stōn′wôl′) *v.i.* **1** In cricket, to play on the defensive so as to secure a draw. **2** *Austral.* To oppose by a policy of obstruction; filibuster: a political term. **3** *U.S. Slang* To act in a calculatedly obstructive way, as by lying or failing to respond to inquiry. —*v.t.* **4** *U.S. Slang* To respond to by stonewalling.

stone wall A wall built of stone; especially, a fence built of stones.

stone·ware (stōn′wâr′) *n.* A variety of very hard, glazed pottery, made from siliceous clay or clay mixed with flint or sand.

stone·work (stōn′wûrk′) *n.* **1** Work concerned with cutting or setting stone; work made of stone. **2** *pl.* A place where stone is shaped or stoneware is made. —**stone′work′er** *n.*

stone·wort (stōn′wûrt′) *n.* Any of a genus (*Chara*) of green algae growing submerged in fresh or brackish waters and often incrusted with deposits of calcium carbonate.

ston·y (stō′nē) *adj.* **ston·i·er, ston·i·est 1** Abounding in stone. **2** Made or consisting of stone. **3** Hard as stone; hence, unfeeling or inflexible. **4** Converting into stone; petrifying; cold and stiff. **5** *Slang* Stone–broke; having no money. —**ston′i·ly** *adv.* —**ston′i·ness** *n.*

stooge (stōōj) *Colloq. n.* **1** An actor placed in the audience to heckle a comedian on the stage. **2** An actor who feeds lines to the principal comedian, acts as a foil for his jokes, etc. **3** Anyone who acts as or is the tool or dupe of another. —*v.i.* **stooged, stooging** To act as a stooge: usually with *for*. [Origin unknown]

stool (stōōl) *n.* **1** A backless and armless seat intended for one person. **2** A low bench or portable support for the feet or for the knees in kneeling. **3** A seat used in defecating; a privy. **4** The matter evacuated from the bowels. **5** *Bot.* **a** A plant from which young plants are produced, as from runners. **b** A stump or root of any kind from which suckers or sprouts shoot up. **c** The shoots from such a root or stump. **6** A decoy, as a bird or likeness of one. —*v.i.* **1** To send up shoots or suckers. **2** To decoy wild fowl with a stool or stools. **3** To void feces. **4** *U.S. Slang* To be a stool pigeon; inform. [OE *stōl*]

stool pigeon 1 A living or artificial pigeon attached to a stool or perch to decoy others. **2** Any decoy, as a person employed to decoy others into a gambling house, etc. **3** *U.S. Slang* An informer or spy, especially for the police.

stoop¹ (stōōp) *v.i.* **1** To bend or lean the body forward and down; bow; crouch. **2** To

stand or walk with the upper part of the body habitually bent forward; slouch. **3** To bend; lean; sink: said of trees, cliffs, etc. **4** To lower or degrade oneself; condescend; deign. **5** To pounce or swoop, as a hawk on prey. **6** *Obs.* To submit; yield. —*v.t.* **7** To bend (one's head, shoulders, etc.) forward. **8** *Obs.* To humble or subdue. See synonyms under BEND¹. —*n.* **1** An act of stooping; a downward and forward bending of the body; also, a habitual forward inclination of the head and shoulders. **2** A decline from dignity or superiority. **3** A swoop, as of a bird of prey. [OE *stūpian*]

stoop² (stōōp) *n. U.S.* **1** Originally, a platform at the door of a house approached by steps and having seats. **2** A small porch or platform at the entrance to a house. [< Du. *stoep*]

stop (stop) *v.* **stopped** or (*chiefly Poetic*) **stopt, stop·ping** *v.t.* **1** To bring (something in motion) to a halt; arrest the progress of: to *stop* an automobile. **2** To prevent the doing or completion of: to *stop* a revolution. **3** To prevent (a person) from doing something; restrain. **4** To keep back, withhold, or cut off, as wages or supplies. **5** To cease doing; desist from; discontinue: *Stop* that! **6** To intercept in transit, as a letter. **7** To block up, obstruct, or clog (a passage, road, etc.): often with *up*. **8** To fill in, cover over, or otherwise close, as a hole, cavity, etc. **9** To close (a bottle, barrel, etc.) with a cork, plug, or other stopper. **10** To stanch (a wound, etc.). **11** To order a bank not to pay or honor: to *stop* a check. **12** To defeat; also, to kill. **13** *Music* To press down (a string) on the fingerboard, or to close (a finger hole) in order to vary pitch. **14** To punctuate. **15** In boxing, etc., to parry. —*v.i.* **16** To come to a halt; cease progress or motion. **17** To cease doing something; pause or desist. **18** To come to an end. See synonyms under ABIDE, ARREST, CEASE, END, HINDER¹, OBSTRUCT, REST¹, SHUT, STAND, SUSPEND. —**to stop off** To stop for a brief stay before continuing on a trip or journey. —**to stop over** *Colloq.* **1** To stay at a place temporarily. **2** To interrupt a journey; make a stopover. —*n.* **1** The act of stopping, or the state of being stopped; a halt; pause; cessation; end. **2** That which stops or limits the range or time of a movement: a camera *stop*; an obstruction or obstacle; a hindrance. **3** *Music* The pressing down of a string or the closing of an aperture on a musical instrument, to change the pitch of the tone emitted; a key, lever, or handle for stopping a string or an aperture; a fret for a guitar. **4** *Music* In an organ, a set of pipes or reeds producing tones of the same quality, and arranged in regular musical progression. **5 a** *Brit.* A punctuation mark; a period. **b** In cables, etc., a period. **6** In joinery, a block, pin, or the like to check sliding motion, as of a drawer. **7** *Naut.* A small line for lashing or fastening anything temporarily on a ship. **8** *Phonet.* **a** Complete blockage of the breath stream (implosion), as with the lips or tongue, followed by a sudden release (explosion). **b** A consonant so produced; a plosive: opposed to *continuant.* The stops in English are the bilabials (p) and (b), the alveolars (t) and (d), and the velars (k) and (g); the nasals (m) and (n) may also be included in this category. **9** In dogs, the short incline between the forepart of the skull and the face. See illustration under DOG. **10** *pl.* A card game in which certain cards, called **stop cards,** terminate play when they appear: a variety of *newmarket.* [OE *-stoppian*, as in *forstoppian* stop up]

stop·cock (stop′kok′) *n.* A faucet or short pipe having a valve for stopping or regulating the passage of liquid, gas, etc.

stop·gap (stop′gap′) *n.* That which stops a gap; also, an expedient.

stop key A key so made that when inserted in one side of a lock no key may be used on the other.

stop knob The knob by which a set of organ pipes is opened.

stop light 1 A red light on a traffic sign, directing a motorist or pedestrian to stop. **2** A red light on the rear of a motor vehicle which shines upon application of the brakes.

stop order An order to an agent or stockbroker to buy or sell a stock at the market only

when it reaches a specified price.

stop·o·ver (stop′ō′vər) *adj.* Giving permission to stop over, as a railway ticket. —*n.* A stopover check, the act of stopping over, or permission to stop over, as from one train to a later train. Also **stop′– off′.**

stop·page (stop′ij) *n.* **1** The act of stopping or the state of being stopped. **2** A deduction from pay to repay something.

stop payment An order to a bank to refuse payment on a certain check.

stop·per (stop′ər) *n.* **1** One who or that which stops up or closes. **2** A plug or cork, as in a bottle. **3** In card games, as bridge, a card that can be used to stop an opponent's successful play of cards of one suit. —*v.t.* To secure or close with a stopper.

stop·ple (stop′əl) *n.* A stopper, plug, cork, or bung. —*v.t.* **·pled, ·pling** To close with or as with a stopple. [ME *stoppel*, prob. < *stoppen* stop]

stop sign A sign in a traffic system, instructing a pedestrian or vehicle to stop.

stop·watch (stop′woch′) *n.* A watch which has a hand indicating fractions of a second and which may be stopped or started by the pressure of a spring: used for timing races, etc.

stor·age (stôr′ij, stō′rij) *n.* **1** The depositing of articles in a warehouse for safekeeping. **2** Space for storing goods. **3** A charge for storing. **4** A section of a computer in which data is held for later use; memory.

STORAGE BATTERY
a. Positive plate.
b. Positive terminal.
c. Vent cap or plug.
d. Negative terminal.
e. Electrolyte space.
f. Separator.
g. Negative plate.

storage battery A connected group of two or more electrolytic cells for the generation of electric energy by the passage of a current which, on being reversed in direction, serves to recharge the cells for another period of use.

sto·rax (stôr′aks, stō′raks) *n.* **1** A fragrant balsam obtained from the wood and inner bark of either of two trees (*Liquidambar orientalis*, or *L. styraciflua*) of Asia Minor: used in medicine and as a perfume. **2** A gum resin obtained from certain trees of a family (*Styracaceae*), especially *Styrax officinalis.* [< L < Gk. *styrax*]

store (stôr, stōr) *v.t.* **stored, stor·ing 1** To put away for future use; to accumulate. **2** To furnish or supply; provide. **3** To place in a warehouse or other place of deposit for safekeeping. —*n.* **1** That which is stored or laid up against future need; hence, a large amount or stock. **2** *pl.* Supplies, as of ammunition, arms, or clothing; necessary articles, especially of food. **3** A place where commodities are stored; warehouse. **4** *U.S.* A place where merchandise of any kind is kept for sale; a shop. See synonyms under HEAP, STOCK. —**department store** A large retail establishment selling various types of merchandise and service, and organized by departments. —**in store** Set apart for the future; forthcoming; impending. —**to set store by** To value or esteem; regard. [Aphetic var. of earlier *astore* < OF *estorer* erect, equip, store < L *instaurare* restore, erect]

store·house (stôr′hous′, stōr′–) *n.* A building in which goods are stored; a warehouse; depository.

store·keep·er (stôr′kē′pər, stōr′–) *n.* **1** A person who keeps a retail store or shop; a shopkeeper. **2** One who has charge of receiving and distributing stores; especially, one in charge of naval or military stores.

store·room (stôr′rōōm′, -rōōm′, stōr′–) *n.* A room in which things are stored, as supplies.

sto·ried¹ (stôr′ēd, stō′rēd) *adj.* Having or consisting of stories, as a building: usually in compounds: a six–*storied* house. Also **sto′· reyed.**

sto·ried[2] (stôr′ēd, stō′rēd) *adj.* **1** Having a notable history. **2** Related in a story. **3** Ornamented with designs representing scenes from history or story.

WHITE STORK
(About 20 inches tall)

sto·ri·ette (stôr′ē·et′, stō′rē-) *n.* A short story or tale.

stork (stôrk) *n.* A wading bird with a long neck and long legs (family *Ciconiidae*), related to the herons and ibises, especially the Old World **migratory** or **white stork** (*Ciconia ciconia*), which often nests on buildings. [OE *storc*]

stork's-bill (stôrks′bil′) *n.* **1** Heronbill. **2** Any species of pelargonium.

storm (stôrm) *n.* **1** A disturbance of the atmosphere, generally a great whirling motion of the air, accompanied by rain, snow, etc. **2** In the Beaufort scale, a wind force of the 11th degree. **3** Figuratively, a furious flight or shower of objects, especially of missiles. **4** A violent outburst, as of passion or excitement: a *storm* of applause or rage. **5** *Mil.* A violent and rapid assault on a fortified place. **6** A violent commotion, as in politics, society, or domestic life. — *v.i.* **1** To blow with violence; rain, snow, hail, etc., heavily: used impersonally: It *stormed* all day. **2** To be very angry; rage. **3** To move or rush with violence or rage: He *stormed* about the room. — *v.t.* **4** *Mil.* To take or try to take by storm. [OE]
Synonyms (noun): agitation, disturbance, tempest. A *storm* is properly a *disturbance* of the atmosphere, with or without rain, snow, hail, or thunder and lightning. Thus we have *rainstorm, snowstorm,* etc., and by extension, *magnetic storm,* etc. A *tempest* is a *storm* of extreme violence, always attended with some precipitation, as of rain, from the atmosphere. In the moral and figurative use *tempest* commonly implies greater intensity. We speak of *agitation* of feeling, *disturbance* of mind, a *storm* of passion, a *tempest* of rage. See WIND. *Antonyms:* calm, hush, peace, serenity, stillness, tranquillity.

storm cellar A cyclone cellar.

storm center 1 *Meteorol.* The center or place of lowest pressure and comparative calm in a cyclonic storm. **2** The central point of a heated argument; the focus of any trouble or turmoil.

storm door A strong outer door for added protection during storms and inclement weather.

storm petrel Any of certain petrels of the North Atlantic; especially, *Hydrobates pelagicus,* thought to portend storm. Also **stormy petrel.**

storm·proof (stôrm′prōōf′) *adj.* Capable of keeping out storms.

storm trooper A member of the Nazi party militia unit, the *Sturmabteilung.*

storm warning A signal, as a flag or light, used to warn mariners of coming storm. Also **storm signal.**

storm window An extra window outside the ordinary one as a protection against storms or for greater insulation against cold.

storm·y (stôr′mē) *adj.* **storm·i·er, storm·i·est 1** Characterized by storms; boisterous; also, turbulent; violent: a *stormy* life. **2** Accompanying storms; also, passionate. See synonyms under BLEAK[1]. [OE *stormig*] — **storm′-i·ly** *adv.* — **storm′i·ness** *n.*

sto·ry[1] (stôr′ē, stō′rē) *n. pl.* **·ries 1** A narrative or recital of an event, or a series of events, whether real or fictitious. **2** A narrative, usually of fictitious events, intended to entertain a reader or hearer; a short tale. **3** An account or allegation of the facts relating to a particular person, thing, or incident: He tells a more plausible *story* of the conflict. **4** A news article in a newspaper or magazine. **5** The material for a news article. **6** An anecdote. **7** *Colloq.* A lie; falsehood. **8** The series of events in a novel, play, etc. **9** Celebrated or romantic legend or history: to live

on in *story.* — *v.t.* **·ried, ·ry·ing 1** To relate as a story. **2** To adorn with designs representing scenes from history, legend, etc. [<OF *estoire* <L *historia.* Doublet of HISTORY.]
Synonyms (noun): allegory, anecdote, incident, narrative, recital, record, relation, tale. *Tale* is nearly synonymous with *story,* but is somewhat archaic; it is used for an imaginative, legendary, or fictitious *recital,* especially if of ancient date; as, a fairy *tale*; also, for an idle or malicious report; as, Do not tell *tales.* See FICTION, HISTORY, REPORT.

sto·ry[2] (stôr′ē, stō′rē) *n. pl.* **·ries** A division in a building comprising the space between two successive floors; a floor; habitable rooms on the same level; also, a horizontal architectural division of a building: also spelled *storey.* [Special use of STORY[1]; ? from earlier sense of "a tier of painted windows or sculptures that narrated an event"]

story board 1 A bulletin board in a newspaper office on which are posted reportorial assignments to specific stories. **2** The set of original drawings illustrating each stage in the sequence of a motion picture, television program, animated cartoon, etc.

sto·ry·tell·er (stôr′ē·tel′ər, stō′rē-) *n.* **1** One who relates stories or anecdotes. **2** *Colloq.* A prevaricator; liar; fibber. — **sto′ry·tell′ing** *n. & adj.*

stout (stout) *adj.* **1** Strong or firm of structure or material; sound; tough. **2** Determined; resolute. **3** Fat; bulky; thick-set. **4** Strong in effects or active qualities; substantial; solid. **5** Having muscular strength; robust. **6** Proud; stubborn. See synonyms under CORPULENT, STAUNCH, STRONG. — *n.* **1** A stout person. **2** A dress or suit made for a stout person.

STORM WARNINGS
A. Daylight signals.   *B.* Night signals.
a. Small-craft warning.   *b.* Gale.   *c.* Whole gale.
d. Hurricane.

3 A strong, very dark porter or ale: also **brown stout.** [<OF *estout* bold, strong <Gmc. Cf. MDu. *stolt* bold.] — **stout′ly** *adv.* — **stout′ness** *n.*

stout-heart·ed (stout′här′tid) *adj.* Brave; courageous. — **stout′heart′ed·ly** *adv.* — **stout′-heart′ed·ness** *n.*

stove (stōv) *n.* **1** An apparatus, usually of metal, in which fuel is consumed for heating or cooking. **2** A drying room or box used in some factories. **3** An artificially heated greenhouse. **4** A pottery kiln. [OE *stofa* a heated room]

stove·pipe (stōv′pīp′) *n.* **1** A pipe, usually of thin sheet iron, for conducting the smoke and gases of combustion from a stove to a chimney flue. **2** *U.S. Colloq.* A tall silk hat: also **stovepipe hat.**

sto·ver (stō′vər) *n.* Fodder or feed for cattle; cornstalks. [<OF *estover.* See ESTOVERS.]

stow (stō) *v.t.* **1** To place or arrange compactly; pack. **2** To fill by packing. **3** To have room for; hold: said of a room, receptacle, etc. **4** *Slang* To stop; cease. **5** *Obs.* To furnish lodging for. — **to stow away 1** To put in a place of safekeeping, hiding, etc. **2** To be a stowaway. [OE *stōwian* <*stōw* a place]

stow·age (stō′ij) *n.* **1** The act or manner of stowing, or the state of being packed away. **2** Space for stowing goods. **3** Charge for stowing goods. **4** The goods stowed.

stow·a·way (stō′ə·wā′) *n.* One who conceals himself, as on a vessel, to obtain free passage.

STP (es′tē′pē′) *n.* A hallucinogenic drug chemically related to mescaline and amphetamine. [<*STP,* a trade name for a gasoline additive supposed to increase engine power]

St. Paul (sānt pôl′) The capital of Minnesota, in the SE part of the State, on the Mississippi River: one of the Twin Cities.

stra·bis·mus (strə·biz′məs) *n. Pathol.* A condition in which the eyes cannot be simultaneously focused on the same spot: when one or both eyes turn inward, the patient is *cross-eyed*; when outward, *walleyed.* [<NL <Gk. *strabismos* < *strabizein* squint < *strabos* twisted] — **stra·bis′mal, stra·bis′mic** *adj.*

stra·bot·o·my (strə·bot′ə·mē) *n. Surg.* The cutting of the eyeball muscles to correct strabismus. [<Gk. *strabos* oblique + -TOMY]

strad·dle (strad′l) *v.* **·dled, ·dling** *v.i.* **1** To stand, walk, or sit with the legs spread apart. **2** To stand wide apart: said of the legs. **3** *Colloq.* To appear to favor both sides of an issue; refuse to commit oneself. — *v.t.* **4** To stand, walk, or sit with the legs on either side of. **5** To spread (the legs) wide apart. **6** *Colloq.* To appear to favor both sides of (an issue). **7** *Mil.* To fire shots both beyond and in front of (a target) so as to determine the range. — *n.* **1** A going, standing, or sitting with legs wide apart; the space between the feet or legs of one who straddles. **2** A noncommittal or vacillating position in any issue. **3** A stock transaction in which the holder obtains the privilege of either delivering or calling for a stock at a fixed price. **4** A long position in some stocks while being short in others. **5** *Mil.* Successive range settings that have bracketed the target. [Freq. of STRIDE] — **strad′dler** *n.* — **strad′dling·ly** *adv.*

strafe (strāf, sträf) *v.t.* **strafed, straf·ing 1** To attack (troops, emplacements, etc.) with machine-gun fire from low-flying airplanes. **2** To bombard or shell heavily. **3** *Slang* To punish. — *n.* A heavy bombardment. [<G *strafen* punish] — **straf′er** *n.*

strag·gle (strag′əl) *v.i.* **·gled, ·gling 1** To wander from the road, main body, etc.; stray. **2** To wander aimlessly about; ramble. **3** To occur at irregular intervals. [? Freq. of obs. *strake* move, go about] — **strag′gler** *n.*

strag·gly (strag′lē) *adj.* **·li·er, ·li·est** Scattered or spread out irregularly.

straight (strāt) *adj.* **1** Extending uniformly in the same direction without curve or bend. **2** Free from kinks; not curly, as hair. **3** Not stooped or inclined; erect, as in posture. **4** Not deviating from truth, fairness, or honesty; accurate; honest; upright; reliable; also, candid. **5** Free from obstruction; uninterrupted; unbroken. **6** Correctly kept, ordered, or arranged. **7** Sold without discount for number or quantity taken. **8** *Colloq.* Adhering without reservation or exception to a particular party or policy; representing the regular or older organization; accepting the whole, as of a plan, party, or policy: a *straight* ticket. **9** In poker, consisting of five cards forming a sequence: a *straight* flush. **10** Having nothing added; unmixed; undiluted: *straight* whisky. **11** *Slang* Conforming to what is accepted as usual, normal, or conventional, especially according to middle-class standards. **12** *Slang* Heterosexual. — *n.* **1** A straight part or piece. **2** The part of a racecourse between the winning post and the last turn. **3** In poker, a numerical sequence of five cards not of the same suit, or a hand containing this. **4** A straight line. **5** *Slang* A conventional person. **6** *Slang* A heterosexual. — *adv.* **1** In a straight line or a direct course. **2** Closely in line; correspondingly. **3** At once; straightway. ◆ Homophone: *strait.* [ME *stregt* <OE *streht,* pp. of *streccan* stretch] — **straight′ly** *adv.* — **straight′ness** *n.*

straight-arm (strāt′ärm′) *v.t.* In football, to ward off (an opposing tackler) with the outstretched arm.

straight·a·way (strāt′ə·wā′) *adj.* Having no curve or turn; straightforward. — *n.* A straight course or track. — *adv.* At once; straightway.

straight·edge (strāt′ej′) *n.* A bar of wood or metal having one edge true to a straight line: used for ruling, etc. — **straight′-edged′** *adj.*

straight·en (strāt′n) *v.t.* 1 To make straight. 2 To lay out (a corpse). — *v.i.* 3 To become straight. — **to straighten out** To restore order to; set right; rectify. — **to straighten up** 1 To free from disorder; make neat; tidy. 2 To stand in erect posture. 3 To reform; become honorable or honest. — **straight′ener** *n.*

straight face A sober, expressionless, or unsmiling face. — **straight–faced** (strāt′fāst′) *adj.*

straight·for·ward (strāt′fôr′wərd) *adj.* Proceeding in a straight course or direct manner; frank. See synonyms under CANDID, CLEAR, HONEST, JUST[1], PLAIN[1]. — **straight′for′ward·ly** *adv.* — **straight′for′ward·ness** *n.*

straight man *U.S. Colloq.* An entertainer who acts as a foil for a comedian.

straight–out (strāt′out′) *adj.* 1 Showing the true sentiments or feelings; unreserved; also, shown without reserve. 2 Real; genuine.

straight ticket 1 A political party ballot or ticket that presents the regular party candidates without addition or change. 2 A ballot cast for all the candidates of one party. Compare SPLIT TICKET.

strain[1] (strān) *v.t.* 1 To pull or draw tight; stretch. 2 To exert to the utmost. 3 To injure by overexertion; sprain; also, to wrench or twist. 4 To deform in structure or shape as a result of pressure or stress. 5 To stretch beyond the true intent, proper limit, etc.: to *strain* a point. 6 To embrace tightly; hug. 7 To pass through a strainer (def. 2). 8 To remove by filtration. 9 *Mech.* To alter in size or shape by applying external force. 10 *Obs.* To force; constrain. — *v.i.* 11 To make violent efforts; strive. 12 To be or become wrenched or twisted. 13 To filter, trickle, or percolate. See synonyms under STRETCH. — **to strain at** 1 To push or pull with violent efforts. 2 To strive for. 3 To scruple or balk at accepting. — *n.* 1 An act of straining or the state of being strained; a violent effort or exertion. 2 The injury due to excessive tension or effort. 3 *Physics* Change of shape or size of a body, especially of a solid, produced by the action of a stress; deformation, temporary or permanent; thrust; force. [<OF *estrein-*, stem of *estreindre* <L *stringere* bind tight]

strain[2] (strān) *n.* 1 Line of descent, or the individuals, collectively, in that line; race; stock. 2 Inborn or hereditary disposition; natural tendency; trace; an element or admixture: to have a heroic *strain* in one's character. 3 *Biol.* A special line of individuals belonging to a certain race or species and maintained at a high standard of perfection by selection: said of animals or plants. 4 *Rare* Distinguishing nature or quality; kind; sort. 5 A section, in hymn tunes, divided off by a double bar; a melody; tune; air. 6 A distinctive portion of a poem; also, a composition in verse. 7 Prevailing tone, style, or manner; mood. [? Var. of ME *strene*, OE *strēon* offspring]

strain·er (strā′nər) *n.* 1 One who or that which strains. 2 A utensil or device, containing meshes or porous parts, through which liquids are passed to separate them from coarse particles. 3 A device used for tightening, strengthening, or stretching.

straining arch Any arch erected to exert a corrective strain or to resist a destructive strain in a building.

straining beam A tie beam receiving a lengthwise pulling stress, and connecting the rafters of a roof with the tops of the queenposts. Also **straining piece.**

strait (strāt) *adj.* 1 Of small transverse dimensions; narrow. 2 *Archaic* Restricted as to space or room; close; tight. 3 Destitute, as of money; needy. 4 *Archaic* Strict; rigorous. 5 *Obs.* Difficult; hard-pressed. — *n.* 1 A narrow passage of water connecting two larger bodies of water. 2 Any narrow pass or passage. 3 A position of perplexity or distress; necessity: frequently plural. 4 *Obs.* An isthmus. ◆ Homophone: *straight.* [<OF *estreit* <L *strictus,* pp. of *stringere* bind tight. Doublet of STRICT.] — **strait′ly** *adv.* — **strait′ness** *n.*

strait·en (strāt′n) *v.t.* 1 To make strait or narrow; contract; restrict. 2 To embarrass, as in finances; also, to distress; hamper. Also **strait.** See synonyms under SCRIMP.

strait·ened (strāt′nd) *adj.* 1 Contracted; narrowed. 2 Suffering privation or hardship, especially from pecuniary difficulties.

strait·jack·et (strāt′jak′it) *n.* 1 A tight jacket of strong canvas, for confining the arms of violent mental patients or prisoners. 2 Anything that unduly confines or restricts. — *v.t.* To confine in or as if in a straitjacket.

strait–laced (strāt′lāst′) *adj.* 1 Tightly laced, as stays; encased in tight corsets. 2 Strict, especially in morals or manners.

stra·min·e·ous (strə·min′ē·əs) *adj.* 1 Straw-colored. 2 Strawlike; chaffy. [<L *stramineus* <*stramen* straw]

stra·mo·ni·um (strə·mō′nē·əm) *n.* 1 The jimsonweed. 2 A drug prepared from the dried leaves and flowering tops of this plant, used as a sedative, especially in asthma. Also **stram·o·ny** (stram′ə·nē). [<NL <Med. L *stramonia,* ? ult. <Tatar *turman,* a medicine for horses]

strand[1] (strand) *n.* A shore or beach; especially, that portion of an ocean shore between high and low tides. See synonyms under BANK[1]. — *v.t. & v.i.* 1 To drive or run aground. 2 To leave or be left in straits or difficulties: usually in the passive. [OE *strand*]

strand[2] (strand) *n.* 1 One of the principal twists or members of a rope. 2 A fiber, hair, or the like. 3 Wires twisted into a cable. 4 Anything plaited or twisted. — *v.t.* 1 To break a strand of (a rope). 2 To make by twisting strands. [? <OF *estran* <Gmc.]

strand line A line marking the boundary between the shore and the ocean, especially a line higher than the present one.

strange (strānj) *adj.* 1 Previously unknown, unseen, or unheard of; unfamiliar. 2 Not according to the ordinary way; unaccountable; remarkable. 3 Pertaining to another or others; of a different class, character, or kind. 4 Foreign; alien. 5 Distant in manner; reserved; shy. 6 Inexperienced; unskilled; unaccustomed. See synonyms under ALIEN, EXTRAORDINARY, ODD, QUEER, RARE[1]. — *adv.* Strangely. [<OF *estrange* <L *extraneus* foreign <*extra* on the outside. Doublet of EXTRANEOUS.] — **strange′ly** *adv.* — **strange′ness** *n.*

stran·ger (strān′jər) *n.* 1 One who is not an acquaintance. 2 An unfamiliar visitor; guest. 3 A foreigner. 4 One unversed in or unacquainted or unfamiliar with something specified: with *to.* 5 *Law* Any person who is neither a party to a transaction nor privy to it. See synonyms under ALIEN. [<OF *estrangier* <*estrange.* See STRANGE.]

stran·gle (strang′gəl) *v.* **·gled, ·gling** *v.t.* 1 To choke to death; throttle; suffocate; stifle. 2 To repress; suppress. — *v.i.* 3 To suffer or die from strangulation. [<OF *estrangler* <L *strangulare* <Gk. *strangalaein* <*strangalē* a halter <*strangos* twisted] — **stran′gler** *n.*

strangle hold 1 In wrestling, a hold which chokes one's opponent: usually forbidden. 2 Any influence or power that chokes freedom or progress.

stran·gles (strang′gəlz) *n. pl.* An infectious bacterial disease of the horse characterized by fever and inflammation of the respiratory mucous membrane.

stran·gu·late (strang′gyə·lāt) *v.t.* **·lat·ed, ·lat·ing** 1 To strangle. 2 *Pathol.* To compress, contract, or obstruct, especially so as to cut off circulation of the blood or flow of fluid. — *adj.* Strangulated. [<L *strangulatus,* pp. of *strangulare.* See STRANGLE.]

stran·gu·lat·ed (strang′gyə·lā′tid) *adj. Pathol.* Characterized by strangulation.

strangulated hernia *Pathol.* A form of hernia in which the protruded organ or part is so tightly constricted as to cut off normal circulation of the blood, with possible necrosis and mortification.

stran·gu·la·tion (strang′gyə·lā′shən) *n.* 1 The act of strangling or the state of being strangled. 2 *Pathol.* The state of being strangulated; constriction of a part, as of the intestine in strangulated hernia, to cut off circulation.

stran·gu·ry (strang′gyə·rē) *n. Pathol.* Difficult and painful urination. [<L *stranguria* <Gk. *strangouria* <*stranx, strangos* a drop + *ouron* urine]

strap (strap) *n.* 1 A long, narrow, and flexible strip of leather or the like, usually having a buckle or other fastener, for binding about objects. 2 A razor strop. 3 A shoulder strap. 4 Something made of, resembling, or used as a strap. 5 A thin metal band or plate. — *v.t.* **strapped, strap·ping** 1 To fasten or bind with a strap. 2 To beat with a strap. 3 To sharpen or strop. 4 *Scot.* To hang. 5 To embarrass financially. [Var. of STROP] — **strap′less** *adj.*

strap hinge A hinge having long leaves, designed for attaching to the flat surfaces of a door and jamb. See illustration under HINGE.

strap·pa·do (strə·pā′dō, -pä′dō) *n. pl.* **·does** 1 A former punishment in which one was drawn up by a rope attached usually to the wrists, and let fall to the length of the rope; also, the machine used. 2 Erroneously, a beating with a strap. [<Ital. *strappata* a pulling, orig. fem. pp. of *strappare* pull]

strap·per (strap′ər) *n.* 1 One who uses a strap or straps. 2 One who bolts the straps to rails. 3 *Colloq.* A strong, tall person. 4 One who grooms horses.

strap·ping (strap′ing) *adj. Colloq.* Large and muscular; robust.

strass (stras) *n.* A lead glass of great brilliance used in the manufacture of gems; paste. [after Josef *Strasser,* 18th century German jeweler]

strasse (stras) *n.* Refuse of silk left in making skeins. [<F *strasse* <Ital. *straccio* rag, something torn <*stracciare* tear, lacerate]

strat·a·gem (strat′ə·jəm) *n.* 1 A maneuver designed to deceive or outwit an enemy in war. 2 A deception; any device for obtaining advantage. See synonyms under ARTIFICE. [<F *stratagème* <L *stratagema* <Gk. *stratēgēma* piece of generalship <*stratēgos* a general <*stratos* army + *agein* lead]

stra·te·gic (strə·tē′jik) *adj.* Of or pertaining to strategy; characterized by, used in, or having relation to strategy. Also **stra·te′gi·cal, strat·e·get·ic** (strat′ə·jet′ik) or **·i·cal.** — **stra·te′gi·cal·ly, strat′e·get′i·cal·ly** *adv.*

strategic material Any of several, chiefly raw, materials essential to national defense and industry, especially those that are wholly lacking or in insufficient supply within a nation's boundaries and have to be obtained from sources outside the country: the stockpiling of *strategic materials.*

stra·te·gics (strə·tē′jiks) *n. pl.* (construed as singular) The art or science of strategy; generalship.

strat·e·gist (strat′ə·jist) *n.* One versed in strategy, or skilled in managing affairs.

strat·e·gy (strat′ə·jē) *n. pl.* **·gies** 1 The science and art of conducting a military campaign by the combination and employment of means on a broad scale for gaining advantage in war; generalship: distinguished from *tactics.* 2 The use of stratagem or artifice, as in business, politics, etc. 3 Skill in management. [<F *stratégie* <Gk. *stratēgia* <*stratēgos* general. See STRATAGEM.]

strati– *combining form* A stratum; of or pertaining to a stratum or to strata: *stratiform.* Also, before vowels, **strat–.** [<L *stratum* a covering]

stra·tic·u·late (strə·tik′yə·lit, -lāt) *adj. Geol.* Arranged in thin layers or strata: said of sedimentary rocks and certain minerals, as the agate. [<NL *straticulum,* dim. of L *stratum* a layer + -ATE[1]] — **stra·tic′u·la′tion** *n.*

strat·i·form (strat′ə·fôrm) *adj.* 1 *Geol.* Having the form of or constituting a stratum. 2 *Anat.* Denoting a fibrous cartilage enclosed in a channel in a bone as a support for tendons. 3 *Meteorol.* Resembling a stratus. [<STRATI- + -FORM]

strat·i·fy (strat′ə·fī) *v.* **·fied, ·fy·ing** *v.t.* 1 To form or arrange in strata. 2 To preserve (seeds) by spreading in alternating layers of earth and sand. — *v.i.* 3 To form in strata. 4 To be formed in strata. [<F *stratifier* <Med. L *stratificare* <L *stratum* layer + *facere* make] — **strat′i·fi·ca′tion** *n.*

stra·tig·ra·phy (strə·tig′rə·fē) *n.* 1 The order and relative position of the strata of the earth's crust. 2 The study or description of such strata; stratigraphic geology. [< STRATI- + -GRAPHY] — **strat·i·graph·ic** (strat′ə·graf′ik) or **·i·cal** *adj.* — **strat′i·graph′i·cal·ly** *adv.*

strat·o·sphere (strat'ə-sfir, strā'tə-) n. *Meteorol.* The portion of the atmosphere lying above the troposphere and beginning at a height of about six miles. In it the systematic fall of temperature with increasing altitude, characteristic of the region below it, ceases, often giving place to a more or less uniform temperature. — **strat'o·spher'ic** (-sfer'ik) *adj.*

stra·tum (strā'təm, strat'əm) n. *pl.* **·ta** (-tə) or **·tums** 1 A natural or artificial layer, bed, or thickness. 2 *Geol.* A more or less homogeneous layer of rock, often in two or more beds, and serving to identify a geological group, system, or series. 3 *Biol.* A sheet or layer of tissue. 4 Something corresponding to a stratum of the earth: a low *stratum* of society. [<L, orig. neut. of *stratus*, pp. of *sternere* spread]

stra·tus (strā'təs, strat'əs) n. *pl.* **·ti** (-tī) *Meteorol.* A cloud of foglike appearance, low–lying and arranged in a uniform layer. See table under CLOUD. [<L, orig. pp. of *sternere* spread]

straw (strô) n. 1 A dry or ripened stalk. 2 Stems or stalks of grain, collectively, after the grain has been thrashed out. 3 A mere trifle or slight indication. 4 A slender tube, originally a wheat straw, now made of paper, glass, etc., used to suck up a beverage. — **the last straw** The final test of patience or endurance; the culminating element in any state of circumstances. — **straw in the wind** A sign or indication of the course of future events. — *adj.* 1 Like or of straw; of straw color. 2 Of no value; worthless; sham. 3 Made of straw. [OE *strēaw* straw] — **straw'y** *adj.*

straw·ber·ry (strô'ber'ē, -bər·ē) n. *pl.* **·ries** 1 The edible fruit of any plant of the genus *Fragaria*, technically neither a fruit nor a berry, but an enlarged fleshy achene receptacle. 2 The plant that bears this fruit, a stemless perennial of the rose family, with radical trifoliolate leaves, usually white flowers on scapes, and slender runners by which it propagates: also **strawberry vine.** [OE *strēaw* straw + BERRY]

strawberry blond A person having reddish–blond hair; a red–headed person.

strawberry bush 1 An upright or straggling shrub (*Euonymus americanus*) of the United States and Canada, with rough, warty, depressed crimson pods and scarlet aril. 2 The wahoo or burningbush.

strawberry shrub A shrub (genus *Calycanthus*), named for the strawberrylike fragrance of its purple or dark–red flowers.

strawberry tomato The ground cherry.

strawberry tree A small evergreen tree (*Arbutus unedo*) of southern Europe, having racemose white flowers and edible fruit resembling strawberries.

straw·board (strô'bôrd', -bōrd') n. Coarse board, made of straw, used for paper boxes and book covers.

straw boss *U.S. Colloq.* In construction work, logging, etc., an under-foreman.

straw man 1 A figure of a man made of straw. 2 A position, as in debate, set forth as one's opponent's view but typically misrepresenting it so that it may be convincingly refuted. 3 A person used to misrepresent or otherwise conceal the real nature of an activity or undertaking.

straw vote A vote taken at a chance gathering to test the strength of opposing candidates; an unofficial test vote.

stray (strā) v.i. 1 To wander from the proper course, an area, group, etc.; straggle; roam. 2 To wander about; rove. 3 To deviate from right or goodness; go astray. See synonyms under RAMBLE, WANDER. — *adj.* 1 Having strayed; straying. 2 Irregular; occasional; casual; unrelated. — n. 1 A domestic animal that has strayed; an estray. 2 A person who is lost or wanders aimlessly. 3 The act of straying or wandering. 4 *pl. Electronics* Electromagnetic waves, affecting a radio receiver, produced by atmospheric electric discharges and electrical storms. [<OF *estraier* wander about, ult. <L *extra vagare* wander outside] — **stray'er** n.

streak (strēk) n. 1 A long, narrow, somewhat irregularly shaped mark, line, or stripe: a *streak* of lightning. 2 A not very marked characteristic; a vein; trace; dash: a *streak* of meanness; also, a transient mood; whim. 3 *Mineral.* The color of the line of powder left when a mineral is rubbed on an unglazed porcelain plate known as a **streak plate.** 4 A strake. 5 A layer or strip: meat with a *streak* of fat and a *streak* of lean. 6 *Bacteriol.* The application of an inoculum in a thin stripe, as across the surface of a culture. 7 *Slang* The act or an instance of streaking (*v.* def. 3). — v.i. 1 To form a streak or streaks. 2 To move, run, or travel at great speed. 3 *Slang* To appear naked in a public place, usually briefly and especially while running, as for a thrill. — v.t. 4 To mark with a streak; form streaks in or on. 5 *Slang* To appear naked in (a public place), usually briefly and especially while running, as for a thrill. [OE *strica.* Akin to STRIKE.] — **streaked** *adj.* — **streak'er** n.

stream (strēm) n. 1 A current or flow of water or other fluid. 2 Anything continuously flowing, moving, or passing, as people. 3 A continuous course or advance; drift; current. 4 Anything issuing out or flowing from a source; a ray. — **on stream** In full commercial production, as an oil refinery, chemical plant, etc. — v.i. 1 To pour forth or issue in a stream. 2 To pour forth a stream: eyes *streaming* with tears. 3 To move in continuous succession; proceed uninterruptedly, as a crowd. 4 To float with a waving movement, as a flag. 5 To move with a trail of light, as a meteor. 6 In mining or dyeing, to wash in running water. [OE *strēam*] — **stream'y** *adj.*

Synonyms (noun): brook, channel, course, creek, current, drift, eddy, flow, flume, flux, race, rill, river, rivulet, run, runlet, runnel, streamlet, tide, watercourse.

stream·er (strē'mər) n. 1 An object that streams forth, or hangs extended. 2 A flag, pennant, or ensign; a long, narrow flag or standard. 3 A stream or shaft of light, such as shoots up from the horizon into or across the sky in the aurora borealis. 4 A newspaper headline that runs across the whole page.

stream·line (strēm'līn') n. 1 The course of a fluid relative to a solid body past which it is moving, especially a course free of turbulence or eddies. 2 Any shape or contour designed to lessen air resistance. — *adj.* 1 Designating an uninterrupted flow or drift. 2 Denoting a form, body, or the like so constructed as to permit an uninterrupted flow of fluid around it: a *streamline* flow, a *streamline* shape, a *streamline* body for a motor car. — v.t. **·lined,** **·lin·ing** 1 To design with a streamline shape. 2 To make more simple, efficient, or up to date, especially by reorganization.

stream·lin·er (strēm'lī'nər) n. A fast, streamlined train.

stream of consciousness *Psychol.* The uninterrupted series of individual conscious states moving continuously as though in a stream. Also **stream of thought.**

stream-of-con·scious·ness technique (strēm'-əv·kon'shəs·nis) A method of writing fiction in which an author objectifies the inward thoughts, feelings, and sometimes sensations of the characters to supplement or replace dialog and narrated action.

street (strēt) n. 1 A public way, with buildings on one or both sides, in a city, town, or village. 2 The highway on which buildings front; also, the roadway for vehicles, between sidewalks. 3 *Colloq.* The people living, habitually gathering, or doing business in a street. — *adj.* 1 Working in the streets: a *street* musician; a *street* beggar. 2 Opening onto the street: a *street* door. 3 Performed or taking place on the street: *street* crime; *street* fair. 4 Habituated to the ways of life in the streets, especially in cities: *street* people. See synonyms under ROAD, WAY. [OE *strǣt* <LL *strata (via)* paved way]

street-walk·er (strēt'wô'kər) n. A prostitute who solicits in the streets. — **street'-walk'ing** n. & adj.

strength (strength) n. 1 The quality or property of being strong; power; muscular force; physical vitality. 2 The capacity of material bodies to sustain the application of force without yielding or breaking; solidity; tenacity; toughness. 3 Power in general; operative energy; ability to do or bear. 4 Binding force or validity, as of a law. 5 Vigor or force of style. 6 Available numerical force in a military unit or other organization. 7 Degree of intensity; vehemence: *strength* of passion. 8 The degree in which a thing possesses its distinctive properties or essential elements; concentration. 9 Potency, as of a drug, chemical, or liquor. 10 Rising prices; firmness of prices. 11 One regarded as an embodiment of sustaining or protecting power; in archaic or poetic use, a fortress. See synonyms under POWER, PROWESS. [OE *strengthu* <*strang* strong]

strength·en (streng'thən) v.t. 1 To make strong. 2 To encourage; hearten. — v.i. 3 To become or grow strong or stronger. See synonyms under CONFIRM. — **strength'en·er** n.

stren·u·ous (stren'yōō·əs) adj. 1 Eagerly pressing or urgent; earnest. 2 Necessitating or marked by strong effort or exertion. [<L *strenuus.* Akin to Gk. *strēnēs* strong.] — **stren'u·ous·ly** adv. — **stren'u·os'i·ty** (-os'ə·tē), **stren'u·ous·ness** n.

strep·to·coc·cus (strep'tə·kok'əs) n. *pl.* **·coc·ci** (-kok'sī) Any of a genus (*Streptococcus*) of Gram–positive, typically non–motile ovoid or spherical bacteria, grouped in long chains, and dividing in one plane, including highly pathogenic species causing many diseases, as pneumonia, erysipelas, etc. See illustration under BACTERIUM. [<NL <Gk. *streptos* twisted + COCCUS] — **strep'to·coc'cal** (-kok'əl), **strep'to·coc'cic** (-kok'sik) *adj.*

strep·to·my·cin (strep'tō·mī'sin) n. A potent antibiotic isolated from a moldlike organism (*Streptomyces griseus*), effective against certain pathogenic bacteria. [<Gk. *streptos* twisted + *mykēs* fungus]

strep·to·thri·cin (strep'tō·thrī'sin, -thris'in) n. A bactericidal substance isolated from a soil fungus (*Actinomyces lavendulae*): used therapeutically in certain intestinal infections. [<NL *Streptothrix*, former genus name <Gk. *streptos* twisted + *thrix* hair + -IN]

stress (stres) n. 1 Special weight, importance, or significance. 2 *Physics* Force exerted between contiguous portions of a body or bodies and generally expressed in pounds per square inch; strain; tension. 3 *Mech.* A force or system of forces which tends to produce deformation in a body on which it acts. 4 Influence exerted forcibly; pressure; compulsion. 5 In pronunciation and oral reading, the relative force with which a sound, syllable, or word is uttered. See also METRICAL STRESS, RHETORICAL STRESS. — v.t. 1 To subject to mechanical stress, as a timber. 2 To put stress or emphasis on; accent, as a syllable. 3 To put into straits or difficulties; distress. [<OF *estrece* <*estrecier* constrain <L *strictus*, pp. of *stringere* draw tight] — **stress'ful** *adj.* — **stress'less** *adj.*

stretch (strech) v.t. 1 To extend or draw out, as to full length or width. 2 To extend or draw out forcibly, especially beyond normal or proper limits: The weight has *stretched* the cable; to *stretch* the truth. 3 To cause to reach, as from one place to another or over an area; extend: They *stretched* telegraph wires across the continent. 4 To put forth, hold out, or extend (the hand, an object, etc.): often with *out*: to *stretch* out the hands in appeal. 5 To draw tight; tighten. 6 To strain or exert to the utmost: to *stretch* every nerve. 7 *Slang* To fell with a blow. — v.i. 8 To reach or extend over an area or from one place to another: The road *stretches* on and on. 9 To become extended, especially beyond normal or proper limits. 10 To extend one's body or limbs, as in relaxing or reaching for something. 11 To lie down and extend one's limbs to full length: usually with *out*. — n. 1 An act of stretching, or the state of being stretched; tension. 2 Extent or reach of that which stretches; scope; especially, an overstrain. 3 A continuous extent of space or time. 4 In racing, the straight part of the track; the straight–away. 5 Direction. 6 *Slang* A term of imprisonment. — *adj.* Capable of being stretched; elastic: said especially of clothing and fabrics: *stretch* socks. [OE *streccan* stretch] — **stretch'a·ble** *adj.*

stretch'i·ness n. — **stretch'y** adj.
  Synonyms (verb): elongate, exaggerate, expand, extend, lengthen, reach, spread, strain, tighten.
stretch·er (strech'ər) n. **1** One who or that which stretches; any device for stretching, as a device for loosening the fit of gloves, shoes, etc., a frame for drying curtains, sweaters, etc., in shape. **2** A frame, as of stretched canvas, for carrying the wounded or dead; a litter. **3** In masonry, a brick or stone lying lengthwise of a course. **4** A tie beam in the frame of a building.
stretch·er–bear·er (strech'ər-bâr'ər) n. One who carries one end of a stretcher or litter. Also **stretch'er·man'** (-man').
stret·to (stret'tō) n. pl. **·ti** (-tē) or **·tos** Music **1** A portion of a fugue, near the close, in which the answer crowds closely on the subject. **2** In an oratorio or operatic piece, the portion at the close accelerated in time to produce a climax: also **stret'ta** (-tä). [<Ital., lit., drawn tight <L strictus. See STRESS.]
strew (strōō) v.t. **strewed, strewed** or **strewn, strew·ing 1** To spread about loosely or at random; scatter; sprinkle. **2** To cover with something scattered or sprinkled. **3** To be scattered over (a surface). [OE *strēawian*]
stri·a (strī'ə) n. pl. **stri·ae** (strī'ē) **1** A narrow streak, stripe, or band of distinctive color, structure, or texture, often parallel with others. **2** Geol. A small groove, channel, or ridge on a rock surface, due to the action of glacier ice. [<L, a groove]
stri·ate (strī'āt) adj. **1** Having fine linear markings; grooved. **2** Constituting a stria or striae. Also **stri'at·ed.** — v.t. **·at·ed, ·at·ing** To mark with striae. [<L *striatus,* pp. of *striare* groove <*stria* a groove]
stri·a·tion (strī-ā'shən) n. **1** The act of striating, or the state of being striated. **2** A striate form or appearance. **3** One of a series of parallel striae, as in a muscle or mineral.
strick·en (strik'ən) adj. **1** Wounded, especially by a missile: a *stricken* hare. **2** Struck down; afflicted, as by calamity or disease: *stricken* with polio. Compare STRIKE v. **3** Advanced or far gone, as in age: *stricken* in years. **4** Having the contents leveled off even with the top of a container. [OE *stricen,* pp. of *strican* strike]
strick·le (strik'əl) n. **1** A straightedge used for striking off an even measure of grain. **2** A template or curved piece of wood used in smoothing a sand or loam mold to form a core. **3** A straightedge, to which emery is applied, for sharpening rotary knives. — v.t. **·led, ·ling** To shape or smooth with a strickle. [OE *stricel*]
strict (strikt) adj. **1** Observing or enforcing rules exactly; also, containing exact or severe rules or provisions; exacting. **2** Strenuously enjoined and maintained; rigidly observed. **3** Exactly defined, distinguished, or applied; not indefinite or loose. **4** Stretched tight; not lax; tense. **5** Close, narrow, and upright; straight: said of the panicles of certain plants. See synonyms under AUSTERE, PRECISE. [<L *strictus,* pp. of *stringere* draw tight. Doublet of STRAIT.] — **strict'ly** adv. — **strict'ness** n.
stric·ture (strik'chər) n. **1** Severe criticism. **2** Pathol. A morbid contraction of some duct or channel of the body. **3** Obs. Strictness. [<L *strictura* <*strictus* strict]
stride (strīd) n. **1** A long and sweeping or measured step; also, the space passed over by such a step. **2** In animal locomotion, an act of progressive motion, completed when all the feet are returned to the same relative positions they occupied at the beginning of the movement. **3** A stage of progress. — **to hit one's stride** To attain one's normal speed. — **to make rapid strides** To make quick progress. — **to take (something) in one's stride** To do (something) without undue effort as part of one's normal activity. — v. **strode, strid·den, strid·ing** v.i. **1** To walk with long steps, as from haste or pride. **2** Archaic To straddle. — v.t. **3** To walk through, along, etc., with long steps. **4** To pass over with a single stride. **5** To straddle; bestride. [OE *strīdan* stride] — **strid'er** n.
stri·dent (strīd'nt) adj. Giving a loud and harsh sound; shrill; grating. [<L *stridens, -entis,* ppr. of *stridere* creak] — **stri'dence, stri'den·cy** n. — **stri'dent·ly** adv.

strid·u·late (strij'ŏŏ-lāt) v.i. **·lat·ed, ·lat·ing** To make a shrill, creaking noise, as a locust, cicada, or the like. [<NL *stridulatus,* pp. of *stridulare* <*stridulus* rattling <*stridere* rattle, rasp] — **strid'u·la'tion** n. — **strid'u·la·to·ry** (-lə·tôr'ē, -tō'rē), **strid'u·lous** adj. — **strid'u·lous·ly** adv. — **strid'u·lous·ness** n.
strife (strīf) n. **1** Angry contention; fighting. **2** Any contest for advantage or superiority; rivalry. **3** The act of striving; strenuous endeavor. See synonyms under BATTLE, FEUD¹, QUARREL¹. [<OF *estrif* <*estriver.* See STRIVE.]
stri·gose (strī'gōs, strī-gōs') adj. **1** Bot. Rough with short, sharp, appressed stiff hairs or bristles, as a leaf; hispid. **2** Zool. Marked with stripes or striae. [<NL *strigosus* <L *striga* a furrow]
strike (strīk) v. **struck, struck** (*chiefly Archaic* **strick·en), strik·ing** v.t. **1** To come into violent contact with; hit; crash into: The car *struck* the wall. **2** To hit with a blow; deal a blow to; smite: It *struck* him in the face. **3** To deal (a blow, etc.). **4** To cause to hit forcibly: He *struck* his hand on the table. **5** To attack; assault: We *struck* the enemy on his left flank. **6** To remove, separate, or take off by or as by a blow: with *off, from,* etc.: *Strike* it from the record. **7 a** To ignite (a match, etc.). **b** To produce (a light, etc.) thus. **8** To form by stamping, printing, etc.; impress; coin. **9** To announce; sound: The clock *struck* two. **10** To fall upon; reach; catch: A sound of crying *struck* his ear. **11** To arrive at; come upon: to *strike* a trail. **12** To discover; find: to *strike* oil. **13** To affect suddenly or in a specified manner: He was *struck* speechless. **14** To come to the mind of; occur to: An idea *strikes* me. **15** To impress in a specified manner; seem to: He *strikes* me as an honest man. **16** To attract the attention of; impress: The dress *struck* her fancy. **17** To assume; take up: to *strike* an attitude. **18** To cause to enter or penetrate deeply or suddenly: to *strike* dismay into one's heart. **19** To lower or haul down; take or let down, as a sail, or a flag in token of surrender. **20** To cease working at in order to compel compliance to a demand, etc. **21** In the theater, to dismantle (a set or scene). **22** To make level (a measure of grain, etc.); strickle. **23** To make and confirm, as a bargain. **24** To harpoon (a whale). **25** To hook (a fish that has taken the lure) by a sharp pull on the line. **26** To arrive at by reckoning: to *strike* a balance. — v.i. **27** To come into violent contact; crash; hit. **28** To deal or aim a blow or blows. **29** To make an assault or attack. **30** To sound from a blow or blows. **31** To be indicated by the sound of blows or strokes: Noon has just *struck.* **32** To ignite. **33** To run aground, as on a reef or shoal: The ship *struck* and heeled over. **34** To lower a flag in token of surrender or in salute. **35** To come suddenly or unexpectedly; chance: with *on* or *upon:* to *strike* upon an unknown path. **36** To take a course; start and proceed: to *strike* for home. **37** To move quickly; dart. **38** To cease work in order to enforce demands, etc. **39** To snatch at or swallow the lure: said of fish. — **to strike camp** To take down the tents of a camp. — **to strike down 1** To fell with a blow. **2** To affect disastrously; incapacitate completely. — **to strike dumb** To astonish; amaze. — **to strike hands** To clasp hands, especially in confirming a bargain. — **to strike home 1** To deal an effective blow. **2** To have telling effect. — **to strike it rich 1** To find a valuable vein or pocket of ore. **2** To come into wealth or good fortune. — **to strike off 1** To remove or take off by or as by a blow or stroke. **2** To cross out or erase by or as by a stroke of the pen. **3** To deduct. — **to strike out 1** To strike off (def. 2). **2** To aim a blow or blows. **3** To originate; devise; contrive. **4** To begin; start. **5** In baseball: **a** To put out (the batter) by pitching three strikes. **b** To be put out because of taking three strikes. — **to strike up 1** To begin to play, sing, or sound, as a band or musical instrument. **2** To start up; begin, as a friendship. — n. **1** An act of striking or hitting; a blow. **2** In baseball, an unsuccessful attempt by the batter to hit the ball; a pitched ball that passes over home plate above the level of the batter's knees and below that of his shoulders; a foul bunt; any foul tip held by the catcher; any ball hit foul except when there

have been two strikes. **3** In bowling, the knocking down by a player of all the pins with the first bowl in any frame. **4** The quitting of work by a body of workers to enforce some demand. **5** A new or unexpected discovery, as of oil or ore. **6** Any unexpected or complete success. **7** A straight-edged implement for leveling something, as grain in a measure; strickle. **8** Geol. The direction, referred to the meridian, of a horizontal line in a given structural plane, or of the intersection of the structural plane with a horizontal surface. **9** In coining, the quantity of coin or the number of medals made or struck at one time. **10** Full measure; hence, excellence. **11** The act of attempting to obtain money or some valuable thing, as by simple request, or by the introduction of a bill in a legislative body for the purpose of being bought off. **12** The sudden rise and taking of the bait by a fish; a bite. — **general strike** Concerted cessation of work on the part of the employees of all or nearly all industries, including public utilities, in a certain town, region, or nation. — **sit-down strike** See SIT-DOWN. [OE *strican* stroke, move. Akin to STREAK.]
strike·break·er (strīk'brā'kər) n. **1** One who takes the place of a workman on strike. **2** A person who supplies workmen to take the place of strikers. — **strike'break'ing** n.
strike fault Geol. A fault lying parallel with the strike of the rocks through which it cuts.
strik·ing (strī'king) adj. Notable; impressive. See synonyms under EXTRAORDINARY. — **strik'ing·ly** adv. — **strik'ing·ness** n.
string (string) n. **1** A slender line, thinner than a cord and thicker than a thread, used for tying or lacing; twine; also, a slender strip, as of cloth or leather; the cord of a bow; prepared wire or catgut for musical instruments. **2** A stringlike organ or formation; a fibrous vegetable formation; an animal nerve or tendon. **3** A thin cord upon which anything is strung; a row or series of things connected by a small cord: a *string* of pearls. **4** A connected series or succession as of things, acts, or events: sometimes implying unusual length: a *string* of carriages; a *string* of lies. **5** U.S. Colloq. A drove or small collection of stock, especially of saddle horses. **6** pl. Stringed instruments, especially those of an orchestra; those who play on these. **7** In billiards, the score; the buttons, strung on a wire, by which the score is kept; the string line; the act of stringing. **8** Archit. **a** A string-course, as of bricks. **b** A stout inclined plank, notched and set edgewise as a support for the steps of a wooden stairway; a ramp or sidepiece of solid-built stairs. **9** In sports, a group of contestants ranked as to skill. **10** The conditions, limitations, or restrictions attached to any proposition, gift, or donation, whereby the terms may not be binding, or whereby the donor retains some control. — **to pull strings** To manipulate or influence others, secretly or underhandedly, to gain some advantage. — v. **strung, string·ing** v.t. **1** To thread, as beads, on or as on a string. **2** To fit with a string or strings, as a guitar. **3** To bind, fasten, or adorn with a string or strings. **4** To tighten the strings of (a musical instrument). **5** To brace; strengthen. **6** To make tense or nervous. **7** To arrange or extend like a string. **8** To remove the strings from (vegetables). **9** Colloq. To hang: usually with *up.* — v.i. **10** To extend, stretch, or proceed in a line or series. **11** To form into strings. **12** In billiards, to drive the cue ball from within the string against the farther cushion and back. — **to string along** Slang **1** To follow with trust or confidence. **2** To fool; deceive; cheat. **3** To keep (someone) waiting or on tenterhooks. [OE *streng* string]
string bass The double bass.
string bean 1 Any of several varieties of beans (genus *Phaseolus*) cultivated for their edible pods, especially *P. vulgaris.* **2** The pod itself. **3** Colloq. A tall, skinny person.
stringed (stringd) adj. **1** Furnished with strings. **2** Produced from stringed instruments. **3** Tied with string.
strin·gent (strin'jənt) adj. **1** Keeping one closely to strict requirements; rigid; severe, as regulations. **2** Hampered by obstructing conditions or scarcity of money; close or tight: The money market is very *stringent.* **3** Convincing; forcible. [<L *stringens, -entis,*

ppr. of *stringere* draw tight] —**strin′gen·cy**, **strin′gent·ness** *n.* —**strin′gent·ly** *adv.*

string·er (string′ər) *n.* **1** A heavy timber, generally horizontal, supporting other members of a structure, and usually running in the direction of the greatest length of the collection of supported members. **2** Any horizontal framing timber, as a tie beam; a stringpiece. **3** A lengthwise timber on which rails are laid, as distinguished from a *cross–tie* or *sleeper.* **4** A news reporter employed on a free–lance basis, often in out–of–town or foreign locations. **5** A person having a specific rating as to excellence, skill, etc.: used in combination: a *second–stringer.*

string·y (string′ē) *adj.* **string·i·er**, **string·i·est 1** Containing fibrous strings. **2** Forming in strings, as thick glue; ropy. **3** Having tough sinews. **4** Tall and wiry in build. —**string′i·ly** *adv.* —**string′i·ness** *n.*

strip[1] (strip) *n.* **1** A narrow piece, comparatively long, as of cloth, wood, etc. **2** A number of stamps attached in a row. **3** A narrow piece of land; a minor civil division in Maine. **4** An act of destruction or spoliation. **5** A comic strip. —**Cherokee strip** A strip of land formerly leased to the Cherokee Indians but now part of Oklahoma. —*v.t.* **stripped, strip·ping** To cut or tear into strips. [? <MLG *strippe* a strap]

strip[2] (strip) *v.* **stripped** (*Rare* **stript**), **strip·ping** *v.t.* **1** To pull the covering, clothing, etc., from; denude; lay bare. **2** To pull off (the covering or clothing). **3** To rob or plunder; spoil. **4** To make bare or empty. **5** To remove; take away. **6** To deprive of something; divest: He was *stripped* of his rank. **7** To separate the leaves of (tobacco) from the stalks. **8** To milk (a cow) dry by a downward stroke and compression of the thumb and forefinger. **9** *Mech.* To damage or break the teeth, thread, etc., of (a gear, bolt, or the like). —*v.i.* **10** To remove one's clothing; undress. **11** *Mech.* To suffer breaking or jamming of the teeth or thread. [ME <OE -*strȳpan*, as in *bestrȳpan* despoil, plunder]

stripe[1] (strip) *n.* **1** A line, band, or long strip of material of different color or finish from the adjacent surface. **2** Distinctive quality or character; kind; sort; also, a certain kind of religious or political belief or opinion: a man of Democratic *stripe.* **3** Striped cloth. **4** *pl.* Prison uniform. **5** A piece of material or braid on the sleeve of a uniform to indicate rank, etc.; a chevron; a service or wound stripe. —*v.t.* **striped, strip·ing** To mark with a stripe or stripes. [<MDu.]

stripe[2] (strip) *n.* **1** A blow struck with a whip or rod, as in flogging. **2** A weal or welt on the skin caused by such a blow. See synonyms under BLOW[2]. [Prob. <LG. Cf. Du. *strippen* whip.]

strip·ling (strip′ling) *n.* A mere youth; a lad. [<STRIP[1] + -LING]

strip mine A mine, especially a coal mine, the seams of which are close to the surface of the earth, and which is worked by stripping away the topsoil and the material beneath it.

strip·per (strip′ər) *n.* **1** One who or that which strips. **2** *Slang* A female performer of a strip–tease. **3** A partially depleted oil well producing few barrels a day: also **stripper well. 4** An owner or operator of a strip mine; also, a worker on a strip mine.

strip–tease (strip′tēz′) *n.* In burlesque, a gradual disrobing by a female performer. —**strip′–teas′er** *n.*

strive (strīv) *v.i.* **strove, striv·en** (striv′ən) or **strived, striv·ing 1** To make earnest effort. **2** To engage in strife; contend; fight. **3** To vie; emulate. See synonyms under CONTEND, ENDEAVOR, STRUGGLE. [<OF *estriver,* prob. <Gmc.] —**striv′er** *n.*

strobe (strōb) *n.* **1** A stroboscope. **2** An electronically controlled device that emits light in very brief, brilliant flashes, used in photography, in the theater, etc.: also **strobe light.**

strob·ic (strō′bik) *adj.* **1** Resembling a top. **2** Seeming to spin: said of concentric circles that appear to spin when moved. [<Gk. *strobos* whirling]

stro·bi·la (strō-bī′lə) *n.* *pl.* ·**lae** (-lē) *Zool.* **1** A stage in the life cycle of a jellyfish char-

acterized by a series of annular plates each of which separates as a new organism. **2** The segmented body of a tapeworm. [<NL <Gk. *strobilē* plug of lint shaped like a fir cone <*strobilos* fir cone, anything twisted <*strobos* twisted, ult. <*strephein* twist]

strob·i·la·tion (strob′ə-lā′shən) *n.* *Zool.* Asexual reproduction by division, as in jellyfish and tapeworms; metameric division.

strob·ile (strob′il) *n.* *Bot.* **1** A multiple fruit consisting of an oblong, oval, or conical mass of dry imbricated scales, as in the pines, spruces, firs, etc.; a cone. **2** A cone-shaped mass of sporophylls producing spore cases, as in the horsetails, clubmosses, etc. Also **strob′il.** [See STROBILA]

stroke (strōk) *n.* **1** The act or movement of striking; a knock; an impact. **2** One of a series of recurring movements, as of oars, a piston, etc.; also, the rate, extent, or manner of such movement. **3** Stroke oar. **4** A single movement, as of the hand, arm, or some instrument, by which something is made or done. **5** A single movement of some instrument, as of a pen or pencil. **6** A blow or any ill effect caused as if by a blow: a *stroke* of misfortune, a *sunstroke.* **7** *Pathol.* An attack of paralysis or apoplexy. **8** A blow or the sound of a blow of a striking mechanism, as of a clock. **9** A sudden or brilliant mental act; feat; coup: a great *stroke* of diplomacy, a *stroke* of wit. **10** A pulsation, as of the heart. **11** A mark or dash of a pen or tool. **12** A light caressing movement; a stroking. See synonyms under BLOW[2], MISFORTUNE. —*v.t.* **stroked, strok·ing 1** To pass the hand over gently or caressingly, or with light pressure. **2** To set the pace for (a rowboat or its crew); act as stroke for. **3** To sound (time), as a gong or clock. [ME *strok, strak* <OE *strācian* strike]

stroke oar 1 The aftmost oar of a boat, whose movement sets the rate of rowing. **2** The person who rows with this oar: also **stroke–oars·man** (strōk′ôrz′mən, -ōrz′-), **strokes·man** (strōks′mən). **3** The position occupied by such an oarsman.

stroll (strōl) *v.i.* **1** To walk in a leisurely or idle manner; saunter. **2** To go from place to place. —*n.* An idle or leisurely walk; a wandering. See synonyms under RAMBLE. [Origin uncertain]

stroll·er (strō′lər) *n.* **1** One who strolls; especially, a strolling showman or player. **2** A tramp. **3** A small, light baby carriage, often collapsible.

stro·ma (strō′mə) *n.* *pl.* ·**ma·ta** (-mə·tə) **1** *Physiol.* The ground substance or connective tissue that forms the framework of an organ or cell. **2** *Bot.* In fungi, the union of mycelial threads into a dense crust on or in which the sporophores are borne. [<Gk. *strōma* bed] —**stro·mat·ic** (strō-mat′ik) *adj.*

stro·mey·er·ite (strō′mī-ə-rīt) *n.* A metallic, lustrous, steel–gray native sulfide of copper and silver, crystallizing in the orthorhombic system. [after F. *Stromeyer,* 1786–1835, German chemist]

strong (strông, strong) *adj.* **1** Physically or bodily powerful; muscular; vigorous. **2** Healthy; robust: a *strong* constitution. **3** Morally powerful; firm; resolute; courageous. **4** Mentally powerful or vigorous. **5** Especially competent or able (in a certain subject or field): *strong* in mathematics. **6** Abundantly or richly supplied (with something): *strong* in trumps; *strong* in literary interest. **7** Solidly made or constituted; not easily destroyed, injured, or strained: *strong* walls, paper, etc. **8** Powerful as a rival or combatant: a *strong* team, army, etc. **9** Easy to defend; difficult to capture: a *strong* hill position. **10** In numerical force: an army 20,000 *strong.* **11** Well able to exert influence, authority, etc.: a *strong* government. **12** Financially sound: a *strong* bank. **13** Powerful in effect: *strong* poison, medicine, etc. **14** Concentrated; not diluted or weak: *strong* coffee. **15** Containing much alcohol: a *strong* drink. **16** Powerful in flavor or odor; also, rank; unpleasant: a *strong* breath. **17** Intense in degree or quality; not mild: a *strong* pulse; *strong* light, heat, etc. **18** Loud and firm: a *strong* voice. **19** Firm; tenacious: a *strong*

grip; a *strong* opinion. **20** Deeply earnest; fervid: a *strong* desire. **21** Cogent; convincing: *strong* evidence. **22** Distinct; marked: definite: a *strong* resemblance. **23** Extreme; high–handed: *strong* measures. **24** Emphatic; not moderate: *strong* language. **25** Moving with great force: said of a wind, stream, or tide; specifically, *Meteorol.,* designating a breeze (No. 6) or a gale (No. 9) on the Beaufort scale. **26** Characterized by steady or rising prices: a *strong* market. **27** *Phonet.* Stressed; accented, as a syllable. **28** *Gram.* In Germanic languages: **a** Of verbs, indicating changes in tense by means of ablaut vowel alteration in the stem, rather than by the addition of inflectional endings; as, English *drink, drank, drunk; write, wrote, written*; German *singen, sang, gesungen*: also called *irregular.* **b** Of nouns and adjectives (in German and Old English), showing distinctive declensional endings for case, number, and gender. For example, in German, a descriptive adjective is used in the strong form when not preceded by a limiting word (*guter Mann*) or when preceded by one having no distinctive case and gender inflection (*mein guter Mann*). Compare WEAK (def. 12). —*adv.* Strongly: usually employed in combination: *strong*-talking. Many self-explaining compound adjectives have *strong* as the first element: *strong*-armed, *strong*-smelling, etc. [OE] —**strong′ly** *adv.*

Synonyms (*adj.*): cohesive, compact, hardy, robust, sinewy, stalwart, stout, stubborn, sturdy, tenacious, vigorous, See FIRM, HEALTHY.

strong–arm (strông′ärm′, strong′-) *Colloq. adj.* Using physical or coercive power: *strong-arm* tactics. —*v.t.* **1** To use physical force upon; assault. **2** To coerce; compel.

strong·bark (strông′bärk′, strong′-) *n.* A small tree (*Bourreria ovata*), native to the West Indies and Florida. The wood is brown, hard, and strong; the berries are edible.

strong·box (strông′boks′, strong′-) *n.* A strongly built chest or safe for keeping valuables.

strong drink Alcoholic liquors.

strong·hold (strông′hōld′, strong′-) *n.* A place that nature or man has made strongly defensible; hence, a refuge.

strong·man (strông′man′, strong′-) *n.* A political leader having considerable or preeminent power, as from a military coup or other extralegal means.

strong–mind·ed (strông′mīn′did, strong′-) *adj.* Having a determined, vigorous mind. —**strong′-mind′ed·ly** *adv.* —**strong′-mind′ed·ness** *n.*

strong·room (strông′rōōm′, -rōōm′, strong′-) *n.* A room especially equipped for the safekeeping of valuables.

strong–willed (strông′wild′, strong′-) *adj.* Having a strong will; decided; often, obstinate.

stron·ti·a (stron′shē-ə) *n.* *Chem.* **1** A grayish-white, infusible strontium monoxide, SrO. **2** Strontium hydroxide, $Sr(OH)_2$. [<NL <STRONTIUM]

stron·ti·an·ite (stron′shē-ən-īt′) *n.* A vitreous, native strontium carbonate, $SrCO_3$, occurring in various forms and colors.

stron·ti·um (stron′shē-əm, -shəm, -tē-əm) *n.* A hard yellowish metallic element (symbol Sr, atomic number 38) of the alkaline earth group, usually occurring with barium and never in the free state. See PERIODIC TABLE. [<NL, from *Strontian,* Argyll, Scotland, where first discovered] —**stron′tic** (-tik) *adj.*

strontium 90 A radioactive isotope of strontium of mass number 90, having a half-life of 28 years, present in used reactor fuel and in the fallout from nuclear explosions, where it constitutes a special hazard because its chemical similarity to calcium results in its being metabolized and accumulated in bone and other living tissues and secretions such as milk.

strop (strop) *n.* **1** A strip of leather or canvas on which to sharpen a razor; also, a rectangular implement with strops on it. **2** A strap. —*v.t.* **stropped, strop·ping** To sharpen on a strop. [OE *stropp* <L *struppus* <Gk. *strophos* a band, cord]

stro·phan·thin (strō-fan′thin) *n.* A bitter, poisonous, crystalline glycoside contained in certain varieties of a tropical plant (genus *Strophanthus*) and resembling digitalis in its action on the heart. [<NL *Strophanthus,* a genus name (<Gk.

strophos cord + *anthos* flower) + -IN]

stro·phe (strō'fē) *n.* **1** In ancient Greek poetry, the verses sung by the chorus in a play while moving from right to left. **2** In classical prosody, the lines of an ode comprising a stanza and alternating with the antistrophe. **3** The first of two alternating metrical systems in a poem. [<Gk. *strophē* a turning, twist <*strephein* turn] — **stroph·ic** (strof'ik, strō'fik) or **·i·cal** *adj.*

stroph·i·ole (strof'ē-ōl, strō'fē-) *n. Bot.* An arillike appendage attached to the base of certain seeds. [<L *strophiolum,* dim. of *strophium* a band <Gk. *strophos* cord <*strephein* twist] — **stroph′i·o·late′** (-lāt′), **stroph′i·o·lat′ed** *adj.*

stroph·u·lus (strof'yə-ləs) *n. Pathol.* Any of various types of miliaria common in children: also called *tooth rash, red gum.* [<NL, dim. of Gk. *strophos* a cord. See STROPHE.]

stroud (stroud) *n.* A coarse, heavy, woolen material used for blankets; also, a blanket made of this material, formerly used for trading with North American Indians. [from *Stroud,* England]

struck jury A jury specially selected by a process in which each party strikes twelve names from a list of forty-eight eligible persons, and the remaining twenty-four are summoned as the panel from which the jury of twelve men is drawn.

struck measure A measure, as of meal, smoothed down: opposed to *heaped measure.*

struc·tur·al (struk'chər-əl) *adj.* **1** Of, pertaining to, possessing, characterized, or caused by structure. **2** *Geol.* Having a form, position, or character determined by the preexistent structure of the earth's crust; tectonic. **3** *Biol.* Morphological. **4** *Chem.* Pertaining to or denoting the spatial arrangements of atoms in a molecule: a *structural* formula. **5** Used in or essential to construction. —**struc'tur·al·ly** *adv.*

structural iron 1 Shapes of iron used in constructing buildings, bridges, etc. **2** Iron cast in shapes for this purpose.

structural steel 1 Steel prepared after the manner of structural iron for use in building. **2** Rolled steel adapted for use in construction: of considerable toughness and strength.

struc·ture (struk'chər) *n.* **1** That which is constructed; a combination of related parts, as a building or machine. **2** *Biol.* The arrangement and functional union of parts, tissues, and organs of a plant or animal. **3** *Geol.* **a** The spatial arrangement of rock strata in a larger formation. **b** The gross physical characteristics of a rock. **4** *Chem.* The disposition of atoms within a molecule or of molecules in a compound. **5** The manner of construction or organization: the social *structure* of a primitive society. **6** *Archaic* The act of constructing. —*v.t.* **·tured, ·tur·ing 1** To form into an organized structure; build. **2** To conceive as a structural whole; ideate: He *structured* the plan before proposing it. See synonyms under FRAME. [<F <L *structura* <*structus,* pp. of *struere* build]

stru·del (strōōd'l, *Ger.* shtrōō'dəl) *n.* A kind of pastry made of a thin sheet of dough, spread with fruit or cheese, nuts, etc., rolled, and baked. [<G, lit., eddy]

strug·gle (strug'əl) *n.* A violent effort or series of efforts; a labored contest; sometimes, a war; battle. See synonyms under ENDEAVOR. [<*v.*] —*v.* **·gled, ·gling** *v.i.* **1** To contend with an adversary in physical combat; fight. **2** To put forth violent efforts; strive: to *struggle* against odds. **3** To make one's way by violent efforts: to *struggle* through mud. —*v.t.* **4** To accomplish with a struggle. [ME *strogelen;* origin unknown] — **strug'gler** *n.* —**strug'gling·ly** *adv.*

Synonyms (verb): battle, contend, contest, endeavor, fight, labor, strain, strive, toil, try, vie, wrestle, writhe.

strum (strum) *v.t. & v.i.* **strummed, strum·ming** To play (on a stringed instrument) without expression; thrum. —*n.* The act of strumming. [Prob. imit.] —**strum'mer** *n.*

stru·ma (strōō'mə) *n. pl.* **·mae** (-mē) **1** *Pathol.* **a** Scrofula. **b** Goiter. **2** *Bot.* A wenlike cushion or swelling of or on an organ, as at the base of the capsule in certain mosses. [<L <*struere* build] —**stru·mat·ic** (strōō-mat'ik), **stru'mose** (-mōs), **stru'mous** (-məs) *adj.*

strum·pet (strum'pit) *n.* A whore; harlot. [? Ult. <OF *strupe* concubinage <L *stuprum* dishonor]

strut (strut) *n.* **1** A proud or pompous step or walk. **2** A compression member in a framework, keeping two others from approaching nearer together, as the vertical members of the wing truss of a biplane. **3** An instrument used in adjusting the plaits of a ruff. —*v.* **strut·ted, strut·ting** *v.i.* To walk pompously, conceitedly, and affectedly. —*v.t.* To brace or support, as a framing or structure, by compression pieces, as struts or posts. [OE *strūtian* be rigid, stand stiffly] —**strut'ter** *n.* —**strut'ting** *adj.* —**strut'ting·ly** *adv.*

stru·thi·ous (strōō'thē-əs) *adj.* **1** Like an ostrich. **2** Pertaining to the *Struthionidae.* [<L *struthio* an ostrich]

strych·nine (strik'nin, -nēn, -nīn) *n.* A white, crystalline, bitter, extremely poisonous alkaloid, $C_{21}H_{22}N_2O_2$, contained in various plants (genus *Strychnos*) of the logania family, especially *S. nuxvomica.* Its salts are used in medicine, chiefly as a neural stimulant; a large dose produces tetanic spasms. Also **strych'ni·a** (-nē-ə), **strych'nin** (-nin). [<F <L *strychnos* <Gk., nightshade]

strych·nin·ism (strik'nin·iz′əm) *n. Pathol.* The morbid condition resulting from the excessive or improper use of strychnine.

Stry·mon (strī'mən) The Greek name for the STRUMA.

stub (stub) *n.* **1** The part of a tree trunk, bush, etc., that remains when the main part is cut down. **2** Any short projecting part or piece; a remnant, as of a pencil, candle, cigarette, cigar, or broken tooth. **3** In a checkbook or the like, one of the inner ends upon which a memorandum is entered, and which remains when the check is detached; also, the detachable coupon of a theater or other ticket. **4** Anything blunt, short, or stumpy, as a worn horseshoe nail or a stub pen. **5** *Obs.* A log; block; blockhead. **6** The title of a row in a statistical table; also, the first or reading column in such a table. —*v.t.* **stubbed, stubbing 1** To strike, as the toe, against a low obstruction or projection. **2** To grub up, as roots; root out. **3** To clear or remove the stubs or roots from. —*adj.* Thick-set; stocky. [OE *stubb*]

stub·ble (stub'əl) *n.* **1** The stubs of grain stalks, sugarcane, etc., covering a field after the crop has been cut. **2** The field itself. **3** Any surface or growth resembling stubble, as short bristly hair or beard. [<OF *stuble,* ult. <L *stipula* stalk] —**stub'bled** *adj.* —**stub'bly** *adj.*

stub·born (stub'ərn) *adj.* **1** Inflexible in opinion or intention; unreasonably obstinate. **2** Not easily handled, bent, or overcome; intractable: *stubborn* facts. **3** Characterized by perseverance or persistence: *stubborn* fighting. See synonyms under HARD, INFLEXIBLE, OBSTINATE, PERVERSE, STRONG. [Prob. OE *stubb* a stump] —**stub'born·ly** *adv.* —**stub'born·ness** *n.*

stuc·co (stuk'ō) *n. pl.* **·coes** or **·cos 1** A fine plaster for walls or their relief ornaments, usually of Portland cement, sand, and a small amount of lime. **2** Any plaster or cement used for the external coating of buildings. —*adj.* Stucco-coated. —*v.t.* **·coed, ·co·ing** To apply stucco to; decorate with stucco. [<Ital. <Gmc. Akin to OHG *stucchi* crust.] —**stuc'co·er** *n.*

stuck-up (stuk'up') *adj. Colloq.* Conceited; very vain; supercilious and arrogant; snobbish. —**stuck'-up'ness** *n.*

stud¹ (stud) *n.* **1** A short intermediate post, as in a building frame; a post to which laths are nailed; a scantling. **2** A knob, round-headed nail, or small protuberant ornament, as an ornamental button in a shirt front. **3** A crosspiece in a link, as in a chain cable. **4** A small pin such as is used in a watch. **5** Stud poker. —*v.t.* **stud·ded, stud·ding 1** To set thickly with small points, projections, or knobs. **2** To be scattered or strewn over: Daisies *stud* the meadows. **3** To support or stiffen by means of studs or upright props. [OE *studu* post]

stud² (stud) *n.* **1** A collection of horses and mares for breeding. **2** The place where they are kept. **3** A collection of horses for riding, hunting, or racing. **4** A stallion: also *studhorse.* —*adj.* **1** Of or pertaining to a stud. **2** Kept for breeding: a *stud* mare. [OE *stōd*]

stud book A record of the pedigree of a stud, or of thoroughbred racing stock collectively.

stu·dent (stōōd'nt, styōōd'nt) *n.* **1** A person engaged in a course of study; especially, one in a secondary school, college or university. **2** One who closely examines or investigates; one devoted to study. See synonyms under SCHOLAR. [<OF *estudiant* <L *studens, -entis,* ppr. of *studere* be eager, apply oneself, study]

stud·horse (stud'hôrs′) *n.* A stallion kept for breeding. Also **stud horse.**

stud·ied (stud'ēd) *adj.* **1** Deliberately and intentionally designed or undertaken; planned; premeditated: a *studied* insult. **2** Acquired or prepared by study. **3** *Rare* Learned; versed. —**stud'ied·ly** *adv.* —**stud'ied·ness** *n.*

stu·di·o (stōō'dē·ō, styōō'-) *n. pl.* **·di·os 1** The workroom of an artist, photographer, etc. **2** A place where motion pictures are filmed. **3** A room or rooms where radio or television programs are broadcast or recorded. [<Ital. <L *studium* zeal <*studere* apply oneself, be diligent]

studio couch A backless couch with a bed frame underneath which may be drawn out and made level with the couch to form a double bed or twin beds.

stu·di·ous (stōō'dē·əs, styōō'-) *adj.* **1** Given to study; devoting oneself to the acquisition of knowledge. **2** Earnest in the use of means; assiduous: *studious* to please. **3** Done with deliberation; studied: *studious* politeness. **4** Favorable to study; for study: *studious* halls. [<L *studiosus* <*studium* zeal. See STUDIO.] —**stu'di·ous·ly** *adv.* —**stu'di·ous·ness** *n.*

stud poker A game of poker in which the cards of the first round are dealt face down and the rest face up, betting opening on the second round.

stud·y (stud'ē) *v.* **stud·ied, stud·y·ing** *v.t.* **1** To apply the mind in acquiring a knowledge of: to *study* physics. **2** To examine; search into: to *study* a problem. **3** To look at attentively; scrutinize: to *study* one's reflection in a mirror. **4** To endeavor to memorize, as a part in a play. **5** To give thought and attention to, as something to be done or devised: often with *out.* —*v.i.* **6** To apply the mind in acquiring knowledge. **7** To follow a regular course of instruction; be a student. **8** To muse; meditate. See synonyms under CONSIDER, EXAMINE, MUSE. — **to study up on** To acquire more complete information concerning, as by investigation. —*n. pl.* **stud·ies 1** The act of studying; the process of acquiring information; application of the mind to books, to art or science, etc. **2** A particular instance or form of mental work. **3** Something to be studied; a branch or department of knowledge. **4** A specific product of studious application. **5** In art, a first sketch; a student's art exercise. **6** A carefully elaborated literary treatment of a subject. **7** A room devoted to study, reading, etc. **8** A studious state of mind; profound thought; absent-mindedness: in a brown *study.* See BROWN STUDY. **9** Earnest endeavor; thoughtful care or its object: Our *study* is to please you. **10** *Music* A composition designed to aid development in technical facility; an étude. See synonyms under EDUCATION, INQUIRY, LEARNING, REFLECTION, TASK, THOUGHT¹. [<OF *estudier* <*estudie* a study <L *studium* zeal. See STUDIO.] —**stud'i·a·ble** *adj.*

stuff (stuf) *v.t.* **1** To fill completely; pack; cram full. **2** To fill (an opening, etc.) with something forced in; plug. **3** To obstruct or stop up; choke. **4** To fill or expand with padding, as a cushion. **5** To fill (a fowl, roast, etc.) with stuffing. **6** In taxidermy, to fill the skin of (a bird, animal, etc.) with a material preparatory to mounting. **7** To fill too full; overload; distend. **8** To fill or cram with food: He *stuffed* himself with oysters. **9** To fill with knowledge, ideas, or attitudes, especially unsystematically: His head is *stuffed* with prejudices. **10** To force or cram, as into a small space. **11** To fill the pores of (a skin or pelt) with a preservative of oil and tallow. —*v.i.* **12** To eat to excess; gluttonize. — **to stuff a ballot box** To put fraudulent votes into a ballot box. [<*n.*] —*n.* **1** The material out of which something may be shaped or made; hence, raw or unwrought material. **2** Figuratively, the fundamental element of anything, material or spiritual. **3** Possessions generally, especially household goods. **4** A worthless collection of things; rubbish; hence, worthless ideas: often used as an interjection: *Stuff* and nonsense! **5** Woven material, especially of wool. **6** Any textile fabric. **7** Any one of various substances, mixtures, or compounds prepared for use, as paper pulp; in leathermaking, dubbing or stuffing. **8** A medicinal mixture or potion. **9** *Scot.* Luggage; belongings; corn; grain. **10** *Slang* Money; means. **11** In journalism, copy ready for the printer or engraver. [<OF *estoffe*, prob. <L *stuppa* tow] — **stuff′er** *n.*

stuffed shirt *Colloq.* A pretentious person; especially, a pompous boob.

stuff·ing (stuf′ing) *n.* **1** The material with which anything is stuffed. **2** A mixture, as of bread or cracker crumbs with meat and seasoning, used in stuffing fowls, etc., for cooking. **3** The process of stuffing anything.

stuff·ing box *Mech.* A device consisting of a chamber affording passage and lengthwise or rotary motion of a piston rod or shaft, while preventing leakage about the moving part by using packing material to fill the free space.

stuff·y (stuf′ē) *adj.* **stuff·i·er, stuff·i·est 1** Badly ventilated. **2** Impeding respiration. **3** *U.S. Colloq.* Angry; sulky. **4** Old-fashioned; stodgy; stiffly precise; strait-laced. — **stuff′i·ly** *adv.* — **stuff′i·ness** *n.*

stul·ti·fy (stul′tə·fī) *v.t.* **·fied, ·fy·ing 1** To cause to appear absurd; give an appearance of foolishness to. **2** To bring to naught; nullify. **3** *Law* To allege to be of unsound mind. [<LL *stultificare* make foolish <L *stultus* foolish + *facere* make] — **stul′ti·fi·ca′tion** *n.* — **stul′ti·fi′er** *n.*

stum (stum) *n.* **1** Unfermented or partly fermented grape juice. **2** Wine revived, as by adding must, to produce increased fermentation; must. — *v.t.* **stummed, stum·ming 1** To stop fermentation in by some admixture. **2** To revive (wine), as by adding must, so as to increase fermentation. [<Du. *stom* must, lit., silent]

stum·ble (stum′bəl) *v.* **·bled, ·bling** *v.i.* **1** To miss one's step in walking or running; trip. **2** To walk or proceed unsteadily or in a blundering manner. **3** To happen upon something by chance: with *across, on, upon,* etc. **4** To fall into sin or error. — *v.t.* **5** To cause to stumble. — *n.* The act of stumbling; hence, a blunder; false step. [Cf. Norw. *stumla* stumble in the dark] — **stum′bler** *n.* — **stum′bling** *adj.* — **stum′bling·ly** *adv.*

stum·bling-block (stum′bling-blok′) *n.* Any obstacle or hindrance; something that may cause one to err: now only figurative.

stump (stump) *n.* **1** That portion of the trunk of a tree left standing when the tree is felled. **2** The part of anything, as of a limb, that remains when the main part has been removed; a stumplike part; a stub. **3** *pl. Colloq.* The legs: chiefly in the phrase **to stir one's stumps. 4** A place or platform where a stump speech is made; hence, any place or platform from which speeches are made; also, political haranguing. **5** *Colloq.* A challenge; a dare. **6** In cricket, any one of the three posts (the **off stump,** the **middle stump,** and the **leg stump**) forming the wicket. **7** A pencil-like soft leather or rubber bar, with conical ends, used to soften drawings of crayon or charcoal or to apply powdered pigments. **8** A short, thick-set person or animal. **9** A heavy step; a clump. — **to be up a stump** To be in trouble or in a dilemma. — **to take the stump** To electioneer in a political campaign. — *adj.* **1** Being or resembling a stump; stumpy. **2** Of or pertaining to political oratory or campaigning: a **stump** speaker, **stump** speech. — *v.t.* **1** To reduce to a stump; truncate; lop. **2** To remove stumps from (land). **3** To canvass (a district) by making political speeches: The candidate **stumped** the State. **4** *Colloq.* To challenge, as to a contest; dare; defy. **5** *Colloq.* To bring to a halt by real or fancied obstacles; nonplus; baffle. **6** To strike against an obstacle; stub, as one's toe. **7** To shade (a drawing) by rubbing with a stump (def. 7). — *v.i.* **8** To go about on or as on stumps; hence, to walk heavily, noisily, and stiffly;

hobble. [<MLG]

stump·age (stum′pij) *n.* **1** Standing timber considered with reference to its value for cutting; also, its price. **2** A tax on lumber cut, rated by the amount cut and the price.

stump·er (stum′pər) *n.* **1** One who or that which stumps. **2** A political speaker. **3** Any problem, situation, etc., beyond one's powers of decision.

stump·y (stum′pē) *adj.* **stump·i·er, stump·i·est 1** Full of stumps. **2** Like a stump; short and thick. — **stump′i·ness** *n.*

stun (stun) *v.t.* **stunned, stun·ning 1** To render unconscious or incapable of action by a blow, fall, etc. **2** To astonish; astound. **3** To daze or overwhelm by loud or explosive noise. — *n.* A stupefying blow, shock, or concussion; also, the condition of being stunned. [<OF *estoner* resound, stun <L *ex-* thoroughly + *tonare* thunder, crash]

stun·ner (stun′ər) *n.* **1** One who or that which stuns. **2** *Slang* A person or thing of extraordinary or surprising qualities, such as beauty.

stun·ning (stun′ing) *adj.* **1** Rendering unconscious. **2** *Colloq.* Surprising; impressive; wonderful; beautiful. — **stun′ning·ly** *adv.*

stunt¹ (stunt) *v.t.* To check the natural development of; dwarf; cramp. — *n.* **1** A check in growth, progress, or development. **2** A stunted animal or thing. [OE *stunt* dull, foolish; prob. infl. in meaning by ON *stuttr* short] — **stunt′ed** *adj.* — **stunt′ed·ness** *n.*

stunt² (stunt) *U.S. Colloq. n.* **1** A sensational feat, as of bodily skill. **2** Any remarkable feat, enterprise, or undertaking. — *v.i.* To perform a stunt or stunts. — *v.t.* To perform stunts with (an airplane, etc.). [Prob. <G *stunde* lesson; orig. college slang]

stunt man In motion pictures, a man employed to perform dangerous actions, such as falling, jumping, etc., often as a temporary substitute for an actor.

stu·pa (stōō′pə) *n.* Tope⁴. [<Skt., heap]

stupe (stōōp, styōōp) *n. Med.* A compress or medicated cloth to be applied to a wound. [<L *stupa, stuppa* tow]

stu·pe·fa·cient (stōō′pə·fā′shənt, styōō′-) *adj.* Having power to stupefy; stupefying: also **stu′pe·fac′tive.** (-fak′tiv). — *n.* Anything that stupefies, as a narcotic. [<L *stupefaciens, -entis,* ppr. of *stupefacere* stun. See STUPEFY.]

stu·pe·fac·tion (stōō′pə·fak′shən, styōō′-) *n.* The act of stupefying or state of being stupefied; stupor. See synonyms under STUPIDITY.

stu·pe·fy (stōō′pə·fī, styōō′-) *v.t.* **·fied, ·fy·ing 1** To dull the senses or faculties of; stun. **2** To amaze; astound. [<F *stupéfier* <L *stupefacere* stun <*stupere* be stunned + *facere* make] — **stu′pe·fied** *adj.* — **stu′pe·fi′er** *n.*

stu·pen·dous (stōō·pen′dəs, styōō-) *adj.* Of prodigious size, bulk, or degree; characterized by any highly impressive feature: a *stupendous* structure, a *stupendous* error. See synonyms under IMMENSE. [<L *stupendus* amazed, orig. gerundive of *stupere* be benumbed, stunned] — **stu·pen′dous·ly** *adv.* — **stu·pen′dous·ness** *n.*

stu·pid (stōō′pid, styōō′-) *adj.* **1** Very slow of apprehension or understanding; dull-witted; sluggish. **2** Affected with stupor; stupefied: *stupid* from drink. **3** Marked by, or resulting from, lack of understanding, reason, or wit; senseless; doltish: *stupid* acts. See synonyms under ABSURD, BRUTISH, FLAT¹, HEAVY. [<L *stupidus* struck dumb <*stupere* be stunned] — **stu′pid·ly** *adv.* — **stu′pid·ness** *n.*

stu·pid·i·ty (stōō·pid′ə·tē, styōō-) *n.* The state, quality, or character of being stupid; great mental dulness. [<L *stupiditas, -tatis* <*stupidus.* See STUPID.]

Synonyms: apathy, dulness, insensibility, obtuseness, slowness, sluggishness, stupefaction, stupor. *Stupidity* is sometimes loosely used for temporary *dulness* or partial *stupor,* but chiefly for innate and chronic *dulness* and *sluggishness* of mental action, *obtuseness* of apprehension, etc. *Apathy* may be temporary, and be dispelled by appeal to the feelings or by the presentation of an adequate motive, but *stupidity* is inveterate and often incurable. Compare APATHY, IDIOCY, STUPOR. *Antonyms:* acuteness, alertness, animation, brilliancy, cleverness, intelligence, keenness, quickness, readiness, sagacity, sense, sensibility.

stu·por (stōō′pər, styōō′-) *n.* **1** A condition of

the body in which the senses and faculties are suspended or greatly dulled, as by drugs or intoxicants. **2** Extreme intellectual or moral dulness; gross stupidity. [<L *stupere* be stunned] — **stu′por·ous** *adj.*

Synonyms: apathy, asphyxia, coma, fainting, insensibility, lethargy, swoon, swooning, syncope, unconsciousness. The *apathy* of disease is a mental state of morbid indifference; *lethargy* is a morbid tendency to heavy and continued sleep, from which the patient may perhaps be momentarily aroused. *Coma* is a deep, abnormal sleep, from which the patient cannot be aroused, or is aroused only with difficulty, a state of profound *insensibility* perhaps with full pulse and deep, stertorous breathing, and is due to brain-oppression. *Syncope* or *swooning* is a sudden loss of sensation and of power of motion, with suspension of pulse and of respiration, and is due to failure of heart action, as from sudden nervous shock or intense mental emotion. *Insensibility* is a general term denoting loss of feeling from any cause, as from cold, intoxication, or injury. *Stupor* is especially profound and confirmed *insensibility,* properly comatose. *Asphyxia* is a special form of *syncope* resulting from partial or total suspension of respiration, as in strangulation or drowning. See STUPIDITY.

stur·dy (stûr′dē) *adj.* **·di·er, ·di·est 1** Possessing rugged health and strength; hardy; enduring; vigorous; lusty: *sturdy* health, *sturdy* blows. **2** Firm and unyielding; resolute: a *sturdy* defense. See synonyms under POWERFUL, STRONG. [<OF *estourdi* dazed, reckless <*estourdir* stun, amaze <LL *exturdire* deafen; ult. origin uncertain] — **stur′di·ly** *adv.* — **stur′di·ness** *n.*

stur·geon (stûr′jən) *n.* A large ganoid fish of northern regions (family *Acipenseridae*), with coarse, edible flesh, especially *Acipenser sturio,* the common sturgeon of both coasts of the Atlantic, which ascends rivers. Sturgeons are the principal source of isinglass and caviar. [<AF *sturgeon,* OF *sturgiun* <Med. L *sturio, -onis* <OHG *sturjo*]

stut·ter (stut′ər) *v.t. & v.i.* To utter or speak with spasmodic repetition, blocking, and prolongation of sounds and syllables, especially those in initial position in a word. — *n.* The act or habit of stuttering. See synonyms under STAMMER. [Freq. of ME *stutten* stutter] — **stut′ter·er** *n.* — **stut′ter·ing** *adj. & n.* — **stut′ter·ing·ly** *adv.*

St. Vi·tus' dance (sānt vī′təs·iz) *Pathol.* Chorea. Also **St. Vitus dance.**

sty¹ (stī) *n. pl.* **sties 1** A pen for swine. **2** Any filthy habitation or place of bestiality or debauchery. — *v.t. & v.i.* **stied, sty·ing** To keep or live in a sty or hovel. [OE *stī, stig*]

sty² (stī) *n. pl.* **sties** *Pathol.* A small, inflamed swelling of a sebaceous gland on the edge of the eyelid. Also **stye.** [<obs. *styanye* <OE *stigend,* ppr. of *stīgan* rise + *ye* eye]

Styg·i·an (stij′ē·ən) *adj.* **1** Pertaining to the river Styx; hence, infernal; dark and gloomy. **2** Inviolable, like the oath, "By the Styx." [<L *Stygius* <Gk. *Stygios* <*Styx* the Styx, prob. <*stygein* hate]

style (stīl) *n.* **1** Manner of expressing thought, in writing or speaking; distinctive or characteristic form of expression: a florid *style;* the *style* of Mark Twain. **2** A good or suitable mode of expression: His writing lacks *style.* **3** A particular form of composition, construction, or appearance, as in art, music, etc.: the Gothic *style;* the American *style* of automobile. **4** The manner in which some action or work is performed: The horse ran in fine *style.* **5** A good or exemplary manner of performing: a team with *style.* **6** A mode of conduct or behavior; a way of living: to

STURGEON
(Length up to 10 feet)

live in makeshift *style.* **7** A fashionable manner

or appearance: to live in *style*. **8** A particular fashion in clothing. **9** A particular type or fashion suitable for or agreeable to a person: That coat is not my *style*. **10** *Printing* The conventions of typography, design, etc., observed in a given printing office. **11** The legal or official title or appellation of a person, organization, etc. **12** A stylus (in any sense). **13** The gnomon of a sundial. **14** *Surg.* A slender probe with a blunt point: also called *stylet*. **15** *Bot.* The prolongation of a carpel or ovary, bearing the stigma. **16** *Zool.* A stylet. **17** A system of arranging the length of the calendar years so as to average that of the true solar year: called **New Style,** when following the arrangement made by Pope Gregory XIII (Gregorian calendar) and used in nearly all Christian countries; and **Old Style** when following the Julian calendar. England adopted the New Style by act of Parliament in 1752. Since 1900 New Style has been 13 days later than Old Style. See synonyms under AIR¹, CUSTOM, DICTION, MANNER, NAME. — *v.* **styled, styl·ing** *v.t.* **1** To name; give a title to. **2** To make consistent in typography, spelling, punctuation, etc., as copy to be printed; stylize. — *v.i.* **3** In ornamentation, to use a style or stylus. ◆ Homophone: *stile*. [<OF <L *stilus, stylus* writing instrument] — **styl′lar, styl′li·form** *adj.* — **styl′er** *n.*

sty·let (stī′lit) *n.* **1** Any slender pointed instrument, as a poniard or stiletto. **2** *Surg.* A style. **3** *Zool.* Any pointed, bristlelike process or appendage. [<F <Ital. *stiletto.* See STILETTO.]

sty·li·form (stī′lə·fôrm) *adj.* Resembling or shaped like a stylus. [<NL *styliformis* <L *stylus* a stylus + *forma* a form]

styl·ish (stī′lish) *adj.* Having style; especially, very fashionable. — **styl′ish·ly** *adv.* — **styl′ish·ness** *n.*

styl·ist (stī′list) *n.* **1** One who is a master of literary or rhetorical style. **2** An adviser concerning style in clothes, interior decoration, etc.

sty·lis·tic (stī·lis′tik) *adj.* Pertaining to style, especially literary style. — *n.* Stylistics. — **sty·lis′ti·cal·ly** *adv.*

sty·lis·tics (stī·lis′tiks) *n. pl.* (construed as singular) The art or study of literary expression.

sty·lite (stī′līt) *n.* One of a class of early religious ascetics who lived most of the time on the tops of pillars, without shelter. The practice was originated by Simeon Stylites in A.D. 420. [<Gk. *stylitēs* <*stylos* column]

styl·ize (stī′līz) *v.t.* **·ized, ·iz·ing** To conform to a distinctive mode or style; conventionalize. Also *Brit.* **styl′ise.** — **styl′i·za′tion** *n.* — **styl′iz·er** *n.*

stylo- *combining form* **1** A pillar: *stylobate.* **2** *Bot. & Zool.* A style; of or related to a style: *stylopodium.* **3** *Anat.* Denoting relationship to a styloid process. Also, before vowels, **styl-.** [<Gk. *stylos* a column, pillar]

sty·lo·bate (stī′lə·bāt) *n.* *Archit.* A continuous base for two or more columns, in contradistinction to a pedestal, which is a base for only one column or object. Compare STEREOBATE. [<L *stylobates* <Gk. *stylobatēs* <*stylos* pillar + *-batēs* a treader <*bainein* walk, step]

STYLOBATE (a)

sty·lo·graph (stī′lə·graf, -gräf) *n.* A fountain pen from which ink is fed to a conical writing point. Also **stylographic pen.** — **sty′lo·graph′ic** or **·i·cal** *adj.*

sty·log·ra·phy (stī·log′rə·fē) *n.* The art or process of writing, engraving, etc., with a stylus or other pointed instrument.

sty·loid (stī′loid) *adj.* Resembling a style or peg; styliform.

styloid process *Anat.* One of various bony processes, as the spine that projects from the base of the temporal bone; a projection on the head of the fibula; the pointed lower extremity of either the radius or the ulna; the proximal end of the third metacarpal bone.

sty·lo·lite (stī′lə·līt) *n.* *Geol.* A small columnar body of the same composition as the surrounding rock. — **sty′lo·lit′ic** (-lit′ik) *adj.*

---

sty·lo·po·di·um (stī′lə·pō′dē·əm) *n.* *pl.* **·di·a** (-dē·ə) *Bot.* The fleshy disk that bears the style in umbelliferous flowers. [<NL]

sty·lus (stī′ləs) *n.* **1** An ancient writing instrument, having one end pointed for writing on wax tablets and the other end blunt for erasure. **2** A pointed instrument for marking or engraving, as on carbons, stencils, etc. **3** The needle of a phonograph or of a sound-recording instrument. [<L]

sty·mie (stī′mē) *n.* A condition obtaining in golf when an opponent's ball lies in the line of the player's putt on the green, the balls being more than six inches apart. — *v.t.* **·mied, ·my·ing** **1** To block (an opponent) by or as by a stymie. **2** To baffle or perplex. Also spelled *stimy.* [Origin uncertain]

styp·sis (stip′sis) *n.* The application or the action of a styptic. [<LL <Gk., a contraction <*styphein* contract]

styp·tic (stip′tik) *adj.* **1** Causing contraction of living tissues, as blood vessels. **2** Preventing hemorrhage; astringent: a *styptic* pencil. Also **styp′ti·cal.** — *n.* A substance or agent that arrests bleeding. [<L *stypticus* <Gk. *styptikos* <*stypsis* a contraction. See STYPSIS.]

Sty·ra·ca·ce·ae (stī′rə·kā′si·ē) *n. pl.* An order of gamopetalous trees or shrubs yielding resins and gums, the storax family, having alternate simple leaves and usually white racemed flowers with a corolla of 4 to 8 united petals. They are found in all parts of the world. [<NL <L *styrax* storax] — **sty′·ra·ca′ceous** (-shəs) *adj.*

sty·rene (stī′rēn, stir′ēn) *n.* *Chem.* A colorless aromatic hydrocarbon, C_8H_8, contained in liquid storax, from which it may be derived by distillation. [<L *styrax* storax + -ENE]

Sty·ro·foam (stī′rə·fōm) *n.* A lightweight, rigid, cellular material formed from a synthetic hydrocarbon polymer: a trade name.

stythe (stīth) *n.* Chokedamp. [OE *stith* harsh]

Styx (stiks) In Greek mythology, the river of hate, one of the five rivers surrounding Hades.

su·a·ble (sōō′ə·bəl) *adj.* Legally subject to civil process; able to be sued. — **su′a·bil′i·ty** *n.*

sua·sion (swā′zhən) *n.* The act of persuading; persuasion: archaic except in the phrase **moral suasion.** [<OF <L *suasio, -onis* <*suadere* persuade] — **sua·sive** (swā′siv), **sua·so·ry** (swā′sər·ē) *adj.*

suave (swäv, swāv) *adj.* Smooth and pleasant in manner; bland; gracious. [<F <L *suavis* sweet] — **suave′ly** *adv.* — **suave′ness** *n.*

suav·i·ty (swä′və·tē, swav′ə-) *n. pl.* **·ties** **1** The state of being suave; urbanity. **2** Something that is suave, bland, or agreeable. [<F *suavité* <L *suavitas, -tatis* <*suavis* sweet]

sub (sub) *n. Colloq.* Short for: **1** A substitute. **2** A subordinate or subaltern. **3** A subway. **4** A submarine.
    Math. Denoting a ratio, the inverse of a given ratio: The *subtriplicate* ratio is the inverse of the ratio of the cube. **7** *Chem.* **a** Present (in a compound) in less than normal amount: *subchloride, suboxide.* **b** Designating a basic salt compound: *subacetate, subcarbonate.*
    Also: *suc-* before *c,* as in *succumb*; *suf-* before *f,* as in *suffer*; *sug-* before *g,* as in *suggest*; *sum-* before *m,* as in *summon*; *sup-* before *p,* as in *support*; *sur-* before *r,* as in *surrogate*; *sus-* before *c, p, t,* as in *susceptible, suspect, sustain.* [<L *sub-* <*sub* under]

sub·a·cute (sub′ə·kyōōt′) *adj.* **1** Somewhat acute. **2** Intermediate between acute and chronic: said of a disease. — **sub′a·cute′ly** *adv.*

sub·aer·i·al (sub′âr′ē·əl, -ā·ir′-) *adj.* Of, pertaining to, or formed at the earth's surface, in open air: contrasted with *aerial, submarine,* and *subterranean.*

sub·al·pine (sub·al′pīn, -pin) *adj.* **1** Lower than alpine. **2** Of or pertaining to mountainous regions near but below the timber line.

sub·al·ter·nate (sub·ôl′tər·nit, -al′-) *adj.* **1** Subordinate; subaltern. **2** Successive, or succeeding by turns. **3** *Bot.* Alternate, with a tendency to become opposite. — *n.* A particular as opposed to a universal proposition. [<Med. L *subalternatus,* pp. of *subalternare.* See SUBALTERNANT.]

sub·a·que·ous (sub·ā′kwē·əs) *adj.* **1** Being, formed, or operating under water; submarine. **2** Occurring under or in water; adapted for use under water. **3** Having an appearance like that produced under water.

---

sub·a·tom·ic (sub′ə·tom′ik) *adj.* Within the atom.

sub·ax·il·lar·y (sub·ak′sə·ler′ē) *adj.* **1** *Bot.* Lying under or beneath the axil. **2** *Anat.* Beneath the armpit.

sub·base·ment (sub′bās′mənt) *n.* An underground story, or any one of several below the first or true basement.

sub·car·ti·lag·i·nous (sub·kär′tə·laj′ə·nəs) *adj. Anat.* **1** Beneath cartilage or under tissue. **2** Partly cartilaginous.

sub·cel·lar (sub′sel′ər) *n.* A cellar under another cellar.

sub·class (sub′klas′) *n. Biol.* A plant or animal division intermediate between a class and an order; superorder.

sub·cla·vi·an (sub·klā′vē·ən) *Anat. adj.* **1** Situated beneath the clavicle. **2** Of or pertaining to the subclavian vessels. — *n.* A subclavian nerve, muscle, vein, etc. [<NL *subclavius* <L *sub-* under + *clavis* a key]

subclavian artery *Anat.* The large main artery that passes under the clavicle to convey blood to the arm.

subclavian groove *Anat.* A groove made by the subclavian artery or vein on the first rib.

subclavian vein *Anat.* That portion of the main venous trunk of the arm that lies under the clavicle.

sub·cli·max (sub·klī′maks) *n.* **1** A stage prior to or below the climax. **2** *Ecol.* **a** Any stage in the development of a plant or animal community determined by agencies other than climate which prevent attainment of the normal climax. **b** Any community so acted upon. — **sub·cli·mac·tic** (sub′klī·mak′tik) *adj.*

sub·clin·i·cal (sub·klin′ə·kəl) *adj.* Not able to be diagnosed by ordinary clinical tests: a *subclinical* infection.

sub·com·mit·tee (sub′kə·mit′ē) *n.* An undercommittee; part of a committee appointed for special work.

sub·con·scious (sub·kon′shəs) *adj.* **1** Only dimly conscious; not clearly discerned by the conscious subject; lacking intellectual clearness. **2** *Psychol.* Denoting such phenomena of mental life as are not attended by full consciousness, as the many automatic processes involved in the performance of familiar actions. — *n.* **1** That portion of mental activity not directly in the focus of consciousness but sometimes susceptible to recall by the proper stimulus. **2** *Psychoanal.* The preconscious. — **sub·con′scious·ly** *adv.* — **sub·con′scious·ness** *n.*

sub·con·ti·nent (sub·kon′tə·nənt) *n.* A great land mass forming part of a continent but having considerable geographical independence, as India.

sub·con·tract (sub·kon′trakt) *n.* A contract subordinate to another contract and assigning part of the work to a third party. — *v.t. & v.i.* (sub′kən·trakt′) To make a subcontract (for); arrange for part or all of (work) to be performed by a third party.

sub·con·trac·tor (sub′kən·trak′tər, -kon′trak-) *n.* One who enters into a contract with a contractor to do work embraced in the latter's contract.

sub·cul·ture (sub·kul′chər) *n.* **1** *Bacteriol.* A culture of bacteria or other material derived from a preexisting culture. **2** *Sociol.* A group having specific patterns of behavior that set it off from other groups within a culture or society.

sub·cu·ta·ne·ous (sub′kyōō·tā′nē·əs) *adj.* **1** Situated, found, or applied beneath the skin. **2** Hypodermic. [< LL *subcutaneus* <L *sub-* under + *cutis* skin] — **sub′cu·ta′ne·ous·ly** *adv.*

sub·dean (sub′dēn′) *n.* An assistant or substitute dean. [<OF *soudeien* <*sou-* SUB- + *deien* a dean]

sub·di·vide (sub′di·vīd′) *v.t. & v.i.* **·vid·ed, ·vid·ing** **1** To divide (a part) resulting from a previous division; divide again. **2** To divide (land) into lots for sale or improvement. [< LL *subdividere* < L *sub-* under + *dividere* DIVIDE]

sub·di·vi·sion (sub′di·vizh′ən) *n.* **1** Division following upon division. **2** A part, as of land, resulting from subdividing. See synonyms under PART.

sub·dom·i·nant (sub·dom′ə·nənt) *n. Music* The tone next below the dominant; fourth tone or degree of a major or minor scale. — *adj.* Less important than the dominant.

sub·duce (sub-dōōs', -dyōōs') v.t. **·duced, ·duc·ing** Obs. **1** To withdraw; take away. **2** To take as a part from a whole; subtract. Also **sub·duct'** (-dukt'). [< L subducere < sub- from + ducere lead] —**sub·duc'tion** (-duk'shən) n.

sub·duc·tion (sub-duk'shən) n. Geol. The sinking of one tectonic plate beneath the edge of another.

sub·due (sub-dōō', -dyōō') v.t. **·dued, ·du·ing 1** To gain dominion over, as by war or force; subjugate; vanquish. **2** To overcome by training, influence, or persuasion; tame. **3** To repress (emotions, impulses, etc.). **4** To reduce the intensity of; soften, as a color or sound. **5** To bring (land) under cultivation. [< OF soduire seduce < L subducere SUBDUCE; infl. in meaning by L subdere overcome] —**sub·du'a·ble** adj. —**sub·du'al** n. —**sub·du'er** n.

Synonyms : beat, break, bridle, conquer, control, crush, master, overbear, overcome, overpower, overwhelm, reduce, repress, subject, suppress, train, vanquish. See CHASTEN, CONQUER, REPRESS.

sub·en·try (sub'en'trē) n. An entry made on a list beneath a major entry.

sub·e·qua·to·ri·al (sub-ē'kwə-tôr'ē-əl, -tō'rē-) adj. **1** Nearly equatorial. **2** Denoting or belonging to a region adjoining the equatorial region.

su·ber·ic (sōō·ber'ik) adj. Of, pertaining to, or derived from cork.

su·ber·in (sōō'bər·in) n. A waxlike, fatty substance formed in cork cells.

su·ber·ize (sōō'bə·rīz) v.t. **·ized, ·iz·ing** To make corky, as cell walls.

su·ber·ose (sōō'bər·ōs) adj. **1** Corky. **2** Of or pertaining to suberin. Also **su'ber·ous** (-əs).

sub·fam·i·ly (sub·fam'ə·lē, -fam'lē) n. pl. **·lies 1** A division of plants or animals next below a family but above the genus. **2** Ling. A division of languages below a family and above a branch.

sub·gla·cial (sub·glā'shəl) adj. Deposited or formed at the bottom of or beneath a glacier.

sub·group (sub'grōōp') n. **1** An inferior order, or one of the biological divisions of an order. **2** Chem. A group that is included within a superior group, as in the periodic table of the elements.

sub·head (sub'hed') n. **1** A heading or title of a subdivision: also **sub·head'ing. 2** An official next below the head in a college or school.

sub·hu·man (sub·hyōō'mən) adj. **1** Less than or imperfectly human. **2** Anthropol. Below the level of the primate type represented by Homo sapiens.

sub·hu·mid (sub·hyōō'mid) adj. Intermediate between semiarid and humid: said especially of a climate with sufficient precipitation to support a moderate to dense growth of tall and short grasses.

sub·in·ci·sion (sub'in·sizh'ən) n. **1** A cutting beneath or under. **2** Among certain primitive peoples, a slitting open of the urethra of the penis.

sub·in·dex (sub·in'deks) n. pl. **·in·dices** (-in'də·sēz) An indicative figure, letter, or sign following and slightly underneath a figure, letter, or sign: in M_n, X_2, Y_4, the subindices are n, 2, and 4.

sub·in·feu·da·tion (sub'in·fyōō·dā'shən) n. **1** The granting of lands by a feudal vassal to a tenant who thus becomes his vassal. **2** The feud or fief resulting from subinfeudation. —**sub·in·feu·da·to·ry** (sub'in·fyōō'də·tôr'ē, -tō'·rē) adj.

su·bi·to (sōō'bē·tō) adv. Music Quickly; suddenly. [< Ital. < L subitus, pp. of subire come or go stealthily < sub- secretly + ire go]

sub·ja·cent (sub·jā'sənt) adj. **1** Situated underneath. **2** Being at a lower elevation. [< L subjacens, -entis, ppr. of subjacere < sub- under + jacere lie] —**sub·ja'cen·cy** n.

sub·ject (sub'jikt) adj. **1** Being under the power of another; owing or yielding obedience to sovereign authority. **2** Exposed to some agency or tendency: subject to headache; a climate subject to storms. **3** Being under discretionary authority: a treaty subject to ratification. —n. **1** One who is under the governing power of another, as of a ruler or government, especially of a monarch. **2** One who or that which is employed or treated in

a specified way, as a body for dissection, a person used in hypnotic experiments, one attacked by or liable to any disease. **3** Something upon which thought or the artistic constructive faculty is employed, as a theme of consideration or the general idea or plan of an artistic work. **4** Gram. The word, phrase, or clause of a sentence about which something is stated or asked in the predicate. **5** Music The melodic phrase on which a composition or a part of it is based. **6** A branch of learning. **7** The originating clause or motive. **8** The ego or self; that of which qualities or attributes are affirmed; substance; essential being; the thinking, feeling agent. **9** Logic In a proposition, that term about which something is affirmed or denied. See PROPOSITION. See synonyms under TOPIC. —v.t. (səb·jekt') **1** To bring under dominion or control; subjugate. **2** To cause to undergo some experience or action. **3** To offer for consideration or approval; submit. **4** To make liable; expose: His inheritance was subjected to heavy taxation. **5** Obs. To place beneath. See synonyms under CONQUER, SUBDUE. [< OF suget, sujet < L subjectus, pp. of subjicere < sub- under + jacere throw; refashioned after L] Synonyms (adj.): dependent, disposed, exposed, inferior, liable, obnoxious, prone, subordinate. Antonyms: clear, exempt, free, supreme, uncontrolled, unrestrained.

sub·jec·tion (səb·jek'shən) n. The act of making subject or bringing into a state of subjection.

sub·jec·tive (səb·jek'tiv) adj. **1** Relating to, or conditioned by, mental states or the ego; proceeding from or taking place within the thinking subject: opposed to objective. **2** Pertaining to the real nature or essence or substance of a person or thing; inherent; essential. **3** Peculiar to an individual; fanciful; illusory. **4** Inclined to be submissive; obedient. **5** Gram. Designating that case of the substantive used to denote its function as subject of a finite verb. **6** In literature and art, giving prominence to the subject or author as treating of his inner experience and emotion. **7** Introspective. —**sub·jec'tive·ly** adv. —**sub·jec'tive·ness, sub·jec·tiv·i·ty** (sub'jek·tiv'ə·tē) n.
◆ Subjective and objective, paired words, are strictly speaking neither synonyms nor antonyms. In scholasticism and philosophies of idealism they are both concerned with the object perceived, but represent different approaches to it. Objective signifies the relating of mental states to an object, that is, to something outside the perceiving mind which is recognized as having an existence outside that mind. Subjective relates to a feeling, attitude, or cognition that is recognized as being a construct within the mind of the perceiver, even though it takes the external object as its point of departure. Different individuals may receive different subjective impressions from the same objective fact. See INHERENT, OBJECTIVE.

sub·jec·tiv·ism (səb·jek'tiv·iz'əm) n. **1** The doctrine that knowledge is merely subjective and relative and is derived from one's own consciousness. **2** The doctrine that we know directly no external object. **3** The doctrine that there is no objective standard, test, or measure of truth; relativism. **4** The doctrine that individual feeling is the standard by which to judge right and wrong. —**sub·jec'tiv·ist** n. —**sub·jec'tiv·is'tic** adj

sub·ju·gate (sub'jōō·gāt) v.t. **·gat·ed, ·gat·ing 1** To bring under dominion; conquer; subdue. **2** To make subservient in any way; enslave. See synonyms under CONQUER. [< L subjugatus, pp. of subjugare < sub- under + jugum a yoke] —**sub'ju·ga'tion** n. —**sub'ju·ga'tor** n.

sub·junc·tive (səb·jungk'tiv) Gram. adj. Of or pertaining to that mood of the finite verb that is used to express a future contingency, a supposition implying the contrary, a mere supposition with indefinite time, or a wish or desire. In English the forms of the subjunctive mood are introduced by conjunctions of condition, doubt, contingency, possibility, etc., as if, though, lest, unless, that, till, or whether, but verbs in conditional clauses are not always in the subjunctive mood, for the

use of these conjunctions with the indicative is very common. —n. **1** The subjunctive mood. **2** A verb form or construction in this mood. [< L subjunctivus < subjunctus, pp. of subjungere SUBJOIN]

sub·king·dom (sub·king'dəm) n. A phylum.

sub·lap·sar·i·an (sub'lap·sâr'ē·ən) n. A believer in the predestinarian view held by moderate Calvinists that God foresaw the fall of man and decreed to save some by election. —adj. Relating to the sublapsarians or to their tenets. [< NL sublapsarius < L sub- consequent upon, under + lapsus a fall] —**sub'·lap·sar'i·an·ism** n.

sub·la·tion (sub·lā'shən) n. Med. The detachment, displacement, or removal of a part. [< L sublatio, -onis < sublatus, pp. to tollere lift up, take away]

sub·lease (sub·lēs') v.t. **·leased, ·leas·ing** To obtain or let (property) on a sublease. —n. (sub'lēs') A lease of property from a tenant or lessee.

sub·let (sub·let', sub'let') v.t. **·let, ·let·ting 1** To let to another (property held on a lease); underlet. **2** To let (work that one has contracted to do) to a subordinate contractor.

sub·le·thal (sub·lē'thəl) adj. Having an effect short of death: a sublethal dose of poison.

sub·li·mate (sub'lə·māt) v. **·mat·ed, ·mat·ing** v.t. **1** Chem. To convert from a solid to a vapor by heat, and then solidify again by cooling, with no apparent intermediate liquefaction. **2** To refine; purify. **3** Psychol. To convert the energy of (primitive impulses) into acceptable social and cultural manifestations. —v.i. **4** To undergo or engage in sublimation. —adj. Sublimated; refined. —n. Chem. The product of sublimation, especially when regarded as purified by the process. [< L sublimatus, pp. of sublimare < sublimis SUBLIME]

sub·li·ma·tion (sub'lə·mā'shən) n. **1** The act or process of sublimating. **2** That which has been sublimated; the pure essence of a thing. **3** Psychol. The transfer of psychic energy into socially acceptable channels of endeavor.

sub·lime (sə·blīm') adj. **1** Characterized by elevation, nobility, or awe; grand; solemn. **2** Preeminent for nobility of character or attainment; majestic; noble: said of persons. **3** Being of the highest degree; supreme; utmost. **4** Poetic Of lofty bearing; haughty; proud; elated. —n. That which is sublime, in any sense: usually with the definite article. —v. **·limed, ·lim·ing** v.t. **1** To make sublime; ennoble. **2** To purify by sublimating. —v.i. To become sublimated. [< L sublimis lofty, prob. < sub- up to, under + limen a lintel] —**sub·lime'ly** adv. —**sub·lim'er** n. —**sub·lim·i·ty** (sə·blim'ə·tē), **sub·lime'ness** n.

Synonyms (adj.): beautiful, exalted, grand, lofty, magnificent, majestic, stately. Sublime represents the ultimate, the quintessence, and is seldom applied to persons. What is beautiful attracts, but what is sublime transcends the beautiful and inspires awe rather than simple delight. Majestic refers exclusively to superficial effect which makes an impression but has no connection with moral greatness. Magnificent denotes the possession at once of greatness, splendor, and richness; as, magnificent array. See GRAND. Antonyms: base, contemptible, insignificant, little, mean, petty, ridiculous.

sub·lim·i·nal (sub·lim'ə·nəl) adj. Psychol. **1** Below the threshold of consciousness: opposed to supraliminal: said of psychophysical changes of too small intensity to produce definite sensations or a clear awareness: a subliminal stimulus. **2** Belonging to the subconscious. [< SUB- + L limen, liminis threshold, trans. of G unter der Schwelle (des Bewusstseins) under the threshold (of consciousness)]

sub·lu·nar·y (sub'lōō·ner'ē, sub·lōō'nər·ē) adj. **1** Situated beneath the moon: also **sub·lu·nar** (sub·lōō'nər). **2** Terrestrial; earthly. [< NL sublunaris < L sub- under + luna the moon]

sub·ma·chine gun (sub'mə·shēn') A lightweight, gas-operated gun, automatic or semi-automatic in action, designed for firing from the shoulder or hip. —**Thompson submachine gun** An air-cooled, .45-caliber submachine gun with automatic firing action:

also called *Tommy gun*: named for its inventor, John T. *Thompson*, 1860–1940, U.S. Army officer.

SUBMACHINE GUN
a. Stock. *b.* Housing. *c.* Barrel.
d. Trigger. *e.* Trigger guard. *f.* Clip.

sub·mar·gin·al (sub·mär'jən·əl) *adj.* **1** Below the margin. **2** Below economic sufficiency: *submarginal* land. **3** *Biol.* Situated close to the margin of an organ or structure.

sub·ma·rine (sub'mə·rēn') *adj.* Existing, done, or operating beneath the surface of the sea: a *submarine* mine: contrasted with *subaerial.* — *n.* (sub'mə·rēn) A boat designed to operate both on, and at various depths below, the surface of the sea, and now often powered by a reactor using nuclear fuel.

sub·max·il·lar·y (sub·mak'sə·ler'ē) *Anat. adj.* **1** Of, pertaining to, or situated beneath the lower jaw. **2** Of or pertaining to one of the salivary glands situated near the angle of the lower jaw. — *n. pl.* **·lar·ies** The lower jaw bone: also **sub·max·il·la** (sub'mak·sil'ə).

sub·me·di·ant (sub·mē'dē·ənt) *n. Music* The sixth tone of a major or minor scale.

sub·merge (səb·mûrj') *v.* **·merged, ·merg·ing** *v.t.* **1** To place under or plunge into water. **2** To cover; hide. — *v.i.* **3** To sink or dive beneath the surface of water. Also **sub·merse'** (-mûrs'). See synonyms under IMMERSE. [<L *submergere*, var. of *summergere* < *sub-* under + *mergere* plunge] — **sub·mer'gence, sub·mer'·sion** (-mûr'shən, -zhən) *n.*

sub·mer·gi·ble (səb·mûr'jə·bəl) *adj.* Capable of being submerged. — **sub·mer'gi·bil'i·ty** *n.*

sub·mersed (səb·mûrst') *adj.* **1** *Bot.* Growing under water. **2** Submerged. [<L *submersus*, pp. of *submergere* SUBMERGE]

sub·mers·i·ble (səb·mûr'sə·bəl) *adj.* That may be submerged. — *n.* A submarine.

sub·mi·cro·scop·ic (sub·mī'krə·skop'ik) *adj.* Below the limit of vision in a microscope.

sub·mis·sion (səb·mish'ən) *n.* **1** The act of submitting; a yielding to the power or authority of another; obedience. **2** The state or quality of being submissive; the spirit of subjection or obedience; an acquiescent temper; humility; resignation; meekness. **3** The act of referring, or the agreement to refer, a matter of controversy to arbitration. **4** *Archaic* Acknowledgment of error.
Synonyms: obedience, patience, resignation, subjection, submissiveness. See PATIENCE.

sub·mis·sive (səb·mis'iv) *adj.* Willing or inclined to submit; yielding; obedient; docile. See synonyms under DOCILE, HUMBLE, OBSEQUIOUS, PASSIVE, SUPPLE. — **sub·mis'sive·ly** *adv.* — **sub·mis'sive·ness** *n.*

sub·mit (səb·mit') *v.* **·mit·ted, ·mit·ting** *v.t.* **1** To place under or yield to the authority, will, or power of another; surrender. **2** To present for the consideration, decision, or approval of others; refer. **3** To present as one's opinion; suggest. — *v.i.* **4** To give up; surrender. **5** To be obedient or submissive; be acquiescent. See synonyms under BEND[1], DEFER, OBEY. [<L *submittere*, var. of *summittere* < *sub-* underneath + *mittere* send] — **sub·mit'tal** *n.* — **sub·mit'ter** *n.*

sub·mon·tane (sub·mon'tān) *adj.* **1** Situated at the foot of a mountain or mountain range. **2** Beneath a mountain. — **sub·mon'tane·ly** *adv.*

sub·nor·mal (sub·nôr'məl) *adj.* **1** Below the normal. **2** *Psychol.* Of less than normal intelligence. — *n.* **1** *Math.* That portion of the axis of a curve included between the ordinate of one of its points and the normal to that point. **2** A subnormal individual. —

sub·o·ce·an·ic (sub'ō·shē·an'ik) *adj.* Occurring, formed, or happening beneath the ocean floor.

sub·or·der (sub'ôr'dər) *n.* **1** *Biol.* A category

of animals or plants next below an order. **2** A subordinate architectural order modifying the principal order, generally for decoration. — **sub·or·di·nal** (sub·ôr'də·nəl) *adj.*

sub·or·di·nate (sə·bôr'də·nit) *adj.* **1** Belonging to an inferior order in a classification; secondary; minor. **2** Subject or subservient to another; inferior in any way. **3** Dependent; joining dependent words to others. See synonyms under AUXILIARY, SUBJECT. — *n.* One who is subordinate; an inferior in rank or official position. — *v.t.* (-nāt) **·nat·ed, ·nat·ing** **1** To make subordinate; assign to a lower order or rank; hence, to hold as of less importance. **2** To make subject or subservient. [<L *subordinatus*, pp. of *subordinare* < *sub-* under + *ordinare* order] — **sub·or'di·nate·ly** *adv.* — **sub·or'di·nate·ness** *n.* — **sub·or'di·na'tion** *n.*

subordinate conjunction See under CONJUNCTION.

sub·or·di·na·tion·ism (sə·bôr'də·nā'shən·iz'əm) *n. Theol.* The doctrine that the second and third persons of the Trinity are inferior to the first person. — **sub·or'di·na'tion·ist** *n.*

sub·or·di·na·tive (sə·bôr'də·nā'tiv) *adj.* Having a tendency to or expressive of subordination.

sub·orn (sə·bôrn') *v.t.* **1** To bribe or procure (someone) to commit perjury. **2** To incite or instigate to an evil act, especially a criminal act. **3** *Obs.* To decorate or adorn. [<L *subornare* < *sub-* secretly + *ornare* equip] — **sub·orn'er** *n.* — **sub·or·na·tion** (sub'ôr·nā'shən) *n.*

sub·phy·lum (sub·fī'ləm) *n. Biol.* A primary division of a phylum, superior to the class.

sub–plot (sub'plot') *n.* A plot subordinate to the principal one in a novel, play, etc.

sub·poe·na (sə·pē'nə, səb-) *n.* A judicial writ requiring a person to appear at a specified time and place under penalty for default. — *v.t.* To notify or summon by writ or subpoena. Also **sub·pe'na.** [<Med. L <L *sub poena* < *sub* under + *poena* penalty]

sub·pre·fect (sub·prē'fekt) *n.* A subordinate prefect; in France, the administrative officer of an arrondissement. — **sub·pre'fec·ture** (-fek·chər) *n.*

sub·prin·ci·pal (sub·prin'sə·pəl) *n.* **1** A vice principal. **2** A rafter or brace next to or auxiliary to one of the main timbers of the frame. **3** *Music* An open diapason sub–bass in an organ.

sub·ra·mose (sub·rā'mōs) *adj. Bot.* **1** Branching moderately, as a plant. **2** Having few branches. [<NL *subramosus* <L *sub-* somewhat, under + *ramosus* RAMOSE]

sub·re·gion (sub'rē'jən) *n.* A subdivision of a region, especially with reference to the distribution of animals. — **sub·re'gion·al** *adj.*

sub·ro·gate (sub'rō·gāt) *v.t.* **·gat·ed, ·gat·ing** **1** To substitute (one thing) for another. **2** To substitute (one person) for another when attributing or assigning rights or appointing to an office. [<L *subrogatus*, pp. of *subrogare* substitute < *sub-* in place of + *rogare* ask] — **sub·ro·ga·tion** (sub'rō·gā'shən) *n.* **1** The succession or substitution of one person or thing by or for another. **2** *Law* The putting of a person who (as a surety) has paid the debt of another in the place of the creditor to whom he has paid it.

sub ro·sa (sub rō'zə) *Latin* Confidentially; in secret: literally, under the rose: because, in Egypt, the rose was the emblem of Horus, (Roman Harpocrates), mistakenly regarded by the Greeks and Romans as the god of silence, for he was often depicted as a child with finger on mouth.

sub·scribe (səb·skrīb') *v.* **·scribed, ·scrib·ing** *v.t.* **1** To write, as one's name, at the end of a document; sign. **2** To sign one's name to as an expression of assent, acceptance, etc.; attest to by signing. **3** To promise, especially in writing, to pay or contribute (a sum of money). — *v.i.* **4** To write one's name at the end of a document. **5** To give sanction, support, or approval; agree. **6** To promise to pay or contribute money. **7** To agree to receive and pay for an article, as a periodical, usually by written agreement: with *to.* [<L *subscribere* < *sub-* underneath + *scribere* write] — **sub·scrib'er** *n.*

sub·script (sub'skript) *adj.* **1** Written following and slightly beneath, as a small letter: iota *subscript.* **2** *Math.* Of a subindex. — *n.* A subscript sign, symbol, or letter. Compare

SUPERSCRIPT. [<L *subscriptus*, pp. of *subscribere.* See SUBSCRIBE.]

sub·scrip·tion (səb·skrip'shən) *n.* **1** The act of subscribing; signature; hence, consent, confirmation, or agreement. **2** That which is subscribed; a signed paper or statement. **3** A signature written at the end of a document. **4** A signed acceptance of religious articles. **5** The individual or total sum or number subscribed for any purpose. **6** A formal agreement or undertaking evinced by signature, as payment of a certain price for the receipt of a magazine, book, ticket, etc. **7** *Archaic* Submission; obedience. **8** The part of a doctor's prescription which gives directions for compounding the ingredients. **9** The sale of books, magazines, tickets, etc., by mail or by personal canvass. — **to take up a subscription** To collect money (for some special purpose or cause) from a large number of people. — **sub·scrip'tive** *adj.* — **sub·scrip'tive·ly** *adv.*

subscription list A list of the names of people and the amounts they have subscribed, as for a periodical, a charity, or other cause.

sub·sec·tion (sub·sek'shən, sub'sek'shən) *n.* A subdivision of a section.

sub·sec·tor (sub·sek'tər, sub'sek'tər) *n.* A portion of a military sector or coastal frontier marked out for convenience in operations.

sub·se·quence (sub'sə·kwəns) *n.* **1** The condition of being subsequent. **2** The act of following. Also **sub'se·quen·cy.**

sub·se·quent (sub'sə·kwənt) *adj.* **1** Following in time, place, or order, or as a result. **2** Succeeding; consequent. [<L *subsequens, -entis,* ppr. of *subsequi* < *sub-* next below + *sequi* follow] — **sub'se·quent·ly** *adv.* — **sub'se·quent·ness** *n.*

sub·ser·vi·ent (səb·sûr'vē·ənt) *adj.* **1** Adapted to promote some end or purpose; being of service; useful as a subordinate. **2** Hence, acting in the interests of another; servile; obsequious; truckling. — *n.* One who or that which subserves. See synonyms under BASE[2]. [<L *subserviens, -entis,* ppr. of *subservire* SUBSERVE] — **sub·ser'vi·ent·ly** *adv.* — **sub·ser'vi·ent·ness, sub·ser'vi·ence, sub·ser'vi·en·cy** *n.*

sub·side (səb·sīd') *v.i.* **·sid·ed, ·sid·ing** **1** To sink to a lower level. **2** To become less violent or agitated; become calm or quiet; abate. **3** To sink to the bottom, as sediment; settle. See synonyms under ABATE, FALL. [<L *subsidere* < *sub-* under + *sidere* settle < *sedere* sit]

sub·sid·ence (səb·sīd'ns, sub'sə·dəns) *n.* **1** The settling of heavy parts to the bottom; precipitation. **2** The sinking of water or other liquids to a lower or usual level: *subsidence* of a flood. **3** A gradual settling into a quiet or inactive state. **4** A gradual settling of the earth to a lower level, because of ground movements or underground workings. [<L *subsidentia* sediment < *subsidere* SUBSIDE]

sub·sid·i·ar·y (səb·sid'ē·er'ē) *adj.* **1** Assisting in an inferior capacity; supplementary; auxiliary; secondary. **2** Of, pertaining to, or in the nature of a subsidy; helping by a subsidy. — *n. pl.* **·ar·ies** **1** One who or that which furnishes supplemental aid or supplies; an auxiliary; assistant. **2** *Music* A theme subordinate to or dependent on the main theme or subject. [<L *subsidiarius* < *subsidium* < *subsidere* SUBSIDE] — **sub·sid'i·ar'i·ly** *adv.*

subsidiary company A company controlled by another company which owns the greater part of its shares.

sub·si·dize (sub'sə·dīz) *v.t.* **·dized, ·diz·ing** **1** To furnish with a subsidy; grant a regular allowance or pecuniary aid to. **2** To obtain the assistance of by a subsidy: now often implying bribery. Also *Brit.* **sub'si·dise.** — **sub'si·di·za'tion** *n.* — **sub'si·diz'er** *n.*

sub·si·dy (sub'sə·dē) *n. pl.* **·dies** **1** Pecuniary aid directly granted by government to an individual or private commercial enterprise deemed beneficial to the public. **2** Formerly, an aid or tax granted by the House of Commons to the king for urgent needs of the kingdom. **3** Any financial assistance afforded by one individual or government to another. [<AF *subsidie*, OF *subside* <L *subsidium* auxiliary forces, aid < *subsidere* SUBSIDE]
Synonyms: aid, allowance, bonus, bounty, gift, grant, indemnity, pension, premium, reward, support, subvention, tribute. A nation grants a *subsidy* to an ally, pays a *tribute* to a conqueror. An *indemnity* is a single reparation

demanded for a specific injury, while a *tribute* may be exacted indefinitely. A nation may also grant a *subsidy* to its own citizens as a means of promoting the public welfare; as, a *subsidy* to a steamship company. The somewhat rare term *subvention* is especially applied to a *grant* of governmental aid to a literary or artistic enterprise. The word *bounty* may be applied to almost any regular or stipulated *allowance* by a government to a citizen or citizens; as, a *bounty* for enlisting in the army, a *bounty* for killing wolves, a land *bounty* to encourage settlement of sparsely populated areas. A *bounty* is reward for a single act; a *pension* is earned by long service.

sub·sist (səb·sist′) *v.i.* **1** To have existence or reality; continue to exist. **2** To remain alive; manage to live. **3** To continue unchanged; abide. **4** To have existence in or by something; inhere. — *v.t. Obs.* **5** To provide with food and clothing; support. See synonyms under LIVE. [<MF *subsister* <L *subsistere* <*sub-* under + *sistere* cause to stand <*stare* stand] — **sub·sist′er** *n.*

sub·sis·tence (səb·sis′təns) *n.* **1** The act of subsisting. **2** That on which one subsists; sustenance; means of support; livelihood. **3** The state of being subsistent; inherent quality. **4** That which subsists; real being. **5** A basis; a logical substance; hypostasis. Also **sub·sis′ten·cy.** [<LL *subsistentia* <*subsistere* SUBSIST]

sub·soil (sub′soil′) *n.* The stratum of earth next beneath the surface soil. — *v.t.* To turn up the subsoil of; plow with a subsoil plow. — **sub′soil′er** *n.*

sub·son·ic (sub·son′ik) *adj.* **1** Designating those sound waves beyond the lower limits of human audibility, or with frequencies of less than about 25 cycles per second; infrasonic. **2** Of, pertaining to, characterized, or operated by such waves. Compare SUPERSONIC.

sub·spe·cies (sub·spē′shēz, -shiz) *n. Biol.* A subdivision of a species, variously ranked but usually distinguished by minor differences in characteristics and by having a particular geographic range within a larger area. [<NL <L *sub-* under + *species* an appearance, sort]

sub·stance (sub′stəns) *n.* **1** The material of which anything is made or constituted. **2** The essential part of anything said or written; put into a brief, condensed statement; the gist or purport. **3** The vital part of that which is spiritual or emotional. **4** Material possessions; wealth; property. **5** That which gives stability or solidity; confidence; ground. **6** *Philos.* The essential nature that underlies phenomena; the permanent cause underlying outward manifestations; that in which qualities or attributes inhere. **7** In Christian Science, Spirit. **8** Any particular kind of material. **9** Essential components or characteristic elements of ideas: The tenets are the same in *substance.* See synonyms under MASS[1]. [<OF <L *substantia* <*substare* be present <*sub-* under + *stare* stand]

sub·stan·dard (sub·stan′dərd) *adj.* **1** Below the standard. **2** Lower than the established rate or authorized requirements.

sub·stan·tial (səb·stan′shəl) *adj.* **1** Solid; strong; firm. **2** Of real worth and importance; of considerable value; valuable. **3** Considerable and sure. **4** Possessed of wealth or sufficient means; responsible. **5** Of or pertaining to substance; having real existence; not illusory; actual; permanent; lasting. **6** Containing or conforming to the essence of a thing; giving the correct idea; essential; material; fundamental. **7** Ample and nourishing. — *n.* **1** That which has substance; a reality. **2** The more important part. — **sub·stan′ti·al′i·ty** (-shē·al′ə·tē), **sub·stan′tial·ness** *n.* — **sub·stan′tial·ly** *adv.*

sub·stan·ti·ate (səb·stan′shē·āt) *v.t.* **·at·ed, ·at·ing** **1** To establish, as a position or a truth, by substantial evidence; verify. **2** To give form to; embody. **3** To make substantial, existent, or real; give substance to. See synonyms under CONFIRM, RATIFY. [<NL *substantiatus,* pp. of *substantiare* establish <L *substantia* SUBSTANCE] — **sub·stan′ti·a′tion** *n.* — **sub·stan′ti·a·tive** *adj.*

sub·stan·tive (sub′stən·tiv) *n.* **1** A noun. **2** Anything used in place of a noun, as a verbal form, phrase, or clause. **3** One who or that which is independent; a self–subsisting person or thing. — *adj.* **1** Capable of being used as a noun. **2** Expressive of or denoting existence: The verb "to be" is called the *substantive* verb. **3** Having substance or reality; hence, lasting. **4** Being an essential part or constituent. **5** Relating to what is essential. **6** Having distinct individuality. **7** Independent in resources; self–supporting, as a country. **8** Of considerable amount; substantial. **9** In dyeing, not needing a mordant. [<OF *substantif* <LL *substantivus* <L *substantia* SUBSTANCE] — **sub′stan·tive·ness** *n.*

sub·stit·u·ent (səb·stich′oo·ənt) *n. Chem.* A radical, atom, or group, substituting or replacing another in a chemical reaction. — *adj.* Of a substituting atom or molecule. [<L *substituens, -entis,* ppr. of *substituere* SUBSTITUTE]

sub·sti·tute (sub′stə·toot, -tyoot) *v.* **·tut·ed, ·tut·ing** *v.t.* **1** To put in the place of another person or thing. **2** To take the place of. — *v.i.* **3** To act as a substitute. **4** *Chem.* To exchange one constituent of a compound for, or replace it with, another. See synonyms under CHANGE. — *n.* **1** One who or that which takes the place or serves in lieu of another. **2** In the American Civil War, one hired to serve in the place of a man drafted into military service. **3** Any substance or material adapted to replace another in a given product or process, or for a specified purpose: Gelatin is a *substitute* for agar, synthetic rubber for cork, etc.: also called *alternative, replacement.* See synonyms under DELEGATE. [<L *substitutus,* pp. of *substituere* <*sub-* in place of + *statuere* set up]

sub·sti·tu·tion (sub′stə·too′shən, -tyoo′-) *n.* **1** The act of substituting, or the state of being substituted. **2** *Chem.* Any reaction which involves the replacement of certain elements or radicals by others: said especially of organic compounds. — **sub′sti·tu′tion·al** *adj.* — **sub′sti·tu′tion·al·ly** *adv.*

sub·strate (sub′strāt) *n.* **1** *Biochem.* The material or substance acted upon by an enzyme or ferment. **2** A substratum. [<SUBSTRATUM]

sub·stra·tum (sub·strā′təm, -strat′əm) *n. pl.* **·stra·ta** (-strā′tə, -strat′ə) **1** An underlying stratum or layer, as of earth or rock; subsoil. **2** That which forms the foundation or groundwork. **3** Matter or mind considered as the ground of qualities and phenomena; the substance possessing attributes. **4** The substance in which something takes root, as vegetable or animal tissue. [<NL <L, pp. neut. of *substernere* spread underneath <*sub-* underneath + *sternere* strew] — **sub·stra′tive** *adj.*

sub·struc·ture (sub·struk′chər, sub′struk′-) *n.* **1** A structure serving as a foundation of a building, etc. **2** Groundwork. **3** The earthen roadway supporting railroad tracks. — **sub·struc′tur·al** *adj.*

sub·sume (səb·soom′) *v.t.* **·sumed, ·sum·ing** **1** To place in some particular class; classify. **2** To include, as the specific or individual in the general. [<NL *subsumere* <L *sub-* underneath + *sumere* take] — **sub·sum′a·ble** *adj.*

sub·sump·tion (səb·sump′shən) *n.* **1** The act of subsuming. **2** That which is subsumed; an assumption; especially, the minor premise of a syllogism as stated after the major premise. **3** Formerly, a narrative of an alleged crime giving minute particulars. [<NL *subsumptio, -onis* <*subsumere* SUBSUME] — **sub·sump′tive** *adj.*

sub·tan·gent (sub·tan′jənt) *n. Geom.* The portion of the axis of a curve cut off between the tangent to a given point and the ordinate of that point. [<NL *subtangens, -entis* <L *sub-* under + *tangens,* ppr. of *tangere* touch]

sub·tem·per·ate (sub·tem′pər·it) *adj.* **1** Pertaining to the colder parts of the temperate zone. **2** Slightly temperate.

sub·ten·ant (sub·ten′ənt) *n.* A person who rents or leases from a tenant; a sublessee. — **sub·ten′an·cy** *n.*

sub·tend (sub·tend′) *v.t.* **1** *Geom.* To extend under or opposite to, as the chord of an arc or the side of a triangle opposite to an angle.

2 *Bot.* To enclose in its axil: A leaf *subtends* a bud. [<L *subtendere* <*sub-* underneath + *tendere* stretch]

sub·tense (sub·tens′) *Geom. n.* **1** A line that subtends an arc or angle. **2** The chord of an arc. — *adj.* Pertaining to or used in estimating distance by measuring the subtended angle. [<NL *subtensa (linea)* (a) subtended (line), pp. fem. of L *subtendere* SUBTEND]

subter- *prefix* Under; less than: opposed to *super-: subteraqueous.* [<L *subter* below, beneath]

sub·ter·fuge (sub′tər·fyooj) *n.* That to which one resorts for escape or concealment; an evasion of an issue; a plan to avoid censure; a false excuse. See synonyms under ARTIFICE, SOPHISTRY. [<L *subterfugium* <*subterfugere* <*subter-* below, in secret + *fugere* flee, take flight]

sub·ter·ra·ne·an (sub′tə·rā′nē·ən) *adj.* **1** Situated or occurring below the surface of the earth: contrasted with *subaerial* and *surficial;* underground. **2** Hidden. Also **sub′ter·ra′ne·al, sub′ter·ra′ne·ous, sub′ter·ra′ne·rene′** (-tə·rēn′).

sub·tile (sut′l, sub′til) *adj.* **1** Having fine structure; delicately formed; ethereal. **2** Characterized by material rarity; rarefied; refined; hence, penetrating; pervasive. **3** Subtle. [<OF *subtil,* alter of *soutil* SUBTLE; refashioned after L] — **sub′tile·ly** *adv.* — **sub′tile·ness** *n.*
Synonym: subtle. *Subtile* and *subtle* have been constantly used as interchangeable by good writers; but there is a present tendency to distinguish them by making *subtile* an attribute of things and *subtle* a characteristic of mind. *Subtle,* the later form of the word, is used preferably when the derogatory sense of crafty is to be expressed. See ACUTE, ASTUTE, FINE[1].

sub·ti·tle (sub′tīt′l) *n.* A subordinate or explanatory title, as in a book, play, or document; a book title repeated, as on top of the first page of the text.

sub·tle (sut′l) *adj.* **1** Characterized by cunning, craft, or artifice; wily; crafty. **2** Keen; penetrative; discriminating: *subtle* humor; overrefined. **3** Apt; skilful. **4** Executed with nice art; ingenious; clever. **5** Insidious; secretly active. **6** Hard to understand; abstruse. **7** Of delicate texture. **8** Subtile. See synonyms under ACUTE, ASTUTE, FINE[1], INSIDIOUS, SUBTILE. [<OF *soutil* <L *subtilis* fine, orig. closely woven <*sub-* under + *tela* a web] — **sub′tle·ness** *n.* — **sub′tly** *adv.*

sub·tle·ty (sut′l·tē) *n. pl.* **·ties** **1** The state or quality of being subtle. **2** The ability to make fine distinctions; keenness of perception. **3** Something subtle, as a nice distinction.

sub·ton·ic (sub·ton′ik) *adj. Phonet.* Sonant or voiced, as certain consonants. — *n.* **1** *Phonet.* A subtonic sound. **2** *Music* The seventh of the scale; a semitone below the tonic.

sub·tract (səb·trakt′) *v.t. & v.i.* To take away or deduct, as a portion from the whole, or one quantity from another. [<L *subtractus,* pp. of *subtrahere* <*sub-* away + *trahere* draw] — **sub·tract′er** *n.*

sub·trac·tion (səb·trak′shən) *n.* **1** The act or process of subtracting; a deducting; something deducted. **2** *Math.* The operation of finding the difference between two quantities (symbol –).

sub·trac·tive (səb·trak′tiv) *adj.* **1** Serving or tending to diminish. **2** *Math.* Having the minus sign; to be subtracted.

subtractive process *Phot.* A method of making two or more negatives through filters which exclude all but a desired color: used in color printing and engraving.

sub·trop·i·cal (sub·trop′i·kəl) *adj.* **1** Of, pertaining to, or designating regions adjacent to the tropical zone. **2** Designating either of two irregular belts of high atmospheric pressure roughly between 30° and 40° latitude, north and south. Also **sub·trop′ic.**

sub·trop·ics (sub·trop′iks) *n. pl.* Subtropical regions.

sub·urb (sub′ûrb) *n.* A place adjacent to a city; in the plural, collectively, environs; outskirts; outlying residential districts; purlieus. [<OF *suburbe* <L *surburbium* <*sub-* near to + *urbs, urbis* a city]

sub·ur·ban (sə·bûr′bən) *adj.* Of or pertaining to a suburb; dwelling or located in a place which is a combination of the rural and urban. — *n.* A suburbanite.

sub·ur·ban·ite (sə·bûr′bən·īt) *n.* A resident of a suburb.

sub·ur·bi·a (sə·bûr′bē·ə) *n.* **1** The social and cultural world of suburbanites. **2** Suburbs or suburbanites collectively.

sub·vene (səb·vēn′) *v.i.* **·vened, ·ven·ing** To come or happen so as to be of aid or support, especially by preventing something; intervene. [<L *subvenire* come to one's assistance < *sub-* up from under + *venire* come]

sub·ven·tion (səb·ven′shən) *n.* **1** The act of subvening; giving of succor; aid. **2** That which aids, especially a grant, as of money; subsidy. See synonyms under SUBSIDY. [<OF *subvencion* <LL *subventio, -onis* <L *subvenire.* See SUBVENE.] — **sub·ven′tion·ar′y** (-er′ē) *adj.*

sub·ver·sion (səb·vûr′shən, -zhən) *n.* **1** The act of subverting, or the state of being subverted; a demolition; overthrow. **2** A cause of ruin. Also **sub·ver′sal** (-səl). See synonyms under RUIN. [<OF <LL *subversio, -onis* <L *subvertere* SUBVERT]

sub·ver·sive (səb·vûr′siv) *adj.* Tending to subvert or overthrow. — *n.* A person who engages in subversion.

sub·vert (səb·vûrt′) *v.t.* **1** To overthrow from the very foundation; destroy utterly. **2** To corrupt; undermine the morals or character of. [<OF *subvertir* <L *subvertere* overturn < *sub-* up from under + *vertere* turn] — **sub·vert′er** *n.* — **sub·vert′i·ble** *adj.*

Synonyms: destroy, extinguish, overthrow, overturn, supersede, supplant. To *supersede* implies the putting of something that is preferred in the place of that which is removed; to *subvert* does not imply substitution. To *supplant* is more often personal, signifying to take the place of another, usually by underhand means; one is *superseded* by authority, *supplanted* by a rival. See ABOLISH. *Antonyms:* conserve, perpetuate, preserve, sustain, uphold.

sub·vit·re·ous (sub·vit′rē·əs) *adj.* Having a luster resembling that of glass, but less brilliant.

sub·way (sub′wā) *n.* **1** An artificial passage below the surface of the ground; specifically, one for traffic, water and gas mains, electric cables, etc. **2** An underground railroad, usually electrically operated; also, a tunnel for such a railroad.

suc– Assimilated var. of SUB-.

suc·ceed (sək·sēd′) *v.i.* **1** To come next in order or sequence; follow; ensue. **2** To come after another into office, ownership, etc.; be the successor: often with *to.* **3** To be successful; accomplish what is attempted or intended; also, formerly, to achieve an end in a specified manner: They *succeeded* badly. **4** *Law* To devolve: said of an estate. — *v.t.* **5** To be the successor or heir of. **6** To come after in time or sequence; follow. [<OF *succeder* <L *succedere* go under, follow after < *sub-* under + *cedere* go] — **suc·ceed′er** *n.*

Synonyms: achieve, attain, flourish, prevail, prosper, thrive, win. To *win* implies that someone loses, but one may *succeed* where no one fails. A solitary swimmer *succeeds* in reaching the shore; if we say he *wins* the shore we place him in competition with the water. Many students may *succeed* in study; a few *win* the special prizes for which all compete. See FOLLOW.

suc·cès d'es·time (sük·se′ des·tēm′) *French* Success marked by the praise of critics but not by widespread popular approval: said of a play, book, etc.

suc·cess (sək·ses′) *n.* **1** A favorable or prosperous course or termination of anything attempted; prosperous or advantageous issue. **2** A successful person or affair. **3** *Obs.* The outcome or result, favorable or unfavorable. **4** *Obs.* Succession. See synonyms under VICTORY. [<L *successus* < *succedere* SUCCEED]

suc·cess·ful (sək·ses′fəl) *adj.* **1** Of persons, obtaining what one desires or intends; especially, having reached a high degree of worldly prosperity. **2** Of things, terminating in or meeting with success; resulting favorably: said of a course of action, etc. See synonyms under AUSPICIOUS, FORTUNATE, HAPPY. — **suc·cess′ful·ly** *adv.* — **suc·cess′ful·ness** *n.*

suc·ces·sion (sək·sesh′ən) *n.* **1** The act of following in order, or the state of being suc-

cessive; a following consecutively. **2** A group of things that succeed in order; a series, either in time or in place; sequence. **3** The act or right of legally or officially coming into a predecessor's office, possessions, etc.; also, the order of so succeeding, or that which is or is to be so taken. **4** The right or act of succeeding to a throne. **5** Descendants collectively; issue. See synonyms under TIME. — **suc·ces′sion·al** *adj.* — **suc·ces′sion·al·ly** *adv.*

suc·ces·sive (sək·ses′iv) *adj.* Following in succession; consecutive. — **suc·ces′sive·ly** *adv.* — **suc·ces′sive·ness** *n.*

suc·ces·sor (sək·ses′ər) *n.* One who or that which follows in succession; especially, a person who succeeds to a throne, property, or office.

suc·cinct (sək·singkt′) *adj.* **1** Reduced or comprised within a narrow compass; terse; concise. **2** Supported by an encircling silken thread, as a butterfly chrysalis. **3** *Archaic* Encircled or held in position by or as by a girdle. See synonyms under TERSE. [<L *succinctus,* pp. of *succingere* < *sub-* underneath + *cingere* gird] — **suc·cinct′ly** *adv.* — **suc·cinct′ness** *n.*

succinic acid *Chem.* Either of two white crystalline isomeric compounds, $C_4H_6O_2$, contained in amber and in certain plants, and also made synthetically.

suc·cor (suk′ər) *n.* **1** Help or relief rendered in danger, difficulty, or distress. **2** One who or that which affords relief. — *v.t.* To go to the aid of; help; rescue. See synonyms under AID, HELP, SERVE. Also *Brit.* **suc′cour.** [<OF *sucurs* <Med. L *succursus* <L *succurrere* < *sub-* up from under + *currere* run] — **suc′cor·a·ble** *adj.* — **suc′cor·er** *n.*

suc·co·ry (suk′ər·ē) *n.* Chicory. [Alter. of *cicoree, sichorie,* earlier vars. of CHICORY; infl. in form by MDu. *sukerie* chicory]

suc·co·tash (suk′ə·tash) *n.* A dish of Indian corn kernels and beans boiled together. [<Algonquian (Narraganset) *misickquatash* an ear of corn]

suc·cu·bus (suk′yə·bəs) *n. pl.* **·bi** (-bī) One of a class of demons in female form fabled to have intercourse with men in their sleep. [<Med. L <LL *succuba* a strumpet <L *succubare* < *sub-* underneath + *cubare* lie]

suc·cu·lent (suk′yə·lənt) *adj.* **1** *Bot.* Juicy; fleshy, as the tissues of certain plants. **2** Rich or vigorous: a *succulent* theme. [<L *succulentus* < *succus* juice] — **suc′cu·lence, suc′cu·len·cy** *n.* — **suc′cu·lent·ly** *adv.*

suc·cumb (sə·kum′) *v.i.* **1** To give way; yield, as to force or persuasion. **2** To die. [<OF *succomber* <L *succumbere* < *sub-* underneath + *cumbere* lie] — **suc·cum′bent** (-bənt) *adj.*

suc·cuss (sə·kus′) *v.t.* To shake suddenly or forcibly. [<L *succussus,* pp. of *succutere* < *sub-* up from under + *quatere* shake] — **suc·cus′sive** *adj.*

suc·cus·sion (sə·kush′ən) *n.* **1** The act of shaking. **2** *Med.* A vigorous shaking of the patient to detect liquids in the thorax or other cavities of the body. Also **suc·cus·sa·tion** (suk′ə-sā′shən). — **suc·cus·sa·to·ry** (sə·kus′ə-tôr′ē, -tō′rē) *adj.*

such (such) *adj.* **1** Of that kind; of the same or like kind: often with *as* or *that* completing the comparison: *Such* wit *as* this is rare. **2** Specifically, being the same as what has been mentioned or indicated: *Such* was the king's command. **3** Being the same in quality: Let the truthful continue *such.* **4** Being the same as something understood by the speaker or the hearer, or purposely left indefinite: a concise and elliptical use by which specification is avoided: the chief of *such* a clan. **5** So extreme, unpleasant, or the like: an emphatic or expletive use: We have come to *such* a pass. — *pron.* **1** Such a person or thing, or (more commonly) such persons or things: by ellipsis of the noun: The friend of *such* as are in trouble. **2** The same; the aforesaid: I bring good tidings, for *such* the general sent. — *adv.* So: *such* destructive criticism. [OE *swelc, swilc, swylc*]

such–and–such (such′ən·such′) *adj.* Being a particular person, thing, or time, not specifically named: He visited *such–and–such* a place. Also **such and such.**

such·like (such′līk′) *adj.* Of a like or similar kind. — *pron.* Persons or things of that kind: mosses, ferns, and *suchlike.*

suck (suk) *v.t.* **1** To draw into the mouth by means of a partial vacuum created by action of the lips and tongue. **2** To draw in or take up in a manner resembling this; inhale; absorb: The sponge *sucked* the water up. **3** To draw liquid or nourishment from with the mouth: to *suck* a lemon; also, to take into and hold in the mouth as if to do this: to *suck* one's thumb. **4** To consume by licking, or by holding in the mouth: to *suck* candy. **5** To bring to a specified state or condition by sucking: He *sucked* the lemon dry. — *v.i.* **6** To draw in liquid, air, etc., by suction. **7** To suckle. **8** To draw in air instead of water, as a defective pump does. **9** To make a sucking sound. — *n.* **1** The act of sucking; suction. **2** That which is sucked or comes by sucking. **3** A slight draft or drink. **4** A mother's milk. **5** A whirlpool or powerful eddy. [OE *sūcan*] — **suck′ing** *adj.* — **suck′ing·ly** *adv.*

suck·er (suk′ər) *n.* **1** One who or that which sucks; a suckler, as a suckling pig or a newly born whale. **2** A North American fresh–water fish (family *Catostomidae*), related to the cyprinoids, having the mouth usually protractile with thick and fleshy lips adapted for sucking in food. **3** *Zool.* An organ by which an animal adheres to other bodies; a suctorial organ. **4** *Slang* A toady; sponger; parasite; hanger-on. **5** *U.S. Slang* A foolish fellow; dolt; one easily deceived; a gull. **6** A piston, as of a syringe or a suction pump; a tube or pipe used for suction. **7** *Bot.* **a** A shoot or branch originating on a subterranean portion of a stem. **b** A shoot or sprout arising from the root near or remote from the trunk of certain trees. **8** A haustorium. **9** A sweetmeat; also, sugar. — *v.t.* To strip of suckers or shoots. — *v.i.* To form or send out suckers or shoots. [<SUCK]

suck·fish (suk′fish′) *n. pl.* **·fish** or **·fish·es 1** A remora. **2** A fish (*Caularchus maeandricus*) of the Pacific coast, with a ventrally placed sucker by which it attaches itself to stones, shells, etc.

suck·le (suk′əl) *v.* **·led, ·ling** *v.t.* **1** To give suck to, as at the breast. **2** To bring up; nourish. — *v.i.* **3** To take nourishment at the breast; suck. [ME *sucklen,* freq. of *suken* SUCK] — **suck′ler** *n.*

suck·ling (suk′ling) *n.* **1** An unweaned mammal. **2** A young, inexperienced person.

su·crate (sōō′krāt) *n. Chem.* A compound in which sucrose or some analogous carbohydrate combines with a base to form a salt: calcium *sucrate.* [<F <*sucre* sugar + *-ate* -ATE³]

su·crose (sōō′krōs) *n. Chem.* **1** Any one of the group of carbohydrates, including cane sugar, milk sugar, maltose, etc., having the common composition $C_{12}H_{22}O_{11}$, and deviating the plane of polarized light to the right. **2** Cane sugar as obtained from the sugarcane, maple, beet, etc. Also called *saccharose.* [<F *sucre* sugar + *-ose* -OSE²]

suc·tion (suk′shən) *n.* **1** The act or process of sucking. **2** The production of a partial vacuum in a space connected with a fluid or gas under pressure. **3** The tendency of a fluid to fill a vacuum contiguous with it. [<OF <L *suctio, -onis* <*sugere* suck]

suction pump A pump operating by suction, consisting of a piston working up and down in a cylinder, both equipped with valves: the most common form of house pump. Compare illustration under FORCE PUMP.

suction stop *Phonet.* A click, as in the Bushman and Hottentot languages. See CLICK (def. 3).

Suc·to·ri·a (suk·tôr′ē·ə, -tō′rē·ə) *n. pl.* A class or subclass of aquatic protozoans having in the adult stage long hollow tentacles for piercing and sucking. [<NL <L *suctus,* pp. of *sugere* suck]

suc·to·ri·al (suk·tôr′ē·əl, -tō′rē·əl) *adj.* **1** Adapted for sucking or for adhesion. **2** *Zool.* Living by sucking; having organs for sucking.

su·dan (sōō·dan′) *adj. Chem.* Designating any of a class of diazo compounds widely used as red and yellow dyes. [from *Sudan*]

Sudan, Republic of the An independent country in NE Africa; 967,500 square miles; capital, Khartoum.

su·dar·i·um (sōō·dâr′ē·əm) *n. pl.* **·dar·i·a** (-dâr′ē·ə) **1** A handkerchief or cloth for drying or removing perspiration; specifically, the sweat cloth or handkerchief of St. Veronica, said to have been miraculously impressed with the features of Jesus when she wiped his face on his way to crucifixion. **2** The napkin about the head of Christ in the tomb. *John* xx 7. **3** Any miraculous picture of Christ; a veronica. **4** A sudatory (def. 2). Also **su·da·ry** (sōō'dər·ē). [< L < *sudor*, *-oris* sweat]

su·da·tion (sōō·dā'shən) *n.* Morbid or excessive sweating. [< L *sudatio*, *-onis* < *sudatus*, pp. of *sudare* sweat]

su·da·to·ry (sōō'də·tôr·ē, -tō'rē) *adj.* **1** Producing perspiration; sudorific. **2** Perspiring. —*n. pl.* **·ries 1** An agent that causes sweating; a sudorific. **2** A sweating bath; specifically, a hot-air room in a Roman bath: also **su·da·to·ri·um**. [< L *sudatorius*]

sudd (sud) *n.* A floating mass of vegetation that frequently obstructs navigation on the White Nile. [< Arabic < *sudd* obstruct]

sud·den (sud'n) *adj.* **1** Happening quickly and without warning: *sudden* death. **2** Hurriedly or quickly contrived, used, or done; hasty. **3** Come upon unexpectedly; causing surprise. **4** Quick–tempered; precipitate; rash. See synonyms under IMPETUOUS, SWIFT[1]. —*n.* The state of being sudden, or that which is sudden: obsolete except in a few phrases. —**all of a sudden, all on a sudden, on a sudden** Without warning; on the spur of the moment. [< AF *sodein*, OF *soudain* < L *subitaneus* < *subitus*, pp. of *subire* come or go stealthily < *sub-* secretly + *ire* go] —**sud'den·ly** *adv.* —**sud'den·ness** *n.*

sudden death 1 Death that occurs suddenly or instantaneously, esp. violently. **2** *Sports* An extra period played in order to break a tie score, in which the first score ends the game.

su·dor·if·ic (sōō·də·rif'ik) *adj.* Causing perspiration. —*n.* A medicine that produces or promotes sweating. [< NL *sudorificus* < L *sudor*, *-oris* sweat + *facere* make]

suds (sudz) *n. pl.* **1** Soapy water worked up into bubbles and froth; foam; lather. **2** *Slang* Beer: so called from its foamy properties. [Prob. < MDu. *sudde*, *sudse* a marsh, marsh water] —**suds'y** *adj.*

sue (sōō) *v.* **sued, su·ing** *v.t.* **1** *Law* **a** To institute proceedings against for the recovery of some right or the redress of some wrong. **b** To prosecute (an action). **c** To seek a grant from (a court). **2** To endeavor to persuade by entreaty; beg; urge; petition. **3** To seek to win in marriage; woo. —*v.i.* **4** To institute legal proceedings. **5** To make entreaty. **6** *Archaic* To pay court; woo. [< AF *suer*, OF *suivre*, ult. < L *sequi* follow] —**su'er** *n.*

suède (swād) *n.* Undressed kid: often attributively: *suède* gloves. [< F *Suède* Sweden, in phrase *gants de Suède* Swedish gloves]

suède fabric A woven or knitted fabric of cotton, rayon, or wool, finished to resemble suède leather: used for sports coats and jackets, linings, gloves, etc.

su·et (sōō'it) *n.* The fatty tissues about the loins and kidneys of sheep, oxen, etc.: used in cookery and for making tallow. [Dim. of AF *sue*, OF *seu* < L *sebum* tallow, fat] —**su'et·y** *adj.*

MEDITERRANEAN SEA

Tel Aviv

Port Said

ISRAEL

SUEZ CANAL

Cairo

EGYPT

Suez

SINAI

JORDAN

Gulf of Suez

Aqaba

SAUDI ARABIA

Gulf of Aqaba

Suez, Isthmus of The neck of land joining Asia and Africa; between the Gulf of Suez

and the Mediterranean; 72 miles wide at its narrowest point; traversed by the **Suez Canal**, a ship canal 107 miles long, 197 feet wide, constructed (1859–69) by Ferdinand de Lesseps.

suf·fer (suf'ər) *v.i.* **1** To feel pain or distress. **2** To be affected injuriously; suffer loss or injury. **3** To undergo punishment; especially, to be put to death. **4** *Archaic* To tolerate or endure pain, injury, etc. —*v.t.* **5** To have inflicted on one; sustain, as an injury or loss. **6** To undergo; pass through, as change. **7** To bear; endure: He cannot *suffer* more pain. **8** To allow; permit: Will he *suffer* us to leave? See synonyms under ALLOW, ENDURE, PERMIT. [< AF *suffrir*, OF *sofrir*, ult. < L *sufferre* < *sub-* up from under + *ferre* bear] —**suf'fer·er** *n.*

suf·fer·ance (suf'ər·əns, suf'rəns) *n.* **1** Permission given or implied by failure to prohibit; negative consent. **2** In customs, a permit for the shipment of certain kinds of goods to specified ports. **3** The act or state of suffering; wretchedness; experience of pain or evil; power to endure. **4** Patience or endurance under suffering; submission; submissiveness. **5** *Rare* Loss; injury; damage. See synonyms under PATIENCE. [< AF, OF *sufrance* < LL *sufferentia* < *sufferre* SUFFER]

suf·fer·ing (suf'ər·ing, suf'ring) *n.* **1** The state of anguish or pain of one who suffers; the bearing of pain, injury, or loss. **2** The pain so borne; distress; loss; injury. See synonyms under AGONY, PAIN. —*adj.* Inured to pain and loss; submissive. —**suf'fer·ing·ly** *adv.*

suf·fice (sə·fīs') *v.* **·ficed, ·fic·ing** *v.i.* To be sufficient or adequate; meet the requirements or answer the purpose. —*v.t.* To be satisfactory or adequate for; satisfy. See synonyms under SATISFY, SERVE. [< OF *suffis-*, stem of *suffire* < L *sufficere* < *sub-* under + *facere* make] —**suf·fic'er** *n.*

suf·fi·cien·cy (sə·fish'ən·sē) *n. pl.* **·cies 1** The state of being sufficient. **2** That which is sufficient; especially, adequate pecuniary means or income; a competency. **3** Full capability or qualification; efficiency. **4** Conceit; self-sufficiency.

suf·fi·cient (sə·fish'ənt) *adj.* **1** Being all that is needful; adequate; enough. **2** *Archaic* Capable; competent. **3** *Obs.* Financially competent; responsible. See synonyms under ADEQUATE, AMPLE, ENOUGH. [< OF < L *sufficiens*, *-entis*, ppr. of *sufficere* SUFFICE] —**suf·fi'cient·ly** *adv.*

suf·fix (suf'iks) *n.* **1** *Ling.* A letter or letters added to the end of a word or root, and functioning as a formative, derivative, or inflectional element, as *–er* in shorter, *–ful* in faithful, *–s* and *–es* in dogs, boxes, *–ed* in loved, *–ness* in kindness, etc. Compare COMBINING FORM, PREFIX. **2** Any added title or the like. **3** *Math.* A subindex. —*v.t.* To add as a suffix; append. [< NL *suffixum* < L *suffixus*, pp. of *suffigere* < *sub-* underneath + *figere* fix. Doublet of SOFFIT.] —**suf'fix·al** *adj.* —**suf·fix·ion** (sə·fik'shən) *n.*

suf·flate (sə·flāt') *v.t.* **·flat·ed, ·flat·ing** *Obs.* To blow up or inflate. [< L *sufflatus*, pp. of *sufflare* < *sub-* up from under + *flare* blow] —**suf·fla'tion** *n.*

suf·fo·cate (suf'ə·kāt) *v.* **·cat·ed, ·cat·ing** *v.t.* **1** To kill by obstructing respiration in any manner. **2** To obstruct or oppress, as by an inadequate supply of air. **3** To stifle; extinguish; smother, as a fire. —*v.i.* **4** To become choked or stifled; die from suffocation. [< L *suffocatus*, pp. of *suffocare* < *sub-* under + *fauces* throat] —**suf'fo·cat'ing·ly** *adv.* —**suf'fo·ca'tion** *n.* —**suf'fo·ca'tive** *adj.*

suf·fra·gan (suf'rə·gən) *Eccl. n.* An auxiliary or assistant bishop, who assists a bishop in the administration of the diocese, or is consecrated for service in a limited portion of the diocese: also **suffragan bishop.** —*adj.* Of or pertaining to a suffragan; assisting; auxiliary; subordinate to an archiepiscopal see. [< AF, OF < Med. L *suffraganeus* < L *suffragari* vote for, support] —**suf'fra·gan·ship'** *n.*

suf·frage (suf'rij) *n.* **1** A vote in support of some measure or candidate; hence, approbation; assent. **2** Voting; also, the right or privilege of voting; franchise: also **political**

suffrage. 3 *Eccl.* Any short intercessory prayer or petition. —**woman suffrage** Political suffrage as belonging to or exercised by women. In the United States suffrage was granted to women in 1920 by the 19th amendment to the Constitution: also **female suffrage.** [< OF < L *suffragium* a voting tablet, vote]

suf·fra·gette (suf'rə·jet') *n. Colloq.* A woman who advocated female suffrage; specifically, a member of a militant organization demanding it. [< SUFFRAGE + -ETTE] —**suf'fra·get'tism** *n.*

suf·fra·gist (suf'rə·jist) *n.* **1** A voter. **2** An advocate of some particular form of suffrage, especially of woman suffrage.

suf·fru·tex (suf'rə·teks) *n. Bot.* **1** An undershrub; a small plant having a decidedly woody stem. **2** An herb with a permanent woody base. [< NL < L *sub-* under, less than + *frutex*, *-icis* a shrub] —**suf'fru·tes'cent** (-tes'ənt) *adj.*

suf·fu·mi·gate (sə·fyōō'mə·gāt) *v.t.* **·gat·ed, ·gat·ing** To fumigate from or as from underneath. [< L *suffumigatus*, pp. of *suffumigare* < *sub-* up from under + *fumigare* FUMIGATE]

suf·fuse (sə·fyōōz') *v.t.* **·fused, ·fus·ing** To overspread, as with a vapor, fluid, or color. [< L *suffusus*, pp. of *suffundere* < *sub-* underneath, up from under + *fundere* pour] —**suf·fu·sive** (sə·fyōō'siv) *adj.*

suf·fu·sion (sə·fyōō'zhən) *n.* **1** The act of welling up or spreading over. **2** The state of being suffused; a blush. **3** That which suffuses: a *suffusion* of blood.

sug·ar (shŏŏg'ər) *n.* **1** A sweet crystalline disaccharide having the formula $C_{12}H_{22}O_{11}$, obtained chiefly from the juice of the sugarcane or sugar beet; called, according to its source, **beet sugar, cane sugar, date sugar, grape sugar, maple sugar,** etc. ◆ Collateral adjective: *saccharine*. **2** Any of a large class of sweet, soluble, optically active carbohydrates which are ketone or aldehyde derivatives of the higher alcohols. They are widely distributed in plants and animals, play an important role in nutrition, and are generally classified on the basis of chemical structure as monosaccharides, disaccharides, trisaccharides. **3** Flattering or honeyed words, especially if used to disguise or soften an unpleasant or severe reality. **4** *Slang* Sweet one: a pet name. —*v.t.* **1** To sweeten, cover, or coat with sugar. **2** To make agreeable or less distasteful, as by flattery. —*v.i.* **3** *U.S. & Can.* To make maple sugar. **4** To form or produce sugar; granulate. [< OF *sucre* < Med. L *succarum*, ult. < Arabic *sukkar*. Prob. related to SACCHARIN.]

sugar beet Any sugar–producing variety of the common garden beet.

sug·ar·bird (shŏŏg'ər·bûrd') *n.* **1** Any bird that sucks the nectar of flowers, as the honey creepers, honey-eaters, sunbirds, etc. **2** The evening grosbeak (*Hesperiphona vespertina*): so named by North American Indians from its fondness for maple sugar.

sugar bush A grove of sugar–maple trees: sometimes designating a grove of 200 or more trees.

sugar camp The collection of cabins and other buildings in a sugar bush where the maple sap is boiled.

sug·ar·cane (shŏŏg'ər·kān') *n.* A tall, stout, perennial grass (*Saccharum officinarum*) of tropical regions with a solid jointed stalk rich in sugar.

sug·ar–coat (shŏŏg'ər·kōt') *v.t.* **1** To cover with sugar. **2** To cause to appear attractive or less distasteful. —**sug'ar–coat'ed** *adj.* —**sug'ar–coat'ing** *n.*

sug·ar–cured (shŏŏg'ər·kyŏŏrd') *adj.* Cured by using sugar in the curing process: said of ham and pork.

sugar daddy *U.S. Slang* A wealthy old man who gives a young woman presents in return for her favors.

sugaring off 1 The boiling of maple sap until it crystallizes into sugar. **2** The time of year at which this is done. **3** A community social gathering to take part in making maple sugar.

sugar loaf 1 A conical mass of hard refined sugar. **2** A conical hat or hill. —**sug'ar–loaf'** *adj.*

sugar maple The maple (*Acer saccharum*) of eastern North America from the sap of which maple sugar is made: also called *hard maple, rock maple.*

sugar pine A tall pine (*Pinus lambertiana*) of the Pacific coast, bearing very large cones and having wood much used in construction work.

sug·ar·plum (shoog'ər·plum') *n.* 1 A small sweetmeat; a small ball or disk of candy; a bon-bon. 2 The shadbush.

sugar tree The sugar maple.

sug·ar·y (shoog'ər·ē) *adj.* 1 Composed of or as of sugar; sweet. 2 Fond of sugar. 3 Figuratively, honeyed; alluring. 4 Granular. — **sug'ar·i·ness** *n.*

sug·gest (səg·jest', sə·jest') *v.t.* 1 To bring or put forward for consideration, action, or approval; propose. 2 To arouse in the mind by association or connection; connote: Hallowe'en *suggests* witches and black cats. 3 To give a hint or indirect suggestion of; intimate: This poem *suggests* a great deal of care and thought. 4 To act as or provide a motive for; prompt: The success of his novel *suggested* a sequel. See synonyms under ALLUDE, IMPORT. [< L *suggestus,* pp. of *suggerere* < *sub-* underneath + *gerere* carry] — **sug·gest'er** *n.*

sug·gest·i·bil·i·ty (səg·jes'tə·bil'ə·tē, sə-) *n.* 1 *Psychol.* Responsiveness to suggestion, normal in children and diminishing in adults, but heightened or abnormal in hypnosis, light sleep, and certain nervous conditions. 2 Readiness to believe and agree without reflection; compliancy of mind and will.

sug·ges·tion (səg·jes'chən, sə·jes'-) *n.* 1 The act of suggesting. 2 A hint; insinuation. 3 The spontaneous calling up of an idea in the mind by a connected idea. 4 *Psychol.* **a** The inducing in a person of some idea, impulse, action, or mode of behavior through a stimulus, verbal or other, coming from another person but independent of critical argument or rational persuasion, as in hypnosis. **b** The idea, impulse, etc., so induced. — *Synonyms:* hint, innuendo, insinuation, intimation. A *suggestion* brings something before the mind less directly than by formal or explicit statement, as by a partial statement, an incidental allusion, an illustration, a question, or the like. *Suggestion* is often used of an unobtrusive statement of one's views or wishes to another, leaving consideration and any consequent action entirely to that person's judgment, and is hence, in many cases, the most respectful way in which to convey one's views to a superior or a stranger. An *intimation* is a *suggestion* in brief utterance, or sometimes by significant act, gesture, or token, of one's meaning or wishes; in the latter case it is often the act of a superior. A *hint* is still more limited in expression and more remote, and is always covert, but frequently with good intent; as, to give one a *hint* of danger or of opportunity. *Insinuation* and *innuendo* usually imply discredit; an *insinuation* is a covert or partly veiled injurious utterance; an *innuendo* is commonly secret as well as sly, as if pointing to something derogatory. See COUNSEL.

sug·ges·tive (səg·jes'tiv, sə-) *adj.* 1 Fitted or tending to suggest; stimulating to thought or reflection. 2 Hinting at indecent thoughts; suggesting the improper. — **sug·ges'tive·ly** *adv.* — **sug·ges'tive·ness** *n.*

su·i·ci·dal (soo'ə·sīd'l) *adj.* Self-destructive; ruinous; pertaining to, or leading to, suicide; fatal to one's prospects or interests. — **su'i·ci'dal·ly** *adv.*

su·i·cide (soo'ə·sīd) *n.* 1 The intentional taking of one's own life. 2 Self-inflicted political, social, or commercial ruin. 3 One who commits self-murder. — *v.i.* **·cid·ed, ·cid·ing** *Colloq.* To commit suicide. [< NL *suicidium* < L *sui* of oneself + *caedere* kill]

su·i gen·e·ris (soo'ī jen'ər·is) *Latin* Literally, of his (her, its) particular kind; forming a kind by itself; unique.

su·int (soo'int, swint) *n.* Natural wool grease from wool-washings: it consists of fatty substances combined with potash salts. [< F < *suer* sweat < L *sudare*]

suit (soot) *n.* 1 A set of outer garments or armor to be worn together. 2 A set of garments consisting of a coat and trousers or skirt, made of the same fabric. 3 An outfit or garment for a particular purpose: a bathing *suit;* a space *suit.* 4 A

group of things of like kind or pattern composing a series or set: now usually *suite.* 5 In card-playing, any one of the four sets of thirteen cards each that make up a pack, as spades, hearts, diamonds, or clubs. 6 *Law* A proceeding in a court of law or chancery in which a plaintiff demands the recovery of a right or the redress of a wrong: a term rarely applied to criminal prosecution. 7 *Archaic* Entreaty; petition; supplication. 8 The courting or courtship of a woman. See synonyms under PRAYER. — **to follow suit.** 1 To play a card identical in suit to the card led. 2 To do as somebody or something else has done; follow an example. — *v.t.* 1 To meet the requirements of, or be appropriate to; be in accord with; befit. 2 To please; satisfy. 3 To render appropriate or accordant; accommodate; adapt. 4 *Archaic* To furnish with clothes. — *v.i.* 5 To be befitting; agree; correspond. 6 To be or prove satisfactory. 7 *Obs.* To clothe oneself. See synonyms under ACCOMMODATE, ADAPT. [< AF *siwte,* OF *sieute,* ult. < L *sequi* follow. Doublet of SUITE.]

suit·a·ble (soo'tə·bəl) *adj.* Capable of suiting; appropriate; applicable; proper. See synonyms under APPROPRIATE, BECOMING, CONVENIENT, EXPEDIENT, GOOD. — **suit'a·bil'i·ty, suit'a·ble·ness** *n.* — **suit'a·bly** *adv.*

suit·case (soot'kās') *n.* A flat, rectangular valise used for carrying clothing, etc.

suite (swēt; *for def.* 3, *also* soot) *n.* 1 A succession of things forming a series; a set of things having a certain dependence upon each other and intended to go or be used together. 2 A number of connected apartments. 3 A set of furniture. 4 A collection of pictures illustrating consecutive events. 5 *Music* A form of instrumental composition formerly consisting of a series of dances, but now often written for an orchestra and varying freely in its construction and movements. 6 A retinue; a company of attendants or followers. ♦ Homophone: *sweet.* [< F < OF *sieute.* Doublet of SUIT.]

suit·ing (soo'ting) *n.* Cloth from which to make entire suits of clothes.

suit·or (soo'tər) *n.* 1 One who institutes a suit in court. 2 A wooer. 3 A petitioner. [< AF *seutor* < LL *secutor, -oris* < L *secutus,* pp. of *sequi* follow]

su·ki·ya·ki (soo'kē·yä'kē, -yak'ē) *n.* A Japanese dish, usually cooked rapidly at the table, made of meat in thin slices, vegetables, and condiments. [< Japanese]

Suk·koth (sook'ōth, sook'ōs) *n. pl.* The feast of Tabernacles, a Jewish holiday beginning on the 15th of Tishri (late September-October): originally a harvest festival: also spelled *Succoth.* Also **Suk'kos, Suk'kot.** [< Hebrew *sukkōth* tabernacles, booths]

sul·cate (sul'kāt, -kit) *adj. Biol.* Having long narrow furrows or channels; grooved; fluted. Also **sul'cat·ed.** [< L *sulcatus,* pp. of *sulcare* plow < *sulcus* a furrow] — **sul·ca'tion** *n.*

sul·cus (sul'kəs) *n. pl.* **·ci** (-sī) 1 A narrow channel or furrow. 2 *Anat.* One of a large number of shallow grooves on the surface of the mammalian brain. [< L]

sulfa- *combining form Chem.* Sulfur; related to or containing sulfur: also spelled *sulpha-.* Also, before vowels, **sulf-,** as in *sulfarsenide.* See also SULFO-. [< SULFUR]

sul·fa·di·a·zine (sul'fə·dī'ə·zēn) *n. Chem.* A white, crystalline, relatively non-toxic derivative of sulfanilamide, $C_{10}H_{10}N_4SO_2$, used in the treatment of infections due to streptococci, pneumococci, and staphylococci.

sul·fa drug (sul'fə) *Chem.* Any of a group of organic compounds consisting mainly of substituted sulfanilamide derivatives and having a wide range of therapeutic effects in the treatment of bacterial infections.

sul·fa·nil·a·mide (sul'fə·nil'ə·mīd, -mid) *n. Chem.* A colorless, crystalline sulfonamide, $C_6H_8N_2O_2S$, originally widely developed and used as a chemotherapeutic agent in the treatment of various bacterial infections. [< SULF(A)- + ANIL(INE) + AMIDE]

sul·fate (sul'fāt) *n. Chem.* A salt of sulfuric acid. Sulfates are widely distributed in nature and are important in the arts and in medicine. — *v.* **·fat·ed, ·fat·ing** *v.t.* 1 To form a sulfate of; treat with a sulfate or sulfuric acid. 2 *Electr.* To form a coating of lead sulfate on (the plate of a secondary battery). 3 To make (red lead) into lead sulfate by the action of sulfuric acid. — *v.i.* 4 To

become sulfated. Also **sul'phate.** [< F < NL *sulfas, -atis* a sulfate < L *sulfur* sulfur]

sulfate process A method for manufacturing tough kraft paper by introducing sulfate of soda in the digesters containing the wood pulp.

sul·fa·thi·a·zole (sul'fə·thī'ə·zōl) *n. Chem.* A sulfanilamide derivative, $C_9H_9N_3O_2S_2$, considered particularly effective in treating certain pneumococcal and staphylococcal infections.

sul·fa·tize (sul'fə·tīz) *v.t.* **·tized, ·tiz·ing** To turn (ores, etc.) into sulfate, by roasting. Also **sul'pha·tize.**

sul·fide (sul'fīd) *n. Chem.* A compound of sulfur with an element or radical. Also **sul'fid** (-fid), **sul'phide, sul'phid.** [< SULF(A)- + -IDE]

sul·fite (sul'fīt) *n. Chem.* A salt or ester of sulfurous acid. Also **sul'phite.** [< SULF(A)- + -ITE²] — **sul·fit'ic** (-fit'ik) *adj.*

sulfite process The production of chemical wood pulp by the use of calcium sulfite.

sulfo- *combining form Chem.* 1 Sulfur; containing sulfur. 2 Denoting the replacement of oxygen by sulfur in a compound. 3 Indicating the presence of the sulfonic or sulfonyl group. Also spelled *sulpho-.* Compare THIO-. [< SULFUR]

Sul·fo·nal (sul'fə·nal, sul'fə·nal') *n.* Proprietary name for a brand of sulfonmethane used in medicine as a sedative and hypnotic.

sul·fon·a·mide (sul·fon'ə·mīd, sul'fən·am'īd, -id) *n. Chem.* Any group of organic compounds containing the univalent radical SO_2NH_2, especially those derived from para-aminobenzene-sulfon-amide, p-$H_2N\cdot C_6H_4\cdot SO_2NH_2$, used in the treatment of certain bacterial infections. [< SULFON(E) + AMIDE]

sulfonic acid *Chem.* Any of several compounds consisting of an organic radical in combination with the sulfonic radical and corresponding to the formula $R\cdot SO_2OH$: used in organic synthesis.

sul·fo·nyl (sul'fə·nil) *n. Chem.* The bivalent radical SO_2: also called *sulfuryl.* [< SULFON(E) + -YL]

sul·fur (sul'fər) *n.* 1 A chemically active, nonmetallic element (symbol S, atomic number 16), under usual conditions consisting of pale yellow crystals but known in many other allotropic forms, and representing an essential constituent of living organisms. See listing under PERIODIC TABLE. 2 Any of various yellowish pieridine butterflies, as the common North American **clouded sulfur** (*Colias philodice*) or the **cloudless sulfur** (*Callidryas eubule*). — **flowers of sulfur** A fine yellow powder obtained by the distillation of sulfur. — *v.t.* To treat or fume, as a wine cask or a hive, with sulfur or with sulfurous acid. Also **sul'phur.** [< AF *sulfre,* OF *soufre* < L *sulfur, -uris*]

sul·fu·rate (sul'fyə·rāt, -fə-) *v.t.* **·rat·ed, ·rat·ing** To sulfurize. [< SULFUR + -ATE¹]

sul·fur·bot·tom (sul'fər·bot'əm) *n.* A very large baleen whale (*Sibbaldius musculus*) found in Atlantic and Pacific waters, having a yellowish belly and attaining an average length of 60–80 feet, with a maximum of about 100 feet.

SULFUR-BOTTOM

sulfur dioxide *Chem.* A colorless, gaseous compound, SO_2, with a sharp odor and readily soluble in water: used in the manufacture of sulfuric acid, in bleaching, as a preservative, etc.

sul·fu·re·ous (sul·fyoor'ē·əs) *adj.* Of or like sulfur. [< L *sulfureus* < *sulfur* sulfur]

sul·fu·ret (sul'fyə·ret) *v.t.* **·ret·ed** or **·ret·ted, ·ret·ing** or **·ret·ting** To sulfurize. — *n.* (-rit) A sulfide. [< F *sulfuret* a sulfide < NL *sulfuretum* < L *sulfur*] — **sul'fu·ret'ed** or **sul'fu·ret'ted** *adj.*

sul·fu·ric (sul·fyoor'ik) *adj. Chem.* Pertaining to or derived from sulfur, especially in its higher valence.

sulfuric acid *Chem.* A colorless, exceedingly corrosive, oily liquid, H_2SO_4, essentially a combination of sulfur trioxide and water, extensively employed in the manufacture of soda, batteries, guncotton, and in almost all chemical operations. Formerly called *vitriol.*

sul·fur·ize (sul'fyə·rīz, -fə-) *v.t.* **·ized, ·iz·ing** **1** To impregnate, treat with, or subject to the action of sulfur. **2** To bleach or fumigate with sulfur. —**sul'fur·i·za'tion** *n.*

sul·fur·ous (sul'fər·əs, sul·fyŏŏr'əs) *adj.* **1** *Chem.* Of, pertaining to, or derived from sulfur: specifically applied to compounds that contain sulfur in its lower valence. **2** Fiery; hellish; blasphemous, as language.

sulfurous acid *Chem.* A compound corresponding to the formula H_2SO_3, and known only in solution and by its salts.

sulfur point *Physics* The boiling point of pure liquid sulfur at standard atmospheric pressure, 444.60° C.: one of the fixed points of the international temperature scale.

sulfur trioxide *Chem.* A compound, SO_3, formed by the union of sulfur dioxide and oxygen in the presence of a catalytic agent. With water, sulfur trioxide forms sulfuric acid; hence, it is often called **sulfuric anhydride.**

sul·fur·y (sul'fər·ē) *adj.* Resembling or suggesting sulfur; sulfureous.

sul·fur·yl (sul'fər·il, -fyə·ril) *n.* Sulfonyl. [< SULFUR + -YL]

sulfuryl chloride *Chem.* A colorless, very pungent liquid compound, SO_2Cl_2, used in the manufacture of dyes, drugs, and poison gas.

sulk (sulk) *v.i.* To be sulky or morose. —*n.* A sulky mood or humor: often plural. [Back formation <SULKY]

sulk·y¹ (sul'kē) *adj.* **sulk·i·er, sulk·i·est** **1** Sullenly cross; doggedly or resentfully ill-humored. **2** Stunted; sluggish: dismal. See synonyms under MOROSE. [? OE (ā)*solcen* slothful, orig. pp. of (ā)*seolcan* be weak, slothful] —**sulk'i·ly** *adv.* —**sulk'i·ness** *n.*

sulk·y² (sul'kē) *n. pl.* **sulk·ies** A light, two-wheeled, one-horse vehicle for one person. —*adj.* Resembling this vehicle: a *sulky* plow. [<SULKY¹; so called because one rides alone]

sul·lage (sul'ij) *n.* **1** Mud or silt deposited by flowing water. **2** Refuse; sewage. [<AF *souiller, soillier* SOIL²; infl. in form by *sully*]

sul·len (sul'ən) *adj.* **1** Obstinately and gloomily ill-humored; morose; glum. **2** Depressing; somber: *sullen* clouds. **3** Slow; sluggish: a *sullen* tread. **4** Melancholy. **5** Ill-omened; threatening. See synonyms under GRIM. [Earlier *solein,* appar. <AF <*sol* SOLE³] —**sul'len·ly** *adv.* —**sul'len·ness** *n.*

sul·ly (sul'ē) *v.* **·lied, ·ly·ing** *v.t.* To mar the brightness or purity of; soil; defile; tarnish. —*v.i.* To become soiled or tarnished: also figuratively. See synonyms under DEFILE, STAIN. —*n. pl.* **·lies** Anything that tarnishes; a stain; spot; blemish. [<MF *souiller* SOIL²]

sulph- For all words so spelled, see the forms beginning SULF-.

sulpha- Var. of SULFA-.

sulpho- Var. of SULFO-.

sul·tan (sul'tən) *n.* **1** The ruler of a Moslem country. **2** A gallinule with deep-blue or purple plumage and white lower tail coverts. *Ionornis martinica* is the purple gallinule or sultan of the warmer parts of America. **3** A small white-crested variety of the domestic fowl, originating in Turkey, having heavily feathered legs and feet. **4** Formerly, any ruler. —**the Sultan** The title of the sovereign of Turkey: office abolished, 1922. [<F <Med. L *sultanus* <Arabic *sultān* a sovereign. dominion]

sul·tan·a (sul·tan'ə, -tä'nə) *n.* **1** A sultan's wife, daughter, sister, or mother: also **sul·tan·ess** (sul'tən·is). **2** The mistress of a king or prince. **3** A variety of raisin from the district of Smyrna, Asia Minor. **4** Sultan (def. 3): also **sul·tan'a·bird'.** [<Ital., fem. of *sultano* a sultan <Arabic *sultān*]

sul·tan·ate (sul'tən·āt, -it) *n.* The authority or territorial jurisdiction of a sultan. Also **sul'tan·ship.**

sul·try (sul'trē) *adj.* **·tri·er, ·tri·est** **1** Hot, moist, and still; close: said of weather.

2 Emitting an oppressive heat; burning; hot with anger. **3** Showing or suggesting passion; sensual. [<obs. *sulter,* var. of SWELTER] —**sul'tri·ly** *adv.* —**sul'tri·ness** *n.*

sum (sum) *n.* **1** The result obtained by addition. **2** The entire quantity, number, or substance; the whole; all: the *sum* total of my means; the *sum* and substance of the case. **3** Any indefinite amount: said chiefly of money. **4** A problem in arithmetic propounded for solution. **5** The summit; topmost or highest point; also, the maximum; the complement. **6** A summary; the pith or essence. See synonyms under AGGREGATE. —*v.* **summed, sum·ming** *v.t.* **1** To present in brief; recapitulate succinctly: usually with *up*: to *sum up* evidence. **2** To add into one total; ascertain the sum of: often with *up.* **3** To ascertain the sum of (the terms of a series). —*v.i.* **4** To make a summation or recapitulation: generally with *up.* ◆ Homophone: *some.* [<AF, OF *summe, somme* <L *summa* (*res*) highest (thing), fem. of *summus* highest]

sum·mand (sum'and) *n.* That which is added; any of the numbers forming part of a sum. [<Med. L *summandus* (*numerus*) (the number) to be added <*summare* add <L *summa.* See SUM.]

sum·ma·rize (sum'ə·rīz) *v.t.* **·rized, ·riz·ing** To make a summary of; sum up; epitomize. Also *Brit.* **sum'ma·rise.** —**sum'ma·ri·za'tion** *n.* —**sum'ma·riz'er** *n.*

sum·ma·ry (sum'ər·ē) *adj.* **1** Giving the substance or sum; greatly condensed; concise. **2** Performed without ceremony or delay; instant; offhand: used specifically in law. —*n. pl.* **·ries** An abridgment or epitome; abstract; compendium. See synonyms under ABRIDGMENT. [<Med. L *summarius* <L *summarium* a summary <*summa.* See SUM.] —**sum·ma·ri·ly** (sum'ər·ə·lē, emphatic sə·mer'ə·lē) *adv.* —**sum'ma·ri·ness** *n.* —**sum'ma·rist** *n.*

sum·mate (sum·āt') *v.t. & v.i.* **·mat·ed, ·mat·ing** **1** To arrive at the sum of (a series). **2** To sum up. [Back formation <SUMMATION]

sum·ma·tion (sum·ā'shən) *n.* **1** The act or operation of obtaining a sum; the computation or statement of an aggregate sum or result; addition. **2** A speech or a portion of a speech summing up the principal points. [<NL *summatio, -onis* <Med. L *summare* add <*summa.* See SUM.]

sum·mer¹ (sum'ər) *n.* **1** The hottest or warmest season of the year: including June, July, and August, in the northern hemisphere. In the southern hemisphere the summer occurs during the months of the northern winter. ◆ Collateral adjective: *estival.* **2** Figuratively, a year of life, especially of early or happy life; a bright and prosperous period. —**Indian summer** A period of mild weather occurring in the autumn, with hazy atmosphere usually along the horizon, and a clear sky. It corresponds to the English St. Luke's or St. Martin's summer. —**St. Luke's summer** or **little summer of St. Luke** A short period of warm weather in England expected for a few days beginning with St. Luke's day, the 18th of October. —**St. Martin's summer** A season of mild weather about St. Martin's day, the 11th of November, corresponding to the American Indian summer. —*v.t.* To keep or care for through the summer. —*v.i.* To pass the summer. —*adj.* Of, pertaining to, or occurring in summer. [OE *sumor, sumer*] —**sum'mer·ly** *adj. & adv.*

sum·mer² (sum'ər) *n. Archit.* **1** A heavy horizontal timber or girder serving as a support for some superstructure in a building, etc.; a lintel. **2** A large stone, as on a column or pilaster, for supporting one or more arches, or any similar structure. **3** A horizontal beam resting upon the walls or external frame of a building, and supporting the ends of

SUMMER (*a*)

joists. [<OF *somier* a pack horse, beam <LL *saumarius* <L *sagmarius* <*sagma* a pack saddle <Gk.]

summer flounder A flounder (*Paralichthys dentatus*) of the Atlantic coast of North America.

sum·mer·house (sum'ər·hous') *n.* A rustic structure, as in a garden, for rest or shade.

summer house A house or cottage in the country or at the seashore, used during the summer.

sum·mer·sault (sum'ər·sôlt), **sum·mer·set** (sum'ər·set) See SOMERSAULT.

summer squash Any of various squashes derived from the variety *Cucurbita pepo melopepo* and picked as vegetables before mature, while their rinds and seeds are tender.

sum·mer·time (sum'ər·tīm') *n.* Summer; the summer season. Also **sum'mer·tide'.**

sum·mer·y (sum'ər·ē) *adj.* Pertaining to or resembling summer.

sum·mit (sum'it) *n.* **1** The highest part; the top; vertex. **2** The highest degree; maximum. **3** The highest level or office, as of a government or business organization. **4** A meeting of executives of the highest level, as heads of government. —*adj.* Of or involving those at the highest level: a *summit* conference. [<OF *sommette,* dim. of *som* a summit, top <L *summum,* neut. of *summus* highest]

Synonyms: acme, apex, cap, climax, crown, height, peak, pinnacle, top, vertex. Antonyms: abyss, base, bottom, chasm, deep, depth, gorge, gulf, pit, vale, valley.

sum·mit·ry (sum'it·rē) *n.* **1** Meetings of officials of the highest rank, as heads of government. **2** The use or dependency upon such meetings to solve international problems.

sum·mon (sum'ən) *v.t.* **1** To order to come; send for. **2** To call together; cause to convene, as a legislative assembly. **3** To order (a person) to appear in court by a summons. **4** To call forth or into action; arouse: usually with *up*: to *summon up* courage. **5** To bid or call on for a specific act: The garrison was *summoned* to surrender. See synonyms under ARRAIGN, CONVOKE. [<AF, OF *somondre* <L *summonere* suggest, hint <*sub-* secretly + *monere* warn] —**sum'mon·er** *n.*

sum·mons (sum'ənz) *n.* **1** A call to attend or act at a particular place or time. **2** *Law* A notice to a defendant summoning him to appear in court: either a judicial writ or process, or a notice signed by the plaintiff or his attorney; any citation issued to a party to an action to appear before a court or judge at chambers. See WRIT OF SUMMONS. **3** A notice to a person requiring him to appear in court as a witness or as a juror. **4** A military demand to surrender. **5** Any signal or sound that is a peremptory call. [<AF *somonse,* OF *sumunse* <*somondre* SUMMON]

su·mo (sōō'mō) *n.* A highly stylized form of wrestling popular in Japan. [<Japanese *sumō*]

sump (sump) *n.* **1** *Mining* **a** A depression sunk below the lowest level in a mine shaft, to receive water and form a pool from which it may be pumped. **b** A sump winze. **2** *Mech.* The lowest part of the crankcase of an internal-combustion engine, acting as a reservoir for lubricating oil. **3** A cesspool or other reservoir for drainage. [<MDu. *somp, sump* a marsh. Akin to SWAMP.]

sump·ter (sump'tər) *n.* A pack animal; beast of burden. [<OF *sometier* a driver of a pack horse, ult. <L *sagma.* See SUMMER².]

sump·tu·ar·y (sump'chōō·er'ē) *adj.* Pertaining to expense; limiting or regulating expenditure, as some laws. [<L *sumptuarius* <*sumptus* expenditure <*sumere* take]

sumptuary law **1** A law limiting or regulating expenditure in order to prevent extravagance and inflation. **2** A law regulating private life on moral or religious grounds.

sump·tu·ous (sump'chōō·əs) *adj.* Involving or showing lavish expenditure; hence, luxurious; magnificent. [<OF *sumptueux, somptueux* <L *sumptuosus* <*sumptus.* See SUMPTUARY.] —**sump'tu·ous·ly** *adv.* —**sump'tu·ous·ness** *n.*

sump·weed (sump'wēd') *n.* Marsh elder.

sun (sun) *n.* **1** The heavenly body that is the center of attraction and the main source of light and heat in the solar system, with a mean distance from the earth of about 93,000,000 miles and a diameter of 864,000 miles. Its mass is 332,000 times that of the earth, but its density only about one-fourth. **2** Any star, especially one that is the center of a system revolving around it. **3** The light and heat radiated from the sun; sunshine. **4** Anything brilliant and magnificent, or that is a source of splendor. **5** The time of the earth's revolution round the sun; a year. **6** The daily appearance of the sun; a day; also, the time of its appearance or shining; sunrise. —**a place in the sun** A dominant position in international affairs; hence, a position in the spotlight; publicity. —*v.* **sunned, sun·ning** *v.t.* **1** To expose to the light or heat of the sun. **2** To warm or dry (something) in the sun. —*v.i.* **3** To bask in the sun; expose oneself to the light or heat of the sun. ◆ Homophone: *son.* [OE *sunne*]

sun·bathe (sun′bāth′) *v.i.* **-bathed, -bath·ing** To bask in the sun, especially as a method of tanning the skin. —**sun′-bath′er** *n.* —**sun′-bath′ing** *n.*

sun·beam (sun′bēm′) *n.* **1** A ray or beam of the sun; light from the sun in a visible path. **2** *pl.* Sunlight.

sun bear A small arboreal bear *(Helarctos malayanus),* inhabiting forests of southeastern Asia. Also called *honey bear.*

sun·bird (sun′bûrd′) *n.* **1** A brilliantly colored oriental singing bird (family *Nectariniidae*) resembling the hummingbird. **2** A sun bittern.

sun bittern Either of two birds of Central and South America (genus *Eurypyga*) related to the rails and herons, having a slender neck and bill, long wings and tail, and moderately long legs.

sun·bon·net (sun′bon′it) *n.* A bonnet of light material with projecting brim and sometimes a cape covering the neck.

sun·burn (sun′bûrn′) *n.* Discoloration or inflammation of the skin, produced by exposure to the sun. —*v.t.* & *v.i.* To affect or be affected with sunburn. —**sun′burnt′, sun′burned′** *adj.*

sun·burst (sun′bûrst′) *n.* **1** A strong burst of sunlight, as through rifted clouds. **2** A brooch or pin with jewels so set around a larger central gem as to suggest sun rays.

sun compass A compass serving to establish Greenwich time in relation to the position of the sun: used chiefly in polar regions, where the magnetic compass is unreliable.

sun·dae (sun′dē) *n.* A refreshment consisting of ice-cream and crushed fruit, flavoring, sirup, nuts, etc. [Prob. < *Sunday*; prob. so called because orig. sold only on that day]

sun dance The greatest ceremonial dance of the Plains Indians, usually a summer solstice ceremony, comprising fast days, dance days, secret rites, and a public performance.

Sun·day (sun′dē, -dā) *n.* The first day of the week; the Lord's day; the Christian Sabbath: sometimes used attributively. See synonyms under SABBATH. [OE *sunnan dæg* < *sunnan* of the sun + *dæg* a day; trans. of LL *dies solis* day of the sun]

sun·der (sun′dər) *v.t.* To break apart; disunite; sever. —*v.i.* To be parted or severed. See synonyms under BREAK, CUT, REND, SEPARATE. —*n.* Division into parts; separation. —**in sunder** Apart; separate from other parts. Compare ASUNDER. [OE *syndrian, sundrian*] —**sun′der·ance** *n.*

sun·dew (sun′dōo′, -dyōo′) *n.* Any of a genus *(Drosera)* of marsh plants that exude a viscid liquid from the tips of the hairs on the leaves. Insects are caught by the secretions and are utilized by the plant for its own nutrition.

sun·di·al (sun′dī′əl) *n.*
A device that measures time and shows the time of day by means of the shadow of a style or gnomon thrown on a dial.

sun disk The winged disk. See under DISK.

sun·dog (sun′dôg′, -dog′) *n.* **1** A parhelion, appearing near the sun, sometimes with a luminous train, due to the presence of ice crystals in the air; a mock sun. **2** A small rainbow lying near the horizon.

sun·down (sun′doun′) *n.* **1** Sunset: originally col-

SUNDIAL

loquial, like *sunup,* but now in good literary usage. **2** A broad-brimmed hat worn by women. [? Contraction of *sun-go-down*]

sun·down·er (sun′dou′nər) *n.* **1** *Colloq.* A tramp. **2** *Austral.* A vagrant who seeks food and lodging at back-country ranches, often about the time of sundown. **3** *Slang* A strict, rigidly uncompromising ship's officer; originally, a ship's captain who granted liberty only until sundown.

sun·dries (sun′drēz) *n. pl.* Items or things too small or too numerous to be separately specified. [<SUNDRY]

sun·drops (sun′drops′) *n.* Any of several American species of evening primrose (genus *Oenothera*), having large yellow flowers, and blooming in the daytime.

sun·dry (sun′drē) *adj.* Of an indefinite small number; various; several; miscellaneous. See synonyms under MANY. [OE *syndrig* separate, private]

sun·fish (sun′fish′) *n. pl.* **·fish** or **·fish·es** **1** A large pelagic plectognath fish (genus *Mola*), having a deep compressed body truncate behind, as *Mola mola* of warm and tropical seas. It has tough and leathery flesh. **2** Any of several North American freshwater perchlike fishes (family *Centrarchidae*) of the genus *Lepomis,* as the pumpkinseed.

SUNFISH *(def. 1)*
(Up to 8 feet in length)

sun·flow·er (sun′flou′ər) *n.* Any of a genus *(Helianthus)* of tall, stout, rough herbs of the composite family, with large leaves and circular heads of flowers, those in the center tubular and usually purple, and those on the margin strap-shaped and bright-yellow; especially, the common sunflower *(H. annuus),* the source of an edible oil, and the State flower of Kansas.

sun·glass (sun′glas′, -gläs′) *n.* **1** A burning glass; a glass used for concentrating the rays of the sun. **2** *pl.* Spectacles that protect the eyes from the glare of the sun by their colored lenses.

sun·glow (sun′glō′) *n.* **1** The rose tint or faint yellow of the sky that precedes sunrise or follows sunset. **2** The warm glow of the sun.

sun·god (sun′god′) *n.* In the religions of some primitive agricultural peoples, a deity conceived of as life-giving and beneficent, and symbolized by the sun, as the ancient Egyptian Ra, ancient Irish Lug, Inti of the Incas, etc.: not to be confused with personifications of the sun in many cosmogonic myths (Greek Helios, for instance) which are mere explanatory etiological tales and do not posit a sun cult.

sunk·en (sung′kən) Obsolete past participle of SINK. —*adj.* **1** Lying at the bottom of a body of water: a *sunken* ship. **2** Located beneath a surface. **3** Lower than the surrounding or usual level: *sunken* gardens. **4** Deeply depressed or fallen in: *sunken* cheeks.

sunk fence A ditch having a retaining wall on one side to divide lands; a ha-ha.

sunk panel A panel so depressed as to form a recess below the surface of its frame.

sun lamp **1** A lamp giving illumination of high intensity, usually reflected by parabolic mirrors: used in motion-picture studios. **2** A lamp radiating ultraviolet rays: used for therapeutic treatments and as a protection against airborne bacteria in operating rooms, etc.

sun·less (sun′lis) *adj.* Dark; cheerless. — **sun′less·ness** *n.*

sun·light (sun′līt′) *n.* The light of the sun.

sun·lit (sun′lit′) *adj.* Lighted by the sun.

sunn (sun) *n.* An East Indian shrub *(Crotalaria juncea)* of the bean family, with bright-yellow flowers and tough, durable fiber: used for making cordage, bagging, and other coarse textiles: also called *Bombay* or *Madras hemp.* Also **sunn hemp.** [<Hind. *san*]

sun·ny (sun′ē) *adj.* **·ni·er, ·ni·est** **1** Filled with the light and warmth of the sun; exposed to the sun. **2** Bright like the sun; of the sun

or sunshine; hence, genial; cheery: a *sunny* smile. See synonyms under BRIGHT, CHEERFUL, HAPPY. — **sun′ni·ly** *adv.* — **sun′ni·ness** *n.*

sunny side **1** The side, as of a hill, facing the sun. **2** The cheerful view of any situation, question, etc.

sun parlor A room enclosed in glass and having a sunny exposure.

sun pillar A column of variously tinted light sometimes seen projecting vertically above or below the sun at sunrise or sunset. It is caused by the reflection of sunlight from small snow crystals.

sun·rise (sun′rīz′) *n.* **1** The daily first appearance of the sun above the horizon, with the atmospheric phenomena just preceding and following. **2** The time at which the sun rises. **3** The east; Orient.

sun·room (sun′rōom′, -rŏom′) *n.* A room built to admit a profusion of sunlight.

sun·scald (sun′skôld′) *n.* A diseased condition of plants induced by exposure to intense sunlight.

sun·scorch (sun′skôrch′) *n.* A scorched or burnt condition of plants.

sun·set (sun′set′) *n.* **1** The apparent daily descent of the sun below the horizon. **2** The time when the sun sets; the early evening. **3** The colors in the sky when the sun sets. **4** The west; Occident. **5** Figuratively, the ending or decline, as of life.

sun·shade (sun′shād′) *n.* Something used as a shade or protection from the rays of the sun, as a parasol, an awning, etc.

sun·shine (sun′shīn′) *n.* **1** The shining light of the sun; the direct rays of the sun. **2** The warmth of the sun's rays. **3** The place where the rays fall. **4** Figuratively, brightness; any cheering influence. — **sun′shin′y** *adj.*

sun·spot (sun′spot′) *n.* **1** *Astron.* One of many dark irregular spots appearing periodically on the surface of the sun: believed to have connection with terrestrial magnetic storms. **2** An incandescent sun lamp used in color photography.

sun·stone (sun′stōn′) *n.* A variety of feldspar; aventurine.

sun·stroke (sun′strōk′) *n.* *Pathol.* A sudden onset of high fever induced by exposure to the sun and often marked by convulsions and coma; insolation. — **sun′struck′** (-struk′) *adj.*

sun tan A bronze-colored condition of the skin, produced by exposure to the sun. — **sun′-tanned′** (-tand′) *adj.*

sun·tans (sun′tanz′) *n. pl.* The lightweight summer uniform made of khaki worn by U.S. Army personnel: officially known as *cotton khakis,* and often called *khakis.* They are worn in the Navy by officers.

sun·up (sun′up′) *n.* Sunrise. [<SUN + UP: on analogy with *sundown*]

sun·wise (sun′wīz′) *adv.* With the sun; in the direction of the sun; clockwise.

sup¹ (sup) *v.t.* & *v.i.* **supped, sup·ping** To take (fluid food) in successive mouthfuls, a little at a time; sip. — *n.* A mouthful or taste of liquid or semiliquid food. [OE *sūpan* drink]

sup² (sup) *v.* **supped, sup·ping** *v.i.* To eat supper. — *v.t. Obs.* To furnish with or invite to supper. [<OF *soper, super*; ult. origin unknown]

su·per¹ (sōo′pər) *n. Colloq.* Shortened form of SUPERINTENDENT.

su·per² (sōo′pər) *n. Slang* Shortened form of SUPERNUMERARY (def. 2).

su·per³ (sōo′pər) *n.* **1** An article of superior size or quality; also, such size or quality. **2** In bookbinding, a thin, starched cotton fabric used in reinforcement. — *adj.* **1** *Slang* First-rate; superfine. **2** Showing excessive loyalty: a *super* American. — *v.t.* To reinforce (a book) with super. [Short for SUPERIOR, SUPERFINE, etc.]

super- *prefix* **1** Above in position; over: *superstructure, superimpose.* **2** *Anat. & Zool.* Situated above, or on the dorsal side of: *superorbital.* **3** Above or beyond; more than: *supersonic, supersensible.* **4** Excessively: *supersaturate.* **5** *Med.* Exceeding the normal: *superacidity.* **6** *Chem.* Denoting a high proportion of the ingredient indicated (now superseded by PER-, BI-): *superphosphate.* **7** Surpassing in power or size all others of its class: *superhighway, supermarket.* In this sense the prefix is sometimes doubled to intensify the degree of superiority: a *super-supernavy* a navy far superior to any other. **8** Extra; additional: *supertax.* [<L *super-* < *super* above, beyond]

su·per·a·ble (sōō′pər·ə·bəl) *adj.* That can be surmounted, overcome, or conquered. [<L *superabilis* < *superare* overcome < *super* over]

su·per·a·bound (sōō′pər·ə·bound′) *v.i.* To abound to excess or to an unusual extent. [<LL *superabundare* <L *super-* exceedingly + *abundare* overflow]

su·per·a·bun·dant (sōō′pər·ə·bun′dənt) *adj.* Excessive; more than sufficient. See synonyms under REDUNDANT. [<LL *superabundans, -antis,* ppr. of *superabundare.* See SUPERABOUND.] — **su′per·a·bun′dance** *n.* — **su′per·a·bun′dant·ly** *adv.*

su·per·a·cid·i·ty (sōō′pər·ə·sid′ə·tē) *n. Med.* An excess of acid, especially in the gastric juices; hyperacidity.

su·per·add (sōō′pər·ad′) *v.t.* To add in addition to something already added. [<LL *superaddere* < *super-* over and above + *addere* ADD] — **su′per·ad·di′tion** (-ə·dish′ən) *n.*

su·per·al·tar (sōō′pər·ôl′tər) *n. Eccl.* **1** A consecrated slab laid on an unconsecrated altar when mass is said in oratories or temporary chapels. **2** Sometimes, incorrectly, a retable. [<Med.L *superaltare* <L *super-* over + *altare* an altar]

su·per·an·nu·ate (sōō′pər·an′yōō·āt) *v.t.* **·at·ed, ·at·ing 1** To retire or retire and pension on account of age: chiefly in past participle. **2** To set aside or discard as obsolete or too old. [<Med.L *superannuatus* more than a year old (said of cattle) <L *super annum* < *super* beyond + *annus* a year] — **su′per·an′nu·at′ed** *adj.* — **su′per·an′nu·a′tion** *n.*

su·per·aq·ual (sōō′pər·ak′wəl, -ā′kwəl) *adj.* Of, pertaining to, or denoting those soils lying just above the water table, from which they derive the greater part of their moisture. [<L *super* above + *aqua* water]

su·perb (sōō·pûrb′, sə-) *adj.* **1** Having grand, impressive beauty; majestic; imposing: a *superb* edifice. **2** Luxurious; rich and costly; elegant. **3** Very good; supremely fine. [<L *superbus* proud < *super-* over] — **su·perb′ly** *adv.* — **su·perb′ness** *n.*

su·per·cal·en·der (sōō′pər·kal′ən·dər) *n.* A calender having a number of polished rollers for giving a high finish to paper. See CALENDER[1]. — *v.t.* To give a high finish to (paper). — **su′per·cal′en·dered** *adj.*

su·per·car·go (sōō′pər·kär′gō) *n. pl.* **·goes** or **·gos** An agent on board ship in charge of the cargo and its sale and purchase. [Alter. of obs. *supracargo* <Sp. *sobrecargo* < *sobre-* over (<L *super-*) + *cargo* CARGO]

SUPERCARRIER OF THE FORRESTAL CLASS

su·per·car·ri·er (sōō′pər·kar′ē·ər) *n.* An aircraft-carrier of exceptional size.

su·per·charge (sōō′pər·chärj′) *v.t.* **·charged, ·charg·ing 1** To adapt (an engine) to develop more power, as by fitting with a supercharger. **2** To charge to excess; overload. — *n.* (sōō′-pər·chärj′) **1** An excess charge, in any sense. **2** *Her.* One charge or device borne on another.

su·per·charg·er (sōō′pər·chär′jər) *n.* A compressor for supplying air or combustible mixture to an internal-combustion engine at a pressure greater than that developed by the suction of the pistons alone.

su·per·cil·i·ar·y (sōō′pər·sil′ē·er′ē) *adj.* **1** Of or pertaining to the eyebrow. **2** Situated over the eyebrow; supraorbital: the *superciliary* arches. [<NL *superciliaris* <L *supercilium* an eyebrow < *super-* above + *cilium* an eyelid]

su·per·cil·i·ous (sōō′pər·sil′ē·əs) *adj.* Exhibiting haughty contempt or indifference; arrogant. See synonyms under HAUGHTY. [<L *superciliosus* < *supercilium.* See SUPERCILIARY.] — **su′per·cil′i·ous·ly** *adv.* — **su′per·cil′i·ous·ness** *n.*

su·per·class (sōō′pər·klas′, -kläs′) *n. Biol.* A division of plants or animals below a phylum but above a class.

su·per·co·lum·nar (sōō′pər·kə·lum′nər) *adj. Archit.* **1** Erected above a colonnade or another column. **2** Having one order placed above another.

su·per·con·duc·tiv·i·ty (sōō′pər·kon′duk·tiv′ə·tē) *n. Electr.* The property, exhibited by certain metals and alloys, of becoming almost perfect conductors of electricity when their temperatures fall below transition points in the neighborhood of absolute zero. — **su′per·con·duc′tive** (-kən·duk′tiv) *adj.* — **su′per·con·duc′tor** *n.*

su·per·cool (sōō′pər·kōōl′) *v.t.* To cool, as a liquid, below the freezing point without solidification.

su·per·dom·i·nant (sōō′pər·dom′ə·nənt) *n. Music* The tone just above the dominant; the sixth or submediant.

su·per·du·per (sōō′pər·dōō′pər) *Slang adj.* Superlative: an intensive formation. — *n.* Anything especially fine. [Reduplication of SUPER[3]]

su·per·e·go (sōō′pər·ē′gō, -eg′ō) *n. Psychoanal.* A largely unconscious element of the personality, regarded as dominating the conscious ego, for which it acts principally in the role of conscience and critic.

su·per·em·i·nent (sōō′pər·em′ə·nənt) *adj.* Excelling or surpassing others; of a superior or remarkable quality; supremely exalted. [<L *supereminens, -entis,* ppr. of *supereminere* rise above < *super-* above + *eminere* rise. See EMINENT.] — **su′per·em′i·nence** *n.* — **su′per·em′i·nent·ly** *adv.*

su·per·e·ro·gate (sōō′pər·er′ə·gāt) *v.i.* **·gat·ed, ·gat·ing** To do more than is required or ordered. [<L *supererogatus,* pp. of *supererogare* < *super-* over and above + *erogare* pay out < *ex-* out + *rogare* ask]

su·per·e·ro·ga·tion (sōō′pər·er′ə·gā′shən) *n.* The performance of an act in excess of the demands or requirements of duty. — **works of supererogation** Good deeds done by saints of the Roman Catholic Church in excess of the requirements of divine law; also, voluntary good deeds performed by men over and above God's commandments.

su·per·e·rog·a·to·ry (sōō′pər·ə·rog′ə·tôr′ē, -tō′rē) *adj.* Of, pertaining to, or of the nature of supererogation; superfluous. Also **su′per·e·rog′a·tive.**

su·per·fam·i·ly (sōō′pər·fam′ə·lē, -fam′lē) *n. pl.* **·lies** *Biol.* A division of plants or animals ranking next above the family but below an order or superorder.

su·per·fe·cun·da·tion (sōō′pər·fē′kən·dā′shən, -fek′ən-) *n. Physiol.* The successive impregnation of two or more ova.

su·per·fe·male (sōō′pər·fē′māl) *n. Biol.* A supersexual organism, characterized in the fruit fly by a ratio of 3 X-chromosomes to 2 sets of autosomes.

su·per·fe·tate (sōō′pər·fē′tāt) *v.i.* **·tat·ed, ·tat·ing** *Physiol.* To conceive again prior to the birth of an embryo or fetus already conceived. [<L *superfetatus,* pp. of *superfetare* < *super-* over and above + *fetus* a foetus]

su·per·fe·ta·tion (sōō′pər·fi·tā′shən) *n.* **1** *Physiol.* **a** The second impregnation of a female already pregnant. **b** The progeny resulting from such second impregnation; hence, any unusual additional growth. **2** *Bot.* Fertilization of the same ovule by two or more kinds of pollen. Also **su′per·foe·ta′tion.**

su·per·fi·cial (sōō′pər·fish′əl) *adj.* **1** Of, pertaining to, lying near, or forming the surface; affecting only the surface. **2** Of or pertaining to only the ordinary and the obvious; not profound; shallow: a *superficial* writer. **3** Marked by partial knowledge; cursory; hasty; slight: *superficial* treatment of a sub-

ject. **4** Not real or genuine. **5** Square: said of measure. [<LL *superficialis* <L *superficies* SUPERFICIES] — **su′per·fi′ci·al′i·ty** (-fish′ē·al′ə·tē), **su′per·fi′cial·ness** *n.* — **su′per·fi′cial·ly** *adv.*

su·per·fi·ci·ar·y (sōō′pər·fish′ē·er′ē) *adj.* **1** Belonging or pertaining to the superficies; superficial. **2** *Law* Situated on another's land, or resulting from such situation.

su·per·fi·ci·es (sōō′pər·fish′i·ēz, -fish′ēz) *n. pl.* **·ci·es 1** A surface or its area; superficial area. **2** External appearance; exterior part. [<L *super-* over + *facies* a face]

su·per·fine (sōō′pər·fīn′) *adj.* **1** Of surpassing fineness and delicacy; of the best quality. **2** Overrefined; unduly elaborate; overnice. [<MF *superfin* < *super-* over (<L) + *fin* FINE[1]] — **su′per·fine′ness** *n.*

su·per·flu·id (sōō′pər·flōō′id) *n. Physics* A peculiar state of matter noted in helium cooled to within a degree of absolute zero: it is characterized by an exceptional heat conductivity, a ready permeation of very dense substances, and the ability to flow upward against gravity: also called *quantum liquid.* — *adj.* (sōō′pər·flōō′id) Of or pertaining to such a state.

su·per·flu·i·ty (sōō′pər·flōō′ə·tē) *n. pl.* **·ties 1** The state of being superfluous; superabundance. **2** That, or that part, which is superfluous. See synonyms under EXCESS. [<OF *superfluité* <Med.L *superfluitas, -tatis* <L *superfluus* excessive < *super-* over + *fluere* flow]

su·per·flu·ous (sōō·pûr′flōō·əs) *adj.* **1** Exceeding what is needed; excessively abundant; surplus. **2** *Music* Augmented: sometimes said of an interval. **3** *Archaic* Supererogatory; officious. **4** *Obs.* Overfed, overequipped, or oversupplied. See synonyms under REDUNDANT, WASTE. [<L *superfluus.* See SUPERFLUITY.] — **su·per′flu·ous·ly** *adv.* — **su·per′flu·ous·ness** *n.*

su·per·fuse (sōō′pər·fyōōz′) *v.* **·fused, ·fus·ing** *v.t.* To pour so as to cover something else, as cod-liver oil on wine. — *v.i.* To be poured over or on something. [<L *superfusus,* pp. of *superfundere* < *super-* over + *fundere* pour] — **su′per·fu′sion** (-fyōō′zhən) *n.*

su·per·heat (sōō′pər·hēt′) *v.t.* **1** To heat to excess; overheat. **2** To raise the temperature of (a vapor not in contact with its liquid) above the saturation point for a given pressure. **3** To heat (a liquid) above the boiling point for a given pressure, but without conversion into vapor. — *n.* (sōō′pər·hēt′) The degree to which steam is superheated, or the heat so imparted.

su·per·heat·er (sōō′pər·hē′tər) *n.* A mechanical contrivance for superheating steam, as by causing it to traverse small tubes in the lower part of a chimney.

su·per·het·er·o·dyne (sōō′pər·het′ər·ə·dīn′) *adj. Electronics* Pertaining to or designating a type of radio reception in which the modulated incoming signals have the frequency of their carrier waves changed to an intermediate (inaudible) frequency, and are then rectified to reproduce the original sounds. — *n.* A radio receiving set for this method of reception. [<SUPER(SONIC) + HETERODYNE]

su·per·high·way (sōō′pər·hī′wā′) *n.* A highway for high-speed traffic, generally with four or more traffic lanes divided by a safety strip.

su·per·hu·man (sōō′pər·hyōō′mən) *adj.* **1** Above the range of human power or skill; above and beyond what is human; miraculous; divine. **2** Beyond normal human ability or power. See synonyms under SUPERNATURAL. — **su′per·hu·man′i·ty** (-hyōō·man′ə·tē) *n.* — **su′per·hu′man·ly** *adv.*

su·per·im·pose (sōō′pər·im·pōz′) *v.t.* **·posed, ·pos·ing 1** To lay or impose upon something else. **2** To add to something else. — **su′per·im·po·si′tion** (-im′pə·zish′ən) *n.*

su·per·in·cum·bent (sōō′pər·in·kum′bənt) *adj.* Resting or lying upon something else. [<L *superincumbens, -entis,* ppr. of *superincumbere* < *super-* over + *incumbere* rest on. See INCUMBENT.] — **su′per·in·cum′bence** or **·ben·cy** *n.*

su·per·in·duce (sōō′pər·in·dōōs′, -dyōōs′) *v.t.* **·duced, ·duc·ing** To introduce additionally; bring in or cause as an addition. [<LL *super-*

inducere cover over, add [<L *super-* over + *inducere* INDUCE] — **su'per·in·duc'tion** (-duk'·shən) *n.*

su·per·in·tend (soō'pər·in·tend') *v.t.* To have the charge and direction of; manage; supervise. [<LL *superintendere* < *super-* over + *intendere* aim at. See INTEND.]

su·per·in·ten·dence (soō'pər·in·ten'dəns) *n.* Direction and management; guiding and controlling supervision. See synonyms under OVERSIGHT.

su·per·in·ten·den·cy (soō'pər·in·ten'dən·sē) *n. pl.* **·cies** 1 The office or rank of a superintendent. 2 Superintendence.

su·per·in·ten·dent (soō'pər·in·ten'dənt) *n.* 1 One whose function is to superintend some particular work, office, or undertaking: a school *superintendent*, road *superintendent*. 2 The person charged with supervising maintenance and repair in an office or apartment building. — *adj.* Of or pertaining to superintendence or a superintendent; superintending. [<LL *superintendens, -entis,* ppr. of *superintendere* superintend]
  Synonyms (noun): conductor, curator, custodian, director, guardian, inspector, intendant, manager, master, overseer, superior, supervisor, warden.

su·pe·ri·or (sə·pir'ē·ər, soō-) *adj.* 1 Surpassing in quantity, quality, or degree; more excellent; preferable; in an absolute sense, of great excellence: a *superior* man. 2 Of higher grade, rank, or dignity. 3 Too great or dignified to be under the influence of something specified; serenely unaffected or indifferent: with *to*: *superior* to envy. 4 Locally higher; more elevated; upper. 5 Situated relatively nearer the top of the head when the body is standing erect: opposed to *inferior.* 6 *Bot.* Situated above or over another organ or part, as an ovary when free from the calyx, or, in an axillary flower, a petal or lip which is the one next to the main axis of the plant. 7 *Printing* Set above the level of the line: said of type; thus, in C⁴Dⁿ, 4 and n are *superior.* 8 *Logic* Of wider application: generic; said of terms, conceptions, and propositions. 9 Supercilious; affecting superiority: a *superior* smile. See synonyms under EXCELLENT, PARAMOUNT, PREDOMINANT. — *n.* 1 One who surpasses another in rank or excellence. 2 The ruler of an ecclesiastical order or house, as an abbey, convent, or monastery. 3 *Printing* A superior letter or character. See synonyms under SUPERINTENDENT. [<OF <L, compar. of *superus* on high, above < *super* above] — **su·pe·ri·or·i·ty** (sə·pir'ē·ôr'ə·tē, -or'-, soō-) *n.* — **su·pe'ri·or·ly** *adv.*

Superior, Lake The northernmost, westernmost, and largest of the Great Lakes, in the United States and Canada; 31,820 square miles; length, 350 miles; width, 160 miles.

su·per·la·tive (sə·pûr'lə·tiv, soō-) *adj.* 1 Elevated to the highest degree; consummate; of supreme excellence or eminence. 2 *Gram.* Expressing or involving the extreme degree: said of a form of comparison of adjectives or adverbs: The *superlative* degree of "wise" is "wisest." See COMPARISON (def. 2). 3 Excessive. — *n.* 1 That which is of the highest possible excellence or superior to all others. 2 *Gram.* The highest degree of comparison of the adjective or adverb; any word or phrase in the superlative degree. [<OF *superlatif* <LL *superlativus* <L *superlatus* excessive < *super-* above + *latus,* pp. to *ferre* carry] — **su·per·la·tive·ly** *adv.* — **su'per·la·tive·ness** *n.*

su·per·male (soō'pər·māl') *n. Biol.* A supersexual individual having, in the fruit fly, a ratio of 1 X–chromosome to 3 sets of autosomes.

su·per·man (soō'pər·man') *n. pl.* **·men** (-men') 1 A hypothetical superior being, characterized by perfection of physique, capacity for power, and a moral nature beyond good and evil, regarded as the product of evolutionary survival of the fittest; the *Übermensch* of Nietzsche. 2 An intellectually and morally improved man; a superior man; one possessing superhuman powers. [Trans. of G *übermensch*]

su·per·mar·ket (soō'pər·mär'kit) *n.* A large store or market selling food and household supplies and operating generally on a self-service, cash-and-carry basis. Also **super market.**

su·per·nal (soō·pûr'nəl) *adj.* 1 Heavenly; celestial. 2 Placed or located above; lofty; overhead; towering. 3 Coming from above or from the sky. [<OF <L *supernus* < *super* over] — **su·per'nal·ly** *adv.*

su·per·na·tant (soō'pər·nā'tənt) *adj.* 1 Floating uppermost, above something, or on the surface. 2 *Chem.* Denoting a liquid from which a precipitate has been thrown down. [<L *supernatans, -antis* < *super-* above + *natare* swim] — **su'per·na·ta'tion** (-nā·tā'·shən) *n.*

su·per·na·tu·ral (soō'pər·nach'ər·əl) *adj.* 1 Existing or occurring through some agency beyond the known forces of nature. 2 Lying outside the sphere of natural law, whether psychic or physical. 3 Believed to be miraculous or caused by the immediate exercise of divine power. 4 Pertaining to the miraculous. — *n.* That which is outside the accepted and known order of nature; that which transcends nature. [<Med. L *supernaturalis* <L *super-* above + *natura* NATURE] — **su'per·nat'u·ral·ly** *adv.* — **su'per·nat'u·ral·ness** *n.*
  Synonyms (adj.): miraculous, preternatural, superhuman. The *supernatural* is above or superior to the known powers of nature; the *preternatural* is aside from or beyond what we have been accustomed to regard as the result of natural law, often in the sense of inauspicious; as, a *preternatural* gloom. *Miraculous* is more emphatic and specific than *supernatural,* as referring to the direct personal intervention of divine power. *Miraculous* might be termed "extranatural," rather than *supernatural.* All that is beyond human power is *superhuman;* as, Prophecy gives evidence of *superhuman* knowledge; the word is sometimes applied to remarkable manifestations of human power, surpassing all that is ordinary. *Antonyms:* common, natural, ordinary, usual.

su·per·nat·u·ral·ism (soō'pər·nach'ər·əl·iz'əm) *n.* 1 The quality of being supernatural. 2 Belief in the supernatural; especially, the doctrine that there is a power not to be identified with nature, but which is the ground of its existences and is manifested in its forces, laws, and events: opposed to *naturalism.* 3 The doctrine of spiritual revelation together with the belief in Providence, the efficacy of prayer, and related doctrines: opposed to *rationalism.* Also spelled *supranaturalism.* — **su'per·nat'u·ral·ist** *adj. & n.* — **su'per·nat'u·ral·is'tic** *adj.*

su·per·nor·mal (soō'pər·nôr'məl) *adj.* 1 *Psychol.* Above the normal in characteristics, properties, or intelligence: a *supernormal* child. 2 Pertaining to or designating phenomena incapable of rigorous scientific explanation but conceivably in accord with still undiscovered natural laws.

su·per·nu·mer·a·ry (soō'pər·noō'mə·rer'ē, -nyoō'-) *adj.* 1 Being beyond a fixed or standard number. 2 Beyond a customary or necessary number; superfluous. — *n. pl.* **·ar·ies** 1 A person or thing in excess of the regular, necessary, or customary number. 2 A stage performer, as in mob scenes or processions, without any speaking part: often contracted to *supe* or *super.* [<LL *supernumerarius* a soldier added to a legion after it is complete <L *super numerum* < *super* over + *numerus* a number]

su·per·or·der (soō'pər·ôr'dər) *n. Biol.* A plant or animal division intermediate between a class and an order.

su·per·pa·tri·ot (soō'pər·pā'trē·ət, -ot) *n.* A person who is or claims to be a great patriot, often one whose patriotic fervor is marked by a readiness to regard dissent as unpatriotic or subversive. — **su'per·pa'tri·ot'ic** *adj.* — **su'per·pa'tri·ot·ism** *n.*

su·per·phos·phate (soō'pər·fos'fāt) *n. Chem.* 1 An acid phosphate. 2 Any fertilizing material mostly consisting of soluble phosphates: *superphosphate* of lime.

su·per·phys·i·cal (soō'pər·fiz'i·kəl) *adj.* Beyond or above the physical.

su·per·pose (soō'pər·pōz') *v.t.* **·posed, ·pos·ing** 1 To lay over or upon something else, as one layer upon another. 2 *Geom.* To suppose (one figure) to be placed upon another so that all like parts coincide. Compare SUPERIMPOSE. 3 *Physics* To combine additively, as forces or wave amplitudes. [<F *superposer* < *super-* over + *poser* POSE¹] — **su'per·pos'a·ble** *adj.* — **su'per·po·si'tion** (-pə·zish'ən) *n.*

su·per·pow·er (soō'pər·pou'ər) *n.* One of a few great, dominant nations characterized by superior economic or military strength and by large population.

su·per·pres·sure (soō'pər·presh'ər) *n.* 1 Excessive pressure under given conditions. 2 *Aeron.* The amount by which the pressure within the gas cell of a dirigible exceeds atmospheric pressure.

su·per·roy·al (soō'pər·roi'əl) *n.* A size of ledger paper, 20 by 28 inches.

su·per·sat·u·rate (soō'pər·sach'oō·rāt) *v.t.* **·rat·ed, ·rat·ing** 1 To saturate to excess or beyond the normal point. 2 To cause (a solution) to contain more of a dissolved substance than can be held under normal conditions of temperature. — **su'per·sat'u·ra'tion** *n.*

su·per·scribe (soō'pər·skrīb') *v.t.* **·scribed, ·scrib·ing** To write or engrave on the outside or on the upper part of; inscribe with a name or address; specifically, to address, as a letter. [<LL *superscribere* <L *super-* over + *scribere* write]

su·per·script (soō'pər·skript') *adj.* Written above or overhead: opposed to *subscript.* — *n.* 1 Superscription. 2 *Math.* An index or other mark following and above a letter or figure, as *a*³, c'. [<LL *superscriptus,* pp. of *superscribere* SUPERSCRIBE]

su·per·scrip·tion (soō'pər·skrip'shən) *n.* 1 The act of superscribing an address on a letter. 2 An upper or outer inscription, as a title or a direction; especially, an address on a letter. 3 That portion of a medical prescription that begins with the word *recipe* (generally abbreviated ℞, and meaning "take"). [<OF <LL *superscriptio, -onis* < *superscribere.* See SUPERSCRIBE.]

su·per·sede (soō'pər·sēd') *v.t.* **·sed·ed, ·sed·ing** 1 To take the place of, as by reason of superior worth, right, or appropriateness; replace; supplant. 2 To put something in the place of; set aside; suspend; annul. See synonyms under SUBVERT. [<OF *superceder* <L *supersedere* sit over, forbear < *super-* above + *sedere* sit] — **su'per·sed'er** *n.* — **su'per·se'dure** (-sē'jər), **su'per·ses'sion** (-sesh'ən) *n.*

su·per·sen·si·ble (soō'pər·sen'sə·bəl) *adj.* Being above or beyond the range of the senses; supersensual; psychical. — **su'per·sen'si·bly** *adv.*

su·per·sen·su·al (soō'pər·sen'shoō·əl) *adj.* 1 Being above the senses; supersensible. 2 Spiritual; ideal. Also **su'per·sen'so·ry** (-sen'sər·ē).

su·per·ser·vice·a·ble (soō'pər·sûr'vis·ə·bəl) *adj.* Trying needlessly or disagreeably to be of service; officious. — **su'per·ser'vice·a·bly** *adv.*

su·per·sex (soō'pər·seks') *n. Biol.* A sterile organism having a mixture of male and female characteristics due to a disturbed ratio of autosomes to X–chromosomes, as in the fruit fly. — **su'per·sex'u·al** (-sek'shoō·əl) *adj.*

su·per·son·ic (soō'pər·son'ik) *adj. Aeron.* Of, pertaining to, or characterized by a speed greater than that of sound: distinguished from *ultrasonic.*

su·per·son·ics (soō'pər·son'iks) *n. pl.* (construed as singular) The science which treats of the phenomena of supersonic speed, with especial reference to their practical applications to aircraft, guided missiles, rockets, etc.: distinguished from *ultrasonics.*

su·per·star (soō'pər·stär') *n.* A public performer, as an actor, singer, or professional athlete, regarded as one of the best or most popular. — **su'per·star'dom** *n.*

su·per·state (soō'pər·stāt') *n.* A state established as the governing power of a union or federation of subordinate states.

su·per·sti·tion (soō'pər·stish'ən) *n.* 1 A belief founded on irrational feelings, especially of fear, and marked by credulity; also, any rite or practice inspired by such belief. 2 Specifically, a belief in a religious system regarded (by others than the believer) as without reasonable support; also, any of its rites. 3 Credulity regarding or reverence for the occult or supernatural, as belief in omens, charms, and signs; loosely, any unreasoning or unreasonable belief or impression. 4 *Obs.* Undue scrupulousness. Also synonym under FANATICISM. [<OF <L *superstitio, -onis* amazement, dread < *super-* over + *stare* stand still]

su·per·sti·tious (soō'pər·stish'əs) *adj.* 1 Disposed to believe in or be influenced by superstitions. 2 Of, pertaining to, or manifesting superstition. — **su'per·sti'tious·ly** *adv.* — **su'-**

per·sti′tious·ness n.

su·per·stra·tum (soo̅′pər·strā′təm, -strat′əm) n. pl. ·stra·ta (-strā′tə, -strat′ə) A layer superimposed upon another; a superficial stratum.

su·per·struct (soo̅′pər·strukt′) v.t. To build or erect upon a foundation.

su·per·struc·ture (soo̅′pər·struk′chər) n. 1 Any structure or any part of a structure above the basement or considered in relation to its foundation. 2 The sleepers, rails, etc., of a railway, as distinguished from the roadbed. 3 Naut. The parts of a ship's structure, especially of a warship, above the main deck. Compare SUBSTRUCTURE.

su·per·sub·tle (soo̅′pər·sut′l) adj. Extremely subtle; oversubtle.

su·per·tank·er (soo̅′pər·tangk′ər) n. A very large tanker capable of carrying a vast cargo, as of oil.

su·per·tax (soo̅′pər·taks′) n. An extra tax in addition to the normal tax; especially, a graded additional tax on incomes above certain amounts; a surtax.

su·per·ton·ic (soo̅′pər·ton′ik) n. Music The tone above the tonic or keynote; the second.

su·per·vene (soo̅′pər·vēn′) v.i. ·vened, ·ven·ing 1 To follow closely upon something; come as something extraneous or additional. 2 To take place; happen. See synonyms under HAPPEN. [<L supervenire <super- over and above + venire come] — su′per·ven′ient (-vēn′yənt) adj. — su′per·ven′tion (-ven′shən) n.

su·per·vise (soo̅′pər·vīz′) v.t. ·vised, ·vis·ing To have a general oversight of; superintend; oversee. [<Med. L supervisus, pp. of supervidere <L super- over + videre see]

su·per·vi·sion (soo̅′pər·vizh′ən) n. 1 The act of supervising; superintendence. 2 The authority to direct or supervise.

su·per·vi·sor (soo̅′pər·vī′zər) n. 1 One who supervises or oversees; a superintendent; an inspector. 2 U.S. A township officer in administrative charge of its business; one of a board of such officers constituting a body having charge of the business of a county; a borough officer who has charge of road repairs, etc. 3 A person supervising teachers of special subjects in a school. 4 Obs. A beholder. — su′per·vi′sor·ship n. — su′per·vi′so·ry (-zər·ē) adj.

su·pi·nate (soo̅′pə·nāt) v.t. & v.i. ·nat·ed, ·nat·ing 1 To make or become supine. 2 To turn, as the hand or forelimb, so that the palm is upward or forward. [<L supinatus, pp. of supinare throw (someone) on the back <supinus SUPINE]

su·pi·na·tion (soo̅′pə·nā′shən) n. Physiol. 1 The act of turning the palm of the hand, or the corresponding surface of the forelimb, upward. 2 The position of a limb so turned: opposed to pronation. 3 The act or state of lying supine.

su·pi·na·tor (soo̅′pə·nā′tər) n. Anat. A muscle of the forearm by which supination is effected.

su·pine (soo̅·pīn′) adj. 1 Lying on the back, or with the face turned upward. 2 Having no interest or care; inactive; indolent; negligent; indifferent; listless. 3 Having an inclined position; sloping, as a hill. [<L supinus <sup-, root of super above] — su·pine′ly adv. — su·pine′ness n.

sup·per (sup′ər) n. The last meal of the day: frequently used of an evening banquet. [<OF soper, super sup, dine] — sup′per·less adj.

sup·plant (sə·plant′, -plänt′) v.t. 1 To take the place of; displace. 2 To take the place of (someone) by scheming, treachery, etc. 3 To replace (one thing) with another; remove; uproot. See synonyms under ABOLISH, SUBVERT. [<OF supplanter <L supplantare trip up <sub- up from below + planta the sole of the foot] — sup·plan·ta·tion (sup′lan·tā′shən) n. — sup·plant′er n.

sup·ple (sup′əl) adj. 1 Easily bent; flexible; pliant: a supple bow. 2 Yielding to the humor or wishes of others; especially, servilely compliant; obsequious. 3 Of the mind, showing adaptability; elastic; easily changing. — v.t. & v.i. ·pled, ·pling To make or become supple. [<OF supple, sople <L supplex, -icis submissive, lit., bending under <sub- under + stem of plicare fold] — sup′ple·ly adv. — sup′ple·ness n.

Synonyms (adj.): compliant, elastic, fawning,

flexible, limber, lissom, lithe, lithesome, obsequious, pliable, pliant, soft, submissive, willowy, yielding. See ACTIVE, OBSEQUIOUS. Antonyms: firm, fixed, inflexible, obstinate, pertinacious, rigid, stiff, stubborn, unbending, unyielding.

sup·ple·jack (sup′əl·jak) n. 1 Any of various woody climbers with tough and lithe stems; specifically, a high–climbing vine (genus Berchemia) of the southern United States. 2 A walking stick made from the wood of such a plant.

sup·ple·ment (sup′lə·ment) v.t. To make additions to; provide for what is lacking in. — n. (-mənt) 1 Something added that supplies a deficiency; especially, an addition to a publication. 2 A supplementary angle. See synonyms under APPENDAGE. [<L supplementum <supplere SUPPLY¹]

sup·pli·ance (sup′lē·əns) n. The act of supplicating; an urgent petition or prayer.

sup·pli·ant (sup′lē·ənt) adj. 1 Entreating earnestly and humbly; beseeching. 2 Manifesting entreaty or submissive supplication. — n. One who supplicates. [<MF, ppr. of supplier <L supplicare SUPPLICATE] — sup′pli·ant·ly adv. — sup′pli·ant·ness n.

sup·pli·cant (sup′lə·kənt) n. One who supplicates; a suppliant. — adj. Asking or entreating humbly; beseeching. [<L supplicans, -antis, ppr. of supplicare SUPPLICATE]

sup·pli·cate (sup′lə·kāt) v. ·cat·ed, ·cat·ing v.t. 1 To ask for humbly or by earnest prayer. 2 To beg something of; entreat. — v.i. 3 To beg or pray humbly; make an earnest request. See synonyms under ASK, PRAY. [<L supplicatus, pp. of supplicare supplicate <sub- under + plicare bend, fold] — sup′pli·ca′tion n. — sup′pli·ca·to·ry (-kə·tôr′ē) adj.

sup·ply¹ (sə·plī′) v. ·plied, ·ply·ing v.t. 1 To give or furnish (something needful or desirable): to supply milk for a city. 2 To furnish with what is needed: to supply an army with ammunition. 3 To provide for adequately; satisfy: to supply a demand. 4 To make up for; make good or compensate for, as a loss or deficiency. 5 To fill (the place of another); also, to fill (an office, etc.) or occupy (a pulpit) as a substitute. — v.i. 6 To take the place of another temporarily. See synonyms under ACCOMMODATE, GIVE, PROVIDE. — n. pl. ·plies 1 That which is or can be supplied; the available aggregate of things needed or demanded. 2 The amount of a commodity offered at a given price or available for meeting a demand. 3 Accumulated stores reserved for distribution, as for an army or a fleet: usually in the plural: He was cut off from his base of supplies. 4 A grant of money to the crown or for the public service; appropriation: usually in the plural. 5 An amount sufficient for a given use; store or quantity on hand. 6 A substitute or temporary incumbent. 7 Obs. Reinforcements. 8 The act of supplying. See synonyms under STOCK. [<OF sopleer, soupleier <L supplere <sub- up from under + ple-, root of plenus full] — sup·pli′er n.

sup·ply² (sup′lē) adv. In a supple manner; supplely. [<SUPPLE]

sup·port (sə·pôrt′, -pōrt′) v.t. 1 To bear the weight of, especially from underneath; hold in position; keep from falling, sinking, etc. 2 To bear or sustain (weight, etc.). 3 To keep (a person, the mind, etc.) from failing or declining; strengthen. 4 To serve to uphold or corroborate (a statement, theory, etc.); substantiate; verify. 5 To provide (a person, institution, etc.) with maintenance; provide for. 6 To give approval or assistance to; uphold; advocate; aid. 7 To endure or tolerate: I cannot support his insolence. 8 To carry on; keep up; maintain: to support a war. 9 In the theater: a To act (a role or part). b To act in a subordinate role to. — n. 1 The act of supporting. 2 One who or that which supports. 3 Subsistence. See synonyms under SUBSIDY. [<OF supporter <L supportare convey <sub- up from under + portare carry] — sup·por′tive adj.

Synonyms (verb): bear, carry, maintain, prop, sustain, uphold. Support and sustain alike signify to hold up or keep up, to prevent from falling or sinking; but sustain has a special sense of continuous exertion or strength, as when we speak of sustained endeavor or a

sustained note; a flower is supported by the stem or a temple roof by arches; the foundations of a great building sustain an enormous pressure; to sustain life implies a greater exigency and need than to support life; to say one is sustained under affliction emphasizes the severity of the trial and the completeness of the upholding more than if we say he is supported. To bear is the most general word, denoting all holding up or keeping up of any object, whether in rest or motion; it refers to something that is a tax upon strength or endurance; as, to bear a strain; to bear pain or grief. To maintain is to keep in a state or condition, especially in an excellent and desirable condition; as, to maintain health, reputation, position, etc. Maintain is a word of more dignity than support; a man supports his family; a state maintains an army or navy. To prop is always partial, signifying to add support to something that is insecure. See ABET, AID, ENDURE, KEEP, LEAN, PROP. Antonyms: abandon, betray, demolish, desert, destroy, drop, overthrow, wreck.

sup·port·a·ble (sə·pôr′tə·bəl, -pōr′-) adj. That may be supported or borne; bearable; endurable. — sup·port′a·ble·ness, sup·port′a·bil′i·ty n. — sup·port′a·bly adv.

sup·pose (sə·pōz′) v. ·posed, ·pos·ing v.t. 1 To think or imagine to oneself as true; believe or believe probable; think; presume. 2 To assume as true for the sake of argument or illustration. 3 To require to exist as true; imply as cause or consequence; involve as an inference: Design in creation supposes the existence of a God. 4 To expect: I am supposed to follow. 5 To presuppose; assume. — v.i. 6 To make a supposition. [<OF suposer <sup- under (<L sub-) + poser POSE¹] — sup·pos′er n.

Synonyms: conjecture, deem, guess, imagine, surmise, think. To suppose is temporarily to assume a thing as true, either with the expectation of finding it so or for the purpose of ascertaining what would follow if it were so. To conjecture is to put together the nearest available materials for a provisional opinion, always with some expectation of finding the facts to be as conjectured. To imagine is to form a mental image of something as existing, while its actual existence may be unknown, or even impossible. To think, in this application, is to hold as the result of thought what is admitted not to be matter of exact or certain knowledge; as, I do not know, but I think this to be the fact: a more conclusive statement than would be made by the use of conjecture or suppose. See GUESS. Antonyms: ascertain, conclude, discover, know, prove.

sup·posed (sə·pōzd′) adj. Accepted as genuine; believed; often, falsely imagined. — sup·pos·ed·ly (-pō′zid·lē) adv.

sup·po·si·tion (sup′ə·zish′ən) n. 1 The act of supposing, or that which is supposed; conjecture. 2 A hypothetical proposition made for the purpose of explaining certain facts, relating them, or of deducing consequences from them; hypothesis. See synonyms under FANCY, GUESS, HYPOTHESIS, IDEA, THOUGHT. [<Med. L suppositio, -onis <L, a substitute <suppositus, pp. of supponere suppose, substitute <sub- under + ponere place] — sup′po·si′tion·al adj. — sup′po·si′tion·al·ly adv.

sup·po·si·tious (sup′ə·zish′əs) adj. Supposed or assumed; hypothetical; also, imaginary.

sup·pos·i·ti·tious (sə·poz′ə·tish′əs) adj. Put in the place of or made to represent, in order to deceive or defraud; spurious. See synonyms under COUNTERFEIT. [<L suppositus. See SUPPOSITION.] — sup·pos′i·ti′tious·ly adv. — sup·pos′i·ti′tious·ness n.

sup·pos·i·tive (sə·poz′ə·tiv) adj. Including or implying supposition; supposed. — n. A conjunction introducing a supposition, as if, or provided. — sup·pos′i·tive·ly adv.

sup·pos·i·to·ry (sə·poz′ə·tôr′ē, -tō′rē) n. pl. ·ries Med. A solid, readily fusible, medicated preparation for introduction into some canal, cavity, or internal organ. [<LL suppositorium, orig. neut. sing. of suppositorius placed underneath or up <L suppositus. See SUPPOSITION.]

sup·press (sə·pres′) v.t. 1 To put an end or stop to; quell; crush, as a rebellion. 2 To stop or prohibit the activities of, as a rival political group; abolish. **3** To withhold from knowledge or publication, as a book, news, etc. **4** To repress, as a groan or sigh. **5** To stop (a hemorrhage, etc.). See synonyms under ABOLISH, HIDE, REPRESS, RESTRAIN, SUBDUE. [<L *suppressus*, pp. of *supprimere* <*sub-* under + *premere* press] — **sup·press′er, sup·pres′sor** n. — **sup·press′i·ble** adj.

sup·pres·sion (sə·presh′ən) n. **1** The act of suppressing, or the state of being suppressed. **2** *Psychoanal.* The deliberate exclusion from consciousness and action of ideas, memories, or emotions, especially those regarded as unpleasant or as socially unacceptable.

sup·pu·rate (sup′yə·rāt) v.i. **·rat·ed, ·rat·ing** To form or generate pus; maturate. [<L *suppuratus*, pp. of *suppurare* <*sub-* under + *pus, puris* pus]

sup·pu·ra·tion (sup′yə·rā′shən) n. **1** The act or process of suppurating. **2** Pus.

sup·pu·ra·tive (sup′yə·rā′tiv) adj. Tending to or producing suppuration. — n. A remedy promoting suppuration.

supra– prefix Above; beyond: *supraliminal*. Used to form adjectives and often the equivalent of *super–* which is preferred in general words. [<L *supra–* < *supra* above, beyond]

su·pra·lap·sar·i·an (sōō′prə·lap·sâr′ē·ən) n. A high Calvinist or holder of the doctrine that predestination preceded creation and the fall of man in the divine order of decrees. See INFRALAPSARIAN. [<NL *supralapsarius* <L *supra–* before + *lapsus* a fall] — **su′pra·lap·sar′i·an·ism** n.

su·pra·lim·i·nal (sōō′prə·lim′ə·nəl) adj. Psychol. Above the threshold of normal consciousness or sensation: opposed to *subliminal*.

su·pra·or·bi·tal (sōō′prə·ôr′bi·təl) adj. Anat. Situated above the orbit of the eye. [<NL *supraorbitalis* <L *supra–* above + *orbita* ORBIT]

su·pra·pro·test (sōō′prə·prō′test) n. Law Acceptance or payment of a bill of exchange by one not a party to it after protest for non-acceptance or non-payment. [<Ital. *sopra protesta* upon protest <*sopra* (<L *supra* above) + *protesta* <L *protestari* PROTEST]

su·pra·tem·po·ral (sōō′prə·tem′pər·əl) Anat. adj. Situated in the upper part of the temporal bone or region. — n. A supratemporal bone.

su·prem·a·cy (sə·prem′ə·sē, sōō-) n. pl. **·cies** The state of being supreme; supreme power or authority. See synonyms under PRECEDENCE, VICTORY. — **royal supremacy** The judicial and executive supremacy of a sovereign as the head of the Christian church within his realm: used especially of English sovereigns.

su·preme (sə·prēm′, sōō-) adj. **1** Highest in power or authority; dominant. **2** Highest in degree, importance, or estimation; most extreme or momentous; utmost: *supreme* devotion. **3** Ultimate; last and greatest. See synonyms under ABSOLUTE, FIRST, IMPERIAL, PARAMOUNT, PREDOMINANT. — **the Supreme Being** God; the Deity. — n. **1** The supreme or highest point; acme. **2** One who is above the rest; a superior; chief. [<L *supremus* highest, superl. of *superus* that is above <*super* above] — **su·preme′ly** adv. — **su·preme′ness** n.

su·prême (sü·prem′) n. French **1** An especially choice portion of breast of fowl, fish, etc.: a culinary term. **2** A rich cream sauce.

sur– prefix A form of the Latin *super–* found in words which came into English through Old French. [<OF *sur–* <L *super–* SUPER-]

su·ra (sōōr′ə) n. A chapter or section of the Koran. [<Arabic *surah*, lit., a step, degree]

su·rah (sōōr′ə) n. A soft, usually twilled, silk fabric, used for women's wear, ties, etc.: now sometimes mixed with rayon. Also **surah silk**. [from *Surat*, India]

sur·base (sûr′bās′) n. Archit. A molding or border above the dado and base of a pedestal or above the baseboard of a room. [<SUR-¹ + BASE¹]

sur·based (sûr′bāst′) adj. Archit. **1** Having a surbase, as a pedestal. **2** Flattened; depressed. **3** Having the rise of the curve less than half the span: a *surbased* arch.

sur·cease (sûr·sēs′, sûr′sēs) n. Absolute cessation; end. — v.t. & v.i. **·ceased, ·ceas·ing** To cease entirely or finally; end. [<AF *sursise* omission, orig. pp. of *surseoir* refrain <L *supersedere* SUPERSEDE]

sur·charge (sûr′chärj′) n. **1** An excessive burden, load, or charge. **2** In chancery law, the showing of an omission of items in an account for which credit ought to be allowed: opposed to *falsification*. **3** An additional or excessive amount charged, especially an unlawful charge; an overcharge. **4** A new valuation or something additional printed on a postage or revenue stamp; also, a stamp so imprinted. — v.t. (sûr·chärj′) **·charged, ·charg·ing** **1** To charge (a person) too much; overcharge. **2** To show an omission of credits in (an account), or of something for which credit should have been allowed. **3** To overload. **4** To fill to excess. **5** To imprint a surcharge on (postage stamps). [<F < *surcharger* <*sur-* over + *charger* <OF *chargier* CHARGE] — **sur·charg′er** n.

sur·cin·gle (sûr′sing·gəl) n. **1** A girth or strap encircling the body of a beast of burden, for holding a saddle, etc. **2** A girdle, as of a cassock. — v.t. **·gled, ·gling** To gird or fasten with a surcingle. [<OF *surcengle* <*sur-* over + L *cingulum* a belt]

sur·coat (sûr′kōt′) n. An outer coat or garment; in the Middle Ages, a loose robe or cloaklike garment worn over armor. [<OF *surcot* <*sur-* over + *cot, cote* a coat]

sur·cu·lose (sûr′kyə·lōs) adj. Bot. Producing or having suckers: said of plants. [<L *surculosus* <*surculus* a twig, sucker, dim. of *surus* a twig]

surd (sûrd) n. **1** Math. An irrational number or quantity, especially an indicated root that can only be approximated, as √2. **2** Phonet. A speech sound made without vibration of the vocal cords. — adj. **1** Math. Incapable of being expressed in rational numbers; irrational. **2** Phonet. Voiceless: opposed to *sonant, voiced*. [<L *surdus* deaf, silent]

sure (shōōr) adj. **1** Not liable to change or failure; firm; unyielding; stable; infallible. **2** Fit, proper, or deserving to be depended on; reliable; trustworthy. **3** Free from doubt; certain; positive. **4** Certain of obtaining, attaining, or retaining something: with of. **5** Safe; secure from danger or harm. **6** Bound to happen. — adv. Colloq. Surely; certainly. — **to be sure** Indeed; certainly. — **to make sure** To make certain; secure. [<OF *sur* <L *securus*. Doublet of SECURE.] — **sure′ness** n. Synonyms (adj.): actual, assured, aware, certain, clear, confident, indisputable, positive, real. See AUTHENTIC, FAITHFUL, SECURE.

sure–fire (shōōr′fīr′) adj. Colloq. Reliable; sure or certain to succeed, win, or come out as expected.

sure–foot·ed (shōōr′fōōt′id) adj. Not liable to fall or stumble; figuratively, not liable to err.

sure·ly (shōōr′lē) adv. **1** Without doubt; certainly. **2** Securely; safely.

sure·ty (shōōr′tē, shōōr′ə·tē) n. pl. **·ties** **1** A person who engages to be responsible for the debt, default, or miscarriage of another; bail. **2** An individual or corporation that, in consideration of the payment of a premium, acts as security for a principal (as a State, city, bank, etc.), against possible loss through the act of an associate or employee who is required to furnish such security. **3** A pledge of money deposited, or of credit given, to secure against loss or damage; security for payment or performance. **4** That which gives security or confidence; ground or basis of certainty or security. **5** The state of being sure; sureness; security; safety; certainty. **6** A sponsor. See synonyms under CERTAINTY, SECURITY. [<OF *surte* <L *securitas, -atis* <*securus* SECURE] — **sure′ty·ship** n.

surf (sûrf) n. **1** The swell of the sea that breaks upon a shore. **2** The foam caused by the billows. — v.i. To ride the surf on a surfboard; engage in surfing. ◆ Homophone: *serf*. [Earlier *suff*, ? var. of SOUGH] — **surf′y** adj.

sur·face (sûr′fis) n. **1** The exterior part or face of anything that has length, breadth, and thickness. **2** That which has length and breadth, but not thickness; a superficies. **3** A superficial aspect; external view or appearance. **4** That portion of the side of a fortification which is bounded by the angle of the nearest bastion and the prolongation of the flank. — v. **·faced, ·fac·ing** v.t. **1** To put a surface on; especially, to make smooth, even, or plain. — v.i. **2** To mine at or near the surface. **3** To rise to the surface, as a submarine. [<F < *sur-* above + *face* FACE] — **surf′ac·er** n.

sur·face–ac·tive (sûr′fis·ak′tiv) adj. Chem. Pertaining to or denoting any of a class of substances which have the property of reducing the surface tension of a liquid in which they are dissolved: said especially of detergents.

surface mail Mail sent by land or sea rather than by air.

surface noise The mechanical noise produced by friction of the needle against the granular surface of a phonograph record.

surface plate Mech. A plate having a very accurate surface: used for testing other surfaces.

surface tension Physics That property of a liquid by virtue of which the surface molecules exhibit a strong inward attraction, thus forming an elastic skin which tends to contract to the minimum area.

sur·fac·tant (sûr·fak′tənt) n. Chem. A surface-active agent or a solute which tends to reduce the surface tension of the solvent, as a soap or detergent. [<SURF(ACE)–ACT(IVE) + -ANT]

surf·bird (sûrf′bûrd′) n. A ploverlike bird (*Aphriza virgata*) of the Pacific coast of America from Alaska to Chile.

surf·board (sûrf′bôrd′, -bōrd′) n. A long, narrow board used in surfing. Compare AQUAPLANE.

surf·boat (sûrf′bōt′) n. A boat of extra strength and buoyancy, for launching and landing through surf. — **surf′boat′man** (-mən) n.

surf duck One of various scoters or sea ducks, especially the surf scoter. Also **surf coot**.

sur·feit (sûr′fit) v.t. **1** To feed to fullness or satiety; overfeed. **2** To supply to satiety. — v.i. **3** To partake of food or drink to excess; overeat. **4** To overindulge. See synonyms under SATISFY. — n. **1** The act of surfeiting oneself; excess in eating or drinking; also, the excessive quantity partaken of. **2** The result of such excess; satiety; superfluity. **3** The state of being surfeited; oppressive fullness of the system caused by excess in eating or drinking. [<OF *sorfait* < *surfaire* overdo < *sur-* above + *faire* make ·<L *facere*]

surf fish Any of a family (*Embiotocidae*) of viviparous sea fishes, perchlike in form, numerous near shore all along the northern Pacific coast of North America.

sur·fi·cial (sûr·fish′əl) adj. Geol. Originally belonging to or being on the surface, as of the earth: contrasted with *subterranean*. [<SURFACE]

surf scoter A North American scoter (*Melanitta perspicillata*). The adult male is black with a white spot on the forehead and the nape. Also **surf′er**.

surge (sûrj) v. **surged, surg·ing** v.i. **1** To rise high and roll onward, as waves; swell or heave. **2** To move or go in a manner suggestive of this: The mob *surged* through the square. **3** To increase or vary suddenly, as an electric current. **4** To slip, as a rope on a windlass. — v.t. **5** To cause to move in surges. **6** To let go suddenly, as a rope or cable. — n. **1** A large swelling wave; billow; also, such billows collectively. **2** The act of surging; a heaving and rolling motion, as of great waves. **3** Naut. The tapered drum of a capstan or windlass around which the rope surges. **4** Electr. A sudden fluctuation of voltage due to lightning, switching, etc. See synonyms under WAVE. ◆ Homophone: *serge*. [<OF *sourge-*, stem of *sourdre* rise <L *surgere*] — **surg′er** n. — **surg′y** adj.

sur·geon (sûr′jən) n. **1** One who practices surgery. **2** A medical officer in the military or naval service; a ship's doctor. **3** A surgeon fish. [<AF *surgien*, var. of OF *cirugien*. See CHIRURGEON.]

surgeon fish A West Indian fish (*Teuthis hepatus*) having erectile lancetlike spines at the sides of the tail.

sur·ger·y (sûr′jər·ē) n. pl. **·ger·ies** **1** The branch of medical science that relates to body injuries, deformities, and morbid conditions that require being remedied by operations or instruments. **2** A place where surgical treatment or advice is regularly given; a surgeon's office; an operating room. **3** The work of a surgeon. **4** The treatment of diseases or injuries to nonhuman organisms by like methods: tree *surgery*. [<OF *surgerie*, contraction of *serurgerie*, ult. <LL *chirurgia* <Gk. *cheirourgia* a handicraft <*cheir, cheiros* the hand + *ergein* work]

sur·gi·cal (sûr'ji·kəl) *adj.* **1** Of or pertaining to surgery. **2** Designating a degree of anesthesia deep enough to permit major surgical operations. — **sur'gi·cal·ly** *adv.*

su·ri·cate (sŏŏr'ə·kāt) *n.* A small burrowing viverrine carnivore (*Suricata tetradactyla*) of South Africa, having only. four toes: often domesticated. [<F *surikate* <Afrikaans, ? <a native South African name]

sur·ly (sûr'lē) *adj.* **·li·er, ·li·est 1** Persistently rude and ill-humored; crabbed; cross; gruff. **2** Characterized by rudeness or gruffness, as a reply. **3** *Obs.* Haughty. See synonyms under HAUGHTY, MOROSE. [Earlier *sirly* like a lord < *sir* a lord + *-ly* like] — **sur'li·ly** *adv.* — **sur'li·ness** *n.*

sur·mise (sər·mīz') *v.* **·mised, ·mis·ing** *v.t.* To infer on slight evidence; guess. — *v.i.* To make a conjecture thus. See synonyms under GUESS, SUPPOSE, SUSPECT. — *n.* (sər·mīz', sûr'mīz) A conjecture made on slight evidence; supposition. See synonyms under GUESS, HYPOTHESIS. [<OF, an accusation, pp. fem. of *surmettre* accuse < *sur-* upon + *mettre* put <L *mittere* send]

sur·mount (sər·mount') *v.t.* **1** To overcome; prevail over (a difficulty, etc.). **2** To mount to the top or cross to the other side of; get over, as an obstacle or mountain. **3** To be or lie over or above. **4** To place something above or on top of; cap. **5** *Obs.* To surpass; exceed. See synonyms under CONQUER. [<OF *surmunter* <Med.L *supermontare* <L *super-* over + *mons, montis* a hill, mountain] — **sur·mount'a·ble** *adj.* — **sur·mount'a·ble·ness** *n.* — **sur·mount'er** *n.*

sur·name (sûr'nām') *n.* A name subjoined to a given or Christian name; hence, a family name. — *v.t.* (sûr'nām', sûr·nām') **·named, ·nam·ing** To give a surname to; call by a surname. [Alter. of obs. *surnoun* <OF *surnom* < *sur-* above, beyond + *nom* a name <L *nomen, -inis*; infl. in form by NAME] — **sur'nam·er** *n.*

sur·pass (sər·pas', -päs') *v.t.* **1** To go beyond or past in degree or amount; exceed; excel. **2** To transcend; be beyond the reach or powers of. [<MF *surpasser* < *sur-* above + *passer* PASS] — **sur·pass'a·ble** *adj.*
Synonyms: eclipse, outdo, outstrip, transcend. See BEAT, LEAD. *Antonyms:* fail, yield.

sur·plice (sûr'plis) *n. Eccl.* A loose white vestment with full sleeves, worn over the cassock by the clergy of the Anglican, Moravian, and Roman Catholic churches, and also by choristers in a vested choir. [<AF *surpliz,* OF *sourpeliz* < Med.L *superpellicium* (*vestimentum*) an overgarment < *super-* over + *pellicia* a fur garment < *pellis* skin]

SURPLICE

sur·plus (sûr'plus) *adj.* Being in excess of what is used or needed. — *n.* **1** That which remains over and above what has been used or is required; overplus; residue. **2** Assets in excess of liabilities. **3** Excess of net assets above the face value of shares of a corporation. **4** A small unorganized tract of land in Maine set apart by State authority. See synonyms under EXCESS. [<OF <Med.L *superplus* < *super-* over and above + *plus* more]

sur·prise (sər·prīz') *v.t.* **·prised, ·pris·ing 1** To cause to feel wonder or astonishment because unusual or unexpected. **2** To come upon suddenly or unexpectedly; take unawares. **3** To attack suddenly and without warning; capture by surprise. **4** To lead unawares, as into doing something not intended: with *into.* **5** To elicit in this manner: They *surprised* the truth from him. — *n.* **1** The act of surprising; a coming upon unawares. **2** A surprised state; astonishment. **3** Something that causes surprise, as a sudden and unexpected event, fact, or gift. Also *Rare* **sur·prize'.** [<OF *surpris,* pp. of *surprendre* < Med.L *superprendere* <L *super-* over + *prehendere* take] — **sur·pris'er** *n.*

sur·re·al·ism (sə·rē'əl·iz'əm) *n.* A movement in 20th century literature and art which attempts to express and exhibit the workings of the subconscious mind, especially as manifested in dreams and uncontrolled by the reason or any conscious process: characterized by the incongruous and startling arrangement and presentation of subject matter. [<F *surréalisme* < *sur-* beyond, above + *réalisme* realism < *réal* REAL] — **sur·re'al·ist** *adj. & n.* — **sur·re'al·is'tic** *adj.* — **sur·re'al·is'ti·cal·ly** *adv.*

sur·ren·der (sə·ren'dər) *v.t.* **1** To yield possession of or power over to another; give up because of demand or compulsion. **2** To give up; abandon, as hope. **3** To give up or relinquish, especially in favor of another; resign. **4** To give (oneself) over to a passion, influence, etc. — *v.i.* **5** To give oneself up, as to an enemy in warfare; yield. — *n.* The act of surrendering one's person to another, or the possession of something to another. [< AF *surrender,* OF *surrendre* < *sur-* over + *rendre* RENDER] — **sur·ren'der·er,** *Law* **sur·ren'der·or** *n.*
Synonyms (verb): abandon, alienate, capitulate, cede, give, relinquish, sacrifice, yield. A state *cedes* territory for a consideration, *surrenders* it to a conqueror; a military commander *abandons* an untenable position or unavailable stores. We *relinquish* a claim, *sacrifice* something precious through error, friendship, or duty, *yield* to convincing reasons, a stronger will, winsome persuasion, or superior force. To *yield* is to give place or give way under pressure, and hence under compulsion; it implies more softness or concession than *surrender.* See ABANDON.

surrender value The reserve value of an insurance policy payable to the insured or to the beneficiary when the policy is discontinued.

sur·rep·ti·tious (sûr'əp·tish'əs) *adj.* **1** Accomplished by secret or improper means; clandestine. **2** Acting secretly or by stealth. [<L *surreptitius, subrepticius* < *subreptus,* pp. of *subripere* steal < *sub-* secretly + *rapere* snatch] — **sur'rep·ti'tious·ly** *adv.* — **sur'rep·ti'tious·ness** *n.*

sur·rey (sûr'ē) *n.* A light pleasure vehicle, having two seats, both facing forward, four wheels, and sometimes a top. [Prob. from *Surrey,* England]

sur·ro·gate (sûr'ə·gāt) *n.* **1** One who or that which is substituted for another; a substitute. **2** *Brit.* A deputy appointed by an ecclesiastical judge to act in his place. **3** A probate judge. — *v.t.* **·gat·ed, ·gat·ing 1** To put in the place of another; substitute; subrogate. **2** To appoint (another) to succeed oneself. [<L *surrogatus* < *subrogatus,* pp. of *subrogare* < *sub-* in place of another + *rogare* ask]

sur·round (sə·round') *v.t.* **1** To extend completely around; be on all sides of; encircle: Chairs *surrounded* the table. **2** To place something completely around; enclose. **3** To shut in or enclose, as enemy troops, on all sides so as to cut off communication or retreat; beset; invest. — *n.* That which surrounds; the surrounding area. [<AF *surunder,* OF *soronder* overflow <LL *superundare* < *super-* over + *undare* rise in waves < *unda* a wave]
Synonyms: compass, encompass, environ, invest. See EMBRACE.

sur·round·ing (sə·roun'ding) *n.* **1** That which surrounds, or any part of it; environment; conditions of life: usually in the plural. **2** The act of one who surrounds. — *adj.* Encompassing; enveloping.

sur·tax (sûr'taks') *n.* An extra or additional tax; specifically, a graduated income tax over and above the usual or fixed income tax, levied on the amount by which net income exceeds a certain sum. — *v.t.* To assess with an extra or additional tax. [<F *surtaxe* < *sur-* above + *taxe* < *taxer* TAX]

sur·veil·lance (sər·vā'ləns, -vāl'yəns) *n.* The act of watching, or the state of being watched; a very close watch; a spying supervision. See synonyms under OVERSIGHT. [<F < *surveiller* superintend < *sur-* over + *veiller* watch <L *vigilare*]

sur·vey (sər·vā') *v.t.* **1** To look at in its entirety; view as from a height. **2** To look at carefully and minutely; scrutinize; inspect. **3** To determine accurately the area, contour, or boundaries of by measuring lines and angles according to the principles of geometry and trigonometry. — *v.i.* **4** To survey land. See synonyms under LOOK. — *n.* (sûr'vā, sər·vā') **1** The operation, act, process, or results of finding the contour, area, boundaries, etc., of a surface. **2** A department or corps for carrying on such operations; also, an area that has been surveyed. **3** A general or comprehensive view; an overlooking. **4** A scrutinizing view; inspection. [<AF *survey-,* stem of *surveier,* OF *sorveir* <Med.L *supervidere* < *super-* over + *videre* look]

sur·vey·ing (sər·vā'ing) *n.* **1** The science and art of determining the area and configuration of portions of the surface of the earth and representing them on maps. **2** The work of one who makes surveys.

sur·vey·or (sər·vā'ər) *n.* **1** One who surveys lands, roads, mines, oil fields, etc.; especially, one engaged in the business of land surveying. **2** One who examines a thing for the purpose of ascertaining its condition, quality, or character; an inspector, as of customs. **3** A customs officer who examines merchandise brought into a port.

sur·vey·or·ship (sər·vā'ər·ship) *n.* The office of a surveyor.

surveyor's level A form of spirit level with telescope and tripod attachment, for use in surveying.

surveyor's measure A system of measurement used in surveying and based on the chain as a unit.

sur·viv·al (sər·vī'vəl) *n.* **1** The act of surviving; an outliving. **2** Something surviving. **3** *Sociol.* The persistence in a society of customs and beliefs originating under circumstances not fully understood or no longer valid. **4** One who or that which lives longer than others. Also *Archaic* **sur·viv'ance.**

survival of the fittest Natural selection.

sur·vive (sər·vīv') *v.* **·vived, ·viv·ing** *v.i.* To live or continue beyond the death of another, the occurrence of an event, etc.; remain alive or in existence. — *v.t.* To live or exist beyond the death, occurrence, or end of; outlive; outlast. See synonyms under LIVE. [<AF *survivre,* OF *sorvivre* <LL *supervivere* < *super-* above, beyond + *vivere* live] — **sur·viv'ing** *adj.* — **sur·vi'vor, sur·viv'er** *n.*

sur·vi·vor·ship (sər·vī'vər·ship) *n.* **1** The state of surviving. **2** *Law* The right of a surviving party, having a joint interest with others in property, to take the whole estate.

sus·cep·ti·bil·i·ty (sə·sep'tə·bil'ə·tē) *n. pl.* **·ties 1** The state or quality of being susceptible to influences or of easily receiving impressions. **2** The ability to receive or be impressed by deep emotions or strong feelings; sensibility. **3** *Physics* The ratio of the magnetization of a material to the magnetic force producing it.

sus·cep·ti·ble (sə·sep'tə·bəl) *adj.* **1** Yielding readily; capable of being influenced, acted on, or determined; unresistant; open; liable: usually with *of* or *to.* **2** Having delicate sensibility; sensitive; impressionable; easily affected. [<Med.L *susceptibilis* <L *suscipere* receive, undertake < *sub-* under + *capere* take] — **sus·cep'ti·ble·ness** *n.* — **sus·cep'ti·bly** *adv.*

sus·lik (sŏŏs'lik) *n.* A sciuroid rodent (*Citellus citellus*) of NE Europe and NW Asia, with a very short tail; a pouched marmot; spermophile. [<Russian]

sus·pect (sə·spekt') *v.t.* **1** To think (a person) guilty as specified on little or no evidence. **2** To have distrust of; doubt: They *suspected* my motives. **3** To have an inkling or suspicion of; think possible: The police *suspect* arson. — *v.i.* **4** To have suspicions. — *adj.* (sus'pekt) Suspected; exciting suspicion. — *n.* (sus'pekt) A person suspected of a crime or other action. [<F *suspecter* <L *suspectus,* pp. of *suspicere* look under, mistrust < *sub-* from under + *specere* look] — **sus·pect'er** *n.*
Synonyms (verb): conjecture, distrust, doubt, mistrust, surmise. See DOUBT, GUESS.

sus·pend (sə·spend') *v.t.* **1** To bar for a time from a privilege, office, or function as a punishment; debar. **2** To cause to cease for a time; interrupt; withhold temporarily: to *suspend* payments on a debt. **3** To hold in a state of indecision or abeyance; withhold or defer action on: to *suspend* a sentence. **4** To hang from a support so as to allow free movement. **5** To sustain in a body of nearly the same specific gravity; keep in suspension, as dust motes in the air. — *v.i.* **6** To stop for a time. **7** To fail to meet obligations; stop payment. [<OF *suspendre* <L *sub-* under + *pendere* hang] *Synonyms:* debar, defer, delay, discontinue, fail, hang, hinder, intermit, interrupt, stay, stop, withhold. See ADJOURN. *Antonyms:* begin, continue, expedite, prolong, protract.

suspended animation Temporary loss of a vital force, simulating death.

sus·pend·er (sə·spen′dər) *n.* **1** One who or that which suspends. **2** One of a pair of straps for supporting the trousers: usually in the plural, **pair of suspenders.** **3** *Brit.* A garter.

sus·pense (sə·spens′) *n.* **1** The state of being uncertain, undecided, or insecure; anxiety. **2** The state of being suspended or stopped temporarily. **3** *Obs.* Cessation. See synonyms under DOUBT. [<OF *suspens, suspense* delay, abeyance <Med. L *suspensum*, orig. pp. neut. of L *suspendere* SUSPEND]

sus·pen·sion (sə·spen′shən) *n.* **1** The act of suspending or hanging. **2** The state of deferment. **3** *Physics* A uniform dispersion of the fine particles of a solid in a liquid which does not dissolve them. Compare BROWNIAN MOVEMENT, COLLOID. **4** Cessation of payments in business; a going into liquidation: the *suspension* of a bank. **5** Any device used for the purpose of suspension, as in a compass. **6** *Mech.* A system of flexible or absorbent members, as springs in a vehicle, intended to insulate the chassis and body against road shocks transmitted by the wheels. **7** *Music* The prolongation of any note of a chord into the succeeding chord, causing at first dissonance which disappears by resolution; the note so prolonged. **8** The act of debarring from an office or its privileges.

suspension bridge See under BRIDGE.

suspension point One of a series of dots used to indicate the omission of words or sentences.

sus·pen·sive (sə·spen′siv) *adj.* **1** Tending to suspend or to keep in suspense. **2** Having the power of suspending operation: a *suspensive* veto. — **sus·pen′sive·ly** *adv.*

sus·pen·sor (sə·spen′sər) *n.* **1** A suspensory bandage. **2** *Bot.* The thread or chain of cells, in flowering plants and certain cryptogams, which produces at its extremity the developing embryo.

sus·pen·so·ry (sə·spen′sər·ē) *adj.* Suspending; sustaining; delaying. — *n. pl.* ·ries A truss, bandage, or supporter.

suspensory ligament *Anat.* A fibrous membrane sustaining the lens of the eye.

sus·pi·cion (sə·spish′ən) *n.* **1** Conjecture; doubt; mistrust; imagining something wrong without proof or clear evidence. **2** *Colloq.* The least particle, as of a flavor. See synonyms under DOUBT. — *v.t. Dial.* To suspect. [<AF *suspecioun*, OF *sospeçon* <Med. L *suspectio, -onis* <L *suspicere.* See SUSPECT.] — **sus·pi′cion·al** *adj.*

sus·pi·cious (sə·spish′əs) *adj.* **1** Inclined to suspect. **2** Questionable. **3** Indicating suspicion. See synonyms under ENVIOUS, EQUIVOCAL. — **sus·pi′cious·ly** *adv.* — **sus·pi′cious·ness** *n.*

sus·pire (sə·spīr′) *v.i.* ·pired, ·pir·ing **1** To sigh. **2** To breathe. [<L *suspirare* <*sub-* up from below + *spirare* breathe] — **sus·pi·ra·tion** (sus′pə·rā′shən) *n.*

sus·tain (sə·stān′) *v.t.* **1** To keep from sinking or falling, especially by bearing up from below; uphold; support. **2** To endure without yielding; withstand. **3** To have inflicted on one; undergo; suffer, as loss or injury. **4** To keep up the courage, resolution, or spirits of; comfort. **5** To keep up or maintain; keep in effect or being: to *sustain* friendly relations. **6** To maintain by providing with food, drink, or other necessities; support. **7** To uphold or support as being true or just. **8** To prove the truth or correctness of; corroborate; confirm. See synonyms under AID, ASSENT, CARRY, CONFIRM, ENDURE, HELP, KEEP, PRESERVE, PROP, SUPPORT. [<OF *sustein-*, stem of *sustenir, sostenir* <L *sustinere* <*sub-* up from under + *tenere* hold] — **sus·tain′a·ble** *adj.* — **sus·tain′er** *n.* — **sus·tain′ment** *n.*

sus·te·nance (sus′tə·nəns) *n.* **1** The act or process of sustaining; especially, maintenance of life or health; subsistence. **2** That which sustains; especially, that which supports life; food. **3** Livelihood; means of support. See synonyms under FOOD, NUTRIMENT. [<AF *sustenaunce*, OF *sostenance* <*sostenir* SUSTAIN]

sus·ten·tion (sə·sten′shən) *n.* **1** Support. **2** The act of being sustained. [<SUSTAIN; on analogy with *retention, detention*, etc.]

su·sur·rant (soo·sûr′ənt) *adj.* Softly murmuring; rustling; whispering. [<L *susurrans, -antis*, ppr. of *susurrare* whisper <*susurrus* a humming, whispering]

su·sur·rate (soo·sûr′āt) *v.i.* ·rat·ed, ·rat·ing To speak softly; whisper. [<L *susurratus*, pp. of *susurrare.* See SUSURRANT.] — **su·sur·ra·tion** (soo′sə·rā′shən) *n.*

su·sur·rus (soo·sûr′əs) *n.* A gentle sibilant murmur; whisper; rustling. [<L, a humming, whispering]

sut·ler (sut′lər) *n.* A peddler who follows an army to sell goods and food to the soldiers. [<Du. *soeteler* a petty tradesman <*soetelen* perform mean duties] — **sut′ler·ship** *n.*

su·tra (soo′trə) *n.* **1** A formulated doctrine, often so short as to be unintelligible without a key; literally, a rule or precept. **2** In Sanskrit literature, a short grammatical rule. **3** *pl.* A collection of writings or aphorisms, as the dialogs of the Buddha, the Laws of Manu. **4** In Buddhism, an extended writing, usually in verse, and often in dialog form, embodying important religious and philosophical propositions, sometimes directly, sometimes in highly allegorical or metaphorical language. Also **sut·ta** (soot′ə). [<Skt. *sûtra* a thread, rule <*siv* sew]

sut·tee (su·tē′, sut′ē) *n.* Formerly, the sacrifice of a Hindu widow on the funeral pyre of her husband: now forbidden; also, the widow so immolated. [<Hind. *satī* <Skt., a faithful wife, fem. of *sat* good, wise, orig. ppr. of *as* be] — **sut·tee′ism** *n.*

sut·tle (sut′l) *adj.* Formerly, taken after the tare has been deducted and before the tret has been allowed; designating that allowance has been made for the container: said of weight. — *n.* Suttle weight. [Earlier var. of SUBTLE]

su·ture (soo′chər) *n.* **1** The junction of two contiguous surfaces or edges along a line by or as by sewing. **2** *Anat.* The interlocking of two bones at their edges, as in the skull. **3** *Zool.* The line of junction between contiguous parts. **4** *Bot.* The line of dehiscence in plants. **5** *Surg.* **a** The act or operation of uniting parts by or as by stitching. **b** The sewing together of the cut or cleft edges of divided parts. **c** The thread, silver wire, or other material used in this operation. — *v.t.* ·tured, ·tur·ing To unite by means of sutures; sew together. [MF <L *sutura* <*sutus*, pp. of *suere* sew] — **su′tur·al** *adj.* — **su′tur·al·ly** *adv.*

su·ze·rain (soo′zə·rān, -rin) *n.* **1** One invested with superior or paramount authority; formerly, a feudal lord. **2** A nation having paramount control over a locally autonomous region. — *adj.* Sovereign; supreme. [<F *sus* above <L *susum, sursum* upwards; on analogy with *souverain* a sovereign] — **su′ze·rain·ty** *n.*

svelte (svelt) *adj.* Slender; slim; willowy. [<F *svelte* <Ital. *svelto* <L *ex-* out + *vellere* pluck]

swab (swob) *n.* **1** One of various utensils consisting essentially of a soft absorbent substance on the end of a handle: used for cleaning, etc. **2** A mop for cleaning decks, floors, etc. **3** A sailor who uses such a mop; a menial; a worthless person. **4** A cylindrical brush for cleaning firearms. **5** *Med.* **a** A bit of sponge or cloth for cleansing the mouth of, or used as a means of applying nourishment or medicine to, a sick person. **b** A specimen of mucus, etc., taken for examination; also, the cotton-wound wire used in obtaining it. — *v.t.* **swabbed, swab·bing** To clean or apply with a swab. Also spelled **swob.** [Back formation <SWABBER]

swad·dle (swod′l) *v.t.* ·dled, ·dling To wrap with a bandage; especially, to wrap (an infant) with a long strip of linen or flannel; swathe. — *n.* A swaddling band. [OE *swæthel* swaddling clothes, a bandage <*swathian* swathe]

swaddling clothes **1** Bands or strips of linen or cloth wound around a newborn infant.

2 A time of immaturity, or the limitations that restrict the immature. Also **swaddling bands, swaddling clouts.**

swag (swag) *n.* **1** *Slang* Property obtained by robbery or theft; plunder; booty. **2** *Austral.* A swagman's bundle or pack. **3** Baggage; luggage. **4** A swaying; a lurch. — *v.i.* **swagged, swag·ging 1** *Brit. Dial.* To swing heavily. **2** *Austral.* To tramp, bearing a swag. **3** To sag; sway; lurch. [Prob. <Scand. Cf. dial. Norw. *svagga* sway.]

swag·bel·ly (swag′bel′ē) *n.* A person having a protuberant abdomen. [<SWAG, *v.* (def. 3) + BELLY] — **swag′bel′lied** *adj.*

swage (swāj) *n.* **1** A tool or form, often one of a pair, for shaping metal by hammering or pressure. **2** An ornamental border or molding. **3** A groove on an anvil for use in shaping metal. **4** A swage block. — *v.t.* **swaged, swag·ing** To shape (metal) with or as with a swage or swage block. [<OF *souage*; ult. origin uncertain]

swage block A heavy iron block or anvil having grooves or holes for shaping metal, heading bolts, etc.: also called *swage.*

swag·ger (swag′ər) *v.i.* **1** To walk with a proud or insolent air; strut. **2** To boast; bluster. — *n.* Braggadocio; expression of superiority in words or deeds. — *adj.* Showy or ostentatious in style, manner, or appearance. [Appar. freq. of SWAG] — **swag′ger·er** *n.* — **swag′ger·ing·ly** *adv.*

swagger coat A sports coat without a belt.

swagger stick A short canelike stick; specifically, one carried by a British soldier when off duty: also called *swanking stick.*

swagger suit A short flared coat and a skirt that matches.

swag·man (swag′man′) *n. pl.* ·men (-men′) *Austral.* One who seeks work, carrying his bundle or swag.

swain (swān) *n.* **1** A youthful rustic; a lover. **2** *Obs.* A squire; a male servant. [<ON *sveinn* a boy, servant] — **swain′ish** *adj.* — **swain′ish·ness** *n.*

swal·low[1] (swol′ō) *v.t.* **1** To cause (food, etc.) to pass from the mouth into the stomach by means of muscular action of the gullet or esophagus. **2** To take in or engulf in a manner suggestive of this; absorb; envelop: often with *up.* **3** To put up with or endure; submit to, as insults. **4** *Colloq.* To believe credulously. **5** To refrain from expressing or giving vent to; suppress. **6** To take back; recant: to *swallow* one's words. — *v.i.* **7** To perform the act or the motions of swallowing. See synonyms under ABSORB. — *n.* **1** That which is swallowed at once; a small amount; a mouthful. **2** The gullet; throat; gorge. **3** The act of swallowing; appetite; inclination. **4** The channel in a hoisting block for the passage of the rope. **5** An abyss; whirlpool; also, a pit. [OE *swelgan* swallow] — **swal′low·er** *n.*

swal·low[2] (swol′ō) *n.* **1** Any of various small, widely distributed passerine birds (family *Hirundinidae*) with short, broad, depressed bill, long, pointed wings, and forked tail: noted for swiftness of flight and migratory habits, as the common **bank swallow** (*Riparia riparia*), the American **tree swallow** (*Iridoprocne bicolor*), and the **barn swallow** (*Hirundo erythrogaster*). ◆ Collateral adjective: *hirundine.* **2** A similar bird, as the swift. [OE *swealwe*]

swal·low·tail (swol′ō·tāl′) *n.* **1** *Colloq.* A man's dress coat with two long, tapering skirts or tails. **2** A butterfly (family *Papilionidae*) having a posterior, tail-like prolongation on each hind wing. — **swal′low-tailed′** *adj.*

swal·low·wort (swol′ō·wûrt′) *n.* **1** A twining perennial herb (*Cynanchum vincetoxicum*) with greenish-white flowers and roots, the latter formerly used in medicine. **2** The common celandine: said to blossom with the arrival of the swallows and to wither when they depart. **3** One of several plants of the milkweed family.

swa·mi (swä′mē) *n.* **1** Master; lord: used by Hindus as a title of respect. **2** A Hindu teacher, especially a religious teacher; a pundit. **3** Loosely, a yogi or fakir. Also **swa′my.** [<Hind. *svāmi* lord, master <Skt. *svāmin*]

swamp (swomp, swômp) *n.* A tract or region of low land saturated with water; a wet bog. Also **swamp′land′** (-land′). ◆ Collateral adjective:

paludal. — *v.t.* **1** To drench or submerge with water or other liquid. **2** To overwhelm with difficulties; crush; ruin. **3** *Naut.* To sink or fill (a vessel) with water. — *v.i.* **4** To sink in water, a swamp, etc. [Cf. LG *swampen* quake (said of a bog). Akin to SUMP.] — **swamp′y, swamp′ish** *adj.*

swamp angel **1** A person who lives in a

swamp blackbird The redwing (def. 1).

swamp boat A small, flat-bottomed, blunt-prowed boat powered by an engine with an airplane propeller mounted high in the stern: used in swampy or boggy areas.

swamp cabbage Skunk cabbage.

swamp·er (swom′pər, swôm′-) *n.* **1** One who lives in a swamp or in a swampy district. **2** One who clears a way in a swamp or forest for skidding logs; also, one who clears away underbrush, fallen trees, and other debris for logging operations.

swamp fever **1** Malaria. **2** An infectious anemia of equine animals, caused by a filtrable virus.

swamp hare A rabbit (*Sylvilagus aquaticus*) frequenting the swamps of the southern United States.

swamp honeysuckle The swamp azalea (*Azalea viscosa*) of the SE United States.

swamp land **1** Land covered with swamps. **2** Fertile, arable land in a swamp.

swamp law Lynch law.

swamp locust The water locust.

swamp maple The red maple of North America (*Acer rubrum*).

swamp oak **1** An oak (*Quercus bicolor*) common in swamps of the eastern United States: also **swamp white oak**. **2** The pin oak.

swamp owl **1** The short-eared owl. **2** The barred owl. See under OWL.

swamp pine Any of certain pines common in swamps or swampy regions; especially, the loblolly pine and the slash pine.

swamp privet See under PRIVET.

swamp sparrow An American sparrow (*Melospiza georgiana*) resembling the song sparrow, inhabiting the swamps of the southern and eastern United States.

swamp willow The pussy willow.

swan¹ (swon, swôn) *n.* **1** A large, web-footed, long-necked bird (subfamily *Cygninae*), allied to but heavier than the goose, and noted for its grace on the water, as the whooper, the trumpeter swan, and the common North American whistling swan (*Cygnus columbiana*). The male is a *cob,* and the female is a *pen.* **2** Figuratively, a poet or singer. [OE]

TRUMPETER SWAN
(Body length from 4
to 4 1/2 feet)

swan² (swon, swôn) *v.i. U.S. Dial.* Swear: chiefly in the phrase *I swan,* an exclamation of amazement. [Prob. < dial. E (Northern) *Is' wan,* lit., I shall warrant, used as euphemism for *swear*]

swan dive A fancy dive performed with head tilted back and arms held like the wings of a swallow until near the water: also called *swallow dive.*

swan·herd (swon′hûrd′, swôn′-) *n.* One who tends swans; especially, a royal officer of England having charge of marking the swans on the Thames which belong to the crown. Also **swan′mas′ter.** Compare SWAN-UPPING.

swank (swangk) *v. & n. Slang* Swagger; bluster. — *adj. Slang* **1** Ostentatiously fashionable; pretentious. **2** *Scot.* Slim; pliant; agile; jolly; lively. Also **swank′y.** [< dial. E. Appar. akin to MLG *swank* flexible, MHG *swanken* sway.] — **swank′i·ly** *adv.* — **swank′i·ness** *n.*

swan maiden In many ancient folk myths, a beautiful fairy maiden able to transform herself into a swan by means of a magic robe, ring, or chain, and living under an enchantment or tabu affecting her life with a human lover.

swan-neck (swon′nek′, swôn′-) *n.* Any of several mechanical contrivances resembling

in outline the neck of a swan.

swan·ner·y (swon′ər-ē, swôn′-) *n.* *pl.* **·ner·ies** A place where swans are bred or kept.

swan·pan (swän′pän′) *n.* A Chinese abacus or frame of beads to aid reckoning: also spelled *schwanpan, shwanpan.* [< Chinese *suan p'an* a reckoning board]

swan's–down (swonz′doun′, swônz′-) *n.* **1** The down of a swan: used for trimming, powder puffs, etc. **2** Canton or cotton flannel. **3** A soft, thick, fine woolen cloth resembling down. Also **swans′down′.**

swan·skin (swon′skin′, swôn′-) *n.* **1** The unplucked skin of a swan. **2** A soft, fine-twilled flannel or cotton fabric having a soft nap. — *adj.* Made of swanskin.

swan·song (swon′sông′, -song′, swôn′-) *n.* A last or dying work, as of a poet or composer: in allusion to the ancient fable that the swan sings a last song before dying.

swan-up·ping (swon′up′ing, swôn′-) *n. Brit.* The annual inspection and marking on the beak of the royal and other privileged young swans or cygnets on the Thames; also, the annual expedition for this purpose.

swap (swop) *v.t. & v.i.* **swapped, swap·ping** *Colloq.* To exchange (one thing for another); trade. — **to swap lies** To exchange tales; tell stories. — *n.* The act of swapping. Also spelled *swop.* [ME *swappen* strike (a bargain), slap; prob. ult. imit. of the sound of clapping the hands, as in bargaining]

sward (swôrd) *n.* **1** Land thickly covered with grass; turf. **2** *Obs.* A skin; rind. Also **swarth** (swôrth). — *v.t. & v.i.* To cover or become covered with sward. [OE *sweard* a skin]

swarm (swôrm) *n.* **1** A large number or body of insects or small living things of any kind. **2** A hive of bees; also, a large number of bees leaving the parent stock at one time, to take up new lodgings, accompanied by a queen. **3** A crowd or throng of persons, animals, or things, especially when in motion or advancing under pressure. **4** *Biol.* A collection of free-swimming unicellular organisms, especially zoospores. See synonyms under FLOCK. — *v.i.* **1** To leave the hive in a swarm: said of bees. **2** To come together, move, or occur in great numbers. **3** To be crowded or overrun; teem: with *with.* **4** *Biol.* To come forth in a swarm. — *v.t.* **5** To fill with a swarm or crowd; throng. [OE *swearm*]

swart (swôrt) *adj.* **1** Swarthy; also, poetically, absolutely black. **2** Malignant; gloomy. Also **swarth** (swôrth). [OE *sweart*] — **swart′ness** *n.*

swarth·y (swôr′thē) *adj.* **swarth·i·er, swarth·i·est** Having a dark hue; of dark or sunburned complexion; tawny; swart. Also **swart′y.** See synonyms under DARK. [Var. of obs. *swarty* < SWART] — **swarth′i·ly** *adv.* — **swarth′i·ness** *n.*

swash (swosh, swôsh) *v.i.* **1** To move or wash noisily, as waves. **2** To swagger. — *v.t.* **3** To splash (water, etc.). **4** To splash or dash water, etc., upon or against. — *n.* **1** The splash of a liquid. **2** A narrow channel through which tides flow. **3** A bar over which the waves pass freely. **4** Swill or wet refuse for pigs. **5** A swaggerer or his behavior. **6** *Slang* Worthless sentimental literature; trash. [Imit.]

swash·buck·ler (swosh′buk′lər, swôsh′-) *n.* A swaggering soldier; a bravo². [< SWASH + BUCKLER; with ref. to striking one's own or one's opponent's shield with a sword] — **swash′buck′ler·ing** *n.* — **swash′buck′ling** *adj. & n.*

swash·er (swosh′ər, swôsh′-) *n.* A blusterer; braggart; bully.

swash·ing (swosh′ing, swôsh′-) *adj.* **1** Splashing. **2** Swaggering; blustering. **3** Crushing; violent.

swash letters Italic special letters having a top or bottom flourish on the side where there is most blank space.

SWASH LETTERS

swas·ti·ka (swos′ti·kə) *n.* **1** A primitive religious ornament or symbol, originally in the form of a gammadion, but variously modified, the most typical being a

Greek cross with the ends of the arms bent at right angles, and prolonged to the length of the upright arms, clockwise, or counterclockwise. See *b* in illustration. It dates back to the Bronze Age in Europe, and still exists as a religious symbol in India, Persia, China, Japan, and among North, Central, and South American Indians: believed to be a token of good luck or blessing. **2** The emblem of the Nazis: as *b* in illustration. See HAKENKREUZ. Compare FYLFOT. Also **swas′ti·ca.** [< Skt. *svastika* < *svastí* well-being, fortune < *sú* good + *astí* being < *as* be]

SWASTIKA
a. Navaho Indian.   *c.* Caucasian.
b. Indian.   *d.* Siberian.
e. Pima Indian.

swat (swot) *v.t.* **swat·ted, swat·ting** To hit with a sharp blow. — *n.* A smart blow. Also spelled *swot.* [Var. of SQUAT, in dial. sense of "squash"]

swatch (swoch) *n.* A strip, as of cloth, especially one cut off for a sample. [< dial. E (Northern), a cloth tally]

swath (swoth, swôth) *n.* **1** A row or line of cut grass. **2** The space cut by a machine or implement in a single course. **3** The width of grass cut by the sweep of a scythe. Also spelled *swathe.* — **to cut a wide swath** To accomplish much; hence, to make a fine impression. [OE *swæth* a track]

swathe (swāth, swäth) *v.t.* **swathed, swath·ing** **1** To bind or wrap, as in bandages; swaddle. **2** To envelop; enwrap; surround. — *n.* A bandage for swathing. [OE *swathian*] — **swath′er** *n.*

swat·ter¹ (swot′ər) *n.* **1** One who or that which crushes with a blow. **2** A perforated rubber or meshed wire device for killing flies. **3** A hard-hitting baseball player.

swat·ter² (swot′ər) *v.i. Dial.* To splash water about, as geese and ducks in drinking. [Imit.]

sway (swā) *v.i.* **1** To swing from side to side or to and fro; oscillate. **2** To bend or incline to one side; lean; veer. **3** To tend in opinion, sympathy, etc. **4** To have influence or control; rule. — *v.t.* **5** To cause to swing from side to side. **6** To cause to bend or incline to one side. **7** *Naut.* To swing into place; hoist, as a yard or mast. **8** To cause (a person, opinion, etc.) to tend in a given way; influence. **9** To cause to swerve; deflect or divert, as from a course of action. **10** *Archaic* **a** To wield, as a weapon or, especially, a scepter. **b** To rule over; govern. See synonyms under GOVERN, INFLUENCE, SHAKE. — *n.* **1** Power exercised in governing; dominion; control. **2** The act of swaying, literal or figurative; a sweeping, swinging, or turning from side to side. **3** Momentum; inclination; bias. **4** Overpowering force or influence. [Prob. fusion of ON *sveigja* bend and LG *swajen* be moved to and fro by the wind]

sway·back (swā′bak′) *n.* **1** A hollow or unnaturally sagging condition of the back, as in a horse. **2** An animal with a swayback.

sway-backed (swā′bakt′) *adj.* **1** Having a sagged or hollow back. **2** Hence, strained or weakened, as by overwork.

swear (swâr) *v.* **swore** (*Obs.* **sware**), **sworn, swear·ing** *v.i.* **1** To make a solemn affirmation with an appeal to God or to some deity, or with invocation of something held sacred, as in attestation of truth or proof of good intentions: He *swore* by all the gods. **2** To make a vow; utter a solemn promise. **3** To use profanity; invoke or mention sacred beings or things irreverently or blasphemously; curse. **4** *Law* To give testimony under oath. — *v.t.* **5** To affirm or assert solemnly by invoking sacred beings or things. **6** To promise with an oath or solemn affirmation; vow. **7** To declare or affirm upon oath: to *swear* treason against a man. **8** To take or utter (an oath). **9** To administer a legal oath to. — **to swear by 1** To appeal to by oath. **2** To have complete confidence in. — **to swear in** To administer a legal oath to. — **to swear off** *Colloq.* To promise to renounce or give up: to *swear off* drink. — **to swear out** To obtain (a warrant for arrest) by making a statement or charge under oath. [OE *swerian*] — **swear′er** *n.*

swear·word (swâr′wûrd′) *n.* A word used in profanity or cursing.

sweat (swet) *v.* **sweat** or **sweat·ed, sweat·ing** *v.i.* **1** To exude or excrete sensible moisture from the pores of the skin; perspire. **2** To exude moisture in drops; ooze. **3** To gather and condense moisture in drops on its surface. **4** To pass through pores or interstices in drops. **5** To ferment, as tobacco leaves. **6** *Colloq.* To work hard; toil; drudge. **7** *Colloq.* To suffer: You will *sweat* for that! — *v.t.* **8** To exude (moisture) from the pores. **9** To gather or condense drops of (moisture). **10** To soak or stain with sweat. **11** To cause to sweat. **12** To cause to work hard. **13** *Colloq.* To force (employees) to work for low wages and under unfavorable conditions. **14** *Slang* To extort money from. **15** To heat (solder, etc.) until it melts. **16** To join, as metal objects, by applying heat after binding together with solder. **17** *Metall.* To heat so as to extract an element that is easily fusible; also, to extract thus. **18** To force moisture from, as wood in a charcoal kiln. **19** To subject to fermentation, as hides or tobacco. **20** To remove particles of (coins) illegally, as by shaking them in a bag. **21** *Slang* To subject to torture or rigorous interrogation for the purpose of extracting information; put through the third degree. — **to sweat (something) out** *Slang* To wait through anxiously and helplessly: to *sweat out* a long delay. — *n.* **1** Sensible perspiration of animals, or any gathering of moisture in minute drops like those of perspiration on the skin. **2** The act or state of sweating; specifically, sweating induced by drugs or artificial means. **3** Figuratively, hard labor; drudgery. **4** *Colloq.* Fuming impatience; worry; hurry. **5** The act or process of causing to sweat, as a short rapid exercise given to a horse or the process of sweating hides or bricks. **6** *Obs.* The sweating sickness. [< OE *swǣtan* < *swāt* sweat] — **sweat′i·ly** *adv.* — **sweat′i·ness** *n.* — **sweat′y** *adj.*

sweat·band (swet′band′) *n.* A band, usually of leather, inside the crown of a hat to protect it from sweat.

sweat·box (swet′boks′) *n.* **1** A device for sweating such products as hides and dried fruits. **2** Any very hot, close room. **3** *Colloq.* Formerly, a narrow cell where an unruly prisoner was confined; now, any place of confinement; specifically, a place where a prisoner is questioned or put through the third degree.

sweat·ed (swet′id) *adj.* **1** Saturated or covered with sweat; that has been made to perspire. **2** Employed in hard work for low pay; overworked and underpaid: *sweated* labor.

sweat·er (swet′ər) *n.* **1** One who or that which sweats; specifically, an employer who underpays and overworks his employees. **2** A jerseylike knitted garment with or without sleeves. **3** A medicine that induces sweating; a sudorific.

sweat gland *Anat.* One of the convoluted tubules that secrete sweat, found in subcutaneous tissue and terminating externally in a small orifice or pore.

sweat shirt A collarless pull-over sweater, sometimes lined with fleece: used by athletes.

sweat·shop (swet′shop′) *n.* A place where work is done under poor conditions, for insufficient wages, and for long hours.

Swe·den (swēd′n) A kingdom in NE Europe, in the eastern part of the Scandinavian peninsula; 173,525 square miles; capital, Stockholm: Swedish *Sverige.*

Swedish clover Alsike.

Swedish massage Massage given in combination with Swedish movements.

Swedish movements A system of muscular movements employed in treating certain diseases or developing the body.

Swedish turnip The rutabaga.

swee·ny (swē′nē) *n.* Atrophy of the shoulder muscles of a horse. [Perhaps < dial. G *schweine* atrophy]

sweep (swēp) *v.* **swept, sweep·ing** *v.t.* **1** To collect, remove, or clear away with a broom, brush, etc. **2** To clear or clean with or as with a broom or brush: to *sweep* a floor; to *sweep* the plains of buffalo. **3** To touch or brush with a motion as of sweeping: Her dress *swept* the ground; to *sweep* the strings of a harp. **4** To pass over or through swiftly, as in searching: His eyes *swept* the sky. **5** To cause to move with an even, continuous action: He *swept* the cape over her shoulders. **6** To move, carry, bring, etc., with strong or continuous force: The flood *swept* the bridge away. **7** To move over or through with strong or steady force: The gale *swept* the bay. **8** To drag the bottom of (a body of water, etc.). — *v.i.* **9** To clean or brush a floor or other surface with a broom, etc. **10** To move or go strongly and evenly, especially with speed: The train *swept* by. **11** To walk with or as with trailing garments: She *swept* into the room. **12** To trail, as a skirt. **13** To extend with a long reach or curve: The road *sweeps* along the lake shore on the north. See synonyms under CLEANSE. — *n.* **1** The act or result of sweeping. **2** The motion of a long stroke or movement: a *sweep* of the hand. **3** The act of clearing out or getting rid of; hence, removal from office or place: a clean *sweep* of the officeholders; also, a clearance. **4** A turning of the eye or of optical instruments over the field of vision. **5** The winning of a great success, as in an election. **6** The range, area, or compass reached by sweeping, as extent of stroke, range of vision, etc.; direction or extent of motion; hence, a curve or bend, as of a scythe blade, etc. **7** One who or that which sweeps. **8** A piece, as of a machine, along which something sweeps. **9** *Brit.* A chimneysweeper. **10** A long, heavy oar. **11** A well sweep. **12** A curved roadway or approach before a building. **13** *pl.* Sweepings, as of a place where precious metals are worked. **14** *Physics* An irreversible process in which a substance settles to thermal equilibrium or tends to do so. **15** In card games, a winning of all the points in a hand, as by taking of all the tricks in whist; in casino, the taking or capture of all the cards on the table. **16** *Colloq.* Sweepstakes. [ME *swepen*, alter. of *swopen* brush away < OE *swāpen*] — **sweep′er** *n.*

sweep·ing (swē′ping) *adj.* **1** Carrying off or clearing away with a driving movement. **2** Carrying all before it; covering a wide area; comprehensive. **3** General and thoroughgoing. — *n.* **1** The action of one who or that which sweeps. **2** *pl.* Things swept up; refuse. — **sweep′ing·ly** *adv.* — **sweep′ing·ness** *n.*

sweep·stakes (swēp′stāks′) *n. pl.* **·stakes 1** A gambling arrangement by which all the sums staked may be won by one or by a few of the betters, as in a horse race. **2** A race for all the stakes. **3** A prize in a sporting contest comprising several stakes. **4** A lottery which offers sweepstakes as prizes. Also **sweep′stake′.**

sweet (swēt) *adj.* **1** Agreeable to the sense of taste; having a flavor like that of sugar; especially, containing or due to sugar in some form. **2** Fresh, as opposed to *salt, sour,* or *rancid*; not fermented or decaying. **3** Gently pleasing to the senses; agreeable to the smell; pleasing in sound; melodious; fair; restful. **4** Agreeable or delightful to the mind; arousing gentle, pleasant emotions. **5** Having gentle, pleasing, and winning qualities; marked by kindness and amiability; dear; beloved. **6** Easy; smooth; noiseless: said of machines or contrivances. **7** Sound; rich; productive: said of soil. **8** Not dry: said of wines. **9** *Chem.* Free from acid, etc. — *n.* **1** The quality of being sweet; sweetness. **2** Something sweet: chiefly in the plural, as confections, preserves, candy. **3** A beloved person; darling. **4** Something agreeable or pleasing; pleasure. **5** A sweet smell; perfume. **6** *Brit.* A dessert. ◆ Homophone: *suite.* [OE *swēte*] — **sweet′ly** *adv.* — **sweet′ness** *n.*

Synonyms (adj.): honeyed, luscious, nectared, saccharine, sugared, sugary.

sweet alyssum A widely cultivated perennial crucifer (*Lobularia maritima*) native to the Mediterranean region, having small, very fragrant white or purple flowers. Also called *alyssum.*

sweet bay 1 Laurel (def. 1). **2** A highly ornamental tree or shrub (*Magnolia virginiana*), with evergreen or deciduous leaves and large handsome flowers.

sweet·bread (swēt′bred′) *n.* The pancreas (**stomach sweetbread**) or the thymus gland (**neck sweetbread** or **throat sweetbread**) of a calf or other animal, when used as food. [< SWEET + BREAD, in obs. sense of "a morsel"]

sweet·bri·er (swēt′brī′ər) *n.* A stout prickly rose (*Rosa eglanteria*) with aromatic leaves. Also **sweet′bri′ar.**

sweet cicely 1 A small European perennial (*Myrrhis odorata*) having white fragrant flowers. **2** A related American herb (genus *Osmorhiza*) with white or purplish flowers and fleshy aromatic root.

sweet corn 1 Any of several varieties of Indian corn rich in sugar, and shriveling when ripe. **2** Indian corn in the milky stage.

sweet·en (swēt′n) *v.t.* **1** To make sweet or sweeter. **2** To make more endurable; lighten. **3** To make pleasant or gratifying. **4** In poker, to increase the chips in (the pot). **5** To add gilt-edge securities to others so as to increase the value of (collateral for a loan). — *v.i.* **6** To become sweet or sweeter. — **sweet′en·er** *n.*

sweet·en·ing (swēt′n·ing) *n.* **1** The act of making sweet. **2** That which sweetens. — **long sweetening** Molasses; treacle. — **short sweetening** Sugar.

sweet fennel Finochio.

sweet fern 1 A shrub of the northern United States and Canada (genus *Comptonia*) with long, fernlike, fragrant leaves. **2** Any of several ferns (genus *Dryopteris*).

sweet·flag (swēt′flag′) *n.* A marsh-dwelling plant (*Acorus calamus*), with sword-shaped leaves and a thick creeping rootstock with an aromatic flavor; the calamus.

sweet·gale (swēt′gāl′) *n.* A branching shrub (*Myrica gale*), with both fertile and sterile flowers in short scaly catkins, and resinous, dotted, fragrant leaves. [< SWEET + GALE[2]]

sweet·gum (swēt′gum′) *n.* **1** A balsamiferous tree (*Liquidambar styraciflua*) of Atlantic North America, the wood of which is sometimes used to imitate mahogany. **2** The balsam or gum yielded by it.

sweet·heart (swēt′härt′) *n.* One who is particularly loved by or as a lover; a lover.

sweet·ing (swē′ting) *n.* **1** A sweet apple. **2** A sweetheart; dear one; darling.

sweet·ish (swē′tish) *adj.* Somewhat sweet; slightly sweet; also, nauseatingly sweet. — **sweet′ish·ly** *adv.* — **sweet′ish·ness** *n.*

sweet·leaf (swēt′lēf′) *n.* The horse sugar.

sweet marjoram Marjoram.

sweet·meat (swēt′mēt′) *n.* **1** A confection, preserve, or the like. **2** A candy or crystallized fruit. **3** *pl.* Very sweet candy, cakes, etc.

sweet pea An ornamental annual climber (*Lathyrus odoratus*) of the bean family cultivated for its fragrant, varicolored flowers.

sweet pepper A mild variety of capsicum used for pickling and as a vegetable.

sweet potato 1 A perennial tropical vine (*Ipomoea batatas*) of the morning-glory family, with rose-violet or pink flowers and a fleshy tuberous root. **2** The root itself, eaten as a vegetable. **3** *Colloq.* An ocarina.

sweets (swēts) *n. pl.* **1** Sweet things to eat, as puddings, cakes, tarts, jellies, etc. **2** The pleasures and gratifying things in life: the *sweets* of success.

sweet·sop (swēt′sop′) *n.* **1** A tropical American tree (*Annona squamosa*) allied to the custard apple. **2** Its egg-shaped, scaly fruit; the sugar apple.

sweet–talk (swēt′tôk′) *Colloq. v.t.* **1** To persuade by coaxing or flattering. — *v.i.* **2** To flatter or coax someone. — **sweet talk**

sweet tooth *Colloq.* A fondness or appetite for candy or sweets.

sweet william A perennial species of pink (*Dianthus barbatus*) with large lanceolate leaves and closely clustered, showy flowers.

swell (swel) *v.* **swelled, swelled** or **swol·len, swell·ing** *v.i.* **1** To increase in bulk or dimension, as by inflation with air or by absorption of moisture; dilate; expand. **2** To increase in size, amount, degree, etc. **3** To grow in volume or intensity, as a sound. **4** To rise in waves or swells, as the sea. **5** To bulge; protrude or belly, as a sail. **6** To become puffed up with pride. **7** To grow within one: My anger *swells* at the sight. —*v.t.* **8** To cause to increase in size or bulk. **9** To cause to increase in amount, extent, or degree. **10** To cause to bulge; belly. **11** To puff with pride. **12** *Music* To sing or play with combined crescendo and diminuendo. —*n.* **1** The act, process, or effect of swelling; expansion. **2** The long continuous body of a wave; a billow; hence, a rise of, or undulation in, the land. **3** A bulge or protuberance. **4** *Music* The union of crescendo and diminuendo; also, the signs (< >) indicating it. **5** A device by which the loudness of a musical instrument, as an organ, may be increased or diminished. **6** *Slang* A person of the ultrafashionable set. See synonyms under WAVE. —*adj.* *Slang* **1** Of or pertaining to swells or ultrafashionable people; hence, in the height of fashion; smart. **2** First-rate; distinctive. [OE *swellan*]

Synonyms (verb): bulge, dilate, distend, enlarge, expand, increase, inflate. See PUFF. *Antonyms:* contract, decrease, dwindle, shrink.

swell·ing (swel'ing) *n.* **1** The act of expanding, inflating, or augmenting. **2** *Pathol.* Morbid enlargement of a part of the body. **3** A protuberance. —*adj.* Increasing; bulging.

swel·ter (swel'tər) *v.i.* **1** To suffer from oppressive heat; perspire from heat. —*v.t.* **2** To cause to swelter. **3** *Obs.* To exude. —*n.* *Rare* A hot, sweltering condition; oppressive humid heat. [Freq. of obs. and dial. *swelt* be faint, die <OE *sweltan* die]

swept·back (swept'bak') *adj.* *Aeron.* Having the front edge (of a wing) tilted backward at an angle with the lateral axis of an airplane. Also called *backswept.*

swept·wing (swept'wing') *n.* A sweptback wing. —*adj.* Having a sweptback wing.

swerve (swûrv) *v.t. & v.i.* **swerved, swerv·ing** To turn or cause to turn aside from a course or purpose; deflect. See synonyms under FLUCTUATE, WANDER. —*n.* The act of swerving; a sudden turning aside. [OE *sweorfan* file or grind away]

swift[1] (swift) *adj.* **1** Traversing space or performing movements in a brief time; rapid; quick. **2** Capable of quick motion; fleet; speedy. **3** Passing rapidly, as time or events; also, coming without warning; unexpected. **4** Acting with readiness; prompt. —*adv.* Quickly: a poetic use. [OE] —**swift'ly** *adv.* **swift'ness** *n.*

Synonyms (adj.): expeditious, fast, fleet, flying, hasty, quick, rapid, speedy, sudden. See IMPETUOUS, NIMBLE. *Antonyms:* deliberate, dilatory, dull, lingering, slow, sluggish, tardy.

swift[2] (swift) *n.* **1** A bird of swallowlike form (family *Micropodidae*), possessing extraordinary powers of flight, including the builders of edible birds' nests (genus *Collocalia*) and the common American swift (*Chaetura pelagica*). **2** One of various small lizards (genera *Sceloporus* and *Uta*) common in the western United States. **3** A reel having an adjustable diameter for winding yarn, etc. **4** The main cylinder of a carding machine; also, a similar part in other machines. [< SWIFT[1]]

CHIMNEY SWIFT

swig (swig) *n. Colloq.* A deep draft. —*v.t. & v.i.* **swigged, swig·ging** *Colloq.* To drink swigs (of). [Origin unknown]

swill (swil) *v.t.* **1** To drink greedily and to excess. **2** *Brit.* To drench, as with water; rinse; wash. —*v.i.* **3** To drink to excess; tope. —*n.* **1** Liquid food for domestic animals; especially, the mixture of liquid and solid food given to swine; garbage. **2** Liquor drunk greedily or grossly; loosely, liquor in general. [OE *swillan, swillian* wash]

swim[1] (swim) *v.* **swam** (*Dial.* **swum**), **swum, swim·ming** *v.i.* **1** To move through water by working the legs, arms, fins, etc. **2** To be supported on water or other liquid; float. **3** To move with a smooth or flowing motion, as

if swimming in water. **4** To be immersed in or covered with liquid; be flooded; overflow. —*v.t.* **5** To cross or traverse by swimming. **6** To cause to swim. See synonyms under FLOAT. —*n.* **1** The action or pastime of swimming. **2** A gliding, swaying motion or movement. **3** The air bladder of a fish; the sound: also **swim bladder, swimming bladder.** **4** *Colloq.* The current of affairs, especially of fashionable life: in the *swim.* [OE *swimman*] —**swim'mer** *n.*

swim[2] (swim) *v.i.* To be dizzy; reel; have a giddy sensation; seem to go round. —*n.* A sudden dizziness; temporary unconsciousness; swoon. [OE *swima* dizziness]

swim·mer·et (swim'ə·ret) *n. Zool.* One of a series of fringed, typically biramous abdominal appendages of a crustacean, adapted for swimming, for aid in respiration, and for carrying the eggs on females. [Dim. of *swimmer*]

swim·ming[1] (swim'ing) *n.* The act of one who swims. —*adj.* **1** Used for swimming; having the capacity of swimming. **2** Watery; flooded with tears, as the eyes. [< SWIM[1]]

swim·ming[2] (swim'ing) *adj.* Affected by dizziness. [< SWIM[2]]

swimming hole A deep hole in a shallow running stream, used for bathing.

swim·ming·ly (swim'ing·lē) *adv.* In a swimming manner; easily, rapidly, and successfully.

swim·suit (swim'sōōt') *n.* A garment designed to be worn while swimming.

swin·dle (swin'dəl) *v.* **·dled, ·dling** *v.t.* **1** To cheat of money or property by deliberate fraud; defraud. **2** To obtain by such means. —*v.i.* **3** To practice fraud; be a swindler. See synonyms under STEAL. —*n.* The act or process of swindling; a cheating; a cheat; fraud; specifically, anything that proves to be inferior to its advertising or appearance. See synonyms under FRAUD. [Back formation <SWINDLER] —**swin'dling** *n.*

swindle sheet *U.S. Slang* An expense account.

swine (swīn) *n. pl.* **swine 1** An omnivorous mammal (family *Suidae*) having a long mobile snout and cloven hoofs. **2** A domesticated hog. **3** A low, greedy, stupid, or vicious person. [OE *swīn*]

SWINE
Nomenclature of anatomical parts.

swine fever Hog cholera.

swine·herd (swīn'hûrd') *n.* A tender of swine.

swine·pox (swīn'poks') *n.* A form of chicken pox affecting swine.

swing (swing) *v.* **swung** (*Dial.* **swang**), **swung, swing·ing** *v.i.* **1** To move to and fro or backward and forward rhythmically, as something suspended; oscillate. **2** To move in a swing (def. 3). **3** To move with an even, swaying motion; walk with vigorous strides. **4** To turn; pivot: We *swung* around and went home. **5** To be suspended; hang. **6** *Colloq.* To be executed by hanging. **7** *Slang* To be very up-to-date and sophisticated, especially in one's amusements and pleasures. **8** *Colloq.* To sing or play with or to have a compelling, usually jazzlike rhythm. **9** *Slang* To be sexually promiscuous. —*v.t.* **10** To cause to move to and fro or backward and forward. **11** To cause to move with a sweeping or circular motion, as a sword, ax, etc.; brandish; flourish. **12** To cause to turn on or as on a pivot or central point. **13** To lift or hoist: They

swung the mast into place. **14** *Colloq.* To bring to a successful conclusion; manage successfully. **15** *Colloq.* To arrange, sing, or play in the style of swing music. —*n.* **1** The action of swinging. **2** A free swaying motion. **3** A contrivance of hanging ropes with a seat on which a person may move to and fro through the air as a pastime. **4** Free course or scope; full liberty or license. **5** Compass; sweep. **6** The movement or rhythm characterizing certain styles of prose and poetry. **7** That which swings or is swung; a swinging blow or stroke. **8** The course of a career or period of activity. **9** Swing music. **10** *Colloq.* A trip or tour. [OE *swingan* scourge, beat up]

swing bridge A bridge constructed to rotate in a horizontal plane to permit the passage of large vessels, etc.

swing·er (swing'ər) *n.* **1** *Slang* A lively and up-to-date person. **2** *Slang* A person who indulges freely in sex.

swing·ing (swing'ing) *adj. Slang* **1** Lively and compelling in effect: a *swinging* jazz quartet. **2** Lively and modern.

swinging door A door that will open in either direction and swing shut when not held.

swin·gle (swing'gəl) *n.* **1** A large, knifelike wooden implement for beating flax: also **swing'-knife. 2** The short wooden bar of a flail; a swiple. —*v.t.* **·gled, ·gling** To cleanse, as flax, by beating with a swingle; scutch. [< MDu. *swinghel.* Akin to SWING.]

swin·gle·tree (swing'-gəl·trē') *n.* A horizontal crossbar, to the ends of which the traces of a harness are attached; a whiffletree or singletree. See illustration under HARNESS. Also **swing·tree** (swing'trē'), **swin'gle·bar'** (-bär').

SWINGLETREE
a. a. Swingletrees.
b. Traces.
c. Double-tree.
d. Plow beam.

swing music 1 A development of jazz after about 1935 which achieved its effects by large bands of musicians, contrapuntal styles, and arranged ensemble playing rather than improvised solo performances. **2** The particular rhythmic quality in such music. Also called *swing.*

swing shift An evening work shift, usually lasting from about 4 p.m. to midnight.

swin·ish (swī'nish) *adj.* Of or like swine; degraded; sensual; beastly. See synonyms under BRUTISH. —**swin'ish·ly** *adv.* —**swin'ish·ness** *n.*

swipe (swīp) *v.t.* **swiped, swip·ing 1** *Colloq.* To give a strong blow; strike with a full swing of the arm. **2** *Slang* To steal; snatch. —*n.* *Colloq.* **1** A hard blow, especially in field games. **2** A well sweep, lever, pump handle, or the like. [Var. of SWEEP]

swirl (swûrl) *v.t. & v.i.* To move or cause to move along in irregular eddies; whirl. —*n.* **1** A whirling along, as in an eddy; whirl. **2** A curl or twist; spiral. [< dial. E (Scottish) *swyrle.* Prob. akin to dial. Norw. *svirla* whirl.]

swish (swish) *v.i.* **1** To move with a sweeping motion and whistling sound, as a whip. —*v.t.* **2** To cause to swish. **3** To thrash; flog. —*n.* **1** A hissing, swishing sound, as of a lash through the air, or the swing of a silk skirt. **2** A movement producing such a sound. **3** An implement, as a broom, used with such a movement. [Imit.]

swiss (swis) *n. Often cap.* A sheer, crisp cotton fabric, similar to muslin, and often dotted or figured, when it is called *dotted swiss.*

Swiss chard Chard (def. 2).

Swiss cheese A pale-yellow cheese with many large holes, made in, or similar to that made in, Switzerland.

Swiss steak A thick cut of steak floured and cooked, often with a sauce of tomatoes and onions.

switch (swich) *n.* **1** A small flexible rod; light whip. **2** A tress of human or false hair, fastened together at one end and used by women in building a coiffure. **3** A mechanism for shifting a railway train or other rail vehicles from one track to another. **4** The act or operation of switching, shifting, or changing. **5** The end of the tail in certain animals, as a cow. **6** *Electr.* A device to make or break a circuit, or transfer a current from one conductor to another. **7** A connecting trench between two lines of defensive trenches. **8** A blow with a switch. See synonyms under STICK. —*v.t.* **1** To whip or lash with or as with a switch. **2** To move, jerk, or whisk suddenly or sharply: The woman *switched* her skirts aside. **3** To turn aside or divert; shift. **4** To exchange: They *switched* plates. **5** To shift, as a railroad car, to another track. **6** *Electr.* To connect or disconnect with a switch. —*v.i.* **7** To turn aside; change; shift. **8** To be shifted or turned. **9** *Dial.* To walk with a jerky or uneven gait. [Earlier *swits*. Akin to LG *zwuske* a thin rod.]

switch·back (swich′bak′) *n.* **1** A railway ascending or descending a steep incline in a series of zigzag tracks. **2** A zigzag mountain road. **3** A railroad at amusement resorts in which the cars are hoisted to a starting point and descend along a circuitous route by gravity.

switch·board (swich′bôrd′, -bōrd′) *n.* A panel or arrangement of panels bearing switches for connecting and disconnecting electric circuits, as a telephone exchange.

switch hitter In baseball, a batter who bats either right- or left-handed.

switch plant A plant in which green shoots take the place of absent or reduced leaves.

switch·yard (swich′yärd′) *n.* A railroad yard for the assembling and breaking up of trains.

Swit·zer·land (swit′sər·lənd) A republic in central Europe; 15,940 square miles; capital, Bern: French *Suisse*, German *Schweiz*, Italian *Svizzera*, Latin *Helvetia*. Also **Swiss Confederation.**

swiv·el (swiv′əl) *n.* **1** A coupling device, link, ring, or pivot that permits either half of a mechanism, as a chain, to rotate independently. **2** A rest on a boat's gunwale, on which a gun may be swept or swung in a horizontal plane. **3** Anything that turns on a pin or headed bolt. **4** A cannon that swings on a pivot: also **swivel gun. 5** The shuttle of a ribbon loom. —*v.* **·eled** or **·elled, ·el·ing** or **·el·ling** *v.t.* **1** To turn on or as on a swivel. **2** To provide with or secure by a swivel. —*v.i.* **3** To turn or swing on or as on a swivel. [ME *swyuel* <OE *swif-*, stem of *swifan* move]

swiv·et (swiv′it) *n. Colloq.* Hurry: anxiety; eager, nervous haste or excitement: Don't be in such a *swivet*. Also **swiv′vet.** [Cf. obs. *swive* copulation <OE *swifan* move] —**swiv′et·ty** *adj.*

swiz·zle (swiz′əl) *n.* One of various compounded intoxicating drinks; specifically, a drink made with rum or other spirit, sugar, bitters, and ice. —*v.t. & v.i.* **·zled, ·zling** *Slang* To guzzle. [Origin unknown] —**swiz′zler** *n.*

swizzle stick 1 A stick, usually with prongs set at right angles to one end, used to mix swizzle by whirling between the palms of the hands. **2** A slender rod of glass, plastic, etc., used to mix drinks.

swoon (swoon) *v.i.* To fall in a faint; faint. —*n.* The act of swooning; a fainting fit. See synonyms under STUPOR. Also, *Obs.*, **swoun, swound.** [ME *swounen*, back formation < *swoweninge* SWOONING]

swoop (swoop) *v.i.* To drop or descend suddenly, as a bird pouncing on its prey. —*v.t.* To take or seize suddenly, as with a swoop. —*n.* A sweeping down or pouncing down, as by a bird of prey: often figuratively. [Var. of obs. *swope* <OE *swāpan* sweep; prob. infl. in form by dial. E *soop* <ON *sōpa*]

sword (sôrd, sōrd) *n.* **1** A weapon consisting of a long blade fixed in a hilt: used for cutting or thrusting, as a rapier, scimitar, or claymore. **2** The power of the sword; sovereignty; the power of life and death; especially, military as opposed to civil power. **3** War; also, the cause of death or ruin. **4** An end bar from which the lay of a hand loom hangs; also, the upright support of the lay of a pow-

er loom. **—at swords' points** Very unfriendly; hostile; ready for a fight. **—to put to the sword** To kill with a sword; slaughter in battle. [OE *sweord*]

sword·bill (sôrd′bil′, sōrd′-) *n.* A tropical American hummingbird (genus *Ensifera*) with a very long, slender bill.

sword·craft (sôrd′kraft′, -kräft′, sōrd′-) *n.* **1** Dexterity or skill in the use of the sword. **2** Exercise of authority by the sword, or by military power.

sword dance 1 A dance among or over naked swords laid on the ground. **2** A dance in which the female dancers pass under a double line of swords crossed over their heads by the men.

sword·fish (sôrd′fish′, sōrd′-) *n. pl.* **·fish** or **·fish·es** A large fish of the open sea (genus *Xiphias*) having the bones of the upper jaw consolidated to form an elongated swordlike process.

SWORDFISH
(Up to 20 feet in length)

sword·grass (sôrd′gras′, -gräs′, sōrd′-) *n.* **1** Any of several grasses or sedges (especially genus *Mariscus*, formerly *Cladium*) with sharp or serrated edges. **2** The sword lily.

sword·knot (sôrd′not′, sōrd′-) *n.* Formerly, a loop of leather used to fasten the. hilt of a sword to the wrist; now, a tassel of cord or ribbon tied to a sword hilt.

sword lily A gladiolus.

sword play 1 Attack and defense with the sword. **2** Skill in fighting with the sword or in fencing; fencing. **—sword′-play·er** *n.*

swords·man (sôrdz′mən, sōrdz′-) *n. pl.* **·men** (-mən) **1** One skilled in the use of or armed with a sword. **2** A soldier. Also **sword′-man. —swords′man·ship, sword′man·ship** *n.*

syb·a·rite (sib′ə·rīt) *n.* A luxurious person; epicure; voluptuary. [<L *Sybarita* <Gk. *Sybaritēs* <*Sybaris* Sybaris]

sy·bo (sī′bō) *n. pl.* **·boes** The cibol or Welsh onion. [< dial. E (Scottish), var. of CIBOL]

syc·a·mine (sik′ə·min) *n.* The mulberry tree (*Morus nigra*) of the New Testament. [<LL *sycaminus* <Gk. *sykaminos* a mulberry tree <Aramaic *shiqmīn*, pl. <Hebrew *shiqmah*]

syc·a·more (sik′ə·môr, -mōr) *n.* **1** A medium-sized bushy tree of Syria and Egypt (*Ficus sycomorus*) allied to the common fig. **2** Any of various plane trees widely distributed in the United States, especially the American sycamore (*Platanus occidentalis*) and the buttonwood of California. **3** An ornamental shade tree of Europe and Asia (*Acer pseudo-platanus*); the sycamore maple. Also *Obs.* **syc′o·more.** [<OF *sicamor* <LL *sycomorus* <Gk. *sykomoros* <*sykon* a fig + *moron* a mulberry]

sy·cee (sī·sē′) *n.* Pure uncoined silver ingots of various weight and size: used by the Chinese as a medium of exchange: also **sycee silver.** —*adj.* Pure; unalloyed. [< dial. Chinese (Cantonese) *sai sze*, var. of Chinese *si szě* fine silk; so called because if pure it may be drawn out into fine threads]

sy·con (sī′kon) *adj. Zool.* Designating a type of sponge having an infolded body wall provided with radial canals for the reception of water, as in the typical genus *Sycon*. [<NL <Gk. *sykon* a fig]

sy·co·ni·um (sī·kō′nē·əm) *n. pl.* **·ni·a** (-nē·ə) *Bot.* An aggregate or multiple fruit in which many flowers have been developed on a fleshy receptacle, which is a flattened disk or forms a nearly closed cavity, as in the fig. [<NL <Gk. *sykon* a fig]

syc·o·phan·cy (sik′ə·fən·sē) *n. pl.* **·cies** The practices of a sycophant; base flattery; fawning.

syc·o·phant (sik′ə·fənt) *n.* **1** A servile flatterer; parasite. **2** *Obs.* An informer; accuser: the original meaning. **3** *Obs.* An impostor; deceiver. [<L *sycophanta* <Gk. *sykophantēs* an informer < *sykon* a fico + *phan-*, stem of

phainein show] —**syc′o·phan′tic** (-fan′tik) or **·ti·cal** *adj.* —**syc′o·phan′ti·cal·ly** *adv.*

Syd·ney (sid′nē) **1** The chief port and capital of New South Wales, Australia. **2** A port on Cape Breton Island, NE Nova Scotia, Canada.

syl·la·bar·y (sil′ə·ber′ē) *n. pl.* **·bar·ies** A list of characters representing syllables; the syllabic characters, collectively, of a language, as Chinese or Japanese, answering the function of an alphabet in writing. [<NL *syllabarium*, neut. of Med. L *syllabarius* <*syllaba* SYLLABLE]

syl·lab·ic (si·lab′ik) *adj.* **1** Of, pertaining to, or consisting of a syllable or syllables. **2** *Phonet.* Designating a consonant capable of forming a complete syllable without a vowel, as *l* in *middle* (mid′l) and *n* in *sudden* (sud′n). See SONORANT. **3** Having every syllable distinctly pronounced. **4** Designating a type of poetry based on a definite number of syllables per line rather than on stress or rhythm. Also **syl·lab′i·cal.** —*n. Phonet.* A syllabic consonant; a sonorant. —**syl·lab′i·cal·ly** *adv.*

syl·la·ble (sil′ə·bəl) *n.* **1** *Phonet.* A word or part of a word uttered in a single vocal impulse, and consisting of a vowel (or diphthong) alone or with one or more consonants, or of a syllabic consonant. An **open syllable** is one ending in a vowel, as the first syllable of *si·lent* (sī′lənt); a **closed syllable** is one ending in a consonant, as the first and third syllables of *cat·a·pult* (kat′ə·pult). **2** A part of a written or printed word corresponding, more or less, to the spoken division. In this dictionary, syllable breaks are indicated by centered dots. **3** The smallest particle of expression; the least detail, mention, or trace: Please don't repeat a *syllable* of what you've heard here. —*v.* **·bled, ·bling** *v.t.* **1** To pronounce the syllables of; utter; speak. **2** *Obs.* To syllabicate. —*v.i.* **3** To pronounce syllables. [<AF *sillable*, OF *sillabe* <L *syllaba* <Gk. *syllabē* <*syllambanein* <*syn-* together + *lambanein* take]

syl·la·bus (sil′ə·bəs) *n. pl.* **·bus·es** or **·bi** (-bī) A concise statement of the main points of a subject; outline, as of a course of study; schedule; epitome; abstract; specifically, a short statement at the beginning of a brief of the legal points involved. [<NL <Med. L *syllabos*, a misprint for L *sittybas*, accusative pl. of *sittyba* label on a book <Gk.]

syl·lep·sis (si·lep′sis) *n. pl.* **·ses** (-sēz) A figure of speech, common in classical Greek and Roman literature, by which an adjective or a verb is made to modify or govern two nouns, but must be understood in a different sense for each noun. This figure conveys a double meaning, often with humorous effect, as in Pope's comment on Queen Anne: Dost sometimes *counsel take* —and sometimes *tea*. Compare ZEUGMA. [<LL *syllepsis* <Gk. *syllēpsis* <*syn-* together + *lēpsis* a taking < *lēb-, lab-*, stem of *lambanein* take] —**syl·lep′tic** *adj.*

syl·lo·gism (sil′ə·jiz′əm) *n.* **1** *Logic* **a** A formula of argument consisting of three propositions. The first two propositions, called *premises*, have one term in common furnishing a logical connection between the two other terms, which are then linked in the third proposition, called the *conclusion*. Example: All men are mortal (*major premise*); kings are men (*minor premise*); therefore, kings are mortal (*conclusion*). In this example, the *major term* is "mortal," the *minor term* is "kings," and the *middle term* is "men." **b** Deductive reasoning. **2** A subtle or crafty argument. [<OF *silogime* <L *syllogismus* <Gk. *syllogismos* <*syllogizesthai* SYLLOGIZE]

syl·lo·gis·tic (sil′ə·jis′tik) *adj.* Pertaining to, or having the nature or form of, a syllogism: also **syl′lo·gis′ti·cal.** —*n.* The art of reasoning by syllogism; the department of logic dealing with syllogisms: also **syl′lo·gis′tics.** —**syl′lo·gis′ti·cal·ly** *adv.*

sylph (silf) *n.* **1** Originally, in the system of Paracelsus, a being, male or female, mortal but without a soul, living in and on the air, and intermediate between material and immaterial beings. **2** A slender, graceful young woman or girl. **3** A South American hummingbird (*Cyanolesbia gorgo*), with a long, forked, brilliantly colored tail. [<NL *sylphes*, pl., ? coined by Paracelsus]

syl·van (sil′vən) *adj.* **1** Of, pertaining to, or

located in a forest or woods. **2** Composed of or abounding in trees or woods. **3** Characteristic of a forest or wood; rustic. — *n.* **1** In mythology, a spirit or deity of the forest. **2** *Archaic* or *Poetic* A person or animal dwelling in the woods. [<MF *sylvain* a sylvan <L *sylvanus, silvanus* < *silva* a wood]

syl·van·ite (sil′vən-īt) *n.* A metallic, steel–gray to silver–white telluride of gold or silver, crystallizing in the monoclinic system: when the crystals are arranged in patterns suggesting runic symbols, it is called *graphic gold, graphic tellurium.* [from (TRAN)SYLVAN(IA) + -ITE¹]

syl·ves·tral (sil-ves′trəl) *adj.* Adapted to growing in woody and shady places, as certain plants; also, relating to the woods; wild. [<L *silvester, silvestris* < *silva* a forest]

Syl·vi·an fissure (sil′vē-ən) *Anat.* A deep fissure that separates the temporal lobe of the cerebrum from the parietal and frontal lobes. [<F *sylvien*, after François de la Boë *Sylvius*, 1614–72, Flemish anatomist]

syl·vite (sil′vīt) *n.* A vitreous, native potassium chloride, crystallizing in the isometric system. Also **syl′vin** (-vin), **syl′vine** (-vin, -vīn), **syl′vin·ite**. [<NL (*sal digestivus*) *sylvii* (digestive salt) of Sylvius + -ITE¹]

sym·bi·ont (sim′bī-ont, -bē-) *n. Biol.* An organism living in a state of symbiosis. Also **sym′bi·on**. [<Gk. *symbioōn, -ontos,* ppr. of *bioein.* See SYMBIOSIS.] — **sym′bi·on′tic** *adj.*

sym·bi·o·sis (sim′bī-ō′sis, -bē-) *n. Biol.* The consorting together or partnership of dissimilar organisms, as of the algae and fungi in lichens. The term ordinarily connotes an association which is mutually advantageous. Compare CONSORTISM. [<NL <Gk. *symbiōsis* a living together, companionship < *symbioein* live together < *symbios* a companion, living together < *syn-* together + *bios* life + *ballein* throw]

sym·bol (sim′bəl) *n.* **1** Something chosen to stand for or represent something else, usually because of a resemblance in qualities or characteristics; an object used to typify a quality, abstract idea, etc.: The oak is a *symbol* of strength. **2** A character, mark, abbreviation, conventional sign, or letter indicating something, as a quantity in mathematics, a substance in chemistry, a planet or celestial body, a quality, operation, relationship, etc. **3** A confession of faith; creed. **4** The disguised representation of an unconscious trend involving a person, object, act, etc. See synonyms under EMBLEM, LETTER, MARK, SIGN, SIMILE. ◆ Homophone: *cymbal.* [<LL *symbolum* <Gk. *symbolon* a mark, token < *symballein* put together < *syn-* together + *ballein* throw]

sym·bol·ae·og·ra·phy (sim′bəl·ē·og′rə·fē) *n.* The drawing up or framing of legal instruments. Also **sym′bol·e·og′ra·phy**. [<Gk. *symbolaiographia* < *symbolaiographos* a notary < *symbolaion* a mark, contract + *graphein* write]

sym·bol·ic (sim-bol′ik) *adj.* **1** Of or pertaining to a symbol or symbols; expressed by a symbol. **2** Serving as signs of relation or connection; relational; connective: distinguished from *presentive*: said of certain classes of words, as prepositions and conjunctions. **3** Characterized by or involving the use of symbols: *symbolic* poetry. Also **sym·bol′i·cal**. — **sym·bol′i·cal·ly** *adv.* — **sym·bol′i·cal·ness** *n.*

symbolic logic A development of formal logic in which the ambiguity of verbal propositions and of operations upon them is reduced to a minimum by the rigorous use of symbols each of which has only one referent within the given context. Also called *mathematical logic.*

sym·bol·ics (sim-bol′iks) *n. pl.* (construed as *singular*) The science or study of symbols or of ancient symbolic rites or creeds.

sym·bol·ism (sim′bəl·iz′əm) *n.* **1** Representation by symbols; treatment or interpretation of things as symbolic; also, the quality of being symbolic. **2** A system of symbols or symbolical representation. **3** The theories and practice of a group of symbolists. **4** Artistic imitation as a means of suggesting or expressing ideal or intangible states or ideas; also, the expression or representation of the invisible by conventional signs or figures.

sym·bol·ist (sim′bəl·ist) *n.* **1** One who uses symbols; one versed or ardent in the interpretation or use of symbols; especially, one who regards the elements in the Eucharist as mere symbols. **2** One of a class of French and Belgian writers and artists of the late 19th century, including Verlaine, Mallarmé and Maeterlinck, who sought to exalt the metaphysical by suggesting ideas and emotions by patterns of color and form and by symbolic meanings of objects, words, and sound.

sym·bol·is·tic (sim′bəl·is′tik) *adj.* **1** Expressed by symbols; characterized by the use of symbols. **2** Of or pertaining to symbolism; symbolic. Also **sym′bol·is′ti·cal**.

sym·bol·ize (sim′bəl·īz) *v.* **·ized**, **·iz·ing** *v.t.* **1** To be a symbol of; represent symbolically; typify. **2** To represent by a symbol or symbols. **3** To treat as symbolic or figurative. — *v.i.* **4** To use symbols. **5** *Psychol.* To transfer emotional values from one person, object, or act to another. Also *Brit.* **sym′bol·ise**. — **sym′bol·i·za′tion** *n.*

sym·bol·o·gy (sim-bol′ə-jē) *n.* The art of representing by, or of interpreting, symbols. [< SYMBO(L) + -LOGY]

sym·met·ri·cal (si-met′ri-kəl) *adj.* **1** Exhibiting symmetry; having harmonious proportions or a correspondence in shape and size of parts; well–balanced; regular: a *symmetrical* structure. **2** *Biol.* Having parts or organs on one side corresponding to those on the other. **3** *Bot.* Regular as to number or shape of parts: said especially of a flower when the parts or divisions in each cycle (that is, the sepals, petals, stamens, and pistils) are of the same number or multiples of the same. **4** *Chem.* Denoting an arrangement of atoms of a molecule at equal relative intervals when graphically represented. **5** *Med.* Affecting corresponding organs or parts similarly. Also **sym·met′ric**. [<SYMMETRY] — **sym·met′ri·cal·ly** *adv.* — **sym·met′ri·cal·ness** *n.*

sym·me·try (sim′ə-trē) *n. pl.* **·tries** **1** Corresponding arrangement or balancing of the parts or elements of a whole in respect to size, shape, and position on opposite sides of an axis or center; hence, loosely, congruity; harmony; also, an instance of such arrangement. **2** The element of beauty in nature or art that results from such arrangement and balancing. **3** *Biol.* Regular arrangement of parts or organs in an animal body so that a division will give halves corresponding in shape, size, function, relative position, etc.; similarity of structure. **4** *Bot.* Equality of number in the whorls of a flower, as of sepals, petals, etc. **5** *Math.* An arrangement of pairs of points in a general system such that the set of lines joining them together is divided into equal parts by a line, a plane, or a point. **6** *Mineral.* The symmetrical distribution of non–parallel but equivalent directions (faces, edges, etc.) in a crystal with reference to certain planes or lines called **planes** or **axes of symmetry**. [<MF *symmetrie* <LL *symmetria* <Gk. < *symmetros* measured together < *syn-* together + *metron* a measure]

Synonyms: agreement, conformity, harmony, order, parity, proportion, regularity, shapeliness. See HARMONY. *Antonyms:* deformity, discordance, disproportion, shapelessness.

sym·pa·thec·to·my (sim′pə·thek′tə·mē) *n. Surg.* The operation of interrupting some portion of the sympathetic nervous system, as by transection or resection of a nerve pathway. [<SYMPATH(ETIC) + -ECTOMY]

sym·pa·thet·ic (sim′pə·thet′ik) *adj.* **1** Pertaining to, expressing, or proceeding from sympathy. **2** Having a fellow feeling for others; sympathizing; compassionate. **3** Being in accord or harmony; congenial. **4** Referring to sounds produced by responsive vibrations. **5** *Anat.* Designating the entire autonomic nervous system. Also **sym′pa·thet′i·cal**. See synonyms under HUMANE. [<NL *sympatheticus* <Gk. *sympathētikos* < *sympatheia*. See SYMPATHY.] — **sym′pa·thet′i·cal·ly** *adv.*

sympathetic nervous system *Anat.* That part of the autonomic nervous system which serves the viscera, glands, heart, blood vessels, and smooth muscles. It consists of a chain of

ganglia on each side of the spinal column between the cervical and sacral regions, connected with nerve plexuses, and in general produces effects opposite to those coming from the parasympathetic system.

sym·path·i·co·to·ni·a (sim-path′i-kō-tō′nē-ə) *n. Physiol.* Increased dominance of the sympathetic nervous system over other body functions, marked by vascular spasm and high blood pressure. [<NL <E *sympathic,* var. of SYMPATHETIC + Gk. *tonos* tension] — **sym·path′i·co·ton′ic** (-ton′ik) *adj.*

sym·pa·thize (sim′pə·thīz) *v.i.* **·thized**, **·thiz·ing** **1** To share the sentiments or ideas of another; have the same feelings as another: with *with.* **2** To feel or express compassion, as for another's sorrow or affliction: with *with.* **3** To be in harmony or agreement. Also *Brit.* **sym′pa·thise**. See synonyms under CONSOLE. — **sym′pa·thiz′er** *n.* — **sym′pa·thiz′ing·ly** *adv.*

sym·pa·thy (sim′pə·thē) *n. pl.* **·thies** **1** The quality of being affected by the state of another with feelings correspondent in kind; a fellow feeling; a mutual affinity or susceptibility; reaction to such relationship. **2** A feeling of compassion for another's sufferings; pity; commiseration. **3** An agreement of affections or inclinations, or a conformity of natural temperaments, which makes persons agreeable to one another; congeniality; accord. **4** That quality of inanimate things by virtue of which they attract or influence one another, or are supposed to do so; affinity: a sense once much used in alchemy and astrology: the *sympathy* of the lodestone for iron. See synonyms under BENEVOLENCE, PITY. [<L *sympathia* <Gk. *sympatheia* < *sympathēs* feeling compassion with another < *syn-* together + *pathos* a feeling, passion]

sympathy strike A strike in which the strikers support the demands of another group of workers but demand nothing for themselves.

sym·pa·try (sim′pə·trē) *n. Ecol.* The distribution of plant and animal species in coextensive areas. [<SYM- + L *patria* fatherland]

sym·phon·ic (sim-fon′ik) *adj.* **1** Relating to or having the form of a symphony: also **sym·pho·net·ic** (sim′fə·net′ik). **2** Agreeing in sound; harmonious.

symphonic poem *Music* A composition in free form for symphony orchestra, composed either as a unit (as Liszt's *Les Préludes* or Strauss's *Death and Transfiguration*) or as a short series of pieces (as Debussy's *La Mer*), and following a descriptive, literary, or "program" outline; a tone poem: a form developed by Liszt in the 19th century.

sym·pho·ni·ous (sim-fō′nē-əs) *adj.* According in sound; harmonious; concordant; agreeing; sounding together or in harmony. — **sym·pho′ni·ous·ly** *adv.*

sym·pho·ny (sim′fə·nē) *n. pl.* **·nies** **1** A harmonious or agreeable mingling of sounds, whether vocal, instrumental, or both; figuratively, any concord or agreeable blending: *symphonies* in gray. **2** *Music* A composition for orchestra, consisting usually of four movements, of which one or more generally follow sonata form, and which are of diverse individuality united by homogeneous elements. **3** A symphony orchestra. [<OF *simphonie* <L *symphonia* <Gk. *symphōnia* < *syn-* together + *phōnē* a sound]

symphony orchestra A large orchestra composed usually of the string, brass, woodwind, and percussion sections needed to present symphonic works.

sym·phy·sis (sim′fə·sis) *n. pl.* **·ses** (-sēz) **1** *Anat.* A junction of two parts of the skeleton, formed either by a growing together (*synostosis*) or by the intervention of cartilage (*synchondrosis*). **2** *Bot.* The union of similar parts, or of parts normally separate. [<NL <Gk., a growing together, esp. of the bones < *syn-* together + *phyein* grow]

sym·plec·tic (sim-plek′tik) *adj. Geol.* Denoting a rock texture formed by the intermingling of two different minerals. [<Gk. *symplektikos* plaiting together < *symplekein* < *syn-* together + *plekein* plait]

sym·po·di·um (sim-pō′dē·əm) *n. pl.* **·di·a** (-dē-ə) *Bot.* A false axis or stem of a plant, morphologically made up of a series of superposed branches imitating a simple stem; a pseudaxis. [<NL <Gk. *syn-* together + *podion*, dim. of *pous*, *podos* a foot] — **sym·po'·di·al** *adj.* — **sym·po'di·al·ly** *adv.*

sym·po·si·um (sim·pō'zē·əm) *n.* **1** A meeting for discussion of a particular subject. **2** A collection of comments or opinions brought together; especially, a series of several brief essays or articles on the same subject by different writers, as in a magazine. **3** In ancient Greece, an after-dinner drinking party, characterized by conversation, music, dancing, and other amusements. **4** Any similar social gathering. Also called *symposiac.* **sym·po'·si·on** (-zē·on) [<L <Gk. *symposion* <*syn-* together + *posis* a drinking <*po-*, stem of *pinein* drink]

symp·tom (simp'təm) *n.* **1** *Pathol.* An organic or functional condition indicating the presence of disease, especially when regarded as an aid in diagnosis. **2** That which serves to point out the existence of something else; any sign, token, or indication. See synonyms under SIGN. [<L *symptoma* <Gk. *symptōma* a chance, a disease <*sympiptein* happen to <*syn-* together + *piptein* fall]

symp·to·mat·ic (simp'tə·mat'ik) *adj.* **1** Pertaining to, of the nature of, or constituting a symptom or symptoms; indicative: Fever is *symptomatic* of inflammation. **2** According to symptoms: a *symptomatic* classification of diseases. Also **symp'to·mat'i·cal.** [<F *symptomatique* <LL *symptomaticus* <Gk. *symptōmatikos* <*symptōma*, *-atos* a symptom] — **symp'to·mat'i·cal·ly** *adv.*

symp·tom·a·tol·o·gy (simp'təm·ə·tol'ə·jē) *n.* **1** The branch of medicine that has for its object the observation and classification of symptoms. **2** The combined symptoms of a disease: also *semeiology, semeiotics.* Compare DIAGNOSIS. [<NL *symptomatologia* <Gk. *symptōma*, *-atos* a symptom + *logos* study]

syn- *prefix* With; together; associated with or accompanying: *syntax, syndrome.* Also: *sy-* before *sc, sp, st,* and *z,* as in *system; syl-* before *l,* as in *syllable; sym-* before *b, p,* and *m,* as in *sympathy; sys-* before *s,* as in *syssarcosis.* [<Gk. <*syn* together]

syn·aer·e·sis (si·ner'ə·sis) See SYNERESIS.

syn·aes·the·sia (sin'is·thē'zhə, -zhē·ə) See SYNESTHESIA. Also

syn·a·gog (sin'ə·gôg, -gog) *n.* **1** A place of meeting for Jewish worship and religious instruction. **2** A Jewish congregation or assemblage for religious instruction and observances. **3** The Jewish religion or communion. Also **syn'a·gogue.** [<OF *sinagoge* <LL *synagoga* <Gk. *synagōgē* an assembly, synagog <*synagein* bring together <*syn-* together + *agein* lead, bring] — **syn'a·gog'i·cal** (-goj'i·kəl), **syn'a·gog'al** (-gôg'əl, -gog'əl) *adj.*

syn·al·gi·a (si·nal'jē·ə) *n.* *Pathol.* Sympathetic pain transmitted to a remote organ through associated nerves. [<NL <Gk. *synalgeein* share in suffering <*syn-* together + *algeein* feel bodily pain <*algos, -eos* bodily pain] — **syn·al'gic** *adj.*

syn·apse (si·naps') *n.* *Physiol.* The junction point of two neurons, across which a nerve impulse passes. [<NL *synapsis* <Gk., a junction <*syn-* together + *hapsis* a joining <*haptein* join]

syn·ap·sis (si·nap'sis) *n.* **1** *Biol.* The conjugation of maternal and paternal chromosomes preceding maturation, or the reduction division in the nucleus; syndesis. **2** A synapse. [<NL. See SYNAPSE.] — **syn·ap'tic** *adj.* — **syn·ap'ti·cal·ly** *adv.*

syn·ar·thro·sis (sin'är·thrō'sis) *n.* *pl.* **·ses** (-sēz) *Anat.* A joint that permits no motion between the parts articulated. Also **syn'ar·thro'di·a** (-dē·ə). [<NL <Gk. *synarthrōsis* <*syn-* together + *arthrōsis* a jointing <*arthron* a joint] — **syn'ar·thro'di·al** — **syn'ar·thro'di·al·ly** *adv.*

syne (singk) See SYNCH.

syn·carp (sin'kärp) *n.* *Bot.* An aggregate fruit composed of several more or less coherent carpels, as in the blackberry, or a multiple fruit, as in the fig. Also **syn·car·pi·um** (sin·kär'pē·əm). [<NL *syncarpium* <*syn-* together + *karpos* a fruit]

syn·car·pous (sin·kär'pəs) *adj. Bot.* Characterized by or characteristic of a syncarp; consisting of united carpels: contrasted with *apocarpous.*

syn·cat·e·gor·e·mat·ic (sin·kat'ə·gôr'ə·mat'ik, -gor'-) *adj.* Pertaining to words that can only

form parts of terms, as adverbs, prepositions, and conjunctions: opposed to *categorematic.* Also **syn·cat'e·gor·e·mat'i·cal.** [<Gk. *katēgorēmatikos* <*synkatēgorēma* <*synkatēgorein* predicate jointly <*syn-* together + *katēgoreein.* See CATEGORY.]

synch (singk) *Slang v.i. & v.t.* To synchronize or cause to be synchronized. — *n.* The state of being synchronous; synchronization: usually in the phrases **in synch** and **out of synch.** [<SYNCHRONIZATION]

syn·chro·mesh (sing'kro·mesh') *n. Mech.* **1** A gear system by which driving and driven members are brought to the same speed before engaging. **2** The mechanism by which this uniform speed of gears is obtained. [<SYNCHRO(NIZED) + MESH]

syn·chro·nic·i·ty (sing'krə·nis'ə·tē) *n.* The temporal coincidence of two or more events linked together by meaning, but without any causal connection; meaningful cross-connection between separate causal chains. [Trans. of G *synchronizität*; used by C. G. Jung]

syn·chro·nism (sing'krə·niz'əm) *n.* **1** The state of being synchronous. **2** Coincidence in time of different events or phenomena; simultaneousness. **3** A tabular grouping of historic personages or events according to their dates. **4** In art, representation in the same picture of events having differing dates. [<LL *synchronismus* <Gk. *synchronismos* <*synchronos* SYNCHRONOUS] — **syn'chro·nis'tic** or **·ti·cal** *adj.* — **syn'chro·nis'ti·cal·ly** *adv.*

syn·chro·nize (sing'krə·nīz) *v.* **·nized, ·niz·ing** *v.i.* **1** To occur at the same time; coincide. **2** To move or operate in unison. — *v.t.* **3** To cause (timepieces) to agree in keeping or indicating time. **4** To cause to operate in unison: to *synchronize* video and audio portions. **5** To assign the same date or period to; make contemporaneous. [<SYNCHRONISM] — **syn'chro·ni·za'tion** *n.* — **syn'chro·niz'er** *n.*

syn·chro·nous (sing'krə·nəs) *adj.* **1** Occurring at the same time; coincident. **2** Happening at the same rate. **3** *Physics* Having the same period or rate of vibration: *synchronous* currents. Also **syn'chro·nal.** [<LL *synchronus* <Gk. *synchronos* <*syn-* together + *chronos* time] — **syn'chro·nous·ly** *adv.* — **syn'chro·nous·ness** *n.*

syn·chro·tron (sing'krə·tron) *n. Physics* An accelerator in which the particles being accelerated travel in nearly constant orbits, the change in orbital period being compensated by a synchronous change in the frequency of the alternating voltage providing the acceleration. [<SYNCHRO(NIZE) + (ELEC)TRON]

syn·clas·tic (sin·klas'tik) *adj.* Having the same kind of curvature in all directions; concave or convex in every direction: said of a surface: opposed to *anticlastic.* [<SYN- + Gk. *klastos* broken <*klaein* break]

syn·cli·nal (sin·klī'nəl) *adj.* **1** Sloping downward on each side toward a common line or point. **2** *Geol.* Dipping downward on each side toward the axis of the fold, as rock strata: opposed to *anticlinal.* Also **syn·clin·i·cal** (sin·klin'i·kəl). — *n.* A syncline. [<Gk. *synklinein* <*syn-* together + *klinein* incline]

syn·cline (sing'klīn) *n. Geol.* **1** A trough or structural basin toward which rocks dip. **2** A synclinal fold. [<Gk. *synklinein.* See SYNCLINAL.]

syn·clit·ism (sing'klə·tiz'əm) *n. Med.* The lateral turning of the fetal head in a natural presentation at childbirth, thus bringing the cranial planes into parallelism with the planes of the maternal pelvis. [<Gk. *syn-* together + *klitikos* <*klinein* incline, turn aside] — **syn·clit'ic** *adj.*

syn·co·pate (sing'kə·pāt) *v.t.* **·pat·ed, ·pat·ing** **1** To contract, as a word, by syncope. **2** *Music* To treat or modify, as a tone, by syncopation. [<LL *syncopatus*, pp. of *syncoparè* affect with syncope <*syncope* SYNCOPE]

syn·co·pa·tion (sing'kə·pā'shən) *n.* **1** The act of syncopating or state of being syncopated; also, that which is syncopated; a dance or rhythm in syncopated time. **2** *Music* The beginning of a tone on an unaccented beat and its continuation through the following accented beat, or the beginning of a tone on the last half of a beat and continuing it through the first half of the next beat; also, the tone so treated, generally receiving an accent. **3** Any music featuring syncopation, as ragtime, jazz, etc. **4** Syncope of a word,

or an example of it.

syn·co·pe (sing'kə·pē) *n.* **1** The elision of a sound or syllable in the middle part of a word, as *e'er* for *ever.* **2** *Music* Syncopation. **3** *Pathol.* Sudden faintness; swooning, with loss of sensation, motion, and consciousness. See synonyms under STUPOR. [Earlier *sincopis* <OF *sincopin*, ult. <LL *syncope* <Gk. *synkopē* <*syn-* together + *kop-*, stem of *koptein* strike, cut; refashioned after LL] — **syn'co·pal, syn·cop·ic** (sin·kop'ik) *adj.*

syn·cre·tism (sing'krə·tiz'əm) *n.* **1** A tendency or effort to reconcile and unite various systems of philosophy or religious opinion on the basis of tenets common to all and against a common opponent. **2** *Ling.* The fusion of two or more inflectional forms which were originally different, as of two cases. [<F *syncrétisme* <NL *syncretismus* <Gk. *synkrētismos* a union of two parties against a third <*synkrētizein* combine] — **syn'cre·tist** *n.* — **syn'cre·tis'tic** or **·ti·cal, syn·cret·ic** (sin·kret'ik) *adj.*

syn·cre·tize (sing'krə·tīz) *v.t.* **·tized, ·tiz·ing** To attempt to blend and reconcile, as various religions or philosophies. [<NL *syncretizare* <Gk. *synkrētizein* combine]

syn·cri·sis (sing'krə·sis) *n.* A figure of speech formed by comparison of opposite persons or things. [<LL <Gk. *synkrisis* <*synkrinein* compare <*syn-* together + *krinein* separate]

syn·dac·tyl (sin·dak'til) *adj. Anat.* Having two or more digits either of the hand or of the foot wholly or partly united; web-footed: also **syn·dac'tyle, syn·dac'ty·lous.** — *n.* A mammal or bird which is syndactyl. [<F *syndactyle* <Gk. *syn-* together + *daktylos* a finger]

syn·dac·tyl·ism (sin·dak'til·iz'əm) *n.* **1** The condition of being syndactyl. **2** The union of two or more digits or toes.

syn·des·mo·sis (sin'des·mō'sis) *n. Anat.* The joining of two portions of the skeleton by means of ligamentous tissue. [<NL <Gk. *syndesmos* a ligament] — **syn'des·mot'ic** (-mot'ik) *adj.*

syn·det·ic (sin·det'ik) *adj.* Serving to unite or connect; connective, as a word. Also **syn·det'i·cal.** [<Gk. *syndetikos* <*syndeein* bind together <*syn-* together + *deein* bind] — **syn·det'i·cal·ly** *adv.*

syn·di·cal·ism (sin'di·kəl·iz'əm) *n.* A social and political theory proposing the taking over of the means of production by syndicates of workers, preferably by means of the general strike, with consequent political control and the disappearance of the bourgeois state. [<F *syndicalisme* <*syndical* of a labor union <*(chambre) syndicale* a labor union <*syndic* a syndic] — **syn'di·cal·ist** *n.* — **syn'di·cal·is'tic** *adj.*

syn·di·cate (sin'də·kit) *n.* **1** An association of individuals united to negotiate some business or to prosecute some enterprise requiring large capital. **2** A combination of persons associated for purchasing manuscripts and selling them again to a number of periodicals, as newspapers, for simultaneous publication. **3** The office or jurisdiction of a syndic; syndics collectively: the original meaning. — *v.t.* (-kāt) **·cat·ed, ·cat·ing** **1** To combine into or manage by a syndicate. **2** To sell for publication in many newspapers or magazines. [<F *syndicat* office of a syndic <*syndic.* See SYNDIC.]

syn·drome (sin'drōm) *n.* **1** *Med.* An aggregate or set of concurrent symptoms together indicating the presence and nature of a disease. **2** A group of traits regarded as being characteristic of a certain type, condition, etc. [<NL <Gk. *syndromē* <*syn-* together + *dramein* run] — **syn·drom·ic** (sin·drom'ik) *adj.*

sy·nec·do·che (si·nek'də·kē) *n.* A figure of speech in which a part is put for a whole or a whole for a part, an individual for a class, or a material for the thing, as a *roof* for a *house,* marble for a *statue.* [<LL <Gk. *synekdochē* <*synekdechesthai* take something with something else <*syn-* together + *ekdechesthai* take from <*ek-* from + *dechesthai* take] — **syn·ec·doch·ic** (sin'ek·dok'ik), **syn'ec·doch'i·cal** *adj.*

syn·e·col·o·gy (sin'ə·kol'ə·jē) *n.* The study of plant and animal communities in relation to their environment; the ecology of organisms taken collectively. [<SYN- + ECOLOGY]

syn·er·e·sis (si·ner'ə·sis) *n.* **1** The coalescence of two vowels or syllables generally pronounced separately, as *seest* for *see-est:* opposed to *dieresis; crasis.* Compare SYNIZESIS. **2** *Chem.* The contraction of a gel, with the expulsion of water or other liquids, as in the clotting of blood. Also spelled *synaeresis.* [< LL *synaeresis* < Gk. *synairesis* a drawing together < *syn-* together + *hairein* take]

syn·er·gism (sin'ər·jiz'əm) *n.* **1** The doctrine that human effort cooperates with divine grace in the salvation of the soul. **2** *Med.* The mutually cooperating action of separate substances which together produce an effect greater than that of any component taken alone, as certain drug mixtures. [< NL *synergismus* < Gk. *synergos* working together < *synergein.* See SYNERGETIC.]

syn·er·gist (sin'ər·jist) *n.* **1** One holding to synergism. **2** A cooperating organ, part, or medicine. —**syn'er·gis'tic** or **·ti·cal** *adj.*

syn·er·gy (sin'ər·jē) *n.* **1** Combined and correlated force; united action. **2** *Med.* Correlation or concurrence of action between different organs in health or disease, or between different drugs. Also **syn·er·gi·a** (si·nûr'jē·ə). [< NL *synergia* < Gk. *synergos.* See SYNERGISM.] —**syn·er'gic** *adj.*

syn·e·sis (sin'ə·sis) *n. Gram.* Construction in accordance with the sense rather than the syntax, as the use of a plural form of a verb with a collective noun to emphasize the individuals in the group. [< Gk., a joining together, understanding < *synienai* perceive < *syn-* together + *hienai* send]

syn·es·the·sia (sin'is·thē'zhə, -zhē·ə) *n. Physiol.* **1** Transferred sensation; sensation produced at a point different from the point of stimulation. **2** The producing of a subjective response normally associated with one sense by stimulation of another sense, as of a color from hearing a certain sound. Also spelled *synaesthesia.* [< NL *synaesthesia* < Gk. *synaisthēsis* joint perception < *synaisthanesthai* perceive simultaneously < *syn-* together + *aisthanesthai* perceive, feel] —**syn'es·thet'ic** (-thet'ik) *adj.*

syn·fu·el (sin'fyōō·əl) *n.* Synthetic fuel.

syn·ga·my (sing'gə·mē) *n. Biol.* The union of male and female gametes in fertilization. [< SYN- + -GAMY] —**syn·gam·ic** (sin·gam'ik), **syn'ga·mous** *adj.*

syn·gen·e·sis (sin·jen'ə·sis) *n. Biol.* **1** Sexual reproduction. **2** The theory that the sexually fertilized germ contains within itself the germs of all future generations: opposed to *epigenesis.* [< NL < Gk. *syn-* together + *genesis* GENESIS] —**syn·ge·net·ic** (sin'jə·net'ik) *adj.*

syn·od (sin'əd) *n.* **1** An ecclesiastical council, stated or special, local or general; hence, any deliberative assembly. **2** *Astron.* A conjunction (def. 2). [OE *synoth* < LL *synodus* < Gk. *synodos,* lit., a coming together < *syn-* together + *hodos* a way; refashioned after MF *synode* < LL]

sy·noe·cious (si·nē'shəs) *adj. Bot.* Having male and female organs, either stamens and pistils or antheridia and archegonia, in the same inflorescence or receptacle, as in most composite plants and many mosses: also spelled *synecious.* [< Gk. *synoikia* living together < *syn-* together + *oikos* a house; formed on analogy with *dioecious, monoecious,* etc.]

syn·o·nym (sin'ə·nim) *n.* **1** A word having the same or almost the same meaning as some other; hence, one of a number of words that have one or more meanings in common: opposite of *antonym.* **2** The equivalent of a word in another language. **3** *Biol.* A scientific name, as of a genus or species, superseded or discarded, as by the law of priority or because of incorrect application. Also **syn·o·nyme.** [< LL *synonymum* < Gk. *synōnymon,* neut. of *synōnymos* having like meaning or name < *syn-* together + *onyma, onoma* a name] —**syn'o·nym'ic** or **·i·cal** *adj.* —**syn'o·nym'i·ty** *n.*

sy·non·y·mous (si·non'ə·məs) *adj.* Being a synonym or synonyms; equivalent or similar in meaning; closely related or nearly alike in significance. Also **syn·o·ny·mat·ic** (sin'ə·ni·mat'ik), **syn'o·nym'ic** (-nim'ik) or **·i·cal.** —**sy·non'·**

y·mous·ly *adv.*
Synonyms: alike, correspondent, corresponding, equivalent, identical, interchangeable, like, same, similar, synonymic. In the strictest sense, *synonymous* words scarcely exist; rarely, if ever, are any two words in any language *equivalent* or *identical* in meaning; where a difference in meaning cannot be easily shown, a difference in usage, often involving connotation, usually exists, so that the words are not *interchangeable.* By *synonymous* words we usually understand words that coincide or nearly coincide in some part of their meaning, and may hence within certain limits be used interchangeably, while outside of these limits they may differ very greatly in meaning and use. To consider *synonymous* words *identical* is fatal to accuracy; to forget that they are *similar,* to some extent *equivalent,* and sometimes *interchangeable,* is destructive of freedom and variety.

sy·non·y·my (si·non'ə·mē) *n. pl.* **·mies 1** The quality of being synonymous; the expressing or extending of an idea by the use of synonyms. **2** The science or systematic collection and study of synonyms; the use and nice discrimination of synonyms: also **syn·o·nym·ics** (sin'ə·nim'iks). **3** A book treating of or discriminating the meaning of synonyms or of allied terms. **4** An index, list, or collection of synonyms, as in scientific. nomenclature. [< LL *synonymia* < Gk. *synōnymia* < *synōnymos.* See SYNONYM.]

sy·nop·sis (si·nop'sis) *n. pl.* **·ses** (-sēz) A general view, as of a subject or its treatment; an abstract; syllabus; a summary. See synonyms under ABRIDGMENT. [< LL < Gk., a general view < *syn-* together + *opsis* a view]

sy·nop·tic (si·nop'tik) *adj.* **1** Giving a general view. **2** Presenting the same or a similar point of view; containing parts that, when compared, are virtually identical: said of the first three Gospels (**Synoptic Gospels**) as distinguished from the fourth. Also **sy·nop'ti·cal.** [< NL *synopticus* < Gk. *synoptikos* < *synopsis* a synopsis] —**sy·nop'ti·cal·ly** *adv.*

sy·nou·si·acs (si·nōō'shē·aks, -nou'-) *n.* That branch of knowledge pertaining to societies: a term used in cataloging, as in libraries. [< Gk. *synousia* society < *synousa,* ppr. fem. of *syneinai* be with < *syn-* together + *einai* be]

sy·no·vi·a (si·nō'vē·ə) *n. Physiol.* The viscid, transparent, albuminous fluid secreted in the interior of joints and at other points where lubrication is necessary. [< NL *sinovia, synovia, synophia;* coined by Paracelsus, appar. < Gk. *syn-* together + L *ovum* an egg < Gk. *ōon*] —**sy·no'vi·al** *adj.*

syn·o·vi·tis (sin'ō·vī'tis) *n. Pathol.* Inflammation of a synovial membrane.

syn·tax (sin'taks) *n.* **1** The arrangement and interrelation of words in grammatical constructions. **2** The branch of linguistics dealing with this. [< F *syntaxe* < LL *syntaxis* < Gk. *syntassein* join together < *syn-* together + *tassein* arrange] —**syn·tac·tic** (sin·tak'tik) or **·ti·cal** *adj.* —**syn·tac'ti·cal·ly** *adv.*

syn·the·sis (sin'thə·sis) *n. pl.* **·ses** (-sēz) **1** The assembling of separate or subordinate parts into a new form; also, the complex whole resulting from this. **2** *Ling.* The combination of radical and formative or inflectional elements in one word, as in *un-think-ing, homewards.* **3** *Logic* **a** Combination of separate elements into a whole, as of species into genera: contrasted with *analysis.* **b** A process of reasoning from the whole to a part, from the general to the particular; deductive reasoning. **4** *Surg.* The operation of reuniting broken or divided parts, as of bones. **5** *Chem.* **a** The building up of compounds from a series of reactions involving elements, radicals, or simpler compounds. **b** The preparation by such means of organic compounds which have specific properties or are identical in certain respects with naturally occurring substances. Compare ANALYSIS. [< L < Gk. < *syntithenai* < *syn-* together + *tithenai* place] —**syn'the·sist** *n.*

syn·the·size (sin'thə·sīz) *v.t.* **·sized, ·siz·ing 1** To unite or produce by synthesis. **2** To apply synthesis to. Also *Brit.* **syn'the·sise.**

syn·thet·ic (sin·thet'ik) *adj.* **1** Pertaining to

or of the nature of synthesis; characterized by or consisting in synthesis; specifically, tending to reduce particulars to inclusive wholes: a *synthetic* mind. **2** *Chem.* Produced by the synthesis of simpler materials or substances: *synthetic* rubber. **3** Artificial; spurious. **4** *Ling.* Describing a language that utilizes inflectional affixes for the expression of relationships between words, as in Latin; inflectional: opposed to *analytic.* Also **syn·thet'i·cal.** —*n.* **1** Anything produced by synthesis. **2** *Chem.* A synthesized compound adapted for use as a substitute for some other material or substance. [< F *synthétique* < NL *syntheticus* < Gk. *synthetikos* < *synthetos* compounded < *syntithenai* < *syn-* together + *tithenai* place] —**syn·thet'i·cal·ly** *adv.*

syn·to·ny (sin'tə·nē) *n. Electr.* **1** The harmonizing or tuning of particular transmitters and receivers each to the other. **2** Resonance. [< Gk. *syntonia* agreement < *syn-* together + *tonos* a tone]

syn·u·ra (sin·yŏŏr'ə) *n. pl.* **·u·rae** (-yŏŏr'ē) Any of a genus (*Synura*) of flagellate protozoans, uniting in subspherical clusters and discharging oil globules. They are common in swamp waters and render drinking water unpalatable by giving it a cucumberlike flavor. [< NL < Gk. *synouros, synoros* bordering on < *syn-* together + *oros* a boundary]

syph·i·lis (sif'ə·lis) *n. Pathol.* An infectious, chronic, venereal disease caused by a spirochete (*Treponema pallidum*) transmissible by direct contact or congenitally. It usually progresses by three stages of increasing severity: primary, secondary, and tertiary. [after *Syphilis, sive Morbus Gallicus,* a Latin poem by Fracastoro, published in 1530, the hero of which, *Syphilus,* a shepherd, was the first sufferer from the disease] —**syph'i·loid, syph'·i·lous** *adj.*

syph·i·lit·ic (sif'ə·lit'ik) *adj.* Relating to or affected with syphilis. —*n.* A person suffering from syphilis. [< NL *syphiliticus* < *syphilis* SYPHILIS]

syph·i·lol·o·gy (sif'ə·lol'ə·jē) *n.* The science of syphilis, its cognate diseases, and their treatment. [< SYPHIL(IS) + -(O)LOGY] —**syph'i·lol'o·gist** *n.*

syph·i·lo·pho·bi·a (sif'ə·lə·fō'bē·ə) *n. Psychiatry* A morbid fear of syphilis. [< SYPHIL(IS) + -(O)PHOBIA] —**syph'i·lo·pho'bic** *adj.*

Syr·i·a (sir'ē·ə) *n.* **1** A former republic, 1941–1958, south of Asia Minor on the NE coast of the Mediterranean, a part of the United Arab Republic from 1958–61; 72,234 square miles; capital, Damascus. *Arabic* **Esh Sham. 2** A former French mandated territory, 1920–1941, roughly comprising Syria (def. 1) and Lebanon. **3** An ancient country including Syria (def. 1), Lebanon, Palestine (def. 2), and adjacent districts of western Asia.

sy·rin·ga (si·ring'gə) *n.* **1** Any of a genus (*Philadelphus*) of ornamental shrubs of the saxifrage family having cream-colored flowers resembling those of the orange in form and fragrance, especially the Lewis mock orange (*P. lewisii*), the State flower of Idaho. **2** Any of a genus (*Syringa*) of ornamental shrubs of the olive family having panicles of showy white or purple flowers; the lilacs. [< NL < Gk. *syrinx, -ingos* a pipe]

SYRINGA
(Plant to 10 feet)

sy·ringe (sir'inj, si·rinj') *n. Med.* An instrument used to withdraw a fluid from a reservoir and eject it in one or more jets or streams. The simplest forms are valveless single-acting devices; other forms consist of an elastic bag supplied with flexible inlet and outlet pipes each having a suitable check valve. —*v.t.* **·inged, ·ing·ing** To spray or inject by a syringe; cleanse or treat with injected fluid. [< Med. L *siringa* < Gk. *syrinx, -ingos* a tube, a pipe]

sy·rin·go·my·e·li·a (si·ring'gō·mī·ē'lē·ə) *n. Pathol.* A morbid condition of the spinal cord, due to the presence of liquid in abnormally formed cavities. [< NL < Gk. *syrinx, -ingos* a

syr·inx (sir′ingks) *n.* **1** *Ornithol.* A special modification of the windpipe serving as the song organ in birds. **2** A tube, pipe, or fistula. **3** Panpipes. [<Gk., a pipe] —**sy·rin·ge·al** (si·rin′jē·əl) *adj.*

syr·phus fly (sûr′fəs) A fly of *Syrphus* or a related genus (family *Syrphidae*). The group is large and widely distributed, and contains many species which deceptively resemble bees and wasps. The larvae of many feed upon harmful plant lice. For illustration see INSECTS (beneficial). Also **syr·phid** (sûr′fid), **syr′phi·an.** [<NL <Gk. *syrphos* a gnat]

syr·up (sir′əp), **syr·up·y** See SIRUP, etc.

sys·sar·co·sis (sis′är·kō′sis) *n. Anat.* The union of bones by means of muscles. [<NL <Gk. *syssarkōsis* <*syssarkoein* unite by or cover over with flesh] —**sys′sar·co′sic, sys′sar·cot·ic** (-kot′ik) *adj.*

sys·tal·tic (sis·tal′tik) *adj. Physiol.* Alternately contracting and dilating: the *systaltic* motion of the heart; pulsatory. Compare PERISTALSIS. [<LL *systalticus* <Gk. *systaltikos* depressing <*systellein* draw together <*syn-* together + *stellein* send]

sys·tem (sis′təm) *n.* **1** Orderly combination or arrangement, as of parts or elements, into a whole; specifically, such combination according to some rational principle; any methodical arrangement of parts. **2** In science and philosophy, an orderly collection of logically related principles, facts, or objects. **3** Any group of facts and phenomena regarded as constituting a natural whole and furnishing the basis and material of scientific investigation and construction: the solar *system.* **4** The connection or manner of connection of parts as related to a whole, or the parts collectively so related; a whole as made up of constitutive parts: a railroad *system.* **5** The state or quality of being in order or orderly; orderliness; method: He works with *system.* **6** *Physiol.* An assemblage of organic structures composed of similar elements and combined for the same general functions: the nervous *system;* also, the entire body, taken as a functional whole. **7** *Physics* An aggregation of matter in, or tending to approach, equilibrium. **8** *Mineral.* One of the six divisions into which

all crystal forms may be grouped, depending upon the relative lengths and mutual inclinations of the assumed crystal axes. **9** *Geol.* A category of rock strata next below a group and above a series and corresponding with a period in the time scale. [<LL *systema* a musical interval <Gk. *systēma, -atos* an organized whole < *syn-* together + *histanai* stand, set up]

Synonyms: manner, method, mode, order, regularity, rule. *Order* in this connection denotes a fact or a result; as, These papers are in *order. Method* denotes a process; *rule* an authoritative requirement or an established course of things; *system,* not merely a law of action or procedure, but a comprehensive plan; *manner* refers to the external qualities of actions, and to those often as settled and characteristic; we speak of a *system* of taxation, a *method* of collecting taxes, the *rules* by which assessments are made; or we say, As a *rule* the payments are heaviest at a certain time of year; a just tax may be made odious by the *manner* of its collection. *Regularity* applies to even disposition of objects or uniform recurrence of acts in a series. There may be *regularity* without *order,* as in the recurrence of paroxysms of disease or insanity; there may be *order* without *regularity,* as in the arrangement of furniture in a room, where the objects are placed at varying distances. *Order* commonly implies the design of an intelligent agent or the appearance or suggestion of such design; *regularity* applies to an actual uniform disposition or recurrence with no suggestion of purpose, and as applied to human affairs is less intelligent and more mechanical than *order.* See BODY, FRAME, HABIT, HYPOTHESIS. *Antonyms:* chaos, confusion, derangement, disarrangement, disorder, irregularity.

sys·tem·at·ic (sis′tə·mat′ik) *adj.* **1** Of, pertaining to, of the nature of, or characterized by system. **2** Acting by system or method; methodical: *systematic* thieving. **3** Forming a system; systematized. **4** Carried out with organized regularity. **5** Taxonomic: *systematic* botany. Also **sys′tem·at′i·cal.** [<LL *systematicus* <LGk. *systēmatikos* <*systēma, -atos* a system] —**sys′tem·at′i·cal·ly** *adv.*

sys·tem·at·ics (sis′tə·mat′iks) *n. pl. (construed*

as singular) **1** The art or principles of classification and nomenclature. **2** *Biol.* The science of the classification of organisms; taxonomy.

sys·tem·a·tism (sis′tə·mə·tiz′əm) *n.* **1** Systematic arrangement or classification. **2** Adherence to or reduction of principles, etc., to a system.

sys·tem·ic (sis·tem′ik) *adj.* **1** Of or pertaining to system or a system; systematic. **2** *Physiol.* Pertaining to or affecting the body as a whole: a *systemic* poison. —**sys·tem′i·cal·ly** *adv.*

systems analysis The technique of reducing complex processes, as of industry, government, research, etc., to basic operations that can be treated quantitatively and reordered into sequences amenable to control. —**systems analyst**

sys·to·le (sis′tə·lē) *n.* **1** *Physiol.* The regular contraction of the heart, especially of the ventricles, that impels the blood outward. Compare DIASTOLE. **2** The shortening of a syllable that is naturally or by position long. [<NL <Gk *systolē* a contraction <*systellein.* See SYSTALTIC.] —**sys·tol·ic** (sis·tol′ik) *adj.*

syz·y·gy (siz′ə·jē) *n. pl.* **·gies 1** *Astron.* One of two opposite points in the orbit of a celestial body when it is in conjunction with or opposition to the sun; especially, the points on the moon's orbit when the moon is most nearly in line with the earth and the sun. **2** The union of parts or organisms. **3** A dipody or group of two feet in one verse. [<LL *syzygia* <Gk., a yoke, conjunction <*syzygos* yoked, paired <*syn-* together + *zeugnynai* yoke <*zygon* a yoke] —**sy·zyg·i·al** (si·zij′ē·əl) *adj.*

SYZYGY
S. Sun's rays. E. Earth. M1, M2. Syzygy of the moon.

Sze·chwan (se′chwän′, su′-) A province of SW and central western China; 338,136 square miles; capital, Chengtu.

T

t, T (tē) *n. pl.* **t's, T's** or **ts, Ts, tees** (tēz) **1** The twentieth letter of the English alphabet, from Greek *tau* (a modification of Phoenician *tau*) and Latin *T.* **2** The sound of the letter *t,* the voiceless alveolar stop. See ALPHABET. —*symbol* Anything shaped like a T. —**to a T** Precisely; with exactness: probably in allusion to a T-square.

T (tē) *adj.* Shaped or having a cross-section like a T, as *T*-beam, *T*-pipe, etc. —*n.* Anything having the shape of a T.

-t Inflectional ending used to indicate past participles and past tenses, as in *bereft, lost, spent:* equivalent to *-ed.*

Ta *Chem.* Tantalum (symbol Ta).

tab (tab) *n.* **1** A flap, strip, tongue, or appendage of something, as a garment. **2** *Colloq.* Tally: to keep *tab.* **3** *Aeron.* An auxiliary airfoil attached to the control surface of an airplane. [Origin uncertain]

tab·a·nid (tab′ə·nid) *n.* Any of a family (*Tabanidae*) of large, bloodsucking insects; a horsefly or deerfly. —*adj.* Of the *Tabanidae.* [<NL, family name <L *tabanus* a horsefly]

tab·ard (tab′ərd) *n.* **1** Formerly, a short, sleeveless or short-sleeved, outer garment. **2** A knight's cape or cloak, worn over his armor and emblazoned with his own arms; also, a similar garment worn by a herald and embroidered with his lord's arms. **3** A banner attached to a trumpet or bugle. [<OF *tabard,* ult. <L *tapete* tapestry]

Ta·bas·co (tə·bas′kō) *n.* A pungent sauce made

from the red-pepper plant (genus *Capsicum*): a trade name.

tab·by (tab′ē) *n. pl.* **·bies 1** Any of several plain-woven fabrics, as a striped or watered taffeta, or a moreen. **2** A garment made of a watered fabric. **3** A brindled or striped cat; popularly, any domestic cat, especially a female. **4** A gossiping old maid. **5** A building material of equal parts of lime and shells, and gravel, mixed with water. —*adj.* **1** Watered; mottled, as a fabric; also, brindled, as a cat. **2** Made of tabby. **3** Woven in the same way as fabric that is to be watered. —*v.t.* **·bied, ·by·ing** To give a wavy or watered appearance to (silk, etc.) by pressure between hot rollers; water; calender. [<F *tabis, atabis* <Arabic *'attābi* <*'Attabi,* name of a quarter of Baghdad where it was manufactured]

tab·er·nac·le (tab′ər·nak′əl) *n.* **1** A tent or similar structure; slight shelter, fixed or portable. **2** Specifically, the portable sanctuary used by the Jews in the wilderness; later, the Jewish temple; hence, any house of worship, especially one of large size and not of specially ecclesiastical architecture: in England, the place of worship of some nonconformists. **3** The human body as the dwelling place of the soul. **4** The ornamental receptacle for the consecrated eucharistic elements, or for the pyx. **5** An ornamental recess or a structure sheltering something. **6** A socket or hinged post to unstep or lower a mast. —*v.i.* **·led, ·ling** To dwell in a tent; hence, to dwell transiently: The soul *tabernacles* in the body. [<OF <L *tabernaculum,* dim. of *taberna* shed] —**tab·er·nac·u·lar** (tab′ər·nak′yə·lər) *adj.*

ta·bes (tā′bēz) *n. Pathol.* **1** Emaciation with general languor, progressive atrophy, and hectic fever; a decline. **2** Locomotor ataxia: also **tabes dor·sa·lis** (dôr·sā′lis). [<L, a wasting away <*tabere* waste away] —**ta·bes·cence** (tə·bes′əns) *n.* —**ta·bes′cent** *adj.* —**ta·bet′ic** (-bet′ik) *n. & adj.* —**tab·id** (tab′id) *adj.*

tab·la·ture (tab′lə·chər) *n.* **1** *Anat.* One of the plates of bony tissue that form the walls of the cranium. **2** A tablelike painting or design. [<F <L *tabula* board]

ta·ble (tā′bəl) *n.* **1** An article of furniture with a flat horizontal top upheld by one or more supports. **2** Such a table around which persons sit for a meal: to set the *table.* **3** The food served or entertainment provided at a meal or dinner. **4** The company of persons at a table. **5** A gaming table, as for roulette, dice, etc. **6** A collection of related numbers, values, signs, or items of any kind, arranged for ease of reference or comparison, often in parallel columns: a *table* of logarithms; a *table* of statistics. **7** A synoptical statement; list: *table* of contents. **8** A tableland; plateau. **9** *Geol.* A horizontal stratum of rock. **10** The flat facet cut across the top of a precious stone. **11** *Archit.* **a** A raised horizontal surface or band of molding on a wall; a string-course. **b** A raised or sunken panel on a wall. **12** In palmistry, the quadrangle formed by four lines of the hand. **13** In backgammon: **a** Either of the two leaves of a backgammon board. **b** *pl. Obs.* Backgammon. **14** *Anat.* One of the flat bony plates forming the inner or outer part of the cranium. **15** A tablet or slab bearing an inscription; especially, one of those which bore the Ten Commandments or certain Roman laws. **—to turn the tables** To thwart an opponent's action and turn the situation to his disadvantage. — *v.t.* **·bled, ·bling 1** To place on a table, as a playing card. **2** To postpone discussion of (a resolution, bill, etc.) until a future time, or for an indefinite period. **3** *Rare* To make into or enter in a list or table; tabulate. [Fusion of OF *table* and OE *tabule*, both < L *tabula* board]

tab·leau (tab′lō, ta·blō′) *n. pl.* **·leaux** (-lōz) or **·leaus** (-lōz) **1** Any picture or picturesque representation; especially, an unexpected situation produced suddenly and dramatically. **2** A tableau vivant. [< F, dim. of *table*. See TABLE.]

ta·bleau vi·vant (tá·blō′ vē·vän′) *pl.* **ta·bleaux vi·vants** (tá·blō′ vē·vän′) *French* A picturelike scene represented by silent and motionless persons standing in appropriate attitudes: also called *living picture.*

ta·ble d'hôte (tab′əl dōt′, tä′bəl) *pl.* **tab·les d'hôte** (tab′əlz dōt, tä′bəlz) **1** A common table for guests, as at a hotel. **2** A complete meal of several specified courses, served in a restaurant at a fixed price. [< F, lit., table of the host]

ta·ble·land (tā′bəl·land′) *n.* A broad, level, elevated region, usually treeless; a plateau; specifically, a precipitous mesa.

table linen Tablecloths, napkins, doilies, etc., made of linen, cotton, etc.

ta·ble·spoon (tā′bəl·spoon′, -spoon′) *n.* A large spoon, larger than a dessertspoon, with a capacity of 15 cc. or three times the capacity of a teaspoon: used for serving food.

usually reckoned as equivalent to half a fluid ounce, 15 cc., or three teaspoonfuls.

tab·let (tab′lit) *n.* **1** A thin leaf or sheet of solid material, as ivory or wood, for writing, painting, or drawing. **2** One of a set of leaves pivoted or joined together at one end and used for writing; also, a set of such leaves; hence, a pad, as of writing paper or note paper. **3** A small table or flat surface, especially one designed for or containing an inscription or design. **4** A small, flat or nearly flat piece of some prepared substance, as chocolate or soap. **5** A definite portion or weight of drug brought by pressure and the addition of a gum into a solid form; a troche or lozenge; also, an electuary. **6** A flat or tablelike surface. [< OF *tablete*, dim. of *table*. See TABLE.]

table tennis A game resembling tennis in miniature, played indoors with a small celluloid ball and wooden paddles on a large table; Ping-pong.

ta·ble·ware (tā′bəl·wâr′) *n.* Ware for table use; dishes, knives, forks, spoons, etc., collectively: called **table furniture** when napery is included.

tab·loid (tab′loid) *n.* A newspaper, one half the size of an ordinary newspaper, in which the news is presented by means of pictures and concise reporting. — *adj.* **1** Compact; concise; condensed. **2** Sensational: *tabloid* journalism. [< TABL(ET) + -OID]

ta·boo (tə·boo′, ta-) See TABU.

ta·bor (tā′bər) *n.* A small drum or tambourine on which a fife-player beats his own accompaniment; a timbrel. — *v.i.* To beat or play on a timbrel or small drum; beat lightly and repeatedly. Also spelled *taber.* Also **ta′bour.** [< OF *tabour*, prob. < Persian *tabīrah* drum] **— ta′bor·er** *n.*

ta·bu (tə·boo′, ta-) *n.* **1** Among primitive peoples, especially the Polynesians, a religious and social interdict against the touching or mentioning of a certain person, thing, or place, the uttering of a certain name, or the performing of a certain action, because it is considered sacred, protective, dangerous, unclean, or possessed of mysterious powers. **2** The system or practice of such interdicts or prohibitions. **3** Any restriction or ban founded on custom or social convention. — *adj.* **1** Consecrated or prohibited by tabu. **2** Banned or forbidden by social authority or convention. — *v.t.* **1** To place under tabu. **2** To exclude; ostracize. Also spelled *taboo.* [< Tonga]

tab·u·lar (tab′yə·lər) *adj.* **1** Pertaining to or consisting of a table or list. **2** Computed from or with a mathematical table. **3** Having a flat surface; tablelike. [< L *tabularis*

< *tabula* table] **— tab′u·lar·ly** *adv.*

tab·u·la ra·sa (tab′yōō·lə rä′sə) *Latin* **1** An empty or clean tablet; a clean slate. **2** The concept of the mind of a newborn child as a blank, to be written on by experience.

tab·u·late (tab′yə·lāt) *v.t.* **·lat·ed, ·lat·ing 1** To arrange in a table or list; to *tabulate* results. **2** To form with a tabular surface. — *adj.* **1** Having a flat surface or surfaces; broad and flat. **2** *Zool.* Having tabulated horizontal plates extending across the visceral cavity: said of certain corals. [< L *tabula* table + -ATE¹] **— tab′u·la′tion** *n.*

tab·u·la·tor (tab′yə·lā′tər) *n.* **1** One who or that which tabulates. **2** A device built into a typewriter with which statistical matter may be speedily written in tabulated form. **3** An automatic high-speed accounting machine for tabulating reports.

tac·a·ma·hac (tak′ə·mə·hak′) *n.* **1** A yellowish resinous substance with a strong odor, derived from various trees and used as incense. **2** Any of the trees producing this substance, especially the balsam poplar (*Populus tacamahaca*) of the United States. Also spelled *tacmahack.* Also **tac′a·ma·hac′a** (-hak′ə), **tac′a·ma·hack′.** [< Sp. *tacamaca, tacamahaca* < Nahuatl *tecomahca*, lit., fetid copal]

ta·cet (tā′set) *Latin* Literally, it is silent: a musical direction for silence.

tach·e·om·e·ter (tak′ē·om′ə·tər) *n.* **1** A tachymeter. **2** A tachometer. [< Gk. *tachos, tacheos* speed + -METER] **— tach′e·om′e·try** *n.*

tach·i·na fly (tak′ə·nə) A fly (family *Tachinidae*) often resembling the house fly, whose larvae develop as parasites in the caterpillar or other insect. For illustration see under INSECTS (beneficial). [< NL *tachina* < Gk. *tachinos* swift]

tach·o·graph (tak′ə·graf, -gräf) *n.* **1** A registering tachometer. **2** The record it makes. [< Gk. *tachos* swiftness + -GRAPH]

ta·chom·e·ter (tə·kom′ə·tər) *n.* **1** An instrument for measuring linear and angular velocity, as of a machine, the flow of a current, blood, etc. **2** A device for indicating the speed of rotation of an engine, etc. [See TACHEOMETER]

ta·chom·e·try (tə·kom′ə·trē) *n.* The art or science of using a tachometer. **— tach·o·met·ric** (tak′ə·met′rik) *adj.*

tachy- *combining form* Speed; swiftness: *tachycardia.* [< Gk. *tachys* swift]

tach·y·car·di·a (tak′i·kär′dē·ə) *n. Pathol.* Abnormal rapidity of the heartbeat, usually indicating a pulse rate above 100 per minute. **— tach′y·car′di·ac** *adj. & n.*

tach·y·graph (tak′ə·graf, -gräf) *n.* **1** A tachygraphic manuscript or symbol. **2** A tachygrapher.

TACHYGRAPHS

Numerals: *Upper* Arabic, A.D. 976;
Lower Modern Shorthand.

tach·y·lyte (tak′ə·līt) *n.* A pitch-black basaltic glass which is rapidly decomposed by acids. [< TACHY- + -LYTE¹; so called because easily decomposed] **— tach′y·lyt′ic** (-lit′ik) *adj.*

ta·chym·e·ter (tə·kim′ə·tər) *n.* **1** A surveying instrument for stadia surveying, having a level, telescope, vertical arc or circle, horizontal compass, and stadia wires. **2** A tachometer.

tac·it (tas′it) *adj.* **1** Existing, inferred, or implied without being directly stated; implied by silence or silent acquiescence. **2** *Law* Not expressed but understood by provision or operation of the law. **3** Silent; emitting no sound; noiseless. ◆ *Homophone: tasset.* [< F *tacite* < L *tacitus*, pp. of *tacere* be silent] **— tac′it·ly** *adv.* **— tac′it·ness** *n.*

Synonyms: implicit, implied, understood, unexpressed, unspoken.

tac·i·turn (tas′ə·tûrn) *adj.* Habitually silent or reserved; disinclined to conversation. [< L *taciturnus* < L *tacere* be silent] **— tac′i·tur′-**

ni·ty *n.* **— tac′i·turn·ly** *adv.*

Synonyms: close, dumb, mute, reserved, reticent, silent, uncommunicative. *Dumb, mute,* and *silent* refer to fact or state; *taciturn* refers to habit and disposition. The talkative person may be stricken *dumb* with terror; the obstinate may remain *mute*; one may be *silent* through preoccupation or set purpose; but the *taciturn* person is averse to the utterance of thought or feeling and to communication with others. One who is *silent* does not speak at all; one who is *taciturn* speaks when compelled, but in a grudging way. *Reserved* suggests more of method and intention than *taciturn*, applying often to some special time or topic. *Reserved* is thus closely equivalent to *uncommunicative*, but is a somewhat stronger word, often suggesting pride or haughtiness, as when we say one is *reserved* toward strangers. *Antonyms:* communicative, free, garrulous, loquacious, talkative, unreserved.

tack¹ (tak) *n.* **1** A small sharp-pointed nail, commonly with tapering sides and a flat head. **2** *Naut.* **a** A rope which holds down the weather clew of a course. **b** The weather clew of a square sail. **c** The lower forward corner of a fore-and-aft sail. **d** A rope by which the lower outer corner of a studdingsail is pulled to the end of the boom. **e** The direction in which a vessel sails when sailing close-hauled, considered in relation to the position of her sails: the starboard *tack* when the wind is coming from the right-hand side. **f** The distance or the course run at one time in such direction. **g** The act of tacking. **h** Any veering of a vessel to one side, as to take advantage of a side wind. **3** A change of policy; a new course of action. **4** A fastening; in needlework, a temporary stitch. **5** In Scots law, a contract; a lease; also, leased land. **6** The saddle, bridle, martingale, etc., used in riding horseback. — *v.t.* **1** To fasten or attach with tacks. **2** To secure temporarily, as with tacks or long stitches. **3** To attach as supplementary; append. **4** *Naut.* **a** To bring (a vessel) momentarily into the wind so as to go on the opposite tack. **b** To navigate (a vessel) to windward by making a series of tacks. — *v.i.* **5** *Naut.* **a** To tack a vessel. **b** To go on the opposite tack, or sail to windward by a series of tacks: said of vessels. **6** To change one's course of action; veer. [< AF *taque*, OF *tache* a nail < Gmc. Doublet of TACHE.] **— tack′er** *n.*

tack² (tak) *n.* Food in general: usually used contemptuously, and often in compounds: *hardtack.* [Origin uncertain]

tack hammer A small hammer for driving tacks.

tack·le (tak′əl, *in nautical usage* tā′kəl) *n.* **1** A rope, pulley, or combination of ropes and pulleys, used for hoisting or moving objects. **2** *Naut.* A mechanism for raising and lowering heavy weights, or managing sails and spars, as on shipboard. **3** A windlass or winch, together with ropes and hooks. **4** The instruments collectively used in any work or sport; gear; equipment: fishing *tackle.* **5** Formerly, the implements of war; weapons. **6** The act of tackling, or seizing and stopping, especially in football. **7** In football, either of two linemen stationed between the guard and end: called **right** and **left tackle. 8** A ship's rigging collectively. — *v.t.* **·led, ·ling 1** To harness (a horse). **2** To deal with; undertake to master, accomplish, or solve: to *tackle* a task or a problem. **3** To seize suddenly and forcefully, usually in order to stop or throw to the ground: to *tackle* a fleeing burglar. **4** In football, to seize and stop (an opponent carrying the ball). [< MLG *takel* < *taken* seize] **— tack′ler** *n.*

tack·ling (tak′ling) *n. Naut.* Tackle, collectively.

tack·y¹ (tak′ē) *adj.* **tack·i·er, tack·i·est** Having adhesive properties; sticky: said especially of surfaces covered with partly dried varnish. Also **tack′ey.** [Prob. < TACK¹, *v.* (def. 2)]

TACKLE
a. Gun.
b. Luff.

tack·y[2] (tak′ē) *adj. U.S. Colloq.* Unfashionable; plain; in bad taste; common. [Cf. dial. G *taklig* untidy]

tac·node (tak′nōd) *n. Math.* A point of osculation. [<L *tactus*, pp. of *tangere* touch + NODE]

ta·co (tä′kō) *n. pl.* **·cos** A fried tortilla folded around any of several fillings, as chopped meat or cheese. [<Sp., wad]

tac·o·nite (tak′ə·nīt) *n. Geol.* A variously tinted ferruginous chert enclosing the iron ores of the Mesabi district in Minnesota. [from *Tacon(ic Mountains)* + -ITE[1]]

tact (takt) *n.* **1** A quick or intuitive appreciation of what is fit, proper, or right; fine or ready mental discernment shown in saying or doing the proper thing, or especially in avoiding what would offend or disturb; skill or facility in dealing with men or emergencies; adroitness; cleverness; address. **2** The sense of touch; feeling; also, a touch or touching. **3** A perception or feeling, other than tactile, of the qualities of things. See synonyms under ADDRESS. [<L *tactus* a touching <*tangere* touch]

tact·ful (takt′fəl) *adj.* Possessing or manifesting tact; considerate. — **tact′ful·ly** *adv.* — **tact′ful·ness** *n.*

tac·tic (tak′tik) *n.* **1** A detail of tactics. **2** *Colloq.* A device or strategem: a clever *tactic.*

tac·ti·cal (tak′ti·kəl) *adj.* **1** Pertaining to or of the nature of tactics. **2** Exhibiting adroit maneuvering. — **tac′ti·cal·ly** *adv.*

tactical unit A military combat unit, running in size from the squad through the army group.

tac·ti·cian (tak·tish′ən) *n.* An expert in tactics; an adroit maneuverer.

tac·tics (tak′tiks) *n. pl.* **1** The science and art of military and naval evolutions; specifically, the art of handling troops in the presence of the enemy or for immediate objectives, as distinguished from *strategy*: construed as singular. **2** Any maneuvering or adroit management to effect an object. [<Gk. *taktika*, pl. of *taktikos* suitable for arranging or organizing <*tassein, tattein* arrange, order]

tac·tile (tak′til, -təl) *adj.* **1** Pertaining to the organs or sense of touch; caused by or consisting of contact; tactual. **2** That may be touched; tangible. [<F <L *tactilis* <*tactus* touch. See TACT.]

tac·til·i·ty (tak·til′ə·tē) *n.* Tangibility.

tac·tion (tak′shən) *n.* **1** The act of touching. **2** The state of being in contact. [<L *tactio, -onis* <*tactus*, pp. of *tangere* touch]

tact·less (takt′lis) *adj.* Without tact. — **tact′less·ly** *adv.* — **tact′less·ness** *n.*

tac·tom·e·ter (tak·tom′ə·tər) *n.* An esthesiometer. [<L *tactus* touch + -METER]

tac·tu·al (tak′chōō·əl) *adj.* **1** Pertaining to the sense or the organs of touch. **2** Derived from or caused by touch. [<L *tactus* touch. See TACT.] — **tac′tu·al·ly** *adv.*

tad (tad) *n.* A little boy or girl; young child. [Prob. short for TADPOLE]

tad·pole (tad′pōl) *n.* The aquatic larva of an amphibian, as a frog or toad, breathing by external gills and having a tail with extended membrane giving it a fishlike form. See FROG. [ME *taddepol* <*tadde* toad + *poll* head]

tae·ni·a (tē′nē·ə) *n.* **1** In classical antiquity, a band, ribbon, or fillet for containing the hair. **2** *Archit.* A band or fillet between the Doric frieze and the architrave. **3** *Anat.* A band or strip of tissue, especially one of several ribbonlike arrangements of white substance in the brain, or one of the three longitudinal muscular bands of the colon. **4** *Zool.* A tapeworm (genus *Taenia*). Also spelled *tenia.* [<L <Gk. *tainia* fillet, tape]

taf·fe·ta (taf′ə·tə) *n.* A fine, glossy, uncorded, somewhat stiff silk fabric: a term variously applied at different times, as to certain silk-and-linen or silk-and-wool mixtures, now also to rayon. — *adj.* Made of or resembling taffeta; also, lacy; filmy; delicate. [<OF *taffetas* <Med. L *taffeta* <Persian *tāftah* <*tāftan* twist]

taff·rail (taf′rāl′) *n. Naut.* **1** The rail around a vessel's stern. **2** The upper part of a vessel's stern. [Alter. of TAFFEREL, after RAIL[1]]

taf·fy (taf′ē) *n.* **1** A confection made from brown sugar or molasses, mixed with butter, boiled down, and pulled into long ropes until it cools sufficiently to hold its shape: also spelled *toffee, toffy.* **2** *Colloq.* Flattery; blarney.

[Origin unknown]

taf·i·a (taf′ē·ə) *n.* A spirituous liquor resembling rum, distilled in the West Indies from impure molasses or from refuse sugar. Also **taf′fi·a.** [<native name, prob. ult. <Malay *tāfia* spirit distilled from molasses]

tag[1] (tag) *n.* **1** Something tacked on or attached to something else; appendage. **2** A label tied or tacked on, as to a trunk; loosely, any label. **3** A loose, ragged edge of anything; tatter. **4** The tail or tip of the tail of any animal. **5** A matted and ragged lock of wool on a sheep; a loose lock of hair. **6** A worthless leaving; remnant; ort. **7** A flap or loop, as for drawing on a boot. **8** An aglet. **9** A decorative flourish, as on a signature. **10** In angling, a piece of bright material surrounding the shank of the hook in an artificial fly. **11** A lamb or yearling sheep. **12** A well-known quotation or saying, as in a song, poem, or book. **13** The refrain of a song or poem; also, the final lines of a speech in a play; catchword; cue. **14** The crowd; rabble: often in the phrases **rag and tag** and **rag, tag, and bobtail.** — *v.* **tagged, tag·ging** *v.t.* **1** To supply, adorn, fit, mark, or label with a tag. **2** To shear away tags from (sheep). **3** To follow closely or persistently. — *v.i.* **4** To follow closely at one's heels: The little boy *tagged* along. [Prob. <Scand. Cf. Sw. *tagg* spike, tooth, Norw. *tagge* tooth.]

tag[2] (tag) *n.* A juvenile game in which the object of the players is to keep from being caught or touched by one, the tagger (usually called "it"), who chases them for that purpose. — *v.t.* **tagged, tag·ging** To overtake and touch, as in the game of tag. [<TAG[1]]

tag day A day on which contributions are solicited for eleemosynary and other institutions: so called from the custom of giving a tag to each donor.

tagged atom *Physics* A radioisotope which betrays its presence in any part of a system into which it has been introduced.

tag·meme (tag′mēm) *n. Ling.* The smallest unit of grammatical form having meaning. [<Gk. *tagma* arrangement + *-eme*, on analogy with *phoneme* and *morpheme*] — **tag·me′mics** *n.*

Ta·hi·ti (tä·hē′tē, tī′tē) The largest island of the Society group; 600 square miles; capital, Papeete; formerly *Otaheite.*

tai·ga (tī′gə) *n.* The far northern coniferous forest of Siberia and by extension of Eurasia and America, extending to the northern limit of trees. [<Russian]

tail[1] (tāl) *n.* **1** The hindmost part or rear end of an animal's body, especially when prolonged beyond the rest of the body. ◆ Collateral adjective: *caudal.* **2** Any slender, flexible, terminal prolongation of the body of a structure: the *tail* of a shirt or kite. **3** *Astron.* The luminous sheaf extending from the nucleus of a comet. **4** The hind, back, or inferior portion of anything. **5** *pl. Colloq.* The reverse side of a coin. **6** The lower end of a stream or pool. **7** Anything of tail-like appearance; a body of persons in single file; a queue; also, a retinue or suite. **8** A pigtail. **9** *Aeron.* One of several fixed horizontal or vertical surfaces of an airplane structure placed at some distance to the rear of the main bearing surfaces. **10** The rear portion of a bomb, projectile, rocket, or guided missile, usually equipped with vanes. **11** The bottom of a printed page. **12** *pl. Colloq.* A man's full-dress suit; also, a swallow-tailed coat. **13** The back end of a wagon. **14** *Colloq.* The trail or course taken by a fugitive: The police were on his *tail.* — *v.t.* **1** To furnish with a tail. **2** To cut off the tail of. **3** To be the tail or end of: to *tail* a procession. **4** To join (one thing) to the end of another. **5** To insert and fasten by one end, as a beam into a wall: with *in* or *on.* **6** *Colloq.* To follow secretly and stealthily; shadow.— *v.i.* **7** To extend or proceed in a line. **8** *Colloq.* To follow close behind. **9** To diminish gradually: His voice *tailed* off. **10** To be inserted and fastened at one end, as a beam. **11** *Naut.* To swing or go aground stern foremost: The ship *tailed* into the wind. — *adj.* **1** Rearmost; hindmost: the *tail* end. **2** Following; coming from behind: a *tail* wind. ◆ Homophone: *tale.* [OE *tægl*] — **tail′less** *adj.*

tail[2] (tāl) *Law adj.* Restricted; limited; abridged; restricted in succession to particular

heirs: an estate *tail.* — *n.* A cutting off, abridgment, or limitation of ownership; an entail: an estate in *tail.* ◆ Homophone: *tale.* [<OF *taillié*, pp. of *taillier* cut]

tail beam Tailpiece (def. 4).

tail coverts *Ornithol.* The feathers that lie at the base of the tail feathers above and below.

tail-first (tāl′fûrst′) *adv.* Backward; with the hind side foremost. Also **tail′fore′most** (-fôr′. mōst, -fōr′-).

tail-gate (tāl′gāt′) *n.* **1** A hinged or vertically sliding board or gate closing the back end of a truck, wagon, etc. Also **tail·board** (tāl′bôrd′, -bōrd′). **2** One of the gates at the lower level of a canal lock. — *v.t. & v.i.* **·gat·ed, ·gat·ing** *U.S. Slang* To drive too close behind for safety: impatient drivers *tailgating* in a no-passing zone.

tail gun A gun mounted in the tail section of an airplane.

tail-heav·y (tāl′hev′ē) *adj.* Having too much weight at the rear: a *tail-heavy* airplane: opposed to *nose-heavy.*

tail·ing (tā′ling) *n.* **1** Refuse or residue from grain after milling, or from ground ore after washing: usually plural. **2** The inner, covered portion of a projecting brick or stone.

tail light A light attached to the rear of a vehicle. Also **tail lamp.**

tai·lor (tā′lər) *n.* One who makes to order or repairs men's or women's outer garments. — *v.i.* **1** To do a tailor's work. — *v.t.* **2** To fit with garments: He is well *tailored.* **3** To work at or make by tailoring: to *tailor* a coat. ◆ Collateral adjective: *sartorial.* [<OF *tailleor* <*taillier* cut <LL *taliare* split, cut, prob. <L *talea* rod]

tailor bee Any of certain leaf-cutting bees (family *Megachilidae*) that line their nests with pieces of leaves.

tai·lor·bird (tā′lər·bûrd′) *n.* A bird (genus *Sutoria*) of Asia and Africa, related to the warblers, that stitches leaves together to form a receptacle for its nest. See illustration under NEST.

tai·lor·ing (tā′lər·ing) *n.* **1** A tailor's trade or occupation. **2** The making or altering of a garment by a tailor. **3** The style and fit resulting from the work of a tailor.

tai·lor-made (tā′lər·mād′) *adj.* Made by a tailor: said especially of women's clothes of a plain, close-fitting, usually heavier type, as for walking, etc.: opposed to *ready-made.* — *n. Colloq.* A commercially prepared cigarette, as opposed to one which is rolled by hand.

tail·piece (tāl′pēs′) *n.* **1** Any endpiece or appendage. **2** In a violin or similar instrument, a piece of wood, as ebony, at the sounding-board end, having the strings fastened to it. **3** *Printing* An ornamental design on the lower blank portion of a short page. **4** A piece inserted by tailing, as a floor timber.

tail·race (tāl′rās′) *n.* **1** That part of a millrace below the water wheel, bearing away the spent water. **2** *Mining* The channel for water to remove tailings.

tail·skid (tāl′skid′) *n. Aeron.* A runner fixed beneath the tail of an airplane.

tail·spin (tāl′spin′) *n.* **1** *Aeron.* The descent of an airplane along a helical path at a steep angle, either by accident or with power of recovery by manipulation of the controls. **2** *Colloq.* A sudden, sharp, emotional upheaval, often resulting in loss of control: He went into a *tailspin* over her.

tail·stock (tāl′stok′) *n.* That standard or stock of a lathe through which passes the non-rotating spindle or dead center.

TAILSPIN

tail wind A wind blowing in the same general direction as the flight of an aircraft or course of a ship.

tain[1] (tān) *n.* **1** Very thin plate. **2** Tinfoil suitable for backing mirrors. [Prob. aphetic var. of F *étain* tin]

tain[2] (tôn) *n.* Literally, a cattle raid; by extension, any of numerous Old Irish epics about a cattle raid. [<Irish *táin*]

Tai·nan (tī′nän′) A city of west central Taiwan.

taint (tānt) *v.t.* **1** To imbue with an offensive, noxious, or deteriorating quality or principle; infect with decay; render corrupt or poisonous. **2** To render morally corrupt or vitiated; contaminate; pollute. **3** *Obs.* To tincture; tinge. — *v.i.* **4** To be or become tainted. See synonyms under POLLUTE. — *n.* **1** A trace or germ of decay; a cause or result of corruption. **2** A moral stain or blemish; spot. [Fusion of aphetic form of ATTAINT and F *teint*, pp. of *teindre* tinge, color <L *tingere*]

Tai·pei (tī′pā′) The capital of Taiwan, in the northern part: Japanese *Taihoku*. Also **Tai′·peh′, T′ai′–pei′.**

Tai·wan (tī′wän′) An island off the coast of SE China, comprising a province, and, together with the Pescadores, the National Republic of China; 13,890 square miles; capital, Taipei; ceded to Japan, 1895–1945: formerly *Formosa*. — **Tai′wan·ese′** (-ēz, -ēs) *n. & adj.*

taj (täj) *n. Persian* A diadem or crown; a headdress of distinction; specifically, a tall cap worn by Moslem dervishes.

take (tāk) *v.* **took, tak·en, tak·ing** *v.t.* **1** To lay hold of; grasp. **2** To get possession of; seize. **3** To seize forcibly; capture; catch. **4** To catch in a trap or snare. **5** To gain in competition; win. **6** To choose; select. **7** To obtain by purchase; buy. **8** To rent or hire; lease: to *take* lodgings. **9** To receive regularly by payment; subscribe to, as a periodical. **10** To assume occupancy of: to *take* a chair. **11** To assume the responsibilities or duties of: to *take* office. **12** To bring or accept into some relation to oneself: He *took* a wife. **13** To assume as a symbol or badge: to *take* the veil. **14** To impose upon oneself; subject oneself to: to *take* a vow. **15** To remove or carry off: with *away*. **16** To remove from the proper place; misappropriate; steal. **17** To remove by death. **18** To subtract or deduct. **19** To be subjected to; undergo: to *take* a beating. **20** To submit to; accept passively: to *take* an insult. **21** To become affected with; contract: He *took* cold. **22** To affect: The fever *took* him at dawn. **23** To captivate; charm or delight: The dress *took* her fancy. **24** To conduct oneself in response to; react to: How did she *take* the news? **25** To undertake to deal with; contend with; handle: to *take* an examination. **26** To consider; deem: I *take* him for an honest man. **27** To understand; comprehend. **28** To strike in a specified place; hit: The blow *took* him on the forehead. **29** *Colloq.* To aim or direct: He *took* a shot at the target. **30** To carry with one; transport; convey: *Take* your umbrella! **31** To lead: This road *takes* you to town. **32** To escort; conduct: Who *took* her to the dance? **33** To receive into the body, as by eating, inhaling, etc.: *Take* a deep breath. **34** To accept, as something offered, due, or given; have conferred on one: to *take* a bribe; to *take* a degree. **35** To let in; admit: The ship is *taking* water; The car will *take* only six people. **36** To indulge oneself in; enjoy: to *take* a nap. **37** To perform, as an action: to *take* a stride. **38** To avail oneself of (an opportunity, etc.). **39** To put into effect; adopt: to *take* measures; to *take* advice. **40** To use up or consume; require as necessary; demand: The piano *takes* too much space; That *takes* a lot of nerve. **41** To make use of; apply: They *took* clubs to him; to *take* pains. **42** To travel by means of: to *take* a train to Boston. **43** To go to; seek: to *take* cover. **44** To ascertain or obtain by measuring, computing, etc.: to *take* a census. **45** To obtain or derive from some source; adopt or copy. **46** To obtain by writing; write down or copy: to *take* notes. **47** To obtain a likeness or representation of, as by drawing or photographing; also, to obtain (a likeness, picture, etc.) in such a manner. **48** To experience; feel: to *take* pride in an achievement. **49** To conceive or feel: She *took* a dislike to him. **50** To become impregnated with; absorb: The cloth will not *take* the pattern. **51** *Slang* To cheat; deceive. **52** *Gram.* To require by construction or usage: The verb *takes* a direct object. — *v.i.* **53** To get possession. **54** To engage; catch, as mechanical parts. **55** To begin to grow; germinate. **56** To have the intended effect: The vaccination *took.* **57** To become popular; gain favor or currency, as a play. **58** To admit of being photographed: His face *takes* well. **59** To detract: with *from.* **60** To become (ill or sick). **61** To make one's way; go. See synonyms under ABSTRACT, ASSUME, CARRY, CATCH. — **to take after 1** To resemble. **2** To follow as an example. — **to take amiss** To be offended by. — **to take at one's word** To believe. — **to take back 1** To regain. **2** To retract. — **to take breath** To pause, as from working. — **to take down 1** To pull down, as a building. **2** To dismantle; disassemble. **3** To humble. **4** To write down; make a record of. — **to take heart** To gain courage or confidence. — **to take in 1** To admit; receive. **2** To lessen in size or scope. **3** To furl or brail (sail). **4** To include; embrace. **5** To understand. **6** To cheat or deceive. **7** To visit as part of a tour: Did you *take* in the Louvre? **8** To receive into one's home for pay, as lodgers or work. — **to take in vain** To use profanely or blasphemously, as the name of a deity. — **to take it 1** To assume; understand. **2** To endure hardship, abuse, etc. — **to take off 1** To remove, as a coat. **2** To carry away. **3** To kill. **4** To deduct. **5** To mimic; burlesque. **6** To rise from the ground or water in starting a flight, as an airplane. **7** To leave; depart. — **to take on 1** To hire; employ. **2** To undertake to deal with; handle. **3** *Colloq.* To exhibit violent emotion. — **to take out 1** To extract; remove. **2** To obtain from the proper authority, as a license or patent. **3** To lead or escort. — **to take over 1** To assume control of. **2** To convey. — **to take place** To happen. — **to take stock 1** To make an inventory. **2** To estimate probability, position, etc.; consider. — **to take the field** To begin a campaign or game. — **to take to 1** To betake oneself to: to *take* to one's bed. **2** To develop the practice of, or an addiction to: He *took* to drink. **3** To become fond of; be attracted by. — **to take to heart 1** To be deeply affected by. — **to take up 1** To raise or lift. **2** To make smaller or less; shorten or tighten. **3** To pay, as a note or mortgage. **4** To accept as stipulated: to *take up* an option. **5** To begin or begin again; resume. **6** To reprove or criticize. **7** To occupy, engage, or consume, as space or time. **8** To acquire an interest in or devotion to: to *take up* a cause. — **to take up with** *Colloq.* To become friendly with; associate with. — *n.* **1** The act of taking, or that which is taken. **2** An uninterrupted run of the camera and sound apparatus in recording any portion of a motion picture. **3** *Slang* The money collected; receipts. **4** The quantity collected at one time: the *take* of fish. [OE *tacan* <ON *taka*]

take–down (tāk′doun′) *adj.* Fitted for being taken apart or down easily: a *take–down* shack; a *take–down* rifle. — *n.* **1** Any article so constructed as to be taken apart easily. **2** The part of a take–down mechanism by means of which it is taken apart or down. **3** *Colloq.* The act of humiliating any one; humiliation.

take–home pay (tāk′hōm′) The remainder of one's wages or salary after tax and other payroll deductions.

take–in (tāk′in′) *n. Colloq.* An act of cheating or hoaxing.

take–off (tāk′ôf′, -of′) *n.* **1** *Colloq.* A satirical representation; caricature. **2** In horsemanship and athletics, the spot at which the feet leave the ground in leaping. **3** *Aeron.* The act of rising from and leaving the ground or water in an aircraft flight.

tak·er (tā′kər) *n.* One who takes; specifically, one who accepts a wager; also, a collector: a ticket *taker.*

take–up (tāk′up′) *n.* **1** *Mech.* A device for taking up lost motion or drawing in the slack of a thing, as in a loom. **2** The act of tightening or taking up.

tak·ing (tā′king) *adj.* **1** Fascinating; captivating. **2** *Colloq.* Contagious; infectious. — *n.* **1** The act of one who takes. **2** The thing or things taken; in fishing, a catch; haul; in the plural, receipts, as of money. **3** *Obs.* Agitation; perplexity; distress. — **tak′ing·ly** *adv.* — **tak′ing·ness** *n.*

tal·a·poin (tal′ə·poin) *n.* **1** A Buddhist priest or monk. **2** A West African monkey (*Cercopithecus talapoin*) of the guenon group, smallest of the Old World monkeys. [<Pg. *talapões*, pl. of *talapão* <Burmese *tala poi* our master]

tal·bot (tôl′bət, tal′-) *n.* A sleuthhound, supposed to be related to the bloodhound. [after *Talbot*, English family name]

talc (talk) *n.* A soft, hydrous magnesium silicate, $H_2Mg_3(SiO_3)_4$, used in making paper, soap, toilet powder, lubricants, etc. Soapstone and French chalk are varieties of talc. — *v.t.* **talcked** or **talced, talck·ing** or **talc·ing** To treat with talc; to *talc* a photographic plate. [<F <Med. L *talcum* <Arabic *talq* <Persian *talk*]

talc·ose (tal′kōs) *adj.* Composed of or containing talc. Also **talc′ous** (tal′kəs).

tal·cum (tal′kəm) *n.* Talc. [<Med. L. See TALC.]

talcum powder Finely powdered and purified talc, used as a dusting agent, filter, and for the relief of chafed skin and prickly heat.

tale (tāl) *n.* **1** That which is told or related; a story; recital. **2** Hence, a connected narrative or account, whether oral or written, of an actual, legendary, or fictitious event or series of events. **3** An idle or malicious report; a piece of gossip. **4** A deliberately untrue story; a lie; falsehood. **5** *Archaic* A counting or enumeration; reckoning; numbering. **6** *Archaic* That which is counted; an amount; total; sum. **7** *Obs.* Speech; talk; also, the language of a country. ◆ Homophone: *tail.* [OE *talu* speech, narrative. Akin to TELL, TALK.]

tale·bear·er (tāl′bâr′ər) *n.* One who tells mischievous tales about other persons. — **tale′·bear′ing** *adj. & n.*

tal·ent (tal′ənt) *n.* **1** Mental endowments or capacities of a superior character; marked mental ability; also, mental ability in general. **2** A particular and uncommon aptitude for some special work or activity; a faculty or gift: a usage founded on a Scriptural parable (*Matt.* xxv 14–30), mental power being considered as a divine trust. **3** People of skill or ability, collectively: the *talent* of stage, screen, and radio. **4** *U.S. Slang* In horse-racing circles, those who make bets or take odds on their individual judgment and responsibility: distinguished from the bookmakers. **5** An ancient weight and denomination of money, varying in weight and value among different nations and in different periods. **6** *Obs.* Inclination; disposition. See synonyms under ABILITY, GENIUS. [OE *talente* appetite, will, inclination <L *talentum*, a sum of money <Gk. *talanton* weight, thing weighed]

tal·ent·ed (tal′ən·tid) *adj.* Having mental ability; gifted. See synonyms under CLEVER.

talent scout One whose business it is to discover talented or exceptionally gifted people, especially those suitable for dramatic or motion-picture careers.

tales·man (tālz′mən) *n. pl.* **·men** (-mən) One summoned to make up a jury when the regular panel is exhausted. [<TALES + MAN]

tale·tel·ler (tāl′tel′ər) *n.* **1** One who tells stories, etc.; a raconteur. **2** A talebearer. — **tale′tell′ing** *adj. & n.*

tal·i·grade (tal′ə·grād) *adj. Zool.* Walking on the outer surface of the foot. [<L *talus* ankle + -GRADE]

tal·i·on (tal′ē·ən) *n.* Retaliation, as a form of justice. [<F <L *talio, -onis* <*talis* such]

tal·i·ped (tal′ə·ped) *adj.* Suffering from or afflicted with talipes; clubfooted. — *n.* A clubfooted person. [See TALIPES]

tal·i·pes (tal′ə·pēz′) *n. Pathol.* **1** Malformation of the foot. **2** A clubfoot. [<NL <L *talus* ankle + *pes, pedis* foot]

tal·i·pom·a·nus (tal′ə·pom′ə·nəs) *n. Pathol.* Clubhand. [<*talipo-* (<TALIPES) + L *manus* a hand]

tal·i·pot (tal′ə·pot) *n.* A stately and valuable East Indian palm (*Corypha umbraculifera*) crowned by large leaves often used as fans, umbrellas, and as a house covering. Also **talipot palm.** [<Bengali *tālipāt* palm leaf <Skt. *tālī* fan palm + *pattra* leaf]

tal·is·man (tal′is·mən, -iz-) *n. pl.* **·mans** **1**

Something supposed to produce or capable of producing extraordinary effects; a charm. **2** An astrological charm or symbol supposed to benefit or protect the possessor, especially by exerting magical or occult influence; in a wider sense, any amulet. [< F < Sp. < Arabic *tilsam, ṭilasm* magic figure < LGk. *telesma* a sacred rite < Gk. *teleein* initiate < *telos* end, completion]

Synonyms: amulet, charm. An *amulet* or *talisman* is strictly a material object; a *charm* may be a movement or a form of words. An *amulet* is ordinarily worn upon the person as a protection against disease, injury, or death. A *talisman* is any object supposed to work wonders, like Aladdin's lamp, whether kept in one's possession or not.

tal·is·man·ic (tal′is·man′ik) *adj.* Exerting magical or occult power. Also **tal′is·man′i·cal.**

talk (tôk) *v.i.* **1** To express or exchange thoughts in audible words; communicate by speech; speak or converse. **2** To communicate by means other than speech: to *talk* with one's fingers. **3** To speak irrelevantly; prate; chatter. **4** To confer; consult. **5** To gossip. **6** To make sounds suggestive of speech. **7** *Colloq.* To give information; inform. — *v.t.* **8** To express in words; utter. **9** To use in speaking; converse in: to *talk* Spanish. **10** To converse about; discuss: to *talk* business. **11** To bring to a specified condition or state by talking: to *talk* one into doing something. **12** To pass or spend, as time, in talking. — **to talk back** To answer impudently. — **to talk big** *Slang* To brag; boast. — **to talk down** To silence by talking; outtalk. — **to talk down to** To speak to (an audience of lower or supposedly lower intelligence than one's own) in simple, obvious words; speak to patronizingly. — **to talk shop** To talk about one's work. — **to talk up 1** To discuss, especially so as to promote; praise; extol. **2** *Colloq.* To speak loudly or boldly. — *n.* **1** The act of talking; conversation; speech, especially when informal. **2** Report, rumor: We heard *talk* of war. **3** That which is talked about; a topic; theme; subject of conversation. **4** A conference for discussion or deliberation; a council. **5** Mere words; verbiage. **6** A language, dialect, or lingo; an argot: baseball *talk.* See synonyms under CONVERSATION. [ME *talken,* prob. freq. of *talen,* OE *talian* reckon, speak. Related to TELL, TALE.]

Synonyms (verb): chat, chatter, converse, discourse, speak. To *talk* is to utter a succession of connected words, ordinarily with the expectation of being listened to. To *speak* is to give articulate utterance even to a single word; the officer *speaks* the word of command, but does not *talk* it. To *chat* is ordinarily to utter in a familiar, conversational way; to *chatter* is to *talk* in an empty, ceaseless way like a magpie. See SPEAK.

talk·a·thon (tô′kə·thon′) *n. Colloq.* A prolonged session of talking, debating, etc. [< TALK + (MAR)ATHON]

talk·a·tive (tô′kə·tiv) *adj.* Given to much talking. See synonyms under GARRULOUS. — **talk′a·tive·ly** *adv.* — **talk′a·tive·ness** *n.*

talk·er (tô′kər) *n.* One who talks; also, a loquacious person.

talk·ie (tô′kē) *n. Colloq.* A motion picture with spoken words and sound effects. Also **talking picture.**

talk·ing-to (tô′king·too′) *n. pl.* **·tos** *Colloq.* A scolding; berating.

talk show A television or radio show in which a well-known personality interviews invited guests, often celebrities, in TV usually before a live audience.

talk·y (tô′kē) *adj.* **talk·i·er, talk·i·est** Talkative.

tall (tôl) *adj.* **1** Having more than average height; high or lofty: a *tall* building. **2** Having specified height: He is five feet *tall.* **3** *Colloq.* Inordinate; extravagant; boastful: *tall* talk; also, unbelievable; remarkable: a *tall* story. **4** *Colloq.* Large; excellent; grand: a *tall* dinner. **5** *Obs.* Handsome; fine; proud. **6** *Obs.* Brave; sturdy; spirited. — *adv. Colloq.* Proudly; handsomely: He walks *tall.* [OE *getæl* swift, prompt] — **tall′ness** *n.*

Tal·la·has·see (tal′ə·has′ē) The capital of Florida, in the northern part.

tall·boy (tôl′boi′) *n.* **1** *Brit.* A highboy. **2** A variety of chimney pot.

Tal·linn (täl′lin) The capital of Estonia, a port

in the NW part, on the Gulf of Finland: German *Reval,* Russian *Revel.* Also **Tal′lin.**

tal·lith (tal′ith, tä′lis) *n.* A fringed mantle of fine linen, originally covering the head and falling over the shoulders, now worn around the shoulders by Jews engaged in prayer. [< Hebrew *tallīth* cover, sheet, robe]

tall oil A fatty resinous liquid obtained as a by-product from wood pulp: it is used as an emulsifying agent in various manufacturing processes. [< Sw. *tallöl* pine oil]

tal·low (tal′ō) *n.* **1** A mixture of the harder animal fats, as of beef or mutton, refined for use in candles, soaps, oleomargarine, etc. **2** A vegetable fat obtained from the bayberry. — *v.t.* **1** To smear with tallow. **2** To fatten. [ME *talgh,* prob. < MLG *talg, talch*] — **tal′low·y** *adj.*

tal·ly (tal′ē) *n. pl.* **·lies 1** A piece of wood on which notches or scores are cut as marks of number. **2** A score or mark; hence, a reckoning; account. **3** A counterpart; duplicate. **4** A mark indicative of tale or number: used to denote one in a series. **5** A label; tag. — *v.* **·lied, ·ly·ing** *v.t.* **1** To score on a tally; mark; record. **2** To reckon; count; estimate: often with *up.* **3** To mark or cut corresponding notches in; cause to correspond. — *v.i.* **4** To correspond; agree precisely; fit: His story *tallies* with yours. **5** To keep score. [< AF *tallie* < L *talea* rod, cutting] — **tal′li·er** *n.*

tal·ly·ho (tal′ē·hō′) *interj.* A huntsman's cry to hounds when the quarry is sighted. — *n.* **1** The cry of "tallyho." **2** A four-in-hand coach. — *v.t.* To urge on, as hounds, with the cry of "tallyho." — *v.i.* To cry "tallyho." [Alter. of F *taïaut,* a hunting cry]

tal·ly·man (tal′ē·mən) *n. pl.* **·men** (-mən) **1** One who keeps a count or a tally, especially of votes. **2** One who keeps a record of number, volume, and measurement, as of timber.

Tal·mud (tal′mud, täl′mŏŏd) *n.* The body of Jewish civil and religious law (and related commentaries and discussion) not comprised in the Pentateuch, commonly including the Mishna and the Gemara, but sometimes limited to the latter. [< Hebrew *talmūdh* instruction < *lāmadh* learn] — **Tal·mud′ic** or **·i·cal** *adj.* — **Tal′mud·ist** *n.*

tal·on (tal′ən) *n.* **1** The claw of a bird or other animal, especially of a bird of prey: often applied figuratively, as to a grasping human hand. **2** A projection on the bolt of a lock on which the key presses in shooting the bolt. **3** In card games, the part of a pack left on the table after the deal; the stock. **4** The heel of a sword blade. [< OF, spur < L *talus* heel] — **tal′oned** *adj.*

ta·lus (tā′ləs) *n. pl.* **·li** (-lī) **1** *Anat.* The astragalus. **2** A slope, as of a tapering wall. **3** *Geol.* The sloping mass of rock fragments below a cliff. Compare SCREE. **4** The slope given to the face of an earthwork or other fortification. [< L, ankle, heel]

tam (tam) *n.* A tam-o'-shanter.

tam·a·ble (tā′mə·bəl) *adj.* Capable of being tamed. Also **tame′a·ble.**

ta·ma·le (tə·mä′lē) *n.* A Mexican dish made of crushed Indian corn and meat, seasoned with red pepper, wrapped in corn husks, dipped in oil, and cooked by steam. Also **ta·mal** (tə·mäl′). [< Am. Sp. *tamales,* pl. of *tamal* < Nahuatl *tamalli*]

ta·man·dua (tə·man′dwə, tä′män·dwä′) *n.* A small arboreal ant-eater (*Tamandua tetra-dactyla*) of Central and South America. Also **tam·an·du** (tam′ən·dŏŏ). [< Pg. < Tupian *taixi* ant + *mondé* catch]

tam·a·rack (tam′ə·rak) *n.* **1** The American larch (*Larix laricina*) common all over northern North America. **2** Its wood: also called *hackmatack.* **3** The lodgepole pine of the Pacific coast. [< Algonquian]

ta·ma·rau (tä′mə·rou′) *n.* A small, dark-brown, short-horned buffalo (genus *Anoa*) of the island of Mindoro, standing about 40 inches high. Also spelled *timarau.* [< native name]

tam·a·rin (tam′ə·rin) *n.* One of various squirrel-like marmosets of Guiana and the Amazon valley; especially, the **silky tamarin** (*Leontocebus rosalia*). [< F < native Cariban name]

tam·a·rind (tam′ə·rind) *n.* **1** A tropical tree (*Tamarindus indica*) of the bean family, with hard yellow wood, pinnate leaves, and showy yellow flowers striped with red. **2** The fruit of

this tree, a flat pod with soft acid pulp used in preserves and as a laxative drink. [< Sp. *tamarindo* < Arabic *tamr hindi* Indian date]

tam·a·risk (tam′ə·risk) *n.* An evergreen shrub (genus *Tamarix*) of the Mediterranean region, western Asia, and India, with slender branches bearing small, pinkish-white flowers in racemes. [< LL *tamariscus,* var. of L *tamarix* a tamarisk]

tam·bour (tam′bŏŏr) *n.* **1** A drum. **2** A light wooden frame, usually circular, on which material for embroidering may be stretched; also, a fabric embroidered on such a frame. **3** A palisade for defending an entrance to a fortified work. — *v.t. & v.i.* To embroider on a tambour. [< F < Arabic *ṭambūr* a stringed instrument; prob. infl. in meaning by OF *tabour* a tabor]

TAMBOURS
a. Snare drum. *b.* Bass drum. *c.* Bongo drums.

tam·bou·rin (tam′bə·rin) *n.* **1** A long, narrow, oblong drum, originating in Provence. **2** A gay, 18th century Provençal dance, or the music accompanying it. [< F, dim. of *tambour*]

tam·bou·rine (tam′bə·rēn′) *n.* A musical instrument like the head of a drum, with jingles in the rim, played by striking it with the hand; a timbrel. [< F]

tame (tām) *adj.* **tam·er, tam·est 1** Having lost its native wildness or shyness; domesticated. **2** In agriculture, brought under or produced by cultivation: *tame* hay or land. **3** Docile; tractable; hence, subdued or subjugated; spiritless; also, gentle; harmless. **4** Lacking in effectiveness; uninteresting; dull; flat; insipid. See synonyms under DOCILE, FLAT, MEAGER. — *v.t.* **tamed, tam·ing 1** To make tame; domesticate. **2** To bring into subjection or obedience; conquer or take the spirit or heart from; render spiritless. **3** To tone down; soften, as glaring colors. See synonyms under RECLAIM. [OE *tam*] — **tame′ly** *adv.* — **tame′ness** *n.* — **tam′er** *n.*

ta·mein (tä·mīn′) *n.* A draped garment, similar to an Indian sari, worn by Burmese women. [< Burmese *thamein*]

tame·less (tām′lis) *adj.* Untamable. — **tame′less·ness** *n.*

tam·is (tam′is) *n.* **1** A strainer of cloth or gauze. **2** A fabric used for straining. Also **tam′my.** [< F, sieve]

tam-o'-shan·ter (tam′ə·shan′tər) *n.* A Scottish cap with a tight headband and a full, flat top, sometimes with a pompon or tassel. [after TAM O' SHANTER]

tamp (tamp) *v.t.* **1** To force down or pack closer by firm, repeated blows. **2** To ram down, as a packing on a charge in a blasthole, in order to increase the explosive effect. — *n.* A tamper. [Back formation < TAMPION]

tam·pa·la (tam′pə·lə) *n.* A horticultural variety of an Asian plant (*Amaranthus tricolor*), cultivated in the United States and esteemed for its edible, spinachlike leaves. [< Hind.]

tam·pan (tam′pan) *n.* A soft-bodied tick (genus *Argas*) of cosmopolitan distribution, a dangerous bloodsucking parasite of poultry whose bite is often injurious to men. Also called *miana bug.* [< native S. African name]

tam·per[1] (tam′pər) *v.i.* **1** To meddle; interfere: usually with *with.* **2** To make changes, especially so as to damage, corrupt, etc.: with *with:* to *tamper* with a manuscript. **3** To use corrupt measures, as bribery; scheme or plot. [Var. of TEMPER] — **tam′per·er** *n.*

tam·per[2] (tam′pər) *n.* **1** One who tamps. **2** An instrument for tamping. **3** *Physics* A reflector (def. 4).

tam·pi·on (tam′pē·ən) *n.* A tompion. [< F *tampon,* nasal var. of *tapon, tape* a bung < Gmc.]

tam·pon (tam′pon) *n. Med.* A plug of cotton

or lint for insertion in a wound or body cavity. — *v.t.* To plug up, as a wound, with a tampon. [See TAMPION]

tam-tam (tum′tum′) *n.* **1** A type of drum, used in the East Indies and western Africa. See TOM-TOM. **2** A Chinese gong. — *v.i.* To play on a tam-tam. [<Hind.; imit. in origin]

tan (tan) *v.* **tanned, tan·ning** *v.t.* **1** To convert into leather, as hides or skins, by treatment with an infusion of tannin obtained from the bark of the oak, hemlock, etc. **2** To make durable or hard, as fishnets or sails. **3** To bronze, as the skin, by exposure to sunlight. **4** *Colloq.* To thrash; flog. — *v.i.* **5** To become tanned, as hides or the skin. — *n.* **1** *Chem.* **a** Tanbark. **b** Tannin. **2** A yellowish-brown color tinged with red. **3** A dark or brown coloring of the skin, resulting from exposure to the sun: a coat of *tan.* — *adj.* **1** Of a yellowish- or reddish-brown; tan-colored. **2** Used in or pertaining to tanning. [OE *tannian* <Med. L *tannare* <*tanum* tanbark, prob. <Celtic. Cf. Breton *tann* oak.]

tan·a·ger (tan′ə·jər) *n.* Any of a family (*Thraupidae*) of arboreal oscine American birds related to the finches and noted for the brilliant plumage of the male. Most of the species are tropical, but a few migrate to the United States, especially the **scarlet tanager** (*Piranga erythromelas*) and the **western tanager** (*P. ludoviciana*). [<NL *tanagra* <Pg. *tangara* <Tupian] — **tan′a·grine** (-grēn) *adj.*

tan·bark (tan′bärk′) *n.* **1** The bark of certain trees, especially oak or hemlock, containing tannin in quantity, and used in tanning leather. **2** Spent bark from the tan vats, used on circus arenas, racetracks, etc.

tan·dem (tan′dəm) *adv.* One in front of or before another: said of two or more persons or things so arranged, and of horses harnessed in single file instead of abreast. — *n.* **1** Two or more horses harnessed and driven in single file; also, such a turnout, including both horses and vehicle. **2** A bicycle with seats for two persons, one behind the other: also **tandem bicycle. 3** Any arrangement of two or more persons or things placed one before another. — *adj.* Consisting of or being two arranged one before another. [<L, at length (of time); used in puns in sense of "lengthwise"]

tang (tang) *n.* **1** A slender shank or tongue projecting from some metal part, as the end of a sword blade or of a chisel, for inserting into or fixing upon a handle, hilt, etc.; also, a tonguelike part, as of a belt buckle. **2** A penetrating taste, flavor, or odor, sometimes a disagreeable one; also, a trace; hint: a *tang* of pepper. **3** Any distinct quality, other than one that is sweet. — *v.t.* To provide with a tang. [<ON *tongi* a point, dagger]

Tan·gan·yi·ka (tan′gən·yē′kə, tang′-), **Lake** A lake in the Great Rift Valley of east central Africa, SW of Victoria Nyanza; 12,700 square miles; 400 miles long; the longest and deepest (4,700 feet) lake in Africa, second deepest fresh-water body in the world.

tan·ge·lo (tan′jə·lō) *n.* *pl.* **·los 1** A loose-skinned orangelike fruit, a hybrid of the tangerine and the pomelo. **2** The tree (genus *Citrus*) on which it grows. [<TANG(ERINE) + (POM)ELO]

tan·gen·cy (tan′jən·sē) *n.* *pl.* **·cies** The state of being tangent. Also **tan′gence.**

tan·gent (tan′jənt) *adj.* **1** *Geom.* Meeting at a point or along a line without further coincidence or intersection: said of either or both of two lines or surfaces so touching. **2** Touching; in contact. — *n.* **1** *Geom.* **a** A line tangent to a curve at any point. **b** The straight line through two coincident points of a curve. **c** The length of a tangent line from the point of contact to the axis of abscissas. **2** *Trig.* One of the functions of an angle; the quotient of the ordinate divided by the abscissa. **3** A sharp change in course or direction. — **to fly** (or **go**) **off on a tangent** *Colloq.* To make a sharp or sudden change in direction or course of action. [<L *tangens, -entis,* ppr. of *tangere* touch]

tan·gen·tial (tan-jen′shəl) *adj.* **1** Of, pertaining to, or moving in the direction of a tangent. **2** Touching slightly. **3** Divergent. Also **tan·gen′tal** (-jen′təl). — **tan·gen·ti·al′i·ty** (-shē-al′-

ə·tē) *n.* — **tan·gen′tial·ly** *adv.*

tan·ger·ine (tan′jə·rēn′) *n.* **1** A small, juicy orange with a loose, easily removed skin; a variety of mandarin (def. 2). **2** A slightly burnt-orange color, like the color of the tangerine. [from *Tangier*]

tan·gi·ble (tan′jə·bəl) *adj.* **1** Perceptible by touch; also, within reach by touch. **2** Figuratively, capable of being apprehended by the mind; of definite shape; not elusive or unreal: *tangible* evidence. **3** *Law* Perceptible to the senses; corporeal; material: *tangible* property. See synonyms under EVIDENT, PHYSICAL. — *n.* **1** That which is tangible. **2** *pl.* Material assets. [<F <L *tangibilis* <*tangere* touch] — **tan·gi·bil′i·ty, tan′gi·ble·ness** *n.* — **tan′gi·bly** *adv.*

Tan·gier (tan·jir′) A port on the northernmost coast of Morocco; formerly an international zone (**Tangier International Zone**; 225 square miles). French **Tan·ger** (tän·zhā′).

tan·gle[1] (tang′gəl) *v.* **·gled, ·gling** *v.t.* **1** To twist or involve in a confused and not readily separable mass. **2** To complicate; ensnare as in a tangle; trap; enmesh. — *v.i.* **3** To be or become entangled. — **to tangle with** *Colloq.* To embroil oneself with. — *n.* **1** A confused intertwining, as of threads or hairs; a snarl. **2** Hence, a state of confusion or complication; a jumbled mess. **3** A state of perplexity or bewilderment. [Nasalized var. of obs. *tagle* <Scand. Cf. dial. Sw. *taggla* disorder.] — **tan′gler** *n.*

tan·gle[2] (tang′gəl) *n.* **1** An edible seaweed (genus *Laminaria*). **2** *Scot.* A tall, lean person. [<ON *thöngull*]

tan·gle·ber·ry (tang′gəl·ber′ē) *n.* *pl.* **·ries** The blue huckleberry (*Gaylussacia frondosa*) of the eastern United States: also called *dangleberry.*

tan·gly (tang′glē) *adj.* Consisting of or being in a tangle.

tan·go (tang′gō) *n.* *pl.* **·gos 1** Any of several Latin-American dances, originally from Argentina, in 2/4 time and characterized by deliberate gliding steps and low dips. **2** Any syncopated tune or melody to which the tango may be danced. — *v.i.* To dance the tango. [<Am. Sp., fiesta <Sp., gipsy dance]

tan·gram (tang′grəm) *n.* A Chinese puzzle consisting of a square card or board cut by straight incisions into different-sized pieces (5 triangles, a square, and a rhomboid) to be combined into a variety of figures. [Arbitrary coinage, after ANAGRAM]

TANGRAM

tang·y (tang′ē) *adj.* **tang·i·er, tang·i·est** Having a tang in taste or odor; pungent.

tan·ist (tan′ist, thôn′-) *n.* Among the ancient Celts, the heir apparent to a chieftainship, elected in the lifetime of a chief from among the chief's kinsmen. [<Irish *tānaiste* second, heir presumptive]

tan·ist·ry (tan′ist·rē, thôn′-) *n.* The succession and life tenure relating to a tanist.

tan·jib (tun·jēb′) *n.* A kind of fine muslin fabric made in India. [<Bengali <Persian *tan-zib,* lit., ornament of the body]

tank (tangk) *n.* **1** A large vessel, basin, or receptacle for holding a fluid. **2** Any natural pool or pond. **3** *Mil.* A heavily armored combat vehicle of the Caterpillar tractor type, propelled by internal-combustion engines and mounting guns of various calibers. — *v.t.* To place or store in a tank. [<Pg. *tanque,* aphetic var. of *estanque* <L *stagnum* pool] — **tank′less** *adj.* — **tank′like** *adj.*

tan·ka (tang′kə) *n.* **1** A Japanese verse form consisting of five lines, of which the first and third have five syllables, and the rest seven. **2** A poem imitating the Japanese tanka in verse form. [<Japanese]

tank·age (tangk′ij) *n.* **1** The act, process, or operation of putting in tanks. **2** The price for storage in tanks. **3** The capacity or contents of a tank. **4** Slaughterhouse waste, as bones and en-

trails, from which the fat has been rendered: used, when dried, as a fertilizer or coarse feed.

tank·ard (tangk′ərd) *n.* A large, one-handled drinking cup, usually made of pewter or silver, often with a cover. [<MDu. *tanckaert* <Med. L *tancardus,* prob. metathetic var. of L *cantharus* tankard, large goblet]

tank destroyer A motor vehicle equipped with an anti-tank gun.

tank·er (tangk′ər) *n.* A cargo vessel especially constructed for the transport of oil and gasoline.

tank farming Hydroponics. — **tank farmer**

tank·ful (tangk′fŏol) *n.* The quantity that fills a tank.

tank town *U.S. Colloq.* A small town where trains stopped to refill from a water tank.

tank trap A camouflaged ditch excavated along the probable route of enemy tanks for the purpose of trapping them.

tan·nage (tan′ij) *n.* The act, process, or operation of tanning.

tan·nate (tan′āt) *n.* *Chem.* A salt or ester of tannic acid.

tanned (tand) Past tense and past participle of TAN.

tan·ner (tan′ər) *n.* One who tans hides.

tan·ner·y (tan′ər·ē) *n.* *pl.* **·ner·ies** A place where leather is tanned.

tan·nic (tan′ik) *adj.* Pertaining to or derived from tannin or tanbark.

tan·nif·er·ous (ta·nif′ər·əs) *adj.* Having or yielding tannin. [<TANNI(N) + -FEROUS]

tan·nin (tan′in) *n.* *Chem.* Any of a group of amorphous, brownish-white, astringent compounds that form shiny scales when extracted, as with water, from gallnuts, sumac, etc. Their principal applications in the arts are in the preparation of ink and the manufacture of leather. Also **tannic acid.** [<F *tanin* <*tan* tan]

tan·ning (tan′ing) *n.* **1** The art or process of converting hides into leather. **2** A bronzing, as of the skin, by exposure to the sun, etc.

tan·sy (tan′zē) *n.* *pl.* **·sies** Any of a genus (*Tanacetum*) of coarse perennial herbs; especially, a species (*T. vulgare*) with yellow flowers and a strongly aromatic and bitter taste, used in medicine for its tonic properties. [<OF *tanesie,* aphetic var. of *athanasie* <LL *athanasia* <Gk., immortality]

tan·ta·lize (tan′tə·līz) *v.t.* **·lized, ·liz·ing** To tease or torment by repeated frustration of hopes or desires. Also *Brit.* **tan′ta·lise.** [from *Tantalus*] — **tan′ta·li·za′tion** *n.* — **tan′ta·liz′er** *n.* — **tan′ta·liz′ing·ly** *adv.*

tan·ta·lum (tan′tə·ləm) *n.* A very hard, heavy, gray, faintly radioactive metallic element (symbol Ta, atomic number 73), nonirritating and unaffected by body liquids, used in alloys and surgical appliances. See PERIODIC TABLE. [<TANTALUS; from its inability to absorb water]

Tan·ta·lus (tan′tə·ləs) In Greek mythology, a rich king, son of Zeus and father of Pelops and Niobe, who was punished in Hades for revealing the secrets of Zeus by being made to stand in water that receded when he tried to drink, and under fruit-laden branches he could not reach.

tan·ta·mount (tan′tə·mount) *adj.* Having equivalent value, effect, or import; equivalent: with *to.* [<AF *tant amunter* amount to as much <L *tantus* as much + OF *amonter* amount. See AMOUNT.]

tan·ta·ra (tan′tə·rä′, tan·tar′ə, -tä′rə) *n.* A quick succession of notes from a horn; also, a hunting cry. [Imit.]

tan·tiv·y (tan·tiv′ē) *adj.* Swift; rapid. — *n. pl.* **·tiv·ies 1** A hunting cry indicating that the chase is at full speed. **2** *Obs.* A rapid, rushing movement. — *adv.* Swiftly; with all speed. [Prob. imit. of the horse's gallop]

tan·trum (tan′trəm) *n.* A petulant fit of passion. [Origin unknown]

Tan·zan·i·a (tan′zə·nē′ə) An independent member of the Commonwealth of Nations consisting of a federation of Tanganyika and Zanzibar in eastern Africa; 362,800 square miles; capital, Dar es Salaam.

Tao·ism (dou′iz·əm, tou′-) *n.* One of the principal religions or philosophies of China, founded about 500 B.C. by Lâo-tse, who taught that happiness could be acquired through obedience to the requirements of man's nature and the simplification of social and political relations, in accordance with the Tao, or Way, the basic principle of the cosmos from which all of nature proceeds. [< Chinese *tao* way, road] —**Tao′ist** *adj.* & *n.* —**Tao·is′tic** *adj.*

tap¹ (tap) *n.* **1** An arrangement for drawing out liquid, as beer from a cask. **2** A faucet or cock; spigot; also, a plug or stopper to close an opening in a cask or other vessel. **3** Liquor drawn from a tap; also, a particular liquor or quality of liquor contained in casks. **4** *Brit.* A place where liquor is served; a bar; taproom. **5** A tool for cutting internal screw threads. **6** A point of connection for an electrical circuit. **7** The act or an instance of wiretapping. —**on tap 1** Contained in a cask; ready for tapping: beer *on tap.* **2** Provided with a tap. **3** Available; ready. —*v.t.* **tapped, tap·ping 1** To provide with a tap or spigot. **2** To pierce or open so as to draw liquid from: to *tap* a sugar-maple tree. **3** To draw (liquid) from a container. **4** To make connection with: to *tap* a gas main. **5** To make connection with secretly: to *tap* a telephone wire. **6** To make an internal screw thread in with a tap: to *tap* a nut. [OE *tæppa*]

tap² (tap) *v.* **tapped, tap·ping** *v.t.* **1** To touch or strike gently. **2** To make or produce by tapping. **3** To apply leather to (the sole or heel of a shoe) in repair. —*v.i.* **4** To strike a light blow or blows, as with the finger tip. —*n.* **1** A gentle or playful blow. **2** Leather, etc., affixed to a shoe sole or heel; also, a metal plate on the toe or heel of a tap-dancer's shoe. **3** *pl.* A military signal by trumpet or beat of drum, sounded after tattoo, for the extinguishing of all lights in soldiers' quarters: often played after a military burial. [< OF *taper*]

ta·pa (tä′pä) *n.* The bark of the Asian paper-mulberry tree (*Broussonetia papyrifera*), used in making a kind of cloth, **tapa cloth.** [< native Polynesian name]

tap·a·der·a (tap′ə-dâr′ə) *n.* The leather hood of the stirrup of a Mexican saddle. Also **tap′a·der′o.** [< Sp., cover < *tapar* stop up]

tap·a·lo (tap′ə-lō) *n. pl.* **·los** A scarf or shawl of coarse cloth worn in Latin-American countries. [< Am. Sp., lit., cover it, imperative of *tapar* cover + *lo* it]

tap-dance (tap′dans′, -däns′) *v.i.* To dance or perform a tap dance. —**tap′-danc′er** *n.*

tap dance A dance, usually solo, in which the dancer emphasizes his steps by tapping the floor with the heels or toes of shoes or clogs designed to make audible the rhythm.

tape (tāp) *n.* **1** A narrow, stout strip of woven fabric. **2** Any long, narrow, flat strip of paper, metal, or the like, as the magnetic strip used in a tape recorder. **3** A tapeline. **4** Red tape. **5** A string or thread stretched breast-high across the finishing point of a racetrack and broken by the winner of the race. —*v.t.* **taped, tap·ing 1** To wrap or secure with tape; also, to bandage: to *tape* a boxer's hands. **2** To measure with or as with a tapeline. **3** To record on magnetic tape. [OE *tæppe* strip of cloth] —**tap′er** *n.*

tape deck An assembly of magnetic head, tape reels, and drive for tape recording and playback.

tape·line (tāp′līn′) *n.* A tape for measuring distances. Also **tape measure.**

ta·per (tā′pər) *n.* **1** A small candle; a burning wick or other light substance giving but feeble illumination. **2** A gradual diminution of size in an elongated object: the *taper* of a mast; also, any tapering object, as a cone. —*v.t.* & *v.i.* **1** To make or become smaller or thinner toward one end. **2** To lessen gradually; diminish: with *off.* —*adj.* Growing small by degrees in one direction. ◆ Homophone: *tapir.* [OE, dissimilated var. of Med. L *papyrus* taper, wick < L, papyrus; from the use of the pith of the papyrus as a wick]

tape-re·cord (tāp′ri·kôrd′) *v.t.* To tape (*v.* def. 3).

tape recorder An electromagnetic apparatus which records by the effect of sound waves upon the particles adhering to a magnetic tape: in the playback the magnetic patterns are reconverted into the original electrical impulses and sound waves.

tap·es·try (tap′is·trē) *n. pl.* **·tries 1** A loosely woven, ornamental fabric used for hangings, in which the woof is supplied by a spindle, the de-

sign being formed by stitches across the warp. **2** Loosely, a fabric imitating this process. —*v.t.* **·tried, ·try·ing** To adorn with tapestry. [< OF *tapisserie* < *tapis* carpet < L *tapete* < Gk. *tapētion,* dim. of *tapēs* rug]

tapestry carpet A carpet in which the fabric is woven after the designs are first printed.

ta·pe·tum (tə-pē′təm) *n. pl.* **·ta** (-tə) **1** *Bot.* A nutrient layer of cells lining the sporangium or the anther of certain plants. **2** *Zool.* A membranous layer, especially the iridescent portion of the choroid coat in certain animals whose eyes shine in the dark. **3** *Anat.* A layer of fibers of the corpus callosum. [< LL < L *tapete* carpet]

tape·worm (tāp′wûrm′) *n.* Any of various cestode worms (class *Cestoda*) with segmented, ribbonlike bodies, parasitic on the intestines of vertebrates; especially, the common pork tapeworm (*Taenia solium*) of man.

taph·e·pho·bi·a (taf′ə-fō′bē-ə) *n. Psychiatry* A morbid fear of being buried alive. [< Gk. *taphē* a grave + -PHOBIA] —**taph′e·pho′bic** *adj.*

taph·on·o·my (taf-on′ə·mē) *n.* The scientific study of the natural processes affecting the formation and modification of fossils. [< Gk. *taphē* grave + -NOMY] —**taph′o·nom′ik** (taf′ə·nom′ik) *adj.*

tap house An inn; tavern; also, a barroom.

tap·i·o·ca (tap′ē·ō′kə) *n.* A nutritious starchy substance having irregular grains, obtained from cassava. [< Sp. < Tupi *tipioca* juice of the cassava < *ty* juice + *pŷa* heart + *ocŏ* be removed]

ta·pir (tā′pər) *n.* A large, ungulate, herbivorous, typically nocturnal mammal (family *Tapiridae*), having short stout limbs and flexible proboscis, with the nostrils near the end. The tapir of South and Central America is brownish-black, that of the Malay Peninsula black and white. ◆ Homophone: *taper.* [< Sp. < Tupi *tapy′ra* tapir]

BRAZILIAN TAPIR
(From 3 to 3 1/2 feet high)

tap·is (tap′ē, tap′is; *Fr.* tå·pē′) *n.* Tapestry, formerly used as a cover of a council table: now only in the phrase **on the tapis** (up for consideration). [< F. See TAPESTRY.]

ta·pis·sier (tá·pē·syä′) *n. French* **1** A tapestry-maker. **2** An upholsterer. —**ta·pis·sière** (tá·pē·syâr′) *n. fem.*

tap·per (tap′ər) *n.* One who or that which taps, in any sense.

tap·pet (tap′it) *n. Mech.* A projecting arm of a mechanism, to operate an unattached part automatically, as to impart the motion of a cam to a valve. [< TAP²]

tappet rod *Mech.* A reciprocating rod bearing one or more tappets.

tap·ping (tap′ing) *n.* **1** The act of one who or that which taps in any sense. **2** Something taken by tapping, or running from a tap.

tap·pit (tap′it) *adj. Scot.* Having a tuft; crested.

tap·pit-hen (tap′it·hen′) *n.* **1** A hen having a topknot. **2** An English pewter measure for liquors, holding three quarts: named for the knob on the lid resembling a hen's topknot. [< dial. E (Scottish) *tappit* topped + HEN]

tap·poon (ta·pōon′) *n.* A semicircular gate of heavy sheet iron, serving as a temporary dam for a small irrigating ditch. [< Sp. *tapón* plug < *tapar* stop up]

tap·room (tap′rōōm′, -rŏŏm′) *n.* A bar; barroom.

tap·root (tap′rōōt′, -rŏŏt′) *n. Bot.* The principal descending root of a plant. —**tap′root′ed** *adj.*

taps (taps) See TAP² (*n.* def. 3).

tap·ster (tap′stər) *n.* One who draws and serves liquor; a bartender. [OE *tæppestre* barmaid]

tar¹ (tär) *n.* **1** A dark, oily, viscid mixture of hydrocarbons, especially phenols, obtained by the dry distillation of resinous woods, coal, etc. **2** Coal tar. Compare ASPHALT, PITCH¹. —*v.t.* **tarred, tar·ring** To cover with or as with tar. —**to tar and feather** To smear with tar and then cover with feathers: an old form of punishment. —*adj.* Made of, derived

from, or resembling tar. [OE *teru*]

tar² (tär) *n. Colloq.* A sailor. [Short for TARPAULIN]

tar·an·tass (tar′ən·tas′) *n.* A large four-wheeled vehicle on longitudinal bars in place of springs and mounted on a sledge in winter. Also **tar′an·tas′.** [< Russian *tarantas*]

tar·an·tel·la (tar′ən·tel′ə) *n.* A lively Neapolitan dance in 6/8 time: once thought to be a remedy for tarantism; also, the music written for it. [< Ital., dim. of *Taranto* Taranto; infl. by *tarantola* a tarantula]

tar·ant·ism (tar′ən·tiz′əm) *n.* A nervous and hysterical disorder characterized by stupor and hypochondria which, it was supposed, could be cured only by inordinate dancing and music; dancing disease. Formerly prevalent in southern Italy, it was believed to follow the bite of a tarantula. [< Ital. *tar·antismo* < *Taranto* Taranto]

ta·ran·tu·la (tə·ran′choo·lə) *n. pl.* **·las** or **·lae** (-lē) **1** A large, hairy, venomous spider (*Lycosa tarentula*) of southern Europe, still popularly but erroneously supposed to cause tarantism by its bite. **2** Any of various large, hairy American spiders (family *Theraphosidae*), especially of the genus *Eurypelma* of the SW United States, dreaded for their painful but not dangerous bite. [< Med. L < Ital. *tarantola* < *Taranto* Taranto]

TARANTULA
(Body from 2 to 3 1/2 inches)

tarantula hawk A large wasp (genus *Pepsis*) which paralyzes tarantulas with its sting and places them in its nest as food for its young. Also **tarantula killer.**

ta·rax·a·cum (tə·rak′sə·kəm) *n.* **1** Any of a genus (*Taraxacum*) of composite plants that includes the dandelion. **2** A medicinal preparation from the dried root of the common dandelion, used as a diuretic and laxative. [< NL < Arabic *tarakhshaqūq* bitter herb]

tar·boosh (tär·bōosh′) *n.* A brimless, usually red, felt cap with colored silk tassel, worn by Moslems. Also **tar·bush′.** [< Arabic *ṭarbūsh*]

tar camphor Naphthalene.

TARBOOSH

tar·di·grade (tär′də·grād) *adj.* **1** Slow in motion or action; stepping or walking slowly. **2** Of or pertaining to a group (*Tardigrada*) of slow-moving microscopical arthropods, the water-bears, found especially in water and damp moss. —*n.* One of the *Tardigrada.* [< F < L *tardigradus* < *tardus* slow + *gradi* walk]

tar·do (tär′dō) *adj. Music* Slow: a direction to performers. [< Ital.]

tar·dy (tär′dē) *adj.* **·di·er, ·di·est 1** Not coming at the appointed time; dilatory; late. **2** Slow; reluctant. See synonyms under SLOW, TEDIOUS. [< F *tardif* < L *tardus* slow] —**tar′di·ly** *adv.* —**tar′di·ness** *n.*

tare¹ (târ) *n.* **1** An unidentified weed that grows among wheat, supposed to be the darnel; hence, a seed of wickedness. *Matt.* xiii 25. **2** Any one of various species of vetch; especially, the common vetch (*Vicia sativa*). ◆ Homophone: *tear¹*. [? < F *tare* defect, rejectable thing. See TARE².]

tare² (târ) *n.* **1** An allowance made to a buyer of goods by deducting from the gross weight of his purchase the weight of the container. **2** *Chem.* An empty flask or vessel used as a counterweight. —*v.t.* **tared, tar·ing** To weigh, as a vessel or package, in order to determine the amount of tare. ◆ Homophone: *tear¹*. [< F < Arabic *ṭarhah* < *ṭaraha* reject, throw away]

targ (tärg) *n.* A device for indicating on a plotting board the changing positions of a target. [Back formation < TARGET]

targe¹ (tärj) *n.* A shield; rarely, a target. [< OF < OE *targa* < ON]

targe² (tärj) *v.t. Scot.* **1** To censure severely; thrash. **2** To cross-question rigidly. **3** To subject to strict discipline.

tar·get (tär′git) *n.* **1** An object presenting a surface that may be used as a mark or butt, as in rifle or archery practice; anything that is shot at. **2** One who or that which is made an object of attack or a center of attention or observation; a butt: He was the *target* of the crowd's sneers. **3** A small, variously shaped and colored signal, usually placed near a railroad track, to indicate the position of the switches. **4** The vane or sliding sight on a surveyor's rod. **5** *Electronics* That electrode of a vacuum tube on which cathode rays are focused and from which X-rays are emitted. **6** A small round shield or buckler; a targe. [OE *targette, targuete,* dim. of *targe* shield. See TARGE[1].]

tar·get·eer (tär'gə·tir') *n.* A soldier armed with a shield.

tar·iff (tar'if) *n.* **1** A schedule of articles of merchandise with the rates of duty to be paid for their importation or exportation. **2** A duty, or duties collectively. **3** The law by which duties are imposed; also, the principles governing their imposition. **4** Any schedule of charges. — *v.t.* **1** To make a list or table of duties or customs on. **2** To fix a price or tariff on. [< Ital. *tariffa* < Arabic *ta'rif* information < *'arafa* know, inform]

tar·la·tan (tär'lə·tən) *n.* A thin, open-mesh transparent muslin, slightly stiffened and often rather coarse. [< F *tarlatane*; ult. origin unknown]

Tar·mac (tär'mak) *n.* A paving material made from coal tar: a trade name.

tarn (tärn) *n.* A small mountain lake. [ME *terne* < ON *tjörn*]

tar·na·tion (tär·nā'shən) *interj.* & *n.* Dial. Damnation: a euphemism. [Blend of TAR-(NAL) + (DAM)NATION]

tar·nish (tär'nish) *v.t.* **1** To dim the luster of. **2** To dim the purity of; stain; disgrace. — *v.i.* **3** To lose luster, as by oxidation; become blemished. See synonyms under DEFILE[1], STAIN. — *n.* **1** Loss of luster; hence, a blemish. **2** The thin film of color on the exposed surface of a metal or mineral. [< OF *terniss-,* stem of *ternir* < *terne* dull, wan] — **tar'nish·a·ble** *adj.*

tarnished plant bug A common, brown-marked hemipterous insect *(Lygus pratensis)* of North America, which attacks many fruits and vegetables. For illustration see INSECTS (injurious).

ta·ro (tä'rō) *n. pl.* **·ros** **1** Any one of several tropical plants (genus *Colocasia*) of the arum family, grown for their edible, cormlike rootstocks. **2** The rootstock of this plant. [< native Polynesian name]

tar·ot (tar'ō, -ət) *n.* One of a set of playing cards with grilled or checkered backs used in Italy as early as the 14th century; also, a game played with such cards in which 22 are trumps and the other 56 are the usual Italian playing cards: used by fortune–tellers and gipsies in foretelling future events. [< F < Ital. *tarocco* < *taroccare* wrangle, play at cards; ult. origin obscure]

tar·pau·lin (tär·pô'lin, tär'pə-) *n.* **1** A waterproof canvas, impregnated with tar, for covering merchandise. **2** A sailor's wide–brimmed storm hat. **3** *Rare* A sailor. [< TAR[1] + PALL[1] + -ING[1]]

tar·pon (tär'pon, -pən) *n. pl.* **·pon** or **·pons** A large marine game fish with conspicuous silvery scales *(Tarpon atlanticus)* of the West Indies and the coast of Florida. [Origin unknown]

tar·ra·did·dle (tar'ə·did'l) *n. Colloq.* A prevarication; lie: also spelled *taradiddle.* [Origin uncertain]

tar·ra·gon (tar'ə·gon) *n.* **1** A European perennial plant *(Artemisia dracunculus)* allied to wormwood, and cultivated for its aromatic leaves which are used as seasoning. **2** The leaves of this plant. [< Sp. *taragona* < Arabic *tarkhun* < Gk. *drakōn* dragon]

tar·ri·er (tar'ē·ər) *n.* One who or that which tarries.

tar·ry[1] (tar'ē) *v.* **·ried, ·ry·ing** *v.i.* **1** To put off going or coming; linger. **2** To remain in the same place; abide; stay. **3** To wait. — *v.t.* **4** *Archaic* To wait for; await: to *tarry* his coming. See synonyms under ABIDE. — *n.* Sojourn; stay. [ME *tarien* vex, hinder, delay, fusion of OE *tergan* vex + OF *targer* delay < LL *tardicare* < L *tardare* delay < *tardus*

slow]

tar·ry[2] (tär'ē) *adj.* Covered with tar; like tar.

tar·sal (tär'səl) *adj.* **1** Of, pertaining to, or situated near the tarsus or ankle. **2** Of or pertaining to the tarsi of the eye. See TARSUS.

tar·si·er (tär'sē·ər) *n.* A small, arboreal, insectivorous East Indian primate *(Tarsius spectrum)* of nocturnal habits, with large eyes and ears, long tail, and adhesive pads on elongated digits: it is the sole member of the suborder *Tarsioidea.* [< F < *tarse* tarsus; so called from its unusually long tarsal bones]

TARSIER

tarso- *combining form* **1** The tarsus; pertaining to the tarsus. **2** The tarsus of the eye; pertaining to the tarsal plate: *tarsoplasty,* plastic surgery of the eyelid. Also, before vowels, **tars-.** [< Gk. *tarsos* flat of the foot, edge of the eyelid]

tar·so·met·a·tar·sus (tär'sō·met'ə·tär'səs) *n. pl.* **·si (-sī)** *Ornithol.* The so-called tarsus of birds; the bone reaching from the tibia to the toes, consisting of the confluent proximal tarsal and metatarsal bones. [< NL]

tar·sus (tär'səs) *n. pl.* **·si (-sī)** **1** *Anat.* **a** The ankle, or, in man, the group of seven bones of which it is composed. **b** A plate of connective tissue in the eyelid. **2** *Zool.* **a** The shank of a bird's leg. **b** The distal part of the leg of certain arthropods. [< NL < Gk. *tarsos* flat of the foot, any flat surface]

tart[1] (tärt) *adj.* **1** Having a sharp, sour taste. **2** Figuratively, severe; cutting; caustic: a *tart* remark. See synonyms under BITTER. [OE *teart*] — **tart'ly** *adv.* — **tart'ness** *n.*

tart[2] (tärt) *n.* **1** A small pastry shell with fruit or custard filling, and without a top crust, as distinguished from a pie. **2** In England, an uncovered fruit pie. **3** *Slang* A girl or woman of loose morality. [< OF *tarte*]

tar·tan[1] (tär'tən) *n.* **1** A woolen fabric having varicolored lines or stripes at right angles, forming a distinctive pattern; a woolen plaid; the characteristic dress of the Scottish Highlanders, each clan having its particular pattern or patterns; hence, any similar pattern; a plaid. **2** A garment made of tartan. — *adj.* Made of tartan; also, striped or checkered in a manner similar to the Scottish tartans. [? < OF *tiretaine* linsey–woolsey]

tar·tan[2] (tär'tən) *n.* **1** A Mediterranean vessel having one mast with a large lateen sail. **2** A variety of long, covered carriage. [< F *tartane* < Arabic *tarīdah,* kind of ship]

tar·tar (tär'tər) *n.* **1** An acid substance deposited from grape juice during fermentation as a pinkish sediment; crude potassium bitartrate. See ARGOL, CREAM OF TARTAR. **2** *Dent.* A yellowish incrustation on the teeth, chiefly calcium phosphate. [< F *tartre* < LL *tartarum* < Med. Gk. *tartaron,* ? < Arabic]

tar·tar·e·ous (tär·târ'ē·əs) *adj.* Resembling tartar.

tar·tare sauce (tär'tər) A fish sauce consisting of mayonnaise, capers, chopped olives, and pickles. Also **tar'tar sauce.**

tar·tar·ic (tär·tar'ik, -tär'ik) *adj.* Pertaining to or derived from tartar or tartaric acid.

tartaric acid *Chem.* Any one of four isomeric organic compounds, $HOOC(CHOH)_2COOH$, differing from each other in their optical properties, especially the dextrorotatory form, occurring in the free state or as a potassium or calcium salt, as in grape juice, various unripe fruits, etc.

tar·tar·ize (tär'tə·rīz) *v.t.* **·ized, ·iz·ing** To impregnate or treat with tartar, cream of tartar, or tartar emetic. — **tar'tar·i·za'tion** *n.*

tar·tar·ous (tär'tər·əs) *adj.* Pertaining to or derived from tartar.

Tartar sable The kolinsky.

tart·let (tärt'lit) *n.* A small tart.

tar·trate (tär'trāt) *n. Chem.* A salt or ester of tartaric acid.

tar·trat·ed (tär'trā·tid) *adj. Chem.* Containing or combined with tartaric acid.

tar·tufe (tär·tŏŏf', *Fr.* tär·tüf') *n.* Any hypocrite or toady. Also **tar·tuffe'.** [after TARTUFE]

Tar·zan (tär'zan, tär·zan') The hero of a series of novels by Edgar Rice Burroughs (1875–1950): an English child of noble birth abandoned in the African jungle, raised by apes, and possessing incredible strength, agility, and a knowledge of the speech of animals. Also **Tarzan of the Apes.**

ta·sim·e·ter (tə·sim'ə·tər) *n.* An electrical apparatus for detecting changes in pressure by the resulting variations in the conductivity of a solid, and so measuring changes, as in length, temperature, or moisture, that produce alteration of pressure. [< Gk. *tasis* extension (< *teinein* stretch) + -METER] — **tas·i·met·ric** (tas'ə·met'rik) *adj.* — **ta·sim'e·try** *n.*

task (task, täsk) *n.* **1** A specific amount of labor or study imposed by authority or required by duty or necessity. **2** Any work voluntarily undertaken and imposed on oneself. **3** An exhausting or vexatious employment; burden. **4** A specific military mission. **5** *Obs.* A tax; duty. — **to take to task** To reprove; lecture. — *v.t.* **1** To assign a task to. **2** To overtax with labor; burden. **3** To censure; reprimand. **4** *Obs.* To tax. [< AF *tasque* < LL *tasca, taxa* < L *taxare* appraise. Related to TAX.]

Synonyms (noun): business, drudgery, job, labor, lesson, stint, toil, work. See TOIL[1].

task·er (tas'kər, täs'-) *n.* **1** A reaper. **2** A thresher of grain. **3** A laborer who performs allotted work.

task force **1** *Mil.* A tactical unit drawn from different branches of the armed services assigned to execute a specific mission. **2** Any group assigned to handle a specific task.

task·mas·ter (task'mas'tər, täsk'mäs'tər) *n.* One who assigns tasks; figuratively, one who or that which loads with heavy burdens.

Tas·ma·nia (taz·mā'nē·ə) An island state in the Commonwealth of Australia, south of Victoria; 26,215 square miles; capital, Hobart; formerly *Van Diemen's Land.* — **Tas·ma'ni·an** *adj.* & *n.*

Tasmanian devil A ferocious burrowing carnivorous marsupial *(Sarcophilus harrisii)* of the dasyure family, with white markings on the black fur.

Tasmanian wolf The thylacine. Also **Tasmanian tiger.**

tas·sel[1] (tas'əl) *n.* **1** A pendent ornament, for curtains, cushions, and the like, consisting of a tuft of loosely hanging threads or cords; formerly, a clasp for holding a cloak. **2** Something resembling a tassel, as the pendent head of some plants or flowers, or the pyramidal inflorescence on a stalk of Indian corn. — *v.* **·seled** or **·selled, ·sel·ing** or **·sel·ling** *v.t.* **1** To provide or adorn with tassels. **2** To form in a tassel or tassels. **3** To remove the tassels from (Indian corn). — *v.i.* **4** To put forth tassels, as Indian corn. [< OF, clasp]

tas·sel[2] (tas'əl) *n.* The tercel.

tas·set (tas'it) *n.* One of a series of overlapping metal plates pendent from the cuirass to protect the waist and thighs: often called *tace.* Also **tasse.** ◆ Homophone: *tacit.* [< F *tassette,* dim. of OF *tasse* a pouch]

taste (tāst) *v.* **tast·ed, tast·ing** *v.t.* **1** To perceive the flavor of (something) by taking into the mouth or touching with the tongue. **2** To take a little of (food or drink); eat or drink a little of. **3** To test the quality of (a product) thus: His business is *tasting* tea. **4** *Archaic* To have a relish for; like. **5** *Obs.* To prove or try by or as by touch. — *v.i.* **6** To take a small quantity into the mouth; take a taste: usually with *of.* **7** To have experience or enjoyment; be or become acquainted through experience: with *of:* to *taste* of great sorrow. **8** To have specified flavor when in the mouth: Sugar *tastes* sweet. — *n.* **1** The sensation excited when a soluble substance comes into contact with any of the taste buds; also, the quality thus perceived; flavor. **2** *Physiol.* Any of the four fundamental sensations, salt, sweet, bitter, or sour, excited alone or in any combination by the sole action of the gustatory nerves. **3** A small quantity tasted, eaten or sipped; a sample: often used figuratively. **4** Special fondness and aptitude for a pursuit; bent; inclination: a *taste* for music. **5** The power or faculty of apprehending and appreciating the beautiful in nature, art, and literature; critical perception or discernment. **6** Style or form with respect to the rules of propriety or etiquette: She behaves in very poor *taste*. **7** Individual preference or liking: That tie suits my *taste*. **8** The act of tasting. **9** *Obs.* The act of examining or testing. See synonyms under RELISH, SAVOR. [< OF *taster* taste, try, feel, prob. ult. < L *taxare* touch, handle, appraise] — **tast′a·ble** *adj.*

taste bud *Physiol.* One of the clusters of cells situated in the mucous membrane chiefly of the tongue and containing sensitive receptors for the discriminatory perception of taste.

taste·ful (tāst′fəl) *adj.* **1** Conforming to taste. **2** Possessing good taste. **3** Savory: a rare use. — **taste′ful·ly** *adv.* —**taste′ful·ness** *n.*

Synonyms: artistic, dainty, delicate, delicious, elegant, esthetic, esthetical, exquisite, fastidious, fine, nice. That which is *elegant* is made so not merely by nature, but by art and culture. *Nice* and *delicate* both refer to exact adaptation to some standard; as regards matters of taste, *delicate* is a higher and more discriminating word than *nice*, and is always used in a favorable sense; a *delicate* distinction is one worth observing; a *nice* distinction may be so, or may be overstrained and unduly subtle. *Esthetic* or *esthetical* refers to beauty or the appreciation of the beautiful, especially from the philosophical point of view. *Exquisite* denotes the utmost perfection of the *elegant* in minute details; we speak of an *elegant* garment, an *exquisite* lace. *Exquisite* is also applied to intense keenness of any feeling; as, *exquisite* pain. *Antonyms:* clumsy, coarse, deformed, disgusting, displeasing, distasteful, fulsome, gaudy, grotesque, harsh, hideous, horrid, inartistic, inharmonious, meretricious, offensive, rude, tawdry.

taste·less (tāst′lis) *adj.* **1** Having no flavor; insipid; dull. **2** Having lost the sense of taste. **3** Devoid of esthetic taste. **4** Lacking, or showing a lack of, good taste. —**taste′less·ly** *adv.* — **taste′less·ness** *n.*

taste·mak·er (tāst′mā′kər) *n.* A person who establishes standards of style or who shapes public opinion.

tast·er (tās′tər) *n.* **1** One who tastes; specifically, one who tests the quality of for trade: a tea-*taster*. **2** A device to assist in testing or sampling. **3** A pipette, or a small, flat, circular metal vessel used in testing wines.

tast·y (tās′tē) *adj.* **tast·i·er, tast·i·est** *Colloq.* **1** Having a fine flavor; savory. **2** Tasteful. — **tast′i·ly** *adv.* —**tast′i·ness** *n.*

tat¹ (tat) *v.* **tat·ted, tat·ting** *v.t.* To make, as an edging, by tatting. —*v.i.* To make tatting. [Back formation < TATTING] —**tat′ter** *n.*

tat² (tat) *n.* A tap or blow: in the phrase **tit for tat.** [? Var. of TAP², *n.*]

ta·ta·mi (tä·tä′mē) *n. pl.* **·mi, ·mis** A floor covering used in a Japanese dwelling, made of rice straw matting.

tat·ou·ay (tat′ōō·ā, tä·tōō′ī) *n.* A large South American armadillo (genus *Cabassous*). [< Sp. *tatuay* < Guarani *tatu-aí* < *tatu* armadillo + *aí* worthless; so called because it is inedible]

tat·ter (tat′ər) *n.* **1** A torn and hanging shred; rag. **2** *pl.* Ragged clothing. —*v.t.* To make ragged; tear into tatters. —*v.i.* To become ragged. [< Scand. Cf. ON *töturr* rags]

tat·ter·de·mal·ion (tat′ər·di·māl′yən, -mal′-) *n.* A person wearing ragged clothes; a ragamuffin. —*adj.* Ragged. [Origin unknown]

tat·tered (tat′ərd) *adj.* **1** Torn into tatters. **2** Clothed in rags; ragged.

Tat·ter·sall check (tat′ər·sôl) A check or plaid design of dark lines on a light ground: used especially in men's vests. Also **Tattersall plaid.** [From a pattern on blankets used in the London market of Richard *Tattersall*, 18th century horse merchant]

tat·ting (tat′ing) *n.* A lacelike threadwork, made by hand; also, the act or process of making it. [Origin unknown]

tat·tle (tat′l) *v.* **·tled, ·tling** *v.i.* **1** To talk idly; prate; chatter. **2** To tell tales about others; gossip. —*v.t.* **3** To reveal by gossiping. See syno-

nyms under BABBLE. —*n.* **1** Idle talk or gossip. **2** Prattling speech, as of children. [Prob. < MDu. *tatelen*] —**tat′tling·ly** *adv.*

tat·tler (tat′lər) *n.* **1** One who tattles; a talebearer; tattletale. **2** Any long-billed bird of the genus *Totanus*, as the redshank and the yellowlegs. **3** The willet. **4** The wandering tattler *(Heteroscelus incanus)*, a shore bird of the Pacific coast of the United States.

tat·tle·tale (tat′l·tāl′) *n.* A talebearer; tattler. — *adj.* Revealing; betraying.

tat·too¹ (ta·tōō′) *v.t.* **1** To prick and mark (the skin) in patterns with indelible pigments. **2** To mark the skin with (designs, etc.) in this way. —*n. pl.* **·toos** A pattern or picture so made. [< Polynesian. Cf. Tahitian, Tongan *tatau*, Marquesan *tatu* < *ta* mark.] —**tat·too′er** *n.* —**tat·too′ing** *n.*

TATTOOING ON MAORI CHIEFTAIN

tat·too² (ta·tōō′) *n.* **1** A continuous beating or drumming. **2** In military or naval usage, a signal by drum or bugle to repair to quarters, usually occurring about 9 p.m. [Var. of earlier *taptoo* < Du. *taptoe* < *tap* tap, faucet + *toe* shut]

tat·ty (tat′ē) *n. pl.* **·ties** *Anglo-Indian* An East Indian matting usually hung in doorways and window openings, and kept wet to cool the air. Also **tat′tie.** [< Hind. *ṭaṭṭī*] —**tat′tied** *adj.*

tau (tou) *n.* **1** The nineteenth letter in the Greek alphabet: (T,τ) equivalent to the English *t*. As a numeral it denotes 300. **2** A lepton having a mass approximately 20 times that of a muon. [< Gk.]

taunt (tônt) *n.* **1** A sarcastic, biting speech or remark; insulting reproach. **2** *Obs.* A butt of contemptuous reproach. See synonyms under SCORN, SNEER. —*v.t.* **1** To reproach with sarcastic or contemptuous words; mock; upbraid. **2** To tease in any way; provoke with taunts. See synonyms under MOCK, RIDICULE, SCOFF. [? < OF *tanter*, var. of *tenter* provoke, tempt. See TEMPT.] —**taunt′er** *n.* —**taunt′ing·ly** *adv.*

tau particle *Physics* A rare, unstable atomic particle of the meson group, positively charged and with a mass about 1,000 times that of the electron.

taupe (tōp) *n.* **1** A mole. **2** The color of moleskin; dark gray, often tinged with brown, purple, or yellow. ◆ Homophone: *tope.* [< F < L *talpa* mole]

tau·rine¹ (tôr′ēn) *adj.* **1** Of or like a bull. **2** Related to or connected with the constellation or sign Taurus. [< L *taurinus* < *taurus* a bull]

tau·rine² (tôr′ēn, -in) *n. Chem.* A colorless crystalline compound, $C_2H_7NSO_3$, contained in the bile and muscles of oxen and other animals: also derived synthetically. [< L *taurus* bull + -INE²]

tauro- *combining form* Bull; ox; bovine. Also, before vowels, **taur-.** [< Gk. *tauros* a bull]

tau·rom·a·chy (tô·rom′ə·kē) *n.* The art of bullfighting. Also **tau·ro·ma·chi·a** (tôr′ə·mā′kē·ə). [< Gk. *tauromachia* < *tauros* a bull + *machesthai* fight]

Taus·sig (tou′sig), **Frank William,** 1859–1940, U.S. political economist.

taut (tôt) *adj.* **1** Hard-drawn; stretched tight. **2** In proper shape; ready; tidy. **3** Tense; tight: *taut* muscles. **4** *Obs.* Filled to distention; firm. [ME *toyt, toht*; origin uncertain] —**taut′ly** *adv.* — **taut′ness** *n.*

taut·en (tôt′n) *v.t. & v.i.* To make or become taut; tighten.

tauto- *combining form* Same; identical: *tautomerism.* Also, before vowels, **taut-.** [< Gk. *tauto* the same]

tau·tog (tô·tôg′, -tog′) *n.* A blackish, edible, labroid fish *(Tautoga onitis)* of the North American Atlantic coast. Also **tau·taug′.** [< Algonquian *tautauog,* pl. of *tautau,* a kind of blackfish]

TAUTOG
(About 16 inches long)

tau·tol·o·gism (tô·tol′ə·jiz′əm) *n.* Use of needlessly repetitious speech, or an instance of it; pleonasm. —

tau·tol′o·gist *n.*

tau·tol·o·gize (tô·tol′ə·jīz) *v.i.* **·gized, ·giz·ing** To repeat needlessly the same idea in different words.

tau·tol·o·gy (tô·tol′ə·jē) *n. pl.* **·gies** Unnecessary repetition of the same idea in different words; pleonasm; also, an instance of such repetition; as, He is writing his own autobiography. See REDUNDANCE. [< LL *tautologia* < Gk. < *tauto* the same + *logos* discourse] —**tau·to·log·ic** (tô′tə·loj′ik) or **·i·cal** *adj.* —**tau′to·log′i·cal·ly** *adv.*

tau·to·mer·ic (tô′tə·mer′ik) *adj.* Having the property of tautomerism.

tau·tom·er·ism (tô·tom′ə·riz′əm) *n. Chem.* The property, exhibited by certain substances and compounds when subjected to appropriate chemical reaction, of assuming either of two interconvertible atomic structures, **tau·to·mers** (tô′tə·mərz), which are in equilibrium with each other. [< TAUTO- + Gk. *meros* part]

tau·tom·er·i·za·tion (tô·tom′ər·ə·zā′shən, -ī·zā′-) *n. Chem.* Conversion into a tautomeric structure.

tau·to·nym (tô′tə·nim) *n.* An instance of tautonymy.

tau·ton·y·my (tô·ton′ə·mē) *n. pl.* **·mies** *Biol.* **1** The possession by two or more distinct plants or animals of the same generic and specific names: prohibited by the rules of scientific nomenclature. **2** Identity of the generic, specific, and subspecific names of a given plant or animal, as *Bison bison bison:* a permitted practice. [< TAUTO- + Gk. *onyma* name] —**tau·to·nym·ic** (tô′tə·nim′ik) *adj.*

tav (täv) *n.* The twenty-second Hebrew letter. Also **taw.** See ALPHABET.

tav·ern (tav′ərn) *n.* **1** A public house where travelers and other guests are accommodated with lodging, food, and drink. **2** A house licensed to retail liquors to be drunk on the premises. [< OF *taverne* < L *taberna* hut, booth]

tav·ern·er (tav′ər·nər) *n. Archaic* A tavernkeeper; also, one who frequents taverns.

taw¹ (tô) *v.t.* **1** To convert into leather by some process other than soaking in tanning liquor, as by using alum and salt. **2** *Brit. Dial.* To torture; vex; also, to harden or prepare. [OE *tawian* prepare, harass] —**taw′er** *n.*

taw² (tô) *n.* **1** A game of marbles. **2** The line from which marble-players shoot. **3** A marble used for shooting. —*v.i.* To shoot a marble or come to the mark before shooting. [< Scand. Cf. ON *taug* string.]

taw·dry (tô′drē) *adj.* **·dri·er, ·dri·est** Showy without elegance; excessively ornamental; gaudy. — *n.* Cheap, pretentious finery. [Short for *tawdry lace,* alter. of *St. Audrey's lace,* a type of silk neckpiece sold at St. Audrey's Fair at Ely, England] —**taw′dri·ly** *adv.* —**taw′dri·ness** *n.*

taw·ny (tô′nē) *adj.* **·ni·er, ·ni·est** Tan-colored; brownish-yellow. Also **taw′ney.** [< AF *taune* < OF *tanné,* pp. of *tanner* tan] —**taw′ni·ness** *n.*

tax (taks) *n.* **1** A compulsory contribution levied upon persons, property, or business for the support of government; by extension, any proportionate assessment, as on the members of a society. **2** A heavy demand on one's powers or resources; an onerous duty or requirement; a burden. —**direct tax** A tax, as on property or income, which the taxpayer cannot shift to another person. —**excise tax** An internal-revenue tax on domestic manufactures, levied before they are sold to the consumer. The term has been extended to include license duties. —**income tax** A tax levied on the income or profits of individuals and of corporations. See CAPITAL LEVY. —**indirect tax** A tax, such as a customs duty, paid by one person but ultimately shifted to the consumer. —**nuisance tax** A tax which yields little benefit in proportion to the amount of discontent it causes. —**single tax** A tax to be obtained from a single source, especially from a levy on land and natural resources, as a substitute for all other forms of taxation. The theory was first proposed by John Locke, and was elaborated and popularized in the 19th century by Henry George. [< *v.*] —*v.t.* **1** To impose a tax on; subject to taxation. **2** *Law* To settle or fix (amounts) as duly chargeable in any judicial matter: to *tax* costs. **3** To subject to a severe demand; impose a burden or load upon; task: He *taxes* my patience. **4** To make an accusation against; charge; also, to blame; censure: usually with *with.* [< OF *taxer* < L *taxare* estimate, appraise. Related to TASK.] —**tax′a·bil′i·ty, tax′a·ble·ness** *n.* —**tax′a·ble** *adj.*

—**tax′a·bly** adv. —**tax′er** n.

Synonyms (noun): assessment, custom, demand, duty, exaction, excise, impost, rate, rating, toll, tribute.

tax·a·ceous (tak·sā′shəs) adj. Bot. Designating or belonging to a widely distributed family (*Taxaceae*) of typically evergreen shrubs and trees, the yew family, having one or two integuments and drupelike or, rarely, cone fruits. [<NL <L *taxus* yew]

tax·a·tion (tak·sā′shən) n. The act of taxing; the amount assessed as a tax.

tax·gath·er·er (taks′gath′ər·ər) n. A collector of taxes. —**tax′gath′er·ing** n. & adj.

tax·i (tak′sē) n. A taxicab. —v. **tax·ied, tax·i·ing** or **tax·y·ing** v.i. **1** To ride in a taxicab. **2** To move along the ground or on the surface of the water under its own power, as an airplane before taking off or after landing. —v.t. **3** To cause (an airplane) to taxi. [<TAXI(CAB)]

tax·i·arch (tak′sē·ärk) n. The commander of a division of an ancient Greek army. [<Gk. *taxiarchēs* <*taxis* division of an army + *archos* leader <*archein* rule]

tax·i·cab (tak′sē·kab′) n. A passenger vehicle, usually an automobile fitted with a taximeter, available for hire. [Short for *taximeter cab*]

taxi dancer U.S. A girl employed by a dance hall or cabaret to dance with patrons for a certain fee. [<*taxi-* hired, as in *taxicab* + DANCER]

tax·i·der·mist (tak′sə·dûr′mist) n. One who practices taxidermy.

tax·i·der·my (tak′sə·dûr′mē) n. The art or process of stuffing and mounting the skins of dead animals for preservation or exhibition. [<Gk. *taxis* arrangement + *derma* skin] —**tax′i·der′mal, tax′i·der′mic** adj.

tax·i·me·ter (tak′si·mē′tər) n. **1** An instrument for measuring distances and recording fares. **2** A taxicab equipped with a taximeter. [<F *taximètre* <*taxe* tariff + *mètre* a meter]

tax·i·plane (tak′sē·plān′) n. An airplane available for hire as a public vehicle.

tax·is (tak′sis) n. **1** Surg. A methodical application of manual pressure, as on a hernial tumor, for restoring the parts to their normal place. **2** Zool. The involuntary movement of an organism or cell, as a zoospore, in response to an external stimulus; specifically, a movement involving locomotion or change of place. Compare TROPISM. **3** In ancient Greece, a body of troops of varying size. **4** Obs. Order; arrangement, as of words in a sentence. [<Gk., arrangement <*tassein* arrange]

-**taxis** *combining form* Order; disposition; arrangement: *thermotaxis*. Also spelled **-taxy**. [<Gk. *taxis* arrangement]

tax·ite (tak′sīt) n. A volcanic rock which has crystallized in such manner as to have a clastic appearance. [<Gk. *taxis* arrangement + -ITE¹] —**tax·it·ic** (tak·sit′ik) adj.

tax·on·o·mist (tak·son′ə·mist) n. One versed in taxonomy. Also **tax·on′o·mer.**

tax·on·o·my (tak·son′ə·mē) n. **1** The department of knowledge that embodies the laws and principles of classification. **2** Biol. The systematic arrangement of plant and animal organisms according to accepted diagnostic criteria which determine their assignment to each of the following major groups, beginning with the most inclusive: kingdom, phylum or division, class, order, family, genus, and species. [<F *taxonomie* <Gk. *taxis* arrangement + *nomos* law] —**tax·o·nom·ic** (tak′sə·nom′ik) or **-i·cal** adj. —**tax′o·nom′i·cal·ly** adv.

tax·pay·er (taks′pā′ər) n. **1** One who pays any tax. **2** A building, the rental from which is intended to cover merely the taxes on the land.

tax title The title conveyed to a purchaser of property sold for non-payment of taxes.

Tb Chem. Terbium (symbol Tb).

T-base (tē′bās′) n. Two strips of wood nailed together in the form of a T and serving as a base for the tripod of a machine-gun.

Tc Chem. Technetium (symbol Tc).

Tchai·kov·sky (chī·kôf′skē), **Peter (Pëtr) Il·ich,** 1840–93, Russian composer.

tchick (chik) n. A sound made by pressing the tongue against the roof of the mouth and sucking it back, as in urging a horse. —v.i. To make a tchick. [Imit.]

Te Chem. Tellurium (symbol Te).

tea (tē) n. **1** An evergreen Asian shrub or small tree *(Thea sinensis),* having a compact head of leathery, toothed leaves and white or pink flowers. **2** The prepared leaves of this plant, or an infusion of them used as a beverage. The difference between **black tea** and **green tea** is the result of manipulation, the latter being withered by steaming, thus retaining the green color, while leaves simply dried turn black. **3** Any infusion, decoction, solution, or extract to be used as a beverage or medicinally: beef *tea.* **4** The leaves of a particular variety of plant, prepared for making a beverage, or for medicinal purposes: senna *tea.* **5** A light evening or afternoon meal; also, a social gathering at which tea is served. [<Chinese *ch'a,* dial. Chinese *t'e*]

tea bag A small porous sack of cloth or paper containing tea leaves, which is immersed in water to make tea.

tea ball 1 A perforated metal ball, filled with tea leaves, to be dropped or suspended in boiling water to make tea. **2** A tea bag.

tea·ber·ry (tē′ber′ē) n. pl. **-ries 1** The wintergreen, whose leaves are sometimes mixed with or used as tea. **2** The berry of this plant.

tea biscuit A biscuit or cracker, usually short and sweetened, served with tea.

tea caddy See CADDY¹ (def. 1).

teach (tēch) v. **taught, teach·ing** v.t. **1** To impart knowledge to by lessons; give instruction to; guide by precept or example; instruct: to *teach* a class. **2** To give instruction in; make known; communicate the knowledge of: to *teach* French. **3** To train by practice or exercise. —v.i. **4** To follow the profession of teaching. **5** To impart knowledge or skill. [OE *tæcan, tæcean*]

Synonyms: discipline, drill, educate, enlighten, indoctrinate, inform, initiate, instruct, nurture, school, train, tutor. To *teach* is to communicate knowledge; to *instruct* is to impart knowledge with special method and completeness; *instruct* has also an authoritative sense nearly equivalent to command. To *educate* is to draw out or develop the mental powers. To *train* is to direct to a certain result powers already existing. *Train* is used in preference to *educate* when the reference is to the inferior animals or to the physical powers of man; as, to *train* a horse; to *train* the hand or eye. To *discipline* is to bring into habitual and complete subjection to authority. To *nurture* is to furnish the care and sustenance necessary for physical, mental, and moral growth; *nurture* is a more tender word than *educate.* See INFORM¹, LEARN.

teach·a·ble (tē′chə·bəl) adj. **1** Capable of being taught; willing to learn; docile. **2** Capable of being imparted by teaching. See synonyms under DOCILE. —**teach′a·bil′i·ty, teach′a·ble·ness** n. —**teach′a·bly** adv.

teach·er (tē′chər) n. One who teaches; specifically, one whose occupation is to teach others. See synonyms under MASTER.

teacher bird 1 The ovenbird. **2** The North American red-eyed vireo. [Imit. of its cry]

teachers' institute See under INSTITUTE.

teach-in (tēch′in′) n. An extended meeting, as at a college or university, during which faculty and students participate in lectures, discussions, etc., on a controversial issue, often as a form of social protest.

teaching (tē′ching) n. **1** The profession of a teacher. **2** That which is taught. See synonyms under DOCTRINE, EDUCATION, NURTURE.

teach·ing machine Any of various manually-operated devices that present educational material in a series of steps designed to enable each student to learn at a rate commensurate with his ability.

tea cozy See COZY, n.

tea·cup (tē′kup′) n. **1** A small cup suitable for serving tea. **2** As much as a teacup will hold: also **tea′cup·ful** (-fŏŏl′).

tea·house (tē′hous′) n. In the Orient, a public place serving tea and other light refreshments.

teak (tēk) n. **1** A large East Indian tree (*Tectona grandis*) of the vervain family, yielding a very hard, durable timber highly prized for shipbuild-

ing. **2** The wood of this tree. [<Malayalam *tēkka*]

tea·ket·tle (tē′ket′l) n. A kettle with a spout, used for boiling water for culinary purposes.

teal (tēl) n. **1** Any of several small, short-necked river ducks (genera *Nettion* and *Querquedula*); especially, the common teal (*N. crecca*) of the Old World and the similar North American **green-winged teal** (*N. carolinense*) having grayish wing coverts and the head slightly crested. **2** A darkish, dull-blue color with a greenish cast. [ME *tele*]

team (tēm) n. **1** Two or more beasts of burden harnessed together: often including harness and vehicle; also, a single horse and vehicle. **2** A set of workers, or players competing in a game: a baseball *team.* **3** Dial. A flock; brood. **4** Obs. Race; lineage. —v.t. **1** To convey with a team. **2** To harness together in a team. —v.i. **3** To drive a team as a business. **4** To form a team: work as a team: to *team* up. —adj. Of or pertaining to a team. ◆ Homophone: *teem.* [OE *tēam* offspring, succession, row. Related to TEEM¹.] —**team′ing** n.

team boat A paddle-wheel ferryboat propelled by horse power.

team·mate (tēm′māt′) n. A fellow player on a team.

team·ster (tēm′stər) n. **1** One who drives or owns a team. **2** One who drives a truck or other commercial vehicle.

team teaching U.S. A method of organizing instruction in schools so that students in a given course are taught by several teachers, each of whom sometimes teaches the whole group and sometimes a part of it.

team·work (tēm′wûrk′) n. **1** Work done by or requiring to be done by or with a team of horses: distinguished from manual labor. **2** Unity of action by the players on an athletic team to further the success of the team. **3** Cooperation.

tea party A social gathering at which tea and light sandwiches or cakes are the principal refreshments.

tea·pot (tē′pot′) n. A vessel with a spout and handle in which tea is made and from which it is served.

tea·poy (tē′poi) n. A small three- or four-legged table for holding a tea service. [<Hind. *tipāī* <*tim* three + Persian *pāē* foot]

tear¹ (târ) v. **tore, torn, tear·ing** v.t. **1** To pull apart, as cloth; part or separate by pulling; rip; rend. **2** To make by rending or tearing: to *tear* a hole in a dress. **3** To injure or lacerate, as skin. **4** To divide; disrupt: a party *torn* by dissension. **5** To distress or torment; anguish: The sight *tore* his heart. —v.i. **6** To become torn or rent. **7** To move with haste and energy. See synonyms under REND. —n. **1** A fissure made by tearing; a rent; an act of tearing. **2** Slang A carouse; a spree; frolic. **3** A rushing motion; to start off with a *tear,* also, any violent outburst, as of anger, enthusiasm, etc. ◆ Homophone: *tare.* [OE *teran*]

tear² (tir) n. **1** A drop of the saline liquid secreted by the lacrimal gland, for moistening the eye. **2** Something resembling or suggesting a drop of the lacrimal fluid. **3** A drop of any liquid. **4** A droplike portion, as of glass, amber, etc. **5** pl. Sorrow; lamentation. ◆ Homophone: *tier.* [OE *tēar*] —**tear′less** adj. —**tear′y** adj.

tear·drop (tir′drop′) n. A tear.

tear·ful (tir′fəl) adj. **1** Weeping abundantly. **2** Causing tears. —**tear′ful·ly** adv. —**tear′ful·ness** n.

tear gas (tir) A lacrimator.

tear·ing (târ′ing) adj. Colloq. **1** Rushing along as in a hurry or rage. **2** Tremendous; mighty.

tear-jerk·er (tir′jûr′kər) n. U.S. Slang A story, play, or motion picture charged with sentimental sadness.

tea·room (tē′rōōm′, -rŏŏm′) n. A restaurant serving tea and other refreshments.

tea rose 1 Any of numerous garden roses thought to be tea-scented, primarily hybrids bred from the Chinese *Rosa odorata.* **2** A yellowish-pink color of many hues.

tear-sheet (târ′shēt′) n. A page torn or cut from a magazine, book, or newspaper, containing matter of particular interest.

tease (tēz) v. **teased, teas·ing** v.t. **1** To annoy or harass with continual importunities, raillery, etc.; pester. **2** To scratch or dress in order to raise the nap, as cloth with teasels. **3** To tear or pull apart with instruments, as tissues in examination. **4** To comb or card, as wool or flax; also, to pick or shred, as hard-packed tobacco. **5** To comb (hair) in such a way as to form fluffy layers and give an effect of fullness. —*v.i.* **6** To annoy a person in a facetious or petty way. See synonyms under AFFRONT. —*n.* **1** One who or that which teases. **2** The act of teasing or the state of being teased. [OE *tǣsan* tease, pluck, pull about] —**teas′ing** *n. & adj.* —**teas′ing·ly** *adv.*

tea·sel (tē′zəl) *n.* **1** A coarse, prickly Old World herb (genus *Dipsacus*) of which the flower head is covered with hooked bracts, especially the **fuller's teasel** (*D. fullonum*). **2** The rough bur of this plant, or a mechanical substitute: used in dressing cloth. —*v.t.* **·seled** or **·selled**, **·sel·ing** or **·sel·ling** To use a teasel on; raise the nap of with a teasel. Also **tea′zel**, **tea′zle**. [OE *tǣsel*] —**tea′sel·er** or **tea′sel·ler** *n.*

TEASEL
(Plant to 5 feet or more)

teas·er (tē′zər) *n.* **1** One who or that which teases, as a machine used for teasing wool. **2** Anything tempting or whetting the appetites. **3** The border at the front of the stage. Compare BORDER.

tea service The articles used in serving tea: a silver *tea service*. Also **tea set**.

tea·shop (tē′shop′) *n.* **1** A tearoom. **2** *Brit.* A lunchroom.

tea·spoon (tē′spoon′, -spoon′) *n.* **1** A small spoon used for stirring tea, etc. **2** As much as a teaspoon will hold, 1/3 of a tablespoon, usually 1 1/3 fluid drams: also **tea′spoon·ful** (-fool′).

teat (tēt) *n.* The protuberance on the breast or udder of most female mammals, through which the milk is drawn; a nipple; pap; dug. [< OF *tete* < Gmc.]

tea wagon A table on wheels for use in serving tea or refreshments.

tech·ne·ti·um (tek·nē′shē·əm) *n.* An intensely radioactive metallic element (symbol Tc, atomic number 43) produced synthetically on earth but found in the spectra of certain stars, the most stable of its isotopes having a half-life of 2.6 million years. See PERIODIC TABLE. [< NL < Gk. *technētos* artificial]

tech·nic (tek′nik) *n.* **1** Technique. **2** *pl.* The theory of an art or of the arts; specifically, the study of the techniques of an art. **3** *pl.* Technical rules, methods, etc. **4** *pl.* Technology. —*adj.* Technical.

tech·ni·cal (tek′ni·kəl) *adj.* **1** Pertaining to some particular art, science, or trade. **2** Peculiar to a specialized field of knowledge. **3** Of or pertaining to the mechanical arts. **4** Employing a specialized vocabulary, as in a treatise or textbook. **5** Considered in terms of an accepted body of rules and regulations: a *technical* defeat. **6** Designating a money market in which prices are for the most part determined by speculation or manipulation. [< Gk. *technikos* < *technē* art] —**tech′ni·cal·ly** *adv.* —**tech′ni·cal·ness** *n.*

tech·ni·cal·i·ty (tek′ni·kal′ə·tē) *n. pl.* **·ties** **1** The state of being technical. **2** The use of technical terms. **3** A technical point peculiar to some profession, art, trade, etc. **4** A petty distinction; quibble. Also **tech′nism.**

technical knockout In boxing, a victory awarded when one fighter has been beaten so severely that the referee discontinues the fight. Abbr. *t.k.o.*, *T.K.O.*, or *TKO*

tech·ni·cian (tek·nish′ən) *n.* **1** One skilled in the handling of instruments or in the performance of tasks requiring specialized training. **2** A rating in the armed services including those qualified for technical work; also, one having such a rating.

Tech·ni·col·or (tek′ni·kul′ər) *n.* A process used in making color motion pictures: a trade name. Also **tech′ni·col·or.**

tech·nique (tek·nēk′) *n.* Working methods or manner of performance, as in art, science, etc. [< F < Gk. *technikos*. See TECHNICAL.]

techno- *combining form* **1** Art; skill; craft: *technology*. **2** Technical; technological. Also, before

vowels, **techn-**. [< Gk. *technē* an art, skill]

tech·noc·ra·cy (tek·nok′rə·sē) *n. pl.* **·cies** **1** A community governed by experts in applied and theoretical science; national government by organized technologists and engineers. **2** A non-political fact-finding body of experts in the various departments of applied and theoretical sciences, whose aim is to re-evaluate industrial output in terms of energy factors. —**tech′no·crat** (tek′nə·krat) *n.* —**tech′no·crat′ic** *adj.*

tech·nog·ra·phy (tek·nog′rə·fē) *n.* **1** Description of the arts and crafts. **2** The scientific study of the development and geographic distribution of technical processes.

tech·nol·a·tor (tek·nol′ə·tər) *n.* One who has an excessive admiration for or belief in technology, especially in relation to social problems; immoderate worship of techniques, gadgets, machinery, and the like. [< TECHNO- + Gk. *latris* servant < *latron* pay, hire] —**tech·nol′a·try** *n.*

tech·no·lith·ic (tek′nə·lith′ik) *adj. Anthropol.* Pertaining to or designating those stone implements which were deliberately fashioned for some intended purpose.

tech·no·log·i·cal (tek′nə·loj′i·kəl) *adj.* Of, pertaining to, associated with, produced or affected by technology, especially in relation to improvements resulting from the application of technical advances in industry, manufacturing, commerce, and the arts. Also **tech′no·log′ic.** —**tech′no·log′i·cal·ly** *adv.*

tech·nol·o·gy (tek·nol′ə·jē) *n.* **1** Theoretical knowledge of industry and the industrial arts. **2** The application of science to the arts. **3** That branch of ethnology which treats of the development of the arts. —**tech·nol′o·gist** *n.*

tech·y (tech′ē) *adj.* **tech·i·er, tech·i·est** Peevishly sensitive; irritable; touchy. Also spelled *tetchy*. [< OF *teche* mark, quality] —**tech′i·ly** *adv.* —**tech′i·ness** *n.*

tec·tol·o·gy (tek·tol′ə·jē) *n.* The branch of morphology that treats of the manner in which organic forms are built up. [< Gk. *tektōn* carpenter, builder + -LOGY] —**tec·to·log′i·cal** (tek′tə·loj′i·kəl) *adj.*

tec·ton·ic (tek·ton′ik) *adj.* **1** Of or pertaining to building or construction. **2** *Geol.* **a** Characteristic of or relating to the structure of the earth's crust, especially as due to deformation. **b** Denoting the forces producing such structures. [< L *tectonicus* < Gk. *tektonikos* < *tektōn* carpenter]

tec·ton·ics (tek·ton′iks) *n. pl.* (*construed as singular*) **1** The science or art of constructing functionally beautiful buildings or things. **2** The geology of earth structure.

tec·tri·ces (tek·trī′sēz, tek′tri-) *n. pl. of* **tec·trix** (tek′triks) *Ornithol.* The wing coverts of a bird. [< NL < L *tectus*, pp. of *tegere* cover] —**tec·tri′cial** (-trish′əl) *adj.*

Te·cum·seh (ti·kum′sə), 1768?–1813, Shawnee chief, an ally of Britain in the War of 1812, during which he was killed.

ted (ted) *v.t.* **ted·ded, ted·ding** To turn over and strew about, or spread loosely for drying, as newly mown grass. [Prob. < Scand. Cf. ON *tethja* spread manure.]

ted·dy (ted′ē) *n. pl.* **·dies** A short undergarment combining chemise and drawers in one. [Origin unknown]

ted·dy bear (ted′ē) A toy bear, usually covered with plush. Also **Teddy bear.** [after *Teddy*, a nickname of Theodore Roosevelt]

Te De·um (tē dē′əm) **1** An ancient Christian hymn beginning with these words. **2** The music to which this hymn is set. **3** Any thanksgiving service in which it is sung. [< L *Te Deum (laudamus)* (we praise) Thee, O God]

te·di·ous (tē′dē·əs) *adj.* **1** Causing weariness; wearisome; boring. **2** *Obs.* Moving slowly. [< LL *taediosus* < L *taedium* tedium, weariness] —**te′di·ous·ly** *adv.* —**te′di·ous·ness** *n.*

Synonyms: dilatory, dreary, dull, fatiguing, irksome, monotonous, slow, sluggish, tardy, tiresome, wearisome. See WEARISOME. *Antonyms:* active, alert, animated, brilliant, energetic, exciting, lively, prompt, quick, stirring, vigorous, vivid.

te·di·um (tē′dē·əm) *n.* Tediousness; wearisomeness. [< L *taedium* < *taedere* vex, weary]

tee¹ (tē) *n.* **1** The letter T. **2** Something resembling the form of the letter T. **3** *Mining* The point of the meeting of two veins lying nearly at right angles to each other without intersecting. —*adj.* T-shaped. [OE *te* < L *te*, name of the letter T]

tee² (tē) *n.* **1** A little cone, as of damp sand or of wood, on which a golf ball is placed in making the first play to a hole. **2** The teeing ground in golf. —*v.t. & v.i.* **teed, tee·ing** To place (the ball) on a tee before striking it. —**to tee off** To strike (the ball) in starting play. [Prob. < TEE³]

tee³ (tē) *n.* In certain games, a mark toward which the balls, quoits, etc., are directed, as in curling. —**to a tee** Exactly; as precisely as possible. [? < TEE¹]

tee⁴ (tē) *n.* A finial in the form of a conventionalized umbrella, used on pagodas, etc. [< Burmese *h'ti* umbrella]

teem¹ (tēm) *v.i.* **1** To be full, as if at the point of producing; be full to overflowing; abound. **2** *Obs.* To bear young. —*v.t.* **3** To produce or bring forth, as offspring: often figuratively. ♦ Homophone: *team*. [OE *tīeman*, prob. < *tēam* progeny. Related to TEAM.] —**teem′er** *n.*

teem² (tēm) *v.i.* To pour; come down heavily: said of rain. —*v.t. Obs.* To pour out; empty. ♦ Homophone: *team*. [< ON *tœma* empty]

teem·ing¹ (tē′ming) *adj.* **1** Prolific; fecund; fruitful; productive. **2** Full; overflowing. **3** Produced in great quantity. See synonyms under FERTILE.

teem·ing² (tē′ming) *adj.* Raining heavily.

teen (tēn) *adj.* Teen-age.

-teen *suffix* Plus ten: used in cardinal numbers from 13 to 19 inclusive: *fifteen*. [OE *-tēne* < *tēn* ten]

teen age The age from 13 to 19 inclusive; hence, adolescence. —**teen′-age** *adj.*

teen-ag·er (tēn′ā′jər) *n.* A person of teen age.

teens (tēnz) *n. pl.* The numbers that end in *-teen*; the years of one's age from 13 to 19 inclusive.

tee·ny (tē′nē) *adj.* **·ni·er, ·ni·est** *Colloq.* Tiny. [Var. of TINY]

teen·y·bop·per (tē′nē·bop′ər) *n. Slang* A modern, hip teen-ager, especially a girl. [< Negro slang *teenybop, teenybopper* a troublesome or tough teen-ager < TEEN(-AGE) + -Y³ + *bop* fight (Cf. BOP¹) + -ER¹]

tee·pee (tē′pē) See TEPEE.

tee shirt (tē) See T-SHIRT.

tee·ter (tē′tər) *v.i.* **1** To see-saw. **2** To walk or move with a swaying or tottering motion. **3** To vacillate; waver. —*v.t.* **4** To cause to teeter. —*n.* **1** An oscillating motion. **2** A see-saw. **3** The spotted sandpiper: so called from its jerky motions. [< dial. E *titter*, prob. < ON *titra* tremble, shiver]

tee·ter-tot·ter (tē′tər·tot′ər) *n.* A see-saw. [< TEETER + TOTTER]

teeth (tēth) Plural of TOOTH.

teethe (tēth) *v.i.* **teethed, teeth·ing** To cut or develop teeth.

teeth·ing (tē′thing) *n.* The process of developing and cutting teeth; dentition.

teething ring A ring of hard rubber, bone, or ivory for a teething baby to bite on.

tee·to·tal (tē·tōt′l) *adj.* **1** Pertaining to total abstinence from intoxicants. **2** Total; entire. [< TOTAL, with emphatic repetition of initial letter] —**tee·to′tal·ism** *n.* —**tee·to′tal·ly** *adv.*

tee·to·tal·er (tē·tōt′l·ər) *n.* One who abstains totally from intoxicants as beverages. Also **tee·to′tal·ist, tee·to′tal·ler.**

tee·to·tum (tē·tō′təm) *n.* **1** A kind of top having lettered and numbered sides: used in the game of put and take. **2** A child's toy, often four-sided, pierced by a peg and spun by the fingers. Also spelled *totetum*: sometimes called *toddle-top*. [< T-*totum* < *T* + L *totus* all; from the fact that the side marked with a T wins the entire stake]

Tef·lon (tef′lon) *n.* A chemically resistant, heat-stable plastic polymer of fluorine and ethylene having wide application in industry and electronics: a trade name.

teg·men (teg′mən) *n. pl.* **·mi·na** (-mə·nə) **1** A covering or coat. **2** *Bot.* The soft inner covering of a seed. Also **teg′u·men** (-yə·min). [< L < *tegere* cover] —**teg′mi·nal** *adj.*

Te·gu·ci·gal·pa (tā·gōō′sē·gäl′pä) The capital of Honduras, in the SW part of the country.

teg·u·la (teg′yə·lə) *n. pl.* **·lae** (-lē) A tile. [< L *tegula* roof tile < *tegere* cover]

teg·u·lar (teg′yə·lər) *adj.* **1** Pertaining to or resembling tiles. **2** Arranged like tiles. **3** Formed of overlapping plates or scales. Also **teg′u·lat·ed.** —**teg′u·lar·ly** *adv.*

teg·u·ment (teg′yə·mənt) *n.* A covering or envelope; an integument. [< L *tegumentum* < *tegere* cover] —**teg·u·men·ta·ry** (teg′yə·men′tər·ē), **teg′u·men′tal** *adj.*

te·hee (tē·hē′) *v.i.* **-heed, -hee·ing** To laugh frivolously or with derision; titter; giggle. —*interj.* An imitative exclamation. —*n.* A restrained laugh; titter. [Imit.]

Te·he·ran (te′ə·rän′, -ran′; *Persian* te·hrän′) The capital of Iran, in the north central part; Roosevelt, Churchill, and Stalin conferred here in November, 1943. Also **Te·hran′.**

te ig·i·tur (tē ij′ə·tər) The prayer or paragraph beginning the canon of the mass in Latin liturgies. [< L, *thee therefore*]

teil (tēl) *n.* **1** The linden. **2** The terebinth pistache (*Pistacia terebinthus*) of the Bible. Also called **teyl tree.** [< OF < L *tilia tree*]

tek·non·y·my (tek·non′ə·mē) *n. Anthropol.* The custom of renaming a parent after his or her child. [< Gk. *teknon child* + *onyma, onoma name*]

tek·tite (tek′tīt) *n. Geol.* Any of numerous small, rounded, glassy objects found in scattered geographical areas and thought to originate in collisions with cosmic bodies. [< Gk. *tēktos molten* + -ITE¹]

tel- Var. of TELO-¹

te·la (tē′lə) *n. pl.* **-lae** (-lē) **1** A tissue or weblike membrane. **2** *Anat.* One of the thin membranes (**tela choroidea**), prolongations of the pia mater, that cover the third and fourth ventricles of the brain. [< L, *web*]

tel·aes·the·sia (tel′əs·thē′zhə, -zhē·ə) See TELESTHESIA.

tel·a·mon (tel′ə·mon) *n. pl.* **tel·a·mo·nes** (tel′ə·mō′nēz) *Archit.* A male figure used as a pillar to support an entablature, etc. Compare ATLANTES, CARYATID. [< L < Gk. *telamōn* < *tlēnai bear*]

TELAMON

tel·an·gi·ec·ta·sia (tel·an′jē·ek·tā′zhə, -zhē·ə) *n. Pathol.* Permanent dilatation of the small arteries or capillaries, producing a vascular tumor: often seen in the form of maternal birthmarks; wine spots. Also **tel·an·gi·ec·ta·sis** (tel′ən·jē·ek′tə·sis). [< NL < Gk. *telos end* + *angeion vessel* + *ekstasis dilatation*] — **tel·an′gi·ec·tat′ic** (-tat′ik) *adj.*

tel·au·to·gram (tel·ô′tə·gram) *n.* A record made by a telautograph.

tel·au·to·graph (tel·ô′tə·graf, -gräf) *n.* An electromagnetically operated device for reproducing writing or drawings at a distance.

Tel A·viv (tel′ ə·vēv′) The largest city of Israel, on the Mediterranean: since 1950 includes Jaffa.

tel·e·car·di·o·gram (tel′ə·kär′dē·ə·gram′) *n.* A cardiogram electrically produced at a distance from the subject.

tel·e·cast (tel′ə·kast, -käst) *v.t. & v.i.* **·cast** or **·cast·ed, ·cast·ing** To broadcast by television. —*n.* A program broadcast by television.

tel·e·com·mu·ni·ca·tion (tel′ə·kə·myoo′nə·kā′shən) *n.* **1** The art and science of communicating at a distance, especially by means of electromagnetic impulses, with or without wires, as in radio, radar, television, telegraphy, telephony, etc. Also **tel′e·com·mu′ni·ca′·tions.** **2** Any message so transmitted.

tel·eg·no·sis (tel′əg·nō′sis) *n.* Knowledge of remote happenings by other than normal sensory means, as by clairvoyance. [< TELE- + Gk. *gnōsis knowing*]

tel·e·gram (tel′ə·gram) *n.* A message sent by telegraph. [< TELE- + -GRAM]

tel·e·graph (tel′ə·graf, -gräf) *n.* Any of various devices, systems, or processes for transmitting messages or signals to a distance, especially any form of such apparatus utilizing electromagnetic impulses transmitted by conducting wires between sending and receiving points. —*v.t.* **1** To send (a message) by telegraph. **2** To communicate with by telegraph. —*v.i.* **3** To transmit a message by

telegraph. [< TELE- + -GRAPH]

te·leg·ra·pher (tə·leg′rə·fər) *n.* One who is employed in sending telegrams or is skilled in telegraphy. Also **te·leg′ra·phist.**

tel·e·graph·ic (tel′ə·graf′ik) *adj.* Of or pertaining to the telegraph; transmitted by means of telegraphy. Also **tel′e·graph′i·cal.** — **tel′e·graph′i·cal·ly** *adv.*

tel·e·gra·phone (tə·leg′rə·fōn) *n.* An instrument for recording and reproducing sound, similar in principle to the tape recorder but adapted for connection with a transmitter or microphone. [< TELE- + -GRA(PH) + -PHONE]

tel·e·graph·o·scope (tel′ə·graf′ə·skōp) *n.* An instrument for transmitting and reproducing a picture telegraphically. [< TELE- + GRAPHO- + -SCOPE]

te·leg·ra·phy (tə·leg′rə·fē) *n.* **1** The process of conveying messages by telegraph. **2** The art or science of the construction and operation of telegraphs.

tel·e·ki·ne·sis (tel′ə·ki·nē′sis) *n.* **1** Movement of an object or inanimate body without apparent external cause. **2** The alleged power of a spiritualist medium to bring about such movements without direct or observable contact. — **tel′e·ki·net′ic** (-net′ik) *adj.*

tel·e·lec·tric (tel′i·lek′trik) *adj.* Denoting the transmission, as of music, to a distance by electricity. [< TEL(E)- + ELECTRIC]

tel·e·mark (tel′ə·märk) *n.* In skiing, a turn effected by shifting the weight to one advanced ski and turning its tip inward: used to change direction or stop quickly. [from *Telemark*, Norway]

tel·e·me·chan·ics (tel′ə·mə·kan′iks) *n.* **1** The theory and practice of operating mechanisms from a distance. **2** Remote control operation, as by electromagnetic and radio impulses.

te·lem·e·ter (tə·lem′ə·tər, tel′ə·mē′tər) *n.* **1** An apparatus for determining distances by the measurement of angles. **2** An electrical apparatus for indicating or measuring various quantities and for transmitting the data to a distant point. — **te·lem′e·try** *n.* — **tel·e·met·ric** (tel′ə·met′rik) *adj.*

tel·e·mo·tor (tel′ə·mō′tər) *n.* A hydraulic or electrical device by which power is applied at a distance, especially in operating the steering gear of a vessel by turning the wheel on the bridge.

tel·en·ceph·a·lon (tel′en·sef′ə·lon) *n. Anat.* The terminal division of the neural tube of the embryo from which are developed the cerebral hemispheres and olfactory lobes; the endbrain. [< TEL(E)- + ENCEPHALON] — **tel·en·ce·phal·ic** (tel′en·si·fal′ik) *adj.*

te·le·ol·o·gy (tel′ē·ol′ə·jē, tē′lē-) *n.* **1** The branch of cosmology that treats of final causes. See FINAL CAUSE. **2** The philosophical and biological doctrine of design which holds that the phenomena of organic life and development can be explained by conscious or purposive causes directed to definite ends and not by mechanical causes; vitalism as opposed to *mechanism*. **3** The explanation of nature in terms of utility or purpose, especially divine purpose; the study of a creative design in the processes of nature. [< NL *teleologia* <Gk. *telos, teleos* end + *logos* discourse] — **tel′e·o·log′i·cal** (-ə·loj′i·kəl) or **tel′e·o·log′ic** *adj.* — **tel′e·o·log′i·cal·ly** *adv.* — **tel′e·ol′o·gist** *n.*

tel·e·ost (tel′ē·ost, tē′lē-) *n.* Any of a large and widely distributed group or order (*Teleostei*) of fishes having true bones: distinguished from cyclostomes and elasmobranchs. —*adj.* Of, pertaining to, or having the characteristics of the teleosts. Also **tel′e·os′te·an.** [< Gk. *telos* end + *osteon* bone]

te·lep·a·thy (tə·lep′ə·thē) *n.* The supposed communication of one mind with another at a distance by other than normal sensory means; thought-transference. [< TELE- + -PATHY] — **tel·e·path·ic** (tel′ə·path′ik) *adj.* — **tel′e·path′i·cal·ly** *adv.* — **tel·ep′a·thist** *n.*

tel·e·phone (tel′ə·fōn) *n.* An instrument for reproducing sound or speech at a distant point, by the electromagnetic transmission of variable audio frequencies over a conducting wire or other communication channel. — **wireless telephone** A radiotelephone. — *v.* **·phoned, ·phon·ing** *v.t.* **1** To send by telephone, as a message. **2** To communicate with by tele-

phone. —*v.i.* **3** To communicate by telephone. [< TELE- + -PHONE] — **tel′e·phon′er** *n.*

tel·e·phon·ic (tel′ə·fon′ik) *adj.* **1** Of or pertaining to the telephone. **2** Conveying sound to a great distance. Also **tel′e·phon′i·cal.** — **tel′e·phon′i·cal·ly** *adv.*

tel·e·pho·no·graph (tel′ə·fō′nə·graf, -gräf) *n.* A combination of a phonograph and a telephone receiver by which telephone messages can be recorded and then reproduced. — **tel′e·pho′no·graph′ic** *adj.*

te·leph·o·ny (tə·lef′ə·nē) *n.* The art or process of communicating by telephone, with or without wires directly connecting the terminal points.

tel·e·pho·to (tel′ə·fō′tō) *adj.* **1** Denoting a combination of lenses which produces a large image of a distant object in a camera; telephotographic. **2** Pertaining to telephotography.

tel·e·pho·to·graph (tel′ə·fō′tə·graf, -gräf) *n.* **1** A picture transmitted by wire or radio. **2** A picture made with a telephoto lens. — **tel′e·pho′to·graph′ic** *adj.*

tel·e·pho·tog·ra·phy (tel′ə·fə·tog′rə·fē) *n.* **1** The art of producing photographic images of distant objects on a larger scale than is possible with an ordinary camera. **2** The reproduction of photographs or other picture material by radio or wire communication.

tel·e·ran (tel′ə·ran) *n. Telecom.* A system of air navigation which combines the principles of television and radar, the information being gathered by ground stations and transmitted to all aircraft within range. [< TELE- (def. 2) + R(A-DAR) A(IR) N(AVIGATION)]

tel·e·scope (tel′ə·skōp) *n.* **1** An optical instrument for enlarging the image of a distant object, consisting of an object glass for collecting light beams from the object and an eyepiece for viewing the image. The **refracting telescope** transmits the rays to a focus through a combination of lenses called the object glass; the **reflecting telescope** brings them to a focus by reflection from a concave

REFRACTING TELESCOPE
Yerkes Observatory
40 inch.

mirror. **2** A valise or traveling bag that shuts with one section inside the other, and thus can be extended, like a telescope. — *v.* **·scoped, ·scop·ing** *v.t.* **1** To drive or slide together so that one part fits into another in the manner of the sections of a small telescope. **2** To crush by driving something into or upon. **3** To represent in a compressed or shortened form, as a period of time. —*v.i.* **4** To crash or be forced into one another, as railroad cars in a collision. [< TELE- + -SCOPE]

tel·e·scop·ic (tel′ə·skop′ik) *adj.* **1** Pertaining to the telescope. **2** Visible only through a telescope. **3** Far-seeing. **4** Having sections that slide within or over one another. Also **tel′e·scop′i·cal.** — **tel′e·scop′i·cal·ly** *adv.*

tel·e·scop·tics (tel′ə·skop′tiks) *n. pl.* (construed as singular) The art of designing, constructing, and using telescopes.

te·les·co·py (tə·les′kə·pē) *n.* The art of using or making telescopes. — **te·les′co·pist** *n.*

tel·e·script (tel′ə·skript) *n.* A script written or adapted for a television program. [< TELE- (def. 2) + SCRIPT]

tel·e·spec·tro·scope (tel′ə·spek′trə·skōp) *n.* **1** A combined telescope and spectroscope. **2** A spectroscope for attachment to a telescope.

tel·e·ster·e·o·scope (tel′ə·ster′ē·ə·skōp′, -stir′-) *n.* An optical instrument that presents images of objects at a distance from the observer in enhanced relief.

tel·es·the·sia (tel′is·thē′zhə, -zhē·ə) *n.* Susceptibility to stimuli coming from a distance and beyond the normal range of the senses: also spelled *telaesthesia*. [< NL < Gk. *tēle* far + *aisthēsis* feeling] —**tel′es·thet′ic** (-thet′ik) *adj.*

tel·e·stich (tel′ə·stik, tə·les′tik) *n.* An acrostic in which the significant letters are at the ends of the lines. [< Gk. *telos* end + *stichos* line]

tel·e·ther·a·py (tel′ə·ther′ə·pē) *n. Med.* 1 Treatment by radiation administered in massive doses at a distance from the body. 2 The prescribing of medical treatment by telephone, letter, etc.: also called **absent treatment.**

tel·e·ther·mom·e·ter (tel′ə·thûr·mom′ə·tər) *n.* Any apparatus used to indicate the temperature of a distant point, as a thermocouple. —**tel′e·ther·mom′e·try** *n.*

tel·e·thon (tel′ə·thon) *n.* A long telecast, usually to raise funds for a charity. [< TELE- + (MARA)THON]

tel·e·tran·scrip·tion (tel·ə·tran·skrip′shən) *n.* A method for transcribing television programs on films for subsequent presentation; also, the transcription itself.

tel·e·type (tel′ə·tīp) *v.t. & v.i.* **·typed, ·typ·ing** To communicate (with) by teletypewriter or Teletype. —*n.* A teletypewriter. —**tel′e·typ′er** *n.*

tel·e·type·writ·er (tel′ə·tīp′rī′tər) *n.* A telegraphic instrument resembling a typewriter, by which the work done on one machine is simultaneously typed on electrically connected typewriters a distance away.

te·leu·to·spore (tə·lōō′tə·spôr, -spōr) *n. Bot.* The one- or two-celled, usually stalked, thick-walled spore produced as the final stage in the growth of rust fungi. [< Gk. *teleutē* fulfilment + SPORE] —**te·leu′to·spor′ic** (-spôr′ik, -spor′ik) *adj.*

tel·e·view (tel′ə·vyōō) *v.t. & v.i.* To observe by means of television. —**tel′e·view′er** *n.*

tel·e·vise (tel′ə·vīz) *v.t. & v.i.* **·vised, ·vis·ing** To transmit or receive by television.

tel·e·vi·sion (tel′ə·vizh′ən) *n.* The exact and continuous transmission of visual images, still or in motion but without permanent recording, for instantaneous viewing at a distance: effected by a combined optical and electrical system for converting light waves into corresponding electrical impulses which are reconverted into their visual form in a receiving set. —**tel′e·vi′sion·al, tel′e·vi′sion·ar′y** (-vizh′ən·er′ē) *adj.*

tel·ex (tel′iks) *n.* 1 A communication system using teletypewriters connected by wire through exchanges which operate automatically. 2 A message sent by such a system. —*v.t.* To send by telex. [< TEL(ETYPEWRITER) + EX(CHANGE)]

tel·fer (tel′fər) See TELPHER.

tel·ford (tel′fərd) *adj.* Designating a road made of large broken stone packed with smaller pieces, covered with a layer of finely broken stone or gravel, and rolled hard and smooth. —*n.* A road having such a surface. [after Thomas *Telford*, 1757–1834, Scottish engineer]

tel·ford·ize (tel′fər·dīz) *v.t.* **·ized, ·iz·ing** To make or cover (a road) with a telford surface.

tel·har·mo·ni·um (tel′här·mō′nē·əm) *n.* An instrument by which an operator at a central station playing on a keyboard controlling alternating electric currents is able to produce music at a distance. [< TEL(E)- + HARMONIUM] —**tel′har·mon′ic** (-mon′ik) *adj.* —**tel·har′mo·ny** (-här′mə·nē) *n.*

tel·ic (tel′ik, tē′lik) *adj.* Connected with, tending toward, or denoting a purpose; teleological. [< Gk. *telikos* < *telos* end] —**tel′i·cal·ly** *adv.*

te·li·o·stage (tē′lē·ə·stāj′, telē-) *n. Bot.* The last stage in the life cycle of rust fungi. [< TELIUM + STAGE]

te·li·um (tē′lē·əm, tel′ē-) *n. Bot.* The sorus of the teliostage of the rust fungi. [< NL < Gk. *telos, teleos* end] —**te′li·al** *adj.*

Tell (tel), **William** A legendary Swiss hero in the struggle for independence from Austria. He refused to salute the governor's cap, which had been set up as a symbol of Austrian authority, and was forced to shoot an apple off his son's head with bow and arrow.

tell·er (tel′ər) *n.* 1 One who relates or informs. 2 A person who receives or pays out money, as in a bank. 3 A person appointed to collect and count ballots in a legislative body or other assembly.

tell·ing (tel′ing) *adj.* Producing a great effect; im-

pressive; effective; striking. See synonyms under VIVID. —**tell′ing·ly** *adv.*

tell·tale (tel′tāl′) *adj.* 1 Tattling; talebearing. 2 Betraying. —*n.* 1 One who improperly gives information concerning the private affairs of others; a tattler. 2 That which conveys information, especially in an involuntary way; a token. 3 An instrument or device, usually automatic, for giving information as to number, position, condition, etc. 4 A row of dangling straps or ropes suspended above a railway track to warn anyone standing on a car roof of the approach of a low overhead structure. 5 A clock to record the times of coming and going, as of workmen, or as a watchman's clock. 6 An index showing the position of a vessel's helm. 7 A yellowlegs or tattler.

tel·lu·rate (tel′yə·rāt) *n. Chem.* A salt of telluric acid.

tel·lu·ri·an (te·lōōr′ē·ən, tel·yōōr′-) *adj.* Of or pertaining to the earth or its inhabitants. —*n.* An inhabitant of the earth. [< L *tellus, -uris* the earth]

tel·lu·ric (te·lōōr′ik, tel·yōōr′-) *adj.* 1 Of or pertaining to the earth; terrestrial; earthly. 2 *Chem.* Derived from or containing tellurium, especially in its higher valence.

telluric acid *Chem.* A weak acid, H_6TeO_6, obtained by oxidizing tellurium. It is analogous to sulfuric acid.

tel·lu·ride (tel′yə·rīd, -rid) *n. Chem.* A compound of tellurium with an element or an organic radical: *telluride* of lead.

tel·lu·rite (tel′yə·rīt) *n.* 1 A white or yellow native tellurium dioxide, TeO_2. 2 *Chem.* A salt of tellurous acid.

tel·lu·ri·um (te·lōōr′ē·əm, tel·yōōr′-) *n.* A brittle element (symbol Te, atomic number 52) having some metallic properties, rarely found native. See PERIODIC TABLE. [< NL < L *tellus, -uris* the earth]

tel·lu·rize (tel′yə·rīz) *v.t.* **·rized, ·riz·ing** To cause to combine with tellurium.

tel·lur·nick·el (tel·ər·nik′əl) *n.* Melonite. [< TELLUR(IUM) + NICKEL]

tel·lu·rous (tel′yər·əs, te·lōōr′əs, tel·yōōr′-) *adj. Chem.* Of, pertaining to, or derived from tellurium, especially in its lower valence: *tellurous* acid, H_2TeO_3.

tel·o·blast (tel′ə·blast) *n. Zool.* A large cell at the growing end of the embryo, in annelids, etc., which produces rows of smaller cells. [< TELO-[1] + -BLAST]

tel·o·dy·nam·ic (tel′ə·dī·nam′ik, -di-) *adj.* Of, related to, or employed in the transmission of power to a distance, specifically by cables and pulleys. [< TELO-[2] + DYNAMIC]

tel·o·lec·i·thal (tel′ə·les′ə·thəl) *adj. Biol.* Having the nutritive part of the yolk at one pole: said of ova, as of birds, with unequal or partial segmentation. [< TELO-[1] + LECITHAL]

tel·o·phase (tel′ə·fāz) *n. Biol.* The closing phase of mitosis, when the cell divides and the daughter nuclei are formed. [< TELO-[1] + PHASE]

tel·pher (tel′fər) *n.* A light car suspended from cables and usually propelled by electricity: used for aerial transportation. —*v.t.* To transport by telpher. Also spelled *telfer.* [< TEL(E)- + Gk. *pherein* bear] —**tel′pher·ic** *adj.* —**tel′pher·age** (-ij) *n.*

tel·son (tel′sən) *n. Zool.* The last abdominal segment of the body of an arthropod, as of a lobster, shrimp, or scorpion. [< Gk. *telson* boundary]

tem·blor (tem·blôr′) *n. pl.* **·blors** or **·blo·res** (-blô′rās) An earthquake. [< Sp.]

tem·e·rar·i·ous (tem′ə·râr′ē·əs) *adj.* Unreasonably adventurous; rash; reckless. [< L *temerarius* < *temere* rashly] —**tem′e·rar′i·ous·ly** *adv.* —**tem′e·rar′i·ous·ness** *n.*

te·mer·i·ty (tə·mer′ə·tē) *n.* Venturesome or foolish boldness; rashness; disregard of personal danger or consequences. [< L *temeritas, -tatis* < *temere* rashly]

Synonyms: audacity, foolhardiness, hardihood, hastiness, heedlessness, precipitancy, precipitation, presumption, rashness, recklessness, venturesomeness. *Rashness* applies to the actual impulsive rushing into danger without counting the cost; *temerity* denotes the needless exposure of oneself to peril because of lack of foresight. *Rashness* is used chiefly of bodily acts, *temerity* often of mental or social matters. We say it is

amazing that one should have had the *temerity* to make a statement which could be readily proved a falsehood; in such use *temerity* is often closely allied to *hardihood, audacity,* or *presumption. Venturesomeness* dallies on the edge of danger and experiments with it; *foolhardiness* rushes in for want of sense, *heedlessness* for want of attention, *rashness* for want of reflection, *recklessness* from disregard of consequences. *Antonyms:* care, caution, circumspection, cowardice, hesitation, timidity, wariness.

tem·per (tem′pər) *n.* 1 Heat of mind or passion; disposition to become angry; also, a fit of anger. 2 Quality of mind with reference to the passions, emotions, or affections; disposition. 3 Composure of mind; equanimity; self-command; calmness: used only in the phrases **to keep,** or **to lose, one's temper.** 4 *Metall.* The condition of a metal as regards hardness and brittleness, especially when due to heating and sudden cooling. 5 Consistency due to mixture, as of mortar, etc. 6 Lime or an equivalent used in clarifying sugar. 7 An alloy, as that added to tin to make pewter. 8 *Obs.* Constitutional condition, resulting, according to the ancients, from the proportion in which the four humors were mixed. 9 *Archaic* A mean; medium. [< *v.*] — *v.t.* 1 To bring to a state of moderation or suitability, as by addition of another quality; free from excess; moderate; mitigate: to *temper* justice with mercy. 2 To bring to the proper consistency, texture, etc., by moistening and working: to *temper* clay. 3 To bring (metal) to a required hardness and elasticity by heating and suddenly cooling. 4 *Music* To adjust the tones of (an instrument) by temperament; tune. 5 *Obs.* To adjust. — *v.i.* 6 To be or become tempered. [Fusion of OE *temprian* mingle, regulate and OF *temprer, tremper* soak, temper (steel), both < L *temperare* combine in due proportion. For sense development of the noun defs. 1, 2, and 3, see def. 8.] — **tem′per·a·bil′i·ty** *n.* — **tem′per·a·ble** *adj.* — **tem′per·er** *n.*

Synonyms (noun): constitution, disposition, frame, grain, humor, mood, nature, organization, temperament. See ANGER, CHARACTER. *Synonyms (verb):* accommodate, adapt, adjust, appease, assuage, attemper, calm, fit, moderate, modify, mollify, pacify, qualify, restrain, soften, soothe.

tem·per·a (tem′pər·ə, *Ital.* tem′pä·rä) *n.* 1 A painting medium which is essentially an emulsion prepared by any of numerous recipes, and composed characteristically of oil usually thickened, with or without a resin such as dammar varnish, and egg and water. 2 The method of painting by this medium, which falls into three principal divisions: *unvarnished tempera, varnished tempera,* and *tempera,* as underpainting for oil glazes: widely used in the Renaissance and revived in modern times, sometimes in combination with oil techniques. [< Ital. < *temperare* temper < L]

tem·per·a·ment (tem′pər·ə·mənt, -prə-) *n.* 1 The characteristic physical and mental peculiarities of an individual as manifested in his reactions. 2 *Music* The tuning of an instrument so that the intervals of the scale shall follow a suitable law of succession. 3 Mental constitution; make-up; disposition. 4 Adjustment or compromise. 5 *Obs.* Temperature. See synonyms under CHARACTER, TEMPER. [< L *temperamentum* proper mixture < *temperare* mix in due proportions]

tem·per·ance (tem′pər·əns) *n.* 1 The state or quality of being temperate; habitual moderation, especially in the indulgence of any appetite. 2 Specifically, the principle and practice of total abstinence from intoxicants. 3 *Obs.* Calmness; self-control. See synonyms under ABSTINENCE. — *adj.* 1 Of or pertaining to public places where alcoholic beverages are not sold. 2 Of, relating to, practicing, or promoting total abstinence from intoxicants. [< OF < L *temperantia,* orig. neut. pl. of *temperans, -antis,* ppr. of *temperare* mix in due proportions]

tem·per·ate (tem′pər·it) *adj.* 1 Observing moderation or self-control; specifically, by extension, not indulging in intoxicating liquors. 2 Moderate as regards temperature; free from extremes of heat or cold; mild. 3 Characterized by moderation or the absence of extremes; not excessive. **4** Calm; restrained; self-controlled. **5** *Music* Tempered: said of an interval or scale. See synonyms under SOBER. [<L *temperare* mix in due proportions] — **tem′per·ate·ly** *adv.* — **tem′per·ate·ness** *n.*

tem·per·a·ture (tem′pər·ə·chər, -prə-) *n.* **1** Condition as regards heat or cold. **2** The degree of heat in a body or substance, as measured on the graduated scale of a thermometer. See table below. **3** Sensible heat of the human body; also, excess of this above the normal. **4** *Obs.* Constitution; temperament; mixture; temperateness; temperance. [<L *temperatura* due measure < *temperatus.* See TEMPERATE.]

To convert from Fahrenheit to Celsius (Centigrade): Subtract 32 from the Fahrenheit reading, multiply by 5, and divide the product by 9. *Example:* $65°$ F. $-32 = 33$; $33 \times 5 = 165$; $165 \div 9 = 18.3°$ C. To convert from Celsius to Fahrenheit: Multiply the Celsius reading by 9, divide the product by 5, add 32. *Example:* $30°$ C. $\times 9 = 270$; $270 \div 5 = 54$; $54 + 32 = 86°$ F.

CONVERSION TABLE

Fahrenheit	Celsius	Fahrenheit	Celsius
500	260.0	−10	−23.3
400	204.4	−20	−28.9
300	149.0	−30	−34.4
212	100.0	−40	−40.0
200	93.3	−50	−45.6
100	37.8	−60	−51.1
90	32.2	−70	−56.7
80	26.7	−80	−62.2
70	21.1	−90	−67.8
60	15.6	−100	−73.3
50	10.0	−200	−129.0
40	4.4	−300	−184.0
32	0.0	−400	−240.0
30	−1.1	*−459.4	−273.0
20	−6.6		
10	−12.2		
0	−17.8	*Absolute zero	

tem·pered (tem′pərd) *adj.* **1** Having temper or a temper, in any sense; mostly in compounds: quick-*tempered*, ill-*tempered.* **2** *Music* Adjusted in pitch to some mean temperament. **3** Moderated by admixture. **4** Having the right degree of hardness and elasticity: well-*tempered* steel.

tem·per·pin (tem′pər·pin′) *n.* **1** A wooden screw used to regulate the motion of a spinning wheel. **2** A tuning peg of a violin.

tem·pest (tem′pist) *n.* **1** An extensive and violent wind, usually attended with rain, snow, or hail. **2** A violent commotion or agitation; a fierce tumult. See synonyms under STORM. — *v.t.* To agitate violently; affect as a tempest does. [<OF *tempeste* <L *tempestas* space of time, weather < *tempus* time]

tem·pes·tu·ous (tem·pes′choo·əs) *adj.* Stormy; turbulent; violent. [<OF *tempestueux* <LL *tempestuosus* <L *tempestas* weather. See TEMPEST.] — **tem·pes′tu·ous·ly** *adv.* — **tem·pes′tu·ous·ness** *n.*

tem·plate (tem′plit) *n.* **1** A pattern or gage, as of wood or metal, used as a guide in shaping something or in checking the accuracy of work. **2** In building, a stout stone or timber for distributing weight or thrust. **3** A wedge for a building block under a ship's keel. Also spelled *templet.* [<F *templette* stretcher, dim. of *temple* small timber <L *templum*]

tem·ple[1] (tem′pəl) *n.* **1** A stately edifice consecrated to one or more deities and forming a seat of their worship. **2** An edifice dedicated to public worship; especially, in the United States, a Reform synagog. **3** In France, a Protestant church. **4** Figuratively, any place considered as occupied by God; specifically, a sanctified human body. **5** A building erected and dedicated for the administration of Mormon ordinances; a Mormon church. — **the Temple 1** Either of two medieval establishments in London and Paris, once occupied by the Knights Templar. In London, since 1185, the district lying between Fleet Street and the Thames river, the site of the **Inner** and **Middle Temple.** See INNS OF COURT. **2** Any of three successive sacred

edifices built in Jerusalem for the worship of Jehovah. [OE *tempel* <L *templum* temple]

tem·ple[2] (tem′pəl) *n.* The region on each side of the head above the cheek bone. [<OF <L *tempora,* pl. of *tempus* temple]

tem·ple[3] (tem′pəl) *n.* An attachment to a loom that serves to keep the last woven part of the fabric stretched and to prevent chafing of the warp. [<F <L *templum* a small timber]

tem·po (tem′pō) *n.* *pl.* **·pos** or **·pi** (-pē) **1** *Music* Relative speed at which a composition is rendered; time; rhythm of a tune. **2** Characteristic manner or style; rate of speed or activity in general. [<Ital. <L *tempus* time]

tem·po·ral[1] (tem′pər·əl) *adj.* **1** Pertaining to affairs of the present life, as contrasted with those of a future life; earthly, as opposed to heavenly. **2** Pertaining to or limited by time; transitory, as opposed to eternal. **3** Related to or concerned with worldly affairs; worldly; material, as opposed to spiritual. **4** Pertaining to civil law or authority; lay; secular: contrasted with *clerical.* **5** *Gram.* Of, pertaining to, or denoting time: *temporal* conjunctions. See synonyms under PROFANE. — **lords temporal** English, Scottish, and Irish lay peers with seats in the House of Lords. [<OF *temporel* <L *temporalis* < *tempus, temporis* time] — **tem′po·ral·ly** *adv.* — **tem′po·ral·ness** *n.*

tem·po·ral[2] (tem′pər·əl) *adj. Anat.* Of, pertaining to, or situated at the temple or temples: the *temporal* bone. [<L *temporalis* < *tempora.* See TEMPLE[2].]

tem·po·ral[3] (tem′pər·äl′) *n. SW U.S.* A field or portion of land; a farm, especially one not requiring irrigation. [<Sp. *temporal* storm, tempest; ? < *terreno de temporal* land where heavy rains fall]

tem·po·rar·y (tem′pə·rer′ē) *adj.* **1** Lasting or intended to be used for a short time only; transitory; of passing interest: opposed to *permanent.* **2** *Obs.* Contemporary. See synonyms under TRANSIENT. [<L *temporarius* < *tempus, temporis* time] — **tem′po·rar′i·ly** *adv.* — **tem′po·rar′i·ness** *n.*

TEMPLE OF HORUS, EDFU, BEGUN 237 B.C.
Greco-Egyptian style.

tem·po·rize (tem′pə·rīz) *v.i.* **·rized, ·riz·ing 1** To act evasively so as to gain time or put off decision or commitment. **2** To give real or apparent compliance to the circumstances; comply. **3** To parley so as to gain time: with *with.* **4** To effect a compromise; negotiate: with *with* or *between.* Also **tem′po·rise.** [<F *temporiser* <L *temporis* time] — **tem·po·ri·za′tion** *n.* — **tem′po·riz′er** *n.* — **tem′po·riz′ing·ly** *adv.*

tempt (tempt) *v.t.* **1** To attempt to persuade (a person) to do wrong, as by promising pleasure or gain. **2** To be attractive to; invite: Your offers do not *tempt* me. **3** To provoke or risk provoking: to *tempt* fate. **4** *Obs.* To test; prove. See synonyms under ALLURE. [< OF *tempter, tenter* <L *temptare, tentare* test, try, prob. intens. of *tendere* stretch] — **tempt′a·ble** *adj.* — **tempt′er** *n.* — **tempt′ress** *n. fem.*

temp·ta·tion (temp·tā′shən) *n.* **1** That which tempts, especially to evil. **2** The state of being tempted, or enticed to evil; the act of tempting or testing. **3** A state of mental conflict between heavenly and infernal influences.

tempt·ing (temp′ting) *adj.* Alluring; attractive; seductive. — **tempt′ing·ly** *adv.* — **tempt′ing·ness** *n.*

ten (ten) *n.* **1** The cardinal number following nine and preceding eleven, or any of the symbols or combinations of symbols (10, x, X) used to represent it. **2** Anything containing or representing ten units or members; a play-

ing card marked with ten pips; also, a ten-dollar bill. — *adj.* Being or consisting of one more than nine; decennary. [OE]

ten·a·ble (ten′ə·bəl) *adj.* Capable of being held, maintained, or defended. [<F <*tenir* hold <L *tenere*] — **ten′a·bil′i·ty, ten′a·ble·ness** *n.* — **ten′a·bly** *adv.*

ten·ace (ten′ās) *n.* The combination in the same hand of the best and third best cards (**major tenace**) or of the second and fourth best cards (**minor tenace**) of any suit. [<Sp. *tenaza* pincers, tongs < *tenaz* tenacious <L *tenax, tenacis.* See TENACIOUS.]

te·na·cious (ti·nā′shəs) *adj.* **1** Having great cohesiveness of parts; tough. **2** Adhesive; sticky. **3** Holding or tending to hold strongly, as opinions, rights, etc.: followed by *of;* hence, stubborn; obstinate; unyielding; persistent. **4** Apt to retain; strongly retentive, as memory. See synonyms under STRONG. [<L *tenax, tenacis* holding fast < *tenere* hold, grasp, embrace] — **te·na′cious·ly** *adv.* — **te·na′cious·ness** *n.*

te·nac·i·ty (ti·nas′ə·tē) *n.* **1** The state or quality of being tenacious. **2** That quality of a body in consequence of which it resists being pulled or forced apart.

te·nac·u·lum (ti·nak′yə·ləm) *n. pl.* **·la** (-lə) *Surg.* A hooked instrument for seizing and holding parts of the body, as arteries, during surgical operations. [<LL, holder <L *tenax, tenacis.* See TENACIOUS.]

te·naille (te·nāl′) *n.* A low outwork, usually with one or two reentering angles, in the main ditch between two bastions. — *v.t.* To equip with tenailles. Also **te·nail′.** [<F <LL *tenacula,* pl. of *tenaculum.* See TENACULUM.]

ten·an·cy (ten′ən·sē) *n. pl.* **·cies 1** The holding of lands or tenements by any form of title; occupancy. **2** The period of holding or occupying lands, tenements, or office; temporary possession. **3** A habitation or dwelling place held of another.

ten·ant (ten′ənt) *n.* **1** One who holds or possesses lands or property by any kind of title; especially, one who holds under another; a lessee. **2** A defendant in an action concerning real property. **3** A dweller in any place; an occupant. — *v.t.* To hold as tenant; occupy. — *v.i.* To be a tenant. [<F, orig. ppr. of *tenir* hold <L *tenere*] — **ten′ant·a·ble** *adj.* — **ten′ant·less** *adj.*

tench (tench) *n.* A European fresh-water cyprinoid fish (*Tinca tinca*), very tenacious of life, and having small, deeply embedded scales. [<F *tenche* <LL *tinca* tench]

tend[1] (tend) *v.i.* **1** To have an aptitude, tendency, or disposition; incline: He *tends* to talk too much. **2** To have influence toward a specified result; lead or conduce: Education *tends* to refinement. **3** To go in a certain direction. [<OF *tendre* <L *tendere* extend, tend]

tend[2] (tend) *v.t.* **1** To attend to the needs or requirements of; take care of; minister to: to *tend* a fire. **2** To watch over; look after: to *tend* children. **3** To watch (a vessel at anchor) with the intention of so managing her when the tide changes as to prevent fouling the anchor and chain. — *v.i.* **4** To be in attendance; serve or wait: with *on* or *upon.* **5** *Colloq.* To give attention or care: with *to.* [Aphetic var. of ATTEND]

ten·dance (ten′dəns) *n.* **1** The act of tending; attendance; service. **2** *Archaic* Attendants collectively. Also **ten′dence.**

ten·den·cy (ten′dən·sē) *n. pl.* **·cies 1** The state of being directed toward some purpose, end, or result; inclination; bent; aptitude. **2** That which tends to produce some specified effect. **3** Bias; propensity. **4** Trend of a speech; purpose of a story. See synonyms under AIM, DIRECTION, INCLINATION. [<Med. L *tendentia,* orig. neut. pl. of *tendens, -entis,* ppr. of *tendere* extend, tend]

ten·den·tious (ten·den′shəs) *adj.* Having a purposed aim or intentional tendency. [<G *tendenziös* <*tendenz* tendency <Med. L *tendentia.* See TENDENCY.] — **ten·den′tious·ly** *adv.* — **ten·den′tious·ness** *n.*

ten·der[1] (ten′dər) *adj.* **1** Yielding easily to force that tends to crush, bruise, break, or injure; soft or delicate. **2** Easily chewed or cut:

said of food, especially meat. **3** Delicate or weak; not strong or hardy. **4** Youthful and delicate; not strengthened by maturity: a *tender* age. **5** Characterized by or expressive of a delicate sensibility; kind; affectionate; gentle: *tender* mercy; a *tender* father. **6** Capable of arousing sensitive feelings; touching: *tender* memories; a *tender* sight. **7** Susceptible to spiritual or moral feelings: a *tender* conscience. **8** Painful if touched; easily pained: a *tender* sore. **9** Of delicate effect or quality; soft: a *tender* light. **10** Requiring deft or delicate treatment; ticklish; touchy: a *tender* subject. **11** *Naut.* Careening too easily under sail: said of a ship. See synonyms under BLAND, FRAGILE, FRIENDLY, HUMANE, MERCIFUL. —*v.t.* To make tender; soften. [<OF *tendre* <L *tener, teneris*] —**ten′der·ly** *adv.* —**ten′der·ness** *n.*

ten·der² (ten′dər) *v.t.* **1** To present for acceptance, as a resignation; offer. **2** *Law* To proffer, as money, in payment, in discharge of a debt, or to fulfil a contract. —*n.* **1** The act of tendering; an offer; specifically, in law, a formal offer of satisfaction. **2** That which is offered as payment, especially money: legal *tender.* [<F *tendre* <L *tendere* extend, tend] —**ten′der·er** *n.*

tend·er³ (ten′dər) *n.* **1** A vessel used to bring supplies, passengers, and crew back and forth between a larger vessel and a nearby shore; also, a vessel which services another at sea. **2** A boat used to carry provisions, etc., to whalers and lighthouses. **3** A vehicle attached to the rear of a steam locomotive to carry fuel and water for it. **4** One who tends or ministers to. [<TEND²]

ten·der·foot (ten′dər·fŏŏt′) *n. pl.* **·foots** or **·feet** (-fēt′) *U.S.* **1** A newcomer in the West; one not yet inured to the hardships of or not yet experienced in the life of the plains, the mining camp, etc.; a greenhorn: opposed to *longhorn.* **2** Any inexperienced person. **3** A boy scout in the beginning class or group. —*adj.* Inexperienced; also, made up of inexperienced people: a *tenderfoot* gang.

ten·der·ize (ten′də·rīz) *v.t.* **·ized, ·iz·ing** To make tender, as meat.

ten·der·loin (ten′dər·loin′) *n.* The tender part of the loin of beef, pork, etc., lying close to the ventral side of the lumbar vertebrae.

ten·di·nous (ten′də·nəs) *adj.* **1** Of, pertaining to, resembling, or formed by a tendon. **2** Having or full of tendons; sinewy. [<F *tendineux* <Med. L *tendo, -inis.* See TENDON.]

ten·don (ten′dən) *n. Anat.* One of the bands of tough, fibrous connective tissue forming the termination of a muscle and serving to transmit its force to some other part; a sinew. [<Med. L *tendo, -inis* <Gk. *tenōn* a sinew < *tenein* stretch]

ten·dril (ten′dril) *n. Bot.* One of the slender, leafless, coiling organs which serve a climbing plant as a means of attachment to a wall, tree trunk, or other supporting surface. [<F *tendrillon,* dim. of *tendron* sprout <*tendre* tender; infl. in meaning by F *tendre* stretch] —**ten′dril·lar, ten′dril·ous** *adj.*

ten·e·brae (ten′ə·brē) *n. pl.* The matins and lauds of Thursday, Friday, and Saturday of Holy Week, sung on the afternoon or evening of the preceding days. [<L, shadows]

ten·e·ment (ten′ə·mənt) *n.* **1** A room, or set of rooms, designed for one family. See TENEMENT HOUSE. **2** *Law* Anything of a permanent nature that may be held by one person of another as property, as land, houses, offices, rents, franchises, etc. **3** A house or building; especially, a dwelling house rented or intended for rent; a tenement house. **4** Figuratively, an abode. [<OF <LL *tenementum* tenure <L *tenere* hold] —**ten′e·men′ta·ry** (-men′tər·ē), **ten′e·men′tal** (-men′təl) *adj.*

tenement house A building or house, usually of inferior type and situated in the poorer sections of a city, rented, leased, or let, to be occupied as the home of three or more families living independently of one another, or by more than two families on a floor, all having a common right in stairways, yards, etc.

te·nen·dum (ti·nen′dəm) *n. Law* The clause in a deed in which, before the abolition of feudal tenures, the tenure was defined: now part of the habendum clause. See HABENDUM. [<L,

that which must be held, gerundive of *tenere* hold]

te·nes·mus (ti·nes′məs, -nez′-) *n. Pathol.* A painful straining and ineffectual effort to evacuate the bladder or the bowels. [<NL <L *tenesmos* a straining <Gk. *teneismos* <*teinein* stretch] —**te·nes′mic** *adj.*

ten·et (ten′it, tē′nit) *n.* An opinion, principle, dogma, or doctrine that a person or organization believes or maintains as true. See synonyms under DOCTRINE. [<L, he holds < *tenere* hold]

te·ni·a·cide (tē′nē·ə·sīd′) *n.* A substance which destroys tapeworms, as the oleoresin of certain ferns, carbon tetrachloride, etc.: also spelled *taeniacide.* Also **te′ni·a·fuge′** (-fyōōj′) [<L *taenia* <Gk. *tainia* tapeworm + -CIDE] —**te′ni·a·ci′dal** *adj.*

te·ni·a·sis (ti·nī′ə·sis) *n. Pathol.* Any morbid or toxemic condition due to the presence of tapeworms in the body: also spelled *taeniasis.* [<Gk. *tainia* tapeworm + -IASIS]

Ten·nes·see (ten′ə·sē′) A State in the SE United States; 42,246 square miles; capital, Nashville; entered the Union June 1, 1796; nicknamed *Volunteer State:* abbr. TN

ten·nis (ten′is) *n.* A game played by striking a ball to and fro with rackets over a net stretched perpendicularly across a space called a court. It has two forms, **court tennis,** played indoors in a specially prepared building, and **lawn tennis,** played out-of-doors on a court of grass, clay, concrete, etc. [<AF *tenetz* take, receive, imperative of *tenir* hold; from the call of the server]

TENNIS COURT — PLAN AND DIMENSIONS

Te·noch·ti·tlán (tā·nōkh′tē·tlän′) The capital of the ancient Aztec Empire, on the site of Mexico City.

ten·on (ten′ən) *n.* A projection on the end of a timber, etc., for inserting in a socket to form a joint. —*v.t.* **1** To form a tenon on. **2** To join by a mortise and tenon. [<F <*tenir* hold]

ten·o·ni·tis (ten′ə·nī′tis) *n. Pathol.* Inflammation of a tendon. [<NL <Gk. *tenōn* a tendon]

ten·or (ten′ər) *n.* **1** A settled course or manner of progress. **2** Course of thought; general purport. **3** *Law* The purport or substance and effect of a document; an exact transcript, as of a record. **4** General character and tendency; nature. **5** The highest adult male voice (except the falsetto); a singer having such a voice, or a part to be sung by it. **6** An instrument playing the part intermediate between the bass and the alto; especially, the viola. **7** In bell ringing, the lowest bell, irrespective of peal. —*adj.* **1** Of or pertaining to a tenor. **2** Having a relation to other instruments that the tenor bears to other musical parts: a *tenor* violin. [<OF *tenour* <L *tenor* a course <*tenere* hold; in def. 5, so called because this voice originally sang or "held" the melody]

ten·or·ite (ten′ə·rīt) *n.* Native oxide of copper, occurring in minute black scales; black copper. [after Prof. G. *Tenore,* president (1841) of Naples Academy]

te·nor·rha·phy (ti·nôr′ə·fē, -nor′-) *n. Surg.* Suture of the ends of a divided tendon. [<TENO- + -RRHAPHY]

te·not·o·my (ti·not′ə·mē) *n. Surg.* The operation of cutting a tendon. [<TENO- + -TOMY]

ten·pen·ny (ten′pen′ē, -pə·nē) *adj.* **1** Valued at tenpence. **2** Designating the size of nails three inches long. See -PENNY.

ten·pins (ten′pinz′) *n.* A game, played in a bowling alley, in which the players attempt to bowl down ten pins set up at the far end of the alley.

tense¹ (tens) *adj.* **1** Stretched tight; taut. **2**

Under mental or nervous strain; strained. **3** *Phonet.* Pronounced with the tongue and its muscles taut, as (ē) and (ōō); narrow: opposed to *lax.* —*v.t. & v.i.* tensed, tens·ing To make or become strained or drawn tight. [<L *tensus,* pp. of *tendere* stretch] —**tense′ly** *adv.* —**tense′ness** *n.*

tense² (tens) *n.* A form of a verb that relates it to time viewed either as finite past, present, or future, or as non-finite. —**sequence of tenses** In inflected languages, the customary choice of tense for a verb that follows another in a sentence, particularly in reported or indirect discourse. ◆ The general principle of sequence of tenses in English is that present follows present and past follows past. Thus, the tense of the subordinate clause tends to shift back to agree with the tense of the main verb. "He *wants* to go," becomes, in indirect discourse, "They said that he *wanted* to go." However, if continued, habitual, future, or universal action is expressed, the present tense may be retained in the subordinate clause: They told me that he *is* still in town; Columbus proved that the world *is* round. The present tense is also retained in the subordinate clause for emphasis: They just learned he *is* going after all. In subordinate clauses of purpose the general rule of tense sequence holds true: We *are working* so that we *can* go to Europe; We *worked* so that we *could* go to Europe. In conditional sentences expressing a simple fact or open question, the main and subordinate verbs remain independent: If he *said* that, I *can't* prove it. However, sequence of tenses is strictly observed in a highly improbable or contrary-to-fact statement. Time present is then expressed by the use of the past tense: If he *had* any sense, he *wouldn't drive* that car. Time past is expressed by the past perfect tense: If I *had had* my wits about me, I *would have* telephoned immediately. [< OF *tens* <L *tempus* time, tense]

ten·si·ble (ten′sə·bəl) *adj.* **1** Extensible. **2** Capable of being made tense; tensile.

ten·sile (ten′sil, *Brit.* ten′sīl) *adj.* **1** Of or pertaining to tension. **2** Capable of extension. **3** Producing tones from stretched strings: said instruments. [<NL *tensilis* <L *tensus.* See TENSE¹.] —**ten·sil·i·ty** (ten·sil′ə·tē) *n.*

tensile strength *Physics* The resistance of a material to forces of rupture and longitudinal stress: usually expressed in pounds or tons per square inch.

ten·sim·e·ter (ten·sim′ə·tər) *n.* An instrument for measuring the tension of gases; a manometer. [<*tensi-* (<TENSION) + -METER]

ten·sion (ten′shən) *n.* **1** The act of stretching; the condition of being stretched tight. **2** Mental strain; intense nervous anxiety. **3** Any strained relation, as between governments. **4** *Physics* **a** Stress on a material caused by pulling: opposed to *compression,* and distinguished from *torsion.* **b** The condition of a body when acted on by such stress. **5** The expansive force of a gas. **6** A regulating device, as that on a sewing machine to regulate the tightness of the thread. **7** *Electr.* Electromotive force; also, electric potential. [< L *tensio, -onis* <*tensus.* See TENSE¹.] —**ten′sion·al** *adj.*

ten·sor (ten′sər, -sôr) *n.* **1** *Anat.* A muscle that stretches a part. **2** *Math.* A vector quantity which may be fully described only with reference to more than three components. [<NL <L *tensus.* See TENSE¹.]

tent¹ (tent) *n.* A shelter of canvas or the like, supported by poles and fastened by cords to pegs (called **tent pegs**) driven into the ground. —*v.t.* To cover with or as with a tent. —*v.i.* To pitch a tent; camp out. [<F *tente* <LL *tenta,* orig. neut. pl. of *tentus,* pp. of *tendere* stretch. Cf. L *tentorium* awning.]

TENTS
a. Pup tent. *b.* Pyramid tent. *c.* Wall tent.

tent² (tent) *Surg. n.* A small roll, as of lint, placed in a wound or orifice to prevent its closing. —*v.t.* To keep open with a tent; also, to probe. [<F *tente* <*tenter* test, probe <L *tentare*]

tent³ (tent) *Scot. v.t.* **1** To pay attention to; observe. **2** To hinder; prevent. **3** To attend upon; look after. —*n.* **1** Attention; note; heed. **2** An open–air wooden pulpit. —**tent′·less** *adj.*

tent⁴ (tent) *n.* A deep–red wine obtained chiefly from Spain. [<Sp. *tinto* deep–colored <L *tinctus* dyed. See TINT.]

ten·ta·cle (ten′tə·kəl) *n.* **1** *Zool.* A protruding flexible process or appendage (usually of the head) of invertebrate animals, functioning as an organ of touch, prehension, or motion. Some examples are the hollow fleshy processes about the mouth of a polyp communicating with the body cavity, the eyestalks of a gastropod, and the arms of a cuttlefish, especially one of the two longer arms of a decapod. **2** *Bot.* A sensitive glandular hair, as on the leaves of the sundew. **3** Something resembling a tentacle; a tendril. Also **ten·tac·u·lum** (ten·tak′yə·ləm). [<L *tentaculum* < *tentare* touch, try] —**ten·tac′u·lar** *adj.*

effect is secured. [<F <L *tentatio, -onis* <*tentare* try. See TEMPT.]

ten·ta·tive (ten′tə·tiv) *adj.* **1** Used in making a trial; provisional or conjectural; experimental and subject to change. **2** *Med.* Based on subjective and objective symptoms: said of a diagnosis subject to change. —*n.* An experiment; conjecture. [<Med. L *tentativus* <*tentatus,* pp. of *tentare* try, probe] —**ten′ta·tive·ly** *adv.* —**ten′ta·tive·ness** *n.*

tent caterpillar The gregarious larva of several North American moths (family *Lasiocampidae*) that spins a large silken web which shelters the colony, especially the **orchard caterpillar** (genus *Malacosoma*).

tented arch A fingerprint pattern in which the skin ridges have an upward thrust in the shape of a tent, arranging themselves on both sides of a spine or axis.

ten·ter (ten′tər) *n.* **1** A frame or machine for stretching cloth to prevent shrinkage while drying. **2** *Obs.* A tenterhook. —*v.t.* To stretch on or as on a tenter. —*v.i.* To be or admit of being stretched thus. [<L *tentus* extended. See TENT¹.]

ten·ter·hook (ten′tər·hook′) *n.* A sharp hook for holding cloth while being stretched on a tenter. —**to be on tenterhooks** To be in a state of anxiety or suspense.

tenth (tenth) *adj.* **1** Next in order after the ninth. **2** Designating one of ten equal parts. —*n.* **1** One of ten equal parts. **2** *Music* An interval compounded of an octave and a third; a note separated from another by this interval. **3** An organ stop tuned a tenth above the diapasons. **4** A tax of one tenth of one's income; a tithe. [ME *tenthe*] —**tenth′ly** *adv.*

ten·u·ous (ten′yōō·əs) *adj.* **1** Thin; slim; delicate; also, weak; flimsy. **2** Having slight density; rare: opposed to *dense.* See synonyms under FINE. [<L *tenuis* thin] —**ten′u·ous·ly** *adv.* —**ten′u·ous·ness, ten·u·i·ty** (ten·yōō′ə·tē, ti·nōō′-) *n.*

ten·ure (ten′yər) *n.* **1** A holding, as of land. **2** The act of holding in general, or the state of being held. **3** The term during which a thing is held, as an office. **4** The conditions or manner of holding. See synonyms under OCCUPATION. [<F <*tenir* hold <L *tenere*] —**ten·u·ri·al** (ten·yŏŏr′ē·əl) *adj.* —**ten·u′ri·al·ly** *adv.*

te·nu·to (te·nōō′tō) *adj. Music* Sustained; held for the full time. [<Ital.]

te·nu·to·mark (te·nōō′tō·märk′) *n. Music* A horizontal stroke over a note or chord that is to be held for its full value.

te·o·cal·li (tē′ə·kal′ē, *Sp.* tā′ō·kä′yē) *n.* **1** A temple peculiar to the ancient Mexicans and Central Americans, usually erected on a truncated pyramid. **2** A mound of similar form. Also **te·o·pan** (tā′ō·pän′). [<Sp. <Nahuatl, house of the god <*teotl* a god + *calli* house]

te·o·sin·te (tē′ə·sin′tē) *n.* A stout, hardy perennial grass (*Euchlaena mexicana*), closely allied to Indian corn, and used for fodder. [<Sp. <Nahuatl *teocentli,* lit., divine maize <*teotl* a god + *centli* corn]

te·pee (tē′pē) *n.* A conical tent of the North American Plains Indians, usually covered with skins or other material: also spelled *teepee, tipi.* [<Dakota *tīpi* <*ti* dwell + *pi* used for]

tep·e·fy (tep′ə·fī) *v.t.* & *v.i.* **·fied, ·fy·ing** To make or become tepid. [<L *tepefacere* make tepid <*tepere* be lukewarm + *facere* make] —**tep′e·fac′tion** (-fak′shən) *n.*

TEPEE
Western Plains Indian.

teph·rite (tef′rīt) *n.* An ash-gray to black volcanic rock, essentially an alkaline andesite, with either nepheline or leucite. [<L *tephritis* <Gk. *tephra* ashes]

te·phro·sin (tə·frō′sin) *n. Chem.* A white crystalline compound, $C_{23}H_{22}O_7$, extracted from the leaves of a leguminous plant (*Tephrosia vogeli*), from derris, and cube: used as a fish poison. [<NL <Gk. *tephros* ash-colored <*tephra* ashes]

te·phro·sis (tə·frō′sis) *n.* Cremation; incineration. [<NL <Gk. *tephrōsis* <*tephra* ashes]

tep·id (tep′id) *adj.* Moderately warm; lukewarm, as a liquid. [<L *tepidus* <*tepere* be lukewarm] —**te·pid·i·ty** (tə·pid′ə·tē), **tep′id·ness** *n.* —**tep′id·ly** *adv.*

tep·i·dar·i·um (tep′ə·dâr′ē·əm) *n. pl.* **·dar·i·a** (-dâr′ē·ə) In the Roman baths, the intermediate apartment between the cold- and the hot-bath rooms. [<L <*tepidus.* See TEPID.]

ter·a·phim (ter′ə·fim) *n. pl. sing.* **ter·aph** (ter′əf) or **ter·a·phim** Images, small idols, or household gods consulted as oracles by some of the ancient Hebrews: used as a plural or collective singular in the Bible. [<Hebrew *terāphīm*]

ter·a·tism (ter′ə·tiz′əm) *n. Biol.* A monstrosity; especially, a malformed human or animal fetus. [<Gk. *teras* monster]

ter·a·to·gen (ter′ə·tə·jən, tə·rat′ə·jən) *n. Biol.* An agent, esp. a drug, that produces monsters or abnormal organisms.

ter·a·tog·e·ny (ter′ə·toj′ə·nē) *n. Biol.* The production of monsters or abnormal organisms. Also **ter′a·to·gen′e·sis** (-tō·jen′ə·sis). [<TERATO- + -GENY] —**ter′a·to·gen′ic** (-tō·jen′ik) *adj.*

ter·a·tol·o·gy (ter′ə·tol′ə·jē) *n.* The branch of biology and medicine treating of abnormal growths or monstrosities. [<TERATO- + -LOGY] —**ter′a·to·log′ic** (-tō·loj′ik) or **·i·cal** *adj.* —**ter′a·tol′o·gist** *n.*

ter·bi·a (tûr′bē·ə) *n. Chem.* Oxide of terbium, Tb_2O_3.

ter·bi·um (tûr′bē·əm) *n.* A silvery gray metallic element (symbol Tb, atomic number 65) belonging to the lanthanide series, occurring in gadolinite and other rare earths. See PERIODIC TABLE. [<NL <*Ytterby,* a town in Sweden] —**ter′bic** *adj.*

terbium metal One of a group in the lanthanide series of elements, including gadolinium, europium, and terbium.

ter·cel (tûr′səl) *n.* A male falcon, especially the peregrine falcon: also spelled *tassel.* Also **terce·let** (tûrs′lit). [<OF <L *tertius* third; said to be so called because every third egg in a falcon's nest was thought to produce a male]

ter·cen·te·nar·y (tûr′sen′tə·ner′ē, tûr′sen·ten′ər·ē) *adj.* Of or pertaining to a period of 300 years or to a 300th anniversary. —*n. pl.* **·nar·ies** The 300th anniversary. Also *tricentennial.* Also **ter·cen·ten·ni·al** (tûr′sen·ten′ē·əl).

ter·cet (tûr′sit, tûr·set′) *n.* **1** *Music* A triplet. **2** A group of three lines riming together or connected with adjacent triplets by double or triple rime. [<F <Ital. *terzetto,* dim. of *terzo* <L *tertius* third]

ter·e·bene (ter′ə·bēn) *n. Chem.* A colorless, aromatic liquid hydrocarbon mixture of terpenes from oil of turpentine: used as an antiseptic and expectorant. [<TEREB(INTH) + (TERP)ENE]

ter·e·bic (te·reb′ik, -rē′bik) *adj. Chem.* Of, pertaining to, or derived from a white crystalline

acid, $C_7H_{10}O_4$, derived from oil of turpentine. [<TEREBINTH]

ter·e·binth (ter′ə·binth) *n.* A small tree (*Pistacia terebinthus*) with winged pinnate leaves resembling those of the common ash but smaller: the original source of turpentine. [<L *terebinthus* <Gk. *terebinthos*]

ter·e·bin·thine (ter′ə·bin′thin) *adj.* Of or pertaining to the terebinth or turpentine. Also **ter′e·bin′thic.**

te·re·do (tə·rē′dō) *n.* One of a genus (*Teredo*) of marine mollusks (family *Teredinidae*); a shipworm. [<L, borer <Gk. *terēdōn* <*terein* rub hard, bore]

te·rete (tə·rēt′, ter′ēt) *adj.* Cylindrical and slightly tapering; round in cross-section. [<L *teres, teretis* round, rounded off < *terere* rub]

ter·fa (tûr′fə) *n.* An edible fungus (genera *Terfezia* and *Tirmania*) of the deserts of North Africa, having a subterranean fruit body resembling truffles and eaten by the Arabs. [<Arabic *tirfāsh* truffle]

ter·gal (tûr′gəl) *adj.* Of or pertaining to the tergum; dorsal.

ter·gem·i·nate (tər·jem′ə·nit) *adj. Bot.* Having three pairs of forked leaflets. [<TER- + GEMINATE]

ter·gi·ver·sate (tûr′ji·vər·sāt) *v.i.* **·sat·ed, ·sat·ing** **1** To be evasive; equivocate or prevaricate. **2** To change sides, attitudes, etc.; become a renegade; apostatize. [<L *tergiversatus,* pp. of *tergiversari* <*tergum* back + *versare* turn] —**ter′gi·ver·sa′tor** *n.*

ter·gi·ver·sa·tion (tûr′ji·vər·sā′shən) *n.* **1** Evasion of a point, as by prevarication or subterfuge. **2** Fickleness or insincerity of conduct; shiftiness.

ter·gum (tûr′gəm) *n. Zool.* The back or dorsal part of an arthropod. [<L]

term (tûrm) *n.* **1** A word or expression used to designate some definite thing; a technical expression: a scientific *term.* **2** Any word or expression conveying some conception or thought: a *term* of reproach; to speak in general *terms.* **3** *pl.* The conditions or stipulations according to which something is to be done or acceded to: the *terms* of sale; peace *terms.* **4** *pl.* Mutual relations; footing: usually preceded by *on* or *upon:* England was on friendly *terms* with France. **5** *Math.* **a** The antecedent or consequent of a ratio. **b** The numerator or denominator of a fraction. **c** One of the quantities of an algebraic expression that are connected by the plus and minus signs. **d** One of the quantities which compose a series or progression. **6** *Logic* **a** In a proposition, either of the two parts, the subject and predicate, which are joined by a copula. **b** Any of the three elements of a syllogism, each of which appears twice. In a syllogism, the **major term** is the predicate of both the major premise and the conclusion. The **minor term** is the subject of both the minor premise and the conclusion. See SYLLOGISM. **7** A fixed period or definite length of time: a *term* of office. **8** One of the periods of the year appointed for holding instruction in colleges and schools. **9** *Law* **a** One of the prescribed periods of the year during which a court may hold a session. **b** A specific extent of time during which a termor may hold an estate. **c** A space of time allowed a debtor to meet his obligation. **10** *Med.* The time for childbirth. **11** *Archaic* An utmost limit; boundary. **12** *Archit.* A pillar of tapering form, ending in a sculptured head or bust. —*v.t.* To designate by means of a term; name or call. [<OF *terme* <L *terminus* a limit]

Synonyms (noun): article, condition, expression, member, name, phrase, word. *Term* in its figurative use always retains something of its literal sense of a boundary or limit. The *articles* of a contract or other instrument are simply the portions into which it is divided for convenience; the *terms* are the essential statements on which its validity depends—as it were, the landmarks of its meaning or power; a *condition* is a contingent *term,* which may become fixed upon the happening of some contemplated event. In logic a *term* is one of the essential members of a proposition, the boundary of statement in some one direction. Thus in general use *term* is more restricted than *word, expression,* or *phrase*; a *term* is a *word* that limits meaning to a fixed point of statement or to a special class of subjects; as, when we speak of the definition of *terms,* that is of the key *words* in any discussion; or we say "that is a legal or scientific *term.*" See BOUNDARY, DICTION.

ter·ma·gant (tûr′mə·gənt) *n.* A scolding or abusive woman; shrew. —*adj.* Violently abusive and quarrelsome; vixenish. [<TERMAGANT] —**ter′ma·gan′cy** *n.*

term·er (tûr′mər) *n.* **1** *Law* A termor. **2** *Colloq.* A prisoner serving a certain term: usually with an ordinal: a first-*termer.*

ter·mi·nal (tûr′mə·nəl) *adj.* **1** Pertaining to or creative of a boundary, limit, or terminus: a *terminal* railroad station. **2** Pertaining to the delivery or storage of freight or baggage: *terminal* charges. **3** Pertaining to a term or name. **4** Situated at or forming the end of a series or part. **5** *Bot.* Borne at the end of a stem or branch. **6** Of, pertaining to, or occurring in or at the end of a period of time; of a fixed period. —*n.* **1** That which terminates; a terminating point or part; termination; end. **2** *Electr.* One of the two free ends of a conductor, particularly if proceeding from an electric source, as a battery or dynamo. **3** *Archit.* A terminal figure or pedestal; terminus. **4** The edges or planes that form the end of a crystal. **5** A railroad terminus. **6** *pl.* Charges for the use of terminal facilities, or for the handling of freight at railroad terminuses. **7** *Physiol.* The end structure or end of a neuron or nerve fiber. [<F <LL *terminalis* <L *terminus* boundary] —**ter′mi·nal·ly** *adv.*

terminal rime The riming of a word or group of syllables at the end of a verse with that at the end of another verse in the same stanza or poem.

terminal velocity *Physics* The velocity acquired by a freely falling body when the resistance of the medium equals the weight of the body.

ter·mi·nate (tûr′mə·nāt) *v.* **·nat·ed, ·nat·ing** *v.t.* **1** To put an end to or stop to. **2** To form the conclusion of; finish. **3** To bound or limit. —*v.i.* **4** To have an end; come to an end. See synonyms under ABOLISH, CEASE, END. [<L *terminatus,* pp. of *terminare* end, limit <*terminus* a limit]

ter·mi·na·tion (tûr′mə·nā′shən) *n.* **1** The act of setting bounds or limits. **2** The act of ending or concluding. **3** That which bounds or limits; close; end; limit in time or space. **4** Outcome; result; conclusion. **5** The final letters or syllable of a word; a suffix. See synonyms under BOUNDARY, END.

ter·mi·na·tion·al (tûr′mə·nā′shən·əl) *adj.* Of, pertaining to, or formative of a syllable or other termination; formed by suffixes.

ter·mi·na·tive (tûr′mə·nā′tiv) *adj.* Designed or tending to terminate; determining; definitive; bounding; conclusive. —**ter′mi·na′tive·ly** *adv.*

ter·mi·na·tor (tûr′mə·nā′tər) *n.* **1** One who or that which terminates. **2** *Astron.* The boundary between the illuminated and dark portions of the moon or of a planet.

ter·mi·nism (tûr′mə·niz′əm) *n.* **1** *Theol.* The doctrine that God has ordained a limit in the life of each man and of mankind beyond which the opportunity for salvation is lost. **2** A form of nominalism; specifically, the doctrine of William of Ockham, who stated that universals are abstract terms or predicables, rather than either real existents or mere vocal sounds. [<L *terminus* term]

ter·mi·nol·o·gy (tûr′mə·nol′ə·jē) *n.* **1** The study or the use of terms. **2** The technical terms used in a science, art, trade, etc. **3** Nomenclature. [<L *terminus* + -LOGY] — **ter′mi·no·log′i·cal** (-nə·loj′i·kəl) *adj.* —**ter′·mi·no·log′i·cal·ly** *adv.* —**ter′mi·nol′o·gist** *n.*

ter·mi·nus (tûr′mə·nəs) *n.* *pl.* **·nus·es** or **·ni** (-nī) **1** The final point or goal; end; terminal. **2** The farthermost station on a railway; also, the town in which such station is situated. **3** A boundary or border; also, a boundary mark. See synonyms under END. [<L]

ter·mite (tûr′mīt) *n.* A white ant. Also *termes.* For illustration see INSECTS (injurious). [<L *termes, termitis*]

term·less (tûrm′lis) *adj.* **1** Of boundless extent or duration. **2** Independent of conditions; unconditional. **3** *Archaic* Incapable of being expressed by terms; indescribable.

term·or (tûr′mər) *n.* *Law* A person who holds lands or tenements for a definite number of years or for life.

tern¹ (tûrn) *n.* Any of several gull-like birds (subfamily *Sterninae*), having the bill pointed and the mandibles co-terminal, smaller than most gulls, with wings more pointed, and the tail usually deeply forked; especially, the common tern (*Sterna hirundo*) of the Atlantic coasts, white with a black cap, and the least or minute tern (*S. antillarum*). ◆ Homophones: *terne, turn.* [< Scand. Cf. Dan. *terne* tern.]

BLACK TERN
(Body length about 10 inches; wingspread, 25 inches)

tern² (tûrn) *n.* **1** That which is composed of three; specifically, three numbers in a lottery that, when drawn together, secure a large prize. **2** In New England, a three-masted schooner. ◆ Homophones: *terne, turn.* [<L *terni* by threes <*ter* thrice]

ter·na·ry (tûr′nər·ē) *adj.* **1** Formed or consisting of three; grouped in threes. **2** *Math.* Containing three variables; also, pertaining to systems of notation, having three as a base, or radix. **3** *Chem.* Having three separate parts, as atoms, elements, etc. **4** *Metall.* Made of an alloy which contains three metals. —*n.* *pl.* **·ries** A group of three; a triad. [<L *ternarius* <*terni* by threes]

ter·nate (tûr′nāt) *adj.* **1** Classified or arranged in threes. **2** *Bot.* Trifoliolate; consisting of threes. [<NL *ternatus* <L *terni* by threes] —**ter′nate·ly** *adv.*

terne (tûrn) *v.t.* **terned, tern·ing** To cover with a thin layer of lead and tin. —*n.* Terne plate. ◆ Homophones: *tern, turn.* [<F *terne* dull; from the resulting finish]

terne plate Steel plate with a coating of lead and tin, having a dull finish and inferior in quality to standard tin plate.

ter·ni·on (tûr′nē·ən) *n.* **1** A set of three. **2** A section of a book composed of three sheets in double folds, or 12 pages. [<L *terni* by threes]

ter·pene (tûr′pēn) *n.* *Chem.* Any of a class of isomeric hydrocarbons, $C_{10}H_{16}$, contained chiefly in the essential oils of coniferous plants. [<*terp(entin),* earlier form of TURPENTINE + -ENE]

ter·pin·e·ol (tər·pin′ē·ōl, -ol) *n.* *Chem.* A colorless, unsaturated, tertiary alcohol, $C_{10}H_{17}OH$, derived from the essential oils of various plants and also made synthetically: it has an odor of lilacs and is used in perfumery. [<*terpin,* earlier form of TERPENE + -OL¹]

ter·pi·nol (tûr′pə·nōl, -nol) *n.* An oily, colorless, liquid mixture of various terpenes, having an odor of hyacinth. [See TERPINEOL]

ter·ra al·ba (ter′ə al′bə) **1** Pipe clay. **2** The pigment made from ground gypsum. **3** Magnesia. **4** A grade of kaolin used as an adulterant of paints. [<L, white earth]

ter·race (ter′is) *n.* **1** An artificial raised level space, as of lawn, having one or more vertical or sloping sides; also, such levels collectively. **2** A raised level supporting a row of houses, or the houses occupying such a position. **3** The flat roof of an Oriental or Spanish house. **4** A relatively narrow step in the face of a steep natural slope. **5** An open gallery; balcony. —*v.t.* **·raced, ·rac·ing** To form into or provide with a terrace or terraces. [<OF <Ital. *terraccia* <L *terra* earth]

ter·ra cot·ta (ter′ə kot′ə) **1** A hard, durable, kiln-burnt clay, reddish-brown in color and usually unglazed: widely used as a structural material and also, in glazed and colored forms, for tiles, building façades, etc. **2** A statue or figure made of this clay. **3** A brownish-orange color resembling that of terra cotta. [<Ital., cooked earth]

ter·rain (te·rān′, ter′ān) *n.* **1** Battleground, or a region suited for defense, fortifications, etc. **2** A piece or plot of ground; a region or territory viewed with regard to its suitability for some particular purpose. **3** A terrane. [<F <L *terrenum* <*terrenus* earthen <*terra* earth]

ter·rane (te·rān′, ter′ān) *n.* **1** *Geol.* A continuous formation or continuous series of related formations; an area of particular

rocks. **2** A tract or region considered with reference to some special purpose. [<F *terrain.* See TERRAIN.]

ter·ra·pin (ter′ə·pin) *n.* One of the several North American edible tortoises (family *Testudinidae*); especially, the diamond-back terrapin. [<Algonquian]

DIAMOND-BACK TERRAPIN
(Shell from 4 to 7 inches)

ter·ra·que·ous (te·rā′kwē·əs) *adj.* Composed of, living in, or consisting of, both land and water. [<L *terra* earth, land + AQUEOUS]

ter·rar·i·um (te·râr′ē·əm) *n.* *pl.* **·rar·i·ums** or **·rar·i·a** (-râr′ē·ə) **1** A small enclosure or box with glass sides for live lizards, growing plants, etc. **2** A vivarium for land animals. [<L *terra* earth + -ARIUM, on analogy with *aquarium*]

ter·raz·zo (ter·rät′sō) *n.* Flooring made of small pieces of marble or colored stone set in concrete. Also **ter·raz′zo Ve·ne·zia·no** (vä′nā·tsyä′nō). [<Ital. <L *terra* earth]

ter·rene (te·rēn′) *adj.* **1** Pertaining to earth; earthy. **2** Earthly; worldly; mundane. —*n.* **1** The surface of the earth. **2** The earth; a land or terrain. [<L *terrenus* <*terra* earth]

terre·plein (ter′plān) *n.* **1** The upper surface of a rampart behind the parapet, on which the guns are mounted. **2** An embankment with a level top. [<F *terre* earth + *plein* level]

ter·res·tri·al (tə·res′trē·əl) *adj.* **1** Belonging to the earth: opposed to *celestial* or *cosmic.* **2** Pertaining to land or earth: *terrestrial* magnetism. **3** *Biol.* Living on or growing in the earth or land: opposed to *aquatic, aerial,* etc. **4** Belonging to or consisting of land, as distinct from water, trees, etc. **5** Worldly; mundane. —*n.* An inhabitant of the earth. [<L *terrestris* <L *terra* land] —**ter·res′tri·al·ly** *adv.* —**ter·res′tri·al·ness** *n.*

ter·ret (ter′it) *n.* **1** One of two metal rings projecting from the saddle of a harness, through which the reins are passed. **2** A ring for attaching a leash to a dog's collar, etc. Also **ter′rit.** [ME *toret* <F *touret* small wheel, dim. of *tour* a turn]

terre-ten·ant (ter′ten′ənt) *n.* *Law* **1** The person who is in actual possession of lands. **2** The owner or holder of the legal estate in lands. Also spelled *ter-tenant.* [<AF *terre tenant* holding land <F *terre* (<L *terra* land) + *tenaunt* holding, ppr. of *tenir* hold <L *tenere*]

terre-verte (ter′vert′) *n.* **1** An earthy silicate resembling glauconite and used as a green pigment by artists. **2** Glauconite. [<F *terre verte* green earth]

ter·ri·ble (ter′ə·bəl) *adj.* **1** Of a nature to excite terror; appalling. **2** *Colloq.* Characterized by excess; severe; extreme. **3** Inspiring awe. See synonyms under AWFUL, FORMIDABLE, FRIGHTFUL, GRIM. [<F <L *terribilis* <*terrere* terrify] —**ter′ri·ble·ness** *n.* —**ter′ri·bly** *adv.*

ter·ric·o·lous (te·rik′ə·ləs) *adj.* *Biol.* Living on or in the ground. Also **ter·ric′o·line** (-lēn, -lin). [<L *terricola* earth dweller <*terra* earth + *colere* dwell]

ter·ri·er¹ (ter′ē·ər) *n.* A small, active, wiry dog of several breeds, formerly used to hunt burrowing animals and noted for the courage and eagerness with which it "goes to earth" in pursuit of its quarry. See AIREDALE, DANDIE DINMONT, SCHNAUZER. [<OF <L *terrarius* pertaining to earth. See TERRIER².]

ter·ri·er² (ter′ē·ər) *n.* *Law* **1** A land survey setting forth in detail the number of acres, names of tenants, etc., in a given district: the *terrier* of glebe lands. **2** A book containing the lists of the lands either of a private person or a corporation; a rent roll. [<OF, list of tenants <LL *terrarius* a roll describing landed property <L, pertaining to land <*terra* land]

ter·rif·ic (tə·rif′ik) *adj.* **1** Arousing or calculated to arouse great terror or fear. **2** *Colloq.* Excessive; extreme; tremendous. See synonyms under AWFUL, FRIGHTFUL. —**ter·rif′i·cal·ly** *adv.*

ter·ri·fy (ter′ə·fī) *v.t.* **·fied, ·fy·ing** To fill with extreme terror. See synonyms under FRIGHTEN. [<L *terrificare* <*terrificus* causing fear <*terrere* frighten + *facere* make]

ter·rig·e·nous (te·rij′ə·nəs) *adj.* **1** Produced

from or of the earth. **2** *Geol.* Derived from the land: said of marine deposits formed of material washed from the land, as contrasted with those of organic, chemical, or other origin, formed in the sea. **3** Earthborn. Also **ter·ri·gene** (ter′ə·jēn). [<L *terrigenus* < *terra* earth + *gignere* be born]

ter·rine (te·rēn′) *n.* **1** An earthenware jar containing some delicacy for the table and sold with its contents: a *terrine* of preserved ginger. **2** A kind of ragout or stew. Also spelled *terreen, terrene.* [<F <LL *terrineus* made of earth <L *terra* earth. Doublet of TUREEN.]

ter·ri·to·ri·al (ter′ə·tôr′ē·əl, -tō′rē-) *adj.* **1** Pertaining to a territory or territories; limited to a particular territory. **2** Designating military forces intended for territorial defense. **3** Belonging to a particular locality. **4** Organized or intended primarily for national defense: a *territorial* reserve. — **ter′ri·to′ri·al·ly** *adv.*

ter·ri·to·ri·al·ism (ter′ə·tôr′ē·əl·iz′əm, -tō′rē-) *n.* The organizations, theories, or doctrines of the territorial systems. — **ter′ri·to′ri·al·ist** *n.*

ter·ri·to·ri·al·i·ty (ter′ə·tôr′ē·al′ə·tē, -tō′rē-) *n.* Territorial condition, status, or position.

ter·ri·to·ri·al·ize (ter′ə·tôr′ē·əl·īz′, -tō′rē-) *v.t.* **·ized, ·iz·ing** **1** To enlarge by annexation of territory. **2** To reduce to the political status of a territory. **3** To distribute among certain territories. — **ter′ri·to′ri·al·i·za′tion** *n.*

territorial jurisdiction *Law* The sovereign jurisdiction exercised by a state over all lands, waters, persons, and properties within its boundaries.·

territorial system **1** A system of church government in which all inhabitants of a territory are required to belong to the same religion as the civil ruler. **2** Local organization for militia service. **3** Landlordism; a system giving predominance to landowners.

territorial waters The belt of sea under a state's territorial jurisdiction: formerly, the range of a cannon shot, or three miles: now often controversial. Also **territorial sea.**

ter·ri·to·ry (ter′ə·tôr′ē, -tō′rē) *n. pl.* **·ries** **1** The domain over which a sovereign state exercises jurisdiction. **2** Any considerable tract of land; a region; district; figuratively, sphere; province. **3** An area assigned for a special purpose: the *territory* of a commercial traveler. [<L *territorium* < *terra* earth]

ter·ror (ter′ər) *n.* **1** An overwhelming impulse of fear; extreme fright or dread. **2** That which or one who causes extreme fear. **3** *Colloq.* An intolerable nuisance: That child is a holy *terror.* See synonyms under ALARM, FEAR, FRIGHT. [<F *terreur* <L *terror* fright < *terrere* frighten]

ter·ror·ism (ter′ə·riz′əm) *n.* **1** The act of terrorizing. **2** A system of government that seeks to rule by intimidation. **3** Unlawful acts of violence committed in an organized attempt to overthrow a government.

ter·ror·ist (ter′ər·ist) *n.* **1** One who adopts or supports a policy of terrorism. **2** A Jacobin or Republican of the French Revolution of 1789, especially during the Reign of Terror. **3** A member of political extremist groups in czarist Russia. **4** An alarmist; a scaremonger. — **ter′ror·is′tic** *adj.*

ter·ror·ize (ter′ə·rīz) *v.t.* **·ized, ·iz·ing** **1** To reduce to a state of terror; terrify. **2** To coerce through intimidation. Also *Brit.* **ter′ror·ise.** — **ter′ror·i·za′tion** *n.* — **ter′ror·iz′er** *n.*

ter·ry (ter′ē) *n. pl.* **·ries** **1** The loop raised for the nap in weaving pile fabrics. **2** A pile dressmaking fabric in which the loops are uncut: also **terry cloth.** **3** A looped cotton fabric, very water-absorbent, used chiefly for towels and beach robes. [Prob. <F *tiré,* pp. of *tirer* draw <L *trahere*]

terse (tûrs) *adj.* **1** Elegantly concise; short and to the point. **2** Rubbed to a polish; clean; polished; refined. [<L *tersus,* pp. of *tergere* rub off, rub down] — **terse′ly** *adv.* — **terse′ness** *n.*
  Synonyms: brief, compact, compendious, concise, condensed, laconic, pithy, sententious, short, succinct. Anything *short* or *brief* is of relatively small extent. That which is *concise* is trimmed down, and that which is *condensed* is, as it were, pressed together, so as to include as much as possible within a small space. That which is *compendious* gathers the substance of a matter into a few weighty and effective words. *Succinct* writing is taut and lean without extraneous detail. *Summary* implies compression to the utmost, often to the point of abruptness; as, a *summary* statement or a *summary* dismissal. That which is *terse* has an elegant and finished completeness within the smallest possible compass. A *sent: tentious* style is one abounding in maxims or short, pithy phrases. A *pithy* utterance gives the gist of a matter effectively, whether in rude or elegant style. *Antonyms:* diffuse, lengthy, long, prolix, tedious, verbose, wordy.

ter·ten·ant (ter′ten′ənt) See TERRE-TENANT.

ter·tial (tûr′shəl) *Ornithol. adj.* Of or pertaining to the third row of flight feathers in a bird's wing. — *n.* A tertiary feather. [<L *tertius* third < *ter* thrice]

ter·tian (tûr′shən) *adj.* Recurring every third day, reckoned inclusively, hence every alternate day. — *n.* *Pathol.* A disease, the paroxysms of which return every other day; a tertian fever. [<L *(febris) tertiana* tertian (fever) < *tertius* third]

ter·ti·ar·y (tûr′shē·er′ē, -shə·rē) *adj.* **1** Third in point of time, number, degree, or standing. **2** Tertial. **3** *Eccl.* Pertaining to the third order of a religious body. **4** *Chem.* **a** Having three substituted atoms or radicals: a *tertiary* amine. **b** Denoting a radical in which three bonds of the combining carbon atoms are directly connected with three other carbon atoms: *tertiary* butyl. — *n. pl.* **·ar·ies** **1** *Ornithol.* One of the feathers attached to the humerus joint of the wing of a bird. **2** Any member of the third order of a monastic body. [<L *tertiarius* < *tertius* third]

ter·ti·um quid (tûr′shē·əm kwid) *Latin* **1** A third something; an indefinite or undefined thing related in some way to two definite or known things. **2** A mediating factor between essentially opposite things.

ter·za–ri·ma (ter′tsä·rē′mä) *n. pl.* **ter·ze–ri·me** (ter′tsä·rē′mā) A form of Italian triplet, in iambic decasyllables or hendecasyllables, in

Welsh Terrier   Airedale   Lakeland Terrier   Irish Terrier

West Highland White Terrier   Cairn Terrier   Yorkshire Terrier   Skye Terrier

Norwich Terrier   Dandie Dinmont   Boston Terrier   Bull Terrier

Scottish Terrier   Schnauzer   Wire-haired Fox Terrier   Smooth-haired Fox Terrier

Bedlington Terrier   Manchester Terrier   Sealyham Terrier   Kerry Blue Terrier

which the middle line of the first triplet rimes with the first and third lines of the following triplet: used by Dante in the *Divine Comedy*. [<Ital., third or triple line]

ter·zet·to (ter·tset′tō) *n. pl.* **·ti** (-tē) *Music* A short composition for three performers or singers; a trio. [See TERCET]

tes·sel·late (tes′ə·lāt) *v.t.* **·lat·ed, ·lat·ing** To construct in the style of checkered mosaic; lay or adorn with squares or tiles, as pavement. [<L *tessellatus* checkered <*tessella*, dim. of *tessera* cube. See TESSERA.] — **tes′sel·lat′ed** *adj.*

tes·sel·la·tion (tes′ə·lā′shən) *n.* **1** Tessellated work. **2** The art or act of doing such work.

tes·ser·a (tes′ər·ə) *n. pl.* **·ser·ae** (-ər·ē) **1** A small square, as of stone, glass, etc., used in mosaic work. **2** A small object, often a square or cube, as of bone or wood, used as a die in gambling or as a token, voucher, or the like. [<L <dial. Gk. (Ionic) *tesseres* four]

tes·ser·act (tes′ər·akt) *n. Math.* **1** A construct intended to illustrate graphically or in the form of a model the general appearance of a four-dimensional figure. **2** A hypercube bounded by 8 cubes or cells, with 16 vertices, 24 faces, and 32 edges. [<dial. Gk. (Ionic) *tesseres* four + *aktis* ray]

test[1] (test) *v.t.* **1** To subject to a test or trial; try. **2** *Chem.* **a** To refine, as gold or silver, by means of lead, as in the process of cupellation. **b** To examine by means of some reagent, as in testing for sulfuric acid. — *v.i.* **3** *Chem.* To undergo testing; also, to show specified qualities or properties under testing: The alcohol *tested* 75 percent. See synonyms under EXAMINE. — *n.* — *n.* **1** Subjection to conditions that disclose the true character of a person or thing in relation to some particular quality. **2** An examination made for the purpose of proving or disproving some matter in doubt, as mental condition. **3** A criterion or standard of judgment. **4** An oath or other confirmatory evidence of principles or belief. **5** *Chem.* **a** A reaction by means of which the identity of a compound or one of its constituents may be determined. **b** Its agent or the result. **6** An earthen vessel similar to a cupel, formerly used in testing metals. **7** A series of questions, problems, etc., intended to measure the extent of knowledge, aptitudes, intelligence, and other mental traits: an intelligence *test*. See synonyms under PROOF. [<OF, a cupel, pot <L *testum* an earthen vessel <*testa* potsherd, shell] — **test′a·ble** *adj.*

test[2] (test) *n.* **1** *Zool.* A rigid external case or covering of many invertebrates, as a sea urchin or mollusk; a shell. **2** *Bot.* A testa. [<L *testa* shell]

test[3] (test) *v.t.* To attest. [<OF *tester* bequeath <L *testari* be a witness. See TESTAMENT.]

tes·ta (tes′tə) *n. pl.* **·tae** (-tē) **1** *Bot.* The outer, usually hard and brittle coat or integument of a seed. **2** *Zool.* A test. [See TEST[2]]

tes·ta·ce·an (tes·tā′shē·ən, -shən) *adj.* Pertaining or belonging to an order (*Testacea*) of rhizopods enclosed in a single-chambered cell. [<NL <L *testaceum* shellfish <*testaceus*. See TESTACEOUS.]

tes·ta·ceous (tes·tā′shəs) *adj.* **1** Of or derived from shells or shellfish. **2** Having a hard shell. **3** Dull brick–red or brownish–yellow. [<L *testaceus* of shell, brick <*testa* a shell]

tes·ta·cy (tes′tə·sē) *n. Law* The state of being testate or of having left a will at death: opposed to *intestacy*.

tes·ta·ment (tes′tə·mənt) *n.* **1** The written declaration of one's last will: usually **last will and testament.** In strictness, a testament differs from a will in that it bequeaths personal property only, but the words are commonly used interchangeably. **2** In Biblical use, a covenant; dispensation. [<F <L *testamentum* <*testari* testify <*testis* a witness] — **tes′ta·men′tal** *adj.*

tes·ta·men·ta·ry (tes′tə·men′tər·ē) *adj.* **1** Derived from, bequeathed by, or set forth in a will. **2** Appointed or provided by, or done in accordance with, a will. **3** Pertaining to a will, or to the administration or settlement of a will; testamental. **4** *Often cap.* Pertaining to a Testament.

tes·tate (tes′tāt) *adj.* Having made a will

before decease. [<L *testatus*, pp. of *testari* be a witness. See TESTAMENT.]

tes·ta·tor (tes·tā′tər, tes′tā·tər) *n.* **1** The maker of a will. **2** One who has died leaving a will. [<L] — **tes·ta′trix** (-triks) *n. fem.*

test·er[1] (tes′tər) *n.* One who tests; a device for testing.

tes·ter[2] (tes′tər) *n.* A flat canopy over a tomb, pulpit, or bed. [<OF *testiere* <*teste* head <L *testa* shell, skull]

tes·ter[3] (tes′tər) *n. Obs.* A silver coin of the Tudor period, originally equal to twelve pence, later worth sixpence. [<OF *teston* coin <*teste* head. See TESTER[2].]

TESTER

tes·ti·cle (tes′ti·kəl) *n. Biol.* One of the two genital glands of the male in which the spermatozoa and certain internal secretions are formed; a testis. [<L *testiculus*, dim. of *testis* testicle]

tes·tic·u·late (tes·tik′yə·lit, -lāt) *adj.* **1** Shaped or formed like a testicle. **2** Solid and ovate, like the roots of certain orchids. **3** Having organs like testicles. [<L *testiculus* + -ATE[1]]

tes·ti·fi·ca·tion (tes′tə·fə·kā′shən) *n.* **1** The act of testifying or the giving of testimony. **2** The testimony given. — **tes′ti·fi·ca′tor** *n.*

tes·ti·fy (tes′tə·fī) *v.* **·fied, ·fy·ing** *v.i.* **1** To make solemn declaration of truth or fact. **2** *Law* To give testimony; bear witness. **3** To serve as evidence or indication: Her rags *testified* to her poverty. — *v.t.* **4** To bear witness to; affirm positively. **5** *Law* To state or declare on oath or affirmation. **6** To be evidence or indication of. **7** To make known publicly; declare. See synonyms under AFFIRM, AVOW. [<L *testificari* <*testis* witness + *facere* make] — **tes′ti·fi′er** *n.*

tes·ti·mo·ni·al (tes′tə·mō′nē·əl) *n.* **1** A formal token of regard. **2** A written certificate; an acknowledgment of services or worth; a letter of recommendation. — *adj.* Pertaining to or constituting testimony or a testimonial. [<L *testimonialis* <*testimonium*. See TESTIMONY.]

tes·ti·mo·ny (tes′tə·mō′nē) *n. pl.* **·nies** **1** A statement or affirmation of a fact, as before a court; evidence; proof. **2** The aggregate of proof offered in a case. **3** The act of testifying; attestation. **4** Public declaration regarding some experience. **5** The Decalog; the Old Testament Scriptures. [<L *testimonium* <*testis* a witness] — **tes′ti·mo′nied** *Obs. adj.*

Synonyms: affidavit, affirmation, attestation, deposition, proof, witness. *Testimony,* in legal as well as in common use, denotes the statements of witnesses. *Deposition* and *affidavit* denote *testimony* reduced to writing. The *deposition* differs from the *affidavit* in that the latter is voluntary and without cross-examination, while the former is made under interrogatories and subject to cross-examination. *Evidence* is a broader term, including the *testimony* of witnesses and all facts of every kind that tend to prove a thing true; we have the *testimony* of a traveler that a fugitive passed this way; his footprints in the sand are additional *evidence* of the fact. Compare PROOF.

tes·tis (tes′tis) *n. pl.* **·tes** (-tēz) A testicle. [<L]

tes·ton (tes′tən, tes·tōōn′) *n. Obs.* **1** A European silver coin: so called from the head on the obverse side. **2** A French coin of the 16th century. **3** An English silver coin; a tester. Also **tes·toon** (tes·tōōn′). [<F <Ital. *testone*, aug. of *testa* head <L, skull]

tes·tos·ter·one (tes·tos′tə·rōn) *n. Biochem.* A male sex hormone, $C_{19}H_{28}O_2$, isolated as a white crystalline substance from the testes, and also made synthetically. [<TESTIS + STER(OL) + -ONE]

test paper 1 *Chem.* A paper saturated with some reagent that readily changes color when exposed to certain others, as litmus paper. **2** A list of questions, problems, etc., for the testing of students.

test pilot An aviator who flies airplanes of new design to test their performance under various conditions.

test tube A glass tube, open at one end, and usually with a rounded bottom, used in making chemical or biological tests.

tes·tu·di·nal (tes·tōō′də·nəl, -tyōō′-) *adj.* Pertaining to or like a turtle or tortoise shell: also **tes·tu′di·nate.** [<L *testudo, -inis* tortoise]

tes·ty (tes′tē) *adj.* **·ti·er, ·ti·est** Having an irritable disposition; touchy. See synonyms under FRETFUL. [<AF *testif* heady <OF *teste* head <L *testa* skull] — **tes′ti·ly** *adv.* — **tes′ti·ness** *n.*

te·tan·ic (ti·tan′ik) *adj.* Relating to or productive of tetanus: also **te·tan′i·cal.** — *n.* A drug capable of causing convulsions, as strychnine or nux vomica.

tet·a·nus (tet′ə·nəs) *n.* **1** *Pathol.* An acute infectious disease caused by a bacillus (*Clostridium tetani*) and characterized by rigid spasmodic contraction of various voluntary muscles, especially that form affecting the muscles of the jaw, called *lockjaw.* **2** *Physiol.* A state of contraction in a muscle excited by a rapid series of shocks. [<L <Gk. *tetanos* spasm <*teinein* stretch]

tetarto– *combining form* Four; fourth. Also, before vowels, **tetart–.** [<Gk. *tetartos* fourth <*tettares* four]

te·tar·to·he·dral (ti·tär′tō·hē′drəl) *adj.* Possessing one fourth of the planes necessary for true symmetry: said of crystals.

teth·er (teth′ər) *n.* **1** Something used to check or confine, as a rope for fastening an animal. **2** The range, scope, or limit of one's powers or field of action. — **at the end of one's tether** At the extreme end or limit of one's resources. — *v.t.* To fasten or confine by a tether. [ME *tethir* <Scand. Cf. ON *tiodhr* a tether.]

tetra– *combining form* Four; fourfold: *tetrachord.* Also, before vowels, **tetr–.**

tet·ra·ba·sic (tet′rə·bā′sik) *adj. Chem.* **1** Containing four atoms of hydrogen replaceable by a base or basic radicals: said of certain acids. **2** Denoting a compound with four atoms of a univalent metal or the equivalent.

tet·ra·cene (tet′rə·sēn) *n. Chem.* A yellow, solid, nitrogen compound, $C_9H_8N_{10}$, used as a sensitizer or combustion initiator in priming compositions. Also *tetrazine.*

tet·ra·chlo·ride (tet′rə·klōr′id, -id, -klō′rīd, -rid) *n. Chem.* A compound containing four atoms of chlorine. Also **tet′ra·chlo′rid** (-klôr′id, -klō′rid).

tet·ra·chord (tet′rə·kôrd) *n. Music* **1** A scale series of half an octave. **2** The interval of a perfect fourth. [<Gk. *tetrachordon* a musical instrument <*tetras* group of four + *chordē* string] — **tet′ra·chor′dal** *adj.*

te·trac·id (te·tras′id) *Chem. adj.* Denoting a base which is capable of combination with four molecules of a monobasic acid to form a salt or ester. — *n.* A base having four replaceable hydroxyl radicals. [<TETR(A)- + ACID]

tet·ra·cy·cline (tet′rə·sī′klin) *n. Chem.* A nitrogenous compound, $C_{22}H_{24}N_2O_8$, isolated as a yellow, odorless, crystalline powder from certain species of a soil bacillus (genus *Streptomyces*). It forms the base of several antibiotics, as Aureomycin and Terramycin. [<*tetracyclic*, containing four atomic rings + -INE]

tet·rad (tet′rad) *n.* **1** A collection of four, or the number four. **2** An atom, radical, or element that is quadrivalent. **3** *Biol.* The group of four chromatids into which two bivalent chromosomes divide in the last stages of meiosis. **4** A crystal having an axis showing fourfold symmetry. [<Gk. *tetras, -ados* group of four]

te·trad·y·mite (te·trad′ə·mīt) *n.* A soft, metallic, pale steel-gray, bismuth telluride, Bi_2Te_3, crystallizing in the rhombohedral system. [<G *tetradymit* <Gk. *tetradymos* fourfold; from its occurring in compound twin crystals]

tet·ra·dyn·a·mous (tet′rə·din′ə·məs, -dī′nə-) *adj. Bot.* Having six stamens, of which four, arranged in opposite pairs, are longer than the other two and inserted above them, as in flowers of the mustard family. [<TETRA- + Gk. *dynamis* power]

tet·ra·eth·yl·lead (tet′rə·eth′il·led′) *n.* An extremely toxic liquid compound, $Pb(C_2H_5)_4$, having an antiknock effect when added in small amounts to motor fuels. Also **tetraethyl lead.** Also called *lead tetraethyl.*

tet·ra·gon (tet′rə·gon) *n. Geom.* A plane figure having four angles; a quadrangle. [<Gk. *tetragonon* a quadrangle <*tetra-* four + *gōnia* an-

tet·rag·o·nal (tet·rag′ə·nəl) *adj.* 1 Being or pertaining to a tetragon; having four angles; quadrangular. 2 Belonging to or designating a crystal system characterized by four alternately dissimilar planes of symmetry intersecting at angles of 45 degrees and a fifth symmetrical plane at right angles to the others.

tet·ra·gram (tet′rə·gram) *n.* A word of four letters.

tet·ra·he·dral (tet′rə·hē′drəl) *adj.* 1 Of or pertaining to a tetrahedron. 2 Made up of or having four sides. [< Gk. *tetraedros.* See TETRAHEDRON.]

tet·ra·he·drite (tet′rə·hē′drīt) *n.* A steel-gray, fine-grained mineral, usually a sulfide of copper and antimony but having other elements, found in tetrahedral crystals. [< TETRAHEDRON]

tet·ra·he·dron (tet′rə·hē′drən) *n. pl.* **·dra** (-drə) 1 *Geom.* A solid bounded by four plane triangular faces. 2 An anti-tank obstacle shaped like a pyramid. [< Gk. *tetraedron,* neut. of *tetraedros* < *tetra-* four + *hedra* base]

TETRAHEDRON

tet·ral·o·gy (te·tral′ə·jē) *n. pl.* **·gies** 1 A group of four dramas, three tragic and one satyric, presented together at the festivals of Dionysus at Athens. 2 Hence, any series of four related dramatic, fictional, or operatic works. [< Gk. *tetralogia* < *tetra-* four + *logos* word, speech]

tet·tram·er·ous (te·tram′ər·əs) *adj.* 1 Having four parts. 2 *Bot.* Having the parts or organs in four; arranged in fours or multiples of four: often written 4-merous. 3 *Zool.* Having four joints; having four-jointed tarsi. Also **te·tram′er·al.** [< Gk. *tetramerēs* four-parted < *tetra-* four + *meros* part]

tet·ram·e·ter (te·tram′ə·tər) *adj.* Having four measures. In classical trochaic, iambic, and anapestic verse a measure consists of two feet (a dipody); hence, a trochaic tetrameter contains eight feet to the line. In English, a tetrameter has four feet or measures. —*n.* A verse (line) thus composed. [< LL *tetrametrus* < Gk. *tetrametros* < *tetra-* four + *metron* measure]

tet·ra·morph (tet′rə·môrf) *n.* The union of the four attributes of the four Evangelists in one composite figure, winged, and standing on winged wheels of fire, the wings being full of eyes. [< Gk. *tetramorphon* four-shaped < *tetra-* four + *morphē* form]

tet·ra·pet·al·ous (tet′rə·pet′l·əs) *adj. Bot.* Having four petals.

tet·ra·pod (tet′rə·pod) *adj.* Four-footed. [< NL *tetrapodus* < Gk. *tetrapous, tetrapodos* four-footed < *tetra-* four + *pous* foot]

te·trap·o·dy (te·trap′ə·dē) *n. pl.* **·dies** A group of four feet, as a colon, meter, or verse containing that number. [< Gk. *tetrapodia* < *tetrapous.* See TETRAPOD.] —**tet·ra·pod·ic** (tet′rə·pod′ik) *adj.*

tet·rap·ter·ous (te·trap′tər·əs) *adj. Biol.* Having four wings, as certain fruits and insects. [< NL *tetrapterus* < Gk. *tetrapteros* four-winged < *tetra-* four + *pteron* wing]

tet·ra·py·lon (tet′rə·pī′lon). *n. Archit.* A structure having four gateways or penetrated by two intersecting passages, as some arches. [< Gk. *tetrapylos* with four gates < *tetra-* four + *pylē* a gate]

tet·rarch (tet′rärk, tē′trärk) *n.* 1 The governor of one of four divisions of a country or province. 2 A tributary prince under the Romans; a subordinate ruler. 3 Anciently, in the Greek army, the commander of a subdivision of a phalanx. [< LL *tetrarcha* < L *tetrarches* < Gk. *tetrarchēs* < *tetra-* four + *archos* ruler] —**tet·rar·chy** (tet′rär·kē, tē′trär-), **tet·rarch·ate** (tet′rär·kāt, -kit, tē′trär-) *n.*

tet·ra·seme (tet′rə·sēm) *n.* A long syllable or a foot equal to four short syllables. [< TETRA- + Gk. *sēma* sign] —**tet′ra·se′mic** *adj.*

tet·ra·spore (tet′rə·spôr, -spōr) *n. Bot.* An asexual spore produced by certain algae: named from the fact that often four are produced together from a mother cell.

tet·ra·stich (tet′rə·stik) *n.* A poem or stanza of four lines; a quatrain. [< TETRA- + Gk. *stichos* row, line] —**tet′ra·stich′ic** *adj.*

te·tras·ti·chous (te·tras′tə·kəs) *adj. Bot.* Four-

ranked; having organs, as leaves on a stem, arranged in four vertical rows or ranks.

tet·ra·style (tet′rə·stīl) *adj.* Having four pillars. —*n. Archit.* 1 A temple having four columns in the front or end row. 2 Any building or structure having four pillars in a row or rows. [< L *tetrastylos* < Gk. < *tetra-* four + *stylos* column]

tet·ra·syl·la·ble (tet′rə·sil′ə·bəl) *n.* A word of four syllables. —**tet′ra·syl·lab′ic** or **-i·cal** *adj.*

tet·ra·tom·ic (tet′rə·tom′ik) *adj. Chem.* 1 Containing four atoms. 2 Containing four replaceable univalent atoms or molecules. 3 Quadrivalent.

tet·ra·va·lent (tet′rə·vā′lənt) *adj. Chem.* Quadrivalent.

Teu·ton·ic (too·ton′ik, tyoo-) *adj.* 1 Of or pertaining to the Teutons; especially, designating the blond peoples of northern Europe, formerly including the Angles, Saxons, Danes, Normans, Norwegians, the Goths, Franks, Lombards, Vandals, etc.; now embracing also the English, Germans, Dutch, etc. 2 Of or pertaining to that subfamily of Indo-European languages now called *Germanic,* including Gothic, the Scandinavian languages, and all the High and Low German languages and dialects, among which are German, Dutch, Flemish, and English. —*n.* The Germanic subfamily of languages.

Teu·ton·ism (toot′n·iz′əm, tyoot′n-) *n.* 1 A custom or mode of expression peculiar to Germans or Teutons; Germanism: also **Teu·ton·i·cism** (too·ton′ə·siz′əm, tyoo-). 2 A belief in the superiority of the Teutonic race. 3 Teutonic character and civilization. —**Teu′ton·ist** *n.*

tex·as (tek′səs) *n. U.S.* The uppermost structure on a river steamboat, containing the pilot house, officers' cabins, etc.; often, a row of staterooms behind the pilot house, or having the pilot house set on top of it. [from *Texas*; so called from the former custom of naming staterooms after the States, those of the officers being the largest]

Tex·as (tek′səs) A State in the SW United States, bordering on Mexico and the Gulf of Mexico; 267,339 square miles; capital, Austin; entered the Union Dec. 29, 1845; nicknamed *Lone Star State:* abbr. TX —**Tex′an** *n. & adj.*

Texas Ranger 1 A member of the mounted State police force of Texas. 2 Originally, one of a band of armed and mounted men organized in Texas to fight Indians and keep order on the frontiers.

Texas sparrow A plain, olive-backed fringilline bird *(Arremonops rufivirgatus)* found in Mexico and southern Texas.

text (tekst) *n.* 1 The actual or original words of an author; the body of matter on a written or printed page, as distinguished from notes, commentary, illustrations, etc. 2 A written or printed version of the matter of an author's works: the folio *text* of Shakespeare. 3 Any one of various recensions that are taken to represent the authentic words, or portion of the words, of the original Scriptures. 4 A verse of Scripture, particularly when cited as the basis of a discourse or sermon. 5 Any subject of discourse; a topic; theme. 6 One of several styles of letters or types. 7 A textbook. [< OF *texte* < L *textus* fabric, structure < *texere* weave]

text·book (tekst′book′) *n.* A book used as a standard work or basis of instruction in any branch of knowledge; schoolbook; manual.

tex·tile (teks′til, -til) *adj.* 1 Pertaining to weaving or woven fabrics. 2 Such as may be woven; manufactured by weaving. —*n.* 1 A woven fabric; textile material. 2 Material capable of being woven. [< L *textilis* < *textus* fabric. See TEXT.]

tex·tu·al (teks′choo·əl) *adj.* 1 Pertaining to, contained in, or based on the text of a book, especially of the Scriptures; literal; word for word. 2 Versed in texts. [< OF *textuel* < *texte.* See TEXT.] —**tex′tu·al·ly** *adv.*

tex·tu·al·ism (teks′choo·əl·iz′əm) *n.* 1 Rigid adherence to the letter of a text. 2 The method or principles of textual criticism.

tex·tu·al·ist (teks′choo·əl·ist) *n.* 1 A close adherent to the letter of a text. 2 One who is versed in or cites texts readily.

tex·tu·ar·y (teks′choo·er′ē) *adj.* 1 Contained in a text. 2 Of, belonging to, or adhering to a text. —*n. pl.* **·ar·ies** A textualist.

tex·ture (teks′chər) *n.* 1 The arrangement or character of the threads, etc., of a woven fabric. 2 The mode of union or disposition of elementary constituent parts, as in a photograph, or surface of paper, etc.; minute structure or make; structural order. 3 The structure, especially as regards detail, of a work of art. 4 Any woven fabric; a web. [< L *textura* < *textus* fabric. See TEXT.] —**tex′tur·al** *adj.* —**tex′tur·al·ly** *adv.*

Th *Chem.* Thorium (symbol Th).

-th[1] *suffix of nouns* 1 The act or result of the action expressed in the root word: *growth.* 2 The state or quality of being what is indicated in the root word: *health.*

-th[2] *suffix* Used in ordinal numbers: *tenth.* Also, after vowels, *-eth,* as in *fortieth.* [OE *-tha, -the*]

Thai (tī) *n.* 1 The people collectively of Thailand, Laos, and parts of Burma, including the Laos, Shan, and Siamese. 2 A family of languages spoken by these people: considered by some a branch of the Sino-Tibetan family. —*adj.* Of or pertaining to the Thai, their culture, or their languages. Also spelled *Tai.*

Thai·land (tī′land) A constitutional monarchy in SE Asia; 198,404 square miles; capital, Bangkok: formerly *Siam. Thai* **Mu·ang Thai** (moo′äng tī′).

thal·a·men·ceph·a·lon (thal′ə·men·sef′ə·lon) *n. Anat.* Diencephalon. [< THALAM(US) + ENCEPHALON]

tha·lam·ic (thə·lam′ik) *adj.* Of or pertaining to a thalamus, especially to the optic thalamus.

thal·a·mus (thal′ə·məs) *n. pl.* **·mi** (-mī) 1 *Anat.* The optic thalamus. 2 *Bot.* The receptacle of a flower. [< L < Gk. *thalamos* chamber]

thal·as·se·mi·a (thal′ə·sē′mē·ə) *n.* Any of a group of mild-to-fatal anemias accompanied by varying bone deformities, enlargement of the spleen and other signs, resulting from an inborn error in the synthesis of globin; limited largely to persons of Mediterranean origin. [< Gk. *thalassa* sea + -EMIA **thal′as·se′mic** *adj.*

tha·las·sic (thə·las′ik) *adj.* 1 Of or pertaining to the seas. 2 Pelagic; oceanic. [< Gk. *thalassa* sea]

thalasso- *combining form* The sea; of or pertaining to the sea: *thalassophobia.* Also, before vowels, **thalass-.** Also **thalassi-.** [< Gk. *thalassa* the sea]

thal·as·sog·ra·phy (thal′ə·sog′rə·fē) *n.* Oceanography. [< THALASSO- + -GRAPHY]

tha·las·so·pho·bi·a (thə·las′ə·fō′bē·ə) *n.* Morbid fear of the sea. [< THALASSO- + -PHOBIA]

tha·ler (tä′lər) See TALER.

thal·i·do·mide (thə·lid′ə·mīd) *n. Med.* A mild sedative, illegalized when its use by pregnant women resulted in birth anomalies.

thal·lic (thal′ik) *adj. Chem.* Of, pertaining to, or derived from thallium, especially in its higher valence.

thal·line (thal′ēn, -in) *n. Chem.* A white, crystalline, synthetic alkaloid, $C_{10}H_{13}NO$: its salts are used as antipyretics and antiseptics.

thal·li·um (thal′ē·əm) *n.* A soft, heavy, toxic metallic element (symbol Tl, atomic number 81) resembling lead. See PERIODIC TABLE. [< NL < Gk. *thallos* a green shoot; from the bright green line in its spectrum, which led to its discovery]

thal·loid (thal′oid) *adj.* Resembling a thallus. Also **thal·loi·dal** (thə·loid′l).

thal·lo·phyte (thal′ə·fīt) *n.* Any plant belonging to a major division or phylum of plants *(Thallophyta),* comprising the bacteria, fungi, algae, and lichens. Many of the forms are unicellular and those more highly developed are without true roots, stems, or leaves. [< *thallo-* (< THALLUS) + -PHYTE] —**thal′lo·phyt′ic** (-fit′ik) *adj.*

thal·lous (thal′əs) *adj. Chem.* Derived from thallium, especially in its lower valence. Also **thal·li·ous** (thal′ē·əs).

thal·lus (thal′əs) *n. pl.* **·lus·es** or **·li** (-ī) *Bot.* A plant body without true root, stem, or leaf, as in thallophytes. [< L, a shoot < Gk. *thallos* < *thallein* bloom]

Tham·muz (täm′mooz, tam′uz) See TAMMUZ.

than (than, *unstressed* thən) *conj.* 1 When, as, or if compared with: after an adjective or adverb to express comparison between what precedes and what follows: I am stronger *than* he (is); I know her better *than* (I know) him. **2** Except; but: used after *other, else,* etc: no other *than* you. *Than* is sometimes considered a preposition in the one phrase, *than whom:* an eminent judge *than whom* no other is more just. [OE *thanne* then]

than·age (thā′nij) *n.* **1** In early English law, the state, jurisdiction, or office of a thane. **2** The land held by a thane or the tenure by which he held it. Also spelled *thenage.* [< AF *thaynage* < OE *thegn* a thane]

thanato- *combining form* Death; of or pertaining to death: *thanatophobia.* Also, before vowels, **thanat-.** [< Gk. *thanatos* death]

than·a·toid (than′ə·toid) *adj.* Resembling death; deadly.

than·a·to·pho·bi·a (than′ə·tə·fō′bē·ə) *n.* Morbid fear of death. [< THANATO- + PHOBIA] — **than′a·to·pho′bic** *adj.*

than·a·top·sis (than′ə·top′sis) *n.* A musing or meditation upon death; a view of death. [< THANAT(O)- + -OPSIS]

thane (thān) *n.* **1** Originally, a warrior companion of an English king before the Conquest. **2** Later, a man who ranked above an ordinary freeman or ceorl (churl) but below an earl or nobleman. **3** *Scot.* The chief of a clan; a baron; one of the old nobility in the service of the king. Also spelled **thegn.** [OE *thegn*]

thank (thangk) *v.t.* **1** To express gratitude to; give thanks to. **2** To hold responsible; blame: often used ironically. [OE *thancian* < *thanc* thanks, thought]

thank·ful (thangk′fəl) *adj.* **1** Deeply sensible of favors received; grateful. **2** Done or made to express thanks; manifesting thanks. — **thank′ful·ly** *adv.* — **thank′ful·ness** *n.*

thank·less (thangk′lis) *adj.* **1** Not feeling or expressing gratitude; ungrateful; unresponsive. **2** Not gaining or likely to gain thanks; unthanked; unappreciated. — **thank′less·ly** *adv.* — **thank′less·ness** *n.*

thanks (thangks) *n. pl.* Expressions of gratitude; grateful acknowledgement. — *interj.* My thanks to you; I thank you. — **thanks to 1** Thanks be given to. **2** Because of.

thanks·giv·ing (thangks′giv′ing) *n.* **1** The act of giving thanks, as to God; the expression of gratitude. **2** A form of words or worship in recognition of divine mercies. **3** A public celebration in recognition of divine favor. **4** A day set apart for such celebration.

Thanksgiving Day *U.S.* The fourth Thursday in November, set apart as an annual festival of thanksgiving to God for the year's blessings. Also **Thanksgiving.**

that (that, *unstressed* thət) *adj. pl.* **those 1** Pertaining to some person or thing previously mentioned, understood, or specifically designated: *that* man. **2** Denoting something more remote in place, time, or thought: correlative to *this.* — *pron.* **1** As a demonstrative, the person or thing implied, mentioned, or understood; or the person or thing there or in the second place: *That* is the dress I like. **2** As a relative, who or which: used as a correlative to *such* or *so.* ♦ In earlier English, *that* was the relative pronoun, *who, what,* and *which* being only interrogatives until they gradually assumed the force of relatives, and in some uses superseded *that.* When the relative clause qualifies or makes an addition to the main clause, *who* or *which* is generally preferred, whereas *that* usually introduces a restrictive clause. Thus we say: Washington, *who* was the first president, is often called Father of his Country. But: *The* Washington *that* emigrated to this country was his ancestor. — *adv.* **1** *Colloq.* In such a manner or degree; so. **2** To that extent: I can't see *that* far. — *conj. That* is used primarily to connect a subordinate clause with its principal clause, with the following meanings: **1** As a fact that: introducing a fact: I tell you *that* it is so. **2** So that; in order that: I tell you *that* you may know. **3** For the reason that; seeing that; because: She wept *that* she was growing old. **4** As a result: introducing a result, consequence, or effect: He bled so profusely *that* he died. **5** At which time; when: It was only yesterday *that* I saw him. **6** Introducing an exclamation: O *that*

he would come! See synonyms under BUT. — **so that 1** To the end that. **2** With the result that. **3** Provided. See THOSE. [OE *thæt,* neut. of *se* the]

thatch (thach) *n.* **1** A covering of reeds, straw, etc., arranged on a roof so as to shed water. **2** Any of various palms whose leaves are used for thatching, especially those of the genera *Thrinax* and *Sabal.* **3** Any of certain tall, coarse American grasses (genus *Spartina*) of the northern Atlantic coasts. — *v.t.* To cover with a thatch. [OE *thæc* cover] — **thatch′er** *n.* — **thatch′y** *adj.*

thau·ma·tol·o·gy (thô′mə·tol′ə·jē) *n.* The scientific study of miracles. [< THAUMATO- + -LOGY]

thau·ma·trope (thô′mə·trōp) *n.* An optical toy or instrument in which pictures on opposite sides of a card appear to blend together when the card is rapidly twirled. [< Gk. *thauma* wonder + -TROPE]

thau·ma·turge (thô′mə·tûrj) *n.* One who performs wonders or miracles; a wonder-worker; magician. Also **thau′ma·tur′gist.** [< Gk. *thaumatourgos* < *thauma* wonder + *ergon* work]

thau·ma·tur·gy (thô′mə·tûr′jē) *n.* Magic; the performance or working of wonders or miracles. — **thau′ma·tur′gic** or **·gi·cal** *adj.*

thaw (thô) *v.i.* **1** To melt or dissolve; become liquid or semi-liquid, as snow or ice. **2** To rise in temperature so as to melt ice and snow: said of weather and used impersonally. **3** To become less cold and unsociable. — *v.t.* **4** To cause to thaw. See synonyms under MELT. — *n.* **1** The act of thawing, or the state of being thawed. **2** Warmth of weather such as melts things frozen; also, figuratively, state of warmer feeling or expression. [OE *thawian*] — **thaw′er** *n.*

the[1] (*stressed* thē; *unstressed before a consonant* thə; *unstressed before a vowel* thi) *definite article* or *adj. The* is opposed to the indefinite article *a* or *an,* and is used, especially before nouns, to render the modified word more particular or individual. It is used specifically: **1** When reference is made to a particular person, thing, or group: *The* natives are getting restless; He left *the* room. **2** To give an adjective substantive force, or render a notion abstract: *the* quick and *the* dead; *the* doing of the deed. **3** Before a noun to make it generic: *The* dog is a friend of man. **4** With the force of a possessive pronoun: He kicked me in *the* (my) leg. **5** To give distributive force: equivalent to *a, per, each,* etc.: a dollar *the* volume. **6** *Scot.* & *Irish* To designate the head of a clan or group: *the* MacIntosh. **7** To designate a particular one as emphatically outstanding: usually stressed in speech and italicized in writing: He is *the* officer for the command. **8** As part of a title: *The* Duke of York. [OE *the,* later form of *se*]

the[2] (thə) *adv.* By that much; by so much; to this extent: *the* more, *the* merrier: used to modify words in the comparative degree. [OE *thy,* oblique case of *se* the]

the·a·ceous (thē·ā′shəs) *adj. Bot.* Designating a family (*Theaceae*) of shrubs and trees having alternate, simple leaves, large flowers, and a typically capsular fruit; the tea family. [< NL < *Thea,* genus name < dial. Chinese *t'e* tea; incorrectly taken by Linnaeus as "divine herb" < Gk. *thea* a goddess]

the·an·throp·ic (thē′ən·throp′ik) *adj.* **1** Being both divine and human. **2** Having or pertaining to a nature both divine and human. Also **the′an·throp′i·cal.** [< Gk. *theanthrōpos* < *theos* god + *anthrōpos, -ōpou* man]

the·an·thro·pism (thē·an′thrə·piz′əm) *n.* **1** The doctrine of the manifestation of God in man, or of the union of the divine and human in Christ. **2** The ascription of human characteristics to a deity; anthropomorphism. **3** Belief in the possibility of the combination in one being of a nature both human and divine. — **the·an′thro·pist** *n.*

the·ar·chy (thē′är·kē) *n. pl.* **·chies 1** Government by God or by a god. **2** A theocracy. **3** A body or class of deities. [< Gk. *thearchia* < *theos* god + *archein* rule]

the·a·ter (thē′ə·tər) *n.* **1** A building especially adapted to dramatic, operatic, or spectacular representations; playhouse. **2** The theatrical world and everything relating to it. **3** A room or hall arranged with seats that rise as they recede from a platform, especially adapted to lectures, surgical demonstrations, etc. **4** Any

place of semicircular form with seats rising by easy gradations. **5** Any place or region that is the scene of events: a *theater* of operations in war. Also **the′a·tre.** [< OF *theatre* < Gk. *theatron* < *theasthai* behold]

the·at·ri·cal (thē·at′ri·kəl) *adj.* **1** Pertaining to the theater or to dramatic performances. **2** Designed for show, display, or effect; showy; artificial. **3** Suited to dramatic presentation. **4** Like the manner of actors; histrionic. Also **the·at′ric.** — *n. pl.* Dramatic performances: especially when given by amateur performers. [< LL *theatricus* < Gk. *theatrikos* < *theatron.* See THEATER.] — **the·at′ri·cal·ly** *adv.* — **the·at′ri·cal·ness** *n.*

the·at·rics (thē·at′riks) *n. pl. (construed as singular)* The art of bringing about effects appropriate for dramatic performances.

the·ba·ine (thē′bə·ēn, thi·bā′ēn, -in) *n. Chem.* A silvery-white, poisonous, crystalline alkaloid, $C_{19}H_{21}O_3N$, found in opium and resembling strychnine in action: also called *paramorphine.* Also **the′ba·in** (-in). [from Egyptian *Thebes,* where a kind of opium was produced + -INE[2]]

Thebes (thēbz) **1** The ancient capital of Upper Egypt; Luxor and Karnak occupy part of its site on the Nile: Greek *Diospolis.* **2** The chief city of ancient Boeotia, Greece; destroyed in 336 B.C. by Alexander the Great: also **The·bae** (thē′bē). **3** A commercial city in east central Greece on the site of ancient Thebes; important in the Middle Ages: Greek **The·vai** or **Thi·vai** (thē′vā). — **The·ban** (thē′bən) *adj. & n.*

the·ca (thē′kə) *n. pl.* **·cae** (-sē) **1** A sheath or case. **2** *Anat.* The investment of the spinal cord formed by the dura mater, sometimes called *theca vertebralis.* **3** *Bot.* A spore case, sac, or capsule. [< L < Gk. *thēkē* case] — **the′cal** *adj.*

thee (thē) *pron.* **1** The objective case of *thou.* **2** *Thou:* used generally by Quakers with a verb in the third person singular: *Thee* knows my mind. [OE *thē,* accusative case of *thū* thou]

theft (theft) *n.* **1** The act of thieving; larceny. **2** *Rare* That which is stolen. [OE *thēoft, thīefth*]

the·ine (thē′ēn, -in) *n. Chem.* The alkaloid found in the tea plant: chemically identical with caffeine. Also **the′in** (-in). [< F *théine* < NL *thea* tea < dial. Chinese *t'e*]

their (thâr) *pronominal adj.* The possessive case of the pronoun *they* employed attributively; belonging or pertaining to them: *their* homes. [ME < ON *theirra* of them]

theirs (thârz) *pron.* **1** The possessive case of *they,* used predicatively; belonging or pertaining to them: That house is *theirs.* **2** The things or persons belonging or relating to them: our country and *theirs.* — **of theirs** Belonging or pertaining to them; their: the double possessive. [< THEIR + -s, on analogy with *his*]

the·ism[1] (thē′iz·əm) *n.* **1** Belief in, or in the existence of, God, a god, or gods: opposed to *atheism.* **2** Belief in a personal God as creator and supreme ruler of the universe, who transcends his creation but works in and through it in revealing himself to men. Compare DEISM, PANTHEISM. **3** Belief in one god; monotheism: opposed to *polytheism.* **4** Formerly, deism. **5** *Philos.* The doctrine that one supreme reality, intrinsically complete and perfect, is the final ground and source of everything other than itself: a doctrine resembling monotheism and some types of monism, but opposed to atheism, agnosticism, deism, materialism, pantheism, and polytheism. [< Gk. *theos* god] — **the′ist** *n.* — **the·is′tic** or **·ti·cal** *adj.* — **the·is′ti·cal·ly** *adv.*

the·ism[2] (thē′iz·əm) *n. Pathol.* The toxic effects of excessive tea-drinking. [< NL *thea* tea. See THEINE.]

the·li·tis (thi·lī′tis) *n. Pathol.* Inflammation of the nipple. [< NL < Gk. *thēlē* teat + -ITIS]

them (them, *unstressed* thəm) *pron.* The objective case of *they.* [ME *theim* < ON, to them]

the·mat·ic (thē·mat′ik) *adj.* **1** Of, constituting, or pertaining to a theme or themes. **2** *Ling.* Constituting a stem. Also **the·mat′i·cal.** — **the·mat′i·cal·ly** *adv.*

theme (thēm) *n.* **1** A subject of discourse; a

topic to be discussed or developed in speech or writing; hence, any topic. 2 An essay or dissertation; loosely, a brief composition in any form, written as an exercise. 3 *Ling.* The stem of a word, to which are attached the inflectional endings, consisting of the root unmodified or with some internal change and, often, a thematic vowel common to the particular stem class. 4 A melodic subject usually developed with variations in a musical composition. 5 One of the administrative divisions of the Byzantine Empire. See synonyms under TOPIC. [<OF *teme* <L *thema* <Gk. *the-*, stem of *tithenai* place]

them·selves (them'selvz', unstressed thəm-) *pron.* Emphatic or reflexive form of THEY, THEM: the plural of HIMSELF, HERSELF, ITSELF.

then (then) *adv.* 1 At that time. 2 Soon or immediately afterward; next in space or time. 3 At another time: often introducing a sequential statement following *now, at first,* etc. — *conj.* 1 For that reason; as a consequence; accordingly. 2 In that case: I will *then,* since you won't. — *adj.* Being or acting in, or belonging to, that time: the *then* secretary of state. — *n.* A specific time already mentioned or understood; that time. [OE *thanne*]

the·nar (thē'när) *n. Anat.* 1 The palm of the hand. 2 The prominence on the palm at the base of the thumb. — *adj.* Of or pertaining to the palm of a hand or the sole of a foot: also **the'nal.** [<Gk. *thenar* palm of the hand]

thence (thens) *adv.* 1 From that place. 2 From the circumstance, fact, or cause; therefore. 3 From that time; after that time. 4 *Archaic* Away from there; elsewhere; absent. [ME *thannes* <OE *thanon* from there + *-s³*]

thence·forth (thens'fôrth', -fôrth', thens'fôrth', -fôrth') *adv.* From that time on; thereafter.

the·o·bro·mine (thē'ə·brō'mēn, -min) *n. Chem.* A bitter, colorless, crystalline alkaloid, $C_7H_8N_4O_2$, resembling caffeine, contained in cacao beans: used in medicine as a diuretic and myocardial stimulant. [<THEOBROM(A) + -INE²]

the·o·cen·tric (thē'ə·sen'trik) *adj.* Having God for its center; proceeding from and returning to God.

the·oc·ra·cy (thē·ok'rə·sē) *n. pl.* **·cies** 1 A state, polity, or group of people that claims a deity as its ruler, as ancient Israel after the Exodus. 2 Government of a state by a god, or by a priestly class claiming to have divine authority, as in the Papacy. [<Gk. *theokratia* <*theos* god + *krateein* rule] — **the·o·crat·ic** (thē'ə·krat'ik) or **·i·cal** *adj.*

the·oc·ra·sy (thē·ok'rə·sē) *n.* 1 The mingling of several deities or divine attributes in one personality. 2 The mystical intimacy or union of the soul with God. [<LGk. *theokrasia* <Gk. *theos* god + *krasis* mingling]

the·o·crat (thē'ə·krat) *n.* 1 A theocratic or divine ruler. 2 An advocate of theocracy.

the·od·i·cy (thē·od'ə·sē) *n. pl.* **·cies** 1 Justification of the divine providence by the attempt to reconcile the existence of evil with the goodness and sovereignty of God: a term established by Leibnitz in 1710. 2 The branch of philosophy that treats of the being, perfections, and government of God and the immortality of the soul. [<F *théodicée* <Gk. *theos* god + *dikē* justice]

the·od·o·lite (thē·od'ə·līt) *n.* One of several surveying and astronomical instruments for measuring horizontal and vertical angles by means of a small telescope turning on both a horizontal and a vertical axis. [An arbitrary formation] — **the·od·o·lit·ic** (-lit'ik) *adj.*

the·og·o·ny (thē·og'ə·nē) *n.* The generation or genealogy of the gods, especially as recited in ancient poetry. [<Gk. *theogonia* <*theos* god + *gonos* generation <*gignesthai* be born] — **the·o·gon·ic** (thē'ə·gon'ik) *adj.* — **the·og'o·nist** *n.*

the·o·lo·gi·an (thē'ə·lō'jē·ən, -jən) *n.* One versed in theology, especially that of the Christian church; a professor of divinity; a divine.

the·o·log·i·cal (thē'ə·loj'i·kəl) *adj.* 1 Pertaining or relating to theology. 2 Linked to, based on, or referring to divine revelation. 3

Pertaining to the exposition or expounders of theology. Also **the·o·log'ic.** — **the·o·log'i·cal·ly** *adv.*

the·ol·o·gize (thē·ol'ə·jīz) *v.* **·gized, ·giz·ing** *v.t.* To devise or fit (something) into a system of theology. — *v.i.* To reason theologically. Also *Brit.* **the·ol'o·gise.**

the·ol·o·gy (thē·ol'ə·jē) *n. pl.* **·gies** 1 The study of religion, culminating in a synthesis or philosophy of religion; also, a critical survey of religion, especially of the Christian religion. 2 A body of doctrines concerning God, including his attributes and relations with man; especially, such a body of doctrines as set forth by a particular church or religious group: Catholic *theology*. [<OF *theologie* <LL *theologia* <Gk. <*theos* god + *logos* discourse]

the·om·a·chy (thē·om'ə·kē) *n.* 1 A combat with the gods, as that waged by the Titans. 2 A battle among the gods. [<Gk. *theomachia* <*theos* god + *machē* combat]

the·o·mor·phic (thē'ə·môr'fik) *adj.* Having the form or likeness of God. [<Gk. *theomorphos* <*theos* god + *morphē* form]

the·o·mor·phism (thē'ə·môr'fiz·əm) *n.* The doctrine that man has the likeness or form of God.

the·o·pa·thet·ic (thē'ō·pə·thet'ik) *adj.* Pertaining to or of the nature of theopathy: *theopathetic* mysticism. Also **the·o·path·ic** (thē'ə·path'ik).

the·op·a·thy (thē·op'ə·thē) *n.* Religious emotion aroused by meditation on God; mystical ecstasy. [<Gk. *theopathia* the suffering of God <*theos* a god + *path-*, stem of *paschein* suffer]

the·oph·a·ny (thē·of'ə·nē) *n. pl.* **·nies** A manifestation or appearance of a deity or of the gods to man. [<L *theophania* <Gk. <*theos* god + *phainein* show]

the·o·phyl·line (thē'ə·fil'ēn, -in) *n. Chem.* A white, bitter, crystalline alkaloid, $C_7H_8O_2N_4$, obtained from tea leaves and also made synthetically: it is an isomer of theobromine. [<NL *thea* tea + Gk. *phyllon* leaf + -INE²]

THEODOLITE
a. Striding level. *b.* Vertical limb and vernier. *c.* Telescope. *d.* Plate bubble. *e.* Horizontal limb and vernier. *f.* Clamp and tangent screw. *g.* Lower clamp screw. *h.* Tangent screw. *i.* Leveling screw.

the·o·rem (thē'ər·əm, thir'əm) *n.* 1 A proposition demonstrably true or acknowledged as such. 2 *Math.* **a** A proposition setting forth something to be proved. **b** A proposition that has been proved or assumed to be true. **c** A rule or statement of relations formulated in symbols. [<F *théorème* <Gk. *theōrēma* sight, theory <*theōreein* look at] — **the·o·re·mat·ic** (thē'ər·ə·mat'ik), **the·o·rem'ic** (-ə·rem'ik) *adj.*

the·o·ret·ic (thē'ə·ret'ik) *n.* 1 Theory, as distinct from practice. 2 *pl.* Theoretical matters; specifically, the theoretical aspect of a science. — *adj.* Theoretical.

the·o·ret·i·cal (thē'ə·ret'i·kəl) *adj.* 1 Of, relating to, or consisting of theory. 2 Relating to knowledge or pure science without reference to its application: compare EXPERIMENT (def. 3). 3 Existing only in theory; hypothetical. 4 Addicted to theorizing; unaffected by practical considerations; hence, impractical; visionary. Also *theoretic.* — **the·o·ret'i·cal·ly** *adv.*

the·o·re·ti·cian (thē'ər·ə·tish'ən) *n.* One who deals with the speculative, hypothetical, or ideal rather than with the practical and executive aspects of a subject.

the·o·rize (thē'ə·rīz) *v.i.* **·rized, ·riz·ing** To form or express theories; speculate. Also **the'o·rise.** — **the·o·ri·za'tion** *n.* — **the'o·riz'er** *n.*

the·o·ry (thē'ər·ē, thir'ē) *n. pl.* **·ries** 1 A plan or scheme existing in the mind only, but based on principles verifiable by experiment or observation. 2 A body of the fundamental principles underlying a science or the application of a science: the *theory* of relativity. 3 Abstract knowledge of any art, as opposed to the practice of it. 4 A proposed explanation or hypothesis designed to account for any phenomenon. 5 Loosely, mere speculation or hypothesis; an individual idea or guess. 6 *Math.* An arrangement of results, or a body of theorems, presenting a systematic view of some subject: the *theory* of functions. 7 The science of musical composition, as distinguished from the art of execution. See synonyms under HYPOTHESIS, IDEA. [<F *théorie* <Gk. *theōria* view, speculation <*theōreein* look at]

the·os·o·phy (thē·os'ə·fē) *n.* Mystical speculation applied to deduce a philosophy of the universe. In its modern phase, a system that claims to embrace the essential truth underlying all systems of religion, science, and philosophy. Its doctrines resemble closely those of Buddhism and Brahmanism, teaching the existence of an omnipotent, infinite, eternal, and immutable principle transcending the power of human conception, and the identity of all souls, through the cycle of incarnation with a universal spirit. [<Med. L *theosophia* <Gk. <*theosophos* wise in divine matters <*theos* god + *sophos* wise] — **the·o·soph·ic** (thē'ə·sof'ik) or **·i·cal** *adj.* — **the'o·soph'i·cal·ly** *adv.* — **the·os'o·phist** *n.*

ther·a·peu·tic (ther'ə·pyōō'tik) *adj.* 1 Having healing qualities; curative. 2 Pertaining to therapeutics. Also **ther'a·peu'ti·cal.** [<NL *therapeuticus* <Gk. *therapeutikos* <*therapeutēs* an attendant <*therapeuein* serve, take care of <*therapōn* an attendant] — **ther'a·peu'ti·cal·ly** *adv.*

ther·a·peu·tics (ther'ə·pyōō'tiks) *n. pl.* (construed as singular) 1 The department of medical science that treats of remedies for disease and their application. 2 The art and science of healing. — **ther'a·peu'tist** *n.*

ther·a·py (ther'ə·pē) *n. pl.* **·pies** 1 The treatment of disease by drugs or other curative processes: chiefly used in compounds: *hydrotherapy.* 2 Healing or curative quality. [<NL *therapia* <Gk. *therapeia* <*therapeuein* take care of. See THERAPEUTIC.] — **ther'a·pist** *n.*

there (thâr) *adv.* 1 In or at that place; in a place other than that of the speaker: opposed to *here.* 2 To, toward, or into that place; thither. 3 At that stage or point of action or proceeding. 4 In that respect, relation, or connection. [OE *thâr*]

◆ *There* is also used: as a pronominal expletive introducing a clause or sentence, the subject usually following the verb: *There* once lived three bears; with independent phrases or clauses, as an equivalent of *that,* expressing encouragement, approval, etc.: *There's*

a little dear; as an exclamation expressing triumph, etc.: *There!* I told you so.
there·a·bout (thâr'ə·bout') *adv.* Near that number, quantity, degree, place, or time; approximately. Also **there'a·bouts'.**
there·af·ter (thâr'af'tər, -äf'-) *adv.* 1 Afterward; from that time on. 2 Accordingly.
there·a·gainst (thâr'ə·genst') *adv.* Against or in opposition to that thing; on the other hand.
there·at (thâr'at') *adv.* At that event, place, or time; at that incentive; upon that.
there·by (thâr'bī') *adv.* 1 Through the agency of that. 2 Connected with that. 3 Conformably to that. 4 Nearby; thereabout. 5 By it or that; into possession of it or that: How did you come *thereby*?
there·for (thâr'fôr') *adv.* For this, that, or it; in return or requital for this or that: We return thanks *therefor*.
there·fore (thâr'fôr', -fōr') *adv. & conj.* For that or this reason; on that ground or account; hence; consequently: He did not run fast enough; *therefore* he lost the race.
  Synonyms (conj.): accordingly, because, consequently, hence, since, then, thence, whence, wherefore. *Therefore* is the most precise and formal word for expressing the direct conclusion of a chain of reasoning; *then* carries a similar but slighter sense of inference, which it gives incidentally rather than formally; as, If this is true, *then* we can go. *Consequently* denotes a direct result, but more frequently of a practical than a theoretical kind; as, Important matters demand my attention; *consequently* I shall not sail today. *Accordingly* denotes correspondence, which may or may not be consequence; it is often used in narration; as, The soldiers were eager and confident; *accordingly* they sprang forward at the word of command. *Thence* is a word of more sweeping inference than *therefore*, applying not merely to a single set of premises but often to all that has gone before, including the reasonable inferences that have not been formally stated. *Wherefore* is the correlative of *therefore*, and *whence* of *hence* or *thence*, appending the inference or conclusion to the previous statement without a break. Compare synonyms for BECAUSE.
there·from (thâr'frum', -from') *adv.* From this, that, or it; from this or that time, place, state, event, or thing.
there·in (thâr'in') *adv.* 1 In that place. 2 In that time, matter, or respect.
there·in·af·ter (thâr'in·af'tər, -äf'-) *adv.* In a subsequent part of that (book, document, speech, etc.).
there·of (thâr'uv', -ov') *adv.* 1 Of or relating to this, that, or it. 2 From or because of this or that cause or particular; therefrom.
there·on (thâr'on', -ôn') *adv.* 1 On this, that, or it. 2 Thereupon; thereat.
there·to (thâr'tōō') *adv.* 1 To this, that, or it. 2 In addition; furthermore. Also **there'·un·to'** (-un·tōō').
there·un·der (thâr'un'dər) *adv.* 1 Under this or that. 2 Less, as in number. 3 In a lower or lesser status or rank.
there·up·on (thâr'ə·pon', -ə·pôn') *adv.* 1 Upon that; upon it. 2 Following upon or in consequence of that. 3 Immediately following; at once.
there·with (thâr'with', -with') *adv.* 1 With this, that, or it. 2 Thereupon; thereafter; immediately afterward.
the·ri·an·thro·pism (thir'ē·an'thrə·piz'əm) *n.* Representation of preternatural beings in combined forms of man and beast, especially in primitive polytheistic worship: the religions of *therianthropism.* [<Gk. *thērion* wild beast + *anthrōpos, -ōpou* man] — **the'ri·an·throp'ic** (-an·throp'ik) *adj.*
the·ri·o·mor·phic (thir'ē·ə·môr'fik) *adj.* Beastlike in form: *theriomorphic* gods. Also **the'ri·o·mor'phous.** [<Gk. *thērion* wild beast + *morphē* form]
therm (thûrm) *n.* 1 A unit of heat used as a basis for the sale of illuminating gas in England, equal to 100,000 British thermal units. 2 One thousand great calories. 3 The great calorie. 4 The lesser calorie. Also **therme.** [<Gk. *thermē* heat]
ther·mal (thûr'məl) *adj.* 1 Pertaining to, determined by, or measured by heat. 2 Hot or warm. Also **ther'mic.** — **ther'mal·ly** *adv.*
thermal barrier *Aeron.* The limit imposed

upon the operating speed of jet engines, rockets, motors, and the like by temperatures above the melting point of their materials.
thermal diffusion 1 The diffusion of heat. 2 *Physics* A method for the separation of isotopes by passing a gas through a vertical tube containing an electrically heated wire which produces a concentration of the heavier components at the bottom and of the lighter components at the top.
therm·el (thûr'mel) *n.* A thermocouple or group of thermocouples when used to determine temperatures. [<Gk. *thermē* heat]
therm·es·the·sia (thûr'mis·thē'zhə, -zhē·ə) *n. Physiol.* The ability to recognize changes of temperature; temperature sensitivity. Also **therm'aes·the'sia.** [<THERM(O)- + ESTHESIA]
therm·i·on (thûrm'ī'ən, thûr'mē·ən) *n. Physics* An electrically charged particle emitted by a heated body: it may be either positive or negative. [<THERM(O)- + ION] — **therm·i·on·ic** (thûr'mē·on'ik) *adj.*
therm·i·on·ics (thûr'mē·on'iks) *n. pl. (construed as singular)* The science and practical application of thermionic phenomena.
thermionic tube A vacuum tube emitting thermions from a heated electrode. Also *Brit.* **thermionic valve.**
therm·is·tor (thər·mis'tər) *n. Electr.* A small, compact thermometric device consisting of a semiconducting material having a large temperature coefficient of resistance: widely used in the measurement of microwave power, of temperatures, and as a protective device in circuits. [<THERM(O)- + (RES)ISTOR]
ther·mit (thûr'mit) *n.* A mixture composed of finely divided aluminum and oxide of iron, chromium, or manganese. When such a mixture is brought to a sufficient temperature, the oxygen of the oxide unites with the aluminum, producing an intense heat. Also **ther'mite** (-mīt). [<Gk. *thermē* heat]
ther·mo·bar·o·graph (thûr'mō·bar'ə·graf, -gräf) *n.* An apparatus for measuring the pressure and temperature of a gas simultaneously.
ther·mo·ba·rom·e·ter (thûr'mō·bə·rom'ə·tər) *n.* 1 An apparatus for measuring atmospheric pressure by the boiling point of water: used in determining altitudes. 2 A form of barometer that can be inverted and made to serve as a thermometer.
ther·mo·cau·ter·y (thûr'mō·kô'tər·ē) *n.* Cautery by means of heated wires or points.
ther·mo·chem·is·try (thûr'mō·kem'is·trē) *n.* The branch of chemistry that treats of the relations between chemical reactions and the evolution and absorption of heat observed to accompany them. — **ther'mo·chem'i·cal** (-kem'·i·kəl) *adj.* — **ther'mo·chem'ist** *n.*
ther·mo·cline (thûr'mō·klīn) *n.* A gradient indicating marked changes in temperature with depth, especially between discontinuous layers of ocean waters.
ther·mo·cou·ple (thûr'mō·kup'əl) *n.* A pair of dissimilar metals so joined as to produce a thermoelectric effect when the contact surfaces are at different temperatures. Also **ther'mo·e·lec'tric couple.**
ther·mo·dy·nam·ics (thûr'mō·dī·nam'iks, -di-) *n. pl. (construed as singular)* That branch of physical science which treats of the relations between heat and energy, especially the convertibility of one into the other and the mechanical work involved. — **ther'mo·dy·nam'ic** or **·i·cal** *adj.* — **ther'mo·dy·nam'i·cist** (-nam'ə·sist) *n.*
ther·mo·e·lec·tric·i·ty (thûr'mō·i·lek'tris'ə·tē) *n.* Electricity generated by differences of temperature, especially between two different metals in contact when one of the junctions is heated.
ther·mo·e·lec·tro·mo·tive (thûr'mō·i·lek'trə·mō'tiv) *adj.* Of, pertaining to, or designating electromotive force caused by difference of temperature.
ther·mo·gal·va·nom·e·ter (thûr'mō·gal'və·nom'·ə·tər) *n.* A combination of a galvanometer and a thermocouple used to measure minute variations of temperature.
ther·mo·gen·e·sis (thûr'mō·jen'ə·sis) *n.* The production of heat, especially of animal heat by organic action. — **ther'mo·gen'ic, ther·mog'·e·nous** (thər·moj'ə·nəs), **ther'mo·ge·net'ic** (-jə·net'ik) *adj.*
ther·mo·graph (thûr'mə·graf, -gräf) *n.* An instrument for recording temperature varia-

tions; a self-registering thermometer.
ther·mog·ra·phy (thər·mog'rə·fē) *n.* 1 Photography by means of heat waves emitted by an object which has been coated with luminescent paint and exposed to ultraviolet light. 2 *Printing* Any process of reproducing written or printed characters that employs heat. — **ther·mo·graph·ic** (thûr'mə·graf'ik) *adj.*
ther·mo·hal·ine (thûr'mō·hal'ēn, -īn, -in) *adj.* Pertaining to or characterized by variations in the temperature and salinity of sea water. [<THERMO- + Gk. *hals* salt + -INE[1]]
ther·mo·junc·tion (thûr'mō·jungk'shən) *n.* The point of contact between the pair of conductors forming a thermocouple.
ther·mo·kin·e·mat·ics (thûr'mō·kin'ə·mat'iks) *n. pl. (construed as singular)* The study of heat in motion or of the motive power of heat.
ther·mo·la·bile (thûr'mō·lā'bil) *adj. Biochem.* Decomposed, destroyed, affected, or liable to be adversely affected by heat, as some enzymes and toxins: opposed to *thermostable.* [<THERMO- + LABILE]
ther·mo·lu·mi·nes·cence (thûr'mō·lōō'mə·nes'·əns) *n.* 1 The emission of light from a substance or material under the action of heat. 2 A luminous effect in rock crystals from which electrons displaced by radioactivity have been released at definite temperatures, with or without pressure: sometimes indicative of the age of sedimentary rocks. — **ther'mo·lu'mi·nes'cent** *adj.*
ther·mol·y·sis (thər·mol'ə·sis) *n.* 1 *Chem.* The resolution of a compound substance into its component elements by the application of heat. 2 *Physiol.* The dissipation of heat from the animal body by physical processes. [<THERMO- + -LYSIS] — **ther·mo·lyt·ic** (thûr'mə·lit'ik) *adj.*
ther·mo·mag·net·ic (thûr'mō·mag·net'ik) *adj.* Of or pertaining to the relations between heat and magnetism.
ther·mom·e·ter (thər·mom'ə·tər) *n.* An instrument for measuring the temperature of a substance, body, or space. The ordinary thermometer consists of a graduated glass capillary tube or stem with a bulb containing mercury which expands or contracts as the temperature rises or falls. The **differential thermometer** has two air bulbs connected by a U-tube, containing colored liquid, so that when the bulbs are exposed to different temperatures a shifting of the liquid in the tube will be caused by the difference of expansion of air in the bulbs. A **resistance thermometer** indicates, by means of the change in electrical conductivity of wires with temperature, the temperature of any given wire or its environment. — **clinical thermometer** A thermometer accurately calibrated for determining body temperature, especially of a person. [<THERMO- + METER]
ther·mom·e·try (thər·mom'ə·trē) *n.* The measurement of temperature, or the art thereof, by means of the thermometer; specifically, the use of the thermometer in medical diagnosis. — **ther·mo·met·ric** (thûr'mō·met'rik) or **·ri·cal** *adj.* — **ther'mo·met'ri·cal·ly** *adv.*
ther·mo·mo·tor (thûr'mō·mō'tər) *n.* A heat engine; especially, a hot-air engine. Compare MOTOR.
ther·mo·nu·cle·ar (thûr'mō·nōō'klē·ər, -nyōō'-) *adj. Physics* Pertaining to or characterized by the mass-energy reactions involving the fusion of light atomic nuclei subjected to very high temperatures, especially with reference to stellar energy and the hydrogen bomb.
ther·mo·phil·ic (thûr'mō·fil'ik) *adj.* Fond of heat: used mainly of certain bacteria. Also **ther'mo·phile** (-fil, -fīl). [<THERMO- + Gk. *philos* loving]
ther·mo·pile (thûr'mō·pīl) *n.* A group of thermocouples acting jointly to produce electric energy, especially when used with a galvanometer to measure heat.
ther·mo·plas·tic (thûr'mō·plas'tik) *adj.* Plastic in the presence of or under the application of heat: said especially of certain synthetic molding materials. — *n.* A thermoplastic substance or material.
thermos bottle (thûr'məs) A container shaped like a bottle or flask, having two walls separated by a vacuum which serves to insulate the contents so that they retain their temperature.
ther·mo·scope (thûr'mə·skōp) *n.* An instrument for detecting changes or differences of

ther·mo·set·ting (thûr′mō-set′ing) *adj.* Having the property of assuming a fixed shape after being molded under heat, as certain phenol and other synthetic resins.

ther·mo·si·phon (thûr′mō-sī′fən) *n.* A device consisting of siphon tubes to increase or induce circulation by making use of temperature differential in a water–cooling system, as in that of an internal–combustion engine.

ther·mo·sta·ble (thûr′mō-stā′bəl) *adj.* 1 Resistant to heat, as certain plastics and chemicals. 2 *Biochem.* Unaffected by moderate heats; denoting immune substances, as certain toxins or ferments, which may be heated to 55° C. without loss of special properties: opposed to *thermolabile.* Also **ther′mo·sta′bile.** — **ther′·mo·sta·bil′i·ty** (-stə-bil′ə-tē) *n.*

ther·mo·stat (thûr′mə-stat) *n.* A device for the automatic regulation of temperature by means of a relay utilizing the expansion and contraction caused by temperature changes in certain metals: used for actuating fire alarms, opening or closing dampers, regulating steam pressures, etc. [<THERMO- + Gk. *statos* standing] — **ther′mo·stat′ic** *adj.* — **ther′mo·stat′i·cal·ly** *adv.*

ther·mo·stat·ics (thûr′mō-stat′iks) *n. pl. (construed as singular)* The science that deals with the equilibrium of heat.

THERMOSTAT
a. Bimetal bar.
b. Contact points.
c. Control knob.

ther·mo·tank (thûr′mō-tangk′) *n.* A tank or box in which steam, water, air, or the like circulates through pipes and thus heats or cools the air passing through the tank.

ther·mo·tax·is (thûr′mō-tak′sis) *n. Biol.* 1 The regulation or normal adjustment of the animal heat in an organism. 2 The determination of movement by heat. — **ther′mo·tax′ic, ther′mo·tac′tic** (-tak′tik) *adj.*

ther·mo·ten·sile (thûr′mō-ten′sil) *adj.* Relating to variation of tensile strength caused by temperature.

therm·o·ther·a·py (thûr′mō-ther′ə-pē) *n. Med.* The treatment of disease by the application of heat.

ther·mot·ics (thər-mot′iks) *n. pl. (construed as singular)* The science of heat. [<Gk. *thermotēs* heat]

ther·mot·ro·pism (thər-mot′rə-piz′əm) *n. Biol.* 1 The property or phenomenon of movement in growing plants or other organisms brought about by the influence of heat or cold. 2 The attraction or repulsion from a source of heat evinced by some bacteria. — **ther·mo·trop·ic** (thûr′mō-trop′ik) *adj.*

the·ro·phyte (thir′ə-fit) *n. Bot.* An annual plant which completes its life cycle in one vegetative season. [<Gk. *theros* summer + -PHYTE]

the·ro·pod (thir′ə-pod) *n.* Any of a suborder (*Theropoda*) of saurischian dinosaurs of the Triassic and Cretaceous periods, including the true carnivorous types, as *Allosaurus* and *Tyrannosaurus.* — *adj.* Of or pertaining to the *Theropoda.* [<NL *Theropoda* <Gk. *thēr, thēros* a wild beast + *pous, podos* foot] — **the·rop·o·dan** (thi·rop′ə-dən) *adj. & n.*

the·sau·ro·sis (thē′sô-rō′sis) *n. Pathol.* A condition marked by the storage in the body of excessive amounts of normal or foreign substances. [<Gk. *thēsauros* treasure + -OSIS]

the·sau·rus (thi-sôr′əs) *n. pl.* **·sau·ri** (-sôr′ī) 1 A place where treasure is laid up; a storehouse. 2 A repository of words or knowledge; hence, a lexicon or cyclopedia. [<L <Gk. *thēsauros* treasure house. Doublet of TREASURE.]

the·sis (thē′sis) *n. pl.* **·ses** (-sēz) 1 A proposition. 2 Specifically, a formal proposition, advanced and defended by argumentation. 3 A formal treatise on a particular subject, especially, a dissertation presented by a candidate for an academic degree. 4 In early prosody, that part of a foot which had the ictus or stress. 5 In later Roman usage and in modern prosody, the unaccented part of a foot; also, the depression of the voice in pronouncing it. See ARSIS. 6 *Logic* An affirmative proposition; a premise or postulate, as opposed to a hypothesis. 7 *Music* The down beat; the accented part of a measure. [<L <Gk., a placing, proposition <*tithenai* put, place]

the·ta (thā′tə, thē′tə) *n.* The eighth letter in the Greek alphabet (Θ, ϑ, θ): equivalent in classical Greek to *t* + *h,* as in *right–hand,* but in modern Greek to spirant *th,* as in *thin.* [<Gk. *thēta*]

the·ur·gy (thē′ûr-jē) *n. pl.* **·gies** 1 Divine or supernatural intervention in human affairs. 2 The working of miracles through divine or supernatural aid. 3 Magic, as practiced by the Neo–Platonists, by means of which miraculous effects were supposedly produced through the intervention of beneficent spirits; white magic. [<Gk. *theourgia* <*theourgos* divine worker <*theos* god + *ergon* work] — **the·ur·gic** (thē-ûr′jik), **the·ur·gi·cal** *adj.* — **the·ur′gi·cal·ly** *adv.* — **the·ur′gist** *n.*

thew (thyōō) *n.* 1 A sinew or muscle, especially when strong or well-developed. 2 *pl.* Bodily strength or vigor. [ME *theawes* good qualities, strength <OE *thēau* habit, characteristic quality] — **thew′y** *adj.*

they (thā) *pron.* 1 The persons, beings, or things previously mentioned or understood: the nominative plural of *he, she, it.* 2 People in general; men: *They* say rain is expected. [<ON *their,* pl. of *sā* this, that]

they'd (thād) Contraction of: 1 They had. 2 They would.

they'll (thāl) They will: a contraction.

they're (thâr) They are: a contraction.

they've (thāv) They have: a contraction.

thi·a·mine (thī′ə-mēn, -min) *n. Biochem.* A white crystalline compound, $C_{12}H_{18}ON_4SCl_4$; vitamin B_1, found in various natural sources, as cereal grains, green peas, liver, egg yolk, etc., and also made synthetically. Thiamine is the anti–beriberi vitamin. Also **thi′a·min** (-min). [<THI- + -AMINE]

thi·a·zine (thī′ə-zēn, -zin) *n. Chem.* One of a class of organic ring compounds of one atom of nitrogen, one of sulfur, and four of carbon. Also **thi′a·zin** (-zin). [<THI- + -AZINE]

thi·a·zole (thī′ə-zōl) *n. Chem.* A colorless, stable, liquid compound, C_3H_3NS, whose derivatives yield dyestuffs and certain sulfa drugs. Also **thi′a·zol** (-zōl, -zol). [<THI- + AZOLE]

thick (thik) *adj.* 1 Having relatively large depth or extent from one surface to its opposite; having the dimension that is commonly least, comparatively great; not thin: distinguished from *long* and *broad.* 2 Having a specified dimension of this kind, whether great or small: an inch *thick.* 3 Arranged compactly; close: a *thick* forest; also, following at brief intervals; frequent, as blows, raindrops, etc. 4 Set or furnished closely or abundantly with objects; abounding. 5 Having considerable density or consistency; dense; hence, turbid; impure; heavy. 6 Overcharged with vapor; foggy; misty. 7 Lacking quickness of apprehension; dull; stupid. 8 Indistinct; muffled: a *thick* sound; also, guttural; husky; throaty. 9 *Colloq.* Very friendly; intimate. 10 *Colloq.* Excessive; going too far; being beyond the bounds of what is tolerable. — *adv.* In a thick manner; placed or following closely. — **to lay it on thick** *Colloq.* 1 To overstate; exaggerate. 2 To praise fulsomely. — *n.* 1 The dimension of thickness; the thickest part. 2 The thickest or most intense time or place of anything: the *thick* of the fight. — **through thick and thin** Through good times and bad; loyally; through good fortune and adversity. [OE *thicce*] — **thick′ly** *adv.*

Synonyms (adj.): close, cloudy, compact, condensed, dense, dull, foggy, gross, hazy, inspissate, misty, muddy, turbid. See BLUNT.

thick·en (thik′ən) *v.t. & v.i.* 1 To make or become thick or thicker. 2 To make or become more intricate or intense: The plot *thickens.* — **thick′en·er** *n.*

thick·et (thik′it) *n.* A thick growth, as of underbrush, through which a passage is not easily effected; a coppice; jungle. [OE *thiccet* <*thicce* thick]

thick·ness (thik′nis) *n.* 1 The state or quality of being thick. 2 The dimension or measure of a solid other than its length or width. 3 A sheet, layer, etc., as of paper.

thick–skinned (thik′skind′) *adj.* 1 Having a thick skin; pachydermatous. 2 Insensitive; callous to hints or insults.

thick–wit·ted (thik′wit′id) *adj.* Stupid; obtuse; dense.

thief (thēf) *n. pl.* **thieves** (thēvz) 1 One who takes something belonging to another; one who steals. 2 *Law* One guilty of simple or compound larceny, embezzlement, or swindling. 3 That which causes loss: Procrastination is the *thief* of time. See synonyms under ROBBER. [OE *thēof*]

thieve (thēv) *v.* **thieved, thiev·ing** *v.t.* To take by theft; purloin; steal. — *v.i.* To be a thief; commit theft. [OE *thēofian*]

thigh (thī) *n.* 1 The leg between the hip and the knee of man or the corresponding portion in other animals. ◆ Collateral adjective: *femoral.* 2 The femur of an insect. [OE *thēoh*]

thig·mot·ro·pism (thig·mot′rə-piz′əm) *n. Biol.* Involuntary response to mechanical stimulation of any kind, as displayed by many insects and by the tendrils, leaves, etc., of certain plants. [<Gk. *thigma* touch + TROPISM] — **thig·mo·trop·ic** (thig′mə-trop′ik) *adj.*

thill (thil) *n.* One of the shafts of a vehicle, between which a horse is harnessed. [OE *thille* board]

thim·ble (thim′bəl) *n.* 1 A caplike cover with a pitted surface, worn in sewing to protect the end of the finger that pushes the needle. 2 *Mech.* A sleeve through which a bolt passes, or which unites two rods, tubes, or the like. 3 *Naut.* a A metal anti–chafing ring forming a guard over a loop or eye in a sail. b The metal piece about which a rope is bent and spliced to the main body of the rope to form an eye. [OE *thȳmel* <*thūma* thumb]

thim·ble·ber·ry (thim′bəl-ber′ē) *n. pl.* **·ries** Any of certain American raspberries or blackberries having a thimble-shaped fruit; especially, the blackcap raspberry, the **fragrant thimbleberry** (*Rubus odoratus*), and the **western thimbleberry** (*R. parviflorus*).

thim·ble·rig (thim′bəl-rig′) *n.* 1 A swindling trick in which a pea or ball is shifted by sleight of hand from one to another of three inverted thimble–shaped cups. 2 A gambler who operates a thimblerig. — *v.t.* **·rigged, ·rig·ging** To cheat by or as by thimblerig. — **thim′ble·rig′ger** *n.*

thim·ble·weed (thim′bəl-wēd′) *n.* Any of various plants (genus *Rudbeckia*) with thimble-shaped receptacles, as the rudbeckia and the American wood anemone.

thin (thin) *adj.* **thin·ner, thin·nest** 1 Having opposite surfaces relatively close to each other; being of little depth or width; not thick. 2 Lacking roundness or plumpness of figure; lean; slender. 3 Having the component parts or particles scattered or diffused; not dense or abundant; sparse; rare: *thin* ranks, *thin* gas. 4 Having little body or substance; of a loose texture; hence, insufficient to conceal or cover: *thin* clothing; flimsy: a *thin* excuse. 5 Having little or no consistency, as a liquid: *thin* molasses. 6 Lacking in essential ingredients or qualities: *thin* blood. 7 Having little volume or richness; shrill or metallic, as a voice. 8 Not abundantly supplied or furnished; bare; scant: a *thin* table. 9 Not having sufficient contrasts of shade to print well: said of a photographic negative. 10 Lacking vigor or force; feeble; superficial: *thin* wit. See synonyms under FINE[1], GAUNT, MEAGER. — *v.t. & v.i.* **thinned, thin·ning** To make or become thin or thinner. [OE *thynne*] — **thin′ly** *adv.* — **thin′ness** *n.*

thine (thīn) *pron.* 1 The possessive case of thou, used predicatively; belonging or pertaining to thee: *Thine* is the kingdom. 2 The things or persons belonging or pertaining to thee. — **of thine** Belonging or relating to thee; thy: the double possessive. — *pronominal* *adj. Archaic* Thy: *thine* eyes. [OE *thīn,* genitive of *thū* thou]

thing (thing) *n.* **1** That which exists or is conceived to exist as a separate entity; an entity; being. **2** That which is designated, as contrasted with the word or symbol used to denote it. **3** A matter or circumstance; an affair; concern: *Things* have changed. **4** An act or deed; transaction: That was a shameless *thing* to do. **5** A statement or expression; utterance: to say the right *thing.* **6** An idea; opinion; notion: Stop putting *things* in her head. **7** A quality; attribute; characteristic: Kindness is a precious *thing.* **8** An inanimate object, as distinguished from a living organism. **9** An organic being: usually with a qualifying word: Every living *thing* dies. **10** An object that is not or cannot be described or particularized: The *thing* disappeared in the shadows. **11** A person, regarded in terms of pity, affection, or contempt: that poor *thing;* You stupid *thing!* **12** *pl.* Possessions; belongings: to pack one's *things.* **13** *pl.* Clothes; especially, outer garments: Take off your *things* and stay awhile. **14** A piece of literature, art, music, etc.: He read a few *things* by Byron. **15** The proper or befitting act or result: with *the:* That was not the *thing* to do. **16** The important or remarkable point: with *the:* The *thing* we learned from the war was this. **17** *Law* A subject or property or dominion, as distinguished from a person. — **to do one's (own) thing** *Slang* To express oneself by doing what one wants to do or can do well or is in the habit of doing. — **to see things** To have hallucinations. [OE *thing,* cause, assembly. Akin to THING².]

think¹ (thingk) *v.* **thought** (thôt), **think·ing** *v.t.* **1** To produce or form in the mind; conceive mentally: to *think* evil thoughts. **2** To examine in the mind; meditate upon, or determine by reasoning: He was *thinking* what to do next; to *think* a plan through. **3** To believe; consider: I *think* him guilty. **4** To expect; anticipate: They did not *think* to meet us. **5** To bring to mind; remember; recollect: I cannot *think* what he said. **6** To have the mind preoccupied by: to *think* business morning, noon, and night. **7** To intend; purpose: Do they *think* to rob me? — *v.i.* **8** To use the mind or intellect in exercising judgment, forming ideas, etc.; engage in rational thought; reason. **9** To have a particular opinion, sentiment, or feeling: I don't *think* so. — **to think better of 1** To abandon a course of action; alter one's intentions: I was going to call but I *thought better* of it. **2** To form a better opinion of. — **to think fit, proper, right,** etc. To regard as worth doing. — **to think nothing of 1** To have a low opinion of; ignore. **2** To consider easy to do. — **to think of 1** To bring to mind; remember; recollect. **2** To conceive in the mind; invent; imagine. **3** To have a specified opinion or attitude toward; regard. **4** To be considerate of; have regard for. — **to think over** To reflect upon; ponder. — **to think up** To devise, arrive at, or invent by thinking. — *n.* An act of thinking; a thought. [OE *thencean;* influenced in form by THINK²]

think² (thingk) *v.i.* To seem; appear: now obsolete except with the pronoun as indirect object in the combinations *methinks. methought.* [OE *thyncan* seem]

think·ing (thingk'ing) *adj.* **1** Exercising the mental capacities. **2** Capable of such exercise; rational. — *n.* **1** Mental action; thought. **2** The product of such action, as an idea. See synonyms under REFLECTION, THOUGHT. — **think'ing·ly** *adv.*

thin·ner (thin'ər) *n.* **1** One who or that which thins. **2** A liquid, as turpentine or petroleum spirits, mixed with paint in order to give it a proper consistency for working.

thin-skinned (thin'skind') *adj.* **1** Having a thin skin. **2** Hence, easily hurt or offended; sensitive.

thi·o·a·ce·tic (thī'ō-ə-sē'tik, -ə-set'ik) *adj. Chem.* Designating a yellow, fuming, pungent acid, C_2H_4OS, used in ammonia solutions as a precipitant of metals. [<THIO- + ACETIC]

thi·o·al·de·hyde (thī'ō-al'də-hīd) *n. Chem.* An aldehyde containing sulfur as a substitute for oxygen.

thi·o·bac·te·ri·um (thī'ō-bak-tir'ē-əm) *n.* Any of an order (*Thiobacteriales*) of bacteria which utilize the sulfur of decaying organic

matter.

thi·o·car·bam·ide (thī'ō-kär-bam'īd, -id, -kär'bə-mīd) *n.* Thiourea. [<THIO- + CARBAMIDE]

thi·o·cy·a·nate (thī'ō-sī'ə-nāt) *n. Chem.* A salt or ester of thiocyanic acid.

thi·o·cy·an·ic (thī'ō-sī-an'ik) *adj. Chem.* Designating or pertaining to a colorless liquid acid, HSCN, soluble in water and having a pungent odor. [<THIO- + CYANIC]

thi·o·gen (thī'ə·jen) *n.* A bacterial organism producing sulfur. [<THIO- + -GEN]

thi·ol (thī'ōl, -ol) *n. Chem.* Any of a class of sulfur compounds which are analogs of the alcohols and have the general formula RSH, in which R is a hydrocarbon radical: used largely in compounding, as *ethanethiol,* C_2H_5SH. Formerly called *mercaptan.* [<THI- + -OL¹]

thi·on·ic (thī-on'ik) *adj. Chem.* **1** Of, pertaining to, containing, or derived from sulfur. **2** Denoting any of a group of unstable acids having the general formula $H_2S_nO_6$. [<Gk. *theion* sulfur]

thi·o·nine (thī'ə·nēn, -nin) *n. Chem.* A dark-green thiazine derivative, $C_{12}H_9N_3S$, made by synthesis, with a glistening metallic luster that yields purplish colors to silk and wool. Also **thi'o·nin** (-nin). [<Gk. *theion* sulfur + -INE²]

thi·o·nyl (thī'ə·nil) *n. Chem.* The bivalent sulfur radical SO: also called *sulfinyl.* [<Gk. *theion* sulfur + -YL]

thi·o·phene (thī'ə·fēn) *n. Chem.* A colorless liquid hydrocarbon, C_4H_4S, with an odor resembling that of benzene, found in coal tar and also made by synthesis. Also **thi'o·phen** (-fen). [<THIO- + PH(ENYL) + -ENE]

thi·o·sin·a·mine (thī'ō-sin-am'in, -sin'ə-mēn) *n. Chem.* A crystalline compound, $C_4H_8N_2S$, formed by the union of allyl mustard oil and alcohol with ammonia: used in photography. Also **thi'o·sin·am'in** (-am'in). [<THIO- + Gk. *sin(api)* mustard + AMINE]

thi·o·sul·fate (thī'ō-sul'fāt) *n. Chem.* A salt of thiosulfuric acid.

thi·o·sul·fu·ric (thī'ō-sul-fyŏor'ik) *adj. Chem.* Designating or pertaining to an unstable acid, $H_2S_2O_3$, known chiefly by its salts, which have extensive applications in bleaching and photography.

thi·o·u·re·a (thī'ō-yŏo-rē'ə) *n. Chem.* A white, solid compound, NH_2CSNH_2, prepared from urea by replacement of oxygen by sulfur: used in organic synthesis, in photography, and as an insecticide: also called *thiocarbamide.* [<THIO- + UREA]

third (thûrd) *adj.* **1** Next in order after second: the ordinal of *three.* **2** Being one of three equal parts. — *n.* **1** One of three equal parts of anything. **2** The person or thing coming after the second, as in a series. **3** *pl. Law* The third part of a husband's personal estate, allotted to the widow in case of his dying intestate and leaving an heir; also, loosely, a dower. **4** A unit of time or of an arc, equal to one sixtieth of a second. **5** *Music* **a** The interval between any note and the next note but one above it on a diatonic scale, known as a **major third** when such interval is two whole steps or degrees of the staff, and as a **minor third** when it is a step and a half. **b** A note separated by this interval from any other, considered in relation to that other; specifically, the third above the keynote. **c** Two notes at this interval written or sounded together, or the consonance so produced. **6** In baseball, the third base. — *adv.* In the third order, rank, or place: also, in formal discourse, **third'ly.** [OE *thridda* < *thrī* three]

third base In baseball, the third base reached by the runner, at the left-hand angle of the infield. Compare illustration under BASEBALL.

third class 1 In the U.S. postal system, a classification of mail that includes all miscellaneous printed matter but not newspapers and periodicals legally entered as second class. **2** A classification of accommodations on some ships and trains, usually the cheapest and least luxurious available; formerly, on a ship, steerage; also, the passengers traveling in this classification.

third degree 1 *Colloq.* Severe or brutal examination of a prisoner by the police for the purpose of securing information or a confession; hence, any brutal treatment. **2** In Freemasonry, the degree of Master Mason.

third estate The commons or common people; the third political class of a kingdom, following the nobility and the clergy. See under ESTATE.

third eyelid The nictitating membrane.

third person The person or thing spoken of, or the grammatical form indicating such person or thing.

third rail An insulated rail placed as a conductor on the track of an electric railway, from which the current is taken by means of a contact device, the running rails acting as return conductors. — **third'-rail'** *adj.*

Third Reich See under REICH.

third world 1 Any or all of the underdeveloped countries in the world, especially such countries in Asia or Africa that are not aligned with either the Communist or non-Communist nations. **2** Those not resident in the countries of the third world but collectively identified with their peoples, as because of ideology, ethnic background, or disadvantaged status. Also **Third World.**

thirst (thûrst) *n.* **1** A distressful feeling of dryness in the throat and mouth, accompanied by an increasingly urgent desire for liquids. **2** The physiological condition which produces this feeling. **3** Any eager desire; a longing or craving: a *thirst* for glory. See synonyms under APPETITE. — *v.i.* **1** To feel thirst; be thirsty. **2** To have an eager desire or craving; long; yearn. [OE *thurst*] — **thirst'er** *n.*

thir·teen (thûr'tēn') *n.* The cardinal number preceding fourteen and following twelve, or any of the symbols (13, xiii, XIII) which represent it. — *adj.* Consisting of or being one more than twelve. [OE *thrēotēne*]

thir·teenth (thûr'tēnth') *adj.* **1** Third in order after the tenth: the ordinal of *thirteen.* **2** Being one of thirteen equal parts. — *n.* **1** One of thirteen equal parts. **2** The next one after the twelfth.

thir·ti·eth (thûr'tē-ith) *adj.* **1** Tenth in order after the twentieth: the ordinal of *thirty.* **2** Being one of thirty equal parts. — *n.* **1** One of thirty equal parts of anything. **2** The tenth in order after the twentieth.

thir·ty (thûr'tē) *n.* The cardinal number preceding thirty-one and following twenty-nine; thrice ten; also, any of the symbols (30, xxx, XXX) used to represent it. — *adj.* Consisting of or being ten more than twenty, or thrice ten; tricennial. [OE *thrītig*]

thir·ty-sec·ond note (thûr'tē-sek'ənd) *Music* A note having one thirty-second of the time of a whole note; a demisemiquaver.

thir·ty-two·mo (thûr'tē-tōo'mō) *n. pl.* **-mos** A sheet of paper folded so as to make 32 leaves about 3 1/8 by 4 3/4 inches; hence a book or pamphlet having 32 leaves to the sheet. — *adj.* Having 32 leaves to a sheet. Commonly written *32mo.*

this (this) *adj. pl.* **these 1** That is near or present, either actually or in thought: *This* house is for sale; I shall be there *this* evening. **2** That is understood or has just been mentioned: *This* offense justified my revenge. **3** That is nearer than or contrasted with something else: opposed to *that: This* tree is still alive, but that one is dead; He ran *this* way and that. **4** These: used of a number or collection considered as a whole: He has been dead *this* fourteen nights. — *pron.* **1** The person or thing near or present, being understood or just mentioned: *This* is where I live; *This* is the guilty man. **2** The person or thing nearer than or contrasted with something else: opposed to *that: This* is a better painting than that. **3** The idea, statement, etc., about to be made clear: I will say *this:* he is a hard worker. — *adv.* To this degree; thus or so: I was not expecting you *this* soon. [OE]

this·tle (this'əl) *n.* **1** One of various vigorous prickly plants (genera *Carduus, Cirsium, Cnicus,* and *Onopordum*) with cylindrical or globular heads of tubular purple flowers; especially, the **bull thistle** (*Cirsium lanceolatum*) of Scotland, and the **Canada thistle** (*Cirsium canadense*). **2** Any of several prickly plants of other genera. [OE *thistel*] — **this'tly** *adj.*

thistle butterfly A butterfly (*Vanessa cardui*) resembling the painted beauty but having usually four eyespots on the under side of each wing: also called *painted lady.*

this·tle·down (this'əl·doun') *n.* The pappus of

a thistle; the ripe silky fibers from the dry flower of a thistle.

thix·ot·ro·py (thik·sot′rə·pē) *n. Chem.* The property possessed by certain gels of liquefying under the action of vibrating forces. [<Gk. *thixis* touch + *tropē* turning] — **thix·o·trop·ic** (thik′sə·trop′ik) *adj.*

thole[1] (thōl) *n.* A pin or pair of pins serving as a fulcrum for an oar in rowing. Also **thole pin.** [OE *thol* pin]

thole[2] (thōl) *v.t. & v.i. Archaic* To endure; suffer; tolerate. [OE *tholian* suffer]

Tho·mism (tō′miz·əm, thō′-) *n.* The doctrine of St. Thomas Aquinas, who attempted to combine Aristotelian metaphysics, ontology, logic, and method with Christian theology into one comprehensive system, including theology, natural philosophy, esthetics, ethics, psychology, and politics. He held that human reason was the faculty by which men apprehended many truths, but that the divinely revealed truths necessary for salvation could be known only through faith; that reason was distinct from faith, though not opposed to it when rightly used; and that reason served faith by preparing men's minds to receive revealed truth, by expounding and systematizing that truth, and by defending it against attack. The system of dogmatic theology constructed by St. Thomas remains the standard within the Roman Catholic Church, and has had a wide influence in many other communions. — **Tho′·mist** *adj. & n.* — **Tho·mis′·tic** or **·ti·cal** *adj.*

thong (thông, thong) *n.* **1** A narrow strip, properly of leather, as for tying or fastening. **2** A whiplash. [OE *thwang* thong]

tho·rac·ic (thô·ras′ik, thō-) *adj.* Of, relating to, or situated in or near the thorax. [<NL *thoracicus* <Gk. *thōrax* the chest]

thoracic duct *Anat.* The canal emptying into the left subclavian vein which collects the lymph from parts of the body below the diaphragm.

tho·ra·co·plas·ty (thôr′ə·kō·plas′tē, thō′rə-) *n. Surg.* An operation for the removal and replacement of several ribs in order to provide a thoracic cavity within which the underlying lung is kept permanently collapsed: used in the treatment of tuberculosis. [<THORACO- + -PLASTY]

tho·rax (thôr′aks, thō′raks) *n. pl.* **tho·rax·es** or **tho·ra·ces** (thôr′ə·sēz, thō′rə-) **1** *Anat.* The part of the body between the neck and the abdomen, enclosed by the ribs. **2** *Entomol.* The middle region of the body of an insect, between the head and the abdomen. **3** *Zool.* The corresponding region of the body in other arthropods. [<L <Gk. *thōrax*]

THORAX
a Manubrium.
b Gladiolus.
c Ensiform cartilage.
d Clavicle.
e Scapula.
f Sternal ribs.
g False ribs.
h Floating ribs.
i Costal arch.
j Costal cartilage.

Tho·reau (thôr′ō, thō′rō, thə·rō′), **Henry David,** 1817–1862, U.S. author.

tho·ri·a (thôr′ē·ə, thō′rē·ə) *n.* A white, very heavy oxide of thorium, ThO₂, used with zirconia and other earths in the mantle of Welsbach's incandescent lamp. [<NL <thorium THORIUM]

tho·ri·a·nite (thôr′ē·ə·nīt, thō′rē-) *n.* A black radioactive mineral composed chiefly of thorium, cerium, and uranium oxides.

tho·ri·um (thôr′ē·əm, thō′rē-) *n.* A gray, radioactive metallic element (symbol Th, atomic number 90) of the actinide series, about as abundant as lead in the lithosphere. See PERIODIC TABLE. [after *Thor*] — **tho·ric** *adj.*

thorium series The succession of radioactive nuclides stemming from the decay of thorium of mass number 232 and terminating in the stable lead isotope of mass number 208.

thorn (thôrn) *n.* **1** An indurated, leafless spine or sharp-pointed process from a branch. **2** One of

various other sharp processes, as the spine of a porcupine. **3** Any of various thorn-bearing shrubs or trees; especially, any of a genus (*Crataegus*) of rosaceous plants, as the hawthorn. **4** Anything or anyone that occasions discomfort, pain, or annoyance; a vexation. **5** The name of the Old English rune þ ; also, the corresponding Icelandic character: equivalent originally to *th*, both voiced and unvoiced, but finally only to the unvoiced sound, as in *thorn*, from which it derives its name. *Y* or *y* is sometimes used as a makeshift for it in early English, as in the contraction yᶜ. Compare EDH. — *v.t.* To pierce or prick with a thorn. [OE] — **thorn′less** *adj.*

thorn apple 1 Jimsonweed: so called from its spiny capsule. **2** Any plant of the same genus. **3** The fruit of the hawthorn; a haw.

thorn·back (thôrn′bak′) *n.* **1** A European ray (*Raia clavata*) whose back is studded with short stout spines. **2** The common European spider crab (*Maia squinado*). **3** Any of certain American skates or sticklebacks. **4** *Brit. Slang.* An old maid.

thorn·bill (thôrn′bil′) *n.* Any of certain bright-colored hummingbirds of South America (genera *Rhamphomicron* and *Chalcostigma*) characterized by a long, sharp bill.

thorn tree 1 The hawthorn. **2** The honey locust.

tho·ron (thôr′on, thō′ron) *n.* An isotope of radon emanating from thorium, having mass number 220 and a half-life of 54.5 seconds. [<NL THOR(IUM) + -*on*, as in *neon*]

thor·ough (thûr′ō, thûr′ə) *adj.* **1** Carried to completion; thoroughgoing: a *thorough* search; also, carrying (a task) to completion; persevering: a very *thorough* worker. **2** Marked by careful attention throughout; not superficial; hence, complete; perfect. **3** Completely (such and such); through and through: a *thorough* nincompoop. **4** Painstakingly conforming to a standard. **5** *Obs.* Going or passing through. See synonyms under RADICAL. —*adv. & prep. Obs.* Through. Also *Obs.* **thor′o.** [Emphatic var. of THROUGH] — **thor′ough·ly** *adv.* —**thor′ough·ness** *n.*

THOROUGH-BASS
The numbers under the bass indicate the notes of the chords in the treble.

thor·ough·bass (thûr′ō·bās′) *n. Music* **1** A bass part accompanied by shorthand marks, as numerals, below the staff, to indicate the general harmony: now disused. **2** Loosely, the science of harmony or the art of harmonic composition.

thorough brace A strong leather strap extending under each side of the body of a carriage and serving as a support and a spring. —**thor′ough·braced′** *adj.*

thor·ough·bred (thûr′ō·bred′, thûr′ə-) *n.* **1** Pure stock. **2** *Colloq.* A person of culture and good breeding. —*adj.* **1** Belonging to the strain of horses known as Thoroughbred. **2** Bred from pure stock. **3** Possessing the traits of a thoroughbred.

thor·ough·fare (thûr′ō·fâr′, thûr′ə-) *n.* **1** A frequented way or course; especially, a road or street through which the public have unobstructed passage; highway. **2** A traveling or passing through, or the right or possibility of doing so; a passage: now chiefly in the phrase *no thoroughfare.* **3** An outlet to an enclosed place, as to a court. **4** Any place through which much traffic passes, as a strait, river, or other waterway. See synonyms under ROAD, WAY. [ME *thurghfare* <OE *thurh* through + *faru* going]

thor·ough·paced (thûr′ō·pāst′, thûr′ə-) *adj.* **1** Perfectly trained, as a horse. **2** Hence, thoroughgoing; accomplished: a *thorough-paced* villain.

thor·ough·pin (thûr′ə·pin′) *n.* Dropsical swelling

of the sheath of the tendon of a flexor muscle connected with the hock of a horse: it appears on both sides of the leg, as if the latter had been pierced by a pin. Also **thor′ough·shot** (-shot′).

thor·ough·wort (thûr′ō·wûrt′, thûr′ə-) *n.* **1** A stout, hairy herb, the boneset, 2 to 5 feet high, with white flowers, common in the United States and Canada. **2** Any other eupatorium.

thorp (thôrp) *n.* A hamlet; small cluster of houses in the country: now chiefly in names of places. Also **thorpe.** [OE. Akin to DORP.]

THOROUGHWORT
(Plant to 5 feet high)

Thors·havn (tôrs·houn′) Capital of the Faeroe Islands, in the central part of the group.

those (thōz) *adj. & pron.* Plural of THAT. [OE *thās*]

Thoth (thōth, tōt) In Egyptian mythology, the god of wisdom, inventor of art, science, and letters: identified with the Greek *Hermes Trismegistus*: represented with the head of an ibis or a dog.

Thoth·mes (thōth′mēz, tōt′mes) Any of several Egyptian kings, between 1587–1328 B.C.: also *Thuthmose.*

thou (thou) *pron.* The person spoken to, as denoted in the nominative case: archaic except in Biblical, homiletic, elevated, or poetic language, in prayers to a deity, or in certain dialects. [OE *thū*]

THOTH

though (thō) *conj.* **1** Notwithstanding the fact that: introducing a clause expressing an actual fact. **2** Conceding or granting that; even if: introducing a clause assumed or admitted as supposedly true. **3** And yet; still; however: introducing a modifying clause or statement added as an afterthought: I am well, *though* I do not feel very strong. **4** Notwithstanding what has been done or said; nevertheless: But they have, *though.* As used in this sense, *though* is sometimes regarded as a conjunctive adverb. Also spelled *tho.* Compare HOWEVER. See synonyms under BUT[1]. [Prob. fusion of OE *thēah* and ON *tho*]

thought[1] (thôt) *n.* **1** The act or process of using the mind actively and deliberately; meditation; cogitation. **2** The product of thinking; an idea, concept, judgment, opinion, or the like. **3** Intellectual activity of a specific kind: Greek *thought.* **4** Consideration; attention; heed: to take *thought* on how to do something. **5** Intention or idea of doing something; plan; design: All *thought* of returning was abandoned. **6** Expectation; anticipation: He had no *thought* of finding her there. **7** A trifle; a small amount: Be a *thought* more cautious. [<THOUGHT[2]]

Synonyms: cogitation, conception, conclusion, consideration, contemplation, deliberation, fancy, idea, imagination, judgment, meditation, musing, notion, opinion, reflection, reverie, speculation, study, supposition, thinking, view. See IDEA, MIND, REFLECTION.

thought[2] (thôt) Past tense and past participle of THINK. [OE *thôht*]

thought·ful (thôt′fəl) *adj.* **1** Full of thought; meditative: a *thoughtful* face. **2** Showing, characterized by, or employed in thought; promotive of thought. **3** Attentive; careful; especially, manifesting regard for others; considerate: often with *of* or an infinitive: *thoughtful* of one's reputation: *thoughtful* to lay up a store for winter. — **thought′ful·ly** *adv.* — **thought′ful·ness** *n.*

Synonyms: attentive, careful, circumspect, considerate, heedful, mindful, provident. An *attentive* person waits upon another to supply what is needed or desired. A *thoughtful* person provides in advance for needs and wishes not yet manifested. A *considerate* person carefully spares another all that would harm, grieve, or annoy; one who is *circumspect* carefully avoids all that might compromise himself. See SEDATE. *Antonyms:* careless, gay, giddy, heedless, inadvertent, inattentive, inconsiderate, neglectful, negligent, reckless, remiss.

thought·less (thôt′lis) *adj.* 1 Manifesting lack of thought or care; heedless; also, giddy. 2 Stupid. See synonyms under IMPROVIDENT, IMPRUDENT. — **thought′less·ly** *adv.* — **thought′·less·ness** *n.*

thought–trans·fer·ence (thôt′trans·fûr′əns) *n.* Telepathy.

thou·sand (thou′zənd) *n.* The cardinal number following 999; one hundred times ten, or any of the symbols (1,000, m, M) used to represent it; also, loosely, an indefinitely large number. — *adj.* Consisting of a hundred times ten; millenary. [OE *thusend*] — **thou′sand·fold′** (-fōld′) *adj. & adv.*

Thousand Islands A group of 1,500 islets in an expansion of the upper St. Lawrence River, near Lake Ontario.

thou·sandth (thou′zəndth) *adj.* 1 Last in a series of a thousand: an ordinal numeral. 2 Being one of a thousand equal parts. — *n.* 1 One of a thousand equal parts. 2 The next in order after the 999th.

thrall (thrôl) *n.* 1 A person in bondage; a slave; serf; hence, figuratively, one controlled by a passion or vice. 2 The condition of bondage; thraldom. — *v.t. Archaic* To reduce to thraldom; enslave. — *adj.* Held in subjection; enslaved. [OE *thræl* <ON]

thrash (thrash) *v.t.* 1 To thresh, as grain. 2 To beat as if with a flail; flog; whip. 3 To defeat utterly. — *v.i.* 4 To move or swing about with flailing, violent motions. 5 *Naut.* To work to windward, against the tide, etc. See synonyms under BEAT. — **to thrash out** To discuss fully and to a conclusion. — *n.* 1 The act of thrashing. 2 In swimming, a kick used with the crawl and back strokes. [Dial. var. of THRESH]

thrash·er[1] (thrash′ər) *n.* 1 One who or that which thrashes. 2 *Agric.* A threshing machine. 3 The thresher shark.

thrash·er[2] (thrash′ər) *n.* Any of several long-tailed American songbirds (genus *Toxostoma*) resembling the thrushes and related to the mockingbirds, especially the common eastern **brown thrasher** (*T. rufum*), colored foxy-red with black spots. [<dial. E *thresher* <THRUSH[1]]

thra·son·i·cal (thrā·son′i·kəl) *adj.* Characterized by boasting or ostentation; bragging; boastful. [<L *Thraso*, a braggart soldier in Terence's *Eunuch* <Gk. *Thrason* < *thrasus* rash] — **thra·son′i·cal·ly** *adv.*

thread (thred) *n.* 1 A very slender cord or line composed of two or more yarns or filaments, as of flax, cotton, silk, or other fibrous substance, twisted together. 2 A filament of any substance, as of metal, glass, or tissue; a hair. 3 A fine stream or beam: a *thread* of light. 4 A fine line of color. 5 Anything suggestive of a thread; something that runs a continuous course through a series, serving to give sequence to the whole: the *thread* of his discourse. 6 *Mining* A very thin seam or vein of ore. 7 *Mech.* The spiral ridge of a screw. 8 Thread of life. — *v.t.* 1 To pass a thread through the eye of: to *thread* a needle. 2 To arrange or string on a thread, as beads. 3 To cut a thread on or in, as a screw. 4 To make one's way through or over: to *thread* a maze. 5 To make (one's way) carefully. 6 To be present throughout; pervade. — *v.i.* 7 To make one's way carefully; step. 8 To drop from a fork or spoon in a fine thread: said of boiling sirup when it has reached a certain consistency. — *adj.* Pertaining to, resembling, or made of thread; filar. [OE *thrǣd*] — **thread′er** *n.* — **thread′like′** *adj.*

thread·bare (thred′bâr′) *adj.* 1 Worn so that the threads show, as a rug or garment. 2 Clad in worn garments. 3 Commonplace; hackneyed. See synonyms under COMMON, TRITE. — **thread′bare′ness** *n.*

thread feather *Ornithol.* An extremely slender feather, having the vane rudimentary or absent; filoplume.

thread·fin (thred′fin′) *n.* A fish of tropical

---

seas (family *Polynemidae*), having three or more threadlike rays below the pectoral fins. Also **thread′fish′**.

thread mark A marking made in paper currency by running colored silk fibers in with the pulp, as a safeguard against counterfeiting. Compare GRANITE PAPER, SILK PAPER.

thread·worm (thred′wûrm′) *n.* A threadlike nematode worm; a pinworm or filaria.

threat (thret) *n.* 1 A declaration of an intention to inflict injury or pain; a menace. 2 An announcement or omen of impending danger or evil. 3 A menace or danger of any sort. — *v.t. Archaic* To threaten. [OE *thrēat* crowd, oppression]

threat·en (thret′n) *v.t.* 1 To utter menaces or threats against. 2 To be menacing or dangerous to. 3 To be ominous or portentous of. 4 To utter threats of (injury, vengeance, etc.). — *v.i.* 5 To utter threats. 6 To have a menacing aspect; lower: The rising waters seemed to *threaten*. [OE *thrēatnian* urge, compel] — **threat′en·er** *n.* — **threat′en·ing·ly** *adv.*

Synonym: menace. *Threaten* is applied alike to vast and trivial matters; *menace* only to those of moment. Either persons or things may *threaten*; *menace* is chiefly used of persons or of things personified. One may *threaten* by word or act; *menace* is for the most part limited to actions or concrete things; one *threatens* another with death; he *menaces* him with a revolver.

three (thrē) *n.* 1 The cardinal number following two and preceding four, or any of the symbols (3, iii, III) used to represent it. 2 Any group of three persons or things; a playing card with three pips. — *adj.* Being one more than two; ternary. [OE *thri*]

three–base hit (thrē′bās′) A fair hit in baseball that enables the batter to reach third base without the help of an error. Also **three′–bag′ger** (-bag′ər).

three–cent piece (thrē′sent′) A copper and nickel coin of the United States from 1865–1890.

three–col·or (thrē′kul′ər) *adj.* Pertaining to or denoting a process of color printing based on three primary colors, each of which is transferred to the printing surface from a separate, accurately registered plate.

three–deck·er (thrē′dek′ər) *n.* 1 A vessel having three decks or gun decks. 2 Any structure having three levels. 3 A sandwich made with three slices of bread.

three–phase (thrē′fāz′) *adj. Electr.* Designating a combination of alternating currents or circuits each of which differs in phase by one third of a cycle or 120 degrees.

three–piled (thrē′pīld′) *adj.* 1 Having a triple pile or nap: said of velvet; also, figuratively, costly or extravagant. 2 Clad in or wearing such velvet; hence, wealthy. 3 Piled in a set or sets of three.

three–ply (thrē′plī′) *adj.* Consisting of three thicknesses, strands, layers, etc.

three–point landing (thrē′point′) 1 *Aeron.* A perfect airplane landing, with the front wheels and tail skid or wheel touching the ground simultaneously. 2 Any successful outcome.

three–quar·ter binding (thrē′kwôr′tər) A style of bookbinding having the strip of leather over the back and corners projecting to a greater width than in half-binding.

three·score (thrē′skôr′, -skōr′) *adj. & n.* Sixty.

three·some (thrē′səm) *adj.* Performed by three; triple: a *threesome* reel. — *n.* A golf match in which one plays against two, the latter playing one ball between them alternately.

three–square (thrē′skwâr′) *adj.* Having three plane faces of equal width: said especially of certain files of triangular cross-section.

threm·ma·tol·o·gy (threm′ə·tol′ə·jē) *n.* The science of breeding animals and plants. [< Gk. *thremma, -atos* a nursling + -LOGY]

thren·o·dy (thren′ə·dē) *n. pl.* **·dies** An ode or song of lamentation; a dirge. Also **thren′ode** (-ōd). [<Gk. *thrēnōidia* <*thrēnos* lament + *ōidē* song] — **thre·no·di·al** (thri·nō′dē·əl), **thre·nod·ic** (thri·nod′ik) — **thren′o·dist** *n.*

thre·o·nine (thrē′ə·nēn, -nin) *n. Biochem.* A crystalline amino acid, $C_4H_9NO_3$, isolated as a product of the hydrolysis of certain proteins and regarded as an essential to proper nutrition.

thresh (thresh) *v.t.* 1 To beat stalks of

(ripened grain) with a flail or machine so as to separate the grain from the straw or husks. 2 To beat; flog. — *v.i.* 3 To thresh grain. 4 To move or thrash about. — **to thresh out** (or over) To discuss fully and to a conclusion. — *n.* The act of threshing; a threshing. [OE *therscan*] — **thresh′ing** *n.*

thresh·old (thresh′ōld, -hōld) *n.* 1 The plank, timber, or stone lying under the door of a building; doorsill. 2 The entrance, entering point, or beginning of anything: the *threshold* of the 20th century. 3 *Physiol.* The point at which a stimulus, as of a nerve or muscle, just produces a response; especially, the minimum degree of stimulation necessary for conscious perception: the *threshold* of consciousness: also called *limen*. ◆ Collateral adjective: *liminal*. [OE *therscold*]

thrift (thrift) *n.* 1 Care and wisdom in the management of one's resources; frugality. 2 A flourishing condition; vigorous growth, as of a plant. 3 Any of a genus (*Armeria*, formerly *Statice*) of tufted herbs of the north temperate zone growing on mountains and the seashore; especially, the common thrift (*A. maritima*), having white or pink flower heads. 4 *Obs.* The state of one who thrives; prosperity. 5 *Scot. & Brit. Dial.* Effort; occupation; work. [<ON. Akin to THRIVE.] — **thrift′less** *adj.* — **thrift′less·ly** *adv.* — **thrift′·less·ness** *n.*

Synonyms: gain, profit, prosperity. See FRUGALITY.

thrill (thril) *v.t.* 1 To cause to feel a sudden wave of emotion; move to great or tingling excitement. 2 To cause to vibrate or tremble. — *v.i.* 3 To feel a sudden wave of emotion or excitement. 4 To vibrate or tremble; quiver. See synonyms under SHAKE. — *n.* 1 A tremor of feeling or excitement. 2 A pulsation. 3 *Med.* An abnormal vibratory or tremulous resonance perceived in auscultation; fremitus. [Metathetic var. of THIRL[1]] — **thrill′ing** *adj.* — **thrill′ing·ly** *adv.*

thrive (thrīv) *v.i.* **throve** (thrōv) or **thrived**, **thrived** or **thriv·en** (thriv′ən), **thriv·ing** 1 To prosper; be successful, especially by being thrifty. 2 To grow with vigor; flourish. See synonyms under FLOURISH, SUCCEED. [<ON *thrīfast*, orig. reflexive of *thrīfa* grasp. Akin to THRIFT.] — **thriv′er** *n.* — **thriv′ing·ly** *adv.*

throat (thrōt) *n.* 1 The anterior part of the neck, extending from the back of the mouth and containing the epiglottis, larynx, trachea, and pharynx. 2 Anything resembling a throat; an entrance, inlet, or orifice: the *throat* of a bottle. 3 *Naut.* The end of a gaff nearest the mast. — *v.t.* 1 *Rare* To utter in a guttural tone. 2 To provide with a throat; channel; groove. [OE *throte*]

HUMAN THROAT
a. Soft palate.
b. Tonsils.
c. Pharynx.
d. Epiglottis.
e. Vocal cords.
f. Larynx.
g. Esophagus.

throb (throb) *v.i.* **throbbed**, **throb·bing** 1 To beat or pulsate rhythmically, as the heart; especially, to beat rapidly or violently; palpitate. 2 To feel or show emotion. — *n.* 1 The act or state of throbbing. 2 A pulsation or beat, especially one caused by excitement or emotion. [? Imit.] — **throb′ber** *n.*

throe (thrō) *n.* 1 A violent pang or pain; agony: said especially of the pains of death and childbirth. 2 Any agonized or agonizing activity. See synonyms under AGONY, PAIN. — *v.t. & v.i.* **throed, throe·ing** *Rare* To put in, suffer, or undergo agony. ◆ Homophone: throw. [ME *throwe*, prob. fusion of OE *throwian* suffer and *thrāwan* twist, throw]

throm·bin (throm′bin) *n. Biochem.* The enzyme present in blood serum that reacts with fibrinogen to form fibrin in the process of clotting. [<THROMBUS]

throm·bo·cyte (throm′bə·sīt) *n.* A blood platelet. [<Gk. *thrombos* clot + -CYTE]

throm·bo·plas·tin (throm′bō·plas′tin) *n. Biochem.* A complex substance present in the blood and other animal tissues, which reacts with calcium ions to give prothrombin. Also **throm·bo·kin·ase** (-kin′ās, -kī′nās). [<Gk. *thrombos* clot + -PLAST + -IN] — **throm′bo·plas′tic** *adj.*

throm·bo·sis (throm·bō′sis) *n. Pathol.* Local coagulation of blood in the heart, arteries, veins, or capillaries, forming by its clot an obstruction to circulation. [<NL <Gk. *thrombōsis* < *thrombos* clot] — **throm·bot′ic** (-bot′ik) *adj.*

throne (thrōn) *n.* **1** The royal chair occupied by a sovereign on state occasions. **2** The chair of state of a pope or of some other dignitary, as a cardinal, archbishop, or bishop. **3** Royal estate or dignity; sovereign power. **4** One invested with sovereign power; sometimes, the rank or authority of any high dignitary. **5** *pl.* The third of the nine orders of angels in the celestial hierarchy. — *v.t. & v.i.* **throned, thron·ing** To place or sit on a throne; enthrone; exalt. [<OF *trone* <L *thronus* <Gk. *thronos* seat]

throng (thrông, throng) *n.* **1** A multitude of people crowded closely together. **2** Any numerous collection. — *v.t.* **1** To crowd into and occupy fully; jam. **2** To press or crowd upon. — *v.i.* **3** To collect or move in a throng. See synonyms under JAM[1]. [OE *gethrang*]
Synonyms (noun): concourse, crowd, host, jam, mass, multitude, press. A *crowd* is a company of persons filling to excess the space they occupy and pressing inconveniently upon one another; the total number in a *crowd* may be great or small. *Throng* implies that the persons are numerous as well as pressed or pressing closely together; there may be a dense *crowd* in a small room, but there cannot be a *throng. Host* and *multitude* both imply vast numbers, but a *multitude* may be diffused over a great space so as to be nowhere a *crowd; host* is a military term, and properly denotes an assembly too orderly for crowding. *Concourse* signifies a spontaneous gathering of many persons moved by a common impulse, and suggests less massing and pressure than is indicated by the word *throng.* Compare ASSEMBLY, COMPANY.

throt·tle (throt′l) *n.* **1** The throat or windpipe. **2** *Mech.* A valve controlling the supply of steam to a steam engine, or of vaporized fuel to the cylinders of an internal-combustion engine: also **throttle valve. 3** The lever which operates the throttle valve: also **throttle lever.** — *v.t.* **·tled, ·tling 1** To press or constrict the windpipe or throat of; strangle; choke or suffocate. **2** To silence, stop, or suppress by or as by choking. **3** To reduce or shut off the flow of (steam, or fuel in an internal-combustion engine). **4** To reduce the speed of by means of a throttle; slow down. — *v.i.* **5** To suffocate; choke. [Dim. of ME *throte* throat] — **throt′tler** *n.*

through (thrōo) *prep.* **1** From end to end, side to side, or limit to limit of; into at one side, end, or point, and out of at another. **2** Covering, entering, or penetrating all parts of; throughout; also, over the surface of. **3** From the first to the last of; during the time or period of. **4** In the midst of; here and there upon or in. **5** By way of: He departed *through* the door. **6** By means of; by the instrumentality or aid of. **7** Having reached the end of, especially with success: He got *through* his examinations easily. **8** On account of; because or as a result of. See synonyms under BY. — *adv.* **1** From one end, side, surface, etc., to or beyond another. **2** From beginning to end. **3** To a termination or conclusion, especially a successful one: to pull *through.* **4** Completely; entirely: He is wet *through.* — **through and through** Thoroughly; completely. — *adj.* **1** Going from beginning to end without stops or with very few stops, and without reshipment or change: a *through* train; also, pertaining to or serving an entire distance or route: a *through* ticket. **2** Extending from one side or surface to another. **3** Unobstructed; open; clear: a *through* road. **4** Arrived at an end; finished: Are you *through* with my pen? **5** At the end of all relations or dealings: He is *through* with his old friends. Also spelled

thru. [OE *thurh*]

through·put (thrōo′poot′) *n.* The quantity of raw materials which may be processed for intended final use in a given time, as in an oil refinery or a chemical plant.

throw (thrō) *v.* **threw** (thrōo), **thrown, throw·ing** *v.t.* **1** To propel through the air by means of a sudden straightening or whirling of the arm. **2** To propel or hurl: The mortar *threw* shells into the town. **3** To put hastily or carelessly: He *threw* a coat over his shoulders. **4** To direct or project (light, shadow, a glance, etc.). **5** To bring to a specified condition or state by or as by throwing: to *throw* the enemy into a panic. **6** To cause to fall; overthrow: The horse *threw* its rider. **7** In wrestling, to force the shoulders of (an opponent) to the ground. **8** To cast (dice). **9** To make (a specified cast) with dice. **10** To cast off or shed; lose: The horse *threw* a shoe. **11** *Colloq.* To lose purposely, as a race. **12** To give birth to (young): said of domestic animals. **13** To move, as a lever or switch, in connecting or disconnecting a circuit, mechanism, etc.; also, to connect or disconnect in this manner. **14** *Slang* To give (a party, etc.). **15** In card games, to play or discard. **16** In ceramics, to shape on a potter's wheel. **17** To spin (filaments, as of silk) into thread. — *v.i.* **18** To cast or fling something. — **to throw away 1** To cast off; discard. **2** To waste; squander. — **to throw back** To revert to ancestral characteristics. — **to throw cold water on** To discourage. — **to throw in 1** To cause (gears or a clutch) to mesh or engage. **2** To contribute; add. **3** To join with others. — **to throw off 1** To cast aside; reject; spurn. **2** To rid oneself of. **3** To do or utter in an offhand manner. **4** To disconnect, as a machine; release. — **to throw oneself at** To strive to gain the affections or love of. — **to throw oneself into** To engage or take part in vigorously. — **to throw oneself on** (or **upon**) To entrust oneself to; rely on. — **to throw open 1** To open suddenly or completely, as a door. **2** To free from restrictions or obstacles. — **to throw out 1** To put forth; emit. **2** To cast out or aside; discard; reject. **3** To utter as if accidentally: to *throw out* hints. **4** In baseball, to retire (a runner) by throwing the ball to the base toward which he is advancing. — **to throw over 1** To overturn. **2** To discard. — **to throw together** To put together hastily or roughly. — **to throw up 1** To erect hastily. **2** To give up; relinquish. **3** To vomit. **4** *Colloq.* To mention or repeat, as a fault or taunt. — *n.* **1** An act of throwing or hurling; a cast; fling. **2** The distance over which a missile may be thrown: a stone's *throw.* **3** A cast of dice, or the resulting number; hence, a hazard; venture. **4** *Mech.* **a** The radius of the circle described by a crank, cam, or the like. **b** The travel or extent of reciprocating motion obtainable, as from a crank, piston, slide valve, etc. **5** A scarf used for draping an easel or picture frame; also, a woman's scarf or boa. **6** *Geol.* **a** A faulting, or dislocation of rock strata. **b** The amount of vertical displacement produced by dislocation of strata. **7** The sudden fluctuation of a magnetic needle when the force is suddenly changed. **8** The distance from a motion-picture projector to the screen. **9** In wrestling, a flooring of one's opponent so that both his shoulders touch the mat simultaneously for ten seconds. ◆ *Homophone: throe.* [OE *thrāwan* turn, twist, curl] — **throw′er** *n.*

throw·back (thrō′bak′) *n.* **1** *Biol.* **a** Reversion to an earlier ancestral or primitive type, phase, or condition of physical being or development. **b** An example of such reversion. **2** Anything returned for revision, correction, redirection, etc.

thrum[1] (thrum) *v.* **thrummed, thrum·ming** *v.t.* **1** To play on or finger (a stringed instrument) idly and without expression. **2** To drum or tap monotonously or listlessly. **3** To recite or repeat in a droning, monotonous way. — *v.i.* **4** To thrum a stringed instrument. **5** To sound when played thus, as a guitar. **6** *Scot.* To purr. — *n.* Any monotonous drumming. [Prob. imit.]

thrum[2] (thrum) *n.* **1** The fringe of warp threads remaining on a loom beam after the web has

been cut off; also, one of such threads. **2** Any loose thread or fringe, or a tuft of filaments or fibers; a tassel. **3** *pl.* Coarse or waste yarn. **4** *pl. Naut.* Bits of rope yarn for sewing on canvas to make chafing gear or collision mats. **5** *Bot.* A threadlike organ or part of a flower; stamen. **6** *Scot.* A bit; particle: I don't care a *thrum.* **7** *Scot.* A tangle. — *v.t.* **thrummed, thrum·ming. 1** To cover or trim with thrums or similar appendages. **2** *Naut.* To insert bits of rope yarn in (canvas) to produce a rough surface or mat to be used to prevent chafing. [OE *-thrum* ligament, as in *tungethrum* the ligament of the tongue]

thrush[1] (thrush) *n.*
Any one of many migratory, passerine birds of the family *Turdidae,* having typically a long and slightly graduated tail, long wings, and spotted under parts. The robin, **hermit thrush** (*Hylocichla guttata*), **wood thrush** (*H. mustelina*), and the European **song thrush** (*Turdus philomelus*) are examples. ◆ Collateral adjective: *turdine.* [OE *thrysce*]

WOOD THRUSH
(To 8 1/2 inches in length)

thrush[2] (thrush) *n.* **1** *Pathol.* A vesicular disease of the mouth, lips, and throat caused by a fungus (*Monilia albicans*): generally confined to infants. **2** A disease of a horse's foot characterized by suppuration. Also called *sprue.* [Cf. Dan. *tröske,* Sw. *trosk* a mouth disease]

thrust (thrust) *v.* **thrust, thrust·ing** *v.t.* **1** To push or shove with force or sudden impulse. **2** To pierce with a sudden forward motion; stab, as with a sword or dagger. **3** To interpose; put in. — *v.i.* **4** To make a sudden push or thrust. **5** To force oneself on or ahead; push one's way; crowd: with *through, into, on,* etc. See synonyms under DRIVE, PUSH. — *n.* **1** A sudden and forcible push, especially with a long, pointed weapon: distinguished from *cut.* **2** A vigorous attack; sharp onset. **3** *Engin.* A stress or strain tending to push a member of a structure outward or sidewise: the *thrust* of an arch. **4** The driving force exerted by certain propulsive devices, as a jet or rocket engine, an airplane's or ship's propeller, etc. **5** Salient force or meaning: the *thrust* of his remarks. **6** *Geol.* A rock fault due to horizontal compression; also, the plane of such a fault. [<OE *thrȳsta*] — **thrust′er** *n.*

thrust fault *Geol.* A fault resulting from horizontal compression in which the hanging wall appears to have moved upward, with a corresponding shortening of the entire rock mass: opposed to *gravity fault.* Also called *reverse fault.*

thu·ja (thōo′jə) *n.* Any of a genus (*Thuja*) of evergreen trees and shrubs of the pine family, including the arborvitae, source of the medicinal oil of thuja. Also spelled *thuya.* [<NL <Gk. *thyia,* an African tree]

thu·li·um (thōo′lē·əm) *n.* A soft, silvery-gray metallic element (symbol Tm, atomic number 69), the least abundant of the lanthanide series. See PERIODIC TABLE. [from THULE]

thumb (thum) *n.* **1** The inner digit of a limb when set apart from and apposable to the other fingers; especially, the short, thick digit on the radial side of the human hand; the pollex. **2** *Ornithol.* The first radial digit of the wing of certain birds. **3** The division in a glove or mitten that covers the thumb. **4** *Archit.* An ovolo. — **all thumbs** *Colloq.* Clumsy with the hands; not deft. — **thumbs down** A sign of negation or disapproval. — **under one's thumb** Under one's influence or power. — *v.t.* **1** To press, rub, soil, or wear with the thumb in handling, as the pages of a book. **2** To perform with or as with the thumbs; hence, to do or handle clumsily. **3** To run through the pages of (a book, manuscript, etc.,) rapidly and perfunctorily. **4** To solicit or obtain (a ride) in an automobile by standing by

add, āce, câre, pälm; end, ēven; it, īce; odd, ōpen, ôrder; tŏŏk, pōōl; up, bûrn; ə = a in *above,* e in *sicken,* i in *clarity,* o in *melon,* u in *focus;* yōō = u in *fuse;* oi, oil; ou, pout; ch, check; g, go; ng, ring; th, thin; ᵺ, this; zh, vision. Foreign sounds à, œ, ü, kh, ń; and ◆: see page xx. < from; + plus; ? possibly.

the road and indicating with the thumb the direction one wishes to go; also, to make (one's way) thus: He *thumbed* his way to New York. [OE *thūma*]

thumb index A series of scalloped indentations cut along the right-hand edge of a book and labeled to indicate its various sections.

thumb·ling (thum′ling) *n.* A diminutive being; dwarf. Compare FINGERLING.

thumb·nut (thum′nut′) *n.* A threaded nut having one or more wings or projections for screwing by the thumb and fingers; wing-nut. See illustration under NUT.

thumb·screw (thum′skrōō′) *n.* 1 A screw to be turned by thumb and fingers. See illustration under SCREW. 2 An instrument of torture for compressing the thumb or thumbs.

thumb·stall (thum′stôl) *n.* A covering or sheath, as of leather, for the thumb.

thump (thump) *n.* A blow with a blunt or heavy object; also, the sound made by such a blow; a dull thud. See synonyms under BLOW. —*v.t.* 1 To beat or strike so as to make a heavy thud or thuds. 2 *Colloq.* To beat or defeat severely. —*v.i.* 3 To strike with a thump. 4 To make a thump or thumps; pound or throb. [Imit.] —**thump′er** *n.*

thumps (thumps) *n. pl.* 1 Hiccups in a horse. 2 A lung disease in swine, caused by infestation with the larvae of a roundworm (genus *Ascaris*). [< THUMP; from the sound of the contractions of the diaphragm]

thun·der (thun′dər) *n.* 1 The sound that accompanies lightning, caused by the sudden heating and expansion of the air along the path of the lightning flash. 2 Any loud, rumbling or booming noise, suggestive of thunder. 3 An awful denunciation or threat; a vehement or powerful utterance, oratorical or other. 4 *Rare* A lightning stroke; thunderbolt. —**to steal one's thunder** To take for one's own use anything especially popular or effective originated by another: said especially of an argument. —*v.i.* 1 To give forth a peal or peals of thunder: used impersonally: It *thunders.* 2 To make a noise like thunder. 3 To utter vehement denunciations or threats. —*v.t.* 4 To utter or express with a noise like or suggestive of thunder: The cannon *thundered* defiance. [OE *thunor*] —**thun′der·er** *n.*

thun·der·bird (thun′dər·bûrd′) *n.* An enormous bird believed to produce thunder by flapping its wings, lightning by opening and closing its eyes, and rain by allowing a huge lake to run off its back: common to the folklore of the North American Indians of the Plains and the Canadian forests.

thun·der·bolt (thun′dər·bōlt′) *n.* 1 One electric discharge accompanied by a clap of thunder: formerly conceived of as a molten ball or bolt hurled by the lightning flash. 2 Any person or thing acting with or as with the force and speed or destructiveness of lightning.

thun·der·cloud (thun′dər·kloud′) *n.* A dark, heavy mass of cloud highly charged with electricity.

thun·der·head (thun′dər·hed′) *n.* A rounded mass of cumulus cloud, either silvery-white or dark with silvery edges, often developing into a thundercloud.

thunder snake The house snake: so called because forced out of its hole by heavy rain.

thun·der·squall (thun′dər·skwôl′) *n.* A squall accompanied by thunder.

thun·der·storm (thun′dər·stôrm′) *n.* A local storm accompanied by lightning and thunder.

thun·der·struck (thun′dər·struk′) *adj.* 1 Struck by lightning. 2 Amazed, astonished, or confounded, as with fear, surprise, or the like. Also **thun′der·strick·en** (-strik′ən).

thu·ri·ble (thōōr′ə·bəl) *n.* A censer. [< L *thuribulum* < *thus, thuris* frankincense]

thu·ri·fer (thōōr′ə·fər) *n.* A censer-bearer; an acolyte or altar boy who carries a thurible. [< *thus, thuris* frankincense + *ferre* bear, carry]

thu·rif·er·ous (thōō·rif′ər·əs) *adj.* Yielding or bearing incense.

Thurs·day (thûrz′dē, -dā) *n.* The fifth day of the week. [Fusion of OE *Thunres dæg* day of Thunor and ON *Thórsdagr* day of Thor; trans. of LL *dies*

Jovis day of Jove]

thus (thus) *adv.* 1 In this or that or the following way or manner. 2 To such degree or extent; so: *thus* far. 3 In these circumstances or conditions; in this case; therefore. [OE]

thwart (thwôrt) *v.t.* 1 To prevent the accomplishment of, as by interposing an obstacle; also, to prevent (one) from accomplishing something; foil; frustrate; balk. 2 *Obs.* To move or place over or across. See synonyms under BAFFLE, HINDER[1]. —*n.* An oarsman's seat extending athwart a boat. —*adj.* 1 Lying, moving, or extending across something; transverse. 2 *Obs.* Perverse or cross-grained; ill-natured. —*adv. & prep.* Athwart. [< ON *thvert*, neut. of *thverr* transverse] —**thwart′er** *n.*

thy (thī) *pronominal adj.* The possessive case of the pronoun *thou* used attributively; belonging or pertaining to thee: *Thy* kingdom come. [Apocopated var. of THINE]

thy·la·cine (thī′lə·sin, -sin) *n.* A nearly extinct, carnivorous, doglike marsupial *(Thylacinus cynocephalus)* of Tasmania, grayish-brown with dark transverse bands on the hinder part of the back: also called Tasmanian wolf, zebra wolf. [< NL < Gk. *thylax, thylakos* pouch]

THYLACINE
(About 18 inches high at the shoulder)

thyme (tīm) *n.* Any of a genus *(Thymus)* of small shrubby plants of the mint family, having aromatic leaves and cultivated for seasoning in cookery; especially, the **wild thyme** *(T. serpyllum).* [< F *thym* < L *thymum* < Gk. *thymon*] —**thym′y** *adj.*

thym·e·la·e·a·ceous (thim′ə·lē·ā′shəs) *adj. Bot.* Designating a family *(Thymelaeaceae)* of apetalous trees or shrubs having very tough bark; the mezereon family. [< NL, family name < L *thymelaea* < Gk. *thymelaia* < *thymon* thyme + *elaia* olive tree]

thy·mol (thī′mōl, -mol, thī′-) *n. Chem.* A crystalline compound, $C_{10}H_{13}OH$, contained in certain volatile oils, as those of thyme and horsemint, and also made synthetically: used as an antiseptic. [< THYME + -OL[2]]

thymol iodide *Chem.* A reddish-brown mixture of iodine derivatives and thymol, used as a deodorant and antiseptic.

thy·mus (thī′məs) *n. Anat.* A lymphoid organ of glandular character and unknown function, developed in the region of the neck in many vertebrates. In man and other mammals it lies at the root of the neck, just above the heart, and is most prominent in the young. It is the neck sweetbread of calves and lambs. [< NL < Gk. *thymos*]

thy·re·oid (thī′rē·oid) *adj.* Thyroid.

thyro- *combining form Med & Surg.* The thyroid; of or related to the thyroid: *thyrotropin.* Also, before vowels, **thyr-.** Also **thyreo-.** [< Gk. *thyreoeidēs* thyroid]

thy·ro·hy·oid (thī′rō·hī′oid) *adj. Anat.* Having a relationship to the thyroid gland and the hyoid bone: the *thyrohyoid* ligament. See illustration under LARYNX. [< THYRO- + HYOID]

thy·roid (thī′roid) *adj.* 1 Relating or pertaining to the thyroid cartilage or the thyroid gland. 2 Shaped like a shield; also, having a shield-shaped marking. —*n.* 1 The thyroid cartilage or gland. 2 The dried and powdered thyroid gland of certain domesticated food animals, used in the treatment of myxedema, goiter, obesity, and other disorders. [< Gk. *thyreoeidēs* shield-shaped < *thyreos* large shield + *eidos* form]

thyroid cartilage *Anat.* The largest cartilage of the larynx, composed of two blades whose juncture in front forms the Adam's apple.

thy·roid·ec·to·my (thī′roid·ek′tə·mē) *n. Surg.* Excision of the thyroid gland. [< THYROID + -ECTOMY]

thyroid gland *Anat.* A bilobate endocrine gland situated in front of and on each side of the trachea, close to the larynx. It secretes thyroxin, vitally important in growth and in the prevention of such disorders as goiter, cretinism, etc.

thy·roid·i·tis (thī′roid·ī′tis) *n. Pathol.* Inflammation of the thyroid gland.

thy·ro·tox·i·co·sis (thī′rō·tok′sə·kō′sis) *n. Pa-*

thol. A morbid or diseased condition resulting from excessive activity of the thyroid gland, as in exophthalmic goiter. [< THYRO- + TOXICOSIS] —**thy·ro·tox′ic** (-tok′sik) *adj.*

thy·rot·ro·pin (thī·rot′rə·pin) *n. Biochem.* A hormone from the anterior lobe of the pituitary gland, regarded as having an affinity for the thyroid gland. [< THYRO- + -TROP(E) + -IN]

thy·rox·in (thī·rok′sin) *n. Biochem.* A white, odorless, crystalline compound, $C_{15}H_{11}O_4NI_4$, obtained as the hormone of the thyroid gland and also made synthetically: used in the treatment of thyroid disorders. Also **thy·rox′ine** (-sēn, -sin). [< THYR(O) + OXY- + -IN] —**thy·rox·in·ic** (thī′rok·sin′ik) *adj.*

thyr·soid (thûr′soid) *adj. Bot.* Resembling or shaped like a thyrsus. Also **thyr·soi·dal** (thûr′soid′l).

thyr·sus (thûr′səs) *n. pl.* **·si** (-sī) 1 A staff wreathed in ivy and crowned with a pine cone or a bunch of ivy leaves with grapes or berries: an attribute of Dionysus and the satyrs. 2 *Bot.* A branched panicle in which the middle branches are longer than those above or below them, as in the lilac and grape. [< L < Gk. *thyrsos*]

thy·sa·nu·ran (thī′sə·nōōr′ən, --nyōōr′-, this′ə-) *adj.* Designating or belonging to an order *(Thysanura)* of primitive wingless insects, including the silverfish and the firebrat. —*n.* One of the *Thysanura.* [< NL, name of the order < Gk. *thysanos* fringe + *oura* tail] —**thy′sa·nu′rous** *adj.*

thy·self (thī·self′) *pron.* Emphatic or reflexive form of the second person singular pronouns *thee* and *thou*: I love thee for *thyself.*

ti[1] (tē) *n. Music* In solmization, a syllable representing the seventh note of the diatonic scale: formerly called *si.* [See GAMUT]

ti[2] (tē) *n.* One of several Asian trees (genus *Cordyline*) of the lily family, especially the **ti palm** *(C. terminalis)* of eastern Asia, having many foliage forms. [< Polynesian]

ti·ar·a (tī·âr′ə, tē·är′ə, -ar′ə) *n.* 1 The pope's triple crown, emblematic of his claim to spiritual and temporal authority; hence, the papal dignity. Compare MITER. 2 The upright headdress worn by the ancient Persian kings. 3 A coronet or form of headdress denoting princely rank; also, anything in imitation of it worn for personal adornment. 4 A Phrygian cap for men and women, long, conical, and falling over the brow: found in Greco-Roman art as the attribute of Paris, Mithras, and others. [< L < Gk. *tiara* Persian headdress]

PAPAL TIARA

Ti·bet (ti·bet′) A former independent theocracy of central Asia, south of the Sinkiang-Uigur Autonomous Region, China, and north of India, Nepal, Sikkim, and Bhutan; incorporated, 1950–1957, in China, as the **Tibetan Autonomous Region**; about 470,000 square miles; capital, Lhasa; Chinese *Sitsang:* also *Thibet. Tibetan* **Pö** (pœ).

Ti·bet·an (ti·bet′n) *adj.* Of or pertaining to Tibet, the Tibetans, or to their language, religion, or customs. —*n.* 1 One of the native Mongoloid people of Tibet, now intermixed with Chinese and various peoples of India. 2 The Sino-Tibetan language of Tibet. Also spelled *Thibetan.*

tib·i·a (tib′ē·ə) *n. pl.* **tib·i·ae** (tib′i·ē) or **tib·i·as** 1 *Anat.* The inner and larger of the two bones of the leg below the knee; the shin bone. See illustration under FOOT. 2 *Entomol.* The fourth or penultimate joint of the leg of an insect, between the femur and the tarsus. 3 An ancient flute or pipe provided with holes for the fingers, originally made of an animal's leg bone. [<L] — **tib′i·al** *adj.*

tic (tik) *n.* 1 An involuntary spasm or twitching of muscles, usually of the face and sometimes of neurotic origin. 2 Tic douloureux. [<F]

tick[1] (tik) *n.* 1 A light recurring sound made by a watch, clock, or similar mechanism. 2 *Brit. Colloq.* The length of time occupied by one tick of a watch or clock: I'll be through in five *ticks.* 3 A mark, as a dot or dash, used in checking off something. — *v.i.* To make or sound a tick or ticks; make a recurrent clicking sound, as a running watch or clock. — *v.t. Brit.* To mark or check with ticks. — **to tick off** *Brit. Colloq.* To tell off. [Prob. imit.]

tick[2] (tik) *n.* 1 One of numerous flat, leathery, bloodsucking arachnids (order *Acarida*) that attack the skin of man and other animals; especially, the **cattle tick** (*Margaropus annulatus*), causative agent of Texas fever. 2 Any of certain two-winged or wingless parasitic insects (family *Hippoboscidae*), as the **sheep ticks** and **bat ticks.** [Cf. LG *tieke,* G *zecke* a tick]

tick[3] (tik) *n.* 1 The stout outer covering of a mattress; also, the material for such covering. 2 *Colloq.* Ticking. [Earlier *teke, tyke,* ult. <L *teca, theca* <Gk. *thēke* a case]

tick·er (tik′ər) *n.* 1 One who or that which ticks. 2 A telegraphic receiving instrument which records stock quotations on a paper ribbon (**ticker tape**). 3 *Slang* A watch. 4 *Slang* The heart.

tick·et (tik′it) *n.* 1 A note or notice; a memorandum; also, a slip of paper containing a notice or memorandum. 2 A card with words or characters on it showing that the holder is entitled to something, as transportation in a public vehicle, admission to a theater, or the like. 3 A certificate or license, as of an airplane pilot or the captain of a ship. 4 A label or tag for attachment or identification. 5 a A list of candidates of a single party on a ballot: the Democratic *ticket.* b The group of candidates running for the offices of a party. — *v.t.* 1 To fix a ticket to; label. 2 To present or furnish with a ticket or tickets. [<MF *etiquet* a little note <OF *estiquette* <*estiquer* stick, fix <OLG *stekan.* Doublet of ETIQUETTE.]

tick fever Any of several fevers caused by ticks, especially the Texas fever of cattle, and Rocky Mountain spotted fever, transmitted to man by the bite of a wood tick.

tick·le (tik′əl) *v.* **·led, ·ling** *v.t.* 1 To excite the nerves of by touching or scratching on some sensitive spot, producing a thrilling sensation resulting in spasmodic laughter or twitching; titillate. 2 To arouse or excite agreeably; please: Compliments *tickle* our vanity. 3 To amuse or entertain; delight. 4 To move, stir, or get by or as by tickling. — *v.i.* 5 To have or experience a thrilling or tingling sensation: My foot *tickles.* — *n.* The sensation produced by tickling; titillation; also, the touch or action producing such sensation. [ME *tikelen,* ? metathetic var. of ON *kitla* tickle]

tick·le-grass (tik′əl·gras′, -gräs′) *n.* Rough bent grass (*Agrostis hiemalis*).

tickler coil In radio, a coil of the regenerative type coupled in series with the plate circuit and employed to intensify sound on a receiving circuit by means of a feedback action.

tick·lish (tik′lish) *adj.* 1 Sensitive to tickling. 2 Liable to be upset; unstable; also, easily offended; sensitive. 3 Attended with risk; difficult; delicate. — **tick′lish·ly** *adv.* — **tick′lish·ness** *n.*

tickseed sunflower A square-stemmed species of bur marigold (genus *Bidens*), with a panicle of large-rayed yellow flowers.

tick-tack (tik′tak′) *n.* 1 A recurrent sound like that of the ticking of a clock. 2 Anything that makes a tapping or rattling noise; specifically, a device for making a rattling noise against a window or door, worked from

a distance: used in playing pranks. [Imit. reduplication of TICK[1]]

tick trefoil Any of several leguminous plants (genus *Desmodium*) whose leaves and pods cling to the coats of animals and to clothing. [<TICK[2] + TREFOIL]

tid·al (tīd′l) *adj.* 1 Of, pertaining to, or influenced by the tides; periodically flowing and ebbing: a *tidal* river. 2 Dependent on the rise of the tide as to time of starting or leaving: a *tidal* steamship.

tidal wave 1 Any great incoming rise of waters along a shore, caused by windstorms at sea or by excessively high tides. 2 A tsunami. 3 A great movement in popular feeling or in the affairs of men.

tide (tīd) *n.* 1 The periodic rise and fall of the surface of the ocean, and of the waters connected with the ocean, caused by the attraction of moon and sun. In each lunar day of 24 hours and 51 minutes there are two high tides and two low tides, alternating at equal intervals of flood and ebb. **Spring tides** are high tides above the average, occurring when the moon is new or full; **neap tides** are high tides below the average, occurring when the moon is in the first or third quarter. See FLOOD, EBB. 2 Anything that comes like the tide at flood; the time at which something is most flourishing. 3 The natural drift or tendency of events; also, a current; stream. 4 Season; time; especially, a season of the ecclesiastical year: used chiefly in composition and in the phrase *time and tide: Christmastide.* 5 *Archaic* A suitable or favorable occasion; opportunity. See synonyms under STREAM. — *v.* **tid·ed, tid·ing** *v.i.* 1 To ebb and flow like the tide. 2 To float with the tide. — *v.t.* 3 To carry or help like a boat buoyed up by the tide: Charity *tided* us over the depression. 4 To surmount; survive; endure, as a difficulty: with *over:* to *tide* over hard times. [OE *tīd* a period, season] — **tide′less** *adj.*

tide-land (tīd′land′) *n.* Land alternately covered and uncovered by the tide.

tide-waiter (tīd′wā′tər) *n.* A customs officer who boards vessels entering port, to enforce customs regulations.

tide-wa·ter (tīd′wô′tər, -wot′ər) *n.* Water which inundates land at high tide; also, water affected by the tide on the seacoast or in a river; hence, loosely, the seacoast. — *adj.* Pertaining to the tidewater; also, situated on the seacoast: the *tidewater* country.

tide-way (tīd′wā′) *n.* A channel where the tide runs.

ti·dings (tī′dingz) *n. pl.* (*sometimes construed as singular*) A report or information; news. [OE *tīdung;* infl. in meaning by· ON *tithindi* news, a message]

  Synonyms: advice, information, intelligence, news. *News* is the most general of these words, signifying something that has either just happened or just become known. *Advices* are communications of fact by a trusted informant with the design of guiding or influencing the action of the recipient; the word signifies *news* with a practical purpose and value. *Intelligence* is *news* or *information,* often secret *information,* specifically communicated, usually in certain form. See NEWS.

ti·dy (tī′dē) *adj.* **·di·er, ·di·est** 1 Marked by neatness and order; trim. 2 Of an orderly disposition. 3 *Colloq.* Moderately large; considerable: a *tidy* sum. 4 *Colloq.* Tolerable; fairly good. See synonyms under NEAT[1]. — *v.t.* & *v.i.* **ti·died, ti·dy·ing** To make (things) tidy; put (things) in order. — *n. pl.* **·dies** A light, detachable covering, to protect the back or arms of a chair or sofa. [ME *tidi* <OE *tīd* time] — **ti′di·ly** *adv.* — **ti′di·ness** *n.*

ti·dy-tips (tī′dē·tips′) *n. pl* **·tips** Any of a genus (*Layia*) of ornamental annual plants of California, having yellow flower heads tipped with white; especially, *L. elegans.*

tie (tī) *v.* **tied, ty·ing** *v.t.* 1 To fasten with cord, rope, etc., the ends of which are then drawn into a knot. 2 To draw the parts of together or into place by a cord or band fastened with a knot: to *tie* one's shoes. 3 To form (a knot). 4 To form a knot in, as string. 5 To fasten, attach, or join in any way. 6 To restrain or confine; restrict; bind. 7 **a** To equal (a com-

petitor) in score or achievement. **b** To equal (a competitor's score). 8 *Colloq.* To unite in marriage. 9 *Music* To unite by a tie. — *v.i.* 10 To make a tie or connection. 11 To make the same score; be equal. See synonyms under BIND. — **to tie down** To hinder; restrict. — **to tie up** 1 To fasten with rope, string, etc. 2 To wrap, as with paper, and then fasten with string, cord, etc. 3 To moor (a vessel). 4 To block; hinder. 5 To have or be already committed, in use, etc., so as to be unavailable. — *n.* 1 A flexible bond or fastening secured by drawing the ends into a knot or loop. 2 Any bond or obligation, mental, moral, or legal: *ties* of affection. 3 An exact equality in number, as of a score, votes, etc.; hence, a contest which neither side wins; a draw. 4 Something that is tied or intended for tying, as a shoelace, necktie, or the like. 5 *Engin.* A structural member fastening parts together and receiving tensile stress: distinguished from a *strut.* 6 *Music* A curved line placed over or under two musical notes of the same pitch on the staff to make them represent one tone length. 7 *pl.* Low shoes fastened with lacings: Oxford *ties.* 8 One of a set of timbers laid crosswise on the ground as supports for railroad tracks. [OE *tīgan* bind <*tēah, tēag* a rope]

tie beam A timber that serves as a tie in a roof, etc.

tie-dye (tī′dī′) *v.t.* **-dyed, -dye·ing** To create designs on fabric by tying parts of it in clumps that will not absorb the dye. — *n.* 1 The process of decorating fabrics by tie-dying. 2 Fabric so decorated; also, a design so made.

tie-in sale A sale in which the buyer, in order to get the article he wants, is required to buy a second article.

tie·man·nite (tē′mə·nīt) *n.* A metallic, steel-to lead-gray, opaque mercuric selenide, HgSe. [<G *tiemannit,* after W. Tiemann, 19th c. German mineralogist, its discoverer]

Tien Shan (tyen′ shän′) A mountain chain of central Asia, chiefly in the Tadzhik S.S.R., Kirghiz S.S.R., and Sinkiang-Uigur Autonomous Region, China; highest point, 24,406 feet.

Tien·tsin (tin′tsin′, *Chinese* tyen′jin′) A port near the Gulf of Chihli, NE China; formerly included in Hopeh Province; since 1935, an independent municipality under direct control of the central government; the leading transportation and industrial center of northern China.

tier (tir) *n.* A rank or row in a series of things placed one above another. — *v.t.* & *v.i.* To place or rise in tiers. — *Homophone: tear.* [Earlier *tire* <OF, a sequence <*tirer* draw, elongate]

tierce (tirs) *n.* 1 A former liquid measure equivalent in the United States to 42 wine gallons; a third of a pipe or butt. 2 A cask holding this amount, intermediate between a hogshead and a barrel. 3 In card games, a sequence of three cards of the same suit. 4 In fencing, the third standard position from which a guard, parry, or thrust can be made. 5 *Eccl.* The third canonical hour, nine a.m., or the office or service of that hour: often called *undernsong.* 6 *Music* An interval of a third. 7 A set of three. [<OF *tierce, terce* a third <L *tertia,* fem. of *tertius*]

Tier·ra del Fue·go (tyer′ä del fwā′gō) 1 An archipelago at the southern tip of South America, belonging to Chile and to Argentina; separated from the mainland by the Strait of Magellan; total, 27,476 square miles: 7,996 square miles in Argentina, the rest in Chile. 2 The largest island of the group; 18,000 square miles: 7,750 square miles in Argentina, the rest in Chile.

tie-up (tī′up′) *n.* 1 A situation, resulting from a strike, the breakdown of machinery, etc., in which further progress or operation is impossible: a *tie-up* in traffic. 2 *Dial.* The part of a barn where cows and oxen are kept.

tiff[1] (tif) *n.* 1 A peevish display of irritation; a pet; huff. 2 A light quarrel; a spat. — *v.i.* To be in or have a tiff. [Prob. imit.]

tiff[2] (tif) *Obs. n.* A small draft of liquor; a sip; drink. — *v.t.* To sip; taste. [Cf. ON *thefr* a smell, taste]

---

add, āce, câre, pälm; end, ēven; it, īce; odd, ōpen, ôrder; tŏŏk, pōōl; up, bûrn; ə = a in *above,* e in *sicken,* i in *clarity,* o in *melon,* u in *focus;* yōō = u in *fuse,* oi, oil; ou, pout; ch, check; g, go; ng, ring; th, thin; t͡h, this; zh, vision. Foreign sounds á, œ, ü, kh, ṅ; and ◆: see page xx. <*from;* + *plus;* ? *possibly.*

tif·fa·ny (tif′ə·nē) *n. pl.* **·nies** 1 A very thin transparent cotton gauze. 2 Formerly, a very thin silk. [<OF *tifinie, tiphanie* Epiphany <LL *theophania* THEOPHANY; ? so called because its transparency manifests the wearer]

ti·ger (tī′gər) *n.* 1 A large carnivorous feline mammal (*Felis tigris*) of Asia, with vertical black wavy stripes on a tawny body and black bars or rings on the limbs and tail. 2 One of several other large ferocious animals, as the South American jaguar or the African leopard; also, the thylacine of Tasmania. 3 A fierce, cruel person. 4 *U.S.* An additional cheer or yell (often the word "tiger") given at the conclusion of a round of cheering. [<OF *tigre* <L *tigris* <Gk., ?< Avestan *tīghri* an arrow, a dart]

BENGAL TIGER
(About 6 1/2 feet long; tail, 3 feet)

tiger beetle Any of certain very active, predacious beetles (genus *Cicindela*) having spotted or striped wings, which dart upon their prey from a concealment. For illustration see INSECTS (beneficial).

tiger cat 1 A wildcat, resembling, but smaller than, the tiger, as the Asian **marbled tiger cat** (*Felis marmorata*), the African serval, the American ocelot, and the margay. 2 A domestic cat having striped markings.

ti·ger-eye (tī′gər·ī′) *n.* 1 A gemstone, usually the mineral crocidolite altered by oxidation, showing a beautiful chatoyant luster. One variety is called *hawk's-eye*. Also **ti′ger's-eye′**. 2 A tiger cat.

ti·ger·ish (tī′gər·ish) *adj.* Of, pertaining to, or resembling the tiger or its habits; predacious; bloodthirsty: also spelled *tigrish*.

tiger lily 1 A tall cultivated lily (*Lilium tigrinum*) from China, with nodding orange flowers spotted with black. 2 Any of various lilies with similar flowers, especially the leopard lily (*L. pardalinum*).

tiger moth A stout-bodied moth (family *Arctiidae*) with striped or spotted wings.

tight (tīt) *adj.* 1 So closely held together or constructed as to be impervious to fluids; not leaky: a *tight* roof; a *tight* vessel. 2 Firmly fixed or fastened in place; secure. 3 Fully stretched, so as not to be slack; taut; tense: *tight* as a drum. 4 Strict; stringent: a *tight* schedule. 5 Fitting closely; especially, fitting too closely: said of a garment, shoe, cork, etc. 6 *Colloq.* Difficult to cope with; troublesome: a *tight* spot; a *tight* squeeze. 7 *Colloq.* Parsimonious; tight-fisted; close. 8 Characterized by a feeling of constriction: a *tight* cough. 9 *Slang* Drunk; intoxicated. 10 Evenly matched: said of a race or contest. 11 Difficult to obtain because of scarcity or financial restrictions: said of money or of commodities. 12 Straitened from lack of money or commodities: a *tight* market. 13 Yielding very little or no profit: said of a bargain. —*adv.* 1 Firmly; securely: Hold me *tight*. 2 Closely; with much constriction: The dress fits too *tight*. —**to sit tight** To remain firm in one's position; refrain from budging. [ME *thight*, appar. <Scand. Cf. ON *thēttr* dense.] —**tight′·ly** *adv.* —**tight′ness** *n.*

tight-fist·ed (tīt′fis′tid) *adj.* Stingy; parsimonious.

tight-lipped (tīt′lipt′) *adj.* Having the lips held tightly together; hence, unwilling to talk; reticent or secretive.

tight·rope (tīt′rōp′) *n.* A tightly stretched rope on which acrobats perform. —*adj.* Pertaining to or performing on a tightrope: a *tightrope* walker.

tights (tīts) *n. pl.* Skin-fitting garments, commonly for the legs and lower torso.

tig·lic (tig′lik) *adj. Chem.* 1 Derived from croton oil. 2 Designating a white, crystalline, poisonous acid, $C_5H_8O_2$, contained in an ester in croton oil. Also **tig·lin·ic** (tig·lin′ik). [<NL (*Croton*) *tiglium* the croton oil plant, prob. ult. <Gk. *tilos* thin feces; so called because of its purgative properties]

ti·gress (tī′gris) *n.* A female tiger.

tike (tīk) *n.* 1 A low-bred dog; a cur. 2 *Scot.* An uncouth fellow; a boor. 3 *Colloq.* A small child. Also spelled *tyke*. [<ON *tīk* a bitch]

til (til, tēl) *n.* Sesame. [<Hind. <Skt. *tilá*]

til·bur·y (til′ber·ē) *n. pl.* **·bur·ies** A form of gig seating two persons. [after *Tilbury*, an early 19th c. London coachmaker who invented it]

til·de (til′də, -dē) *n.* 1 A sign (~) used in Spanish over *n* to indicate nasal palatalization or the sound of *ny*, as in *cañon*, canyon. 2 The same sign (usually called **til**) used in Portuguese over a vowel or the first vowel of a dipthong to indicate nasalization, as in *lã*, *Camões*. [<Sp. <L *titulus* superscription, title]

tile (tīl) *n.* 1 A thin piece or plate of baked clay, sometimes decorated, used for covering roofs, floors, etc., and as an ornament. 2 A short earthenware pipe, used in forming sewers. 3 Tiles collectively; tiling. 4 *Colloq.* A high silk hat. —*v.t.* **tiled, til·ing** 1 To cover with tiles. 2 To secure against intrusion; specifically, in Freemasonry, to place the doorkeeper or tiler at the door of (a lodge) to keep out unauthorized persons. [OE *tigule, tigele*, ult. <L *tegula* <*tegere* cover]

tile·fish (tīl′fish′) *n. pl.* **·fish** or **·fishes** A large marine fish (*Lopholatilus chamaeleonticeps*) of the western Atlantic, marked with large yellow spots, and esteemed as food. [<NL (*Lophola*)*til*(*us*), genus name; infl. by *tile*, because its markings resemble ornamental tiles]

til·i·a·ceous (til′ē·ā′shəs) *adj. Bot.* Designating or belonging to a widely distributed family (*Tiliaceae*) of trees, shrubs, and herbs, the linden family, having clusters of often fragrant flowers. [<NL <L *tiliaceus* <*tilia* the linden tree]

til·ing (tī′ling) *n.* 1 The act, operation, or system of using tiles for roofing or drainage. 2 Tiles collectively; tiling. 3 Something made of or faced with tiles.

till¹ (til) *v.t. & v.i.* To put and keep (soil) in order for the production of crops, as by plowing, harrowing, hoeing, sowing, etc.; cultivate. [OE *tilian* strive, acquire] —**till′a·ble** *adj.*

till² (til) *prep.* 1 To the time of; up to; until: He slept till noon. 2 Before: with the negative: He couldn't leave *till* today. 3 *Scot. & Brit. Dial.* To; unto; as far as. —*conj.* 1 Up to such time as; until: *till* death do us part. 2 Before: with the negative: They couldn't go *till* the carriage came for them. [OE *til* <ON *til*]

till³ (til) *n.* A drawer, compartment, or tray; a money drawer. [Earlier *tille*, prob. <ME *tillen, tyllen* draw]

till⁴ (til) *n. Geol.* An unassorted, commingled, and chiefly unstratified mass of clay, sand, pebbles, and boulders, deposited by masses of ice. [Var. of ME *thill*, ? <OE *thille* a board, flooring]

till·age (til′ij) *n.* The cultivation of land. See synonyms under AGRICULTURE. [<TILL¹ + -AGE]

til·land·si·a (ti·land′zē·ə) *n.* Any of a genus (*Tillandsia*) of mainly epiphytic bromeliaceous plants of tropical America and the southern United States, having narrow, entire, often scurfy leaves, and flowers in a terminal spike. [<NL, after Elias *Tillands*, 18th c. Swedish botanist]

till·er¹ (til′ər) *n.* One who or that which tills; a plowman; a farmer. [<TILL¹]

till·er² (til′ər) *n.* 1 A lever to turn a rudder. 2 A means of guidance. [<OF *telier* stock of a crossbow <Med. L *telarium* a weaver's beam <L *tela* a web; prob infl. in meaning by ME *tillen* draw]

till·er³ (til′ər) *n.* 1 A shoot from the base of a stem; sucker. 2 A sapling. —*v.i.* To put forth stems from the root; send forth new shoots. [Prob. OE *telgor* a twig <*telga* a branch]

tilt¹ (tilt) *v.t.* 1 To cause to rise at one end or side; incline at an angle; slant; lean; tip. 2 To aim or thrust, as a lance. 3 To charge or overthrow in a tilt or joust. 4 To hammer or forge with a tilt hammer. —*v.i.* 5 To incline at an angle; lean. 6 To contend with the lance; engage in a joust. See synonyms under TIP¹. —*n.* 1 An inclination from the vertical or horizontal position; slant; slope; also, the act of inclining, or the state of being

inclined. 2 A medieval sport in which mounted knights, charging with lances, endeavored to unseat each other. 3 Any encounter resembling or suggestive of that between two tilting knights; hence, a quarrel; dispute; altercation; also, a thrust or blow, as with a lance. 4 A tilt hammer. 5 A seesaw. 6 The American black-necked stilt. —**at full tilt** At full speed; at full charge. [ME *tylten* be overthrown, totter <OE *tealt* unsteady] —**tilt′er** *n.*

tilt² (tilt) *n.* A canvas canopy or awning on a boat, wagon, booth, or the like. —*v.t.* To furnish or cover with an awning or tilt. [Var. of ME *tild, teld*, OE *teld* a tent]

tilt roof A round-topped roof: so called from its resemblance to the canopy or tilt of a covered wagon.

tilt-up (tilt′up′) *n.* The spotted sandpiper: so called from its teetering habits.

tim·bal (tim′bəl) *n.* 1 A kettledrum. 2 *Entomol.* The drumlike, sound-producing, folding membrane of the shrilling organ of a male cicada or harvest fly. Also spelled *tymbal*. [<F *timbale*, appar. alter. of *attabale* <Sp. *atabal* ATABAL]

tim·ber (tim′bər) *n.* 1 Wood suitable for building purposes, prepared for use. 2 Growing or standing trees; also, woodland. 3 A single piece of squared wood prepared for use or already in use. 4 Any principal beam in a vessel's framing. 5 The wooden part or handle of any implement. 6 Loosely, the materials for any structure; hence, also, human material: That boy has good *timber* in him. See synonyms under STICK. —*v.t.* To provide or shore with timber. [OE] —**tim′ber·er** *n.*

tim·ber-head (tim′bər·hed′) *n. Naut.* 1 An end of a timber projecting above the deck, and used for attaching lines, etc. 2 An upright post fastened to the deck at the point where a timber's end would come.

timber hitch *Naut.* A knot by which a rope is fastened around a spar.

timber line 1 The upper limit of tree growth on mountains and in arctic regions; the line above which no trees grow. 2 The boundary line of a tract of timber. —**tim′ber-line′** (-līn′) *adj.*

timber wolf The large gray or brindled wolf (*Canis occidentalis*) of the forests of the northern United States and Canada: distinguished from the *coyote* or *prairie wolf*.

tim·ber·work (tim′bər·wûrk′) *n.* Work constructed of wood, especially the framing of a structure.

TIMBER WOLF
(About 4 feet long; 26 inches high)

tim·bre (tim′bər, tam′-; *Fr.* taṅ′br′) *n.* 1 The inherent quality of tone which serves to distinguish one musical instrument or voice from another and renders it unique: sometimes called *tone color*. 2 In acoustics, the character or quality of a sound that is produced by the relative number and strength of its harmonics: distinguished from *intensity* (amplitude of vibrations) and *pitch* (frequency of vibrations). 3 *Phonet.* The degree of resonance of a voiced sound, especially a vowel. [<F <OF, a small bell, sound of a bell, orig. a timbrel <L *tympanum* a kettledrum <Gk. *tympanon*]

tim·breled (tim′brəld) *adj.* Chanted to the accompaniment of a timbrel. Also **tim′brelled.**

time (tīm) *n.* 1 The general idea, relation, or fact of continuous or successive existence; infinite duration or its measure. 2 A definite portion of duration; a moment; period; season. 3 A considerable period marked off by some special characteristics; era. 4 The portion of duration allotted to some specific purpose, as that allotted to human life or to any particular life, military service, a prison sentence, etc. 5 The length of an apprenticeship. 6 Period of gestation. 7 A portion of duration available or sufficient for, or allotted to, some special purpose or event; also, leisure: I have no *time* to read. 8 Indefinite duration viewed in the concrete as measurable and terminable, but not precisely limited: You build for *time*, we for eternity. 9 A general term indicating a subdivision of one of the

grander divisions of geological history. **10** A point in duration; date; occasion; especially, the hour of death or of travail: Your *time* has come! **11** A portion of duration considered as having some quality or experience of its own, personal or general: in the latter sense usually in the plural: *Times* are hard. **12** A system of reckoning or measuring duration, especially with reference to the rotation and revolution of the earth, or to the movements of the celestial bodies. See also DAYLIGHT-SAVING TIME, STANDARD TIME, and lists given below. **13** A case of recurrence or repetition: many a *time*, three *times* a day. **14** The temporal relation of a verb. **15** *Music* **a** The characteristic tempo suited to a particular style of composition. **b** The division of musical composition into measures of equal length; rhythm: common *time*, triple *time*. Rhythms which are divisible by two are called **duple** or **common time**, as 2/2, 2/4, 2/8, 4/2, 4/4, 4/8, etc. Rhythms which are divisible by three are called **triple time**, as 3/2, 3/4, 3/8. **Compound triple times** are 9/4, 9/8, 9/16, 5/4, and 5/8. **16** A measured interval in verse; a unit of duration in rhythmical utterance; a mora. **17** One of the Aristotelian unities of the drama. See under UNITY. **18** Period during which work has been, or remains to be done; also, the amount of pay due one, especially on an hourly rate: *time* and a half for overtime. **19** Rate of movement, as in dancing, marching, etc.; tempo. **20** *pl.* In arithmetic, the fact or process of being multiplied or added to or by: Five *times* four is twenty; also, the multiplication sign ×. **21** Fit or proper occasion: This is no *time* to quibble. **— at the same time 1** At the same moment. **2** Despite that; however; nevertheless. **— at times** Now and then. **— to bring to time** To call to account; discipline; force to conform. **— to have a time** To experience unusual pleasure, difficulty, etc. **— high time** The expiration of, or a time past the expiration of, a period of which something should have been accomplished. **— in time 1** While time permits or lasts; before it is too late. **2** In the progress of time; ultimately. **— to keep time 1** To indicate time correctly, as a clock; run in time, as a train. **2** To make regular or rhythmic movements in unison with another or others. **3** To render a musical composition in proper time or rhythm. **4** To make a record of the number of hours worked by an employee or employees. **— to make a fuss** To make a fuss or to-do. **— to make time 1** To gain time; especially, to make up for lost time by extra speed, as a train. **2** To perform, achieve, or arrive in a certain time: to *make* good *time*. **3** *Slang* To impress or influence favorably: with *with*. **— on time 1** Promptly; according to schedule: The train left *on time*. **2** Paid for, or to be paid for, later or in instalments. **— adj. 1** Of or pertaining to time. **2** Devised so as to operate, explode, etc., at a specified time: a *time* bomb, *time* lock. **3** Payable at, or to be paid for at, a future date. **— v.t. timed, tim·ing 1** To regulate as to time. **2** To cause to correspond in time: They *timed* their steps to the music. **3** To choose or arrange the time or occasion for: He *timed* his arrival for five o'clock. **4** To mark the rhythm or measure of. **5** To assign metrical or rhythmic qualities to (a syllable or note). **6** To ascertain or record the speed or duration of: to *time* a horse or a race. [OE *tīma*]
— civil time (or **civil day**) The 24-hour period extending from midnight to midnight: generally divided into two sections of 12 hours each, but in navigation, aeronautics, and other technical uses reckoned from 0 (midnight) to 24 hours. The same reckoning now applies to *astronomical time.*
— Greenwich mean time See CIVIL TIME.
— Greenwich time Time as reckoned from the zero meridian of Greenwich, England. To each hour in advance of, or behind, Greenwich time there corresponds a difference of 15 degrees longitude east or west of the Greenwich meridian.
— mean time Time reckoned from the hour angle of the mean sun; the *mean solar day* is the 24-hour interval between two successive lower transits of the mean sun across the

meridian of a place and corresponds exactly with civil time.
— solar time Time reckoned from the hour angle of the central point of the sun's disk; the *apparent solar day* is the slightly variable interval between two successive lower transits of the sun across the meridian of a place, noon being the moment of upper transit or the hour angle plus 12 hours.
— zone time Time corresponding to that within a zone of 7 1/2 degrees on either side of a meridian; used in the determination of a ship's longitude.
Synonyms (noun): age, date, duration, epoch, era, period, season, sequence, succession. *Sequence* and *succession* apply to events viewed as following one another; *time* and *duration* denote something conceived of as enduring while events take place and acts are done. According to the necessary conditions of human thought, events are contained in *time* as objects are in space, *time* existing before the event, measuring it as it passes, and still existing when the event is past. *Duration* and *succession* are more general words than *time*; we can speak of infinite or eternal *duration* or *succession*, but *time* is commonly contrasted with eternity. *Time* is measured or measurable *duration*.

time-card (tīm′kärd′) *n.* A card for recording the time of arrival and departure of an employee.

time clock A clock equipped for automatically recording times of arrival and departure, or for actuating release mechanisms, as on vault doors, etc.

time exposure *Phot.* A film exposure made at spaced intervals by two separate manual operations of the shutter instead of automatically.

time immemorial A considerable and indefinite length of time; specifically, in law, time beyond legal memory, now reckoned at twenty years: the period of the statute of limitations relating to reality.

time-keep·er (tīm′kē′pər) *n.* **1** One who or that which keeps time. **2** One who declares the time in a race, game, athletic match, etc., or records the hours worked by employees. **3** A railroad train starter. **4** A timepiece.

time·less (tīm′lis) *adj.* **1** Independent of, or unaffected by, time; unending. **2** *Archaic* Untimely. **3** Not assigned or limited to any special time, era, or epoch; without a date. See synonyms under ETERNAL. **— time′less·ly** *adv.* **— time′less·ness** *n.*

time lock A lock, having a clock mechanism attached, so devised as to prevent its being unlocked before a specified time.

time-out (tīm′out′) *n.* **1** A short recess requested by a team during play. **2** Any interval of rest taken during the course of a regular period of work. Also **time out.**

time·piece (tīm′pēs′) *n.* A chronometer; a clock, or watch.

tim·er (tī′mər) *n.* **1** A timekeeper, or one who gives or officially records time. **2** A stopwatch, as for timing a race. **3** A device attached in an adjustable form to an internal-combustion engine so as to time the spark automatically.

time-serv·er (tīm′sûr′vər) *n.* One who yields to the apparent demands of the time, without reference to principle; a temporizer. Also **time′pleas′er** (-plē′zər). **— time′-serv′ing** *adj. & n.*

time-shar·ing (tīm′shâr′ing) *n.* **1** simultaneous use of a single large computer by many people at one time through individual terminals. **2** Joint use of a condominium or other vacation property, whereby each user occupies the property for a specified portion of the year.

time signature *Music* A sign placed at the beginning of a composition, immediately after the key signature, to indicate the rhythm or time.

Times Square A square in New York City formed by the intersection of Broadway and Seventh Avenue, extending from 42nd to 45th street; by extension, the area around it, the city's entertainment district.

time-ta·ble (tīm′tā′bəl) *n.* A tabular statement of the times at which certain things, as arrivals and departures of trains, boats, high and low tides, etc., are to take place.

time-work (tīm′wûrk′) *n.* Work paid for on the basis of a set wage per hour, day, week, etc. —

time′work′er *n.*

time-worn (tīm′wôrn′, -wōrn′) *adj.* Showing the ravages of time; affected by time.

time zone One of the 24 established divisions or sectors into which the globe is divided for convenience in reckoning standard time from the meridian of Greenwich: each sector represents 15 degrees of longitude, or a time interval of 1 hour. See table below. See also STANDARD TIME.

WORLD TIME ZONES

Each zone comprises (with certain geographic adjustments) an area 7½ degrees on each side of the reference longitude from Greenwich, and the zone number is equivalent to the number of hours later (−) or earlier (+) than Greenwich time. The places given in parentheses are for convenience of reference.

Zone No. East of Greenwich		Longitude from Greenwich	Zone No. West of Greenwich	
0	(Greenwich)	0°	0	(Greenwich)
− 1	(Berlin)	15°	+ 1	(Iceland)
− 2	(Leningrad)	30°	+ 2	(Azores)
− 3	(Baghdad)	45°	+ 3	(Rio de Janeiro)
− 4	(Bokhara)	60°	+ 4	(Halifax)
− 5	(Bombay)	75°	+ 5	(Washington)
− 6	(Lhasa)	90°	+ 6	(Chicago)
− 7	(Singapore)	105°	+ 7	(Denver)
− 8	(Manila)	120°	+ 8	(Vancouver)
− 9	(Kyoto)	135°	+ 9	(Dawson)
− 10	(Melbourne)	150°	+ 10	(Tahiti)
− 11	(Kamchatka)	165°	+ 11	(Nome)
− 12	(Fiji Is.)	180°	+ 12	(Samoa)

(International Date Line)

tim·id (tim′id) *adj.* Shrinking from danger or publicity; easily frightened; shy; lacking self-confidence. See synonyms under FAINT, PUSILLANIMOUS. [< L *timidus* < *timere* fear] **— ti·mid·i·ty** (ti·mid′ə·tē), **tim′id·ness** *n.* **— tim′id·ly** *adv.*

tim·ing (tī′ming) *n.* **1** In music, oratory, acting, etc., the act or art of regulating the speed of performance, utterance, etc., so as to accentuate the impressiveness of certain parts; also, the effect produced by such regulation. **2** In certain sports, as swimming, boxing, etc., the regulation of the speed of a blow or stroke so that it reaches its highest effectiveness at just the right moment.

WORLD TIME ZONES
The system of keeping standard time at sea has been adopted by most of the world's navies.

ti·moc·ra·cy (tī·mok′rə·sē) *n. pl.* **·cies 1** A state in which the honor attaching to the position of ruler becomes an object of contention, and is sought by the ambitious with intrigue, rather than accepted as a trust. **2** A state in which honors are bestowed according to property owned. [< OF *tymocracie* < Med. L *timocratia* < Gk. *timokratia* < *timē* honor + *krateein* rule] **— ti·mo·crat·ic** (tī′mə·krat′ik) or **·i·cal** *adj.*

tim·or·ous (tim′ər·əs) *adj.* **1** Fearful of danger; timid. **2** Indicating or produced by fear. See synonyms under PUSILLANIMOUS. [< OF *timoureus, temeros* < Med. L *timorosus,* ult. < L *timor, -oris* fear] **— tim′or·ous·ly** *adv.* **— tim′or·ous·ness** *n.*

tim·pa·ni (tim′pə·nē) *n. pl. sing.* **·pa·no** (-pə·nō) Kettledrums; a set of kettledrums in an orchestra: also spelled *tympani.* [< Ital., pl. of *timpano* < L *tympanum* a drum < Gk. *tympanon*] **— tim′pa·nist** *n.*

tin (tin) *n.* **1** A metallic element (symbol Sn,

atomic number 50) having at least two allotropic forms, the more common being a soft, lustrous, white metal used in making alloys and protective coatings. See PERIODIC TABLE. **2** Tin plate. **3** An article of tinware; a box or container made of tin. **4** *Brit.* A tin container for preserved foods; a can. **5** *Slang* Money. —*v.t.* **tinned, tin·ning 1** To coat or cover with tin or tin plate. **2** To pack or put up in tins. —*adj.* Made of tin [OE]

tin·a·mou (tin′ə·mōō) *n.* Any of certain South American birds (family *Tinamidae*), resembling quails, and hunted as game birds. [< F < Cariban *tinamu*]

tinct (tingkt) *v.t.* To tinge; tint. —*adj. Poetic* Slightly tinged. —*n.* **1** *Poetic* A tint. **2** *Obs.* A tincture; specifically, the elixir vitae. [< L *tinctus,* pp. of *tingere* dye, color]

tinc·to·ri·al (tingk·tôr′ē·əl, -tō′rē-) *adj.* **1** Of or pertaining to color or hue. **2** Affording or imbuing with tint or color. [< L *tinctorius* < *tinctus.* See TINCT.]

tinc·ture (tingk′chər) *n.* **1** A solution, usually in alcohol, of some principle used in medicine. **2** A tinge of color; tint. **3** A slight flavor superadded; modicum; spice. **4** That part of a substance which is extracted by a solvent. **5** One of the metals, colors, or furs used in heraldic description. —*v.t.* **·tured, ·tur·ing 1** To impart a slight hue or tinge to. **2** To imbue with flavor, odor, etc. **3** To imbue with a specified moral or mental quality. [< L *tinctura* a dyeing < *tinctus.* See TINCT.]

tin·der (tin′dər) *n.* Any readily combustible substance, as charred linen or touchwood, that will ignite (without explosion) on contact with a spark. [OE *tynder*] —**tin′der·y** *adj.*

tin·der·box (tin′dər·boks′) *n.* **1** A portable metallic box containing tinder, and usually flint and steel to ignite it. **2** A highly inflammable mass of material. **3** A person with an easily excitable temper.

tine (tīn) *n.* A spike or prong, as of a fork or of an antler. [OE *tind*] —**tined** *adj.*

tin·e·a (tin′ē·ə) *n.* **1** Any of a genus (*Tinea*) of small, narrow-winged moths, including the case-making clothes moth (*T. pellionella*). **2** *Pathol.* Ringworm; any fungous skin disease. [<NL <L, a moth, gnawing worm]

tin·e·id (tin′ē·id) *adj.* Of or pertaining to a family (*Tineidae*) of moths. —*n.* One of the *Tineidae.* [<NL < *Tinea* TINEA]

tin·foil (tin′foil′) *n.* Tin or an alloy of tin made into thin sheets for use as wrapping material and in decoration.

ting (ting) *n.* A single high metallic sound, as of a small bell. —*v.t. & v.i.* To give forth or cause to give forth a ting. [Imit.]

tinge (tinj) *v.t.* **tinged, tinge·ing** or **ting·ing 1** To imbue with a faint trace of color; impart a tint to. **2** To impart a slight characteristic quality of some other element to. See synonyms under STAIN. —*n.* **1** A faint trace of added color. **2** A quality or peculiar characteristic imparted to something by the slight admixture of some foreign element. [< L *tingere* dye]

tin·gle (ting′gəl) *v.* **·gled, ·gling** *v.i.* **1** To experience a prickly, stinging sensation, as the skin from exposure to cold, or the ears from a sharp blow. **2** To cause such a sensation. —*v.t.* **3** To cause to tingle. —*n.* **1** A prickly, stinging sensation; a tingling. **2** A jingle or tinkling. [Appar. var. of TINKLE] —**tin′gler** *n.* —**tin′gly** *adj.*

tink·er (tingk′ər) *n.* **1** An itinerant mender of domestic tin utensils, as pots and pans. **2** Loosely, one who does repairing work of any kind; a jack-of-all-trades. **3** A clumsy workman; a botcher. **4** The act of roughly repairing; hasty workmanship. **5** A young mackerel about two years old. **6** The chub mackerel. **7** The razor-billed auk. —*v.i.* **1** To work as a tinker. **2** To work in a clumsy, makeshift fashion on anything. **3** To potter; fuss. —*v.t.* **4** To mend as a tinker. **5** To repair clumsily or inexpertly. [Var. of earlier *tinekere* a worker in tin]

tin·kle (ting′kəl) *v.* **·kled, ·kling** *v.i.* **1** To produce slight, sharp, metallic sounds, as a small bell. —*v.t.* **2** To cause to tinkle. **3** To summon or signal by a tinkling. —*n.* A sharp, clear, tinkling sound. [Freq. of TINK] —**tin′kling** *adj. & n.* —**tin′kly** *adj.*

tin·ner (tin′ər) *n.* **1** A miner employed in tin

mines. **2** A maker of or dealer in tinware; a tinsmith.

tin·ni·tus (ti·nī′təs) *n. Pathol.* A subjective ringing, rushing, or buzzing sound in the ears, not caused by any external stimulus. [<NL <L < *tinnire* ring]

tin·ny (tin′ē) *adj.* **·ni·er, ·ni·est 1** Pertaining to, composed of, or abounding in tin. **2** Sounding as if a tin pan were being struck: a *tinny* sound. **3** Tasting of tin, as food from a can. —**tin′ni·ly** *adv.* —**tin′ni·ness** *n.*

tin-pan (tin′pan′) *adj.* Noisy; clanging; inharmonious; tinny. Also **tin′-pan′ny.**

tin-plate (tin′plāt′) *v.t.* **·plat·ed, ·plat·ing** To plate with tin. —**tin′-plat′er** *n.*

tin plate Sheet iron or steel plated with tin.

tin·sel (tin′səl) *n.* **1** Very thin glittering bits of brass, copper, and other cheap metals, used for display and to ornament articles of dress; also, the thin metal from which they are cut. **2** A fabric in which such spangles or bits of metal are woven, or to which they are attached; also, a fabric or yarn containing gold or silver thread. **3** Anything sparkling and showy, with little real worth; superficial adornment and brilliancy. —*adj.* **1** Made or covered with tinsel. **2** Of tinsel-like qualities; superficially brilliant; tawdry. —*v.t.* **·seled** or **·selled, ·sel·ing** or **·sel·ling 1** To adorn or decorate with or as with tinsel. **2** To give a metallic appearance to (ceramic ware) by washing with a metallic substance. [<MF *étincelle* <OF *estincelle* <L *scintilla* a spark]

tin·smith (tin′smith′) *n.* One who works with tin or tin plate.

tin spirits *Chem.* A solution of a tin salt in acid, used in dyeing.

tint (tint) *n.* **1** A variety of color; tincture; specifically, a tendency toward or slight admixture of a different color; tinge: red with a blue *tint.* **2** A gradation or shading of a color made by dilution with white to lessen its chroma and saturation. **3** Any color having a brilliance higher than that of median gray. **4** In engraving, an effect of light, shade, texture, etc., produced by the spacing of lines or by hatching. **5** An impression from a block bearing a design to be printed in a faint color as a background: used on checks as a safeguard against erasure. —*v.t.* **1** To give a tint to; tinge. **2** In engraving, to form a tint upon. See synonyms under STAIN. [Alter. of TINCT; ? infl. in form by Ital. *tinta* color] —**tint′er** *n.*

tin·tin·nab·u·lar (tin′ti·nab′yə·lər) *adj.* Characterized by tinkling, as of bells. Also **tin′tin·nab·u·lar′y, tin′tin·nab′u·lous.**

tin·type (tin′tīp′) *n.* A photograph taken on a sensitized film supported on a thin sheet of enameled tin or iron; a ferrotype.

tin·work (tin′wûrk′) *n.* **1** Articles made of tin; work with tin. **2** *pl.* A place or establishment where tin is manufactured or mined.

ti·ny (tī′nē) *adj.* **·ni·er, ·ni·est** Very small; minute; wee. See synonyms under LITTLE, MINUTE², SMALL. [< obs. *tine* a small amount, bit + -Y³; ult. origin unknown]

-tion *suffix of nouns* **1** Action or process of: *rejection.* **2** Condition or state of being: *completion.* **3** Result of: *connection.* Also *-ation,* *-cion, -ion, -sion, -xion.* [<F *-tion* <OF *-cion* <L *-tio, -tionis*]

tip¹ (tip) *n.* A slanting or inclined position; a tilt. —*v.* **tipped, tip·ping** *v.t.* **1** To cause to lean by lowering or raising one end or side; cant; tilt. **2** To overturn or upset: often with *over.* —*v.i.* **3** To become tilted; slant. **4** To overturn; topple: with *over.* [ME *tipen* overturn; origin unknown] —**tip′per** *n.*

Synonyms (verb): cant, careen, heel, incline, lean, list, slant, slope, tilt. To *tilt* or *tip* is to throw out of a horizontal position by raising one side or end or lowering the other. *Slant* and *slope* are said of things somewhat fixed or permanent in a position out of the horizontal or perpendicular: the roof *slants,* the hill *slopes. Incline* is a more formal word for *tip,* and also for *slant* or *slope.* To *cant* is to set slantingly; in many cases *tip* and *cant* might be interchanged, but *tip* is more temporary, often momentary; one *tips* a pail so that the water flows over the edge; a mechanic *cants* a table by making or setting one side higher than the other. *Careen, heel,* and *list* are used of vessels which from any cause, as leakage, shifting of cargo, etc., are off an even keel.

tip² (tip) *v.t.* **tipped, tip·ping 1** To strike lightly, or with something light; tap. **2** In baseball, to strike (the ball) a light, glancing blow. —*n.* A tap; light blow. [Earlier *tippe,* prob. <LG. Cf. Du. *tippen* tap.]

tip³ (tip) *n.* ′**1** A small gift of money for services rendered, given to a servant, waiter, porter, or the like. **2** A friendly, helpful hint; specifically, secret information presumed to increase a better's or speculator's chance of winning. [< *v.*] —*v.* **tipped, tip·ping 1** To give a small gratuity to. **2** *Colloq.* To give secret information to, as in betting and speculation: often with *off.* —*v.i.* **3** To give tips. [Orig. < thieves' cant, ? <TIP²] —**tip′·per** *n.*

tip⁴ (tip) *n.* **1** The point or extremity of anything tapering; end: the *tip* of the tongue. **2** A piece or part made to form the end of anything, as a nozzle, ferrule, etc. **3** The upper part of a hat crown; also, the lining in the upper part of the crown. —*v.t.* **tipped, tip·ping 1** To furnish with a tip. **2** To form the tip of. **3** To cover or adorn the tip of. [Prob. <MDu., a point]

tip-cart (tip′kärt′) *n.* A cart having a body that can be tipped for unloading.

tip-cat (tip′kat′) *n.* A game played with a stick or bat and a small piece of wood pointed at the ends and called a *cat,* which the batter hits lightly into the air and then hits again, trying to drive it as far as possible; also, the cat. [<TIP¹ + CAT]

Tip·pe·ca·noe River (tip′ē·kə·nōō′) A river in north central Indiana, flowing 166 miles NW, west, and SW to the Wabash River near Lafayette; scene of General W. H. Harrison's victory over Indians, 1811.

tip·pet (tip′it) *n.* **1** An outdoor covering for the neck, or neck and shoulders, hanging well down in front. **2** *Eccl.* A long scarf worn by clergymen in the Anglican Church. **3** A ruff of feathers on birds, etc. [Prob. dim. of TIP⁴]

tip·ple¹ (tip′əl) *v.t. & v.i.* **·pled, ·pling** To drink (alcoholic beverages) frequently and habitually. —*n.* Liquor consumed in tippling. [Cf. Norw. *tipla* drip, tipple] —**tip′pler** *n.*

tip·ple² (tip′əl) *n.* **1** An apparatus for tipping loaded cars. **2** The place where such tipping is done. [< dial. E *tipple* topple, freq. of TIP¹]

tip·staff (tip′staf′, -stäf′) *n.* **1** *pl.* **·staffs** In England, a sheriff's subordinate; bailiff; constable; also, a court crier. **2** *pl.* **·staves** (-stāvz′) A staff having a metal tip: a badge of office. [<TIP(PED) STAFF]

tip·ster (tip′stər) *n. Colloq.* One who sells tips for betting, as on a race. [<TIP³]

tip·sy (tip′sē) *adj.* **·si·er, ·si·est 1** Befuddled with drink, but not really drunk; partially intoxicated; high. **2** Tippy; shaky; also, crooked; askew. [<TIP¹] —**tip′si·ly** *adv.* —**tip′si·ness** *n.*

tip·toe (tip′tō′) *n.* **1** The tip of a toe, or the tips of all the toes collectively. **2** Topmost height; also, alertness of expectation: usually in the phrase **to be on tiptoe** or **a-tiptoe,** to be eagerly expectant. —*v.i.* **·toed, ·toe·ing** To walk on tiptoe; go stealthily. —*adj.* **1** Standing on tiptoe. **2** Quiet; gentle; stealthy. —*adv.* On tiptoe, in any sense.

ti·rade (tī′rād, tə·rād′) *n.* **1** A prolonged declamatory outpouring, as of censure. **2** *Music* A diatonic run, filling the interval between two musical notes. [<F < Ital. *tirata* a volley, pp. of *tirare* fire, pull]

ti·rail·leur (tir′ə·lûr′, *Fr.* tē·rá·yœr′) *n.* A sharpshooter; skirmisher. [<F]

Ti·ra·na (tē·rä′nə) The capital of Albania, in the central part. Also **Ti·ra′në.**

tire¹ (tīr) *v.* **tired, tir·ing** *v.t.* **1** To reduce the strength of, as by toil; weary; fatigue. **2** To reduce the interest or patience of, as with tediousness. —*v.i.* **3** To become weary or exhausted. **4** To lose patience, interest, etc. —**to tire of** To become weary of or impatient with. —**to tire out** To weary completely. —*n. Dial.* The sensation of fatigue; weariness. [OE *tiorian, tēorian*]

Synonyms (verb): exhaust, fag, fatigue, harass, jade, weary. To *tire* is to reduce one's strength in any degree by exertion; one may be *tired* just enough to make rest pleasant, or even unconsciously *tired,* becoming aware of the fact only when he ceases the exertion. One who is *fatigued* suffers from painful lack of strength as the result of overtaxing; an invalid may be *fatigued* with very slight exertion; when one is *wearied*, the painful lack of strength is the result of long-continued demand or strain; one is *exhausted* when the strain has been so severe and continuous as utterly to consume the strength, so that further exertion is for the time impossible. One is *fagged* by drudgery; he is *jaded* by incessant repetition of the same act until it becomes increasingly difficult or well-nigh impossible; as, a horse is *jaded* by a long and unbroken journey. See WEAR[1].

tire[2] (tīr) *n.* **1** A band or hoop surrounding the rim of a wheel. **2** A flexible tube, usually of inflated rubber, set in a rim and protected by an outer covering: used on automobiles, bicycles, etc., to reduce vibration. —*v.t.* **tired, tir·ing** To furnish with a tire; put a tire on. Also, *Brit.*, **tyre.** [Special use of TIRE[4]]

tire[3] (tīr) *Archaic v.t.* **1** In falconry, to rend and devour; draw; pull. —*v.i.* **2** To prey. **3** To be preoccupied; dote; gloat. [< OF *tirer*; ult. origin uncertain]

tire[4] (tīr) *Obs. v.t.* To attire; dress; adorn. —*n.* **1** A tiara; headdress. **2** Attire. [Aphetic var. of AT-TIRE]

tire[5] (tīr) *n.* A volley of cannon; a broadside. [< OF *tir* < *tirer* draw, shoot; ult. origin uncertain]

tired (tīrd) *adj.* Weary; exhausted; jaded; fatigued. [Orig. pp. of TIRE[1]] —**tired′ly** *adv.* —**tired′ness** *n.*

tire·less (tīr′lis) *adj.* Proof against fatigue; untiring. See synonyms under INDEFATIGABLE. [< TIRE[1] + -LESS] —**tire′less·ly** *adv.* —**tire′less·ness** *n.*

tire·some (tīr′səm) *adj.* Tending to tire, or causing one to tire; tedious. See synonyms under TEDIOUS, TROUBLESOME, WEARISOME. —**tire′some·ly** *adv.* —**tire′some·ness** *n.*

tire-wom·an (tīr′wŏŏm′ən) *n. pl.* **·wom·en** (-wim′in) *Obs.* A lady's maid; an abigail. Also **tir′ing-wom′an.** [< TIRE[4] + WOMAN]

'tis (tiz) It is: a contraction.

ti·sane (ti-zan′, *Fr.* tē-zàn′) *n.* a slightly medicated decoction, usually of herbs, prepared for the sick; a ptisan. [< F < L *ptisana* a ptisan]

Tish·ri (tish′rē) The first month of the Hebrew calendar. See CALENDAR (Hebrew). Also **Tis·ri** (tiz′rē). [< Hebrew < Aramaic *tishrī* < *sherā* begin; infl. by Babylonian *tashrītu* the seventh month, first month of the second half of the year]

tis·sue (tish′ōō) *n.* **1** Any light or gauzy textile fabric, usually of silk; originally, cloth interwoven with gold or silver thread. **2** *Biol.* One of the elementary aggregates of cells and their products, developed by plants and animals for the performance of a particular function: connective *tissue*. **3** A connected or interwoven series; chain; fabrication: a *tissue* of lies. **4** Tissue paper. —*v.t.* **·sued, ·su·ing** *Rare* **1** To make into tissue. **2** To adorn with tissue; weave. [< OF *tissu* a rich stuff, orig. pp. of *tistre* weave < L *texere*]

tissue culture The science and art of growing body tissues in a culture medium.

tis·sued (tish′ōōd) *adj.* **1** Clad in tissue. **2** Variegated.

tissue paper Very thin, unsized, almost transparent paper for wrapping delicate articles, protecting engravings, etc.

tit[1] (tit) *n.* **1** A titmouse. **2** One of various other small birds, as a titlark, etc. [Short for TITMOUSE, TITLARK, etc.]

tit[2] (tit) *n.* A light blow; tap: chiefly in the phrase *tit for tat.* [Var. of TIP[2]]

tit[3] (tit) *n.* Teat; breast; nipple. [OE *titt*]

tit[4] (tit) *n.* **1** A small or worn-out horse; a nag. **2** *Slang* A young woman or girl: a disrespectful term. [ME, a little thing, ? < Scand. Cf. dial. Norw. *titta* little girl.]

ti·tan (tīt′n) *n.* Any person having gigantic strength or size; a giant. —*adj.* Titanic. [after *Tītan*] —**ti′tan·ess** *n. fem.*

Ti·tan (tīt′n) **1** In Greek mythology, one of a race of giant gods, children of Uranus and Gaea, who were vanquished and succeeded by the Olympian gods, who imprisoned them in Tartarus. **2** Helios: so called by some Latin poets.

ti·tan·ate (tīt′ə-nāt) *n. Chem.* A salt or ester of titanic acid. [< TITAN(IC)[2] + -ATE[3]]

ti·tan·ic[1] (tī-tan′ik) *adj.* Gigantic; huge; tremendous. [< Gk. *titanikos* < *Titanes* the Titans]

ti·tan·ic[2] (tī-tan′ik, ti-) *adj. Chem.* Of or pertaining to titanium, especially in its higher valence. [< TITAN(IUM) + -IC]

titanic acid *Chem.* **1** A white pulverulent titanium dioxide, TiO₂, found native as rutile, etc.: a common constituent of iron ores: also **titanic oxide. 2** One of various weak acids derived from titanium ioxide.

ti·tan·if·er·ous (tīt′ən-if′ər-əs) *adj.* Containing or yielding titanium. [< TITAN(IUM) + -(I)FER-OUS]

ti·tan·ite (tīt′ən-īt) *n.* Sphene. [< G *titanit* < *titanium* titanium]

ti·ta·ni·um (tī-tā′nē-əm) *n.* An abundant, light, strong, lustrous metallic element (symbol Ti, atomic number 22), never found uncombined, used in certain alloys. See PERIODIC TABLE. [< NL < L *Titani* the Titans < Gk. *Titanes*; named on analogy with *uranium*]

ti·tan·o·there (tī′tən-ə-thir′, tī-tā′nə-, ti-) *n. Paleontol.* Any of an extinct family (*Titanotheri·idae*) of large, odd-toed ungulates resembling the rhinoceros and common in the Lower Eocene of the Tertiary period. [< NL < Gk. *Titan* a Titan + *thērion*, dim. of *thēr* a wild beast]

ti·tan·ous (tīt′ən-əs, tī-tan′əs, ti-) *adj. Chem.* Of or pertaining to titanium, especially in its lower valence. [< TITAN(IUM) + -OUS[2]]

ti·ter (tīt′ər, tē′-) *n. Chem.* **1** The strength or concentration of a solution as determined by titration. **2** The temperature at which a molten fatty acid or wax solidifies. Also spelled *titre*. [< F *titre* the fineness of gold or silver alloy]

tit for tat Retaliation in kind; blow for blow. [? Alter. of *tip for tap*; ? infl. in form by MF *tant pour tant* tit for tat]

tith·a·ble (tī′thə-bəl) *adj.* Liable to be tithed, as property.

tithe (tīth) *n.* **1** A tax or assessment of one tenth, especially when payable in kind; loosely, any ratable tax. **2** Specifically, in England, a tenth part of the yearly proceeds arising from lands and from the personal industry of the inhabitants, for the support of the clergy and the church. **3** The tenth part of anything; hence, a small part. —*v.t.* **tithed, tith·ing 1** To give or pay a tithe, or tenth part of. **2** To tax with tithes. [ME *tithe, tethe*, OE *tēotha, tēogotha* a tenth] —**tith′er** *n.*

tith·ing (tī′thing) *n.* **1** The act of levying tithes. **2** A tenth part. **3** In old English law, a civil division composed of ten freeholders and their families.

tith·ing·man (tī′thing·mən) *n. pl.* **·men** (-mən) **1** Anciently, in England, the chief of a tithing; more recently, a constable. **2** In the New England colonies, an officer for enforcing Sunday observance and order.

ti·ti[1] (tē′tē) *n.* **1** An evergreen or small tree (*Cliftonia monophylla*) with fragrant white flowers, native in swamps of the southern United States. **2** Any of a genus (*Cyrilla*) of related trees of tropical America; especially, the **white titi** (*C. racemiflora*). [< Sp. < Aymaran]

ti·ti[2] (tē-tē′) *n.* One of several small South American monkeys (genus *Callicebus*). [< Sp. *titi* < Guarani *titi*]

ti·tian (tish′ən) *n.* A reddish-yellow color much used by Titian, especially in painting women's hair. —*adj.* Having or pertaining to the color of titian. [after *Titian*]

Ti·ti·ca·ca (tē′tē-kä′kä), **Lake** The largest lake in South America, in the Andes between SE Peru and west central Bolivia; 3,200 square miles; elevation, 12,500 feet; the highest large lake in the world.

tit·il·lant (tit′ə-lənt) *n.* An excitant. [< L *titillans, -antis*, ppr. of *titillare* tickle]

tit·il·late (tit′ə-lāt) *v.t.* **·lat·ed, ·lat·ing 1** To cause a tickling sensation in. **2** To excite pleasurably in any way. [< L *titillatus*, pp. of *titillare* tickle]

tit·i·vate (tit′ə-vāt) *v.t. & v.i.* **·vat·ed, ·vat·ing** *Colloq.* To put on decorative touches; smarten; dress up: also spelled *tittivate*. [Earlier *tidivate, tiddivate*. ? < TIDY, on analogy with *cultivate*] —**tit′i·va′tion** *n.*

ti·tle (tīt′l) *n.* **1** *Law* **a** The means whereby the owner of lands has the just possession of his property; the union of possession, the right of possession, and the right of property in lands and tenements; also, the legal evidence of one's right of property, or the means by or source from which one's right to property has accrued: *title* by purchase. **b** The distinguishing form of words that heads or opens a legal document or statute; also, the opening clause containing the name of the court in which any action is pending, together with the names of the parties, etc. A claim based on an acknowledged or alleged right: What is his *title* to credence? **3** A section or division of a statute, legal document, treatise, or the like. **4** An inscription that serves as a name for designating something, as a book or legal document. **5** A name; descriptive designation. **6** An appellation significant of office, rank, etc.; especially, a designation of nobility. **7** In or near Rome, a church or parish headed by a cardinal: so called because dedicated to or named after the title of some martyr or saint. **8** A source of maintenance, as a patrimony, or a place of duty, especially with income attached, a right or nomination to which is a canonical prerequisite to ordination. **9** In some sports, supremacy; championship: to play for the *title*. See synonyms under NAME. —*v.t.* **·tled, ·tling 1** To give a name to; entitle; call. **2** To confer an honorary title upon; ennoble. [< OF < L *titulus* a label, an inscription. Doublet of TITTLE.] —**ti′tle·less** *adj.*

title page A page containing the title of a work and the names of its author and its publisher.

title role The character in a play, opera, or motion picture for whom it is named.

tit·mouse (tit′mous′) *n. pl.* **·mice** (-mīs′) Any of several small oscine birds (family *Paridae*) related to the nuthatches; especially, the **tufted titmouse** (*Baeolophus bicolor*) of the United States, having a conspicuous crest. [Alter. of ME *titmose* < *tit-* little + *mose*, alter. of OE *māse* a titmouse; infl. in form by MOUSE]

TITMOUSE
(About 5 1/2 inches long)

Ti·to (tē′tō), **Marshal,** 1891?–1980, Yugoslav guerrilla leader in World War II; premier 1945–53; president 1953–80; real name *Josip Broz*.

Ti·to·grad (tē′tô-gräd) The capital of Montenegro in southern Yugoslavia: formerly **Pod·go·ri·ca** (pod′gô-rē′tsä).

ti·trate (tī′trāt, tit′rāt) *v.t. & v.i.* **·trat·ed, ·trat·ing** *Chem.* To determine the strength of (a solution) by means of standard solutions or by titration. [< F *titrer* < *titre*. See TITER.]

ti·tra·tion (tī-trā′shən, ti-) *n. Chem.* The process of determining the strength or concentration of a given solution by adding to it measured amounts of a standard solution until the desired chemical reaction has been effected.

tit·ter (tit′ər) *v.i.* To laugh in a suppressed way, as from nervousness or in ridicule; snicker; giggle. —*n.* The act of tittering; a giggling. [Imit.] —**tit′ter·er** *n.* —**tit′ter·ing·ly** *adv.*

tit·tle (tit′l) *n.* **1** The minutest quantity; iota. **2** Originally, a very small mark in writing, as the dot over an *i*, etc.; any diacritical mark. [< L *titulus*. Doublet of TITLE.]

tit·tup (tit′əp) *v.i.* **·tuped or ·tupped, ·tup·ing or ·tup·ping** To act in a restless or lively manner; dance along; prance. —*n.* A prancing or curveting action, indicating gaiety or frolicsomeness; a caper. [Appar. imit. of hoof beats]

tit·u·ba·tion (tich′ŏŏ-bā′shən, tit′yə-) *n. Pathol.* A stumbling; tottering; a disturbance of equilibrium resulting in the stumbling gait characteristic of spinal disease. [< L *titubatio, -onis* < *titubatus*, pp. of *titubare* stagger]

tit·u·lar (tich'ŏŏ·lər, tit'yə-) *adj.* **1** Existing in name or title only; nominal. **2** Pertaining to a title. **3** Bestowing or taking title. See TITLE (def. 8). —*n.* One having a title in virtue of which he holds an office or benefice, whether he performs its duties or not; in ecclesiastical law, one holding a sinecure title. Also **tit'u·lar'y** (-ler'ē). [< L *titulus* a title] —**tit'u·lar·ly** *adv.*

Tlax·ca·la (tläs·kä'lä) A state of central Mexico; 1,555 square miles; capital, Tlaxcala.

Tm *Chem.* Thulium (symbol Tm).

tme·sis (tmē'sis, mē'sis) *n.* The separation of the elements of a compound word by an intervening word, as in the phrase *to us ward,* meaning "toward us." [< L < Gk. *tmēsis* a cutting < *temnein* cut]

to (tŏŏ, *unstressed* tə) *prep.* **1** In a direction toward or terminating in: going *to* town. **2** Opposite, in contact with, or near: face *to* face; Hold me *to* your breast. **3** Intending or aiming at; having as an object or purpose: Come *to* my rescue. **4** Resulting in; having as a condition or effect: frozen *to* death; flattered *to* his ruin. **5** Belonging in connection or accompaniment with; denoting the relation of things made to go together or between which there is correspondence: the key *to* the barn; March *to* the music. **6** In honor of: Drink *to* me only with thine eyes. **7** In comparison, correspondence, or agreement with: often denoting ratio: 9 is *to* 3 as 21 *to* 7; four quarts *to* the gallon. **8** Until; approaching as a limit; denoting the end of a period of time, or a time not reached: *to* my dying day; five minutes *to* one. **9** For the utmost duration of; as far as: a miser *to* the end of his days. **10** In respect of; concerning: blind *to* her charms; a speech *to* the point. **11** In close application toward: Buckle down *to* work; Fall *to* dinner. **12** For; with regard for: The contest is open *to* everyone. **13** Noting an indirect or limiting object after verbs, adjectives, or nouns, and designating the recipient of the action: taking the place of the dative case in other languages: Give the ring *to* me; That fact is not apparent *to* me. **14** By: known *to* the world. **15** From the point of view of: It seems *to* me. **16** *Dial.* At or in (a place): He is not *to* home now. **17** *Colloq.* With: The land was planted *to* potatoes. **18** About; involved in: That's all there is *to* it. ◆ *To* also serves to indicate the infinitive, and is often used elliptically for it: You may come if you care *to.* See synonyms under AT, INTO. —*adv.* **1** To or toward something. **2** In a direction, position, or state understood or implied; especially, shut or closed: Pull the door *to.* **3** Into a normal condition; into consciousness: She soon came *to.* **4** *Naut.* With head to the wind: said of a sailing vessel: to lie *to.* **5** Upon the matter at hand; into action or operation: They fell *to* with good will. **6** Nearby; at hand. —**to and fro** In opposite or different directions; back and forth. [OE *tō*]

toad (tōd) *n.* **1** A tailless, jumping, insectivorous amphibian (family *Bufonidae*), resembling the frog but without teeth in the upper jaw, and resorting to water only to breed. **2** Some similar amphibian; especially, the Surinam toad *(Pipa pipa)* or the European midwife toad *(Alytes obstetricans).* **3** Any person regarded scornfully or contemptuously. [OE *tādige*]

TOAD
(Species vary from 2 to 6 inches)

toad-eat·er (tōd'ē'tər) *n.* A fawning parasite; a sycophant. [Orig. an assistant to a charlatan, who ate, or pretended to eat, toads (held to be poisonous) to show the efficacy of a patent medicine]

toad·fish (tōd'fish') *n. pl.* **·fish** or **·fish·es** Any of a family *(Batrachoididae)* of fishes with scaleless skin and mouth and head resembling those of a toad.

toad·flax (tōd'flaks') *n.* **1** A common, showy perennial weed *(Linaria vulgaris)* of the figwort family, having terminal spikes of spurred yellow flowers marked with an orange spot: also called *butter-and-eggs.* **2** Any other plant of the genus *Linaria.* [So called because spotted like toads and having a flaxlike foliage]

toad·stone[1] (tōd'stōn') *n. Dial.* A volcanic rock,

generally decomposed, occurring in limestone in Derbyshire, England. [? So called from a resemblance of its markings to those of a toad]

toad·stone[2] (tōd'stōn') *n.* A natural or artificial stone resembling a toad in color and form, and long believed to be formed in a toad: worn as a talisman. [< TOAD + STONE; trans. of L *batrachites* < Gk.]

toad·stool (tōd'stōōl') *n.* **1** Any one of many umbrella-shaped fungi, growing on decaying vegetable matter, common in woods and damp places; a mushroom. **2** *Colloq.* A poisonous mushroom.

toad·y (tō'dē) *n. pl.* **toad·ies** An obsequious flatterer; a fawning, servile person; a toad-eater. —*v.t.* & *v.i.* **toad·ied, toad·y·ing** To act the toady (to). ◆Homophone: *tody.* [Short for TOAD EATER] —**toad'y·ish** *adj.* —**toad'y·ism**

toast[1] (tōst) *v.t.* **1** To brown before or over a fire; especially, to brown (bread or cheese) before a fire or in a toaster. **2** To warm thoroughly before a fire. —*v.i.* **3** To become warm or toasted. —*n.* Sliced bread browned in a toaster or at a fire; toasted bread. [< OF *toster* roast, grill < L *tostus* < *torrere* parch, roast]

toast[2] (tōst) *n.* **1** The act of drinking to someone's health or to some sentiment. **2** The person or sentiment named in thus drinking: She was the *toast* of the town. —*v.t.* To drink to the health of or in honor of. —*v.i.* To drink a toast or toasts. [< TOAST[1] in obs. sense of "a spiced piece of toast put in a drink to flavor it"]

toast·er[1] (tōs'tər) *n.* A device for making toast.

toast·er[2] (tōs'tər) *n.* One who proposes a toast.

toast·mas·ter (tōst'mas'tər, -mäs'tər) *n.* A person who, at public dinners, announces the toasts, calls upon the various speakers, etc. —**toast' mis'tress** (-mis'tris) *n. fem.*

to·bac·co (tə·bak'ō) *n. pl.* **·cos** or **·coes 1** An annual plant of the nightshade family (genus *Nicotiana*), especially *N. tabacum,* the chief source of the tobacco of commerce, originally of tropical America, but now cultivated in various parts of the world. **2** Its leaves prepared in various ways, as for smoking, chewing, snuffing, etc. **3** The use of tobacco for smoking. **4** The various products prepared from tobacco leaves, as cigarettes, cigars, etc. [< Sp. *tabaco* < Cariban, a tube or pipe in which the natives smoked tobacco]

TOBACCO
(Plant to 8 feet or more)

tobacco heart *Pathol.* A cardiac disorder brought about by excessive smoking and characterized by a rapid or uneven pulse; nicotinism.

tobacco worm Either of two large green worms *(Protoparce sexta* and *P. quinquemaculata)* with white stripes and a slender horn at the rear end of the body, destructive to tobacco plants.

To·ba·go (tō·bā'gō) See TRINIDAD AND TOBAGO.

to·bog·gan (tə·bog'ən) *n.* **1** A light sledlike vehicle, consisting of a long thin board or boards curved upward at the forward end: used for transporting goods or coasting, especially on prepared slides. **2** A luge. —*v.i.* **1** To coast on a toboggan. **2** To move downward swiftly: Wheat prices *tobogganed.* [< dial. F (Canadian) *tabagan* a sleigh < Algonquian. Cf. Micmac *tobākun.*] —**bog'gan·er, to·bog'gan·ist** *n.*

toboggan slide A slope prepared for coasting with toboggans: often a winding track with banked curves.

to·by (tō'bē) *n. pl.* **·bies 1** A mug or jug for ale or beer, often made in the form of an old man wearing a three-cornered hat. **2** *Colloq.* A form of stogie cigar. [< TOBY]

TOBY JUG

toc·ca·ta (tə·kä'tə, *Ital.* tôk·kä'tä) *n. Music* A rapid free composition for piano, organ, or other keyboard instrument, often preceding a fugue. [< Ital., lit., a touching, orig. pp. fem. of *toccare* touch]

toco- *combining form* Child; pertaining to children or to childbirth: *tocology.* Also, before

vowels, **toc-.** [< Gk. *tokos* child, childbirth]

to·col·o·gy (tō·kol'ə·jē) *n.* The science and art of midwifery; obstetrics: also spelled *tokology.* [< TOCO- + -LOGY]

to·coph·er·ol (tō·kof'ə·rōl, -rol) *n.* Any of a group of chemically related compounds occurring naturally in many vegetable oils and including some that exhibit the biological activity of vitamin E. [< TOCO- + Gk. *pherein* bear + -OL[1]; so called because thought to be effective against sterility]

toc·sin (tok'sin) *n.* **1** A signal sounded on a bell; alarm. **2** An alarm bell. [< MF < OF *toquassen* < Provençal *tocasenh* < *tocar* strike, touch + *senh* a bell < LL *signum* a signal bell < L, a sign]

tod (tod) *n.* **1** A bushy clump. **2** A former weight for wool, about 28 pounds. [ME *todde,* prob. < LG. Cf. East Frisian *todde* small load]

to·day (tə·dā') *adv.* **1** On or during this present day. **2** At the present time; nowadays. —*n.* The present day, time, or age. Also **to-day'.** ◆ Collateral adjective: *hodiernal.* [OE *tō dœg* < *tō* to + *dœg* a day]

tod·dle (tod'l) *v.i.* **·dled, ·dling** To walk unsteadily and with short steps, as a little child. —*n.* The act of toddling; a child's walk; also, a stroll. [? Freq. of TOTTER] —**tod'dler** *n.*

tod·dy (tod'ē) *n. pl.* **·dies 1** A drink made with spirits, hot water, sugar, and a slice of lemon. **2** The sap or juice that flows from the incised spathes of certain East Indian palms; also, a spirituous liquor distilled from it. The principal palms yielding toddy are called **toddy palms,** as the wild date of India *(Phoenix sylvestris).* [< Hind. *tārī* toddy (def. 2) < *tār* palm tree < Skt. *tāla* a palmyra]

to-do (tə·dōō') *n. Colloq.* Confusion or bustle, as on account of something disturbing; a demonstration; a fuss. [OE *to-dōn* < *to-* asunder + *dōn* do, put]

to·dy (tō'dē) *n. pl.* **·dies** Any of numerous very small insectivorous West Indian birds (genus *Todus*) related to the kingfishers; especially, the **green tody** *(Todus godus)* of Jamaica, bright green with a scarlet throat. ◆Homophone: *toady.* [< F *todier* < L *todus,* a kind of small bird]

toe (tō) *n.* **1** One of the digits of the foot; also, the forward part of the foot, as distinguished from the *heel.* **2** That portion of a shoe, boot, sock, stocking, skate, or the like that covers, or corresponds in position with, the toes. **3** The lower end or projection of something, resembling or suggestive of a toe. **4** *Mech.* **a** A pivot or journal in a bearing. **b** A horizontally projecting arm on a stem, as for operating a valve, raised by a cam or lifted. **5** The end of the head of a golf club. **6** In a railroad switch, the space between the rails at the unchanneled end of a frog. —**on one's toes** Alert; wide-awake. —**to tread on (someone's) toes** To offend (a person); trespass on (someone's) feelings, opinions, prejudices, etc. —*v.* **toed, toe·ing** *v.t.* **1** To touch with the toes: to *toe* the line. **2** To kick with the toes. **3** To furnish with a toe. **4** To drive (a nail or spike) obliquely; also, to attach (beams, etc.) end to end, by nails driven thus. **5** To strike (a golf ball) with the toe of the club. —*v.i.* **6** To stand or walk with the toes pointing in a specified direction: to *toe* out. —**to toe the mark** To touch a certain line or mark with the toes preparatory to starting a race; hence, to abide by the rules; conform to discipline or a standard. [OE *tā*] —**toe'less** *adj.*

toe cap A cap covering for the tip or toe of a boot or shoe. See illustration under SHOE.

toed (tōd) *adj.* **1** Having toes: chiefly in composition: pigeon-*toed.* **2** Fastened or fastening by obliquely driven nails; also, driven obliquely, as a nail.

toe dance A dance performed on tiptoe.

toe·hold (tō'hōld') *n.* **1** In climbing, a small space which supports the toes. **2** Any means of entrance, support, or the like; a footing: The Marines gained a *toehold* on the island. **3** A hold in which a wrestler bends back the foot of his opponent.

toe·nail (tō'nāl') *n.* **1** A nail growing on the toe. **2** A nail driven obliquely to hold the foot of a stud or brace. —*v.t.* To fasten with obliquely driven nails.

toft (tôft, toft) *n. Brit.* **1** Land once occupied as a messuage, on which the buildings have decayed or been burned; a homestead. **2** A hillock or knoll. [OE, a homestead < ON *topt, tupt*]

to·fu (tō′fōō) *n.* A soft, cheeselike, protein-rich food made from soybean milk curds. [< Jap.]

tog (tog) *Colloq. n.* **1** A coat. **2** *pl.* Clothes; outfit: football *togs.* — *v.t.* **togged, tog·ging** To dress; clothe: often with *up* or *out.* [Short for vagabond's cant *togemans, togman* coat, cloak < F *toge* a toga < L *toga*]

to·ga (tō′gə) *n. pl.* ·**gas** or ·**gae** (-jē) **1** The distinctive outer garment worn in public by a citizen of ancient Rome. **2** Any gown or cloak characteristic of a calling or profession: the lawyer's *toga.* [< L *tegere* cover]

to·gaed (tō′gəd) *adj.* Robed in the toga; hence, classical and stately. Also **to·gat·ed** (tō′gā·tid).

to·ga vi·ri·lis (tō′gə vi·rī′lis) *Latin* The toga assumed by a male citizen of ancient Rome at the age of 14 as a token of manhood.

ROMAN TOGA

to·geth·er (tōō·geth′ər, tə-) *adv.* **1** Into union or contact with each other; conjointly. **2** In the same place or at the same spot; with each other; in company. **3** At the same moment of time; simultaneously. **4** Without cessation or intermission. **5** With one another; mutually. [OE *tōgœdere, tōgadore* < *tō* to + *gœdre* together. Akin to GATHER.]

to·geth·er·ness (tōō·geth′ər·nis, tə-) *n.* The state of being associated or united.

tog·gle (tog′əl) *n.* **1** A pin, or short rod, properly attached in the middle, as to a rope, and designed to be passed through a hole or eye and turned. **2** A toggle iron. **3** A toggle joint. — *v.t.* ·**gled, ·gling** To fix, fasten, or furnish with a toggle or toggles. [Prob. nautical var. of dial. *tuggle,* appar. freq. of TUG]

toggle iron A harpoon, as for killing whales, so arranged as to turn crosswise when it enters the animal's body. Also **toggle harpoon.**

toggle joint *Mech.* A joint having a central hinge like an elbow, and operable by applying the power at the junction, thus changing the direction of motion and giving indefinite mechanical pressure.

TOGGLE JOINT Level Type

toggle switch *Electr.* A switch in the form of a projecting lever whose movement through a small arc opens or closes an electric circuit.

To·go (tō′gō) An independent republic in western Africa; 22,008 square miles; capital, Lomé: formerly French Togoland, a United Nations Trust Territory. — **To′go·lese′** (-lēs, -lēz) *adj. & n.*

toil[1] (toil) *n.* **1** Fatiguing work; labor; hence, any oppressive task. **2** Any notable work accomplished by labor. **3** *Obs.* Strife; struggle. — *v.i.* **1** To work arduously; labor painfully and tiringly. **2** To progress or make one's way with slow and labored steps. — *v.t.* **3** To accomplish or obtain by toil. See synonyms under STRUGGLE. [< AF *toil* a dispute, OF *tooil* trouble < AF *toiler* strive, OF *tooillier* soil, agitate < L *tudiculare* stir about < *tudicula* a machine for bruising olives, dim. of *tudes* a mallet] — **toil′er** *n.*

Synonyms (*noun*): drudgery, labor, stent, stint, task, travail, work. *Work* is exertion of body or mind that taxes the powers for the accomplishment of some end. The term is a broad one; *work* may be light and pleasant, or severe and exhausting. *Labor* is always strenuous; it is hard *work. Toil* is still more severe. One may enjoy *work* and be cheerful in *labor,* but *toil* oppresses. *Drudgery* is often applied to menial service, but also to any *work* that is not only hard, but dull and mechanical. A *task* is a definite amount of *work* appointed and required by another; yet we sometimes speak of a *task* which one imposes upon himself; this in popular language is called a *stint* or *stent.* See TASK, WORK. *Antonyms:* amuse-

ment, ease, idleness, leisure, play, recreation, relaxation, repose, rest.

toil[2] (toil) *n.* A net, snare, or other trap: now generally used figuratively and commonly in the plural. [< MF *toiles* nets < *toile* cloth < OF *teile* < L *tela* a web]

toile (twäl) *n.* A sheer linen fabric; also, a fine cretonne with scenic designs printed in one color. [< F. See TOIL[2].]

toi·let (toi′lit) *n.* **1** A fixture in the shape of a bowl, used for urination and defecation. **2** A lavatory or watercloset; also, a bathroom. **3** The act or process of dressing oneself; formerly, especially of dressing the hair. **4** Attire; toilette; also, a toilette or costume. — *adj.* Used in dressing or grooming: *toilet* articles. [< F *toilette* orig. a cloth dressing gown, dim. of *toile* cloth. See TOIL[2].]

toi·let·ry (toi′lit·rē) *n. pl.* ·**ries** Any of the several articles used in making one's toilet, as soap, comb, brush, etc.

toi·lette (toi·let′, *Fr.* twȧ·let′) *n.* **1** The act or process of grooming oneself, usually including bathing, hair-dressing, application of cosmetics and perfume, and costuming. **2** A person's actual dress or style of dress; also, any specific costume or gown: an elaborate *toilette.* [< F. See TOILET.]

toilet water A scented liquid containing a small amount of alcohol, used in or after the bath, after shaving, etc.

To·ke·lau (tō′kə·lou′) A New Zealand island group north of Samoa; 4 square miles: also *Union Islands.*

to·ken (tō′kən) *n.* **1** Anything indicative of some other thing; a visible sign; indication; evidence: in *token* of respect. **2** A symbol: This gift is a *token* of my affection. **3** *Obs.* A signal. **4** Some tangible proof or evidence of a statement or of one's identity, authority, etc. **5** A memento; keepsake; souvenir. **6** A characteristic mark or feature. **7** A piece of metal issued as currency and having a face value greater than its actual value. **8** A piece of metal issued by a transportation company and good for one fare. See synonyms under EMBLEM, MARK[1], SIGN, TRACE[1]. — *v.t.* To evidence by a token; betoken. — *adj.* Done or given as a token, especially in partial fulfilment of an obligation or engagement: a *token* payment. [OE *tācen, tācn*]

to·kened (tō′kənd) *adj. Obs.* Marked by spots: the *tokened* pestilence. [< TOKEN, in obs. sense "a spot on the body indicating disease"]

to·ken·ism (tō′kən·iz·əm) *n.* The policy of attempting to meet certain obligations or conditions by symbolic or token efforts.

To·kyo (tō′kē·ō, *Japanese* tō·kyō) The capital of Japan, a port on **Tokyo Bay,** an inlet of the Philippine Sea in central Honshu, Japan: formerly *Edo* or *Yedo.* Also **To′ki·o.**

to·lan (tō′lan) *n.* A white crystalline unsaturated hydrocarbon, $C_{14}H_{10}$, prepared by synthesis. Also **to·lane** (tō′lān). [< TOL(UENE) + -ANE[2]]

told (tōld) Past tense and past participle of TELL.

tole[1] (tōl) *v.t.* **toled, tol·ing 1** *Dial.* To draw as with a lure; entice; decoy. **2** *Obs.* To pull; drag; draw. Also spelled *toll.* [Var. of TOLL[2]]

tole[2] (tōl) *n.* A metalware, enameled or lacquered in various colors and frequently gilded: esteemed as an ornamental material. Also **tôle.** ◆ Homophone: *toll.* [< F *tôle* sheet iron, dial. var. of *table* a table]

tol·er·a·ble (tol′ər·ə·bəl) *adj.* **1** Passably good; commonplace. **2** Endurable; capable of being borne. **3** Allowable. **4** *Colloq.* In passably good health. [< OF < L *tolerabilis* able to endure < *tolerare* endure] — **tol′er·a·ble·ness** *n.* — **tol′er·a·bly** *adv.*

tol·er·ance (tol′ər·əns) *n.* **1** The character, state, or quality of being tolerant. **2** Indulgence or forbearance in judging the opinions, customs, or acts of others; freedom from bigotry or from racial or religious prejudice. **3** The act of enduring, or the capacity for endurance. **4** *Mech.* A fractional allowance for variations from the specified standard weight, dimensions, etc., of mechanical constructions. **5** A legally permissible variation from the standard of weight, fineness, etc., of coins: also called *remedy.* **6** *Med.* Natural or acquired ability to endure without ill effects large or increasing amounts of specified sub-

stances, particularly drugs.

tol·er·ant (tol′ər·ənt) *adj.* **1** Of a long-suffering disposition. **2** Indulgent; liberal. **3** *Med.* Capable of taking with impunity unusual or excessive doses of dangerous drugs. [< F < L *tolerans, -antis,* ppr. of *tolerare* endure] — **tol′er·ant·ly** *adv.*

tol·er·ate (tol′ə·rāt) *v.t.* ·**at·ed, ·at·ing 1** To allow to be or be done without active opposition. **2** To concede, as the right to opinions or participation. **3** To bear, sustain, or be capable of enduring or sustaining. **4** *Med.* To endure, as a poisonous amount of dose, with impunity. See synonyms under ABIDE, ALLOW, ENDURE, PERMIT. [< L *toleratus,* pp. of *tolerare* endure] — **tol′er·a′tive** *adj.* — **tol′er·a′tor** *n.*

tol·er·a·tion (tol′ə·rā′shən) *n.* **1** The act or practice of tolerance. **2** The recognition of the rights of the individual to his own opinions and customs, as in matters pertaining to religious worship, when they do not interfere with the rights of others or with decency and order. **3** The spirit and desire to be tolerant in matters of opinion; forbearance; freedom from bigotry or race prejudice.

tol·i·dine (tol′ə·dēn, -din) *n. Chem.* One of several isomeric bases, $(CH_3 \cdot C_6H_3 \cdot NH_2)_2$, derived from dimethyl benzidine: one form is used in making dyes. Also **tol′i·din** (-din). [< TOL(UOL) + (BENZ)IDINE]

toll[1] (tōl) *n.* **1** A fixed compensation for some privilege granted or service rendered, especially for one granted in a general or public way, as passage on a bridge or turnpike, or that taken by a miller for grinding grain (commonly a portion of the grain). **2** The right to levy such charge. **3** Something taken or elicited like a toll; price: The train wreck took a heavy *toll* of lives. **4** A due charged for the privilege of shipping or landing goods. **5** A charge for transportation of goods, especially by rail or canal. **6** A charge for a long-distance telephone call. See synonyms under TAX. — *v.t.* To take as a toll. — *v.i.* To take or exact a toll. ◆ Homophone: *tole.* [OE, ? < LL *toloneum* < L *telonium* < Gk. *telōnion* a customhouse < *telōnes* a tax collector < *telos* a tax]

toll[2] (tōl) *v.t.* **1** To cause (a bell) to sound slowly and at regular intervals. **2** To announce thus; especially, to announce (a death, funeral, etc.) by tolling. **3** To call or summon by tolling. **4** To decoy (game, especially ducks). **5** *Rare* To entice. — *v.i.* **6** To sound slowly and at regular intervals. — *n.* The sound of a bell rung slowly and with single, regularly repeated strokes. ◆ Homophone: *tole.* [Prob. < TOLL[1], in obs. sense of "pull, draw"]

toll·bar (tōl′bär′) *n.* A tollgate, properly one with a single bar.

toll bridge A bridge at which toll for passage is paid.

toll call A long-distance telephone call, charged for at more than local rates.

toll·er (tō′lər) *n.* **1** One who tolls a bell. **2** A bell used for tolling. **3** A small dog trained to toll or decoy ducks.

toll·gate (tōl′gāt′) *n.* A gate at the entrance to a bridge, or on a road, at which toll is paid.

toll line A telephone line or channel, as between two central offices in different exchanges, for the use of which a toll is charged; a long-distance circuit.

Tol·stoy (tōl′stoi, tōl′-; *Russian* tol·stoi′), **Count Leo Nikolaevich,** 1828–1910, Russian novelist and social reformer. Also **Tol′stoi.**

tol·u·ate (tol′yōō·āt) *n. Chem.* A salt or ester of a toluic acid. [< TOLU(IC) + -ATE[3]]

To·lu·ca (tō·lōō′kä) The capital of Mexico state, central Mexico. Also **Toluca de Ler·do** (thä ler′thō).

tol·u·ene (tol′yōō·ēn) *n. Chem.* A limpid hydrocarbon, $C_6H_5CH_3$, of the aromatic series, homologous with benzene, and obtained from coal tar by distillation: it is used in making dyestuffs and explosives. [< TOLU + -ENE; so called because orig. obtained from tolu]

to·lu·ic (tə·lōō′ik, tol′yōō·ik) *adj. Chem.* Designating or pertaining to any one of four isomeric acid derivatives of toluene, $C_8H_8O_2$, occurring as white crystalline compounds. [< TOLU(ENE) + -IC]

tom·a·hawk (tom′ə-
hôk) *n.* A war weap-
on used by the
Algonquian Indians
of North America,
originally a carved
club about three
feet long, having a
knob of solid wood
on the end in which
a piece of bone or
metal was inserted;
later, the light ax
or hatchet-shaped
weapon with an
iron blade obtained
in trade with Euro-
peans. Tomahawks
were either thrown
or wielded in the hand. — *v.t.* To strike or kill
with a tomahawk. [<Algonquian *tamahak,*
short for *tamahaken* a cutting utensil < *tamahaken* he uses for cutting < *tamaham* he cuts]

PIPE TOMAHAWKS
a. Cree.   *b.* Iroquois.
c. Omaha. *d.* Osage.

tom·al·ley (tom′al-ē) *n.* The liver of the lobster,
turning green when cooked: considered a great
delicacy. Also **to·mal·ly** (tə-mal′ē). [Prob.
<Cariban]

to·man (tō-män′) *n.* A Persian gold coin of
varying value: formerly a money of account.
[<Persian *tūmān, tumān, tuman* <Turki, lit.,
ten thousand]

to·ma·tin (tə-mā′tin, -mä′-) *n.* An antibiotic
extracted from the leaves and plants of the
tomato plant and also from the leaf juices
of potatoes and green peppers. [<TOMAT(O)
+ -IN]

to·ma·to (tə-mā′tō, -mä′-) *n. pl.* ·**toes** 1 The
pulpy edible berry, yellow or red when ripe, of
a tropical American perennial plant (*Lyco-
persicon esculentum*) of the nightshade family,
highly esteemed as a vegetable. 2 The plant
itself. 3 *U.S. Slang* A girl or woman. [<Sp.
tomate <Nahuatl *tomatl*]

tomato fruitworm The bollworm.

tomb (tōōm) *n.* 1 A place for the burial of the
dead; a vault; grave. 2 A place where the
dead lie. 3 Death itself. 4 A tombstone.
— *v.t.* To entomb; bury; inter. [<AF *tumbe,*
OF *tombe* <LL *tumba* <Gk. *tymbos* a
mound]

tom·bac (tom′bak) *n.* Any of several copper-
and-zinc alloys used to make gongs and bells
in the East, and cheap jewelry in Europe:
often spelled *tambac.* Also **tom′back, tom′·
bak.** [<F <Pg. <Malayan *tambāga* copper
<Skt. *tāmraka*]

tom·boy (tom′boi) *n.* A girl of romping and
boisterous conduct; hoyden. [<TOM + BOY]
— **tom′boy′ish** *adj.* — **tom′boy′ish·ness** *n.*

tomb·stone (tōōm′stōn) *n.* A stone, usually
inscribed, marking a place of burial.

tom·cat (tom′kat′) *n.* A male cat. [after *Tom,*
a male cat, hero of *The Life and Adventures
of a Cat,* 1760, a very popular anonymous
work]

tom·cod (tom′kod) *n.* Any of several small
edible fishes (genus *Microgadus*) common on
the Atlantic coast of North America. [<TOM
+ COD]

tome (tōm) *n.* A volume, particularly if large;
originally, one of a series of volumes. [<MF
<L *tomus* <Gk. *tomos* a fragment, volume <
temnein cut]

-tome *combining form* A cutting instrument
(of a specified kind): *microtome.* [<Gk. *tomos*
a cutting < *temnein* cut]

to·men·tose (tə-men′tōs, tō′men-tōs) *adj. Biol.*
Covered with matted woolly hairs; flocculent.
Also **to·men′tous** (-təs). [<L *tomentosus* <
tomentum a stuffing for cushions]

to·men·tum (tə-men′təm) *n. pl.* ·**ta** (-tə) 1
Anat. A network of small blood vessels of the
pia mater where applied to the brain or spinal
cord. 2 *Bot.* A form of pubescence composed of matted woolly hairs. [<L. See
TOMENTOSE.]

tom·fool (tom′fōōl′) *n.* 1 An idiotic or silly
person. 2 An amusing trifler. — *adj.* Ridiculous; very stupid. [after *Tom Fool,* a name
formerly applied to mental defectives]

tom·ful·ler (tom′fōōl′ər) *n.* Sour or fermented
hominy prepared as food: originally a Choctaw Indian dish. Also **tom′ful′la** (-fōōl′ə),
tom fuller. [<Choctaw *tahfula* hominy]

tom·my (tom′ē) *n. pl.* ·**mies** Provisions or
goods given instead of money in payment of
wages; also, the system of paying workmen

partly or entirely in kind. [Short for *tommy-
shop,* a store run on the truck system]

to·mo·dro·mic (tō′mə-drō′mik, -drom′ik) *adj.*
Having a flight path which cuts athwart a
moving target; heading to cut or intercept:
said of guided missiles. [<Gk. *tomos* cutting
(< *temnein* cut) + *dromos* a running <
dramein run]

to·mog·ra·phy (tō-mog′rə-fē) *n. Med.* X-ray
photography of a predetermined plane of the
body, with a blurring or elimination of details
in other planes. [<Gk. *tomos* a slice (< *temnein* cut) + (PHOTO)GRAPHY]

to·mor·row (tə-môr′ō, -mor′ō) *adv.* On or for
the next day after today. — *n.* The next day
after today; the morrow. Also **to·mor′row.**
[OE *tō morgen* < *tō* to + *morgen* morning,
morrow]

tom·pi·on (tom′pē-ən) *n. Mil.* A stopper, as the
plug put into the mouth of a cannon, to
exclude moisture, etc.: also called *tampion.*
[Var. of TAMPION]

tom·tit (tom′tit′) *n.* 1 A tit; titmouse. 2 Any
of various small birds, as a chickadee or a
wren. [<TOM + TIT¹]

tom-tom (tom′tom′) *n.* 1 The native drum of
India, Africa, etc., variously shaped, and
usually beaten with the hands. 2 A percussion instrument of monotonous tone, used in
some modern orchestras for special effects.
3 A copper or copper-alloy disk-shaped
instrument sounded with a felt-covered hammer or stick; a Chinese gong. Also spelled
tam-tam. [<Hind. *tamtam,* imit. of the instrument's sound]

-tomy *combining form* 1 *Surg.* A cutting of a
(specified) part or tissue: *osteotomy.* 2 A
(specified) kind of cutting or division: *dichotomy.* [<Gk. *tomē* a cutting < *temnein* cut]

ton¹ (tun) *n.* 1 Any of several large measures
of weight; particularly, the **short ton** of 2000
pounds avoirdupois, commonly used in the
United States and Canada; the **long ton** of
2240 pounds of Great Britain; or the **metric
ton** of 1000 kilograms. 2 A unit for reckoning
the displacement or weight of vessels, 35 cubic
feet of sea water weighing about one long ton:
called **displacement ton.** 3 A unit for reckoning the freight-carrying capacity of a ship,
usually equivalent to 40 cubic feet of space
but varying with the cargo: called **freight ton,
measurement ton.** 4 A unit for reckoning
the internal capacity of merchant vessels for
purposes of registration, equivalent to 100
cubic feet or 2.832 cubic meters: called
register ton. [Var. of TUN; infl. in form by OF
tonne a cask]

ton² (tôn) *n. French* Tone; style; the prevailing
fashion; vogue.

-ton *suffix* Town: used in place names:
Charleston, Brockton. [OE *-tun* < *tun* a town]

to·nal (tō′nəl) *adj.* Of or pertaining to tone or
tonality. — **to′nal·ly** *adv.*

to·nal·ite (tō′nəl·īt) *n.* A quartz–mica diorite.
Also **to′nal·yte.** [from *Tonale,* in the Tirol,
where it was first described]

to·nal·i·ty (tō-nal′ə-tē) *n. pl.* ·**ties** 1 *Music*
The quality and peculiarity of a tonal system;
the melodic and harmonic relations between
the tones of a scale or system of tones; a key
or mode. 2 The general color scheme or
collective tones of a painting. 3 Tonicity.

to-name (tōō′nām′) *n. Scot.* 1 Some special
distinguishing name; nickname. 2 A surname. [<tō-nama]

to·na·pha·si·a (tō′nə-fā′zhē-ə, -zhə) *n. Psychiatry* Inability to recall a familiar tune; musical
aphasia. [<NL <L *tonus* TONE + Gk. *aphasia*
inability to speak]

tone (tōn) *n.* 1 Sound in relation to quality,
volume, duration, and pitch. 2 *Physics* A
sound having a definite pitch, and due to
vibration of a sounding body. The pitch of a
tone depends on rate of vibration and its force
on amplitude of vibration; its timbre is a complex resultant of concomitant vibration. If the
vibration is simple harmonic motion the tone
is pure; if there are complex components, the
one of lowest pitch is the **fundamental tone**
and the other components, in a simple ratio
to the lowest, are **partial tones** or *overtones.*
The combined result of all the partial tones
gives the quality or *timbre* of the tone. 3
Music **a** The timbre, or peculiar characteristic
sound, as of a voice or instrument. **b** The
interval corresponding to one degree of the
scale or staff; two semitones: sometimes called

a **major tone** or **whole tone,** in distinction from
a *semitone.* 4 A predominating disposition;
especially, a frame or condition of mind;
mood. 5 **a** Characteristic style or tendency;
tenor; quality: a want of moral *tone.* **b** Style
or distinction; elegance: The party had *tone.*
6 Vocal inflection as expressive of feeling:
a *tone* of pity. 7 *Ling.* A musical intonation
or modulation of the voice by which a word
or phrase may be changed in meaning or function: Peking Chinese distinguishes four *tones.*
8 *Phonet.* **a** The acoustical pitch, or change
in pitch, of a phrase or sentence: In English,
a questioning is indicated by a rising *tone.*
b Special stress or accent given to one syllable of a word, or to one of the words in a
sentence or phrase. 9 The prevailing effect of
a picture, due to the management of chiaro-
scuro and to the effect of light upon the quality
of color. 10 A shade, hue, tint, or degree
of a particular color, or some slight modification of it: a deep *tone* of yellow; red
with a purplish *tone.* 11 *Phot.* The shade or
color of a photographic positive picture; also,
the color of a negative film. 12 *Physiol.* The
general condition of the body with reference
to the vigorous and healthy discharge of its
functions. See synonyms under SOUND¹. — *v.*
toned, ton·ing *v.t.* 1 To give tone to; modify
in tone. 2 To tune or modify with reference
to musical quality, as an instrument. 3 To
intone in monotonous recitative; intone. 4 To
alter the color or increase the brilliancy of
(a photographic print) by a chemical bath.
— *v.i.* 5 To assume a certain tone or hue.
6 To blend or harmonize, as in tone or shade.
— **to tone down** 1 To subdue the tone of (a
painting). 2 To moderate in quality or tone.
— **to tone up** 1 To raise in quality or strength.
2 To elevate in pitch. 3 To gain in vitality.
[<OF *ton* <L *tonus* <Gk. *tonos* a pitch of
voice, a stretching < *teinein* stretch] — **ton′er** *n.*

tone poem A symphonic poem.

tong¹ (tông, tong) *v.t.* To gather, collect, or
seize with tongs. — *v.i.* To use or fish with
tongs. [<TONGS]

tong² (tông, tong) *n.* A Chinese closed society;
in the United States, a secret society composed of Chinese. [<Chinese *t'ang* a hall,
meeting place]

Ton·ga (tong′gə) *n.* A Polynesian language
spoken in the Tonga Islands.

Ton·ga Islands (tong′gə) An island group SE
of the Fiji Islands in the South Pacific, comprising an independent Polynesian kingdom
under British protection; total, 270 square
miles; capital, Nukualofa: also *Friendly Islands.*

Ton·ga·land (tong′gə-land) A region of Zulu-
land on the Mozambique Channel.

tongs (tôngz, tongz) *n. pl. (sometimes construed
as singular)* 1 An implement for grasping,
holding, or lifting objects, consisting usually
of a pair of pivoted levers: also called **pair
of tongs.** 2 One of various grasping mechanisms. [OE *tang, tange*]

tongue (tung) *n.* 1 A protrusile, freely moving
organ situated in the mouth of most vertebrates and supported by the hyoid bone: most
completely developed in mammals, where it is
important in taking in and masticating food,
as one of the organs of taste, and in man as an
organ of speech. ◆ Collateral adjective: *lingual.*

2 An organ or part of the mouth of various
insects and fishes, having a similar shape or
function. 3 An animal's tongue, as of beef,
prepared as food. 4 The power of speech or
articulation: to lose one's *tongue.* 5 Manner
or style of speaking: a smooth *tongue.* 6 Mere
speech, as contrasted with fact or deed.
7 Utterance; talk; discourse. 8 A language,
vernacular, or dialect. 9 *Archaic* A people or
race, regarded as having its own language: a
Biblical use. 10 Anything resembling an
animal tongue in appearance, shape, or function. 11 A slender projection of land, as a
cape or small promontory. 12 A long narrow
bay or inlet of water. 13 A jet of flame. 14 A
strip of leather for closing the gap in the front
of a laced shoe. 15 The fastening pin of a
brooch or buckle. 16 *Music* The free or
vibrating end of a reed in a wind instrument.
17 The clapper of a bell. 18 The harnessing
pole of a horse-drawn vehicle. 19 The
pointed, movable rail in a street railway
switch. 20 *Mech.* Any flange or projecting
part of a machine or mechanical device. 21 A
projecting edge or tenon of a board for in-

sertion into a corresponding groove of another board, thus forming a **tongue-and-groove joint. 22** A spike on a sword blade on which the hilt is secured. **23** The movable arm of a bevel. **24** A small, young sole. See synonyms under LANGUAGE. — **gift of tongues** See under GIFT. — **to hold one's tongue** To keep silent. — **with tongue in cheek** With mental reservations; facetiously; insincerely. — *v.* **tongued, tongu·ing** *v.t.* **1** To use the tongue in playing (a wind instrument) so as to produce marcato or staccato effects; also, to modify the sound of (a flute, cornet, etc.) by the use of the tongue. **2** To touch or lap with the tongue. **3 a** To cut a tongue on (a board). **b** To join or fit by a tongue-and-groove joint. **4** *Poetic* To utter; articulate. **5** *Archaic* To reproach; chide. — *v.i.* **6** To use the tongue in playing a wind instrument. **7** To talk or prattle. **8** To extend as a tongue. [OE *tunge*. Akin to LANGUAGE.]

TONGUE
AND
GROOVE

tongue-tie (tung'tī') *n.* Abnormal shortness of the frenum of the tongue, whereby its motion is impeded or confined. — *v.t.* **1** To deprive of speech or the power of speech, or of distinct articulation. **2** To bewilder or amaze so as to render speechless. — **tongue'-tied'** *adj.*

ton·ic (ton'ik) *adj.* **1** Having power to invigorate or build up; bracing. **2** Pertaining to tone or tones; specifically, in music, pertaining to the keynote. **3** In art, denoting the general color effect and the light and shade in a picture or scene. **4** *Physiol.* **a** Of or pertaining to tension, especially muscular tension. **b** Rigid; unrelaxing: *tonic* spasm. **5** *Ling.* **a** Of or pertaining to musical intonations or modulations of words, sentences, etc. **b** Designating languages which distinguish

TONGS
a, b, c, d. Blacksmith's tongs.
e. Rail tongs. *f.* Ice tongs.

words of identical or very similar form by variations in tone or pitch, as Chinese. **6** *Phonet.* **a** Stressed, as a syllable. **b** *Obs.* Voiced. — *n.* **1** *Med.* A drug that gradually restores the normal tone of organs from a condition of debility. **2** Whatever imparts vigor or tone. **3** The basic note of a key; keynote. [<Gk. *tonikos* < *tonos* sound, tone]

tonic accent 1 An accent that is spoken or pronounced rather than written. **2** *Phonet.* Emphasis placed on a syllable or sound by raising or changing the pitch of the voice.

to·nic·i·ty (tō-nis'ə·tē) *n.* **1** The state of being tonic; tone. **2** *Physiol.* The peculiar elastic condition of healthy tissue; tonus. **3** Health and vigor generally.

tonic sol-fa A system of teaching, writing, and reading music, especially vocal music, that lays particular stress on the tonal relations of the various elements of the key. The initials of the syllables used in solmization are employed to write its scale. [<TONIC + SOL[1] + FA]

to·night (tə·nīt') *adv.* **1** In or during the present or coming night. **2** *Obs.* Last night. — *n.* The night that follows this day; also, the present night. Also **to-night'.** [OE *tō niht* < *tō* to + *niht* night]

ton·nage (tun'ij) *n.* **1** The cubic capacity of a merchant vessel expressed in tons of 100 cubic feet each. **2** The freight-carrying capacity of a vessel. **3** The aggregate freightage of a collection of vessels, especially of a country's merchant marine, as represented by

their registered cubic capacity. **4** A tax levied on vessels at a given rate per ton. **5** The total weight of materials produced, mined, or transported. [<OF < *tonne* a ton, tun]

ton·o·graph (ton'ə·graf, -gräf, tō'nə-) *n.* A recording tonometer. [<TONO- + GRAPH]

to·nom·e·ter (tō·nom'ə·tər) *n.* **1** An instrument to measure strains within a liquid that tend to pull the particles asunder. **2** An accurately pitched tuning fork or set of forks; any instrument for determining the pitch of a tone. **3** An instrument for measuring tension in the eyeball or varying pressure of the blood.

to·nom·e·try (tō·nom'ə·trē) *n.* The art of using a tonometer. — **ton·o·met·ric** (ton'ə·met'rik, tō'nə-) *adj.*

ton·o·plast (ton'ə·plast) *n. Biol.* An inner plasmic membrane lining the vacuole of a cell and controlling the osmotic pressure. [<TONO- + -PLAST]

ton·o·scope (ton'ə·skōp, tō'nə-) *n.* An instrument by which a player or singer can observe departures from pitch or tone.

ton·sil (ton'səl) *n. Anat.* One of two oval lymphoid organs situated on either side of the passage from the mouth to the pharynx. [<L *tonsillae* the tonsils] — **ton'sil·lar, ton'sil·ar** *adj.*

ton·sil·lec·to·my (ton'sə·lek'tə·mē) *n. Surg.* Removal of a tonsil. [<TONSIL + -ECTOMY]

ton·sil·li·tis (ton'sə·li'tis) *n. Pathol.* Inflammation of the tonsils. — **ton'sil·lit'ic** (-lit'ik) *adj.*

ton·sil·lo·tome (ton·sil'ə·tōm) *n.* An instrument used for cutting away a portion of the tonsils. [< *tonsillo-* (<TONSIL) + -TOME]

ton·sure (ton'shər) *n.* **1** The shaving of the head, or of the crown of the head, as of a priest or monk, or the state of being thus shaven; hence, the priestly office. **2** That part of a priest's or monk's head left bare by shaving. — *v.t.* **·sured, ·sur·ing** To shave the head of. [<OF <L *tonsura* a shearing < *tonsus.* See TONSORIAL.] — **ton'sured** *adj.*

ton·tine (ton'tēn, ton·tēn') *n.* **1** A form of collective life annuity, the individual profits of which increase as the number of survivors diminishes, the final survivor taking the whole. **2** The subscribers to such an annuity, collectively. **3** The share of a single subscriber. [<F, after Lorenzo *Tonti*, a Neapolitan banker who introduced it into France in about 1653]

to·nus (tō'nəs) *n.* **1** Tonicity. **2** *Physiol.* **a** The ability of a muscle to contract in response to a stimulus. **b** A condition of prolonged muscular spasm. [<L, TONE]

too (tōō) *adv.* **1** In addition; likewise; also: *beautiful and good too.* **2** In excessive quantity or degree; more than sufficiently: *too long and too technical.* **3** In a degree beyond extremity or endurance; extremely: I am *too* happy for you. **4** *Colloq.* Indeed: an intensive, often used to reiterate a contradicted statement: You are *too* going! [Stressed var. of OE *tō* to]

tool (tōōl) *n.* **1** A simple mechanism or implement, as a hammer, saw, spade, or chisel, used chiefly in the direct manual working, moving, shaping, or transforming of material. **2** A power-driven apparatus, as a lathe, used for cutting and shaping the parts of a machine. **3** The cutting or shaping part of such an apparatus. **4** A bookbinder's hand stamp used in lettering or ornamenting book covers. **5** A person used to carry out the designs of others or another; a dupe. **6** *Law* Any instrument or apparatus necessary to the efficient prosecution of one's profession or trade. — *v.t.* **1** To shape, mark, or ornament with a tool. **2** To provide with tools. **3** *Colloq.* To drive, as an automobile, or convey (a person) by driving. **4** In bookbinding, to ornament or impress designs upon with a roller bearing a pattern. — *v.i.* **5** To work with a tool or tools. **6** *Colloq.* To drive or travel in a vehicle. [OE *tōl*]

Synonyms (noun): apparatus, appliance, implement, instrument, machine, mechanism, utensil. A *tool* is both contrived and used for extending the force of an intelligent agent to something that is to be operated upon. An

instrument is anything through which power is applied and a result produced; in general usage, the word is of considerably wider meaning than *tool*; as, a piano is a musical *instrument*. Instruments is the word usually applied to *tools* used in scientific pursuits; as, we speak of a surgeon's or an optician's *instruments*. An *implement* is a mechanical agency considered with reference to some specific purpose to which it is adapted; as, an agricultural *implement, implements* of war. *Implement* is a less technical term than *tool*. A *utensil* is that which may be used for some special purpose; the word is especially applied to articles used for domestic or agricultural purposes; as, kitchen *utensils*, farming *utensils*. *Mechanism* is a word of wide meaning, denoting any combination of mechanical devices for united action. A *machine* in the most general sense is any mechanical *instrument* for the conversion of motion; in this sense a lever is a *machine*; but in more commonly accepted usage a *machine* is distinguished from a *tool* by its complexity, and by the combination and coordination of powers and movements to produce results.

tool-mak·er (tōōl'mā'kər) *n.* A maker of tools.

toon (tōōn) *n.* **1** The fine, close-grained red wood of an East Indian tree (*Toona ciliata*) of the mahogany family, used for furniture, boxes, and construction. **2** The tree itself. [<Hind. *tun, tūn* <Skt. *tunna*]

toot (tōōt) *v.i.* **1** To blow a horn, whistle, etc., especially with short blasts. **2** To give forth a blast or toot, as a horn. **3** To make a similar sound. — *v.t.* **4** To sound (a horn, etc.) with short blasts. **5** To sound (a blast, etc.). — *n.* **1** A short note or blast on a horn. **2** *Slang* A spree; especially, a drinking spree. [? <MLG *tuten*; prob. orig. imit.] — **toot'er** *n.*

tooth (tōōth) *n. pl.* **teeth** (tēth) **1** One of the hard, dense structures in the mouth of a vertebrate, used for seizing and chewing food, as offensive and defensive weapons, etc. It consists chiefly of dentine or ivory, invested on the outer surface and crown with enamel, and a root embedded in the gum, with a small opening leading into a pulp cavity richly supplied with blood vessels and nerves. ◆ Collateral adjective: *dental*. **2** One of various hard calcareous or chitinous bodies of the oral or gastric regions of invertebrates. **3** Any one of various small toothlike projections.

TEETH OF HUMAN ADULT
A. Cross-section of a molar.
B. Left upper jaw. *C.* Left lower jaw.
A. a. Crown. *b.* Enamel. *c.* Pulp cavity. *d.* Dentine.
e. Cement. *f.* Roots.
B. & C. g. Incisors. *h.* Canines. *i.* Bicuspids.
j. Molars. *k.* Wisdom teeth.

4 *Zool.* A process near the hinge of a bivalve shell. **5** *Bot.* One of the processes in the peristome of a moss. **6** Something resembling a tooth in form or use; specifically, a projecting point, pin, tine, or cog, as on a saw, comb, fork, rake, or gearwheel. **7** Appetite, liking, or taste (for something): She has a sweet *tooth.* **8** *pl.* That part which opposes, as in the gnawing, biting, or piercing manner of a tooth; the face of opposition, especially when involving resistance or risk: the *teeth* of the wind; He disobeyed them in their *teeth.* **9** *pl.* Means of enforcement: to put *teeth* into a law. **10** In paper or painting grounds, coarseness; irregularity of surface. — **armed to the teeth** Completely or heavily armed. — **by the skin of one's teeth** Barely; by the narrowest possible margin. — **in the teeth of** Directly against, counter to, or in defiance of. — **to put teeth into** To provide (something) with strength or power. **— to show one's teeth** To display a disposition to fight; threaten. **— to throw (or cast) in one's teeth** To fling at one, as a challenge or taunt. **—** *v.t.* **1** To supply with teeth, as a rake or saw. **2** To give a serrated edge to; indent. **—** *v.i.* **3** To become interlocked, as gear-wheels; to gear. [< ON *tóth, tódh*]

tooth·brush (tōōth′brush′) *n.* A small brush used for cleaning the teeth.

tooth·paste (tōōth′pāst′) *n.* A paste used in cleaning the teeth.

tooth·shell (tōōth′shel′) *n.* A burrowing mollusk (genus *Dentalium*), having a long, very slender tubular shell.

tooth·wort (tōōth′wûrt′) *n.* **1** Any of a genus (*Dentaria*) of spring-blooming herbs of the mustard family, with compound toothed leaves and terminal clusters of white or purplish flowers. **2** Any of a genus (*Lathraea*) of small, parasitic plants having rootstocks covered with white scales instead of leaves.

top¹ (top) *n.* **1** The uppermost or highest part, end, side, or surface of anything. **2** That end or part of anything, regarded as the higher or upper extremity: the *top* of the street. **3** A lid or cover: a bottle *top*. **4** The roof of a vehicle, as an automobile. **5** The crown of the head: from *top* to toe. **6** *pl.* The above-ground part of a plant producing root vegetables. **7** The highest degree or reach: at the *top* of one's voice; the *top* of one's ambition. **8** The highest or most prominent place or rank: at the *top* of one's profession. **9** One who is highest in rank or position: the *top* of one's class. **10** The choicest or best part: the *top* of the crop. **11** In bridge, the highest card in a suit. **12** In billiards, tennis, golf, etc.: **a** A stroke in which the player hits the ball above the center or on the upper half. **b** The forward spinning motion imparted to the ball by such a stroke. **13** *Naut.* A platform at the head of the lower section of a ship's mast, used as a place to stand and for extending the topmast rigging. **14** *Chem.* The most volatile part of a substance in distillation. **15** *Scot.* **a** The hair on one's head. **b** A bird's crest. **c** A horse's forelock. **d** A bunch of hair, wool, flax, etc. See synonyms under SUMMIT. **— to blow one's top** *Slang* **1** To break out in a rage; flare up. **2** To go insane. **— adj. 1** Of or pertaining to the top or upper part. **2** Forming or comprising the top or upper part. **3** Highest in rank or quality; chief: *top* authors. **4** Greatest in amount or degree: *top* prices. **— v. topped, top·ping** *v.t.* **1** To remove the top or upper end of; prune. **2** To provide with a top, cap, etc. **3** To form the top of. **4** To reach or pass over the top of; surmount. **5** To surpass or exceed. **6** *Chem.* To take away the most volatile part of by distillation. **7** In golf, tennis, etc.: **a** To hit the upper part of (the ball) in making a stroke. **b** To make (a stroke) thus. **—** *v.i.* **8** To top someone or something. **— to top off 1** To put something on the top of. **2** To complete; finish. [OE]

top² (top) *n.* A toy of wood or metal, with a point on which it is made to spin, as by the unwinding of a string, a spring, etc. [OE]

to·paz (tō′paz) *n.* **1** A native fluosilicate of aluminum, often found in yellow prismatic crystals valued as gemstones. **2** The yellow sapphire, a highly prized corundum of Ceylon: also called **Oriental topaz. 3** Citrine (def. 2). **4** Either of two large tropical American hummingbirds (*Topaza pyra* and *T. pella*) with brilliant green-and-gold plumage. **5** A brownish-gold color, the color of the mineral. [< OF *topaze, topace* < L *topazus* < Gk. *topazos*]

to·paz·o·lite (tō·paz′ə·līt) *n.* A variety of andradite, yellow or sometimes green. [< Gk. *topazos* topaz + -LITE]

top·boot (top′bōōt′) *n.* A boot with a high top, sometimes ornamented with materials different from the rest of the boot. **— top′-boot′ed** *adj.*

top buggy A buggy with a top that may be raised or folded back.

top·coat (top′kōt′) *n.* A lightweight overcoat.

top dressing *Agric.* A dressing of manure not to be plowed under the surface of a field.

tope¹ (tōp) *v.t.* **toped, top·ing** To drink (alcoholic beverages) excessively and frequently. ◆ Homophone: *taupe.* [? Related to earlier *top* tilt, turn over]

tope² (tōp) *n. Dial.* A small European shark or dogfish (genus *Galeorhinus*). ◆ Homophone: *taupe.* [? < dial. E (Cornish); ult. origin unknown]

to·pec·to·my (tō·pek′tə·mē, tə-) *n. Surg.* An operation in which certain prefrontal cortical areas of the brain are removed. [< TOP(O)- + -ECTOMY]

to·pek (tō′pek) *n.* A North American Indian or Eskimo hut of weeds, twigs, and animal skins. [< Eskimo *toopik, tupek* a tent]

To·pe·ka (tə·pē′kə) The capital of Kansas, on the Kansas River in the NE part.

top·e·po (tə·pep′ō) *n. pl.* **·pep·oes 1** A hybrid plant obtained by crossing the Chinese pepper with a variety of tomato, cultivated for its edible fruit. **2** The fruit itself. [< TO(MAT)O + PEP(PER)]

top-flight (top′flīt′) *adj.* Of the highest quality; outstanding; superior.

top·gal·lant (tə·gal′ənt, top′gal′ənt) *n. Naut.* **1** The mast, sail, yard, or rigging immediately above the topmast and topsail. **2** The parts of a deck that are higher than the rest. **— adj.** Pertaining to the topgallants. [< TOP¹ + GALLANT; with ref. to "making a gallant show" compared with the lower tops]

top·ham·per (top′ham′pər) *n. Naut.* **1** Spars and rigging usually kept aloft. **2** The light upper sails and rigging. **3** Casks, cables, rigging, etc., encumbering the deck. [< TOP¹ + HAMPER¹, *n.*] **— top′-ham′pered** *adj.*

top hat A high silk hat for men.

top-heav·y (top′hev′ē) *adj.* Having the top or upper part too heavy for the lower part; ill-proportioned; impracticable. **— top′heav′i·ness** *n.*

to·phus (tō′fəs) *n. pl.* **·phi** (-fī) **1** *Dent.* Tartar of the teeth. **2** *Pathol.* A deposit of urates around and at the surface of joints in persons affected with gout. **3** *Mineral.* Any natural calcareous tufa. [< L, tufa]

to·pi (tō·pē′, tō′pē) *n.* A hat or helmet, especially a light helmet made of pith: also spelled *topee.* [< Hind. *topī*]

to·pi·ar·y (tō′pē·er′ē) *adj.* Arranged or trimmed in, or making use of, fantastic shapes of shrubs and evergreen trees, as in gardening, etc. **— n. pl. ·ar·ies** A topiary garden. [< L *topiarius* concerning ornamental gardening < *topia opera* ornamental gardening < Gk. *topion,* dim. of *topos* a place]

top·ic (top′ik) *n.* **1** A subject of discourse or of a treatise; any matter treated of in speech or writing; a theme for discussion. **2** *pl.* In rhetorical invention, the part that treats of the selection and arrangement of the proofs; also, the places or classes in which the various kinds of proofs are to be found. **3** A subdivision of an outline or a treatise. **— adj. Obs.** Topical. [< L *topica* < Gk. (*ta*) *topica,* lit., (matters) concerning commonplaces, title of a work by Aristotle, neut. pl. of *topikos* of a place < *topos* a place, commonplace]

Synonyms (noun): division, head, issue, matter, motion, point, proposition, question, subject, theme. Since a *topic* for discussion is often stated in the form of a *question, question* has come to be extensively used to denote a debatable *topic,* especially of a practical nature; as, the labor *question.* In deliberative assemblies the *motion* or other matter for consideration is known as the *question;* a member is required to speak to the *question.* In speaking or writing the general *subject* or *theme* may be termed the *topic,* but it is more usual to apply the latter term to the subordinate *divisions, points,* or *heads* of discourse; as, To enlarge on this *topic* would carry me far from my *subject.*

top·i·cal (top′i·kəl) *adj.* **1** Pertaining to a topic. **2** Of the nature of merely probable argument. **3** Belonging to a place or spot; local. **4** Pertaining to matters of present interest: a *topical* song. **5** *Med.* Local. **— top′i·cal·ly** *adv.*

top·knot (top′not′) *n.* **1** A crest, tuft, or knot on the top of the head, as of feathers on the head of a bird. **2** The hair of the human head when worn as a high knot. **3** A knot or bow worn by women, as a headdress, etc.

top·less (top′lis) *adj.* **1** Lacking a top. **2** Nude from the waist up, or characterized by such nudity. **3** Being without a covering for the breasts: a *topless* bathing suit. **4** So high that no top can be seen. **— top′less·ness** *n.*

top·most (top′mōst′) *adj.* Being at the very top.

top-notch (top′noch′) *adj. Colloq.* Excellent; best. **— top′-notch′er** *n.*

topo- *combining form* A place or region; regional: *topography.* Also, before vowels, **top-.** [< Gk. *topos* a place]

to·pog·ra·pher (tə·pog′rə·fər) *n.* An expert in topography.

to·pog·ra·phy (tə·pog′rə·fē) *n.* **1** The detailed description of particular places. **2** The art of representing on a map the physical features of a place. **3** The physical features, collectively, of a region. **4** Topographic surveying. [< TOPO- + -GRAPHY] **— top·o·graph·ic** (top′ə·graf′ik) or **·i·cal** *adj.* **— top′o·graph′i·cal·ly** *adv.*

to·pol·o·gy (tə·pol′ə·jē) *n.* **1** The branch of geometry which studies those properties of figures or solid bodies which remain invariant under all continuous deformation: also called *analysis situs.* **2** *Med.* The relation between the forward part of the fetus and the birth canal. [< TOPO- + -LOGY] **— top·o·log·ic** (top′ə·loj′ik) or **·i·cal** *adj.*

top·o·nym (top′ə·nim) *n.* **1** *Anat.* The name of a region of the body, as distinguished from an organ. **2** Any name derived from the name of a place. [< TOPO- + Gk. *onoma, onyma* a name] **— top′o·nym′ic** or **·i·cal** *adj.*

to·pon·y·my (tə·pon′ə·mē) *n. pl.* **·mies 1** The nomenclature of anatomical regions. **2** The science or study of place names, or a register of place names.

top·o·type (top′ə·tīp) *n. Biol.* A plant or animal specimen selected from the locality typical of the species. [< TOPO- + TYPE]

top·ping (top′ing) *adj.* **1** Towering high above; eminent; distinguished. **2** Making great pretensions; arrogant; domineering. **3** *Brit. Colloq.* Excellent; first-rate. **— n. 1** The act of one who tops, in any sense. **2** That which forms the top of anything.

topping lift *Naut.* A rope extending from the lower masthead to the outer end of a boom, for hoisting or supporting the boom.

top·ple (top′əl) *v.* **·pled, ·pling** *v.t.* **1** To push over and cause to totter or fall by its own weight; overturn. **—** *v.i.* **2** To totter and fall, as by its own weight. **3** To lean or jut out, as if about to fall. [Freq. of TOP¹, *v.*]

tops (tops) *adj. Slang* Excellent; first-rate.

top·sail (top′səl, top′sāl′) *n. Naut.* **1** In a square-rigged vessel, a square sail set next above the lowest sail of a mast. **2** In a fore-and-aft-rigged vessel, a square or triangular sail carried above the gaff of a lower sail.

top-se·cret (top′sē′krit) *adj. U.S.* Designating defense information requiring the strictest measures of secrecy and safeguard. Compare SECRET (*adj.* def. 5), CONFIDENTIAL (def. 4).

top·side (top′sīd′) *n. Naut.* The portion of a ship above the main deck. **— adv.** To or on the upper parts of a ship: He is going *topside.*

top·soil (top′soil′) *n.* The surface soil of land: distinguished from *subsoil.* **—** *v.t.* To remove the surface soil of (an area or region).

top·stone (top′stōn′) *n.* A capstone.

toque (tōk) *n.* **1** A small, close-fitting, brimless hat worn by women. **2** The tall conical headdress formerly worn by the doges of Venice. **3** A black velvet cap, ornamented with eagle's plumes and furnished with a band and brim: worn by both sexes in France before the Restoration. Also **to·quet** (tō·kā′). [< F, a cap < Sp. *toca* < Basque *tauka,* a kind of cap]

to·rah (tôr′ə, tō′rə) *n.* In Hebrew literature, a law; also, counsel or instruction proceeding from a specially sacred source. Also **to′ra.** [< Hebrew *tōrāh* an instruction, law < *yārāh* throw, show, instruct]

To·rah (tôr′ə, tō′rə) *n.* The Mosaic law; the Pentateuch.

tor·bern·ite (tôr′bərn·īt) See under URANITE. [< G *torbernit, torberit* < NL *torbernus,* after *Torber* Bergmann, 18th c. Swedish chemist]

torch (tôrch) *n.* **1** A source of light, as from flaming pine knots, or from some material dipped in tallow or oil, and fixed at the end of a handle or pole. **2** Anything that illuminates or brightens: the *torch* of science. **3** A portable device giving off an intensely hot flame and used for burning off paint, melting solder, etc. **4** *Brit.* A flashlight. **— to carry a (or the) torch for** *Slang* To continue to love (someone), though the love is unrequited. [<OF *torche*, ult. <L *torquere* twist; so called because early torches were made of twisted tow dipped in pitch]

torch·bear·er (tôrch′bâr′ər) *n.* **1** One who carries a torch. **2** One who imparts knowledge, truth, etc. **3** *Colloq.* One loud in his praise of a friend.

torchlight procession A parade of persons carrying torches, usually a political demonstration.

tor·chon lace (tôr′shon, *Fr.* tôr-shôn′) **1** A coarse, durable bobbin lace in simple geometrical designs made of linen thread. **2** An imitation of this made by machine. [<F *torchon* a dishcloth < *torcher* wipe]

torch song A popular love song, slow and melancholy, expressing sadness and hopeless yearning. [<phrase "carry a torch for." See under TORCH.]

torch·wood (tôrch′wŏŏd′) *n.* **1** Any of a genus (*Amyris*) of tropical American shrubs and small trees, especially *A. balsamifera*. **2** Its bright-burning, fragrant wood.

to·reu·tics (tə-rŏō′tiks) *n. pl.* (construed as singular) The art of working in ornamental relief or intaglio, especially in metal. [<Gk. *toreutikos* < *toreuein* work in relief, bore] — **to·reu′tic** *adj.*

tor·ic (tôr′ik, tor′-) *adj.* Of, pertaining to, or resembling a torus; segmental.

toric lens *Optics* A lens in which one of the surfaces is a segment of a torus: used for eyeglasses because of its special refracting powers.

to·ri·i (tôr′i-ē, tō′ri-ē) *n.* The gateway of a Shinto temple or of a shrine: properly comprising two uprights with one straight crosspiece, and another above with a concave lintel. [<Japanese]

TORII

tor·ment (tôr′ment) *n.* **1** Intense bodily pain or mental anguish; agony; torture. **2** One who or that which torments. **3** The inflicting of torture. **4** *Archaic* Any device for inflicting torture, as the rack; also, the torture inflicted. **5** Hell. See synonyms under AGONY, PAIN. — *v.t.* (tôr-ment′) **1** To subject to excruciating physical or mental suffering; torture. **2** To make miserable; afflict or vex grievously. **3** To harass or tease. **4** To distort; also, to throw into violent agitation. See synonyms under PERSECUTE. [<AF *turment*, OF *torment, tourment* <L *tormentum* a rack, orig. a machine for hurling missiles by means of torsion < *torquere* twist] — **tor·ment′ing·ly** *adv.* — **tor·ment′ing·ness** *n.*

tor·men·til (tôr′men-til) *n.* A slender, trailing, Old World herb (*Potentilla erecta*), with yellow flowers. Its root, a powerful astringent, has been used in treating diarrhea and dysentery, and also in tanning. [<OF *tormentille* < Med. L *tormentilla*, dim. of L *tormentium* TORMENT; so called because used as a pain killer]

tor·men·tor (tôr-men′tər) *n.* **1** One who or that which torments. **2** A movable panel of sound-insulating material for controlling the acoustics on a sound stage outside of the field of the camera. **3** A movable piece of theater scenery at either side and back of the proscenium arch to mask sidelights and downstage entrances and exits. Also **tor·ment′er.**

tor·na·do (tôr-nā′dō) *n. pl.* **·does** or **·dos** **1** A whirling wind of exceptional violence, usually associated with thunderstorms and accompanied by a pendulous, funnel-shaped cloud marking the narrow path of greatest destruction. **2** A violent thunderstorm or squall of the west coast of Africa. **3** A hurricane or violent windstorm of the tropical Atlantic. See synonyms under CYCLONE. [Alter. of *ternado*, prob. alter. of Sp. *tronada* a thunderstorm < *tronar* thunder <L *tonare*; infl. in form by Sp. *tornar* turn, because characterized by shifting or whirling winds] — **tor·nad′ic** (-nad′ik) *adj.*

to·roid (tôr′oid, tō′roid) *n.* **1** *Geom.* **a** A surface generated by the rotation of any closed plane curve, as a circle or ellipse, about an axis lying in its plane. **b** The solid produced by such a surface. **2** *Electr.* An electromagnetic coil wound upon a ring of

circular cross-section. [<TOR(US) + -OID] — **to·roi′dal** *adj.*

To·ron·to (tə-ron′tō) The capital of Ontario province, Canada, on Lake Ontario; a leading industrial center.

to·rose (tôr′ōs, tō′rōs, tô-rōs′, tō-) *adj.* **1** Having protuberances; bulging. **2** *Bot.* Knobby; cylindrical and swollen at intervals. Also **to·rous** (tôr′əs, tō′rəs). [<L *torosus* < *torus* a swelling] — **to·ros·i·ty** (tô-ros′ə-tē) *n.*

tor·pe·do (tôr-pē′dō) *n. pl.* **·dos** or **·does** **1** A device or apparatus containing an explosive to be fired by concussion or otherwise. **2** A self-propelling, cigar-shaped projectile for carrying a powerful detonating charge under water to a hostile vessel. **3** A submarine mine. **4** A cartridge placed on a railway track and exploded by the weight of a train passing over it, the report serving as a warning signal to the train crew. **5** A cartridge exploded in an oil or gas well to start or increase the flow. **6** A toy of gravel and a fulminating powder wrapped in paper, and exploded by being dashed against some hard surface. **7** A ray fish (*Torpedo ocellata*) having an electric apparatus with which it stuns or kills its prey; a crampfish; numbfish. **8** *Colloq.* A gangster, especially an armed bodyguard prepared to attack or kill without warning. — **aerial torpedo** A torpedo projectile, moving under its own power and usually released from low-flying aircraft at fixed or floating targets. — *v.t.* **·doed, ·do·ing** To damage or sink (a vessel) with a torpedo or torpedos. [<L, stiffness, numbness < *torpere* be numb]

torpedo boat A small, swift, lightly armed and armored surface vessel equipped with one or more tubes for the discharge of torpedos.

torpedo tube A tube in a torpedo boat or other war vessel, through which torpedos are launched.

tor·pid[1] (tôr′pid) *adj.* **1** Having lost sensibility or power of motion, partially or wholly, as a hibernating animal. **2** Dormant; numb. **3** Sluggish; apathetic; dull. See synonyms under LIFELESS, NUMB. [<L *torpidus* < *torpere* be numb] — **tor·pid·i·ty** (tôr-pid′ə-tē), **tor′pid·ness** *n.* — **tor′pid·ly** *adv.*

tor·pid[2] (tôr′pid) *n.* **1** An eight-oared, clinker-built racing boat for the second crew at Oxford University; also, one of its crew. **2** *pl.* The Lenten races in which such boats take part. [<TORPID[1]; so called because the second crew consisted of awkward or very young oarsmen]

tor·por (tôr′pər) *n.* **1** Complete or partial insensibility; stupor. **2** Apathy; torpidity. [<L < *torpere* be numb] — **tor·po·rif·ic** (tôr′pə-rif′ik) *adj.*

tor·quate (tôr′kwit, -kwāt) *adj. Zool.* Having a torque or ring, as of color, about the neck; collared. [<L *torquatus* having a collar < *torques* See TORQUES.]

torque[1] (tôrk) *n.* **1** *Mech.* **a** Anything that causes or tends to cause torsion in a body; the moment of forces that causes rotation or twisting. **b** The rotary force in a mechanism. **c** The degree of smoothness in the conversion of reciprocating into rotary motion. **2** *Optics* The rotatory effect upon the plane of polarization produced by the passage of light through certain liquids and crystals. [<L *torquere* twist]

torque[2] (tôrk) *n.* A necklace, armlet, or collar of wire, usually twisted: worn especially by ancient Gauls and Britons: also spelled *torc*. [<L *torques*. See TORQUES.]

tor·ques (tôr′kwēz) *n. Zool.* A natural ring or collar, of feathers or hair, on the neck of a bird or other animal. [<NL <L, a twisted collar < *torquere* twist]

tor·re·fy (tôr′ə-fī, tor′-) *v.t.* **·fied, ·fy·ing** To dry or roast by exposure to heat, as ores or drugs. Also **tor′ri·fy.** [<MF *torréfier* <L *torrefacere* < *torrere* dry, parch + *facere* make] — **tor′re·fac′tion** (-fak′shən) *n.*

tor·rent (tôr′ənt, tor′-) *n.* **1** A stream of water flowing with great velocity or turbulence. **2** Any similar stream, as of lava. **3** Any abundant or tumultuous flow: a *torrent* of rain; a *torrent* of abuse. — *adj.* Like a torrent; pouring forth with violence. [<OF <L *torrens, -entis,* lit., boiling, burning, ppr.

of *torrere* parch]

tor·ren·tial (tô-ren′shəl, to-) *adj.* **1** Of, pertaining to, or resulting from the action of a torrent or torrents. **2** Figuratively, suggestive of a torrent in rapidity and volume; outpouring; overpowering: *torrential* passion. — **tor·ren′tial·ly** *adv.*

tor·rid (tôr′id, tor′-) *adj.* **1** Exposed to the full force of the sun's heat; sultry. **2** Having power to parch or burn; scorching; burning; hot and dry. [<L *torridus* < *torrere* parch] — **tor·rid·i·ty** (tô-rid′ə-tē, to-), **tor′rid·ness** *n.* — **tor′rid·ly** *adv.*

torrid zone See under ZONE.

tor·sade (tôr-sād′) *n.* **1** A molded ornament resembling a twisted cable. **2** A twisted cord for draperies. [<F <Med. L *torsus,* var. of L *tortus,* pp. of *torquere* twist]

tor·si·bil·i·ty (tôr′sə-bil′ə-tē) *n.* Capacity for undergoing torsion, measured by the amount of torsion produced.

tor·sion (tôr′shən) *n.* **1** The act of twisting, or the state of being twisted. **2** *Mech.* Deformation of a body, as a thread or rod, by twisting, one end being held fast while the other is subjected to a torque around its length as an axis. **3** The force with which a twisted cord or cable tends to return to its former position: distinguished from *tension*. [<OF <LL *torsio, -onis,* var. of L *tortio, -onis < tortus,* pp. of *torquere* twist] — **tor′sion·al** *adj.* — **tor′sion·al·ly** *adv.*

torsion balance An instrument for determining very minute forces by measuring the angle through which an arm turns before the resisting force of torsion acts upon the supporting wire or filament.

torsion bar A solid or laminated bar or rod, anchored on one end, which acts as a spring when subjected to torsion (def. 2). — **tor′sion-bar′** *adj.*

tor·so (tôr′sō) *n. pl.* **·sos** or **·si** (-sē) **1** The trunk of a human body. **2** In sculpture, a statue deprived of head and limbs. **3** Any fragmentary or defective thing. [<Ital., a stalk, core, trunk of a body <L *thyrsus* a stalk <Gk. *thyrsos* a thyrsus]

tort (tôrt) *n. Law* Any private or civil wrong by act or omission for which a civil suit can be brought, but not including breach of contract. [<OF <L *tortus*. See TORSION.]

torte (tôrt, *Ger.* tôr′tə) *n.* A rich cake variously made of butter, eggs, fruits, and nuts. [<G]

tort·fea·sor (tôrt′fē′zər) *n. Law* One who has committed a tort; a wrongdoer. [<OF *tortfesor, tortfaiseur < tort* a wrong, tort + *fesor, faiseur* a doer < *faire* do <L *facere*]

tor·ti·col·lis (tôr′tə-kol′is) *n. Pathol.* A spasmodic affection of the muscles of the neck which draws the head to one side; wryneck. [<NL <L *tortus* twisted + *collum* neck] — **tor′ti·col′lar** *adj.*

tor·tile (tôr′til) *adj.* Twisted up into a coil. [<L *tortilis < tortus* twisted. See TORSION.] — **tor·til·i·ty** (tôr-til′ə-tē) *n.*

tor·toise (tôr′təs) *n.* **1** A turtle; chelonian; specifically, one of a terrestrial or fresh-water species, or a terrestrial as distinguished from an aquatic species. **2** A testudo. — **giant tortoise** Any of several species of very large herbivorous land tortoises (family *Testudinidae*), especially those found on the Galápagos Islands, which may reach a length of four feet and weigh 600 pounds. [Earlier *tortuce* < Med. L *tortuca,* ult. <L *tortus* twisted; so called from its crooked feet]

GIANT TORTOISE
(Largest specimens: up to 5 1/2 feet long by 4 1/2 feet wide)

tortoise beetle A small, iridescent beetle

(family *Chrysomelidae*) having a tortoiselike form.

tortoise shell 1 The shell of a marine turtle, especially of the hawkbill, valuable in the arts. 2 A cat having fur mottled with black and yellow like the shell of a tortoise. — **tor'·toise–shell'** *adj.*

tor·tri·cid (tôr'trə-sid) *n.* Any of a large family (*Tortricidae*) of small, usually bright–colored moths with rectangular fore wings, including many important pests of fruit and forest trees. — *adj.* Of or pertaining to the *Tortricidae.* [<NL <*Tortrix,* type genus <L *tortus.* See TORSION.]

tor·tu·os·i·ty (tôr'chŏŏ-os'ə-tē) *n.* 1 The quality or state of being tortuous, or an instance of it. 2 A bend or twist; winding.

tor·tu·ous (tôr'chŏŏ-əs) *adj.* 1 Consisting of or abounding in irregular bends or turns; twisting. 2 Figuratively, morally irregular or crooked; not straightforward; devious. [<AF <L *tortuosus* <*tortus.* See TORSION.] — **tor'tu·ous·ly** *adv.* — **tor'tu·ous·ness** *n.*

tor·ture (tôr'chər) *n.* 1 Infliction of or subjection to extreme physical pain. 2 A former judicial mode of getting evidence by inflicting pain. 3 Great mental suffering; agony. 4 Something that causes severe pain. 5 A violent perversion or straining. See synonyms under AGONY, PAIN. — *v.t.* **·tured, ·tur·ing** 1 To inflict extreme pain upon; cause to suffer keenly in body or mind; specifically, to put to judicial torture. 2 To twist or turn into an abnormal form; distort; wrench. [<OF <L *tortura,* lit., a twisting <*tortus.* See TORSION.] — **tor'tur·er** *n.*

to·rus (tôr'əs, tō'rəs) *n.* *pl.* **to·ri** (tôr'ī, tō'rī) 1 *Archit.* A large convex molding, nearly semicircular in cross–section: used in bases as the lowest molding, or in columns above the plinth. 2 *Anat.* A rounded ridge, as on the occipital bone of the skull. 3 *Bot.* The swollen end of a flowerstalk which bears the floral leaves; the receptacle. 4 *Geom.* The surface or solid generated by the rotation of a conic section about an axis in its own plane. [<L, lit., a swelling]

To·ry (tôr'ē, tō'rē) *n.* *pl.* **To·ries** 1 A historical English political party, successor to the Cavaliers and opponent of the Whigs; since about 1832 called the Conservative party. 2 One who at the period of the American Revolution adhered to the cause of British sovereignty over the colonies. 3 A very conservative person: also **tory.** — **To'ry·ism** *n.*

toss (tôs, tos) *v.t.* 1 To throw, pitch, or fling about. 2 To make restless; agitate; disturb. 3 To throw with the hand, especially with the palm of the hand upward; pitch. 4 To lift with a quick motion, as the head. 5 To bandy about, as something discussed. 6 To toss up with. See to TOSS UP, below. — *v.i.* 7 To be moved or thrown about; be flung to and fro, as a ship in a storm. 8 To throw oneself from side to side; roll about restlessly, as in sleep. 9 To go quickly or angrily, as with a toss of the head. 10 To toss up a coin. — **to toss (or peak) oars** To raise the oars out of the rowlocks to a vertical position. — **to toss off** 1 To drink at one draft. 2 To utter, write, or do in an offhand manner. — **to toss up** To throw a coin into the air to decide a wager or choice by the way in which it falls. — *n.* 1 The act of tossing; specifically, a gentle throwing from the hand; a pitch; also, the distance over which a thing is tossed. 2 A quick upward or backward movement of the head; any quick jerk. 3 The state of being tossed about; excitement; agitation. 4 A toss–up or wager. 5 *Scot.* A belle; a toast. [Prob. <Scand. Cf. dial. Norw. *tossa* spread, strew.] — **toss'er** *n.*

to·tal (tōt'l) *n.* The whole sum or amount; the whole, especially when considered as an aggregate of parts or elements. See synonyms under AGGREGATE, MASS[1]. — *adj.* 1 Constituting a whole, without diminution or division; being a total: the sum *total.* 2 Extending throughout the whole; comprising everything; complete; perfect: a *total* loss. — *v.* **·taled** or **·talled, ·tal·ing** or **·tal·ling** *v.t.* 1 To ascertain the total of. 2 To come to or reach as a total; amount to. — *v.i.* 3 To amount: often with *to.* [<OF <Med. L *totalis* <L *totus* all] — **to'tal·ly** *adv.*

total depravity The condition defined by the

doctrine that human nature has no tendency to piety or spirituality, but has the opposite tendency, every faculty having an innate taint: one of the five points of Calvinism. Compare ORIGINAL SIN.

total emission *Physics* The maximum emission of electrons from the cathode of a thermionic or vacuum tube.

to·tal·i·tar·i·an (tō-tal'ə-târ'ē-ən) *adj.* Designating or characteristic of a government controlled exclusively by one party or faction, which suppresses all opposition and criticism and controls and regiments all social, cultural, and economic activity in the country to advance its political aims. — *n.* An adherent of totalitarian government. [<TOTALIT(Y) + -ARIAN] — **to·tal'i·tar'i·an·ism** *n.*

to·tal·i·ty (tō-tal'ə-tē) *n.* 1 An aggregate of parts or individuals. 2 The state of being whole or entire. 3 *Astron.* The state or period of an eclipse while it is total. Also **to'tal·ness.** See synonyms under AGGREGATE, MASS[1].

to·tal·ize (tōt'l-īz) *v.t.* **·ized, ·iz·ing** To collect into or ascertain as an aggregate; make total. — **to'tal·i·za'tion** *n.*

to·tal·iz·er (tōt'l-ī'zər) *n.* A pari–mutuel machine.

total reflection *Optics* The complete reflection of a ray of light passing from a denser to a less dense medium.

to·ta·quine (tō'tə-kwin) *n.* A mixture of the alkaloids from cinchona bark, including an effective percentage of quinine: used in the treatment of malaria. [<NL *totaquina* <L *tota,* fem. of *totus* all + Quechua *(quin)quina* cinchona bark]

tote (tōt) *Colloq. v.t.* **tot·ed, tot·ing** 1 To carry or bear on the person, as a burden. 2 To carry, transport, or haul, as supplies. 3 In arithmetic, to carry. 4 To wear habitually: He *totes* a gun. — *n.* 1 The act of toting. 2 A load or haul. [Prob. <West African] — **tot'er** *n.*

to·tem (tō'təm) *n.* 1 Among many primitive peoples, especially the North American Indians, an animal, plant, or other natural object believed to be ancestrally related to a tribe, clan, or family group or to be its tutelar spirit. 2 The representation of such an animal, plant, or object taken as an emblem or symbol. 3 The name or symbol of a person, clan, or tribe. [<Algonquian. Cf. Ojibwa *ototeman* his relations.] — **to·tem·ic** (tō-tem'ik) *adj.*

to·tem·ism (tō'təm-iz'əm) *n.* 1 Belief in totems and the practices associated therewith. 2 The system of dividing a tribe into sibs or clans according to their totems. [<TOTEM + -ISM] — **to'tem·is'tic** *adj.*

totem pole A post or pole, usually of cedar and sometimes as much as 50 feet high, carved or painted with totemic symbols, erected outside an Indian house or as a memorial to a deceased, especially among the Indians of the NW American coast. Also **totem post.**

toth·er (tuth'ər) *pron. Colloq.* The other; other. Also **t'oth'er.** [ME *the tother* < *thet other* the other]

TOTEM POLE

toti– *combining form* Whole; wholly: *totipalmate.* [<L *totus* whole]

to·ti·pal·mate (tō'ti-pal'māt) *adj. Ornithol.* Wholly webbed; having all four toes joined by a web, as pelicans. [<TOTI– + PALMATE] — **to'ti·pal·ma'tion** (-pal-mā'shən) *n.*

to·tip·o·tence (tō-tip'ə-təns) *n. Biol.* Power to regenerate the whole of an organism, or some one part, from a fragment. [<TOTI– + potence, var. of POTENCY] — **to·tip'o·tent** *adj.*

tot·ter (tot'ər) *v.i.* 1 To walk feebly and unsteadily. 2 To shake or waver, as if about to fall; be unsteady. — *n.* The act of tottering. See synonyms under SHAKE. [Prob. <Scand. Cf. Norw. *totra, tutra* quiver.] — **tot'ter·er** *n.* — **tot'ter·y** *adj.*

tou·can (tōō'kan, tōō-kän') *n.* A large, fruit-eating bird of tropical America (family

TOUCAN
(About 12 inches over–all)

Rhamphastidae) with brilliant plumage and an immense thin–walled beak. [<F <Pg. *tucano* <Tupian *tucana*]

touch (tuch) *v.t.* 1 To place the hand, finger, etc., in contact with. 2 To be in or come into contact with. 3 To bring into contact with something else. 4 To hit or strike lightly; tap. 5 To lay the hand or hands on. 6 To border on; adjoin. 7 To come to; reach. 8 To attain to; equal. 9 To mark or delineate lightly, as with a brush or pen. 10 To modify by adding fine strokes or lines; retouch. 11 To color slightly: The sun *touched* the clouds with gold. 12 To affect injuriously; taint: Vegetables *touched* by frost. 13 To affect by contact; act upon: The drill could not *touch* the steel. 14 To affect the emotions of; soften; move. 15 To move to anger; irritate. 16 To strike the strings or keys of (a musical instrument); play on. 17 To play (a tune). 18 To relate to; concern: This quarrel *touches* you. 19 To treat or discuss in passing; deal with. 20 To have to do with, use, or partake of: I will not *touch* this food. 21 *Slang* To borrow money from. 22 *Slang* To steal. 23 *Geom.* To be tangent to. 24 *Obs.* To test, as gold with a touchstone. — *v.i.* 25 To touch someone or something. 26 To come into or be in contact. See synonyms under REACH. — **to touch at** To stop briefly at (a port or place) in the course of a journey or voyage. — **to touch off** 1 To cause to explode; detonate; fire. 2 To cause to happen or occur. — **to touch on** (or **upon**) 1 To relate to; concern. 2 To treat briefly or in passing. — **to touch up** 1 To strike or prod gently; rouse. 2 To add finishing touches or corrections to. — *n.* 1 The act or process of touching or coming in contact with (something). 2 The act or state of being touched. 3 That one of the special senses that gives the impression of contact with external material objects or their impact upon the body. ◆ Collateral adjective: *tactile.* 4 The sensation conveyed by touching something: a smooth *touch.* 5 *Med.* **a** Examination by feeling; palpation. **b** Digital examination of the vagina in obstetrics. 6 A stroke; hit; blow: to give a ball a slight *touch.* 7 A stroke of wit, ridicule, etc.: He felt the *touch* of her wit. 8 In art, any slight or delicate effort or effect, as of a brush, pen, or chisel; a light stroke or mark: to apply the finishing *touches* to a painting. 9 Any slight detail or effort given to anything, as to a literary work. 10 The manner or style in which an artist, workman, or author executes his work: a master's *touch*; a freedom of *touch.* 11 A trace; tinge; hint; infusion: a *touch* of irony; a *touch* of autumn. 12 A slight attack or twinge: a *touch* of rheumatism; a *touch* of remorse. 13 A small quantity or dash: to apply a *touch* of perfume. 14 Close communication, contact, or sympathy: to keep in *touch* with; to lose *touch* with. 15 A test; trial: to put something to the *touch* of proof. 16 *Music* **a** In the pianoforte, the resistance made to the fingers by the keys. **b** The manner in which a player presses the keyboard. 17 In Rugby football and soccer, the ground just outside the touch lines. 18 An official stamp impressed upon ware made of gold, silver, or pewter, to testify to its fineness. 19 *Obs.* A touchstone, or the method of assaying by the use of a touchstone. 20 *Slang* A sum of money obtained, usually from a friend or acquaintance, by borrowing or mooching. 21 *Slang* A request for such a sum of money: to make a *touch.* 22 *Slang* A person who is an easy mark for a loan or gift of money: usually with an attributive word: a soft *touch*; an easy *touch.* [<OF *tochier, tuchier*; prob. ult. imit.] — **touch'a·ble** *adj.* — **touch'a·ble·ness** *n.* — **touch'er** *n.*

touch and go 1 An uncertain, risky, or precarious state of things; a narrow escape. 2 An instantaneous or rapid action.

touch·back (tuch'bak') *n.* In football, the act of touching the ball to the ground behind the player's own goal line when the impetus that sent the ball over the goal line was given to it by an opponent.

touch·down (tuch'doun') *n.* A scoring play in football in which the ball is held on or over the opponent's goal line and is there declared dead.

tou·ché (tōō·shā') *French adj.* In fencing, touched by the point of an opponent's foil. —*interj.* You've scored a point! That argument struck home!: an exclamation used to indicate an opponent's success.

touched (tucht) *adj.* 1 That has been subjected to contact. 2 Slightly unbalanced in mind; crack–brained.

touch·hole (tuch'hōl') *n.* The orifice in old–fashioned cannon or firearms through which the powder was ignited.

touch·ing (tuch'ing) *adj.* Appealing to the susceptibilities; affecting; pathetic. See synonyms under PITIFUL. —*n.* 1 The act of one who touches. 2 The sense of touch. —*prep.* With regard to; concerning; with respect to. —**touch'ing·ly** *adv.* —**touch'ing·ness** *n.*

touch lines The side boundary lines of a Rugby football or soccer field.

touch·stone (tuch'stōn') *n.* 1 A fine–grained dark stone, as jasper, formerly used to test the fineness of gold by the color of the streak made on the stone. 2 A criterion or standard by which the qualities of something are tested.

touch·wood (tuch'wŏod') *n.* 1 Wood, decayed or thoroughly dried, for use as tinder; punk. 2 Dried fungi or fungous growth; amadou.

tough (tuf) *adj.* 1 Susceptible of great tension or strain without breaking; also, of a close texture. 2 Not easily separated; tenacious; viscid; ropy. 3 Possessing great physical endurance: a *tough* constitution. 4 Possessing moral or intellectual endurance; steadfast; persistent; also, stubborn. 5 Irreclaimably vicious; disreputable; vulgar. 6 Difficult to accomplish; laborious; also, severe. 7 Hard to believe; incredible. —*n.* A lawless person; a rowdy; ruffian. [OE *tōh*] —**tough'·ly** *adv.* —**tough'ness** *n.*

tough·en (tuf'ən) *v.t.* & *v.i.* To make or become tough or tougher. —**tough'en·er** *n.*

tou·pee (tōō·pā', -pē') *n.* 1 A little tuft or lock of hair. 2 A curl or lock of hair worn as a false front or at the top of a wig. 3 A wig worn to cover baldness or a bald spot. [<F *toupet* <OF *toup, top* a tuft of hair, prob. <Gmc.]

tour (tŏor) *n.* 1 A round trip or journey or a rambling excursion. 2 A passing around; circuit for inspection or sightseeing. 3 A turn or shift, as of service. See synonyms under JOURNEY. —**grand tour** A tour of the principal cities of Europe, customary in the 17th and 18th centuries for young English gentlemen as a supplement to their education: chiefly used in the expression *to make the grand tour.* —*v.t.* 1 To make a tour of; travel. 2 To present on a tour: to *tour* a play. —*v.i.* 3 To go on a tour. [<MF <OF *tor, tors* <L *tornus* a lathe <Gk. *tornos*; infl. in meaning by OF *tourner* TURN]

tour·bil·lion (tŏor·bil'yən) *n.* 1 A whirling wind or a vortex, or something resembling them. 2 A kind of rocket with a spiral flight. [<MF *tourbillon* a whirlwind <OF *torbeillon* <L *turbo, -inis*]

tour·ism (tŏor'iz·əm) *n.* 1 Traveling as a recreation. 2 Touring groups; tourists. 3 The organization and guidance of tourists. —**tour·is'tic** *adj.*

tour·ist (tŏor'ist) *n.* One who makes a tour or a pleasure trip. —*adj.* Of or suitable for tourists.

tourist class A class of accommodations for steamship passengers, lower than cabin class.

tour·ma·line (tŏor'mə·lēn, -lin) *n.* A complex borosilicate of aluminum, with a vitreous to resinous luster and found commonly black or brownish or bluish–black, but sometimes blue, green, red, or colorless. The transparent variety, when cut, is esteemed as a gemstone. Also spelled *turmaline.* Also **tour'ma·lin** (-lin). [<F, ult. <Singhalese *tōramalli* carnelian]

tour·na·ment (tûr'nə·mənt, tŏor'-) *n.* 1 In medieval times, a pageant in which two opposing parties of men in armor contended on horseback, with blunted weapons, in mock combat. 2 The jousts, sports, or contests in which such combatants engaged. 3 A comparatively recent sport of skilled horsemen, who tilt at rings suspended in the air, seeking to bear them off on their lances. 4 Any contest of skill involving a number of competitors and a series of games: a chess *tournament.* 5 An encounter, at arms: Don Quixote's *tournament* with the barber. Also *tourney.* [<OF *torneiement, tornoiement* <*torneier, tornoier* tourney, ult. <L *tornare.* See TURN.]

tour·ney (tûr'nē, tŏor'-) *v.i.* To take part in a tournament; tilt. —*n.* A tournament. [<OF *torneier.* See TOURNAMENT.]

tour·ni·quet (tŏor'nə·ket, -kā, tûr'-) *n. Surg.* A bandage, etc., for stopping the flow of blood through an artery by compression. [<F <*tourner* TURN]

tour of duty *Mil.* The hours or period of time during which a member of the armed services is on official duty, or assigned to a particular duty: the 24-hour *tour of duty* as officer of the day.

tou·sle (tou'zəl) *v.t.* **·sled, ·sling** To disarrange or disorder, as the hair or dress. —*n.* 1 *Scot.* A tussle; also, a rude dalliance. 2 A tousled mass or mop of hair. Also **tou'zle.** [Freq. of TOUSE]

tout (tout) *Colloq. v.i.* 1 To solicit patronage, customers, votes, etc. 2 To spy on a race horse so as to gain information for betting; act as a tout. —*v.t.* 3 To solicit; importune. 4 a To spy on (a race horse) to gain information for betting. b To sell information concerning (a race horse). —*n.* 1 One who touts. 2 In horse-racing, a spy who sells information regarding horses entered for a race. 3 One who solicits business. 4 A spy for a robber. [OE *tōtian, tȳtan* peep, look out]

tout·er (tou'tər) *n.* 1 One who plies or solicits customers or supporters obtrusively: a *touter* for a candidate for election. 2 *Colloq.* A runner.

tow¹ (tō) *n.* A short, coarse hemp or flax fiber prepared for spinning. [Prob. OE *tōw-* for spinning, as in *tōwlic* pertaining to spinning]

tow² (tō) *v.t.* To pull or drag by a rope or chain; drag or pull along. See synonyms under DRAW. —*n.* 1 The act of towing, or the state of being towed. 2 That which is towed, as barges by a tugboat. 3 That which tows. 4 A rope or cable used in towing; towline. —**to take in tow** To take in charge for or as for towing; take under protection; take charge of. [OE *togian*]

to·ward (tôrd, tōrd, tə·wôrd') *prep.* 1 In the direction of; facing. 2 With respect to; regarding: his attitude *toward* women. 3 In anticipation of or as a contribution to; for: He is saving *toward* his education. 4 Near in point of time; approaching; about: arriving *toward* evening. 5 Tending to result in; designed or likely to achieve: a struggle *toward* mutual understanding. Also **to·wards'.** See synonyms under AT. —*adj.* (tôrd, tōrd) *Archaic or Rare* 1 Ready to do or learn; apt. 2 Docile. 3 In progress: used predicatively. 4 Impending or imminent. [OE *tōweard* <*tō* to + *-weard* -ward] —**to·ward'ness** *n.*

to·ward·ly (tôrd'lē, tōrd'-) *Archaic adj.* 1 Ready to do or learn; compliant; docile. 2 Favorable; promising; propitious.

tow·a·way (tō'ə·wā) *n.* The act of towing away a vehicle, especially one illegally parked. —*adj.* Of or pertaining to the towing away of such vehicles: the city *towaway* policy.

tow·el (toul, tou'əl) *n.* 1 A cloth or paper for drying anything by wiping. 2 An altar cloth. —*v.t.* **·eled** or **·elled, ·el·ing** or **·el·ling** To wipe or dry with a towel. [<OF *toaille,* prob. < OHG *dwahila* a washcloth <*dwahan* wash]

tow·er (tou'ər) *n.* 1 A structure very tall in proportion to its other dimensions, and frequently forming part of a large building; properly, a structure larger than a pinnacle, and less tapering than a steeple. 2 A tall, wooden, movable structure from which besiegers formerly stormed a fortress. 3 A place of security or defense; fortified place; citadel. —*v.i.* 1 To rise or stand like a tower; extend to a great height. 2 To fly directly upward, as some birds. [Fusion of OE *torr* (<L *turris*) and OE *tūr* <OF *tor, tur* <L *turris*]

tow·ered (tou'ərd) *adj.* 1 Furnished with towers for ornament or defense. 2 Rising like a tower.

tow·er·ing (tou'ər·ing) *adj.* 1 Like a tower; lofty; hence, very high or great: also **tow'er·y.** 2 Rising or increasing to a high pitch of violence or intensity; furious. See synonyms under HIGH.

Tower of London A group of buildings comprising a fortress and palace on the north bank of the Thames, built in 1078 around the original tower (the White Tower) and used as a royal residence, a political prison, and a museum.

tower of silence A circular tower with central well, having a high outer wall, and inner platform on which the Parsees expose the bodies of their dead to be eaten by vultures, so that the bodies may be dissipated without polluting the earth: also called *dakhma, dokhma.*

tow·head (tō'hed') *n.* 1 A head of very light-colored or flaxen hair, or a person having such hair. 2 *U.S.* A wooded sandbar or newly formed island in a river. [<TOW¹ + HEAD] —**tow'-head'ed** *adj.*

tow·hee (tou'hē, tō'-) *n.* An American bird related to the buntings and the sparrows, especially the **Alabama towhee** *(Pipilo erythrophthalmus)* and the **green-tailed towhee** *(Oberholseria chlorura)* of the western United States. Also **towhee bunting.** [Imit. of one of its notes]

tow·line (tō'līn') *n.* A line, rope, or chain used in towing.

town (toun) *n.* 1 Any considerable collection of dwellings and other buildings larger than a village and comprising a geographical and political community unit, but not incorporated as a city. 2 The local government of such a community; also, the voters, the representatives, or the inhabitants collectively. 3 A subdivision of a county, usually rural, that may include a number of villages and towns; a township. 4 In New England, a local unit governing itself through a town meeting. 5 *Brit.* Originally, a collection of dwellings enclosed for security within some form of fortification; subsequently, any collection of dwelling houses larger than a village. ◆Collateral adjective: *oppidan.* 6 A closely settled urban district as contrasted with the open country: *town* and country. 7 The city or town nearest to where one lives: a trip to *town;* also, the downtown or business section of a city or town. 8 A group of prairie-dog burrows. —**on the town** 1 Dependent on municipal charity. 2 *Slang* On a round of pleasure in the city. —**to go to town** *Slang* To succeed in the highest degree. —**to paint the town red** *Slang* To carouse. —*adj.* 1 Of or pertaining to, like, situated in, or for use in town: *town* clothes. 2 Supported by town funds: a *town* library. [OE *tūn, tuun* an enclosure, group of houses]

town clerk An official who keeps the records of a town.

town crier A person appointed to make proclamations through the streets of a town.

town farm A farm maintained by town or township funds for the poor or indigent.

town hall The building containing the public offices of a town and used for meetings of the town council and other official business.

town house 1 A residence in a town or city. 2 A town hall. 3 *U.S. Obs.* a An almshouse; workhouse. b A town prison.

town marshal 1 An officer of a town police force. 2 In the American colonies, an officer who levied and collected taxes, fines, etc.

town meeting 1 A general assemblage of the people of a town. 2 An assembly of qualified voters for the purpose of transacting town business; also, the voters assembled.

town·ship (toun'ship) *n.* 1 *U.S.* a A territorial subdivision of a county with certain corporate powers of municipal government for local purposes; also, the corporation or government thereof. b In New England, a local political unit governed by a town meeting. 2 A unit of area in surveys of U.S. public lands, normally six miles square, subdivided into 36 sections of one square mile each. 3 *Brit.* Anciently, an organized group of families forming the political unit of early society which existed prior to the parish. [OE *tūnscipe < tūn* a village, group of houses]

towns·man (tounz′mən) *n. pl.* **·men** (-mən) **1** A resident of a town; also, a fellow citizen. **2** In New England, a town officer; a selectman. **3** In a school or college town, one who lives in the town as contrasted with a student or teacher in the school or college.

tow·path (tō′path′, -päth′) *n.* A path along a river or canal used by men, horses, or mules towing boats; a towing path.

tow·rope (tō′rōp′) *n.* A heavy rope or cable used in towing. Also called *towline*.

tow truck (tō) A truck equipped to tow other vehicles.

tow·y (tō′ē) *adj.* Composed of, like, or containing tow. [< TOW¹]

tox·al·bu·min (tok′sal·byoō′min) *n. Biochem.* Any protein substance having toxic properties, as snake venom, ricin, certain bacterial cultures, etc. [< TOX(IC) + ALBUMIN]

tox·a·phene (tok′sə·fēn) *n.* A waxy chlorinated hydrocarbon, C₁₀H₁₀Cl, used as a pesticide. [< TOX(IC) + PHEN(YL)]

tox·e·mi·a (tok·sē′mē·ə) *n. Pathol.* A poisoned condition of the body caused by the absorption of bacterial toxins from a local source of infection and their distribution by the blood. Also **tox·ae′mi·a.** [< NL < Gk. *toxicon* a poison + *haima* blood] —**tox·e′mic, tox·ae′mic** *adj.*

tox·ic (tok′sik) *adj.* **1** Pertaining to poison; poisonous. **2** Due to or caused by poison or a toxin. Also **tox′i·cal.** [< Med. L *toxicus* poisoned; poisonous < L *toxicum* a poison, orig. a poison for arrows < Gk. *toxicon (pharmakon)* (a poison) for arrows < *toxa* arrows < *toxon* a bow] —**tox′i·cal·ly** *adv.*

tox·i·cant (tok′sə·kənt) *adj.* **1** Possessing poisonous qualities. **2** Producing a poisonous effect. — *n.* A toxic substance; poison; also, an intoxicant. [< LL *toxicans, -antis,* ppr. of *toxicare* smear with poison < L *toxicum.* See TOXIC.]

tox·i·ca·tion (tok′sə·kā′shən) *n.* **1** The act of poisoning. **2** The state of being poisoned. **3** Poisoning.

tox·ic·i·ty (tok·sis′ə·tē) *n.* **1** The quality of being toxic. **2** The degree or intensity of virulence of a poison.

tox·i·co·gen·ic (tok′sə·kō·jen′ik) *adj.* **1** Producing poisons or toxins. **2** Generated or formed by toxic matter.

tox·i·col·o·gy (tok′sə·kol′ə·jē) *n.* The science that treats of the origin, nature, properties, and effects of poisons, of their detection in the organs or tissues, of their antidotes, and of the treatment of diseases due to poisoning. [< F *toxicologie*] — **tox′i·co·log′i·cal** (-kō·loj′i·kəl) *adj.* — **tox′i·co·log′i·cal·ly** *adv.* — **tox′i·col′o·gist** *n.*

tox·i·co·ma·ni·a (tok′sə·kō·mā′nē·ə, -mān′yə) *n.* A morbid desire to take poison. [< TOXICO- + -MANIA]

tox·i·co·pho·bi·a (tok′sə·kō·fō′bē·ə) *n.* A morbid fear of poison or of being poisoned: also called *iophobia, toxiphobia.* [< TOXICO- + -PHOBIA] — **tox′i·pho′bic** *adj.*

tox·in (tok′sin) *n.* **1** Any of a class of more or less unstable poisonous compounds elaborated by animal, vegetable, or bacterial organisms and acting as causative agents in many diseases, usually after an incubation period. **2** Any toxic matter generated in living or dead organisms. Also **tox·ine** (tok′sēn). [< TOX(IC) + -IN]

tox·o·phil (tok′sə·fil) *adj. Biol.* Having an affinity for or being in harmony with a toxin. Also **tox′o·phile** (-fīl, -fil). [< *toxo-* (< TOXIN) + -PHIL]

tox·o·plas·mo·sis (tok′sō·plaz·mō′sis) *n.* A diseased condition resulting from the presence of or infection by sporozoan parasites (genus *Toxoplasma*) which act principally upon the nervous system of certain animals and sometimes of man. [< NL < *Toxoplasma,* genus name]

toy (toi) *n.* **1** An article constructed for the amusement of children; a plaything; hence, any trifling or diverting object; an ornament; trinket. **2** Any diminutive object imitating a larger one and fitted for entertainment and instruction. **3** *Obs.* Wanton play; dalliance. **4** A small dog bred to extreme smallness and kept as a pet: also **toy dog.** **5** *Scot.* A head covering for women that hangs loosely over the shoulders; a toy-mutch. **6** *Obs.* A dance

tune. **7** *Archaic* A quaint utterance, idle tale, or anecdote; fancy; jest. See synonyms under GAUD. — *v.i.* To trifle; play. — *adj.* Resembling a toy; of miniature size. [Prob. fusion of ME *toye* flirtation, sport + Du. *tuig* tools, stuff] — **toy′er** *n.* — **toy′ish** *adj.*

to·yon (tō′yən) *n.* An evergreen shrub (*Photinia arbutifolia*) indigenous to the Pacific coast of North America, having white flowers, followed by persistent berries of a bright red color; California holly. [< Sp. *tollón* < N. Am. Ind. (Mexican)]

tra·be·at·ed (trā′bē·ā′tid) *adj. Archit.* **1** Having an entablature. **2** Having beams or long stones as lintels instead of an arch. Also **tra′be·ate** (-it, -āt). [Irregularly formed < L *trabs, trabis* a beam]

tra·bec·u·la (trə·bek′yə·lə) *n. pl.* **·lae** (-lē) **1** A small supporting band or bar. **2** *Anat.* The interwoven bands of connective tissue that form the supporting framework of an organ, as the spleen. **3** *Bot.* A row or plate of sterile cells extending across the cavity in the sporangium of a moss. [< L, dim. of *trabs, trabis* a beam] — **tra·bec′u·lar** *adj.*

trace¹ (trās) *n.* **1** A vestige or mark left by some past event or agent, especially when regarded as a sign or clue. **2** A barely detectable quantity, quality, token, or characteristic; touch. **3** *Chem.* A proportion or ingredient too small to be weighed (often abbreviated *tr.*): *a trace* of soda. **4** An imprint or mark indicating the passage of a person or thing, as a footprint, etc. **4** A path or trail through woods or forest beaten down by men or animals. **5** A lightly drawn line; something traced. **6** The point or line on a map or on the ground indicating the position of a trench, an aircraft flight path, etc. **7** The path of a tracer bullet. **8** *Psychol.* An engram. — *v.* **traced, trac·ing** *v.t.* **1** To follow the tracks, course, or development of. **2** To follow (tracks, a course of development; etc.). **3** To discover or ascertain by examination or investigation; find out or determine. **4** To draw; sketch. **5** To copy (a drawing, etc.) on a superimposed transparent sheet. **6** To form (letters, etc.) with careful strokes. **7** To mark with an impressed design; chase. **8** To imprint (a pattern or design). **9** To mark or record by a curved or broken line. **10** To go or move over, along, or through. — *v.i.* **11** To make one's way; proceed. **12** To have its origin; go back in time. [< OF *tracier,* ult. < L *tractus* a dragging, a track < *trahere* draw] — **trace′a·ble** *adj.* — **trace′a·bil′i·ty, trace′a·ble·ness** *n.* — **trace′a·bly** *adv.* — **trace′less** *adj.*

Synonyms (noun): footmark, footprint, footstep, mark, memorial, remains, remnant, sign, token, track, vestige. A *vestige* is always slight compared with that whose existence it recalls; as, Scattered mounds containing human implements are *vestiges* of a former civilization. A *vestige* is always a part of that which has passed away; a *trace* may be merely the *mark* it has made, or some slight evidence of its presence or of the effect it has produced; as, *Traces* of game were observed by the hunter. See CHARACTERISTIC, MARK¹.

trace² (trās) *n.* **1** One of two side straps or chains for connecting the collar of a harness with the swingletree. **2** *Mech.* A link or connecting bar hinged at each end to other pieces of a mechanism, to transmit motion from one part to another. — **to kick over the traces** To throw off control; become unmanageable. — *v.t.* **traced, trac·ing** To fasten, as with traces. [< OF *traiz, trais,* pl. of *trait* a dragging, a leather harness < L *tractus.* See TRACE¹.]

trac·er (trā′sər) *n.* **1** One who or that which traces. **2** One of various instruments used in tracing drawings, etc. **3** An inquiry forwarded from one point to another, to trace missing mail matter, etc. **4** *Surg.* An instrument for laying bare and tracing the course of nerves, muscles, etc. **5** One who searches for lost property, as on railroads. **6** *Mil.* **a** A chemical incorporated in certain types of ammunition used for ranging, signaling, or incendiary purposes. **b** A tracer bullet. **7** *Med.* A radioisotope introduced into the body for the purpose of following the processes of metabolism, the course or location of a disease, etc. **8** A message that describes a person or thing wanted, as by the police.

tracer bullet A bullet which leaves a line of smoke or fire in its wake, thus indicating its course for correction of aim.

trac·er·y (trā′sər·ē) *n. pl.* **·er·ies 1** Ornamental stonework formed of ramifying lines. **2** Any work resembling this.

tra·che·a (trā′kē·ə) *n. pl.* **·che·ae** (-ki·ē) **1** *Anat.* The duct, composed of membrane and incomplete cartilaginous rings, by which air passes from the larynx to the bronchi and the lungs; the windpipe. **2** *Zool.* One of the passages by which air is conveyed from the exterior in air-breathing arthropods, as insects and arachnids. **3** *Bot.* A duct or vessel in plants, particularly one having spiral markings. [< Med. L < LL *trachia* < Gk. *(artēria) tracheia* a rough (artery), fem. of *trachys* rough] — **tra′che·al** *adj.*

tra·che·id (trā′kē·id) *n. Bot.* An elongated, taper-pointed, woody plant cell, especially when marked with bordered pits and serving for support, as in the pine family. [< G *tracheïde* < Med. L *trachea* the trachea] — **tra·che·i·dal** (trə·kē′ə·dəl) *adj.*

tra·che·os·co·py (trā′kē·os′kə·pē) *n. Med.* Instrumental inspection of the windpipe. — **tra′che·o·scop′ic** (-ō-skop′ik) *adj.* — **tra′che·os′co·pist** *n.*

tra·che·ot·o·my (trā′kē·ot′ə·mē) *n. Surg.* The operation of making an incision into the windpipe. — **tra′che·ot′o·mist** *n.*

tra·cho·ma (trə·kō′mə) *n. Pathol.* A contagious virus disease of the eye characterized by hard papillary elevations or granular excrescences on the inner surface of the eyelids, with inflammation of the lining; granular conjunctivitis. [< NL < Gk. *trachōma, -atos* roughness < *trachys* rough] — **tra·chom·a·tous** (trə·kom′ə·təs) *adj.*

track (trak) *n.* **1** A mark or trail left by the passage of anything: the *track* of a storm. **2** A footprint or series of footprints. **3** Any regular path; course: the *track* of a comet round the sun. **4** Any kind of racecourse; also, sports performed on such a course; track athletics. **5** A set of rails or a rail on which something may travel; specifically, the pair of metal rails on which a railway train or tramway runs; also, the rail or pair of rails with its ties, bolts, etc.; by extension, the whole trackway. **6** A trace or vestige. **7** A sequence of events; a succession of ideas. **8** Awareness of the progress or sequence; count; record: to keep *track* of. **9** Tread (def. 2). See synonyms under MARK¹, ROAD, TRACE¹, WAY. **10** A course or trail leading to a desired goal: to be on the right *track.* **11** One of a pair of endless metal belts by means of which certain vehicles, as tanks, are capable of moving over a variety of surfaces. **12** In education, any of two or more classes covering the same course of study, segregated according to the students' preparation or ability and taught at correspondingly different levels. — **to make tracks** To hurry; run away in haste. — **in one's tracks** Right where one is; on the spot. — **to jump the track 1** To leave the rails, as a railroad engine or car. **2** To depart from any usual course or procedure. — *v.t.* **1** To follow the tracks of; trail. **2** To discover and follow up or out, by means of marks or indications. **3** To make tracks upon or with: to *track* snow through a house. **4** To traverse, as on foot: to *track* the wild forests. **5** To furnish with rails or tracks. — *v.i.* **6** To measure a certain distance between wheels. **7** To have the wheels equal in span or gage to the wheels of another vehicle. **8** To run in the same track; be in alinement. — *adj.* Pertaining to or performed on a track. [< OF *trac,* prob. < Gmc. Cf. Du. *trek* pull.] — **track′er** *n.* — **track′a·ble** *adj.*

track·age (trak′ij) *n.* **1** Railroad tracks collectively. **2** The right of one company to use the track system of another company. **3** The charge for this right. **4** A towing, especially of a vessel in a canal, with a rope from the towpath.

track detector *Physics* A device for showing the ionization paths of subatomic particles, as the cloud chamber.

track events The races at an athletic meet: distinguished from *field events.* Also **track athletics.**

track·man (trak'mən) *n. pl.* **·men** (-mən) *U. S.* A person employed to inspect regularly the condition of a section of railroad track. Also **track·walk·er** (trak'wôk'ər).

track meet An athletic contest made up of track events.

tract[1] (trakt) *n.* **1** An extended area, as of land or water. **2** Continued duration, as of time. **3** *Anat.* An extensive region of the body, especially one comprising a system of parts or organs: the alimentary *tract.* [<L *tractus* a drawing out, duration < *trahere* draw. Doublet of TRAIT.]

tract[2] (trakt) *n.* **1** A short treatise, as on some question of religion or morals; a propaganda leaflet. **2** An anthem sometimes substituted for the Alleluia: so styled because, instead of being treated antiphonally, it is sung *tractim* (continuously) and as a solo: also **trac'tus.** [Short for TRACTATE]

tract·a·ble (trak'tə·bəl) *adj.* **1** Easily led or controlled; manageable; docile. **2** Readily worked or handled; malleable. See synonyms under DOCILE. [<L *tractabilis* < *tractare* handle, freq. of *trahere* draw] — **tract'a·bly** *adv.* — **tract'a·ble·ness, tract·a·bil'i·ty** *n.*

trac·tile (trak'til) *adj.* That can be drawn out; ductile. [<L *tractilis* < *tractus.* See TRACE[1].] — **trac·til'i·ty** *n.*

trac·tion (trak'shən) *n.* **1** The act of drawing, as by motive power over a surface. **2** The state of being drawn, or the power employed. **3** *Physiol.* Contraction, as of a muscle. **4** Adhesive or rolling friction, as of wheels on a track. [<Med. L *tractio, -onis* <L *tractus.* See TRACE[1].] — **trac'tion·al** *adj.*

trac·tor (trak'tər) *n.* **1** A machine or instrument for pulling or drawing. **2** A powerful, motor-driven vehicle, usually having heavy treads, used, as on farms, to draw a plow, reaper, etc. **3** An automotive vehicle with a driver's cab, used to haul trailers, etc. **4** A traction engine. **5** *Aeron.* **a** An airplane with the propeller or propellers situated in front of the supporting surface to pull it through the air: also **tractor airplane. b** The propeller of a tractor airplane. [<NL <L *tractus.* See TRACE[1].]

trade (trād) *n.* **1** A business, particularly a skilled or specialized handicraft; a craft. **2** Mercantile traffic; commerce. **3** A bargain; deal; also, an exchange; specifically, a corrupt bargain in patronage between political-party leaders. **4** The people following a particular calling. **5** The amount of business or exchange done in a particular place; a firm's customers. **6** Customary pursuit; occupation. **7** *Brit.* **a** The submarine service of the Royal Navy. **b** The liquor traffic. **8** *Obs.* A trail or track. **9** *Obs.* A course, path, passage, or way. **10** *Obs.* Custom, habit, or practice. **11** A trade wind: usually in the plural. See synonyms under BUSINESS, SALE, TRAFFIC. — *v.* **trad·ed, trad·ing** *v.t.* To dispose of by bargain and sale; now, especially, to barter; exchange. — *v.i.* To engage in commerce or in business transactions of bargain and sale. — **to trade in** To give in exchange as payment or part payment. — **to trade off** To get rid of by exchange or trading. — **to trade on** To take advantage of. [<MLG, a track. Akin to TREAD.]

trade acceptance A bill of exchange drawn by the seller of goods on the purchaser who accepts the draft by writing across the face of it when and where it is payable.

trade book An edition of a book designed for ordinary sale to the general public, as distinguished from a textbook, limited or de luxe edition, etc.

trade–in (trād'in') *n.* Something given or accepted in payment or part payment for something else; an exchange.

trade journal A periodical publishing news and discussions of a particular trade or business.

trade·mark (trād'märk') *n.* A name, symbol, design, device, or word, or any combination thereof, used by a merchant or manufacturer to identify his goods and distinguish them from those made or sold by others. A trademark may or may not be legally registered as such — *v.t.* **1** To label with a trademark. **2** To register as a trademark. — **trade'marked'** *adj.*

trade name **1** The name by which an article, process, service, or the like is designated in trade. **2** A name given by a manufacturer to designate a proprietary article, sometimes having the status of a trademark or of a copyrighted and patented proprietary name. **3** A style or a name of a business house acquired by purchase from a retiring firm or trader.

trade-off (trād'ôf', -of') *n.* **1** A giving up of something, as an objective or advantage, in exchange for something else: a *trade-off* of higher pay for longer vacations. **2** The relationship that characterizes such an exchange; a compromise or adjustment between opposing elements or positions: the *trade-off* between taxation and improved public services.

trad·er (trā'dər) *n.* **1** One who trades. **2** Any vessel employed in a particular trade. **3** A member of a stock exchange who trades for himself, and not for customers.

trade rat A pack rat.

trad·es·can·ti·a (trad'əs·kan'shē·ə, -shə) *n.* Any of a genus (*Tradescantia*) of perennial American herbs, often having grasslike leaves and showy flowers with ephemeral petals. [<NL, after John *Tradescant,* died in 1638, English traveler and naturalist]

trade union An organized association of workmen formed for the protection and promotion of their common interests, especially with regard to wages, hours, and working conditions. Also **trades union.** — **trade'–un'ion·ism** *n.* — **trade'–un'ion·ist** *n.*

trade wind Either of two steady winds blowing in the same course toward the equator from about 30° N and S latitude, one from the northeast on the north, the other from the southeast on the south side of the equatorial line.

trad·ing (trā'ding) *adj.* **1** Carrying on trade. **2** Corrupt; venal: said of officials. **3** *Obs.* Pursuing a steady course.

trading post A building or small settlement in unsettled territory where a trader or trading company has set up a station for barter (usually in furs) with North American Indians or other natives.

trading stamp See under STAMP.

tra·di·tion (trə·dish'ən) *n.* **1** The transmission of knowledge, opinions, doctrines, customs, practices, etc., from generation to generation, originally by word of mouth and by example. **2** That which is so transmitted; a body of beliefs and usages handed down from generation to generation; also, any particular story, belief, or usage so handed down; hence, remembrance, or recollection existing as by transmission. **3** That body of Christian doctrine, handed down through successive generations and held by some churches to belong to the deposit of faith, even if it may not be found in the Holy Scripture. **4** Among the Jews, an unwritten code said to have been revealed to Moses on Mount Sinai at the time of the delivery of the Decalog and handed down through the oral teaching of prophets and doctors of the law. **5** The record of the acts and utterances of Mohammed, known as the *Sunna.* **6** A custom so long continued that it has almost the force of a law. **7** *Law* Delivery of possession. [<OF *tradicion* <L *traditio, -onis* a delivery, surrender < *traditus,* pp. of *tradere* deliver < *trans-* across + *dare* give. Doublet of TREASON.] — **tra·di'tion·er, tra·di'tion·ist** *n.*

tra·di·tion·al·ism (trə·dish'ən·əl·iz'əm) *n.* **1** A system of faith founded on tradition. **2** Adherence to tradition; especially, undue reverence for tradition in religious matters.

tra·duce (trə·dōōs', -dyōōs') *v.t.* **·duced, ·duc·ing** To misrepresent wilfully the conduct or character of; defame; slander. See synonyms under ASPERSE, REVILE. [<L *traducere* transport, bring into disgrace < *trans-* across + *ducere* lead] — **tra·duc'er** *n.* — **tra·duc'i·ble** *adj.* — **tra·duc'ing·ly** *adv.* — **tra·duc·tion** (trə·duk'shən) *n.*

tra·du·cian·ism (trə·dōō'shən·iz'əm, -dyōō'-) *n.* The doctrine that the soul, equally with the body, is produced and begotten by the parent or parents: distinguished from *creationism* and *preexistence.* [<LL *traducianus* <L *tradux, -icis* a shoot for propagation < *traducere.* See

TRADUCE.] — **tra·du'cian·ist** *n.* — **tra·du'cian·is'tic** *adj.*

traf·fic (traf'ik) *n.* **1** The exchange of goods, wares, etc.; the business of buying and selling, between individuals or communities; trade. **2** The business of transportation, as by railroad. **3** The subjects of transportation collectively; the things carried. **4** A business procedure; transaction; hence, intercourse. **5** The passing of pedestrians and vehicles along a road; the flow of telephone messages, etc. **6** Unlawful or improper trade: *traffic* in stolen goods. — *v.i.* **·ficked, ·fick·ing 1** To engage in buying and selling; do business, especially illegally: with *in.* **2** To have dealings: with *with.* [<MF *trafic, trafique* <Ital. *traffico* < *trafficare* <L *trans-* across + Ital. *ficcare* thrust in <L *figere* fasten] — **traf'fick·er** *n.*

Synonyms (*noun*): business, commerce, trade. *Commerce* is the broadest and noblest term of this group. *Trade* may be local; *commerce* is always extended and is between members of distinct communities, states, or nations; as, foreign, interstate, or intrastate *commerce*; foreign, domestic, or free-port *trade. Traffic* is local, as between different parts of one city or between two or more cities. *Trade* may be largely by letter or telegram, etc.; *traffic* involves the actual passing to and fro of persons or commodities and may be applied directly to persons when considered as in some way a source of gain: the passenger *traffic* of a railroad. *Traffic* always suggests stir and bustle: the din of *traffic*; one may say dull *trade,* but scarcely dull *traffic.* Compare synonyms for BUSINESS.

traffic circle A circular intersection, where traffic is maintained in one direction, so constructed as to allow vehicles to enter or leave it at any of the converging roads, or to change course, without interruption of the flow of traffic.

traffic light A signal light which, by changing color, directs the flow of traffic along a road or highway.

trag·a·canth (trag'ə·kanth) *n.* **1** A white or reddish gum obtained from various species of Old World leguminous herbs (genus *Astragalus*), especially *A. gummifer* of SW Asia: used in pharmacy and the arts. **2** Any of the shrubs yielding this gum. [<MF *tragacante* <L *tragacantha* <Gk. *tragakantha* a tragacanth shrub < *tragos* a male goat + *akantha* a thorn]

trag·e·dy (traj'ə·dē) *n. pl.* **·dies 1** A form of drama in which the protagonist, having some quality of greatness (and, in Greek, Roman, and Renaissance tragedy, in high place) comes to disaster through some flaw (which may be a noble fault) in his nature that interacts with the fabric of events (the plot) to bring about his inevitable downfall or death, the action being managed in a way to produce pity and fear in the spectator and to effect a catharsis of these feelings. The failure to achieve this leads to **tragedy manquée,** which falls short of true tragedy. To the outcome of death or madness usual in ancient and Renaissance tragedy, modern tragedy adds the possibility of frustration and unfulfilment from which there seems no escape. Opposed to *comedy.* **2** A fatal event or course of events; murder, especially one involving dramatic incidents. **3** A very terrible or sorrowful fate or end. **4** The art or theory of acting or composing tragedy. [<OF *tregedie, tragedie* <L *tragoedia* <Gk. *tragōidia* appar. < *tragos* a goat + *ōidē* a song; semantic development uncertain]

trag·ic (traj'ik) *adj.* **1** Involving death or calamity; causing suffering; fatal; terrible. **2** Pertaining to or having the nature of tragedy. **3** Appropriate to or like tragedy, especially in drama. Also **trag'i·cal.** [<L *tragicus* <Gk. *tragikos* pertaining to tragedy < *tragos* a goat] — **trag'i·cal·ly, trag'ic·ly** *adv.* — **trag'i·cal·ness** *n.*

trag·i·com·e·dy (traj'i·kom'ə·dē) *n. pl.* **·dies** A drama in which tragic and comic scenes are intermingled. [<MF *tragi–comédie* <LL *tragicomoedia* <L *tragico–comoedia* < *tragicus* TRAGIC + *comoedia* COMEDY] — **trag'i·com'ic** or **·i·cal** *adj.* — **trag'i·com'i·cal·ly** *adv.*

tra·gus (trā′gəs) n. pl. ·gi (-jī) Anat. A flattened, somewhat conical eminence of the auricle in front of the opening of the external ear. [<LL <Gk. tragos the hairy part of the ear, a he-goat; so called because of the hairs on it]

trail (trāl) v.t. 1 To draw along lightly over a surface; also, to drag or draw after: to trail a robe. 2 To follow the trail of; trace; track. 3 Mil. To carry, as a rifle, by grasping it in the right hand just above the balance, with the muzzle to the front and the butt nearly touching the ground. 4 To tread or force down, as grass into a pathway. 5 Naut. To allow (the oars) to drift alongside the boat. —v.i. 6 To hang or float loosely. 7 To grow along the ground or over rocks, bushes, etc., in a loose, creeping way. 8 To follow behind loosely; stream. 9 To saunter leisurely along; move heavily. 10 To lag behind; straggle; remain in the rear. —n. 1 The track left by anything that has moved or been drawn or dragged over any surface. 2 The track or indications followed by a huntsman or by a dog in hunting; the scent. 3 The path worn by persons or by animals; particularly, a route made by repeated passage through a wilderness. 4 Anything drawn behind or in the wake of something; a train; specifically, the train of a dress or gown. 5 Mil. The inclined stock of a gun carriage, or extension of the stock that rests on the ground when the piece is not limbered up: when divided longitudinally into two parts, it is called a **split trail. —to hit** (or take) **the trail** To set out on a journey. [<AF trailler haul, tow a boat <L tragula a dragnet <trahere draw]

trail·er (trā′lər) n. 1 One who or that which trails. 2 A vehicle without automotive power designed to be coupled with a cab or tractor and used to haul freight, household goods, etc. 3 A vehicle usually drawn by an automobile or truck and equipped to serve as living quarters. 4 A preview (def. 2).

trailing arbutus An evergreen perennial (Epigaea repens) of the heath family, bearing clusters of fragrant pink flowers; the mayflower: the State flower of Massachusetts.

trailing edge Aeron. The rear edge of an airfoil or propeller blade.

trail rope 1 A guiderope. 2 A rope used for dragging or towing. 3 A rope attached to a horse's halter or tied around its neck, but allowed to drag while the horse grazes. 4 Mil. A prolonge.

train (trān) n. 1 Anything drawn out to a length, or any series of things drawn along. 2 A continuous line of coupled railway cars. 3 A series, succession, or set of connected things; a sequence; especially, an assemblage of people or objects drawn up processionally or in orderly disposition. 4 A retinue or body of retainers; suite. 5 Something pulled along with and in the track of another. 6 An extension of a dress skirt, trailing behind the wearer. 7 Proper order; due course. 8 Mech. A series of parts acting upon each other, as for transmitting motion: also called drive train, power train. 9 Mil. a The variation of the axis of a gun in a horizontal plane. b Collectively, the men, animals, and vehicles attached to a military body for the transportation of its ammunition, supplies, etc. 10 A succession or line of wagons and pack animals en route. 11 A line of gunpowder or other combustible laid to conduct fire to a charge, mine, or the like. See synonyms under PROCESSION. —v.t. 1 To bring to a requisite standard, as of conduct or skill; by protracted and careful instruction; specifically, to mold the character of; educate; instruct: sometimes with up. 2 To render skilful or proficient, as a mechanic or soldier. 3 To make obedient to orders or capable of performing tricks, as an animal. 4 To bring into a required physical condition by means of a course of diet and exercise: to train a man for a boat race. 5 To lead into taking a particular course; develop into a fixed shape: to train a plant on a trellis. 6 To put or point in an exact direction; bring to bear; aim, as a cannon. 7 Obs. To mislead; entice. 8 Obs. To draw along; trail. —v.i. 9 To undergo a course of training. 10 To give a course of training; drill. See synonyms under LEARN, SUBDUE, TEACH. [Fusion of OF traïne a dragging and traïn a series, procession, both

<traïner, trahiner draw <L trahere] —train′a·ble adj. —train′less adj.

train·a·si·um (trā·nā′zē-əm) n. A structure of bars crossing and intersecting one another to form ladders, tunnels, etc.: used in developing the muscles, as in military training. [<TRAIN + (GYMN)ASIUM]

train·er (trā′nər) n. 1 One who trains. 2 One who directs and superintends a course of physical training, or who supervises the physical condition of members of an athletic team. 3 An apparatus or device used in training: a Link trainer. 4 One who trains a cannon; specifically, in the U.S. Navy, the member of the gun's crew who gives direction to the gun. 5 One who trains animals for shows, contests, animal acts, etc.

train·ing (trā′ning) n. 1 Systematic instruction and drill. 2 The condition of being physically fit for the performance of an athletic exercise or contest; also, the act or science of bringing one to such a condition. See synonyms under EDUCATION, LEARNING, NURTURE.

training school A school for practical instruction and drill; specifically, a school in which students receive special vocational or technical instruction and practice.

training ship A vessel on which apprentice seamen and cadets are educated in seamanship, navigation, etc.

train·mas·ter (trān′mas′tər, -mäs′-) n. A railroad official supervising some division or subdivision of a rail line.

train oil Oil obtained from the fat of whales, especially from the right whale, and from cod livers, etc. [Earlier trane <MDu. traen extracted oil]

traipse (trāps) v.i. traipsed, traips·ing Colloq. To walk about in an idle or aimless manner: go on foot: also spelled trapes. [Earlier trapass, prob. <OF trapasser, var. of trespasser TRESPASS]

trait (trāt) n. 1 A distinguishing feature or quality of mind or character. 2 A line, stroke, or touch. See synonyms under CHARACTERISTIC. [<F <MF traict <L tractus. Doublet of TRACT¹.]

trai·tor (trā′tər) n. 1 One who betrays a trust; especially, one who commits treason. 2 Hence, one who acts deceitfully and falsely. [<OF traitre, traitor <L traditor. See TRADITOR.] —trai′tor·ism n. Obs. —trai′tress (-tris) n. fem.

trai·tor·ous (trā′tər-əs) adj. 1 Inclined to treason. 2 Involving treason. See synonyms under PERFIDIOUS. —trai′tor·ous·ly adv. — trai′tor·ous·ness n.

tra·ject (trə-jekt′) v.t. To throw or cast over, through, or across, as a beam of light; transmit. [<L trajectus, pp. of trajicere <trans-over + jacere throw] —tra·jec′tion n.

tra·jec·to·ry (trə-jek′tər-ē) n. pl. ·ries 1 The path described by an object or body moving in space. 2 The path of a projectile after leaving the muzzle of a gun. 3 Geom. a A curve which cuts a set of curves at the same angle. b A surface which passes through a given set of points. [<Med. L trajectorius <L trajectus. See TRAJECT.]

tral·a·ti·tion (tral′ə·tish′ən) n. Obs. The use of a word or expression in a figurative sense; metaphor. [<L tralatio, -onis <tralatus, pp. to transferre TRANSFER]

tral·a·ti·tious (tral′ə-tish′əs) adj. 1 Traditional; legendary. 2 Not literal; figurative; metaphorical.

tram¹ (tram) n. 1 Brit. A tramway. 2 A street railway car for passengers; a tramcar. 3 A four-wheeled vehicle for conveying coals to or from a pit's mouth. —v.t. **trammed, tram·ming** To convey in a tramcar. [Short for TRAMROAD]

tram² (tram) n. 1 A trammel. 2 Mech. Accuracy or trueness of adjustment. Compare TRAMMEL. —v.t. **trammed, tram·ming** To use a trammel in adjusting (any part). [Short for TRAMMEL]

tram³ (tram) n. A thick silk thread used for the cross threads of the best silks and velvets. Also **trame.** [<F trame <OF traime a woof <L trama a woof]

tram·line (tram′līn′) n. Brit. A street-car line.

tram·mel (tram′əl) n. 1 That which limits freedom or activity; an impediment; hindrance. 2 A fetter, shackle, or bond, particularly of such kind as is used in teaching a horse to amble. 3 An instrument whose parts slide on

a rod, especially one bearing pointers, for use as a compass, or for describing ellipses. 4 A gage for adjusting machine parts. 5 A two-piece hook, adjustable for length, used to suspend cooking pots from a fireplace crane. 6 A net formed of three layers, the central one being of finer mesh in order to catch the fish which pass through either of the others: also **trammel net.** —v.t. **·meled** or **·melled, ·mel·ing** or **·mel·ling** 1 To hinder or obstruct; restrict. 2 To entangle in or as in a snare; imprison. Also **tram′el** or **tram′ell.** [<OF tramail a net <LL tramaculum, tremaculum <L tri- three + macula a mesh] —**tram′mel·er** or **tram′mel·ler** n.

tra·mon·tane (trə-mon′tān, tram′ən-tān) adj. 1 Situated beyond the mountains; ultramontane; hence, barbarous; foreign. 2 Coming from the other side of the mountains. —n. A foreigner or barbarian; originally, a resident beyond the mountains. [<Ital. tramontana north wind, polestar <L transmontanus beyond the mountains <trans- over + mons, montis a mountain]

tramp (tramp) v.i. 1 To walk or wander, especially as a tramp or vagabond. 2 To walk heavily or firmly. —v.t. 3 To walk or wander through. 4 To walk on heavily; trample. —n. 1 A heavy continued tread. 2 The sound produced by continuous and heavy marching or walking. 3 A long stroll on foot. 4 One who walks from place to place; a vagrant; vagabond. 5 A steam vessel that goes from port to port picking up freight wherever it can be obtained: also **tramp steamer.** 6 A metal plate on a shoe to protect it from wear or from a spade in digging. [ME trampen <Gmc. Cf. LG trampen.]

tramp·er (tram′pər) n. One who or that which tramps; specifically, a vagabond.

tram·ple (tram′pəl) v. **·pled, ·pling** v.t. To tread on heavily; injure, violate, or encroach upon by or as by tramping. —v.i. To tread heavily or ruthlessly; tramp. —n. The act or sound of treading under foot. [ME trampelen, freq. of trampen TRAMP] —**tram′pler** n.

tram·po·line (tram′pə-lin) n. 1 An acrobatic performance on stilts. 2 A heavy mat or net used in acrobatic exhibitions. Also **tram′po·lin.** [<Ital. trampoli stilts]

trampoline trainer A section of strong canvas stretched on a frame, on which a person may bound or spring: used in training for body control and acrobatics.

tram·road (tram′rōd′) n. A road with wheel tracks of stone, wood, or metal; especially, a railroad in a mine. [<dial. E tram a rail, wagon shaft (prob. <LG traam a beam, shaft) + ROAD]

trance (trans, träns) n. 1 A state in which the soul seems to have passed out of the body; an ecstasy; rapture. 2 Psychol. A condition between sleep and waking characterized by dissociation, involuntary movements, and automatisms of behavior, as in hypnosis and mediumistic seances. 3 A dreamlike state marked by bewilderment and an insensibility to ordinary surroundings. 4 A state of deep abstraction. See synonyms under DREAM. —v.t. **tranced, tranc·ing** To entrance, usually in a figurative sense; enchant. [<OF transe passage, dread of coming evil <transir pass, die, benumb <L transire. See TRANSIENT.]

tran·gam (trang′gəm) n. Obs. A worthless person or thing; a knick-knack or trinket. Also **tran·kum** (trang′kəm). [Origin uncertain]

tran·quil (trang′kwil) adj. **·quil·er** or **·quil·ler, ·quil·est** or **·quil·lest** 1 Free from agitation or disturbance; calm: said of persons. 2 Quiet and motionless: said of things. See synonyms under CALM, PACIFIC, SEDATE. [<L tranquillus quiet] —**tran′quil·ly** adv. —**tran′quil·ness** n.

tran·quil·ize (trang′kwəl-īz) v.t. & v.i. **·ized, ·iz·ing** To make or become tranquil. Also **tran′quil·lize,** Brit. **tran′quil·lise.** —**tran′quil·i·za′tion** n.
Synonyms: allay, appease, assuage, calm, compose, hush, lull, moderate, pacify, quell, quiet, soothe, still. See ALLAY. *Antonyms:* agitate, alarm, arouse, disturb, excite, inflame, rouse, stimulate, stir.

tran·quil·iz·er (trang′kwəl-ī′zər) n. 1 One who or that which tranquilizes. 2 Med. An ataractic drug. Also **tran′quil·liz·er.**

tran·quil·li·ty (trang·kwil′ə-tē) n. The state of being tranquil; rest; quiet. Also **tran·quil′i·ty.** See synonyms under APATHY, REST.

trans– *prefix* **1** Across; beyond; through; on the other side of; as in:

transarctic	transequatorial
transborder	transfrontier
transchannel	transisthmian
transdesert	transpolar

In adjectives and nouns of place, the prefix may signify "on the other side of" (opposed to *cis-*) or "across; crossing." Through long usage, certain of these are written as solid words, as *transalpine, transatlantic*; otherwise, words in this class, unless by contrary official usage, are properly written with a hyphen, as in:

trans–American	trans–Germanic
trans–Andean	trans–Himalayan
trans–Arabian	trans–Iberian
trans–Baltic	trans–Mediterranean
trans–Canadian	trans–Siberian

2 Through and through; changing completely; as in:

transcolor	transfashion

3 Surpassing; transcending; beyond; as in:

transconscious	transmundane
transempirical	transnational
transhuman	transphysical
transmaterial	transrational
transmental	

4 *Anat.* Across; transversely; as in:

transcortical	transocular
transduodenal	transthoracic
transfrontal	transuterine

[< L < *trans* across, beyond, over]

trans·act (trans·akt′, tranz-) *v.t.* **1** To carry through; accomplish; do. — *v.i. Rare* To do business. [< L *transactus*, pp. of *transigere* drive through, accomplish < *trans-* through + *agere* drive, do] — **trans·ac′tor** *n.*

Synonyms: accomplish, act, conduct, do, negotiate, perform, treat. There are many acts that one may *do, accomplish*, or *perform* unaided; what he *transacts* is by means of or in association with others; one may *do* a duty, *perform* a vow, *accomplish* a task, but he *transacts* business, since that always involves the agency of others. To *negotiate* and to *treat* are likewise collective acts, but *negotiate* implies deliberation with adjustment of mutual claims and interests, while *transact* implies execution. Nations may *treat* of peace without result, but when a treaty is *negotiated* peace is secured; the citizens of the two nations are then free to *transact* business with one another.

trans·ac·tion (trans·ak′shən, tranz-) *n.* **1** The management of any affair. **2** Something transacted; an affair; a business deal. **3** *pl.* Published reports, as of a society. — **trans·ac′tion·al** *adj.*

Synonyms: act, action, affair, business, deed, doing, proceeding. A man's *acts* or *deeds* may be exclusively his own; his *transactions* involve the agency or participation of others. A *transaction* is something completed; a *proceeding* is or is viewed as something in progress; but since *transaction* is often used to include the steps leading to the conclusion, while *proceedings* may result in *action*, the dividing line between the two words becomes sometimes quite faint. Both *transactions* and *proceedings* are used of the records of a deliberative body, especially when published. See ACT.

trans·al·pine (trans·al′pin, -pīn, tranz-) *adj.* **1** On the other side of the Alps, especially from Rome. **2** Crossing or extending across the Alps. **3** Of or pertaining to the country or the people beyond the Alps. — *n.* A native of or a resident beyond the Alps. [< L *transalpinus* < *trans-* across + *alpinus* alpine < *Alpes* the Alps]

Transalpine Gaul The section of Gaul on the northern side of the Alps.

trans·at·lan·tic (trans′ət·lan′tik, tranz′-) *adj.* **1** On the other side of the Atlantic. **2** Across or crossing the Atlantic.

trans·berke·li·an (trans·bûrk′lē·ən) *adj. Physics* Of or pertaining to unstable radioactive elements beyond berkelium, atomic No. 97, as californium, einsteinium, fermium, mendelevium, and nobelium. [< TRANS- + BERKE-

L(IUM) + -IAN]

trans·ca·lent (trans·kā′lənt) *adj.* Permitting or facilitating the passage of heat. [< TRANS- + L *calens, -entis*, ppr. of *calere* be hot] — **trans·ca′len·cy** *n.*

trans·cei·ver (tran·sē′vər) *n. Electronics* A radio unit, usually for portable or mobile service, containing equipment for both transmission and reception. [< TRANS(MITTER) + (RE)CEIVER]

tran·scend (tran·send′) *v.t.* **1** To rise above in excellence or degree. **2** To overstep or exceed, as a limit. — *v.i.* **3** To be surpassing; excel. See synonyms under SURPASS. [< L *transcendere* surmount < *trans-* beyond, over + *scandere* climb] — **tran·scend′i·ble** *adj.*

tran·scen·dent (tran·sen′dənt) *adj.* **1** Of very high and remarkable degree; surpassing; superexcellent. **2** *Philos.* In Kantianism, lying beyond the bounds of all possible human experience; hence, beyond knowledge. **3** *Theol.* Pertaining to God as exalted above the universe; beyond limitation; hence, perfect. See synonyms under EXCELLENT, TRANSCENDENTAL. — *n.* That which is transcendent or surpassingly great or remarkable. [< L *transcendens, -entis*, ppr. of *transcendere* TRANSCEND] — **tran·scen′dence** *n.* — **tran·scen′dent·ly** *adv.* — **tran·scen′dent·ness** *n.*

tran·scen·den·tal (tran′sen·den′təl) *adj.* **1** Of very high degree; transcendent. **2** Pertaining to or being a transcendent; not included in any of the categories. See CATEGORY. **3** *Philos.* **a** In Kant's system, of an a priori character; transcending experience but not knowledge. **b** Rising above the common notions of men; with the Cartesians, pertaining to body and spirit alike. **4** Wildly speculative; above, beyond, or contrary to common sense. **5** *Math.* That cannot be formed by the five fundamental operations of algebra, each performed a finite number of times. — **tran′scen·den′tal·ly** *adv.*

Synonyms: instinctive, intuitive, original, primordial, transcendent. *Intuitive* truths are those which are in the mind independently of all experience, not being derived from experience nor limited by it. All *intuitive* truths or beliefs are *transcendental*. But *transcendental* is a wider term than *intuitive*, including all within the limits of thought that is not derived from experience, as the ideas of space and time. *Transcendent, transcendental*, and *intuitive* are opposed to *empirical*; or, according to the philosophy of Kant, *transcendent* is opposed to *immanent*, and *transcendental* to *empirical*. See MYSTERIOUS.

tran·scen·den·tal·ism (tran′sen·den′təl·iz′əm) *n.* **1** The state or quality of being transcendental. **2** In common usage, that which, in philosophy or religion, is vague, visionary, or sublimated. **3** *Philos.* The doctrine that man can attain knowledge which goes beyond or transcends appearances or phenomena. In the Kantian sense, transcendentalism affirmed the existence of a priori principles of cognition. The New England movement, as represented by Emerson and others, has been characterized by the exaltation of the spiritual in a general sense over the material, and the immanence of the divine in all creation. — **tran′scen·den·tal·ist** *n. & adj.*

tran·scribe (tran·skrīb′) *v.t.* **·scribed, ·scrib·ing** **1** To write over again; copy or recopy in handwriting or typewriting from an original or from shorthand notes. **2** *Telecom.* To make an electrical recording of for use on a later radio program. **3** To adapt (a musical composition) for a change of instrument or voice. [< L *transcribere* < *trans-* over + *scribere* write] — **tran·scrib′a·ble** *adj.* — **tran·scrib′er** *n.*

tran·script (tran′skript) *n.* **1** A copy made directly from an original. **2** Any copy. **3** A copy of a student's academic record, listing courses taken and grades received. See synonyms under DUPLICATE. [Fusion of OF *transcrit* (pp. of *transcrire* transcribe < L *transcribere*) and L *transcriptus*, pp. of *transcribere* TRANSCRIBE]

tran·scrip·tion (tran·skrip′shən) *n.* **1** The act of transcribing; a copying. **2** A copy; transcript. **3** *Telecom.* An electrical recording made for the purpose of a later radio broad-

cast. **4** *Music* The adaptation of a composition for some instrument or voice other than that for which it was written. — **tran·scrip′tion·al, tran·scrip′tive** *adj.*

trans·cul·tu·ra·tion (trans·kul′chə·rā′shən) *n. Anthropol.* **1** The processes, resulting in the development of new cultural phenomena and the disappearance of old, involved in the transition of a group or a people from one culture context to another. **2** The transition itself. [< TRANS- + *culturation* development of a culture < CULTUR(E) + -ATION] — **trans·cul′tu·ra·tive** *adj.*

trans·duc·er (trans·dōō′sər, -dyōō′-, tranz-) *n. Physics* Any device whereby the energy of one power system may be transmitted to another system, whether of the same or a different type. [< L *transducere*, var. of *traducere*. See TRADUCE.]

tran·sept (tran′sept) *n. Archit.* One of the lateral members or projections between the nave and choir of a cruciform church: commonly distinguished as the *north* and *south* transepts. [< Med. L *transeptum*, short for L *transversum septum* < *transversus* TRANSVERSE + *septum* an enclosure] — **tran·sep′tal** *adj.*

trans·fer (trans·fûr′, trans′fər) *v.* **·ferred, ·fer·ring** *v.t.* **1** To carry, or cause to pass, from one person, place, etc., to another. **2** To make over possession of to another. **3** To convey (a drawing) from one surface to another, as by specially prepared paper. — *v.i.* **4** To transfer oneself. **5** To be transferred. **6** To change from one car or line to another on a transfer. **7** To shift one's enrollment as a student from one educational institution to another. See synonyms under CONVEY. — *n.* (trans′fər) **1** The act of transferring, or the state of being transferred. **2** That which is transferred; specifically, in art, lithography, etc., a design conveyed or to be conveyed, as by copying ink or pressure, in reverse, from one surface to another. **3** A place, method, or means of transfer. **4** A ticket, entitling a passenger on one car or boat to ride on another, as on a connected line, with or without paying an additional fare; also, the place where such transfer is made. **5** A delivery of title or property from one person to another. **6** The exchange of a person from one organization to another, from one military division to another, from one school to another, etc. **7** An order transferring money or securities. [< OF *transferer* < L *transferre* < *trans-* across + *ferre* carry] — **trans·fer′a·bil′i·ty** *n.* — **trans·fer′a·ble** *adj.*

trans·fer·ence (trans·fûr′əns) *n.* **1** Transfer. **2** *Psychoanal.* **a** The reproduction of the repressed or forgotten experiences of early childhood, accompanied by a transfer of emotions from the original object or person to another. **b** Displacement (def. 7). [< NL *transferentia* < L *transferens, -entis*, ppr. of *transferre* TRANSFER] — **trans·fer·en′tial** (trans′fə·ren′shəl) *adj.*

trans·fig·ure (trans·fig′yər) *v.t.* **·ured, ·ur·ing** **1** To change the outward form or appearance of. **2** To make glorious. See synonyms under CHANGE. [< L *transfigurare* change the shape of < *trans-* across + *figura* shape] — **trans′·fig·u·ra′tion, trans·fig′ure·ment** *n.*

trans·fi·nite (trans·fī′nīt) *adj.* **1** Beyond the finite. **2** *Math.* Of, pertaining to, or characterizing the properties of a set of numbers whose cardinality is not expressible by any finite number.

trans·fix (trans·fiks′) *v.t.* **1** To pierce through; impale. **2** To fix in place by impaling. **3** To make motionless, as with horror, amazement, etc. See synonyms under PIERCE. [< L *transfixus*, pp. of *transfigere* < *trans-* through, across + *figere* fasten] — **trans·fix′ion** (-fik′shən) *n.*

trans·flu·ent (trans·flōō′ənt) *adj.* **1** Flowing across or through. **2** *Her.* Flowing through the arches of a bridge. [< L *transfluens, -entis*, ppr. of *transfluere* < *trans-* across + *fluere* flow]

trans·form (trans·fôrm′) *v.t.* **1** To give a different form to; change the character of. **2** To alter the nature of; convert. **3** *Math.* To change (one expression or operation) into another equivalent to it or having similar properties. **4** *Electr.* **a** To change the potential or the type of, as a current from higher to lower voltage, or from alternating to direct. **b** To alter the energy form of, as electrical into mechanical. **5** In alchemy, to transmute. — *v.i.* **6** To be or become changed in form or character. See synonyms under CHANGE. [<L *transformare* <*trans-* over + *formare* form <*forma* a form] — **trans·form'·a·ble** *adj.*

trans·form·er (trans·fôr'mər) *n.* **1** One who or that which transforms. **2** *Electr.* A device for altering the strength and potential of a current; especially, a form of induction coil used in alternating-current systems of electrical distribution, by which a current of high voltage is transformed to one of lower voltage, or vice versa: classed accordingly either as **step-down** or **step-up transformers.**

trans·form·ism (trans·fôr'miz·əm) *n. Biol.* **1** The theory of the development of one species from another through gradual modifications and without the intervention of special acts of creation. **2** Any doctrine or example of evolution.

trans·fuse (trans·fyōōz') *v.t.* **-fused, ·fus·ing** **1** To pour, as a fluid, from one vessel to another. **2** To cause to be imparted or instilled. **3** *Med.* To transfer (blood) from one person or animal to another. [<L *transfusus,* pp. of *transfundere* <*trans-* across + *fundere* pour] — **trans·fus'er** *n.* — **trans·fus'·i·ble, trans·fu·sive** (trans·fyōō'siv) *adj.*

trans·fu·sion (trans·fyōō'zhən) *n.* **1** The act of pouring from one vessel into another; hence, transference; transmission. **2** *Med.* **a** The transfer of blood from one person or animal to the veins or arteries of another. **b** A similar transfer of any other fluid, as a saline solution.

trans·gress (trans·gres', tranz·) *v.t.* **1** To break over the bounds of, as a law; violate. **2** To pass beyond or over (limits); exceed; trespass. — *v.i.* **3** To break a law; sin. See synonyms under BREAK. [Appar. <OF *transgresser* <L *transgressus,* pp. of *transgredi* <*trans-* across + *gradi* step] — **trans·gress'i·ble** *adj.* — **trans·gress'ing·ly** *adv.* — **trans·gres'sor** *n.*

trans·gres·sion (trans·gresh'ən, tranz·) *n.* **1** The act of transgressing; sin. **2** An overpassing. **3** *Geol.* An overlap. See synonyms under OFFENSE, SIN[1].

trans·gres·sive (trans·gres'iv, tranz·) *adj.* Apt to transgress; faulty; culpable. — **trans·gres'·sive·ly** *adv.*

tran·sience (tran'shəns) *n.* The quality of existing for a short time only; also, something that is transient: the *transience* of life. Also **tran'sien·cy.**

tran·sient (tran'shənt) *adj.* **1** Passing before the vision in a brief time; of short duration; brief; hasty. **2** Not permanent; temporary; casual. **3** *Obs.* Proceeding from one place or object to another; imparted. — *n.* One who or that which is transient; specifically, a lodger or boarder who remains for a short time. [<L *transiens, -euntis,* ppr. of *transire* <*trans-* across + *ire* go] — **tran'sient·ly** *adv.* — **tran'sient·ness** *n.*

Synonyms (*adj.*): brief, ephemeral, evanescent, fleeting, flitting, flying, fugitive, momentary, passing, short, temporary, transitory. A thing is *transient* which in fact is not lasting; a thing is *transitory* which by its very nature must soon pass away; a thing is *temporary* which is intended to last or be made use of but a little while; as, a *transient* joy; this *transitory* life; a *temporary* chairman. That which is *ephemeral,* literally lasting but for a day, is looked upon as at once slight and perishable, and the word carries often a suggestion of contempt; with no solid qualities or worthy achievement a pretender may sometimes gain an *ephemeral* popularity. That which is *fleeting* is viewed as in the act of passing swiftly by, and that which is *fugitive* as eluding attempts to detain it; that which is *evanescent* is in the act of vanishing even while we gaze, as the hues of the sunset. *Antonyms:* abiding, enduring, eternal, everlasting, immortal, imperishable, lasting, permanent, perpetual, persistent, undying, unfading.

tran·si·gent (tran'sə·jənt) *n.* A person who is willing to compromise or to be brought to terms. [<L *transigens, -entis,* ppr. of *transigere* settle. See TRANSACT.]

tran·sil·i·ent (tran·sil'ē·ənt) *adj.* Leaping or passing abruptly from one thing or condition to another; saltatory; spanning; extending over. [<L *transiliens, -entis,* ppr. of *transilire* <*trans-* across + *salire* leap] — **tran·sil'i·ence** *n.*

trans·il·lu·mi·nate (trans'i·lōō'mə·nāt, tranz'-) *v.t.* **·nat·ed, ·nat·ing** *Med.* To cause light to pass through (an organ or part of the body) to reveal its condition.

tran·sis·tor (tran·zis'tər, -sis'-) *n. Electronics* **1** A semiconductor device having three terminals and the property that the current between one pair of them is a function of the current between another pair. **2** A transistorized radio. [<TRANS(FER) (RES)ISTOR]

tran·sit (tran'sit, -zit) *n.* **1** The act of passing over or through; passage. **2** The act of carrying across or through; conveyance. **3** A specific passage or route; also, a traveler through a country. **4** *Astron.* **a** The passage of one heavenly body over the disk of another. **b** The moment of passage of a celestial body across the meridian: when in that half of the meridian containing the zenith it is *superior* or *upper* transit; when in that half containing the nadir it is *inferior* or *lower* transit. **5** A transit compass. See synonyms under JOURNEY, MOTION. [<L *transitus* <*transire* cross. See TRANSIENT.]

transit instrument 1 An astronomical telescope mounted in the plane of the meridian and turning on a fixed east-and-west axis: used to determine the time of passage of an object over the meridian. **2** A transit compass.

tran·si·tion (tran·zish'ən) *n.* **1** Passage from one place, condition, or action to another; change. **2** *Music* A passing modulation, an abrupt change of key, or a passage leading from one theme to another. **3** The time, period, or place of such passage; also, its product or result. See synonyms under CHANGE, MOTION. — **tran·si'tion·al, tran·si'tion·ar'y** (-er'ē) *adj.* — **tran·si'tion·al·ly** *adv.*

tran·si·tive (tran'sə·tiv) *adj.* **1** *Gram.* Having, requiring, or terminating upon a direct object; also, expressing an action performed by a subject or agent, that passes over to or takes effect on some person or thing as its object. **2** Having the power of passing; effecting transition. — *n. Gram.* A transitive verb. [<LL *transitivus* <L *transitus* transit. See TRANSIT.] — **tran'si·tive·ly** *adv.* — **tran'si·tive·ness, tran'si·tiv'i·ty** *n.*

transitive verb A verb whose action, performed by a subject or agent, requires or terminates upon a direct object. The verbs in the following are transitive: *catch* the ball; he *shot* the gun; they *shot* the traitor; cats *climb* trees; we *speak* French.

tran·si·to·ry (tran'sə·tôr'ē, -tō'rē) *adj.* Existing for a short time only; transient. See synonyms under TRANSIENT. [<OF *transitoire* <L *transitorius* having, allowing passage through <*transitus.* See TRANSIT.] — **tran'si·to'ri·ly** *adv.* — **tran'si·to'ri·ness** *n.*

trans·late (trans·lāt', tranz·, trans'lāt, tranz'-) *v.* **·lat·ed, ·lat·ing** *v.t.* **1** To give the sense or equivalent of, as a word or an entire work, in another language; change into another language. **2** To interpret; explain in other words. **3** To remove, as an ecclesiastic, from one office to another. **4** To change into another form; transform. **5** To convey or remove from one place to another, as a human being from earth to heaven without natural death. **6** *Archaic* To transport; enrapture. **7** *Mech.* To impart to (any body) motion in which all the parts follow the same direction. **8** To retransmit, as a message, by means of a telegraphic relay. — *v.i.* **9** To act as translator; also, to admit of translation: This book *translates* easily. **10** To give form to ideas. See synonyms under INTERPRET. [? <OF *translater* <L *translatus,* pp. to *transferre* TRANSFER] — **trans·lat'a·ble** *adj.* — **trans·lat'a·ble·ness** *n.*

trans·la·tion (trans·lā'shən, tranz·) *n.* **1** The act of translating, or the state of being translated. **2** A transfer from one language to another; a turning of a foreign literary composition into the vernacular; a reproduction of a work in a language different from the original. **3** *Mech.* Motion in which all the parts of a body follow the same direction: distinguished from *rotation.* **4** Automatic resending of a telegraphic message to a more distant point. See synonyms under DEFINITION. — **trans·la'tion·al** *adj.*

trans·la·tor (trans·lā'tər, tranz·, trans'lā·tər, tranz'-) *n.* **1** One who translates; also, an interpreter. **2** A telegraph repeater. — **trans·la·to·ri·al** (trans'lə·tôr'ē·əl, -tō'rē-, tranz'-) *adj.*

trans·lit·er·ate (trans·lit'ə·rāt, tranz·) *v.t.* **·at·ed, ·at·ing** To represent, as a word, by the alphabetic characters of another language having the same sound: distinguished from *translate.* [<TRANS- + L *litera* a letter] — **trans·lit·er·a'tion** *n.*

trans·lo·ca·tion (trans'lō·kā'shən, tranz'-) *n.* **1** A shift in position. **2** *Genetics* The attachment of a part of a chromosome to another chromosome, with resulting changes in the arrangement of the genes.

trans·lu·cent (trans·lōō'sənt, tranz-) *adj.* Allowing the passage of light, but not permitting a clear view of any object; semitransparent. See synonyms under CLEAR, TRANSPARENT. [<L *translucens, -entis,* ppr. of *translucere* <*trans-* through, across + *lucere* shine] — **trans·lu'cence, trans·lu'cen·cy** *n.* — **trans·lu'cent·ly** *adv.*

trans·lu·nar (trans·lōō'nər, tranz-) *adj.* **1** Situated beyond the moon. **2** Ethereal; visionary. Also **trans·lu'na·ry** (-nər·ē). [<TRANS- + L *luna* the moon]

trans·lu·vi·al (trans·lōō'vē·əl, tranz-) *adj.* Pertaining to or characterized by progressive leaching, with some erosion: said of soils. [<TRANS- + (AL)LUV(IUM) + -IAL]

trans·ma·rine (trans'mə·rēn', tranz'-) *adj.* **1** Beyond the sea. **2** Born or found overseas. **3** Crossing the sea. [<L *transmarinus* <*trans-* across + *mare* the sea]

trans·mi·grate (trans·mī'grāt, tranz-, trans'mə-, tranz'-) *v.i.* **·grat·ed, ·grat·ing** **1** To migrate, as from one place or condition to another; pass from one country or jurisdiction to another. **2** To pass into another body, as the soul at death. [<L *transmigratus,* pp. of *transmigrare* <*trans-* across + *migrare* migrate] — **trans·mi'gra·tor** *n.* — **trans·mi·gra·to·ry** (trans·mī'grə·tôr'ē, -tō'rē, tranz-) *adj.*

trans·mi·gra·tion (trans'mi·grā'shən, -mə-, tranz'-) *n.* The act of transmigrating; especially, the assumed passing of the soul from one body, after death, to another; metempsychosis. — **trans'mi·gra'tion·ism** *n.*

trans·mis·si·ble (trans·mis'ə·bəl, tranz-) *adj.* That may be transmitted. Also **trans·mit'ti·ble** (-mit'ə·bəl). — **trans·mis'si·bil'i·ty** *n.*

trans·mis·sion (trans·mish'ən, tranz-) *n.* **1** The act of transmitting. **2** The state of being transmitted. **3** That which is transmitted. **4** *Mech.* **a** A device that transmits power from the engine of an automobile to the driving wheels and varies the speed ratios between them. The principal types are **automatic transmission,** in which the speed ratios are automatically selected and engaged (see also FLUID DRIVE), and **manual transmission,** in which the speed ratios are selected and engaged by hand. **b** The gears for changing speed. [<L *transmissio, -onis* <*transmissus,* pp. of *transmittere* TRANSMIT]

trans·mis·sive (trans·mis'iv, tranz-) *adj.* **1** Derivable. **2** Tending to transmit; capable of sending or being sent through. **3** Derived; transmitted.

trans·mit (trans·mit', tranz-) *v.t.* **·mit·ted, ·mit·ting** **1** To send from one place or person to another; forward or convey; dispatch. **2** To pass on by heredity; transfer. **3** To serve as a medium of passage for; conduct. **4** To send out by means of radio waves. **5** To cause (light, sound, etc.) to pass through a medium. **6** *Mech.* To convey (force, motion, etc.) from one part or mechanism to another. See synonyms under CARRY, CONVEY, SEND[1]. [<L *transmittere* <*trans-* across + *mittere* send] — **trans·mit'tal** *n.*

trans·mit·ter (trans·mit'ər, tranz-) *n.* **1** One who or that which transmits. **2** A telegraphic sending instrument. **3** That part of a telephone into which a person talks. **4** That part of a radio or television system which produces, modulates, and transmits radio-frequency waves.

trans·mog·ri·fy (trans·mog'rə·fī, tranz-) *v.t.* **·fied, ·fy·ing** To convert into a different shape; transform. [A humorous coinage; ? alter. of TRANSMIGRATE] — **trans·mog'ri·fi·ca'tion** *n.*

trans·mu·ta·tion (trans′myōō·tā′shən, tranz′-) *n.* **1** The act of transmuting. **2** In alchemy, the supposed change of a baser metal into one of greater value, as of lead into gold. **3** *Physics* The change of one element into another through alteration of its nuclear structure, as in radioactivity or by bombardment with high–energy particles, etc. **4** *Biol.* Successive change of form; transformism. See synonyms under CHANGE. — **trans′mu·ta′tion·al, trans·mut′a·tive** (trans·myōō′tə·tiv, tranz′-) *adj.*

trans·mute (trans·myōōt′, tranz-) *v.t.* **·mut·ed, ·mut·ing** To change in nature or form; alter in essence. Also **trans·mu′tate.** See synonyms under CHANGE. [<L *transmutare* < *trans-* across + *mutare* change] — **trans·mut′a·ble** *adj.* — **trans·mut′a·bil′i·ty, trans·mut′a·ble·ness** *n.* — **trans·mut′a·bly** *adv.* — **trans·mut′er** *n.*

trans·o·ce·an·ic (trans′ō·shē·an′ik, tranz′-) *adj.* **1** Lying beyond or over the ocean. **2** Crossing the ocean.

tran·som (tran′səm) *n.* **1** A horizontal piece framed across an opening; a lintel. **2** A window above such a bar, especially a small window above a door. **3** A horizontal construction dividing a window into stages. **4** A tie beam. **5** *Naut.* A beam running across and forming part of the stern frame of a ship. **6** The horizontal crossbar of a gallows or cross. [<L *transtrum* a crossbeam < *trans* across] — **tran′somed** *adj.*

transom window 1 A window divided into stages by transoms. **2** A window over a door transom and often hinged to it.

trans·pa·cif·ic (trans′pə·sif′ik) *adj.* **1** Crossing the Pacific Ocean. **2** Situated across or beyond the Pacific.

trans·par·en·cy (trans·pâr′ən·sē, -pâr′-) *n. pl.* **·cies 1** The quality of being transparent. **2** Something, as a picture on glass, intended to be viewed by shining a light through it. **3** *Phot.* The light–transmitting power of a sensitized negative. **4** Simplicity. Also **trans·par′ence.**

trans·par·ent (trans·pâr′ənt, -pâr′-) *adj.* **1** Admitting the passage of light, and of clear views of objects beyond; pervious to light: *transparent* glass: distinguished from *translucent.* **2** Figuratively, easy to see through or understand; hence, without guile; frank. **3** Diaphanous. **4** Luminous; bright. [<Med. L *transparens, -entis* <L *trans-* across + *parere* appear, be visible] — **trans·par′ent·ly** *adv.* — **trans·par′ent·ness** *n.*
Synonyms: clear, diaphanous, limpid, lucid, pellucid, translucent. Whatever offers no obstruction to the vision is *clear; limpid, lucid,* and *pellucid* refer to a shining, sparkling clearness. A *transparent* body allows the forms and colors of objects beyond to be seen through it; a *translucent* body allows light to pass through, but may not permit forms and colors to be distinguished; plate glass is *transparent,* ground glass is *translucent. Limpid* refers to a liquid clearness, or that which suggests it; as, *limpid* streams. See CANDID, CLEAR, EVIDENT, MANIFEST, PLAIN[1]. *Antonyms:* cloudy, dark, dim, obscure, opaque, turbid.

tran·spic·u·ous (tran·spik′yōō·əs) *adj.* Transparent. [<Med. L *transpicuus* <L *transpicere* look, see through < *trans-* through + *specere* look]

tran·spi·ra·tion (tran′spə·rā′shən) *n.* A transpiring or exhalation, as through a porous substance or through the tissues of a plant.

tran·spire (tran·spīr′) *v.* **·spired, ·spir·ing** *v.t.* **1** *Physiol.* To send off through the excretory organs, as of the skin and lungs; exhale. — *v.i.* **2** *Physiol.* To be emitted, as through the skin; be exhaled, as moisture or odors. **3** To become known. **4** *Colloq.* To happen; occur. [<F *transpirer* <L *trans-* across, through + *spirare* breathe]

trans·plant (trans·plant′, -plänt′) *v.t.* **1** To remove and plant in another place. **2** To remove and settle or establish for residence in another place. **3** *Surg.* To transfer (an organ or tissue) from its original site to another part of the body or to another individual. — *n.* (trans′plant′, -plänt′) **1** That which is transplanted, as a seedling or an organ of

the body. **2** A transplanting. [<LL *transplantare* <L *trans-* across + *plantare* plant]
— **trans′plan·ta′tion** *n.* — **trans·plant′er** *n.*

trans·pond·er (trans·pon′dər) *n. Electronics* A device that receives a signal from one telecommunication circuit and transmits the corresponding signal to another circuit: used in conjunction with an interrogator. Also called *pulse repeater.* [<TRANS(MITTER) + (RES)PONDER]

trans·port (trans·pôrt′, -pōrt′) *v.t.* **1** To carry or convey from one place to another. **2** To carry into banishment, especially beyond the sea. **3** To carry away with emotion. **4** *Obs.* To take out of the world; kill. See synonyms under CARRY, CONVEY, RAVISH. — *n.* (trans′. pôrt, -pōrt) **1** The state of being transported, as with rapture. **2** *pl.* The varied and recurrent emotions that characterize such a state. **3** Transportation. **4** A vessel, rolling stock, or other means of conveyance used by a government to transport troops, military supplies, etc. **5** The act of transporting convicts. **6** A deported convict. **7** *Aeron.* An airplane used to transport passengers, mail, etc. See synonyms under ENTHUSIASM, RAPTURE. [<MF *transporter* <L *transportare* < *trans-* across + *portare* carry] — **trans·port′er** *n.*

trans·por·ta·tion (trans′pər·tā′shən) *n.* **1** The act of transporting; conveyance. **2** The sending away of a convict to a remote place. **3** Vehicles used in transporting; also, charge for conveyance. **4** A ticket, pass, or other printed matter entitling a passenger to travel on a railroad train, street car, etc.

trans·pose (trans·pōz′) *v.t.* **·posed, ·pos·ing 1** To reverse the order or change the place of; interchange. **2** *Math.* To transfer (a term) with a changed sign from one side of an algebraic equation to the other, so as not to destroy the equality of the members. **3** To change in place or order, as a word in a sentence. **4** *Music* To write or play in a different key. **5** To transport. **6** *Obs.* To transform. [<OF *transposer* <L *trans-* over + OF *poser.* See POSE[1].] — **trans·pos′a·ble** *adj.* — **trans·pos′er** *n.*

trans·sex·u·al (trans·sek′shōō·əl, -sek′shəl) *n.* A person who is genetically and physically of one sex but who identifies psychologically with the other and may seek treatment by surgery or with hormones to bring the physical sexual characteristics into conformity with the psychological preference. — *adj.* Of, for, or characteristic of transsexuals. — **trans·sex′u·al·ism** *n.*

tran·sub·stan·ti·ate (tran′səb·stan′shē·āt) *v.t.* **·at·ed, ·at·ing 1** To change from one substance into another; transmute; transform. **2** *Theol.* To change the substance of (the bread and wine of the Eucharist) into the body and blood of Christ. [<Med. L *transubstantiatus,* pp. of *transubstantiare* <L *trans-* over + *substantia* substance]

tran·sub·stan·ti·a·tion (tran′səb·stan′shē·ā′. shən) *n.* **1** *Theol.* The conversion of the substance of the eucharistic elements into that of Christ's body and blood: a doctrine of the Greek and Roman Catholic churches. Compare CONSUBSTANTIATION, IMPANATION. **2** A change of anything into something essentially different. — **tran′sub·stan′ti·a′tion·al·ist** *n.*

tran·sude (tran·sōōd′) *v.i.* **·sud·ed, ·sud·ing** To pass through the pores or tissues, as of a membrane. [<NL *transudare* <L *trans-* across, through + *sudare* sweat] — **tran·su′. da·to·ry** (-də·tôr′ē, -tō′rē) *adj.*

Trans·vaal (trans·väl′, tranz-) A province of NE Republic of South Africa; 110,450 square miles; seat of government, Pretoria.

trans·val·ue (trans·val′yōō, tranz-) *v.t.* **·ued, ·u·ing 1** To appraise the value of, as conduct, morals, beliefs, and the like, in accordance with principles at variance with accepted or conventional standards. **2** *Psychoanal.* To attach to an idea or complex of ideas a disproportionate emotional value, as in dreams, schizophrenia, etc. — **trans′val·u·a′tion** *n.*

trans·ver·sal (trans·vûr′səl, tranz-) *adj.* Transverse. — *n. Geom.* A straight line intersecting a system of lines.

trans·verse (trans·vûrs′, tranz-) *adj.* **1** Lying

or being across; athwart. **2** *Anat.* Placed across the long axis of a part: a *transverse* muscle. — *n.* (*also* trans′vûrs, tranz′-) **1** That which is transverse. **2** *Geom.* That axis of a conic section which passes through its foci. [<L *transversus* lying across, pp. of *transvertere < trans-* across + *vertere* turn] — **trans·verse′ly** *adv.*

transverse process *Anat.* A long process extending laterally from a vertebra.

transverse wave *Physics* A wave whose component particles oscillate in a direction perpendicular to the line of propagation.

trans·ves·tite (trans·ves′tit, tranz-) *n.* One who wears the clothes of the opposite sex. [<L *trans-* over + *vestire* to clothe + -ITE] — **trans·ves′tism, trans·ves′ti·tism** (-ves′tə·tiz′. əm) *n.*

Tran·syl·va·ni·a (tran′sil·vā′nē·ə) A region and former province in central Rumania; 24,000 square miles; formerly the eastern part of Hungary. — **Tran·syl·va′ni·an** *adj.* & *n.*

trap[1] (trap) *n.* **1** A device for catching game or other animals, as a pitfall or a baited device so arranged that a slight disturbance causes it to close or fall and thus kill or capture the victim. **2** A contrivance for hurling clay pigeons or glass balls into the air for sportsmen to shoot at. **3** Any artifice by which a person may be betrayed or taken unawares. **4** *Mech.* A U– or S–bend in a pipe, etc., for stopping return flow, as of noxious gas. **5** A trap door. **6** *Colloq.* A light, two–wheeled carriage suspended by springs. **7** A rattletrap. **8** *pl.* Traps. **9 a** The game of trap ball. **b** A pivoted piece of wood, resembling a low shoe, used in the game of trap ball to throw a ball into the air. **10** In some games, especially golf, an obstacle or hazard: a water *trap,* sand *trap.* **11** *U.S. Slang* The mouth: Shut your *trap.* — *v.* **trapped, trapping** *v.t.* **1** To catch in a trap; ensnare. **2** To provide with a trap. **3** To stop or hold by some obstruction: said of a liquid. — *v.i.* **4** To set traps for game; be a trapper. [<OE *treppe, træppe*]

trap[2] (trap) *n.* **1** *pl. Colloq.* Personal effects, as luggage; also, household goods. **2** A trapping. — *v.t.* **trapped, trapping** To adorn with trappings; bedeck. [Orig. a cloth covering for a horse, alter. of OF *drap* a cloth, covering <Med. L *drappus;* ult. origin uncertain]

trap[3] (trap) *n. Geol.* A dark, fine-grained igneous rock, often of columnar structure, as basalt, dolerite, etc.: also called *traprock.* [<Sw. *trapp* <*trappa* a stair; so called from the steplike arrangement of this rock in other rock]

trap-door spider (trap′dôr′, -dōr′) A large spider (family *Ctenizidae*) that inhabits a vertical, tubular pit in the ground, covered by a circular trap door hinged at one side to the silken lining of the tube, especially *Bothriocyrtum californica* of the SW United States.

tra·peze (trə·pēz′, tra-) *n.* **1** A short swinging bar, suspended by two ropes, for various gymnastic exercises. **2** *Geom.* A trapezium. [<F *trapèze* <NL *trapezium* a trapezium]

tra·pe·zi·um (trə·pē′zē·əm) *n. pl.* **·zi·a** (-zē·ə) **1** *Geom.* **a** A four-sided plane figure of which no two sides are parallel. **b** In England, a quadrilateral of which two sides are parallel; a trapezoid. **2** *Anat.* **a** The bone of the distal row of the carpus situated on the radial side at the base of the thumb. **b** A band of transverse fibers found in the pons Varolii of the brain. **3** *Astron.* The four brightest stars in the nebula of Orion, at the angles of a trapezium. [<NL <Gk. *trapezion,* dim. of *trapeza* a table, lit., a four-footed (bench) <*tetra-* four + *peza* foot]

TRAPEZIUM

tra·pe·zi·us (trə·pē′zē·əs) *n. Anat.* Either of a pair of large, flat, triangle-shaped muscles on the upper back and neck.

trap·e·zo·he·dron (trap′ə·zō·hē′drən, trə·pē′-) *n. pl.* **·dra** (-drə) A crystal figure bounded by six, eight, or twelve faces, each having unequal intercepts on all axes. [<NL <*trapezium* a trapezium + Gk. *hedra* a base]

trap·e·zoid (trap′ə·zoid) *n.* **1** *Geom.* **a** A quadrilateral of which two sides are parallel. **b** In England, a plane quadrilateral of which no two sides are parallel; a trapezium. **2** *Anat.* An irregular bone in the second row of the carpus, at the end of the forefinger. [< NL *trapezoides* < Gk. *trapezoeidēs* tablelike < *trapeza* a table + *eidos* a form] —**trap′e·zoi′dal** *adj.*

trap net A fishing net having a funnel-shaped entrance into an oblong net pen from which egress is almost impossible.

trap·ping (trap′ing) *n.* **1** An ornamental housing or harness for a horse. **2** *pl.* Adornments of any kind; embellishments; superficial dress. See synonyms under CAPARISON. [< TRAP²]

traps (traps) *n. pl.* Percussion instruments, such as drums, cymbals, etc. [< TRAP¹ (def. 8)]

trash¹ (trash) *n.* **1** Worthless or waste matter of any kind; rubbish. **2** That which is broken or lopped off, as loppings of trees. **3** The lowest grade of tobacco. **4** The dry refuse of sugarcane after the juice has been expressed. **5** A worthless person, or one of ill repute. —*v.t.* **1** To free from trash. **2** To strip of leaves; prune; lop. **3** To regard as trash; discard. [Cf. dial. Norw. *trask* lumber, trash, baggage]

trash² (trash) *n.* **1** Something fastened to an animal's neck to serve as a check. **2** A clog; collar; leash; any hindrance. —*v.t.* To keep in check with a leash, trash, or halter. [< OF *trachier,* var. of *tracier.* See TRACE¹.]

trass (tras) *n.* A gray, yellow, or whitish earth, related to pozzuolana, common in volcanic districts: used in preparation of a hydraulic cement. [< G < Du. *tras* < earlier *taras.* Akin to TERRACE.]

trau·ma (trô′mə, trou′-) *n. pl.* **·mas** or **·ma·ta** (-mə·tə) **1** *Pathol.* Any injury to the body caused by shock, violence, etc.; a wound. **2** *Psychiatry* A severe emotional shock having a deep, often lasting effect upon the personality. **3** A traumatism. [< NL < Gk. *trauma, -atos* a wound]

trau·mat·ic (trô·mat′ik) *adj.* **1** Of or pertaining to trauma. **2** Connected with or resulting from shock, a wound, or wounds. [< LL *traumaticus* < Gk. *traumatikos* < *trauma, -atos* a wound] —**trau·mat′i·cal·ly** *adv.*

trau·ma·to·pho·bi·a (trô′mə·tə·fō′bē·ə) *n.* A morbid fear of injury. [< *traumato-* (< Gk. *trauma* a wound) + -PHOBIA]

trau·mat·ro·pism (trô·mat′rə·piz′əm) *n. Biol.* The growth or involuntary movement of an organism as determined by an injury. [< TRAUMA + TROPISM]

trav·ail (trav′āl, trə·vāl′) *v.t.* **1** To weary. —*v.i.* **2** To suffer the pangs of childbirth. **3** To toil; labor. —*n.* **1** Labor in childbirth. **2** Anguish or distress in achievement. **3** Hard or agonizing labor. **4** Physical agony. See synonyms under TOIL¹. [< OF < *travaillier* labor, toil, ult. < LL *trepalium* a three-pronged instrument of torture < *tres, tria* three + *palus* a stake]

trave (trāv) *n. Obs.* **1** A frame to confine a beast of burden while being shod. **2** A crossbeam; transom. [< OF < L *trabs, trabis* a beam]

trav·el (trav′əl) *v.* **trav·eled** or **·elled, trav·el·ing** or **·el·ling** *v.i.* **1** To go from one place to another or from place to place; make a journey or tour. **2** To proceed; advance. **3** To go about from place to place as a traveling salesman. **4** *U.S. Colloq.* To move with speed. **5** To pass or be transmitted, as light, sound, etc. **6** *Mech.* To move in a fixed path, as part of a mechanism. —*v.t.* **7** To move or journey across or through; traverse. —*n.* **1** The act of traveling; a journeying: chiefly in the plural. **2** *pl.* A narration of things experienced or observed in traveling. **3** A moving or progress of any kind. **4** *Mech.* Movement or length of stroke. **5** The passage of people and vehicles to, over, or past a certain place. **6** Tourists, collectively. **7** Distance traveled; mileage. See synonyms under JOURNEY. [Var. of TRAVAIL¹] —**trav′el·ing** or **·el·ling** *adj. & n.*

trav·eled (trav′əld) *adj.* **1** Having made many journeys, especially to distant lands. **2** Experienced as the result of travel. **3** Frequented or used by travelers: a *traveled* district. Also

trav′elled.

trav·el·er (trav′əl·ər, trav′lər) *n.* **1** One who travels or journeys from place to place. **2** An animal or thing considered with reference to its mode or speed of movement. **3** A traveling salesman; specifically, a drummer: also **commercial traveler. 4** *Naut.* **a** A metal ring or thimble running freely on a rope, rod, or spar. **b** A bar affixed to the deck, along which a ring or thimble slides. **5** A traveling crane or other moving device for transporting heavy objects. **6** In the theater, an overhead rod or pipe in the flys of the stage from which small spotlights are suspended and made available for unusual lighting effects. **7** The rings and track for drawn curtains. Also **trav′el·ler.**

trav·el·ing (trav′əl·ing, trav′ling) *adj.* **1** Designed or used for travel: a *traveling* bag. **2** Itinerant: a *traveling* tinker. **3** Portable; movable. **4** *Mech.* **a** Running or sliding along a fixed course, as a ring or thimble. **b** Constructed with a part that travels.

traveling crane A hoisting and transporting apparatus which moves along a supporting frame or bridge, the frame itself moving on tracks. Compare illustration under GANTRY.

trav·e·log (trav′ə·lôg, -log) *n.* A lecture or discourse on or an account of travel, usually illustrated pictorially. Also **trav′e·logue.** [< TRAVEL, on analogy with *monolog, dialog,* etc.]

trav·erse (trav′ərs, trə·vûrs′) *v.* **·ersed, ·ers·ing** *v.t.* **1** To pass over, across, or through. **2** To move back and forth over or along. **3** To examine carefully; survey or scrutinize. **4** To oppose; thwart. **5** To turn (a gun, lathe, etc.) to right or left; swivel. **6** *Law* To make denial of; in legal pleading, to deny and tender issue upon, as a matter of fact alleged by the opposite party; impeach the validity of an inquest of office. **7** *Naut.* To brace (a yard) fore and aft. —*v.i.* **8** To move back and forth. **9** To move across; cross. **10** To turn; swivel. **11** In fencing, to slide one's

TRAVERSE (def. 13)

blade toward the hilt of an opponent's sword while maintaining pressure on it. —*n.* (trav′ərs) **1** A part, as of a machine or structure, that traverses, as a crosspiece, crossbeam, transom, or the like. **2** *Archit.* A gallery or loft communicating with opposite sides of a building. **3** Something serving as a screen or barrier. **4** *Geom.* A transversal. **5** The act of traversing or traveling; a journey; passage. **6** *Mech.* Sidewise travel, as of the tool in a slide rest. **7** The act of traversing or denying; a denial; in legal pleading, a formal denial. **8** *Naut.* A zigzag track of a vessel while beating to windward. **9** A short line surveyed from a main line, to establish the position of a side point. **10** *Mil.* A bank of earth thrown up, as from a trench, to afford protection from gunfire. **11** Something that obstructs, vexes, or thwarts. **12** A path cut transversely in the side of a cliff or mountain; also, the cliff across which a path is cut. **13** A sled having a long board connecting two or more sleds or two or more sets of runners. —*adj.* (trav′ərs) Transverse; lying or being across. —*adv.* (trav′ərs, trə·vûrs′) Transversely; crosswise. [< OF *traverser* < LL *traversare, transversare* < L *transversus* TRANSVERSE] —**trav′ers·a·ble** *adj.* —**trav·er·sal** (trav′ər·səl, trə·vûr′səl) *n.* —**trav′ers·er** *n.*

trav·es·ty (trav′is·tē) *n. pl.* **·ties 1** A grotesque imitation; burlesque. **2** In literature, a burlesque treatment of a lofty subject. See synonyms under CARICATURE. —*v.t.* **·tied, ·ty·ing** To make a travesty on; burlesque; parody. [< MF *travesti,* pp. of *(se) travestir* disguise (oneself) < Ital. *travestire* disguise]

tra·vois (trə·voi′) *n. pl.* **·vois** (-voiz′) or **·vois·es** (-voi′ziz) A primitive sled constructed of two poles which serve as shafts for a dog or other draft animal and which drag on the ground, bearing a frame for the load: used by North

TRAVOIS

American Indians and lumbermen in logging: also spelled *travail.* Also **tra·voise′** (-voiz′). [< dial. F (Canadian), alter. of F *travail,* a frame in which horses are held while being shod <OF]

trawl (trôl) *n.* **1** A stout line, sometimes over a mile long, anchored and buoyed, and having hanging from it many lines frequently spaced and bearing baited hooks: also called *trotline.* **2** A great net shaped like a flattened bag, for towing on the bottom of the ocean by a boat. —*v.t.* To drag, as a net to catch fish. —*v.i.* To fish with a trawl line, trawl net, or the like. [Cf. MDu. *traghel* a dragnet; prob. infl. by *trail*] —**trawl′ing** *n.*

tray (trā) *n.* **1** A flat shallow utensil or bowl with raised edges, for various uses. **2** A shallow box without a cover, used in trunks and otherwise. **3** A kind of flat board with a low rim, made of wood, metal, or other material, and used for carrying or holding articles; also, its contents. ◆ Homophone: *trey.* [OE *treg, trig* a wooden board]

treach·er·ous (trech′ər·əs) *adj.* **1** Traitorous; perfidious. **2** Having a good appearance, but bad in character or nature; untrustworthy; affording unsafe footing: a *treacherous* path. See synonyms under INSIDIOUS, PERFIDIOUS, ROTTEN. —**treach′er·ous·ly** *adv.* —**treach′er·ous·ness** *n.*

treach·er·y (trech′ər·ē) *n. pl.* **·er·ies** Violation of allegiance, confidence, or plighted faith; perfidy; treason. See synonyms under FRAUD. [<OF *trecherie, tricherie* < *tricher, trechier* cheat]

trea·cle (trē′kəl) *n.* **1** The sirup obtained in refining sugar. **2** Molasses. **3** A saccharine fluid of certain plants. **4** Originally, a compound used as an antidote. **5** *Obs.* A panacea. [<OF *triacle* < L *theriaca* < Gk. *thēriakē* a remedy for poisonous bites < *thērion,* dim. of *thēr* a wild beast] —**trea′cly** *adj.*

tread (tred) *v.* **trod** (*Archaic* **trode**), **trod·den** or **trod, tread·ing** *v.t.* **1** To step or walk on, over, along, etc.: to *tread* the floor. **2** To press with the feet; trample: to *tread* grass. **3** To accomplish in walking or in dancing: to *tread* a measure. **4** To copulate with: said of male birds. —*v.i.* **5** To place the foot down; walk. **6** To press the ground or anything beneath the feet: usually with *on.* —**to tread water** In swimming, to keep the body erect and the head above water by moving the feet up and down as if walking. —*n.* **1** The act or manner of treading; a walking or stepping. **2** That on which something treads or rests in moving, or which affords space for or as for treading. **3** The part of a wheel that bears upon the ground or rails. **4** The outer surface of an automobile tire, or the distance between opposite wheels. **5** The part of a rail on which the wheels bear. **6** The cicatricle or chalaza of an egg. **7** The impression made by a foot, a tire, etc. **8** The flat part of a step in stairs. [OE *tredan*] —**tread′er** *n.* —**tread′ing** *n.*

tread·mill (tred′mil′) *n.* **1** A mechanism rotated by the walking motion of one or more persons: formerly used as a prison punishment. **2** A somewhat similar mechanism operated by a quadruped. **3** Toilsome effort; monotonous routine.

trea·son (trē′zən) *n.* **1** Betrayal, treachery, or breach of allegiance or of obedience toward the sovereign or government. Treason against the United States is declared by the Constitution (Article 3, section 3) to "consist only in levying war against them, or in adhering to their enemies, giving them aid and comfort." **2** A breach of faith; treachery. See synonyms under FRAUD. [< AF *treyson,* OF *traïson* < L *traditio, -onis* a betrayal, delivery. Doublet of TRADITION.]

treas·ure (trezh′ər) *n.* **1** The precious metals; money; jewels. **2** Riches accumulated or possessed; a stock or store of anything; wealth. **3** Something very precious. See synonyms under WEALTH. —*v.t.* **·ured, ·ur·ing 1** To lay up in store; accumulate. **2** To retain carefully, as in the mind: generally with *up.* **3** To set a high value upon; prize. See synonyms under CHERISH. [<OF *tresor* <L *thesaurus.* Doublet of THESAURUS.]

treas·ur·er (trezh′ər·ər) *n.* **1** One who has the care of treasure or of a treasury. **2** An officer legally authorized to receive, care for, and disburse public revenues upon lawful orders. **3** A similar custodian of the funds of a society or a corporation.

treas·ur·y (trezh′ər-ē) *n.* *pl.* **·ur·ies** **1** The place of receipt and disbursement of public revenue, or of funds belonging to a corporation. **2** A repository, especially of words, as a dictionary or thesaurus. — **Department of the Treasury** An executive department of the U. S. government (established in 1789), headed by the Secretary of the Treasury, which superintends and manages the national finances, controls the coinage and printing of money, and supervises the Coast Guard (except when it is a part of the Navy, in wartime or when the president directs), the Bureau of Narcotics, and the Secret Service. Also **Treasury Department.** [<OF *tresorie* < *tresor* TREASURE]

treat (trēt) *v.t.* **1** To conduct oneself toward in a specified manner: He *treated* her shamefully. **2** To look upon or regard in a specified manner: They *treat* the matter as a joke. **3** To subject to chemical or physical action, as for altering or improving. **4** To give medical or surgical attention to. **5** To deal with in writing or speaking; handle. **6** To deal with or develop (a subject in art) in a specified manner or style. **7** To pay for the entertainment, food, or drink of. — *v.i.* **8** To handle a subject in writing or speaking: usually with *of.* **9** To carry on negotiations; negotiate. **10** To pay for another's entertainment. See synonyms under TRANSACT. — *n.* **1** Something that gives unusual pleasure. **2** Entertainment of any kind furnished gratuitously to another. **3** *Colloq.* One's turn to pay for refreshment or entertainment, especially for drinks. [<OF *tretier*, *traitier* < L *tractare*. See TRACTABLE.] — **treat′a·ble** *adj.* — **treat′er** *n.* — **treat′ing** *n.*

trea·tise (trē′tis) *n.* **1** An elaborate, formal, and systematic literary composition presenting a serious subject in all its parts: distinguished from an *essay* in being longer, more exhaustive, and less popular, and from a *monograph* in being less full and complete. **2** *Obs.* A story; tale. [<AF *tretiz*, OF *traitier* TREAT]

treat·ment (trēt′mənt) *n.* **1** The act, mode, or process of treating anything, as a raw material, substance, or product. **2** *Med.* The management of illness, by the use of drugs, dieting, or other means designed to bring relief or effect a cure. **3** In motion pictures and television, an expanded synopsis of a story, used in planning, writing, or marketing a play or scenario.

trea·ty (trē′tē) *n.* *pl.* **·ties** **1** A formal agreement or compact, duly concluded and ratified, between two or more states. **2** *Obs.* The act of negotiating for an agreement; also, the agreement so made. **3** *Obs.* An entreaty. [<AF *treté*, OF *traitié*, pp. of *traitier* TREAT]

treb·le (treb′əl) *v.t.* & *v.i.* **·led**, **·ling** To multiply by three; triple. — *adj.* **1** Threefold; triple. **2** Soprano. — *n.* **1** *Music* The soprano; the highest register of the compass of an instrument; a soprano singer. **2** High, piping sound. **3** A musical instrument of treble pitch; a violin. [<OF < L *triplus*. Doublet of TRIPLE.] — **treb′le·ness** *n.* — **treb′ling** *n.* — **treb′ly** *adv.*

treb·u·chet (treb′yŏŏ·shet) *n.* A medieval catapultike device for throwing heavy missiles. The missile, on the long arm of a lever, was hurled with great force by the sudden descent of a heavy weight on the short arm. Also **treb′uck·et** (-uk·it). [<OF < *trebucher* trip, fall]

tree (trē) *n.* **1** A perennial woody plant having usually a single self-supporting trunk, with branches and foliage growing at some distance above the ground, the whole ranging from about ten feet to as high as 300 feet. ◆ Collateral adjective: *arboreal.* **2** Any shrub or plant that assumes treelike shape or dimensions. **3** Something whose outline resembles that of a tree: a genealogical *tree*; a branching diagram; a treelike group of crystals. **4** A timber or heavy piece of wood, as in a framing: usually in composition: *axletree*, *boot–tree*, etc. **5** A gibbet; also, a cross. — **up a ʌree** *Colloq.* In a posi-

tion from which there is no retreat; cornered; caught; also, in an embarrassing position. — *v.t.* **treed**, **tree·ing** **1** To force to climb or take refuge in a tree: to *tree* an opossum. **2** *Colloq.* To get the advantage of; corner. **3** To stretch, as a boot, on a boot-tree. [OE *trēow*, *trīow*, *trēo*]

tree fern Any of various ferns (families *Cyatheaceae* and *Dicksoniaceae*) with large fronds and woody trunks that often attain a treelike size.

tree frog An arboreal amphibian (family *Hylidae*), having the toes dilated with viscous, adhesive disks. Also **tree toad.**

tree heath An evergreen shrub of southern Europe (*Erica arborea*) about 4 feet high, with white flowers: also called brier.

TREE FROG
(Species vary from 1 to 5 inches)

tree kangaroo Any of various kangaroos (genus *Dendrolagus*) of Australia and New Guinea adapted for tree-dwelling.

tree of heaven A large ornamental tree (*Ailanthus altissima*) of eastern Asia. It has large green flowers, those on the male trees being very ill–scented; ailanthus.

tree of knowledge of good and evil In the Bible, a tree in Eden whose fruit Adam and Eve were forbidden to eat. *Gen.* iii 3, 6. Also **tree of knowledge.**

tree of life **1** Arborvitae. **2** In the Bible: **a** A tree in the garden of Eden whose fruit conferred immortality. *Gen.* iii 22. **b** A similar tree in heaven. *Rev.* xxii 2.

tree sparrow A North American sparrow (*Spizella arborea*) which nests in Canada and migrates southward in winter: also called **Canada sparrow.**

tree surgery The treatment of disease conditions and decay in trees by operative methods.

tre·foil (trē′foil) *n.* **1** Any one of the clovers (genus *Trifolium*), so called from the trifoliolate leaves. **2** Certain other plants with trifoliolate leaves, as the black medic. **3** A three–lobed architectural ornamentation. [< AF *trifoil*, OF *trefeuil* <L *trifolium*]

tre·ha·la (tri·hä′lə) *n.* *Biochem.* A carbohydrate substance forming the pupal case of certain weevils (genus *Larixus*) and deposited upon Asian plants of the genus *Echinops.* [<NL <Turkish *tīqālah*]

trek (trek) *v.* **trekked**, **trek·king** *v.i.* **1** In South Africa, to travel by ox wagon. **2** To travel; migrate. — *v.t.* **3** In South Africa, to draw (a vehicle or load): said of an ox. — *n.* **1** An organized migration, as for the founding of a colony. **2** A journey; also, a stage in a journey. **3** The act of pulling. — **Great**

trel·lis (trel′is) *n.* **1** A crossbarred grating or lattice, used as a screen or a support for vines, etc. **2** A summerhouse or other structure of trelliswork. — *v.t.* **1** To interlace so as to form a trellis. **2** To furnish with or fasten on a trellis. [<OF *treliz*, *trelis* <L *trilix*, *trilicis* of three threads < *tri-* three + *licium* a thread]

trem·a·tode (trem′ə·tōd) *n.* One of a class (*Trematoda*) of typically parasitic flatworms, including the liver flukes. [<NL <Gk. *trēmatōdēs* perforated < *trēma*, *-atos* a hole + *eidos* form] — **trem′a·toid** (-toid) *adj.*

trem·ble (trem′bəl) *v.i.* **·bled**, **·bling** **1** To shake involuntarily, as with fear or weakness; be agitated. **2** To have slight, irregular vibratory motion, as from some jarring force; quiver; shake. **3** To feel anxiety or fear. **4** To quaver, as the voice. See synonyms under QUAKE, SHAKE. — *n.* **1** The act or state of trembling. **2** *pl.* A debilitating disease of cattle and sheep, possibly caused by eating certain plants, and communicated to man as the milk sickness. [<OF *trembler* <LL *tremulare* < *tremulus* tremulous < *tremere* tremble, shake] — **trem′bler** *n.* — **trem′bling** *adj.* & *n.* — **trem′bling·ly** *adv.* — **trem′bly** *adj.*

tre·men·dous (tri·men′dəs) *adj.* **1** Causing or fitted to cause astonishment by its magni-

tude, force, etc.: a *tremendous* blow; awe-inspiring; terrible. **2** *Colloq.* Extraordinarily big; remarkable. See synonyms under FORMIDABLE. [<L *tremendus* to be trembled at < *tremere* tremble] — **tre·men′dous·ly** *adv.* — **tre·men′dous·ness** *n.*

trem·e·tol (trem′ə·tōl, -tol) *n.* An oily, poisonous alcohol isolated from certain plants, as the white snakeroot, and believed to be the cause of trembles in sheep. [<L *tremere* tremble + -OL[1]]

trem·o·lite (trem′ə·līt) *n.* A light–colored calcium–magnesium amphibole, $CaMg_3Si_4O_{12}$. [from *Tremola*, Switzerland, where it was first found + -ITE[1]]

trem·o·lo (trem′ə·lō) *n.* *pl.* **·los** *Music* **1** A vibrating, beating, or throbbing sound produced vocally or instrumentally. **2** The mechanism for causing this effect in organ tones. [<Ital., trembling <L *tremulus.* See TREMBLE.]

trem·or (trem′ər, trē′mər) *n.* **1** A quick, vibratory movement caused by an external impulse; a shaking; also, a succession of such movements. **2** Any involuntary quivering or trembling of the body or limbs; a shiver. **3** *Pathol.* An involuntary and continued quivering or shaking of the whole or some part of the body: a form of paralysis. **4** Any trembling, quivering effect. See synonyms under FEAR. [<OF, fear, a trembling <L < *tremere* tremble]

trench (trench) *n.* **1** A long narrow excavation in the ground; ditch. **2** A long irregular ditch, lined with a parapet of the excavated earth, to protect troops: often with a descriptive word: *communication*, *reserve*, *shelter*, or *supply trench.* — *v.t.* **1** To dig a trench or trenches in. **2** *Mil.* To fortify with trenches; construct trenches against. **3** To cut deep furrows in; ditch. **4** To confine in a trench, as water; entrench. — *v.i.* **5** To cut or dig trenches. **6** To cut; carve. **7** To encroach. [<OF *trenche* a cutting, gash < *trenchier* cut, ult. <L *truncare* lop off < *truncus* a tree trunk]

trench coat A loose–fitting overcoat of rainproof fabric with removable lining, several pockets, and a belt.

trench·er (tren′chər) *n.* **1** A wooden plate formerly used at table; originally, a square piece of board used to cut food on. **2** *Archaic* The food served on trenchers; hence, the table or its pleasures. **3** *Obs.* A thick slice of bread used as a platter. [<AF *trenchour*, OF *tranchouoir* < *trenchier*. See TRENCH.]

trench·er·man (tren′chər·mən) *n.* *pl.* **·men** (-mən) **1** A feeder; eater; especially, one who enjoys food. **2** A table companion: also **trench′er·mate′** (-māt′). **3** A hanger–on; parasite.

trench fever *Pathol.* A remittent rickettsial fever transmitted by body lice and characterized by headache, nausea, high temperature, profuse sweating, muscular pains, and neuralgic pains in the legs. It attacked soldiers assigned to prolonged service in trenches during World War I.

trench foot *Pathol.* A disease of the feet caused by continued dampness and cold, and characterized by discoloration, weakness, and sometimes gangrene.

trench mortar Any of various portable, muzzleloading mortars designed for firing a projectile at a high trajectory. Also **trench gun.**

trench mouth *Pathol.* A mildly contagious disease of the mouth, gums, and sometimes the larynx and tonsils, caused by a soil bacillus; Vincent's angina.

TRENCH MORTAR
A. Shell. *B.* 8 mm. mortar. *a.* Base plate. *b.* Tube. *c.* Sight. *d.* Bipod.

trend (trend) *v.i.* To have or take a general course or direction; incline. — *n.* General course or direction; bent. [OE *trendan* roll]

Treng·ga·nu (treng·gä′nōō) A State of Malaya in the southern part on the South China Sea; 5,050 square miles; capital, Kuala Trengganu.

Trent (trent) The third longest river of England, flowing 170 miles SE and NE from NW Staffordshire, to a confluence with the Ouse, forming the Humber.

Trent, Council of A council of the Roman Catholic Church, held at intervals in Trent, Italy, from 1545 to 1563: it condemned the leading doctrines of the Reformation.

trente–et–qua·rante (trän·tā·ká·ränt′) *n.* A gambling game played with cards laid out in two rows on a table, the top row representing "black" and the lower, "red." The players, who play against the bank, win if the row of cards they have chosen totals, in pips, nearer 31 than the other. Compare ROUGE ET NOIR. [<F, thirty and forty]

Tren·ton (tren′tən) The capital of New Jersey, on the Delaware River at the west central border of the State.

tre·pan (tri·pan′) *n.* **1** An early form of the trephine. **2** A large rock-boring tool. — *v.t.* ·panned, ·pan·ning **1** *Mech.* To use a trepan upon. **2** *Surg.* To subject to the operation of trephining. **3** To cut a hole partly through, as the back of a brush, for the insertion of bristles. Also **trep·a·nize** (trep′ə·nīz). [<OF, a borer <Med. L *trepanum* a crown saw <Gk. *trypanon* a borer <*trypaein* bore] — **trep·a·na·tion** (trep′ə·nā′shən) *n.* — **tre·pan′ner** *n.*

tre·phine (tri·fīn′, -fēn′) *n. Surg.* A cylindrical saw for removing a piece of bone from the skull, to relieve pressure, etc. — *v.t.* ·phined, ·phin·ing To operate on with a trephine. [Earlier *trafine* <L *tres fines* three ends; infl. in form by *trepan*[1]]

trep·i·da·tion (trep′ə·dā′shən) *n.* **1** A state of agitation from fear. **2** An involuntary trembling. **3** *Obs.* Confused haste. **4** *Obs.* A vibrating or vibration, as of leaves. Also **trep·id·i·ty** (tri·pid′ə·tē). See synonyms under FEAR. [<L *trepidatio, -onis* <*trepidatus*, pp. of *trepidare* hurry, be alarmed <*trepidus* alarmed]

tres·pass (tres′pəs, -pas′) *v.i.* **1** *Law* To violate wilfully and forcibly the personal or property rights of another; commit a trespass: with *on* or *upon.* **2** To pass the bounds of propriety or rectitude, to the injury of another; intrude offensively; encroach: with *on* or *upon.* **3** To violate a positive law, rule, or custom: with *against.* — *n.* **1** Any voluntary transgression of law or rule of duty; any offense done to another. **2** *Law* Any wrongful act accompanied with force, either actual or implied, as wrongful entry on another's land, whereby another is injuriously treated; also, an action for trespass. See synonyms under AGGRESSION, ATTACK, OFFENSE. [<OF *trespasser* pass beyond, across <Med. L *trans-passare* <L *trans-* across, beyond + *passare* PASS] — **tres′pass·er** *n.*

tress (tres) *n.* **1** A lock, curl, or ringlet of human hair, especially when abundant: applied also, figuratively, to adornment suggesting tresses. **2** *pl.* The hair of a woman or girl, especially when worn loose. [<OF *tresce* <LL *tricia*; ult. origin uncertain] — **tress′y** *adj.*

tres·sure (tresh′ər) *n. Her.* A bearing around the edge of a shield; modified or double orle, generally ornamented with fleurs-de-lis. Also **tres′sour.** [<OF *tresseor, tressure* <*tresce* a tress] — **tres′sured** *adj.*

tres·tle (tres′əl) *n.* **1** A beam or bar supported by four divergent legs, for bearing platforms, etc. **2** An open braced framework for supporting the horizontal stringers of a railway bridge, etc. **3** In carpentry, an intervening stud. **4** A trestletree. **5** *pl.* The props of a vessel on the ways. [<OF *trestel* <L *transtrum.* See TRANSOM.]

tres·tle·work (tres′əl·wûrk′) *n.* **1** Trestles collectively. **2** A bridge made of trestles or braced framework, especially of wood. Also **tres′tling.**

tret (tret) *n.* A former allowance to purchasers for waste due to transportation. [<AF, OF *tret,* var. of *traict.* See TRAIT.]

trev·is (trev′is) *n.* **1** A bar or beam. **2** A crosspiece; partition. [Var. of TRAVERSE]

tri·ac·id (trī·as′id) *n. Chem.* An acid containing three hydroxyl radicals which are re-placeable by acid radicals.

tri·ad (trī′ad) *n.* **1** A group of three persons or things. **2** *Music* A chord of three tones or notes; often the common chord, consisting of a fundamental tone with its third and fifth higher. A **major triad** has a major third and a perfect fifth; a **minor triad** has a minor third and a perfect fifth. **3** *Chem.* **a** A trivalent atom or radical. **b** One of a group of three elements having similar chemical properties, as chlorine, bromine, and iodine. [<L *trias, -adis* <Gk. *trias, -ados* <*treis* three] — **tri·ad′ic** *adj. & n.*

tri·age (trī′ij, trē·äzh′) *n. Med.* The sorting out of a group of sick and wounded persons and classifying them according to a system of priorities for the treatment of mass casualties under conditions of limited medical resources and personnel. [<OF <*trier* pick out, sort]

tri·ag·o·nal (trī·ag′ə·nəl) *adj.* Having three angles; triangular. [Var. of TRIGONAL, on analogy with *tetragonal, pentagonal,* etc.]

tri·al (trī′əl, trīl) *n.* **1** The act of testing or proving by experience or use. **2** The state of being tried or tested by suffering: the hour of *trial.* **3** Experimental treatment or action performed to determine a result: to learn by *trial* and error. **4** An experience, person, or thing that puts strength, patience, or faith to the test. **5** An attempt or effort to do something; a try: to make a *trial.* **6** The examination, before a tribunal having assigned jurisdiction, of the facts or law involved in an issue in order to determine that issue. **7** A former method of determining guilt or innocence by subjecting the accused to physical tests of endurance, as by ordeal or by combat with his accuser. **8** *Brit.* An academic or licensing examination. See synonyms under ENDEAVOR, MISFORTUNE, PROOF. — **on trial** In the process of being tried or tested. — *adj.* **1** Of or pertaining to a trial or trials. **2** Made or performed in the course of trying or testing: a *trial* trip. **3** Used in testing: a *trial* specimen. [<AF <*trier* TRY]

trial balance In double-entry bookkeeping, a draft or statement of the debit and credit footings or balances of each account in the ledger.

trial balloon **1** A balloon released in order to test atmospheric and meteorological conditions, as wind velocities, air currents, etc. **2** Any tentative plan or scheme advanced to test public reaction.

trial jury A jury impaneled to try a civil or criminal case: also called *petit* or *petty jury.*

tri·a·morph (trī′ə·môrf) *n.* Any mineral or other substance that crystallizes in three different forms. [<L *tres, tria* three + Gk. *morphē* form] — **tri′a·mor′phous** *adj.*

tri·an·gle (trī′ang′gəl) *n.* **1** *Geom.* A figure,

TRIANGLE
a. Scalene. *b.* Isosceles. *c.* Equilateral.
d. Right-angled. *e.* Obtuse.

especially a plane figure, bounded by three sides, and having three angles. **2** Something resembling such a figure in shape or arrangement. **3** A flat drawing implement for making parallel or diagonal lines, etc. **4** A group or set of three; a triad. **5** A situation involving three persons: the eternal *triangle.* **6** *Music* A musical instrument of percussion, consisting of a resonant bar bent into a triangle and open at one corner, sounded by being struck with a small metal rod. [<OF <L *triangulum* <*triangulus* three-cornered <*tri-* three + *angulus* an angle]

tri·an·gu·lar (trī·ang′gyə·lər) *adj.* **1** Pertaining to, like, or bounded by a triangle: also **tri′an·gled.** **2** Concerned with or pertaining to three things, parties, or persons. [<LL *triangularis* <L *triangulum* a triangle] — **tri·an·gu·lar′i·ty** (-lar′ə·tē) *n.* — **tri·an′gu·lar·ly** *adv.*

tri·an·gu·late (trī·ang′gyə·lāt) *v.t.* ·lat·ed, ·lat·ing **1** To divide into triangles. **2** To survey by triangulation. **3** To give triangular shape to. — *adj.* Marked with triangles. [<L *triangulum* a triangle + -ATE[1]]

tri·an·gu·la·tion (trī·ang′gyə·lā′shən) *n.* The laying out and accurate measurement of a network of triangles, especially on the surface of the earth, as in surveying.

tri·ar·chy (trī′är·kē) *n. pl.* ·chies Government by three persons, or a country so governed; a triumvirate. [<Gk. *triarchia* <*tri-* three + *archein* rule]

Tri·as·sic (trī·as′ik) *adj. Geol.* Of or pertaining to the lowest of the three geological periods comprised in the Mesozoic era. — *n.* The Triassic period or rock system, following the Permian and succeeded by the Jurassic. Also **Tri·as** (trī′əs). [<LL *trias.* See TRIAD.]

tri·at·ic stay (trī·at′ik) *Naut.* A device consisting of two pendants connected by a span, and attached respectively to the foremast head and mainmast head of a ship: used principally for hoisting boats in and out of a vessel.

tri·a·tom·ic (trī′ə·tom′ik) *adj. Chem.* **1** Containing only three atoms in the molecule. **2** Containing three replaceable univalent atoms. **3** Trivalent.

tri·a·zole (trī′ə·zōl, trī·az′ōl) *n.* One of four five-membered ring compounds, $C_2H_3N_3$, in which nitrogen atoms have replaced two CH groups. [<TRI- + AZ(O)- + OLE[1]]

trib·ade (trib′əd) *n.* A female homosexual, especially one who assumes the role of the male; a Lesbian. [<MF <L *tribas, -adis* <Gk. *tribas, -ados* <*tribein* rub]

tri·ba·sic (trī·bā′sik) *adj. Chem.* **1** Containing three atoms of hydrogen replaceable by a base or basic radical: said of certain acids. **2** Having three hydroxyl groups in the molecule.

tribe (trīb) *n.* **1** A division, class, or group of people, varying ethnologically according to the circumstances from which their separation or distinction is supposed to originate. **2** Among primitive peoples, a group or aggregation of persons, usually consanguineous and endogamous, under one chief, characterized by its own culture, and having a name, a dialect, a government, and usually a territory of its own: Kaffir *tribes.* **3** In ancient states, an ethnic, hereditary, or political division of a united people: the *tribes* of Athens or of Israel. **4** A division of freeholders with a right to vote in certain of the ancient Roman councils. The Latins, Sabines, and Etruscans probably represented primitive clan divisions, to which Servius Tullius added a fourth when making his territorial division of Rome. Outside the city the spread of tribal organizations was coincident with the founding of new colonies. **5** A number of persons of any class or profession taken together: often derogatory or contemptuous: the theatrical *tribe.* **6** *Biol.* A group of plants or animals of indefinite rank. **7** Among stockbreeders, the descendants of a particular female bearer through females. See synonyms under PEOPLE. [Fusion of OF *tribu* (<L *tribus* a tribe) and L *tribus*] — **tri′bal** *adj.* — **tri′bal·ly** *adv.*

trib·o·e·lec·tric (trib′ō·i·lek′trik) *adj.* Of, pertaining to, or characterized by frictional electricity, as when a glass rod is rubbed with flannel. [<*tribo-* (<Gk. *tribein* rub) + ELECTRIC] — **trib′o·e·lec·tric′i·ty** (-i·lek′tris′ə·tē) *n.*

trib·o·lu·mi·nes·cence (trib′ō·lōō′mə·nes′əns) *n.* Luminescence produced by crushing or grinding certain substances, as glass. [<*tribo-* (<Gk. *tribein* rub) + LUMINESCENCE] — **trib′o·lu′mi·nes′cent** *adj.*

trib·u·la·tion (trib′yə·lā′shən) *n.* A condition of affliction and distress; suffering; also, that which causes it. See synonyms under GRIEF, MISFORTUNE. [<OF *tribulacion* <LL *tribulatio, -onis* <L *tribulatus,* pp. of *tribulare* thrash <*tribulum* a threshing floor <*tri-,* root of *terere* rub, grind]

tri·bu·nal (tri·byōō′nəl, trī-) *n.* **1** A court of justice; any judicial body, as a board of arbitrators. **2** The seat set apart for judges, magistrates, etc. [<L <*tribunus* TRIBUNE]

trib·une[1] (trib′yōōn, *Brit.* trī′byōōn) *n.* **1** In Roman history, a magistrate chosen by the plebeians to protect them against patrician oppression. **2** One of various civil or military officers of later times; any champion of the people: as the title of a newspaper, often pronounced tri·byōōn′. [<L *tribunus,* lit., head of a tribe <*tribus* a tribe] — **trib′u·nar′y** (-yə·ner′ē), **trib′u·ni′cial** (-yə·nish′əl), **trib′u·ni′cian** *adj.*

trib·une[2] (trib′yōōn) *n.* **1** A raised floor for

a Roman magistrate's chair. **2** A bishop's throne. **3** A rostrum or platform. [<MF <Ital. *tribuna* <L *tribunal* a tribunal]

trib·u·tar·y (trib′yə·ter′ē) *adj.* **1** Bringing supply; contributory; subsidiary: a *tributary* stream. **2** Offered or due as tribute; having the character of tribute: a *tributary* payment. **3** Paying tribute; hence, subordinate, as a state. — *n. pl.* **·tar·ies** **1** A person or state paying tribute; a dependent. **2** A stream flowing into another; an affluent. [<L *tributarius* <*tributum*. See TRIBUTE.] — **trib′u·tar′i·ly** *adv.* — **trib′u·tar′i·ness** *n.*

trib·ute (trib′yo̅o̅t) *n.* **1** Money or other valuables paid by one state or ruler to another as an acknowledgment of submission or as the price of peace and protection, or by virtue of some treaty; also, the taxes imposed to raise money to make such payment. **2** The obligation or necessity of making such gift or payment; the state of being tributary. **3** Anything given, paid, or rendered as by a subordinate to a superior; figuratively, that which is due to worth, affection, or duty; contribution; tax; gift; offering; meed: I must render my *tribute* of praise. See synonyms under SUBSIDY, TAX. [<L *tributum*, neut. of *tributus*, pp. of *tribuere* pay, allot]

trice (trīs) *v.t.* **triced, tric·ing** To raise with a rope; also, to tie or lash: usually with *up*. — *n.* An instant: only in the phrase *in a trice*. [<MDu. *trisen* hoist]

tri·cen·ni·al (trī·sen′ē·əl) *adj.* Of or pertaining to the number thirty; taking place every thirtieth year. [<L *tricennium* a period of thirty years <*tricies* thirty times + *annus* a year]

tri·ceps (trī′seps) *n. Anat.* A muscle having three heads; specifically, the large muscle at the back of the upper arm, of which the function is to extend the forearm. [<L *triceps, -cipitis* three-headed <*tri-* three + *caput, capitis* a head]

tri·chi·a·sis (tri·kī′ə·sis) *n. Pathol.* **1** A condition of ingrowing hairs about an orifice, especially ingrowing eyelashes. **2** The presence of hairlike filaments in the urine. [<LL *trichiasis* <Gk. <*trichiaein* be hairy <*thrix, trichos* hair]

tri·chi·na (tri·kī′nə) *n. pl.* **·nae** (-nē) A small nematode parasitic worm (*Trichinella spiralis*) that in its larval stage sometimes infests the muscles of man, swine, and other mammals. [<NL <Gk. *trichinos* of hair <*thrix, trichos* hair]

trich·i·no·sis (trik′ə·nō′sis) *n. Pathol.* The disease produced by trichinae in the intestines and muscles of the body. Also **trich′i·ni′a·sis** (-nī′ə·sis). [<TRICHINA + -OSIS] — **trich′i·nosed, trich′i·not′ic** (-not′ik), **trich′i·nous** *adj.*

trich·ite (trik′īt) *n.* **1** *Mineral.* A microscopic crystallite, curved, bent, or zigzag in form, found in volcanic rocks. **2** *Bot.* One of the needle-shaped, radial crystals occurring in starch grains. **3** *Zool.* A rodlike organ surrounding the mouth and gullet of certain ciliate protozoa. [<G *trichit* <Gk. *thrix, trichos* hair] — **tri·chit·ic** (tri·kit′ik) *adj.*

tri·chlo·ro·eth·yl·ene (trī·klôr′ō·eth′əl·ēn, -klō′rō-) *n. Chem.* A colorless, odorless, volatile liquid, C_2HCl_3, used in organic synthesis, in chemical manufactures, and as a general anesthetic. Also **tri′chlor·eth′yl·ene** (trī′klôr-).

trich·o·bac·te·ri·a (trik′ō·bak·tir′ē·ə) *n.* A group of bacteria which includes forms possessing flagella.

trich·o·cyst (trik′ə·sist) *n. Biol.* **1** A stinging capsule containing a protrusible hairlike body; found in various protozoans. **2** A thread cell. — **trich′o·cys′tic** *adj.*

trich·o·gyne (trik′ə·jīn, -jin) *n. Bot.* The slender threadlike portion of the procarp in red algae which receives the male fertilizing bodies. [<TRICHO- + Gk. *gynē* a woman, female]

trich·oid (trik′oid) *adj.* Having the form or appearance of hair. [<Gk. *trichoeidēs* <*thrix, trichos* a hair + *eidos* form]

tri·chol·o·gy (tri·kol′ə·jē) *n.* The sum of knowledge concerning the hair.

tri·cho·ma (tri·kō′mə) *n. pl.* **·ma·ta** (-mə·tə) **1** *Pathol.* **a** Entropion. **b** Matted and crusted hair; plica polonica. **2** *Bot.* One of the

threads or filaments of filamentous algae: also spelled *trichome*. [<NL <Gk. *trichōma* growth of hair <*trichoein* cover with hair <*thrix, trichos* hair] — **tri·chom′ic** (-kom′ik) *adj.*

trich·ome (trik′ōm, trī′kōm) *n. Bot.* **1** Any surface appendage or epidermal outgrowth in a plant, comprising hairs, bristles, prickles, scales, root hairs, etc. **2** A trichoma (def. 2). [<Gk. *trichōma*. See TRICHOMA.]

tri·cho·sis (tri·kō′sis) *n. Pathol.* Any morbid condition of the hair. [<NL <Gk. *trichōsis* growth of hair <*trichoein*. See TRICHOMA.]

tri·chot·o·my (trī·kot′ə·mē) *n.* **1** Division into three parts. **2** *Logic* The threefold division of a genus or class. **3** *Theol.* The division of human nature into body, soul, and spirit. [<Gk. *tricha* threefold + -TOMY] — **trich·o·tom·ic** (trik′ə·tom′ik), **tri·chot′o·mous** *adj.* — **tri·chot′o·mous·ly** *adv.*

tri·chro·ism (trī′krō·iz′əm) *n.* The property of a crystal of transmitting light of different colors in three different directions. [<Gk. *trichroos* of three colors <*tri-* three + *chroia* color, skin] — **tri·chro·ic** (trī·krō′ik) *adj.*

tri·chro·mat·ic (trī′krō·mat′ik) *adj.* Of, pertaining to, having, or using three colors, as the normal eye, the three-color process in photography and printing, etc. Also **tri′chrome**, **tri·chro·mic** (trī·krō′mik). [<TRI- + CHROMATIC] — **tri·chro′ma·tism** (-mə·tiz′əm) *n.*

trick (trik) *n.* **1** A device for getting an advantage by deception; a petty artifice. **2** A malicious, injurious, or annoying act: a dirty *trick*. **3** A practical joke; prank: the *tricks* of schoolboys. **4** A particular habit or manner; characteristic; trait; also, a vicious habit. **5** A peculiar skill or knack. **6** An act of legerdemain; a feat of jugglery: conjurer's *tricks*. **7** In card games, the whole number of cards played in one round. **8** The turn of one sailor at the helm; a turn or spell of duty; a railroad or factory shift. **9** *Colloq.* A toy; trifle; plaything; a child. See synonyms under ARTIFICE, FRAUD. — **to do** (or **turn**) **the trick** *Slang* To produce the desired result. — *v.t.* **1** To deceive or cheat; delude. **2** To dress or array; adorn: with *up* or *out*. — *v.i.* **3** To practice trickery or deception. See synonyms under DECEIVE. [<AF *trique*, OF *triche* deceit <*trichier* cheat, prob. ult. <L *tricare, tricari* trifle, play tricks <*tricae* trifles, tricks] — **trick′er** *n.* — **trick′less** *adj.*

trick·er·y (trik′ər·ē) *n. pl.* **·er·ies** **1** The practice of tricks; artifice; stratagem; wiles. **2** Dressing up; decorations. See synonyms under DECEPTION.

trick·ing (trik′ing) *n.* The act of dressing up; also, ornaments. — *adj. Obs.* Given to tricks; tricky.

trick·le (trik′əl) *v.* **·led, ·ling** *v.i.* **1** To flow or run drop by drop or in a very thin stream. **2** To move, come, go, etc., slowly or bit by bit. — *v.t.* **3** To cause to trickle. — *n.* The act or state of trickling, or that which trickles. [ME *triklen*, prob. alter. of *striklen*, freq. of *striken* strike] — **trick′ly** *adj.*

trick·y (trik′ē) *adj.* **trick·i·er, trick·i·est** **1** Disposed to or characterized by trickery; deceitful. **2** Vicious, as an animal. **3** Intricate; requiring or showing adroitness or skill in making: *tricky* clothes. See synonyms under INSIDIOUS. Also *Scot.* **trick′ie**. — **trick′i·ly** *adv.* — **trick′i·ness** *n.*

tri·clin·ic (trī·klin′ik) *adj.* Describing a crystal form having three unequal and dissimilar axes with oblique intersections. [<TRI- + Gk. *klinein* incline + -IC]

tri·col·or (trī′kul′ər) *adj.* Having or characterized by three colors: also **tri′col′ored**. — *n.* **1** A flag of three colors; the French national flag of blue, white, and red vertical bands. **2** The tricolor cockade of the French Revolutionists. Also *Brit.* **tri′col′our**. [<F *tricolore* <LL *tricolor* <L *tri-* three + *color* color]

tri·corn (trī′kôrn) *n.* A hat with the brim turned up on three sides, worn during the 17th and 18th centuries by both men and women: used improperly in the form *tricorne* for the two-cornered hat of the French gendarmes. See BICORN. — *adj.* Three-horned; three-pronged; having three hornlike processes. [<F *tricorne* <L *tricornis* three-horned <*tri-* three + *cornu* a horn]

tri·cos·tate (trī·kos′tāt) *adj. Biol.* Having three ribs or costae. [<TRI- + L *costa* a rib + -ATE¹]

tri·cot (trē′kō, *Fr.* trē·kō′) *n.* **1** A hand-knitted or woven fabric, or a machine-made imitation thereof. **2** A soft ribbed cloth. **3** A tight-fitting garment worn by ballet dancers. [<F, knitting <*tricoter* knit, ? ult. <LG *striken* make movements]

tri·crot·ic (trī·krot′ik) *adj. Med.* Having three distinct rhythmic waves in succession, as the pulse: also **tri·cro·tous** (trī′krə·təs). [<TRI- + Gk. *kroteein* knock, beat] — **tri·crot·ism** (trī′krə·tiz′əm) *n.*

tri·cus·pid (trī·kus′pid) *adj.* **1** Having three cusps or points, as a molar tooth or a valve of the heart. **2** Of or pertaining to the tricuspid valve. Also **tri·cus′pi·dal**. [<L *tricuspis, -idis* three-pointed <*tri-* three + *cuspis, -idis* a point]

tricuspid valve *Anat.* A three-segmented valve which controls the flow of blood from the right atrium to the right ventricle of the heart.

tri·cy·cle (trī′sik·əl) *n.* **1** A three-wheeled vehicle of the velocipede class. **2** A motorcycle with three wheels. [<F <*tri-* three + Gk. *kyklos* a circle]

tri·cy·clic (trī·sī′klik, -sik′lik) *adj.* Having or characterized by three cycles or identical units of structure: a *tricyclic* chemical compound.

tri·dac·tyl (trī·dak′til) *adj. Anat.* Possessing three fingers or toes. [<Gk. *tridaktylos* <*tri-* three + *daktylos* a digit]

tri·dec·ane (trī·dek′ān) *n. Chem.* A light, colorless, liquid hydrocarbon, $C_{13}H_{28}$, of the methane series, having an odor like turpentine. [<TRI- + DECANE]

tri·dent (trīd′nt) *n.* **1** A three-pronged implement or weapon, the emblem of Neptune (Poseidon); hence, dominion over the sea. **2** The three-pronged spear with which the Roman retiarius was armed. **3** A fishspear with three prongs. **4** *Geom.* A plane cubic curve somewhat resembling a three-pronged spear. — *adj.* Having three teeth or prongs: also **tri·den·tate** (trī·den′tāt), **tri·den′tat·ed**. [<L *tridens, -dentis* <*tri-* three + *dens, dentis* a tooth]

tri·di·men·sion·al (trī′di·men′shən·əl) *adj.* Of three dimensions; having length, breadth, and thickness. — **tri′di·men′sion·al′i·ty** *n.*

tri·di·ur·nal (trī′dī·ûr′nəl) *adj.* Occurring every three days or lasting three days.

tried (trīd) *adj.* **1** Tested; trustworthy, as a friend or a formula. **2** Freed of impurities, as metal or oil. **3** Rendered, as fat.

tri·en·ni·al (trī·en′ē·əl) *adj.* **1** Taking place every third year. **2** Lasting three years. — *n.* **1** A ceremony or event observed or celebrated every three years; a third anniversary. **2** A plant lasting three years. — **tri·en′ni·al·ly** *adv.*

tri·en·ni·um (trī·en′ē·əm) *n. pl.* **·en·ni·ums** or **·en·ni·a** (-ē·ə) A period of three years. [<L <*tri-* three + *annus* a year]

tri·fle (trī′fəl) *v.* **·fled, ·fling** *v.i.* **1** To treat something as of no value or importance; dally: with *with*. **2** To act or speak frivolously or idly; jest. **3** To play; toy. **4** To pass time idly; idle. — *v.t.* **5** To pass (time) in an idle and purposeless way. — *n.* **1** Anything of very little value or importance. **2** A light confection, usually made of alternate layers of macaroons or ladyfingers with sugared fruit, covered with a custard and topped with meringue or whipped cream. **3** A variety of pewter. — **a trifle** Slightly; to a small extent: a *trifle* short. [<OF *truffler*, var. of *truffer* deceive, jeer at <*trufle*, dim. of *trufe* a cheating, mockery; ult. origin unknown] — **tri′fler** *n.*

tri·fling (trī′fling) *adj.* **1** Frivolous. **2** Insignificant. See synonyms under CHILDISH, IDLE, INSIGNIFICANT, LITTLE, RIDICULOUS, VAIN. — **tri′fling·ly** *adv.*

tri·fo·cal (trī·fō′kəl) *adj.* **1** Having three foci. **2** *Optics* Pertaining to or describing a lens ground in three segments, for near, intermediate, and far vision respectively.

tri·fo·li·ate (trī·fō′lē·it, -āt) *adj. Bot.* Having three leaves or leaflike processes. Also **tri·fo′li·at′ed**. [<TRI- + FOLIATE]

tri·fo·li·o·late (trī·fō′lē·ə·lāt′) *adj. Bot.* Having three leaflets.

tri·fo·li·um (trī·fō′lē·əm) *n.* Any of a genus (*Trifolium*) of small plants of the bean family, the clovers, with trifoliolate leaves, and purple, red, white, or yellow flowers. [<NL <L < *tri-* three + *folium* a leaf]

tri·fo·ri·um (trī·fôr′- ē·əm, -fō′rē-) *n. pl.* **·fo·ri·a** (-fôr′ē·ə, -fō′- rē·ə) *Archit.* A gallery above the arches of the nave in a church. [<Med. L <L *tri-* three + *foris* a door] — **tri·fo′ri·al** *adj.*

TRIFORIUM

tri·formed (trī′- fôrmd′) *adj.* 1 Having three forms or shapes. 2 Consisting of three parts or divisions. Also **tri′- form.** — **tri·form′i·ty** *n.*

tri·fur·cate (trī·fûr′kāt) *adj.* Three-forked; trichotomous. Also **tri·fur′cat·ed.** — **tri·fur·ca·tion** (trī′fər·kā′shən) *n.*

trig¹ (trig) *adj.* 1 Characterized by tidiness; trim; neat. 2 Strong; sound; firm. 3 In a depreciative sense, correct; precise; prim. 4 Faithful; trustworthy; dependable. 5 Active; alert. 6 Full; inflated. — *v.t.* **trigged, trig·ging** To make trig or neat; dress finely or smartly: often with *out* or *up.* [<ON *tryggr* true, trusty] — **trig′ly** *adv.* — **trig′ness** *n.*

trig² (trig) *v.t.* **trigged, trig·ging** 1 To check, as with a skid; obstruct; stop. 2 To shore; prop. — *n.* A check or brake, as a skid or drag for a wheel. [? <ON *tryggja* make firm]

tri·gem·i·nal (trī·jem′ə·nəl) *adj.* 1 Being in three parts; threefold; triple. 2 Of or pertaining to the trigeminus: *trigeminal* neuralgia. — *n.* The trigeminus. [<L *trigeminus* born three at a time < *tri-* three + *geminus* a twin]

tri·gem·i·nus (trī·jem′ə·nəs) *n. pl.* **·ni** (-nī) *Anat.* The fifth cranial or trifacial nerve, the great nerve of sensation for the face and head. [<NL <L. See TRIGEMINAL.]

trig·ger (trig′ər) *n.* 1 The fingerpiece of a gunlock or pistol-lock, for releasing the hammer. 2 A catch or small lever doing similar service in a trap or other mechanism. — **quick on the trigger** 1 Quick to shoot. 2 Quick to act in response to a suggestion; quick-witted; alert. — *v.t.* To cause or precipitate. [Earlier *tricker* <Du. *trekker* < *trekken* pull, tug at]

trig·ger·fish (trig′ər- fish′) *n. pl.* **·fish** or **·fish·es** A plectognath fish (genus *Balistes*) found mainly in the tropical Pacific region, with an ovate body covered with large, rough scales: named from the triggerlike second spine of the dorsal fin.

TRIGGERFISH
(About 12 inches long)

tri·glyph (trī′glif) *n. Archit.* An ornament in a Doric frieze consisting of a tablet with three parallel vertical channels or glyphs, and standing on each side of the metopes. [<L *triglyphus* <Gk. *triglyphos* thrice grooved < *tri-* three + *glyphē* a carving < *glyphein* carve, engrave]

tri·gon (trī′gon) *n.* 1 A triangle; especially, the triangle of reference used in trilinear coordinates. 2 One of four parts of the zodiac, each consisting of three signs. 3 In Greek and Roman antiquity, a triangular lyre or harp of triangular form. [<L *trigonum* <Gk. *trigōnon,* orig. neut. of *trigōnos* three-angled < *tri-* three + *gōnia* an angle]

trig·o·nal (trig′ə·nəl) *adj.* 1 Pertaining to or in the form of a trigon; triangular; three-cornered. 2 Characterized, in the hexagonal crystal system, by having a principal (vertical) axis of threefold symmetry. Also **trig′o·nous.** — **trig′o·nal·ly** *adv.*

trig·o·nom·e·ter (trig′ə·nom′ə·tər) *n.* 1 An instrument for solving triangles mechanically. 2 *Obs.* An expert in trigonometry.

trigonometric functions Certain functions of an angle or arc used in trigonometry. The most commonly used are: sine, cosine, tangent, cotangent, secant, cosecant. In illustration *A* the functions of the angle θ are defined as ratios or fractions. They are:

$$\text{sine } \theta = \frac{AB}{AC} \qquad \text{cosecant } \theta = \frac{AC}{AB}$$

$$\text{cosine } \theta = \frac{CB}{AC} \qquad \text{secant } \theta = \frac{AC}{CB}$$

$$\text{tangent } \theta = \frac{AB}{CB} \qquad \text{cotangent } \theta = \frac{CB}{AB}$$

The functions may be represented also as lines by constructing the reference triangle in a circle whose radius is taken as unity, and drawing additional lines as in *B*. The *sine* is then AB, the *cosine* CB, the *tangent* ED, the *cotangent* GF, the *secant* CE, and the *cosecant* CF.

TRIGONOMETRIC FUNCTIONS

These are all spoken of as the sine, cosine, etc., of the arc AD as well as of the angle θ. Other, less common, trigonometric functions are: versed sine, coversed sine, exsecant, and haversine. These functions are expressed as follows:

versed sine θ (or versine θ) = 1 − cosine θ
coversed sine θ (or versed cosine θ) = 1 − sine θ
exsecant θ = secant θ − 1
haversine θ = 1/2 versine θ

trig·o·nom·e·try (trig′ə·nom′ə·trē) *n.* The branch of mathematics that treats of the relations of the sides and angles of triangles and of the methods of applying these relations in the solution of problems involving triangles: widely used in navigation, surveying, etc. [<NL *trigonometria* <Gk. *trigōnon* a triangle + *metron* measure] — **trig·o·no·met·ric** (trig′ə·nō·met′rik) or **·ri·cal** *adj.* — **trig·o·no·met′ri·cal·ly** *adv.*

tri·graph (trī′graf, -gräf) *n.* A group of three letters representing one articulate sound: *eau* in *beau;* also, the sound thus represented. [<TRI- + -GRAPH] — **tri·graph′ic** *adj.*

tri·he·dron (trī·hē′drən) *n. pl.* **·dra** (-drə) *Geom.* A figure having three plane surfaces meeting at a point. [<NL <Gk. *tri-* three + *hedra* a base] — **tri·he′dral** *adj.*

tri·hy·brid (trī·hī′brid) *n. Biol.* A hybrid whose parents differ from each other in respect to three pairs of contrasting Mendelian characters.

tri·hy·dric (trī·hī′drik) *adj. Chem.* Pertaining to or designating a compound containing three hydroxyl groups. Also **tri·hy·drox·y** (trī′hī·drok′sē). [<TRI- + HYDR(OXYL) + -IC]

tri·ju·gate (trī′jōō·gāt, trī·jōō′gāt, -git) *adj. Bot.* Having three pairs of leaflets. Also **tri·ju·gous** (trī′jōō·gəs, trī·jōō′gəs). [<L *trijugus* threefold < *tri-* three + *jugum* a yoke]

tri·lat·er·al (trī·lat′ər·əl) *adj.* Having three sides. [<L *trilaterus* < *tri-* three + *latus, lateris* a side] — **tri·lat′er·al·ly** *adv.*

tri·lin·e·ar (trī·lin′ē·ər) *adj.* Pertaining to, referring to, or bounded by three lines.

tri·lin·gual (trī·ling′gwəl) *adj.* Derived from, composed of, or using three languages: a *trilingual* discourse. Also **tri·lin′guar.** [<L *trilinguis* < *tri-* three + *lingua* a tongue]

trill (tril) *v.t.* 1 To sing or play in a quavering or tremulous tone. 2 *Phonet.* To articulate with a trill. — *v.i.* 1 To utter, make, or give forth a quavering or tremulous sound. 2 *Music* To execute a trill or shake. — *n.* 1 A tremulous utterance of successive tones, as of certain insects or birds; a warble. 2 *Music* A quick alternation of two notes either a tone or a semitone apart; shake. 3 *Phonet.* A rapid vibration of a speech organ, as of the tip of the tongue against the alveolar ridge or the uvula against the back of the tongue, as in the articulation of *rr* in Spanish. 4 A consonant or word so uttered. Also spelled *thrill.* [<Ital. *trillare,* prob. <Gmc.]

tril·ling (tril′ing) *n.* A compound crystal made up of three individuals. [Cf. Dan. *trilling* a triplet]

tril·lion (tril′yən) *n.* A cardinal number; in the French and United States system of numeration, 1 followed by 12 zeros; in the English and German system, 1 followed by 18 zeros. — *adj.* Numbering a trillion. [<MF < *tri-* three + *million* million] — **tril′lionth** *adj. & n.*

tril·li·um (tril′ē·əm) *n.* Any of a genus (*Trillium*) of North American herbs of the lily family,

with a stout stem, rising from a short rootstock and bearing a whorl of three leaves and a solitary flower. The fruit is a red or purple berry. [<NL <L *tri-* three; so called because of its three leaves]

tri·lo·bate (trī·lō′bāt, trī′lə·bāt) *adj.* 1 Three-lobed. 2 *Bot.* Having three lobes, as some leaves. Also **tri·lo′bal, tri·lo′bat·ed, tri′lobed.**

tri·lo·bite (trī′lə·bīt) *n. Paleontol.* Any of a subclass or group (*Trilobita*) of early Paleozoic marine arthropods related to the crustaceans, having a flattened body divided into a variable number of segments covered by a hard dorsal shield marked in three lobes. [<NL *Trilobites* <Gk. *tri-* three + *lobos* a lobe] — **tri·lo·bit′ic** (-bit′ik) *adj.*

tri·loc·u·lar (trī·lok′yə·lər) *adj.* Having three cells or chambers. [<TRI- + L *loculus* a small receptacle, dim. of *locus* a place]

tril·o·gy (tril′ə·jē) *n. pl.* **·gies** A group of three literary or dramatic compositions, each complete in itself, but continuing the same general subject. [<Gk. *trilogia* < *tri-* three + *logos* a discourse]

trim (trim) *v.* **trimmed, trim·ming** *v.t.* 1 To put in or restore to order; make neat by clipping, pruning, etc. 2 To remove by cutting: usually with *off* or *away.* 3 To put ornaments on; decorate. 4 In carpentry, to smooth; dress. 5 *Colloq.* a To chide; rebuke. b To punish or thrash; beat. c To defeat. d To cheat; victimize. 6 *Naut.* a To adjust (sails or yards) for sailing. b To cause (a ship) to sit well in the water by adjusting cargo, ballast, etc. 7 *Aeron.* To bring (an airplane) to level or balanced flight by adjusting control surfaces. 8 *Obs.* To furnish; equip. — *v.i.* 9 *Naut.* a To be or remain in equilibrium: said of a ship. b To adjust sails or yards for sailing. 10 To act so as to appear to favor opposing sides in a controversy. — *n.* 1 State of adjustment or preparation; fitting condition; orderly disposition: All was in good *trim.* 2 Condition as to general appearance; dress; style. 3 *Naut.* Fitness for sailing: said of a vessel in reference to disposition of ballast, masts, cargo, etc. 4 *Naut.* Actual or comparative degree of immersion: said of a vessel. 5 Particular character or nature; kind; stripe. 6 The moldings, etc., as about the doors of a building; also, the hardware trimmings of a house, such as hinges, window fastenings, etc. 7 Ornament; trapping; dress. 8 Material rejected or cut out, as sections from a motion-picture film. 9 In advertising, window dressing or display. 10 The interior furnishings of an automobile body. 11 *Aeron.* The position of an aircraft relative to balanced flight. — *adj.* **trim·mer, trim·mest** 1 Adjusted to a nicety; being in perfect order; handsomely equipped or of stylish and smart appearance; spruce; precise; jaunty. 2 Excellently fit; nice; pretty; fine. See synonyms under NEAT¹, STAUNCH. — *adv.* In a trim manner: also **trim′ly.** [OE *trymman* arrange, strengthen < *trum* steadfast, strong] — **trim′ness** *n.*

tri·mer (trī′mər) *n. Chem.* A compound formed by the union of three molecules of another compound or substance, as benzene from acetylene. [<TRI- + Gk. *meros* a part]

trim·er·ous (trim′ər·əs) *adj.* 1 Composed of three similar parts. 2 *Bot.* Three-parted. 3 *Entomol.* Having three joints, as the tarsus of an insect: often written 3-*merous.* [<TRI- + Gk. *meros* a part]

tri·mes·ter (trī·mes′tər) *n.* A three-month period; quarter. [<F *trimestre* <L *trimestris* < *tri-* three + *mensis* a month] — **tri·mes′- tral, tri·mes′tri·al** *adj.*

trim·e·ter (trim′ə·tər) *adj.* In prosody, consisting of three measures or of lines containing three measures. — *n.* 1 A verse consisting of three measures, as the iambic trimeter. 2 In classical prosody, a line or verse consisting of three dimeters, or six feet. [<L *trimetrus* <Gk. *trimetros* < *tri-* three + *metron* a measure]

trimetric projection *Geom.* A three-dimensional geometric projection in which each dimension is measured on a separate scale and according to arbitrarily assigned angles.

tri·met·ro·gon (trī·met′rə·gon) *n.* A high-speed system of aerial topographic photography, in which a unit of three cameras takes simultaneous pictures of one area, from three positions, one vertical and two at matching oblique angles. — *adj.* Of or pertaining to this system or camera unit. [<TRI- + METRO- + -GON]

trim·ming (trim'ing) n. 1 Something added for ornament or to give a finished appearance or effect. 2 Material attached to a garment, etc., for ornamentation or effect. 3 pl. Articles or equipment; fittings, as the hardware of a house. 4 pl. The usual or proper accompaniments or condiments of an article or food. 5 pl. That which is removed by trimming, cutting, or clipping; in shearing, wool from the shanks. 6 A severe reproof or a chastisement; flogging; beating. 7 Colloq. A defeat. 8 The act of one who trims.

tri·morph (trī'môrf) n. 1 A substance existing or occurring in three forms. 2 One of the forms in which such a substance exists. [<Gk. trimorphos having three forms < tri- three + morphē a form]

tri·mor·phism (trī-môr'fiz-əm) n. 1 Bot. The existence on the same plant of three distinct forms of flowers as regards the relative lengths of stamens and pistils. 2 Mineral. The property of crystallizing in three series of fundamentally different forms with the same ultimate chemical composition. 3 Zool. Difference of species in form, color, etc., characterizing three distinct types. — **tri·mor'phic, tri·mor'phous** adj.

tri·nal (trī'nəl) adj. 1 Of or pertaining to three. 2 Having three parts; threefold. [<LL trinalis <L trinus three each < tres, tria three]

tri·na·ry (trī'nər·ē) adj. Made up of three parts or proceeding by threes; ternary. [<LL trinarius of three kinds <L trinus. See TRINAL.]

trine (trīn) adj. 1 Threefold; triple: also trinal. 2 In astrology, relating to or situated in trine; auspicious. — n. 1 A compound in three parts or elements; a trio; triad. 2 Her. A charge composed of three objects. 3 In astrology, the aspect of two planets when 120° apart. — v.t. Obs. In astrology, to place or join in trine. [<OF trin, trine <L trinus. See TRINAL.]

Trin·i·dad and To·ba·go (trin'ə·dad, tō·bā'gō, Span. trē'nē·thäth') An independent member of the Commonwealth of Nations, in the West Indies NE of Venezuela, comprising the islands of **Trinidad**; 1,864 square miles; and **Tobago**; 116 square miles; capital, Port-of-Spain, on Trinidad.

tri·ni·trate (trī·nī'trāt) n. Chem. A nitrate containing three nitric-acid radicals in combination: bismuth trinitrate.

tri·ni·tro·ben·zene (trī·nī'trō·ben'zēn) n. Chem. A yellow crystalline compound, $C_6H_3(NO_2)_3$, occurring in three forms, one of which is highly explosive.

tri·ni·tro·cre·sol (trī·nī'trō·krē'sōl, -sol) n. Chem. A yellow crystalline organic compound, $C_8H_8N_3O_7$, used as an explosive. [<TRI- + NITRO- + CRESOL]

tri·ni·tro·phe·nol (trī·nī'trō·fē'nōl, -nol) n. Picric acid. [<TRI- + NITROPHENOL]

tri·ni·tro·tol·u·ene (trī·nī'trō·tol'yōō·ēn) n. Chem. A high explosive, $C_7H_5N_3O_6$, made by treating toluene with nitric acid: used for filling high explosive shells, for it melts readily and can be poured safely and rapidly: also called TNT, trotyl. Also **tri·ni'tro·tol'u·ol** (-yōō·ōl, -ol). [<TRI- + NITRO- + TOLUENE]

trin·i·ty (trin'ə·tē) n. pl. **·ties** 1 In art, a symbolic representation of the Trinity. 2 The state or character of being three; also, any union of three parts or elements in one; a trio; triad. [<OF trinite <LL trinitas <L, a triad < trinus. See TRINAL.]

Trin·i·ty (trin'ə·tē) n. 1 Theol. A threefold personality existing in the one divine being or substance; the union in one God of Father, Son, and Holy Spirit as three infinite persons. 2 Trinity Sunday.

trin·ket (tring'kit) n. 1 Any small ornament, as of jewelry. 2 Any small article forming part of an outfit. 3 A trifle; a trivial object; a toy. 4 Obs. A knife. See synonyms under GAUD. [<AF trenquet, OF trenchet a toy knife, ornament, < trenchier. See TRENCH.]

tri·no·dal (trī·nōd'l) adj. Bot. Having three nodes or nodal points.

tri·no·mi·al (trī·nō'mē·əl) adj. 1 Biol. Of, having, or employing three terms or names—the generic, the specific, and the subspecific

or varietal, as Lynx rufus texensis, the Texas bobcat. 2 Math. Consisting of three terms connected by plus or minus signs or both. — n. 1 An algebraic expression consisting of three terms connected by plus or minus signs or both, as $3x + y - 27z$. 2 A trinomial name. Also **tri·nom'i·nal** (-nom'ə·nəl), **tri·on'y·mal** (-on'ə·məl). [<TRI- + (BI)NOMIAL]

tri·o (trē'ō, for def. 1 also trī'ō) n. pl. **tri·os** 1 Any three things grouped or associated together. 2 Music a A composition for three performers. b The second part of a minuet or scherzo, of a march, and of dance forms generally. c A group of three musicians who render trios. [<F <Ital. < tre three <L tres, tria]

tri·ode (trī'ōd) n. Electronics A three-element vacuum tube, containing an anode, cathode, and a control grid or electrode. [<TRI- + (ELECTR)ODE]

tri·oe·cious (trī-ē'shəs) adj. Bot. Having in different plants of the same species male, female, and hermaphrodite flowers: also spelled triecious. Also **tri·oi'cous** (-oi'kəs). [<NL Trioecia, order name <Gk. tri- three + oikos a house] — **tri·oe'cious·ly** adv.

tri·o·let (trī'ə·lit) n. A stanza of eight lines on two rimes, the first line repeated as the fourth and seventh and the second as the eighth. Its rime scheme is abaaaabab. [<F, dim. of trio TRIO]

tri·ose (trī'ōs) n. Biochem. A monosaccharide whose molecule contains three atoms of carbon and three of oxygen. [<TRI- + -OSE²]

tri·ox·ide (trī·ok'sīd, -sid) n. Chem. An oxide containing three atoms of oxygen in combination: iron trioxide, Fe_2O_3. Also **tri·ox'id** (-sid).

trip (trip) n. 1 A short journey; excursion; jaunt. 2 A misstep or stumble occasioned by losing the balance or striking the foot against an object. 3 An active, nimble step or movement. 4 The number of fish caught in an excursion. 5 A single tack to windward. 6 Mech. A pawl or similar device that trips, or the action of such a device. 7 A sudden catch, especially of the legs and feet, as of a wrestler. 8 A blunder; mistake. 9 Slang a The hallucinations and other sensations experienced by a person taking a psychedelic drug. b Any intense, usually personal experience. See synonyms under JOURNEY. — v. **tripped, trip·ping** v.i. 1 To stumble. 2 To move quickly with light or small steps; saunter. 3 To commit an error; make a false step; go astray. 4 Mech. To run past the nicks or dents in the ratchet escape wheel of a timepiece. 5 Slang To experience the effects of a psychedelic drug: often with out. — v.t. 6 To cause to stumble: often with up. 7 To detect and expose in an error; defeat the purpose of. 8 To perform (a dance) lightly. 9 Mech. To set free or in operation by releasing a stay, catch, trigger, etc. 10 Naut. a To loosen, as an anchor, from the bottom by a long rope or cable. b To hoist (the topmast) so as to prepare it for being lowered. c To tilt (a yard) similarly. [OF treper, triper leap, trample, ? <MDu. trippen trip, hop]

tri·par·tite (trī·pär'tīt) adj. 1 Divided into three parts or divisions; threefold: a tripartite leaf: also **tri·part·ed** (trī'pär·tid). 2 Law Pertaining to or executed between three parties. 3 Math. Homogeneous in three sets of variables. [<L tripartitus < tri- three + partitus, pp. of partiri divide] — **tri·par'tite·ly** adv.

tripe (trīp) n. 1 A part of the stomach of a ruminant, as the ox, used for food. 2 Colloq. Contemptible or worthless stuff; an inferior, mean, or offensive thing. [<OF tripe, trippe <Arabic tharb entrails, a net]

tri·pe·dal (trī'pə·dəl, trī·pēd'l, trip'ə·dəl) adj. Having three feet; three-footed. [<L tripedalis < tri- three + pes, pedis foot]

tri·pet·al·ous (trī·pet'l·əs) adj. Bot. Having three petals.

tri·phase (trī'fāz) adj. Electr. Having or employing three phases, as in an alternating current.

tri·phen·yl·meth·ane (trī·fen'əl·meth'ān) n. Chem. A hydrocarbon, $(C_6H_5)_3CH$, occurring in colorless leaflets: used in organic synthesis and in the manufacture of dyes. [<TRI- +

PHENYL + METHANE]

tri·phib·i·an (trī·fib'ē·ən) adj. Describing a joint military and naval operation which utilizes terrestrial, marine, and aerial weapons.

triph·thong (trif'thông, -thong, trip'-) n. 1 A combination of three vowel sounds in one syllable, as in one pronunciation of fire. 2 A trigraph composed of vowels, as in beau. [<TRI- + (DI)PHTHONG] — **triph·thon'gal** adj.

triph·y·lite (trif'ə·līt) n. A greenish-gray, bluish, transparent to translucent phosphate of iron and lithium, crystallizing in the orthorhombic system. Also **triph'y·line** (-lin, -lēn). [<TRI- + Gk. phylē a tribe + -ITE¹; so called because it contains three bases]

tri·pin·nate (trī·pin'āt) adj. Bot. Thrice pinnate, as when the pinnae of a bipinnate leaf become again pinnate in certain ferns. Also **tri·pin'nat·ed**. — **tri·pin'nate·ly** adv.

tri·plane (trī'plān) n. An airplane having three supporting surfaces arranged one above the other.

tri·ple (trip'əl) v. **·led, ·ling** v.t. 1 To make threefold in number or quantity. — v.i. 2 To be or become three times as many or as large. 3 In baseball, to make a triple. — adj. 1 Consisting of three things united or of three parts; threefold. 2 Multiplied by three; thrice said or done. 3 Archaic Third. — n. 1 A set or group of three. 2 In baseball, a three-base hit. [<MF <L triplus <Gk. triploos threefold. Doublet of TREBLE.] — **trip'ly** adv.

tri·ple-ex·pan·sion (trip'əl·ik·span'shən) adj. Designating a compound steam engine constructed with three cylinders of graduated sizes in which the steam is successively expanded.

triple measure Music A measure of three beats, the first accented, the second and third unaccented.

tri·ple-nerved (trip'əl·nûrvd') adj. Bot. Three-nerved; having three principal nerves arising from or near the base, as certain leaves.

trip·let (trip'lit) n. 1 A group of three of a kind. 2 One of three children born at one birth. 3 A group of three rimed lines. 4 Music A group of three notes performed in the time of two. 5 A bicycle for three. [<TRIPLE, on analogy with doublet]

tri·ple·tail (trip'əl·tāl') n. A large edible marine fish (Lobotes surinamensis) of warm seas, with soft dorsal and anal fins extended backward, suggesting additional tails.

tri·plex (trī'pleks, trip'leks) adj. Having three parts; threefold. — n. Music Triple measure. [<L < tri- three + plicare fold]

trip·li·cate (trip'lə·kit) adj. Threefold; made in three copies. — n. A third thing corresponding to two others of the same kind or three similar things collectively: a document signed in triplicate. — v.t. (-kāt) **·cat·ed, ·cat·ing** To make three times as much or as many; treble. [<L triplicatus, pp. of triplicare triple < triplex TRIPLEX] — **trip'li·cate·ly** adv.

tri·plic·i·ty (tri-plis'ə·tē) n. pl. **·ties** 1 Threefold character. 2 A group or combination of three; a triad; a triplet. 3 In astrology, a combination of three of the twelve signs of the zodiac. [<LL triplicitas, -tatis <L triplex, -icis TRIPLEX]

trip·lite (trip'līt) n. A brown or black, translucent to opaque, fluophosphate of iron and manganese. [<G triplit <Gk. triploos triple; with ref. to its three cleavages]

trip·lo·blas·tic (trip'lə·blas'tik) adj. Biol. Having or characterized by three germ layers, as the embryos of the higher animals. [<Gk. triploos triple + BLASTIC]

trip·lo·pi·a (trip·lō'pē·ə) n. Pathol. A defect of vision in which objects are seen tripled. [<NL <Gk. triploos threefold + ōps, ōpos eye]

tri·pod (trī'pod) n. 1 A utensil or article having three feet or legs. 2 A three-legged stand, as for supporting a camera, compass, or other instrument. [<L tripus, -podis <Gk. tripous < tri- three + pous foot]

trip·o·dy (trip'ə·dē) n. pl. **·dies** A verse or meter having three feet. [<TRI- + (DI)PODY]

Trip·o·li (trip'ə·lē) 1 One of the two capitals (with Bengasi) and the largest city of Libya, a port on the central Mediterranean and the capital of Tripolitania province: Phoenician *Oea.* **2** A port of NW Lebanon on the Mediterranean: ancient **Trip·o·lis** (trip′ə·lis). —**Tri·pol·i·tan** (tri·pol′ə·tən) *adj.* & *n.* —**Trip′o·line** (-lin) *adj.*

tri·pos (trī′pos) *n.* **1** An honors examination held at Cambridge University, England, especially in mathematics. **2** *Obs.* A tripod. [Appar. alter. of L *tripus* TRIPOD]

trip·per (trip′ər) *n.* **1** One who trips in any sense. **2** *Brit. Colloq.* One who makes trips; a tourist or traveler. **3** *Mech.* A trip or tripping mechanism, as a device on a railroad track which operates a catch on a passing train to give a signal or alarm.

trip·pet (trip′it) *n. Mech.* A cam, toe, or projecting piece, designed to strike some other piece at fixed intervals. [< TRIP, *v.*]

trip·ping (trip′ing) *n.* **1** The act of one who or that which trips. **2** A light dance. —*adj.* Light; nimble; easy; stepping. —**trip′ping·ly** *adv.*

trip·tane (trip′tān) *n. Chem.* A hydrocarbon compound, C_7H_{16}, derived from butane and having a very high octane number. [Contraction of *tripentane* < TRI- + PENTANE]

triptane number An improved measure of the efficiency of a motor fuel, expressed in terms of a blend of normal heptane and triptane, each containing a specified amount of tetraethyl lead.

trip·ter·ous (trip′tər·əs) *adj. Bot.* Having three wings or winglike processes, as certain seeds. [< TRI- + Gk. *pteron* a wing, on analogy with *dipterous*]

trip·tych (trip′tik) *n.* **1** A picture, carving, or work of art on three panels side by side. **2** Three pictures associated in their subjects and placed side by side in compartments. **3** A writing tablet in three sections, made of various laminate materials. Also **trip′ty·ca** (-ti·kə), **trip′ty·chon** (-ti·kon). [< Gk. *triptychos* threefold < *tri-* three + *ptyx, ptychos* a fold < *ptyssein* fold]

tri·pu·di·ate (trī·pyōō′dē·āt) *v.i.* -**at·ed**, -**at·ing** To dance, especially in a measured way. [< L *tripudiatus*, pp. of *tripudiare* < *tripudium* a religious dance, prob. < *tri-* three + *pes, pedis* foot] —**tri·pu·di·a′tion** *n.*

tri·quet·rous (trī·kwet′rəs, -kwē′trəs) *adj.* **1** Three-sided. **2** Having three acute or salient angles. **3** Three-cornered, as certain stems and bones. [< L *triquetrus*]

tri·ra·di·ate (trī·rā′dē·āt) *adj.* Having three rays or radiate branches: the *triradiate* sulcus of the brain. Also **tri·ra′di·al**, **tri·ra′di·at·ed**. —**tri·ra′di·al·ly**, **tri·ra′di·ate·ly** *adv.*

tri·sac·cha·ride (trī·sak′ə·rīd, -rid) *n. Biochem.* Any of a class of saccharides which yield three monosaccharide molecules when subjected to hydrolysis, as raffinose. Also **tri·sac′cha·rid** (-rid).

tri·sect (trī·sekt′) *v.t.* To divide into three parts, especially as, in geometry, into three equal parts. [< TRI- + L *sectus*, pp. of *secare* cut] —**tri·sect′ed** *adj.* —**tri·sec′tion** (-sek′shən) *n.* —**tri·sec′tor** *n.*

tri·seme (trī′sēm) *n.* A syllable or foot consisting of or equivalent to three morae or short syllables, as the tribrach, iambus, and trochee. —*adj.* Consisting of or equal to three morae or short syllables: also **tri·se·mic** (trī·sē′mik). [< Gk. *trisēmos* < *tri-* three + *sēma* a sign]

tri·sep·al·ous (trī·sep′əl·əs) *adj. Bot.* Having three sepals.

tri·sep·tate (trī·sep′tāt) *adj. Biol.* Having three septa.

tris·kel·i·on (tris·kel′ē·ən) *n. pl.* ·**kel·i·a** (-kel′ē·ə) A symbolic figure charaterized by three lines or three human legs radiating from a common center. It is used as the arms of the Isle of Man. Also **tris·cele** (tris′sēl), **tris·kele** (tris′kēl). [< Gk. *triskelēs* of three legs < *tri-* three + *skelos* a leg]

TRISKELION

tris·mus (triz′məs, tris′-) *n. Pathol.* Tetanic spasm causing rigid closure of the jaws; lockjaw. [< NL < Gk. *trismos* a gnashing of teeth, a grinding] —**tris′mic** *adj.*

tris·oc·ta·he·dron (tris·ok′tə·hē′drən) *n. pl.* ·**dra** (-drə) **1** A solid having 24 equal faces corresponding by threes to the faces of an octahedron.

2 A holohedral isometric crystal included under 24 equal isosceles triangular faces with eight planes meeting at the extremities of the rectangular axes: also **trigonal trisoctahedron. 3** An isometric holohedron included under 24 similar and equal trapeziform faces; a trapezohedron: also **tetragonal trisoctahedron.** [< Gk. *tris* thrice (< *treis* three) + OCTAHEDRON.] —**tris·oc′ta·he′dral** *adj.*

tri·spo·rous (trī·spôr′əs, -spō′rəs) *adj. Bot.* Having three spores. Also **tri·spor′ic** (-spôr′ik, -spor′ik). [< TRI- + -SPOROUS]

trist·ful (trist′fəl) *adj. Archaic* Sad; gloomy; sorrowful. [< *obs. trist* sad < OF *triste* < L *tristis*] —**trist′ful·ly** *adv.*

tris·ti·chous (tris′tə·kəs) *adj.* **1** Three-ranked. **2** *Bot.* Having parts, as leaves, arranged in three vertical rows. [< Gk. *tristichos* three-rowed < *tri-* three + *stichos* a row]

tri·stim·u·lus (trī·stim′yə·ləs) *adj.* **1** Having, pertaining to, or caused or characterized by three distinct stimuli. **2** In color analysis, designating an instrument or method for measuring a color stimulus in terms of three selected primary stimuli.

tri·sty·lous (trī·stī′ləs) *adj. Bot.* Having three styles.

tri·sul·fide (trī·sul′fīd, -fid) *n. Chem.* A sulfide containing three atoms of sulfur in combination. Also **tri·sul′fid** (-fid), **tri·sul′phide, tri·sul′phid.**

tri·syl·la·ble (trī·sil′ə·bəl) *n.* A word of three syllables. —**tri·syl·lab·ic** (trī′si·lab′ik) or ·**i·cal** *adj.* —**tri′syl·lab′i·cal·ly** *adv.*

tri·tag·o·nist (trī·tag′ə·nist) *n.* In Greek drama, the actor who played the third part; hence, also, a third-rate actor. [< Gk. *tritagōnistēs* < *tritos* third + *agōnistēs* a contender, actor < *agōnizesthai* contend < *agōn* a contest]

trit·an·o·pi·a (trit′ən·ō′pē·ə) *n. Pathol.* Impairment of vision for blue and yellow; blue blindness. Also **trit·an·op′si·a** (-op′sē·ə). [< NL < Gk. *tritos* third′ + ANOPIA] —**trit′an·op′tic** (-op′tik) *adj.*

trite (trīt) *adj.* **1** Used so often as to be hackneyed; made commonplace by repetition. **2** *Archaic* Worn-out; frayed. [< L *tritus*, pp. of *terere* rub] —**trite′ly** *adv.* —**trite′ness** *n.*

Synonyms: common, commonplace, hackneyed, musty, rusty, stale, stereotyped, threadbare, worn. See COMMON. *Antonyms:* bright, brilliant, fresh, new, original, racy, striking, telling, vivid.

tri·the·ism (trī′thē·iz′əm) *n. Theol.* The doctrine of the separate existence of three Gods: sometimes opprobriously applied to belief in the distinct personality of the Father, the Son, and the Holy Spirit. [< TRI- + Gk. *theos* a god] —**tri′the·ist** *n.* —**tri′the·is′tic** or ·**ti·cal** *adj.*

trit·i·ca·le (trit′ə·kā′lē) *n.* A hybrid grain produced for its high protein content by crossing wheat and rye. [< L *triticum* wheat + *secale* rye]

trit·i·um (trit′ē·əm, trish′ē·əm) *n.* An unstable isotope of hydrogen having atomic mass 3 and a half-life of about 12.5 years. [< NL < Gk. *tritos* third]

tri·ton[1] (trīt′n) *n.* Any of a genus (*Triton*) of marine gastropods with many gills and a trumpet-shaped shell. [< NL < L, Triton]

tri·ton[2] (trī′ton) *n.* The nucleus of an atom of tritium. [< TRIT(IUM) + (ELEC-TR)ON]

Tri·ton (trīt′n) **1** In Greek mythology: **a** A son of Poseidon (Neptune) and Amphitrite, represented with a man's head and upper body and a dolphin's tail. **b** One of a race of attendants of the sea gods. **2** *Her.* A merman; also, a Neptune holding a trident. —**Tri′ton·ess** *n. fem.*

tri·tone (trī′tōn) *n. Music* An augmented fourth, as containing three whole tones. [< Med. L *tritonus* < Gk. *tritonos* < *tri-* three + *tonos*. See TONE.]

trit·u·rate (trich′ə·rāt) *v.t.* ·**rat·ed**, ·**rat·ing** To reduce to a fine powder or pulp by grinding or rubbing; pulverize. —*n.* **1** That which has been triturated. **2** A trituration (def. 3). [< LL *trituratus*, pp. of *triturare* thresh < L *tritura* a rub-

TRITON

bing, threshing < *tritus*. See TRITE.] —**trit·u·ra·ble** (trich′ər·ə·bəl) *adj.* —**trit′u·ra′tor** *n.*

trit·u·ra·tion (trich′ə·rā′shən) *n.* **1** The act of triturating; reduction to a very fine powder by grinding or rubbing, as in a mortar. **2** The process of reducing to a pulp. **3** A triturated preparation, especially one in which 10 parts of a medicinal substance are triturated with 90 parts of milk sugar: also *triturate.*

tri·umph (trī′əmf) *v.i.* **1** To win a victory; be victorious. **2** To be successful. **3** To rejoice over a victory; exult. **4** To celebrate a triumph, as a victorious Roman general. —*v.t.* **5** *Obs.* To conquer. See synonyms under REJOICE. —*n.* **1** In Roman antiquity, the religious pageant of the entry of a victorious consul, dictator, or pretor into Rome: given only for a decisive victory over a foreign enemy. **2** Exultation over victory. **3** The condition of being victorious; victory. **4** *Obs.* A trump card. **5** *Obs.* Any public spectacular display, procession, or pageant. See synonyms under HAPPINESS, VICTORY. [< OF *triumpher* < L *triumphare* < *triumphus* a triumph < Gk. *thriambos* a processional hymn to Dionysus] —**tri′umph·er** *n.*

tri·um·phal (trī·um′fəl) *adj.* **1** Of, pertaining to, or of the nature of a triumph. **2** Celebrating a victory.

triumphal arch A large monumental arch erected in ancient or modern times to commemorate any great victory or achievement.

tri·um·phant (trī·um′fənt) *adj.* **1** Exultant for or as for victory. **2** Crowned with victory; victorious. **3** *Obs.* Of supreme magnificence or beauty; glorious. **4** *Obs.* Triumphal. [< L *triumphans, -antis*, ppr. of *triumphare* TRIUMPH] —**tri·um′phant·ly** *adv.*

tri·um·vir (trī·um′vər) *n. pl.* ·**virs** or ·**vi·ri** (-və·rī) One of three men united in public office or authority, as in ancient Rome. [< L < *trium virorum* of three men < *tres, trium* three + *vir* a man] —**tri·um′vi·ral** *adj.*

tri·um·vi·rate (trī·um′vər·it, -və·rāt) *n.* **1** A group or coalition of three men who unitedly exercise authority or control; government by triumvirs. **2** The office of a triumvir; also, the triumvirs collectively. **3** A group of three men; a trio. [< L *triumviratus* < *triumvir* TRIUMVIR]

tri·une (trī′yōon) *adj.* Three in one: said of the Godhead. —*n.* A group of three things united; a triad; a trinity in unity. [< TRI- + L *unus* one]

tri·u·ni·ty (trī·yōo′nə·tē) *n.* Trinity.

tri·va·lent (trī·vā′lənt, triv′ə·lənt) *adj. Chem.* Having a valence or combining value of three. [< TRI- + L *valens, -entis*, ppr. of *valere* be strong] —**tri·va′lence, tri·va′len·cy** *n.*

tri·valve (trī′valv′) *adj.* Having three valves, as a shell. —*n.* A trivalve shell.

triv·et (triv′it) *n.* A short, usually three-legged stand for holding cooking vessels in a fireplace, a heated iron, or a hot dish on a table: also *trevet.* [OE *trefet* < L *tripes, -pedis* three-footed < *tri-* three + *pes, pedis* a foot]

triv·i·al (triv′ē·əl) *adj.* **1** Of little value or importance; trifling; insignificant. **2** Such as is found everywhere or every day; ordinary; commonplace. **3** Occupied with trifles; of low ability or wit; unscholarly. See synonyms under CHILDISH, INSIGNIFICANT, LITTLE, RIDICULOUS, VAIN, VENIAL. [< L *trivialis* of the crossroads, commonplace < *trivium* a crossing of three roads < *tri-* three + *via* a road] —**triv′i·al·ism** *n.* —**triv′i·al·ly** *adv.*

triv·i·um (triv′ē·əm) *n.* In medieval schools, the course in the liberal arts embracing grammar, logic, and rhetoric. Compare QUADRIVIUM. [< Med. L < L. See TRIVIAL.]

tri·week·ly (trī·wēk′lē) *adj.* & *adv.* **1** Occurring three times a week. **2** Sometimes, done or occurring every third week.

Tro·bri·and Islands (trō′brē·änd) A volcanic island group off the eastern tip of New Guinea; a dependency of the Australian Trust Territory of Papua and New Guinea; total, 175 square miles.

tro·car (trō′kär) *n. Surg.* A sharp-pointed instrument used with a cannula to drain off internal fluids. Also **tro′char.** [< F *troquart, trois-quarts* < *trois* three + *carre* face; so called because of its triangular shape]

tro·cha (trō′chä) *n.* **1** A path; road. **2** An obstruction on a road, to hinder an enemy; a military cordon. [< Sp.]

tro·cha·ic (trō-kā'ik) *adj.* Pertaining to, containing, or composed of trochees: a *trochaic* foot or verse. — *n.* A trochaic verse or line. [<MF *trochaïque* <L *trochaicus* <Gk. *trochaikos* < *trochaios* TROCHEE]

tro·chal (trō'kəl) *adj.* 1 Shaped like a wheel; rotiform. 2 Trochilic. [<Gk. *trochos* a wheel]

tro·chan·ter (trō-kan'tər) *n.* 1 *Anat.* One of several bony processes on the upper thigh bone. 2 *Entomol.* The small second segment of an insect's leg. [<MF <Gk. *trochantēr* < *trechein* run]

tro·che (trō'kē) *n.* A medicated lozenge, usually circular. [Alter. of obs. *trochisk* <MF *trochisque* a lozenge <L *trochiscus* <Gk. *trochiskos* a small wheel, a lozenge < *trochos* a wheel < *trechein* run]

tro·chee (trō'kē) *n.* In prosody, a foot comprising a long and short syllable (–◡), or, in modern verse, an accented syllable followed by an unaccented one. [<L *trochaeus* <Gk. *trochaios (pous)* a running (foot) < *trechein* run]

tro·chil·ic (trō-kil'ik) *adj.* 1 Of the nature of or pertaining to rotary motion. 2 Capable of such motion. [<Gk. *trochilos* a pulley, taken as var. of *trochos* a wheel < *trechein* run]

troch·i·lus (trok'ə-ləs) *n. pl.* ·li (-lī) 1 The crocodile bird: also **tro·chil** (trō'kil, trok'il). **troch'i·los** (-los). 2 A hummingbird (family *Trochilidae*). 3 One of various small warblers or warblerlike birds. [<L *trochilus* a crocodile bird <Gk. *trochilos* < *trechein* run]

troch·le·a (trok'lē-ə) *n. pl.* ·le·ae (-li-ē) *Anat.* A grooved pulleylike surface, permitting smooth motion, as between the humerus and ulna. [<L, a pulley <Gk. *trochilia, trochileia* < *trechein* run]

troch·le·ar (trok'lē-ər) *adj.* 1 *Anat.* Of, pertaining to, or situated near a trochlea. 2 Of the nature of a pulley. 3 Short, cylindrical, compressed, and contracted in the middle of its circumference like a pulley block. [<NL *trochlearis* <L *trochlea* TROCHLEA]

tro·choid (trō'koid) *adj.* Rotating upon its own axis; pivotal: also **tro·choi'dal**. — *n. Math.* A plane curve traced by a point on a circle or on its extended radius as the circle rolls, without slipping, on a straight line: when the point is on the circumference of the circle, the curve traced is a cycloid. [<Gk. *trochoeidēs* round, wheel–like < *trochos* a wheel + *eidos* form, shape] — **tro·choi'dal·ly** *adv.*

troch·o·phore (trok'ə-fôr, -fōr) *n. Zool.* A pear–shaped larval form of certain aquatic invertebrates, as annelids, brachiopods, and mollusks. Also **troch'o·sphere** (-sfir). [<Gk. *trochos* a wheel + -PHORE]

trog·lo·dyte (trog'lə-dīt) *n.* 1 A prehistoric cave man. 2 Figuratively, a hermit; anyone of primitive or degenerate habits. 3 An anthropoid ape, as the gorilla. 4 The wren. [<L *troglodyta* <Gk. *trōglodytēs* < *trōglē* a hole + *dyein* go into] — **trog'lo·dyt'ic** (-dit'ik), **trog'lo·dyt'i·cal** *adj.*

tro·gon (trō'gon) *n.* A tropical American bird (family *Trogonidae*) noted for its resplendent plumage. [<NL <Gk. *trōgōn,* ppr. of *trōgein* gnaw]

troilus butterfly The green–clouded or spicebush swallowtail butterfly (*Papilio troilus*) of eastern North America. [after *Troilus*]

Trojan horse 1 In classical legend, a large, hollow wooden horse, described in Vergil's *Aeneid,* filled with Greek soldiers and left at the Trojan gates: when it was brought within the walls the soldiers emerged at night and admitted the Greek army, who burned the city: also called *wooden horse.* 2 *Mil.* The infiltration of military men into a potentially hostile region for the purpose of nullifying resistance against attack: compare FIFTH COLUMN.

Trojan War In Greek legend, the ten years' war waged by the confederated Greeks under their king, Agamemnon, against the Trojans to recover Helen, the wife of Menelaus, who had been abducted by Paris: celebrated especially in the *Iliad* and the *Odyssey.* See APPLE OF DISCORD.

troke (trōk) *Scot. n.* 1 Exchange; also, articles of trade; small wares; truck. 2 Familiar intercourse or acquaintance. — *v.t. & v.i.* To exchange; barter. Also spelled *troak, trock.*

troll[1] (trōl) *v.t.* 1 To cause to roll; revolve. 2 To sing in succession, as in a round or catch. 3 To sing in a full, hearty manner. 4 To fish for with a moving lure, as from a moving boat. 5 To move (the line or lure) in fishing. 6 *Obs.* To pass around, as a bottle or decanter. — *v.i.* 7 To roll; turn. 8 To sing a tune, etc., in a full, hearty manner. 9 To be uttered in such a way. 10 To fish with a moving lure. 11 *Obs.* To move about; ramble. — *n.* 1 A catch or round. 2 A rolling movement or motion; hence, repetition or routine. 3 In fishing, a spoon or other lure. [? <OF *troller* quest, wander <Gmc. Cf. MHG *trollen* walk with short steps.] — **troll'er** *n.*

troll[2] (trōl) *n.* In Scandinavian folklore, a giant; later, a friendly but often mischievous dwarf. Also **trold** (trōld). [<ON]

trol·ley (trol'ē) *n. pl.* ·leys 1 A grooved metal wheel for rolling in contact with an electric conductor (the **trolley wire**), to convey the current to an electric vehicle. 2 In a subway system, a bow or shoe adapted to the same purpose attached to a current–taker operating through a slot in the track: also **trolley wheel.** 3 A car or system so operated. 4 A small truck or car for conveying material, as in a factory, mine, etc.: also spelled *trawley.* 5 A small cart for serving food and drink: tea *trolley.* 6 *Brit. Dial.* A small hand or donkey cart. 7 A parcels carrier. 8 The mechanism of a traveling crane. 9 A small car running on tracks and worked by a lever operated by hand: used by workmen on a railway. — *v.t. & v.i.* To convey or travel by trolley. Also spelled *trolly.* [<TROLL[1]]

trolley bus A passenger conveyance operating without rails, propelled electrically by current taken from an overhead wire by means of a trolley: also called *trackless trolley.* Also **trolley coach.**

trolley car A car arranged with a trolley and motor for use on an electric railway operated by the trolley system.

troll·ing (trō'ling) *n.* The method or act of fishing by dragging a hook and line, as behind a boat and near the surface: usually with a spoon bait or the like. [<TROLL[1]]

trol·lop (trol'əp) *n.* 1 A slatternly woman. 2 A prostitute. [<dial. E (Scottish) <ME *trollen* roll about; prob. infl. in meaning by *trull*] — **trol'lop·ish, trol'lop·y, trol'lop·ing** *adj.*

trom·bic·u·li·a·sis (trom·bik'yə·lī'ə·sis) *n. Pathol.* Infestation with mites of the genus *Trombicula,* the chiggers. Also **trom·bic'u·lo'sis** (-lō'sis). [<NL *Trombicula* + -IASIS]

trom·bone (trom'bōn, trom·bōn') *n.* A powerful brass wind instrument of the trumpet family possessing a complete chromatic scale. It consists of a cupped mouthpiece and a long tube bent twice upon itself, the outer bend being a U–shaped slide, by the motion of which the length of the vibrating air column may be so adjusted as to produce any note within its compass. [<Ital., aug. of *tromba* a trumpet] — **trom'bon·ist** *n.*

TROMBONE

trom·mel (trom'əl) *n. Metall.* A perforated steel plate, usually cylindrical in form, used for sifting or screening rock, ore, etc. [<G, a drum]

trom·o·ma·ni·a (trom'ə·mā'nē·ə, -mān'yə) *n.* Delirium tremens. [<NL <Gk. *tromos* a trembling + *mania* madness]

trompe (tromp) *n.* 1 *Metall.* An apparatus that supplies a blast of air, as to a forge, by the action of a thin column of water falling through a large, long tube and thus carrying air by entanglement. 2 An arched and vaulted structure that supports a portion of a building.

Also **tromp.** [<F, lit., a trumpet]

tro·na (trō'nə) *n.* A vitreous, gray or white, monoclinic hydrous sodium carbonate, $Na_2CO_8HNaCO_8 \cdot 2H_2O$. [<Sw., appar. <Arabic *ṭrōn,* short for *natrūn* NATRON]

troop (trōōp) *n.* 1 An assembled company; gathering; a herd or flock. 2 *Usually pl.* A body of soldiers; soldiers collectively. 3 The cavalry unit of formation, corresponding to a company of infantry. 4 A body of Boy Scouts consisting of four patrols of eight scouts each. 5 Formerly, a troupe: a company of actors. See synonyms under ARMY. — *v.i.* 1 To move along or gather as a troop or as a crowd. 2 *Archaic* To associate; consort. — *v.t.* 3 To form into troops. 4 *Brit. Mil.* To carry ceremoniously before troops: to *troop* the colors. ◆ Homophone: *troupe.* [<OF *trope* <LL *troppus* a flock <Gmc.]

tro·pa·co·caine (trō'pə·kō·kān', -kō'kān, -kō'kə·ēn) *n. Chem.* A white crystalline compound, $C_{15}H_{19}O_2N,$ obtained from Java coca leaves and also made synthetically from atropine and hyoscine: used as an anesthetic. [<(*benzoylpseudo)trop(eine),* its chemical name + COCAINE]

tro·par·i·on (trō·pâr'ē·on) *n. pl.* ·par·i·a (-pâr'ē·ə) In the Greek Church, a stanza of, or the several stanzas constituting, a hymn. [<Gk., dim. of *tropos.* See TROPE.]

trope (trōp) *n.* 1 The figurative use of a word. 2 Loosely and less properly, a figure of speech; figurative language in general. 3 A short distinguishing cadence interpolated in Gregorian melodies. 4 An interpolated phrase that was occasionally inserted in various parts of the mass prior to the 16th century. [<F <L *tropus* a figure of speech <Gk. *tropos* a turn < *trepein* turn]

tro·pe·ine (trō'pē·in, -ēn) *n. Chem.* An ester of tropine, from which it is formed by the action of certain organic acids. Also **tro'pe·in** (-in). [Alter. of TROPINE]

tro·pe·o·lin (trō·pē'ə·lin) *n. Chem.* Any of several orange azo dyes formed by the action of diazosulfuric acids on phenols. Also **tro·pae'o·lin.** [<TROPAEOL(UM) + -IN; so called because their hues resemble those of the flower]

troph·al·lax·is (trof'ə·lak'sis) *n. Biol.* The free exchange of food substances among individuals, considered as an essential factor in the life cycle of certain insects, especially army ants. [<NL <Gk. *trophē* food + *allaxis* an exchange] — **troph'al·lac'tic** (-lak'tik) *adj.*

troph·ic (trof'ik) *adj.* Pertaining to nutrition and its processes. Also **troph'i·cal.** [<Gk. *trophikos* < *trophē* nourishment < *trephein* nourish] — **troph'i·cal·ly** *adv.*

tropho– *combining form* Nutrition; nourishment; of or pertaining to food or nutrition: *trophoplasm.* Also, before vowels, **troph–.** [<Gk. *trophē* food, nourishment < *trephein* feed, nourish]

troph·o·blast (trof'ə·blast) *n. Biol.* The ectodermal layer of cells in the embryo that establishes relation with the uterus and is concerned in the nutrition of the embryo and fetus. Also **troph'o·derm** (-dûrm). [<TROPHO- + -BLAST] — **troph'o·blas'tic** *adj.*

troph·o·gen·e·sis (trof'ə·jen'ə·sis) *n. Biol.* The production of variations among plants and animals by differences in food and nutrition, as distinguished from genetic factors. Also **tro·phog·e·ny** (trō·foj'ə·nē). — **troph'o·gen'ic** *adj.*

troph·o·plasm (trof'ə·plaz'əm) *n. Biol.* 1 The nutritive or vegetative substance of the cell, as distinguished from the idioplasm. 2 Formerly, a cytoplasmic substance distinguished from the archiplasm. — **troph'o·plas'mic** *adj.*

tro·phot·ro·pism (trō·fot'rə·piz'əm) *n. Bot.* The movement or curvature, as toward or away from nutrient substances, induced in a growing plant by the influence of the chemical nature of its surroundings. — **troph'o·trop'ic** (trof'ə·trop'ik) *adj.*

troph·o·zo·ite (trof'ə·zō'īt) *n. Zool.* A parasitic sporozoan at the stage of entering the blood cell of its host, feeding on the nutritive material in the blood. [<TROPHO- + Gk. *zōion* an animal + -ITE[1]]

tro·phy (trō'fē) *n. pl.* ·phies 1 Anything taken from an enemy and displayed or treasured in proof of victory; hence, a memento of victory or success: *trophies* of the chase. **2** An ancient Roman memorial of victory in imitation of the Greek tropaeum, but a permanent structure, decorated with arms or beaks of ships suspended over the undecorated parts. **3** An ornamental group of objects hung together on a wall, or any collection of objects typical of some event, art, industry, or branch of knowledge. **4** A memento or memorial. **5** *Archit.* A group of arms and armor carved in marble or cast in bronze rising from a circular or quadrangular stepped base. [<MF *trophée* <L *trophaeum, tropaeum* <Gk. *tropaion* < *tropē* a defeat, turning < *trepein* turn, rout]

-trophy *combining form* A (specified) kind of nutrition or nurture: *hypertrophy*. Corresponding adjectives end in *-trophic*. [<Gk. *trophē*. See TROPHO-.]

trop·ic (trop′ik) *n.*
1 *Geog.* Either of two parallels of latitude at a distance from the equator, north and south, equal to the obliquity of the ecliptic, or 23° 27′, on which the sun is seen in the zenith on the days of its greatest declination: called respectively **tropic of Cancer** and **tropic of Capricorn**. **2** *Astron.* **a** Either of two corresponding parallels of declination in the celestial sphere similarly named, and respectively 23° 27′ north or south from the celestial equator. **b** Either of the two points in the celestial sphere where the sun reaches its maximum distance north or south of the celestial equator; a solstice. **3** *pl.* The regions of the earth's surface between the tropics of Cancer and Capricorn, where the sun crosses the zenith twice in the course of the year: with the definite article; the torrid zone. — *adj.* Of or pertaining to the tropics; tropical. [<L *tropicus* <Gk. *tropikos (kyklos)* the tropical (circle), pertaining to the turning of the sun at the solstice < *tropē* turn. See TROPHY.]

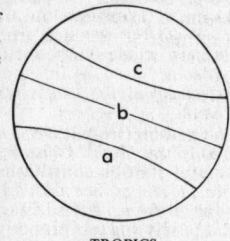

TROPICS
a. Tropic of Capricorn.
b. Equator.
c. Tropic of Cancer.

-tropic *combining form* Having a (specified) tropism; turning or changing in a (particular) way, or in response to a (given) stimulus: *chemotropic, phototropic.*

trop·i·cal (trop′i·kəl) *adj.* **1** Of, pertaining to, or characteristic of the tropics. **2** Of the nature of a trope or metaphor; changed from the original to a figurative meaning. — **trop′i·cal·ly** *adv.*

trop·i·cal·ize (trop′i·kəl·īz′) *v.t.* **·ized, ·iz·ing** To adapt, as clothing, war equipment, ships, etc., for service in tropical areas. — **trop′i·cal·i·za′tion** *n.*

tropic bird A long-winged, oceanic, ternlike bird (genus *Phaëthon*), found mostly in the tropics, having the two middle tail feathers elongated.

tro·pine (trō′pēn, -pin) *n. Chem.* A colorless crystalline alkaloid, $C_8H_{15}NO$, with a tobacco odor, formed when atropine is hydrolyzed. Also **tro′pin** (-pin). [<ATROPINE]

tro·pism (trō′piz·əm) *n. Biol.* **1** The involuntary response of an organism, or of any of its parts, to an external stimulus. **2** Any automatic reaction to a stimulus. [<Gk. *tropē* a turning] — **tro·pis·tic** (trō·pis′tik) *adj.*

tro·pol·o·gy (trō·pol′ə·jē) *n.* **1** The use of tropical or figurative language. **2** Consideration or treatment of the Scriptures both literally and figuratively, or as having a double sense. **3** A treatise on figures of speech. [<LL *tropologia* <Gk. *tropos* TROPE + *logos* discourse] — **trop·o·log·ic** (trop′ə·loj′ik) or **·i·cal** *adj.* — **trop·o·log′i·cal·ly** *adv.*

trop·o·pause (trop′ə·pôz) *n. Meteorol.* A transition zone in the atmosphere between the troposphere and the stratosphere at which the fall of temperature with increasing height abruptly ceases. [<TROPO(SPHERE) + Gk. *pausis* a ceasing]

tro·poph·i·lous (trō·pof′ə·ləs) *adj. Ecol.* Adapted to extreme conditions of moisture or of heat: said of plants. [<Gk. *tropos* a turning, change + *philos* loving; with ref. to

adaptation to seasonal changes]

trop·o·phyte (trop′ə·fīt) *n. Ecol.* Any of the plants that adapt themselves to seasonal changes of dryness or cold and also of moisture: they form the highest type of temperate-zone plants, as the deciduous trees. [<Gk. *tropos* a turning, change + -PHYTE] — **trop′o·phyt′ic** (-fit′ik) *adj.*

trop·o·sphere (trop′ə·sfir) *n. Meteorol.* The region of the atmosphere from the earth's surface to the tropopause, having a height of from six to twelve miles and characterized by decreasing temperature with increasing altitude. [<F *troposphère* <Gk. *tropos* a turning + F *sphère* <L *sphaera* <Gk. *sphaira*]

trop·po (trop′ō, *Ital.* trôp′pō) *adv. Music* Too much: andante ma non *troppo* (andante but not too much). [<Ital.]

-tropous *combining form* Turned in a specified way: *anatropous*. Corresponding nouns end in *-tropy*.

-tropy *combining form* **1** -tropism. **2** A state of being turned. See -TROPOUS. [<Gk. *trope* a turning < *trepein* turn]

trot (trot) *n.* **1** A progressive motion of a quadruped, in which each diagonal pair of legs is alternately lifted, thrust forward, and placed upon the ground almost simultaneously, the body of the animal being entirely unsupported twice during each stride; the sound of this gait. **2** A race for trotters. **3** A little child; toddler: a term of endearment. **4** Steady going or movement, implying persistence and diligence: I have been on the *trot* all day. **5** *Colloq.* A literal translation of a foreign-language text, used as an aid in study or in examination; a crib; pony. — *v.* **trot·ted, trot·ting** *v.i.* **1** To go at a trot. **2** To go quickly; hurry. — *v.t.* **3** To cause to trot. **4** To ride at a trotting gait. — **to trot out** To bring forth for inspection, approval, etc. [<OF *troter* <OHG *trottōn* tread]

troth (trôth, trōth) *n.* **1** Good faith; fidelity; also, the act of pledging fidelity; especially, betrothal. **2** Truth; verity. — *v.t. Archaic* To betroth; pledge. [ME *trowthe, trouthe*, var. of OE *trēowth* truth]

Trot·sky (trot′skē), **Leon**, 1879-1940, Russian Bolshevist leader; exiled 1929; murdered: real name *Lev Davidovitch Bronstein*.

Trot·sky·ism (trot′skē·iz′əm) *n.* The doctrines of Trotsky and his followers; especially, his belief in "permanent revolution" or the theory that Communism to succeed must be international. — **Trot′sky·ist** *n.*

trot·ter (trot′ər) *n.* **1** One who or that which trots; a trotting horse; specifically, a horse trained to trot for speed. **2** *Colloq.* An animal's foot: a pig's *trotters.*

trou·ba·dour (trōō′bə·dôr, -dōr, -dōōr) *n.* One of a class of lyric poets, sometimes including wandering minstrels and jongleurs, originating in Provence in the 11th century and flourishing in southern France, northern Italy, and eastern Spain during the 12th and 13th centuries. Compare TROUVÈRE. See synonyms under POET. [<MF <Provençal *trobador* < *trobar* compose, invent, find; ult. origin uncertain]

trou·ble (trub′əl) *n.* **1** The state of being distressed, annoyed, or confused; also, grief; affliction; disturbance. **2** A person, circumstance, or event that occasions difficulty or perplexity; the vexation thus occasioned; annoyance; worry; civil unrest or agitation. **3** Toilsome exertion; pains. **4** Any serious or permanent diseased condition: lung *trouble*. See synonyms under ANXIETY, CARE, GRIEF, MISFORTUNE, PAIN. — *v.* **led, ·ling** *v.t.* **1** To cause mental agitation to; distress; worry. **2** To agitate or disturb; stir up or roil, as water. **3** To inconvenience or incommode. **4** To annoy or pester; bother. **5** To cause physical pain or discomfort to; afflict. — *v.i.* **6** To take pains; bother. **7** To worry. See synonyms under PERPLEX. [<OF *truble, turble* < *turbler* <L *turbula* a mob, dim. of *turba* a crowd] — **troub′ler** *n.* — **troub′ling·ly** *adv.*

trou·ble-shoot·er (trub′əl·shōō′tər) *n.* **1** A mechanic; a repairman. **2** One who locates difficulties and seeks to remove them. **3** A person trained to find and eliminate trouble in the operation of a machine, process, or the like; a maintenance man. — **troub′le-shoot′ing** *n.*

troub·le·some (trub′əl·səm) *adj.* **1** Causing

trouble; vexatious; burdensome; trying; afflictive: a *troublesome* business. **2** Marked by violence; tumultuous. **3** Greatly agitated or disturbed; troublous. — **troub′le·some·ly** *adv.* — **troub′le·some·ness** *n.*

Synonyms: afflictive, annoying, arduous, burdensome, difficult, galling, harassing, hard, importunate, intrusive, irksome, laborious, painful, perplexing, teasing, tiresome, trying, vexatious, wearisome. *Antonyms:* amusing, cheering, easy, entertaining, grateful, gratifying, helpful, light, pleasant.

trough (trôf, trof; *Dial.* trôth, troth) *n.* **1** A long, narrow, open receptacle for conveying a fluid or for holding food or water for animals. **2** A long, narrow channel or depression, as between ridges on land or waves at sea. **3** A gutter for rain water fixed under the eaves of a building. [OE *trog*]

trounce (trouns) *v.t.* **trounced, trounc·ing** **1** To beat or thrash severely; punish. **2** *Colloq.* To defeat. [<OF *tronce* a thick piece of wood <L *truncus* stem, trunk] — **trounc′ing** *n.*

troupe (trōōp) *n.* A company of actors or other performers. — *v.i.* **trouped, troup·ing** To travel as one of a company of actors or entertainers. ◆ Homophone: *troop*. [<MF <OF *trope* TROOP] — **troup′er** *n.*

trou·sers (trou′zərz) *n. pl.* A man's garment, covering the body from the waist to the ankles or knees and divided so as to make a separate covering for each leg. Also **trow′sers.** [Blend of obs. *trouse* breeches (<Irish *triubhas*) and DRAWERS]

trousse (trōōs) *n.* **1** A collection of small implements in a sheath or case. **2** A case containing knives, tweezers, etc., fastened to the belt: a surgeon's *trousse*. [<F. See TRUSS.]

trous·seau (trōō·sō′, trōō′sō) *n. pl.* **·seaux** (-sōz′, -sōz) **1** A bride's outfit, especially of clothing. **2** *Obs.* A bundle; truss. [<F < *trousse* a packed collection of things. See TRUSS.]

trout (trout) *n.* **1** A salmonoid fish mostly found in fresh waters and highly esteemed as a game and food fish. The **brown trout** or **river trout** (*Salmo trutta*), attaining a length of 30 inches, is common in Europe; the **cut-throat trout** (*S. clarkii*), and the **rainbow trout** or steelhead (*S. gairdnerii*) are species of western North America. The **speckled trout** or **brook trout** (*Salvelinus fontinalis*) is common in eastern North America. **2** A fish resembling, or supposed to resemble, the above, as the greenling. [OE *truht* <LL *tructus, tructa* <Gk. *trōktēs* a nibbler < *trōgein* gnaw]

tro·ver (trō′vər) *n. Law* An action to recover the value of personal property of the plaintiff wrongfully withheld or converted by another to his own use: originally an action of trespass against one who found the goods of another, and refused to give them up; the finding, however, became a fiction. [<OF, find; ult. origin uncertain]

trow·el (trou′əl, troul) *n.* **1** A flat-bladed, sometimes pointed implement having an offset handle; used by masons, plasterers, and molders. **2** A small concave scoop with a handle; used in digging about small plants, potting them, etc. **3** A molder's smoothing tool. — *v.t.* **·eled** or **·elled, ·el·ing** or **·el·ling** To apply, dress, or form with a trowel. [<OF *truele* <LL *truella* <L *trulla*, dim. of *trua* a stirring spoon, ladle] — **trow′el·er** or **trow′el·ler** *n.*

TYPES OF TROWELS
a. Garden. *b.* Circle. *c.* Corner.
d. Brick. *e.* Plastering.

troy (troi) *n.* A system of weights in which 12 troy ounces make a pound, used by jewelers in England and the United States. See under WEIGHT. Also **troy weight.** [from *Troyes*; with ref. to a weight used at a fair held there]

Troy (troi) **1** The site of nine superimposed

ruined cities in NW Asia Minor: the seventh stratum, a Phrygian city of perhaps about 1200 B.C., the scene of the *Iliad*, was also called *Ilium, Ilion*. **2** A city on the Hudson River in eastern New York.

tru·an·cy (trōō'ən·sē) *n. pl.* **·cies** The state or habit of being truant; an act of playing truant. Also **tru'ant·ry**.

tru·ant (trōō'ənt) *n.* One who absents himself, especially from school, without leave. — *v.i.* To play the truant. — *adj.* **1** Playing truant; idle. **2** Relating to or characterizing a truant. [<OF, a vagabond, prob. <Celtic]

truce (trōōs) *n.* **1** An agreement between belligerents for a temporary suspension of hostilities; an armistice. **2** Temporary cessation or intermission. [Plural of ME *trew*, OE *truwa* faith, a promise. Akin to TRUE, TRUST.]

truck[1] (truk) *n.* **1** One of several forms of strong vehicles, variously constructed, for moving bulky articles, freight, etc.; a dray; a stout automotive vehicle on rubber tires able to carry heavy loads. **2** A two-wheeled barrowlike vehicle with a forward lip and no sides, for use in moving barrels, boxes, etc., by hand. **3** A two-, three-, four-, or sometimes six-wheeled vehicle used about railway stations, for moving trunks, etc.: distinguished as **baggage truck, freight truck,** or **wagon truck. 4** Any of numerous small, flat-topped cars moved by pushing or pulling and used in stores. **5** *Brit.* An open or platform freight car. **6** *Naut.* A disk at the upper extremity of a mast or flagpole through which the halyards of signals are run. **7** A wheel: the original sense, now rare, and usually implying a small tireless wheel. — *v.t.* **1** To carry on a truck. — *v.i.* **2** To carry goods on a truck. **3** To drive a truck. [Appar. <L *trochus* a hoop <Gk. *trochos* a wheel < *trechein* run]

truck[2] (truk) *v.t. & v.i.* To exchange or barter; also, to peddle. — *n.* **1** Commodities for sale. **2** *U.S.* Garden produce for market: often in compounds: *truck* farming, etc. **3** *Colloq.* Rubbish; worthless articles collectively. **4** Barter. **5** *Colloq.* Intercourse; dealings: I will have no *truck* with him. [<OF *troquer* barter; origin unknown]

truck·age[1] (truk'ij) *n.* **1** Money paid for conveyance of goods on trucks. **2** Such conveyance. [<TRUCK[1] + -AGE]

truck·age[2] (truk'ij) *n.* Exchange; barter. [<TRUCK[2] + -AGE]

truck·er[1] (truk'ər) *n.* One who drives or supplies trucks or moves commodities in trucks: also called *truckman*.

truck·er[2] (truk'ər) *n.* **1** *U.S.* A market gardener; a truck farmer. **2** One who barters or sells commodities; a hawker.

truck farm *U.S.* A farm on which vegetables are produced for market. [<TRUCK[2] + FARM] — **truck farming**

truck·head (truk'hed') *n.* The terminal to which supplies are brought by truck and from which they are distributed to the required points. [< TRUCK[1] + HEAD; on analogy with *railhead*]

truck house Formerly, a building used to store articles used in trading with the Indians. Also **trucking house.**

truck·le (truk'əl) *v.* **·led, ·ling** *v.i.* **1** To yield meanly or weakly: with *to*. **2** To roll on truckles or casters. — *v.t.* **3** To cause to roll on truckles or casters. — *n.* **1** A small wheel. **2** *Dial.* A trundle bed. [<AF *trocle, trokle* <L *trochlea*. See TROCHLEA.] — **truck'ler** *n.* — **truck'ling·ly** *adv.*

truck·man (truk'mən) *n. pl.* **·men** (-mən) A dealer in truck; one who trucks or trades.

truck system The practice of paying wages to workmen in goods instead of money.

truc·u·lent (truk'yə·lənt) *adj.* **1** Of savage character; awakening terror; cruel; ferocious. **2** Scathing; harsh; violent: said of writing or speech. [<L *truculentus* <*trux, trucis* fierce] — **truc'u·lent·ly** *adv.*

trudge (truj) *v.i.* **trudged, trudg·ing** To walk wearily or laboriously; plod. — *n.* A tiresome walk or tramp. [Earlier *tredge, tridge*; origin uncertain] — **trudg'er** *n.*

true (trōō) *adj.* **tru·er, tru·est** **1** Faithful to fact or reality; not false or erroneous: a *true*

judgment or proposition. **2** Being real or natural; genuine, not counterfeit: a *true* specimen, *true* gold. **3** Faithful to friends, promises, or principles; loyal; steadfast: *true* love, a *true* friend. **4** Conformable to an existing standard type or pattern; exact: a *true* copy. **5** Accurate, as in shape, dimensions, or position: a *true* fit, a *true* circle. **6** Faithful to the requirements of law or justice; legitimate: the *true* king. **7** Faithful to truth; trustful; honest: a *true* man. **8** Faithful to the promise or predicted event; correctly indicative: a *true* sign. **9** *Biol.* **a** Possessing all the attributes of a developed organ or structure of its class; complete. **b** Of pure strain or pedigree: a *true* collie dog. **c** Conformed to the structure of the type; properly so called: said of a plant or animal, as distinguished from others improperly so called: a *true* locust. **10** Exactly correspondent in pitch or key; in perfect tune: His voice is *true*. See synonyms under AUTHENTIC, CORRECT, FAITHFUL, GOOD, HONEST, JUST[1], MORAL, RIGHT, PURE. — *n.* **1** Truth; covenant; pledge. **2** *pl.* **trues** or **truce** *Obs.* An armistice or truce. — **in** (or **out of**) **true** In (or not in) line of adjustment: said of a mark or part, as in a drawing or a machine. — *adv.* **1** In truth; truly. **2** In a true and accurate manner: The wheel runs *true*. **3** Conformably to the ancestral type: in the phrase *to breed true*. — *v.t.* **trued, tru·ing** To bring to conformity with a standard or requirement; form or adjust, as with geometrical precision: to *true* a frame or a tool. [OE *trēowe*. Akin to TRUCE, TRUST.] — **true'ness** *n.*

true bill *Law* **1** The endorsement by a grand jury on a bill of indictment which they find to be sustained by the evidence. **2** A bill so endorsed.

true copy An exact, verbatim transcript of any document, report, etc.; especially, one certified as correct by a qualified authority.

true level A surface that is everywhere perpendicular to a plumb line, as that of a liquid at rest.

true·love (trōō'luv') *n.* **1** One truly beloved; a sweetheart: used also adjectively. **2** *Obs.* Truelovers' knot. **3** The herb-Paris, so called because its four leaves are set together in the form of a truelovers' knot.

true·lov·ers' knot (trōō'luv'-ərz) A complicated double knot, a symbol of fidelity in love.

true·pen·ny (trōō'pen'ē) *n. Archaic* **1** Originally, a coin of genuine metal. **2** A trusty or genuine person; an honest fellow.

TRUELOVERS'
KNOT

true time Mean time, or mean solar time.

truf·fle (truf'əl, trōō'fəl) *n.* Any of various fleshy underground fungi (genus *Tuber*), regarded as a choice table delicacy. [<OF *trufe, truffe*, prob. <Ital. *truffa*, ult. <L *tuber* a tuber]

tru·ism (trōō'iz·əm) *n.* An obvious or self-evident truth; a platitude. See synonyms under AXIOM.

tru·ly (trōō'lē) *adv.* **1** In conformity with fact. **2** With accuracy. **3** With loyalty or fidelity. **4** *Archaic* Surely; verily. **5** Lawfully; legally.

Tru·man (trōō'mən), **Harry S**, 1884–1972, president of the United States 1945–1953.

trump (trump) *n.* **1** In various card games, a card of the suit selected to rank above all others temporarily. **2** The suit thus determined: usually in the plural. **3** *Colloq.* A very acceptable and agreeable person; good fellow. — *v.t.* **1** To take (another card) with a trump. **2** To surpass; excel; beat. — *v.i.* **3** To play a trump. — **to trump up** To make up or invent for a fraudulent purpose. [Alter. of TRIUMPH]

trump·er·y (trum'pər·ē) *n. pl.* **·er·ies 1** Worthless finery. **2** Rubbish; nonsense. **3** Deceit; trickery. See synonyms under GAUD. — *adj.* Having a showy appearance, but valueless. [<OF *tromperie* <*tromper* TRUMP[1], v.]

trum·pet (trum'pit) *n.* **1** A soprano wind instrument with a flaring bell and a long metal tube. The tube was formerly always straight, but now may recurve singly or

doubly. **2** A powerful reed stop in an organ. **3** Something resembling a trumpet in form. **4** A tube for collecting and conducting sounds to the ear; an ear trumpet. **5** A loud penetrating sound like that of a trumpet; trumpeting. **6** *pl.* A pitcherplant (*Sarracenia flava*) of the southern United States having trumpet-shaped leaves. **7** *Obs.* A trumpeter. — *v.t.* **1** To sound or proclaim by or as by trumpet; publish abroad. — *v.i.* **2** To blow a trumpet. **3** To give forth a sound as if from a trumpet. [<OF *trompette*, dim. of *trompe* TRUMP[2]]

TRUMPET

trumpet creeper A woody vine (*Campsis radicans*) of the southern United States, with scarlet trumpet-shaped flowers. Also **trumpet vine.**

trum·pet·er (trum'pit·ər) *n.* **1** One who sounds a trumpet. **2** One who publishes something loudly abroad. **3** A large South American bird, related to the cranes; especially, the golden-breasted trumpeter (*Psophia crepitans*), often domesticated. **4** A large North American wild swan (*Cygnus buccinator*), having a clarionlike cry: now very scarce: also **trumpeter swan. 5** One of a breed of domestic pigeons.

trumpet flower Any of various plants having trumpet-shaped flowers, as the trumpet creeper, the trumpet honeysuckle.

trumpet honeysuckle A twining honeysuckle (*Lonicera sempervirens*) with oblong leaves and trumpet-shaped flowers, scarlet without and yellow within.

trumpet tree A West Indian and South American tree (*Cecropia peltata*) whose hollow branches are used for musical instruments. Also **trum'pet·wood'** (-wŏŏd').

trun·cate (trung'kāt) *v.t.* **·cat·ed, ·cat·ing** To cut the top or end from. — *adj.* **1** Truncated. **2** *Biol.* Appearing as though cut or broken squarely off, as the end of certain leaves and shells, the tail of certain birds, the caudal fin of some fishes, etc. [<L *truncatus*, pp. of *truncare* <*truncus* TRUNK] — **trun·ca·tion** (trung·kā'shən) *n.*

trun·cat·ed (trung'kā·tid) *adj.* **1** Cut off; shortened. **2** Describing a cone or pyramid whose vertex is cut off by a plane usually parallel to the base. **3** *Mineral.* Having the edges or angles cut off, as certain crystals. **4** *Biol.* Truncate.

trun·cheon (trun'chən) *n.* **1** A short, heavy stick; a baton; club; staff. **2** The baton of a military officer or marshal. **3** A tree whose branches have been lopped off to hasten growth; tree trunk: the original meaning. **4** *Obs.* A short club or cudgel; a spear shaft. **5** *Brit.* A policeman's club. — *v.t.* To beat as with a truncheon; cudgel. [<OF *trunçun, tronchon* a stump, ult. <L *truncus* TRUNK]

TRUNCATED
PYRAMID

trun·dle (trun'dəl) *n.* **1** A small broad wheel, as of a caster. **2** The act, motion, or sound of trundling. **3** A trundle bed. **4** A lantern wheel. **5** *Obs.* A small low-wheeled vehicle; truck. — *v.t. & v.i.* **·dled, ·dling 1** To roll along, as a hoop. **2** To rotate. [Var. of TRINDLE] — **trun'dler** *n.*

trunk (trungk) *n.* **1** The main stem or stock of a tree, as distinguished from its branches or roots. **2** The human body, apart from the head, neck, and limbs; the torso. **3** *Entomol.* The thorax. **4** *Anat.* The main stem of a nerve, blood vessel, or lymphatic. **5** The main line of a communication or transportation system. **6** The circuit connecting two telephone exchanges. **7** The main body, line, or stem of anything, as distinct from its appendages. **8** A proboscis, as of an elephant. **9** A large box or case used for packing and carrying clothes or other articles, as for a journey. **10** A large compartment at the rear of an automobile, used for storage. **11** *pl.* A close–fitting garment covering the loins and often part of the thighs, worn by male swimmers, athletes, etc. **12** *pl. Obs.* Trunk hose. **13** *Mech.* **a** A trough, chute, or conduit. **b** A large hollow piston in which a connecting rod moves. **14** *Naut.* **a** The well for the centerboard of a vessel. **b** A casing connecting the hatchways of two or more decks and forming a shaft. **c** Any structure placed on the upper deck of a ship, as for shelter. **15** *Archit.* The shaft of a column. See synonyms under BODY. — *adj.* Being or belonging to a trunk or main body: a *trunk* railroad. [<OF *tronc* <L *truncus* stem, trunk, orig. adj., mutilated; def. 8 infl. in meaning by F *trompe* a trumpet]

trunk·fish (trungk′fish′) *n.* *pl.* **·fish** or **·fish·es** A plectognath fish (family *Ostraciidae*) of warm seas, characterized by a body covering of hard, bony plates.

TRUNKFISH

trun·nion (trun′yən) *n.* **1** One of two opposite cylindrical projections from the sides of a cannon, forming an axis on which it is elevated or depressed. **2** A similar support on which the cylinders of some engines oscillate. [<F *trognon* the core of a fruit, a stump, trunk; ult. origin unknown]

truss (trus) *n.* **1** *Med.* A bandage or support for a rupture. **2** A braced framework of ties, beams, or bars, usually arranged in a series of triangles, as for the support of a roof, airplane, or bridge. **3** A bundle, especially of hay or straw. In England, 56 pounds of old or 60 pounds of new hay make a *truss*; 36 pounds make a *truss* of straw. **4** *Naut.* A heavy iron piece by which a lower yard is attached to a mast. **5** *Bot.* A compact terminal cluster of flowers. **6** *Archit.* A projection from the face of a wall, used to support a cornice; a large corbel; a bracket or modillion. **7** A pack; package. — *v.t.* **1** To tie or bind; fasten: often with *up.* **2** To support by a truss; brace, as a roof. **3** To fasten the wings of (a fowl) with skewers or twine before cooking. **4** To fasten, tighten, or tie around one, as a garment or laces. **5** To hang, as a criminal: with *up.* [<OF *trusse, trousse* <*trousser, trusser* pack up, bundle, prob. <L *torca* a bundle <*torques.* See TORQUES.] — **truss′er** *n.*

truss·ing (trus′ing) *n.* **1** A system of diagonal tension rods and struts for strengthening or stiffening a structure, as a railway car or a vessel's hull. **2** Trusses collectively. **3** The act of one who trusses. **4** A bracing with ties, struts, or the like.

trust (trust) *n.* **1** A confident reliance on the integrity, veracity, or justice of another; confidence; faith; also, the person or thing so trusted. **2** Something committed to one's care for use or safekeeping; a charge; responsibility. **3** The state or position of one who has received an important charge. **4** A confidence in the reliability of persons or things without careful investigation. **5** Credit, in the commercial sense. **6** *Law* The confidence, or the obligation arising from the confidence, re-

posed in a person (called the *trustee*) to whom the legal title to property is conveyed for the benefit of another (the *cestui que trust*), that he will faithfully apply the property according to such confidence; also, the beneficial title or ownership of property of which the legal title is in another. ◆ Collateral adjective: *fiducial.* **7** The property or thing held in trust; also, the relation subsisting between the holder and the property so held. **8** A permanent combination, now illegal, for the purpose of controlling the production, price, etc., of some commodity or the management, profits, etc., of some business; also, a trust company. Compare CARTEL, CORNER, MONOPOLY, POOL², SYNDICATE. **9** Confident expectation; belief; hope. **10** Custody; care; keeping. **11** *Obs.* Trustworthiness. — *v.t.* **1** To have trust in; rely upon. **2** To commit to the care of another; entrust. **3** To commit something to the care of: with *with.* **4** To allow to do something without fear of the consequences. **5** To expect with confidence or with hope. **6** To believe. **7** To allow business credit to. — *v.i.* **8** To place trust or confidence; rely: with *in.* **9** To hope: with *for.* **10** To allow business credit. — *to trust to* To depend upon; confide in. — *adj.* Held in trust: *trust* property, *trust* money. [<ON *traust,* lit., firmness. Akin to TRUCE, TRUE.] — **trust′er** *n.* — **trust′less** *adj.*

Synonyms (noun): assurance, belief, confidence, credence, expectation, faith, hope. See ASSURANCE, BELIEF, FAITH.

Synonyms (verb): believe, commit, confide, hope. See COMMIT, LEAN¹. *Antonyms:* despair, disbelieve, discredit, distrust, doubt, mistrust, suspect.

trust company An incorporated institution empowered by its charter to accept and execute trusts, as provided by law, to receive deposits of money and other personal property and issue obligations therefor, and to lend money on real and personal securities.

trus·tee (trus·tē′) *n.* **1** One who holds property in trust; especially, in popular usage, one of a body of men, often elective, who hold the property and manage the affairs of a church or public institution. **2** One in whose hands property is attached by a trustee process. — *v.t.* **·teed, ·tee·ing** **1** *Law* To attach by trustee process (the property of a debtor in the hands of a third person). **2** To place (property) in the care of a trustee.

trustee process A statutory remedy whereby a creditor may reach property or assets of his debtor in the hands of a third person.

trus·tee·ship (trus·tē′ship) *n.* **1** The post or function of a trustee. **2** Supervision and control of a trust territory by a country or countries commissioned by the United Nations; also, the territory so controlled.

Trust Territory An area, usually a former colonial possession, governed by a member state of the United Nations as an Administering Authority reporting to the United Nations Trusteeship Council functioning under the authority of the General Assembly with the exception that the trusteeships of the areas designated as strategic are supervised by the Security Council after first having approved the trust agreements. Trust Territories in-

clude former League of Nations mandates. Also **trust territory, UN Trust Territory.** The independence of the Cameroons, Somaliland, Tanganyika, and Togoland in 1960–61 and of Western Samoa in 1962 reduced the Trust Territories to:

Trust Territory	Administered by
Nauru	Australia on behalf of Australia, New Zealand, and the United Kingdom
(Papua and) New Guinea	Australia
Ruanda-Urundi	Belgium
Trust Territory of the Pacific Islands (a strategic territory)	United States

truth (trooth) *n.* *pl.* **truths** (troothz, trooths) **1** The state or character of being true in relation to being, knowledge, or speech. **2** Conformity to fact or reality. **3** Conformity to rule, standard, model, pattern, or ideal. **4** Conformity to the requirements of one's being or nature; steadfastness; sincerity. **5** That which is true; a statement or belief which corresponds to the reality. **6** A fact as the object of correct belief; reality. **7** A tendency or disposition to speak or tell only what is true; veracity. **8** The quality of being true; fidelity; constancy. **9** In the fine arts, faithfulness to the facts of nature, history, or life. **10** *Obs.* Right, according to divine law. See synonyms under FIDELITY, JUSTICE, VERACITY, VIRTUE. [OE *trēowth* <*treowe* true] — **truth′less** *adj.* — **truth′less·ness** *n.*

truth·ful (trooth′fəl) *adj.* Veracious, as a person; true, as a narrative; veridical. See synonyms under CANDID. — **truth′ful·ly** *adv.* — **truth′ful·ness** *n.*

try (trī) *v.* **tried, try·ing** *v.t.* **1** To make an attempt to do or accomplish; undertake; endeavor. **2** To make experimental use or application of: often with *out*: to *try* a new pen. **3** To subject to a test; put to proof. **4** To put severe strain upon; tax, as the eyes. **5** To subject to trouble or tribulation; afflict. **6** To extract by rendering or melting; refine: often with *out*: to *try* out oil. **7** *Law* **a** To determine the guilt or innocence of by judicial trial. **b** To examine or determine judicially, as a case. — *v.i.* **8** To make an attempt; put forth effort. **9** To make an examination or test. See synonyms under CHASTEN, ENDEAVOR, EXAMINE, STRUGGLE. — **to try on** To put on (a garment) to test it for fit or appearance. — **to try out** To attempt to qualify: He *tried out* for the football team. — *n.* *pl.* **tries** **1** The act of trying; trial; experiment. **2** In Rugby football, the act of touching the ball down behind an opponent's goal, which scores three points. [<OF *trier* sift, pick out, prob. <LL *tritare* thresh <L *tritus.* See TRITE.] — **tri′er** *n.*

trying plane A long plane used to true up the edges of boards to be joined; a jointer. Also **try plane.**

try·lon (trī′lon) *n.* A three–sided pylon: used as part of the main gateway to the New York World's Fair, 1939. [<TR(I)- + (P)YLON]

try·ma (trī′mə) *n.* *pl.* **·ma·ta** (-mə·tə) *Bot.* A drupelike, commonly two–celled fruit with a bony nucleus and a fleshy, leathery, or fibrous dehiscent or separating exocarp, as the hickory nut and walnut. [<NL <Gk. *tryma, trymē* a hole < *tryein* wear away]

try·out (trī′out′) *n.* *U.S. Colloq.* A test of ability, as of an actor or athlete, often in competition with others.

tryp·a·no·some (trip′ə·nə·sōm′) *n.* Any of a genus (*Trypanosoma*) of flagellate infusorians infesting the blood of man and some lower animals. They destroy the red corpuscles, and cause serious and even fatal diseases, as the sleeping sickness. Also **tryp′a·no·so′ma** (-sō′·mə). [<Gk. *trypanon* a borer + -SOME²]

tryp·a·no·so·mi·a·sis (trip′ə·nō·sō·mī′ə·sis) *n.* *Pathol.* Any disease caused by the presence in the body of trypanosomes. Also **tryp′a·no·so′ma·to′sis** (-sō′mə·tō′sis). [<TRYPANOSOME + -IASIS]

tryp·ars·am·ide (trip′är·sam′id, -īd, trip·är′sə·mid, -mid) *n.* *Chem.* A colorless crystalline compound, $C_8H_{10}O_4N_2AsNa$, used in the treatment of trypanosomiasis and certain forms of syphilis. [<TRYP(ANOSOME) + ARS(ENIC) + AMIDE]

tryp·sin (trip′sin) *n.* *Biochem.* A proteolytic enzyme contained in the pancreatic juice.

Collar   Bowstring   Hammer-beam
Deck (short span)   Deck (long span)   Warren
Pegram   Dome   Mansard

TYPES OF TRUSSES

[<G <Gk. *tripsis* a rubbing (< *tribein* rub) + (PEP)SIN] — **tryp′tic** (-tik) *adj.*

tryp·sin·o·gen (trip·sin′ə·jen) *n. Biochem.* The substance secreted by the pancreas and converted into trypsin by the action of intestinal enzymes. [<*trypsino*- <TRYPSIN + -GEN]

tryp·to·phan (trip′tə·fan) *n. Biochem.* A crystalline amino acid, $C_{11}H_{12}O_2N_2$, contained in variable amounts in most proteins and associated with the digestive functions. Also **tryp′to·phane** (-fān). [< *tryptic* (<TRYPSIN) + -*phan*, var. of -PHANE]

try·sail (trī′səl, -sāl′) *n. Naut.* A small sail bent to a gaff abaft the foremast and mainmast of a ship: also called *spencer*. [< nautical phrase *(at) try* lying to in a storm + SAIL]

try square A carpenter's square having usually a wooden stock and a steel blade.

tryst (trist, trīst) *v.t.* **1** To agree to meet. **2** To appoint (a time), as for meeting. **3** To arrange for in advance; engage. **4** *Obs.* To trust. — *v.i.* **5** To agree upon some place or time of meeting. — *n.* **1** An appointment to meet, or the meeting place agreed upon: also **tryst′ing. 2** *Scot.* A market. **3** *Scot.* A journey in company. Also **tryste.** [<OF *triste, tristre* an appointed station in hunting, prob. < Scand.] — **tryst′er** *n.*

tryst·ed (tris′tid, trī′stid) *adj.* Agreed upon.

tset·se (tset′sē, tsē′tsē) *n.* **1** A small bloodsucking fly (*Glossina morsitans*) of southern Africa whose bite transmits disease in cattle, horses, etc. **2** A related species (*G. palpalis*), which transmits the parasite that causes sleeping sickness. For illustration see INSECTS (injurious). Also spelled *tzetze.* Also **tsetse fly.** [<Afrikaans <Bantu]

tsu·na·mi (tsōō·nä′mē) *n.* An extensive and often very destructive ocean wave caused by a violent submarine earthquake: erroneously called a tidal wave. [<Japanese, a storm wave < *tsu* port, harbor + *nami* wave]

Tsu·shi·ma (tsōō·shē′mä) A Japanese island in Korea Strait; 271 square miles, including 42 offshore islets; scene of a naval battle in the Russo–Japanese War in which the Russian fleet was destroyed, 1905.

tsu·tsu·ga·mu·shi disease (tsōō·tsōō′gä·mōō′·shē) *Pathol.* A rickettsial fever endemic in Japan and the Orient, caused by a microorganism (*Rickettsia orientalis*) transmitted to man by the infected larvae of a mite (genus *Trombicula*): also called *Japanese river fever, river fever, scrub typhus.* [<Japanese *tsutsuga-mush*, a small Japanese mite < *mushi* a bug]

tub (tub) *n.* **1** A broad, open-topped vessel, usually of wood, and formed with staves, bottom, hoops, and handles on the side. **2** A bathtub. **3** *Brit. Colloq.* A bath taken in a tub. **4** The amount that a tub contains. **5** Anything resembling a tub, as a broad, clumsy boat: contemptuous or humorous. **6** A small cask. **7** A bucket for bringing ore or coal up a shaft; also, an underground tram. **8** A keeve. **9** A sweating in a tub. — *v.t. & v.i.* **tubbed, tub′bing** To wash, bathe, or place in a tub. [<MDu. *tubbe*] — **tub′ba·ble** *adj.* — **tub′ber** *n.*

tu·ba (tōō′bə, tyōō′-) *n.* *pl.* **·bas** or **·bae** (-bē) **1** A large bass instrument of the saxhorn family. **2** An ancient Roman war trumpet. **3** A powerful reed stop in an organ. [<L, a war trumpet]

tu·bal (tōō′bəl, tyōō′-) *adj.* **1** Relating to a tube. **2** *Anat.* Pertaining to the Fallopian tube.

tu·bate (tōō′bāt, tyōō′-) *adj.* Of the form of or provided with a tube; tubular. [<NL *tubatus* <L *tubus* a pipe]

TUBA

tub·by (tub′ē) *adj.* **·bi·er, ·bi·est** **1** Resembling a tub in form; round and fat; corpulent. **2** Lacking resonance when struck; sounding dull or wooden, as a musical instrument.

tube (tōōb, tyōōb) *n.* **1** A long hollow cylindrical body of metal, glass, rubber, etc., generally used for the conveyance of something through it; a pipe. **2** The principal part of a gun. **3** Any similar device having a tube or tubelike part, as a telescope. **4** *Biol.* Any elongated hollow part or organ, as the united part of a gamopetalous corolla or a gamosepalous calyx. **5** A subway or a tunnel. **6** An electron, thermionic, or vacuum tube. **7** The tubular space enclosing lines of magnetic force or induction. **8** A collapsible metal cylinder for containing paints, toothpaste, glue, and the like. — *v.t.* **tubed, tub·ing 1** To fit or furnish with a tube. **2** To enclose in a tube or tubes. **3** To make tubular. [<F <L *tubus* a tube] — **tube′less** *adj.* — **tub′er** *n.*

tube foot *Zool.* An ambulacral sucker; one of the small vascular locomotor processes exserted through the ambulacral pores of echinoderms.

tu·ber (tōō′bər, tyōō′-) *n.* **1** *Bot.* A short, thickened portion of an underground stem, as in the potato or artichoke. **2** *Anat.* A swelling or prominence; tubercle. [<L, a swelling]

tu·ber·cle (tōō′bər·kəl, tyōō′-) *n.* **1** A small rounded eminence or nodule. **2** *Bot.* A minute swelling on the roots of leguminous plants, which contains a micro–organism believed to absorb nitrogen from the air for the use of the plant. **3** *Pathol.* A small granular tumor formed within an organ from morbid or infected matter: in the lungs, the seat of pulmonary consumption. **4** *Anat.* A small knoblike excrescence, especially on the skin or on a bone. [<L *tuberculum*, dim. of *tuber* a swelling] — **tu·ber·cu·loid** (tōō·bûr′kyə·loid, tyōō′-) *adj.*

tubercle bacillus The rod-shaped, Grampositive bacterium (*Mycobacterium tuberculosis*) which is the cause of tuberculosis in man.

tu·ber·cu·lar (tōō·bûr·kyə·lər, tyōō-) *adj.* **1** Affected with tubercles; nodular. **2** Tuberculous. — *n.* One affected with tuberculosis.

tu·ber·cu·late (tōō·bûr′kyə·lit, -lāt) *adj.* **1** Nodular. **2** Affected with tubercles; tuberculous. Also **tu·ber′cu·lat′ed.** [<NL *tuberculatus* <L *tuberculum* TUBERCLE] — **tu·ber′cu·la′tion** *n.*

tu·ber·cu·lin (tōō·bûr′kyə·lin, tyōō′-) *n.* *Bacteriol.* A sterile liquid prepared from attenuated cultures of the tubercle bacillus, used especially as a test for tuberculosis in children and animals. Also **tu·ber′cu·line** (-lin, -lēn). [<L *tuberculum* TUBERCLE + -IN]

tuberculo– *combining form* **1** Tuberculosis; of or pertaining to tuberculosis; tuberculous. **2** The tubercle bacillus. Also, before vowels, **tubercul–.** [<L *tuberculum*, dim. of *tuber* a swelling]

tu·ber·cu·lo·sis (tōō·bûr·kyə·lō′sis, tyōō′-) *n.* *Pathol.* A communicable disease caused by infection with the tubercle bacillus, characterized by the formation of tubercles within some organ or tissue: when affecting the lungs, known as **pulmonary tuberculosis.** [<NL <L *tuberculum* TUBERCLE + -OSIS]

tu·ber·cu·lous (tōō·bûr′kyə·ləs, tyōō′-) *adj.* Of, pertaining to, or affected with tuberculosis.

tu·ber·if·er·ous (tōō′bə·rif′ər·əs, tyōō′-) *adj.* Bearing or producing tubers. [<TUBER + -(I)FEROUS]

tube·rose¹ (tōōb′rōz′, tyōōb′-, tōō′bə·rōs′, tyōō′-) *n.* A bulbous plant (*Polianthes tuberosa*) of the amaryllis family, bearing a long raceme of fragrant white flowers. [<NL *Tuberosa*, species name <L *tuberosus* knobby < *tuber* a swelling]

tu·ber·ose² (tōō′bər·ōs, tyōō′-) *adj.* Tuberous. [<TUBER + -OSE]

tu·ber·os·i·ty (tōō′bə·ros′ə·tē, tyōō′-) *n.* *pl.* **·ties** **1** The state of being tuberous. **2** A swelling or protuberance. **3** *Anat.* A large, rough eminence on a bone, as for the attachment of a muscle.

tu·ber·ous (tōō′bər·əs, tyōō′-) *adj.* **1** Bearing projections or prominences. **2** Resembling tubers. **3** *Bot.* Bearing tubers.

tuberous root *Bot.* One of the tuberlike parts of a multiple or fascicled fleshy root, as in the dahlia.

tu·bi·form (tōō′bə·fôrm, tyōō′-) *adj.* Having the form of a tube; tubular. [<*tubi*- (<TUBE) + -FORM]

tub·ing (tōō′bing, tyōō′-) *n.* **1** Tubes collectively. **2** A piece of tube or material for tubes. **3** Material for pillowcases. **4** The act of making tubes.

Tu·bu·ai Islands (tōō′bōō·ī′) An island group south of the Society Islands, comprising a part of French Oceania; 115 square miles: also *Austral Islands.*

tu·bu·lar (tōō′byə·lər, tyōō′-) *adj.* **1** Having the form of a tube; tube–shaped. **2** Made up of or provided with tubes. **3** Pertaining to or sounding as if produced in a tube. [<L *tubulus* TUBULE]

tu·bu·late (tōō′byə·lāt, tyōō′-) *v.t.* **·lat·ed, ·lat·ing 1** To shape or fashion into a tube. **2** To furnish with a tube. — *adj.* Shaped like or into a tube; also, provided with a tube: also **tu′bu·lat′ed.** [<L *tubulatus* tubular < *tubulus* TUBULE] — **tu′bu·la′tor** *n.*

tu·bu·li·flo·rous (tōō′byə·lə·flôr′əs, -flō′rəs, tyōō′-) *adj.* *Bot.* Having tubular florets: said of composite plants with all the florets tubular. [< *tubuli*- (TUBULE) + -FLOROUS]

tu·bu·lous (tōō′byə·ləs, tyōō′-) *adj.* **1** Tube-shaped; tubular. **2** *Bot.* Having tubular florets. **3** Consisting of or containing small tubes. Also **tu′bu·lose** (-lōs).

tu·bu·lure (tōō′byə·lər, tyōō′-) *n.* The short open tube of a retort, receiver, or bell jar. [<F <L *tubulus* TUBULE]

tuck (tuk) *n.* **1** A fold made in a garment usually horizontal. **2** A flap forming a continuation of one side of a book cover, and inserted in a loop or pocket in the other side. **3** *Naut.* That part of a vessel's hull where the after planks meet. **4** *Brit. Slang* Food. **5** *U.S. Slang* Stamina; determination. [< *v.*] — *v.t.* **1** To fold under; thrust or press in the ends or edges of. **2** To wrap or cover snugly. **3** To thrust or press into a close place; cram; hide. **4** To make tucks in, by folding and stitching. — *v.i.* **5** To contract; draw together. **6** To make tucks. [Fusion of OE *tūcian* ill-treat, lit., tug and MDu. *tucken* pluck]

tuck·a·hoe (tuk′ə·hō) *n.* An underground fungus (*Poria cocos*) with a brown edible sclerotium: found in the southern United States: also *Indian bread* or *Virginia truffle.* [<Algonquian (Virginian) *tockawhoughe*]

tuck·er¹ (tuk′ər) *n.* **1** One who or that which tucks. **2** A covering, formerly worn over the neck and shoulders by women. **3** *Austral.* Food. [<TUCK¹]

tuck·er² (tuk′ər) *v.t. Colloq.* To weary completely; exhaust: usually with *out.* [Freq. of TUCK¹, *v.*]

Tu·dor (tōō′dər, tyōō′-) *adj.* **1** Of or pertaining to the **Tudors,** an English royal family descended from Sir Owen Tudor, a Welshman who married Catherine of Valois, widow of Henry V. See the table of sovereigns under ENGLAND. **2** Designating or pertaining to the architecture, poetry, etc., developed during the reigns of the Tudors.

Tudor architecture The latest phase of the Perpendicular style, developed under the Tudors to make houses more livable. It employed large windows, many fireplaces, large bays, steep roofs, flattened arches, much carving, and paneling. The house plan was generally a quadrangle, an H or an E.

Tues·day (tōōz′dē, -dā, tyōōz′-) *n.* The third day of the week; the day after Monday. [OE *tīwesdæg* day of Tiw <*Tīw*, an ancient Teutonic deity + *dæg* a day; trans. of LL *dies Martis* Mars's day]

tu·fa (tōō′fə, tyōō′-) *n.* **1** A variety of calcium carbonate with cellular structure, as deposited from springs and streams. **2** Tuff. [<Ital. *tufa, tufo* <L *tofus, tophus*] — **tu·fa·ceous** (tōō·fā′shəs, tyōō′-) *adj.*

tuff (tuf) *n.* A volcanic rock composed of material varying in size from fine sand to coarse gravel: used for building. [<MF *tufe, tuffe* <Ital. *tufo* TUFA] — **tuff·a′ceous** *adj.*

tuft (tuft) *n.* **1** A collection or bunch of small, flexible parts, as hair, grass, or feathers, held together at the base. **2** A clump or knot; frequently, a cluster of threads drawn tightly through a quilt, mattress, or upholstery to secure the stuffing. **3** A gold tassel formerly worn by titled undergraduates at Oxford and Cambridge universities; also, a student who wears such a tuft. — *v.t.* **1** To separate or form into tufts. **2** To cover or adorn with tufts. —*v.i.* **3** To form tufts. [<OF *tuffe*, prob. <Gmc.] —**tuft′er** *n.* —**tuft′y** *adj.*

tuft·ed (tuf′tid) *adj.* **1** Having, or adorned with, a tuft; crested: the *tufted* duck. **2** Forming a tuft or dense cluster; cespitose.

tuft·hunt·er (tuft′hun′tər) *n. Archaic* **1** Originally, a student at Oxford or Cambridge who sought association with titled students distinguished by gold tufts on their hats. **2** One who seeks the acquaintance of persons of rank; a snob; sycophant; parasite. —**tuft′hunt′ing** *n. & adj.*

tug (tug) *v.* **tugged, tug·ging** *v.t.* **1** To pull at with effort; strain at. **2** To pull, draw, or drag with effort. **3** To tow with a tugboat. —*v.i.* **4** To pull strenuously: to *tug* at an oar. **5** To strive; toil; struggle. See synonyms under DRAW. —*n.* **1** An act of tugging; a violent pull. **2** A strenuous contest; a struggle; wrestle. **3** A tugboat. **4** A trace of a harness; also, *Scot.*, rawhide: formerly used in making traces. **5** *Brit.* A colleger or member of the king's foundation at Eton College. **6** *Brit. Dial.* A high-wheeled cart for carrying logs, etc., slung beneath its axles. [ME *toggen*, intens. of OE *téon* tow; infl. by ON *toga* draw] —**tug′ger** *n.*

tug·boat (tug′bōt′) *n.* A small, compact, ruggedly built vessel operated by steam or other power and designed for towing: also called *towboat.*

tug of war **1** A contest in which a number of persons at one end of a rope pull against a like number at the other end, each side endeavoring to drag the other across a line marked between. **2** A laborious effort; supreme contest.

tuille (twēl) *n.* In armor, a steel protection for the thighs, attached by straps to the tassets. [<MF <OF *tieule* <L *tegula* a tile]

tu·i·tion (tōō·ish′ən, tyōō-) *n.* **1** The act or business of teaching any branch of learning; instruction. **2** The charge or payment for instruction. **3** *Archaic* Guardianship; care. See synonyms under EDUCATION, LEARNING, NURTURE. [<AF *tuycioun*, OF *tuicion* <L *tuitio, -onis* a guard, guardianship < *tuitus*, pp. of *tueri* look at, watch] —**tu·i′tion·al, tu·i′tion·ar′y** (-er′ē) *adj.*

tu·la·re·mi·a (tōō′lə·rē′mē·ə) *n.* A disease of rodents, especially rabbits, caused by a micro-organism (*Pasteurella tularensis*) which may be transmitted to man by flies and certain insects, producing an undulant fever; rabbit fever. Also **tu′la·rae′mi·a.** [<NL, from *Tulare* County, California + Gk. *haima* blood]

tu·le (tōō′lē) *n.* A large bulrush (*Scirpus acutus*) of the sedge family growing on damp or flooded land in the southwestern United States. [<Sp. <Nahuatl *tullin*]

tu·lip (tōō′lip, tyōō′-) *n.* **1** Any of numerous hardy bulbous herbs (genus *Tulipa*) of the lily family, bearing variously colored bell-shaped flowers. **2** A bulb or flower of this plant. [<F *tulipe* <OF *tulipan* <Turkish *tulibald* <Persian *dulband* a turban]

tu·lip-tree (tōō′lip·trē′, tyōō′-) *n.* **1** A large magnoliaceous tree (*Liriodendron tulipifera*) of the eastern United States, with greenish cup-shaped flowers. **2** Any of various other trees having tuliplike flowers.

tu·lip-wood (tōō′lip·wōod′, tyōō′-) *n.* **1** The wood of the tuliptree. **2** Any of several ornamental cabinet woods yielded by various trees: so called from their color or markings. **3** Any of the trees themselves.

Tul·la·more (tul′ə·môr′, -mōr′) The county town of County Offaly, Ireland.

tum·ble (tum′bəl) *v.* **·bled, ·bling** *v.i.* **1** To roll or toss about. **2** To perform acrobatic feats, as somersaults, etc. **3** To fall violently or awkwardly. **4** To move in a careless or headlong manner; stumble. **5** *Colloq.* To understand; comprehend: with *to.* **6** *Metall.* To smooth, clean, or polish, as castings, by friction with each other or with a polishing material, in a rotating box or barrel. —*v.t.* **7** To toss carelessly; cause to fall. **8** To throw into disorder or confusion; rumple. —*n.* **1** The act of tumbling; a fall. **2** A state of disorder or confusion. [ME *tumbel*, freq. of *tumben*, OE *tumbian* fall, leap] —**tum′bling** *n.*

tum·ble·bug (tum′bəl·bug′) *n.* A scarabaeid beetle that rolls up a ball of dung to enclose its eggs.

tumble gear *Mech.* A type of reversing gear comprising a rocking frame adapted to bring either of two idlers into mesh with the driving gear.

TUMBLE GEAR
a. Rocking frame.

tum·ble-home (tum′bəl·hōm′) *n. Naut.* The inward inclination of a vessel's hull above the line of extreme breadth.

tum·bler (tum′blər) *n.* **1** A drinking glass without a foot; also, its contents. The base was formerly rounded, so that the glass would not stand upright. **2** One who or that which tumbles; especially, an acrobat or contortionist. **3** One of a breed of domestic pigeons noted for the habit of turning forward somersaults during flight. **4** A greyhound used formerly in coursing. **5** In a lock, a latch that engages a bolt and prevents its being shot in either direction unless the tumbler is raised by the key bit. **6** In a firearm lock, a piece attached to the hammer and receiving the thrust of the mainspring. **7** A tumbling box. **8** *Mech.* **a** A piece of metal that projects from a revolving or rocking shaft and communicates motion to another piece. **b** The rocking frame in a tumble gear. **9** *Scot.* A light cart. **10** A child's toy, so formed and weighted as to rock at the slightest touch.

tum·ble-weed (tum′bəl·wēd′) *n.* Any of various plants which, when withered, break from the root and are driven about by the wind, widely scattering their seed.

tumbling box *Metall.* A box, usually cylindrical and mounted on a horizontal shaft, in which articles, as castings, are cleaned by friction against each other and the walls of the box. Also **tumbling barrel.**

tum·brel (tum′bril) *n.* **1** *Obs.* A two-wheeled military covered cart for carrying tools, ammunition, etc. **2** A farmer's cart; especially, a boxlike cart for carrying and dumping dung. **3** A rude cart in which prisoners were taken to the guillotine during the French Revolution. **4** Formerly, a ducking stool set on wheels. Also **tum′bril.** [<OF *tomberel* < *tomber* fall, ult. <Gmc.]

TUMBREL

tu·me·fa·cient (tōō′mə·fā′shənt, tyōō′-) *adj.* Producing or tending to produce tumefaction; causing a swelling.

tu·me·fac·tion (tōō′mə·fak′shən, tyōō′-) *n.* **1** Any puffing up of a part, especially as in a tumor. **2** A swelling; puffiness. **3** The act of tumefying; state of being tumefied.

tu·mes·cence (tōō·mes′əns, tyōō-) *n.* **1** The state or quality of being swollen. **2** The act or process of becoming tumid, as an organ or part of the body. **3** That which is swollen.

tu·mes·cent (tōō·mes′ənt, tyōō-) *adj.* **1** Swelling; somewhat tumid. **2** Beginning to swell. [<L *tumescens, -entis,* ppr. of *tumescere,* inceptive of *tumere* swell]

tu·mid (tōō′mid, tyōō′-) *adj.* **1** Swollen; enlarged; protuberant. **2** Inflated or pompous in style; bombastic. **3** Bursting; teeming. [<L *tumidus* < *tumere* swell] —**tu′mid·ly** *adv.*

tu·mor (tōō′mər, tyōō′-) *n.* **1** *Pathol.* A local swelling on or in any part of the body, especially from some autonomous morbid growth of tissue which may or may not become malignant; a neoplasm. **2** *Obs.* High-sounding words or style; bombast. **3** *Obs.* A swelling of any kind, as of water. Also *Brit.* **tu′mour.** —**fatty tumor** Lipoma. [<OF *tumour* <L *tumor* a swelling < *tumere* swell] —**tu′mor·ous** *adj.*

tu·mu·lar (tōō′myə·lər, tyōō′-) *adj.* Having the form of a mound.

tu·mu·lose (tōō′myə·lōs′, tyōō′-) *adj.* Full of mounds or hills. Also **tu′mu·lous.** [<L *tumulosus* <*tumulus* a mound] —**tu·mu·los′i·ty** (-los′ə·tē) *n.*

tu·mult (tōō′mult, tyōō′-) *n.* **1** The commotion, disturbance, or agitation of a multitude; an uproar; turbulence; hubbub. **2** Any violent commotion or agitation, as of the mind. [<OF *tumulte* <L *tumultus* <*tumere* swell]

Synonyms: agitation, bluster, bustle, commotion, confusion, disorder, disturbance, ferment, flurry, hubbub, hurly-burly, noise, outbreak, racket, riot, turbulence, turmoil, uproar. See NOISE, QUARREL[1], REVOLUTION. *Antonyms:* calmness, peace, quiet, repose, tranquillity.

tu·mul·tu·ous (tōō·mul′chōō·əs, tyōō-) *adj.* **1** Characterized by tumult; disorderly. **2** Causing or affected by tumult or agitation; agitated or disturbed. Also **tu·mul′tu·ar′y** (-er′ē). See synonyms under NOISY, TURBULENT, VIOLENT. —**tu·mul′tu·ous·ly,** **tu·mul′tu·ar′i·ly** *adv.* —**tu·mul′tu·ous·ness, tu·mul′tu·ar′i·ness** *n.*

tu·mu·lus (tōō′myə·ləs, tyōō′-) *n. pl.* **·li** (-lī) A sepulchral mound, often of great size. Compare BARROW[2], CAIRN. [<L, a mound <*tumere* swell]

tun (tun) *n.* **1** A large cask. **2** A brewers' fermenting vat. **3** The amount of malt liquor fermented at one operation; a brew. **4** A varying measure of capacity, usually equal to 252 gallons. —*v.t.* **tunned, tun·ning** **1** To put into a cask or tun. **2** To add to a liquor, as for flavoring. [OE *tunne*]

tu·na[1] (tōō′nə) *n.* A tunny. Also **tuna fish.** [<Am. Sp., ult. <L *thunnus* TUNNY]

tu·na[2] (tōō′nə) *n.* **1** A tropical American prickly pear (*Opuntia tuna*), or its edible fruit. **2** One of a number of other prickly pears. [<Am. Sp., prob. <Taino]

tun·a·ble (tōō′nə·bəl, tyōō′-) *adj.* **1** That may be put in tune. **2** Being in tune. **3** *Obs.* Tuneful; musical. Also **tune′a·ble.** —**tun′a·ble·ness** *n.* —**tun′a·bly** *adv.*

tun·dra (tun′drə, tōōn′-) *n.* A rolling, treeless, often marshy plain of Siberia, arctic North America, etc. [<Russian <Lapp]

tune (tōōn, tyōōn) *n.* **1** A melodious succession of musical tones adjusted to some measure and constituting one whole; a melody or air. **2** A setting for a hymn or psalm used in worship. **3** The state or quality of being in the proper pitch or key. **4** Concord or unison. **5** Suitable temper or humor; state of mind. **6** *Obs.* A musical tone or sound. —**to change one's tune** To assume a different manner or style. —**to the tune of** To the serious or exorbitant amount of: *to the tune of* a thousand dollars. —*v.* **tuned, tun·ing** *v.t.* **1** To adjust to a musical standard; put in tune; attune. **2** To adapt to a particular tone, expression, or mood. **3** To bring into harmony or accord. **4** To utter or express musically; sing. —*v.i.* **5** To be in harmony. —**to tune in** To adjust a radio receiver to the frequency of (a station, broadcast, etc.). —**to tune out** To adjust a radio receiver to exclude (interference, a station, etc.). —**to tune up** **1** To bring (musical instruments) to a common pitch. **2** To adjust (a machine, engine, etc.) to proper working order. [Var. of TONE] —**tun′ing** *adj. & n.*

tune·ful (tōōn′fəl, tyōōn′-) *adj.* Musically disposed; melodious; musical. —**tune′ful·ly** *adv.* —**tune′ful·ness** *n.*

tune·less (tōōn′lis, tyōōn′-) *adj.* **1** Not being in tune. **2** Not employed in making music; silent. **3** Lacking in rhythm, melody, etc. —**tune′less·ly** *adv.* —**tune′less·ness** *n.*

tun·er (tōō′nər, tyōō′-) *n.* **1** One who or that which tunes. **2** One who puts musical instruments, as pianos, in tune. **3** *Telecom.* A radio receiver without audio-frequency amplifiers, speaker, etc.

tune-up (tōōn′up′, tyōōn′-) *n. Colloq.* An adjustment to bring a motor or other device into proper operating condition.

tung oil (tung) A yellow, ill-smelling oil extracted from the seeds of the Chinese **tung tree** (*Aleurites fordi*), now cultivated in the U.S.: used in paints, varnishes, etc., as a highly effective drying agent, and also as a waterproofing agent. [<Chinese *t'ung* the tung tree]

tung·sten (tung′stən) *n.* A gray, brittle, metallic element (symbol W, atomic number 74) having about the same density as gold and the highest melting point of any metal, much used in the manufacture of filaments for electric lamps and tools. See PERIODIC TABLE. [<Sw. <*tung* weighty + *sten* stone] —**tung·sten·ic** (tungsten′ik) *adj.*

tungsten lamp An incandescent electric lamp having a filament of metallic tungsten.

tungsten steel A hard, tenacious steel that contains tungsten.

tung·stic (tung′stik) *adj. Chem.* Of, pertaining to, derived from, or containing tungsten, especially in its highest valence. [< TUNGST(EN) + -IC]

tungstic acid *Chem.* Either of two acids consisting of tungsten oxide combined with water, and uniting with bases to form salts; especially, the yellow crystalline monohydrate, H_2WO_4.

tung·stite (tung′stīt) *n.* A yellow or yellowish-green native tungsten trioxide, WO_3. Also **tungstic ocher.**

tu·nic (tōō′nik, tyōō′-) *n.* 1 Among the ancient Greeks and Romans, a body garment, with or without sleeves, reaching to the knees: worn usually without a girdle. 2 A modern outer garment gathered at the waist, as a short overskirt or a blouse. 3 A surcoat worn over armor. 4 A tunica. 5 *Bot.* Any loose membranous skin enveloping an organ, as a seed coat. 6 *Brit.* The undercoat worn by soldiers, policemen, etc. 7 A bishop's tunicle; a dalmatic. [< F *tunique* < L *tunica* < Semitic]

tu·ni·ca (tōō′nə·kə, tyōō′-) *n. pl.* **·cae** (-sē) *Biol.* A covering or investing part; a mantle of tissue, as of the kidney, ovaries, etc.; tunic. [< NL < L, a tunic]

tu·ni·cate (tōō′nə·kit, -kāt, tyōō′-) *n.* Any of a subphylum (Tunicata or Urochordata) of small marine chordates characterized by the presence of a notochord and tail in the larval stage only and by the secretion of a tough envelope, or tunic, enclosing the body of the adult, as ascidians and salps. —*adj.* 1 Pertaining to or resembling a tunicate. 2 Covered with a tunic or tunica. 3 *Bot.* Having concentric coats, as an onion. [< NL *tunicata* < L *tunicata* (*animalia*) coated (animals), neut. pl. of *tunicatus*, pp. of *tunicare* clothe with a tunic < *tunica* a tunic]

tu·ni·cle (tōō′ni·kəl, tyōō′-) *n.* 1 A light or fine tunic. 2 A slight natural covering. 3 A short ecclesiastical vestment. [< L *tunicula*, dim. of *tunica* a tunic]

tuning fork A fork-shaped piece of steel which vibrates with a definite frequency when struck: used to measure the pitch of musical tones.

Tu·nis (tōō′nis, tyōō′-) 1 A former Barbary state of northern Africa. 2 The capital and chief port of Tunisia, on the Mediterranean.

Tu·ni·sia (tōō·nish′ə, -nish·ē·ə, -nē′zhə, tyōō′-) A republic in northern Africa, proclaimed July, 1957; 48,195 square miles; capital, Tunis; formerly, Tunis.

tun·nage (tun′ij) *n. Brit.* Tonnage.

tun·nel (tun′əl) *n.* 1 An artificial subterranean passageway or gallery, especially one under a hill, etc., as for a railway. 2 Any similar passageway under or through something. 3 A funnel. The main flue or shaft of a chimney or the like. 5 An adit or level in a mine. —*v.* **·neled** or **·nelled**, **·nel·ing** or **·nel·ling** *v.t.* 1 To make a tunnel through. 2 To shape or make in the form of a tunnel: to *tunnel* a passage. —*v.i.* 3 To make a tunnel. [Fusion of OF *tonnelle* a partridge net and *tonel*, dim. of *tonne* a cask] —**tun′nel·er** *n.* **tun′nel·ler** *n.*

tun·ny (tun′ē) *n. pl.* **·nies** 1 A large, oily, marine fish (family *Thunnidae*) related to

GREAT TUNNY

the mackerel, especially the **great tunny** (*Thunnus thynnus*) of warm seas, sometimes weighing 1,500 pounds. 2 One of various related fishes, as the albacore and the California horse mackerel (*Trachurus symmetricus*). [< OF *thon* < L *thunnus* < Gk. *thynnos*]

tu·pe·lo (tōō′pə·lō) *n. pl.* **·los** 1 One of several trees of Asia and the southeastern United States (genus *Nyssa*), especially the sourgum or blackgum. 2 The wood of any of these trees. [< Muskhogean]

Tu·pi (tōō·pē′) *n. pl.* **Tu·pis** or **Tu·pi** 1 A member of any of a group of South American Indian tribes, comprising the northern branch of the Tupian stock, and occupying the Amazon, Tapajós, and Xingú valleys. 2 The language spoken by the Tupis, used as a lingua franca along the Amazon: also called *Neengatu.* [< Tupian, a comrade]

tuque (tōōk, tyōōk) *n.* A Canadian cap consisting of a knitted cylindrical bag with tapered ends, worn by thrusting one end inside the other, for tobogganing, etc. [< dial. F (Canadian) < F *toque* TOQUE]

tu·ra·cou (tōō′rä·kōō′) *n.* An African bird (*Turacus fischeri*) related to the cuckoo, remarkable for its red-and-green plumage: also called *touraco.* [< F *touraco* < native West African name]

Tu·ra·ni·an (tōō·rā′nē·ən, tyōō′-) *adj.* Of or pertaining to a large family of agglutinative languages of Europe and northern Asia, neither Indo-European nor Semitic, specifically known as the Ural-Altaic languages, or any of the people who speak them. —*n.* 1 One whose mother tongue is a Ural-Altaic language; a person of Ural-Altaic stock. 2 The Ural-Altaic languages collectively. 3 Theoretically, one of an unknown nomadic people who antedated the Aryans in Europe and Asia. [< Persian *Tūrān*, a country north of the Oxus River]

tur·ban (tûr′bən) *n.* 1 An Oriental head covering consisting of a sash or shawl, twisted about the head or about a cap. 2 Any similar headdress. 3 A round-crowned brimless hat for women or children. [< F *turban, turbant* < Pg. *turbante* < Turkish *tülbend*, dial. alter. of *dülbend* < Persian *dulband* < *dul* a turn + *band* a band] —**tur′baned** (-bənd) *adj.*

tur·ba·ry (tûr′bər·ē) *n. pl.* **·ries** 1 In English law, the liberty of digging turf or peat upon another's ground. 2 A place where turf or peat is dug. [< AF *turberie*, OF *tourberie* < *tourbe* peat < LG *turf, turv* turf]

tur·bel·lar·i·an (tûr′bə·lâr′ē·ən) *n.* Any of a class (Turbellaria) of motile aquatic flatworms having a ciliated epidermis and sometimes brilliantly colored: includes the planarians. [< NL < L *turbellae* a tumult, pl. dim. of *turba* a crowd]

tur·beth (tûr′bəth), **tur·bith** See TURPETH.

tur·bid (tûr′bid) *adj.* 1 Having the sediment or lees stirred up; cloudy; muddy. 2 Being in a state of confusion; disturbed. See synonyms under THICK. [< L *turbidus* < *turbare* trouble < *turba* a crowd] —**tur′bid·ly** *adv.* —**tur′bid·ness, tur·bid·i·ty** (tûr·bid′ə·tē) *n.*

tur·bi·nal (tûr′bə·nəl) *adj.* Spirally coiled; turbinate; top-shaped. —*n.* A turbinate bone or cartilage. [< L *turbo, -inis* a whirlwind, top]

tur·bi·nate (tûr′bə·nit, -nāt) *adj.* 1 Top-shaped; also, spinning like a top. 2 *Zool.* Tapering from a broad base to the apex, as certain spiral shells. 3 *Anat.* Pertaining to one of the thin, curved bones on the walls of the nasal passages. Also **tur′bi·nat·ed.** [< L *turbinatus* < *turbo, -inis* a whirlwind]

tur·bine (tûr′bin, -bīn) *n.* An engine consisting of one or more rotary units, mounted on a shaft and usually provided with a series of curved vanes, actuated by the reaction, impulse, or suction of steam, water, gas, or other fluid under pressure. [< F < L *turbo, -inis* a whirlwind, top]

TURBINE
Type used in an electric-light plant.

tur·bo·fan (tûr′bō·fan′) *n. Aeron.* 1 A compressor having ducted fans which supply air to a jet engine. 2 The engine using such a fan.

tur·bo·gen·er·a·tor (tûr′bō·jen′ə·rā′tər) *n.* An electric power-generating machine adapted for direct coupling to a steam turbine.

tur·bo·jet (tûr′bō·jet′) *n. Aeron.* 1 A gas turbine which drives the air compressor and auxiliaries of certain types of jet engines. 2 The engine itself.

tur·bo·prop (tûr′bō·prop′) *n. Aeron.* 1 A gas turbine connecting directly with the propeller. 2 An engine having such a turbine. [< TURBO- + PROP(ELLER)]

tur·bo·su·per·charg·er (tûr′bō·sōō′pər·chär′jər) *n. Aeron.* A compact, highly efficient supercharging device utilizing exhaust gases, for use on aircraft engines operating at very high altitudes.

tur·bot (tûr′bət) *n. pl.* **·bot** or **·bots** 1 A large European flatfish (*Psetta maxima*) esteemed as food. 2 One of various related flatfishes. [< AF *turbut*, OF *tourbout*, ? < OSw. *törnbut* < *törn* a thorn + *but* the butt]

tur·bu·lent (tûr′byə·lənt) *adj.* 1 Being in violent agitation or commotion. 2 Inclined to rebel; insubordinate. 3 Having a tendency to disturb or throw into confusion. [< MF < L *turbulentus* full of disturbance < *turbare.* See TURBID.] —**tur′bu·lent·ly** *adv.*

   Synonyms: agitated, blustering, boisterous, disorderly, disturbed, insurgent, mutinous, obstreperous, rebellious, refractory, riotous, seditious, tumultuous, wild. See NOISY, VIOLENT

tur·di·form (tûr′də·fôrm) *adj.* Thrushlike in form or structure. [< L *turdus* a thrush + -FORM]

tur·dine (tûr′dīn, -dīn) *adj.* 1 Belonging or pertaining to a large and widely distributed family (*Turdidae*) of singing birds, including thrushes and bluebirds. 2 Pertaining to the subfamily (*Turdinae*) which includes the true thrushes. [< NL, subfamily name < L *turdus* a thrush]

tu·reen (tōō·rēn′, tyōō′-) *n.* A deep, covered dish, as for soup. [Earlier *terrene* < F *terrine.* Doublet of TERRINE.]

turf (tûrf) *n. pl.* **turfs** (*Archaic* **turves**) 1 A mass of matted roots of grass and other fine plants filling the upper stratum of certain soils; a sod. 2 Peat. 3 Loosely, a grass plot. 4 A racecourse; horse-racing: in the phrase **the turf.** 5 *Slang* a A home territory, especially that of a youthful street gang, defended against invasion by rival gangs. b Any place regarded possessively as the center of one's activity or interest: Philadelphia is his *turf.* —*v.t.* To cover with turf; sod. [OE] —**turf′y** *adj.*

turf·man (tûrf′mən) *n. pl.* **·men** (-mən) A man who is devoted to or connected with horse-racing.

tur·ges·cence (tûr·jes′əns) *n.* 1 The process of swelling up; the state of being swollen. 2 Hence, empty pompousness; inflation. Also **tur·ges′cen·cy.** [< Med.L *turgescentia* < *turgescens, -entis*, ppr. of *turgescere*, inceptive of *turgere* swell] —**tur·ges′cent** *adj.* —**tur·ges′cent·ly** *adv.*

tur·gid (tûr′jid) *adj.* 1 Unnaturally distended, as by contained air or liquid; swollen. 2 Figuratively, inflated; bombastic; tumid: a *turgid* tale of woman wronged. [< L *turgidus* < *turgere* swell] —**tur′gid·ly** *adv.*

tur·gid·i·ty (tûr·jid′ə·tē) *n.* 1 The state or quality of being turgid. 2 *Biol.* The internal pressure of a cell against its enclosing membrane. Also **tur·gid·ness** (tûr′jid·nis).

tur·gite (tûr′jīt) *n.* A fibrous, earthy iron ore, found as a reddish-black or dark-red ferric hydroxide. [from *Turginsk*, a copper mine in the Ural Mountains]

tur·gor (tûr′gər) *n.* 1 The state of being turgid; turgidity. 2 *Physiol.* The normal condition of the blood vessels and of cells distended by their protoplasmic contents: also **vital turgor.** [< LL < L < *turgere* swell]

Turk (tûrk) *n.* 1 A native or inhabitant of Turkey; an Ottoman. 2 One of any of the peoples speaking any of the Turkic languages, and ranging from the Adriatic to the Sea of Okhotsk: believed to be of the same ultimate extraction as the Mongols. 3 Loosely, a Moslem. 4 A Turkish horse.

Tu·ke·stan A region of central Asia that extended from the Caspian Sea to the Gobi

Desert and was divided by the Pamir and Tien Shan mountain systems, incorporating the Kazakh, Kirghiz, Tadzhik, Turkmen, and Uzbek S.S.R. (called Soviet Central Asia) during the era pf tje Soviet Union; and Chinese Turkestan, comprising the Sinkiang-Uigur Autonomous Region.

tur·key (tûr′kē) *n. pl.* **·keys** **1** A large American bird (family *Meleagridae*) related to the pheasant, having the head naked and the tail extensible upward and sideward; especially, the American domesticated turkey (*Meleagris gallopavo*): much esteemed as food. **2** A guinea fowl. **3** *U. S. Slang* A play (occasionally, a motion picture) that is a failure. [Short for *turkey cock* the guinea fowl, from *Turkey*; later applied erroneously to the American bird]

Tur·key (tûr′kē) A republic of Asia Minor and SE Europe; 296,108 square miles (Turkey in Asia, known as *Anatolia*, 287,043 square miles, Turkey in Europe, 9,065 square miles); capital, Ankara.

Tur·ki (tŏŏr′kē) *adj.* **1** Of or pertaining to any of the languages included in the Turkic subfamily of Altaic languages. **2** Of or pertaining to any of the peoples speaking any of these languages, as the Osmanlis and Chuvashes of Turkey, NW Persia, Transcaucasia, etc., and the Asian Tatar tribes, as the Uigurs, Uzbeks, Kipchaks, Turkomans, etc., of Mongolia and Turkestan. — *n.* **1** The Turkic languages. **2** A member of any of the Turki peoples.

Turk·ic (tûr′kik) *n.* A subfamily of the Altaic family of languages, including Osmanli or Turkish, Azerbaijani, Uzbek, Chuvash, Yakut, etc. — *adj.* Pertaining to this linguistic subfamily, or to any of the peoples speaking these languages.

Turk·man *n. pl.* **·mans** **1** A member of the ethnic group in Turkmenistan, descended from the nomadic tribes that inhabited the land during the Persian Empire. Also spelled **Turkcoman.** **Turk′·man.** [Persian *Turkuman* one like a Turk] - *adj. & n.* **-Turk·o·manic.**

Turk·me·ni·stan A country of Central Asia; capital Ashkhabad; pop. 3,714,000.

Turks and Cai·cos Islands (tûrks, kā′kəs) An archipelago SE of the Bahamas, comprising a dependency of Jamaica in The West Indies; 202 square miles.

tur·mer·ic (tûr′mər·ik) *n.* **1** The root of an East Indian plant (*Curcuma longa*) of the ginger family, used as a condiment, aromatic stimulant, dyestuff, etc. **2** The plant. **3** Any of several plants resembling turmeric. — *adj.* Of, pertaining to, or saturated with turmeric. [Earlier *tarmaret*, ? <F *terre mérite* deserving earth <Med. L *terra merita*; ult. origin uncertain]

turmeric paper A paper, yellow from saturation with the extract of turmeric, used as a test for alkalis, turning it brown, and for boric acid, turning it red-brown: also called *curcuma paper.*

tur·moil (tûr′moil) *n.* Confused motion; disturbance; tumult. See synonyms under TUMULT. — *v.t. & v.i. Archaic* To be or cause to be in a state of turmoil. [? <OF *tremouille* hopper of a mill <L *tremere* tremble; prob. infl. in form by *turn* and *moil*]

turn (tûrn) *v.t.* **1** To give a rotary motion to; cause to rotate, as about an axis. **2** To change the position of, as by rotating: to *turn* a trunk on its side. **3** To move so that the upper side becomes the under: to *turn* a page. **4** To bring the subsoil of to the surface, as by plowing or spading. **5** To alter (a garment) by reversing the material: to *turn* a cuff. **6** To reverse the arrangement or order of; cause to be upside down. **7** To upset mentally; dement or distract; infatuate. **8** To revolve mentally; ponder: often with *over*. **9** To sprain or strain: to *turn* one's ankle in running. **10** To nauseate (the stomach). **11** To shape (an object revolving in a lathe, etc.) in rounded form by application of a cutting tool. **12** To give rounded or curved form to. **13** To give graceful or finished form to: to *turn* a phrase. **14** To perform by revolving: to *turn* cartwheels. **15** To bend, curve, fold, or twist. **16** To bend or blunt (the edge of a knife, etc.). **17** To change or transform; convert: to

turn water into wine. **18** To translate: to *turn* French into English. **19** To exchange for an equivalent: to *turn* stocks into cash. **20** To adapt to some use or purpose; apply: to *turn* information to good account. **21** To cause to become as specified: The sight *turned* him sick. **22** To change the color of. **23** To make sour or rancid; ferment or curdle. **24** To change the direction of. **25** To direct or aim; point. **26** To change the direction or focus of (thought, attention, etc.). **27** To deflect or divert: to *turn* a blow. **28** To repel: to *turn* a charge. **29** To go around or to the other side of: to *turn* a corner. **30** To pass or go beyond: to *turn* twenty-one. **31** To cause or compel to go; send; drive: to *turn* a beggar from one's door. **32** To keep circulating in trade: to *turn* goods or money. **33** *Obs.* To pervert. — *v.i.* **34** To move around an axis or center; rotate; revolve. **35** To move completely or partially on or as if on an axis: He *turned* and ran. **36** To change position; also, to roll from side to side, as in bed. **37** To take a new direction: We *turned* north. **38** To reverse position; become inverted. **39** To reverse direction or flow: The tide has *turned.* **40** To change the direction or focus of one's thought, attention, etc.: Let us *turn* to the next problem. **41** To depend; hinge: with *on* or *upon*. **42** To be affected with giddiness; whirl, as the head. **43** To become upset or nauseated, as the stomach. **44** To change attitude, sympathy, or allegiance: to *turn* on one's neighbors. **45** To rebel; act in retaliation: The worm *turns*; to *turn* on one's persecutors. **46** To become transformed; change: The water *turned* into ice. **47** To become as specified: His hair *turned* gray. **48** To change color: said especially of leaves. **49** To become sour, rancid, or fermented, as milk or wine. **50** *Naut.* To tack or put about. **51** *Obs.* To vacillate. See synonyms under BEND, CHANGE, REVOLVE. — **to turn against** To become or cause to become opposed or hostile to. — **to turn an honest dollar** (or **penny**) To earn money honestly. — **to turn down 1** To diminish the flow, volume, etc., of: *Turn down* the gas. **2** *Colloq.* **a** To reject or refuse, as a proposal, or request. **b** To refuse the request, proposal, etc., of. — **to turn in 1** To fold or double. **2** To bend or incline inward. **3** To deliver; hand over. **4** *Colloq.* To go to bed. — **to turn off 1** To stop the operation, flow, etc., of. **2** To leave the direct road; make a turn. **3** To deflect or divert. **4** *Brit.* To dismiss; discharge. — **to turn on 1** To set in operation, flow, etc.: to *turn on* an engine. **2** *Slang* To take or experience the mental and perceptual effects of taking a psychedelic drug, as marijuana, LSD, etc. **3** *Slang* To arrange for (someone) to take or be affected by such a drug. **4** *Slang* To evoke in (someone) a profound or rapt response, as though under the influence of a psychedelic drug: Baroque music really *turned* him *on*. — **to turn out 1** To turn inside out. **2** To eject or expel; put out. **3** To dismiss or discharge. **4** To turn off (def. 1). **5** To bend or incline outward. **6** To produce by work or toil; make. **7** To come or go out, as for duty or service. **8** To prove (to be); be found. **9** To become or result. **10** To equip or fit; dress. **11** *Colloq.* To get out of bed. — **to turn over 1** To change the position of; invert. **2** To upset; overturn. **3** To hand over; transfer or relinquish. **4** To do business to the amount of. **5** To invest and get back (capital). **6** To use in trade or exchange; buy and then sell: to *turn over* merchandise. — **to turn tail** To run away; flee. — **to turn to 1** To set to work. **2** To seek aid from. **3** To refer or apply to. — **to turn up 1** To bring or fold the under side upward. **2** To bend or incline upward. **3** To bring or be brought to view by plowing, digging, etc.; find or be found. **4** To increase the flow, volume, etc., of. **5** To put in an appearance; arrive. — *n.* **1** The act of turning, or the state of being turned. **2** A change to another direction, motion, or position: a *turn* of the tide. **3** A deflection or deviation from a course; a bend; a change in policy or trend: a *turn* of fortune. **4** The point at which a change takes place: a *turn* for the better in a crisis or an illness. **5** Motion about or as about a center; a rotation or revolution:

the *turn* of a crank. **6** Favorable, fitting, or regular time or chance in some succession or rotation, or the work it offers; a job; also, a round; spell: one's *turn* to read, a *turn* of work. **7** Characteristic form or style; distinguishing shape; mold; cast: the *turn* of an ankle or sentence. **8** Disposition; tendency; manner: a humorous *turn*; a knack or special ability: a *turn* for study. **9** A deed performed, regarded as aiding or injuring another: an ill *turn*; also, an advantage proposed or gained: It served his *turn*. **10** A walk, drive, or trip to and fro; promenade: a *turn* in the park. **11** A trip back and forth in taking a load of anything: *turns* made to a mill; also, the load so taken. **12** A round in a skein or coil. **13** *Music* An instrumental or vocal embellishment formed by a group of four notes rapidly performed, the first a tone above and the third a tone below the principal tone, which occupies the second and fourth positions. In an *inverted* **turn** the tones are reversed in order. **14** *Colloq.* A spell of dizziness or faintness; a shock to the nerves, as from alarm: It gave her quite a *turn*. **15** A variation or difference in type or kind. **16** A short theatrical act of any description; also, in sport, a contest; a bout. **17** A twist, as of a rope, around a tree or post. **18** A transaction on the stock exchange, involving purchase and sale, or the reverse; also, any business transaction. **19** In infantry drill, a maneuver in which a line of troops changes the direction of its front, usually in preparation for marching. — **at every turn** On every occasion; constantly. — **by turns 1** In alternation or sequence. **2** At intervals. — **in turn** One after another; in proper order or sequence. — **out of turn** Not in proper order or prescribed order or sequence. — **to a turn** Just right; perfectly or exactly: said especially of cooked food, in allusion to the turning of the spit in roasting. — **to take turns** To act, play, etc. in proper order. ◆ Homophones: *tern. terne.* [Fusion of OE *tyrnan* and *turnian* and OF *turner*, all <L *tornare* turn in a lathe < *turnus* a lathe <Gk. *tornos*]

turn-a-bout-face (tûrn′ə·bout′fās′) *n.* A change from one loyalty or viewpoint to another; adoption of new opinions or policy: also *turnabout.*

turn·a·round (tûrn′ə·round′) *n.* **1** The time required for maintenance, refueling, discharging or loading cargo, etc., during a round trip of a truck, ship, aircraft, etc. **2** A space, as in a driveway, large enough for the turning around of a vehicle. **3** A shift or reversal of a trend, procedure, development, etc.

turn·buck·le (tûrn′. buk′əl) *n. Mech.* A form of coupling so threaded that when connected lengthwise between two metal rods it may be turned so as to regulate the distance between them.

TURNBUCKLES
a. Insulated for electric wires.
b. Type for metal tie rods.
c. For window shutters.

turn·er¹ (tûr′nər) *n.* One who turns; specifically, one who fashions objects with a lathe. **turn·er²** (tûr′nər) *n.* A gymnast; a member of a turnverein. [<G <*turnen* engage in gymnastics <F *turner* turn]

turn·er·y (tûr′nər·ē) *n. pl.* **·er·ies** **1** A place where lathework is carried on. **2** The act or process of turning, or articles and ornamentation made with a lathe.

turn indicator In motor vehicles, any device, as a flashing light, which enables the driver to signal his intention to turn.

turn·ing (tûr′ning) *n.* **1** The act of one who turns. **2** The art of shaping wood, metal, etc., in a lathe. **3** Any deviation from a straight or customary course; a winding; bend.

turning point 1 The point of a decisive change in direction of action; a crisis. **2** The point at which the direction of a motion is reversed. **3** A marked object toward which a surveying instrument is sighted from each of two positions in the process of leveling.

tur·nip (tûr′nip) *n.* **1** The fleshy globular edible root of either of two brassicaceous biennial herbs, *Brassica rapa* and the rutabaga. **2** Either of the plants. [Earlier *turnepe*, ? <F *tour* a turn, rotation (<L *tornus* a lathe)

+ ME *nepe* <L *napus* a turnip; with ref. to its round shape]

turn·key (tûrn′kē′) *n.* One who has charge of the keys of a prison; a jailer. —*adj.* Of, pertaining to, or being, by prearrangement with a buyer, a product or service in complete readiness for use when purchased: a *turnkey* housing project.

turn·out (tûrn′out′) *n.* **1** An act of turning out or coming forth. **2** An assemblage of persons; attendance. **3** A quantity produced; output. **4** Array; equipment; outfit. **5** A railroad siding. **6** The movement of a vehicle from a line of traffic to pass other vehicles. **7** A section of narrow road widened to permit vehicles to pass one another. **8** A carriage or wagon with its horses and equipage. **9** *Brit.* A labor strike; also, a striker.

turn·o·ver (tûrn′ō′vər) *n.* **1** The act or process of turning over; an upset or overthrow, as of a vehicle. **2** A change or revolution: a *turnover* in affairs. **3** A small pie or tart made by covering half of a circular crust with fruit, jelly, or the like, and turning the other half over on top. **4** The amount of business accomplished, or of work achieved; turnout. **5** A completed commercial transaction or course of business; also, the money receipts of a business for a given period. **6** The rate at which persons hired by a given establishment within a given period are replaced by others; also, the number of persons hired. —*adj.* **1** Designed for turning over or reversing. **2** Capable of being turned over or folded down. **3** Made with a part folded down: a *turnover* collar.

turn·pike (tûrn′pīk′) *n.* **1** A road on which there are tollgates. **2** Loosely, any highway: also **turnpike road**. **3** A tollbar or tollgate. **4** *Obs.* A turnstile. See synonyms under ROAD. [ME *turnpyke* a spiked road barrier <TURN, *v.* + *pyke* PIKE¹]

turn·sole (tûrn′sōl′) *n.* **1** Any of several plants supposed to turn their flowers toward the sun; especially, the heliotrope and the sunflower. **2** Litmus. **3** One of various other blue coloring matters obtained from certain lichens and herbs. [<OF *tournesole* <Ital. *tornasole* < *tornare* turn (<L) + *sole* the sun <L *sol*]

turn·spit (tûrn′spit′) *n.* **1** One who turns a spit; a menial. **2** A dog formerly used in a treadmill to turn a roasting spit.

turn·stile (tûrn′stīl′) *n.* **1** A kind of gate or closure consisting of a vertical post and horizontal arms which by revolving permit persons, but not cattle, to pass; also, one that permits persons to pass in one direction only. **2** A similar device for registering the number of persons entering a building or for automatically admitting passengers to subways, buses, etc., on the deposit of fares.

turn·stone (tûrn′stōn′) *n.* A ploverlike migratory bird (genus *Arenaria*) of northern regions: so called from its habit of turning over stones to obtain its food; especially, the **ruddy turnstone** (*A. interpres*) and the **black turnstone** (*A. melanocephala*) of North America.

turn·ta·ble (tûrn′tā′bəl) *n.* **1** A rotating platform arranged to turn a section of a bridge in order to open a passage for ships. **2** Such a platform to turn a locomotive, car, etc.: also *Brit.* **turn′plate′** (-plāt′). **3** A small rotating disk in a microscope. **4** A rotating table in a show window. **5** The disk which carries a phonograph record.

tur·pen·tine (tûr′pən-tīn′) *n.* **1** A resinous, oily mixture of various pinenes exuding from any one of several coniferous trees, especially the longleaf pine (*Pinus palustris*). **2** The semi-fluid resin of the terebinth: also **Chian turpentine**. —**oil of turpentine** The colorless essential oil formed when turpentine is distilled with steam and consisting of a mixture of terpenes: widely used in industry, medicine and the arts. —*v.t.* **·tined, ·tin·ing** **1** To put turpentine with or upon; saturate with turpentine. **2** To obtain crude turpentine from (a tree). [<OF *turbentine* <L *terebinthinus* of the terebinth tree < *terebinthus* the terebinth <Gk. *terebinthos*]

tur·pi·tude (tûr′pə-tōōd, -tyōōd) *n.* Inherent baseness; vileness; depravity, or any action showing depravity. [<MF <L *turpitudo*,

-*inis* < *turpis* vile]

tur·quoise (tûr′koiz, -kwoiz) *n.* **1** A blue or green hydrous aluminum phosphate, H_5Al_2 PO_8, colored by copper: found massive, and in its highly polished blue varieties esteemed as a gemstone. **2** A light, greenish blue, the color of the turquoise: also **turquoise blue**. Also spelled *turkois*. Also *Obs.* **tur·quois** (tûr·koiz′). [<MF (*pierre*) *turquoise* Turkish (stone) <OF *turqueise*, fem. of *turqueis* Turkish; so called because first imported through Turkey]

tur·ret (tûr′it) *n.* **1** A small tower, often merely ornamental, rising above a larger structure, as on a castle. **2** *Mil.* A rotating armed tower, large enough to contain a powerful gun or guns and gunners, forming part of a man-of-war or of a fort; a similar enclosed structure in a tank or a bombing or combat airplane. **3** The clerestory of a railway car. **4** In ancient warfare, a high wooden structure, supported on slides or wheels, intended to enable besiegers to surmount the walls against which it was pushed. **5** *Mech.* In a lathe, a cylinder fitted with sockets or chucks for the reception of various tools, any one of which may be presented in succession in the axial line of the work: also **turret head**. [<OF *torete*, dim. of *tor* TOWER]

tur·ret·ed (tûr′it-id) *adj.* **1** Provided with turrets. **2** Having the form of a turret. **3** *Zool.* Having a long spire, as certain shells.

turret lathe A power-driven metalworking machine having a rotating turret head holding various tools, each of which in turn processes the material.

tur·ric·u·late (tə-rik′yə-lit, -lāt) *adj.* **1** Having or resembling a turret or turrets. **2** Turreted or having a spire: said of shells. [<L *turricula*, dim. of *turris* a tower + -ATE¹]

tur·tle (tûr′təl) *n.* **1** Any of numerous reptiles (order *Chelonia*) having a horny, toothless beak, and characterized by a short, stout body covered above and below with a bony carapace and plastron respectively, into which all the members may be drawn for protection; tortoise; specifically, a marine species as distinguished from a terrestrial or fresh-water species. **2** The flesh of certain varieties of turtle, served as food. **3** A stout frame in the form of a segment of a cylinder, used to hold the type in a type-revolving web press. —**green turtle** An important food turtle (*Chelonia*

TURTLES
a. Wood turtle. *b.* Emyd. *c.* Trionychid.

mydas) of wide distribution in tropical and semitropical seas: so called from the greenish color of its flesh. —**to turn turtle** To overturn; capsize. —*v.i.* **·tled, ·tling** To hunt for or catch turtles. [Appar. alter. of Sp. *tortuga* <Med. L *tortuca* TORTOISE; infl. in form by TURTLE²]

tur·tle·back (tûr′təl-bak′) *n.* **1** *Naut.* An arched covering, resembling the shell of a turtle, built over the main deck of a ship as protection against heavy seas: usually at the bow or stern. Also **turtle deck. 2** *Archeol.* A rude, chipped stone implement whose facets resemble the sculptured carapace of a turtle. [<TURTLE¹ + BACK]

turtle dove 1 An Old World dove (genus *Streptopelia*), noted for its affection for its mate and young. **2** One of other pigeons, as the mourning dove. [<TURTLE² + DOVE]

tur·tle·head (tûr′təl-hed′) *n.* Any species of a genus (*Chelone*) of hardy American herbs of

the figwort family, with large white or purple flowers.

turtle neck A high collar that fits snugly about the neck, usually rolled or turned over double: used especially on athletic sweaters. —**tur·tle-neck′** *adj.*

tur·tle-peg (tûr′təl-peg′) *n.* A small, sharp, steel spike attached to a line and loosely mounted upon a shaft which is thrown like a harpoon to capture sea turtles.

Tuscan order A Roman order of architecture resembling Roman Doric but having bolder moldings, no decorated details, and no triglyphs.

Tus·ca·ny (tus′kə-nē) A region and former duchy of west central Italy; 8,876 square miles; chief city, Florence: Italian *Toscana*.

Tus·ca·ro·ra (tus′kə-rôr′ə, -rō′rə) *n. pl.* **·ra** or **·ras** One of a tribe of North American Indians of Iroquoian stock formerly living in North Carolina, now surviving in New York and Ontario. They joined the Five Nations in 1722.

Tus·cu·lum (tus′kyə-ləm) An ancient ruined city of Latium, SE of Rome. — **Tus′cu·lan** *adj.*

tush¹ (tush) *interj.* An exclamation expressing disapproval, impatience, etc.

tush² (tush) See TUSK.

tushed (tusht) *adj.* Having tushes or tusks.

tusk (tusk) *n.* **1** A long, pointed tooth, as in the boar, walrus, or elephant. **2** A sharp, projecting, toothlike point. **3** A shoulder on a tenon, to strengthen it at its base; also, a tenon having such a shoulder. —*v.t.* **1** To gore with the tusks. **2** To root up with the tusks. Also *tush.* [Metathetic var. of OE *tux*] —**tusked** (tuskt) *adj.* —**tusk′less** *adj.* —**tusk′like′** *adj.*

tusk·er (tus′kər) *n.* An elephant or wild boar with developed tusks.

tusk tenon A tenon strengthened by a step or steps, or by a shoulder. [<TUSK (def. 3) + TENON]

tus·sah (tus′ə) *n.* **1** A wild and semi-domesticated Asian silkworm (*Antheraea paphia*) which spins large cocoons of brownish or yellowish silk. **2** The silk, or the tough, durable fabric woven from it. Also **tus′sa**, **tus·sar** (tus′ər), **tus′seh, tus′ser, tus·sore** (tus′ôr, -ōr), **tus′sur**. [<Hind. *tasar* <Skt. *tasara, trasara*, lit., a shuttle]

tus·sis (tus′is) *n. Pathol.* A cough: bronchial *tussis.* [<NL <L] —**tus′sal, tus′sive** *adj.*

tus·sle (tus′əl) *v.t.* & *v.i.* **·sled, ·sling** To fight or struggle in a vigorous, determined way; engage in a tussle. —*n.* A disorderly struggle, as in sport; scuffle. [Var. of TOUSLE]

tus·sock (tus′ək) *n.* **1** A tuft or clump of grass or sedge. **2** A tuft, as of hair or feathers. Also **tus′suck.** [Prob. dim. of obs. *tusk* a tuft of hair, ? <TUSK] —**tus′sock·y** *adj.*

tussock moth Any of various robust, medium-sized moths (family *Lymantriidae*) whose larvae bear tufts of hairs and are very destructive of broad-leaved deciduous trees, as the gipsy moth.

Tut-ankh-a-men (tōōt′ängk-ä′min) Egyptian pharaoh who reigned 1358–1350 B.C.

tu·te·lage (tōō′tə-lij, tyōō′-) *n.* **1** The state of being under a tutor or guardian. **2** The act or office of a guardian; guardianship. **3** The act of tutoring; instruction. [<L *tutela* a watching, guardianship < *tutus* safe < *tueri* watch, guard]

tu·te·lar (tōō′tə-lər, tyōō′-) *adj.* **1** Invested with guardianship. **2** Pertaining to a guardian. Also **tu′te·lar′y** (-ler′ē).

tu·te·nag (tōō′tə-nag, tyōō′-) *n.* **1** A white alloy, with varying proportions of copper, zinc, and nickel. **2** Zinc or spelter. Also

tu·tor (tōō′tər, tyōō′-) *n.* **1** One who instructs another in one or more branches of knowledge; a private teacher. 2 A college teacher who gives individual instruction. 3 *Brit.* A college official entrusted with the tutelage and care of undergraduates assigned to him. 4 *Law* A guardian of a minor or of a woman. — *v.t.* 1 To act as tutor to; instruct; teach; train. 2 To have the guardianship of. 3 To treat severely or sternly, as a tutor might; discipline. — *v.i.* 4 To do the work of a tutor. 5 To be tutored or instructed. See synonyms under TEACH. [<AF, OF *tutour* <L *tutor* a watcher, guardian < *tutus*. See TUTELAGE.] — tu·to·ri·al (tōō-tôr′ē-əl, -tō′rē-, tyōō-) *adj.*

tutorial system A system of education, generally collegiate, in which each student is assigned to a tutor, who directs his studies and has general supervision over his instruction.

tu·tor·ship (tōō′tər-ship, tyōō′-) *n.* 1 The office of a tutor or of a guardian. 2 Tutelage.

tut·ti (tōō′tē) *Music adj.* All: a term used to indicate that all performers are to take part: contrasted with *solo*. — *n.* A composition, piece, movement, or passage to be performed by all the voices and instruments together: contrasted with *solo*. [<Ital., pl. of *tutto* all]

tut·ty (tut′ē) *n.* An impure zinc oxide obtained as a sublimate in the flues of zinc-smelting furnaces: used as a polishing powder. [<OF *tutie* <Arabic *tūtiya* oxide of zinc, ? <Persian]

tu·tu (tü·tü′) *n. French* A short, full, projecting skirt consisting of many layers of sheer fabric, worn by ballet dancers.

tux·e·do (tuk·sē′dō) *n.* *pl.* ·dos 1 A man's semi-formal dinner coat without tails. 2 The suit of which the coat is a part. Also **Tux·e′. do.** [from *Tuxedo* Park, N.Y.; so called because first worn at the country club there]

Tuxt·la (tōōst′lä) The capital of Chiapas state, southern Mexico, in the west central part of the state. Also **Tuxtla Gu·tiér·rez** (gōō-tyär′räs).

twad·dle (twod′l) *v.t. & v.i.* ·dled, ·dling To talk foolishly and pretentiously. See synonyms under BABBLE. — *n.* Pretentious, silly talk; also, a twaddler. [Prob. alter. of TWATTLE] — **twad′dler** *n.*

twain (twān) *adj. Archaic* Two: rare except in poetic usage. See synonyms under BOTH. — *n.* 1 A couple; two. 2 In river navigation, two fathoms or twelve feet. [OE *twēgen*, masculine of *twa* two]

Twain (twān), **Mark** See MARK TWAIN.

twang (twang) *v.t. & v.i.* twanged, twang·ing 1 To make or cause to make a sharp, vibrant sound, as a bowstring. 2 To utter or speak with a harsh, nasal sound. — *n.* 1 A sharp, vibrating sound, as of a tense string plucked. 2 A sharp, nasal sound of the voice. 3 A sound resembling either of the foregoing. Also *tang*. [Imit.] — **twang′y** *adj.*

tway·blade (twā′blād) *n.* Any one of various hardy terrestrial orchids (genera *Listera* or *Liparis*) with two radical leaves: also spelled *twyblade*. [<archaic *tway* two, var. of TWAIN + BLADE]

tweak (twēk) *v.t.* To pinch and twist sharply; twitch. — *n.* A twisting pinch; twitch. [Var. of dial. *twick*, OE *twiccan* twitch] — **tweak′y** *adj.*

tweed (twēd) *n.* 1 A soft woolen fabric with a homespun surface: often woven in two or more colors to effect a check or plaid pattern. 2 A tweed suit or coat. — **Harris tweed** A homespun woolen cloth, usually of mixed colors, made at Harris in the Hebrides. [Alter. of dial. E (Scottish) *tweel*, var. of TWILL; prob. infl. in form by *Tweed* river, which flows through the district where it is woven]

twee·dle[1] (twēd′l) *v.* ·dled, ·dling *v.t.* 1 To play (a musical instrument) casually or carelessly. 2 To wheedle; cajole. — *v.i.* 3 To produce a series of shrill tones. 4 To play a musical instrument casually or carelessly. — *n.* A sound resembling the tones of a violin. [Imit. of the sound of a reed pipe]

twee·dle[2] (twēd′l) *v.* ·dled, ·dling *v.t.* To handle carelessly. — *v.i.* To wriggle. [Var. of TWIDDLE]

twee·dle·dum and twee·dle·dee (twēd′l·dum′, twēd′l·dē′) Two things between which there is the slightest possible distinction: from John Byrom, *On the Feuds between Handel and Bononcini* (1723). [Orig. imit. of low- and high-pitched musical instruments, respectively]

tweet (twēt) *v.i.* To utter a thin, chirping note. — *n.* A twittering or chirping. Also **tweet′. tweet′.** [Imit.]

tweet·er (twē′tər) *n. Electronics* A loudspeaker used to reproduce the treble register in high-fidelity sound equipment: distinguished from *woofer*. [<TWEET]

tweeze (twēz) *v.t.* tweezed, tweez·ing *Colloq.* To handle, pinch, pluck, etc., with tweezers. [Back formation <TWEEZERS]

tweez·ers (twē′zərz) *n. pl.* 1 Small pincers for tiny objects: often called **a pair of tweezers.** 2 *Obs.* A set of surgeon's instruments; also, a surgeon's instrument case. [Alter. of *tweezes*, pl. of *tweeze*, earlier *etweese* a case of small instruments <F *étuis*, pl. of *étui* ÉTUI]

twelfth (twelfth) *adj.* 1 Second in order after the tenth: the ordinal of *twelve*. 2 Being one of twelve equal parts. — *n.* 1 One of twelve equal parts; the quotient obtained by dividing by twelve. 2 *Music* An interval compounded of an octave and a fifth. [OE *twelfta*]

Twelfth–day (twelfth′dā′) *n.* The festival of the Epiphany, the twelfth day after Christmas.

Twelfth–night (twelfth′nīt′) *n.* The eve (Jan. 5th) of Twelfth–day, or the evening before Epiphany; sometimes, the evening (Jan. 6th) of Epiphany. — *adj.* Of or pertaining to Twelfth–night.

twelve (twelv) *adj.* Consisting of twice six: a cardinal numeral. — *n.* The sum of ten and two, or the symbols (12, xii, XII) representing it. — **the Twelve** The twelve apostles. See APOSTLE (def. 1). [OE *twelf*]

Twelve Apostles 1 A governing body of the Mormon Church, composed of twelve high officials. 2 The twelve disciples of Jesus: more commonly *the Twelve.*

twelve·mo (twelv′mō) *adj. & n.* Duodecimo.

twelve·month (twelv′munth′) *n.* A year.

twelve–tone (twelv′tōn′) *adj. Music* Of, pertaining to, or composed in a system or technique developed by Arnold Schönberg, in which any particular series of twelve tones containing all twelve of the tones of the chromatic scale is used in various permutations as the basis of composition, usually without reference to a fixed tonal center; dodecaphonic.

twen·ti·eth (twen′tē·ith) *adj.* 1 Tenth in order after the tenth: the ordinal of *twenty.* 2 Being one of twenty equal parts. — *n.* One of twenty equal parts; the quotient of a unit divided by twenty. [OE *twentigotha* < *twentig* twenty]

twen·ty (twen′tē) *adj.* 1 Consisting of twice ten; vicenary. 2 *Archaic* A considerable but indefinite number. — *n. pl.* ·ties The sum of ten and ten, or the symbols (20, xx, XX) representing it. [OE *twentig*] — **twen′ty·fold′** *adj.*

Twenty–fourth Amendment An amendment to the Constitution of the United States prohibiting the denial or abridgment of the right to vote in elections for Federal office by reason of failure to pay any poll tax or other tax: ratified in 1964.

twen·ty–one (twen′tē·wun′) *n.* Vingt-et-un: a card game.

twerp (twûrp) *n. Slang* A small, contemptible person. [Cf. obs. *twirk* twitch, var. of TWIRL]

Twi (twē) *n.* A Sudanic language spoken by African Negroes in Ghana: also called *Ashanti*: also spelled *Tshi.*

twi– *prefix* Two; double; twice: *twibil.* Also spelled *twy–.* [OE, double <*twa* two]

twi·bil (twī′bil) *n.* 1 An ax with two cutting edges. 2 A double–bladed battle–ax. 3 A garden tool like an ax; a mattock. Also **twi′. bill.** [OE <*twi–* two + *bill* an ax]

twice (twīs) *adv.* 1 Two times. 2 In double measure; doubly. [OE *twiges*, gen. of *twiga* twice]

twice–laid (twīs′lād′) *adj.* 1 Made from the yarns of old or used rope. 2 Made from remnants or refuse.

twid·dle (twid′l) *v.* ·dled, ·dling *v.t.* 1 To twirl idly; toy or play with. — *v.i.* 2 To revolve or twirl. 3 To toy with something idly. 4 To be busy about trifles. — *n.* A gentle twirling, as of the fingers. [Prob. <ON *tridla* stir; ? infl. in meaning by TWIRL and FIDDLE] — **twid′. dler** *n.*

twi·er (twī′ər) Altered form of TUYÈRE.

twig[1] (twig) *n.* A small shoot or branchlet of a tree. ◆ Collateral adjective: *viminal.* [OE *twigge*] — **twig′less** *adj.*

twig blight 1 Any of various bacterial or fungous infections of plants which attack the

twigs, resulting in extreme decay. 2 Dieback.

twig borer The larva of a lepidopterous insect (*Anarsia lineatella*) which bores into the twigs of certain fruit trees, as the peach, plum, and apricot, with destructive effect.

twigged (twigd) *adj.* Having shoots or twigs.

twig·gen (twig′ən) *adj.* Made of twigs; wicker.

twig·gy (twig′ē) *adj.* Like, or abounding in, twigs.

twi·light (twī′līt) *n.* 1 The light diffused over the sky after sunset and before sunrise (especially, in popular use, the former) which is caused by the reflection of sunlight from the higher portions of the atmosphere. 2 Any faint light; shade; obscurity: the *twilight* of the groves. 3 Indistinct apprehension or perception: the *twilight* of doubt or barbarism. 4 A hazy or obscure condition following the waning of past glory, achievements, etc.: the *twilight* of the gods. — *adj.* 1 Pertaining or peculiar to twilight; crepuscular. 2 Imperfectly or faintly lighted; shaded; dim. [ME *twylight* <OE *twi–* (<*twa* two) + LIGHT; used in sense of "the light between the two," i.e., between day and night]

twilight arch The arch that bounds the brightest region of twilight.

twilight sleep *Med.* A light or partial anesthesia, induced artificially, as by injection of morphine and scopolamine, in which the patient loses the power to remember present events and sensations: sometimes used to relieve childbirth pains. [Trans. of G *dämmerschlaf*]

TWILL
Enlarged to show weave.

twill (twil) *n.* 1 One of the three foundation systems of weaves, in which the shuttle carries the woof thread over one and under two or more warp threads, producing the characteristic diagonal ribs or lines in fabrics. 2 A fabric woven with a twill; twilled cloth. — *v.t.* To weave (cloth) so as to produce diagonal lines or ribs on the surface. [Var. of ME *twile*, OE *twili* a twilled fabric <*twi–* <*twa* two, partial trans. of L *bilix* having a double thread]

twin (twin) *n.* 1 One of two young produced at the same birth. 2 The counterpart or exact mate of another. 3 An intergrowth of two or more crystals of the same substance according to some definite law, a single plane or axis usually being common to the different individuals. — **the Twins** Castor and Pollux, the two brightest stars in the constellation Gemini; also, the constellation. — *adj.* 1 Being, or standing in the relation of, a twin or twins. 2 Consisting of, forming, or being one of a pair of similar and closely related objects; double; twofold. — **the Twin Cities** St. Paul and Minneapolis. — *v.* twinned, twin·ning *v.i.* 1 To bring forth twins. 2 To be matched or equal; agree. 3 *Archaic* To be born as a twin. — *v.t.* 4 To bring forth as twins. 5 To couple; match. 6 *Scot.* To separate: also twine (twīn). [Fusion of OE *twinn*, *getwinn* (< *twi–* <*twa* two) and ON *tvinnr*, *tvennr* double]

twin bed One of a pair of single beds.

twin·ber·ry (twin′ber′ē, *n. pl.* ·ries 1 The partridgeberry. 2 A North American shrub (*Lonicera involucrata*) with elliptic leaves, yellowish–red flowers, and shining black berries.

twine[1] (twīn) *v.* twined, twin·ing *v.t.* 1 To twist together, as threads. 2 To form by such twisting. 3 To coil or wrap about something. 4 To encircle by winding or wreathing. 5 To enfold; embrace. — *v.i.* 6 To interlace; become twined. 7 To proceed in a winding course; meander. See synonyms under BEND, TWIST. — *adj.* Of or like twine. — *n.* 1 A string composed of two or more strands twisted together; loosely, any small cord. 2 The act of twining or entwining. 3 A form or conformation produced by twining. 4 An interweaving or interlacing. 5 *Obs.* A twisting about; spin. [OE *twin* a twisted double thread < *twi–* double < *twa* two] — **twin′er** *n.*

twin·flow·er (twin′flou′ər) *n.* A trailing evergreen plant (genus *Linnaea*) of the honeysuckle family, as the Old World *L. borealis*, with fragrant rose or white bell-shaped flowers growing in pairs, and its American variety, *L. borealis americana.*

twinge (twinj) *v.t. & v.i.* **twinged, twing·ing** To affect with or suffer a sudden pain or twinge. — *n.* A sharp, darting, local pain; twitch; also, a mental pang. See synonyms under PAIN. [OE *twengan* pinch]

twi·night (twī′nīt′) *adj.* Beginning in the late afternoon and continuing, under artificial light, into the night, as baseball games or other outdoor contests. [Blend of TWILIGHT and NIGHT]

twin·kle (twing′kəl) *v.* **·kled, ·kling** *v.i.* **1** To shine with fitful, intermittent gleams, as a star. **2** To be bright, as with amusement: Her eyes *twinkled.* **3** To wink or blink; open and shut with a quick, involuntary motion. **4** To move rapidly to and fro; flicker: *twinkling* feet. — *v.t.* **5** To emit or cause to flash out, as gleams of light. **6** To move (the eyelids) quickly and repeatedly. — *n.* **1** A tremulous gleam of light; sparkle; glimmer. **2** A quick or repeated movement of the eyelids; also, a wink or sparkle of the eye. **3** An instant; a twinkling. See synonyms under LIGHT¹. [OE *twinclian*] — **twin′kler** *n.*

twin·kling (twing′kling) *n.* **1** The act of scintillating. **2** A wink or twinkle. **3** The act of winking, or the time required for it. **4** A moment. See synonyms under LIGHT.

twin-leaf (twin′lēf′) *n.* A small perennial herb (*Jeffersonia diphylla*) of the barberry family native in eastern North America, having solitary white flowers and leaves divided into kidney-shaped leaflets.

twinned (twind) *adj.* **1** Produced at one birth; twin. **2** Formed by twinning, as a crystal.

twin·ning (twin′ing) *n.* **1** The production of two young at one birth; the bearing of twins. **2** Close union or combination; coupling of two related objects. **3** The formation of twin crystals, each the counterpart of the other.

twin-screw (twin′skroō′) *adj.* Of a vessel, having two propeller shafts, one on each side of the keel, and two propellers, normally turning in opposite directions. — *n.* (twin′skroō′) Such a vessel.

twirl (twûrl) *v.t. & v.i.* **1** To whirl or rotate. **2** In baseball, to pitch. — *n.* **1** A whirling motion, or a quick twisting action, as of the fingers. **2** A curl; twist; coil. [Alter. of ME *tirlen,* var. of *trillen* TRILL²; appar. infl. by *whirl*] — **twirl′er** *n.*

twist (twist) *v.t.* **1** To wind (strands, etc.) around each other. **2** To form by such winding: to *twist* thread. **3** To give spiral, circular, or semicircular form to, as by turning at either end. **4** To force out of natural shape; distort or contort. **5** To distort the meaning of. **6** To confuse; perplex. **7** To wreathe, twine, or wrap. **8** To cause to revolve or rotate. **9** To impart spin to (a ball) so that it moves in a curve. — *v.i.* **10** To become twisted. **11** To move in a winding course; meander or bend. **12** To squirm; writhe. — *n.* **1** The act, manner, or result of twisting or turning on an axis. **2** The state of being twisted. **3** *Physics* **a** A torsional strain. **b** The angle of torsion, as of a rod or bar. **4** A curve; turn; bend; winding: This path is full of *twists* and turns. **5** A contortion or twisting of a facial or bodily feature: a smile with a certain *twist.* **6** A wrench; strain, as of a joint or limb: He fell and gave his ankle a *twist.* **7** A peculiar or perverted inclination, bent, or attitude: the *twist* of a criminal's mind. **8** A distortion; deviation; wresting: a *twist* of meaning. **9** Thread or cord made of tightly twisted or braided strands. **10** *Naut.* One of the strands of a rope. **11** A twisted roll of bread. **12** Tobacco twisted in the form of a large cord. **13** In baseball, billiards, tennis, etc.: **a** A spin or whirling motion given to a ball by a certain stroke or throw. **b** The stroke or throw producing such a spin. **c** The act or knack of imparting such a spin. [ME *twisten* divide in two, combine two, prob. <OE *-twist* a rope, as in *mæst-twist* a rope to stay a mast < *twi-double* < *twa* two]

Synonyms (verb): bend, contort, crook, encircle, entwine, twine, wreathe. To *twist* is to bend a thing somewhat spirally upon itself.

To *twine* is to *bend* it around some other object. Wrestlers *twine* their arms about each other, but if a combatant's arm is *twisted* it is likely to disable him. An iron shaft may be *twisted* out of shape, but not *twined*; the groove of a rifle barrel is *twisted*, not *twined*; a wreath is *twined* around one's temples, but not *twisted.* Compare BEND, PERVERT.

twist drill *Mech.* A drill or bit whose body is cut with deep spiral grooves to carry out the chips.

twist·er (twis′tər) *n.* **1** One who or that which twists. **2** A ball, as in cricket, bowled with a twist. **3** In baseball, a curve; also, one who pitches a curve. **4** *U.S.* A tornado.

twit (twit) *v.t.* **twit·ted, twit·ting** To taunt, reproach, or annoy by reminding of a mistake, fault, etc. — *n.* A taunting allusion; reproach. [Aphetic var. of ME *atwite,* OE *ætwitan* taunt < *æt-* at + *witan* accuse] — **twit′ter** *n.*

twitch (twich) *v.t.* **1** To pull sharply; pluck with a jerky movement. **2** In lumbering, to drag or skid (logs) along the ground with a chain. — *v.i.* **3** To tug or move with a quick, spasmodic jerk, as a muscle. — *n.* **1** A sudden involuntary contraction of a muscle. **2** A sudden jerk or pull. [ME *twicchen.* Akin to OE *twiccian* pluck.] — **twitch′ing·ly** *adv.*

twit·ter (twit′ər) *v.i.* **1** To utter a series of light chirping or tremulous notes, as a bird. **2** To titter. **3** *Brit. Dial.* To be excited; tremble. — *v.t.* **4** To utter or express with a twitter. — *n.* **1** A succession of light, tremulous sounds. **2** *Bot.* A disease of plants caused by insects. [Imit.]

twit·ter (twit′ər) *v.t.* Spin or twist unevenly. [< earlier *twit,* a fault or entanglement in thread; ult. origin uncertain]

two (tōō) *adj.* Being one more than one, or a unit taken once again; binary: a cardinal numeral. See synonyms under BOTH. — *n.* **1** The sum of one and one: a cardinal number. **2** Any symbol or set of symbols (2, ii, II) for this number. — **in two** Bisected; bipartite; asunder; apart. [OE *twā, tū*]

two-base hit (tōō′bās′) In baseball, a hit in which the batter reaches second base without benefit of an error. Also **two′-bag′ger.**

two-by-four (tōō′bī-fôr′, -fōr′) *adj.* **1** Measuring two inches by four inches. **2** *U.S. Slang* Of trifling size or significance; narrow or limited. — *n.* (tōō′bī-fôr′, -fōr′) A piece of lumber measuring two inches by four inches before finishing: much used in building.

two-cy·cle (tōō′sī′kəl) *adj.* Designating a type of internal-combustion engine in which the piston completes its work in two strokes.

two-edged (tōō′ejd′) *adj.* Having an edge on each side; cutting both ways.

two-faced (tōō′fāst′) *adj.* **1** Having two faces. **2** Double-dealing; insincere; of dissimulating tendency. — **two′-fac′ed·ly** (-fā′sid-lē, -fāst′lē) *adv.*

two-fold (tōō′fōld′) *adj.* Double. — *adv.* In a twofold manner or degree; doubly.

two-hand·ed (tōō′han′did) *adj.* **1** Requiring both hands at once. **2** Constructed for use by two persons. **3** Ambidextrous. **4** Having two hands.

two-mast·er (tōō′mas′tər, -mäs′-) *n.* A ship with two masts.

two-name (tōō′nām′) *adj.* Bearing two names or signatures.

two-name paper A negotiable paper, bearing either two signatures or one signature and one endorsement.

two-ply (tōō′plī′) *adj.* **1** Made of two united webs; woven double: a *two-ply* carpet. **2** Made of two strands or two thicknesses of material.

Two Sic·i·lies (sis′ə-lēz), **The** A kingdom formed by the union of Sicily with Naples in 1130; incorporated with Italy in 1861.

two·some (tōō′səm) *n.* **1** Two persons together. **2** A match with one player on each side. — *adj.* **1** Performed or participated in by two, as a dance. **2** Comprising two or a pair.

two-spot (tōō′spot′) *n.* **1** A playing card having two pips; a deuce. **2** *U.S. Slang* An unimportant person. **3** *U.S. Slang* A two-dollar bill. **4** *U.S. Slang* A two-year prison sentence.

two-step (tōō′step′) *n.* A round dance consisting of a sliding step in 2/4 time; also, the

music for it.

two-up (tōō′up′) *n. Austral.* A gambling game in which two, or sometimes three, pennies are tossed; also called *swy.*

two-way (tōō′wā′) *adj.* **1** Having an arrangement that will permit a fluid to be directed in either of two channels: specifically said of cocks and valves. **2** *Math.* Having a double mode of variation. **3** Permitting traffic in either direction: a *two-way* street.

ty·ing (tī′ing) *n.* The act of fastening, or a fastening, as a ribbon or cord.

ty·lo·sis (tī-lō′sis) *n. pl.* **·ses** (-sēz) **1** *Bot.* A bladderlike enlargement of a plant cell, intruding within the cavity of a vessel from the wall of a contiguous growing cell. **2** The formation of calluses, especially on the skin. **3** The callus so formed. [<Gk. *tylōsis* < *tylos* a lump, callus]

tymp (timp) *n. Metall.* A water-cooled block of refractory material or of cast iron, as the top of the opening between the crucible and the forehearth of a blast furnace. [Short for TYMPAN]

tym·pan (tim′pən) *n.* **1** *Printing* A thickness (or, more usually, several thicknesses), as of paper, on the impression surface of a printing press: used to improve the quality of the presswork. **2** *Archit.* A tympanum. **3** A membrane or other thin sheet tightly stretched. **4** A drum. [<OF <L *tympanum.* See TYMPANUM.]

tym·pan·ic (tim-pan′ik) *adj.* **1** Like or of the nature of a drum. **2** Of or pertaining to the middle ear.

tympanic bone *Anat.* An incomplete bony ring that surrounds the external auditory canal.

tympanic membrane *Anat.* The drumhead membrane separating the middle ear from the external ear; the eardrum. See illustration under EAR.

tym·pa·ni·tes (tim′pə-nī′tēz) *n. Pathol.* Swelling of the abdomen due to accumulation of gas. [<LL <Gk. *tympanitēs* < *tympanon.* See TYMPANUM.] — **tym′pa·nit′ic** (-nit′ik) *adj.*

tym·pa·ni·tis (tim′pə-nī′tis) *n. Pathol.* Inflammation of the mucous membrane lining the tympanum. [<NL <L *tympanum* a drum]

tym·pa·num (tim′pə-nəm) *n. pl.* **-na** (-nə) **1** *Anat.* The middle ear; also, the tympanic membrane. **2** *Archit.* An ornamental space, as over a doorway, bounded by an arch or within the coping of a pediment. **3** A large drum wheel fitted with buckets for raising water from a flowing stream. **4** An ancient form of drum. **5** *Electr.* The diaphragm in a telephone. Also spelled *timpanum.* [<NL <L, a drum <Gk. *tympanon* < *typtein* beat]

type (tīp) *n.* **1** Something that represents or symbolizes something else; an image; emblem; symbol. **2** *Theol.* That by which something is prefigured. **3** An object representative of, or embodying the characteristics of, a class or group. **4** *Biol.* **a** The general plan of an organism, with special reference to those structural and physiological characteristics which make it representative of a group, species, class, etc. **b** An individual considered as representative of members of the next higher category in a biological system of classification: the *type* of a genus, family, order, etc. **5** A variety of some physiological substance as determined by specific differences in properties and in mode of action when compared with another variety of the same substance: a blood *type.* **6** *Printing* A piece or block of metal or of wood, bearing on its upper surface, usually in relief, a letter or character for use in printing; also, such pieces collectively. See AGATE, PICA, POINT SYSTEM. **7** A distinctive sign; stamp; mark. **8** A plan to which proposed work or action should conform, as in fine arts; a standard or model. **9** In coinage, the characteristic device on either side of a medal or coin. See synonyms under EMBLEM, EXAMPLE, LETTER, MODEL, SIGN. — *v.* **typed, typ·ing** *v.t.* **1** To assign to a particular type or role, as an actor. **2** To determine the type of; identify: to *type* a blood sample. **3** To typewrite. **4** To represent; typify. **5** To prefigure. — *v.i.* **6** To typewrite. [<MF <L *typus* <Gk. *typos* an

impression, figure, type < *typtein* strike]

-type *combining form* **1** Representative form; stamp; type: *prototype.* **2** Used in or produced by printing, photography, or other duplicating processes, or by type: *Linotype, collotype.* [<Gk. *typos* stamp]

type·face (tīp′fās′) *n. Printing* **1** Face (def. 8). **2** A set of type of a particular design.

type genus *Biol.* A genus that combines the essential characteristics of the higher group (as a family) to which it belongs; the representative genus after which a family is named.

type–high (tīp′hī′) *adj. Printing* Designating the standard height of type *(height–to–paper)* from base to the level of the printing surface; in the United States, 0.918 of an inch: also *letter–high.*

type line One of the innermost ridges that circumscribe the pattern area of a fingerprint and assist in its identification.

type metal The alloy of which type is made, usually of lead, tin, and antimony.

type–script (tīp′skript′) *n.* Matter which has been typewritten: also called *typoscript.* [< TYPE(WRITTEN) + SCRIPT]

type·set·ter (tīp′set′ər) *n.* **1** A compositor. **2** A machine for composing type. —**type′set′ting** *n. & adj.*

type species *Biol.* The plant or animal species regarded as most typical of the genus to which its name is given; a genotype.

type specimen *Biol.* The individual plant or animal on whose description the distinguishing characters of a species are based.

type·writ·er (tīp′rī′tər) *n.* **1** A machine for producing printed characters as a substitute for writing: it usually has a keyboard, depression of the keys serving to impress a type upon the paper through the medium of an inked ribbon. **2** A typist.

type·writ·ing (tīp′rī′ting) *n.* **1** The act or operation of using a typewriter. **2** Work done by such process.

ty·pha (tī′fə) *n.* **1** The cat–tail. **2** A fiber resembling kapok prepared from the spikes of the cat–tail, for use in life preservers, pillows, etc. [<NL < *typhē* a cat–tail]

typh·li·tis (tif·lī′tis) *n. Pathol.* Inflammation of the cecum. [<NL <Gk. *typhlos* blind] —**typh·lit′ic** (-lit′ik) *adj.*

typh·lol·o·gy (tif·lol′ə·jē) *n.* The branch of medicine and pathology that deals with blindness. [<TYPHLO- + -LOGY]

typh·lo·sis (tif·lō′sis) *n.* Blindness. [<NL <Gk. *typhlōsis* < *typhlos* blind]

typho– *combining form* Typhus; typhoid: *typhogenic.* Also, before vowels, **typh-.** [<Gk. *typhos* smoke, stupor]

ty·pho·gen·ic (tī′fə·jen′ik) *adj.* Producing typhus.

ty·phoid (tī′foid) *adj.* **1** Pertaining to or resembling typhoid fever: also **ty·phoi′dal, ty′phose** (-fōs). **2** Resembling typhus. —*n.* Typhoid fever. [<TYPH(US) + -OID]

typhoid bacillus A motile, flagellated, Gram-negative bacterium *(Eberthella* or *Salmonella typhosa),* usually introduced into the body by food or drink: the bacillus that causes typhoid fever.

typhoid carrier A person who, with few or none of the clinical symptoms of infection, carries the typhoid bacillus and can communicate it to others in its active form. Also **ty·pho·phore** (tī′fə·fôr, -fōr).

typhoid fever *Pathol.* An acute, infectious fever caused by the typhoid bacillus and

characterized by severe intestinal disturbances, a typical eruption of bright rose–red spots on the chest and abdomen, and great physical prostration.

ty·phoi·din (tī·foi′din) *n. Bacteriol.* A culture of the typhoid bacillus, used as a test for passive or active infection. [<TYPHOID + -IN]

ty·pho·ma·lar·i·al (tī′fō·mə·lâr′ē·əl) *adj. Pathol.* Describing a fever resembling that of typhoid but believed to be malarial in origin. [<TYPHO- + MALARIAL]

ty·pho·ma·ni·a (tī′fə·mā′nē·ə, -mān′yə) *n. Pathol.* The delirious state associated with typhoid fever or typhus. Also **ty·pho·ni·a** (tī-fō′nē·ə).

ty·phoon (tī·fōōn′) *n.* A tropical storm of cyclonic force and peculiar violence, occurring in the western Pacific and the China Sea. See synonyms under CYCLONE. [< dial. Chinese *tai feng,* lit., big wind; infl. by obs. *typhon* a whirlwind (<Gk. *typhōn* a hurricane) and by obs. *tuphan, tufan* a typhoon <Arabic *tūfān,* ? ult. from the same Gk. source]

ty·phus (tī′fəs) *n. Pathol.* An acute, contagious, rickettsial disease caused by a micro-organism *(Rickettsia prowazeki)* and marked by high fever with eruption of red spots, cerebral disorders, and extreme prostration; typhus fever: also called *Brill's disease.* **Epidemic typhus** is transmitted by the bite of the body louse, and **endemic** or **murine typhus** by the bite of the rat flea. [<NL <Gk. *typhos* smoke, a stupor < *typhein* smoke] —**ty′phous** *adj.*

typ·i·cal (tip′i·kəl) *adj.* **1** Having the nature or character of a type; constituting a type or pattern; symbolic. **2** Conforming to the essential features of a species, group, class, etc.; characteristic. Also **typ′ic:** also *typal.* See synonyms under NORMAL. [<Med. L *typicalis* <L *typicus* <Gk. *typikos* < *typos* TYPE] —**typ′i·cal·ly** *adv.* —**typ′i·cal·ness** *n.*

typ·i·fy (tip′ə·fī) *v.t.* **·fied, ·fy·ing** **1** To represent by a type; signify, as by an image or token. **2** To constitute a type or serve as a characteristic example of. — **typ′i·fi·ca′tion** (-fə·kā′shən) *n.* —**typ′i·fi′er** *n.*

ty·po·graphed (tī′pə·graft, -gräft) *adj.* Printed from type, or from plates in which the design is raised above the level of the body of the plate.

ty·po·graph·i·cal (tī′pə·graf′i·kəl) *adj.* Pertaining to, concerned with, or effected by typography or printing. Also **ty′po·graph′ic.** — **ty′po·graph′i·cal·ly** *adv.*

ty·pog·ra·phy (tī·pog′rə·fē) *n.* **1** The arrangement of composed type. **2** The style and appearance of printed matter. **3** The act or art of composing and printing from types. [<TYPO- + -GRAPHY]

ty·pol·o·gy (tī·pol′ə·jē) *n.* The study of types, as in systems of classification. [<TYPO- + -LOGY]

ty·ra·mine (tī′rə·mēn′, tir′ə-) *n. Chem.* A white, crystalline, nitrogenous compound, C₈H₁₁ON, found in ergot, ripe cheese, and putrefying animal tissue: the hydrochloride is used in medicine. [<TYR(OSINE) + AMINE]

ty·ran·ni·cal (ti·ran′i·kəl, tī-) *adj.* Of or like a tyrant; harsh; despotic; arbitrary. Also **ty·ran′nic.** See synonyms under ABSOLUTE, ARBITRARY. — **ty·ran′ni·cal·ly** *adv.* — **ty·ran′ni·cal·ness** *n.*

ty·ran·ni·cide (ti·ran′ə·sīd, tī-) *n.* **1** The slayer of a tyrant. **2** The slaying of a tyrant. [<F <L *tyrannicida* < *tyrannus* a tyrant + *caedere* kill; def. 2 <L *tyrannicidium*]

tyr·an·nize (tir′ə·nīz) *v.* **·nized, ·niz·ing** *v.i.* **1** To exercise power cruelly or unjustly. **2** To rule as a tyrant; have absolute power. —*v.t.* **3** To treat tyrannically; domineer. Also *Brit.* **tyr′an·nise.** [<MF *tyranniser* <LL *tyrannizare* <Gk. *tyrannizein* < *tyrannos* a tyrant] — **tyr′an·niz′er** *n.*

ty·ran·no·saur·us (ti·ran′ə·sôr′əs, tī-) *n. Paleontol.* A carnivorous dinosaur *(Tyrannosaurus rex)* inhabiting North America in the Cretaceous period: it was characterized by its huge bulk, massive jaws, and ability to walk erect on its hind legs. [<NL <Gk. *tyrannos* a tyrant + *sauros* a lizard]

tyr·an·nous (tir′ə·nəs) *adj.* Despotic, tyrannical. See synonyms under ARBITRARY. — **tyr′an·nous·ly** *adv.* — **tyr′an·nous·ness** *n.*

tyr·an·ny (tir′ə·nē) *n. pl.* **·nies** **1** Absolute power arbitrarily or unjustly administered; despotism. **2** An arbitrarily cruel exercise of power; a tyrannical act. **3** In Greek history, the office or the administration of a tyrant. **4** Severity; roughness. [<OF *tirannie* <L *tyrannia* < *tyrannus* a tyrant]

ty·rant (tī′rənt) *n.* **1** One who rules oppressively or cruelly; a despot. **2** One who exercises absolute power without legal warrant, whether ruling well or ill: the original meaning in ancient Greece. [<OF *tiran, tyran* <L *tyrannus* <Gk. *tyrannos* a master, a usurper]

tyrant flycatcher Any American flycatcher (family *Tyrannidae),* as the kingbird, pewee, etc.

tyre (tīr) See TIRE².

Tyrian dye **1** A purple or crimson dyestuff obtained by the ancient Greeks and Romans from certain mollusks of the genus *Murex.* **2** A violet–purple color of high saturation and low brilliance. Also **Tyrian purple.**

ty·ro (tī′rō) *n. pl.* **·ros** One who is in the rudiments of any study or the preliminary stage of any occupation; a beginner; novice: also spelled *tiro.* [<Med. L <L *tiro* a recruit]

Tyr·o·lese (tir′ə·lēz′, -lēs′) See TIROLESE.

Ty·ro·lienne (tē·rō·lyen′) *n.* A ländler. [<F, fem. of *tyrolien* Tyrolean]

Ty·rone (ti·rōn′) A county of Ulster, western Northern Ireland; 1,218 miles; county town, Omagh.

ty·ro·sin·ase (tī′rō·si·nās′, tir′ō-) *n. Biochem.* A plant and animal enzyme which converts tyrosine into dark pigments, as melanin. [< TYROSIN(E) + -ASE]

ty·ro·sine (tī′rə·sēn, -sin, tir′ə-) *n. Biochem.* A white crystalline amino acid, C₉H₁₁O₃N, formed by the hydrolysis of many plant and animal proteins. [<Gk. *tyros* cheese + -INE²]

ty·ro·sin·o·sis (tī′rō·sin·ō′sis, tir′ō-) *n. Pathol.* A disorder caused by defective metabolism of tyrosine in the body. [<TYROSIN(E) + -OSIS]

ty·ro·thri·cin (tī′rō·thrī′sin, -thris′in) *n.* An antibiotic isolated from a soil bacterium *(Bacillus brevis):* similar to gramicidin and used therapeutically in localized infections. [<TYRO-(SINE) + Gk. *thrix, trichos* a hair + -IN]

Tyrr (tür, tir) See TYR.

Tyr·rhe·ni·an Sea (ti·rē′nē·ən) The part of the Mediterranean between Italy, Sardinia, Corsica, and Sicily. [<Gk. *Tyrrhēnia* Tuscany]

Tyr·tae·us (tûr·tē′əs) Greek poet of the seventh century B.C.

Tyu·men (tyōō·men′, *Russian* tyōō·myān′y′) A city in western Asiatic Russian S.F.S.R.

Tyu·zen·zi (chōō·zen·jē) See CHUZENJI.

tzet·ze (tset′sē) See TSETSE.

U

u, U (yōō) *n. pl.* **u's, U's** or **Us** (yōōz) **1** The twenty–first letter of the English alphabet: from Greek *upsilon.* In Roman it was written V and had both consonant and vowel value. In English U was formerly the uncial or cursive form of V; gradually V came to be preferred in initial position in writing, and, as the sound at the beginning of a word is ordinarily consonantal, U was finally restricted to vowel use. **2** Any sound of the letter *u.* See ALPHA-

BET. —*symbol* **1** *Chem.* Uranium (symbol U). **2** Anything shaped like a U.

Uau·pés (wou·pās′) A river in SE Colombia and NW Brazil, flowing 500 miles SE to the Río Negro: also *Vaupés.*

U·ban·gi (ōō·bäng′gē) A river of central Africa, flowing 1,400 miles from NE Belgian Congo to the Congo river and forming part of the boundary between the Belgian Congo and French Equatorial Africa.

u·bi·e·ty (yōō·bī′ə·tē) *n.* The state of being in a place; local relation. [<NL *ubietas, -tatis* <L *ubi* where]

u·biq·ui·tar·i·an (yōō·bik′wə·târ′ē·ən) *n.* One who has ubiquitous existence.

U·biq·ui·tar·i·an (yōō·bik′wə·târ′ē·ən) *n.* A believer in the omnipresence of the human nature of Christ and, as a consequence, in his necessary actual bodily presence in the Eucharist. Also **U·bi·quar·i·an** (yōō′bə·kwâr′-

ē·ən), U′bi·quist, U·biq′ui·tist.

u·biq·ui·tous (yoō·bik′wə·təs) *adj.* Existing, or seeming to exist, everywhere at once; omnipresent. Also **u·biq′ui·tar′y** (-ter′ē). — **u·biq′·ui·tous·ly** *adv.* — **u·biq′ui·tous·ness** *n.*

u·biq·ui·ty (yoō·bik′wə·tē) *n.* **1** The state of being in an indefinite number of places at once; omnipresence real or seeming. **2** The state of existing always without beginning or end. [<F *ubiquité* <L *ubique* everywhere]

u·bi su·pra (yoō′bī soō′prə) *Latin* Where (mentioned) above.

U-boat (yoō′bōt′) *n.* A German submarine. [<G *U-boot,* contraction of *Unterseeboot,* lit., undersea boat]

U-bolt (yoō′bōlt′) *n.* A bolt bent like the letter U, and fitted with a screw and nut at each end.

U·che·an (yoō·chē′ən) *n.* A North American Indian linguistic stock, consisting only of the Yuchi tribe.

U·dai·pur (oō·dī′poōr, oō′dī-) **1** A former princely state of the Rajputana States, India; since 1948 merged with the State of Rajasthan; 13,170 square miles: also *Mewar.* **2** A city of southern Rajasthan, India; formerly capital of Udaipur state.

U·day Shan·kar (oō′dī shän·kär′), born 1900, Indian dancer.

ud·der (ud′ər) *n.* A large, pendulous, milk-secreting gland having nipples or teats for the suckling of offspring, as in cows. [OE *ūder*]

Ud·murt Autonomous Soviet Socialist Republic (oōd′moōrt, oōd-moōrt′) An administrative division of east central European Russian S.F.S.R.; 16,300 square miles; capital, Izhevsk.

u·do (oō′dō) *n.* A bushy plant (*Aralia cordata*) of Japan and China which, when young, yields edible shoots. [<Japanese]

u·dom·e·ter (yoō·dom′ə·tər) *n.* A pluviometer. [<L *udus* moist + -METER] — **u·do·met·ric** (yoō′də·met′rik) *adj.* — **u·dom′e·try** *n.*

Ue·le (we′lā) A river of NE Belgian Congo, flowing 700 miles north, NW, and west to a confluence with the Bomu at the border of French Equatorial Africa, forming the Ubangi: also *Welle.*

U·fa (oō·fä′) **1** A city on the Byelaya river in eastern European Russian S.F.S.R.; capital of Bashkir Autonomous S.S.R. **2** A river in eastern European Russian S.F.S.R., flowing 599 miles NW and SW from the southern Urals to the Byelaya river at Ufa.

UFO Unidentified flying object: an official U. S. Air Force designation. Compare FLYING SAUCER.

U·gan·da (yoō·gan′də, oō·gän′dä) An independent member of the Commonwealth of Nations in east central Africa; 93,981 square miles; capital, Kampala.

ug·li·fy (ug′lə·fī) *v.t.* **·fied, ·fy·ing** To make ugly. — **ug′li·fi·ca′tion** (-fə·kā′shən) *n.*

ug·ly (ug′lē) *adj.* **·li·er, ·li·est** **1** Displeasing to the esthetic feelings, as from lack of grace or proportion; distasteful in appearance; ill-looking; unsightly. **2** Repulsive to the moral sentiments; revolting. **3** Bad in character or consequences, as a rumor or a wound. **4** *Colloq.* Ill-tempered; quarrelsome. **5** Portending storms; threatening: said of the weather. [<ON *uggligr* dreadful < *uggr* fear] — **ug′li·ly** *adv.* — **ug′li·ness** *n.*

ugly duckling 1 In Hans Christian Andersen's story, *The Ugly Duckling,* a young swan hatched by a duck, belittled and persecuted by all the ducks for his strange appearance, until he grew into the most beautiful bird on the pond. **2** Any ill-favored or unpromising child who unexpectedly grows into a beauty or a wonder.

U·gri·an (oō′grē·ən, yoō′-) *n.* **1** A member of any of the Finno-Ugric peoples of Hungary and western Siberia, including the Ostyaks, Voguls, and Magyars. **2** Ugric. — *adj.* Of or pertaining to the Ugrians, their culture, or their languages.

U·gric (oō′grik, yoō′-) *n.* A branch of the Finno-Ugric subfamily of Uralic languages, comprising Magyar (Hungarian), Ostyak, and Vogul. — *adj.* Of or pertaining to any of these languages.

uh·lan (oō′län, oō·län′, yoō′lən) *n.* **1** A cavalry-man and lancer of a type originating in eastern

Europe, formerly prominent in European armies, notably the German. **2** One of a body of Tatar militia. Also spelled *ulan.* [<G <Polish <Turkish *ōghlān* lad, servant]

Uh·land (oō′länt), **Johann Ludwig,** 1787–1862, German poet.

Ui·gur (wē′goōr) *n.* **1** One of a Turkic people who ruled in Mongolia and East Turkestan from the eighth to the twelfth century, now the majority of the population of the Sinkiang–Uigur Autonomous Region, NW China. **2** The Turkic language of these people. — **Ui·gu·ri·an** (wē·goōr′ē·ən), **Ui·gu·ric** (wē·goōr′ik) *adj.*

u·in·tah·ite (yoō·in′tə·īt) *n.* A variety of asphalt common in Utah: often called *gilsonite.* Also **u·in′ta·ite.** [from *Uinta Mountains*]

U·in·ta Mountains (yoō·in′tə) A range in NE Utah and SW Wyoming; highest point, 13,498 feet (the highest point in Utah).

uit·land·er (īt′län·dər, oit′-; *Afrikaans* œit′·län·dər) *n. Afrikaans* A foreigner; formerly, in the South African Republic, a foreign white resident.

u·ku·le·le (yoō′kə·lā′lē, *Hawaiian* oō′koō·lā′lä) *n.* A guitar-like musical instrument having four strings. [<Hawaiian, flea <*uku* insect + *lele* jump; from the movements of the fingers in playing]

U·lan (oō′län, oō·län′, yoō′lən) See UHLAN.

U·lan Ba·tor (oō′·län bä′tôr) The capital of the Mongolian People's Republic: formerly *Urga:* Chinese *Kulun.*

UKULELE

U·lan Ho·to (oō′län khō′tō) The capital of Inner Mongolian Autonomous Region, northern China, in the NE part of the Region: Chinese *Wulanhaote:* formerly *Wangyehmiao.* Also *Khoto.*

U·lan–U·de (oō′län·oō·dé′de) The capital of Buryat–Mongol Autonomous S.S.R., in SE central Asiatic Russian S.F.S.R., SE of Baikal lake.

ul·cer (ul′sər) *n.* **1** *Pathol.* An open sore on an external or internal surface of the body, usually accompanied by disintegration of tissue with the formation of pus. **2** Figuratively, a corroding fault or vice; corruption; evil. [<L *ulcus, ulceris*]

ul·cer·ate (ul′sə·rāt) *v.t. & v.i.* **·at·ed, ·at·ing** To make or become ulcerous. [<L *ulceratus,* pp. of *ulcerare* <*ulcus, ulceris* ulcer] — **ul′cer·a′tive** *adj.*

ul·cer·a·tion (ul′sə·rā′shən) *n.* **1** The forming of an ulcer, or the condition of being affected with ulcers. **2** An ulcer, or ulcers collectively.

ul·cer·ous (ul′sər·əs) *adj.* **1** Resembling an ulcer. **2** Affected with ulcers. — **ul′cer·ous·ly** *adv.* — **ul′cer·ous·ness** *n.*

-ule *suffix of nouns* Small; little: used to form diminutives: *granule.* [<F *-ule* <L *-ulus, -ula, -ulum,* diminutive suffix]

u·le·ma (oō′lə·mä′) *n.* **1** In Moslem countries, a council or college of learned officials (priests, judges, or scholars) who are trained in Moslem religion and law, and interpret the Koran. **2** Hence, any Moslem scholar. [<Turkish *'ulema* <Arabic *'ulamā,* pl. of *'alim* wise <*'alama* know]

-ulent *suffix of adjectives* Abounding in; full of (what is indicated in the main element): *opulent, truculent.* Corresponding nouns are formed in **-ulence,** as in *opulence, truculence.* [<L *-ulentus*]

Ul·fi·las (ul′fi·ləs), A.D. 311?–383, bishop of the Goths; translated the Bible into Gothic: also spelled *Wulfila.* Also **Ul′fi·la** (-lə).

ul·lage (ul′ij) *n.* The quantity that a vessel, as a wine cask, lacks of being full; wantage. [<AF *ulliage,* OF *ouillage* <*ouiller* fill up (to the bunghole) <*ueil* eye, bunghole <L *oculus* eye]

Ulm (oōlm) A city on the Danube River in central eastern Baden–Württemberg, SW

West Germany.

ul·ma·ceous (ul·mā′shəs) *adj. Bot.* Designating or belonging to a family (*Ulmaceae*) of shrubs and trees of the order *Urticales,* the elm family, widely distributed in temperate and tropical regions, and characterized by alternate simple leaves, apetalous bisexual or unisexual flowers, and a compressed fruit. [<NL, family name <L *ulmus* elm]

ul·na (ul′nə) *n. pl.* **·nae** (-nē) or **·nas** *Anat.* In vertebrates above fishes, that one of the two long bones of the forearm or foreleg which forms a joint with the radius and is on the same side as the little finger or fifth digit. [<L, elbow] — **ul′nar** *adj.*

-ulose *suffix of adjectives* Marked by or abounding in: widely used in scientific and technical terms: *ramulose.* Compare –ULOUS (def. 2). [<L *-ulosus,* adjective suffix]

U·lot·ri·chi (yoō·lot′rə·kī) *n. pl.* In the classification of Huxley, a subdivision of the human species, characterized by woolly or crispy hair. Also **U·lot′ri·ches** (-kēz). [<NL *Ulotriches* <Gk. *oulothrix, oulotrichos* woolly-haired <*oulos* woolly + *thrix* hair] — **u·lot′ri·chous** (-kəs) *adj.*

-ulous *suffix of adjectives* **1** Tending to do or characterized by (what is indicated by the main element): *tremulous, ridiculous.* **2** Full of: *meticulous, populous.* Compare –ULOSE. [<L *-ulus* and *-ulosus,* adjective suffixes]

ul·ster (ul′stər) *n.* A very long, loose overcoat, sometimes belted at the waist: made originally of frieze from Ulster, Ireland.

Ul·ster (ul′stər) A former province of northern Ireland comprising the nine counties listed below; 8,331 square miles. In 1925 six of the counties (Antrim, Armagh, Downe, Fermanagh, Londonderry, Tyrone: 5,238 square miles) became Northern Ireland and three (Cavan, Donegal, Monaghan: 3,093 square miles) the Province of Ulster of the Republic of Ireland. — **Ul′ster·man** (-mən) *n.*

Ulster cycle The older and more famous of the two cycles of Old Irish epic and romance. The manuscripts date from the seventh and eighth centuries, but celebrate the Ireland and Irish heroes of the first century, and depict a civilization of barbaric splendor that dates back centuries earlier. See FENIAN CYCLE, TAIN BO CUAILGNE.

ul·te·ri·or (ul·tir′ē·ər) *adj.* **1** More remote; not so pertinent as something else to the matter spoken of: applied to immaterial things: *ulterior considerations;* also, intentionally unrevealed; hidden: *ulterior motives.* **2** Following; succeeding; later in time, or secondary in importance. **3** Lying beyond or on the farther side of a certain bounding line. [<L, compar. of *ulter* beyond] — **ul·te′ri·or·ly** *adv.*

ul·ti·ma (ul′tə·mə) *n.* The last syllable of a word. [<L, fem. of *ultimus* last]

ul·ti·mate (ul′tə·mit) *adj.* **1** Beyond which there is no other; last of a series; final. **2** Fundamental or essential; hence, not susceptible of further analysis; elementary; primary. **3** Most distant; farthest; extreme. **4** *Mech.* Designating the maximum strength of a body, or a strain of the least intensity sufficient to cause rupture. — *n.* **1** The final result; last step; conclusion. **2** A fundamental or final fact. [<LL *ultimatus,* orig. pp. of *ultimare* come to an end <*ultimus* farthest, last, superl. of *ulter* beyond] — **ul′ti·mate·ness** *n.*

ul·ti·mate·ly (ul′tə·mit·lē) *adv.* In the end; at last; finally.

ul·ti·ma Thu·le (ul′tə·mə thoō′lē, toō′lē) **1** Farthest Thule: in ancient geography, the northernmost habitable regions of the earth. **2** Any distant, unknown region. **3** The

ULNA
A. Front view.
B. Back view.
a. Elbow joint.
b. Ulna.
c. Radius.
d. Wrist.

ul·ti·ma·tum (ul′tə·mā′təm, -mä′-) *n.* *pl.* **·tums** or **·ta** (-tə) **1** A final statement, as concerning terms or conditions; in diplomacy, the final terms offered by one party during negotiations concerning a treaty, the rejection of which by the other party will result in breaking off all negotiation; loosely, a last proposal, offer, concession, or demand. **2** Anything ultimate. [<NL <LL, neut. of *ultimatus*. See ULTIMATE.]

ul·ti·mo (ul′tə·mō) *adv.* *Latin* In the last month; shortened to *ult.*, following a date: the 15th *ult.*: distinguished from *proximo* (*prox.*) or *instant* (*inst.*).

ul·ti·mo·gen·i·ture (ul′tə·mō·jen′ə·chər) *n.* The rule whereby the youngest son takes the inheritance: the opposite of *primogeniture*. [<L *ultimus* last + GENITURE]

ul·tra (ul′trə) *adj.* Going beyond the bounds of moderation; extreme; extravagant. —*n.* One who holds extreme opinions; a radical. [<L, beyond, on the other side]

ul·tra·cen·tri·fuge (ul′trə·sen′trə·fyōōj) *n.* A centrifuge whose rotor, sometimes driven by blasts of hydrogen, will exert a force of about one million times gravity: used for high precision scientific and laboratory work. — **ul′tra·cen′tri·fu·ga′tion** (-fyōō·gā′shən) *n.*

ul·tra·fil·ter (ul′trə·fil′tər) *n.* *Chem.* A filter having extremely minute pores, as a living membrane or a film of gelatin on filter paper: used to sift out colloidal particles which pass through ordinary filters. — **ul′tra·fil·tra′tion** (-fil·trā′shən) *n.*

ul·tra·high frequency (ul′trə·hī′) Any wave frequency between 300 and 3,000 megahertz. Abbr. *uhf, UHF.*

ul·tra·ist (ul′trə·ist) *n.* One who in opinions or conduct goes beyond moderation; a radical; an extremist. —*adj.* Radical; extreme: also **ul′tra·is′tic.** —**ul′tra·ism** *n.*

ul·tra·ma·rine (ul′trə·mə·rēn′) *n.* **1** A deep, usually purplish-blue, permanent pigment made by treating the powdered mineral lapis lazuli. **2** A similar pigment made largely by synthesis from kaolin, silica, soda, sulfur, and charcoal: also called *new blue, French blue.* **3** The color of ultramarine. —*adj.* Being beyond or across the sea. [<Med. L *ultramarinus* <L *ultra* beyond + *marinus* marine]

ul·tra·mi·crom·e·ter (ul′trə·mī·krom′ə·tər) *n.* A micrometer designed for measurements requiring a high order of precision and accuracy.

ul·tra·mi·cro·scope (ul′trə·mī′krə·skōp) *n.* An optical instrument for detecting objects too small to be seen with an ordinary microscope, by means of an intense beam of light thrown from the side upon the spot to be examined.

ul·tra·mun·dane (ul′trə·mun′dān) *adj.* Extending beyond the world, the solar system, or the present life. [<L *ultramundanus*]

ul·tra·na·tion·al·ism (ul′trə·nash′ən·əl·iz′əm) *n.* Extreme devotion to or support of national, as opposed to international, interests or considerations. —**ul′tra·na′tion·al** *adj.* —**ul′tra·na′tion·al·ist** *n.* & *adj.* —**ul′tra·na′tion·al·is′tic** *adj.*

ul·tra·pho·tic (ul′trə·fō′tik) *adj.* *Physics* Denoting wavelengths of radiant energy beyond the visible region of the spectrum, as ultraviolet and infrared.

ul·tra·son·ic (ul′trə·son′ik) *adj.* *Physics* Pertaining to or designating sound waves having a frequency above the limits of audibility, or in excess of about 20 kilocycles per second: distinguished from *supersonic.*

ul·tra·son·ics (ul′trə·son′iks) *n.* *pl. (construed as singular)* The study of acoustic phenomena in the frequency range above that of audibility.

ul·tra·sound (ul′trə·sound′) *n.* *Physics.* Sound having a frequency above the limits of audibility, or in excess of 20 kilocycles per second.

ul·tra·vi·o·let (ul′trə·vī′ə·lit) *adj.* *Physics* Lying beyond the violet end of the visible spectrum: said of high-frequency light waves more refrangible than the violet and having wavelengths ranging from about 3,900 angstroms to the upper limits of X-rays. Compare INFRARED.

ul·tra vi·res (ul′trə vī′rēz) *Latin* **1** *Law* Beyond the lawful capacity or powers: said especially of corporations as to acts or contracts not within the scope of the powers conferred upon them and which are *ipso facto* void: applied also to the acts which although within their powers have been done without their required consent, as in the case of powers delegated to directors. **2** Figuratively, not permissible; forbidden: a colloquial use.

ul·u·late (yōōl′yə·lāt, ul′-) *v.i.* **·lat·ed, ·lat·ing** To howl, hoot, or wail. [<L *ululatus*, pp. of *ululare* howl] —**ul′u·la′tion** *n.*

um·bel (um′bəl) *n.* *Bot.* An indeterminate inflorescence in which a number of nearly equal pedicels radiate from a small area at the top of a very short axis, giving an umbrellalike appearance. [<L *umbella* a parasol, dim. of *umbra* shadow. Related to UMBRELLA.]

um·bel·late (um′bə·lit, -lāt) *adj.* Disposed in or resembling umbels. Also **um′bel·lar, um′bel·lat·ed.** [<NL *umbellatus*]

um·bel·lif·er·ous (um′bə·lif′ər·əs) *adj.* **1** Bearing umbels. **2** Designating or pertaining to an important and widely distributed family (*Umbelliferae*) of herbs and some shrubs, the parsley or carrot family, comprising many plants used as food, for flavoring, and in medicine. [<NL, family name <L *umbella* parasol + *ferre* bear]

um·bel·lu·late (um·bel′yə·lit, -lāt) *adj.* Having or disposed in umbellules.

um·bel·lule (um′bəl·yōōl, um·bel′-) *n.* *Bot.* A small or secondary umbel. [<NL *umbellula*, dim. of L *umbella* parasol]

um·ber¹ (um′bər) *n.* A chestnut- to liver-brown hydrated ferric oxide, containing some manganese oxide and clay: used as a pigment; also, the color. When in its natural state it is known as **raw umber,** and when heated, so as to produce a reddish-brown, as **burnt umber.** —*adj.* Of or pertaining to umber; of a dusky hue; brownish. —*v.t.* To color with umber; darken, as by staining. [<F (*terre d'*)*ombre* <Ital. *ombra*, prob. <L *Umbra*, fem. of *Umber* of Umbria, where originally found; ? infl. in Ital. by *ombra* shadow, shade <L *umbra*]

um·ber² (um′bər) *n.* **1** Shade; hence, some indefinite dark color. **2** The grayling. [<F *ombre* <L *umbra* shadow]

um·bil·i·cal (um·bil′i·kəl) *adj.* **1** Pertaining to or situated near the umbilicus. **2** Placed near the navel; central. —*n.* **1** A long, flexible tube that serves as a connecting device, conduit for air, power, communication, etc., for an astronaut or aquanaut when outside the craft. **2** A similar device used as a source of fuel, etc., for a spacecraft before launching. [<LL *umbilicalis* <L *umbilicus* navel]

umbilical cord *Anat.* The ropelike tissue connecting the navel of the fetus with the placenta.

um·bil·i·cate (um·bil′ə·kit, -kāt) *adj.* **1** Resembling a navel, as by having a central depression or mark. **2** Having an umbilicus or navel-shaped depression, as a shell. Also **um·bil′i·cat·ed.** —**um·bil′i·ca′tion** *n.*

um·bil·i·cus (um·bil′ə·kəs, um′bə·lī′kəs) *n.* *pl.* **·ci** (-sī) **1** *Anat.* The depression at the middle of the abdomen where the umbilical cord of the fetus was attached; the navel. **2** *Zool.* An indention or depression at the axial base of a spiral shell, as in many gastropods. **3** *Ornithol.* Either of the apertures (inferior and superior) of the calamus of a feather. **4** *Bot.* A navel-shaped depression; a hilum. [<L]

um·bles (um′bəlz) *n. pl.* The entrails of a deer; humbles. [Var. of NUMBLES]

um·bo (um′bō) *n. pl.* **um·bo·nes** (um·bō′nēz) or **·bos 1** The boss or projecting spike in the center of a shield. **2** *Zool.* An elevation, boss, or knob, as the prominence of a bivalve shell near the hinge, or the plate of an echinoderm. **3** *Bot.* The top of the cap of certain fungi. **4** *Anat.* The surface of the tympanic membrane at the point of attachment to the malleus. [<L] —**um′bo·nal, um·bon·ic** (um·bon′ik) *adj.*

um·bra (um′brə) *n. pl.* **·brae** (-brē) **1** That region of a shadow from which the direct light is entirely cut off. **2** *Astron.* **a** In an eclipse, that part of the shadow of the earth or moon within which the moon or the sun is entirely hidden. See PENUMBRA. **b** The inner dark portion of a sunspot. [<L, shadow]

um·brage (um′brij) *n.* **1** Resentment, as at being obscured by another. **2** A sense of injury; offense: now usually in **to give** (or **take**) **umbrage. 3** That which gives shade, as a leafy tree. **4** *Poetic* Shade or shadow cast. See synonyms under PIQUE. [<F *ombrage* <L *umbraticus* shady <*umbra* shade]

um·brel·la (um·brel′ə) *n.* **1** A light portable canopy on a folding frame, carried as a protection against sun or rain. **2** *Zool.* The contractile, jellylike portion of the body of a medusa expanded like a bell or umbrella. **3** Something serving as a cover or shield, or as a means of linking together various things under a common designation or sponsoring agency: the expanding *umbrella* of nuclear power; various theater groups appearing under the *umbrella* of UNESCO. —*adj.* Being or serving as an umbrella (def. 3): an *umbrella* organization; an *umbrella* statement. [<Ital. *ombrella,* alter. (after *ombra* shade) of L *umbrella* parasol. Related to UMBEL.]

umbrella bird Any of several South American birds (genus *Cephalopterus*), the male of which has a broad crest likened to an umbrella. *C. ornatus* has lustrous black plumage with an umbrellalike crest of blue, hairlike feathers.

umbrella leaf A smooth perennial herb (*Diphylleia cymosa*) of the barberry family, with a single large peltate leaf, one to two feet across, and a terminal cyme of white flowers. It is found in the southern United States.

umbrella palm A palm (*Hedyscepe canterburyana*) having pinnate leaves, native to Lord Howe Island in the British Solomons.

umbrella tree 1 A small magnolia (*Magnolia tripetala*) of the southern United States, with fragrant white flowers and oval leaves 16 to 30 inches long, crowded in an umbrellalike whorl at the ends of the branches. **2** Any one of several other trees with large, round cordate leaves.

um·brel·la·wort (um·brel′ə·wûrt) *n.* A typically North American herb (genus *Allionia*) with the flowers enclosed in a three- or four-parted involucre.

um·brif·er·ous (um·brif′ər·əs) *adj.* Affording or making a shade; umbrageous. [<L *umbrifer* <*umbra* shade + *ferre* bear] —**um·brif′er·ous·ly** *adv.*

um·laut (ōōm′lout) *n.* **1** *Ling.* **a** The change in quality of a vowel sound caused by its partial assimilation to a vowel or semivowel (often later lost) in the following syllable; vowel mutation: primarily a phenomenon of the Germanic languages. English plurals showing internal vowel modification, such as *feet* and *geese,* are a result of this process. **b** A vowel which has been so altered, as *ä, ö,* and *ü* in German. **2** In German, the two dots (¨) put over a vowel modified by umlaut: short for **umlaut-mark.** —*v.t.* To modify by umlaut or mutation. [<G, change of sound <*um* about + *laut* sound]

Um·nak Island (ōōm′nak) One of the Fox Islands in the Aleutian Islands; 83 miles long, 2 to 18 miles wide.

um·pir·age (um′pīr·ij, -pə·rij) *n.* The office or function of an umpire. Also **um′pire·ship.**

um·pire (um′pīr) *n.* **1** *Law* A person called upon to settle a disagreement in opinion between arbitrators. **2** In general, anything by which a question in controversy is settled. **3** In various games, as baseball, a person chosen to enforce the rules of the game, and in case of controversy to settle disputed points. See synonyms under JUDGE. —*v.t.* & *v.i.* **·pired, ·pir·ing** To decide as umpire; act as umpire (of or in). [Apheic alter. of ME *noumpere* <OF *nonper* odd, uneven (i.e., third) <*non* not + *per* even, equal]

UN See UNITED NATIONS.

un-¹ *prefix* Not; opposed to. [OE] ◆ **Un-¹** is used to express negation, lack, incompleteness or opposition. It is freely attached to adjectives and adverbs, less often to nouns. See UN-².

un-² *prefix* Back. [OE *un-, on-, and-*] ◆ **Un-²** is used to express reversal of the action of verbs, or to form verbs from nouns indicating removal from the state or quality expressed by the noun, or sometimes to intensify the force of negative verbs. Beginning at the foot of this page will be found a partial list of words which are formed with un-¹ and un-². Other compounds of these prefixes, with strongly positive, specific, or special meanings, will be found in vocabulary place. In the verbs in the list *un-* gives the sense of reversal: *unchain* "to loose the chains of." In the nouns and the adjectives usually it has negative or privative force. Thus, *unburdened* may be regarded as an adjective meaning "not burdened," or as a participle of the verb *unburden*, meaning "relieved of a burden." *In-* as a prefix of adjectives expresses in usage more of negation, *un-* more of mere lack or privation: a child's *unartistic* speech, a writer's *inartistic* diction. In general, *in-* is more confined to words of Latin origin.

Pronunciations may be ascertained by consulting the second element in its vocabulary place.

un·a·ble (un·ā′bəl) *adj.* **1** Lacking the necessary power or resources; not able: usually used with an infinitive: *unable* to walk. **2** Lacking mental capacity; incompetent. **3** *Obs.* Feeble; helpless. — **un·a·bil·i·ty** (un′ə·bil′ə·tē) *Obs.* — **un·a′bly** *Obs. adv.*

un·a·bridged (un′ə·brijd′) *adj.* Not abridged; not being a shorter or condensed version of another work; original and complete in itself: an *unabridged* dictionary.

un·ac·com·mo·dat·ed (un′ə·kom′ə·dā′tid) *adj.* **1** Not made suitable; ill-adapted or -adjusted. **2** Being without accommodations or conveniences.

un·ac·com·mo·dat·ing (un′ə·kom′ə·dā′ting) *adj.* Not disposed to accommodate; unobliging.

un·ac·com·plished (un′ə·kom′plisht) *adj.* **1** Having fallen short of accomplishment; not done or finished. **2** Lacking accomplishments.

un·ac·count·a·ble (un′ə·koun′tə·bəl) *adj.* **1** Impossible to be accounted for; inexplicable; hence, remarkable; extraordinary. **2** Exempt from supervision or control; irresponsible. — **un′ac·count′a·ble·ness** *n.* — **un′ac·count′a·bly** *adv.*

un·ac·count·ed-for (un′ə·koun′tid-fôr′) *adj.* Unexplained; not accounted for.

un·ac·cus·tomed (un′ə·kus′təmd) *adj.* **1** Not made familiar by use or by practice: *unaccustomed* to hardship. **2** Not familiar or well known; strange: an *unaccustomed* sight. — **un′ac·cus′tomed·ness** *n.*

un·ad·vised (un′əd·vīzd′) *adj.* **1** Not advised; not having received advice. **2** Rash or imprudent; lacking consideration. — **un′ad·vis′ed·ly** (-vī′zid-lē) *adv.* — **un′ad·vis′ed·ness** *n.*

un·af·fect·ed (un′ə·fek′tid) *adj.* **1** Not showing affectation; natural; sincere; real. **2** Not influenced or changed. See synonyms under SIMPLE. — **un′af·fect′ed·ly** *adv.* — **un′af·fect′ed·ness** *n.*

Un·a·las·ka Island (un′ə·las′kə, ōō′nə-) One of the SW Fox Islands of the Aleutian Islands; 30 miles long, 6 to 30 miles wide.

un·al·ien·a·ble (un·āl′yən·ə·bəl) *adj. Obs.* Inalienable.

un·al·loyed (un′ə·loid′) *adj.* Free from alloy or admixture; pure; also, figuratively, perfectly complete; absolute: *unalloyed* content.

un-A·mer·i·can (un′ə·mer′ə·kən) *adj.* Not having characteristics of persons or things native to the United States; lacking in patriotism and national feeling toward the United States; not consistent with American ideals, objectives, spirit, etc.

un·a·neled (un′ə·nēld′) *adj. Obs.* Not having received extreme unction. [<UN-¹ + ANELE]

u·na·nim·i·ty (yōō′nə·nim′ə·tē) *n.* The state of being unanimous; complete agreement in opinion or purpose. See synonyms under HARMONY. [<OF *unanimité* <L *unanimitas, -tatis* <*unanimus*. See UNANIMOUS.]

u·nan·i·mous (yōō·nan′ə·məs) *adj.* **1** Sharing the same views or sentiments; consentient; harmonious. **2** Establishing or expressive of unanimity; showing or resulting from the assent of all concerned: the *unanimous* voice of the jury. [<L *unanimus, unanimis* <*unus* one + *animus* mind] — **u·nan′i·mous·ly** *adv.* — **u·nan′i·mous·ness** *n.*

un·ap·peal·a·ble (un′ə·pēl′ə·bəl) *adj.* **1** Admitting no appeal to a higher court: an *unappealable* case. **2** That cannot be appealed from; conclusive; final.

un·ap·pro·pri·at·ed (un′ə·prō′prē·ā′tid) *adj.* Not set apart for special use; not taken possession of by or formally granted to a particular person or company.

un·ap·proved (un′ə·prōōvd′) *adj.* **1** Not regarded with approval; not approved. **2** *Obs.* Not verified by proof; not proved.

un·apt (un·apt′) *adj.* **1** Not likely or inclined. **2** Not suitable or qualified. **3** Not ready-witted. — **un·apt′ly** *adv.* — **un·apt′ness** *n.*

un·ar·gued (un·är′gyōōd) *adj.* **1** Not argued; undebated. **2** Undisputed. **3** *Obs.* Not censured: a Latinism.

un·armed (un·ärmd′) *adj.* **1** Not armed; without weapons. **2** Having no sharp, hard projections, as spines, prickles, plates, etc.: said of plants and animals.

un·as·sum·ing (un′ə·sōō′ming) *adj.* Unpretentious; modest. — **un′as·sum′ing·ly** *adv.*

un·at·tached (un′ə·tacht′) *adj.* **1** Not attached. **2** *Law* Not held or seized, as in satisfaction of a judgment. **3** In the armed forces, not assigned to a regiment or company.

u·nau (yōō·nō′, -nô′, ōō·nou′) *n.* The common two-toed sloth of Brazil (genus *Choloepus*). [<F <Tupian]

u·na vo·ce (yōō′nə vō′sē) *Latin* Unanimously; with one voice.

un·a·void·a·ble (un′ə·voi′də·bəl) *adj.* **1** That cannot be avoided; inevitable. **2** That cannot be made null and void; not voidable. See synonyms under NECESSARY.

un·a·ware (un′ə·wâr′) *adj.* **1** Giving no heed; not cognizant, as of something specified. *Poetic* Carelessly unmindful; inattentive; heedless. — *adv. Obs.* Unawares.

un·backed (un·bakt′) *adj.* **1** Never having borne a rider, as a horse; unbroken. **2** Left without backers or support; not supported financially; also, in sports, not wagered on. **3** Without a back, as a stool.

un·baked (un·bākt′) *adj.* **1** Not baked; insufficiently baked. **2** Immature; crude.

un·bal·ance (un·bal′əns) *v.t.* ·anced, ·anc·ing **1** To deprive of balance. **2** To disturb or derange.

un·bal·anced (un·bal′ənst) *adj.* **1** Not in a state of equilibrium. **2** In bookkeeping, not adjusted so as to balance. **3** Lacking mental balance; unsound; erratic.

un·bal·last·ed (un·bal′əs·tid) *adj.* **1** Not steadied by ballast. **2** Not firm; wavering.

un·bar (un·bär′) *v.* ·barred, ·bar·ring *v.t.* To remove the bar from. — *v.i.* To become unlocked or unbarred; open.

un·barbed (un·bärbd′) *adj.* **1** Not fitted or made with barbs. **2** *Obs.* Untrimmed; unbarbered.

un·bat·ed (un·bā′tid) *adj. Archaic* **1** Not bated or blunted by having a button on the point, as a lance or other thrusting weapon. **2** Unabated; undiminished.

un·bear (un·bâr′) *v.t.* ·beared, ·bear·ing To free from the pressure of the checkrein, as a horse.

un·be·com·ing (un′bi·kum′ing) *adj.* **1** Not becoming; unsuited to the wearer, place, or surroundings: an *unbecoming* robe. **2** Not befitting; not worthy of. **3** Not decorous; improper. — **un′be·com′ing·ly** *adv.* — **un′be·com′ing·ness** *n.*

un·be·known (un′bi·nōn′) *adj.* Unknown: used with *to*. Also **un′be·knownst′** (-nōnst′).

un·be·lief (un′bi·lēf′) *n.* **1** Absence of positive belief; incredulity. **2** A refusal to believe; belief in a contrary proposition; disbelief, as in religion. **3** In Scriptural use, lack of faith in God's promises. See synonyms under DOUBT.

un·be·liev·er (un′bi·lē′vər) *n.* **1** One who withholds belief. **2** One who has no religious faith. **3** One having a religion different from that of the speaker or writer; specifically, a non-Christian. See synonyms under SKEPTIC.

un·bend (un·bend′) *v.* ·bent, ·bend·ing *v.t.* **1** To relax, as from exertion or formality: to *unbend* the mind. **2** To straighten (something bent or curved). **3** To relax, as a bow, from tension. **4** *Naut.* **a** To loose; untie, as a rope. **b** To detach or remove (a sail) from a spar or stay. — *v.i.* **5** To become free of restraint or formality; relax. **6** To become straight or nearly straight again.

un·bend·ing (un·ben′ding) *adj.* Not bending easily; stiff; hence, unyielding; resolute; firm,

as character. — *n.* Relaxation. — **un·bend′-ing·ly** *adv.* — **un·bend′ing·ness** *n.*

un·bi·ased (un·bī′əst) *adj.* Having no bias; especially, having no mental bias; not prejudiced or warped; impartial. Also **un·bi′assed.** — **un·bi′ased·ly** *adv.* — **un·bi′ased·ness** *n.*

un·bid·den (un·bid′n) *adj.* **1** Not commanded; not invited: an *unbidden* guest. **2** Not called forth; spontaneous: *unbidden* thoughts. Also **un·bid′.**

un·bind (un·bīnd′) *v.t.* ·bound, ·bind·ing **1** To free from bindings; undo; hence, to release. **2** To remove, as something that binds; unfasten. See synonyms under RELEASE. [OE *unbindan*]

un·bit·ted (un·bit′id) *adj.* Not furnished with or restrained by a bit or bridle; uncontrolled.

un·blenched (un·blencht′) *adj. Obs.* Not dismayed or confounded.

un·blessed (un·blest′) *adj.* **1** Not having been blessed or admitted to blessedness or divine favor. **2** Unhappy. **3** Unhallowed or unholy; evil.

un·blood·y (un·blud′ē) *adj.* **1** Not stained by blood; hence, not attended with slaughter, as a conflict. **2** Not of a bloodthirsty disposition.

un·blush·ing (un·blush′ing) *adj.* Not blushing; immodest; shameless. — **un·blush′ing·ly** *adv.*

un·bod·ied (un·bod′ēd) *adj.* **1** Having no body; immaterial. **2** Disembodied.

un·bolt (un·bōlt′) *v.t.* To release, as a door, by withdrawing a bolt; unlock; open. — *v.i. Obs.* To remove a bolt or bar; hence, to expose something to view; make explanation.

un·bolt·ed (un·bōl′tid) *adj.* Not fastened by bolts; not bolted.

un·boned (un·bōnd′) *adj.* **1** Without bones. **2** Not having had the bones removed.

un·bon·net (un·bon′it) *v.t. & v.i.* To remove the bonnet or other covering from (the head); uncover. — **un·bon′net·ed** *adj.*

un·born (un·bôrn′) *adj.* **1** Not yet born; of a future time or generation; future. **2** Not in existence.

un·bos·om (un·bōōz′əm, -bōō′zəm) *v.t.* To reveal, as one's thoughts or secrets; disclose or give vent to: often used reflexively. — *v.i.* To say what is troubling one; tell one's thoughts, feelings, etc. — **un·bos′om·er** *n.*

un·bound·ed (un·boun′did) *adj.* **1** Having no bounds; of unlimited extent; very great; boundless. **2** Having no boundary, as a line that returns into itself or a closed surface. **3** Going beyond bounds; unrestrained. — **un·bound′ed·ly** *adv.* — **un·bound′ed·ness** *n.*

un·bowed (un·boud′) *adj.* Not bent; not bowed or subdued; proud in defeat or adversity.

un·brace (un·brās′) *v.t.* ·braced, ·brac·ing **1** To free from bands or braces. **2** To free from tension; loosen. **3** To weaken; make feeble.

un·breathed (un·brēthd′) *adj.* **1** Not breathed; hence, not whispered, or spoken; not communicated to another. **2** *Obs.* Unexercised; not practiced.

un·bred (un·bred′) *adj.* **1** Devoid of good breeding; ill-bred. **2** Not taught; untrained: sometimes followed by *to*: *unbred* to spinning. **3** *Obs.* Unbegotten; not born.

un·bri·dled (un·brīd′ld) *adj.* **1** Having no bridle on: an *unbridled* horse. **2** Without restraint; unrestrained; unruly: an *unbridled* tongue; *unbridled* license. — **un·bri′dled·ly** *adv.* — **un·bri′dled·ness** *n.*

un·bro·ken (un·brō′kən) *adj.* **1** Not broken; whole; entire: an *unbroken* seal. **2** Unviolated: *unbroken* faith; an *unbroken* promise. **3** Uninterrupted; regular; smooth: *unbroken* sleep; an *unbroken* prairie. **4** Not weakened; strong; firm. **5** Not broken to harness or service, as a draft animal. **6** Not disarranged or thrown out of order. Also *Obs.* **un·broke′.** — **un·bro′ken·ly** *adv.* — **un·bro′ken·ness** *n.*

un·buck·le (un·buk′əl) *v.t. & v.i.* ·led, ·ling To unfasten the buckle or buckles (of).

un·bur·den (un·bûr′dən) *v.t.* To free from a burden; relieve. Also *Archaic* **un·bur′then** (-thən).

un·but·ton (un·but′n) *v.t.* To unfasten the button or buttons of.

un·caged (un·kājd′) *adj.* **1** Not locked up in

a cage; free. **2** Released from a cage; freed.

un·called (un·kôld′) *adj.* Not in response to a summons; without being asked or demanded.

un·called-for (un·kôld′fôr′) *adj.* Unnecessary; gratuitous; not justified by circumstances; discourteous.

un·can·ny (un·kan′ē) *adj.* **1** Exciting superstitious fear; weird; unnatural; eerie. **2** So good as to seem almost supernatural in origin: *uncanny* accuracy. **3** *Scot.* Dangerous; severe, as a wound. — **un·can′ni·ly** *adv.* — **un·can′ni·ness** *n.*

un·cap (un·kap′) *v.* **·capped, ·cap·ping** *v.t.* To take off the cap or covering of. — *v.i.* To remove the hat or cap, as in respect.

un·ca·pa·ble (un·kā′pə·bəl) *adj. Obs.* Incapable.

un·cer·e·mo·ni·ous (un′ser·ə·mō′nē·əs) *adj.* Informal; abrupt; discourteous. — **un′cer·e·mo′ni·ous·ly** *adv.*

un·cer·tain (un·sûr′tən) *adj.* **1** Not certain; that cannot be relied upon; variable; changeful; fitful; erring: an *uncertain* friend; *uncertain* weather; an *uncertain* shot. **2** That cannot be certainly predicted; being of doubtful issue. **3** Not having certain knowledge or assured conviction. **4** Not surely or exactly known: a lady of *uncertain* age. **5** Having no exact or precise significance: *uncertain* phraseology. See synonyms under EQUIVOCAL, PRECARIOUS, VAGUE. — **un·cer′tain·ly** *adv.*

un·cer·tain·ty (un·sûr′tən·tē) *n. pl.* **·ties 1** The state of being uncertain; doubt; also **un·cer′tain·ness. 2** A doubtful matter; a contingency. See synonyms under DOUBT.

uncertainty principle *Physics* A statement of the impossibility of exactly determining at any given instant or by a single operation more than one magnitude or quantity, as the velocity, position, etc., of an electron: also called *indeterminacy principle.*

un·chain (un·chān′) *v.t.* To release from a chain; set free.

un·charged (un·chärjd′) *adj.* **1** Not loaded. **2** Not attacked or accused. **3** Not required or asked to pay a price or meet an expense. **4** Having no electrical charge.

un·char·i·ta·ble (un·char′ə·tə·bəl) *adj.* Not charitable; harsh in judgment; censorious. — **un·char′i·ta·ble·ness** *n.* — **un·char′i·ta·bly** *adv.*

un·chris·tian (un·kris′chən) *adj.* **1** Unbecoming to a Christian. **2** Foreign to Christianity; hence, uncharitable, ungracious, rude, etc. **3** Non-Christian; pagan.

un·church (un·chûrch′) *v.t.* **1** To deprive of membership in a church; expel from a church. **2** To excommunicate. **3** To deny the validity of the sacraments and order of, as a sect.

un·cial (un′shəl, -shē·əl) *adj.* Pertaining to or consisting of a form of letters found in manuscripts from the fourth to the eighth century, and resembling modern capitals but more rounded. — *n.* **1** An uncial letter. **2** An uncial manuscript. [< L *uncialis* inch-high < *uncia* inch, ounce]

UNCIALS

a. Greek uncials — fifth century.
b. Latin uncials — circa A.D. 700.

un·ci·form (un′sə·fôrm) *adj.* Shaped like a hook; hooklike. — *n.* The unciform bone. [< L *uncus* hook + -FORM]

unciform bone *Anat.* A bone of the distal row of the wrist on the ulnar side, articulating with the fourth and fifth metacarpals.

unciform process *Anat.* **1** A projection upon the anterior surface of the unciform bone. **2** The uncinate process.

un·ci·na·ri·a·sis (un′si·nə·rī′ə·sis) *n. Pathol.* Ancylostomiasis. [< NL < *Uncinaria*, genus name < L *uncinus* a hook, barb, dim. of *uncus* hook]

un·ci·nate (un′sə·nit, -nāt) *adj. Biol.* Hooked or bent at the end; having a hooked appendage. Also **un′ci·nal, un′ci·nat·ed.** [< L *uncinatus* < *uncinus,* dim. of *uncus* hook]

uncinate process *Anat.* A hooklike process on the eth-

UNCINATE APPENDAGES

moid bone.

un·cir·cum·cised (un·sûr′kəm·sīzd) *adj.* Not circumcised; Gentile; heathen.

un·cir·cum·ci·sion (un′sûr·kəm·sizh′ən) *n.* **1** The state of being uncircumcised. **2** Those not circumcised; in Scripture, the Gentiles.

un·civ·il (un·siv′əl) *adj.* **1** Wanting in civility; discourteous; ill-bred. **2** *Obs.* Uncivilized. See synonyms under BLUFF, HAUGHTY. — **un·civ′il·ly** *adv.*

un·civ·i·lized (un·siv′ə·līzd) *adj.* Destitute of civilization; barbarous. See synonyms under BARBAROUS.

un·clad (un·klad′) *adj.* Without clothes; naked.

un·clasp (un·klasp′, -kläsp′) *v.t.* **1** To release from a clasp. **2** To release the clasp of. — *v.i.* **3** To become released from a clasp.

un·cle (ung′kəl) *n.* **1** The brother of one's father or mother; also, the husband of one's aunt. ◆ Collateral adjective: *avuncular.* **2** An elderly man: used in direct address. **3** *Colloq.* A pawnbroker. [< F *oncle* < L *avunculus* a mother's brother, orig. dim. of *avus* grandfather]

un·clean (un·klēn′) *adj.* **1** Not clean; foul. **2** Characterized by impure thoughts; unchaste; depraved. **3** Ceremonially impure. See synonyms under FOUL. — **un·clean′ness** *n.*

un·clean·ly (un·klen′lē) *adj.* **1** Lacking cleanliness. **2** Impure; indecent; not chaste. [< UN-[1] + CLEANLY, *adj.*] — **un·clean′li·ness** *n.*

un·clear (un′klir′) *adj.* **1** Not clear. **2** Not easily understandable; confused or muddled: His point was *unclear* to me.

un·clench (un·klench′) *v.t. & v.i.* To relax or open from a clenched condition. Also **un·clinch′** (-klinch′)

Uncle Re·mus (rē′məs) In Joel Chandler Harris's folk tales, an old southern Negro who tells the stories of Br'er Rabbit, Br'er Fox, and others to a small white boy.

Uncle Sam The personification of the government of the United States or of the people of the United States: represented as a tall, lean man with chin whiskers, wearing a plug hat, blue swallow–tailed coat, and red–and–white striped pants. See BROTHER JONATHAN.

Uncle Tom 1 The chief character in Harriet Beecher Stowe's *Uncle Tom's Cabin,* a faithful, elderly Negro slave. **2** *U.S. Slang* A Negro who toadies or truckles to white men: a contemptuous term.

un·cloak (un·klōk′) *v.t.* **1** To remove the cloak or covering from. **2** To unmask; expose. — *v.i.* **3** To remove one's cloak or outer garments.

un·close (un·klōz′) *v.t. & v.i.* **·closed, ·clos·ing 1** To open or set open. **2** To reveal; disclose. — **un·closed′** *adj.*

un·cock (un·kok′) *v.t.* **1** To release and let down the hammer of (a firearm) without exploding the charge. **2** To restore to usual position, as a hat.

un·coil (un·koil′) *v.t. & v.i.* To unwind or become unwound.

un·coined (un·koind′) *adj.* **1** Not fabricated; natural. **2** Not minted.

un·com·fort·a·ble (un·kum′fər·tə·bəl, -kumpf′· tə·bəl) *adj.* **1** Not at ease; feeling discomfort. **2** Causing uneasiness or disquietude, physical or mental; disquieting. — **un·com′· fort·a·bly** *adv.*

un·com·mer·cial (un′kə·mûr′shəl) *adj.* **1** Not engaged or versed in commerce. **2** Conflicting with the spirit of commerce.

un·com·mit·ted (un′kə·mit′id) *adj.* **1** Not committed; specifically, not performed or done. **2** Not entrusted. **3** Not bound by a pledge.

un·com·mon (un·kom′ən) *adj.* Unusual; remarkable. See synonyms under EXTRAORDINARY, ODD, RARE. — **un·com′mon·ly** *adv.*

un·com·mu·ni·ca·tive (un′kə·myōō′nə·kə·tiv, -nə·kā′tiv) *adj.* Not communicative; not disposed to talk, either to express oneself or to give information; reserved; taciturn.

un·com·pro·mis·ing (un·kom′prə·mī′zing) *adj.* Making or admitting of no compromise; inflexible; strict. — **un·com′pro·mis′ing·ly** *adv.* — **un·com′pro·mis′ing·ness** *n.*

un·con·cern (un′kən·sûrn′) *n.* Absence of or freedom from concern or anxiety; indifference. See synonyms under APATHY.

un·con·cerned (un′kən·sûrnd′) *adj.* Undisturbed; not anxious; indifferent. — **un·con·cern′ed·ly** (-sûr′nid·lē) *adv.* — **un·con·cern′ed·ness** *n.*

un·con·di·tion·al (un′kən·dish′ən·əl) *adj.* Limited by no conditions; absolute. See synonyms under ABSOLUTE. — **un′con·di′tion·al·ly** *adv.*

unconditional surrender The unconditional acceptance of military defeat by a warring enemy power, subject only to terms to be subsequently imposed by the victors.

un·con·di·tioned (un′kən·dish′ənd) *adj.* **1** Not restricted; unconditional. **2** In metaphysics, not limited by conditions of space or time; free from relation; unrelated; absolute. **3** *Psychol.* Not having a reaction or reflex developed by a specified condition or conditions; not acquired; natural. **4** Admitted to a school, college, or higher class without condition.

un·con·form·a·ble (un′kən·fôr′mə·bəl) *adj.* **1** Not conforming or conformable; inconsistent. **2** *Geol.* Showing unconformity. — **un′con·form′a·bil′i·ty, un′con·form′a·ble·ness** *n.* — **un′con·form′a·bly** *adv.*

un·con·form·i·ty (un′kən·fôr′mə·tē) *n. pl.* **·ties 1** Want of conformity; nonconformity. **2** *Geol.* **a** A lack of continuity between groups of stratified rocks in contact, indicative of a gap in the stratigraphic record. **b** The contact layer between such groups.

un·con·scion·a·ble (un·kon′shən·ə·bəl) *adj.* **1** Going beyond customary or reasonable bounds. **2** Not governed by sense or prudence; unconscientious; devoid of conscience. **3** *Law* Inequitable. — **un·con′scion·a·ble·ness** *n.* — **un·con′scion·a·bly** *adv.*

un·con·scious (un·kon′shəs) *adj.* **1** Temporarily deprived of consciousness. **2** Not cognizant; unaware: with *of: unconscious* of his charm. **3** Not known or felt to exist; not produced or accompanied by conscious effort: *unconscious* thought. **4** Not endowed with consciousness or a mind. — *n. Psychoanal.* That extensive area of the psyche which is not in the immediate field of awareness and whose content, when consisting of repressed material, may affect the personality through dreams, morbid fears and compulsions, forms of behavior, etc.: with *the.* — **un·con′scious·ly** *adv.* — **un·con′scious·ness** *n.*

un·con·sol·i·dat·ed (un′kən·sol′ə·dā′tid) *adj. Geol.* Not compact or solid, as rock or soil material in a form of loose aggregation.

un·con·sti·tu·tion·al (un′kon·sti·tōō′shən·əl, -tyōō′-) *adj.* Contrary to or violative of the constitution or fundamental law of a state. — **un′con·sti·tu′tion·al′i·ty** *n.* — **un′con·sti·tu′tion·al·ly** *adv.*

un·con·trol·la·ble (un′kən·trō′lə·bəl) *adj.* Beyond control; ungovernable. See synonyms under REBELLIOUS, VIOLENT. — **un′con·trol′la·ble·ness, un′con·trol′la·bil′i·ty** *n.* — **un′con·trol′la·bly** *adv.*

un·con·ven·tion·al (un′kən·ven′shən·əl) *adj.* Not adhering to conventional rules; informal; free. — **un′con·ven′tion·al′i·ty** *n.* — **un′con·ven′tion·al·ly** *adv.*

un·con·vert·ed (un′kən·vûr′tid) *adj.* **1** Not converted. **2** *Theol.* Impenitent; without saving faith.

un·count·ed (un·koun′tid) *adj.* **1** Not counted. **2** Beyond counting; innumerable.

un·cou·ple (un·kup′əl) *v.* **·led, ·ling** *v.t.* **1** To disconnect or unfasten. **2** To set loose; unleash (dogs). — *v.i.* **3** To break loose. — **un·coup′led** (-kup′əld) *adj.*

un·couth (un·kōōth′) *adj.* **1** Marked by awkwardness or oddity; outlandish; ungainly; unrefined; rough. **2** Not common; not wellknown. **3** Mysterious; alarming. See synonyms under AWKWARD, BARBAROUS, RUSTIC. [OE *uncûth* unknown < *un-* not + *cûth,* pp. of *cunnan* know] — **un·couth′ly** *adv.* — **un·couth′ness** *n.*

un·cov·e·nant·ed (un·kuv′ə·nən·tid) *adj.* **1** Not bound by a covenant or promise; not having entered into a covenant or league. **2** Not guaranteed by a covenant: used specifically to describe divine grace or mercy not promised by a covenant.

un·cov·er (un·kuv′ər) *v.t.* **1** To remove the covering from. **2** To make known; reveal; disclose. **3** In military tactics, to expose successively, as lines of formation. — *v.i.* **4** To remove a covering; raise or remove the hat, in token of respect.

un·cov·ered (un·kuv′ərd) *adj.* **1** Not covered; devoid of covering. **2** Not covered by collateral security.

un·cre·ate (un'krē·āt') *v.t.* **·at·ed**, **·at·ing** To deprive of existence.

un·cre·at·ed (un'krē·ā'tid) *adj.* **1** Not yet created or brought into being. **2** *Philos.* Not created; self-existent.

unc·tion (ungk'shən) *n.* **1** The act of anointing, as with oil. **2** *Eccl.* **a** A ceremonial anointing with oil, as in consecration or dedication. **b** The sacramental rite of anointing the sick, reserved in the Roman Catholic Church for those in danger of death: also called *extreme unction.* **3** The act of treating medicinally by anointing. **4** A substance used in anointing, as an unguent or a salve; something that soothes or palliates. **5** The quality or characteristic of speech, especially in religious discourse, that awakens or is intended to awaken deep sympathetic feeling; sometimes, effusive or affected emotion. [< F *onction* < L *unctio, -onis* < *ungere* anoint] — **unc'·tion·less** *adj.*

unc·tu·ous (ungk'chōō·əs) *adj.* **1** Having the characteristics of an unguent; greasy. **2** Characterized by deep sympathetic feeling. **3** Characterized by affected emotion; hence, oily-tongued; unduly suave. **4** Being greasy or soapy to the touch, as certain minerals. **5** Soft; rich in organic matter, as certain soils. **6** Having plasticity, as clay. [< Med. L *unctuosus* < L *unctum* ointment, orig. neut. pp. of *ungere* anoint] — **unc'tu·ous·ly** *adv.* — **unc'·tu·ous·ness** *n.* — **unc·tu·os·i·ty** (-chōō·os'ə·tē) *n.*

un·damped (un·dampt') *adj. Physics* Pertaining to or designating those electromagnetic oscillations which continue without change in amplitude: *undamped* radio waves.

un·daunt·ed (un·dôn'tid, -dän'-) *adj.* Not daunted; fearless; intrepid. See synonyms under BRAVE. — **un·daunt'ed·ly** *adv.* — **un·daunt'ed·ness** *n.*

un·dé (un'dā) *adj. Her.* Wavy; undulating: said of an ordinary or of the lines dividing the shield. Also **un'dée**, **un'dy** (-dē). [< OF < L *unda* wave]

un·dec·a·gon (un·dek'ə·gon) *n.* A figure that has eleven angles and eleven sides. [< L *undecim* eleven + -GON]

un·de·ceiv·a·ble (un'di·sē'və·bəl) *adj.* **1** That cannot be deceived. **2** *Obs.* Not deceitful.

un·de·ceive (un'di·sēv') *v.t.* **·ceived**, **·ceiv·ing** To free from deception, error, or illusion.

un·de·ceived (un'di·sēvd') *adj.* **1** Not deceived. **2** Freed from error or deception.

un·de·cen·ni·al (un'di·sen'ē·əl) *adj.* **1** Pertaining to a period of eleven years or to the eleventh year. **2** Lasting eleven years, or occurring or celebrated on the eleventh year or every eleven years. Also **un'de·cen'na·ry** (-sen'ər·ē). [< L *undecim* eleven + *annus* year]

un·de·cid·ed (un'di·sī'did) *adj.* **1** Not having the mind made up. **2** Not decided upon; not determined. See synonyms under IRRESOLUTE. — **un·de·cid'ed·ly** *adv.*

un·decked (un·dekt') *adj.* **1** Having no ornaments; not decked out. **2** Having no deck, as a vessel.

un·dec·u·ple (un·dek'yə·pəl) *adj.* **1** Consisting of eleven. **2** Having eleven parts or members; elevenfold. **3** Taken by elevens. — *n.* A number or sum eleven times as great as another. — *v.t. & v.i.* **·pled**, **·pling** To multiply by eleven; make or become eleven times as large. [< L *undecim* eleven, on analogy with *decuple*]

un·de·cu·pli·cate (un'də·kyōō'plə·kit, -kāt) *adj.* **1** Elevenfold. **2** Raised to the eleventh power. — *v.t. & v.i.* (-kāt) **·cat·ed**, **·cat·ing** To multiply by eleven; undecuple. — *n.* One of eleven like things. — **un'de·cu'pli·cate·ly** *adv.* — **un'de·cu'pli·ca'tion** *n.*

un·de·mon·stra·tive (un'di·mon'strə·tiv) *adj.* Not demonstrative; not characterized by show of feeling.

un·de·ni·a·ble (un'di·nī'ə·bəl) *adj.* **1** That cannot be denied; indisputably true; obviously correct: an *undeniable* fact. **2** Unquestionably good; excellent: His reputation was *undeniable.* — **un'de·ni'a·bly** *adv.*

un·der (un'dər) *prep.* **1** Beneath, so as to have something directly above; covered by: layer *under* layer. **2** In a place lower than; at the foot or bottom of: *under* the hill. **3** Beneath the shelter of: *under* the paternal roof. **4** Beneath the concealment, guise, or assumption of: *under* a false name. **5** Less than in

number, degree, age, value, or amount: *under* 10 tons. **6** Inferior to in quality, character, or rank. **7** Beneath the domination of; owing allegiance to; subordinate or subservient to: *under* the Nazi flag. **8** Subject to the guidance, tutorship, or direction of: He studied *under* Mendelssohn. **9** Subject to the moral obligation of: a statement *under* oath; subject to the sanction of; with the liability or certainty of incurring: *under* penalty of the law. **10** Subject to the influence or pressure of: *under* the circumstances; swayed or impelled by: *under* fear of death. **11** Driven or propelled by: *under* sail, *under* steam. **12** Included in the group or class of; found in the matter titled or headed: See *under* History. **13** Being the subject of: *under* medical treatment. **14** During the period of; in the reign of; pending the administration of. **15** By virtue of; authorized, substantiated, attested, or warranted by: *under* his own signature. **16** In conformity to or in accordance with; having regard to. **17** Planted or sowed with: an acre *under* wheat. See synonyms under BENEATH. — *adv.* **1** In or into a position below something; underneath. **2** In or into an inferior or subordinate degree or rank. **3** So as to be covered or hidden; in or into concealment. **4** Less than the required or appointed amount. — **to go under** To fail or collapse, as a business venture. — *adj.* **1** Situated or moving under something else; lower or lowermost: an *under* layer. **2** *Zool.* Ventral: the *under* side of a rattlesnake. **3** Subordinate; lower in rank or authority. **4** Insufficient; less than usual, standard, or prescribed. **5** Held in subjection or restraint: used predicatively: Hold your emotions *under.* [OE]

un·der·a·chieve (un'dər·ə·chēv') *v.i.* **·chieved**, **·chiev·ing** To fail to achieve the approximate level of performance, especially in school studies, commensurate with one's abilities as indicated by testing. — **un'der·a·chieve'ment**, **un'der·a·chiev'er** *n.*

under a cloud Overshadowed by reproach or distrust.

un·der·age (un'dər·āj') *adj.* Not of a requisite age; immature.

un·der·arm (un'dər·ärm') *adj.* Situated or placed under the arm: the *underarm* section of a blouse. — *n.* The armpit.

un·der·arm (un'dər·ärm') *adj. & adv.* In various sports, as tennis, baseball, etc., delivered with the hand lower than the elbow.

un·der·bel·ly (un'dər·bel'ē) *n. pl.* **·lies** **1** The lower region of the belly. **2** Any similar unprotected part: the soft *underbelly* of Europe.

un·der·bid (un'dər·bid') *v.t.* **·bid**, **·bid·ding** **1** To bid lower than, as in a competition. **2** In auction bridge, to fail to bid the full value of (a hand). — **un'der·bid'der** *n.*

un·der·bred (un'dər·bred') *adj.* **1** Of impure breed; not thoroughbred. **2** Lacking in good breeding. See synonyms under VULGAR.

un·der·brush (un'dər·brush') *n.* Small trees and shrubs growing beneath forest trees; undergrowth. Also **un'der·bush** (-bōōsh').

un·der·buy (un'dər·bī') *v.t.* **·bought**, **·buy·ing** **1** To buy at a price lower than that paid by (another). **2** To pay less than the value for.

un·der·car·riage (un'dər·kar'ij) *n.* **1** The framework supporting the body of a structure, as an automobile. **2** The principal landing gear of an aircraft.

un·der·charge (un'dər·chärj') *v.t.* **·charged**, **·charg·ing** **1** To make an inadequate charge for. **2** To load with an insufficient charge, as a gun. — *n.* (un'dər·chärj') An inadequate or insufficient charge.

un·der·class (un'dər·klas, -kläs) *n. Sociol.* The group in a society so hopelessly poverty-stricken and so unorganized as to be beneath any apparent social class structure.

un·der·class·man (un'dər·klas'mən, -kläs'-) *n. pl.* **·men** (-mən) A freshman or sophomore in a school or college.

un·der·clay (un'dər·klā') *n.* A layer of clay underlying a coal seam, often containing the roots of ancient coal-forming plants: also called *seatstone.*

un·der·clothes (un'dər·klōz', -klōthz') *n. pl.* Clothes designed for underwear, or to be worn

next the skin. Also **un'der·cloth'ing.**

un·der·coat (un'dər·kōt') *n.* **1** A coat worn under another. **2** Underfur. **3** A layer of paint, varnish, etc., beneath another layer: also **un'der·coat'ing.** — *v.t.* To provide with an undercoat (def. 3).

un·der·cool (un'dər·kōōl') *v.t.* To supercool.

un·der·cov·er (un'dər·kuv'ər) *adj.* Secret; surreptitious; specifically, engaged in spying or secret investigation: an *undercover* man.

under cover Secretively; surreptitiously.

un·der·cov·ert (un'dər·kuv'ərt) *n. Ornithol.* A wing covert.

un·der·croft (un'dər·krôft', -kroft') *n.* A subterranean chamber, vault, or passage. [< UNDER + obs. *croft* vault, ult. < L *crypta* crypt]

un·der·cur·rent (un'dər·kûr'ənt) *n.* **1** A current, as of water or air, below another or below the surface. **2** A hidden drift or tendency, as of popular sentiments.

un·der·cut (un'dər·kut') *n.* **1** The act or result of cutting under. **2** The tenderloin. **3** A slanting cut in a sawed log. **4** A notch cut in the side of a tree so that it will fall toward that side when sawn through. **5** Any part that is cut away below: the *undercut* of a carriage. **6** In sports, a cut or backspin imparted to the ball by an underhand or downward stroke. — *v.t.* (un'dər·kut') **·cut**, **·cut·ting** **1** To cut under. **2** To cut away a lower portion of so as to leave a part overhanging: The river *undercut* its banks. **3** To work or sell for lower payment than (a rival). **4** In golf, to impart backspin to (the ball) by striking it obliquely downward. **5** In tennis, to use an underhand stroke in cutting (the ball). **6** To lessen or destroy the effectiveness or impact of; undermine. — *adj.* **1** Having the parts in relief cut under. **2** Done by undercutting.

un·der·de·vel·oped (un'dər·di·vel'əpt) *adj.* **1** Not sufficiently developed. **2** Below a normal or adequate standard in the development of industry, resources, agriculture, etc.: an *underdeveloped* country.

un·der·do (un'dər·dōō') *v.t. & v.i.* **·did**, **·done**, **·do·ing** To do less than is expected or needed.

un·der·dog (un'dər·dôg', -dog') *n.* **1** The dog that is losing, has lost, or is at a disadvantage in a dogfight. **2** The weaker or worsted person. **3** Anyone in a position of inferiority.

un·der·done (un'dər·dun') *adj.* **1** Insufficiently done. **2** Not cooked to the full.

un·der·drive (un'dər·drīv') *n. Mech.* A gearing device which turns a drive shaft at a speed less than that of the engine: opposed to *overdrive.*

un·der·em·ployed (un'dər·əm·ploid') *adj.* Unable to get a full-time or regular job; employed part of the time or working too few hours. — **un'der·em·ploy'ment** *n.*

un·der·es·ti·mate (un'dər·es'tə·māt) *v.t.* **·mat·ed**, **·mat·ing** To put too low an estimate or valuation upon (things or people). See synonyms under DISPARAGE. — *n.* (-mit) **1** An insufficiently high opinion. **2** An estimate below the just value or expense. — **un'der·es'ti·ma'tion** *n.*

un·der·ex·pose (un'dər·ik·spōz') *v.t.* **·posed**, **·pos·ing** *Phot.* To expose (a film) less than is required for proper development. — **un'der·ex·posed'** *adj.* — **un'der·ex·po'sure** (-spō'zhər) *n.*

un·der·feed (un'dər·fēd') *v.t.* **·fed**, **·feed·ing** **1** To feed insufficiently. **2** To supply fuel for (an engine) from beneath.

under fire Engaged in a battle; exposed to fire; being attacked: said of troops.

un·der·foot (un'dər·fōōt') *adv.* **1** Beneath the feet; down on the ground; immediately below. **2** In the way.

un·der·fur (un'dər·fûr') *n.* The coat of dense, fine hair forming the main part of a pelt.

un·der·gar·ment (un'dər·gär'mənt) *n.* A garment to be worn under the ordinary outer garments.

un·der·gird (un'dər·gûrd') *v.t.* **·girt** or **·gird·ed**, **·gird·ing** To fasten or gird, as by something that passes underneath.

un·der·glaze (un'dər·glāz') *adj.* Used in or suitable for porcelain decoration: said of painting in vitrifiable pigment before the glaze is applied.

un·der·go (un'dər·gō') *v.t.* **·went**, **·gone**, **·go·ing** **1** To be subjected to; have experience of; suffer. **2** To bear up under; endure. **3** *Obs.*

To exist under. See synonyms under ENDURE.

un·der·grad·u·ate (un'dər·graj'ōo·it) *n.* A student of a university or college who has not taken the bachelor's degree.

un·der·ground (un'dər·ground') *adj.* 1 Situated, done, or operating beneath the surface of the ground. 2 Hence, done in secret; clandestine. — *n.* 1 That which is beneath the surface of the ground, as a passage or space. 2 A railway operated in a system of tunnels beneath the ground. 3 A group secretly organized to resist or oppose those in control of a government or country. 4 An avant-garde movement in art, cinema, journalism, etc., generally considered to be in opposition to conventional culture or society and whose works are usually experimental, erotic, o: radical in style, content, or purpose: used with *the.* — *adv.* (un'dər·ground') 1 Beneath the surface of the ground: to work *underground.* 2 Secretly.

Underground Railroad A system of cooperation among anti–slavery people, before 1861, for assisting fugitive slaves to escape to Canada and the free States.

un·der·grown (un'dər·grōn') *adj.* Not fully grown; undersized.

un·der·growth (un'dər·grōth') *n.* 1 A growth of smaller plants among larger ones; specifically, a thicket or coppice in or as in a forest. 2 Condition of being undergrown. 3 A close growth of hair beneath and finer than the outer growth of a pelt.

un·der·hand (un'dər·hand') *adj.* 1 Done or acting in a treacherously secret manner; unfair; sly. 2 In baseball, cricket, etc., underarm. — *adv.* Underhandedly; slily.

un·der·hand·ed (un'dər·han'did) *adj.* Clandestinely carried on; underhand. — **un'der·hand'ed·ly** *adv.* — **un'der·hand'ed·ness** *n.*

un·der·hung (un'dər·hung') *adj.* 1 *Anat.* Protruding from beneath, as a lower jaw: said of persons, dogs, etc., with a jaw protruding beyond the upper jaw. 2 Underslung.

un·der·laid (un'dər·lād') *adj.* 1 Laid underneath; supporting. 2 Supported by or having something lying or placed underneath.

un·der·lay (un'dər·lā') *v.t.* **·laid, ·lay·ing** 1 To place (one thing) under another. 2 To furnish with a base or lining. 3 *Printing* To support or raise by underlays. — *n.* (un'dər·lā') 1 *Printing* A piece of paper, etc., placed under certain parts of a printing form, to bring them to the proper level. 2 *Mining* An inclination, as of a lode. 3 A wager made at odds unfavorable to the better: opposed to *overlay.*

un·der·lease (un'dər·lēs') *n.* A lease of premises by a lessee; sublease.

un·der·let (un'dər·let') *v.t.* **·let, ·let·ting** 1 To lease (premises already held on lease); sublet. 2 To lease at less than the usual rate.

un·der·lie (un'dər·lī') *v.t.* **·lay, ·lain, ·ly·ing** 1 To lie below or under. 2 To be the ground or support of: the principle that *underlies* a scheme. 3 To constitute a first or prior claim or lien over: A first mortgage *underlies* a second. 4 To be subject, answerable, or liable to. [OE *underlicgan*]

un·der·line (un'dər·līn') *v.t.* **·lined, ·lin·ing** 1 To mark with a line underneath; underscore. 2 To emphasize. — *n.* A line underneath, as beneath a printed or written word or syllable to indicate emphasis or stress.

un·der·lin·en (un'dər·lin'ən) *n.* Linen underwear; any underwear.

un·der·ling (un'dər·ling) *n.* A subordinate; an inferior; a servile person.

un·der·ly·ing (un'dər·lī'ing) *adj.* 1 Lying under: *underlying* strata. 2 Hence, figuratively, fundamental: *underlying* principles. 3 Prior in claim or lien. See UNDERLIE (def. 3).

un·der·men·tioned (un'dər·men'shənd) *adj.* Mentioned below in a writing.

un·der·mine (un'dər·mīn', un'dər·mīn) *v.t.* **·mined, ·min·ing** 1 To excavate beneath; dig a mine or passage under: to *undermine* a fortress. 2 To weaken by wearing away at the base. 3 To weaken or impair secretly or by degrees: to *undermine* the influence or the health of someone. See synonyms under WEAKEN. — **un'der·min'er** *n.*

un·der·most (un'dər·mōst') *adj.* Having the lowest place or position.

un·der·neath (un'dər·nēth', -nēth') *adv.* 1 In a place below. 2 On the under or lower side. See synonyms under BENEATH. — *prep.* 1 Beneath; under; below. 2 Under the form or

appearance of. 3 Under the authority of; in the control of. — *adj.* Lower. — *n.* The lower or under part or side. [OE *underneothan*]

un·der·nour·ish (un'dər·nûr'ish) *v.t.* To provide with nourishment insufficient in amount or quality for proper health and growth. — **un'der·nour'ish·ment** *n.*

un·dern·song (un'dərn·sông', -song') *n.* Tierce (def. 5). [OE *undern* midday, midday meal + SONG]

un·der·pants (un'dər·pants') *n. pl.* An undergarment worn over the loins and sometimes extending over the thighs or lower legs.

un·der·pass (un'dər·pas', -päs') *n.* A passage beneath; the section of a way or road that passes under railway tracks or under another road.

un·der·pay (un'dər·pā') *v.t.* **·paid, ·pay·ing** To pay insufficiently.

un·der·pin (un'dər·pin') *v.t.* **·pinned, ·pin·ning** 1 To support, as a wall or structure, from below, especially when a previous support is removed, by inserting a prop or pier. 2 To corroborate; support.

un·der·pin·ning (un'dər·pin'ing) *n.* 1 Material or framework used to support a wall or building from below. 2 *Often pl.* Something used or functioning as a basis or foundation.

un·der·pitch (un'dər·pich') *adj. Archit.* Designating a main vault intersected by another at a lower level. [<UNDER- + PITCH², *n.* (def. 3)]

un·der·plant (un'dər·plant', -plänt') *v.t. Rare* To plant young trees under (existing trees).

un·der·plot (un'dər·plot') *n.* 1 A subsidiary literary or dramatic plot; an episode. 2 A piece of roguery or trickery; an underhand action. — **un'der·plot'ter** *n.*

un·der·priv·i·leged (un'dər·priv'ə·lijd) *adj.* At a social or economic disadvantage; specifically, through economic cause, not privileged to enjoy certain rights theoretically possessed by all members of a community or state.

un·der·pro·duc·tion (un'dər·prə·duk'shən) *n.* Production below capacity or below requirements; abnormally low production. Compare OVERPRODUCTION.

un·der·proof (un'dər·prōof') *adj.* Having less strength than proof spirit.

un·der·prop (un'dər·prop') *v.t.* **·propped, ·prop·ping** To prop from below; support.

un·der·quote (un'dər·kwōt') *v.t.* **·quot·ed, ·quot·ing** 1 To undersell or offer to undersell, as goods or stocks. 2 To underbid.

un·der·rate (un'dər·rāt') *v.t.* **·rat·ed, ·rat·ing** To rate too low; underestimate. See synonyms under DISPARAGE.

un·der·run (un'dər·run') *v.t.* **·ran, ·run, ·run·ning** 1 To run or pass beneath. 2 *Naut.* To examine (a line, hawser, etc.) from below by drawing a boat along beneath it.

un·der·score (un'dər·skôr', -skōr') *v.t.* **·scored, ·scor·ing** To draw a line below, as for indicating emphasis; underline. — *n.* (un'dər·skôr', -skōr') A line drawn beneath a word, etc., as for emphasis.

un·der·sea (un'dər·sē') *adj.* Existing, carried on, or adapted for use beneath the surface of the sea: *undersea* exploration; an *undersea* oil well. — *adv.* Beneath the surface of the sea: also **un'der·seas'**.

un·der·sell (un'dər·sel') *v.t.* **·sold, ·sell·ing** 1 To sell at a lower price than. 2 To sell for less than the real value. — **un'der·sell'er** *n.*

un·der·set¹ (un'dər·set') *v.t.* **·set, ·set·ting** 1 To prop up; support. 2 *Brit.* To underlet; sublet.

un·der·set² (un'dər·set') *n.* An undercurrent.

un·der·set·ter (un'dər·set'ər) *n.* 1 An underpinning prop or support. 2 *Brit.* One who sublets.

un·der·shap·en (un'dər·shā'pən) *adj.* Below normal size; imperfectly formed.

un·der–sher·iff (un'dər·sher'if) *n.* A deputy sheriff, especially one upon whom the sheriff's duties devolve in his absence.

un·der·shirt (un'dər·shûrt') *n.* A garment worn beneath the shirt, generally of cotton, wool and cotton, or silk.

un·der·shot (un'dər·shot') *adj.* 1 Propelled by water that flows underneath: said of a water wheel. 2 Projecting; having a projecting lower jaw or teeth: said especially of a bulldog.

UNDERSHOT WATER WHEEL

un·der·side (un'dər·sīd') *n.* The lower or under side or surface.

un·der·sign (un'dər·sīn') *v.t.* To sign at the foot of; subscribe: used chiefly in the past participle. — **the undersigned** The subscriber or subscribers to a document.

un·der·sized¹ (un'dər·sīzd') *adj.* Of less than the normal or average size.

un·der·sized² (un'dər·sīzd') *adj.* Insufficiently sized, as paper.

un·der·skirt (un'dər·skûrt') *n.* 1 A skirt worn beneath another; a petticoat. 2 The foundation skirt of a draped gown.

un·der·sleeve (un'dər·slēv') *n.* A sleeve worn beneath another, especially when of contrasting color and showing through slashes or openings.

un·der·slung (un'dər·slung') *adj.* Having the springs fixed to the axles from below, instead of resting upon them: said of certain automobiles.

un·der·soil (un'dər·soil') *n.* Subsoil.

un·der·song (un'dər·sông', -song') *n.* 1 A subordinate strain or subdued melody. 2 An underlying meaning.

un·der·sparred (un'dər·spärd') *adj. Naut.* Having too few, too short, or too slight spars or masts.

un·der·spin (un'dər·spin') *n.* In golf, a backward spin imparted to the ball.

un·der·stand (un'dər·stand') *v.* **·stood, ·stand·ing** *v.t.* 1 To come to know the meaning or import of; apprehend. 2 To perceive the nature or character of: I do not *understand* her. 3 To have comprehension or mastery of: Do you *understand* German? 4 To be aware of; realize: She *understands* her position. 5 To have been told; believe: I *understand* that she went home. 6 To take or suppose to mean: How am I to *understand* that remark? 7 To accept as a condition or stipulation: It is *understood* that the tenant will provide his own heat. 8 To supply in thought when unexpressed, as the subject of a sentence. — *v.i.* 9 To have understanding; comprehend. 10 To be informed; believe. See synonyms under APPREHEND, KNOW, PERCEIVE, SOLVE. — **to understand each other** To be in agreement; be privately in sympathy with each other. [OE *understandan* <*under-* under + *standan* stand] — **un'der·stand'a·ble** *adj.* — **un'der·stand'a·bly** *adv.*

un·der·stand·ing (un'dər·stan'ding) *n.* 1 The act of one who understands, or the resulting state; intellectual apprehension; mental discernment; comprehension. 2 The power by which one understands. 3 The sum of the mental powers by which knowledge is acquired, retained, and extended; the power of apprehending relations and making inferences from them. 4 The facts or elements of a case as apprehended by any one intelligence; an individual view of a case; opinion. 5 An agreement between two or more persons; an informal or confidential compact; also, the subject of such compact; the thing agreed on; sometimes, an arrangement or settlement of differences, or of disputed points: That was not our *understanding*; They have come to an *understanding.* — *adj.* Possessing comprehension and good sense. — **un'der·stand'ing·ly** *adv.* — **un'der·stand'ing·ness** *n.*

Synonyms (noun): apprehension, comprehension, discernment, intellect, intelligence, judgment, mind, perception, reason. See INTELLECT, MIND, WISDOM.

un·der·state (un'dər·stāt') *v.* **·stat·ed, ·stat·ing** *v.t.* 1 To state with less force than the truth warrants or allows. 2 To state, as a number or dimension, as less than the true one. — *v.i.* 3 To make an understatement.

un·der·state·ment (un'dər·stāt'mənt) *n.* A statement covering less than the truth or fact.

un·der·stood (un'dər·stood') Past tense and past participle of UNDERSTAND. — *adj.* Taken for granted; agreed upon by all.

un·der·strap·per (un'dər·strap'ər) *n.* An underling; a subordinate agent.

un·der·strap·ping (un'dər·strap'ing) *adj.* Subordinate; inferior.

un·der·stra·tum (un'dər·strā'təm, -strat'əm) *n. pl.* **·stra·ta** (-strā'tə, -strat'ə) An underlying stratum; substratum, literal or figurative.

un·der·stud·y (un'dər·stud'ē) *v.t. & v.i.* **·stud·ied, ·stud·y·ing** 1 To study (a part) in order to be able, if necessary, to take the place of the actor playing it. **2** To act as an understudy to (another actor). — *n.* *pl.* **stud·ies** **1** An actor or actress who can take the place of another actor in a given role when necessary. **2** A person prepared to perform the work or fill the position of another.

un·der·take (un'dər·tāk') *v.* **·took**, **·tak·en**, **·tak·ing** *v.t.* **1** To take upon oneself; agree or attempt to do; begin. **2** To contract to do; pledge oneself to. **3** To guarantee or promise. **4** To take under charge or guidance. **5** *Obs.* To enter into combat with. — *v.i.* **6** To make oneself responsible or liable; be surety: with *for.* See synonyms under ENDEAVOR.

un·der·tak·er (un'dər·tā'kər for def. 1; un'dər·tā'kər for def. 2) *n.* **1** One who undertakes any work or enterprise; especially, a contractor. **2** One whose business it is to arrange for burying the dead and to conduct funerals.

un·der·tak·ing (un'dər·tā'king; *for def. 3* un'·dər·tā'king) *n.* **1** The act of one who undertakes any task or enterprise. **2** The thing undertaken; an enterprise; task. **3** The management of funerals; the business of an undertaker. **4** An engagement, promise, or guaranty.

under tenant A tenant of a tenant; one who holds premises by a lease from one who is himself a lessee.

under the rose Sub rosa.

under the weather *Colloq.* **1** Depressed by unpleasant weather; hence, somewhat ill; indisposed. **2** Inebriated; drunk. **3** In financial straits.

under the yoke In subjection.

un·der·thrust (un'dər·thrust') *n.* *Geol.* **1** A deformation of the earth's crust in which a mass of rock is pushed beneath an overlying mass. **2** The intruded rock mass itself.

un·der·tint (un'dər·tint') *n.* A subdued tint.

un·der·tone (un'dər·tōn') *n.* **1** A tone of lower pitch or loudness than is usual; the tone of a subdued voice; sometimes, a whisper. **2** A subdued shade of a color, as when spread thinly on a white surface; also, a color upon which other colors have been imposed and which is seen through them, modifying their effect. **3** A meaning or suggestion implied but not expressed. **4** An underlying stability in the price level of some stocks.

un·der·took (un'dər·tŏŏk') Past tense of UN-DERTAKE.

un·der·tow (un'dər·tō') *n.* **1** The flow of water beneath and in a direction opposite to the surface current. **2** The backward undercurrent below the surf.

un·der·trick (un'dər·trik') *n.* In certain card games, a trick required to make the number declared, but not taken.

un·der·trump (un'dər·trump') *v.t.* To play to (a previous card in the same trick) a trump lower than one already played by another player; also, to trump with too low a trump, and so be overtrumped.

un·der·val·ue (un'dər·val'yōō) *v.t.* **·ued**, **·u·ing** **1** To value too lightly; underrate; underestimate. **2** *Obs.* To hold inferior: with *to* before the object compared. See synonyms under DISPARAGE. — **un'der·val'u·a'tion** *n.*

un·der·vest (un'dər·vest') *n.* *Brit.* An undershirt.

un·der·waist (un'dər·wāst') *n.* A waist to be worn under another waist.

un·der·wa·ter (un'dər·wô'tər, -wot'ər) *adj.* **1** Being, occurring, or used below the surface of a body of water: *underwater research.* **2** Below the water line of a ship. — *n.* The region or environment below the surface of water. — *adv.* Below the surface of water.

un·der·way (un'dər·wā') *adv.* **1** In progress: The meeting was already *underway.* **2** Into operation or motion: to get the fund drive *underway.* Also **under way.**

un·der·wear (un'dər·wâr') *n.* Garments worn underneath the ordinary outer garments.

un·der·weight (un'dər·wāt') *adj.* Having less than the normal weight. — *n.* Insufficiency of weight; also, weight below normal.

un·der·went (un'dər·went') Past tense of UN-DERGO.

un·der·wing (un'dər·wing') *n.* *Entomol.* One of the posterior pair of wings in an insect.

underwing moth A large noctuid moth (genus *Catocala*), whose front wings are an

inconspicuous brown or gray.

un·der·wood (un'dər·wŏŏd') *n.* Low trees and brush growing among large forest trees.

un·der·work (un'dər·wûrk') *v.t.* **1** To work for lower wages than. **2** To exact too little work from. **3** *Obs.* To weaken or injure by underhand contrivances; undermine. — *v.i.* **4** To do too little work. — *n.* (un'dər·wûrk') Subordinate, unimportant, or routine work.

un·der·world (un'dər·wûrld') *n.* **1** In Greek and Roman mythology, the abode of the dead; Hades; Orcus. **2** In later folklore, sometimes a beautiful country under the earth or sea; also, fairyland, sometimes entered through a well. **3** The antipodes; also, all beneath the horizon. **4** The sublunary world; the earth. **5** The debased, criminal, or degenerate components of the social order; the world of crime and vice; gangsterdom.

un·der·write (un'dər·rīt') *v.* **·wrote**, **·writ·ten**, **·writ·ing** *v.t.* **1** To write beneath; subscribe. **2** In finance, to execute and deliver (a policy of insurance on specified property, especially marine property); insure; assume (a risk) by way of insurance. **3** To engage to buy, at a determined price and time, all or part of the stock in (a new enterprise or company) that is not subscribed for by the public; loosely, to guarantee or assume responsibility for, as an enterprise. **4** To undertake to pay, as a subscription or written pledge of money. — *v.i.* **5** To act as an underwriter; especially, to issue a policy of insurance. [OE *under·wrītan,* trans. of L *subscribere*]

un·der·writ·er (un'dər·rī'tər) *n.* **1** A body corporate or a person in the insurance business; one who sets up the premium for a risk. **2** One who underwrites (def. 3) an issue of stocks, bonds, or the like.

un·de·sign·ing (un'di·zī'ning) *adj.* Without ulterior purpose or selfish plan; artless; sincere.

un·de·ter·mined (un'di·tûr'mind) *adj.* **1** Not decided or fixed. **2** Not determined.

un·dine (un·dēn', un'dēn, -dīn) *n.* *Med.* A small glass cup or flask for irrigating the eye. [<L *unda* wave + -INE¹; from its wavy profile]

un·di·rect·ed (un'di·rek'tid, -dī-) *adj.* **1** Unguided, or uninformed as to direction. **2** Not addressed: said of a letter.

un·dis·posed (un'dis·pōzd') *adj.* **1** Not sold, settled, placed, or otherwise decided: frequently with *of.* **2** *Obs.* Disinclined. — **un'·dis·pos'ed·ness** (-pō'zid·nis) *n.*

un·do (un·dōō') *v.t.* **·did**, **·done**, **·do·ing** **1** To cause to be as if never done; reverse, annul, or cancel. **2** To loosen or untie. **3** To unfasten and open. **4** To bring to ruin; destroy. **5** *Obs.* To solve, as a riddle. [OE *undōn*] — **un·do'er** *n.*

un·do·ing (un·dōō'ing) *n.* **1** Reversal of what has been done. **2** Destruction; ruin; cause of ruin. **3** The action of unfastening, loosening, opening, etc. **4** *Psychoanal.* The abolition of painful experiences by the unconscious, resulting in obliviousness to the unacceptable fact.

un·done¹ (un·dun') *adj.* **1** Untied; unfastened. **2** Ruined. [Orig. pp. of UNDO]

un·done² (un·dun') *adj.* Not done. [<UN-¹ + DONE]

un·doubt·ed (un·dou'tid) *adj.* **1** Assured beyond question; being beyond a doubt. **2** Not viewed with distrust; unsuspected. See synonyms under INCONTESTABLE. — **un·doubt'ed·ly** *adv.*

un·draw (un·drô') *v.t.* & *v.i.* **·drew**, **·drawn**, **·draw·ing** To draw open, away, or aside.

un·dress (un·dres') *v.t.* **1** To divest of clothes; strip. **2** To remove the dressing or bandages from, as a wound. **3** To divest of special attire; disrobe. — *v.i.* **4** To remove one's clothing. — *n.* **1** Ordinary attire; negligee, as opposed to full or evening dress; specifically, the military or naval uniform worn by officers when not on parade or at functions necessitating full dress. **2** Comfortable, informal clothing. **3** Nudity: in a state of *undress.* — *adj.* (un'dres') Pertaining to everyday attire; hence, informal.

un·dressed (un·drest') *adj.* **1** Not dressed. **2** Not treated or dressed: said of kid leather.

un·due (un·dōō', -dyōō') *adj.* **1** Excessive;

disproportionate. **2** Not justified by law; illegal. **3** Not due; in process of becoming due, but not yet demandable. **4** Not appropriate; improper.

un·du·lant (un'dyə·lənt, -də-) *adj.* Undulating; fluctuating. [<L *undul(atus)* + -ANT]

undulant fever *Pathol.* A persistent and wasting infectious disease of wide distribution, caused by a bacterium (genus *Brucella*) which is usually transmitted to man in the milk of cows and goats. The disease is marked by fluctuating or recurrent fever, with swelling of the joints, neuralgic pains, profuse perspiration, and enlargement of the spleen: also called *brucellosis, Malta fever, Mediterranean fever.*

un·du·late (un'dyə·lāt, -də-) *v.* **·lat·ed**, **·lat·ing** *v.t.* **1** To cause to move like a wave or in waves. **2** To give a wavy appearance to. — *v.i.* **3** To move like a wave or waves. **4** To have a wavy form or appearance. — *adj.* (-lit, -lāt) **1** Wavy. **2** Having wavelike markings, as of color. See synonyms under FLUCTUATE. [<L *undulatus* undulated, ult. < *unda* wave]

un·du·lat·ing (un'dyə·lā'ting, -də-) *adj.* Having the appearance of waves; vibrating; wavy.

un·du·la·tion (un'dyə·lā'shən, -də-) *n.* **1** The act of undulating; a waving or sinuous motion; a wave. **2** An appearance as of waves; a gentle rise and fall. **3** *Physics* The continuous propagation of waves through a medium. — **un'du·la·to'ry** (-lə·tôr'ē, -tō'rē) *adj.*

un·du·la·tus (un'dyə·lā'təs, -də-) *n.* *Meteorol.* A variety of stratocumulus cloud characterized by elongated wavelike undulations, sometimes in different directions. [<NL <L. See UNDULATE.]

un·du·ly (un·dōō'lē, -dyōō'-) *adv.* **1** Excessively. **2** In violation of a moral or of a legal standard; unjustly.

un·dy·ing (un·dī'ing) *adj.* Immortal.

un·earned (un·ûrnd') *adj.* Not earned by labor; also, undeserved.

unearned increment See under INCREMENT.

un·earth (un·ûrth') *v.t.* **1** To dig or root up from the earth. **2** To reveal; discover.

un·earth·ly (un·ûrth'lē) *adj.* **1** Not earthly; sublime. **2** Supernatural; terrifying; weird; terrible. **3** Ridiculously unconventional; inconvenient, or unpleasant; preposterous: at this *unearthly* hour. — **un·earth'li·ness** *n.*

un·ease (un·ēz') *n.* Mental or emotional discomfort, dissatisfaction, anxiety, etc.

un·eas·y (un·ē'zē) *adj.* **·eas·i·er**, **·eas·i·est** **1** Deprived of ease; disturbed; unquiet. **2** Not affording ease or rest; uncomfortable; causing discomfort. **3** Showing embarrassment or constraint; strained. **4** *Obs.* Difficult. — **un·eas'i·ly** *adv.* — **un·eas'i·ness** *n.*

un·eath (un·ēth') *adv.* *Obs.* Scarcely; hardly; not easily. [OE *unēathe* not easily]

un·em·ploy·a·ble (un'əm·ploi'ə·bəl) *adj.* Not employable. — *n.* A person who, because of illness, age, mental or physical incapacity, or other reason, cannot be employed.

un·em·ployed (un'əm·ploid') *adj.* **1** Having no occupation; out of work. **2** Not put to use or turned to account; uninvested: *unemployed* resources. See synonyms under IDLE, VACANT. — *n.* A jobless person: with *the,* unemployed persons collectively. — **un'em·ploy'ment** *n.*

un·en·cum·bered funds (un'en·kum'bərd) **1** Funds not designated for any specific use; general funds. **2** Funds not pledged in connection with present or future obligations.

un·e·qual (un·ē'kwəl) *adj.* **1** Not having equivalent or equal extension, duration, or properties; not equal in strength, ability, wealth, status, or other respects. **2** Inadequate for the purpose; insufficient: with *to.* **3** Not balanced; disproportioned; inequitable; unfair. **4** Wanting in uniformity; varying; irregular. **5** *Bot.* Unsymmetrical; *unequal* distribution. **6** Involving poorly matched competitors or contestants: an *unequal* contest. — **un·e'qual·ly** *adv.*

un·e·qualed (un·ē'kwəld) *adj.* Not equaled or matched; unrivaled; supreme. Also **un·e'qualled.**

un·e·quiv·o·cal (un'i·kwiv'ə·kəl) *adj.* Understandable in only one way; distinct; plain.

See synonyms under ABSOLUTE, CLEAR, PLAIN.
— un'e·quiv'o·cal·ly adv.

un·err·ing (un·ûr'ing, -er'-) adj. Making no mistakes; not erring: also, sure; accurate; infallible. — un·err'ing·ly adv.

UNESCO (yōō·nes'kō) The United Nations Educational, Scientific and Cultural Organization, established November, 1946, to "advance mutual knowledge and understanding of peoples," promote popular education, and assist in the diffusion of knowledge. Also Unesco.

un·es·sen·tial (un'ə·sen'shəl) adj. 1 Not absolutely required; not of prime importance. 2 Unimportant. 3 Void of essence, real or apparent. — un'es·sen'tial·ly adv.

un·e·vac·u·a·ble (un'i·vak'yōō·ə·bəl) adj. Not capable of being removed or evacuated, as in a military action or air raid.

un·e·ven (un·ē'vən) adj. 1 Not even, smooth, or level; rough. 2 Not level, parallel, or perfectly horizontal. 3 Not divisible by two without remainder; odd: said of numbers. 4 Not uniform; variable; spasmodic. 5 Obs. Not having correspondence; not balanced; not fair or just; also, ill-suited; not matched. See synonyms under IRREGULAR, ROUGH. — un·e'ven·ly adv. — un·e'ven·ness n.

un·e·vent·ful (un'i·vent'fəl) adj. Devoid of noteworthy events; quiet.

un·ex·am·pled (un'ig·zam'pəld) adj. So great, remarkable, or striking as to have no precedent or analogy; without a parallel example.

un·ex·cep·tion·a·ble (un'ik·sep'shən·ə·bəl) adj. That cannot be objected to; irreproachable. — un'ex·cep'tion·a·ble·ness n. — un'ex·cep'tion·a·bly adv.

un·ex·cep·tion·al (un'ik·sep'shən·əl) adj. 1 Being no exception; ordinary. 2 Subject to no exception: unexceptional orders.

un·ex·pect·ed (un'ik·spek'tid) adj. Coming without warning; not expected: said especially of things of such a kind that one would not naturally expect them; sudden; strange and unforeseen. — the unexpected Unexpected things or events collectively; that which is unforeseen. — un'ex·pect'ed·ly adv. — un'ex·pect'ed·ness n.

un·ex·pe·ri·enced (un'ik·spir'ē·ənst) adj. 1 Not experienced; not had, undergone, possessed, or known: unexperienced pain. 2 Lacking experience; inexperienced.

un·ex·pres·sive (un'ik·spres'iv) adj. 1 Not having expression; inexpressive. 2 Obs. Inexpressible. — un'ex·pres'sive·ly adv.

un·fail·ing (un·fā'ling) adj. 1 Giving or constituting a supply that never fails; inexhaustible: an unfailing spring. 2 Always fulfilling requirements; not falling short of need, hope, or expectation. 3 Sure; infallible. — un·fail'ing·ly adv. — un·fail'ing·ness n.

un·fair (un·fâr') adj. 1 Marked by dishonesty or fraud; showing partiality or prejudice; not fair: unfair dealing. 2 Not compatible with law and justice; illegal: unfair competition. 3 Obs. Not pleasing or comely. See synonyms under BAD. [OE unfæger ugly] — un·fair'ly adv. — un·fair'ness n.

un·faith·ful (un·fāth'fəl) adj. 1 Manifesting lack or absence of faith; unworthy of trust; perfidious; faithless; not true to marriage vows: an unfaithful husband. 2 Not true to a standard or to an original; not accurate or exact: an unfaithful description. 3 Obs. Not having religious faith; unbelieving; infidel. See synonyms under PERFIDIOUS. — un·faith'ful·ly adv. — un·faith'ful·ness n.

un·fa·mil·iar (un'fə·mil'yər) adj. 1 Not familiarly knowing: I am unfamiliar with it. 2 Not familiarly known: an unfamiliar face. — un'fa·mil·i·ar·i·ty (-mil'ē·ar'ə·tē) n. — un'fa·mil'iar·ly adv.

un·fast·en (un·fas'ən, -fäs'-) v.t. To untie; loosen; open. — v.i. To become untied.

un·fa·thered (un·fä'thərd) adj. 1 Having no acknowledged father; hence, illegitimate. 2 Unauthenticated.

un·fa·vor·a·ble (un·fā'vər·ə·bəl) adj. Not favorable; unpropitious; adverse. Also Brit. un·fa'vour·a·ble. — un·fa'vor·a·ble·ness n. — un·fa'vor·a·bly adv.

Unfederated Malay States Former collective name for the states of Perlis, Kedah, Kelanton, Trengganu, and Johore, now States of Malaya in Malaysia.

un·feel·ing (un·fē'ling) adj. 1 Not sympathetic; hard; cruel. 2 Obs. Destitute of feeling or

sensation. See synonyms under HARD. — un·feel'ing·ly adv. — un·feel'ing·ness n.

un·feigned (un·fānd') adj. Not feigned; not pretended; sincere; genuine.

un·fel·lowed (un·fel'ōd) adj. 1 Unequaled; unmatchable. 2 Alone; without a companion.

un·fit (un·fit') v.t. ·fit·ted or ·fit, ·fit·ting To deprive of requisite fitness, skill, etc.; disqualify. — adj. 1 Having no fitness; unsuitable. 2 Not appropriate; improper. 3 Not completely trained; not in best condition: said of race horses. — un·fit'ly adv. — un·fit'ness n.

un·fix (un·fiks') v.t. 1 To unfasten; loosen; detach. 2 To unsettle.

un·flap·pa·ble (un·flap'ə·bəl) adj. Characterized by unshakable composure; imperturbable. — un·flap'pa·bil'i·ty n.

un·fledged (un·flejd') adj. 1 Not yet fledged; immature, as a young bird. 2 Inexperienced: an unfledged orator.

un·flesh·ly (un·flesh'lē) adj. Not corporeal, worldly, or sensual; ethereal; spiritual.

un·flinch·ing (un·flin'ching) adj. Done without shrinking; steadfast; brave. — un·flinch'ing·ly adv. — un·flinch'ing·ness n.

un·fold (un·fōld') v.t. 1 To open or spread out (something folded). 2 To lay open to view. 3 To make clear by detailed explanation; explain: to unfold a plan. 4 To develop. — v.i. 5 To become opened; expand. 6 To become manifest. See synonyms under AMPLIFY, INTERPRET, SOLVE. [OE unfealdan]

un·for·get·ta·ble (un'fər·get'ə·bəl) adj. Not forgettable; memorable. — un'for·get'ta·bly adv.

un·formed (un·fôrmd') adj. 1 Devoid of shape or form; not fully developed in character; crude. 2 Unorganized.

un·for·tu·nate (un·fôr'chə·nit) adj. 1 Having ill fortune; not prosperous; unsuccessful. 2 Causing or attended by ill fortune; disastrous. See synonyms under BAD. — n. 1 One who is unfortunate. 2 Specifically, one who has lapsed from virtue; a prostitute. — un·for'tu·nate·ly adv. — un·for'tu·nate·ness n.

un·found·ed (un·foun'did) adj. 1 Resting on no solid foundation; groundless; baseless. 2 Not founded or established. — un·found'ed·ly adv.

un·fre·quent·ed (un'fri·kwen'tid) adj. Rarely or never visited or frequented.

un·friend·ed (un·fren'did) adj. Without friends. — un·friend'ed·ness n.

un·friend·ly (un·frend'lē) adj. 1 Unkindly disposed; inimical; hostile. 2 Not favorable or propitious. See synonyms under INIMICAL. — adv. In an unfriendly manner. — un·friend'li·ness n.

un·frock (un·frok') v.t. 1 To divest of a frock or gown. 2 To depose, as a monk or priest, from ecclesiastical rank.

un·fruit·ful (un·frōōt'fəl) adj. 1 Bearing no fruit; having no offspring; barren. 2 Having no useful results; fruitless: an unfruitful line of thought. — un·fruit'ful·ly adv. — un·fruit'·ful·ness n.

un·fumed (un·fyōōmd') adj. 1 Not fumigated. 2 Obs. Undistilled.

un·fund·ed (un·fun'did) adj. Not funded: said of a debt.

un·furl (un·fûrl') v.t. & v.i. 1 To unroll, as a flag; spread out; expand. 2 To unfold. — un·furled' adj.

un·gain·ly (un·gān'lē) adj. Lacking grace or ease; clumsy. See synonyms under AWKWARD. — adv. In an awkward manner. — un·gain'·li·ness n.

Un·ga·va (ung·gä'və, -gä'və) A district of northern Quebec province, extending south of Ungava Bay, and including part of Labrador; 239,780 square miles: also New Quebec.

Ungava Bay An inlet of Hudson Strait in northern Quebec province; 200 miles long, 160 miles wide at the mouth.

Ungava Peninsula A peninsula of northern Quebec province between Ungava Bay and Hudson Bay; 400 miles long, 350 miles wide.

un·gen·er·ous (un·jen'ər·əs) adj. 1 Not generous; illiberal; niggardly; unkind or harsh in judging others. — un·gen'er·ous·ly adv.

un·gift·ed (un·gif'tid) adj. 1 Not gifted or endowed with talent. 2 Not having received gifts.

un·god·ly (un·god'lē) adj. 1 Having no reverence for God; impious; wicked. 2 Unholy; sinful. 3 Colloq. Outrageous. — adv. In an ungodly manner. — un·god'li·ness n.

un·got·ten (un·got'n) adj. 1 Not begotten. 2 Not obtained; not acquired.

un·gov·ern·a·ble (un·guv'ər·nə·bəl) adj. That cannot be governed; refractory; unruly. See synonyms under PERVERSE, REBELLIOUS, VIOLENT. — un·gov'ern·a·ble·ness n. — un·gov'ern·a·bly adv.

un·gra·cious (un·grā'shəs) adj. 1 Lacking in graciousness of manner; unmannerly. 2 Not pleasing; offensive; unacceptable. 3 Obs. Odious. — un·gra'cious·ly adv. — un·gra'cious·ness n.

un·grate·ful (un·grāt'fəl) adj. 1 Feeling or showing a lack of gratitude; not thankful. 2 Not pleasant; disagreeable. 3 Unrewarding; yielding no return. — un·grate'ful·ly adv. — un·grate'ful·ness n.

un·gual (ung'gwəl) adj. Having, resembling, or pertaining to a hoof, claw, or nail. [<L unguis hoof, claw, nail]

un·guard (un·gärd') v.t. To deprive of a guard; expose.

un·guard·ed (un·gär'did) adj. 1 Having no guard; being without protection. 2 Done or spoken without proper caution; careless: unguarded speech. — un·guard'ed·ly adv. — un·guard'ed·ness n.

un·guent (ung'gwənt) n. Any ointment for local application; a salve or cerate. [<L unguentum < unguere anoint]

un·guen·tar·y (ung'gwən·ter'ē) adj. Of, for, like, or pertaining to unguents.

un·guic·u·late (ung·gwik'yə·lit, -lāt) adj. 1 Zool. Having claws, as a carnivorous mammal. 2 Bot. Having a stalklike or clawlike base, as the petals of pinks. — n. A mammal having claws, as distinguished from an ungulate or cetacean. [<NL unguiculatus <L unguiculus fingernail, dim. of unguis nail]

un·gui·form (ung'gwi·fôrm) adj. Claw-shaped; hooked; unciform. [<L unguis nail + -FORM]

un·gui·nous (ung'gwi·nəs) adj. Resembling, containing, or consisting of oil or fat; unctuous. [<L unguinosus < unguen, -inis ointment]

un·guis (ung'gwis) n. pl. ·gues (-gwēz) 1 A nail, claw, hoof, or talon. 2 A structure resembling a nail. 3 Bot. A claw or lower contracted part of a petal. [<L, nail]

un·gu·la (ung'gyə·lə) n. pl. ·lae (-lē) 1 Zool. A hoof, claw, nail, or talon. 2 Surg. An instrument for removing a dead fetus from the womb. 3 Geom. That which is left of a cone or cylinder when the top is cut off by a plane oblique to the base: so called from its resemblance to a horse's hoof. 4 Bot. An unguis. [<L, hoof < unguis nail]

UNGULATE FEET
a. Hind foot of horse.
b. Foot of a stag.
c. Forefoot of Indian rhinoceros.
d. Side view of stag foot, showing false hoof at e.

un·gu·late (ung'gyə·lit, -lāt) adj. 1 Having hoofs; hoof-shaped. 2 Designating, pertaining to, or belonging to a large division (Ungulata) of hoofed, herbivorous mammals, including the elephant, rhinoceros, horse, cony, hog, and all the ruminants. — n. A hoofed mammal. [<LL ungulatus <L ungula hoof]

un·gu·li·grade (ung'gyə·lə·grād') adj. Walking on hoofs, as a horse or cow. [<L ungula hoof + -GRADE]

un·hal·low (un·hal'ō) v.t. To profane; desecrate.

un·hal·lowed (un·hal'ōd) adj. 1 Left secular. 2 Not sacred. 3 Unholy; wicked.

un·hand (un·hand') v.t. To remove one's hand from; release from the hand or hands; let go.

un·hand·y (un·han'dē) adj. 1 Inconvenient;

hard to handle. **2** Clumsy; lacking in manual skill. —**un·hand'i·ly** *adv.*

un·hap·py (un·hap'ē) *adj.* **·pi·er, ·pi·est** **1** Subject to conditions that prevent or destroy happiness; sad; depressed. **2** Causing or constituting misery, unrest, or dissatisfaction: *unhappy* circumstances. **3** Characterized by or exhibiting ill fortune; unfortunate; unpropitious. **4** Exhibiting lack of tact or judgment; inappropriate; inopportune. **5** *Obs.* Evil. See synonyms under BAD, SAD. —**un·hap'pi·ly** *adv.* —**un·hap'pi·ness** *n.*

un·har·bored (un·här'bərd) *adj.* **1** Having no harbor, shelter, or cover. **2** *Obs.* Not affording shelter. Also *Brit.* **un·har'boured.**

un·har·ness (un·här'nis) *v.t.* **1** To remove the harness from; unyoke; release. **2** To remove the armor from.

un·hat (un·hat') *v.* **·hat·ted, ·hat·ting** *v.i.* To take off one's hat, especially to show respect or in worship. —*v.t.* To remove the hat from.

un·health·y (un·hel'thē) *adj.* **·health·i·er, ·health·i·est** **1** Lacking health, vigor, or wholesomeness; sickly; unsound: *unhealthy* animals or plants; also, indicating such a condition: *unhealthy* signs. **2** Loosely, insalubrious; injurious to health. **3** Morally or spiritually unsound, defective, or pernicious: *unhealthy* fiction. —**un·health'i·ly** *adv.* —**un·health'i·ness** *n.*

un·heard (un·hûrd') *adj.* **1** Not perceived by the ear. **2** Not granted a hearing. **3** Obscure; unknown.

un·heard-of (un·hûrd'uv', -ov') *adj.* Not known of before; unknown or unprecedented.

un·helm (un·helm') *v.t.* To remove the helmet or helm of. —*v.i.* To remove one's helmet.

un·hinge (un·hinj') *v.t.* **·hinged, ·hing·ing** **1** To take from the hinges. **2** To remove the hinges of. **3** To detach; dislodge. **4** To throw into confusion; disorder. **5** To make unstable; unsettle, as the mind.

un·hitch (un·hich') *v.t.* To unfasten.

un·ho·ly (un·hō'lē) *adj.* **·ho·li·er, ·ho·li·est** **1** Not hallowed. **2** Lacking purity; wicked; sinful. See synonyms under PROFANE, SINFUL. [OE *unhālig*] —**un·ho'li·ly** *adv.* —**un·ho'li·ness** *n.*

un·hook (un·hŏok') *v.t.* **1** To remove from a hook. **2** To unfasten the hook or hooks of. —*v.i.* **3** To become unhooked.

un·hoped (un·hōpt') *adj.* Not hoped (for); unexpected; exceeding hope: chiefly in the compound **un·hoped'-for'.**

un·horse (un·hôrs') *v.t.* **·horsed, ·hors·ing** **1** To throw from a horse. **2** To dislodge; overthrow. **3** To remove a horse or horses from: to *unhorse* a vehicle.

un·hou·seled (un·hou'zəld) *adj. Obs.* Not having received the last sacraments. [<UN-¹ + HOUSEL + -ED²]

un·hur·ried (un·hûr'ēd) *adj.* Leisurely; not hurried.

un·husk (un·husk') *v.t.* **1** To strip the husk from. **2** To expose; lay open.

uni- *combining form* One; single; one only: *unifoliate.* [<L *unus* one]

U·ni·at (yōo'nē·at) *n.* A member of any community of Eastern Christians that acknowledges the supremacy of the pope at Rome, but retains its own liturgy, ceremonies, and rites: also called *United Armenian, United Greek.* Compare LATIN CHURCH. —*adj.* Of the Uniats or their faith. Also **U'ni·ate** (-it, -āt). [<Russian *uniyat* < *uniya* union <L *unus* one; from being in union with the Roman Catholic Church]

u·ni·ax·i·al (yōo'nē·ak'sē·əl) *adj.* **1** Having one axis. **2** Doubly refracting and having only a single optical axis, as crystals of the tetragonal and hexagonal systems. **3** *Bot.* Unbranched, as a primary stem terminating in a flower.

u·ni·cam·er·al (yōo'nə·kam'ər·əl) *adj.* Consisting of but one chamber, as a legislature.

u·ni·cel·lu·lar (yōo'nə·sel'yə·lər) *adj. Biol.* Consisting of a single cell, as a protozoan; one-celled.

u·ni·col·or (yōo'nə·kul'ər) *adj.* Of one color.

u·ni·corn (yōo'nə·kôrn) *n.* **1** A fabulous horselike animal with one horn. **2** A two-horned animal, identified with the urus, so called in the early English versions of the Bible to render the Latin and Greek mistranslations of the Hebrew *re' ēm*: translated as *wild ox* in the Revised Version. *Deut.* xxxiii 17. [<OF *unicorne* <L *unicornis* one-horned < *unus* one + *cornu* a horn]

UNICORN

u·ni·cos·tate (yōo'nə·kos'tāt) *adj.* **1** Having a single principal costa, rib, or nervure. **2** *Bot.* Having a midrib, as a leaf.

u·ni·cy·cle (yōo'nə·sī'kəl) *n.* A cycle or velocipede having a single wheel propelled by pedals.

un·i·de·aed (un'ī·dē'əd) *adj.* Not having ideas; frivolous.

u·ni·di·rec·tion·al (yōo'nə·di·rek'shən·əl, -dī-) *adj.* **1** Moving in the same direction. **2** Designed or equipped to operate best in only one direction, as a radio antenna. **3** *Electr.* Of or pertaining to a direct current.

u·ni·fi·a·ble (yōo'nə·fī'ə·bəl) *adj.* That can be unified.

u·nif·ic (yōo·nif'ik) *adj.* Unifying.

unified field theory *Physics* **1** Any mathematically rigorous generalization which will combine two or more physical theories in a form permitting accurate inclusive predictions not deducible from one theory alone, as the electromagnetic theory of Maxwell. **2** Such a generalization, as tentatively formulated by Einstein, to unify the theories of electromagnetism, gravitation, and relativity.

u·ni·fi·lar (yōo'nə·fī'lər) *adj.* **1** Possessing but a single thread. **2** Utilizing only one suspending thread.

u·ni·flo·rous (yōo'nə·flôr'əs, -flō'rəs) *adj. Bot.* One-flowered.

u·ni·fo·li·ate (yōo'nə·fō'lē·it, -āt) *adj. Bot.* Having one leaf.

u·ni·fo·li·o·late (yōo'nə·fō'lē·ə·lit, -lāt) *adj. Bot.* Having a single leaflet, as the compound leaves of the orange.

u·ni·form (yōo'nə·fôrm) *adj.* **1** Being the same or alike, as in form, appearance, quantity, quality, degree, or character; not varying: *uniform* temperature. **2** Agreeing with each other; harmonious; accordant; consonant: *uniform* tastes. See synonyms under ALIKE. —*n.* A dress or suit of uniform style and appearance worn by members of the same organization, service, etc., as soldiers, sailors, postmen, etc. See synonyms under DRESS. —**dress uniform** A military or naval uniform worn at social or ceremonial events. —*v.t.*

To put into or clothe with a uniform. [<F *uniforme* <L *uniformis* < *unus* one + *forma* form] —**u'ni·form·ness** *n.* —**u'ni·form·ly** *adv.*

u·ni·for·mal·ize (yōo'nə·fôr'məl·īz) *v.t.* **·ized, ·iz·ing** To bring into a uniform system; render uniform.

Uniform Code of Military Justice The code of laws and related procedures enacted in 1951 by the U. S. Congress for the government of the personnel of the armed services: supersedes the former Army *Articles of War* and the *Articles for the Government of the Navy.*

u·ni·formed (yōo'nə·fôrmd) *adj.* Dressed in uniform.

u·ni·form·i·tar·i·an·ism (yōo'nə·fôr'mə·târ'ē·ən·iz'əm) *n. Geol.* The doctrine that essential uniformity in causes and effects, forces and phenomena, has prevailed in all ages of the world's physical history, and that the activities of the past were similar in mode and intensity to those of the present: opposed to *catastrophism.* —**u'ni·form'i·tar'i·an** *adj. & n.*

u·ni·form·i·ty (yōo'nə·fôr'mə·tē) *n. pl.* **·ties** **1** The state or quality of being uniform, or an instance of it; consistency throughout; lack of diversity. **2** Conformity or compliance, as in opinions or religion. **3** Monotony; sameness.

u·ni·fy (yōo'nə·fī) *v.t.* **·fied, ·fy·ing** To cause to be a unit; make uniform; unite; cause to be one. [<F *unifier* <LL *unificare* <L *unus* one + *facere* make] —**u'ni·fi·ca'tion** (-fə·kā'shən) *n.* —**u'ni·fi'er** *n.*

u·ni·gen·i·ture (yōo'nə·jen'ə·chər) *n.* The state of being an only child, or, in theology, of being the only begotten Son.

u·nij·u·gate (yōo·nij'ŏo·gāt, yōo'nə·jōo'git, -gāt) *adj. Bot.* Having one pair, as of leaflets: said especially of a pinnate leaf. [<UNI- + JUGATE]

u·ni·lat·er·al (yōo'nə·lat'ər·əl) *adj.* **1** One-sided; relating to one side only; made, undertaken, done, or signed by only one of two or more people or parties. **2** *Law* Binding or obligatory on one party only. **3** Arranged or growing on one side only, as a plant or animal organ. **4** *Med.* Affecting but one side of the body. **5** Relating to or tracing ancestry on one side only.

u·ni·lit·er·al (yōo'nə·lit'ər·əl) *adj.* Comprising but one letter.

u·ni·loc·u·lar (yōo'nə·lok'yə·lər) *adj. Biol.* Having or consisting of one cell or chamber, as an anther, ovary, etc.

U·ni·mak Island (yōo'nə·mak) The most northeasterly of the Fox Islands in the NE Aleutian Islands; 70 miles long.

un·im·peach·a·ble (un'im·pē'chə·bəl) *adj.* Not to be called in question as regards truth, honesty, etc.; faultless; blameless. —**un'im·peach'a·bly** *adv.*

un·im·proved (un'im·prōovd') *adj.* **1** Not improved; not bettered or advanced: *unimproved* health. **2** Having no improvements; not cleared, cultivated, or built upon: *unimproved* land. **3** Not made anything of; unused: *unimproved* opportunities. **4** *Obs.* Not proved or tried.

un·in·gen·ious (un'in·jēn'yəs) *adj.* **1** Lacking ingenuity; not possessed of inventiveness. **2** *Obs.* Uningenuous.

un·in·gen·u·ous (un'in·jen'yōo·əs) *adj.* Not ingenuous; sly or designing.

un·in·tel·li·gent (un'in·tel'ə·jənt) *adj.* **1** Not intelligent; characterized by lack of intelligence. **2** Unwise; ignorant. —**un'in·tel'li·gence** *n.*

un·in·ter·est·ed (un·in'tər·is·tid, -tris-) *adj.* **1** Having no interest in, as in property.

unknowable	unlevel	unlocated	unmangled	unmaternal	unmentionability	unmodish
unknowing	unlevied	unlocked	unmanifested	unmatted	unmentioned	unmoistened
unlabeled,	unlibidinous	unlovable	unmanipulated	unmatured	unmercenary	unmold
unlabelled	unlicensed	unloved	unmannered	unmeant	unmerchantable	unmolested
unladylike	unlifelike	unloveliness	unmannish	unmeasurable	unmerited	unmollified
unlamented	unlighted	unloverlike	unmannishly	unmeasured	unmethodical	unmolten
unlash	unlikable,	unloving	unmanufacturable	unmechanical	unmilitary	unmortgaged
unlashed	unlikeable	unlubricated	unmanufactured	unmedicated	unmilled	unmotivated
unlaundered	unlined	unlying	unmarketable	unmeditated	unmingle	unmounted
unleased	unlink	unmagnified	unmarred	unmelodious	unmingled	unmourned
unled	unliquefiable	unmaidenly	unmarriageable	unmelted	unmirthful	unmovable
unlessened	unliquefied	unmailable	unmarried	unmenaced	unmistaken	unmoved
unlessoned	unlit	unmalleable	unmastered	unmendable	unmitigable	unmown
unlet	unliveliness	unmanageable	unmatched	unmended	unmixed,	unmurmuring
unletted	unlively	unmanful	unmated	unmensurable	unmixt	

add,āce,câre,pälm; end,ēven; it,īce; odd,ōpen,ôrder; tŏok,pōol; up,bûrn; ə = a in *above,* e in *sicken,* i in *clarity,* o in *melon,* u in *focus;* yōō = u in *fuse;* oi,oil; ou,pout; ch,check; g,go; ng,ring; th,thin; ŧħ,this; zh,vision. Foreign sounds à,œ,ü,kh,ń; and ◆: see page xx. <from; + plus; ? possibly.

2 Taking no interest in; indifferent; unconcerned.

un·ion (yōōn′yən) *n.* **1** The act of uniting, or the state of being united; a joining; coalescence; junction. **2** That which is constituted as one by the combination of elements previously separate; a coalition; confederation; league. **3** A combination of co–laborers for the joint and mutual protection of their common interests. See TRADE UNION. **4** *Brit.*

PIPE UNION

An amalgamation of parishes for administration of poor relief; also, a workhouse administered by such a union. **5** Agreement in sentiment or action; harmony; concord; unanimity. **6** The joining of two persons in marriage, or the resulting state of wedlock. **7** A device emblematic of union borne in the canton of a flag, as the three crosses in a British ensign; the canton itself containing such device, sometimes used separately as a flag, as the blue canton with white stars in the flag of the United States, and the Union Jack of Great Britain. **8** A coupling or connection for pipes or rods. **9** A fabric made of two or more materials, as cotton and wool. **10** *Obs.* A pearl of extraordinary worth. —*adj.* Of, pertaining to, or adhering to a union, particularly a political or trade union. [<F <LL *unio, -onis* <L *unus* one. Doublet of ONION.]

Synonyms (noun): coalition, combination, conjunction, junction, juncture, oneness, unification, unity. *Unity* is *oneness*, the state of existing as essentially one, especially of that which never has been divided or of that which cannot be conceived of as resolved into parts; as, the *unity* of the human soul. *Union* is a bringing together of things that have been distinct, so that they combine or coalesce to form a new whole, or the state or condition of things thus brought together; in a *union* the separate individuality of the things united is never lost sight of; we speak of the *union* of the parts of a fractured bone. See ALLIANCE, ASSOCIATION, ATTACHMENT, HARMONY, MARRIAGE. *Antonyms:* analysis, contrariety, decomposition, disconnection, disjunction, dissociation, disunion, division, divorce, separation, severance.

Un·ion (yōōn′yən) *n.* **1** The United States regarded as a national unit: with *the.* **2** The Union of South Africa. —*adj.* Of, pertaining to, or loyal to the United States, especially the Federal government during the Civil War: a *Union* soldier; He was *Union* to the core.

union card **1** A card certifying that the person named belongs to a certain labor union. **2** A card certifying that the shop named hires only union labor.

union catalog A library catalog combining the catalogs of more than one library, usually in a single alphabetical list.

union down Reversed, as a flag, so as to have the union or canton at the lower edge: a signal of distress.

Union Islands See TOKELAU ISLANDS.

un·ion·ism (yōōn′yən·iz′əm) *n.* **1** The principle of combination for unity of purpose and action. **2** Trade–unionism. **3** Adherence to or advocacy of political union between states, as opposed to secession. —**un′ion·is′tic** *adj.*

un·ion·ist (yōōn′yən·ist) *n.* **1** An advocate of union or unionism. **2** A member of a trade union.

Un·ion·ist (yōōn′yən·ist) *n.* **1** One who before and during the Civil War in the United States supported the Union cause and opposed secession; a Union man. **2** One of those opposed to loosening the formal ties between Great Britain and Ireland, whether belonging to the Conservatives or the branch of the Liberals (**Liberal Unionists**) that separated from their party in 1886 in opposition to the advocates of Home Rule for Ireland. From this time the term *Unionists* began to come into use, at first to signify both the Conservative and the Liberal Unionist parties, and later, as the distinction between the two wings gradually grew smaller, the Conservative Party.

un·ion·ize (yōōn′yən·īz) *v.* **·ized, ·iz·ing** *v.t.* To cause to join, or to organize into a union, especially a trade union. — *v.i.* To become a member of or organize a trade union. —**un′·ion·i·za′tion** *n.*

union jack A flag consisting of the union or canton only.

Union Jack The British national flag. It is a combination of the flags of England, Scotland, and Ireland.

Union of South Africa Former name of the Republic of South Africa.

Union of Soviet Socialist Republic The former federal union of 26 constituent republics of eastern Europe and northern Asia extending from the Artic Ocean to the Black Sea and east to the Pacific, dissolved into independent nations in 1991-1993; formerly **Soviet Russia, Soviet Union,** abbr. **U.S.S.R., USSR.**

union shop An industrial establishment in which only members of a trade union are employed.

union station A railroad station or depot used by two or more railroad lines.

union suit A one–piece undergarment consisting of shirt and drawers.

Union Territory In India, under the provisions of the States Reorganization Act, which came into effect November 1, 1956, a division of India administered by the central government, rather than governing itself as a State. The six Union Territories of India are the Andaman and Nicobar Islands, Delhi, Himachal Pradesh, the Laccadive Islands, Manipura, and Tripura; Pondicherry is also temporarily administered as a Union Territory.

u·ni·pa·ren·tal (yōō′nə·pə·ren′təl) *adj.* Having or produced by one parent only; asexual.

u·nip·a·rous (yōō·nip′ər·əs) *adj.* **1** *Bot.* Having but one axis or stem. **2** Bringing forth but one offspring at a time, or not having borne more than one. [<UNI- + -PAROUS]

u·ni·per·son·al (yōō′nə·pûr′sən·əl) *adj.* **1** Manifested or existing in but one person. **2** *Gram.* Used in only one person, especially the third person singular; impersonal.

u·ni·pet·al·ous (yōō′nə·pet′l·əs) *adj.* *Bot.* Having only one petal.

u·ni·pla·nar (yōō′nə·plā′nər) *adj.* Lying or taking place in one plane.

u·ni·po·lar (yōō′nə·pō′lər) *adj.* **1** *Physics* Showing only one kind of polarity. **2** *Anat.* Having or operating by means of, one pole: said especially of nerve cells having only one process.

u·nique (yōō·nēk′) *adj.* **1** Being the only one of its kind; being without equal; singular; uncommon; rare. **2** Not complicated with other things. **3** Sole. See synonyms under ODD, QUEER, RARE. [<F <L *unicus* <*unus* one] —**u·nique′ly** *adv.* —**u·nique′·ness** *n.*

u·ni·sep·tate (yōō′nə·sep′tāt) *adj.* Having a single septum or partition.

u·ni·sex (yōō′nə·seks′) *Colloq. adj.* For, appropriate to, or having characteristics of both sexes: *unisex* fashions. —*n.* The embodiment or integration of qualities, characteristics, etc., of both sexes, as in appearance, clothes, or activities.

u·ni·sex·u·al (yōō′nə·sek′shŏō·əl) *adj.* **1** Of one sex: specifically said of flowers and animals having one kind of sexual organs only. **2** *Colloq.* Of or having to do with unisex.

u·ni·son (yōō′nə·sən, -zən) *n.* **1** A condition of perfect agreement and accord; harmony. **2** *Colloq.* Of or having to do with unisex. or voices perform the same part; unity of pitch; also, the interval of one or more octaves. See synonyms under HARMONY, MELODY. [<L *unisonus* having a single sound <*uni-* one + *sonus* a sound]

u·nis·o·nal (yōō·nis′ə·nəl) *adj.* Being in unison. Also **u·nis′o·nant.** —**u·nis′o·nal·ly** *adv.*

u·nit (yōō′nit) *n.* **1** A single person or thing regarded as an individual but belonging to an entire group. **2** A body or group considered as a single whole among a plurality of similars. **3** A standard quantity with which others of the same kind are compared for purposes of measurement and in terms of which their magnitude is stated. **4** *Math.* A quantity whose measure is represented by the number 1; a least whole number; specifically, in arithmetic, the number 1 itself; unity. **5** *Med.* The quantity of a drug, vaccine, serum, or antigen required to produce a given effect. **6** A fundamental quantity used in calculating how much scholastic work a student has finished. [Short for UNITY]

unit angle A radian.

u·ni·tar·i·an (yōō′nə·târ′ē·ən) *n.* One who rejects the doctrine of the Trinity; a non-Trinitarian monotheist. —*adj.* Pertaining to a unit. [<NL *unitarius* unitary]

U·ni·tar·i·an (yōō′nə·târ′ē·ən) *n.* A member of a Protestant denomination which rejects the doctrine of the Trinity, but accepts the ethical teachings of Jesus and emphasizes complete freedom of religious opinion, the importance of personal character, and the independence of each local congregation. —*adj.* Pertaining to the Unitarians, or to their teachings. —**U′ni·tar′i·an·ism** *n.*

u·ni·tar·i·an·ism (yōō′nə·târ′ē·ən·iz′əm) *n.* Any unitary system.

u·ni·tar·y (yōō′nə·ter′ē) *adj.* **1** Pertaining to a unit; characterized by, based on, or pertaining to unity. **2** Having the nature of a unit; whole.

unit cell *Crystall.* Cell (def. 6).

unit character *Genetics* One of two or more contrasting characters which is transmitted as a unit and without modification.

u·nite (yōō·nīt′) *v.* **u·nit·ed, u·nit·ing** *v.t.* **1** To join together so as to form a whole; combine; compound. **2** To bring into close connection, as by legal, physical, marital, social, or other tie; join in action, interest, etc. **3** To attach permanently or solidly; cause to

unmusical	unnoted	unobtruding	unornamental	unparental	unperceivable	unphonetic
unmuzzle	unnoticeable	unobtrusive	unornate	unperceived	unpicked
unmuzzled	unnoticed	unobtrusiveness	unparted	unperceiving	unpicturesque
unmystified	unnurtured	unoccasioned	unorthodox	unpartisan,	unperfected	unpierced
unnail	unobjectionable	unoffended	unorthodoxy	unpartizan	unperformed	unpile
unnamable,	unobliged	unoffending	unostentatious	unpasteurized	unperplexed	unpitying
unnameable	unobliging	unoffensive	unowned	unpatched	unpersuadable	unplaced
unnamed	unobnoxious	unoffered	unoxidized	unpatented	unpersuaded	unplagued
unnaturalized	unobscured	unofficious	unpacified	unpatriotic	unpersuasive	unplait
unnavigable	unobservant	unoiled	unpacker	unpaved	unperturbed	unplanned
unnavigated	unobserved	unopen	unpainful	unpeaceable	unperused	unplanted
unneeded	unobserving	unopened	unpalatable	unpeaceful	unphilanthropic	unplayed
unneedful	unobstructed	unopposed	unpalatably	unpedigreed	unphilological	unpleasing
unnegotiable	unobtainable	unoppressed	unpardonable	unpen	unphilosophic	unpledged
unneighborly	unobtained	unordained	unpardonably	unpenetrated	unphilosophical	unpliable
				unpardoned	unpensioned	

adhere; combine. —*v.i.* **4** To become or be merged into one; be consolidated; combine. **5** To join together for action; act in conjunction; concur. [< LL *unitus*, pp. of *unire* make one < L *unus* one]

Synonyms: amalgamate, blend, cement, cohere, combine, compound, conjoin, connect, consolidate, fuse, join, link, merge. See MIX. Compare ADD, COMPLEX. **Antonyms:** disconnect, disjoin, disrupt, dissociate, dissolve, divide, separate, sever.

u·nit·ed (yōō·nī′tid) *adj.* Incorporated into one; allied; combined; harmonious. **—u·nit′·ed·ly** *adv.* **—u·nit′ed·ness** *n.*

United Arab Republic A former republic formed in 1958 by the merger of the republics of Egypt and Syria; after the withdrawal of Syria in 1961, the official name for EGYPT.

United Armenian A Uniat.

United Church of Christ A Protestant denomination formed in 1957 by a union of the Congregational Christian Churches and the Evangelical and Reformed Church.

United Greek A Uniat.

United Kingdom 1 The kingdom of the British Isles, comprising Great Britain, Northern Ireland, the Isle of Man, and the Channel Islands; 94,284 square miles; capital, London: officially **United Kingdom of Great Britain and Northern Ireland. 2** Formerly, Great Britain and Ireland (1801–1922).

United Nations 1 A coalition to resist the military aggression of the Axis Powers in World War II, formed of 26 national states in January, 1942. **2** An international organization of sovereign states (originally called the **United Nations Organization**) created by the United Nations Charter drafted in September–October, 1944, at Dumbarton Oaks and adopted at San Francisco in May and June, 1945: the 26 states of the United Nations coalition and 25 others form the original membership.

Membership (1945): Argentina, Australia, Belgium, Belorussian S.S.R., Bolivia, Brazil, Canada, Chile, China (Taiwan), Colombia, Costa Rica, Cuba, Czechoslovakia, Denmark, Dominican Republic, Ecuador, Egypt, El Salvador, Ethiopia, France, Greece, Guatemala, Haiti, Honduras, India, Iran, Iraq, Lebanon, Liberia, Luxembourg, Mexico, Netherlands, New Zealand, Nicaragua, Norway, Panama, Paraguay, Peru, Philippines, Poland, Saudi Arabia, South Africa (Union of South Africa), Syria, Turkey, Ukrainian S.S.R., United Kingdom, United States, Uruguay, U.S.S.R., Venezuela, Yugoslavia; (1946) Afghanistan, Iceland, Sweden, Thailand; (1947) Pakistan, Yemen; (1948) Myanmar (Burma); (1949) Israel; (1950) Indonesia; (1955) Albania, Austria, Bulgaria, Finland, Hungary, Ireland, Italy, Jordan, Kampuchea (Cambodia), Laos, Libya, Nepal, Portugal, Romania, Spain, Sri Lanka (Ceylon); (1956) Japan, Morocco, Sudan, Tunisia; (1957) Ghana, Malaysia (Malaya); (1958) Guinea; (1960) Benin (Dahomey), Burkina Faso (Upper Volta), Cameroon, Central African Republic, Chad, Congo, Côte d'Ivoire (Ivory Coast), Cyprus, Gabon, Madagascar, Mali, Niger, Nigeria, Senegal, Somalia, Togo, Zaire (Belgian Congo); (1961) Mauritania, Mongolia, Sierra Leone, Tanzania (Tanganyika, merged in 1964 with Zanzibar, member 1963); (1962) Algeria, Burundi, Jamaica, Rwanda, Trinidad and Tobago, Uganda; (1963) Kenya, Kuwait; (1964) Malawi, Malta, Zambia; (1965) Gambia, Mal-

dives, Singapore; (1966) Barbados, Botswana, Guyana, Lesotho; (1967) Democratic Yemen; (1968) Equatorial Guinea, Mauritius, Swaziland; (1970) Fiji; (1971) Bahrain, Bhutan, China (People's Republic, replaced Taiwan), Oman, Qatar, United Arab Emirates; (1973) Bahamas, Germany (German Democratic Republic and Federal Republic of); (1974) Bangladesh, Grenada, Guinea-Bissau; (1975) Cape Verde, Comoros, Mozambique, Papua New Guinea, São Tome and Príncipe; Suriname; (1976) Angola, Samoa, Seychelles; (1977) Djibouti, Vietnam; (1978) Dominica, Solomon Islands; (1979) St. Lucia; (1980) St. Vincent and the Grenadines, Zimbabwe; (1981) Antigua and Barbuda, Belize, Vanuatu; (1983) St. Kitts and Nevis; (1984) Brunei. Also called *UN.*

United Nations Trust Territory See TRUST TERRITORY.

United Presbyterian Church in the United States of America The largest U.S. Presbyterian body, formed in 1958 by the merger of two separate churches.

United Press A news-collecting and -distributing organization, merged in 1958 with the International News Service to form the **United Press International.**

United Society of Believers in Christ's Second Appearing See SHAKER.

United States The United States of America.

United States Army, Navy, Air Force, etc. See under ARMY, NAVY, AIR FORCE, etc.

United States of America A federal republic of North America, including 50 states, and the District of Columbia, the Canal Zone, Puerto Rico, the Virgin Islands of the United States, American Samoa, Guam, Wake, and several other scattered islands of the Pacific; total area, about 3,720,407 square miles; capital, Washington, in the District of Columbia. **—conterminous United States** The 48 contiguous States and the District of Columbia. **—continental United States** The District of Columbia and the 49 States on the continent of North America. Also *America, the States, United States:* abbr. *U.S.A., U.S., US.*

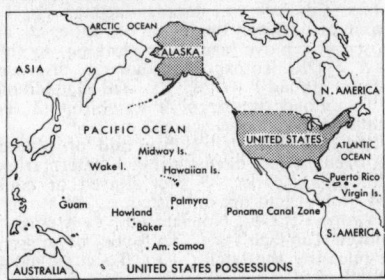

unit factor *Biol.* A gene controlling the inheritance of a unit character.

unit fraction See under FRACTION.

u·ni·tive (yōō′nə·tiv) *adj.* Productive of or promoting union; having power to unite; characterized by union.

u·ni·tize (yōō′nə·tīz) *v.t.* **·tized, ·tiz·ing** To form into a whole; unify.

unit modifier A conventional or improvised compound used adjectively before a substantive. Examples: *blue-green* algae, *bitter-sweet* chocolate, *suit-coat* pattern, *situation-comdey* plot, *storm-window* installation, *contour-plowing*

method, *most-favored-nation* clause. ♦The use of the hyphen in the unit modifier is to avoid ambiguity in a word sequence where the relationship is not immediately apparent from context: The house had faded red-brick walls (faded walls of red brick, *not* faded red walls of brick). The hyphen here is to be considered a nonce use and not as a spelling form or variant.

Unit rule *U.S.* A rule in a national convention of the Democratic party, requiring that, if so instructed by a State party convention, the vote of an entire delegation shall be determined by a majority of its members.

u·ni·ty (yōō′nə·tē) *n. pl.* **·ties 1** The state, property, or product of being united, physically, socially, or morally; oneness: opposed to *division, plurality.* **2** Union, as of constituent parts or elements: national *unity.* **3** Agreement of parts; harmonious adjustment of constituent elements; sameness of character: the *unity* of two writings. **4** The fact of something's being a whole that is more than or different from its parts or their sum. **5** Singleness of purpose or action. **6** A state of general good feeling; mutual understanding; concord: brethren dwelling together in *unity.* **7** *Math.* **a** The number one; the ratio of two equal quantities. **b** The element of a number system that leaves any number unchanged under multiplication, that is, a number e such that $ex = xe = x$ for all $x.$ **8** In literature and the arts, combination into a homogeneous artistic whole, exhibiting oneness of purpose, thought, spirit, and style, with subordination of all parts to the general effect. **9** In the drama, observance, complete or partial, of the law of dramatic unities. **10** Identity. See synonyms under HARMONY, UNION. **— the law of dramatic unities** The law of Aristole that in a drama there must be unity of action, unity of time, and unity of place. These unities were strictly observed by the French classical dramatists of the 17th century, but were violated by Shakespeare and certain of the German playwrights. [< F *unité* < L *unitas* < *unus* one]

U·ni·ty (yōō′nə·tē) *n.* A religious philosophy, based on the teachings of Jesus Christ, stating that man is inseparable from the spirit of God within him, and that through prayerful realization of this spirit he can obtain healing of all life's inharmonies in mind, body, etc.: founded in 1889.

Unity of the Brethren See MORAVIAN.

u·ni·va·lent (yōō′nə·vā′lent) *adj.* **1** *Chem.* Having a valence or combining value of one; monovalent. **2** *Biol.* Pertaining to or designating a single unpaired chromosome. **—u′ni·va′lence, u′ni·va′len·cy** *n.*

u·ni·valve (yōō′nə·valv′) *adj.* Having only one valve, as a mollusk. Also **u′ni·val′vate, u′ni·valved′.** **—n. 1** A mollusk having a univalve shell; a gastropod. **2** A shell of a single piece. **— u′ni·val′vu·lar** (-val′vyə-lər) *adj.*

u·ni·ver·sal (yōō′nə·vûr′səl) *adj.* **1** Prevalent or common everywhere or among all things or persons specified or implied: a *universal* belief; *universal* suffrage; a *universal* language. **2** Of or including everyone: a *universal* church. **3** Applicable to all cases: a *universal* law; a *universal* cure. **4** Accomplished or interested in a vast variety of subjects or activities: Leonardo da Vinci was a *universal* genius. **5** Of, pertaining to, or occuring throughout the universe: a *universal* being. **6** *Mech.* Adapted or adaptable to a great variety of uses, shapes, etc., as certain machines or machine parts. **7** *Logic* **a** Including all the individuals of a class or genus; generic. **b** In a proposition, predicable of all the individuals denoted by the subject: opposed to *particular*: "All men are mortal" is a *universal* proposition. See synonyms under COMMON, GENERAL. —*n.* **1** *Logic* **a** A universal proposition. **b** One of the five predicables, that is, genus, species, difference, property, and accident, known collectively as the *universals*. **c** A general or abstract concept considered as having absolute reality or mental or nominal existence. **2** Any general or universal notion or idea. **3** A metaphysical being which preserves its identity in spite of the changes through which it passes, as the ego. [<OF <L *universalis* < *universus*. See UNIVERSE.] — **u′ni·ver′sal·ly** *adv.* — **u′ni·ver′sal·ness** *n.*

universal developer *Phot.* A developer adapted for use with various types of films, plates, or papers.

universal donor One whose blood belongs to group O and may be transfused with little or no danger of agglutination into a person belonging to any of the four blood groups.

U·ni·ver·sal·ism (yōō′nə·vûr′səl·iz′əm) *n. Theol.* The doctrine that all souls will finally be saved and that good will triumph universally.

U·ni·ver·sal·ist (yōō′nə·vûr′səl·ist) *adj.* Pertaining to Universalism or Universalists. — *n.* A believer in the doctrines of Universalism, or a member of the Universalist denomination.

u·ni·ver·sal·i·ty (yōō′nə·vər·sal′ə·tē) *n.* **1** The state of being all-embracing. **2** Unrestricted fitness or adaptability.

u·ni·ver·sal·ize (yōō′nə·vûr′səl·īz) *v.t.* **·ized, ·iz·ing** To make universal.

universal joint *Mech.* A joint that permits both connected parts of a machine to be turned in any direction within definite limits; specifically, a coupling for connecting two shafts, etc., so as to permit angular motion in all directions. Also **universal coupling**.

UNIVERSAL JOINT

u·ni·verse (yōō′nə·vûrs) *n.* **1** The aggregate of all existing things; the whole creation embracing all celestial bodies and all of space; the cosmos. **2** In restricted sense, the earth. **3** Human beings collectively; mankind. **4** *Logic* All objects, collectively, that are the subjects of consideration at once: also **universe of discourse**. **5** *Stat.* All the instances in a given class: contrasted with *sample*. [<F *univers* <L *universum*, neut. of *universus* turned, combined into one, all collectively < *unus* one + *versus*, pp. of *vertere* turn]

u·ni·ver·si·ty (yōō′nə·vûr′sə·tē) *n. pl.* **·ties** **1** An educational institution for higher instruction or for the examination of students already instructed. Universities arose in Europe in the Middle Ages and were first essentially ecclesiastic. Their functions gradually became specialized, some dividing into several *faculties,* each of which took charge of some one great branch of instruction, or into *colleges,* as now in the older English universities, where the relation of the university to the college is similar to that of a federal government to its component states. In the United States the word has been used loosely, chiefly to mean a collection of educational associations including a college (which offers degrees in general subjects) and several more advanced and specialized faculties, either professional, as law, medicine, etc., or academic, as history or mathematics. **2** All the students of such an in-

stitution. **3** *Brit. Colloq.* A university team or crew.

u·ni·ver·son (yōō′nə·vûr′son) *n. Physics* A hypothetical primordial entity originally containing the entire mass of the universe and whose splitting simultaneously gave rise to the cosmos and to its balanced opposite, the anticosmos. [<UNIVERSE]

u·niv·o·cal (yōō·niv′ə·kəl) *adj.* Having but one proper sense or meaning. — *n.* A word that has but one meaning. [<LL *univocus* <L *unus* one + *vox* voice]

un·just (un·just′) *adj.* **1** Not legitimate, fair, or just; wrongful. **2** Unrighteous; acting contrary to right and justice. **3** *Archaic* Faithless. **4** *Archaic* Dishonest. — **un·just′ly** *adv.* — **un·just′ness** *n.*

un·kempt (un·kempt′) *adj.* **1** Not combed; neglected; untidy. **2** Without polish; rough. [<UN-¹ + *kempt* combed, pp. of dial. *kemb,* var. of COMB] — **un·kempt′ness** *n.*

un·kenned (un·kend′) *adj. Scot.* & *Brit. Dial.* Unknown. Also **un·kend′, un·kent′** (-kent′).

un·ken·nel (un·ken′əl) *v.t.* **1** To drive or release from a kennel or lair. **2** To bring to light; disclose.

un·kind (un·kīnd′) *adj.* Showing lack of kindness; unsympathetic; harsh; cruel. [OE *uncynde* strange, unnatural] — **un·kind′ly** *adv.* — **un·kind′ness** *n.*

un·known (un·nōn′) *adj.* **1** Not known; not apprehended mentally; not recognized, as a fact or person. **2** Not ascertained; incalculable. See synonyms under MYSTERIOUS, SECRET. — *n.* An unknown person or quantity. — **the Great Unknown** Life after death; future life.

Unknown Soldier One of the unidentified dead of World War I who is honored as a symbol of all his compatriots who died in action; extended to include unknown dead of World War II and the Korean conflict.

un·la·bored (un·lā′bərd) *adj.* **1** Produced without strain or effort; seemingly free and easy; natural. **2** Uncultivated by labor; unworked; untilled. Also *Brit.* **un·la′boured.**

un·lace (un·lās′) *v.t.* **·laced, ·lac·ing** **1** To loosen or unfasten the lacing of; untie. **2** To loosen or remove (armor or clothing) in this way. **3** *Obs.* To expose to damage; disgrace.

un·lade (un·lād′) *v.t.* & *v.i.* **·lad·ed, ·lad·ing** **1** To unload the cargo of (a ship). **2** To unload or discharge (cargo, etc.).

un·laid (un·lād′) *adj.* **1** Not laid or placed; not fixed. **2** Not having parallel watermarked lines: *unlaid* paper. **3** Not allayed or pacified. **4** Not laid up; untwisted, as the strands of a rope. **5** *Obs.* Not laid out, as a corpse.

un·latch (un·lach′) *v.t.* To open or unlock by releasing the latch. — *v.i.* To come open or unlocked.

un·law·ful (un·lô′fəl) *adj.* Contrary to or in violation of law; illegal; illicit; also, illegitimate. See synonyms under CRIMINAL. — **un·law′ful·ly** *adv.* — **un·law′ful·ness** *n.*

un·lay (un·lā′) *v.t.* & *v.i.* **·laid, ·lay·ing** To untwist: said specifically of the strands of a rope. [<UN-² + LAY¹ (def. 21)]

un·lead (un·led′) *v.t.* **1** To strip of lead. **2** *Printing* To remove the leads from between (lines of type matter).

un·lead·ed (un·led′id) *adj.* **1** Not supplied or weighted with lead. **2** *Printing* Having no leads between the lines; not spaced with leads.

un·learn (un·lûrn′) *v.t.* **·learned** or **·learnt, ·learn·ing** To dismiss from the mind (something learned); forget.

un·learn·ed (un·lûr′nid) *adj.* **1** Not learned; not possessed of or characterized by learn-

ing; illiterate; ignorant; untaught. **2** Unworthy or unsuggestive of a scholar; not like the production of a learned man. **3** (un·lûrnd′) Not acquired by learning or study. See synonyms under IGNORANT.

un·leash (un·lēsh′) *v.t.* To set free from or as from a leash.

un·leav·ened (un·lev′ənd) *adj.* Not leavened: said specifically of the bread used at the feast of the Passover.

un·less (un·les′) *conj.* **1** If it be not a fact that; supposing that . . . not; except that: *Unless* we persevere, we shall lose. **2** *Obs.* For fear that; lest. — *prep.* Save; except; excepting: with an implied verb: *Unless* a miracle, he'll not be back in time. See synonyms under BUT. [Earlier *onlesse (that)* in a less case <ON + LESS]

un·let·tered (un·let′ərd) *adj.* Not educated; not lettered; illiterate.

un·like (un·līk′) *adj.* Having little or no resemblance; different. See synonyms under ALIEN, CONTRARY, HETEROGENEOUS. — *adv.* In another manner: with *to* expressed or implied. By the ellipsis of *to* it approaches prepositional use. [ME *unliche*] — **un·like′·ness** *n.*

un·like·ly (un·līk′lē) *adj.* **1** Improbable. **2** Not inviting or promising success. — *adv.* Improbably. — **un·like′li·ness, un·like′li·hood** *n.*

un·lim·ber (un·lim′bər) *v.t.* & *v.i.* To disconnect (a gun or caisson) from its limber; prepare for action.

un·lim·it·ed (un·lim′it·id) *adj.* **1** Having no limits in space, number, or time; unbounded; endless; unnumbered. **2** Not limited by restrictions; unconfined: *unlimited* authority. **3** Not limited by exceptions or qualifications; undefined. — **un·lim′it·ed·ly** *adv.* — **un·lim′it·ed·ness** *n.*

un·liq·ui·dat·ed (un·lik′wə·dā′tid) *adj.* **1** *Law* Unascertained as to amount; undetermined or not settled: *unliquidated* damages. **2** Not yet eliminated from the living: said of the survivors of attempted genocide.

un·list·ed (un·lis′tid) *adj.* Not listed; specifically, noting stocks quoted in the unlisted department of a stock exchange, but not admitted to dealings on the floor of the New York Stock Exchange.

un·live (un·liv′) *v.t.* **·lived, ·liv·ing** To live so as to wipe out the effects of (a former period of life); undo by living; live down.

un·load (un·lōd′) *v.t.* **1** To remove the load or cargo from. **2** To take off or discharge (cargo, etc.). **3** To relieve of something burdensome or oppressive. **4** To withdraw the charge of ammunition from. **5** *Colloq.* To dispose of, especially by selling in large quantities. — *v.i.* **6** To discharge freight, cargo, or other burden.

un·load·er (un·lō′dər) *n.* One who or that which unloads; specifically, a contrivance for unloading something, as hay or coal.

un·lock (un·lok′) *v.t.* **1** To unfasten (something locked). **2** To open or undo; release. **3** To lay open; reveal or disclose. — *v.i.* **4** To become unlocked.

un·looked-for (un·lŏŏkt′fôr′) *adj.* Not anticipated; unexpected.

un·loose (un·lōōs′) *v.t.* **·loosed, ·loos·ing** To release from fastenings; set loose or free. See synonyms under RELEASE.

un·loos·en (un·lōō′sən) *v.t.* To loose; unloose.

un·love·ly (un·luv′lē) *adj.* Unattractive; disagreeable; ugly.

un·luck·y (un·luk′ē) *adj.* **·luck·i·er, ·luck·i·est** **1** Not favored by luck; unfortunate. **2** Resulting in or attended by ill luck; causing misfortune; disastrous. **3** Ill-omened; inauspicious: an *unlucky* day. See synonyms under

BAD. — **un·luck'i·ly** *adv.* — **un·luck'i·ness** *n.*

un·make (un·māk') *v.t.* **·made, ·mak·ing** **1** To reverse the making of; reduce to the original condition or form. **2** To ruin; destroy. **3** To depose, as from a position of authority.

un·man (un·man') *v.t.* **·manned, ·man·ning** **1** To cause to lose courage or fortitude; dishearten. **2** To render unmanly or effeminate. **3** To deprive of virility; emasculate; castrate. **4** To remove the men from, as a ship or fortress.

un·man·ly (un·man'lē) *adj.* **1** Not masculine; effeminate; not virile; not courageous. **2** Not gentlemanly; not honorable. — **un·man'li·ness** *n.*

un·manned (un·mand') *adj.* **1** Not manned. **2** Deprived of virility or manhood. **3** *Obs.* Unaccustomed to men; untamed: said of hawks. **4** Uninhabited.

un·man·ner·ly (un·man'ər·lē) *adj.* Lacking manners; rude. — *adv.* Impolitely. — **un·man'·ner·li·ness** *n.*

un·marked (un·märkt') *adj.* **1** Bearing no mark; having no distinctive mark. **2** *Electr.* Denoting that pole of a magnet which points south. **3** Not noticed. **4** Not examined; hence, uncorrected; ungraded: *unmarked* test papers.

un·mask (un·mask', -mäsk') *v.t.* **1** To remove a mask from. **2** To reveal; disclose. — *v.i.* **3** To remove one's mask or disguise.

un·mean·ing (un·mē'ning) *adj.* **1** Having no meaning: an *unmeaning* speech or look. **2** Having no expression; not displaying intelligence. — **un·mean'ing·ly** *adv.* — **un·mean'·ing·ness** *n.*

un·meet (un·mēt') *adj.* Not meet, adapted, or suitable; not proper or fit; unbecoming. [OE *unmǣte*] — **un·meet'ly** *adv.* — **un·meet'·ness** *n.*

un·men·tion·a·ble (un·men'shən·ə·bəl) *adj.* Not proper to be mentioned or discussed; embarrassing; shameful; disgraceful. — **un·men'·tion·a·ble·ness** *n.* — **un·men'tion·a·bly** *adv.*

un·men·tion·a·bles (un·men'shən·ə·bəlz) *n. pl.* Things or articles not ordinarily discussed or mentioned; usually, undergarments; formerly, trousers; pants.

un·mer·ci·ful (un·mûr'sə·fəl) *adj.* **1** Showing no mercy; cruel; pitiless; unconscionable. **2** Extreme; exorbitant. — **un·mer'ci·ful·ly** *adv.* — **un·mer'ci·ful·ness** *n.*

un·mew (un·myoo') *v.t.* To release from confinement; set free.

un·mind·ful (un·mīnd'fəl) *adj.* Not keeping in mind; neglectful; inattentive. — **un·mind'ful·ly** *adv.* — **un·mind'ful·ness** *n.*

un·mis·tak·a·ble (un'mis·tā'kə·bəl) *adj.* That cannot be mistaken for something else; evident; clear; obvious. See synonyms under CLEAR, EVIDENT, MANIFEST. — **un'mis·tak'a·bly** *adv.*

un·mi·ter (un·mī'tər) *v.t.* To divest of a miter; deprive of the office of bishop. Also **un·mi'tre.**

un·mit·i·gat·ed (un·mit'ə·gā'tid) *adj.* **1** Not mitigated or lightened in effect; unabated; unassuaged: *unmitigated* sorrow. **2** As bad as can be; unconscionable: an *unmitigated* rogue. — **un·mit'i·gat·ed·ly** *adv.*

un·mod·u·lat·ed (un·moj'ŏŏ·lā'tid) *adj.* **1** Without modulation. **2** *Telecom.* Denoting a carrier wave of constant amplitude, as during a pause in broadcasting.

un·moor (un·moor') *Naut. v.t.* **1** To loose the moorings of; release from moorings: to *unmoor* a ship. **2** To release all but one anchor of (a vessel formerly moored by two or more). — *v.i.* **3** To cast off moorings.

un·mor·al (un·môr'əl, -mor'-) *adj.* Having no moral sense or relation; not pertaining to morality; distinguished from *amoral* and *immoral.* — **un·mo·ral·i·ty** (un'mə·ral'ə·tē) *n.*

un·mor·tise (un·môr'tis) *v.t.* **·tised, ·tis·ing** **1** To loosen; loosen the mortised joints of. **2** To separate.

un·muf·fle (un·muf'əl) *v.* **·fled, ·fling** *v.t.* **1** To take the covering from. **2** To remove the muffling of (a drum, oar, etc.). — *v.i.* **3** To remove that which muffles.

un·nat·u·ral (un·nach'ər·əl) *adj.* **1** Contrary to the laws of nature; opposed to what is natural. **2** Contrary to the common laws of morality or decency; monstrous; inhuman: *unnatural* crimes. **3** Destitute of natural feeling. **4** Not consistent with nature; artificial: *unnatural* acting. See synonyms under FACTITIOUS, IRREGULAR. — **un·nat'u·ral·ly** *adv.* — **un·nat'u·ral·ness** *n.*

un·nec·es·sary (un·nes'ə·ser'ē) *adj.* Not required; not necessary. — **un·nec'es·sar'i·ly** *adv.* — **un·nec'es·sar'i·ness** *n.*

un·nerve (un·nûrv') *v.t.* **·nerved, ·nerv·ing** To deprive of strength, firmness, self-control, or courage; unman. See synonyms under WEAKEN.

un·num·bered (un·num'bərd) *adj.* **1** Not counted. **2** Innumerable. **3** Not assigned a number; not marked with a number.

u·no an·i·mo (yoo'nō an'ə·mō) *Latin* With one mind; unanimously; in agreement.

un·oc·cu·pied (un·ok'yə·pīd) *adj.* **1** Empty; not dwelt in; uninhabited: an *unoccupied* house. **2** Idle; unemployed; not put to use: an *unoccupied* day.

un·of·fi·cial (un'ə·fish'əl) *adj.* **1** Not of an official character. **2** Not in an official capacity. **3** Not in the regular list of the pharmacopoeia.

un·or·gan·ized (un·ôr'gən·īzd) *adj.* **1** Not organized. **2** Not living; inorganic; structureless. **3** Not unionized. Also *Brit.* **un·or'gan·ised.**

un·o·rig·i·nal (un'ə·rij'ə·nəl) *adj.* Not original.

un·pack (un·pak') *v.t.* **1** To open and take out the contents of. **2** To take out of the container, as something packed. **3** To remove a load or pack from; unload. — *v.i.* **4** To unpack a trunk, goods, etc.

un·paid (un·pād') *adj.* **1** Not met or discharged, as a debt. **2** Not receiving pay; serving without pay. **3** Having wages remaining due.

un·paired (un·pârd') *adj.* **1** Not paired; not forming one of a pair; not matched. **2** *Anat.* **a** Having no corresponding part in the opposite half of the body. **b** Situated in the median plane of the body.

un·par·al·leled (un·par'ə·leld) *adj.* Without parallel; unmatched; unprecedented.

un·par·lia·men·ta·ry (un'pär·lə·men'tər·ē) *adj.* Not parliamentary; contrary to the rules that govern deliberative or legislative bodies. — **un'par·lia·men·ta·ri·ly** *adv.* — **un'par·lia·men'ta·ri·ness** *n.*

un·peg (un·peg') *v.t.* **·pegged, ·peg·ging** To remove the peg or pegs from; unfasten.

un·peo·ple (un·pē'pəl) *v.t.* **·pled, ·pling** To depopulate.

un·peo·pled (un·pē'pəld) *adj.* **1** Uninhabited. **2** Depopulated.

un·per·fo·rat·ed (un·pûr'fə·rā'tid) *adj.* **1** Not perforated. **2** In philately, imperforate.

un peu (œṅ pœ') *French* A little; somewhat.

un·pick (un·pik') *v.t.* **1** To undo by removing the stitches; also, to remove (stitches). **2** To open with a pick or picklock.

un·pin (un·pin') *v.t.* **·pinned, ·pin·ning** **1** To remove the pins from. **2** To unfasten by removing pins.

un·pleas·ant (un·plez'ənt) *adj.* Disagreeable; objectionable; not pleasing. — **un·pleas'ant·ly** *adv.*

un·pleas·ant·ness (un·plez'ənt·nis) *n.* **1** The quality, character, or condition of being unpleasant or disagreeable. **2** Any disagreeable experience or event; a disagreement or quarrel. — **the late unpleasantness** The American Civil War: now chiefly humorous; by extension, any recent war.

un·plumbed (un·plumd') *adj.* **1** Not sounded; not explored fully; unfathomed. **2** Not furnished with plumbing.

un·poised (un·poizd') *adj.* Not poised or balanced.

un·pol·i·cied (un·pol'ə·sēd) *adj.* **1** Having no established system of civil polity. **2** *Obs.* Unguided by reason or prudence; impolitic.

un·pol·i·tic (un·pol'ə·tik) *adj.* Impolitic.

un·polled (un·pōld') *adj.* Not registered: an *unpolled* vote or voter; not having voted at an election.

un·pop·u·lar (un·pop'yə·lər) *adj.* Having no popularity; generally disliked or condemned. — **un·pop'u·lar·ly** *adv.* — **un·pop'u·lar'i·ty** (-lar'·ə·tē) *n.*

un·prac·ticed (un·prak'tist) *adj.* **1** Being without practice; inexperienced. **2** Not carried out in practice; not used. **3** Not yet tried.

un·prec·e·dent·ed (un·pres'ə·den'tid) *adj.* Being without precedent; preceded by no similar case; unexampled. See synonyms under EXTRAORDINARY. — **un·prec'e·dent'ed·ly** *adv.*

un·prej·u·diced (un·prej'ŏŏ·dist) *adj.* **1** Free from prejudice or bias; impartial. **2** Not impaired, as a right. See synonyms under CANDID.

un·pre·med·i·tat·ed (un'pri·med'ə·tā'tid) *adj.* **1** Not planned beforehand; undesigned: *unpremeditated* assault. **2** Not previously considered or thought of. — **un'pre·med'i·tat'ed·ly** *adv.* — **un'pre·med'i·ta'tion** *n.*

un·pre·pared (un'pri·pârd') *adj.* **1** Having made no preparations: an *unprepared* student. **2** Not brought into a state of preparation; not yet ready: Dinner is still *unprepared.* **3** Done or carried out without preparation; impromptu: an *unprepared* speech. — **un·pre·par·ed·ly** (un'pri·pâr'id·lē) *adv.* — **un'pre·par'·ed·ness** *n.*

un·priced (un·prīst') *adj.* **1** Having no fixed price. **2** Priceless.

un·prin·ci·pled (un·prin'sə·pəld) *adj.* Destitute of conscientious scruples; unscrupulous; wicked. See synonyms under BAD, IMMORAL. — **un·prin'ci·pled·ness** *n.*

un·print·a·ble (un·prin'tə·bəl) *adj.* Not fit to be printed.

un·priz·a·ble (un·prī'zə·bəl) *adj. Obs.* **1** Of worth beyond estimation; invaluable. **2** Not prized; valueless.

un·pro·duc·tive (un'prə·duk'tiv) *adj.* **1** Producing little or nothing; barren, literally or figuratively. **2** *Econ.* Not adding to exchangeable value: *unproductive* labor. — **un'pro·duc'·tive·ly** *adv.* — **un'pro·duc'tive·ness** *n.*

un·pro·fes·sion·al (un'prə·fesh'ən·əl) *adj.* **1** Having no profession; also, lay; amateur. **2** Violating the rules or ethical code of a profession; not up to the standard of a profession: *unprofessional* work. — **un'pro·fes'sion·al·ly** *adv.*

un·prof·it·a·ble (un·prof'it·ə·bəl) *adj.* Productive of no profit; serving no desirable purpose; fruitless; futile: *unprofitable* conversation; an

unsafe	unsatiating	unscholarlike	unseconded	unsew	unshorn	unsized
unsafely	unsatisfactory	unscholarly	unsectarian	unsewn	unshrinkable	unskeptical
unsaintly	unsatisfied	unschooled	unsecured	unsexual	unshrinking	unslacked
unsalability,	unsatisfying	unscientific	unseeing	unshaded	unshriven	unslaked
unsaleability	unsaved	unscorched	unsegmented	unshakable	unshrouded	unsleeping
unsalable,	unsawed	unscorned	unselected	unshaken	unshrunk	unslumbering
unsaleable	unsawn	unscoured	unselective	unshamed	unshunned	unsmiling
unsalaried	unsayable	unscourged	unselfish	unshapely	unshut	unsmirched
unsalted	unscabbarded	unscratched	unselfishly	unshared	unsifted	unsmoked
unsanctified	unscaled	unscreened	unsent	unshaved	unsigned	unsoaked
unsanctioned	unscanned	unscriptural	unsentimental	unshaven	unsilenced	unsober
unsanitary	unscarred	unsculptured	unserved	unshed	unsimilar	unsocial
unsated	unscented	unsealed	unserviceable	unshelled	unsingable	unsoiled
unsatiable	unsceptical	unseaworthiness	unserviceably	unsheltered	unsinkable	unsold
unsatiated	unscheduled	unseaworthy	unset	unshod	unsisterly	unsoldierlike

unprofitable transaction. **—un·prof'it·a·ble·ness** *n.* **—un·prof'it·a·bly** *adv.*

un·pro·nounce·a·ble (un'prə-noun'sə-bəl) *adj.* 1 Not easy to pronounce, especially properly. 2 Not fit to be mentioned.

un·pro·vid·ed (un'prə-vī'did) *adj.* 1 Not furnished or provided: with *with*, formerly with *of*: to be *unprovided* with suitable raiment. 2 Not fittingly prepared; not ready: *unprovided* for a sudden change. **—un'pro·vid'ed·ly** *adv.*

un·qual·i·fied (un·kwol'ə-fīd) *adj.* 1 Being without the proper qualifications; unfit. 2 Having failed to qualify; lacking legal power or authority. 3 Without limitation or restrictions; absolute; entire: *unqualified* approval. **—un·qual'i·fied'ly** *adv.* **—un·qual'i·fied'ness** *n.*

un·ques·tion·a·ble (un·kwes'chən-ə-bəl) *adj.* Too certain or sure to admit of question; being beyond a doubt; indisputable. See synonyms under INCONTESTABLE, NOTORIOUS. **—un·ques'tion·a·bly** *adv.*

un·ques·tioned (un·kwes'chənd) *adj.* 1 Not called in question; undoubted. 2 Not to be frustrated or opposed; indisputable. 3 Not interrogated.

un·qui·et (un·kwī'ət) *adj.* 1 Not at rest; disturbed; restless, in mind or physically. 2 Causing unrest or discomfort. **—un·qui'et·ly** *adv.* **—un·qui'et·ness** *n.*

un·quote (un·kwōt') *v.t. & v.i.* **·quot·ed, ·quot·ing** To close (a quotation).

un·rav·el (un·rav'əl) *v.* **·eled** or **·elled, ·el·ing** or **·el·ling** *v.t.* 1 To separate the threads of, as a tangled skein or knitted article. 2 To free from entanglement; unfold; explain, as a mystery or a plot. **—***v.i.* 3 To become unraveled. See synonyms under INTERPRET.

un·read (un·red') *adj.* 1 Not informed by reading; ignorant. 2 Not yet perused.

un·read·y (un·red'ē) *adj.* 1 Being without readiness or alertness; not apt or quick to see or appreciate. 2 Not in a condition to act effectively; unprepared. **—un·read'i·ly** *adv.* **—un·read'i·ness** *n.*

un·re·al (un·rē'əl, -rēl') *adj.* Having no reality, actual existence, or substance; having no genuineness; insincere; artificial; also, fanciful; visionary. **—un·re·al·i·ty** (un'rē·al'ə·tē) *n.* **—un·re'al·ly** *adv.*

un·rea·son (un·rē'zən) *n.* Lack or absence of reason; irrationality; also, absurdity; nonsense.

un·rea·son·a·ble (un·rē'zən·ə·bəl) *adj.* 1 Acting without or contrary to reason. 2 Not according to reason; irrational. 3 Exceeding what is reasonable; immoderate; exorbitant. See synonyms under ABSURD, IMMODERATE. **—un·rea'son·a·ble·ness** *n.* **—un·rea'son·a·bly** *adv.*

un·rea·son·ing (un·rē'zən·ing) *adj.* So intolerant, or so unaccompanied by reason or control, as to be obstinate, blind, or wild.

un·reck·on·a·ble (un·rek'ən·ə·bəl) *adj.* That cannot be reckoned or computed; unlimited.

un·reel (un·rēl') *v.t. & v.i.* To unwind, as from a reel.

un·reeve (un·rēv') *v.* **·reeved** or **·rove** (*for pp.* also **·rov·en**), **·reev·ing** *Naut.* *v.t.* 1 To take out or withdraw (a rope) from a block, thimble, deadeye, etc. **—***v.i.* 2 To become unreeved. 3 To unreeve a rope.

un·re·flec·tive (un'ri·flek'tiv) *adj.* Not given to reflection; not thoughtful.

un·re·gen·er·ate (un'ri·jen'ər·it) *adj.* Not having been changed spiritually by regeneration; remaining unreconciled to God; loosely, sinful. Also **un're·gen'er·at·ed** (-ā'tid). **—un're·gen'er·a·cy** (-ə·sē) *n.* **—un're·gen'er·ate·ly** *adv.*

un·re·lent·ing (un'ri·len'ting) *adj.* 1 Continuing to be severe; pitiless; inexorable. 2 Not diminishing, or not changing, in pace, effort, speed, etc. **—un're·lent'ing·ly** *adv.*

un·re·li·a·ble (un'ri·lī'ə·bəl) *adj.* That cannot be relied upon; not dependable. **—un're·li'·a·bil'i·ty, un're·li·a·ble·ness** *n.* **—un're·li'a·bly** *adv.*

un·re·li·gious (un'ri·lij'əs) *adj.* 1 Irreligious; hostile to religion. 2 Having no religion; not connected with religion.

un·re·mit·ting (un'ri·mit'ing) *adj.* Incessant; not relaxing. **—un're·mit'ting·ly** *adv.* **—un're·mit'ting·ness** *n.*

un·re·proved (un'ri·prōōvd') *adj.* 1 Not censured or blamed; not reproved. 2 Not liable to reproof; above reproach.

un·re·serve (un'ri·zûrv') *n.* Absence of reserve; freedom of style or manner.

un·re·served (un'ri·zûrvd') *adj.* 1 Given or done without reserve. 2 Having no reserve of manner; informal; open; frank. See synonyms under CANDID, IMPLICIT. **—un·re·serv·ed·ly** (un'ri·zûr'vid·lē) *adv.* **—un're·serv'ed·ness** *n.*

un·re·spec·tive (un'ri·spek'tiv) *adj. Obs.* 1 Undiscriminating. 2 Inattentive; heedless. 3 Common; not restricted.

un·re·spit·ed (un·res'pit·id) *adj.* 1 Not postponed; not respited, as from a sentence of the law. 2 *Obs.* Having no intermission.

un·re·spon·sive (un'ri·spon'siv) *adj.* Showing no reaction or response; unsympathetic. **—un're·spon'sive·ly** *adv.* **—un're·spon'sive·ness** *n.*

un·rest (un·rest') *n.* 1 Restlessness, especially of the mind. 2 Trouble; turmoil: used with regard to public or political conditions and suggesting premonitions of revolt.

un·re·strained (un'ri·strānd') *adj.* Not restrained; free; not controlled. **—un·re·strain·ed·ly** (un'ri·strā'nid·lē) *adv.*

un·rid·dle (un·rid'l) *v.t.* **·dled, ·dling** To solve, as a mystery.

un·ri·fled¹ (un·rī'fəld) *adj.* Smooth-bored, as a gun.

un·ri·fled² (un·rī'fəld) *adj.* Not rifled, seized, or plundered.

un·rig (un·rig') *v.t.* **·rigged, ·rig·ging** *Naut.* To strip of rigging.

un·right·eous (un·rī'chəs) *adj.* 1 Not righteous; wicked; sinful. 2 Contrary to the law of right; unjust. See synonyms under SINFUL. **—un·right'eous·ly** *adv.* **—un·right'eous·ness** *n.*

un·rip (un·rip') *v.t.* **·ripped, ·rip·ping** To separate by ripping; rip or cut open.

un·ripe (un·rīp') *adj.* 1 Not arrived at maturity; not ripe; immature. 2 Premature. 3 Not ready; not prepared. [OE, *untimely*] **—un·ripe'ness** *n.*

un·ri·valed (un·rī'vəld) *adj.* Having no rival or competitor; unequaled; matchless. Also **un·ri'valled.**

un·roll (un·rōl') *v.t.* 1 To spread or open (something rolled up). 2 To exhibit to view. 3 *Rare* To remove from a roll or register. **—***v.i.* 4 To become unrolled.

un·root (un·rōōt', -rŏŏt') *v.t.* To uproot.

un·ruf·fled (un·ruf'əld) *adj.* 1 Not disturbed or agitated emotionally; calm. 2 Not ruffled or made rough physically.

un·ru·ly (un·rōō'lē) *adj.* Disposed to resist rule or discipline; intractable; ungovernable. See synonyms under RESTIVE. **—un·ru'li·ness** *n.*

un·sad·dle (un·sad'l) *v.t.* **·dled, ·dling** 1 To remove a saddle from. 2 To remove from the saddle; unhorse.

un·said (un·sed') *adj.* Not said; not spoken.

un·sat·u·rat·ed (un·sach'ə·rā'tid) *adj.* 1 Falling short of saturation, as a solution. 2 *Chem.* Not combined to the greatest possible extent; capable of uniting with certain other elements or compounds to form additional compounds.

un·sa·vor·y (un·sā'vər·ē) *adj.* 1 Having a disagreeable taste or odor. 2 Suggesting something disagreeable, offensive, or unclean;

also, morally bad: an *unsavory* reputation. 3 *Obs.* Having no savor; tasteless; odorless. Also *Brit.* **un·sa'vour·y. —un·sa'vor·i·ly** *adv.* **—un·sa'vor·i·ness** *n.*

un·say (un·sā') *v.t.* **·said, ·say·ing** To retract (something said).

un·scathed (un·skāthd') *adj.* Uninjured.

un·scram·ble (un·skram'bəl) *v.t.* **·bled, ·bling** *Colloq.* To resolve the confused, scrambled, or disordered condition of.

un·screw (un·skrōō') *v.t.* 1 To remove the screw or screws from. 2 To remove or detach by withdrawing screws, or by turning. **—***v.i.* 3 To permit of being unscrewed.

un·scru·pu·lous (un·skrōō'pyə·ləs) *adj.* Not scrupulous; having no scruples; unprincipled. **—un·scru'pu·lous·ly** *adv.* **—un·scru'pu·lous·ness** *n.*

un·seal (un·sēl') *v.t.* 1 To break or remove the seal of. 2 To open (that which has been sealed or closed).

un·seam (un·sēm') *v.t.* To open the seam or seams of.

un·search·a·ble (un·sûr'chə·bəl) *adj.* That cannot be searched or explored; hidden; mysterious. **—un·search'a·bly** *adv.*

un·sea·son·a·ble (un·sē'zən·ə·bəl) *adj.* Not being in the proper season or not being in time; inappropriate; ill-timed. **—un·sea'son·a·ble·ness** *n.* **—un·sea'son·a·bly** *adv.*

un·sea·soned (un·sē'zənd) *adj.* 1 Not seasoned; not flavored. 2 Immature; unripe; not properly aged. 3 Not habituated. **—un·sea'soned·ness** *n.*

un·seat (un·sēt') *v.t.* 1 To remove from a seat or fixed position. 2 To unhorse. 3 To deprive of office or rank; depose.

un·seem·ly (un·sēm'lē) *adj.* **·li·er, ·li·est** Unbecoming; indecent; not handsome. **—***adv.* In an unseemly fashion. **—un·seem'li·ness** *n.*

un·seen (un·sēn') *adj.* Not seen; not evident; invisible; not previously seen or prepared, as a passage for translation.

un·set·tle (un·set'l) *v.* **·tled, ·tling** *v.t.* 1 To move from a fixed or settled condition. 2 To confuse; disturb. **—***v.i.* 3 To become unsteady or unfixed. See synonyms under DISPLACE.

un·sex (un·seks') *v.t.* 1 To deprive of the distinctive qualities of a sex; especially, to render unfeminine or unwomanly. 2 To castrate.

un·shack·le (un·shak'əl) *v.t.* **·led, ·ling** To unfetter; free from shackles. **—un·shack'led** *adj.*

un·shap·en (un·shā'pən) *adj.* Not shaped; imperfectly formed; badly shaped. Also **un·shaped'.**

un·sheathe (un·shēth') *v.t.* **·sheathed, ·sheath·ing** To take from or as from a scabbard or sheath; bare.

un·ship (un·ship') *v.t.* **·shipped, ·ship·ping** 1 To unload from a ship or other vessel; also, to dismiss from a ship. 2 To remove from the place where it is fixed or fitted, as a rudder or oar.

un·sick·er (un·sik'ər) *adj. Scot.* Insecure; unreliable; undependable. **—un·sick'er·ness** *n.*

un·sight·ed (un·sī'tid) *adj.* 1 Not sighted; not in view. 2 Having no sight, as a cannon. 3 Not aimed with the assistance of a sight, as a shot.

un·sight·ly (un·sīt'lē) *adj.* **·li·er, ·li·est** Offensive to the sight; ugly. **—un·sight'li·ness** *n.*

unsight unseen Sight unseen: former usage.

un·skaithed (un·skāthd') *adj. Scot.* Unscathed.

un·skil·ful (un·skil'fəl) *adj.* 1 Lacking or not evincing skilfulness; awkward. 2 *Obs.* Lacking in discernment; ignorant. Also **un·skill'ful. —un·skil'ful·ly** *adv.* **—un·skil'ful·ness** *n.*

---

unsoldierly	unspeculative	unsquandered	unsterilized	unsuggestive	unsustained	untalented
unsolicited	unspelled	unsquared	unstick	unsuited	unswayed	untalked–of
unsolicitous	unspent	unstack	unstigmatized	unsullied	unsweetened	untamable,
unsolid	unspilled	unstainable	unstinted	unsunk	unswept	untameable
unsoluble	unspilt	unstained	unstitched	unsunned	unswerving	untame
unsolvable	unspiritual	unstamped	unstrained	unsupportable	unsworn	untamed
unsolved	unspirituality	unstandardized	unstressed	unsupported	unsymmetrical	untangled
unsophistication	unspiritually	unstarched	unstripped	unsupportedly	unsympathetic	untanned
unsorted	unspiritualness	unstarred	unstuffed	unsuppressed	unsympathizing	untapped
unsought	unspoiled	unstatesmanlike	unstung	unsure	unsystematic	untarnished
unsounded	unspoilt	unsteadfast	unsubdued	unsurmountable	unsystematized	untasted
unsoured	unspoken	unsteadily	unsubmissive	unsurpassable	untack	untaxable
unsowed	unsportsmanlike	unsteadiness	unsubscribed	unsurpassed	untactful	untaxed
unsown	unsprinkled	unsteady	unsubstantiated	unsusceptible	untainted	unteachable
unspecified	unsprung	unstemmed	unsuccess	unsuspicious	untaken	untechnical

un·skilled (un·skild') *adj.* **1** Destitute of skill or dexterity in artisan's work; good only for common labor: an *unskilled* workman. **2** Produced without or not requiring special skill or training; untrained. **3** Destitute of practical knowledge; unskilful.

un·sling (un·sling') *v.t.* **·slung**, **·sling·ing 1** To remove, as a rifle, from a slung position. **2** *Naut.* To take the slings from.

un·snap (un·snap') *v.t.* **·snapped**, **·snap·ping** To undo the snap or snaps of; unfasten.

un·snarl (un·snärl') *v.t.* To disentangle.

un·so·cia·ble (un·sō'shə·bəl) *adj.* **1** Not sociable; not inclined to seek the society of others. **2** Not congenial or in accord: an *unsociable* group. **3** Not encouraging social intercourse. — **un·so'cia·bil'i·ty, un·so'cia·ble·ness** *n.* — **un·so'cia·bly** *adv.*

un·sol·der (un·sod'ər) *v.t.* **1** To disunite or take apart (something soldered). **2** To separate; sunder.

un·son·sie (un·son'sē) *adj. Scot.* Unlucky; disagreeable. Also **un·son'cy, un·son'sy.**

un·so·phis·ti·cat·ed (un'sə·fis'tə·kā'tid) *adj.* **1** Not sophisticated; showing inexperience or naiveté; artless; simple. **2** Free from adulteration; genuine; pure. See synonyms under CANDID, RUSTIC. — **un'so·phis'ti·cat'ed·ly** *adv.* — **un'so·phis'ti·cat'ed·ness** *n.*

un·sound (un·sound') *adj.* **1** Lacking in soundness; not having material strength and solidity; weak; rotten. **2** Not sound in health; diseased. **3** Not logically valid; erroneous; in religion, heterodox. **4** Disturbed; not profound: said of sleep. — **un·sound'ly** *adv.* — **un·sound'ness** *n.*

un·spar·ing (un·spâr'ing) *adj.* **1** Not sparing or saving; lavish; liberal. **2** Showing no mercy. — **un·spar'ing·ly** *adv.* — **un·spar'ing·ness** *n.*

un·speak (un·spēk') *v.t.* **spoke**, **·spo·ken**, **·speak·ing** To retract (something said); take back.

un·speak·a·ble (un·spē'kə·bəl) *adj.* **1** That cannot be expressed; unutterable: *unspeakable* joy. **2** Extremely bad or objectionable: an *unspeakable* crime. **3** Mute. — **un·speak'·a·ble·ness** *n.* — **un·speak'a·bly** *adv.*

un·spe·cial·ized (un·spesh'əl·īzd) *adj.* **1** Not specialized. **2** *Biol.* Not set apart for a special function or purpose; generalized. Also *Brit.* **un·spe'cial·ised.**

un·sphere (un·sfir') *v.t.* **·sphered**, **·spher·ing** To take out of its sphere or place.

un·spot·ted (un·spot'id) *adj.* **1** Not marked or marred with spots. **2** Not morally tainted; immaculate; free from blemishes; perfect. **3** Ceremonially clean. See synonyms under PURE. — **un·spot'ted·ness** *n.*

un·sprung weight (un·sprung') In automobiles, the weight of components not supported by the suspension, as the wheel assemblies: opposed to *sprung weight.*

un·sta·ble (un·stā'bəl) *adj.* **1** Lacking in stability or firmness; not stable. **2** Having no fixed purposes; easily influenced; inconstant: an *unstable* character. **3** *Chem.* Readily decomposable, as certain compounds. **4** Subject to a radical change by the application of a slight force: *unstable* equilibrium. See FICKLE, PRECARIOUS. — **un·sta'ble·ness** *n.* — **un·sta'bly** *adv.*

un·state (un·stāt') *v.t.* **·stat·ed**, **·stat·ing 1** To divest of statehood. **2** To deprive of dignity, rank, or office.

un·steel (un·stēl') *v.t.* To deprive of steel–like quality; disarm; soften.

un·step (un·step') *v.t.* **·stepped**, **·step·ping** To take out of a step or socket: to *unstep* a mast.

un·stop (un·stop') *v.t.* **·stopped**, **·stop·ping 1** To remove a stop or stopper from. **2** To open by removing obstructions; clear. **3** To open the stops of (an organ).

un·stopped (un·stopt') *adj.* **1** Not stopped; unobstructed. **2** *Phonet.* Of consonants, not stopped; capable of being prolonged: said of the continuants, as (z) and (l).

un·stowed (un·stōd') *adj.* **1** Not stowed or filled, as a ship, with cargo. **2** Lying loose in the hold or on deck, as cargo

un·strap (un·strap') *v.t.* **·strapped**, **·strap·ping** To unfasten or loosen the strap or straps of.

un·strat·i·fied (un·strat'ə·fīd) *adj. Geol.* Not deposited in beds or strata, as igneous rocks.

un·stri·at·ed (un·strī'ā·tid) *adj.* Without striations; smooth–textured, as certain muscles.

un·string (un·string') *v.t.* **·strung**, **·string·ing 1** To remove from a string, as pearls. **2** To take the string or strings from. **3** To loosen the string or strings of, as a bow or guitar. **4** To relax, as if by loosening; weaken: usually in the passive: Her nerves were *unstrung.*

un·striped (un·stript') *adj.* **1** Not striped; unstriated. **2** *Anat.* Denoting certain muscles that act independently of the will, as the heart muscles. See under MUSCLE.

un·strung (un·strung') *adj.* **1** Having the strings removed or relaxed. **2** Unnerved; emotionally upset; weakened; relaxed.

un·stud·ied (un·stud'ēd) *adj.* **1** Not planned; unpremeditated. **2** Not stiff or artificial; natural. **3** Not acquainted through study; unversed: with *in.* See synonyms under SIMPLE.

un·sub·stan·tial (un'səb·stan'shəl) *adj.* **1** Lacking solidity, strength, or weight. **2** Having no valid basis. **3** Having no bodily existence; fanciful. — **un'sub·stan'tial·ly** *adv.* — **un'sub·stan'ti·al'i·ty** (-shē·al'ə·tē) *n.*

un·suc·cess·ful (un'sək·ses'fəl) *adj.* Having or meeting with no success: said of persons or their acts: *unsuccessful* in business, an *unsuccessful* attempt. — **un'suc·cess'ful·ly** *adv.* — **un'suc·cess'ful·ness** *n.*

un·suit·a·ble (un·sōō'tə·bəl) *adj.* Not suitable; unfitting. — **un·suit·a·bil·i·ty** (un'sōō·tə·bil'ə·tē), **un·suit'a·ble·ness** *n.* — **un·suit'a·bly** *adv.*

un·sung (un·sung') *adj.* **1** Not celebrated in song or poetry; obscure. **2** Not yet sung, as a song.

un·sus·pect·ed (un'sə·spek'tid) *adj.* **1** Not suspected, as of evil; not under suspicion. **2** Not imagined or known to exist.

un·sus·pect·ing (un'sə·spek'ting) *adj.* Having no suspicion; trusting.

un·swathe (un·swāth') *v.t.* **·swathed**, **·swath·ing** To remove swathings from; free from swathings.

un·swear (un·swâr') *v.t.* **·swore**, **·sworn**, **·swear·ing** To revoke (an oath); retract; abjure.

un·tan·gle (un·tang'gəl) *v.t.* **·gled**, **·gling** To free from entanglement or embarrassment; resolve.

un·taught (un·tôt') *adj.* Not having been instructed; ignorant.

un·teach (un·tēch') *v.t.* **·taught**, **·teach·ing 1** To cause to forget or to disbelieve what has been taught. **2** To cause to be forgotten or disbelieved.

un·ten·a·ble (un·ten'ə·bəl) *adj.* **1** That cannot be maintained: *untenable* theories. **2** Incapable of being defended or held, as a fortress. — **un·ten'a·ble·ness** *n.*

un·tent·ed (un·ten'tid) *adj.* **1** Having no tents. **2** *Obs.* Not kept open or dressed, as a wound.

Un·ter den Lin·den (ŏŏn'tər den lin'dən) A famous avenue in East Berlin; literally, under the lindens.

Un·ter·wal·den (ŏŏn'tər·väl'dən) A canton of central Switzerland; 296 square miles.

un·thanked (un·thangkt') *adj.* **1** Not thanked. **2** *Obs.* Not received with thankfulness.

un·thank·ful (un·thangk'fəl) *adj.* **1** Not grateful. **2** Not received with thanks; unwelcome. — **un·thank'ful·ly** *adv.* — **un·thank'ful·ness** *n.*

un·think (un·thingk') *v.t.* **·thought**, **·think·ing** To retract in thought; change the mind concerning.

un·think·ing (un·thingk'ing) *adj.* **1** Not having the power of thought. **2** Lacking thoughtfulness, care, or attention; heedless; inconsiderate. See synonyms under IMPRUDENT. — **un·think'ing·ly** *adv.* — **un·think'ing·ness** *n.*

un·thread (un·thred') *v.t.* **1** To remove the thread from, as a needle. **2** To find one's way out of, as a maze.

un·ti·dy (un·tī'dē) *adj.* **·di·er**, **·di·est** Showing or characterized by lack of tidiness. [ME *untīdi*] — **un·ti'di·ly** *adv.* — **un·ti'di·ness** *n.*

un·tie (un·tī') *v.* **·tied**, **·ty·ing** *v.t.* **1** To loosen or undo, as a knot or knotted rope. **2** To free from that which binds or restrains. — *v.i.* **3** To become untied. See synonyms under RELEASE. [OE *untīgan*] — **un·tied'** *adj.*

un·til (un·til') *prep.* **1** Up to the time of; till: We will wait *until* midnight. **2** Before: used with a negative: The music doesn't begin *until* nine. **3** *Scot. & Brit. Dial.* Unto. — *conj.* **1** To the time when: *until* I die. **2** To the place or degree that: Walk east *until* you reach the river. **3** Before: with a negative: He couldn't leave *until* the car came for him. [ME *untill* < *und*- up to, as far as + TILL]

un·time·ly (un·tīm'lē) *adj.* Coming before time or not in proper time; unseasonable; ill–timed: also *Scot.* **un·time'ous.** — *adv.* Before the proper time; inopportunely.

un·ti·tled (un·tīt'ld) *adj.* **1** Having no right (to a throne). **2** Having no title, as a book. **3** Having no title of distinction: *untitled* nobility.

un·to (un'tōō) *prep.* **1** *Poetic & Archaic* To: used in all senses except to indicate the infinitive. **2** *Archaic* Until. — *conj. Obs.* Up to the extent or time that; until. [ME *un*-, *und*- up to, as far as + TO, on analogy with *until*]

un·told (un·tōld') *adj.* **1** That cannot be told, revealed, or described; inexpressible: *untold* misery. **2** That cannot be numbered or estimated; hence, of great number or extent: *untold* numbers; *untold* treasure. **3** Not told.

un·touch·a·bil·i·ty (un'tuch·ə·bil'ə·tē) *n.* The character or state of being untouchable.

un·touch·a·ble (un·tuch'ə·bəl) *adj.* **1** Inaccessible to the touch; out of reach; intangible; unrivaled; unapproachable. **2** Forbidden to the touch. **3** Unpleasant, disgusting, vile, or dangerous to touch; that should not be touched. — *n.* In India, a member of the lowest caste; one whose touch was formerly counted as pollution by Hindus of higher station.

un·to·ward (un·tôrd', -tōrd') *adj.* **1** Causing annoyance or hindrance; vexatious. **2** Not yielding readily; refractory; perverse. **3** *Obs.* Uncouth; ungraceful. See synonyms under PERVERSE. — **un·to'ward·ly** *adv.* — **un·to'ward·ness** *n.*

un·trav·eled (un·trav'əld) *adj.* **1** Not passed over, as a road. **2** Not having traveled; hence, narrow in ideas; provincial. Also **un·trav'elled.**

un·tread (un·tred') *v.t.* **·trod**, **·trod·den** or **·trod**, **·tread·ing** To retrace.

un·tried (un·trīd') *adj.* **1** Not tried or tested. **2** Not tried in court.

un·trimmed (un·trimd') *adj.* **1** Not adorned

untempered	untillable	untranslatable	untuneful	unvail	unvitrified	unweakened
untenanted	untilled	untranslated	unturned	unvalidated	unvocal	unweaned
untended	untinged	untransmitted	untwilled	unvanquished	unvolatilized	unwearable
unterrified	untired	untrapped	untwisted	unvaried	unvulcanized	unweary
untested	untiring	untraversable	untypical	unvarying	unwakened	unwearying
untether	untouched	untraversed	un–uniformed	unveiled	unwalled	unweathered
unthatched	untraceable	untreasured	un–uniformly	unventilated	unwanted	unweave
untheatrical	untraced	untrim	un–united	unveracious	unwarlike	unwed
unthinkable	untracked	untroubled	unurged	unverifiable	unwarmed	unwedded
unthoughtful	untractable	untrustiness	unusable	unverified	unwarned	unweeded
unthought–of	untrained	untrusty	unutilizable	unversed	unwashed	unwelded
unthrift	untrammeled,	untuck	unutilized	unvexed	unwasted	unwetted
unthriftiness	untrammelled	untufted	unuttered	unvext	unwasting	unwhetted
unthrifty	untransferable	untunable	unvaccinated	unvisited	unwatched	unwhipped
unthrone	untransferred	untuned	unvacillating	unvitiated	unwavering	unwhipt

with trimmings: an *untrimmed* hat. **2** Not made trim or orderly; not clipped or pruned: an *untrimmed* tree. **3** *Obs.* Virgin.

un·trod·den (un·trod'n) *adj.* Not having been trodden upon; hence, unfrequented. Also **un·trod'.**

un·true (un·trōō') *adj.* **1** Lacking truth; not true; not corresponding with fact. **2** Not conforming to rule or standard. **3** Not adhering to faith, pledge, or duty; disloyal. See synonyms under BAD, PERFIDIOUS. **— un·tru'ly** *adv.*

un·truss (un·trus') *v.t.* **1** To loosen or free from or as from a truss; unfasten; undo. **2** *Obs.* To take off (breeches); undress.

un·trust·ful (un·trust'fəl) *adj.* **1** Not trusting or trustful. **2** Not to be trusted; untrustworthy.

un·trust·wor·thy (un·trust'wûr'thē) *adj.* Worthy of no trust; unreliable. See synonyms under BAD, PERFIDIOUS. **— un·trust'wor'thi·ness** *n.* **— un·trust'wor'thi·ly** *adv.*

un·truth (un·trōōth') *n. pl.* **-truths** (-trōōths', -trōōthz') **1** The quality or character of being untrue; want of veracity. **2** *Obs.* Lack of fidelity; disloyalty. **3** Something that is not true; a falsehood; lie. See synonyms under DECEPTION, LIE. [OE *untrēowth*]

un·truth·ful (un·trōōth'fəl) *adj.* Not truthful; untrue; not veracious. **— un·truth'ful·ly** *adv.* **— un·truth'ful·ness** *n.*

un·tu·tored (un·tōō'tərd, -tyōō'-) *adj.* Having had no tutor or teacher; hence, uninstructed; raw. See synonyms under IGNORANT.

un·twine (un·twīn') *v.* **·twined, ·twin·ing** *v.t.* To undo (something twined); unwind by disentangling. **— v.i.** To become untwined.

un·twist (un·twist') *v.t. & v.i.* To separate or open by a movement the reverse of twisting; untwine and untwine.

U·nun·gun (ōō·nŏŏng'gŏŏn) *n. pl.* Literally, people: the collective name for two Eskimo tribes, the Unalaskans and the Atkans, inhabiting the Aleutian Islands; the Aleuts.

un·used (un·yōōzd') *adj.* **1** Not made use of; disused; also, never having been used. **2** Not accustomed or wont: with *to*.

un·u·su·al (un·yōō'zhŏō·əl) *adj.* Of a character, kind, number, or size not usually met with. See synonyms under EXTRAORDINARY, ODD, RARE. **— un·u'su·al·ly** *adv.* **— un·u'su·al·ness** *n.*

un·ut·ter·a·ble (un·ut'ər·ə·bəl) *adj.* **1** That cannot be uttered; too great or deep for verbal expression; ineffable: *unutterable* bliss. **2** Unpronounceable. **— un·ut'ter·a·ble·ness** *n.* **— un·ut'ter·a·bly** *adv.*

un·val·ued (un·val'yōōd) *adj.* **1** Not valued; neglected; unappreciated. **2** Not having a fixed value; not appraised. **3** *Obs.* Inestimable.

un·var·nished (un·vär'nisht) *adj.* **1** Having no covering of varnish. **2** Having no embellishment; plain: the *unvarnished* truth.

un·veil (un·vāl') *v.t.* To remove the veil or covering from; disclose to view; reveal. **— v.i.** To remove one's veil; reveal oneself.

un·voice (un·vois') *v.t.* **·voiced, ·voic·ing** *Phonet.* To pronounce (a voiced sound) without vibration of the vocal cords; devocalize.

un·voiced (un·voist') *adj.* **1** Not expressed. **2** *Phonet.* Not voiced; rendered voiceless: The final (v) in "have" is often heard *unvoiced* in "have to": also *devoiced.*

un·voic·ing (un·voi'sing) *n. Phonet.* The change of a voiced consonant to its unvoiced counterpart, as of (b) to (p).

un·war·rant·a·ble (un·wôr'ən·tə·bəl, -wor'-) *adj.* That cannot be warranted; unjustifiable; indefensible. **— un·war'rant·a·bly** *adv.*

un·war·rant·ed (un·wôr'ən·tid, -wor'-) *adj.* **1** Having no warrant; unwarrantable; unjustifiable. **2** Being without warranty or guarantee.

un·war·y (un·wâr'ē) *adj.* Taking no precautions against accident or danger; especially, not realizing the necessity of such precautions; incautious. **— un·war'i·ly** *adv.* **— un·war'i·ness** *n.*

un·wea·ried (un·wir'ēd) *adj.* **1** Not tired. **2** Indefatigable.

un·wel·come (un·wel'kəm) *adj.* **1** Not welcome; not desired: an *unwelcome* guest. **2** Causing no satisfaction: *unwelcome* news. **— un·wel'come·ly** *adv.* **— un·wel'come·ness** *n.*

un·well (un·wel') *adj.* **1** Somewhat ill; ailing. **2** Menstruating; indisposed by reason of menstruation: a euphemism. See synonyms under SICKLY. **— un·well'ness** *n.*

un·wept (un·wept') *adj.* **1** Not lamented or wept for, as a deceased person. **2** Not shed, as tears.

un·whole·some (un·hōl'səm) *adj.* **1** Deleterious to physical or mental health. **2** Unsound in quality or condition; diseased or decayed: *unwholesome* provisions. **3** Impaired in health; sickly in appearance: an *unwholesome* look. **4** Not contributing to moral health; pernicious: *unwholesome* literature. See synonyms under BAD, NOISOME. **— un·whole'some·ly** *adv.* **— un·whole'some·ness** *n.*

un·wield·y (un·wēl'dē) *adj.* Moved or managed with difficulty, as from great size or awkward shape; bulky; clumsy. **— un·wield'i·ly** *adv.* **— un·wield'i·ness** *n.*

un·willed (un·wild') *adj.* **1** Not willed or intended; spontaneous. **2** Being without, or deprived of, purpose or will.

un·will·ing (un·wil'ing) *adj.* **1** Not willing; reluctant; loath. **2** Done with reluctance. **3** *Obs.* Not intended; involuntary. See synonyms under RELUCTANT. **— un·will'ing·ly** *adv.* **— un·will'ing·ness** *n.*

un·wind (un·wind') *v.* **·wound, ·wind·ing** *v.t.* **1** To reverse the winding of; untwist or wind off; uncoil. **2** To disentangle. **— v.i.** **3** To become unwound.

un·wise (un·wīz') *adj.* Acting with, or showing, lack of wisdom; injudicious; foolish. [OE *unwīs*] **— un·wise'ly** *adv.* **— un·wis'dom** (-wiz'dəm) *n.*

un·wish (un·wish') *v.t.* **1** To retract (something wished); stop wishing. **2** To wish (something) not to be. **3** *Obs.* To destroy or do away with by wishing.

un·wished (un·wisht') *adj.* **1** Not desired or wished. **2** Unwelcome.

un·wit·ting (un·wit'ing) *adj.* **1** Having no knowledge or consciousness of the thing in question; unknowing or unconscious. **2** Unintentional. [OE *unwitende*] **— un·wit'ting·ly** *adv.*

un·wont·ed (un·wun'tid, -won'-) *adj.* **1** Not according to wont or custom; unusual; uncommon. **2** *Obs.* Not accustomed; unfamiliar. See synonyms under EXTRAORDINARY. **— un·wont'ed·ly** *adv.* **— un·wont'ed·ness** *n.*

un·world·ly (un·wûrld'lē) *adj.* **1** Not motivated by worldly values or interests; spiritually minded. **2** Unearthly; spiritual; not belonging to this world. **— un·world'li·ness** *n.*

un·wor·thy (un·wûr'thē) *adj.* **1** Not worthy or deserving of something specified: usually with *of.* **2** Not befitting or becoming: often with *of;* wrong; improper: conduct *unworthy* of a gentleman. **3** Lacking worth or merit; unfit; wrong; contemptible. See synonyms under BAD, SINFUL. **— un·wor'thi·ly** *adv.* **— un·wor'thi·ness** *n.*

un·wrap (un·rap') *v.* **·wrapped, ·wrap·ping** *v.t.* To take the wrapping from; open; undo. **— v.i.** To become unwrapped.

un·wrin·kle (un·ring'kəl) *v.t.* **·kled, ·kling** To free from wrinkles; smooth.

un·writ·ten (un·rit'n) *adj.* **1** Not reduced to writing; not written down; oral; traditional. **2** Having no writing upon it; blank.

unwritten law **1** A rule or custom established by general usage: an *unwritten law* of gentlemanly decorum. **2** Law which rests on custom and judicial decision, and not on a written command, decree, or statute. See COMMON LAW under LAW. **3** A custom in some communities granting a measure of immunity to those who commit criminal acts of revenge in support of personal or family honor, especially in cases of seduction, adultery, etc.

un·yoke (un·yōk') *v.* **·yoked, ·yok·ing** *v.t.* **1** To release from a yoke. **2** To separate; part. **— v.i.** **3** To become unyoked. **4** To stop work; cease. [OE *ungeocian*]

un·yoked (un·yōkt') *adj.* **1** Not subjected to or not wearing a yoke. **2** Freed from a yoke. **3** *Obs.* Unrestrained; licentious.

up (up) *adv.* **1** Toward a higher place or level: opposed to *down.* **2** In or on a higher place; above the horizon. **3** Toward that which is figuratively or conventionally higher: **a** To or at a higher price: Barley is *up.* **b** To or at a higher rank: people who have come *up* in the world. **c** To or at a greater size or larger amount: to swell *up.* **d** To or at a higher musical pitch. **e** To or at a place that is locally or arbitrarily regarded as higher: *up* north. **4** To a vertical position; standing; on one's feet. **5** Risen from bed. **6** So as to be level (to) or even (with) in space, time, degree, or amount: *up* to date; *up* to the brim. **7** In or into commotion or activity; in progress: They were stirred *up* to mutiny; to be *up* in arms. **8** Into existence: to draw *up* a document; to turn *up.* **9** In or into prominence; under consideration: The question was *up* for debate. **10** Into or in a place of safekeeping; aside: Fruits are put *up* in glass jars. **11** At an end or close: Your time is *up.* **12** Completely; wholly: Houses were burned *up;* The brooks dried *up.* **13** In baseball and cricket, at bat: He made but one hit in three times *up.* **14** In tennis and other sports: **a** In the lead; ahead: said of a player or team. **b** Apiece; alike: said of a score. **15** Bound for: said of a ship: *up* for Panama. **16** Running for as a candidate: Jones is *up* for mayor. **17** On trial before a magistrate: *up* for manslaughter. **18** *Naut.* Shifted to windward, as a tiller. **— all up with** At an end for; no further hope for. **— to be up against** *Colloq.* To meet with; be face to face with. **— to be up against it** *Colloq.* To be in difficulty; have financial trouble. **— to be up to 1** *Colloq.* To be doing or plotting; be about to do: What is he *up to?* **2** To be equal to; be capable of: I'm not *up to* moving all this furniture today. **3** To be incumbent upon; be dependent upon: It's *up to* him to save us. **— adj. 1** Moving, sloping, or directed upward or in a direction arbitrarily regarded as upward. **2** At stake, as in gambling: to have money *up* on a horse race. **3** *Colloq.* Going on; taking place: What's *up?* **4** *Colloq.* In a state acquainted (with), equal (to), or a match (for); of a kind or character capable (of): He is *up* in that subject. **5** In golf: **a** In' advance of the opponent or opponents: with a number indicating the extent (in holes) of such advance: three *up* and four to play: opposed to *down.* **b** Struck so as to travel as far as or beyond the hole: said of the ball. **6** Rising, risen, overflowing, or at flood: The moon is *up;* The river is *up.* **— up and around** *Colloq.* Sufficiently recovered to walk, as following an illness or injury; on one's feet again; convalescent and ambulatory. **— up to no good** Engaged in or contemplating some mischief or improper act. **— prep. 1** From a lower to a higher point or place of, on, or along; toward a higher condition or rank on or in: *up* the social ladder. **2** To or at a point farther above or along: The farm is *up* the road. **3** From the coast toward the interior of (a country, as being higher); from the mouth toward the source of (a river): to sail *up* a river. **4** At, on, or near the height or top of: said of position or situation. **— n.** One who or that which is up, as elevated ground, an ascent or upward movement, state of prosperity, etc.: usually plural. **— ups and downs** Changes of fortune or circumstance. **— v. upped, up·ping** *Colloq. v.t.* **1** To increase; make larger; cause to rise. **2** To put or take up. **— v.i.** **3** To rise. [OE]

up- *combining form* As an element in solidemes *up* has adverbial force with various meanings, as in the following examples:

1 To a higher place or level:

upbear	upflow	upsend
upbearer	upgaze	upshoot
upborne	upgoing	upsoar
upbuilder	upgrow	upstare
upbuilding	upheap	upstep
upclimb	upleap	upsurge
upcoil	uppile	upswell
upcurl	upraiser	uptilt
upcurve	upreach	uptoss
updart	upreaching	upvomit
updive	uprise	upwaft
upfling	uprush	upwreathe

unwifelike	unwinning	unwomanlike	unwooed	unworn	unwounded	unwrung
unwifely	unwithered	unwomanly	unworkable	unworshiped,	unwoven	unyielding
unwincing	unwithering	unwon	unworked	unworshipped	unwreathe	unyouthful
unwinking	unwitnessed	unwooded	unworkmanlike	unwound	unwrought	unzealous

2 To a greater size or larger amount:

| upbulging | upflashing | uplight |
| upflaring | upflooding | upswell |

3 To a vertical position:

| upprop | upstand | upsticking |

4 In or into commotion or activity:

| upboil | upbubbling | upstir |

5 Completely; wholly:

| upbind | upfold | upgird |
| updry | upgather | uphoard |

up-and-coming (up′ənd·kum′ing) *adj.* Enterprising; energetic; promising.

U·pan·i·shad (ōō·pän′ə·shad, -pä′nə·shäd) *n.* *Sanskrit* Literally, a philosophical treatise; one of the treatises forming the third division of the Vedas, dealing with the nature of man and the universe.

u·par·na (ōō·pär′nə) *n.* A silk or muslin scarf, interwoven with gold or silver threads, worn as a shawl by men and as a shawl or veil by women in India. [< Hind.]

u·pas (yōō′pəs) *n.* **1** A tall evergreen moraceous tree *(Antiaris toxicaria)* of the island of Java, with an acrid, milky, poisonous juice. **2** The poisonous sap of this tree, used by natives in the manufacture of arrow poison; also, a similar poison from the **upas-tieute**, a climbing shrub (genus *Strychnos*) of the family *Loganiaceae*. **3** Hence, something morally deadly. [< Malay *(pohon) upas* poison (tree)]

up·beat (up′bēt′) *n.* *Music* An unaccented beat; the beat at which the hand is raised. —*adj.* Optimistic; confident.

up·bow (up′bō′) *n.* An upward stroke of the violin bow, indicated in score by the symbol **V**: opposed to *down-bow*.

up·braid (up·brād′) *v.t.* To reproach for some wrongdoing; scold or reprove. —*v.i.* To utter reproaches. See synonyms under REPROVE, REVILE. [OE *upbregdan* < *up-* up + *bregdan* weave, twist] —**up·braid′er** *adj.* —**up·braid′ing** *n.* —**up·braid′ing·ly** *adv.*

up·bring·ing (up′bring′ing) *n.* Rearing and training received by a person during childhood.

up·bye (up′bī) *adv. Scot.* A little farther on; up the way. Also **up′by**.

up·cast (up′kast′, -käst′) *adj.* Cast, turned, or directed upward. —*n.* **1** A casting or throwing upward; that which is so cast. **2** An airshaft in a mine. **3** An upward current of air, as in a mine shaft. **4** *Scot.* An upset, or a reproach.

up·chuck (up′chuk′) *Colloq. v.t. & v.i.* To vomit. —*n.* Vomit.

up·com·ing (up′kum′ing) *adj.* Forthcoming; coming soon.

up·coun·try (up′kun′trē) *Colloq. n.* Country somewhat distant from the seashore or from lowlands; inland country. —*adj.* Living in, from, or characteristic of inland places. —*adv.* (up′kun′trē) In, into, or toward the interior: to move *up-country*.

up·date (up·dāt′) *v.t.* **·dat·ed**, **·dat·ing** To bring up to date; to revise, with corrections, additions, etc., as a textbook or manual: to *update* an encyclopedia.

up·end (up′end′) *v.t. & v.i.* To set or stand on end.

up·front (up′frunt′) *adj. Colloq.* Out in the open; unconcealed.

up·grade (up′grād′) *n.* An upward incline or slope. —*v.t.* (up·grād′) **·grad·ed**, **·grad·ing** **1** To improve the breed of (animals) by the introduction of a higher strain. **2** To raise to a higher grade, rank, or responsibility, as an employee.

up·growth (up′grōth′) *n.* **1** The process of growing up. **2** That which grows or has grown up.

up·heav·al (up·hē′vəl) *n.* **1** The act of upheaving, or the state of being upheaved. **2** *Geol.* An elevation of the earth's surface due to a warping of large rock masses. **3** Overthrow or violent disturbance of the established social order.

up·heave (up·hēv′) *v.* **·heaved** or **·hove**, **·heav·ing** *v.t.* To heave or raise up. —*v.i.* To be raised or lifted.

up·held (up·held′) Past tense and past participle of UPHOLD.

up·hill (up′hil′) *adv.* Up or as up a hill or an ascent; against difficulties. —*adj.* **1** Going up a hill or an ascent; sloping upward. **2** Attended with difficulty or exertion. —*n.* (up′hil′) An upward slope; rising ground.

up·hold (up·hōld′) *v.t.* **·held**, **·hold·ing** **1** To hold up; raise. **2** To keep from falling or sinking. **3** To give aid or support to; encourage. **4** To regard with approval. See synonyms under ABET, AID, ASSENT, CONFIRM, HELP, JUSTIFY, PRESERVE, SUPPORT. —**up·hold′er** *n.*

up·hol·ster (up·hōl′stər) *v.t.* **1** To fit, as furniture, with coverings, cushioning, etc. **2** To provide or adorn with hangings, curtains, etc., as an apartment. **3** To furnish with a covering of any kind. [Back formation < UPHOLSTERER]

up·hol·ster·er (up·hōl′stər·ər) *n.* One who furnishes upholstery; one who upholsters. [< obs. *upholster*, alter. of ME *upholder* a tradesman + -ER[1]]

up·hol·ster·y (up·hōl′stər·ē, -strē) *n. pl.* **·ster·ies** **1** Goods used in upholstering. **2** Textile decoration of an apartment. **3** The act, art, or business of upholstering.

u·phroe (yōō′frō, yōō′·rō) See EUPHROE.

up·keep (up′kēp) *n.* The act or state of maintenance; also, means or cost of maintenance.

up·land (up′lənd, -land′) *n.* **1** The higher portions of a region, district, farm, etc. **2** The country in the interior. —*adj.* **1** Pertaining to an upland; higher in situation. **2** Pertaining to or situated in inland districts.

upland plover See under PLOVER.

up·lift (up·lift′) *v.t.* **1** To lift up, or raise aloft; elevate. **2** To raise the tone of; put on a higher plane, mentally or morally. See synonyms under HEIGHTEN, RAISE. —*adj.* (up′lift′) Uplifted: a rare form. —*n.* (up′lift′) **1** The act of raising; the fact of being raised. **2** A movement upward. **3** *Geol.* An upheaval. **4** Mental or spiritual stimulation or elevation. **5** A social movement aiming to improve, morally or esthetically, the condition of the underprivileged. **6** A brassiere designed to lift and support the breasts. —**up·lift′er** *n.*

up·most (up′mōst′) *adj.* Uppermost.

up·on (ə·pon′, ə·pôn′) *prep.* **1** On, in all its meanings. **2** On, in an elevated position: *upon* the throne. **3** On, by motion upward: to get *upon* a roof. —*adv.* On: completing a verbal idea: The paper has been written *upon*. Also *Scot.* **up·o′**. See synonyms under ABOVE. [ME]

◆ *Upon* now differs little in use from *on*, the former being sometimes used for reasons of euphony and also preferably when motion into position is involved, the latter when merely rest or support is to be indicated. When *upon* has its original meaning of *up* and *on*, it is written as two words, *up* having its adverbial force: Let us go *up on* the roof.

up·per (up′ər) *adj.* **1** Higher than something else; being above. **2** Higher in place: opposed to *lower*. **3** Higher in station or dignity; superior: opposed to *inferior*: the *upper* house. —**to get the upper hand** To get the advantage. —*n.* **1** That part of a boot or shoe above the sole: the vamp. **2** *pl.* Cloth gaiters. **3** *Slang* Any of various drugs that stimulate the central nervous system, as amphetamines. —**on one's uppers** *Colloq.* **1** Having worn out the soles of one's shoes. **2** At the end of one's resources. [ME, orig. compar. of UP]

Up·per (up′ər) *adj. Geol.* Designating a later period or a later formation of a specified period: the *Upper* Cambrian.

Upper Austria A province of northern Austria; 4,624 square miles; capital, Linz. *German* **O·ber·ös·ter·reich** (ō′bər·œs′tə·rīkh).

Upper Bavaria An administrative division of southern Bavaria, West Germany; 6,308 square miles; capital, Munich. *German* **O·ber·bay·ern** (ō′bər·bī′ərn).

upper berth The top berth in a ship, railroad sleeping-car, cabin, etc., where two bunks or beds are built one above the other.

Upper Burma See BURMA, UNION OF.

Upper Canada A former British province (1791 to 1840) in the southern part of Ontario province, Canada.

upper case 1 Case[2] (def. 3). **2** Capital letters.

upper class The socially or economically superior group in society. —**up′per-class′** (-klas′, -kläs′) *adj.*

upper classman A junior or senior in a school or college.

upper crust *Colloq.* That portion of society assuming or thought of as having more social standing by reason of wealth or ancestry.

up·per·cut (up′ər·kut′) *n.* In boxing, a blow upward from the waist or hip, delivered under or inside the opponent's guard. —*v.t. & v.i.* **·cut**, **·cut·ting** To strike with an uppercut.

Upper Egypt See under EGYPT.

Upper Franconia An administrative division of NE Bavaria, Germany; 2,897 square miles; capital, Bayreuth. *German* **O·ber·fran·ken** (ō′bər·fräng′kən).

upper hand The advantage.

Upper House The branch, in a bicameral legislature, where membership is more restricted, as the U.S. Senate and the English House of Lords. Also **upper house**.

up·per·most (up′ər·mōst′) *adj.* **1** Highest in place, rank, authority, or vantage ground. **2** First to come into the mind: one's *uppermost* thoughts. Also *upmost*. —*adv.* In the highest place; also, first, as in time.

Upper New York Bay An arm of the Atlantic at the junction of the Hudson and the East River, joined to Newark Bay and Long Island Sound.

Upper Peninsula The northern part of Michigan, between Lake Superior and Lake Michigan; 16,538 square miles; 320 miles long, 125 miles wide.

Upper Silesia A former province of eastern Germany, now in western Poland.

Upper Vol·ta (vol′tə), **Republic of the** An independent republic of the French Community in western Africa; 105,900 square miles; capital, Ouagadougou; formerly the French overseas territory of Upper Volta.

up·pish (up′ish) *adj. Colloq.* Inclined to be self-assertive; assuming; pretentious; snobbish. Also **up′pi·ty**. —**up′pish·ly** *adv.* —**up′pish·ness** *n.*

up·raise (up·rāz′) *v.t.* **·raised**, **·rais·ing** To lift up; elevate. Also **up·rear′** (-rir′).

up·right (up′rīt′) *adj.* **1** Being in a vertical position; erect. **2** Morally correct; especially, just and honest. See synonyms under GOOD, HONEST, INNOCENT, JUST, MORAL, PURE, VIRTUOUS. —*n.* **1** Something having a vertical position, as an upright timber or piano. **2** The state of being upright: a post out of *upright*. **3** In football, one of the goal posts. —*adv.* Vertically; honestly; sincerely; justly. [OE *upriht* < *up-* up + *riht* right] —**up′right·ly** *adv.* —**up′right·ness** *n.*

upright piano See under PIANO.

up·rise (up·rīz′) *v.i.* **·rose**, **·ris·en**, **·ris·ing** **1** To get up; rise, as from a seat or from sleep. **2** To be or become erect. **3** To go upward; ascend. **4** To increase; swell. **5** To rise into view. **6** To rise in revolt. —*n.* (up′rīz′) **1** The act of rising; ascent. **2** An upward slope; upgrade.

up·ris·ing (up·rī′zing, up′rī′zing) *n.* **1** The act of rising. **2** Revolt; insurrection. **3** An ascent; a slope; acclivity.

up·riv·er (up′riv′ər) *adj. & adv.* On or toward the upper part of a river. —*n.* A region located up-river.

up·roar (up′rôr′, -rōr′) *n.* Violent disturbance and noise; tumult. See synonyms under NOISE, TUMULT. —*v.* (up·rôr′, -rōr′) *Obs. v.i.* To make an uproar. —*v.t.* To throw into uproar or confusion. [< Du. *oproer* < *op-* up + *roeren* stir]

up·roar·i·ous (up·rôr′ē·əs, -rōr′ē-) *adj.* Accompanied by or making uproar. See synonyms under NOISY. —**up·roar′i·ous·ly** *adv.* —**up·roar′i·ous·ness** *n.*

up·root (up·rōōt′, -rōōt′) *v.t.* To tear up by the roots; eradicate; destroy utterly. See synonyms under EXTERMINATE. —**up·root′al** *n.* —**up·root′er** *n.*

up·rouse (up·rouz′) *v.t.* **·roused**, **·rous·ing** To rouse up, as from sleep.

Up·sa·la (up·sä′lə, *Sw.* ōōp′sä·lä) A city in eastern Sweden; site of Upsala University, founded 1477, one of world's oldest universities. Also **Upp·sa′la**.

up·scale (up′skāl′) *adj.* Higher than average in income and cultural appreciation: *upscale* attitudes.

up·set (up·set′) *v.* **·set**, **·set·ting** *v.t.* **1** To overturn. **2** To throw into confusion or disorder. **3** To disconcert; derange or disquiet. **4** To defeat, especially unexpectedly: Navy *upset* Army. **5** To shorten and thicken (metal) by hammering or by pressure: to *upset* a bolt to form a head or to *upset* the metal tire of a wheel. **6** To swage (the ends of the teeth of a saw). —*v.i.* **7** To become overturned. —*adj.* (*also* up′set′) Set up; required: in the phrase **upset price,** a price at which property is offered for sale, as by an auctioneer, as the lowest selling price. —*n.* (up′set′) The act of upsetting, or the state of being upset. —**up·set′ter** *n.*

up·shot (up′shot′) *n.* The final outcome. See synonyms under CONSEQUENCE.

up·side (up′sīd′) *n.* The upper side or part.

up·side-down (up′sīd′doun′) *adj.* Having the upper side down; in disorder. —*adv.* With the upper side down; in disorder. [Alter. of ME *up so down* up as if down]

up·si·lon (yōōp′sə·lon, *Brit.* yōōp·sī′lən) *n.* The twentieth letter and sixth vowel in the Greek alphabet (Y, υ): having the sound of French *u,* Latin and Old English *y.* It is transliterated in English as *u* or *y.* See Y. [< Gk. *ypsilon* smooth y]

up·spring (up′spring′) *n.* **1** A leap up into the air. **2** *Obs.* An upstart. —*v.i.* **·sprang** *or* **·sprung, ·sprung, ·spring·ing** To spring up.

up·stage (up′stāj′) *n.* The half of a stage, from left to right, extending from the center to the backdrop. —*adj.* **1** Pertaining to the back half of a stage. **2** *Colloq.* Conceited; haughty; stuck-up; supercilious. —*adv.* Toward or on the back half of a stage. —*v.t.* **·staged, ·stag·ing** To steal a scene from (another actor).

up·stairs (up′stârz′) *adj.* Pertaining to an upper story. —*n.* The upper story; the part of a building above the ground floor. —*adv.* In, to, or toward an upper story. —**to kick upstairs** To promote so as to get out of the way.

up·stand·ing (up·stan′ding) *adj.* Standing up; erect; hence, honest; upright; straightforward.

up·start (up′stärt′) *v.i.* To start or spring up suddenly. —*adj.* (up′stärt′) **1** Suddenly raised to prominence, wealth, or power. **2** Characteristic of a parvenu; vulgar. —*n.* (up′stärt′) One who has suddenly risen from a humble position to consequence; a parvenu.

up·state (up′stāt′) *U.S. adj.* Of, from, or designating that part of a State lying outside, usually north, of the principal city. —*n.* The outlying, usually northern, sections of a State. —*adv.* In or toward the outlying or northern sections of a State. —**up′stat′er** *n.*

up·stream (up′strēm′) *adv.* Toward the upper part of a stream; against the current; toward or at a place nearer the source.

up·stroke (up′strōk′) *n.* An upward stroke.

up·sweep (up′swēp′) *n.* **1** A sweeping up or upward. **2** The upturning of the lower jaw, as in the bulldog. —*v.t.* & *v.i.* (up·swēp′) **·swept, ·sweep·ing** To brush or sweep upward.

up·swept (up′swept′) *adj.* Of or pertaining to a style of hairdressing in which the hair is swept upward smoothly in the back and piled high on the top of the head.

up·swing (up′swing′) *n.* **1** A swinging upward. **2** An improvement. —*v.i.* (up·swing′) **·swung, ·swing·ing** To swing upward; improve.

up·take (up′tāk′) *n.* **1** The act of lifting or taking up. **2** A boiler flue that unites the combustion gases and carries them toward the smokestack. **3** An upward ventilating shaft in a mine. **4** Mental comprehension; understanding.

up·throw (up′thrō′) *n.* **1** A throwing upward; an upheaval. **2** *Geol.* An upward displacement of the rock on one side of a fault.

up·thrust (up′thrust′) *n.* **1** An upward thrust. **2** *Geol.* An upheaval (usually violent) of rocks in the earth's crust.

up·tight (up′tīt′) *adj. U.S. Slang* Uneasy, anxious, or tense; nervous. Also **up′-tight′, up tight.** —**up′tight′ness** *n.*

up to See under UP.

up-to-date (up′tə-dāt′) *adj.* Having the latest information, fashion, manner, or improvement: an *up-to-date* dictionary.

up to date To the present time.

up·town (up′toun′) *adv.* In or toward the upper part of a town. —*adj.* Pertaining to or resident in the upper part of a town or city, or that part which is conventionally regarded as the upper part, usually the residence section.

up·turn (up·tûrn′) *v.t.* To turn up or over, as sod with the plow; hence, to overturn; upset. —*n.* (up′tûrn′) A turning upward; an increase.

up·ward (up′wərd) *adv.* **1** In or toward a higher place; in an ascending course or direction; toward the source: to look *upward;* to trace a stream *upward.* **2** With increase or advancement; toward a higher price: Prices tended *upward.* **3** In excess; more: children five years old and *upward.* **4** Toward that which is better, nobler, or holier. **5** In the upper parts. Also **up′wards.** —**upward of** *or* **upwards of** Higher than or in excess of. —*adj.* Turned or directed toward a higher place. [OE *upweard* < *up-* up + *-weard* -WARD] —**up′ward·ly** *adv.*

Ur (ûr) An ancient city of Sumer, southern Mesopotamia, the site of which is on the Euphrates in SE Iraq. Old Testament **Ur of the Chal·dees** (kal·dēz′, kal′dēz).

ur-[1] Var. of URO-[1].

ur-[2] Var. of URO-[2].

u·ra·chus (yōōr′ə·kəs) *n. Anat.* A canal connecting the bladder of the fetus with the allantois. [< NL. *Gk. ourachos* urinary canal of a fetus < *ouron* urine + *echein* hold]

u·rae·mi·a (yōō·rē′mē·ə), **u·rae·mic** (yōō·rē′mik) See UREMIA, etc.

u·rae·us (yōō·rē′əs) *n.* The emblem of the sacred serpent (haje) in the headdress of Egyptian divinities and kings: a symbol of sovereignty. [< NL. < Gk. *ouraios* of a tail < *oura* tail]

URAEUS

U·ral (yōōr′əl, *Russian* ōō·räl′) A river in SE European Russian S.F.S.R., and SW Kazakh S.S.R., considered as forming part of the traditional boundary between Asia and Europe and flowing 1,574 miles south and west from the Ural Mountains to the Caspian Sea.

U·ral-Al·ta·ic (yōōr′əl·al·tā′ik) *n.* A hypothetical family of languages embracing almost all the agglutinative languages of Europe and northern Asia, comprising the Uralic (Finno-Ugric, Samoyedic) and Altaic (Turkic, Mongolian, Manchu-Tungusic) subfamilies. —*adj.* **1** Of or pertaining to the Ural and Altai mountain ranges. **2** Of, pertaining to, or designating the Ural-Altaic languages, or any of the peoples speaking any of these languages. Also called *Turanian, Ugro-Altaic.*

U·ral·ic (yōō·ral′ik) *n.* A family of agglutinative languages comprising the Finno-Ugric and Samoyedic subfamilies: by some classified with Altaic in one great Ural-Altaic family. —*adj.* Of or pertaining to this linguistic family. Also **U·ra·li·an** (yōō·rā′lē·ən).

u·ral·ite (yōōr′əl·īt) *n.* A pyroxene altered to amphibole. [from *Ural* Mountains] —**u·ral·it·ic** (-it′ik) *adj.*

U·ral Mountains A mountain system in Russia the traditional boundary between Asia and Europe; 1,300 miles long, from the Artic Ocean to the Kazakhstan border; highest peak 6,217 feet.

U·ralsk (ōō·rälsk′) A city on the Ural river in NW Kazakh S.S.R.

u·ra·nal·y·sis (yōōr′ə·nal′ə·sis) See URINALYSIS.

U·ra·ni·a (yōō·rā′nē·ə) **1** The Muse of astronomy. **2** The heavenly one: an epithet of Aphrodite. [< L. < Gk. *Ourania* < *ouranios* heavenly < *ouranos* heaven] —**U·ra′ni·an** *adj.*

u·ran·ic (yōō·ran′ik) *adj. Chem.* Pertaining to or derived from uranium, especially in its higher valence. [< Gk. *ouranos* heaven]

u·ran·i·nite (yōō·ran′ə·nīt) *n.* A greenish-black, opaque uranium mineral containing also lead, nitrogen, helium, thorium, radium, and certain rare earths, occurring in octohedral crystals. In the massive form it is called *pitchblende.* [< URANIUM]

u·ran·ism (yōōr′ən·iz′əm) *n.* Homosexuality: opposed to *dionism.* [< Gk. *Ourania* URANIA (def. 2)]

u·ra·nite (yōōr′ə·nīt) *n.* Any of several uranium minerals, especially uranium phosphates, torbernite or copper uranite, autunite or lime uranite. —**u′ra·nit′ic** (-nit′ik) *adj.*

u·ra·ni·um (yōō·rā′nē·əm) *n.* A heavy, toxic, silvery-white, radioactive metallic element (symbol U, atomic number 92) occurring in various minerals in equilibrium with a variety of disintegration products, and in certain of its isotopes constituting the fuel for nuclear reactors. See PERIODIC TABLE. [< URANUS]

uranium series *Physics* A series of radioactive elements beginning with uranium of mass 238 and a half-life of 4.5×10^{10} years and continuing through successive disintegrations to the stable isotope of lead of mass 206.

urano- *combining form Astron.* The heavens; of or pertaining to the heavens, or to celestial bodies: *uranography.* Also, before vowels, **uran-.** [< Gk. *ouranos* heaven]

u·ra·nog·ra·phy (yōōr′ə·nog′rə·fē) *n.* Scientific description of the celestial bodies; the making of celestial globes and maps: also spelled *ouranography.* —**u′ra·nog′ra·pher** *or* **·phist** *n.* —**u′ra·no·graph′ic** (-nō-graf′ik) *or* **·i·cal** *adj.*

u·ra·nous (yōōr′ə·nəs) *adj. Chem.* Of or pertaining to uranium, especially in its lower valence.

U·ra·nus (yōōr′ə·nəs) **1** In Greek mythology, the son and husband of Gaea (Earth) and father of the Titans, Furies, and Cyclopes: overthrown by his son Kronos: also spelled *Ouranos.* **2** *Astron.* A planet of the solar system; seventh in distance from the sun. Its mean distance from the sun is 1,781 millions of miles, its sidereal period about 84 terrestrial years, and its diameter about 29,600 miles. It has four satellites. See PLANET. [< L < Gk. *Ouranos* < *ouranos* heaven]

u·ra·nyl (yōōr′ə·nil) *n. Chem.* The bivalent radical UO_2, found in many uranium compounds. [< URANIUM + -YL]

u·ra·re (yōō·rä′rē) *n.* Curare: also called *oorali.* Also **u·ra′ri.**

U·ra·ri·coe·ra (ōō·rä′rē·kwä′rə) A river in northern Brazil, flowing 300 miles east from the Venezuela border to the Río Branco.

u·rase (yōōr′ās) See UREASE.

u·rate (yōōr′āt) *n. Chem.* A salt of uric acid.

U·ra·wa (ōō·rä·wä) A city of central Honshu island, Japan.

ur·ban (ûr′bən) *adj.* Pertaining to, characteristic of, including, or constituting a city; situated or dwelling in a city. [< L *urbanus.* See URBANE]

Ur·ban (ûr′bən) Name of eight popes. —**Urban II,** 1042?–99, pope 1088–99; preached the First Crusade.

urban district A subdivision, for administrative purposes, of a shire of England, Wales, or Northern Ireland.

ur·bane (ûr·bān′) *adj.* **1** Characterized by or having refinement, especially in manner; polite; courteous; suave: opposed to *rustic.* **2** *Obs.* Urban. See synonyms under POLITE. [< L *urbanus* of a city < *urbs, urbis* a city] —**ur·bane′ly** *adv.* —**ur·bane′ness** *n.*

ur·ban·ism (ûr′bən·iz′əm) *n.* **1** Life in the cities; the manner of life of urban dwellers. **2** The study of urban life, often with special attention to the physical environment. **3** The advocacy of living in a city. —**ur′ban·ist** *n.* —**ur·ban·is·tic** (ûr′bən·is′tik) *adj.*

ur·ban·ite (ûr′bən·īt) *n.* A city-dweller.

ur·ban·i·ty (ûr·ban′ə·tē) *n. pl.* **·ties 1** The character or quality of being urbane; refined or elegant courtesy; strictly, the city quality, from the assumption that life in the city results in superior refinement. **2** *Obs.* Polished humor or wit. [< L *urbanitas, -tatis* < *urbs, urbis* a city]

ur·ban·i·za·tion (ûr′bə·nə·zā′shən) *n.* **1** The act or process of urbanizing an area or a rural group of people. **2** The quality or state of being urbanized. Also *Brit.* **ur·ban·i·sa′tion.**

ur·ban·ize (ûr′bən·īz) *v.t.* **·ized, ·iz·ing 1** To cause (an area) to assume the characteristics of a city: to *urbanize* a suburb. **2** To cause (people) to adopt an urban life style. Also *Brit.* **ur′ban·ise.**

ur·ban·ol·o·gy (ûr′bə·nol′ə·jē) *n.* The study of problems peculiar to cities. —**ur·ban·ol′o·gist** *n.*

urban renewal The planned upgrading of a deteriorating urban area, usually using public funds and coordinated by a local government.

urban sprawl The uncontrolled spread of urban housing, shopping centers, etc., into rural or undeveloped areas close to a city.

ur·bi·cul·ture (ûr′bə·kul′chər) *n.* The study of the proper development, planning, and use of cities, especially in relation to the needs of their inhabitants. [<L *urbs; urbis* a city + CULTURE]

ur·bi et or·bi (ûr′bī et ôr′bī) *Latin* To the city (Rome) and to the world: used in official announcements, as papal bulls.

Urbs Ve·tus (ûrbz vē′təs) The ancient Latin name for ORVIETO.

ur·ce·o·late (ûr′sē·ə·lit, -lāt′) *adj. Bot.* Pitcher- or urn–shaped, as a corolla. [<L *urceolus*, dim. of *urceus* pitcher]

ur·chin (ûr′chin) *n.* 1 A roguish, mischievous boy. 2 A cylinder in a carding machine. 3 A hedgehog. 4 A sea urchin. 5 *Obs.* An elf, as often assuming the form of a hedgehog. —*adj. Obs.* Elfish; mischievous. [ME *irchoun* <OF *irechon, ireçon* <L *ericius* hedgehog + *er* hedgehog]

Ur·du (ōor′dōo, ōor·dōo′, ûr′dōo) *n.* A variety of Hindustani used by the Moslems, containing many Arabic and Persian elements and written in the Arabic alphabet: the official language of Pakistan. Also spelled *Oordoo.* [<Hind. *urdū*, short for (*zaban–i–*) *urdū* (language of the) camp <Turkish *ordū* camp <Persian *urdū*. Related to HORDE.]

-ure *suffix of nouns* 1 The act, process, or result of: *pressure.* 2 The function, rank, or office of: *prefecture.* 3 The means or instrument of: *ligature.* [<F <L *-ura*]

u·re·a (ōor′ē·ə) *n. Biochem.* A very soluble colorless crystalline compound, $CO(NH_2)_2$, formed by the oxidation of nitrogenous compounds in the body, and also made synthetically: used in medicine and in the making of plastics. Also called *carbamide.* [<NL <F *urée* <Gk. *ouron*] — **u·re′al** *adj.*

urea resin Any of a class of thermosetting resins obtained by the reaction of urea and formaldehyde in the presence of certain modifying agents.

u·re·ase (ōor′ē·ās, -āz) *n. Biochem.* An enzyme which promotes the hydrolysis of urea, with the formation of ammonium carbonate. [<UREA + -ASE]

U·red·i·na·les (ōor·red′ə·nā′lēz) *n. pl.* An order of fungi characterized by a branched, septate mycelium and the formation of reddish or yellow spores; the rust fungi. [<NL <L *uredo, -inis* blast, blight <*urere* burn]

u·re·din·i·um (ōor′ə·din′ē·əm) *n. Bot.* The spore fruit of a rust fungus which produces the uredospores. Also **u·re·di·um** (ōor·rē′dē·əm), **u′re·do·so′rus** (-dō·sôr′əs, -sō′rəs). [<NL <L *uredo, -inis* blight. See UREDO.]

u·re·do (ōor·rē′dō) *n.* 1 The uredo stage. 2 Urticaria. [<L, blight <*urere* burn]

u·re·do·spore (ōor·rē′də·spôr, -spōr) *n. Bot.* A unicellular thin–walled spore produced as a repeating generation in summer as part of the life cycle of a rust fungus. Also **u·re·din·i·o·spore** (ōor′ə·din′ē·ə·spôr′, -spōr′).

uredo stage *Bot.* The stage in the life history of certain rust fungi during which uredospores are produced.

u·re·ide (ōor′ē·īd, -id) *n. Chem.* Any of several nitrogenous compounds derived from urea and an acid or aldehyde by the removal of water.

u·re·mi·a (ōor·rē′mē·ə) *n. Pathol.* An abnormal condition of the blood due to the presence of urea with other urinary constituents ordinarily excreted by the kidneys. Also *uraemia, urinemia.* [<NL <UR-¹ + -EMIA] — **u·re′mic** *adj.*

-uret *suffix Chem.* Used to denote a compound: now replaced by *–ide.* [<F <*-ure* -URE]

u·re·ter (ōor·rē′tər) *n. Anat.* The duct by which urine passes from the kidney to the bladder or the cloaca. [<NL <Gk. *ourētēr* <*ourein* urinate] — **u·re′ter·al, u·re·ter·ic** (ōor′ə·ter′ik) *adj.*

u·re·ter·ec·to·my (ōor·rē′tə·rek′tə·mē) *n. Surg.* Excision of all or part of the ureter. [<URETER(O)- + -ECTOMY]

uretero- *combining form Med.* A ureter; of or related to a ureter. Also, before vowels, **ureter-.** [<Gk. *ourētēr* <*ourein* urinate]

u·re·than (ōor′ə·than′, yōo·reth′ən) *n. Chem.* 1 A white crystalline compound, $C_3H_7NO_2$, derived from carbamic acid by substituting ethyl for the hydrogen of the hydroxyl group: some of its derivatives are used as hypnotics and sedatives: also called *ethylurethane.*

2 Any ester of carbamic acid. Also **u·re·thane** (yōor′ə·thān′, yōo·reth′ān). [<UR(EA) + ETHAN(E)]

u·re·thra (yōo·rē′thrə) *n. Anat.* The duct by which urine is discharged from the bladder of most mammals, and which, in males, carries the seminal discharge. [<LL <Gk. *ourēthra* <*ouron* urine] — **u·re′thral** *adj.*

u·re·thri·tis (yōor′ə·thrī′tis) *n. Pathol.* Inflammation of the urethra. [<NL] — **u′re·thrit′ic** (-thrit′ik) *adj.*

urethro- *combining form Med.* The urethra; of or pertaining to the urethra: *urethroscope.* Also, before vowels, **urethr-.** [<Gk. *ourēthra* the urethra]

u·re·thro·scope (yōo·rē′thrə·skōp) *n. Med.* An instrument for examining the urethra. — **u·re′thro·scop′ic** (-skop′ik) *adj.* — **u·re·thros·co·py** (yōor′ə·thros′kə·pē) *n.*

u·ret·ic (yōo·ret′ik) *adj. Med.* 1 Diuretic. 2 Of or pertaining to the urine; urinary. [<LL *ureticus* <Gk. *ourētikos* <*ouron* urine]

U·rey (yōor′ē), **Harold Clayton,** born 1893, U. S. chemist.

Ur·fa (ōor·fä′) A city in southern Turkey in Asia, near the Syrian border: ancient *Edessa.*

Ur·fé (dür·fā′), **Honoré d',** 1568–1625, French novelist.

Ur·ga (ōor′gä) The former name for ULAN BATOR.

urge (ûrj) *v.* **urged, urg·ing** *v.t.* 1 To drive or force forward; impel; push. 2 To plead with or entreat earnestly, as with arguments or explanations: He *urged* them to accept the plan. 3 To press or argue the doing, consideration, or acceptance of; advocate earnestly. 4 To move or force to some course or action; constrain. 5 To stimulate or excite; incite; intensify. 6 To ply or use vigorously, as oars. — *v.i.* 7 To present or press arguments, claims, etc. 8 To exert an impelling or prompting force. See synonyms under ACTUATE, PERSUADE, PIQUE, PLEAD, PUSH, QUICKEN. — *n.* 1 A strong impulse to perform a certain act. 2 The act of urging; the state of being urged. [<L *urgere* drive, urge]

Ur·gel (ōor·hel′) A city in Lérida, NE Spain, in the Pyrenees SW of Andorra; seat of a bishop who is joint suzerain of Andorra.

ur·gen·cy (ûr′jən·sē) *n. pl.* **·cies** 1 The quality of being urgent. 2 Pressure by entreaty; pressure of necessity. 3 The act of urging. 4 Something urgent. See synonyms under NECESSITY.

ur·gent (ûr′jənt) *adj.* 1 Characterized by urging or importunity; requiring prompt attention; pressing; imperative. 2 Eagerly importunate or insistent. [<F <L *urgens, -entis,* ppr. of *urgere* drive] — **ur′gent·ly** *adv.*

Synonyms: importunate, pertinacious, pressing, solicitous.

-urgy *combining form* Development of or work with a (specified) material or product: *metallurgy, chemurgy, zymurgy.* [<Gk. *-ourgia* <*ergon* work]

U·ri (ōor′ē) A canton in central Switzerland; 415 square miles; capital, Altdorf.

-uria *combining form Pathol.* A (specified) condition of the urine: usually used to indicate disease or abnormality: *hematuria, dysuria.* [<NL <Gk. *-ouria* <*ouron* urine]

U·ri·ah (yōo·rī′ə) A masculine personal name. Also *Ital.* **U·ri·a** (ōo·rē′ä), **U·ri·as** (*Ger.* ōo·rē′äs, *Lat.* yə·rī′əs), *Fr.* **U·rie** (ü·rē′). [<Hebrew, God is light]

—**Uriah** A Hittite captain in the Israelite army, husband of Bathsheba, treacherously sent to his death by David. II *Sam.* xi 15–17.

Uriah Heep An unctuous, fawning, scheming character in Dickens's *David Copperfield;* hence, an odious hypocrite.

u·ric (yōor′ik) *adj.* Of, pertaining to, or derived from urine. [<F *urique*]

uric acid *Biochem.* A white, almost insoluble dibasic acid, $C_5H_4N_4O_3$, of varying crystalline forms, found in small quantity in human urine. It is a product of the incomplete oxidation of animal tissue and animal diet, and forms the nucleus of most urinary and renal calculi.

urico- *combining form* Uric acid; of or related to uric acid: *uricolysis,* the splitting up of uric acid. Also, before vowels, **uric-.** [<URIC]

U·ri·el (yōor′ē·əl) A masculine personal name. [<Hebrew, light of God]

—**Uriel** One of the seven archangels of Christian legend: in Milton's *Paradise Lost,* represented as "regent of the sun."

U·rim (yōor′im) *n. pl.* 1 Objects mentioned in the Old Testament (*Ex.* xxviii 30, etc.) in connection with the breastplate of the high priest: generally in the phrase **Urim and Thummim,** supposed to have been precious stones used in casting lots, one signifying an affirmative and the other a negative answer. 2 In Mormon theology, with the Thummim, the sacred objects used by seers under divine direction, especially those used by Joseph Smith in translating the *Book of Mormon.* [<Hebrew *ūrīm* fires <*ūr* shine]

u·ri·nal (yōor′ə·nəl) *n.* 1 A toilet or closet convenience or fixture for men's use in urination; also, a private place containing such conveniences for public use, as in a park. 2 A receptacle for urine; a glass receptacle, as a bottle, used in the inspection of urine. [<OF <Med. L *urinale,* orig. neut. of L *urinalis* pertaining to urine <*urina* urine]

u·ri·nal·y·sis (yōor′ə·nal′ə·sis) *n. pl.* **·ses** (-sēz) Chemical analysis of the urine: also spelled *uranalysis.* [<NL <URIN(O)- + (AN)ALYSIS]

u·ri·nar·y (yōor′ə·ner′ē) *adj.* Of, pertaining to, or concerned in the production and excretion of urine: the *urinary* organs. — *n. pl.* **·nar·ies** 1 A reservoir for storing urine, etc., for use as manure. 2 A urinal.

urinary calculus *Pathol.* A concretion formed in the urinary passages; the stone.

u·ri·nate (yōor′ə·nāt) *v.i.* **·nat·ed, ·nat·ing** To void or pass urine. [<Med. L *urinatus,* pp. of *urinare* pass urine <*urina* urine] — **u′ri·na′tion** *n.*

u·rine (yōor′in) *n.* A pale–yellow fluid secreted from the blood of mammals by the kidneys, stored in the bladder, and voided through the urethra: the principal vehicle by which nitrogenous and saline matters are removed from the system. [<F <L *urina*]

u·ri·ne·mi·a (yōor′ə·nē′mē·ə) *n.* Uremia. Also **u′ri·nae′mi·a.** [<URIN(O)- + -EMIA] — **u′ri·ne′mic** or **·nae′mic** *adj.*

u·ri·nif·er·ous (yōor′ə·nif′ər·əs) *adj.* Concerned in the conveyance of urine.

urino- *combining form* Urine. Also, before vowels, **urin-,** as in *urinalysis.* [<L *urina* urine]

u·ri·no·gen·i·tal (yōor′ə·nō·jen′ə·təl) *adj.* Urogenital.

u·ri·nos·co·py (yōor′ə·nos′kə·pē) *n. pl.* **·pies** Uroscopy.

u·ri·nous (yōor′ə·nəs) *adj.* Of, pertaining to, containing, or resembling urine. Also **u′ri·nose** (-nōs).

Ur·mi·a (ōor′mē·ə), **Lake** The largest lake of Iran, between Tabriz and the Turkish border; in summer, 1,500 square miles; in winter, 2,300 square miles; 90 miles long, 30 miles wide: also *Rizaiyeh.* Persian **U·ru·mi·yeh** (ōo·rōo·mē·ye′).

urn (ûrn) *n.* 1 A rounded or angular vase having a foot, variously used in antiquity as a receptacle for the ashes of the dead, a water vessel, measure, etc. 2 A vessel for preserving the ashes of the dead; a grave. 3 In ancient Rome, a receptacle used to hold lots drawn in voting. 4 A vase–shaped receptacle having a faucet, and designed for keeping tea, coffee, etc., hot, as by means of a spirit lamp. ◆ Homophones: *earn, erne.* [<F *urne* <L *urna*]

URN
In park at Versailles.

uro-¹ *combining form* Urine; pertaining to urine or to the urinary tract: *urology.* Also, before vowels, **ur-.** [<Gk. *ouron* urine]

uro-² *combining form* A tail; of or related to the tail; caudal: *uropod.* Also, before vowels, **ur-.** [<Gk. *oura* a tail]

u·ro·bil·in (yōor′ə·bil′in, -bī′lin) *n. Biochem.* A brownish, resinous bile pigment, found in urine and sometimes in the blood. [<URO-¹ + BILE + -IN]

u·ro·chord (yŏŏr'ə·kôrd) *n. Zool.* The noto-chord or central axis of larval ascidians and certain adult tunicates. [<URO-² + CHORD²] —**u'ro·chor'dal** *adj.*

U·ro·chor·da·ta (yŏŏr'ō·kôr·dā'tə) *n. pl.* The tunicates. [<NL <URO-² + CHORDATA]

u·ro·chrome (yŏŏr'ə·krōm) *n. Biochem.* The yellow pigment which gives to urine its characteristic color.

u·rochs (yŏŏr'oks) *n.* The urus. [<G]

U·ro·de·la (yŏŏr'ə·dē'lə) *n. pl.* Caudata. [<NL <URO-² + Gk. *dēlos* visible]

u·ro·gen·i·tal (yŏŏr'ō·jen'ə·təl) *adj.* Of or pertaining to the urinary and genital organs and their functions.

u·ro·gen·i·tals (yŏŏr'ō·jen'ə·təlz) *n. pl.* The urogenital organs.

u·rog·e·nous (yŏŏ·roj'ə·nəs) *adj.* Producing or promotive of the urinary secretion. [<URO-¹ + -GENOUS]

u·ro·lith (yŏŏr'ə·lith) *n. Pathol.* A urinary calculus. [<URO-¹ + -LITH¹] —**u'ro·lith'ic** *adj.*

u·ro·li·thi·a·sis (yŏŏr'ō·li·thī'ə·sis) *n. Pathol.* Any diseased condition due to the formation of urinary calculi. [<NL <URO-¹ + LITHIASIS]

u·rol·o·gy (yŏŏ·rol'ə·jē) *n.* The branch of medical science that relates to the urine and to the genitourinary tract in health and in disease. —**u·ro·log·ic** (yŏŏr'ə·loj'ik) or **·i·cal** *adj.* —**u·rol'o·gist** *n.*

u·ro·pod (yŏŏr'ə·pod) *n. Zool.* An abdominal or caudal limb or appendage of an arthropod, especially one of the posterior pairs of pleopods in a crustacean. [<URO-² + -POD] —**u·rop·o·dal** (yŏŏ·rop'ə·dəl), **u·rop'o·dous** *adj.*

u·ro·pyg·i·al (yŏŏr'ə·pij'ē·əl) *adj.* Of or pertaining to the uropygium.

uropygial gland *Ornithol.* The gland at the base of a bird's tail, secreting an oily substance used to preen the feathers.

u·ro·pyg·i·um (yŏŏr'ə·pij'ē·əm) *n. Ornithol.* The terminal part of the body supporting the tail feathers of a bird; rump. [<NL <Gk. *ouropygion*, alter. (after *oura* tail) of *orrhopygion* < *orrhos* end of the os sacrum + *pygē* rump]

u·ros·co·py (yŏŏ·ros'kə·pē) *n. Med.* Diagnosis by examination of the urine. [<URO-¹ + -SCOPY] —**u·ro·scop·ic** (yŏŏr'ə·skop'ik) *adj.* —**u·ros'co·pist** *n.*

U·ro·tro·pin (yŏŏr'ə·trō'pin) *n.* Proprietary name for a brand of methenamine.

u·ro·xan·thin (yŏŏr'ə·zan'thin) *n.* Indican (def. 2). [<URO-¹ + XANTHIN]

Ur·quhart (ûr'kərt), **Sir Thomas**, 1611–60, Scottish author; translator of Rabelais.

ur·sa (ûr'sə) *n. Latin* A she-bear: used in the phrases *Ursa Major* and *Ursa Minor.*

Ursa Major *Astron.* The Great Bear, a large northern constellation containing the seven conspicuous stars called the Septentriones, including the two Pointers, Dubhe and Merak, which point to the polestar: also called *Big Dipper, the Dipper, Charles's Wain.* See CONSTELLATION.

URSA MAJOR AND URSA MINOR
a. Ursa Major. *b.* Ursa Minor. *c.* Polestar.

Ursa Minor *Astron.* The Little Bear, a northern constellation including the polestar: also called *Little Dipper, Dog's Tail.* See CONSTELLATION.

ur·si·form (ûr'sə·fôrm) *adj.* Having the form of a bear. [<L *ursus* bear + -FORM]

ur·sine (ûr'sīn, -sin) *adj.* 1 Pertaining to or like a bear. 2 Clothed with dense bristles, as certain caterpillars. [<L *ursinus* < *ursus* bear]

ursine howler See HOWLER (def. 3).

Ur·spra·che (ŏŏr'shprä'khə) *n. German* A primitive, original, or parent language; particularly, a hypothetical primitive Indo-European language.

Ur·su·la (ûr'syə·lə, -sə-, *Du.* ŏŏr'sŏŏ·lä) A feminine personal name. Also *Fr.* **Ur·sule** (ûr·sül'), *Ger., Sw.* **Ur·sel** (ŏŏr'səl), *Sp.* **Ur·so·la** (ŏŏr'sō·lä). [<L, little she-bear]

—**Ursula, Saint** A Cornish princess of the fourth or fifth century, martyred, according to legend, with eleven thousand virgins at Cologne by the Huns.

Ur·su·line (ûr'syə·lin, -sə-, -līn) *adj.* Pertaining to St. Ursula or to an order of nuns founded in 1537 by St. Angela Merici: they are engaged chiefly in the education of girls. — *n.* An Ursuline nun.

Ur·text (ŏŏr'tekst) *n. German* Earliest or primary form of a written text.

ur·ti·ca·ceous (ûr'tə·kā'shəs) *adj. Bot.* Belonging to a widely distributed family (*Urticaceae*) of trees, shrubs, or herbs, the nettle family, some of which are provided with sharp, stinging hairs. [<NL <L *urtica* nettle]

ur·ti·car·i·a (ûr'tə·kâr'ē·ə) *n. Pathol.* A disease of the skin, variously caused, characterized by evanescent, rounded elevations resembling wheals raised by a whip, and attended with intense itching; nettle rash; hives. [<NL <L *urtica* nettle] —**ur'ti·car'i·al** or **·i·ous** *adj.*

ur·ti·cate (ûr'tə·kāt) *v.t. & v.i.* **·cat·ed, ·cat·ing** To sting, as with nettles. [<Med. L *urticatus,* pp. of *urticare* sting < *urtica* nettle]

ur·ti·ca·tion (ûr'tə·kā'shən) *n. Med.* 1 Formerly, the act, process, or effect of whipping with nettles as a stimulant, as in paralysis. 2 A tingling or burning sensation. 3 The development of urticaria.

U·ru·bam·ba (ŏŏ'rŏŏ·väm'bä) A river in southern Peru, flowing about 450 miles NW and north from the Andes of SE Peru to the Ucayali in central Peru.

U·ru·guay (yŏŏr'ə·gwā, *Sp.* ŏŏ'rŏŏ·gwī') 1 A republic of SE South America, on the Atlantic; 72,172 square miles; capital, Montevideo. 2 A river in SE South America, flowing 1,000 miles SW to the Río de la Plata. —**U'ru·guay'an** *adj. & n.*

U·rum·chi (ŏŏ'rŏŏm'chē') The capital of the Sinkiang–Uigur Autonomous Region, NW China. Also **U'rum'tsi'**.

U·run·di (ŏŏ·rŏŏn'dē) A former district of German East Africa; since 1923, the southern county of Ruanda–Urundi; 10,658 square miles.

u·rus (yŏŏr'əs) *n.* An extinct, long-horned, wild ox of Germany (*Bos primigenius*), so named by Julius Caesar; also called *aurochs, urochs.* [<L <Gmc. Cf. OHG *ur.*]

u·ru·shi·ol (ŏŏr'ŏŏ·shē·ōl', -ol') *n.* A poisonous, irritant liquid, the active principle of poison ivy and the Japanese lac tree. [<Japanese *urushi* lacquer + -OL²]

us (us) *pron.* The objective case of WE. [OE *ūs*]

us·a·ble (yŏŏ'zə·bəl) *adj.* 1 Capable of being used. 2 That can be used conveniently. Also **use'a·ble.** —**us'a·ble·ness** *n.* —**us'a·bly** *adv.*

us·age (yŏŏ'sij, -zij) *n.* 1 The manner of using or treating a person or thing; treatment; also, the act of using. 2 Customary or habitual practice, or something permitted by it or done in accordance with it; custom or a custom: an act permitted by *usage;* ancient *usages.* 3 *Law* Uniform practice. 4 The way of using words, speech patterns, etc., that is general and established among the majority of the native speakers and writers of a language. 5 *Obs.* Conduct; behavior. See synonyms under HABIT. —**nonjurors' usages** In English and Scottish history, certain ceremonies, including mixing wine with water, prayer for the dead, trine immersion at baptism, the chrism at confirmation, anointing of the sick, etc., adopted by the nonjurors. [<OF <Med. L *usaticum* <L *usus.* See USE.]

us·ance (yŏŏ'zəns) *n.* 1 A period of time, variable as between various countries, which, by commercial usage, is allowed, exclusive of days of grace, for payment of bills of exchange, especially foreign. 2 *Econ.* An income derived from the possession of wealth in any way it may be invested. 3 *Obs.* Employment; use. 4 *Obs.* Interest on money. 5 *Obs.* Custom. Also *Obs.* **us'aunce.** [<OF <*us* <L *usus.* See USE.]

use (yŏŏz) *v.* **used, us·ing** *v.t.* 1 To employ for the accomplishment of a purpose; make use of. 2 To put into practice or employ habitually; make a practice of: to *use* diligence in business. 3 To expend the whole of; consume: often with *up.* 4 To conduct oneself toward; treat: to *use* one badly. 5 To make familiar by habit or practice; accustom; inure: usually in the past participle: He is *used* to exposure. 6 To partake of; smoke or chew: He does not *use* tobacco. — *v.i.* 7 To do something customarily or habitually; be accustomed or wont: now only in the past tense as an auxiliary to form a phrase equivalent to a frequentative past tense: I *used* to go there. See synonyms under EMPLOY, OCCUPY. — *n.* (yŏŏs) 1 The act of using; application or employment to an end, particularly a good or useful end; the fact or condition of being employed. 2 Suitableness or adaptability to an end; serviceableness: the *uses* of adversity. 3 Way or manner of using. 4 Occasion or need to employ; necessity: I have no *use* for it; purpose; function. 5 Habitual practice or employment; the fact of being habitually used; custom; usage. 6 Any special form, ceremony, or ritual of public worship, or any individual service that arose in or was perpetuated by a church, diocese, or branch of a church: Sarum *use,* Roman *use,* York *use.* Compare LITURGY. 7 *Law* The permanent equitable right that a beneficiary has to the enjoyment of the rents and profits of lands and tenements of which the legal title and possession are vested in another in trust for the beneficiary. 8 *Obs.* Ordinary experience or occurrence. 9 Usury. See synonyms under CUSTOM, HABIT, OCCUPATION, SERVICE, UTILITY. [<OF *user* <L *usus,* pp. of *uti* use]

use·ful (yŏŏs'fəl) *adj.* Serviceable; serving a use or purpose, especially a valuable one; productive of good; beneficial. —**use'ful·ly** *adv.* —**use'ful·ness** *n.*
Synonyms: adapted, advantageous, available, beneficial, conducive, convenient, favorable, good, helpful, profitable, salutary, serviceable, suitable, suited. See CONVENIENT, EXPEDIENT, GOOD. Compare UTILITY. *Antonyms:* see synonyms for USELESS.

use·less (yŏŏs'lis) *adj.* Unserviceable; being of no use; not serving, or not capable of serving, any beneficial purpose. —**use'less·ly** *adv.* —**use'less·ness** *n.*
Synonyms: abortive, bootless, fruitless, futile, ineffectual, nugatory, null, profitless, unavailing, unprofitable, unserviceable, vain, valueless, worthless. That which is *bootless, fruitless,* or *profitless* fails to accomplish any valuable result; that which is *abortive, ineffectual,* or *unavailing* fails to accomplish a result that it was, or was supposed to be, adapted to accomplish. That which is *useless, futile,* or *vain* is inherently incapable of accomplishing a specified result. *Useless* in the widest sense signifies not of use for any valuable purpose, and is thus closely similar to *valueless* and *worthless. Fruitless* is more final than *ineffectual,* as applying to the sum or harvest of endeavor. That which is *useless* lacks fitness for a purpose; that which is *vain* lacks imaginable fitness. See VAIN, WASTE. *Antonyms:* see synonyms for USEFUL.

us·er (yŏŏ'zər) *n.* 1 One who or that which uses. 2 *Law* The exercise or enjoyment of a right.

Ush·ant (ush'ənt) An island off NW France, comprising the westernmost point of France; 5 miles long, 2 miles wide: French *Île d'Ouessant.*

U·shas (ŏŏ'shəs, ŏŏ·shäs') In Hindu mythology, the goddess of the dawn.

ush·er (ush'ər) *n.* 1 One who acts as doorkeeper, as of a court or other assemblyroom. 2 An officer whose duty it is to introduce strangers or walk before a person of rank. 3 One who conducts persons to seats, etc., as in a church or theater. 4 *Brit.* An underteacher. — *v.t.* 1 To act as an usher to; escort; conduct. 2 To precede as a harbinger; be a forerunner of. [<OF *uissier* <L *ostiarius* doorkeeper < *ostium* door]

ush·er·ette (ush'ə·ret') *n.* A female usher, as in a theater.

Usk (usk) A river in SW England and SE

Wales, flowing 60 miles east, SE, and south from the eastern border of Carmarthenshire to the Bristol Channel at Newport.

Üs·küb (üs·küp′) The Turkish name for SKOPLJE.

Us·ku·da·ma (ōōs′kōō·dā′mə) An ancient name for ADRIANOPLE.

Üs·kü·dar (üs′kü·där′) A Turkish city on the Asian side of the Bosporus opposite Istanbul: also *Scutari.*

Us·nach (ōōsh′nə) In old Irish legend, a famous warrior, father of three even more famous sons.

Us·pal·la·ta (ōōs′pä·yä′tä) A pass over the Andes between Santiago, Chile, and Mendoza, Argentina; elevation, 12,650 feet: also *La Cumbre.*

us·que·baugh (us′kwə·bô) *n.* A distilled spirit, as whisky: so called in Ireland and Scotland. Also **us′qua·bae, us′que, us′que·bae.** [< Irish and Scottish Gaelic *uisge–beatha* < *uisge* water + *beatha* life]

Ussh·er (ush′ər), **James,** 1581–1656, Irish bishop and theologian.

Us·su·ri (ōō·sōō′rē) A river forming part of the boundary between northeastern most China and southeasternmost U.S.S.R., and flowing 365 miles north from the SW Sikhote–Alin Range to the Amur at Khabarovsk.

U·sta·ši (ōō·stä′shē) A Croat fascist party in World War II supported by the German and Italian governments. Also **U·sta′chi.**

Us·ti·la·go (us′tə·lā′gō) *n.* A genus of smut fungi (order *Ustilaginales*) which attack the tissues of many plants, especially cereals, as *U. zeae,* destructive of corn, *U. tritici,* parasitic on wheat, etc. [< NL < LL < L *ustulatus* scorched. See USTULATE.]

Us·ti nad La·bem A city on the Elbe in NW Bohemia, the Czech Republic.

us·tion (us′chən) *n.* **1** The act of burning, or the state of being burnt. **2** *Med.* Cauterization by burning. [< L *ustio, -onis* < *ustus,* pp. of *urere* burn]

us·tu·late (us′chōō·lit, -lāt) *adj.* Scorched, burned, or colored as if by burning or scorching. [< L *ustulatus,* pp. of *ustulare* scorch, freq. of *urere* burn]

us·tu·la·tion (us′chōō·lā′shən) *n.* **1** The act of burning or searing. **2** In pharmacy, the drying of substances by heat preparatory to pulverization. **3** The burning of wine.

u·su·al (yōō′zhōō·əl) *adj.* Such as occurs in the ordinary course of events; frequent; common. [< OF < LL *usualis* < L *usus* use. See USE.] —**u′su·al·ly** *adv.* —**u′su·al·ness** *n.*

   Synonyms: accustomed, common, customary, everyday, familiar, frequent, general, habitual, normal, ordinary, prevailing, prevalent, regular, wonted. In strictness, *common* and *general* apply to the greater number of individuals in a class; but both words are in good use as applying to the greater number of instances in a series, so that it is possible to speak of one person's *common* practice or *general* custom, but *ordinary* or *usual* would in such case be preferable. See COMMON, FREQUENT, GENERAL, HABITUAL, NORMAL. *Antonyms:* exceptional, extraordinary, infrequent, out–of–the–way, rare, singular, strange, uncommon, unusual.

u·su·fruct (yōō′zyōō·frukt, yōō′syōō-) *n. Law* The right of using the property of another and of drawing the profits it produces without wasting its substance. [< LL *usufructus* < L *ususfructus* < *usus et fructus* use and fruit]

u·su·fruc·tu·ar·y (yōō′zyōō·fruk′chōō·er′ē, yōō′·syōō-) *n. pl.* **·ar·ies** One who holds property for use by usufruct, as a tenant. —*adj.* Of, pertaining to, or having the nature of a usufruct. [< LL *usufructuarius* < *usufructus.* See USUFRUCT.]

u·su·rer (yōō′zhər·ər) *n.* **1** One who practices usury; one who lends money, especially at an exorbitant or illegal rate. **2** *Obs.* One who lends money on interest; any money–lender. [< OF *usurier* < Med. L *usurarius* < L *usura* use, usury. See USURY.]

u·su·ri·ous (yōō·zhōōr′ē·əs) *adj.* Practicing usury; having the nature of usury. —**u·su′ri·ous·ly** *adv.* —**u·su′ri·ous·ness** *n.*

u·surp (yōō·zûrp′, -sûrp′) *v.t.* **1** To seize and hold (the office, rights, or powers of another)

without right or legal authority; take possession of by force. **2** To take arrogantly, as if by right. —*v.i.* **3** To practice usurpation; encroach: with *on* or *upon.* See synonyms under ASSUME. [< OF *usurper* < L *usurpare* make use of, usurp, ? < O *usususe* + *rapere* seize] —**u·surp′er** *n.* —**u·surp′ing·ly** *adv.*

u·sur·pa·tion (yōō′zər·pā′shən, -sər-) *n.* **1** The act of usurping: said especially of unlawful or forcible seizure of kingly power. **2** *Law* The wrongful intrusion into or unjust exercise of the privileges of any office, franchise, or right of another.

u·su·ry (yōō′zhər·ē) *n. pl.* **·ries** **1** The act or practice of exacting a rate of interest beyond what is allowed by law. **2** *Obs.* The lending of money at interest; interest in general. **3** *Law* A premium paid for the use of money beyond the rate of interest established by law. [< OF *usure* < L *usura* < *usus,* pp. of *uti* use]

u·sus lo·quen·di (yōō′səs lō·kwen′dī) *Latin* Usage in speaking.

ut (ōōt) *n.* The first note in the Guido scale: now commonly *do.* [See GAMUT]

U·tah (yōō′tô, -tä) A State of the western United States; 84,916 square miles; capital, Salt Lake City; entered the Union Jan. 4, 1896; nickname, *Beehive State:* abbr. UT — **U′tah·an** *adj.* & *n.*

U·ta·ma·ro (ōō·tä·mä·rō), **Kitagama,** 1754?–1806, Japanese engraver and designer of color prints.

ut dic·tum (ut dik′təm) *Latin* As said or directed.

Ute (yōōt, yōō′tē) *n.* One of a group of tribes of North American Indians of Shoshonean stock, including the Uncompahgre, Kaviawach, and Uinta, formerly living in Utah, Colorado, and New Mexico: now on reservations in Colorado and Utah.

u·ten·sil (yōō·ten′səl) *n.* A vessel, tool, implement, etc., serving a useful purpose, especially for domestic or farming use. See synonyms under TOOL. [< OF *utensile* < L *utensilis* fit for use < *utens,* ppr. of *uti* use]

u·ter·ine (yōō′tər·in, -īn) *adj.* **1** Pertaining to the uterus. **2** Born of the same mother, but having a different father. [< LL *uterinus* born of the same mother]

u·ter·i·tis (yōō′tə·rī′tis) *n. Pathol.* Metritis. [< NL]

utero- *combining form* The uterus; of or pertaining to the uterus. Also, before vowels, **uter-,** as in *uteritis.* [< L *uterus* the uterus]

u·ter·us (yōō′tər·əs) *n. pl.* **u·ter·i** (yōō′tər·ī) **1** *Anat.* The organ of a female mammal in which the young are protected and developed before birth; the womb. In the higher mammals the uterus is single, but in the lower, as marsupials and monotremes, it is double. **2** *Zool.* Any differentiated portion of an oviduct found in various animals, other than mammals, serving as a repository for the development and nourishment of the eggs or the young during the embryonic stage. [< L]

Ut·gard (ōōt′gärd) In Norse mythology, the abode of Utgard–Loki.

Ut·gard–Lo·ki (ōōt′gärd·lō′kē) In Norse mythology, an invulnerable giant.

U·ther (yōō′thər) A legendary king of Britain; father of Arthur. See ARTHUR, KING; IGRAINE; PENDRAGON.

U·ti·ca (yōō′tə·kə) **1** An ancient city, 20 miles NW of Carthage in northern Africa; site 18 miles north of modern Tunis. **2** A city of central New York, on the Mohawk River.

u·tile (yōō′til) *adj.* Useful: now rare. [< L *utilis* < *uti* use]

u·til·i·tar·i·an (yōō·til′ə·târ′ē·ən) *adj.* **1** Relating to utility; especially, placing utility above beauty or the amenities of life. **2** Pertaining to or advocating utilitarianism. —*n.* **1** An advocate of utilitarianism. **2** One devoted to mere material utility.

u·til·i·tar·i·an·ism (yōō·til′ə·târ′ē·ən·iz′əm) *n.* **1** *Philos.* A system that holds usefulness to be the end and criterion of action; specifically, the ethical doctrine that actions derive their moral quality from their usefulness as means to some end, especially as means productive of happiness or unhappiness. Jeremy

Bentham, James Mill, and John Stuart Mill (who coined the word *utilitarianism*), understood by it the ethical theory which makes the pleasure or happiness of the individual or of mankind the end and criterion of the morally good and right. **2** The doctrine, in civics and politics, that the greatest happiness of the greatest number should be the sole end and criterion of all public action. **3** Devotion to mere material interests and aims.

u·til·i·ty (yōō·til′ə·tē) *n. pl.* **·ties 1** Fitness for some desirable, practical purpose; serviceableness; also, that which is necessary. **2** Fitness to supply the natural needs of man. **3** In philosophy, the happiness of mankind; the greatest happiness of the greatest number; the utilitarianism expounded by J. S. Mill. **4** *Obs.* Use; profit. **5** A public service, as gas, water, or other service. **6** *pl.* Shares of utility company stocks. [< F *utilité* < L *utilitas* < *utilis* useful < *uti* use]

   Synonyms: advantage, advantageousness, avail, benefit, expediency, policy, profit, serviceableness, use, usefulness. *Utility* is somewhat more abstract and philosophical than *usefulness* or *use,* and is often employed to denote adaptation to produce a valuable result, while *usefulness* denotes the actual production of such result. We contrast beauty and *utility.* We say of an invention its *utility* is questionable, or, on the other hand, its *usefulness* has been proved by ample trial, or, I have found it of *use. Expediency* (literally, the getting the foot out) refers primarily to escape from or avoidance of some difficulty or trouble. *Policy* is often used in a kindred sense, more positive than *expediency,* but narrower than *utility,* as in the proverb "Honesty is the best *policy.*" See PROFIT, SERVICE. *Antonyms:* disadvantage, folly, futility, impolicy, inadequacy, inexpediency, inutility, unprofitableness, worthlessness.

utility man 1 A regular member of a theatrical company who must be prepared, on short notice, to go on in any of the less important parts. **2** In baseball, a member of a team who acts as a substitute.

u·til·ize (yōō′təl·īz) *v.t.* **·ized, ·iz·ing** To make useful or serviceable; turn to practical account; make use of. Also *Brit.* **u′til·ise.** —**u′til·i·za·ble** *adj.* —**u′til·i·za′tion** *n.* —**u′til·iz′er** *n.*

ut in·fra (ut in′frə) *Latin* As below.

u·ti pos·si·de·tis (yōō′tī pos′ə·dē′təs) *Latin* In international law, the principle that the parties to a war retain what they possessed at its close, unless otherwise provided by treaty; literally, as you possess.

ut·most (ut′mōst) *adj.* **1** Of the highest degree or the largest amount or number; greatest; uttermost. **2** Being at the farthest limit or most distant point; most remote; last. —*n.* The greatest possible extent; the most possible. See synonyms under END. [OE *ūtmest*]

U·to–Az·tec·an (yōō′tō·az′tek·ən) *n.* One of the chief linguistic stocks of North American Indians, formerly occupying two large regions of the NW and SW United States, comprising three branches (Shoshonean, Piman, and Nahuatlan) and embracing about fifty tribes: still surviving in the United States and Mexico. —*adj.* Of or pertaining to this linguistic stock.

u·to·pi·a (yōō·tō′pē·ə) *n.* **1** Any state, condition, or place of ideal perfection. **2** A visionary, impractical scheme for social improvement. [from *Utopia*]

U·to·pi·a (yōō·tō′pē·ə) An imaginary island described as the seat of a perfect social and political life in a romance by Sir Thomas More, published in 1516. [< NL < Gk. *ou* not + *topos* place]

u·to·pi·an (yōō·tō′pē·ən) *adj.* Excellent, but existing only in fancy or theory; ideal. See synonyms under IMAGINARY. —*n.* One who advocates impractical reforms; a visionary.

U·to·pi·an (yōō·tō′pē·ən) *adj.* Pertaining to or like Utopia. —*n.* A dweller in Utopia.

u·to·pi·an·ism (yōō·tō′pē·ən·iz′əm) *n.* Highly idealistic and impractical views, especially about social problems.

U·trecht (yōō'trekt, *Du.* ü'trekht) **1** A province of central Netherlands; 511 square miles. **2** Its capital, scene of the signing of a treaty (1713) ending the War of the Spanish Succession.

u·tri·cle (yōō'tri·kəl) *n.* **1** *Anat.* A small saclike cavity, especially the larger of two found in the bony vestibule of the inner ear. **2** *Bot.* **a** A small fruit having an inflated pericarp, as in the pigweed. **b** An air cell, as in certain aquatic plants. [<L *utriculus*, dim. of *uter* skin bag]

u·tric·u·lar (yōō·trik'yə·lər) *adj.* **1** Resembling a utricle or small sac. **2** Bladderlike; bearing or provided with utricles. Also **u·tric'u·late** (-lit, -lāt).

u·tric·u·li·tis (yōō·trik'yə·lī'tis) *n. Pathol.* Inflammation of a utricle, as of the inner ear. [<NL]

u·tric·u·lus (yōō·trik'yə·ləs) *n.* *pl.* **·li** (-lī) Utricle. [<L]

U·tril·lo (ōō·trē'lyō, ōō·tril'ō; *Fr.* ü·trē·lō'), **Maurice,** 1883–1955, French painter.

ut su·pra (ut sōō'prə) *Latin* As above: abbreviated *ut sup.*

Ut·tar Pra·desh (ŏŏt'ər prə·dāsh') A constituent State of northern India, formed in 1950; 113,409 square miles; capital, Lucknow: formerly *United Provinces of Agra and Oudh.*

ut·ter[1] (ut'ər) *v.t.* **1** To give out or send forth with audible sound; express; say. **2** *Law* To put in circulation; now, especially, to deliver or offer (something forged or counterfeit) to another. **3** *Obs.* To give vent to in any way; give forth; emit. **4** *Obs.* To issue or deliver, as merchandise, in the course of trade. See synonyms under SPEAK. [ME *outre*, freq. of *obs. out* say, speak out] — **ut'ter·a·ble** *adj.* — **ut'ter·er** *n.*

ut·ter[2] (ut'ər) *adj.* **1** Realized or developed to the last degree; absolute; total: *utter misery.* **2** Being or done without conditions or qualifications; unqualified; final; per-

emptory; absolute: *utter* denial. **3** *Obs.* Outer; remote. [OE *ūttra,* orig. compar. of *ūt* out]

ut·ter·ance[1] (ut'ər·əns) *n.* **1** The act of uttering; vocal expression; manner of speaking; also, the power of speech. **2** A thing uttered or expressed. See synonyms under REMARK.

ut·ter·ance[2] (ut'ər·əns) *n. Obs.* The bitter end; the uttermost; the last extremity; death: in the phrase **to the utterance.** [Var. of OUTRANCE]

ut·ter·ly (ut'ər·lē) *adv.* In a complete manner; entirely; thoroughly.

ut·ter·most (ut'ər·mōst') *adj. & n.* Utmost.

U-tube (yōō'tōōb', -tyōōb') *n.* A tube bent into U form, especially such a tube made of glass for laboratory use.

U-turn (yōō'tûrn') *n. Colloq.* A continuous turn which reverses the direction of a vehicle on a road.

u·va (yōō'və) *n. Bot.* A succulent fruit having a central placenta, as a grape. [<L, grape]

u·var·ov·ite (ōō·vär'ôf·īt) *n.* An emerald-green calcium–chromium garnet. [after Count S. *Uvarov,* 1785–1855, Russian nobleman]

u·va–ur·si (yōō'və·ûr'sī) *n.* A trailing plant, the bearberry (def. 1). [<L, bear's grape]

u·ve·a (yōō'vē·ə) *n. Anat.* **1** The inner, colored layer of the iris. **2** The iris, ciliary muscle, and choroid coat. [<Med. L <L *uva* grape] — **u've·al** *adj.*

U·vé·a (ōō·vā'ä) The largest island of the Wallis archipelago, capital of the protectorate; 7 miles long, 4 miles wide.

u·ve·i·tis (yōō'vē·ī'tis) *n. Pathol.* Inflammation of the uvea or iris. [<NL <UVEA] — **u'·ve·it'ic** (-it'ik) *adj.*

u·ve·ous (yōō'vē·əs) *adj.* **1** Resembling a grape or a cluster of grapes. **2** Uveal. [<L *uva* grape]

u·vu·la (yōō'vyə·lə) *n.* *pl.* **·las** or **·lae** (-lē) *Anat.* **1** The pendent fleshy portion of the soft palate. **2** Either of two other similar

processes, one at the neck of the bladder and the other on the under side of the cerebellum. [<LL, dim. of *uva* grape]

u·vu·lar (yōō'vyə·lər) *adj.* **1** Pertaining to or of the uvula. **2** *Phonet.* Produced by vibration of, or with the back of the tongue near or against, the uvula. — *n. Phonet.* A uvular sound.

u·vu·li·tis (yōō'vyə·lī'tis) *n. Pathol.* Inflammation of the uvula. [<NL]

Ux·bridge (uks'brij) An urban district of Middlesex, England, NW of London.

Ux·mal (ōōz·mäl', ōōsh-, ōōs-) An ancient Mayan city of Yucatán, SE Mexico; site, 40 miles south of Mérida.

ux·or (uk'sôr) *n. Latin* Wife: abbreviated *ux.*

ux·o·ri·al (uk·sôr'ē·əl, -sō'rē-, ug·zôr'ē·əl, -zō'rē-) *adj.* **1** Of, pertaining to, characteristic of, or becoming to a wife. **2** Uxorious. [<L *uxorius* <*uxor* wife]

ux·o·ri·cide (uk·sôr'ə·sīd, -sō'rə-, ug·zôr'ə-, -zō'rə-) *n.* **1** The act of murdering or killing one's wife; wife-murder. **2** One who murders his wife. [<L *uxor* wife + -CIDE] — **ux·or'i·ci'dal** (-sīd'l) *adj.*

ux·o·ri·ous (uk·sôr'ē·əs, -sō'rē-, ug·zôr'ē-, -zō'rē-) *adj..* Fatuously or foolishly devoted to one's wife; showing extreme or foolish fondness for one's wife. [<L *uxorius* <*uxor* wife] — **ux·o'ri·ous·ly** *adv.* — **ux·o'ri·ous·ness** *n.*

Uz·bek 1 A member of a Turkic people dominant in Uzbekistral Mountainsan; a native or inhabitant of Uzbekistan. **2** The Turkic language of Uzbeks; the national language of Uzbekjstan.

Uz·bek·i·stan A republic in Asia. 172,000 square miles, pop. 21,000,000; capital Tashkent.

Uz·bek Soviet Socialist Republic A former republic of the U.S.S.R. in Central Asia.

U·zhok A pass of the Carpathian Mountains in SW Ukraine. *Polish* U·zok. *Hungarian* U·zsok.

V

v, V (vē) *n.* *pl.* **v's** or **V's**, **vs** or **Vs**, **vees** (vēz) **1** The twenty-second letter of the English alphabet; ultimately from Phoenician *vau,* vocalized by the Greeks into *upsilon,* and used by the Romans in the form V with the value of a semivowel (w) and, later, a consonant (v). In English it was used interchangeably with the character *u* until fairly modern times. Compare U, W. **2** The sound of the letter *v,* the voiced, labiodental fricative. See ALPHABET. *n.* **1** A V-shaped piece, or two pieces at an acute angle, as part of a construction: also **vee. 2** *Colloq.* A five-dollar bill. — *symbol* **1** The Roman numeral five. See under NUMERAL. **2** *Chem.* Vanadium (symbol V). **3** *Electr.* Volt. **4** Anything shaped like a V.

V–1 (vē'wun') *n.* The robot bomb used against England by the Germans in World War II. See ROBOT BOMB under BOMB. [<G *vergeltungswaffe eins* retaliation weapon 1]

V–2 (vē'tōō') *n.* A rocket bomb carrying a bomb load of one ton or more, and able to travel about 200 miles from its launching site: used against England by the Germans in World War II. [<G *vergeltungswaffe zwei* retaliation weapon 2]

Vaal (väl) A river of the Republic of South Africa, forming part of the boundary between the Orange Free State and the Transvaal and flowing 750 miles SW and west, from near the Swaziland border in SE Transvaal, to the Orange River near Kimberley.

Vaa·sa (vä'sä) A port of western Finland on the Gulf of Bothnia. *Swedish* Va'sa.

vacan·cy (vā'kən·sē) *n.* *pl.* **·cies 1** The state of being vacant; vacuity; emptiness; specifically, emptiness of mind. **2** That which is vacant, empty, or unoccupied; empty space. **3** An interruption of continuity of thought or space; a gap; chasm. **4** An unoccupied post, place, or office; a place destitute of an

incumbent. **5** *Rare* Unoccupied time; leisure.

va·cant (vā'kənt) *adj.* **1** Containing or holding nothing; being without contents or occupants; especially, devoid of occupants; empty. **2** Occupied with nothing; unemployed; unencumbered; free. **3** Being or appearing without intelligence; inane. **4** Having no incumbent; unfilled: a *vacant* office. **5** *Law* Unoccupied or unused, as land; also, abandoned; having neither claimant nor heir, as an estate. **6** Free from cares. **7** Devoid of thought; unreflecting. [<F <L *vacans, -antis,* ppr. of *vacare* be empty] — **va'cant·ly** *adv.*

Synonyms: blank, empty, unemployed, unfilled, unoccupied, vacuous, void, waste. That is *empty* which contains nothing; that is *vacant* which is without that which has filled or might be expected to fill it; *vacant* has extensive reference to rights or possibilities of occupancy. A *vacant* room may not be *empty,* and an *empty* house may not be *vacant. Void* and *devoid* are rarely used in the literal sense, but are for the most part confined to abstract relations, *devoid* being followed by *of,* and having with that addition the effect of a prepositional phrase: The article is *devoid* of sense; The contract is *void* for want of consideration. *Waste,* in this connection, applies to that which is made so by devastation or ruin, or gives an impression of desolation, especially as combined with vastness, probably from association of the words *waste* and *vast; waste* is applied also to uncultivated or unproductive land, if of considerable extent; we speak of a *waste* tract or region. *Vacuous* refers to the condition of being *empty* or *vacant,* regarded as continuous or characteristic. See BLANK, IDLE. *Antonyms:* brimful, brimmed, brimming, busy, crammed, crowded, full, gorged, inhabited, jammed, occupied, overflowing, packed, replete.

va·can·ti·a bo·na (vā·kan'shē·ə bō'nə) *Latin*

Goods without an owner; escheated goods.

va·cate (vā'kāt) *v.* **·cat·ed, ·cat·ing** *v.t.* **1** To make vacant; surrender possession of by removal. **2** To set aside; annul. **3** To give up (a position or office); quit. — *v.i.* **4** To leave an office, position, place, etc. **5** *Colloq.* To go away; leave. See synonyms under CANCEL. [<L *vacatus,* pp. of *vacare* be empty]

va·ca·tion (vā·kā'shən) *n.* **1** An intermission of activity, employment, or stated exercises, as for recreation or rest; a holiday. **2** *Law* The period of time intervening between stated terms of court. **3** The intermission of the course of studies and exercises in an educational institution. **4** The act of vacating. **5** *Obs.* The time during which an office is vacant. — *v.i.* To take a vacation. [<F <L *vacatio, -onis* freedom from duty <*vacatus.* See VACATE.] — **va·ca'tion·er** *n.*

va·ca·tion·ist (vā·kā'shən·ist) *n.* One who is taking a vacation or staying at a resort; a tourist.

vac·ci·nal (vak'sə·nəl) *adj.* Of the nature of or relating to vaccine or vaccination.

vac·ci·nate (vak'sə·nāt) *v.* **·nat·ed, ·nat·ing** *Med. v.t.* To inoculate with a vaccine as a preventive or therapeutic measure; especially, to inoculate against smallpox. — *v.i.* To perform the act of vaccination. [<VACCIN(E) + -ATE[2]]

vac·ci·na·tion (vak'sə·nā'shən) *n. Med.* The act or process of vaccinating, especially against smallpox.

vac·ci·na·tion·ist (vak'sə·nā'shən·ist) *n. Med.* An advocate of vaccination.

vac·ci·na·tor (vak'sə·nā'tər) *n. Med.* **1** One who vaccinates. **2** An instrument used for vaccination.

vac·cine (vak'sēn, -sin) *n.* **1** The virus of cowpox, as prepared for or introduced by vaccination: usually lymph, dried or fluid, or part of the crust from a pustule. **2** Any inoculable immunizing agent; a preparation containing bacteria so treated as to give immunity from specific diseases when injected into the subject. — *adj.* **1** Pertaining to or derived from cows. **2** Pertaining to cowpox or vaccination. [<L *vaccinus* pertaining to a cow <*vacca* cow]

vaccine point *Med.* A sharp-pointed piece of bone, ivory, or the like, coated with vaccine for inoculation purposes.

vac·cin·i·a (vak·sin′ē·ə) *n. Pathol.* Cowpox. Also **vac·ci·na** (vak·sī′nə). [<NL <L *vacci̇·us*. See VACCINE.]

vac·cin·i·a·ceous (vak·sin′ē·ā′shəs) *adj. Bot.* Pertaining or belonging to a genus (*Vaccinium*; family *Ericaceae* or *Vacciniaceae*) of shrubs with cylindrical or globular flowers and small blue, black, or red berries, including the blueberry, huckleberry, and cranberry. [<NL <L *vaccinium* blueberry]

vac·ci·ni·za·tion (vak′sə·nə·zā′shən, -nī·zā′-) *n. Med.* Repeated inoculation with a vaccine.

vac·cin·o·ther·a·py (vak′sən·ō·ther′ə·pē) *n. Med.* Treatment by bacterial vaccines.

vac·il·late (vas′ə·lāt) *v.i.* **·lat·ed**, **·lat·ing** **1** To sway one way and the other; totter; waver. **2** To fluctuate. **3** To waver in mind; be irresolute. See synonyms under FLUCTUATE. [<L *vacillatus*, pp. of *vacillare* waver] — **vac′il·la′tion** *n.*

vac·il·lat·ing (vas′ə·lā′ting) *adj.* Inclined to waver; uncertain; wavering. Also **vac′il·lant**, **vac′il·la·to·ry** (-lə·tôr′ē, -tō′rē). — **vac′il·lat′ing·ly** *adv.*

vac·u·a (vak′yōō·ə) Plural of VACUUM.

va·cu·i·ty (va·kyōō′ə·tē) *n. pl.* **·ties** **1** The state of being a vacuum; emptiness. **2** Vacant space; a void. **3** Freedom from mental exertion; idleness. **4** Lack of intelligence; stupidity. **5** Nothingness. **6** An inane or idle thing or statement: His speech was weakened by *vacuities.* [<F *vacuité* <L *vacuitas, -tatis* <*vacuus* empty]

vac·u·o·lat·ed (vak′yōō·ə·lā′tid) *adj. Biol.* Having one or more vacuoles. — **vac′u·o·la′tion** *n.*

vac·u·ole (vak′yōō·ōl) *n. Biol.* A minute cavity containing air, a watery fluid, or a chemical secretion of the protoplasm, found in an organ, tissue, or cell. [<F <L *vacuum,* neut. of *vacuus* empty]

vac·u·ous (vak′yōō·əs) *adj.* **1** Having no contents; containing no matter; empty. **2** Lacking intelligence; blank. **3** Idle; unoccupied. See synonyms under VACANT. [<L *vacuus*] — **vac′u·ous·ly** *adv.* — **vac′u·ous·ness** *n.*

vac·u·um (vak′yōō·əm, -yōōm) *n. pl.* **·u·ums** or **·u·a** (-yōō·ə) **1** *Physics* **a** A space absolutely devoid of matter. **b** A space from which air or other gas has been exhausted to a very high degree. **2** A partial diminution of the normal atmospheric pressure. **3** A void; an empty feeling. — *adj.* **1** Of, or used in the production of, a vacuum. **2** Exhausted or partly exhausted of gas, air, or vapor. **3** Operated by suction to produce a vacuum. — *v.t. & v.i. Colloq.* To clean with a vacuum cleaner. [<L, neut. of *vacuus* empty]

vacuum bottle A bottle having a double wall separated by a vacuum which permits the contents to be kept cold or hot for an appreciable period. Also **vacuum flask.**

vacuum cleaner A machine for cleaning floors, carpets, furnishings, etc., by the suction of an air current.

vacuum fan A fan producing suction or an incomplete vacuum.

vacuum gage A gage containing mercury for testing the pressure consequent on producing a vacuum, as in a condenser. Also **vacuum gauge.**

vacuum pump A pulsometer.

vacuum tube *Electronics* **1** A sealed glass tube exhausted of air to a high degree and containing electrodes between which electric discharges may be passed. **2** An electron tube.

vacuum valve *Brit.* A vacuum tube.

va·de in pa·ce (vā′dē in pä′sē) *Latin* Go in peace.

va·de me·cum (vā′dē mē′kəm) *Latin* Go with me; hence, anything carried for constant use, as a guidebook, manual, or bag. Also **va′de·me′cum**, **va′de-me′cum.**

Va·duz (fä·dōōts′) The capital of the princi-

---

pality of Liechtenstein, near the Rhine, SE of St. Gall, Switzerland.

vae vic·tis (vē vik′təs) *Latin* Woe to the vanquished.

vag·a·bond (vag′ə·bond) *n.* **1** One who wanders from place to place without visible means of support; a tramp. **2** One without a settled home; a wanderer; nomad. **3** A worthless fellow; rascal. — *adj.* **1** Pertaining to a vagabond; nomadic. **2** Having no definite residence; wandering; irresponsible. **3** Driven to and fro; aimless. [<F <L *vagabundus* <*vagus* wandering] — **vag′a·bond′age** *n.* — **vag′a·bond′ish** *adj.* — **vag′a·bond′ism** *n.*

vagabond neurosis Dromomania.

va·gar·y (və·gâr′ē) *n. pl.* **·gar·ies** A wild fancy; extravagant notion. See synonyms under FANCY, WHIM. [<obs. *vagary, v.,* wander <L *vagari*]

va·gi·na (və·jī′nə) *n. pl.* **·nas** or **·nae** (-nē) **1** *Anat.* **a** A sheath or sheathlike covering. **b** The canal leading from the external genital orifice in female mammals to the uterus. **2** *Zool.* The terminal portion of the oviduct of various invertebrates. **3** *Bot.* A tubular part surrounding another, as the basal portion of a leaf around a stem. [<L, a sheath]

vag·i·nal (vaj′ə·nəl, və·jī′-) *adj.* **1** Pertaining to or like a sheath; thecal. **2** Pertaining to the vagina.

vag·i·nate (vaj′ə·nit, -nāt) *adj.* **1** Having a sheath. **2** Formed into a sheath; tubular. Also **vag′i·nat′ed.** [<NL *vaginatus* <L *vagina* sheath]

vag·i·nec·to·my (vaj′ə·nek′tə·mē) *n. Surg.* **1** Removal or obliteration of the vaginal canal. **2** Resection of the serous membrane of the testis: also **vag′i·na·lec′to·my** (-nə·lek′tə·mē). [<VAGIN(O)- + -ECTOMY]

vag·i·nis·mus (vaj′ə·niz′məs, -nis′-) *n. Pathol.* Spasm of the sphincter muscle of the vagina with extreme sensitivity of the adjacent parts. [<NL]

vag·i·ni·tis (vaj′ə·nī′tis) *n. Pathol.* Inflammation of the vagina. [<NL]

vagino– *combining form Med.* The vagina; of or pertaining to the vagina. Also, before vowels, **vagin–**, as in *vaginectomy.* [<L *vagina* a sheath, the vagina]

va·gi·tus (və·jī′təs) *n.* The first cry of the newborn infant. [<L, pp. of *vagire* cry, squall]

va·go·to·ni·a (vā′gə·tō′nē·ə) *n. Pathol.* Excessive or morbid excitability of the vagus nerve, characterized by vasomotor instability, involuntary spasms, sweating, and constipation. [<NL <*vagus* the vagus nerve + Gk. *tonos* tone, tension] — **va′go·ton′ic** (-ton′ik) *adj.*

va·gran·cy (vā′grən·sē) *n. pl.* **·cies** The state, condition, or action of a vagrant. Also **va′grant·ness.**

va·grant (vā′grənt) *n.* **1** A person without a settled home; an idle wanderer; vagabond; tramp. **2** A roving person; wanderer. — *adj.* **1** Wandering about as a vagrant. **2** Pertaining to one who or that which wanders; nomadic. **3** Having a wandering course; capricious; wayward. [ME *vagraunt,* alter. of AF *wakerant* <OF *wacrant,* ppr. of *wacrer* walk, wander <Gmc.; infl. in form by L *vagari* wander] — **va′grant·ly** *adv.*

va·grom (vā′grəm) *adj. Obs.* Vagrant. [Alter. of VAGRANT; used by Dogberry in Shakespeare's *Much Ado About Nothing*]

vague (vāg) *adj.* **1** Lacking definiteness or precision. **2** Of uncertain source or authority: a *vague* rumor. **3** Not clearly recognized, understood, stated, or felt. **4** *Obs.* Roving; vagrant. **5** Shadowy; hazy. [<F <L *vagus* wandering] — **vague′ly** *adv.* — **vague′ness** *n.*

Synonyms: ambiguous, doubtful, dreamy, indefinite, indeterminate, indistinct, lax, loose, obscure, uncertain, undetermined, unsettled.

va·gus (vā′gəs) *n. pl.* **·gi** (-jī) *Anat.* Either of the tenth pair of cranial nerves originating in the medulla oblongata and sending branches to the lungs, heart, stomach, and most of the abdominal viscera; the pneumogastric nerve. Also **vagus nerve.** [<L, wandering]

Váh (väkh) A river in western Slovakia, Czechoslovakia, flowing 245 miles SW to the Danube: German *Waag.*

vail[1] (vāl) *n. & v.t. Obs.* Veil.

---

vail[2] (vāl) *Obs. v.i.* To be of use; avail. — *n.* **1** *Usually pl.* A gratuity or tip; a perquisite, often corrupt. **2** A windfall; find. **3** Advantage; proceeds; profit. ♦ Homophones: *vale, veil.* [Aphetic var. of AVAIL] — **vail′a·ble** *adj.*

vail[3] (vāl) *v.t. Archaic* **1** To let fall; lower, as the topsail, in salute or submission. **2** To take off (the hat, etc.) in respect or submission. ♦ Homophones: *vale, veil.* [Aphetic form of obs. *avale* <F *avaler* lower <*à val* down <L *ad vallem*, lit., to the valley]

vain (vān) *adj.* **1** Elated with self-admiration; greedy of applause. **2** Characterized by frivolity. **3** Ostentatious; showy: said of things. **4** Unproductive; worthless; fruitless; useless. **5** Without any substantial foundation; empty; unreal. — **in vain** **1** To no purpose; without effect. **2** In an irreverent or disrespectful manner: to take the Lord's name *in vain.* ♦ Homophones: *vane, vein.* [<F <L *vanus* empty] — **vain′ly** *adv.* — **vain′ness** *n.*

Synonyms: abortive, baseless, delusive, empty, fruitless, futile, idle, ineffectual, profitless, shadowy, trifling, trivial, unavailing, useless, vapid, worthless. *Vain* keeps the etymological idea through all changes of meaning; a *vain* endeavor is *empty* of result, or of adequate power to produce a result, a *vain* pretension is *empty* or destitute of support, a *vain* person has a conceit that is *empty* or destitute of adequate cause or reason. See USELESS. *Antonyms:* effective, efficient, firm, potent, powerful, real, solid, sound, substantial, valid, valuable, worthy.

vain·glo·ry (vān·glôr′ē, -glō′rē) *n.* Excessive or groundless vanity; also, vain pomp; boastfulness. See synonyms under PRIDE. [<OF *vaine gloire* <Med. L *vana gloria* empty pomp, show] — **vain·glo′ri·ous** *adj.* — **vain·glo′ri·ous·ly** *adv.* — **vain·glo′ri·ous·ness** *n.*

vair (vâr) *n.* **1** *Her.* One of the furs represented by rows of small shield-shaped figures. **2** *Obs.* A fur used for the garments of the nobility (14th century). [<F <LL *varius* ermine <L *varius* parti-colored, various]

Va·lais (và·le′) A canton in southern Switzerland, in the upper Rhône valley; 2,021 square miles; capital, Sion: German *Wallis.*

val·ance (val′əns, vā′ləns) *n.* **1** A drapery hanging from the tester of a bedstead. **2** A short, full drapery across the top of a window. **3** A damask used for upholstering. — *v.t.* **·anced**, **·anc·ing** To furnish with or as with drapery, or a valance. [Prob. <OF *avalant,* ppr. of *avaler* descend] — **val′anced** *adj.*

Val·dai Hills (väl·dī′) A low plateau and group of hills in western European Russian S.F.S.R.; maximum height, 1,053 feet.

Val·de·mar (väl′də·mär) See WALDEMAR.

Val d'Aos·ta (väl dä·ôs′tä) An autonomous region of NW Italy bordering on France and Switzerland; 1,260 square miles; capital, Aosta.

Val·di·via (val·div′ē·ə, *Sp.* bäl·dē′vyä), **Pedro de**, 1500?-54, Spanish conqueror of Chile.

vale[1] (vāl) *n.* **1** A valley; a low-lying tract of land: now chiefly poetic. **2** A trough or channel. See synonyms under VALLEY. ♦ Homophones: *vail, veil.* [<OF *val* <L *vallis*]

va·le[2] (vā′lē) *interj. Latin* Farewell; literally, be in good health.

val·e·dic·tion (val′ə·dik′shən) *n.* A bidding farewell. See synonyms under FAREWELL. [<L *valedictus,* pp. of *valedicere* say farewell <*vale* farewell, orig. imperative of *valere* be well + *dicere* say]

val·e·dic·to·ri·an (val′ə·dik·tôr′ē·ən, -tō′rē-) *n.* One who delivers a valedictory; specifically, a student who delivers a valedictory at the graduating exercises of an educational institution: usually the member of the graduating class whose rank in scholarship is highest.

val·e·dic·to·ry (val′ə·dik′tər·ē) *adj.* Pertaining to a leave-taking. — *n. pl.* **·ries** A parting address, as by a member (ordinarily the first in rank) of a graduating class. See synonyms under FAREWELL.

va·lence (vā′ləns) *n. Chem.* **1** The property possessed by an element or radical of combining with or replacing other elements or radicals in definite and constant proportion. **2** The number of atoms of hydrogen (or its equivalent), taken as unity, with which an atom or radical can combine, or which it can

---

add,āce,câre,pälm; end,ēven; it,īce; odd,ōpen,ôrder; tŏŏk,pōōl; up,bûrn; ə = a in *above,* e in *sicken,* i in *clarity,* o in *melon,* u in *focus;* yōō = u in *fuse;* oi,oil; ou,pout; ch,check; g,go; ng,ring; th,thin; ŧh,this; zh,vision. Foreign sounds á,œ,ü,kh,ń; and ♦: see page xx. <from; + plus; ? possibly.

replace. It varies with different elements, and with certain elements in different compounds. **3** *Med.* The combining power of certain substances or bodies, as serums, chromosomes, and the like. Also **va′len·cy.** [<LL *valentia* strength, orig. neut. pl. of L *valens, -entis,* ppr. of *valere* be well, be strong]

valence electron *Chem.* One of the electrons in the outermost shell of an atom, regarded as being responsible for the chemical reaction of an element.

va·len·ci·a (və·len′shē·ə, -shə) *n.* A woven fabric with wool weft and silk or cotton warp. [from VALENCIA]

Va·len·ci·a (və·len′shē·ə, -shə; *Sp.* bä·len′thyä) **1** A region and former Moorish kingdom of eastern Spain on the Mediterranean; 8,996 square miles. **2** A province of eastern Spain, center of the Valencia region; 4,155 square miles. **3** A port of eastern Spain, the chief city of Valencia region and capital of Valencia province. **4** A city of north central Venezuela.

Va·len·ci·ennes (və·len′sē·enz′, *Fr.* vå·län·syen′) *n.* A kind of bobbin lace with a floral pattern, originally made at Valenciennes. Also **Valenciennes lace, Val lace.**

Va·len·ciennes (vå·län·syen′) A city of northern France on the Escaut in Nord department.

Va·lens (vā′lenz) 328?–378, Roman emperor of the East 364–378.

val·en·tine (val′ən·tīn) *n.* **1** A letter or token of affection sent, often anonymously, to a person of the opposite sex on St. Valentine's Day (Feb. 14), the anniversary of the beheading of this martyr by the Romans. **2** A sweetheart. [<OF]

Val·en·tine (val′ən·tīn) A masculine personal name. Also **Va·len·tin** (*Russian* vä·lyen·tyin′; *Ger.* vä′len·tēn; *Sw.* vä′len·tēn′; *Fr.* vå·län·tan′), *Sp.* **Va·len·tín** (bä′len·tēn′), *Pg.* **Va·len·tim** (vä′len·tēn′), *Ital.* **Va·len·ti·no** (vä·len·tē′nō), *Lat.* **Va·len·ti·nus** (val′ən·tī′nəs), *Du.* **Va·len·tijn** (vä′len·tīn). [<L, well, healthy]
—**Valentine, Saint,** Christian martyr of the third century A.D.

Val·en·tin·i·an (val′ən·tin′ē·ən) Name of three Roman emperors.
—**Valentinian I,** 321–375, reigned 364–375.
—**Valentinian II,** 372?–392, reigned 375–392.
— **Valentinian III,** 419–455, reigned 425–455: full name *Flavius Placidus Valentinianus.*

Va·le·ra (və·ler′ə), **Éamon de** See under DE VAL-ERA.

val·er·ate (val′ə·rāt) *n. Chem.* A salt of valeric acid. Also **va·le·ri·an·ate** (və·lir′ē·ən·āt′).

Va·le·ri·a (və·lir′ē·ə, *Ital.* vä·ler′yä) A feminine personal name. Also *Fr.* **Va·lé·rie** (vå·lā·rē′), *Ger.* **Va·le·ri·e** (vä·lā′rē·ə). [<L, strong]

va·le·ri·an (və·lir′ē·ən) *n.* **1** Any of a genus (*Valeriana*) of perennial herbs having flowers in cymes and roots often strong-smelling, especially the garden heliotrope. **2** The dried root of the garden heliotrope, which has been used as a sedative and carminative. [<OF *valeriane* <Med. L *valeriana,* appar. ult. <*Valerius* a personal name]

Va·le·ri·an (və·lir′ē·ən) Anglicized name of *Publius Licinius Valerianus,* 193?–260?, Roman emperor 254?–260?.

va·le·ri·a·na·ceous (və·lir′ē·ə·nā′shəs) *adj. Bot.* Pertaining to a family (*Valerianaceae*) of herbs, including valerian. [<NL <Med. L *valeriana* VALERIAN]

va·ler·ic (və·ler′ik, -lir′-) *adj.* **1** Of, pertaining to, or derived from valerian. **2** *Chem.* Pertaining to or designating one of four isomeric acids, $C_5H_{10}O_2$, of which two are found in valerian: all are made synthetically. Also **va·le·ri·an·ic** (və·lir′ē·an′ik).

Va·lé·ry (vå·lā·rē′), **Paul Ambroise,** 1871–1945, French poet and philosopher.

val·et (val′it, val′ā; *Fr.* vå·le′) *n.* **1** A gentleman's personal servant. **2** A man servant in a hotel who performs personal services for patrons. —*v.t. & v.i.* To serve or act as a valet. [<F, a groom <OF *vaslet, varlet,* dim. of *vasal* vassal. Doublet of VARLET.]

va·let de cham·bre (vå·le′ də shäɴ′br′) *pl.* **va·lets de cham·bre** (vå·le′) *French* A valet.

Va·let·ta (və·let′ə) See VALLETTA.

val·e·tu·di·nar·i·an (val′ə·tōō′də·nâr′ē·ən, -tyōō′-) *n.* A chronic invalid; one unduly solicitous about his health. —*adj.* Seeking to recover health; infirm. Also **val′e·tu′di·nar′y.** [<L *valetudinarius* infirm <*valetudo, -inis* health, ill

health <*valere* be well] —**val′e·tu′di·nar′i·an·ism** *n.*

val·gus (val′gəs) *adj.* Knock-kneed or bow-legged. —*n. Pathol.* An abnormal eversion of the foot, as by a depression of the arch. [<L, bow-legged]

Val·hal·la (val·hal′ə) **1** In Norse mythology, the great hall into which the souls of heroes fallen bravely in battle were borne by the valkyries and received and feasted by Odin. **2** An edifice wherein the remains or memorials of deceased heroes of a nation are placed. Also **Val·hall** (val·hal′): also spelled *Walhalla.* [<NL <ON *valhöll,* genitive of *valhallar* hall of the slain <*valr* the slain + *höll* hall]

val·iant (val′yənt) *adj.* **1** Strong and intrepid; powerful and courageous. **2** Performed with valor; bravely conducted; heroic. See synonyms under BRAVE. [<OF *vailant,* ppr. of *valoir* be strong <L *valere*] —**val′iant·ly** *adv.* — **val′iant·ness, val′iance, val′ian·cy** *n.*

val·id (val′id) *adj.* **1** Based on evidence that can be supported; sound; just; sufficient and effective in law. **2** *Obs.* Strong. **3** *Stat.* Having a high degree of correlation with its criterion: distinguished from *reliable.* [<F *valide* <L *validus* powerful <*valere* be strong] —**val′id·ly** *adv.* — **val′id·ness** *n.*

Synonyms: cogent, conclusive, convincing, efficacious, efficient, good, incontestable, irrefragable, irrefutable, just, logical, solid, sound, substantial, sufficient, undeniable, weighty. See POWERFUL. Antonyms: see synonyms for VAIN.

val·i·date (val′ə·dāt) *v.t.* **·dat·ed, ·dat·ing 1** To make valid; ratify and confirm. **2** To declare legally valid; legalize. See synonyms under RAT-IFY. —**val′i·da′tion** *n.*

va·lid·i·ty (və·lid′ə·tē) *n.* **1** The state or quality of being valid; soundness, as in law or reasoning; efficacy. **2** *Archaic* Health; strength. **3** *Obs.* Worth.

val·ine (val′ēn) *n. Biochem.* An essential amino acid, $C_5H_{11}O_2N$, occurring in most proteins. [<VAL(ERIC) + -INE[2]]

va·lise (və·lēs′) *n.* A portable receptacle for clothes and toilet articles; traveling bag. [<F <Ital. *valigia;* ult. origin uncertain]

val·kyr·ie (val·kir′ē, val′kir·ē) *n.* In Norse mythology, one of the maidens who ride through the air and choose heroes from among those slain in battle, and carry them to Valhalla. Also **val′kyr, Val·kyr′ie.** [<ON *valkyrja,* lit., chooser of the slain <*valr* the slain + stem of *kjōsa* choose, select] —**val·kyr′i·an** *adj.*

Val·la·do·lid (val′ə·dō′lid, *Sp.* bä′lyä·thō′lēth) **1** A province of north central Spain; 3,221 square miles. **2** A city of central Spain, former capital of Castile and capital of Valladolid province.

val·la·tion (və·lā′shən) *n.* **1** The art of planning or erecting fortifications. **2** A rampart. [<L *vallatio, -onis* <L *vallare* protect with a wall <*vallum* a wall] —**val·la·to·ry** (val′ə·tôr′ē, -tō′rē) *adj.*

val·lec·u·la (və·lek′yə·lə) *n. pl.* **·lae** (-lē) **1** A furrow or depression. **2** *Anat.* A deep sulcus (**vallecula cerebelli**) enclosing the median lobe on the inferior surface of the cerebellum; also, a depression on the back of the tongue on either side of the epiglottis. **3** *Bot.* A groove or furrow, as those between the ridges on the fruit of plants of the parsley family. [<NL, var. of L *vallicula,* dim. of *vallis* a valley] —**val·lec′u·lar, val·lec′u·late** (-lit, -lāt) *adj.*

Val·let·ta (və·let′ə) The capital of Malta, a port on the SE coast; site of a major British naval base: also *Valetta.*

val·ley (val′ē) *n.* **1** A depression of the earth's surface, as one through which a stream flows; level or low land between mountains, hills, or high lands; also, the people who inhabit a valley. **2** *Archit.* **a** The gutter or angle formed by the meeting of the two roof slopes. **b** An interval in a vault, or the space between vault ridges as seen from above. **3** A vallecula. [<OF *valee* <*val* <L *vallis* a valley]

Synonyms: canyon, dale, dell, dingle, glen, gorge, gulch, gully, ravine, vale.

Valley Forge A village in SE Pennsylvania, scene of Washington's winter encampment, 1777–78, in the American Revolution.

Valley of Ten Thousand Smokes A region in Katmai National Monument, southern Alaska, punctuated by thousands of small volcanoes; 72 square miles.

Val·lom·bro·sa (väl′lôm·brō′zä) A resort town near Florence, Italy, in the Apennines.

Val·my (vål·mē′) A village in NE France, near Reims; scene of a French victory over the Prussians, 1792.

Va·lois (vå·lwå′) A medieval county and former duchy of northern France.

Va·lois (vå·lwå′) A French dynasty; began 1328 with Philip VI of Valois, ended with Henry III, 1589.

Va·lo·na (və·lô′nä) An ancient port on the **Bay of Valona,** an inlet of the Strait of Otranto in SW Albania (15 miles long, 3 miles wide): formerly *Avlona:* Albanian *Vlona.*

va·lo·ni·a (və·lō′nē·ə) *n.* The dried acorn cups of the Old World **valonia oak** (*Quercus macrolepis*), used as a tanning material. [<Ital. *vallonea* <Modern Gk. *balania* an evergreen oak, pl. of *balani* an acorn <Gk. *balanos*]

val·or (val′ər) *n.* Intrepid courage, especially in warfare; personal bravery. Also *Brit.* **val′our.** See synonyms under PROWESS. [<OF *valour* <LL *valor* worth <*valere* be strong]

val·or·i·za·tion (val′ər·ə·zā′shən, -ī·zā′-) *n.* The maintenance by governmental action of an artificial price for any product. [<Pg. *valorização* <*valor* value <LL. See VALOR.]

val·or·ize (val′ə·rīz) *v.t.* **·ized, ·iz·ing** To subject to valorization. Also *Brit.* **val′or·ise.**

val·or·ous (val′ər·əs) *adj.* Courageous; valiant. —**val′or·ous·ly** *adv.* —**val′or·ous·ness** *n.*

Val·pa·rai·so (val′pə·rā′zō, -sō, -rī′-) A port of central Chile; the most important port on the west coast of South America. *Spanish* **Val·pa·ra·í·so** (bäl′pä·rä·ē′sō).

val·u·a·ble (val′yōō·ə·bəl, val′yə·bəl) *adj.* **1** Having financial worth, price, or value; costly. **2** Of a nature or character capable of being valued or estimated: These goods are *valuable* by money. **3** Having moral worth, value, or importance; very serviceable; worthy; estimable: a *valuable* friend. See synonyms under EXCELLENT, GOOD, IMPORTANT. —*n. Usually pl.* An article of value, as a piece of jewelry. —**val′u·a·ble·ness** *n.* — **val′u·a·bly** *adv.*

val·u·a·tion (val′yōō·ā′shən) *n.* **1** The act of valuing. **2** Estimated worth or value; appraisement; price. **3** Personal estimation; judgment of merit or character: to set a high *valuation* on one's skill or power.

val·u·a·tor (val′yōō·ā′tər) *n.* One who makes appraisals; an appraiser.

val·ue (val′yōō) *n.* **1** The desirability or worth of a thing; intrinsic worth; utility. **2** *Often pl.* Something regarded as desirable, worthy, or right, as a belief, standard, or precept: the *values* of a democratic society. **3** The rate at which a commodity is potentially exchangeable for others; a fair return in service, goods, etc.; worth in money; market price; also the ratio of utility to price; a bargain. **4** Attributed or assumed valuation; esteem or regard. **5** Exact meaning; signification; import: the *value* of the words "will" and "shall." **6** *Music* The relative length of a tone as signified by a note. **7** *Math.* The quantity, magnitude, or number an algebraic symbol or expression is supposed to denote. **8** Rank in a system of classification. **9** In the graphic arts, the relation of the elements of a picture, as light and shade, to one another, especially with reference to their distribution and interdependence, apart from the idea of hue. **10** *Phonet.* The special quality of the sound represented by a written character: the *values* of the letter *e.* See synonyms under PRICE, PROFIT. —**book value** The value of property or stock as shown by the books of the company that owns it; the value of stock of a corporation based on the profit or loss shown by its books, and distinguished from the face, market, or artificially created value. —**face value 1** The value stated on the face of a bond, coin, note, etc. **2** Seeming or apparent value: a promise taken at its *face value.* —**par value** The nominal value, or value printed on a security or stock: not necessarily the market value of the shares. —*v.t.* **·ued, ·u·ing 1** To estimate the value or worth of; assess; appraise. **2** To regard highly; esteem; prize. **3** To place a relative estimate of value or desirability upon: to *value* honor more than life. See synonyms under APPRECIATE, CHERISH. [<OF *valu,* pp. of *valoir* be worth <L *valere*] —**val′ue·less** *adj.* —**val′u·er** *n.*

val·ue-add·ed tax (val′yōō·ad′id) A tax levied on each stage of a product's manufacture and marketing, from the raw material to the final retailer, the ultimate burden being placed on the consumer in the form of higher prices.

val·ued (val'yōōd) *adj.* **1** Regarded or estimated; hence, much or highly esteemed: a *valued* friend. **2** Having a value: a many-*valued* function.

valued policy An insurance policy in which the value of property or cargo is agreed on and inserted as the amount of damages in case of total loss.

val·val (val'vəl) *adj.* Of or pertaining to a valve. Also **val'var** (-vər).

val·vate (val'vāt) *adj.* **1** Serving as or like a valve; having a valve; valvular. **2** *Bot.* Touching by contiguous edges but not overlapping: applied to most dehiscent capsules in which the component parts separate like valves, to certain anthers, and to the petals or sepals of many flowers in estivation. [< L *valvatus* with folding doors < *valva*. See VALVE.]

valve (valv) *n.* **1** *Mech.* Any contrivance or arrangement that permits the flow of a liquid, gas, vapor, or loose material in either of two directions, and closes against its return. **2** *Obs.* One of a pair of folding doors. **3** *Anat.* A structure formed by one or more loose folds of the lining membrane of a vessel or other organ, preventing or retarding the flow of a fluid in one direction and allowing it in another. **4** *Zool.* **a** One of the parts of a shell, as of a mollusk. **b** A covering plate or one of two or more external pieces forming a sheath, as for an ovipositor. **5** *Bot.* **a** One of the parts into which a capsule splits in dehiscence. **b** One of the halves of an anther after its opening. **6** *Electr.* A device for controlling the direction of flow of a current, as an electrolytic cell, or a vacuum tube. **7** *Brit.* A radio tube. **8** A device in certain brass-wind instruments for lengthening the air column and lowering the pitch of the instrument's scale, by turning the air current from the main tube into an additional side tube. —*v.t.* **valved, valv·ing** To furnish with valves; control the flow of by a valve. [< L *valva* leaf of a door] —**valve'less** *adj.*

GATE VALVE
Cross-section.
a. Screw.
b. Gate closed.

valve-in-head engine (valv'in-hed') An internal-combustion engine having overhead valves; an overhead-valve engine. See OVERHEAD VALVE.

valve·let (valv'lit) *n.* A little valve; a valvule, as of a pericarp.

val·vu·lar (val'vyə·lər) *adj.* **1** Pertaining to or of the nature of a valve, as of the heart. **2** Having valves; acting as a valve.

val·vule (val'vyōōl) *n.* A small valve; a structure like a small valve. Also **val'vu·la** (-vyə·lə). [< F < Med. L *valvula*, dim. of L *valva* a door]

val·vu·li·tis (val'vyə·lī'tis) *n. Pathol.* Inflammation of any membrane that serves as a valve in the organs or channels of circulation. [< NL < Med. L *valvula* VALVULE + -ITIS]

vam·brace (vam'brās) *n.* Armor for the forearm from the elbow to the wrist: also, *Obs., vantbrace.* [Var. of *vantbrace* < AF *vantbras*, OF *avant-bras* < *avant* in front of + *bras* arm] — **vam'braced** *adj.*

va·moose (va·mōōs') *v.t. & v.i.* **·moosed, ·moos·ing** *U.S. Slang* To leave hastily or hurriedly; quit. Also **va·mose'** (-mōs'). [< Sp. *vamos* let us go]

vamp[1] (vamp) *n.* **1** The piece of leather forming the upper front part of a boot or shoe. **2** Something added to give an old thing a new appearance. **3** *Music* A simple improvised accompaniment. —*v.t.* **1** To provide with a vamp. **2** To repair or patch. **3** *Music* To improvise an accompaniment to. —*v.i.* **4** *Music* To improvise accompaniments. [< OF *avampie* forepart of the foot < *avant* before + *pied* foot] —**vamp'er** *n.*

vamp[2] (vamp) *Slang v.t.* To seduce or prey upon (a man) by utilizing one's feminine charms. —*v.i.* To play the vamp. —*n.* An unscrupulous

flirt or coquette. See VAMPIRE (def. 2). [Short for VAMPIRE]

vam·pire (vam'pīr) *n.*
1 A living corpse that rises from its grave at night to feed upon the living, usually by sucking the blood: a widespread folk belief originating in primitive cannibalism but developed primarily in Slavic folklore. It is not a demon or a ghost, but the physical body of one who has died; it cannot be exorcised, but must be disinterred and either burned or fastened in the grave with a stake through its heart. Belief in vampires still exists in Slavic Europe, Hungary, Greece, and Iceland. Bram Stoker's *Dracula* is a famous treatment of the subject. **2** A man or woman who preys upon persons of the opposite sex; especially, a woman who brings her lover to a state of poverty or degradation. **3** A large bat (genera *Desmodus* and *Diphylla*) of South or Central America, which drinks the blood of horses, cattle, and, sometimes, men: more fully **true vampire.** **4** An insectivorous or frugivorous bat (genera *Phyllostomus* and *Vampyrum*) formerly supposed to suck blood: a **false vampire.** [< F < G *vampir* < Slavic] —**vam·pir'ic** (-pir'ik), **vam·pir'ish** (-pīr'ish) *adj.*

ALBINO VAMPIRE
(Bats vary from 2 to 28 inches in body length)

vam·pir·ism (vam'pī·riz'əm, -pə-) *n.* **1** Belief in vampires. See VAMPIRE (def. 1). **2** The act or practice of a vampire; bloodsucking. **3** The practice of extortion or of preying upon others.

van[1] (van) *n.* **1** A large covered wagon or vehicle, for removing furniture, household goods, etc.; a caravan. **2** *Brit.* A closed railway car for luggage, etc.; also, a vehicle, open or covered, used for carrying light goods. [Short for CARAVAN]

van[2] (van) *n.* **1** An advance guard, as of an army, or foremost division of a fleet. **2** The leaders of a movement; those at the front of any line or unit. [Short for VANGUARD]

van[3] (van) *n.* A fan or winnowing machine; hence, a wing. [Dial. var. of FAN[1]]

van[4] (vän) *prep. Dutch* Of; from: used with Dutch family names, originally designating where the family came from or received its name.

Van (vän) Singular of VANIR.

Van (vän) A town on the eastern shore of **Lake Van** (1,453 square miles) in eastern Turkey in Asia.

van·a·date (van'ə·dāt) *n. Chem.* A salt or ester of vanadic acid. Also **va·na·di·ate** (və·nā'dē·āt).

va·nad·ic (və·nad'ik) *adj. Chem.* Of, pertaining to, or derived from vanadium, especially in its higher valence.

vanadic acid *Chem.* Any of several acids known only in their salts, as *meta*-vanadic acid, a yellow compound, HVO_3, used as a pigment and a substitute for gold bronze.

va·nad·i·nite (və·nad'ə·nīt) *n.* A native vanadate and chloride of lead, found in opaque prismatic crystals of red and yellow color. [< VANAD(IUM) + -IN + -ITE[1]]

va·na·di·um (və·nā'dē·əm) *n.* A soft, ductile, toxic, lustrous metallic element (symbol V, atomic number 23) difficult to separate from its compounds, used in alloys. See PERIODIC TABLE. [< NL < ON *Vanadis*, a name of the Norse goddess Freya]

vanadium steel Steel containing from .1 to .25 per cent of vanadium to increase its tensile strength.

van·a·dous (van'ə·dəs) *adj. Chem.* Of, pertaining to, or derived from vanadium, especially in its lower valence. Also **va·na·di·ous.**

Van Allen radiation A high-intensity radiation consisting of charged atomic particles circling the earth in an inner and outer belt conforming to the earth's magnetic field.

Van·brugh (van·brōō', van'brə), **Sir John,** 1664–1726, English playwright and architect.

Van Bu·ren (van byōōr'ən), **Martin,** 1782–1862, eighth president of the United States 1837–41.

Van·cou·ver (van·kōō'vər) **1** A port of SW British Columbia opposite **Vancouver Island,** the largest island off the western coast of North America, comprising part of British Columbia; 12,408 square miles. **2** A city of SW Washington on the Columbia River.

Van·cou·ver (van·kōō'vər), **George,** 1758?–1798, English navigator.

Vancouver, Mount A peak on the Yukon-Alaska border in the St. Elias Mountains; 15,700 feet.

van·dal (van'dəl) *n.* A ruthless plunderer; wilful destroyer of what is beautiful or artistic. —*adj.* Being a vandal; barbarous. [< VANDAL] — **van·dal·ic** (van·dal'ik) *adj.*

Van·dal (van'dəl) *n.* One of a Germanic people from a region between the Vistula and Oder rivers, south of the Baltic, who invaded the western Roman Empire in the fourth century. At the beginning of the fifth century, they ravaged Gaul and overran Spain and North Africa. In 455 they pillaged the city of Rome, destroying many artistic and literary treasures. Their kingdom, established in North Africa with Carthage as its capital, was overthrown in 534 by the Byzantines under Belisarius. —**Van·dal·ic** (van·dal'ik) *adj.* —**Van'dal·ism** *n.*

van·dal·ism (van'dəl·iz'əm) *n.* Hostility to or wilful destruction of artistic works, or of property in general.

Van·den·berg (van'dən·bûrg), **Arthur Hendrick,** 1884–1951, U.S. statesman. —**Hoyt,** 1899–1954, U.S. Air Force general.

Van·der·bilt (van'dər·bilt), **Cornelius,** 1794–1877, U.S. capitalist: called "Commodore Vanderbilt."

Van Die·men Gulf (van dē'mən) An arm of the Timor Sea between Northern Territory and Melville Island, Australia; 90 miles long, 50 miles wide. [after Anthony *Van Diemen,* 1593–1645, Dutch admiral]

Van Die·men's Land (van dē'mənz) The former name for TASMANIA.

Van Do·ren (van dôr'ən, dōr'ən), **Carl,** 1885–1950, U.S. writer and editor. —**Mark,** 1894–1972, U.S. poet, writer, and critic; brother of preceding.

Van Dyck (van dīk'), **Anthony,** 1599–1641, Flemish painter. Also **Van·dyke'.**

Van·dyke (van·dīk') *adj.* Of or pertaining to Anthony Van Dyck (or Vandyke), or to his style; also, of or pertaining to the dress or fashions represented in the paintings of Van Dyck. —*n.* **1** A painting by Van Dyck. **2** A Vandyke cape, collar, or beard.

Van Dyke (van dīk'), **Henry,** 1852–1933, U.S. clergyman, educator, and author.

Vandyke beard A peaked or pointed beard resembling those depicted in Van Dyck's paintings.

Vandyke brown A deep-brown pigment, a king of bog-earth or peat color used by the painter Van Dyck; any of the various brown pigments, as those resembling burnt umber.

Vandyke collar A broad, deep collar or cape of fine linen and lace resembling those represented in portraits by Van Dyck. Also **Vandyke cape.**

vane (vān) *n.* **1** A thin plate, pivoted out of center, on a vertical rod, to indicate the direction of the wind; a weathercock: also **wind vane.** **2** A slender flag or streamer used for the same purpose. **3** An arm or blade, as of a windmill, propeller, projectile, etc. **4** *Ornithol.* The web of a feather. **5** The target on a leveling rod. **6** The sight on a quadrant, compass, or similar instrument, by which the direction of the object viewed is determined. **7** One of the plates or strips of metal fixed in the tail of a bomb, guided missile, or the like, to provide stability or guidance. **8** *Obs.* A flag; pennon. ◆ Homophones: *vain, vein.* [Dial. var. of *fane* a small flag, OE *fana* a flag] —**vaned** *adj.*

WINDMILL VANES

Vane (vān), **Sir Henry,** 1613–62, English

Puritan statesman; executed on charge of treason.

Vä·ner (vā′nər), **Lake** See VENER, LAKE.

van Eyck (van īk′) See EYCK, VAN.

vang (vang) n. Naut. One of two guy ropes from the end of a gaff to the deck: used to steady the gaff. [<Du., a catch <vangen catch]

van Gogh (van gō′, gôkh′; Du. vän khokh′), **Vincent**, 1853–90, Dutch painter.

van·guard (van′gärd) n. 1 The advance guard of an army; the van. 2 Hence, one who or that which is foremost. [<OF avangarde, var. of avantgarde <avant before + garde guard]

Vanguard n. The second U.S. artificial satellite, launched from Cape Canaveral, Fla., on March 17, 1958, to a maximum altitude of 2,513 miles: diameter, 6.4 inches; weight, 3.25 pounds; equipment, two radio transmitters.

va·nil·la (və·nil′ə) n. 1 Any of a genus (Vanilla) of tall climbing orchids of tropical America. 2 The long dehiscent capsule of one species (V. planifolia) of this genus. 3 A flavoring extract made from these capsules. [<NL <Sp. vainilla, dim. of vaina sheath, pod <L vagina sheath; so called from the little pods that contain its seeds]

vanilla plant An erect perennial herb (Trilisa odoratissima) of the composite family growing in SE United States: the leaves have a vanilla odor when bruised: also called hound's-tongue.

va·nil·lic (və·nil′ik) adj. Of, pertaining to, or derived from vanilla or vanillin.

va·nil·lin (və·nil′in) n. Chem. A colorless crystalline compound, $C_8H_8O_3$, contained in vanilla, of which it is the odoriferous principle: also made synthetically. Also **va·nil′line** (-in, -ēn).

Va·nir (vä′nir) sing. **Van** (vän) In Norse mythology, an early race of fertility deities, of whom the names Njord, Frey, and Freya survive: later combined with the Aesir.

van·ish (van′ish) v.i. 1 To disappear from sight; fade away; depart. 2 To pass out of existence; be annihilated. 3 Math. To become equal to zero. — n. Phonet. The slight terminal sound of certain vowels, as the faint (ōō) heard after the (ō) in go. [Aphetic var. of OF esvanniss-, stem of esvanir <L evanescere fade away. See EVANESCE.] — **van′ish·er** n.

van·i·tas van·i·ta·tum (van′ə·tas van′ə·tā′təm) Latin Vanity of vanities.

van·i·ty (van′ə·tē) n. pl. **·ties** 1 The condition or character of being vain; a feeling of shallow pride; conceit; ambitious display; ostentation; show. 2 The quality or state of being vain or empty, or destitute of reality, etc. 3 That which is vain or unsubstantial. 4 A vanity bag or box. 5 A dressing-table. See synonyms under ARROGANCE, EGOTISM, LEVITY, PRIDE. [<OF vanité <L vanitas, -tatis <vanus empty, vain]

vanity bag or **box** A bag or box containing face powder, rouge, puff, mirror, etc. Also **vanity**.

Vanity Fair 1 In Bunyan's Pilgrim's Progress, a fair depicting the world as a scene of vanity and folly. 2 A novel by W. M. Thackeray, satirizing the weaknesses and follies of human nature. 3 The world of fashion and frivolity.

Van Loon (van lōn), **Hendrik Willem**, 1882–1944, U.S. author and lecturer born in Holland.

van·ner (van′ər) n. Brit. A truck driver; one who drives a van.

van·quish (vang′kwish, van′-) v.t. 1 To defeat in battle; overcome; conquer. 2 To suppress or overcome (a feeling or emotion): to vanquish lust. 3 To defeat, as in argument; confute. See synonyms under BEAT, CONQUER, SUBDUE. [<OF veinquiss-, stem of veinquir conquer <L vincere] — **van′quish·a·ble** adj. — **van′quish·er** n.

Van Rens·se·laer (van ren′sə·lər, -lir), **Stephen**, 1764–1839, U.S. general and politician.

Van·sit·tart (van·sit′ərt), **Robert Gilbert**, 1881–1957, first Baron Vansittart, British diplomat.

van·tage (van′tij) n. 1 Superiority over a competitor, as in means of attack; advantage. 2 In lawn tennis, the state of the game when either player has scored a point after deuce. 3 An opportunity; chance. [Aphetic var. of OF avantage ADVANTAGE] — **van′tage·less** adj.

vantage ground A position or condition which gives one an advantage.

vantage point A strategic position affording perspective; point of view.

vant·brace (vant′brās) See VAMBRACE.

van't Hoff (vänt hôf), **Jacobus Henricus**, 1852–1911, Dutch physical chemist.

van't Hoff's law Chem. A statement that the osmotic pressure of a substance in solution approximately equals the pressure it would have in a gaseous state at the same temperature and volume as the solution. [after J. H. van't Hoff]

Va·nu·a Le·vu (vä′nōō·ä lā′vōō) Second largest of the Fiji Islands; 2,137 square miles.

van·ward (van′wərd) adj. Pertaining to or situated in the van or front: vanward regiments.

Van·zet·ti (van·zet′ē), **Bartolomeo**, 1888–1927, Italian anarchist active in the United States. See SACCO, NICOLA.

vap·id (vap′id) adj. 1 Having lost sparkling quality and flavor. 2 Flat; dull; insipid. See synonyms under FLAT, VAIN. [<L vapidus insipid] — **va·pid·i·ty** (və·pid′ə·tē), **vap′id·ness** n. — **vap′id·ly** adv.

va·por (vā′pər) n. 1 Moisture in the air; especially, visible floating moisture, as light mist. 2 Any light, cloudy substance in the air, as smoke or fumes. 3 Any substance in the gaseous state, which, under ordinary conditions, is usually a liquid or solid. 4 A gas below its critical temperature. 5 That which is fleeting and unsubstantial. 6 A remedial agent applied by inhalation; also, a substance vaporized for use in industries. 7 Boastful swagger; vaporing. 8 pl. Depression of spirits; hypochondria. — v.t. 1 To vaporize. — v.i. 2 To emit vapor. 3 To evaporate. 4 To make idle boasts; brag. Also Brit. **va′pour**. [<AF vapour, OF vapeur <L vapor steam] — **va′por·a·bil·i·ty** n. — **va′por·a·ble** adj. — **va′por·er** n.

vapor density Physics 1 The density of a substance in the state of vapor, reaching its maximum before the substance passes into the liquid state. 2 The density of a gas or vapor as compared with that of hydrogen at the same temperature and pressure.

va·por·es·cence (vā′pə·res′əns) n. The process of forming mist or vapor. — **va′por·es′cent** adj.

vapori– combining form Vapor; of or related to vapor, steam, etc.: vaporimeter. Also, before vowels, **vapor–**. [<L vapor steam]

va·por·if·ic (vā′pə·rif′ik) adj. Producing vapors. [<NL vaporificus <L vapor, -oris steam + facere make]

va·por·im·e·ter (vā′pə·rim′ə·tər) n. An instrument for determining vapor pressure.

va·por·ing (vā′pər·ing) adj. Boasting; swaggering. — n. The act of boasting or talking pretentiously. — **va′por·ing·ly** adv.

va·por·ish (vā′pər·ish) adj. 1 Somewhat like vapor. 2 Somewhat hypochondriac.

va·por·i·za·tion (vā′pər·ə·zā′shən, -ī·zā′-) n. 1 The act or process of vaporizing, or the state of being vaporized. 2 Med. Treatment with vapors.

va·por·ize (vā′pə·rīz) v.t. & v.i. **·ized**, **·iz·ing** To convert or be converted into vapor. — **va′por·iz′a·ble** adj.

va·por·iz·er (vā′pə·rī′zər) n. 1 One who or that which vaporizes. 2 An atomizer.

va·por·ous (vā′pər·əs) adj. 1 Of or like vapor; foggy; misty; ethereal. 2 Full of vapors; hypochondriac; also, producing vapors; flatulent. 3 Vainly imaginative; whimsical. Also **va′por·y**. — **va·por·os·i·ty** (vā′pər·os′ə·tē) n. — **va′por·ous·ly** adv. — **va′por·ous·ness** n.

vapor pressure Physics The pressure of a confined vapor when it is in equilibrium with its liquid at any specific temperature. Also **vapor tension**.

va·que·ro (vä·kā′rō) n. pl. **·ros** (-rōz, Sp. -rōs) A herdsman; cowboy. [<Sp. <vaca cow <L vacca]

var (vär) n. Electr. The reactive volt-ampere. [<V(OLT) + A(MPERE) + R(EACTIVE)]

va·ra (vä′rä) n. A Spanish and Portuguese measure of length, varying from 2.7 to 3.6 feet. — **square vara** A varying measure of surface. [<Sp. and Pg., lit., a rod <L, a forked pole <varus bent]

Va·rang·er Fjord (vä·rang′ər) An inlet of the Barents Sea in NE Norway; 60 miles long, 3 to 35 miles wide.

Va·ran·gi·an (və·ran′jē·ən) n. A Norse rover; one of a group of predatory Scandinavian seamen who, in the ninth century, sailed down the Volga into the Caspian Sea and

established a dynasty in Caucasia. [<Med. L Varangus <Med. Gk. Barangos <Slavic, ult. <ON Væringi an ally <várar pledges]

va·ra·ni·an (və·rā′nē·ən) n. One of a family of lizards (Varanidae) with tongue sheathed at the root and forked at the tip; a monitor: also **var·a·nid** (var′ə·nid) — adj. Of or pertaining to the Varanidae. [<NL Varanus < Arabic waran a monitor lizard]

Var·dar (vär′där) A river of southern Yugoslavia and NE Greece, flowing 230 miles NE and SE to the Gulf of Salonika near Salonika: Greek Axios.

va·reuse (và·rœz′) n. French A loose, woolen jacket, similar to a peajacket.

Var·gas (vär′gəs), **Getulio**, 1883–1954, provisional president of Brazil 1930–34; president 1934–45 and 1951–54; forced out of office.

vari– combining form Various; different: variform, varicolored. Also **vario–**. [<L varius varied]

var·i·a·ble (vâr′ē·ə·bəl) adj. 1 Having the capacity of varying; alterable; mutable. 2 Having a tendency to change; not constant; fickle. 3 Having no definite value as regards quantity. 4 Biol. Prone to variation from a normal or established type: said of plants and animals. See synonyms under FICKLE, IRREGULAR, MOBILE[1]. — n. 1 That which is liable to change. 2 Math. a A quantity susceptible of fluctuating in value or magnitude under different conditions. b A symbol representing one of a group of objects. 3 Meteorol. A shifting wind or winds; also, in the plural, places where such winds are common. [<OF <L variabilis <variare VARY] — **var′i·a·bil′i·ty**, **var′i·a·ble·ness** n. — **var′i·a·bly** adv.

variable star See under STAR.

variable zone A temperate zone.

var·i·ance (vâr′ē·əns) n. 1 The act of varying, or the state of being variant; difference; discrepancy; hence, dissension; discord. 2 Law a A disagreement between the allegations in the pleadings and the proof in an essential matter. b A material disagreement between the writ beginning an action and the declaration or complaint. 3 Stat. The square of the standard deviation. 4 Chem. Degree of freedom. See synonyms under QUARREL[1].

var·i·ant (vâr′ē·ənt) adj. 1 Having or showing variation; varying; differing. 2 Tending to vary; variable; changing. 3 Restless; fickle; inconstant. 4 Differing from a standard or type; discrepant. See synonyms under HETEROGENEOUS. — n. 1 A thing that differs from another in form only; especially, a different spelling, pronunciation, or form of the same word. 2 A variate. [<OF <L varians, -antis, ppr. of variare VARY]

var·i·ate (vâr′ē·āt) v.t. & v.i. Obs. To vary. — n. 1 That which varies; a variable. 2 Stat. The magnitude or value of a variable. [<L variatus, pp. of variare VARY]

var·i·a·tion (vâr′ē·ā′shən) n. 1 The act, process, state, or result of varying; modification; diversity. 2 The extent to which a thing varies. 3 Inflection, as of declensions or conjugations; also, change in certain vowel sounds. 4 A repetition of the essential features of a musical theme or melody with fanciful embellishments. 5 Astron. a An inequality in the moon's motion. b Any change in the elements of an orbit. 6 Biol. Deviation in structure or function from the type or parent form of an organism, as by heredity or in response to conditions of environment. 7 Stat. Dispersion. See synonyms under CHANGE, DIFFERENCE. [<F] — **var′i·a′tion·al** adj.

var·i·cel·la (var′ə·sel′ə) n. Pathol. Chicken pox. [<NL, dim. of variola. See VARIOLA.]

var·i·cel·late (var′ə·sel′it, -āt) adj. Zool. Marked with small varices, as certain shells. [<NL varicella, dim. of L varix a varicose vein]

var·i·cel·loid (var′ə·sel′oid) adj. Resembling varicella: varicelloid smallpox.

varico– combining form Med. A vein; of or related to veins, especially to varicose veins: varicotomy. Also, before vowels, **varic–**. [<L varix, varicis a varicose vein]

var·i·ces (var′ə·sēz) Plural of VARIX.

var·i·co·cele (var′ə·kō·sēl′) n. Pathol. A tumor formed by varicose veins of the spermatic cord. [<NL <L varix, -icis a varicose vein + Gk. kēlē a tumor]

var·i·col·ored (vâr′i·kul′ərd) *adj.* Variegated in color; parti-colored; diversified; of various colors. Also *Brit.* **var′i·col′oured.**

var·i·cose (var′ə·kōs) *adj. Pathol.* Abnormally dilated or contorted, as veins. [<L *varicosus* < *varix, -icis* a varicose vein]

var·i·co·sis (var′ə·kō′sis) *n. Pathol.* A condition in which there are varicose veins; varicosity. [<NL]

var·i·cos·i·ty (var′ə·kos′ə·tē) *n. pl.* **·ties** *Pathol.* 1 The condition of being varicose. 2 A varix.

var·i·cot·o·my (var′ə·kot′ə·mē) *n. Surg.* Excision of a varix or of a varicose vein. [< VARICO- + -TOMY]

var·ied (vâr′ēd) *adj.* 1 Partially or repeatedly altered. 2 Consisting of diverse sorts. 3 Differing from one another. 4 Varicolored. See VARY. — **var′ied·ly** *adv.*

varied thrush A robinlike bird of the western United States (*Ixoreus naevius*) with a plump, rust-colored body, black or gray wings, and a dark band across the breast.

var·i·e·gate (vâr′ē·ə·gāt′) *v.t.* **·gat·ed, ·gat·ing** 1 To mark with different colors or tints; dapple; spot; streak. 2 To make varied; diversify. — *adj.* Variegated. [<LL *variegatus*, pp. of *variegare* variegate < *varius* various + *agere* drive, do]

var·i·e·gat·ed (vâr′ē·ə·gā′tid) *adj.* 1 Having diverse colors; varied in color, as with streaks or blotches. 2 Having or exhibiting different forms, styles, or varieties. 3 *Bot.* Designating a type of inflorescence: see illustration under INFLORESCENCE.

var·i·e·ga·tion (vâr′ē·ə·gā′shən) *n.* 1 The act of variegating, or the state of being variegated. 2 Diversity of colors.

va·ri·e·tal (və·rī′ə·təl) *adj. Biol.* Of, pertaining to, or of the nature of a distinct variety: opposed to *specific* or *generic.* — **va·ri′e·tal·ly** *adv.*

va·ri·e·ty (və·rī′ə·tē) *n. pl.* **·ties** 1 The state or character of being various or varied; diversity. 2 A collection of diverse things; an assortment of unlike objects. 3 The possession of different characteristics by one individual. 4 A limited class of things that differ in certain common peculiarities from a larger class to which they belong; sometimes, an example of such a sort or kind. 5 *Biol.* An individual, or a group of individuals of a species, that differs from the type in certain characters capable of perpetuation, and that is usually fertile with any other member of the species; a subdivision of a species; subspecies. See synonyms under CHANGE. [<MF *variété* <L *varietas* < *varius* various]

variety shop 1 A store having a great variety of merchandise for sale, as hardware, dry-goods, notions, toys, and other small wares. 2 A general store. Also **variety store.**

variety show A theatrical show consisting of a series of short acts or numbers, including songs, dances, dramatic sketches, acrobatic feats, animal acts, etc.; a vaudeville show.

var·i·form (vâr′ə·fôrm) *adj.* Of diverse form; having different shapes.

vario– Var. of VARI-.

var·i·o·coup·ler (vâr′ē·ə·kup′lər) *n. Electr.* A tuning coil in which the secondary winding is mounted to rotate within the primary winding. It resembles the variometer.

va·ri·o·la (və·rī′ə·lə) *n. Pathol.* Smallpox. [< Med. L, a pustule <L *varius* speckled] — **va·ri′o·lar, va·ri′o·lous** *adj.*

var·i·o·late (vâr′ē·ə·lāt′) *v.t.* **·lat·ed, ·lat·ing** To vaccinate with smallpox virus. — **var′i·o·la′tion, var′i·o·li·za′tion** *n.*

var·i·ole (vâr′ē·ōl) *n.* 1 A foveola. 2 A spherulite or variolite. [<F <Med. L *variola.* See VARIOLA.]

var·i·o·lite (vâr′ē·ə·līt′) *n.* A dense, finely crystalline variety of basalt, characterized by whitish spheroid granules. [<G *variolit* < Med. L *variola.* See VARIOLA.]

var·i·o·lit·ic (vâr′ē·ə·lit′ik) *adj.* 1 Of, pertaining to, or containing variolite. 2 Spotted.

var·i·o·loid (vâr′ē·ə·loid′) *Pathol. n.* A mild form of smallpox, occurring after vaccination or in persons who have had smallpox. — *adj.* 1 Resembling smallpox. 2 Pertaining to varioloid.

var·i·om·e·ter (vâr′ē·om′ə·tər) *n. Electr.* 1 An instrument used to determine the variation of magnetic force at different times or at different places, usually by means of a needle suspended within the magnetic field. 2 A variable inductance device composed of two coils connected in series, one of which revolves within the other, and capable of controlling the strength of a current. [< VARIO- + -METER]

var·i·o·rum (vâr′ē·ôr′əm, -ō′rəm) *adj.* Having notes or comments by different critics or editors. — *n.* 1 An edition containing various versions of a text, usually with notes and commentary. 2 A text or edition, especially the complete works of a classical author, containing various notes and comments: also **variorum edition.** [<L *(cum notis) variorum* (with the notes) of various persons]

var·i·ous (vâr′ē·əs) *adj.* 1 Characteristically different from one another; diverse. 2 Being more than one and easily distinguishable; several. 3 Many-sided; variform. 4 Having a changeable or inconstant nature; unfixed. 5 Having a diversity of appearance; variegated. See synonyms under HETEROGENEOUS, MANY. [<L *varius*] — **var′i·ous·ly** *adv.* — **var′i·ous·ness** *n.*

Vari–Typ·er (vâr′i·tī′pər) *n.* A compact, electrically operated, self-justifying composing machine for the rapid preparation of copy for all kinds of printing reproduction: a trade name.

var·ix (vâr′iks) *n. pl.* **var·i·ces** (vâr′ə·sēz) 1 *Pathol.* **a** Permanent dilatation of a vein or other vessel of circulation. **b** A vessel thus distorted, as a varicose vein. 2 *Zool.* A ridge marking the former position of the outer lip of certain univalve shells. [<L, a varicose vein]

var·let (vär′lit) *n.* 1 *Archaic* A low menial or subordinate; formerly, a page. 2 A knave or scoundrel. [<OF, a groom. Doublet of VALET.]

var·let·ry (vär′lit·rē) *n.* The rabble; the mob.

var·mint (vär′mənt) *n. Dial.* Any person or animal considered as troublesome; vermin. [Alter. of VERMIN] — **var′mint·ry** *n.*

Var·na (vär′nä) A major seaport on the Black Sea in eastern Bulgaria: formerly (1949–58) called *Stalin.*

var·nish (vär′nish) *n.* 1 A solution of certain gums or resins in alcohol, linseed oil, etc., used to produce a shining, transparent coat on a surface. 2 Any natural or artificial product resembling varnish. 3 Outward show, or any superficial polish, as of politeness. — *v.t.* 1 To cover with varnish. 2 To give a smooth or glossy appearance to. 3 To improve the appearance of; polish. 4 To hide by a deceptive covering or appearance; gloss over. [<OF *vernis* <Med. L *vernicium* sandarac <Med. Gk. *bernikē*, prob. from Gk. *Berenikē*, a city in Cyrenaica] — **var′nish·a·ble** *adj.* — **var′nish·er — var′nish·ing** *n.*

varnish tree 1 A tree of China and Japan (*Toxicodendron vernicifluum*) yielding a milky juice suitable for making varnish. 2 The candlenut tree.

Var·ro (Var′ō), **Marcus Terentius,** 116–27? B.C., Roman scholar and author.

var·si·ty (vär′sə·tē) *n. pl.* **·ties** *Colloq.* 1 *Brit.* University. 2 The team that represents a university, college, or school in any activity, as in football, debating, etc. [Aphetic alter. of UNIVERSITY]

Var·u·na (var′ōō·nə, vûr′-) In the earliest (Vedic) Hindu mythology, the god of the sky, creator and supreme god of the universe; later, in the Puranas, the god of the waters.

var·us (vâr′əs) *n. Pathol.* A malformation in which a bone or joint is turned away from its normal position. [<NL *varus*, growing inward, bandy-legged]

Var·us (vâr′əs), **Publius Quintilius,** died A.D. 9, Roman general, commander in Germany; defeated by Arminius.

varve (värv) *n.* One of a series of finely stratified seasonal deposits, as of clay or shale: often useful in determining the age of geological formations. [<Sw. *varv* a layer]

var·y (vâr′ē) *v.* **var·ied, var·y·ing** *v.t.* 1 To change the form, nature, substance, etc., of; modify. 2 To cause to be different from one another. 3 To impart variety to; diversify. 4 *Music* To embellish (a melody) by changes of rhythm, harmony, etc. — *v.i.* 5 To become changed in form, nature, substance, etc. 6 To be diverse or different; differ. 7 To deviate; depart: with *from.* 8 To change in succession; alternate. 9 *Math.* To be subject to continual change. 10 *Biol.* To undergo variation. See synonyms under CHANGE, FLUCTUATE. [<OF *varier* <L *variare* < *varius* various, diverse] — **var′i·er** *n.*

varying hare Any of certain hares whose coats turn white in the winter, specifically the American *Lepus americanus.*

vas (vas) *n. pl.* **va·sa** (vā′sə) *Biol.* A vessel or duct. [<L, vessel, dish]

vas– Var. of VASO-.

Va·sa·ri (vä·zä′rē), **Giorgio,** 1511–74, Italian painter, architect, and biographer of artists.

vas·cu·lar (vas′kyə·lər) *adj. Biol.* 1 Of, pertaining to, consisting of, or containing vessels or ducts, as blood vessels, etc. 2 Having vessels. 3 Richly supplied with blood vessels. Also **vas′cu·lose** (-lōs), **vas′cu·lous** (-ləs). [<L *vasculum,* dim. of *vas* vessel] — **vas′cu·lar′i·ty** (-lar′ə·tē) *n.* — **vas′cu·lar·ly** *adv.*

vascular bundle Bundle (def. 4).

vascular tissue *Bot.* Plant tissue made up of vessels or ducts through which the sap is conveyed.

vas·cu·lum (vas′kyə·ləm) *n. pl.* **·la** (-lə) 1 A small box used in plant collecting. 2 *Bot.* An ascidium. [<L, little vessel]

vas def·er·ens (vas def′ər·ənz) *Anat.* The duct by which semen is conveyed from the epididymis to the seminal vesicles. [<NL <L *vas* vessel + *deferens* leading down]

vase (vās, vāz, väz) *n.* An urnlike vessel, usually rounded and generally of greater height than width, ordinarily used as an ornament or for holding flowers. [<F <L *vas* vessel]

va·sec·to·my (və·sek′tə·mē) *n. Surg.* Removal of a portion of the vas deferens. [<VAS- + -ECTOMY]

Vas·e·line (vas′ə·lēn, -lin) *n.* Proprietary name for various semisolid hydrocarbons derived from petroleum: a brand of petrolatum.

Vash·ti (vash′tī) In the Bible, the queen of Ahasuerus, of Persia, whom he divorced because she refused to come to a royal banquet as commanded. *Esther* i 10–21.

Va·si·lev·ski (vä′sē·lyef′skē), **Alexander Mikhailovich,** born 1901, Russian marshal and chief of general staff in World War II.

vaso– *combining form* 1 *Physiol.* A vessel, especially a blood vessel: *vasomotor.* 2 *Med.* The vas deferens: *vasosection,* the severing of the vas deferens. Also, before vowels, *vas–.* [<L *vas* a vessel]

vas·o·con·stric·tor (vas′ō·kən·strik′tər) *adj. Physiol.* Causing constriction of a blood vessel when stimulated. — *n.* A nerve or drug causing such constriction.

vas·o·den·tine (vas′ō·den′tēn, -tin) *n.* Dentine in which the capillaries have remained wide enough to give passage to the blood.

vas·o·di·la·tor (vas′ō·di·lā′tər) *adj. Physiol.* Causing dilatation of a blood vessel, as certain nerves or drugs.

vas·o·mo·tor (vas′ō·mō′tər) *adj. Physiol.* Producing movement, either of contraction or dilatation, in the walls of vessels.

vas·sal (vas′əl) *n.* 1 One who held land of a superior lord by a feudal tenure; a liegeman or feudal tenant. 2 A dependent, retainer, or servant of any kind; a slave or bondman. — *adj.* Having the character of or pertaining to a vassal; tributary; hence, servile. [<OF <Med. L *vassallus* <LL *vassus* a servant <Celtic]

vas·sal·age (vas′əl·ij) *n.* 1 The condition, duties, and obligations of a vassal; also, the feudal system. 2 Servitude in general. 3 Lands held by feudal tenure; a fief. 4 Vassals collectively.

vas·sal·ize (vas′əl·īz) *v.t.* **·ized, ·iz·ing** To reduce to vassalage; use as a vassal.

vast (vast, väst) *adj.* 1 Of great extent; immense; enormous; huge; also, very spacious. 2 Very great in number, quantity, or amount. 3 Very great in degree, intensity, or importance. 4 *Obs.* Wide and waste; desolate; desert. See synonyms under IMMENSE, LARGE. — *n.* 1 A boundless space; immensity. 2 *Brit. Dial.* A great quantity. [<L, waste, empty, vast. Related to WASTE.] — **vast′ly** *adv.*

—**vast'ness, vas·ti·tude** (vas'tə·tood, -tyood, väs'-) *n.*

vas·ta·tion (vas·tā'shən) *n.* **1** Purification by the spiritual burning away of evil. **2** *Obs.* Devastation. [< L *vastatio, -onis* < *vastare* lay waste < *vastus* waste, empty]

Väs·ter·ås (ves·tər·ōs') A city of east central Sweden; an industrial center: formerly *Vesterås.*

vas·ti·ty (vas'tə·tē, väs'-) *n. pl.* **·ties** Vastness; immensity. [< F *vastité* < *vaste* large]

vast·y (vas'tē, väs'-) *adj. Poetic* Vast. [< VAST]

vat (vat) *n.* A large vessel, tub, or cistern, especially for holding liquids and dyeing materials. —*v.t.* **vat·ted, vat·ting** To put into a vat; treat in a vat. [OE *fæt*]

vat dye *Chem.* A dye produced by oxidation, and resistant to sunlight and washing.

Va·té(vä'tē) See EFATE.

vat·ic (vat'ik) *adj.* Pertaining to or proceeding from a prophet or seer; oracular; prophetic; inspired: *vatic* dicta, *vatic* lips. Also **vat'i·cal.** [< L *vates* prophet]

Vat·i·can (vat'ə·kən) *n.* **1** The papal palace in Vatican City, Rome. **2** The papal government, as distinguished from the Quirinal, or Italian civil government. —**Council of the Vatican** An ecumenical council, 1869–70, at the Vatican which declared the pope's infallibility, when speaking *ex cathedra,* to be a dogma of the church. [from L *Vaticanus* Vatican Hill in Rome]

Vatican City A sovereign papal state within the city of Rome, established June 10, 1929; 108.7 acres, including the Vatican and St. Peter's Church, along with the square in front of it; twelve buildings outside this area, both in and outside Rome, enjoy extraterritorial rights: Italian *Città del Vaticano.*

Vat·i·can·ism (vat'ə·kən·iz'əm) *n.* The ecclesiastical system and the tenet based on the supremacy and infallibility of the pope.

vat·i·cide (vat'ə·sīd) *n.* The killing of a prophet; also, a prophet-slayer. [< L *vates* prophet +-CIDE]

va·tic·i·nal (və·tis'ə·nəl) *adj.* Prophetic.

va·tic·i·nate (və·tis'ə·nāt) *v.t. & v.i.* **·nat·ed, ·nat·ing** To prophesy; foretell. [< L *vaticinatus,* pp. of *vaticinari* prophesy < *vates* prophet]—**va·tic'i·na'tion** *n.* —**va·tic'i·na'tor** *n.* —**va·tic'i·na·to·ry** (-nə·tôr'ē, -tō'rē) *adj.*

Vät·ter (vet'ər), **Lake** The second largest lake in Sweden, in the south central part; 733 square miles: formerly *Vetter. Swedish* **Vät·tern** (vet'ərn).

Va·tu·tin (vä·too'tin), **Nikolai,** 1901?–44, Russian general in World War II.

vau (väv) See VAV.

Vau·ban (vō·bän'), **Marquis de,** 1633–1707, Sébastien le Prestre, French military engineer.

vau·che·ri·a·ceous (vō·kir'ē·ā'shəs) *adj. Bot.* Belonging or pertaining to a genus (*Vaucheria*) of green algae consisting of long and usually branched filaments which grow in feltlike masses in shallow water and on muddy banks: often called *green felt.* [< NL, after Jean Pierre *Vaucher,* 1763–1841, Swiss botanist]

Vau·cluse (vō·klüz') A department in Provence, SE France; 1,381 square miles; capital, Avignon.

Vaud (vō) A canton in west central Switzerland; 1,239 square miles; capital, Lausanne: German *Waadt.*

vau·de·ville (vô'də·vil, vōd'vil) *n.* **1** A miscellaneous theatrical entertainment consisting of a slight dramatic sketch or pantomime interspersed with songs and dances; a series of short sketches, songs, dances, acrobatic feats, etc., having no dramatic connection; a variety show; also, a theater presenting such shows. **2** A street ballad; originally, a satirical or topical popular song. [< F, alter. of (*chanson de) Vau de Vire* (song of) the valley of the Vire river (in Normandy), where Basselin, the best-known composer of such songs, lived]

Vau·dois (vō·dwä') *n. pl.* **·dois** (-dwä') **1** An inhabitant, or the inhabitants collectively, of the Swiss canton of Vaud. **2** The dialect of this canton.

Vau·dois (vō·dwä') *n. pl.* The Waldenses.

Vaughan (vôn), **Henry,** 1622–95, English poet.

Vaughan Williams, Ralph, 1872–1958, English composer.

vault[1] (vôlt) *n.* **1** An arched apartment or chamber; also, any subterranean compartment; cellar. **2** An arched structure; arched ceiling or roof. **3** Any vaultlike covering; the sky. **4** An arched roof of a cavity. **5** An underground room or compartment for storing wine, valuables, etc. **6** A burial chamber. —*v.t.* **1** To form with a vaulted roof; cover with or as with a vault. **2** To construct in the form of a vault. [< OF *volte, vaute,* ult. < L *volutus,* pp. of *volvere* turn about, roll]—**vault'ed** *adj.*

TYPES OF VAULTS
a. Cloister or cove. *b.* Groin.
c. Welsh or underpitch.

vault[2] (vôlt) *v.t.* **1** To leap over, especially with the aid of a pole or with the hands resting on something. **2** To mount with a leap, as a horse. —*v.i.* **3** To leap; spring. **4** To do a curvet. See synonyms under LEAP. —*n.* **1** A leap or bound; a springing leap, as one made with the aid of a pole. **2** The curvet of a horse. [< OF *volter* leap, gambol, ? ult. < L *volutus,* pp. of *volvere* turn about, roll] —**vault'er** *n.*

vault·ing[1] (vôl'ting) *n.* **1** Vaulted work, or vaults collectively. **2** The work or art of building a vault.

vault·ing[2] (vôl'ting) *adj.* **1** That overleaps; hence, unduly confident or presumptuous: *vaulting* ambition. **2** That can be used in vaulting, as in gymnastics.

vaunt (vônt, vänt) *v.i.* To speak boastfully. —*v.t.* To boast of. See synonyms under FLAUNT. —*n.* Boastful assertion or ostentatious display. See synonyms under OSTENTATION. [< OF *vanter* < LL *vanitare* brag < L *vanus* empty, vain]— **vaunt'er** *n.* —**vaunt'ing** *n.* —**vaunt'ing·ly** *adv.*

vaunt-cour·i·er (vänt'koor'ē·ər, vônt'-) *n.* **1** Archaic A horseman or soldier sent in advance of an army. **2** A forerunner; precursor; herald. [< F *avant-coureur*]

vaunt·ie (vôn'tē) *adj. Scot.* Boastful. Also **vaunt'y, vawnt'ie.**

Vaux (vō) A village west of Château-Thierry in north central France; point of furthest German advance on the road to Paris in World War I, 1918.

vav (väv) *n.* The sixth Hebrew letter: also spelled *vau.* Also **vaw.** See ALPHABET.

vav·a·sor (vav'ə·sôr, -sôr) *n.* **1** The rank of a principal vassal next below a baron. **2** A vassal holding lands from a great vassal, and having other vassals under him. Also **vav'a·sour** (-soor). [< OF *vavassour* < LL *vassus vassorum* vassal of vassals]

va·ward (vä'wərd) *adj. Obs.* Vanward. [Alter. of obs. *avantward* < AF *avantwarde,* OF *avant-garde* vanguard]

VCR A videocassette recorder.

V-day (vē'dā') *n.* A day of victory; in World War II, **V-E Day** (vē'ē'dā') (officially May 8, 1945), the date of victory of the United Nations in Europe, and **V-J Day** (vē'jā'dā') (officially Sept. 2, 1945, Tokyo time), the date of their victory in the Pacific.

Ve·a·dar (vē'ä·där, vä'-) A Hebrew month. See CALENDAR(Hebrew).

veal (vēl) *n.* **1** The flesh of a calf considered as food. **2** *Obs.* A calf. —**bob veal** The flesh of a calf so young as to be unfit for food. [< OF *viel* calf < L *vitellus,* dim. of *vitulus* calf]

Veb·len (veb'lən), **Thorstein Bunde,** 1857–1929, U.S. economist and sociologist.

vec·tion (vek'shən) *n. Med.* The carrying of a disease organism from an infected to a well person. [< L *vectio, -onis* a conveyance, carrying < *vehere* carry]

vec·tor (vek'tər) *n.* **1** *Math.* **a** A line representing a physical quantity that has magnitude and direction in space, as velocity, acceleration or force: distinguished from *scalar.* **b** A radius vector. **2** *Med.* A carrier of pathogenic micro-organisms from one host to another: The anopheles mosquito is a *vector* of the malaria parasite. [< L, carrier < *vehere* carry]—**vec·to·ri·al** (vek·tôr'ē·əl, -tō'rē-) *adj.*

vectorial angle *Math.* A polar angle.

vec·tur·ism (vek'chə·riz'əm) *n. U.S.* The hobby of collecting old transportation tokens from bus and trolley lines. [< L *vecturus* fare, passage money < *vehere* carry]—**vec'tur·ist** *n.*

Ve·da (vā'də, vē'-) *n.* The body of ancient Indian sacred writings, dating from the second millennium B.C., which form the Hindu scriptures; specifically, the four major collections included in this literature: **Rigveda,** containing sacrificial hymns addressed to the gods; **Yajurveda,** containing liturgical formulas; **Samaveda,** a group of hymns chiefly in honor of Indra; and **Aharvaveda,** a large collection of charms and incantations. [< Skt., knowledge]—**Ve·da·ic** (vi·dā'ik) *adj.* —**Ve·da·ism** (vā'də·iz'əm, vē'-) *n.*

Ve·dan·ta (vi·dän'tə, -dan'-) *n.* Any of several schools of Hindu religious philosophy based on the Upanishads; especially, the monistic system of Shankara which teaches the worship of Brahma as the creator and soul of the universe. [< Skt. < *Veda* Veda +*anta* end]—**Ve·dan'tic** *adj.* —**Ve·dan'tism** *n.* —**Ve·dan'tist** *n.*

Ved·da (ved'ə) *n.* One of a primitive people of Ceylon of doubtful classification, slender, dark, small, with heavy, wavy hair, having both Caucasoid and Australoid traits, but not typically either: by some anthropologists thought to be remnants of an original Indo-Australoid race. Also **Ved'dah.** [< Singhalese, hunter]

Ved·der (ved'ər), **Elihu,**1836–1923, U.S. painter and illustrator.

ve·dette (vi·det') *n.* **1** A mounted sentinel placed in advance of an outpost. **2** A small vessel used to watch the movements of the enemy: also **vedette boat. 3** *Colloq.* In France, a female movie star. Also spelled *vidette.* [< F < Ital. *vedetta,* alter. (after *vedere* see) of *veletta,* dim. of Sp. *vela* vigil < L *vigilare* watch]

Ve·dic (vā'dik, vē'-) *adj.* Of or pertaining to the Vedas or the language in which they were written. —*n.* Vedic Sanskrit.

Vedic Sanskrit See under SANSKRIT.

vee (vē) *n.* **1** The sound or the shape of the letter V. **2** Anything shaped like the letter V. **3** *U.S. Slang* A five-dollar bill. —*adj.* V-shaped.

veep (vēp) *n. Slang* A vice president; specifically, the vice president of the United States. [< *V.P.,* abbr. of vice president]

veer[1] (vir) *v.i.* **1** *Naut.* To turn to another course; wear ship. **2** To change direction by a clockwise motion, as the wind. **3** To shift from one position to another; be variable or fickle. —*v.t.* **4** To change the direction of. See synonyms under CHANGE, FLUCTUATE, WANDER. —*n.* A change in direction; a swerve. [< F *virer* turn]

veer[2] (vir) *v.t. & v.i. Naut.* To let out or allow (a rope, anchor chain, etc.) to run out to a certain length. [< MDu. *vieren* slacken]

veer·y (vir'ē) *n. pl.* **veer·ies** A melodious tawny thrush (*Hylocichla fuscescens*) of eastern North America: also called *Wilson's thrush.* [Prob. imit.]

Ve·ga (vē'gə, vā'-) A star, Alpha in the constellation Lyra; 0.14 magnitude. [< Med. L < Arabic (*al-Nasr) al-Waqi* the falling (vulture)]

Ve·ga (vā'gə, *Sp.* bā'gä), **Lope de,**1562–1635, Spanish dramatist and poet: full name Lope Felix de Vega Carpio.

veg·e·ta·ble (vej'ə·tə·bəl, vej'tə-) *n.* **1** The edible part of any herbaceous plant, raw or cooked, chiefly when served with an entree, or before the dessert. **2** Any member of the vegetable kingdom; a plant. **3** *Colloq.* A person who is mindless, apathetic, or passive. See synonyms under FRUIT. —*adj.* **1** Pertaining to plants, especially garden or farm vegetables. **2** Derived from, of the nature of, or resembling plants. **3** Made from or consisting of vegetables. **4** *Colloq.* Showing little mental activity; vacant. [< OF < LL *vegetabilis* full of life < L *vegetare* animate < *vegetus* vigorous, lively < *vegere* be lively]

vegetable butter See BUTTER[1] (def. 2).

vegetable fibers Textile fibers such as cotton, flax, kapok, jute, ramie, etc.

vegetable ivory Ivory nut.

vegetable kingdom The domain of nature that includes all organisms classified as plants. Compare ANIMAL KINGDOM, MINERAL KINGDOM.

vegetable marrow 1 A plant of the gourd family (*Cucurbita pepo*), having a tender, edible fruit. **2** The fruit, esteemed as a vegetable: also called *marrow squash*.

vegetable oyster The salsify.

vegetable silk A cottonlike material obtained from the seed pods of a Brazilian tree (*Chorisia speciosa*) and used for stuffing cushions, etc.

vegetable sponge A luffa.

vegetable tallow Any of several fatty vegetable substances, variously derived, resembling tallow, and used locally for making candles, soap, etc.

vegetable wax Any wax derived from a plant.

veg·e·tal (vej′ə·təl) *adj.* **1** Of or pertaining to plants or vegetables; vegetative. **2** Characterizing those vital processes which are common to plants and animals, especially as distinguished from sensation and volition. [<L *vegetus* lively, vigorous. See VEGETABLE.]

veg·e·tant (vej′ə·tənt) *adj.* **1** Invigorating; vivifying; stimulating growth. **2** Vegetating; plantlike. [<L *vegetans, -antis*, ppr. of *vegere* be active, lively]

veg·e·tar·i·an (vej′ə·târ′ē·ən) *adj.* **1** Pertaining to or advocating the eating of only vegetable foods. **2** Exclusively vegetable, as a diet. — *n.* One who holds or practices vegetarianism: also **veg·e·tist** (vej′ə·tist).

veg·e·tar·i·an·ism (vej′ə·târ′ē·ən·iz′əm) *n.* The theory or practice of eating only vegetables and fruits. Also **veg′e·tism.**

veg·e·tate (vej′ə·tāt) *v.i.* **·tat·ed, ·tat·ing** **1** To grow, as a plant. **2** To live in a monotonous, passive way. **3** *Pathol.* To increase in size. [<L *vegetatus*, pp. of *vegetare* animate. See VEGETABLE.]

veg·e·ta·tion (vej′ə·tā′shən) *n.* **1** The process of vegetating. **2** Plant life in the aggregate. **3** *Pathol.* An excrescence on the body; an abnormal or fibrous growth. **4** A plantlike growth. — **veg′e·ta′tion·al** *adj.*

veg·e·ta·tive (vej′ə·tā′tiv) *adj.* **1** Of, pertaining to, or exhibiting the processes of plant life. **2** Growing or capable of growing as plants; productive. **3** Having a mere physical existence; showing but little mental activity. **4** Asexual. **5** Concerned with growth and nutrition. **6** Functioning involuntarily or unconsciously: a *vegetative* process. Also **veg·e·tive** (vej′ə·tiv). — **veg′e·ta′tive·ly** *adv.* — **veg′e·ta′tive·ness** *n.*

Ve·glia (ve′lyä) The Italian name for KRK.

ve·he·ment (vē′ə·mənt) *adj.* **1** Arising from or marked by impetuosity of feeling or passion; ardent. **2** Acting with great force or energy; energetic; violent; furious. See synonyms under ARDENT, EAGER, HOT, VIOLENT. [<OF <L *vehemens, -entis* impetuous, rash; ult. origin uncertain] — **ve′he·mence, ve′he·men·cy** *n.* — **ve′he·ment·ly** *adv.*

ve·hi·cle (vē′ə·kəl) *n.* **1** That in or on which anything is carried; especially, a contrivance fitted with wheels or runners for carrying something; a conveyance, as a car or sled. **2** *Med.* A medium, as a liquid, with which is mixed some other substance that it may be applied or administered more easily; an excipient. **3** The medium with which pigments are mixed in painting. **4** Anything by means of which something else, as power, thought, etc., is transmitted or communicated; a device used to transmit an effect. [<F *véhicule* <L *vehiculum* <*vehere* carry, ride] — **ve·hic·u·lar** (vi·hik′yə·lər) *adj.*

Vehm·ge·richt (fām′gə·rikht) *n.* *pl.* **·rich·te** (-rikh′tə) An institution peculiar to Germany, especially Westphalia, from about 1150 to 1568, consisting of irregular tribunals. Civil cases were tried openly, but serious crimes, such as heresy, witchcraft, murder, etc., were tried by night in secret session. [<G <*fehm* judgment, punishment + *gericht* law, court]

Ve·ii (vē′yī) An ancient Etruscan city in central Italy, destroyed by Romans, 396 B.C.; site, 10 miles NW of Rome.

veil (vāl) *n.* **1** A piece of thin and light fabric, worn over the face or head for concealment, protection, or ornament. **2** Any piece of fabric used to conceal an object; a screen; curtain; mask. **3** Figuratively, that which conceals from inspection; a disguise; pretext. **4** A velum. **5** A caul. **6** The life of a nun; vows made by a nun. — **to take the veil** To become a nun. — *v.t.* **1** To cover with a veil. **2** To hide; disguise. See synonyms under

HIDE[1], MASK[1], PALLIATE. Also, *Obs., vail.* ♦ Homophones: *vail, vale*. [<OF *veile* <L *velum* piece of cloth, sail] — **veiled** *adj.* — **veil′er** *n.*

veil·ing (vā′ling) *n.* **1** The act of covering with a veil. **2** Material for veils. **3** A veil.

vein (vān) *n.* **1** *Anat.* One of the muscular tubular vessels that convey blood to the heart; loosely, any blood vessel. ♦ Collateral adjective: *venal.* **2** *Entomol.* One of the radiating supports of an insect's wing; a rib or nerve. **3** *Bot.* One of the slender vascular bundles that form the framework of a leaf. **4**

VEINING OF SILVER
MAPLE LEAF

Geol. The filling of a fissure or fault in a rock, particularly if deposited by aqueous solutions. **5** A lode. **6** A bed or shoot of ore parallel with the fault. **7** A long, irregular, colored streak, as in wood, marble, etc. **8** A distinctive trait; a specific tendency or disposition. **9** A temporary state of mind; humor; mood. **10** A cavity; cleft; fissure. **11** A crevice or natural channel through which water trickles. — *v.t.* **1** To furnish or fill with veins. **2** To streak or ornament with veins. **3** To extend over or throughout as veins. ♦ Homophones: *vain, vane.* [<OF *veine* <L *vena* blood vessel] — **vein′less** *adj.* — **vein′y** *adj.*

veined (vānd) *adj.* **1** Having veins. **2** Marked with or abounding in veins. **3** Marked with streaks of another color.

vein·ing (vā′ning) *n.* **1** A vein or network of veins. **2** A streaked or veined surface.

vein·let (vān′lit) *n.* A small vein.

vein·stone (vān′stōn′) *n.* Gangue.

Ve·la (vē′lə) A southern constellation, formerly part of the larger one, Argo Navis. [<L, veil]

ve·la·men (və·lā′mən) *n.* *pl.* **·lam·i·na** (-lam′ə·nə) **1** *Anat.* Any membrane, covering, or integument. **2** *Bot.* An envelope consisting of several layers of empty cells, forming the outer covering of the aerial roots of certain orchids and arums. Also **vel·a·men·tum** (vel′ə·men′təm). [<L, covering <*velare* veil]

ve·lar (vē′lər) *adj.* **1** Of or pertaining to a velum, especially the soft palate. **2** *Phonet.* Formed with the back of the tongue touching or near the soft palate, as (k) in *cool*, (g) in *go*. — *n.* *Phonet.* A velar sound. [<L *velaris* <*velum* sail, curtain]

ve·lar·ize (vē′lə·rīz) *v.* **·ized, ·iz·ing** *Phonet. v.t.* To modify (a sound) by raising the back of the tongue toward the soft palate. — *v.i.* To be modified to a velar sound.

ve·lar·i·um (və·lâr′ē·əm) *n.* *pl.* **·lar·i·a** (-lâr′ē·ə) *Latin* The awning spread over the seats in ancient Roman theaters or amphitheaters.

Ve·lás·quez (və·las′kwiz, *Sp.* bā·läs′kāth), **Diego Rodriguez de Silva y,** 1599–1660, Spanish painter. Also **Ve·láz·quez** (bā·läth′-kāth).

ve·late (vē′lāt, -lit) *adj.* *Biol.* Having a velum on one side. [<L *velatus*, pp. of *velare* veil]

ve·la·tion (vē·lā′shən) *n.* **1** The forming of a velum. **2** The act of veiling, or the state of being veiled; hence, concealment; mystery.

veldt (velt, felt) *n.* In South Africa, open country or pasture land; grassland having few shrubs or trees. Low-lying wooded land is known as **bush veldt**, and the high treeless plains as **high veldt**. Also **veld**. [<Afrikaans *veld* <Du., field]

vel·i·ger (vel′ə·jər) *n.* *Zool.* The larva of a mollusk at the stage succeeding the trochophore and when it has a ciliated swimming membrane or membranes. [<LL *veliger* sail-bearing <L *velum* sail + *gerere* bear]

ve·lig·er·ous (və·lij′ər·əs) *adj.* Bearing a velum or membranous partition.

Ve·li·ki Kvar·ner (ve′li·kē kvär′nər) An arm of the Adriatic Sea, SE of Istria, in NW Croatia, Yugoslavia: also *Gulf of Quarnero. Italian* **Gol·fo di Quar·ne·ro** (gôl′fô dē kwär·nā′rō).

vel·i·ta·tion (vel′ə·tā′shən) *n.* A petty skirmish; a wordy controversy. [<L *velitatio*,

-onis <*velitatus*, pp. of *velitari* skirmish <*veles, velitis* a foot soldier]

ve·li·tes (vē′lə·tēz) *n.* *pl.* Light-armed Roman soldiers used as skirmishers in ancient legions. [<L, pl. of *veles* foot soldier]

vel·le·i·ty (ve·lē′ə·tē) *n.* *pl.* **·ties** A very low degree of desire or volition, not leading to action; a mere wish. [<Med. L *velleitas, -tatis* <L *velle* wish]

vel·li·cate (vel′ə·kāt) *v.t.* & *v.i.* **·cat·ed, ·cat·ing** To twitch or pluck. [<L *vellicatus*, pp. of *vellicare* twitch, freq. of *vellere* pluck] — **vel′li·ca′tion** *n.* — **vel′li·ca′tive** *adj.*

vel·lum (vel′əm) *n.* **1** Fine parchment made from the skins of calves: used for expensive binding, printing, etc. **2** A manuscript written on such parchment. **3** Paper made to resemble parchment. [<OF *velin, vellin* <*veel, viel* calf. See VEAL.]

ve·lo·ce (vā·lō′chā) *adv.* *Music* Rapidly; in quick tempo; swiftly. [<Ital., swift]

ve·loc·i·pede (və·los′ə·pēd) *n.* **1** An early form of bicycle or tricycle; also, a child's tricycle. **2** A light handcar or vehicle propelled by hands or feet and used along railroad tracks. [<L *velox, velocis* swift + -PEDE]

ve·loc·i·ty (və·los′ə·tē) *n.* *pl.* **·ties** **1** The state of moving swiftly; rapid motion; celerity; speed. **2** *Physics* **a** The rate of change of position in a moving object. **b** The rate of motion in a stated direction: a vector quantity: distinguished from *speed.* [<L *velocitas, -tatis* <*velox* swift]

velocity of escape *Physics* The minimum velocity at which any particle or object would permanently escape the gravitational field of a body of stated mass: on the earth this velocity is approximately 7 miles per second. See table under PLANET.

ve·lo·drome (vē′lə·drōm) *n.* A racecourse, as for bicycles. [<L *velox* speedy + -DROME]

ve·lours (və·lōor′) *n.* *pl.* **·lours** A soft, velvet-like, closely woven cotton or wool fabric having a short, thick pile. Also **ve·lour′.** [<F. See VELURE.]

ve·lou·té (və·lōo·tā′) *n.* *French* A rich white sauce made by thickening chicken or veal stock with flour and butter. Also **sauce velouté.**

ve·lum (vē′ləm) *n.* *pl.* **·la** (-lə) **1** *Biol.* A thin membranous covering or partition, as in certain jellyfishes, and in mushrooms. **2** *Anat.* The soft palate. See PALATE. [<L]

ve·lure (və·lōor′) *n.* **1** Velvet, or a fabric resembling velvet; specifically, a heavy fabric of linen, silk, or jute, used for hangings, table covers, and the like. **2** A velvet or silk pad for smoothing a silk hat. — *v.t.* **·lured, ·lur·ing** To smooth with a soft pad, as a hat. [<F *velours* <L *villosus* shaggy <*villus* shaggy hair]

ve·lu·ti·nous (və·lōo′tə·nəs) *adj.* *Bot.* Covered with close, soft hairs, like the pile of velvet; velvety. [<NL *velutinus* <Med. L *velutum*, var. of *velvetum*. See VELVET.]

vel·ver·et (vel′və·ret′) *n.* A velvet fabric with cotton backing.

vel·vet (vel′vit) *n.* **1** A fabric, properly of silk, now sometimes made of cotton or one of the synthetics, closely woven and having on one side a thick, short, smooth pile: called **pile velvet** when the pile is formed of loops, and **cut velvet** when the pile is of single threads. **2** The furry skin covering a growing antler. — **chiffon velvet** A very soft, lightweight velvet having the pile pressed flat. — *adj.* **1** Made of velvet. **2** Smooth and soft to the touch; velvety. [<Med. L *velvetum*, ult. <L *villus* shaggy hair]

velvet carpet A carpet having a pile longer than a Brussels carpet but cut in the manner of a Wilton carpet: also **tapestry velvet carpet.**

vel·vet·een (vel′və·tēn′) *n.* **1** A cotton fabric, with a short, close pile like velvet. **2** *pl.* Clothes, especially trousers, made of this material. [<VELVET] — **vel′vet·eened′** *adj.*

vel·vet·leaf (vel′vit·lēf′) *n.* **1** Any one of several plants, especially the Indian mallow. **2** A tropical climbing shrub (*Cissampelos pareira*) of the moonseed family, the bark of which yields a variety of pareira brava.

vel·vet·y (vel′vit·ē) *adj.* **1** Like velvet; smooth and soft to appearance or touch. **2**

Mild and smooth to the taste: *velvety* liqueur.

ve·na (vē′nə) *n.* *pl.* **·nae** (-nē) *Anat.* A vein. [<L]

ve·na ca·va (vē′nə kā′və) *n.* *pl.* **ve·nae ca·vae** (vē′nē kā′vē) *Anat.* Either of the two great venous trunks (called *superior* and *inferior*) emptying into the right auricle of the heart. See illustration under HEART. [<L, hollow vein]

ve·nal¹ (vē′nəl) *adj.* **1** Ready to sell honor or principle, or to accept a bribe; mercenary; purchasable: said of persons. **2** Subject to sordid bargaining or to corrupt influences; salable. **3** Characterized by corruption and venality. [<L *venalis* < *venum* sale] — **ve′nal·ly** *adv.*

Synonyms: hireling, mercenary, purchasable, salable. *Mercenary* has especial application to character or disposition; as, a *mercenary* spirit; *mercenary* motives—that is, a spirit or motives to which money is the chief consideration or the moving principle. Thus, etymologically, the *mercenary* can be hired, while the *venal* are openly or actually for sale; *hireling* signifies serving for hire or pay, or having the spirit or character of one who works or of that which is done directly for hire or pay. The *hireling*, the *mercenary*, and the *venal* are alike in making principle, conscience, and honor of less account than gold or sordid considerations; but the *mercenary* and *venal* may be simply open to the bargain and sale which the *hireling* has already consummated. A public officer who makes his office tributary to private speculation is *mercenary*; if he receives a stipulated recompense for administering his office at the behest of some leader, faction, corporation, or the like, he is both *hireling* and *venal*; if he sells essential advantages, without subjecting himself to any direct domination, his course is *venal*, but not *hireling*. *Antonyms:* disinterested, honest, honorable, incorruptible, patriotic, unpurchasable.

ve·nal² (vē′nəl) *adj.* Of or pertaining to the veins; venous. [<L *vena* vein]

ve·nal·i·ty (vē·nal′ə·tē) *n.* *pl.* **·ties** The state or character of being basely or improperly influenced by sordid considerations; prostitution, as of talents, office, etc., for gain or reward; willingness to accept bribes. [<L *venalitas, -tatis*]

ve·nat·ic (vē·nat′ik) *adj.* **1** Of, used in, or pertaining to hunting. **2** Living by or fond of hunting. Also **ven·a·to·ri·al** (ven′ə·tôr′ē·əl, -tō′rē-). [<L *venaticus* < *venatus,* pp. of *venari* hunt] — **ve·nat′i·cal** *adj.* — **ve·nat′i·cal·ly** *adv.*

ve·na·tion (vē·nā′shən) *n.* *Biol.* **1** The particular arrangement of veins, as in a leaf. **2** The distribution of veins in an organism or part, as an insect wing, etc. [<L *vena* a vein]

vend (vend) *v.t.* **1** To sell. **2** To utter (an opinion); publish. — *v.i.* **3** To be a vender. **4** To be sold. [<F *vendre* <L *vendere* < *venum* sale + *dare* give] — **ven·di·tion** (ven-dish′ən) *n.*

ven·dace (ven′dis) *n.* A small whitefish (*Coregonus vandesius*) of some British lakes. Also **ven′dis.** [<F *vandoise* dace]

ven·dee (ven-dē′) *n.* The person or party to whom something, especially land, is sold.

Ven·dée (vän-dā′) A region and department in western France on the Bay of Biscay; scene of a royalist revolt, 1793–95; 2,708 square miles. — **Ven·de·an** (ven-dē′ən) *adj.* & *n.*

Ven·dé·miaire (vän-dā-myâr′) See under CALENDAR (Republican).

vend·er (ven′dər) *n.* One who sells; a peddler or hawker; vendor.

ven·det·ta (ven-det′ə) *n.* Private warfare or feud, as in revenge for a murder, injury, etc.; a blood feud in which the relatives of the killed or injured person take vengeance on the offender or his relatives. It is still prevalent in Sicily, Corsica, and Montenegro, and, to some extent, in certain other districts. [<Ital. <L *vindicta* vengeance]

vend·i·ble (ven′də·bəl) *adj.* Capable of being vended or sold; marketable. — *n.* A thing exposed for sale. [<L *vendibilis* < *vendere* sell] — **vend′i·bil′i·ty, vend′i·ble·ness** *n.* — **vend′i·bly** *adv.*

Ven·dôme (vän·dôm′) A town and former duchy in north central France.

ven·dor (ven′dər) The common legal spelling of VENDER.

ven·due (ven·dōō′, -dyōō′) *n.* A public sale or auction. [<F, orig. fem. pp. of *vendre* sell]

ve·neer (və·nir′) *n.* **1** A thin layer, as of choice wood, upon a commoner surface; a layer of superior material for overlaying a cheaper one. **2** Any of the thin layers glued together to strengthen plywood. **3** Figuratively, mere outside show or elegance. — *v.t.* **1** To cover (a surface) with veneers; overlay for decoration or finer finish. **2** To glue together to form plywood. **3** To conceal, as something disagreeable or coarse, with an attractive or deceptive surface. [Earlier *fineer* <G *furnieren* inlay <F *fournir* furnish] — **ve·neer′er** *n.*

ve·neer·ing (və·nir′ing) *n.* **1** The art of applying veneer. **2** Material used for veneers. **3** A facing or surface of veneer.

ven·e·punc·ture (ven′ə·pungk′chər) See VENIPUNCTURE.

Ve·ner (vē′nər), **Lake** The largest lake of Sweden, in the SW part; 2,141 square miles; 90 miles long, 5 to 46 miles wide: also *Vaner.* Swedish **Vä·nern** (ve′nərn).

ven·er·a·ble (ven′ər·ə·bəl) *adj.* **1** Meriting or commanding veneration; worthy of reverence: now usually implying age. **2** Exciting reverential feelings because of sacred or elevated associations. **3** Revered: used as a title for an archdeacon in Anglican churches, and for those beatified in the Roman Catholic Church. See synonyms under ANCIENT¹. [<OF <L *venerabilis* < *venerari* revere] — **ven·er·a·ble·ness, ven′er·a·bil′i·ty** *n.* — **ven′er·a·bly** *adv.*

ven·er·ate (ven′ə·rāt) *v.t.* **·at·ed, ·at·ing** To look upon or regard with respect and deference; revere. [<L *veneratus,* pp. of *venerari* revere]

Synonyms: adore, honor, respect, revere, reverence. In the highest sense, to *revere* or *reverence* is to hold in mingled love and honor with something of sacred fear; to *revere* is a wholly spiritual act; to *reverence* is often, but not necessarily, to give outward expression to the reverential feeling; we *revere* or *reverence* the divine majesty. *Revere* is a stronger word than *reverence* or *venerate.* To *venerate* is to hold in exalted honor without fear, and is applied to objects less removed from ourselves than those we *revere,* being said especially of aged persons, of places or objects having sacred associations, and of abstractions; we *venerate* an aged friend or some great cause, as that of civil or religious liberty; we do not *venerate* God, but *revere* or *reverence* him. We *adore* with a humble yet free outflowing of soul. See ADMIRE, DEFER. *Antonyms:* contemn, despise, disdain, dishonor, disregard, scorn, slight, spurn.

ven·er·a·tion (ven′ə·rā′shən) *n.* **1** The act of venerating; reverence; profound respect combined with awe, evoked by the high character or wisdom of a person. **2** The act of worshiping; worship.

Synonyms: adoration, awe, dread, reverence. *Awe* is inspired by that in which there is sublimity or majesty so overwhelming as to awaken a feeling akin to fear; in *awe,* considered by itself, there is no element of esteem or affection, but a sense of the vastness, power, or grandeur of the object. *Dread* is a shrinking apprehension or expectation of possible harm awakened by any one of many objects or causes; in its higher uses *dread* approaches the meaning of *awe,* but with more of chilliness and cowering, and without that subjection of soul to the grandeur and worthiness of the object that is involved in *awe. Reverence* and *veneration* are less overwhelming than *awe* or *dread,* and suggest something of esteem, affection, and personal nearness. We may feel *awe* of that which we cannot reverence, as a grandly terrible ocean storm; *awe* of the divine presence is more distant and less trustful than *reverence. Veneration* is commonly applied to things which are not subjects of *awe. Adoration,* in its full sense, is loftier than *veneration,* less restrained and awed than *reverence,* and with more of the spirit of direct, active, and joyful worship. See REVERENCE. Compare VENERATE. *Antonyms:* contempt, disdain, dishonor, disregard, scorn.

ve·ne·re·al (və·nir′ē·əl) *adj.* **1** Pertaining to or proceeding from sexual intercourse. **2** Communicated by sexual relations with an infected person: a *venereal* disease. **3** Pertaining to or curative of diseases so communicated. **4** Infected with venereal disease. [<L *venereus* < *Venus, -eris,* the goddess of love]

venereal disease *Pathol.* One of several diseases propagated directly or indirectly by sexual intercourse, as syphilis, gonorrhea, and chancroid.

ve·ne·re·ol·o·gy (və·nir′ē·ol′ə·jē) *n.* The study and treatment of venereal diseases. — **ve·ne′re·ol′o·gist** *n.*

ven·er·y¹ (ven′ər·ē) *n.* Sexual indulgence, especially when excessive. [<L *Venus, -eris,* the goddess of love]

ven·er·y² (ven′ər·ē) *n.* *pl.* **·er·ies** The hunting of game; the sport of hunting; the chase. [<F *venerie* < *vener* hunt <L *venari* hunt]

ven·e·sec·tion (ven′ə·sek′shən) *n.* *Surg.* Phlebotomy. [<Med. L *venae sectio* cutting of a vein]

Ve·ne·ti·a (və·nē′shē·ə, -shə) **1** An ancient division of the Roman Empire comprising that part of Italy between the Po river and the Alps. **2** Venezia. **3** Veneto.

Ve·ne·tian (və·nē′shən) *adj.* Pertaining to Venice, or to the medieval school of architecture developed there. — *n.* **1** A native of Venice. **2** *Colloq.* A Venetian blind. **3** A heavy braid or tape used on Venetian blinds.

Venetian blind A flexible window screen that may be raised or lowered, having overlapping horizontal slats so fastened on webbing or tape as to regulate, exclude, or admit light.

Venetian carpet A worsted carpet for stairs and hallways, commonly of a simple striped pattern.

Venetian glass A delicate and fine glassware originally made at or near Venice.

Venetian red Red ocher. See under OCHER.

Venetian school 1 A school of painting originating in and near Venice in the 15th century and distinguished by richness of coloring, as in the work of Titian, Tintoretto, Giorgione, etc. **2** A school of Italian architecture.

Ve·net·ic (və·net′ik) *n.* **1** A member of an ancient people of NE Italy. **2** Their Indo-European language, possibly related to Illyrian and Messapian. — *adj.* Of or pertaining to these people or their language.

Ve·ne·to (vā′nā·tō) A region of northern and NE Italy; 7,093 square miles; capital, Venice.

Ve·ne·zia (vā·nā′tsyä) **1** The Italian name for VENICE. **2** A province in Veneto, northern Italy; 949 square miles; capital, Venice.

Venezia Giu·lia (jōō′lyä) A former region of NE Italy including Trieste, Rijeka, and Istria; 3,370 square miles; divided 1947 between Italy (180 square miles), Yugoslavia (2,891 square miles), and the Free Territory of Trieste (298 square miles, later also divided).

Ven·e·zue·la (ven′ə·zwē′lə, -zōō·ā′lə; *Sp.* bā′nā·swā′lä) A republic in northern South America; 352,143 square miles; capital, Caracas. — **Ven′e·zue′lan** *adj.* & *n.*

Venezuela, Gulf of See under MARACAIBO.

ven·geance (ven′jəns) *n.* **1** The infliction of a deserved penalty; retributive punishment. **2** In a bad sense, wrathful avenging of a wrong; revenge. **3** *Obs.* Mischief; evil. See synonyms under REVENGE. — **with a vengeance** With great force or violence; extremely; to an unusual extent. [<AF <OF *venger* avenge <L *vindicare* defend, avenge < *vindex, vindicis* claimant, protector]

venge·ful (venj′fəl) *adj.* Prone to inflict vengeance; vindictive. — **venge′ful·ly** *adv.* — **venge′ful·ness** *n.*

ve·ni·al (vē′nē·əl, vēn′yəl) *adj.* That may be pardoned or overlooked; excusable. [<OF <L *venialis* < *venia* forgiveness, mercy] — **ve′ni·al′i·ty** (-al′ə·tē), **ve′ni·al·ness** *n.* — **ve′ni·al·ly** *adv.*

Synonyms: excusable, pardonable, slight, trivial. Aside from its technical ecclesiastical use, *venial* is always understood as marking some fault comparatively *slight* or *trivial.* A *venial* offense is one readily overlooked; a *pardonable* offense requires more serious consideration, but on deliberation is found to be susceptible of pardon. *Excusable* is scarcely applied to offenses, but to matters open to doubt or criticism rather than direct censure; so used, it often falls little short of justifiable; as, I suppose, under those circumstances, his action was *excusable*. *Antonyms*: inexcusable, mortal, unpardonable.

venial sin *Theol.* A pardonable offense, or an unpremeditated one: opposed to *mortal* or *deadly* sin.

Ven·ice (ven'is) A port in NE Italy, built on 118 islands in the **Lagoon of Venice**, the NW part of the **Gulf of Venice**, the northern sector of the Adriatic between Istria and the Po river delta: Italian *Venezia*.

Ve·ni Cre·a·tor (vē'nī krē·ā'tər) *Latin* A hymn to the Holy Ghost: so called from its beginning, *Veni Creator Spiritus* (Come, Creator Spirit).

ven·i·punc·ture (ven'ə·pungk'chər) *n. Surg.* The operation of puncturing a vein: also spelled *venepuncture*. [<L *vena* vein + PUNC- TURE]

ve·ni·re (vi·nī'rē) *n. Law* A writ issued to the sheriff for summoning persons to serve as a jury in court: from its phrase *venire facias* (that you cause to come). [<L]

ve·ni·re·man (vi·nī'rē·mən) *n. pl.* **·men** (-mən) A juryman; one summoned to be on a jury.

ven·i·son (ven'ə·zən, -sən; *Brit.* ven'zən) *n.* **1** Deer flesh used for food. **2** *Obs.* The flesh of any edible game. [<F *venaison* <L *venatio*, *-onis* hunting < *venatus*, pp. of *venari* hunt]

venison bird *Canadian* The Canada jay.

Ven·i·te (vi·nī'tē) *n.* The 95th psalm, used as a canticle in various liturgies: from its first word. [<L, come, imperative of *venire* come]

ve·ni, vi·di, vi·ci (vē'nī, vī'dī, vī'sī; wā'nē, wē'dē, wē'kē) *Latin* I came, I saw, I conquered: words used by Julius Caesar to report his victory over Pharnaces, king of Pontus, to the Roman Senate.

Ve·ni·ze·los (ve'nē·ze'lōs), **Eleftherios**, 1864– 1936, Greek statesman; premier 1917–20 and 1928–32.

ven·om (ven'əm) *n.* **1** The poisonous fluid that certain animals, as serpents and scorpions, secrete, and which produces toxic effects when introduced into the system by a bite or sting. **2** Something harmful; hence, malignity; spite. **3** Any poison. — *v.t.* To imbue with poison; envenom. [<OF *venim* <L *venenum* poison] — **ven'om·er** *n.*

ven·om·ous (ven'əm·əs) *adj.* **1** Having glands secreting venom. **2** Able to give a poisonous sting; virulent; noxious. **3** Working harm; baneful. **4** Malignant; spiteful. See synonyms under MALICIOUS. — **ven'om· ous·ly** *adv.* — **ven'om·ous·ness** *n.*

ve·nose (vē'nōs) *adj.* **1** Having numerous or prominent veins, as a leaf; veiny. **2** Venous. [<L *venosus*]

ve·nos·i·ty (vi·nos'ə·tē) *n.* **1** An excess of venous blood in a part. **2** A plentiful supply of blood vessels.

ve·nous (vē'nəs) *adj. Physiol.* **1** Of, pertaining to, contained, or carried in a vein or veins. **2** Designating the blood carried by the veins and distinguished from arterial blood by its darker color, absence of oxygen, and presence of carbon dioxide. **3** Marked with or having veins. [<L *venosus* < *vena* vein] — **ve'nous·ly** *adv.* — **ve'nous·ness** *n.*

vent (vent) *n.* **1** An opening, commonly small, for the passage of fluids, gases, etc.; hence, an outlet of any kind: also **vent hole.** **2** The act of giving utterance, as to passion; expression; escape; passage: now usually in the phrase **to give vent to.** **3** *Zool.* The external opening of the alimentary canal, especially of animals below mammals; the anus. **4** A touchhole of a gun. — *v.t.* **1** To give expression to: to *vent* one's rage. **2** To relieve, as by giving vent to emotion. **3** To permit to escape at a vent, as a gas. **4** To make a vent in, as a mold. [ME *fent* <OF *fente* cleft < *fendre* cleave <L *findere* split]

vent·age (ven'tij) *n.* **1** A small opening. **2** A finger hole in a musical instrument. [<VENT]

ven·tail (ven'tāl) *n.* The adjustable front of a helmet, permitting complete defense of the face in combat. [<OF *ventaile* < *vent* wind]

vent·er¹ (ven'tər) *n.* One who vents.

ven·ter² (ven'tər) *n.* **1** The belly or stomach. **2** Any protuberant part. **3** The womb. **4** A hollowed part, as of a bone. [<L, stomach]

ven·ti·duct (ven'tə·dukt) *n.* An air passage, especially a subterranean ventilating passage. [<L *ventus* wind + DUCT]

ven·ti·late (ven'tə·lāt) *v.t.* **·lat·ed, ·lat·ing** **1** To produce a free circulation of air in, as by means of open shafts, windows, doors, etc.; admit fresh air into. **2** To provide with a vent. **3** To make widely known; expose to examination and discussion. **4** To oxygenate, as blood. **5** *Obs.* To winnow; fan, as wheat. [<L *ventilatus*, pp. of *ventilare* fan < *ventus* wind] — **ven'ti·lat·ing, ven'ti· la'tion** *n.* — **ven'ti·la'tive** *adj.*

ven·ti·la·tor (ven'tə·lā'tər) *n.* **1** One who or that which ventilates. **2** A device or arrangement for supplying fresh air. — **ven'· ti·la·to·ry** (-lə·tôr'ē, -tō'rē) *adj.*

Ven·ti·mi·glia (ven'tē·mē'lyä) An Italian port on the Gulf of Genoa NE of Nice; an important international railroad station.

Ven·tôse (vän·tōz') See under CALENDAR (Republican).

ven·trad (ven'trad) *adv. Biol.* Toward the belly or undersurface. [<L *venter* belly]

ven·tral (ven'trəl) *adj.* **1** *Biol.* **a** Of, pertaining to, or situated on or near the abdomen or abdominal surface of an animal. **b** On or toward the lower surface of the body: the *ventral* plates of a serpent: opposed to *dorsal*. **2** *Bot.* Pertaining to the surface of a petal, carpel, etc., that faces the center of a flower. — *n.* One of the paired fins on the underside of fishes, homologous with the hind limb of higher vertebrates: in full, **ventral fin.** [<L *ventralis* < *venter, ventris* belly] — **ven'tral·ly** *adv.*

ven·tri·cle (ven'trə·kəl) *n. Anat.* **1** Any of various cavities in the body, as of the brain, the spinal cord, or between the true and false vocal cords in the larynx. **2** One of the two lower chambers of the heart, from which blood received from the atria is forced into the arteries. [<L *ventriculus*, dim. of *venter, ventris* belly]

ven·tri·cose (ven'trə·kōs) *adj.* **1** Having a protruding belly. **2** Swelling out or inflated on one side or in the middle; bellied; distended. Also **ven'tri·cous** (-kəs). [<NL *ventricosus* <L *venter, ventris* belly] — **ven'tri· cos'i·ty** (-kos'ə·tē) *n.*

ven·tric·u·lar (ven·trik'yə·lər) *adj.* **1** Of, pertaining to, or of the nature of a ventricle. **2** Swollen and distended; ventricose.

ven·tric·u·lose (ven·trik'yə·lōs) *adj.* Slightly ventricose. [<L *ventriculosus* < *ventriculus*. See VENTRICLE.]

ven·tri·lo·qui·al (ven'trə·lō'kwē·əl) *adj.* Pertaining to, resembling, or practicing ventriloquism. Also **ven·tril'o·qual** (ven·tril'ə·kwəl), **ven·tril'o·quous.** — **ven'tri·lo'qui·al·ly** *adv.*

ven·tril·o·quism (ven·tril'ə·kwiz'əm) *n.* The art or practice of speaking in such a manner that the sounds seem to come from some source other than the person speaking. Also **ven·tril'o·quy** (-kwē). [<L *venter* belly + *loqui* speak] — **ven·tril'o·quist** *n.* — **ven· tril'o·quis'tic** *adj.*

ven·tril·o·quize (ven·tril'ə·kwīz) *v.t. & v.i.* **·quized, ·quiz·ing** To speak as a ventriloquist. Also *Brit.* **ven·tril'o·quise.**

ventro- combining form *Anat.* The abdomen; related to or near the abdomen; ventral. [<L *venter, ventris* the belly, abdomen]

Vents·pils (vents'pils) A port on the Baltic Sea in NW Latvia: German *Windau*.

ven·ture (ven'chər) *v.* **·tured, ·tur·ing** *v.t.* **1** To expose to chance or risk; hazard; stake. **2** To run the risk of; brave. **3** To express at the risk of denial or refutation: to *venture* a suggestion. **4** To place or send on a chance, as in a speculative business enterprise. **5** *Obs.* To trust as an agent or doer; rely on. — *v.i.* **6** To take a risk; dare. — *n.* **1** The staking of a thing upon a contingency; a risk; hazard. **2** An undertaking attended with risk; a business speculation. **3** That which is ventured; especially, property risk. **4** That which is unforeseen and hazardous; chance; fortune: a rare usage. See synonyms under HAZARD. — **at a venture** At hazard; at random; without aim or thought. [Aphetic form of ADVEN- TURE] — **ven'tur·er** *n.*

ven·ture·some (ven'chər·səm) *adj.* **1** Bold; daring. **2** Involving hazard; risky. See synonyms under BRAVE, IMPRUDENT. — **ven'ture· some·ly** *adv.* — **ven'ture·some·ness** *n.*

ven·tur·ous (ven'chər·əs) *adj.* **1** Adventur-

ous; willing to take risks and brave dangers; bold. **2** Hazardous; risky; dangerous. See synonyms under IMPRUDENT. — **ven'tur·ous·ly** *adv.* — **ven'tur·ous·ness** *n.*

ven·ue (ven'yōō) *n. Law* **1** The place or neighborhood where a crime is committed or a cause of action arises; the county or political division from which the jury must be summoned and in which the trial must be held. **2** The clause, usually at the beginning of a declaration or indictment, indicating the county in which the proceeding is pending. **3** A clause in an affidavit, stating where it was made and sworn to. — **change of venue** The change of the place of trial, for good cause shown, from one county to another. [<OF, orig. fem. pp. of *venir* come <L *venire*]

ven·ule (ven'yōōl) *n.* A small vein; veinlet, as of an insect. [<L *venula*, dim. of *vena* vein] — **ven'u·lar** (-yə·lər) *adj.*

ven·u·lose (ven'yə·lōs) *adj.* Having numerous veinlets, as a leaf. Also **ven'u·lous** (-ləs). [<VENULE]

ve·nus (vē'nəs) *n.* A bivalve having three hinge teeth in each valve, as the quahaug. [<VENUS; from the resemblance of the lunula of the closed valve to the vulva]

Ve·nus (vē'nəs) **1** In Roman mythology, the goddess of spring, bloom, and beauty: identified with the Greek *Aphrodite*. **2** A statue or painting of Venus. **3** A lovely woman. **4** *Astron.* The second planet from the sun, the most brilliant object in the heavens except the sun and the moon. It moves in an orbit between those of Mercury and Earth at a mean distance from the sun of about 67,000,- 000 miles, completing a revolution in 224.7 days. Its diameter is about 7,700 miles and it has no satellites. **5** *Obs.* In alchemy, the metal copper. [<L]

Ve·nus·berg (vē'nəs·bûrg, *Ger.* vā'nŏŏs·berkh) In medieval German legend, a mountain in the dark recesses of which Venus lured men to sensuous pleasures. See TANNHÄUSER.

Venus flytrap A plant (*Dionaea muscipula*), with clustered leaves the blades of which instantly close upon insects or other objects lighting upon them: found native chiefly in the sandy bogs of eastern North and South Carolina. Also **Ve·nus's·fly·trap** (vē'nəs· iz·flī'trap').

VENUS FLYTRAP
(From 4 to 14 inches tall)

Venus of Mi·lo (mē'lō) A marble statue of Venus, nude above the thighs and with the arms missing, discovered in 1820 on the island of Milo: now in the Louvre. Also **Venus de Milo.**

Ve·nus's·comb (vē'nəs·iz·kōm') *n.* A European plant (*Scandix pecten-veneris*) with white flowers in numerous umbels, and lobed leaves suggestive of a comb: often called *shepherd's-needle, devil's-darning-needle*.

Ve·nus's·gir·dle (vē'nəs·iz·gûr'dəl) *n.* A ctenophore of warm seas, having a transparent body that shimmers with blue, green, or violet colors.

Ve·nus's·hair (vē'nəs·iz·hâr') *n.* A maidenhair fern (*Adiantum capillus-veneris*) having a black stipe and branches.

ver·a (ver'ə, var'ə) *adj. & adv. Scot.* Very.

Ve·ra (vir'ə) A feminine personal name. [<Slavic, faith]

ve·ra·cious (və·rā'shəs) *adj.* **1** Habitually disposed to speak the truth; truthful. **2** Conforming to or expressing truth; true; accurate. [<L *verax, veracis* < *verus* true] — **ve·ra'- cious·ly** *adv.* — **ve·ra'cious·ness** *n.*

ve·rac·i·ty (və·ras'ə·tē) *n. pl.* **·ties** **1** The habitual regard for truth; truthfulness; honesty. **2** Agreement with truth; accuracy, or fact; trueness. **3** That which is true; truth. [<F *véracité* <L *verax*. See VERACIOUS.]

Synonyms: candor, fact, frankness, honesty, ingenuousness, reality, truth, truthfulness, verity. *Truth* is primarily and *verity* is always a quality of thought or speech, especially of speech, as in exact conformity to *fact*. *Veracity* is properly a quality of a person, the habit of speaking and the disposition to speak the *truth. Truthfulness* is a quality that may inhere either in a person or in his statements or beliefs. *Candor, frankness, honesty,* and *ingenuousness* are closely allied with *veracity,* and *fact, reality,* and *verity* with *truth,* while *truthfulness* may accord with either. *Truth* in a secondary sense may be applied to intellectual action or moral character, in the former case becoming a close synonym of *veracity:* She knows him to be a man of *truth. Antonyms:* deceit, deception, delusion, duplicity, error, fabrication, fallacy, falsehood, falsity, fiction, guile, imposture, lie, untruth.

Ve·ra·cruz (ver′ə·krōōz′, *Sp.* bā′rä·krōōs′, -krōōth′) 1 A coast state in eastern Mexico; 27,752 square miles; capital, Jalapa. 2 Its chief city, a port on the Gulf of Mexico: officially **Veracruz Lla·ve** (yä′vä).

ve·ran·da (və·ran′də) *n.* An open portico, gallery, or balcony, usually roofed, along the outside of a building; a porch or stoop. Compare LOGGIA. Also **ve·ran′dah.** [<Hind. *varandā* <Pg. *varanda* railing, balustrade, prob. < *vara* rod, pole <L *vara* forked pole]

ve·ra·no (və·rä′nō) *n.* The dry midwinter season in tropical America. [<Sp., lit., summer]

ve·rat·ric acid (və·rat′rik) *Chem.* A colorless crystalline acid, $C_9H_{10}O_4$, contained in sabadilla seeds and also made synthetically. [<L *veratrum* hellebore]

ve·rat·ri·dine (və·rat′rə·dēn, -din) *n. Chem.* A yellowish, amorphous alkaloid, $C_{36}H_{51}$-$O_{11}N$, contained in sabadilla seeds. Also **ve·rat′ri·din** (-din). [<L *veratrum* hellebore + -ID(E) + -INE²]

ver·a·trine (ver′ə·trēn, -trin) *n. Chem.* A white or grayish-white, amorphous (rarely crystalline), extremely poisonous mixture of alkaloids, contained in sabadilla seeds: used in medicine as an analgesic in neuralgia and rheumatism. Also **ve·ra·tri·a** (və·rā′trē·ə), **ver′a·trin** (-trin), **ver′a·tri′na** (-trī′nə). [<L *veratrum* hellebore + INE²]

ver·a·trize (ver′ə·trīz) *v.t.* **·trized, ·triz·ing** To treat with veratrine so as to produce its toxic effects.

ve·ra·trum (və·rä′trəm) *n.* Hellebore (def. 2). [<L]

verb (vûrb) *n. Gram.* 1 One of a class of words which assert, declare, or predicate something; that part of speech which expresses existence, action, or occurrence, as the English words *be, collide, think.* 2 Any word or construction functioning similarly. [<F *verbe* <L *verbum* word. Akin to WORD.]

ver·bal (vûr′bəl) *adj.* 1 Of, pertaining to, or connected with words; concerned with words rather than the ideas they convey: *verbal* distinctions. 2 Uttered by the mouth; expressed in words orally; not written: a *verbal* communication; a *verbal* contract or agreement. 3 Having word corresponding with word; literal: a *verbal* translation. 4 *Gram.* **a** Partaking of the nature of or derived from a verb: a *verbal* noun. **b** Used to form verbs: a *verbal* prefix. — *n. Gram.* A noun directly derived from a verb, in English often having the form of the present participle, and signifying the act or process of what is expressed in the verb root; as, there shall be *weeping* and *wailing* and *gnashing* of teeth; also, an infinitive used as a noun; as, *to err* is human: also **verbal noun.** Compare GERUND. [<F <LL *verbalis* <L *verbum* word] — **ver′bal·ly** *adv.*

Synonyms (adj.): literal, oral, vocal. These words, whose etymology would make them similar in meaning, are differentiated in usage by their applications. *Oral* (L *os* the mouth) signifies uttered through the mouth or (in common phrase) by word of mouth; *vocal* (L *vox* the voice) signifies of or pertaining to the voice, uttered or modulated by the voice, and especially uttered with or sounding with full, resonant voice; *literal* (L *litera* a letter) signifies consisting of or expressed by letters, or according to the letter in the broader sense of the exact meaning or requirement of the words used; what is called "the letter of the law" is its *literal* meaning without going behind what is expressed by the letters on the page. Thus *oral* applies to that which is given by spoken words in distinction from that which is written or printed; as, *oral* tradition; an

oral examination. By this rule we should in strictness speak of an *oral* contract or an *oral* message, but *verbal* contract and *verbal* message, as indicating that which is spoken rather than by written word, have become fixed in the language. A *verbal* translation may be *oral* or written, so that it is word for word; a *literal* translation follows the construction and idiom of the original as well as the words; thus a *literal* translation is more than one that is merely *verbal;* both *verbal* and *literal* are opposed to *free.* In the same sense, of attending to words only, we speak of *verbal* criticism, a *verbal* change. *Vocal* has primary reference to the human voice; as, *vocal* sounds, *vocal* music; *vocal* may be applied within certain limits to inarticulate sounds given forth by other animals than man; as, The woods were *vocal* with the songs of birds; *oral* is never so applied.

ver·bal·ism (vûr′bəl·iz′əm) *n.* A verbal remark or expression; sometimes, a meaningless form of words; wordiness.

ver·bal·ist (vûr′bəl·ist) *n.* One who deals with words or is skilled in the use and meanings of words; a critic of words.

ver·bal·ize (vûr′bəl·īz) *v.* **·ized ·iz·ing** *v.t.* 1 *Gram.* To make a verb of; change into a verb. 2 To express in words. — *v.i.* 3 To speak or write verbosely. — **ver′bal·i·za′tion** *n.* — **ver′bal·iz′er** *n.*

ver·ba·tim (vər·bā′tim) *adv.* In the exact words; word for word. [<LL <L *verbum* word]

ver·ba·tim et lit·e·ra·tim (vər·bā′tim et lit′ə·rā′tim) *Latin* Word for word and letter for letter.

ver·be·na (vər·bē′nə) *n.* Any of a genus (*Verbena*) of American garden plants having dense terminal spikes of showy, often fragrant flowers. [<L, foliage, vervain. Doublet of VERVAIN.]

ver·be·na·ceous (vûr′bə·nā′shəs) *adj.* Belonging to a family (*Verbenaceae*) of herbs, shrubs, and trees, the verbena family, having opposite or whorled leaves and more or less two-lipped or irregular corollas. [<NL, family name <L *verbena* vervain]

ver·bi·age (vûr′bē·ij) *n.* Use of many words without necessity; wordiness; verbosity. See synonyms under CIRCUMLOCUTION, DICTION. [<F <*verbier* gabble <*verbe.* See VERB.]

verb·i·fy (vûr′bə·fī) *v.t.* **·fied, ·fy·ing** To form into or use as a verb.

ver·big·er·ate (vər·bij′ə·rāt) *v.i.* **·at·ed, ·at·ing** *Psychiatry* To repeat meaningless words, phrases, or sentences over and over, as in certain forms of schizophrenia. [<L *verbigerare* chatter, babble < *verbum* word + *gerere* carry on, conduct] — **ver·big′er·a′tion** *n.*

ver·bose (vər·bōs′) *adj.* Using or containing a wearisome and unnecessary number of words; wordy. See synonyms under GARRULOUS. [<L *verbosus* <*verbum* word] — **ver·bose′ly** *adv.* — **ver·bose′ness** *n.*

ver·bos·i·ty (vər·bos′ə·tē) *n.* *pl.* **·ties** The state or quality of being verbose; wordiness.

ver·bo·ten (fər·bōt′n) *adj. German* Forbidden; authoritatively prohibited.

ver·bum sat sa·pi·en·ti (vûr′bəm sat sā′pē·en′tī) *Latin* A word to the wise is sufficient: abbr. *verbum sap.*

Ver·cin·get·o·rix (vûr′sin·jet′ər·iks) Gallic chieftain, leader of rebellion against Julius Caesar, who put him to death in 45 B.C.

Ver·dan·di (vər·dän′dē) One of the Norns.

ver·dant (vûr′dənt) *adj.* 1 Green with vegetation; covered with grass or green leaves; fresh. 2 Immature in experience; unsophisticated. See synonyms under FRESH, RUSTIC. [<F *verdoyant,* ppr. of *verdoyer* grow green, ult. <L *viridis* green] — **ver′dan·cy** *n.* — **ver′·dant·ly** *adv.*

verd antique (vûrd) 1 A variety of serpentine. 2 Dark-green andesite porphyry containing crystals of feldspar: also **Oriental verd antique.** 3 A green coating that forms on ancient bronzes. [<OF *verd antique* ancient green]

Verde (vûrd), **Cape** The westernmost point of Africa, in Senegal, a peninsula about 20 miles long, up to 7 miles wide: also *Cape Vert.*

ver·der·er (vûr′dər·ər) *n.* An officer in charge of the royal forests in early England. Also **ver′der·or.** [<AF *verder,* OF *verdier* <Med. L *viridarius* <L *viridis* green]

Ver·di (ver′dē), **Giuseppe,** 1813–1901, Italian composer.

ver·dict (vûr′dikt) *n.* 1 The decision of a jury in an action. 2 A conclusion expressed; an opinion. [<AF *verdit,* OF *voirdit* <L *vere dictum* truly said < *verus* true + *dictum,* pp. of *dicere* say; later refashioned after L]

ver·di·gris (vûr′də·grēs, -gris) *n.* 1 *Chem.* A green basic acetate of copper obtained by treating copper with acetic acid: used as a pigment, for dyeing and calico printing, in medicine, and in the preparation of other copper pigments. 2 The green or bluish patina formed on copper, bronze, or brass surfaces after long exposure to the air. [<OF *verd de Grice, vert de Grece,* lit., green of Greece]

ver·din (vûr′din) *n.* A small, brightly-colored titmouse (*Auriparus flaviceps*) with a yellow head, of the southwestern United States and northern Mexico. [<F, yellowhammer]

ver·di·ter (vûr′də·tər) *n.* 1 A pigment made by grinding a basic copper carbonate; bice: azurite yields **blue verditer,** malachite yields **green verditer.** 2 Verdigris. [<OF *verd de terre,* lit., green of earth]

Ver·dun (vâr·dun′, *Fr.* ver·dœn′) A town on the Meuse in NE France; scene of heroic French resistance to German attack during several battles of World War I, 1916. Also **Verdun-sur-Meuse** (-sür-mœz′).

ver·dure (vûr′jər) *n.* 1 The fresh greenness of growing vegetation, or such vegetation itself. 2 A tapestry representing trees and other vegetation. [<F <*verd* green <L *viridis*] — **ver′dure·less** *adj.*

ver·dur·ous (vûr′jər·əs) *adj.* Covered with verdure; verdant. — **ver′dur·ous·ness** *n.*

ver·e·cund (ver′ə·kund) *adj. Rare* Modest; bashful; coy; shy. [<L *verecundus*]

Ve·ree·ni·ging (fə·rē′nə·khing) A city in the southern Transvaal, Republic of South Africa, on the Vaal: site of the signing of the treaty concluding the Boer War, 1902.

Ver·ein (fer·īn′) *n. German* A society; association: often compounded, as in *Turnverein.*

Ve·re·shcha·gin (vyi·ryish·chä′gin), **Vasili Vasilevich,** 1842–1904, Russian genre painter.

verge¹ (vûrj) *n.* 1 The extreme edge of something having defined limits; brink; margin. 2 A bounding or enclosing line; a circlet; ring; also, the space enclosed. 3 A stick or rod, or something having this shape; a wand or staff as a symbol of authority or emblem of office. 4 *Obs.* In England, a stick or wand which tenants held in the hand while swearing fealty to their lord. 5 The spindle of a balance wheel, especially in an old-fashioned vertical escapement. 6 *Archit.* **a** A column shaft. **b** The projecting edge of the tiling on a gable. 7 In old English law, the area over which the authority of an official extended. See synonyms under BOUNDARY, MARGIN. — *v.i.* **verged, verg·ing** 1 To be contiguous or adjacent. 2 To form the limit or verge. [<F, rod, stick <L *virga* twig]

verge² (vûrj) *v.i.* **verged, verg·ing** 1 To come near; approach; border: often with *on:* His speech *verges* on the chaotic. 2 To tend; slope; incline. [<L *vergere* bend, turn]

verg·er (vûr′jər) *n.* 1 An official who carries a verge before a scholastic, legal, or ecclesiastical dignitary; specifically, in English cathedrals and collegiate churches, one who carries the mace before the dean or canons. 2 *Brit.* One in charge of the interior of a cathedral or church; usher. 3 *Obs.* A master of ceremonies. [<F <*verge* rod]

Ver·gil (vûr′jil) Anglicized name of *Publius Vergilius Maro,* 70–19 B.C., Roman epic poet. Also spelled *Virgil.*

Ver·gil·i·an (vər·jil′ē·ən) *adj.* Pertaining to or in the style of Vergil: also spelled *Virgilian.*

ver·glas (vər·gläs′) *n. French* A thin, slippery coating of ice on rock: a mountaineering term.

ve·rid·i·cal (və·rid′i·kəl) *adj.* Telling or expressing the truth; truthful; accurate. Also **ve·rid′ic.** [<L *veridicus* speaking the truth < *verus* true + *dicere* say] — **ve·rid′i·cal′i·ty** (-kal′ə·tē) *n.* — **ve·rid′i·cal·ly** *adv.*

ver·i·fi·ca·tion (ver′ə·fə·kā′shən) *n.* 1 The act of verifying, or the state of being verified. 2 *Law* An oath appended to an account, petition, or plea, as to the truth of the facts stated in it; also, at common law, the formal statement at the end of a plea, "and this he is ready to verify."

ver·i·fi·ca·tive (ver′ə·fə·kā′tiv) *adj.* Aiding or resulting in verification.

ver·i·fy (ver′ə·fī) v.t. **·fied, ·fy·ing 1** To prove to be true or accurate; substantiate; confirm. **2** To test or ascertain the accuracy or truth of. **3** *Law* **a** To affirm under oath. **b** To add a confirmation to. [< OF *verifier* < Med. L *verificare* make true < *verus* true + *facere* make] —**ver′i·fi′a·ble** *adj.* —**ver′i·fi′er** *n.*

ver·i·ly (ver′ə·lē) *adv.* **1** In truth; assuredly; certainly. **2** Sincerely and truly; really; confidently. [< VERY]

ver·i·sim·i·lar (ver′ə·sim′ə·lər) *adj.* Appearing or seeming to be true; likely; probable. [< L *verisimilis* < *verus* true + *similis* like] —**ver′i·sim′i·lar·ly** *adv.*

ver·i·si·mil·i·tude (ver′ə·si·mil′ə·tōōd, -tyōōd) *n.* **1** Appearance of truth; likelihood. **2** That which resembles truth. See synonyms under PROBABILITY. [< L *verisimilitudo* < *verisimilis*. See VERISIMILAR.]

ver·ism (ver′iz·əm) *n.* A style in art and literature that follows the theory that reality should be rigidly represented, even when it is ugly or vulgar. [< L *verus* true] —**ver′ist** *n. & adj.* —**ve·ris·tic** (və·ris′tik) *adj.*

ver·i·ta·ble (ver′ə·tə·bəl) *adj.* Conforming to truth or fact; genuine; true; real. See synonyms under AUTHENTIC. [< F *vérité*. See VERITY.] —**ver′i·ta·ble·ness** *n.* —**ver′i·ta·bly** *adv.*

ver·i·tas (ver′ə·tas) *n. Latin* Truth.

ver·i·ty (ver′ə·tē) *n. pl.* **·ties 1** The quality of being correct or true as a statement or representation of reality. **2** A true statement; a fact; truth. See synonyms under VERACITY. [< F *vérité* < L *veritas* truth < *verus* true]

ver·juice (vûr′jōōs) *n.* **1** The sour juice of green fruit, as of unripe grapes. **2** Sharpness or sourness of disposition or manner; acidity. [< OF *verjus* < *vert* green + *jus* juice]

Ver·kho·yansk Range (vir·khō·yänsk′) A mountain system in northern Yakut Autonomous S.S.R. north of the Arctic Circle; highest point, 8,000 feet.

Ver·laine (ver·len′), **Paul**, 1844–96, French poet.

Ver·meer (vər·mâr′), **Jan**, 1632–75, Dutch painter.

ver·meil (vûr′mil) *n.* **1** Silver or bronze gilt. **2** A transparent water varnish. **3** An orange-red garnet. **4** *Poetic* Vermilion, or the color of vermilion. —*adj.* Of a bright-red color. [< L *vermiculus*, dim. of *vermis* worm, the cochineal insect]

vermi– *combining form* A worm; of or related to a worm, or to worms: *vermiform.* [< L *vermis* a worm]

ver·mi·cel·li (vûr′mə·sel′ē, *Ital.* ver′mē·chel′lē) *n.* A food paste made into slender wormlike cords thinner than spaghetti or macaroni. [< Ital., lit., little worms, pl. of *vermicello* < L *vermiculus*. See VERMEIL.]

ver·mi·ci·dal (vûr′mə·sīd′l) *adj.* Destructive of intestinal worms; anthelmintic.

ver·mi·cide (vûr′mə·sīd) *n.* Any substance that kills worms; specifically, any medicine or drug destructive of intestinal worms. [< VERMI– + -CIDE]

ver·mic·u·lar (vər·mik′yə·lər) *adj.* **1** Pertaining to a worm; having the form or motion of a worm. **2** Like the tracks of a worm. [< L *vermicularis* < *vermiculus*, dim. of *vermis* worm] —**ver·mic′u·lar·ly** *adv.*

vermicular work 1 A form of rusticated masonry simulating worm tracks. **2** Ornamental work consisting of winding tracks in mosaic work. Also **vermiculated work.**

ver·mic·u·late (vər·mik′yə·lāt) *v.t.* **·lat·ed, ·lat·ing 1** To adorn with tracery simulating the tracks of worms. **2** To make worm-eaten; infest with worms. —*adj.* **1** Wormlike or covered with wormlike markings. **2** Having the motions of a worm; insinuating; wavy. **3** Worm-eaten. [< L *vermiculatus*, pp. of *vermiculate* be worm-eaten < *vermiculus*, dim. of *vermis* a worm]

VERMICULAR WORK

ver·mic·u·la·tion (vər·mik′yə·lā′shən) *n.* **1** Wormlike motion, as of the intestines. **2** Vermicular ornamentation. **3** The state of being wormy. **4** A track left by worms. **5** A fine wavy color marking, as on a bird.

ver·mic·u·lite (vər·mik′yə·līt) *n.* A laminated hydrous silicate, derived chiefly as an alteration product of biotite, phlogopite, and other micaceous minerals. [< L *vermiculus*, dim. of *vermis* worm + -ITE[1]]

ver·mic·u·lose (vər·mik′yə·lōs) *adj.* **1** Worm-eaten; wormy. **2** Worm-shaped; wormlike. Also **ver·mic′u·lous** (-ləs). [< LL *vermiculosus* < L *vermiculus*, dim. of *vermis* worm]

ver·mi·form (vûr′mə·fôrm) *adj.* Like a worm in shape. [< Med. L *vermiformis* < L *vermis* a worm + *forma* a form]

vermiform appendix *Anat.* A slender, wormlike diverticulum, 3 to 6 inches long, protruding from the end of the cecum in man and certain other mammals.

vermiform process *Anat.* **1** Either surface of the median lobe of the cerebellum. **2** The vermiform appendix.

ver·mi·fuge (vûr′mə·fyōōj) *n.* Any remedy that destroys intestinal worms. —*adj.* Anthelmintic. [< F *vermis* a worm + *fugare* expel]

ver·mil·ion (vər·mil′yən) *n.* **1** A brilliant, durable red pigment consisting of mercuric sulfide, obtained native by grinding the mineral cinnabar to a fine powder, or artificially, as by treating a mixture of mercury and sulfur with potassium hydroxide. **2** The color of the pigment, an intense orange red. —*adj.* Of a bright-red color. —*v.t.* To color with vermilion; dye bright red. [< OF *vermeilon, vermillon* < *vermeil* VERMEIL]

ver·min (vûr′min) *n. pl.* **·min 1** Noxious small animals or parasitic insects, as lice, fleas, worms, rats, mice, etc. **2** *Brit.* Certain animals injurious to game, as weasels, owls, etc. **3** A repulsive or noxious human being, or such persons collectively. [< OF < L *vermis* a worm]

ver·mi·nate (vûr′mə·nāt) *v.i.* **·nat·ed, ·nat·ing** To produce or breed vermin, especially parasitic vermin. —**ver′mi·na′tion** *n.*

ver·mi·nous (vûr′mə·nəs) *adj.* **1** Infested with vermin. **2** Affected with intestinal worms, or caused, as a disease, by vermin. **3** Of the nature of vermin.

Ver·mont (vər·mont′) A State in NE United States; 9,609 square miles; capital, Montpelier; entered the Union March 4, 1791; nickname, *Green Mountain State*: abbr. VT —**Ver·mont′er** *n.*

ver·mou·lu (ver·mōō·lü′) *adj. French* Worm-eaten.

ver·mouth (vûr′mōōth, vər·mōōth′) *n.* A liqueur made from white wine flavored with aromatic herbs. Also **ver′muth.** [< F *vermout* < G *wermuth* wormwood]

ver·nac·u·lar (vər·nak′yə·lər) *n.* **1** The native language of a locality. **2** The common daily speech of the people, as opposed to the literary language. **3** The vocabulary or jargon of a particular profession or trade: to speak the medical *vernacular.* **4** An idiomatic word or phrase. **5** The common name of a plant or animal as distinguished from its scientific designation. See synonyms under LANGUAGE. —*adj.* **1** Originating in or belonging to one's native land; indigenous: said of a language, idiom, etc. **2** Using the colloquial native tongue, rather than the literary language: *vernacular poets.* **3** Written in the language indigenous to a country or people: a *vernacular* translation of the Bible. **4** Characteristic of a specific locality or country; local: *vernacular* arts. **5** *Rare* Peculiar to a particular region; endemic: a *vernacular* disease. **6** Designating the common name of a plant or animal. [< L *vernaculus* domestic, native < *verna* a home-born slave, a native] —**ver·nac′u·lar·ly** *adv.*

ver·nac·u·lar·ism (vər·nak′yə·lə·riz′əm) *n.* **1** A vernacular term or idiom. **2** The use of the vernacular as opposed to classic or literary language.

ver·nal (vûr′nəl) *adj.* **1** Belonging to, appearing in, or appropriate to spring. **2** Pertaining to youth; having a springlike freshness. [< L *vernalis* < *vernus* belonging to spring < *ver* spring] —**ver′nal·ly** *adv.*

vernal equinox See under EQUINOX.

ver·nal·ize (vûr′nəl·īz) *v.t.* **·ized, ·iz·ing** To accelerate the growth of (a plant) by subjecting the seeds to artificial treatment, as by moistening at a low temperature. —**ver′nal·i·za′tion** *n.*

vernal point The vernal equinox. See under EQUINOX.

ver·na·tion (vər·nā′shən) *n. Bot.* The disposition of leaves within the leaf bud, as regards their folding, coiling, etc. [< NL *vernatio, -onis* < *vernare* flourish < *ver* spring]

Verne (vûrn, *Fr.* vern), **Jules**, 1828–1905, French writer of science fiction.

Ver·ner (vér′nər), **Karl Adolph**, 1846–96, Danish philologist.

Verner's Law A law regarding certain consonant changes in Germanic languages, set forth by Karl Verner in 1876, stating that certain exceptions to Grimm's Law are due to a still wider law, namely, the position of the primary accent in the parent language. It shows that original Indo-European voiceless plosives *p, t, k,* which, according to Grimm's Law became in Germanic the voiceless fricatives *f, th* (as in *thin*), *h,* became, instead, except in specific combinations, the corresponding voiced fricatives and, ultimately, the voiced plosives, *b, d, g,* if the original Indo-European tonic stress was not on the immediately preceding syllable. This statement can be illustrated in English by the distinction in final consonant between *death* and *dead.* The same process operated for the Indo-European *s,* which became *z,* and finally *r,* as can be seen in English *was* and *were, raise* and *rear.*

ver·ni·cose (vûr′nə·kōs) *adj. Bot.* Appearing as if varnished, as some leaves. [< NL *vernicosus* < Med. L *vernicium* VARNISH]

ver·ni·er (vûr′nē·ər) *n.* **1** The small, movable, auxiliary scale for obtaining fractional parts of the subdivisions of a fixed scale on a theodolite, barometer, sextant, gage, or other measuring instrument. **2** *Mech.* An auxiliary device to insure fine adjustments in precision instruments. [after Pierre *Vernier*]

Ver·nier (ver·nyä′), **Pierre**, 1580?–1637, French mathematician.

ver·nis·sage (ver′nē·sázh′) *n.* The opening day of an exhibition of oil paintings to which critics are often invited: also called *varnishing day.* [< F < *vernir* varnish; because the painters varnish their works on this day]

Ver·no·le·ninsk (vyer′nə·lyä′nyinsk) A former name for NIKOLAEV.

Ver·non (vûr′nən), **Edward**, 1684–1757, English admiral.

Ver·nyi (vyer′nē) A former name for ALMA-ATA.

Ve·ro·na (və·rō′nə, *Ital.* vā·rō′nä) A city in Veneto, NE Italy. —**Ver·o·nese** (ver′ə·nēz′, -nēs′) *adj. & n.*

Ver·o·nal (ver′ə·nəl) *n.* Proprietary name for a brand of barbital.

Ve·ro·ne·se (vā′rō·nā′zā), **Paolo**, 1528–88, Venetian painter; real name *Cagliari.*

ve·ron·i·ca[1] (və·ron′i·kə) *n.* The speedwell. [< Med. L, appar. after St. *Veronica*]

ve·ron·i·ca[2] (və·ron′i·kə) *n.* A cloth said to have been miraculously impressed with the face of Christ on his way to Calvary, handed to him by a woman named Veronica to wipe the perspiration from his face; also, the representation of the face on this handkerchief; hence, a cloth or handkerchief having on it a representation of Christ's face. See SUDARIUM. [< Med. L < LL *veraiconica,* prob. < L *verus* true + Gk. *eikōn* an image, likeness]

ve·ron·i·ca[3] (və·ron′i·kə, *Sp.* bā·rō′nē·kä) *n.* In bullfighting, a maneuver in which the torero faces the bull and holds the cape directly in front of himself. [< Sp.]

Ve·ron·i·ca (və·ron′i·kə, *Ital.* vä·rō·nē′kä) A feminine personal name. Also *Fr.* **Vé·ro·nique** (vā·rō·nēk′). [See VERONICA[2]]

—**Veronica, Saint** A legendary follower of Christ, upon whose handkerchief a picture of Christ's features is said to have appeared.

Ver·ra·za·no (ver′rä·tsä′nō), **Giovanni da**, 1480?–1528?, Italian navigator.

Ver·roc·chio (ver·rōk′kyō), **Andrea del**, 1435–88, Florentine sculptor and painter.

ver·ru·ca (ve·rōō′kə) *n. pl.* **·cae** (-sē) **1** *Med.*

A wart. 2 *Biol.* A wart or wartlike elevation on animals or plants. [<L, a wart, orig. a steep place]

ver·ru·ca·no (ver'ə·kā'nō) *n.* A hard conglomerate of quartz cemented by various siliceous materials, usually colored. [<Ital., from Mount *Verruca* near Pisa]

ver·ru·cose (ver'ə·kōs) *adj.* Abounding in wartlike elevations; warty. Also **ver'ru·cous** (-kəs). [<L *verrucosus* < *verruca* a wart] — **ver'ru·cos'i·ty** (-kos'ə·tē) *n.*

Ver·sailles (vər·sī', -sālz'; *Fr.* ver·sä'y') A city of north central France, 11 miles SW of Paris; site of the palace of Louis XIV; scene of the signing of a treaty (1919) between the Allies and Germany after World War I.

ver·sant (vûr'sənt) *n. Geog.* 1 An entire area having a general slope in one direction. 2 The general aspect or slope of any portion of country; inclination. [<F, ppr. of *verser* overturn, pour <L *versare,* freq. of *vertere* turn]

ver·sa·tile (vûr'sə·til) *adj.* 1 Having an aptitude for new tasks or occupations; many-sided. 2 Subject to change; inconstant; variable. 3 Freely swinging or turning: said of an anther part so slightly attached to its support that it readily swings to and fro. 4 Capable of being turned forward or backward, as the toe of a bird; movable in every direction, as insect antennae. [<F <L *versatilis* < *versare,* freq. of *vertere* turn] — **ver'sa·tile·ly** *adv.* — **ver'sa·til'i·ty, ver'sa·tile·ness** *n.*

vers de so·ci·é·té (ver' də sō·syä·tā') *French* A form of light verse characterized by grace, elegance, and wit.

verse (vûrs) *n.* 1 A single metrical or rhythmical line made up of a number of feet, arranged according to a specific rule. 2 A group of metrical lines; a stanza. 3 Metrical composition as distinguished from prose; poetry. 4 **a** Composition in meter; versification. **b** A specified type of metrical composition; type of meter or metrical structure: iambic *verse.* 5 One of the short divisions of a chapter of the Bible; also, a short division of any composition. 6 The solo part of a song, anthem, or other piece. See synonyms under METER[2], POETRY. — *v.t.* & *v.i.* **versed, vers·ing** *Rare* To versify. [Fusion of OE *fers* and OF *vers,* both <L *versus* a turning, a verse < *vertere* turn]

versed (vûrst) *adj.* 1 Thoroughly acquainted; having ready skill; proficient. 2 Turned about; reversed. [<L *versatus,* pp. of *versari* occupy oneself]

versed sine, ver·sine (vûr'sīn) See under SINE[1]. [<NL *sinus versus* < *sinus* a sine + L *versus,* pp. of *vertere* turn]

verse·mon·ger (vûrs'mung'gər, -mong'-) *n.* A writer of inferior verses; poetaster.

ver·si·cle (vûr'si·kəl) *n.* 1 A little verse. 2 One of a series of lines said or sung alternately by minister and people. [<L *versiculus,* dim. of *versus* VERSE]

ver·si·col·or (vûr'si·kul'ər) *adj.* 1 Showing a variety of colors; variegated. 2 Changing from one color to another in different lights; iridescent. Also *Brit.* **ver'si·col'our.** [<L *versus,* pp. of *vertere* turn + *color* color]

ver·sic·u·lar (vər·sik'yə·lər) *adj.* Relating to verses, especially Biblical verses; marking the division into verses. [<L *versiculus* VERSICLE]

ver·sie·ra (ver·syä'rä) *n. Math.* The witch of Agnesi. See WITCH OF AGNESI. [<Ital., a ghost, hobgoblin]

ver·si·fy (vûr'sə·fī) *v.* **·fied, ·fy·ing** *v.t.* 1 To change from prose into verse. 2 To narrate or treat in verse. — *v.i.* 3 To write poetry; make verses. [<OF *versifier, versifier* <L *versificare* < *versus* VERSE + *facere* make] — **ver'si·fi·ca'tion** (-fə·kā'shən) *n.* — **ver'si·fi'er** *n.*

ver·sion (vûr'zhən, -shən) *n.* 1 That which is translated or rendered from one language into another; a translation; a translation of the original Hebrew and Greek of the Old and New Testaments, or any part of them, into some other tongue. 2 A description of something as modified by the relator. 3 *Med.* **a** The manual turning of a fetus in the womb so as to secure proper delivery. **b** Displacement of the uterus in which the organ is deflected without bending upon itself. 4 *Obs.* A transformation; conversion. [<MF <Med.L *versio, -onis* a turning <L *vertere* turn] — **ver'sion·al** *adj.*

vers li·bre (ver lē'br') *French* Free verse.

ver·so (vûr'sō) *n. pl.* **·sos** 1 A left-hand page of a book, piece of music, or sheet of folded paper: also called *reverso.* Compare RECTO. 2 The reverse of a coin or medal. Compare OBVERSE. [<L *verso (folio)* a turned (leaf), ablative neut. sing. pp. of *vertere* turn]

verst (vûrst) *n.* A Russian measure of distance: about two thirds of a mile, or 1.067 kilometers. [<F *verste* and G *werst* <Russian *versta,* orig. a line]

ver·sus (vûr'səs) *prep.* 1 Against: used in naming or entitling actions in courts: plaintiff *versus* defendant; in contests: Dempsey *versus* Tunney: usually contracted to *v.* or *vs.* 2 Considered as the alternative of: free trade *versus* high tariffs. [<L, toward, turned toward, orig. pp. of *vertere* turn]

vert (vûrt) *n.* 1 In English forest law, anything that grows and bears green leaves within a forest, especially thick coverts; also, the right to cut green or growing wood in a forest. 2 *Her.* The color or tincture green. [<MF *vert, verd* <L *viridis* green]

Vert (ver), **Cape** See VERDE, CAPE.

ver·te·bra (vûr'tə·brə) *n. pl.* **·brae** (-brē) or **·bras** *Anat.* One of the segmented bones of the spinal column. In man and the higher vertebrates, each vertebra, with its semicylindrical central body and attached processes, articulates with those on either side by means of elastic fibrous pads. [<L, a joint, a vertebra < *vertere* turn]

HUMAN VERTEBRAE

A. Sixth thoracic vertebra.

B. Third lumbar vertebra.

a. Spinous process.   *f.* Pedicle.
b. Lamina.   *g.* Vertebral foramen.
c. Inferior articular process.   *h.* Body.
d. Transverse process.   *i.* Facet for rib.
e. Superior articular process.   *j.* Demi-facet for rib.

ver·te·bral (vûr'tə·brəl) *adj.* 1 Pertaining to or of the nature of a vertebra. 2 Having, or composed of, vertebrae.

vertebral column The spinal column; the backbone.

ver·te·brate (vûr'tə·brāt, -brit) *adj.* 1 Having a backbone or spinal column. 2 Pertaining to or characteristic of vertebrates. 3 Vertebral. — *n.* Any of a primary division or subphylum (*Vertebrata*) of animals, of the phylum *Chordata,* characterized by a spinal column, as fishes, birds, mammals, and a few primitive forms in which a notochord represents the backbone. [<L *vertebratus* jointed < *vertebra* VERTEBRA]

ver·te·bra·tion (vûr'tə·brā'shən) *n.* 1 The formation of vertebrae. 2 Segmentation like that of the spinal column.

ver·tex (vûr'teks) *n. pl.* **·tex·es** or **·ti·ces** (-tə·sēz) 1 The highest point or summit of anything; apex; top. 2 *Astron.* **a** The zenith. **b** The point in the sky toward or from which a group of stars appears to be moving. 3 The top of the head; also, in craniometry, the top of the arch of the skull. 4 *Math.* **a** The point of intersection of the sides of an angle. **b** The point opposite to, and farthest from, the base. **c** The intersection of three or more edges of a polyhedron. [<L, the top < *vertere* turn]

ver·ti·cal (vûr'ti·kəl) *adj.* 1 Of or pertaining to the vertex. 2 Occupying a position directly above or overhead; being at the highest point. 3 Directed perpendicularly to the plane of the horizon; upright; plumb. 4 Of or pertaining to the crown of the head. 5 *Bot.* **a** Perpendicular to the surface or to the axis of support. **b** In the direction of the axis of growth; lengthwise. 6 *Econ.* Of or pertaining to a business concern that undertakes a process from raw material to consumer: a *vertical* trust. — *n.* 1 A vertical line, plane, or circle. 2 An upright beam or rod in a truss. [<MF <L *verticalis* < *vertex, -icis* VERTEX] — **ver'ti·cal'i·ty** (-kal'ə·tē), **ver'ti·cal·ness** *n.* — **ver'ti·cal·ly** *adv.*

vertical circle *Astron.* A great circle perpendicular to the plane of the horizon.

ver·ti·ces (vûr'tə·sēz) Plural of VERTEX.

ver·ti·cil (vûr'tə·sil) *n. Biol.* A set of organs, as leaves or tentacles, disposed in a circle around an axis; whorl; a volution of a spiral shell. [<L *verticillus* a whorl, dim. of *vertex, -icis* VERTEX]

ver·ti·cil·las·ter (vûr'tə·si·las'tər) *n. Bot.* An inflorescence or flower cluster with the flowers seemingly in a whorl, but composed of a pair of dense sessile cymes in the axils of opposite leaves, as in most mints. [<NL <L *verticillus* VERTICIL + -ASTER]

ver·tic·il·late (vər·tis'ə·lit, -lāt, vûr'tə·sil'it, -āt) *adj.* 1 Arranged in a verticil or whorl. 2 Having parts so arranged; whorled. Also **ver·tic'il·lat'ed.** [<NL *verticillatus* <L *verticillus* VERTICIL] — **ver·tic'il·late·ly** *adv.*

ver·tic·i·ty (vər·tis'ə·tē) *n.* Tendency to move toward the north, as manifested by a magnetic needle. [<NL *verticitas, -tatis* <L *vertex, -icis* VERTEX]

ver·tig·i·nous (vər·tij'ə·nəs) *adj.* 1 Affected by vertigo; dizzy. 2 Turning round; whirling; revolving. 3 Liable to cause giddiness. [<L *vertiginosus* < *vertigo, -inis* VERTIGO] — **ver·tig'i·nous·ly** *adv.* — **ver·tig'i·nous·ness** *n.*

ver·ti·go (vûr'tə·gō) *n. pl.* **·goes** or **ver·tig·i·nes** (vər·tij'ə·nēz) *Pathol.* Any of a group of disorders, variously caused, in which a person feels as if he or his surroundings are whirling around; dizziness. [<L, lit., a turning around < *vertere* turn]

Ver·tum·nus (vər·tum'nəs) In Roman mythology, the god of the changing seasons and growing plants; husband of Pomona: also *Vortumnus.*

Ver·u·la·mi·um (ver'yŏŏ·lā'mē·əm) The ancient Roman name for ST. ALBANS.

Ve·rus (vir'əs), **Lucius Aurelius,** 130–169, Roman emperor 161–169.

ver·vain (vûr'vān) *n.* Any of various plants (genus *Verbena*), congeners of the common cultivated ornamental verbenas, as the American blue vervain (*V. hastata*), or the common European vervain (*V. officinalis*). [<OF *verveine* <L *verbena.* Doublet of VERBENA.]

verve (vûrv) *n.* 1 Enthusiasm or energy, especially as manifested in artistic production; hence, spirit; vigor. 2 *Rare* Special bent or talent. [<F, prob. <L *verba,* pl. of *verbum* a word]

ver·vet (vûr'vit) *n.* A South African monkey (genus *Cercopithecus*), grayish-green speckled with black, and with reddish-white cheeks and belly. [<F <*ver(t)* green (<L *viridis*) + (*gri*)*vet* a grivet; so called because of its color]

ver·y (ver'ē) *adv.* 1 In a high degree; in large measure; extremely: *very* generous. 2 Exactly: the *very* same thought. ◆ Some grammarians feel that *very* may properly be used before a participle only when the latter precedes the noun it modifies, as in *a very agitated speech;* when the participle is used after some form of the verb *to be,* another adverb is interposed, as in *He was very much* (or *greatly*) *agitated.* However, the construction without the adverb is now widely accepted with participles of emotion or feeling, and is often found, as well, with some participles describing physical condition, as in *They were very disturbed; His face is very changed in aspect.* — *adj.* **ver·i·er, ver·i·est** 1 Absolute; actual; simple; utter: said of truth. 2 Suitable; right: the *very* tool we need. 3 Unqualified; utter; complete: a *very* rogue. 4 Selfsame; identical: my *very* words. 5 The (thing) itself: used as an intensive equivalent to *even:* The *very* stones cry out. 6 *Obs.* True: *very* God; also, truthful; veracious. [<AF *verrai,* OF *verai* <L *verus* true]

very high frequency Any wave frequency from 30 to 300 megahertz. Abbr. *vhf, VHF.*

Ver·y light (ver'ē, vir'ē) A brilliant signal flare discharged from a special type of pistol, the **Very pistol.** [after E. W. *Very,* 1847–1910, U.S. naval officer and inventor]

Ve·sa·li·us (vi·sā'lē·əs), **Andreas,** 1514–64, Belgian physician; founder of modern anatomy.

ves·i·ca (vi·sī'kə) *n. pl.* **·cae** (-sē) A bladder. [<L]

ves·i·cal (ves'i·kəl) *adj.* Of, pertaining to, supplying, or affecting the bladder.

ves·i·cant (ves'i·kənt) *adj.* Blister-producing. — *n.* 1 That which produces blisters; a blister. **2** A chemical warfare agent which attacks the skin, as mustard gas or lewisite: also called *blister gas*. [<NL *vesicans, -antis,* ppr. of *vesicare* raise blisters <L *vesica* a blister, bladder]

ve·si·ca pis·cis (vi·sī′kə pis′kis, pīsis) The pointed oval aureole used by medieval sculptors and painters to enclose the figure of Christ, the Virgin Mary, or an apostle.

ves·i·cate (ves′i·kāt) *v.* **·cat·ed, ·cat·ing** *v.t.* To raise blisters on. — *v.i.* To become blistered; blister, as the skin. [<NL *vesicatus,* pp. of *vesicare.* See VESICANT.]

ves·i·ca·to·ry (ves′i·kə·tôr′ē, və·sik′ə·tôr·ē, -tō′rē) *adj.* Capable of producing blisters; vesicant. — *n. pl.* **·ries** Any substance, as an ointment or plaster, that causes a blister.

ves·i·cle (ves′i·kəl) *n.* **1** Any small bladderlike cavity, cell, or cyst. **2** A small sac, containing gas or fluid. **3** *Pathol.* Any small rounded elevation of the cuticle containing a clear liquid; a blister. **4** *Bot.* A small bladderlike cavity filled with air. **5** *Geol.* A small spherical cavity found commonly in volcanic rocks. [<L *vesicula,* dim. of *vesica* a bladder]

vesico- *combining form Med.* The urinary bladder; of or pertaining to the urinary bladder: *vesicotomy,* a cutting into the bladder. Also, before vowels, **vesic-.** [<L *vesica* a bladder]

ve·sic·u·la (və·sik′yə·lə) *n. pl.* **·lae** (-lē) A little bladder; vesicle. [<L, VESICLE]

ve·sic·u·lar (və·sik′yə·lər) *adj.* **1** Of, pertaining to, composed of, or resembling vesicles. **2** Bearing or containing vesicles or air bladders. [<L *vesicula* VESICLE] — **ve·sic′u·lar·ly** *adv.*

ve·sic·u·late (və·sik′yə·lāt) *v.t.* & *v.i.* **·lat·ed, ·lat·ing** To make or become vesicular or vesiculate. — *adj.* (-lit, -lāt) Full of or having vesicles; also, vesicular. [Back formation < *vesiculated* <NL *vesiculatus* <L *vesicula* VESICLE] — **ve·sic′u·la′tion** *n.*

Vesle (vel) A river in NE France, flowing 90 miles NW from the badlands of Champagne, NE of Châlons-sur-Marne, through Reims to the Aisne east of Soissons.

Ve·son·ti·o (və·son′shē·ō) The ancient name for BESANÇON.

Ve·soul (və·zōōl′) A city in eastern France, capital of Haute-Saône department.

Ves·pa·sian (ves·pā′zhən) Anglicized name of *Titus Flavius Vespasianus,* A.D. 9–79, Roman emperor 69–79.

ves·per (ves′pər) *n.* **1** A bell that calls to vespers: also **vesper bell. 2** An evening service, prayer, or song. **3** *Obs.* Evening. — *adj.* Pertaining to or suitable for evening or vespers. [<L, the evening star]

Ves·per (ves′pər) The evening star; Hesperus; the planet Venus when an evening star. [<L]

ves·per·al (ves′pər·əl) *adj.* Pertaining to evening or the service of vespers. — *n.* **1** A book of the music and office of vespers. **2** A cover for an altar cloth.

ves·pers (ves′pərz) *n. pl. Often cap.* **1** *Eccl.* The sixth in order of the canonical hours. **2** *Eccl.* A service of worship in the late afternoon or evening; specifically, in the Anglican church, Evening Prayer; in the Roman Catholic Church, a public service on Sundays or holy days at which the office of vespers is said or sung. **3** The hour of vespers, usually about sunset. [<OF *vespres* <Med. L *vesperae* <L *vespera* evening]

vesper sparrow An American sparrow (*Pooecetes gramineus*) distinguished by the partial whiteness of its outer tail feathers: so called from its evening song.

ves·per·til·i·o·nine (ves′pər·til′ē·ə·nīn′, -nin) *adj.* Belonging to a family (*Vespertilionidae*) of insectivorous bats. [<L *vespertilio, -onis* a bat + -INE[1]] — **ves′per·til′i·o·nid** *adj.* & *n.*

ves·per·tine (ves′pər·tin, -tīn) *adj.* **1** Pertaining to or occurring in the evening. **2** Flying, opening, etc., in the evening, as a bat, flower, etc. **3** Descending toward the horizon at the sunset hour. Also **ves′per·ti′nal** (-tī′nəl). [<L *vespertinus* < *vesper* VESPER]

ves·pi·ar·y (ves′pē·er′ē) *n. pl.* **·ar·ies** A nest of social wasps or its colony. [<L *vespa* a wasp + (AP)IARY]

ves·pid (ves′pid) *n.* Any of a large family (*Ves-*

pidae) of hymenopterous insects, including social wasps and hornets. — *adj.* Of or pertaining to the *Vespidae.* [<NL <L *vespa* a wasp] — **ves′pi·form** (-pə·fôrm) *adj.*

ves·pine (ves′pīn, -pin) *adj.* Of or pertaining to wasps. [<L *vespa* a wasp + -INE[1]]

Ves·puc·ci (ves·pōōt′chē), **Amerigo,** 1451–1512, Italian navigator for whom America was named.

ves·sel (ves′əl) *n.* **1** A hollow receptacle of any form or material, especially one capable of holding a liquid. **2** A ship or craft designed to float on the water: usually one larger than a rowboat; also, an airship. **3** *Biol.* A duct or canal for containing or transporting a body fluid, as an artery, vein, etc. **4** *Bot.* A water-conducting tube in plants. **5** Figuratively, a person viewed as having capacity or fitness to receive or contain something; one who receives: chiefly in religious use: a *vessel* of mercy or of wrath. [<OF <L *vascellum,* dim. of *vas* a vessel]

vest (vest) *n.* **1** A short sleeveless jacket worn by men and sometimes by women under the coat; waistcoat; originally, a kind of cassock: in England chiefly a trade term. **2** A close jacket formerly worn by women; now, an extra piece of trimming on the front of the body or waist of a woman's dress, usually V-shaped. **3** An undervest or undershirt. **4** Clothing of any kind; vesture; array; dress. **5** *Obs.* An ecclesiastical vestment. — *v.t.* **1** To confer (ownership, authority, etc.) upon some person or persons: usually with *in.* **2** To place ownership, control, or authority with (a person or persons). **3** To clothe or robe, as with vestments. — *v.i.* **4** To clothe oneself, as in vestments. **5** To be or become vested; devolve. [<F *veste* <Ital. <L *vestis* clothing, a garment]

ves·ta (ves′tə) *n.* A friction match of wax; a short wax taper; a wooden match. [after *Vesta*]

Ves·ta (ves′tə) **1** In Roman mythology, the goddess of the hearth and the hearth fire, protectress of the state and custodian of the sacred fire tended by the vestals: identified with the Greek *Hestia.* **2** A minor planet.

ves·tal (ves′təl) *n.* **1** One of the virgin priestesses of Vesta: also **vestal virgin. 2** A woman of pure character; a virgin; nun. — *adj.* **1** Pertaining to Vesta. **2** Suitable for a vestal or a nun; hence; chaste. [<L *vestalis* <*Vesta* Vesta]

vest·ed (ves′tid) *adj.* **1** Having vestments; robed. **2** *Law* Held by a tenure subject to no contingency; complete; established by law as a permanent right: *vested* interests.

vest·ee (ves·tē′) *n.* **1** An imitation blousefront worn in the front of a suit or dress. **2** A broadcloth garment without sleeves worn with a formal riding habit. [Dim. of VEST]

Ves·ter·å·len (ves′tər·ô′lən) A Norwegian archipelago in the Norwegian Sea north of the Lofoten Islands; total, about 1,200 square miles. Also **Ves′ter·aa′len.**

ves·ti·ar·y (ves′tē·er′ē) *adj.* Pertaining to clothes. — *n. pl.* **·ar·ies** *Obs.* A vestry; robing-room. [<OF *vestiairie* <Med. L *vestiarium.* See VESTRY.]

ves·tib·u·lar (ves·tib′yə·lər) *adj.* Pertaining to or like a vestibule. Also **ves·tib′u·late** (-lit, -lāt).

ves·ti·bule (ves′tə·byōōl) *n.* **1** A small antechamber between the outer door of a building and an interior one; an entrance hall; lobby. **2** An enclosed passage from one railway passenger car to another. **3** Formerly, a walled place before the entrance to a Roman or Greek house; later, a porch. **4** *Anat.* Any one of several chambers or channels adjoining or communicating with others: the *vestibule* of the ear. — *v.t.* **·buled, ·bul·ing 1** To provide with a vestibule or vestibules. **2** To couple (railroad cars) and connect by vestibules. [<L *vestibulum* an entrance hall] — **ves′ti·buled** *adj.*

vestibule train A passenger train with enclosed platforms connected by flexible walls and roof, forming a weatherproof passageway between connected cars, called **vestibule cars.**

ves·tige (ves′tij) *n.* **1** A visible trace, impression, or a sensible evidence or sign, of something absent, lost, or gone; trace; originally, a footprint; track. **2** *Biol.* A part or organ,

small or degenerate, but well developed and functional in ancestral forms of organisms. See synonyms under MARK[1], TRACE[1]. [<F <L *vestigium* a footprint]

ves·tig·i·al (ves·tij′ē·əl) *adj.* Of, or of the nature of a vestige; surviving in small or degenerate form. — **ves·tig′i·al·ly** *adv.*

ves·tig·i·um (ves·tij′ē·əm) *n. pl.* **·tig·i·a** (-tij′ē·ə) A vestigial part; vestige. [<L, a footprint]

vest·ment (vest′mənt) *n.* **1** An article of dress; clothing or covering; particularly, a garment or robe of state or office. **2** *Eccl.* **a** One of the ritual garments of the clergy, especially one worn at the Eucharist. **b** A chasuble. See synonyms under DRESS. [<OF *vestement* <L *vestimentum* clothes <*vestire* clothe] — **vest′ment·al** *adj.*

vest–pock·et (vest′pok′it) *adj.* **1** Small enough to fit in a vest pocket; very small; diminutive: a *vest-pocket* edition. **2** Much smaller than standard or usual size: a *vest-pocket* battleship.

vest–pock·et park A small urban park, often on a vacant lot.

ves·try (ves′trē) *n. pl.* **·tries 1** A room where vestments are put on or kept. **2** A room for altar linens, sacred vessels, etc., attached to a church and often called a *sacristy.* **3** A room in a church used for Sunday school, meetings, as a chapel, etc. **4** In the Anglican church: **a** A body administering the affairs of a parish or congregation; also, a meeting of such a body. **b** In English parishes, a business meeting of all the parishioners or their representatives. **5** A place of meeting for the parish vestry; a vestry hall. [<AF *vestrie,* OF *vestiarie* <Med. L *vestiarium* a wardrobe <L *vestis* a garment]

ves·try·man (ves′trē·mən) *n. pl.* **·men** (-mən) A member of a vestry.

ves·ture (ves′chər) *n.* **1** Something that covers; garments; clothing; a robe. **2** *Law* All that covers land, except trees. **3** A covering or envelope. See synonyms under DRESS. — *v.t.* **·tured, ·tur·ing** To cover or clothe with vesture; vest; robe; envelop: usually in the past participle. [<OF *vestir* cloth <L *vestire* clothe]

ve·su·vi·an (və·sōō′vē·ən) *n.* **1** Vesuvianite. **2** A kind of match or fusee which burns with a spluttering flame: used for lighting cigars, etc. [from *Vesuvius*]

ve·su·vi·an·ite (və·sōō′vē·ən·īt′) *n.* A vitreous, brown to green, translucent hydrous silicate of calcium and aluminum, with traces of iron and magnesium: also called *idocrase.*

Ve·su·vi·us (və·sōō′vē·əs) The only active volcano on the European mainland; on the Bay of Naples, Italy; 3,891 feet. *Italian* **Ve·su·vio** (vā·zōō′vyō). — **Ve·su′vi·an** *adj.*

vet (vet) *Colloq. n.* A veterinary surgeon. — *v.* **vet·ted, vet·ting** *v.t.* **1** To treat as a veterinarian does. **2** *U.S. Slang* To criticize or emend: to *vet* a manuscript. — *v.i.* **3** To treat animals medically. [Short for VETERINARIAN]

vetch (vech) *n.* **1** Any of a genus (*Vicia*) of climbing herbaceous vines of the bean family, especially the common broadbean, grown for fodder. **2** A leguminous European plant (*Lathyrus sativus*) yielding edible seeds. — **bitter vetch** A species of vetch (*V. ervilia*) of which the seeds contain a bitter, poisonous alkaloid: also called *ers.* [<AF *veche, vecce* <L *vicia*]

vetch·ling (vech′ling) *n.* A plant (genus *Lathyrus*), nearly allied to the vetches; especially, a European species (*L. pratensis*), naturalized in the United States. [Dim. of VETCH]

vet·er·an (vet′ər·ən, vet′rən) *n.* **1** One who is much experienced in any service, especially a soldier or an ex-soldier. **2** A member of the armed forces who has been in active service. — *adj.* **1** Having had long experience or practice; old in service. **2** Belonging to or suggestive of a veteran. **3** Long continued; extending over a long period. [<MF <L *veteranus* < *vetus, veteris* old]

Veterans Administration An agency of the U.S. government which administers all federal laws relating to the relief of former members of the military and naval services.

Veterans Day A U.S. national holiday honoring veterans of the armed forces, held on November 11, the anniversary of the date in 1918 when the Allies granted an armistice to the Central Powers in World War I. Formerly called *Armistice Day*.

Veterans of Foreign Wars A society of ex-servicemen who have served in the United States Army, Navy, or Marine Corps in a war with and in a foreign country: founded 1899.

vet·er·i·nar·i·an (vet′ər·ə·nâr′ē·ən, vet′rə-) *n.* A practitioner of veterinary medicine or surgery. [<L *veterinarius* VETERINARY]

vet·er·i·nar·y (vet′ər·ə·ner′ē, vet′rə-) *adj.* Pertaining to the diseases or injuries of animals, and to their treatment by medical or surgical means. — *n. pl.* **·nar·ies** A veterinarian; a veterinary surgeon. [<L *veterinarius* pertaining to beasts of burden < *veterinus* < *veterina* beasts of burden, ult. < *vehere* carry]

vet·i·ver (vet′ə·vər) *n.* **1** An Asian grass (*Vetiveria zizanioides*) grown in Florida and the SE United States. **2** Its aromatic roots, used for weaving mats, fans, etc., and as a source of vetiver oil, an ingredient of perfumes. [<F *vétyver* <Tamil *veṭṭivēru*, lit., a root that is dug up < *vēr* a root]

Vet·lu·ga (vet·lōō′gə) A river in central European Russian S.F.S.R., flowing 500 miles west, north, and south to the Volga.

ve·to (vē′tō) *v.t.* **·toed, ·to·ing 1** To refuse executive approval of (a bill passed by a legislative body). **2** To forbid or prohibit authoritatively; refuse consent to. — *n. pl.* **·toes 1** The prerogative in a chief executive of refusing to approve a legislative enactment by withholding his signature. **2** The act of vetoing; also, the official communication containing a refusal to approve a bill. **3** Any authoritative prohibition. [<L, I forbid] — **ve′to·er** *n.*

veto message A message giving the reasons of the chief executive for refusing his approval of a proposed law.

veto power 1 The right or power possessed by a branch of the government to forbid or refuse approval of projects proposed by another department. **2** A power vested in the chief executive to prevent the enactment of bills passed by the legislature.

Vet·ter (vet′ər), **Lake** A former spelling for VÄTTER, LAKE.

vex (veks) *v.t.* **1** To provoke to anger or displeasure by small irritations; irritate; annoy. **2** To trouble or afflict. **3** To throw into commotion; agitate. **4** To make a subject of dispute: a *vexed* question. See synonyms under PIQUE[1]. [<OF *vexer* <L *vexare* shake]

vex·a·tion (vek·sā′shən) *n.* **1** The act of vexing, or the state of being vexed; irritation. **2** That which vexes; annoyance; affliction; cause of trouble or distress. See synonyms under CHAGRIN, IMPATIENCE.

vex·a·tious (vek·sā′shəs) *adj.* **1** Being a source of vexation. **2** Full of vexation; harassing; annoying. See synonyms under TROUBLESOME, WEARISOME. — **vex·a′tious·ly** *adv.* — **vex·a′tious·ness** *n.*

vexed (vekst) *adj.* **1** Harassed; troubled; irritated; agitated; disturbed. **2** Much debated; contested: a *vexed* question. — **vex·ed·ly** (vek′sid·lē) *adv.* — **vex′ed·ness** *n.*

vex·il (vek′sil) *n.* A vexillum (def. 2). [Short for VEXILLUM]

vex·il·lar·y (vek′sə·ler′ē) *n. pl.* **·lar·ies** A standard-bearer. — *adj.* **1** Of or pertaining to a vexillum: also **vex′il·lar** (-lər). **2** Of or pertaining to a standard or ensign. [<L *vexillarius* a standard-bearer < *vexillum* VEXILLUM]

vex·il·late (vek′sə·lit, -lāt) *adj.* Having a vexillum or vexilla.

vex·il·lol·o·gy (veks′ə·lol′ə·jē) *n.* The study of flags. [<L *vexillum* flag, standard + -LOGY] — **vex′il·lo·log′ic** or **·i·cal** *adj.* — **vex′il·lol′o·gist** *n.*

vex·il·lum (vek·sil′əm) *n. pl.* **vex·il·la** (vek·sil′ə) **1** In Roman antiquity, a square flag, or standard; hence, a company or troop of soldiers serving under a separate standard. **2** *Bot.* The large upper petal of a papilionaceous flower. **3** *Ornithol.* The web of a feather. [<L < *vehere* carry]

vi·a (vī′ə, vē′ə) *prep.* By way of; by a road passing through: He went to Boston *via* New Haven. [<L, ablative sing. of *via* a way]

Vi·a Ap·pi·a (vī′ə ap′ē·ə) The ancient Latin name for the APPIAN WAY.

vi·a·ble (vī′ə·bəl) *adj.* Capable of living and developing normally, as a newborn infant, a seed, etc. [<F < *vie* life <L *vita*] — **vi′a·bil′i·ty** *n.*

Vi·a Do·lo·ro·sa (vī′ə dol′ō·rō′sə) *Latin* The road traveled by Jesus to Golgotha; literally, the sorrowful way.

vi·a·duct (vī′ə·dukt) *n.* A bridgelike structure, especially a large one of arched masonry, to carry a roadway or the like over a valley or ravine. Compare AQUEDUCT. [<L *via* a way + (AQUE)DUCT]

VIADUCT
Roman aqueduct, Nîmes, France.

Vi·a Fla·min·i·a (vī′ə flə·min′ē·ə) The Latin name for the FLAMINIAN WAY.

vi·al (vī′əl) *n.* A small bottle for liquids, commonly cylindrical; also, more widely, any bottle: also spelled *phial*. — **to pour out the vials of wrath upon** To inflict retribution or vengeance on. See *Rev.* xvi. — *v.t.* **·aled** or **·alled, ·al·ing** or **·al·ling** To put or keep in or as in a vial. [<OF *viole* <L *phiala* a saucer <Gk. *phialē* a shallow cup]

vi·a me·di·a (vī′ə mē′dē·ə) *Latin* A middle way.

vi·and (vī′ənd) *n.* **1** An article of food, especially meat. **2** *pl.* Victuals; provisions; food. See synonyms under FOOD. [<AF *viaunde*, OF *viande*, ult. <L *vivenda*, neut. pl. gerundive of *vivere* live]

vi·at·ic (vī·at′ik) *adj.* Of or pertaining to a journey or to traveling. Also **vi·at′i·cal.** [<L *viaticus* < *via* a way]

vi·at·i·cum (vī·at′ə·kəm) *n. pl.* **·ca** (-kə) or **·cums 1** *Eccl.* The Eucharist, as given on the verge of death. **2** In ancient Rome, the provision of necessaries for an official journey of a magistrate; later, provisions for any journey. [<L, traveling money, neut. sing. of *viaticus* < *via* a way. Doublet of VOYAGE.]

vi·a·tor (vī·ā′tər) *n. pl.* **vi·a·to·res** (vī′ə·tôr′ēz, -tō′rēz) A traveler; wayfarer. [<L < *via* a way]

vibes (vībz) *n.pl. (usu. construed as sing. for def. 2) Slang* **1** Vibrations. See VIBRATION (def. 3). **2** A vibraphone.

Vi·borg (vē′bôr·y′) The Swedish name for VYBORG.

vi·brac·u·lum (vī·brak′yə·ləm) *n. pl.* **·la** (-lə) *Zool.* One of the slender, whiplike defensive organs of the cells of many polyzoans. [<NL < L *vibrare* shake] — **vi·brac′u·lar** *adj.* — **vi·brac′u·loid** *adj.*

vi·bran·cy (vī′brən·sē) *n. pl.* **·cies** The state or character of being vibrant; resonance.

vi·brant (vī′brənt) *adj.* **1** Having, showing, or resulting from vibration; vibrating; resonant. **2** Throbbing; pulsing: a nation *vibrant* with enthusiasm. **3** Energetic; vigorous. **4** *Phonet.* Produced with vibration of the vocal cords; voiced. — *n. Phonet.* A speech sound made with vibration of the vocal cords; a voiced sound. [<L *vibrans, -antis*, ppr. of *vibrare* shake] — **vi′brant·ly** *adv.*

vi·bra·phone (vī′brə·fōn) *n.* A type of marimba in which a pulsating sound is produced by motor-driven valves in the resonators. Also **vi′bra-harp′** (-härp′). [<VIBRA(TO) + -PHONE]

vi·brate (vī′brāt) *v.* **·brat·ed, ·brat·ing** *v.i.* **1** To move or swing back and forth, as a pendulum. **2** To move back and forth rapidly; quiver. **3** To sound: The note *vibrates* on the ear. **4** To be emotionally moved; thrill. **5** To vacillate; waver, as between choices. — *v.t.* **6** To cause to move or swing back and forth. **7** To cause to quiver or tremble. **8** To send forth (sound, etc.) by vibration. **9** To measure by each vibration: a pendulum *vibrating* seconds. See synonyms under QUAKE, SHAKE. [<L *vibratus* < *vibrare* shake]

vi·bra·tile (vī′brə·til, -tīl) *adj.* **1** Adapted to, having, or used in vibratory motion. **2** Pertaining to or resembling vibration.

vi·bra·til·i·ty (vī′brə·til′ə·tē) *n.* Capability, or quality, of being vibratile.

vi·bra·tion (vī·brā′shən) *n.* **1** The act of vibrat-

ing; oscillation. **2** *Physics* **a** A periodic, usually rapid back-and-forth motion of a particle, as of electrons in an atom, or the parts of an elastic or rigid body suddenly released from tension. **b** Any physical process characterized by cyclic variations in amplitude, intensity, or the like, as wave motion or an electric field. **c** A single complete oscillation. **3** *pl. Slang* One's emotional response to an aura felt to surround a person or thing, especially when considered in or out of harmony with oneself: good *vibrations*. — **vi·bra′tion·al** *adj.*

vi·bra·to (vē·brä′tō) *n. Music* A trembling or pulsating effect, not confined to vocal music, caused by rapid variation of emphasis on the same tone: properly distinguished from *tremolo*, where there is an alternation of tones. [<Ital., pp. of *vibrare* vibrate <L, shake]

vi·bra·tor (vī′brā·tər) *n.* **1** One who or that which vibrates. **2** An electrically operated massaging apparatus. **3** *Electronics* **a** An electromagnetic switch mechanism for converting direct into alternating current by continuously vibrating impulses. **b** An oscillator (def. 3).

vi·bra·to·ry (vī′brə·tôr′ē, -tō′rē) *adj.* Pertaining to, causing, or characterized by vibration. Also **vi′bra·tive** (-tiv).

vib·ri·o (vib′rē·ō) *n.* Any of a genus (*Vibrio*) of motile, rodlike bacteria in which the cells are but slightly sinuous and have one or more flagellae at each end; especially, the Gram-negative **comma vibrio** (*V. comma*), found in the intestines of cholera victims. [<NL <L *vibrare* shake]

vib·ri·oid (vib′rē·oid) *adj.* Resembling a vibrio. — *n.* A vibrioid body. [<VIBRI(O) + -OID]

vi·bris·sa (vī·bris′ə) *n. pl.* **·bris·sae** (-bris′ē) *Biol.* **1** One of the stiff, coarse hairs found in the nostrils of man and about the mouth of many other mammals, as the cat: they often function as tactile organs. **2** One of the vaneless, hairlike rictal feathers of many insectivorous birds, especially flycatchers. [<L *vibrissae* hairs in a man's nostrils < *vibrare* shake]

vi·bro·scope (vī′brə·skōp) *n.* A device for observing and recording vibrations, especially those of harmonic character.

vi·bro·tro·pism (vī′brə·trō′piz·əm) *n. Biol.* The involuntary response of an organism to a vibratory stimulus. [< *vibro-* (<VIBRATE) + -TROPISM] — **vi′bro·trop′ic** (-trop′ik) *adj.*

vi·bur·num (vī·bûr′nəm) *n.* Any of a large and widely distributed genus (*Viburnum*) of shrubs or small trees of the honeysuckle family, bearing small flowers and berrylike fruit; especially, the dockmackie, the sheepberry, and the hobble-bush. [<L, the wayfaring tree]

vic·ar (vik′ər) *n.* **1** In general, one who is authorized to perform functions, especially religious ones, in the stead of another; a substitute in office. **2** Hence, an agent; deputy. **3** *Brit.* The priest of a parish of which the main revenues are appropriated or impropriated by a layman, the priest himself receiving but a stipend; any incumbent of a parish who is not a rector. **4** In the Roman Catholic Church, a substitute or representative of an ecclesiastical person; in a strict sense, one whose jurisdiction is confined to the external forum. **5** In some parishes of the Protestant Episcopal Church, the clergyman who is the head of a chapel; also, a clergyman having charge of a church or mission as the bishop's deputy. [<AF *vikere, vicare*, OF *vicaire* <L *vicarius* a substitute < *vicis* a change]

vic·ar·age (vik′ər·ij) *n.* **1** The benefice, office, or duties of a vicar. **2** A vicar's residence or household.

vicar apostolic In the Roman Catholic Church, formerly, a bishop or archbishop appointed by the pope to act in his stead in a given district; more recently, a titular bishop exercising episcopal jurisdiction where there is no see canonically.

vicar fo·rane (fō·rān′, fō-) In the Roman Catholic Church, a clergyman appointed by a bishop, having a limited jurisdiction over the inferior clergy in the parishes constituting the deanery; a rural dean. [<VICAR + Med. L *foraneus* outside the episcopal city, rural <L *foras* out of doors]

vicar general 1 In the Roman Catholic Church, a functionary appointed by the bishop as assistant or representative in certain matters of jurisdiction, but without power to perform the specific function of the episcopal order. **2** In the Church of England, an official assisting the bishop or archbishop in ecclesiastical causes. **3** In English history, the ecclesiastical vicegerent of the king: a title bestowed on Thomas Cromwell by Henry VIII.

vi·car·i·al (vī·kâr′ē·əl, vi-) *adj.* **1** Vicarious; delegated. **2** Belonging to, relating to, or acting as a vicar.

vi·car·i·ate (vī·kâr′ē·it, -āt, vi-) *n.* A delegated office or power; specifically, the office or authority of a vicar. Also **vic·ar·ate** (vik′ər·it).

vi·car·i·ous (vī·kâr′ē·əs, vi-) *adj.* **1** Made or performed by substitution; suffered or done in place of another; substitutionary: a *vicarious* sacrifice; also, enjoyed or felt by a person as a result of his imagined participation in an experience that is not his own: *vicarious* gratification. **2** Filling the office of or acting for another. **3** Of, pertaining to, or belonging to a vicar or deputy; deputed; delegated. **4** *Med.* Performing, as an organ, the functions of another; substitutive; also, occurring in an abnormal situation: *vicarious* menstruation. [< L *vicarius.* See VICAR.] — **vi·car′i·ous·ly** *adv.* — **vi·car′i·ous·ness** *n.*

vic·ar·ly (vik′ər·lē) *adj.* Resembling or pertaining to a vicar.

vicar of Christ The pope, regarded as Christ's representative on earth.

vic·ar·ship (vik′ər·ship) *n.* The office or position of a vicar.

vice[1] (vīs) *n.* **1** A moral blemish or taint; an immoral habit or trait: the *vice* of intemperance. **2** Habitual indulgence in degrading or harmful appetites; deviation from moral rectitude; depravity. **3** Something that mars; a defect; blemish. **4** A physical deformity, taint, or imperfection. **5** A bad trick, as of a horse. See synonyms under SIN[1]. — **inherent vice** In insurance, a hazard arising from a preexistent condition not manifest when the commodity was insured and therefore not covered by the insurance policy: Eggs of worms were the *inherent vice* that ruined the cargo of hides. ◆ Homophone: *vise.* [< OF < L *vitium* a fault]

vice[2] (vīs) See VISE.

vice[3] (vīs) *adj.* Acting in the place of; substitute; deputy: *vice* president. — *n.* One who acts in the place of another; a substitute; deputy.

— **vi·ce** (vī′sē) *prep.* Instead of; in the place of. [< L, ablative of *vicis* change]

Vice may appear as a combining form in hyphemes or as the first element in two-word phrases:

vice–chair	vice–ministry
vice chairman	vice principal
vice–chairmanship	vice–principalship
vice dean	vice rector
vice–government	vice–rectorship
vice governor	vice–reign
vice–governorship	vice–wardenship

vice admiral A commissioned officer in the Navy or Coast Guard who ranks next above a rear admiral and next below an admiral. [< AF *visadmirail,* OF *visamiral* < *vis-* in place (< L *vice*) + *admiral, amiral* an admiral]

vice-ad·mir·al·ty (vīs′ad′mər·əl·tē) *n.* The area under or office of a vice admiral.

vice chancellor **1** *Law* A judge in equity courts subordinate to the chancellor. **2** A deputy chancellor in a university. [< OF *vichancelier* < Med. L *vicecancellarius* < L *vice* in place + LL *cancellarius* a chancellor] — **vice′-chan′cel·lor·ship′** *n.*

vice consul One who exercises consular authority, either as the substitute or as the subordinate of a consul. — **vice–con·su·lar** (vīs′kon′sə·lər) *adj.* — **vice–con·su·late** (vīs′·kon′sə·lit) *n.* — **vice′-con′sul·ship** *n.*

vice·ge·ren·cy (vīs·jir′ən·sē) *n. pl.* **·cies** **1** The office or authority of a vicegerent; the fact of ruling as a vicegerent or deputy. **2** A district ruled by a vicegerent.

vice·ge·rent (vīs·jir′ənt) *n.* One duly authorized to exercise the powers of another; a deputy; vicar. — *adj.* Acting in the place of another, usually in the place of a superior. [< Med. L *vicegerens, -entis* < L *vice* in place + *gerens,*

-entis, ppr. of *gerere* carry, manage] — **vice·ge′ral** *adj.*

vic·e·nar·y (vis′ə·ner′ē) *adj.* **1** Consisting of or pertaining to twenty. **2** Relating to a system of notation based upon twenty. [< L *vicenarius* < *viceni* twenty each < *viginti* twenty]

vi·cen·ni·al (vī·sen′ē·əl) *adj.* Occurring once in twenty years; also, lasting or existing twenty years. [< L *vicennium* a twenty-year period < *vicies* twenty times + *annus* a year]

Vi·cen·te (Pg. vē·sen′tə, Sp. bē·then′tā) Portuguese and Spanish form of VINCENT.

Vi·cen·za (vē·chen′tsä) **1** A province in Veneto, northern Italy; 1,051 square miles. **2** A city in NE Italy, capital of Vicenza province: ancient **Vi·cen·ti·a** (vi·sen′shē·ə).

vice president An officer ranking next below a president, and acting, on occasion, in his place. The vice president of the United States is elected at the same time and in the same manner as the president, and is designated by the Constitution to be president of the Senate and to succeed the president in case of that officer's death, resignation, removal, or inability. — **vice–pres·i·den·cy** (vīs′prez′ə·dən·sē) *n.* — **vice′–pres′i·den′tial** (-prez′ə·den′shəl) *adj.*

vice·re·gal (vīs·rē′gəl) *adj.* Of or relating to a viceroy, his office, or his jurisdiction. Also **vice·roy′al** (-roi′əl). — **vice·re′gal·ly** *adv.*

vice regent A deputy regent. — **vice′–re′gent** (-rē′jənt) *adj.*

vice·roy (vīs′roi) *n.* **1** One who rules a country, colony, or province by the authority of his sovereign or king. **2** A North American nymphalid butterfly (*Basilarchia archippus*), orange-red with black markings and a row of white marginal spots. The larva feeds on the willow, poplar, and certain other trees. [< MF *viceroy, visroy* < *vice-, vis-* in place (< L *vice*) + *roy* a king, ult. < L *rex, regis*]

vice·roy·al·ty (vīs·roi′əl·tē) *n.* **1** The office or authority of a viceroy. **2** The term of office of a viceroy. **3** A district ruled or governed by a viceroy. Also **vice′roy·ship.**

vice squad A police division charged with combating illegal prostitution, perversion, gambling, and other vices.

vi·ce ver·sa (vī′sē vûr′sə, vīs′) The order being changed; the relation of terms being reversed; conversely. [< L]

Vi·cha·da (bē·chä′thä) A river in eastern Colombia, flowing 400 miles east to the Orinoco at the Venezuela border.

Vi·chy (vē·shē′) A resort city in central France; provisional capital of France during German occupation, World War II.

vi·chy·ssoise (vē′shē·swäz′) *n.* A potato cream soup flavored with leeks, celery, etc., usually served cold with a sprinkling of chives. [< F, of Vichy < *Vichy* Vichy]

Vichy water (vish′ē) The effervescent mineral water from the springs at Vichy, France; any mineral water resembling it. Also **Vi′chy, vi′chy.**

vic·i·nage (vis′ə·nij) *n.* **1** Neighboring places collectively; vicinity. **2** The state of being a neighbor or neighbors. See synonyms under NEIGHBORHOOD. [< OF *visenage, vicenage* < L *vicinus* nearby]

vic·i·nal (vis′ə·nəl) *adj.* **1** Neighboring; adjoining; near. **2** *Mineral.* Designating a crystal form closely approximating one of the fundamental forms. **3** *Chem.* Designating a benzene derivative in which the substituted elements or radicals are in consecutive order on the benzene ring. [< L *vicinalis* < *vicinus* a neighbor, orig. nearby]

vicinal planes In crystallography, crystal planes which may approximate or take the place of the fundamental planes.

vicinal road A local road, as distinguished from one between towns.

vic·i·nism (vis′ə·niz′əm) *n. Ecol.* Plant variation resulting from the proximity of other plants.

vi·cin·i·ty (vi·sin′ə·tē) *n. pl.* **·ties** **1** Nearness in space or relationship; proximity. **2** A region adjacent or near; neighborhood; vicinage. See synonyms under NEIGHBORHOOD. [< L *vicinitas, -tatis* < *vicinus* nearby]

vi·cious (vish′əs) *adj.* **1** Addicted to vice; corrupt in conduct or habits; wicked; depraved. **2** Partaking of what is base, low, and vile; morally injurious; evil. **3** Unruly

or dangerous; refractory, as an animal. **4** Defective or faulty: *vicious* arguments. **5** Impure or incorrect; corrupted, as a text, manuscript, etc. **6** Noxious; poisonous; foul, as water, air, etc. **7** *Colloq.* Marked by malice or spite; malignant: a *vicious* lie. See synonyms under CRIMINAL, IMMORAL, IRREGULAR, RESTIVE. [< OF < L *vitiosus* < *vitium* a fault] — **vi′cious·ly** *adv.* — **vi′cious·ness** *n.*

vicious circle **1** The process or predicament that arises when the solution of a problem creates a new problem and each successive solution adds another problem. **2** *Logic* Argument in a circle. See under CIRCLE. **3** *Med.* The accelerating effect of one disease upon another when the two are coexistent.

vi·cis·si·tude (vi·sis′ə·tōod, -tyōod) *n.* **1** *pl.* Irregular changes or variations, as of conditions or fortune: the *vicissitudes* of life. **2** A change; especially, a complete change; mutation or mutability. **3** Alternating change or succession, as of the seasons. See synonyms under CHANGE. [< MF < L *vicissitudo* < *vicis* a turn, change]

vi·cis·si·tu·di·nar·y (vi·sis′ə·tōo′də·ner′ē, -tyōo′-) *adj.* Marked by or subject to change or alternation. Also **vi·cis′si·tu′di·nous.**

Vicks·burg (viks′bûrg) A city in western Mississippi on the Mississippi River; besieged and taken by the Union army in the Civil War, 1863.

vi·con·ti·el (vī·kon′tē·əl) *adj. Obs.* Of or pertaining to a viscount or sheriff. [< AF, OF *vicontal* < *viconte* a viscount]

vic·tim (vik′tim) *n.* **1** A living creature sacrificed to some deity or as a religious rite. **2** A person sacrificed in the pursuit of some object; one who is injured or killed, as by misfortune or calamity. **3** A sufferer from any diseased condition or morbid feeling. **4** One who is swindled; a dupe. [< L *victima* a beast for sacrifice]

vic·tim·ize (vik′tim·īz) *v.t.* **·ized, ·iz·ing** To make a victim of, especially by defrauding or swindling; dupe; cheat. See synonyms under ABUSE. — **vic′tim·i·za′tion** *n.* — **vic′tim·iz′er** *n.*

vic·tor (vik′tər) *n.* One who vanquishes an enemy; one who is successful in any struggle or contest; winner; conqueror. — *adj.* Pertaining to a victor; victorious; triumphant: the *victor* nation. [< AF *victor, victour,* OF *victeur* < L *victus,* pp. of *vincere* conquer]

Synonyms (*noun*): conqueror, master, vanquisher, winner. A *victor* wins in a single battle or contest; a *conqueror* wins by subjugating his opponents in many battles or campaigns.

Vic·tor (vik′tər, *Fr.* vēk·tôr′) A masculine personal name. [< L, a conqueror]

Vic·tor Em·man·u·el (vik′tər i·man′yōo·əl) Name of three Italian kings.

— **Victor Emmanuel I,** 1759–1824, king of Sardinia 1820–21.

— **Victor Emmanuel II,** 1820–78, king of Sardinia 1849–61, and first king of Italy 1861–78.

— **Victor Emmanuel III,** 1869–1947, king of Italy 1900–46.

vic·to·ri·a (vik·tôr′ē·ə, -tō′rē·ə) *n.* **1** A low, light, four-wheeled carriage, with a calash top, a seat for two persons over the rear axle, and a raised driver's seat. **2** A passenger automobile with a calash top which usually covers the rear seat only. [after Queen *Victoria*]

VICTORIA

Vic·to·ri·a (vik·tôr′ē·ə, -tō′rē·ə) A feminine personal name.

— **Victoria,** 1819–1901, queen of Great Britain 1837–1901.

Victoria **1** A state of SE Australia; 87,884 square miles; capital, Melbourne. **2** The capital of British Columbia, a port at the southern extremity of Vancouver Island. **3** A port on Hong Kong Island, capital of Hong Kong colony, China. **4** A province of SE Southern Rhodesia; 21,028 square miles.

Victoria, Lake The largest lake in Africa

Victoria, Mount   1084   vigilant

and the second largest fresh-water body in the world, situated between Kenya, Uganda and Tanzania; 26,828 square miles. Also *Victoria Nyanza.*

Victoria, Mount 1 The highest peak of the Owen Stanley Range, SE New Guinea; 13,240 feet. **2** The highest peak of the Chin Hills, Upper Burma; 10,018 feet.

Victoria Cross See under CROSS.

Victoria Desert The southern belt of the Western Australian desert, south of the Gibson Desert: also *Great Victoria Desert.*

Victoria Falls A cataract on the Zambesi River between Zambia and Zimbabwe; 343 ft. high; over a mile wide; discovered by Livingstone in 1855.

Victoria Island An island in SW Franklin district, Northwest Territories, Canada; 80,340 square miles.

Victoria Land A part of Antarctica south of New Zealand, east of the Ross Sea, and west of Wilkes Land, consisting of a series of snow-covered mountains; highest point, 13,350 feet.

Vic·to·ri·an (vik·tôr′ē·ən, -tō′rē-) *adj.* **1** Of or relating to Queen Victoria, or to her reign. **2** Pertaining to or characteristic of the ideals and standards of morality and taste prevalent during the reign of Queen Victoria; prudish; conventional; narrow. **3** Of or pertaining to Victoria, Australia. — *n.* **1** Anyone, especially an author, contemporary with Queen Victoria. **2** An article of furniture, dress, or the like, identified with or dating from the Victorian age.

Victoria Nile See under NILE.

Vic·to·ri·an·ism (vik·tôr′ē·ən·iz′əm, -tō′rē-) *n.* The state or quality of being Victorian, as in style or moral outlook.

Victoria Ny·an·za (nī·an′zə, nyän′zä) See VICTORIA, LAKE.

Victoria River A river in western Northern Territory, Australia, flowing 350 miles NE, north, and west to the Timor Sea.

Victoria waterlily Any of a genus *(Victoria)* of very large tropical American waterlilies, having leaves often five feet in diameter, and huge, showy, crimson-and-white flowers.

vic·to·ri·ous (vik·tôr′ē·əs, -tō′rē-) *adj.* **1** Having won victory; conquering; triumphant. **2** Bringing victory: distinguished by victory; instrumental in bringing victory. **3** Relating to victory. — **vic·to′ri·ous·ly** *adv.* — **vic·to′ri·ous·ness** *n.*

vic·to·ry (vik′tər·ē) *n. pl.* **·ries 1** The state of being a victor. **2** The overcoming of an enemy or of any difficulty. [< OF *victorie, victoire* < L *victoria* < *victor* VICTOR]
Synonyms: achievement, advantage, conquest, mastery, success, supremacy, triumph. *Victory* is the state resulting from the overcoming of an opponent or opponents in any contest, or from the overcoming of difficulties, obstacles, evils, etc., considered as opponents or enemies. In the latter sense any hard-won *achievement, advantage,* or *success* may be termed a *victory.* In *conquest* and *mastery* there is implied a permanence of state that is not implied in *victory. Triumph,* originally denoting the public rejoicing in honor of a *victory,* has come to signify also an exultant, complete, and glorious *victory.* Compare CONQUER. *Antonyms:* defeat, disappointment, disaster, failure, frustration, miscarriage, overthrow, retreat, rout.

Victory Medal Either of two bronze medals awarded to all who served in the U.S. armed forces in World War I or World War II, worn with the **Victory Ribbon,** combining six colors of the rainbow.

Vic·tro·la (vik·trō′lə) *n.* A make of phonograph: a trade name.

vict·ual (vit′l) *n.* **1** *pl.* Food for human beings, as prepared for eating: except in dialect, seldom used in any but a humorous or depreciatory sense: also spelled *vittles.* **2** *Obs.* Provisions of any kind. See synonyms under FOOD. — *v.* **·ualed** or **·ualled, ·ual·ing** or **·ual·ling** *v.t.* **1** To furnish with victuals. — *v.i.* **2** To lay in supplies of food. **3** *Rare* To eat; feed. [< OF *vitaile* < LL *victualia* provisions, neut. pl. of L *victualis* of food < *victus* food]

vict·ual·age (vit′l·ij) *n. Rare* Victuals; victualing.

vict·ual·er (vit′l·ər) *n.* **1** One who supplies or sells victuals; specifically, one engaged in supplying an army, navy, or ship with provisions; a commissary; sutler. **2** An innkeeper. **3** A victualing ship. Also **vict′ual·ler.**

---

vi·cu·ña (vi·kōōn′yə,-kyōō′nə, vī-) *n.* **1** A small ruminant *(Lama vicugna)* of the high Andes related to the llama and alpaca, having fine and valuable wool. **2** A fiber and textile made from this wool, or some substitute. Also **vi·cu′gna,** [< Sp. < Quechua]

vicuña cloth Soft cloth made of vicuña wool.

vi·de (vī′dē) See: used to make a reference or direct attention to: *vide* p. 36. [< L, imperative sing. of *videre* see]

vi·de an·te (vī′dē an′tē) *Latin* See before.

vi·de in·fra (vī′dē in′frä) *Latin* See below.

Vi·de·la (bē·thä′lä), **Gabriel González** See GONZÁLEZ-VIDELA.

vi·de·li·cet (vi·del′ə·sit) *adv.* To wit; that is to say; namely: abbr. *viz.* [< L < *videre licet* it is permitted to see]

vid·e·o (vid′ē·ō) *adj.* **1** Of or, pertaining to television, especially to the picture portion of a program. Compare AUDIO. **2** Producing a signal convertible into a television picture: a *video* cassette. — *n.* A television image or the electric signal corresponding to it. [< L, I see]

vid·e·o·cas·sette (vid′ē·ō·kə·set′) *n.* A cassette for use in a television set that contains film or videotape.

videocassette recorder An electronic device for recording and playing back of the images and sounds on a videocassette.

vid·e·o·disc (vid′ē·ō·disk) *n.* A disc for recording both image and sound to be replaced through a television set.

vid·e·o·gen·ic (vid′ē·ō·jen′ik) *adj.* Having such characteristics, as coloration, form, etc., as appear effectively in television: also *telegenic.*

vid·e·o·tape (vid′ē·ō·tāp′) *n.* A recording of a television program on magnetic tape. — *v.t.* **·taped, ·tap·ing** To make such a recording.

vi·de post (vī′dē pōst′) *Latin* See after; see what follows.

vi·de su·pra (vī′dē sōō′prə) *Latin* See above.

vi·dette (vi·det′) See VEDETTE.

vi·de ut su·pra (vī′dē ut sōō′prə) *Latin* See what is written above.

vie (vī) *v.* **vied, vy·ing** *v.i.* **1** To strive for superiority; put forth effort to excel or outdo others, as in a race: with *with* or *for.* — *v.t.* **2** *Obs.* To wager; bet. [< MF *envier* invite, challenge < L *invitare* invite]

Vied·ma (vyed′mä, *Sp.* byeth′mä) The capital of Río Negro province, in SE central Argentina near the Atlantic.

Vi·en·na (vē·en′ə) A city on the Danube, capital of Austria, in the NE part: German *Wien.*

Vienne (vyen) **1** A city in SE France, on the Rhône. **2** A river of west central France, flowing 230 miles west and north to the Loire. **3** A department of west central France; 2,719 square miles; capital, Poitiers.

Vi·en·nese (vē′ə·nēz′, -nēs′) *adj.* Belonging or relating to Vienna, or to its inhabitants. — *n. pl.* **·nese** A native or citizen of Vienna.

Vien·nois (vye·nwá′) An ancient county of SE France.

Vien·tiane (vyań·tyán′) A city on the Mekong river, the administrative capital of Laos, in the NW central part on the Thailand border.

Vie·ques Island (byä′käs) An island belonging to and east of Puerto Rico; 52 square miles.

Vier·wald·stät·ter See (fir′vält·shtet′ər zā) The German name for the LAKE OF LUCERNE.

vi et ar·mis (vī et är′mis) *Latin.* With force and arms.

Vi·et·cong (vē·et′kông′, vē′et-; vē·et·kong′, vē′et-) *n.* **1** The Communist guerrilla force in South Vietnam during the Vietnamese war. **2** A member of this force. — *adj.* Of or having to do with the Vietcong. Also **Viet Cong.**

Vi·et·minh (vē·et·min′, vē′et·min′) *n.* **1** The Communist party in Vietnam. **2** A member of this party. Also **Viet Minh.**

VICUÑA
(Up to 3 feet high at the shoulder)

Vi·et·nam (vē·et·näm′) A country in Indochina, comprising the former **Democratic Republic of Vietnam (North Vietnam)** and the **Republic of Vietnam (South Vietnam);** united under North Vietnamese leadership in 1975; 129,623 sq. mi.; capital Hanoi.

Vi·et·nam·ese (vē·et′nä·mēz′, -mēs′) *adj.* Of or pertaining to Vietnam. — *n.* **1** A person born or living in Vietnam. **2** The Austro-Asiatic language spoken in Vietnam.

view (vyōō) *n.* **1** The act of seeing; survey; inspection. **2** Mental examination or inspection. **3** Power of seeing, or range of vision; reach of perception or insight; range or scope of thought. **4** That which is seen; a spectacle; prospect. **5** A representation of a scene; especially, a landscape; also, a sketch; design; plan. **6** Reference to something regarded as the object of action; intention; purpose. **7** Manner of looking at things; opinion; judgment; belief: What are your *views* on this subject? **8** *Obs.* Appearance; aspect; show. See synonyms under PURPOSE, SCENE, THOUGHT[1]. — **in view of** In consideration of. — **on view** Open to the public; set up for public inspection. — **with a view to** With the aim or purpose of. — *v.t.* **1** To look at; see; behold. **2** To look at carefully; scrutinize; examine. **3** To survey mentally; consider. See synonyms under EXAMINE, LOOK. [< OF *veue,* orig. pp. of *veoir* see < L *videre*] — **view′er** *n.*

view-hal·loo (vyōō′hə·lōō′) *n.* A shout uttered by a huntsman when a fox breaks cover. Also **view′-hal·lo′ (-lō′), view′-hal·loa′.**

view·less (vyōō′lis) *adj.* **1** Devoid of a view; that cannot be viewed. **2** Having no views or opinions. **3** Invisible; unseen.

view·point (vyōō′point′) *n.* Point of view.

view·y (vyōō′ē) *adj.* **1** *Colloq.* Having visionary ideas or peculiar views; visionary. **2** Appearing good at first sight; showy.

Vi·gée-Le·brun (vē·zhä′lə·broeń′), **Marie Anne,** 1755–1842, French painter.

vi·ges·i·mal (vī·jes′ə·məl) *adj.* **1** Twentieth. **2** Of or pertaining to twenty; proceeding by twenties. [< L *vigesimus,* var. of *vicesimus* < *viceni.* See VICENARY.]

vig·il (vij′əl) *n.* **1** The act or state of keeping awake; a nightlong watch; watchfulness. **2** *Eccl.* **a** The eve of a holy day, especially the eve of a fast day. **b** *pl.* Religious devotions on such an eve. **3** *Usually pl.* Any nocturnal devotions. [< AF *vigile* < L *vigilia* < *vigil* awake]

vig·il·am·bu·lism (vij′əl·am′byə·liz′əm) *n. Psychol.* A state in which a person, while awake, is unconscious of his surroundings: a condition resembling somnambulism. [< L *vigil* awake + *ambulare* walk]

vig·i·lance (vij′ə·ləns) *n.* **1** The quality of being vigilant; alertness; watchfulness in guarding against danger or providing for safety. **2** A morbid watchfulness; insomnia. See synonyms under CARE.

vigilance committee 1 A body of men self-organized for the maintenance of order and the administration of summary justice in communities where regular authority is lacking or inefficient, especially in lawless sections of the western United States. **2** Formerly, in the southern United States, a group of white citizens organized to terrify and control Negroes and abolitionists.

vig·i·lant (vij′ə·lənt) *adj.* Characterized by vigilance; being on the alert; watchful; heedful; wary. [< MF < L *vigilans, -antis,* ppr. of *vigilare* keep awake < *vigil* awake] — **vig′i·lant·ly** *adv.* — **vig′i·lant·ness** *n.*
Synonyms: active, alert, awake, careful, cautious, circumspect, heedful, mindful, sleepless, wakeful, wary, watchful, wide-awake. *Vigilant* implies more sustained activity and more intelligent volition than *alert.* One is *vigilant* against danger; he may be *alert* or *watchful* for good as well as against evil; he is *wary* in view of suspected stratagem, trickery, or treachery. A person may be *wakeful* because of some merely physical excitement or excitability, as through insomnia; yet he may be utterly careless and negligent in his wakefulness, the reverse of *watchful*; a person who is truly *watchful* must keep himself *wakeful* while on watch, in which case *wakeful* has something of mental quality. *Watchful,* from the English, and *vigilant,* from the Latin, are almost exact equivalents; but *vigilant* has a

somewhat sharper definiteness and somewhat more of a suggestion of volition; one may be habitually *watchful*; one is *vigilant* of set purpose and for direct cause. See ALERT. *Antonyms*: careless, drowsy, dull, heedless, inattentive, incautious, inconsiderate, neglectful, negligent, oblivious, thoughtless, unwary.

vig·i·lan·te (vij′ə·lan′tē) *n.* One who belongs to a vigilance committee. Also **vigilance man.** [<Sp., vigilant <L *vigilans* VIGILANT]

vi·gnette (vin·yet′) *n.* **1** Originally, a running ornament of leaves and tendrils, as in Gothic architecture. **2** A decorative or illustrative design placed on or before the title page of a book, at the end or beginning of a chapter, etc.; also, in medieval manuscript, an ornamented capital letter. **3** An engraving, photograph, or the like, having a background that shades off gradually. **4** A word–picture which delineates something subtly and delicately. — *v.t.* **·gnet·ted, ·gnet·ting 1** To make with a gradually shaded background or border, as a photograph. **2** To ornament with vignettes. [<F, dim. of *vigne* a vine]

vi·gnet·ter (vin·yet′ər) *n.* **1** A device, as a shaded paper with an oval hole in the center, used by photographers in printing vignettes. **2** One who makes vignettes: also **vi·gnet′tist.**

Vi·gno·la (vē·nyō′lä), **Giacomo da** See BAROZZI.

Vi·gny (vē·nyē′), **Comte Alfred Victor de,** 1799–1863, French poet, dramatist, and novelist.

Vi·go (vē′gō, *Sp.* bē′gō) A port of Pontevedra province, on **Vigo Bay,** an inlet of the Atlantic in NW Spain (18 miles long, 1/2 to 10 miles wide).

vig·or (vig′ər) *n.* **1** Active strength or force, physical or mental. **2** Vital or natural power, as in a healthy animal or plant. **3** Forcible exertion of strength; energy; intensity. **4** *Legal* force; validity. Also *Brit.* **vig′our. — in vigor** *Law* In operation; effective. [<AF *vigur, vigour,* OF *vigor* <L < *vigere* be lively, thrive]

vi·go·ro·so (vē′gō·rō′sō) *adj. Music* Vigorous; energetic: a direction. [<Ital.]

vig·or·ous (vig′ər·əs) *adj.* **1** Full of physical or mental vigor; robust. **2** Marked by or accompanied by vigor; performed or done with vigor; showing vigor; energetic. See synonyms under ACTIVE, FRESH, HEALTHY, POWERFUL, STRONG, VIVID. — **vig′or·ous·ly** *adv.* — **vig′or·ous·ness** *n.*

Vii·pu·ri (vē′pŏō·rē) The Finnish name for VYBORG.

Vi·ja·ya·na·gar (vij′ə·yə·nug′ər) **1** A former princely state in the Rajputana States, India; since 1949 a part of Bombay State; 135 square miles. **2** A village of northern Bombay State, India, formerly capital of Vijayanagar state.

vi·king (vī′king) *n.* One of the Scandinavian warriors who harried the coasts of Europe from the eighth to the tenth centuries; a pirate; sea rover. Also **Vi′king.** [<ON *vīkingr* a pirate, ? <OE and Frisian *wicing* < *wīc* a camp <L *vicus* a village]

Vi·la (vē′lä) The capital of the New Hebrides condominium, on Efate.

vi·la·yet (vē′lä·yet′) *n.* An administrative division of Turkey. [<Turkish *vilāyet* <Arabic *wilāyat* < *wāli* a governor]

vile (vīl) *adj.* **vil·er, vil·est 1** Morally base, despicable, or loathsome; shamefully wicked; sinful; corrupt; filthy; disgusting. **2** Of little worth or account; mean. **3** Objectionable in any way; disagreeable: a general term of derogation. See synonyms under BAD[1], BASE[2], BRUTISH, COMMON, CRIMINAL, IMMORAL, INFAMOUS, SINFUL, VULGAR. [<AF, OF, fem. of *vil* <L *vilis* cheap] — **vile′ly** *adv.* — **vile′ness** *n.*

vil·i·a·co (vil′ē·ä′kō) *n. Obs.* A villain; scoundrel. [<Ital., ult. <L *vilis* cheap]

vil·i·fy (vil′ə·fī) *v.t.* **·fied, ·fy·ing 1** To speak of as vile; defame; slander; traduce. **2** To make base or vile; degrade. [<LL *vilificare* <L *vilis* cheap + *facere* make] — **vil′i·fi·ca′tion** (-fə·kā′shən) *n.* — **vil′i·fi′er** *n.*

vil·i·pend (vil′ə·pend) *v.t.* **1** To think or speak of disparagingly; depreciate. **2** To vilify; defame. [<OF *vilipender* <L *vilipendere* < *vilis* cheap + *pendere* weight]

vill (vil) *n.* In old English law, a village; hamlet; township; also, a manor. [<AF *vill,* OF

vile, ville a country house, village <L *villa.* See VILLA.]

vil·la (vil′ə) *n.* Originally, a country house with some suggestion of opulence; now, a suburban or rural residence. See synonyms under HOUSE. [<Ital. <L, a country house, farm, dim. of *vicus* a village]

Vil·la (vē′yä, *Sp.* bē′yä), **Francisco,** 1877–1923, Mexican revolutionary leader called "Pancho": real name *Doroteo Arango.*

Vil·la Bens (bē′lyä bäns) Capital of the Southern Protectorate of Morocco, Spanish West Africa, on the SW coast; until 1940, capital of Spanish Sahara: formerly *Cabo Jubi.*

Vil·la Cis·ne·ros (bē′lyä thēs·nä′rōs) The capital of Río de Oro, Spanish West Africa, on the central western coast near the tropic of Cancer.

vil·la·dom (vil′ə·dəm) *n. Brit.* Villas collectively; also, their occupants; the world of suburban villas.

vil·lage (vil′ij) *n.* **1** A collection of houses in a rural district, smaller than a town but larger than a hamlet, and usually arranged according to a regular plan. Villages may or may not be incorporated. **2** In some States, a municipality smaller than a city. Compare TOWNSHIP. **3** A collection of habitations of animals: a gopher *village.* **4** The inhabitants of a village, collectively; the villagers. **5** An encampment or community of North American Indians or Eskimos: permanent, or sometimes temporary, during a migration or for a season. — *adj.* Of, pertaining to, or characteristic of a village. [<OF <L *villaticum,* neut. sing. of *villaticus* pertaining to a villa < *villa* a villa]

village community An agricultural community with a simple organization, such as was found in early England, Germany, Russia, India, etc.; specifically, a free, self-dependent, communal group, regarded by many writers as the political unit out of which the modern state developed.

vil·lag·er (vil′ij·ər) *n.* One who lives in a village.

vil·lage·ry (vil′ij·rē) *n. Obs.* A collection of villages.

Vil·la·her·mo·sa (bē′yä·er·mō′sä) The capital of Tabasco state, SE Mexico.

vil·lain (vil′ən) *n.* **1** One who has committed or is disposed to commit any flagitious or disgraceful crime or series of crimes; a scoundrel; rogue: often used jocosely: He's a little *villain.* **2** A character in a novel, play, etc., who represents such a person and is the opponent of the hero or protagonist; also, an actor who regularly portrays such a character. **3** A villein. **4** *Obs.* A countryman; boor; clown; rustic. — *adj.* **1** Base; vile. **2** Of low birth; occupying a low station in life. ♦ Homophone: *villein.* [<AF, OF *vilein, vilain* a farm servant <LL *villanus* <L *villa* a villa]

vil·lain·age (vil′ən·ij) *n.* See VILLEINAGE.

vil·lain·ess (vil′ən·is) *n.* A female villain.

vil·lain·ous (vil′ən·əs) *adj.* **1** Having the nature of a villain. **2** Marked by extreme depravity. **3** *Colloq.* Very bad; disgusting; abominable: said of things: *villainous* words. See synonyms under BAD[1], INFAMOUS. — **vil′lain·ous·ly** *adv.* — **vil′lain·ous·ness** *n.*

vil·lain·y (vil′ən·ē) *n. pl.* **·lain·ies 1** The quality or condition of being villainous; moral depravity. **2** Conduct befitting a villain; a villainous act; a crime. **3** *Obs.* Villeinage; servitude. **4** *Obs.* A low or miserable condition or state. See synonyms under ABOMINATION.

Vil·la-Lo·bos (vē′lə·lō′bŏōsh, -bŏōs), **Heitor,** 1887–1959, Brazilian composer and conductor.

vil·lan·age (vil′ən·ij) *n.* **1** Villeinage. **2** *Obs.* Villainy. [Var. of VILLEINAGE]

vil·la·nel·la (vil′ə·nel′ə, *Ital.* vēl′lä·nel′lä) *n. pl.* **·nel·le** (-nel′ē, *Ital.* -nel′lä) **1** A light, rustic part song, or dance accompanying it. **2** An early form of madrigal, popular in Naples during the sixteenth century. [<Ital., fem. dim. of *villano* <LL *villanus.* See VILLAIN.]

vil·la·nelle (vil′ə·nel′) *n.* A verse form, originally French, in 19 lines and 2 rimes, arranged in five tercets and a concluding quatrain. [<F <Ital. *villanella* a villanella]

Vil·lard (vi·lärd′), **Oswald Garrison,** 1872–1949, U.S. journalist.

Vil·lars (vē·làr′), **Duc Claude Louis Hector de,** 1653–1734, French marshal.

vil·lat·ic (vi·lat′ik) *adj.* Of or pertaining to a villa, farm, or village; rural. [<L *villaticus.* See VILLAGE.]

vil·lein (vil′ən) *n.* In the manorial system of feudal times, a member of any of the classes of freemen ranking below the thanes; more specifically, a free peasant ranking below a socman but above a cotter. By the 13th century the term *villein* was applied to a class of serfs who were regarded as freemen in respect to their legal relations with all persons except their lord, whose slaves they were. — *adj. Obs.* Relating to villeins; low-born. ♦ Homophone: *villain.* [<AF, OF *vilein, vilain.* See VILLAIN.]

vil·lein·age (vil′ən·ij) *n.* In feudal law, the tenure by which villeins held land; also, the status or condition of a villein: also spelled *villanage.* Also **vil′len·age.**

Ville·neuve (vēl′nœv′), **Pierre Charles Jean Baptiste Silvestre de,** 1763–1806, French admiral.

Vil·liers (vil′ərz), **George** See BUCKINGHAM.

vil·li·form (vil′ə·fôrm) *adj.* **1** Having the form of a villus. **2** Resembling nap, as of plush, as the teeth of fishes when numerous, small, and close together in velvety bands. [<NL *villiformis* <L *villus* tuft of hair + *forma* form]

Vil·lon (vē·yôn′), **François,** 1431–85?, French poet: real name *François de Montcorbier.*

vil·los·i·ty (vi·los′ə·tē) *n. pl.* **·ties 1** The state or condition of being villous. **2** A villous surface or coating. **3** A villus.

vil·lous (vil′əs) *adj.* **1** Covered with short, soft hairs; nappy. **2** Covered with or having villi. Also **vil′lose** (-ōs). [<L *villosus* < *villus* tuft of hair] — **vil′lous·ly** *adv.*

vil·lus (vil′əs) *n. pl.* **vil·li** (vil′ī) **1** *Anat.* One of the short, hairlike processes found on certain membranes, as of the small intestine, where they aid in the digestive process. **2** *Bot.* One of the long, close, rather soft hairs on the surface of certain plants. [<L, a tuft of hair, shaggy hair, var. of *vellus* a fleece, wool]

Vil·na (vil′nə, *Russian* vēl′nä) The capital of Lithuania, in the SE part: Polish *Wilno.* Also **Vil·ni·us** (vil′nē·əs), **Vil·nyus** (vil′nyəs).

Vi·lyui (vyē·lyŏō′ē) A river in western Yakut Autonomous S.S.R., flowing 1,512 miles east to the Lena.

vim (vim) *n.* Force or vigor; energy; spirit. [<L, accusative of *vis* power]

vi·men (vī′mən) *n. pl.* **vim·i·na** (vim′ə·nə) *Bot.* A long, flexible shoot or branch. [<L *vimen, -inis* a twig < *viere* bend together, plait]

vim·i·nal (vim′ə·nəl) *adj. Rare* Pertaining to twigs; made of or producing twigs. [<L *vimen, -inis.* See VIMEN.]

Vim·i·nal (vim′ə·nəl) One of the seven hills on which ancient Rome was built.

vi·min·e·ous (vī·min′ē·əs) *adj.* **1** Having or resembling long, flexible shoots or branches. **2** Composed of twigs. [<L *vimineus* < *vimen, -inis.* See VIMEN.]

Vi·my (vē·mē′) A town in Pas-de-Calais department, northern France, near **Vimy Ridge,** scene of fierce fighting in World War I, 1915–1917.

vin (vaṅ) *n. French* Wine.

vin– Var. of VINI–.

vi·na (vē′nä) *n.* An East Indian musical instrument with seven steel strings stretched on a long, fretted fingerboard over two gourds. [<Hind. *vīṇā* <Skt.]

VINA OF BENARES

vi·na·ceous (vī·nā′shəs) *adj.* **1** Of or pertaining to wine or grapes. **2** Of the color of red wine. [<L *vinaceus* < *vinum* wine]

Vi·ña del Mar (bē′nyä ᵺel mär′) A city on the Pacific in central Chile; a beach resort and industrial and agricultural center.

vin·ai·grette (vin′ə·gret′) *n.* **1** An ornamental

box or bottle, with a perforated top, for holding vinegar, smelling salts, or a pungent drug: also *vinegarette.* **2** Vinaigrette sauce. [<F, dim. of *vinaigre* vinegar]

vinaigrette sauce A vinegar and savory herb sauce served with fish and cold meats.

vi·nasse (vi·nas´) *n.* A residual product containing potassium salts, obtained from the winepress or from beets after the sugar has been extracted. [<F]

Vin·cennes (vin·senz´, *Fr.* vañ·sen´) **1** A city on the Wabash River in SW Indiana; site of French mission established in 1702. **2** A city just east of Paris, France.

Vin·cent (vin´sənt, *Fr.* vañ·sän´) A masculine personal name. Also *Ger.* **Vin·cenz** (vin´sents), *Ital.* **Vin·cen·zo** (vin·chen´tsō). [<L, conquering]

— **Vincent de Paul, Saint,** 1574?–1660, French Roman Catholic priest, founder of several charitable organizations.

Vin·cen·tian (vin·sen´shən) *n.* A member of a Roman Catholic order founded in 1625 by St. Vincent de Paul. See LAZARIST.

Vincent's infection *Pathol.* Trench mouth. Also **Vincent's angina, Vincent's disease.** [after J. H. *Vincent,* 1862–1950, French physician]

Vin·ci (vēn´chē), **Leonardo da** See LEONARDO DA VINCI.

vin·ci·ble (vin´sə·bəl) *adj.* That may be conquered or overcome; conquerable. [<L *vincibilis < vincere* conquer] — **vin´ci·bil´i·ty, vin´ci·ble·ness** *n.*

vin·cu·lum (vingk´yə·ləm) *n. pl.* **·la** (-lə) **1** A bond of union. **2** *Anat.* A confining band of fascia. **3** *Math.* A straight line drawn over several algebraic terms, or a brace uniting them to show that all are to be operated on together. [<L < *vincire* bind]

Vin·dhya Pra·desh (vind´hyə prə·dāsh´) A former State of central India, incorporated in Madhya Pradesh State, 1956; 24,600 square miles; capital, Rewa.

Vin·dhya Range (vind´hyə) A chain of hills in central India; highest point, 3,400 feet.

vin·di·ca·ble (vin´də·kə·bəl) *adj.* That may be vindicated; justifiable.

vin·di·cate (vin´də·kāt) *v.t.* **·cat·ed, ·cat·ing 1** To clear of accusation, censure, suspicion, etc. **2** To support or maintain, as a right or claim, against denial, opposition, etc. **3** To serve to justify. **4** *Rare* To lay claim to. **5** *Obs.* To avenge; punish. **6** *Obs.* To set free; rescue. See synonyms under AVENGE, JUSTIFY. [<L *vindicatus,* pp. of *vindicare* avenge, claim] — **vin´di·ca´tor** *n.*

vin·di·ca·tion (vin´də·kā´shən) *n.* The act of vindicating, or the state of being vindicated; justification; defense. See synonyms under APOLOGY, DEFENSE.

vin·di·ca·tive (vin´də·kā´tiv) *adj.* That contributes to vindication; that vindicates or serves to vindicate.

vin·di·ca·to·ry (vin´də·kə·tôr´ē, -tō´rē) *adj.* **1** Bringing to vindication; justificatory. **2** Punitive; avenging.

vin·dic·tive (vin·dik´tiv) *adj.* **1** Having a revengeful spirit; of a revengeful character. **2** *Obs.* Punitive. [<L *vindicta* a revenge] — **vin·dic´tive·ly** *adv.* — **vin·dic´tive·ness** *n.*

vine (vīn) *n.* **1** Any of a large and widely distributed group of plants having a slender, weak stem that may clasp or twine about a support by means of tendrils, leaf petioles, etc. **2** The stem itself. **3** A grapevine. [<OF *vigne, vine* <L *vinea* vineyard < *vinum* wine]

vine·dress·er (vīn´dres´ər) *n.* One who trims or prunes grapevines.

vin·e·gar (vin´ə·gər) *n.* **1** An acid liquid obtained by the acetous fermentation of alcoholic liquids, as cider, beer, wine, etc., and used as a condiment and preservative. **2** *Med.* A preparation of dilute acetic acid. **3** Anything metaphorically sour or soured, as a face; acerbity, as of speech. [<OF *vyn egre, vinaigre < vin* wine (<L *vinum*) + *aigre, egre* sour <L *acer* sharp] — **vin´e·gar·ish** *adj.*

vinegar eel A small nematode worm (*Anguillula aceti*) common in vinegar, sour paste, and similar fermenting liquids. Also **vinegar worm.**

vin·e·gar·ette (vin´ə·gə·ret´) See VINAIGRETTE (def. 1).

vinegar fly A fruit fly (def. 2).

vin·e·gar·roon (vin´ə·gə·rōōn´) *n.* The whip-tailed scorpion (*Mastigoproctus giganteus*) of the SW United States and Mexico, so called

from its odor when alarmed: erroneously supposed to be venomous. Also **vin´e·ge·rone´** (-rōn´). [<Sp. *vinagre* vinegar < *vino* wine (<L *vinum*) + *agrio* sour <L *acer* sharp]

vin·e·gar·y (vin´ə·gər·ē) *adj.* **1** Being like or suggestive of vinegar; sour; acid. **2** Crabbed; of a sour disposition.

Vine·land (vīn´lənd) See VINLAND.

vin·er·y (vī´nər·ē) *n. pl.* **·er·ies 1** A greenhouse for grapes; grapery. **2** Vines in general.

vine·yard (vin´yərd) *n.* **1** A large collection of cultivated grapevines. **2** Figuratively, a field for labor, especially spiritual culture or labor. [Earlier *wineyard,* OE *wīngeard;* infl. in form by VINE]

vine·yard·ist (vin´yər·dist) *n.* One who grows or cultivates grapevines.

vingt-et-un (vañ·tā·œn´) *n.* A game of cards played with a full pack, the object being to draw cards on which the aggregate number of spots shall reach as near as possible to but not exceed 21. Also called *twenty-one, blackjack.* [<F, twenty-one]

vini- *combining form* Wine; of or pertaining to wine or to wine grapes: *viniculture, viniferous:* also, before vowels, *vin-.* Also *vino-.* [<L *vinum* wine]

vi·nic (vī´nik, vin´ik) *adj.* Of, pertaining to, or derived from wine: *vinic* alcohol. [<L *vinum* wine]

vin·i·cul·ture (vin´ə·kul´chər) *n.* The cultivation of grapes for winemaking. — **vin´i·cul´tur·al** *adj.*

vin·i·cul·tur·ist (vin´ə·kul´chər·ist) *n.* One engaged in viniculture.

vi·nif·er·ous (vī·nif´ər·əs) *adj.* Producing wine. [<VINI- + -FEROUS]

vin·i·fi·ca·tor (vin´ə·fə·kā´tər) *n.* An apparatus for receiving and condensing the vapor of alcohol that rises from the fermenting must during the making of wine. [<VINI- + L *-ficator* a maker < *facere* make]

Vin·land (vin´lənd) A name given to part of the coast of North America by Norse voyagers: also *Vineland.*

Vin·ni·tsa (vin´it·sə, *Russian* vyēn´nyē·tsə) A city on the Bug river in SW central Ukrainian S.S.R.

Vi·no·gra·doff (vē´nə·grä´dôf), **Sir Paul Gavrilovich,** 1854–1925, Russian jurist and medieval historian, active in England.

vi·nom·e·ter (vi·nom´ə·tər, vī-) *n.* A hydrometer for measuring the percentage of alcohol in wine. [<VINO- + -METER]

vin or·di·naire (vañ ôr·də·nâr´) *French* A cheap wine; literally, ordinary wine.

vi·nos·i·ty (vī·nos´ə·tē) *n.* **1** The state or quality of being vinous. **2** The general character of a wine, including the bouquet, flavor, body, etc. **3** Addiction to or fondness for wine. [<LL *vinositas, -tatis* <L *vinosus* VINOUS]

vi·nous (vī´nəs) *adj.* **1** Pertaining to, characteristic of, or having the qualities of wine. **2** Caused by, affected by, or addicted to wine. **3** Wine-colored. [<L *vinosus < vinum* wine]

Vin·son (vin´sən), **Fred M.,** 1890–1953, U.S. administrator and jurist; chief justice of the United States 1946–53.

vin·tage (vin´tij) *n.* **1** The yield of a vineyard or wine-growing district for one season. **2** The visible fruit of vineyards. **3** The harvesting of a vineyard and the first steps in the making of wine. **4** Wine, especially wine of high quality. **5** The year or the region in which a particular wine is produced. **6** *Colloq.* The type or kind current or appropriate at a particular time or in a particular season of the past: a joke of *ancient vintage.* [<AF *vintage,* alter. of *vendage, vendage,* OF *vendage* <L *vindemia < vinum* wine + *demere* remove < *de-* off + *emere* take; infl. in form by *vintner*]

vin·tag·er (vin´tij·ər) *n.* A harvester of grapes.

vintage wine Wine of an exceptionally good year, especially a dated champagne or port.

vint·ner (vint´nər) *n.* A wine merchant, especially at wholesale. [<OF *vinetier, vinotier < vinot,* dim. of *vin* wine <L *vinum*]

vin·y (vī´nē) *adj.* Pertaining to, like, of, full of, or yielding vines.

vi·nyl (vī´nəl) *n. Chem.* The univalent radical, $CH_2{:}CH$, derived from ethylene, especially when used in organic synthesis. [<L *vinum* wine + -YL]

vinyl acetate *Chem.* A colorless liquid, C_4H_6-

O_2, used as a starting point in the synthesis of various resins and plastics.

vinyl alcohol *Chem.* A hypothetical unstable alcohol, C_2H_4O, derived from acetylene.

vinyl chloride *Chem.* A compound of vinyl and chlorine, C_2H_3Cl, used in the production of synthetic fibers.

vinyl polymer *Chem.* Any of a class of organic compounds obtained by the polymerization of vinyl compounds.

vi·ol (vī´əl) *n.* **1** Any member of a family of stringed musical instruments, predecessors of the violin family, originating in the later Middle Ages and passing out of use in the 18th century, having usually six strings, and played with a bow. **2** A stringed instrument of the violin class. See BASS VIOL. [Earlier *vielle* <AF, OF <Med. L *vidula* <Gmc.; infl. in form by OF *viole*]

vi·o·la (vē·ō´lə, vī-; *Ital.* vyō´lä) *n.* **1** A four-stringed musical instrument of the violin family, somewhat larger than the violin, and tuned a fifth lower, with a graver and less brilliant tone. Its four strings are tuned in fifths. **2** A medieval viol. **3** An organ stop of eight-foot length and tone, producing stringlike tones. [<Ital., orig. a viol <Med. L *vidula* <Gmc.]

Vi·o·la (vī´ō·lə, vē´-, vī·ō´lə) A feminine personal name. Also **Vi·o·lan·te** (*Pg.* vē´ō·län´tə, *Sp.* bē´ō·län´tä), *Gér.* **Vi·o·le** (vē·ō´lə). [<L, a violet]

— **Viola** The heroine in Shakespeare's *Twelfth Night.*

vi·o·la·ble (vī´ō·lə·bəl) *adj.* That may be violated. [<L *violabilis < violare* VIOLATE] — **vi´o·la·ble·ness, vi´o·la·bil´i·ty** *n.* — **vi´o·la·bly** *adv.*

vi·o·la·ceous (vī´ō·lā´shəs) *adj.* **1** Having a violet hue. **2** *Bot.* Of or pertaining to the violet or the violet family (*Violaceae*) of herbs, shrubs, and trees. [<L *violaceus < viola* a violet]

vi·o·la da gam·ba (vyō´lä dä gäm´bä) **1** The bass of the viol family, held between the legs, and having a range and tone similar to those of the violoncello: also *bass viol.* **2** An organ stop producing tones akin to those of the viola da gamba and usually having an eight-foot length and tone. [<Ital., viola of the leg]

vi·o·late (vī´ō·lāt) *v.t.* **·lat·ed, ·lat·ing 1** To break or infringe, as a law, oath, agreement, etc. **2** To treat irreverently; profane, as a holy place. **3** To break in upon; disturb. **4** To ravish; rape. **5** To do violence to; offend grossly; outrage. **6** *Obs.* To treat roughly; abuse. [<L *violatus,* pp. of *violare* use violence < *vis* force] — **vi´o·la´tor** *n.*

Synonyms: abuse, debauch, defile, deflower, desecrate, hurt, injure, outrage, pollute, profane, rape, ravish. See ABUSE, POLLUTE.

vi·o·la·tion (vī´ō·lā´shən) *n.* The act of violating, or the state of being violated.

vi·o·la·tive (vī´ō·lā´tiv) *adj.* Having a tendency to violate; violating; involving violation.

vi·o·lence (vī´ō·ləns) *n.* **1** The quality or state of being violent; intensity; fury; also, an instance of violent action. **2** Violent or unjust exercise of power; injury; outrage; desecration; profanation. **3** *Law* Physical force unlawfully exercised; an act tending to intimidate or overawe by causing apprehension of bodily injury. **4** The perversion or distortion of the meaning of a text, word, or the like; unjustified alteration of wording. [<AF, OF <L *violentia < violentus* violent]

Synonyms: acuteness, boisterousness, eagerness, fierceness, force, fury, impetuosity, injury, intensity, outrage, passion, poignancy, rage, severity, sharpness, vehemence, violation, wildness, wrath. See OUTRAGE. *Antonyms:* calmness, feebleness, forbearance, gentleness, meekness, mildness, patience, self-command, self-control, self-restraint.

vi·o·lent (vī´ō·lənt) *adj.* **1** Proceeding from or marked by great physical force or roughness; sudden; forcible. **2** Caused by or exhibiting intense emotional or mental excitement; passionate; impetuous; fierce. **3** Characterized by intensity of any kind; extreme: *violent* heat. **4** Marked by unjust exercise of force; harsh; severe: to take *violent* measures. **5** Resulting from external force or injury; not in the ordinary course of nature: a *violent* death. **6** Tending to pervert the meaning or sense: a *violent* construction. [<OF <L *violentus* <*vis* force] — **vi·o·lent·ly** *adv.*

Synonyms: acute, boisterous, fierce, forceful, frantic, frenzied, fuming, furious, immoderate, impetuous, intense, irate, mad, maniacal, outrageous, passionate, poignant, raging, raving, severe, sharp, tumultuous, turbulent, uncontrollable, ungovernable, vehement, wild. See FIERCE, HOT, IMMODERATE, TURBULENT.

violent presumption *Law* An inference based on evidence that is so strong as to be almost conclusive.

vi·o·les·cent (vī'ə·les'ənt) *adj.* Having a tinge of violet color. [<L *viola* a violet + -ESCENT]

vi·o·let (vī'ə·lit) *n.* **1** Any of a widely distributed genus (*Viola*) of herbaceous perennial herbs, bearing flowers typically of a purplish-blue color; especially, the common **garden violet** (*V. odorata*). The violet is the State flower of Illinois, New Jersey, Rhode Island, and Wisconsin. **2** Any of several similar plants: the dog's-tooth *violet*. **3** A color seen at the end of the spectrum, opposite the red and beyond the blue; also, a pigment of this color. —*adj.* Of the color of violet. [<OF *violette*, dim. of *viole* <L *viola* a violet]

violet rays High-frequency radiation from the violet end of the visible spectrum: distinguished from *ultraviolet*.

vi·o·lin (vī'ə·lin') *n.*
1 A musical instrument having four strings and a sounding box of seasoned wood, and played by means of a bow; a fiddle. It is the treble member of the **violin family**, which includes the viola, violoncello, and double-bass, and is distinguished in its modern form by its fully molded belly and back. **2** A violinist, especially in an orchestra: He is second *violin*. [< Ital. *violino*, dim. of *viola* a viola]

vi·o·lin·ist (vī'ə·lin'ist) *n.* One who plays the violin.

vi·ol·ist (vī'əl·ist) *n.* One who plays the viol or viola.

Viol·let–le–Duc (vyô·le'lə·dük'), **Eugène Emmanuel**, 1814–79, French architect and archeologist.

vi·o·lon·cel·list (vē'ə·lən·chel'ist) *n.* One who plays the violoncello: usually abbreviated to *cellist* or *'cellist*.

vi·o·lon·cel·lo (vē'ə·lən·chel'ō) *n. pl.* **·los** A bass instrument of the violin family, having four strings tuned an octave lower than the viola, and held between the performer's knees when played: commonly called *cello* or *'cello*. [<Ital., dim. of *violone* a bass viol, aug. of *viola*. See VIOLA.]

vi·o·lo·ne (vyō·lō'nä) *n.* **1** The double-bass of the viol family, playing an octave lower than the viola da gamba: the immediate ancestor of the modern double-bass, which replaces the true double-bass of the violin family. **2** An organ stop with stringlike tone quality, having a 16-foot length and tone. **3** A small-scaled organ stop of eight-foot length and tone. [< Ital., aug. of *viola* a viol. See VIOLA.]

vi·os·ter·ol (vī·os'tər·ōl, -ol) *n.* Irradiated ergosterol, a vitamin D preparation variously used in medicine. [<(ULTRA)VIO(LET) + (ERGO)STEROL]

vi·per (vī'pər) *n.* **1** Any of a family (*Viperidae*) of venomous Old World snakes, especially the common European viper or adder (*Vipera berus*), about two feet long and variously colored; also, the African puff adder, and the horned viper. **2** One of a family (*Crotalidae*)

of typically American poisonous snakes, the **pit vipers**, including the rattlesnake, copperhead, and fer–de–lance, which are characterized by a small depression between the nostril and the eye. **3** Any poisonous or allegedly poisonous snake. **4** A venomous, malicious, treacherous, or spiteful person. **5** *U.S. Slang* A marihuana smoker. [<OF *vipere, vipre* < L *vipera*, contraction of *vivipara* <*vivus* living + *parere* bring forth] —**vi·per·ine** (vī'pər·in, -pə·rin) *adj.* —**vi'per·ish** *adj.*

vi·per·ous (vī'pər·əs) *adj.* **1** Snakelike; viperine. **2** Venomous. —**vi'per·ous·ly** *adv.*

vi·per's–bu·gloss (vī'pərz·byōō'glôs, -glos) *n.* Blueweed.

vir·a·gin·i·ty (vir'ə·jin'ə·tē) *n. Psychiatry* The assumption by a woman of male characteristics and reactions. [<L *virago, -inis* VIRAGO]

vi·ra·go (vi·rā'gō, vī-) *n. pl.* **·goes** or **·gos 1** A turbulent woman; vixen. **2** *Obs.* A woman of extraordinary size and courage; a female warrior; Amazon. [<L, manlike woman <*vir* a man]

vi·ral (vī'rəl) *adj. Med.* Of, pertaining to, caused by, or resembling a virus.

Vir·chow (vir'khō), **Rudolf**, 1821–1902, German pathologist.

vir·e·lay (vir'ə·lā) *n.* A form of old French verse, arranged in any of various arbitrary orders; especially, a verse form having only two rimes throughout; also, a form in which each stanza has two rimes, one repeated from the preceding stanza and a new one that will be repeated in the next. Also *French* **vire·lai** (vēr·le'). [<OF *virelai*, prob. alter. of *vireli, virli* a refrain of old dance songs]

vir·e·o (vir'ē·ō) *n. pl.* **·os** Any of various small, insectivorous birds (family *Vireonidae*), predominantly dull–green and grayish, which make slight, cup–shaped, pensile nests; a greenlet. The **red–eyed vireo** (*Vireo olivaceus*), the **yellow–throated vireo** (*V. flavifrons*), the **white–eyed vireo** (*V. griseus*), the **blue–headed** or **solitary vireo** (*V. solitarius*) and the **warbling vireo** (*V. gilvus*) are common in the United States. Many of the species are noted for their song. [<L, a kind of small bird, ? the greenfinch]

vir·e·o·nine (vir'ē·ə·nin', -nin) *adj.* Characteristic of or pertaining to a vireo and related birds. —*n.* A vireo or related bird. [<L *vireo, -onis*. See VIREO.]

vir·es·cence (vi·res'əns) *n.* **1** The state or condition of becoming green. **2** *Bot.* Abnormal assumption of green by the usually bright-colored organs of plants, as when petals become green like ordinary leaves.

vi·res·cent (vi·res'ənt) *adj.* Greenish or becoming green. [<L *virescens, -entis*, ppr. of *virescere* grow green <*vir* be green]

vir et ux·or (vir et uk'sôr) *Latin* Husband and wife.

vir·ga (vûr'gə) *n. Meteorol.* Drooping streamers or wisps of precipitation from clouds, usually of the altocumulus and altostratus types. [< L, twig, streak in the sky]

vir·gate (vûr'git, -gāt) *adj.* **1** Long, straight, and slender like a wand. **2** *Bot.* Bearing or producing many small twigs. [<L *virga* a twig, rod]

vir·gate (vûr'git, -gāt) *n.* An early English measure of land, varying greatly (15, 20, 24, 30, and sometimes 40 acres) in different parts of England. [<Med. L *virgata (terrae)* a virgate (of land) <L *virga* a rod]

Vir·gil (vûr'jəl), **Vir·gil·i·an** (vər·jil'ē·ən) See VERGIL, etc.

vir·gin (vûr'jin) *n.* **1** A person, especially a young woman, who has never had sexual intercourse; a maiden. **2** A chaste young girl or unmarried woman; a spinster. **3** *Eccl.* **a** A member of a religious community who has taken a vow of chastity; a nun. **b** A chaste, unmarried woman honored for her piety or virtue: used as an epithet of saints: St. Cecilia, *virgin* and martyr. **4** Any female animal before its first copulation. **5** *Entomol.* A female insect producing fertile eggs by parthenogenesis. —*adj.* **1** Being a virgin. **2** Consisting of virgins: a *virgin* band. **3** Pertaining or suited to a virgin; chaste; maidenly. **4** Uncorrupt; pure; undefiled: *virgin* whiteness. **5** Not hitherto used, touched, tilled, or worked upon by man: *virgin* soil; *virgin* forest. **6** Not

previously processed, manufactured, or acted upon; new: *virgin* rubber; *virgin* wool. **7** Obtained from the first pressing (of olives, nuts, etc.) without the use of heat: said of an oil. **8** *Metall.* Produced directly from ore, or at the primary smelting: *virgin* silver. **9** *Mining* Occurring in native form; unalloyed; unmixed: *virgin* gold. **10** First: a ship's *virgin* voyage. **1** Untrained; lacking experience or contact with: waters *virgin* of ships. **12** *Zool.* Parthenogenetic. [<OF *virgine* <L *virgo, -inis* a maiden]

Vir·gin (vûr'jin) **1** Mary, the mother of Jesus: usually with *the:* also, **the Virgin Mary, the Blessed Virgin. 2** The constellation Virgo. See CONSTELLATION.

vir·gin·al (vûr'jin·əl) *adj.* Related to, like, or suited to a virgin; pure; modest; maidenly. [< OF <L *virginalis* <*virgo, -inis* a virgin]

VIRGINAL, LATE 16TH CENTURY

vir·gin·al (vûr'jin·əl) *n.* A legless keyboard musical instrument of the 16th and 17th centuries, predecessor of the harpsichord: often in the plural, sometimes called a **pair of virginals.** [<OF, VIRGINAL[1]; ? so called from its use by young men and girls]

virgin birth 1 *Zool.* Parthenogenesis. **2** *Usually cap. Theol.* The doctrine that Jesus Christ was conceived by divine agency and born without impairment of the virginity of his mother Mary.

vir·gin·hood (vûr'jin·hŏŏd) *n.* Virginity.

Vir·gin·ia (vər·jin'yə) A middle Atlantic State of the United States; 40,815 square miles; capital, Richmond; entered the Union June 25, 1788, one of the original thirteen States; nickname, *Old Dominion:* abbr. VA Original name: *Commonwealth of Virginia.*

Virginia cowslip A smooth perennial herb (*Mertensia virginica*) of the eastern United States, with clusters of blue or purple tubular flowers. Also **Virginia bluebell.**

Virginia creeper A common American climbing vine (*Parthenocissus* or *Ampelopsis quinquefolia*) of the grape family, with compound toothed leaves, small green flowers, and inedible blue berries: also called *American ivy, woodbine.*

Virginia deer A large, graceful, white–tailed deer (*Odocoileus virginianus*), native in the eastern United States and as far west as the Great Plains.

Virginia dogwood The flowering dogwood: State flower of Virginia. See under DOGWOOD.

Virginia Key Northernmost of the Florida Keys, one mile south of Miami Beach; about 2 miles long.

Vir·gin·ian (vər·jin'yən) *adj.* **1** Of, pertaining to, or from Virginia. **2** Of, pertaining to, or designating the language of certain Algonquian North American Indians of eastern Virginia, North Carolina, and Maryland, especially of the Powhatan confederacy, formerly dwelling on the James River, Virginia. —*n.* A native or citizen of Virginia.

Virginia nightingale The cardinal bird.

Virginia rail fence A worm fence; a stake-and–rider.

Virginia reel A country dance in which the performers stand in two parallel lines facing one another and perform various figures, usually at the direction of a caller.

Virginia truffle Tuckahoe.

Virginia trumpet flower The trumpet creeper.

Virgin Islands A group of islands in the West Indies, east of Puerto Rico; divided into the **Virgin Islands of the United States,** an unincorporated territory comprising the

The violin diagram labels:

VIOLIN
a. Scroll.
b. Peg box.
c. Peg.
d. Nut.
e. Fingerboard.
f. Neck plate.
g. Sound holes.
h. Bridge.
i. Tailpiece.
j. Chin rest.
k. Button.

islands of St. Thomas, St. John, and St. Croix, and adjacent islets, purchased from Denmark in 1917; 133 square miles; capital, Charlotte Amalie, on St. Thomas: formerly *Danish West Indies*; and the BRITISH VIRGIN ISLANDS; total area, 200 square miles.

vir·gin·i·ty (vǝr·jin'ǝ·tē) *n. pl.* **·ties** 1 The state of being a virgin; maidenhood; virginal chastity. 2 The state of being unsullied or unused.

vir·gin·i·um (vǝr·jin'ē·ǝm) *n.* Former name of an element now identified as francium. [from the State of Virginia]

Virgin Mary Mary, the mother of Jesus.

Virgin River A river in Utah, Arizona, and Nevada, flowing 200 miles SW to Lake Mead.

vir·gin's-bow·er (vûr'jinz·bou'ǝr) *n.* A species of clematis (*Clematis virginiana*) bearing white flowers in leafy panicles.

Vir·go (vûr'gō) 1 A zodiacal constellation south of Ursa Major and Boötes; the Virgin. See CONSTELLATION. 2 The sixth sign of the zodiac. See illustration under ZODIAC. [<L, a virgin]

vir·gu·late (vûr'gyǝ·lit, -lāt) *adj.* Diminutively virgate; like a small rod. [<L *virgula*. See VIRGULE.]

vir·gule (vûr'gyōol) *n.* A slanting line (/) used to indicate a choice between two alternatives, as in the phrase *and/or*. See SOLIDUS. [<L *virgula*, dim. of *virga* a rod]

vir·i·des·cent (vir'ǝ·des'ǝnt) *adj.* Greenish, or becoming slightly green. [<LL *viridescens*, *-entis*, ppr. of *viridescere* become green < *viridis* green] — **vir'i·des'cence** *n.*

vi·rid·i·an (vǝ·rid'ē·ǝn) *n.* A durable bluish-green pigment consisting of hydrated chromic oxide. [<L *viridis* green]

vi·rid·i·ty (vǝ·rid'ǝ·tē) *n.* Fresh greenness, as of vegetation; verdure. [<L *viriditas*, *-tatis* greenness, verdure < *viridis* green]

vir·ile (vir'ǝl) *adj.* 1 Having the characteristics of manhood. 2 Having the vigor or strength of manhood; sturdy, intrepid, and forceful; masculine. 3 Capable of procreation. See synonyms under MASCULINE. [<OF < L *virilis* < *vir* a man]

vir·il·ism (vir'ǝl·iz'ǝm) *n.* 1 The appearance in a woman of secondary male sexual and physical characteristics. 2 Female hermaphroditism.

vi·ril·i·ty (vǝ·ril'ǝ·tē) *n. pl.* **·ties** The state, character, or quality of being virile.

vi·rip·o·tent (vǝ·rip'ǝ·tǝnt) *adj.* 1 Sexually mature. 2 Nubile. [<LL *viripotens*, *-entis* < L *vir*, *viri* a man + *potens*, *-entis* able, powerful]

virl (vûrl) *n. Scot.* A ring around a column; a band; a ferrule.

vi·rol·o·gy (vǝ·rol'ǝ·jē, vī-) *n.* The study of viruses, especially in their relation to disease. [< *viro-* (<VIRUS) + -LOGY] — **vi·rol'o·gist** *n.*

Vir·ta·nen (vir'tä·nen), **Artturi Ilmari**, 1895–1973, Finnish biochemist.

vir·tu (vǝr·tōō', vûr'tōō) *n.* 1 Rare, curious, or beautiful quality: generally in the phrase **objects** or **articles of virtu.** 2 A taste for such objects. 3 Such objects collectively. [<Ital. *virtù* <L *virtus*. See VIRTUE.]

vir·tu·al (vûr'chōō·ǝl) *adj.* 1 Being in effect, but not in form or appearance; having potency, validity, or essential qualities: opposed to *apparent* or *nominal.* 2 *Obs.* Potent; effective; energizing. [<Med. L *virtualis* <L *virtus.* See VIRTUE.] — **vir·tu·al'i·ty** (-al'ǝ·tē) *n.* — **vir'tu·al·ly** *adv.*

virtual focus See under FOCUS.

virtual image See under IMAGE.

vir·tue (vûr'chōō) *n.* 1 The disposition to conform to the law of right; moral excellence; rectitude. 2 The practice of moral duties and the abstinence from immorality and vice: a life devoted to *virtue.* 3 Sexual purity; chastity, especially in women. 4 A particular moral excellence, especially one of those considered to be of special importance and classified by Plato as the four **cardinal virtues** (justice, temperance, prudence, and fortitude), to which the Christian scholastic moralists added the three **theological virtues** (faith, hope, and charity or love). The latter are sometimes called the **supernatural** or **Christian virtues** and the former the **natural virtues,** and all seven are opposed to the Seven Deadly Sins. 5 Any admirable quality, merit, or accomplishment: Patience

is a *virtue.* 6 Active quality; power; efficacy; especially, medical efficacy; potency. 7 The quality of manliness; strength; valor. 8 *pl.* The fifth of the nine orders of angels in the celestial hierarchy. — **by** (or **in**) **virtue of** By or through the fact, quality, force, or authority of. [<OF *vertu* <L *virtus* strength, bravery < *vir* man]

Synonyms: chastity, duty, excellence, faithfulness, goodness, honesty, honor, integrity, justice, morality, probity, purity, rectitude, righteousness, rightness, truth, uprightness, virtuousness, worth, worthiness. *Virtue* is *goodness* that is victorious through trial, perhaps through temptation and conflict. *Goodness* may be much less than *virtue,* as lacking the strength that comes from trial and conflict, or it may be more than *virtue,* as rising above the possibility of temptation and conflict. *Virtue* is human; we do not predicate it of God. *Morality* is conformity to the moral law in action, whether in matters concerning ourselves or others, whether with or without right principle. *Honesty* and *probity* are used especially of one's relations to his fellow men, *probity* being to *honesty* much what *virtue* is to *goodness; probity* is *honesty* tried and proved, especially in those things that are beyond the reach of legal requirement; above the commercial sense, *honesty* may be applied to the highest truthfulness of the soul to and with itself. *Integrity,* in the full sense, is moral wholeness; when used of contracts and dealings, it has reference to inherent character and principle, and denotes more than conventional *honesty. Purity* is freedom from all admixture, especially of that which debases. *Duty,* the rendering of what is due to any person or in any relation, is the fulfilment of moral obligation. *Rectitude* and *righteousness* denote conformity to the standard of right; *righteousness* is used especially in the religious sense. *Uprightness* refers especially to conduct. Compare INNOCENCE, JUSTICE, RELIGION. *Antonyms:* evil, vice, viciousness, wrong. See synonyms for SIN.

vir·tu·os·i·ty (vûr'chōō·os'ǝ·tē) *n. pl.* **·ties** 1 The state of being a virtuoso; the technical mastery of an art, as music. 2 A taste for the fine arts, especially the taste of a dilettante. 3 Virtuosi collectively.

vir·tu·o·so (vûr'chōō·ō'sō) *n. pl.* **·si** (-sē) or **·sos** 1 A master of technique, as a skilled musician; one who displays virtuosity. 2 A connoisseur; a collector or lover of curios or works of art. 3 *Obs.* A savant; a scientist; learned person. [<Ital., skilled, learned <LL *virtuosus* full of excellence <L *virtus.* See VIRTUE.]

vir·tu·ous (vûr'chōō·ǝs) *adj.* 1 Characterized by, exhibiting, or having the nature of virtue; morally pure and good; chaste: now said especially of women. 2 Potent; efficacious. — **vir'tu·ous·ly** *adv.* — **vir'tu·ous·ness** *n.*

Synonyms: blameless, chaste, correct, dutiful, equitable, estimable, excellent, exemplary, good, honest, just, pure, right, righteous, upright, worthy. See GOOD, INNOCENT, JUST, MODEST, MORAL, PURE. *Antonyms:* see synonyms for CRIMINAL, SINFUL.

vir·tu·te of·fi·ci·i (vǝr·tōō'tē ǝ·fish'ē·ī, vǝr·tyōō'tē) *Latin* By virtue of office.

vir·u·lence (vir'yǝ·lǝns, vir'ǝ-) *n.* 1 The quality of being virulent. 2 Extreme bitterness or malignity. 3 The power of bacteria and other micro-organisms to overcome the resistance of the host.

vir·u·lent (vir'yǝ·lǝnt, vir'ǝ-) *adj.* 1 Manifesting or partaking of the nature of virus; exceedingly noxious. 2 Very bitter in enmity. 3 *Med.* Actively poisonous or infective; malignant. 4 Having or exhibiting virulence. See synonyms under BITTER[1], MALICIOUS. [<L *virulentus* full of poison < *virus* a poison] — **vir'u·lent·ly** *adv.*

vi·rus (vī'rǝs) *n.* 1 Venom; snake poison. 2 Any virulent substance developed by morbid processes within an animal body, and capable of transmitting a specific disease, as smallpox: when inoculated in an attenuated form it is called a *vaccine.* 3 Any of a class of filter-passing, pathogenic agents, chiefly protein in composition but often reducible to crystalline form, and typically inert except when in contact with certain living cells: also

filtrable virus. 4 An illness caused by such an agent. 5 Figuratively, a moral taint; a corrupting influence. 6 Bitterness of mind; acrimony; malice. [<L, poison, slime]

vis (vis) *n. pl.* **vi·res** (vī'rēz) *Latin* Force; potency.

vi·sa (vē'zǝ) *n.* 1 An official endorsement, as on a passport, certifying that it has been found correct and that the bearer may proceed. 2 A signature of approval, as by an authorized inspecting officer. — *v.t.* **·saed,** **·sa·ing** 1 To put a visa on. 2 To give a visa to. Also spelled *visé.* [<F <L, fem. sing. pp. of *videre* see]

vis·age (viz'ij) *n.* The face or look of a person, or of an animal; distinctive aspect. [<OF < vis a face <L *visus* a look < *videre* see]

vis·aged (viz'ijd) *adj.* Having a visage of some character indicated.

vis·ard (viz'ǝrd) See VIZARD.

vis-à-vis (vē'zǝ·vē', *Fr.* vē·zȧ·vē') *n.* 1 One of two persons or things that face each other, as in dancing. 2 A seat having an S-shaped back so arranged that two persons can sit side by side, but facing in opposite directions. — *adj. & adv.* Face to face. [<F, face to face]

Vi·sa·yan (vē·sä'yǝn) *n.* 1 One of the native people of the Philippines, occupying the Visayan Islands and northern Mindanao. 2 The language of these people, belonging to the Indonesian subfamily of Austronesian languages. — *adj.* Of or pertaining to the Visayans or their language. Also spelled *Bisayan.*

Vi·sa·yan Islands (vē·sä'yǝn) A group of the central Philippines, comprising Bohol, Cebu, Leyte, Masbate, Negros, Panay, Samar, Romblon, and the islets adjacent to them; total 23,621 square miles: also *Bisayan Islands.* Also **Vi·sa'yas** (-yǝs).

Visayan Sea A part of the Pacific in the central Philippines, bounded by the Visayan Islands.

Vis·by (vēs'bü) A port on western Gotland island, SE Sweden: German *Wisby.*

vis·ca·cha (vis·kä'chǝ) *n.* 1 A large burrowing rodent (*Lagostomus maximus*) of the South American pampas, related to the chinchilla, with three-toed hind feet. 2 An allied genus (*Lagidium*) of the Andes, resembling the gray squirrel but with large rabbitlike ears. [<Sp. <Quechuan *uiscacha*]

vis·cer·a (vis'ǝr·ǝ) *n. pl. sing.* **vis·cus** (vis'kǝs) 1 *Anat.* The internal organs, especially those of the great cavities of the body, as the stomach, lungs, heart, etc. ◆ Collateral adjective: *splanchnic.* 2 Commonly, the intestines. [<L, pl. of *viscus, visceris* an internal organ]

vis·cer·al (vis'ǝr·ǝl) *adj.* 1 Pertaining to the viscera. 2 Abdominal.

Visch·er (fish'ǝr), **Peter,** 1455?–1529, German sculptor.

vis·cid (vis'id) *adj.* Sticky or adhesive; mucilaginous; viscous. See synonyms under ADHESIVE. [<LL *viscidus* <L *viscum* birdlime, mistletoe] — **vis'cid·ly** *adv.* — **vis'cid·ness** *n.*

vis·cid·i·ty (vi·sid'ǝ·tē) *n.* The quality or state of being viscid.

vis·coi·dal (vis·koid'l) *adj.* Somewhat viscid.

Vis·con·ti (vēs·kôn'tē) A Lombard family which ruled Milan from 1277 to 1447.

vis·cose (vis'kōs) *n.* A thick, honeylike substance produced by the action of caustic soda and carbon disulfide upon cellulose: an important source of rayon. — *adj.* 1 Viscous. 2 Of, pertaining to, containing, or made from viscose. [<LL *viscosus* VISCOUS]

viscose rayon Rayon formed from fibers composed of regenerated cotton or wood-pulp cellulose which has been coagulated or solidified from a solution of cellulose xanthate.

vis·co·sim·e·ter (vis'kǝ·sim'ǝ·tǝr) *n.* An apparatus for determining the viscosity of liquids. Also **vis·com·e·ter** (vis·kom'ǝ·tǝr). [<VIS-COSI(TY) + -METER]

vis·cos·i·ty (vis·kos'ǝ·tē) *n. pl.* **·ties** 1 The state, quality, property, or degree of being viscous. 2 *Physics* That property of fluids by virtue of which they offer resistance to flow or to any change in the arrangement of their molecules. Compare POISE[2].

vis·count (vī'kount) *n.* 1 In England, a title of nobility between earl and baron. 2 In continental Europe, a title next below that of count; also, the son or younger brother of a count. 3 Formerly, a representative or deputy of a count or earl in the government of a district; specifically, in English use, a sheriff. [<AF *viscounte*, OF *visconte* <*vis-* in place (<L *vice*) + *counte, conte* COUNT²]

vis·count·cy (vī′kount·sē) *n. pl.* ·**cies** The rank, title, or dignity of a viscount. Also **vis′count·ship, vis′count·y.**

vis·count·ess (vī′koun·tis) *n.* The wife of a viscount, or a peeress holding the title in her own right.

vis·cous (vis′kəs) *adj.* 1 Glutinous; semifluid; sticky. 2 Imperfectly fluid, as warm tar. See synonyms under ADHESIVE. [<L *viscosus* <L *viscum* birdlime, mistletoe] — **vis′cous·ly** *adv.* — **vis′cous·ness** *n.*

vis·cus (vis′kəs) Singular of VISCERA.

vise (vīs) *n.* A clamping device, usually of two jaws made to be closed together with a screw, lever, or the like, for grasping and holding a piece of work. — *v.t.* **vised, vis·ing** To hold, force, or squeeze in or as in a vise. ◆ Homophone: *vice.* Also spelled *vice.* [<OF *vis* a screw <L *vitis* vine; with ref. to the spiral growth of vine tendrils]

MACHINIST'S VISE
Cross-section.

vi·sé (vē′zā) See VISA.

Vish·nu (vish′nōō) In Hindu theology, the second god of the trinity (Brahma, Vishnu, and Siva), known as "the Preserver"; of his many incarnations the most famous is as Krishna.

VISHNU

vis·i·bil·i·ty (viz′ə·bil′ə·tē) *n. pl.* ·**ties** 1 Condition, capability or degree of being seen. 2 *Meteorol.* The condition of the atmosphere as affecting the distance at which objects can be seen and identified. 3 *Physics* The ratio of the luminous flux of a given wavelength to the radiant energy producing it.

vis·i·ble (viz′ə·bəl) *adj.* 1 Perceivable by the eye; capable of being seen. 2 Apparent at sight; evident. 3 At hand; available; manifest. See VISIBLE SUPPLY. 4 Accessible to visitors; prepared or disposed to be seen or visited. 5 Constructed so that certain parts can be seen by the operator: a *visible* typewriter. See synonyms under EVIDENT, MANIFEST. [<OF <L *visibilis* <*visus*, pp. of *videre* see] — **vis′i·ble·ness** *n.* — **vis′i·bly** *adv.*

visible speech Phonetic symbols devised by Alexander Melville Bell to represent every possible utterance of the organs of speech.

visible supply The total of the known available supply of any commodity, as wheat in elevators and in shipment.

Vis·i·goth (viz′ə·goth) *n.* One of the western Goths, a Teutonic people that invaded the Roman Empire in the third and fourth centuries and settled in France and Spain. See OSTROGOTH. [<LL *Visigothus* <Gmc.; ? lit., the western Goths] — **Vis′i·goth′ic** *adj.*

vi·sion (vizh′ən) *n.* 1 The faculty or sense of sight, localized in the eye, which, with its receptors and associated organs, is normally adapted to receive the stimulus of radiant energy within a certain range of wavelengths. 2 That which is or has been seen; also, something or someone beautiful or delightful: She is a *vision* of loveliness. 3 A mental representation of or as of external objects or scenes, as in sleep; an apparition; dream; fantasy; specifically, an inspired revelation. 4 Some product of the fancy or imagination; an imaginary or unreal thing: *visions* of sugarplums. 5 The ability to anticipate and make provision for future

events; foresight. 6 Insight; imagination. See synonyms under DREAM. — *v.t.* To see in or as in a vision. [<OF <L *visio, -onis* <*visus,* pp. of *videre* see]

vi·sion·al (vizh′ən·əl) *adj.* Of, pertaining to, or consisting of vision or a vision. — **vi′sion·al·ly** *adv.*

vi·sion·ar·y (vizh′ən·er′ē) *adj.* 1 Not founded on fact; imaginary; impracticable. 2 Affected by fantasies; dreamy; impractical. 3 Associated with apparitions, dreams, etc. See synonyms under FANCIFUL, IDEAL, IMAGINARY, ROMANTIC. — *n. pl.* ·**ar·ies** 1 One who has visions. 2 A dreamer; an impractical schemer. — **vi′sion·ar′i·ness** *n.*

vis·it (viz′it) *v.t.* 1 To go or come to see (a person) from friendship, courtesy, on business, etc.; make a call on. 2 To go or come to (a place, etc.), as for transacting business or for touring: to *visit* the Louvre. 3 To be a guest of; stay with temporarily: I *visited* them for several days. 4 To go or come to so as to make official inspection or inquiry: to *visit* a military school. 5 To come upon or afflict. 6 To inflict punishment upon or for. 7 To comfort or bless: The Lord hath *visited* His people. — *v.i.* 8 To make a visit; pay a call or calls. 9 To inflict punishment or vengeance. See synonyms under AVENGE. — *n.* 1 The act of going or coming to see a person or thing, especially with some formality and with the intention of staying some time; a sojourn in a place or with a person; a call or stay. 2 *Colloq.* A talk or friendly chat. 3 An authoritative personal call for inspection and examination or discharge of an official or professional duty. — **right of visit** See RIGHT OF SEARCH. [<OF *visiter* <L *visitare* go to see, freq. of *visare* <*visus,* pp. of *videre* see]

vis·it·a·ble (viz′it·ə·bəl) *adj.* 1 Subject to visitation or punishment. 2 Agreeable to visitors, as a country or region. 3 Having a social position.

vis·it·ant (viz′ə·tənt) *n.* 1 A visitor; that which comes and goes or makes a transient appearance. 2 A migratory animal or bird at a particular region. 3 A visitor as if from another sphere; a supernatural being. — *adj.* Acting as a visitor; paying visits. [<MF <L *visitans, -antis,* ppr. of *visitare* VISIT]

vis·i·ta·tion (viz′ə·tā′shən) *n.* 1 The act or fact of visiting; a visit; also, the state or circumstance of being visited. 2 The visit of a bishop to his diocese; an official or authoritative inspection and examination of a foundation, institution, or establishment to set affairs to rights, correct abuses, enforce laws or rules, etc. 3 In Biblical and religious use, a visit of blessing or affliction; a blessed *visitation* from on high; a dreadful *visitation* of famine. 4 *Obs.* The purpose or object of a visit. 5 The resorting of birds or animals to unusual places. See synonyms under MISFORTUNE. — **vis′i·ta′tion·al** *adj.*

Vis·i·ta·tion (viz′ə·tā′shən) *n.* A religious festival held on July 2 in honor of the visit of the Virgin Mary to Elizabeth. *Luke* i 40.

vis·i·ta·to·ri·al (viz′ə·tə·tôr′ē·əl, -tō′rē-) *adj.* Of or pertaining to visitation; done · under an official right of visitation. Also **vis′i·to′·ri·al.**

visiting card A calling card.

vis·i·tor (viz′ə·tər) *n.* One who visits. Also **vis′it·er.**

Vis·la (vēs′lä) The Russian name for the VISTULA.

vis ma·jor (vis mā′jər) *Latin* 1 Irresistible or uncontrollable force; inevitable accident. 2 *Law* An unavoidable accident: in civil law, nearly the same as, but broader than, an act of God.

vis med·i·ca·trix na·tu·rae (vis med′ə·kā′triks nə·choor′ē) *Latin* The curative power of nature.

vi·sor (vī′zər, viz′ər) *n.* 1 A projecting piece on a cap shielding the eyes. 2 In ancient armor, the front piece of a helmet which protected the upper part of the face and could be raised. — *v.t.* To mask; cover with a visor. Also spelled *vizor.* [<AF *viser,* OF *visiere* <*vis* face. See VISAGE.]

vis·ta (vis′tə) *n.* 1 A view or prospect, as

along an avenue; an outlook. 2 A mental view embracing a series of events. [<Ital. <L *visus,* pp. of *videre* see]

Vis·tu·la (vis′chōo·lə) The longest river in Poland, flowing 678 miles north from the Carpathian Mountains to the **Vistula Lagoon** (German *Frisches Haff*), a coastal inlet (332 square miles; about 60 miles long, 7 to 11 miles wide) of the Gulf of Danzig: German *Weichsel,* Russian *Visla.*

vis·u·al (vizh′ōō·əl) *adj.* 1 Pertaining to, resulting from, or serving the sense of sight; ocular. 2 Perceptible by sight; visible. 3 Optical: the *visual* focus of a lens. 4 Produced or induced by mental images: a *visual* conception. [<MF <LL *visualis* <L *visus* a sight <*videre* see]

visual field The total area visible to the unmoving eye or eyes at any given moment.

vis·u·al·i·ty (vizh′ōō·al′ə·tē) *n. pl.* ·**ties** 1 The quality or condition of being visual; mental visibility. 2 That which is or may be perceived by or as by vision.

vis·u·al·ize (vizh′ōō·əl·īz′) *v.* ·**ized, ·iz·ing** *v.t.* To form a mental image of; picture in the mind. — *v.i.* To form mental images. Also *Brit.* **vis′u·al·ise′.** — **vis′u·al·ism** *n.* — **vis′u·al·i·za′tion** *n.*

vis·u·al·iz·er (vizh′ōō·əl·ī′zər) *n.* 1 One who visualizes. 2 One whose mental images are formed chiefly by visualization: also **vis′u·al·ist** (-ist).

visual purple *Biochem.* A complex reddish-purple protein present in the rods of the vertebrate retina: it is an important factor in the process of vision, especially at night: also called *rhodopsin.*

visual yellow *Biochem.* The pigmented protein into which visual purple is changed by the action of light: heat acts upon it to produce vitamin A: also called *retinene.*

vis vi·tae (vis vī′tē) *Latin* The force of life; vitality. Also **vis vi·ta·lis** (vī·tā′lis).

vi·ta·ceous (vī·tā′shəs) *adj. Bot.* Designating or belonging to a family (*Vitaceae*) of mostly woody and climbing vines, the grape family, having alternate leaves, inconspicuous greenish flowers in clusters, and berry-like fruit. [<NL, family name <L *vitis* a vine]

vi·tal (vīt′l) *adj.* 1 Pertaining to life. 2 Essential to or supporting life. 3 Affecting life; fatal to life: a *vital* error or wound. 4 Necessary to existence or continuance; necessary; essential; life-sustaining. 5 Relating to the facts of life, as births, deaths, etc.: *vital* statistics. [<OF <L *vitalis* <*vita* life] — **vi′tal·ly** *adv.*

vital force A form of energy regarded as acting independently of all physical and chemical forces in the causation of life and in the development of living phenomena. Also **vital principle.**

vi·tal·ism (vīt′l·iz′əm) *n.* 1 The doctrine that life had its origin and support in some principle that is neither material nor organic. 2 *Philos.* A movement represented by Henri Bergson, which upholds the principles of freedom and self-determination and the creative power of the human consciousness. It places intuition above intellect, and considers the universe as living and self-evolving without predestined development or end. Compare BERGSONISM, ÉLAN VITAL. 3 *Biol.* The theory that organic growth is due to forces that operate only in living organisms and differ in kind from the chemical and physical forces at work in the inorganic world: opposed to *mechanism.* — **vi′tal·ist** *n.* — **vi′tal·is′tic** *adj.*

vi·tal·i·ty (vī·tal′ə·tē) *n.* 1 The state of being vital; vital force; the principle of life; animation; life. 2 Power of continuing in force or effect. See synonyms under LIFE.

vi·tal·ize (vīt′l·īz) *v.t.* ·**ized, ·iz·ing** To make vital; endow with life or energy; animate. — **vi′tal·i·za′tion** *n.* — **vi′tal·iz′er** *n.*

vi·tals (vīt′lz) *n. pl.* 1 The parts necessary to life, as the heart and brain: used also figuratively. 2 The parts essential to the health, maintenance, etc., of anything.

vital statistics Quantitative data relating to certain aspects and conditions of human life, especially in relation to large population groups.

vi·ta·mer (vī′tə-mər) *n. Biochem.* Any dietary factor or other substance that possesses the activity of a given vitamin or acts to counteract a vitamin deficiency, as carotenoid in human subjects. [<VITA(MIN) + Gk. *meros* a part]

vi·ta·min (vī′tə-min) *n. Biochem.* Any of a group of complex organic substances found in minute quantities in most natural foodstuffs, and closely associated with the maintenance of normal physiological functions in man and animals. Numerous forms have been isolated and described under special names. Also **vi·ta·mine** ·(-mēn, -min). [<L *vita* life + AMINE] — **vi′ta·min′ic** *adj.*

vitamin A The fat-soluble vitamin occurring in green and yellow vegetables, dairy products, liver oil, and fish oil: it prevents atrophy of epithelial tissue and protects against night blindness.

vitamin B complex A group of water-soluble vitamins widely distributed in plants and animals, most members of which have special names.

vitamin B₁ Thiamine.

vitamin B₂ Riboflavin.

vitamin B₆ Pyridoxine.

vitamin B₁₂ A vitamin extracted from liver and believed to be protective against pernicious anemia.

vitamin C Ascorbic acid.

vitamin D The anti-rachitic vitamin occurring chiefly in fish-liver oils. Many closely related forms are known.

vitamin D₁ An impure mixture of calciferol and lumisterol.

vitamin D₂ Calciferol.

vitamin D₃ A form of vitamin D₂ found principally in fish-liver oils.

vitamin E The anti-sterility vitamin, found in whole grain cereals, seeds of legumes, corn and cottonseed oils, egg yolks, meat, and milk: known to be a mixture of alpha–, beta–, and gamma–tocopherols.

vitamin G Riboflavin.

vitamin H Biotin.

vitamin K₁ A vitamin, found in green leafy vegetables, which promotes the clotting of blood: also called *phylloquinone.*

vitamin K₂ A form of vitamin K₁ prepared from fishmeal.

vi·ta·min·ol·o·gy (vī′tə-min-ol′ə-jē) *n.* The scientific study of vitamins. [<VITAMIN + -(O)LOGY]

vitamin P The factor present in citrus juices along with vitamin C; citrin. It promotes the normal permeability of capillary walls.

vi·ta·scope (vī′tə-skōp) *n.* A device by which pictures taken by the kinetoscope are enlarged and exhibited on a screen. [<L *vita* life + -SCOPE]

Vi·tebsk (vē′tepsk) A city on the Western Dvina river in NE Belorussian S.S.R.

vi·tel·lin (vi-tel′in, vī-) *n. Biochem.* A phosphoprotein occurring in the yolk of eggs. [<VITELL(US) + -IN]

vi·tel·line (vi-tel′in, vī-) *adj.* 1 Of or pertaining to the food yolk of an egg. 2 Of a dull yellow, approaching red; of the color of the yolk of eggs. — *n.* The yolk of an egg. [<Med. L *vitellinus* <L *vitellus* VITELLUS]

vi·tel·lus (vi-tel′əs, vī-) *n.* The egg yolk. [<L, orig. dim. of *vitulus* a calf]

vi·tesse (vē-tes′) *n. French* Speed: used especially in the phrases **grande vitesse** (gränd), fast express, and **pe·tite vitesse** (pə-tēt′), ordinary express, or freight, etc.

vi·ti·ate (vish′ē-āt) *v.t.* ·at·ed, ·at·ing 1 To impair the use or value of; spoil. 2 To debase or corrupt. 3 To render legally ineffective: Fraud *vitiates* a contract. See synonyms under CORRUPT, DEFILE¹, POLLUTE. [<L *vitiatus*, pp. of *vitiare* <*vitium* a fault] — **vi·ti·a·ble** (vish′ē-ə-bəl) *adj.* — **vi′ti·a′tion** *n.* — **vi′ti·a′tor** *n.*

vi·ti·at·ed (vish′ē-ā′tid) *adj.* Contaminated; rendered defective; invalidated.

vit·i·cul·ture (vit′ə-kul′chər, vī′tə-) *n.* 1 The science and art of grape-growing. 2 The culture of the vine. [<L *vitis* a vine + CULTURE] — **vit′i·cul′tur·al** *adj.* — **vit′i·cul′tur·er, vit′i·cul′tur·ist** *n.*

Vi·ti Le·vu (vē′tē lā′vōō) The largest of the Fiji Islands; 4,010 square miles; capital, Suva.

vit·i·li·go (vit′ə-lī′gō) *n. Pathol.* A skin disease characterized by a partial privation of color in spots, with a tendency to increase in size;

piebald skin; leukoderma. [<L *vitiligo* tetter <*vitium* a fault]

Vi·tim (vi-tēm′, *Russian* vē-tyēm′) A river in NE Buryat-Mongol Autonomous S.S.R., flowing 1,132 miles to the Lena.

Vi·to·ri·a (vē-tôr′ē·ə, *Sp.* bē·tō′ryä) A city in north central Spain, capital of a Basque province.

Vi·tó·ria (vē-tô′ryə) The capital of Espírito Santo state, SE central Brazil; a port on the Atlantic coast.

vit·rain (vit′rān) *n.* A variety of bituminous coal having a vitreous appearance and a structure characterized by narrow, compact, crystalline bands. [<L *vitrum* glass, on analogy with *fusain* (def. 2)]

vit·re·ous (vit′rē-əs) *adj.* 1 Pertaining to glass; glassy. 2 Obtained from glass. 3 Resembling glass in some property or properties; vitriform. 4 Pertaining to the vitreous humor. [<L *vitreus* <*vitrum* glass] — **vit′re·os′i·ty** (-os′ə-tē), **vit′re·ous·ness** *n.*

vitreous electricity Electricity generated by rubbing glass with silk: regarded as positive.

vitreous humor *Anat.* The transparent jelly-like tissue that fills the ball of the eye and is enclosed by the hyaloid membrane. Also **vitreous body.**

vi·tres·cence (vi-tres′əns) *n.* The state of becoming vitreous.

vi·tres·cent (vi-tres′ənt) *adj.* 1 Capable of being turned into glass. 2 Tending to become glass. [<L *vitrum* glass + -ESCENT]

vi·tres·ci·ble (vi-tres′ə-bəl) *adj.* Capable of forming a viscous, glasslike layer under the action of great heat, as certain crushed minerals. [<VITRESC(ENT) + -IBLE]

vitri– *combining form* Glass; of or pertaining to glass; crystalline: *vitriform.* Also, before vowels, **vitr–.** [<L *vitrum* glass]

vit·ric (vit′rik) *adj.* Pertaining to or like glass.

vit·ri·fac·ture (vit′rə-fak′chər) *n.* The manufacture of vitreous or vitrified wares, as glass. [<VITRI– + (MANU)FACTURE]

vit·ri·fi·ca·tion (vit′rə-fə-kā′shən) *n.* 1 The process of vitrifying. 2 The state of being vitrified. 3 A vitrified object. Also **vit′ri·fac′tion** (-fak′shən).

vit·ri·form (vit′rə-fôrm) *adj.* Having a glassy appearance; glasslike.

vit·ri·fy (vit′rə-fī) *v.t.* & *v.i.* ·fied, ·fy·ing To change into glass or a vitreous substance; make or become vitreous. [<MF *vitrifier* <L *vitrum* glass + *facere* make] — **vit′ri·fi′a·ble** *adj.*

vit·rine (vit′rin) *n.* A glass showcase for art objects. [<F <*vitre* glass <L *vitrum*]

vit·ri·ol (vit′rē-ōl, -əl) *n.* 1 *Chem.* a Sulfuric acid, originally made from green vitriol: more commonly called **oil of vitriol.** b Any sulfate of a heavy metal, as **green vitriol,** from iron; **blue vitriol,** from copper; **white vitriol,** from zinc. 2 Anything sharp or caustic, as sarcasm. — *v.t.* ·oled or ·olled, ·ol·ing or ·ol·ling 1 To injure (a person) with vitriol. 2 To subject (anything) to the agency of vitriol. [<OF <Med. L *vitriolum* <L *vitrum* glass; so called because of its glassy appearance]

vit·ri·ol·ic (vit′rē-ol′ik) *adj.* 1 Derived from a vitriol. 2 Corrosive, burning, or caustic.

vit·ri·ol·ize (vit′rē-əl·īz′) *v.t.* ·ized, ·iz·ing 1 To corrode, injure, or burn with sulfuric acid. 2 To convert into or impregnate with vitriol. — **vit′ri·ol·i·za′tion** *n.*

Vi·tru·vi·us (vi-trōō′vē·əs) Roman architect, military engineer, and writer of the first century B.C.; full name, *Marcus Vitruvius Pollio.* — **Vi·tru′vi·an** *adj.*

vit·ta (vit′ə) *n. pl.* **vit·tae** (vit′ē) 1 A fillet or band for the head; specifically, a sacred or sacrificial headband or chaplet worn by brides, vestals, priests, poets, and sacrificial victims. 2 *Bot.* An oil tube; a tube or canal in the fruit of plants of the parsley family, containing an aromatic oil. 3 *Zool.* A band or stripe, as of color. [<L *viere* plait]

vit·tate (vit′āt) *adj.* 1 Having or bearing vittae or a vitta. 2 Striped.

vit·tles (vit′lz) See VICTUAL.

Vit·to·rio (vit-tô′ryō) Italian form of VICTOR.

Vit·to·rio E·ma·nu·e·le (vit-tô′ryō ā-mä-nwā′lā) See VICTOR EMMANUEL.

Vit·to·rio Ve·ne·to (vit-tô′ryō ve′nā-tō) A city in NE Italy: scene of an Italian victory and armistice in World War I, November 3, 1918.

vit·u·line (vich′ōō-līn, -lin) *adj.* Pertaining

to, of, or like a calf or veal. [<L *vitulinus* <*vitulus* a calf]

vi·tu·per·ate (vī-tōō′pə-rāt, -tyōō′-, vi-) *v.t.* ·at·ed, ·at·ing To find fault with abusively; rail at; berate; scold. See synonyms under ABUSE. [<L *vituperatus,* pp. of *vituperare* blame, scold <*vitium* a fault + *parare* prepare] — **vi·tu′per·a′tion** *n.* — **vi·tu′per·a′tive** *adj.* — **vi·tu′per·a′tive·ly** *adv.* — **vi·tu′per·a′tor** *n.*

vi·va (vē′vä) *interj.* Live! Long live!: a shout of applause; an acclamation or salute. [<Ital., 3rd person sing. present subjunctive of *vivere* live <L]

vi·va·ce (vē-vä′chā) *adv. Music* Lively; quickly; briskly. Also **vi·va′ce·men′te** (-mān′tā). [<Ital. <L *vivax.* See VIVACIOUS.]

vi·va·cious (vi-vā′shəs, vī-) *adj.* 1 Full of life and spirits; lively; active. 2 *Obs.* Tenacious of life. [<L *vivax, vivacis* <*vivere* live] — **vi·va′cious·ly** *adv.* — **vi·va′cious·ness** *n.*

Synonyms: animated, brisk, cheerful, frolicsome, gay, jocose, jocund, lively, merry, mirthful, pleasant, sparkling, spirited, sportive. See ALIVE, SPRIGHTLY. *Antonyms:* dead, dreary, dull, heavy, inanimate, lifeless, monotonous, moody, spiritless, stolid, stupid.

vi·vac·i·ty (vi-vas′ə-tē, vī-) *n. pl.* ·ties 1 The state or quality of being vivacious. 2 Sprightliness, as of temper or behavior; liveliness. 3 A vivacious act, expression, etc.

Vi·val·di (vē-väl′dē), **Antonio,** 1675?-1743, Italian violinist and composer.

vi·van·dière (vē-vän-dyâr′) *n.* Formerly, a woman who supplied provisions and liquors to troops in the field, as in the French army. [<F, fem. of *vivandier* a sutler, ult. <L *vivenda.* See VIAND.]

vi·var·i·um (vī-vâr′ē·əm) *n. pl.* ·var·i·a (-vâr′ē·ə) or ·var·i·ums A place for keeping or raising live animals, fish, or plants, as a park, pond, aquarium, cage, etc. Also **viv·a·ry** (viv′ər·ē). [<L, orig. neut. of *vivarius* concerning live things <*vivus* alive <*vivere* live]

vi·va vo·ce (vī′və vō′sē) *Latin* By spoken word; orally: used both as an adverb and adjective.

vive (vēv) *French interj.* Live! Long live!: used in acclamation: opposed to *à bas.*

vive la ré·pu·blique (vēv lä rā-pü-blēk′) *French* Long live the republic!

vive le roi (vēv lə rwä′) *French* Long live the king!

vi·ver·rine (vī-ver′īn, -in, vi-) *adj.* Belonging or pertaining to a family (*Viverridae*) of small carnivores including civets and mongooses. — *n.* A civet. [<NL *viverrinus* <L *viverra* a ferret]

vi·vers (vī′vərz) *n. pl. Scot.* Food; provisions.

vives (vīvz) *n. pl.* A morbid enlargement of the submaxillary glands of the horse: also called *fives.* [Earlier *avives* <OF <Sp, *avivas* <Arabic *addhíba* <*al* the + *dhíba* a she-wolf]

Viv·i·an (vī-vē·ən, *Ger.* vē′vē·än) A personal name. Also **Viv·i·en** (viv′ē·ən, *Fr.* vē-vyän′), *Fr.* fem. **Vi·vienne** (vē-vyen′), *Ital.* fem. **Vi·vi·a·na** (vē-vyä′nä) [<L, lively] — **Vivian** In Arthurian romance, the wily mistress of Merlin, who imprisons him by his own magic: also known as *the Lady of the Lake, Nimue.* Also **Vivien, Viviane.**

viv·id (viv′id) *adj.* 1 Having an appearance of vigorous life; intense: said of colors having intense luminosity. 2 Producing or fitted to evoke lifelike imagery or suggestion. 3 Acting or exercised with lively interest; keen; clearly felt; strongly expressed. [<L *vividus* lively <*vivere* live] — **viv′id·ly** *adv.* — **viv′id·ness** *n.*

Synonyms: animated, bright, brilliant, clear, graphic, intense, keen, lively, luminous, quick, sprightly, stirring, telling, vigorous. See GRAPHIC. *Antonyms:* dim, dreary, dull, gloomy, heavy, lifeless, prosy, spiritless, stupid.

viv·i·fy (viv′ə-fī) *v.t.* ·fied, ·fy·ing 1 To give life to; animate; vitalize. 2 To make more vivid or striking. [<OF *vivifier* <LL *vivificare* <L *vivus* alive + *facere* make] — **viv′i·fi·ca′tion** (-fə-kā′shən) *n.* — **viv′i·fi′er** *n.*

vi·vip·a·rous (vi-vip′ər-əs) *adj.* 1 *Zool.* Bringing forth living young, as most mammals: contrasted with *oviparous.* 2 *Bot.* Producing bulbs or seeds that germinate while still attached to the parent plant; proliferous. [<L *viviparus* <*vivus* alive + *parere* bring forth] — **vi·vip′a·rous·ly** *adv.* — **vi·vip′a·rous·ness, vi·vi·par·i·ty** (viv′ə-par′ə-tē) *n.*

viv·i·sect (viv′ə·sekt) *v.t.* To dissect or operate upon (a living animal), with a view to exposing its physiological processes. — *v.i.* To practice vivisection. [Back formation <VIVISECTION] — **viv′i·sec′tor** *n.*

viv·i·sec·tion (viv′ə·sek′shən) *n.* 1 The dissection of a living animal. 2 Experimentation on living animals by means of operations designed to promote knowledge of physiological and pathological processes. [<L *vivus* living, alive + *sectio, -onis* a cutting. See SECTION.] — **viv′i·sec′tion·al** *adj.* — **viv′i·sec′tion·ist** *n.* & *adj.*

vix·en (vik′sən) *n.* 1 A turbulent, quarrelsome woman; shrew. 2 A female fox. [ME *fixen* a she-fox, fem. of OE *fox*] — **vix′en·ish** *adj.* — **vix′en·ly** *adj.* & *adv.*

viz·ard (viz′ərd) *n.* A mask; visor: also spelled *visard.* [Alter. of VISOR]

viz·ard·ed (viz′ərd·id) *adj.* Masked; disguised or protected by a vizard.

Viz·ca·ya (vēs·kä′yä, *Sp.* bēth·kä′yä) The Spanish name for BISCAY.

Viz·e·tel·ly (viz′ə·tel′ē) **Frank Horace,** 1864–1938, U.S. lexicographer and encyclopedist born in England.

vi·zier (vi·zir′, viz′yər) *n.* A high official of a Moslem country, especially of the old Turkish Empire; a minister of state. Also **vi·zir′.** — **grand vizier** The highest dignitary in Moslem countries; the prime minister. [<Turkish *vezir* <Arabic *wazīr* a counselor, orig. a porter < *wazara* carry]

vi·zier·ate (vi·zir′it, -āt, viz′yər·it, -yə·rāt) *n.* The office or dignity of a vizier. Also **vi·zier′al·ty, vi·zier′ship, vi·zir′ate, vi·zir′ship.**

vi·zor (vī′zər, viz′ər) *n.* The movable upper front piece of a helmet protecting the eyes. See VISOR.

Vlad·i·mir (vlad′ə·mir, *Russian* vlä·dyē′mir), 956?–1015, first Christian Russian ruler.

Vlad·i·mir (vlad′ə·mir, *Russian* vlä·dyē′mir) A city in central European Russian S.F.S.R., NE of Moscow.

VIZOR
15th century.

Vla·di·vos·tok (vlad′ə·vos·tok′, -vos′tok; *Russian* vlä′dyē·vos·tôk′) A port on the Sea of Japan in extreme SE Asiatic Russian S.F.S.R.

Vla·minck (vlà·maṅk′), **Maurice de,** 1876–1958, French painter.

Vlis·sing·en (vlis′ing·ən) The Dutch name for FLUSHING.

Vlo·na (vlō′nä) The Albanian name for VALONA.

Vl·ta·va (vul′tä·vä) A river in central Bohemia, Czechoslovakia, flowing 267 miles north from the Bohemian Forest, through Prague, to the Elbe: German *Moldau.*

V-mail (vē′māl′) *n.* Mail written on special forms, transmitted overseas in World War II on microfilm, and enlarged at point of reception for final delivery. [<V(ICTORY) + MAIL[1]]

vo·ca·ble (vō′kə·bəl) *n.* 1 A word, chiefly as regarded in relation to its sound or combination of sounds instead of its meaning. 2 A vocal sound. — *adj.* Utterable. [<F <L *vocabulum* a name <*vocare* call <*vox* voice]

vo·cab·u·lar·y (vō·kab′yə·ler′ē) *n. pl.* **·lar·ies** 1 A list of words or of words and phrases, especially one arranged in alphabetical order and defined or translated; a lexicon; glossary. 2 All the words of a language. 3 A sum or aggregate of the words used or understood by a particular person, class, etc., or employed in some specialized field of knowledge. 4 The range of expression at a person's disposal, especially in art. [<LL *vocabularius* <L *vocabulum.* See VOCABLE.]

vocabulary entry 1 A word or term given in a vocabulary. 2 A word, term, or phrase entered in a dictionary, in some readily distinguishable type, for purposes of definition or identification. Vocabulary entries may be listed in alphabetical place (main entries), run in within a main entry (additional parts of speech, inflected forms, idioms, etc.), run on at the end of an entry (derivatives and related words), listed under a word, prefix, or combining form (self-explanatory compounds and two-word phrases), or entered in a special

section of the book. In this dictionary, all vocabulary entries are shown in boldface type or preceded by a boldface em-dash.

vo·cal (vō′kəl) *adj.* 1 Of or pertaining to the voice; uttered by the voice; oral: *vocal* protests. 2 Having voice; endowed with the power of utterance: *vocal* creatures. 3 Composed for or performed by the voice: a *vocal* score. 4 Concerned in the production of voice: the *vocal* organs. 5 Full of voices or sounds; resounding: The air was *vocal* with their cries. 6 Eloquent without need of speech: the *vocal* beauty of the Parthenon. 7 Freely expressing oneself in speech; readily given to voicing opinions: the *vocal* segment of the populace. 8 *Phonet.* a Voiced; sonant, as *b, d, g,* distinguished from *p, t, k.* b Pertaining to or like a vowel; vocalic. See synonyms under VERBAL. — *n. Phonet.* 1 A vowel. 2 A voiced consonant. [<L *vocalis* speaking, sounding <*vox, vocis* a voice. Doublet of VOWEL.] — **vo′cal·ly** *adv.*

VOCAL CORDS
a. Open. *b.* Closed. *c.* Voice. *d.* Whisper.

vocal cords Two membranous bands extending from the thyroid cartilage of the larynx. The edges of these bands, when drawn tense, are caused to vibrate by the passage of air from the lungs, thereby producing voice; the degree of tension of the cords controls the pitch of the voice.

vo·cal·ic (vō·kal′ik) *adj.* Consisting of, like, or relating to vowel sounds.

vo·ca·lise (vō·kä·lēz′) *n. Music* A practice exercise for singers designed to develop flexibility and control of pitch and tonal beauty, usually employing vowels or Italian syllables. [<F]

vo·cal·ism (vō′kəl·iz′əm) *n.* 1 Vocalization. 2 A vocalic sound; also, a vowel system. 3 Singing; also, the technique of singing.

vo·cal·ist (vō′kəl·ist) *n.* A singer, especially one who has a cultivated voice.

vo·cal·ize (vō′kəl·īz) *v.* **·ized, ·iz·ing** *v.t.* 1 To make vocal; utter, say, or sing; make sonant. 2 To provide a voice for; render articulate. 3 To mark with vowel points, as a Hebrew text. 4 *Phonet.* a To change to or use as a vowel: to *vocalize* y. b To voice. — *v.i.* 5 To produce sounds with the voice, as in speaking or singing. 6 *Phonet.* To be changed to a vowel. — **vo′cal·i·za′tion** *n.* — **vo′cal·iz′er** *n.*

vo·ca·tion (vō·kā′shən) *n.* 1 A stated or regular occupation; a calling. 2 A call to, or fitness for, a certain career, especially a religious position. 3 The work or profession for which one has a sense of special fitness. See synonyms under BUSINESS. [<L *vocatio, -onis* <*vocatus,* pp. of *vocare* call] — **vo·ca′tion·al** *adj.* — **vo·ca′tion·al·ly** *adv.*

vocational adviser One who diagnoses the personal characteristics of people with the view of suggesting suitable vocations for them; a specialist in vocational guidance. Also **vocational expert.**

vocational school See under SCHOOL.

voc·a·tive (vok′ə·tiv) *adj.* 1 Pertaining to or used in the act of calling. 2 *Gram.* In some inflected languages, denoting the case of a noun, pronoun, or adjective used in direct address: The name "Brutus" is in the *vocative* case in "Et tu, Brute." — *n. Gram.* 1 The vocative case. 2 A word in this case. [<F, fem. of *vocatif* <L *vocativus* <*vocare* call]

vo·ces (vō′sēz) Plural of VOX.

vo·cif·er·ant (vō·sif′ər·ənt) *adj.* Vociferous; clamorous; uttering loud cries. — *n.* A vociferous person. [<L *vociferans, -antis,* ppr. of *vociferari.* See VOCIFERATE.] — **vo·cif′er·ance** *n.*

vo·cif·er·ate (vō·sif′ə·rāt) *v.t.* & *v.i.* **·at·ed, ·at·ing** To cry out with a loud voice; exclaim noisily; shout; bawl. See synonyms under CALL. [<L *vociferatus,* pp. of *vociferari* cry out <*vox, vocis* a voice + *ferre* carry] — **vo·cif′er·a′tion** *n.* — **vo·cif′er·a′tor** *n.*

vo·cif·er·ous (vō·sif′ər·əs) *adj.* Making a loud outcry; clamorous. See synonyms under NOISY. — **vo·cif′er·ous·ly** *adv.* — **vo·cif′er·ous·ness** *n.*

vod·ka (vod′kə, *Russian* vôd′kä) *n.* A colorless alcoholic liquor, originally made in Poland and Russia, usually made from fermented wheat mash. [<Russian, dim. of *voda* water]

voe (vō) *n. Scot.* A small bay, creek, or inlet.

Vo·gel·kop (vō′gəl·kôp′) A peninsula of NW Netherlands New Guinea, connected to the mainland by an isthmus 20 miles wide; about 225 miles east to west, about 135 miles north to south.

vogue (vōg) *n.* 1 The prevalent way or fashion; popular temporary usage: often preceded by *in.* 2 Popular favor; popularity. [<F, fashion, orig. rowing <*voguer* row <Ital. *vogare* <MHG *wogen* sail <*woge* a wave]

Vo·gul (vō′gool) *n.* 1 One of a Finno–Ugric people of the Ural Mountains. 2 The Ugric language of these people.

voice (vois) *n.* 1 The sound produced by the vocal organs of a person or animal; also, the quality or character of such sound: a melodious *voice.* 2 The power or faculty of vocal utterance; speech. 3 A sound suggesting vocal utterance or speech: the *voice* of the wind. 4 Opinion or choice expressed; also, the right of expressing a preference or judgment: to have a *voice* in the affair. 5 Instruction; admonition; teaching: the *voice* of nature. 6 A speaker; also, a person or agency by which the thought, wish, or purpose of another is expressed: This journal is the *voice* of the teaching profession. 7 Expression of thought, opinion, feeling, etc.: to give *voice* to one's ideals. 8 *Phonet.* The sound produced by vibration of the vocal cords, as heard in the utterance of vowels and certain consonants, as (g), (m),(v): distinguished from *whisper,* and also from *breath,* as heard in (k), (sh), (f). 9 Musical tone produced by vibration of the vocal cords and resonating in the cavities of the throat and head; also, the ability to sing, or the state of the vocal organs with regard to this ability: to be in poor *voice.* 10 *Gram.* The relation of the action expressed by the verb to the subject, or the form of the verb indicating this relationship. In English, as in most Indo–European languages, a distinction between an *active* and a *passive* voice is made, indicating, respectively, that the subject of the sentence is either performing the action or is being acted upon. (Active: *He wrote the letter.* Passive: *The letter was written by him.*) In Greek and Sanskrit verbs, there is, in addition, a *middle* voice, representing the subject as acting upon himself directly, or in his own interest. 11 *Obs.* Report; rumor; fame. — **with one voice** With one accord; unitedly; unanimously. — *v.t.* **voiced, voic·ing** 1 To put into speech; give expression to; utter. 2 *Music* To regulate the tones of; tune, as the pipes of an organ. 3 *Phonet.* To utter with voice or sonance. [<OF *vois* <L *vox, vocis*]

voiced (voist) *adj.* 1 Having a voice; expressed by voice. 2 *Phonet.* Uttered with vibration of the vocal cords, as (b), (d), (z); sonant: opposed to *surd, voiceless.*

voice·ful (vois′fəl) *adj.* Having vocal quality.

voice·less (vois′lis) *adj.* 1 Having no voice, speech, or suffrage. 2 *Phonet.* Produced without voiced breath, as (p), (t), (s); surd: opposed to *sonant, voiced.* — **voice′less·ly** *adv.*

voice-o·ver (vois′ō′vər) *n.* In motion pictures and television programs, the voice of a narrator or announcer speaking off camera.

voice part A single part, as a melody written for the voice and either sung, or played by a solo instrument, in a concerted composition.

voice·print (vois′print′) *n.* A record of a speech sound, consisting of a complex pattern of wavy lines corresponding to the various pitches used in the utterance.

void (void) *adj.* 1 Not occupied by matter or by visible matter; empty. 2 Destitute; clear or free: with *of: void* of reason, *void* of offense.

3 Unoccupied, as a house or room; having no incumbent. **4** Having no legal force or validity; incapable of confirmation or ratification; invalid; null. **5** Producing no effect; useless. See synonyms under VACANT. — *n.* **1** An empty space; a vacuum. **2** A breach of surface or matter; a disconnecting space. **3** Empty condition or feeling; a blank. — *v.t.* **1** To make void or of no effect; annul. **2** To empty or remove (contents); evacuate, as urine. **3** *Archaic* To leave empty or vacant. [<OF *voide*, fem. of. *voit*, ult. <LL *vocuus* empty <L *vacuus*] — **void′er** *n.*

void·a·ble (voi′də·bəl) *adj.* **1** Capable of being made void: A *voidable* contract is valid unless annulled. **2** That may be evacuated. — **void′·a·ble·ness** *n.*

void·ance (void′ns) *n.* **1** The act of voiding, evacuating, ejecting, or emptying. **2** The state or condition of being void; vacancy: *voidance* of a benefice. [<AF *voidaunce*, OF *vuidance* < *voider* empty < *voit* VOID]

void·ed (voi′did) *adj.* **1** Made empty or void; cleared of contents; having a vacant space. **2** *Her.* Having the central area removed, so as to leave only an outline through which the field is visible: said of a charge, as a cross.

voi·là (vwà·là′) *interj. French* There! behold! literally, see there.

voi·là tout (vwà·là tōō′) *French* That is all; there is the whole matter.

voile (voil, *Fr.* vwàl) *n.* A fine, sheer cotton, silk, wool, or rayon fabric like heavy veiling: used for summer dresses and curtains. [<F, a veil <OF *veile* VEIL]

voir dire (vwàr dēr′) *Law* A legal oath administered to a witness to be examined, to make true answers to the questions to be asked him regarding his competency. [<OF *voir* truth + *dire* say]

voix (vwà) *n. French* The voice.

voix cé·leste (vwà sā·lest′) *French* An organ stop consisting of two ranks of soft flue stops which produce a waving effect; literally, heavenly voice.

Voj·vo·di·na An autonomous province of NE Yugoslavia, included in Serbia as its northern part and bordering on Hungary and Romania; 8,683 square miles; capital Novi Sad. Also **Voy′vo·di·na, Vol′vo·di·na.**

vo·lant (vō′lənt) *adj.* **1** Passing through the air; flying, or able to fly. **2** Characterized by lightness and quickness; nimble. **3** *Her.* Flying, as a bird or bee. [<OF, ppr. of *voler* fly <L *volare*]

vo·lan·te (vō·län′tā) *adj. Music* Swift and light. [<Ital., ppr. of *volare* fly <L]

Vo·la·pük (vō′lə·pük′) *n.* A proposed universal language, invented in 1879 by Johann M. Schleyer, a German priest. [<Volapük *vol* world + *pük* speech] — **Vo′la·pük′ist** *n.*

vo·lar[1] (vō′lər) *adj.* Used in flying; pertaining to flight. [<L *volare* fly]

vo·lar[2] (vō′lər) *adj.* Pertaining to the sole of the foot or palm of the hand. [<L *vola* sole, palm]

vol·a·tile (vol′ə·til) *adj.* **1** Evaporating rapidly at ordinary temperatures on exposure to the air; capable of being vaporized. **2** Easily influenced; fickle; changeable. **3** Transient; fleeting; ephemeral. **4** *Obs.* Flying, or able to fly. See synonyms under MOBILE[1]. [<OF *volatil* <L *volatilis* < *volare* fly]

volatile oil Any oil that may be readily vaporized, especially one distilled from plants: distinguished from *fixed oil.*

volatile salts Salts that volatilize without residue; sal volatile.

vol·a·til·i·ty (vol′ə·til′ə·tē) *n.* **1** The state or quality of being volatile. **2** The property of being freely or rapidly diffused in the atmosphere. Also **vol′a·tile·ness.**

vol·a·til·ize (vol′ə·til·īz′) *v.t. & v.i.* **·ized, ·iz·ing** **1** To make or become volatile. **2** To pass off or cause to pass off in vapor; evaporate. — **vol′a·til·iz′a·ble** *adj.* — **vol′a·til·i·za′tion** *n.* — **vol′a·til·iz′er** *n.*

vol·au·vent (vôl·ō·vän′) *n. French* A patty shell of light puff paste filled with a ragout of meat, fowl, or fish.

vol·can·ic (vol·kan′ik) *adj.* **1** Of, pertaining to, or characteristic of a volcano or volcanoes. **2** Produced by a volcano or by igneous action: distinguished from *plutonic.* — **vol·can·ic·i·ty** (vol′kə·nis′ə·tē) *n.* — **vol·can′·i·cal·ly** *adv.*

volcanic glass An igneous rock of volcanic origin and glassy texture having cooled too quickly to crystallize, as obsidian.

volcanic rocks Rocks formed by the consolidation of lava from volcanoes.

vol·can·ism (vol′kən·iz′əm) *n.* The conditions, phenomena, or science of volcanoes or volcanic action.

vol·can·ist (vol′kən·ist) *n.* One who studies, or is expert on volcanoes; a volcanologist.

vol·can·ize (vol′kən·īz) *v.t.* **·ized, ·iz·ing** To subject to the action and effects of volcanic heat. — **vol′can·i·za′tion** *n.*

vol·ca·no (vol·kā′nō) *n. pl.* **·noes** or **·nos** *Geol.* An opening in the earth's surface surrounded by an accumulation of ejected material, forming a hill or mountain, from which heated matter is or has been ejected: known in the former case as *active,* and in the latter as *dormant* or *extinct.* [<Ital. <L *Volcanus, Vulcanus* Vulcan]

Volcano Islands Three small islands, including Iwo Jima, in the western Pacific south of the Bonin Islands, administered by the United States; total, 11 square miles; held by Japan, 1887–1945. *Japanese* **Ka·zan Ret·to** (kä·zän ret·tō).

vol·can·ol·o·gy (vol′kən·ol′ə·jē) *n.* The scientific study of volcanoes. — **vol′can·o·log′i·cal** (-ə·loj′i·kəl) *adj.* — **vol′can·ol′o·gist** *n.*

vole[1] (vōl) *n.* Any of a genus (*Microtus*) of short-tailed, mouselike or ratlike rodents; especially, the common European field mouse or the North American meadow mouse. [Short for earlier *vole mouse* <*vole* a field (<Norw. *voll*) + MOUSE]

vole[2] (vōl) *n.* In some card games, as écarté, a winning of all the tricks in a deal; hence, the entire range; a slam. — **to go the vole** To risk all for great gains. [<F, appar. <*voler* fly <L *volare*]

vol·er·y (vol′ər·ē) *n. pl.* **·er·ies** A large bird cage; aviary; also, the birds in it. [<F *volerie* a flying <*voler.* See VOLE[2].]

Vol·ga The longest river in Europe, in central European Russia, flowing 2,290 miles east and south from the Valdai Hills to its delta, the Volga Basin (approximately 2,500 square miles), on the Caspian Sea.

Vol·hyn·i·a (vol·hin′ē·ə, vo·lin′ē·ə) A historical region, formerly in Poland, in NW Ukrainian S.S.R.; about 27,230 square miles. *Russian* **Vo·lyn** (vo·lin′y′), *Polish* **Wo·łyń** (vô′win·y′). — **Vol·hyn′ian** *adj.*

vol·i·tant (vol′ə·tənt) *adj.* Flying, or having power to fly; volant. [<L *volitans, -antis,* ppr. of *volitare,* freq. of *volare* fly]

vol·i·ta·tion (vol′ə·tā′shən) *n.* The act or power of flying; flight. [<L *volitatus,* pp. of *volitare.* See VOLITANT.] — **vol′i·ta′tion·al** *adj.*

vo·li·tient (və·lish′ənt) *adj.* Exercising the will, or having freedom of will; willing; voluntary. [<VOLITI(ON) + -ENT] — **vo·li′tien·cy** *n.*

vo·li·tion (və·lish′ən) *n.* **1** The act or faculty of willing; exercise of the will; especially, the termination of a process of deliberation or vacillation of purpose by a decision or choice. **2** The faculty of will by which the powers are directed toward the attainment of a chosen end; willpower. **3** That which is specifically willed or determined upon. [<F <Med. L *volitio, -onis* <L *vol-,* stem of *velle* will] — **vo·li′tion·al** *adj.* — **vo·li′tion·al·ly** *adv.*

vol·i·tive (vol′ə·tiv) *adj.* **1** Of, pertaining to, or originating in the will. **2** Expressing a wish or permission.

Vol·khov **1** A river of NW European Russia, flowing 140 miles NE from Lake Ilmen, through Novgorod to Lake Ladoga. **2** A town on the Volkhov river in Russia. Also **Vol′khof.**

Volks·lied (fôlks′lēt′) *n. pl.* **·lied·er** (-lē′dər) *German* A folk song; popular song.

vol·ley (vol′ē) *n.* **1** A simultaneous discharge of many missiles; also, the missiles so discharged. **2** Any discharge of many things at once: a *volley* of oaths. **3** In tennis, a return of the ball before it touches the ground. **4** In soccer, a kick given the ball before its rebound. **5** In cricket, a ball bowled so that it strikes the head of the wicket before it touches the ground. — *v.t. & v.i.* **·leyed, ·ley·ing** **1** To discharge or be discharged in a volley; let fly together. **2** In tennis, to return (the ball) without allowing it to touch the ground. **3** In soccer, to kick (the ball) before its rebound; in cricket, to bowl (a ball) full pitch. [<MF *volée,* pp. fem. of *voler* fly <L *volare*]

volley ball A game in which a number of players on both sides of a high net endeavor to keep a large ball in motion with the hands from side to side without letting it drop; also, the ball used. Also **vol·ley·ball** (vol′ē·bôl′).

Vo·log·da **1** A city in northwest Russia; an industrial and dairy center; capital of a 15th century principality. **2** A region (oblast) in northwest Russia.

Vo·los (vō′los) A port city on the **Gulf of Volos,** an inlet of the Aegean in SE Thessaly, Greece (about 20 miles long and wide); the principal port of Thessaly and capital of Magnesia nome.

vo·lost (vō′lost) *n.* A district having one joint administrative assembly; a rural soviet; formerly, a canton. [<Russian *volost′*]

vol·plane (vol′plān) *v.i.* **·planed, ·plan·ing** To glide in an airplane. — *n.* An airplane glide. [<F *vol plané* gliding flight <*vol* flight + *plané,* pp. of *planer* glide, soar] — **vol′plan·ist** *n.*

Vol·scian (vol′shən) *adj.* Of or pertaining to the **Vol·sci** (vol′sī), a warlike people of ancient Italy, subdued by the Romans about 350 B.C. — *n.* **1** One of the Volsci. **2** Their language, belonging to the Sabellian branch of the Italic languages.

Vol·stead Act (vol′sted) An act to enforce the Eighteenth (Prohibition) Amendment to the Constitution of the United States, and defining intoxicating liquors as those containing more than one half of one percent of alcohol by volume: effective 1920–33. [after Representative Andrew J. *Volstead,* 1860–1947, of Minnesota] — **Vol′stead·ism** *n.*

Vol·sun·ga Sa·ga (vol′sŏong·gə sä′gə) A prose version of the legends of the dwarf race, the Nibelungs, and Sigurd, the grandson of Volsung. See NIBELUNGENLIED. [<ON *Völsunga saga,* lit., saga of the Volsungs]

volt[1] (vōlt) *n.* The unit of electromotive force, or that difference of potential which, when steadily applied to a conductor whose resistance is one ohm, will produce a current of one ampere. Abbr. *v., V.* [after Alessandro *Volta*]

volt[2] (vōlt) *n.* **1** In horse-training, a gait in which the horse moves partially sidewise round a center with the head turned out; a circular tread. **2** In fencing, a sudden leap to avoid a thrust. [<F *volte* a turn <Ital. *volta,* orig. fem. of *volvere* turn <L]

vol·ta (vol′tə, *Ital.* vôl′tä) *n. pl.* **·te** (-tä) *Music* A turning; a time: used mainly in phrases. — **prima volta** First time. — **seconda volta** Second time. — **una volta** Once. [<Ital. See VOLT[2].]

Vol·ta (vol′tä) The principal river of Ghana, formed by the confluence, in north central Ghana, of the **Black Volta** and **White Volta,** and flowing 300 miles (with Black Volta, about 800 miles) SE to the Bight of Benin.

Vol·ta (vôl′tä), **Count Alessandro,** 1745–1827, Italian physicist and pioneer in electricity.

volt·age (vōl′tij) *n.* Electromotive force expressed in volts: the *voltage* of a current.

vol·ta·ic (vol·tā′ik) *adj.* **1** Pertaining to electricity developed through chemical action or contact; galvanic: a *voltaic* battery; *voltaic* cell. **2** Of or pertaining to Alessandro Volta. [after Alessandro *Volta*]

voltaic battery An assembly of voltaic cells which operate as a unit in generating an electric current.

voltaic cell Cell (def. 5).

voltaic couple A pair of dissimilar, usually metallic, substances which will produce an electric current when immersed in an electrolyte.

voltaic pile An arrangement of dissimilar metal disks, placed alternately and having between them paper moistened with acids for the generation of an electric current. Also *galvanic pile.*

Vol·taire (vol·târ′, *Fr.* vôl·târ′), **François Marie Arouet de,** 1694–1778, French author and philosopher.

volt·a·ism (vol′tə·iz′əm) *n.* The act of producing an electric current by the chemical action of a liquid on dissimilar metals; galvanism. [after Alessandro *Volta*]

volt·am·e·ter (vol·tam′ə·tər) *n.* A coulometer. [<VOLTA(IC) + -METER]

volt·am·me·ter (vôlt′am′mē′tər) *n.* A wattmeter. [<VOLT(AGE) + AM(PERAGE) + -METER]

volt–am·pere (vôlt′am′pir) *n.* A watt: so called because it is the rate of working in an electric circuit when the current is one ampere and the potential one volt.

volte–face (volt·fäs′, *Fr.* vôlt·fäs′) *n.* 1 A turning about so as to face in the opposite direction. 2 A complete change of attitude or reversal of opinion. [<F <Ital. *volta faccia* < *volta* a turning + *faccia* a face <L *facies*]

vol·ti (vôl′tē) *interj. Music* Turn; specifically, a direction to turn the leaf. [<Ital., imperative sing. of *voltare* turn < *volta*. See VOLT².]

vol·ti·geur (vôl·tē·zhœr′) *n.* One who vaults; a tumbler; formerly, in the French army, a skirmisher in a light infantry regiment. [<F < *voltiger* hover, vault <Ital. *volteggiare* < *volta.* See VOLT².]

volt·me·ter (vôlt′mē′tər) *n.* An instrument for determining the voltage or potential difference existing between any two points, generally consisting of a calibrated galvanometer wound with a coil of high resistance.

Vol·tur·no (vôl·tŏŏr′nō) The chief river of southern Italy, arising in the Apennines and flowing 109 miles to the Tyrrhenian Sea NW of Naples.

vol·u·ble (vol′yə·bəl) *adj.* 1 Having a flow of words or fluency in speaking; talkative; garrulous. 2 Turning readily or easily; revolving; apt or formed to roll. 3 Twining, as a plant. [<MF <L *volubilis* easily turned < *volutus,* pp. of *volvere* turn] — **vol′u·bil′i·ty, vol′u·ble·ness** *n.* — **vol′u·bly** *adv.*

vol·ume (vol′yŏŏm, -yəm) *n.* 1 A collection of sheets of paper bound together; a book; a separately bound part of a work; anciently, a written roll, a scroll, as of papyrus or vellum. 2 Sufficient matter to fill a volume. 3 Something of a swelling form; coil; fold or turn. 4 A large quantity; a considerable amount. 5 Space occupied, as measured by cubic units, that is, cubic centimeters, cubic feet, etc. 6 The amount of space included by the bounding surfaces of a solid. 7 *Music* Fullness or quantity of sound or tone. — **to speak volumes** To be full of meaning; express a great deal. [<OF *volum* <L *volumen* a roll, scroll < *volutus.* See VOLUBLE.]

vol·umed (vol′yŏŏmd, -yəmd) *adj.* 1 Rounded or swelling in form: *volumed* mists. 2 Having bulk or quantity. 3 Being in one or more volumes: a two-*volumed* history.

vo·lu·me·ter (və·lŏŏ′mə·tər) *n.* An instrument for measuring the volume of a gas by the amount of liquid displaced by it in a graduated vessel, under known conditions of pressure and temperature. [<VOLU(ME) + -METER]

vol·u·met·ric (vol′yə·met′rik) *adj. Chem.* Of or pertaining to measurement of substances by comparison of volumes or by volumetric analysis. Also **vol′u·met′ri·cal.** — **vol′u·met′ri·cal·ly** *adv.* — **vo·lu·me·try** (və·lŏŏ′mə·trē) *n.*

volumetric analysis *Chem.* The quantitative analysis of a substance by determining the amount of a standard solution required to effect a reaction in a known quantity of the substance.

vo·lu·mi·nos·i·ty (və·lŏŏ′mə·nos′ə·tē) *n.* The state or quality of being voluminous; especially, copiousness or prolixity.

vo·lu·mi·nous (və·lŏŏ′mə·nəs) *adj.* 1 Consisting of many volumes; capable of filling several volumes; also, of great bulk. 2 Writing or having written much; productive. 3 Having coils, folds, convolutions, or windings. [<LL *voluminosus* <L *volumen, -inis* a roll] — **vo·lu′mi·nous·ly** *adv.* — **vo·lu′mi·nous·ness** *n.*

vol·un·ta·rism (vol′ən·tə·riz′əm) *n.* 1 The theory that will is the ultimate principle or constituent of reality, both in experience and development of the individual, and in the constitution and evolution of the universe. 2 The theory that will is the fundamental psychic factor. Compare VITALISM. — **vol′un·ta·rist** *n.* — **vol′un·ta·ris′tic** *adj.*

vol·un·tar·y (vol′ən·ter′ē) *adj.* 1 Proceeding from the will or from one's own free choice: *voluntary* murder; specifically, unconstrained; intentional; volitional. 2 Endowed with, possessing, or exercising will or free choice: a *voluntary* donor. 3 Effected by choice or volition; acting without constraint. 4 Subject to or directed by the will, as a muscle or movement. 5 Of or relating to voluntaryism. 6 *Law* Unconstrained of will; done without compulsion; performed without legal obligation; also, done without valuable consideration; gratuitous. See synonyms under SPONTANEOUS. — *n. pl.* **·tar·ies** 1 Any work or performance not compelled or imposed by another. 2 *Music* a An organ solo, often improvised, played before, during, or after a service. b *Rare* A piece of music, usually spontaneous, played or sung as a prelude. 3 *Obs.* A volunteer. [<OF *voluntaire* <L *voluntarius* < *voluntas* will] — **vol′un·tar′i·ly** *adv.* — **vol′un·tar′i·ness** *n.*

vol·un·tar·y·ism (vol′ən·ter′ē·iz′əm) *n.* The principle that religious and educational institutions should be supported by voluntary contributions. — **vol′un·tar′y·ist** *n.*

voluntary system A system of freely given support in distinction from state support of religious or educational institutions.

vol·un·teer (vol′ən·tir′) *n.* 1 One who enters into any service of his own free will. 2 One who voluntarily enters military service, but is then subject to the same regulations and discipline as other soldiers: opposed to *conscript.* 3 *Law* One who takes title under a deed made without valuable consideration; also, a voluntary agent or actor in a transaction. — *adj.* 1 Pertaining to or composed of volunteers; voluntary. 2 Springing up naturally or spontaneously, as from fallen or self-sown seed: a *volunteer* growth. — *v.t.* To offer to give or do. — *v.i.* To enter or offer to enter into some service or undertaking of one's free will; enlist. [< obs. F *voluntaire* <OF, VOLUNTARY]

Volunteers of America A religious and philanthropical organization founded in the United States in 1896 by Commander and Mrs. Ballington Booth, who resigned from the Salvation Army for that purpose.

Volunteer State Nickname of TENNESSEE.

vo·lup·tu·ar·y (və·lup′chŏŏ·er′ē) *adj.* Pertaining to or promoting sensual indulgence and luxurious pleasures. — *n. pl.* **·ar·ies** One addicted to sensual pleasures; a sensualist. [<L *voluptuarius* < *voluptas* pleasure]

vo·lup·tu·ous (və·lup′chŏŏ·əs) *adj.* 1 Belonging to, producing, exciting, or yielding sensuous gratification. 2 Pertaining to or devoted to the enjoyment of pleasures or luxuries; luxurious; sensual. 3 Having a full and beautiful form, as a woman. [<OF *voluptueux* <L *voluptuosus* full of pleasure < *voluptas* pleasure] — **vo·lup′tu·ous·ly** *adv.* — **vo·lup′tu·ous·ness** *n.*

vo·lute (və·lōōt′) *n.* 1 *Archit.* A spiral scroll–like ornament, as in Ionic capitals; a scroll. 2 *Zool.* One of the whorls or turns of a spiral shell. — *adj.* 1 Rolled up; forming spiral curves. 2 Having a spiral form, as a machine part. [<F <L *voluta* a scroll, orig. fem. pp. of *volvere* turn]

VOLUTE

vo·lut·ed (və·lōō′tid) *adj.* Having a volute or flat spiral scroll.

volute spring *Mech.* A flat metallic spring coiled in a spiral conical form.

vo·lu·tion (və·lōō′shən) *n.* 1 A spiral turn or twist; convolution. 2 A whorl of a spiral shell. 3 A revolving movement.

vol·va (vol′və) *n. Bot.* That part of the sheath enclosing certain young mushrooms which, on being ruptured in the course of growth, forms a cuplike appendage at the base of the stem. [<L *volvere* wrap, turn]

vol·vu·lus (vol′vyə·ləs) *n. pl.* **·li** (-lī) *Pathol.* Obstruction of the intestines caused by twisting. [<NL <L *volvere* turn]

vo·mer (vō′mər) *n. Anat.* 1 A bone of the face situated between the nasal passages on the median line in vertebrates above fishes. 2 A bone of the roof of the mouth in fishes, behind the premaxillaries. [<NL <L *vomer* a plow] — **vo·mer·ine** (vō′mər·in, vom′ər-) *adj.*

vom·i·ca (vom′i·kə) *n. pl.* **·cae** (-sē) *Pathol.* 1 A collection of purulent matter within an organ. 2 An ulcerous cavity, especially in the lungs. 3 Expectoration of putrid matter. [<L, a boil, ulcer < *vomere* vomit]

vom·it (vom′it) *v.i.* 1 To throw up or eject the contents of the stomach through the mouth. 2 To issue with violence from any hollow place; be ejected. — *v.t.* 3 To throw up or eject from the stomach, as food. 4 To discharge or send forth copiously or forcibly: The volcano *vomited* smoke. — *n.* 1 Matter that is ejected, as from the stomach in vomiting. 2 A sickness which is characterized by vomiting. 3 An emetic. 4 The act of vomiting. [<L *vomitare,* freq. of *vomere* vomit] — **vom′it·er** *n.*

vomiting gas Chlorpicrin.

vom·i·tive (vom′ə·tiv) *adj.* Causing vomiting. — *n.* An emetic.

vom·i·to (vom′ə·tō, *Sp.* vō′mē·tō) *n. Pathol.* Yellow fever; black vomit. Also **vomito ne·gro** (nē′grō, *Sp.* nā′grō). [<Sp. *vómito* <L *vomitus,* pp. of *vomere* vomit]

vom·i·to·ry (vom′ə·tôr′ē, -tō′rē) *adj.* Efficacious in producing vomiting. — *n. pl.* **·ries** 1 An emetic. 2 An opening or vent through which matter is discharged. 3 In a Roman amphitheater, one of the entrances from the encircling arcades to the passages leading to the seats.

vom·i·tu·ri·tion (vom′ə·chŏŏ·rish′ən) *n. Pathol.* 1 Violent vomiting with the ejection of but little matter; retching. 2 Vomiting with but small effort; repeated vomiting. [<F <L *vomitus* a vomiting < *vomere* vomit]

von (von, *Ger.* fôn, *unstressed* fən) *prep. German* Of; from: used in German and Austrian family names as an attribute of nobility, corresponding to the French *de.*

voo·doo (vōō′dōō) *n.* 1 A primitive religion of West African origin, found among Haitian and West Indian Negroes and the Negroes of the southern United States, characterized by belief in sorcery and the use of charms, fetishes, witchcraft, etc. 2 A witch doctor; a Negro conjurer who practices voodoo. 3 A voodoo charm or fetish. — *adj.* Of or pertaining to the beliefs, ceremonies, or practices of voodoo. — *v.t.* To put a spell upon after the manner of a voodoo; bewitch. [<Creole *voudou* <Ewe *vodu*]

voo·doo·ism (vōō′dōō·iz′əm) *n.* 1 The religion of voodoo. 2 Belief in or practice of this religion. — **voo′doo·ist** *n.* — **voo′doo·is′tic** *adj.*

-vora *combining form Zool.* Used to denote orders or genera when classified according to their food: *Carnivora.* An individual member of such an order or genus is denoted by -**vore.** [<NL <L -*vorus.* See -VOROUS.]

vo·ra·cious (vô·rā′shəs, vō-, və-) *adj.* 1 Eating with greediness; ravenous. 2 Greedy; rapacious. 3 Ready to swallow up or engulf. 4 Insatiable; immoderate. See synonyms under GREEDY. [<L *vorax, -acis* < *vorare* devour] — **vo·ra′cious·ly** *adv.* — **vo·rac·i·ty** (vô·ras′ə·tē, vō-, və-), **vo·ra′cious·ness** *n.*

Vor·arl·berg (fôr′ärl·berkh) An autonomous province of western Austria, bordering on Germany, Switzerland, and Liechtenstein; 1,004 square miles; capital, Bregenz.

Vor·i·ai Spor·a·des (vô′rē·e spô·rä′thes) The Greek name for the NORTHERN SPORADES. See under SPORADES.

vor·la·ge (fôr′lä·gə) *n.* In skiing, a posture in which the body leans forward, beyond the perpendicular to the incline. [<G, lit., a lying

forward <*vorlagern* extend forward <*vor-forward* + *lagern* lie, lay]

Vo·ro·nezh (vo·rô′nesh) A city in SW European Russian S.F.S.R.; a major industrial center.

Vo·ro·shi·lov (vo′ro·shē′lôf), **Klement Efremovich,** 1881–1969, Russian politician; marshal in World War II.

Vo·ro·shi·lov·grad (vo′ro·shē′lôf·grät) See LUGANSK.

-vorous *combining form* Consuming; eating or feeding upon: *omnivorous, carnivorous.* [<L *-vorus* <*vorare* devour]

vor·tex (vôr′teks) *n.* *pl.* **·tex·es** or **·ti·ces** (-tə·sēz) 1 A mass of rotating or whirling fluid, especially when sucked spirally toward the center; a whirlpool; an eddy. 2 A portion of fluid whose particles have rotary motion. [<L, var. of *vertex* top, point]

vor·ti·cal (vôr′ti·kəl) *adj.* Of, like, or causing a vortex. [<L *vortex, -icis* a vortex] — **vor′·ti·cal·ly** *adv.*

vor·ti·cose (vôr′tə·kōs) *adj.* Rotating rapidly; whirling; vortical. [<L *vorticosus* <*vortex, -icis* a vortex]

vor·tig·i·nous (vôr·tij′ə·nəs) *adj.* Moving as in a vortex. [<L *vortigo, -inis,* var. of *vertigo* a spinning]

Vor·tum·nus (vôr·tum′nəs) See VERTUMNUS.

Vosges Mountains (vōzh) A mountain chain in eastern France; highest peak, 4,672 feet.

Vos·toch·no-Si·bir·sko·ye Mo·re (vos·toch′nô·sē·bir′skô·yə mô′rə) See SIBERIAN SEA, EAST.

vo·ta·ry (vō′tər·ē) *n.* *pl.* **·ries** 1 One devoted to some particular worship, pursuit, study, etc. 2 A worshiper, as of an idol. Also **vo′ta·rist.** — *adj.* Consecrated by a vow or promise; votive. [<L *votus,* pp. of *vovere* vow] — **vo′ta·ress, vo′tress** *n. fem.*

vote (vōt) *n.* 1 A formal expression of will or opinion in regard to some question submitted for decision, as in electing officers, passing resolutions, etc. 2 That by which such choice is expressed, as a show of hands, or ballot. 3 The result of an election; also, votes in the aggregate: the foreign *vote.* 4 The right to vote. 5 A voter. 6 *Obs.* A wish, vow, or prayer. — **casting vote** A deciding vote given by the chairman of an assembly in cases where the votes of the members tie. — *v.* **vot·ed, vot·ing** *v.t.* 1 To enact or determine by vote. 2 To cast one's vote for: to *vote* a straight ticket. 3 To elect or defeat by vote. 4 *Colloq.* To declare by general agreement: to *vote* a concert a success. — *v.i.* 5 To cast one's vote; express opinion or preference by or as by a vote. — **to vote down** To defeat or suppress by voting against. — **to vote in** To elect. [<L *votum* a vow, wish, orig. pp. neut. of *vovere* vow. Doublet of vow.] — **vot′er** *n.*

vote–get·ter (vōt′get′ər) *n.* 1 A person with ability to win votes. 2 A campaign slogan, platform, etc., that draws votes. — **vote′-get′ting** *n.* & *adj.*

voting precinct An election district.

vo·tive (vō′tiv) *adj.* Dedicated by a vow; performed in fulfilment of a vow. [<L *votivus* <*votum.* See VOTE.] — **vo′tive·ly** *adv.* — **vo′tive·ness** *n.*

votive mass A mass not rubrically assigned to a particular day, but said at the choice of the priest.

vouch (vouch) *v.i.* 1 To give one's own assurance or guarantee; bear witness: with *for:* I will *vouch* for their honesty. 2 To serve as assurance or proof: with *for:* The evidence *vouches* for his innocence. — *v.t.* 3 To bear witness to; attest or affirm. 4 To cite as support or justification, as a precedent, authority, etc. 5 To uphold by satisfactory proof or evidence; substantiate. 6 *Law* To call upon or summon (a person) to defend a title. 7 *Obs.* To call to witness. — *n.* A declaration that attests; an assertion. [<OF *vocher, voucher* <L *vocare* call <*vox, vocis* a voice]

vouch·ee (vou·chē′) *n. Law* A person who is called into an action to warrant or defend a title.

vouch·er (vou′chər) *n.* 1 Any material thing (as a writing) that serves to vouch for the truth of something, or attest an alleged act, especially the receipt of money. 2 One who vouches for another; a witness. 3 In early English law, the calling in of a person, or the person called in, as warrantor, to defend a title.

vouch·safe (vouch′sāf′) *v.* **·safed, ·saf·ing** *v.t.*

1 To grant, as with condescension; permit; deign. 2 *Obs.* To assure or guarantee. — *v.i.* 3 To condescend; deign. [<VOUCH + SAFE] — **vouch′safe′ment** *n.*

vous·soir (vōō·swär′) *n. Archit.* A stone in an arch shaped to fit its curve. [<OF *vausoir, volsoir* curvature of a vault, ult. <L *volutus.* See VOLUBLE.]

vow (vou) *n.* 1 A solemn promise to God or to a deity or saint to perform some act or make some gift or sacrifice: generally made in a time of peril or need, and on the condition of the fulfilment of some petition or in return for special divine favor: the *vow* of Jephthah. 2 A solemn engagement to adopt a certain course of life, pursue some end, observe some moral precept, or surrender oneself to a higher life of holiness; also, a pledge of faithfulness: marriage *vows.* 3 A solemn and emphatic affirmation. See synonyms under OATH. — **to take vows** To enter a religious order. — *v.t.* 1 To promise solemnly; especially, to promise to God or to some deity. 2 To declare with assurance or solemnity. 3 To make a solemn promise or threat to do, inflict, etc. — *v.i.* 4 To make a vow. [<AF *vu,* OF *vo, vou* <L *votum.* Doublet of VOTE.] — **vow′er** *n.*

vow·el (vou′əl) *n.* 1 *Phonet.* A voiced speech sound produced by the relatively unimpeded passage of air through the mouth, altering in quality according to the shape of the resonance cavity: distinguished from *consonant.* Vowels may be characterized by the height of the tongue (high, mid, low), the place of articulation (front, central, back), the tension of the tongue muscles (tense, lax), and the presence of lip rounding; as, *a* is a high, back, tense, rounded vowel. 2 A letter indicating such a sound, as *a, e, i, o,* or *u.* — *adj.* Of or pertaining to a vowel; vocal. [<OF *vouele* <L *vocalis (littera)* vocal (letter) <*vox, vocis* a voice, sound. Doublet of VOCAL.]

vow·el·ize (vou′əl·īz) *v.t.* **·ized, ·iz·ing** To supply with vowel points or signs: to *vowelize* a Hebrew text. — **vow′el·i·za′tion** *n.*

vowel point One of a system of diacritical marks written above or below the consonants in Hebrew and certain other Semitic languages to indicate the vowel sound following the consonant.

vox (voks) *n.* *pl.* **vo·ces** (vō′sēz) Voice; especially, in music, a voice; part. [<L]

vox an·gel·i·ca (voks an·jel′i·kə) 1 An organ stop of two ranks of pipes, one of which is tuned slightly sharper than the other, so that beats are produced giving a tremulous effect; voix céleste: also **vox cae·les·tis** (si·les′tis). 2 A single–rank stop of soft, sweet quality. [<L, an angelic voice]

vox clan·des·ti·na (voks klan′des·tī′nə) *Latin* A secret voice; a whisper.

vox hu·ma·na (voks hyōō·mā′nə) A reed stop with very short pipes used for clarinet tones in an organ. [<L, a human voice]

vox po·pu·li (voks pop′yə·lī) *Latin* The voice of the people; public sentiment.

voy·age (voi′ij) *n.* 1 A journey by water, especially by sea: commonly used of a somewhat extended journey by water; formerly, any journey: a *voyage* across the sea. 2 A journey in an airship. 3 A book describing a voyage or voyaging: Hakluyt's *Voyages.* 4 Any enterprise or project; also, course. See synonyms under JOURNEY. — *v.* **·aged, ·ag·ing** *v.i.* To make a voyage; journey by water. — *v.t.* To travel over. [<OF *veiage, voiage* <L *viaticum.* Doublet of VIATICUM.] — **voy′ag·er** *n.*

voy·age·a·ble (voi′ij·ə·bəl) *adj.* Navigable.

vo·ya·geur (vwä·yȧ·zhœr′) *n.* *pl.* **·geurs** (-zhœr′) *French* An employee of Hudson's Bay Company, engaged in carrying men, supplies, etc., between remote trading posts; also, a Canadian boatman or fur trader.

vo·yeur (vwä·yûr′) *n.* One who is sexually gratified by looking at sexual objects or acts. [<F <*voir* see] — **vo·yeur′ism** *n.*

V–par·ti·cle (vē′pär′ti·kəl) *n. Physics* A hyperon.

vrai·sem·blance (vre·sän·bläns′) *n. French* A show or appearance of truth; verisimilitude. [<F <*vrai* true + *semblance* appearance]

Vry·burg (frī′bûrg) The capital of Bechuanaland, Republic of South Africa.

VT fuze A proximity fuze. [<V(ARIABLE) T(IME)]

VTOL (vē′tôl) *n. Aeron.* An aircraft that takes off and lands vertically.

Vuel·ta A·ba·jo (vwel′tä ä·bä′hō) A region including all Cuba west of Havana.

vug (vug, vōōg) *n. Mining* An opening in a mineral vein into which crystals often project. Also **vugg, vugh.** [<Cornish *vooga* a cave] — **vug′gy** *adj.*

Vuil·lard (vwē·yȧr′), **Jean Édouard,** 1868–1940, French painter.

Vul·can (vul′kən) In Roman mythology, the god of fire and of metallurgy: identified with the Greek *Hephaestus.*

vul·ca·ni·an (vul·kā′nē·ən) *adj.* 1 Volcanic: also **vul·can·ic** (vul·kan′ik). 2 Of or pertaining to Plutonism; plutonic. [<L *Vulcanius* pertaining to Vulcan <*Vulcanus* Vulcan]

Vul·ca·ni·an (vul·kā′nē·ən) *adj.* 1 Relating to Vulcan or to the art of working in metals. 2 Wrought by Vulcan or by Vulcan's art. Also **Vul·can·ic** (vul·kan′ik).

vul·can·ite (vul′kən·īt) *n.* A dark–colored hard variety of India rubber that has been subjected to vulcanization: also called *hard rubber.* — *adj.* Made of vulcanite. [after *Vulcan*]

vul·can·i·za·tion (vul′kən·ə·zā′shən, -ī·zā′-) *n.* 1 The process of treating crude India rubber with sulfur or sulfur compounds in varying proportions and at different temperatures, thereby increasing its strength and elasticity, yielding either soft rubber or vulcanite. 2 A similar process applied to other substances.

vul·can·ize (vul′kən·īz) *v.t.* & *v.i.* **·ized, ·iz·ing** To subject to or undergo the process of vulcanization. [after *Vulcan*] — **vul′can·iz′a·ble** *adj.* — **vul′can·iz′er** *n.*

vulcanized fiber A cellulose material made from cotton and linen rags passed through a solution of zinc chloride, or sometimes of sulfuric acid.

vul·can·ol·o·gy (vul′kən·ol′ə·jē) *n.* Volcanology. [<L *Vulcanus* of Vulcan + -(O)LOGY] — **vul′·can·o·log′i·cal** (-ə·loj′i·kəl) *adj.* — **vul′can·ol′o·gist** *n.*

vul·gar (vul′gər) *adj.* 1 Pertaining to the common people; plebeian; general; popular. 2 Pertaining to or characteristic of the people at large, as distinguished from the privileged or educated classes; coarse; boorish; offensive to good taste or sensitive feelings; low. 3 Written in or translated into the common language or dialect; vernacular. — *n. Obs.* 1 The common people. 2 The vernacular tongue. [<L *vulgaris* <*vulgus* the common people] — **vul′gar·ly** *adv.*

Synonyms (*adj.*): base, broad, coarse, gross, ignoble, inelegant, inferior, loose, low, mean, obscene, obscure, offensive, rude, unauthorized, underbred, vile. See COMMON. **Antonyms:** aristocratic, chaste, choice, cultivated, cultured, dainty, elegant, high–bred, learned, literary, lofty, polite, refined, select, stylish.

vulgar fraction A common fraction. See under FRACTION.

vul·gar·i·an (vul·gâr′ē·ən) *n.* A person of vulgar tastes or manners; especially, a wealthy person with coarse ideas or low standards.

vul·gar·ism (vul′gə·riz′əm) *n.* 1 Vulgarity. 2 A word, phrase, or expression that is in common colloquial or unrefined usage, though not necessarily coarse or gross: distinguished from those in literary or standard usage.

vul·gar·i·ty (vul·gar′ə·tē) *n.* *pl.* **·ties** 1 The quality or character of being vulgar; low condition in life; commonness. 2 Lack of refinement in conduct or speech, or an instance of it; coarseness. Also **vul′gar·ness.**

vul·gar·ize (vul′gə·rīz) *v.t.* **·ized, ·iz·ing** To make vulgar. Also *Brit.* **vul′gar·ise.** — **vul′gar·i·za′tion** *n.* — **vul′gar·iz′er** *n.*

Vulgar Latin See under LATIN.

vul·gate (vul′gāt) *adj.* Common; popular; usual; generally accepted; in common use. — *n.* 1 The vulgar tongue; colloquial everyday speech. 2 Any commonly accepted text. [<L *vulgatus* common, orig. pp. of *vulgare* make common <*vulgus* the common people]

Vul·gate (vul′gāt) *n.* 1 St. Jerome's Latin version of the Bible, now revised and used as the authorized version by the Roman Catholics. Jerome translated the Gospels into Latin, then the vernacular or vulgar tongue, about A.D. 383, the remaining New Testament somewhat later, and the Old Testament from the Hebrew between 390 and 405. The Sistine edition of the Vulgate, published under Pope Clement VIII in 1592–93, is the source of the modern revision of the Douai version ordered by Pius X in 1908. — *adj.* Belonging or relating to the Vulgate. [<Med. L *vulgata* (*editio*) the popular (edition), fem. of L *vulgatus* common]

vul·go (vul′gō) *adv. Latin* Commonly; popularly.

vul·ner·a·ble (vul′nər·ə·bəl) *adj.* 1 That may be wounded; capable of receiving injuries. 2 Liable to attack; assailable. 3 In contract bridge, having won one game of a rubber, and hence subject to doubled penalties if contract is not fulfilled. [<LL *vulnerabilis* wounding <L *vulnerare* wound <*vulnus, -eris* a wound] — vul′ner·a·bil′i·ty, vul′ner·a·ble·ness *n.* — vul′ner·a·bly *adv.*

vul·ner·ar·y (vul′nə·rer′ē) *adj.* Tending to cure wounds. — *n. pl.* ·ries A healing application for wounds, as a preparation of medicinal plants. [<L *vulnerarius* <*vulnus, -eris* a wound]

Vul·pec·u·la (vul·pek′yə·lə) A small northern constellation lying between Cygnus and Aquila; the Fox: sometimes called **Vulpecula cum An·se·re** (kum an′sə·rē) (*The Little Fox with the Goose*). See CONSTELLATION. [<L, dim. of *vulpes* a fox]

vul·pec·u·lar (vul·pek′yə·lər) *adj.* Of or pertaining to a fox, especially a young one; vulpine.

vul·pi·cide (vul′pə·sīd) *n.* 1 One who kills a fox otherwise than by hunting. 2 The act of killing a fox when not hunting it with hounds. [<L *vulpes, -is* a fox + -CIDE] — vul′pi·ci′dal (-sīd′l) *adj.*

vul·pine (vul′pin, -pīn) *adj.* 1 Pertaining to a fox; resembling foxes. 2 Like a fox; sly; crafty; cunning. [<L *vulpinus* < *vulpes* a fox]

vul·pi·nite (vul′pə·nīt) *n.* A scaly variety of anhydrite from Vulpino, Italy.

vul·ture (vul′chər) *n.*
1 Any of various large birds of prey (family *Cathartidae* or *Vulturidae*) related to the eagles, hawks, and falcons, having the head and neck naked or partly naked, and feeding mostly on carrion; especially, the common **turkey vulture,** or buzzard, and the tropical American **king vulture** (*Gypagus papa*), strikingly colored, with black wings and tail. 2 Some-

VULTURE
(From 30 to 55 inches; wingspread from 7 to 11 feet)

thing or someone that preys upon a person in the manner of a vulture. [<AF *vultur,* OF *voltour* <L *vultur, vulturius*] — vul·tur·ine (vul′chə·rīn, -chər·in), vul′tur·ous *adj.*

vul·va (vul′və) *n. pl.* ·vae (-vē) *Anat.* The external genital parts of the female, including the labia majora and minora, the clitoris, and the area between the clitoris and the labia minora. [<L, a covering, womb] — vul′val, vul′var *adj.* — vul′vi·form (-və·fôrm) *adj.*

Vyat·ka (vyät′kə) 1 A former name for KIROV. 2 A river in east central European Russian S.F.S.R., flowing 849 miles north, SW, and SE from the central Ural foothills to the Kama.

Vy·borg (vē′bôrg, *Russian* vī′berk) A port on the Gulf of Finland in NW Russian S.F.S.R. near the Finnish border. Swedish *Viborg,* Finnish *Viipuri.*

Vy·cheg·da (vī′chəg·də) A river in northern European Russian S.F.S.R., flowing 700 miles south and west to the Northern Dvina.

vy·ing (vī′ing) *adj.* That vies or contends. — vy′ing·ly *adv.*

Vy·shin·ski (vī·shin′skē), **Andrei,** 1883–1954, U.S.S.R. lawyer and politician: also *Vishinski.*

W

w, W (dub′əl·yōō, -yōō) *n. pl.* w's, W's or ws, Ws or doub·le·yous 1 The 23rd letter of the English alphabet; double u: a ligature of vv or uu. It first came into English writing as a substitution by Norman scribes of the 11th century for the Old English rune *wen,* which later dropped completely out of use. 2 The sound of the letter *w,* a voiced bilabial velar semivowel before vowels (*we, wage, worry*), and a *u*-glide in diphthongs (*how, allow, dew, review*). It is silent before *r* (*wrist, write, wrong*), and is often lost internally (*two, sword, answer*). ◆ The combination *wh-* (in Old English spelled *hw-*) is pronounced in this dictionary as (hw); many educated speakers of English, however, use simple (w) instead, and this pronunciation should be inferred as an acceptable variant in every case. Some speakers normally use still a third sound here, a voiceless allophone of (w) heard also after voiceless consonants, as in *sweet, twin,* etc. See ALPHABET. — *symbol* 1 *Chem.* Tungsten (symbol W, for *wolfram*). 2 *Electr.* Watt.

wa' (wä) *n. Scot.* Wall.

Waadt (vät) The German name for VAUD.

Waag (väkh) The German name for the VAH.

Waal (väl) The southern branch of the Rhine in the Netherlands, flowing 52 miles west from the Rhine proper to the Maas.

Waals (väls), **Johannes Diderik van der,** 1837–1923, Dutch physicist.

wab (wäb) *n. Scot.* A web.

Wa·bash (wô′bash) A river in western Ohio and north central and western Indiana, forming part of the boundary between Indiana and Illinois and flowing 475 miles NW, west, SW, and south from western Ohio to the Ohio River at the SW corner of Indiana.

wab·ble¹ (wob′əl) *n., v.t. & v.i.* Wobble. [Var. of WOBBLE] — wab′bler *n.* — wab′bly *adj.*

WAC (wak) *n.* A member of the Women's Army Corps. [<W(OMEN'S) A(RMY) C(ORPS)]

Wace (wäs, wās), 1100?–75, Anglo-Norman poet.

wack·e (wak′ə) *n.* A brown earthy or clayey variety of basaltic rock. [<G <MHG, a large stone <OHG *waggo* a pebble]

wack·y (wak′ē) *adj.* wack·i·er, wack·i·est *Slang* Extremely irrational or impractical; erratic; screwy. [Prob. <WHACK; with ref. to the mental impairment caused by repeated blows on the head]

Wa·co (wā′kō) A manufacturing city in central Texas.

wad¹ (wod) *n.* 1 A small compact mass of any soft or flexible substance, especially as used for stuffing, packing, or lining; also, a lump; mass: a *wad* of hair; also, a chew of tobacco; or a portion the right size for chewing. 2 A piece of paper, cloth, or leather used to hold in a charge of powder in a muzzleloading gun; also, a pasteboard or paper disk to hold powder and shot in place in a shotgun shell. 3 Fibrous material for stopping up breaks, leakages, etc.; wadding. 4 *Colloq.* A large amount. 5 *Colloq.* A roll of banknotes; hence, money; wealth. 6 A hydrated oxide of manganese and other metals. — *v.* wad·ded, wad·ding *v.t.* 1 To press (fibrous substances, as cotton) into a mass or wad. 2 To roll or fold into a tight wad, as paper. 3 To pack with wadding for protection, as valuables, or to stuff or line with wadding. 4 To place a wad in, as a gun; hold in place with a wad. — *v.i.* 5 To form into a wad. [Cf. Sw. *vadd* a wad] — wad′dy *adj.*

wad² (wod) *n. Scot.* A pledge; wager.

wad³ (wod) *v.t. & v.i. Scot.* To wed.

wad⁴ (wäd, wod) *v. Scot.* Would.

Wa·dai (wä·dī′) A former independent sultanate of north central Africa; now part of central and eastern Chad; 94,225 square miles: French *Ouadaï.*

wad·ding (wod′ing) *n.* 1 Wads collectively. 2 Any substance, as carded cotton, used as material for wads. 3 The act of applying a wad or wads.

Wad·ding·ton (wod′ing·tən), **Mount** The highest mountain in British Columbia, in the SW part; 13,260 feet.

wad·dle (wod′l) *v.i.* ·dled, ·dling 1 To walk with short steps, swaying from side to side. 2 To move clumsily; totter. — *n.* The act of waddling; a clumsy rocking walk, like that of a duck. [Freq. of WADE] — wad′dler *n.* — wad′dly *adj.*

wad·dy (wod′ē) *n. pl.* ·dies *Austral.* 1 A thick war club used by the aborigines. 2 A walking stick; piece of wood. — *v.t.* ·died, ·dy·ing To strike with a waddy. [< native Australian pronunciation of *wood*]

wade (wād) *v.* wad·ed, wad·ing *v.i.* 1 To walk through water or, by extension, any substance more resistant than air, as mud, sand, etc. 2 To proceed slowly or laboriously: to *wade* through a lengthy book. 3 *Obs.* To go; proceed. — *v.t.* 4 To pass or cross, as a river, by walking on the bottom; walk through; ford. — to wade in (or into) *Colloq.* To attack or begin energetically or vigorously. — *n.* 1 The act of wading. 2 A ford. [OE *wadan* go]

wad·er (wā′dər) *n.* 1 One who wades. 2 A long-legged wading bird, as a snipe, plover, or stork. 3 *pl.* High waterproof boots, worn especially by anglers.

wa·di (wä′dē) *n. pl.* ·dies 1 In Arabia and northern Africa, a river or valley; a ravine containing the bed of a watercourse, usually dry except in the rainy season. 2 An oasis. Also **wa′dy.** [<Arabic *wādī*]

Wa·di Hal·fa (wä′dē häl′fə) A city on the Nile in the northern Sudan near the Egyptian border; the northern gateway to the Sudan.

Wad·jak (wä′jək) A village in central Java.

Wadjak man A hominid (*Homo wadjakensis*), probably of the third interglacial period, and represented solely by two skulls found near Wadjak, Java, in 1891: of larger cranial capacity than earlier types but otherwise controversial because of the crushed condition of the remains and inadequate investigation at the site.

wad·mal (wod′məl) *n. Obs.* A thick, coarse, hairy, durable woolen cloth, used by the poor of northern Europe for garments. Also **wad′maal, wad′mol.** [<ON *vathmāl* woolen fabric]

wad·na (wod′nə) *Scot.* Would not.

wad·set (wod′set) *n.* In Scots law, a pledge, as of land, as security for a debt. — *v.t.* ·set·ted, ·set·ting In Scots law, to mortgage.

wad·set·ter (wod′set′ər) *n. Scot.* One receiving a wadset.

wae (wā) *n. Scot.* Woe. — wae′ness *n.*

wae·ful (wā′fool) *adj. Scot.* Woeful; sad. Also **wae′fu** (-foo).

wae·sucks (wā′suks) *interj. Scot.* Alas! Also **wae′suck.** [<WAE + alter. of SAKE]

WAF (waf, wäf) *n.* A member of the Women in the Air Force. [<W(OMEN IN THE) A(IR) F(ORCE)]

Wafd (woft) *n.* A nationalist party in Egypt founded about 1919. [<Arabic, a deputation] — Wafd′ist *n. & adj.*

wa·fer (wā′fər) *n.* 1 A very thin crisp biscuit, cooky, or cracker; also, a small disk of candy. 2 *Eccl.* A small flat disk of unleavened bread stamped with a cross or the letters IHS, and used in the Eucharist in some churches; the sacred host. 3 A thin hardened disk of gelatin, flour, isinglass, or other suitable substance, used for sealing letters, attaching papers, or receiving the impression of a seal. 4 *Med.* **a** A thin double layer of dried paste enclosing a pill or capsule. **b** A suppository. 5 A disk of priming material used in early artillery. —v.t. To attach, seal, or fasten with a wafer. [<AF *wafre* <MLG *wafel*. Akin to WAFFLE.]

waff[1] (waf, wäf) *Scot. & Brit. Dial. v.t. & v.i.* To wave. —n. **1** The act of waving. **2** A light ailment. **3** A gust; puff. **4** A glimpse; sight. **5** A spirit or ghost. [Var. of WAVE]

waff[2] (waf, wäf) *Scot. adj.* **1** Low-born; worthless; inferior. **2** Strayed; solitary. —n. A tramp; vagrant.

waff·ie (wäf'ē) *n. Scot.* A tramp.

waf·fle[1] (wof'əl, wô'fəl) *n.* A batter cake, crisper than a pancake, baked in a waffle iron marked with regular indentations. [< Du. *wafel* a wafer. Akin to WAFER.]

waf·fle[2] (wof'əl, wô'fəl) *v.i.* **·fled, ·fling** *Colloq.* **1** *Chiefly Brit.* To speak or write nonsense. **2** To avoid giving a direct answer. —n. *Chiefly Brit.* Nonsense; twaddle. [<obs. *woff*, *waff* to yelp]

waffle iron A type of utensil for cooking waffles, consisting of two metal griddles, hinged together, and usually marked with indentations so as to give a large heating surface when closed on each other: now usually made of aluminum and heated electrically.

waft[1] (waft, wäft) *v.t.* **1** To carry or bear gently or lightly over air or water; float. **2** To convey as if on air or water. —v.i. **3** To float, as on the wind. —n. **1** The act of one who or that which wafts. **2** A breath or current of air; also, a passing odor. [Back formation < *wafter*, in obs. sense, "an escort ship" <Du. *wachter* a guard < *wachten* guard]

waft[2] (waft, wäft) *n.* **1** A signal flag or pennant, sometimes used to indicate the direction of the wind to a ship's helmsman. **2** A signal made with a flag or pennant. —v.t. *Obs.* **1** To signal or beckon to with the hand. **2** To turn; direct, as a glance. [Alter. of dial. E *waff*, var. of WAVE]

waft[3] (waft, wäft) *n. Scot.* Woof; weft.

waft·age (waf'tij, wäf'-) *n.* Conveyance by wafting.

waft·er (waf'tər, wäf'-) *n.* **1** One who or that which wafts. **2** A form of fan or revolving disk used in a blower.

waf·ture (waf'chər, wäf'-) *n.* **1** A wafting or waving motion. **2** Conveyance by wafting. **3** That which is wafted, as an odor.

wag[1] (wag) *v.* **wagged, wag·ging** *v.t.* **1** To cause to move lightly and quickly from side to side or up and down; oscillate; swing: The dog *wags* its tail. **2** To move (the tongue) in talking. —v.i. **3** To move lightly and quickly from side to side or up and down. **4** To move busily in animated talk or gossip: said of the tongue. **5** To proceed at a regular pace: Life *wags* on. **6** To waddle. **7** *Brit. Slang* To play truant. —n. The act or motion of wagging: a *wag* of the head. [ME *waggen*, prob. <Scand. Cf. Sw. *vagga* rock a cradle. Akin to OE *wagian* oscillate.]

wag[2] (wag) *n.* A droll or humorous fellow; a wit; joker. [Short for obs. *waghalter* <WAG[1] + HALTER[1]]

wage (wāj) *v.t.* **waged, wag·ing** **1** To engage in and maintain vigorously; carry on: to *wage* war. **2** *Obs.* To pledge; put down as security; hence, to wager; bet. **3** *Obs.* To attempt; risk. **4** *Brit. Dial.* To pay a salary to; hire; employ. —n. **1** Payment for service rendered, especially the pay of artisans or laborers receiving a fixed sum by the day, week, or month, or for a certain amount of work; hire. **2** *pl.* The remuneration received by labor as distinguished from that received by capital, including the expenses incurred for superintendence and management, called respectively **wages of superintendence** and **wages of management.** **3** Figuratively, produce; yield. **4** *Obs.* A pledge; gage; also, the state of being pledged: to lay one's fortune in *wage*. See synonyms under SALARY. See LIVING WAGE, MINIMUM WAGE. [<AF *wagier*, OF *guagier* pledge < *gage* a pledge. Doublet of GAGE[2].] ◆ The plural of *wage* is sometimes construed as a singular: The *wages* of sin *is* death.

Wage may appear as a combining form in hyphemes or solidemes, or as the first element in two-word phrases:

wage board	wage floor
wage ceiling	wage–freeze
wage–control	wage–labor
wage differential	wage law
wage–driver	wage level

wage–incentive	wage–slave
wage–increase	wage–slavery
wage–paying	wage structure
wage rate	wagework

wage–earn·er (wāj'ûr'nər) *n.* One who works for wages.

wa·ger (wā'jər) *v.t. & v.i.* To stake (something) on an uncertain event; bet. —n. **1** An agreement between persons that something, as money, shall be delivered over to one of them on the happening or not happening of an uncertain event; a bet. **2** The thing so pledged. **3** The act of giving a pledge. [<AF *wageure* < *wagier*. See WAGE.] — **wa'ger·er** *n.*

wager of law Anciently, a mode of trial whereby a defendant acquitted himself of a debt by taking his oath that he owed the plaintiff nothing, and having eleven compurgators present to swear that they believed his oath to be true.

wage scale **1** A scale or series of amounts of wages paid for similar duties. **2** The scale of wages paid by a single employer.

wage·work·er (wāj'wûr'kər) *n.* An employee receiving wages.

wag·ger·y (wag'ər-ē) *n. pl.* **·ger·ies** **1** Mischievous jocularity; drollery. **2** A jest; joke. See synonyms under WIT[1]. [<WAG[2] + -ERY]

wag·gish (wag'ish) *adj.* **1** Being or acting like a wag. **2** Said or done in waggery. See synonyms under JOCOSE. — **wag'gish·ly** *adv.* — **wag'gish·ness** *n.*

wag·gle (wag'əl) *v.* **·gled, ·gling** *v.t.* To cause to move with rapid to–and–fro motions; wag; swing: The duck *waggles* its tail. —v.i. To totter; wobble. —n. The act of waggling or wagging. [Freq. of WAG[1]] — **wag'gling·ly** *adv.* — **wag'gly** *adj.*

Wag·ner (väg'nər), **(Wilhelm) Richard,** 1813–83, German composer, poet, and critical writer.

Wag·ner·esque (väg'nə·resk') *adj.* Similar to or suggestive of the works or style of Richard Wagner.

Wag·ne·ri·an (väg·nir'ē·ən) *adj.* Relating to Richard Wagner or to his style, theory, or works. —n. One who advocates or accepts the theories of Richard Wagner; also, one who admires his works.

Wag·ner·ism (väg'nə·riz'əm) *n.* The theory of Richard Wagner regarding music drama, as exemplified in the construction and rendition of his own works. Its chief point, especially that in which it differs from the method of the old Italian composers of opera, is its abundant use of the leitmotif for cumulative dramatic effect and its insistence on the equal participation of music, both vocal and orchestral, poetry, scenic effect, and dramatic action, no one of these being subordinate.

Wag·ner–Jau·regg (väg'nər–you'rek), **Julius,** 1857–1940, Austrian neurologist and psychiatrist. Also **Wag'ner von Jau'regg.**

wag·on (wag'ən) *n.* **1** A strong four–wheeled vehicle used to carry heavy loads of freight. Compare DRAY, WAIN. **2** An open four–wheeled vehicle for carrying hay, corn, etc.: a farm *wagon.* **3** A light four–wheeled vehicle used for various business purposes, as a grocer's *wagon.* **4** *Brit.* A railway freight car. **5** A covered four–wheeled vehicle used as living quarters by gipsies, traveling showmen, etc. **6** *Obs.* A chariot. **7** *Colloq.* A patrol wagon. **8** A station wagon. **9** *Slang* An automobile. **10** A child's four–wheeled toy cart. **11** *Astron.* Charles's Wain. **12** A stand on wheels or casters for serving food or drink: a tea *wagon.* — **on the (water) wagon** *Colloq.* Abstaining from alcoholic beverages. — **to fix (someone's) wagon** *Slang* To even scores with; obtain revenge on: I'll *fix your wagon!* —v.t. To carry or transport in a wagon. Also *Brit.* **wag'gon.** [<Du. *wagen.* Akin to WAIN.]

wag·on·age (wag'ən·ij) *n.* **1** The amount paid for conveyance in a wagon. **2** Wagons collectively. Also *Brit.* **wag'gon·age.**

wagon bed The body of a wagon.

wag·on·er (wag'ən·ər) *n.* **1** One whose business is driving wagons. **2** *Obs.* A charioteer. Also *Brit.* **wag'gon·er.**

Wag·on·er (wag'ən·ər) **1** Charles's Wain. See under WAIN. **2** The constellation Auriga.

wag·on·ette (wag'ən·et') *n.* A light wagon, with or without a cover, with lengthwise

seats facing inward and a crosswise seat in front for the driver. Also **wag'on·et.** [Dim. of WAGON.]

wag·on–head·ed (wag'ən·hed'id) *adj. Archit.* Having a semicylindrical head or top, resembling the top of a covered wagon; having a round–arched roof.

wa·gon–lit (vá·gôn·lē') *n. pl.* **–lits** (-lē') *French* A sleeping–car on a French railway.

wag·on·load (wag'ən·lōd') *n.* The amount that a wagon can carry.

wagon train **1** A train or line of wagons. **2** A group of wagons and families typical of those which formerly traveled together to settle new regions, especially in the western United States. **3** The equipment of a military force for the carriage of ammunition, provisions, etc.

Wa·gram (vä'gräm) A village NE of Vienna, Austria; scene of Napoleon's victory over the Austrians, 1809.

wag·some (wag'səm) *adj. Rare* Waggish.

wag·tail (wag'tāl') *n.* **1** Any of several small singing birds (genus *Motacilla*), named from their habit of jerking the tail; especially, the **yellow wagtail** (*M. flava*) of Asia and eastern Alaska. **2** Any of certain American birds that wag the tail when walking on the ground, especially the ovenbird and the water thrush.

Wa·ha·bi (wä·hä'bē) *n.* A believer in Wahabiism. Also **Wa·ha'bee, Wah·ha'bi.**

Wa·ha·bi·ism (wä·hä'bē·iz'əm) *n.* A puristically orthodox Moslem sect of Arabia, related to the Sunnites, founded by Abdul–Wahhab; the religion of the ruling family of Saudi Arabia.

wah·con·da (wä·kon'dä) See WAKANDA.

wa·hoo[1] (wä·hōō', wä'hōō) *n.* A deciduous North American shrub or small tree (*Euonymus atropurpureus*) with finely toothed leaves, purple flowers, and scarlet fruit: also called *burningbush.* [<Siouan (Dakota) *wanhu*, lit., arrowwood]

wa·hoo[2] (wä·hōō', wä'hōō) *n.* **1** The American winged elm (*Ulmus alata*). **2** The white basswood (*Tilia heterophylla*). **3** The cascara buckthorn. [<Muskhogean (Creek) *uhawhu* the winged elm]

Wai·chow (wī'jō') A former name for WAI-YEUNG.

waif (wāf) *n.* **1** A homeless, neglected wanderer; a stray. **2** *Law* Something stolen and then abandoned by the thief in his flight to avoid arrest. **3** Anything found and unclaimed, the owner being unknown. **4** A nautical signal; a waft. —v.t. To throw away; cast off, as a waif. —adj. Stray; wandering; homeless. [<AF *waif*, OF *gaif*, prob. <Scand. Cf. ON *veif* something flapping < *veifa* wave.]

Wai·ki·ki (wī'kē·kē, wī'kē·kē') A section of Honolulu; site of a resort beach on Honolulu harbor, SE Oahu, Hawaii.

wail (wāl) *v.t. & v.i.* To grieve with mournful cries; lament; cry out in sorrow. —n. A prolonged, high–pitched sound of lamentation; a shrill moan of grief; also, any mournful sound, as of the wind. ◆ Homophone: *wale.* [<ON *væla* wail < *væ, vei* woe] — **wail'er** *n.*

wail·ful (wāl'fəl) *adj.* **1** Deeply sorrowing; mournful. **2** Making a mournful sound.

Wailing Wall A wall on the western side of the traditional site of Solomon's temple in Jerusalem, reputedly containing fragments of Herod's temple (20 B.C.), a place of prayer, formerly of lamentation, for Jews: also *Western Wall.*

wain (wān) *n.* An open, four–wheeled wagon for hauling heavy loads. — **Charles's Wain** Seven bright stars in Ursa Major; the Dipper: also **the Wain**: sometimes called the *Wagoner.* ◆ Homophone: *wane.* [OE *wægn, wēn.* Akin to WAGON.]

wain·scot (wān'skət, -skot) *n.* **1** A facing for inner walls, usually of wood, but sometimes of marble or other material: usually paneled and of elaborate workmanship. **2** *Brit.* A superior quality of imported oak used for paneling; also, a piece of such wood. **3** The lower part of an inner wall, when finished with material different from the rest of the wall. —v.t. **·scot·ed** or **·scot·ted, ·scot·ing** or **·scot·ting** To face or panel with wainscot. [<MLG *wagenschot* < *wagen* a wagon + *schot* a wooden partition]

wain·scot·ing (wān'skət·ing, -skot-) *n.* Material

for a wainscot; a wainscot; wainscots collectively. Also **wain′scot·ting.**

wain·wright (wān′rīt) *n.* A maker of wagons.

Wain·wright (wān′rīt), **Jonathan,** 1883–1953, U. S. general.

Wai·pa·hu (wī·pä′hōō) A city of southern Oahu, Hawaii, on Pearl Harbor, NW of Honolulu.

wair (wâr) See WARE³.

waist (wāst) *n.* **1** The narrow part of the body between the chest and the hips. **2** The middle part or section of any object, especially if of less diameter than the ends: the *waist* of a violin. **3** *Naut.* That section of a ship between the quarter-deck and the forecastle. **4** The central section of an airplane. **5** That part of a woman's dress or other garment covering the body from the waistline to the neck or shoulders; a bodice; also, an undergarment for children, to which other garments may be buttoned. **6** A waistband. ◆ Homophone: *waste.* [ME *wast.* Akin to OE *wæstm* growth.]

waist·band (wāst′band′, -bənd) *n.* A band encircling the waist, especially a band inside the top of a skirt or the upper part of trousers.

waist·cloth (wāst′klôth′, -kloth′) See LOINCLOTH.

waist·coat (wāst′kōt′, wes′kit) *n.* **1** A man's garment, now commonly sleeveless, buttoning in front and extending just below the waistline; a vest. **2** A similar garment worn by women. **3** A long vest formerly worn with trunk and hose under a slip doublet.

waist·coat·ing (wāst′kō′ting, wes′kit·ing) *n.* A textile fabric specially designed for men's waistcoats.

waist·er (wās′tər) *n. Rare* An apprentice or new hand on a whaling vessel, placed at work in the ship's waist to learn his duties.

waist·ing (wās′ting) *n.* Any material suitable for making waists.

waist·line (wāst′līn′) *n.* The line of the waist, between the ribs and the hips; in dressmaking, the line at which the skirt of a dress meets the waist.

wait (wāt) *v.i.* **1** To stay or remain in expectation, as of an anticipated action or event: with *for, until,* etc. **2** To be or remain in readiness. **3** To remain temporarily neglected or undone. **4** To perform duties of personal service or attendance; especially, to act as a waiter or waitress: She *waits* at table. — *v.t.* **5** To stay or remain in expectation of: to *wait* one's turn. **6** *Colloq.* To put off or postpone; defer; delay: Don't *wait* breakfast for me. **7** *Obs.* To attend; escort. **8** *Obs.* To attend as a result or consequence. See synonyms under ABIDE, LINGER. — **to wait on** (or **upon**) **1** To act as a servant or attendant to. **2** To go to see; call upon; visit. **3** To attend as a result or consequence. — **to wait up** To delay going to bed in anticipation of the arrival of someone. — *n.* **1** The act of waiting, or the time spent in waiting; delay. **2** An ambush or trap; snare: to lie in *wait* for a victim. **3** A member of a musical band organized to play and sing in the streets, at night or dawn: now applied only to those who sing carols in the streets at Christmastime. **4** *Obs.* A watchman or guard. [<AF *waitier,* OF *guaitier* <OHG *wahtēn* watch < *wahta* a guard]

wait-a-bit (wāt′ə·bit′) *n.* Any one of various plants with sharp or hooked thorns that catch and tear the clothing, and thus detain those who would pass through them, as the greenbrier or the prickly ash. [Trans. of Afrikaans *wacht-een-beetje*]

Waite (wāt), **Morrison Remick,** 1816–88, U. S. jurist; chief justice of the Supreme Court 1874–88.

wait·er (wā′tər) *n.* **1** One who waits upon others, as in a restaurant. **2** One who awaits something. **3** A tray for dishes, etc. **4** *Obs.* A watchman or keeper.

wait·ing (wā′ting) *n.* The act or business of a waiter; attendance. — **in waiting** In attendance, especially at court. — *adj.* That waits; expecting.

waiting list A list of people waiting to be admitted to some institution, as a school or club, or to some privilege or opportunity.

waiting room A room for the use of persons waiting, as for a railroad train, a doctor, dentist, or the like.

wait·ress (wā′tris) *n.* A woman or girl employed to wait on guests at table, as in a restaurant.

waive (wāv) *v.t.* **waived, waiv·ing 1** To give up or relinquish a claim to. **2** To refrain from insisting upon or taking advantage of; forgo. **3** To put off; postpone; delay. **4** *Law* To surrender, abandon, or relinquish voluntarily, either expressly or by implication, as a claim, privilege, or right. **5** *Obs.* To reject; cast off; abandon; desert. ◆ Homophone: *wave.* [<AF *weyver,* OF *gaiver* abandon <AF *weyf, waif* WAIF]

waiv·er (wā′vər) *n. Law* The voluntary relinquishment of a right, privilege, or advantage; also, the instrument which evidences such relinquishment. [<AF, var. of *weyver* abandon. See WAIF.]

Wai·yeung (wī′yüng′) A city in eastern Kwangtung province, China; a river port on the Tung, east of Canton: formerly *Waichow.*

wa·kan·da (wä·kän′dä) *n.* Among the Sioux, the great power or supreme being behind the world: identical with Algonquian *manito:* also spelled *wahconda.* [<Siouan]

Wa·ka·ya·ma (wä·kä·yä·mä) A port of southern Honshu island, Japan.

wake¹ (wāk) *v.* **woke** or **waked, waked** (*Dial.* **wok·en**), **wak·ing** *v.i.* **1** To be roused from sleep or slumber. **2** To be or remain awake. **3** To become active or alert after being inactive or dormant. **4** *Dial.* To keep watch or guard at night; especially, to hold a wake (def. 1). **5** *Obs.* To feast or revel late into the night. — *v.t.* **6** To rouse from sleep or slumber; awake. **7** To rouse or stir up; excite: to *wake* evil passions. **8** *Dial.* To keep a vigil over; especially, to hold a wake over. See synonyms under STIR¹. — *n.* **1** A watch over the body of a dead person through the night, just before the burial, by the relatives and friends: common among the Irish, and often accompanied by conviviality. **2** Formerly, in the Anglican Church, a dedication festival or anniversary celebration of a parish church, preceded by a night vigil in the church. **3** The act of refraining from sleep, especially on a festive or solemn occasion. **4** *Obs.* The act of waking, or the state of being awake; vigil. [Fusion of OE *wacan* awake and *wacian* be awake. Akin to WATCH.]

◆ **awake, awaken, wake, waken** These four verbs, so similar in basic meaning, offer a confusing variety of choices in actual use. In the imperative, *Wake up!* is the familiar and homely form; the other three would be felt as poetic. *Awake* and *wake* have checkered form-histories. In the King James Bible, Shakespeare, and Milton, only the inflected forms in *-ed* are found. But *awake* and *wake* each had a strong verb as well as a weak one in its ancestry, and in the late seventeenth century the alternative inflected forms *awoke, awoken,* and *woke, woken* emerged, reinforced by analogy with *break, broke, broken,* etc. These alternative forms have led to uncertainty and confusion in usage. For the past tense of *awake, awoke* is usual; *awaked* tends to be felt as Biblical. *Awoke* as the past participle is rare, and *awaked* seems awkward to some; what happens in practice is a borrowing of the past participle from *awaken.* For *wake,* the more usual past is *woke* (or *woke up*); *waked* in the intransitive is also standard, but in the transitive sense it is dialectal, referring to holding a vigil or wake: They *waked* old Tim on Thursday night. Real uncertainty arises over the form to choose for the past participle of *wake.* In British (or dialectal American) usage, *woken,* or, for the phrasal verb, *woken up* is used: He had *woken* (or *woken up*) early. American usage here employs *waked (up),* or if this is felt as awkward, particularly in the passive, the past participle is borrowed from *waken* or *awaken:* What *woke* her? She was *awakened* (or *wakened*) by the noise of the crash.

wake² (wāk) *n.* **1** The track left by a vessel passing through the water. **2** Any course passed over. — **in the wake of 1** Following close behind. **2** In consequence of. [<ON *vök* an opening in ice]

Wake·field (wāk′fēld) **1** A county borough in southern Yorkshire, England; scene of Lancastrian victory in the Wars of the Roses, 1460. **2** The birthplace of George Washington, an estate in SE Virginia.

wake·ful (wāk′fəl) *adj.* **1** Remaining awake, especially at the ordinary time of sleep; not sleeping or sleepy. **2** Watchful; alert. **3** Unable to sleep; restless; suffering from insomnia. **4** Arousing from or as from sleep. See synonyms under VIGILANT. — **wake′ful·ly** *adv.* — **wake′ful·ness** *n.*

Wake Island (wāk) A U. S. naval and air base, comprising a coral atoll and three islands in the North Pacific, acquired by the United States in 1898; 4 square miles; about 4 1/2 miles long, 2 1/4 miles wide; occupied by Japanese forces, 1941–45.

wake·less (wāk′lis) *adj.* Uninterrupted; unbroken: a *wakeless* sleep.

wak·en (wā′kən) *v.t.* **1** To rouse from sleep; awake. **2** To rouse to alertness or activity. — *v.i.* **3** To cease sleeping; wake up. **4** *Obs.* To keep awake; also, to keep watch. [OE *wæcnan, wacnian*]

wak·en·er (wā′kən·ər) *n. Archaic* One who or that which awakens.

wake·rife (wāk′rīf) *adj. Scot.* or *Obs.* Wakeful; alert. — **wake′rife·ness** *n.*

wake·rob·in (wāk′rob′in) *n.* **1** The cuckoo pint. **2** Any species of trillium; the mooseflower. **3** The jack-in-the-pulpit.

wakf (wukf) *n.* In Moslem law, the inalienable dedication of property in trust for the service of God or charitable uses; also, the property so dedicated. [<Arabic *waqf*]

wa·kif (wu′kif) *n.* One who makes a wakf.

wa·ki·ki (wä′ki·kē) *n.* Shell money of the South Sea Islands. [<Melanesian]

Waks·man (waks′mən), **Selman Abraham,** 1888–1973, U.S. microbiologist; discovered streptomycin.

Wa·la·chi·a (wo·lā′kē·ə) See WALLACHIA.

Wał·brzych (vä′ōō·bzhikh) A city in SW Poland, in former Lower Silesia; a coalmining and manufacturing center. *German* **Wal·den·burg** (väl′dən·bŏŏrkh).

Wal·che·ren (väl′khə·rən) An island at the mouth of the Scheldt river in SW Netherlands; the westernmost island of Zeeland province; 80 square miles.

Wal·deck (väl′dek) An administrative district of Hesse; 420 square miles; formerly a principality of western Germany, a state of the German Republic (1918–29), and a Prussian province (1929–45).

Wal·de·mar (väl′də·mär) Name of four kings of Denmark: also *Valdemar.*

— **Waldemar I,** 1131–82, king 1157–82: called "Waldemar the Great."

— **Waldemar II,** 1170–1241, king 1202–41; greatly extended Danish territory: called "Waldemar the Victorious."

Wal·den·ses (wol·den′sēz) *n. pl.* A sect of religious dissenters founded about 1170 by Peter Waldo or Valdo, a rich merchant of Lyons, France. Waldo and his disciples sought to restore the church to its early purity and poverty, but were excommunicated by Pope Alexander III, and severely persecuted. [<Med. L *Waldenses* of (Peter) *Waldo*] — **Wal·den′si·an** *adj.* & *n.*

wald·grave (wôld′grāv) *n.* **1** An old German title of nobility. **2** Originally, the lord or intendant of a forest. Compare LANDGRAVE, MARGRAVE. [<G *waldgraf* < *wald* a wood + *graf* a count]

Wald·heim (vält′hīm′), **Kurt,** born 1918, Austrian statesman; secretary general of the United Nations 1972–.

Wal·do (wôl′dō), **Peter** Late 12th century French religious reformer: also *Valdo, Valdez.* See WALDENSES.

Wal·dorf salad (wôl′dôrf) A salad made of chopped celery, apples, and walnuts, and garnished with lettuce and mayonnaise. [from the first *Waldorf*-Astoria Hotel, New York City]

Wald·stät·ter, Die Vier (dē fēr vält′shtet′ər) Lucerne, Schwyz, Unterwalden and Uri, the forest cantons of Switzerland: the original cantons of the Swiss federation.

Wald·teu·fel (väl′toi·fəl), **Émile,** 1837–1915, French composer born in Alsace.

add, āce, câre, pälm; end, ēven; it, īce; odd, ōpen, ôrder; tŏŏk, pool; up, bûrn; ə = a in *above,* e in *sicken,* i in *clarity,* o in *melon,* u in *focus;* yōō = u in *fuse;* oi, oil; ou, pout; ch, check; g, go; ng, ring; th, thin; ṯh, this; zh, vision. Foreign sounds à, œ, ü, kh, ṅ; and ◆: see page xx. < from; + plus; ? possibly.

wale[1] (wāl) *n.* **1** A stripe or ridge made on living flesh by a rod, whip, or stick; a wheal. **2** *Naut.* One of certain strakes of outer planking running fore and aft on a vessel: the channel *wales.* **3** A ridge or rib on the surface of cloth; hence texture; grain. — *v.t.* **waled, wal·ing** **1** To raise wales or stripes on by striking, as with a lash; flog; beat. **2** To manufacture, as cloth, with a ridge or rib. **3** To weave, as wickerwork, with several rods together. **4** To protect, fasten, or hold with wales. ◆ Homophone: *wail.* [OE *walu*]

wale[2] (wāl) *Dial. & Scot. n.* A choice or preference of one thing from among others; also, the best; the cream. — *adj.* Well-selected; choice. — *v.t.* **waled, wal·ing** To choose; select; hence, to woo. ◆ Homophone: *wail.* [<ON *val* choice]

wal·er (wā′lər) *n. Anglo-Indian* A horse imported to India from New South Wales, Australia, for cavalry service; also, any horse from Australia.

Wales (wālz) A peninsula of SW Britain, comprising a principality of England, with which it has been politically united since 1536; 8,016 square miles.

Wal·fish Bay (wôl′fish) See WALVIS BAY.

Wal·hal·la (wal·hal′ə, -hä′lä, val-) See VALHALLA.

walk (wôk) *v.i.* **1** To advance on foot in such a manner that one part of a foot is always on the ground; of quadrupeds, to advance in such a manner that two or more feet are always on the ground. **2** To move or go on foot for exercise or amusement. **3** To proceed or advance slowly. **4** To move in a manner suggestive of walking, as a piece of masonry subjected to wind pressure. **5** To act or live in some manner: to *walk* in peace. **6** To return to earth and appear, as a ghost. **7** In baseball, to advance to first base on balls. **8** In basketball, to take more than two steps while holding the ball. **9** *Obs.* To be in continual motion. — *v.t.* **10** To pass through, over, or across at a walk: to *walk* the floor. **11** To cause to go at a walk; lead, ride, or drive at a walk: to *walk* a horse. **12** To force or help to walk. **13** To accompany on a walk. **14** To bring to a specified condition by walking. **15** To measure or survey by traversing on foot: to *walk* a boundary. **16** To cause to move with a motion resembling a walk: to *walk* a trunk on its corners. **17** In baseball, to allow to advance to first base on balls. **18** In basketball, to take more than two steps while holding (the ball). — **to walk off** **1** To depart, especially abruptly or without warning. **2** To get rid of (fat, drunkenness, etc.) by walking. — **to walk off with** **1** To win. **2** To steal. — **to walk out** *Colloq.* **1** To go out on strike. **2** To keep company with *with* or *together.* — **to walk out on** *Colloq.* To forsake; desert. — **to walk over** **1** In certain sports, to walk over the course without a competitor so as to perform the technicality of winning; hence, to gain an easy victory. **2** To defeat easily; overwhelm. — *n.* **1** The act of walking, as for enjoyment or recreation; a stroll. **2** Manner of walking; gait; specifically, the gait of a horse in which two or more feet are always on the ground. **3** Method or way of living; behavior. **4** Chosen profession or habitual sphere of action: the different *walks* of life. **5** Distance as measured by the time taken by one who walks: It's an hour's *walk* to my house. **6** A place laid out or set apart for walking or resorted to by those who walk; a path, avenue, promenade, or sidewalk for pedestrians. **7** A ropewalk. **8** The formation of, or space between, two lines or rows of plants or trees, as in a coffee plantation. **9** A piece of ground set apart for the feeding and exercise of domestic animals; range; pasture: a *sheepwalk.* **10** A hawker's or vender's district or route; a beat. **11** A contest of speed in walking. **12** In baseball slang, a base on balls. [OE *wealcan* roll, toss] — **walk′ing** *adj. & n.*

walk·a·bout (wôk′ə·bout′) *n. Austral.* A wandering, apparently aimless journey over long distances. — **to go walkabout** To wander.

walk·a·round (wôk′ə·round′) *n.* **1** A rhythmic Negro dance performed by a group walking around in a large circle; also, the music

composed for this dance. **2** A dance of this kind performed on the stage; also, the music for it.

walk·a·way (wôk′ə·wā′) *n.* A contest won without serious opposition.

walk·er (wôk′ər) *n.* **1** One who or that which walks. **2** A shoe used for walking.

Walk·er, John, 1732–1807, English lexicographer and actor. — **William,** 1824–60, U.S. filibuster in Lower California and Nicaragua.

walk·ie-talk·ie (wô′kē·tô′kē) *n. Telecom.* A portable radio set, equipped for both sending and receiving, and light enough to be carried by one man. Also spelled *walky-talky.*

walking bass An insistently reiterated bass figure, usually in eighth notes, used in boogie-woogie music.

walking beam *Mech.* In a vertical engine, a horizontal beam that transmits power to the crankshaft through the connecting rod.

WALKING BEAM

walking delegate See under DELEGATE.

walking fern A tufted evergreen fern (*Camptosorus rhizophyllus*) with fronds ending in long tapering tips which take root and thus give rise to new plants. Also **walking leaf.**

walking papers Notice of dismissal from employment, office, position, etc.

walking stick **1** A staff or cane carried in the hand. **2** Any of a family (*Phasmidae*) of insects having legs, body, and wings resembling one of the twigs among which it lives.

walk-on (wôk′on′, -ôn′) *n.* An actor who plays a bit part or merely walks on the stage; also, the part.

walk-out (wôk′out′) *n. Colloq.* **1** The act of walking out. **2** A workmen's strike.

walk-o·ver (wôk′ō′vər) *n.* **1** A horse race in which there is only one horse entered, and which can thus be won by going over the course at a mere walk. **2** An easy or unopposed success.

walk-up (wôk′up′) *Colloq. n.* An apartment house having no elevator. — *adj.* Having no elevator.

Wal·kü·re (väl·kü′rə), **Die** *German* The second music drama in Richard Wagner's tetralogy, *Der Ring des Nibelungen.* See RING OF THE NIBELUNG, VALKYRIE.

walk·way (wôk′wā′) *n.* A sidewalk; a passage; a garden path.

wal·kyr·ie (wal·kir′ē, val-) *n.* A valkyrie. [OE *wælcyrie,* lit., a chooser of the slain]

walk·y-talk·y (wô′kē·tô′kē) See WALKIE-TALKIE.

.wall (wôl) *n.* **1** A continuous structure, as of stone or brick, designed to enclose an area, to provide defense or security, or to be the surrounding exterior of a house or a partition between rooms or halls; also, a fence of stone or brickwork, surrounding or separating yards, fields, etc. ◆ Collateral adjective: *mural.* **2** A barrier or rampart constructed for defense; in the plural, fortifications. **3** A sea wall; levee. **4** The side of any cavity, vessel, or receptacle; a parietal surface: the *walls* of the abdomen. **5** Something suggestive of a wall or barrier: a *wall* of bayonets. See synonyms under RAMPART. — **to drive, push,** or **thrust to the wall** To force (one) to an extremity; crush. — **to go to the wall** To be pressed or driven to an extremity; be forced to yield. — **to take the wall** To take the inner side of the walk; hence, to take a rude advantage. — *v.t.* **1** To provide, surround, protect, etc., with or as with a wall or walls. **2** To fill or block up a wall: often with *up.* — *adj.* Of or pertaining to a wall; hanging or growing on a wall [OE *weall, wall* <L *vallum* a rampart < *vallus* a stake, palisade]

Wall may appear as the first element in two-word phrases:

wall arcade	wall bracket	wall crane
wall arch	wall case	wall engine
wall berry	wall casing	wall face
wall border	wall clock	wall garden
wall box	wall coping	wall map

wall mosaic	wall plant	wall tower
wall moss	wall plug	wall tree
wall nook	wall top	wall vase

wal·la·by (wol′ə·bē) *n. pl.* **·bies** Any of various medium-sized to small kangaroos of Australia and New Guinea, ranging from the rock wallaby (genus *Petrogale*), to the **pademelon wallaby,** about the size of a rabbit. [<Australian *wolaba*]

Wal·lace (wol′is), **Alfred Russel,** 1823–1913, English naturalist. — **(Richard Horatio) Edgar,** 1875–1932, English novelist. — **Henry Agard,** 1888–1965, U.S. vice president 1941–1944; agriculturist, editor, and politician. — **Lewis,** 1827–1905, U.S. general, administrator, and author: known as *Lew Wallace.* — **Sir William,** 1272?–1305, Scottish national hero; executed by the English.

Wal·lach (väl′äkh), **Otto,** 1847–1931, German chemist.

Wal·la·chi·a (wo·lā′kē·ə) A historic region and former principality in southern and SE Rumania; 29,575 square miles; chief city, Bucharest: also *Walachia.* — **Wal·la′chi·an** *adj. & n.*

wal·lah (wä′lä) *n. Anglo-Indian* A person engaged in a specified occupation or activity, as a merchant, vender, agent, worker, or servant; popularly and somewhat contemptuously, a man or fellow. Also **wal′la.** — **punka-wallah** The servant whose job it is to keep the punka in motion. [<Hind. *-vālā,* suffix indicating a personal agent]

wal·la·roo (wol′ə·rōō′) *n.* A species of large kangaroo (*Macropus robustus*). Also **wallaroo kangaroo.** [<Australian *wolarū*]

Wal·la·sey (wol′ə·sē) A county borough in NW Cheshire, England, on the Mersey river opposite, and forming part of the port of, Liverpool.

Wal·la-wal·la (wol′ə·wol′ə) *n.* One of a small tribe of North American Indians of Shahaptian linguistic stock of the NW Pacific coast: now on a reservation in Oregon.

Wal·la Wal·la (wol′ə wol′ə) A city in SE Washington near the Oregon border on the Walla Walla River.

Walla Walla River A river in NE Oregon and SW Washington, flowing 60 miles NW to the Columbia River.

wall·board (wôl′bôrd′, -bōrd′) *n.* A material composed of several layers of compressed wood chips and pulp, molded and sized for use as a substitute for wooden boards and plaster.

wall-creep·er (wôl′krē′pər) *n.* A small, brilliantly colored Old World bird (*Tichodroma muraria*) that obtains its insect prey by creeping on cliffs and walls.

Wal·len·stein (wol′ən·stīn, *Ger.* vol′ən·shtīn), **Albrecht Wenzel Eusebius von,** 1583–1634, Duke of Friedland; Austrian general in the Thirty Years' War.

Wal·ler (wol′ər), **Edmund,** 1606–87, English poet.

wal·let (wol′it) *n.* **1** A pocketbook, usually of leather, for holding unfolded banknotes, personal papers, etc.; a billfold. **2** A leather or canvas bag for tools, etc. **3** A knapsack. **4** *Obs.* Any baggy protuberance hanging loosely. [ME *walet,* ? metathetic var. of *watel* a bag, basket <OE *watul* a wattle]

wall·eye (wôl′ī′) *n.* **1** An eye in which the iris is light-colored or white. **2** An eye in which the cornea is opaque and whitish; also, leukoma of the cornea. **3** A large staring eye, usually one showing much white, because of divergent strabismus. **4** Any of several walleyed fishes, as the walleyed pike or perch, the alewife, or the walleyed pollack. [Back formation <WALL-EYED]

wall·eyed (wôl′īd′) *adj.* **1** Affected with divergent strabismus. **2** Having a whitish or grayish eye; also, affected with leukoma of the cornea. **3** Squinting. **4** Having large, staring eyes, as a fish. **5** *Slang* Drunk. [<ON *valdeygthr,* alter. of *vagl eygr* <*vagl* a film on the eye + *eygr* having eyes <*auga* eye]

walleyed pike An American fresh-water percoid fish (genus *Stizostedion*) of the Great Lakes, having large eyes, esteemed as a game fish. Also **walleyed perch.**

walleyed pollack A coal-black North American pollack (*Pollachius fucensis*) of Pacific waters.

walleyed surf fish A sooty fish (*Hyperprosopon argenteus*) common in California waters.

wall fern The common polypody.

wall·flow·er (wôl′flou′ər) *n.* 1 Any of a genus (*Cheiranthus*) of European herbs of the mustard family, in particular the popular garden perennial *C. cheiri*, having fragrant yellow, orange, or red flowers. 2 An Australian desert shrub (genus *Gastrolobium*). 3 *Colloq.* A man or woman at a party who remains sitting or standing by the wall, presumably for want of a dancing partner.

WALL-FLOWER (Varies from 1 to 3 feet high)

wall fruit Fruit grown and ripened close to a wall or fence.

wal·lie (wol′ē) *n. Scot.* A valet.

Wal·lis and Fu·tu·na Islands (wol′is, fōō·tōō′na) Two closely connected protectorates NE of Fiji Islands, both dependencies of New Caledonia, including the chief islands of Uvéa, Futuna, and Alofi; total, 75 square miles.

wall lizard A gecko.

Wal·lo·ni·an (wo·lō′nē·ən) *adj.* Of or pertaining to the Walloons or the dialect spoken by them. — *n.* 1 A Walloon. 2 The French dialect of the Walloons.

Wal·loon (wo·lōōn′) *n.* 1 One of a people inhabiting southern and southeastern Belgium and the adjoining regions of France, originally descended from the ancient Belgae. 2 Their language, a dialect of French. 3 One of the Huguenot colonists who came to the United States from Artois, France. — *adj.* Of or pertaining to the Walloons or their dialect.

wal·lop (wol′əp) *v.t. Colloq.* 1 To beat soundly; thrash. 2 To hit with a hard blow. 3 To defeat soundly. — *v.i. Dial.* or *Colloq.* 4 To move quickly and strenuously; gallop. 5 To move in an awkward, floundering manner; waddle. — *n. Brit. Dial. & Scot.* A lively rolling motion; a gallop. 2 *Colloq.* A severe blow. [<AF *waloper*, OF *galoper*. Doublet of GALLOP.]

wal·lop·er (wol′əp·ər) *n. Colloq.* 1 One who wallops. 2 Something astounding or amazing; an extraordinary statement or act; a whopper.

wal·lop·ing (wol′əp·ing) *Colloq. adj.* Extraordinarily large; whopping: a *walloping* lie. — *n.* A beating; whipping.

wal·low (wol′ō) *v.i.* 1 To roll about, as in mud, snow, etc.; flounder: the hippopotamus *wallows* in the mud. 2 To move with a heavy, rolling motion, as a ship in a storm. 3 To live or indulge complacently or wantonly: to *wallow* in sensuality or wealth. — *n.* 1 The act of wallowing. 2 A pool, mudhole, or slough in which animals wallow; also, any depression or hollow made by or suggesting such use. [OE *wealwian*] — **wal′low·er** *n.*

wall·pa·per (wôl′pā′pər) *n.* Paper specially prepared and printed in colors and designs, for covering walls and ceilings of rooms. — *v.t.* To cover or provide with wallpaper.

wall pellitory See PELLITORY.

wall plate 1 A horizontal timber on a wall, for bearing the ends of joists, girders, etc. 2 *Mech.* A plate for attaching a bearing or the like to a wall.

wall rock *Mining* The non-metalliferous rock between two lodes.

wall rocket A British perennial (*Diplotaxis tenuifolia*) of the mustard family, with large yellow flowers.

wall rue A small delicate spleenwort (*Asplenium ruta-muraria*) growing on walls and cliffs.

Walls·end (wôlz′end) *n.* A size or grade of coal for household purposes. [from *Wallsend*, England]

Walls·end (wôlz′end) A municipal borough in SE Northumberland, England, on the Tyne just NE of Newcastle-on-Tyne.

Wall Street 1 A street in lower Manhattan, New York City: the financial center of the United States. 2 American financiers collectively, their interests, power, etc., or the American financial world.

wall tent A tent having vertical sides and peaked top.

wal·ly (wā′lē, wol′ē) See WALY[1].

wal·ly-drai·gle (wā′lē·drā′gəl, wol′ē-) *n. Scot.* 1 The youngest in a family; also, a young bird in the nest. 2 Any feeble or ill-grown creature. Also **wal′ly·drag′** (-drag, -dräg′).

wal·nut (wôl′nut′, -nət) *n.* 1 Any of various deciduous, typically European and Asian trees (genus *Juglans*), cultivated as ornamental shade trees and valued for their timber and their edible nuts; especially, the **black walnut** (*J. nigra*) of the eastern United States, and the **English, Persian, Circassian,** or **Caucasian walnut** (*J. regia*). 2 The wood or nut of any of these trees. 3 The shagbark hickory, or its nut. 4 The color of the wood of any of these trees, especially of the black walnut, a very dark brown; also, the color of the shell of the English walnut, a dull, medium yellowish brown: also called **walnut brown.** [OE *walhhnutu, wealh hnutu* < *wealh* foreign + *hnutu* a nut]

BLACK WALNUT
a. Catkin.
b. Shuck, nut inside.
c. Nut, shuck removed.

Wal·pole (wôl′pōl, wol′-), **Horace,** 1717-97, fourth earl of Orford; English author and wit; son of Sir Robert Walpole. — **Sir Hugh Seymour,** 1884-1941, English novelist. — **Sir Robert,** 1676-1745, first earl of Orford; English statesman.

Wal·pur·gis Night (väl·pŏŏr′gis) The night before May 1, originally dedicated to St. Walpurga, an English nun of the eighth century who founded religious houses in Germany: associated in German folklore with a witches' Sabbath on the Brocken. Also *German* **Wal·pur·gis·nacht′** (-näkht′). [<G *Walpurgisnacht*]

wal·rus (wôl′rəs, wol′-) *n.* A large, marine, seal-like mammal (family *Odobenidae*) of arctic seas, with flexible hind limbs, tusklike canines in the upper jaw, and a thick, heavy neck; especially, the common Atlantic walrus (*Odobenus rosmarus*). — *adj.* 1 Belonging or pertaining to a walrus. 2 Designating a type of mustache suggestive of the coarse bristles on the muzzle of a walrus. [<Du. *walrus* <Scand. Cf. Dan. *hyalros,* ? <ON *hrosshvalr,* lit., a horse whale.]

WALRUS (Body to 10 feet; weight to 3,000 pounds)

Wal·sall (wôl′sôl) A county borough in southern Staffordshire, England.

Wal·sing·ham (wôl′sing·əm), **Sir Francis,** 1530?-90, English statesman.

Wal·ter (wôl′tər, *Ger.* väl′tər) A masculine personal name. Also *Ger., Sw.* **Wal·ther** (väl′tər). [<Gmc., ruler of the army]

Wal·ter (väl′tər), **Bruno,** 1876-1962, German orchestra conductor active in the United States: real name *Bruno Schlesinger*.

Wal·ter (wôl′tər), **John,** 1739-1812, English journalist; founder of the London *Times.*

Wal·tham (wôl′thəm) An industrial city in eastern Massachusetts on the Charles River west of Boston.

Wal·tham·stow (wôl′thəm·stō, -təm-) A municipal borough of SW Essex, England, NE of London.

Wal·ther von der Vo·gel·wei·de (väl′ter fôn der fō′gəl·vī′də), 1170?-1230?, German minnesinger.

Wal·ton (wôl′tən), **Izaak,** 1593-1683, English author. — **William Turner,** born 1902, English composer.

waltz (wôlts) *n.* 1 A round dance executed to music in triple time. 2 The music for such a dance, or any composition written in the triple time characteristic of the waltz. — *v.i.* 1 To dance a waltz. 2 To move quickly: He *waltzed* out of the room. — *v.t.* 3 To cause to waltz. — *adj.* Pertaining to, or typical of, the waltz: *waltz* time. [<G *walzer* < *walzen* waltz, roll] — **waltz′er** *n.*

Wal·vis Bay (wôl′vis) 1 An inlet of the Atlantic in South-West Africa. 2 An enclave in South-West Africa, administered by that territory, but an integral part of the Cape of Good Hope Province, Union of South Africa; on Walvis Bay; 374 square miles. 3 A port in this enclave: also *Walfish Bay. Afrikaans* **Wal·vis·baai** (wôl′vis·bī′).

wa·ly[1] (wā′lē, wol′ē) *Scot. adj.* 1 Beautiful; pleasing; excellent. 2 Strong; robust; vigorous. — *n. pl.* **·lies** 1 Something pleasing to the eye; a toy; ornament. 2 Good luck. 3 *pl.* Finery. Also spelled *wally.*

wa·ly[2] (wā′lē) *interj. Dial. & Scot.* Alas!: an expression of sorrow or lament.

wam·ble (wom′əl, wam′-) *Dial. v.i.* **·bled, ·bling** 1 To move unsteadily; roll. 2 To twist or turn; writhe. 3 *Obs.* To feel nausea; be giddy or faint. — *n.* 1 A rolling gait. 2 A rolling or upheaving of the stomach; nausea. [ME *wamlen.* Cf. Dan. *vamle* feel nausea, Norw. *vamla* stagger.] — **wam′bling·ly** *adv.* — **wam′bly** *adj.*

wame (wām) *n. Scot.* The abdomen; belly; womb.

wame·fou (wām′fōō) *n. Scot.* A bellyful. Also **wame′fu′, wame′ful** (-fōōl).

wamp·ish (wom′pish) *v.t. Scot.* To toss or throw about; wave; brandish.

wam·pum (wom′pəm, wôm′-) *n.* 1 Beads made of the interior parts of shells, formerly used as currency among North American Indians and between the Indians and white settlers: used loose, strung on strings, and also made into belts, scarfs, etc. The strings were often worn as ornaments, necklaces, bracelets, etc. The belts, woven with symbolic designs, were used in rituals, official communications, proposals, ratification of treaties, alliances, etc. The beads were either black, dark-purple, or white, the last being specifically **wam′pum·peag** (-pēg). The dark beads were double the value of the white. See SEAWAN. 2 *Colloq.* Money. [<Algonquian *wampum(peage),* lit., a white (string of beads)]

WAMPUM
The historic Pennwampum — Iroquois Indian.

wampum snake The hoop snake: so called from its coloring.

wa·mus (wô′məs, wom′əs) *n.* A cardigan; a heavy outer jacket of strong, coarse cloth, worn in the United States. Also **wam′mus, wam′pus** (-pəs). [<Du. *wammes,* short for *wambuis* <OF *wambois* a leather doublet <OHG *wamba* the belly]

wan[1] (won) *adj.* 1 Pale, as from sickness or anxiety; pallid; livid; careworn; of a sickly hue. 2 Having a gloomy aspect; dismal; dark: said of scenes or landscapes. 3 *Obs.* Sad; mournful. 4 Faint; feeble: a *wan* smile. See synonyms under GHASTLY, PALE[2]. — *v.t. & v.i.* **wanned, wan·ning** To make or become wan. — *n. Rare* The quality of being wan; paleness. [OE *wann* dark, gloomy] — **wan′ly** *adv.* — **wan′ness** *n.*

wan[2] (won) Obsolete past tense of WIN.

Wan·a·mak·er (won′ə·mā′kər), **John,** 1838-1922, U.S. merchant.

wand (wond) *n.* 1 A slender, flexible rod waved by a magician, conjurer, or legerdemain artist; also, any rod indicating an office or function of the bearer, as a scepter. 2 A musician's baton. 3 A thin, flexible stick or twig; also, a willow shoot; osier. 4 In archery, a slat used as a mark and placed at varying distances for men and women.

See synonyms under STICK. [<ON *vöndr*. Akin to WIND[2].]

wan·der (won'dər) *v.i.* **1** To move or travel about without destination or purpose; roam; rove. **2** To go casually or by an indirect route; idle; stroll. **3** To extend in an irregular course; twist or meander. **4** To turn from a true or direct course; stray. **5** To deviate in conduct or opinion; go astray. **6** To think or speak deliriously or irrationally. — *v.t.* **7** *Poetic* To wander through or across. — *n.* The act of wandering; a ramble. [OE *wandrian*] — **wan'der·er** *n.* — **wan'der·ing** *adj.* — **wan'der·ing·ly** *adv.*

Synonyms (verb): deviate, digress, diverge, err, ramble, range, roam, rove, stray, swerve, veer. To *wander* is to move in an indefinite or indeterminate way which may or may not be a departure from a prescribed way; to *deviate* is to turn from a prescribed or right way, physically, mentally, or morally, usually in an unfavorable sense; to *diverge* is to turn from a course previously followed or that something else follows, and has no unfavorable implication; to *digress* is used only with reference to speaking or writing; to *err* is used of intellectual or moral action. To *swerve* or *veer* is to turn suddenly from a prescribed or previous course, and often but momentarily; *veer* is more capricious and repetitious; the horse *swerves* at the flash of a sword; the wind *veers*; the ship *veers* with the wind. To *stray* is to go in a somewhat purposeless way aside from the regular path or usual limits or abode, usually with unfavorable implication; cattle *stray* from their pastures; an author *strays* from his subject. *Stray* is in most uses a lighter word than *wander*. *Ramble* in its literal use is always a word of pleasant suggestion, but in its figurative use somewhat contemptuous; as, *rambling* talk. See RAMBLE.

wandering albatross A large, whitish, black-winged, web-footed sea bird (*Diomedea exulans*), having extraordinary powers of flight.

wandering jew 1 A perennial trailing herb (*Tradescantia fluminensis*) of the spiderwort family, with hairy white flowers and vivid green leaves sometimes striped with yellow. **2** A related plant (*Zebrina pendula*) with red or white flowers and striped leaves.

Wandering Jew See under JEW.

wandering kidney A floating kidney.

wan·der·lust (won'dər·lust', *Ger.* vän'dər·lŏŏst) *n.* An impulse to travel; restlessness combined with a sense of adventure. [<G *wandern* travel + *lust* joy]

wan·der·oo (won'də·rōō') *n.* **1** A large black monkey (*Macaca silenus*) of western India, having a heavy whitish mane. **2** A Ceylonese langur (*Presbytis cephalopterus*). [<Singhalese *vanduru*, pl. of *vandurā* the Ceylonese langur <Skt. *vānara* a monkey]

wan·dle (won'dəl, -əl) *adj. Dial.* Supple; nimble. [Back formation <OE *wandlung* changeableness]

Wands·worth (wondz'wûrth) A metropolitan borough in SW London, England.

wane (wān) *v.i.* **waned, wan·ing 1** To diminish in size and brilliance: opposed to *wax*. **2** To decline or decrease gradually; draw to an end. — *n.* **1** Decrease, as of power, prosperity, or reputation. **2** The decrease of the moon's visible illuminated surface; also, the period of such decrease. **3** The beveled edge of a board sawn from a log; also, the bark or defective portion on the edge or corner of a board. ◆ Homophone: *wain*. [OE *wanian* lessen]

wane·y (wā'nē) *adj.* Having a beveled edge, as the wane of a plank: also spelled *wany*. [<WANE, *n.* (def. 3)]

Wang·a·nu·i (wông'ə·nōō'ē) A port of southern North Island, New Zealand.

wan·gle (wang'gəl) *v.* **·gled, ·gling** *Colloq. v.t.* **1** To obtain or make by indirect or irregular methods; contrive: to *wangle* an introduction to a celebrity. **2** To manipulate or adjust, especially dishonestly. **3** To wriggle or wag. — *v.i.* **4** To resort to indirect, irregular, or dishonest methods. **5** To wriggle. [? Alter. of WAGGLE] — **wan'gler** *n.*

Wan·hsien (wän'shyen') A city on the Yangtze River, eastern Szechwan province, central China; a major commercial port NE of Chungking.

wan·i·gan (won'ə·gən) *n.* In American logging

camps: **1** A storage chest for clothing, etc. **2** A shanty fitted with sleeping and cooking accommodations. Also **wan·gan** (won'gən), **wan'gun, wan'ni·gan.** [Earlier *wangan* <Algonquian *atawangan* < *atawan* buy, sell]

wan·ion (won'yən) *n. Archaic* Disaster, or bad luck; a curse: used only in the phrases **in a wanion, with a wanion,** etc. [Alter of dial. ME (Northern) *waniand*, ppr. of *wanien* wane]

Wan·kel engine (väng'kəl, wäng'-) A light, compact type of internal-combustion engine having combustion chambers bounded by the wall of a shallow cylinder and the sides of a triangular piston that rotates in one direction inside it. Also **Wan'kel.** [<F. *Wankel*, 1902-, German inventor]

Wan·ne–Eick·el (vän'ə·ī'kəl) A city in west central North Rhine–Westphalia NW of Bochum, West Germany.

Wan·stead and Wood·ford (won'sted, -stid, wood'fərd) A municipal borough in Essex, England, NE of London.

want (wont, wônt) *v.t.* **1** To feel a desire or wish for. **2** To wish; desire: used with the infinitive: Your friends *want* to help you. **3** To be deficient in; lack; be without. **4** To be lacking to the extent of: He *wants* three inches of six feet. **5** *Brit.* To need; require. — *v.i.* **6** To have need: usually with *for*. **7** To be needy or destitute. **8** *Rare* To be lacking or absent. — *n.* **1** Lack or absence of something; scarcity; shortage. **2** Privation; destitution; need. **3** Something that is lacking or needed; a need. **4** A conscious or felt need of something; a craving. [Prob. <ON *vanta* be lacking] — **want'er** *n.*

Synonyms (noun): absence, dearth, default, defect, deficiency, lack, necessity, need, privation, scantiness, scarceness, scarcity. See NECESSITY, POVERTY. *Antonyms:* abundance, affluence, fullness, luxury, plenty, wealth.

wa'n't (wont, wônt) Was not: a dialectal contraction.

want ad *Colloq.* An advertisement in a newspaper for something wanted, as hired help, a job, a lodging, etc.

want·age (won'tij, wôn'-) *n.* Whatever is lacking; deficiency.

want column A column of want ads in a newspaper or other periodical.

want·ing (won'ting, wôn'-) *adj.* **1** Not at hand; missing; lacking: One juror is still *wanting*. **2** Marked by lack or deficiency; not coming up to need or expectation: He was found *wanting*. **3** *Colloq.* Deficient in intellect; feeble-minded. — **wanting in** Deficient in. — *prep.* With the exception of; less; save; minus.

wan·ton (won'tən) *adj.* **1** Dissolute; unchaste; licentious; lewd; lustful. **2** Recklessly inconsiderate, heartless, or unjust; evincing a malicious nature: *wanton* savagery; also, unprovoked: a *wanton* murder. **3** Of vigorous and abundant growth; rank. **4** Extravagant; running to excess; unrestrained: *wanton* speech. **5** Not bound or tied; loose: *wanton* curls; also, frolicsome; prankish. **6** *Obs.* Refractory; rebellious. — *v.i.* **1** To act wantonly or playfully; revel or sport. **2** To grow luxuriantly. — *v.t.* **3** To waste wantonly. — *n.* **1** A lewd or licentious person, especially a woman. **2** A playful or frolicsome person or animal. **3** A trifler; dallier. **4** *Obs.* A person who has been much indulged; a pet. [ME *wantoun* <OE *wan* deficient + ME *towen*, OE *togen*, pp. of *tēon* bring up, educate] — **wan'ton·ly** *adv.* — **wan'ton·ness** *n.*

Synonyms (adj.): airy, free, frisky, frolicsome, gay, loose, merry, playful, reckless, sportive, unbridled, uncurbed, unrestrained, wandering, wild. See IMMODEST. *Antonyms:* austere, demure, discreet, reserved, sedate, thoughtful.

wan·y (wā'nē) See WANEY.

wap[1] (wop, wap) *Dial.* or *Archaic v.t. & v.i.* **wapped, wap·ping 1** To whip; beat; strike. **2** To flutter or flap, as wings. — *n.* **1** A stroke; blow. **2** A quarrel; fight. **3** A storm. [Prob. var. of WHOP]

wap[2] (wop, wop) *Dial. v.t.* **wapped, wap·ping** To wrap; tie; bind. — *n.* A wrapping. [? Alter. of WARP]

wap·en·shaw (wop'ən·shô, wap'-) *n. Scot.* A show of weapons; review of weapons. Also **wap'in·schaw, wap'pen·schaw'ing.**

wap·en·take (wop'ən·tāk, wap'-) *n.* An old administrative and judicial subdivision of some English counties, equivalent to the

hundred of most counties. [OE *wǣpengetæc* <ON *vápnatak* a (symbolical) flourish of weapons denoting confirmation of the decisions of an assembly < *vápna*, genitive pl. of *vápn* a weapon + *tak* a taking]

wap·i·ti (wop'ə·tē) *n.* A large North American deer (*Cervus canadensis*): usually *elk*. [<Algonquian. Cf. Shawnee *wapiti* pale, white.]

wap·per–jawed (wop'ər·jôd') *adj. U. S. Dial.* **1** Having a wry or undershot jaw. **2** Out of true; askew.

WAPITI
(About 5 feet high at the shoulders; antler spread to 3 feet)

war[1] (wôr) *n.* **1** A contest between or among nations or states, or between different parties in the same state, carried on by force and with arms. **2** Any act or state of hostility; enmity; strife; also, a contest or conflict. **3** *Poetic* **a** A battle. **b** The supplies and paraphernalia of war. **c** Armed troops; an army. See table MAJOR WARS OF HISTORY on page 1417. **4** The science or art of military operations; strategy. — *v.i.* **warred, war·ring 1** To wage war; fight or take part in a war. **2** To be in any state of active opposition; contend; strive. — *adj.* Of or pertaining to, used in, or resulting from war. [OE *wyrre, werre* <AF *werre* <OHG *werra* strife, confusion]

War may appear as a combining form in hyphemes or solidemes, or as the first element in two-word phrases:

war–blasted	war–making
war–born	war march
war–breeder	war–marked
war–breeding	war neurosis
war bride	war office
war–broken	war party
war budget	war prisoner
war chant	war–production
war chief	war–proof
war cloud	war–ridden
war code	war–risk
warcraft	war service
war–debt	war–shaken
war–disabled	war song
war dog	war–stirring
war drum	war–swept
war–famed	war talk
war–footing	war tax
war gains	wartime
war–god	war–torn
war–goddess	war–tossed
war–hardened	war traitor
war–impoverished	war vessel
war insurance	war–wasted
war law	war–wearied
war leader	war–weary
war loan	war–work ·
war–loving	war–worker
war–machine	war–worn
war–made	warworthy
war–maimed	war–wounded
war–maker	war zone

war[2] (wär) *Dial. v.t.* To guard against; ware. — *adj.* Cautious; wary. [Var. of WARE[2]]

war[3] (wär) *adj. & adv. Scot. & Brit. Dial.* Worse.

War·beck (wôr'bek), **Perkin,** 1474–99. Walloon impostor and pretender to the English throne; hanged.

war belt Among certain North American Indians, a belt of wampum bearing symbolic figures or designs, sent by one tribe to another or passed from tribe to tribe, as a message declaring war, summoning a group of tribes to war, invoking aid in war, etc.

War between the States The United States Civil War: used especially in the former Confederate States.

war bird Among certain North American Indians, the golden eagle: so called because its feathers were worn in the war bonnet.

war·ble[1] (wôr'bəl) *v.* **bled, ·bling** *v.t.* **1** To sing with trills and runs, or with tremulous vibrations. **2** To celebrate in song. — *v.i.* **3** To sing with trills, etc. **4** To make a liquid,

1101

MAJOR WARS OF HISTORY

NAME	CONTESTANTS (victor shown first)	NOTABLE BATTLES	TREATIES
Greco-Persian Wars 499–478 B.C.	Greek states—Persia	Marathon, 490; Thermopylae, Salamis, 480; Plataea, 479	
Peloponnesian War 431–404 B.C.	Sparta—Athens	Syracuse, 415; Cyzicus, 410; Aegospotami, 405	Peace of Nicias, 421
First Punic War 264–241 B.C.; Second Punic War 218–201 B.C.; Third Punic War 149–146 B.C.	Rome—Carthage	Drepanum, 249; Aegates, 241 Lake Trasimene, 217, Cannae, 216; Zama, 202	
Islamic Invasion of Europe 630–19th century	Christianity—Islam	Constantinople, 717–718; Tours, 732; Manzikert, 1071; Hattin, 187; Lepanto, 1571; Vienna, 1524, 1683; Zenta, 1697	Pruth, 1711; Kutchuk—Kanardjii, 1774; Sistova, 1791
Norman Conquest 1066	Normandy—England	Hastings, 1066	
Crusades 1096–1291	Christianity—Islam (indecisive)	Jerusalem, 1099; Acre, 1191	
Hundred Years' War 1338–1453	England—France	Crécy, 1346; Poitiers, 1356; Agincourt, 1415; Siege of Orléans, 1428–39	
Wars of the Roses 1455–85	Lancaster—York (indecisive)	St. Albans, 1455	
Thirty Years' War 1618–48	Catholics—Protestants	Leipzig, Breitenfeld, 1631; Lützen, 1632	Westphalia, 1648
Civil War (English) 1642–46	Roundheads—Cavaliers	Marston Moor, 1643; Naseby, 1645	
War of the Spanish Succession 1701–14	England, Austria, Prussia, Netherlands—France, Spain	Blenheim, 1704	Utrecht, 1713
War of the Austrian Succession 1740–48	France, Prussia, Sardinia, Spain—Austria, England	Dettingen, 1743; Fontenoy, 1745	Aix-la-Chapelle, 1748
French & Indian War 1755–63	England—France	Plains of Abraham, 1759; Montreal, 1760	
Seven Years' War 1756–63	Prussia—Austria, France, Russia	Rossbach, Leuthen, 1757	Hubertusberg, 63
Revolutionary War 1775–83	American Colonies—England	Lexington, Concord, Bunker Hill, 1775; Saratoga, 1777; Yorktown, 1781	Paris, 1783
Napoleonic Wars 1796–1815	England, Austria, Russia, Prussia, etc.—France	Nile, 1798; Trafalgar, 1805; Jena, Auerstädt, 1806; Leipzig, 1813 Waterloo, 1815	Campoformio, 1797; Tilsit, 1807; Schönbrunn, 1809; Paris, 1814–15; Vienna, 1815
War of 1812 1812–15	Unites States—England	Lake Erie, 1813; New Orleans, 1815	Ghent, 1814
War of Independence (Greek) 1821–29	Greece, England, Sweden, Russia—Turkey	Navarino, 1827	London, 1827
Mexican War 1846–48	United States—Mexico	Resaca de la Palma, 1846; Chapultepec, 1847	Guadalupe Hidalgo, 1848
Crimean War 1854–56	Turkey, England, France, Sardinia—Russia	Sevastopol, 1854	Paris, 1856
Civil War (United States) 1861–65	Union (North)—Confederate States (South)	Bull Run, 1861; Antietam, 1862; Chancellorsville, Gettysburg, Vicksburg, Chattanooga, 1863; Wilderness, 1864	
Franco-Prussian War 1870–71	Prussia—France	Sedan, 1870	Versailles, 1871
Spanish-American War 1898	United States—Spain	Manila Bay, Santiago, 1898	Paris, 1898
Boer War 1899–1902	England—Transvaal Republic & Orange Free State	Ladysmith, 1899	Vereeniging, 1902
Russo-Japanese War 1904–1905	Japan—Russia	Port Arthur, Mukden, Tsushima, 1905	Portsmouth, 1905
First Balkan War 1912–13; Second Balkan War 1913	Bulgaria, Serbia, Greece, Montenegro—Turkey	Scutari, 1912; Salonika, 1912; Adrianople, 1912	London, 1913; Bucharest, 1913
World War I 1914–18	Allies—Central Powers	Dardanelles, 1915; Verdun, Somme, Jutland, 1916; Caporetto, 1917; Vittorio Veneto, Amiens, Marne, Ypres, 1918	Versailles, Saint-Germain, Neuilly, 1919; Trianon, Sèvres, 1920; Lausanne, 1923
Civil War (Spanish) 1936–39	Insurgents—Loyalists	Teruel, 1937; Ebro River, 1938	
World War II 1939–45	Allies—Axis 1939–45	Dunkirk 1940; Crete, 1941; El Alamein, 1942; Tunis, 1943; Stalingrad, 1942–43; Kharkov, 1943; Cassino, 1943–44; Saint-Lô, 1944; Rhine, Ruhr, Berlin, 1945	Potsdam, 1945
	Allies—Japan 1941–45	Pearl Harbor, 1941; Bataan, 1941–42; Singapore, Coral Sea, Midway Island, Guadalcanal, 1942; Bismarck Sea, Tarawa, 1943; Leyte Gulf, 1944; Philippines, 1944–45; Okinawa, 1945	San Francisco, 1951
Korean War 1950–52	United Nations—North Korea	Inchon, Pyongyang, 1950; Seoul, 1951	Panmunjom, 1953
Vietnam War 1957–75	North Vietnam—South Vietnam, United States	Tet Offensive, Saigon, 1968	Paris, 1973

add,āce,câre,pälm; end,ēven; it,īce; odd,ōpen,ôrder; to͝ok,po͞ol; up,bûrn; ə = a in *above*, e in *sicken*, i in *clarity*, o in *melon*, u in *focus* ; yo͞o = u in *fuse*, oi,oil; ou,pout; ch,check; g,go; ng,ring; th,thin; th,this; zh,vision. Foreign sounds à,œ,ü,kh,ṅ; and ◆: see page xx. <from; + plus; ? possibly.

murmuring sound, as a stream. **5** *U.S.* To yodel. See synonyms under SING. — *n.* The act of warbling; a carol; song. [<AF *werbler*, OF *guerbler* < *werble* a warble <OHG *werbel* something that revolves. Akin to WHIRL.]

war·ble² (wôr′bəl) *n.* **1** A hard swelling on the back of a horse, caused by the chafing of the saddle. **2** A boil or swelling under the hide of a horse, cow, deer, or the like, caused by the maggot of a botfly or warblefly. **3** A warblefly. [Cf. obs. Sw. *varbulde* < *var* pus + *bulde* a tumor] — **war′bled** *adj.*

war·ble·fly (wôr′bəl·flī′) *n. pl.* **·flies** Any of a family (*Hypodermatidae*) of dipterous insects resembling the botflies, whose larvae produce swellings under the hides of cattle, horses, etc. [<WARBLE² + FLY²]

war·bler (wôr′blər) *n.* **1** One who or that which warbles; a songster. **2** Any of a family (*Sylviidae*) of plain-colored, mostly Old World birds allied to the kinglets and noted for their song, as the whitethroat. **3** Any of a large and varied family (*Compsothlypidae*) of small American insectivorous birds, usually brilliantly colored and with little powers of song, as the **summer** or **yellow warbler** (*Dendroica aestiva*), the redstart, ovenbird, and water thrush. Also **wood warbler.**

war bonnet The ceremonial head dress of the North American Plains Indians, consisting of a rawhide cap fitting the head and extending down the back to the heels, the crown and the extension being decorated with feathers of the golden eagle.

War·burg (vär′boŏrkh), **Otto Heinrich,** born 1883, German physiologist and chemist.

War College One of four colleges in the United States giving advanced instruction to experienced military, naval, and air officers; specifically, the **Army War College,** Carlisle Barracks, Pennsylvania, under the Department of the Army; the **Naval War College,** Newport, Rhode Island, under the Navy Department; and the **Air War College,** near Montgomery, Alabama, under the Department of the Air Force. The **National War College,** Washington, D.C., operating under the Joint Chiefs of Staff, prepares officers of the armed services, the State Department, and other executive departments for duties concerned with national security.

war correspondent A newspaper reporter or representative of some other periodical engaged to write up the scenes of combat from direct observation.

war cry A rallying cry used by combatants in a war, or by participants in any contest.

ward (wôrd) *n.* **1** The act of guarding; protection. **2** The state of being under a guard or guardian; custody; confinement; also, guardianship; control. **3** A guarded or protected place; a prison; jail; also, a division or subdivision of a jail or hospital: the maternity *ward.* **4** A territorial division of a city, made for convenience of government; also, in certain northern counties of England, a division equivalent to a hundred or wapentake. **5** A person who is in the charge or under the protection of a guardian. **6** An instrument or means of defense; a protection. **7** A defensive attitude or movement, as in fencing; guard. **8** A projection inside a lock, designed to obstruct the turning of any key other than the proper one; also, a corresponding notch in the bit of a key. **9** In feudal law, a minor under the care or protection of a guardian. **10** A warden; overseer. **11** A local congregation within the Mormon Church. **12** *Obs.* A company of men detailed to defend or guard; a garrison; watch. See synonyms under SHELTER. — *v.t.* **1** To repel or turn aside, as a thrust or blow: usually with *off.* **2** To put in a ward; keep in safety. **3** *Archaic* To guard; protect. [OE *weard* a watching < *weardian* watch, guard; infl. in some senses by AF *warde,* OF *garde* <Gmc.]

-ward *suffix* Toward; in the direction of: *upward, homeward.* Also **-wards.** [OE *-weard, -weardes* at, toward]

Ward (wôrd), **Artemas,** 1727-1800, American Revolutionary general. — **Artemus** Pseudonym of Charles Farrar Browne, 1834-67, U.S. humorist. — **Mary Augusta,** 1851-1920, *née* Arnold, English novelist: known as *Mrs. Humphrey Ward.*

war dance A dance of savage tribes before going to war or in celebration of a victory.

war·den¹ (wôr′dən) *n.* **1** One who keeps ward;

a warder or gatekeeper. **2** A chief officer, as in a prison. **3** In England, the head of certain colleges. **4** In Connecticut, the chief executive of a borough. **5** A churchwarden. See synonyms under SUPERINTENDENT. [<AF *wardein,* OF *gardein, guarden* <Gmc. Doublet of GUARDIAN.]

war·den² (wôr′dən) *n.* A variety of pear used chiefly for cooking. Also **War′den.** [ME *wardon,* prob. <AF *warder,* OF *garder* keep <Gmc.]

war·den·ry (wôr′dən·rē) *n. pl.* **·ries** The office, functions, or jurisdiction of a warden. Also **war′den·ship** (-ship).

War Department A former executive department of the U.S. government (1789-1947) in charge of matters relating to the Army and (later) the Army Air Force: now absorbed into the Department of Defense.

ward·er (wôr′dər) *n.* **1** A keeper; guard; sentinel; watchman. **2** An official staff or baton; a truncheon. **3** A prison official; warden. [<AF *wardere* < *warder,* var. of OF *guarder* guard, keep]

ward–heel·er (wôrd′hē′lər) *n. U.S. Slang* A hanger-on of a political boss, who does minor tasks, canvasses votes, etc. [<WARD (def. 4) + HEELER (def. 1)]

ward–hold·ing (wôrd′hōl′ding) *n.* The holding of lands by military tenure: distinguished from *feu.*

ward·ress (wôrd′ris) *n.* A female warden.

ward·robe (wôrd′rōb′) *n.* **1** A large upright cabinet for wearing apparel; formerly, a large clothes closet or room, where clothes were also made and repaired. **2** All the garments of any one person. **3** In a noble or royal household, the department responsible for clothing, jewelry, etc. **4** The costumes of a theater or theatrical troupe. **5** The styles of a particular season taken collectively: the spring *wardrobe.* [<AF *wardrobe,* OF *garderobe* < *warder* keep + *robe* a robe, dress]

ward·room (wôrd′rōom′, -rŏom′) *n.* On a warship, the quarters allotted to the commissioned officers above the rank of ensign, excepting the commander, who has his own quarters; especially, the dining-room of these officers; also, these officers regarded as a group.

ward·ship (wôrd′ship) *n.* **1** The state of a ward; pupilage. **2** In feudal law, the right by which the lord had the custody of the bodies, and the custody and profits of the lands, of minor heirs of a deceased tenant.

ware¹ (wâr) *n.* **1** Articles of the same class; especially, manufactured articles: used collectively, often in composition: *tableware, glassware.* **2** *pl.* Articles of commerce; goods; merchandise; products. **3** Pottery; ceramic articles; earthenware. ♦ Homophone: *wear.* [OE *waru*]

ware² (wâr) *v.t.* **wared, war·ing** To beware of: used mainly in the imperative: *Ware* the dog. — *adj. Obs.* Conscious; aware; hence, on one's guard; cautious. ♦ Homophone: *wear.* [Fusion of OE *warian* beware and AF *warer,* OF *garer* <Gmc. Akin to WARN.]

ware³ (wâr) *v.t. Scot.* To expend; lay out; also, to lavish; squander: also spelled *wair.* ♦ Homophone: *wear.*

ware·house (wâr′hous′) *n.* **1** A storehouse for goods or merchandise. **2** *Brit.* A large wholesale shop. — *v.t.* **·housed** (-houzd′), **·hous·ing** (-hou′zing) To place or store in a warehouse, especially in a bonded warehouse.

ware·house·man (wâr′hous′mən) *n. pl.* **·men** (-mən) One who makes a business of storing goods.

ware·room (wâr′rōom′, -rŏom′) *n.* A room for the storage, exhibition, or sale of goods or wares.

war·fare (wôr′fâr′) *n.* **1** The waging or carrying on of war; conflict with arms; war. **2** Struggle; strife.

War·field (wôr′fēld), **David,** 1866-1951, U.S. actor.

War for Southern Independence See CIVIL WAR (AMERICAN) in table under WAR.

war game 1 Kriegspiel. **2** *pl.* Practice maneuvers imitating the conditions of actual warfare.

war hawk One who advocates war; a jingo.

war·head (wôr′hed′) *n. Mil.* **1** An ogive-shaped chamber in the nose of a torpedo, containing the charge of high explosive. **2** A similar chamber in a bomb, guided missile, or the like.

war horse 1 A heavy horse used in warfare.

a charger. **2** *Colloq.* A veteran; especially, an aggressive or veteran politician.

war·i·son (war′ə·sən) *n.* **1** A signal for assault: an erroneous use. **2** Reward; healing. [<AF *warison,* OF *garison* wealth, possession]

wark¹ (wärk) *n. Scot.* Work.

wark² (wärk) *Scot. & Brit. Dial. n.* Ache; pain. — *v.i.* To suffer pain; ache; throb.

war·like (wôr′līk′) *adj.* **1** Disposed to engage in war; belligerent. **2** Relating to, used in, or suggesting war. **3** Threatening war; belligerent; hostile.

Synonyms: martial, military, soldierlike, soldierly. *Antonyms:* civil, effeminate, meek, pacific, peaceful, unmilitary, unsoldierlike, unsoldierly, unwarlike.

war·lock¹ (wôr′lok′) *n.* A wizard; sorcerer; also, a demon. [OE *wǣrloga* a traitor, foe, devil < *wǣr* a covenant + *lēogan* lie, deny]

war·lock² (wôr′lok′) *n.* A scalp lock worn by the warriors of certain North American Indian tribes. [<WAR + LOCK²]

war·lord (wôr′lôrd′) *n.* **1** A leader or high-ranking officer in a militaristic nation. **2** The warlike ruler or leader of a local region or group of bandits, especially in the Orient.

warm (wôrm) *adj.* **1** Moderately hot; having, or characterized by, heat somewhat greater than temperate: *warm* water; a *warm* climate. **2** Imparting heat: a *warm* fire. **3** Imparting, promoting, or preserving warmth; preventing loss of bodily heat: a *warm* coat. **4** Having a feeling of heat somewhat greater than ordinary: *warm* from exertion. **5** Possessing or marked by ardor, zeal, liveliness, enthusiasm, or cordiality: a *warm* argument; *warm* wishes. **6** Excited; agitated; also, vehement; passionate: a *warm* temper. **7** United by ardent affection: *warm* friends; also, amorous; loving. **8** Having predominating tones of red or yellow: opposed to *cool.* **9** Recently made; fresh: a *warm* trail; hence, near a hidden object, as in certain games of children. **10** *Colloq.* Uncomfortable by reason of annoyances or danger: They made the town *warm* for him. **11** Characterized by brisk activity: a *warm* skirmish. **12** *Colloq.* Rich; wealthy. — *v.t.* **1** To make warm; heat slightly: often with *up.* **2** To make ardent or enthusiastic; interest. **3** To fill with kindly feeling: The sight *warms* my heart. — *v.i.* **4** To become warm. **5** To become ardent or enthusiastic: often with *up* or *to.* **6** To become kindly disposed or friendly: with *to* or *toward.* — *n. Colloq.* The state or sensation of being or becoming warm; warmth; a heating. [OE *wearm*] — **warm′ly** *adv.* — **warm′ness** *n.*

warm–blood·ed (wôrm′blud′id) *adj.* **1** Having warm blood: said of animals, as mammals and birds, that preserve a nearly uniform and high body temperature, whatever the surrounding medium; homoiothermal. **2** Enthusiastic; ardent; passionate.

warm·er (wôr′mər) *n.* One who or that which warms.

warm front *Meteorol.* The irregular boundary line between an advancing mass of warm air and the underlying colder air mass.

warm–heart·ed (wôrm′här′tid) *adj.* Kind; affectionate.

warming pan A closed metal pan with a long handle, containing live coals or hot water, for warming a bed.

warm·ish (wôr′mish) *adj.* Rather warm.

war·mon·ger (wôr′mung′gər, -mong′-) *n.* One who propagates warlike ideas; a jingo. — **war′mon′ger·ing** *adj. & n.*

Warm Springs A resort town in western Georgia; site of an institution for the study and treatment of poliomyelitis; here Franklin D. Roosevelt died, 1945.

warmth (wôrmth) *n.* **1** The state, quality, or sensation of being warm. **2** Ardor or fervidness of disposition or feeling; excitement of temper or mind. **3** The effect produced by warm colors. [ME *wermthe,* ult. <OE *wearm* warm]

Synonyms: animation, ardor, cordiality, eagerness, earnestness, emotion, energy, enthusiasm, excitement, fervidness, fervor, geniality, glow, heat, intensity, irascibility, life, passion, vehemence, zeal. Compare ENTHUSIASM. *Antonyms:* coldness, coolness, frigidity, iciness, indifference, insensibility, torpor.

warm-up (wôrm′up′) *n. Colloq.* The act of exercising or limbering up just before a game, contest, etc.

warn (wôrn) v.t. **1** To make aware of impending or possible harm; put on guard; caution. **2** To advise; admonish; counsel. **3** To inform; give notice in advance. **4** To notify (a person) to stay, go, or keep: with *off*, *away*, etc. See synonyms under ADMONISH. [OE *warenian*, *wearnian*. Akin to WARE².] — **warn'er** n.

warn·ing (wôr'ning) n. **1** The act of one who warns, or that which he communicates; notice of danger. **2** That which warns or admonishes. See synonyms under COUNSEL, EXAMPLE. — adj. Serving as a warning. — **warn'ing·ly** adv.

war nose The end of a projectile or shell which carries the detonating device.

War of American Independence *Brit.* The American Revolution.

War of Independence The American Revolution.

War of Secession The Civil War in the United States.

War of the Rebellion The Civil War in the United States: used especially in the States that adhered to the Union.

War of the Spanish Succession See table under WAR.

War of 1812 See table under WAR.

warp (wôrp) v.t. **1** To turn or twist out of shape, as by shrinkage or heat. **2** To turn from a correct or proper course; give a twist or bias to; corrupt; pervert. **3** To stretch or arrange (yarn) so as to form a warp. **4** *Naut.* To move (a vessel) by hauling on a rope or cable, which is usually fastened to something stationary, as a pier or anchor. **5** *Aeron.* To change the curvature of (an airfoil or wing) by twisting, so as to bring the airplane into balance. — v.i. **6** To become turned or twisted out of shape, as wood in drying. **7** To turn or deviate from a correct or proper course; go astray. **8** *Naut.* To move by means of ropes fastened to a pier, anchor, etc. See synonyms under BEND¹. — n. **1** The state of being warped or twisted out of shape; a twist or distortion, especially in a piece of wood. **2** A mental or moral deviation or aberration; bias. **3** The threads that run the long way of a fabric, crossing the woof. **4** The heavy cords forming the carcass of a pneumatic tire. **5** *Naut.* A light cable used for warping a ship or boat; a towline or towrope. **6** A length of rope yarn or rope. [OE *weorpan* throw] — **warp'er** n.

war paint 1 Paint applied to faces and bodies by North American Indians and other primitive peoples in token of going to war. **2** Hence, any preparation for battle. **3** *Colloq.* Any front assumed to intimidate an adversary or increase self-confidence. **4** *Colloq.* Rouge and other cosmetics applied to the person; hence, full dress and personal adornment; finery; also, official garb or regalia.

war·path (wôr'path', -päth') n. The route taken by an attacking party of American Indians; the state of war; also, a war expedition. — **on the warpath 1** On a warlike expedition; at war. **2** Ready for a fight; thoroughly angry; ready to begin hostilities.

warp beam The roller or beam in a loom on which the warp is wound.

war·plane (wôr'plān') n. An airplane equipped for fighting.

war·pow·er (wôr'pou'ər) n. The armed potential of a country; capacity of a nation's manpower and resources for waging war.

war powers Certain powers granted under the Constitution of the United States to the national government or to the chief executive in time of war, to prosecute war and act in all contingent emergencies.

war·rant (wôr'ənt, wor'-) n. **1** *Law* A judicial writ or order authorizing arrest, search, seizure, or any other designated act in aid of the administration of justice. **2** Something which assures or attests; a voucher; evidence; guarantee. **3** That which gives authority for some course or act; sanction; justification: What *warrant* have you for that statement? **4** A certificate of appointment given to army and navy officers of rank lower than commissioned officers. See under OFFICER. **5** A document giving a certain authority; specifically, a document authorizing receipt or pay-

ment of money: a dividend *warrant*. See synonyms under PRECEDENT. — v.t. **1** To assure or guarantee the quality, accuracy, certainty, or sufficiency of: to *warrant* a title to property. **2** To assure or guarantee the character or fidelity of; pledge oneself for. **3** To guarantee against injury, loss, etc. **4** To be sufficient grounds for; justify: The facts did not *warrant* your action. **5** To give legal authority or power to, so as to secure against harm; empower; authorize. **6** *Colloq.* To say confidently; feel sure. See synonyms under JUSTIFY. [<AF *warant*, OF *guarant* <Gmc.] — **war'rant·a·ble** adj. — **war'rant·a·bly** adv. — **war'rant·er** n.

war·ran·tee (wôr'ən·tē', wor'-) n. *Law* The person to whom a warranty is given.

warrant officer See under OFFICER.

war·rant·or (wôr'ən·tôr, wor'-) n. *Law* One who makes or gives a warranty to another.

war·ran·ty (wôr'ən·tē, wor'-) n. pl. **·ties 1** *Law* An assurance or undertaking by the seller of property, express or implied, that the property is or shall be as it is represented or promised to be. **2** In conveyancing, a covenant in a deed whereby the grantor binds himself and his heirs to secure to the grantee the estate conveyed to him. **3** In insurance law, a stipulation or engagement on the part of the insured that the facts in relation to the risk are as stated by him. **4** Authorization; warrant. **5** *Dial.* Security; guaranty. [<AF *warantie*, OF *guarantie* <OF *guarant* a warrant. Doublet of GUARANTY.]

War·re·go River (wor'i·gō) A river in east central Australia, flowing 495 miles SW to the Darling River.

war·ren (wôr'ən, wor'-) n. **1** A place where rabbits live and breed in communities. **2** An enclosure for keeping small game; also, a place for keeping fish in a river. **3** An obscure crowded place of habitation. **4** In English law, a franchise, either by prescription or royal grant, to keep in an enclosure "beasts and fowls of warren," that is, animals that are by nature wild. See also FREEWARREN. [<AF *warenne* a game park, a rabbit warren < *warir* preserve <Gmc.]

War·ren (wôr'ən, wor'-), **Earl**, 1891–1974, U.S. administrator; chief justice of the U.S. Supreme Court 1953–1969. — **Joseph**, 1741–75, American physician and general. — **Robert Penn**, born 1905, U.S. poet, novelist, and educator.

war·ren·er (wôr'ən·ər, wor'-) n. The keeper of a warren.

Warren hoe A pointed garden hoe: used to make furrows for seeds: a trade name. See illustration under HOE.

war·ri·gal (wär'ə·gəl) n. *Austral.* **1** One who or that which is considered wild or uncivilized. **2** The dingo. Also **war'ra·gal.** [< native Australian *warregal* dog, savage]

War·ring·ton (wôr'ing·tən, wor'-) A county borough in southern Lancashire, England, on the Mersey east of Liverpool.

war·ri·or (wôr'ē·ər, -yər, wor'-) n. A man engaged in or experienced in warfare; one devoted to a military life. — adj. Military; martial. [<AF *werreieor* <*werreier* make war <*werre* WAR]

war-risk insurance (wôr'risk') Insurance written by the government of the United States for military and naval personnel.

war·saw (wôr'sô) n. **1** A fish, the black grouper (*Garrupa nigrita*) of the South Atlantic and Gulf of Mexico. **2** A jewfish (*Promicrops guttatus*) of tropical American waters. [Alter. of Sp. *guasa*; prob. infl. in form by *Warsaw*]

War·saw (wôr'sô) The capital of Poland, on the Vistula, in the east central part of the country. *Polish* **War·sza·wa** (vär·shä'vä).

war·ship (wôr'ship') n. Any vessel used in naval combat; especially, an armored vessel.

war·sle (wär'səl) n., v.t. & v.i. *Scot.* Wrestle. Also **war'stle.** — **war'sler** n.

Wars of the Roses See table under WAR.

wart (wôrt) n. **1** A small, usually hard and non-malignant excrescence formed on and rooted in the skin. **2** A spongy excrescence found on the pasterns of a horse. **3** A hard glandular protuberance on a plant. [OE *wearte*]

War·ta (vär'tä) A river in NW Poland, flowing 492 miles north and west to the Oder. *German* **War·the** (vär'tə).

Wart·burg (värt'bŏŏrkh) A castle in the former state of Thuringia, SW of Eisenach, SW East Germany, where Luther translated the New Testament (1521–22).

wart·hog (wôrt'hôg', -hog') n. An African veldt wild hog (*Phacochoerus aethiopicus*) having warty excrescences on the face and large tusks in both jaws.

WARTHOG
(From 2 to 2 1/2 feet at the shoulder)

War·ton (wôr'tən), **Thomas**, 1728–90, English literary historian, critic, and poet laureate.

wart·y (wôr'tē) adj. **wart·i·er, wart·i·est 1** Characterized by having warts: *warty*-flowered panic grass. **2** Of the nature of warts.

war whoop A yell made by American Indians, as a signal for attack or to terrify their opponents in battle.

War·wick (wôr'ik, wor'-) **1** A county of central England; 983 square miles. Also **War'wick·shire** (-shir). **2** A municipal borough of central Warwick on the Avon; county town of Warwick.

War·wick (wôr'ik, wor'-), **Earl of**, 1428–71, Richard Neville, Earl of Salisbury, English statesman and soldier: called the "Kingmaker."

war·y (wâr'ē) adj. **war·i·er, war·i·est 1** Carefully watching and guarding. **2** Shrewd; wily. See synonyms under POLITIC, VIGILANT. [<WARE², adj.] — **war'i·ly** adv. — **war'i·ness** n.

was (woz, wuz, *unstressed* wəz) First and third person singular, past indicative of BE. [OE *wæs*, first and third person sing. of *wesan* be]

Wa·satch Plateau (wô'sach) A high tableland of central Utah at the southern end of the Wasatch Range; highest point 12,300 feet.

Wasatch Range A section of the Rocky Mountains in SE Idaho and northern Utah; highest point, 12,008 feet.

wase (wāz) n. *Obs.* or *Dial.* A wisp or bundle of hay, straw, or the like; especially, a cushion of such material for use between the head and a load borne thereon.

wash (wosh, wôsh) v.t. **1** To cleanse by immersing in or applying water or other liquid, often with rubbing or scrubbing. **2** To purify from pollution, defilement, or guilt. **3** To wet or cover with water or other liquid. **4** To flow against or over; lave: a beach *washed* by the ocean. **5** To carry away or remove by the action of water: with *away*, *off*, *out*, etc. **6** To form or wear by erosion: The storm *washed* gulleys in the hillside. **7** To purify, as gas, by passing through a liquid. **8** To coat with a thin or watery layer of color. **9** To cover with a thin coat of metal. **10** *Mining* **a** To subject (gravel, earth, etc.) to the action of water so as to separate the ore, etc. **b** To separate (ore, etc.) thus. **11** *Aeron.* To warp. — v.i. **12** To wash oneself. **13** To wash clothes, etc., in water or other liquid. **14** To withstand the effects of washing: That calico will *wash*. **15** *Brit. Colloq.* To undergo testing successfully: That story won't *wash*. **16** To flow with a lapping sound, as waves. **17** To be carried away or removed by the action of water: with *away*, *off*, *out*, etc. **18** To be eroded by the action of water. See synonyms under CLEANSE, PURIFY. — **to wash out** *Slang* **1** To fail and be dropped from a course, especially in military flight training. **2** To damage (an aircraft) irreparably, especially in landing. — n. **1** The act or process of washing; cleansing; ablution. **2** A number of articles, as of clothing, set apart for washing or being washed at one time; a washing; laundry. **3** Liquid or semi-liquid refuse; especially, waste food from the kitchen; swill. **4** A preparation used in washing or coating; specifically, a liquid cosmetic or a mouthwash; also, a water-color or India-ink pigment for spreading lightly and evenly on a drawing or picture. **5** The breaking of a body of water upon the shore, or the sound made by waves breaking or surging against a surface; swash. **6** Erosion of soil or earth by the action of rain or running water. **7** Backwash. **8** *Aeron.* Local air currents set up by the passing of an airplane. **9** An area washed by a sea or river; also, the shallow part of a river or ah arm of the sea; a marsh; bog. **10** Material collected and deposited by water, as in the bed of a river or along its banks. **11** *U.S.* The dry bed of a stream; an arroyo. **12** Fermented liquor ready for the distillery. — *adj.* Washable; that may be washed without injury: *wash* fabrics. [OE *wæscan, wascan*]

Wash (wosh, wôsh), **The** An inlet of the North Sea on the eastern coast of England between Norfolk and Lincolnshire; 20 miles long, 15 miles wide.

wash·a·ble (wosh′ə·bəl, wôsh′-) *adj.* That may be washed without fading or injury.

wash–and–wear (wosh′ən·wâr′, wôsh′-) *adj.* Designating or pertaining to a garment or fabric so treated as to require little or no ironing after washing.

wash·board (wosh′bôrd′, -bôrd′, wôsh′-) *n.* **1** A board or frame having a corrugated surface on which to rub clothes while washing them. **2** *Naut.* A thin plank adjusted to turn the wash of the sea from a deck or port of a ship.

wash bowl A basin or bowl, either portable or stationary, used for washing the hands and face. Also **wash basin.**

wash·cloth (wosh′klôth′, -kloth′, wôsh′-) *n.* A small cloth used for washing the body.

wash·day (wosh′dā′, wôsh′-) *n.* A day of the week set aside for doing household washing.

washed–out (wosht′out′, wôsh′-) *adj.* **1** Faded; colorless; pale. **2** *Colloq.* Exhausted; worn-out; tired.

washed–up (wosht′up′, wôsh′-) *adj. Slang* Finished; done with; through.

wash·er (wosh′ər, wô′shər) *n.* **1** One who washes. **2** *Mech.* A small, flat, perforated disk of metal, leather, or wood, used for placing beneath a nut or at an axle bearing or joint, to serve as a cushion, to relieve friction, etc. **3** A machine for washing (ore or clothes). **4** A device for purifying gases; a scrubber.

wash·er·man (wosh′ər·mən, wô′shər-) *n. pl.* **·men** (-mən) A laundryman.

wash·er·wom·an (wosh′ər·wŏŏm′ən, wô′shər-) *n. pl.* **·wom·en** (-wim′in) A laundress.

wash·ing (wosh′ing, wô′shing) *n.* **1** The act of one who washes. **2** Things (as clothing) washed on one occasion, or collected during a certain time. **3** That which is retained after being washed: a *washing* of ore. **4** A thin coating of metal: The forks had received only one *washing* of silver. **5** The sale of stock or other securities at a stock exchange between parties of one interest, in order to create a fictitious activity. — *adj.* Used in or intended for washing.

washing soda Sodium carbonate.

Wash·ing·ton (wosh′ing·tən, wô′shing-) **1** A State in NW United States, adjoining Canada; 68,192 square miles; capital, Olympia; entered the Union Nov. 11, 1889; nickname, *Evergreen State*: abbr. *Wash.* **2** A city coextensive with the District of Columbia and capital of the United States. — **Wash′ing·to′·ni·an** (-tō′nē·ən) *adj. & n.*

Wash·ing·ton (wosh′ing·tən, wô′shing-), **Booker Taliaferro,** 1856–1915, U.S. Negro educator. — **George,** 1732–99, American patriot, soldier, and statesman; first president of the United States 1789–97. — **Martha,** 1731–1802, *née* Dandridge (Mrs. Daniel Parke Custis 1749–57), wife of George Washington.

Washington, Lake A lake in west central Washington, near Seattle; 20 miles long.

Washington, Mount The highest peak of the White Mountains of New Hampshire; 6,288 feet.

Washington palm The fan palm (*Washingtonia filifera*) of California and the Colorado desert.

Washington pie A layer cake with a filling of cream or jam.

Washington's Birthday The anniversary of George Washington's birth, February 22: a legal holiday in most States of the United States.

Wash·i·ta River (wosh′ə·tô, wô′shə-) **1** See

OUACHITA RIVER. **2** A river in Texas and Oklahoma, flowing 450 miles SE and east from the Texas Panhandle near the Oklahoma border to Lake Texoma; formerly flowed 40 miles further to the Red River.

wash–out (wosh′out′, wôsh′-) *n.* **1** A considerable erosion of earth by the action of water; also, the excavation thus made; a gully or gulch. **2** *Aeron.* A decrease in the angle of incidence of an airplane wing toward the tip. **3** *Slang* A hopeless or total failure.

wash–rag (wosh′rag, wôsh′-) *n.* A washcloth.

wash·room (wosh′rŏŏm′, -rŏŏm′, wôsh′-) *n.* A lavatory.

wash sale On a stock exchange, the buying of stock by the seller's agents, to mislead as to the real demand.

wash·stand (wosh′stand′, wôsh′-) *n.* A piece of furniture used for holding the utensils for ablutions; a stand for wash bowl, pitcher, etc.

wash·tub (wosh′tub′, wôsh′-) *n.* A tub used for washing.

wash·wom·an (wosh′wŏŏm′ən, wôsh′-) *n. pl.* **·wom·en** (-wim′in) A washerwoman.

wash·y (wosh′ē, wô′shē) *adj.* **wash·i·er, wash·i·est** **1** Overly wet; sodden; water–logged. **2** Bringing rain: said of weather or wind. **3** Wanting in substance, solidity, stamina, or force; wishy–washy; feeble. **4** Sweating: said of horses. — **wash′i·ness** *n.*

was·n't (woz′ənt, wuz′-) Was not.

wasp (wosp, wôsp) *n.* Any of numerous hymenopterous insects, chiefly of the superfamilies *Sphecoidea* and *Vespoidea,* of which the workers and females are provided with effective stings. The typical social wasps construct papery nests of masticated vegetable material; they feed on fruits, the nectar of flowers, and on insects. The solitary wasps construct nests of mud or sand. ◆ Collateral adjective: *vespine.* [OE *wæsp*]

WASP (wosp, wôsp) *n. Slang* A white Protestant American. [From the initial letters of the words "white Anglo–Saxon Protestant"]

wasp·ish (wos′pish, wôs′-) *adj.* **1** Having a nature like a wasp; irritable; irascible. **2** Having a wasplike form or slender waist. See synonyms under FRETFUL. — **wasp′ish·ly** *adv.* — **wasp′ish·ness** *n.*

wasp waist A person's waist, so slender as to suggest that of a wasp. — **wasp–waist·ed** (wosp′wās′tid, wôsp′-) *adj.*

wasp·y (wos′pē, wôs′-) *adj.* **wasp·i·er, wasp·i·est** Like a wasp; waspish.

was·sail (wos′əl, was′-, wo·sāl′) *n.* **1** An ancient salutation or toast; an expression of good will in festivities, especially when pledging someone's health. See DRINK–HAIL. **2** The liquor prepared for a wassail; especially, a mixture of ale and wine with sugar, roasted apples, spices, etc. **3** A festivity at which healths are drunk; a carousal. **4** *Brit.* A convivial song. — *v.i.* To take part in a wassail; carouse. — *v.t.* To drink the health of; toast. [ME *wæs hæil* <ON *ves heill* be whole (*i.e.,* in good health)] — **was′sail·er** *n.*

Was·ser·mann (väs′ər·män), **August von,** 1866–1925, German physician and bacteriologist. — **Jakob,** 1873–1934, German novelist.

Wasserman reaction A diagnostic test for syphilis, based on testing the serum of the blood for syphilitic antibodies. Also **Wassermann test.** [after August von *Wasserman*]

wast[1] (wost, *unstressed* wəst) Archaic second person singular, past indicative of BE: used with *thou.*

wast[2] (wast) *adj. Scot.* West.

wast·age (wās′tij) *n.* That which is lost by leakage, wear, waste, etc.

waste (wāst) *adj.* **1** Cast aside as worthless or of no practical value; used; worn out; discarded. **2** Excreted; cast out of an animal body, as food, etc. **3** Not under cultivation; untilled; hence, unproductive; unoccupied. **4** Made desolate; ruined; dismal; gloomy. **5** Containing or conveying waste products. **6** Produced in excess of consumption; superfluous: *waste* energy. **7** *Obs.* Wasteful; lavish. — **to lay waste** To destroy utterly. — *v.* **wast·ed, wast·ing** *v.t.* **1** To use or expend thoughtlessly, uselessly, or without return; be prodigal or extravagant of; squander. **2** To cause to lose strength, vigor, or bulk; make weak or feeble. **3** To use up; exhaust; consume. **4** To fail to use or take advantage of, as an opportunity. **5** To lay

waste; desolate; devastate. — *v.i.* **6** To lose strength, vigor, or bulk; become weak or feeble: often with *away.* **7** To diminish or dwindle gradually. **8** To pass gradually: said of time. See synonyms under SQUANDER, WEAR[1]. — *n.* **1** The act of wasting or squandering, or the state of being wasted; useless or unnecessary expenditure. **2** A place or a region that is devastated or made desolate; wilderness; desert. **3** A continuous, gradual diminishing of strength, vigor, or substance by use or wear. **4** The act of laying waste or devastating; ravage: the *waste* of war. **5** Something rejected as worthless or unneeded; specifically, tangled spun cotton thread, the refuse of a textile factory; also, steam or other fluid that escapes without being used. **6** Garbage; rubbish; trash. **7** The waste products of the soil due to erosion by chemical or human action and carried out to sea by running water. **8** A wasting disease; specifically, consumption. ◆ Homophone: *waist.* [<AF *waster,* ult. <L *vastare* lay waste <*vastus* desert, desolate. Related to VAST.]

Synonyms (adj.): excess, extra, redundant, refuse, superfluous, useless, valueless, worthless. See BLEAK, VACANT. *Antonyms:* choice, good, precious, useful, valuable.

Synonyms (noun): chaff, debris, dregs, dross, leavings, offal, offscouring, refuse, remains, scum, sediment. See EXCESS, LOSS.

Waste may appear as a combining form in hyphemes or solidemes, or as the first element in two–word phrases, with the meaning: containing or conveying refuse or waste; as in:

waste bin	waste sluice
waste–collector	waste trap
waste gate	waste–water
waste heap	wasteway
waste pit	wasteyard

waste·bas·ket (wāst′bas′kit, -bäs′-) *n.* A basket for paper scraps and other waste.

waste·ful (wāst′fəl) *adj.* **1** Prone to waste; extravagant. **2** Causing waste; ruinous. — **waste′ful·ly** *adv.* — **waste′ful·ness** *n.*

waste·land (wāst′land′) *n.* A barren or desolate land.

waste paper Paper thrown away as worthless. Also **waste·pa·per** (wāst′pā′pər). — **waste′–pa′per** *adj.*

waste–paper basket A wastebasket.

waste pipe A pipe for carrying off waste-water, etc.

wast·er (wās′tər) *n.* One who wastes; a wastrel.

wast·ing (wās′ting) *adj.* **1** Producing emaciation; sapping the strength; enfeebling: a *wasting* fever. **2** Laying waste; devastating.

wast·rel (wās′trəl) *n.* **1** An abandoned child; a waif. **2** A waster; a profligate; spendthrift. [Dim. of WASTER]

wast·ry (wās′trē) *Scot.* or *Obs. adj.* Wasteful. — *n.* Wastefulness: also **waste′rie, wast′·rie, wast′rife.**

wat[1] (wat) *adj. Scot.* **1** Intemperate. **2** Wet.

wat[2] (wot) *n.* A hare. [Prob. from *Wat,* nickname for WALTER]

wa·tap (wä·täp′) *n.* Roots of the spruce, cedar, pine, etc., used by North American Indians to sew bark for canoes and other objects. Also **wa·ta·pe** (wä·tä′pe). [<Algonquian (Narraganset) *wattap* a root of a tree]

watch (woch) *v.i.* **1** To be constantly on the alert; give earnest heed; be observant, vigilant, or attentive. **2** To look attentively; observe. **3** To wait expectantly for something; be in a state of expectation: with *for.* **4** To do duty as a guard or sentinel; serve as a watchman. **5** To have in one's care or keeping; guard; tend. **6** To be awake; go without sleep; keep vigil. — *v.t.* **7** To keep under observation; look at steadily and attentively; observe. **8** To follow the course of mentally; keep informed concerning. **9** To be alert for; wait for expectantly: to *watch* one's opportunity. **10** To keep watch over; guard. See synonyms under ABIDE, LOOK. — *n.* **1** The act of watching; wakefulness with close and continuous attention; careful observation; vigil. **2** One of the divisions of the night made in ancient times: with the Hebrews, one third; with the Romans, one fourth; hence, any indefinite waking period which marks the passage of the night. **3** Position or service as a guard or sentry. **4** *Obs.* Vigilance; a vigil; wake. **5** One or more persons set to watch; a watchman or set of watchmen; sentinel; guard. **6** The place occupied by or assigned to a guard. **7** The period of time during which a guard is on duty. **8** *Naut.* **a** One of the two divisions of a ship's officers and crew, performing duty in alternation. **b** The period of time during which each division is on duty: four hours, except the dog-watches, from 4 to 6 and from 6 to 8 p.m., which are interposed daily to shift night duty from one watch to the other alternately. **9** A small, portable timepiece, actuated by a coiled spring, for keeping and indicating time. **10** *Obs.* A candle marked into equal sections, each of which burns a known length of time. **11** *Obs.* The cry of a watchman. **12** *Obs.* Wakefulness; the state of staying or being awake. See synonyms under OVERSIGHT. [OE *waeccan.* Akin to WAKE¹.]

watch cap In the U.S. Navy, a small, knitted woolen cap of navy blue worn by enlisted men during cold weather.

watch·case (woch′kās′) *n.* **1** The protecting case of a watch: usually of gold or silver. **2** *Obs.* A sentry box.

watch·cry (woch′krī′) *n. pl.* **·cries** A slogan; a watchword.

watch·dog (woch′dôg′, -dog′) *n.* A dog kept to guard a building or other property.

watch·er (woch′ər) *n.* **1** One who watches; especially, one who watches by a sickbed, deathbed, or corpse. **2** One who watches the voting at the polls on election day to detect dishonest practices.

watch·ful (woch′fəl) *adj.* **1** Vigilant. **2** *Obs.* Wakeful. See synonyms under ALERT, VIGILANT. — **watch′ful·ly** *adv.* — **watch′ful·ness** *n.*

watch·guard (woch′gärd′) *n.* A chain, cord, or ribbon attached to a watch and fastened to the clothing.

watch·mak·er (woch′mā′kər) *n.* One who makes or repairs watches.

watch·man (woch′mən) *n. pl.* **·men** (-mən) **1** Formerly, one of a group of men appointed to keep watch or patrol the streets of a town or village at night. **2** Anyone who keeps watch or guard; especially, a man employed to guard a building, etc., at night.

watch night New Year's Eve.

watch·tow·er (woch′tou′ər) *n.* A tower upon which a sentinel is stationed.

watch·word (woch′wûrd′) *n.* **1** A secret password. **2** A rallying cry or maxim.

Wa·ten·stedt-Salz·git·ter (vä′tən-shtet-zälts′-git-ər) A city in SE Lower Saxony, north central West Germany.

wa·ter (wô′tər, wot′ər) *n.* **1** A colorless limpid liquid compound of hydrogen and oxygen, H_2O, in the proportion of two volumes of hydrogen to one of oxygen, or by weight of approximately 2 parts of hydrogen to 16 of oxygen. Water has its maximum density at 4° C. or 39° F., one cubic centimeter weighing a gram. It freezes at 0° C. or 32° F., and boils at 100° C. or 212° F. **2** Any body of water, as a lake, river, or a sea; in Scotland, a small river. **3** Any one of the aqueous or liquid secretions of animals; also, perspiration, tears, urine, etc. **4** Any preparation of water holding a gaseous or volatile substance in solution. **5** The transparency or luster of a precious stone or a pearl; hence, excellence; purity. **6** An undulating sheen given to certain fabrics, as silk, etc. **7** In commerce and finance, stock issued without increase of paid-in capital to represent it. — **above water** Out of danger; secure. — **hard water** Water containing in solution salts of calcium and magnesium, especially the sulfates or bicarbonates of these elements: so called because of the difficulty of obtaining a soap lather with such water. — **soft water** Water free from the salts of calcium and magnesium, as rain water and water found in sandstone districts. — *v.t.* **1** To pour water upon; irrigate. **2** To provide with water for drinking; give water to. **3** To dilute or weaken with water: often with *down.* **4** To give an undulating sheen to the surface of (silk, linen, etc.) by uneven pressure after

damping and heating. **5** To enlarge the number of shares of (a stock company) without increasing the paid-in capital in proportion. **6** To provide with streams: used in the passive participle. — *v.i.* **7** To secrete or discharge water, tears, etc. **8** To fill with saliva, as the mouth, from desire for food. **9** To drink water. **10** To take in water, as a locomotive. [OE *wæter.* Akin to OTTER.]
Water may appear as a combining form in hyphemes or solidemes, or as the first element in two-word phrases:

water–analysis	water–laden
water barge	water–locked
water–bearing	water pail
water bottle	waterplane
water–bound	water plant
water bucket	water police
water–carrier	water problem
water–carrying	water project
water cask	water pump
water channel	water–quenched
water content	water–resistant
water–deposited	water resources
water diver	water–rolling
water–drain	water–rot
water–drawer	water–rotted
water–drinker	water–route
water–drinking	water–scarcity
water flow	water–sealed
water–flushed	water service
water fountain	water–soaked
waterfree	water–sodden
water–girt	water source
water–gray	water tap
water–green	water trough
water heater	water turbine
waterhole	water–walled
water insect	water–washed
water jar	water–wasting

water adder 1 The water moccasin. **2** The water snake.

wa·ter·age (wô′tər·ij, wot′ər-) *n. Brit.* Conveyance of merchandise by water; also, the fee paid for such transportation.

wa·ter·back (wô′tər·bak′, wot′ər-) *n.* A coil or chamber for heating water in the back of a range or other stove.

water balance *Biol.* The preservation of a nearly uniform water content in an organism, especially a plant.

water bear See under TARDIGRADE.

Wa·ter·bear·er (wô′tər·bâr′ər, wot′ər-) The constellation Aquarius.

water bearing *Mech.* A journal bearing in which water under pressure does the work of a lubricant.

wa·ter·bed (wô′tər·bed′, wot′ər-) *n.* A bed with a water-filled container serving as a mattress, adjustable in firmness and often heated.

water beetle Any of several aquatic beetles (especially of the families *Dytiscidae, Hydrophilidae* or *Gyrinidae*), having legs flattened and fringed with hairs for swimming.

water bird Any bird living on or near water.

water biscuit A plain cracker or biscuit of flour, shortening, and water.

water blink In arctic regions, a cloud or spot on the horizon arising from and indicating the presence of open water: a sign of the breaking up of winter.

water blister A blister containing limpid watery matter.

wa·ter·bloom (wô′tər·bloom′, wot′ər-) *n.* The sudden appearance of large masses of blue-green algae in bodies of fresh water.

wa·ter·borne (wô′tər·bôrn′, -bōrn′, wot′ər-) *adj.* **1** Floating on water. **2** Transported or carried by water: *water-borne* commerce.

wa·ter·brain (wô′tər·brān′, wot′ər-) *n.* A disease of sheep characterized by staggering as from giddiness; gid.

water brake *Mech.* A brake, formerly used on steam locomotives, formed by using water pressure to provide a braking effect.

wa·ter·brash (wô′tər·brash′, wot′ər-) *n. Pathol.* Pyrosis; heartburn.

wa·ter·buck (wô′tər·buk′, wot′ər-) *n.* **1** Either of two large African antelopes (genus *Kobus*), frequenting the neighborhood of rivers and swimming with ease; especially, *K. ellipsiprymnus* of south central Africa. **2** Any

of several similar antelopes. [<Du. *waterbok*]

water buffalo 1 A buffalo (*Bubalus bubalus*) of India, the largest of wild cattle, attaining a height of 6 feet at the withers and a very wide spread of horns. When domesticated it becomes a useful draft animal. **2** The carabao. Also called *Indian buffalo.*

WATER BUFFALO
(Spread of horns
up to 9 feet)

water bug 1 The Croton bug. **2** Any of various hemipterous bugs (family *Belostomatidae*) which live in the water, especially the large species (*Lethocerus americanus*) common in North America. **3** The water scorpion.

Wa·ter·bu·ry (wô′tər·ber′ē, wot′ər-) A city in SW Connecticut; an industrial center, especially of the brass industry.

water chestnut 1 The hard horned edible fruit of an aquatic plant (*Trapa natans*). **2** The plant itself: also **water caltrop, wa′ter·nut′.**

water chinkapin 1 The American or yellow lotus (*Nelumbium pentapetalum*). **2** One of its edible nutlike seeds. Also **water chinquapin.**

wa·ter·clock (wô′tər·klok′, wot′ər-) *n.* Any device, as a clepsydra, for measuring time by the fall or flow of water.

WATER CHINKAPIN
a. Flower. *b.* Leaf.
c. Fruit.

wa·ter·clos·et (wô′tər·kloz′it, wot′ər-) *n.* A room or closet having a hopper flushed and discharged by means of water, used as a privy; also, the hopper and its trap.

wa·ter·col·or (wô′tər·kul′ər, wot′ər-) *adj.* Of, pertaining to, used with, or executed in water colors.

water color 1 A color prepared for painting with water as the medium, as distinguished from one to be used with oil, tempera, etc., as the medium, and characterized by the fact that the result may be either transparent or opaque. **2** That branch of painting in which water colors are used, or the method of using them. **3** A picture or painting done in water colors.

wa·ter·cool (wô′tər·kool′, wot′ər-) *v.t.* To cool by means of water, as by using a water jacket on an internal-combustion engine. — **wa′ter·cooled′** *adj.* — **wa′ter·cool′ing** *adj. & n.*

water cooler A vessel or apparatus for cooling and dispensing drinking water: often operated electrically.

wa·ter·course (wô′tər·kôrs′, -kōrs′, wot′ər-) *n.* **1** A stream of water; river; brook; a stream having a bed and banks. **2** The course or channel of a stream of water; a canal. See synonyms under STREAM.

wa·ter·craft (wô′tər·kraft′, -kräft′, wot′ər-) *n.* **1** Skill in sailing boats or in aquatic sports. **2** Any boat or ship; also, sailing vessels collectively.

water crake 1 The spotted crake. **2** The water ouzel. See under OUZEL.

wa·ter·cress (wô′tər·kres′, wot′ər-) *n.* A creeping perennial herb (*Rorippa nasturtium-aquaticum*) of the mustard family, having pinnate leaves and white flowers. It grows in springs and clear cool streams and is cultivated for use as salad.

water culture Hydroponics.

water cure 1 *Med.* Hydropathy. **2** *Colloq.* A kind of torture in which large quantities of water are put forcibly down the victim's throat.

water cushion A pool of water maintained to absorb the impact of water, as from the spillway of a dam.

water dog 1 A dog that takes readily to the water, as the water spaniel. **2** A dog trained to retrieve water fowl. **3** *Colloq.* An old sailor.

Wa·ter·ee (wô′tə·rē′) The lower course of the

CATAWBA RIVER, flowing about 75 miles from north central South Carolina to a junction with the Congaree, forming the Santee.

water elm The planer tree.

wa·ter·er (wô'tər·ər, wot'ər-) *n.* 1 One who waters, in any sense. 2 Any contrivance used for watering.

wa·ter·fall (wô'tər·fôl', wot'ər-) *n.* 1 A cataract; cascade. 2 *Colloq.* A chignon suggesting a cascade. [OE *wætergefeall*]

water fence A fence built into or across a stream, or one extending into the water on the shore of a lake or the sea, to prevent cattle, horses, etc., from passing around it.

wa·ter·find·er (wô'tər·fīn'dər, wot'ər-) *n.* A dowser who tries to locate underground water with a divining rod. See RHABDOMANCY.

wa·ter·flea (wô'tər·flē', wot'ər-) *n.* Any of numerous minute, fresh-water crustaceans (family *Daphniidae*), about the size of a flea, which swim with a jumping motion.

Wa·ter·ford (wô'tər·fərd, wot'ər-) 1 A maritime county in eastern Munster province, Ireland; 710 square miles. 2 Its county town, a port on **Waterford Harbor**, an inlet of the Atlantic in southern Ireland; 15 miles long.

water fowl 1 A bird that lives on or about the water, especially a swimming game bird. 2 Such birds collectively.

wa·ter·front (wô'tər·frunt', wot'ər-) *n.* 1 Real property abutting on or overlooking a natural body of water. 2 That part of a town which fronts on a body of water. 3 A coil or chamber for heating water in the front of a range or other stove.

water gage A gage indicating the level of water in a boiler, etc. Also **water gauge.**

water gall 1 A hollow in the earth made by a flood, etc.; a washout. 2 A partial rainbow: also, *Scot., weather gall.* [<WATER + GALL²]

water gap A deep ravine in a mountain ridge giving passage to a stream.

water gas A highly poisonous mixture of hydrogen and carbon monoxide produced by forcing steam over white-hot carbon (as coal or coke): used for cooking and heating, and when carbureted, as an illuminant. — **wa·ter·gas** (wô'tər·gas', wot'ər-) *adj.*

wa·ter·gate (wô'tər·gāt', wot'ər-) *n.* Floodgate (def. 1).

wa·ter·glass (wô'tər·glas', -gläs', wot'ər-) *n.* 1 A waterclock; clepsydra. 2 A glass-bottomed tube or box for examining objects lying or moving under water. 3 A substance composed of sodium silicate, potassium silicate, or both, soluble in hot water: used in preserving eggs, as a facing for walls, etc. 4 A water gage on a steam boiler, etc. 5 A vessel for holding water; a drinking glass.

wa·ter·gum (wô'tər·gum', wot'ər-) *n.* 1 The American sourgum or tupelo tree. 2 Any of several trees of the myrtle family, especially a tall, slender, ornamental shrub (*Tristania laurina*) native to Australia, with opposite leaves and yellow flowers.

water hammer 1 The concussion of confined water when its flow is suddenly arrested, as when a faucet is suddenly closed. 2 The hammering sound caused in pipes containing water when live steam is admitted. 3 A sealed tube void of air but containing water which strikes against the ends of the tube with a sharp knocking sound when shaken: used to demonstrate the equal rate of fall of solids and liquids in a vacuum.

water haul 1 In fishing, an empty haul of the net. 2 Any fruitless attempt or effort.

water hemlock Any of a genus (*Cicuta*) of poisonous, typically North American flowering herbs of the carrot family; especially, the **spotted water hemlock** (*C. maculata*) of the United States, highly injurious to livestock, and the Old World species (*C. virosa*).

water hen 1 Any of several coots or gallinules that frequent ponds and streams; especially, the moorhen. 2 The American coot (*Fulica americana*).

water hyacinth An aquatic herb of tropical America (*Eichornia crassipes*) with pendulous branched roots and a whorl of floating glossy leaves containing a cluster of bluish-purple to lilac and white flowers.

water ice 1 An ice made with water, sugar, and fruit juice. 2 Ice formed by the freezing of water as distinguished from that formed by the packing together of snow.

wa·ter·inch (wô'tər·inch', wot'ər-) *n.* An old unit of hydraulic measure based on the discharge of water from a round hole with a diameter of one inch: reckoned at fourteen pints a minute.

wa·ter·ing (wô'tər·ing, wot'ər-) *n.* 1 The act of one who waters. 2 The process of producing a wavy ornamental effect. — *adj.* 1 Sprinkling; irrigating; that waters. 2 Situated near the shore or near mineral springs: a *watering* place.

watering cart A cart carrying a barrel or large tank of water: used for sprinkling streets.

watering place 1 A place where water can be obtained, as a spring; also, a place by a road where horses can be watered. 2 A health resort having mineral springs; also, a pleasure resort near the water.

watering pot A tin can having a spout fitted with a perforated nozzle: used for watering flowers, etc.

wa·ter·ish (wô'tər·ish, wot'ər-) *adj.* Resembling water; watery; hence, weak.

wa·ter·jack·et (wô'tər·jak'it, wot'ər-) *v.t.* To encase in or fit with a water jacket.

water jacket A casing containing water and surrounding a cylinder or mechanism, especially the cylinder block of an internal-combustion engine, for keeping it cool.

water jump A water barrier, as a pool, stream, or ditch, to be jumped over by the horses in a steeplechase.

water leaf Any of a genus (*Hydrophyllum*) of delicate biennial or perennial herbs with white or blue flowers, growing in the woods of North America.

wa·ter·less (wô'tər·lis, wot'ər-) *adj.* Without water; arid; dry.

wa·ter·lev·el (wô'tər·lev'əl, wot'ər-) *adj.* Following the course of a river: a *water-level* route.

water level 1 The level of still water in the sea or in any other body of water. 2 A water table. 3 *Naut.* A ship's water line. 4 A leveling instrument in which water serves to determine the horizontal line.

wa·ter·lift (wô'tər·lift', wot'ər-) *n.* The transportation of personnel, equipment, and supplies by water, with special reference to the 1950 military campaign in Korea.

wa·ter·lil·y (wô'tər·lil'ē, wot'ər-) *n.* *pl.* ·lil·ies 1 Any plant of a genus (*Nymphaea*) of showy aquatic herbs of temperate and tropical regions, with large floating leaves and flowers; especially, the fragrant **white waterlily** (*N. odorata*) of the eastern United States. 2 The yellow pondlily (*Nuphar luteum*) of the same family. 3 The Victoria waterlily.

water line 1 *Naut.* That part of the hull of a ship which corresponds with the water level at various loads. 2 Water level. 3 A river or system of waterways affording transportation.

water locust A small species of the American honey locust (*Gleditsia aquatica*) growing in southern swamps and boglands: also called *swamp locust.*

wa·ter·logged (wô'tər·lôgd', -logd', wot'ər-) *adj.* 1 Heavy and unmanageable on account of the leakage of water into the hold, as a ship. 2 Water-soaked; saturated with water. [<WATER + LOG *v.*, in obs. sense of "to reduce to the condition of a log"]

Wa·ter·loo (wô'tər·loo, wô'tər·loo') A village in central Belgium; scene of Napoleon's final defeat by Wellington and Blücher, June 18, 1815; hence, final and decisive defeat; a complete reverse.

water lot 1 A building lot fronting on a body of water, as a river, harbor, etc. 2 A lot or piece of ground wholly or partially covered by water, or a piece of marsh or swamp land designated to be filled in for use.

water main A large conduit for carrying water, especially one laid underground.

wa·ter·man (wô'tər·mən, wot'ər-) *n.* *pl.* ·men (-mən) A man who plies for hire with a boat or small vessel on the water; a boatman. — **wa'ter·man·ship'** *n.*

water marigold An aquatic plant (*Bidens becki*) with terminal heads of yellow flowers.

wa·ter·mark (wô'tər·märk', wot'ər-) *n.* 1 A mark showing the extent to which water rises; especially, the line marking the limit of the ebb and flow of the tide. 2 A series of translucent lines, letters, or designs made in paper by shaping the wires of the dandy rolls over which the paper passes while still in a pulpous state; also, the metal pattern which produces these markings. — *v.t.* 1 To impress (paper) with a watermark. 2 To impress as a watermark.

wa·ter·mel·on (wô'tər·mel'ən, wot'ər-) *n.* 1 The large edible fruit of a trailing plant (*Citrullus vulgaris*) of the gourd family, containing a many-seeded red or pink pulp and a refreshing sweet, watery juice. 2 The plant on which this fruit grows.

water meter An instrument for registering the amount of water flowing through a pipe, etc.

water milfoil Any of a genus (*Myriophyllum*) of aquatic herbs with graceful, feathery leaves.

water mill A mill operated by waterpower.

water moccasin The cottonmouth.

water motor 1 A turbine operated by water-power. 2 A water wheel.

water nymph In classical mythology, any nymph or goddess living in or guarding a body of water; a naiad, Nereid, Oceanid, etc.

water oak A species of oak (*Quercus nigra*) growing near swamps and streams in the eastern United States.

water of Ayr See AYR STONE.

water of crystallization *Chem.* Water forming part of crystallized salts, from which it may be eliminated by heat, often with loss of crystalline structure. Also **water of hydration.**

water of life A rare and mysterious water that restores the dead to life. The human hope and belief that death can be overcome is expressed in the water-of-life motif in the peasant folklore of every European country, in the myths of the ancient Persians, Greeks, Romans, Hebrews, Hindus, in Japanese mythology, and in the folk tales of all primitive peoples, as the Polynesians, North and South American Indians, etc.

water ouzel See under OUZEL.

water ox A water buffalo.

wa·ter·part·ing (wô'tər·pär'ting, wot'ər-) *n.* A watershed.

wa·ter·pep·per (wô'tər·pep'ər, wot'ər-) *n.* Any of several species of knotweed, especially the common smartweed.

water pimpernel 1 The brookweed. 2 The common pimpernel.

water plantain Any of a genus (*Alsima*) of common, smooth, aquatic herbs with leaves like those of the plantain, especially the North American species (*A. plantago-aquatica*).

water polo A game played in a swimming pool by two teams of seven swimmers each, who push or throw a round, buoyant ball toward opposite goals.

wa·ter·pow·er (wô'tər·pou'ər, wot'ər-) *n.* 1 The power of water derived from its gravity or its momentum as applied to the driving of machinery. 2 A descent or fall in a stream from which motive power may be obtained.

water pox *Pathol.* Varicella.

wa·ter·proof (wô'tər·prōōf', wot'ər-) *adj.* 1 Proof against water. 2 Impervious to water. 3 Coated with some substance, as rubber, which resists the passage of water. — *n.* 1 Material or fabric rendered impervious to water. 2 *Brit.* A raincoat or other garment made of such fabric. — *v.t.* To render water-proof.

water purslane 1 An herb (*Isnardia* or *Ludwigia palustris*) of the evening-primrose family, procumbent and creeping in muddy places and floating in water. 2 An aquatic plant (*Didiplis* or *Peplis diandra*) growing in swampy ground in the U. S.

water ram A hydraulic ram.

water rat 1 The American muskrat. 2 The European water vole (*Microtus amphibius*). 3 Any of a subfamily (*Hydromyinae*) of aquatic rodents of New Guinea, Australia, and the Philippines. 4 *Slang* A thief or tough who frequents the waterfront.

water repellent *Chem.* Any of various chemicals, as an emulsion of aluminum acetate, used to make textiles, leather, and other porous materials resistant to wetting by water but which does not waterproof or impair their desirable properties. — **wa·ter·re·pel·lent** (wô'tər·ri·pel'ənt, wot'ər-) *adj.*

wa·ter·right (wô'tər·rīt', wot'ər-) *n.* 1 The right to draw upon a water supply. 2 The right to use or navigate a particular body of water. Also **water right.**

water sapphire A rich blue variety of iolite often worn as an ornament. [Trans. of F *saphir d'eau*]

wa·ter·scape (wô'tər·skāp, wot'ər-) *n.* A sea or other water view, as distinguished from a land-scape. [< WATER + (LAND)SCAPE]

water scorpion Any of numerous hemipterous insects of aquatic habits (family *Nepidae*), having raptorial front legs and a long breathing tube at the end of the abdomen.

wa·ter·shed (wô'tər·shed', wot'ər-) *n.* **1** The line of separation between two contiguous drainage valleys. **2** The whole region from which a river receives its supply of water. **3** A decisive turning point profoundly affecting or altering what follows it.

wa·ter·shield (wô'tər·shēld', wot'ər-) *n.* **1** An aquatic American herb (*Brasenia schreberi*) of the waterlily family, with the stems and the under sides of the leaves covered with a viscid jelly. **2** Any plant of a kindred genus (*Cabomba*), especially the fanwort.

wa·ter·sick (wô'tər·sik', wot'ər-) *adj.* Unproductive because of excessive irrigation: said of land.

wa·ter·side (wô'tər·sīd', wot'ər-) *n.* The shore of a body of water; the water's edge. —*adj.* **1** Of, pertaining to, or living or growing by the water's edge. **2** Working by the waterside, as a stevedore.

wa·ter·ski (wô'tər·skē', wot'ər-) *v.i.* **-skied**, **-ski·ing** To glide over water on water-skis, while being towed by a motorboat. —*n.* A broad, ski-like runner with a fitting to hold the foot: worn in the sport of water-skiing. —**wa'ter·ski'er** *n.* —**wa'ter·ski'ing** *n.*

water snake **1** A serpent of aquatic habits. **2** Any of a genus (*Natrix*) of harmless North American snakes that live chiefly in water.

wa·ter·soak (wô'tər·sōk', wot'ər-) *v.t.* To fill the pores or crevices of with water; soak in water.

wa·ter·sol·u·ble (wô'tər·sol'yə·bəl, wot'ər-) *adj.* *Biochem.* Soluble in water: said especially of certain organic compounds.

water spaniel The Irish water spaniel. See under SPANIEL.

water speedwell A common plant (*Veronica anagallis-aquatica*) of the composite family, growing in damp places.

wa·ter·spout (wô'tər·spout', wot'ər-) *n.* **1** A moving, whirling column of spray and mist, with masses of water in the lower parts, accumulated because of a tornado at sea or on other large bodies of water. **2** A pipe for the free discharge of water, especially one connecting with the gutters of a roof: also called *rainspout.*

water sprite A water nymph.

water starwort Any of a widely distributed genus (*Callitriche*) of herbaceous aquatic plants, especially *C. autumnalis,* common in the United States.

water station A place beside a railroad where there is a water tank for supplying locomotives with water.

water strider Any of a family (*Gerridae*) of hemipterous insects with elongate middle and hind legs adapted for darting over the surface of water.

water supply **1** The water available for the use of a community or region. **2** The means for supplying it, as reservoirs, lakes, etc. —**wa·ter-sup·ply** (wô'tər·sə·plī', wot'ər-) *adj.*

water system **1** A river with all its tributaries, considered as a hydrologic unit. **2** Water supply.

water table **1** *Archit.* A projecting ledge, molding, or string-course, running along the sides of a building to shed the rain. **2** The surface marking the upper level of a water-saturated zone extending beneath the ground to depths determined by the thickness of the permeable strata.

water tank A large cistern of wood or metal, as upon an engine or building, for storing or supplying water.

water thrush **1** Any of certain American warblers (genus *Seiurus*), frequenting swamps and streams; especially, the common or **northern water thrush** (*S. noveboracensis*), olive-brown above, yellowish beneath, with dusky streaks and a buffy superciliary line, or the **Louisiana water thrush** (*S. motacilla*), with a pure-white superciliary line. **2** The water ouzel.

water tiger The larva of the diving beetle.

wa·ter·tight (wô'tər·tīt', wot'ər-) *adj.* **1** So closely made that water cannot enter or leak through. **2** Constructed so as to be impermeable; without loopholes: a *watertight* legal document.

Wa·ter·ton Lakes National Park (wô'tər·tən) A national park in SW Alberta, Canada; 204 square miles; adjoining Glacier National Park, Montana, forming with it the **Waterton-Glacier International Peace Park**; total area, 1,800 square miles; highest U.S. point, 10,448 feet; highest Canadian point, 9,600 feet; established 1932.

water tower **1** A standpipe or tower, often of considerable height, used as a reservoir for a system of water distribution. **2** A vehicular tower-like structure having an extensible vertical pipe from which water can be played on a burning building from a great height.

wa·ter-tube boiler (wô'tər·tōōb', -tyōōb', wot'ər-) A type of boiler in which continuously heated water circulates through a series of tubes communicating with a steam chamber.

water turkey The snakebird.

water vapor The vapor of water, especially when found below the boiling point, as in the atmosphere. Compare STEAM.

wa·ter·vas·cu·lar system (wô'tər·vas'kyə·lər, wot'ər) A closed system unique in echinoderms consisting of water-filled canals and reservoirs which serve in locomotion and also in some species in respiration, excretion, and sensory reception.

water wave **1** An undulating effect of the hair, artificially produced when the hair is wet, and usually set by drying with heat. **2** A wave of water; a billow.

wa·ter·way (wô'tər·wā', wot'ər-) *n.* A river, channel, or other stream of water as a means of communication; water route.

wa·ter·weed (wô'tər·wēd', wot'ər-) *n.* **1** A submerged aquatic perennial (*Anacharis canadensis*), having whitish flowers. **2** Any of various other aquatic plants, as the pondweed.

water wheel **1** A wheel so equipped with floats, buckets, etc., that it may be turned by flowing water. See OVERSHOT WHEEL. **2** A noria.

water wings A waterproof, wing-shaped fabric device that may be inflated with air and used as a support for the body while swimming or learning to swim.

water witch **1** One who claims to discover underground springs with the use of a divining rod or hazel wand. **2** Any of various quick-diving water birds, as certain grebes.

water witching The use of a divining rod to discover water; rhabdomancy.

wa·ter·works (wô'tər·wûrks', wot'ər-) *n. pl.* **1** A display or pageant presented on floats; a display of fountains in operation. **2** A system of machines, buildings, and appliances for furnishing a water supply, especially for a city; also, any mill or factory run by waterpower. **3** *Slang* **a** Tears: usually in the phrase *to turn on the waterworks.* **b** Rain.

wa·ter·worn (wô'tər·wôrn', -wōrn', wot'ər-) *adj.* Worn smooth by running or falling water.

wa·ter·y (wô'tər·ē, wot'ər·ē) *adj.* **1** Containing or discharging water; brimming; tearful; soft and flabby. **2** Resembling water; thin or liquid. **3** Consisting of or pertaining to water. —**wa'ter·i·ness** *n.*

Wat·ford (wot'fərd) A municipal borough in Hertford, England, NW of London.

Wat·ling Island (wot'ling) See SAN SALVADOR. Also **Wat'lings Island.**

Wat·son (wot'sən), **John,** 1850–1907, Scottish minister and author: pseudonym, *Ian Maclaren.* —**John Broadus,** 1878–1958, U.S. psychologist. —**Sir William,** 1858–1935, English poet.

Wat·son-Watt (wot'sən-wot'), **Sir Robert Alexander,** born 1892, Scottish physicist.

watt (wot) *n.* The practical unit of electric power, activity, or rate of work: equivalent to 10^7 ergs or one joule per second, or approximately 1/746 of a horsepower; a volt-ampere. [after James *Watt*]

Watt (wot), **James,** 1736–1819, Scottish inventor and engineer.

wat·tage (wot'ij) *n.* **1** Amount of electric power in terms of watts. **2** The total number of watts needed to operate an appliance.

Wat·teau (wä·tō', wot'ō) *adj.* Of or pertaining to Antoine Watteau, or the costumes shown in his pictures.

Wat·teau (wä·tō', *Fr.* và·tō'), **Jean Antoine,** 1684–1721, French painter.

Watteau back A style of women's dress in which the fullness of the back is confined at the neck in plaits or gathers, and falls from there to the waistline.

Wat·ten·scheid (vät'ən·shīt) A city of east central North Rhine-Westphalia, central West Germany; a coal-mining and manufacturing center in the Ruhr.

Wat·ter·son (wot'ər·sən), **Henry,** 1840–1921, U.S. editor and journalist.

watt·hour (wot'our') *n.* Electrical energy equivalent to that represented by one watt acting for one hour.

wat·tle (wot'l) *n.* **1** A frame of rods or twigs woven together; a hurdle or other wickerwork. **2** A twig or withe, especially as used for interweaving with others; also, collectively, material for fences, hurdles, roofs, etc. **3** A naked, fleshy process, often wrinkled and brightly colored, hanging from the throat of a bird or snake. **4** A pendent fold of skin on the throat or neck of some domestic swine. **5** A barbel of a fish. **6** Any one of various acacias of Australia, Tasmania, and South Africa: so called by the early colonists, who used the branches to make hurdles. **7** *pl.* Rods for supporting thatch on a roof. —*v.t.* **·tled**, **·tling** **1** To weave or twist, as twigs, into a network. **2** To form, as baskets, by intertwining flexible twigs. **3** To bind together with wattles. —*adj.* Made of or covered with wattles; formed by wattling. [OE *watul*]

wat·tle·bird (wot'l·bûrd') *n.* Any of several large Australian honey-eaters (genus *Anthochaera*), having conspicuous wattles about the head and face.

wat·tled (wot'ld) *adj.* **1** Made with wattles. **2** Having a wattle, as a bird. **3** *Her.* Having wattles, comb, or gills of a tincture different from that of the body.

watt·less (wot'lis) *adj.* *Electr.* Denoting an alternating current, or the component of such a current, which is neutralized by the originating electromotive force and which for that reason does not produce any power.

watt·me·ter (wot'mētər) *n.* An instrument for measuring in watts the rate of doing electrical work: also called *voltammeter.*

Watts (wots), **George Frederick,** 1817–1904, English painter and sculptor. —**Isaac,** 1674–1748, English theologian and hymn writer.

Watts-Dun·ton (wots'dun'tən). **Theodore,** 1832–1914, English critic and poet.

Wa·tu·si (wä·tōō'sē) *n. pl.* **·si** One of a pastoral, Bantu-speaking people of east central Africa.

Wau (wou) A town in the Territory of New Guinea, NE New Guinea, a gold-mining center reached only by air.

Waugh (wô), **Alec,** born 1898, English novelist and travel writer. —**Evelyn,** 1903–1966, English novelist and critic; brother of preceding.

wauk[1] (wôk) *v.i. Scot.* To full cloth.

wauk[2] (wôk) *v.t. Scot.* To wake; watch over.

waul (wôl) *v.i.* To give a prolonged, plaintive cry like that of a cat: also spelled *wawl.* [Imit.]

waur (wôr) *adj. Scot.* Worse.

wave (wāv) *v.* **waved,** **wav·ing** *v.i.* **1** To move freely back and forth or up and down, as a flag in the wind; undulate or fluctuate. **2** To be moved back and forth or up and down as a signal; also, to make a signal by moving something thus. **3** To have an undulating shape or form; be sinuous: Her hair *waves.* —*v.t.* **4** To cause to move back and forth or up and down: to *wave* a banner. **5** To form with an undulating surface, edge, or outline. **6** To give a wavy appearance to; water, as silk. **7** To form into waves or undulations: to *wave* one's hair. **8** To signal by waving something: He *waved* me aside. **9** To express by waving something: to *wave* farewell. See

synonyms under FLAUNT, SHAKE. — *n.* **1** A ridge or undulation moving on the surface of a liquid, the particles composing it having an oscillatory motion usually in the form of closed or nearly closed curves in a plane at right angles to the direction of movement of the ridge itself. **2** *Physics* One of the complete vibratory impulses set up by a disturbance propagated through the particles of a body or elastic medium, as a rope, air, or water. Each impulse, as in the transmission of light or sound, has characteristics of length, frequency, duration, etc., determined by the nature of the disturbance in the medium involved. **3** One of the rising curves on an undulatory edge or surface; one of a series of curves: amber *waves* of grain. **4** Something that comes, like a wave, with great volume or power; a flood; a period of marked activity or excitement: a *wave* of enthusiasm. **5** A wavelike stripe or undulation impressed on a surface, as on watered silk; also, a wavelike tress or curl of hair. **6** *Poetic* Any body of water; the sea. **7** The act of waving; a sweeping or undulating motion, as with the hand or a flag. **8** One of a series, as of groups or events, occurring or moving with wavelike fluctuations: He went ashore with the first *wave* of Marines. **9** A progressive change in temperature or in barometrical condition passing over a large area: a heat *wave*. ◆ Homophone: *waive*. [OE *wafian*] — **wav′er** *n.*
Synonyms (noun): billow, breaker, ripple, surge, swell, undulation, vibration.

Wave (wāv) *n.* A member of the WAVES. [Back formation from WAVES (taken as a pl.)]

wave cloud *Meteorol.* A cloud consisting of parallel bands or ridges, separated by strips of clear sky, due to air currents occurring at the bounding plane between two strata of the atmosphere.

wave front The leading surface of a wave as it advances through a medium.

wave-guide (wāv′gīd′) *n.* **1** Any system of material boundaries by which the direction of waves may be controlled. **2** *Electronics* A device, typically an arrangement of hollow metal pipes of varying size and cross-section, through which high-frequency electromagnetic waves may be guided as required.

wave-length (wāv′length′) *n.* *Physics* The distance, measured along the line of propagation, between two points representing similar phases of two consecutive waves. It is a fundamental unit in the study of radiant energy.

wave-less (wāv′lis) *adj.* Having no waves; tranquil. See synonyms under PACIFIC.

wave-let (wāv′lit) *n.* A little wave.

Wa-vell (wā′vəl), **Sir Archibald Percival**, 1883–1950, first Earl Wavell, Viscount Wavell of Cyrenaica and Tripolitania, British field marshal and administrator in World War II.

wa-vel-lite (wā′və-līt) *n.* A vitreous, translucent, hydrous aluminum phosphate, crystallizing in the orthorhombic system. [after Dr. William *Wavell*, died 1829, English physician, its discoverer]

wave mechanics The branch of physics which investigates the wave characteristics ascribed to the atom and its associated particles, and seeks to explain physical processes in terms of these characteristics as revealed by the quantum theory of atomic structure.

wave-me-ter (wāv′mē′tər) *n.* An apparatus for determining wavelengths and wave frequencies, as in a radio circuit.

wave number *Physics* The number of electromagnetic waves in a space of 1 centimeter, equal to the frequency of the wave divided by the velocity of light: it is the reciprocal of the wavelength.

wave-off (wāv′ôf′, -of′) *n.* *Aeron.* The act of denying landing privileges to an approaching aircraft, usually an aircraft making a faulty approach for landing on an aircraft carrier.

wa-ver (wā′vər) *v.i.* **1** To move one way and the other; sway; flutter. **2** To be uncertain or undecided; show irresolution; vacillate. **3** To show signs of falling back or giving way; reel; falter. **4** To flicker; gleam. **5** To quaver; tremble. See synonyms under FLUCTUATE, QUAKE, SHAKE. — *n.* A wavering. ◆ Homophone: *waiver*. [< ME *waveren*, freq. of OE *wafian* wave] — **wa′ver-er** *n.* — **wa′ver-ing** *adj.* — **wa′ver-ing-ly** *adv.*

Wa-ver-ley Novels (wā′vər-lē) A series of historical novels by Sir Walter Scott, published 1814–1831.

WAVES (wāvz) *n.* A corps of women in the U. S. Navy, which includes all women except nurses; officially, *Women in the United States Navy* (1946). [< W(omen) A(ppointed for) V(oluntary) E(mergency) S(ervice), an earlier name]

wave train A series of waves sent out at regular intervals from a vibrating body.

wave trap 1 *Telecom.* A device, usually connected with the antenna, for improving the selectivity of a radio receiver by cutting out undesired wave frequencies. **2** A widening inward of the distance between the sides of adjoining piers to allow for the spreading of storm waves.

wa-vey (wā′vē) *n.* The snow goose. [Var. of WAVY; so called because faintly streaked on head, neck, and back with darker plumage]

wav-y (wā′vē) *adj.* **wav-i-er, wav-i-est 1** Full of waves; ruffled by or raised into waves. **2** Undulatory; waving. **3** Unstable; wavering. — **wav′i-ly** *adv.* — **wav′i-ness** *n.*

wawl (wôl) See WAUL.

wax¹ (waks) *n.* **1** A yellow fatty solid excreted from the abdominal rings of bees and used by them to build honeycombs; beeswax. It has a honeylike odor and a balsamic taste; becomes plastic with the heat of the hand; is insoluble in water, but is almost completely dissolved by boiling alcohol. **2** Any of a class of plant and animal substances consisting of the esters of fatty acids and alcohols other than glycerol, and including spermaceti and carnauba wax; specifically, a substance derived from the fruit of the wax myrtle or bayberry. **3** A solid mineral substance resembling wax, as ozocerite or paraffin. **4** A substance used for joining surfaces, sealing documents, etc.; sealing wax. **5** A mixture of pitch and tallow or some resinous composition used by shoemakers to wax their thread. **6** Earwax; cerumen. **7** *U. S.* The sap of the sugar maple after being boiled down and cooled. **8** A substance resembling beeswax secreted by certain scale insects. — *v.t.* To coat or treat with wax. — *adj.* Made of or pertaining to wax. [OE *weax*]

wax² (waks) *v.i.* **waxed, waxed** (*Poetic* **wax-en**), **wax-ing 1** To become larger gradually; increase in size or numbers; grow: said specifically of the moon as it approaches fullness: opposed to *wane*. **2** To become as specified: to *wax* angry. [OE *weaxan* grow]

wax³ (waks) *v.t.* *Colloq.* To record phonographically: to *wax* a folk song. [< WAX¹; so called because wax was formerly used in making phonograph records]

wax⁴ (waks) *n.* *Colloq.* A tantrum; fit of bad temper. [? < phrase *wax angry*]

wax bean A variety of string bean (*Phaseolus vulgaris*) cultivated in the United States: also called *butter bean*.

wax-ber-ry (waks′ber′ē) *n.* *pl.* **·ries 1** The wax myrtle, or bayberry. **2** Its wax-covered fruit. **3** The snowberry.

wax-bill (waks′bil′) *n.* **1** Any of various small Old World seed-eating birds of the weaverbird family (genus *Estrilda*), having beaks resembling sealing wax. **2** The Java sparrow.

wax-en (wak′sən) *adj.* **1** Resembling wax. **2** Consisting wholly or in part of wax; covered with wax. **3** Pale; pallid: a *waxen* complexion; also, pliable or impressible as wax.

wax end A stout thread, or the end of a thread, made stiff and pointed with shoemakers' wax, or waxed and twisted with a bristle, as for the purpose of sewing shoes. Also **waxed end.**

wax myrtle Any of a genus (*Myrica*) of North American shrubs or small trees, especially *M. cerifera*, having fragrant leaves and small berries covered with white wax, often used in making candles: also called *bayberry*, *candleberry*.

wax palm 1 A South American palm (*Ceroxylon andicola*) with pinnate leaves, having a lofty straight trunk covered with a waxy, whitish, resinous substance. **2** A Brazilian palm (*Copernicia cerifera*) whose young leaves yield the carnauba wax of commerce.

wax paper Paper coated or treated with wax and used to protect against moisture. Also **waxed paper.**

wax plant The Indian pipe.

wax-weed (waks′wēd′) *n.* An annual, clammy, hairy herb (*Cuphea petiolata*) of the loose-

strife family with irregular purplish axillary flowers.

wax-wing (waks′-wing′) *n.* Any of various crested passerine birds (family *Bombycillidae*) of America and Asia, having soft, mainly brown plumage, and the tips of the secondary wing feathers tipped with horny appendages resembling red or yellow sealing wax; especially, the two best-known North American species, the **cedar waxwing** (*Bombycilla cedrorum*), and the larger **Bohemian waxwing** (*B. garrula pallidiceps*).

CEDAR WAXWING
(About 7 inches long)

wax-work (waks′wûrk′) *n.* **1** Work produced in wax; particularly, ornaments or life-size figures of wax. **2** *pl.* A collection of such figures.

wax-work-er (waks′wûr′kər) *n.* One who works in wax; one who makes waxwork.

wax-worm (waks′wûrm′) *n.* A honeycomb moth.

wax-y (wak′sē) *adj.* **wax-i-er, wax-i-est 1** Resembling wax in appearance, consistency, or adhesive qualities; waxen; pliable; impressionable. **2** Having the dull whitish or yellowish color of wax; pale; pallid; bloodless. **3** Made of or abounding in wax; rubbed with wax; waxed. **4** *Pathol.* Characterized by the formation of an insoluble, waxlike protein in certain organs of the body, as the kidney; amyloid. — **wax′i-ness** *n.*

way (wā) *n.* **1** Direction; turn; route; line of motion or progress: Which *way* is the city? **2** A path, course, or track leading from one place to another or along which one goes; a road, street, highway, lane, path, or the like. **3** Space or room to advance or work: Make *way* for the king. **4** Length of space passed over; hence, distance in general: a little *way* off: often, popularly or dialectally, *ways* **5** Passage from one place to another; hence, onward movement; headway; progress. **6** A customary or habitual manner or style; a manner peculiar to an individual, class, or people: the British *way* of doing things. **7** A chosen line or plan of action; a procedure; method: In what *way* will you accomplish this? **8** A point of relation; particular: He erred in two *ways*. **9** A course of life or experience: the *way* of sin. **10** *Colloq.* Vocation; line of business; profession. **11** *Colloq.* State of health: to be in a bad *way*. **12** A course wished for or resolved upon; something which one resolves to do: Have it your *way*. **13** The range of one's notice or observation: An accident threw it in his *way*. **14** *Naut.* **a** The movement of a vessel through the water; forward motion; headway. **b** *pl.* A tilted framework of timbers upon which a ship slides when launched. **15** The direction of the weave in textile goods. **16** *Law* A right of way. **17** *Mech.* A longitudinal guide for material being worked upon, or for a moving table bearing the work. **18** *Colloq.* Neighborhood, or route taken to go home: He lives out of my *way*. — **by the way** In passing; incidentally. — **by way of 1** With the object or purpose of; to serve as: *by way of* introduction. **2** Through; via: We went home *by way of* Main Street. — **out of the way 1** Removed, as an obstruction; unable to hinder or impede. **2** Out of the proper course; hence, remarkable; unusual; also, improper; wrong: Has he done anything *out of the way*? **3** Out of place; lost; mislaid; remote. — **under way** In motion; well along; making progress. — *adv.* *Colloq.* Away; very far; all the great distance: He went *way* to Denver. ◆ Homophone: *weigh*. [OE *weg*]
Synonyms (noun): alley, avenue, bridlepath, channel, course, driveway, highroad, highway, lane, pass, passage, path, pathway, road, route, street, thoroughfare, track. Wherever there is room for an object to proceed, there is a *way*. A road (originally a *ride*way) is a prepared way for traveling with horses or vehicles, a *way* suitable to be traversed only by foot-passengers or by animals being called a *path*, *bridlepath*, or *track*; as, The *roads* in that country are mere *bridlepaths*. A road may be private: a *highway* or *highroad* is public,

highway being a specific name for a *road* legally set apart for the use of the public forever; a *highway* may be over water as well as over land. A *route* is a line of travel, and may be over many *roads*. A *street* is in some center of habitation, as a city, town, or village; when it passes between rows of dwellings, the country *road* becomes the village *street*. An *avenue* is a long, broad, and imposing or principal *street*. *Track* is a word of wide signification; we speak of a goat-*track* on a mountainside, a railroad *track*, a racetrack, the *track* of a comet; on a traveled *road* the line worn by regular passing of hoofs and wheels is called the *track*. A *passage* is between any two objects or lines of enclosure, a *pass* commonly between mountains. A *driveway* is within enclosed grounds, as of a private residence. A *channel* is a *waterway*. A *thoroughfare* is a *way* through. See AIR[1], DIRECTION, ROAD.

way back *Colloq.* Long ago. [Short for AWAY BACK]

way·bill (wā′bil′) *n.* A list describing or identifying goods or naming passengers carried by a common carrier, as a railroad, train, steamer, or other public vehicle.

way·far·er (wā′fâr′ər) *n.* One who journeys along a way on foot.

way·far·ing (wā′fâr′ing) *adj. & n.* Journeying; being on the road.

way freight Freight taken on or put off at way stations; also, a freight train stopping at way stations and handling such goods: distinguished from *through freight.*

way·go·ing (wā′gō′ing) *adj.* Pertaining to one's going away; going away; departing.

way-going crop *Law* A crop sown by a tenant during his term, but ripening after its expiration. [Short for *away-going crop*]

Way·land (wā′lənd) In Teutonic and English mythology, an invisible blacksmith with magical powers: in German folklore spelled *Wieland.* Also **Wayland (the) Smith.**

way·lay (wā′lā′) *v.t.* **·laid, ·lay·ing** **1** To lie in ambush for and attack, as in order to rob. **2** To accost on the way. [<WAY + LAY[1], on analogy with MHG *wegelagen* < *wegelage* an ambush] — **way′lay′er** *n.*

Wayne (wān), **Anthony,** 1745–96, American Revolutionary general: called "Mad Anthony" Wayne.

way passenger A passenger getting on or off a public conveyance, as a train, steamship, bus, etc., at a way station; a local passenger.

-ways *suffix of adverbs* In a (specified) manner, direction, or position: *noways, sideways:* often equivalent to –WISE. Also **-way.** [<WAY + -s[3]]

ways and means Means or methods of accomplishing an end or defraying expenses; specifically, in legislation, methods of raising funds for the use of the government.

way·side (wā′sīd′) *adj.* Pertaining to the side of a road; growing or being near the wayside. — *n.* The side or edge of the road or highway.

way station Any station between principal stations, especially on a railroad; a local station.

way train A train stopping at way stations; a local train.

way·ward (wā′wərd) *adj.* **1** Wandering away; wilful; froward. **2** Without definite way or course; unsteady; vacillating; capricious. **3** Unexpected or unwished for: a *wayward* fortune. See synonyms under PERVERSE. [ME *weiward,* short for *aweiward* < *awei* away + -WARD] — **way′ward·ly** *adv.* — **way′ward·ness** *n.*

way·worn (wā′wôrn′, -wōrn′) *adj.* Fatigued by travel.

Wa·zir·i·stan (wä-zir′i-stän′) A tribal region in NW central Pakistan on the Afghanistan border; 5,214 square miles.

we (wē) *pron.* **1** The persons speaking or writing as they denote themselves, or a single person writing or speaking when referring to himself and one or more others: the nominative case. **2** A single person denoting himself, as a sovereign, editor, writer, or speaker, when wishing to give his words an impersonal character. [OE]

weak (wēk) *adj.* **1** Lacking in physical strength; wanting in energy, activity, or vigor; feeble; debilitated. **2** Insufficiently resisting stress; incapable of supporting weight: a *weak* link

or bridge. **3** Lacking in strength of will or stability of character; yielding easily to temptation; pliable. **4** Ineffectual, as from deficient supply: *weak* artillery support. **5** Lacking in power or sonorousness: a *weak* voice. **6** Lacking a specified component or components in the usual or proper amount; of less than customary strength or potency: *weak* tea, a *weak* tincture. **7** Lacking the power or ability to perform properly its function: a *weak* heart. **8** Lacking in mental or moral strength; liable to err or fail through feebleness of conception or vacillation of judgment. **9** Showing or resulting from poor judgment or a want of discretion or firmness: a *weak* plan; unable to persuade or convince: a *weak* argument. **10** Lacking in influence or authority: a *weak* state. **11** Deficient in strength, durability, skill, experience, or the like. **12** *Gram.* In Germanic languages: **a** Of verbs, forming the past tense and past participle by the addition of a dental suffix to the present stem; as, English *ask, asked; sight, sighted;* German *leben, lebte, gelebt.* Some weak verbs in English show vowel change in the stem (as in *leave, left*), but in such cases the change is due to factors other than ablaut. Also called *regular.* **b** Of nouns and adjectives (in German and Old English), inflected in the less full manner originally restricted to stems ending in –*n.* Weak nouns and adjectives in Old English characteristically terminate in –*a* in the masculine singular (*nama* name) and –*e* in the feminine singular (*tunge* tongue). In German, a descriptive adjective appears in the weak form when preceded by a limiting word, such as the definite article, having strong inflection (*der gute Mann*). Compare STRONG (def. 28). **13** *Phonet.* Unstressed; unaccented, as a syllable or sound. **14** *Phot.* Thin; wanting in contrast: a *weak* negative. **15** In prosody, designating a verse ending in which the accent falls on a word or syllable otherwise without stress. **16** Declining in price; without an active market: The wheat market is *weak.* **17** Wanting in impressiveness or interest: a *weak* play or book. See synonyms under FAINT, FRAGILE, PUSILLANIMOUS, SICKLY. ◆ Homophone: *week.* [<ON *veikr.* Akin to OE *wac.*] — **weak′ly** *adv.* — **weak′ness** *n.*

Weak may appear as a combining form in hyphemes or as the first element in two-word phrases; as in:

weak–backed	weak–nerved
weak–bodied	weak point
weak–built	weak side
weak–eyed	weak–sighted
weak–growing	weak–spirited
weak–handed	weak–stemmed
weak–headed	weak–throated
weak–headedness	weak–toned
weak–hearted	weak–voiced
weak–limbed	weak–walled
weak–looking	weak–willed
weak–made	weak–winged
weak–mindedness	weak–witted

weak·en (wē′kən) *v.t. & v.i.* To make or become weak or weaker. — **weak′en·er** *n.* *Synonyms:* debilitate, depress, enervate, enfeeble, impair, invalidate, lower, paralyze, reduce, relax, sap, undermine, unnerve. See IMPAIR.

weak·fish (wēk′fish′) *n.* *pl.* **·fish** or **·fish·es** Any of various American marine food fishes (genus *Cynoscion*), especially the common variety (*C. regalis*), frequenting coastal waters of the eastern United States.

weak-kneed (wēk′nēd′) *adj.* Weak in the knees; hence, without resolution, strong purpose, or energy; spineless.

weak·ling (wēk′ling) *n.* A feeble person or animal. — *adj.* Having no natural strength or vigor.

weak·ly (wēk′lē) *adj.* **·li·er, ·li·est** Sickly; feeble; weak. See synonyms under SICKLY.

weak-mind·ed (wēk′mīn′did) *adj.* **1** Indecisive; unable to say no. **2** Feeble-minded.

weak·ness (wēk′nis) *n.* **1** The state, condition, or quality of being weak. **2** A characteristic indicating feebleness. **3** A slight failing; a fault.

weak sister *Colloq.* **1** The weakling in any group; specifically, one who cannot be de-

pended on to stand firm against opposition. **2** Any ineffectual person.

weak spot **1** Any spot having less strength than the contiguous area, as in a fabric, fence, etc. **2** The most vulnerable part of an argument, proposition, etc. **3** The weakest or least dependable person on a team, in a group, etc.

weal[1] (wēl) *n.* **1** A sound or healthy state, either of persons or things; prosperity; welfare. **2** *Obs.* The body politic, state, or nation: now only in the phrase, *public weal.* **3** *Obs.* Wealth; worldly store. [OE *wela.* Akin to WELL.]

weal[2] (wēl) *n.* A discolored ridge or stripe on the skin, as from the blow of a whip; a wheal. [Var. of WALE[1]; infl. in form by obs. *wheal* a pustule]

weald (wēld) *n.* An exposed forest area; waste woodland; also, an open region; down. [OE, a forest]

Weald (wēld), **The** A district of SE England between the North and South Downs in Kent, Surrey and Sussex counties; formerly forested, now primarily agricultural.

wealth (welth) *n.* **1** A large aggregate of real and personal property; an abundance of those material or worldly things that men desire to possess; riches; also, the state of being rich. **2** *Econ.* All material objects which have economic utility; also, in the private sense, all property possessing a monetary value. **3** Great abundance of anything: a *wealth* of learning. **4** *Obs.* Weal; well-being. — **personal wealth** Those faculties, energies, and habits which contribute to personal industrial efficiency. [ME *welthe* < *wele* weal, on analogy with *health*]
Synonyms: abundance, affluence, comfort, competence, competency, fortune, funds, goods, independence, lucre, mammon, money, opulence, pelf, plenty, possession, produce, property, riches, substance, treasure. See PROPERTY. *Antonyms:* see synonyms for POVERTY.

wealth·y (wel′thē) *adj.* **wealth·i·er, wealth·i·est** **1** Possessing wealth; affluent. **2** More than sufficient; abounding. — **wealth′i·ly** *adv.* — **wealth′i·ness** *n.*

wean[1] (wēn) *v.t.* **1** To transfer (the young of any animal) from dependence on its mother's milk to another form of nourishment. **2** To estrange from former habits or associations; alienate the affections of: usually with *from.* [OE *wenian* accustom]

wean[2] (wēn) *n. Scot.* A baby; infant.

wean·er (wē′nər) *n.* **1** One who weans. **2** A muzzle used in weaning a calf.

wean·ling (wēn′ling) *adj.* Freshly weaned. — *n.* A child or animal newly weaned.

weap·on (wep′ən) *n.* **1** Any implement of war or combat, as a sword, gun, etc. **2** Figuratively, any means that may be used against an adversary. **3** *pl.* The thorns or prickles of plants, or the stings, claws, etc., of animals. See synonyms under ARMS. [OE *wǣpen*] — **weap′on·less** *adj.*

weap·oned (wep′ənd) *adj.* Furnished with weapons; bearing arms.

weap·on·eer (wep′ən·ir′) *n.* A person concerned with the design, improvement, production, and use of weapons, especially of the atomic and thermonuclear type.

wear[1] (wâr) *v.* **wore, worn, wear·ing** *v.t.* **1** To carry or have on the person as a garment, ornament, etc. **2** To have or bear on the person habitually or as a practice: He *wears* a derby. **3** To have in one's appearance or aspect; exhibit: He *wears* a scowl. **4** To bear habitually in a specified manner; carry: He *wears* his age well; She *wears* her hair in a chignon. **5** To display or fly: A ship *wears* its colors. **6** To impair, waste, or consume by use or constant action. **7** To cause or produce by scraping, rubbing, etc.: to *wear* a hole in a coat. **8** To bring to a specified condition by wear: to *wear* a sleeve to tatters. **9** To exhaust the strength or patience of; weary. — *v.i.* **10** To be impaired or diminished gradually by use, rubbing, etc. **11** To withstand the effects of use, wear, etc., as specified: The vest *wears* well. **12** To become as specified from use or attrition: His patience is *wearing* thin. **13** To pass gradually or

tediously: with *on* or *away*. The day *wears on*. — **to wear out** 1 To make·or become worthless by use: The cloak is *worn out.* 2 To waste gradually; use up: He *wears out* patience. 3 To tire or exhaust. — *n.* 1 The act of wearing, or the state of being worn: the worse for *wear.* 2 The material or articles of dress worn or made to be worn; a fashion: silk for summer *wear;* also in compounds: *footwear, underwear.* 3 The destructive effect of use or work; impairment from use or time. 4 Capacity for resistance to use or impairment; endurance; lasting quality; durability. ◆ Homophone: *ware.* [OE *werian*] — **wear'a·ble** *adj.* — **wear'er** *n.*
Synonyms (verb): abrade, chafe, consume, deteriorate, diminish, fret, fritter, impair, rub, tire, waste.

wear² (wâr) *v.* **wore, worn, wear·ing** *Naut. v.t.* To change the course of (a vessel), so as to bring the wind to the other side, by turning it through an arc in which its head points momentarily directly to leeward. — *v.i.* To go about with the wind astern. Compare TACK¹. ◆ Homophone: *ware.* [Prob. alter. of VEER¹; infl. in form by *wear¹*]

wear·a·ble (wâr'ə·bəl) *adj.* That can be worn. — *n. pl.* Garments.

wear and tear Loss by the service, exposure, decay, or injury incident to ordinary use.

wea·ri·ful (wir'i·fəl) *adj.* Tiresome; wearisome. — **wea'ri·ful·ly** *adv.* — **wea'ri·ful·ness** *n.*

wea·ri·less (wir'i·lis) *adj.* Unwearying; untiring.

wear·ing (wâr'ing) *adj.* 1 Fatiguing; exhausting; wasting: *wearing* trials. 2 Capable of being, or designed to be, worn. — **wear'ing·ly** *adv.*

wearing apparel Clothing; garments.

wear·ish (wâr'ish) *adj. Obs.* or *Dial.* 1 Insipid; watery. 2 Wizened; shrunk; withered. [ME *werische*; origin uncertain] — **wear'ish·ly** *adv.* — **wear'ish·ness** *n.*

wea·ri·some (wir'i·səm) *adj.* Causing fatigue; tiresome. — **wea'ri·some·ly** *adv.* — **wea'ri·some·ness** *n.*
Synonyms: annoying, fatiguing, irksome, laborious, tedious, tiresome, vexatious, wearing, weary. See TEDIOUS, TROUBLESOME. *Antonyms:* cheering, enlivening, inspiring, inspiriting, restful, reviving, rousing, soothing, stirring, thrilling.

wea·ry (wir'ē) *adj.* **·ri·er, ·ri·est** 1 Worn with exertion, vexation, or suffering; tired; fatigued. 2 Discontented or vexed by continued endurance, or by something disagreeable: usually with *of: weary* of life. 3 Indicating or characteristic of fatigue: a *weary* sigh. 4 Causing weariness; wearisome. — *v.t. & v.i.* **·ried, ·ry·ing** To make or become weary. See synonyms under TIRE¹. [OE *wērig*] — **wea'ri·ly** *adv.* — **wea'ri·ness** *n.*

wea·sand (wē'zənd) *n. Archaic* The windpipe; in general, the throat: often spelled *wizen.* Also *Scot.* **wea'son.** [OE *wāsend*]

wea·sel (wē'zəl) *n.* Any of certain small, slender, reddish-brown, carnivorous mammals (genus *Mustela*) that prey on smaller mammals and birds. In northern regions their fur turns white in winter. [OE *wesle*]

weasel word A word that weakens a statement by rendering it ambiguous or equivocal: term popularized by Theodore Roosevelt.

weath·er (weth'ər) *n.* 1 The general atmospheric condition, as regards temperature, moisture, winds, or other meteorological phenomena. 2 The common phenomena of wind, rain, cold, heat, cloudiness, or storm. 3 Bad weather; storm. — **to keep one's weather eye open** *Colloq.* To be alert. — **under the weather** *Colloq.* 1 Ailing; ill. 2 Somewhat intoxicated. — *v.t.* 1 To expose to the action of the weather. 2 To discolor, crumble, or otherwise affect by action of the weather. 3 To pass through and survive, as a crisis. 4 To slope, as a roof,

WEASEL
(Head and body from 6 to 7 inches)

so as to shed water. 5 *Naut.* To pass to windward of: to *weather* Cape Fear. — *v.i.* 6 To undergo changes resulting from exposure to the weather. 7 To resist the action of the weather. — *adj.* Facing the wind; windward: opposed to *lee.* ◆ Homophone: *wether.* [OE *weder*]
Weather may appear as a combining form in hyphemes or solidemes, or as the first element in two–word phrases:

weather–bitten	weather report
weather–bleached	weather–reporter
weather–blown	weather–reporting
weather–burnt	weather–rotted
weather–driven	weather–scarred
weather–eaten	weathersick
weather forecast	weather–tanned
weather–hardened	weathertight
weather–observer	weather–tough
weather–observing	weather–withstanding

weath·er·beat·en (weth'ər·bēt'n) *adj.* Bearing the effects of exposure to weather.

weath·er·board (weth'ər·bôrd', -bōrd') *n.* 1 A board for the outside covering of wooden buildings, usually feather–edged and nailed so as to form lap joints with the boards above and below and thus shed rain; a clapboard. 2 *Naut.* The windward side of a vessel. — *v.t.* To fasten weatherboards on.

weath·er·board·ing (weth'ər·bôr'ding, -bōr'-) *n.* 1 Weatherboards collectively, or material for making them. 2 The outer wooden covering of the walls and roof of a building.

weath·er·bound (weth'ər·bound') *adj.* Detained by unfavorable weather, as a vessel in port.

Weather Bureau A bureau of the Department of Commerce in Washington, D.C., for meteorological observation, the diffusion of information concerning the weather, etc.

weath·er·cast (weth'ər·kast', -käst') *n.* A radio or television broadcast reporting on weather conditions. [<WEATHER + (BROAD)CAST] — **weath'er·cast'er** *n.*

weath·er·cock (weth'ər·kok') *n.* 1 A vane, properly one in the semblance of a cock, which turns to indicate the direction of the wind; a weathervane. 2 A fickle person or variable thing.

weath·er·drome (weth'ər·drōm') *n. Meteorol.* A large, floating structure resembling an airdrome, permanently anchored in offshore waters to serve as a weather station.

WEATHERCOCK

weath·ered (weth'ərd) *adj.* 1 Affected by exposure to the atmosphere; seasoned. 2 *Archit.* Sloped to prevent water lodging on the surface, as woodwork or stonework. 3 Worn, shaped, or stained by exposure in the atmosphere: said of rocks. 4 Denoting wood that has been artificially colored to represent weathering.

weather gage 1 *Naut.* The advantage to a ship or yacht of receiving the wind first; a position to the windward. 2 Any advantage gained.

weath·er·glass (weth'ər·glas', -gläs') *n.* A meteorological instrument for indicating the state of the weather; especially, a common barometer.

weath·er·ize (weth'ə·rīz) *v.t.* **·ized, ·iz·ing** To process (fabrics, leather, etc.) chemically or otherwise, so as to make impervious or highly resistant to moisture or other effects of severe weather.

weath·er·ly (weth'ər·lē) *adj. Naut.* Capable of keeping close into the wind without drifting to leeward.

weath·er·man (weth'ər·man') *n.*, *pl.* **·men** (-men') *n. Colloq.* A meteorologist, especially one concerned with daily weather conditions and reports.

weather map *Meteorol.* A map or chart compiled periodically from official sources and indicating, for a given region and specified time, various components of the weather, as temperature, atmospheric pressure, wind velocity, rain, snow, cloud formations, etc.

weath·er·proof (weth'ər·proof') *adj.* Capable of withstanding rough weather without appreciable deterioration. — *v.t.* To make weatherproof.

weather station A station or office where meteorological observations are taken and recorded.

weath·er·strip (weth'ər·strip') *n.* A narrow strip of material to be placed over or in crevices, as at doors and windows, to exclude drafts, rain, etc.: also **weath'er·strip'ping.** — *v.t.* **-stripped, -strip·ping** To equip or fit with weather–strips.

weath·er·vane (weth'ər·vān') *n.* A vane; weathercock.

weath·er·vi·sion (weth'ər·vizh'ən) *n.* A system which combines television and radar in the rapid dissemination of weather data to aircraft. [<WEATHER + (TELE)VISION]

weath·er·wise (weth'ər·wīz') *adj.* Experienced in observing or predicting the weather.

weath·er·worn (weth'ər·wôrn', -wōrn') *adj.* Worn by exposure to the weather.

weave (wēv) *v.* **wove** or (*esp. for defs.* 7 *and* 10) **weaved, wo·ven** or *less frequently* **wove, weav·ing** *v.t.* 1 To form, produce, or manufacture as a textile, by interlacing threads or yarns; especially, to make by interlacing woof threads among warp threads in a loom. 2 To form by interlacing strands, strips, twigs, etc.: to *weave* a basket. 3 To produce by combining details or elements: to *weave* a story. 4 To bring together so as to form a whole: to *weave* fancies into theories. 5 To twist or introduce into, about, or through something else: to *weave* ribbons through one's hair. 6 To spin (a web). 7 To make or effect by side–to–side movements: to *weave* one's way. — *v.i.* 8 To make cloth, etc., by weaving. 9 To become woven or interlaced. 10 To move with a side–to–side motion. — *n.* A particular method or style of weaving. — **plain** or **taffeta weave** A weave in which each filling yarn passes successively over and under each warp yarn, forming an even surface. — **satin weave** An irregular weave in which the warp or filling yarns pass over a number of yarns of the other set before interweaving, thus forming a smooth, unbroken, lustrous surface. — **twill weave** A strong weave having a distinct diagonal line or rib, caused by the passage of the filling yarns over one warp yarn and under two or more. [OE *wefan.* Akin to WEB, WEFT.]

WEAVES
Simple figured. Leno. Five–shaft satin.

weav·er (wē'vər) *n.* 1 One who weaves. 2 A weaverbird.

weav·er·bird (wē'vər·bûrd') *n.* Any of various finchlike birds (family *Ploceidae*) of the warmer parts of Asia, Africa, and Australia, that construct intricately woven nests.

weaver's bottom *Pathol.* An inflamed condition of the tissue over the ischium, or seat bone, arising from long sitting.

weaver's hitch A sheet bend. Also WEAVER'S KNOT.

web (web) *n.* 1 Textile fabric, especially as in the piece or as being woven in a loom. 2 A long sheet or roll of material formed like a web of cloth; especially, a roll of paper as it comes from the mill. 3 The network of delicate threads spun by a spider to entrap its prey; a cobweb. 4 Any complex network: a *web* of highways; anything artfully contrived or elaborated into a trap or snare: a *web* of espionage. 5 *Zool.* A membrane or fold of skin connecting the digits of an animal, as in aquatic birds, otters, bats, frogs, etc. 6 *Ornithol.* The series of barbs on either side of the shaft of a feather; the vane. 7 *Mech.* A plate or sheet, as of metal, connecting the heavier sections, ribs, frames, etc., of any tool or mechanical element. 8 The plate between the flange and head of a railroad rail. 9 *Archit.* The part of a ribbed vault between the ribs. 10 *Anat.* A membrane; tissue; tela. 11 A thin metal plate, as the blade of a saw or sword, or the bit of a key. — **pin and web** A darkening speck on the cornea, with a film spreading fanwise from the cornea. — *v.t.* **webbed, web·bing** **1** To provide with a web. **2** To cover or surround with a web; entangle. [OE. Akin to WEAVE, WEFT.]

Webb (web), **Beatrice**, 1858–1943, *née* Potter, English economist and sociologist; wife of Sidney James Webb. — **Mary**, 1881–1927, *née* Meredith, English novelist. — **Sidney James**, 1859–1947, Baron Passfield, English economist and sociologist.

webbed (webd) *adj.* **1** Having a web. **2** Having the digits united by a membrane.

web·bing (web'ing) *n.* **1** A woven strip of strong fiber, as for girths, seat bottoms, etc. **2** Any woven texture; the structure of a web.

web·by (web'ē) *adj.* **·bi·er, ·bi·est** **1** Relating to or consisting of a web or membrane. **2** Palmate.

we·ber (vā'bər, wē'bər) *n. Physics* **1** The mks unit of magnetic flux, equal to 100,000,000 maxwells. **2** *Obs.* Coulomb. **3** *Obs.* Ampere. [after Wilhelm Eduard *Weber*]

We·ber (vā'bər), **Ernst Heinrich**, 1795–1878, German physiologist. — **Baron Karl Friedrich Ernst von**, 1786–1826, German composer. — **Wilhelm Eduard**, 1804–91, German physicist; brother of Ernst Heinrich Weber.

web·foot (web'fŏŏt') *n.* **1** A foot with webbed toes. **2** A web-footed bird or animal. **3** The condition of being web-footed.

web-foot·ed (web'fŏŏt'id) *adj.* Having the toes connected by a membrane, as many aquatic animals and birds.

web press A printing press which is fed from a continuous roll of paper instead of sheets.

web·ster (web'stər) *n. Obs.* A weaver. [OE *webbestre*, fem. of *webba* a weaver]

Web·ster (web'stər), **Daniel**, 1782–1852, U.S. statesman. — **John**, 1580?–1625, English dramatist. — **Noah**, 1758–1843, U.S. lexicographer.

Web·ste·ri·an (web-stir'ē-ən) *adj.* Of or pertaining to Daniel or Noah Webster.

web·worm (web'wûrm') *n.* Any of various caterpillars, usually gregarious and very destructive of foliage, which build large silken webs or tents for shelter; especially, the common **garden webworm** (*Loxostege similalis*).

wecht (wekht) *n. Scot.* Weight.

wed (wed) *v.* **wed·ded, wed·ded** or **wed, wed·ding** *v.t.* **1** To take as one's husband or wife; marry. **2** To unite or give in matrimony; join in wedlock. **3** To attach as if in marriage; join securely: chiefly in the past participle, with *to*: *wedded* to his job. — *v.i.* **4** To take a husband or wife; marry. [OE *weddian* pledge]

we'd (wēd) **1** We had. **2** We would.

Wed·dell Sea (wed'l) An embayment of the South Atlantic in Antarctica, SE of the Palmer Peninsula and of South America.

wed·ding (wed'ing) *n.* **1** The ceremony of a marriage with the attendant nuptial festivities; also, the ceremony alone; originally, a betrothal. **2** The anniversary or celebration of a marriage. Such weddings are named from the character of the presents regarded as appropriate: golden *wedding* (50th); for list, see under ANNIVERSARY. See synonyms under MARRIAGE. [OE *weddung* < *weddian* pledge]

wedding cake A very rich fruit or pound cake served at a wedding reception, and also often divided among absent friends.

We·de·kind (vā'də·kint), **(Benjamin) Frank·lin**, 1864–1918, German poet and playwright.

wedge (wej) *n.* **1** One of the so-called mechanical powers, consisting of a double inclined plane; specifically, a V-shaped piece of metal, wood, etc., used for splitting substances, raising weights, and the like. **2** Anything in the form of a wedge, as a piece of pie; specifically, a formation, as of soldiers or football players, arranged like a wedge. **3** A right triangular prism, having one very acute angle. **4** Any one of the triangular characters used in cuneiform writing. **5** *Meteorol.* **a** A wedge-shaped area of high barometric pressure as shown on a weather map. **b** An air mass advancing in the form of a wedge. **6** Any action or procedure which facilitates a change in policy, entrance, intrusion, etc.: also **entering**

wedge. — *v.* **wedged, wedg·ing** *v.t.* **1** To force apart or split with or as with a wedge; rend; rive. **2** To compress or fix in place with a wedge. **3** To crowd or squeeze (something). — *v.i.* **4** To force oneself or itself in like a wedge. [OE *wecg*]

wedg·ie (wej'ē) *n. Colloq.* A kind of shoe worn by women, having a wedge-shaped piece making a solid sole, flat on the ground from heel to toe.

Wedg·wood (wej'wŏŏd') *n.* Any of various fine, hard earthenwares invented by Josiah Wedgwood, characterized by an unglazed, tinted clay background bearing small, finely detailed, classical figures in cameo relief applied in white paste. It is typically tinted either light or dark blue, but **Wedgwood bamboo ware** (yellow), **Wedgwood basalt** (black), and **Wedgwood queen's** (cream-colored) are also famous. Also **Wedgwood ware.**

Wedg·wood (wej'wŏŏd), **Josiah**, 1730–95, English potter; inventor of the ware bearing his name. — **Josiah Clement**, 1872–1943, first Baron Wedgwood of Barlaston, English naval architect and statesman; great-great-grandson of the preceding: called the "Father of the Labour Party."

Wedgwood blue Either of two shades of blue, a light grayish blue and a dark reddish blue: the typical blues of the Wedgwood wares.

wedg·y (wej'ē) *adj.* Having the form or uses of a wedge; cuneal.

wed·lock (wed'lok) *n.* The ceremony of marriage, or the state of being married; matrimony. See synonyms under MARRIAGE. [OE *wedlāc* < *wed* a pledge + *-lāc*, suffix of nouns of action]

Wednes·day (wenz'dē, -dā) *n.* The fourth day of the week. [OE *Wōdnes dæg* day of Woden, trans. of LL *Mercurii dies* day of Mercury]

wee (wē) *adj.* **we·er, we·est** Very small; tiny. — *n. Scot.* A short time or space; a bit: *bide a wee.* [ME *wei*, OE *wēg, wēge* a quantity]

weed[1] (wēd) *n.* **1** Any unsightly or troublesome plant that grows in abundance; especially, any coarse, herbaceous plant growing to injurious excess on cultivated or fallow ground where it is not wanted, as dock, ragweed, etc. **2** *Colloq.* Tobacco: usually with *the*; also, a cigarette or cigar. **3** Any worthless animal or thing; specifically, a horse that is unfit for racing or breeding. **4** The stem and leaves of any useful plant as distinguished from its flower and fruit: The plant runs to *weed.* **5** *Obs.* Thick, luxuriant growth, as of underbrush or shrubs. — *v.t.* **1** To pull up and remove weeds from: to *weed* a garden. **2** To remove (a weed): often with *out.* **3** To remove (anything regarded as harmful or undesirable): with *out.* **4** To rid of anything harmful or undesirable. — *v.i.* **5** To remove weeds, etc. [OE *wēod*] — **weed'less** *adj.*

weed[2] (wēd) *n.* **1** A token of mourning, as a band of crape, worn as part of the dress: He wore a *weed* on his hat; especially in the plural, a widow's mourning garb. **2** *Obs.* Any article of clothing. [OE *wǣd, wǣde* a garment]

Weed (wēd), **Thurlow**, 1797–1882, U.S. journalist and politician.

weed·er (wē'dər) *n.* **1** One who weeds. **2** An implement for removing weeds.

weeding hoe A narrow-bladed hoe for weeding: usually with prongs on the end opposite the blade. See illustration under HOE.

weed·y (wē'dē) *adj.* **weed·i·er, weed·i·est** **1** Having or containing a growth of weeds; abounding in weeds. **2** Of or pertaining to a weed or weeds. **3** Resembling a weed; weedlike, as in rapid, ready growth. **4** *Colloq.* Gawky; awkward; ungainly: *weedy* youths. — **weed'i·ly** *adv.* — **weed'i·ness** *n.*

wee folk The fairies, elves, etc.

Wee·haw·ken (wē'hô·kən) A township in NE New Jersey opposite the Hudson River from New York City; scene of the fatal wounding of Alexander Hamilton in a duel with Aaron Burr, 1804.

week (wēk) *n.* **1** A period of seven successive days; especially, such a period beginning with Sunday. **2** The period of time within a week devoted to work: The office has a 35-hour *week.* **3** A period of seven days preceding or following any given day or date: *a week* from

Tuesday. ◆ Homophone: *weak.* [OE *wicu, wice*]

week·day (wēk'dā') *n.* Any day of the week except Sunday.

week·end (wēk'end') *n.* The end of the week; specifically, the time from Friday evening or Saturday noon to the following Monday morning. — *v.i.* To pass the week-end: We *week-ended* in the country.

week-end·er (wēk'en'dər) *n.* One who goes on week-end vacation trips.

Week·ley (wēk'lē), **Ernest**, 1865–1954, English lexicographer and etymologist.

week·ly (wēk'lē) *adv.* Once a week; especially, at regular seven-day intervals. — *adj.* **1** Of or pertaining to a week or to weekdays. **2** Done or occurring once a week; also, reckoned by the week; hebdomadal. — *n. pl.* **·lies** A publication issued once a week.

weel (wēl) *adj., adv., & interj. Scot.* Well.

Weems (wēmz), **Mason Locke**, 1759–1825, American clergyman and biographer: known as *Parson Weems.*

ween (wēn) *v.t. & v.i. Archaic* To suppose; guess; fancy. [OE *wēnan* think]

ween·di·jo (wēn'də·jō) See WINDIGO.

ween·ie (wē'nē) *n. Colloq.* A wiener.

weep[1] (wēp) *v.* **wept, weep·ing** *v.i.* **1** To manifest grief or other strong emotion by shedding tears: to *weep* for joy. **2** To mourn; lament: with *for.* **3** To give out or shed water or other liquid in drops, as the stems of some plants under pressure; bleed. — *v.t.* **4** To weep for; mourn or bewail. **5** To shed (tears, or drops of other liquid). **6** To bring to a specified condition by weeping: to *weep* oneself to sleep. — *n.* The act of weeping, or a fit of tears. [OE *wēpan*]

weep[2] (wēp) *n.* A lapwing; pewit. [Imit.]

weep·er (wē'pər) *n.* **1** One who weeps, as a hired mourner. **2** A long piece of black crape worn as a sign of mourning, customarily hanging down from the hat. **3** A pendant of moss, as from a branch. **4** A hole through which water may drip.

weep·ing (wē'ping) *adj.* **1** That weeps; crying; tearful. **2** Having slim, pendulous branches: the *weeping* ash.

weeping ash A variety of the common European ash (*Fraxinus excelsior pendula*) with drooping branches.

WEEPING WILLOW
a. Leaves. *b.* Catkin. *c.* Tree.

weeping willow An Old World willow (*Salix babylonica*), remarkable for its long, slender, pendulous branches.

weet (wēt) *n.* **1** The imitation of the call of various birds. **2** The peetweet, or common European sandpiper. [Imit.]

wee·ver (wē'vər) *n.* Any of various edible marine fishes (genus *Trachinus*), having upward-looking eyes and sharp dorsal and opercular spines, with which they can inflict serious wounds. [<AF *wivre*, OF *guivre*, orig. a serpent, dragon <L *vipera* a viper]

wee·vil (wē'vəl) *n.* **1** Any of numerous small beetles (family *Curculionidae*) with elongated snoutlike heads which bear the mouth parts at the end and the antennae along the sides: also called *curculio.* Weevil larvae feed on plants and plant products, especially flowers, fruits, and trees; many are serious pests. **2** Any insect injurious to stored grain. [OE *wifel* a beetle] — **wee'vil·y, wee'vil·ly** *adj.*

weft (weft) *n.* **1** The cross-threads in a web

of cloth; woof. **2** A woven fabric; web. [OE. Akin to WEAVE, WEB.]

Wehr·macht (vâr′mäkht) *n. German* The armed forces, collectively, of Germany: literally, defense force.

Wei (wā) A river in NW central China, flowing 540 miles east from SE Kansu province to the Yellow River.

Weich·sel (vīkh′səl) The German name for the Vistula.

wei·ge·la (wī·gē′lə, -jē′-, wī′jə·lə) *n.* Any of a large genus (*Weigela*) of deciduous Asian shrubs of the honeysuckle family; especially, *W. florida*, cultivated extensively in the United States for its profusion of dark rose-purple flowers. [<NL, after Dr. C. E. *Weigel*, 1748–1831, German physician]

weigh[1] (wā) *v.t.* **1** To determine the weight of, as by measuring on a scale or balance. **2** To balance or hold in the hand so as to estimate weight or heaviness. **3** To measure (a quantity or quantities of something) according to weight: with *out.* **4** To consider carefully; estimate the worth or advantages of: to *weigh* a proposal. **5** To press or force down by weight or heaviness; burden or oppress: with *down.* **6** To raise or hoist: now only in the phrase *to weigh anchor.* **7** *Obs.* To think well of; esteem; regard. — *v.i.* **8** To have weight; be heavy to a specified degree: She *weighs* ninety pounds. **9** To have influence or importance: The girl's testimony *weighed* heavily with the jury. **10** To be burdensome or oppressive: with *on* or *upon:* What *weighs* on your mind? **11** *Naut.* **a** To raise anchor. **b** To begin to sail. See synonyms under CONSIDER, DELIBERATE, EXAMINE. **— to weigh in 1** Of a prize fighter or other contestant, to be weighed before a contest. **2** In racing, to be weighed, as a jockey, after a race. **— to weigh one's words** To consider one's words carefully before speaking them. **— to weigh out** In racing, to be weighed, as a jockey, before a race. ◆ Homophone: *way.* [OE *wegan* weight, carry, lift] **— weigh′er** *n.*

weigh[2] (wā) *n.* Way: used in the phrase *under weigh* by mistaken analogy with *aweigh.* See AWEIGH. ◆ Homophone: *way.* [Var. of WAY; infl. in form by *weigh*[1], in phrase "weigh anchor"]

weight (wāt) *n.* **1** The measure of the force with which bodies tend toward the earth's center, or the quality thus measured. The weight of a body is a product of its mass and the acceleration due to gravity. **2** Any object or mass which weighs a definite or specific amount. **3** A definite mass of brass, iron, or other metal, used in weighing machines as a standard; any unit of heaviness, as a pound, ounce, etc. **4** Any mass used as a counterpoise or to exert pressure by force of gravity: a *paperweight.* **5** Burden; pressure; oppressiveness: the *weight* of care; the *weight* of an attack. **6** Any quantity of heaviness, expressed indefinitely or in terms of standard units. **7** The relative tendency of any mass toward a center of superior mass: the *weight* of a planet. **8** A scale or graduated system of standard units of weight: avoirdupois *weight.* See tables below; see also under METRIC SYSTEM. **9** Influence; importance; consequence: a man of *weight.* **10** The comparative heaviness of clothes, as appropriate to the season: summer *weight.* **11** *Stat.* **a** The relative value of an item in a statistical compilation. **b** The frequency of its occurrence among related items, or the number used to express such frequency. — *v.t.* **1** To add weight to; make heavy. **2** To oppress or burden. **3** To adulterate or treat (fabrics or other merchandise) with cheap foreign substances. **4** *Stat.* To give weight to. [OE *wiht, gewiht*]

Synonyms (noun): burden, gravity, heaviness, import, load, moment. See LOAD.

AVOIRDUPOIS WEIGHT

27.34+ grains (gr.)	=	1 dram (dr. av.)
16 drams av.	=	1 ounce (oz. av.)
16 ounces av.	=	1 pound (lb., lbs. av.)
2000 pounds av.	=	1 short ton (sh. tn.)
2240 pounds av.	=	1 long ton (l. tn.)

TROY WEIGHT

24 grains	=	1 pennyweight (dwt.)
20 pennyweight	=	1 ounce (oz. t.)
12 ounces	=	1 pound (lb., lbs. t.)

weight·less (wāt′lis) *adj.* **1** Having little or no heaviness. **2** Subject to little or no gravitational force. **— weight′less·ly** *adv.* **— weight′-less·ness** *n.*

weight·y (wā′tē) *adj.* **weight·i·er, weight·i·est 1** Having great weight; ponderous. **2** Having power to move the mind; cogent. **3** Of great importance. **4** Influential, as in public affairs. **5** Burdensome. See synonyms under HEAVY, IMPORTANT. **— weight′i·ly** *adv.* — **weight′i·ness** *n.*

Wei·hai (wā′hī′) A port and naval base in NE Shantung province, NE China; leased with the surrounding area (285 square miles) to Great Britain, 1898–1930. Formerly **Wei·hai·wei** (wā′hī′wā′).

Wei·mar (vī′mär) A city in SW East Germany, formerly capital of Thuringia.

Wei·mar·an·er (vī′mər·ä′nər) *n.* A breed of dog of the hound type, blue- or amber-eyed, gray in color, used for hunting and as a watchdog. [from *Weimar*, Germany, where the breed originated]

weir (wir) *n.* **1** An obstruction placed in a stream to raise the water, divert it into a millrace or irrigation ditches, or form a fish pond; a dam. **2** A series of wattled enclosures in a stream, to catch fish. [OE *wer* < *werian* dam up]

Weir (wir), **Robert Walter**, 1803–89, and his sons, **John Ferguson**, 1841–1926, and **Julian Alden**, 1852–1919, U. S. painters.

weird (wird) *adj.* **1** Concerned with the unnatural or with witchcraft; unearthly; uncanny. **2** Pertaining to or having to do with fate or the Fates. **— the Weird Sisters 1** The Fates. **2** The three witches in Shakespeare's *Macbeth.* — *n. Scot.* **1** One's allotted fate; fortune. **2** Destiny; fate. **3** One of the Fates. **4** A prophecy; prediction. **5** A spell; enchantment. [OE *wyrd* fate]

weird·o (wir′dō) *n. pl.* **·os** *Slang* A person who is strange or eccentric. Also **weird′ie, weird′y** (-dē).

Weis·mann (vīs′män), **August,** 1834–1914, German biologist. — **Weis·man·ni·an** (vīs·män′ē·ən) *adj. & n.*

Weis·mann·ism (vīs′män·iz′əm) *n.* The theory of evolution, as propounded by August Weismann, which asserts the continuity of the germ plasm within but in isolation from the soma, and denies the heritability by offspring of characters acquired by the parents during their lifetime.

weiss beer (vīs) A light, whitish beer, brewed usually from wheat. [<G *weissbier* pale Berlin beer, lit., white beer]

Weis·sen·fels (vī′sən·fels) A city in south central East Germany.

Weiss·horn (vīs′hôrn) A peak in southern Switzerland; 14,804 feet.

Weiz·mann (wīts′mən, vīts′män), **Chaim,** 1874–1952, Israeli chemist and Zionist leader; first president of Israel 1948–52; born in Russian Poland.

we·jack (wē′jak) *n.* The fisher or pekan. [<Algonquian. Cf. Cree *otchek.*]

we·ka (wē′kə, wā′-) *n.* A wingless rail (genus *Ocydroma*) of New Zealand, now nearly extinct; also called **woodhen.** [<Maori]

welch (welch, welsh) See WELSH.

Welch (welch, welsh) See WELSH.

Welch (welch), **William Henry,** 1850–1934, U.S. pathologist and sanitarian.

wel·come (wel′kəm) *adj.* **1** Admitted gladly to a place or festivity; received cordially: a *welcome* guest. **2** Producing satisfaction or pleasure; pleasing: *welcome* tidings. **3** Made free to use or enjoy: She is *welcome* to my purse. See synonyms under AGREEABLE, DELIGHTFUL. — *n.* The act of bidding or making welcome; a hearty greeting given or cordial reception accorded to a guest or visitor. **— to wear out one's welcome** To come so often or to linger so long as no longer to be welcome. — *v.t.* **·comed, ·com·ing 1** To give a welcome to; greet gladly or hospitably. **2** To receive with pleasure: to *welcome* constructive advice. [OE *wilcuma* < *will-* will, pleasure + *cuma* a guest; infl. in form by WELL[2] and COME, on analogy with OF *bien venu*] — **wel′come·ly** *adv.* — **wel′come·ness** *n.* — **wel′com·er** *n.*

weld[1] (weld) *v.t.* **1** To unite, as two pieces of metal, with or without pressure, by the application of heat along the area of contact. **2** To bring into close association or connection. — *v.i.* **3** To admit of being welded. — *n.* The consolidation of pieces of metal by welding; also, the closed joint so formed. [Alter of WELL[1], *v.*] — **weld′a·bil′·i·ty** *n.* — **weld′a·ble** *adj.* — **weld′er** *n.*

weld[2] (weld) *n.* **1** An erect Old World annual (*Reseda luteola*), formerly cultivated for dyers' use: also called *yellowweed.* **2** The yellow pigment obtained from it: also spelled *woald.* [ME *welde.* Cf. MLG *walde*, MDu. *woude.*]

wel·fare (wel′fâr) *n.* **1** The condition of faring well; exemption from pain or discomfort; prosperity; also, condition, as regards well-being: Inquire concerning thy brethren's *welfare.* **2** Organized efforts by a community or organization to improve the social and economic condition of a group or class: also **welfare work. 3** Money, food, clothing, etc., given to those in need; relief. **— on welfare** Receiving money, food, clothing, etc., from a local or other government because of need. [ME *wel fare* < *wel* well + *fare* a going <OE *faran* go]

Welfare Island An island in the East River, New York City; 139 acres; site of two municipal hospitals: formerly *Blackwell's Island.*

welfare state A state or polity in which the government assumes a large measure of responsibility for the social welfare of its members, as through unemployment and health insurance, etc.

wel·kin (wel′kin) *n. Archaic* or *Poetic* **1** The vault of the sky; the heavens. **2** The air. [OE *wolcn, wolcen* a cloud]

well[1] (wel) *n.* **1** A hole or shaft sunk into the earth to obtain a fluid, as water, oil, brine, or natural gas. **2** A spring of water; a place where water issues from the ground; a fountain. **3** A source of continued supply, or that which issues forth continuously; a wellspring: a *well* of learning. **4** A depression, cavity, or vessel resembling a well: an *inkwell.* **5** A cavity in the lower part of some sorts of furnaces to receive falling metal. **6** In an English law court, the railed-in space between the bench and the bar, reserved for solicitors. **7** *Archit.* **a** The vertical opening contained within a winding staircase. **b** A similar opening descending through floors, or a deep enclosed space in a building for light or ventilation: an air *well;* an elevator *well.* **8** *Naut.* The boxed-in space in a vessel's hold, enclosing the pumps. **9** A compartment admitting water, in which fish are preserved alive. — *v.i.* To pour forth or flow up, as water in a spring. — *v.t.* To gush: Her eyes *welled* tears. [OE *wielle* < *weallan* boil, bubble up]

well[2] (wel) *adv.* **bet·ter, best 1** Satisfactorily; favorably; according to one's wishes: Everything goes *well.* **2** In a good or correct manner; properly; excellently; expertly: to dance or speak *well.* **3** Suitably; befittingly; with reason or propriety: I cannot *well* remain here. **4** In a successful manner; prosperously; also, agreeably or luxuriously: He lives *well.* **5** Intimately: How *well* do you know him? **6** To a large or proper extent or degree; plentifully: a *well*-stocked larder. **7** Completely; wholly. **8** Far; at some distance: He lagged *well* behind us. **— as well 1** Also; in addition. **2** With equal effect or consequence: He might just *as well* have sold it. **— as well as 1** As satisfactorily as. **2** To the same degree as. **3** In addition to. — *adj.* **1** Satisfactory; rightly done or arranged; fortunate; suitable; gratifying: also used in the predicate position: It is *well.* **2** Having physical health; free from ailment of mind or body. **3** Prosperous; comfortable. — *interj.* An exclamation used to express surprise, expectation, resignation, doubt, indignation, etc., or merely to preface a remark. [OE *wel.* Akin to WEAL.]

Synonyms (adj.): advantageous, beneficial, convenient, desirable, excellent, expedient, favorable, fortunate, good, happy, lucky, prosperous. See HEALTHY. *Antonyms:* see synonyms for BAD.

Well may appear as a combining form in hyphemes when joined to participles to form unit modifiers; thus, predicatively, His words were *well* chosen; but attributively, his *well-chosen* words. The following examples are self-explanatory:

well-accepted	well-acquainted
well-accustomed	well-acted
well-acknowledged	well-adjusted

well–administered	well–knit
well–aimed	well–liked
well–aired	well–looking
well–armed	well–loved
well–armored	well–made
well–arranged	well–managed
well–assorted	well–mannered
well–assured	well–measured
well–attested	well–ordered
well–attired	well–paid
well–authenticated	well–phrased
well–behaved	well–placed
well–beloved	well–planned
well–built	well–pleased
well–chaperoned	well–pleasing
well–chosen	well–poised
well–considered	well–prepared
well–contented	well–preserved
well–covered	well–proportioned
well–cultivated	well–recognized
well–defended	well–regulated
well–defined	well–remembered
well–deserving	well–rooted
well–digested	well–seasoned
well–disciplined	well–selected
well–done	well–skilled
well–dressed	well–spent
well–earned	well–stocked
well–educated	well–swept
well–established	well–timed
well–financed	well–trained
well–fitted	well–trimmed
well–formed	well–understood
well–fortified	well–used
well–fought	well–versed
well–furnished	well–wooded
well–governed	well–worded
well–handled	well–worn
well–informed	well–woven
well–judged	well–written
. well–kept	well–wrought

we'll (wel) We shall;)we will: a contraction.

Wel·land (wel'ənd) A city in southern Ontario, on the **Welland Ship Canal**, a waterway (28 miles long) connecting Lake Ontario with Lake Erie.

well–ap·point·ed (wel'ə-poin'tid) *adj.* Properly equipped; excellently furnished.

well·a·way (wel'ə-wā') *interj. Obs.* Woe is me! alas! Also **well'a·day'**. [OE *wei lā wei,* alter. of *wā lā wā* woe! lo! woe!; infl. in form by ON *vei* woe]

well–bal·anced (wel'bal'ənst) *adj.* Evenly balanced; adjusted with reference to welfare.

well–be·ing (wel'bē'ing) *n.* A condition of happiness or prosperity; welfare.

well–born (wel'bôrn') *adj.* Of good lineage.

well–bred (wel'bred') *adj.* **1** Well brought up; polite. **2** Of good ancestry; of good or pure stock.

well–curb (wel'kûrb') *n.* The frame or stone ring around the mouth of a well.

well–dis·posed (wel'dis·pōzd') *adj.* Favorably inclined.

well–do·er (wel'dōō'ər) *n.* **1** A performer of moral and social duties. **2** *Scot. & Brit. Dial.* One who is prosperous or well–to–do. — **well'–do'ing** *adj. & n.*

Wel·le (we'lā) See UELE.

well enough Tolerably good or satisfactory. — **to let well enough alone** To leave things as they are lest the result of interference be worse.

Welles (welz), **Gideon,** 1802–78, U.S. politician and writer. — **(George) Orson,** born 1915, U.S. actor and producer. — **Sumner,** 1892–1961, U.S. diplomat.

Welles·ley (welz'lē), **Richard Colley,** 1760–1842, first Marquis of Wellesley, British statesman; brother of the Duke of Wellington.

well–fa·vored (wel'fā'vərd) *adj.* Of attractive appearance; comely; handsome. Also *Brit.* **well'–fa'voured.**

well–fed (wel'fed') *adj.* Plump; fat; sleek.

well–fixed (wel'fikst') *adj. Colloq.* Affluent; well–to–do.

well–found (wel'found') *adj.* **1** Found to meet expectations. **2** Well equipped.

well–found·ed (wel'foun'did) *adj.* Based on fact: *well–founded* suspicions.

well–groomed (wel'grōōmd') *adj.* **1** Carefully curried, as a horse. **2** Carefully dressed and scrupulously neat; having a fashionable, sleek appearance.

well–ground·ed (wel'groun'did) *adj.* **1** Ade-

quately schooled in the elements of a subject. **2** Well–founded.

well·head (wel'hed') *n.* A natural source supplying water to a spring or well.

well–heeled (wel'hēld') *adj. Slang* Plentifully supplied with money. [< WELL² + HEEL¹, *v.* (def. 6)]

Wel·ling·ton (wel'ing·tən) The capital of New Zealand, a port on southern North Island.

Wel·ling·ton (wel'ing·tən), **Duke of,** 1769–1852, Arthur Wellesley, British general; defeated Napoleon at Waterloo; prime minister; born in Ireland.

Wellington boot A high boot covering the leg as far as the knee in front but cut away behind.

well–in·ten·tioned (wel'in·ten'shənd) *adj.* Having good intentions; well–meant: often with connotation of failure or of clumsy or harmful execution.

well–known (wel'nōn') *adj.* Widely known; famous.

well–mean·ing (wel'mē'ning) *adj.* Having good intentions. — **well'–meant'** (-ment') *adj.*

well met Welcome.

well–nigh (wel'nī') *adv.* Very nearly; almost.

well–off (wel'ôf', -of') *adj.* In comfortable circumstances; wealthy; fortunate.

well–read (wel'red') *adj.* Having a wide knowledge of literature or books; having read much: usually with *in.*

Wells (welz) A municipal borough in east central Somerset, England; noted for its 12th century cathedral.

Wells (welz), **Henry,** 1805–78, U.S. express operator; organized Wells, Fargo & Co. in 1852. — **H(erbert) G(eorge),** 1866–1946, English author.

wells·ite (welz'īt) *n.* A vitreous hydrated silicate of barium, calcium, potassium, and aluminum, crystallizing in the monoclinic system. [after H. L. *Wells,* 1855–1924, U.S. chemist]

well–spo·ken (wel'spō'kən) *adj.* **1** Fitly or excellently said. **2** Of gentle speech and manners.

well·spring (wel'spring') *n.* **1** An inexhaustible fountain. **2** A source of continual supply.

well sweep A long tapering pole swung on a pivot attached to a high post, and having the bucket suspended from one end, for use in drawing water.

well–thought–of (wel'thôt'uv', -ov') *adj.* In good repute; esteemed; respected.

WELL SWEEP

well–to–do (wel'tə·dōō') *adj.* In prosperous circumstances; evincing a state of comfort or wealth.

well–wish·er (wel'wish'ər) *n.* One who wishes well, as to another. — **well'–wish'ing** *adj. & n.*

Wels·bach (welz'bak, *Ger.* vels'bäkh), **Baron Carl Auer von,** 1858–1929, Austrian chemist and inventor.

Welsbach burner A burner of the Bunsen type, having a cotton–gauze mantle impregnated with thoria and ceria, so arranged that upon ignition of a mixture of gases the mantle becomes incandescent. [after Baron Carl A. von *Welsbach*]

welsh (welsh, welch) *v.t. & v.i. Slang* **1** To cheat by failing to pay a bet or debt. **2** To avoid fulfilling (an obligation). Also spelled *welch.* [? Back formation < *welsher,* prob. < *Welsher* a Welshman, with ref. to supposed national traits]

Welsh (welsh, welch) *adj.* Pertaining to Wales, its people, or their language. — *n.* **1** The natives of Wales, a people of Celtic stock: with *the*: also called *Cymry.* **2** The language of Wales, belonging to the Brythonic or Cymric group of the Celtic subfamily of Indo–European languages: also called *Cymric.* Also spelled *Welch.* [OE *Welisc < wealh* a foreigner (one not of Saxon origin)] — **Welsh'·man** *n.*

Welsh cor·gi (kôr'gē) *n.* Either of two ancient breeds of a Welsh working dog, characterized by a long body, short legs, and erect ears:

the **Cardigan Welsh corgi** has a long tail, the **Pembroke Welsh corgi** a short tail. [< Welsh < *corr* dwarf + *ci* dog]

Welsh rabbit A concoction of melted cheese cooked in cream or milk, often with ale or beer added, and served hot on toast or crackers. ◆ The form *rarebit* was a later development and is the result of mistaken etymology.

welt (welt) *n.* **1** A strip of material, covered cord, etc., applied to a seam to cover or strengthen it. **2** In shoemaking, a strip of leather set into the seam between the edges of the upper and the outer sole. **3** In carpentry, a batten or strip made fast over a flush seam. **4** A wale or stripe raised on the skin by a blow. — *v.t.* **1** To sew a welt on or in; decorate with a welt. **2** *Colloq.* To flog severely, so as to raise welts or wales. [ME *welte, walt.* Cf. OE *weltan* roll.]

Welt·an·schau·ung (velt'än·shou'ŏŏng) *n. German* Literally, world viewing; philosophy of life: a comprehensive philosophy regarding the cosmos; ideology.

Welt·an·sicht (velt'än·zikht) *n. German* Literally, world view; a special view or interpretation of reality, seen as a whole.

wel·ter¹ (wel'tər) *v.i.* **1** To roll about; wallow. **2** To lie or be soaked in some fluid, as blood. **3** To surge or move tumultuously, as the sea. — *n.* **1** A rolling movement, as of waves; hence, commotion. **2** That in which weltering is done; a wallow. [<MDu. *welteren*]

wel·ter² (wel'tər) *adj.* Designating or pertaining to a horse race in which welterweights are carried. [< *welter* a heavyweight (horseman), ? <WELT, *v.* (def. 2)]

welter race A horse race in which heavy weights are imposed on the horses, in order to permit amateur jockeys to ride.

wel·ter·weight (wel'tər·wāt') *n.* **1** The weight (regularly 28, sometimes 40 pounds, in addition to weight for age) borne by a horse running in a welter race; hence, loosely, a heavyweight. **2** A boxer whose fighting weight is between 135 and 147 pounds. [< *welter* a heavyweight + WEIGHT]

Welt·lit·e·ra·tur (velt'lit'ə·rä·tōōr') *n. German* World literature.

Welt·po·li·tik (velt'pō·li·tēk') *n. German* International politics; world policy.

Welt·schmerz (velt'shmerts) *n. German* World–weariness; melancholy pessimism over the state of the world; romantic discontent.

Wem·bley (wem'blē) A municipal borough of Middlesex, England, 8 miles NW of London.

Wemyss (wēmz) A parish on the Firth of Forth, central Fifeshire, Scotland.

wen¹ (wen) *n.* **1** *Pathol.* Any encysted tumor containing a suetlike substance, occurring commonly on the scalp. **2** Any protuberance. [OE *wenn, wænn*] — **wen'nish, wen'ny** *adj.*

wen² (wen) *n.* The old English rune Þ, replaced by modern English w. [OE, var. of *wynn* joy]

Wen·ces·laus (wen'səs·lôs), 1361–1419, Holy Roman Emperor 1378–1400; king of Bohemia 1378–1419. Also **Wen'ces·las** (-läs), *Ger.* **Wenzel** (ven'tsəl), **Wen·zes·laus** (ven'tsəs·lous).

wench (wench) *n.* **1** A young peasant woman; also, a female servant; maid. **2** Any young woman; girl; maiden. **3** *Archaic* A prostitute; strumpet. — *v.i.* To keep company with strumpets. [ME *wenche,* short for *wenchel* <OE *wencel* a child, servant]

Wen·chow (wen'chou', *Chinese* wun'jō') A port on the Wu (def. 2) and chief city of SE Chekiang province, central eastern China.

wend (wend) *v.t. & v.i.* To direct (one's course); go. [OE *wendan*]

Wend (wend) *n.* One of a Slavic people now occupying the region between the Elbe and Oder rivers in Saxony and Prussia; a Sorb. [<G *Wende, Winde*]

Wen·dat (wen'dat) See WYANDOT.

Wen·dell (wen'dəl), **Barrett,** 1855–1921, U.S. scholar.

Wend·ish (wen'dish) *adj.* Of or pertaining to the Wends or their language; Sorbian. — *n.* The West Slavic language of the Wends; Sorbian. Also **Wend'ic.**

went (went) An obsolete past tense and past participle of *wend,* now used as past tense of GO.

wen·tle·trap (wen′tǝl·trap′) *n.* Any of a genus (*Epitonium*) or family (*Epitoniidae*) of mollusks, having a white, turreted, many-whorled shell. [<Du. *wenteltrap* a spiral staircase or shell]

wept (wept) Past tense and past participle of WEEP.

were (wûr, *unstressed* wǝr) Plural and second person singular past indicative, and past subjunctive singular and plural of BE. [OE *wǣre, wǣron*, pt. forms of *wesan* be]

we're (wir) We are: a contraction.

wer·en't (wûr′ǝnt) Were not: a contraction.

were·wolf (wir′woolf′, wûr′-) *n. pl.* **·wolves** (-woolvz′) In European folklore, a human being transformed into a wolf by bewitchment, or one having power to assume wolf form at will. Also **wer′wolf**. [OE *werwulf* man-wolf < *wer* a man + *wulf* a wolf]

Wer·fel (ver′fǝl), **Franz**, 1890–1945, German novelist, poet, and dramatist.

wer·geld (wûr′geld) *n.* In Anglo-Saxon and Teutonic law, a fine or pecuniary compensation for crime against the person, especially for homicide, paid by the kindred of the slayer to those of the slain. Also **were′gild** (-gild), **wer′gelt** (-gelt). [OE, lit., man-yield, *i.e.*, man-price < *wer* a man + *geld, gield* yield]

Wer·ner (ver′nǝr), **Alfred**, 1866–1919, Swiss chemist.

wer·ner·ite (wûr′nǝr·īt) *n.* Scapolite. [after A. G. Werner, 1750–1817, German mineralogist]

wert (wûrt, *unstressed* wǝrt) Archaic second person singular, past tense of both indicative and subjunctive of BE: used with *thou*.

Wes·cott (wes′kot), **Glenway**, born 1901, U.S. novelist and poet.

we'se (wēz) 1 *Dial.* We is: a mistake for *we are*: *We'se* going. 2 *Scot.* We shall.

We·ser (vā′zǝr) A river in east and north central West Germany, flowing 300 miles north to the North Sea.

Wes·ley (wes′lē, *Brit.* wez′lē), **Charles**, 1707?–1788, English clergyman and hymn writer; brother of John Wesley. —**John**, 1703–91, English clergyman; founder of Methodism.

Wes·ley·an (wes′lē·ǝn, *Brit.* wez′lē·ǝn) *adj.* Of or pertaining to the Wesleys, especially John Wesley, as the founder of Methodism. —*n.* A disciple of John Wesley; a Methodist. —**Wes′·ley·an·ism** *n.*

Wes·sex (wes′iks) The ancient kingdom of the West Saxons, including modern Berkshire, Dorset, Hampshire, Somerset, and Wiltshire in southern England.

west (west) *n.* **1** The point of the compass at which the sun sets at the equinox, directly opposite *east*. See COMPASS CARD. **2** Any direction, region, or part of the horizon near that point. —**the West 1** The countries lying west of Asia and Turkey; the Occident. **2** The western hemisphere, discovered by explorers sailing westward from Europe. **3** The Western Roman Empire. **4** In the United States: **a** Formerly, the region west of the Allegheny Mountains. **b** The region west of the Mississippi, especially the northwestern part of this region. —*adj.* **1** To, toward, facing, or placed in the west; western. **2** Coming from the west: the *west* wind. **3** Designating or located in that part of a church directly opposite the altar. —*adv.* In or toward the west; in a westerly direction. —**go West, young man** Go settle in the unsettled western regions of the United States, a land of little competition and unusual opportunity: advice usually attributed to Horace Greeley. [OE]

West (west), **Benjamin**, 1738–1820, American painter. —**Rebecca** Pseudonym of Cicily Isabel Fairfield, born 1892, English novelist and critic.

West Bengal See under BENGAL.

west·bound (west′bound′) *adj.* Going westward. Also **west′bound′**.

West Brom·wich (brum′ich, -ij) A county borough in southern Stafford, England, just NW of Birmingham.

west by north One point north of west on the mariner's compass. See COMPASS CARD.

west by south One point south of west on the mariner's compass. See COMPASS CARD.

West·cott (west′kot), **Edward Noyes**, 1846–1898, U.S. banker and novelist.

West End The western part of London, England; includes parks and a fashionable shopping district and notable residential section.

west·er (wes′tǝr) *v.i.* To turn, trend, or shift to the west.—*n.* A wind, especially a storm, blowing from the west. [<WEST + -ER⁵]

west·er·ing (wes′tǝr·ing) *adj.* Moving or turning westward: the *westering* sun. —*n.* Movement or declension toward the west.

west·er·ly (wes′tǝr·lē) *adj.* **1** In, toward, or of the west. **2** From the west: a *westerly* wind. —*n. pl.* **·lies** A wind blowing from the west. —*adv.* **1** From the west. **2** Toward the west. —**west′er·li·ness** *n.*

Wes·ter·marck (ves′tǝr·märk), **Edward Alexander**, 1862–1939, Finnish anthropologist.

west·ern (wes′tǝrn) *adj.* **1** Being in the west; of, pertaining to, or directed toward the west. **2** Coming from the west: the *western* winds. —*n.* **1** A westerner. **2** A type of fiction or motion picture using cowboy and pioneer life in the western United States as its material.

West·ern (wes′tǝrn) *adj.* **1** Proceeding from or characteristic of the West; Occidental. **2** Belonging or pertaining to the Western Church: *Western* ritual. **3** Of or pertaining to the western part of the United States of America. —*n.* A person identified with or belonging to the Western Church.

Western Australia The largest state of the Commonwealth of Australia, including all of the Australian continent west of 129° E.; about 975,920 square miles; capital, Perth.

Western Church The medieval church of the Western Roman Empire, now the Roman Catholic Church: distinguished from the church of the Eastern Empire, now the Greek or Eastern Church.

Western Dvina See DVINA (def. 2).

west·ern·er (wes′tǝr·nǝr) *n.* One who dwells in a western region, especially in the western United States.

western frontier Formerly, that part of the United States bordering on the west in still unsettled regions.

western hemisphere See under HEMISPHERE.

Western Islands The Hebrides.

west·ern·ism (wes′tǝr·niz′ǝm) *n.* An expression or practice peculiar to the West, especially the western United States.

west·ern·ize (wes′tǝr·nīz) *v.t.* **·ized, ·iz·ing** To make western in characteristics, habits, etc. —**west′ern·i·za·tion** *n.*

Western Ocean In ancient geography, the ocean lying westward of the known world; hence, the Atlantic Ocean.

Western Reserve A region now comprising ten counties in the NE portion of Ohio, on Lake Erie from the Pennsylvania border to near Sandusky, Ohio, reserved by Connecticut for her settlers when she ceded her western lands to the Federal Government in 1786, but relinquished in 1800.

Western (Roman) Empire The part of the Roman Empire west of the Adriatic, which existed as a separate empire from 395 A.D. until the fall of Rome in 476 A.D.

Western Samoa See SAMOA.

Western Turkestan See under TURKESTAN.

Western Wall Wailing Wall.

West Flanders A province of western Belgium; 1,249 square miles; capital, Bruges.

West Germanic See under GERMANIC.

West Germany See under GERMANY.

West Ham A county borough in Essex, England; a NE suburb of London.

West Har·tle·pool (här′tǝl·pool) A county borough on the North Sea in SE Durham, England.

West Indies A series of island groups separating the North Atlantic from the Caribbean, between North and South America, divided into the *Bahamas*, the *Greater Antilles*, and the *Lesser Antilles*. —**West Indian**

West Indies, The A former federation of British colonies in the Caribbean, including Antigua, Barbados, Dominica, Grenada, Jamaica, Montserrat, St. Lucia, St. Vincent, Trinidad and Tobago, and St. Christopher, Nevis and Anguilla; formed January, 1958; dissolved May 31, 1962.

west·ing (wes′ting) *n.* **1** Distance accomplished toward the west. **2** *Naut.* The amount by which a ship has increased her west longitude from a specified meridian.

West·ing·house (wes′ting·hous), **George**, 1846–1914, U.S. inventor.

West Ir·i·an (ir′ē·ǝn) A province of Indonesia comprising the western part of New Guinea and several adjacent islands, the former *Netherlands New Guinea;* capital, Kotabaru: also **West New Guinea.**

West Lo·thi·an (lō′thē·ǝn) A county in SE Scotland on the Firth of Forth; 120 square miles; county town, Linlithgow: formerly *Linlithgowshire.*

West·meath (west′mēth) An inland county of Leinster province, Ireland; 681 square miles; county town, Mullingar.

West·min·ster (west′min·stǝr) A city and borough in the county of London, England, on the north bank of the Thames; London's largest borough; site of the Houses of Parliament and Buckingham Palace.

Westminster Abbey A Gothic church in Westminster, London, begun in A.D. 1050; burial place of English kings and notables.

West·mor·land (west′môr·lǝnd, -mǝr-; *Brit.* west′mǝr·lǝnd) A county in the Lake District, NW England; 789 square miles; county town, Appleby.

west–north·west (west′nôrth′west′, *in nautical usage* west′nôr·west′) *adj., adv., & n.* Midway between west and northwest. See COMPASS CARD.

Wes·ton su·per Ma·re (wes′tǝn soo′pǝr mä′rē, mâr′) A resort and municipal borough on Bristol Channel, in NE Somerset, England.

West Pakistan 1 A province of Pakistan comprising all of Pakistan west of the Republic of India with the exception of the **Federal District of Pakistan** around and including Karachi (812 square miles); formed in 1955 by the merger of the former provinces of Baluchistan, North-West Frontier Province, Punjab and Sind, along with Bahawalpur, Khairpur, and the other princely states in the area; 309,424 square miles; capital, Lahore. **2** Formerly, the region comprising all of the western portion of Pakistan, including the four former provinces, the princely states, and the present federal district; 310,236 square miles.

West·pha·li·a (west·fā′lē·ǝ) A former province of Prussia, since 1945 a part of North Rhine–Westphalia, West Germany; scene of the signing of a treaty by France, Sweden, and the Holy Roman Empire at the end of the Thirty Years' War, 1648; 7,806 square miles; capital, Münster. German **West·fa·len** (vest·fä′lǝn). —**West·pha′li·an** *adj. & n.*

West Point A U.S. military reservation on the Hudson River in SE New York; seat of the United States Military Academy.

West Prussia A former province of Prussia; since 1945 under Polish administration; capital, Danzig. German **West·preus·sen** (vest′·prois′ǝn).

West Quod·dy Head (kwod′ē) The easternmost point of continental United States, a promontory on the Atlantic coast of Maine near the Canadian border.

Wes·tra·li·a (wes·trā′lē·ǝ, -trāl′yǝ) A contraction of WESTERN AUSTRALIA. —**Wes·tra′li·an** *adj. & n.*

West Riding An administrative division of SW York, England; 2,936 square miles; capital, Wakefield.

West River The chief river of southern China, flowing 1,250 miles east from eastern Yünnan province (900 miles as the Hungshui to its confluence with the Yü) to the South China Sea: Chinese *Si Kiang.*

West Saxon The dialect of Old English spoken in Wessex: preserved in most of the literature of the period.

west–south·west (west′south′west′, *in nautical usage* west′sou·west′) *adj., adv., & n.* Midway between west and southwest. See COMPASS CARD.

West Spitsbergen The largest island of the Spitsbergen group, NW Svalbard; about 15,000 square miles.

West Virginia A State of the east central United States; 24,181 square miles; capital, Charleston; entered the Union June 20, 1863; nickname, *Panhandle State:* abbr. WV. —**West Virginian**

West·wall (west′wôl) See LIMES (def. 2).

west·ward (west′wǝrd) *adj.* Tending, moving, lying, or facing toward the west. —*adv.* Toward the west: also **west′wards.** [OE *westweard* < *west* the west] —**west′ward·ly** *adv.*

wet (wet) *adj.* **wet·ter, wet·test 1** Moistened

or saturated with water or other liquid; consisting of or covered with moisture. **2** Marked by showers or by heavy rainfall; rainy: the *wet* season. **3** Not dry: *wet* varnish. **4** *Colloq.* Favoring or not prohibiting the manufacture and sale of alcoholic beverages: a *wet* State; also, opposed to prohibition. **5** Preserved in liquid; also, bottled in alcohol, as laboratory specimens. **6** *Chem.* Treated or separated by means of liquid reagents. — **all wet** *Slang* Quite wrong; crazy; mistaken: He's *all wet.* — *n.* **1** Water; moisture; wetness. **2** Showery or rainy weather; rain. **3** *Colloq.* One · opposed to prohibition. — *v.t. & v.i.* **wet** or **wet·ted, wet·ting** To make or become wet. — **to wet one's whistle** *Colloq.* To take a drink. [OE *wǣt*] — **wet'ly** *adv.* — **wet'·ness** *n.* — **wet'ta·ble** *adj.* — **wet'ter** *n.*

We·tar (wē'tär) One of the southern Molucca Islands, Indonesia, north of Portuguese Timor; 1,400 square miles.

wet·back (wet'bak') *n. U.S. Colloq.* A Mexican laborer who enters the United States illegally. [So called from those who swim or wade across the Rio Grande]

wet-blank·et (wet'blang'kit) *v.t.* To discourage; depress.

wet blanket A discouragement, or one who discourages any proceedings.

weth·er (weth'ər) *n.* A castrated ram. ◆ Homophone: *weather.* [OE]

wet-nurse (wet'nûrs') *n.* A woman who is hired to suckle the child of another woman.

wet pack *Med.* A method of reducing fever or of relieving a disturbed neurotic condition by wrapping the patient in wet sheets.

wet suit A skin–tight rubber garment worn by divers, surfers, etc., to retain body warmth in cold waters.

Wet·ter·horn (vet'ər·hôrn) A mountain of three peaks in the Bernese Alps, Switzerland; 12,153 feet.

wet·ting agent (wet'ing) *Chem.* Any of a class of substances that, by reducing surface tension, enable a liquid to spread more readily over a solid surface to which it is applied: a form of detergent.

we've (wēv) We have: a contraction.

Wex·ford (weks'fərd) **1** A maritime county of SE Leinster province, Ireland; 908 square miles. **2** Its county town, a port on **Wexford Harbor,** an inlet of St. George's Channel in SE Ireland.

Wey·den (wī'dən), **Roger van der,** 1399?–1464, Flemish painter.

Wey·gand (ve·gän'), **Maxime,** 1867–1965, French general in World Wars I and II.

Wey·man (wā'mən), **Stanley,** 1855–1928, English novelist.

Wey·mouth (wā'məth) A port in southern Dorset, England; the old part of the present municipal borough of **Weymouth and Melcombe Regis.**

wha (hwä) *pron. Scot.* Who.

whack (hwak) *v.t. & v.i.* **1** *Colloq.* To strike sharply; beat; hit. **2** *Slang* To share: often with *up.* **3** *Slang* To drive (mules or oxen). — *n.* **1** *Colloq.* A sharp, resounding stroke or blow. **2** The noise made by such a blow. **3** *Slang* A share; portion. **3** *Slang* A turn; a chance; a try. — **to have a whack at** *Slang* **1** To give a blow to. **2** To have a chance or turn at; to have a chance to try. — **out of whack** *Slang* Out of order. [? Var. of THWACK]

whack·er (hwak'ər) *n.* **1** One who whacks. **2** The driver of a mule team. **3** *Colloq.* A whopper.

whack·ing (hwak'ing) *Colloq. adj.* Strikingly large; whopping. — *adv.* Very; extremely.

whai·sle (hwā'zəl) *v.i. Scot.* To breathe hard or roughly; wheeze. Also **whai'zle.**

whale[1] (hwāl) *n.* **1** A cetaceous mammal of fishlike form, especially one of the larger pelagic species, as distinguished from dolphins and porpoises. Whales have the fore limbs developed as broad flattened paddles, the hind limbs absent, and a thick layer of fat or blubber immediately beneath the skin. The principal types are the toothless or whalebone whales (suborder *Mysticeti*), and the toothed whales (suborder *Odontoceti*). **2** *Colloq.* Something extremely good or large: a *whale* of a party. — *v.i.* **whaled, whal·ing**

To engage in the hunting of whales. [OE *hwæl*]

whale[2] (hwāl) *v.t.* **whaled, whal·ing** *Colloq.* To strike as if to produce wales or stripes; flog; wale. [Var. of WALE[1], *v.*]

whale·back (hwāl'bak') *n.* A steamship having a convex main deck, used on the Great Lakes in passenger and freight traffic.

whale·boat (hwāl'bōt') *n.* A long, deep rowboat, sharp at both ends, often steered with an oar: so called because first used in whaling, now carried on steamers as lifeboats.

WHALEBOAT

whale·bone (hwāl'bōn') *n.* **1** The horny substance developed in plates from the palate of the whalebone whales; baleen. **2** A strip of whalebone, used in stiffening dress bodies, corsets, etc.

whale iron A harpoon.

whale·man (hwāl'mən) *n. pl.* **·men** (-mən) One who hunts whales; a whaler.

whal·er (hwā'lər) *n.* **1** A person or a vessel engaged in whaling. **2** A whaleboat.

Whales (hwālz), **Bay of** An inlet of the Antarctic Ocean in Ross Shelf Ice just north of Little America.

whale shark A very large pelagic shark (*Rhineodon typus*) somewhat resembling the basking shark in its habits but often reaching a length of 50 feet: it has a spotted body and very small teeth adapted for feeding on plankton.

whal·ing (hwā'ling) *n.* The industry of capturing whales. — *adj. Slang* Huge; whopping.

whaling station A place on shore to which whales are taken to be flensed and the oil tried out.

wham·my (hwam'ē) *n. pl.* **·mies** *U.S. Slang* **1** A gesture made by extending in parallel the index and little finger from the closed fist and pointing toward the person or object intended: an ancient form of hexing (*mano cornuta,* sign of the horns). If the fingers of both hands are used, the fists being in contact, it is a *double whammy.* **2** A jinx; hex: to put the *whammy* on someone. [<*wham,* colloq. interjection imit. of the sound of a hard blow]

Wham·po·a (hwäm'pō'ä') The deep–water port for Canton in southern Kwangtung province, China, on an island in the Canton River.

whang[1] (hwang) *v.t. & v.i. Colloq.* To beat or sound with a resounding noise. — *n. Colloq.* A beating or banging; heavy blow; whack. [Imit.]

whang[2] (hwang) *n.* **1** A buckskin thong or one made of a deer sinew. **2** Whang leather. **3** *Scot.* A big slice, as of bread or cheese; a chunk. — *v.t.* **1** To beat as with a thong; lash. **2** To beat or strike violently. **3** *Scot. & Dial.* To fling; throw violently; hurl. **4** *Scot.* To slice, usually in large pieces. [Var. of OE *thwang* a thong]

whang·ee (hwang·ē') *n.* **1** Any of a genus (*Phyllostachys*) of tall woody Asian grasses related to the bamboo. **2** A cane or stick made of the stalk of one of these plants. [<Chinese *huang* bamboo sprout]

whang leather A leather, usually of deerskin, made for lacings, thongs, etc. [<WHANG[2] + LEATHER]

Whang·poo (hwang'pōō') See HWANGPOO.

whap (hwap), **whap·per** (hwap'ər), etc. See WHOP, etc.

wharf (hwôrf) *n. pl.* **wharves** (hwôrvz) or **wharfs** **1** A structure of masonry or timber erected on the shore of a harbor, river, or the like, alongside which vessels may lie to load or unload cargo, passengers, etc.; also, any landing place for vessels, as a pier or quay. **2** *Obs.* A river bank; also, the seashore.

— *v.t.* **1** To moor to a wharf. **2** To provide or protect with a wharf or wharves. **3** To deposit or store on a wharf. [OE *hwearf, hwerf* a dam]

wharf·age (hwôr'fij) *n.* **1** Charge for the use of a wharf. **2** Wharf accommodations for shipping.

wharf boat A barge or float with a platform used as a landing stage for men and freight on rivers where the water level is changeful: usually connected with the shore or levee by a bridge.

wharf·in·ger (hwôr'fin·jər) *n.* One who keeps a wharf for landing goods and collects wharfage fees. [Earlier *wharfager* + intrusive *n*]

wharf rat **1** A rat that inhabits wharves; especially, the brown or Norway rat. **2** *U.S. Slang* A man or boy who loiters habitually about wharves, especially with thievish or other criminal intent.

Whar·ton (hwôr'tən), **Edith Newbold,** 1862–1937, *née* Jones, U.S. novelist.

wharve (hwôrv) See WHERVE.

wha's (hwäz), **whase** (hwāz) *pron. Scot.* Whose.

what (hwot, hwut) *adj.* **1** In interrogative construction, asking for information that will specify the person or thing qualified by it: Of *what* person do you speak? **2** How surprising, ridiculous, great, or the like: used in exclamation to express excess or something exceptional in the person or thing qualified: commendatory or the reverse according to circumstances: *What* genius! *What* a noise that boy is making! **3** How much: an ambiguous use: *What* cash has he? — *pron.* **1** Which circumstance, event, relation, or the like: asking for some specification concerning persons or things referred to: an interrogative pronoun used in absolute interrogation: Who and *what* is he? When used of persons, it ordinarily implies some shade of contempt. In this sense *what* is used elliptically for "What did you say?" or in surprise or indignation: *What!* did he really say that? Formerly it was used as a common introductory expletive like *well,* especially in a summons, as in the phrase *what ho!* **2** That which: a double relative, equivalent to a demonstrative followed by a simple relative: Tell me *what* it is; *What* followed occupied little time. **3** *Dial.* or *Illit.* That or which: a simple relative: a donkey *what* wouldn't go. — **what for 1** Why: *What* did you do that *for?* **2** *Slang* Physical punishment or verbal rebuke: He took the bully outside and gave him the *what for.* — *adv.* **1** In what respect; to what extent: *What* are you profited? **2** In some measure; partly: usually followed by *with: What* with the heat, and *what* with the noise, it is distracting. **3** For what reason; why. **4** How extraordinarily! how!: an exclamatory or intensive use. — *conj.* **1** So far as; as well as: He did *what* he could at the time. **2** That: especially in the phrase *but what.* [OE *hwæt,* neut. of *hwa* who]

what-all (hwot'ôl', hwut'-) *pron. Colloq.* Whatever; everything.

Whate·ly (hwāt'lē), **Richard,** 1787–1863, English prelate and logician.

what·ev·er (hwot'ev'ər, hwut'-) *pron.* **1** As a compound relative, the whole that; anything that; no matter what: often added for emphasis to a negative assertion: *whatever* makes life dear; I do not want anything *whatever.* **2** *Colloq.* What: usually interrogative: *Whatever* were you saying? Also *Poetic* **what'e'er** (-âr').

what-not (hwot'not', hwut'-) *n.* **1** An ornamental set of shelves for holding bric–à–brac, etc. **2** Anything you please; something or other.

what·so·ev·er (hwot'sō·ev'ər, hwut'-) *adj. & pron.* Whatever: a slightly more formal usage. Also *Poetic* **what'so·e'er** (-âr').

whaup[1] (hwäp, hwôp) *n. Scot. & Brit. Dial.* A curlew. [Imit.]

whaup[2] (hwäp, hwôp) *Scot. v.i.* **1** To fuss about noisily. **2** To whine; whistle. — *n.* **1** A whistle or cry. **2** A pod; capsule. **3** A clumsy lout; also, a scamp. **4** An outcry; a fuss.

wheal (hwēl) *n.* A discolored ridge on the skin, as from hives or the stroke of a whip;

also, a whelk. ◆Homophone: *wheel.* [Alter. of WALE¹]

wheat (hwēt) *n.* **1** A grain yielding an edible flour, the annual product of a cereal grass (genus *Triticum*): the most important of the cereals, it is excelled only by rice in the number of people by whom it is used as a staple food. **2** The plant that produces this grain, especially *Triticum aestivum* and varieties, a tall, slender annual or biennial of cosmopolitan distribution, bearing at its summit an imbricated spike of usually four-flowered spikelets called the ear or head. **3** A wheatfield; a crop of wheat. [OE *hwǣte*]

WHEAT
a. Ear of bearded wheat.
b. Ear of beardless wheat.
c, d. Grain: front and back of *b.*

wheat·ear (hwēt'ir) *n.* A thrushlike bird (*Oenanthe oenanthe*) of the northern parts of the northern hemisphere, related to the whinchat, ash-gray above and white below, with the wings, sides of head, and tip of tail black. [Earlier *wheatears* < WHITE + *ers, eeres* rump]

wheat·en (hwēt'n) *adj.* Belonging to or made of wheat.

Wheat·ley (hwēt'lē), **Phillis**, 1753?–84, American Negro poet born in Africa.

Wheat·stone (hwēt'stōn), **Sir Charles**, 1802–1875, English physicist.

Wheat·stone bridge (hwēt'stōn) *Electr.* An instrument for the measurement of differential resistance in an electric current. Also **Wheatstone's bridge.** [after Sir Charles *Wheatstone*]

wheat·worm (hwēt'wûrm') *n.* A threadworm (*Tylenchus tritici*) destructive of wheat. Also **wheat eelworm.**

WHEATSTONE BRIDGE
a. Galvanometer.
b. Battery.
c, d. Bridge.
R¹, R² Resistances to be compared.
R³, R⁴ Known resistances which can be varied. When galvanometer shows no current, $R^1R^2 = R^3R^4$.

whee·dle (hwēd'l) *v.* **·dled, ·dling** *v.t.* **1** To persuade or try to persuade by flattery, cajolery, etc.; coax. **2** To obtain by cajoling or coaxing. —*v.i.* **3** To use flattery or cajolery. [? OE *wǣdlian* beg, be poor < *wǣdl* poverty] —**whee'dler** *n.* —**whee'dling·ly** *adv.*

wheel (hwēl) *n.* **1** A circular rim and hub connected by spokes or rays in one structure, or a disk, capable of rotating on a central axis and used to reduce friction and facilitate movement or transportation, as in vehicles, or to act with a rotary motion, as in machines. **2** Anything resembling or suggestive of a wheel; a disk or a circle, or any circular object or formation. **3** An instrument or device having a wheel or wheels as its distinctive characteristic, as a bicycle, a steering wheel or steering gear, or the like. **4** An old instrument of torture or execution, consisting of a wheel to which the limbs of the victim were tied and then broken with an iron bar; also, the death so inflicted. **5** The wheel with which the goddess of fortune is represented, symbolizing the vicissitudes and uncertainty of human fate. **6** A turning; revolution; rotation. **7** Figuratively, that which imparts or directs motion or controls activity; the moving force: the *wheels* of democracy. **8** A turning of a body of troops or a swinging of a line of ships in which a change of direction is accomplished while the different units keep in alinement. **9** A rotating firework; a pinwheel or catherine wheel. **10** A refrain of a song. **11** The rotating disk used in various gambling games, especially roulette; hence, roulette. —**Pelton wheel**

A device consisting of a wheel which carries on it a succession of cupshaped buckets, and is made to rotate by the impingement of high-pressure jets of water on the buckets, the form of which is such as to prevent the accumulation of dead water. —**wheels within wheels** An intricate series of motives or influences, acting and reacting on one another. —*v.t.* **1** To move or convey on wheels. **2** To cause to turn on or as on an axis; pivot or revolve. **3** To perform with a circular movement. **4** To provide with a wheel or wheels. —*v.i.* **5** To turn on or as on an axis; pivot; rotate or revolve. **6** To take a new direction or course of action; change attitudes, opinions, etc.: often with *about.* **7** To move in a circular or spiral course. **8** To roll or move on wheels. —**to wheel and deal** *Slang* To act freely, aggressively, and often unscrupulously, as in the arrangement of a business or political deal. —*adj.* **1** Pertaining to or shaped like a wheel. **2** Harnessed to a vehicle directly in front of the wheels: said of a draft animal when there is a leader or leaders in front. ◆Homophone: *wheal.* [OE *hwēol*]

wheel and axle *Mech.* A wheel or drum mounted on an axle with a rope wound about the drum so that a slight pull on one end of the rope will raise a disproportionately heavy weight attached to the other: one of the so-called simple machines.

wheel animalcule A rotifer.

wheel·bar·row (hwēl'bar'ō) *n.* A boxlike vehicle ordinarily with one wheel and two handles, for moving small loads. —*v.t.* To convey in a wheelbarrow.

wheel·base (hwēl'bās') *n.* The distance from the center of the back axle to the center of the front axle, as in an automobile.

wheel·bug (hwēl'bug') *n.* A large hemipterous insect (*Arilus cristatus*) of the southern United States, which preys upon caterpillars and other soft-bodied insects: so called from a semicircular crest on the thorax resembling a cogwheel.

wheel·chair (hwēl'châr') *n.* A mobile chair mounted between large wheels, for the use of invalids. Also **wheel chair.**

wheeled (hwēld) *adj.* **1** Having wheels; furnished with a wheel or wheels: often in compounds: a *two-wheeled* cart. **2** Effected or borne by wheels: *wheeled* transportation.

wheel·er (hwē'lər) *n.* **1** One who wheels. **2** A wheelhorse or other draft animal working next the wheel. **3** Something furnished with a wheel or wheels: a side-*wheeler.*

Wheel·er (hwē'lər), **Joseph**, 1836–1906, American Confederate general.

wheel·er-deal·er (hwē'lər-dē'lər) *n.* *Slang* One who wheels and deals.

wheel·horse (hwēl'hôrs') *n.* **1** A horse harnessed to the pole or shafts when there is a leader or leaders in front; hence, one who does the heaviest work. **2** In politics, a person bearing great responsibility, or one to be greatly depended upon.

wheel·house (hwēl'hous') *n.* **1** A small house on the deck of a vessel in which the steering wheel is located; a pilothouse. **2** A paddle box.

wheel·ing (hwē'ling) *n.* **1** The act of one who wheels, especially of one riding a bicycle. **2** The condition of the roads, as regards traveling on wheels. **3** A rotating movement; a turning.

Wheel·ing (hwē'ling) A port on the Ohio River in NW West Virginia; an industrial center.

wheel lock 1 An old form of lock for small arms, in which a small steel wheel, actuated by a spring and released by a trigger, produced sparks by rotating against a flint. **2** A lock or catch for stopping a vehicle wheel.

wheel·man (hwēl'mən) *n.* *pl.* **·men** (-mən) **1** The man who steers a vessel. **2** A bicyclist. Also **wheels'man.**

Whee·lock (hwē'lok), **Eleazar**, 1711–79, U.S. clergyman and educator.

wheel window See ROSE WINDOW.

wheel·work (hwēl'wûrk') *n. Mech.* The gearing and arrangement of wheels in a machine or mechanical device.

wheel·wright (hwēl'rīt') *n.* A man whose business is making or repairing wheels and wheeled vehicles.

wheen (hwēn) *n. Scot. & Dial.* A few.

wheeze (hwēz) *v.t. & v.i.* **wheezed, wheez·ing** To breathe or utter with a husky, whistling sound. —*n.* **1** A wheezing sound. **2** A whispering sound so exaggerated as to give rise to the sound popularly called a "stage whisper." **3** *Colloq.* A popular tale, saying, or trick, especially an ancient one. [Prob. < ON *hvæsa* hiss] —**wheez'er** *n.* —**wheez'ing·ly** *adv.*

wheez·y (hwē'zē) *adj.* **wheez·i·er, wheez·i·est** Subject to wheezing, or making a wheezing sound. —**wheez'i·ly** *adv.* —**wheez'i·ness** *n.*

whelk¹ (hwelk) *n.* Any of several large marine snails found in temperate waters, having whorled shells and preying on other mollusks or scavenging; a popular food in Europe. [OE *weoloc*]

whelk² (hwelk) *n.* A swelling, protuberance, or pustule; wheal; especially, a pimple or eruption of pimples on the face. [OE *hwylca* a pustule < *hwelian* suppurate]

whelk·y¹ (hwel'kē) *adj.* **whelk·i·er, whelk·i·est 1** Protuberant; rounded. **2** Shelly. Also spelled *welky.* [< WHELK¹]

whelk·y² (hwel'kē) *adj.* **whelk·i·er, whelk·i·est** Marked with pustules or whelks. [< WHELK²]

whelm (hwelm) *v.t.* **1** To cover with water or other fluid; submerge; engulf. **2** To overpower; overwhelm. —*v.i.* **3** To roll with engulfing force. [Prob. blend of OE *helmian* cover and *gehwelfan* bend over]

whelp (hwelp) *n.* **1** One of the young of a dog, wolf, lion, or other beast of prey; sometimes, a dog of any age. **2** A worthless young fellow; a cub; puppy: used contemptuously. **3** *Mech.* **a** One of series of longitudinal ridges on a windlass or capstan. **b** One of the teeth of a sprocket wheel. —*v.t. & v.i.* To give birth (to): said of dogs, lions, etc. [OE *hwelp*]

COMMON WHELK (About 4 inches)

when (hwen) *adv.* **1** Interrogatively, at what or which time: *When* did you arrive? **2** Conjunctively: **a** At which: the time *when* we went on the picnic. **b** At which or what time: They watched till midnight *when* they fell asleep. **c** As soon as: He laughed *when* he heard it; You may play *when* you finish work. **d** Although: He walks *when* he might ride. **e** At the time that; while: *when* you were in church; *when* we were young. **f** If; considering that: *When* in doubt, ask; How can I buy it *when* I have no money? **g** After which; then: We had just awakened *when* you called. —*pron.* What or which time: since *when*; till *when.* —*n.* The time; date: I don't know the *when* or the circumstances. [OE *hwanne, hwænne*]

when·as (hwen'az') *conj. Obs.* **1** Whereas; while. **2** When. Also **when that.**

whence (hwens) *adv.* **1** Interrogatively, from what place or source; of what origin: *Whence* and what art thou? *Whence* is the correlative of *thence.* **2** Conjunctively: **a** From what or which place, source, or cause; from which: the place *whence* these sounds arise. **b** To which place; where: Return *whence* you came. **c** For which reason; wherefore. [ME *whannes, whennes*, adverbial genitive of *whanne,* OE *hwanne* whence]

whence·so·ev·er (hwens'sō·ev'ər) *adv. & conj.* From whatever place, cause, or source.

when·e'er (hwen·âr') *adv. & conj. Poetic* Whenever.

when·ev·er (hwen·ev'ər) *adv. & conj.* At whatever time.

when·so·ev·er (hwen'sō·ev'ər) *adv. & conj.* At what time soever; whenever.

where (hwâr) *adv.* **1** Interrogatively: **a** At or in what place, relation, or situation: *Where* is my book? **b** To what place or end; whither: *Where* are you going? **c** From what place; whence: *Where* did you get that hat? **2** Conjunctively: **a** At or in which place, or what place; at the place in which: *where* men gather. **b** To a place or situation in or to which; whither: Let us go *where* the mountains and the trees are. ◆ *Where* is the correlative of *there.* In composition with a preposition, *where* has sometimes the force of an interrogative pronoun and sometimes that of a relative: *Wherein* was he wrong? *Wherein* he was much deceived. — *pron.* The place in which: The accident occurred 100 yards from *where* we stood. — *n.* Place; locality. [OE *hwǣr*]

where·a·bouts (hwâr′ə-bouts′) *adv.* **1** Near or at what place; about where. **2** *Obs.* About which; concerning which. Also *Rare* **where′·a·bout′**. — *n.* The place in or near which a person or thing is.

where·as (hwâr′az′) *conj.* **1** Since the facts are such as they are; seeing that: often used in the preamble of a resolution, etc. **2** The fact of the matter being that; when in truth: implying opposition to a previous statement. — *n.* *pl.* **·as·es** A clause or item beginning with the word "whereas."

where·at (hwâr′at′) *adv.* **1** Interrogatively, at what: *Whereat* are you angry? **2** Conjunctively, at which; for which reason; whereupon: He won the race, *whereat* we were delighted.

where·by (hwâr′bī′) *adv.* **1** Interrogatively, by what; how. **2** Conjunctively, by, near, or through which.

where·e′er (hwâr′âr′) *adv.* *Poetic* Wherever.

where·fore (hwâr′fôr′, -fōr′) *adv.* **1** Interrogatively, for what reason; what for; to what end; why: *Wherefore* didst thou doubt? **2** Conjunctively, for which reason. See synonyms under THEREFORE. — *n.* The cause; reason: the whys and *wherefores*. [<WHERE + FOR]

where·from (hwâr′frum′, -from′) *conj.* From which; whence.

where·in (hwâr′in′) *adv.* **1** Interrogatively, in what; in what particular or regard: *Wherein* is the error? **2** Conjunctively, in which thing, place, circumstance, etc.: a state *wherein* there is discord.

where·in·to (hwâr′in·tōō′) *adv.* **1** Interrogatively, into what. **2** Conjunctively, into which: the gulf *whereinto* he sailed.

where·of (hwâr′uv′, -ov′) *adv.* **1** Interrogatively, of or from what: *Whereof* did you partake? **2** Conjunctively, of which or whom: the house *whereof* he is the head.

where·on (hwâr′on′, -ôn′) *adv.* **1** Interrogatively, on what or whom. **2** Conjunctively, on which: a rock *whereon* to build.

where·so·ev·er (hwâr′sō·ev′ər) *adv. & conj.* **1** In or to whatever place; wherever. **2** Whithersoever. **3** Whencesoever.

where·som·ev·er (hwâr′səm·ev′ər) *adv. & conj.* *Dial.* Wherever; wheresoever. [<WHERE + SOMEVER < *som* ever, just (<Scand.) + EVER]

where·through (hwâr′thrōō′) *adv. & conj.* Through which.

where·to (hwâr′tōō′) *adv.* **1** Interrogatively, to what place or end: *Whereto* serves avarice? **2** Conjunctively, to which or to whom; whither: the grave *whereto* we haste. Also *Archaic* **where′·un·to′**.

where·up·on (hwâr′ə·pon′, -ə·pôn′) *adv.* **1** Interrogatively, upon what; whereon. **2** Conjunctively, upon which or whom; in consequence of which; after which: *whereupon* they took in sail.

wher·ev·er (hwâr′ev′ər) *adv. & conj.* In, at, or to whatever place; wheresoever.

where·with (hwâr′with′, -with′) *adv.* **1** Interrogatively, with what: *Wherewith* shall I do it? **2** Conjunctively, with which; by means of which: *wherewith* we abated hunger. — *pron.* That with or by which: with the infinitive: I have not *wherewith* to do it. — *n.* The requisites; wherewithal.

where·with·al (hwâr′with·ôl′) *n.* The necessary means or resources; especially, the necessary money: with the definite article. — *adv. & pron.* (hwâr′with·ôl′) Wherewith.

wher·ry (hwer′ē) *n.* *pl.* **·ries** **1** A light, fast rowboat used on inland waters. **2** *Brit.* A decked fishing vessel with two sails. **3** An open rowboat for racing or exercise, built for one person. **4** *Brit.* A very broad, light barge. — *v.t. & v.i.* **·ried, ·ry·ing** To transport in or use a wherry. [? <WHIR; with ref. to rapid movement]

wherve (hwûrv) *n.* In spinning, a pulley on the spindle: also spelled *wharve*. [OE *hweorfa*]

whet (hwet) *v.t.* **whet·ted, whet·ting** **1** To sharpen, as a knife, by friction. **2** To make more keen or eager; excite; stimulate, as the appetite. — *n.* **1** The act of whetting. **2** Something that whets. [OE *hwettan*] — **whet′ter** *n.*

wheth·er (hweth′ər) *conj.* As the first alternative; in case; if: introducing an alternative clause, followed by a correlative *or*, or *or whether*; sometimes also introducing a single alternative, the other, usually a negative, being implied: Tell us *whether* you are going (or not). — *pron.* Which: properly of two, less exactly of more than two: an archaism used interrogatively and relatively. — **whether or no** Regardless; in any case. [OE *hwæther, hwether*]

whet·slate (hwet′slāt′) *n.* A hard, fine-grained siliceous rock used for whetstones.

whet·stone (hwet′stōn′) *n.* A fine-grained stone for whetting knives, axes, etc. [OE *hwetstān* < *hwettan* whet + *stān* a stone]

whew (hwyōō) *interj.* An exclamatory sound, expressive usually of amazement, dismay, relief, admiration (real or feigned), or discomfort (from the heat). [Imit. of whistling]

Whew·ell (hyōō′əl), **William**, 1794–1866, English scientist and philosopher.

whey (hwā) *n.* A clear, straw-colored liquid that separates from the curd when milk is curdled, as in making cheese. [OE *hwæg, hweg*] — **whey′ey, whey′ish** *adj.*

whey-face (hwā′fās′) *n.* Formerly, a face or person pale as if from fear; now, one of pale, sallow complexion. — **whey′-faced′** *adj.*

which (hwich) *pron. & adj.* **1** Interrogatively, what individual person or thing, or group of persons or things collectively, of a certain number or class: asking for the indication or definite description. In this sense *which* is used both substantively and adjectively, singular and plural: *Which* shall I take? *Which* apple do you want? *Which* mammals are carnivorous? **2** As a relative pronoun, that particular one or ones of a certain number or class of impersonal beings or things: pointing out or definitely fixing upon that which is designated in the antecedent word, phrase, or clause to which it is related: now generally as a substantive, but sometimes as an adjective: He raised his hand, *which* gesture attracted my attention. *Which* as a relative now refers only to animals, without distinction of masculine or feminine, or to things without life; it was formerly used for persons, even in the most exalted sense, as "Our Father, *which* art in heaven." **3** Also relatively, the one that: often equivalent to the use of the interrogative in a dependent question: used substantively or adjectively: Tell me *which* (or *which* apple) you prefer. [OE *hwelc, hwilc*]

which·ev·er (hwich′ev′ər) *pron. & adj.* Whether one or another (of two or of several); no matter which. Also **which′so·ev′er**.

whick·er (hwik′ər) *v.i. & n.* Whinny. [Imit.]

whid[1] (hwid) *Scot. n.* A brisk, nimble, scurrying movement. — *v.i.* **whid·ded, whid·ding** To move nimbly: said of small animals.

whid[2] (hwid) *Scot. n.* **1** A fib; lie. **2** A quarrel. **3** A word. — *v.i.* **whid·ded, whid·ding** To tell a lie; fib.

whid·ah bird (hwid′ə) An African weaverbird (subfamily *Viduinae*), the male of which has the tail greatly lengthened in the breeding season: formerly called *widow bird.* Also **whid′ah, whidah finch**: also spelled *whydah.* [Alter. of *widow bird*; infl. in form by *Whid-ah* former name of Ouidah, a seaport in French West Africa, near which this bird is commonly found]

whiff (hwif) *n.* **1** Any sudden or slight gust or puff of air. **2** A gust or puff of odor: a *whiff* of onions. **3** A sudden expulsion of breath or smoke from the mouth; a puff. **4** An inhalation, as of smoke. — *v.t.* **1** To drive or blow with a whiff or puff. **2** To exhale or inhale in whiffs. **3** To smoke, as a pipe. — *v.i.* **4** To blow or

WHIDAH BIRD
(From 12 to 14 inches over all)

move in whiffs or puffs. **5** To exhale or inhale whiffs. [Alter. of ME *weffe* an offensive odor; imit.] — **whiff′er** *n.*

whif·fet (hwif′it) *n. Colloq.* **1** A trifling, useless person; whippersnapper: in slight contempt. **2** A small, snappish dog. **3** A little whiff. [? Dim. of WHIFF]

whif·fle (hwif′əl) *v.* **·fled, ·fling** *v.i.* **1** To blow with puffs or gusts; shift about, as the wind. **2** To vacillate; veer. — *v.t.* **3** To blow or dissipate with or as with a puff. [Freq. of WHIFF]

whif·fler (hwif′lər) *n.* **1** One who fluctuates or shuffles in argument; a trifler. **2** One who whiffs tobacco. **3** A piper; fifer. — **whiff′·fler·y** *n.*

whif·fle·tree (hwif′əl·trē′) *n.* A swingletree: also called *whippletree.* [Var. of WHIPPLETREE]

whig[1] (hwig) *v.i. Scot.* To drive onward; move along easily; jog.

whig[2] (hwig) *n. Dial.* **1** Sour whey. **2** Buttermilk. [Var. of OE *hweg* whey]

Whig (hwig) *n.* **1** An American colonist who supported the Revolutionary War in the 18th century: opposed to *Tory*; later, a member of a party opposed to the Democratic and succeeded by the Republican party in 1856. **2** A member of the Liberal party in England in the 18th and 19th centuries, as opposed to a *Tory* or *Conservative.* **3** In earlier usage, a Presbyterian rebel of the west of Scotland in the 17th century: thus named in derision; also, after the Restoration (1660), a Roundhead, as opposed to a Cavalier. — *adj.* Consisting of or supported by Whigs. [Prob. short for WHIGGAMORE] — **Whig′gish** *adj.* — **Whig′gish·ly** *adv.* — **Whig′gish·ness** *n.*

Whig·ga·more (hwig′ə·môr, -mōr) *n.* **1** A member of a body of insurgents who in 1648 marched on Edinburgh and opposed the compromise with Charles I. **2** In the later 17th century, a Scotch Presbyterian; a Whig (def. 3). Also **Whig′a·more**. [Prob. <dial. E (Scottish) *whiggamaire* < *whig* a cry to urge on a horse + *mere* a horse]

Whig·ger·y (hwig′ər·ē) *n.* *pl.* **·ger·ies** The doctrines of Whigs. Also **Whig′gism.**

whig·ma·lee·rie (hwig′mə·lir′ē) *n. Scot.* A small or useless ornament; gewgaw; also, a whim. Also **whig′ma·lee′ry, whig′me·lee′rie.**

while (hwīl) *n.* **1** A short time; also, a period of time, or time in general: Stay and rest a *while.* **2** Time or pains expended on a thing; trouble; labor: only in the phrase *worth while* or *worth one's while.* — **between whiles** From time to time. — **the while** At the same time: He went about his work and sang *the while.* — *conj.* **1** During the time that; as long as. **2** At the same time that; although: *While* he found fault, he also praised. **3** *Colloq.* Whereas: This man is short, *while* that one is tall. **4** *Brit. Dial.* Until; till. — *v.t.* **whiled, whil·ing** To cause to pass lightly and pleasantly; spend; pass: usually with *away*: to *while* away the time. [OE *hwīl*]

whiles (hwīlz) *Archaic* or *Dial. adv.* Occasionally; at intervals. — *conj.* While; during the time that.

whi·lom (hwī′ləm) *Archaic adj.* Being once upon a time; former. — *adv.* **1** Formerly; at one time. **2** At times. [OE *hwīlum* at times, dative pl. of *hwīl* a while]

whilst (hwīlst) *conj.* While: an old form still widely used, especially in England. [ME *whilest* < *whiles,* genitive of WHILE + *-t*]

whim (hwim) *n.* **1** A sudden, unexpected, and unreasonable deviation of the mind from its usual or natural course; caprice; freak. **2** An old form of mine hoist, run by horsepower. [Short for earlier *whim-wham* a trifle, ? < Scand. Cf. ON *hvima* wander with the eyes.] *Synonyms:* caprice, crotchet, fancy, freak, humor, kink, quirk, vagary, whimsy, wrinkle. See FANCY.

whim·brel (hwim′brəl) *n.* A small northern curlew with a white rump, especially a species (*Numenius phaeopus*) of northern portions of the eastern hemisphere. [? <obs. *whimp* whimper, prob. imit. of its cry]

whim·per (hwim′pər) *v.i.* To cry or whine with plaintive broken sounds. — *v.t.* To utter with a whimper. — *n.* A low, broken, whining cry; whine. [Imit.] — **whim′per·er** *n.* — **whim′per·ing** *n.* — **whim′per·ing·ly** *adv.*

whim·si·cal (hwim′zi·kəl) *adj.* **1** Having eccentric ideas; capricious. **2** Oddly constituted; fantastic; quaint. See synonyms under FICKLE, ODD, QUEER. — **whim′si·cal·ly** *adv.* — **whim′·si·cal·ness** *n.*

whim·si·cal·i·ty (hwim′zi·kal′ə·tē) *n. pl.* ·**ties** **1** Whimsicalness. **2** A singularity. **3** A quaint, fanciful, or odd idea or its expression.

whim·sy (hwim′zē) *n. pl.* ·**sies** **1** A whim; caprice; freak. **2** Tenuously fanciful humor. Also **whim′sey.** See synonyms under WHIM. [Prob. related to WHIM]

whin¹ (hwin) *n.* Furze; gorse. [Prob. <Scand. Cf. Dan. & Norw. *hvine* a kind of grass.]

whin² (hwin) *n.* Whinstone. [< dial. E (Scottish) *quin*; ult. origin uncertain]

whin·chat (hwin′chat) *n.* A small, Old World, thrushlike singing bird (*Saxicola rubetra*), streaked with brown above and rufous below. [<WHIN¹ + CHAT¹]

whine (hwīn) *v.* **whined, whin·ing** *v.i.* **1** To utter a low, plaintive, nasal sound expressive of grief or distress. **2** To complain in a mean or childish way. — *v.t.* **3** To utter with a whine. — *n.* The act or sound of whining; any peevish complaint. [OE *hwīnan* whiz] — **whin′er** *n.* — **whin′ing·ly** *adv.* — **whin′y** *adj.*

whinge (hwinj) *v.i.* **whinged, whinge·ing** *Austral. Slang* To complain; whine.

whing·er (hwing′ər) *n. Brit. Dial.* A dirk, used at meals or as a weapon; a hanger. See HANGER. Also **whing′ar.** [Prob. var. of WHINYARD]

whin·ny¹ (hwin′ē) *v.* ·**nied,** ·**ny·ing** *v.i.* To neigh, especially in a low or gentle way. — *v.t.* To express with a whinny. — *n. pl.* ·**nies** The cry or call of a horse; a neigh. [<WHINE]

whin·ny² (hwin′ē) *adj.* ·**ni·er,** ·**ni·est** Abounding in whin or furze. [<WHIN¹]

whin·stone (hwin′stōn) *n.* Any very hard, dark–colored rock, as basalt or chert. [<WHIN² + STONE]

whin·yard (hwin′yərd) *n. Dial.* **1** One of certain ducks, especially the pochard. **2** A hanger or sword. [Earlier *whyneherd,* ? <OE *hwīnan* whiz; the duck is so called because of the swordlike shape of its bill]

whip (hwip) *v.* **whipped** or **whipt, whip·ping** *v.t.* **1** To strike with a lash, rod, strap, etc. **2** To punish by striking thus; flog. **3** To drive or urge with lashes or blows: with *on, up, off,* etc. **4** To strike in the manner of a whip: The wind *whipped* the trees. **5** To attack with scathing criticism; berate; flay. **6** To beat, as eggs or cream, to a froth. **7** To seize, move, jerk, throw, etc., with a sudden motion: with *away, in, off, out,* etc. **8** In fishing, to make repeated casts upon the surface of (a stream, etc.). **9** To wrap (rope, cable, etc.) with light line so as to prevent chafing or wear; serve. **10** To wrap or bind about something. **11** To form, as a flat seam, by laying two selvages of a fabric together and sewing with a loose overcast or overhand stitch. **12** *U.S. Colloq.* To defeat; overcome, as in a contest. **13** *Naut.* To hoist by means of a whip (def. 5). — *v.i.* **14** To go, come, move, or turn suddenly and quickly: with *away, in, off, out,* etc. **15** To thrash about in a manner suggestive of a whip: pennants *whipping* in the wind. **16** In fishing, to make repeated casts with rod and line. — **to whip in 1** To keep from scattering, as hounds in a hunt. **2** To keep together or united, as a political party. — **to whip up 1** To excite; arouse. **2** *Colloq.* To prepare quickly, as a meal. — *n.* **1** An instrument consisting of a lash attached to a handle, used for driving draft animals or for administering punishment. **2** One who handles a whip expertly; a driver. **3** A stroke, blow, or cut with a whip. **4** A member of a legislative body appointed unofficially to enforce the discipline and look after the interests of his party: often called **party whip;** also, a call made upon members of a legislature by such a person to bring or keep them in their places at a given time, as when a vote or division may be expected. **5** *Mech.* A simple form of hoisting apparatus, consisting of a rope passing over an elevated single pulley, and used for lifting light objects. **6** One who operates such an apparatus. **7** A huntsman who whips in the hounds to control them; a whipper-in. **8** *Electr.* A vibrating spring that whips back and forth, closing different circuits in electrical apparatus. **9** A dish or

dessert containing cream or eggs whipped to a froth: prune *whip.* **10** A thrashing motion, as of a rope or wire suddenly broken. **11** Flexibility in the shaft of a golf club. **12** An arm of a windmill. **13** *Obs.* or *Scot.* An attack of illness; also, a sudden movement; a single swift attack or blow. [ME *wippen, hwippen.* Cf. MDu. *wippen* swing, leap, dance.]

whip·cord (hwip′kôrd) *n.* **1** A strong, hard-twisted, sometimes braided hempen cord, used in making whiplashes. **2** A cord of catgut. **3** A twill-weave fabric, similar to gabardine, but with a more pronounced diagonal rib on the right side: used for riding habits and other outdoor garments.

whip·graft (hwip′graft′, -gräft′) *v.t. Bot.* To graft by fitting a tongue cut on the cion to a slit cut slopingly in the stock. — **whip′graft′·age, whip′graft′ing** *n.*

whip·hand (hwip′hand′) *n.* **1** The hand that wields the whip; in riding or driving, the right hand. **2** An instrument or means of mastery; advantage: She, not he, has the *whiphand.*

whip·lash (hwip′lash′) *n.* The flexible striking part of a whip.

whiplash injury An injury to the upper spine or base of the brain caused by a sudden jolting of the neck, as in an automobile collision.

whip·per (hwip′ər) *n.* One who whips.

whip·per–in (hwip′ər·in′) *n.* **1** In hunting, one employed to assist the huntsman and to enforce obedience among the hounds. **2** A political or parliamentary whip.

whip·per·snap·per (hwip′ər·snap′ər) *n.* A pretentious but insignificant person. [? Extension of *whipsnapper* a cracker of whips]

whip·pet (hwip′it) *n.* **1** A swift dog resembling an English greyhound in miniature, characterized by a long, narrow head, long arched back, smooth, close coat, and a long, tapering tail. **2** A small, light, speedy tank used in World War I: also **whippet tank.** **3** Anything suggestive of a whippet, as in size, speed, etc. [Dim. of WHIP; so called with ref. to its rapid movement]

WHIPPET
(From 23 to 28 inches high at the shoulder)

whip·ping (hwip′ing) *n.* **1** The act of one who whips; castigation; state or fact of being flogged or defeated. **2** Material used to bind the head of a rope, or to bind the head to the shaft of a golf club.

whipping boy Formerly, a boy brought up as companion to a prince or other noble youth, and punished in his stead for all misdeeds; now, anyone who receives punishment deserved by another.

whipping post The fixture to which those sentenced to flogging are secured; hence, legal punishment by flogging.

Whip·ple (hwip′əl), **George Hoyt,** born 1878, U.S. pathologist. — **William,** 1730–85, American Revolutionary general; signed Declaration of Independence.

whip·ple·tree (hwip′əl·trē′) *n.* A swingletree. [Prob. <WHIP]

whip·poor·will (hwip′ər·wil) *n.* A small nocturnal bird (*Caprimulgus vociferus*), allied to the goatsuckers, common in the eastern United States. [Imit. of its reiterated cry]

whip·saw (hwip′sô′) *n.* A thin, narrow, tapering ripsaw about six feet long. — *v.t.* ·**sawed,** ·**sawed** or ·**sawn,** ·**saw·ing 1** To saw with a whipsaw. **2** In faro, to beat (an opponent) in two bets, one to win and one to lose, at the same time. **3** To get the best of (an opponent) in spite of every effort he makes.

whip scorpion Any of various scorpionlike arachnids (family *Thelyphonidae*) having an abdomen terminating in a slender appendage like a whiplash, and lacking a sting; especially, the vinegarroon.

whip·stall (hwip′stôl′) *Aeron. n.* The stalled condition of a sharply climbing airplane in which the nose whips violently downward. — *v.i.* To bring about or go into a whipstall.

whip·stitch (hwip′stich′) *v.t.* To sew or gather with overcast stitches, as the turned edge of a ruffle; overcast. — *n.* **1** An overcast stitch in whipping an edge or seam. **2** A tailor.

whip·stock (hwip′stok′) *n.* That part of a whip to which the lash is attached; a whip handle.

whipt (hwipt) Alternative past tense and past participle of WHIP.

whip·worm (hwip′wûrm′) *n.* A nematode (*Trichuris trichiura*), with the posterior part of the body thickened: found in the human cecum.

whir (hwûr) *v.t. & v.i.* **whirred, whir·ring** To fly, move, or whirl with a buzzing sound. — *n.* **1** A whizzing, swishing sound, as that caused by the sudden rising of birds. **2** Confusion; bustle. Also **whirr.** [Prob. <Scand. Cf. Dan. *hvivre.* Akin to WHIRL.]

whirl (hwûrl) *v.i.* **1** To turn or revolve rapidly, as about a center. **2** To turn away or aside quickly. **3** To move or go swiftly. **4** To have a sensation of spinning: My head *whirls.* — *v.t.* **5** To cause to turn or revolve rapidly. **6** To carry or bear along with a revolving motion: The wind *whirled* the dust into the air. **7** *Obs.* To hurl. — *n.* **1** A swift rotating or revolving motion. **2** Something whirling, as a cloud of dust. **3** Confusion; turmoil. [Prob. <ON *hvirfla* revolve. Akin to WARBLE¹.]

whirl·a·bout (hwûrl′ə·bout′) *n.* Anything that turns swiftly around or about; a whirligig.

whirl·er (hwûr′lər) *n.* **1** One who or that which whirls. **2** A rotating hook or reel used in ropemaking.

whirl·i·gig (hwûr′lə·gig′) *n.* **1** Any toy or small device that revolves rapidly on an axis. **2** A merry-go-round. **3** Anything that performs quick revolutions or moves in a cycle: the *whirligig* of time. **4** Any of a family (*Gyrinidae*) of water beetles that frequent the surface of smooth water and move in swift circles: also **whirligig beetle.** **5** A trifling ornament, as one used by printers; also, a fanciful notion. [< *whirly* (<WHIRL) + GIG¹ (def. 4)]

whirl·pool (hwûrl′pool′) *n.* **1** An eddy or vortex where water moves with a gyrating sweep, as from the meeting of two currents. **2** Any disturbance from such causes, whether accompanied by vortical motion or not.

whirl·wind (hwûrl′wind′) *n.* **1** A moving atmospheric vortex; a funnel-shaped column of air, with a rapid circular and upward spiral motion around a vertical or inclined axis, causing waterspouts, sand pillars, and dust whirls. **2** Any violent rushing or rotatory movement. See synonyms under CYCLONE. — *adj.* Extremely swift or impetuous: a *whirlwind* courtship.

whirl·y·bird (hwûr′lē·bûrd′) *n. Colloq.* A helicopter. [< *whirly* (<WHIRL) + BIRD]

whir·ry (hwûr′ē) *v.t. & v.i.* ·**ried,** ·**ry·ing** *Scot.* To hurry.

whish¹ (hwish) *v.i.* To move with a sibilant, whistling sound. — *n.* A swishing sound like that made by cutting the air with a pliant rod. [Imit.]

whish² (hwish) *interj.* Hush! silence! Also **whisht** (hwisht). [Alter. of HUSH; infl. in form by WHISHT]

whisht (hwisht, hwist, wisht; *Scot.* hwusht) *Scot. v.t.* To hush. — *v.i.* To be silent. — *n.* The slightest sound; a whisper. — **to hold one's whisht** To be or remain silent.

whisk (hwisk) *v.t.* **1** To bear along or sweep with light movements, as of a small broom or a fan: often with *away* or *off:* to *whisk* flies away. **2** To cause to move with a quick sweeping motion. **3** To beat or mix with a quick movement, as eggs, cream, etc. — *v.i.* **4** To move quickly and lightly. — *n.* **1** A light stroke; a sudden, sweeping movement. **2** A little broom or brush. **3** A little bunch, as of straw, feathers, etc.; wisp. **4** A small culinary instrument for rapidly whipping (cream, etc.) to a froth. **5** A neckerchief of lawn or lace formerly worn by women. [Prob. <Scand. Cf. Dan. *viske* wipe, rub.]

whisk·broom (hwisk′broom′, -broom′) *n.* A small, short-handled broom for brushing clothing, etc.

whisk·er (hwis′kər) *n.* **1** *pl.* The hair that grows on the sides of a man's face, as distinguished from that on his lips, chin, and throat; loosely, the beard or any part of the beard; also, formerly, a mustache. **2** A hair from the whiskers or beard. **3** One of the long, bristly hairs on the sides of the mouth of some animals, as the cat, or a similar formation of bristles, as about the mouth of a bird; a vibrissa. **4** One who or that which whisks; formerly, a switch. **5** One of two small projecting spars or booms on the side of a bowsprit, to extend the jib or flying-jib guys: also **whisker boom.** — **whisk′ered, whisk′er·y** *adj.* —**whisk′er·less** *adj.*

whis·ky (hwis′kē) *n. pl.* **·kies 1** An alcoholic liquor obtained by the distillation of a fermented starchy compound, usually a grain. Whisky is often named (sometimes improperly) from the substance from which it is made, as **corn whisky, rye whisky,** etc.; or from the place or country of production, as **Bourbon whisky, Irish whisky,** etc. **2** A drink or portion of whisky. Compare USQUEBAUGH. —*adj.* Pertaining to or made of whisky. Also **whis′key.** [Short for *usquebaugh* < Irish *uisgebeatha,* lit., water of life < *uisge* water + *beatha* life]

whis·ky-jack (hwis′kē-jak′) *n.* The gray or Canada jay (*Perisoreus canadensis*), common in the northern forests of North America, about lumber camps, etc. [Alter. of earlier *whisky-john,* alter. of Algonquian (Cree) *wiskatjan*]

whis·per (hwis′pər) *n.* **1** A low, soft, sibilant voice; articulated but not sonant breath; also, a low, rustling sound, as of waves or leaves. See VOICE. **2** A whispered utterance; secret communication; hint; insinuation. —*v.i.* **1** To speak in a whisper. **2** To talk cautiously or furtively; plot or gossip. **3** To make a low, rustling sound, as leaves. —*v.t.* **4** To utter in a whisper. **5** To speak to in a whisper. [OE *hwisprian*] —**whis′per·er** *n.* —**whis′per·ing** *n. & adj.* —**whis′per·ing·ly** *adv.* —**whis′per·y** *adj.*

whist [1] (hwist) *n.* A game of cards played by four persons with a full pack of 52 cards, opposite players being partners: all the cards are played in each hand, the highest card of the suit led played in each of the 13 tricks, or a card of the trump suit, or the highest trump played, winning such trick. Every trick above the sixth counts one point. See CONTRACT BRIDGE under BRIDGE[2]. [Alter. of earlier *whisk;* ult. origin unknown]

whist[2] (hwist) *interj.* Hush! be still! —*adj.* Silent or quiet; mute. See also WHISHT. [Prob. imit.]

whis·tle (hwis′əl) *n.* **1** A device for producing a shrill, musical sound, operated on the principle of forcing a current of air, steam, or the like, through a pipe or tube of narrowed aperture or against a thin edge. **2** A musical sound, more or less shrill, made without the use of the vocal cords, by sending the breath through a small orifice formed by contracting the lips; also, the act of making this sound. **3** The sound produced by a whistle, or any sound suggestive of it, as the sound of wind rushing by an object, or of a flying missile, or the shrill cry of some birds. **4** A summons or call made by a whistle: The dog comes at his master's *whistle.* **5** *Slang* The mouth and throat: to wet one's *whistle.* **6** The short, loud cry of a male moose or elk. —*v.* **·tled, ·tling** *v.i.* **1** To make a sound or series of sounds like a whistle. **2** To cause a sharp, shrill sound by swift passage through the air, or by passage past an edge or through an orifice: The bullets *whistled* over our heads. **3** To blow or sound a whistle. —*v.t.* **4** To produce, as a tune or melody, by whistling. **5** To call, manage, or direct by whistling. **6** To send with a whistling sound. —**to whistle for** To go without; fail to get. [OE *hwistle* a shrill pipe]

whis·tler (hwis′lər) *n.* **1** One who or that which whistles. **2** A large gray marmot (*Marmota caligata*) of NW North America. **3** One of various birds, as the American goldeneye or the English widgeon: so called from the noise of their wings in flight.

Whis·tler (hwis′lər), **James Abbott McNeill,** 1834–1903, U.S. artist and etcher. —**Whis·tle·ri·an** (hwis·lir′ē·ən) *adj.*

whistle stop *U.S. Colloq.* A small town, where a train stops only on signal. —**whis·tle-stop** (hwis′əl-stop′) *adj.*

whistle blower one who informs authorities of malfeasance in government or business

whit (hwit) *n.* The smallest particle; speck: usually with a negative: not a *whit* abashed. See synonyms under PARTICLE. [Var. of WIGHT[1], as

used in phrases *any wight, no wight,* OE *ænig wiht, nān wiht* a little amount]

Whit·by (hwit′bē) A port on the North Sea in the North Riding, NE York, England.

white (hwit) *adj.* **whit·er, whit·est 1** Having the color produced by reflection of all the rays of the solar spectrum, as from a finely powdered surface; having the color of new snow: opposed to *black.* **2** Light or comparatively light in color; specifically, light-colored as opposed to *red: white* wine. **3** Bloodless; ashen: *white* with rage. **4** Very fair; blond. **5** Silvery, hoary, or gray, as with age. **6** Covered with snow; snowy. **7** Made of silver; also unburnished, as silverwork. **8** Habited in white clothing: *white* nuns. **9** Not intentionally wicked or evil; not malicious or harmful: a *white* lie. **10** Figuratively, free from spot or stain; innocent: a *white* soul. **11** Incandescent; being at white heat. **12** Blank; unmarked by ink: said of a space in an advertisement or the like. **13** Belonging to a racial group characterized by light-colored skin; especially, Caucasian. **14** Of, pertaining to, or controlled by white men: the *white* power structure. **15** *Colloq.* Fair and honorable; straightforward; honest. **16** Propitious; auspicious: a rare meaning. **17** In certain European countries, constitutional; conservative, as a party; opposed to the radicals or revolutionaries. See synonyms under PALE[2]. —*n.* **1** That color seen when sunlight is reflected without sensible absorption of any of the visible rays of the spectrum; the color in the scale of grays which is entirely without hue and is the opposite of *black.* **2** The state or condition of being white; whiteness; figuratively, innocence; truth. **3** The white or light-colored part of something; specifically, the albumen of an egg, or the white part of the eyeball. **4** Anything that is white or nearly white, as cloth or garments; in the plural, a white uniform or outfit: The sailor wore his summer *whites.* **5** White wine. **6** A white paint or pigment; hence, by comparison, a color approaching pure white in its effect. **7** In chess or checkers, the white or light men, or the player who has them. **8** *pl.* Flour made from the finest and whitest part of the wheat. **9** *pl. Printing* Blank spaces in a picture, plate, mold, etc. **10** In archery, the outermost ring of a target; also, a hit on that ring, scoring one point. **11** A member of the so-called white race. **12** In some European countries, a member of a party opposed to the radicals or revolutionaries; a conservative. **13** *pl. Pathol.* Leukorrhea. **14** A breed of animal, especially a swine, that is white in color. —*v.t.* **whit·ed, whit·ing 1** To make white; whiten; bleach. **2** *Printing* To make or leave blank spaces in, as between lines or about an illustration: often with *out:* to *white* out a column. [OE *hwīt*]

White (hwit), **Andrew,** 1832–1918, U.S. educator, historian, and diplomat. —**Byron Raymond,** born 1917, U.S. lawyer; associate justice of the Supreme Court 1962– . —**E(lwyn) B(rooks),** born 1899, U.S. writer and editor. —**Gilbert,** 1720–93, English naturalist and antiquary. —**Peregrine,** 1620–1704, first child of English parentage born in New England. —**Stanford,** 1853–1906, U.S. architect. —**William Allen,** 1868–1944, U.S. editor.

white alkali 1 The product obtained from soda ash during the manufacture of carbonate of soda, dissolved in water, clarified, and freed from moisture by evaporation. **2** Pure soda ash.

white ant A small, whitish, isopterous insect, the termite, closely resembling the true ant in general appearance and social habits: it exists in tropical and warmer temperate regions, and does much damage to wooden structures, furniture, etc., by boring. For illustration see INSECTS (injurious) —**to white ant** *Austral.* To undermine or sabotage.

white-ant·er (hwit′ant′ər) *n. Austral.* One who undermines or sabotages.

white·bait (hwit′bāt′) *n.* **1** The young of various clupeoid fishes, especially of sprat and herring, served as a delicacy. **2** One of various species of silversides of fresh and salt waters of the United States.

white bear The polar bear.

white birch 1 The North American birch (*Betula papyrifera*) with thin, white bark resembling paper. **2** The common European birch (*Betula pendula, B. pubescens*), having an ash-colored bark; also, a related Asian species (*B. platyphylla*).

WHITE BIRCH
a. Leaf. *b.* Fruit.
(Tree 20 to 30 feet tall, rarely 40)

white blood cell Leukocyte.

white book In some European countries and in Japan, a formal report issued by a government on some special subject; in England an alternate of the bluebook: so called from the colors of the bookbinding.

white brant The snow goose.

white bryony A species of bryony (*Bryonia alba*) common in Europe.

white·cap (hwit′kap′) *n.* **1** A foam-crested wave. **2** One of several birds having white about the head.

White·cap (hwit′kap′) *n.* Formerly, in the Middle West and southward, one of a lawless, secret organization of men, who, under the pretense of regulating public morals, imposed lynch-law rule upon individuals who incurred their ill will: so named from their white caps or hoods.

white cedar 1 An evergreen tree (*Chamaecyparis thyoides*) of the cypress family, growing in moist places along the Atlantic coast. **2** Its soft, easily worked wood. **3** The arborvitae.

White·chap·el (hwit′chap·əl) A district in Stepney borough, eastern London, England; the older Jewish quarter.

white clover A common variety (*Trifolium repens*) of clover, with white flowers.

white coal Water considered as a source of power.

white-col·lar (hwit′kol′ər) *adj.* Pertaining to or designating salaried workers in occupations which demand a well-dressed appearance.

white comb A contagious disease of poultry, caused by a fungus (*Lophophyton gallinae*), and marked by the formation of grayish patches on the comb and a breaking off of the feathers.

white corpuscle Leukocyte.

white crane The whooping crane (*Grus americana*) of North America, which is pure white when adult.

white curlew The white ibis (*Guara alba*) of the southern United States.

whit·ed sepulcher (hwit′id) A hypocrite; a person with a pleasing outward aspect, but corrupted thoughts. Matt. xxiii 27.

white elephant 1 A rare pale-gray variety of Asian elephant held sacred by the Burmese and Siamese. **2** Anything rare, expensive, and difficult to keep; a burdensome possession.

white-eye (hwit′ī′) *n.* **1** The white-eyed vireo (*Vireo griseus*) of North America. **2** Any of numerous small singing birds (*Zosterops* and related genera), mostly of the Old World tropics: named from the circle of white feathers around the eye.

white-eyed (hwit′īd′) *adj.* Having the iris of the eye white or colorless, as an albino.

white-faced (hwit′fāst′) *adj.* **1** Pallid in countenance; pale. **2** Having a white mark or spot on the face or front of the head: the *white-faced* hornet. **3** Having a white facing or exposed surface, as a skirt.

white feather A mark of cowardice, full-blooded gamecocks being said to have no white feathers.

White·field (hwit′fēld), **George,** 1714–70, English preacher; a founder of Methodism.

white·fish (hwit′fish′) *n. pl.* **·fish** or **·fish·es 1** A salmonoid food fish (genus *Coregonus*) of North America, living mostly in lakes and having teeth minute or absent. **2** One of various other species of fish, as the menhaden, the European whiting, or the silver salmon (*Oncorhynchus kisutch*). **3** A tropical marine food fish of California (*Caulolatilus princeps*). **4** The young of the bluefish. **5** The beluga.

white flag 1 A flag of truce. **2** A signal of surrender when hoisted over a fortified position or a body of men.

white flax Gold-of-pleasure.

white-foot-ed mouse (hwīt′fŏŏt′id) The deer mouse.

White Friar A Carmelite: so called from the color of his cloak.

White-fri-ars (hwīt′frī′ərz) The neighborhood surrounding the site of a former Carmelite monastery in Fleet Street, London.

white frost Hoar frost.

white gerfalcon The gerfalcon in the phase when its plumage is of a conspicuous, highly prized white color.

white gold An alloy of gold with a white metal, usually nickel and zinc, sometimes palladium.

white-gum (hwīt′gum′) n. 1 An Australian eucalyptus with a white bark. 2 The American sweetgum.

White-hall (hwīt′hôl) 1 A former royal palace near Westminster Abbey. 2 A street in Westminster, London, where a number of government offices are located. 3 The British government.

White-head (hwīt′hed), **Alfred North,** 1861-1947, English mathematician and philosopher, active in the United States.

white heat 1 The temperature at which a body becomes incandescent. 2 A condition of extreme anger or emotional strain.

White-horse (hwīt′hôrs) The capital of Yukon Territory on the upper Yukon River. Also **White Horse.**

white-hors-es (hwīt′hôr′siz) n. pl. Foam-crested waves; white caps (def. 1).

white-hot (hwīt′hot′) adj. 1 Exhibiting the condition of white heat. 2 Colloq. Extremely angry.

White House, The 1 The official residence of the president of the United States, at Washington, D.C.: a white building in American colonial style, officially called the *Executive Mansion.* 2 The executive branch of the United States government.

white lead 1 A poisonous white pigment composed of lead carbonate and hydrated lead oxide and prepared by several processes: also called *ceruse.* 2 Native carbonate of lead; cerusite. See LEAD.

white leather Whiteleather.

white lie See under LIE.

white-liv-ered (hwīt′liv′ərd) adj. 1 Having a pale and feeble look. 2 Base; cowardly; envious.

white lupine A white-flowered variety (*Lupinus albus*) of lupine, grown in Europe for forage.

white-ly (hwīt′lē) adv. With a pale appearance; so as to look white.

white mahogany Primavera.

white man 1 A person belonging to a racial group characterized by light-colored skin: territory first settled by *white men* in 1740. 2 A male member of the so-called white race.

white man's burden The alleged duty of the white peoples to spread culture among the so-called backward peoples of the world: phrase originated by Rudyard Kipling.

white maple Any of certain maples having a whitish bark, as the silver maple (*Acer saccharinum*) and red maple (*A. rubrum*), both of North America.

white matter Anat. That portion of the brain and spinal cord that is composed mainly of medullated nerve fibers, giving it a white appearance: contrasted with *gray matter.*

white meat 1 The light-colored meat or flesh of animals, as veal or the breast of turkey. 2 Obs. Food made from milk, butter, cheese, eggs, and other animal products.

white metal See under METAL.

White Mountains 1 A range of the Appalachians in north central New Hampshire; highest peak, 6,288 feet. 2 A range of mountains in eastern Arizona; highest point, 11,590 feet. 3 A range of mountains in eastern California and SW Nevada; highest point, 14,242 feet.

whit-en (hwīt′n) v.t. & v.i. To make or become white; blanch; bleach. See synonyms under BLEACH. — **whit′en-er** n.

white-ness (hwīt′nis) n. 1 The state of being white; freedom from stains or darkness of surface. 2 Pallor from emotion or from illness. 3 Cleanness or pureness of heart; innocence.

White Nile See NILE.

white oak 1 A North American oak (*Quercus alba*) of the eastern United States, with long leaves having from five to nine entire, rounded lobes. 2 Either of two related species, the swamp white oak (*Q. bicolor*) and the Oregon white oak (*Q. garryana*). 3 The British oak (*Q. petraea*). 4 The wood of any species of white oak.

WHITE OAK
a. Leaf. *b.* Blossom. *c.* Acorn.

white of egg Egg white.

white-out (hwīt′out′) n. Meteorol. An atmospheric condition in arctic regions in which a blending of clouds and snow cover produces a uniform milky whiteness characterized by the absence of shadow and the invisibility of all but very dark objects.

white paper A government publication on some subject of less importance than that treated in a white book or a bluebook. See WHITE BOOK, BLUEBOOK.

White Pass A pass in the Coast Mountains, on the border between SE Alaska and NW British Columbia; elevation 2,888 feet.

white pepper See under PEPPER.

white perch A small food fish (*Morone americana*) related to the sea basses, found in Atlantic coastal waters and sometimes landlocked in streams of the United States.

white pine 1 A pine (*Pinus strobus*) widely distributed in eastern North America, with soft, bluish-green leaves in clusters of five. The cone and tassel of this tree are the State emblem of Maine. 2 The light, soft wood of this tree. 3 Any of several varieties of this pine.

white-pine weevil (hwīt′pīn′) A weevil (*Pissodes strobi*) of NE North America which feeds on the leading shoots of white pine and other conifers. For illustration see INSECTS (injurious).

white plague Pathol. Tuberculosis, especially of the lungs.

white poplar 1 A large, rapidly growing Old World tree (*Populus alba*), often planted in the United States for shade or for its ornamental leaves, which are green above and clothed with a silvery-white down beneath; the silver poplar. 2 The aspen.

white potato The common potato.

white rabbit The varying hare.

white race The Caucasoid ethnic division of mankind.

white rat 1 Any albino rat. 2 One of a special breed of albino Norway rats much used in biological and medical experimentation.

White River 1 A river in northern and eastern Arkansas and SW Missouri, flowing 690 miles to the Mississippi. 2 A river in Nebraska and southern South Dakota, flowing 507 miles NE to the Missouri.

White Russian See under RUSSIAN.

White Russian S.S.R. See BELORUSSIAN SOVIET SOCIALIST REPUBLIC. Also **White Russia.**

White Sands National Monument A government reservation in southern New Mexico; 219 square miles; established 1933.

white sapphire A variety of translucent, colorless corundum.

White Sea An inlet of the Barents Sea in NW European U.S.S.R.; 36,680 square miles. *Russian* **Be-lo-e Mo-re** (bye′lə-yə mô′ryə).

white slave A girl forced into or held in prostitution. — **white–slave** (hwīt′slāv′) adj.

White–slave Act The Mann Act.

white-slav-er (hwīt′slā′vər) n. One who procures or engages in white-slavery.

white-slav-er-y (hwīt′slā′vər-ē) n. The business or practice of forced prostitution.

white-smith (hwīt′smith′) n. 1 A worker in white metals, as a tinsmith. 2 A finisher,

polisher, or galvanizer of iron. Compare BLACKSMITH.

white spruce A spruce (*Picus glauca*) of Canada and the northern United States.

white squall Meteorol. A small whirlwind occurring in the tropics, having no accompanying cloud and often making ocean waters foam-white.

white-tail (hwīt′tāl′) n. 1 The white-tailed deer. 2 The wheatear.

white-tailed deer (hwīt′tāld′) The common North American deer (*Odocoileus virginianus*), having a moderately long tail white on the underside: also called *Virginia deer.*

white-throat (hwīt′thrōt′) n. One of various Old World warblers, especially the common or **greater whitethroat** (*Sylvia cinerea*), with gray head, white throat, and rufous wings.

white-throat-ed sparrow (hwīt′thrō′tid) A common North American sparrow (*Zonotrichia albicollis*), with a prominent white patch on the throat.

white tie 1 A white bow tie, worn with a swallowtail coat. 2 A swallowtail coat and its correct accessories: the phrase is used on invitations, etc., to indicate formal attire.

white trash Poor whites: an offensive term.

white turnip The common turnip (*Brassica rapa*).

white vitriol Hydrated zinc sulfate, $ZnSo_4 \cdot 7H_2O$, widely used in medicine as an emetic, astringent, and antiseptic.

white-wash (hwīt′wosh′, -wôsh′) n. 1 A mixture of slaked lime and water, sometimes with salt, whiting, and glue added, used for whitening walls, etc. 2 A toilet preparation for whitening the skin. 3 Figuratively, a report falsely ascribing virtues, suppressing adverse evidence, etc. 4 A failure to score in a game. — v.t. 1 To coat with whitewash. 2 To gloss over; hide. 3 Colloq. In sports, to defeat without allowing the losing side to score. See synonyms under BLEACH. — **white′wash′er** n.

white wax Paraffin.

white-weed (hwīt′wēd′) n. The oxeye daisy.

white whale The beluga.

white-wing (hwīt′wing′) n. 1 One of the members of the Department of Sanitation of New York City: so called because they formerly wore white uniforms. 2 Any person who wears a white uniform. 3 The surf duck.

white–winged dove (hwīt′wingd′) A dove (*Melopelia asiatica*) of the SW United States with a conspicuous white patch on the wings.

white-wood (hwīt′wŏŏd′) n. 1 Any of various trees yielding a whitish timber, as the basswood, the tuliptree, the cottonwood, the wild cinnamon, etc. 2 The wood of these trees.

Whi-tey (hwī′tē, wī′-) n. pl. -teys U.S. Slang 1 The white man, especially when considered as the oppressor or enemy of the Negro. 2 A white man: an offensive term. Also **whi′·tey.**

whith-er (hwith′ər) adv. 1 As a relative, to which or what: approaching a conjunctive use: the village *whither* we went. 2 As an interrogative, to which or to what place. 3 Wheresoever; whithersoever. 4 To what degree or extent. [OE *hwider*]

whith-er-so-ev-er (hwith′ər-sō-ev′ər) adv. To whatever place.

whit-ing[1] (hwī′ting) n. A pure white chalk, levigated and washed for use in making putty and whitewash, as a pigment, and for polishing.

whit-ing[2] (hwī′ting) n. 1 A small European gadoid food fish (*Merlangus merlangus*) without a barbel. 2 The hake (def. 1). 3 Any of several silvery sciaenoid fishes (genus *Menticirrhus*), especially the Carolina whiting (*M. americanus*), common on the coast of the southern United States. 4 The menhaden. [<MDu. *wijting* < *wit* white]

whit-ish (hwī′tish) adj. Somewhat white or, especially, very light gray. — **whit′ish-ness** n.

whit-leath-er (hwīt′leth′ər) n. Leather tawed with alum to render it pliable; white leather. [<WHITE + LEATHER]

whit-low (hwīt′lō) n. Pathol. An inflammatory tumor, especially on the terminal phalanx of a finger, seated between the epidermis and true skin; a felon. [ME *whitflaw*, appar. <WHITE + FLAW[1]]

Whit-man (hwīt′mən), **Marcus,** 1802-47, U.S. missionary massacred by Indians in Oregon. — **Walt,** 1819-92, U.S. poet.

Whit-Mon-day (hwit'mun'dē, -dā) *n.* The Monday next following Whitsunday: observed in England as a holiday. Also **Whit'mon'day, Whit'sun-Mon'day.** [On analogy with WHITSUNDAY]

Whit-ney (hwit'nē), **Eli,** 1765-1825, American inventor. — **Gertrude,** 1877?-1942, *née* Vanderbilt, U. S. sculptress. — **Josiah Dwight,** 1819-96, U. S. geologist. — **William Dwight,** 1827-94, U. S. philologist; brother of Josiah Dwight.

Whit-ney (hwit'nē), **Mount** A peak of the southern Sierra Nevada Range in eastern California; 14,496 feet; highest point in the United States.

whit-rack (hwit'rak) *n. Dial. & Scot.* A weasel. [ME *whitratt* <WHITE + RAT]

Whit-sun (hwit'sən) *n.* Whitsunday: frequently used in composition: *Whitsun*-ale, *Whitsun*-week. [ME *witsonen, whitsone* < *whitsondei* WHITSUNDAY]

Whit-sun-day (hwit'sun'dē, -dā) *n.* The seventh Sunday after Easter: a church festival commemorating Pentecost. [OE *Hwīta Sunnandæg,* lit., white Sunday; so called from the white robes worn by recently baptized persons on that day]

Whit-sun-week (hwit'sən-wēk') *n.* The week that begins with Whitsunday. Also **Whit'sun-tide'** (-tīd')

Whit-ta-ker (hwit'ə-kər), **Charles E(vans),** born 1901, U. S. jurist; associate justice of the U. S. Supreme Court 1957-1962.

whit-ter (hwit'ər) *n. Scot.* **1** A copious draft of liquor, etc. **2** Anything weak. **3** Chatter; loquacity. **4** A token; sign.

Whit-ti-er (hwit'ē-ər) A port of southern Alaska on Prince William Sound.

Whit-ti-er (hwit'ē-ər), **John Greenleaf,** 1807-1892, U. S. poet.

Whit-ting-ton (hwit'ing-tən), **Richard,** 1358?-1423, English tradesman; lord mayor of London, 1397, 1406, and 1419.

whit-tle¹ (hwit'l) *v.* **-tled, -tling** *v.t.* **1** To cut or shave bits from (wood, a stick, etc.). **2** To make or shape by carving or whittling. **3** To reduce or wear away by paring a little at a time: with *down, off, away,* etc.: to *whittle* down costs. — *v.i.* **4** To whittle wood, usually as an aimless diversion. See synonyms under CUT. [< *n.*] — *n. Dial. & Scot.* A knife; especially, a sheath knife worn at the belt, or any large knife. [Alter. of ME *thwitel* <OE *thwitan* cut] — **whit'tler** *n.*

whit-tle² (hwit'l) *n. Dial.* **1** A blanket. **2** A shaggy mantle formerly worn by countrywomen. Also **whittle shawl.** [OE *hwītel* < *hwīt* white]

whit-tlings (hwit'lingz) *n. pl.* The fine chips and shavings made with a whittle or by a whittler.

Whit-Tues-day (hwit'tōōz'dē, -dā, -tyōōz'-) *n.* The day after Whit-Monday. Also **Whit'sun-Tues'day.** [On analogy with WHITSUNDAY]

whiz (hwiz) *v.* **whizzed, whiz-zing** *v.i.* **1** To make a hissing and humming sound while passing rapidly through the air. **2** To move or pass with such a sound. — *v.t.* **3** To cause to whiz. — *n.* **1** A sibilant sound with some sonant character, such as is produced by a missile passing through the air. **2** *Slang* Any person or thing of extraordinary excellence or ability. **3** *Slang* A bargain. **4** *Slang* A celebration; a spree. Also **whizz.** [Imit.]

whiz-bang (hwiz'bang') *n. Slang* A high-explosive shell; also, a firecracker that explodes with a loud noise. Also **whizz'-bang'.**

who (hōō) *pron. possessive case* **whose;** *objective case* **whom 1** As an interrogative, which or what person or persons. **2** As a relative, that: pointing out or fixing upon a particular person or persons, and identifying the subject or object in a relative clause with that of the principal clause. **3** As a compound relative, he, she, or they that: *Who* steals my purse steals trash. — **as who should say** As one who should say; as if one should say. [OE *hwa, hwā*]

   ◆ In modern usage, *who* as a relative is applied only to persons, *which* only to animals or to inanimate objects, *that* to persons or things indifferently. *Whose* is correctly used as the possessive of *which,* as well as of *who,* especially where the phrase *of which*

would seem awkward: the man *whose* house was sold; a peak *whose (of which* the) summit seeks the sky. The use of *whom* as an interrogative pronoun in initial position, as in *Whom* did you see?, is supported by some grammarians, but the more natural *Who* did you see? *Who* did you give the book to? are in wider use and are now considered acceptable. However, when used after a verb or preposition, *whom* is still required, as in To *whom* did you give it? You saw *whom?* See also usage note under THAT (pronoun).

whoa (hwō) *interj.* Stop! stand still! [Var. of HO]

who-dun-it (hōō-dun'it) *n. Colloq.* A type of mystery fiction or dramatic production which challenges the reader or auditor to detect the perpetrator of a crime. [<WHO + DONE + IT; coined by Donald Gordon in 1930 in *American News of Books*]

who-ev-er (hōō-ev'ər) *pron.* Any one without exception; any person who.

whole (hōl) *adj.* **1** Containing all the parts necessary to make up a total; undivided and undiminished; entire; complete. **2** Having all the essential or original parts in their proper constitution; unbroken and uninjured; sound; intact. **3** Specifically, in or having regained sound health; hale. **4** Having the same parents; full, as opposed to *half-:* a *whole* brother. **5** *Colloq.* Each one of (something); all: He ate the *whole* batch of cookies. **6** *Math.* Integral. — **on the whole** Taking one thing with another. — **out of whole cloth** Fabricated; made up, without foundation in truth or fact, as a story or lie. — *n.* **1** All the parts or elements entering into and making up a thing. **2** An organization of parts making a unity or system; an organism. See synonyms under AGGREGATE, MASS¹. ◆ Homophone: *hole.* [OE (Northumbrian) *hol,* var. of *hāl.* Related to HALE².]

whole blood 1 Full blood. **2** Blood as taken direct from the body, especially that used in transfusions.

whole brother See under BROTHER.

whole gale *Meteorol.* A gale of force 10 on the Beaufort scale.

whole-heart-ed (hōl'här'tid) *adj.* Done or experienced with all earnestness; characteristically sincere, sound, generous, or kind. — **whole'heart'ed-ly** *adv.* — **whole'heart'ed-ness** *n.*

whole-hog (hōl'hôg', -hog') *adj. Colloq.* Thoroughgoing.

whole hog *Colloq.* **1** The whole of anything: to believe in the *whole hog,* accept the *whole hog.* **2** Reliance or approval; trust: We don't put the *whole hog* on them. — **to go the whole hog** *Colloq.* To do something thoroughly; become involved without reservation.

whole milk Milk containing all its constituents: distinguished from *skim milk.*

whole-ness (hōl'nis) *n.* Entireness; completeness.

whole note *Music* A semibreve. See NOTE *n.* (def. 12).

whole number *Math.* A unit or a number composed of units; an integral number or integer: distinguished from *fraction* and *mixed number.*

whole-sale (hōl'sāl') *n.* The sale of goods by the piece or in large bulk or quantity: opposed to *retail.* — *adj.* **1** Selling in quantity, not at retail: a *wholesale* druggist. **2** Done in buying and selling in quantity: the *wholesale* trade. **3** Pertaining to wholesale trade: the *wholesale* price. — Hence, made or done on a large scale; made or done indiscriminately: *wholesale* murder. — *adv.* In bulk or quantity; hence, indiscriminately: to make the medical profession *wholesale.* — *v.t. & v.i.* **-saled, -sal-ing** To sell at wholesale. [ME *holesale* < *by hole sale* in large quantities] — **whole'sal'er** *n.*

whole sister See under SISTER.

whole snipe See under SNIPE.

whole-some (hōl'səm) *adj.* **1** Tending to promote health; salubrious; healthful: *wholesome* air or food. **2** Favorable to virtue and well-being; salutary; sound; beneficial. **3** Healthy; physically, mentally, and morally sound: a *wholesome* girl. **4** Indicative or characteristic of health: *wholesome* red cheeks. **5** Safe; free from danger or risk: This is not a *wholesome* situation. **6** *Obs.* Auspi-

cious; favorable. See synonyms under HEALTHY. [ME *holsum* < *hol* WHOLE + OE *-sum* -SOME¹] — **whole'some-ly** *adv.* — **whole'some-ness** *n.*

whole-souled (hōl'sōld') *adj.* Feeling or acting with one's whole heart; devoted; generous.

whole-wheat (hōl'hwēt') *adj.* Made from wheat grain and bran.

who'll (hōōl) Who will; who shall: a contraction.

whol-ly (hō'lē, hōl'lē) *adv.* **1** Completely; totally. **2** Exclusively; only.

whom (hōōm) *pron.* The objective case of WHO. [OE *hwam,* dative of *hwā* who]

whom-ev-er (hōōm-ev'ər), **whom-so** (hōōm'sō'), **whom-so-ev-er** (hōōm'sō-ev'ər) Objective cases of WHOEVER, WHOSO, etc.

whoop (hōōp, hwōōp, hwŏŏp) *v.i.* **1** To utter loud cries, as of excitement, rage, or exultation. **2** To hoot, as an owl. **3** To make a loud, gasping inspiration, as after a paroxysm of coughing. — *v.t.* **4** To utter with a whoop or whoops. **5** To call, urge, chase, etc., with whoops; hoot. — **to whoop up 1** To arouse enthusiasm in or for; ballyhoo. **2** To raise, as a price, or sum of money. — **to whoop it (or things) up 1** *Slang* To make noisy revelry. **2** To arouse enthusiasm. — *n.* **1** A shout of excitement, encouragement, or exultation; also, a hoot of derision. **2** A signal halloo or a guiding call, as to incite dogs or men in the chase. **3** A loud, convulsive inspiration after a paroxysm of coughing in whooping cough; a sonorous indrawing of breath. **4** An owl's hoot. — *interj.* Hurrah! halloo! [Imit.]

whoop-ee (hwōō'pē, hwŏŏp'ē) *Slang interj.* An exclamation of joy, excitement, etc. — *n.* A hilarious, festive time. — **to make whoopee** To have a noisy, festive time. [<WHOOP]

whoop-er (hōō'pər, hwŏŏ'pər, hwŏŏp'ər) *n.* **1** One who or that which whoops. **2** A large Old World swan (*Cygnus cygnus*). **3** The white crane: so called from its loud cry.

whoop-ing cough (hōō'ping, hŏŏp'ing) *Pathol.* A contagious respiratory disease of bacterial origin chiefly affecting children, marked in its final stage by recurrent paroxysms of violent coughing, ending with a whoop; pertussis.

whooping crane See under CRANE.

whop (hwop) *Colloq. n.* A blow or fall, or the resulting noise. — *v.* **whopped, whop-ping** *v.t.* **1** To strike or beat. **2** To defeat convincingly. — *v.i.* **3** To drop or fall suddenly; flop. Also spelled *whap.* [Var. of WAP¹]

whop-per (hwop'ər) *n. Colloq.* **1** One who whops. **2** Something large or remarkable, especially a surprising falsehood. Also spelled *whapper.*

whop-ping (hwop'ing) *adj.* Unusually large; excessively exaggerated.

whore (hôr) *n.* A prostitute. — *v.* **whored, whor-ing** *v.i.* **1** To have illicit sexual intercourse, especially with a prostitute. **2** To be a whore. — *v.t.* **3** To make a whore of; corrupt; debauch. ◆ Homophone: *hoar.* [OE *hōre,* prob. <ON *hōra*]

whore-dom (hôr'dəm, hōr'-) *n.* **1** The practice of illicit sexual intercourse. **2** Whores collectively. **3** In the Bible, idolatry. [Prob. <ON *hōrdōmr*]

whore-house (hôr'hous', hōr'-) *n.* A house of prostitution.

whore-mas-ter (hôr'mas'tər, -mäs'-, hōr'-) *n.* **1** A procurer; pander. **2** A whoremonger.

whore-mon-ger (hôr'mung'gər, -mong'-, hōr'-) *n.* **1** A man who has intercourse with whores. **2** A pander.

whore-son (hôr'sən, hōr'-) *n. Obs.* The son of a whore: commonly, a term of contempt. [ME *hores son,* trans. of AF *fiz a putain*]

whor-ish (hôr'ish, hōr'ish) *adj.* Addicted to unlawful sexual indulgences; unchaste; lewd. — **whor'ish-ly** *adv.* — **whor'ish-ness** *n.*

whorl (hwûrl, hwôrl) *n.* **1** The flywheel of a spindle; wherve. **2** *Bot.* A set of leaves, etc., on the same plane with one another; distributed in a circle; a verticil. **3** *Zool.* A turn or volution, as of a spiral shell. **4** Any of the convoluted ridges of a fingerprint. [ME *wharwyl,*

WHORL (def. 2)

whorwhil, appar. vars. of WHIRL; infl. in form by *wharve*]

whorled (hwûrld, hwôrld) *adj.* Furnished with or arranged in whorls.

whort (hwûrt) *n.* The whortleberry, or its fruit. Also **whor·tle** (hwûr′təl). [OE *horta* a whortleberry.]

whor·tle·ber·ry (hwûr′təl·ber′ē) *n.* *pl.* **·ries** 1 A European variety of blueberry (*Vaccinium myrtillus*); the bilberry. 2 Its blue–black fruit. 3 The huckleberry. [Dial. var. of HURTLEBERRY.]

whose (hōoz) The possessive case of WHO and often of WHICH. See under WHO. [OE *hwæs*, genitive of *hwā* who]

whose·so·ev·er (hōoz′sō·ev′ər) Possessive case of WHOSOEVER.

who·so (hōo′sō) *pron.* Whoever; any person who. [Reduced form of OE *swā hwā swā*, generalized form of *hwā* who]

who·so·ev·er (hōo′sō·ev′ər) *pron.* Any person whatever; who; whoever.

why (hwī) *adv.* 1 For what cause, purpose, or reason; wherefore: used interrogatively: *Why* did you go? 2 Because of which; for which; the reason or cause for which: used relatively: I don't know *why* he went; I know no reason *why* he went. — *n.* *pl.* **whys** 1 An explanatory cause; reason; cause. 2 A puzzling problem; riddle; enigma. — *interj.* An introductory expletive, sometimes denoting surprise. [OE *hwī, hwȳ*, instrumental case of *hwæt* what]

whyd·ah (hwid′ə), **whydah bird** See WHIDAH BIRD.

wi' (wi) *prep.* *Scot.* With.

wich (wich) See WITCH².

Wich·i·ta (wich′ə·tô) *n.* A member of a North American Indian confederacy of Caddoan linguistic stock, formerly inhabiting Oklahoma and Texas.

Wich·i·ta (wich′ə·tô) A city on the Arkansas River in south central Kansas; a center of the food and oil industries.

Wichita River A river in Texas, flowing 250 miles NE to the Red River.

wick¹ (wik) *n.* A band of loosely twisted or woven fibers, as in a candle or lamp, acting by capillary attraction to convey oil or other illuminant to a flame. [OE *wēoca*] — **wick′ing** *n.*

wick² (wik) *Scot.* *v.t.* In curling, to strike (a stone) obliquely. — *n.* 1 In curling, an opening surrounded by stones already played. 2 A creek; inlet.

wick³ (wik) *n.* A village or town: now mostly in composition, often as **-wich**: *Woolwich*. [OE *wīc*, appar. <L *vicus*]

wick·ed (wik′id) *adj.* 1 Evil in principle and practice; vicious; sinful; depraved. 2 Mischievous; roguish. 3 Noxious; pernicious. 4 Troublesome; painful. See synonyms under BAD, CRIMINAL, IMMORAL, INFAMOUS, PROFANE, SINFUL. [ME < *wikke, wicke*, appar. <OE *wicca* a wizard] — **wick′ed·ly** *adv.*

wick·ed·ness (wik′id·nis) *n.* 1 The quality of being wicked; moral depravity; sin; vice; crime: opposed to *goodness*. 2 A wicked thing or act; wicked conduct: to work *wickedness*.

wick·er (wik′ər) *adj.* Made of twigs, osiers, etc. — *n.* 1 A pliant young shoot or rod; twig; osier. 2 Ware made of such shoots. [Prob. <Scand. Cf. dial. Sw. *viker* < *vika* bend.]

wick·er·work (wik′ər·wûrk′) *n.* A fabric or texture, as a basket, made of woven twigs, osiers, etc.; basketwork.

wick·et (wik′it) *n.* 1 A small door or gate subsidiary to or made within a larger entrance. 2 A small opening in a door. 3 A small sluicegate in a canal lock or at the end of a millrace. 4 In cricket, an arrangement of three upright rods called *stumps* set near together, with two crosspieces called *bails* laid over the top; also, the place at which the wicket is set up; the right or turn of each batsman at the wicket; the playing pitch between the wickets: a fast *wicket*; an inning that is not finished or not begun: The eleven won by three *wickets*, that is, the two men at bat and one yet to go in. 5 In croquet, an arch, usually of wire. [<AF *wiket*, OF *guichet*, prob. <Gmc.]

wick·et–keep·er (wik′it·kē′pər) *n.* In cricket, the fielder stationed immediately behind the wicket which is being bowled at.

wick·i·up (wik′ē·up) *n.* A loosely constructed hut of certain North American Indian tribes: distinguished from *tepee* or *wigwam*: also spelled *wikiup*. [<Algonquian. Cf. Sac and Fox *wikiyap* a lodge.]

Wic·liffe (wik′lif), **Wic·lif, Wic·liff·ite**, etc. See WYCLIF, etc.

Wick·low (wik′lō) A maritime county of eastern Leinster province, Ireland; 782 square miles; county town, Wicklow.

wic·o·py (wik′ə·pē) *n.* *pl.* **·pies** 1 The leatherwood. 2 The basswood. 3 Any of several species of willow herb. [<Algonquian. Cf. Cree *wikupiy*.]

wid·der·shins (wid′ər·shinz) See WITHERSHINS.

wid·dle (wid′l) *v.t.* & *n.* *Dial.* & *Scot.* Wriggle; struggle; waddle.

wid·dy¹ (wid′ē) *n.* *pl.* **·dies** *Scot.* A halter of withes; withy; hangman's noose; hence, the gallows. Also **wid′die.**

wid·dy² (wid′ē) *n.* *pl.* **·dies** *Dial.* Widow. [Var. of WITHY]

wide (wīd) *adj.* **wid·er, wid·est** 1 Having relatively great extent between sides; broad, as opposed to *narrow*. 2 Extended far in every direction; ample; spacious: a *wide* expanse. 3 Having a specified degree of width or breadth: an inch *wide*. 4 Distant from the desired or proper point by a great extent of space; remote; wild: *wide* of the mark. 5 Figuratively, having intellectual breadth; considering questions from all points of view; liberal: a man of *wide* views. 6 Fully open; expanded or extended: *wide* eyes. 7 *Phonet.* Lax. 8 Comprehensive; inclusive: *wide* learning. 9 Loose; ample; roomy: *wide* breeches. 10 In the stock exchange, exhibiting a considerable range between high and low, or bid and offered prices: a *wide* opening. See synonyms under LARGE. — *n.* 1 In cricket, a ball bowled too far over or on either side of the wicket to be within the batsman's reach. 2 Breadth of extent; also, a broad, open space. — *adv.* 1 To a great distance; extensively. 2 Far from the mark. 3 To the greatest extent; fully open. [OE *wīd*] — **wide′ly** *adv.* — **wide′ness** *n.*

◆ Various self-explaining compounds have *wide* as their first element: **wide′–arched′, wide′–branched′, wide′–brimmed′**, etc.

wide–an·gle lens (wīd′ang′gəl) *Phot.* A type of camera lens designed and ground to permit an angle of view wider than that of the ordinary lens, or more than 50 degrees.

wide–a·wake (wīd′ə·wāk′) *adj.* Marked by vigilance and alertness; keen. See synonyms under ALERT, VIGILANT. — *n.* A soft, broadbrimmed felt hat: also **wide′–a·wake′ hat.**

wide–eyed (wīd′īd′) *adj.* 1 With the eyes wide open, as if gazing intently in wonder or surprise. 2 Marked by an innocent readiness to believe or admire; uninformed or unsophisticated: *wide–eyed* trust of any stranger she happened to meet.

.wid·en (wīd′n) *v.t.* & *v.i.* To make or become wide or wider. See synonyms under AMPLIFY. — **wid′en·er** *n.*

wide–o·pen (wīd′ō′pən) *adj.* 1 Opened wide: The gates are *wide–open*. 2 *Colloq.* Remiss in the enforcement of laws which regulate various forms of vice, as gambling, prostitution, etc.: a *wide–open* city.

wide–spread (wīd′spred′) *adj.* Extending over a large space or territory; general: a *widespread* belief. Also **wide′spread′.**

widge·on (wij′ən) *n.* Any of a genus (*Mareca*) of river ducks with short bill and wedge-shaped tail; especially, the **American widgeon**, or baldpate (*M. americana*), esteemed as a game bird: also spelled *wigeon*. [Cf. MF *vigeon* a wild duck.]

Wi·dor (vē·dôr′), **Charles Marie**, 1845–1937, French organist and composer.

wid·ow (wid′ō) *n.* 1 A woman who has lost her husband by death and has not remarried. 2 In some card games, an additional hand dealt to the table; also, a kitty. 3 *Printing* An incomplete line of type ending a paragraph; especially, a single line or less at the top of a page or column. — *v.t.* 1 To make a widow of; deprive of a husband: usually in the past participle: a woman *widowed* by war. 2 To deprive of something desirable; bereave. 3 *Rare* To survive as the widow of. 4 *Rare* To recognize as a widow; give the rights of

a widow to. — *adj.* Widowed. [OE *widewe, wuduwe*]

widow bird A whidah bird. [<NL *Vidua*, genus name, trans. of Pg. *viuva*, lit., a widow]

wid·ow·er (wid′ō·ər) *n.* A man whose wife is dead, and who has not married again. [ME *widwer* < *widwe*, OE *widewe* a widow]

wid·ow·hood (wid′ō·hŏod) *n.* The state or condition of being a widow, or, rarely, of being a widower; also, the period during which one is a widow.

widow's cruse An endless or inexhaustible supply: in allusion to the stories in I *Kings* xvii 10–16, and II *Kings* iv 1–7.

widow's mite See MITE².

widow's peak See PEAK¹.

width (width) *n.* 1 Dimension or measurement of an object taken from side to side, or at right angles to the length. 2 Wideness; the state or fact of being wide. 3 Something that has width; specifically, in dressmaking, one of the several pieces of material used in making a garment. [<WIDE, on analogy with *breadth*]

width·wise (width′wīz′) *adv.* In the direction of the width; from side to side. Also **width′way′** (-wā′), **width′ways′.**

Wi·du·kind (vē′dŏo·kint) See WITTEKIND.

wiel (wēl) *n.* *Scot.* An eddy; pool.

Wie·land (vē′länt), **Christoph Martin**, 1733–1813, German poet, novelist, and translator. — **Heinrich**, 1877–1957, German chemist.

wield (wēld) *v.t.* 1 To use or handle, as a weapon or instrument, especially with full command and effect. 2 To exercise (authority, power, influence, etc.). 3 *Obs.* To exercise authority over; command. [Fusion of OE *wealdan* cause and OE *wildan* rule] — **wield′a·ble** *adj.* — **wield′er** *n.*

wield·y (wēl′dē) *adj.* **wield·i·er, wield·i·est** Easily handled; wieldable: opposed to *unwieldy*.

Wie·licz·ka (vye·lech′kä) A town 7 miles SE of Cracow, Poland; a salt–mining center since the 11th century.

Wien (vēn) The German name for VIENNA.

Wien (vēn), **Wilhelm**, 1864–1928, German physicist.

wie·ner (wē′nər) *n.* *U.S.* A kind of sausage, often shorter than a frankfurter, made of beef and pork: often called *weenie*. Also **wie·ner–wurst** (wē′nər·wûrst′, *Ger.* vē′nər·vŏorst′). [Short for G *wiener-(wurst)* Vienna (sausage)]

Wie·ner schnit·zel (vē′nər shnit′səl) A breaded veal cutlet, seasoned or garnished in any of several ways, as with capers, anchovies, a fried egg, or the like. [<G <*Wiener* Viennese + *schnitzel* a cutlet, dim. of *schnitz* a slice <*schneiden* cut]

Wieprz (vyepsh) A river in central Poland, flowing 194 miles NW to the Vistula.

Wies·ba·den (vēs′bä·dən) The capital of Hesse, West Germany, on the Rhine west of Frankfurt: site of a famous spa.

wife (wīf) *n.* *pl.* **wives** (wīvz) 1 A woman joined to a man in lawful wedlock; a spouse: the correlative of *husband*. ◆ Collateral adjective: *uxorial*. 2 A grown woman; adult female: usually in composition or in certain phrases: *housewife*, old *wives'* tales. — **to take (a woman) to wife** To marry (a woman). [OE *wīf*] — **wife′dom, wife′hood** *n.* — **wife′less** *adj.* — **wife′ly** *adj.*

wife–carl (wīf′kärl) *n.* *Scot.* A man who meddles with household affairs, especially such as belong naturally to women.

wig (wig) *n.* An artificial covering of hair for the head, so constructed as to form an imitation of the natural growth or to act as a coiffure. — *v.t.* **wigged, wig·ging** 1 To furnish with a wig or wigs. 2 *Brit. Colloq.* To censure severely; berate or scold, especially in public. [Short for PERIWIG]

wig·an (wig′ən) *n.* A stiff, canvaslike fabric used for stiffening the borders of garments. [from *Wigan*, where originally made]

BARRISTER'S WIG

Wig·an (wig′ən) A county borough in south central Lancashire, England.

wig·eon (wij′ən) See WIDGEON.

wigged (wigd) *adj.* Furnished with or wearing a wig.

wig·ger·y (wig′ər·ē) *n.* *pl.* **·ger·ies** 1 A peruke;

wig; also, wigs collectively. **2** Excessive formality; red-tapism. **3** The material of a wig; false hair.

Wig·gin (wig′in), **Kate Douglas**, *née* Smith, 1856–1923, U.S. educator and novelist.

wig·ging (wig′ing) *n. Brit. Colloq.* A rebuke; a scolding.

wig·gle (wig′əl) *v.t. & v.i.* **·gled, ·gling** To move or cause to move quickly and irregularly from side to side; squirm; wriggle. — *n.* The act of wiggling. [? <MLG *wiggelen*] —**wig′gly** *adj.*

wig·gler (wig′lər) *n.* **1** One who or that which wiggles. **2** The larva of a mosquito; a wiggletail.

Wig·gles·worth (wig′əlz·wûrth), **Michael**, 1631–1705, American divine and poet.

wig·gle·tail (wig′əl·tāl′) *n.* **1** The larva of a mosquito. **2** A tadpole.

wight[1] (wīt) *n.* A person; creature: usually an archaic or humorous term. [OE *wiht* a creature]

wight[2] (wīt) *adj. Obs.* Full of prowess; strong and valiant; active; swift. [<ON *vigt*, neut. of *vigr* able to fight]

Wight (wīt), **Isle of** An island in the English Channel just off the southern coast of England, comprising an administrative county of Hampshire; 147 square miles.

Wig·man (vikh′män), **Mary**, born 1886, German dancer; leading pioneer of modern dance.

Wig·ner (wig′nər), **Eugene Paul**, born 1902, U.S. physicist born in Hungary.

Wig·town (wig′tən) A county in SW Scotland; 487 square miles; county town, Wigtown. Also **Wig′town·shire** (-shir).

wig·wag (wig′wag′) *v.t. & v.i.* **·wagged, ·wagging 1** To move briskly to and fro; wag. **2** To send (a message) by hand flags, torches, etc. — *n.* The act or art of signaling with such flags, etc., or the message so sent. [< dial. E *wig* wiggle + WAG[1]] — **wig′wag′ger** *n.*

wig·wam (wig′wom, -wôm) *n.* **1** A dwelling or lodge of the North American Indians of Algonquian stock, used in the area from Canada to North Carolina and in the Great Lakes regions: commonly an arbor-shaped or conical framework of poles covered with bark, rush matting, or hides. **2** By extension, a family of Indians. **3** A dwelling or lodge of North American Indians of other than Algonquian stock: a misuse by early travelers. **4** *Slang* A public building used for political gatherings, mass meetings, etc. — **the Wigwam** Tammany Hall. [<Algonquian (Ojibwa) *wigwaum*, lit., their dwelling]

WIGWAM
Eastern North
American Indian.

wik·i·up (wik′ē·up) See WICKIUP.

Wil·ber·force (wil′bər·fôrs, -fōrs), **William**, 1759–1833, English abolitionist and philanthropist.

Wil·bur (wil′bər) A masculine personal name. [<Gmc., ? resolute protection]

Wil·cox (wil′koks), **Ella**, *née* Wheeler, 1855?–1919, U.S. poet and author.

wild (wīld) *adj.* **1** Inhabiting the forest or open field; not domesticated or tamed; living in a state of nature: a *wild* horse; shy and easily startled: The deer are *wild*. **2** Growing or produced without care or culture; not cultivated: *wild* flowers. **3** Being in the natural state: being without civilized inhabitants or cultivation; desert; waste: *wild* prairies. **4** Living without any civilization and in a rude, savage way; uncivilized: the *wild* men of Borneo. **5** Boisterous; in a bad sense, dissolute; prodigal; in a milder sense, frolicsome and gay. **6** Affected with or originating violent disturbances, as of the elements or of human passions; stormy; turbulent: a *wild* night, a *wild* crowd. **7** Showing reckless want of judgment; rashly imprudent; extravagant: a *wild* speculation. **8** Fantastically irregular or disordered; odd in arrangement or effect; strange or weird: a *wild* imagination, *wild* dress. **9** Eager and excited, as by reason of joy, fear, desire, etc.: She was *wild* with delight. **10** Excited to frenzy or distraction; roused to

fury or desperation; crazed or crazy: The mosquitoes are driving me *wild*. **11** Being or going far from the proper course or from the mark aimed at; erratic; wide of the mark: a *wild* ball, a *wild* guess. **12** In some card games, having its value arbitrarily determined by the dealer or holder: to play poker with fours *wild*. **13** *Slang* **a** Terrific; great: a *wild* party. **b** Showy; jazzy: a *wild* necktie. See synonyms under ABSURD, BLEAK[1], FIERCE, INSANE, ROMANTIC, TURBULENT, VIOLENT, WANTON. — *n.* An uninhabited or uncultivated place; a waste; wilderness. — **the wild** The wilderness; also, the free, natural, wild life: the call of *the wild*. — *adv.* **1** Wildly. **2** Without control; unrestrainedly: The locomotive is running *wild*. [OE *wilde*] — **wild′ly** *adv.* — **wild′ness** *n.*

wild allspice The spicebush.

wild boar The native hog (*Sus scrofa*) of continental Europe, southern Asia, and North Africa, and formerly of Great Britain.

wild brier 1 Any species of rose in the wild state. **2** The dog rose. **3** The sweetbrier.

wild carrot An umbelliferous herb (*Daucus carota*) from which the cultivated carrot is derived; Queen Anne's lace.

wild·cat (wīld′kat′) *n.* **1** A small, undomesticated feline carnivore (*Felis sylvestris*) of Europe, resembling the domestic cat, but larger and stronger. **2** The North American bobcat (genus *Lynx*). **3** One of several other small felines, as the ocelot and serval. **4** Figuratively, an aggressive, quick-tempered person. **5** An unattached locomotive and its tender, used on special work, as when sent out to haul a train, etc. **6** A successful oil well drilled in an area previously unproductive. **7** A tricky or unsound business venture; specifically, a worthless mine. Also **wild cat.** — *adj.* **1** Unsound; risky; especially, financially unsound or risky: a *wildcat* venture. **2** Illegal; made, produced, or carried on without official sanction or authorization. **3** Not running on schedule time; also, running wild or without control, as a railroad train or engine. — *v.t. & v.i.* **·cat·ted, ·cat·ting** To drill for oil in (an area not known to be productive). — **wild′cat′ting** *n. & adj.*

wildcat bank Prior to the passage of the National Bank Act of 1863–64, a bank operating with insufficient capital to redeem its circulating notes.

wildcat bill A note of a wildcat bank.

wildcat mine A worthless mine; especially, one represented to possible investors as being profitably productive.

wildcat strike A strike unauthorized by regular union procedure.

wild·cat·ter (wīld′kat′ər) *n.* **1** A promoter of mines of doubtful value. **2** One who develops oil wells in unproved territory. **3** One who manufactures illicit whisky.

wild cherry Any of certain species of cherry found growing wild; especially, the wild black cherry (*Prunus serotina*) and the chokecherry.

Wilde (wīld), **Oscar Fingall O'Flahertie Wills**, 1856–1900, Irish poet and playwright.

wilde·beest (wīld′bēst, wil′də-; *Du.* vil′də·bāst) *n.* A gnu. [<Afrikaans <Du. *wild* wild + *beeste* a beast]

wil·der (wil′dər) *Poetic v.t.* **1** To bewilder. **2** To lead astray; mislead. — *v.i.* **3** To be bewildered. **4** To wander; stray. [Prob. back formation <WILDERNESS] — **wil′der·ment** *n.*

Wil·der (wil′dər), **Thornton Niven**, 1897–1975, U.S. novelist and playwright.

wil·der·ness (wil′dər·nis) *n.* **1** An uncultivated, uninhabited, or barren region. **2** A waste, as of an ocean. **3** A multitudinous and confusing collection: a *wilderness* of curiosities. **4** *Obs.* Wildness. [OE *wilder* a wild beast (< *wilde* wild + *deor* an animal, deer) + -NESS]

Wil·der·ness (wil′dər·nis), **The** A region in NE Virginia; scene of a Civil War battle, 1864.

wild·fire (wīld′fīr′) *n.* **1** A raging, destructive fire: now generally in phrases like *to spread like wildfire*. **2** A composition of inflammable materials, or the flame produced by it, very hard to put out; Greek fire. **3** A phosphorescent luminousness; ignis fatuus. **4** *Obs.* A spreading inflammation of the skin; erysipelas. **5** A skin disease of sheep with inflammation.

wild flax 1 Toadflax. **2** Gold-of-pleasure.

wild-flow·er (wīld′flou′ər) *n.* **1** Any uncultivated flower. **2** The plant growing it. Also **wild flower.**

wild-fowl (wīld′foul′) *n.* Wild game birds, especially wild ducks and geese. Also **wild fowl.**

wild gean (gēn) **1** A European wild cherry (*Prunus avium*), yielding a fine cabinet wood. **2** Its small dark fruit, the mazzard cherry. [<WILD + dial. E *gean* the wild cherry <OF *guine*, prob. <Gmc.]

wild goose An undomesticated goose, as the English graylag, or the Canada goose.

wild-goose chase (wīld′gōōs′) Pursuit of the unknown or unattainable; a bootless enterprise.

wild honeysuckle The pinkster flower.

wild hyacinth 1 The eastern camas (*Camassia scilloides*) of the United States. **2** The wood hyacinth.

wild indigo Any of a genus (*Baptisia*) of perennial North American herbs, especially one (*B. tinctoria*) having yellow flowers and a root which yields a purgative glycoside.

wild·ing (wīl′ding) *adj.* Growing wild; uncultivated; undomesticated. — *n.* **1** An uncultivated plant; a fruit tree on its own roots growing among grafted trees. **2** A cultivated plant that has sprung up spontaneously; an escape (def. 4). **3** A creature not conforming to type.

wild lettuce 1 A tall, yellow-flowered herb (*Lactuca virosa*) found in the northern United States. **2** The round-leaved wintergreen (*Pyrola rotundifolia*). **3** The prickly lettuce (*Lactuca serriola*).

wild-life (wīld′līf′) *n.* Wild animals, trees, and plants collectively, especially as objects of government conservation. — *adj.* Pertaining to wild animals, trees, and plants collectively.

wild·ling (wīld′ling) *n.* An uncultivated plant or flower; a wild animal. [<WILD + -LING[1]]

wild madder 1 Madder (def. 1). **2** Either of two herbs (genus *Galium*) of the madder family, the white bedstraw (*G. mollugo*) and the dye bedstraw (*G. tinctorium*).

wild mandrake The May apple.

wild mare 1 A nightmare. **2** A see-saw.

wild mustard An annual herb (*Brassica kaber*) of the mustard family, frequently growing as a weed, whose seeds are sometimes used as a substitute for mustard and its leaves cooked as greens: also called *charlock*.

wild oat 1 An uncultivated grass (genus *Avena*); especially, the common European meadow weed (*A. fatua*). **2** *pl.* Indiscretions of youth.

wild olive Any of various trees resembling the olive or bearing an olivelike fruit.

wild pansy The European heartsease (*Viola tricolor*), from which the common garden pansy is derived.

wild parsley 1 Any of a genus (*Lomatium*) of perennial herbs of the carrot family, especially the nine-leaf species (*L. simplex*), valued as a forage plant in the western United States: also called *biscuitroot*. **2** Lovage.

wild parsnip 1 The parsnip in its uncultivated, weedlike form. **2** A perennial herb (*Angelica lyalli*) of the carrot family, resembling the water hemlock but non-poisonous and useful as a forage plant.

wild pink An American catchfly (*Silene caroliniana*) with white or rose-colored flowers and long spatulate or lanceolate flowers.

wild rice 1 A tall aquatic grass of North America (*Zizania aquatica*). **2** The grain of this plant: formerly used as food by North American Indians, now esteemed as a table delicacy: also called *Indian rice*.

wild rose Any of various uncultivated roses of the north temperate zone, as the sweetbrier.

wild rubber Rubber as extracted from the rubber tree (genus *Hevea*) in its wild state.

wild rye A tall perennial grass (genus *Elymus*), widely distributed in temperate regions.

wild sage 1 The sagebrush of the western United States. **2** The Old World vervain sage (*Salvia verbeneca*) known as wild clary.

wild spinach 1 A goosefoot sometimes used as a substitute for spinach. **2** One of several other spinaceous plants.

wild turkey A large North American turkey

(*Meleagris gallopavo silvestris*) formerly ranging east of the Rocky Mountains from southern Canada to Florida and Mexico, and first domesticated in Mexico.

wild vanilla A smooth, erect, perennial herb (*Trilisa odoratissima*) of the composite family, found in the SE United States. Its leaves give off an odor of vanilla.

wild wall A soundproof movable wall used on motion-picture sets: also called *jockey wall*.

Wild West The western United States, especially in its early period of Indian fighting, pioneer conditions, and lawlessness.

Wild West show A circus or a feature of a circus presenting feats of Indian and cowboy horsemanship; also, a rodeo.

wild·wood (wīld′wo͝od′) *n.* Natural forest land.

wild yam An uncultivated species of yam (*Dioscorea villosa*) of the eastern United States; the colic root.

wile (wīl) *n.* **1** An act or a means of cunning deception; also, any beguiling trick or artifice. **2** Craftiness; cunning. See synonyms under ARTIFICE. — *v.t.* **wiled**, **wil·ing** **1** To lure, beguile, or mislead. **2** To pass divertingly, as time: usually with *away*: by confusion with *while*. [OE *wīl*, prob. <Scand. Cf. ON *vēl* an artifice.]

Wi·ley (wī′lē), **Harvey Washington**, 1844–1930, U.S. chemist.

Wil·fred (wil′frid) A masculine personal name. Also **Wil′frid**. [<Gmc., willing peace]

wil·ful (wil′fəl) *adj.* **1** Bent on having one's own way; headstrong; self-willed. **2** Resulting from the exercise of one's own will; voluntary; intentional. Also spelled *willful*. See synonyms under PERVERSE. — **wil′ful·ly** *adv.* — **wil′ful·ness** *n.*

Wil·helm (vil′helm) German form of WILLIAM. — **Wilhelm I**, 1797–1888, king of Prussia 1861–88 and emperor of Germany 1871–88. — **Wilhelm II**, 1859–1941, emperor of Germany 1888–1918.

Wil·hel·mi·na (wil′hel·mē′nə) A feminine personal name. Also **Wil·hel·mine** (wil′hel·mēn, *Fr.* vē·lel·mēn′, *Ger.* vil′hel·mē′nə). [Fem. of WILHELM] — **Wilhelmina**, 1880–1962, queen of the Netherlands 1890–1948; abdicated in favor of her daughter Juliana: full name *Wilhelmina Helena Pauline Maria of Orange-Nassau*.

Wil·helms·ha·ven (vil′helms·hä′fən) A port on the North Sea in former Oldenburg state, Lower Saxony, NW West Germany.

Wil·helm·stras·se (vil′helm·shträ′sə) **1** A street in Berlin on which the German foreign office and government offices were formerly located. **2** Formerly, the German government, especially its foreign policies.

Wilkes (wilks), **Charles**, 1798–1877, U.S. admiral and Antarctic explorer. — **John**, 1727–97, English politician.

Wilkes–Bar·re (wilks′bar·ē) A city on the Susquehanna River in NE Pennsylvania, an industrial and coal-mining center.

Wilkes Land (wilks) Part of Antarctica on the Indian Ocean south of Australia, between Queen Mary Coast and George V Coast; site of the south magnetic pole in its eastern part.

Wil·kins (wil′kinz), **Sir George Hubert**, 1888–1958, Australian aviator and explorer. — **Mary Eleanor** See FREEMAN, MARY E. WILKINS. — **Roy**, born 1901, U.S. civil rights leader for Negroes.

Wil·kin·son (wil′kən·sən), **James**, 1757–1825, American Revolutionary general and politician.

will¹ (wil) *n.* **1** The power of conscious, deliberate action; the faculty by which the rational mind makes choice of its ends of action, and directs the energies in carrying out its determinations; in popular usage, choice, purpose, or directive effort. **2** The act or experience of exercising this faculty; a volition or a choice. **3** Strong determination; practical enthusiasm; energy of character: He works with a *will*; also, self-control. **4** That which has been resolved or determined upon; a purpose. **5** Power to dispose of a matter arbitrarily; discretion. **6** *Law* The legal declaration of a man's intentions as to his estate after his death; the written instrument by which someone declares his desires for the distribution of his property. **7** A conscious inclination toward any end or course; a wish. **8** A request or command. — **at will** As one pleases. — *v.* **willed**, **will·ing**; third per-

son singular, present indicative **wills** *v.t.* **1** To decide upon; choose. **2** To resolve upon as an action or course; determine to do. **3** To give, devise, or bequeath by a will. **4** To control, as a hypnotized person, by the exercise of will. **5** *Archaic* To have a wish for; desire. — *v.i.* **6** To exercise the will. [OE *willa*] — **will′a·ble** *adj.*

Synonyms (*noun*): decision, desire, disposition, inclination, resolution, volition, wish. *Will* is a word of wide range of meaning, and both as faculty and act has been the subject of many and various theories; in popular language *will* is often equivalent to *desire* or *inclination*, as when we speak of doing something against our *will*. *Volition* is a word of scientific precision, denoting the determinative element of *will*.

will² (wil) *v.* Present *sing.* & *pl.*: **will** (*Archaic* **thou wilt**); past: **would** (*Archaic* **thou would·est** or **wouldst**) As an auxiliary verb *will* is used with the infinitive without *to*, or elliptically without the infinitive, to express: **1** Futurity: They *will* arrive by dark. ◆ See usage note under SHALL. **2** Willingness or disposition: Why *will* you not tell the truth? **3** Capability or capacity: The ship *will* survive any storm. **4** Custom or habit: He *will* sit for hours and brood. **5** *Colloq.* Probability or inference: I expect this *will* be the main street. — *v.t.* & *v.i.* To wish or have a wish; desire: What *wilt* thou? As you *will*. [OE *willan*]

Wil·lam·ette River (wi·lam′it) A river in NW Oregon, flowing 190 miles north to the Columbia River.

Wil·lard (wil′ərd), **Emma**, 1787–1870, *née* Hart, U.S. pioneer in education for women. — **Frances Elizabeth Caroline**, 1839–98, U.S. temperance advocate.

Will·cocks (wil′koks), **Sir William**, 1852–1932, English engineer.

willed (wild) *adj.* Having a will, especially one of a given character: mostly in composition: self-*willed*.

wil·lem·ite (wil′əm·īt) *n.* A vitreous or resinous orthosilicate of zinc, crystallizing in the hexagonal system and occurring in many colors. [<Du. *willemit*, after *Willem I* William of Orange]

Wil·lem·stad (wil′əm·stät, vil′-) A town on Curaçao, capital of Netherlands Antilles.

will·er (wil′ər) *n.* One who wills.

Willes·den (wilz′dən) A municipal borough in Middlesex, England, NW of London.

wil·let (wil′it) *n.* A large, light-colored shore bird (*Catoptrophorus semipalmatus*) of North America, related to the snipes. [Short for *pill-will-willet*, imit. of the cry of the bird]

will·ful (wil′fəl), **will·ful·ly**, **will·ful·ness** See WILFUL, etc.

will I, nill I or **will he, nill he** or **will ye, nill ye** Willingly or unwillingly; without choice. See WILLY-NILLY.

Wil·liam (wil′yəm) A masculine personal name. Also *Du.* **Wil·lem** (vil′əm). See also WILHELM. [<Gmc., resolute protection] — **William I**, 1027–87, invaded England, 1066; king of England 1066–87: known as *William the Conqueror*. — **William II**, 1056–1100, king of England 1087–1100: known as *William Rufus*. — **William III**, 1650–1702, stadholder of Holland 1672–1702; invited to England; ruled 1689–1702 jointly with his wife Mary. — **William IV**, 1765–1837, king of England 1830–37. — **William of Malmesbury**, 1095?–1143? English historian. — **William of Orange**, 1533–84, founded the Dutch republic; stadholder 1579–84: called "William the Silent."

Wil·liams (wil′yəms), **Roger**, 1603?–83, English clergyman; founded Rhode Island. — **Roger John**, born 1893, U.S. biochemist. — **Tennessee**, born 1914, U.S. playwright: original name *Thomas Lanier Williams*. — **William Carlos**, 1883–1963, U.S. poet, novelist, playwright, and physician.

Wil·liams·burg (wil′yəmz·bûrg) A town in eastern Virginia; founded in 1693; capital of Virginia (1699–1779); restored to condition of the colonial period.

wil·lies (wil′ēz) *n. pl. Slang* Nervousness; jitters; the creeps: with *the*. [? <WILLY-NILLY; with ref. to a state of indecision]

will·ie·waught (wil′ē·wäht) *n. Scot.* A draft of liquor. Also **will′ie·waucht**.

will·ing (wil′ing) *adj.* **1** Having the mind favorably inclined or disposed. **2** Answering to demand or requirement; compliant. **3** Gladly proffered or done; hearty. **4** Of or pertaining to the faculty or power of choice; volitional. See synonyms under SPONTANEOUS. — **will′ing·ly** *adv.* — **will′ing·ness** *n.*

Wil·lis (wil′is), **Nathaniel Parker**, 1806–67, U.S. writer and editor.

wil·li·waw (wil′ē·wô) *n.* A sudden, violent blast of wind moving seaward down the slope of a mountainous coast, especially in the Strait of Magellan. [Origin unknown]

Will·kie (wil′kē), **Wendell Lewis**, 1892–1944, U.S. lawyer and political leader.

will-o'-the-wisp (wil′ə-thə-wisp′) *n.* **1** Ignis fatuus. **2** Any elusive or deceptive object. — *adj.* Deceptive; fleeting; misleading. [Earlier *Will with the wisp*]

wil·low (wil′ō) *n.* **1** Any of a large genus (*Salix*) of shrubs and trees related to the poplars, having generally smooth branches and often long, slender, pliant, and sometimes pendent branchlets. **2** The soft white wood of the willow. **3** *Colloq.* Something made of willow wood, especially a baseball or cricket bat. **4** A machine for giving a preliminary cleaning to cotton, flax, hemp, wool, etc., by means of long spikes projecting from a revolving cone or cylinder. — *v.t.* To clean, as cotton, wool, etc., with a willow. — *adj.* Of or pertaining to the willow; made of willow wood. [OE *wilige*, *welig*] — **wil′low·ish** *adj.*

wil·low·er (wil′ō·ər) *n.* One who or that which willows.

willow herb **1** Any of a genus (*Epilobium*) of perennial herbs of the evening-primrose family, especially the fireweed (*E. angustifolium*), having scattered, willowlike leaves and large, pink flowers. **2** The purple loosestrife (*Lythrum salicaria*).

willow oak **1** An oak (*Quercus phellos*) of the eastern United States, having long, slender, entire leaves resembling willow leaves. **2** The laurel oak (*Q. laurifolia*).

willow pattern A decorative design introduced on household china in England in 1780 and since extremely popular: so called from the willow tree, usually blue on a white background, which appears in the design.

wil·low·ware (wil′ō·wâr′) *n.* China decorated with the willow pattern.

wil·low·y (wil′ō·ē) *adj.* **1** Abounding in willows. **2** Having supple grace of form or carriage. See synonyms under SUPPLE.

will·pow·er (wil′pou′ər) *n.* Ability to control oneself; determination; firmness of mind.

Will·stät·ter (vil′shtet·ər), **Richard**, 1872–1942, German organic chemist.

will·y¹ (wil′ē) *adj. Obs.* Willing; also, propitious. [Cf. ON *viljugr*]

will·y² (wil′ē) *v.t.* **·lied**, **·ly·ing** To willow, as cotton, flax, hemp, etc.

will·yard (wil′yərd) *adj. Scot.* Wilful; also, abashed; bewildered. Also **will′yart** (-yärt).

wil·ly-nil·ly (wil′ē-nil′ē) *adj.* Having no decisiveness; uncertain; irresolute. — *adv.* Willingly or unwillingly. [Earlier *will I, nill I*: whether I will or not]

willy willy *Austral.* **1** A violent storm of wind and rain on the NW coast of Australia: also called *cockeye bob*. **2** A brief but violent duststorm.

Wil·ming·ton (wil′ming·tən) **1** A port of entry on the Delaware River in northern Delaware. **2** A port of entry in SE North Carolina.

Wil·no (vil′nô) The Polish name for VILNA.

Wil·son (wil′sən), **Alexander**, 1766–1813, American ornithologist born in Scotland. — **Charles Thomson Rees**, 1869–1959, Scottish physicist. — **Edmund**, 1895–1972, U.S. critic, author, and dramatist. — **Henry**, 1812–75, U.S. statesman. — **James**, 1742–98, American patriot, signed Declaration of Independence. — **John**, 1785–1854, Scottish poet: pseudonym *Christopher North*. — **(Thomas) Woodrow**, 1856–1924, U.S. educator and statesman; president of the United States 1913–21.

Wil·son (wil′sən), **Mount** A peak in SW California, near Pasadena; 5,710 feet; site of a famous observatory.

Wilson Dam A power dam in the Tennessee River at Muscle Shoals, NW Alabama; 137 feet high, 4,862 feet long; forms **Lake Wilson** (25 square miles; 15 1/2 miles long, 1 1/2 miles wide) over Muscle Shoals.

Wilson's petrel The storm petrel. [after Alexander *Wilson*]

Wilson's phalarope A shore bird (*Steganopus tricolor*) which breeds in northern North America and winters as far south as the Falkland Islands. [after Alexander *Wilson*]

Wilson's plover The ring plover (*Charadrius wilsonia*) of the southern United States and South America. [after Alexander *Wilson*]

Wilson's snipe Snipe (def. 1). [after Alexander *Wilson*]

Wilson's thrush The veery. [after Alexander *Wilson*]

Wilson's warbler A small, very active flycatcher (*Wilsonia pusilla*) of eastern North America, black-crowned with a yellow and olive-green body. [after Alexander *Wilson*]

wilt[1] (wilt) *v.i.* **1** To lose freshness; droop or become limp, as a flower that has been cut or that has not been watered. **2** To lose energy and vitality; become faint or languid: We *wilted* under the hot sun. **3** To lose courage or spirit; subside suddenly. — *v.t.* **4** To cause to droop or wither. **5** To cause to lose vitality and energy. — *n.* **1** The act of wilting; also, languor; faintness. **2** An infectious and virulent disease sometimes epidemic among certain caterpillars and insect larvae, which are reduced to a liquefied mass by its ravages: also **wilt disease**. [Prob. dial. var. of obs. *welk* wither. Cf. MDu. *welken* wither.]

wilt[2] (wilt) Archaic second person singular, present tense of WILL[2], used with *thou*.

Wil·ton (wil′tən) *n.* A kind of carpet resembling the Brussels carpet, but having the loops of the pile cut, thus giving it a velvety texture: originally made at Wilton, England. Also **Wilton carpet, Wilton rug.**

Wilt·shire (wilt′shir) *n.* One of a breed of long-horned sheep raised in Wiltshire, England.

Wilt·shire (wilt′shir) A county in southern England; 1,345 square miles; county town, Salisbury. Shortened form **Wilts.**

Wiltshire cheese A variety of Cheddar cheese.

wi·ly (wī′lē) *adj.* **·li·er, ·li·est** Full of or characterized by wiles; sly; cunning. See synonyms under INSIDIOUS, POLITIC. — **wi′li·ly** *adv.* — **wi′·li·ness** *n.*

wim·ble (wim′bəl) *n.* Anything that bores a hole, especially if turned by hand, as a gimlet, auger, brace and bit, or the like. — *v.t.* **·bled, ·bling** To bore or pierce, as with a wimble. [< AF, OF *guimbel* < MLG *wiemel.* Akin to GIMLET.]

Wim·ble·don (wim′bəl·dən) A town and municipal borough SW of London in NE Surrey, England; scene of international tennis matches.

wim·ple (wim′pəl) *n.* **1** A cloth, as of linen or silk, wrapped in folds around the neck close under the chin and over the head, exposing only the face: formerly worn as a protection by women outdoors, and still by nuns. **2** *Scot.* A fold; plait; also, a curve; a winding turn, as in a river or road. — *v.* **·pled, ·pling** *v.t.* **1** To cover or clothe with a wimple; veil. **2** To make or fold into plaits, as a veil. **3** To cause to move with slight undulations; ripple. **4** *Obs.* To deceive; hoodwink. — *v.i.* **5** To lie in plaits or folds. **6** To ripple. [OE *wimpel*]

WIMPLE
14th
century.

Wims·hurst machine (wimz′hûrst) A machine for the generation of static electricity by means of two insulated rotating disks carrying a number of equally spaced strips of conducting material which, by friction, build up an electrostatic charge. [after James *Wimshurst*, 1832–1903, English engineer, its inventor]

win[1] (win) *v.* **won** (*Obs.* **wan**), **won, win·ning** *v.i.* **1** To gain a victory; be victorious; prevail, as in a contest: May the best man *win*. **2** To succeed in an effort or endeavor. **3** To succeed in reaching or attaining a specified end or condition; get: often with *across, over, through,* etc.: The fleet *won* through the storm. **4** *Obs.* To fight; struggle. — *v.t.* **5** To be successful in; gain victory in: to *win* a game; to *win* an argument. **6** To gain in competition

or contest: to *win* the blue ribbon. **7** To gain by effort, persistence, etc.: to *win* fame or fortune. **8** To influence so as to obtain the good will or favor of: often with *over*: His eloquence *won* the audience; We *won* him over to our side. **9** To secure the love of; gain in marriage: He wooed and *won* her. **10** To succeed in reaching; attain: to *win* the harbor. **11** To make (one's way), especially with effort. **12** To capture; take possession of. **13** To earn or procure, as a living: to *win* support from poor soil. **14** *Mining* **a** To extract, as ore or coal, or metal from ore. **b** To reach and open (a deposit, vein, etc.); prepare for mining. See synonyms under ALLURE, CONQUER, GAIN[1], GET, OBTAIN, PERSUADE, SUCCEED. — **to win out** *Colloq.* To succeed to the fullest extent or expectation. — *n.* **1** A victory; success. **2** Profit; winnings. [OE *winnan* contend, labor]

win[2] (win) *v.t. Scot. & Irish* **1** To winnow. **2** To cure, as hay.

win[3] (win) *n. Scot.* Wind.

win·cey (win′sē) *n.* A fabric woven with cotton or linen warp and woolen filling. [Short for *wincey-woolsey,* alter. of LINSEY-WOOLSEY]

wince[1] (wins) *v.i.* **winced, winc·ing** To shrink back or start aside, as from a blow or pain; flinch. — *n.* The act of wincing. [< AF *wenchier* (assumed), var. of OF *quenchier* avoid < Gmc.] — **winc′er** *n.*

wince[2] (wins) *n.* A dyer's winch or windlass. [Var. of WINCH[1]]

winch[1] (winch) *n.* **1** A windlass, particularly one used for hoisting, as on a truck or the mast of a crane, derrick, etc., having usually one or more hand cranks geared to a drum around which the rope or chain winds. **2** A crank with a handle, used to impart motion to a grindstone or the like. — *v.t.* To move, hoist, or haul with or as with a winch. [OE *wince*] — **winch′er** *n.*

WINCH

winch[2] (winch) *v.i. Obs.* To wince; flinch. [See WINCE[1].]

Win·ches·ter (win′ches·tər) **1** The county town of Hampshire, England; known for its 11th century cathedral. **2** A city of northern Virginia near eastern West Virginia; scene of several Civil War battles, 1862 and 1864.

Winchester rifle A breechloading, lever-action, repeating rifle with a tubular magazine under the barrel, first produced in 1866: a trade name. Also **Winchester.** [after Oliver F. *Winchester,* 1810–80, U. S. industrialist]

Winck·el·mann (vingk′əl·män), **Johann Joachim,** 1717–68, German archeologist and art critic.

wind[1] (wind, *Poetic* wīnd) *n.* **1** Any movement of air, especially a natural horizontal movement; air in motion naturally. See BEAUFORT SCALE. **2** Any powerful or destructive wind; a tornado; hurricane. **3** The direction from which a wind blows; one of the cardinal points of the compass: They gathered from the four *winds.* **4** Air in motion by artificial means: the *wind* of a bullet, *wind* from a bellows. **5** Air pervaded by a scent: The deer got *wind* of the hunter; hence, figuratively, a suggestion or intimation: to get *wind* of a plot. **6** The power of breathing or respiring; breath: He lost his *wind* in the race. **7** Breath as expended in words, especially as having more sound than sense; idle chatter; also, vanity; conceit. **8** *pl.* The wind instruments of an orchestra; also, the players of these instruments. See WIND INSTRUMENT. **9** The gaseous product of indigestion; flatulence. **10** In pugilism, the pit of the stomach where a blow may cause temporary stoppage of breath: He was hit in the *wind.* — **in the wind** **1** Impending; astir; afoot. **2** Inebriated; drunk. — **in the wind's eye** Directly opposed to the point from which the wind blows. — **to break wind** To expel gas through the

anus. — **to get wind of** To receive a hint of. — **to have in the wind** To be on the track or scent of; be in pursuit of. — **to have the wind of** To be to windward of; hence, to have an advantage over. — **to have the wind up** To be apprehensive; be alarmed or wary. — **to sail close to the wind** To sail in a direction as near as possible to that from which the wind blows; hence, to come near to the limit, as of a danger line; also, to manage or live economically. — *v.t.* (wind) **1** To follow by scent; to catch a scent of on the wind. **2** To exhaust the breath of, as by fast driving or walking. **3** To allow to recover breath by resting. **4** To expose to the wind, as in ventilating. [OE]

wind[2] (wīnd) *v.* **wound** (*Rare* **wind·ed**), **wind·ing** *v.t.* **1** To coil or pass (thread, rope, etc.) around some object or fixed core; twine; wreathe. **2** To encircle or cover with something, as by coiling or wrapping: to *wind* a spool with thread or a pillar with garlands. **3** To continue or renew the motion of, as a clock, by coiling a spring, cord, etc. **4** To cause to turn and twist. **5** To make (one's) way) by a turning and twisting course. **6** To introduce carefully or deviously; insinuate: He *wound* himself into my confidence. **7** To raise or hoist, as by means of a capstan or windlass. — *v.i.* **8** To move in a turning, twisting course; change direction; meander. **9** To coil or twine about some central object or core. **10** To move in a circular or spiral course: The hawk *wound* into the sky. **11** To proceed carefully or deviously; gain an end by indirect or subtle methods. **12** To warp; twist: This board *winds* badly. — **to wind down** To decrease or be decreased gradually; de-escalate: to *wind down* a war. — **to wind up** **1** To coil or wind round and round. **2** To put in readiness for action; excite; arouse. **3** To bring to conclusion or settlement; close, as a business: He *wound up* his affairs. **4** In baseball, to swing the arm preparatory to pitching. **5** To hoist. — *n.* The act of winding, or the condition of being wound; a winding bend, turn, or twist. [OE *windan.* Akin to WAND.] — **wind′a·ble** *adj.*

wind[3] (wind, wīnd) *v.t.* **wind·ed** (*erroneously* **wound**), **wind·ing** **1** To blow, as a horn; sound. **2** To give (a call or signal), as with a horn. [< WIND[1]; infl. by *wind*[2]]

wind·age (win′dij) *n.* **1** The rush of air caused by the rapid passage of an object, as a projectile or a railway train. **2** Deflection of an object, as a bullet, from its natural course due to wind pressure. **3** In a muzzleloading rifled gun, the difference between the diameter of a projectile and the bore through which it is discharged; also, in a smoothbore gun, the space between the surface of the bore and the projectile. **4** *Mech.* The free air space between any moving piece and the socket or bore in which it travels. **5** A contusion caused by sudden compression of air due to the passing of gunshot nearby. **6** *Naut.* The surface offered to the wind by a vessel.

Win·dau (vin′dou) The German name for VENTSPILS.

wind·bag (wind′bag′) *n.* **1** A wordy talker. **2** A bellows. **3** *Slang* The chest.

wind–blown (wind′blōn′) *adj.* **1** Tossed or blown by the wind. **2** Having a permanent direction of growth as determined by prevailing winds: said of plants and trees. **3** Pertaining to an irregular hair arrangement causing the hair in front to appear as if blown forward by the wind.

wind–borne (wind′bôrn′, -bōrn′) *adj.* Carried or transported by the wind.

wind–bound (wind′bound′) *adj.* Delayed by contrary winds.

wind·break (wind′brāk′) *n.* Anything, as a hedge, fence, etc., that protects from or breaks the force of the wind.

wind·break·er (wind′brā′kər) *n.* A sports jacket for outer wear, having a close–fitting or elastic waistband and cuffs. [< *Windbreaker,* a trade name]

wind–bro·ken (wind′brō′kən) *adj.* Asthmatic; broken–winded: said of a horse.

Wind Cave National Park (wind) A region containing a large limestone cavern in the Black Hills in SW South Dakota; 41 square miles; established 1903.

wind·cone (wind'kōn') n. A windsock.

wind·ed (win'did) adj. 1 Exposed to the wind or air, or spoiled by such exposure. 2 Breathless, as from work or exercise; out of breath.

wind·er[1] (wīn'dər) n. 1 One who or that which winds. 2 That upon which or from which thread, etc., may be wound. 3 A step in winding stairs. 4 A twining plant. 5 An appliance for winding up a spring.

wind·er[2] (wīn'dər, win'dər) n. One who winds a horn, bugle, etc.

Win·der·mere (win'dər·mir) An urban district in Westmorland, England.

Windermere, Lake The largest lake in England, in Westmorland and Lancashire; 10 1/2 miles long by 1 mile wide.

wind·fall (wind'fôl') n. 1 Something, as ripening fruit, brought down by the wind; a heap of trees blown down by wind. 2 A tract of land on which trees have been felled by the wind. 3 A piece of unexpected good fortune.

wind·flaw (wind'flô) n. A sharp gust of wind.

wind·flow·er (wind'flou'ər) n. 1 The anemone. 2 The rue anemone. [Trans. of Gk. *anemōnē* the anemone < *anemos* the wind]

wind gage A scale on a gunsight to allow for windage (def. 2). Also **wind gauge.**

wind·gall (wind'gôl') n. A soft swelling near the pastern joint of a horse. [< WIND + GALL[2]; so called because formerly thought to contain wind] —**wind'galled'** adj.

wind gap A notch or ravine in a mountain ridge, moderately deep, but not deep enough to give passage to a watercourse.

wind harp An Eolian harp.

Wind·hoek (vint'hōōk) The capital of South-West Africa, in the central part.

wind·hov·er (wind'huv'ər) n. Brit. The kestrel: so called from its habit of hovering in the face of the wind.

win·di·go (win'di·gō) n. In the mythology of certain Algonquian North American Indians, especially in the Labrador and Ojibwa districts, an evil demon; also, a mythical tribe of cannibals believed by the Chippewa to inhabit an island in Hudson Bay: also spelled *weendijo*. [< Algonquian (Ojibwa) *weendigo* a cannibal]

wind·ing[1] (wīn'ding) n. 1 The act or condition of one who or that which winds; a spiral turning or coiling. 2 A bend or turn, or a series of them. 3 A warp or twist from a plane surface. 4 Electr. The manner in which the wire is wound in a coil, as on the armature of a dynamo. 5 A defective gait of horses in which one leg seems to wind around the other. —adj. 1 Turning spirally about an axis or core. 2 Having bends or lateral turns. 3 Twisting from a plane.

wind·ing[2] (wīn'ding) n. A boatswain's signal.

winding frame A device or machine for winding, as a reel.

wind·ing·ly (wīn'ding·lē) adv. In a winding manner.

winding sheet (wīn'ding) The sheet that wraps a corpse.

wind instrument (wind) A musical instrument whose sounds are produced by vibrations of air injected by the lungs or by mechanical bellows. Those blown by air from the lungs are known as **wood-wind instruments** or **woodwinds,** consisting of the flutes, oboes, clarinets, etc., and the **brass-wind instruments** or **brasses,** consisting of the horns, trumpets, trombones, tubas, etc. Those in which the vibration of the air column is induced by bellows are the various types of organ, accordion, etc.

wind·jam·mer (wind'jam'ər) n. 1 Naut. A merchant sailing vessel, as distinguished from a steamship. 2 A member of its crew. 3 Slang A chatterbox; a loquacious person.

wind·lass (wind'ləs) n. Any of several devices for hauling or lifting, especially that form familiar in well curbs, consisting of a drum or barrel on which the hoisting rope winds, and turned by means of cranking. —**Chinese** or **differential windlass** A horizontal wheel and axle having two drums of different di-

DIFFERENTIAL
WINDLASS

ameters on the same axis, one of which pays out as the other winds up, the power being increased in inverse proportion to the difference between the diameters. —v.t. & v.i. To raise or haul with a windlass. [Alter. of ME *windas* < ON *vindass* < *vinda* wind + *ass* a beam; infl. in form by WINDLE[2]]

win·dle[1] (win'dəl) n. A basket. [OE *windel* a basket < *windan* plait, twist]

win·dle[2] (win'dəl) Scot. & Brit. Dial. v.t. & v.i. To wind. —n. Something used for winding or turning. [Freq. of WIND[2]]

wind·less (wind'lis) adj. 1 Without wind; breezeless; calm. 2 Being out of breath.

win·dle·straw (win'dəl·strô') n. Scot. & Brit. Dial. 1 A withered stalk of any one of several grasses, used in plaiting or ropemaking. 2 A feeble, unhealthy person. 3 The white-throat warbler. Also **win·dle·strae** (-strā'). [OE *windelstrēaw*, ? < *windel* basket + *strēaw* straw]

wind·ling (wind'ling) n. 1 Dial. That which is torn off by the wind, as a branch of a tree. 2 Scot. A bottle of straw. [< WIND[1] + -LING[1]]

wind·mill (wind'mil') n. 1 A mill consisting of a tower within which is a shaft having at the top a horizontal axis which bears a rudder at one end and at the other a system of adjustable slats, wings, or sails which, in revolving, transmit motion to a pump, millstone, or the like. 2 Anything resembling a windmill. 3 An imaginary wrong, evil, or foe: usually in the phrase, **to fight** (or **tilt at**) **windmills,** in allusion to Don Quixote's combat with windmills, which he mistook for giants.

win·dow (win'dō) n. 1 An opening in the wall of a building, to admit light or air, capable of being opened and closed, and including, architecturally, the casement, sash, panes, etc.; in common usage, sometimes, the sash alone: Raise the *window.* 2 A windowpane. 3 Anything resembling or suggesting a window; a windowlike aperture: The eyes are the *windows* of the soul. 4 A transparent patch through which the address of an envelope can be read. —v.t. 1 To provide with a window or windows. 2 To fill with holes resembling windows. [< ON *vindauga* < *vindr* wind + *auga* an eye]

window box 1 One of the grooves along the sides of a window frame for the weights that counterbalance a lifting sash. 2 A box, generally long and narrow, along a window ledge or sill, for growing plants.

win·dow-dress·ing (win'dō-dres'ing) n. 1 The act or the art of arranging merchandise attractively in shop and store windows; also, the goods so displayed; hence, anything superficially attractive. 2 A business report that unduly stresses favorable conditions. 3 Anything added or done to make something else more attractive: The prosecution of the thieves was mere *window-dressing* for his campaign for governor. —**win'dow-dress'er** n.

win·dow·pane (win'dō-pān') n. A single sheet of glass for a window. Also **window pane.**

window seat A seat in the recess of a window.

window shade A flexible fabric shade, usually mounted on a spring roller, used to regulate light at a window.

win·dow-shop (win'dō-shop') v.i. **-shopped, -shop·ping** To look at goods shown in store windows without buying them. —**win'dow-shop'per** n. —**win'dow-shop'ping** n. & adj.

wind·pipe (wind'pīp') n. The duct by which the breath is carried to and from the lungs; the trachea.

Wind River Range (wind) A range of the Rocky Mountains in west central Wyoming; highest point, 13,787 feet, highest point in Wyoming.

wind rose Meteorol. A diagram indicating the direction and relative velocities of the wind in a given locality by means of lines of varying length radiating from a common center.

wind·row (wind'rō') n. 1 A long ridge or pile of hay or grain raked together preparatory to building into cocks. 2 A row of Indian corn made by setting two rows together. 3 A wind-swept line of dust, surf,

leaves, etc. 4 A deep furrow made for planting. 5 Land on which the trees have been felled by the wind; sometimes, a tornado track: also **wind slash.** —v.t. To rake or shape into a windrow. —**wind'row'er** n.

wind sail 1 Naut. A canvas tube or funnel with a spreading opening at one side of the top that may be stayed to face the wind: used to conduct fresh air below decks. 2 A sail on the arm of a windmill.

wind scale See BEAUFORT SCALE.

wind·shake (wind'shāk') n. A defect in wood; anemosis.

wind·shield (wind'shēld') n. 1 Any arrangement for breaking the force of the wind against an object. 2 A transparent screen of glass or similar material, attached in front of the occupants of an automobile, airplane, etc., as protection against wind and weather. 3 A covering for a chimney.

wind·sock (wind'sok') n. Meteorol. A large, conical bag, open at both ends, mounted on a pivot, and used to indicate the direction of the wind by the current of air which blows through it; a drogue: also called *windcone.*

Wind·sor (win'zər) Name of the royal family of Great Britain since July 27, 1917, when it was officially changed from *Saxe-Coburg-Gotha.*

Wind·sor (win'zər) 1 A municipal borough in eastern Berkshire, England; site of **Windsor Castle,** a residence of the English sovereigns since the time of William the Conqueror. Officially **New Windsor.** 2 A city on the Detroit River in SE Ontario, Canada, opposite Detroit, Michigan.

Wind·sor (win'zər), **Duke of** See EDWARD VIII.

Windsor chair A wooden chair, with or without arms, common in England and America in the 18th century, typically with a spindle back, turned, slanting legs, and a flat or saddle seat.

Windsor tie A wide, soft necktie knotted loosely in a double bow, usually of black silk cut on the bias.

COMB-BACKED WINDSOR CHAIR

wind·storm (wind'stôrm') n. A violent wind, usually with little or no precipitation.

wind·suck·er (wind'suk'ər) n. A horse that cribs. —**wind'suck'ing** n. & adj.

wind tee (wind) A T-shaped weathervane, especially one located on or near an aircraft landing field.

wind tunnel Aeron. A tunnel-like structure in which the effects of artificially produced winds may be investigated, as on airplane wings and other surfaces.

wind-up (wīnd'up') n. 1 The act of concluding or closing. 2 A conclusion; a final act or part. 3 In baseball, the swing of the arm preparatory to pitching the ball.

wind·ward (wind'wərd) adj. Being on the side exposed to the wind. —n. The direction from which the wind blows. —**to windward of** Advantageously placed with respect to. —adv. In the direction from which the wind blows: opposed to *leeward.*

Wind·ward Islands (wind'wərd) A West Indies island group north of Trinidad, comprising four British colonies, all federating units of The West Indies, on the islands of Dominica, Grenada, St. Lucia, and St. Vincent, together with the Grenadines; 820 square miles; capital, St. George's, on Grenada. The French island of Martinique; Barbados, a British colony; and three islands of the Netherlands Antilles, Aruba, Bonaire, and Curaçao, are also sometimes included in this group.

Windward Passage The strait between Cuba and Hispaniola in the West Indies; 50 miles wide.

wind·y (win'dē) adj. **wind·i·er, wind·i·est** 1 Pertaining to, consisting of, or abounding in wind; stormy; tempestuous: *windy* weather. 2 Exposed to the wind; wind-swept: high on a *windy* hill. 3 Suggestive of wind; boisterous;

swift: *windy* emotions. **4** Producing, due to, or troubled with gas in the stomach or intestines; producing or affected with flatulence; flatulent: *windy* food. **5** Given to or expressed in bombast; pompous, loquacious, or bragging: *windy* talk, a *windy* orator. See synonyms under BLEAK[1]. — **wind′i·ly** *adv.* —**wind′i·ness** *n.*

Windy City A nickname for CHICAGO.

wine (wīn) *n.* **1** The fermented juice of the grape, containing various percentages of alcohol by volume, commonly used as a beverage and in cooking. Wines are often classified as dry or sweet, red or white, still or sparkling. Fortified wines have brandy added, and contain alcohol of from 16 to 23 percent. **2** By extension, the fermented juice of some fruit other than the grape: elderberry *wine;* sometimes, a fermented vegetable juice: dandelion *wine.* **3** The effects of drinking too much wine; intoxication. **4** A convivial gathering at which wine and other liquors are served; a wine party. **5** A medicinal preparation in which wine is used as the menstruum: *wine* of opium. **6** Any color resembling the color of wine, especially of a red wine, usually a dark, purplish red. —**Adam's wine** Water. —**new wine in old bottles** Any dynamic new thing, as a doctrine, theory, etc., which cannot be restricted by older forms or customs: with reference to *Matt.* ix 17. —*v.* **wined, win·ing** *v.t.* To entertain or treat with wine. —*v.i.* To drink wine. [OE *wīn* < L *vinum*]

wine-bib·bing (wīn′bib′ing) *adj.* Addicted to excessive drinking of wine. —*n.* The habitual, excessive drinking of wine. —**wine′bib′ber** *n.*

wine card The list of alcoholic drinks for sale at a hotel or restaurant.

wine cellar A storage space for wines; also, the wines stored.

wine-col·ored (wīn′kul′ərd) *adj.* Having the color of red wine.

wine fly Any fly (as of the genus *Piophila*) whose larva lives in wine or other fermented liquor.

wine gallon See under GALLON.

wine-glass (wīn′glas′, -gläs′) *n.* A small goblet from which to drink wine.

wine-glass·ful (wīn′glas·fŏŏl′, -gläs-) *n. pl.* **·fuls** The amount a wineglass will hold, approximately equivalent to two fluid ounces or four tablespoonfuls.

wine-grow·er (wīn′grō′ər) *n.* One who cultivates a vineyard and makes wine; a viticulturist. —**wine′grow′ing** *adj. & n.*

wine measure A system of liquid measures formerly used for wines and spirits in which the gallon was equal to the present U.S. gallon.

wine palm Any palm from which palm wine is obtained.

wine-press (wīn′pres′) *n.* An apparatus or a place where the juice of grapes is expressed. —**wine′press′er** *n.*

wine purple A hue of purple consisting of 50 percent red, 33 percent black, and 17 percent blue.

win-er·y (wī′nər·ē) *n. pl.* **·er·ies 1** An establishment for making wine. **2** A room for fining and storing wines.

Wine·sap (wīn′sap) *n.* An American variety of red winter apple.

wine-skin (wīn′skin′) *n.* The skin of some domestic quadruped kept as entire as possible and made into a tight bag for containing wine: much used in the Orient.

wine·sop (wīn′sop′) *n.* Any farinaceous foodstuff steeped or sopped in wine, as bread or cake.

wine steward An attendant in a restaurant or hotel who takes orders for wines, and who is in charge of the wine cellar.

wine-tast·er (wīn′tās′tər) *n.* A person who tastes wine to judge its quality.

wine vinegar A vinegar made from wine.

wine whey *Brit.* A beverage made of wine and curdled milk.

Win-fre·da (win-frē′də) Latin form of WIN-IFRED. Also *Du.* **Win·fried** (vin′frēt), *Sw.* **Winfrid** (vin′frid).

wing (wing) *n.* **1** An organ of flight; specifically, one of the anterior movable pair of appendages of a bird or bat, homologous with the forelimbs of vertebrates but adapted for flight. **2** An analogous organ in insects and some other animals. **3** One of the pectoral fins of a flying fish. **4** *Slang* An arm; specifically, in baseball, the arm used for throwing or pitching. **5** Something regarded

as conferring the power of swift motion or performing some function of a wing: on *wings* of song. **6** Flight or passage by or as by wings; also, the means or act of flying: to take *wing.* **7** Anything resembling or suggestive of a wing in form, function, or appearance; specifically, one of a pair of pneumatic planes for aid in swimming; a shoulder ornament. **8** The flare of a moldboard plowshare; also, the curved mudguard or fender of an automobile. **9** Something moved by or moving in the wind, as the vane of a windmill or a winnowing fan. **10** *Mil.* Either division of a military force on either side of the center. **11** An analogous formation in certain outdoor games, as hockey or football. **12** Either of two extremist groups or factions in a political or other organization: the left *wing.* **13** *Archit.* A part attached to a side; especially, a projection or extension of a building on the side of the main portion. **14** A sidepiece at the top of an armchair. **15** A side section of something that shuts or folds, as a double door, a screen, etc. **16** In fortifications, one of the sides connecting an outwork with the main fort. **17** *Anat.* An ala: a *wing* of the nose. **18** *Bot.* Any thin membranous or foliaceous expansion of an organ, as of certain stems, seeds, samaras, etc. **19** *Zool.* One of the lateral finlike expansions of the foot of a pteropod. **20** One of the sides of a stage; a small platform at either side of the stage; also, a piece of scenery for the side. **21** *Aeron.* One of the sustaining surfaces of an airplane. **22** A tactical and administrative unit of the U.S. Air Force, under the direction of a wing commander, larger than a group and smaller than a command. **23** A shore dam or jetty for narrowing a channel; also, an extension of a dam at either end, usually built at an angle. —**on** (or **upon**) **the wing** In flight; as, a bird *on the wing;* hence, just about to go; departing; also, journeying. —**to take wing** To fly away. —**under one's wing** Under one's protection. —*v.t.* **1** To pass over or through in flight. **2** To accomplish by flying: the eagle *winged* its way. **3** To enable to fly. **4** To cause to go swiftly; speed: Hope *winged* his steps. **5** To transport by flight. **6** To provide with wings for flight; also, to feather (an arrow). **7** To supply with a side body or part: The house was *winged* on both sides. **8** To wound (a bird) in a wing; hence, to disable by a minor wound: I *winged* him in the arm. —*v.i.* **9** To fly; soar. [< ON *vœngr*]

wing and wing *Naut.* With sails spread or boomed out on each side like wings: said of a fore-and-aft vessel running downwind.

wing-back (wing′bak′) *n.* In football, the position taken by one (**single wingback**) or two (**double wingback**) of the backs behind or beyond the ends; also, the back so posted.

wing-bow (wing′bō′) *n.* A distinctive mark of color on the bend of the wing in a domestic fowl.

wing chair A large armchair, upholstered throughout, with high back and side pieces designed as protection from drafts.

wing cover The elytron of an insect. Also **wing case.**

wing covert *Ornithol.* One of the small close feathers clothing the bend of a bird's wing and covering the insertion of the flight feathers. Those of the lining of the wing are called *undercoverts.*

WING CHAIR

winged (wingd, *Poetic* wing′id) *adj.* **1** Having wings. **2** Passing swiftly; soaring; lofty; rapt. **3** Alive with creatures having wings. **4** (wingd) *Colloq.* Wounded or disabled in or as in the wing.

winged bean A tropical leguminous plant (*Psophocarpus tetragonolobus*) having a pod with a wing along four edges, cultivated for the nutrients provided by the foliage, roots, and fruit.

winged wolf A harpy (def. 2).

wing flap *Aeron.* A control surface hinged to an airplane wing, used primarily to increase lift and to retard the speed.

wing-foot·ed (wing′fŏŏt′id) *adj.* Rapid; swift.

wing-less (wing′lis) *adj.* Having no wings, or having aborted wings.

wing-let (wing′lit) *n.* An alula.

wing loading *Aeron.* The over-all weight of a fully loaded airplane divided by the area of the supporting surface, exclusive of the stabilizer and elevators. Also **wing load.**

wing-nut (wing′nut′) *n.* A thumbnut.

wing-o·ver (wing′ō′vər) *n. Aeron.* A flight maneuver in which an airplane at the top of a climbing turn and just before stalling is put into a dive before resuming normal flight in the direction from which it started.

wing rail A guardrail, as at a railway switch.

wing skid *Aeron.* A device set beneath the wing tip of an airplane to guard the tip against contact with the ground.

wing-spread (wing′spred′) *n.* The distance between the tips of the fully extended wings of a bird, insect, or airplane.

wing walk *Aeron.* A reinforced section of an airplane wing, used as a walking strip.

Win-i·fred (win′ə·frid) A feminine personal name. Also **Win′e·fred, Win′i·frid.** [< Welsh *Gwenfrewi* a white wave]

wink (wingk) *v.i.* **1** To close and open the eye or eyelids quickly. **2** To draw the eyelids of one eye together, as in conveying a hint or making a sign. **3** To shut one's eyes, especially in ignoring; pretend not to see: usually with *at.* **4** To emit fitful gleams; twinkle. —*v.t.* **5** To close and open (the eye or eyelids) quickly. **6** To move, force, etc., by winking: with *away, off,* etc. **7** To signify or express by winking. —*n.* **1** The act of winking. **2** The time necessary for a wink. **3** A twinkle. **4** A hint conveyed by winking. **5** A short nap: especially in the phrase **forty winks.** [OE *wincian* close the eyes]

Win-kel-ried (ving′kəl-rēt), **Arnold von** A 14th century Swiss patriot.

wink-er (wing′kər) *n.* **1** One who winks. **2** A blinder for a horse. **3** *Slang* An eyelash. **4** A small secondary bellows for use with an organ. **5** The nictitating membrane, as of a bird. **6** The muscle by which winking is done. **7** *pl. Slang* Spectacles.

win-kle (wing′kəl) *n.* A periwinkle[1]. [Short for PERIWINKLE[1]]

win·na (win′ə) *Scot.* Will not.

Win-ne-ba-go (win′ə-bā′gō) *n. pl.* **·gos** or **·goes** One of a tribe of North American Indians of Siouan linguistic stock, formerly occupying what is now eastern Wisconsin, south of Green Bay, where many still survive.

Win-ne-ba-go (win′ə-bā′gō), **Lake** The largest lake in Wisconsin, in the eastern part; 215 square miles; 30 miles long.

Win-ne-pe-sau-kee (win′ə-pə-sô′kē), **Lake** The largest lake in New Hampshire, in the east central part; 25 miles long, 12 miles wide. Also **Win′ni-pe-sau′kee.**

win·ner (win′ər) *n.* One who or that which wins.

win·ning (win′ing) *adj.* **1** Successful in achievement, especially in competition. **2** Capable of winning or charming; attractive; winsome. —*n.* **1** The act of one who wins. **2** That which is won: usually in the plural. **3** A new opening in a mine; also, a section of a mine prepared for working. —**win′ning·ly** *adv.* —**win′ning·ness** *n.*

winning gallery In court tennis, the grille or square opening in the penthouse in the rear of the hazard court: so named because a ball played into it counts as a win.

winning hazard See HAZARD *n.* (def. 6).

winning post The post or goal at the end of a racecourse.

Win-ni·peg (win′ə·peg) The capital of Manitoba, Canada, on the Red River in the SE part.

Winnipeg, Lake A lake in south central Manitoba, Canada; 240 miles long, 55 miles wide; 9,398 square miles.

Winnipeg goldeye *Canadian* The goldeye.

Win-ni-pe-go-sis (win′ə-pə-gō′sis), **Lake** A lake in western Manitoba, Canada, west of Lake Winnipeg; 125 miles long, 25 miles wide; 2,086 square miles.

Winnipeg River A river in NW Ontario and

add,āce,câre,pälm; end,ēven; it,īce; odd,ōpen,ôrder; tŏŏk,pōōl; up,bûrn; ə = a in *above*, e in *sicken*, i in *clarity*, o in *melon*, u in *focus*; yōō = u in *fuse*, oi,oil; ou,pout; ch,check; g,go; ng,ring; th,thin; th,this; zh,vision. Foreign sounds à,œ,ü,kh,ń; and ♦: see page xx. < from; + plus; ? possibly.

SE Manitoba, flowing 200 miles NW from Lake of the Woods to Lake Winnipeg.

win·nock (win′ək) *n. Scot.* A window.

win·now (win′ō) *v.t.* **1** To separate (grain, etc.) from the chaff by means of wind or a current of air. **2** To blow away (the chaff) thus. **3** To examine so as to separate good from bad; analyze minutely; sift. **4** To separate (what is valuable) from what is valueless, or to eliminate (what is valueless) from what is valuable; distinguish, sort: often with *out*. **5** To blow upon; cause to flutter. **6** To beat or fan (the air) with the wings. **7** To scatter by blowing; disperse. **8** *Rare* To proceed along (a course) by flapping the wings. —*v.i.* **9** To separate grain from chaff. **10** To fly; flap. —*n.* **1** Any device used in winnowing grain. **2** The act of winnowing; also, a vibrating motion caused by a current of air. [OE *windwian* < *wind* the wind] —**win′now·er** *n.*

win·o (wī′nō) *n. pl.* **·noes** or **·nos** *U.S. Slang* A drunkard who habitually drinks sweet, fortified wines. [< WINE]

Wins·low (winz′lō), **Edward,** 1595–1655, English Puritan, governor of Plymouth Colony.

win·some (win′səm) *adj.* Having a winning appearance or manner; pleasing; attractive; rarely, joyous. See synonyms under AMIABLE, LOVELY. [OE *wynsum* < *wyn* joy] —**win′some·ly** *adv.* —**win′some·ness** *n.*

Win·sor (win′zər), **Justin,** 1831–97, U.S. historian and librarian.

Win·ston (win′stən) A masculine personal name. [Orig. from *Winston*, a hamlet near Cirencester, England]

Win·ston-Sa·lem (win′stən·sā′ləm) A city in NW central North Carolina; one of the world's chief tobacco centers.

win·ter (win′tər) *n.* **1** The coldest season of the year, extending from the end of autumn to the beginning of spring: in the northern hemisphere, astronomically from the winter solstice, December 21, to the vernal equinox, March 21, but popularly regarded as including December, January, and February. ◆ Collateral adjectives: *hibernal, hiemal.* **2** Any time compared to winter, as being marked by lack of life, warmth, and cheer. **3** A year as including the winter season: used in reckoning the age of elderly persons: a man of ninety *winters.* —*v.i.* To pass the winter: We *wintered* in Bermuda. —*v.t.* To care for, feed, or protect during the winter: to *winter* animals or plants. —*adj.* **1** Pertaining to or taking place in winter; hibernal. **2** Suitable to or characteristic of winter. [OE] —**win′ter·er** *n.* —**win′terish** *adj.* —**win′ter·less** *adj.*

winter aconite A European tuberous-rooted, hardy, flowering garden herb (*Eranthis hyemalis*) of the crowfoot family, 5 to 8 inches high, with bright-yellow sessile flowers and oblong anthers.

win·ter·ber·ry (win′tər·ber′ē) *n. pl.* **·ries** Any of several North American shrubs (genus *Ilex*) of the holly family, bearing bright-red berrylike drupes about the size of a pea; especially, the smooth winterberry (*I. laevigata*) of the eastern United States.

win·ter·bourne (win′tər·bôrn′, -bōrn′, -bŏŏrn′) *n.* A stream flowing only during excessive rain fall, as in winter, when water at the source rises above a certain level. [OE *winter burna* < *winter* + *burna* a stream]

win·ter·feed (win′tər·fēd′) *v.t.* **-fed, -feed·ing** To feed (stock) during the time when grazing is impossible.

win·ter·green (win′tər·grēn) *n.* **1** A small evergreen plant (*Gaultheria procumbens*) of eastern North America, bearing a cluster of aromatic oval leaves and white, bell-shaped flowers surrounded by red berries (often called *teaberries* or *checkerberries*). **2** Oil of wintergreen: a colorless, volatile oil extracted from the leaves of the true wintergreen, used as a flavor and in medicine: often called *Gaultheria oil.* **3** Any of various English low evergreen herbs (genus *Pyrola*). In the United States they are sometimes called *shinleaf* or **English** or **false wintergreen.** [On analogy with Du. *wintergroen;* so called because it is an evergreen]

winter itch Frost itch.

win·ter·ize (win′tə·rīz) *v.t.* **-ized, -iz·ing** To prepare or equip for winter.

win·ter·kill (win′tər·kil′) *v.t. & v.i.* To die or kill by exposure to extreme cold: said of plants and grains. —**win′ter·kill′ing** *adj. & n.*

win·ter·ly (win′tər·lē) *adj.* Wintry; cheerless.

winter melon A hardy, cold-resistant muskmelon (*Cucumis melo,* variety *inodorus*).

winter squash Any of various varieties of squash having a tough rind that is resistant to spoilage.

Win·ter·thur (vin′tər·tŏŏr) A city of northern Switzerland NE of Zurich; a rail and industrial center.

win·ter·tide (win′tər·tīd′) *n. Poetic* Winter. Also **win′ter·time′** (-tīm′).

winter wheat Wheat planted before snowfall and harvested the following summer.

Win·throp (win′thrəp), **John,** 1588–1649, English Puritan; governor of Massachusetts Colony. —**John,** 1606–76, governor of Connecticut Colony; son of the preceding.

win·try (win′trē) *adj.* **·tri·er, ·tri·est** Belonging to winter; cold; frosty; brumal. Also **win′ter·y** (-tər·ē). —**win′tri·ly** *adv.* —**win′tri·ness** *n.*

win·y (wī′nē) *adj.* **win·i·er, win·i·est** Having the taste or qualities of wine.

winze[1] (winz) *n. Mining* A small inclined shaft from one level of a mine to another. [Earlier *winds,* ? < *wind* a windlass, fusion of MDu. *winde* a windlass and WIND[2]]

winze[2] (winz) *n. Scot.* An oath.

wipe (wīp) *v.t.* **wiped, wip·ing 1** To subject to slight friction or rubbing, usually with some soft, absorbent material. **2** To remove by rubbing lightly; brush: usually with *away* or *off.* **3** To move, apply, or draw for the purpose of wiping: He *wiped* his hand across his brow. **4** To apply solder to a piece of greased cloth or leather; solder with a wiper or pad: to *wipe* a joint. See synonyms under CLEANSE. —**to wipe out** To remove or destroy utterly; annihilate. —*n.* **1** The act of wiping or rubbing. **2** *Slang* A sweeping blow or stroke; a swipe. **3** *Mech.* A wiper or cam. **4** *Slang* A handkerchief. **5** *Slang* A jeer; jibe. [OE *wīpian.* Akin to WISP.]

wip·er (wī′pər) *n.* **1** One who wipes. **2** An article designed or used for wiping. **3** *Mech.* A cam having one or more slightly curved projections serving, when mounted on a rock shaft or rotating shaft, to give a reciprocating (usually vertical) motion to another part. **4** *Electr.* A moving member of an electrical device which makes contact with the terminals. **5** One who cleans locomotives in a roundhouse.

wire (wīr) *n.* **1** A slender rod, strand, or thread of ductile metal, usually formed by drawing through dies or holes. **2** Something made of wire, as a fence, a bar of a cage, or a snare made for catching small animals. **3** A telegraph cable. **4** The telegraph system as a means of communication. **5** A telegram. **6** The screen of a papermaking machine. **7** A fine metallic thread, a cobweb, or one of a set of ruled lines, in the focus of a telescope. **8** *Ornithol.* A long slender filament of the plumage of various birds. **9** *pl.* A secret means of exerting influence: to pull the *wires:* from the analogy with the system of hidden wires by which puppets are operated. **10** An imaginary line marking the finish of a racecourse. —**to lay wires for** To prepare for. —**under wire** Fenced. —*v.* **wired, wir·ing** *v.t.* **1** To fasten with wire. **2** To furnish or equip with wiring: The studio was *wired* for sound. **3** In croquet, to place (a ball) so that the wire of an arch will be between it and another ball. **4** To catch, as a rabbit, with a snare of wire. **5** *Colloq.* To transmit or send by electric telegraph: to *wire* an order. **6** *Colloq.* To send a telegram to: Will you *wire* John? **7** To place on wire, as beads. —*v.i.* **8** *Colloq.* To telegraph. [OE *wīr*]

wire cloth A fabric of woven wire, as for strainers, window screens, etc.

wire coat An outer coat, as of some dogs, of dense stiff hair.

wire-danc·er (wīr′dan′sər, -dän′-) *n.* One who performs feats of balancing, etc., upon a wire stretched in mid-air: also called *wirewalker.* —**wire′-danc′ing** *n.*

wire-draw (wīr′drô′) *v.t.* **-drew, -drawn, -draw·ing 1** To draw, as a metal rod, through a

series of holes of diminishing diameter to produce a wire. **2** To treat (a subject) with excessive subtlety or overrefinement. —**wire′-draw′er** *n.* —**wire′-draw′ing** *n.*

wire gage 1 A gage for measuring the diameter of round wire, usually a round plate with slots on its periphery numbered according to an arbitrary standard, or a long graduated plate with a slot of diminishing width. **2** A standard system of sizes for wire. Also **wire gauge.**

wire gauze A material of a gauzelike structure made of interwoven strands of wire.

wire glass See under GLASS.

wire-grass (wīr′gras′, -gräs′) *n.* **1** A European grass (*Poa compressa*) having slender, compressed stems, cultivated in the United States and Canada: also called *Canada bluegrass.* **2** Any one of several similar grasses.

wire-haired griffon (wīr′hârd′) A griffon (def. 2).

wire·less (wīr′lis) *adj.* **1** Without wire or wires; having no wires. **2** *Brit.* Radio. —*n.* **1** The wireless telegraph or telephone system, or a message transmitted by either. **2** *Brit.* Radio. —*v.t. & v.i. Brit.* To communicate (with) by wireless telegraphy; radio.

wireless telegraphy or **telephony** Telegraphy or telephony without wires connecting the points of transmission and reception, the message being transmitted through space by electromagnetic waves; radio communication.

wire-man (wīr′mən) *n. pl.* **·men** (-mən) **1** A man who has to do with wire. **2** One who handles wire for telegraph lines, etc.; a wirer.

wire mark The faint impression left on paper by the wires of the mold during manufacture.

wire netting Netting made of wire, as window screens, fences, etc.

Wire-pho·to (wīr′fō′tō) *n. pl.* **·tos** An apparatus and method for transmitting and receiving photographs by wire: a trade name.

wire-pull·er (wīr′pŏŏl′ər) *n.* One who pulls wires, as of a puppet; hence, one who uses secret means to control others or gain his own ends; an intriguer.

wire-pull·ing (wīr′pŏŏl′ing) *n.* **1** The pulling of wires, as in a puppet show. **2** The use of secret influence to obtain an end.

wir·er (wīr′ər) *n.* **1** A trapper who snares with wire contrivances. **2** A wireman.

wire recorder A device for recording sounds on an uncoiling fine wire by magnetic registration of variations in the flow of electrical current from a microphone: these sounds are reproduced as the magnetized wire is passed back between the poles of the electromagnet.

wire rope A rope of wires firmly wound together.

wire-sonde (wīr′sond′) *n. Meteorol.* A type of radiosonde for use at low altitudes, the required data being transmitted by wire to ground stations. [< WIRE + (RADIO)SONDE]

wire-spun (wīr′spun′) *adj.* Wire-drawn; spun or drawn out too fine; overrefined.

wire-tap (wīr′tap′) *n.* **1** A device used to make a connection with a telephone or telegraph wire to listen to or record the message transmitted. **2** The act of wiretapping. —*v.t.* **-tapped, -tap·ping 1** To connect a wiretap to. **2** To monitor by the use of a wiretap. —**wire′tap′per** *n.*

wire-walk·er (wīr′wô′kər) *n.* A wire-dancer.

wire wheel In automobiles, a wheel in which slender metal spokes, usually in a criss-cross pattern, connect the hub and rim.

wire-work (wīr′wûrk′) *n.* **1** Small articles made of wire cloth. **2** Wire fabrics in general. —**wire′work′er** *n.*

wire-works (wīr′wûrks′) *n. pl.* **·works 1** A factory where wire or articles of wire are made. **2** A shop where wire is woven and manufactured into protective screens, filters, or the like.

wire-worm (wīr′wûrm′) *n.* **1** The cylindrical brown to whitish larva of a click beetle, with a stiff, wiry texture: some species are common in fields, where they damage the roots of plants. For illustration see INSECTS (injurious). **2** A millipede.

wire-wove (wīr′wōv′) *adj.* **1** Denoting a high grade of paper with a smooth writing surface. **2** Woven of wire.

wir·ing (wīr′ing) *n.* An entire system of wire installed for the distribution of electric power, as for lighting, heating, radio, engine ignition, or the like.

wir·ra (wir′ə) *interj.* An exclamation of sorrow or despair. [Earlier O *wirra*, partial trans. of Irish *a Muire* O Mary]

wir·y (wir′ē) *adj.* **wir·i·er, wir·i·est 1** Having great resisting power; thin, but tough and sinewy: said of persons. **2** Like wire; stiff. — **wir′i·ly** *adv.* —**wir′i·ness** *n.*

wis (wis) *v.t. Obs.* To suppose; think. [<IWIS]

Wis·by (wiz′bē, *Ger.* viz′bē) The German name for VISBY.

Wis·con·sin (wis·kon′sən) A State of the Great Lakes region of the United States; 56,154 square miles; capital, Madison; entered the Union May 29, 1848; nickname, *Badger State*: abbr. WI —**Wis·con′sin·ite** (-īt) *n.*

Wisconsin River A river in central Wisconsin, flowing 430 miles south and SW to the Mississippi.

wis·dom (wiz′dəm) *n.* **1** The power of true and right discernment; conformity to the course of action dictated by such discernment. **2** Good practical judgment; common sense. **3** A high degree of knowledge; learning. **4** A wise saying. [OE *wisdōm* <*wis* wise]

Synonyms: attainment, depth, discernment, discretion, enlightenment, erudition, foresight, information, insight, judgment, judiciousness, knowledge, learning, lore, prescience, profundity, prudence, reason, reasonableness, sagacity, sense, skill, understanding. *Enlightenment, erudition, information, knowledge, learning,* and *skill* are acquired, as by study or practice. *Insight, judgment, profundity* or *depth, reason, sagacity, sense,* and *understanding* are native qualities of mind, but are capable of increase by cultivation. *Wisdom* is mental power acting upon the materials that fullest *knowledge* gives in the most effective way. There may be what is termed "practical *wisdom*" that looks only to material results; but in its full sense *wisdom* implies the highest exercise of all the faculties. *Prudence* is a more negative form of the same virtue and largely with a view of avoiding loss and injury. *Judgment,* the power of forming decisions, is broader and more positive than *prudence,* leading one to do, as readily as to refrain from doing; but *judgment* is more limited in range and less exalted in character than *wisdom. Skill* is far inferior to *wisdom,* consisting largely in the practical application of acquired *knowledge,* power, and habitual processes, or in the ingenious contrivance that makes such application possible. In the making of something perfectly useless there may be great *skill,* but no *wisdom.* Compare KNOWLEDGE, PRUDENCE. *Antonyms:* absurdity, error, fatuity, folly, foolishness, idiocy, imbecility, imprudence, indiscretion, miscalculation, misjudgment, nonsense, shallowness, silliness, stupidity.

wisdom literature The didactic books of the Old Testament, comprising Proverbs and Ecclesiastes, and the book of Wisdom and Ecclesiasticus in the Apocrypha.

Wisdom of Jesus, the Son of Si·rach (sī′rak) Ecclesiasticus.

Wisdom of Solomon A book of the Old Testament Apocrypha, consisting of a hymn in praise of wisdom: ascribed by tradition to Solomon, but probably dating from the first or second century B.C.

wisdom tooth The last molar tooth on either side of the upper and lower jaws in man, appearing between the 17th and 22d year. —**to cut one's wisdom teeth** To acquire mature judgment by age and experience.

wise[1] (wīz) *adj.* **wis·er, wis·est 1** Possessed of wisdom; seeing clearly what is right and just; having sound judgment concerning one's highest interests, and in one's own conduct choosing the best end and the best means for reaching that end; in a lower sense, sagacious; also, shrewd or calculating. **2** Marked by wisdom; prudent; sensible. **3** Having great learning; erudite. **4** Suited to a man of wisdom; sage. **5** Having practical knowledge of the arts or sciences. **6** Versed in mysterious things. **7** *Colloq.* Aware of; onto: *wise* to his motives. —**to get wise** *Slang* To know the true facts. —*v.t. Slang* To make cognizant of; inform. —**to wise up** *Slang* To make or become aware, informed, or sophisticated. [OE *wīs*] —**wise′ly** *adv.* —**wise′ness** *n.*

Synonyms: deep, discerning, enlightened, erudite, intellectual, intelligent, judicious, knowing, profound, rational, reasonable, sagacious, sage, sapient, solid, sound, thoughtful. See EXPEDIENT, POLITIC, SAGACIOUS. *Antonyms:* see synonyms for ABSURD, IGNORANT.

wise[2] (wīz) *n.* Way of doing; manner; method: chiefly in phrases: **in any wise, in no wise,** etc. [OE *wise* manner. Akin to GUISE.]

wise[3] (wīz) *v.t. & v.i. Dial. & Scot.* or *Obs.* To incline; turn. [OE *wisian*]

-wise *suffix of adverbs & nouns* **1** In a (specified) way or manner: *no wise, likewise.* **2** In a (specified) direction or position: *lengthwise, clockwise:* often equivalent to *-ways.* **3** *Colloq.* With reference to: *Moneywise,* the job is worth considering. [OE *wise* manner, fashion]

Wise (wīz), **Stephen Samuel,** 1872–1949, U.S. rabbi born in Hungary.

wise·a·cre (wīz′ā′kər) *n.* **1** One who affects great wisdom. **2** A wise man; sage. [< MDu. *wijsseggher* a soothsayer; infl. in form by ACRE]

wise·crack (wīz′krak′) *Slang n.* A smart or supercilious remark. —*v.i.* To utter a smart remark. —**wise′crack′er** *n.* —**wise′crack′ing** *adj. & n.*

wise·ling (wīz′ling) *n. Rare* One who pretends to or affects wisdom.

Wise·man (wīz′mən), **Nicholas Patrick Stephen,** 1802–65, English cardinal and author born in Spain.

wis·er·ite (wīs′ər·īt) *n. Mineral.* A hydrous carbonate of manganese, yellowish–white to gray in color, found in Switzerland. [after D. F. Wiser, 19th c. Swiss mineralogist]

wise woman A woman skilled in magic; a soothsayer; sorceress; a witch, usually benevolent, who deals in charms against disease, misfortune, etc.

wish (wish) *n.* **1** A desire or longing, usually for some definite thing. **2** An expression of such a desire; petition. **3** Something wished for. **4** *Psychoanal.* An impulse, tendency, or striving toward the satisfaction of some need, especially when originating in or generated by the unconscious. See synonyms under WILL[1]. [< *v.*] —*v.t.* **1** To have a desire or longing for; crave; want: usually with a clause or infinitive as object: We *wish* to be sure. **2** To desire a specified condition or state for (a person or thing): I *wish* this day were over. **3** To invoke upon or for someone: I *wished* him good luck. **4** To bid: to *wish* someone good morning. **5** To request or entreat: I *wish* you would tell me what you are whispering about; also, to command. —*v.i.* **6** To have or feel a desire; yearn; long: usually with *for:* to *wish* for a friend's return. **7** To make or express a wish. —**to wish on** To impose (something or someone) on a person. [OE *wӯscan*]

wish·bone (wish′bōn′) *n.* The forked bone formed by the united clavicles of a carinate bird; the furcula: so called from the old belief that when pulled apart by two persons, each making a wish, the one who gets the longer part will have his wish fulfilled. See MERRYTHOUGHT.

wish·ful (wish′fəl) *adj.* Having a wish or desire; full of longing. —**wish′ful·ly** *adv.* —**wish′ful·ness** *n.*

wish fulfilment 1 The satisfaction of a wish. **2** *Psychoanal.* The illusory realization of a strongly motivated, often unconscious and repressed aim by mental processes divorced from or not in accord with reality.

wish·ton·wish (wish′tən·wish) *n.* **1** The prairie dog. **2** The whippoorwill: incorrect use by James Fenimore Cooper. [<Caddoan; orig. prob. imit.]

wish–wash (wish′wosh′, -wôsh′) *n.* Any thin, weak, insipid drink; slops. [Varied reduplication of WASH]

wish·y–wash·y (wish′ē·wosh′ē, -wôsh′ē) *adj. Colloq.* **1** Thin; diluted, as liquor. **2** Lacking in solidity, consistence, or vigor; unsubstantial.

Wis·mar (vis′mär) A port on the Baltic in NW East Germany, in the former state of Mecklenburg.

wisp (wisp) *n.* **1** A small bunch, as of hay, straw, or hair. **2** A small bit; a mere indication: a *wisp* of vapor. **3** A whiskbroom. **4** A

will–o′–the–wisp. —*v.t.* **1** To dress, brush, or groom with a wisp or whisk. **2** To fold and lightly twist into a wisp or wisplike form; rumple; crumple. [ME *wisp, wips.* Akin to WIPE.] —**wisp′y** *adj.*

wisp·ish (wis′pish) *adj.* Like or having the nature of a wisp.

wist (wist) Past tense and past participle of WIT[2].

wis·tar·i·a (wis·târ′ē·ə) *n.* **1** Any of a genus (*Wistaria*) of woody twining shrubs of the bean family, with pinnate leaves, elongated pods, and handsome clusters of blue, purple, or white flowers. The two best–known species are the **Chinese wistaria** (*W. sinensis*) and the later blossoming **Japanese wistaria** (*W. floribunda*). The common spelling **wis·te·ri·a** (wis·tir′ē·ə, -târ′-) was the one originally given by the botanist Nuttall. **2** A shade of dull, purplish blue. [after Caspar *Wistar,* 1761–1818, U.S. anatomist]

WISTARIA

Wis·ter (wis′tər), **Owen,** 1860–1938, U.S. novelist.

wist·ful (wist′fəl) *adj.* **1** Wishful; longing. **2** Musing; pensive. [Appar. <obs. *wistly* intently; infl. in form by *wishful*] —**wist′ful·ly** *adv.* —**wist′ful·ness** *n.*

wist·less (wist′lis) *adj. Obs.* Inattentive; unobservant.

wit[1] (wit) *n.* **1** The power of knowing or perceiving; intelligence; ingenuity; sagacity; keen or good sense. **2** The power or faculty of rapid and accurate observation; the power of comprehending and judging. **3** *pl.* The mental faculties, as of perception and understanding: to use one's *wits;* also, the mental faculties with regard to their state of balance: out of her *wits.* **4** The ready perception and happy expression of unexpected or amusing analogies or other relations between apparently incongruous ideas; sudden and ingenious association of ideas or words causing delight and surprise; loosely, any form of humor which expresses irony or satire by a happy association of words. **5** One who has a keen perception of the incongruous or ludicrous and makes skilful use of it in writing or speaking; also, a clever conversationalist; one gifted in repartee or clever sayings. **6** Significance; meaning; import. **7** *Obs.* Mental activity. —**at one's wits' end** At the limit of one's devices and resources; not knowing what to do. —**to live by one's wits** To make a living by using one's practical intelligence and resourcefulness, often in unscrupulous or fraudulent ways. [OE]

Synonyms: banter, drollery, facetiousness, fun, humor, jest, jocularity, joke, playfulness, pleasantry, raillery, waggery, waggishness. *Wit* is the quick perception of unusual or commonly unperceived analogies or relations between things apparently unrelated; it depends on the production of a diverting, entertaining, or merrymaking surprise. The analogies with which *wit* plays are often superficial or artificial; *humor* deals with real analogies of an amusing or entertaining kind, or with traits of character that are seen to have a comical side. *Wit* is keen, sudden, brief, and sometimes severe; *humor* is deep, thoughtful, sustained, and kindly. *Pleasantry* is lighter and less vivid than *wit. Fun* denotes the merry results produced by any fortuitous occasion of mirth, and is pronounced and often hilarious. *Antonyms:* gravity, seriousness, sobriety, solemnity, stolidity.

wit[2] (wit) *v.t. & v.i.* Present indicative: I **wot,** thou wost, he **wot,** *pl.* **wite(n);** *pt.* and *pp.* **wist;** *ppr.* **wit·ting** *Archaic* To be or become aware (of); learn; know. —**to wit** That is to say; namely; scilicet: used, especially in legal documents, to introduce a detailed statement or an explanation. [OE *witan* know]

wit·an (wit′ən) *n. pl.* **1** Members of the national council in Saxon England. **2** The council itself. [OE, councilors, pl. of *wita* a wise man, witness]

witch[1] (wich) *n.* **1** A person who practices

sorcery; a sorcerer or sorceress; one having supernatural powers in the natural world, especially to work evil, and usually by association with evil spirits or the devil; formerly applied to men, women, and children, now generally restricted to women. **2** An ugly, malignant old woman; a hag. **3** A bewitching or fascinating woman or girl. — *v.t.* **1** To overcome by witchcraft; work an evil spell upon. **2** To effect by witchcraft or sorcery. **3** To fascinate or bewitch; enchant. [OE *wicce* a witch, fem. of *wicca* a wizard < *wiccian* bewitch]

witch² (wich) *n.* The wych-elm: also spelled *wich, wych.* [OE *wice* < *wican* bend]

witch alder A shrub (*Fothergilla gardeni*) resembling the witch hazel in its fruit and the alder in its leaves. It is found along shady swamps from Virginia to Florida. [< WITCH² + ALDER]

witch broom Leaf curl. [< WITCH¹ + BROOM]

witch·craft (wich′kraft′, -kräft′) *n.* **1** The practices or powers of witches or wizards, especially when regarded as due to dealings with evil spirits or the devil; black magic; sorcery; also, an instance of such practices. **2** Extraordinary influence or fascination; witchery. See synonyms under SORCERY.

witch doctor **1** Among certain primitive peoples of Africa, especially the Kaffirs, a medicine man skilled in detecting witches and counteracting evil spells; hence, any medicine man or magician. **2** One who professes to heal or cure by sorcery; a hex.

witch·dom (wich′dəm) *n. Rare* Witchcraft.

witch–elm (wich′elm′) *n.* The wych-elm. [< WITCH² + ELM]

witch·er·y (wich′ər-ē) *n. pl.* **·er·ies** **1** Witchcraft. **2** Power to charm; fascination.

witch·es′-broom (wich′iz-broōm′, -broŏm′) *n.* A compact broomlike growth of portions of various trees and shrubs, characterized by excessive multiplication of branches, and due in some cases to the presence of parasitic fungi: also called *hexenbesen.* Also **witch′-broom′.**

witches′ Sabbath In medieval folklore, a midnight orgy of demons and witches, which in German folklore is believed to occur on May Day eve or Walpurgis Night: also called *sabbat.*

witch·et·ty (wich′it-ē) *n.* The grub of a longicorn beetle, living in the roots of shrubs, in decayed timber, or in the earth, which is roasted and eaten by Australian aborigines. [< Australian]

witch–find·er (wich′fīn′dər) *n.* Formerly, one employed to seek and obtain information against witches.

witch·grass (wich′gras′, -gräs′) *n.* **1** The panic grass, common in sandy soils and cultivated fields, with a very loose, pyramidal, compound hairy panicle. **2** The couchgrass. [Alter. of QUITCHGRASS]

witch hazel **1** A shrub (*Hamamelis virginiana*) of the United States and Canada, with several branching crooked trunks and small yellow flowers. **2** An ointment and fluid extract used as a remedy for bruises, sprains, etc., derived from the bark and dried leaves of this shrub. **3** The wych-elm. Also *wych-hazel.* [< WITCH² + HAZEL]

witch hunt An investigation of persons ostensibly to uncover subversive activities, but intended for ulterior motives, such as harassing political opposition.

witch·ing (wich′ing) *adj.* Having power to enchant; weird; fascinating. — *n.* Witchcraft; sorcery. — **witch′ing·ly** *adv.*

witch·mon·ger (wich′mung′gər, -mong′-) *n.* One who deals with witches or believes in witchcraft.

witch moth Any of several moths (family *Noctuidae*) of nocturnal habits and typically somber appearance; especially, the large black witch moth (*Erebus odora*) of South and North America.

witch of A·gne·si (ä·nyā′zē) *Math.* The plane curve of the equation $x^2y = 4a^2(2a-y)$: it is symmetric with respect to the *y*-axis and asymptotic to the *x*-axis. Also called the *versiera.* [after Donna Maria Gaetani *Agnesi*, 1718–1799, Italian mathematician]

wite (wīt) *n. Scot. & Brit. Dial.* **1** A penalty; fine. **2** A reproach; blame. **3** A guilty action; fault. [OE *wīte*]

wit·e·na·ge·mot (wit′ə·nə·gə·mōt′) *n.* The assembly of the witan. [OE *witena gemōt* councilors' assembly]

with (with, with) *prep.* **1** In the company of; as a member or associate of. **2** Next to; beside: Walk *with* me. **3** Having; bearing: a hat *with* a feather. **4** Characterized or marked by; characteristically possessed of: the house *with* green shutters; a man *with* brains. **5** In a manner characterized by; exhibiting: to dance *with* grace. **6** Among: counted *with* the others. **7** During; in the course of: We forget *with* time. **8** From; so as to be separated from: to part *with* the past; to dispense *with* luxury. **9** Against: to struggle *with* an adversary. **10** In the opinion of: That is all right *with* me. **11** Because of; as a consequence of: faint *with* hunger. **12** In charge of; in possession of: Leave the key *with* the janitor; I have my fiddle *with* me. **13** Using; by means or aid of: to write *with* a pencil. **14** By adding or having as a material or quality: trimmed *with* lace; endowed *with* beauty. **15** Under the influence of: confused *with* drink. **16** In spite of: *With* all his money, he could not buy health. **17** At the same time as: to go to bed *with* the chickens. **18** In the same direction as: to drift *with* the crowd. **19** In regard to; in the case of: Be gentle *with* the horse; I am angry *with* them. **20** Onto; to: Join this tube *with* that one. **21** In proportion to: His fame grew *with* his achievements. **22** In support of: He voted *with* the Left. **23** Of the same opinion as: I'm *with* you there! **24** Compared to; contrasted to: Consider this picture *with* that one. **25** Immediately after; following: *With* that, he slammed the door. **26** Having received or been granted: *With* your consent I'll go now. [OE]

with– *prefix* **1** Against: *with*stand. **2** Back; away: *with*hold. [OE *with-* < *with* against]

with·al (with-ôl′, with-) *Archaic adv.* With the rest; in addition. — *prep.* With: intensive form used after its object and at the end of the clause: a bow to shoot *withal.* [ME *with alle* < *with + alle* all]

with·draw (with-drô′, with-) *v.* **·drew, ·drawn, ·draw·ing** *v.t.* **1** To draw or take away; remove. **2** To take back, as an assertion or a promise; recall. **3** To keep or abstract from use. — *v.i.* **4** To draw back; retire. See synonyms under ABSTRACT, SEPARATE. [< WITH- + DRAW] — **with·draw′al, with·draw′ment** *n.*

with·draw·ing (with-drô′ing, with-) *adj.* Stretching back or away; receding.

withdrawing room **1** A room behind another room for retirement. **2** A drawing room.

withe (wīth, with, with) *n.* **1** A willowy, supple twig. **2** A band made of twisted flexible shoots, straw, or the like. **3** An elastic handle for a tool. — *v.t.* **withed, with·ing** To bind with withes. [OE *withthe*]

with·er (with′ər) *v.i.* **1** To become limp or dry, as a plant when cut down or deprived of moisture. **2** To waste, as flesh. **3** To droop or languish. — *v.t.* **4** To cause to become limp or dry. **5** To abash, as by a scornful glance. [Appar. var. of WEATHER, *v.*]

Synonyms: blast, blight, collapse, droop, shrink, shrivel. See DIE¹. *Antonyms:* bloom, develop, expand, flourish, freshen, grow, luxuriate, swell.

With·er (with′ər), **George,** 1588–1667, English poet. Also **With′ers.**

with·er·ite (with′ə·rīt) *n.* A white, translucent barium carbonate, $BaCO_3$, occurring massive or in orthorhombic crystals. [after Dr. Wm. *Withering,* 1741–99, English physician, who first described and analyzed it]

withe rod A shrub (*Viburnum cassinoides*) of the honeysuckle family, growing in swamps from Newfoundland to New Jersey and Minnesota.

WITCH OF AGNESI

with·ers (with′ərz) *n. pl.* **1** The highest part of the back of the horse between the shoulder blades. **2** The similar part in some other animals, as the deer and ox. [OE *withre* resistance < *wither* against; so called because the horse opposes this part against the load he pulls]

with·er·shins (with′ər·shinz) *adv. Scot.* In the opposite direction; in a reversed way. Also spelled *widdershins, widershins.*

With·er·spoon (with′ər·spoōn), **John,** 1722–94, American educator born in Scotland; signed Declaration of Independence.

with·hold (with-hōld′, with-) *v.* **·held, ·hold·ing** *v.t.* **1** To hold back; restrain. **2** To keep back; decline to grant. — *v.i.* **3** To refrain; forbear. See synonyms under KEEP, RETAIN, SUSPEND. [< WITH- + HOLD] — **with·hold′er** *n.*

withholding tax That part of an employee's wages or salary which is deducted as an instalment on his income tax.

with·in (with-in′, with-) *adv.* **1** In the inner part; interiorly. **2** Inside the body, heart, or mind. **3** Indoors. — *prep.* **1** In the inner or interior part or parts of; inside: *within* the house. **2** In the limits, range, or compass of (a specified time, space, or distance): *within* a mile of here; *within* ten minutes' walk. **3** Not exceeding (a specified quantity): Live *within* your means. **4** In the reach, limit, or scope of: *within* my power. See synonyms under AT. [OE *withinnan* < *with* with + *innan* in]

with·in·doors (with-in′dôrz′, -dōrz′, with-) *adv.* Inside a building.

with·it (with′it) *adj. Slang* **1** In touch with modern habits, fashions, trends, etc.; up-to-date; hip. **2** Lively and modern; swinging. Also **with it.**

with·out (with-out′, with-) *prep.* **1** Not having, as the result of loss, privation, negation, etc.; lacking: *without* money; *without* a home. **2** In the absence of: We must manage *without* help. **3** Free from: *without* fear. **4** At, on, or to the outside of. **5** Outside of or beyond the limits of: living *without* the pale of civilization. **6** With avoidance of: He listened *without* paying attention. **7** *Obs.* Besides. — *adv.* **1** In or on the outer part; externally. **2** Out of doors. — *conj. Dial.* Unless; except. [OE *withūtan* < *with* with + *ūtan* out]

without day Sine die.

with·out·doors (with-out′dôrz′, -dōrz′, with-) *adv.* Out of doors; outside.

with·stand (with-stand′, with-) *v.* **·stood, ·stand·ing** *v.t.* To oppose with any force; resist successfully. — *v.i.* To make resistance; endure. See synonyms under OPPOSE. [OE *withstandan* < *with-* against + *standan* stand] — **with·stand′er** *n.*

with·y (with′ē, with′ē) *adj.* Made of withes; flexible and tough. — *n. pl.* **with·ies** **1** A rope made of withes. **2** A withe. [< WITHE]

wit·less (wit′lis) *adj.* Lacking in wit; foolish. — **wit′less·ly** *adv.* — **wit′less·ness** *n.*

wit·ling (wit′ling) *n.* A person who has little wit or understanding. [< WIT¹ + -LING¹]

wit·ness (wit′nis) *n.* **1** An act or fact of attestation to a fact or an event; testimony; evidence. **2** A person who has seen or knows something, and is therefore competent to give evidence concerning it; a spectator. **3** That which serves as or furnishes evidence or proof. **4** *Law* One who has knowledge of facts relating to a given cause and is subpoenaed to testify; also, a person who has signed his name to an instrument executed by another in order that he may testify to the genuineness of the maker's signature. See synonyms under SPECTATOR, TESTIMONY. — *v.t.* **1** To see or know by personal experience. **2** To furnish or serve as evidence of. **3** To give testimony to. **4** To be the site or scene of: This spot has *witnessed* many heinous crimes. **5** *Law* To see the execution of (an instrument) and subscribe to it for the purpose of establishing its authenticity. — *v.i.* **6** To give evidence; testify. See synonyms under AVOW. [OE *witnes* knowledge, testimony] — **wit′ness·er** *n.*

witness stand The platform in a courtroom from which a witness gives evidence.

wit·ney (wit′nē) *n.* A heavy woolen fabric, preshrunk and napped, used for blankets and coats. [from *Witney,* England, where it was first manufactured]

Wit·te (vit′ə), **Count Sergei Yulievitch,** 1849–1915, Russian statesman, diplomat, and financier.

wit·ted (wit'id) *adj.* Having wit: used principally in compounds with the meaning having (a specified kind of) wit: quick-*witted*, half-*witted*.

Wit·te·kind (vit'ə-kint), died in battle 807?, leader of the Saxons against Charlemagne. Also spelled *Widukind*.

Wit·ten (vit'n) A city on the Ruhr in North Rhine–Westphalia, Germany.

Wit·ten·berg (vit'n-bûrg, *Ger.* vit'n-berkh) A city on the Elbe river in central East Germany, in the former state of Saxony–Anhalt; the Protestant Reformation originated here, 1517.

Witt·gen·stein (vit'gən-shtīn), **Ludwig**, 1889–1951, Austrian philosopher active in England.

Witt·gen·stein Island (vit'gən-shtīn) A former name for FAKARAVA.

wit·ti·cism (wit'ə-siz'əm) *n.* A witty saying. [<WITTY, on analogy with *criticism*; coined by Dryden]

wit·ting[1] (wit'ing) *adj.* Aware; done consciously, with knowledge and responsibility. [<WIT[2]]

wit·ting[2] (wit'ing) *n. Obs.* Knowledge; information. [<ON *vitand* consciousness < *vita* know]

wit·ting·ly (wit'ing-lē) *adv.* With knowledge and by design; knowingly and designedly.

wit·tol (wit'l) *n. Obs.* A contented cuckold; a husband who is aware of, but indifferent to, his wife's infidelity. [ME *wetewold* < *wete* know + (*coke*)*wold* cuckold]

wit·ty (wit'ē) *adj.* **·ti·er**, **·ti·est** **1** Given to making original or clever speeches; quick at repartee; humorous. **2** Displaying or full of wit. See synonyms under HUMOROUS. [OE *wittig* wise] — **wit'ti·ly** *adv.* — **wit'ti·ness** *n.*

Wit·wa·ters·rand (wit-wä'tərs-ränt, -rand) A region of southern Transvaal on a rocky ridge near Johannesburg; 1,000 square miles; site of the world's richest gold fields: also *The Rand.*

witz·chour·a (wits-chŏŏr'ə) *n.* A mantle with large sleeves and a wide collar, worn in the early 19th century. [<F *vitchoura* <Polish *wilczura* a wolf-skin coat < *wilk* a wolf]

wive (wīv) *v.* **wived**, **wiv·ing** *v.t.* **1** To furnish with a wife. **2** To marry. — *v.i.* **3** To marry a woman. [OE *wīfian* < *wīf* a wife, woman]

wi·vern (wī'vərn) *n. Her.* A two-legged, winged dragon, with barbed and knotted tail: often spelled *wyvern.* Also **wi'ver**. [<AF *wivre,* OF *guivre* a dragon, serpent, var. of *vivre* <L *vipera*]

WIVERN

wives (wīvz) Plural of WIFE.

wiz (wiz) *n. Slang* A wizard (def. 2). [Short for WIZARD]

wiz·ard (wiz'ərd) *n.* **1** One supposed to be in league with the devil; a male witch; sorcerer. **2** *Colloq.* A very skilful or clever person: He's a *wizard* with machinery. **3** *Obs.* A wise man; sage. — *adj.* **1** Having magical powers. **2** Fascinating; enchanting. [ME *wysard* < *wys,* OE *wīs* wise]

wiz·ard·ry (wiz'ərd·rē) *n.* The practice or methods of a wizard.

wiz·en[1] (wiz'ən) *v.t.* & *v.i.* To become or cause to become withered; shrivel. — *adj.* Wizened; shrunken; shriveled. [OE *wisnian* dry up, wither]

wiz·en[2] (wiz'ən) *n. Dial.* or *Obs.* The weasand. Also **wiz'zen**.

wiz·ened (wiz'ənd) *adj.* Shrunken; withered; dried up.

Wło·cła·wek (vwô-tswä'vek) A city on the Vistula in central Poland; a manufacturing center. *Russian* **Vlo·tslavsk** (vlo-tsläfsk').

woad (wōd) *n.* **1** An Old World herb (*Isatis tinctoria*) of the mustard family; dyer's-weed. **2** The blue dyestuff obtained from its leaves. [OE *wād*] — **woad'ed** *adj.*

woad·wax·en (wōd'wak'sən) *n.* Dyer's-broom: also spelled *woodwaxen.*

woald (wōld) See WELD[2].

wob·ble (wob'əl) *v.* **·bled**, **·bling** *v.i.* **1** To move or sway unsteadily, as a top while rotating at a low speed. **2** To show indecision or unsteadiness; waver; vacillate. — *v.t.* **3** To cause to wobble. — *n.* An unsteady motion, as that of unevenly balanced rotating bodies. Also spelled *wabble.* [? <LG *wabbeln*] —

wob'bler *n.* — **wob'bling** *adj.* — **wob'bling·ly** *adv.* — **wob'bly** *adj.*

wobble pump A hand pump.

wob·bly (wob'lē) *n. pl.* **·blies** *U.S. Slang* A member of the Industrial Workers of the World (I.W.W.). [Appar. mispronunciation of *w* in *I.W.W.*]

Wode·house (wŏŏd'hous, wōd'-), **Sir P(elham) G(renville)**, 1881–1975, English humorous novelist.

Wo·den (wōd'n) The Old English name for Odin, the chief Norse god. Wednesday is named for Woden. Also **Wo'dan**.

woe (wō) *n.* **1** Overwhelming sorrow; grief. **2** Heavy affliction or calamity; disaster: His *woes* are many. — *interj.* Alas! used to proclaim disaster or to express sorrow, to denounce, or invoke censure. Also **wo.** [OE *wa* misery]

woe·be·gone (wō'bi-gôn', -gon') *adj.* Overcome with woe; mournful; sorrowful. Also **wo'be·gone'.** See synonyms under SAD.

woe·ful (wō'fəl) *adj.* **1** Accompanied by or causing woe; direful. **2** Expressive of sorrow; doleful. **3** Deserving condemnation; paltry; miserable; mean. Also **woe'some, wo'ful.** See synonyms under PITIFUL, SAD. — **woe'ful·ly** *adv.* — **woe'ful·ness** *n.*

Wo·ë·vre (vō·e'vr') A tableland in NE France, near Verdun; scene of severe fighting in World War I, 1915 and 1918.

Wof·fing·ton (wof'ing-tən), **Margaret**, 1714?–1760; English actress born in Dublin: commonly called "Peg Woffington."

Wöh·ler (vœ'lər), **Friedrich**, 1800–82, German chemist.

wok (wok) *n.* A Chinese cooking pan, as of iron, aluminum, or copper, with handles and a rounded bottom, usually equipped with a separate metal ring to prevent tipping. [< Chinese]

wo·kas (wō'kəs) *n.* A yellow waterlily (*Nuphar polysepalum*) of western North America, having small seeds formerly roasted and eaten by the Klamath Indians. [<Klamath]

woke (wōk) Past tense of WAKE[1].

wok·en (wō'kən) Dialectal past participle of WAKE[1].

Wol·cott (wŏŏl'kət), **Oliver**, 1726–97, American statesman; signed Declaration of Independence.

wold (wōld) *n.* An undulating tract of open upland; down or moor. [OE *wald* a forest]

Wolds (wōldz), **the** A range of hills in Lincolnshire and Yorkshire, England, parallel to the coast, north and south of the Humber; highest point, 800 feet.

wolf (wŏŏlf) *n. pl.* **wolves** (wŏŏlvz) **1** Any of a genus (*Canis*) of large carnivorous mammals related to the dog, especially the common European species (*C. lupus*) or the timber wolf of North America. ◆ Collateral adjective: *lupine.* **2** Any ravenous, cruel, or rapacious person or thing; hence, popularly, a philanderer. **3** *Entomol.* The destructive larva of various beetles and moths. **4** The harsh, dissonant sound of certain chords on a keyed instrument, as an organ or piano, when tuned by a system of unequal temperament; in bowed instruments, a harsh, discordant sound caused by defective vibration of one or more notes of a scale. — **to cry wolf** To give a false alarm. — **to keep the wolf from the door** To avert want or starvation. — *v.t.* To devour ravenously; gulp down: He *wolfed* his food. [OE *wulf*]

Wolf (wŏŏlf) The constellation Lupus.

Wolf (vôlf), **Friedrich August**, 1759–1824, German classical scholar. — **Hugo**, 1860–1903, Austrian composer.

wolf·ber·ry (wŏŏlf'ber'ē) *n. pl.* **·ries** A shrub (*Symphoricarpos occidentalis*) of the honeysuckle family, with pinkish, bell-shaped flowers and white berries in spikes, growing in the western United States.

Wolf Cub A member of the division of Boy Scouts for boys between 8 and 11 years of age.

wolf dog **1** A large dog for hunting wolves. **2** A cross between a wolf and a dog.

Wolfe (wŏŏlf), **Charles**, 1791–1823, Irish poet. — **James**, 1727–59, English general; defeated the French under Montcalm at Quebec; both he and Montcalm were killed. — **Thomas Clayton**, 1900–38, U.S. novelist.

Wolff (vôlf), **Christian von**, 1679–1754, German philosopher. — **Kaspar Friedrich**, 1733–1794, German anatomist.

Wolf–Fer·ra·ri (vôlf'fer·rä'rē), **Ermanno**, 1876–1948, Italian composer.

Wolff·i·an (wŏŏlf'fē·ən) *adj.* Pertaining to or named after the German anatomist Kaspar F. Wolff.

Wolffian body *Anat.* The mesonephros.

wolf fish A large fish (*Anarhichas lupus*) of the North Atlantic, with powerful teeth adapted for crushing shellfish.

Wolf·gang (vôlf'gäng) *German* A masculine personal name. [<G, a wolf's progress]

wolf·hound (wŏŏlf'hound') *n.* Either of two breeds of large dogs, the **Russian wolfhound** or *borzoi* and the **Irish wolfhound**, a dog resembling the Great Dane, trained, or originally intended, to catch and kill wolves.

wolf·ish (wŏŏlf'ish) *adj.* **1** Having the qualities of a wolf; rapacious; savage. **2** *Colloq.* Ravenously hungry. — **wolf'ish·ly** *adv.* — **wolf'ish·ness** *n.*

wolf pack A number of submarines which cooperate in making concerted attacks on enemy ships or convoys.

wolf·ram (wŏŏl'frəm) *n.* **1** Wolframite. **2** Tungsten. [<G, prob. < *wolf* a wolf + *rahm* cream, soot]

wolf·ram·ite (wŏŏl'frəm·īt) *n.* A submetallic, grayish-black or brown tungstate of iron and manganese, crystallizing in the monoclinic system. It is important commercially as a source of tungsten and its compounds. [<G *wolframit* < *wolfram* tungsten]

Wol·fram von Esch·en·bach (vôl'främ fôn esh'ən-bäkh), 1165?–1220?, German poet.

wolf's–bane (wŏŏlfs'bān') *n.* **1** A species of aconite; monkshood. **2** A species of European arnica (*Arnica montana*), used as a lotion for bruises. **3** The silk vine. [Trans. of NL *lycoctonum* <Gk. *lykoctonon,* lit., a wolf-slayer < *lykos* a wolf + *kteinein* kill]

Wol·las·ton (wŏŏl'əs·tən), **William Hyde**, 1766–1828, English chemist and physicist.

wol·las·ton·ite (wŏŏl'əs·tən·īt') *n.* A vitreous, white, translucent calcium silicate, crystallizing in the monoclinic system. [after Dr. W. H. *Wollaston*]

Wolse·ley (wŏŏlz'lē), **Garnet Joseph**, 1833–1913, first Viscount Wolseley, British general.

Wol·sey (wŏŏl'zē), **Thomas**, 1475?–1530, English cardinal and statesman.

wolv·er (wŏŏl'vər) *n.* One who hunts wolves.

Wol·ver·hamp·ton (wŏŏl'vər·hamp'tən) A county borough and industrial center in southern Stafford, England.

wol·ver·ine (wŏŏl'və·rēn') *n.* A rapacious and cunning carnivore (genus *Gulo*) of northern forests, with stout body and limbs and bushy tail. Also **wol'ver·ene'.** [Dim. of WOLF]

WOLVERINE
(Body to 3 feet long; tail, 1 1/2 feet)

Wolverine State Nickname of MICHIGAN.

wolves (wŏŏlvz) Plural of WOLF.

wom·an (wŏŏm'ən) *n. pl.* **wom·en** (wim'in) **1** An adult human female. **2** The female part of the human race; women collectively. **3** Womanly character; femininity: usually with *the.* **4** As applied to a man, one who is effeminate, timid, or weak. **5** A female attendant or servant. **6** A paramour or kept mistress. **7** *Colloq.* A wife. — *adj.* **1** Feminine; characteristic of women. **2** Female: when used with a plural noun, usually *women*: *women* students. **3** Affecting or pertaining to women. — *v.t. Obs.* To play the part of a woman in or in reference to. [OE *wifmann* < *wif* a wife + *mann* a human being]

wom·an·hood (wŏŏm'ən·hŏŏd) *n.* **1** The state of a woman or of womankind. **2** Women collectively.

wom·an·ish (wŏŏm'ən·ish) *adj.* Characteristic of a woman; effeminate. See synonyms under FEMININE. — **wom'an·ish·ly** *adv.* — **wom'an·ish·ness** *n.*

wom·an·ize (wŏŏm'ən·īz) *v.* **·ized**, **·iz·ing** *v.t.*

To make effeminate or womanish. —*v.i. Colloq.* To consort with women illicitly.

wom·an·kind (woom′ən·kīnd′) *n.* Women collectively.

wom·an·ly (woom′ən·lē) *adj.* Having the qualities natural, suited, or becoming to a woman; feminine. —*adv.* In a feminine manner; like a woman. —**wom′an·li·ness** *n.*

woman suffrage See under SUFFRAGE. — **wom′an·suf′fra·gist** *n.*

womb (woom) *n.* **1** The organ in which the young of higher mammals are developed; the uterus. **2** The place where anything is engendered or brought into life. **3** A cavity viewed as enclosing something. **4** *Obs.* The belly or stomach. [OE *wamb, womb* the belly]

wom·bat (wom′bat) *n.* An Australian nocturnal marsupial (family *Vombatidae*) resembling a small bear. [< Australian]

wombed (woomd) *adj.* Having a womb; hence, hollow; capacious; cavernous. Also **womb′y.**

wom·en (wim′in) Plural of WOMAN.

wom·en·folk (wim′in·fōk′) *n. pl.* Women collectively. Also **wom′en·folks′.**

Women in the Air Force A corps of women in the U.S. Air Force, including all women except nurses and medical specialists. Abbr. *WAF* or *W.A.F.*

Women's Army Corps A corps of women in the U.S. Army, composed of all women except nurses and medical specialists. Abbr. *WAC* or *W.A.C.*

women's rights The rights of women to enjoy equal legal rights and privileges with men, as of suffrage, property, and education.

wom·er·a (wom′ər·ə) *n.* A stick used by Australian aborigines for throwing javelins, spears, etc.: also **woomera.** [< Australian]

won (wun) Past tense and past participle of WIN.

won·der (wun′dər) *n.* **1** A feeling of mingled surprise and curiosity; astonishment. **2** That which causes wonder; a prodigy; a strange thing; a miracle. See synonyms under PRODIGY. —**nine days' wonder** Something that excites public wonder for a short time. —*v.t.* **1** To have a feeling of doubt and strong curiosity in regard to. —*v.i.* **2** To be affected or filled with wonder; marvel. **3** To be doubtful; query mentally. —*adj.* Spectacularly successful: a *wonder* drug. [OE *wundor*] — **won′der·er** —**won′der·ing** *adj.* — **won′der·ing·ly** *adv.*

won·der·ful (wun′dər·fəl) *adj.* Of a nature to excite wonder; marvelous. —**won′der·ful·ly** *adv.* — **won′der·ful·ness** *n.*

won·der·land (wun′dər·land′) *n.* A realm of fairy romance or wonders.

won·der·ment (wun′dər·mənt) *n.* **1** The emotion of wonder; surprise. **2** Something wonderful; a marvel.

Wonder State Nickname for ARKANSAS.

won·der·strick·en (wun′dər·strik′ən) *adj.* Suddenly smitten with wonder or admiration. Also **won′der·struck′** (-struk′).

won·der·work (wun′dər·wûrk′) *n.* A work inspiring wonder; miracle. —**won′der·work′er** *n.* — **won′der·work′ing** *adj.*

won·drous (wun′drəs) *adj.* Commanding wonder; wonderful; marvelous. —*adv.* Surprisingly. [Alter. of ME *wonders,* genitive of WONDER] — **won′drous·ly** *adv.* —**won′drous·ness** *n.*

won·ky (wong′kē) *adj. Brit. Slang* Unsteady; liable to break down; shaky; feeble. [Prob. OE *wancol* shaky]

Won·san (woen·sän) A port in eastern Korea: Japanese *Gensan.*

wont (wunt, wōnt) *v.* **wont, wont** or **wont·ed, wont·ing** *v.t.* **1** To accustom or habituate: used reflexively. —*v.i.* **2** To be accustomed; be used. **3** *Obs.* To dwell. [< *adj.*] —*adj.* Doing habitually; accustomed; used. —*n.* Ordinary manner of doing or acting; habit. See synonyms under

HABIT. [OE *gewunod,* pp. of *gewunian* be accustomed]

won't (wōnt) Will not: a contraction of Middle English *woll not.* Also *Scot.* **won·na** (wun′nə).

wont·ed (wun′tid, wōn′-) *adj.* **1** Commonly used or done; habitual. **2** Habituated; accustomed; at ease; at home. See synonyms under HABITUAL, USUAL.

woo[1] (woo) *v.t.* **1** To make love to, especially so as to marry; court. **2** To entreat earnestly; beg. **3** To invite; solicit; seek. —*v.i.* **4** To pay court; make love. See synonyms under ADDRESS. [OE *wōgian*]

woo[2] (woo) *n. Scot.* Wool.

wood[1] (wood) *n.* **1** A large and compact collection of trees; a forest; grove: also **woods. 2** The tough, fibrous material, composed mainly of cellulose and lignin, which forms the xylem of trees and shrubs and constitutes the bulk of their stems and branches under the bark. **3** The hard substance of a tree or shrub, whether as growing or as cut for use, for building, fuel, etc.; lumber; timber. **4** Something made of wood. **5** *pl.* A rural district; backwoods. —**to knock wood** To tap on a piece of wood or a wooden object as a charm against bad luck, especially while making an optimistic statement. —*adj.* **1** Made of wood; wooden. **2** Made for using or holding wood: a *wood* stove. **3** Living or growing in woods: the *wood* anemone. —*v.t.* **1** To furnish with wood for fuel. **2** To convert into a forest; plant with trees. —*v.i.* **3** To take on a supply of wood. [OE *widu, wiodu*]

wood[2] (wood) *Obs. v.i.* To act like a maniac; rave. —*adj.* Furious; frantic; raging; mad. [OE *wōd* insane]

Wood (wood), **Grant,** 1892–1942, U.S. painter. —**Leonard,** 1860–1927, U.S. physician, army officer, and colonial administrator.

wood alcohol Methanol, especially if produced by the destructive distillation of wood.

wood anemone Any of several small plants (genus *Anemone*), growing in woodlands and blooming in the early spring, especially the common American species (*A. quinquefolia*), and the common European species (*A. nemorosa*).

wood betony 1 The common lousewort (*Pedicularis canadensis*) of the eastern United States, with yellow or reddish flowers. **2** The common betony (*Stachys officinalis*).

wood·bin (wood′bin′) *n.* A box or crib for holding firewood.

wood·bine (wood′bīn) *n.* **1** The common European honeysuckle. **2** The Virginia creeper. [OE *wudubind < wudu* wood + *bindan* bind]

wood·block (wood′blok′) *n.* **1** A block of wood prepared for engraving. **2** A woodcut.

wood block 1 A block of wood for paving, etc. **2** *Music* A percussion instrument consisting of a hollow block of wood struck with a drumstick.

wood·bor·er (wood′bôr′ər, -bōr′ər) *n.* Any of a large family (*Buprestidae*) of brilliantly colored beetles whose larvae are very destructive of trees. For illustration see INSECTS (injurious).

wood·carv·ing (wood′kär′ving) *n.* **1** The art of carving wood, especially for decoration. **2** A carving in wood. —**wood′carv′er** *n.*

wood·chat (wood′chat) *n.* **1** A European butcherbird (*Lanius collorio*) with reddish plumage and a notched beak. **2** Any of several Asian birds (genera *Ianthia* and *Larvivora*) of the thrush family. [Prob. partial trans. of G *waldkatze* the butcherbird, lit., wood cat]

wood·chuck (wood′chuk) *n.* A marmot (*Marmota monax*) of eastern North America; a ground hog. [Prob. alter. of WE·JACK; infl. in form by WOOD[1] and CHUCK[1]]

wood coal 1 Charcoal made from wood: also **wood charcoal. 2** Lignite.

wood·cock (wood′kok′) *n.* **1** A small European game bird (*Scolopax rusticola*), having the thighs entirely feathered. **2** A related North American bird (*Philohela minor*). **3** *Obs.* A dolt; fool.

wood·craft (wood′kraft′, -kräft′) *n.* **1** Skill in such things as belong to woodland life, such as hunting or trapping; the faculty of finding

WOODCHUCK
(Head and body to 14 inches; tail, 5 inches)

one's way, and living comfortably in the wilderness. **2** Skill in woodwork or in constructing articles of wood. —**wood′crafts′man** (-krafts′mən, -kräfts′-) *n.*

wood·cut (wood′kut′) *n.* **1** An engraving on wood. **2** A print from such a block.

wood·cut·ter (wood′kut′ər) *n.* One who cuts or chops wood. —**wood′cut′ting** *n.*

wood·ed (wood′id) *adj.* Having a supply of wood; abounding with trees.

wood·en (wood′n) *adj.* **1** Made of wood: *wooden* tools. **2** Like a block of wood; stupid; mechanical; stiff; awkward. **3** Dull; spiritless. —**wood′en·ly** *adv.* —**wood′en·ness** *n.*

wood engraving 1 The art of cutting designs on wood for printing; the making of woodcuts. **2** A block thus engraved or a print therefrom. — **wood engraver**

wood·en·head (wood′n·hed′) *n. Colloq.* A stupid person; blockhead. —**wood′en·head′ed** *adj.*

wooden horse See TROJAN HORSE (def. 1).

wooden Indian 1 A carved and painted wooden figure of a North American Indian, usually in a standing position, formerly placed in front of cigar stores as an advertisement. **2** An inarticulate, sluggish, or dull person.

wooden nutmeg 1 An imitation nutmeg: proverbially used by New England (especially Connecticut) traders. **2** Any deceptive device.

wood·en·shoe dance (wood′n·shoo′) The trasko.

wood·en·ware (wood′n·wâr′) *n.* Dishes, vessels, bowls, etc., made of wood: said especially of household utensils.

wood grouse The capercaillie.

wood·hen (wood′hen′) *n.* A weka.

wood·hoo·poe (wood′hoo′pō) *n.* Any of a genus (*Phoeniculus*) of gregarious, insect-eating birds with metallic green, blue, or purple plumage, related to the hoopoes in the family Upupidae but lacking a crest and restricted to African forests.

wood·house (wood′hous′) *n.* A house or shed for storing firewood. Also called *woodshed.*

wood hyacinth A small European squill (*Scilla nonscripta*), with clusters of bell-shaped blue, white, or pink flowers.

wood ibis A very large storklike bird (*Mycteria americana*) with a white body, glossy black tail, and naked head, common in wooded swamps of South America and the southern United States.

wood·ie (wood′ē) *n. Scot.* The gallows; a hangman's rope: used humorously.

wood·land (wood′lənd, -land′) *n.* Land occupied by or covered with wood or trees; timberland. — *adj.* (-lənd) Belonging to or dwelling in the woods. —**wood′land·er** *n.*

woodland caribou See under CARIBOU.

wood·lark (wood′lärk′) *n.* A European passerine bird (*Lullula arborea*) resembling the skylark but with a sweeter note.

wood lot A plot of land devoted to the growing of forest trees or consisting of woodland.

wood louse Any of numerous small terrestrial flat-bodied crustaceans (genera *Oniscus, Porcellion,* and others) commonly found under old logs; a sow bug or pill bug.

wood·man (wood′mən) *n. pl.* **·men** (-mən) **1** A woodcutter; lumberman. **2** A forester; also, a dweller in forests. **3** A hunter of forest game. Also *woodsman.*

wood·note (wood′nōt′) *n.* A simple, artless, or natural song, as of a wild bird.

wood nymph 1 A goddess or nymph of the forest; a dryad. **2** Any of several South American hummingbirds (genus *Thalurania*). **3** A butterfly of the family Satyridae, including species usually brown in color and with eyelike spots on the wings. They occur in woods and are not attracted to flowers.

wood·peck·er (wood′pek′ər) *n.* Any of a large family (*Picidae*) of birds related to the flickers, having stiff tail feathers to aid in climbing, strong claws, and a sharp, chisel-like bill for drilling holes in woodin search of insects; especially, the red-headed

RED-HEADED WOODPECKER
(9 to 9 1/2 inches long)

woodpecker (*Melanerpes erythrocephalus*) of North America, which has the head and upper breast deep red and the tail black, tipped with white; and the **pileated woodpecker** of North America (*Ceophloeus pileatus*) with a scarlet crest, white throat, white wing markings, and a large yellowish bill.

wood pewee Pewee (def. 1).

wood pigeon 1 The cushat. **2** The wild band-tailed pigeon (*Columba fasciata*) of the western United States.

wood·pile (wŏŏd′pīl′) *n.* A pile of wood, especially of wood cut or split in sizes for burning in a fireplace or stove.

wood pitch The final residuum of wood tar.

wood·print (wŏŏd′print′) *n.* A woodcut.

wood pulp Wood reduced to a pulp, as by grinding to a powder and digesting with chemicals: used for making paper.

wood pussy *Colloq.* A skunk.

wood rat A pack rat.

wood·ruff (wŏŏd′ruf′) *n.* Any of several common European woodland herbs (genus *Asperula*) of the madder family, especially the **sweet-scented woodruff** (*A. odorata*), used to flavor wine and in perfumery. [OE *wudurofe* < *wudu* wood]

woods (wŏŏdz) *n. pl.* A forest or wooded area.

Woods, Lake of the See LAKE OF THE WOODS.

wood·screw (wŏŏd′skrŏŏ′) *n.* A screw with a thread of coarse pitch, used for fastening pieces against wood. See illustration under SCREW.

wood·shed (wŏŏd′shed′) *n.* A woodhouse.

woods·i·a (wŏŏd′zē·ə) *n.* Any of a genus (*Woodsia*) of small tufted ferns, found in rocky places. [after Joseph *Woods*, 1776–1864, English botanist]

woods·man (wŏŏdz′mən) *n. pl.* **·men** (-mən) **1** A woodman. **2** A man skilled in woodcraft.

wood sorrel Oxalis.

wood spirit Wood alcohol or methanol.

Wood·stock (wŏŏd′stok) A municipal borough of central Oxfordshire, England.

wood sugar Xylose.

woods·y (wŏŏd′zē) *adj. Colloq.* Of, pertaining to, or dwelling in the woods; suggesting the woods: a *woodsy* fragrance.

wood tar A tar produced by the dry distillation of wood: it contains turpentine, resins, oils, creosote, and other hydrocarbons, and yields pyroligneous acid.

wood thrush 1 A large, common woodland thrush of North America (*Hylocichla mustelina*), noted for the vigor and sweetness of its song. **2** The missel thrush.

wood tick Any of certain ticks found in the woods, especially *Dermacentor variabilis* which transfers itself from underbrush to passing animals or human beings.

wood·turn·ing (wŏŏd′tûr′ning) *n.* The process or art of shaping blocks of wood into various forms by means of a lathe. —**wood′turn′er** *n.*

wood vinegar 1 Impure acetic acid from the distillation of wood. **2** Pyroligneous acid.

wood violet The bird's-foot violet.

wood·wax·en (wŏŏd′wak′sən) See WOAD-WAXEN.

wood·wind (wŏŏd′wind′) *n.* A musical wind instrument made of wood. See WIND INSTRUMENT. —*adj.* Pertaining to or characteristic of a wooden wind instrument.

wood·work (wŏŏd′wûrk′) *n.* **1** The wooden parts of any structure, especially interior wooden parts, as moldings or doors. **2** Work made of wood. —**wood′work′er** *n.* —**wood′work′ing** *n.*

wood·worm (wŏŏd′wûrm′) *n.* A worm or larva dwelling in or that bores in wood.

wood·y (wŏŏd′ē) *adj.* **wood·i·er**, **wood·i·est 1** Of the nature of wood; containing wood; ligneous. **2** Pertaining to wood; resembling wood. **3** Wooded; abounding with woods; sylvan. —**wood′i·ness** *n.*

woo·er (wŏŏ′ər) *n.* One who woos; a lover.

woof[1] (wŏŏf) *n.* **1** The weft of a woven fabric; the threads that are carried back and forth across the fixed threads of the warp in a loom. **2** The texture of a fabric. [OE *ōwef*]

woof[2] (wŏŏf) *n.* A sound made in imitation of the growl or low suppressed bark of a dog or bear. [Imit.]

woof·er (wŏŏf′ər) *n. Electronics* A loudspeaker used to reproduce the bass register in high-fidelity sound equipment, generally in connection with a tweeter. [< WOOF[2]]

wool (wŏŏl) *n.* **1** The soft, curly or crisped hair obtained from the fleece of sheep and some allied animals, especially that from domesticated sheep, noted for its felting properties and which provides the widest range of fibers for yarns and textiles. **2** The under-fur of a fur-bearing animal. **3** Short kinky or crisp human hair. **4** Material or garments made of wool. **5** Something resembling or likened to wool. —**all wool and a yard wide** Perfect in quality and quantity; hence, one hundred percent genuine. —**to pull the wool over one's eyes** To delude or deceive one. —*adj.* Made of or pertaining to wool or woolen material. [OE *wull*]

wool-clip (wŏŏl′klip′) *n.* The amount of wool clipped from the sheep in one year.

wool-dyed (wŏŏl′dīd′) *adj.* Dyed before the wool has been spun into yarn: said of fabrics.

wool·en (wŏŏl′ən) *adj.* **1** Consisting wholly or in part of wool; like wool. **2** Pertaining to wool or its manufacture. —*n.* Cloth or clothing made of wool: especially in the plural. Also **wool′len.**

Woolf (wŏŏlf), **(Adeline) Virginia,** 1882–1941, *née* Stephen, English novelist and essayist.

wool fat Lanolin. Also **wool grease.**

wool·fell (wŏŏl′fel′) *n.* The pelt of a sheep or other wool-bearing animal with the wool still on it. [< WOOL + FELL[4]]

wool·gath·er·ing (wŏŏl′gath′ər·ing) *n.* Any trivial or purposeless employment; especially, idle reverie: from gathering wool caught on bushes, which required much wandering to collect even a little. —*adj.* Idly indulging in fancies. —**wool′gath′er·er** *n.*

wool·grow·er (wŏŏl′grō′ər) *n.* A person who raises sheep for the production of wool. —**wool′grow′ing** *adj.*

Wooll·cott (wŏŏl′kət), **Alexander,** 1887–1943, U.S. journalist and critic.

Wool·ley (wŏŏl′ē), **Sir (Charles) Leonard,** 1880–1960, English archeologist.

wool·ly (wŏŏl′ē) *adj.* **·li·er, ·li·est 1** Consisting of, covered with, or resembling wool; wool-bearing. **2** Soft and vaporous; lacking clearness; not sharply detailed; fuzzy; blurry. **3** Having a rounded and somewhat fleecy appearance, as clouds. **4** Having a growth of wool-like hairs. **5** Resembling the roughness and excitement of the West: usually in the phrase *wild and woolly.* —*n. pl.* **·lies** A garment made of wool; especially, woolen underwear. Also **wool′y.** —**wool′li·ness, wool′iness** *n.*

woolly bear The larva of any of several tiger moths: so called because covered with long dense hairs.

wool·pack (wŏŏl′pak′) *n.* **1** A bag or wrapper of canvas, cotton, etc., for packing a bale of wool. **2** A bale or bundle of wool. **3** *Meteorol.* A cumulus cloud.

wool·sack (wŏŏl′sak′) *n.* **1** A sack of wool. **2** The seat of the lord chancellor in the English House of Lords, a cushion stuffed with wool. **3** The office of lord high chancellor.

wool·sta·pler (wŏŏl′stā′plər) *n.* A dealer in or sorter of wool. —**wool′-sta′pling** *adj. & n.*

Wool·wich (wŏŏl′ich, -ij) A metropolitan borough of London on the south bank of the Thames.

Wool·worth (wŏŏl′wûrth), **Frank Winfield,** 1852–1919, U.S. merchant; developed the five-and-ten-cent store.

woom·e·ra (wŏŏ′mər·ə) *n.* A womera.

Woon·sock·et (wŏŏn·sok′it) A city in NE Rhode Island on the Blackstone River.

woo·ra·li (wŏŏ·rä′lē) *n.* Curare. Also **woo·ra′ri** (-rē). [Var. of CURARE]

Woo·sung (wŏŏ′sŏŏng′) The outer port of Shanghai, China, at the mouth of the Hwang-poo, north of Shanghai.

wooz·y (wŏŏ′zē) *adj. Slang* **1** Befuddled, especially with drink. **2** Fuzzy. [Prob. < *wooze*, var. of OOZE] —**wooz′i·ly** *adv.* —**wooz′i·ness** *n.*

wop (wop) *n. Slang* An Italian: a derogatory term. [? < dial. Ital. (Sicilian) *guapo* a dandy < Sp.]

Worces·ter (wŏŏs′tər) **1** A midland county in England; 699 square miles. Also **Worces′ter-shire** (-shir). **2** Its county town, famous for its 14th century cathedral. **3** A city in central Massachusetts, second largest in the State; an industrial, rail, and university center.

Worces·ter (wŏŏs′tər), **Joseph Emerson,** 1784–1865, U.S. lexicographer.

Worcester china A very fine china or porcelain made in Worcester, England, from 1751: also **Worcester porcelain,** and called **Royal Worcester** by royal warrant.

Worcestershire sauce A piquant sauce made originally in Worcester, England, from vinegar and many other ingredients. Also **Worcester sauce.**

word (wûrd) *n.* **1** A speech sound or combination of sounds which has come to signify and communicate a particular idea or thought, and which functions as the smallest meaningful unit of a language when used in isolation. There are **basic** or **radical words** as *master, man,* **derivative words** as *masterful, manly,* **inflectional words** as *masters, men,* and **compound words** as *masterpiece, manpower,* etc. In terms of modern linguistics, a word may be a single morpheme (a free form, as *master*) or a union of morphemes (free and bound forms, as *masters, masterful, masterpiece*). **2** The letters or characters that stand for a significant vowel sound. **3** A vocable considered only as a sound: ideas rather than *words.* **4** *Usually pl.* Conversation; talk: a man of few *words.* **5** A brief remark; hence, a short and pithy saying. **6** A communication or message: Send him *word.* **7** A command, signal, or direction: Give the *word* to start. **8** A promise; hence, good faith: a man of his *word.* **9** A party cry; watchword. **10** *pl.* Language used in anger, rebuke, or otherwise emotionally: They had *words.* See synonyms under TERM. —*v.t.* To express in a word or words, especially in selected words; phrase. [OE. Akin to VERB.]

Word (wûrd) *n.* **1** The Logos; the Son of God. **2** Divine Wisdom, as in *John* i. **3** The Scriptures as an embodiment of divine revelation.

word·age (wûr′dij) *n.* Words collectively.

word blind·ness *n.* Alexia.

word·book (wûrd′bŏŏk′) *n.* **1** A collection of words; vocabulary; lexicon; dictionary. **2** An opera libretto.

word deafness Inability to understand speech, resulting from disease of the cortical center: a form of aphasia.

word for word In the exact words; literally; verbatim.

word·i·ly (wûr′də·lē) *adv.* In a wordy manner; verbosely. —**word′i·ness, word′ish·ness** *n.*

word·ing (wûr′ding) *n.* The act or style of expressing in words; phraseology; also, words used; expression. See synonyms under DICTION.

word·less (wûrd′lis) *adj.* Having no words; dumb; silent.

word play 1 Repartee; fencing with words. **2** Subtle discussion on words and their meaning. **3** Play on words.

word processing The production of typewritten documents through the use of computer tapes and other automated equipment.

word square An arrangement of a set of words in rectangular form, so that they can be read in either horizontal or vertical lines, as in the accompanying example.

F	R	E	T
R	E	A	R
E	A	S	E
T	R	E	E

Words·worth (wûrdz′wûrth), **William,** 1770–1850, English poet; laureate 1843–50.

word·watch·er (wûrd′woch′ər) *n.* A close observer of words and their ways.

word·y (wûr′dē) *adj.* **word·i·er, word·i·est 1** Of the nature of words; verbal. **2** Expressed in many words. **3** Given to the use of words; verbose; prolix.

wore (wôr, wōr) Past tense of WEAR[1] & WEAR[2].

work (wûrk) *n.* **1** Continued exertion or activity directed to some purpose or end; especially, manual labor; hence, opportunity for labor; occupation. **2** That upon which labor is expended; an undertaking; task. **3** That which is produced by or as by labor; specifically, an engineering structure; fortification; a design produced with a needle; also, a product of mental labor, as a book or opera. **4** A manufacturing or other industrial establishment: usually in the plural. **5** *pl.* Running gear or machinery, as of a watch. **6**

Manner of working, or style of treatment; management; workmanship. **7** *pl.* Moral duties considered as external acts, especially as meritorious. **8** A froth or foam produced by fermentation in making vinegar, etc. **9** A feat or deed. **10** *Physics* A transference of energy from one body to another, resulting in the motion or displacement of the body acted upon, in the direction of the acting force: it is expressed as the product of the force and the amount of displacement in the line of its action. —*v.* **worked** (*Archaic* **wrought**), **work·ing** *v.i.* **1** To perform work; labor; toil. **2** To be employed in some trade or business. **3** To perform a function; operate: The machine *works* well. **4** To prove effective or influential; succeed: His stratagem *worked.* **5** To move or progress gradually or with difficulty: He *worked* up in his profession. **6** To become as specified, as by gradual motion: The bolts *worked* loose. **7** To have some slight improper motion in functioning: The wheel *works* on the shaft. **8** To move from nervousness or agitation: His features *worked* with passion. **9** To undergo kneading, hammering, etc.; be shaped: Copper *works* easily. **10** To ferment. **11** *Naut.* To labor in a heavy sea so as to loosen seams and fastenings: said of a ship. —*v.t.* **12** To cause or bring about; effect; accomplish: to *work* a miracle. **13** To cause to function; direct the operation of: to *work* a machine. **14** To make or shape by toil or skill. **15** To prepare, as by manipulating, hammering, etc.: to *work* dough. **16** To decorate, as with embroidery or inlaid work. **17** To cause to be productive, as by toil: to *work* a mine. **18** To cause to do work: He *works* his employees too hard. **19** To cause to be as specified, usually with effort: We *worked* the timber into position. **20** To make or achieve by effort: He *worked* his way to the top of his profession; to *work* one's passage on a ship. **21** To carry on some activity in (an area, etc.); cover: to *work* a stream for trout. **22** To solve, as a problem in arithmetic. **23** To cause to move from nervousness or excitement: to *work* one's jaws. **24** To excite; provoke: He *worked* himself into a passion. **25** To influence or manage, as by insidious means; lead. **26** To cause to ferment. **27** *Colloq.* To practice trickery upon; cheat; swindle. **28** *Colloq.* To make use of for one's own purposes; use. —**to work in** To put in; insert or be inserted. —**to work off** To get rid of, as extra flesh by exercise. —**to work on** (or **upon**) **1** To try to influence or persuade. **2** To influence or affect. —**to work out 1** To make its way out or through. **2** To effect by work or effort; accomplish. **3** To exhaust, as a mineral vein or a subject of inquiry. **4** To discharge, as a debt, by labor rather than by payment of money. **5** To develop; form, as a plan. **6** To solve. **7 a** To prove effective or successful. **b** To result as specified. —**to work up 1** To excite; rouse, as rage or a person to rage. **2** To form or shape by working; develop. **3** To make one's or its way. [OE *weorc*] —*Synonyms (noun):* achievement, action, business, deed, doing, drudgery, employment, exertion, labor, occupation, performance, product, production, toil. *Work* is the generic term for any continuous application of energy toward an end; *work* may be hard or easy. *Labor* is hard and wearing *work; toil* is straining and exhausting *work.* *Work* is also used for any result or working, physical or mental; as, a *work* of art; a *work* of genius. In this connection, *work* has special uses, which *labor* and *toil* do not share. *Drudgery* is plodding, irksome, and often menial *work.* See ACT, BUSINESS, PRODUCTION, TASK, TOIL¹. *Antonyms:* ease, idleness, leisure, recreation, relaxation, repose, rest, vacation.

-work *combining form* **1** A product made from a (specified) material: *paperwork, brickwork.* **2** Work of a (given) kind: *piecework.* **3** Work performed in a (specified) place: *housework.* [< WORK]

work·a·ble (wûr′kə·bəl) *adj.* **1** Of a nature to be operated, as a machine. **2** Practicable, as a plan. **3** That can be developed, as a mine. **4** Able to work. **5** That can be worked upon or influenced. —**work′a·bil′i·ty, work′a·ble·ness** *n.*

work·a·day (wûr′kə·dā′) *adj.* **1** Of, pertaining to, or suitable for working days; everyday. **2** Commonplace; prosaic. [Alter. of ME *werkeday* < *werke,* OE *weorca* work + DAY; infl. in form by NOWADAYS]

work·a·hol·ic (wûrk′ə·hol′ik, -hôl′ik) *n.* A person who works to excess.

work·bag (wûrk′bag′) *n.* A bag for holding tools or materials, as for needlework.

work·bench (wûrk′bench′) *n.* A bench for work, as that of a carpenter, machinist, etc.

work·book (wûrk′bŏŏk′) *n.* **1** A booklet based on a course of study and containing problems and exercises which a student works out directly on the pages. **2** A manual containing operating instructions. **3** A book for recording work performed or planned.

work·box (wûrk′boks′) *n.* A small bag or box for needlework, etc.

work·day (wûrk′dā′) *n.* **1** Any day not a Sunday or holiday; a working day. **2** The part of the day or number of hours of one day spent in work. —*adj.* Workaday.

work·er (wûr′kər) *n.* **1** One who or that which performs work; specifically, a laborer as distinguished from a *capitalist.* **2** An individual female of an insect colony, as a true ant, a bee, or a white ant, with undeveloped sexual organs.

work·fare (wûrk′fâr′) *n.* Welfare that is conditional upon assigned work or training by those receiving payments.

work·fel·low (wûrk′fel′ō) *n.* A companion in work.

work·folk (wûrk′fōk′) *n. pl.* Manual laborers.

work·house (wûrk′hous′) *n.* **1** *Brit.* A house for paupers able to work; an almshouse. **2** An industrial prison for petty offenders.

work·ing (wûr′king) *adj.* **1** Engaged actively in some employment. **2** That works, or performs its function: This is a *working* model. **3** Sufficient for use or action: They formed a *working* agreement. **4** Relating to or occupied by work: a *working* day. **5** Throbbing with pain; also, twitching: said especially of the face muscles. **6** Fermenting, as wine. —*n.* **1** The act or operation of any person or thing that works, in any sense. **2** That part of a mine or quarry where excavation is going on or has gone on.

working capital 1 That part of the finances of a business available for its operation. **2** The amount of quick assets which exceed current liabilities.

working day A workday.

working drawing In engineering, etc., a drawing made to scale, as of a part of a machine or building, for the direction of workmen, contractors, etc.

work·ing·man (wûr′king·man′) *n. pl.* **-men** (-men′) A male worker; laborer.

working papers An age certificate and other official papers certifying that a minor may be legally employed.

working substance *Mech.* The fluid, as steam, or gasoline vapor, under pressure, that serves to operate a prime mover. Also **working fluid.**

work·ing·wom·an (wûr′king·wŏŏm′ən) *n. pl.* **-wom·en** (-wim′in) A female worker; laborer.

work·less (wûrk′lis) *adj.* Jobless; unemployed.

work·load (wûrk′lōd′) *n.* The amount of work apportioned to a person, machine, or department over a given period.

work·man (wûrk′mən) *n. pl.* **-men** (-mən) One who earns his bread by manual labor; an artisan; mechanic; workingman. —**work′man·ly** *adj.*

work·man·like (wûrk′mən·līk′) *adj.* Like or befitting a skilled workman; skilfully done. —**work′man·ly** *adv.*

work·man·ship (wûrk′mən·ship) *n.* **1** The art or skill of a workman, or the quality of work. **2** The work or result produced by a worker.

work of art A product of the fine arts, especially painting and sculpture, but including artistic, literary, and musical productions.

work·out (wûrk′out′) *n.* A test, trial, practice performance, etc., to discover, maintain, or increase ability for some work or competition, as a practice boxing bout, a fast turn around a track by a horse, runner, etc.

work·peo·ple (wûrk′pē′pəl) *n. pl.* People employed in work, especially in manual labor; working people.

work·place (wûrk′plās′) *n.* A place where a person works.

work·room (wûrk′rŏŏm′, -rŏŏm′) *n.* A room where work is performed.

works (wûrks) *n.* **1** A manufacturing establishment including buildings and equipment: a gas *works.* **2** *Slang* The whole of anything; the kit and caboodle; everything: the whole *works.* —**to give (someone) the works** *Slang* To maul; kill by shooting. —**to shoot the works** *Slang* To make a supreme effort; risk one's all in one single attempt.

works council A committee of employed workers organized by an employer to discuss company and industrial problems and relations; a company union or similar group.

work·sheet (wûrk′shēt′) *n.* **1** A sheet of paper on which practice work or rough drafts of problems are written. **2** A sheet of paper used to record work schedules and operations.

work·shop (wûrk′shop′) *n.* **1** A building or room where any work is carried on; workroom. **2** A seminar or single session for training, discussion, etc., in a specialized field: a writer's *workshop.*

work·ta·ble (wûrk′tā′bəl) *n.* A table with drawers and other conveniences for use while working, especially while sewing.

work·up (wûrk′up′) *n.* A thorough study of a sick person's symptoms and bodily condition.

work·week (wûrk′wēk′) *n.* The total number of hours worked in a week; also, the number of working hours in a week.

world (wûrld) *n.* **1** The earth; the terraqueous globe; the universe (of which the earth was once supposed to be the center); any similar orb; a part of the earth: the Old *World.* **2** A division of existing or created things belonging to the earth; natural grand division: the mineral, vegetable, or animal *world.* **3** The human inhabitants of the earth; mankind. **4** A definite class of people having certain interests or activities in common: the scientific *world;* a sphere or domain: the *world* of letters. **5** Man regarded socially; the public; hence, public or social life and intercourse. **6** The practices, usages, and ways of men: He knows the *world.* **7** A total of things as pertaining to or affecting an individual man; a career among men; one's experience in life: to begin the *world* anew. **8** The course of events as affecting one personally; individual condition or circumstances: How goes the *world* with you? Your *world* is changed then. **9** A scene of existence or of affairs regarded from a moral or religious point of view; secular affairs; worldly aims, pleasures, or people collectively; earthly existence; mortal life. **10** Figuratively, great quantity, number, or size: a *world* of trouble. —**for all the world** In every respect. —**on top of the world** *Colloq.* Elated. —**to bring into the world** To give birth to. [OE *weorold*]

World may appear as a combining form in hyphemes or as the first element in two-word phrases; as in:

world affairs	world love
world battle	world-old
world builder	world order
world-changing	world peace
world citizen	world politics
world commerce	world price
world conflict	world problem
world-conquering	world-rejoicing
world destroyer	world-renowned
world-domination	world report
world dominion	world revolution
world empire	world sadness
world-encircling	world-shaking
world-famed	world state
world-famous	world struggle
world hero	world trade
world history	world-wandering
world leader	world-winning

World Court See PERMANENT COURT OF INTERNATIONAL JUSTICE under COURT.

world·ling (wûrld′ling) *n.* One who lives merely for this world; a worldly-minded person.

world·ly (wûrld′lē) *adj.* **·li·er, ·li·est 1** Pertaining to the world; mundane; earthly; not spiritual. **2** Devoted to temporal things; secular. **3** Sophisticated; worldly-wise. **4** *Obs.* Lay, as opposed to clerical. —*adv.* In a worldly manner. See synonyms under PROFANE. —**world′li·ness** *n.*

world·ly-mind·ed (wûrld′lē-mīn′did) *adj.* Absorbed in the things of this world. —**world′ly-mind′ed·ly** *adv.* —**world′ly-mind′ed·ness** *n.*

world·ly-wise (wûrld′lē-wīz′) *adj.* Wise in the

ways and affairs of the world; sophisticated.

world power A state or organization whose policy and action are of world-wide influence.

world series In baseball, the games played at the finish of the regular schedule between the champion teams of the American and National Leagues, the first team to win four games being adjudged world's champions. Also **world's series**.

world's fair An international exhibit of the folk crafts and arts, agricultural and industrial products, and scientific progress of various countries.

world soul 1 The hypothetical soul of the world; the All–Soul, conceived of after the analogy of the indwelling soul of man. 2 The principle that animates and informs the physical world. Also **world spirit**.

world's people Worldly people; those not belonging to some specific religious sect or group: a term used especially by the Friends.

World War See table under WAR.

world-wea·ry (wûrld′wir′ē) adj. ·ri·er, ·ri·est Dissatisfied with life and its conditions; weary and tired of this life.

world-wide (wûrld′wīd′) adj. Extended throughout the world.

world without end Forever.

worm (wûrm) n. 1 A small, legless, invertebrate crawling animal, with an elongated, soft, and usually naked body, as a flatworm, roundworm, or annelid. ◆ Collateral adjective: *vermicular*. 2 A small creeping animal with short or undeveloped feet, as an insect larva, a grub, angleworm, etc. 3 Figuratively, that which suggests the action or habit of a worm as eating away or as an agent of decay or destruction, as remorse, death, etc. 4 A despicable or despised person; also, a feeble mortal. 5 Something conceived to be like a worm. 6 A screw thread. 7 A worm screw. 8 The spiral part of a corkscrew. 9 A spiral part in a still. 10 An organ or part that resembles a worm in shape, as the lytta of the dog or the vermiform process. 11 pl. An intestinal disorder due to the presence of parasitic worms. 12 The windings of a log road made to lessen the steepness of a grade. 13 The zigzag course of a log fence or a rail fence. — v.t. 1 To insinuate (oneself or itself) in a wormlike manner; effect as by crawling: with *in* or *into*: to *worm* one's way. 2 To draw forth by artful means, as a secret: with *out*. 3 To remove worms from. 4 To wind yarn, etc., along (a rope) so as to fill up the grooves between the strands. 5 To remove the lytta or worm from, as a dog. — v.i. 6 To move or progress slowly and stealthily. [OE *wyrm*] — **worm′er** n.

Worm (vôorm), **Olaus**, 1588–1654, Danish anatomist and physician.

worm-eat·en (wûrm′ēt′n) adj. Eaten or bored through by worms.

worm fence See under FENCE.

worm gear 1 Mech. A worm wheel having teeth shaped so as to mesh with a worm screw. 2 A worm wheel.

worm·hole (wûrm′hōl′) n. The hole made by a worm or a wormlike animal, as in plants, earth, or stone. — **worm′holed′** adj.

WORM GEAR

Wor·mi·an (wôr′mē-ən) adj. Relating to or discovered by Olaus Worm.

Wormian bones Anat. Small bones occasionally lying along the lines of the cranial sutures.

wor·mil (wûr′məl) n. A warblefly or botfly larva. [Var. of dial. *warnel*, OE *wernægel*]

worm·root (wûrm′rōōt′, -rōot′) n. Pinkroot.

Worms (wûrmz, Ger. vôrms) A city on the Rhine in Rhenish Hesse, SW West Germany; scene of the Diet of Worms (1521) by which Martin Luther was pronounced a heretic.

worm screw Mech. A short threaded portion of a shaft constituting an endless screw formed to mesh with a worm wheel.

worm·seed (wûrm′sēd′) n. 1 The seeds of any of various plants used as a vermifuge. 2 The

plants themselves; especially, santonica, and a species of goosefoot (*Chenopodium ambrosioides*).

worm wheel Mech. A toothed wheel gearing with a worm screw.

worm·wood (wûrm′wood′) n. 1 Any of a genus (*Artemisia*) of European herbs or small shrubs related to the sagebrush, especially a common species (*A. absinthium*), aromatic, tonic, bitter, and used in making absinthe. 2 That which embitters or makes bitter; bitterness. [Alter. of obs. *wermod* <OE; infl. in form by *worm* and *wood*[1]]

worm·y (wûr′mē) adj. **worm·i·er, worm·i·est** 1 Infested with or injured by worms. 2 Of or pertaining to worms; resembling a worm. 3 Earthy; groveling. — **worm′i·ness** n.

worn (wôrn, wōrn) Past participle of WEAR. — adj. 1 Affected by attrition or any similar continuous action. 2 Used, as a garment; showing the effects of anxiety, etc., as the mind; hackneyed, as phrases. 3 Exhausted or spent; used up.

worn-out (wôrn′out′, wōrn′-) adj. 1 Used until without value for its purpose. 2 Thoroughly tired; exhausted.

wor·ri·cow (wûr′ē-kou′) n. Scot. A hobgoblin; the devil; any hideous object or person; bugbear; a scarecrow.

wor·ri·some (wûr′i-səm) adj. Causing worry or anxiety.

wor·rit (wûr′it) n. Colloq. Worry; vexation. [Appar. alter. of WORRY]

wor·ry (wûr′ē) v. ·ried, ·ry·ing v.i. 1 To be uneasy in the mind; feel anxiety about something; fret. 2 To pull or tear at something with the teeth: with *at*. 3 Colloq. To advance or manage despite trials or difficulties: with *along* or *through*. — v.t. 4 To cause to feel uneasy in the mind; trouble. 5 To bother; pester. 6 To mangle or kill by biting, shaking, or tearing with the teeth. 7 Scot. or Obs. To strangle; choke. See synonyms under PERSECUTE. — n. pl. ·ries A state of anxiety; vexation. See synonyms under ANXIETY, CARE. [OE *wyrgan* strangle] — **wor′ri·er** n. — **wor′ri·ment** n.

worse (wûrs) Used as comparative of *bad, ill, evil*, and the like. — adj. 1 Bad or ill in a greater degree; more evil, unworthy, etc. 2 Physically ill in a greater degree. 3 Less favorably situated as to means and circumstances. — n. Something worse; disadvantage; loss. — adv. 1 In a manner more evil or ill. 2 With greater intensity, severity, etc. 3 Decreasingly; less. [OE *wyrsa*]

wors·en (wûr′sən) v.t. & v.i. To make or become worse.

wors·er (wûr′sər) adj. & adv. Worse: a former redundant form of the comparative, on the analogy of *lesser*: now regarded as a vulgarism.

wors·et (wûr′sit) adj. & n. Scot. Worsted.

wor·ship (wûr′ship) n. 1 The act or feeling of adoration or homage; the paying of religious reverence, as in prayer, praise, etc. 2 The act or feeling of deference, respect, or honor toward virtue, power, or the like. 3 Excessive or ardent admiration; also, the object of such love or admiration. 4 A title of honor in addressing persons of station. See synonyms under RELIGION, REVERENCE. — v. ·shiped or ·shipped, ·ship·ing or ·ship·ping v.t. 1 To pay an act of worship to; venerate; adore. 2 To treat with intense or exaggerated admiration or affection. 3 Obs. To honor. — v.i. 4 To perform acts or have sentiments of worship. [OE *weorthscipe* < *weorth* worthy] — **wor′ship·er, wor′ship·per** n.

Synonyms (verb): adore, deify, exalt, honor, idolize, revere, reverence. See PRAISE. *Antonyms*: abhor, abjure, abominate, blaspheme, curse, denounce, detest, renounce, revile, scoff, scorn.

wor·ship·ful (wûr′ship·fəl) adj. 1 Worthy of honor; entitled to respect by reason of character or position: applied to dignitaries, as magistrates, etc. In Freemasonry, it is part of a specific official title, as of masters. 2 Esteemed; distinguished; honorable. 3 Giving reverence; adoring. — **wor′ship·ful·ly** adv. — **wor′ship·ful·ness** n.

worst (wûrst) Used as the superlative of *bad, ill*, or *evil*. — adj. Bad, ill, or evil in the

highest degree. — in the worst way Slang Very much. — n. The most evil state or result. — at worst On the most pessimistic estimate. — to get the worst of it To be defeated or put at a disadvantage. — adv. In the worst or most extreme manner or degree. — v.t. To get the advantage over; defeat; vanquish. See synonyms under BEAT, CONQUER. [OE *wyrsta*]

wors·ted (woos′tid, wûr′stid) n. 1 Woolen yarn spun from long staple, with fibers combed parallel and twisted hard. 2 A lightly twisted woolen yarn. 3 A tightly woven or smooth fabric made from worsted yarns, as gabardine or serge. — adj. Consisting of or made from this yarn. [from *Worsted*, former name of a parish in Norfolk, north of Norwich, England]

wort (wûrt) n. 1 A plant or herb: usually in combination: *liverwort, navelwort*. 2 The sweet, unfermented infusion of malt that becomes beer when fermented. [OE *wyrt* a root, a plant]

worth[1] (wûrth) n. 1 That quality which renders a thing useful or desirable; value or excellence of any kind; hence, market value. 2 That quality or combination of qualities that makes one deserving of esteem; mental and moral excellence. 3 Wealth. — adj. 1 Having value; equal in value (to); exchangeable (for). 2 Deserving (of): in either a good or bad sense. 3 Having possessions to the value of: He is *worth* a million. — for all it is worth To the utmost. — for all one is worth With every effort possible; to the utmost of one's capacity. [OE *weorth*]

Synonyms (noun): character, desert, excellence, integrity, merit, preciousness, value. See PRICE, VIRTUE.

worth[2] (wûrth) v.i. To betide or befall: now only in phrases, as *woe worth the day*, etc. [OE *weorthan* come to be]

-worth combining form Of the value of: *pennyworth*. [OE *weorth* worth]

Wor·thing (wûr′thing) A municipal borough on the coast of southern Sussex, southern England, west of Brighton.

worth·less (wûrth′lis) adj. Having no worth; having no utility or value; destitute of dignity, virtue, or standing. See synonyms under BAD[1], BASE[2], USELESS, VAIN, WASTE. — **worth′less·ly** adv. — **worth′less·ness** n.

worth·while (wûrth′hwīl′) adj. Sufficiently important to occupy the time; of enough value to repay the effort. ◆ This compound originated from the phrase *worth the while* and it is firmly established as a solideme in American usage. In British usage it is usually a hyphene: *worth-while*. — **worth′while′ness** n.

wor·thy (wûr′thē) adj. ·thi·er, ·thi·est 1 Possessing worth; deserving of respect or honor; having valuable or useful qualities. 2 Having such qualities as to be deserving of or adapted to some specified thing; fit; suitable: followed by *of* (rarely *for*), sometimes by an infinitive and rarely by the object directly. 3 Obs. Well deserved; fitting. See synonyms under BECOMING, EXCELLENT, GOOD, MORAL, VIRTUOUS. — n. pl. ·thies 1 A person of eminent worth. 2 Humorously, a person of local note; a character. [ME *wurthi, worthi*] — **wor′thi·ly** adv. — **wor′thi·ness** n.

-worthy combining form 1 Meriting or deserving: *trustworthy*. 2 Valuable as; having worth as: *newsworthy*. 3 Fit for: *seaworthy*. [OE *wyrthe* worthy]

wot (wot) Present tense, first and third person singular, of WIT[2].

Wot·ton (wot′n), **Sir Henry**, 1568–1639, English diplomat and poet.

would (wood) Past tense of WILL, expressing desire, condition, or what might be expected: used also to express determination: He *would* go, I couldn't stop him. [OE *wolde*, pt. of *willan* will]

◆ **would & should** Anybody dealing in ifs, as–ifs, promises, threats, hopes, wishes, or similar feelings and attitudes about the real or imagined future, will find himself making plentiful use of *would* and/or *should*, which do duty to express the vestigial and fast vanishing subjunctive mood. As to which one to use, the distinctions are subtle and fine-drawn and at several points British usage calls for *should* where American practice is to use *would,* although *would* has not here displaced *should* to the extent that *shall* has given way to *will* (see usage note under SHALL vs. WILL). (1) In simple factual conditions, for example, British usage calls for *should* in the first person in the conclusion: If he failed, I *should* (U.S. *would*) still support him. (2) When one of these modal auxiliaries is to be used in the first person preceding such verbs as *like, prefer, care, be glad,* etc., British usage holds firmly to *should;* but American, Scottish, and Irish usage calls for *would:* We *would* (Brit. & formal U.S. *should*) like to have you come to dinner next Tuesday. *Would* in this example represents true present time. (3) *Would* is the true past expressing an act of will mostly in negations or expressions of indifference: They asked him to wait, but he *would* not (was unwilling to comply). (4) *Would* can also convey customary or habitual action in the past: He *would* take her gifts every time he called. Except for these rare instances in which *would* is used as a true past, it is usually confined to the purposes of the subjunctive. (5) It may express an act of will under projected or imagined conditions: (I, You, He) *wouldn't* tolerate that insult even if it were offered with smiling politeness. (6) When no condition is expressed, *would* in the second and third person often lacks even a vestigial trace of any act of will: She *would* be no more than second choice in the matrimonial sweepstakes. (7) When *would* is stressed with the voice it may indicate (a) an element of malign fate or misfortune: She *would* be the one to lose her take-home fare; or (b) the notion of persistent contrariness: You *would* insist on bumping your head against a stone wall twice! (8) In conditions contrary to fact, *would* is used in conclusion without any feeling of volition involved: Had he left sooner he *would* have heard less to his discredit. If I had been able to dodge the small souls around the commission, I *would* (Brit. *should*) have got a third share in the radio station. (9) *Would* may also express probability in cases where some contingency or hypothesis is unexpressed: "He was very boastful." "He *would* be." (10) Finally, there is the matter of the idiomatic use of *would* and *should* in indirect or reported discourse. In most cases, if the direct utterance used *shall,* the reported discourse employs *should.* Similarly, if it was *will* in the direct utterance, *would* is used in the indirect discourse. If obligation is involved, *should* must be used. Except in this area of obligation, *would* is the more common form in American usage.

would-be (wŏŏd′bē′) *adj.* Desiring or professing to be: a *would-be* poet.

would·n't (wŏŏd′nt) Would not: a contraction.

wound[1] (wŏŏnd, *Poetic* wound) *n.* **1** A hurt or injury caused by violence; especially, a cut, bruise, stab, etc.; a trauma. **2** A breach or cut of the bark or substance of a tree or plant. **3** Hence, any injury or cause of pain or grief, as to the feelings, honor, etc. — *v.t.* & *v.i.* To inflict a wound or wounds (upon); cause injury or grief (to); hurt. See synonyms under AFFRONT, HURT, PIQUE[1]. [OE *wund*] — **wound′ed** *adj.* — **wound′less** *adj.*

wound[2] (wound) Past tense and past participle of WIND[2].

Wou·ter (wou′tər) Dutch form of WALTER.

wove (wōv) Past tense and alternative past participle of WEAVE.

wo·ven (wō′vən) Past participle of WEAVE.

wove paper Paper carrying the marks of the wire gauze on which it was laid during finishing.

wow (wou) *interj.* An exclamation of wonder, surprise, pleasure, or pain. — *n. Slang* An extraordinary success. — *v.t. Slang* To be extraordinarily successful with.

wow·ser (wou′zər) *n. Australian Slang* One who is opposed to Sunday amusements, sports, etc.; a hypocritical censor of the lesser vices; a meddlesome puritan or sanctimonious reformer. [Origin unknown]

wrack[1] (rak) *n.* **1** Marine vegetation and floating material cast ashore by the sea, as seaweed or eelgrass; kelp. **2** The state of being wrecked; ruin; destruction: chiefly in the phrase **wrack and ruin.** **3** Shipwreck. **4** *Scot. & Brit. Dial.* Weeds. — *v.t.* & *v.i.* To wreck or be wrecked. ◆ Homophone: *rack.* [Fusion of OE *wræc* punishment, revenge and MDu. *wrak* a wreck]

wrack[2] (rak) *n.* A rack of clouds; any floating vapor. Compare RACK[3]. [Var. of RACK[3]]

wraith (rāth) *n.* **1** An apparition of a person thought to be alive, seen shortly before or shortly after his death. **2** Any specter, ghost, or apparition. [< dial. E (Scottish), alter. of *warth* < ON *vörthr* a guardian < *vartha* guard]

wrang (rang) *adj.* & *n. Scot.* Wrong.

Wran·gel (vrän′gil), **Ferdinand Petrovich von,** 1794?–1870, Russian explorer. Also **Wran′gell.**

Wran·gell (rang′gəl), **Mount** An active volcano (14,005 feet) in the western Wrangell Mountains, a range in SE Alaska; highest peak, 16,208 feet.

Wran·gell Island (rang′gəl) **1** An island of the Alexander Archipelago, SE Alaska; 30 miles long, 5 to 14 miles wide. **2** An island in the western Chukchi Sea off NE Siberia; part of Khabarovsk territory, Asiatic Russian S.F.S.R.; 75 miles long, 45 miles wide; 1,740 square miles. Also **Wran′gel Island.** *Russian* O·strov Vran·ge·ly (ô′strôf vrän′gi·lyə).

wran·gle (rang′gəl) *v.* **·gled, ·gling** *v.i.* **1** To argue or dispute noisily and angrily; brawl. — *v.t.* **2** To argue; debate. **3** To herd or round up, as livestock on a range. See synonyms under CONTEND. — *n.* An angry or noisy dispute; a quarrel. See synonyms under ALTERCATION, DISPUTE, QUARREL[1]. [Cf. LG *wrangeln* quarrel, freq. of *wrangen* struggle]

wran·gler (rang′glər) *n.* **1** One who wrangles. **2** At Cambridge University, England, one who has taken the highest mathematical honors. **3** A herdsman on a range.

wrap (rap) *v.* **wrapped** or **wrapt, wrap·ping** *v.t.* **1** To surround and cover by something folded or wound about; swathe; enwrap. **2** To cover with paper, etc., folded about and secured. **3** To wind or fold (a covering) about something. **4** To surround so as to obscure; blot out or conceal; envelop. **5** To fold, wind, or draw together. — *v.i.* **6** To be or become twined or coiled: with *about, around,* etc. — *n.* **1** An article of dress drawn or folded about a person; a wrapper. **2** *pl.* Outer garments collectively, as cloaks, scarfs, etc. **3** A blanket. [ME *wrappen;* origin uncertain]

wrap·a·round windshield (rap′ə·round) In automobiles, a windshield curving back into the sides of the body, thus providing a greater field of vision.

wrap·per (rap′ər) *n.* **1** A paper enclosing a newspaper, magazine, or similar packet for mailing or otherwise. **2** A detachable paper cover to protect the binding of a book. **3** A loose flowing outer garment; a dressing gown. **4** A tobacco leaf of high quality enclosing a cigar or plug of tobacco. **5** One who wraps articles.

wrap·ping (rap′ing) *n.* A covering; something in which an object is wrapped.

wrap·ras·cal (rap′ras′kəl) *n.* A long loose overcoat fashionable during the 18th century.

wrapt (rapt) Erroneous spelling of RAPT.

wrasse (ras) *n.* Any of a group of spiny-finned food fishes (family *Labridae*) of warm tropical seas, often highly colored; especially, the tautog. [<Cornish *wrach* < *gwrach,* orig., an old woman]

wrath (rath, räth; *Brit.* rôth) *n.* **1** Determined and lasting anger; extreme or violent rage; fury; vehement indignation. **2** An act done in violent rage. See synonyms under ANGER, VIOLENCE. — *v.t.* & *v.i. Obs.* To make or become angry. — *adj. Obs.* Wroth; angry. [OE *wræththu* < *wrath* wroth]

Wrath (rath, räth), **Cape** A promontory at the NW extremity of Scotland in NW Sutherland.

wrath·ful (rath′fəl, räth′-) *adj.* **1** Full of wrath; extremely angry. **2** Springing from or expressing wrath. — **wrath′ful·ly** *adv.* — **wrath′ful·ness** *n.*

wrath·y (rath′ē, räth′ē) *adj.* **wrath·i·er, wrath·i·est** **1** Disposed to wrath. **2** *Colloq.* Wroth. — **wrath′i·ly** *adv.* — **wrath′i·ness** *n.*

wreak (rēk) *v.t.* **1** To inflict or exact, as vengeance. **2** To satiate; give free expression to, as a feeling or passion. ◆ Homophone: *reek.* [OE *wrecan* drive, avenge]

wreath (rēth) *n.* **1** A twisted band, as of flowers, commonly circular, as for a crown or chaplet. **2** Any curled band of circular

or spiral shape, as of smoke or snow. [OE *writha* <*writhan* writhe] — **wreath′y** *n.*

Wreath (rēth) See CORONA AUSTRALIS.

wreathe (rēth) *v.* **wreathed, wreath·ing** *v.t.* **1** To form into a wreath, as by twisting or twining. **2** To adorn or encircle with or as with wreaths. **3** To envelop; cover: His face was *wreathed* in smiles. — *v.i.* **4** To take the form of a wreath. **5** To twist, turn, or coil, as masses of cloud. See synonyms under TWIST. [Earlier *wrethe,* back formation <ME *wrethen,* var. of *writhen,* pp. of *writhen* writhe; infl. by *wreath*]

wreck (rek) *v.t.* **1** To cause the destruction or wreck of, as a vessel; shipwreck. **2** To bring ruin, damage, or destruction upon. **3** To tear down, as a building; dismantle. — *v.i.* **4** To suffer wreck; be ruined. **5** To engage in wrecking, as for plunder or salvage. See synonyms under RUIN. [< *n.*] — *n.* **1** The act of wrecking, or the state of being wrecked; the ruin of anything, especially if effected violently. **2** That which has been wrecked or ruined, as a vessel or an army; hence, an emaciated person. **3** Wreckage; shipwreck. **4** *Law* Property cast upon land by the sea, either broken portions of a wrecked vessel or cargo from it. ◆ Homophone: *reck.* [<AF *wrec, wrech,* OF *warec* <ON (assumed) *wrek* < *wrekan* drive]

wreck·age (rek′ij) *n.* **1** The act of wrecking, or the state of being wrecked; wrecked material. **2** Broken or disordered remnants or fragments from a wreck.

wreck·er (rek′ər) *n.* **1** One who causes wreck, destruction, or frustration of any sort. **2** One employed in tearing down and removing old buildings. **3** A person, train, car, or machine that clears away wrecks. **4** One employed to recover disabled vessels or wrecked cargoes for the owners; also, a vessel employed in this service; a salvager. **5** One who lures ships to destruction by false lights on the shore in order to plunder the wreck. **6** One who ruins something valuable, as a bank or a railroad, especially for his own profit.

wreck·ful (rek′fəl) *adj. Poetic* Causing wreck; involving ruin.

wrecking company **1** A business organization that salvages wrecked ships. **2** A business organization that tears down and removes old buildings.

wren (ren) *n.* **1** Any of numerous small passerine birds (family *Troglodytidae*) having short rounded wings and a short tail, including the common **house wren** (*Troglodytes aëdon*), the **Carolina wren** (*Thryothorus ludovicianus*), **Bewick's wren** (*Thryomanes bewicki*) of North America, and the European wren (*Nannus troglodytes*). **2** Any one of numerous similar birds. [OE *wrenna*]

Wren (ren), **Sir Christopher,** 1632–1723, English architect. — **Percival Christopher,** 1885–1941, English novelist.

wrench (rench) *n.* **1** A violent twist; hence, a twist causing pain or injury; sprain. **2** Any strain or sudden and violent tension; sudden and violent emotion. **3** Any perversion or distortion of an original meaning. **4** A tool for twisting or turning bolts, nuts, pipe, etc.

TYPES OF WRENCHES

a. Engineer's wrench.   *e.* Pipe wrench.
b. Socket wrench.   *f.* Ratchet wrench.
c. Bicycle wrench.   *g.* Offset wrench.
d. Monkey wrench.   *h.* S-wrench.

— *v.t.* **1** To twist violently; turn suddenly by force; wrest. **2** To twist forcibly so as to cause strain or injury; sprain. **3** To twist from the proper meaning, intent, or use. — *v.i.* **4** To give a twist or wrench. [OE *wrenc* a trick. Akin to WRINKLE[1].]

Wrens (renz) *n. pl. Brit. Colloq.* Women's Royal Naval Service, an organization to relieve men of certain shore duties connected with the Royal Navy: so called from the initial letters *W,R,N,S,* plus *E.*

wrest (rest) *v.t.* **1** To pull or force away by violent twisting or wringing; wrench. **2** To turn from the true meaning, character, intent, or application; distort; pervert. **3** To seize forcibly by violence, extortion, or usurpation. — *n.* **1** An act of wresting; a violent twist. **2** A misapplication or perversion. **3** A crooked act; wile. **4** A key for tuning a stringed instrument, as a harp. ◆ Homophone: *rest.* [OE *wrǣstan*] — **wrest'er** *n.*

wres·tle (res'əl) *v.* **·tled, ·tling** *v.i.* **1** To engage in wrestling. **2** To struggle, as for mastery; contend. — *v.t.* **3** To engage in (a wrestling match), or wrestle with. **4** To throw (a calf) and hold it down for branding. — *n.* A wrestling match; a hard struggle. [OE *wrǣstlian,* freq. of *wrǣsten* wrest]

wres·tler (res'lər) *n.* One who wrestles; especially, a person who competes in wrestling matches.

wres·tling (res'ling) *n.* A sport or exercise in which each of two unarmed contestants endeavors to throw the other to the ground or force him into a certain fallen position.

wretch(rech) *n.* **1** A base, vile, or contemptible person; despicable character. **2** A miserable or unhappy person; also, sometimes, any person or creature viewed with pity. ◆ Homophone: *retch.* [OE *wrecca* an outcast < *wrecan* drive]

wretch·ed (rech'id) *adj.* **1** Sunk in dejection; profoundly unhappy. **2** Causing misery or grief. **3** Mean; paltry; worthless; unsatisfactory in ability or quality. **4** Despicable; contemptible. See synonyms under BAD[1], BASE[2], PITIFUL. — **wretch'ed·ly** *adv.* — **wretch'ed·ness** *n.*

wrig·gle (rig'əl) *v.* **·gled, ·gling** *v.i.* **1** To twist in a sinuous manner; squirm; writhe. **2** To proceed as by twisting or crawling. **3** To make one's way by evasive or indirect means. — *v.t.* **4** To cause to wriggle. — *n.* The motion of one who or that which wriggles; a squirm. [< MLG *wriggeln,* freq. of *wriggen* twist] — **wrig'gly** *adj.*

wrig·gler (rig'lər) *n.* **1** Someone or something that wriggles. **2** A mosquito larva.

wright (rīt) *n.* **1** One who does mechanical or constructive work. **2** An artificer or workman: used chiefly in compounds: *shipwright.* ◆ Homophones: *right, rite, write.* [OE *wyrhta*]

Wright (rīt), **Frank Lloyd,** 1867–1959, U.S. architect. — **Harold Bell,** 1872–1944, U.S. novelist. — **Joseph,** 1855–1930, English philologist and lexicographer. — **Orville,** 1871–1948, U.S. pioneer in aviation, with his brother **Wilbur,** 1867–1912. — **Richard,** 1908–1960, U.S. novelist. — **Willard Huntington,** 1888–1939, U.S. writer and art critic: pseudonym *S. S. Van Dine.*

wring (ring) *v.* **wrung** (*Rare* **wringed**), **wring·ing** *v.t.* **1** To squeeze or compress by twisting; turn and strain with force; pass (clothes) through a wringer. **2** To squeeze or press out, as water, by twisting. **3** To extort; acquire by extortion. **4** To distress; torment. **5** To twist or wrest violently out of shape or place: to *wring* his neck. **6** *Obs.* To pervert; distort. — *v.i.* **7** To writhe or squirm, as with anguish. **8** To perform the action of wringing. ◆ Homophone: *ring.* [OE *wringan*]

wring·bolt (ring'bōlt') A ring bolt. [Earlier *wrainbolt,* var. of *ring bolt*]

wring·er (ring'ər) *n.* **1** One who or that which wrings. **2** A contrivance used to press water out of fabrics after washing; also, the operator of such a machine.

wrin·kle[1] (ring'kəl) *n.* **1** A small ridge or prominence, as on a smooth surface; a crease; fold. **2** Specifically, a small fold or crease in the skin, usually produced by age or by excessive exposure to the elements. **3** A ripple; little wave. — *v.t. & v.i.* **·kled, ·kling** To contract or be contracted into wrinkles or

ridges; pucker. [OE *wrincle.* Akin to WRENCH.] — **wrin'kly** *adj.*

wrin·kle[2] (ring'kəl) *n. Colloq.* A curious or ingenious notion or device; happy thought; a novelty, as in dress. See synonyms under WHIM. [Prob. dim. of OE *wrenc* a trick]

wrist (rist) *n.* **1** The part of the arm immediately adjoining the hand; the carpus. ◆ Collateral adjective: *carpal.* **2** The part of a glove or garment that covers the wrist. **3** A wrist pin. [OE, prob. < *wrīthan* writhe]

wrist·band (rist'band', -bənd, riz'-) *n.* The band of a sleeve that covers the wrist or ends a shirt sleeve.

wrist–drop (rist'drop') *n. Pathol.* Paralysis of the forearm, usually due to lead poisoning.

wrist·let (rist'lit) *n.* **1** A flexible band worn on the wrist for ornament or warmth. **2** A bracelet. **3** *Slang* A handcuff.

wrist·lock (rist'lok') *n.* In wrestling, a hold whereby an opponent is made helpless by twisting his arm with a grip at the wrist.

wrist pin *Mech.* **1** A pin holding together the piston and connecting rod of a steam engine. **2** A similar pin in the cross-head of an internal-combustion engine.

wrist watch A watch set in a leather or metal wristlet and worn at the wrist.

writ[1] (rit) *n.* **1** *Law* A written order, under seal, issued by a court, and commanding the person to whom it is addressed to do or not to do some act. **2** That which is written: now chiefly in the phrase **Holy Writ,** meaning the Bible. [OE, a writing < *wrītan* write]

writ[2] (rit) Archaic or dialectal past tense and past participle of WRITE.

write (rīt) *v.* **wrote** (*Archaic* or *Dial.* **writ**), **written** (*Archaic* or *Dial.* **writ**), **writ·ing** *v.t.* **1** To trace or inscribe (letters, words, numbers, symbols, etc.) on a surface with pen or pencil, or by other means. **2** To describe in writing: to *write* one's impressions of a journey. **3** To communicate by letter: Be sure to *write* all the news; He *writes* that he will be home soon. **4** To communicate with by letter: He *writes* her every day. **5** To produce by writing; be the author or composer of. **6** To draw up; draft: to *write* one's will; to *write* a check. **7** To cover or fill with writing: to *write* two full pages. **8** To leave marks or evidence of: Anxiety is *written* on his face. **9** To spell or inscribe as specified: He *writes* his name with two *n's.* **10** To entitle or designate in writing: He *writes* himself "General." **11** To underwrite: to *write* an insurance policy. — *v.i.* **12** To trace or inscribe letters, etc., on a surface, as of paper. **13** To write a letter or letters; communicate in writing. **14** To be engaged in the occupation of a writer or author. **15** To produce a specified quality of writing. See synonyms under INSCRIBE. — **to write down** **1** To put into writing. **2** To injure or depreciate in writing. — **to write in** **1** To insert in writing, as in a document. **2** To cast (a vote) for one not listed on a ballot by inserting his name in writing. — **to write off** **1** To cancel or remove (claims, debts, etc.) from an open account. **2** To acknowledge the loss or failure of. — **to write out** **1** To put into writing. **2** To write in full or complete form. — **to write up** **1** To describe fully in writing; put in written form: to *write up* a report. **2** To praise fully or too fully in writing. **3** In accounting, to put an unusually high value upon. ◆ Homophones: *right, rite, wright.* [OE *wrītan*]
◆ *Writ,* the archaic or dialectal past participle of *write,* is now used chiefly in the phrase **writ large,** written or shown on a grand scale: *a name writ large in history.*

write–off (rīt'ôf', -of') *n.* **1** A cancellation. **2** An amount canceled or noted as a loss.

writ·er (rī'tər) *n.* **1** One who writes. **2** One who engages in literary composition. **3** That which writes or assists in writing: used in composition: *typewriter.*

writer's cramp *Pathol.* Spasmodic contraction of the muscles of the fingers and hand, caused by excessive writing. Also **writer's palsy** or **spasm.**

write–up (rīt'up') *n. Colloq.* A written description, record, or account, usually laudatory, as of a person, theatrical performance, etc.

writhe (rīth) *v.t. & v.i.* **writhed, writh·ing** To twist with violence; wrench; distort, as the body, face, or limbs in pain. — *n.* An act of writhing; a contortion. See synonyms under STRUGGLE. [OE *wrīthan*] — **writh'er** *n.*

writh·en (rīth'ən) Obsolete past participle of WRITHE. — *adj. Poetic* Twisted; distorted.

writ·ing (rī'ting) *n.* **1** The act of one who writes. **2** The characters so made; chirography; handwriting. **3** Anything written or expressed in letters, especially a literary production. **4** *Law* A written instrument: words, or characters that stand for words or ideas, traced on some substance, as paper, wood, or stone, with an implement, as a pen, pencil, or brush, or by some other device, as stamping, printing, or engraving. **5** The profession or occupation of a writer. **6** The practice, art, form, or style of literary composition.

writing machine A typewriter.

writ·ing–mas·ter (rī'ting·mas'tər, -mäs'-) *n.* A teacher of penmanship.

writing paper Paper prepared to receive ink in writing.

writ of error *Law* A commission by which the judges of one court are authorized to examine a record upon which a judgment was given in another court, and to affirm or reverse the judgment according to law.

writ of prohibition *Law* A writ issued by a superior court to an inferior court, commanding it to desist from proceeding in a matter not within its jurisdiction.

writ of right *Law* **1** Formerly, in England, a writ in an action for the purpose of establishing a title to real estate. **2** A similar common–law writ.

writ of summons *Law* The writ by which, in modern practice, a civil action is commenced; a written order to an authorized officer to notify a person to appear in court to answer a complaint.

writ·ten (rit'n) Past participle of WRITE.

Wro·claw (vrô'tswäf) A city in SW Poland, on the Oder; a German city from the 13th century; part of Prussia 1741–1945; a major industrial center: German *Breslau.*

wrong (rông, rong) *adj.* **1** Deviating from moral rectitude as prescribed by civil or divine law or by conscience; immoral. **2** Not just, proper, or equitable according to a standard, code, or convention; incongruous; improper. **3** Deviating from fact and truth; not according to reality; erroneous; mistaken: a *wrong* estimate. **4** Not in accordance with rule or appropriateness; improper; incorrect: to enter the *wrong* store. **5** Deviating from the proper design, intention, or requirement; unsuitable: the *wrong* side of cloth; the *wrong* letter in a word. **6** Unsatisfactory: a *wrong* reply. — **to go wrong** **1** To lapse from the strict path of rectitude. **2** To turn out badly; go astray. — **on the wrong side of** (30, 40, etc.) Older than (30, etc.). See synonyms under IMMORAL, SINFUL. — *adv.* In a wrong direction, place, or manner; awry or amiss; erroneously. — *n.* **1** That which is contrary to justice or rectitude; an injury; mischief. **2** Hence, some particular form of disobedience or non-conformity to lawful authority, human or divine. **3** *Law* An invasion or violation of one's legal rights; specifically, a crime; a tort. See synonyms under INJURY, INJUSTICE, SIN[1]. — *v.t.* **1** To violate the rights of; inflict injury or injustice upon. **2** To impute evil to unjustly; misrepresent: If you think so, you *wrong* him. **3** To seduce (a woman). **4** To treat dishonorably; malign. **5** *Scot.* To injure. See synonyms under ABUSE. [OE *wrang* twisted < ON *rangr* awry, unjust] — **wrong'ness** *n.*

wrong·do·er (rông'dōō'ər, rong'-) *n.* One who commits a fault or crime. — **wrong'do'ing** *n.*

wrong·er (rông'ər, rong'-) *n.* One who commits an offense, injury, or trespass.

wrong font *Printing* The wrong font or type face: indicated by the abbreviation *w.f.* in marking printers' proofs.

wrong·ful (rông'fəl, rong'-) *adj.* **1** Characterized by wrong or injustice; injurious; unjust. **2** Unlawful; illegal. — **wrong'ful·ly** *adv.* — **wrong'ful·ness** *n.*

wrong–head·ed (rông'hed'id, rong'-) *adj.* Having perverted judgment; perverse; obstinate.

—**wrong′–head′ed·ly** *adv.* —**wrong′–head′ed·ness** *n.*

wrong·ly (rông′lē, rong′-) *adv.* In a wrong manner; erroneously; falsely.

wrote (rōt) Past tense of WRITE.

wroth (rôth) *adj.* Filled with anger; angry. —*n. Obs.* Anger. [OE *wrǣth*]

wrought (rôt) Archaic past tense and past participle of WORK. —*adj.* **1** Beaten or hammered into shape by tools: *wrought* gold. **2** Worked; molded. **3** Made with delicacy; elaborated carefully. **4** Made; fashioned; formed: The cathedral was *wrought* by skilled hands. [ME *wrogt*, var. of *worht*, pp. of *wirchen* work]

wrought iron Commercially pure iron, prepared from pig iron and easily forged and welded into various shapes.

wrought up Excited.

wrung (rung) Past tense and past participle of WRING.

wry (rī) *adj.* **wri·er, wri·est 1** Bent to one side or out of position; contorted; askew; also, made by twisting or distorting the features: a *wry* smile. **2** Hence, deviating from that which is right or proper; perverted, as a course or an interpretation; warped. —*v.t.* **wried, wry·ing** To twist; contort. ◆ Homophone: *rye.* [ME *wrye* < OE *wrigian* move, tend] —**wry′ly** *adv.* —**wry′ness** *n.*

Wry may appear as a combining form in hyphemes, with the meaning of adjective definition 1:

> wry–eyed wry–looking wry–set
> wry–faced wry–mouthed wry–toothed

wry·neck (rī′nek′) *n.* **1** A bird (genus *Jynx*) resembling and allied to the woodpeckers, with the habit of twisting its head and neck. **2** A rheumatic affection in the muscles of the neck; torticollis. **3** One having a twisted neck; a person afflicted with torticollis.

Wu (wōō) The chief river of Kweichow province, south central China, comprising the upper course of the Kien and flowing over 5000 miles NE, north, and NW into the Kien proper in SE Szechwan province.

Wu (wōō), **C. C.,** 1886–1934, Chinese statesman and diplomat: full name *Wu Ch'ao-ch'u.*

Wu·chang (wōō′chäng′) A formerly independent city and former capital of Hupeh province, China, on the Yangtze river, now part of Wuhan.

Wuch·er·er·i·a (vukh′ə·rer′ē·ə) *n.* A genus of parasitic nematode worms, especially *W. bancrofti,* the causative agent of elephantiasis. [after Otto *Wucherer,* 1820–73, German physician]

wud (wud) *adj. Scot.* Mad; insane.

Wu·han (wōō′hän′) A city comprising the three formerly independent cities of Hankow, Hanyang, and Wuchang on the Yangtze river, capital of Hupeh province, east central China: also *Han Cities.*

Wu·hu (wōō′hōō′) A port on the Yangtze river in central Anhwei province, central eastern China.

wul·fen·ite (wōōl′fən·īt) *n.* A resinous or hard, yellow, brown, or red molybdate of lead, $PbMoO_4$, usually occurring in tabular crystals. [after F. X. von *Wulfen,* 1728–1805, Austrian mineralogist]

Wul·fi·la (wōōl′fə·lə) See ULFILAS.

wun (wun) *Scot.* Won. —*v.t. & v.i.* To win. —*n.* Wind.

Wundt (vōōnt), **Wilhelm Max,** 1832–1920, German psychologist and physiologist. —**Wundt′i·an** *adj.*

wun·na (wun′nə) *Scot.* Will not.

Wup·per·tal (vōōp′ər·täl) A city in SW central North Rhine–Westphalia, west central West Germany, formed by the union of the cities of Barmen and Elberfeld.

Würm (vürm) See GLACIAL EPOCH.

Würm·see (vürm′zā) See STARNBERGERSEE.

Würt·tem·berg (wûr′təm·bûrg, *Ger.* vür′təm·berkh) A former state of SW Germany; 7,532 square miles; capital, Stuttgart; divided after 1945 into Württemberg–Baden and Württemberg–Hohenzollern, which merged in 1951, along with Baden, to form the state of Baden–Württemberg.

Würt·tem·berg–Ba·den (wûr′təm·bûrg·bäd′. *Ger.* vür′təm·berkh·bä′den) A former state of SW Germany in the Federal Republic (1949) formed in 1945 by the union of northern Württemberg and northern Baden; 6,062 square miles; capital, Stuttgart; in 1951 the states Baden, Württemberg–Baden and Württemberg–Hohenzollern merged to form the state of Baden–Württemberg; 13,800 square miles; capital, Stuttgart.

Würt·tem·berg–Ho·hen·zol·lern (wûr′təm·bûrg·hō′ən·zol′ərn, *Ger.* vür′təm·berkh·hō′ən·tsôl′ərn) A state of SW Germany in the Federal Republic (1949); formed in 1945 by the union of southern Württemberg and the former Prussian province of Hohenzollern; 4,018 square miles; capital, Tübingen; merged into the state of Baden–Württemberg in 1951.

Würz·burg (wûrts′bûrg, *Ger.* vürts′bŏŏrkh) A city in Lower Franconia, NW Bavaria, SW central West Germany.

Wu·sih (wōō′shē′) A city of southern Kiangsu province, central eastern China.

Wu T'ing–fang (wōō′ ting′fäng′), 1841–1922, Chinese reformer and diplomat; father of C. C. Wu.

Wu·wei (wōō′wā′) A city in central Kansu province, north central China.

Wy·an·dot (wī′ən·dot) *n.* One of a tribe of North American Indians of Iroquoian stock, formerly very powerful in the Ohio valley and lake regions: descendants of a group of fugitive Hurons who called themselves *Wendat:* presently settled in Oklahoma. Also **Wy′an·dotte.**

Wy·an·dotte (wī′ən·dot) *n.* One of an American breed of domestic fowls. [after the *Wyandot* Indians]

Wy·att (wī′ət), **Sir Thomas,** 1503–42, English poet and diplomat.

wych (wich) See WITCH[2].

wych–elm (wich′elm′) *n.* **1** A wide–spreading elm (*Ulmus glabra*), with large, dull–green leaves, common in England, Ireland, and Scotland: also called *Scotch elm.* **2** Witch hazel. Also *witch.* [< *wych,* var. of WITCH[2] +ELM]

Wych·er·ley (wich′ər·lē), **William,** 1640?–1716, English dramatist and poet.

wych–ha·zel (wich′hā′zəl) *n.* **1** Witch hazel. **2** Wych–elm. [Var. of WITCH HAZEL]

Wyc·lif (wik′lif), **John,** 1324?–84, English reformer; first translator, with assistants, of the entire Bible into English. Also spelled *Wiclif, Wickliffe, Wycliffe.* —**Wyc′lif·ite** *adj. & n.*

wye (wī) *n.* The letter Y, or something Y–shaped.

Wye (wī) A river of SE Wales and SW England, flowing 130 miles SE from SW Montgomery to the Severn estuary.

Wyld (wild), **Henry Cecil Kennedy,** 1870–1945, English philologist and lexicographer.

wyle (wil) *v.t. Scot.* or *Obs.* To beguile; wile.

Wy·lie (wī′lē), **Elinor Morton,** 1885–1928, *née* Hoyt, U.S. poet and novelist: married name *Mrs. William Rose Benét.* —**Philip Gordon,** 1902–1971, U.S. author.

wy·lie–coat (wī′lē·kōt′, wil′ē-, wul′ē-) *n. Scot.* A boy's flannel underdress; also, a flannel petticoat.

Wy·o·ming (wī·ō′ming) A State in the NW United States; 97,914 square miles; capital, Cheyenne; entered the Union July 10, 1890; nickname, *Equality State:* abbr. WY —**Wy·o′ming·ite** *n.*

Wyoming Valley A valley along the north branch of the Susquehanna River in NE Pennsylvania; scene of a massacre of settlers by Indians and Tories, 1778; chief city, Wilkes-Barre.

Wythe (with), **George,** 1726–1806, American jurist; signer of the Declaration of Independence.

wy·vern (wī′vərn) See WIVERN.

X

x, X (eks) *n. pl.* **x's** or **X's, xs** or **Xs, ex·es** (ek′siz) **1** The 24th letter of the English alphabet: from the ancient western Greek alphabets of Chalcis, Boeotia, and Elis, and Roman *X.* **2** The sound of the letter *x:* in English variously sounded as (ks), as in *axle, box, next;* (gz), as in *executive, exert;* (ksh), as in *noxious;* (gzh), as in *luxurious;* and initially, always (z) as in *xenophobe, xylophone, Xanthippe.* See ALPHABET.—symbol **1** The Roman numeral ten. See under NUMERAL. **2** *Math.* The principal unknown quantity; hence, anything unknown. **3** A mark shaped like an X, representing the signature of one who cannot write. **4** A mark used in diagrams, maps, etc., to place some event or substance, or to point out something to be emphasized. **5** A symbol used to indicate a kiss. **6** Anything shaped like an X. —**X marks the spot** *Colloq.* "Here": used in diagrams, maps, or the like, to indicate a specific locality.

xan·thate (zan′thāt) *n. Chem.* A salt or ester of xanthic acid. [<XANTH(IC) + -ATE³]

xan·the·in (zan′thē·in) *n. Biochem.* A water-soluble yellow coloring matter found in the cell sap of some plants. [< F *xanthéine* <Gk. *xanthos* yellow]

xan·the·las·ma (zan′thə·laz′mə) *n. Pathol.* A form of xanthoma marked by the appearance of small yellowish disks on the eyelids. [< NL < Gk. *xanthos* yellow + *elasmos* a metal plate]

Xan·thi·an (zan′thē·ən) *adj.* Relating to Xanthus.

xan·thic (zan′thik) *adj.* **1** Having a yellow or yellowish color. **2** *Chem.* Of or pertaining to xanthin or xanthine. [< F *xanthique* <Gk. *xanthos* yellow]

xanthic acid *Chem.* Any of a group of unstable, colorless, liquid thio compounds made by decomposing a xanthate with a dilute acid.

xan·thin (zan′thin) *n. Biochem.* An insoluble yellow pigment found in yellow flowers. [<G <Gk. *xanthos* yellow]

xan·thine (zan′thēn, -thin) *n. Biochem.* A white, crystalline, nitrogenous compound, $C_5H_4N_4O_2$, contained in blood, urine, and other animal secretions, and in some plants. It leaves a yellow residue when evaporated with nitric acid. [< F <Gk. *xanthos* yellow]

Xan·thip·pe (zan·tip′ē) The wife of Socrates; renowned as a shrew. Also **Xan·tip′pe.**

xantho– *combining form* Yellow: *xanthophyll.* Also, before vowels, **xanth–.** [<Gk. *xanthos* yellow]

xan·tho·car·pous (zan′thō·kär′pəs) *adj. Bot.* Yellow–fruited.

xan·tho·chroid (zan′thə·kroid) *Anthropol. adj.* Characterized by a light–colored or fair complexion. —*n.* One who exhibits xanthochroid characteristics. [<XANTHO- + Gk. *chroa* color + -OID]

xan·tho·ma (zan·thō′mə) *n. Pathol.* A skin disease marked by the presence of small yellowish disks formed by the deposit of lipoids. [<XANTH- + -OMA]

xan·tho·phyll (zan′thə·fil) *n. Biochem.* A yellow pigment, $C_{40}H_{56}O_2$, contained in plants and related to carotene. Also **xan′tho·phyl.** [< F *xanthophylle* <Gk. *xanthos* yellow + *phyllon* a leaf]

xan·thop·si·a (zan·thop′sē·ə) *n. Pathol.* A disorder of vision in which all objects appear yellow. [<NL <Gk. *xanthos* yellow + *opsis* a sight]

xan·thous (zan′thəs) *adj.* **1** Yellow. **2** *Anthropol.* **a** Of or pertaining to the yellow–skinned or Mongoloid type of mankind. **b** Of or relating to that variety of mankind that has yellowish, brown, or auburn hair, including the Teutons and Scandinavians; blond. Opposed to *melanous*. [< XANTH(O)- + -OUS]

Xan·thus (zan′thəs) An ancient, ruined city of Lycia, SW Turkey in Asia, near the Mediterranean.

Xa·vi·er (zā′vē·ər, zav′ē-; *Sp.* hä·vyer′), **Saint Francis**, 1506–52, Spanish Jesuit missionary in the Orient; founder, with Ignatius Loyola, of the Society of Jesus: called "the Apostle of the Indies." —**Xa·ve·ri·an** (zā·vir′ē·ən) *adj. & n.*

X-chro·mo·some (eks′krō′mə·sōm) *n.* A sex chromosome.

Xe *Chem.* Xenon (symbol Xe).

xe·bec (zē′bek) *n.* A small, three-masted Mediterranean vessel, with both square and lateen sails: formerly used by Algerine pirates: also spelled *zebec*. [Earlier *chebec* < F < Sp. *jabeque, xabeque* < Arabic *shabbāk*]

xe·ni·a (zē′nē·ə) *n. Bot.* The influence of the pollen of one species upon the maternal tissues of another species after hybrid fertilization: a phenomenon observed particularly in maize, which often shows blue kernels in a yellow-seeded variety pollinated by a blue-seeded one. [< NL < Gk. *xenia* hospitality < *xenos* a guest]

xe·ni·al (zē′nē·əl) *adj.* Of or pertaining to hospitality. [< Gk. *xenia*. See XENIA.]

xeno- *combining form* Strange; foreign; different: *xenophobia*. Also, before vowels, **xen-**. [< Gk. *xenos* a stranger]

Xe·noc·ra·tes (zi·nok′rə·tēz), 396?–314 B.C., Greek philosopher.

xe·nog·a·my (zi·nog′ə·mē) *n. Biol.* Cross-fertilization. —**xe·nog′a·mous** *adj.*

xen·o·gen·e·sis (zen′ə·jen′ə·sis) *n. Biol.* **1** Abiogenesis. **2** Metagenesis. **3** The fancied production of an organism unlike either of its parents. Also **xe·nog·e·ny** (zi·noj′ə·nē). —**xen′o·ge·net′ic** (-jə·net′ik), **zen′o·gen′ic** *adj.*

xe·no·gloss·i·a (zē′nə·glô′sē·ə, -glos′ē·ə) *n.* In psychic research, the alleged power of a person to communicate with others in a language which he has never learned. [< NL < Gk. *xenos* strange + *glōssa* a tongue]

xen·o·lith (zen′ə·lith) *n. Geol.* A rock fragment enclosed in a larger mass of igneous rock.

xen·o·mor·phic (zen′ə·môr′fik) *adj. Mineral.* Not having its own characteristic form, but having an irregular shape that is imposed by the interference of surrounding minerals: said of the constituents of a crystalline rock.

xe·non (zē′non) *n.* A colorless, odorless, almost inert gaseous element (symbol Xe, atomic number 54) occurring in small traces in the atmosphere. See PERIODIC TABLE. [< Gk., neut. of *xenos* strange]

Xe·noph·a·nes (zi·nof′ə·nēz) Sixth century B.C. Greek philosopher and poet.

xen·o·phobe (zen′ə·fōb) *n.* A person who hates or distrusts strangers or foreigners.

xen·o·pho·bi·a (zen′ə·fō′bē·ə) *n.* Dislike of strangers or foreigners.

Xen·o·phon (zen′ə·fən), 435?–355? B.C., Greek historian and soldier.

Xe·res (hā′rās, *older* shā′rās, sher′es) The former name for JEREZ.

Xé·rez (hā′rās, -rāth), **Francisco de**, 1504–1547?, Spanish historian of the conquest of Peru.

xer·ic (zer′ik, zir′ik) *adj.* Of, pertaining to, or characterized by extreme dryness; arid.

xero- *combining form* Dry; dryness: *xerophyte*. Also, before vowels, **xer-**. [< Gk. *xēros* dry]

xe·ro·chore (zir′ə·kôr, -kōr) *n. Ecol.* A region of extreme dryness; the desert areas of the earth, collectively. —**xe′ro·chor′ic** (-kôr′ik, -kor′ik) *adj.*

xe·ro·der·ma (zir′ō·dûr′mə) *n. Pathol.* Roughness and dryness of the skin, with scaly desquamation. [< NL < Gk. *xēros* dry + *derma* skin] —**xe′ro·der·mat′ic** (-dər·mat′ik), **xe′ro·der′ma·tous** (-dûr′mə·təs) *adj.*

Xe·ro·form (zir′ō·fôrm) *n.* Proprietary name for a yellow powder containing bismuth and tribromphenol in equal quantities: used as an intestinal and surgical antiseptic.

xe·rog·ra·phy (zi·rog′rə·fē) *n.* A method of printing by electrostatic attraction in which a negatively charged ink powder is sprayed upon the positively charged copy area of a

metal plate, whence it is transferred to the positively charged printing surface. —**xe·ro·graph·ic** (zir′ō·graf′ik) *adj.* —**xe·rog′raph·er** *n.*

xe·ro·mor·phy (zir′ō·môr′fē) *n. Bot.* The form or structure of the plant by which it is protected from desiccation. [< XERO- + Gk. *morphē* form] —**xe′ro·mor′phic** *adj.*

xe·roph·i·lous (zi·rof′ə·ləs) *adj. Bot.* Growing in or adapted to drought: said of plants living in dry, hot climates, as the cactus.

xe·roph·thal·mi·a (zir′əf·thal′mē·ə) *n. Pathol.* Inflammation with thickening of the lining membrane of the eye, but without liquid discharge: associated with conjunctivitis and a lack of vitamin A. [< NL < Gk. *xēros* dry + *ophthalmos* an eye]

xe·ro·phyte (zir′ə·fīt) *n. Bot.* A plant adapted to dry conditions of air and soil. —**xe′ro·phyt′ic** (-fit′ik) *adj.*

xe·ro·print·ing (zir′ō·prin′ting) *n.* A simplified variation of xerography which uses a suitably prepared plate on a rotating cylinder.

xe·ro·sere (zir′ə·sir) *n. Ecol.* The series of changes in the succession of the plant formation found upon dry soil. [< XERO- + SERE²]

xe·ro·sis (zi·rō′sis) *n. Pathol.* A condition of abnormal dryness of a part; specifically, a dry, thickened, and scaly condition of the skin or mucous membrane of a part. [< NL < Gk. *xēros* dry] —**xe·rot′ic** (-rot′ik) *adj.*

xe·ro·tro·pism (zir′ō·trō′piz·əm) *n. Bot.* The tendency of plants, or plant parts, to alter their position so as to protect themselves from desiccation. —**xe′ro·trop′ic** *adj.*

Xer·ox (zir′oks) *n.* A xerographic process for producing copies of printed or pictorial matter: a trade name. —*v.t.* To make or reproduce by Xerox. Also **xer′ox**.

Xerx·es (zûrk′sēz), 519?–465? B.C., Persian king 486?–465; invaded Greece, but was defeated at Salamis 480 B.C.

Xho·sa (kō′sä) *n.* The Bantu language of the Kaffirs, closely related to Zulu: also called *Kaffir.* also spelled *Xosa*.

xi (zī, sī; *Gk.* ksē) *n.* The fourteenth letter in the Greek alphabet (Ξ, ξ): equivalent to English *x* or *z*. [< Gk.]

Xin·gú (shing·gōō′) A river in northern and central Brazil, flowing 1,230 miles north from central Mato Grosso to the Amazon at the head of its delta.

-xion Var. of -TION.

xiphi- *combining form* A sword; of or pertaining to a sword: *xiphisternum*. Also, before vowels, **xiph-**. [< Gk. *xiphos* a sword]

xiph·i·ster·num (zif′ə·stûr′nəm) *n. pl.* **-na** (-nə) *Anat.* The lower segment or ensiform process of the sternum. Also *xiphoid*. [< NL < Gk. *xiphos* a sword + *sternon* the breastbone]

xiph·oid (zif′oid) *adj.* Shaped like a sword: the *xiphoid* cartilage at the lower end of the breastbone. —*n.* The xiphisternum.

xiph·o·su·ran (zif′ə·sŏŏr′ən) *n.* Any of an order (*Xiphosura*) of primitive arachnids having a horseshoe-shaped carapace and a long swordlike tail; a king crab. —*adj.* Of or pertaining to the *Xiphosura*. [< NL < Gk. *xiphos* a sword + *oura* a tail]

Xmas Christmas: popular abbreviation. [< *X*, abbr. for *Christ* < Gk. *X*, chi, the first letter of *Christos* Christ + -MAS]

Xo·chi·mil·co (sō′chi·mēl′kō) A resort city south of Mexico City in Federal District, central Mexico; famous for its "floating gardens."

Xo·sa (kō′sä) See XHOSA.

XP Chi and rho: The first two letters of ΧΡΙΣΤΟΣ, the Greek word for Christ: introduced by Constantine the Great as an emblem of Christ.

X-ray (eks′rā′) *v.t.* To examine, diagnose, or treat with X-rays. —*n.* A picture made with X-rays; roentgenogram: also **X-ray photograph**.

X-rays (eks′rāz′) *n. pl.* Electromagnetic radiations of extremely short wavelength, emitted from a substance when it is bombarded by a stream of electrons moving at a sufficiently high velocity, as in a Coolidge tube. Their great penetrating power, ionizing effect, and property of acting on photographic plates have many useful applications, especially in the detection, diagnosis,

and treatment of certain organic disorders, chiefly internal. Also called *Roentgen rays*. [Trans. of G *X-strahlen*, name coined by Roentgen, their discoverer, because their nature was unknown]

X-ray therapy Medical treatment by the use of X-rays.

Xu·thus (zōō′thəs) In Greek legend, son of Hellen and ancestor of the Ionians.

xy·lan (zī′lan) *n. Biochem.* A yellow, gummy hemicellulose found in straw, oat hulls, peanut shells, and other plant wastes: it yields xylose on hydrolysis. [< Gk. *xylon* wood]

xy·lem (zī′ləm) *n.* The chief fluid-transporting and supportive tissue in vascular plants, made up of various arrangements of tracheids, parenchyma, fibers, and associated cells. [< G < Gk. *xylon* wood]

xy·lene (zī′lēn) *n. Chem.* Any one of three isomeric colorless hydrocarbons, $C_6H_4(CH_3)_2$, contained in coal tar and wood tar. A mixture of the three yields a colorless, inflammable liquid used as a solvent and in medicine as an antiseptic. Also **xy′lol** (-lōl, -lol). [< Gk. *xylon* wood + -ENE]

xy·lic (zī′lik) *adj.* Of, pertaining to, or derived from xylene. [< XYL(ENE) + -IC]

xylic acid *Chem.* One of six isomeric crystalline carboxyl derivatives of xylene, C_8H_9COOH.

xy·li·dine (zī′li·dēn, -din, zil′ə-) *n. Chem.* Any of six isomeric amino derivatives of xylene, $C_8H_{11}N$: they are homologs of aniline, and are used in the synthesis of certain dyes. Also **xy′li·din** (-din). [< XYL(ENE) + -ID(E) + -INE²]

xylo- *combining form* Wood; of or pertaining to wood; woody: *xylocarpous*. Also, before vowels, **xyl-**. [< Gk. *xylon* wood]

xy·lo·car·pous (zī′lō·kär′pəs) *adj. Bot.* Having a hard, woody fruit.

xy·lo·graph (zī′lə·graf, -gräf) *n.* **1** An engraving on wood, or a print from such engraving. **2** An impression obtained from the grain of wood, as used for surface decoration. —**xy′lo·graph′ic** or **-i·cal** *adj.* —**xy·log·ra·pher** (zī·log′rə·fər) *n.*

xy·log·ra·phy (zī·log′rə·fē) *n.* **1** Wood engraving, especially of the 15th century. **2** Printing with wood engravings. **3** Painting or printing on wood for decorative purposes. **4** The making of prints or impressions showing the grain of wood.

xy·loid (zī′loid) *adj.* Of, pertaining to, or resembling wood.

xy·loph·a·gous (zī·lof′ə·gəs) *adj.* Feeding on or boring in wood, as insect larvae. [< XYLO- + -PHAGOUS] —**xy·lo·phage** (zī′lə·fāj) *n.*

xy·lo·phone (zī′lə·fōn) *n.* A musical instrument consisting of a row of parallel wooden bars graduated in length to form a musical scale and struck by small mallets or sounded by rubbing. [< XYLO- + -PHONE] —**xy·loph·o·nist** (zī·lof′ə·nist) *n.*

XYLOPHONE

xy·lose (zī′lōs) *n. Chem.* A pentose, $C_5H_{10}O_5$, obtained by treating xylan with sulfuric acid; wood sugar: the levorotatory form is used in the synthesis of vitamin C. [< XYL(AN) + -OSE²]

xy·lot·o·mous (zī·lot′ə·məs) *adj.* Adapted to cutting or boring wood, as an insect. [< XYLO- + Gk. *tomē* a cutting < *temnein* cut]

xy·lot·o·my (zī·lot′ə·mē) *n.* The preparation of wood for examination by microscope, as for scientific purposes. [< XYLO- + -TOMY] —**xy·lot′o·mist** *n.*

xy·lyl (zī′lil) *n. Chem.* The univalent radical, $(CH_3)_2C_6H_3$, derived from xylene. [< XYL(ENE) + -YL]

xy·ly·lene (zī′lə·lēn) *n. Chem.* The bivalent radical, C_8H_8, contained in xylene. [< XYLYL + -ENE]

xyst (zist) *n.* **1** In classical antiquity, a hall or covered portico used by athletes for their exercises: chiefly for use in stormy weather.

2 A garden walk or terrace. [< L *xystus* < Gk. *xystos,* orig. scraped, polished < *xyein* scrape, polish]

xys·ter (zis'tər) *n.* A surgical instrument for scraping bones. [< NL < Gk. *xystēr* a scraper, < *xyein* scrape]

Y

y, Y (wī) *n. pl.* **y's, Y's,** or **ys, Ys** or **wyes** (wīz) **1** The 25th letter of the English alphabet: ultimately from Phoenician *vau,* Greek *upsilon.* The Romans took it from the Greek alphabet sometime in the first century B.C. and used it as a vowel. **2** The sound of the letter *y.* Initial *y* (introducing either a vowel or a syllable) is a voiced palatal semivowel, as in *yet, you, yonder, beyond.* Final *y* is either a vowel, pronounced (ē), as in *honey, pretty, steady;* a diphthong, pronounced (ī), as in *fly, my;* or the final glide of a diphthong, as in *gray, obey, annoy.* Internal *y* is pronounced as a vowel (i), as in *lyric, myth, syllable;* a diphthong (ī), as in *lyre, type, psychic;* an *r*-colored central vowel (ûr) or (ər), as in *myrtle, martyr.* See ALPHABET.

Y (wī) *n.* **1** Something similar to a Y in shape. **2** A branch pipe, forked pipe, or coupling in the shape of the letter Y. **3** A forked piece, often with the branches curved, usually one of a pair, serving as a rest or support, as for some part of a sighting instrument.
—*symbol Chem.* Yttrium (symbol Y).

y- *prefix* Used in Middle English as a sign of the past participle, as an intensive, or without perceptible force: *yclad, yclept.* It survives (as *a*-) in such words as *alike, aware,* etc. Also spelled *i-,* as in *iwis.* [OE *ge*-]

-y¹ *suffix of adjectives* Being, possessing, or resembling what is expressed in the main element: *stony, rainy.* Also *-ey,* when added to words ending in *y,* as in *clayey, skyey.* [OE *-ig*]

-y² *suffix* The quality or state of being: *victory:* often used in abstract nouns formed from adjectives in *-ous* and *-ic.* [< F *-ie* < L *-ia;* also < Gk. *-ia, -eia*]

-y³ *suffix* Little; small: *kitty:* often used in nicknames or to express endearment, as in *Tommy.* [Prob. < dial. E (Scottish) < OF *-i, -e,* dim. suffixes]

Ya·an (yä'än') A city in west central Szechwan province, western China.

yab·ber (yab'ər) *n. Austral. Colloq.* Speech; talk; jabber. [< Australian *yabba* < *ya* speak]

Ya·blo·noi Range (yi·blə·noi') Part of the watershed between the Arctic and Pacific drainage areas, in SE Asiatic Russian S.F.S.R.; highest peak, 5,280 feet. Also **Ya·blo·no·vy** (yi'·blə·nô'vē).

yacht (yot) *n.* A relatively small vessel specially built or fitted for private pleasure excursions, as distinguished from war or commerce. —*v.i.* To cruise, race, or sail in a yacht. [< Du. *jaghte,* short for *jaghtschip* a pursuit ship < *jaght* hunting (< *jagen* hunt) + *schip* a ship]

yacht club A club of yachtsmen.

yacht·ing (yot'ing) *n.* The act, practice, or pastime of sailing in or managing a yacht.

yachts·man (yots'mən) *n. pl.* **·men** (-mən) One who owns or sails a yacht; a devotee of yachting. Also **yacht'er, yacht'man.** —**yachts'wom·an** (-wŏŏm'ən) *n. fem.*

yachts·man·ship (yots'mən·ship) *n.* The art of managing a yacht; skill in yachting. Also **yacht'man·ship.**

yack·er (yak'ər) *n. Austral. Slang* Work, especially hard work: also spelled *yakker.*

Yad·kin River (yad'kin) The upper course of the Pee Dee River, flowing 204 miles NE and SE from NW to south central North Carolina.

yaff (yaf) *v.i. Brit. Dial.* To bark like a dog when excited; hence, to speak sharply; scold.

yaf·fle (yaf'əl) *n.* The green woodpecker. [Imit. of its cry]

yag·ger (yag'ər) *n. Scot.* An itinerant peddler; wanderer; ranger.

ya·gua·run·di (yä'gwə·run'dē) See JAGUA-RONDI.

yah¹ (yä, ya) *interj.* An exclamation of disgust; bah.

yah² (yä, yâ) *interj. Colloq.* Yes. [Alter. of YES; infl. in form by G *ja* yes]

Ya·ha·ta (yä·hä·tä) See YAWATA.

ya·hoo (yä'hŏŏ, yä'-, yä·hŏŏ') *n.* **1** Any person of low or vicious instincts. **2** An awkward fellow; a bumpkin. [< YAHOO]

Ya·hoo (yä'hŏŏ, yä'-, yä·hŏŏ') *n.* One of an imaginary race of brutes possessing human form and vices, described by Swift in *Gulliver's Travels.* See HOUYHNHNM.

Yah·weh (yä'we) In the Old Testament, the national god of Israel; God: a modern transliteration of the Tetragrammaton. See JEHOVAH. Also spelled *Jahveh, Jahwe.* Also **Yah·veh** (yä've). [< Hebrew *YHWH*]

Yah·wism (yä'wiz·əm) *n.* **1** The ancient Hebrew religion centered on the monotheistic worship of Yahweh. **2** The use of the name Yahweh for God. Also spelled *Jahvism, Jahwism.* Also **Yah'vism** (-viz·əm).

Yah·wist (yä'wist) *n.* In Biblical criticism, the writer supposed to have written those parts of the Hexateuch in which God is mentioned as Yahweh (erroneously Jehovah). Compare ELOHIST. Also spelled *Jahvist, Jahwist.* Also **Yah'vist** (-vist).

Yah·wis·tic (yä·wis'tik) *adj.* **1** Of or relating to Yahwist or Yadwism. **2** Characterized by the use of the name Yahweh (or Jehovah) for God. Compare ELOHISTIC. Also spelled *Jahvistic, Jahwistic.* Also **Yah·vis'tic** (-vis'-).

yaird (yârd) *n. Scot.* **1** A yard (36 inches). **2** A garden; courtyard; churchyard.

yak (yak) *n.* A large bovine ruminant (*Bos grunniens*) of the higher regions of central Asia: it has long hair fringing the shoulders, sides, and tail, and is often domesticated. [< Tibetan *gyag*]

Yak·i·ma (yak'ə·mə) A city on the Yakima River in southern Washington.

YAK
(From 5 to 5 1/2 feet high at the shoulder)

Yakima River A river in central and southern Washington, flowing 203 miles SE from the Cascade Range to the Columbia River.

yak·ker (yak'kər) *n.* Yacker.

Ya·ko (yä'kŏŏ) See JACO.

Ya·kof (yä·kôf') Russian form of JAMES.

Ya·kut (yä·kŏŏt') *n.* **1** One of a people living in the Yakut Autonomous S.S.R. **2** The Turkic language of these people.

Ya·kut Autonomous Soviet Socialist Republic (yä·kŏŏt') An administrative division of NE Asiatic Russian S.F.S.R.; 1,181,971 square miles; capital, Yakutsk.

Ya·kutsk (yä·kŏŏtsk') A city on the Lena river; capital of Yakut Autonomous S.S.R.

yald¹ (yäd, yôd) See YELD.

yald² (yäd, yôd) *adj. Scot.* Athletic; supple; active: also spelled *yauld.*

Yale (yāl), **Elihu,** 1649–1721, English merchant; benefactor of Yale College (now Yale University); born in America. —**Linus,** 1821–68, U.S. locksmith.

Yal·ta (yäl'tə, yôl'-) A port on the Black Sea in the southern Crimea, U.S.S.R.; scene of a conference of Roosevelt, Churchill, and Stalin in February, 1945.

Ya·lu (yä'lŏŏ') A river forming part of the boundary between Manchuria, NE China, and Korea, and flowing 500 miles SW to the Yellow Sea: Japanese *Oryokko.*

Ya·lung (yä'lŏŏng') A river in Szechwan province, China, flowing 800 miles south from SE Tsinghai province to the Yangtze, on the border of Yünnan province.

yam (yam) *n.* **1** The fleshy, edible, tuberous root of any of a genus (*Dioscorea*) of climbing tropical plants. **2** Any of the plants growing this root. **3** A large variety of the sweet potato. **4** *Scot.* A potato. [< Pg. *inhame* < Senegal *nyami* eat]

Ya·ma·ga·ta (yä·mä·gä·tä), **Prince Aritomo,** 1838–1922, Japanese general.

Ya·mal Peninsula (ye·mäl') A peninsula of Asiatic Russian S.F.S.R. between the Kara Sea and Ob Gulf, about 400 miles long, up to 140 miles wide.

Ya·ma·mo·to (yä·mä·mō·tō), **Isoroku,** 1884–1943, Japanese admiral.

Ya·ma·shi·ta (yä·mä·shē·tä), **Tomoyuki,** 1885–1946, Japanese general; captured Singapore (February) and Philippines (May) 1942; executed as war criminal; called "the Tiger of Malaya."

Yam·bol (yäm'bôl) A city of east central Bulgaria: also *Jambol.* Turkish **Yam·bo·li** (yäm'bô·lē').

yam·mer (yam'ər) *v.i. Colloq.* **1** To complain peevishly; whine, whimper. **2** To howl; roar; shout. —*v.t.* **3** To utter peevishly; complain. [OE *gēomrian* lament < *gēomor* sorrowful; infl. in form by MDu. *jammeren* complain]

ya·men (yä'mən) *n. Chinese* The office or official residence of a public functionary, as a mandarin; also, any department of the public service: the *yamen* of public justice. Also **ya'mun.**

Ya·nam (yə·num') A city and former French settlement in NE Andhra Pradesh State, SE India. *French* **Ya·na·on** (yä·nä·ôn').

yang (yang) *n.* In Chinese philosophy and art, the male element, source of life and heat, represented symbolically by a circular diagram bisected by an S-curve, one half red (*yang*), the other half black (*yin*): originated during the Han Dynasty: opposed to *yin.* Also **Yang.** [< Chinese]

Yang (yang), **C(hen) N(ing),** born 1922, U.S. physicist born in China.

Yang·chow (yäng'jō') A city in central Kiangsu province, eastern China.

Yang·tze (yang'tsē', *Chinese* yäng'tse') The longest river of Asia and China, flowing 3,430 miles from the Tibetan highlands to the East China Sea near Shanghai; forms border between Tibetan Autonomous Region and Szechwan province. Also **Yang'tze-Ki·ang'** (-kē·ang', *Chinese* jē·äng'), **Yangtse-Kiang.**

Ya·ni·na (yä'nē·nä) See IOANNINA.

yank (yangk) *v.t.* **1** To jerk or pull suddenly. — *v.i.* **2** To give a pull or jerk. **3** *Brit.* To be vigorously active. **4** *Brit.* To jabber; scold. —*n.* **1** *Colloq.* A sudden sharp pull; jerk. **2** *Scot.* A sharp blow or slap; buffet. [? < dial. E (Scottish) *yank* a sharp sudden blow]

Yank (yangk) *n. & adj. Colloq.* Yankee. [Short for YANKEE]

Yan·kee (yang'kē) *n.* **1** Originally, a native or inhabitant of New England. **2** A Northerner; especially, a Federal soldier during the Civil War: so called in the South. **3** Any citizen of the United States; an American: a foreign, chiefly British, usage. —*adj.* **1** Of or pertaining to the Yankees. **2** *Brit.* American. [Prob. back formation < *Jan Kees* (taken as a plural), John Cheese, orig. a nickname for a Hollander; later applied by Dutch colonists in New York to English settlers in Connecticut]

Yan·kee·dom (yang′kē·dəm) *n.* **1** New England or the northern States as opposed to southern. **2** The United States as a whole. **3** Yankees collectively or as a class.

Yankee Doodle A song, of many humorous verses, popular in pre-Revolutionary times and one of the national airs of the United States.

Yan·kee·ism (yang′kē·iz′əm) *n.* **1** Yankee characteristics collectively. **2** A Yankee word, trait, or idiom, especially as restricted to New England.

Yan·kee·land (yang′kē·land′) *n. Colloq.* **1** The United States. **2** New England or the northern States as opposed to the southern.

yank·ing (yang′king) *adj.* **1** Inclined to jerk or pull sharply, as a horse. **2** *Scot.* Active; enterprising.

Yan·tra (yän′trä) A river in northern Bulgaria, flowing 168 miles NE to the Danube.

Ya·oun·dé (yä·ōōn·dā′) The capital of French Cameroons, central western Africa; a trading, manufacturing, and educational center.

yap (yap) *n.* **1** *Slang* Talk; jabber. **2** *Slang* A rowdy or bumpkin. **3** A bark or yelp. **4** A worthless dog. —*v.i.* **yapped, yap·ping 1** *Slang* To prate; jabber. **2** *Colloq.* To bark or yelp, as a cur. [Imit. of a dog's bark]

Yap (yäp, yap) An island group in the western Carolines; 80 square miles: formerly *Guap.*

ya·pon (yä′pon) See YAUPON.

Ya·qui (yä′kē) *n.* One of a tribe of North American Indians belonging to the Piman branch of the Uto-Aztecan linguistic stock, now living in southern Sonora, Mexico.

Ya·qui (yä′kē) A river in NW Mexico, flowing 420 miles SW and south from the Sierra Madre Occidental to the Gulf of California; the largest river of Sonora state.

Yar·bor·ough (yär′bûr·ō, *Brit.* yär′bər·ə) *n.* A whist or bridge hand with no card above a nine. [after an earl of *Yarborough,* who bet against the occurrence of such a hand]

yard¹ (yärd) *n.* **1** The standard English and American measure of length: 3 feet, or 36 inches, or 0.914 meter. **2** A yardstick. **3** *Naut.* A long, slender, tapering spar set crosswise on a mast and used to support sails. [OE *gyrd* a rod, a measure of length]

yard² (yärd) *n.* **1** A tract of ground enclosed or set apart. **2** An enclosure, usually small and near a residence or other building; by extension, the grounds near a house, college, or university, whether enclosed or not. **3** An enclosure used for some specific work: often in composition: a *brickyard, shipyard.* **4** An enclosure or piece of ground adjacent to a railroad station, used for making up trains and for storing the rolling stock. **5** The winter pasturing ground of deer and moose: a moose *yard.* **6** An enclosure for animals, poultry, etc. —*v.t.* To put or collect into or as into a yard. —*v.i.* To gather into an enclosure or yard. [OE *geard* an enclosure]

yard·age¹ (yär′dij) *n.* The amount or length of something in yards, as of silk. [< YARD¹]

yard·age² (yär′dij) *n.* The use or charge for a yard in handling cattle as they are moved to and from railway cars. [< YARD²]

yard·arm (yärd′ärm′) *n. Naut.* Either end of a yard of square sail.

yard·grass (yärd′gras′, -gräs′) *n.* A coarse, widely distributed, annual grass (*Eleusine indica*); goosegrass.

yard·man¹ (yärd′mən) *n. pl.* **·men** (-mən) *Naut.* A sailor who works on the yards.

yard·man² (yärd′mən) *n. pl.* **·men** (-mən) A man employed in a yard, especially on a railroad.

yard·mas·ter (yärd′mas′tər, -mäs′-) *n.* A railroad official having charge of a yard.

yard·stick (yärd′stik′) *n.* **1** A graduated measuring stick a yard in length. **2** A measure or standard of comparision. Also **yard′wand′** (-wond′).

yare (yâr) *adj. Archaic & Dial.* **1** Responding quickly to the helm; manageable: said of a ship. **2** Brisk; prompt. **3** Prepared; ready. —*adv. Obs.* With dispatch; quickly; soon. [OE *gearu* ready] —**yare′ly** *adv.*

Yar·kand (yär·kand′) **1** A town and oasis of SW Sinkiang-Uigur Autonomous Region, NW China: Chinese *Soche.* **2** A river of SW Sinkiang-Uigur Autonomous Region, NW China, flowing 500 miles NE from the Karakoram range to the Tarim.

Yar·mouth (yär′məth) **1** A port at the entrance to the Bay of Fundy in SW Nova Scotia, Canada. **2** See GREAT YARMOUTH. England.

yarn (yärn) *n.* **1** Any spun material, natural or synthetic, prepared for use in weaving, knitting, or crocheting. **2** Continous strands of spun fiber, as wool, cotton, linen, silk, jute, or rayon. **3** A quantity of such spun material. **4** *Colloq.* A long, exciting story of adventure, often of doubtful truth: a sailor spinning a *yarn.* —*v.i. Colloq.* To tell a yarn or yarns. [OE *gearn*]

Ya·ro·slavl (yä′rō·slav′əl) A city on the Volga in north central European Russian S.F.S.R.

yar·row (yar′ō) *n.* A genus (*Achillea*) of perennial carduaceous herbs of Europe and North America; especially, the common yarrow or milfoil, with small white flowers and a pungent odor and taste. [OE *gearwe*]

yar·rup (yar′əp) *n.* Flicker². [Imit. of its song]

yash·mak (yäsh·mäk′, yash′mak) *n.* The double veil or covering for the face worn by Moslem women when in public. Also **yash·mac′, yas·mak′.** [< Arabic *yashmaq*]

yat·a·ghan (yat′ə·gan, -gən; *Turkish* yä′tä·gän′) *n.* A Turkish sword or scimitar with a double-curved blade and a handle without a guard: often called *ataghan.* Also **yat′a·gan.** [< Turkish *yātāghan*]

TURKISH YATAGHAN

yaud (yäd, yôd) *n. Scot.* An old mare. See JADE.

yauld¹ (yôd, yäd, yäld) See YALD².

yauld² (yäld) See YELD.

yaup (yôp) See YAWP.

yau·pon (yô′pən) *n.* A bushy evergreen shrub (*Ilex vomitoria*) of the holly family, found in the southern United States, where its leaves were used for tea and by the North Carolina Indians for their celebrated *black drink:* also spelled *yapon, youpon, yupon.* [< Siouan (Catawba) *yopún,* dim. of *yop* a bush]

Ya·va·ri (yä′vä·rē′) See JAVARI. Also **Ya′va·ry′.**

yaw (yô) *v.i.* **1** *Naut.* To steer wildly or out of its course, as a ship when struck by a heavy sea. **2** To move unsteadily or irregularly. **3** *Aeron.* To deviate from the flight path by angular displacement about the vertical axis; fishtail. —*v.t.* **4** To cause to yaw. —*n.* **1** A movement of a ship or aircraft by which it temporarily alters its course. **2** Irregular, unsteady, or deviating motion. [Cf. ON *jaga* move to and fro]

Ya·wa·ta (yä·wä·tä) A city of northern Kyushu island, Japan: also *Yahata.*

yawl¹ (yôl) See YOWL.

yawl² (yôl) *n.* **1** A fore-and-aft rigged two-masted vessel similar to a ketch but having the mizzen- or jiggermast aft of the rudder post. **2** A ship's small boat; jolly-boat. **3** A small fishing boat. [Appar. < Du. *jol,* orig. a boat used in Jutland]

yawl-rigged (yôl′rigd′) *adj. Naut.* Having two masts, the after one very small and stepped astern of the rudder post, and both rigged with fore-and-aft sails.

GAFF–RIGGED YAWL

yaw-me·ter (yô′mē′tər) *n. Aeron.* An instrument for measuring the angle of yaw in an aircraft.

yawn (yôn) *v.i.* **1** To open the mouth wide, either voluntarily, as an animal seeking its prey, or involuntarily, with a long, full inspiration of the breath, usually as the result of drowsiness, fatigue, or boredom. **2** To be or stand wide open, especially as ready to engulf or receive something: A chasm *yawned* below. —*v.t.* **3** To express or utter with a yawn. —*n.* **1** A wide opening of the mouth, especially as from weariness. **2** The act of opening wide. [Prob. fusion of OE *geonian* yawn and *gānian* gape] —**yawn′er** *n.*

yawp (yôp) *v.i.* **1** To bark or yelp. **2** *Colloq.* To gape; yawn audibly. **3** *Brit. Colloq.* To shout; bawl; talk loudly. —*n.* **1** A bark or yelp. **2** A shout; noise; noisy talking; also, a loud, uncouth outcry. **3** *Scot.* The scream of a bird, especially when in distress. **4** *Scot.* A cough. Also spelled *yaup.* [Imit.] —**yawp′er** *n.*

yaws (yôz) *n. pl.* (also construed as *sing.*) A contagious tropical disease caused by a spirochete (*Treponema pertenue*) and superficially resembling syphilis in first appearing as a skin eruption. Also called *frambesia.* [< Cariban *yáya*]

yay (yä) *U.S. Dial. adj.* **1** This many; this much. **2** Ever so many: for *yay* years. —*adv.* **1** To this extent. **2** Ever so: *yay* big. [Cf. G *je* ever]

Yazd (yäzd) See YEZD.

Yaz·oo River (yaz′ōō) A river in west central Mississippi, flowing 189 miles SW to the Mississippi at Vicksburg.

Yb *Chem.* Ytterbium (symbol Yb).

Y-car·ti·lage (wī′kär′tə·lij) *n. Anat.* A piece of cartilage shaped like the letter Y, situated at the bottom of the socket of the hip joint.

Y-chro·mo·some (wī′krō′mə·sōm) *n.* A sex chromosome.

y·clept (i·klept′) *adj. Archaic* Called; named: now a humorous term. Also **y·cleped′.** [OE *geclypod,* pp. of *clypian* call]

ye¹ (the) *The:* an archaic contraction in which the *y* represents the thorn (*þ*) of the Old and Middle English alphabet. Often printed **yͤ.**

ye² (yē) *pron. Archaic* The persons addressed: now confined almost exclusively to poetic or formal pulpit style. Historically *ye* is only a nominative form: "Blessed are *ye* when men shall revile *you.*" *Matt.* v 11. [OE *ge,* nominative pl.]

yea (yä) *adv.* **1** Yes: used to express affirmation or assent: in this sense now superseded by *yes.* **2** Not only so, but more so: to intensify or amplify a meaning: fifty, *yea,* a hundred: an archaic term. **3** In reality; verily: a form of introduction in a sentence. **4** So as to be realized: All the promises of God in him are *yea* and Amen; truly; really: a use of the Authorized Version of the Bible. —*n.* An expression of affirmation; an affirmative vote; by extension, one who casts such a vote. [OE *gēa*]

ye·ah (ye′ə) *adv. Slang* Yes. [< YES]

yeal·ing (yē′ling) *n. Scot.* A contemporary; an equal in age: also spelled *yeelin.*

yean (yēn) *v.t. & v.i.* To bring forth (young), as a goat or sheep. [OE (assumed) *gēanian*]

yean·ling (yēn′ling) *n.* The young of a goat or sheep. —*adj.* Young; newly born.

year (yir) *n.* **1** The period of time in which the earth completes a revolution around the sun: about 365 days, used as a unit of time, and divided into 12 months. It is now reckoned as beginning January 1 and ending December 31. **2** Any period of 12 months. **3** The period of time during which a planet revolves around the sun. **4** *pl.* Length or time of life; age; sometimes, old age: active for his *years.* —**astronomical year** The period between two passages of the sun through the same equinox, which determines the changing seasons. Its length is 365 days, 5 hours, 48 minutes, 46 seconds. Also **equinoctial, natural, solar,** or **tropical year.** —**calendar, civil,** or **legal year** The period of time from midnight of December 31 to the same hour twelve months thereafter. Formerly, in England, the legal year began with March 25, but historic years were counted from January 1. In 1751 the English Parliament prescribed that the legal year should begin with the first of January, 1752. — **common year** That of 365 days, approaching most nearly in the number of days to the astronomical year. The leap year has 366 days. — **fiscal year** A financial year of a national treasury or of a business at the end of which accounts are balanced; any twelve–month period used as a basis of business reckoning. — **lunar year** That of thirteen months, one month being added at intervals to make the mean length of the astronomical year, as in the Hebrew calendar. — **sidereal year** The period of 365 days, 6 hours, 9 minutes, 9 seconds, in which the sun apparently returns to the same position among the stars. It is longer than the astronomical year, owing to the precession of the equinoxes. — **Sothic year** The fixed solar year of the Egyptians, consisting of 365 days and 6 hours: so called because determined by the heliacal rising of the Dog Star (Sothis). [OE *gēar*]

year·book (yir′boŏk′) *n.* A book published annually, presenting information about the previous year.

year·ling (yir′ling) *n.* A young animal past its first year and not yet two years old; specifically, a colt or filly a year old dating from January 1 of the year of foaling. — *adj.* Being a year old.

year·long (yir′lông′, -long′) *adj.* Continuing through a year.

year·ly (yir′lē) *adj.* 1 Included within a year's time. 2 Occurring once a year; annual. 3 Continuing or lasting for a year: a *yearly* subscription. — *adv.* Once a year; annually.

yearn (yûrn) *v.i.* 1 To desire something earnestly; long: with *for.* 2 To be deeply moved; feel sympathy. [OE *giernan, geornan.* Akin to OE *georn* eager.]

yearn·ing (yûr′ning) *n.* A strong emotion of longing or desire, especially with tenderness. — **yearn′ing·ly** *adv.*

yeast (yēst) *n.* 1 A substance consisting of minute cells of ascomycetous fungi (genus *Saccharomyces*) that clump together, forming a yellow, frothy, viscous growth which, in contact with saccharine liquids, develops or increases by germination, producing fermentation by means of enzymes, in which process alcohol and carbon dioxide are produced, as in the brewing of beer and the raising of bread. 2 Such a substance mixed with flour or meal, and sold commercially. 3 Any of a family (*Saccharomycetaceae*) of yeast–forming fungi. 4 Froth or spume. 5 Figuratively, mental or moral ferment: the *yeast* of youth. — *v.i.* To foam; froth. [OE *gist*]

yeast cake A mixture of living yeast cells and starch in compressed form suitable for use in baking or brewing.

yeast powder Dried and powdered yeast used as a leavening agent.

yeast·y (yēs′tē) *adj.* 1 Of, pertaining to, or resembling yeast. 2 Causing or characterized by fermentation. 3 Restless; unsettled; frivolous. 4 Covered with or consisting mainly of froth or foam. 5 Light or unsubstantial. — **yeast′i·ness** *n.*

Yeats (yāts), **William Butler,** 1865–1939, Irish poet, dramatist, and essayist.

Ye·do (ye·dō) A former name for Tokyo.

yeel·in (yē′lin) See YEALING.

yegg (yeg) *n. Slang* An itinerant burglar; a criminal tramp; a safe–cracker; loosely, any burglar. Also **yegg′man.** [Prob. < earlier *yekkman* a beggar in San Francisco's Chinatown < dial. Chinese *yekk* a beggar]

Ye·gor·yevsk (yə·gôr′yəfsk) A city in west central European Russian S.F.S.R.; a cotton milling center: also *Egorevsk.*

Ye·hsien (ye′shyen′) A city of NE Shantung province, NE China, near the Gulf of Chihli.

yeld (yeld) *adj. Scot.* Not giving milk; barren: also spelled *yald, yauld.* Also **yell.**

Yel·ga·va (yel′gə·və) See JELGAVA.

yelk (yelk) *n. Dial.* Yolk.

yell (yel) *v.t. & v.i.* To shout; scream; roar; also, to cheer. See synonyms under CALL, ROAR. — *n.* 1 A sharp, loud, inarticulate cry, as of pain, terror, anger, etc. 2 A rhythmic cheer composed of a prearranged set of words and shouted by a group in unison. [OE *gellan, giellan*] — **yell′er** *n.*

yell·och (yel′əkh) *v.i. & n. Scot.* Yell; scream.

yel·low (yel′ō) *adj.* 1 Having the color of ripe lemons, or sunflowers. 2 Changed to a sal-

---

low color by age, sickness, or the like: a paper *yellow* with age. 3 Having a sallow complexion, as a member of the Mongoloid ethnic group. 4 Jaundiced; hence, melancholy; jealous. 5 Sensational, especially offensively so: said of newspapers: *yellow* journalism. 6 *Colloq.* Cowardly; mean; dishonorable. — *n.* 1 The color of the spectrum between green and orange, including wavelengths centering at about 5,890 angstroms; the color of ripe lemons. 2 Any pigment or dyestuff having such a color. 3 The yolk of an egg. 4 *pl.* Any of various unrelated plant diseases in which there is stunting of growth and yellowing of the foliage; especially, an infectious virus disease of peach, nectarine, apricot, and almond trees. 5 *pl.* Jaundice, especially a variety that affects domestic animals. 6 *pl. Obs.* Jealousy; hence, a jealous frame of mind. — *v.t. & v.i.* To make or become yellow. [OE *geolu*] — **yel′low·ly** *adv.* — **yel′low·ness** *n.*

yel·low·bark (yel′ō·bärk′) *n.* Calisaya.

yel·low–bel·lied (yel′ō·bel′ēd) *adj.* 1 *Slang* Cowardly; yellow. 2 Having a yellow underside: *yellow–bellied* sapsucker.

yellow–bellied glider The fluffy glider.

yel·low–bird (yel′ō·bûrd′) *n.* 1 The goldfinch (def. 2). 2 The yellow warbler.

yellow daisy The black–eyed Susan.

yel·low–dog contract (yel′ō·dôg′, -dog′) A contract with an employer in which an employee agrees not to join a labor union.

yellow fever *Pathol.* An acute, infectious intestinal disease of tropical and semitropical regions, caused by a filtrable virus transmitted by the bite of a mosquito (genus *Aëdes*). It is characterized by hemorrhages, jaundice, vomiting, and fatty degeneration of the liver. Also *yellow jack.*

yel·low–ham·mer (yel′ō·ham′ər) *n.* 1 An Old World bunting (*Emberiza citrinella*) with the sides of the head, neck, and breast bright yellow, the back yellow and black, and the top of the head and tail feathers blackish. 2 The flicker or golden–winged woodpecker. [Alter. of earlier *yelambre,* prob. <OE *geolo* yellow + *amore,* a kind of bird]

yel·low·ish (yel′ō·ish) *adj.* Somewhat yellow. — **yel′low·ish·ness** *n.*

yellow jack 1 A carangoid fish (*Caranx bartholomaei*) of the West Indies and Florida. 2 The flag of the quarantine service. 3 Yellow fever.

yellow jacket Any of various social wasps (genus *Vespa*) with bright–yellow markings.

yellow jasmine or **jessamine** A smooth twining shrub (*Gelsemium sempervirens*) with bright–yellow flowers.

yellow journal A cheaply sensational newspaper or other publication. [So called from the use of yellow ink in printing a cartoon strip, "The Yellow Kid," in the *New York Journal,* commencing Oct. 18, 1896]

yellow lead ore Wulfenite.

yel·low·legs (yel′ō·legz′) *n.* 1 Either of two North American sandpipers (genus *Totanus*) with long yellow legs: the **greater,** or **winter, yellowlegs** (*T. melanoleucus*), or the **lesser yellowlegs** (*T. flavipes*). 2 *U.S. Colloq.* Formerly, in the U.S. Army, a cavalry soldier.

yellow metal 1 A brass consisting of 60 parts copper and 40 parts zinc. 2 Gold.

yellow perch Perch² (def. 1).

yellow peril The political power of the peoples of eastern Asia, conceived of as threatening white supremacy.

yellow pine 1 Any of various American pines, as the Georgia or loblolly pine. 2 Their tough, yellowish wood.

yellow poplar The tuliptree.

yellow race The Mongoloid ethnic division of mankind.

Yellow River See HWANG HO.

yel·lows (yel′ōz) See YELLOW (*n.* defs. 4 and 5).

Yellow Sea An arm of the Pacific between Korea and the eastern coast of China; 400 miles long, 400 miles wide: Chinese *Hwang Hai.*

yellow spot *Anat.* A small yellowish spot in the retina, the region of most acute vision.

Yellowstone Falls Two waterfalls of the Yellowstone River in Yellowstone National Park: **Upper Yellowstone Falls,** 109 feet; **Lower Yellowstone Falls,** 308 feet.

Yellowstone National Park The largest and oldest of the United States national parks,

---

at the junction of Wyoming, Montana, and Idaho, largely in NW Wyoming; 3,458 square miles; established, 1872.

Yel·low·stone River (yel′ō·stōn) A river in NW Wyoming, SE Montana, and NW North Dakota, flowing 671 miles NW to the Missouri River and passing through Yellowstone National Park where it forms **Yellowstone Lake,** 20 miles long, 14 miles wide; 140 square miles.

yellow streak A personality trait combining cowardice, treachery, and meanness.

yel·low·tail (yel′ō·tāl′) *n.* 1 Any of various fishes having a yellowish tail. 2 A carangoid fish (genus *Seriola*), especially the **California yellowtail** (*S. dorsalis*). 3 A California rockfish (*Sebastodes flavidus*). 4 The menhaden.

yel·low·throat (yel′ō·thrōt′) *n.* Any of various American warblers (genus *Geothlypis*), especially the **Maryland yellowthroat** (*G. trichas*), olive–green, with yellow throat and breast.

yel·low–throat·ed warbler (yel′ō·thrō′tid) A warbler (*Dendroica petechia*) of wooded regions of the southern United States.

yellow waterlily A yellow variety of pondlily (genus *Nuphar*).

yel·low·weed (yel′ō·wēd′) *n.* 1 Any of various goldenrods; especially, the Canada goldenrod (*Solidago canadensis*). 2 The bulbous crowfoot (*Ranunculus bulbosus*). 3 The European ragwort (*Senecio jacobaea*). 4 Weld² (def. 1).

yel·low·wood (yel′ō·woŏd′) *n.* 1 The yellowish wood of a tree (*Cladrastis lutea*) of the southern United States, with smooth bark and showy white flowers; gopherwood. The wood yields a yellow dye. 2 The tree. 3 Any one of several other trees with yellowish wood, as the Osage orange, buckthorn, smoketree, or the like.

yel·low·y (yel′ō·ē) *adj.* Yellowish.

yellow yel·dring (yel′drin) *Dial.* The yellowhammer. [<YELLOW + var. of dial. É *yowlring* < *yowlo* yellow + RING]

yelp (yelp) *v.i.* To utter a sharp or shrill cry; give a yelp. — *v.t.* To express by a yelp or yelps. — *n.* 1 A sharp, shrill cry; a sharp, crying bark, as of a dog in distress. 2 The sharp, staccato cry of the turkey hen. [OE *gielpan* boast] — **yelp′er** *n.*

yelp·ing (yel′ping) *n.* The act of one who yelps; utterance of quick, sharp cries or barks, as of a dog; also, the sounds so uttered.

Yem·en (yem′ən) A kingdom of the SW Arabian peninsula; 75,000 square miles; capitals, Sana and Ta'iz; joined United Arab States, 1958. — **Yem·e·ni** (yem′ə·nē), **Yem·e·nite** (yem′ə·nīt) *adj. & n.*

yen¹ (yen) *Slang n.* An ardent longing or desire; an intense want; an infatuation. — *v.i.* yenned, yen·ning To yearn; long. [<Chinese, opium, smoke]

yen² (yen) *n.* The monetary unit of the Japanese, containing 100 sen. [<Japanese <Chinese *yüan* round, a dollar]

Ye·nan (ye′nän′) A city in northern Shensi province, north central China; a commercial center; headquarters of the Chinese Communist party, 1937–47; formerly (1913–1948) *Fushih.*

Yen·geese (yeng′gēz) *n. pl.* White people; specifically, English settlers in New England. [Appar. N. Am. Ind. alter. of ENGLISH]

Yen·i·sei (yen′ə·sā′) A river in central Asiatic Russian S.F.S.R., flowing 2,364 miles NW through Yenisei Bay to Yenisei Gulf (90 miles wide), its estuary in the Arctic Ocean: also *Enisei.*

Yen·i·seisk (yen′ə·sāsk′) A city on the Yenisei river in central Krasnoyarsk territory, central Asiatic Russian S.F.S.R.

yen·ta (yen′tə) *n.* A female gossip or meddler. Also **yen′teh.** [<Yiddish]

Yen·tai (yen′tī′) A port on the Yellow Sea in NE Shantung province, NE China, on the northern coast of the Shantung peninsula: formerly *Chefoo.*

yeo·man (yō′mən) *n. pl.* **·men** (-mən) 1 *Brit.* A freeholder next under the rank of gentleman; in early times, one who owned a small landed estate; in modern usage, a farmer, especially one who cultivates his own farm; loosely, a man of the common people. 2 A petty officer in the U. S. Navy, Coast Guard, or Army Transport Service, who performs clerical duties. 3 *Brit.* One of the higher–class attendants in the service of a nobleman or of royalty: a *yeoman* of the crown; sometimes, a servitor of lower rank: a *yeoman* of the chamber, the buttery, etc. **4** *Brit.* A member of the yeomanry cavalry; also, a Yeoman of the (Royal) Guard. **5** *Obs.* One who acts as an assistant in a subordinate capacity; a helper; journeyman. [ME *yeman, yoman,* prob. contraction of *yengman* a young man < OE *geong* young + *mann* a man]

yeo·man·ly (yō′mən-lē) *adj.* Pertaining to or resembling a yeoman; of yeoman's rank; brave; rugged; staunch. —*adv.* Like a yeoman; bravely; staunchly.

Yeoman of the (Royal) Guard A member of the special bodyguard of the English royal household, consisting of one hundred yeomen chosen from the best rank below the gentry, and first appointed by Henry VII. See BEEFEATER.

yeo·man·ry (yō′mən-rē) *n.* **1** The collective body of yeomen; freemen; farmers. **2** *Brit.* A home guard of volunteer cavalry, created in 1761, consisting of gentlemen and gentlemen farmers, known since 1901 as the **Imperial yeomanry.** In 1907 it became a part of the Territorial Army.

yeoman's service Faithful and useful support or service; loyal assistance in need. Also **yeoman service.**

yep (yep) *adv. Colloq.* Yes. [Alter. of YES]

-yer Var. of -IER.

yer·ba (yâr′bə, yûr′-) *n.* Maté (def. 1). [< Sp. *yerba (maté)* the herb (maté)]

Yer·ba Bue·na Island (yâr′bə bwā′nə, yûr′-) An island of 300 acres in San Francisco Bay, California; mid-point of the San Francisco-Oakland Bay Bridge.

yerb tea (yûrb, yärb) *Dial.* Herb tea. [< *yerb,* dial. var. of HERB + TEA]

Ye·re·men·ko (yi·ryi·myen′kə), **Andrei Ivanovich,** born 1892, Russian general; broke the siege of Stalingrad in World War II.

Ye·re·van (ye′re·vän′) The Armenian name for ERIVAN.

yerk (yûrk) *Obs.* or *Dial. v.t. & v.i.* **1** To tie with a jerk; bind tightly. **2** To crack, as a whip. **3** To beat; lash; excite. **4** To jerk; to kick, as a horse. —*n.* A jerk; a smart blow.

Yer·kes (yûr′kēz), **Charles Tyson,** 1837–1905, U.S. financier. —**Robert Mearns,** 1876–1956, U.S. psychobiologist.

yes (yes) *adv.* As you say; truly; just so: a reply of affirmation or consent: opposed to *no,* and equivalent to a repetition of the words of a question or command in the form of an assertion. The word is sometimes used to enforce by repetition or addition something that precedes. —*n. pl.* **yes·es** or **yes·ses** A reply in the affirmative. —*v.t. & v.i.* **yessed, yes·sing** To say "yes" (to). [OE *gēse,* prob. < *gēa* yea + *sī,* third person sing. present subj. of *bēon* be]

ye'se (yēs) *Scot.* You shall; ye shall.

Ye·sil Ir·mak (ye·shēl′ ir·mäk′) A river in northern Turkey in Asia, flowing 260 miles NW to the Black Sea: ancient *Iris.*

Ye·sil·köy (ye′shēl·kœē′) The Turkish name for SAN STEFANO.

yes man *Colloq.* One who agrees without criticism; a servile, acquiescent assistant or subordinate; a toady.

yester- *prefix* Pertaining to the day before the present; by extension of the preceding, used of longer periods than a day: *yesteryear.* [< YESTER(DAY)]

yes·ter·day (yes′tər·dē, -dā′) *n.* **1** The day preceding today. **2** Loosely, the near past. —*adv.* **1** On the day last past. **2** At a recent time. [OE *geostran dæg* < *geostran* yesterday + *dæg* day]

yes·ter·eve·ning (yes′tər·ēv′ning) *n.* The evening of yesterday. Also **yes′ter·eve′, yes′·ter·e′ven** (-ē′vən), **yes·treen** (yes·trēn′).

yes·ter·morn·ing (yes·tər·môr′ning) *n.* The morning of yesterday. Also **yes′ter·morn′.**

yes·tern (yes′tərn) *adj. Archaic* Of or pertaining to yesterday. [< YESTER(DAY), on analogy with *eastern, western,* etc.]

yes·ter·night (yes′tər·nīt′) *n. Archaic & Poetic* The night last past. —*adv.* In or during the night last past. [OE *geostran* yesterday + *niht* night]

yes·ter·noon (yes′tər·nōōn′) *n.* The noon of yesterday.

yes·ter·week (yes′tər·wēk′) *n.* Last week.

yes·ter·year (yes′tər·yir′) *n.* Last year. [Trans. of F *antan;* coined by D. G. Rossetti]

yet (yet) *adv.* **1** In addition; besides; further: often with a comparative. **2** Before or at some future time; eventually: He will *yet* succeed. **3** In continuance of a previous state or condition; still: I can hear him *yet.* **4** At the present time; now: Don't go *yet.* **5** After all the time that has or had elapsed: Are you not ready *yet?* **6** Up to the present time; heretofore: commonly with a negative: He has never *yet* lied to me. **7** Than that which has been previously affirmed: with a comparative: It was hot yesterday; today it is hotter *yet.* **8** As much as; even: He did not believe the reports, nor *yet* the evidence. —**as yet** Up to now. —*conj.* **1** Nevertheless; notwithstanding: I speak to you peaceably, *yet* you will not listen. **2** But: He is willing, *yet* unable. **3** Although: active, *yet* ill. See synonyms under BUT[1], NOTWITHSTANDING. [OE *gīet, gīeta*]

Synonyms (adverb): besides, further, hitherto, now, still. *Yet* and *still* have many closely related senses, and, with verbs of past time, are often interchangeable; we may say "while he was *still* a child." *Yet,* like *still,* often applies to past action or state extending to and including the present time, especially when joined with *as;* we can say "He is feeble *as yet,*" or "He is *still* feeble," with scarcely appreciable difference of meaning, except that the former statement implies somewhat more of expectation than the latter. *Yet* with a negative applies to completed action, often replacing a positive statement with *still:* "He has not gone *yet*" is nearly the same as "He is here *still.*" *Yet* has a reference to the future which *still* does not share; "We may be successful *still*" implies that we may continue to enjoy in the future such success as we are winning now.

yet·i (yet′ē) *n.* The abominable snowman. [< Tibetan]

yett (yet) *n. Scot.* A gate.

YEW

yew (yōō) *n.* **1** Any one of several evergreen trees or shrubs (genus *Taxus*), with flat, lanceolate, dark-green leaves and a red berrylike fruit; especially, the **European** or **English yew** *(T. baccata),* a medium-sized coniferous tree of slow growth and long life, with spreading horizontal branches and dense dark-green foliage. **2** The hard, fine-grained, durable wood of the common yew, of a purplish or deep-brown color. **3** A bow made from the wood of the yew tree. —*Homophones: ewe, you.* [OE *ēow, īw*]

Yezd (yezd) A city in central Iran: also *Yazd.*

Ye·zo (ye·zō) The former name for HOKKAIDO.

Yg·dra·sil (ig′drə·sil) In Norse mythology, the huge ash tree whose roots and branches bind together heaven, earth, and hell: also spelled *Igdrasil.* Also **Yg′dra·sill, Ygg′dra·sill.**

Y·gerne (i·gûrn′) See IGRAINE.

Y-gun (wī′gun′) *n. Mil.* A gun having two barrels set at an angle, used for discharging depth bombs against enemy submarines, and mounted aft, usually on a destroyer. [So called because shaped like a Y]

YHWH Yahweh. See JEHOVAH.

Yid·dish (yid′ish) *n.* A Germanic language derived from the Middle High German spoken in the Rhineland in the thirteenth and fourteenth centuries, now spoken primarily by Jews in Poland, Lithuania, the Ukraine, and Rumania, and by Jewish immigrants from those regions in other parts of the world. It contains elements of Hebrew and the Slavic languages, and is written in slightly modified Hebrew characters. —*adj.* **1** Of or pertaining to Yiddish; written or spoken in Yiddish. **2** *Slang* Jewish. [< G *jüdisch* Jewish]

yield (yēld) *v.t.* **1** To give forth by a natural process, or as a result of labor or cultivation: The field will *yield* a good crop. **2** To give in return, as for investment; furnish: The bonds *yield* five percent interest. **3** To give up, as to superior power; surrender; relinquish: often with *up:* to *yield* a fortress; to *yield* oneself up to one's enemies. **4** To concede or grant: to *yield* precedence; to *yield* consent. **5** *Obs.* To pay, repay, or reward. —*v.i.* **6** To provide a return; produce; bear. **7** To give up; submit; surrender. **8** To give way, as to pressure or force; bend, collapse, etc. **9** To assent or comply, as under compulsion; consent: We *yielded* to their persuasion. **10** To give place, as through inferiority or weakness: with *to:* We will *yield* to them in nothing. See synonyms under ALLOW, BEND[1], DEFER[2], OBEY, PRODUCE, SURRENDER. —*n.* **1** The amount yielded; product; result, as of cultivation or mining. **2** The profit derived from invested capital. **3** The proceeds of a tax after the expenses of collection and administration have been deducted. **4** *Mil.* The explosive force of an atomic or thermonuclear bomb as expressed in kilotons or megatons. See synonyms under HARVEST, PRODUCT. [OE *gieldan, geldan* pay] —**yield′er** *n.*

yield·ing (yēl′ding) *adj.* Disposed to yield; flexible; obedient. See synonyms under DOCILE, SUPPLE. —**yield′ing·ly** *adv.* —**yield′ing·ness** *n.*

yield point *Physics* The amount of stress, measured in unit area, under which a given material, as a rod of metal, will exhibit permanent deformation; the point at which a stress or strain just exceeds the elastic strength of the material. Also **yield strength.**

yill (yil) *n. Scot.* Ale.

yin[1] (yin) *n. Scot.* One.

yin[2] (yin) *n.* In Chinese philosophy and art, the female element, which stands for darkness, cold, and death. Compare YANG. Also **Yin.** [< Chinese]

yince (yins) *adv. Scot.* Once.

Yin-chwan (yin′chwän′) A city of NE Kansu province, NW central China; capital (1928–1954) of former Ningsia province: formerly (until 1945) *Ningsia.*

Ying-kow (ying′kō′) A port on the Gulf of Liaotung in SW Lianoing province, NE China.

yip (yip) *n.* A yelp, as of a dog. —*v.i.* **yipped, yip·ping** To yelp. [Imit.]

yird (yird) *n. Scot.* Earth. Also **yirth** (yûrth).

yirr (yûr) *v.i. Scot.* To snarl; yell; growl, as a dog.

yit (yit) *adv. & conj. Dial. & Obs.* Yet. [Var. of YET]

-yl *suffix Chem.* Used to denote a radical, especially a univalent one: *ethyl, butyl.* [< Gk. *hylē* wood, matter]

y·lang-y·lang (ē′läng-ē′läng) *n.* **1** A tree *(Cananga odorata)* of Malaysia; the Malayan custard apple. **2** A perfume derived from the greenish-yellow flowers of this tree. Also spelled *ilang-ilang.* [< Tagalog *álang-ílang* flowers of flowers]

Y-lev·el (wī′lev′əl) *n.* A combined telescope and spirit level on a Y-shaped mounting which may be rotated: used in surveying, etc.

Y·mir (ē′mir, ü′mir) In Norse mythology, the progenitor of the giants, formed of frost and fire, out of whose body the gods created the world. Also **Y′mer.**

y·nogh (i·nuf′) *adj. & adv. Obs.* Enough. Also **y·nough′, y·now** (i·nou′, i·nō′). [ME, enough, OE *genōg*]

yod (yōd, *Hebrew* yōd) *n.* The tenth Hebrew letter. Also **yodh.** See ALPHABET. [< Hebrew *yōdh,* lit., a hand]

yo·del (yōd′l) *n.* A melody or refrain sung to meaningless syllables, with abrupt changes from chest to head tones and the reverse: common among Swiss and Tirolese mountaineers. —*v.t. & v.i.* **·deled** or **·delled, ·del·ing** or **·del·ling** To sing with a yodel, changing the voice quickly from its natural tone to a falsetto and back. Also **yo′dle.** [< G *jodeln,* lit., utter the syllable *jo*] —**yo′del·er, yo′del·ler, yo′dler** *n.*

yo·ga (yō′gə) *n.* A Hindu system of mystical and ascetic philosophy which involves withdrawal from the world and abstract meditation upon any object, as the Supreme Spirit, with the purpose of identifying one's consciousness with the object. [<Hind. <Skt., lit., union] — **yo′gic** adj.

yogh (yōkh) n. A Middle English letter which represented a voiced or voiceless palatal fricative, or a voiced velar fricative. It is variously spelled in Modern English as y, as in lay, w, as in law, and gh, as in daughter and enough.

yo·gi (yō′gē) n. A follower of the yoga philosophy; an ascetic or adept, supposed to possess magical powers. Also **yo′gee, yo′gin.** [<Hind. yogī <Skt. yogin <yoga yoga]

yo·gurt (yō′gŏŏrt) n. A thick, curdled milk treated with cultures of bacteria regarded as beneficial to the intestines: also called matzoon. Also **yo′ghurt, yo′ghourt.** [<Turkish yŏghurt]

yoicks (yoiks) interj. A cry formerly used in foxhunting to urge on the hounds: also hoicks. [Earlier hoik, var. of hike; prob. imit.]

YOKE (def. 1)

yoke (yōk) n. **1** A curved timber with attachments used for coupling draft animals, as oxen, usually having a bow at each end to receive the neck of the animal. **2** Any of many similar contrivances, as a frame fitted for a person's shoulders from the ends of which are suspended burdens intended to balance, as pails of milk. **3** Naut. A crosspiece on a rudder head, carrying yoke lines for steering. **4** Mech. A strap, clamp, clip, slotted piece, or the like, serving to confine, guide, or guard the movement of a part of a machine or mechanism. **5** A crossbar suspended from the collars in double harness for supporting the tongue or pole. **6** A part of a garment designed to support a plaited or gathered part, as at the hips or shoulders, giving shape to the garment. **7** That which binds or connects; a bond: the yoke of love. **8** In ancient Rome, a device consisting of two upright spears with a third laid transversely across them, under which a conquered army was made to march. **9** Servitude, or some visible mark of it; bondage. **10** sing. & pl. A couple; pair; team: a yoke of oxen. **11** Obs. The amount of land a yoke of oxen can plow in a day. **12** Scot. The time required for a yoke of oxen to accomplish a specified amount of work; hence, a part of the day. — v. **yoked, yok·ing** v.t. **1** To attach by means of a yoke, as draft animals; put a yoke upon. **2** To join with or as with a yoke; couple or link. **3** To join in marriage. **4** Rare To bring into bondage; enslave. — v.i. **5** To be joined or linked; unite. [OE geoc]

yoke·fel·low (yōk′fel′ō) n. A mate or companion in labor. Also **yoke′mate′** (-māt′).

yo·kel (yō′kəl) n. A countryman; country bumpkin: a contemptuous term. [? <dial. E, a green woodpecker, a yellowhammer] — **yo′·kel·ish** adj.

yok·ing (yō′king) n. **1** The act of one who yokes. **2** Scot. As much work as is done by a yoke of draft animals at a time.

Yok·kai·chi (yōk·kī·chē) A city of central southern Honshu island, Japan, on Ise Bay.

Yo·ko·ha·ma (yō′kə·hä′mə) A port on Tokyo Bay in central Honshu island, Japan.

Yo·ko·su·ka (yō′kə·sŏŏ′kə) A port at the entrance to Tokyo Bay, central Honshu island, Japan.

yol·dring (yōl′drin) n. Scot. & Brit. Dial. A species of bunting, the yellowhammer (def. 1). Also **yol′ding** (-ding), **yol′drin.** [Var. of earlier yowlring <ME yowlow yellow + RING]

yolk (yōk, yōlk) n. **1** The yellow portion of an egg. **2** Biol. That portion of the contents or substance of the ovum which is used for the nourishment and formation of the embryo, consisting of fat or oil drops, etc., as distinguished from the albumen or white of an egg. ◆ Collateral adjective: vitelline. **3** A fine yellow soapy exudation in sheep's wool. [OE geol(o)ca, lit., (the) yellow part <geolu yellow]

yolk·y (yō′kē, yōl′kē) adj. **yolk·i·er, yolk·i·est 1** Of or pertaining to a yolk. **2** Affected with or containing yolk: yolky wool.

yom (yom, yōm) n. Hebrew Day: used in designating days of feast or fasting: Yom Kippur.

Yom Kip·pur (yom kip′ər, Hebrew yōm kip′. ŏŏr) The Jewish Day of Atonement: the 10th of Tishri (September–October). It is marked by continuous prayer and fasting for 24 hours from sundown on the evening previous. [<Hebrew yōm kipūr day of atonement]

yon (yon) adj. & adv. Archaic, Dial. & Poetic Yonder; that or those over there: yon fine house. [OE geon]

yond (yond) adj. & adv. Archaic & Dial. Yonder. [OE geond across; infl. in meaning by yon]

yon·der (yon′dər) adj. Being at a distance indicated. — adv. In that place; there: Do you see that tree yonder? [ME, prob. extension of yone, OE geon yon]

yo·ni (yō′nē) n. The female organ of generation: the symbol under which Shakti is worshiped in India. [<Skt.]

yon·ker (yong′kər) See YOUNKER.

yont (yont) prep. Scot. Beyond.

yore (yôr, yōr) n. Old time; time long past: in days of yore. — adv. Obs. Long ago; in olden times. [OE geara formerly, prob. orig. genitive pl. of gear year]

Yor·ick (yôr′ik, yor′-) A court jester to the king of Denmark, mentioned in Shakespeare's Hamlet.

York (yôrk) A royal house of England that reigned from 1461–85; a branch of the Plantagenet line.

York (yôrk) **1** A maritime county in NE England; the largest county in England; 6,080 square miles; divided into East, West, and North Riding: also Yorkshire. **2** Its county town, a city on the Ouse, famous for its Norman cathedral: capital of Roman Britain as Eboracum.

York (yôrk), **Alvin Cullum,** 1887–1964, U.S. soldier and hero in World War I.

York (yôrk), **Cape 1** The northernmost point of Australia, in Queensland on Torres Strait. **2** A promontory of NW Greenland on Baffin Bay at the western end of Melville Bay; site of major meteorites, discovered by Peary.

York boat Canadian A type of heavy cargo canoe used by the Hudson's Bay Company. [after York factory on Hudson Bay]

Yorke Peninsula (yôrk) A promontory of southern South Australia; 160 miles long, 35 miles wide. Also **Yorke's Peninsula.**

York·ist (yôr′kist) n. An adherent of the house of York.

York River An estuary in SE Virginia, flowing into Chesapeake Bay; 40 miles long, 1 to 2 1/2 miles wide.

York·shire (yôrk′shir, -shər) See YORK (def. 1).

York·shire pudding (york′shir, -shər) A batter pudding baked in the drippings of roasting meat, often in the same pan.

York·town (yôrk′toun) A town in SE Virginia on the York River; scene of Cornwallis's surrender to Washington in 1781.

Yo·ru·ba (yō′rŏŏ·bä) n. **1** A Negro belonging to an extensive linguistic family of the African Slave Coast between the lower Niger and Dahomey rivers. Many North American Negroes are of Yoruba descent. **2** The language of the Yoruba, one of the dominant tongues of the Sudanic family. — **Yo′ru·ban** adj.

Yo·ru·ba (yō′rŏŏ·bä) A former native state in SW Nigeria.

Yo·sem·i·te National Park (yō·sem′ə·tē) A government reservation in east central California noted for its scenic grandeur; 1,183 square miles; highest point, 13,095 feet; established in 1890.

Yosemite Valley A gorge in the western Sierra Nevada mountains in Yosemite National Park in east central California; 7 miles long, 1 mile wide; including **Yosemite Falls,** a triple cataract (Upper Fall, 1,430 feet; Lower Fall, 320 feet; total drop, with intermediate cascades, 2,425 feet).

Yo·shi·hi·to (yō·shē·hē·tō), 1879–1926, emperor of Japan 1912–26.

Yo·su (yō·sŏŏ) A port of southern South Korea. Japanese Rei·sui (rā·syē).

you (yŏŏ) pron. **1** The person or persons, animal or animals, personified thing or things addressed, in either the nominative or objective case: as a subject, always linked with a plural verb. **2** Colloq. One; anyone: You

learn by trying. [OE ēow, dative and accusative pl. of ge ye]

you′d (yŏŏd) You had; you would: a contraction.

you′ll (yŏŏl) You will: a contraction.

young (yung) adj. **young·er** (yung′gər), **young·est** (yung′gist) **1** Being in the early period of life or growth; having existed a short or comparatively short time; not old. **2** Not having progressed far; newly formed: The day was young. **3** Pertaining to youth or early life. **4** Full of vigor or freshness. **5** Being without experience; immature. **6** Denoting the younger of two persons having the same name or title; junior. **7** Geol. Having the characteristics of an early stage in the geological cycle: said of a river or of certain land forms. **8** Radical or progressive in social or political aims: used with proper names: the Young Turks, Young Italy. See synonyms under FRESH, NEW, YOUTHFUL. — n. **1** Young persons as a group; youth collectively. **2** Offspring, especially of animals. — **with young** With child; pregnant. [OE geong]

Young (yung), **Arthur Henry,** 1866–1943, U.S. cartoonist. — **Brigham,** 1801–77, U.S. Mormon leader. — **Edward,** 1683–1765, English poet. — **Francis Brett,** 1884–1954, English novelist. — **Mahonri Mackintosh,** 1877–1957, U.S. sculptor. — **Owen D.,** 1874–1962, U.S. lawyer and industrialist. — **Thomas,** 1773–1829, English physicist. — **Whitney Moore, Jr.,** 1921–1971, U.S. civil rights leader for Negroes.

young·ber·ry (yung′ber′ē) n. pl. **·ries** A type of large dark-red berry, hybridized from a trailing blackberry and a dewberry, found in the western United States. [after B. M. Young, U.S. horticulturist]

young blood Youth; young people.

younger hand In card games, the hand next to the leader: also called pone: opposed to eldest hand.

young-eyed (yung′īd′) adj. Having youthful eyes or fresh vision; bright-eyed.

young·ish (yung′ish) adj. Rather young.

young·ling (yung′ling) n. **1** A young person, animal, or plant. **2** An inexperienced person. — adj. Young. [OE geongling]

Young Plan The plan, adopted in 1929, whereby the amount of German reparations for World War I was finally determined. [after Owen D. Young]

Young Pretender See STUART, CHARLES EDWARD.

young·ster (yung′stər) n. **1** A young person; a child; youth; sometimes, also, a colt or other young animal. **2** Colloq. A junior military officer. [<YOUNG + -STER, infl. by younker]

Youngs·town (yungz′toun) A city in NE Ohio; a major steelmaking center.

youn·ker (yung′kər) n. **1** A German squire. **2** Colloq. A youngster. **3** A young gentleman; knight. Also spelled yonker. [<MDu. jonckher a young gentleman <jonc young + here a lord, master]

you·pon (yŏŏ′pən) See YAUPON.

your (yôr, yŏŏr) pronominal adj. The possessive case of the pronoun you employed attributively; belonging or pertaining to you: your fate. [OE ēower, genitive of ge ye]

you′re (yŏŏr, yôr) You are: a contraction.

yours (yôrz, yŏŏrz) pron. **1** The possessive case of you used predicatively; belonging or pertaining to you: This room is yours. **2** The things or persons belonging or pertaining to you: as many as quiet as yours; God bless you and yours. — **of yours** Belonging or relating to you; your: the double possessive. [ME youres]

your·self (yŏŏr·self′, yôr-) pron. pl. **·selves** (-selvz′) A reflexive and often emphatic form of the pronoun of the second person. Yourself is employed as a simple objective: This rests with yourself, or in apposition with you: You did it yourself. Its use as a subject nominative is obsolete. Yourself is also used reflexively: You've cut yourself, and, rarely, as a substantive: You're not yourself today. Also Scot. **your·sel′.**

youth (yŏŏth) n. pl. **youths** (yŏŏths, yŏŏthz) **1** The state or condition of being young. **2** The period when one is young; that part of life between childhood and manhood; adolescence. **3** The early period of being or development, as of a movement. **4** A young man: in this sense with plural: several youths: used, also, as a collective noun: the youth of the land. [OE geoguth]

youth·ful (yōōth′fəl) *adj.* **1** Pertaining to youth; characteristic of youth; hence, buoyant; fresh; vigorous. **2** Having youth; being still young; immature. **3** Not far advanced; early; new. **4** *Geol.* Young. —**youth′ful·ly** *adv.* —**youth′ful·ness** *n.*
   Synonyms : boyish, childish, childlike, girlish, juvenile, puerile, young. *Boyish, childish,* and *girlish* are used in a good sense of those to whom they properly belong, but in a bad sense of those from whom more maturity is to be expected; *childish* eagerness or glee is pleasing in a child, but unbecoming in a man; *puerile* in modern use is distinctly contemptuous. *Juvenile* and *youthful* are commonly used in a favorable and kindly sense in their application to those still *young; youthful* may have a favorable import as applied to any age, as when we say the old man still retains his *youthful* ardor, vigor, or hopefulness; *juvenile* in such use would belittle the statement. See FRESH, NEW.

you've (yōōv) You have: a contraction.

yow (you) See YOWL.

yowe (yō) *n. Obs. & Dial.* A ewe. Also **yow** (yō). [Dial. var. of EWE]

yow·ie (yō′ē) *n. Scot.* A small ewe. [Dim. of YOWE]

yowl (youl) *v.i.* To utter a yowl; howl; yell. —*n.* A loud, prolonged, wailing cry; a howl. Also spelled *yawl, yow.* [Cf. ON *gaula* howl, yell]

yo-yo (yō′yō) *n. pl.* **-yos** A wheel-like toy with a deep central groove around which is looped a string connecting the toy with the operator's finger. As the toy spins up and down the string it may be put through a variety of movements by manipulation of the string. **2** *Slang* A compromising person; one whose political ideas and opinions change as necessary for personal advantage. [Origin unknown]

Y·pres (ē′pr′) A town in NW Belgium; site of three major battles of World War I, 1914, 1915, 1917. *Flemish* **Ie·per** (yā′pər); popularly spelled **Wi·pers** (wī′pərz) by British soldiers in World War I.

Yp·si·lan·ti (ip′sə·lan′tē, *Gk.* ēp′sē·län′tē), **Alexander,** 1792–1828, Greek patriot. —**Demetrios,** 1793–1832, Greek patriot; brother of the preceding.

Yp·si·lan·ti (ip′sə·lan′tē) a city in southeastern Michigan; pop. 30,000.

Y·quem (ē·kem′) *n.* A highly esteemed Sauterne wine. [from Château *Yquem,* an estate in SW France]

Y·sa·bel (ē·sä·bel′) See SANTA ISABEL.

Y·ser (ē·zer′) A river in northern France and western Belgium, flowing 48 miles NE from near St. Omer through Nord department and West Flanders to the North Sea at Nieuport.

Y·seult (i·sōōlt′) See ISEULT.

Ys·sel (ī′səl) See IJSSEL.

Ys·trad·y·fod·wg (ŭs′träd·i·vod′ŏōg) See RHONDDA.

Y-track (wī′trak′) *n.* A track at approximately right angles to a line of railroad, and connected with it by two switches: used in place of a turntable.

yt·ter·bi·a (i·tûr′bē·ə) *n. Chem.* White ytterbium oxide, Yb₂O₃.

yt·ter·bi·um (i·tûr′bē·əm) *n.* A metallic element (symbol Yb, atomic number 70) occurring in minute amounts in ores containing other rare-earth elements. See PERIODIC TABLE. [< NL, from *Ytterby,* a town in Sweden where gadolinite was first found] —**yt·ter′bic** *adj.*

yt·tri·a (it′rē·ə) *n. Chem.* A white insoluble earth, yttrium sesquioxide, Y₂O₃. [< NL, from *Ytterby.* See YTTERBIUM.]

yt·tric (it′rik) *adj. Chem.* Of, pertaining to, or derived from yttrium, especially in its higher valence. [< YTTR(IUM) + -IC]

yt·trif·er·ous (i·trif′ər·əs) *adj.* Yielding or containing yttrium. [< YTTRI(UM) + -FEROUS]

yt·tri·um (it′rē·əm) *n.* A metallic element (symbol Y, atomic number 39) found in association with rare-earth elements. See PERIODIC TABLE. [< NL < YTTRIA]

Yü(yü) A river of southern China, flowing 500 miles east from eastern Yünnan through southern Kwangsi to a confluence with the Hungshui, forming the West River proper: also *Siang.*

yu·an (yōō·än′, *Chinese* yü′än′) *n.* The monetary unit of China. Also **yuan dollar.** Also called *Taiwan dollar.* [< Chinese *yüan,* lit., a circle]

Yü·an (yü′än′) A river in NW Hunan province, SE central China, flowing 540 miles NE and east from western Kweichow province to Tungting Lake. Also **Yü·en** (yü′en′).

Yü·an Shih-k'ai (yü′än′ shē′kī′), 1859–1916, Chinese general; president of the Chinese Republic 1912–1916.

Yu·bi (yōō′bē), **Cape** See JUBY, CAPE.

Yu·ca·tán (yōō′kə·tan′, *Sp.* yōō′kä·tän′) **1** A peninsula of SE Mexico and NE Central America (including British Honduras and part of Guatemala); 70,000 square miles; separated from Cuba by **Yucatán Channel,** a strait between Yucatán and Cuba, connecting the Gulf of Mexico with the Caribbean; 135 miles wide. **2** A state in SE Mexico at the NW end of the peninsula; 13,706 square miles; capital, Mérida.

yuc·ca (yuk′ə) *n.* **1** Any of a large genus (*Yucca*) of liliaceous plants of the southern United States, Mexico, and Central America, generally found in dry, sandy places, having a woody stem, usually very short, but sometimes arborescent, which bears a large panicle of white, bell-shaped, drooping flowers emerging from a crown of sword-shaped leaves. **2** The flower of this plant, the State flower of New Mexico. [< NL < Sp. *yuca* < Taino]

yucca moth A moth (*Tegeticula* or *Pronuba yuccasella*) whose larvae feed on yucca seed pods.

Yu·chi (yōō′chē) *n.* One of a tribe of North American Indians, the one tribe comprising the Uchean linguistic stock, formerly dwelling along the Savannah River in eastern Georgia. In 1836 they migrated with the Creeks to what is now Oklahoma.

YUCCA
(Plant from 2 to 10 feet tall)

Yu·ga (yōō′gə) *n.* An age; cycle; a period of long duration according to Hindu thought. Each **Mahâ-yuga** or great age of the world, consisting of 4,320,000 years, is subdivided into four *Yugas* or ages: **Krita-yuga** (1,728,000 years), **Treta-yuga** (1,296,000 years), **Dvâpara-yuga** (864,000 years), and **Kali-yuga** (432,000 years), which began in 3094 B.C. These ages decrease successively in excellence; the life of man is supposed to last for 400 years in the first, 300 years in the second, 200 years in the third, and 100 years in the present or Kali age. Also **Yug** (yōōg). [< Skt., an age, yoke]

Yu·go·sla·vi·a A country of SE Europe; capital Belgrade; with two territories; Montenegro and Serbia. Formerly (1918-1929) the Kingdom of the Serbs, Croats, and Slovenes, which was formed by the union of Serbia and Montenegro with former Austro-Hungarian provinces; (1929-1941) the Kingdom of Yugoslavia; (1941-1945) occupied by Axis Powers; (1945-1992) Federal Republic of Yugoslavia, which comprised the six states of Bosnia and Herzegovina, Croatia, Macedonia, Montenegro, Serbia, and Slovinia. During the civil war of the 1990's the republic divided into sparate regions and countries. Yugoslavia was formed out of the territories of Montenegro and Serbia. - *n & adj.* Yu'go•slav, Yu'go•sla'vi•an - *adj.* Yu'go•slav'ic.

Yu·it (yōō′it) *n.* One of the Eskimos inhabiting northeastern Siberia. Compare INNUIT. [< Eskimo, men]

Yu·ka·wa (yōō·kä·wä), **Hideki,** born 1907, Japanese physicist.

Yu·kon (yōō′kon) A territory in NW Canada between Alaska and the Northwest Territories; 207,076 square miles; capital, Whitehorse.

Yu·kon River (yōō′kon) A river in NW Canada and central Alaska, flowing 1,979 miles to the Bering Sea.

Yule (yōōl) *n.* Christmas time, or the feast celebrating it. [OE *geōl(a)* Christmas day, Christmastide]

yule candle A large candle formerly used to light Christmas festivities.

Yule Day *Dial.* or *Scot.* Christmas Day.

yule log A large log or block of wood, brought in with much ceremony, and made the foundation of the Christmas Eve fire. Also **yule block, yule clog.**

Yule·tide (yōōl′tīd′) *n.* Christmas time.

Yu·ma (yōō′mə) *n.* One of a tribe of North American Indians, the dominant tribe of the Yuman linguistic stock, formerly living along the Gila and Colorado rivers in northern Mexico and Arizona and in SE California: now on a reservation in California.

Yu·man (yōō′mən) *n.* A North American Indian linguistic stock of the SW United States and NW Mexico, including the Mohave and Yuma tribes.

Yün·nan (yōō′nän′, *Chinese* yün′nän′) A province of SW China; 154,014 square miles; capital, Kunming.

yu·pon (yōō′pən) See YAUPON.

Yup·pie (yup′ē) *n. pl.* **·pies** *Slang* A member of the young, professional segment of the population. [< Y(OUNG) U(RBAN) P(ROFESSIONAL) + -IE]

Yur·ev (yōōr′yəf) The Russian name for TARTU.

Yu·zov·ka (yōō′zəf·kə) The former name for STALINO.

Z

z, Z (zē, *Brit.* zed) *n. pl.* **z's, Z's** or **zs, Zs** or **zees** (zēz) **1** The 26th letter of the English alphabet: from Phoenician *zayin,* Greek *zeta,* Roman *Z.* It was not used by the Romans until about the first century B.C. **2** The sound of the letter *z,* a voiced alveolar fricative corresponding to the voiceless *s.* See ALPHABET.

Z (zē) *n.* Something resembling a letter Z in shape: sometimes written *zee.*

Zab·rze (zäb′zhe) A city in southern Poland, formerly (1742–1945) in Upper Silesia: German *Hindenburg.*

Za·ca·te·cas (sä′kä·tā′käs) A state in central Mexico; 28,117 square miles; capital, Zacatecas.

za·ca·tón (sä′kä·tōn′, *Sp.* thä′kä·tōn′) *n.* A species of muhly grass (*Muhlenbergia macroura*) found in Mexico, the roots of which are often used in making brushes: also called *Mexican broomroot, whisk grass.* [< Sp. < *zacate* forage, grass, hay < Nahuatl *zacatl*]

Zac·chae·us (za·kē′əs) A masculine personal name. Also **Zac·che·us** (za·kē′əs), *Fr.* **Za·chée** (zä·shā′), *Ital.* **Za·che·o** (dzä·kā′ō). [< Hebrew, remembrance of the Lord]—**Zacchaeus** A wealthy publican at whose house Jesus dined in Jericho. *Luke* xix 2.

Zach (zak) Diminutive of ZACHARIAH, ZACHARIAS.

Zach·a·ri·ah (zak′ə·rī′ə) A masculine personal

name. Also **Zach·a·ry** (zak'ər·ē), *Dan., Du., Sw.* **Za·cha·ri·as** (zä'kä·rē'äs), *Fr.* **Za·cha·rie** (zȧ·shä·rē'), *Ital.* **Zac·ca·ri·a** (dzäk'kä·rē'ä), *Lat.* **Zach·a·ri·as** (zak'ə·rī'əs), *Sp.* **Za·ca·ri·as** (thä'kä·rē'äs). [< Hebrew, remembrance of the Lord]
—**Zachariah** The last king of Israel of Jehu's race. II *Kings* xiv 29.
—**Zacharias** The father of John the Baptist. *Luke* i 5.
Za·cyn·thus (zə·sin'thəs) The ancient name for ZANTE.
Za·dar (zä'där) A port of western Croatia, Yugoslavia, on the Adriatic; formerly (1918–1947) in Venezia Giulia, Italy: Italian *Zara*.
Za·dok (zā'dok) A masculine personal name. Also *Fr.* **Za·doc** (zȧ·dôk'), *Lat.* **Za·do·cus** (zə·dō'kəs). [< Hebrew, the just]
zaf·fer (zaf'ər) *n.* A blue pigment made by roasting cobalt ores to yield an impure cobalt oxide: used for enamel and for painting on glass. Also **zaf'far, zaf'fir, zaf'fre.** [< Ital. *zaffera*, prob. < Arabic *sufr* copper]
zaf·tig (zäf'tik) *adj. U.S. Slang* Curvaceous.
Zag·a·zig (zag'ə·zig, zä·gä·zēg') A city of SE Lower Egypt.
Za·greb (zä'greb) The capital of Croatia, in NW Yugoslavia; a major industrial center and the second largest city of Yugoslavia: German *Agram*.
Za·gre·us (zā'grē·əs, -grōōs) In Greek mythology, a son of Zeus and Persephone, slain by the Titans and revived as Dionysus. See ORPHIC MYSTERIES.
Zag·ros Mountains (zag'rəs) The chief mountain system of Iran, extending from Azerbaijan to Iranian Baluchistan; highest point, over 14,900 feet.
Za·ha·roff (zä·hä'rəf), **Sir Basil,** 1850?–1936, international financier and armament manufacturer born in Turkey of Greek and Russian parents.
Zah·ran (zä'rän) See DHAHRAN.
zai·bat·su (zī·bät·sōō) *n. Japanese* The wealthy clique of Japan, representing four or five dominant families.
Zaire Republic (zâr) An independent republic in central Africa; 904,754 square miles; capital, Kinshasa: formerly *Belgian Congo, Democratic Republic of the Congo.*
Za·les·ki (zä·les'kē), **August,** 1883–1972, Polish statesman.
Za·ma (zā'mə) An ancient town in Numidia, northern Africa, SW of Carthage: scene of Hannibal's defeat by Scipio Africanus, 202 B.C., ending the strength of Carthage; site of a modern village of north central Tunisia.
za·mar·ra (zä·mär'ə, -mar'ə) *n.* A sheepskin coat worn by Spanish shepherds. Also **za·mar'ro** (-mär'ō, -mar'ō). [< Sp.]
Zam·be·zi (zam·bē'zē) A river in southern Africa, flowing 1,650 miles SE from northwesternmost Northern Rhodesia through Rhodesia (forming the border between Northern and Southern Rhodesia) to the Indian Ocean in Mozambique. Also **Zam·be'si.** *Portuguese* **Zam·be·ze** (zäm·bā'zə).
Zam·bi·a (zam'bē·ə) An independent member of the Commonwealth of Nations in south central Africa; 288,130 square miles; capital, Lusaka: formerly *Northern Rhodesia.*
Zam·bo·an·ga (säm·bō·äng'gä) A port of SW Mindanao, Philippines.
za·mi·a (zā'mē·ə) *n.* Any of a genus *(Zamia)* of palmlike trees and low shrubs of the cycad family, having unbranched stems terminating in a tuft of thick, pinnate, often spiny-edged leaves. [< NL < LL *zamiae,* misreading of L *(nuces) azaniae* pine (nuts)]
za·min·dar (zə·mēn'där') See ZEMINDAR.
Za·mo·ra (thä·mô'rä) **1** An ancient city of NW Spain; capital of Zamora province. **2** A province of NW Spain, bordering on Portugal; 4,081 square miles.
Za·mo·ra y Tor·res (thä·mô'rä ē tôr'räs), **Ni·ceto Alcalá,** 1877–1949, Spanish politician; president of Spain 1931–36.
za·na·na (zə·nä'nə) See ZENANA.
Zang·will (zang'gwil), **Israel,** 1864–1926, English novelist and dramatist.
Zan·te (zan'tē, *Ital.* dzän'tā) **1** The southernmost main island of the Ionian Islands, Greece; 157 square miles: ancient *Zacynthus.* Greek **Za·kyn·thos** (zä·kin'thəs). **2** Its capital, a port on the SE coast.

Zan·thox·y·lum (zan·thok'sə·ləm) *n.* A genus of trees of the rue family with prickly stems, of which some species have medicinal properties. [< NL < Gk. *xanthos* yellow + *xylon* wood]
za·ny (zā'nē) *adj.* **·ni·er, ·ni·est** Absurdly funny; ludicrous. —*n. pl.* **·nies 1** In old comic plays, a clown who imitates the other performers with ludicrous failure. **2** A simpleton; buffoon; fool. [< F *zani* < Ital. *zanni* servants who act as clowns in early Italian comedy < dial. Ital. *Zanni,* var. of *Giovanni* John] —**za'ni·ly** *adv.* —**za'ni·ness** *n.*
Zan·zi·bar (zan'zə·bär, zan'zə·bär') A region of Tanzania consisting of the islands of *Zanzibar* (640 square miles) and *Pemba;* capital, Zanzibar.
zap (zap) *Slang. v.t.* **zapped, zap·ping 1** To kill. **2** To attack; hit; clobber. **3** To confront or impress suddenly and forcefully; astound; overwhelm. —*n.* **1** Vigorous effort; punch. **2** An attack or confrontation.
Za·pa·ta (sä·pä'tä), **Emiliano,** 1877?–1919, Mexican revolutionary leader 1911–1916.
za·pa·te·o (thä'pä·tā'ō) *n.* A Spanish folk dance. [< Sp. < *zapato* a shoe, clog]
Za·po·rozh·e (zə·pə·rôzh'yə) A city on the Dnieper in southern Ukrainian S.S.R.: formerly *Aleksandrovsk, Alexandrovsk.*
Za·ra (zä'rä, *Ital.* dzä'rä) The Italian name for ZADAR.
Za·ra·go·za (thä'rä·gō'thä) The Spanish name for SARAGOSSA.
za·ra·pe (sä·rä'pā) See SERAPE.
Za·ra·thus·tra (zä'rä·thōōs'trä, zar'ə·thōōs'trə) See ZOROASTER.
za·ra·tite (zä'rə·tīt) *n.* A massive, vitreous nickel carbonate found usually as an emerald-green incrustation: also called *emerald nickel.* [< Sp. *zaratita,* after a Señor *Zarate* of Spain]
za·re·ba (zə·rē'bə) *n.* **1** In the Sudan, a stockade, thorn hedge, or other palisaded enclosure for protecting a village or camp: used also as a means of military defense. **2** A village or camp so protected; by extension, any village. Also **za·ree'ba.** [< Arabic *zaribah* a pen for cattle < *zarb* a sheepfold]
zarf (zärf) *n.* A metal cup-shaped holder, of open or ornamental filigree, for a hot coffee cup, used in the Levant. [< Arabic *zarf* a vessel, sheath]
zar·zue·la (thär·thwā'lä) *n. Spanish* A form of lyrical theater in which song is intermingled with spoken dialog; operetta.
za·stru·ga (zə·strōō'gə) *n. pl.* **·gi** (-jē) *Meteorol.* One of a series of long parallel snow ridges formed by the wind on the open plains of Russia: also spelled *sastruga.* [< Russian]
za·yin (zä'yin) *n.* The seventh Hebrew letter. See ALPHABET. [< Hebrew *zāyin*]
Z-bar (zē'bär'), **Z-beam** (zē'bēm') *n.* A Z-iron.
Ze·a (zē'ə) *n.* A genus of tall annual cereal grasses which includes corn or maize. *Zea mays,* Indian corn, is the only species. [< NL < LL, *spelt* < Gk. *zeia* one-seeded wheat]
Ze·a (zē'ə) The medieval name for KEOS.
zeal (zēl) *n.* Ardor for a cause, or, less often, for a person; enthusiastic devotion; fervor. See synonyms under ENTHUSIASM, WARMTH. [< OF *zele* < L *zelus* < Gk. *zēlos* < *zeein* boil]
Zea·land (zē'lənd) A Danish island between the Kattegat and the Baltic Sea, on which Copenhagen is located; the largest island of Denmark, separated from Sweden by the Oresund; 2,709 square miles: German *Seeland,* Danish *Sjaelland.*
zeal·ot (zel'ət) *n.* One who is overzealous; a fanatic; immoderate partisan. [< LL *zelotes* < Gk. *zēlōtēs* < *zēloein* be zealous < *zēlos* zeal]
Zeal·ot (zel'ət) *n.* A member of a fanatical Jewish party (A.D. 6–70) in almost continual revolt against the Romans.
zeal·ot·ry (zel'ət·rē) *n.* The conduct or disposition of a zealot.
zeal·ous (zel'əs) *adj.* Filled with or incited by zeal; enthusiastic. See synonyms under EAGER. —**zeal'ous·ly** *adv.* —**zeal'ous·ness** *n.*
ze·a·xan·thin (zē'ə·zan'thin) *n. Biochem.* A yellow pigment, $C_{40}H_{56}O_2$, related to carotene and obtained in the form of golden-orange leaflets from yellow corn, egg yolk, and green leaves. [< ZEA + XANTH- + -IN]
Zeb·a·di·ah (zeb'ə·dī'ə) A masculine personal name. [< Hebrew, God has bestowed]
ze·bec (zē'bek), **ze·beck** See XEBEC.
Zeb·e·dee (zeb'ə·dē) A masculine personal name. [Contraction of ZEBADIAH]
—**Zebedee** The father of James and John, disciples of Christ. *Matt.* iv. 21.

ze·bra (zē'brə) *n.* Any of various African equine mammals resembling the ass, having a white or yellowish-brown body fully marked with variously patterned, dark-brown or blackish bands; especially, the true or **mountain** zebra *(Equus zebra)* of the Cape of Good Hope Province and Grevy's zebra. *(E. grevyi)* of Abyssinia and northeast Africa.

ZEBRA
(From 10 1/2 to 13 hands high at the withers)

[< Pg. < Bantu (Congo)] —**ze'brine** (-brēn, -brin), **ze'broid** (-broid) *adj.*
zebra wolf The thylacine.
ze·bra·wood (zē'brə·wōōd') *n.* **1** The wood of a large tree *(Connarus guianensis)* of Guiana, light brown in color with dark stripes, used in making furniture. **2** The tree. **3** The striped or banded wood of various other trees.
ze·bu (zē'byōō) *n.* The domesticated ox *(Bos indicus)* of India, China, and East Africa, having a hump on the withers, a large dewlap, and short curved horns: there are many breeds, varying in color, some being reared for milk and flesh, and others for riding and draft. [< F *zébu* < Tibetan]

ZEBU
(From 3 to 4 1/2 feet high at the shoulder)

Zeb·u·lon (zeb'yə·lən) A son of Jacob and ancestor of the tribe of Israel bearing that name. *Gen.* XXX 20. Also **Zeb'u·lun.**
zec·chi·no (tsek·kē'nō) *n. pl.* **·ni** (-nē) A gold coin of the republic of Venice; the sequin. Also **zec·chin** (zek'in), **zech'in.** [< Ital. See SEQUIN.]
Zech·a·ri·ah (zek'ə·rī'ə) A masculine personal name. [Var. of ZACHARIAH]
—**Zechariah** Hebrew prophet of the sixth century B.C., who promoted the rebuilding of the Temple; also, the Old Testament book bearing his name. Also *Zacharias.*
zed (zed) *n. Brit.* The letter z: generally called *zee* in the United States. [< F *zède* < L *zeta* < Gk. *zēta*]
Zed·e·ki·ah (zed'ə·kī'ə) A masculine personal name. [< Hebrew, justice of the Lord]
—**Zedekiah** The last king of Judah, 597–586 B.C.; son of Josiah. II *Kings* xxiv 17.
zed·o·ar·y (zed'ō·er'ē) *n.* The root of a species of turmeric *(Curcuma zedoaria),* used in medicine as a stomachic and as a carminative. [< Med. L *zedoarium* < Arabic *zedwār*]
zee[1] (zē, *Du.* zā) *n. Dutch* Sea: used in geographic names: Zuyder *Zee,* Tappan *Zee.*
zee[2] (zē) *n.* The letter Z, z.
Zee·brug·ge (zē'brōōg·ə, *Flemish* zā'brœkh·ə) A port of NW Belgium on the North Sea in West Flanders province.
Zee·land (zē'lənd, *Du.* zā'länt) A province of SE Netherlands bordering on Belgium and including Walcheren and other islands; 650 square miles.
Zee·man (zā'män), **Pieter,** 1865–1943, Dutch physicist.
Zeeman effect *Physics* The splitting of spectral lines when the source emitting them is placed in a strong magnetic field. [after Pieter *Zeeman*]
ze·in (zē'in) *n. Biochem.* A simple protein derived from corn: it is insoluble in water but soluble in 70 to 80 percent alcohol. [< ZEA + -IN]
Zeit·geist (tsit'gist) *n. German* The spirit of the time; the intellectual and moral tendencies that characterize any age or epoch. [< G < *zeit* time + *geist* spirit]
Zeke (zēk) Diminutive of EZEKIEL.
Ze·lin·ski (zyi·lyēn'skē), **Nikolai,** 1861–1953, Russian chemist.

ze·min·dar (zə·mēn′där′) *n.* In India, a tax farmer, required, under the Mogul rule, to pay a fixed sum for the tract of land assigned him; hence, later, especially in Bengal, a native landlord required to pay a certain land tax to the English government; an owner of the soil: also spelled *zamindar.* [< Hind. < Persian *zamīndār* < *zamīn* earth + *dār* a holder]

Zem·po·al·te·pec (sām′pō·äl′tä·pek′) A peak in Oaxaca, Mexico; 11,142 feet. Also **Zem·po·al·té·petl** (sām′pō·äl·tä′petl).

zemst·vo (zem′stvō, *Russian* zyem′stfō) *n.* A Russian elective district and provincial representative assembly; replaced in 1917 by the soviet system. [< Russian *zemlya* land]

Ze·mun (ze′mōōn) The port section of Belgrade, Yugoslavia, on the Danube; formerly a separate city: German *Semlin.*

ze·na·na (zə·nä′nə) *n.* In India, the women's apartments; the East Indian harem: also spelled *zanana.* [< Hind. *zenāna* belonging to women < Persian *zanāna* < *zan* woman]

Zen Buddhism (zen) A form of meditative Buddhism whose adherents believe in and work toward abrupt enlightenment; much emphasis is placed on the identity of nirvana and samsara, and on direct transmission of the enlightened state from master to pupil, with a minimum of words; scriptures and ritual forms are minimized, while continual meditation and practical physical labor are stressed. It originated in China when late northern Indian Buddhism came into contact with Taoism around A.D. 500, whence it acquired many Taoist features; it then spread to Japan, where it greatly influenced Japanese culture in all areas, especially in the age of the Samurai, whose feudal code, bushido, derived from Zen, as did judo and jiujitsu. [< Japanese *zen* meditation < Chinese *chan* < Skt. *dhyana*]

Zend (zend) *n.* 1 The ancient translation and commentary, in a literary form of Middle Persian (Pahlavi), of the Avesta, the sacred writings of the Zoroastrian religion. 2 Erroneously, the language of the Avesta; Avestan. [< F < Persian, interpretation] —**Zend′ic** *adj.*

Zend-A·ves·ta (zend′ə·ves′tə) *n.* The Avesta, including the later translation and commentary called the Zend. [Alter. of Persian *Avestā-va-Zend* the Avesta with its interpretation < Avestan *Avestā* a sacred text + Persian *zend* interpretation] —**Zend′-A·ves·ta′ic** (-ə·ves·tā′ik) *adj.*

zen·dik (zen·dēk′) *adj.* In Eastern countries, an atheist or heretic; one who practices black magic. [< Arabic *zindīq* an atheist < Persian *zandīq* a fire worshiper]

Zen·ger (zeng′ər), **John Peter,** 1697–1746, American printer and publisher.

ze·nith (zē′nith) *n.* 1 The point in the celestial sphere that is exactly overhead: opposed to *nadir.* 2 The culminating point of prosperity, greatness, etc.; summit. [< OF *cenit* < Arabic *samt (ar-rās)* the path (over the head)]

Ze·no (zē′nō) Either of two ancient Greek philosophers:
—**Zeno of Elea,** 490?–430? B.C., early Greek philosopher, noted for his arguments (paradoxes) against motion and multiplicity.
—**Zeno the Stoic,** 342?–270? B.C., Greek philosopher; founder of the Stoic school.

Ze·no·bi·a (zi·nō′bē·ə) Queen of Palmyra in the third century; conquered and captured by the Roman emperor Aurelian.

ze·o·lite (zē′ə·līt) *n.* A secondary mineral occurring in cavities and veins in eruptive rocks, usually a hydrous silicate of aluminum and sodium: various forms are used as water softeners. [< Sw. *zeolit* < Gk. *zeein* boil + *lithos* stone] —**ze′o·lit′ic** (-lit′ik) *adj.*

Zeph·a·ni·ah (zef′ə·nī′ə) A masculine personal name. [< Hebrew, the Lord has hidden]
—**Zephaniah** Hebrew prophet of the seventh century B.C.; also, the book of the Old Testament bearing his name. Also *Sophonias.*

zeph·yr (zef′ər) *n.* 1 The west wind; poetically, any soft, gentle wind. 2 Worsted or woolen yarn of very light weight used for embroidery, shawls, etc.: also **zephyr worsted.** 3 Figuratively, anything very light and airy. [< L *zephyrus* < Gk. *zephyros*]

zephyr cloth Thin, fine cashmere used for women's clothing.

Zeph·y·rus (zef′ər·əs) In Greek mythology, the west wind: regarded as the mildest and gentlest of all sylvan deities.

Zep·pe·lin (zep′ə·lin, *Ger.* tsep′ə·lēn′) *n.* A large dirigible having a rigid, cigar-shaped body, as originally designed and constructed by Count Ferdinand von Zeppelin.

Zep·pe·lin (zep′ə·lin, *Ger.* tsep′ə·lēn′), **Count Ferdinand von,** 1838–1917, German general; aeronaut and airship builder.

Zer·matt (tser·mät′) A resort village of SE Valais canton, SW Switzerland; elevation, 5,315 feet.

ze·ro (zir′ō, zē′rō) *n. pl.* **ze·ros** or **ze·roes** 1 The numeral or symbol 0; a cipher. ◆ In nontechnical speech, this symbol is often pronounced (ō). 2 *Math.* The element of a number system that leaves any element unchanged under addition, in particular, a real number 0 such that $a + 0 = 0 + a = a$ for any real number a. 3 The point on a scale, as of a thermometer, from which measures are counted. 4 *Mil.* A setting for a gunsight which adjusts both for elevation and wind. 5 The lowest point in any standard of comparison; nullity. —*v.t.* **ze·roed, ze·ro·ing** To adjust (instruments) to an arbitrary zero point for synchronized readings. —**to zero in** 1 To bring an aircraft into a desired position, as for bombing or landing. 2 To adjust the sight of (a gun) by calibrated results of firings. —**to zero in on** 1 To direct gunfire, bombs, etc., toward (a specific target). 2 To concentrate or focus one's energy, attention, etc., on. —*adj.* Without value or appreciable change. [< F *zéro* < Ital. *zero* < Arabic *sifr.* Doublet of CIPHER.]

ze·ro-beat (zir′ō-bēt′) *adj. Electronics* Homodyne.

zero hour 1 The time set for attack or other military operations: also called *H-hour.* 2 Any critical moment.

zest (zest) *n.* 1 Agreeable excitement and keen enjoyment of the mind accompanying exercise, mental or physical. 2 That which imparts such excitement and relish. 3 Specifically, an agreeable and piquant flavor in anything tasted, especially if added to the usual flavor, as that imparted to soups or wines by the essential oil of lemon peel, or by spice; figuratively, increase of enjoyment produced by the addition of any agreeable stimulant. 4 A piece of orange or lemon peel used to flavor anything, or the aromatic oil squeezed from it: a rare usage. See synonyms under APPETITE, RELISH. —*v.t.* To give zest or relish to; make piquant. [< F *zeste* lemon peel (for flavoring)] —**zest′ful** *adj.*

ze·ta (zā′tə, zē′-) *n.* The sixth letter (Z,ζ) in the Greek alphabet, corresponding to English *z,* in ancient Greek sounded *zd* or *dz,* in modern Greek *z.*

Ze·thus (zē′thəs) In Greek mythology, Amphion's twin brother. Also **Ze′thos.** See AMPHION.

Zet·land (zet′lənd) See SHETLAND.

zeug·ma (zōōg′mə) *n.* A rhetorical figure in which an adjective is made to modify, or a verb to govern, two nouns, while applying properly only to one: *She was remembered but they forgotten.* Compare SYLLEPSIS. [< NL < Gk., a yoking < *zeugnymi* yoke]

Zeus (zōōs) In Greek mythology, the supreme deity, ruler of the celestial realm, son of Kronos and Rhea and husband of Hera: identified with the Roman *Jupiter.*

Zeus-Am·mon (zōōs′am′ən) See AMMON.

Zeux·is (zōōk′sis) Greek painter of the late fifth century B.C.

Zhda·nov (zhdä′nôf) A port on the Sea of Azov, SE Ukrainian S.S.R.: formerly *Mariupol.*

Zhda·nov (zhdä′nôf), **Andrei,** 1896–1948, U.S.S.R. politician and general.

Zhi·to·mir (zhi·tô′mir) A city in west central Ukrainian S.S.R.

Zhu·kov (zhōō′kôf), **Georgi,** 1895–1974, U.S.S.R. marshal and statesman.

zib·e·line (zib′ə·līn, -lin) *adj.* Pertaining to the sable; made of sable fur. —*n.* The fur of the sable. Also **zib′el·line.** [< F < OF *sebelin,* ult. < Slavic. Akin to SABLE.]

zib·et (zib′it) *n.* A carnivore, the Asian or Indian civet (*Viverra zibetha*), with the black

markings less distinct and the tail more ringed than the common civet. It is often domesticated. Also **zib′eth.** [< Med. L *zibethum* < Arabic *zabād* a civet]

Zieg·feld (zēg′feld, zig′-), **Florenz,** 1869–1932, U.S. theatrical producer.

zig·gu·rat (zig′ŏŏ·rat)*n.* Among the Assyrians and Babylonians, a terraced temple tower pyramidal in form, each successive story being smaller than the one below, leaving a terrace around each of the floors. Also **zik′ku·rat** (zik′-). [< Assyrian *ziqquratu,* orig. a mountain top]

ZIGGURAT

zig·zag (zig′zag) *n.* A series of short, sharp turns or angles from one side to the other in succession, or something, as a path or pattern, characterized by such angles. —*adj.* Having a series of short alternating turns or angles from side to side: *a zigzag pattern.* —*adv.* In a zigzag manner. —*v.t. & v.i.* **·zagged, ·zag·ging** To form or move in zigzags. [< F < G *zickzack,* prob. reduplication of *zacke* a sharp point]

zig·zag·ger (zig′zag·ər) *n.* 1 One who or that which zigzags. 2 A sewing-machine attachment for stitching appliqué, joining lace and insertion to fabric, etc.

zilch (zilch) *n. Slang* Nothing; naught. [Origin unknown]

zil·lah (zil′ə) *n. Anglo-Indian* A provincial governmental district in India.

zil·lion (zil′yən) *n. Colloq.* A very large, indeterminate number: She said she had a *zillion* things to do before the plane left. [Imit. of *million, trillion,* etc.] —**zil′lionth** *adj.*

Zil·pah (zil′pə) The mother of Gad. *Gen.* xxx 10.

Zim·ba·bwe (zim·bä′bwä) 1 An independent republic in south central Africa, formed in 1980 from the British colony of Southern Rhodesia; 150,869 sq. mi.; capital Harare (Salisbury). See RHODESIA. 2 The site of a ruined city (probably of a Bantu people, dating from the 15th century) of SE Zimbabwe; discovered about 1870.

Zim·ba·list (zim′bə·list, *Russian* zim′bə·lyēst′), **Efrem,** born 1889, U.S. violinist born in Russia.

zinc (zingk) *n.* A bluish-white, lustrous metallic element (symbol Zn, atomic number 30) occurring in various ores and essential in traces for the activity of many plant and animal enzymes. See PERIODIC TABLE. —*v.t.* **zinced** or **zincked, zinc·ing** or **zinck·ing** To coat or cover with zinc; galvanize. [< G *zink;* ult. origin unknown] —**zinc′ic** *adj.* —**zinck′y, zinc′y, zink′y** *adj.*

zinc·al·ism (zingk′əl·iz′əm) *n. Pathol.* Chronic zinc poisoning.

zinc·ate (zingk′āt) *n. Chem.* A salt derived from zinc hydroxide by substitution of a metal for the hydrogen. [< ZINC + -ATE³]

zinc blende Sphalerite.

zinc chloride *Chem.* A white deliquescent compound, $ZnCl_2$, extensively used in medicine, industry, and the arts.

zinc·if·er·ous (zingk·if′ər·əs, zin·sif′ər·əs) *adj.* Yielding zinc, as ore. Also **zink·if′er·ous.** [< ZINC + -(I)FEROUS]

zinc·i·fy (zingk′ə·fī) *v.t.* **·fied, ·fy·ing** To apply zinc to, as by coating or impregnating. [< ZINC + -(I)FY] —**zinc′i·fi·ca′tion** (-fə·kā′shən) *n.*

zinc·ite (zingk′īt) *n.* A deep-red, translucent to subtranslucent zinc oxide, ZnO, crystallizing in the hexagonal system; zinc ore. [< ZINC + -ITE²]

zin·co·graph (zingk′ə·graf, -gräf) *n.* An etching on zinc; a picture obtained by zincography. Also **zin′co·type** (-tīp). [< ZINC + -(O)GRAPH] —**zin·cog·ra·pher** (zing·kog′rə·fər) *n.*

zin·cog·ra·phy (zing·kog′rə·fē) *n.* The art of etching on zinc to produce plates for printing. [< ZINC + -(O)GRAPHY] —**zinc·o·graph·ic** (zingk′ə·graf′ik) or **·i·cal** *adj.*

zinc ointment A medicated ointment containing zinc oxide.

zinc·ous (zingk′əs) *adj. Chem.* Pertaining to or derived from zinc; zincic.

zinc oxide *Chem.* White pulverulent oxide, ZnO, made by burning zinc in air. It is used as a pigment, chiefly as a substitute for white lead, and in medicine as a mild antiseptic.

zinc sulfate *Chem.* A crystalline compound, $ZnSO_4 \cdot 7H_2O$, obtained by the action of sulfuric acid on zinc; white vitriol.

zinc white Zinc oxide used as a pigment.

zin·fan·del (zin′fən·del) *n.* A dry, red or white, claret-type wine made in California. [? from a European place name]

zing (zing) *Colloq. n.* **1** A high-pitched buzzing or humming sound. **2** Energy; vitality. —*v.i.* To make a shrill, humming sound.

zin·ga·ro (tsēng′gä·rō) *n. pl.* **·ri** (-rē) *Italian* A gipsy. Also **zin′ga·no** (-nō). **zin′ga·ra** (-rä) *n. fem.*

zin·gi·ber·a·ceous (zin′jə·bə·rā′shəs) *adj. Bot.* Of or pertaining to a family (*Zingiberaceae*) of monocotyledonous tropical plants, the ginger family, having aromatic rootstocks and including cardamon. Also **zin′zi·ber·a′ceous** (zin′zə-). [< NL, family name < LL *zingiber* GINGER]

Zin·jan·thro·pus (zin·jan′thrə·pəs) *n.* Scientific name of a supposed forerunner of modern man, the evidence consisting of the remains of a skull found in East Africa and thought to be nearly two million years old. [< NL < Arabic *Zinj* eastern Africa + Gk. *anthrōpos* man]

zink·en·ite (zingk′ən·īt) *n.* A metallic steel-gray mineral, $PbSb_2S_4$, crystallizing in the orthorhombic system. Also **zinck′en·ite.** [< G *zinkenit,* after J. K. L. *Zinken,* 1798–1862, German mine director]

zin·ni·a (zin′ē·ə) *n.* Any of a genus (*Zinnia*) of American, chiefly Mexican, herbs of the composite family, having opposite entire leaves and showy flowers; especially, the common zinnia (*Z. elegans*), the State flower of Indiana. [< NL, after J. G. *Zinn,* 1727–59, German professor of medicine]

Zi·nov·iev (zē·nôv′yif), **Grigori,** 1883–1936, U.S.S.R. political leader.

Zins·ser (zin′sər), **Hans,** 1878–1940, U.S. bacteriologist.

Zin·zen·dorf (tsin′tsən·dôrf), **Count Nicholas Ludwig von,** 1700–60, German theologian.

Zi·on (zī′ən) **1** A hill in Jerusalem, the site of the Temple and the royal residence of David and his successors: regarded by the Jews as a symbol for the center of Jewish national culture, government, and religion. **2** The Jewish people. **3** Any place or community considered to be especially under God's rule, as ancient Israel or the Christian church. **4** The heavenly Jerusalem; heaven. Also spelled *Sion.* [OE *Sion* < LL < Gk. *Seōn, Seiōn* < Hebrew *tsiyōn* a hill]

Zi·on·ism (zī′ən·iz′əm) *n.* A movement for a resettlement of the Jews in Palestine. The form which lays stress upon the political questions involved is sometimes called **political Zionism,** and the term **religious Zionism** is used by those Zionists who lay a special stress upon the regeneration of the Holy Land as a center of social and religious influence for Judaism. Also **Zion movement.** —**Zi′on·ist** *adj.* & *n.* —**Zi′on·is′tic** *adj.* —**Zi′on·ite** *n.*

Zion National Park A government reservation in SW Utah; 147 square miles; established in 1919; contains **Zion Canyon,** a gorge ½ mile deep, about 15 miles long.

Zi·on·ward (zī′ən·wərd) *adv.* Toward Zion; Godward; heavenward.

zip (zip) *n.* **1** A sharp, hissing sound, as of a bullet passing through the air. **2** *Colloq.* Energy; vitality; vim. —*v.* **zipped, zip·ping** *v.t.* **1** To fasten with a sliding fastener. —*v.i.* **2** *Colloq.* To be very energetic. **3** To move or fly with a zip. [Imit.]

Zi·pan·gu (zi·pang′gōō) *Japan:* name used by Marco Polo.

ZIP Code (zip) A numerical code devised by the U.S. Post Office to aid in the distribution of domestic mail. Also **Zip Code.** [< Z(ONE) I(MPROVEMENT) P(LAN)]

zip gun A home-made pistol consisting of a small pipe or other tube fastened to a block of wood and equipped with a firing pin actuated by a spring or rubber band.

zip·per (zip′ər) *n.* A slide fastener.

Zip·per (zip′ər) *n.* An overshoe or boot secured with a slide fastener: a trade name.

zip·py (zip′ē) *adj.* **·pi·er, ·pi·est** *Colloq.* Brisk; energetic; lively; snappy.

zir·con (zûr′kon) *n.* **1** An adamantine, variously colored zirconium silicate, $ZrSiO_4$. The transparent reddish variety, called *hyacinth,* is used as a gem, as are also the leaf-green, yellowish, colorless, or smoky varieties called *jargon.* **2** A variety of this mineral having an artificially produced steely-blue color of high brilliance and luster: esteemed as a gem. [< F *zircone* < Arabic *zarqūn* cinnabar < Persian *zargūn* golden < *zar* gold + *gūn* color]

zir·con·ate (zûr′kən·āt) *n. Chem.* A salt formed by replacing hydrogen in zirconium hydroxide with a metal. [< ZIRCON(IUM) + -ATE³]

zir·co·ni·a (zûr·kō′nē·ə) *n. Chem.* A white pulverulent zirconium dioxide, ZrO_2, obtained by heating zirconium to redness in contact with air: when strongly heated it becomes luminous, and it is hence used in certain forms of incandescent burners. [< NL < ZIRCON]

zir·co·ni·um (zûr·kō′nē·əm) *n.* A corrosion-resistant metallic element (symbol Zr, atomic number 40), having five naturally occurring isotopes, of which one is weakly radioactive. See PERIODIC TABLE. [< NL < ZIRCON] —**zir·con′ic** (zûr·kon′ik) *adj.*

Z-i·ron (zē′ī′ərn) *n.* An angle iron of Z form: also called *Z-bar, Z-beam.*

Zis·ka (tsis′kä), **John,** 1360?–1424, Bohemian general; leader of the Hussites. Also *Žiž·ka* (zhish′kä).

zith·er (zith′ər) *n.* A simple form of stringed instrument, having a flat sounding board and from thirty to forty strings that are played by plucking with a plectrum. Also **zith′ern** (-ərn). [< G < L *cithara* < Gk. *kithara.* Doublet of CITHARA and GUITAR.]

zit·tern (zit′ərn) See CITHERN.

zi·zith (tsē·tsēt′, tsi′tsis) *n.* The fringe or tassel formerly worn by Jews on the outer garment (*Num.* xv 38), but now worn on the tallith during prayer. [< Hebrew *tsītsīth*]

ziz·zle (ziz′əl) *v.i.* **·zled, ·zling** *Brit. Dial.* To make a sputtering or hissing sound, as meat when cooking; sizzle. [Imit.]

Zla·to·ust (zlä′tə·ōōst′) A city of SW Asiatic Russian S.F.S.R. in the southern Urals.

zlo·ty (zlô′tē) *n. pl.* **·tys** or **·ty** The monetary unit of Poland. [< Polish, lit., golden]

Zn *Chem.* Zinc (symbol Zn).

zo- Var. of ZOO-.

-zoa *combining form Zool.* Used to denote the names of groups: *Protozoa, Hydrozoa.* An individual in such a group is denoted by **-zoan.** [< NL < Gk. *zōion* an animal]

Zo·an (zō′an) The Old Testament name for TANIS.

zo·an·thro·py (zō·an′thrə·pē) *n.* The obsessive delusion that one has become a beast; lycanthropy. [< NL *zoanthropia* < Gk. *zōion* an animal + *anthropos* a man] —**zo·an·throp′ic** (zō′ən·throp′ik) *adj.*

SIGNS OF THE ZODIAC
Reading clockwise:

A. Vernal equinox: Aries, Taurus, Gemini.
B. Summer solstice: Cancer, Leo, Virgo.
C. Autumnal equinox: Libra, Scorpio, Sagittarius.
D. Winter solstice: Capricorn, Aquarius, Pisces.

zo·di·ac (zō′dē·ak) *n.* **1** An imaginary belt encircling the heavens and extending about 8° on each side of the ecliptic, within which are the orbits of the moon, sun, and larger planets. It is divided into twelve parts, called **signs of the zodiac,** which formerly corresponded to twelve constellations bearing the same names. Now, owing to the precession of the equinoxes, each constellation is in the sign that has the name next following its own. **2** Figuratively, a complete circuit; round. **3** *Rare* A circle or halo; also, a girdle. [< OF *zodiaque* < L *zodiacus* < Gk. (*kyklos*) *zōdiakos* (circle) of animals < *zōdion* a sculptured animal, dim. of *zōion* an animal] —**zo·di·a·cal** (zō·dī′ə·kəl) *adj.*

zodiacal light *Astron.* A cone-shaped tract of faint light lying near the plane of the ecliptic: it may be seen in the west after twilight in winter and spring, or in the east before daybreak from September till January. It is attributed to the reflection of sunlight from a cloud of fine meteoric dust.

Zo·e (zō′ē) A feminine personal name. [< Gk., life]

zo·e·trope (zō′ə·trōp) *n.* A toy having a revolving cylinder with slits through which a series of pictures inside are seen in apparent motion. Compare PHENAKISTOSCOPE. [< Gk. *zōē* life + -TROPE] —**zo·e·trop′ic** (-trop′ik) *adj.*

zo·ic (zō′ik) *adj.* Pertaining to or characterized by animals or animal life. [< Gk. *zōikos* < *zōion* an animal]

zois·ite (zoi′sīt) *n.* A vitreous, transparent to subtranslucent silicate of aluminum and calcium, in which iron sometimes replaces the aluminum. [< G *zoisit,* after Baron *Zois* von Edelstein, 1747–1819, its discoverer]

Zo·la (zō′lə, zō·lä′; *Fr.* zō·lá′), **Émile,** 1840–1902, French writer. —**Zo·la·esque′** (-esk′) *adj.*

zoll·ver·ein (tsôl′fer·īn) *n.* **1** A former trade league constituted by twenty-six German states. **2** Hence, a union of states for tariff purposes. [< G *zoll* a tax, custom + *verein* a union]

Zom·ba (zom′bə) The capital of Nyasaland, Federation of Rhodesia and Nyasaland, in the SE part.

zom·bi (zom′bē) *n.* **1** In West African voodoo cults, the python deity; also, the snake deity of the voodoo cults of Haiti and of the southern United States. **2** The supernatural power by which a dead body is believed to be reanimated; specifically, a corpse reactivated by sorcery, but still dead. **3** Loosely, a ghost. Also **zom′bie.** [< West African. Cf. Bantu (Congo) *zumbi* fetish.] —**zom′bi·ism** *n.*

Zom·bie (zom′bē) *n.* A large, strong cocktail made from several kinds of rum, fruit juices, and liqueur. [< ZOMBI]

zo·nal (zō′nəl) *adj.* Of, pertaining to, exhibiting, or marked by a zone or zones; having the form of a zone. Also **zo′na·ry** (-nər·ē).

zo·nate (zō′nāt) *adj.* **1** Marked with zones or concentric colored bands. **2** *Bot.* Disposed in a single row, as certain tetraspores. Also **zo′nat·ed.** [< ZON(E) + -ATE¹] —**zo·na·tion** (zō·nā′shən) *n.*

zone (zōn) *n.* **1** One of five divisions of the earth's surface, enclosed between two parallels of latitude and named for the prevailing climate. These are the **torrid zone,** extending on each side of the equator 23° 27′; the **temperate** or **variable zones,** included between the parallels 23° 27′ and 66° 33′ on both sides of the equator; and the **frigid zones,** within the parallels 66° 33′ and the poles. **2** In war, a region proscribed for neutrals as being within the range of military or naval operations: a defense *zone,* combat *zone;* also, any region neutralized by agreement of combatants: a demilitarized *zone.* **3** *Ecol.* A belt or area delimited from others by the character of its plant or animal life, its climate, geological formations, etc. **4** A region of land distinguished or set off by some special characteristic: a canal *zone.* **5** *Anat.* A beltlike area distinguished from its surroundings either by structure or appearance.

TERRESTRIAL ZONES

6 *Mineral.* Any series of faces upon a crystal whose planes form a prismatic surface. **7** A belt, stripe, etc., distinguished by color or the like, encircling an object. **8** *Geom.* A portion of the surface of a sphere enclosed between two parallel planes. **9** Originally (now chiefly in poetry), a belt or girdle. **10** The total number of railroad stations situated in a certain area measured from a place whence traffic is shipped; also, a circular area within which a uniform fare is charged by the transportation companies. **11** In the United States parcel post system, any one of the concentric areas within each of which a uniform rate is charged. **12** A postal district in a city. —*v.t.* **zoned, zon·ing 1** To divide into zones; especially, to divide (a city, etc.) into zones which are restricted as to types of construction and activity, as residential, industrial, etc. **2** To encircle with a zone or belt. **3** To mark with or as with zones or stripes. [< MF < L *zona* < Gk. *zōnē* a girdle] —**zoned** *adj.*

zone axis *Mineral.* The imaginary line through a crystal, to which all the faces in a given zone, and the mutual intersections of those faces, are parallel.

zone·less (zōn′lis) *adj.* Having no zone or belt.

zone time See under TIME.

Zon·gul·dak (zóng′gŏŏl·däk′) **1** A port on the Black Sea in NW Turkey in Asia, capital of Zonguldak province; a coal-shipping center. **2** A province of NW Turkey in Asia, bordering on the Black Sea; 2,876 square miles.

zo·nule (zōn′yŏŏl) *n.* A small zone, belt, or ring. Also **zo′nu·la**. [< NL *zonula*, dim. of L *zona* ZONE]

zoo (zōō) *n.* A menagerie. [Short for ZOOLOGICAL GARDEN]

zoo- *combining form* Animal; of or related to animals, or to animal forms: *zoology, zoophyte.* Also, before vowels, *zo-.* [< Gk. *zōion* an animal]

zo·o·chem·is·try (zō′ə·kem′is·trē) *n.* Animal chemistry; specifically, the chemistry of the solids and fluids contained in the animal organism. —**zo′o·chem′i·cal** (-kem′i·kəl) *adj.*

zo·o·ge·o·graph·ic (zō′ə·jē′ə·graf′ik) *adj.* Of, pertaining to, or engaged in zoogeography. Also **zo′o·ge′o·graph′i·cal.** —**zo′o·ge′o·graph′i·cal·ly** *adv.*

zoogeographic realm One of a series of major geographic areas characterized by the dominance of certain animal groups. The principal realms in the classification of A. R. Wallace are: the Palearctic, Nearctic, Neotropical, Ethiopian, Oriental, and Australian. The first two are often considered together as the Holarctic realm.

zo·o·ge·og·ra·phy (zō′ə·jē·og′rə·fē) *n.* **1** The systematic study of the distribution of animals and of the factors controlling it. **2** The study of the relations between special animal groups and the land or aquatic areas in which they predominate. —**zo′o·ge·og′ra·pher** *n.*

zo·o·gloe·a (zō′ə·glē′ə) *n. pl.* **·gloe·ae** (-glē′ē) A colony of bacteria forming a jellylike mass held together by a viscid sheath secreted by themselves. [< NL < Gk. *zōion* an animal + *gloios* sticky stuff]

zo·og·ra·phy (zō·og′rə·fē) *n.* The branch of zoology that describes animals; descriptive zoology. —**zo·og′ra·pher** or **·phist** *n.* —**zo·o·graph·ic** (zō′ə·graf′ik) or **·i·cal** *adj.*

zo·oid (zō′oid) *n.* **1** *Biol.* Any organism, usually very small, capable of spontaneous movement and independent existence, as a spermatozoon. **2** *Zool.* **a** One of the distinct members of a compound or colonial organism, as in a bryozoan. **b** A free-swimming organism produced as a stage in the life cycle of a jellyfish. —*adj.* Having essentially the nature of an animal: also **zo·oi·dal** (zō·oid′l). [< ZO- + -OID]

zo·ol·a·try (zō·ol′ə·trē) *n.* Animal-worship. [< ZOO- + -LATRY] —**zo·ol′at·er** *n.* —**zo·ol′a·trous** *adj.*

zo·o·log·i·cal (zō′ə·loj′i·kəl) *adj.* **1** Of, pertaining to, or occupied with zoology. **2** Relating to or characteristic of animals. Also **zo′o·log′ic.** —**zo′o·log′i·cal·ly** *adv.*

zoological garden A park or garden in which wild animals are kept for exhibition.

zo·ol·o·gy (zō·ol′ə·jē) *n.* **1** The science that treats of animals with reference to their struc-

ture, functions, development, nomenclature, and classification. **2** The animal kingdom, or local examples of it, regarded biologically. **3** A scientific treatise on animals. [< NL *zoologia* < Gk. *zōion* an animal + *logos* a word, discourse] —**zo·ol′o·gist** *n.*

zoom (zōōm) *v.i.* **1** To make a low-pitched but loud humming or buzzing sound. **2** To climb sharply in an airplane, using the energy of momentum. **3** To move a motion picture or TV camera rapidly or adjust the focus, as with a zoom lens, to make an object in view appear to come very close or become much more distant. —*v.t.* **4** To cause to zoom. —*n.* The act of zooming. [Imit.]

zo·om·e·try (zō·om′ə·trē) *n.* Measurement of the parts of animals and determination of their relative magnitude. [< ZOO- + -METRY] —**zo·o·met·ric** (zō′ə·met′rik) *adj.*

zoom lens *Photog.* A lens, used chiefly on television and motion picture cameras, that permits the size of the image to be varied continuously without loss of focus.

zo·o·mor·phism (zō′ə·môr′fiz·əm) *n.* **1** The conception, symbolization, or representation of a man or a god in the form of an animal; also, the attribution of divine or human qualities to animals. **2** The representation of animals or animal forms in art or symbolism. **3** Transformation into animals. In this sense compare BEAST MARRIAGE, SWAN MAIDEN. See also CIRCE. Also **zo′o·mor·phy.** —**zo′o·mor′phic** *adj.*

zo·on (zō′on) *n. pl.* **zo·ons** or **zo·a** (zō′ə) *Biol.* A developed individual of a compound animal or of a simple egg. [< NL < Gk. *zōion* an animal] —**zo·on·al** (zō·on′əl) *adj.*

zo·oph·a·gous (zō·of′ə·gəs) *adj.* Feeding on animals. [< ZOO- + -PHAGOUS]

zo·o·phile (zō′ə·fīl, -fil) *n.* **1** A zoophilous plant. **2** A lover of animals; specifically, one who objects to vivisection; also, one addicted to zoophilism: also **zo·oph·i·list** (zō·of′ə·list). [< ZOO- + -PHILE] —**zo′o·phil′ic** (-fil′ik) *adj.*

zo·oph·i·lism (zō·of′ə·liz′əm) *n.* **1** Fondness for animals. **2** The obtaining of sexual gratification by the fondling of animals. Also **zo·o·phil·i·a** (zō′ə·fil′ē·ə).

zo·oph·i·lous (zō·of′ə·ləs) *adj.* **1** Animal-loving. **2** Adapted for pollination by animals, as certain plants. [< ZOO- + -PHILOUS]

zo·o·pho·bi·a (zō′ə·fō′bē·ə) *n.* A morbid fear of animals. [< ZOO- + -PHOBIA] —**zo′o·pho′bic** *adj.*

zo·o·phyte (zō′ə·fīt) *n.* An invertebrate animal resembling a plant, as a coral or sea anemone. [< ZOO- + -PHYTE] —**zo′o·phyt′ic** (-fit′ik) or **·i·cal** *adj.*

zo·o·plas·ty (zō′ə·plas′tē) *n. Surg.* That operation by which a part of an animal body is grafted on some part of the human body. —**zo′o·plas′tic** *adj.*

zo·o·sperm (zō′ə·spûrm) *n.* **1** A zoospore. **2** A spermatozoon. —**zo′o·sper·mat′ic** (-spər·mat′ik) *adj.*

zo·o·spo·ran·gi·um (zō′ə·spə·ran′jē·əm) *n. pl.* **·gi·a** (-jē·ə) *Bot.* A sporangium producing zoospores. [< NL < Gk. *zōion* an animal + *spora* a seed + *angeion* a vessel]

zo·o·spore (zō′ə·spôr, -spōr) *n.* **1** *Bot.* A motile spore destitute of any cell wall, produced particularly among some algae and fungi: they move sometimes in an ameboid manner, but more frequently they are provided with cilia, by the lashing of which the spore is propelled through the water. **2** *Zool.* A flagellate or ameboid motile cell in certain protozoa. [< ZOO- + SPORE] —**zo′o·spor′ic** (-spôr′ik, -spor′ik), **zo·os·po·rous** (zō·os′pər·əs) *adj.*

zo·ot·o·my (zō·ot′ə·mē) *n.* The anatomy or dissection of animals; comparative anatomy. [< NL *zootomia* < Gk. *zōion* an animal + *tomē* a cutting < *temnein* cut] —**zo·o·tom·ic** (zō′ə·tom′ik) or **·i·cal** *adj.* —**zo′o·tom′i·cal·ly** *adv.* —**zo·ot′o·mist** *n.*

zo·o·tox·in (zō′ə·tok′sin) *n.* A toxin derived from animals, as snake venom, the poison of bee stings, etc.

zoot suit (zōōt) *Slang* A suit having an extra-long coat and baggy trousers narrowing at the ankle. [Origin uncertain]

zo·ri (zō′rē) *n.* A flat, thonged sandal of straw or rubber. [< Japanese]

zor·il (zôr′il, zor′-) *n.* An African musteline carnivore (*Ictonyx striata*) which can emit a noxious odor; the Cape polecat. Also **zo·ril·la** (zə·ril′ə). [< F *zorille* < Sp. *zorrilla* a polecat, dim. of *zorra* a fox]

Zorn (sôrn), **Anders Leonhard,** 1860–1920, Swedish painter, etcher, and sculptor.

Zo·ro·as·ter (zōrō·as′tər) The traditional founder of the ancient Persian religion, believed to have lived about 600 B.C.: also called *Zarathustra.* —**Zo′ro·as′tri·an** *adj. & n.*

Zo·ro·as·tri·an·ism (zōrō·as′trē·ən·iz′əm) *n.* The religious system founded by Zoroaster on the old Aryan folk religion and taught in the Zend-Avesta. It recognizes two creative powers, one good and the other evil, includes the belief in life after death, and teaches the final triumph of good over evil. See AHRIMAN, ORMUZD. Also **Zo′ro·as′trism.**

Zor·ril·la y Mo·ral (thôr·rē′lyä ē mō·räl′), **José,** 1817–93, Spanish poet and dramatist.

Zos·i·mus (zos′ə·məs, zō′sə-) Greek historian of the fifth century A.D.

zos·ter (zos′tər) *n.* **1** An ancient Greek belt or girdle worn especially by men. **2** *Pathol.* Shingles; herpes zoster. [< L < Gk. *zōstēr* a girdle < *zōnynai* gird]

Zou·ave (zōō·äv′, zwäv) *n.* **1** A light-armed French infantryman wearing a brilliant Oriental uniform, originally an Algerian recruit. **2** In the Civil War, a member of a volunteer regiment assuming the name and part of the dress of the French Zouaves. **3** A woman's short, gaily embroidered jacket: also **Zouave jacket.** [< F < Arabic *Zouaoua*, a Kabyle tribe; so called because orig. recruited from this tribe]

zounds (zoundz) *interj.* An exclamation denoting astonishment: also spelled *swounds.* [Short for *God's wounds*]

zoy·si·a (zoi′shə, zoi′sē·ə) *n.* Any grass of a genus (*Zoysia*), used esp. on lawns in warm, dry regions.

Zr *Chem.* Zirconium (symbol Zr).

Zsig·mon·dy (zhig′mŏn·dē), **Richard,** 1865–1929, German chemist born in Austria.

zuc·chet·to (tsŏŏk·ket′tō) *n.* A skullcap worn by ecclesiastics in the Roman Catholic Church: black for a priest, purple for a bishop, red for a cardinal, and white for the pope. Also **zuc·chet′ta.** [Var. of Ital. *zucchetta*, orig. a small gourd, dim. of *zucca* a gourd]

zuc·chi·ni (tsŏŏ·kē′nē, *Ital.* dzōōk·kē′nē) *n.* A type of green summer squash (evolved from *Cucurbita pepo*) of a small cylindrical shape. Also called *Italian squash.* [< Ital., pl. of *zucchino*, dim. of *zucca* a gourd, squash]

Zug (tsŏŏkh) **1** The smallest canton of Switzerland; 92 square miles. **2** Its capital, a town on the Lake of Zug (15 square miles; about 9 miles long), in the north central part of the country. *French* **Zoug** (zōōg).

Zug·spit·ze (tsŏŏk′shpit·sə) The highest mountain in Germany, in the Bavarian Alps on the Austrian border; 9,722 feet.

Zu·lu (zōō′lōō) *n. pl.* **Zu·lus** or **Zu·lu 1** One of a Bantu nation of Natal, South Africa, sometimes included with the Kaffirs. **2** The language of the Zulus, belonging to the Bantu family of agglutinative languages. —*adj.* Of, pertaining to, or characteristic of the Zulus or their language.

Zu·lu·land (zōō′lōō·land′) A district of NE Natal, Union of South Africa, formerly a native kingdom; 10,362 square miles.

zum Bei·spiel (tsŏŏm bī′shpēl) *German* For example: abbreviated *z.B.*

Zu·ñi (zōō′nyē) *n.* **1** One of a tribe of North American Indians of pueblo culture but comprising a distinct linguistic stock; still occupying the big Zuñi pueblo in New Mexico, which is now a reservation. **2** The language of this tribe. —**Zu′ñi·an** *adj. & n.*

Zur·ba·rán (thōōr′bä·rän′), **Francisco de,** 1598–1662, Spanish painter.

Zu·rich (zŏŏr′ik) **1** A canton of NE Switzerland on the border of Baden-Württemberg, West Germany; 667 square miles. **2** Its capital, a city on the northern shore of the Lake of Zurich (35 square miles; 25 miles long) in NE Switzerland. *German* **Zü·rich** (tsü′rikh).

Zuy·der Zee (zī′dər zē, *Du.* zœi′dər zä) A former shallow inlet of the North Sea in NW Netherlands; 80 by 34 miles; enclosed by a dike; drainage projects have reclaimed much of the land and formed Lake Ijssel. Also **Zui'.der Zee.**

Zweig (tsvīg, tsvīkh), **Arnold,** 1887–1968, German novelist. — **Stefan,** 1881–1942, Austrian dramatist and novelist.

Zwick·au (tsvik'ou) A city in the former state of Saxony, central southern East Germany.

zwie·back (zwī'bak, zwē'-, swī'-, swē'-, -bäk; Ger. tsvē'bäk) *n.* A biscuit of wheaten bread or rusk baked yellow in the loaf and later sliced and toasted. [<G, twice baked < *zwie*twice (< *zwei* two) + *backen* bake]

Zwing·li (tsving'lē), **Ulrich,** 1484–1531, Swiss Protestant reformer. Also *Huldreich Zwingli.*

Zwing·li·an (zwing'lē·ən, tsving'-) *adj.* Of or pertaining to the doctrines taught by Zwingli, especially to the doctrine that the Eucharist is simply a memorial or a symbolic commemoration of the death of Christ. — *n.* A follower of Zwingli. — **Zwing'li·an·ism** *n.*

zwit·ter·i·on (tsvit'ər·ī'ən) *n. Physics* An ion which carries both a negative and a positive charge, as in certain amino acids. [<G *zwitter* hybrid, hermaphrodite, mongrel + ION] — **zwit'ter·i·on'ic** (-ī·on'ik) *adj.*

Zwol·le (zvôl'ə) The capital of Overijssel province, north central Netherlands; a manufacturing and dairy center; site of many 15th century buildings.

Zwor·y·kin (zwôr'i·kin), **Vladimir Kosma,** born 1889, U.S. research engineer in electronics; born in Russia.

zyg·a·poph·y·sis (zig'ə·pof'ə·sis) *n. pl.* **·ses** (-sēz) *Anat.* One of the processes, usually disposed in pairs, by which a vertebra articulates with another; an articular process. [<NL <Gk. *zygon* a yoke + *apophysis* a branch. See APOPHYSIS.] — **zyg'a·po·phys'e·al** (-pō·fiz'ē·əl) or **·i·al** *adj.*

zygo– *combining form* Yoke; pair; resembling a yoke, especially in shape: *zygospore.* Also, before vowels, **zyg–.** [<Gk. *zygon* a yoke]

zy·go·dac·tyl (zī'gō·dak'til) *Zool. adj.* Having paired toes, one pair directed forward and the other pair backward, as in parrots and woodpeckers. — *n.* A zygodactyl bird. [<ZYGO- + Gk. *daktylos* a finger]

zy·go·ma (zī·gō'mə) *n. pl.* **·ma·ta** (-mə·tə) *Anat.* **1** The long arch that joins the temporal and malar bones on the side of the skull. **2** The zygomatic bone. **3** The zygomatic process. [<NL <Gk. *zygōma* < *zygon* a yoke] — **zy·go·mat·ic** (zī'gō·mat'ik) *adj.*

zygomatic arch *Anat.* The zygoma.

zygomatic bone *Anat.* The malar bone or cheek bone.

zygomatic process *Anat.* That process of the temporal bone which helps to form the zygomatic arch.

zy·go·mor·phic (zī'gō·môr'fik) *adj. Biol.* Bilaterally symmetrical: said of organisms or parts of organisms divisible into similar halves in only one plane. Also **zy'go·mor'.phous.** [<ZYGO- + -MORPHIC] — **zy'go·mor'.phism** *n.*

zy·go·phyl·la·ceous (zī'gō·fi·lā'shəs) *adj. Bot.* Designating or pertaining to a family *(Zygophyllaceae)* of herbs and shrubs, the caltrop family, having jointed branches, two-foliolate or pinnate stipulate leaves, and axillary white, red, or yellow flowers: mainly tropical in distribution. [<NL <Gk. *zygon* a yoke + *phyllon* a leaf]

zy·go·phyte (zī'gō·fīt) *n. Bot.* A plant in which reproduction is by means of zygospores. [< ZYGO- + -PHYTE]

zy·go·sis (zī·gō'sis) *n. Biol.* The union of gametes or cells; conjugation. [<NL <Gk. *zygōsis* a joining < *zygon* a yoke]

zy·go·spore (zī'gō·spôr, -spōr) *n. Bot.* A spore formed by the conjugation of two similar gametes, as in algae and fungi. Also **zy'go·sperm** (-spûrm). [<ZYGO- + SPORE]

zy·gote (zī'gōt, zig'ōt) *n. Biol.* **1** The product of the union of two gametes. **2** An individual developed from such a union. [<Gk. *zygōtos* yoked < *zygoein* yoke < *zygon* a yoke] — **zy·got·ic** (zī·got'ik) *adj.*

zy·mase (zī'mās) *n. Biochem.* An enzyme, obtained principally from yeast, which induces fermentation by breaking down glucose and related carbohydrates into alcohol and carbon dioxide. [<F <Gk. *zymē* leaven]

zyme (zīm) *n.* **1** A ferment. **2** A disease germ or virus supposed to be the specific cause of a zymotic disease. [<Gk. *zymē* leaven]

zy·mic (zī'mik) *adj.* Relating to or produced by fermentation.

zymo– *combining form* Fermentation; of or related to fermentation: *zymology.* Also, before vowels, **zym–.** [<Gk. *zymē* leaven]

zy·mo·gen (zī'mə·jən) *n.* **1** *Biochem.* A substance that develops into an enzyme when suitably activated, as in the stomach or pancreas. **2** *Biol.* A bacterial organism which produces enzymes or fermentation. Compare PATHOGEN. Also **zy'mo·gene** (-jēn). [<ZYMO- + -GEN]

zy·mo·gen·e·sis (zī'mō·jen'ə·sis) *n. Biochem.* The transformation of a zymogen into an enzyme.

zy·mo·gen·ic (zī'mō·jen'ik) *adj.* **1** Of, pertaining to, or relating to zymogen. **2** Capable of producing a ferment, as yeast. Also **zy·mog·e·nous** (zī·moj'ə·nəs).

zymogenic organism Any micro–organism which causes fermentation, as yeast.

zy·mol·o·gy (zī·mol'ə·jē) *n.* The study of the principles of fermentation and the action of enzymes. [<ZYMO- + -LOGY] — **zy·mo·log·ic** (zī'mə·loj'ik) or **·i·cal** *adj.* — **zy·mol'o·gist** *n.*

zy·mol·y·sis (zī·mol'ə·sis) *n.* Fermentation or the action of enzymes. [<ZYMO- + -LYSIS] — **zy·mo·lyt·ic** (zī'mə·lit'ik) *adj.*

zy·mom·e·ter (zī·mom'ə·tər) *n.* An instrument for measuring the degree of fermentation. [<ZYMO- + -METER]

zy·mo·sis (zī·mō'sis) *n.* **1** Any form of fermentation. **2** *Med.* **a** A fermentation giving rise to a morbid or diseased condition, as by the action of bacteria. **b** Any contagious or infectious disease produced by morbific fermentation; a zymotic disease. [<NL <Gk. *zymōsis* < *zymoein* leaven, ferment < *zymē* leaven]

zy·mot·ic (zī·mot'ik) *adj.* Relating to or produced by or from fermentation, as certain epidemic or contagious diseases. [<Gk. *zymōtikos* < *zymoein.* See ZYMOSIS.]

zy·mur·gy (zī'mûr·jē) *n.* A branch of chemistry treating of processes in which fermentation is the principal feature, as brewing, making of yeast, and winemaking. [<ZYM(O)- + -URGY]

Zy·ri·an Autonomous Region (zir'ē·ən) A former name for the KOMI AUTONOMOUS S.S.R.

Zyr·ya·nevsk A city of NE Kazakhstan near the Russian border.

THESAURUS

A

abandon, v. SYN.-abdicate, abjure, relinquish, renounce, resign, surrender, vacate, waive; desert, forsake, leave, quit. ANT.-defend, maintain, uphold; stay, support.

abase, v. SYN.-debase, degrade, demote, humble, lower.

abate, v. SYN.-assuage, decrease, diminish, lessen, lower, moderate, reduce, suppress. ANT.-amplify, enlarge, increase, intensify, revive.

abbey, n. SYN.-cloister, convent, hermitage, monastery, nunnery, priory.

abbreviate, v. SYN.-abridge, condense, contract, curtail, diminish, lessen, limit, reduce, restrict. ANT.-elongate, extend, lengthen.

abbreviation, n. SYN.-abridgement, contraction, reduction, shortening. ANT.-amplification, enlargement, expansion, extension.

abdicate, v. SYN.-abandon, abjure, relinquish, renounce, resign, surrender, vacate, waive; desert, forsake, leave, quit. ANT.-defend, maintain, uphold; stay, support.

aberrant, a. SYN.-abnormal, capricious, devious, eccentric, irregular, unnatural, unusual, variable. ANT.-fixed, methodical, ordinary, regular, usual.

abet, v. SYN.-aid, assist, encourage, help, incite. ANT.-discourage, hinder, oppose, resist.

abhor, v. SYN.-abominate, despise, detest, dislike, hate, loathe. ANT.-admire, approve, cherish, like, love.

abhorrence, n. SYN.-antipathy, aversion, disgust, disinclination, dislike, distaste, dread, hatred, loathing, repugnance, repulsion, reluctance animosity, detestation, enmity, hostility, ill will, malevolence, rancor. ANT.-affection, attachment, devotion, enthusiasm attraction, friendship, love.

abide, v. SYN.-continue, dwell, endure, live, remain, room, wait, withstand.

ability, n. SYN.-aptitude, aptness, capability, capacity, dexterity, efficiency, faculty, power, qualification, skill, talent. ANT.-disability, incapacity, incompetence, unreadiness.

abject, a. SYN.-contemptible, debased, despicable, disheartening, groveling, ignoble, low, mean, vile, worthless, wretched. ANT.-attractive, decent, laudable; upright.

able, a. SYN.-apt, agile, adept, capable, clever, competent, efficient, experienced, fitted, gifted, qualified, skillful, versatile. ANT.-inadequate, incapable, incompetent, unfitted.

ablution, n. SYN.-bath, cleansing, washing; ceremony, rite.

abnormal, a. SYN.-aberrant, capricious, devious, eccentric, irregular, unnatural, unusual, variable. ANT.-fixed, methodical, ordinary, regular, usual.

abode, n. SYN.-dwelling, home, house.

abolish, v. SYN.-destroy, end, eradicate,

obliterate, overthrow; abrogate, annul, cancel, invalidate, revoke. ANT.-continue, establish, promote, restore, sustain.

abominable, a. SYN.-detestable, execrable, foul, hateful, loathsome, odious, revolting, vile. ANT.-agreeable, commendable, delightful, pleasant.

aboriginal, a. SYN.-ancient, antiquated, early, old, primary, primeval, primitive primordial, pristine. ANT.-civilized, late, modern, modish, sophisticated.

abound, v. SYN.-copious, full, overflow, rich, plenty, plentiful, teem.

above, a. SYN.-aloft, beyond, higher, over, overhead, raised, superior. ANT.-low, below, beneath, under.

abrade, v. SYN.-rub, scrape, wear.

abridge, v. SYN.-abbreviate, condense, contract, curtail, diminish, lessen, limit, reduce, restrict shorten. ANT.-elongate, extend, lengthen.

abridgement, n. SYN.-abbreviation, contraction, reduction, shortening. ANT.-amplification, enlargement, expansion, extension.

abrogate, v. SYN.-cancel, cross out, delete, eliminate, erase, expunge, obliterate; abolish, annul, invalidate.

abrupt, a. SYN.-hasty, precipitate, sudden, unannounced, unexpected; blunt, brusque, curt, rude; craggy, harsh, precipitous, rough, rugged, sharp, steep. ANT.-anticipated, expected; courteous, gradual, smooth.

absent, a. SYN.-abroad, away, departed; absent-minded, abstracted, distracted, inattentive, preoccupied. ANT.-attending, present; attentive, watchful.

absolute, a. SYN.-actual, complete, entire, perfect, pure, ultimate, unconditional, unqualified, unrestricted; arbitrary, authoritative, despotic, tyrannous. ANT.-accountable, conditional, contingent, dependent, qualified.

absolve, v. SYN.-acquit, clear, condone, excuse, forgive, overlook, pardon, release, remit. ANT.-accuse, chastise, condemn, convict, punish.

absorb, v. SYN.-assimilate, consume, digest, engulf, imbibe, swallow up; engage, engross, occupy. ANT.-discharge, dispense, emit, expel, exude.

abstain, v. SYN.-avoid, decline, desist, fast, forbear, forgo, refrain, renounce, shun, withhold. ANT.-continue, indulge, persist.

abstention, n. See **abstinence.**

abstinence, n. SYN.-abstention, continence, denial, fasting, forbearance, moderation, self-denial, sobriety, temperance. ANT.-excess, gluttony, greed, intoxication, self-indulgence.

abstract, v. SYN.-draw from, part, remove, separate, appropriate, purloin, steal; abridge, summarize; ideal, intellectual. ANT.-add, replace, restore, return, unite.

absurd, a. SYN.-foolish, inconsistent, irrational, nonsensical, preposterous, ridiculous, self-contradictory, silly, un-

reasonable. ANT.-consistent, rational, reasonable, sensible, sound.

abundance, n. SYN.-affluence, bounty, overflowing, plenty, profusion, wealth. ANT.-lack, need, want.

abundant, a. SYN.-ample, bountiful, copious, overflowing, plenteous, plentiful, profuse, rich, teeming. ANT.-deficient, insufficient, scant, scarce.

abuse, n. SYN.-aspersion, defamation, desecration, dishonor, disparagement, insult, invective, maltreatment, misuse, outrage, perversion, profanation, reproach, reviling, upbraiding. ANT.-approval, commendation, laudation, plaudit, respect.

abuse, v. SYN.-asperse, defame, disparage, ill-use, malign, revile, scandalize, traduce, vilify; misapply, misemploy, misuse. ANT.-cherish, honor, praise, protect, respect.

academic, a. SYN.-bookish, erudite, formal, learned, pedantic, scholarly, scholastic, theoretical. ANT.-commonsense, ignorant, practical, simple.

accede, v. SYN.-accord, allow, concede, grant, permit; abdicate, acquiesce, capitulate, cede, quit, relent, relinquish, resign, submit, succumb, surrender, waive, yield. ANT.-deny, dissent, oppose, refuse; assert, resist, strive, struggle.

accelerate, v. SYN.-dispatch, expedite, facilitate, forward, hasten, hurry, push, quicken, rush, speed. ANT.-block, hinder, impede, retard, slow.

accent, n. SYN.-beat, emphasis, inflection, intonation.

accept, v. SYN.-acknowledge, admit, agree, allow, assent, concede, confess, get, grant, permit, receive, take, welcome. ANT.-bestow, deny, dismiss, give, impart, reject, discharge, shun, turn away.

acceptable, a. SYN.-agreeable, amiable, charming, gratifying, pleasant, pleasing, pleasurable, suitable, welcome. ANT.-disagreeable, obnoxious, offensive, unpleasant.

access n. SYN.-accessibility, admission, admittance; approach, entrance, passage, path.

accessible, a. SYN.-available handy, obtainable, prepared, ready, usable. ANT.-inaccessible, unavoidable.

accessory, n. SYN.-abettor, accomplice, ally, assistant, associate, confederate. ANT.-adversary, enemy, opponent, rival.

accident, n. SYN.-calamity, casualty, contingency, disaster, fortuity, misfortune, mishap. ANT.-calculation, design, intention, purpose.

accidental, a. SYN.-casual, chance, contingent, fortuitous, incidental, undesigned, unintended. ANT.-calculated, decreed, intended, planned, willed.

acclaim, v. SYN.-applaud, approve, cheer, hail.

accommodate, v. SYN.-adapt, adjust, aid, assist, benefit, conform, fit, gratify, help, serve, suit. ANT.-disturb, misapply, misfit.

accompany, v. SYN.-associate with, attend, chaperone, consort with, convoy, escort, go with. ANT.-abandon, avoid, desert, leave, quit.

accomplice, n. SYN.-abettor, accessory, ally, assistant, associate, confederate. ANT.-adversary, enemy, opponent, rival.

accomplish, v. SYN.-achieve, attain, complete, consummate, do, effect, execute, finish, fulfill, perfect, perform. ANT.-block, defeat, fail, frustrate, spoil.

accord, v. SYN.-agree, grant, harmonize.

accordance, n. SYN.-agreement, coincidence, concord, concurrence, harmony, understanding, unison, bargain, compact, contract, covenant, pact, stipulation. ANT.-difference, disagreement, discord, dissension, variance.

account, n. SYN.-chronicle, description, detail, history, narration, narrative, recital, relation; computation, reckoning, record. ANT.-caricature, confusion, distortion, misrepresentation.

account, v. SYN.-believe, chronicle, consider, deem, esteem, estimate, hold, judge, rate, reckon, regard, think, view; elucidate, explain, expound.

accountability, n. SYN.-amenability, liability, obligation, responsibility, trustworthiness; duty, trust.

accountable, a. SYN.-amenable, answerable, exposed to, liable, reliable, responsible, trustworthy, subject to. ANT.-exempt, careless, negligent, free, immune, independent, irresponsible.

accumulate, v. SYN.-accrue, amass, collect, gather, heap, hoard, increase, store. ANT.-diminish, disperse, dissipate, scatter, waste.

accuracy, n. SYN.-constancy, exactness, fidelity, precision. ANT.-carelessness, imprecision.

accurate, a. SYN.-correct, definite, distinct, exact, faultless, impeccable, precise, proper, right, strict. ANT.-careless, erroneous, false, faulty, untrue, wrong.

accusation, n. SYN.-arraignment, charge, imputation, incrimination, indictment. ANT.-exculpation, exoneration, pardon.

accuse, v. SYN.-arraign, censure, charge, incriminate, indict. ANT.-absolve, acquit, exonerate, release, vindicate.

accustom, v. SYN.-acclimate, familiarize, inure, train. ANT.-ignore, neglect, overlook.

accustomed, a. SYN.-customary, habitual, usual.

ache, n. SYN.-pang, pain, paroxysm, throe, twinge; agony, anguish, distress, grief, suffering. ANT.-comfort, ease, relief, happiness, pleasure. solace.

achieve, v. SYN.-accomplish, acquire, do, effect, execute, gain, obtain, realize, win. ANT.-fail, fall short, lose, miss.

achievement, n. SYN.-deed, exploit, feat, accomplishment, attainment, completion, performance, realization. ANT.-neglect, omission; defeat, failure.

acid, a. SYN.-biting, sharp, sour, tart.

acknowledge, v. SYN.-accept, admit, agree, allow, assent, avow, certify, concede, confess, grant, identify, own, permit, recognize, welcome. ANT.-deny, dismiss, reject, shun.

acquaintance, n. SYN.-cognizance, companionship, familiarity, fellowship, friendship, intimacy, knowledge. ANT.-ignorance, inexperience, unfamiliarity.

acquiesce, v. SYN.-allow, concede, grant, permit; abdicate, accede, acquiesce, capitulate, cede, quit, relent, relinquish, resign, submit, succumb, surrender, waive, yield. ANT.-deny, dissent, oppose, refuse; assert, resist, strive, struggle.

acquire, v. SYN.-assimilate, attain, earn, gain, get, obtain, procure, secure, win. ANT.-forego, forfeit, lose, miss, surrender.

acquisition, n. SYN.-award, donation, earnings, fortune, gain, gift, income, purchase, proceeds, profit, riches, salary, wages.

acquit, v. SYN.-absolve, condone, excuse, forgive, overlook, pardon, repay, release, remit, return. ANT.-accuse, chastise, condemn, convict, punish.

acquittal, n. SYN.-absolution, amnesty, pardon, forgiveness, remission. ANT.-conviction, penalty, punishment, sentence.

acrid, a. SYN.-biting, bitter, caustic, distasteful, galling, grievous, harsh, painful, poignant, pungent, sardonic, severe, sharp, sour, tart. ANT.-bland, delicious, gentle, mellow, pleasant, sweet.

act, n. SYN.-accomplishment, action, deed, doing, execution, feat, operation, performance, transaction; decree, edict, law, statute. ANT.-cessation, deliberation, inactivity, inhibition, intention.

act, v. SYN.-affect, assume, bear, behave, carry, comport, conduct, demean, deport, feign, interact, manage, operate, pretend, profess, sham, simulate.

action, n. SYN.-achievement, activity, deed, exercise, exploit, feat, motion, movement, performance, play, procedure. ANT.-idleness, inactivity, inertia, repose, rest.

activate, v. SYN.-begin, initiate, stimulate.

active, a. SYN.-operative, working; busy, industrious; agile, alert, brisk, lively, nimble, quick, sprightly, supple. ANT.-dormant, inactive; indolent, lazy, passive.

activity, n. SYN.-action, agility, briskness, energy, enterprise, exercise, intensity, liveliness, motion, movement, quickness, rapidity, vigor. ANT.-dullness, idleness, inactivity, inertia, sloth.

actor, n. SYN.-character, entertainer, ham, mime, mimic, performer, player, tragedian.

actual, a. SYN.-authentic, certain, genuine, positive, real, substantial, true, veritable. ANT.-apparent, fictitious, imaginary, supposed, unreal.

actuate, v. SYN.-agitate, drive, impel, induce, instigate, move, persuade, propel, push, shift, stir. ANT.-deter. halt, rest, stay, stop.

acute, a. SYN.-intense, keen, penetrating, poignant, sharp, shrill; crucial, decisive, important, sensitive, vital.

adamant, a. SYN.-firm, hard, immovable, insistent, positive, unyielding.

adage, n. SYN.-aphorism, apothegm, by-word, maxim, motto, proverb, saw, saying.

adapt, v. SYN.-accommodate, adjust, conform, fit, suit. ANT.-disturb, misapply, misfit.

add, v. SYN.-adjoin, affix, append, attach, augment, increase, sum, total. ANT.-deduct, detach, reduce, remove, subtract.

addiction, n. SYN.-fixation, inclination, obsession.

address, v. SYN.-accost, approach, greet, hail, speak to. ANT.-avoid, pass by.

adept, a. SYN.-able, accomplished, clever, competent, cunning, expert, ingenious, practiced, proficient, skilled, skillful, versed. ANT.-awkward, bungling, clumsy, inexpert, untrained.

adequate, a. SYN.-ample, capable, commensurate, enough, fitting, satisfactory, sufficient, suitable. ANT.-deficient, lacking, scant.

adherent, n. SYN.-devotee, disciple, follower, supporter, votary; learner, pupil, scholar, student.

adjacent, a. SYN.-abutting, adjoining, adjunct, bordering, close, contiguous, immediate, impending, near, nearby, neighboring, tangent, touching. ANT.-afar, distant, faraway, removed.

adjoin, v. SYN.-abut, append, border, connect, join, unite. ANT.-divide, separate.

adjourn, v. SYN.-defer, delay, move, postpone, suspend. ANT.-continue, expedite, hasten.

adjunct, n. SYN.-accessory, assistant, helper, modifier. ANT.-thing, primary, principal.

adjust, v. SYN.-accommodate, adapt, arrange, conform, fit, harmonize, modify, refashion, suit. ANT.-disturb, misapply, misfit.

adjutant, n. SYN.-aide, assistant.

administer, v. SYN.-direct, manage, supervise; apply, dispense, dole, give, minister, tender, treat.

administration, n. SYN.-government, management, supervision; directors, executives, officers, supervisors.

admirable, a. SYN.-eminent, fair, honest, honorable, noble, respectable, true, trusty, upright, virtuous; creditable, esteemed, proper, reputable. ANT.-disgraceful, ignominious, infamous, shameful.

admire, v. SYN.-adore, appreciate, approve, esteem, regard, respect, revere, venerate, wonder. ANT.-abhor, despise, dislike.

admissible, a. SYN.-allowable, fair, justifiable, permissible, probable, tolerable, warranted. ANT.-inadmissible, irrelevant, unsuitable.

admit, v. SYN.-accept, acknowledge, agree, allow, assent, concede, confess, grant, permit, welcome. ANT.-deny, dismiss, reject, shun.

admonition, n. SYN.-advice, caution, counsel, exhortation, instruction, recommendation, suggestion, warning; information, intelligence, notification.

adopt, v. SYN.-accept, appropriate, assume, choose, espouse, select, take.

adore, v. SYN.-esteem, honor, love, respect, revere, venerate, worship. ANT.-

despise, hate, ignore.

adorn, v. SYN.-beautify, bedeck, decorate, embellish, garnish, gild, ornament, trim. ANT.-deface, deform, disfigure, mar, spoil.

adroit, a. SYN.-apt, clever, dexterous, quick, quick-witted, skillful, talented, witty; bright, ingenious, sharp, smart. ANT.-awkward, bungling, clumsy, slow, unskilled; dull, foolish, stupid.

adult, a. SYN.-developed, grown, mature.

adulterate, v. SYN.-abase, alloy, corrupt, debase, defile, degrade, deprave, depress, humiliate, impair, lower, pervert, vitiate. ANT.-enhance, improve, raise, restore, vitalize.

advance, v. SYN.-aggrandize, elevate, forward, further, promote, adduce, allege, assign, bring forward, offer, propose, propound, improve, proceed, progress, rise, thrive, augment, enlarge, increase. ANT.-hinder, oppose, retard, retreat, withhold.

advantage, n. SYN.-edge, mastery, superiority; benefit, good, profit, service, utility. ANT.-detriment, handicap, harm, impediment, obstruction.

advantageous, a. SYN.-beneficial, good, helpful, profitable, salutary, serviceable, useful, wholesome. ANT.-deleterious, destructive, detrimental, harmful, injurious.

adventure, n. SYN.-experience, happening, story, tale.

adventurous, a. SYN.-bold, chivalrous, daring, enterprising, foolhardy, precipitate, rash. ANT.-cautious, hesitating, timid.

adversary, n. SYN.-antagonist, competitor, enemy, foe, opponent, rival. ANT.-accomplice, ally, comrade, confederate, friend, teammate.

adverse, a. SYN.-antagonistic, contrary, hostile, opposed, opposite; counteractive, disastrous, unfavorable, unlucky. ANT.-benign, favorable, fortunate, lucky, propitious.

adversity, n. SYN.-accident, affliction, calamity, catastrophe, disaster, distress, hardship, misfortune, mishap, ruin. ANT.-blessing, comfort, prosperity, success.

advertise, v. SYN.-announce, communicate, declare, display, exhibit, proclaim, publicize.

advertisement, n. SYN.-announcement, bulletin, declaration, notification, promulgation. ANT.-hush, muteness, silence, speechlessness.

advice, n. SYN.-admonition, caution, counsel, exhortation, guidance, instruction, recommendation, suggestion, warning; information, intelligence, notification.

advise, v. SYN.-acquaint, apprise, enlighten, impart, inform, instruct, notify, recommend, teach, tell, warn. ANT.-conceal, delude, distract, mislead.

aesthetic, a. SYN.-appreciative, creative, inventive, spiritual.

affable, a. SYN.-affable, civil, communicative, friendly, gregarious, hospitable, outgoing, sociable, social. ANT.-antisocial, disagreeable, hermitic, inhospitable.

affair, n. SYN.-concern, duty, interest, matter, obligation, pursuit, responsibility.

affect, v. SYN.-alter, change, influence, modify, transform; concern, interest, regard; impress, melt, move, soften, subdue, touch; adopt, assume, feign, pretend.

affected, a. SYN.-artificial, ceremonious, dramatic, histrionic, melodramatic, showy, stagy, theatrical. ANT.-modest, subdued, unaffected, unemotional.

affection, n. SYN.-attachment, endearment, fondness, kindness, love, tenderness; disposition, emotion, feeling, inclination. ANT.-aversion, hatred, indifference, repugnance, repulsion.

affidavit, n. SYN.-affirmation, testimony, statement.

affiliate, v. SYN.-ally, associate, combine, conjoin, connect, join, link, mingle, mix. ANT.-disrupt, divide, estrange, separate.

affinity, n. SYN.-attraction, closeness, fondness, liking.

affirm, v. SYN.-assert, aver, declare, maintain, protest, state, swear. ANT.-contradict, demur, deny, dispute, oppose.

affix, v. SYN.-adjoin, administer, allot, annex, append, apply, appropriate, assign, attach, avail, connect, devote, direct, employ, use; bear, pertain, refer, relate; appeal, petition, request, join, stick, unite; associate, attribute. ANT.-detach, disengage, separate, unfasten, untie.

afflict, v. SYN.-burden, encumber, load, oppress, overload, tax, trouble, weigh. ANT.-alleviate, console, ease, lighten, mitigate.

affluence, n. SYN.-abundance, fortune, luxury, money, opulence, plenty, possessions, riches, wealth. ANT.-indigence, need, poverty, want.

affluent, a. SYN.-abundant, ample, bountiful, copious, costly, luxurious, opulent, plentiful, prosperous, rich, sumptuous, wealthy, well-to-do. ANT.-beggarly, destitute, indigent, needy, poor.

affront, n. SYN.-abuse, defiance, indignity, insolence, insult, offense. ANT.-apology, homage, salutation.

afraid, a. SYN.-apprehensive, fainthearted, fearful, frightened, scared, timid, timorous. ANT.-assured, bold, composed, courageous, sanguine.

afterward, a. SYN.-after, eventually, later, subsequently, ultimately.

against, a. SYN.-adverse, facing, opposed, toward, versus.

age, n. SYN.-adolescence, adulthood, dotage, senescence, senility, seniority, youth; antiquity, date, duration, epoch, era, generation, period, span, time. ANT.-childhood, infancy, youth.

agency, n. SYN.-bureau, company, firm, office, representative.

agent, n. SYN.-apparatus, channel, device, instrument, means, medium, tool, utensil, vehicle. ANT.-hindrance, impediment, obstruction, preventive.

aggravate, v. SYN.-heighten, increase, intensify, magnify; annoy, chafe, embitter, exasperate, inflame, irritate, nettle, provoke, vex. ANT.-appease, mitigate, palliate soften, soothe.

aggregate, n. SYN.-amount, collection, conglomeration, entirety, sum, total, whole. ANT.-element, ingredient, part, particular, unit.

aggression, n. SYN.-assault, attack, battle, incursion, invasion, offensive, raid, threat, war.

agile, a. SYN.-active, alert, brisk, deft, flexible, lively, nimble, quick, spirited, sprightly, spry, supple. ANT.-awkward, clumsy, heavy, inert, slow, sluggish.

agitate, v. SYN.-arouse, disconcert, disturb, excite, jar, perturb, rouse, ruffle, shake, trouble. ANT.-calm, ease, placate, quiet.

agitated, a. SYN.-disquieted, disturbed, irresolute, restless, sleepless, uneasy, unquiet; active, roving, transient, wandering. ANT.-at ease, peaceable, quiet, tractable.

agony, n. SYN.-ache, anguish, distress, misery, pain, suffering, throe, torment, torture, woe. ANT.-comfort, ease, mitigation, relief.

agree, v. SYN.-accede, acquiesce, assent, comply, consent; coincide, concur, conform, tally. ANT.-contradict, differ, disagree, dissent, protest.

agreeable, a. SYN.-acceptable, amiable, charming, gratifying, pleasant, pleasing, pleasurable, suitable, welcome. ANT.-disagreeable, obnoxious, offensive, unpleasant.

agreement, n. SYN.-accordance, coincidence, concord, concurrence, harmony, understanding, unison; bargain, compact, contract, covenant, pact, stipulation. ANT.-difference, disagreement, discord, dissension, variance.

agriculture, n. SYN.-agronomy, cultivation, farming, gardening, horticulture, husbandry, tillage.

ahead, a. SYN.-before, first, leading, preceding.

aid, n. SYN.-alms, assistance, backing, comfort, furtherance, help, patronage, relief, succor, support. ANT.-antagonism, counteraction, defiance, hostility, resistance.

aid, v. SYN.-abet, back, further, help, promote, serve, support, sustain, assist, succor, uphold; facilitate, mitigate, relieve, remedy. ANT.-hamper, hinder, impede, prevent resist, thwart; afflict.

ailment, n. SYN.-complaint, disease, disorder, illness, infirmity, malady, sickness. ANT.-health, healthiness, soundness, vigor.

aim, n. SYN.-ambition, aspiration, design, emulation, end, goal, incentive, intent, intention, object, objective, purpose. ANT.-accident, contentment, indifference, indolence, resignation, satisfaction.

aim, v. SYN.-level, point, train; conduct, direct, govern, guide, manage, regulate, rule; bid, command, instruct, order. ANT.-deceive, distract, misdirect, misguide.

aimless, a. SYN.-blind, careless, capricious, drifting, erratic, pointless, purposeless, rambling, unplanned, unpredictable, wandering. ANT.-considered, directed, purposeful, planned.

air, *n.* SYN.-atmosphere, breeze, draft, oxygen, ventilation, wind.

air, *v.* SYN.-cool, freshen, open, ventilate; broadcast, disclose, expose, reveal.

aisle, *n.* SYN.-corridor, course, opening, passage, passageway, path, walk, way.

ajar, *a.* SYN.-agape, unclosed, uncovered, unlocked, unobstructed, available, open, accessible, exposed, public, unrestricted.

alarm, *n.* SYN.-affright, apprehension, consternation, dismay, fear, fright, signal, terror, warning. ANT.-calm, composure, quiet, security, tranquillity.

alarm, *v.* SYN.-affright, appall, astound, daunt, dismay, frighten, horrify, intimidate, scare, startle, terrify, terrorize. ANT.-allay, compose, embolden, reassure, soothe.

alert, *a.* SYN.-alert, anxious, attentive, careful, cautious, circumspect, observant, vigilant, wakeful, wary, watchful. ANT.-careless, inattentive, lax, neglectful, oblivious.

alibi, *n.* SYN.-assertion, defense, excuse, explanation, reply.

alien, *a.* SYN.-adverse, contrasted, exotic, extraneous, foreign, irrelevant, remote, strange, unconnected. ANT.-akin, germane, kindred, relevant.

alienate, *v.* SYN.-divide, estrange, separate, withdraw.

alike, *a.* SYN.-akin, allied, analogous, comparable, correlative, correspondent, corresponding, like, parallel, similar. ANT.-different, dissimilar, divergent, incongruous, opposed.

alive, *a.* SYN.-animate, breathing, conscious, existing, growing, living, mortal. ANT.-dead, inanimate, lifeless.

all, *n.* SYN.-collection, ensemble, entire, everyone, everything, group, total. ANT.-nobody, none, nothing.

allege, *v.* SYN.-advance, affirm, assign, cite, claim, declare, maintain. ANT.-contradict, deny, disprove, gainsay, refute.

allegiance, *n.* SYN.-constancy, devotion, faithfulness, fealty, fidelity. ANT.-disloyalty, falseness, perfidy, treachery.

alleviate, *v.* SYN.-abate, allay, assuage, diminish, extenuate, mitigate, relieve, soften, solace, soothe. ANT.-aggravate, agitate, augment, increase, irritate.

alliance, *n.* SYN.-association, coalition, combination, confederacy, entente, federation, league, partnership, union; compact, covenant, marriage, treaty. ANT.-divorce, schism, separation.

allocate, *v.* See **allot.**

allot, *v.* SYN.-apportion, deal, dispense, distribute, divide, mete; allocate, appropriate, assign, give, grant, measure. ANT.-confiscate, keep, refuse, retain, withhold.

allotment, *n.* SYN.-apportionment, division, fragment, moiety, part, piece, portion, scrap, section, segment, share. ANT.-entirety, whole.

allow, *v.* SYN.-let, permit, sanction, suffer, tolerate; authorize, give, grant, yield; acknowledge, admit, concede. ANT.-forbid, object, protest, refuse, resist.

allowable, *a.* SYN.-admissible, fair, justifiable, permissible, probable, tolerable, warranted. ANT.-inadmissible, irrelevant, unsuitable.

allowance, *n.* SYN.-alimony, annuity, bequest, commission, gift, grant, legacy, pay, stipend, subsidy, wages.

allude, *v.* SYN.-advert, hint, imply, insinuate, intimate, refer, suggest. ANT.-declare, demonstrate, specify, state.

alluring, *a.* SYN.-attractive, bewitching, captivating, charming, enchanting, engaging, fascinating, winning. ANT.-repugnant, repulsive, revolting.

alone, *a.* SYN.-abandoned, deserted, desolate, isolated, lonely, secluded, unaccompanied, unaided; lone, only, single, sole, solitary. ANT.-accompanied, attended, surrounded.

aloof, *a.* SYN.-distant, far, faraway, remote, removed; cold, reserved, stiff, unfriendly. ANT.-close, near, nigh; cordial, friendly.

also, *adv.* SYN.-besides, furthermore, in addition, likewise, moreover, similarly, too.

alter, *v.* SYN.-change, exchange, substitute; convert, modify, shift, transfigure, transform, vary, veer. ANT.-retain; continue, establish, preserve, settle, stabilize.

alteration, *n.* SYN.-change, modification, mutation, substitution, variation, variety, vicissitude. ANT.-monotony, stability, uniformity.

alternate, *n.* SYN.-agent, deputy, lieutenant, proxy, representative, substitute, understudy. ANT.-head, master, principal, sovereign.

alternative, *n.* SYN.-election, option, choice, preference, selection.

altitude, *n.* distance, elevation, height.

always, *adv.* SYN.-constantly, continually, eternally, ever, evermore, forever, incessantly, perpetually, unceasingly. ANT.-fitfully, never, occasionally, rarely, sometimes.

amass, *v.* SYN.-accumulate, assemble, gather, collect, congregate, convene, muster; cull, garner, glean, harvest, pick, reap; conclude, deduce, infer, judge. ANT.-disband, disperse, distribute, scatter, separate.

amateur, *n.* SYN.-apprentice, beginner, dabbler, dilettante, learner, neophyte, novice. ANT.-adept, authority, expert, master, professional.

amazement, *n.* SYN.-astonishment, awe, bewilderment, curiosity, surprise, wonder, wonderment. ANT.-triviality; apathy, expectation, indifference.

ambiguity, *n.* SYN.-distrust, doubt, hesitation, incredulity, scruple, skepticism, suspense, suspicion, unbelief, uncertainty. ANT.-belief, certainty, conviction, determination, faith.

ambiguous, *a.* SYN.-dubious, enigmatical, equivocal, obscure, uncertain, vague. ANT.-clear, explicit, obvious, plain, unequivocal.

ambition, *n.* SYN.-aspiration, eagerness, emulation, goal, incentive, pretension. ANT.-contentment, indifference, indolence, resignation, satisfaction.

ambush, *n.* SYN.-net, pitfall, ruse, snare,

stratagem, trap, trick, wile.

amend, *v.* SYN.-correct, mend, rectify, reform, right; admonish, discipline, punish. ANT.-aggravate, ignore, spoil; condone, indulge.

amiable, *a.* SYN.-agreeable, engaging, friendly, good-natured, gracious, pleasing. ANT.-churlish, disagreeable, hateful, ill-natured, surly.

amicable, *a.* SYN.-affable, companionable, friendly, genial, kindly, neighborly, sociable, social. ANT.-antagonistic, cool, distant, hostile, reserved.

amid, *prep.* See **among.**

among, *prep.* SYN.-amid, amidst, between, betwixt, mingled, mixed, within.

amount, *n.* SYN.-aggregate, number, product, quantity, sum, total, whole.

ample, *a.* SYN.-broad, extensive, great, large, spacious, wide; abundant, bountiful, copious, full, generous, liberal, plentiful, profuse, rich. ANT.-constricted, limited, small; insufficient, lacking, meager.

amplify, *v.* SYN.-accrue, augment, enhance, enlarge, expand, extend, grow, heighten, increase, intensify, magnify, multiply, raise, wax. ANT.-atrophy, contract, decrease, diminish, reduce.

amusement, *n.* SYN.-diversion, entertainment, fun, game, pastime, play, recreation, sport. ANT.-boredom, labor, toil, work.

analogous, *a.* SYN.-akin, alike, allied, comparable, correlative, correspondent, corresponding, like, parallel, similar. ANT.-different, dissimilar, divergent, incongruous, opposed.

analyze, *v.* SYN.-assess, audit, check, contemplate, dissect, examine, inquire, interrogate, notice, question, quiz, review, scan, scrutinize, survey, view, watch. ANT.-disregard, neglect, omit, overlook.

anarchy, *n.* SYN.-chaos, disorder, lawlessness, turmoil.

ancestry, *n.* SYN.-clan, folk, lineage, nation, people, race, stock, strain, tribe.

anchor, *n.* SYN.-ballast, mooring, protection, safeguard, security, tie.

ancient, *a.* SYN.-aged, antiquated, antique, archaic, obsolete, old, old-fashioned, venerable. ANT.-modern, new, young, youthful.

anecdote, *n.* SYN.-account, anecdote, chronicle, fable, fabrication, falsehood, fiction, history, narration, narrative, novel, report, story, tale, yarn.

angelic, *a.* SYN.-beautiful, devout, good, heavenly, lovely, pure, radiant, saintly. ANT.-bad, evil, ugly.

anger, *n.* SYN.-animosity, choler, exasperation, fury, indignation, ire, irritation, passion, petulance, rage, resentment, temper, wrath. ANT.-conciliation, forbearance, patience, peace, self-control.

angry, *a.* SYN.-enraged, exasperated, furious, incensed, indignant, irate, maddened, provoked, wrathful, wroth. ANT.-calm, happy, pleased, satisfied.

anguish, *n.* SYN.-agony, distress, grief, misery, suffering, torment, torture. ANT.-comfort, joy, relief, solace.

animosity, *n.* SYN.-bitterness, enmity,

grudge, hatred, hostility, malevolence, rancor, spite. ANT.-friendliness, good will, love.

angular, a. SYN.-bent, crooked, crotched, forked, jagged, rectangular, staggered, triangular, zig-zag.

animated, a. SYN.-active, alive, expressive, gay, lively, spirited.

animosity, n. SYN.-abhorrence, dislike, hatred.

annihilate, v. SYN.-demolish, destroy, devastate, eradicate, exterminate, extinguish, obliterate, ravage, raze, ruin, wreck. ANT.-construct, establish, make, preserve, save.

announce, v. SYN.-advertise, declare, give out, herald, make known, notify, proclaim, promulgate, publish, report. ANT.-bury, conceal, stifle, suppress, withhold.

announcement, n. SYN.-advertisement, bulletin, declaration, notification, promulgation. ANT.-hush, muteness, silence, speechlessness.

annoy, v. SYN.-bother, chafe, disturb, inconvenience, irk, irritate, molest, pester, tease, trouble, vex. ANT.-accommodate, console, gratify, soothe.

annoying, a. SYN.-bothersome, distressing, disturbing, irksome, troublesome, trying, vexatious. ANT.-accommodating, amusing, gratifying, pleasant.

annul, v. SYN.-destroy, end, eradicate, obliterate, overthrow; abrogate, cancel, invalidate, revoke, cross out, delete, eliminate, erase, expunge, abolish, nullify, quash, repeal, rescind, ANT.-continue, establish, promote, restore, sustain. confirm, enact, enforce, perpetuate

answer, n. SYN.-rejoinder, reply, response, restatement, result, retort, retaliation, solution, total; defense, rebuttal. ANT.-inquiry, questioning, summoning; argument.

antagonistic, a. SYN.-contrary, hostile, opposed, opposite; counteractive, disastrous, unfavorable, unlucky adverse, inimical, unfriendly, warlike. ANT.-benign, favorable, fortunate, lucky, propitious amicable, cordial.

antic, n. SYN.-caper, frolic, trick.

anticipation, n. SYN.-contemplation, expectation, foresight, forethought, hope, preconception, prescience, presentiment. ANT.-doubt, dread, fear, worry.

antipathy, n. SYN.-animosity, antagonism, enmity, hatred, hostility, ill-will, invidiousness, malignity. ANT.-affection, cordiality, friendliness, good will, love.

antiquated, a. SYN.-ancient, archaic, obsolescent, obsolete, old, out-of-date, venerable. ANT.-current, extant, fashionable, modern, recent.

anxiety, n. SYN.-apprehension, care, concern, disquiet, fear, solicitude, trouble, worry, ANT.-assurance, confidence, contentment, equanimity, nonchalance.

anxious, a. SYN.-ardent, avid, enthusiastic, eager, fervent, hot, impassioned, impatient, keen, yearning. ANT.-apathetic, indifferent, unconcerned, uninterested.

apart, a. SYN.-alone, disconnected, dis-

tant, far, isolated, separated.

apathy, n. SYN.-disinterestedness, impartiality, indifference, insensibility, neutrality, unconcern. ANT.-affection, ardor, fervor, passion.

apex, n. SYN.-acme, climax, consummation, culmination, height, peak, summit, zenith. ANT.-anticlimax, base, depth, floor.

apology, n. SYN.-alibi, confession, defense, excuse, explanation, justification. ANT.-accusation, complaint, denial, dissimulation.

apparatus, n. SYN.-agent, channel, device, instrument, means, medium, tool, utensil, vehicle. ANT.-hindrance, impediment, obstruction, preventive.

apparel, n. SYN.-array, attire, clothes, clothing, drapery, dress, garb, garments, raiment, vestments, vesture. ANT.-nakedness, nudity.

apparent, a. SYN.-clear, evident, manifest, obvious, palpable, plain, self-evident, transparent, unambiguous, unmistakable, visible; illusory, ostensible, seeming. ANT.-ambiguous, dubious, indistinct, real, uncertain.

appeal, n. SYN.-beg, entreaty, petition, plea, prayer, request, supplication.

appear, v. SYN.-look, seem; arise, arrive, emanate, emerge, issue. ANT.-be, exist; disappear, vanish, withdraw.

appearance, n. SYN.-advent, apparition, arrival, air, aspect, demeanor, look, manner, mien, fashion, guise, pretense, semblance.

appease, v. SYN.-allay, alleviate, assuage, calm, compose, lull, pacify, placate, quell, quiet, relieve, satisfy, soothe, still, tranquilize. ANT.-arouse, excite, incense, inflame.

appetite, n. SYN.-hunger, relish, stomach, thirst, zest; craving, desire, inclination, liking, longing, passion. ANT.-disgust, distaste, renunciation, repugnance, satiety.

apply, v. SYN.-administer, affix, allot, appropriate, assign, attach, avail, devote, direct, employ, use; bear, pertain, refer, relate; appeal, petition, request.

appoint, v. SYN.-call, denominate, designate, entitle, mention, name, specify. ANT.-hint, miscall, misname.

apportion, v. SYN.-allot, appropriate, assign, dispense, distribute, divide, parcel, partake, partition, portion, share. ANT.-aggregate, amass, combine, condense.

appraise, v. SYN.-assign, assess, calculate, compute, estimate, evaluate, fix, levy, reckon, tax.

appreciate, v. SYN.-admire, cherish, enjoy, esteem, prize, regard, value, appraise, estimate, evaluate, rate, apprehend, comprehend, understand, go up, improve, rise. ANT.-belittle, degrade, depreciate, misapprehend, misunderstand.

appreciative, a. SYN.-beholden, grateful, indebted, obliged, thankful. ANT.-thankless, unappreciative.

apprehend, v. SYN.-arrest, capture, catch, clutch, grasp, grip, lay hold of, seize, snare, trap. ANT.-liberate, lose, release, throw.

apprehension, n. SYN.-anxiety, concern, disquiet, fear, trouble, uneasiness, worry. ANT.-contentment, equanimity, peace, satisfaction.

apprehensive, a. SYN.-afraid, faint-hearted, fearful, frightened, scared, timid, timorous. ANT.-assured, bold, composed, courageous, sanguine.

apprentice, n. SYN.-amateur, beginner, learner, student.

approach, v. SYN.-advance, approximate, come, gain, near, touch. ANT.-depart, leave, recede.

appropriate, a. SYN.-applicable, apt, becoming, fitting, particular, proper, suitable. ANT.-contrary, improper, inappropriate.

appropriation, n. SYN.-allowance, benefaction, bequest, boon, bounty, donation, endowment, gift, grant, subsidy.

approval, n. SYN.-approbation, assent, commendation, consent, endorsement, praise, sanction, support. ANT.-censure, reprimand, reproach, stricture.

approve, v. SYN.-appreciate, commend, like, praise; authorize, confirm, endorse, ratify, sanction. ANT.-criticize, disparage; condemn, nullify.

approximate, a. SYN.-about, almost, guess, imprecise, inexact, rough. ANT.-exact, precise, sure.

apropos, a. SYN.-applicable, apposite, appropriate, apt, fit, germane, material, pertinent, related, relating, relevant, to the point. ANT.-alien, extraneous, foreign, unrelated.

aptitude, n. SYN.-ability, adroitness, aptness, capability, capacity, cleverness, deftness, dexterity, efficiency, facility, faculty, knack, power, qualification, skill, talent. ANT.-disability, inability, incapacity, incompetence, unreadiness.

arbitrary, a. SYN.-absolute, despotic, discretionary, inconsistent, irrational, willful.

arbitrate, v. SYN.-decide, decree, determine; adjudicate, condemn, judge, try, umpire; appreciate, consider, estimate, evaluate, measure, think.

arbitrator, n. SYN.-arbitrator, critic, judge, justice, magistrate, referee, umpire.

archetype, n. SYN.-example, illustration, instance. model, pattern, prototype, sample, specimen. ANT.-concept, precept, principle, rule.

archives, n. pl. SYN.-file, library, museum, repository, vault.

ardent, a. SYN.-eager, enthusiastic, fervent, fervid, fiery, glowing, hot, impassioned, intense, keen, passionate, vehement, zealous. ANT.-apathetic, cool, indifferent, nonchalant.

ardor, n. SYN.-devotion, eagerness, enthusiasm, fervor, fire, passion, rapture, spirit, zeal. ANT.-apathy, disinterest, indifference, unconcern.

arduous, a. SYN.-complicated, demanding, hard, intricate, involved, laborious, obscure, perplexing, toilsome, trying burdensome, difficult, onerous, tough; cruel, harsh, rigorous, severe. ANT.-easy, effortless, facile, simple, gentle, lenient, tender.

area, n. SYN.-locale, locality, location,

place, precinct, region, site, situation, spot, station, territory, township, vicinity, ward.

arena, n. SYN.-amphitheater, coliseum, field, grounds, gymnasium, park,

argue, v. SYN.-debate, discuss, dispute, plead, reason, wrangle; denote, imply, indicate, prove, show. ANT.-ignore, overlook, reject, spurn.

argument, n. SYN.-contention, controversy, debate, disagreement, dispute, quarrel, squabble. ANT.-agreement, concord, decision, harmony.

arid, a. SYN.-dehydrated, desiccated, drained, dry, parched, thirsty; barren, dull, insipid, plain, tedious, tiresome, uninteresting, vapid. ANT.-damp, moist; fresh, interesting, lively.

aristocracy, n. SYN.-elite, gentry, nobility, noblemen, patricians, privileged, rulers. ANT.-commoners, peasants, peons.

armed, a. SYN.-equipped, fortified, loaded, outfitted, protected. ANT.-unprotected, vulnerable.

aroma, n. SYN.-fragrance, fume, incense, odor, perfume, redolence, scent, smell, stench, stink.

arrange, v. SYN.-adjust, assort, classify, dispose, organize, place, regulate; devise, plan, prepare. ANT.-confuse, disorder, disturb, jumble, scatter.

arrangement, n. SYN.-method, mode, order, organization, plan, process, regularity, rule, scheme, system. ANT.-chance, chaos, confusion, disarrangement, disorder, irregularity.

array, n. SYN.-apparel, attire, clothes, clothing, drapery, dress, garb, garments, raiment, vestments, vesture. ANT.-nakedness, nudity.

arrest, v. SYN.-apprehend, check, detain, hinder, interrupt, obstruct, restrain, seize, slow, stop, withhold. ANT.-activate, discharge, free, liberate, release.

arrive, v. SYN.-appear, attain, come, emerge, land, reach, visit. ANT.-depart, exit, leave.

arrogant, a. SYN.-disdainful, haughty, overbearing, proud, stately, supercilious, vain, vainglorious. ANT.-ashamed, humble, lowly, meek.

art, n. SYN.-adroitness, aptitude, cunning, knack, skill, tact; artifice, duplicity, guile, shrewdness, subtlety. ANT.-clumsiness, unskillfulness; forthrightness, honesty, innocence.

article, n. SYN.-object, particular, thing.

articulate, v. SYN.-enunciate, lecture, pronounce, speak, talk, verbalize, vocalize.

artificial, a. SYN.-affected, assumed, bogus, counterfeit, ersatz, fake, feigned, fictitious, phony, sham, spurious, synthetic, unreal. ANT.-genuine, natural, real, true.

artist, n. SYN.-actor, composer, creator, dancer, dramatist, impresario, musician, painter, performer, poet, sculptor, writer.

artistic, a. SYN.-creative, cultured, imaginative, inventive, sensitive, talented.

ascend, v. SYN.-climb, mount, rise, scale, soar, tower. ANT.-descend, fall, sink.

ascertain, v. SYN.-detect, devise, discover, expose, find, find out, invent, learn, originate, reveal. ANT.-cover, hide, lose, mask, screen.

ashamed, a. SYN.-abashed, debased, embarrassed, mortified, shamefaced.

asinine, a. SYN.-absurd, brainless, crazy, foolish, idiotic, irrational, nonsensical, preposterous, ridiculous, senseless, silly, simple. ANT.-judicious, prudent, sagacious, sane, wise.

ask, v. SYN.-beg, claim, demand, entreat, invite, request, solicit; inquire, interrogate, query, question. ANT.-command, dictate, insist, order, reply.

asperse, v. SYN.-abuse, defame, disparage, ill-use, malign, revile, scandalize, traduce, vilify; misapply, misemploy, misuse. ANT.-cherish, honor, praise, protect, respect.

aspiration, n. SYN.-aim, ambition, craving, desire, goal, hope, longing, objective, passion.

aspire, v. SYN.-attempt, endeavor, strive, struggle, undertake, aim, design, intend, mean, try. ANT.-abandon, decline, ignore, neglect, omit.

assail, v. SYN.-assault, attack, besiege, charge, encounter, invade, abuse, censure, impugn. ANT.-aid, defend, protect, repel, resist.

assassinate, v. SYN.-butcher, execute, kill, massacre, murder, put to death, slaughter, slay. ANT.-animate, protect, resuscitate, save, vivify.

assault, v. SYN.-assail, attack, bombard, charge, invade, pound, storm, strike. ANT.-defend, oppose, protect.

assembly, n. SYN.-aggregation, band, brood, bunch, class, cluster, collection, crowd, flock, group, herd, horde, lot, mob, pack, party, set, swarm, throng, troupe.

assent, v. SYN.-accede, acquiesce, agree, comply, consent; coincide, concur, conform, tally. ANT.-contradict, differ, disagree, dissent, protest.

assert, v. SYN.-affirm, allege, aver, claim, declare, express, maintain, state; defend, support, uphold, vindicate. ANT.-contradict, deny, refute.

assess, v. SYN.-appraise, assign, calculate, compute, estimate, evaluate, fix, levy, reckon, tax.

assessment, n. SYN.-assessment, custom, duty, exaction, excise, impost, levy, rate, tax, toll, tribute. ANT.-gift, remuneration, reward, wages.

assign, v. SYN.-allot, apportion, appropriate, ascribe, attribute, cast, designate, distribute, specify. ANT.-discharge, release, relieve, unburden.

assimilate, v. SYN.-absorb, consume, engulf, imbibe, swallow up; engage, engross, occupy. ANT.-discharge, dispense, emit, expel, exude.

assist, v. SYN.-abet, aid, back, further, help, promote, serve, support, sustain. ANT.-hamper, hinder, impede, prevent.

assistance, n. SYN.-aid, alms, backing, furtherance, help, patronage, relief, succor, support. ANT.-antagonism, counteraction, defiance, hostility, resistance.

assistant, n. SYN.-aide, auxiliary, bodyguard, colleague, deputy, helper, henchman, lieutenant, secretary.

associate, n. SYN.-attendant, colleague, comrade, consort, crony, friend, mate, partner. ANT.-adversary, enemy, stranger.

associate, v. SYN.-affiliate, ally, combine, companion, conjoin, connect, join, link, mingle, mix. ANT.-disrupt, divide, estrange, separate.

association, n. SYN.-affinity, alliance, bond, conjunction, connection, link, relationship, tie, union. ANT.-disunion, isolation, separation.

assorted, a. SYN.-diverse, heterogeneous, indiscriminate, miscellaneous, mixed, motley, sundry, varied. ANT.-alike, classified, homogeneous, ordered, selected.

assortment, n. SYN.-change, difference, dissimilarity, diversity, heterogeneity, medley, miscellany, mixture, multifariousness, variety, variousness. ANT.-homogeneity, likeness, monotony, sameness, uniformity.

assuage, v. SYN.-abate, decrease, diminish, lessen, lower, moderate, reduce, suppress. ANT.-amplify, enlarge, increase, intensify, revive.

assume, v. SYN.-appropriate, arrogate, conjecture, take, usurp, adopt, affect, pretend, simulate, wear, postulate, presume, suppose, theorize. ANT.-concede, grant, surrender, doff, demonstrate, prove.

assurance, n. SYN.-assuredness, certainty, confidence, conviction, courage, firmness, security, self-reliance, surety, pledge, promise, word; assertion, declaration, statement. ANT.-bashfulness, humility, modesty, shyness, suspicion.

assure, v. SYN.-corroborate, substantiate, verify; acknowledge, establish, settle; approve, fix, ratify, sanction; strengthen.

astonishment, n. SYN.-admiration, amazement, astonishment, awe, bewilderment, curiosity, marvel, surprise, wonder, wonderment. ANT.-familiarity, triviality; apathy, expectation, indifference.

astound, v. SYN.-amaze, astonish, disconcert, dumbfound, flabbergast, shock, startle, stun, surprise, take aback. ANT.-admonish, caution, forewarn, prepare.

atrocity, n. SYN.-barbarity, brutality, cruelty, inhumanity, outrage, wickedness.

attach, v. SYN.-adjoin, affix, annex, append, connect, join, stick, unite; assign, associate, attribute. ANT.-detach, disengage, separate, unfasten, untie.

attachment, n. SYN.-adherence, affection, affinity, devotion, friendship, liking, regard. ANT.-alienation, aversion, estrangement, opposition, separation.

attack, n. SYN.-aggression, assault, criticism, denunciation, invasion, offense, onslaught; convulsion, fit, paroxysm. ANT.-defense, opposition, resistance, surrender, vindication.

attack, v. SYN.-assail, assault, besiege, charge, encounter, invade, abuse, censure, impugn. ANT.-aid, defend, protect, repel, resist.

attain, v. SYN.-accomplish, achieve, acquire, arrive, effect, gain, get, obtain, procure, reach, secure, win. ANT.-abandon, desert, discard, relinquish.

attempt, n. SYN.-effort, endeavor, essay, experiment, trial, undertaking. ANT.-inaction, laziness, neglect.

attend, v. SYN.-accompany, escort, follow, guard, lackey, protect, serve, tend, watch; be present, frequent.

attention, n. SYN.-alertness, care, circumspection, consideration, heed, mindfulness, notice, observance, watchfulness; application, contemplation, reflection, study. ANT.-disregard, indifference, negligence, omission, oversight.

attentive, a. SYN.-alert, alive, awake, aware, careful, considerate, heedful, mindful, observant, thoughtful, wary, watchful; assiduous, diligent, studious. ANT.-apathetic, indifferent, oblivious, unaware.

attire, n. SYN.-apparel, array, clothes, clothing, drapery, dress, garb, garments, raiment, vestments, vesture. ANT.-nakedness, nudity.

attitude, n. SYN.-air, demeanor, disposition, emotion, inclination, mood, propensity, reaction, standpoint, temper, temperament, viewpoint; aspect, pose, position, posture, stand.

attract, v. SYN.-allure, captivate, charm, enchant, entice, fascinate, lure. ANT.-alienate, deter, repel, repulse.

attractive, a. SYN.-alluring, charming, enchanting, engaging, inviting, magnetic, pleasant, pleasing, seductive, winning. ANT.-forbidding, obnoxious, repellent, repulsive.

attribute, n. SYN.-characteristic, distinction, feature, peculiarity, property, quality, trait.

audacious, a. SYN.-adventurous, bold, brave, courageous, daring, dauntless, fearless, intrepid; brazen, forward, impudent, insolent, pushy, rude; abrupt, conspicuous, prominent, striking. ANT.-cowardly, flinching, timid; bashful, retiring.

audacity, n. SYN.-boldness, effrontery, fearlessness, hardihood, temerity. ANT.-circumspection, fearfulness, humility, meekness.

audible, a. SYN.-clear, discernible, emphatic, heard, loud, plain, resounding.

audience, n. SYN.-assemblage, band, company, crew, group, horde, party, spectators, throng, troop, witnesses.

audit, n. SYN.-check, inspection, report, review, scrutiny.

augment, v. SYN.-accrue, amplify, enhance, enlarge, expand, extend, grow, heighten, increase, intensify, magnify, multiply, raise, wax. ANT.-atrophy, contract, decrease, diminish, reduce.

august, a. SYN.-dignified, grand, grandiose, high, imposing, lofty, magnificent, majestic, noble, pompous,

stately, sublime. ANT.-common, humble, lowly, ordinary, undignified.

austere, a. SYN.-harsh, rigid, rigorous, severe, stern, strict, stringent, unyielding. ANT.-elastic, flexible, resilient, supple, yielding.

authentic, a. SYN.-genuine, pure, real, true, verifiable, accurate, authoritative, correct, reliable, trustworthy. ANT.-counterfeit, erroneous, false, spurious.

author, n. SYN.-columnist, composer, creator, father, inventor, journalist, maker, originator, writer.

authoritarian, a. SYN.-arrogant, dictatorial, doctrinaire, dogmatic, domineering, magisterial, opinionated, overbearing, positive; authoritative, doctrinal, formal. ANT.-fluctuating, indecisive, open-minded, questioning, skeptical.

authority, n. SYN.-control, domination, dominion, force, justification, power, supremacy, authorization, license, permission, sanction, ground, importance, influence, prestige, weight. ANT.-impotence, incapacity, weakness, denial, prohibition.

autobiography, n. SYN.-adventures, biography, experiences, history, journal, letters, life, memoirs.

automated, a. SYN.-automatic, computerized, electronic, mechanical, mechanized, motorized, programmed. ANT.-manual.

autonomous, a. SYN.-emancipated, exempt, free, independent, liberated, unconfined, uncontrolled, unrestricted, unobstructed. ANT.-confined, restrained, restricted; blocked, clogged, contingent, dependent, impeded; subject.

auxiliary, a. SYN.-ancillary, assisting, conducive, furthering, helping, instrumental, subsidiary. ANT.-cumbersome, obstructive, opposing, retarding.

available, a. SYN.-accessible, convenient, handy, obtainable, prepared, ready, usable. ANT.-inaccessible, unavoidable.

avaricious, a. SYN.-covetous, grasping, greedy, rapacious, selfish; devouring, gluttonous, insatiable, ravenous, voracious. ANT.-generous, munificent; full, satisfied.

avenge, v. SYN.-requite, retaliate, revenge, vindicate. ANT.-forgive, pardon, pity, reconcile.

aver, v. SYN.-affirm, assert, declare, maintain, protest, state, swear. ANT.-contradict, demur, deny, dispute, oppose.

average, a. SYN.-fair, intermediate, mean, median, mediocre, medium, middling, moderate, ordinary. ANT.-exceptional, extraordinary, outstanding.

averse, a. SYN.-disinclined, hesitant, loath, reluctant, slow, unwilling. ANT.-disposed, eager, inclined, ready, willing.

aversion, n. SYN.-abhorrence, antipathy, disgust, disinclination, dislike, distaste, dread, hatred, loathing, repugnance, repulsion, reluctance. ANT.-affection, attachment, devotion, enthusiasm.

avert, v. See **avoid.**

avoid, v. SYN.-avert, dodge, escape, eschew, elude, forbear, forestall, free, shun, ward. ANT.-confront, encounter, face, meet, oppose.

awake, a. SYN.-alert, alive, aware, conscious, stirring, up. ANT.-asleep, dozing, napping, unconscious.

aware, a. SYN.-apprised, cognizant, conscious, informed, mindful, observant, perceptive, sensible. ANT.-ignorant, insensible, oblivious, unaware.

away, a. SYN.-abroad, absent, departed, inattentive, preoccupied. ANT.-attending, present; attentive, watchful.

awful, a. SYN.-appalling, dire, dreadful, frightful, horrible, terrible, awe-inspiring, imposing, majestic, solemn. ANT.-commonplace, humble, lowly, vulgar.

awkward, a. SYN.-clumsy, gauche, gawky, inept, rough, unpolished, untoward. ANT.-adroit, graceful, neat, polished, skillful.

axis, n. SYN.-axle, divider, pole, shaft, spindle.

axiom, n. SYN.-adage, aphorism, apothegm, byword, fundamental, maxim, postulate, principle, proverb, saw, saying, theorem, truism.

B

babble, v. SYN.-chatter, gabble, gush, jabber, prattle, rant, rave.

back, a. SYN.-aft, after, astern, behind, following, hind, hindmost, rear. ANT.-ahead, fore, forward, front, head, leading.

backed, a. SYN.-abetted, aided, assisted, boosted, championed, encouraged, established, furthered, propelled, pushed.

backward, a. SYN.-regressive, retrograde, revisionary, dull, sluggish, stupid, disinclined, hesitating, indisposed, loath, reluctant, unwilling, wavering. ANT.-advanced, civilized, progressive.

bad, a. SYN.-baleful, base, deleterious, evil, immoral, iniquitous, noxious, pernicious, sinful, unsound, unwholesome, villainous, wicked. ANT.-excellent, good, honorable, moral, reputable.

badger, v. SYN.-aggravate, annoy, bother, disturb, harass, harry, irritate, molest, nag, pester, plague, provoke, tantalize, taunt, tease, torment, vex, worry. ANT.-comfort, delight, gratify, please, soothe.

baffle, v. SYN.-balk, circumvent, defeat, disappoint, foil, frustrate, hinder, outwit, prevent, thwart. ANT.-accomplish, fulfill, further, promote.

bag, n. SYN.-attaché case, backpack, briefcase, pack, pocketbook, purse, satchel, suitcase, tote.

balance, n. SYN.-composure, equilibrium, poise, stability, steadiness, proportion, symmetry, excess, remainder, remains, residue, rest. ANT.-fall, imbalance, instability, unsteadiness.

balance, v. SYN.-dangle, hang, poise, suspend, swing. ANT.-continue, maintain, persist, proceed, prolong.

bald, a. bare, exposed, naked, nude,

stripped, unclad, uncovered, barren, plain, simple, defenseless, open, unprotected. ANT.-clothed, covered, dressed; concealed; protected.

ban, v. SYN.-debar, forbid, hinder, inhibit, interdict, prevent, prohibit. ANT.-allow, permit, sanction, tolerate.

banal, a. SYN.-commonplace, hackneyed, inane, insipid, trite, vapid. ANT.-fresh, novel, original, stimulating, striking.

band, n. SYN.-circle, circumference, latitude, meridian, orbit, zone; bandage, belt, obi, ring, sash, scarf.

banish, v. SYN.-deport, dismiss, dispel, eject, exclude, exile, expatriate, expel, ostracize, oust. ANT.-accept, admit, harbor, receive, shelter.

banquet, n. SYN.-celebration, dinner, entertainment, feast, festival, regalement.

barbaric, a. See **barbarous.**

barbarous, a. SYN.-barbarian, barbaric, brutal, crude, cruel, inhuman, merciless, remorseless, rude, ruthless, savage, uncivilized, uncultured, unrelenting. ANT.-civilized, humane, kind, polite, refined.

bargain, n. SYN.-agreement, compact, contract, covenant, pact, promise, stipulation, treaty.

barren, a. SYN.-devoid, empty hollow, unfilled, unfurnished, unoccupied, vacant, vacuous, void, worthless. ANT.-full, inhabited, occupied, replete, supplied.

barrier, n. SYN.-barricade, blockade, fence, hindrance, hurdle, impediment, obstacle, obstruction, restriction, wall.

base, a. SYN.-abject, contemptible, despicable, dishonorable, groveling, ignoble, ignominious, low, lowly, mean, menial, servile, sordid, vile, vulgar. ANT.-teemed, exalted, honored, lofty, noble, righteous.

base, n. SYN.-basis, bottom, foundation, ground, groundwork, root, substructure, support, underpinning. ANT.-building, cover, superstructure, top.

bashful, a. SYN.-abashed, coy, diffident, embarrassed, humble, modest, recoiling, retiring, shamefaced, sheepish, shy, timid, timorous. ANT.-adventurous, daring, fearless, gregarious, outgoing.

basic, a. SYN.-elementary, fundamental, primary, rudimentary, simple. ANT.-abstract, abstruse, complex, elaborate, intricate.

basis, n. SYN.-base, bottom, foundation, ground, groundwork, support, underpinning, assumption, postulate, premise, presumption, presupposition, principle. ANT.-derivative, implication, superstructure, trimming.

bath, n. SYN.-bathroom, lavatory, sauna, shower, toilet, tub, washroom.

bathe, v. SYN.-clean, cleanse, launder, rinse, scrub, wash, wet. ANT.-dirty, foul, soil, stain.

battle, n. SYN.-combat, conflict, contest, fight, fray, skirmish, strife, struggle. ANT.-agreement, concord, peace, truce.

battle, v. SYN.-brawl, combat, conflict, contend, dispute, encounter, fight,

quarrel scuffle, skirmish, squabble, struggle, wrangle.

bay, n. SYN.-bayou, cove, gulf, harbor, inlet, lagoon, mouth, sound.

beacon, n. SYN.-beam, flare, guide, lamp, lantern, radar, signal, sonar.

bear, v. SYN.-support, sustain, uphold, allow, brook, endure, permit, stand, suffer, tolerate, undergo; carry, convey, take, transport; produce, spawn, yield. ANT.-avoid, dodge, evade, refuse, shun.

beast, n. SYN.-animal, barbarian, brute, creature, fiend, lout, monster, pervert, savage,

beastly, a. SYN.-abominable, base, brutal, coarse, degraded, depraved, disgusting, low, obscene, repulsive, savage, vulgar. ANT.-kind, nice, pleasant, refined, suave.

beat, v. SYN.-belabor, buffet, dash, hit, knock, pound, pummel, punch, smite, strike, thrash, thump; conquer, defeat, overpower, overthrow, rout, subdue, vanquish, palpitate, pulsate, pulse, throb. ANT.-defend, shield, stroke, fail, surrender.

beautiful, a. SYN.-beauteous, charming, comely, elegant, fair, fine, gorgeous, handsome, lovely, pretty. ANT.-foul, hideous, homely, repulsive, unsightly.

beauty, n. SYN.-attractiveness, charm, comeliness, elegance, fairness, grace, handsomeness, loveliness, pulchritude. ANT.-deformity, disfigurement, eyesore, homeliness, ugliness.

because, conj. SYN.-as, for, inasmuch as, since.

beckon, v. SYN.-call, signal, summon, wave.

bed, n. SYN.-berth, bunk, cot, couch, cradle, hammock, mattress; accumulation, deposit, layer, stratum, vein.

bedlam, n. SYN.-chaos, clamor, commotion, confusion, disorder, tumult, turmoil, uproar. ANT.-order, quiet, serenity.

befoul, v. SYN.-corrupt, contaminate, defile, infect, poison, pollute, sully, taint. ANT.-disinfect, purify.

beg, v. SYN.-adjure, ask, beseech, crave, entreat, implore, importune, petition, pray, request, solicit, supplicate. ANT.-bestow, cede, favor, give, grant.

beget, v. SYN.-breed, create, engender, father, generate, originate, procreate, produce, propagate, sire. ANT.-abort, destroy, extinguish, kill, murder.

beggar, n. SYN.-mendicant, pauper, ragamuffin, scrub, starveling, tatterdemalion, vagabond, wretch.

begin, v. SYN.-arise, commence, enter, inaugurate, initiate, institute, open, originate, start. ANT.-close, complete, end, finish, terminate.

beginner, n. SYN.-apprentice, amateur, dabbler, dilettante, learner, neophyte, novice. ANT.-adept, authority, expert, master, professional.

beginning, n. SYN.-commencement, inception, genesis, opening, origin, outset, source, start. ANT.-close, completion, consummation, end, termination.

behalf, n. SYN.-account, advantage, avail,

benefit, favor, gain, good, interest, profit, service. ANT.-calamity, distress, handicap, trouble.

behave, v. SYN.-act, bear, carry, comport, conduct, demean, deport, interact, manage, operate.

behavior, n. SYN.-action, bearing, carriage, conduct, deed, demeanor, deportment, disposition, manner.

behind, a. SYN.-after, back, delayed, following, trailing; backward, retarded, slow. ANT.-ahead, forward, leading; clever, quick, smart.

behold, v. SYN.-contemplate, descry, discern, distinguish, espy, glimpse, inspect, look at, notice, observe, perceive, scan, scrutinize, see, view, watch, witness.

belief, n. SYN.-certitude, confidence, conviction, credence, faith, feeling, notion, opinion, persuasion, reliance, trust. ANT.-denial, doubt, heresy, incredulity.

believe, v. SYN.-accept, apprehend, conceive, credit, fancy, hold, imagine, support, suppose. ANT.-distrust, doubt, question, reject.

belittle, v. SYN.-decry, depreciate, disparage, derogate, discredit, lower, undervalue minimize, underrate. ANT.-admire, appreciate, esteem. aggrandize, commend, exalt, magnify, praise.

belongings, n. SYN.-commodities, effects, estate, goods, possessions, property, stock, wealth.

beloved, a. SYN.-adored, dear, esteemed, precious, prized, valued; valuable. ANT.-despised, unwanted.

below, prep. SYN.-beneath, lower, under, underneath. ANT.-above, aloft, over, overhead.

bend, v. SYN.-bow, crook, curve, deflect, incline, lean, stoop, turn, twist, influence, mold, submit, yield. ANT.-break, resist, stiffen, straighten.

beneath, prep. SYN.-below, under, underneath. ANT.-above, over.

beneficial, a. SYN.-advantageous, good, helpful, profitable, salutary, serviceable, useful, wholesome. ANT.-deleterious, destructive, detrimental, harmful, injurious.

benefit, n. SYN.-account, advantage, avail, behalf, favor, gain, good, interest, profit, service. ANT.-calamity, distress, handicap, trouble.

benefit, v. SYN.-aid, assist, attend, help, oblige, succor; advance, forward, promote.

benevolence, n. SYN.-altruism, beneficence, charity, generosity, humanity, kindness, liberality, magnanimity, philanthropy, tenderness. ANT.-cruelty, inhumanity, malevolence, selfishness, unkindness.

benevolent, a. SYN.-altruistic, benign, charitable, friendly, generous, humane, kind, liberal, merciful, obliging, philanthropic, tender, unselfish. ANT.-greedy, harsh, malevolent, wicked.

bent, n. SYN.-bending, inclination, leaning, affection, attachment, bent, bias, desire, disposition, penchant, predilection, preference. ANT.-apathy, aversion, distaste, nonchalance, repugnance.

bequeath, v. SYN.-donate, endow, give, will.

bequest, n. SYN.-appropriation, benefaction, boon, bounty, concession, donation, endowment, gift, grant, subsidy.

berate, v. SYN.-admonish, blame, censure, lecture, rebuke, reprehend, reprimand, scold, upbraid, vituperate. ANT.-approve, commend, praise.

besides, prep. SYN.-also, furthermore, in addition, likewise, moreover, similarly, too.

best, a. SYN.-finest, greatest, incomparable, top, unequaled. ANT.-common, ordinary, worst.

bestial, a. SYN.-barbarous, brutal, brutish, carnal, coarse, cruel, ferocious, gross, inhuman, merciless, remorseless, rough, rude, ruthless, savage, sensual. ANT-civilized, courteous, gentle, humane, kind.

bestow, v. SYN.-confer, contribute, deliver, donate, furnish, give, grant, impart, present, provide, supply, ANT.-keep, retain, seize, withdraw.

bet, v. SYN.-gamble, hazard, risk, speculate, venture, wager.

better, v. SYN.-ameliorate, amend, help, improve, rectify, reform. ANT.-corrupt, damage, debase, impair, vitiate.

bevy, n. SYN.-crowd, crush, horde, host, masses, mob, multitude, populace, press, rabble, swarm, throng.

bewilder, v. SYN.-confound, confuse, dumfound, mystify, nonplus, perplex, puzzle. ANT.-clarify, explain, illumine, instruct, solve.

bewildered, a. SYN.-deranged, disconcerted, disordered, disorganized, indistinct, mixed, muddled, perplexed. ANT.-clear, lucid, obvious, organized, plain.

bias, n. SYN.-bent, disposition, inclination, leaning, partiality, penchant, predilection, predisposition, prejudice, proclivity, proneness, propensity, slant, tendency, turn. ANT.-equity, fairness, impartiality, justice.

bicker, v. SYN.-altercate, argue, contend, contest, debate, discuss, dispute, quarrel, squabble, wrangle. ANT.-agree, allow, assent, concede.

big, a. SYN.-august, bulky, colossal, enormous, grand, great,. huge, hulking, immense, large, majestic, massive, monstrous. ANT.-little, petite, small, tiny.

bigoted, a. SYN.-dogmatic, fanatical, illiberal, intolerant, narrow-minded, prejudiced. ANT.-liberal, progressive, radical, tolerant.

bind, v. SYN.-attach, connect, engage, fasten, fetter, join, link, oblige, restrain, restrict, tie. ANT.-free, loose, unfasten, untie.

binding, a. SYN.-cogent, conclusive, convincing, effective, efficacious, legal, logical, powerful, sound, strong, telling, valid, weighty. ANT.-counterfeit, null, spurious, void, weak.

biography, n. SYN.-adventures, biography, experiences, history, journal, letters, life, memoirs.

bit, n. SYN.-amount, fraction, fragment, morsel, part, piece, portion, scrap.

ANT.-all, entirety, sum, total, whole.

bite, v. SYN.-champ, chew, crunch, gnash, gnaw, nibble, nip, pierce, rend, tear.

bitter, a. SYN.-acrid, biting, distasteful, pungent, sour, tart; galling, grievous, painful, poignant; cruel, fierce, relentless, ruthless; acrimonious, caustic, harsh, sardonic, severe. ANT.-delicious, mellow, pleasant, sweet.

bizarre, a. SYN.-abnormal, curious, eccentric, extraordinary, grotesque, irregular, odd, peculiar, quaint, queer, singular, strange, uncommon, unique, unusual. ANT.-common, conventional, familiar, normal, ordinary, regular, typical.

blab, v. SYN.-chatter, confess, divulge, squeal, talk, tell.

black, a. SYN.-dark, dim, gloomy, murky, obscure, shadowy, unilluminated; dusky, opaque, sable, swarthy; dismal, gloomy, mournful, somber, sorrowful; evil, sinister, sullen, wicked; hidden, mystic, occult, secret. ANT.-light, bright, clear; pleasant; lucid.

blackball, v. SYN.-bar, except, exclude, expel, hinder, omit, ostracize, prevent, prohibit, restrain, shut out. ANT.-accept, admit, include, welcome.

blame, v. SYN.-accuse, censure, charge, condemn, implicate, involve, prosecute, rebuke, reproach, slander, upbraid. ANT.-absolve, acquit, exonerate.

blameless, a. SYN.-faultless, holy, immaculate, perfect, pure, sinless. ANT.-blemished, defective, faulty, imperfect.

bland, a. SYN.-boring, dull, flat, insipid, lifeless, tasteless; gentle, mild soothing. ANT.-exciting, interesting, spicy; irritating, stimulating.

blank, a. SYN.-clear, empty, new, open, untouched, vacant, white.

blaze, n. SYN.-burning, combustion, conflagration, fire, flame, glow, heat, warmth.

bleak, a. SYN.-cheerless, dark, dismal, doleful, dreary, dull, funereal, gloomy, lonesome, melancholy, sad, somber. ANT.-cheerful, gay, joyous, lively.

bleakness, n. SYN.-blackness, darkness, gloom, obscurity, shadow; dejection, depression, despondency, melancholy, misery, sadness, woe. ANT.-exultation, frivolity, joy, light, mirth.

blemish, n. SYN.-blot, speck, stain; defect, disgrace, fault, flaw, imperfection, tarnish. ANT.-adornment, embellishment, perfection, purity.

blend, v. SYN.-amalgamate, coalesce, combine, commingle, conjoin, consolidate, fuse, mingle, mix, merge, unify, unite. ANT.-analyze, decompose, disintegrate, separate.

bless, v. SYN.-adore, baptize, celebrate, consecrate, delight, exalt, extol, gladden, glorify. ANT.-blaspheme, curse, denounce, slander.

blessing, n. SYN.-absolution, consecration, miracle, unction; asset, boon, benefit, help, luck, windfall.

blind, a. SYN.-ignorant, oblivious, sightless, undiscerning, unmindful, unseeing; headlong, heedless, rash. ANT.-aware, calculated, discerning, perceiv-

ing, sensible.

bliss, n. SYN.-blessedness, blissfulness, ecstasy, felicity, happiness, joy, rapture. ANT.-grief, misery, sorrow, woe, wretchedness.

blithe, a. SYN.-effervescent, light, resilient; animated, buoyant, cheerful, elated, hopeful, jocund, lively, spirited, sprightly, vivacious. ANT.-dejected, depressed, despondent, hopeless, sullen.

block, v. SYN.-bar, barricade, clog, close, obstruct, stop, delay, impede; hinder. ANT.-clear, open; aid, further, promote.

blond, a. SYN.-attractive, comely, fair, light, pale.

blot, n. SYN.-blemish, speck, stain; defect, disgrace, fault, flaw, imperfection. ANT.-adornment, embellishment, perfection, purity.

blow, n. SYN.-bang, box, clout, cuff, hit, jab, punch, slam, slap, strike, swat, whack.

bluff, v. SYN.-con, deceive, delude, fool, mislead, threaten, trick.

blunt, a. SYN.-dull, edgeless, obtuse, pointless, stolid, thick-witted, unsharpened; abrupt, bluff, brusque, impolite, outspoken, plain, rough, rude, unceremonious. ANT.-polished, polite, suave, subtle, tactful.

blustery, a. SYN.-gusty, inclement, roaring, rough, stormy, tempestuous, turbulent, windy. ANT.-calm, clear, peaceful, quiet, tranquil.

boast, v. SYN.-brag, crow, flaunt, glory, vaunt. ANT.-apologize, deprecate, humble, minimize.

bodily, a. SYN.-animal, base, carnal, corporeal, fleshly, gross, lustful, sensual, voluptuous, worldly, ANT.-exalted, intellectual, refined, spiritual, temperate.

body, n. SYN.-carcass, corpse, remains; form, frame, physique, torso; bulk, corpus, mass; aggregate, association, company, society. ANT.-intellect, mind, soul, spirit.

boisterous, a. SYN.-disruptive, loud, noisy, rude, unruly.

bold, a. SYN.-adventurous, audacious, brave, courageous, daring, dauntless, fearless, intrepid; brazen, forward, impudent, insolent, pushy, rude; abrupt, conspicuous, prominent, striking. ANT.-cowardly, flinching, timid; bashful, retiring.

boldness, n. SYN.-effrontery, audacity, fearlessness, hardihood, temerity. ANT.-circumspection, fearfulness, humility, meekness.

bolt, v. SYN.-bar, clasp, fastening, hook, latch, lock, padlock.

bond, n. SYN.-connection, connective, coupler, juncture, link, tie, union. ANT.-break, gap, interval, opening, split.

bondage, n. SYN.-captivity, confinement, imprisonment, serfdom, servitude, slavery, thralldom, vassalage. ANT.-freedom, liberation.

bonus, n. SYN.-award, bounty, compensation, premium, prize, recompense, remuneration, reward. ANT,-assessment, charge, earnings, punishment, wages.

book, n. SYN.-booklet, brochure, compendium, edition, handbook, manual, monograph, pamphlet, publication, textbook, tract, treatise, volume, work.

bookkeeper, *n.* SYN.-accountant, auditor, clerk, comptroller, controller; treasurer.

boor, *n.* SYN.-boob, bumpkin, lout, peasant, rustic, yokel.

boost, *v.* SYN.-advance, assist, abet, encourage, help, promote, support.

border, *n.* SYN.-boundary, brim, brink, edge, fringe, frontier, limit, margin, outskirts, rim, termination, verge. ANT.-center, core, interior, mainland.

boredom, *n.* SYN.-apathy, doldrums, dullness, ennui, indifference, monotony, tedium, weariness. ANT.-activity, excitement, motive, stimulus.

boring, *a.* SYN.-dense, slow, stupid; blunt, obtuse; commonplace, dull, dismal, dreary, monotonous, sad, tedious. ANT.-animated, lively, sharp; clear, interesting.

borrowed, *a.* SYN.-acquired, adopted, appropriated, copied, imitated, plagiarized, taken.

botch, *v.* SYN.-blunder, bungle, mishandle, mismanage, muddle, ruin, spoil, wreck.

bother, *v.* SYN.-annoy, disturb, harass, haunt, inconvenience, molest, perplex, pester, plague, tease, trouble, upset, worry. ANT.-gratify, please, relieve, soothe.

bottle, *n.* SYN.-canteen, carafe, cruet, decanter, flagon, flask, jar, vial.

bottom, *n.* SYN.-base, basis, foot, foundation, fundament, groundwork. ANT.-apex, peak, summit, top.

bought, *a.* SYN.-acquired, contracted, ordered, procured, purchased, requisitioned.

boulder, *n.* SYN.-rock, slab, stone.

bounce, *v.* SYN.-bolt, bound, hop, jump, leap, ricochet, spring, vault.

bound, *v.* SYN.-circumscribe, confine, enclose, encompass, envelop, fence, limit, surround. ANT.-develop, distend, enlarge, expand, expose, open.

boundary, *n.* SYN.-brim, brink, edge, fringe, frontier, limit, margin, outskirts, rim, termination, verge, border, extremity, hem, periphery. ANT.-center, core, interior, mainland.

bountiful, *a.* SYN.-ample, abundant, copious, overflowing, plenteous, plentiful, profuse, rich, teeming. ANT.-deficient, insufficient, scant, scarce.

bow, *v.* SYN.-bend, crook, curve, deflect, incline, lean, stoop, turn, twist, influence, mold, submit, yield. ANT.-break, resist, stiffen, straighten

brag, *v.* SYN.-bluster, boast, crow, flaunt, flourish, vaunt. ANT.-debase, degrade, demean, denigrate.

brand, *n.* SYN.-mark, scar, stain, stigma, trace, vestige; badge, label, sign; characteristic, feature, indication, property, trait.

brave, *a.* SYN.-adventurous, audacious, bold, chivalrous, courageous, daring, dauntless, fearless, gallant, heroic, intrepid, magnanimous, valiant, valorous. ANT.-cowardly, cringing, fearful, timid, weak.

bravery, *n.* SYN.-boldness, chivalry, courage, fearlessness, fortitude, intre-

pidity, mettle, prowess, resolution. ANT.-cowardice, fear, pusillanimity, timidity.

brazen, *a.* SYN.-adventurous, audacious, bold, brave, courageous, daring, dauntless, fearless, intrepid; forward, impudent, insolent, pushy, rude; abrupt, conspicuous, prominent, striking. ANT.-cowardly, flinching, timid; bashful, retiring.

break, *v.* SYN.-burst, crack, crush, demolish, destroy, fracture, infringe, pound, rack, rend, rupture, shatter, smash, squeeze; disobey, transgress, violate. ANT.-join, mend, renovate, repair, restore.

breed, *n.* SYN.-kind, sort, stock, strain, subspecies, variety. ANT.-homogeneity, likeness, monotony, sameness, uniformity.

breed, *v.* SYN.-bear, beget, conceive, engender, generate, procreate, propagate; foster, nurture, raise, rear, train.

breeding, *n.* SYN.-civilization, culture, cultivation, education, enlightenment, refinement. ANT.-boorishness, ignorance, illiteracy, vulgarity.

breeze, *n.* SYN.-draft, gust, wind, zephyr.

bribe, *n.* SYN.-blackmail, compensation, fee, graft, gratuity, present, protection, reward.

bridge, *n.* SYN.-bond, connection, link, span.

brief, *a.* SYN.-compendious, concise, curt, laconic, pithy, short, succinct, terse; fleeting, momentary, passing, transient. ANT.-extended, lengthy, long, prolonged, protracted.

bright, *a.* SYN.-brilliant, clear, gleaming, lucid, luminous, lustrous, radiant, shining, translucent, transparent; clever, intelligent, witty. ANT.-dark, dull, gloomy, murky, sullen.

brightness, *n.* SYN.-brilliance, brilliancy, effulgence, luster, radiance, splendor. ANT.-darkness, dullness, gloom, obscurity.

brilliant, *a.* See **bright.**

brim, *n.* SYN.-border, edge, lip, margin, rim, top.

bring, *v.* SYN.-carry, convey, transmit, transport; bear, support, sustain. ANT.-abandon, drop.

brisk, *a.* SYN.-cool, fresh, refreshing. ANT.-hackneyed, musty, stagnant.

brittle, *a.* SYN.-breakable, crisp, crumbling, delicate, fragile, frail, splintery. ANT.-enduring, thick, tough, unbreakable.

broad, *a.* SYN.-expanded, extensive, immense, large, sweeping, vast, wide; liberal, tolerant. ANT.-confined, narrow, restricted.

broadcast, *v.* SYN.-air, announce, disseminate, notify, scatter, transmit.

broke, *a.* SYN.-bankrupt, indebted, owing, penniless, poverty-stricken, ruined. ANT.-rich, wealthy.

broken, *a.* SYN.-crushed, destroyed, flattened, fractured, interrupted, reduced, rent, ruptured, separated, shattered, smashed, wrecked. ANT.-integral, repaired, united, whole.

brood, *v.* SYN.-care, fret, grieve, mope, muse, ponder, sulk, think, worry.

brook, *n.* SYN.-rill, rivulet, stream.

broth, *n.* SYN.-brew, concoction, consommé, purée, soup, stock.

brotherhood, *n.* SYN.-brotherliness, fellowship, kindness, solidarity; association, clan, fraternity, society. ANT.-acrimony, discord, opposition, strife.

browbeat, *v.* SYN.-berate, bully, frighten, intimidate, scold, threaten.

browse, *v.* SYN.-examine, glance, peruse, scan, skim.

brutal, *a.* SYN.-barbarous, bestial, brute, brutish, carnal, coarse, cruel, ferocious, gross, inhuman, merciless, remorseless, rough, rude, ruthless, savage, sensual. ANT.-civilized, courteous, gentle, humane, kind.

budget, *v.* SYN.-allocate, allow, estimate, forecast, plan, provide.

build, *n.* SYN.-appearance, configuration, contour, cut, figure, form, frame, guise, image, mold, outline, pattern, shape. ANT.-contortion, deformity, distortion, mutilation.

build, *v.* SYN.-construct, erect, establish, found, raise, rear. ANT.-demolish, destroy, overthrow, raze, undermine.

bulletin, *n.* SYN.-advertisement, announcement, declaration, notification, promulgation. ANT.-hush, muteness, silence, speechlessness.

bulge, *n.* SYN.-appendage, excess, lump, projection, prominence, promontory.

bulk, *n.* SYN.-best, biggest, greater, majority, most. ANT.-least, lesser, fraction, remnant.

bulky, *a.* SYN.-big, cumbersome, large, huge, massive, unwieldy.

bum, *n.* SYN.-beggar, hobo, rover, tramp, vagabond, vagrant, wanderer. ANT.-gentleman, laborer, worker.

bump, *n.* SYN.-bang, clash, crash, hit, jar, jolt, knock, pat, push, shove.

bunch, *n.* SYN.-aggregation, assembly, band, brood, class, cluster, collection, crowd, flock, group, herd, horde, lot, mob, pack, party, set, swarm, throng, troupe.

bungle, *v.* SYN.-blunder, botch, mishandle, mismanage, muddle, ruin, spoil, wreck.

buoyant, *a.* SYN.-effervescent, light, resilient; animated, blithe, cheerful, elated, hopeful, jocund, lively, spirited, sprightly, vivacious. ANT.-dejected, depressed, despondent, hopeless, sullen.

burden, *v.* SYN.-afflict, encumber, load, oppress, overload, tax, trouble, weigh. ANT.-alleviate, console, ease, lighten, mitigate.

burdensome, *a.* SYN.-boring, dilatory, dreary, dull, humdrum, irksome, monotonous, slow, sluggish, tardy, tedious, tire-some, uninteresting, wearisome. ANT.-amusing, entertaining, exciting, interesting, quick.

burglarize, *v.* SYN.-loot, pilfer, pillage, plunder, purloin, rob, snatch, steal, swipe. ANT.-buy, refund, repay, restore, return.

burglary, *n.* SYN.-break in, depredation, larceny, pillage, plunder, robbery, theft.

burn, *v.* SYN.-blaze, char, consume, cremate, incinerate, scald, scorch, sear, singe. ANT.-extinguish, put out, quench.

burst, *v.* SYN.-break, crack, erupt, explode, fracture, rupture, split.

bury, *v.* SYN.-conceal, cover, entomb, hide, immure, inhume, inter, secrete, stash, stow. ANT.-display, expose, open, reveal.

business, *n.* SYN.-art, commerce, employment, engagement, enterprise, job, occupation, profession, trade, trading, vocation, work. ANT.-avocation, hobby, pastime.

busy, *a.* SYN.-working; industrious, alert, brisk, lively, nimble, quick, sprightly, supple, active, assiduous, hard-working, industrious, diligent, persevering. ANT.-dormant, inactive; indolent, lazy, passive, apathetic, indifferent, lethargic, unconcerned.

butchery, *n.* SYN.-carnage, massacre, pogrom, slaughter.

buy, *v.* SYN.-acquire, bargain, get, market, obtain, procure, purchase, secure. ANT.-dispose of, sell, vend.

by, *prep.* SYN.-beside, near, next to; by means of, through, with; according to; from.

C

cabal, *n.* SYN.-collusion, combination, conspiracy, intrigue, machination, plot, treachery, treason.

cabinet, *n.* SYN.-administrators, advisors, assistants, council, committee, ministry.

calamity, *n.* SYN.-adversity, accident, casualty, catastrophe, disaster, misfortune, mishap, ruin. ANT.-advantage, fortune, welfare calculation, design, intention, purpose.

calculate, *v.* SYN.-compute, consider, count, estimate, figure, reckon. ANT.-conjecture, guess, miscalculate.

caliber, *n.* SYN.-attribute, characteristic, distinction, feature, peculiarity, property, quality, trait, caliber, grade, value. ANT.-being, essence, nature, substance.

call, *v.* SYN.-cry, exclaim, hail, shout, signal, yell; convene, invite, muster, request, summon.

callous, *a.* SYN.-hard, impenitent, indurate, insensible, insensitive, obdurate, tough, unfeeling. ANT.-compassionate, sensitive, soft, tender.

calm, *a.* SYN.-appease, composed, dispassionate, imperturbable, pacific, peaceful, placid, quiet, serene, still, tranquil, undisturbed, unruffled. ANT.-excited, frantic, stormy, turbulent, wild.

calm, *n.* SYN.-calmness, hush, peace, quiescence, quiet, quietude, repose, rest, serenity, silence, stillness, tranquility. ANT.-agitation, disturbance, excitement, noise, tumult.

calm, *v.* SYN.-allay, alleviate, assuage, compose, lull, pacify, placate, quell, quiet, relieve, satisfy, soothe, still, tranquilize. ANT.-arouse, excite, incense, inflame.

calumny, *n.* SYN.-aspersion, backbiting, defamation, libel, scandal, slander,

vilification. ANT.-applause, commendation, defense, flattery, praise.

camouflage, *n.* SYN.-cloak, cover, disguise, hide, mask, shroud, veil; deceit, misdirection.

cancel, *v.* SYN.-cross out, delete, eliminate, erase, expunge, obliterate; abolish, abrogate, annul, invalidate, nullify, quash, repeal, rescind, revoke. ANT.-confirm, enact, enforce, perpetuate

candid, *a.* SYN.-frank, free, honest, ingenuous, open, plain, sincere, straightforward, truthful; fair, impartial, just, unbiased. ANT.-contrived, scheming, sly, wily.

candidate, *n.* SYN.-aspirant, competitor, contestant, nominee.

candor, *n.* SYN.-fairness, frankness, honesty, integrity, justice, openness, rectitude, responsibility, sincerity, trustworthiness, uprightness. ANT.-cheating, deceit, dishonesty, fraud, trickery.

capability, *n.* See **capacity**.

capable, *a.* SYN.-able, clever, competent, efficient, fitted, qualified, skillful. ANT.-inadequate, incapable, incompetent, unfitted.

capacity, *n.* SYN.-ability, capability, faculty, power, skill, talent; magnitude, room, size, volume. ANT.-impotence, inability, incapacity, stupidity.

caper, *n.* SYN.-act, activity, escapade, prank, trick.

capital, *n.* SYN.-assets, cash, equipment, property, wealth.

capitulate, *v.* SYN.-abandon, acquiesce, cede, relinquish, renounce, resign, sacrifice, submit, surrender, yield. ANT.-conquer, overcome, resist, rout.

caprice, *n.* SYN.-fancy, humor, inclination, notion, quirk, vagary, whim, whimsy.

capricious, *a.* SYN.-changeable, fickle, fitful, inconstant, restless, unstable, variable. ANT.-constant, reliable, stable, steady, trustworthy.

captivity, *n.* SYN.-bondage, confinement, imprisonment, serfdom, servitude, slavery, thralldom, vassalage. ANT.-freedom, liberation.

capture, *v.* SYN.-apprehend, arrest, catch, clutch, grasp, grip, lay hold of, seize, snare, trap. ANT.-liberate, lose, release, throw.

carcass, *n.* SYN.-body, corpse, remains; form, frame, torso; bulk, corpus, mass. ANT.-intellect, mind, soul, spirit.

care, *n.* SYN.-anxiety, concern, solicitude, worry; attention, caution, circumspection, regard, vigilance, wariness; charge, custody, guardianship, ward. ANT.-disregard, indifference, neglect, negligence.

careful, *a.* SYN.-attentive, exact, finicky, fussy, heedful, meticulous, painstaking, prudent, scrupulous, thorough, thoughtful; cautious, circumspect, discreet, guarded, suspicious, vigilant, wary. ANT.-forgetful, improvident, indifferent, lax.

careless, *a.* SYN.-heedless, imprudent, inattentive, inconsiderate, indiscreet, reckless, thoughtless, unconcerned; desultory, inaccurate, lax, neglectful, negligent, remiss. ANT.-accurate, care-

ful, meticulous, nice.

carelessness, *n.* SYN.-default, disregard, failure, heedlessness, neglect, negligence, omission, oversight, slight, thoughtlessness. ANT.-attention, care, diligence, watchfulness.

caress, *v.* SYN.-coddle, cuddle, embrace, fondle, hug, kiss, pet, stroke. ANT.-annoy, buffet, spurn, tease, vex.

carnal, *a.* SYN.-animal, base, bodily, corporeal, fleshly, gross, lustful, sensual, voluptuous, worldly. ANT.-exalted, intellectual, refined, spiritual, temperate.

carping, *a.* SYN.-caviling, censorious, critical, faultfinding, hypercritical. ANT.-cursory, shallow, superficial, uncritical; appreciative, approving, commendatory, encouraging.

carriage, *n.* SYN.-air, attitude, bearing, cast, demeanor, look, poise, pose, posture, presence.

carry, *v.* SYN.-bring, convey, fetch, move, take, transmit, transport; bear, support, sustain. ANT.-abandon, drop.

carve, *v.* SYN.-chisel, create, fashion, form, model, mold, pattern, shape.

case, *n.* SYN.-bag, box, carton, container, crate, grip, holder, sheath.

cast, *v.* SYN.-fling, hurl, pitch, sling, throw, toss.

caste, *n.* SYN.-category, class, denomination, genre, kind; grade, order, rank, set.

casual, *a.* SYN.-accidental, chance, fortuitous, unexpected; incidental, informal, nonchalant, offhand, relaxed, unconcerned, unpremeditated. ANT.-expected, intended; formal, planned, pretentious.

casualty, *n.* SYN.-accident, calamity, contingency, disaster, fortuity, misfortune, mishap. ANT.-calculation, design, intention, purpose.

catalogue, *n.* SYN.-bulletin, classification, directory, file, listing, record, register.

catastrophe, *n.* SYN.-accident, adversity, affliction, calamity, casualty, devastation, disaster, distress, misfortune, mishap, ruin. ANT.-advantage, blessing, fortune, welfare.

catch, *v.* SYN.-apprehend, arrest, capture, clutch, grasp, grip, lay hold of, seize, snare, trap. ANT.-liberate, lose, release, throw.

catching, *a.* SYN.-communicable, contagious, infectious, pestilential, virulent. ANT.-healthful, hygienic, non-communicable.

category, *n.* SYN.-caste, class, denomination, genre, kind; grade, order, rank, set.

cause, *n.* SYN.-agent, determinant, incentive, inducement, motive, origin, principle, reason, source. ANT.-consequence, effect, end, result.

cause, *v.* SYN.-create, effect, evoke, incite, induce, make, occasion, originate, prompt.

caustic, *a.* SYN.-acrimonious, biting, cutting, derisive, ironic, sarcastic, sardonic, satirical, sneering, taunting. ANT.-affable, agreeable, amiable, pleasant.

caution, *n.* SYN.-care, heed, prudence, vigilance, wariness, watchfulness; admonition, counsel, injunction, warning.

ANT.-abandon, carelessness, recklessness.

cautious, *a.* SYN.-attentive, heedful, prudent, scrupulous, thoughtful; careful, circumspect, discreet, guarded, vigilant, wary. ANT.-forgetful, improvident, indifferent, lax.

cease, *v.* SYN.-abandon, abstain, arrest, check, desist, discontinue, end, halt, quit, stop; give up, relinquish, resign, stop, surrender, terminate; abandon, depart, leave, withdraw. ANT.-continue, endure, occupy, persist, stay.

celebrate, *v.* SYN.-commemorate, keep, observe, solemnize; commend, extol, glorify, honor, laud, praise. ANT.-disregard, overlook; decry, disgrace, dishonor, profane.

celebration, *n.* SYN.-anniversary, carnival, commemoration, ceremony, feast, festival, festivity, holiday, jubilee, observance, revelry, spree.

celebrity, *n.* SYN.-dignitary, hero, leader, luminary, notable, personage, star.

celestial, *a.* SYN.-divine, godlike, heavenly, holy, superhuman, supernatural, transcendent. ANT.-blasphemous, diabolical, mundane, profane, wicked.

cell, *n.* SYN.-cage, compartment, coop, keep, lockup, pen, vault.

censor, *v.* SYN.-abridge, ban, control, edit, forbid, inspect, restrict, suppress, void.

censure, *v.* SYN.-blame, condemn, denounce, reprehend, reproach, reprobate, reprove, upbraid; convict, sentence. ANT.-approve, commend, condone, forgive, praise; absolve, acquit, exonerate, pardon.

center, *n.* SYN.-core, heart, middle, midpoint, midst, nucleus. ANT.-border, boundary, outskirts, periphery, rim.

ceremonious, *a.* SYN.-affected, correct, decorous, exact, formal, methodical, precise, proper, regular, solemn, stiff. ANT.-easy, natural, unconstrained, unconventional.

ceremony, *n.* SYN.-formality, observance, parade, pomp, protocol, rite, ritual, solemnity.

certain, *a.* SYN.-assured, convinced, definite, fixed, indubitable, inevitable, positive, satisfied, secure, sure, undeniable, unquestionable. ANT.-doubtful, probable, questionable, uncertain.

certainty, *n.* SYN.-assurance, assuredness, confidence, conviction, courage, firmness, security, self-reliance, surety, pledge, promise, word, assertion, declaration, statement. ANT.-bashfulness, humility, modesty, shyness, suspicion.

certificate, *n.* SYN.-credential, declaration, endorsement, guarantee, license, testimonial, ticket, warrantee.

certify, *v.* SYN.-aver, attest, declare, state, swear, testify.

challenge, *v.* SYN.-object to, question; brave, dare, defy; call, invite, summon; demand, require.

chance, *a.* SYN.-accidental, casual, contingent, fortuitous, incidental, undesigned, unintended. ANT.-calculated, decreed, intended, planned, willed.

chance, *n.* SYN.-accident, contingency, fortuity, fortune, happening, misfor-

tune, mishap, occasion, occurrence, opening, opportunity, possibility. ANT.-calculation, design, intention, purpose.

chance, *v.* SYN.-accidentally, bechance, befall, betide, coincidence, happen, occur, unexpectedly, risk, take place, transpire.

change, *n.* SYN.-alteration, alternation, modification, mutation, substitution, variation, variety, vicissitude. ANT.-monotony, stability, uniformity.

change, *v.* SYN.-exchange, substitute; alter, convert, modify, remodel, shift, transfigure, transform, vary, veer. ANT.-retain; continue, establish, preserve, settle, stabilize.

changeable, *a.* SYN.-fickle, fitful, inconstant, shifting, unstable, vacillating, variable, wavering. ANT.-constant, stable, steady, unchanging, uniform.

channel, *n.* SYN.-artery, canal, conduit, course, ditch, duct, furrow, gutter, tube, vein.

chaos, *n.* SYN.-anarchy, confusion, disorder, disorganization, jumble, muddle. ANT.-order, organization, system.

chaperone, *v.* SYN.-accompany, attend, escort, go with. ANT.-abandon, avoid.

character, *n.* SYN.-class, description, disposition, individuality, kind, nature, reputation, repute, temperament, sort, standing, style; figure, mark, sign, symbol, representation.

characteristic, *n.* SYN.-attribute, feature, mark, peculiarity, property, quality, trait.

charge, *n.* SYN.-accusation, arraignment, imputation, incrimination, indictment. ANT.-exculpation, exoneration, pardon.

charge, *v.* SYN.-accuse, arraign, censure, incriminate, indict. ANT.-absolve, acquit, exonerate, release, vindicate.

charitable, *a.* SYN.-altruistic, benevolent, benign, friendly, generous, humane, kind, liberal, merciful, obliging, philanthropic, tender, unselfish. ANT.-greedy, harsh, malevolent, wicked.

charity, *n.* SYN.-altruism, beneficence, benevolence, generosity, humanity, kindness, liberality, magnanimity, philanthropy, tenderness. ANT.-cruelty, inhumanity, malevolence, selfishness, unkindness.

charming, *a.* SYN.-alluring, attractive, bewitching, captivating, enchanting, engaging, fascinating, winning. ANT.-repugnant, repulsive, revolting.

chart, *n.* SYN.-diagram, graph, map, outline, plan, poster, presentation.

chase, *v.* SYN.-follow, hunt, persist, pursue, trace, track, trail, seek; drive, scatter. ANT.-abandon, elude, escape, evade, flee.

chaste, *a.* SYN.-decent, demure, guiltless, innocent, modest, moral, proper, pure, sincere, strong, uncorrupted, undefiled, virginal. ANT.-brash, corruptible, foul, polluted, sullied, tainted, tarnished, weak.

chastise, *v.* SYN.-berate, castigate, correct, discipline, pummel, punish, scold, strike, upbraid. ANT.-acquit, exonerate, free, pardon, release.

chat, *n.* SYN.-chatter, colloquy, conference, conspiracy, conversation, dia-

logue, interview, intrigue, parley, plan, plot, scheme, talk.

chat, *v.* SYN.-converse, gossip, jabber, speak, talk, tattle; confer, consult, deliberate, discuss, reason.

chatter, *n.* SYN.-conversation, dialogue, discussion, gossip, rumor, talk. ANT.-correspondence, meditation, silence, writing.

cheap, *a.* SYN.-budget, inexpensive, low-priced, moderate, poor, reasonable, thrifty; beggarly, common, inferior, mean, shabby. ANT.-costly, dear, expensive; dignified, honorable, noble.

cheat, *n.* SYN.-chicanery, con, deception, duplicity, fraud, guile, imposture, swindle, trick; charlatan, cheater, chiseler, conniver, crook, fake, fraud, rogue, swindler, trickster. ANT.-fairness, honesty, integrity, sincerity.

cheat, *v.* SYN.-bilk, circumvent, deceive, defraud, dupe, fool, gull, hoax, hoodwink, outwit, swindle, trick, victimize.

check, *v.* SYN.-analyze, assess, audit, contemplate, dissect, examine, inquire, interrogate, notice, question, quiz, review, scan, scrutinize, survey, view, watch; block, hamper, hinder, impede, obstruct, prevent, resist, restrain, retard, stop, thwart. ANT.-disregard, neglect, omit, overlook; assist, expedite, facilitate, further, promote.

cheer, *v.* SYN.-comfort, consolation, contentment, ease, enjoyment, relief, solace, succor. ANT.-affliction, discomfort, misery, suffering, torment, torture.

cheerful, *a.* SYN.-gay, glad, happy, jolly, joyful, lighthearted, merry, sprightly. ANT.-depressed, glum, mournful, sad, sullen.

cherish, *v.* SYN.-appreciate, hold dear, prize, treasure, value; foster, nurture, sustain. ANT.-dislike, disregard, neglect; abandon, reject.

chief, *a.* SYN.-cardinal, essential, first, foremost, highest, leading, main, paramount, predominant, supreme. ANT.-auxiliary, minor, subordinate, subsidiary, supplemental.

chief, *n.* SYN.-captain, chieftain, commander, head, leader, master, principal, ringleader, ruler, sovereign. ANT.-attendant, follower, servant, subordinate.

childish, *a.* SYN.-adolescent, childlike, foolish, immature, infantile, juvenile, youthful.

chilly, *a.* SYN.-arctic, brisk, cold, cool, crisp, freezing, frigid, frozen, icy, wintry; passionless, phlegmatic, stoical, unfeeling. ANT.-burning, fiery, heated, hot, torrid; ardent, passionate.

chivalrous, *a.* SYN.-brave, courteous, gallant, generous, heroic, noble, polite, valiant. ANT.-base, crass, cowardly, crass, ignoble.

choice, *n.* SYN.-alternative, election, favorite, option, preference, selection.

choose, *v.* SYN.-cull, decide, elect, favor, judge, opt, pick, prefer, select, take. ANT.-refuse, reject.

chronic, *a.* SYN.-continual, continuing, lasting, lingering, perennial, persisting, recurring.

chronicle, *n.* SYN.-account, accounting,

annals, history, narrative, record, report.

chronicle, v. SYN.-account, elucidate, explain, expound, narrate, record, recount, report, tell.

chronological, a. SYN.-classified, consecutive, dated, historical, sequential.

cinema, n. SYN.-film, movie, picture.

circle, n. SYN.-belt, circuit, circumference, cycle, disk, loop, meridian, orbit, ring, sphere, wheel.

circuitous, a. SYN.-crooked, devious, distorted, erratic, indirect, roundabout, swerving, tortuous, wandering, winding; crooked, cunning, tricky. ANT.-direct, straight; honest, straightforward.

circular, a. SYN.-complete, curved, cylindrical, entire, globular, round, spherical.

circumspection, n. SYN.-anxiety, care, concern, solicitude, worry; attention, caution, regard, vigilance, wariness. ANT.-disregard, indifference, neglect, negligence.

circumstance, n. SYN.-cause, condition, contingency, event, fact, factor, happening, incident, occurrence, position, situation.

citation, n. SYN.-charge, summons, ticket; award, certificate, commendation.

cite, v. SYN.-adduce, advance, affirm, allege, assign, claim, declare, extract, maintain, paraphrase, quote, recite, refer, repeat. ANT.-contradict, deny, disprove, gainsay, refute.

citizen, n. SYN.-civilian, commoner, householder, inhabitant, national, native, occupant, resident, subject, taxpayer, voter. ANT.-alien, foreigner, outsider.

city, n. SYN.-metropolis, municipality, town, township, village. ANT.-country, suburb.

civil, a. SYN.-considerate, courteous, cultivated, genteel, polite, refined, urbane, well-bred, well-mannered. ANT.-boorish, impertinent, rude, uncivil, uncouth.

civilization, n. SYN.-cultivation, culture, education, enlightenment, refinement. ANT.-boorishness, ignorance, illiteracy, vulgarity.

claim, n. SYN.-application, declaration, deed, interest, petition, right, suit, title.

claim, v. SYN.-affirm, allege, assert, aver, avow, declare, express, maintain, recite, recount, say, tell, state, utter; defend, support, uphold, vindicate. ANT.-contradict, deny, imply, refute.

clamor, n. SYN.-babel, cry, din, noise, outcry, racket, row, sound, tumult, uproar. ANT.-hush, quiet, silence, stillness.

clan, n. SYN.-brotherhood, fellowship, solidarity; association, clan, fraternity, society. ANT.-acrimony, discord, individual, opposition, strife.

clandestine, a. SYN.-concealed, covert, hidden, latent, private, secret, surreptitious, unknown. ANT.-conspicuous, disclosed, exposed, known, obvious, overt.

clarify, v. SYN.-decipher, elucidate, explain, expound, illustrate, interpret, resolve, unfold, unravel. ANT.-baffle, confuse, darken, obscure.

clarity, n. SYN.-clearness, directness, distinctness, exactness, explicitness, precision, prominence, purity, transparency.

clash, v. SYN.-argue, collide, conflict, differ, disagree, encounter, oppose.

clasp, v. SYN.-cling, clutch, grasp, grip; have, hold, keep, maintain, possess, retain. ANT.-relinquish, vacate.

class, n. SYN.-breed, category, degree, denomination, distinction, genre, family, kind; caste, grade, order, rank, standing, set; elegance, excellence.

classify, v. SYN.-arrange, catalogue, categorize, correlate, grade, group, index, label, order, organize, rank, rate. ANT.-combine, disorganize, mix.

clean, v. SYN.-cleanse, mop, purify, scrub, sweep, wash. ANT.-dirty, pollute, soil, stain, sully.

cleanse, v. SYN.-bathe, clean, launder, mop, purify, sanitize, scald, scrub, sterilize, wash. ANT.-dirty, foul, pollute, soil, stain, sully.

clear, a. SYN.-cloudless, fair, sunny; limpid, transparent; apparent, distinct, evident, intelligible, lucid, manifest, obvious, plain, unmistakable, visible; open, unobstructed. ANT.-cloudy, foul, overcast; ambiguous, obscure, unclear, vague.

clemency, n. SYN.-charity, compassion, forgiveness, grace, leniency, mercy, mildness, pity. ANT.-cruelty, punishment, retribution, vengeance.

clerical, a. SYN.-apostolic, cleric, ecclesiastical, holy, monastic, monkish, ministerial, pontifical, priestly, sacred.

clerk, n. SYN.-assistant, bookkeeper, cashier, recorder, registrar, salesperson, stenographer, teller, timekeeper.

clever, a. SYN.-adroit, apt, dexterous, quick, quick-witted, skillful, talented, witty; bright, ingenious, sharp, smart. ANT.-awkward, bungling, clumsy, slow, unskilled; dull, foolish, stupid.

cleverness, n. SYN.-comprehension, intellect, intelligence, mind, perspicacity, reason, sagacity, sense, understanding; banter, cleverness, fun, humor, irony, pleasantry, raillery, sarcasm, satire, wit, witticism. ANT.-commonplace, platitude, sobriety, solemnity, stupidity.

cliché, n. SYN.-platitude, proverb, saw, saying, slogan.

client, n. SYN.-buyer, customer, patron, user.

climax, n. SYN.-acme, apex, consummation, crown, culmination, end, extremity, height, peak, pinnacle, summit, zenith. ANT.-anticlimax, base, depth, floor.

climb, v. SYN.-ascend, clamber, escalate, mount, rise, scale, soar, tower. ANT.-descend, fall, sink.

cling, v. SYN.-adhere, clasp, clutch, grab, grasp, grip, hold, keep, maintain, retain. ANT.-abandon, loose, relinquish.

clip, v. SYN.-crop, curtail, cut, prune, shorten, snip, trim.

clique, n. SYN.-clan, club, faction, group.

cloak, v. SYN.-clothe, conceal, cover, disguise, envelop, guard, hide, mask, protect, screen, shield, shroud, veil. ANT.-bare, divulge, expose, reveal, unveil.

cloister, n. SYN.-abbey, convent, hermitage, monastery, nunnery, priory.

close, a. SYN.-abutting, adjacent, adjoining, immediate, impending, near, nearby, neighboring; confidential, dear, devoted, intimate. ANT.-afar, distant, faraway, removed.

close, n. SYN.-completion, conclusion, end, finale, settlement, termination; ANT.-beginning, commencement, inception, prelude, start.

close, v. SYN.-occlude, seal, shut; clog, obstruct, stop; cease, complete, conclude, end, finish, terminate. ANT.-open, unbar, unlock; begin, commence, inaugurate, start.

clothes, n. SYN.-apparel, array, attire, clothing, drapery, dress, garb, garments/raiment, vestments, vesture. ANT.-nakedness, nudity.

cloudy, a. SYN.-dark, dim, indistinct, hazy, murky, mysterious, obscure, overcast, shadowy. ANT.-bright, clear, distinct, limpid, sunny.

clue, n. SYN.-evidence, hint, information, mark, sign, spoor, trace, track.

clumsy, a. SYN.-awkward, gauche, inept, rough, unpolished, untoward. ANT.-adroit, graceful, neat, polished, skillful.

clutch, v. SYN.-clasp, cling, grasp, grip; have, hold, keep, maintain, possess, retain. ANT.-relinquish, vacate.

coach, n. SYN.-drill, instill, instruct, prompt, teach, train, tutor.

coalition, n. SYN.-alliance, association, combination, confederacy, entente, federation, league, partnership, union; compact, covenant, marriage, treaty. ANT.-divorce, schism, separation.

coarse, a. SYN.-crude, impure, rough, rugged, unrefined; gross, gruff, immodest, indelicate, rude, unpolished, vulgar. ANT.-fine, polished, refined, smooth; cultivated, cultured, delicate.

coax, v. SYN.-cajole, inveigle, persuade, wheedle.

coerce, v. SYN.-coerce, constrain, drive, enforce, force, impel, oblige. ANT.-allure, convince, induce, persuade, prevent.

coercion, n. SYN.-compulsion, constraint, force, restraint, violence. ANT.-persuasion.

cognizant, a. SYN.-apprised, aware, conscious, informed, mindful, observant, perceptive, sensible. ANT.-ignorant, insensible, oblivious, unaware.

coherent, a. SYN.-articulate, comprehensible, consistent, logical, reasonable, sound, understandable.

coincide, v. SYN.-accede, acquiesce, agree, assent, comply, consent; agree, concur, conform, harmonize, match, tally. ANT.-contradict, differ, disagree, dissent, protest; casual, random.

cold, a. SYN.-arctic, chilly, cool, freezing, frigid, frozen, icy, wintry; apathetic, indifferent, passionless, phlegmatic, reserved, stoical, unconcerned, unfeeling. ANT.-burning, fiery, heated, hot, torrid; ardent, passionate.

collapse, v. SYN.-decline, decrease, deflate, diminish, drop, fall, sink, subside; implode, topple, tumble. ANT.-arise, ascend, climb, mount, soar.

colleague, n. SYN.-associate, attendant, collaborator, companion, comrade, consort, crony, friend, mate, partner. ANT.-adversary, enemy, stranger.

collect, v. SYN.-accumulate, amass, assemble, concentrate, congregate, consolidate, gather, heap, hoard, mass, pile. ANT.-assort, disperse, distribute, divide, dole.

collected, a. SYN.-calm, composed, cool, imperturbable, peaceful, placid, quiet, sedate, tranquil, unmoved. ANT.-agitated, aroused, excited, perturbed, violent.

collection, n. SYN.-aggregate, amount, conglomeration, entirety, sum, total, whole. ANT.-element, ingredient, part, particular, unit.

collision, n. SYN.-battle, combat, conflict, duel, encounter, fight, struggle; contention, controversy, discord, inconsistency, interference, opposition, variance. ANT.-amity, concord, consonance, harmony.

collusion, n. SYN.-cabal, combination, conspiracy, intrigue, machination, plot, treachery, treason.

color, n. SYN.-complexion, dye, hue, paint, pigment, shade, stain, taint, tincture, tinge, tint. ANT.-achromatism, paleness, transparency.

colossal, a. SYN.-elephantine, enormous, gargantuan, gigantic, huge, immense, large, prodigious, vast. ANT.-diminutive, little, minute, small, tiny.

combat, n. SYN.-battle, collision, conflict, duel, encounter, fight, struggle; contention. ANT.-amity, concord, consonance, harmony.

combat, v. SYN.-battle, brawl, conflict, contend, dispute, encounter, fight, quarrel skirmish, struggle.

combination, n. SYN.-alliance, association, coalition, confederacy, entente, federation, league, partnership, union, unification; compact, covenant, marriage, treaty. ANT.-divorce, schism, separation.

combine, v. SYN.-adjoin, amalgamate, associate, attach, blend, conjoin, connect, consolidate, couple, go with, join, link, merge, unite, unify. ANT.-detach, disconnect, disjoin, separate.

comedy, n. SYN.-burlesque, farce, humor, mimicry, satire, slapstick.

comfort, n. SYN.-cheer, consolation, contentment, ease, enjoyment, luxury, plenty, relaxation, relief, rest, restfulness, solace, succor, warmth. ANT.-affliction, discomfort, misery, suffering, torment, torture.

comfort, v. SYN.-aid, alleviate, calm, cheer, console, encourage, gladden, help, solace, soothe, support, sympathize. ANT.-antagonize, aggravate, depress, dishearten.

comfortable, a. SYN.-acceptable, agreeable, contented, gratifying, pleasing, pleasurable, relaxed, restful, soothed, untroubled; cozy, luxurious, protected, rich, roomy, satisfying, sheltered, snug,

spacious, warm, wealthy. ANT.-distressing, miserable, troubled, uncomfortable, wretched; mean, poor, wanting.

comical, a. SYN.-amusing, droll, farcical, funny, humorous, laughable, ludicrous ridiculous, slapstick, witty. ANT.-melancholy, sad, serious, sober, solemn.

coming, a. SYN.-advancing, approaching, anticipated, arriving, close, due, expected, foreseen, imminent, impending, near, nearing, predicted. ANT.-departing, going, leaving.

command, n. SYN.-bidding, decree, dictate, injunction, instruction, law, mandate, order, proclamation, requirement. ANT.-consent, license, permission.

command, v. SYN.-conduct, govern, guide, manage, regulate, rule; bid, charge, direct, instruct, order, tell. ANT.-deceive, distract, misdirect, misguide.

commemorate, v. SYN.-celebrate, honor, remember, solemnize.

commence, v. SYN.-arise, begin, enter, inaugurate, initiate, institute, open, originate, start. ANT.-close, complete, end, finish, terminate.

commencement, n. SYN.-beginning, birth, inception, opening, origin, origination, outset, source, start. ANT.-close, completion, consummation, end, termination.

commend, v. SYN.-acclaim, applaud, appreciate, approve, compliment, extol, flatter, laud, like, praise; authorize, confirm, endorse, ratify, sanction. ANT.-criticize, disparage; condemn, nullify.

commensurate, a. SYN.-adequate, alike, equal, equitable, equivalent, even, fair, judicious, like, proportional, same, similar, uniform. ANT-different, disparate, dissimilar, diverse.

comment, n. SYN.-annotation, assertion, conversation, criticism, declaration, notation, observation, remark, statement, talk, utterance.

comment, v. SYN.-affirm, assert, aver, criticize, interject, mention, note, observe, remark, speak.

commerce, n. SYN.-business, employment, engagement, enterprise, job, occupation, profession, trade, trading, vocation, work. ANT.-avocation, hobby, pastime.

commission, v. SYN.-appoint, authorize, charge, command, delegate, deputize, employ, empower, engage, entrust, hire, ordain, select.

commit, v. SYN.-do, perform, perpetrate; commend, consign, entrust, relegate, trust; bind, obligate, pledge. ANT.-fail, miscarry, neglect; mistrust, release, renounce; free, loose.

commodious, a. SYN.-accessible, appropriate, convenient, fitting, handy, suitable. ANT.-awkward, inconvenient, inopportune, troublesome.

common, a. SYN.-familiar, frequent, general, ordinary, popular, prevalent, universal, usual; low, mean, vulgar. ANT.-exceptional, extraordinary, odd, scarce; noble, refined.

commotion, n. SYN.-agitation, chaos, confusion, disarrangement, disarray, disorder, ferment, jumble, stir, tumult,

turmoil. ANT.-certainty, order, peace, tranquility.

communicable, a. SYN.-catching, contagious, infectious, pestilential, virulent. ANT.-healthful, hygienic, non-communicable.

communicate, v. SYN.-advise, confer, contact, convey, disclose, divulge, impart, inform, notify, relate, reveal, tell, transmit. ANT.-conceal, hide, withhold.

communion, n. SYN.-association, fellowship, intercourse, participation, sacrament, union. ANT.-alienation, non participation.

compact, a. SYN.-constricted, contracted, firm, small, snug, tight; mash, tamp. ANT.-lax, loose, open, relaxed, slack.

compact, n. SYN.-agreement, bargain, compact, contract, covenant, pact, stipulation. ANT.-disagreement, discord, dissension, variance.

companion, n. SYN.-associate, attendant, colleague, comrade, consort, crony, friend, guide, mate, partner, protector. ANT.-adversary, enemy, stranger.

company, n. SYN.-assemblage, band, crew, group, horde, party, throng, troop; association, fellowship, society; corporation, firm. ANT.-dispersion, individual, seclusion, solitude.

comparable, a. SYN.-akin, alike, allied, analogous, correlative, correspondent, corresponding, equivalent, like, parallel, similar. ANT.-different, dissimilar, divergent, incongruous, opposed.

compare, v. SYN.-associate, connect, contrast, critique, describe, differentiate, discriminate, distinguish, equate, examine, link, match, measure, oppose, rate, relate, sample.

comparison, n. SYN.-analogy, association, contrast, correspondence, example, metaphor, parable, relation, resemblance.

compassion, n. SYN.-commiseration, concern, condolence, consideration, empathy, mercy, pity, sensitivity, sympathy, tenderness, warmth. ANT.-brutality, cruelty, hardness, inhumanity, ruthlessness.

compassionate, a. SYN.-affable, benevolent, benign, forbearing, forgiving, gentle, good, humane, indulgent, kind, kindly, merciful, sympathetic, tender, thoughtful. ANT.-cruel, inhuman, merciless, severe, unkind.

compatible, a. SYN.-accordant, agreeing, conforming, congruous, consistent, consonant, constant, correspondent. ANT.-contradictory, discrepant, incongruous, inconsistent, paradoxical.

compel, v. SYN.-coerce, constrain, drive, enforce, force, impel, oblige. ANT.-allure, convince, induce, persuade, prevent.

compensation, n. SYN.-allowance, bonus, commission, consideration, earnings, fee, indemnity, pay, payment, recompense, reimbursement, remuneration, repayment, salary, stipend, wages. ANT.-gift, gratuity, present.

compete, v. SYN.-battle, clash, contest, encounter, engage, face, oppose, rival, spar, strive, struggle, vie.

competent, a. SYN.-able, capable, clever,

efficient, fitted, qualified, skillful. ANT.-inadequate, incapable, incompetent, unfitted.

competitor, n. SYN.-adversary, antagonist, enemy, foe, opponent, rival. ANT.-accomplice, ally, comrade, confederate, friend, teammate.

compile, v. SYN.-accumulate, amass, arrange, assemble, catalogue, collect, correlate, gather, group, index, label, order, organize, rank, rate.

complacent, a. SYN.-contented, happy, pleased, self-satisfied, smug; accommodating, complaisant, compliant, yielding.

complain, v. SYN.-criticize, denounce, deplore, deprecate, disapprove, fuss, grouch, grumble, lament, murmur, object, oppose, protest, regret, remonstrate, repine, whine. ANT.-applaud, approve, praise, rejoice.

complete, a. SYN.-concluded, consummated, detailed, ended, entire, finished, full, perfect, thorough, total, unbroken, undivided. ANT.-imperfect, lacking, unfinished.

complete, v. SYN.-accomplish, achieve, close, conclude, consummate, do, end, execute, finish, fulfill, get done, perfect, perform, terminate.

complex, a. SYN.-complicated, compound, intricate, involved, manifold, perplexing. ANT.-plain, simple, uncompounded.

complexion, n. SYN.-color, coloration, hue, pigment, pigmentation, shade, texture, tone.

complicated, a. SYN.-complex, compound, intricate, involved, perplexing. ANT.-plain, simple, uncompounded.

compliment, n. SYN.-adulation, appreciation, approval, commendation, endorsement, eulogy, flattery, honor, praise, regards, respects, salute, tribute. ANT.-affront, criticism, insult, taunt.

comply, v. SYN.-accede, acquiesce, agree, assent, consent; coincide, concur, conform, tally. ANT.-contradict, differ, disagree, dissent, protest.

component, n. SYN.-division, fragment, moiety, piece, portion, scrap, section, segment, share; element, ingredient, member, organ, part. ANT.-entirety, whole.

compose, v. SYN.-construct, create, fashion, forge, make, mold, produce, shape; constitute, form, make up; arrange, combine, organize; devise, frame, invent. ANT.-destroy, disfigure, dismantle, misshape, wreck.

composed, a. SYN.-calm, collected, cool, imperturbable, peaceful, placid, quiet, sedate, tranquil, unmoved. ANT.-agitated, aroused, excited, perturbed, violent.

composer, n. SYN.-author, creator, father, inventor, maker, originator, writer.

composure, n. SYN.-balance, calmness, carriage, complacence, contentment, control, equanimity, equilibrium, poise, self-control, serenity, tranquility. ANT.-agitation, anger, excitement, rage, turbulence.

compound, v. SYN.-alloy, amalgamate, blend, combine, composite, concoct,, fuse, jumble, mingle, mix. ANT.-dissociate, divide, segregate, separate, sort.

comprehend, v. SYN.-appreciate, apprehend, conceive, discern, grasp, know, learn, perceive, realize, see, understand. ANT.-ignore, misapprehend, mistake, misunderstand.

comprehension, n. SYN.-apprehension, cognizance, conception, discernment, insight, perception, understanding. ANT.-ignorance, insensibility, misapprehension, misconception.

compress, v. SYN.-abbreviate, abridge, compact, condense, consolidate, pack, reduce, shorten, shrink.

comprise, v. SYN.-contain, embody, embrace, encompass, hold, include. ANT.-discharge, emit, exclude; encourage, yield.

compulsion, n. SYN.-dint, energy, force, intensity, might, potency, power, strength, vigor; coercion. ANT.-feebleness, frailty, impotence, weakness; persuasion.

compute, v. SYN.-add, ascertain, calculate, consider, count, derive, divide, divine, estimate, figure, multiply, reckon, subtract. ANT.-conjecture, guess, miscalculate.

comrade, n. SYN.-associate, attendant, colleague, companion, consort, crony, friend, mate, partner. ANT.-adversary, enemy, stranger.

conceal, v. SYN.-cloak, cover, curtain, disguise, envelop, guard, hide, mask, protect, screen, secrete, shield, shroud, suppress, veil, withhold. ANT.-bare, disclose, divulge, expose, reveal, show, uncover, unveil.

concede, v. SYN.-let, permit, suffer, tolerate; authorize, give, grant, yield; acknowledge, admit, allow. ANT.-forbid, object, protest, refuse, resist.

conceit, n. SYN.-complacency, egotism, pride, self-esteem, vanity; caprice, conception, fancy, idea, imagination, notion, whim. ANT.-diffidence, humility, meekness, modesty.

conceited, a. SYN.-proud, vain, vainglorious. ANT.-effective, potent, profitable; meek, modest.

conceive, v. SYN.-begin, comprehend, concoct, contrive, create, design, devise, fabricate, frame, grasp, invent, understand. ANT.-copy, imitate, reproduce.

concentrated, a. SYN.-close, compact, compressed, crowded, dense, thick, undiluted. ANT.-dispersed, dissipated, sparse.

concept, n. SYN.-abstraction, conception, fancy, idea, image, impression, notion, opinion, sentiment, thought. ANT.-entity, matter, object, substance, thing.

conception, n. SYN.-apprehension, cogitation, cognition, comprehension, consideration, fancy, idea, imagination, impression, judgment, memory, notion, opinion, recollection, reflection, sentiment, thought, understanding, view.

concern, n. SYN.-affair, business, matter, transaction; anxiety, care, solicitude, worry. ANT.-apathy, indifference, negligence, unconcern.

concise, a. SYN.-brief, compact, condensed, compendious, curt, incisive, laconic, neat, pithy, short, succinct, summary, terse. ANT.-extended, lengthy, long, prolonged, protracted, verbose, wordy.

conclude, v. SYN.-close, complete, conclusion, consummate, end, finale, finish, fulfill, get done, perfect, settlement, terminate, termination. ANT.-beginning, commencement, inception, prelude, start.

conclusion, n. SYN.-close, completion, end, finale, issue, settlement, termination; decision, deduction, inference, judgment. ANT.-beginning, commencement, inception, prelude, start.

conclusive, a. SYN.-concluding, decisive, ending, eventual, final, last, latest, terminal, ultimate. ANT.-first, inaugural, incipient, original, rudimentary.

concord, n. SYN.-accordance, agreement, coincidence, concurrence, harmony, understanding, unison, bargain, compact, contract, covenant, pact, stipulation. ANT.-difference, disagreement, discord, dissension, variance.

concrete, a. SYN.-definite, firm, positive, precise, real, solid, specific.

concur, v. SYN.-accede, acquiesce, agree, assent, comply, consent; coincide, conform, tally. ANT.-contradict, differ, disagree, dissent, protest.

condemn, v. SYN.-blame, censure, denounce, reprehend, reproach, reprobate, reprove, upbraid; convict, sentence. ANT.-approve, commend, condone, forgive, praise; absolve, acquit, exonerate, pardon.

condense, v. SYN.-abbreviate, abridge, compress, consolidate, compact, dehydrate, reduce, shorten, summarize.

condescend, v. SYN.-accommodate, comply, concede, deign, oblige, patronize.

condition, n. SYN.-case, circumstance, plight, predicament, situation, state; prohibition, provision, requirement, restraint, restriction, stipulation, term.

condition, v. SYN.-adapt, equip, fit, furnish, get ready, make ready, modify, predispose, prepare, provide, qualify, ready.

conditional, a. SYN.-contingent, dependent, depending, relying, subject, subordinate. ANT.-absolute, autonomous, casual, independent, original.

condolence, n. SYN.-commiseration, compassion, empathy, pity, sympathy, tenderness, warmth. ANT.-antipathy, harshness, indifference, malevolence, unconcern.

condone, v. SYN.-accept, allow, excuse, overlook, pardon.

conduct, n. SYN.-action, bearing, behavior, carriage, deed, demeanor, deportment, disposition, manner.

conduct, v. SYN.-direct, escort, guide, lead, steer; control, manage, regulate, supervise.

confederate, n. SYN.-abettor, accessory, accomplice, ally, assistant, associate. ANT.-adversary, enemy, opponent, rival.

confederation, n. SYN.-alliance, association, coalition, combination, confederacy, entente, federation, league, partnership, union; compact, covenant, marriage, treaty. ANT.-schism, separation.

confer, v. SYN.-chat, converse, speak; consult, counsel, deliberate, discuss, negotiate, reason, talk.

conference, n. SYN.-conversation, discussion, gathering, interchange, meeting.

confess, v. SYN.-acknowledge, admit, allow, avow, concede, divulge, grant, own, reveal. ANT.-conceal, deny, disclaim, disown, renounce.

confession, n. SYN.-apology, defense, excuse, explanation, justification. ANT.-accusation, complaint, denial, dissimulation.

confidence, n. SYN.-assurance, assuredness, certainty, conviction, courage, firmness, security, self-reliance, surety, pledge, promise, word, assertion, declaration, statement. ANT.-bashfulness, humility, modesty, shyness, suspicion.

confine, v. SYN.-bound, circumscribe, enclose, encompass, envelop, fence, limit, surround. ANT.-develop, distend, enlarge, expand, expose, open.

confirm, v. SYN.-authenticate, corroborate, substantiate, validate, verify; acknowledge, assure, establish, settle; approve, fix, ratify, sanction; strengthen.

confirmation, n. SYN.-corroboration, demonstration, evidence, proof, test, testimony, trial, validation, verification. ANT.-failure, fallacy, invalidity.

confiscate, v. SYN.-appropriate, capture, catch, purloin, remove, steal, take; grasp, grip, seize; get, obtain, ; claim, demand; adopt, choose, espouse, select.

conflagration, n. SYN.-blaze, burning, combustion, fire, flame, heat.

conflict, n. SYN.-battle, collision, combat, duel, encounter, fight, struggle; contention, controversy, discord, inconsistency, interference, opposition, variance. ANT.-amity, concord, consonance, harmony.

conform, v. SYN.-acclimate, accommodate, adjust, comply, follow, obey, reconcile, suit.

confounded, a. SYN.-abashed, amazed, bewildered, confused, disconcerted, perplexed, puzzled.

confront, v. SYN.-contradict, counteract, defy, face, hinder, obstruct, oppose, resist, thwart, withstand. ANT.-agree, cooperate, submit, succumb, support.

confuse, v. SYN.-bewilder, confound, disorient, disconcert, dumfound, fluster, mislead, misinform, muddle, mystify, nonplus, obscure, perplex, puzzle. ANT.-clarify, explain, illumine, instruct, solve.

confused, a. SYN.-bewildered, chaotic, confounded, deranged, disconcerted, disordered, disorganized, indistinct, jumbled, mistaken, misunderstood, mixed, muddled, perplexed. ANT.-clear, lucid, obvious, organized, plain.

confusion, n. SYN.-agitation, chaos, commotion, disarrangement, disarray,

disorder, ferment, jumble, stir, tumult, turmoil. ANT.-certainty, order, peace, tranquility.

congratulate, v. SYN.-commend, compliment, praise, salute, toast.

congruous, a. SYN.-accordant, agreeing, compatible, conforming, consistent, consonant, constant, correspondent. ANT.-contradictory, discrepant, incongruous, inconsistent, paradoxical.

conjecture, n. SYN.-hypothesis, supposition, theory. ANT.-certainty, fact, proof.

conjecture, v. SYN.-chance, guess, hazard, infer. ANT.-determine, guard, insure, know.

connect, v. SYN.-adjoin, affix, annex, append, associate, attach, couple, join, link, stick, unite; assign, associate. ANT.-detach, disengage, separate, unfasten, untie.

connection, n. SYN.-affinity, alliance, association, bond, conjunction, link, relationship, tie, union. ANT.-disunion, isolation, separation.

conquer, v. SYN.-beat, crush, defeat, humble, master, overcome, quell, rout, subdue, subjugate, surmount, vanquish. ANT.-capitulate, cede, lose, retreat, surrender.

conquest, n. achievement, triumph, victory. ANT.-defeat, failure.

conscientious, a. SYN.-attentive, careful, exact, fastidious, heedful, meticulous, painstaking, prudent, scrupulous, thorough, thoughtful. ANT.-forgetful, improvident, indifferent, lax.

conscious, a. SYN.-alert, alive, apprised, aware, cognizant, discerning, informed, keen, knowing, mindful, observant, perceptive, sensible, understanding, wary. ANT.-ignorant, insensible, oblivious, unaware.

consecrate, v. SYN.-adore, dignify, enshrine, enthrone, exalt, extol, glorify, hallow, honor, revere, sanctify, venerate. ANT.-abuse, debase, degrade, dishonor, mock.

consecrated, a. SYN.-blessed, devout, divine, hallowed, holy, pious, religious, sacred, saintly, spiritual. ANT.-evil, profane, sacrilegious, secular, worldly.

consecutive, a. SYN.-chronological, connected, continuous, progressive, sequential, successive.

consensus, n. SYN.-accord, agreement, opinion.

consent, n. SYN.-approval, authority, authorization, leave, liberty, license, permission, permit. ANT.-denial, opposition, prohibition, refusal.

consent, v. SYN.-accede, acquiesce, agree, assent, comply, coincide, concur, conform, tally. ANT.-contradict, differ, disagree, dissent, protest.

consequence, n. SYN.-conclusion, effect, importance, outcome, result.

consequently, adv. SYN.-accordingly, hence, so, then, thence, therefore.

conservation, n. SYN.-conserving, guarding, keeping, maintenance, preservation, preserving, protecting, protection, safekeeping, saving.

conservative, a. SYN.-careful, constant, conventional, cautious, guarded, inflexible, prudent, sober, steady, traditional,

unchanging, unimaginative, wary.

consider, v. SYN.-contemplate, deliberate, examine, heed, meditate, ponder, reflect, study, weigh; esteem, regard, respect. ANT.-ignore, neglect, overlook.

considerate, a. SYN.-attentive, careful, cautious, charitable, concerned, heedful, kind, provident, prudent, thoughtful; contemplative, introspective, meditative, pensive, reflective. ANT.-heedless, inconsiderate, precipitous, rash, thoughtless.

consideration, n. SYN.-alertness, attention, care, circumspection, heed, kindliness, mindfulness, notice, observance, watchfulness; application, contemplation, reflection, study. ANT.-disregard, indifference, negligence, omission, oversight.

considered, a. SYN.-careful, contemplated, examined, investigated, thoughtful, weighed.

consistent, a. SYN.-accordant, agreeing, compatible, conforming, congruous, consonant, constant, correspondent. ANT.-contradictory, discrepant, incongruous, inconsistent, paradoxical.

consolation, n. SYN.-comfort, contentment, ease, enjoyment, relief, solace, succor. ANT.-affliction, discomfort, misery, suffering, torment, torture.

console, v. SYN.-allay, assuage, cheer, comfort, encourage, solace, soothe. ANT.-annoy, distress, worry.

consolidate, v. SYN.-blend, join, merge, mix, solidify, strengthen, unify, unite.

consort, n. SYN.-associate, colleague, companion, comrade, friend, mate, partner. ANT.-adversary, enemy, stranger.

conspicuous, a. SYN.-clear, distinguished, eminent, illustrious, manifest, noted, noticeable, obvious, outstanding, prominent, salient, striking, visible. ANT.-common, hidden, inconspicuous, obscure.

conspiracy, n. SYN.-cabal, collusion, combination, intrigue, machination, plot, treachery, treason.

constant, a. SYN.-abiding, ceaseless, continual, enduring, faithful, fixed, immutable, invariant, permanent, perpetual, persistent, unalterable, unchanging, uninterrupted, unwavering. ANT.-fickle, mutable, vacillating, wavering.

constantly, adv. SYN.-always, continually, eternally, ever, evermore, forever, invariably, incessantly, perpetually, unceasingly. ANT.-fitfully, never, occasionally, rarely, sometimes.

constituent, n. SYN.-component, element, ingredient, part.

constrain, v. coerce, compel, confine, force, restrain.

constraint, n. SYN.-coercion, compulsion, constriction, destiny, fate, forced, requirement, requisite; awkwardness, embarrassment, shyness. ANT.-choice, freedom, option, uncertainty; confidence.

constrict, v. SYN.-block, check, choke, clog, contract, hamper, restrict, retard, slow, tighten.

construct, v. SYN.-build, erect, fabricate,

form, frame, make, raise. ANT.-demolish, destroy, raze.

construe, v. SYN.-analyze, decipher, decode, deduce, elucidate, explain, explicate, interpret, render, solve, translate, unravel. ANT.-confuse, distort, falsify, misconstrue, misinterpret.

consult, v. SYN.-chat, converse, speak; comment, discourse; argue, confer, conspire, deliberate, discuss, reason, talk.

consummate, a. SYN.-achieve, complete, concluded, ended, entire, finished, full, perfect, thorough, total, unbroken, undivided. ANT.-imperfect, lacking, unfinished.

consummation, n. SYN.-acme, apex, climax, culmination, height, peak, summit, zenith. ANT.-anticlimax, base, depth, floor.

contagious, a. SYN.-catching, communicable, infectious, pestilential, virulent. ANT.-healthful, hygienic, non-communicable.

contain, v. SYN.-accommodate, comprise, embody, embrace, hold, include; repress, restrain. ANT.-discharge, emit, exclude; encourage, yield.

contaminate, v. SYN.-befoul, corrupt, defile, infect, poison, pollute, sully, taint. ANT.-disinfect, purify.

contaminated, a. SYN.-corrupted, crooked, debased, depraved, impure, profligate, putrid, spoiled, tainted, venal, vitiated.

contamination, n. SYN.-ailment, contamination, disease, infection, poison, pollution, taint.

contemplate, v. SYN.-conceive, imagine, picture, recall, recollect, remember; cogitate, deliberate, meditate, muse, ponder, reason, reflect, speculate, think; consider, deem, esteem, judge, opine, reckon, regard, suppose. ANT.-conjecture, forget, guess.

contemplative, a. SYN.-dreamy, introspective, meditative, pensive, reflective, thoughtful. ANT.-heedless, inconsiderate, precipitous, rash, thoughtless.

contemporary, a. SYN.-current, modern, new, novel, present, recent. ANT.-ancient, antiquated, bygone, old, past.

contempt, n. SYN.-contumely, derision, detestation, disdain, hatred, scorn. ANT.-awe, esteem, regard, respect, reverence.

contemptible, a. SYN.-base, despicable, low, mean, sordid, vile, vulgar; malicious, nasty, offensive, selfish. ANT.-admirable, dignified, exalted, generous, noble.

contend, v. SYN.-argue, battle, compete, contest, debate, dispute, fight, rival, struggle, vie; accuse, affirm, assert, aver, claim, testify.

contented, a, SYN.-blessed, cheerful, delighted, fortunate, happy, gay, glad, joyful, joyous, lucky, merry, opportune, pleased, propitious, satisfied. ANT.-blue, depressed, gloomy, morose.

contention, n. SYN.-battle, collision, conflict, duel, encounter, fight, struggle; controversy, discord, inconsistency, opposition, variance. ANT.-amity, concord, consonance, harmony.

contentment, n. SYN.-beatitude, blessedness, bliss, delight, felicity, gladness, happiness, pleasure, satisfaction, well-being. ANT.-despair, grief, misery, sadness, sorrow.

contents, n. SYN.-essence, gist, meaning, significance, substance.

contest, v. SYN.-battle, challenge, contention, debate, dispute, duel, encounter, quarrel, squabble, test, trial. ANT.-agreement, concord, decision, harmony.

contestant, n. SYN.-adversary, challenger, combatant, competitor, opponent, player, rival,

continence, n. SYN.-abstention, abstinence, fasting, forbearance, moderation, self-denial, sobriety, temperance. ANT.-excess, gluttony, greed, intoxication, self-indulgence.

contingent, a. SYN.-conditional, dependent, depending, relying, subject, subordinate. ANT.-absolute, autonomous, casual, independent, original.

continual, a. SYN.-ceaseless, constant, continuous, endless, everlasting, incessant, perennial, perpetual, unceasing, uninterrupted, unremitting. ANT.-interrupted, occasional, periodic, rare.

continue, v. SYN.-advance, extend, proceed; endure, last, remain; persevere, persist, prolong, pursue. ANT.-arrest, check, interrupt; cease, defer, halt, stop, suspend.

contract, n. SYN.-agreement, bargain, compact, covenant, pact, pledge, promise, stipulation, treaty.

contract, v. SYN.-abbreviate, abridge, condense, curtail, diminish, lessen, limit, reduce, recede, restrict, shorten, shrink, shrivel. ANT.-elongate, extend, lengthen.

contradict, v. SYN.-confront, confute, controvert, counter, dispute, gainsay, oppose. ANT.-agree, confirm, support, verify.

contradictory, a. SYN.-contrary, discrepant, illogical, incompatible, incongruous, inconsistent, irreconcilable, paradoxical, unsteady, vacillating, wavering. ANT.-compatible, congruous, consistent, correspondent.

contrary, a. SYN.-adverse, antagonistic, hostile, opposed, opposite; counteractive, disastrous, unfavorable, unlucky. ANT.-benign, favorable, fortunate, lucky, propitious.

contrast, n. SYN.-difference, distinction, divergence, diversity, incompatibility, opposition, variance, variation. ANT.-likeness, similarity, uniformity.

contrast, v. SYN.-compare, differentiate, discriminate, distinguish, oppose.

contribute, v. SYN.-bequeath, bestow, confer, dispense, donate, endow, give, grant, present, proffer, share.

contrite, a. SYN.-penitent, regretful, remorseful, repentant, sorrowful, sorry. ANT.-obdurate, remorseless.

contrition, n. SYN.-compunction, grief, penitence, qualm, regret, remorse, repentance, self-reproach, sorrow. ANT.-complacency, impenitence, obduracy, self-satisfaction.

contrive, v. SYN.-delineate, design, devise, intend, manipulate, outline, plan, plot, prepare, project, scheme.

control, n. SYN.-discipline, order, regulation, restraint, supervision. ANT.-chaos, confusion, turbulence.

control, v. SYN.-administer, check, command, direct, dominate, drive, influence, govern, manage, master, regulate, rule, superintend, supervise; bridle, check, curb, repress, restrain. ANT.-abandon, follow, forsake, ignore, submit.

controversy, n. SYN.-argument, contention, debate, disagreement, discord, dispute, dissonance, quarrel, squabble. ANT.-agreement, concord, decision, harmony.

convene, v. SYN.-assemble, congregate, convoke, gather, meet, sit.

convenient, a. SYN.-accessible, accommodating, adapted, advantageous, appropriate, comfortable, commodious, favorable, fitting, handy, helpful, suitable, timely. ANT.-awkward, inconvenient, inopportune, troublesome.

conventional, a. SYN.-accepted, accustomed, common, customary, established, familiar, normal, ordinary, prevailing, regular, standard, typical, usual. ANT.-alien, strange, unusual.

conversation, n. SYN.-chat, colloquy, conference, dialogue, discussion, gossip, interview, parley, talk.

converse, v. SYN.-blab, chat, discuss, gossip, jabber, mutter, prattle, speak, talk, tattle; confer, consult, deliberate, discuss, reason.

convert, v. SYN.-exchange, substitute; alter, change, modify, shift, transfigure, transform, vary. ANT.-retain; continue, establish, preserve, settle, stabilize.

convey, v. SYN.-bring, carry, transmit, transport; bear. ANT.-abandon, drop.

convict, n. SYN.-criminal, delinquent, felon, malefactor, offender, transgressor.

convict, v. SYN.-blame, censure, condemn, denounce, reprehend, reproach, reprobate, reprove, upbraid; condemn, sentence. ANT.-approve, commend, condone, forgive, praise; absolve, acquit, exonerate, pardon.

conviction, n. SYN.-belief, certitude, confidence, credence, faith, feeling, opinion, persuasion, reliance, trust. ANT.-denial, doubt, heresy, incredulity.

convince, v. SYN.-allure, coax, entice, exhort, incite, induce, influence, persuade, prevail upon, satisfy, urge, win over. ANT.-coerce, compel, deter, dissuade, restrain.

cool, a. SYN.-brisk, chilly, cold, frigid, frosty, nippy, wintry; apathetic, composed, indifferent, passionless, phlegmatic, reserved, stoical, unconcerned, unfeeling. ANT.-burning, fiery, heated, hot, torrid; ardent, passionate.

cooperation, n. SYN.-alliance, coalition, collaboration, concert, confederation, federation, participation.

copious, a. SYN.-abundant, ample, bountiful, overflowing, plenteous, plentiful, profuse, rich, teeming. ANT.-deficient, insufficient, scant, scarce.

copy, *n.* SYN.-duplicate, exemplar, facsimile, imitation, replica, reproduction, transcript. ANT.-original, prototype.

copy, *v.* SYN.-ape, counterfeit, duplicate, imitate, impersonate, mimic, mock, simulate. ANT.-alter, distort, diverge, invent.

cordial, *a.* SYN.-ardent, earnest, friendly, gracious, hearty, sincere, sociable, warm. ANT.-aloof cool, reserved, taciturn.

core, *n.* SYN.-center, heart, middle, midpoint, midst, nucleus. ANT.-border, boundary, outskirts, periphery, rim.

corporal, *a.* SYN.-bodily, carnal, corporeal, somatic; material, natural, physical. ANT.-mental, spiritual.

corporation, *n.* SYN.-company, firm. ANT.-individual.

corpse, *n.* SYN.-body, carcass, remains; form, frame, torso; corpus. ANT.-intellect, mind, soul, spirit.

correct, *a.* SYN.-accurate, exact, faultless, impeccable, precise, proper, right, strict. ANT.-erroneous, false, faulty, untrue, wrong.

correct, *v.* SYN.-aid, amend, help, improve, mend, rectify, reform, remedy, right; admonish, discipline, punish, reprimand. ANT.-aggravate, ignore, ruin, spoil; condone, indulge.

correction, *n.* SYN.-adjustment, alteration, amendment, improvement, instruction, discipline, punishment.

correlative, *a.* SYN.-akin, alike, allied, analogous, comparable, correspondent, corresponding, like, parallel, similar. ANT.-different, dissimilar, divergent, incongruous, opposed.

correspondent, *a.* SYN.-akin, alike, allied, analogous, comparable, correlative, corresponding, like, parallel, similar. ANT.-different, dissimilar, divergent, incongruous, opposed.

corrupt, *a.* SYN.-contaminated, corrupted, crooked, debased, depraved, dishonest, fraudulent, impure, profligate, putrid, spoiled, tainted, unsound, venal, vitiated.

corrupt, *v.* SYN.-abase, adulterate, alloy, contaminate, debase, defile, degrade, deprave, disgrace, dishonor, impair, infect, lower, pervert, spoil, taint, undermine, vitiate. ANT.-enhance, improve, raise, restore, vitalize.

cost, *n.* SYN.-charge, expense, payment, price, value, worth.

council, *n.* SYN.-admonition, advice, caution, counsel, exhortation, instruction, recommendation, suggestion, warning; information, intelligence, notification.

counsel, *n.* SYN.-advice, consultation, elucidation, guidance, information, instruction, opinion; lawyer.

counsel, *v.* SYN.-advise, allude, offer, propose, recommend, refer, suggest. ANT.-declare, demand, dictate, insist.

count, *v.* SYN.-calculate, compute, consider, enumerate, estimate, figure, inventory, reckon. ANT.-conjecture, guess, miscalculate.

counterfeit, *a.* SYN.-artificial, assumed, bogus, ersatz, fake, feigned, fictitious, phony, sham, spurious, synthetic, un-

real. ANT.-genuine, natural, real, true.

courage, *n.* SYN.-audacity, boldness, bravery, chivalry, daring, fearlessness, fortitude, intrepidity, mettle, prowess, resolution. ANT.-cowardice, fear, pusillanimity, timidity.

courageous, *a.* SYN.-adventurous, audacious, bold, brave, chivalrous, daring, dauntless, fearless, gallant, heroic, intrepid, valiant, valorous. ANT.-cowardly, cringing, fearful, timid, weak.

course, *n.* SYN.-avenue, channel, passage, path, road, route, street, thoroughfare, track, trail, walk, way; fashion, form, habit, manner, method, mode, plan, practice, procedure, process, style, system.

courteous, *a.* SYN.-civil, considerate, courtly, cultivated, genteel, polite, refined, urbane, well-bred, well-mannered. ANT.-boorish, impertinent, rude, uncivil, uncouth.

courtesy, *n.* SYN.-affability, consideration, cordiality, courteousness, deference, friendliness, gallantry, geniality, graciousness, kindness, manners, polish, politeness, refinement, respect, tact.

covenant, *n.* SYN.-accordance, understanding, agreement, bargain, compact, contract, pact, stipulation. ANT.-difference, disagreement, discord, dissension, variance.

cover, *v.* SYN.-cloak, clothe, conceal, curtain, disguise, envelop, guard, hide, mask, protect, screen, shield, shroud, veil, wrap. ANT.-bare, divulge, expose, reveal, unveil.

covert, *a.* SYN.-clandestine, concealed, hidden, latent, private, secret, surreptitious, unknown. ANT.-conspicuous, disclosed, exposed, known, obvious.

covetousness, *n.* SYN.-avarice, desire, envy, greed, jealousy. ANT.-generosity, geniality, indifference.

cowardice, *n.* SYN.-alarm, apprehension, consternation, dismay, dread, fear, fright, horror, panic, scare, terror, timidity, trepidation. ANT.-assurance, boldness, bravery, courage, fearlessness.

cower, *v.* SYN.-cringe, crouch, fear, hide, quake, run, shake, shiver, shrink, snivel, tremble.

coy, *a.* SYN.-bashful, demure, diffident, humble, modest, recoiling, retiring, shy, timid. ANT.-daring, gregarious, outgoing.

cozy, *a.* SYN.-luxurious, protected, satisfying, secure, sheltered, snug, warm.

craft, *n.* SYN.-ability, aptitude, competence, dexterity, faculty, skill, talent; avocation, business, career, occupation, vocation, work; airplane, boat, jet, ship.

crafty, *a.* SYN.-artful, astute, clandestine, covert, cunning, foxy, furtive, guileful, insidious, shrewd, sly, stealthy, subtle, surreptitious, tricky, underhanded, wily. ANT.-candid, frank, ingenuous, open, sincere.

cranky, *a.* SYN.-critical, cross, disagreeable, disapproving, fault-finding, fussy, grouchy, hostile, hypercritical, peevish, surly, whiny.

crass, *a.* SYN.-coarse, crude, harsh, rough, uncouth, unpolished, unrefined. ANT.-finished, well-prepared; cultivated, refined.

craving, *n.* SYN.-hunger, relish, stomach, thirst, zest; appetite, desire, inclination, liking, longing, need, passion. ANT.-disgust, distaste, renunciation, repugnance, satiety.

crazy, *a.* SYN.-delirious, demented, deranged, foolish, idiotic, imbecilic, insane, mad, maniacal. ANT.-rational, reasonable, sane, sensible, sound.

create, *v.* SYN.-cause, engender, fashion, form, formulate, generate, invent, make, originate, produce; appoint, constitute, ordain. ANT.-annihilate, demolish, destroy; disband, terminate.

creative, *a.* SYN.-clever, fanciful, fresh, imaginative, inventive, mystical, new, novel, original, poetical, visionary. ANT.-dull, literal, prosaic, unromantic.

credibility, *n.* SYN.-belief, confidence, credence, faith, persuasion, reliance, trust

credible, *a.* SYN.-creditable, honest, honorable, noble, reliable, reputable, trusty, virtuous.

creed, *n.* SYN.-belief, doctrine, dogma, precept, teaching, tenet. ANT.-conduct, deed, performance, practice.

creeping, *a.* SYN.-crawling, inching, faltering, hobbling, limping, skulking, slinking, sneaking.

crest, *n.* SYN.-acme, apex, head, pinnacle, summit, top. ANT.-base, bottom, foot.

crew, *n.* SYN.-assistants, cast, company, gang, group, hands, helpers, seamen, squad, team, troupe, workers.

crime, *n.* SYN.-atrocity, outrage; aggression, crime, injustice, misdeed, misdemeanor, offense, sin, transgression, trespass, vice, wrong. ANT.-gentleness, innocence, morality, right.

criminal, *n.* SYN.-bandit, convict, crook, culprit, delinquent, felon, lawbreaker, malefactor, offender, transgressor.

crippled, *a.* SYN.-defective, deformed, disabled, feeble, halt, hobbling, lame, limping, maimed, weak. ANT.-agile, athletic, robust, sound, vigorous.

crisis, *n.* SYN.-acme, conjuncture, contingency, emergency, exigency, juncture, pass, pinch, predicament, strait. ANT.-calm, equilibrium, normality, stability.

crisp, *a.* SYN.-bracing; brittle, crumbling, delicate, fragile, frail, fresh, splintery. ANT.-enduring, thick, tough, unbreakable.

criterion, *n.* SYN.-gauge, law, measure, principle, proof, rule, standard, test, touchstone. ANT.-chance, fancy, guess, supposition.

critical, *a.* SYN.-accurate, discerning, discriminating, exact, fastidious, particular; captious, carping, caviling, censorious, faultfinding, hypercritical; acute, crucial, decisive, hazardous, important, momentous. ANT.-cursory, shallow, superficial, uncritical; appreciative, approving, commendatory, encouraging; insignificant, unimportant.

criticize, *v.* SYN.-analyze, appraise, evaluate, examine, inspect, scrutinize;

blame, censure, reprehend. ANT.-approve, neglect, overlook.

critique, *n.* SYN.-commentary, criticism, critique, examination, inspection, reconsideration, retrospect, retrospection, review, revision, survey, synopsis.

crony, *n.* SYN.-associate, attendant, colleague, companion, comrade, consort, friend, mate, partner. ANT.-adversary, enemy, stranger.

crooked, *a.* SYN.-corrupt, corrupted, debased, depraved, dishonest, illegal, immoral, impure, profligate, unlawful.

crop, *n.* SYN.-fruit, harvest, proceeds, produce, product, reaping, result, store, yield.

crop, *v.* SYN.-clip, cut, prune, shorten, top, trim.

1cross, *a.* SYN.-angry, annoyed, cantankerous, churlish, complaining, critical, exasperated, fault-finding, incensed, indignant, irate, irritable, maddened, provoked. ANT.-calm, happy, pleased, satisfied.

crowd, *n.* SYN.-bevy, crush, horde, host, masses, mob, multitude, populace, press, rabble, swarm, throng.

crown, *n.* SYN.-apex, chief, crest, head, pinnacle, summit, top, zenith; coronet, diadem, tiara. ANT.-base, bottom, foot, foundation.

crucial, *a.* SYN.-acute, critical, decisive, hazardous, imperative, important, momentous, threatening. ANT.-insignificant, unimportant.

crude, *a.* SYN.-coarse, green, harsh, ill-prepared, raw, rough, unfinished, unpolished, unrefined; crass, uncouth. ANT.-finished, well-prepared; cultivated, refined.

cruel, *a.* SYN.-barbaric, bloodthirsty, brutal, callous, debased, degenerate, depraved, evil, ferocious, heartless, inhuman, malevolent, malignant, merciless, monstrous, remorseless, ruthless, sadistic, savage, sinful, spiteful, tyrannical, unfeeling, unmerciful, vengeful, viscious, wicked. ANT.-benevolent, compassionate, forbearing, gentle, humane, kind, merciful.

cruelty, *n.* SYN.-barbarity, brutality, coercion, domination, ferocity, harshness, indifference, inhumanity, injustice, malice, oppression, persecution, rancor, ruthlessness, sadism, severity, venom, wickedness,

crumb, *n.* SYN.-bit, grain, iota, jot, mite, ort, particle, scrap, shred, smidgen, speck, spot. ANT.-aggregate, bulk, mass, quantity.

crumble, *v.* SYN.-corrode, decay, degenerate, disintegrate, rot, rust.

cry, *n.* SYN.-bellow, call, cheer, clamor, exclamation, holler, hullabaloo, outcry, scream, shout, shriek, whoop, yell.

cry, *v.* SYN.-bawl, bemoan, bewail, blubber, grieve, lament, sob, sorrow, wail, weep, whimper, whine.

cuddle, *v.* SYN.-caress, coddle, embrace, fondle, hug, pet, snuggle. ANT.-annoy, buffet, spurn, tease, vex.

cue, *n.* SYN.-alert, hint, prompt, ready, sign, signal, warning.

cull, *v.* SYN.-choose, elect, opt, pick, select. ANT.-refuse, reject.

culmination, *n.* SYN.-acme, apex, climax, completion, consummation, end, finale, finish, height, peak, summit, zenith. ANT.-anticlimax, base, depth, floor.

culprit, *n.* SYN.-criminal, delinquent, felon, malefactor, offender, transgressor.

cultivation, *n.* SYN.-agriculture, agronomy, farming, gardening, horticulture, husbandry, tillage; breeding, education, enhancement, learning, nurturing, refinement.

culture, *n.* SYN.-breeding, civilization, clan, cultivation, education, enlightenment, family, folklore, folkways, instruction, knowledge, refinement, society. ANT.-boorishness, ignorance, illiteracy, vulgarity.

cultured, *a.* SYN.-accomplished, appreciative, blasé, civilized, cultivated, cultured, educated, enlightened, erudite, experienced, informed, lettered, polished, sophisticated, understanding, urbane, worldly, worldly-wise. ANT.-crude, ingenuous, naive, simple, uncouth.

cunning, *a.* SYN.-clever, crooked, distorted, erratic, indirect, ingenious, roundabout, skillful, swerving, tortuous, wandering, winding; circuitous, crooked, devious, tricky. ANT.-direct, straight; honest, straightforward.

cunning, *n.* SYN.-aptitude, cleverness, faculty, ingeniousness, ingenuity, inventiveness, resourcefulness, skill ANT.-clumsiness, dullness, inaptitude, stupidity.

curb, *v.* SYN.-block, bridle, check, constrain, delay, halt, hinder, hold back, impede, inhibit, limit, repress, restrain, retard, stay, stem, stop, suppress. ANT.-aid, encourage, incite, loosen.

cure, *n.* SYN.-antidote, help, medicant, prescription, remedy, restorative; relief, solution.

curiosity, *n.* SYN.-marvel, miracle, phenomenon, oddity, peculiarity, prodigy, rarity, spectacle, wonder; concern, inquisitiveness, interest, meddling, prying, regard. ANT.-familiarity, triviality.

curious, *a.* SYN.-inquiring, inquisitive, interrogative, meddling, nosy, peeping, peering, prying, questioning, searching, snoopy; odd, peculiar, queer, strange, rare, unique, unusual. ANT.-incurious, indifferent, unconcerned, uninterested; common, ordinary.

current, *a.* SYN.-contemporary, fashionable, latest, modern, new, newest, novel, present, recent. ANT.-ancient, antiquated, bygone, old, past.

curse, *n.* SYN.-anathema, ban, blasphemy, cursing, cuss, damning, denunciation, expletive, fulmination, imprecation, irreverence, oath, profanity, vulgarism; affliction, annoyance, bane, calamity, evil, misfortune, plague.

curse, *v.* SYN.-abuse, blaspheme, damn, denounce, fulminate, imprecate, insult, profane, revile; afflict, annoy, doom, plague, scourge, trouble, vex.

cursory, *a.* SYN.-abbreviated, brief, external, flimsy, frivolous, imperfect, offhand, quick, shallow, short, slight, superficial. ANT.-abstruse, complete, deep, profound, thorough.

curt, *a.* SYN.-abrupt, blunt, brief, brusque, concise, impatient, quick, rude, terse. ANT.-anticipated, courteous, expected.

curtail, *v.* SYN.-abbreviate, abridge, condense, contract, curtail, diminish, lessen, limit, reduce, restrict, shorten. ANT.-elongate, extend, lengthen.

curve, *v.* SYN.-bend, bow, crook, turn, twist. ANT.-straighten.

custodian, *n.* SYN.-attendant, caretaker, cleaner, keeper, porter, superintendent, watchman.

custody, *n.* SYN.-care, charge, guardianship, keeping, supervision, ward. ANT.-neglect, negligence.

custom, *n.* SYN.-characteristic, convention, fashion, formality, habit, manner, mores, observance, practice, precedent, procedure, ritual, routine, rule, style, usage, use, way, wont.

customary, *a.* SYN.-accustomed, characteristic, common, conventional, everyday, familiar, general, habitual, normal, ordinary, procedural, usual. ANT.-abnormal, exceptional, extraordinary, irregular, rare.

customer, *n.* SYN.-buyer, client, consumer, patron, user.

cut, *n.* SYN.-divide, furrow, gash, gouge, groove, hole, incision, mark, nick, notch, opening, separation, slash, slice, slit, wound.

cut, *v.* SYN.-amputate, chop, cleave, dice, dissect, gash, gouge, lop, nick, notch, prune, score, separate, shear, slash, slice, slit, snip, split, trim, wound.

cute, *a.* SYN.-alluring, attractive, captivating, charming, dainty, delicate, elegant, engaging, fascinating, fetching, petite, pleasing, sensitive, slender, slight, winsome.

cylindrical, *a.* SYN.-circular, barrel-shaped, curved, round.

cynic, *n.* SYN.-detractor, doubter, egoist, egotist, misanthrope, mocker, pessimist, satirist, scoffer, sneerer, unbeliever.

cynical, *a.* SYN.-antisocial, acerbic, caustic, derisive, hostile, misanthropic, sardonic, unbelieving, unfriendly, unsociable.

D

dainty, *a.* SYN.-airy, beautiful, delicate, elegant, exquisite, fastidious, feeble, fragile, frail, lacy, lovely, petite, precious, pretty, sensitive, slender, slight, weak; pleasant, pleasing, savory ANT.-brutal, coarse, rude, tough, vulgar.

dam, *n.* SYN.-bank, barrier, dike, ditch, embankment, gate, levee, wall.

dam, *v.* SYN.-bar, barricade, check, choke, clog, close, confine, impede, obstruct, restrict, retard, slow, stop.

damage, *n.* SYN.-adversity, affliction, blemish, breakage, corruption, defacement, deterioration, detriment, erosion, evil, hardship, harm, hurt, illness, infliction, injury, mischief, misfortune, mishap, reverse, suffering, wound, wrong. ANT.-benefit, boon, favor, kindness.

damage, *v.* SYN.-abuse, batter, break, crack, deface, disfigure, harm, hurt, impair, injure, mar, mutilate, ruin, scratch, spoil, tarnish, wreck. ANT.-ameliorate, benefit, enhance, mend, repair.

damaging, *a.* SYN.-deleterious, detrimental, harmful, hurtful, injurious, mischievous. ANT.-advantageous, beneficial, helpful, profitable, salutary.

damages, *n.* SYN.-compensation, cost, indemnification, indemnity, payment, recompense, reimbursement, reparations, repayment, restitution, SYN.-settlement.

danger, *n.* SYN.-hazard, jeopardy, menace, peril, risk, threat, uncertainty. ANT.-defense, immunity, protection, safety.

dangerous, *a.* SYN.-alarming, critical, hazardous, insecure, menacing, perilous, precarious, risky, serious, threatening, unsafe. ANT.-firm, protected, safe, secure.

dare, *v.* SYN.-attempt, brave, challenge, defy, endeavor, hazard. risk, try, undertake, venture; challenge, confront, denounce, mock, oppose, resist, scorn, threaten.

daring, *a.* SYN.-adventurous, bold, brave, chivalrous, courageous, enterprising, fearless, foolhardy, precipitate, rash, risqué, unconventional. ANT.-cautious, hesitating, timid.

dark, *a.* SYN.-black, dim, dull, indistinct, gloomy, murky, obscure, overcast, shadowy, unilluminated, vague; dusky, opaque, sable, swarthy; dismal, gloomy, mournful, somber, sorrowful; evil, sinister, sullen, wicked; hidden, mystic, occult, secret. ANT.-light; bright, clear; pleasant; lucid.

dart, *v.* SYN.-bolt, dash, fling, flit, fly, heave, hurtle, plunge, rush, shoot, speed, spring, spurt, thrust.

dead, *a.* SYN.-deceased, defunct, departed, dull, gone, inanimate, insensible, lifeless, spiritless, unconscious. ANT.-alive, animate, living, stirring.

dash, *n.* SYN.-alacrity, charge, dispatch, hurry, hustle, plunge, run, rush, spurt; hint, little, sprinkling, scattering, touch, trace.

dash, *v.* SYN.-chill, dampen, dismay, discourage; bolt, dart, fly, hurry, race, speed.

data, *n.* SYN.-abstracts, details, evidence, facts, figures, information, reports, results, statistics.

date, *n.* SYN.-day, duration, epoch, era, generation, period, spell, term, year; appointment, assignation, call, engagement, rendezvous, tryst, visit.

daze, *n.* SYN.-astonishment, bewilderment, confusion, distraction, muddle, stupor.

daze, *v.* SYN.-amaze, confound, confuse, dazzle, perplex, puzzle, stun, stupefy.

deafening, *a.* SYN.-loud, noisy, resounding, sonorous, stentorian, vociferous ANT.-dulcet, inaudible, quiet, soft, subdued.

dead, *a.* SYN.-anesthetized, deadened, deceased, defunct, departed, gone, inanimate, inert, lifeless, numb, perished, spent, still, tired, unconscious, wearied, worn.

deaden, *v.* SYN.-anesthetize, benumb, desensitize, dull, impair, numb, paralyze, repress, slow.

deadly, *a.* SYN.-bloodthirsty, dangerous, deathly, destructive, fatal, harmful, injurious, lethal, mortal, violent. ANT.-invigorating, stimulating, vital, wholesome.

deal, *n.* SYN.-affair, agreement, business, compromise, contract, negotiation, pact, pledge, proceeding, transaction, understanding.

dear, *a.* SYN.-beloved, cherished, esteemed, precious, valued; costly, expensive, valuable. ANT.-despised, unwanted; cheap.

death, *n.* SYN.-decease, demise, departure, doom, expiration, extinction, mortality, passing, rest, end. ANT.-beginning, birth, life.

debase, *v.* SYN.-abase, adulterate, alloy, corrupt, defile, degrade, deprave, depress, humiliate, impair, lower, pervert, vitiate. ANT.-enhance, improve, raise, restore, vitalize.

debate, *v.* SYN.-altercate, argue, bicker, contend, contest, differ, discuss, dispute, quarrel, oppose, question, reason, squabble, wrangle; denote, imply, indicate, prove, refute, show. ANT.-agree, allow, assent, concede, ignore, overlook, reject, spurn.

debris, *n.* SYN.-fragments, garbage, litter, pieces, refuse, rubbish, ruins, trash, waste, wreckage.

debt, *n.* SYN.-arrears, bill, deficit, indebtedness, liability, obligation, mortgage, note. ANT.-asset, capital, credit, excess, grace, trust.

decadent, *a.* SYN.-brutal, callous, debased, degenerate, depraved, evil, heartless, immoral, inhuman, malignant, merciless, monstrous, remorseless, ruthless, sadistic, savage, sinful, spiteful, unfeeling, unmerciful, vengeful, viscious, wicked.

decay, *n.* SYN.-blight, collapse, consumption, corrosion, corruption, decadence, decline, decomposition, degeneration, deterioration, disintegration, downfall, failure, putrefaction, ruin, ruination.

decay, *v.* SYN.-blight, decline, decompose, decrease, disintegrate, dwindle, ebb, putrefy, rot, spoil, wane, waste, wither. ANT.-flourish, grow, increase, luxuriate, rise.

deceased, *a.* SYN.-dead, defunct, departed, gone, lifeless. ANT.-alive, animate, living, stirring.

deceit, *n.* SYN.-beguilement, cheat, chicanery, cunning, deceitfulness, deception, duplicity, fraud, guile, sham, trick, wiliness. ANT.-candor, honesty, openness, sincerity, truthfulness.

deceitful, *a.* SYN.-deceptive, delusive, delusory, dishonest, fallacious, false, illusive, misleading, specious. ANT.-authentic, genuine, honest, real, truthful.

deceive, *v.* SYN.-betray, defraud, delude, dupe, ensnare, entrap, fleece, fool, hoodwink, mislead, outwit, rob, swindle, victimize,

decent, *a.* SYN.-adequate, becoming, befitting, comely, decorous, ethical, fit, nice, proper, respectable, seemly, suitable, tolerable, trustworthy, upright, virtuous. ANT.-coarse, gross, indecent, reprehensible, vulgar.

deception, *n.* SYN.-beguilement, betrayal, cheat, chicanery, craftiness, cunning, deceit, deceitfulness, dishonesty, duplicity, fraud, guile, sham, treachery, treason, trickery, wiliness. ANT.-candor, honesty, openness, sincerity, truthfulness

deceptive, *a.* SYN.-deceitful, delusive, delusory, fallacious, false, illusive, misleading, specious. ANT.-authentic, genuine, honest, real, truthful.

decide, *v.* SYN.-adjudicate, choose, close, conclude, determine, end, judge, pick, resolve, select, settle, terminate. ANT.-doubt, hesitate, suspend, vacillate, waver.

decipher, *v.* SYN.-clarify, construe, decode, elucidate, explain, explicate, interpret, render, solve, translate, unravel. ANT.-confuse, distort, falsify, misconstrue, misinterpret.

declaration, *n.* SYN.-acknowledgment, affidavit, affirmation, allegation, announcement, assertion, avowal, communication, disclosure, manifesto, notice, notification, presentation, proclamation, profession, proposition, report, resolution, statement, thesis, utterance.

declare, *v.* SYN.-affirm, allege, announce, assert, aver, broadcast, certify, claim, contend, disclose, express, impart, indicate, maintain, make known, notify, proclaim, profess, promulgate, pronounce, protest, state, swear, tell. ANT.-conceal, hide, repress, suppress, withhold.

decline, *v.* SYN.-incline, slant, slope; descend, sink, wane; decay, decrease, degenerate, depreciate, deteriorate, diminish, dwindle, weaken; refuse, reject. ANT.-ameliorate, appreciate, ascend, increase; accept.

decorate, *v.* SYN.-adorn, beautify, brighten, deck, embellish, enhance, enrich, garnish, ornament, renovate, trim. ANT.-debase, defame, expose, strip, uncover.

decoration, *n.* SYN.-adornment, design, embellishment, garnish, improvement, ornament, ornamentation.

decrease, *v.* SYN.-abate, abbreviate, abridge, check, compress, condense, crumble, curb, curtail, cut, decay, decline, deduct, deflate, degenerate, deteriorate, diminish, dwindle, fade, lessen, lower, melt, pare, prune, reduce, remove, shorten, shrink, shrivel, sink, slacken, subside, subtract, trim, wane. ANT.-amplify, augment, enlarge, expand, grow, increase, multiply.

decree, *n.* SYN.-declaration, edict, mandate, order, proclamation, pronouncement, ruling.

dedicated, *a.* SYN.-addicted, affectionate, ardent, attached, devoted, disposed, earnest, faithful, fond, given up to, inclined, loyal, prone, true, wedded. ANT.-

detached, disinclined, indisposed, untrammeled.

dedication, n. SYN.-affection, ardor, attachment, celebration, consecration, devotion, devoutness, fidelity, love, loyalty, piety, religiousness, zeal. ANT.-alienation, apathy, aversion, indifference, unfaithfulness.

deduct, v. SYN.-decrease, diminish, lessen, reduce, remove, shorten, subtract. ANT.-amplify, enlarge, expand, grow, increase.

deduction, n. SYN.-answer, conclusion, inference, judgment, opinion, reasoning.

deed, n. SYN.-accomplishment, act, action, doing, execution, feat, operation, performance, transaction; agreement, certificate, charter, document, lease, record, voucher, warranty. ANT.-cessation, deliberation, inactivity, inhibition, intention.

deep, a. SYN.-below, beneath, bottomless, immersed, impenetrable, submerged, subterranean; absorbing, abstract, abstruse, acute, buried, difficult, incisive, grave, penetrating, rich.

deepen, v. SYN.-augment, develop, expand, exacerbate, extend, grow, increase, intensify.

deface, v. SYN.-abuse, batter, crack, disfigure, harm, hurt, mar, mutilate, ruin, scratch, spoil, tarnish, wreck. ANT.-ameliorate, benefit, enhance, mend, repair.

defame, v. SYN.-abuse, asperse, disparage, ill-use, libel, malign, revile, scandalize, slander, traduce, vilify. ANT.-cherish, honor, praise, protect, respect.

default, n. SYN.-dereliction, failure, lapse, neglect, omission, oversight, transgression; deficiency, lack, loss, want. ANT.-achievement, success, victory; sufficiency.

defeat, n. SYN.-annihilation, conquest, collapse, destruction, extermination, fall, loss, overthrow, rebuff, reverse, setback, subjugation. ANT.-conquest, triumph, victory.

defeat, v. SYN.-annihilate, beat, conquer, crush, decimate, demolish, humble, master, overcome, overrun, overwhelm, quell, repulse, rout, smash, subdue, subjugate, surmount, thrash, trounce, vanquish. ANT.-capitulate, cede, lose, retreat, surrender.

defect, n. SYN.-blemish, crack, error, failure, fault, flaw, imperfection, mark, mistake, omission, scratch, shortcoming, vice. ANT.-completeness, correctness, perfection.

defend, v. SYN.-fortify, guard, protect, safeguard, screen, shelter, shield; assert, back, espouse, justify, plead, maintain, rationalize, uphold, vindicate. ANT.-assault, attack, deny, oppose, submit.

defense, n. SYN.-barricade, bastille, bastion, bulwark, citadel, dike, fence, fort, fortification, fortress, rampart, refuge, shelter, shield, stockade, stronghold, trench, wall; backing, explanation, guard, justification, precaution, preservation, protection, resistance, safeguard, security, stand.

defer, v. SYN.-adjourn, delay, postpone, shelve, slacken, suspend, waive; accede, comply, concede, obey, submit, yield. ANT.-advance, dispatch, expedite, further, hasten, press, stimulate, urge.

deference, n. SYN.-acclaim, adoration, courtesy, esteem, fame, homage, renown, respect, reverence, veneration, worship.

deficient, a. SYN.-defective, inadequate, incomplete, insufficient, lacking, scanty, short. ANT.-adequate, ample, enough, satisfactory, sufficient.

define, v. SYN.-bound, circumscribe, delimit, establish, fix, limit, mark, outline, set; ascertain, characterize, designate, elucidate, explain, illustrate, interpret, specify. ANT.-confuse, distort; misinform, mislead.

definite, a. SYN.-absolute, categorical, certain, correct, decisive, determined, exact, explicit, fixed, positive, precise, prescribed, specific, unequivocal; bold, clear, crisp, distinct, obvious, plain, sharp, unmistakable, vivid. ANT.-ambiguous, confused, dubious, equivocal, indefinite, obscure; indistinct, hazy, unclear.

deformed, a. SYN.-askew, contorted, crooked, crushed, damaged, disfigured, distorted, irregular, malformed, mangled, warped. ANT.-regular, shapely, well-formed.

defy, v. SYN.-confront, face, hinder, impede, insult, obstruct, oppose, resist, thwart, withstand. ANT.-accede, allow, cooperate, relent, yield.

degenerate, v. SYN.-atrophy, descend, sink, wane; decay, decline, decrease, depreciate, deteriorate, diminish, dwindle, weaken; corrupt, debase, depraved, immoral. ANT.-ameliorate, appreciate, ascend, increase; accept.

degrade, v. SYN.-abase, abash, adulterate, alloy, corrupt, debase, defile, deprave, depress, humble, humiliate, impair, lower, mortify, pervert, shame, vitiate. ANT.-enhance, improve, raise, restore, vitalize.

degree, n. SYN.-caliber, extent, grade, intensity, order, proportion, quality, quantity, range, scope, stage, standing, station, status, step, strength.

delay, v. SYN.-defer, postpone, procrastinate; arrest, detain, hinder, impede, retard, stay; dawdle, linger, loiter, tarry. ANT.-expedite, hasten, precipitate, quicken.

delectable, a. SYN.-delicious, delightful, luscious, palatable, savory, sweet, tasty. ANT.-acrid, distasteful, nauseous, unpalatable, unsavory.

delegate, n. SYN.-agent, alternate, appointee, deputy, emissary, legate, minister, proxy, representative.

delegate, v. SYN.-appoint, assign, authorize, choose, commission, deputize, elect, empower, name, nominate, ordain, select.

deliberate, a. SYN.-calculated, conscious, considered, contemplated, designed, intended, intentional, meant, planned, premeditated, purposeful, studied, voluntary, willful. ANT.-accidental, fortuitous.

deliberate, v. SYN.-consider, contemplate, examine, heed, meditate, ponder, reflect, study, weigh. ANT.-ignore, neglect, overlook.

delicacy, n. SYN.-airiness, daintiness, flimsiness, lightness, smoothness, subtlety, tenderness, transparency; luxury, rarity, tidbit.

delicate, a. SYN.-dainty, elegant, exquisite, fastidious, feeble, frail, sensitive, slender, slight, weak; pleasant, pleasing, savory ANT.-brutal, coarse, rude, tough, vulgar.

delicious, a. SYN.-appetizing, dainty, delectable, delightful, luscious, palatable, rich, savory, sweet, tasty, tempting. ANT.-acrid, distasteful, nauseous, unpalatable, unsavory

delight, n. SYN.-bliss, ecstasy, enjoyment, gladness, happiness, joy, pleasure, rapture, transport. ANT.-annoyance, dejection, melancholy, misery, sorrow.

delighted, a. SYN.-amused, blessed, cheerful, contented, fascinated, fortunate, happy, gay, glad, joyful, joyous, merry, pleased, satisfied. ANT.-blue, depressed, gloomy, morose.

deliver, v. SYN.-commit, give, impart, transfer, yield; announce, communicate, impart, proclaim,. publish; emancipate, free, liberate, release, rescue, save. ANT.-confine, withhold; capture, imprison, restrict.

delusion, n. SYN.-deception, dream, fallacy, fancy, fantasy, hallucination, illusion, mirage, phantom, vision. ANT.-actuality, reality, substance.

demand, v. SYN.-charge, command, direct, order; ask, ask for, challenge, claim, exact, require; inquire, necessitate. ANT.-give, offer, present, tender.

demented, a. SYN.-bemused, crazy, deranged, insane, mad, maniacal, psychotic, unbalanced, unsound.

demolish, v. SYN.-annihilate, destroy, devastate, eradicate, exterminate, extinguish, obliterate, ravage, raze, ruin, wreck. ANT.-construct, establish, make, preserve, save.

demonstrate, v. SYN.-display, exhibit, show; establish, evince, manifest, prove. ANT.-conceal, hide.

denial, n. SYN.-disapproval, disavowal, disclaimer, dismissal, dissent, negation, rejection, repudiation.

denounce, v. SYN.-accuse, blame, castigate, censure, charge, condemn, implicate, incriminate, indict, prosecute, rebuke, reprehend, reprimand, reproach, reprobate, reprove, revile, scold, upbraid. ANT.-approve, commend, condone, forgive, praise.

dense, a. SYN.-close, compact, compressed, concentrated, crowded, solid, thick; dull, obtuse, slow, stupid. ANT.-dispersed, dissipated, sparse; clever, quick.

deny, v. SYN.-contradict, contravene, controvert, disagree, gainsay, refute; abjure, disallow, disavow, disown, forbid, refuse, repudiate, withhold. ANT.-affirm, assert, concede, confirm.

depart, v. SYN.-abandon, desert, exit, flee, forsake, give up, go, leave, quit, retire, withdraw. ANT.-abide, arrive, enter, remain, stay, tarry.

departure, *n.* SYN.-departing, embarkation, evacuation, exit, exodus, getaway, going, leaving, parting, starting. ANT.-arrival, landing.

dependable, *a.* SYN.-certain, reliable, safe, secure, sure, tried, trustworthy, trusty. ANT.-dubious, fallible, questionable, uncertain, unreliable.

dependent, *a.* SYN.-conditional, contingent, depending, relying, subject, subordinate. ANT.-absolute, autonomous, casual, independent, original.

depict, *v.* SYN.-characterize, describe, draw, explain, narrate, paint, picture, portray, recount, relate, represent, sketch. ANT.-caricature, misrepresent, suggest.

depleted, *a.* SYN.-consumed, destroyed, dissipated, emptied, exhausted, spent, squandered, wasted.

deposit, *v.* SYN.-accumulate, bank, entrust, hoard, invest, keep, save, secure, store. ANT.-pay, spend, withdraw.

depraved, *a.* SYN.-base, corrupted, crooked, debased, dishonest, fraudulent, impure, low, mean, profligate, putrid, spoiled, tainted, unsound, venal.

depreciate, *v.* SYN.-descend, sink, wane; decay, decline, decrease, degenerate, deteriorate, diminish, dwindle, weaken; refuse, reject. ANT.-ameliorate, appreciate, ascend, increase; accept.

depress, *v.* SYN.-dampen, darken, degrade, discourage, dishearten, dismay, dull, mock, mortify, sadden; lower, reduce, squash.

depression, *n.* SYN.-blues, dejection, despair, desperation, despondency, discouragement, doldrums, gloom, hopelessness, melancholy, misery, oppression, pessimism, sorrow, trouble, unhappiness, worry. ANT.-confidence, elation, hope, optimism.

deputy, *n.* SYN.-aide, agent, alternate, appointee, assistant, delegate, emissary, legate, lieutenant, minister, proxy, representative.

derision, *n.* SYN.-banter, disdain, gibe, irony, jeering, mockery, raillery, ridicule, sarcasm, satire, scorn, sneering.

derivation, *n.* SYN.-beginning, birth, commencement, cradle, foundation, inception, origin, root, source, spring, start. ANT.-end, harvest, issue, outcome, product.

descend, *v.* SYN.-decline, degenerate, dip, drop, plunge, settle, sink, slip, tumble, wane. ANT.-ascend, increase.

describe, *v.* SYN.-characterize, depict, explain, narrate, portray, recount, relate.

describe, *v.* SYN.-characterize, depict, elucidate, illuminate, illustrate, narrate, picture, portray, relate, summarize.

description, *n.* SYN.-account, characterization, chronicle, depiction, detail, history, narration, narrative, portrayal, recital, relation, report. ANT.-caricature, confusion, distortion, misrepresentation.

desert, *v.* SYN.-abandon, defect, forsake, leave, quit. ANT.-defend, maintain, uphold; stay, support.

deserter, *n.* SYN.-betrayer, defector, delinquent, fugitive, runaway, traitor, truant.

desertion, *n.* SYN.-abandonment, defection, departure, escape, flight, renunciation, treason.

design, *n.* SYN.-blueprint, concept, delineation, diagram, draft, drawing, outline, pattern, plan, sketch, treatment; artfulness, contrivance, cunning, plotting, scheming; intent, intention, objective, purpose. ANT.-result; candor, sincerity; accident, chance.

design, *v.* SYN.-contrive, create, devise, invent, plan, scheme; intend, mean, purpose; draw, outline, sketch.

designate, *v.* SYN.-appoint, choose, denote, disclose, indicate, intimate, manifest, reveal, select, show, signify, specify, verify. ANT.-conceal, distract, divert, falsify, mislead.

desire, *n.* SYN.-ambition, appetite, aspiration, attraction, craving, hungering, inclination, longing, lust, propensity, urge, wish, yearning, yen. ANT.-abomination, aversion, distaste, hate, loathing.

desire, *v.* SYN.-choose, covet, crave, long for, want, wish; ask, seek, solicit.

desist, *v.* SYN.-abstain, arrest, bar, cease, check, close, cork, discontinue, end, halt, hinder, impede, interrupt, obstruct, plug, seal, stop, terminate. ANT.-begin, proceed, promote, speed, start.

desolate, *a.* SYN.-abandoned, bare, bleak, deserted, forlorn, forsaken, lonely, solitary, uninhabited, waste, wild. ANT.-attended, cultivated, fertile.

despair, *n.* SYN.-depression, desperation, despondency, discouragement, gloom, hopelessness, pessimism ANT.-confidence, elation, hope, optimism.

desperate, *a.* SYN.-audacious, daring, despairing, despondent, determined, hopeless, reckless, wild. ANT.-assured, composed, confident, hopeful, optimistic.

desperation, *n.* SYN.-anxiety, depression, despair, despondency, discouragement, distress, gloom, hopelessness, pessimism. ANT.-confidence, elation, hope, optimism.

despicable, *a.* SYN.-base, contemptible, low, mean, sordid, vile, vulgar; malicious, nasty, offensive, selfish. ANT.-admirable, dignified, exalted, generous, noble.

despise, *v.* SYN.-abhor, abominate, detest, dislike, hate, loathe. ANT.-admire, approve, cherish, like, love.

despondent, *a.* SYN.-dejected, depressed, disconsolate, dismal, dispirited, doleful, gloomy, glum, melancholy, moody, sad, somber, sorrowful; grave, pensive. ANT.-cheerful, happy, joyous, merry.

despotic, *a.* SYN.-absolute, arbitrary, authoritative, brutal, cruel, odious, oppressive, repressive, severe, tyrannical. ANT.-accountable, conditional, contingent, dependent, qualified.

destined, *a.* SYN.-compelled, fated, foreordained, forthcoming, inevitable, inexorable, predetermined.

destiny, *n.* SYN.-consequence, doom, for-

tune, lot, portion; fate, issue, necessity, outcome, result.

destitute, *a.* SYN.-impecunious, indigent, needy, penniless, poor, poverty-stricken; scanty, shabby. ANT.-affluent, opulent, rich, wealthy.

destroy, *v.* SYN.-annihilate, demolish, devastate, eradicate, exterminate, extinguish, liquidate, obliterate, ravage, raze, ruin, wreck. ANT.-construct, establish, make, preserve, save.

destroyed, *a.* SYN.-broken, crushed, eradicated, flattened, fractured, reduced, rent, ruptured, shattered, smashed, wrecked. ANT.-integral, repaired, united, whole.

destructive, *a.* SYN.-baneful, deadly, deleterious, detrimental, devastating, fatal, injurious, noxious, pernicious, ruinous. ANT.-beneficial, constructive, creative, profitable, salutary.

detail, *n.* SYN.-circumstance, item, minutia, part, particular; detachment, party, squad. ANT.-generality.

detail, *v.* SYN.-analyze, catalogue, enumerate, itemize, narrate, recapitulate, recite, recount, relate, report, summarize.

detain, *v.* SYN.-arrest, delay, hinder, hold, impede, inhibit, keep, restrain, retard, stay. ANT.-expedite, hasten, precipitate, quicken.

detect, *v* SYN.-ascertain, devise, discover, expose, find, find out, invent, learn, originate, reveal. ANT.-cover, hide, lose, mask, screen.

detention, *n.* SYN.-arrest, custody, confinement, constraint, imprisonment, restraint, seizure.

determinant, *n.* SYN.-agent, cause, incentive, inducement, motive, origin, principle, reason, source. ANT.-consequence, effect, end, result.

determination, *n.* SYN.-conviction, courage, decision, firmness, fortitude, obstinacy, perseverance, persistence, resolution, resolve, steadfastness, tenacity, will. ANT.-inconstancy, indecision, vacillation.

determine, *v* SYN.-conclude, decide, end, fix, resolve, settle; ascertain, learn, verify; incline, induce, influence; condition, define, limit; compel, necessitate.

detest, *v.* SYN.-abhor, abominate, despise, dislike, hate, loathe. ANT.-admire, approve, cherish, like, love.

detestable, *a.* SYN.-abominable, disgusting, execrable, foul, hateful, loathsome, odious, revolting, vile. ANT.-agreeable, commendable, delightful, pleasant.

detriment, *n.* SYN.-damage, evil, harm, hurt, ill, infliction, injury, mischief, misfortune, mishap, wrong. ANT.-benefit, boon, favor, kindness.

detrimental, *a.* SYN.-damaging, deleterious, harmful, hurtful, injurious, mischievous. ANT.-advantageous, beneficial, helpful, profitable, salutary.

develop, *v* SYN.-advance, amplify, create, cultivate, elaborate, enlarge, evolve, expand, extend, mature, perfect, promote, unfold. ANT.-compress, contract, restrict, stunt, wither.

development, *n.* SYN.-elaboration, expansion, unfolding, unraveling; evolution, growth, maturing, progress. ANT.-abbreviation, compression, curtailment.

deviate, v. SYN.-bend, crook, deflect, digress, diverge, divert, sidetrack, stray, wander. ANT.-continue, follow, persist, preserve. remain.

device, n. SYN.-apparatus, appliance, channel, contraption, contrivance, instrument, means, medium, tool, utensil, vehicle; artifice, craft, design, plan, plot, scheme, trick, wile. ANT.-hindrance, impediment, obstruction, preventive.

devious, a. SYN.-circuitous, crooked, distorted, erratic, indirect, roundabout, swerving, tortuous, wandering, winding; crooked, cunning, foxy, insidious, shrewd, tricky. ANT.-direct, straight; honest, straightforward.

devoted, a. SYN.-addicted, affectionate, ardent, attached, constant, dedicated, disposed, dutiful, earnest, faithful, fond, given up to, inclined, loyal, prone, true, wedded. ANT.-detached, disinclined, indisposed, untrammeled.

devotion, n. SYN.-affection, ardor, attachment, consecration, dedication, devoutness, fidelity, love, loyalty, piety, religiousness, zeal. ANT.-alienation, apathy, aversion, indifference, unfaithfulness.

devout, a. SYN.-devoted, godly, holy, pietistic, pious, religious, reverent, sanctimonious, spiritual, theological. ANT.-atheistic, impious, profane, secular, skeptical.

dexterity, n. SYN.-ability, adroitness, aptitude, aptness, capability, capacity, cleverness, deftness, facility, efficiency, faculty, power, qualification, skill, skillfulness, talent. ANT.-awkwardness, clumsiness, disability, inability, incapacity, incompetence, ineptitude, unreadiness.

dialect, n. SYN.-cant, diction, idiom, jargon, lingo, language, phraseology, slang, speech, tongue, vernacular. ANT.-babble, drivel, gibberish, nonsense.

dialogue, n. SYN.-chat, colloquy, conference, conversation, exchange, interview, meeting, negotiation, parley, remarks, talk, tête-à-tête.

dictator, n. SYN.-autocrat, despot, leader, lord, master, mogul, oppressor, overlord, persecutor, taskmaster, tyrant.

diction, n. SYN.-articulation, eloquence, enunciation, fluency, language, locution, style, vocabulary.

die, v. SYN.-cease, decay, decease, decline, depart, expire, fade, languish, perish, sink, succumb, wane, wither. ANT.-begin, flourish, grow, live, survive.

differ, v. SYN.-alter, change, conflict, contrast, deviate, diverge, diversify, modify, qualify, vary; argue, contradict, disagree, dispute, dissent, object, oppose, quarrel.

difference, n. SYN.-disparity, dissimilarity, distinction, divergence, separation, variety, variance; disagreement, discord, dissension, estrangement. ANT.-identity, resemblance, similarity; agreement, harmony.

different, a. SYN.-contrary, dissimilar, distinct, divergent, diverse, incongruous, opposite, unlike, variant; divers, miscellaneous, sundry, various. ANT.-alike, congruous, identical, same, similar.

differentiate, v. SYN.-descry, detect, discern, discriminate, distinguish, observe, perceive, recognize, see, separate. ANT.-confound, confuse, mingle, omit, overlook.

difficult, a. SYN.-arduous, challenging, complicated, demanding, formidable, hard, intricate, involved, laborious, obscure, perplexing, strenuous, thorny, toilsome, troublesome, trying. ANT.-easy, effortless, facile, simple.

difficulty, n. SYN.-adversity, annoyance, complication, crisis, distress, embarrassment, frustration, hardship, hindrance, impasse, impediment, irritation, knot, misfortune, obstacle, obstruction, predicament, scrape, setback, snag, struggle, trouble.

dig, v. SYN.-burrow, delve, dredge, excavate, uncover, undermine.

dignified, a. SYN.-aristocratic, august, courtly, distinguished, elegant, formal, noble, proud, regal, reserved, solemn, somber, stately, sublime. ANT.-base, crass, rude, undignified.

dignity, n. SYN.-air, bearing, culture, elegance, nobility, pride, quality, refinement, restraint, stateliness, style.

digress, v. SYN.-deviate, diverge, divert, shift, sidetrack, stray, wander. ANT.-continue, follow, persist, preserve. remain.

dilate, v. SYN.-amplify, augment, broaden, distend, enlarge, expand, increase, magnify, widen. ANT.-abridge, contract, diminish, restrict, shrink.

dilemma, n. SYN.-complication, difficulty, fix, impasse, predicament, plight, scrape, situation, strait. ANT.-calmness, comfort, ease, satisfaction.

diligent, a. SYN.-active, alert, assiduous, busy, careful, earnest, hard-working, industrious, patient, persevering, quick. ANT.-apathetic, careless, indifferent, lethargic, unconcerned.

dim, a. SYN.-faded, faint, indistinct, pale, shadowy; feeble, languid, wearied; irresolute, weak. ANT.-conspicuous, glaring; strong, vigorous; forceful.

diminish, v. SYN.-abate, assuage, curtail, decline, decrease, dwindle, lessen, lower, moderate, reduce, shorten, suppress, wane. ANT.-amplify, enlarge, expand, grow, increase, intensify, revive.

din, n. SYN.-babel, clamor, cry, noise, outcry, racket, row, sound, tumult, uproar. ANT.-hush, quiet, silence, stillness.

dip, v. SYN.-bathe, baptize, douse, duck, dunk, lower, plunge, steep, submerge; ladle, scoop, spoon; decline, incline, recede, sink, slant, slope, tilt.

diplomacy, n. SYN.-adroitness, dexterity, discretion, finesse, knack, poise, savoir faire, skill, tact. ANT.-awkwardness, blunder, incompetence, rudeness, vulgarity.

diplomatic, a. SYN.-adroit, discreet, discriminating, judicious, politic, tactful.

ANT.-boorish, churlish, coarse, gruff, rude.

dire, a. SYN.-appalling, calamitous, catastrophic, deadly, dreadful, frightful, ghastly, grim, grisly, gruesome, hideous, horrible, terrible, threatening.

direct, a. SYN.-straight, undeviating, unswerving; erect, unbent, upright; fair, honest, honorable, just, square. ANT.-circuitous, winding; bent, crooked; dishonest.

direct, v. SYN.-aim, level, point, train; conduct, govern, guide, manage, regulate, rule, show; bid, command, instruct, order. ANT.-deceive, distract, misdirect, misguide.

direction, n. SYN.-bearing, course, inclination, tendency, trend, way; administration, management, superintendence; guidance, instruction, order.

dirty, a. SYN.-filthy, foul, grimy, muddy, soiled, squalid; indecent, nasty, obscene; base, contemptible, despicable, low, mean, pitiful, shabby. ANT.-clean, neat, presentable; pure, wholesome.

disabled, a. SYN.-crippled, defective, deformed, feeble, halt, hobbling, lame, limping, maimed, unconvincing, unsatisfactory, weak. ANT.-agile, athletic, robust, sound, vigorous.

disagreement, n. SYN.-altercation, argument, bickering, challenge, conflict, contention, controversy, difference, discord, dispute, dissent, dissentience, feud, objection, protest, quarrel, spat, squabble, variance, wrangle. ANT.-acceptance, agreement, assent, compliance, harmony, peace, reconciliation.

disappear, v. SYN.-depart, desert, disintegrate, dissipate, dissolve, escape, evaporate, fade, flee, vanish.

disappoint, v. SYN.-disillusion, dismay, displease, dissatisfy, fail, frustrate, mislead.

disappointed, a. SYN.-annoyed, despondent, discontented, disillusioned, dissatisfied, disturbed, irritated, unsatisfied.

disappointing, a. SYN.-inadequate, ineffective, inferior, insufficient, failing, lame, mediocre, ordinary, second-rate, uninteresting.

disapprove, v. SYN.-condemn, criticize, denounce, disparage, object, oppose, resist.

disaster, n. SYN.-accident, adversity, calamity, casualty, catastrophe, defeat, emergency, failure, misadventure, mishap, ruin, setback, tragedy. ANT.-advantage, fortune, welfare.

disavow, v. SYN.-abandon, forego, forsake, quit, relinquish, resign; deny, disclaim, disown, reject, renounce, retract, revoke. ANT.-defend, maintain, uphold; acknowledge, assert, recognize.

discard, v. SYN.-abandon, discharge, dismiss, eject, expel, reject, renounce, repudiate.

discern, v. SYN.-descry, detect, determine, differentiate, discriminate, distinguish, observe, perceive, recognize, see, separate. ANT.-confound, confuse, mingle, omit, overlook.

discerning, a. SYN.-accurate, critical, discriminating, exact, fastidious, particular, perceptive. ANT.-cursory, shallow, superficial, uncritical.

discernment, n. SYN.-acumen, insight, intuition, penetration, perspicuity. ANT.-obtuseness.

discharge, v. SYN.-banish, belch, discard, dismiss, eject, emanate, emit, exile, expel, fire, liberate, oust, release, remove, send off, shed, shoot, spurt, terminate, vent. ANT.-accept, detain, recall, retain.

disciple, n. SYN.-adherent, believer, devotee, follower, supporter, votary; learner, pupil, scholar, student.

discipline, n. SYN.-control, order, regulation, restraint, self-control; exercise, instruction, practice, training; correction, punishment. ANT.-chaos, confusion, turbulence.

disclaim, v. SYN.-abandon, forego, forsake, quit, relinquish, resign; deny, disavow, disown, reject, renounce, retract, revoke. ANT.-defend, maintain, uphold; acknowledge, assert, recognize.

disclose, v. SYN.-betray, divulge, expose, identify, impart, reveal, show, testify, uncover. ANT.-cloak, conceal, cover, hide, obscure.

disconsolate, a. SYN.-cheerless, dejected, depressed, despondent, dismal, doleful, downcast, gloomy, lugubrious, melancholy, mournful, sad, somber, sorrowful. ANT.-cheerful, glad, happy, joyous, merry.

discontinue, v. SYN.-adjourn, interrupt, postpone, stay, suspend. ANT.-continue, maintain, persist, proceed, prolong.

discourage, v. SYN.-appall, dampen, daunt, demoralize, deter, dissuade, dull, forbid, hinder, inhibit, prevent, repress, warn.

discourteous, a. SYN.-blunt, boorish, gruff, impolite, impudent, insolent, rough, rude, saucy, surly, uncivil, vulgar; coarse, crude, ignorant, rough, savage, unpolished, fierce, harsh, inclement, tumultuous, violent. ANT.-civil, genteel, polished; courtly, dignified, noble, stately; calm, mild, peaceful.

discover, v. SYN.-ascertain, catch, create, detect, determine, devise, discern, expose, find, find out, glimpse, identify, invent, learn, observe, originate, perceive, recognize, reveal, uncover, unearth. ANT.-cover, hide, lose, mask, screen.

discreet, a. SYN.-cautious, circumspect, considerate, diplomatic, discerning, discriminating, guarded, judicious, politic, prudent, reserved, sensible, strategic, tactful, wary, watchful. ANT.-boorish, churlish, coarse, gruff, rude.

discrepant, a. SYN.-contradictory, contrary, illogical, incompatible, incongruous, inconsistent, irreconcilable, paradoxical. ANT.-compatible, congruous, consistent, correspondent.

discretion, n. SYN.-calculation, care, caution, concern, consideration, deliberation, diplomacy, discrimination, foresight, forethought, heed, prudence, responsibility, tact.

discriminate, v. SYN.-differentiate, distinguish, segregate, separate. ANT.-

mingle, overlook.

discriminating, a. SYN.-accurate, critical, discerning, exact, fastidious, particular. ANT.-cursory, shallow, superficial, uncritical.

discrimination, n. SYN.-discernment, intelligence, judgment, perception, perspicacity, sagacity, taste, understanding, wisdom; bigotry, isolation, persecution. ANT.-arbitrariness, senselessness, stupidity, thoughtlessness.

discuss, v. SYN.-chat, converse, speak, tattle; argue, comment, contest, declaim, debate, discourse, dispute; confer, consult, deliberate, explain, reason, talk.

discussion, n. SYN.-chat, conference, consultation, conversation, debate, dialogue, discourse, exchange, gossip, lecture, report, symposium, talk. ANT.-correspondence, meditation, silence, writing.

disdain, n. SYN.-contempt, contumely, derision, detestation, hatred, scorn. ANT.-awe, esteem, regard, respect, reverence.

disease, n. SYN.-ailment, complaint, disorder, illness, infirmity, malady, sickness. ANT.-health, healthiness, soundness, vigor.

diseased, a. SYN.-ill, indisposed, infirm, morbid, sick, unhealthy, unwell. ANT.-healthy, robust, sound, strong, well.

disgrace, n. SYN.-abashment, chagrin, humiliation, mortification; dishonor, disrepute, ignominy, odium, opprobrium, scandal, shame. ANT.-dignity, glory, honor, praise, renown.

disgraceful, a. SYN.-discreditable, dishonorable, disreputable, ignominious, scandalous, shameful. ANT.-teemed, honorable, renowned, respectable.

disguise, n. SYN.-affectation, cloak, deception, garb, mask, pretense, pretension, pretext, semblance, simulation, subterfuge. ANT.-actuality, fact, reality, sincerity, truth.

disguise, v. SYN.-cloak, conceal, cover, hide, mask, screen, secrete, suppress, veil, withhold. ANT.-disclose, divulge, expose, reveal, show, uncover.

dishonest, a. SYN.-corrupt, corrupted, crooked, debased, deceitful, deceiving, deceptive, depraved, fraudulent, immoral, profligate, treacherous, underhanded.

dishonor, n. SYN.-humiliation, mortification; disgrace, disrepute, ignominy, odium, opprobrium, scandal, shame. ANT.-dignity, glory, honor, praise, renown.

disintegrate, v. SYN.-decay, decompose, decrease, dwindle, putrefy, rot, spoil, waste. ANT.-flourish, grow, increase, luxuriate.

dislike, n. SYN.-abhorrence, animosity, antipathy, aversion, detestation, disgust, dislike, disinclination, distaste, dread, enmity, hatred, hostility, loathing, malevolence, rancor, repugnance, repulsion, reluctance. ANT.-affection, attachment, attraction, devotion, enthusiasm, friendship, love.

dislike, v. SYN.-abhor, abominate, deplore, despise, detest, disapprove, hate,

loathe, revulse. ANT.-admire, approve, cherish, like, love.

disloyal, a. SYN.-apostate, faithless, false, perfidious, recreant, traitorous, treacherous, treasonable. ANT.-constant, devoted, loyal, true.

dismal, a. SYN.-bleak, cheerless, dark, doleful, dreary, dull, funereal, gloomy, lonesome, melancholy, sad, somber. ANT.-cheerful, gay, joyous, lively.

dismiss, v. SYN.-banish, discard, discharge, eject, exile, expel, fire, oust, reject, release, remove, send off, terminate. ANT.-accept, detain, recall, retain.

disobedient, a. SYN.-defiant, forward, insubordinate, rebellious, refractory, undutiful, unruly. ANT.-compliant, dutiful, obedient, submissive.

disobey, v. SYN.-balk, decline, defy, differ, disagree, disregard, ignore, rebel, refuse, resist, revolt, transgress, violate. ANT.-follow, fulfill, obey.

disorder, n. SYN.-agitation, anarchy, chaos, commotion, confusion, disarrangement, disarray, disorganization, ferment, jumble, muddle, stir, tumult, turmoil. ANT.-certainty, order, organization, peace, system, tranquility.

disorganization, n. SYN.-anarchy, chaos, confusion, disorder, jumble, muddle. ANT.-order, organization, system.

disorganized, a. SYN.-bewildered, confused, deranged, disconcerted, disordered, indistinct, mixed, muddled, perplexed. ANT.-clear, lucid, obvious, organized, plain.

disparage, v. SYN.-belittle, decry, depreciate, derogate, discredit, lower, minimize, undervalue. ANT.-aggrandize, commend, exalt, magnify, praise.

dispatch, v. SYN.-cast, discharge, dispatch, emit, impel, propel, send, throw, transmit. ANT.-bring, get, hold, receive, retain.

dispel, v. SYN.-diffuse, disperse, disseminate, dissipate, scatter, separate. ANT.-accumulate, amass, assemble, collect, gather.

dispense, v. SYN.-allot, apportion, deal, distribute, divide, mete; allocate, appropriate, assign, give, grant, measure. ANT.-confiscate, keep, refuse, retain, withhold.

disperse, v. SYN.-diffuse, dispel, disseminate, dissipate, scatter, separate. ANT.-accumulate, amass, assemble, collect, gather.

displace, v. SYN.-dislodge, move, remove, shift, transfer, transport; discharge, dismiss, eject; oust, vacate. ANT.-leave, remain, stay; retain.

display, v. SYN.-arrange, disclose, exhibit, expose, flaunt, open, parade, present, reveal, show, spread out, uncover, unveil. ANT.-conceal, cover, disguise, hide.

disposition, n. SYN.-action, bearing, behavior, bent, bias, carriage, conduct, demeanor, deportment, inclination, leaning, manner, partiality, penchant, predilection, predisposition, prejudice, proclivity, proneness, propensity, slant, tendency, turn. ANT.-equity, fairness, impartiality, justice.

dispute, n. SYN.-altercation, argument,

conflict, contention, controversy, debate, disagreement, discussion, misunderstanding, quarrel, squabble. ANT.-agreement, concord, decision, harmony.

dispute, v. SYN.-altercate, argue, bicker, contend, contest, debate, disagree, discuss, quarrel, squabble, wrangle. ANT.-agree, allow, assent, concede.

disregard, v. SYN.-ignore, neglect, omit, overlook, skip, slight. ANT.-include, notice, regard.

disreputable, a. SYN.-discreditable, disgraceful, dishonorable, ignominious, scandalous, shameful. ANT.-teemed, honorable, renowned, respectable.

dissent, n. SYN.-challenge, difference, disagreement, dissentience, noncompliance, nonconformity, objection, protest, rejection, remonstrance, variance. ANT.-acceptance, agreement, assent, compliance.

dissimilar, a. SYN.-different, distinct, divergent, diverse, incongruous, opposite, unlike, variant; divers, miscellaneous, sundry, various. ANT.-alike, congruous, identical, same, similar.

dissipate, v. SYN.-despoil, destroy, devastate, strip; consume, corrode, dispel, lavish, misuse, scatter, spend, squander, waste, wear out; decay, diminish, dwindle, pine, conserve, wither. ANT.-accumulate, economize, preserve, save.

distant, a. SYN.-far, faraway, remote, removed; aloof, cold, reserved, stiff, unfriendly. ANT.-close, near, nigh; cordial, friendly.

distinct, a. SYN.-apparent, clear, evident, intelligible, lucid, manifest, obvious, plain, unmistakable, visible; open, unobstructed. ANT.-ambiguous, obscure, unclear, vague.

distinction, n. SYN.-attribute, characteristic, feature, peculiarity, property, quality, trait; eminence, fame, honor, luster, notability, reputation. ANT.-being, essence, nature, substance; disgrace, disrepute, obscurity.

distinctive, v. SYN.-eccentric, exceptional, extraordinary, odd, rare, singular, strange, striking, unusual; characteristic, individual, particular, peculiar, special, unique. ANT.-common, general, normal, ordinary.

distinguish, v. SYN.-descry, detect, differentiate, discern, discriminate, observe, perceive, recognize, see, separate. ANT.-confound, confuse, mingle, omit, overlook.

distinguished, a. SYN.-branded, characterized, conspicuous, differentiated, distinct, identified, marked, separate, unique; elevated, eminent, famed, famous, glorious, illustrious, noted, notorious, outstanding, prominent, renowned, singular. ANT.-common, obscure, ordinary, unimportant, unknown.

distort, v. SYN.-alter, deceive, embellish, falsify, fib, lie, misconstrue, misinterpret, mislead, pervert, prevaricate, rig; bend, buckle, contort, crush, deform, twist, warp, wrench.

distress, n. SYN.-agony, anguish, anxiety, discomfort. grief, misery, pain, sorrow,

suffering, torment, torture, tribulation, worry, . ANT.-comfort, joy, relief, solace.

distribute, v. SYN.-allot, apportion, bestow, deal, dispense, disperse, divide, dole, issue, mete, scatter, share, spread; classify, group, sort.

district, n. SYN.-area, community, division, domain, neighborhood, place, province, quarter, region, section, territory.

distrust, n. SYN.-ambiguity, doubt, hesitation, incredulity, scruple, skepticism, suspense, suspicion, unbelief, uncertainty. ANT.-belief, certainty, conviction, determination. faith.

disturb, v. SYN.-agitate, alarm, annoy, confuse, decompose, derange, interrupt, perplex, perturb, rattle, rouse, trouble, unsettle, vex, worry. ANT.-order, pacify, quiet, settle, soothe.

disturbance, n. SYN.-agitation, bother, clamor, disruption, eruption, racket, riot, stir, turbulence, turmoil, uproar.

disturbing, a. SYN.-alarming, annoying, bothersome, disquieting, distressing, foreboding, frightening, ominous, perturbing, startling, threatening, troublesome, trying, upsetting.

diverse, a. SYN.-different, dissimilar, divergent, incongruous, opposite, unlike, variant; assorted, divers, miscellaneous, sundry, various. ANT.-alike, congruous, identical, same, similar.

diversity, n. SYN.-assortment, change, difference, dissimilarity, heterogeneity, medley, miscellany, mixture, multifariousness, variety, variousness. ANT.-homogeneity, likeness, monotony, sameness, uniformity.

divert, v. SYN.-avert, deflect, deviate, swerve, turn; alter, change, redirect, transmute. ANT.-arrest, fix, stand, stop; continue, proceed; endure, perpetuate.

divide, v. SYN.-carve, chop, cleave, cut, detach, part, rend, separate, sever, splinter, split, sunder, tear; allocate, allot, apportion, deal out, dispense, distribute, share. ANT.-combine, convene, gather, join unite.

divine, a. SYN.-celestial, godlike, hallowed, heavenly, holy, sacred, superhuman, supernatural, transcendent. ANT.-blasphemous, diabolical, mundane, profane, wicked.

divulge, v. SYN.-betray, disclose, expose, impart, inform, reveal, show, uncover. ANT.-cloak, conceal, cover, hide, obscure.

do, v. SYN.-accomplish, achieve, act, create, complete, conclude, consummate, effect, execute, finish, fulfill, perform, settle, terminate; carry on, conduct, discharge, labor, transact, work; observe, perform, practice; make, produce, work; answer, serve, suffice.

docile, a. SYN.-adaptable, compliant, obedient, pliant, submissive, tame, teachable, tractable, yielding. ANT.-mulish, obstinate, stubborn, ungovernable, unruly.

doctrinaire, a. SYN.-opinionated, overbearing, positive; authoritative, theoretical, visionary. ANT.-fluctuating, indecisive, open-minded, questioning, skeptical.

doctrine, n. SYN.-belief, concept, convention, creed, dogma, precept, principle, teaching, tenet, tradition. ANT.-conduct, deed, performance, practice.

document, n. SYN.-account, archive, chronicle, letter, memorandum, minutes, note, paper, permit, record, report, register; testimonial, trace, verification, vestige.

dogma, n. SYN.-creed, doctrine, precept, tenet. ANT.-conduct, deed, performance, practice.

dogmatic, a. SYN.-arbitrary, arrogant, authoritarian, bigoted, confident, determined, dictatorial, doctrinaire, domineering, emphatic, fanatical, intolerant, magisterial, narrow-minded, obstinate, opinionated, overbearing, positive; authoritative, doctrinal, formal. ANT.-fluctuating, indecisive, open-minded, questioning, skeptical.

dole, v. SYN.-allot, apportion, deal, dispense, distribute, divide, measure, mete, parcel, scatter, share, spread.

doleful, a. SYN.-bleak, cheerless, dark, dismal, dreary, dull, funereal, gloomy, lonesome, melancholy, sad, somber. ANT.-cheerful, gay, joyous, lively.

domain, n. SYN.-country, district, division, dominion, land, place, province, quarter, region, section, territory.

dominate, v. SYN.-command, control, dictate, direct, domineer, govern, influence, manage, regulate, rule, subjugate, superintend, tyrannize. ANT.-abandon, follow, forsake, ignore, submit.

domination, n. SYN.-ascendancy, control, mastery, predominance, rule, sovereignty, supremacy, sway, transcendence. ANT.-inferiority.

donation, n. SYN.-appropriation, benefaction, bequest, boon, charity, endowment, favor, gift, grant, gratuity, largess, offering, present, subsidy. ANT.-deprivation, earnings, loss, purchase.

done, a. SYN.-accomplished, completed, executed, over, perfected, performed, realized, through, settled. ANT.-failed, incomplete, unfinished.

donor, n. SYN.-benefactor, contributor, giver, patron, sponsor, subscriber.

doomed, a. SYN.-condemned, cursed, fated, foreordained, predestined, sentenced.

dormant, a. SYN.-idle, inactive indolent, inert, lazy, quiescent, quiet, slothful, still, unemployed, unoccupied. ANT.-active, employed, industrious, occupied, working.

doubt, n. SYN.-ambiguity, apprehension, disbelief, distrust, hesitation, incredulity, misgiving, mistrust, scruple, skepticism, suspense, suspicion, unbelief, uncertainty. ANT.-belief, certainty, conviction, determination. faith.

doubt, v. SYN.-hesitate, question, uncertain, waver; distrust, mistrust, puzzled, suspect, wonder. ANT.-believe, confide, decide, rely on, trust.

dour, a. SYN.-crabby, fretful, gloomy, glum, moody, morose, sulky, surly. ANT.-amiable, gay, joyous, merry, pleasant.

drab, *a.* SYN.-colorless, dingy, dreary, dull, homely, monotonous, plain.

draw, *v.* SYN.-drag, haul, pull, tow, tug; extract, remove, take out, unsheathe; allure, attract, entice, induce, lure, persuade; delineate, depict, sketch, trace; compose, draft, formulate, write; deduce, derive, get, infer, obtain; extend, lengthen, prolong, protract, stretch. ANT.-alienate, contract, drive, propel, shorten.

drawing, *n.* SYN.-cartoon, engraving, etching, illustration, image, likeness, picture, portrait, portrayal, rendering, representation, resemblance, scene, schematic, sketch, view.

dread, *n.* SYN.-alarm, apprehension, awe, fear, foreboding, horror, reverence, terror. ANT.-assurance, boldness, confidence, courage.

dreadful, *a.* SYN.-appalling, awful, dire, fearful, frightening, frightful, ghastly, hideous, horrible, horrid, repulsive, terrible. ANT.-beautiful, enchanting, enjoyable, fascinating, lovely.

dream, *n.* SYN.-apparition, hallucination, idea, image, nightmare, trance.

dream, *v.* SYN.-conceive, conjure, fancy, hallucinate, idealize, imagine, picture, visualize.

dreary, *a.* SYN.-bleak, cheerless, dark, dismal, doleful, dull, funereal, gloomy, lonesome, melancholy, sad, somber. ANT.-cheerful, gay, joyous, lively.

dress, *n.* SYN.-apparel, array, attire, clothes, clothing, drapery, ensemble, garb, garments, habit, raiment, trappings, vestments, vesture. ANT.-nakedness, nudity.

drift, *n.* SYN.-bent, bias, digression, inclination, leaning, tendency, tenor, trend,

drill, *n.* SYN.-activity, application, conditioning, employment, exercise, exertion, lesson, operation, performance, practice, preparation, repetition, task, training, use. ANT.-idleness, indolence, relaxation, repose, rest.

drive, *v.* SYN.-coerce, compel, constrain, encourage, enforce, force, hasten, impel, incite, induce, instigate, oblige, press, stimulate, urge. ANT.-allure, convince, persuade, prevent.

droll, *a.* SYN.-amusing, comical, farcical, funny, humorous, laughable, ludicrous ridiculous, witty; curious, odd, queer. ANT.-melancholy, sad, serious, sober, solemn.

drop, *v.* SYN.-collapse, decline, decrease, descend, diminish, fall, sink, subside; stumble, topple, tumble; droop, extend downward, hang. ANT.-arise, ascend, climb, mount, soar; steady.

drunk, *a.* SYN.-drunken, high, inebriated, intoxicated, tight, tipsy. ANT.-clearheaded, sober, temperate.

dry, *a.* SYN.-arid, dehydrated, desiccated, drained, parched, thirsty; barren, dull, insipid, plain, tedious, tiresome, uninteresting, vapid. ANT.-damp, moist; fresh, interesting, lively.

dull, *a.* SYN.-dense, obtuse, retarded, slow, stupid; blunt, blunted, toothless, unsharpened; commonplace, dingy, dismal, drab, dreary, gloomy, insipid,

plain, sad, sober, somber; banal, boring, common, dry, flat, hackneyed, heavy, monotonous, ordinary, pointless, prosaic, repetitious, routine, senseless, tedious, tiresome, trite, uninspiring, uninteresting, vapid. ANT.-animated, lively, sharp; clear, interesting.

dumb, *a.* SYN.-brainless, crass, dense, dull, foolish, inarticulate, obtuse, senseless, stupid, witless. ANT.-alert, bright, clever, discerning, intelligent.

dunk, *v.*. SYN.-dip, douse, immerse, plunge, sink, submerge.

duplicate, *n.* SYN.-carbon, copy, exemplar, facsimile, imitation, likeness, replica, reproduction, transcript. ANT.-original, prototype.

duplicate, *v.* SYN.-copy, counterfeit, iterate, recapitulate, reiterate, repeat, replicate, reproduce.

durability, *n.* SYN.-endurance, fortitude, intensity, might, potency, power, stamina, stoutness, strength, sturdiness, toughness. ANT.-feebleness, frailty, infirmity, weakness.

durable, *a.* SYN.-abiding, changeless, constant, enduring, fixed, indestructible, lasting, permanent, stable, strong, unchangeable. ANT.-ephemeral, temporary, transient, transitory, unstable.

duration, *n.* SYN.-continuance, interval, length, limit, period, season, span, term, time.

duty, *n.* SYN.-accountability, burden, charge, compulsion, contract, obligation, responsibility; assessment, custom, exaction, excise, impost, levy, rate, revenue, tax, toll, tribute. ANT.-choice, exemption, freedom; gift, remuneration, reward, wages.

dwelling, *n.* SYN.-abode, apartment, domicile, flat, habitat, hearth, home, house, hovel, manor, mansion, quarters, residence, seat.

dying, *a.* SYN.-expiring, fading, failing, going, perishing, sinking.

dynamic, *a.* SYN.-active, changing, charismatic, compelling, effective, energetic, forceful, influential, live, potent, productive, progressive, vigorous, vital, vivid.

E

each, *a.* SYN.-all, any, individual, particular, specific; apiece, every, individually, proportionately, respectively, singly.

eager, *a.* SYN.-anxious, ardent, avid, enthusiastic, fervent, hot, impassioned, impatient, keen, yearning. ANT.-apathetic, indifferent, unconcerned, uninterested.

eagerly, *a.* SYN.-actively, anxiously, earnestly, fervently, gladly, heartily, intently, willingly, zealously.

early, *a.* SYN.-ahead, beforehand, preceding, premature, prompt, punctual, quick, speedy, unexpected. ANT.-belated, late, over-due, tardy.

earn, *v.* SYN.-achieve, acquire, attain, derive, deserve, gain, get, merit, obtain, realize, win. ANT.-consume, forfeit, lose, spend, waste.

earned, *a.* SYN.-deserved, merited, proper, suitable. ANT.-improper, undeserved, unmerited.

earnest, *a.* SYN.-candid, frank, genuine, heartfelt, honest, open, sincere, straightforward, true, truthful, unfeigned, upright. ANT.-affected, dishonest, hypocritical, insincere, untruthful.

earth, *n.* SYN.-continent, country, domain, field, island, land, plain, region, tract; earth, orb, planet, sphere; dirt, ground, humus, loam, soil.

ease, *v.* SYN.-allay, alleviate, assuage, calm, comfort, facilitate, lighten, mitigate, pacify, peace, rest, relieve, soften, soothe, unburden. ANT.-confound, distress, disturb, trouble, worry.

easily, *a.* SYN.-efficiently, effortlessly, freely, readily, simply, smoothly; doubtless, unquestionably.

easy, *a.* SYN.-facile, light, manageable, paltry, pleasant, relaxed, simple, slight, uncomplicated. ANT.-arduous, demanding, difficult, hard.

eat, *v.* SYN.-bite, chew, consume, devour, dine, gorge, nibble, swallow; corrode, decay, rust, squander, waste.

ebb, *n.* SYN.-abatement, decline, decrease, lessening, reduction, regression, shrinkage, wane.

ebb, *v.* SYN.-abate, decline, decrease, recede, retreat, subside, wane.

eccentric, *a.* SYN.-bizarre, curious, distinctive, odd, peculiar, quaint, queer, singular, strange, unique, unusual. ANT.-common, familiar, normal, regular, typical.

economical, *a.* SYN.-careful, close, frugal, mean, miserly, niggardly, provident, prudent, saving, sparing, thrifty; cheap, inexpensive, moderate, reasonable. ANT.-extravagant, improvident, lavish, prodigal, wasteful; expensive, overpriced.

economize, *v.* SYN.-conserve, husband, manage, pinch, save, scrimp, skimp, stint.

ecstasy, *n.* SYN.-delight, exaltation, gladness, rapture, transport; frenzy, madness, trance. ANT.-depression, melancholy.

edge, *n.* SYN.-border, boundary, brim, brink, extremity, hem, margin, periphery, rim, verge; intensity, keenness, sharpness, sting. ANT.-center, interior; bluntness, dullness.

edgy, *a.* SYN.-cross, grouchy, irritable, nervous, peevish, touchy. ANT.-calm, serene.

edict, *n.* SYN.-act, decree, demand, law, ordinance, statute.

edit, *v.* SYN.-alter, arrange, compile, correct, polish, rearrange, revise, rewrite, select; condense, cut, delete, trim; distribute, issue, publish, regulate.

editorial, *n.* SYN.-article, column, essay, feature; opinion, viewpoint.

educate, *v.* SYN.-discipline, inculcate, inform, instill, instruct, school, train, teach, tutor. ANT.-misguide, misinform.

educated, *a.* SYN.-accomplished, civilized, cultured, enlightened, informed, instructed, intelligent, lettered, literate, polished, prepared, scholarly, taught, trained.

education, *n.* SYN.-cultivation, development, instruction, knowledge, learning, schooling, study, training, tutoring.

effect, *n.* SYN.-aftermath, consequence, outcome, results.

effect, *v.* SYN.-accomplish, achieve, attain, cause, complete, consummate, do, execute, finish, fulfill, perfect, perform. ANT.-block, defeat, fail, frustrate, spoil.

effective, *a.* SYN.-capable, competent, efficient, potent, practical, productive, serviceable, telling, useful.

effects, *n.* SYN.-assets, belongings, estate, holdings, possessions, property.

efficiency, *n.* SYN.-ability, capability, competency, effectiveness, efficacy, potency, skillfulness, ANT.-inability, ineptitude, wastefulness.

efficient, *a.* SYN.-adept, capable, competent, dynamic, effective, effectual, efficacious, expedient, practiced, productive, proficient, skillful, streamlined. ANT.-incompetent, ineffectual, inefficient, unskilled.

effort, *n.* SYN.-attempt, endeavor, essay, exertion, trial; labor, pains, strain, strife, struggle, toil, trouble, undertaking.

effortless, *a.* SYN.-easy, offhand, simple, smooth, unconstrained.

effrontery, *n.* SYN.-assurance, audacity, boldness, impertinence, impudence, insolence, presumption, rudeness, sauciness. ANT.-diffidence, politeness, subserviency, truckling.

egotism, *n.* SYN.-arrogance, conceit, overconfidence, pride, self-confidence, self-esteem, vanity. ANT.-diffidence, humility, meekness, modesty.

egotistic, *a.* SYN.-arrogant, boastful, conceited, overbearing, pretentious, proud, self-centered, selfish, self-satisfied, vain.

elaborate, *a.* SYN.-decorated, elegant, embellished, flashy, gaudy, luxurious, showy; complex, complicated, extensive, intricate.

elaborate, *n.* SYN.-comment, develop, embellish, explain, expound, particularize.

elastic, *a.* SYN.-compliant, flexible, lithe, pliable, pliant, resilient, supple, tractable. ANT.-brittle, hard, rigid, stiff, unbending.

elder, *n.* SYN.-ancestor, counselor, dignitary, patriarch, senior, superior, veteran.

elderly, *a.* SYN.-aged, declining, old, patriarchal, venerable

elect, *v.* SYN.-choose, name, opt, pick, select. ANT.-refuse, reject.

elegance, *n.* SYN.-beauty, charm, comeliness, courtliness, culture, fairness, grace, handsomeness, loveliness, polish, politeness, pulchritude, splendor, sophistication. ANT.-deformity, disfigurement, eyesore, homeliness, ugliness.

elegant, *a.* SYN.-beauteous, beautiful, charming, comely, fair, fine, handsome, lovely, ornate, pretty. ANT.-foul, hideous, homely, repulsive, unsightly.

elementary, *a.* SYN.-basic, fundamental, introductory, primary, rudimentary, simple. ANT.-abstract, abstruse, complex, elaborate, intricate.

elevate, *v.* SYN.-exalt, heighten, hoist, lift, raise, uplift; promote. ANT.-abase, depreciate, depress, destroy, lower.

elevated, *a.* SYN.-high, lofty, tall, towering; eminent, exalted, proud. ANT.-small, stunted, tiny; base, low, mean.

eligible, *a.* SYN.-acceptable, authorized, available, fit, qualified, satisfactory, suitable, suited. ANT.-ineligible, unfit, unsuitable.

eliminate, *v.* SYN.-abolish, discard, dislodge, disqualify, eject, eradicate, erase, exclude, expel, exterminate, extirpate, oust, remove. ANT.-accept, admit, include, involve.

elongate, *v.* SYN.-distend, distort, expand, extend, lengthen, protract, spread, strain, stretch. ANT.-contract, loosen, shrink, slacken, tighten.

elite, *n.* SYN.-aristocracy, chosen, nobility, privileged, royalty, selected, society, wealthy.

eloquence, *n.* SYN.-appeal, articulation, delivery, diction, expressiveness, fluency, poise, power, wit.

elude, *v.* SYN.-abscond, avert, avoid, dodge, escape, eschew, evade, flee, forbear, forestall, free, shun, ward. ANT.-confront, encounter, face, meet, oppose.

emanate, *v.* SYN.-belch, breathe, discharge, eject, emit, expel, exude, hurl, radiate, shed, shoot, spurt, vent.

emancipate, *v.* SYN.-deliver, discharge, free, let go, liberate, release, set free. ANT.-confine, imprison, oppress, restrict, subjugate.

embargo, *n.* SYN.-ban, injunction, penalty, prohibition, punishment, restriction, sanction.

embarrass, *v.* SYN.-abash, chagrin, discomfit, distress, entangle, fluster, hamper, hinder, mortify, perplex, rattle, shame, trouble. ANT.-cheer, encourage, help, relieve.

embarrassing, *a.* SYN.-annoying, awkward, delicate, distressing, flustering, inauspicious, mortifying, shameful, touchy, uncomfortable, unpleasant.

embarrassment, *n.* SYN.-abashment, chagrin, clumsiness, confusion, discomfiture, distress, humiliation, mortification, unease; indebtedness, poverty. ANT.-composure, self-confidence.

embellish, *v.* SYN.-adorn, beautify, deck, decorate, enhance, enrich, garnish, ornament, trim. ANT.-debase, defame, expose, strip, uncover.

embezzle, *v.* SYN.-forge, misappropriate, pilfer, steal.

emblem, *n.* SYN.-badge, crest, design, flag, image, insignia, mark, seal, sign, symbol.

embody, *v.* SYN.-accommodate, combine, comprise, contain, embrace, hold, include, incorporate, integrate, unitize. ANT.-discharge, emit, exclude.

embrace, *v.* SYN.-clasp, hug; accept, adopt, espouse, receive, welcome; comprehend, comprise, contain, embody, include, incorporate, subsume. ANT.-reject, renounce, repudiate, scorn, spurn.

emerge, *v.* SYN.-appear, arise, arrive, emanate, issue. ANT.-be, exist; disappear, vanish, withdraw.

emergency, *n.* SYN.-contingency, crisis, exigency, jam, juncture, pass, pinch, predicament, scrape, strait, urgency.

emigrant, *n.* SYN.-alien, colonist, émigré, exile, expatriot, foreigner, migrant, refugee.

emigration, *n.* SYN.-crossing, departure, displacement, exodus, expatriation, flight, journey, migration, shift, trek, voyage, wandering.

eminent, *a.* SYN.-celebrated, conspicuous, distinguished, elevated, famous, glorious, illustrious, noted, prominent, renowned. ANT.-common, obscure, ordinary, unimportant, unknown.

emissary, *n.* SYN.-agent, ambassador, consul, delegate, deputy, envoy, intermediary, proxy, representative.

emit, *v.* SYN.-belch, breathe, discharge, eject, emanate, erupt, expel, hurl, ooze, shed, shoot, spew, spurt, squirt, vent.

emotion, *n.* SYN.-affection, agitation, feeling, passion, perturbation, sentiment, trepidation, turmoil. ANT.-calm, dispassion, indifference, restraint, tranquility.

emotional, *a.* SYN.-demonstrative, excitable, fervent, hysterical, high-strung, impetuous, irrational, maudlin, neurotic, overwrought, passionate, sensitive, sentimental, temperamental. ANT.-calm, rational, tranquil, unruffled.

empathy, *n.* SYN.-feeling, insight, pity, understanding.

emphasize, *v.* SYN.-accent, accentuate, articulate, dramatize, highlight, stress, underscore.

emphatic, *a.* SYN.-definitive, dogmatic, earnest, energetic, forceful, pointed, positive, powerful, stressed, strong.

employ, *v.* SYN.-adopt, apply, avail, busy, devote, engage, manipulate, occupy, operate, use, utilize. ANT.-banish, discard, discharge, reject.

employed, *a.* SYN.-active, busy, engaged, hired, laboring, occupied, operating, performing, used, utilized, working.

employee, *n.* SYN.-agent, assistant, flunky, hireling, laborer, lackey, servant, worker.

employer, *n.* SYN.-boss, business, company, corporation, executive, manager, owner, proprietor; operator, user.

employment, *n.* SYN.-business, engagement, function, occupation, service, vocation, work. ANT.-idleness, leisure, slothfulness.

empty, *a.* SYN.-bare, barren, devoid, hollow, senseless, unfilled, unfurnished, unoccupied, vacant, vacuous, vain, void, worthless. ANT.-full, inhabited, occupied, replete, supplied.

empty, *v.* SYN.-deplete, drain, dump, evacuate, exhaust, leak, pour, spill.

enact, *v.* SYN.-constitute, decree, institute, legislate, ordain, order, pass, ratify.

enchant, *v.* SYN.-allure, bewitch, captivate, charm, enrapture, enthrall, entice, entrance, fascinate,

enclose, *v.* SYN.-bound, circumscribe, confine, encompass, envelop, fence, limit, surround. ANT.-develop, distend, enlarge, expand, expose, open.

encounter, *n.* SYN.-battle, collision, combat, conflict, duel, fight, meeting, struggle. ANT.-amity, concord, consonance, harmony.

encounter, *v.* SYN.-collide, confront, engage, greet, intersect, meet. ANT.-cleave, disperse, part, scatter, separate.

encourage, *v.* SYN.-animate, cheer, countenance, embolden, exhilarate, favor, foster, hearten, impel, incite, promote, sanction, stimulate, support, urge. ANT.-reject, deter, discourage, dispirit, dissuade.

encouraged, *a.* SYN.-cheered, confident, enlivened, enthusiastic, heartened, inspired, revived, roused.

encouragement, *n.* SYN.-backing, comfort, reassurance, support.

encroach, *v.* SYN.-infringe, intrude, invade, penetrate, trespass, violate. ANT.-abandon, evacuate, relinquish, vacate.

end, *n.* SYN.-aim, cessation, close, completion, conclusion, culmination, expiration, extremity, finish, fulfillment, intention, object, purpose, realization, result, termination, terminus, tip. ANT.-beginning, commencement, inception, introduction.

end, *v.* SYN.-close, complete, conclude, consummate, execute, finish, fulfill, get done, perfect, terminate.

endanger, *v.* SYN.-expose, hazard, imperil, jeopardize, peril; risk. ANT.-insure, protect, secure.

endeavor, *n.* SYN.-attempt, effort, enterprise, exertion, trial; labor, strain, strife, struggle, toil.

endless, *a.* SYN.-boundless, eternal, illimitable, immeasurable, immense, incalculable, infinite, interminable, unbounded, unlimited, vast. ANT.-bounded, circumscribed, confined, finite, limited.

endorse, *v.* SYN.-affirm, approve, praise, recommend, sanction, sign, support, underwrite.

endorsement, *n.* SYN.-approbation, approval, assent, commendation, consent, praise, sanction, support. ANT.-censure, reprimand, reproach, stricture.

endow, *v.* SYN.-bequeath, bestow, contribute, donate, give, grant, subsidize.

endurance, *n.* SYN.-forbearance, fortitude, long-suffering, patience, perseverance, resignation, tolerance. ANT.-impatience, nervousness, restlessness, unquiet.

endure, *v.* SYN.-bear, brook, experience, suffer, sustain, tolerate, undergo; abide, continue, last, persist, remain, survive. ANT.-fail, falter, succumb; disperse, wane.

enduring, *a.* SYN.-abiding, ceaseless, constant, continual, durable, eternal, faithful, firm, fixed, immutable, invariant, lasting, permanent, perpetual, persistent, stable, steadfast, unalterable, unchanging, unwavering. ANT.-changeable, fickle, irresolute, mutable, vacillating, wavering.

enemy, *n.* SYN.-adversary, antagonist, competitor, foe, opponent, rival. ANT.-accomplice, ally, comrade, confederate, friend.

energetic, *a.* SYN.-active, animated, blithe, brisk, frolicsome, lively, spirited, sprightly, supple, vigorous, vivacious. ANT.-dull, insipid, listless, stale, vapid.

enforce, *v.* SYN.-administer, compel, demand, dictate, impel, oblige, require.

energy, *n.* SYN.-dint, force, might, potency, power, strength, vigor. ANT.-feebleness, frailty, impotence, weakness; persuasion.

engage, *v.* SYN.-commission, contract, employ, hire, retain, secure; absorb, bewitch, captivate, charm, engross, fascinate.

engaged, *a.* SYN.-absorbed, busy, employed, occupied, working.

engender, *n.* SYN.-cause, create, fashion, form, formulate, generate, invent, make, originate, produce. ANT.-annihilate, demolish, destroy; disband, terminate.

engross, *v.* SYN.-assimilate, consume, engulf, swallow up; absorb, engage, occupy. ANT.-discharge, dispense, emit, expel, exude.

enhance, *v.* SYN.-amplify, embellish, heighten, improve, increase, inflate, magnify.

enigma, *n.* SYN.-ambiguity, conundrum, mystery, problem, puzzle, riddle. ANT.-answer, clue, key, resolution, solution.

enjoyment, *n.* SYN.-amusement, comfort, delight, ecstasy, entertainment, gladness, gratification, happiness, joy, pleasure, rapture, satisfaction. ANT.-affliction, annoyance, dejection, melancholy, misery, pain, sorrow, suffering, trouble, vexation.

enlarge, *v.* SYN.-amplify, augment, broaden, dilate, distend, expand, increase, magnify, spread, swell, widen. ANT.-abridge, contract, diminish, restrict, shrink.

enlighten, *v.* SYN.-brighten, clarify, educate, elucidate, illuminate, illumine, illustrate, inform, irradiate, show, teach. ANT.-complicate, confuse, darken, obfuscate, obscure.

enlist, *v.* SYN.-enroll, induce, join, obtain, procure, volunteer; employ, engage, hire, recruit, retain.

enmity, *n.* SYN.-animosity, antagonism, antipathy, hatred, hostility, ill-will, invidiousness, malice, malignity. ANT.-affection, cordiality, friendliness, good will, love.

ennoble, *v.* SYN.-aggrandize, consecrate, dignify, elevate, exalt, extol, glorify, hallow, raise. ANT.-debase, degrade, dishonor, humble, humiliate.

enormous, *a.* SYN.-colossal, elephantine, gargantuan, gigantic, huge, immense, large, prodigious, vast. ANT.-diminutive, little, minute, small, tiny.

enough, *a.* SYN.-abundant, adequate, ample, commensurate, fitting, plenty, satisfactory, sufficient, suitable. ANT.-deficient, lacking, scant.

enrage, *v.* SYN.-affront, agitate, anger, annoy, arouse, bait, chafe, goad, inflame, incense, infuriate, madden, provoke, vex.

enrich, *v.* SYN.-adorn, embellish, improve.

ensue, *v.* SYN.-succeed, come next; trail;

follow, result. ANT.-precede; guide, lead; avoid, elude, flee; cause.

entangle, *v.* SYN.-embroil, entwine, envelop, implicate, include, incriminate, involve, ravel, snare. ANT.-disconnect, disengage, extricate, separate.

entente, *n.* SYN.-alliance, association, coalition, combination, confederacy, federation, league, partnership, union; compact, covenant, marriage, treaty. ANT.-divorce, schism, separation.

enterprise, *n.* SYN.-art, business, commerce, employment, engagement, job, occupation, profession, trade, trading, vocation, work. ANT.-avocation, hobby, pastime.

enterprising, *a.* SYN.-adventurous, bold, chivalrous, clever, daring, precipitate, rash. ANT.-cautious, hesitating, timid.

entertain, *v.* SYN.-consider, contemplate, harbor, hold; amuse, beguile, cheer, delight, divert, gladden, please, regale. ANT.-annoy, bore, disgust, disturb, repulse.

entertainment, *n.* SYN.-amusement, diversion, fun, game, pastime, play, recreation, sport. ANT.-boredom, labor, toil, work.

enthusiasm, *n.* SYN.-ardor, devotion, earnestness, excitement, fanaticism, fervency, fervor, inspiration, intensity, vehemence, warmth, zeal. ANT.-apathy, detachment, ennui, indifference, unconcern.

enthusiastic, *a.* SYN.-absorbed, anxious, ardent, avid, delighted, eager, ecstatic, enraptured, excited, exhilarated, fascinated, fervent, fevered, hot, impassioned, impatient, keen, thrilled, yearning. ANT.-apathetic, indifferent, unconcerned, uninterested.

entice, *v.* SYN.-allure, attract, captivate, charm, enchant, fascinate, lure. ANT.-alienate, deter, repel, repulse.

entire, *a.* SYN.-all, complete, intact, integral, perfect, total, undivided, unimpaired, whole. ANT.-deficient, imperfect, incomplete, partial.

entrance, *n.* SYN.-access, doorway, entry, inlet, opening, portal; admission, arrival, debut, entry, induction, penetration. ANT.-departure, exit.

entreaty, *n.* SYN.-appeal, invocation, petition, plea, prayer, request, suit, supplication.

entrust, *v.* SYN.-commend, commit, consign, relegate, trust; bind, obligate, pledge. ANT.-fail, miscarry, neglect; mistrust, release, renounce; free, loose.

envious, *a.* SYN.-begrudging, covetous, desirous, greedy, jealous, resentful.

environment, *n.* SYN.-background, conditions, habitat, scene, setting, surroundings.

envoy, *n.* SYN.-agent, ambassador, consul, delegate, deputy, emissary, intermediary, proxy, representative.

envy, *n.* SYN.-covetousness, jealousy, malevolence, malice, rivalry, spitefulness. ANT.-generosity, geniality, indifference.

episode, *n.* SYN.-circumstance, event, happening, incident, issue; occurrence, outcome.

epoch, *n.* SYN.-age, antiquity, date, era,

generation, period, time.

equal, *a.* SYN.-alike, commensurate, equitable, equivalent, even, identical, impartial, like, proportionate, regular, same, uniform, unvarying. ANT.-different, disparate, dissimilar, diverse.

equal, *n.* SYN.-complement, counterpart, double, likeness, match, parallel, peer, twin.

equality, *n.* SYN.-balance, equilibrium, evenness, fairness, impartiality, parity, symmetry, uniformity.

equalize, *v.* SYN.-balance, even, level, match.

equilibrium, *n.* SYN.-balance, composure, poise, stability, steadiness, proportion, symmetry. ANT.-fall, imbalance, instability, unsteadiness.

equip, *v.* SYN.-fit out, furnish, provide, supply; afford, give. ANT.-denude, despoil, divest, strip.

equipment, *n.* SYN.-apparatus, gear, implements, machinery, material, paraphernalia, supplies, tools, trappings, utensils.

equitable, *a.* SYN.-fair, honest, impartial, just, reasonable, unbiased. ANT.-dishonorable, fraudulent, partial.

equity, *n.* SYN.-fairness, impartiality, justice, justness, law, rectitude, right; investment, money, property. ANT.-inequity, partiality, unfairness, wrong.

equivalent, *a.* SYN.-coincident, equal, identical, indistinguishable, like, same. ANT.-contrary, disparate, dissimilar, distinct, opposed.

equivocal, *a.* SYN.-ambiguous, dubious, enigmatical, equivocal, obscure, uncertain, vague. ANT.-clear, explicit, obvious, plain, unequivocal.

era, *n.* SYN.-age, antiquity, date, epoch, generation, period, time.

eradicate, *v.* SYN.-erase, eliminate, expel, extirpate, oust, remove. ANT.-accept, admit, include, involve.

erase, *v.* SYN.-cancel, cross out, delete, eliminate, expunge, obliterate; abolish, abrogate, annul, invalidate, nullify, quash, repeal, rescind, revoke. ANT.-confirm, enact, enforce, perpetuate

erect, *a.* SYN.-straight, unbent, upright, vertical. ANT.-bent, crooked.

erect, *v.* SYN.-build, construct, establish, fabricate, found, raise. ANT.-demolish, destroy, overthrow, raze, undermine.

erratic, *a.* SYN.-eccentric, inconsistent, irregular, random, unpredictable.

erroneous, *a.* SYN.-amiss, askew, awry, fallacious, false, faulty, inaccurate, incorrect, mistaken, unprecise, untrue; improper, inappropriate, unsuitable, wrong. ANT.-correct, right, true; suitable; proper.

error, *n.* SYN.-blunder, fallacy, fault, inaccuracy, mistake, slip. ANT.-accuracy, precision, truth.

erudite, *a.* SYN.-academic, bookish, learned, pedantic, scholarly, scholastic, theoretical. ANT.-common-sense, ignorant, practical, simple.

erudition, *n.* SYN.-discretion, foresight, information, insight, intelligence, judgment, knowledge, learning, prudence, reason, sagacity, sageness, sense, wisdom. ANT.-foolishness, ignorance, im-

prudence, nonsense, stupidity.

escape, *n.* SYN.-avoidance, breakout, departure, evasion, flight, release.

escape, *v.* SYN.-abscond, decamp, flee, fly; avert, avoid, elude, evade, shun. ANT.-catch, confront, face, invite, meet.

eschew, *v.* SYN.-avert, avoid, dodge, escape, elude, forbear, forestall, free, shun, ward. ANT.-confront, encounter, meet, oppose.

escort, *v.* SYN.-accompany, associate with, attend, chaperone, consort with, convoy, go with, guard, guide, protect. ANT.-abandon, avoid, desert, leave, quit.

especially, *a.* SYN.-abnormally, extraordinarily, notably, particularly, remarkably, unusually; chiefly, mainly, primarily.

essay, *n.* SYN.-composition, subject, text, theme, thesis, topic.

essence, *n.* SYN.-basis, core, fundamentals, gist, heart, pith, root, substance.

essential, *a.* SYN.-basic, fundamental, imperative, important, indispensable, intrinsic, necessary, requisite, vital. ANT.-expendable, extrinsic, optional, peripheral.

establish, *v.* SYN.-form, found, institute, organize, raise; confirm, fix, ordain, sanction, settle, strengthen; prove, substantiate, verify. ANT.-abolish, demolish, overthrow, unsettle, upset; disprove, refute.

estate, *n.* SYN.-belongings, bequest, commodities, effects, goods, lands, manor, merchandise, possessions, property, stock, wealth; inheritance. ANT.-deprivation, destitution, poverty, privation, want.

esteem, *v.* SYN.-admire, appreciate, honor, prize, regard, respect, revere, reverence, value, venerate; consider, deem, hold, regard, think. ANT.-abhor, depreciate, dislike, scorn.

esteemed, *a.* SYN.-dear, honored, precious, respected, valued. ANT.-despised, unwanted; cheap.

esthetic, *a.* SYN.-artistic, beautiful, creative, emotional, natural, pleasant.

estimate, *v.* SYN.-appraise, assess, calculate, compute, consider, count, evaluate, figure, fix, guess, levy, reckon.

eternal, *a.* SYN.-ceaseless, deathless, endless, everlasting, immortal, infinite, perpetual, timeless, undying. ANT.-ephemeral, finite, mortal, temporal, transient.

eternally, adv. SYN.-always, constantly, continually, eternally, ever, evermore, forever, incessantly, perpetually, unceasingly. ANT.-fitfully, never, occasionally, rarely, sometimes.

ethereal, *a.* SYN.-celestial, divine, ghostly, holy, immaterial, incorporeal, religious, sacred, spiritual, supernatural, unearthly, unworldly. ANT.-carnal, corporeal, material, mundane, physical.

ethical, *a.* SYN.-decent, good, honorable, just, moral, pure, right, righteous, scrupulous, virtuous. ANT.-amoral, libertine, licentious, sinful, unethical.

evacuate, *v.* SYN.-abandon, desert, empty, leave, vacate.

evade, *v.* SYN.-avert, avoid, deceive, dodge, elude, escape, lie, shun. ANT.-catch, confront, face, invite, meet.

evaluate, *v.* SYN.-analyze, appraise, assess, assign, calculate, compute, criticize, estimate, evaluate, examine, inspect, rate, scrutinize.

evaporate, *v.* SYN.-disappear, dissipate, dissolve, fade, vanish.

even, *a.* SYN.-balance, flat, level, smooth, uniform.

evenly, *a.* SYN.-equally, equitably, fairly, impartially, justly, proportionately, symmetrically.

event, *n.* SYN.-circumstance, episode, happening, incident, issue, occasion, occurrence, phenomenon; consequence, end, outcome, result.

ever, adv. SYN.-always, constantly, continually, eternally, evermore, forever, incessantly, perpetually, unceasingly. ANT.-fitfully, never, occasionally, rarely, sometimes.

everlasting, *a.* SYN.-ceaseless, deathless, endless, eternal, immortal, infinite, perpetual, timeless, undying. ANT.-ephemeral, finite, mortal, temporal, transient.

every, *a.* SYN.-all, each.

evidence, *n.* SYN.-confirmation, corroboration, demonstration, proof, testimony, verification. ANT.-fallacy, invalidity.

evident, *a.* SYN.-apparent, clear, conspicuous, indubitable, manifest, obvious, open, overt, patent, unmistakable. ANT.-concealed, covert, hidden, obscure.

evil, *a.* SYN.-bad, baleful, base, deleterious, immoral, iniquitous, noxious, pernicious, sinful, unsound, unwholesome, villainous, wicked. ANT.-excellent, good, honorable, moral, reputable.

evil, *n.* SYN.-crime, iniquity, offense, sin, transgression, ungodliness, vice, wickedness, wrong. ANT.-goodness, innocence, purity, righteousness, virtue.

evolve, *v.* SYN.-create, develop, elaborate, enlarge, expand, mature, unfold. ANT.-compress, contract, restrict, stunt, wither.

exact, *a.* SYN.-accurate, correct, definite, distinct, precise, strict, unequivocal; ceremonious, formal, prim, rigid, stiff. ANT.-erroneous, loose, rough, vague; careless, easy, informal.

exaggerate, *v.* SYN.-amplify, caricature, embroider, enlarge, expand, heighten, magnify, misrepresent, overstate, stretch. ANT.-belittle, depreciate, minimize, understate.

exalt, *v.* SYN.-aggrandize, consecrate, dignify, elevate, ennoble, erect, extol, glorify, hallow, raise. ANT.-debase, degrade, dishonor, humble, humiliate.

exalted, *a.* SYN.-dignified, elevated, eminent, grand, illustrious, lofty, majestic, noble, stately. ANT.-base, low, mean, plebeian, vile.

examination, *n.* SYN.-audit, exploration, inquiry, interrogation, investigation, observation, query, quest, question, research, scrutiny, test, trial. ANT.-disregard, inactivity, inattention, negligence.

examine, *v.* SYN.-analyze, assess, audit,

check, contemplate, dissect, inquire, interrogate, notice, probe, question, quiz, review, scan, scrutinize, survey, view, watch. ANT.-disregard, neglect, omit, overlook.

example, n. SYN.-archetype, illustration, instance. model, pattern, prototype, sample, specimen. ANT.-concept, precept, principle, rule.

exasperate, v. SYN.-aggravate, annoy, chafe, embitter, inflame, irritate, nettle, provoke, vex. ANT.-appease, mitigate, palliate soften, soothe.

exasperation, n. SYN.-annoyance, chagrin, irritation, mortification, pique, vexation. ANT.-appeasement, comfort, gratification, pleasure.

exceed, v. SYN.-beat, excel, outdo, pass, surpass, transcend.

excellent, a. SYN.-conscientious, exemplary, honest, moral, pure, reliable, virtuous, worthy; admirable, commendable, genuine, good, precious, safe, sound, valid; benevolent, gracious, humane, kind; agreeable, cheerful, friendly, genial, pleasant; fair, honorable, immaculate; auspicious, beneficial, favorable, profitable, useful; able, capable, efficient, expert, proficient, skillful.

exception, n. SYN.-exclusion, omission, preclusion; anomaly, deviation, unusual case; affront, objection, offense. ANT.-inclusion, rule, standard.

exceptional, a. SYN.-choice, incomparable, precious, rare, scarce, singular, uncommon, unique. ANT.-customary, ordinary, usual; abundant, commonplace, numerous, worthless.

excess, n. SYN.-abundance, extravagance, immoderation, intemperance, profusion, superabundance, superfluity, surplus. ANT.-dearth, deficiency, lack, paucity, want.

excessive, a. SYN.-abundant, copious, extravagant, exuberant, immoderate, improvident, lavish, luxuriant, overflowing, plentiful, prodigal, profuse, wasteful. ANT.-economical, meager, poor, skimpy, sparse.

exchange, v. SYN.-change, substitute; alter, convert, transfigure, transform. ANT.-retain; continue, establish, preserve, settle, stabilize.

excite, v. SYN.-agitate, arouse, awaken, disquiet, disturb, incite, irritate, provoke, rouse, stimulate, stir up. ANT.-allay, calm, pacify, quell, quiet.

exclaim, v. SYN.-call out, cry, cry out, ejaculate, shout, vociferate. ANT.-intimate, whisper, write.

exclude, v. SYN.-bar, blackball, except, expel, hinder, omit, ostracize, prevent, prohibit, reject, restrain, shut out. ANT.-accept, admit, include, welcome.

exclusive, a. SYN.-clannish, fashionable, private, restricted, segregated, select.

excusable, a. SYN.-allowable, forgivable, pardonable, plausible, reasonable, trivial, understandable.

excuse, n. SYN.-alibi, apology, defense, explanation, justification, reason. ANT.-accusation, complaint, denial, dissimulation.

excuse, v. SYN.-absolve, acquit, condone,

exculpate, exempt, forgive, free, justify, overlook, pardon, remit. ANT.-convict, prosecute, punish, retaliate, revenge.

execrable, a. SYN.-abominable, detestable, foul, hateful, loathsome, odious, revolting, vile. ANT.-agreeable, commendable, delightful, pleasant.

execution, n. SYN.-accomplishment, act, action, deed, doing, feat, operation, performance, transaction. ANT.-cessation, deliberation, inactivity, inhibition, intention.

exemplar, n. SYN.-copy, duplicate, example, facsimile, imitation, model, replica, reproduction, specimen. ANT.-original, prototype.

exemplary, a. SYN.-faultless, excellent, honest, honorable, ideal, immaculate, moral, perfect, pure, reliable, supreme, virtuous. ANT.-faulty, imperfect.

exercise, n. SYN.-activity, application, drill, employment, exertion, lesson, operation, performance, practice, task, training, use. ANT.-idleness, indolence, relaxation, repose, rest.

exhaust, v. SYN.-bore, fatigue, jade, tire, tucker, wear out, weary. ANT.-amuse, invigorate, refresh, restore, revive.

exhausted, a. SYN.-fatigued, spent, tired, wearied, weary, worn. ANT.-fresh, hearty, invigorated, rested.

exhaustion, n. SYN.-enervation, fatigue, languor, lassitude, tiredness, weariness. ANT.-freshness, rejuvenation, restoration, vigor, vivacity.

exhibit, v. SYN.-display, expose, flaunt, parade, present, reveal, show, spread out; demonstrate, evidence, prove, verify. ANT.-conceal, cover, disguise, hide.

exhibition, n. SYN.-array, display, exposition; demonstration, flourish, ostentation, parade, show, spectacle, splurge.

exile, n. SYN.-banishment, deportation, expatriation, expulsion, extradition, ostracism, proscription. ANT.-admittance, recall, reinstatement, retrieval, welcome.

existence, n. SYN.-being, life, liveliness, spirit, vitality, vivacity. ANT.-death, demise.

exorbitant, a. SYN.-excessive, extravagant, immoderate, unreasonable.

exotic, a. SYN.-alien, different, extrinsic, foreign, outstanding, strange, unusual.

expand, v. SYN.-augment, develop, distend, enlarge, extend, grow, increase, swell. ANT.-contract, diminish, shrink, wane.

expanse, n. SYN.-area, extent, magnitude, measure, range, reach, scope, size.

expansion, n. SYN.-development, elaboration, unfolding, unraveling; evolution, growth, maturing, progress. ANT.-abbreviation, compression, curtailment.

expatriation, n. SYN.-banishment, deportation, exile, expulsion, extradition, ostracism, proscription. ANT.-admittance, recall, reinstatement, retrieval, welcome.

expect, v. SYN.-anticipate, await, contemplate, demand, hope for, suppose. ANT.-despair of.

expectation, n. SYN.-anticipation, contemplation, expectancy, foresight, forethought, hope, optimism, preconception, prescience, presentiment. ANT.-doubt, dread, fear, worry.

expedient, n. SYN.-convenient, desirable, practical, suitable, useful.

expedite, v. SYN.-accelerate, dispatch, facilitate, forward, hasten, hurry, push, quicken, rush, speed. ANT.-block, hinder, impede, retard, slow.

expedition, n. SYN.-cruise, incursion, jaunt, journey, passage, pilgrimage, safari, tour, travel, trip, voyage.

expel, v. SYN.-banish, discharge, dismiss, disown, excommunicate, exile, expatriate, ostracize, oust, proscribe; dislodge, eject, eliminate, void. ANT.-admit, favor, include, recall.

expend, v. SYN.-consume, employ, exhaust, pay, spend, use.

expense, n. SYN.-budget, charge, cost, debt, expenditure, liability, price.

expensive, a. SYN.-costly, high-priced, precious; dear, prized, valuable. ANT.-cheap, mean, poor; trashy, worthless.

experience, n. SYN.-background, judgment, knowledge, maturity, practice, seasoning, training, wisdom.

experiment, v. SYN.-analyze, assay, examine, explore, inspect, investigate, probe, research, sample, test, try.

expert, a. SYN.-able, accomplished, adept, clever, competent, cunning, ingenious, practiced, proficient, skilled, skillful, versed. ANT.-awkward, bungling, clumsy, inexpert, untrained.

expire, v. SYN.-cease, conclude, decease, die, end, finish, perish, stop, terminate. ANT.-begin, live, survive.

explain, v. SYN.-clarify, decipher, elucidate, expound, illustrate, interpret, resolve, unfold, unravel. ANT.-baffle, confuse, darken, obscure.

explanation, n. SYN.-alibi, apology, clarification, confession, defense, elucidation, excuse, justification, recapitulation, report. ANT.-accusation, complaint, denial, dissimulation.

explicit, a. SYN.-clear, definitive, express, lucid, manifest, specific. ANT.-ambiguous, equivocal, implicit, obscure, vague.

exploit, n. SYN.-achievement, deed, feat, accomplishment, attainment, performance, realization. ANT.-neglect, omission; defeat, failure.

exploit, v. SYN.-apply, avail, employ, manipulate, operate, use, utilize; consume, exhaust, expend; handle, manage, treat. ANT.-ignore, neglect, overlook, waste.

explore, v. SYN.-examine, hunt, inspect, seek, test.

explorer, n. SYN.-adventurer, forerunner, searcher, trailblazer, pioneer, voyager.

explosive, a. SYN.-fiery, forceful, frenzied, hysterical, raging, savage, uncontrollable, violent.

expose, v. SYN.-air, bare, betray, debunk, disclose, display, open, reveal, show, unmask.

exposed, a. SYN.-disclosed, discovered, revealed, unclosed, uncovered; accessible, open, public, unrestricted; candid, frank, honest, overt, plain.

expound, v. SYN.-clarify, decipher, elucidate, explain, illustrate, interpret, resolve, unfold, unravel. ANT.-baffle, confuse, darken, obscure.

express, a. SYN.-clear, definitive, explicit, lucid, manifest, specific. ANT.-ambiguous, equivocal, implicit, obscure, vague.

express, v. SYN.-affirm, assert, avow, claim, declare, explain, propound, recite, recount, say, specify, state, tell, utter. ANT.-conceal, deny, imply, retract.

expressive, a. SYN.-bright, brilliant, dramatic, intense, spirited, stirring, striking; animated, clear, demonstrative, eloquent, fresh, graphic, lively, lucid, vivid. ANT.-dull, vague; dim, dreary, dusky.

extend, v. SYN.-distend, distort, elongate, expand, lengthen, protract, spread, stretch. ANT.-contract, loosen, shrink, slacken, tighten.

extended, a. SYN.-drawn out, elongated, lasting, lengthy, lingering, long, prolix, prolonged, protracted, tedious, wordy. ANT.-abridged, brief, concise, short, terse.

extensive, a. SYN.-broad, expanded, large, sweeping, vast, wide; liberal. ANT.-confined, narrow, restricted.

extending, a. SYN.-continuing, perpetual, ranging, reaching, spreading, stretching.

extent, n. SYN.-amount, area, compass, degree, expanse, limit, length, magnitude, measure, range, reach, scope, size, stretch.

exterior, n. SYN.-cover, facade, face, front, outer, surface, veneer. ANT.-back, interior, rear.

extol, v. SYN.-aggrandize, celebrate, elevate, ennoble, observe; commend, exalt, glorify, hallow, honor, laud, praise, raise. ANT.-disregard, overlook; decry, disgrace, dishonor, profane.

extra, a. SYN.-added, additional, another, auxiliary, other, reserve, spare.

extract, v. SYN.-dislodge, eject, oust, remove, vacate; withdraw. ANT.-leave, remain, stay; retain.

extradition, n. SYN.-banishment, deportation, exile, expatriation, expulsion, ostracism, proscription. ANT.-admittance, recall, reinstatement, retrieval, welcome.

extraneous, a. SYN.-alien, contrasted, extraneous, foreign, irrelevant, remote, strange, unconnected. ANT.-akin, germane, kindred, relevant.

extraordinary, a. SYN.-exceptional, marvelous, peculiar, rare, remarkable, singular, uncommon, unusual, wonderful. ANT.-common, frequent, ordinary, usual.

extravagance, n. SYN.-excess, immoderation, intemperance, profusion, superabundance, superfluity, surplus. ANT.-dearth, deficiency, lack, paucity, want.

extravagant, a. SYN.-abundant, copious, excessive, exuberant, immoderate, improvident, lavish, luxuriant, overflowing, plentiful, prodigal, profuse, wasteful. ANT.-economical, meager, poor, skimpy, sparse.

extreme, a. SYN.-acute, exacting, excessive, harsh, inordinate, intense, radical, relentless, rigorous, severe, unmitigated, unreasonable, unyielding. ANT.-genial, indulgent, yielding.

F

fable, n. SYN.-allegory, chronicle, fiction, legend, myth, parable, saga, tale. ANT.-fad, history.

fabricate, v. SYN.-build, construct, erect, form, frame, make, manufacture, raise; contrive, devise, fake, lie, prevaricate. ANT.-demolish, destroy, raze.

facade, n. SYN.-appearance, deceit, face, front, look, mask.

face, n. SYN.-countenance, mug, visage; assurance, audacity; cover, exterior, front, surface. ANT.-timidity; back, interior, rear.

facilitate, v. SYN.-aid, allay, alleviate, assuage, calm, comfort, ease, lighten, mitigate, pacify, relieve, soothe. ANT.-confound, distress, disturb, trouble, worry.

facility, n. SYN.-ability, adroitness, cleverness, cunning, deftness, dexterity, ingenuity, knack, readiness, skill, skillfullness; building, company, plant, tools. ANT.-awkwardness, clumsiness, inability, ineptitude.

facsimile, n. SYN.-copy, duplicate, facsimile, imitation, replica, reproduction, transcript. ANT.-original, prototype.

fact, n. SYN.-actuality, certainty, reality, truth; act, circumstance, deed, event, incident, occurrence. ANT.-fiction, supposition, theory; delusion, falsehood.

faction, n. SYN.-division, fragment, moiety, piece, portion, section, segment; component, element, ingredient, member, organ; concern, interest, part, party, side. ANT.-entirety, whole.

factual, a. SYN.-accurate, authentic, exact, genuine, specific, true.

faculty, n. SYN.-ability, aptitude, aptness, capability, capacity, dexterity, efficiency, power, qualification, skill, talent. ANT.-disability, incapacity, incompetence, unreadiness.

fad, n. SYN.-craze, curiosity, fashion, gimmick, innovation, novel, oddity, style, vogue.

faded, a. SYN.-dim, faint, indistinct, pale; feeble, languid, wearied; irresolute, timid, weak. ANT.-conspicuous, glaring; strong, vigorous; brave, forceful.

fail, v. SYN.-blunder, cease, crash, decline, default, deteriorate, disappoint, falter, fizzle, flag, flop, founder, miss.

failure, n. SYN.-fiasco, miscarriage; default, dereliction, omission; decay, decline; deficiency, lack, loss, want. ANT.-achievement, success, victory; sufficiency.

faint, a. SYN.-dim, faded, indistinct, pale; feeble, languid, wearied; irresolute, timid, weak. ANT.-conspicuous, glaring; strong, vigorous; brave, forceful.

fair, a. SYN.-bright, clear, light; attractive, blond, comely, lovely; equitable, honest, impartial, just, reasonable, unbiased; average, mediocre, passable.

ANT.-foul, ugly; dishonorable, fraudulent, partial; excellent, first-rate, worst.

fairness, n. SYN.-decency, equity, honesty, impartiality, integrity, justice, justness, law, truth, rectitude, right. ANT.-inequity, partiality, unfairness, wrong.

faith, n. SYN.-confidence, credence, dependence, reliance, trust; belief, creed, doctrine, dogma, persuasion, religion, tenet; constancy, fidelity, loyalty. ANT.-doubt, incredulity, mistrust, skepticism; infidelity.

faithful, a. SYN.-conscientious, constant, dependable, devoted, honest, incorruptible, loyal, staunch, steadfast, true; accurate, genuine, reliable, trusty. ANT.-disloyal, false, fickle, treacherous, untrustworthy.

faithless, a. SYN.-apostate, disloyal, false, perfidious, recreant, traitorous, treacherous, treasonable. ANT.-constant, devoted, loyal, true.

fake, a. SYN.-affected, artificial, assumed, bogus, counterfeit, ersatz, fabrication, feigned, fictitious, imitation, phony, sham, spurious, synthetic, unreal. ANT.-genuine, natural, real, true.

fall, v. SYN.-collapse, decline, decrease, descend, diminish, drop, sink, subside; stumble, topple, tumble; droop, extend downward, hang. ANT.-arise, ascend, climb, mount, soar; steady.

fallacy, n. SYN.-ambiguity, error, fault, inaccuracy, inconsistency, mistake, paradox, slip. ANT.-accuracy, precision, truth.

falling, a. SYN.-declining, decreasing, descending, diminishing, dropping, ebbing, plunging, sinking, tumbling.

false, a. SYN.-amiss, deceitful, dishonest, disloyal, erroneous, fallacious, faulty, inaccurate, incorrect, lying, mistaken, treacherous, underhanded, untrue, wrong; bogus, copied, counterfeit, fabricated, faked, forged, pseudo, spurious, synthetic, . ANT.-correct, right, true.

falsehood, n. SYN.-deception, delusion, equivocation, exaggeration, fib, fiction, illusion, lie, prevarication, untruth. ANT.-axiom, canon, fact, truism.

falsify, v. SYN.-alter, counterfeit, deceive, lie, misrepresent. ANT.-confirm, establish, prove.

falter, v. SYN.-delay, demur, doubt, hesitate, pause, scruple, stammer, stutter, vacillate, waver. ANT.-continue, decide, persevere, proceed, resolve.

fame, n. SYN.-acclaim, credit, distinction, eminence, glory, honor, notoriety, renown, reputation. ANT.-disrepute, ignominy, infamy, obscurity.

familiar, a. SYN.-acquainted, aware, cognizant, conversant, intimate, knowing, versed; affable, amicable, close, courteous, friendly, informal, sociable, unreserved; accustomed, common, commonplace, customary, everyday, homespun, prosaic, simple, unsophisticated, well-known. ANT.-affected, cold, distant, reserved, unfamiliar.

familiarity, n. SYN.-acquaintance, fellowship, friendship, sociability; frankness, informality, intimacy, liberty, unre-serve. ANT.-constraint, distance, haughtiness, presumption, reserve.

family, n. SYN.-ancestry, clan, descendants, extraction, forbears, genealogy, genre, group, heirs, house, kin, kindred, kinsfolk, lineage, pedigree, progeny, relations, relationship, relatives, tribe, type. ANT.-disconnection, foreigners, strangers.

famished, a. SYN.-craving, hungry, ravenous, starved, thirsting, voracious. ANT.-full, gorged, sated, satiated; satisfied.

famous, a. SYN.-acclaimed, celebrated, distinguished, eminent, glorious, illustrious, influential, noted, notorious, prominent, recognized, renowned, well-known. ANT.-hidden, ignominious, infamous, obscure, unknown.

fanatical, n. SYN.-arbitrary, dogmatic, frenzied, intolerant, narrow-minded, obsessed, obstinate, passionate, stubborn, zealous.

fanciful, a. SYN.-dreamy, fantastic, fictitious, ideal, idealistic, imaginative, maudlin, mawkish, picturesque, poetic, romantic, sentimental. ANT.-factual, literal, matter-of-fact, practical, prosaic.

fancy, a. SYN.-adorned, capricious, elaborate, elegant, embellished, gaudy, ostentatious, showy.

fancy, n. SYN.-caprice, conception, creation, dream, fantasy, idea, imagination, invention, notion, whimsy.

fantastic, a. SYN.-capricious, extravagant, farfetched, freakish, outlandish, preposterous, ridiculous, whimsical, wonderful. ANT.-conventional, ordinary, routine.

fantasy, n. SYN.-caprice, dream, fancy, hallucination, illusion, imagination, vision, whim.

far, a. SYN.-away, distant, faraway, remote, removed. ANT.-close, near, nigh; cordial, friendly.

farewell, n. SYN.-departure, good-by, leave-taking, valediction. ANT.-greeting, salutation, welcome.

farming, n. SYN.-agriculture, agronomy, cultivation, gardening, horticulture, husbandry, tillage.

fascinate, v. SYN.-attract, beguile, bewitch, captivate, charm, delight, enamor, enchant, enrapture, enthrall, entice, intoxicate, lure, overpower, overwhelm, stimulate, titillate. ANT.-alienate, deter, disgust, displease, repel, repulse, tire.

fascinating, a. SYN.-alluring, appealing, attractive, bewitching, captivating, charming, delightful, enchanting, engaging, seductive, winning. ANT.-repugnant, repulsive, revolting.

fashion, n. SYN.-approach, convention, custom, mode, practice, style, usage; craze, fad, vogue.

fashion, v. SYN.-construct, create, forge, form, make, mold, produce, shape; compose, constitute, make up; arrange, combine, organize; devise, frame, invent. ANT.-destroy, disfigure, dismantle, misshape, wreck.

fast, a. SYN.-expeditious, fleet, quick, rapid, speedy, swift; constant, firm, in-

flexible, secure, solid, stable, steadfast, steady, unswerving, unyielding. ANT.-slow, sluggish; insecure, loose, unstable, unsteady.

fasten, v. SYN.-affix, anchor, attach, bind, fix, link, place, secure, set, stick, tie. ANT.-displace, remove, unfasten.

fastidious, a. SYN.-accurate, critical, discerning, discriminating, exact, particular. ANT.-cursory, shallow, superficial, uncritical.

fat, a. SYN.-chubby, corpulent, heavy, husky, obese, paunchy, plump, portly, pudgy, rotund, stocky, stout, thickset. ANT.-gaunt, lean, slender, slim, thin.

fatal, a. SYN.-deadly, destructive, disastrous, final, lethal, mortal, predestined. ANT.-life-giving; divine, immortal.

fate, n. SYN.-consequence, doom, fortune, lot, portion; circumstance, destiny, issue, karma, necessity, outcome, result.

father, v. SYN.-beget, create, engender, father, generate, originate, procreate, produce, propagate, sire. ANT.-abort, destroy, extinguish, kill, murder.

fatigue, n. SYN.-enervation, exhaustion, languor, lassitude, tiredness, weariness. ANT.-freshness, rejuvenation, restoration, vigor, vivacity.

fatigued, a. SYN.-bored, exhausted, faint, jaded, spent, tired, wearied, weary, worn. ANT.-fresh, hearty, invigorated, rested.

fault, n. SYN.-blemish, defect, error, failure, flaw, imperfection, mistake, omission, shortcoming, vice, weakness. ANT.-completeness, correctness, perfection.

faultless, a. SYN.-complete, entire, finished, full, utter, whole; blameless, holy, immaculate, perfect, pure, sinless; consummate, excellent, ideal, superlative, supreme; absolute, downright, unqualified, utter. ANT.-deficient, incomplete, lacking; blemished, defective, faulty, imperfect.

faulty, a. SYN.-blemished, damaged, defective, deficient, flawed, imperfect, tainted, unsound; inadequate, incomplete, insufficient, substandard, unfit, unsatisfactory. ANT.-complete, perfect, whole.

favor, n. SYN.-advantage, bias, exemption, immunity, liberty, license, partiality, preference, prerogative, privilege, right, sanction; accommodation, boon, courtesy, kindness. ANT.-disallowance, inhibition, prohibition, restriction.

favor, v. SYN.-animate, cheer, countenance, embolden, encourage, exhilarate, hearten, impel, incite, inspirit, urge; esteem, foster, like, prefer, prize, promote, sanction, stimulate, support ANT.-reject, deter, discourage, dispirit, dissuade.

favorite, a. SYN.-beloved, cherished, pet, popular, preferred, prevailing, prevalent. ANT.-unpopular.

fealty, n. SYN.-allegiance, constancy, devotion, faithfulness, fidelity, loyalty. ANT.-disloyalty, faithlessness, perfidy, treachery.

fear, n. SYN.-alarm, apprehension, consternation, cowardice, dismay, dread, fright, horror, panic, scare, terror, ti-

midity, trepidation. ANT.-assurance, boldness, bravery, courage, fearlessness.

fearful, a. SYN.-afraid, apprehensive, fainthearted, frightened, scared, timid, timorous. ANT.-assured, bold, composed, courageous, sanguine.

fearless, a. SYN.-adventurous, audacious, bold, brave, courageous, daring, dauntless, intrepid; brazen, forward. ANT.-cowardly, flinching, timid; bashful, retiring.

feasible, a. SYN.-credible, likely, plausible, possible, practicable, practical, probable. ANT.-impossible, impracticable, visionary.

feast, n. SYN.-banquet, celebration, dinner, entertainment, festival, regalement.

feature, n. SYN.-attribute, characteristic, mark, peculiarity, property, quality, trait; highlight, innovation, specialty.

fecund, a. SYN.-bountiful, fertile, fruitful, luxuriant, plenteous, productive, prolific, rich, teeming. ANT.-barren, impotent, sterile, unproductive.

feeble, a. SYN.-decrepit, delicate, enervated, exhausted, faint, forceless, impaired, infirm, languid, powerless, puny, weak. ANT.-forceful, lusty, stout, strong, vigorous.

feed, v. SYN.-cater, cram, dine, encourage, fatten, feast, nourish, nurture, provide, stock, stuff, supply, support, sustain.

feel, v. SYN.-accept, acknowledge, believe, consider, deem, observe, perceive, savor, sense, think; caress, clutch, fondle, grip, grope, handle, paw, press, squeeze.

feeling, n. SYN.-awareness, consciousness, perception, reaction, sensation, sensibility; affection, emotion, intuition, judgment, passion, sensibility, sentiment, sympathy, tenderness; impression, opinion. ANT.-anesthesia; coldness, imperturbability, insensibility; fact.

feign, v. SYN.-act, affect, assume, fabricate, pretend, profess, sham, simulate. ANT.-display, exhibit, expose, reveal.

felicity, n. SYN.-beatitude, blessedness, bliss, contentment, delight, gladness, happiness, pleasure, satisfaction, well-being. ANT.-despair, grief, misery, sadness, sorrow.

fellowship, n. SYN.-amity, brotherhood, brotherliness, camaraderie, communion, friendliness, intimacy, solidarity, togetherness; alliance, association, brotherhood, clan, club, fraternity, society. ANT.-acrimony, discord, opposition, strife.

felon, n. SYN.-convict, criminal, culprit, delinquent, malefactor, offender, transgressor.

feminine, a. SYN.-delicate, fair, female, gentle, girlish, ladylike, maidenly, sensitive, tender, womanish, womanly. ANT.-male, manly, mannish, masculine, virile.

ferment, n. SYN.-agitation, chaos, commotion, confusion, stir, tumult, turmoil. ANT.-certainty, order, peace, tranquility.

ferocious, *a.* SYN.-barbarous, bestial, brutal, brute, brutish, carnal, coarse, cruel, fierce, gross, inhuman, merciless, remorseless, rough, rude, ruthless, savage, sensual. ANT.-civilized, courteous, gentle, humane, kind.

fertile, *a.* SYN.-bountiful, fecund, fruitful, luxuriant, plenteous, productive, prolific, rich, teeming. ANT.-barren, impotent, sterile, unproductive.

fervent, *a.* SYN.-ardent, eager, enthusiastic, fervid, fiery, glowing, hot, impassioned, intense, keen, passionate, vehement, zealous. ANT.-apathetic, cool, indifferent, nonchalant.

fervor, *n.* SYN.-ardor, devotion, earnestness, enthusiasm, excitement, fanaticism, fervency, inspiration, intensity, vehemence, warmth, zeal. ANT.-apathy, detachment, ennui, indifference, unconcern.

festive, *a.* SYN.-blithe, cheerful, gay, gleeful, hilarious, jolly, jovial, joyous, lively, merry, mirthful, sprightly. ANT.-gloomy, melancholy, morose, sad, sorrowful.

fetish, *n.* SYN.-compulsion, craze, fixation, mania, obsession, passion; amulet, charm, talisman.

fetter, *v.* SYN.-attach, bind, connect, fasten, join, link, restrain, restrict, tie. ANT.-free, loose, unfasten, untie.

feud, *n.* SYN.-affray, altercation, argument, bickering, contention, disagreement, dispute, quarrel, spat, squabble, wrangle. ANT.-agreement, friendliness, harmony, peace, reconciliation.

few, *a.* SYN.-any, inconsiderable, meager, negligible, rare, scant, scanty, scattering, some, sparse, thin, trifling.

fickle, *a.* SYN.-capricious, changeable, fitful, inconstant, restless, unstable, variable. ANT.-constant, reliable, stable, steady, trustworthy.

fiction, *n.* SYN.-allegory, fable, fabrication, falsehood, invention, narrative, novel, romance, story, tale. ANT.-fact, history, reality, truth, verity.

fictitious, *a.* SYN.-affected, artificial, assumed, bogus, counterfeit, ersatz, fake, feigned, phony, sham, spurious, synthetic, unreal, untrue. ANT.-genuine, natural, real, true.

fidelity, *n.* SYN.-allegiance, constancy, devotion, faithfulness, fealty, loyalty; accuracy, exactness, precision. ANT.-disloyalty, faithlessness, perfidy, treachery

field, *n.* SYN.-acreage, ground, land, meadow, pasture, patch, plain, plot, range, region, soil, tract; domain, estate, farm, realm.

fiend, *n.* SYN.-barbarian, beast, brute, demon, devil, maniac, monster; addict, aficionado, fan, fanatic, junkie.

fierce, *a.* SYN.-angry, boisterous, enraged, forceful, frenzied, frightening, furious, impetuous, monstrous, passionate, powerful, raging, raving, savage, turbulent, untamed, vehement, violent, wild; acute, awful, extreme, intense, severe, violent. ANT.-calm, feeble, gentle, quiet, soft.

fiery, *a.* SYN.-burning, hot, scalding, scorching, torrid, warm; ardent, fer-

vent, fiery, hot-blooded, impetuous, intense, passionate; peppery, pungent. ANT.-cold, cool, freezing, frigid; apathetic, impassive, indifferent, passionless, phlegmatic; bland.

fight, *n.* SYN.-altercation, battle, brawl, clash, combat, conflict, confrontation, contention, dispute, encounter, feud, fracas, quarrel, scuffle, skirmish, strife.

fight, *v.* SYN.-argue, attack, battle, brawl, combat, conflict, contend, debate, dispute, encounter, grapple, oppose, quarrel, scuffle, skirmish, squabble, struggle, tussle, wrangle.

fighter, *n.* SYN.-aggressor, antagonist, assailant, bully, competitor, contender, opponent, rival.

figurative, *a.* SYN.-allegorical, illustrative, metaphorical.

figure, *n.* SYN.-appearance, build, cast, configuration, contour, cut, form, frame, guise, image, mold, outline, pattern, shape. ANT.-contortion, deformity, distortion, mutilation.

figure, *v.* SYN.-calculate, compute, consider, count, estimate, number, reckon. ANT.-conjecture, guess, miscalculate.

fill, *v.* SYN.-fill up, occupy, pervade; furnish, replenish, stock, store, supply; content, glut, gorge, pack, sate, satiate, satisfy, stuff. ANT.-deplete, drain, empty, exhaust, void.

filling, *n.* SYN.-contents, dressing, filler, insides, lining, padding, stuffing, wadding.

film, *n.* SYN.-celluloid, cinema, filmstrip, image, movie, negative, photograph, picture, portrayal, print, representation, slide, transparency; coating, covering, fabric, gauze, membrane, skin.

filter, *v.* SYN.-clarify, clean, distill, filtrate, purify, refine, separate, sift, strain; seep, trickle.

filth, *n.* SYN.-contamination, dirt, garbage, grime, impurity, muck, pollution, sewage, slop, trash.

filthy, *a.* SYN.-dirty, foul, grimy, muddy, soiled, squalid. ANT.-clean, neat, presentable.

final, *a.* SYN.-concluding, conclusive, decisive, ending, eventual, last, latest, terminal, ultimate. ANT.-embryonic, first, inaugural, incipient, original, rudimentary.

finally, *a.* SYN.-at last, conclusively, decisively, definitely, irrevocably, permanently, ultimately.

find, *v.* SYN.-ascertain, detect, devise, discern, discover, encounter, expose, find out, learn, locate, notice, reveal, uncover. ANT.-cover, hide, lose, mask, screen.

fine, *a.* SYN.-choice, dainty, delicate, elegant, exquisite, nice, pure, refined, splendid, subtle; beautiful, handsome, pretty; minute, powdered, pulverized, sharp, slender, small, thin. ANT.-blunt, coarse, large, rough, thick.

finish, *v.* SYN.-accomplish, achieve, close, complete, conclude, consummate, do, end, execute, fulfill, get done, perfect, perform, terminate.

finished, *a.* SYN.-accomplished, ceased, complete, concluded, consummated, done, ended, executed, finalized, full,

perfect, settled, stopped, thorough, total, unbroken, undivided. ANT.-imperfect, lacking, unfinished.

fire, *n.* SYN.-blaze, burning, combustion, conflagration, embers, flame, glow, heat, sparks, warmth. ANT.-cold; apathy, quiescence.

firm, *a.* SYN.-constant, durable, enduring, established, fixed, hardy, immovable, immutable, lasting, permanent, secure, stable, staunch, steadfast, steady, strong, sturdy, tough, unwavering; callous, incorruptible, obdurate, stubborn. ANT.-changeable, erratic, irresolute, vacillating, variable.

firm, *n.* SYN.-association, business, company, concern, corporation, partnership. ANT.-dispersion, individual.

first, *a.* SYN.-beginning, earliest, initial, original, primary, prime, primeval, primitive, pristine; chief, foremost. ANT.-hindmost, last, latest; least, subordinate.

fit, *a.* SYN.-applicable, appropriate, becoming, befitting, beneficial, comely, competent, decent, decorous, desirable, equitable, fitting, likely, proper, qualified, respectable, rightful, seemly, suitable, suited, tolerable; healthy, robust, trim. ANT.-awkward, brash, gross, illtimed, improper, inappropriate, unqualified.

fit, *v.* SYN.-accommodate, adapt, adjust, agree, belong, conform, harmonize, match, relate, suit. ANT.-clash, disturb, misapply, misfit.

fitting, *a.* SYN.-applicable, appropriate, apt, becoming, particular, proper, suitable. ANT.-contrary, improper, inappropriate.

fix, *v.* SYN.-affix, attach, bind, fasten, link, place, plant, secure, set, stick, tie; define, determine, establish, limit, set, settle; adjust, correct, mend, patch, rectify, regulate, rejuvenate, repair. ANT.-displace, remove, unfasten; alter, change, disturb, modify; damage, mistreat.

fixed, *a.* SYN.-abiding, ceaseless, constant, continual, enduring, faithful, immutable, invariant, permanent, perpetual, persistent, unalterable, unchanging, unwavering; adjusted, corrected, improved, mended, restored. ANT.-fickle, mutable, vacillating, wavering.

flagrant, *a.* SYN.-disgraceful, glaring, gross, heinous, outrageous, overt, shameful.

flamboyant, *a.* SYN.-adorned, bombastic, decorated, elaborate, flashy, lavish, ornate, ostentatious, resplendent, showy, superficial

flame, *n.* SYN.-brightness, fire, flare, illumination, light, radiance. ANT.-darkness, gloom, obscurity, shadow.

flash, *n.* SYN.-burst, flicker, glimmer, glitter, illumination, impulse, moment, reflection, spark, sparkle, vision, wink.

flashy, *a.* SYN.-elaborate, flamboyant, gaudy, ornate, ostentatious, showy, superficial.

flat, *a.* SYN.-even, horizontal, level, low, plane, smooth; boring, pointless, prosaic, tedious, unanimated; dull, flavorless, insipid, stale, tasteless, unsavory, vapid; absolute, downright, positive, unqualified. ANT.-broken, hilly, irregular, sloping; exciting, racy; savory, tasty.

flattery, n. SYN.-adulation, applause, commendation, compliment, eulogy, fawning, praise, tribute. ANT.-affront, criticism, insult, taunt.

flaunt, v. SYN.-boast, brag, crow, display, glory, flourish, parade, show, vaunt. ANT.-apologize, deprecate, humble, minimize.

flavor, n. SYN.-relish, savor, style, tang, taste.

flaw, n. SYN.-blemish, blot, scar, speck, stain; defect, error, fault, imperfection, mistake, omission, shortcoming, vice. ANT.-adornment, embellishment, perfection, purity.

flee, n. SYN.-abscond, decamp, escape, fly, hasten, run away. ANT.-appear, arrive, remain, stay.

fleet, a. SYN.-expeditious, fast, quick, rapid, speedy, swift. ANT.-slow, sluggish.

fleeting, a. SYN.-brief, ephemeral, evanescent, momentary, short-lived, temporary, transient. ANT.-abiding, immortal, lasting, permanent, timeless.

flexible, a. SYN.-compliant, ductile, elastic, formative, impressionable, limber, lithe, pliable, pliant, resilient, supple, tractable, yielding. ANT.-brittle, hard, rigid, stiff, unbending.

flighty, a. SYN.-capricious, erratic, fickle, frivolous, inconstant, unstable, volatile, whimsical. ANT.-disciplined, reliable, restrained.

flimsy, a. SYN.-decrepit, fragile, frail, inadequate, weak; ineffectual, poor, superficial.

flippant, a. SYN.-disrespectful, facetious, frivolous, impertinent, impudent, offhand, rude, saucy, smart.

flop, v. SYN.-blunder, bomb, fail, falter, flunk, founder, miscarry; flap, flounder, flounce, jerk, quiver, squirm, wiggle, wriggle.

flourish, v. SYN.-burgeon, flower, grow, increase, luxuriate, prosper, thrive; brandish, display, flaunt, gesture, parade, vaunt, wave; adorn, decorate, embellish.

flow, v. SYN.-gush, run, spout, spurt, stream; come, emanate, issue, originate, proceed, result; abound, be copious.

flowing, a, SYN.-ample, complete, copious, extensive, plentiful, sweeping; full, loose, voluminous. ANT.-depleted, devoid, empty, vacant; insufficient, lacking, partial.

fluctuate, v. SYN.-change, hesitate, oscillate, undulate, vacillate, vary, waver. ANT.-adhere, decide, persist, resolve, stick.

fluent, a. SYN.-articulate, eloquent, garrulous, glib, mellifluent, persuasive, smooth, talkative, vocal, wordy; copious, flowing.

fluid, a. SYN.-flowing, fluent, juicy, liquid, running, watery. ANT.-congealed, frozen, solid, stiff.

fluster, v. SYN.-abash, chagrin, discom-

fit, distress, embarrass, entangle, hamper, hinder, mortify, perplex, rattle, trouble. ANT.-cheer, encourage, help, relieve

fly, v. SYN.-flit, float, flutter, glide, hover, mount, sail, soar; dart, rush, shoot, spring; abscond, decamp, escape, flee, run away. ANT.-descend, fall, plummet, sink.

foil, v. SYN.-baffle, balk, circumvent, defeat, disappoint, frustrate, hinder, outwit, prevent, thwart. ANT.-accomplish, fulfill, further, promote.

folk, n. SYN.-clan, community, culture, nation, society, tribe.

follow, v. SYN.-succeed, come next; comply, heed, obey, observe; adopt, copy, imitate; accompany, attend; chase, pursue, trail; ensue, result. ANT.-precede; guide, lead; avoid, elude, flee; cause.

follower, n. SYN.-adherent, admirer, advocate, attendant, backer, believer, companion, devotee, disciple, helper, henchman, member, partisan, participant, pupil, successor, supporter, votary, witness. ANT.-chief, head, leader, master.

folly, n. SYN.-foolishness, imbecility, silliness; absurdity, extravagance, imprudence, indiscretion. ANT.-sense, wisdom; judgment, prudence, reasonableness.

fond, a. SYN.-affectionate, attached, dedicated, devoted, disposed, given up to, inclined, prone, wedded. ANT.-detached, disinclined, indisposed, untrammeled.

fondle, v. SYN.-caress, coddle, cuddle, embrace, hug, kiss, pet. ANT.-annoy, buffet, spurn, tease, vex.

fondness, n. SYN.-affection, attachment, endearment, kindness, love, tenderness; disposition, emotion, feeling, inclination. ANT.-aversion, hatred, indifference, repugnance, repulsion.

food, n. SYN.-diet, edibles, fare, feed, meal, nutriment, provisions, rations, repast, sustenance, viands, victuals. ANT.-drink, hunger, starvation, want.

fool, n. SYN.-buffoon, clown, harlequin, jester; blockhead, dolt, dunce, idiot, imbecile, nincompoop, numbskull, oaf, simpleton. ANT.-genius, philosopher, sage, scholar.

foolish, a. SYN.-absurd, asinine, brainless, crazy, idiotic, irrational, nonsensical, preposterous, ridiculous, senseless, silly, simple. ANT.-judicious, prudent, sagacious, sane, wise.

forbear, v. SYN.-abstain, cease, desist, omit, refrain, spare, stop, withhold. ANT.-continue, indulge, persist.

forbid, v. SYN.-ban, bar, block, deny, debar, disallow, embargo, hinder, inhibit, interdict, prevent, prohibit, restrain. ANT.-allow, authorize, permit, recommend, sanction, tolerate.

force, n. SYN.-dint, emphasis, energy, intensity, might, potency, power, strength, vigor; coercion, compulsion, constraint, dominance, violence. ANT.-feebleness, frailty, impotence, weakness; persuasion.

force, v. SYN.-coerce, command, compel, constrain, demand, drive, enforce, im-

pel, impose, insist, make, oblige, order, require. ANT.-allure, convince, induce, persuade, prevent.

forceful, a. SYN.-cogent, commending, dominant, firm, forcible, fortified, hale, hardy, impregnable, mighty, potent, powerful, robust, sinewy, strong, sturdy, tough. ANT.-brittle, delicate, feeble, fragile, insipid.

foreboding, n. SYN.-anticipation, apprehension, dread, expectation, fear, feeling, premonition, prescience, presentiment.

forecast, n. SYN.-anticipation, augury, conjecture, divination, estimate, guess, prediction, prognosis, prognostication, projection, prophecy.

foreign, a. SYN.-alien, contrasted, exotic, extraneous, imported, irrelevant, outlandish, remote, strange, unconnected, unknown. ANT.-akin, germane, kindred, relevant.

foreigner, n. SYN.-alien, immigrant, newcomer, outsider, stranger. ANT.-acquaintance, associate, countryman, friend, neighbor.

foresight, n. SYN.-anticipation, carefulness, contemplation, expectation, forethought, hope, preconception, prescience, presentiment, prudence. ANT.-doubt, dread, fear, worry.

foretell, v. SYN.-augur, divine, forecast, foresee, portend, predict, prophesy.

forever, adv. SYN.-always, constantly, continually, eternally, ever, evermore, forever, incessantly, perpetually, unceasingly. ANT.-fitfully, never, occasionally, rarely, sometimes.

forge, v. SYN.-coin, copy, counterfeit, duplicate, fabricate, falsify, imitate, reproduce; create, fabricate, fashion, make, produce.

forgery, n. SYN.-bogus, copy, counterfeit, fabrication, fake, hoax, phony.

forgive, v. SYN.-absolve, acquit, condone, excuse, exonerate, forget, overlook, pardon, release, remit. ANT.-accuse, chastise, condemn, convict, punish.

forgiveness, n. SYN.-absolution, acquittal, amnesty, clemency, leniency, mercy, pardon, remission. ANT.-conviction, penalty, punishment, sentence.

forlorn, a. SYN.-abandoned, alone, comfortless, deserted, desolate, disconsolate, destitute, distressed, forgotten, forsaken, heartbroken, miserable, pitiable, sad, wretched. ANT.-contented, fortunate, happy.

form, n. SYN.-approach, ceremony, conformity, custom, formality, manner, method, practice, procedure, ritual, system; appearance, arrangement, configuration, design, fashion, formation, structure.

form, v. SYN.-construct, create, fashion, forge, make, mold, produce, shape; compose, constitute, make up; arrange, combine, organize; devise, frame, invent. ANT.-destroy, disfigure, dismantle, misshape, wreck.

formal, a. SYN.-affected, ceremonious, correct, decorous, exact, methodical, precise, proper, regular, solemn, stiff; external, outward, perfunctory. ANT.-easy, natural, unconstrained, unconventional; heartfelt.

formed, *a.* SYN.-built, carved, created, cultivated, developed, established, modeled, molded, patterned, shaped.

former, *a.* SYN.-aforesaid, antecedent, earlier, erstwhile, late, once, onetime, preceding, previous, prior. ANT.-consequent, following, later, subsequent, succeeding.

formulate, *v.* SYN.-compose, create, draw, engender, fashion, form, frame, generate, invent, make, originate, prepare, produce. ANT.-annihilate, demolish, destroy; disband, terminate.

fornication, *n.* SYN.-adultery, carnality, debauchery, lechery, lewdness, licentiousness, promiscuity.

forsake, *v.* SYN.-abandon, abdicate, abjure, abstain, relinquish, renounce, resign, surrender, vacate, waive; desert, leave, quit. ANT.-defend, maintain, uphold; stay, support.

forthcoming, *a.* SYN.-anticipated, approaching, coming, destined, expected, fated, imminent, impending, inevitable, near, prospective.

fortified, *a.* SYN.-armed, armored, defended, enclosed, guarded, protected, secured, walled.

fortitude, *n.* SYN.-boldness, bravery, chivalry, courage, durability, fearlessness, intrepidity, mettle, might, potency, power, prowess, stamina, stoutness, strength, sturdiness, resolution, toughness. ANT.-cowardice, fear, pusillanimity, timidity.

fortuity, *n.* SYN.-accident, chance, contingency, exigency, incidence, luck, mishap. ANT.-calculation, design, intention, purpose.

fortunate, *a.* SYN.-advantageous, auspicious, benign, blessed, favored, felicitous, flourishing, fortuitous, happy, lucky, propitious, prosperous, successful. ANT.-cheerless, condemned, illfated, persecuted, unlucky.

fortune, *n.* SYN.-accident, break, chance, fate, fluke, lot, luck, windfall; assets, bundle, estate, inheritance, mint, money, possessions, property, riches, treasure, wealth.

forward, *n.* SYN.-beginning, introduction, overture, preamble, preface, prelude, prologue, start. ANT.-completion, conclusion, end, epilogue, finale.

forward, *v.* SYN.-advance, further, promote; improve, proceed, progress, rise, thrive. ANT.-hinder, oppose, retard, retreat, withhold.

fossil, *a.* SYN.-ancient, antique, archaic, out-of-date, prehistoric, venerable.

foster, *v.* SYN.-advance, cherish, cultivate, encourage, favor, further, help, nourish, nurture, raise, retain, support, sustain. ANT.-abandon, dislike, disregard, neglect, reject.

foul, *a.* SYN.-dirty, filthy, grimy, muddy, soiled, squalid; indecent, nasty, obscene; base, contemptible, despicable, low, mean, pitiful, shabby. ANT.-clean, neat, presentable; pure, wholesome.

found, *v.* SYN.-begin, create, endow, erect, establish, form, institute, organize, raise. ANT.-abolish, demolish, overthrow, unsettle, upset.

foundation, *n.* SYN.-base, basis, bedrock, bottom, footing, ground, groundwork, root, substructure, support, underpinning; authority, data, facts, justification, observation, reason; association, charity, company, endowment, establishment, institute, institution, organization, society. ANT.-building, cover, superstructure, top.

fracture, *v.* SYN.-break, burst, cleave, crack, crush, demolish, destroy, rend, rupture, separate, sever, shatter, shear, smash, split. ANT.-join, mend, renovate, repair, restore.

fragile, *a.* SYN.-breakable, brittle, delicate, exquisite, feeble, fine, frail, infirm, weak. ANT.-durable, hardy, strong, sturdy, tough.

fragment, *n.* SYN.-division, moiety, part, piece, portion, remnant, scrap, section, segment, share; component, element, faction, fraction, ingredient. ANT.-entirety, whole.

fragrance, *n.* SYN.-aroma, bouquet, essence, incense, odor, perfume, scent, smell.

frail, *a.* SYN.-breakable, brittle, dainty, delicate, feeble, fragile, infirm, weak. ANT.-durable, hardy, strong, sturdy, tough.

frame, *v.* SYN.-build, conceive, construct, contrive, devise, erect, fabricate, form, make, outline, sketch. ANT.-demolish, destroy, raze.

frank, *a.* SYN.-artless, blunt, bold, candid, direct, familiar, free, forthright, honest, open, outspoken, plain, sincere, straightforward, truthful; fair, impartial, just, unbiased, uninhibited, . ANT.-contrived, scheming, sly, wily.

frantic, *a.* SYN.-crazy, delirious, deranged, desperate, distracted, excited, frenzied, mad, raging, rash, reckless, raving, wild. SYN.-calm, composed, serene.

fraternity, *n.* SYN.-brotherliness, fellowship, kindness, solidarity; association, brotherhood, clan, society. ANT.-acrimony, discord, opposition, strife.

fraternize, *v.* SYN.-associate, consort, hobnob, join, mingle, mix, socialize. ANT.-dissociate, divide, segregate, separate, sort.

fraud, *n.* SYN.-artifice, cheat, chicanery, deceit, deception, duplicity, guile, imposition, imposture, misrepresentation, racket, sham, swindle, trick, trickery; charlatan, cheat, fake, impostor, pretender, quack. ANT.-fairness, honesty, integrity, sincerity.

freak, *n.* SYN.-aberration, curiosity, monstrosity, oddity, rarity; abnormal, bizarre, capricious, erratic odd, peculiar, strange, unusual.

free, *a.* SYN.-autonomous, emancipated, exempt, freed, independent, liberated, unconfined, unrestricted; clear, loose, open, unfastened, unobstructed; immune, uninfected; artless, careless, easy, familiar, frank; bounteous, bountiful, complimentary, generous, gratis, liberal, munificent. ANT.-confined, restrained, restricted; blocked, clogged, impeded; subject; illiberal, parsimonious, stingy.

free, *v.* SYN.-absolve, acquit, deliver, discharge, disentangle, dismiss, emancipate, let go, liberate, loosen, pardon, release, rid, set free, untie. ANT.-confine, imprison, oppress, restrict, subjugate.

freedom, *n.* SYN.-exemption, familiarity, immunity, impunity, independence, latitude, leeway, liberation, liberty, license, privilege, unrestraint. ANT.-bondage, compulsion, constraint, necessity, servitude.

freely, *a.* SYN.-abundantly, deliberately, easily, extravagantly, frankly, intentionally, loosely, openly, profusely, spontaneously, unhindered, voluntarily, willingly.

freezing, *a.* SYN.-arctic, chilly, cold, cool, frigid, frosty, frozen, icy, polar, wintry. ANT.-burning, fiery, heated, hot, torrid.

freight, *n.* SYN.-burden, cargo, encumbrance, goods, load, packages, shipment.

frenzied, *a.* SYN.-frantic, impetuous, irregular, mad, turbulent, wanton, wayward, wild; boisterous, stormy, tempestuous; extravagant, foolish, giddy, rash, reckless. ANT.-civilized, gentle; calm, placid, quiet.

frequent, *a.* SYN.-common, continual, general, habitual, incessant, often, periodic, persistent, repeated, usual. ANT.-exceptional, rare, recurrent, regular, scanty, solitary, unique.

frequent, *v.* SYN.-attend, hang out, haunt, visit.

frequently, *adv.* SYN.-commonly, generally, often, recurrently, regularly, repeatedly. ANT.-infrequently, occasionally, rarely, seldom, sporadically.

fresh, *a.* SYN.-modern, new, novel, original, recent; additional, further; bracing brisk, cool, invigorating, refreshing, stimulating; artless, green, inexperienced, natural, raw, unskilled, untrained. ANT.-decayed, faded, hackneyed, musty, stagnant.

fretful, *a.* SYN.-fractious, ill-natured, ill-tempered, irritable, peevish, petulant, snappish, testy, touchy, waspish. ANT.-affable, genial, good-natured, good-tempered, pleasant.

friend, *n.* SYN.-acquaintance, ally, associate, chum, colleague, companion, compatriot, comrade, confidant, crony, intimate; accomplice, advocate, backer, defender, patron, supporter, well-wisher. ANT.-adversary, enemy, stranger.

friendly, *a.* SYN.-affable, affectionate, amiable, amicable, attentive, civil, close, companionable, congenial, cordial, devoted, familiar, gracious, helpful, intimate, kind, kindly, neighborly, pleasant, sociable, social, sympathetic, warm-hearted. ANT.-aloof, antagonistic, cool, distant, hostile, reserved.

friendship, *n.* SYN.-acquaintance, affection, association, brotherhood, camaraderie, cognizance, companionship, congeniality, devotion, esteem, familiarity, fellowship, friendship, harmony, intimacy, kindliness, kindness, sympathy. ANT.-ignorance, inexperience, unfamiliarity.

fright, *n.* SYN.-affright, alarm, apprehension, consternation, dread, fear, horror, panic, scare, terror, trepidation. ANT.-assurance, boldness, calm, composure, bravery, courage, fearlessness, quiet, security, tranquillity.

frighten, *v.* SYN.-affright, alarm, appall, astound, badger, daunt, dismay, disturb, horrify, intimidate, panic, petrify, scare, startle, terrify, terrorize, threaten. ANT.-allay, compose, embolden, reassure, soothe.

frightened, *a.* SYN.-afraid, apprehensive, disturbed, fainthearted, fearful, horrified, intimidated, scared, terrified, timorous. ANT.-assured, bold, composed, courageous, sanguine.

frigid, *a.* SYN.-arctic, chilly, cold, cool, freezing, frosty, frozen, icy, wintry; indifferent, passionless, phlegmatic, stoical, unfeeling. ANT.-burning, fiery, heated, hot, torrid; ardent, passionate.

frisky, *a.* SYN.-active, alive, animated, boisterous, dapper, dashing, gleeful, jaunty, lively, playful, spirited.

frivolous, *a.* SYN.-childish, cursory, dizzy, exterior, flighty, flimsy, foolish, imperfect, paltry, petty, shallow, slight, superficial, trifling, trivial, unimportant. ANT.-abstruse, complete, deep, profound, thorough.

frolic, *v.* SYN.-caper, cavort, gamble, gambol, play, revel, rollick, romp, sport; execute, perform.

front, *n.* SYN.-anterior, bow, exterior, facade, face, foreground, frontage, nose, prow, vanguard; appearance, aspect, carriage, countenance, demeanor, expression, mask, mien, presence. ANT.-back, posterior, rear.

frontier, *n.* SYN.-border, boundary, brim, brink, edge, fringe, hinterland, limit, outskirts, rim, termination, verge. ANT.-center, core, interior, mainland.

frozen, *a.* SYN.-arctic, chilled, cold, freezing, frigid, frosted, frosty, iced, icy, wintry. ANT.-burning, fiery, heated, hot, torrid.

frugal, *a.* SYN.-careful, economical, niggardly, parsimonious, provident, prudent, saving, spare, sparing, stingy, temperate, thrifty. ANT.-extravagant, intemperate, self-indulgent, wasteful.

frustrate, *v.* SYN.-baffle, balk, bewilder, circumvent, confuse, defeat, disappoint, foil, hinder, mystify, nonplus, outwit, perplex, prevent, thwart. ANT.-accomplish, fulfill, further, promote.

fulfill, *v.* SYN.-accomplish, achieve, complete, comply, conclude, consummate, discharge, effect, execute, finish, perform, terminate.

full, *a.* SYN.-abundant, ample, complete, copious, crammed, entire, extensive, filled, gorged, lavish, packed, perfect, plentiful, replete, satiated, satisfied, saturated, soaked, sufficient; baggy, flowing, loose, voluminous; broad, detailed, exhaustive, ranging, unlimited. ANT.-depleted, devoid, empty, vacant; insufficient, lacking, partial.

fully, *a.* SYN.-abundantly, adequately, amply, completely, entirely, perfectly, sufficiently, thoroughly, well, wholly.

fun, *n.* SYN.-amusement, antic, caper, comedy, diversion, enjoyment, entertainment, festivity, foolery, frolic, game, glee, jest, lark, laughter, mirth, pastime, play, pleasure, prank, recreation, relaxation, romp, sport, trifling.

function, *n.* SYN.-business, capacity, duty, employment, faculty, office, province, purpose, service, utility; banquet, celebration, meeting, party, reception, social.

function, *v.* SYN.-act, do, go, move, officiate, operate, perform, run, work.

fund, *n.* SYN.-accumulation, donation, endowment, hoard, provision, reserve, stock, store, supply.

fundamental, *a.* SYN.-absolute, basic, cardinal, central, crucial, elemental, elementary, essential, first, important, intrinsic, key, precise, primary, rudimentary, simple, specific. ANT.-abstract, abstruse, auxiliary, common, complex, dispensable, elaborate, intricate, secondary, subordinate, unimportant.

funds, *n.* SYN.-assets, capital, cash, collateral, currency, money, reserves, resources, revenue, savings, wealth, wherewithal

funny, *a.* SYN.-amusing, comic, comical, droll, entertaining, facetious, farcical, hilarious, humorous, jocular, laughable, ludicrous ridiculous, whimsical, witty; curious, odd, peculiar, queer, strange, suspicious, unusual. ANT.-melancholy, sad, serious, sober, solemn.

furious, *a.* SYN.-agitated, angry, enraged, exasperated, incensed, indignant, irate, maddened, provoked, raging, tumultuous, wrathful, wroth; extreme, frantic, frenetic, frenzied, intense. ANT.-calm, happy, pleased, satisfied.

furnish, *v.* SYN.-appoint, endow, equip, fit, fit out provide, purvey, stock, supply; afford, cater, give, produce, yield. ANT.-denude, despoil, divest, strip.

further, *v.* SYN.-advance, aggrandize, elevate, forward, promote, bring forward, offer, propose, propound, proceed, progress, rise, thrive, augment, enlarge, increase. ANT.-hinder, oppose, retard, retreat, withhold.

furor, *n.* SYN.-agitation, bedlam, clamor, commotion, disturbance, excitement, rumpus, shouting, stir, tumult.

fury, *n.* SYN.-anger, choler, fierceness, indignation, ire, irritation, passion, petulance, rage, resentment, temper, turbulence, vehemence, violence, wrath. ANT.-conciliation, forbearance, patience, peace, self-control.

fusion, *n.* SYN.-combination, concurrence, incorporation, joining, solidarity, unification, union; alliance, amalgamation, coalition, concert, confederacy, league, marriage. ANT.-division, schism, separation; disagreement, discord.

fussy, *a.* SYN.-careful, conscientious, demanding, exact, exacting, fastidious, meticulous, particular, precise.

futile, *a.* SYN.-abortive, bootless, empty, fruitless, idle, ineffective, ineffectual, pointless, unavailing, unproductive, unsatisfactory, useless, valueless, vain, vapid, worthless. ANT.-effective, potent, profitable.

G

gab, *v.* SYN.-babble, chatter, discuss, gossip, jabber, prate, prattle, ramble, speak, talk.

gaily, *a.* SYN.-brightly, brilliantly, colorfully, extravagantly, jovially, joyfully, joyously, gaudily, showily, spiritedly.

gain, *n.* SYN.-accrual, accumulation, addition, advantage, benefit, favor, goods, increase, interest, profit, profits. ANT.-calamity, distress, handicap, trouble.

gain, *v.* SYN.-achieve, acquire, advance, approach, attain, augment, benefit, earn, get, improve, net, obtain, procure, profit, progress, reach, secure, win. ANT.-forfeit, lose, surrender.

gale, *n.* SYN.-blow, gust, hurricane, squall, storm, typhoon, wind.

gallant, *a.* SYN.-bold, brave, chivalrous, courageous, courtly, daring, dauntless, fine, intrepid, magnificent, noble, polite, splendid, valiant.

gallery, *n.* SYN.-arcade, balcony, grandstand, mezzanine, veranda; audience, onlookers, public, spectators; exhibit, hall, museum, salon, showroom, wing.

game, *n.* SYN.-amusement, contest, diversion, fun, match, merriment, pastime, play, recreation, sport. ANT.-business drudgery, hardship, labor, work.

gap, *n.* SYN.-aperture, breach, break, cavity, fissure, gulf, hole, opening, orifice, pore, rift, void; arroyo, canyon, chasm, gulch, gully, hollow, ravine; hiatus, interim, intermission, lag, lull, pause, recess.

garb, *n.* SYN.-appearance, fashion, form, guise, mode, style, uniform; attire, clothes, garments, vestments.

garish, *a.* SYN.-colorful, flashy, gaudy, loud, ornate, ostentatious, showy, spirited, tawdry.

garment, garments, *n.* SYN.-apparel, array, attire, clothes, clothing, drapery, dress, garb, raiment, vestments, vesture. ANT.-nakedness, nudity.

garnish, *v.* SYN.-adorn, beautify, deck, decorate, embellish, enrich, ornament, trim. ANT.-debase, defame, expose, strip, uncover.

garrulous, *a.* SYN.-articulate, chattering, chatty, communicative, effusive, glib, loquacious, talkative, verbose, voluble. ANT.-laconic, reticent, silent, taciturn, uncommunicative.

gash, *n.* SYN.-cut, slash, slit, wound.

gate, *n.* SYN.-barrier, entrance, entry, inlet, opening, passage, portal.

gather, *v.* SYN.-accumulate, amass, associate, assemble, collect, congregate, convene, hoard, muster, rally, reunite, swarm; cull, garner, glean, harvest, pick, pluck, reap, select, sort; assume, conclude, deduce, infer, judge, learn. ANT.-disband, disperse, distribute, scatter, separate.

gathered, *a.* SYN.-assembled, collected, congregated, convened, convoked, grouped, joined, massed, met, rallied, thronged, united.

gathering, *n.* SYN.-assembly, association, caucus, committee, company, conclave, conference, congregation, convention, convocation, council, crowd, flock, herd, legislature, meet, reunion, society, throng, turnout.

gaudy, *a.* SYN.-colorful, flashy, garish, loud, meretricious, ornate, ostentatious, showy, spirited, tasteless, tawdry, vulgar.

gaunt, *a.* SYN.-emaciated, haggard, lank, lean, scrawny, skinny, slender, slight, slim, spare, tenuous, thin. ANT.-broad, bulky, fat, thick, wide.

gay, *a.* SYN.-cheerful, frolicsome, glad, happy, jolly, jovial, joyful, joyous, lighthearted, merry, sprightly, vivacious. ANT.-depressed, glum, mournful, sad, sullen.

gear, *n.* SYN.-accouterments, equipment, material, outfit, rigging, tackle, things.

gem, *n.* SYN.-bauble, jewel, ornament, stone; cherished, prized, treasured.

general, *n.* SYN.-broad, common, comprehensive, customary, ecumenical, extensive, inclusive, ordinary, popular, prevalent, regular, ubiquitous, universal, usual, widespread; imprecise, indefinite, inexact, vague. ANT.-exceptional, rare, singular; definite, particular, specific.

generate, *v.* SYN.-afford, bear, bestow, breed, cause, create, engender, form, impart, induce, make, pay, produce, supply, yield.

generation, *n.* SYN.-age, antiquity, date, epoch, era, period, span, time; creation, formation, invention, procreation, production. ANT.-childhood, infancy, youth; breeding, creation, procreation, reproduction.

generous, *a.* SYN.-altruistic, beneficent, charitable, giving, lavish, liberal, magnanimous, munificent, noble, openhanded, philanthropic, unselfish; abundant, ample, bountiful, copious, flowing, overflowing, plentiful. ANT.-covetous, greedy, miserly, selfish, stingy.

genial, *a.* SYN.-affable, agreeable, amicable, companionable, cordial, friendly, hearty, kindly, neighborly, pleasant, sociable, social. ANT.-antagonistic, cool, distant, hostile, reserved.

genius, *n.* SYN.-ability, aptitude, brains, capability, creativity, faculty, gift, inspiration, intellect, intelligence, originality, sagacity, talent, wisdom; adept, gifted, intellectual, prodigy, proficient. ANT.-ineptitude, obtuseness, shallowness, stupidity; dolt, dullard, moron.

genre, *n.* SYN.-category, class, grade, kind, order, rank, set, sort, variety.

gentle, *a.* SYN.-amiable, benign, calm, considerate, cultivated, disciplined, docile, kind, mild, peaceful, placid, pliant, polite, refined, relaxed, respectable, sensitive, serene, soft, soothing, tame, temperate, tender, tractable, well-bred. ANT.-fierce, harsh, rough, savage, violent.

gently, *a.* SYN.-benevolently, carefully, cautiously, considerately, delicately, sensitively, tenderly.

genuine, *a.* SYN.-accurate, actual, authentic, bona fide, certain, certified, legitimate, natural, original, precise,

positive, proven, real, sincere, tested, true, unadulterated, unaffected, valid, veritable. ANT.-artificial, bogus, counterfeit, false, sham.

germ, *n.* SYN.-antibody, bacteria, contagion, infection, microbe, pest, virus; ailment, contamination, disease, poison, pollution, taint; beginning, genesis, inception, origin, seed, source.

gesture, *n.* SYN.-indication, motion, portent, sign, signal, symbol, token; appearance, attitude, concession, display, formality, posture.

get, *v.* SYN.-achieve, acquire, attain, earn, gain, get, obtain, procure, purchase, reach, realize, receive, secure, seize, take, win; apprehend, comprehend, grasp, learn, perceive, understand, . ANT.-forfeit, leave, lose, renounce, surrender.

ghastly, *a.* SYN.-abhorrent, cadaverous, deathlike, disgusting, dreadful, frightful, grisly, gruesome, hideous, horrible, repulsive, shocking.

ghost, *n.* SYN.-apparition, demon, phantom, shade, specter, spirit, spook, vision; hint, shadow, suggestion.

giant, *a.* SYN.-colossal, enormous, gigantic, huge, immense, large, monstrous, tremendous.

gift, *n.* SYN.-award, benefaction, bequest, boon, bounty, charity, donation, endowment, favor, grant, gratuity, handout, largess, legacy, offering, present, token; ability, aptitude, capability, capacity, faculty, forte, genius, power, talent. ANT.-deprivation, earnings, loss, purchase; incapacity, ineptitude, stupidity.

gigantic, *a.* SYN.-broad, colossal, elephantine, enormous, gargantuan, huge, immense, large, prodigious, tremendous, vast. ANT.-diminutive, little, minute, small, tiny.

giggle, *n.* SYN.-cackle, chortle, chuckle, laugh, snicker, snigger, titter.

girl, *n.* SYN.-child, coed, damsel, lassie, maid, maiden, miss, young lady, young woman.

gist, *n.* SYN.-basis, connotation, core, drift, essence, explanation, heart, implication, import, intent, interpretation, meaning, meat, point, purport, purpose, sense, significance, signification, substance.

give, *v.* SYN.-assign, award, bequeath, bestow, confer, contribute, deliver, donate, endow, furnish, grant, impart, issue, offer, present, provide, render, supply. ANT.-keep, retain, seize, withdraw.

glad, *a.* SYN.-cheerful, contented, delighted, exhilarated, exulting, gratified, happy, jovial, joyous, lighthearted, merry, pleased. ANT.-dejected, depressed, despondent, melancholy, sad.

gladly, *a.* SYN.-blissfully, cheerfully, cordially, delightfully, enthusiastically, gaily, gleefully, happily, heartily, joyfully, joyously, lovingly, passionately, readily, sweetly, warmly, willingly.

gladness, *n.* SYN.-beatitude, blessedness, bliss, contentment, cheer, delight, felicity, gaiety, glee, happiness, merriment, pleasure, satisfaction, well-being. ANT.-

despair, grief, misery, sadness, sorrow.

glance, *n.* SYN.-behold, eye, gaze, glimpse, look, observe, regard, scan, see, survey, view. ANT.-avert, miss, overlook, stare.

glare, *v.* SYN.-blind, dazzle, gleam, radiate, shine; frown, glower, scowl, stare.

gleam, *v.* SYN.-beam, flash, flicker, glare, glimmer, glisten, glitter, glow, shimmer, shine, sparkle, twinkle.

glib, *a.* SYN.-artful, articulate, diplomatic, facile, fluent, polished, sleek, slick, smooth, suave, superficial, urbane. ANT.-bluff, blunt, harsh, rough, rugged.

glide, *v.* SYN.-coast, descend, drift, float, flow, fly, slide, slip, slither, soar, waft.

gloom, *n.* SYN.-blackness, bleakness, darkness, dimness, obscurity, shadow; apprehension, dejection, depression, despair, despondency, foreboding, grief, malaise, melancholy, misery, misgiving, mourning, pessimism, sadness, sorrow, woe. ANT.-exultation, frivolity, joy, light, mirth.

gloomy, *a.* SYN.-bleak, cheerless, dark, dejected, depressed, despondent, disconsolate, dismal, dispirited, doleful, dreary, dull, funereal, glum, lonesome, melancholy, moody, sad, somber, sorrowful. ANT.-cheerful, gay, happy, joyous, lively, merry.

glorify, *v.* SYN.-acclaim, adore, aggrandize, bless, commend, consecrate, dignify, enshrine, enthrone, exalt, extol, hallow, honor, laud, revere, venerate. ANT.-abuse, debase, degrade, dishonor, mock.

glorious, *a.* SYN.-admirable, celebrated, distinguished, elevated, esteemed, exalted, excellent, grand, gratifying, high, honorable, honored, illustrious, lofty, magnificent, majestic, memorable, noble, notable, praiseworthy, raised, splendid, sublime, supreme. ANT.-base, ignoble, low, ordinary, ridiculous.

glory, *n.* SYN.-admiration, adoration, deference, dignity, esteem, fame, homage, honor, praise, renown, respect, reverence, worship; beauty, brilliance, grandeur, magnificence, majesty, pomp, radiance, resplendence, richness; exult, rejoice, triumph. ANT.-contempt, derision, disgrace, dishonor, reproach.

glow, *v.* SYN.-blaze, flicker, glare, gleam, glimmer, glisten, glitter, radiate, scintillate, shimmer, shine, sparkle, twinkle.

glum, *a.* SYN.-dejected, depressed, despondent, disconsolate, dismal, dispirited, doleful, dour, fretful, gloomy, melancholy, moody, morose, plaintive, sad, somber, sorrowful, sulky, sullen, surly. ANT.-amiable, cheerful, happy, joyous, merry, pleasant.

glut, *v.* SYN.-clog, congest, fill up, inundate, occupy, overstock, pervade; cram, devour, feast, fill, gorge, overeat, sate, satiate, satisfy, stuff. ANT.-deplete, drain, empty, exhaust, void.

go, *v.* SYN.-depart, exit, fade, flee, leave, move, proceed, quit, retire, run, vacate, vanish, walk, withdraw; advance, continue, endeavor, journey, operate, perform, persevere, persist, proceed, progress, travel ANT.-arrive, come, enter, stand, stay.

goad, *v.* SYN.-coerce, drive, encourage, force, impel, induce, press, prod, prompt, push, stimulate, spur, urge, whip; bully, instigate, needle, provoke, tease.

goal, *n.* SYN.-aim, ambition, aspiration, craving, design, desire, hope, intent, intention, longing, object, objective, plan, passion.

godlike, *a.* SYN.-almighty, boundless, celestial, divine, eternal, excellent, heavenly, holy, invincible, omnipotent, spiritual, superhuman, supernatural, transcendent, universal. ANT.-blasphemous, diabolical, mundane, profane, wicked.

godly, *a.* SYN.-angelic, divine, devout, holy, pious, righteous, spiritual.

going, *v.* SYN.-auspicious, flourishing, growing, operating, profitable, running, successful, thriving; bound, destined, directed.

gone, *a.* SYN.-abandoned, departed, disappeared, disintegrated, dissipated, dissolved, extinct, left, moved, removed, retired, vanished, withdrawn.

good, *a.* SYN.-able, admirable, agreeable, benevolent, capable, cheerful, commendable, conscientious, efficient, exemplary, expert, fair, friendly, genial, gracious, honest, honorable, humane, kind, moral, pleasant, proficient, pure, reliable, skillful, virtuous, worthy; excellent, genuine, immaculate, precious, safe, sound, valid; auspicious, beneficial, favorable, profitable, useful; adequate, ample, sufficient.

gossip, *n.* SYN.-babble, chatter, hearsay, meddling, news, rumor, scandal, slander; backbiter, blabbermouth, chatterbox, meddler, muckraker, snoop, tattler.

govern, *v.* SYN.-administer, command, conduct, control, dictate, direct, handle, legislate, manage, oversee, regulate, reign, rule, superintend, supervise, sway, tyrannize. ANT.-acquiesce, assent, obey, submit, yield.

graceful, *a.* SYN.-adroit, agile, controlled, dexterous, elegant, flowing, fluid, lithe, natural, nimble, pliant, poised, skilled, smooth, sprightly, supple, willowy; artistic, balanced, beautiful, comely, dainty, delicate, elegant, exquisite, harmonious, neat, pretty, slender, trim. ANT.-awkward, clumsy, deformed, gawky, ungainly.

gracious, *a.* SYN.-agreeable, amiable, condescending, cordial, courteous, courtly, earnest, engaging, elegant, friendly, good-natured, hearty, hospitable, kind, patronizing, pleasing, polite, sincere, warm. ANT.-churlish, disagreeable, hateful, ill-natured, surly.

grade, *n.* SYN.-caliber, category, class, denomination, genre, kind, order, rank, set; attribute, characteristic, distinction, feature, peculiarity, property, quality, trait, value. ANT.-being, essence, nature, substance.

gradual, *a.* SYN.-continuous, creeping, dawdling, delaying, deliberate, leisurely, slow, sluggish, unhurried. ANT.-fast, quick, rapid, speedy, swift.

grandeur, *n.* SYN.-amplitude, beauty, brilliance, ceremony, dignity, greatness, immensity, impressiveness, luxury, magnificence, pomp, resplendence, richness, splendor, stateliness, vastness.

grandiose, *a.* SYN.-august, dignified, grand, high, imposing, lofty, magnificent, majestic, noble, ostentatious, pretentious, pompous, showy, stately, sublime. ANT.-common, humble, lowly, ordinary, undignified.

grant, *n.* SYN.-allowance, appropriation, benefaction, bequest, boon, bounty, concession, donation, endowment, gift, gratuity, present, reward, subsidy.

grant, *v.* SYN.-allocate, allot, apportion, appropriate, assign, award, bestow, bequeath, confer, dispense, distribute, divide, give, measure, mete; accord, allow, concede, grant, permit, yield. ANT.-confiscate, keep, refuse, retain, withhold.

graph, *n.* SYN.-chart, design, diagram, plan, plot, sketch.

graphic, *a.* SYN.-clear, colorful, comprehensive, depicted, descriptive, detailed, distinct, drawn, eloquent, explicit, forcible, illustrated, moving, outlined, pictured, picturesque, portrayed, sketched, striking, strong, telling, visual.

grasp, *v.* SYN.-capture, catch, clutch, grip, lay hold of, seize; comprehend, follow, perceive, understand. ANT.-liberate, lose, release.

grateful, *a.* SYN.-appreciative, beholden, gracious, indebted, obliged, pleased, thankful. ANT.-heedless, rude, thankless, unappreciative, unmindful.

gratifying, *a.* SYN.-acceptable, agreeable, amusing, comfortable, convenient, cozy, delightful, enjoyable, pleasant, pleasing, pleasurable, relaxed, restful, welcome. ANT.-distressing, miserable, troubling, uncomfortable, wretched.

grave, *a.* SYN.-consequential, critical, dangerous, important, momentous, ominous, serious, weighty; dignified, sedate, serious, sober, solemn, staid, thoughtful. ANT.-insignificant, trifling, trivial; flighty, frivolous, light, merry.

grave, *n.* SYN.-barrow, catacomb, crypt, mound, pit, sepulcher, tomb, vault.

great, *a.* SYN.-big, enormous, gigantic, huge, immense, large, vast; countless, numerous; celebrated, eminent, famed, illustrious, prominent, renowned; critical, important, momentous, serious, vital, weighty; august, dignified, elevated, grand, majestic, noble; excellent, fine, magnificent. ANT.-diminutive, little, minute, small; common, obscure, ordinary, unknown; menial, paltry.

greedy, *a.* SYN.-avaricious, covetous, grasping, mercenary, miserly, niggardly, parsimonious, rapacious, selfish, stingy, tight; devouring, gluttonous, insatiable, intemperate, ravenous, voracious. ANT.-generous, munificent; full, satisfied.

green, *a.* SYN.-artless, callow, fresh, immature, ignorant, inexperienced, innocent, naive, natural, new, novice, raw, unsophisticated, untrained, young,

youthful. ANT.-decayed, faded, hackneyed, musty, stagnant.

greet, *v.* SYN.-accost, acknowledge, address, approach, bow, hail, nod, receive, recognize, salute, speak to, welcome. ANT.-avoid, pass by.

gregarious, *a.* SYN.-affable, civil, communicative, congenial, convivial, friendly, gay, genial, hospitable, jovial, merry, outgoing, sociable, social. ANT.-antisocial, disagreeable, hermitic, inhospitable.

grief, *n.* SYN.-affliction, anguish, desolation, distress, gloom, heartache, lamentation, malaise, melancholy, misery, mourning, pain, regret, remorse, sadness, sorrow, trial, tribulation, unhappiness, woe. ANT.-comfort, consolation, happiness, joy, solace.

grievance, *n.* SYN.-affliction, burden, complaint, damage, detriment, encumbrance, hardship, harm, injury, mischief, injustice, ordeal, prejudice, trial, wrong. ANT.-benefit, improvement, repair.

grieve, *v.* SYN.-agonize, bemoan, bewail, deplore, depress, distress, lament, mourn, sadden, sorrow, suffer, weep. ANT.-carouse, celebrate, rejoice, revel.

grieved, *a.* SYN.-afflicted, aggrieved, depressed, distressed, hurt, pained, sad, sorrowful, sorry, vexed. ANT.-cheerful, delighted, splendid.

grim, *a.* SYN.-appalling, austere, bleak, crusty, dire, forbidding, frightful, gloomy, glowering, glum, grouchy, grumpy, harsh, morose, scowling, severe, sour, stern, sullen, sulky,

grip, *v.* SYN.-capture, catch, clasp, clench, clutch, embrace, grab, grasp, hold, seize, snare, squeeze, trap. ANT.-liberate, loose, release, throw.

groceries, *n.* SYN.-comestibles, edibles, food, foodstuffs, perishables, produce, staples.

gross, *a.* SYN.-aggregate, entire, total, whole; brutal, enormous, glaring, grievous, manifest, plain; coarse, crass, earthy, indelicate, lewd, obscene; rough, rude, vulgar; big, bulky, corpulent, fat, great, large, obese, . ANT.-proper, refined; appealing, comely, delicate.

grotesque, *a.* SYN.-abnormal, deformed, distorted, hideous, malformed, repulsive, ugly; absurd, fantastic, ludicrous, outrageous, ridiculous, scary.

grouch, *n.* SYN.-bear, complainer, crank, growler, grumbler, sourpuss.

grouch, *v.* SYN.-complain, grouse, grumble, lament, murmur, mutter, protest, remonstrate, repine, whine. ANT.-applaud, approve, praise, rejoice.

group, *n.* SYN.-aggregation, assembly, band, brood, bunch, class, cluster, collection, crowd, flock, herd, horde, lot, mob, pack, party, set, swarm, throng, troupe.

grovel, *v.* SYN.-abase, beg, cower, crawl, flatter, kneel, kowtow, obey, prostrate, snivel, stoop, surrender, wheedle, yield.

grow, *v.* SYN.-advance, alter, build, develop, distend, enlarge, evolve, expand, extend, flourish, gain, germinate, increase, mature, mount, multiply, progress, spread, sprout, swell, thrive. ANT.-atrophy, contract, decay, diminish, shrink, wane.

growth, *n.* SYN.-augmentation, development, elaboration, evolution, expansion, increase, maturing, progress, unfolding, unraveling. ANT.-abbreviation, compression, curtailment.

gruff, *a.* SYN.-abrupt, blunt, brusque, churlish, coarse, crude, curt, discourteous, harsh, rough, rude, severe, short, uncivil, unpolished. ANT.-calm, placid, tranquil, unruffled; civil, courteous, gentle, mild.

guarantee, *n.* SYN.-assurance, bail, bond, earnest, guaranty, pawn, pledge, promise, security, surety, token, warrant, warrantee.

guarantee, *v.* SYN.-affirm, assure, attest, confirm, endorse, insure, pledge, reassure, secure, stake, support, vouch, wager, warrant.

guard, *n.* SYN.-bulwark, defense, protection, safeguard, safety, security, shelter, shield; defender, guardian, protector, sentinel, sentry, watchman..

guard, *v.* SYN.-cloak, conceal, cover, curtain, defend, envelop, hide, protect, safeguard, screen, shelter, shield, shroud, veil; attend, check, observe, oversee, patrol, picket, superintend, supervise, tend, watch. ANT.-bare, divulge, expose, reveal, unveil; desert, disregard, forsake, ignore, leave, neglect.

guardian, *n.* SYN.-baby-sitter, curator, custodian, defender, guard, keeper, nursemaid, overseer, parent, preserver, protector, regent, sentinel, sentry, trustee.

guess, *n.* SYN.-assumption, conjecture, estimate, hypothesis, notion, opinion, presumption, speculation, supposition, suspicion, theory.

guess, *v.* SYN.-assume, believe, conjecture, estimate, hypothesize, imagine, predicate, presume, reckon, speculate, suppose, surmise, suspect, theorize, think.

guidance, *n.* SYN.-administration, care, conduct, control, direction, execution, instruction, leadership, management, supervision.

guide, *n.* SYN.-conductor, director, escort, guru, helmsman, lead, leader, pathfinder, pilot, scout.

guide, *v.* SYN.-conduct, direct, escort, instruct, lead, manage, pilot, point, teach, train, steer.

guile, *n.* SYN.-beguilement, chicanery, cunning, deceit, deceitfulness, deception, duplicity, fraud, trick, wiliness. ANT.-candor, honesty, openness, sincerity, truthfulness.

guilt, *n.* SYN.-blame, culpability, fault, liability; compunction, contrition, remorse, shame.

guilty, *a.* SYN.-censured, charged, condemned, damned, derelict, impeached, incriminated, indicted, judged, liable, sentenced; ashamed, contrite, sorrowful, remorseful.

gullible, *a.* SYN.-artless, credulous, guileless, innocent, naive, simple, trustful, trusting.

gypsy, *n.* SYN.-bohemian, itinerant, maverick, nomad, nonconformist, outcast, rover, traveler, vagabond, wanderer.

H

habit, *n.* SYN.-addiction, bent, characteristic, convention, custom, disposition, fashion, fixation, manner, mode, observance, penchant, practice, routine, tradition, turn, usage, use, way, wont; clothes, costume, dress, garb.

habitual, *a.* SYN.-accustomed, automatic, common, continual, established, fixed, frequent, general, ingrained, often, periodic, perpetual, persistent, recurrent, regular, repeated, repetitious, routine, usual. ANT.-exceptional, rare, scanty, solitary, unique.

hackneyed, *a.* SYN.-banal, common, ordinary, overused, pedestrian, prosaic, stale, stereotyped, trite. ANT.-fresh, modern, momentous, novel, stimulating.

hag, *n.* SYN.-crone, fishwife, harridan, shrew, virago, witch.

hairy, *a.* SYN.-bearded, bewhiskered, bristly, downy, fluffy, furry, fuzzy, hirsute, shaggy, unshorn, whiskered.

hall, *n.* SYN.-anteroom, armory, assembly, auditorium, ballroom, chamber, church, clubroom, corridor, dormitory, entry, foyer, gallery, gym, gymnasium, hallway, lobby, lounge, room, salon, theater.

hallow, *v.* SYN.-aggrandize, bless, consecrate, dedicate, dignify, elevate, ennoble, erect, exalt, extol, glorify, worship, raise. ANT.-debase, degrade, dishonor, humble, humiliate.

hallowed, *a.* SYN.-blessed, consecrated, divine, holy, sacred, sacrosanct.

hallucination, *n.* SYN.-aberration, allusion, apparition, chimera, fantasy, ghost, illusion, phantasm, specter, vision.

halt, *v.* SYN.-abstain, arrest, bar, block, cease, check, contravene, curb, desist, discontinue, end, hinder, impede, interrupt, obstruct, quell, stall, stem, stop, suspend, terminate. ANT.-begin, proceed, promote, speed, start.

handicap, *n.* SYN.-affliction, block, disability, disadvantage, hindrance, impairment, impediment, inability, incapacity, limitation, obstacle, penalty, weakness. ANT.-ability, capability, power, strength.

handle, *v.* SYN.-advise, check, control, examine, feel, finger, manage, manipulate, operate, supervise, touch, wield, work.

handsome, *a.* SYN.-aristocratic, athletic, attractive, beautiful, charming, clean-cut, comely, dapper, elegant, fair, fine, gracious, jaunty, noble, personable, princely, robust, stately, well-dressed; ample, considerable, generous, magnanimous. ANT.-foul, hideous, homely, repulsive, unsightly.

handy, *a.* SYN.-accessible, advantageous, appropriate, convenient, fitting, helpful, near, suitable, timely, usable, valuable; able, adept, dexterous, ingenious, resourceful, skillful. ANT.-awkward, in-

convenient, inopportune, troublesome; clumsy, inept, unskilled.

hanging, *a.* SYN.-attached, dangling, drooping, flapping, hovering, projecting, swaying, swinging, waving; deadlocked, iffy, pending, tentative, uncertain, unresolved.

haphazard, *a.* SYN.-capricious, careless, casual, erratic, infrequent, incidental, irregular, loose, offhand, random, slipshod, uncoordinated, unplanned.

happen, *v.* SYN.-bechance, befall, betide, chance, ensue, occur, take place, transpire.

happening, *n.* SYN.-accident, affair, circumstance, event, incident, instance, moment, occasion.

happily, *a.* SYN.-agreeably, brightly, cheerfully, freely, gaily, gladly, graciously, joyfully, pleasantly,

happiness, *n.* SYN.-beatitude, blessedness, bliss, contentment, delight, felicity, gaiety, gladness, glee, joy, pleasure, satisfaction, well-being. ANT.-despair, grief, misery, sadness, sorrow.

happy, *a.* SYN.-blissful, carefree, cheerful, congenial, contented, delighted, ecstatic, elated, exuberant, gay, glad, intoxicated, jesting, joyful, joyous, jubilant, laughing, merry, smiling, sparkling; apt, befitting, blessed, favored, fortunate, lucky, opportune, propitious, prosperous. ANT.-blue, depressed, gloomy, morose.

harass, *v.* SYN.-aggravate, annoy, badger, bother, disturb, harry, irritate, molest, nag, pester, plague, provoke, tantalize, taunt, tease, torment, vex, worry. ANT.-comfort, delight, gratify, please, soothe.

hard, *a.* SYN.-compact, firm, impenetrable, rigid, solid, strong, tempered, unyielding; arduous, burdensome, complex, difficult, formidable, intricate, laborious, onerous, perplexing, puzzling, strenuous, tough, trying; callous, cruel, exacting, harsh, oppressive, rigorous, severe, stern, strict, unfeeling, unmerciful. ANT.-brittle, elastic, flabby, fluid, plastic, soft; easy, effortless, facile; simple; gentle, lenient, tender.

harden, *v.* SYN.-clot, coagulate, compact, crystallize, fossilize, freeze, petrify, solidify, stiffen; acclimate, accustom, discipline, fortify, toughen.

hardship, *n.* SYN.-affliction, burden, calamity, difficulty, distress, grief, misery, misfortune, ordeal, pain, problem, sorrow, suffering, test, trial, tribulation, trouble, woe. ANT.-alleviation, consolation, ease, pleasure.

harm, *n.* SYN.-damage, detriment, evil, hurt, ill, infliction, injury, mischief, misfortune, mishap, wrong. ANT.-benefit, boon, favor, kindness.

hardy, *a.* SYN.-acclimatized, bold, conditioned, courageous, dauntless, firm, fit, hale, hardened, healthy, hearty, robust, rugged, solid, sound, sturdy, tough. ANT.-delicate, feeble, fragile, weak.

harm, *v.* SYN.-damage, disfigure, hurt, impair, injure, maltreat, mar, spoil, wound; abuse, affront, dishonor, insult, wrong. ANT.-ameliorate, benefit, help, preserve; compliment, praise.

harmful, *a.* SYN.-corrupting, damaging, deleterious, detrimental, destructive, evil, hurtful, injurious, malignant, menacing, painful, ruinous, sinister, subversive, toxic, unhealthy, virulent. ANT.-advantageous, beneficial, helpful, profitable, salutary.

harmless, *a.* SYN.-disarmed, docile, friendly, impotent, innocent, innocuous, passive, powerless, pure, reliable, safe, secure, sterile, trustworthy. ANT.-dangerous, hazardous, insecure, perilous, unsafe.

harmony, *n.* SYN.-accordance, agreement, coincidence, compatibility, concord, concurrence, congruence, congruity, equanimity, peace, rapport, understanding, unison. ANT.-difference, disagreement, discord, dissension, strife, variance.

harsh, *a.* SYN.-cacophonous, clashing, discordant, dissonant, grating, jangling, jarring, rasping, shrill; austere, acrimonious, blunt, brusque, coarse, gruff, rigorous, rough, rugged, severe, strict, stringent. ANT.-melodious, tuneful; gentle, mild, smooth, soft.

harvest, *n.* SYN.-crop, fruit, gathering, proceeds, produce, product, reaping, result, store, yield.

harvest, *v.* SYN.-acquire, amass, collect, cull, gain, garner, gather, glean, pick, reap. ANT.-lose, plant, sow, squander.

haste, *n.* SYN.-abruptness, alacrity, bustle, carelessness, dispatch, excitement, flurry, hurry, hustle, impatience, impetuosity, rashness, recklessness.

hasten, *v.* SYN.-accelerate, expedite, goad, hurry, hustle, precipitate, press, push, quicken, rush, scoot, scramble, scurry, speed, stimulate, urge. ANT.-delay, detain, hinder, retard, tarry.

hasty, *a.* SYN.-abrupt, brisk, careless, fast, fleet, foolhardy, hurried, impetuous, indiscreet, lively, precipitate, quick, rapid, rash, reckless, speedy, sudden, swift, thoughtless, unannounced, unexpected. ANT.-anticipated, expected; courteous, gradual, smooth.

hate, *v.* SYN.-abhor, abominate, despise, detest, dislike, loathe, resent, scorn, spurn. ANT.-admire, approve, cherish, like, love.

hateful, *a.* SYN.-abominable, abusive, detestable, execrable, foul, insulting, loathsome, nasty, odious, offensive, repugnant, revolting, vile. ANT.-agreeable, commendable, delightful, pleasant.

hatred, *n.* SYN.-abhorrence, abomination, alienation, animosity, antagonism, antipathy, bitterness, contempt, detestation, disgust, dislike, enmity, grudge, hostility, ill will, loathing, malevolence, prejudice, rancor, repugnance, venom. ANT.-affection, attraction, friendship, love.

haughty, *a.* SYN.-arrogant, disdainful, egotistical, lofty, overbearing, proud, stately, supercilious, vain, vainglorious. ANT.-ashamed, humble, lowly, meek.

haunt, *v.* SYN.-annoy, bedevil, beset, bother, frighten, harass, hound, obsess, pester, plague, possess, terrify, terrorize, trouble, worry, vex.

have, *v.* SYN.-control, hold, occupy, own,

possess, retain. ANT.-abandon, lose, renounce, surrender.

haven, *n.* SYN.-asylum, harbor, hermitage, hideaway, port, refuge, retreat, sanctuary, shelter.

hazard, *n.* SYN.-chance, danger, jeopardy, peril, risk, uncertainty, venture. ANT.-defense, immunity, protection, safety.

hazard, *v.* SYN.-chance, conjecture, dare, endanger, gamble, imperil, jeopardize, peril, risk, speculate, try, venture. ANT.-determine, guard, insure, know.

hazardous, *a.* SYN.-chancy, dangerous, menacing, perilous, precarious, risky, speculative, threatening, uncertain, unsafe. ANT.-firm, protected, safe, secure.

hazy, *a.* SYN.-ambiguous, blurred, cloudy, dim, dull, foggy, indefinite, indistinct, misty, murky, obscure, smoky, uncertain, unclear, undetermined, unsettled, vague, veiled. ANT.-clear, explicit, lucid, precise, specific.

head, *n.* SYN.-authority, chief, commander, director, leader, master, principal, ruler; acme, crest, peak, pinnacle, summit, top; climax, crisis, conclusion, culmination, ending, finale. ANT.-follower, subordinate, underling; base, bottom, foot.

head, *v.* SYN.-command, direct, govern, lead, manage, oversee, precede, supervise.

heading, *n.* SYN.-banner, caption, headline, legend, preface, streamer, title.

heal, *v.* SYN.-attend, cure, medicate, purify, regenerate, rehabilitate, remedy, renew, restore, salve, soothe, treat. ANT.-damage, harm, infect, injure.

healthful, *a.* SYN.-beneficial, bracing, clean, fresh, healing, hygienic, invigorating, nourishing, nutritious, preventive, pure, regenerative, salubrious, sanitary, stimulating, sustaining, unpolluted, untainted, wholesome.

healthy, *a.* SYN.-able-bodied, blooming, fit, hale, hardy, hearty, hygienic, invigorating, normal, nourishing, robust, salubrious, salutary, sound, strong, vigorous, virile, well, wholesome. ANT.-delicate, diseased, frail, infirm; injurious, noxious.

hear, *v.* SYN.-apprehend, attend, detect, eavesdrop, hearken, heed, listen, overhear, perceive, regard.

hearing, *n.* SYN.-audience, audit, audition, conference, consultation, interview, meeting, review, test, trial, tryout.

heart, *n.* SYN.-center, core, crux, essence, middle, midpoint, midst, nucleus; bravery, courage, fortitude, gallantry, mettle, nerve, valor. ANT.-border, boundary, outskirts, periphery, rim.

heartache, *n.* SYN.-affliction, anguish, despair, distress, grief, lamentation, misery, mourning, sadness, sorrow, trial, tribulation, woe. ANT.-comfort, consolation, happiness, joy, solace.

heartbroken, *a.* SYN.-comfortless, disconsolate, distressed, doleful, forlorn, melancholy, miserable, pitiable, sorrowful, wretched. ANT.-contented, fortunate, happy.

hearten, *v.* SYN.-assure, cheer, em-

bolden, encourage, enthuse, exhilarate, favor, foster, impel, incite, inspire, promote, reassure, stimulate, support, urge. ANT.-deter, discourage, dispirit, dissuade, reject.

hearty, *a.* SYN.-ardent, authentic, cheery, cordial, eager, earnest, enthusiastic, genial, gracious, hale, healthy, jovial, profuse, robust, sincere, sociable, sound, strong, unrestrained, warm, well, wholehearted, wholesome, zealous. ANT.-aloof cool, reserved, taciturn.

heat, *v.* SYN.-boil, char, cook, fry, roast, scald, scorch, sear, singe, warm.

heathen, *n.* SYN.-atheist, barbarian, infidel, nonbeliever.

heavenly, *a.* SYN.-celestial, divine, godlike, holy, superhuman, supernatural, transcendent. ANT.-blasphemous, diabolical, mundane, profane, wicked.

heavy, *a.* SYN.-bulky, hefty, huge, massive, ponderous, portly, stout, weighty; burdensome, cumbersome, depressing, distressing, gloomy, grave, grievous, harsh, oppressive, serious, troublesome, trying; boring, clumsy, dull, listless, ponderous, slow, sluggish, tedious, tiresome; complicated, complex, concentrated, difficult, important, intense, momentous, obscure, pithy, serious, trying. ANT.-animated, brisk, light.

heckle, *v.* SYN.-badger, bait, bother, harass, pester, ridicule, tease, torment.

heed, *n.* SYN.-alertness, attention, care, consideration, mindfulness, notice, observance, watchfulness. ANT.-disregard, indifference, negligence, omission, oversight.

heed, *v.* SYN.-attend, consider, contemplate, deliberate, examine, listen, mark, mind, notice, obey, ponder, reflect, study, weigh. ANT.-ignore, neglect, overlook.

heedless, *a.* SYN.-blind, careless, hasty, headlong, ignorant, impetuous, impulsive, oblivious, rash, unaware, undiscerning, unmindful, unseeing. ANT.-aware, calculated, discerning, perceiving, sensible.

height, *n.* SYN.-apex, climax, culmination, elevation, extent, peak, prominence, stature, summit, zenith. ANT.-anticlimax, base, depth, floor.

heighten, *v.* SYN.-aggravate, amplify, augment, elevate, emphasize, enhance, exalt, increase, intensify, lift, magnify, raise, uplift. ANT.-appease, lessen, lower, mitigate, palliate soften, soothe.

help, *n.* SYN.-advice, aid, assistance, backing, comfort, encouragement, furtherance, guidance, patronage, relief, succor, support. ANT.-antagonism, counteraction, defiance, hostility, resistance.

help, *v.* SYN.-abet, accommodate, advise, advocate, aid, assist, back, bolster, encouragement, facilitate, foster, further, mitigate, promote, relieve, remedy, succor, support, uphold. ANT.-afflict, hinder, impede, oppose, resist, thwart.

helpful, *a.* SYN.-accommodating, advantageous, beneficial, essential, good, invaluable, kind, obliging, practical, profitable, salutary, serviceable, useful, valuable, wholesome. ANT.-deleterious, destructive, detrimental, harmful, ineffective, injurious, useless.

hence, adv. SYN.-accordingly, consequently, so, then, thence, therefore.

heretic, n. SYN.-apostate, cynic, dissenter, dissident, nonconformist, schismatic, sectarian, sectary, skeptic, unbeliever.

heritage, n. SYN.-ancestry, birthright, estate, inheritance, legacy, lot; convention, culture, custom, endowment, fashion, tradition.

hero, n. SYN.-champion, conqueror, master, model, protagonist, protector, star.

heroic, a. SYN.-adventurous, audacious, bold, brave, chivalrous, courageous, daring, dauntless, desperate, drastic, excessive, extreme, fearless, gallant, great, intrepid, magnanimous, noble, valiant, valorous. ANT.-cowardly, cringing, fearful, timid, weak.

hesitant, a. SYN.-averse, diffident, disinclined, doubtful, irresolute, loath, reluctant, skeptical, slow, uncertain, unwilling. ANT.-disposed, eager, inclined, ready, willing.

hesitate, v. SYN.-consider, defer, delay, deliberate, demur, doubt, falter, pause, ponder, scruple, stammer, stop, stutter, vacillate, wait, waver, weigh. ANT.-continue, decide, persevere, proceed, resolve.

hesitation, n. SYN.-ambiguity, dawdling, delaying, distrust, doubt, faltering, halting, incredulity, indecision, irresolution, pause, procrastination, scruple, skepticism, stammering, suspicion, unbelief, uncertainty. ANT.-belief, certainty, conviction, determination, faith.

hidden, a. SYN.-clandestine, clouded, concealed, covert, disguised, eclipsed, latent, obscured, potential, private, quiescent, secluded, secret, shadow, shrouded, suppressed, surreptitious, undeveloped, unseen. ANT.-conspicuous, evident, explicit, manifest, visible.

hide, v. SYN.-cloak, conceal, cover, curtain, disguise, mask, screen, secrete, shelter, shroud, suppress, veil, withhold. ANT.-disclose, divulge, expose, reveal, show, uncover.

high, a. SYN.-elevated, lofty, tall, towering; distinguished, eminent, exalted, important, preeminent, prominent, proud. ANT.-small, stunted, tiny; base, low, mean.

hinder, v. SYN.-arrest, bar, block, bottleneck, burden, check, delay, encumber, foil, frustrate, hamper, handicap, impede, inhibit, interrupt, neutralize, obstruct, prevent, resist, restrain, retard, stall, stop, thwart. ANT.-assist, expedite, facilitate, further, promote.

hint, n. SYN.-allusion, clue, cue, implication, inference, inkling, innuendo, insinuation, intimation, reference, reminder, taste, tip, trace. ANT.-affirmation, declaration, statement.

hint, v. SYN.-advert, allude, foreshadow, imply, infer, insinuate, intimate, mention, prompt, refer, suggest. ANT.-declare, demonstrate, specify, state.

hire, v. SYN.-appoint, charter, commis-

sion, delegate, employ, engage, enlist, lease, retain, use, utilize. ANT.-banish, discard, discharge, reject.

history, n. SYN.-account, annals, antiquity, archives, chronicle, evidence, memoir, records, writings.

hit, v. SYN.-bash, beat, buffet, bump, collide, cuff, hurt, jab, knock, pelt, pound, pummel, punch, rap, slap, smack, smite, sock, strike, thump, whack.

hoard, n. SYN.-accumulation, cache, riches, stockpile, store, treasure, wealth.

hoard, v. SYN.-accumulate, acquire, keep, save, stash, store, stow.

hoarse, a. SYN.-harsh, husky, grating, gruff, guttural, rasping, raucous, rough, scratchy, thick, throaty.

hoax, n. SYN.-antic, artifice, deceit, deception, fabrication, fraud, joke, ploy, prank, ruse, stratagem, stunt, swindle, subterfuge, trick, wile. ANT.-candor, exposure, honesty, openness, sincerity.

hobby, n. SYN.-activity, amusement, avocation, craft, diversion, fancy, pastime, relaxation, sideline, whimsy.

hold, v. SYN.-adhere, attach, clasp, cling, clutch, continue, endure, fasten, grasp, grip, have, keep, last, maintain, occupy, own, persist, possess, remain, retain, stick, support, sustain; check, confine, contain, curb, detain, hinder, restrain; believe, consider, deem, embrace, entertain, espouse, esteem, think. ANT.-abandon, relinquish, surrender, vacate.

hole, n. SYN.-abyss, aperture, breach, break, burrow, cavity, chasm, cleft, crack, cranny, crater, fissure, fracture, gap, gash, gorge, gulf, incision, opening, orifice, perforation, pit, pore, puncture, ravine, rent, rupture, shaft, slit, split, tear, tunnel, void.

hollow, a. SYN.-depressed, empty, unfilled, vacant, vacuous, void; false, hypocritical, insincere, vain. ANT.-full, solid, sound; genuine, sincere.

holy, a. SYN.-angelic, blessed, consecrated, dedicated, devout, divine, godly, good, hallowed, humble, just, moral, pious, religious, reverent, righteous, sacred, saintly, sanctified, spiritual, venerable. ANT.-evil, profane, sacrilegious, secular, worldly.

home, n. SYN.-abode, apartment, base, chalet, domicile, dwelling, flat, habitat, hearth, homestead, house, household, hovel, lodging, mansion, quarters, residence, seat, shelter.

homely, a. SYN.-coarse, ill-favored, inelegant, plain, repellent, simple, ugly, unattractive, uncomely, unrefined; cozy, crude, modest, simple, snug, unpretentious. ANT.-attractive, beautiful, fair, handsome, pretty.

honest, a. SYN.-above-board, candid, conscientious, decent, factual, fair, genuine, honorable, just, legitimate, moral, open, realistic, scrupulous, sincere, sound, straightforward, true, trustworthy, truthful, unreserved, upright, virtuous. ANT.-deceitful, dishonest, fraudulent, lying, tricky.

honesty, n. SYN.-candor, character, con-

science, fairness, fidelity, frankness, goodness, integrity, justice, morality, openness, rectitude, reliability, responsibility, sincerity, trustworthiness, uprightness, virtue. ANT.-cheating, deceit, dishonesty, fraud, trickery.

honor, n. SYN.-admiration, adoration, deference, dignity, distinction, esteem, faith, fame, glory, homage, praise, renown, recognition, reference, reputation, repute, respect, reverence, trust, veneration, worship. ANT.-contempt, derision, disgrace, dishonor, reproach.

honor, v. SYN.-admire, adore, celebrate, commemorate, esteem, extol, glorify, keep, laud, observe, praise, regard, respect, revere, solemnize, value, venerate, worship. ANT.-decry, disgrace, dishonor, disregard, overlook, profane.

honorable, a. SYN.-admirable, creditable, dignified, distinguished, eminent, equitable, esteemed, estimable, ethical, fair, honest, illustrious, just, noble, proper, reputable, respectable, true, trusty, upright, virtuous. ANT.-disgraceful, ignominious, infamous, shameful.

hope, n. SYN.-anticipation, assurance, belief, confidence, desire, dream, expectancy, expectation, faith, goal, longing, optimism, reliance, trust, wish. ANT.-despair, despondency, pessimism.

hopeless, a. SYN.-desperate, disastrous, fatal, foreboding, impossible, incurable, irreversible, lost, pointless, tragic, vain, worthless.

hopelessness, n. SYN.-depression, despair, desperation, despondency, discouragement, gloom, grief, heartache, pessimism, sorrow, torture. ANT.-confidence, elation, hope, optimism.

horde, n. SYN.-band, bevy, crowd, crush, gathering, group, host, masses, mob, multitude, pack, populace, press, rabble, swarm, throng.

horrible, a. SYN.-abominable, appalling, awful, deplorable, dire, disgusting, dreadful, fearful, frightful, ghastly, hideous, horrid, odious, offensive, repulsive, shameful, shocking, terrible. ANT.-beautiful, enchanting, enjoyable, fascinating, lovely.

horror, n. SYN.-abomination, alarm, antipathy, apprehension, aversion, awe, dread, fear, foreboding, fright, hatred, loathing, panic, repugnance, terror. ANT.-assurance, boldness, confidence, courage.

hostile, a. SYN.-adverse, antagonistic, conflicting, hateful, inimical, opposed, repugnant, unfriendly, warlike. ANT.-amicable, cordial, favorable.

hostility, n. SYN.-abhorrence, animosity, aversion, bitterness, dislike, enmity, grudge, hatred, ill will, malevolence, rancor, spite. ANT.-friendliness, good will, love.

hot, a. SYN.-baking, blazing, blistering, burning, flaming, parching, scalding, scorching, sizzling; ardent, fervent, fiery, hot-blooded, impetuous, intense, passionate, torrid; acrid, biting, peppery, piquant, pungent, spicy. ANT.-cold, cool, freezing, frigid; apathetic, impassive, indifferent, passionless, phlegmatic; bland.

however, *adv.* SYN.-but, nevertheless, notwithstanding, still, yet.

hue, *n.* SYN.-color, complexion, pigment, shade, stain, tincture, tinge, tint. ANT.-achromatism, paleness, transparency.

hug, *v.* SYN.-caress, clinch, coddle, cuddle, embrace, squeeze. ANT.-buffet, spurn.

huge, *a.* SYN.-ample, big, capacious, colossal, enormous, extensive, giant, great, immense, large, mammoth, tremendous, vast, wide. ANT.-little, mean, short, small, tiny.

humane, *a.* SYN.-benevolent, charitable, clement, compassionate, forbearing, forgiving, humanitarian, kind, kindhearted, kindly, lenient, merciful, softhearted, sympathetic, tender, tenderhearted, tolerant, understanding, warmhearted. ANT.-brutal, cruel, pitiless, remorseless, unfeeling.

humanity, *n.* SYN.-altruism, beneficence, benevolence, charity, compassion, generosity, kindness, liberality, love, magnanimity, philanthropy, sympathy, tenderness, understanding. ANT.-cruelty, inhumanity, malevolence, selfishness.

humble, *a.* SYN.-compliant, deferential, diffident, lowly, meek, mild, modest, ordinary, passive, plain, quiet, simple, submissive, unassuming, unpretentious. ANT.-arrogant, boastful, haughty, proud, vain.

humble, *v.* SYN.-abase, abash, break, chasten, crush, debase, degrade, demean, humiliate, mortify, shame, subdue. ANT.-elevate, exalt, honor, praise.

humiliate, *v.* See **humble**

humiliation, *n.* SYN.-abasement, chagrin, mortification, shame; disgrace, dishonor, disrepute, embarrassment, ignominy, mortification, scandal, shame. ANT.-dignity, glory, honor, praise, renown.

humor, *n.* SYN.-amusement, comedy, facetiousness, fun, irony, jocularity, joke, pleasantry, sarcasm, satire, waggery, wit; disposition, mood, temper, tendency, temperament, vagary, whim. ANT.-gravity, seriousness, sorrow.

humor, *v.* SYN.-comfort, coddle, gratify, indulge, pamper, placate, please, spoil.

humorous, *a.* SYN.-amusing, comic, comical, droll, entertaining, farcical, funny, laughable, ludicrous ridiculous, whimsical, witty. ANT.-melancholy, serious, sober, solemn.

hunch, *n.* SYN.-clue, feeling, foreboding, idea, intuition, notion, portent, premonition, prescience; bulge, bump, hump, protuberance.

hunger, *n.* SYN.-appetite, craving, desire, inclination, liking, longing, passion, relish, thirst, yearning, zest. ANT.-disgust, distaste, renunciation, repugnance, satiety.

hungry, *a.* SYN.-craving, famished, ravenous, starved, thirsting, voracious; avid, greedy, longing. ANT.-full, gorged, sated, satiated; satisfied.

hunt, *v.* SYN.-chase, explore, follow, hound, inquire, investigate, pursue, probe, ransack, rummage, scour, scrutinize, search, seek, stalk, trail, trace,

track.

hurl, *v.* SYN.-cast, fling, heave, pitch, propel, throw, thrust, toss. ANT.-draw, haul, hold, pull, retain.

hurry, *v.* SYN.-accelerate, dash, expedite, hasten, precipitate, quicken, race, rush, scoot, speed. ANT.-delay, detain, hinder, retard, tarry.

hurt, *n.* SYN.-damage, detriment, disservice, harm, injury, mischief, grievance, injustice, prejudice, wound, wrong. ANT.-benefit, improvement, repair.

hurt, *v.* SYN.-abuse, affront, damage, disfigure, dishonor, distress, harm, impair, injure, insult, lash, mar, smite, spoil, wound, wrong. ANT.-ameliorate, benefit, compliment, help, praise, preserve.

hush, *n.* SYN.-calm, lull, peace, quiet, serenity, silence, stillness.

hustle, *v.* SYN.-hasten, hurry, race, rush, scramble.

hygienic, *a.* SYN.-clean, decontaminated, disinfected, healthy, pure, sanitary, wholesome. ANT.-contaminated, diseased, infected, injurious, noxious, unsanitary.

hypocrisy, *n.* SYN.-bigotry, cant, deceit, dissimulation, pretense, sanctimony. ANT.-candor, frankness, honesty, openness, truth.

hypothesis, *n.* SYN.-assumption, conjecture, law, notion, postulate, supposition, theory. ANT.-certainty, fact, proof.

hysterical, *a.* SYN.-delirious, demonstrative, distraught, emotional, excitable, fervent, frenzied, overwrought, possessed, raging, raving, uncontrolled.

I

idea, *n.* SYN.-abstraction, belief, concept, conception, fancy, image, impression, notion, opinion, sentiment, theory, thought. ANT.-entity, matter, object, substance, thing.

ideal, *a.* SYN.-exemplary, fancied, faultless, imaginary, perfect, supreme, unreal, utopian, visionary. ANT.-actual, faulty, imperfect, material, real.

idealistic, *a.* SYN.-dreamy, extravagant, fanciful, fantastic, fictitious, ideal, imaginative, maudlin, mawkish, picturesque, poetic, romantic, sentimental. ANT.-factual, literal, matter-of-fact, practical, prosaic.

identical, *a.* SYN.-coincident, equal, equivalent, indistinguishable, like, same, twin. ANT.-contrary, disparate, dissimilar, distinct, opposed.

identify, *v.* SYN.-acknowledge, apprehend, avow, concede, confess, own, perceive, recognize, recollect, remember. ANT.-disown, renounce, repudiate.

ideology, *n.* SYN.-belief, convictions, culture, dogma, ethics, ideas, philosophy, tenets.

idiot, *n.* SYN.-buffoon, clown, harlequin, jester; blockhead, dolt, dunce, fool, imbecile, nincompoop, numbskull, oaf, simpleton. ANT.-genius, philosopher, sage, scholar.

idiotic, *a.* SYN.-absurd, asinine, brainless, crazy, foolish, irrational, nonsensical, preposterous, ridiculous, sense-

less, silly, simple. ANT.-judicious, prudent, sagacious, sane, wise.

idle, *a.* SYN.-dormant, inactive, indolent, inert, fallow, lazy, slothful, unemployed, unoccupied; insignificant, trifling, trivial, unimportant. ANT.-active, employed, engaged, industrious, occupied, working.

idol, *n.* SYN.-deity, figurine, icon, image, statue, symbol, totem; beloved, favorite, hero, model.

ignominious, *a.* SYN.-abject, base, contemptible, despicable, dishonorable, groveling, ignoble, ignominious, low, lowly, mean, menial, shameful, sordid, vile, vulgar. ANT.-teemed, exalted, honored, lofty, noble, righteous.

ignorant, *a.* SYN.-coarse, crude, dense, dumb, illiterate, oblivious, shallow, superficial, uncultured, uneducated, uninformed, unlearned, unlettered, untaught, vulgar. ANT.-cultured, educated, erudite, informed, literate.

ignore, *v.* SYN.-disdain, disregard, neglect, omit, overlook, skip, slight. ANT.-include, notice, regard.

ill, *a.* SYN.-afflicted, ailing, diseased, indisposed, infirm, morbid, sick, unhealthy, unwell; bad, evil, naughty, wicked. ANT.-healthy, robust, sound, strong, well; good.

illegal, *a.* SYN.-criminal, dishonest, illegitimate, illicit, outlawed, prohibited, unlawful, wrongful. ANT.-honest, lawful, legal, permitted.

illicit, *a.* SYN.-banned, illegal, illegitimate, outlawed, prohibited, unauthorized, unlawful. ANT.-allowed, authorized, lawful, legal, permitted.

illness, *n.* SYN.-ailment, complaint, disease, disorder, infirmity, malady, sickness. ANT.-health, healthiness, soundness, vigor.

illogical, *a.* SYN.-absurd, contradictory, fallacious, groundless, implausible, inconsistent, incongruous, irrational, untenable.

illuminate, *v.* SYN.-brighten, clarify, edify, elucidate, enlighten, explain, illumine, illustrate, inform, irradiate. ANT.-complicate, confuse, darken, obfuscate, obscure.

illusion, *n.* SYN.-apparition, delusion, dream, fantasy, hallucination, mirage, phantom, vision. ANT.-actuality, reality, substance.

illusive, *a.* SYN.-apparent, deceptive, delusive, delusory, fallacious, false, misleading, ostensible, presumable, seeming, specious. ANT.-authentic, genuine, real, truthful.

illustration, *n.* SYN.-drawing, effigy, engraving, etching, image, landscape, likeness, painting, panorama, picture, portrayal, print, rendering, representation, resemblance, scene, sketch, view.

illustrious, *a.* SYN.-august, celebrated, dignified, distinguished, elevated, eminent, excellent, famed, famous, fine, grand, great, magnificent, majestic, noble, prominent, renowned. ANT.-common, menial, obscure, ordinary, paltry, unknown.

image, *n.* SYN.-concept, conception, idea, notion, perception; copy, effigy, figure, form, icon, idol, likeness, picture, representation, semblance, statue.

imagination, *n.* SYN.-awareness, conception, creation, daydream, fancy, fantasy, idea, insight, invention, inventiveness, notion, wit.

imaginative, *a.* SYN.-artistic, clever, creative, fanciful, inventive, mystical, poetical, sublime, talented, visionary. ANT.-dull, literal, prosaic, unromantic.

imagine, *v.* SYN.-assume, believe, conceive, conjecture, dream, envision, fancy, guess, opine, perceive, picture, pretend, suppose, surmise, think.

imbecile, *n.* SYN.-blockhead, dolt, dunce, fool, idiot, jerk, moron, nincompoop, numbskull, oaf, simpleton. ANT.-genius, philosopher, sage, scholar.

imbibe, *v.* SYN.-absorb, assimilate, consume, drink, ingest, guzzle, partake, receive, swallow. ANT.-discharge, dispense, emit, expel, exude.

imitate, *v.* SYN.-ape, copy, counterfeit, duplicate, echo, impersonate, mimic, mirror, mock, parallel, reflect, reproduce, simulate. ANT.-alter, distort, diverge, invent.

imitation, *n.* SYN.-copy, duplicate, exemplar, facsimile, fake, forgery, replica, reproduction, simulation, transcript. ANT.-original, novelty, prototype.

immature, *a.* SYN.-callow, childish, childlike, green, innocent, juvenile, naive, provincial, puerile, raw, silly, unseasoned, unsophisticated, young, youthful. ANT.-aged, elderly, mature, old, senile.

immeasurable, *a.* SYN.-boundless, endless, eternal, immense, indefinite, infinite, interminable, limitless, unbounded, unlimited, vast. ANT.-bounded, circumscribed, confined, finite, limited.

immediately, adv. SYN.-directly, forthwith, instantaneously, instantly, now, presently, promptly, straight-away. ANT.-distantly, hereafter, later, shortly, sometime.

immense, *a.* SYN.-colossal, elephantine, enormous, gargantuan, gigantic, huge, large, prodigious, tremendous, vast. ANT.-diminutive, little, minute, small, tiny.

immerse, *v.* SYN.-dip, douse, dunk, plunge, sink, submerge; absorb, bury, engage, engross, involve. ANT.-elevate, recover, uplift.

immigration, *n.* SYN.-arrival, colonization, journey, migration, relocation, settlement. ANT.-displacement, emigration, exodus.

imminent, *a.* SYN.-approaching, close, coming, impending, menacing, near, nigh, overhanging, threatening. ANT.-afar, distant, improbable, remote, retreating.

immoderation, *n.* SYN.-dissipation, excess, extravagance, glut, intemperance, luxuriance, overindulgence, profusion, superabundance, superfluity, surplus. ANT.-dearth, deficiency, lack, paucity, want.

immoral, *a.* SYN.-anti-social, bad, corrupt, debased, debauched, dissolute, indecent, libertine, licentious, profli-

gate, shameless, sinful, unprincipled, vicious, wicked. ANT.-chaste, high-minded, noble, pure, virtuous.

immortal, *a.* SYN.-ageless, deathless, endless, eternal, everlasting, imperishable, indestructible, infinite, permanent, perpetual, timeless, undying. ANT.-ephemeral, finite, mortal, temporal, transient.

immune, *a.* SYN.-excused, exempt, free, freed, independent, liberated, unaffected, unconfined, unrestricted.

immunity, *n.* SYN.-exemption, freedom, immunization, impunity, privilege, resistance, right.

immutable, *a.* SYN.-abiding, ceaseless, consistent, constant, continual, enduring, even, faithful, fixed, invariable, permanent, perpetual, persistent, steady, unalterable, unchanging, uniform, unwavering. ANT.-fickle, mutable, vacillating, wavering.

impair, *v.* SYN.-damage, deface, diminish, harm, hurt, injure, lessen, mar, spoil. ANT.-ameliorate, benefit, enhance, mend, repair, vitiate.

impart, *v.* SYN.-bestow, cede, communicate, confer, convey, disclose, divulge, give, grant, inform, notify, relate, relinquish, reveal, tell, transmit. ANT.-conceal, hide, withhold.

impartial, *a.* SYN.-detached, dispassionate, equitable, fair, honest, just, reasonable, unbiased. ANT.-dishonorable, fraudulent, partial.

impartiality, *n.* SYN.-candor, disinterestedness, equality, fairness, indifference, insensibility, justice, neutrality, objectivity. ANT.-bias, favoritism, prejudice.

impasse, *n.* SYN.-deadlock, delay, draw, halt, stalemate, standoff, standstill.

impeach, *v.* SYN.-accuse, arraign, challenge, charge, cite, criticize, denounce, discredit, incriminate, question. ANT.-absolve, acquit, clear, exonerate.

impede, *v.* SYN.-arrest, bar, block, check, clog, delay, deter, encumber, frustrate, hamper, hinder, interrupt, obstruct, restrain, retard, stop, thwart. ANT.-advance, assist, further, help, promote.

impediment, *n.* SYN.-bar, barrier, block, check, difficulty, handicap, hindrance, limitation, obstacle, obstruction, setback, snag. ANT.-aid, assistance, backing, encouragement, guidance, help, relief, support.

impel, *v.* SYN.-coerce, compel, drive, enforce, force, incite, motivate, oblige, prod, push, spur, urge. ANT.-allure, convince, induce, persuade, prevent.

impending, *a.* SYN.-approaching, close, immediate, imminent, menacing, nigh, overhanging, threatening. ANT.-distant, improbable, remote, retreating.

impenetrable, *a.* SYN.-compact, firm, hard, impervious, inscrutable, inviolable, rigid, solid; tough. ANT.-flabby, plastic, soft.

imperative, *a.* SYN.-cogent, compelling, critical, crucial, exigent, immediate, impelling, important, importunate, insistent, instant, necessary, pressing, serious, urgent; aggressive, autocratic, bossy commanding, domineering, imperial, masterful, powerful. ANT.-insig-

nificant, petty, trifling, trivial, unimportant; feeble, impotent, powerless, weak, yielding.

imperceptible, *a.* SYN.-ambiguous, blurred, cryptic, dim, esoteric, inaudible, indistinct, indistinguishable, invisible, obscure, shadowy, indiscernible, unseen. ANT.-evident, perceptible, seen, visible.

imperfection, *n.* SYN.-blemish, defect, deformity, error, failure, fault, flaw, mistake, omission, shortcoming, vice. ANT.-completeness, correctness, perfection.

impersonate, *v.* SYN.-ape, copy, counterfeit, duplicate, imitate, mimic, mock, portray, pose, pretend, represent, simulate. ANT.-alter, distort, diverge, invent.

impertinence, *n.* SYN.-affront, audacity, boldness, disrespectfulness, effrontery, impudence, inappropriateness, injury, insolence, insult, offense, rudeness, sauciness, slight, slur. ANT.-diffidence, politeness, subserviency.

impertinent, *a.* SYN.-abusive, arrogant, brazen, contemptuous, discourteous, impolite, impudent, insolent, insulting, offensive, rude, saucy. ANT.-considerate, courteous, polite, respectful.

impetus, *n.* SYN.-cause, force, impulse, incentive, pressure, push, stimulus, thrust.

impetuous, *a.* SYN.-blind, careless, hasty, headlong, heedless, impulsive, irrational, passionate, quick, rash, uncontrolled, unreasonable. ANT.-calculating, cautious, reasoning.

implicate, *v.* SYN.-accuse, associate, blame, charge, cite, concern, condemn, hint, imply, include, involve, link, relate, suggest. ANT.-absolve, acquit, exonerate, ignore.

implicit, *a.* SYN.-absolute, accurate, assured, certain, confident, definite, doubtless, positive, satisfied, unequivocal, unquestionable; alluded, indicated, inferred, insinuated, intended, meant, suggested, tacit, understood.

implore, *v.* SYN.-adjure, appeal, ask, beg, beseech, crave, entreat, importune, petition, plead, pray, request, solicit, supplicate. ANT.-bestow, cede, favor, give, grant.

imply, *v.* SYN.-connote, infer, insinuate, involve, mean, signify, suggest. ANT.-assert, express, state.

impolite, *a.* SYN.-arrogant, blunt, boorish, brazen, coarse, crude, discourteous, gruff, impudent, insolent, insulting, moody, primitive, rough, rude, saucy, surly, uncivil, unpolished, vulgar. ANT.-civil, genteel, polished; courtly, dignified, noble, stately.

importance, *n.* SYN.-emphasis, gravity, heaviness, import, influence, pressure, significance, stress, value, weight. ANT.-buoyancy, levity, lightness; insignificance, triviality.

important, *a.* SYN.-consequential, critical, decisive, grave, influential, material, meaningful, momentous, paramount, pressing, primary, prominent, relevant, significant, substantial, valuable, weighty. ANT.-commonplace, foolish, insignificant, irrelevant, little, mean, paltry, petty, trivial.

imposing, *a.* SYN.-august, dignified, exciting, grand, grandiose, high, impressive, lofty, magnificent, majestic, noble, overwhelming, pompous, stately, stirring, sublime, substantial. ANT.-common, humble, lowly, ordinary, undignified.

impossible, *a.* SYN.-fruitless, futile, hopeless, impractical, inaccessible, inconceivable, unattainable, unworkable, useless, vain.

impression, *n.* SYN.-concept, conjecture, feeling, image, notion, opinion, perception, sensation, sense, supposition, understanding; dent, indentation, mark, scar. ANT.-fact, insensibility, reality.

impressive, *a.* SYN.-absorbing, affecting, arresting, august, beautiful, commanding, dazzling, dramatic, eloquent, exciting, extraordinary, forceful, gorgeous, grand, grandiose, imposing, inspiring, magnificent, majestic, moving, notable, overpowering, profound, remarkable, splendid, stirring, striking, sumptuous, superb, thrilling, touching. ANT.-commonplace, ordinary, regular, unimpressive.

improve, *v.* SYN.-ameliorate, amend, augment, better, correct, enhance, enrich, help, modernize, progress, rectify, refine, reform, update. ANT.-corrupt, damage, debase, impair, vitiate.

improvement, *n.* SYN.-advance, advancement, alteration, amendment, betterment, development, enhancement, enrichment, growth, modernization, progress, progression, reformation, renovation, reorganization. ANT.-decline, delay, regression, relapse, retrogression.

imprudent, *a.* SYN.-careless, excessive, heedless, immoderate, improvident, inattentive, indiscreet, inordinate, lavish, lax, neglectful, negligent, prodigal, reckless, remiss, thoughtless. ANT.-accurate, careful, meticulous, nice.

impudence, *n.* SYN.-assurance, audacity, boldness, brass, cheek, discourtesy, effrontery, impertinence, insolence, nerve, presumption, rudeness, sauciness, temerity. ANT.-diffidence, politeness, subserviency, truckling.

impudent, *a.* SYN.-bold, brazen, discourteous, forward, fresh, impertinent, insolent, pushy, rude. ANT.-cowardly, flinching, timid; bashful, retiring.

impulsive, *a.* SYN.-careless, hasty, heedless, impetuous, offhand, passionate, quick, rash, spontaneous, unconstrained. ANT.-calculating, cautious, reasoning.

impure, *a.* SYN.-adulterated, contaminated, corrupt, corrupted, crooked, debased, depraved, diluted, dirty, immoral, profligate, putrid, spoiled, tainted, unclean, unsound, venal, vitiated.

inability, *n.* SYN.-disability, failure, handicap, impotence, incapacity, incompetence, weakness. ANT.-ability, capability, power, strength.

inaccurate, *a.* SYN.-amiss, askew, awry,

distorted, erroneous, fallacious, false, faulty, imprecise, inexact, incorrect, mistaken, unprecise, untrue, wrong. ANT.-correct, right, true.

inactive, *a.* SYN.-dead, dormant, idle, indolent, inert, lazy, sluggish, slothful, stagnant, still, torpid, unemployed, unoccupied. ANT.-active, employed, industrious, occupied, working.

inadequate, *a.* SYN.-bare, defective, deficient, imperfect, incomplete, ineffective, insufficient, lacking, little, meager, scanty, scarce, short, spare, sparse, sufficient, wanting, weak. ANT.-adequate, ample, enough, satisfactory, sufficient.

inadvisable, *a.* SYN.-improper, imprudent, inappropriate, injudicious, unsuitable, unwise, wrong. ANT.-appropriate, correct, recommended, suitable.

inane, *a.* SYN.-absurd, dumb, foolish, pointless, ridiculous, silly, stupid.

inanimate, *a.* SYN.-dead, deceased, defunct, inert, insensible, lifeless, senseless, spiritless, unconscious, unfeeling. ANT.-alive, animate, living, spirited, stirring.

inattentive, *a.* SYN.-away, absent, absent-minded, abstracted, careless, distracted, forgetful, heedless, indifferent, indiscreet, neglectful, preoccupied, slack. ANT.-attending, present; attentive, watchful.

incapacity, *n.* SYN.-disability, handicap, impotence; inability, incompetence, weakness. ANT.-ability, capability, power, strength.

incentive, *n.* SYN.-aim, bait, consideration, enticement, impetus, inducement, instigation, motive, rationale, reason, stimulation.

inception, *n.* SYN.-beginning, cause, commencement, derivation, opening, origin, outset, root, source, start. ANT.-close, completion, consummation, end, termination.

incessant, *a.* SYN.-ceaseless, constant, continual, continuous, endless, everlasting, nonstop, perennial, perpetual, persistent, unceasing, uninterrupted, unremitting. ANT.-interrupted, occasional, periodic, rare.

incident, *n.* SYN.-circumstance, condition, episode, event, fact, happening, occurrence, situation.

incidental, *a.* SYN.-accidental, ancillary, casual, chance, fortuitous, lucky, random, secondary, subordinate, supplemental, unplanned.

incinerate, *v.* SYN.-burn, char, consume, cremate, incinerate, scorch, sear, singe. ANT.-extinguish, put out, quench.

incisive, *a.* SYN.-acute, biting, brief, concise, condensed, crisp, cutting, neat, penetrating, pithy, succinct, summary, terse. ANT.-casual, lengthy, prolix, verbose, wordy.

incite, *v.* SYN.-arouse, cause, encourage, excite, foment, galvanize, goad, induce, inspire, instigate, prompt, provoke, rouse, spur, stimulate, urge. ANT.-bore, pacify, quiet, soothe.

inclination, *n.* SYN.-angle, bending, incline, lean, pitch, slope, tilt; affection,

attachment, bent, bias, desire, disposition, leaning, liking, penchant, predilection, preference, propensity. ANT.-antipathy, apathy, aversion, coldness, dislike, distaste, indifference, nonchalance, repugnance, unconcern.

include, *v.* SYN.-accommodate, admit, combine, comprise, contain, cover, embody, embrace, entail, hold, incorporate, involve. ANT.-bar, discharge, emit, exclude, omit.

included, *a.* SYN.-admitted, combined, counted, entered, incorporated, inserted, merged, noted, numbered

incongruous, *a.* SYN.-absurd, alien, bizarre, contradictory, contrary, discrepant, inappropriate, incompatible, inharmonious, paradoxical, strange, unfitting, unsuitable. ANT.-consistent, harmonious, logical, proper, sensible.

inconsistency, *n.* SYN.-conflict, contention, controversy, deviation, difference, disagreement, discord, discrepancy, disparity, paradox, variance. ANT.-amity, concord, consonance, harmony.

inconsistent, *a.* SYN.-contradictory, changeable, contrary, discrepant, erratic, fickle, illogical, incompatible, incongruous, irreconcilable, paradoxical, unstable, unsteady, vacillating, wavering. ANT.-compatible, congruous, consistent, correspondent, harmonious, suitable.

inconspicuous, *a.* SYN.-blurred, cloudy, dim, faded, faint, indistinct, murky, obscure, quiet, sly, subtle.

inconstant, *a.* SYN.-capricious, changeable, fickle, fitful, shifting, uncertain, unreliable, unstable, vacillating, variable, wavering. ANT.-constant, stable, steady, unchanging, uniform.

inconvenient, *a.* SYN.-annoying, awkward, bothersome, difficult, disturbing, troublesome, untimely. ANT.-convenient, opportune, welcome.

incorporate, *v.* SYN.-add, blend, combine, consolidate, embody, fuse, include, join, merge, unite.

increase, *v.* SYN.-accrue, aggrandize, amplify, augment, boost, broaden, build, deepen, develop, dilate, enhance, enlarge, expand, extend, grow, heighten, intensify, lengthen, magnify, multiply, raise, supplement, thicken, wax, widen. ANT.-atrophy, contract, decrease, diminish, lessen, reduce.

incredible, *a.* SYN.-extraordinary, implausible, improbable, inconceivable, suspect, unbelievable, unimaginable, unthinkable. ANT.-believable, convincing, probable, rational.

indebted, *a.* SYN.-accountable, appreciative, beholden, grateful, gratified, obligated, obliged, responsible, thankful. ANT.-thankless, unappreciative.

indecent, *a.* SYN.-coarse, dirty, disgusting, filthy, gross, immodest, immoral, impure, indelicate, lascivious, lewd, nasty, obscene, offensive, pornographic, shameless, smutty, sordid. ANT.-decent, modest, pure, refined.

indefinite, *a.* SYN.-ambiguous, dim, equivocal, hazy, indecisive, indistinct, inexact, obscure, uncertain, unclear, vague; boundless, endless, eternal, infinite, unlimited.

indelible, *a.* SYN.-abiding, enduring, impressive, lasting, memorable, permanent, unforgettable.

independence, *n.* SYN.-autonomy, exemption, freedom, immunity, liberation, liberty, license, privilege, unrestraint. ANT.-bondage, captivity, compulsion, constraint, necessity, servitude, submission.

independent, *a.* SYN.-alone, autonomous, free, self-reliant, separate, unconstrained, uncontrolled, unrestrained, unrestricted, voluntary. ANT.-contingent, dependent, enslaved, restricted.

indestructible, *a.* SYN.-abiding, changeless, constant, durable, enduring, fixed, lasting, imperishable, permanent, stable, unchangeable. ANT.-ephemeral, temporary, transient, transitory, unstable.

indicate, *v.* SYN.-announce, attest, betoken, connote, denote, designate, disclose, hint, imply, insinuate, intimate, manifest, mark, point, reveal, say, show, signify, specify, suggest, symbolize, verify. ANT.-conceal, contradict, distract, divert, falsify, misdirect, mislead.

indication, *n.* SYN.-clue, evidence, gesture, hint, implication, mark, omen, portent, proof, sign, signal, symbol, symptom, token.

indictment, *n.* SYN.-accusation, allegation, arraignment, censure, charge, complaint, imputation, incrimination, reproach. ANT.-exculpation, exoneration, pardon.

indifference, *n.* SYN.-aloofness, apathy, callousness, coldness, coolness, detachment, disdain, disinterestedness, heedlessness, impartiality, insensibility, insensitivity, neutrality, nonchalance, unconcern. ANT.-affection, ardor, attention, compassion, concern, enthusiasm, feeling, fervor, heed, importance, inclination, passion.

indifferent, *a.* SYN.-aloof, apathy, callous, cold, cool, detached, distant, heartless, impassive, mediocre, nonchalant, reserved, unemotional, unfeeling, unmoved, unsympathetic; average, common, conventional, fair, mediocre, ordinary, passable, undistinguished. ANT.-aroused, concerned, warm; exceptional, outstanding.

indigence, *n.* SYN.-destitution, distress, insolvency, necessity, need, penury, poverty, privation, want. ANT.-abundance, affluence, plenty, riches, wealth.

indigenous, *a.* SYN.-congenital, domestic, endemic, inborn, inherent, innate, local, native, natural.

indigent, *a.* SYN.-broke, destitute, distressed, impoverished, insolvent, needy, poor, poverty-stricken.

indignation, *n.* SYN.-anger, exasperation, ire, irritation, outrage, passion, resentment, temper, umbrage, wrath. ANT.-conciliation, forbearance, patience, peace, self-control.

indignity, *n.* SYN.-abuse, affront, betrayal, defilement, insolence, insult, mistreatment, offense, violation. ANT.-apology, homage, salutation

indirect, *a.* SYN.-circuitous, crooked, cunning, devious, distorted, erratic, implied, meandering, oblique, obscure, rambling, roundabout, sinister, swerving, tricky, tortuous, wandering, winding. ANT.-direct, honest, straight, straightforward.

indiscreet, *a.* SYN.-extravagant, foolish, hasty, naive, precipitate, rash, reckless, silly, tactless.

indiscretion, *a.* SYN.-absurdity, extravagance, folly, foolishness, imprudence, silliness. ANT.-judgment, prudence, reasonableness, sense, wisdom.

indispensable, *a.* SYN.-basic, essential, fundamental, imperative, important, intrinsic, necessary, needed, required, requisite, vital. ANT.-expendable, extrinsic, optional, peripheral.

indistinct, *a.* SYN.-abstruse, ambiguous, blurred, cloudy, cryptic, dark, dim, dusky, enigmatic, mysterious, obscure, unintelligible, unknown, vague. ANT.-bright, clear, distinct, lucid.

individual, *a.* SYN.-definite, distinct, distinctive, exclusive, marked, particular, personal, private, select, separate, singular, special, specific, unique. ANT.-common, general, ordinary, universal.

individuality, *n.* SYN.-character, description, disposition, distinctiveness, habit, identity, idiosyncrasy, kind, manner, nature, peculiarity, personality, reputation, repute, singularity.

indoctrinate, *v.* SYN.-convince, edify, enlighten, influence, initiate, instruct, orient, teach, train, tutor.

indomitable, *a.* SYN.-dauntless, impregnable, insurmountable, invincible, invulnerable, unassailable, unconquerable. ANT.-powerless, puny, vulnerable, weak.

induce, *v.* SYN.-begin, cause, create, effect, engender, evoke, generate, incite, influence, instigate, make, muster, occasion, originate, persuade, produce, prompt, spur, start, urge.

inducement, *n.* SYN.-cause, incentive, incitement, motive, principle, purpose, reason, spur, stimulus. ANT.-action, attempt, deed, effort, result.

indulge, *v.* SYN.-allow, cater, coddle, entertain, gratify, humor, pamper, permit, placate, please, suffer, tolerate.

indurate, *a.* SYN.-callous, cold, hard, hardened, heartless, impenitent, inured, insensible, insensitive, obdurate, tough, unfeeling. ANT.-compassionate, sensitive, soft, tender.

industrious, *a.* SYN.-active, assiduous, busy, diligent, hard-working, intent, patient, persevering. ANT.-apathetic, careless, indifferent, lethargic, unconcerned.

inebriated, *a.* SYN.-drunk, drunken, high, intoxicated, tight, tipsy. ANT.-clearheaded, sober, temperate.

ineffective, *a.* SYN.-debilitated, decrepit, delicate, feeble, impotent, infirm, illogical , inadequate, lame, poor, vague; irresolute, pliable, vacillating, wavering, weak; assailable, defenseless, exposed, vulnerable. ANT.-potent, powerful, robust, strong, sturdy.

inept, *a.* SYN.-awkward, clumsy, dumb,

foolish, graceless, inappropriate, ridiculous, unfitting, unsuited. ANT.-adroit, appropriate, apt, competent, fit, skillful, suitable.

inertia, *n.* SYN.-idleness, inactivity, indolence, laziness, listlessness, passivity, sluggishness.

inequity, *n.* SYN.-bias, favoritism, grievance, inclination, iniquity, injury, injustice, partiality, unfairness, wrong. ANT.-equity, justice, lawfulness, righteousness.

inevitable, *a.* SYN.-assured, certain, definite, destined, fated, fixed, impending, indubitable, ordained, positive, predestined, secure, sure, unavoidable, undeniable, unquestionable. ANT.-doubtful, indeterminate, possible, probable, questionable, uncertain.

inexpensive, *a.* SYN.-cheap, common, economical, fair, inferior, low-priced, mean, moderate, modest, poor, reasonable, shabby, thrifty. ANT.-costly, dear, expensive.

inexperienced, *a.* SYN.-amateur, artless, fresh, green, innocent, naive, new, raw, uncultivated, unskilled, untrained, untried, youthful.

inexplicable, *a.* SYN.-abnormal, bizarre, cryptic, dark, dim, enigmatical, extraordinary, hidden, incomprehensible, inscrutable, mysterious, mystical, obscure, occult, peculiar, recondite, secret, strange, unusual. ANT.-clear, explained, obvious, plain, simple.

infect, *v.* SYN.-adulterate, befoul, contaminate, corrupt, defile, pervert, poison, pollute, sully, taint. ANT.-disinfect, purify.

infection, *n.* SYN.-ailment, contagion, contamination, disease, germ, pest, poison, pollution, taint, virus.

infectious, *a.* SYN.-catching, communicable, contagious, pestilential, virulent. ANT.-healthful, hygienic, non-communicable.

inference, *n.* SYN.-conclusion, consequence, corollary, deduction, judgment, reason, result, supposition. ANT.-assumption, foreknowledge, preconception, presupposition.

inferior, *a.* SYN.-common, lesser, lower, mediocre, minor, poor, poorer, secondary, subordinate, substandard. ANT.-better, greater, higher, superior.

infest, *v.* SYN.-defile, fill, flood, infect, invade, jam, overrun, pack, plague, press, pollute, ravage, spread, swarm, teem.

infinite, *a.* SYN.-boundless, countless, endless, eternal, illimitable, immeasurable, immense, incalculable, inexhaustible, interminable, limitless, unbounded, unlimited, vast. ANT.-bounded, circumscribed, confined, finite, limited, restricted.

infirm, *a.* SYN.-decrepit, delicate, enervated, exhausted, faint, feeble, forceless, impaired, languid, powerless, puny, weak. ANT.-forceful, lusty, stout, strong, vigorous.

infirmity, *n.* SYN.-ailment, complaint, debility, disease, disorder, frailty, illness, malady, malaise, sickness, weakness. ANT.-health, healthiness, soundness, vigor.

inflame, *v.* SYN.-aggravate, arouse, disturb, excite, gall, grate, incense, provoke, rile, stimulate.

inflate, *v.* SYN.-balloon, bloat, boost, enlarge, exaggerate, exalt, expand, fill, magnify, overestimate, stretch, swell.

inflection, *n.* SYN.-accent, articulation, emphasis, enunciation, intonation, pronunciation, tone.

inflexibility, *n.* SYN.-firmness, obstinacy, rigidity, stability, stiffness, stubbornness, tenacity, toughness.

inflexible, *a.* SYN.-determined, dogged, firm, headstrong, immovable, implacable, intractable, obdurate, obstinate, pertinacious, resolute, rigid, steadfast, stubborn, taut, unbending, uncompromising, unyielding. ANT.-amenable, compliant, docile, submissive, yielding.

influence, *n.* SYN.-authority, command, control, domination, effect, esteem, importance, prestige, power, prominence, weight. ANT.-impotence, inferiority, subjection, timidity.

influence, *v.* SYN.-activate, actuate, affect, bias, control, convince, direct, impel, impress, incite, induce, influence, inspire, mold, persuade, shape, stir, sway, train.

influential, *a.* SYN.-consequential, convincing, critical, decisive, effective, forceful, grave, important, material, momentous, powerful, prominent, relevant, significant, substantial. ANT.-insignificant, irrelevant, mean, petty, trivial.

inform, *v.* SYN.-acquaint, advise, apprise, enlighten, familiarize, impart, instruct, notify, relate, squeal, tattle, teach, tell, testify, warn. ANT.-conceal, delude, distract, mislead.

informal, *a.* SYN.-congenial, easy, familiar, intimate, natural, offhand, ordinary, relaxed, simple, spontaneous, unceremonious, unofficial. ANT.-ceremonious, conventional, distant, formal, precise, proper, reserved, restrained.

informality, *n.* SYN.-closeness, familiarity, frankness, friendliness, intimacy, liberty, unconstrained, unreserved. ANT.-constraint, distance, haughtiness.

information, *n.* SYN.-data, evidence, facts, figures, knowledge, learning, material, statistics.

infrequent, *a.* SYN.-exceptional, limited, occasional, rare, scarce, seldom, singular, uncommon, unique, unusual. ANT.-abundant, commonplace, frequent, numerous, often, ordinary, usual.

infuriate, *v.* SYN.-anger, enrage, madden, provoke

ingenious, *a.* SYN.-acute, adroit, apt, astute, bright, clever, dexterous, keen, original, quick, quick-witted, sharp, skillful, smart, talented, witty. ANT.-awkward, bungling, clumsy, dull, foolish, slow, stupid, unskilled.

ingenuity, *n.* SYN.-ability, aptitude, artifice, cleverness, cunning, faculty, imagination, ingeniousness, inventiveness, resourcefulness, skill ANT.-clumsiness, dullness, inaptitude, stupidity.

ingenuous, *a.* SYN.-artless, candid,

frank, free, guileless, honest, innocent, instinctive, naive, open, plain, simple, sincere, spontaneous, straightforward, truthful. ANT.-contrived, scheming, sly, wily.

ingredient, *n.* SYN.-additive, component, constituent, element, part.

inhabit, *v.* SYN.-abide, dwell, fill, live, occupy, permeate, possess, reside, stay. ANT.-abandon, release, relinquish.

inhabitant, *n.* SYN.-dweller, native, occupant, resident.

inherent, *a.* SYN.-congenital, inborn, inbred, innate, instinctive, intrinsic, native, natural, real. ANT.-acquired, external, extraneous, extrinsic, superficial.

inhibit, *v.* SYN.-arrest, ban, bridle, check, constrain, curb, discourage, forbid, frustrate, hinder, limit, obstruct, prohibit, repress, restrain, stop, suppress. ANT.-adopt, aid, allow, authorize, consent, encourage, grant, incite, loosen.

inhuman, *a.* SYN.-barbarous, brutal, callous, cruel, ferocious, heartless, malignant, merciless, monstrous, pitiless, ruthless, satanic, savage. ANT.-benevolent, compassionate, forbearing, gentle, humane, kind, merciful.

iniquitous, *a.* SYN.-bad, baleful, base, corrupt, deleterious, depraved, evil, immoral, noxious, pernicious, sinful, unjust, unsound, unwholesome, villainous, wicked. ANT.-excellent, good, honorable, moral, reputable.

iniquity, *n.* SYN.-corruption, depravity, evil, inequity, injury, injustice, sin, unfairness, wrong. ANT.-equity, justice, lawfulness, righteousness.

initial, *a.* SYN.-beginning, earliest, elementary, first, inaugural, introductory, original, primary, prime, primeval, primitive, pristine; chief, foremost, leading, primary. ANT.-hindmost, last, latest; least, subordinate.

initiate, *v.* SYN.-arise, begin, commence, inaugurate, induct, install, instate, institute, introduce, launch, open, originate, propose, sponsor, start. ANT.-close, complete, end, finish, terminate.

injure, *v.* SYN.-abuse, affront, batter, damage, disfigure, dishonor, harm, hurt, impair, insult, maltreat, mar, spoil, wound, wrong. ANT.-ameliorate, benefit, compliment, help, praise, preserve.

injurious, *a.* SYN.-abusive, damaging, defamatory, deleterious, derogatory, detrimental, destructive, harmful, hurtful, inequitable, insulting, libelous, offensive, slanderous, unfair, unjust. ANT.-advantageous, beneficial, good, helpful, profitable, salutary, useful.

injury, *n.* SYN.-abrasion, affliction, blemish, damage, detriment, grievance, harm, hurt, impairment, injustice, laceration, mischief, outrage, prejudice, slight, wound, wrong. ANT.-aid, assistance, benefit, improvement, relief, repair, service.

injustice, *n.* SYN.-abuse, breach, crime, grievance, inequity, iniquity, injury, transgression, unfairness, villainy, wrong. ANT.-equity, fairness, honest,

impartiality, integrity, just, justice, lawfulness, right, righteousness.

innate, *a.* SYN.-ancestral, congenital, hereditary, inborn, inbred, inherent, inherited, innate, intrinsic, intuitive, native, natural, real. ANT.-acquired, external, extraneous, extrinsic.

innocent, *a.* SYN.-artless, blameless, faultless, forthright, guileless, harmless, honest, innocuous, lawful, legitimate, naive, pure, simple, sinless, unblemished, undefiled, virtuous ANT.-corrupt, culpable, guilty, sinful, unrighteous.

innocuous, *a.* SYN.-harmless, innocent, safe.

inquire, *v.* SYN.-ask, interrogate, investigate, probe, pry, query, question, search. ANT.-command, dictate, insist, order, reply.

inquiring, *a.* SYN.-curious, inquisitive, interrogative, meddling, nosy, peeping, peering, prying, searching, snoopy. ANT.-incurious, indifferent, unconcerned, uninterested.

inquiry, *n.* SYN.-examination, exploration, inquest, interrogation, investigation, probe, query, quest, question, research, scrutiny. ANT.-assumption, conjecture, disregard, guess, inactivity, inattention, intuition, negligence, supposition.

inquisitive, *a.* SYN.-curious, inquiring, interested, interrogative, nosy, peeping, peering, prying, questioning, searching, snoopy. ANT.-incurious, indifferent, unconcerned, uninterested.

insane, *a.* SYN.-crazy, daft, delirious, demented, deranged, frenzied, lunatic, mad, maniacal, psychotic, touched. ANT.-rational, reasonable, sane, sensible, sound.

insanity, *n.* SYN.-aberration, compulsion, craziness, delirium, dementia, derangement, frenzy, hysteria, lunacy, madness, mania, obsession, psychosis. ANT.-rationality, sanity, stability.

insecurity, *n.* SYN.-anxiety, doubt, indecision, uncertainty, vulnerability; danger, exposure, hazard, jeopardy, liability, peril, pitfall, vulnerability.

insensitive, *a.* SYN.-callous, hard, impenitent, indurate, insensible, obdurate, obstinate, remorseless, tough, unfeeling. ANT.-compassionate, sensitive, soft, tender.

inseparable, *a.* SYN.-attached, connected, indivisible, integrated, integral, joined, united.

insight, *n.* SYN.-acumen, awareness, discernment, discretion, intuition, penetration, perception, perspicuity, recognition, sense, understanding. ANT.-obtuseness.

insignificant, *a.* SYN.-frivolous, irrelevant, paltry, petty, small, trifling, trivial, unimportant, worthless. ANT.-important, momentous, serious, weighty.

insincere, *a.* SYN.-deceitful, dishonest, hypocritical, pretentious, shifty, superficial.

insinuate, *v.* SYN.-allude, connote, hint, imply, intimate, involve, mean, signify, suggest. ANT.-assert, express, state.

insipid, *a.* SYN.-banal, bland, dull, flat,

prosaic, stale, tasteless, uninteresting, vapid. ANT.-exciting, racy, savory, tasty.

insist, v. SYN.-allege, ask, assert, charge, claim, contend, demand, expect, maintain.

insistent, a. SYN.-determined, obstinate, persistent, relentless, resolute, tenacious, unrelenting.

insolence, n. SYN.-arrogance, audacity, boldness, defiance, disdain, effrontery, haughtiness, impertinence, impudence, loftiness, presumption, pride, rudeness, sauciness. ANT.-diffidence, politeness, subserviency, truckling.

insolent, a. SYN.-abusive, arrogant, bold, brazen, contemptuous, defiant, disrespectful, haughty, impertinent, impudent, insulting, offensive, overbearing, proud, rude. ANT.-considerate, courteous, polite, respectful.

inspect, v. SYN.-ascertain, determine, examine, eye, fathom, gaze, investigate, look, observe, probe, regard, scan, see, stare, survey, view, watch, witness. ANT.-avert, hide, miss, overlook.

inspection, n. SYN.-critique, examination, retrospect, retrospection, review, survey, synopsis, test.

inspiration, n. SYN.-ability, aptitude, bent, creativity, faculty, genius, gift, hunch, impulse, inclination, intellect, motivation, notion, originality, sagacity, stimulus, talent, whim. ANT.-ineptitude, obtuseness, shallowness, stupidity.

inspire, v. SYN.-animate, encourage, enliven, hearten, invigorate, motivate, spark, spur, stimulate.

instability, n. SYN.-changeability, fickleness, fluctuation, imbalance, immaturity, inconsistency, transience, vacillation.

install, v. SYN.-build, establish, inaugurate, induct, initiate, introduce.

instance, n. SYN.-case, example, illustration, occurrence, representation, sample, situation, specimen.

instantaneous, a. SYN.-abrupt, hasty, immediate, rapid, sudden, unexpected. ANT.-anticipated, gradual, slowly.

instantly, adv. SYN.-directly, forthwith, immediately, instantaneously, now, presently, promptly, straight-away. ANT.-distantly, hereafter, later, shortly, sometime.

instinctive, a. SYN.-automatic, extemporaneous, impulsive, inborn, inherent, innate, intuitive, offhand, spontaneous, subconscious, voluntary, willing. ANT.-compulsory, forced, planned, prepared, rehearsed.

institute, v. SYN.-establish, form, found, organize, raise. ANT.-abolish, demolish, overthrow, unsettle, upset.

instruct, v. SYN.-brief, command, direct, educate, guide, help, inculcate, inform, instill, order, school, teach, train, tutor. ANT.-misguide, misinform.

instruction, n. SYN.-admonition, advice, caution, counsel, exhortation, recommendation, suggestion; information, intelligence, notification.

instrument, n. SYN.-agent, apparatus, device, means, medium, tool, utensil, vehicle. ANT.-hindrance, impediment,

obstruction, preventive.

instrumental, a. SYN.-contributory, effective, helpful, useful.

insubordinate, a. SYN.-defiant, disobedient, mutinous, rebellious, refractory, seditious, undutiful, unruly. ANT.-compliant, dutiful, obedient, submissive.

insubstantial, a. SYN.-ephemeral, ethereal, flimsy, immaterial, inconsequential, insignificant, insubstantial, intangible, negligible, tenuous, trifling, trivial, unimportant.

insufficient, a. SYN.-low, undersized; deficient, inadequate, lacking, limited, meager, short, skimpy, thin, wanting, weak. ANT.-abundant, ample, enough, extended, protracted.

insulation, n. SYN.-alienation, covering, isolation, loneliness, protector, quarantine, retirement, seclusion, segregation, separation, solitude, withdrawal. ANT.-association, communion, connection, fellowship, union.

insult, n. SYN.-abuse, affront, derision, discourtesy, indignity, insolence, invective, libel, offense, ridicule, scorn, slander, slap, slur. ANT.-apology, homage, praise, salutation

insult, v. SYN.-abuse, affront, belittle, dishonor, hurt, injure, libel, mock, offend, revile, ridicule, slander, slur, taunt, wound, wrong. ANT.-compliment, praise.

insulting, a. SYN.-abusive, contemptuous, degrading, humiliating, impertinent, nasty, offensive, outrageous.

intangible, a. SYN.-ethereal, hypothetical, immaterial, incorporeal, vague, vaporous.

integrated, a. SYN.-blended, combined, mixed, synthesized, united.

integrity, n. SYN.-candor, fairness, frankness, goodness, honesty, honor, justice, morality, openness, perfection, principle, rectitude, responsibility, sincerity, trustworthiness, uprightness, virtue. ANT.-cheating, corruption, deceit, disgrace, dishonesty, duplicity, fraud, meanness, trickery.

intellect, n. SYN.-ability, acumen, brain, intelligence, mentality, mind, propensity, reason, sense, talent, understanding. ANT.-emotion, feeling, passion.

intelligence, n. SYN.-comprehension, discernment, information, knowledge, perspicacity, reason, sense, understanding

intelligent, a. SYN.-alert, astute, bright, clever, contemplative, discerning, discriminating, enlightened, intellectual, keen, knowledgeable, perceptive, profound, quick, reasonable, reasoning, smart, well-informed. ANT.-dull, foolish, insipid, obtuse, slow, stupid.

intend, v. SYN.-aim, aspire, contrive, delineate, design, determine, devise, expect, mean, outline, plan, plot, prepare, project, propose, resolve, scheme.

intense, a. SYN.-acute, animated, bright, brilliant, clear, concentrated, deep, earnest, expressive, fervent, fresh, graphic, heightened, impassioned, intensive, keen, lively, lucid, piercing, powerful, profound, severe, stinging,

striking, strong, vivid. ANT.-dim, dreary, dull, dusky, vague.

intensify, v. SYN.-amplify, augment, compound, confound, emphasize, enhance, enlarge, exacerbate, expand, extend, grow, heighten, increase, magnify, multiply, raise, sharpen, strengthen, wax. ANT.-atrophy, contract, decrease, diminish, reduce.

intensity, n. SYN.-ardor, concentration, depth, emphasis, fervor, force, magnitude, passion, power, severity, stress, vehemence, vigor.

intent, a. SYN.-engrossed, firm, rapt, resolute, steadfast.

intent, n. SYN.-aim, delineation, design, focus, import, intention, meaning, objective, outline, plan, purpose, significance. ANT.-accident, chance.

intention, n. SYN.-aim, contrivance, delineation, design, draft, end, intention, objective, outline, plan, plotting, purpose, scheming. ANT.-accident, candor, chance, result.

intentional, a. SYN.-conscious, considered, contemplated, deliberate, designed, intended, premeditated, studied, voluntary, wanton, willful. ANT.-accidental, fortuitous.

intercept, v. SYN.-ambush, block, catch, interfere, overtake, reach.

interest, n. SYN.-attention, concern, curiosity, regard; advantage, benefit, claim, gain, percentage, profit, share, stake.

interested, a. SYN.-absorbed, affected, attentive, attracted, biased, curious, drawn, engrossed, impressed, inquiring, inquisitive, inspired, involved, moved, prying, nosy, responsive, stimulated, stirred, touched.

interesting, a. SYN.-absorbing, amusing, arresting, captivating, enchanting, engaging, enticing, exciting, fascinating, impressive, pleasing, satisfying

interfere, v. SYN.-compete, conflict, contend, interpose, interrupt, intervene, meddle, mix in, monkey, pry, question, tamper, vie.

interior, a. SYN.-center, central, inmost, inner, internal, intrinsic, inward. ANT.-adjacent, exterior, external, outer.

interject, v. SYN.-include, inject, insert, interpose, introduce.

interjection, n. SYN.-cry, exclamation, utterance.

interminable, a. SYN.-boundless, ceaseless, dull, endless, eternal, illimitable, immeasurable, immense, infinite, monotonous, unbounded, unlimited, vast. ANT.-bounded, circumscribed, confined, finite, limited.

intermittent, a. SYN.-broken, disconnected, erratic, irregular, periodic, recurrent, spasmodic.

internal, a. SYN.-constitutional, domestic, indigenous, inherent, innate, inside, inward, organic, private.

interpose, v. SYN.-arbitrate, inject, insert, intercede, interfere, interject, intervene, introduce, intrude, meddle, mediate. ANT.-avoid, disregard, overlook.

interpret, v. SYN.-clarify, construe, decipher, decode, define, diagnose, elucidate, explain, explicate, portray, render, solve, translate, unravel. ANT.-confuse, distort, falsify, misconstrue, misinterpret.

interpretation, n. SYN.-account, analysis, commentary, definition, description, diagnosis, explanation, portrayal, rendering, representation, translation, version.

interrogate, v. SYN.-ask, audit, check, examine, inquire, pump, query, question, quiz. ANT.-disregard, omit, overlook.

interrupt, v. SYN.-adjourn, break, check, defer, delay, discontinue, interfere, interject, intervene, intrude, postpone, stay, suspend. ANT.-continue, maintain, persist, proceed, prolong.

intervene, v. SYN.-arbitrate, intercede, interfere, interpose, meddle, mediate, negotiate. ANT.-avoid, disregard, overlook.

intimacy, n. SYN.-affection, closeness, familiarity, fellowship, frankness, friendship, informality, liberty, love, sociability, warmth. ANT.-constraint, distance, haughtiness, reserve.

intimate, a. SYN.-affectionate, chummy, close, confidential, familiar, friendly, loving, near, personal, private. ANT.-ceremonious, conventional, distant, formal.

intimation, n. SYN.-allusion, connotation, hint, implication, indication, inference, innuendo, insinuation, reminder, suggestion. ANT.-affirmation, declaration, statement.

intolerant, a. SYN.-biased, bigoted, dogmatic, fanatical, narrow, narrow-minded, opinionated, parochial, prejudiced. ANT.-liberal, progressive, radical, tolerant.

intoxicate, v. SYN.-befuddle, confuse, elate, excite, exhilarate, inebriate, invigorate, muddle, stimulate, thrill.

intoxicated, a. SYN.-drunk, drunken, high, inebriated, tight, tipsy; elated, euphoric, excited, exhilarated, infatuated, stimulated. ANT.-clearheaded, sober, temperate; calm, cool, unconcerned.

intricate, a. SYN.-abstract, abstruse, complex, complicated, compound, involved, perplexing, puzzling. ANT.-plain, simple, uncomplicated.

intrigue, n. SYN.-artifice, cabal, conspiracy, design, machination, plan, plot, scheme, stratagem.

intriguing, a. SYN.-appealing, attractive, charming, engaging, entertaining, fascinating, interesting, pleasing.

intrinsic, a. SYN.-congenital, inborn, inbred, ingrained, inherent, innate, native, natural, real. ANT.-acquired, external, extraneous, extrinsic.

introduce, v. SYN.-add, advance, begin, inaugurate, initiate, insert, insinuate, institute, interject, offer, present, propose,

introduction, n. SYN.-admittance, baptism, beginning, debut, forward, initiation, overture, preamble, preface, prelude, presentation, prologue, start. ANT.-completion, conclusion, end, epilogue, finale.

introductory, a. SYN.-basic, beginning, early, initial, opening, original, preparatory, primary, starting.

intrude, v. SYN.-encroach, impose, infringe, intervene, invade, penetrate, trespass, violate. ANT.-abandon, evacuate, relinquish, vacate.

intuition, n. SYN.-acumen, clue, discernment, feeling, hunch, insight, penetration, perspicuity, premonition, prescience, presentiment. ANT.-obtuseness.

intuitive, a. SYN.-automatic, natural, spontaneous; clairvoyant, discerning, insightful, perceptive.

invade, v. SYN.-assault, attack, encroach, infringe, intrude, penetrate, raid, storm, transgress, trespass, violate. ANT.-abandon, evacuate, relinquish, vacate.

invalid, a. SYN.-defective, erroneous, fallacious, groundless, illogical, irrational, null, void.

invalidate, v. SYN.-annul, belie, cancel, contradict, deny, discredit, negate, nullify, refute, reject, repeal, revoke, void.

invaluable, a. SYN.-expensive, inestimable, precious, priceless, valuable. ANT.-cheap, useless, worthless.

invariable, a. SYN.-changeless, consistent, constant, static, unchanging, uniform.

invasion, n. SYN.-aggression, assault, attack, incursion, offensive, onslaught, raid. ANT.-defense, opposition, resistance, surrender.

invective, n. SYN.-abuse, aspersion, censure, defamation, denunciation, desecration, dishonor, disparagement, insult, outrage, perversion, profanation, reproach, reviling, scorn, upbraiding, vituperation. ANT.-approval, commendation, laudation, plaudit, respect.

invent, v. SYN.-conceive, concoct, contrive, create, design, devise, discover, fabricate, fashion, forge, frame, originate, plan. ANT.-copy, imitate, reproduce.

inventive, a. SYN.-bright, clever, creative, fanciful, imaginative, resourceful, visionary. ANT.-dull, literal, prosaic, unromantic.

inventiveness, n. SYN.-ability, adroitness, cleverness, cunning, dexterity, expertise, faculty, imagination, ingeniousness, ingenuity, resourcefulness, skill. ANT.-clumsiness, dullness, inaptitude, stupidity.

invert, v. SYN.-change, overthrow, overturn, reverse, subvert, transpose, unmake, upset. ANT.-maintain, stabilize.

investigate, v. SYN.-analyze, examine, explore, ferret, inquire, interrogate, look, probe, question, research, scour, scrutinize, search, seek, study, test.

investigation, n. SYN.-examination, exploration, inquiry, interrogation, query, quest, question, research, scrutiny. ANT.-disregard, inactivity, inattention, negligence.

invincible, a. SYN.-impregnable, indomitable, insurmountable, invulnerable, unassailable, unconquerable. ANT.-powerless, puny, vulnerable, weak.

invigorate, v. SYN.-animate, energize, enliven, excite, exhilarate, rejuvenate, revive, stimulate.

invigorating, a. SYN.-bracing, cool, exhilarating, fresh, quickening, refreshing, stimulating.

invisible, a. SYN.-ethereal, imperceptible, indistinguishable, intangible, obscure, undiscernible, unseen. ANT.-evident, perceptible, seen, visible.

invitation, n. SYN.-attraction, encouragement, lure, offer, overture, request, summons, temptation.

invite, v. SYN.-ask, attract, beg, bid, draw, entice, implore, lure, persuade, petition, request, solicit, summon, tempt.

inviting, a. SYN.-alluring, appealing, attractive, bewitching, captivating, encouraging, fascinating, magnetic, tempting.

involve, v. SYN.-comprise, embrace, embroil, entangle, envelop, implicate, include, incriminate. ANT.-disconnect, disengage, extricate, separate.

involved, a. SYN.-absorbed, complex, complicated, compound, elaborate, implicated, intricate, mesmerized, perplexing. ANT.-plain, simple, uncompounded.

invulnerable, a. SYN.-impenetrable, impervious, impregnable, indomitable, insurmountable, invincible, steadfast, unassailable, unconquerable. ANT.-powerless, puny, vulnerable, weak.

irate, a. SYN.-angry, enraged, furious, incensed, mad, raging.

ire, n. SYN.-anger, animosity, choler, frenzy, fury, indignation, irritation, passion, petulance, rage, raving, resentment, temper, vehemence, wrath. ANT.-conciliation, forbearance, patience, peace, self-control.

irk, v. SYN.-annoy, beset, bother, chafe, disturb, inconvenience, irritate, molest, pester, tease, torment, trouble, vex, worry. ANT.-accommodate, console, gratify, soothe.

ironic, a. SYN.-caustic, contradictory, contrary, cynical, derisive, incongruous, mocking, paradoxical, sardonic, scathing.

irrational, a. SYN.-absurd, contradictory, fallacious, foolish, illogical, inconsistent, nonsensical, preposterous, ridiculous, silly, specious, unreasonable, untenable. ANT.-consistent, rational, reasonable, sensible, sound.

irregular, a. SYN.-aberrant, abnormal, capricious, devious, divergent, eccentric, fitful, inconstant, intermittent, random, sporadic, unequal, uneven, unnatural, unusual, variable. ANT.-fixed, methodical, ordinary, regular, usual.

irrelevant, a. SYN.-alien, contrasted, extraneous, foreign, inapplicable, pointless, remote, strange, unconnected. ANT.-akin, germane, kindred, relevant.

irresistible, a. SYN.-alluring, charming compelling, enchanting, enticing, fascinating, invincible, overwhelming, tantalizing, tempting.

irresolute, a. SYN.-assailable, bending, inadequate, ineffective, insecure, pliable, pliant, undecided, unstable, unsteady, vacillating, vulnerable, wavering, weak, yielding. ANT.-potent, powerful, robust, strong, sturdy.

irresponsible, a. SYN.-capricious, fickle, flighty, immoral, loose, rash, shiftless, thoughtless, unreliable, unstable.

irritable, a. SYN.-choleric, excitable, fiery, hasty, hot, irascible, peevish, petulant, sensitive, snappish, tense, testy, touchy. ANT.-agreeable, calm, composed, tranquil.

irritant, n. SYN.-aggravation, annoyance, bother, inconvenience, nuisance, pest.

irritate, v. SYN.-annoy, bother, chafe, disturb, gall, harass, harry, haze, irk, molest, pester, provoke, tease, torment, trouble, vex. ANT.-accommodate, console, gratify, soothe.

irritation, n. SYN.-annoyance, bother, displeasure, exasperation, pique, stress, vexation. ANT.-appeasement, comfort, gratification, pleasure.

isolated, a. SYN.-alone, apart, deserted, desolate, lone, lonely, only, remote, secluded, segregated, separate, single, sole, solitary, withdrawn. ANT.-accompanied, attended, surrounded.

isolation, n. SYN.-alienation, detachment, insulation, loneliness, privacy, quarantine, retirement, seclusion, segregation, separation, solitude, withdrawal. ANT.-association, communion, connection, fellowship, union.

issue, v. SYN.-abound, come, discharge, emanate, emerge, emit, flow, gush, originate, release, run, spout, spurt, stream, vent.

itinerant, a. SYN.-drifting, nomadic, roaming, roving, wandering.

itinerant, n. SYN.-nomad, tramp, vagabond, vagrant, wanderer.

J

jabber, n. SYN.-babble, chatter, drivel, gibberish, nonsense, patter, twaddle.

jaded, a. SYN.-cold, impassive, indifferent, nonchalant, numbed, weary.

jam, n. SYN.-difficulty, predicament, problem, trouble.

jam, v. SYN.-compress, crowd, crush, jostle, mob, pack, press, ram, squeeze.

jammed, a. SYN.-blocked, caught, congested, crowded, frozen, obstructed, overflowing, swarming, wedged.

jargon, n. SYN.-cant, colloquialism, dialect, idiom, language, lingo, patter, phraseology, slang, speech, tongue, vernacular. ANT.-babble, drivel, gibberish, nonsense.

jaunt, n. SYN.-excursion, journey, junket, pilgrimage, tour, trip, voyage, walk.

jealous, a. SYN.-apprehensive, demanding, doubting, envious, mistrustful, possessive, resentful, suspicious, vigilant, watchful.

jealousy, n. SYN.-covetousness, distrust, envy, invidiousness, mistrust, possessiveness, resentfulness, resentment, suspicion. ANT.-geniality, indifference, liberality, tolerance.

jeer, v. SYN.-boo, deride, flout, gibe, insult, mock, ridicule, scoff, sneer, taunt. ANT.-compliment, flatter, laud, praise.

jeering, n. SYN.-banter, derision, gibe, insult, irony, mockery, raillery, ridicule, sarcasm, satire, sneering.

jeopardize, v. SYN.-endanger, expose, hazard, imperil, peril, risk, venture. ANT.-guard, insure.

jerk, n. SYN.-convulsion, flick, jiggle, quiver, tic, twitch; ass, fool, nincompoop, rascal, scamp, scoundrel, simpleton.

jester, n. SYN.-buffoon, clown, fool, harlequin. ANT.-philosopher, sage, scholar.

jewel, n. SYN.-adornment, bangle, bauble, gem, ornament, trinket.

job, n. SYN.-assignment, business, career, chore, employment, errand, function, labor, mission, obligation, occupation, pursuit, position, post, profession, situation, stint, task, toil, work, undertaking, vocation.

join, v. SYN.-accompany, adjoin, assemble, associate, attach, cement, clamp, combine, conjoin, connect, consolidate, contact, couple, fuse, link, marry, touch, unite, weld. ANT.-detach, disconnect, disjoin, separate.

joined, a. SYN.-allied, affiliated, associated, attached, banded, blended, cemented, combined, connected, coupled, fused, involved, linked, melded, mingled, unified, united, wed.

joke, v. SYN.-banter, fool, frolic, jest, josh, kid, laughter, play, pun, quip, tease, trick.

jolly, a. SYN.-cheerful, gay, glad, happy, jovial, joyful, joyous, lighthearted, merry, mirthful, sprightly. ANT.-depressed, glum, mournful, sad, sullen.

jolt, v. SYN.-bounce, jar, quake, rock, shake, shudder, tremble, vibrate, waver.

journey, n. SYN.-cruise, expedition, jaunt, passage, pilgrimage, safari, tour, travel, trip, venture, voyage.

journey, v. SYN.-drive, go, jaunt, ramble, ride, roam, rove, tour, travel, trek. ANT.-stay, stop.

jovial, a. SYN.-affable, amiable, congenial, convivial, cordial, friendly, happy, jocular, jolly, merry.

joy, n. SYN.-bliss, delight, ecstasy, elation, exultation, festivity, gaiety, glee, felicity, happiness, jubilation, levity, merriment, mirth, pleasure, rapture, rejoicing, transport. ANT.-affliction, depression, despair, grief, sorrow.

joyful, a. SYN.-blessed, cheerful, contented, delighted, fortunate, gay, glad, happy, joyous, lucky, merry, opportune, propitious. ANT.-blue, depressed, gloomy, morose.

joyous, a. SYN.-blithe, cheerful, festive, gay, gleeful, hilarious, jolly, jovial, lively, merry, mirthful, sprightly. ANT.-gloomy, melancholy, morose, sad, sorrowful.

judge, n. SYN.-adjudicator, arbitrator, critic, justice, magistrate, referee, umpire.

judge, v. SYN.-; adjudicate, arbitrate, condemn, try, umpire; appreciate, consider, decide, decree, deem, determine, estimate, evaluate, measure, think.

judgment, n. SYN.-acuity, appraisal, as-

sessment, awareness, belief, comprehension, consideration, conviction, discernment, discrimination, finding, grasp, intelligence, knowledge, mentality, opinion, perspicacity, profundity, prudence, rationality, sagacity, taste, understanding, view, wisdom. ANT.-arbitrariness, senselessness, stupidity, thoughtlessness.

judicious, a. SYN.-discreet, expedient, intelligent, politic, practical, prudent, rational, sensible, sober, sound, wise. ANT.-blind, foolish, ill-advised, hasty, rash.

jumble, n. SYN.-agitation, chaos, clutter, commotion, confusion, disarrangement, disarray, disorder, ferment, medley, mixture, stir, tumult, turmoil. ANT.-certainty, order, peace, system, tranquility.

jumble, v. SYN.-amalgamate blend, combine, commingle, concoct, confound, confuse, mess, mingle, mix, muddle. ANT.-classify, dissociate, divide, file, isolate, segregate, separate, sort, straighten.

jump, v. SYN.-bolt, bound, caper, hop, jerk, leap, skip, spring, start, vault.

just, a. SYN.-appropriate, apt, fair, good, honest, honorable, equitable, honorable, impartial, legal, legitimate, proper, righteous, rightful, scrupulous, sincere, trustworthy, truthful, upright, virtuous. ANT.-deceitful, dishonest, fraudulent, lying, tricky.

justice, n. SYN.-equity, fairness, impartiality, integrity, justness, law, rectitude, right, virtue. ANT.-inequity, partiality, unfairness, wrong.

justifiable, a. SYN.-admissible, allowable, defensible, fair, fit logical, permissible, probable, proper, tolerable, warranted. ANT.-inadmissible, irrelevant, unsuitable.

justify, v. SYN.-absolve, acquit, assert, clear, defend, excuse, exonerate, support, uphold, vindicate. ANT.-abandon, accuse, blame, convict.

K

keen, a. SYN.-acute, anxious, ardent, bright, clever, cunning, cutting, discerning, eager, excited, incisive, intent, interested, quick, piercing, sensitive, shrewd, wily, witty, zealous. ANT.-slow, sluggish; dull, inattentive, unaware.

keep, v. SYN.-celebrate, commemorate, conserve, continue, guard, honor, maintain, observe, own, possess, preserve, protect, reserve, retain, save, support, sustain, tend; confine, detain, hold, restrain, store. ANT.-abandon, discard, dismiss, forsake, ignore, neglect, reject, relinquish.

kidnap, v. SYN.-abduct, capture, grab, pirate, shanghai, snatch, steal, waylay.

kill, v. SYN.-assassinate, butcher, dispatch, execute, exterminate, liquidate, massacre, murder, sacrifice, slaughter, slay; cancel, halt, forbid, negate, nullify, prohibit, stop, veto. ANT.-animate, protect, resuscitate, save, vivify.

kin, n. SYN.-connection, family, kinsman, relation, relative, sibling.

kind, *a.* SYN.-accommodating, affable, benevolent, benign, charitable, compassionate, considerate, forbearing, gentle, good, helpful, humane, indulgent, kindly, loving, merciful, obliging, solicitous, sympathetic, tender, thoughtful, understanding. ANT.-cruel, inhuman, merciless, severe, unkind.

kind, *n.* SYN.-breed, character, class, classification, denomination, designation, family, genus, race, sort, species, stock, strain, type, variety.

kindness, *n.* SYN.-altruism, benevolence, charity, compassion, consideration, courtesy, friendliness, generosity, goodness, helpfulness, humanity, mercy, philanthropy, sympathy, tact, tenderness, thoughtfulness, understanding. ANT.-cruelty, harshness, injury, malevolence, selfishness.

kindred, *a.* SYN.-alike, allied, assimilated, associated, family, germane, kin, like, related, similar

kindred, *n.* SYN.-affinity, clan, consanguinity, family, folks, house, kin, kinsfolk, relations, relationship, relatives, tribe. ANT.-disconnection, foreigners, strangers.

kingdom, *n.* SYN.-country, domain, dominion, empire, lands, nation, possessions, principality, realm, state, territory.

kinship, *n.* affiliation, affinity, alliance, cohesion, connection, familiarity, family, intimacy, kin, kindred, relationship, unity.

kiss, *v.* SYN.-caress, coddle, cuddle, embrace, greet, fondle, hug, pet. ANT.-annoy, buffet, spurn, tease, vex.

knack, *n.* SYN.-ability, adroitness, aptitude, capability, cleverness, cunning, deftness, dexterity, endowment, facility, genius, gift, ingenuity, readiness, skill, skillfulness, talent. ANT.-awkwardness, clumsiness, inability, ineptitude.

knife, *n.* SYN.-bayonet, blade, broadsword, cutter, dagger, dirk, edge, lance, machete, point, poniard, razor, saber, scalpel, scimitar, scythe, sickle, stiletto, sword.

knit, *v.* SYN.-affiliate, braid, cable, connect, crochet, intertwine, net, ossify, web

knot, *n.* SYN.-bond, bunch, clinch, cluster, conundrum, crowd, difficulty, entanglement, group, perplexity, snarl, tangle, tie, twist.

know, *v.* SYN.-acquaint, appreciate, apprehend, ascertain, befriend, cognize, comprehend, differentiate, discern, distinguish, experience, familiarize, fathom, perceive, recognize, see, understand. ANT.-dispute, doubt, ignore, suspect.

knowing, *a.* SYN.-acute, awake, aware, clever, cognizant, conscious, intelligent, sharp.

knowingly, *a.* SYN.-consciously, deliberately, intentionally, willfully.

knowledge, *n.* SYN.-apprehension, awareness, cognizance, education, enlightenment, erudition, expertise, information, intelligence, learning, lore, mation, intelligence, learning, lore, scholarship, science, understanding,

wisdom. ANT.-ignorance, illiteracy, misunderstanding, stupidity.

known, *a.* SYN.-accepted, acknowledged, admitted, certified, disclosed, established, familiar, learned, noted, prominent, proverbial, public, recognized, revealed.

L

label, *n.* SYN.-classification, description, identification, mark, marker, name, stamp, sticker, tag.

labor, *n.* SYN.-diligence, drudgery, effort, employment, endeavor, exertion, industry, striving, task, toil, travail, undertaking, work; childbirth, parturition. ANT.-idleness, indolence, leisure, recreation.

lacking, *a.* SYN.-deficient, destitute, inadequate, incomplete, insufficient, needed, scant, scanty, short. ANT.-adequate, ample, enough, satisfactory, sufficient.

lag, *n.* SYN.-cessation, retardation, slowdown, slowing, slowness.

lame, *a.* SYN.-crippled, defective, deformed, disabled, feeble, halt, hobbling, limping, maimed, unconvincing, unsatisfactory, weak. ANT.-agile, athletic, robust, sound, vigorous.

lament, *v.* SYN.-bemoan, bewail, deplore, grieve, mourn, repine, wail, weep.

land, *n.* SYN.-acreage, area, continent, country, domain, earth, estate, expanse, farm, field, ground, island, nation, plain, property, province, realm, region, soil, terrain, tract, turf.

land, *v.* SYN.-alight, arrive, berth, disembark, dock,

language, *n.* SYN.-cant, dialect, diction, idiom, jargon, lingo, phraseology, slang, speech, tongue, vernacular. ANT.-babble, drivel, gibberish, nonsense.

languish, *v.* SYN.-decline, desire, deteriorate, droop, dwindle, fade, fail, flag, pine, shrink, shrivel, sink, waste, weaken, wilt, wither. ANT.-refresh, rejuvenate, renew, revive.

lapse, *n.* SYN.-backsliding, blunder boner, degeneration, error, mistake, slip.

larceny, *n.* SYN.-burglary, crime, depredation, embezzlement, fraud, pillage, plunder, robbery, theft, thievery.

large, *a.* SYN.-ample, big, capacious, colossal, considerable, cumbersome, enormous, extensive, extravagant, grand, great, huge, immense, lavish, massive, substantial, vast, wide. ANT.-little, mean, short, small, tiny.

largely, *a.* SYN.-chiefly, essentially, mainly, mostly, predominantly, primarily, principally.

last, *a.* SYN.-climactic, closing, concluding, crowning, decisive, ending, extreme, final, hindmost, latest, terminal, ultimate, utmost. ANT.-beginning, first, foremost, initial, opening.

lasting, *a.* SYN.-abiding, enduring permanent

late, *a.* SYN.-behind, belated, delayed, overdue, slow, tardy; advanced, contemporary, modern, new, recent. ANT.-

early, timely.

latent, *a.* SYN.-concealed, dormant, hidden, inactive, potential, quiescent, secret, undeveloped, unseen. ANT.-conspicuous, evident, explicit, manifest, visible.

laugh, *n.* SYN.-amusement, cackle, chortle, chuckle, giggle, guffaw, jeer, merriment, mirth, mock, roar, scoff, snicker, titter.

laughable, *a.* SYN.-amusing, comic, comical, droll, funny, humorous, ludicrous.

launch, *v.* SYN.-begin, drive, inaugurate, introduce, originate, propel, start.

launched, *a.* SYN.-begun, driven, sent, started.

lavish, *a.* SYN.-excessive, extravagant, generous, improvident, plentiful, unstinting, wasteful.

lavish, *v.* SYN.-consume, dissipate, expend, misuse, profligate, scatter, spend, squander, waste. ANT.-accumulate, economize, preserve, save.

law, *n.* SYN.-act, code, constitution, decree, edict, enactment, injunction, order, ordinance, rule, ruling, statute.

lawful, *a.* SYN.-allowable, authorized, constitutional, enacted, legal, legalized, legitimate, permissible, permitted, rightful. ANT.-criminal, illegal, illegitimate, illicit, prohibited.

lawless, *a.* SYN.-barbarous, fierce, savage, tempestuous, uncivilized, violent, uncontrolled, untamed, wild.

lax, *a.* SYN.-careless, desultory, inaccurate, indifferent, neglectful, negligent, remiss, slack. ANT.-accurate, careful, meticulous.

lay, *a.* SYN.-earthly, laic, secular, temporal, worldly; amateur, beginner, novice, neophyte. ANT.-ecclesiastical; experienced, trained.

lay, *v.* SYN.-arrange, deposit, dispose, place, put, set. ANT.-disarrange, disturb, mislay, misplace, remove.

layman, *n.* SYN.-amateur, dilettante, nonprofessional, novice.

layout, *n.* SYN.-arrangement, blueprint, design, draft, organization, plan, scheme, strategy.

lazy, *a.* SYN.-idle, inactive, indifferent, indolent, inert, remiss, slothful, sluggish, supine, torpid. ANT.-active, alert, assiduous, diligent.

lead, *v.* SYN.-allure, beat, conduct, control, convince, direct, entice, escort, excel, guide, induce, influence, manage, outstrip, persuade, pilot, precede, regulate, steer, supervise, surpass.

leader, *n.* SYN.-captain, chief, chieftain, commander, conductor, director, guide, head, manager, master, principal, ruler. ANT.-attendant, follower, servant, subordinate, underling.

leadership, *n.* SYN.-administration, authority, control, direction, guidance, influence, management, power, superiority

league, *n.* SYN.-alliance, association, brotherhood, club, coalition, combination, confederacy, entente, federation, fellowship, fraternity, partnership, union.

league, *v.* SYN.-band, combine, confederate, cooperate, unite.

lean, *v.* SYN.-bend, incline, list, sag, slant, slope, tend; depend, rely, trust. ANT.-erect, raise, rise, straighten.

leaning, *n.* SYN.-bent, bias, drift, inclination, partiality, penchant, predisposition, proclivity, proneness, propensity, tendency, trend. ANT.-aversion, deviation, disinclination.

leap, *v.* SYN.-bound, caper, clear, hop, hurdle, jump, spring, start, surmount, vault.

learn, *v.* SYN.-acquire, ascertain, determine, discover, get, master, memorize, understand, unearth.

learned, *a.* SYN.-able, academic, accomplished, adept, cultured, educated, enlightened, erudite, experience, expert, informed, intelligent, knowing, lettered, pedantic, professional, professorial, proficient, profound, sagacious, scholarly, skilled, trained, wise. ANT.-foolish, illiterate, shallow, simple.

learning, *n.* SYN.-cognizance, education, erudition, information, knowledge, lore, scholarship, science, understanding, wisdom. ANT.-ignorance, illiteracy, misunderstanding, stupidity.

least, *a.* SYN.-infinitesimal, microscopic, minimal, minute, slightest, smallest, tiniest, trivial, unimportant.

leave, *v.* SYN.-abandon, abscond, depart, desert, embark, emigrate, flee, forsake, go, move, quit, relinquish, renounce, retire, vacate, withdraw. ANT.-abide, remain, stay, tarry.

lecture, *v.* SYN.-address, admonish, declaim, discourse, expound, harangue, preach, reason, reprimand, scold, speak, spout, talk, teach, upbraid.

led, *a.* SYN.-accompanied, escorted, guided, taken, taught.

legal, *a.* SYN.-allowable, authorized, constitutional, decreed, fair, forensic, just, lawful, legalized, legitimate, licit, permissible, right, rightful, sanctioned, sound, statutory, warranted. ANT.-criminal, illegal, illegitimate, illicit, prohibited.

legend, *n.* SYN.-allegory, chronicle, fable, fiction, myth, parable, saga, story, tradition. ANT.-fad, history.

legendary, *a.* SYN.-allegorical, apocryphal, celebrated, created, fabulous, famous, fanciful, historical, imaginary, immortal, invented, mythical, mythological, romantic, storied, traditional.

legible, *a.* SYN.-clear, comprehensible, conspicuous, distinct, intelligible, lucid, perceptible, plain, sharp, visible.

legitimate, *a.* SYN.-authentic, authorized, bona fide, correct, genuine, justifiable, lawful, legal, licit, logical, official, proper, proven, real, reasonable, regular, rightful, sanctioned, sensible, sincere, statutory, true, unadulterated, unaffected, valuable, veritable, warranted. ANT.-artificial, bogus, counterfeit, false, sham.

leisure, *n.* SYN.-calm, ease, freedom, intermission, pause, peace, quiet, recess, recreation, relaxation, repose, respite, rest, tranquility. ANT.-agitation, commotion, disturbance, motion, tumult.

leisurely, *a.* SYN.-dawdling, delaying, deliberate, dull, gradual, laggard, lethar-

gic, premeditated, slow, slowly, sluggish. ANT.-fast, quick, rapid, speedy, swift.

lend, *v.* SYN.-accommodate, adjust, advance, allow, comply, confer, conform, contribute, entrust, furnish, give, grant, impart, loan, oblige, present, supply.

length, *n.* SYN.-dimension, distance, duration, expanse, interval, measure, period, range, reach, season, span, stretch.

lengthen, *v.* SYN.-attenuate, draw, elongate, extend, prolong, protract, stretch. ANT.-contract, shorten.

leniency, *n.* SYN.-charity, clemency, compassion, forgiveness, grace, indulgence, mercy, mildness, patience, pity, understanding. ANT.-cruelty, punishment, retribution, vengeance.

lenient, *a.* SYN.-clement, compassionate, forbearing, forgiving, humane, indulgent, kind, merciful, tender, tolerant. ANT.-brutal, cruel, pitiless, remorseless, unfeeling.

lessen, *v.* SYN.-abate, curtail, decline, decrease, deduct, degrade, diminish, dwindle, ease, fade, lighten, lower, reduce, shorten, shrink, subtract, truncate, wane. ANT.-amplify, enlarge, expand, grow, increase.

lessening, *a.* SYN.-abating, declining, decreasing, dwindling, ebbing, falling, reducing, shrinking, waning, weakening.

lesser, *a.* SYN.-diminutive, inferior, insignificant, minor, negligible, petty, secondary, trivial.

lesson, *n.* SYN.-assignment, drill, education, example, explanation, guide, instruction, lecture, model, schooling, study, teaching, tutoring.

let, *v.* SYN.-allow, approve, authorize, condone, consent, permit, tolerate.

lethargy, *n.* SYN.-apathy, daze, inactivity, indolence, languor, numbness, passivity, sloth, stupefaction, stupor, torpor. ANT.-activity, alertness, liveliness, readiness, wakefulness.

letter, *n.* SYN.-character, mark, sign, symbol, type; communication, dispatch, epistle, memorandum, message, missive, note, report, writ.

level, *a.* SYN.-aligned, balanced, equal, equivalent, even, flat, flush, horizontal, plane, smooth, stable, steady, uniform. ANT.-broken, hilly, irregular, sloping.

levy, *n.* SYN.-assessment, custom, duty, exaction, excise, impost, rate, tax, toll, tribute. ANT.-gift, remuneration, reward, wages.

lewd, *a.* SYN.-carnal, coarse, debauched, dirty, disgusting, dissolute, filthy, gross, impure, indecent, obscene, offensive, pornographic, prurient, ribald, smutty. ANT.-decent, modest, pure, refined.

liability, *n.* SYN.-accountability, burden, debt, disadvantage, encumbrance, obligation, pledge, responsibility,

liable, *a.* SYN.-accountable, amenable, answerable, bound, exposed, likely, obliged, prone, responsible, sensitive, subject. ANT.-exempt, free, immune, independent, protected.

libel, *n.* SYN.-aspersion, backbiting, cal-

umny, defamation, denigration, lie, scandal, slander, vilification. ANT.-applause, commendation, defense, flattery, praise.

liberal, *a.* SYN.-abundant, ample, bountiful, broad-minded, expanded, extensive, impartial, indulgent, large, left, progressive, radical, reform, sweeping, tolerant, unconventional, understanding, vast, wide. ANT.-confined, narrow, restricted.

liberate, *v.* SYN.-deliver, discharge, emancipate, free, loose, release, set free. ANT.-confine, imprison, oppress, restrict, subjugate.

liberated, *a.* SYN.-autonomous, discharged, dismissed, emancipated, exempt, free, freed, independent, loose, open, unconfined, unobstructed, unrestricted. ANT.-confined, restrained, restricted; blocked, impeded.

liberty, *n.* SYN.-autonomy, deliverance, freedom, holiday, immunity, independence, leave, license, leisure, permission, privilege, self-government, vacation. ANT.-captivity, imprisonment, submission; constraint.

library, *n.* SYN.-archives, books, collection, den, manuscripts, museum, studio, study.

license, *n.* SYN.-consent, excess, exemption, freedom, grant, immoderation, immunity, independence, latitude, liberation, liberty, permit, prerogative, privilege, right, sanction, unrestraint, warrant. ANT.-bondage, compulsion, constraint, necessity, servitude.

lie, *n.* SYN.-delusion, equivocation, fabrication, falsehood, fib, fiction, illusion, invention, prevarication, untruth. ANT.-axiom, canon, fact, truism.

lie, *v.* SYN.-deceive, distort, equivocate, exaggerate, falsify, fib, mislead, misrepresent, prevaricate.

life, *n.* SYN.-activity, animation, being, buoyancy, energy, entity, existence, growth, liveliness, mortality, spirit, vigor, vitality, vivacity. ANT.-death, demise, dullness, languor, lethargy.

lifeless, *a.* SYN.-dead, deceased, defunct, departed, dull, expired, extinct, gone, inactive, inanimate, inert, insensible, insipid, listless, passive, sluggish, spiritless, torpid, unconscious. ANT.-alive, animate, living, stirring.

lift, *v.* SYN.-elevate, exalt, heave, heighten, hoist, raise, uplift; recall, repeal, rescind, revoke. ANT.-depreciate, depress, lower.

light, *a.* SYN.-animated, blithe, buoyant, cheerful, elated, effervescent, lively, resilient, spirited, sprightly, vivacious. ANT.-dejected, depressed, despondent, hopeless, sullen.

light, *n.* SYN.-beam, brightness, dawn, flame, gleam, illumination, incandescence, lamp, luminosity, radiance, shine; enlightenment, insight, knowledge, understanding. ANT.-darkness, gloom, obscurity, shadow.

lighten, *v.* SYN.-allay, alleviate, cheer, console, ease, lessen, mitigate, reduce, unburden

like, *a.* SYN.-analogous, coincident, comparable, equal, equivalent, identical, indistinguishable, resembling, same, similar, uniform. ANT.-contrary, disparate, dissimilar, distinct, opposed.

like, v. SYN.-admire, approve, esteem, love; enjoy, fancy, relish, savor.

likely, a. SYN.-anticipated, apparent, appropriate, credible, encouraging, expected, feasible, hopeful, possible, promising, reasonable.

likeness, n. SYN.-affinity, analogy, congruence, correspondence, facsimile, image, parity, representation, resemblance, semblance, similarity, similitude. ANT.-difference, distinction, variance.

limit, n. SYN.-border, bound, boundary, confine, edge, end, extent, limitation, restraint, restriction, terminus. ANT.-boundlessness, endlessness, extension, infinity, vastness.

limitation, n. SYN.-barrier, check, condition, control, defect. deficiency, failing, fault, flaw, frailty, hindrance, inadequacy, obstruction, restriction, stipulation, stricture.

limp, a. SYN.-bending, feeble, flaccid, flimsy, frail, limber, pliable, pliant, relaxed, supple, yielding.

limpid, a. SYN.-clear, cloudless, crystalline, lucid, pure, transparent, unclouded. ANT.-cloudy; ambiguous, obscure, unclear, vague.

line, n. SYN.-arrangement, band, border, course, file, groove, limit, mark, path, queue, road, route rank, row, seam, stripe, streak, string, succession.

lineage, n. SYN.-ancestry, blood, breed, clan, descent, folk, line, nation, parentage, pedigree, people, race, species, stock, strain, tribe.

linger, v. SYN.-abide, amble, bide, dawdle, delay, drift, hesitate, lag, loiter, procrastinate, remain, rest, saunter, stay, stroll, tarry, wait. ANT.-act, expedite, hasten, leave.

link, n. SYN.-bond, connection, connective, coupler, juncture, loop, ring, splice, tie, union. ANT.-break, gap, interval, opening, split.

link, v. SYN.-adjoin, attach, combine, conjoin, connect, couple, join, loop, splice, tie, unite. ANT.-detach, disconnect, disjoin, separate.

lip, n. SYN.-brim, edge, flange, margin, portal, rim.

liquid, a. SYN.-flowing, fluent, fluid, juicy, liquor, molten, viscous, watery, wet. ANT.-congealed, gaseous, solid.

liquidate, v. SYN.-abolish, annihilate, assassinate, cancel, destroy, eliminate, eradicate, execute, obliterate, purge, reimburse, remove, repay.

list, n. SYN.-agenda, catalogue, directory, docket, index, muster, register, roll, roster, slate, tally.

list, v. SYN.-arrange, catalogue, enumerate, index, record, tabulate, tally; careen, incline, lean, tilt.

listen, v. SYN.-attend, hear, hearken, heed, learn, list, mark, mind, note, notice, obey, overhear. ANT.-disregard, ignore, reject, scorn.

listless, a. SYN.-apathetic, indifferent, indolent, languid, lethargic, passive, slow, sluggish, torpid.

literal, a. SYN.-accurate, complete, correct, exact, precise, true, verbatim, veritable.

literate, a. SYN.-educated, erudite, intelligent, learned, lettered, scholarly,

little, a. SYN.-diminutive, insignificant, miniature, minor, minute, paltry, petite, petty, puny, slight, small, tiny, trivial, wee; bigoted, mean, selfish, stingy. ANT.-big, enormous, huge, immense, large.

livelihood, n. SYN.-business, career, living, means, support, sustenance, vocation, work.

lively, a. SYN.-active, alive, animated, blithe, brisk, energetic, frolicsome, spirited, sprightly, spry, supple, vigorous, vivacious; bright, brilliant, clear, fresh, glowing, sparkling, vivid. ANT.-dull, insipid, listless, stale, vapid.

load, n. SYN.-burden, cargo, charge, encumbrance, obligation, onus, responsibility, trust, weight.

load, v. SYN.-burden, encumber, oppress, overload, recharge, resupply, stack, supply, tax, trouble, weigh. ANT.-alleviate, console, ease, lighten, mitigate.

loaf, v. SYN.-dawdle, idle, loiter, loll, lounge, relax

loathe, v. SYN.-abhor, abominate, despise, detest, dislike, hate. ANT.-admire, approve, cherish, like, love.

loathsome, a. SYN.-abominable, detestable, execrable, foul, hateful, odious, revolting, vile. ANT.-agreeable, commendable, delightful, pleasant.

locale, n. area, district, locality, place, region, site, spot, territory, vicinity.

locality, n. SYN.-area, district, environs, neighborhood, place, position, province, range, region, section, sector, sphere, zone. ANT.-distance, remoteness.

locate, v. SYN.-discover, find, pinpoint, position, recover; dwell, inhabit, reside, settle.

location, n. SYN.-area, discovering, finding, locale, locality, place, point, position, region, site, situation, spot, station, vicinity, whereabouts.

lock, n. SYN.-bar, bolt, catch, clasp, closure, fastening, hook, latch, padlock; curl, plait, ringlet, tress, tuft.

lodge, n. SYN.-cabin, chalet, cottage, hostel, house, inn, resort, shelter; association, brotherhood, club, society.

lofty, a. SYN.-august, dignified, grand, grandiose, high, imposing, magnificent, majestic, noble, pompous, stately, sublime. ANT.-common, humble, lowly, ordinary, undignified.

logic, n. SYN.-deduction, discernment, induction, intellect, judgment, rationalism, reason, understanding.

logical, a. SYN.-cogent, coherent, conclusive, convincing, effective, efficacious, powerful, probable, rational, sound, strong, telling, valid, weighty. ANT.-counterfeit, null, spurious, void, weak.

loiter, v. SYN.-dally, dawdle, lag, linger, pause, remain, shuffle, tarry, trail, wait.

lone, a. SYN.-alone, apart, deserted, desolate, isolated, lonely, only, secluded, single, sole, solitary, unaided.

ANT.-accompanied, attended, surrounded.

loneliness, n. SYN.-alienation, detachment, isolation, privacy, refuge, retirement, retreat, seclusion, solitude. ANT.-exposure, notoriety, publicity.

lonely, a. SYN.-abandoned, alone, deserted, desolate, forsaken, friendless, isolated, secluded. ANT.-accompanied, attended, surrounded.

long, a. SYN.-elongated, extended, extensive, lasting, lengthy, lingering, prolix, prolonged, protracted, tedious, wordy. ANT.-abridged, brief, concise, short, terse.

look, v. SYN.-anticipate, behold, discern, examine, eye, gaze, glance, hunt, inspect, observe, regard, scan, scrutinize, see, seek, stare, survey, view, watch, witness. ANT.-avert, hide, miss, overlook.

looks, n. SYN.-appearance, aspect, bearing, countenance, demeanor, features, manner.

loose, a. SYN.-careless, corrupt, detached, disengaged, dissolute, free, heedless, imprecise, indefinite, lax, limp, promiscuous, slack, unbound, unfastened, unrestrained, untied, vague, wanton. ANT.-fast, inhibited, restrained, tight.

lose, v. SYN.-drop, fail, forfeit, mislay, misplace, succumb, surrender, yield.

loser, n. SYN.-defeated, dispossessed, dud, failure, flop, prey, ruined, victim, washout.

lost, a. SYN.-adrift, astray, bewildered, condemned, confused, consumed, dazed, defeated, destroyed, distracted, doomed, forfeited, gone, missing, misspent, perplexed, preoccupied, squandered, used, vanquished, wasted. ANT.-anchored, found, located.

lot, n. SYN.-circumstance, consequence, destiny, fate, fortune, issue, outcome, portion, result; acreage, parcel, plat, plot, tract.

loud, a. SYN.-blaring, booming, brash, clamorous, deafening, noisy, offensive, resonant, resounding, sonorous, stentorian, vociferous ANT.-dulcet, inaudible, quiet, soft, subdued.

lounge, v. SYN.-languish, loaf, loll, relax, rest, sprawl.

lousy, a. SYN.-bad, disliked, horrible, offensive, pedicular, undesirable, unwanted.

love, n. SYN.-adoration, affection, ardor, attachment, beloved, darling, devotion, endearment, fondness, passion, rapture. ANT.-aversion, dislike, enmity, hatred, indifference.

love, v. SYN.-adore, caress, cherish, embrace, fancy, hug, idolize, prize, treasure. ANT.-detest, loathe, spurn.

loveliness, n. SYN.-appeal, attractiveness, beauty, charm, comeliness, elegance, fairness, grace, handsomeness, pulchritude. ANT.-deformity, disfigurement, eyesore, homeliness, ugliness.

lovely, a. SYN.-beauteous, beautiful, charming, comely, elegant, fair, fine, handsome, pretty. ANT.-foul, hideous, homely, repulsive, unsightly.

loving, a. SYN.-affectionate, amorous, attentive, caring, close, concerned, considerate, devoted, familiar, generous, intimate, near, passionate, solicitous, tender, thoughtful. ANT.-ceremonious, conventional, distant, formal.

low, *a.* SYN.-abject, base, coarse, contemptible, crude, dejected, depressed, despicable, dishonorable, dispirited, groveling, ignoble, ignominious, inferior, lowly, mean, menial, plebeian, rude, servile, sordid, vile, vulgar. ANT.-teemed, exalted, honored, lofty, noble, righteous.

lower, *a.* SYN.-inferior, minor, poorer, secondary, subordinate. ANT.-better, greater, higher, superior.

lower, *v.* SYN.-abase, corrupt, debase, degrade, deprave, depress, impair, pervert, vitiate. ANT.-enhance, improve, raise, restore, vitalize.

lowly, *a.* SYN.-humble, ignoble, meek, menial, servile, unpretentious.

loyal, *a.* SYN.-ardent, attached, constant, dedicated, devoted, disposed, earnest, faithful, fond, inclined, prone, staunch, true, trustworthy, wedded. ANT.-detached, disinclined, indisposed, untrammeled.

loyalty, *n.* SYN.-allegiance, constancy, dependability, devotion, faith, faithfulness, fealty, fidelity, obedience, support. ANT.-disloyalty, falseness, perfidy, treachery.

lucid, *a.* SYN.-apparent, bright, brilliant, clear, cloudless, distinct, evident, intelligible, limpid, luminous, manifest, obvious, open, plain, radiant, rational, sane, shining, transparent; unmistakable, unobstructed, visible. ANT.-cloudy; ambiguous, obscure, unclear, vague.

lucky, *a.* SYN.-advantageous, auspicious, benign, favored, felicitous, fortuitous, happy, lucky, propitious, successful. ANT.-cheerless, condemned, ill-fated, persecuted, unlucky.

luminous, *a.* SYN.-bright, brilliant, clear, gleaming, lucid, lustrous, radiant, shining. ANT.-dark, dull, gloomy, murky, sullen.

lunacy, *n.* SYN.-craziness, delirium, dementia, derangement, frenzy, insanity, madness, mania, psychosis. ANT.-rationality, sanity, stability.

lure, *v.* SYN.-allure, attract, charm, draw, enchant, entrap, entice, fascinate, induce, lure, persuade, seduce, tempt. ANT.-alienate, contract, drive, propel.

lurk, *v.* SYN.-creep, crouch, hide, prowl, skulk, slink, sneak, steal.

luscious, *a.* SYN.-delectable, delicious, delightful, palatable, savory, sweet, tasty. ANT.-acrid, distasteful, nauseous, unpalatable, unsavory

lush, *a.* SYN.-dense, extensive, lavish, luxurious, opulent, ornate, profuse, rich.

lust, *n.* SYN.-appetite, aspiration, craving, desire, hungering, longing, passion, sensuality, urge, wish, yearning. ANT.-abomination, aversion, distaste, hate, loathing.

luster, *n.* SYN.-brightness, brilliance, brilliancy, effulgence, glory, gloss, polish, radiance, sheen, splendor. ANT.-

darkness, dullness, gloom, obscurity.

lustful, *a.* SYN.-animal, base, carnal, corporeal, fleshly, gross, sensual, voluptuous, worldly. ANT.-exalted, intellectual, refined, spiritual, temperate.

lusty, *a.* SYN.-bold, energetic, hardy, healthy, hearty, robust, stout, strong, sturdy, vigorous, virile. ANT.-effeminate, emasculated, weak.

luxuriant, *a.* SYN.-abundant, ample, bountiful, copious, exuberant, fecund, fertile, fruitful, luxurious, opulent, ornate, plentiful, profuse, prolific, rich. ANT.-barren, sterile, unfruitful, unproductive.

luxurious, *a.* SYN.-affluent, bounteous, bountiful, lavish, opulent, ornate, plenteous plentiful, replete, rich, sumptuous. ANT.-deficient, insufficient, rare, scanty, scarce.

luxury, *n.* SYN.-abundance, affluence, fortune, money, opulence, plenty, possessions, riches, wealth. ANT.-indigence, need, poverty, want.

M

machine, *n.* SYN.-appliance, automaton, contrivance, device, implement, instrument, movement, organization, robot.

mad, *a.* SYN.-angry, crazy, delirious, demented, enraged, exasperated, furious, incensed, insane, lunatic, maniacal, provoked, wrathful. ANT.-calm, happy, healthy, pleased, sane, sensible.

made, *a.* SYN.-built, created, fashioned, formed, manufactured, shaped.

madly, *a.* SYN.-crazily, hastily, hurriedly, rashly, wildly.

madness, *n.* SYN.-craziness, delirium, dementia, derangement, frenzy, insanity, lunacy, mania, psychosis. ANT.-rationality, sanity, stability.

magic, *n.* SYN.-charm, conjuring, enchantment, hex, legerdemain, necromancy, occultism, sorcery, voodoo, witchcraft, wizardry.

magical, *a.* SYN.-astral, charmed, cryptic, enchanted, enchanting, entrancing, fascinating, miraculous, mysterious, mystical, mythical, spellbinding, spiritualistic, supernatural, uncanny.

magnanimous, *a.* SYN.-beneficent, charitable, exalted, forgiving, generous, giving, honorable, liberal, lofty, munificent, noble, openhanded, unselfish. ANT.-covetous, greedy, miserly, selfish, stingy.

magnetic, *a.* SYN.-alluring, appealing, attractive, captivating, charming, fascinating, inviting, irresistible.

magnificent, *a.* SYN.-brilliant, dazzling, dignified, exalted, extraordinary, grand, imposing, lavish, luxurious, majestic, noble, splendid, stately

magnify, *v.* SYN.-amplify, augment, enhance, enlarge, exaggerate, expand, extend, grow, heighten, increase, intensify, overstate, stretch, wax. ANT.-belittle, depreciate, minimize, understate.

magnitude, *n.* SYN.-amplitude, bigness, bulk, consequence, dimensions, eminence, enormity, expanse, extent, greatness, importance, largeness,

mass, quantity, significance, size, volume.

maim, *v.* SYN.-cripple, disable, disfigure, hurt, lame, mutilate, scar.

main, *a.* SYN.-cardinal, chief, dominant, essential, first, foremost, highest, leading, paramount, predominant, principal, significant. ANT.-auxiliary, minor, subordinate, subsidiary, supplemental.

mainly, *a.* SYN.-chiefly, essentially, largely, mostly, predominantly, primarily, principally.

maintain, *v.* SYN.-affirm, allege, assert, claim, contend, continue, declare; defend, hold, justify, keep, preserve, support, sustain, uphold, vindicate. ANT.-deny, discontinue, neglect, oppose, resist.

majestic, *a.* SYN.-august, dignified, exalted, grand, grandiose, high, imposing, lofty, magnificent, noble, pompous, regal, stately, sublime. ANT.-common, humble, lowly, ordinary, undignified.

make, *v.* SYN.-assemble, build, cause, compel, construct, create, establish, execute, fashion, form, gain, generate, manufacture, mold, plan, produce, shape. ANT.-break, demolish, destroy, undo, unmake.

makeshift, *n.* SYN.-alternative, equivalent, expedient, replacement, stopgap, substitute. ANT.-master, original, prime, principal.

malady, *n.* SYN.-ailment, complaint, disease, disorder, illness, infirmity, sickness. ANT.-health, healthiness, soundness, vigor.

malevolence, *n.* See **malice.**

malice, *n.* SYN.-animosity, enmity, grudge, hatred, ill will, malevolence, malignity, rancor, spite. ANT.-affection, kindness, love, toleration.

malicious, *a.* SYN.-bitter, evil-minded, hostile, malevolent, malignant, rancorous, spiteful, virulent, wicked. ANT.-affectionate, benevolent, benign, kind.

malign, *v.* SYN.-abuse, accuse, asperse, defame, disparage, ill-use, insult, libel, revile, scandalize, slander, traduce, vilify. ANT.-cherish, honor, praise, protect, respect.

malignant, *a.* SYN.-dangerous, destructive, growing, harmful, lethal, malicious, rancorous, vicious, virulent.

malleable, *a.* SYN.-flexible, impressionable, pliant, soft, supple, yielding. ANT.-hard, rigid, rough, tough, unyielding.

manage, *v.* SYN.-administer, arrange, command, conduct, contrive, control, direct, dominate, educate, engineer, govern, guide, influence, lead, manipulate, officiate, oversee, pilot, regulate, rule, superintend, train. ANT.-abandon, follow, forsake, ignore, misdirect, misguide, submit.

manageable, *a.* SYN.-adaptable, compliant, controllable, docile, flexible, gentle, governable, humble, obedient, orderly, teachable, tractable.

manager, *n.* SYN.-administrator, coach, director, executive, handler, mentor, supervisor, trainer.

mandate, *n.* SYN.-command, decree, dictate, order, ordinance, regulation.

mandatory, *a.* SYN.-compulsory, imperative, obligatory, required, requisite.

maneuver, *n.* SYN.-action, design, execution, movement, operation, performance, plan, plot, proceeding, ruse, scheme, stratagem, tactics, trick. ANT.-cessation, inaction, inactivity, rest.

maneuver, *v.* SYN.-conspire, contrive, design, devise, intrigue, manage, manipulate, plan, plot, scheme, trick.

mania, *n.* SYN.-craze, enthusiasm, excitement, fad, frenzy, lunacy, madness, obsession.

manifest, *a.* SYN.-apparent, clear, distinct, evident, intelligible, lucid, obvious, open, plain, unmistakable, unobstructed, visible. ANT.-ambiguous, obscure, unclear, vague.

manifest, *v.* SYN.-confirm, declare, demonstrate, denote, designate, disclose, display, exhibit, indicate, prove, reveal, show, signify, specify. ANT.-conceal, distract, divert, falsify, mislead.

manipulate, *v.* SYN.-command, control, direct, govern, guide, handle, lead, manage, mold, shape.

manner, *n.* SYN.-custom, fashion, habit, method, mode, practice, style, way.

manners, *n.* SYN.-air, appearance, aspect, behavior, carriage, conduct, demeanor, deportment, look.

mansion, *n.* SYN.-castle, chateau, estate, manor, palace, residence, villa.

manufacture, *v.* SYN.-assemble, build, construct, fabricate, fashion, form, make, produce.

manuscript, *n.* SYN.-article, book, composition, document, essay, original, script, text, writing.

many, *a.* SYN.-divers, manifold, multifarious, multitudinous, numerous, several, sundry, various. ANT.-few, infrequent, meager, scanty, scarce.

map, *n.* SYN.-blueprint, chart, diagram, graph, outline, plan, plat, projection, sketch.

mar, *v.* SYN.-blemish, bruise, damage, deface, harm, hurt, injure, maim, ruin, scratch, spoil. ANT.-ameliorate, benefit, enhance, mend, repair.

marine, *a.* SYN.-maritime, nautical, naval, ocean, oceanic.

mark, *n.* SYN.-badge, brand, characteristic, distinction, emblem, feature, imprint, indication, label, property, scar, sign stain, stigma, symptoms, trace, trademark, trait, vestige.

mark, *v.* SYN.-brand, characterize, imprint, inscribe, label, tag; behold, descry, discover, distinguish, heed, notice, note, observe, perceive, recognize, regard, remark, see. ANT.-disregard, ignore, overlook, skip.

marriage, *n.* SYN.-espousal, matrimony, nuptials, union, wedding, wedlock. ANT.-celibacy, divorce, virginity.

marvelous, *a.* SYN.-astonishing, exceptional, extraordinary, peculiar, rare, remarkable, singular, uncommon, unusual, wonderful. ANT.-common, frequent, ordinary, usual.

masculine, *a.* SYN.-bold, hardy, lusty, male, manly, mannish, robust, strong, vigorous, virile. ANT.-effeminate, emas-

culated, feminine, unmanly, weak, womanish.

mask, *v.* SYN.-cloak, conceal, cover, disguise, hide, screen, secrete, suppress, veil, withhold. ANT.-disclose, display, divulge, expose, reveal, show, uncover.

mass, *n.* SYN.-accumulation, aggregate, body, bulk, chunk, collection, company, conglomerate, crowd, heap, hunk, mob, piece, pile, portion, rabble, section, stack. ANT.-intellect, mind, soul, spirit.

massacre, *n.* SYN.-atrocity, butchery, carnage, holocaust, killing, murder, pogrom, slaughter.

massacre, *v.* SYN.-annihilate, butcher, execute, exterminate, kill, liquidate, murder, slaughter, slay. ANT.-animate, protect, resuscitate, save, vivify.

masses, *n.* SYN.-crowd, mob, multitude, people, populace, proletariat, rabble.

massive, *a.* SYN.-bulky, burdensome, cumbersome, enormous, gigantic, heavy, huge, immense, imposing, impressive, monumental, ponderous, tremendous, weighty. ANT.-light, small.

master, *n.* SYN.-adept, authority, boss, chief, commander, employer, expert, head, leader, lord, maestro, manager, overseer, owner, proprietor, ruler, sage, teacher. ANT.-servant, slave.

mastery, *n.* SYN.-authority, command, control, domination, expertise, influence, jurisdiction, predominance, proficiency, skill, sovereignty, supremacy, sway, transcendence. ANT.-inferiority.

match, *v.* SYN.-balance, coordinate, equalize, equate, harmonize, liken, mate, pair, unite.

mate, *n.* SYN.-associate, buddy, colleague, companion, complement, comrade, consort, crony, counterpart, friend, partner, spouse. ANT.-adversary, enemy, stranger.

material, *a.* SYN.-bodily, corporeal, palpable, physical, real, sensible, solid, tangible; consequential, considerable, essential, germane, important, momentous, relevant, significant, substantial, weighty. ANT.-mental, metaphysical, spiritual; immaterial, insignificant.

material, *n.* SYN.-component, data, element, facts, figures, information, matter, stuff, substance; cloth, fabric, textile.

matrimony, *n.* SYN.-espousal, marriage, nuptials, union, wedding, wedlock. ANT.-celibacy, divorce, virginity.

matter, *n.* SYN.-element, material, stuff, substance, thing; affair, business, cause, concern, essence, focus, interest, occasion, situation, subject, theme, thing, topic, undertaking; consequence, difficulty, distress, importance, moment, perplexity, trouble. ANT.-immateriality, phantom, spirit.

mature, *a.* SYN.-adult, aged, complete, consummate, cultivated, developed, finished, full-grown, matured, mellow, old, ready, ripe, sophisticated. ANT.-crude, green, immature, raw, undeveloped.

mature, *v.* SYN.-age, culminate, develop, evolve, grow, mellow, perfect, ripen, season.

maxim, *n.* SYN.-adage, axiom, epithet, foundation, precept, principle, proverb, saying.

meager, *a.* SYN.-lacking, lean, scant, slight, stinted, wanting.

mean, *a.* SYN.-base, coarse, common, contemptible, despicable, low, malicious, mercenary, nasty, offensive, plebeian, selfish, shabby, sordid, stingy, treacherous, undignified, vile, vulgar. ANT.-admirable, dignified, exalted, generous, noble.

mean, *n.* SYN.-average, center, medium, middle, midpoint.

meander, *v.* SYN.-ramble, stroll, turn, twist, wander, wind.

meaning, *n.* SYN.-acceptation, connotation, drift, explanation, gist, implication, import, intent, interpretation, purport, purpose, sense, significance, signification.

meaningful, *a.* SYN.-consequential, explicit, important, material, pithy, profound, significant, substantial, useful.

meaningless, *a.* SYN.-insignificant, nonsensical, senseless, trivial, unimportant.

means, *n.* SYN.-agent, apparatus, approach, backing, channel, device, instrument, medium, method, mode, property, resources, substance, support, tool, utensil, vehicle, way, wealth. ANT.-hindrance, impediment, obstruction, preventive.

measure, *n.* SYN.-action, maneuver, move, procedure, proceeding; capacity, criterion, dimension, gauge, law, magnitude, mass, quantity, principle, proof, rule, size, standard, test, volume. ANT.-chance, fancy, guess, supposition.

meddle, *v.* SYN.-encroach, interfere, intervene, interpose, interrupt, intrude, monkey, pry, snoop, tamper.

mediocre, *a.* SYN.-average, common, fair, intermediate, mean, median, medium, middling, moderate, ordinary. ANT.-exceptional, extraordinary, outstanding.

meditate, *v.* SYN.-cogitate, consider, contemplate, deem, deliberate, muse, imagine, picture, plot, ponder, reason, recall, recollect, reflect, remember, speculate, study, think, weigh. ANT.-disregard, ignore, neglect, overlook.

meditation, *n.* SYN.-contemplation, examination, reflection, thought.

meek, *a.* SYN.-compliant, demur, docile, gentle; mild, passive, reserved, resigned, serene, shy, subdued, submissive, tame, timid, unassuming. ANT.-fierce, savage, spirited, wild; animated, exciting, lively, spirited.

meet, *v.* SYN.-assemble, collect, collide, confront, congregate, convene, converge, encounter, engage, face, find, greet, intersect. ANT.-cleave, disperse, part, scatter, separate.

melancholy, *a.* SYN.-dejected, depressed, despondent, disconsolate, dismal, dispirited, doleful, gloomy, glum, grave, moody, pensive, sad, somber, sorrowful, unhappy, wistful. ANT.-cheerful, happy, joyous, merry.

melodramatic, *a.* SYN.-affected, artificial, ceremonious, dramatic, emotive, histrionic, showy, stagy, theatrical. ANT.-modest, subdued, unaffected, unemotional.

mellow, *a.* SYN.-aged, cultured, genial, gentle, good-natured, jovial, mature, quiet, peaceful, perfected, ripe, soft, sweet. ANT.-crude, green, immature, raw, undeveloped.

melodramatic, *a.* SYN.-artificial, exaggerated, overdone, overemotional, sensational, theatrical.

melody, *n.* SYN.-air, aria, ballad, composition, lyric, music, song, strain, tune.

melt, *v.* SYN.-decrease, disintegrate, dissolve, dwindle, fade, liquefy, soften, thaw, vanish.

member, *n.* SYN.-affiliate, component, constituent, element, ingredient, organ, part; faction, party, side. ANT.-entirety, whole.

memorable, *a.* SYN.-decisive, distinguished, eventful, exceptional, great, impressive, lasting, momentous, monumental, notable, noteworthy, outstanding, remarkable, significant, singular, unforgettable, unusual.

memorandum, *n.* SYN.-directive, letter, message, memo, missive, note, summary.

memorial, *n.* SYN.-commemoration, memento, monument, remembrance, souvenir.

memory, *n.* SYN.-consciousness, image, recall, recollection, remembrance, reminiscence, retrospection, vision. ANT.-forgetfulness, oblivion.

menace, *n.* SYN.-caution, danger, hazard, intimidation, peril, threat.

menace, *v.* SYN.-impend, intimidate, loom, portend, threaten.

mend, *v.* SYN.-ameliorate, amend, better, correct, improve, fix, patch, reconstruct, rectify, refit, reform, remedy, renew, repair, restore, sew. ANT.-deface, destroy, hurt, injure, rend.

menial, *a.* SYN.-abject, base, common, humble, low, mean, servile.

menial, *n.* SYN.-attendant, domestic, flunky, footman, hireling, lackey, minion, serf, servant.

mentality, *n.* SYN.-brain, comprehension, disposition, faculties, inclination, intellect, intelligence, intention, judgment, liking, mind, psyche, purpose, reason, understanding, will, wish, wit. ANT.-body, corporeality, materiality, matter.

mention, *v.* SYN.-cite, declare, disclose, discuss, divulge, impart, infer, intimate, introduce, notice, quote, remark, specify, state, suggest.

mercenary, *a.* SYN.-avaricious, corrupt, greedy, miserly, niggardly, parsimonious, penurious, selfish, sordid, stingy, tight, venal. ANT.-generous, honorable, liberal.

merchant, *n.* SYN.-businessman, dealer, exporter, importer, retailer, shopkeeper, storekeeper, trader, tradesman, wholesaler.

merciful, *a.* SYN.-clement, compassionate, forbearing, forgiving, gentle, gracious, humane, indulgent, kind, lenient, mild, tender, tolerant. ANT.-brutal, cruel, pitiless, remorseless, unfeeling.

merciless, *a.* SYN.-barbarous, bestial,

brutal, brute, brutish, carnal, coarse, cruel, ferocious, gross, inhuman, pitiless, remorseless, rough, rude, ruthless, savage, sensual. ANT-civilized, courteous, gentle, humane, kind.

mercy, *n.* SYN.-charity, clemency, compassion, forgiveness, grace, leniency, mildness, pity. ANT.-cruelty, intolerance, punishment, retribution, selfishness, vengeance.

mere, *a.* SYN.-bare, insignificant, minor, scant, small.

merely, *a.* SYN.-but, exactly, hardly, just, only, solely.

merge, *v.* SYN.-amalgamate, blend, coalesce, combine, commingle, conjoin, consolidate, fuse, join, mingle, mix, unify, unite. ANT.-decompose, divide, disintegrate, separate.

merit, *n.* SYN.-credit desert, due, effectiveness, efficacy, entitlement, excellence, goodness, integrity, morality, probity, rectitude, value, virtue, worth. ANT.-corruption, fault, lewdness, sin, vice.

merit, *v.* SYN.-achieve, acquire, attain, deserve, earn, gain, get, justify, obtain, rate, warrant, win. ANT.-consume, forfeit, lose, spend, waste.

merited, *a.* SYN.-adequate, appropriate, condign, deserved, earned, fitting, proper, suitable. ANT.-improper, undeserved, unmerited.

merry, *a.* SYN.-blithe, cheerful, festive, gay, gleeful, hilarious, jolly, jovial, joyous, lively, mirthful, sprightly. ANT.-gloomy, melancholy, morose, sad, sorrowful.

mess, *n.* SYN.-chaos, clutter, confusion, congestion, difficulty, disorder, hodgepodge, jumble, melange, muddle, predicament, snag, unpleasantness, untidiness.

message, *n.* SYN.-annotation, comment, directive, information, letter, memorandum, missive, note, observation, remark, tidings.

messenger, *n.* SYN.-angel, bearer, courier, crier, emissary, envoy, herald, minister, prophet, runner.

messy, *a.* SYN.-dirty, disorderly, rumpled, sloppy, slovenly, untidy.

metaphor, *n.* SYN.-allegory, comparison, correlation, likening, resemblance, similarity, substitution. symbolism.

metaphorical, *a.* SYN.-allegorical, figurative, symbolic.

metaphysical, *a.* SYN.-abstract, mystical, spiritual, supernatural, transcendent.

mete, *v.* SYN.-allocate, allot, apportion, assign, deal, dispense, distribute, divide, dole, give, grant, measure, parcel. ANT.-confiscate, keep, refuse, retain, withhold.

method, *n.* SYN.-arrangement, design, fashion, manner, mode, order, plan, procedure, process, routine, style, system, technique, way. ANT.-confusion, disorder.

methodical, *a.* SYN.-accurate, careful, correct, definite, distinct, exact, orderly, regulated, strict, systematic, unequivocal; ceremonious, formal, precise, prim, rigid, stiff. ANT.-erroneous, loose, rough, vague; careless, easy, in-

formal.

mettle, *n.* SYN.-ardor, boldness, bravery, character, chivalry, courage, disposition, fearlessness, fortitude, intrepidity, nerve, pluck, prowess, resolution, spirit, temperament. ANT.-cowardice, fear, pusillanimity, timidity.

microscopic, *a.* SYN.-detailed, exact, infinitesimal, little, miniature, minute, particular, precise, small, tiny. ANT.-enormous, huge, large.

middle, *n.* SYN.-center, central, core, heart, intermediate, mean, median, midpoint, nucleus. ANT.-border, boundary, outskirts, periphery, rim.

midst, *n.* SYN.-center, core, heart, middle. midpoint, nucleus. ANT.-border, boundary, outskirts, periphery, rim.

might, *n.* SYN.-ability, dynamism, energy, force, intensity, potency, power, strength, vigor. ANT.-inability, weakness.

mighty, *a.* SYN.-firm, forceful, forcible, fortified, hale, hardy, impregnable, potent, powerful, robust, sinewy, strong, sturdy, tough. ANT.-brittle, delicate, feeble, fragile, insipid.

migrate, *v.* SYN.-emigrate, immigrate, leave, move.

mild, *a.* SYN.-bland, gentle, kind, meek, moderate, peaceful, soft, soothing, tender. ANT.-bitter, fierce, harsh, rough, severe.

militant, *a.* SYN.-aggressive, bellicose, belligerent, combative, contentious, firm, forceful, inflexible, obstinate, offensive, positive, quarrelsome, resolute, rigid, unbending.

militant, *n.* SYN.-activist, demonstrator, protester, radical.

mimic, *v.* SYN.-ape, copy, exaggerate, imitate, impersonate, mock, pantomime, parody, simulate. ANT.-alter, distort, diverge, invent.

mind, *n.* SYN.-brain, faculties, intellect, intelligence, judgment, memory, mentality, psyche, reason, recall, sense, soul, spirit, understanding, wit; belief, bias, disposition, inclination, intention, judgment, liking, proclivity, purpose, temper, will, wish, wont. ANT.-body, corporeality, materiality, matter.

mind, *v.* SYN.-attend, behave, heed, listen, mark, note, notice, obey, regard.

mindless, *a.* SYN.-asinine, brainless, careless, foolish, heedless, idiotic, inattentive, indifferent, oblivious, senseless, simple, stupid.

mingle, *v.* SYN.-amalgamate, blend, coalesce, combine, commingle, conjoin, consolidate, mix, merge, unify, unite. ANT.-analyze, decompose, disintegrate, separate.

miniature, *a.* SYN.-baby, diminutive, little, petite, small, tiny.

minimize, *v.* SYN.-contract, decrease, diminish, lessen, reduce.

minister, *n.* SYN.-chaplain, clergyman, cleric, curate, deacon, parson, pastor, preacher, prelate, priest, rector, vicar; ambassador, consul, diplomat, statesman.

minister, *v.* SYN.-aid, attend, comfort, heal, help, sustain, tend.

minor, *a.* SYN.-inconsequential, inferior,

insignificant, lesser, lower, poorer, secondary, subordinate. ANT.-better, greater, higher, superior.

minute, a. SYN.-detailed, exact, fine, microscopic, miniature, particular, precise, tiny. ANT.-enormous, huge, large; general.

miraculous, a. SYN.-awesome, extraordinary, incredible, marvelous, metaphysical, phenomenal, preternatural, prodigious, spiritual, stupefying, superhuman, supernatural, unearthly, wondrous. ANT.-common, human, natural, physical, plain.

mirage, n. SYN.-apparition, delusion, dream, fantasy, hallucination, illusion, phantom, vision. ANT.-actuality, reality, substance.

mirror, v. SYN.-embody, epitomize, exemplify, illustrate, reflect, represent, symbolize, typify.

misbehave, v. SYN.-blunder, defy, disobey, fail, offend, rebel, sin, trespass.

miscarriage, n. SYN.-default, dereliction, failure, fiasco, malfunction, mistake, omission. ANT.-achievement, success, victory; sufficiency.

miscellaneous, a. SYN.-assorted, different, dissimilar, diverse, heterogeneous, indiscriminate, mixed, motley, odd, sundry, varied. ANT.-alike, classified, homogeneous, ordered, selected.

mischief, n. SYN.-damage, detriment, evil, fault, harm, hurt, ill, infliction, injury, malice, misconduct, misfortune, mishap, naughtiness, transgression, vandalism, wrong. ANT.-benefit, boon, favor, kindness.

misconception, n. SYN.-delusion, error, misapprehension, misinterpretation, mistake, misunderstanding.

miser, n. SYN.-cheapskate, skinflint, tightwad.

miserable, a. SYN.-afflicted, comfortless, disconsolate, distressed, forlorn, heartbroken, pitiable, sickly, suffering, tormented, troubled, wretched; abject, contemptible, despicable, low, mean, paltry, worthless. ANT.-contented, fortunate, happy; noble, significant.

miserly, a. SYN.-acquisitive, avaricious, greedy, niggardly, parsimonious, penurious, stingy, tight. ANT.-altruistic, bountiful, extravagant, generous, munificent.

misery, n. SYN.-agony, anguish, desolation, distress, grief, sadness, sorrow, suffering, torment, trial, tribulation, trouble, unhappiness, woe. ANT.-delight, elation, fun, joy, pleasure.

misfortune, n. SYN.-accident, adversity, affliction, calamity, catastrophe, disaster, distress, hardship, mishap, ruin, unpleasantness. ANT.-blessing, comfort, prosperity, success.

misgiving, n. SYN.-cynicism, distrust, doubt, mistrust, skepticism, suspicion.

misguided, a. SYN.-confused, deceived, delinquent, misled, mistaken, wayward.

mislead, v. SYN.-beguile, betray, cheat, deceive, defraud, delude, dupe, fool, misrepresent, outwit, trick, victimize.

misleading, a. SYN.-ambiguous, deceitful, deceptive, delusive, delusory, dubious, equivocal, fallacious, false, illusive, specious, unclear, vague. ANT.-authentic, genuine, honest, real, truthful.

misplace, v. SYN.-confuse, displace, disturb, lose, mislay, remove.

miss, n. SYN.-blunder, error, failure, fumble, mishap, mistake, slip.

missed, a. SYN.-desired, craved, gone, hidden, needed, neglected, strayed, mislaid, misplaced, unseen, wanted.

mistake, n. SYN.-blunder, error, fallacy, fault, inaccuracy, inadvertence, inattention, misapprehension, misconception, misprint, mistake, misunderstanding, neglect, omission, oversight, slip. ANT.-accuracy, precision, truth.

mistaken, a. SYN.-confounded, confused, deceived, deluded, duped, erroneous, faulty, fooled, imprecise, inaccurate, incorrect, misguided, misinformed, misled, untrue, wrong. ANT.-correct, right, true.

mistreat, v. SYN.-abuse, bully, harm, injure, maltreat, wrong.

mistress, n. SYN.-caretaker, concubine, courtesan, housekeeper, lover, manager, mother, paramour, wife.

misty, a. SYN.-dim, drizzly, foggy, hazy, murky, obscure, rainy, shrouded.

misuse, v. SYN.-abuse, asperse, defame, disparage, malign, misapply, misemploy, revile, scandalize, traduce, vilify. ANT.-cherish, honor, praise, protect, respect.

mitigate, v. SYN.-abate, allay, alleviate, assuage, diminish, extenuate, relieve, soften, solace, soothe. ANT.-aggravate, agitate, augment, increase, irritate.

mix, v. SYN.-alloy, amalgamate blend, combine, commingle, compound, concoct, confound, fuse, jumble, mingle; associate, consort, fraternize, join. ANT.-dissociate, divide, segregate, separate, sort.

mixture, n. SYN.-assortment, blend, combination, diversity, heterogeneity, medley, miscellany, multifariousness, variety, variousness. ANT.-homogeneity, likeness, monotony, sameness, uniformity.

mob, n. SYN.-bevy, crowd, crush, horde, host, masses, multitude, populace, press, rabble, swarm, throng.

mock, a. SYN.-counterfeit, fake, false, feigned, forged, fraudulent, pretended, sham.

mock, v. SYN.-caricature, challenge, dare, defy, deride, flout, gibe, imitate, jeer, mimic, ridicule, scoff, sneer, taunt. ANT.-compliment, flatter, laud, praise.

mockery, n. SYN.-banter, derision, gibe, irony, jeering, raillery, ridicule, sarcasm, satire, sneering.

model, n. SYN.-archetype, copy, example, ideal, guide, mold, pattern, prototype, specimen, standard, type. ANT.-imitation, production, reproduction.

moderate, a. SYN.-average, balanced, calm, careful, considered, cool, deliberate, disciplined, frugal, gentle, judicious, modest, reserved, restrained, tepid, tranquil.

moderate, v. SYN.-abate, appease, assuage, calm, decline, decrease, diminish, modulate, restrain; arbitrate, chair, preside, referee, regulate.

moderation, n. SYN.-balance, caution, constraint, continence, discretion, forbearance, restraint, temperance.

modern, a. SYN.-chic, contemporary, current, late, latest, new, novel, present, recent, stylish. ANT.-ancient, antiquated, bygone, old, past.

modest, a. SYN.-bashful, demure, diffident, humble, meek, moderate, proper, reasonable, reserved, restrained, retiring, shy, simple, unassuming, unpretentious, virtuous. ANT.-arrogant, bold, conceited, forward, immodest, ostentatious, proud.

modesty, n. SYN.-constraint, control, decency, diffidence, dignity, humility, inhibition, innocence, meekness, reserve, restraint, temperance.

modification, n. SYN.-adjustment, alteration, alternation, change, substitution, transformation, variation, variety. ANT.-monotony, stability, uniformity.

modify, v. SYN.-adjust, alter, change, convert, curb, exchange, limit, mitigate, qualify, shift, substitute, temper, transfigure, transform, vary. ANT.-retain; continue, establish, preserve, settle, stabilize.

mold, v. SYN.-arrange, cast, combine, compose, constitute, construct, convert, create, devise, fashion, forge, form, frame, influence, invent, make, organize, pattern, produce, shape, transfigure, transform. ANT.-destroy, disfigure, dismantle, misshape, wreck.

molest, v. SYN.-annoy, attack, bother, chafe, disturb, frighten, inconvenience, intrude, irk, irritate, meddle, pester, scare, tease, terrify, trouble, vex. ANT.-accommodate, console, gratify, soothe.

momentary, a. SYN.-brief, concise, curt, ephemeral, fleeting, laconic, meteoric, passing, pithy, quick, short, succinct, terse, transient. ANT.-extended, lengthy, long, prolonged, protracted.

momentous, a. SYN.-consequential, critical, decisive, grave, important, influential, material, pressing, prominent, relevant, significant, weighty. ANT.-insignificant, irrelevant, mean, petty, trivial.

monarch, n. SYN.-autocrat, despot, governor, king, lord, master, prince, ruler, sovereign.

monastery, n. SYN.-abbey, cloister, convent, hermitage, nunnery, priory, refuge, retreat. monopolize

monotonous, a. SYN.-boring, burdensome, dilatory, dreary, dull, humdrum, irksome, slow, sluggish, tardy, tedious, tiresome, uninteresting, wearisome. ANT.-amusing, entertaining, exciting, interesting, quick.

monster, n. SYN.-beast, brute, chimera, demon, fiend, freak, miscreant, monstrosity, villain, wretch.

monstrous, a. SYN.-abnormal, atrocious, colossal, dreadful, enormous, fantastic, frightful, gigantic, great, grotesque, hideous, horrible, large, massive, prodigious, repulsive, stupendous, unusual.

monument, n. SYN.-commemoration,

landmark, masterpiece, memorial, remembrance, souvenir.

monumental, *a.* SYN.-classic, enormous, grand, great, immense, impressive, lofty, majestic, massive, memorable.

mood, *n.* SYN.-attitude, bent, caprice, disposition, humor, propensity, temper, temperament, tendency, whim.

mope, *v.* SYN.-brood, despair, fret, grieve, pine, sorrow, sulk.

moral, *a.* SYN.-chaste, courteous, decent, ethical, good, honorable, just, kindly, principled, proper, pure, respectable, right, righteous, scrupulous, trustworthy, truthful, virtuous. ANT.-amoral, libertine, licentious, sinful, unethical.

morale, *n.* SYN.-assurance, confidence, resolve, spirit.

morality, *n.* SYN.-chastity, decency, ethics, goodness, honesty, integrity, morals, probity, purity, rectitude, righteousness, virtue. ANT.-corruption, fault, lewdness, sin, vice.

morals, *n.* SYN.-belief, custom, dogma, mores, standards.

morbid, *a.* SYN.-aberrant, depressed, gloomy, gruesome, melancholic, morose, sullen; ailing, diseased, sickly, unhealthy.

morose, *a.* SYN.-crabbed, dejected, dour, downhearted, fretful, gloomy, glum, melancholy, moody, sad, sorrowful, sulky, surly, unhappy. ANT.-amiable, gay, joyous, merry, pleasant.

mortal, *a.* SYN.-deadly, destructive, fatal, final, killing, lethal, malignant, poisonous; ephemeral, frail, human, momentary, perishable, temporal. ANT.-lifegiving; divine, immortal.

mostly, *a.* SYN.-chiefly, customarily, especially, frequently, generally, often, particularly, regularly.

motherly, *a.* SYN.-devoted, gentle, kind, loving, maternal, protective, supporting, sympathetic, tender, watchful.

motion, *n.* SYN.-action, activity, change, gesture, move, movement, sign, stirring; plan, proposal, proposition, suggestion. ANT.-equilibrium, immobility, stability, stillness.

motivate, *v.* SYN.-arouse, begin, cause, encourage, goad, ignite, induce, instigate, prompt, start, whet.

motive, *n.* SYN.-cause, grounds, impulse, incentive, incitement, inducement, principle, purpose, reason, spur, stimulus.

motley, *a.* SYN.-assorted, diverse, heterogeneous, indiscriminate, miscellaneous, mixed, mottled, multicolored, sundry, varied, variegated. ANT.-alike, classified, homogeneous, ordered, selected.

motto, *n.* SYN.-adage, aphorism, axiom, credo, maxim, principle, rule, saying, sentiment, slogan, tenet, truism.

mount, *v.* SYN.-ascend, climb, grow, increase, rise, scale, tower; frame, secure, set. ANT.-descend, fall, sink.

mourn, *v.* SYN.-bemoan, bewail, deplore, grieve, lament, suffer, weep. ANT.-carouse, celebrate, rejoice, revel.

move, *v.* SYN.-actuate, advance, agitate, arouse, drive, excite, impel, impress, induce, influence, instigate, persuade, proceed, propel, propose, push, recommend, shift, stimulate, stir, suggest, sway, transfer. ANT.-deter, halt, rest, stay, stop.

moved, *a.* SYN.-carried, conveyed, departed, disturbed, excited, recommended, shifted, stimulated, taken, transferred.

movement, *n.* SYN.-action, activity, change, gesture, inclination, motion, move, progress, rhythm, tempo, tendency. ANT.-equilibrium, immobility, stability, stillness.

much, *a.* SYN.-abundant, ample, considerable, plentiful, profuse, substantial.

muddled, *a.* SYN.-addled, bewildered, confused, disconcerted, disordered, disorganized, indistinct, mixed, perplexed. ANT.-clear, lucid, obvious, organized, plain.

muddy, *a.* SYN.-cloudy, confused, dark, indistinct, murky, obscure.

multitude, *n.* SYN.-army, crowd, host, legion, mob, throng. ANT.-few, handful, paucity, scarcity.

mundane, *a.* SYN.-earthly, laic, lay, normal, ordinary, practical, routine, secular, temporal, worldly. ANT.-ecclesiastical, religious, spiritual, unworldly.

municipality, *n.* SYN.-borough, city, community, district, town, village.

murder, *v.* SYN.-assassinate, butcher, destroy, execute, kill, mar, massacre, ruin, slaughter, slay, spoil. ANT.-animate, protect, resuscitate, save, vivify.

murky, *a.* SYN.-cloudy, dark, dim, dusky, gloomy, obscure, shadowy.

murmur, *n.* SYN.-complaint, grumble, mumble, mutter, plaint, rumor, whimper.

murmur, *v.* SYN.-babble, complain, grouse, growl, grumble, moan, mumble, rumble, trickle, whisper.

museum, *n.* SYN.-archive, depository, gallery, library, treasury.

music, *n.* SYN.-air, consonance, harmonics, harmony, melody, song, symphony, tune.

muss, *n.* SYN.-chaos, confusion, disorder, mess, muddle, turmoil.

muss, *v.* SYN.-crumple, dishevel, disturb, jumble, ruffle, tousle.

must, *n.* SYN.-condition, contingency, obligation, provision, requisite, requirement.

muster, *v.* SYN.-accumulate, amass, assemble, collect, congregate, convene, gather, marshal, summon. ANT.-disband, disperse, distribute, scatter, separate.

mute, *a.* SYN.-inarticulate, dumb, hushed, noiseless, peaceful, quiet, silent, still, taciturn, tranquil. ANT.-clamorous, loud, noisy, raucous.

mutiny, *n.* SYN.-agitation, commotion, coup, insurrection, overthrow, rebellion, revolt, revolution, sedition, uprising.

mutual, *a.* SYN.-collective, communal, common, correlative, interchangeable, joint, public, reciprocal, shared. ANT.-dissociated, separate, unrequited, unshared.

myriad, *a.* SYN.-endless, indefinite, innumerable, multiple, variable.

mysterious, *a.* SYN.-cabalistic, cryptic, dark, dim, enigmatic, esoteric, hidden, incomprehensible, inexplicable, inscrutable, mystical, obscure, occult, recondite, secret, strange. ANT.-clear, explained, obvious, plain, simple.

mystery, *n.* SYN.-cabal, conundrum, enigma, problem, puzzle, riddle, secret. ANT.-answer, clue, key, resolution, solution.

mystical, *a.* See **mysterious.**

mystique, *n.* SYN.-attitude, characteristics, nature, style.

myth, *n.* SYN.-allegory, chronicle, fable, fiction, legend, parable, saga. ANT.-fad, history.

N

nag, *v.* SYN.-aggravate, annoy, badger, bother, disturb, harass, harry, irritate, pester, plague, provoke, tantalize, taunt, tease, torment, vex, worry. ANT.-comfort, delight, gratify, please, soothe.

naive, *a.* SYN.-artless, callow, candid, fanciful, frank, guileless, ingenuous, innocent, instinctive, natural, open, provincial, romantic, simple, spontaneous, unaffected, unsophisticated. ANT.-crafty, cunning, sophisticated, worldly.

naked, *a.* SYN.-bare, defenseless, exposed, mere, nude, open, plain, simple, stripped, unclad, uncovered, unprotected; bald, barren, unfurnished. ANT.-clothed, covered, dressed; concealed; protected.

name, *n.* SYN.-appellation, denomination, designation, epithet, style, surname, title; acclaim, character, distinction, eminence, fame, honor, note, renown, reputation, repute. ANT.-misnomer, namelessness; anonymity.

name, *v.* SYN.-address, appoint, baptize, call, characterize, christen, classify, denominate, entitle, enumerate, identify, indicate, label, mention, specify. ANT.-hint, miscall, misname.

named, *a.* SYN.-appointed, commissioned, delegated, designated, nominated, ordained, picked, selected.

nap, *n.* SYN.-catnap, doze, drowse, nod, repose, rest, sleep, slumber, snooze.

narrate, *v.* SYN.-declaim, deliver, describe, detail, enumerate, mention, recapitulate, recite, recount, rehearse, relate, repeat, tell.

narrative, *n.* SYN.-account, chronicle, description, detail, history, narration, recital, relation, story, yarn. ANT.-caricature, confusion, distortion, misrepresentation.

narrow, *a.* SYN.-close, confined, cramped, meager, slender, slim, spare, tight; bigoted, dogmatic, fanatical, illiberal, intolerant, narrow-minded, opinionated, parochial, prejudiced. ANT.-liberal, progressive, radical, tolerant.

nasty, *a.* SYN.-base, contemptible, defiled, despicable, disagreeable, disgusting, foul, gross, horrid, low, malicious, mean, nauseous, offensive, repellent, revolting, sordid, unpleasant, vile, vulgar. ANT.-admirable, amiable, attractive, decent, delightful, dignified, exalted, generous, nice, noble, pleasant.

nation, n. SYN.-commonwealth, community, country, domain, dominion, kingdom, nationality, people, populace, principality, realm, republic, state.

nationalism, n. SYN.-allegiance, chauvinism, loyalty, provincialism, patriotism.

native, a. SYN.-aboriginal, congenital, domestic, endemic, fundamental, hereditary, inborn, indigenous, inherent, innate, natural, original.

natural, a. SYN.-actual, characteristic, common, congenital, crude, fundamental, general, genetic, genuine, ingenuous, inherent, innate, intrinsic, involuntary, native, normal, original, real, regular, simple, spontaneous, tangible, typical, unaffected, unconstrained, unfeigned, usual. ANT.-affected, artificial, embellished, forced, formal.

nature, n. SYN.-character, class, description, disposition, essence, individuality, kind, qualifications, reputation, repute, sort, standing, temperament.

nautical, a. SYN.-marine, maritime, naval, ocean, oceanic.

near, a. SYN.-adjacent, approaching, beside, bordering, close, coming, contiguous, expected, imminent, impending, neighboring, nigh, proximate; dear, familiar, intimate. ANT.-distant, far, removed.

neat, a. SYN.-clear, dapper, deft, exact, nice, orderly, precise, prim, smart, spruce, systematic, taut, tidy, trim, unadulterated, undiluted. ANT.-dirty, disheveled, sloppy, slovenly, unkempt.

necessary, a. SYN.-compulsory, essential, expedient, fundamental, indispensable, inevitable, needed, obligatory, requisite, unavoidable. ANT.-accidental, casual; contingent, nonessential, optional.

necessity, n. SYN.-compulsion, demand, exigency, fundamental, need, qualification, requirement, requisite, want. ANT.-choice, freedom, luxury, option, uncertainty.

need, v. SYN.-claim, covet, crave, demand, desire, lack, require, want, wish.

needless, a. SYN.-groundless, pointless, superfluous, unnecessary, useless.

negate, v. SYN.-annul, belie, cancel, contradict, impugn, repeal, retract.

neglect, n. SYN.-carelessness, default, dereliction, disregard, failure, heedlessness, indifference, negligence, omission, oversight, slight, thoughtlessness. ANT.-attention, care, diligence, watchfulness.

neglect, v. SYN.-affront, disregard, ignore, insult, omit, overlook, procrastinate, slight. ANT.-do, guard, perform, protect, satisfy.

negligence, n. SYN.-carelessness, default, dereliction, disregard, failure, heedlessness, neglect, nonchalance, omission, oversight, slight, thoughtlessness. ANT.-attention, care, diligence, watchfulness.

negligent, a. SYN.-careless, delinquent, derelict, desultory, heedless, imprudent, inaccurate, inattentive, lax, neglectful, remiss, thoughtless, unconcerned. ANT.-accurate, careful, meticulous, precise.

negotiate, v. SYN.-arbitrate, bargain, barter, conciliate, confer, consult, intercede, mediate, parley, referee.

neighbor, n. SYN.-acquaintance, associate, friend.

neighbor, v. SYN.-abut, adjoin, border, touch, verge.

neighborhood, n. SYN.-adjacency, block, district, environs, locality, nearness, vicinity. ANT.-distance, remoteness.

neighborly, a. SYN.-affable, amicable, companionable, congenial, friendly, genial, helpful, hospitable, kindly, sociable, social. ANT.-antagonistic, cool, distant, hostile, reserved.

nerve, n. SYN.-audacity, courage, fortitude, impudence, intrepidity, mettle, presumption, resolution, spirit, temerity.

nerves, n. SYN.-anxiety, apprehension, emotion, misgivings, strain, stress, tension.

nervous, a. SYN.-excitable, impatient, irritable, moody, restless, sensitive, tense, touchy, uneasy, unstable.

network, n. SYN.-arrangement, channels, complex, labyrinth, mesh, net, structure, system, tangle, web.

neurotic, a. SYN.-deranged, disturbed, erratic, irrational, troubled, unstable.

neutral, a. SYN.-detached, disinterested, impartial, inactive, indifferent, nonpartisan, unbiased.

new, a. SYN.-contemporary, current, fashionable, fresh, late, modern, newfangled, novel, original, recent, unique. ANT.-ancient, antiquated, archaic, obsolete, old.

news, n. SYN.-account, advice, copy, description, discovery, enlightenment, information, intelligence, message, narration, publication, report, tidings.

nice, a. SYN.-agreeable, amiable, considerate, courteous, cultured, genial, good, gracious, obliging, pleasant, pleasing, refined.

niche, n. SYN.-alcove, corner, cranny, cubbyhole, nook, recess.

nick, n. SYN.-dent, gouge, indentation, mar, notch, score, scrape, scratch.

niggardly, a. SYN.-avaricious, cheap, greedy, miserly, parsimonious, penurious, stingy, tight. ANT.-altruistic, bountiful, extravagant, generous, munificent.

nimble, a. SYN.-active, agile, alert, bright, brisk, clever, flexible, lively, quick, spry, supple. ANT.-clumsy, heavy, inert, slow, sluggish.

noble, a. SYN.-courtly, cultivated, dignified, distinguished, elevated, eminent, exalted, grand, illustrious, imposing, impressive, lofty, lordly, majestic, refined, stately, virtuous. ANT.-base, low, mean, plebeian, vile.

nod, v. SYN.-acknowledge, assent, concur, consent, greet.

noise, n. SYN.-babel, clamor, cry, din, outcry, racket, row, sound, tumult, uproar. ANT.-hush, quiet, silence, stillness.

noisy, a. SYN.-cacophonous, clamorous, deafening, loud, resounding, sonorous, stentorian, vociferous ANT.-dulcet, inaudible, quiet, soft, subdued.

nonchalant, a. SYN.-aloof, apathetic, calm, casual, composed, detached, impassive, unconcerned. ANT.-active, attentive, emotional, enthusiastic.

nonconformist, n. dissenter, eccentric, maverick, radical, rebel.

nonexistent, a. SYN.-fictitious, imaginary, unreal.

nonsensical, a. SYN.-absurd, foolish, inconsistent, irrational, ludicrous, meaningless, preposterous, ridiculous, self-contradictory, silly, unreasonable. ANT.-consistent, rational, reasonable, sensible, sound.

normal, a. SYN.-common, conventional, customary, natural, ordinary, regular, steady, systematic, typical, uniform, unvaried, usual. ANT.-abnormal, erratic, exceptional, rare, unusual.

nosy, a. SYN.-curious, inquiring, inquisitive, interrogative, meddling, peeping, peering, prying, searching, snoopy. ANT.-incurious, indifferent, unconcerned, uninterested.

notable, a. SYN.-celebrated, conspicuous, distinguished, eminent, famous, notable, remarkable, striking, unusual.

note, n. SYN.-indication, mark, sign, symbol, token; annotation, comment, letter, memorandum, message, observation, remark.

noted, a. SYN.-celebrated, distinguished, eminent, famous, glorious, illustrious, renowned, well-known. ANT.-hidden, ignominious, infamous, obscure, unknown.

notice, n. SYN.-alertness, attention, cognizance, heed, mindfulness, observance, watchfulness; advertisement, announcement, circular, declaration, notification, proclamation, sign, warning. ANT.-disregard, indifference, negligence, omission, oversight.

notice, v. SYN.-attend, behold, descry, distinguish, heed, mark, note, observe, perceive, recognize, regard, remark, see. ANT.-disregard, ignore, overlook, skip.

notify, v. SYN.-advise, announce, apprise, caution, communicate, convey, disclose, enlighten, inform, herald, mention, proclaim, reveal, telephone, tell, warn, write. ANT.-conceal, delude, distract, mislead.

notion, n. SYN.-assumption, belief, fancy, idea, impression, inkling, opinion, sentiment, thought, whim.

novel, n. SYN.-allegory, fiction, narrative, romance, story, tale. ANT.-fact, history, reality, truth, verity.

novice, n. SYN.-amateur, apprentice, beginner, learner, neophyte. ANT.-adept, authority, expert, master, professional.

now, n. SYN.-immediate, present, today.

nuance, n. SYN.-difference, gradation, shade, subtly, variation.

nude, a. SYN.-bare, exposed, naked, stripped, unclad, uncovered. ANT.-clothed, covered, dressed.

nudge, v. SYN.-bump, dig, jab, poke, tap, touch.

nuisance, n. SYN.-aggravation, annoyance, bother, irritation, pest, vexation.

nullify, v. SYN.-abolish, abrogate, annul, cancel, cross out, delete, eliminate, erase, expunge, invalidate, obliterate, quash, repeal, rescind, revoke. ANT.-confirm, enact, enforce, perpetuate

numb, *a.* SYN.-anesthetized, apathetic, callous, deadened, disinterested, lethargic, unfeeling.

number, *n.* SYN.-aggregate, amount, count, extent, enumeration, estimate, measure, portion, quantity, sum, total, volume. ANT.-nothing, nothingness, zero.

numerous, *a.* SYN.-divers, manifold, many, multifarious, multitudinous, several, sundry, various. ANT.-few, infrequent, meager, scanty, scarce.

nuptials, *n.* SYN.-espousal, marriage, matrimony, union, wedding, wedlock. ANT.-celibacy, divorce, virginity.

nurture, *v.* SYN.-cherish, feed, nourish, nurse, prize, sustain, treasure, value. ANT.-abandon, disregard, neglect, reject.

nutriment, *n.* SYN.-diet, edibles, feed, food, meal, provisions, rations, repast, sustenance, viands, victuals. ANT.-drink, hunger, starvation, want.

nymph, *n.* SYN.-dryad, fairy, goddess, mermaid, sprite.

O

oath, *n.* SYN.-affidavit, declaration, deposition, pledge, promise, testimony, vow.

obdurate, *a.* SYN.-callous, hard, impenitent, indurate, insensible, insensitive, tough, unfeeling. ANT.-compassionate, sensitive, soft, tender.

obedient, *a.* SYN.-compliant, deferential, dutiful, loyal, submissive, tractable, yielding. ANT.-insubordinate, intractable, obstinate, rebellious.

obese, *a.* SYN.-chubby, corpulent, fat, paunchy, plump, portly, pudgy, rotund, stocky, stout, thickset. ANT.-gaunt, lean, slender, slim, thin.

object, *n.* SYN.-article, particular, thing; aim, design, end, goal, intention, mark, objective, purpose. ANT.-shadow, spirit, vision; consequence, result.

object, *v.* SYN.-abominate, disagree, disapprove, oppose, protest, reject, remonstrate. ANT.-acquiesce, approve, assent, comply, concur.

objection, *n.* SYN.-challenge, difference, disagreement, dissent, dissentience, protest, remonstrance. ANT.-acceptance, agreement, assent, compliance.

objective, *n.* SYN.-aim, ambition, aspiration, craving, design, desire, end, goal, hope, intent, intention, object, passion, purpose.

obligate, *v.* SYN.-bind, commit, consign, entrust, force, oblige, pledge, relegate, trust. ANT.-free, loose, neglect, release, renounce.

obligation, *n.* SYN.-accountability, bond, compulsion, contract, debt, duty, engagement, responsibility. ANT.-choice, exemption, freedom.

oblige, *v.* SYN.-coerce, compel, constrain, drive, enforce, force, impel; accommodate, aid, assist, favor, help, please. ANT.-allure, convince, exempt, induce, persuade; annoy, forsake.

obliterate, *v.* SYN.-annihilate, demolish,

destroy, devastate, eradicate, exterminate, extinguish, ravage, raze, ruin, wreck. ANT.-construct, establish, make, preserve, save.

oblivious, *a.* SYN.-blind, ignorant, preoccupied, undiscerning, unmindful, unseeing. ANT.-aware, calculated, discerning, perceiving, sensible.

obnoxious, *a.* SYN.-annoying, disagreeable, displeasing, impertinent, insulting, nasty, odious, offensive

obscene, *a.* SYN.-coarse, dirty, disgusting, filthy, gross, impure, indecent, lewd, offensive, pornographic, smutty. ANT.-decent, modest, pure, refined.

obscure, *a.* SYN.-abstruse, ambiguous, cloudy, cryptic, dark, dim, dusky, enigmatic, indistinct, mysterious, unintelligible, vague. ANT.-bright, clear, distinct, lucid.

observance, *n.* SYN.-ceremony, formality, parade, pomp, protocol, rite, ritual, solemnity; awareness, cognizance, heed, notice, observation.

observant, *a.* SYN.-alert, assiduous, attentive, aware, careful, considerate, diligent, discerning, heedful, mindful, perceptive, sensitive, thoughtful, wakeful, wary, watchful. ANT.-apathetic, careless, inattentive, indifferent, oblivious, unaware.

observe, *v.* SYN.-behold, detect, discover, examine, eye, inspect, mark, note, notice, perceive, recognize, see, view, watch; celebrate, commemorate, honor, keep, solemnize; express, mention, remark, utter. ANT.-disregard, ignore, neglect, overlook.

obsession, *n.* SYN.-compulsion, craze, fascination, fixation, mania, passion.

obsolete, *a.* SYN.-ancient, antiquated, archaic, obsolescent, old, out-of-date, venerable. ANT.-current, extant, fashionable, modern, recent.

obstacle, *n.* SYN.-bar, barrier, block, check, difficulty, hindrance, impediment, obstruction, snag. ANT.-aid, assistance, encouragement, help.

obstinate, *a.* SYN.-contumacious, determined, dogged, firm, headstrong, immovable, inflexible, intractable, obdurate, pertinacious, stubborn, uncompromising, unyielding. ANT.-amenable, compliant, docile, submissive, yielding.

obstruct, *v.* SYN.-bar, barricade, block, clog, close, delay, impede, hinder, stop. ANT.-aid, clear, further, open, promote.

obtain, *v.* SYN.-acquire, assimilate, attain, collect, earn, get, glean, gather, procure, reap, recover, secure, win. ANT.-forego, forfeit, lose, miss, surrender.

obtuse, *a.* SYN.-blunt, boring, commonplace, dense, dull, slow, stupid, tedious. ANT.-animated, lively, sharp; clear, interesting.

obvious, *a.* SYN.-apparent, clear, conspicuous, distinct, evident, manifest, palpable, patent, plain, prominent, self-evident, unmistakable, visible. ANT.-abstruse, concealed, hidden, obscure.

occupation, *n.* SYN.-business, commerce, employment, engagement, enterprise, job, profession, trade, vocation, work. ANT.-avocation, hobby, pastime.

occupy, *v.* SYN.-absorb, busy, dwell, fill, have, hold, inhabit, keep, possess, remain. ANT.-abandon, release, relinquish.

occur, *v.* SYN.-appear, arise, bechance, befall, betide, chance, happen, transpire.

occurrence, *n.* SYN.-circumstance, episode, event, happening, incident, issue.

odd, *a.* SYN.-bizarre, curious, eccentric, peculiar, quaint, queer, singular, strange, unique, unusual. ANT.-common, familiar, normal, regular, typical.

odious, *a.* SYN.-abject, base, debased, depraved, despicable, foul, ignoble, loathsome, low, mean, obscene, revolting, sordid, vicious, vile, vulgar, wicked, worthless, wretched. ANT.-attractive, decent, honorable, laudable, upright.

odor, *n.* SYN.-aroma, fetidness, fragrance, fume, incense, perfume, redolence, scent, smell, stench, stink.

offend, *v.* SYN.-annoy, antagonize, bother, insult, slight.

offense, *n.* SYN.-aggression, affront, atrocity, crime, indignity, injustice, insult, outrage, misdeed, sin, transgression, trespass, vice, wrong. ANT.-gentleness, innocence, morality, right.

offensive, *a.* SYN.-disagreeable, disgusting, distressing, dreadful, foul, horrid, invidious, nauseous, nasty, repugnant, unpleasant.

offer, *n.* SYN.-bid, overture, proposal, proposition, suggestion, tender. ANT.-acceptance, denial, rejection, withdrawal.

offer, *v.* SYN.-advance, exhibit, extend, present, proffer, propose, sacrifice, tender, volunteer. ANT.-accept, receive, reject, retain, spurn.

offering, *n.* SYN.-alms, charity, contribution, donation, gift, present, sacrifice.

office, *n.* SYN.-building, cubicle, facility, site, station, suite; berth, incumbency, job, place, position, post, rank, situation, standing, status.

often, *adv.* SYN.-commonly, frequently, generally, recurrent, repeatedly. ANT.-infrequently, occasionally, rarely, seldom, sporadically.

old, *a.* SYN.-aged, ancient, antiquated, antique, archaic, elderly, obsolete, old-fashioned, senile, superannuated, venerable. ANT.-modern, new, young, youthful.

omen, *n.* SYN.-augury, foretoken, gesture, indication, mark, portent, presage, sign, symbol, token, warning.

ominous, *a.* SYN.-dire, forbidding, foreboding, gloomy, grim, menacing, portentous, threatening.

omission, *n.* SYN.-default, deletion, failure, neglect, oversight. ANT.-attention, inclusion, insertion, notice.

omit, *v.* SYN.-cancel, delete, disregard, drop, eliminate, exclude, ignore, miss, neglect, overlook, skip. ANT.-enter, include, insert, introduce, notice.

onslaught, *n.* SYN.-aggression, assault, attack, criticism, denunciation, invasion, offense. ANT.-defense, opposition, resistance, surrender, vindication.

open, *a.* SYN.-accessible, agape, ajar,

available, candid, clear, disengaged, exposed, frank, free, honest, overt, passable, plain, public, unclosed, uncovered, unlocked, unobstructed, unoccupied, unrestricted.

open, v. SYN.-exhibit, expand, spread, unbar, unfasten, unfold, unlock, unseal. ANT.-close, conceal, hide, shut.

opening, n. SYN.-abyss, aperture, cavern, cavity, chasm, gap, gulf, hole, pore, slit, slot, void.

operate, v. SYN.-act, function, employ, interact, manage, manipulate, proceed, run, use, utilize.

operation, n. SYN.-action, agency, control, effort, enterprise, execution, handling, instrumentality, maneuver, manipulation, performance, proceeding, running, surgery, working. ANT.-cessation, inaction, inactivity, rest.

operative, a. SYN.-active, effective, serviceable, working. ANT.-dormant, inactive.

opinion, n. SYN.-belief, conviction, decision, feeling, idea, impression, judgment, notion, persuasion, sentiment, view. ANT.-fact, skepticism, misgiving, knowledge.

opinionated, a. SYN.-arrogant, authoritarian, bigoted, doctrinaire, dogmatic, domineering, magisterial, obstinate, overbearing, positive, stubborn. ANT.-fluctuating, indecisive, open-minded, questioning, skeptical.

opponent, n. SYN.-adversary, antagonist, challenger, competitor, contestant, enemy, foe, rival. ANT.-ally, comrade, confederate, teammate.

opportunity, n. SYN.-chance, contingency, freedom, fortune, happening, occasion, opening, possibility, probability. ANT.-disadvantage, hindrance, obstacle.

oppose, v. SYN.-argue, bar, combat, confront, contradict, counteract, debate, defy, deny, disapprove, hinder, mutiny, obstruct, protest, rebel, resist, thwart, withstand. ANT.-agree, cooperate, submit, succumb, support.

opposed, a. SYN.-adverse, antagonistic, contrary, hostile, opposite. ANT.-benign, favorable.

opposition, n. SYN.-conflict, contention, controversy, discord, encounter, fight, interference, struggle. ANT.-amity, concord, consonance, harmony.

oppress, v. SYN.-afflict, harass, harry, hound, persecute, plague, torment, torture, vex, worry. ANT.-aid, assist, comfort, encourage, support.

optimism, n. SYN.-anticipation, confidence, expectancy, expectation, faith, hope, trust. ANT.-despair, despondency, pessimism.

option, n. SYN.-alternative, choice, election, preference, selection.

opulence, n. SYN.-abundance, affluence, fortune, luxury, money, plenty, possessions, riches, wealth. ANT.-indigence, need, poverty, want.

oral, a. SYN.-literal, spoken, verbal, vocal. ANT.-documentary, recorded, written.

ordain, v. SYN.-appoint, cause, constitute, create, engender, fashion, form, formulate, generate, invent, make,

originate, produce. ANT.-annihilate, demolish, destroy, disband, terminate.

ordeal, n. SYN.-affliction, examination, experiment, hardship, misery, misfortune, suffering, test, trial, tribulation, trouble. ANT.-alleviation, consolation.

order, n. SYN.-arrangement, class, method, plan, rank, regularity, sequence, series, succession, system; bidding, command, decree, dictate, injunction, instruction, mandate, requirement. ANT.-confusion, disarray, disorder, irregularity; consent, license, permission.

order, v. SYN.-bid, command, conduct, direct, govern, guide, instruct, manage, regulate, rule. ANT.-misdirect, misguide.

orderly, a. SYN.-arranged, methodical, neat, organized, systematic, tidy.

ordinary, a. SYN.-accustomed, common, conventional, customary, familiar, habitual, normal, plain, regular, typical, usual, vulgar. ANT.-extraordinary, marvelous, remarkable, strange, uncommon.

organization, n. SYN.-arrangement, method, mode, order, plan, process, regularity, rule, scheme, system. ANT.-chance, chaos, confusion, disarrangement, disorder, irregularity.

organize, v. SYN.-arrange, assort, classify, devise, place, plan, prepare, regulate, sort. ANT.-confuse, disorder, disturb, jumble, scatter.

origin, n. SYN.-beginning, birth, commencement, cradle, derivation, foundation, inception, source, spring, start. ANT.-end, harvest, issue, outcome, product.

original, a. SYN.-first, initial, primary, primeval, primordial, pristine; creative, fresh, inventive, new, novel. ANT.-derivative, later, modern., subsequent, terminal; banal, plagiarized, trite.

originate, v. SYN.-arise, begin, cause, commence, create, engender, establish, fashion, form, formulate, found, generate, inaugurate, initiate, institute, invent, make, organize, originate, produce, start; appoint, constitute, ordain. ANT.-annihilate, complete, demolish, destroy, disband, end, finish, terminate.

ornament, n. SYN.-adornment, decoration, embellishment, garnish, ornamentation.

ornate, a. SYN.-adorned, embellished, flashy, gaudy, lavish, showy, stylish, tawdry, trimmed

oscillate, v. SYN.-change, fluctuate, undulate, swing, vary, waver. ANT.-adhere, persist, resolve, stick.

ostentation, n. SYN.-boasting, display, flourish, pageantry, parade, pomp, show, vaunting. ANT.-humility, modesty, reserve, unobtrusiveness.

ostracize, v. SYN.-bar, blackball, except, exclude, expel, prevent, prohibit, restrain, shut out. ANT.-accept, admit, include, welcome.

oust, v. SYN.-banish, depose, discharge, dismiss, eject, evict, expel, overthrow, remove.

outline, n. SYN.-brief, contour, deline-

ation, draft, figure, form, plan, profile, silhouette, sketch.

outrageous, a. SYN.-abominable, atrocious, disgraceful, exorbitant, heinous, infamous, notorious, scandalous, shameless, shocking.

outsider, n. SYN.-alien, foreigner, immigrant, newcomer, stranger. ANT.-acquaintance, associate, countryman, friend, neighbor.

outspoken, a. SYN.-abrupt, bluff, blunt, brusque, candid, direct, frank, impertinent, impolite, insulting, plain, rough, rude, unceremonious. ANT.-polished, polite, suave, subtle, tactful.

overcast, a. SYN.-cloudy, dark, dim, murky, shadowy. ANT.-bright, clear, distinct, limpid, sunny.

overcome, v. SYN.-beat, conquer, crush, defeat, humble, master, quell, rout, subdue, subjugate, surmount, vanquish. ANT.-capitulate, cede, lose, retreat, surrender.

overload, v. SYN.-afflict, burden, encumber, load, oppress, tax, trouble, weigh. ANT.-alleviate, console, ease, lighten, mitigate.

overlook, v. SYN.-disregard, exclude, ignore, miss, neglect, omit, pass, pass over, skip. ANT.-enter, include, insert, introduce, notice.

overseer, n. SYN.-employer, foreman, head, leader, manager, master, owner, proprietor, superintendent, supervisor. ANT.-servant, slave; amateur.

oversight, n. SYN.-error, inadvertence, inattention, mistake, neglect, omission; charge, control, inspection, management, superintendence, supervision, surveillance. ANT.-attention, care, observation, scrutiny.

overturn, v. SYN.-destroy, overcome, replace, rout, ruin, supplant, upset. ANT.-conserve, maintain, preserve, uphold.

overthrow, v. SYN.-demolish, destroy, overcome, overturn, rout, ruin, supplant, upset, vanquish. ANT.-build, conserve, construct, preserve, uphold.

overwhelmed, a. SYN.-beaten crushed, extinguished, obliterated, ravaged, swamped; affected, impressed, moved, touched.

P

pacific, a. SYN.-calm, composed, dispassionate, imperturbable, peaceful, placid, quiet, serene, still, tranquil, undisturbed, unruffled. ANT.-excited, frantic, stormy, turbulent, wild.

pacify, v. SYN.-allay, alleviate, appease, assuage, calm, compose, lull, placate, quell, quiet, relieve, satisfy, soothe, still, tranquilize. ANT.-arouse, excite, incense, inflame.

packed, a. SYN.-crammed, filled, full, gorged, replete, satiated, soaked, stuffed, tamped. ANT.-depleted, devoid, empty, vacant; insufficient, lacking, partial.

pact, n. SYN.-accordance, agreement, bargain, compact, concord, concurrence, contract, covenant, stipulation, understanding. ANT.-difference, disagreement, discord, dissension, variance.

pageant, n. SYN.-array, celebration, display, exhibition, exposition, parade.

pain, n. SYN.-ache, agony, anguish, distress, grief, pang, paroxysm, suffering, throe, twinge. ANT.-comfort, ease, relief, happiness, pleasure. solace.

painful, a. SYN.-acrimonious, biting, bitter, caustic, distasteful, galling, grievous, harsh, poignant, sardonic, severe. ANT.-delicious, mellow, pleasant, sweet.

painting, n. SYN.-illustration, landscape, likeness, panorama, picture, portrait, portrayal, rendering, representation, scene, view.

pale, a. SYN.-anemic, ashen, blanched, haggard, pallid, sickly, wan.

pamper, v. SYN.-coddle, humor, indulge, spoil.

panic, n. SYN.-alarm, apprehension, dread, fear, fright, horror, terror, trembling. ANT.-calmness, composure, serenity, tranquility.

parable, n. SYN.-allegory, anecdote, fable, legend, narrative, story, tale, yarn.

parade, n. SYN.-cavalcade, ceremony, cortege, file, pageant, procession, review, train.

paradox, n. SYN.-ambiguity, contradiction, enigma, mystery, puzzle.

paradoxical, a. SYN.-ambiguous, contradictory, curious, discrepant, illogical, incompatible, incongruous, inconsistent, ironic, irreconcilable, obscure, puzzling, strange. ANT.-compatible, congruous, consistent, correspondent.

parallel, a. SYN.-akin, alike, allied, analogous, comparable, correlative, correspondent, corresponding, equal, like, similar. ANT.-different, dissimilar, divergent, incongruous, opposed.

parched, a. SYN.-arid, burned, dehydrated, desiccated, dry, thirsty, withered. ANT.-damp, moist.

pardon, n. SYN.-absolution, acquittal, amnesty, exoneration, forgiveness, remission. ANT.-conviction, penalty, punishment, sentence.

pardon, v. SYN.-absolve, acquit, condone, excuse, forgive, overlook, release, remit. ANT.-accuse, chastise, condemn, convict, punish.

park, n. SYN.-boulevard, common, esplanade, green, lawn, plaza, preserve, promenade, reservation, square, tract.

parley, n. SYN.-chat, colloquy, conference, conversation, dialogue, discourse, discussion, encounter, interview, meeting, negotiation, talk.

part, n. SYN.-allotment, apportionment, component, division, element, fragment, ingredient, member, moiety, piece, portion, scrap, section, segment, share; character, lines, role. ANT.-entirety, whole.

part, v. SYN.-break, cleave, detach, divide, separate, sever, sunder; allot, apportion, distribute, mete, parcel, share. ANT.-combine, convene, gather, join unite.

partake, v. SYN.-appropriate, cooperate, experience, participate, receive, share.

partiality, n. SYN.-affection, bent, bias, favoritism, fondness, inclination, leaning, predisposition, preference, preju-

dice, taste, tendency. ANT.-dislike, equality, fairness, impartiality, justice, proof, reason.

participation, n. SYN.-allotment, dividend, interest, quota, part, proportion; association, communion, encouragement, fellowship, intercourse, sacrament, sharing, union. ANT.-alienation, non participation.

particle, n. SYN.-atom, bit, corpuscle, crumb, grain, iota, jot, mite, scrap, shred, smidgen, speck. ANT.-aggregate, bulk, mass, quantity.

particular, a. SYN.-characteristic, distinctive, individual, peculiar, specific; singular, unusual; circumstantial, detailed, exact, minute, specific; careful, choosy, fastidious, finicky, squeamish. ANT.-comprehensive, general, universal; ordinary; general, rough; undiscriminating.

particular, n. SYN.-circumstance, detail, feature, item, minutia, point, specification. ANT.-generality.

partisan, n. SYN.-adherent, attendant, devotee, disciple, follower, henchman, successor, supporter, votary. ANT.-chief, head, leader, master.

partner, n. SYN.-accomplice, ally, associate, attendant, cohort, colleague, companion, comrade, consort, crony, friend, mate, spouse. ANT.-adversary, enemy, stranger.

passable, a. SYN.-acceptable, admissible, average, fair, mediocre, marginal. ANT.-excellent, first-rate, worst.

passion, n. SYN.-affection, craving, desire, emotion, feeling, lust, sentiment, trepidation, turmoil. ANT.-calm, dispassion, indifference, restraint, tranquility.

passionate, a. SYN.-ardent, burning, excitable, fervent, fervid, fiery, glowing, hot, impetuous, impassioned, intense, irascible, moving, tempestuous, vehement. ANT.-apathetic, calm, cool, deliberate, quiet.

passive, a. SYN.-acquiescent, enduring, idle, inactive, inert, patient, quiet, relaxed, resigned, stoical, submissive. ANT.-active, aggressive, alert, dynamic, energetic, hostile, impatient.

pastime, n. SYN.-amusement, avocation, contest, diversion, fun, game, hobby match, merriment, play, recreation, sport. ANT.-business drudgery, hardship, labor, work.

patent, a. SYN.-apparent, clear, conspicuous, evident, indubitable, manifest, obvious, open, overt, unmistakable. ANT.-concealed, covert, hidden, obscure.

path, n. SYN.-avenue, channel, course, passage, road, route, street, thoroughfare, track, trail, walk, way.

pathetic, a. SYN.-affecting, moving, piteous, pitiable, poignant, sad, touching. ANT.-comical, funny, ludicrous.

patience, n. SYN.-composure, endurance, forbearance, fortitude, long-suffering, perseverance, resignation. ANT.-impatience, nervousness, restlessness.

patient, a. SYN.-composed, forbearing, indulgent, long-suffering, passive, resigned, stoical, uncomplaining. ANT.-

chafing, clamorous, high-strung, hysterical, turbulent.

patron, n. SYN.-advocate, ally, backer, benefactor, champion, friend, helper, protector.

patronizing, a. SYN.-condescending, contemptuous, disdainful, disparaging, egotistic, overbearing, scornful.

pause, v. SYN.-delay, deliberate, demur, doubt, falter, hesitate, interrupt, reflect, rest, suspend, vacillate, waver. ANT.-continue, decide, persevere, proceed.

pay, n. SYN.-allowance, compensation, consideration, earnings, fee, payment, proceeds, recompense, return, salary, stipend, wages. ANT.-gift, gratuity, present.

peace, n. SYN.-calm, calmness, hush, quiescence, quiet, quietude, repose, serenity, silence, stillness, tranquility; cease fire, disarmament, treaty, truce. ANT.-agitation, disturbance, excitement, noise, tumult; hostility, war.

peaceful, a. SYN.-calm, gentle, mild, pacific, placid, quiet, serene, still, tranquil, undisturbed. ANT.-agitated, disturbed, noisy, turbulent, violent.

peak, n. SYN.-acme, apex, climax, consummation, crown, culmination, height, summit, top, zenith. ANT.-anticlimax, base, depth, floor.

peculiar, a. SYN.-characteristic, distinctive, eccentric, exceptional, extraordinary, individual, odd, particular, rare, singular, special, strange, striking, unusual. ANT.-common, general, normal, ordinary.

peculiarity, n. SYN.-attribute, characteristic, feature, mark, property, quality, trait.

pedantic, a. SYN.-academic, bookish, erudite, formal, learned, scholarly, scholastic, theoretical. ANT.-commonsense, ignorant, practical, simple.

peevish, a. SYN.-fractious, fretful, ill-natured, ill-tempered, irritable, petulant, snappish, testy, touchy, waspish. ANT.-affable, genial, good-natured, good-tempered, pleasant.

penalty, n. SYN.-chastisement, fine, forfeiture, punishment, retribution; disadvantage, handicap. ANT.-compensation, pardon, remuneration, reward.

penance, n. SYN.-amends, atonement, compensation, expiation, mortification, purgation, reparation, repentance, restitution, suffering.

penetrating, a. SYN.-abstruse, deep, discerning, perspicacious, profound, recondite, solemn. ANT.-shallow, slight, superficial, trivial.

penitent, a. SYN.-apologetic, contrite, regretful, remorseful, repentant, sorrowful, sorry. ANT.-obdurate, remorseless.

pensive, a. SYN.-contemplative, dreamy, introspective, meditative, reflective, thoughtful. ANT.-heedless, inconsiderate, precipitous, rash, thoughtless.

people, n. SYN.-clan, community, folk, humanity, humankind, mankind, masses, multitude, nation, populace, proletariat, public, rabble, race, tribe.

perceive, v. SYN.-apprehend, comprehend, conceive, discern, note, notice, observe, recognize, see, understand. ANT.-ignore, miss, overlook.

perceptible, *a.* SYN.-appreciable, apprehensible, discernible, measurable, practical, reasonable, sensible, understandable. ANT.-absurd, impalpable, imperceptible, stupid.

perception, *n.* SYN.-apprehension, cognizance, comprehension, conception, discernment, insight, understanding. ANT.-ignorance, insensibility, misapprehension, misconception.

perceptive, *a.* SYN.-alert, astute, aware, cognizant, conscious, discerning, keen, mindful, observant, sensitive, shrewd, wise. ANT.-oblivious, unaware.

perfect, *a.* SYN.-absolute, blameless, complete, consummate, downright, entire, excellent, faultless, finished, full, holy, ideal, immaculate, pure, sinless, superlative, supreme, unqualified, utter, whole. ANT.-blemished, defective, deficient, faulty, imperfect, incomplete, lacking.

perfection, *n.* SYN.-accuracy, completion, consummation, fulfillment, ideal, paragon, precision, realization, standard, ultimate.

perform, *v.* SYN.-accomplish, achieve, act, complete, discharge, do, entertain, execute, finish, fulfill, impersonate, play, pretend, render, transact.

performance, *n.* SYN.-accomplishment, act, demonstration, entertainment, exhibition, play, production, show, spectacle.

perfunctory, *a.* SYN.-artificial, careless, cursory, dull, mechanical, stiff. ANT.-easy, heartfelt, natural, unrestrained.

peril, *n.* SYN.-danger, hazard, jeopardy, risk. ANT.-defense, immunity, protection, safety.

perilous, *a.* SYN.-critical, dangerous, hazardous, insecure, menacing, precarious, risky, threatening, unsafe. ANT.-firm, protected, safe, secure.

period, *n.* SYN.-age, date, duration, epoch, era, interim, season, span, spell, term, time.

periphery, *n.* SYN.-border, boundary, extremity, frontier, limit, outpost, perimeter.

perish, *v.* SYN.-cease, decay, decease, depart, die, expire. ANT.-begin, flourish, grow, live, survive.

permanent, *a.* SYN.-abiding, changeless, constant, durable, enduring, fixed, indestructible, lasting, stable, unchangeable. ANT.-ephemeral, temporary, transient, transitory, unstable.

permeate, *v.* SYN.-fill, infiltrate, penetrate, pervade, run through, saturate.

permissible, *a.* SYN.-admissible, allowable, fair, probable, tolerable, warranted. ANT.-inadmissible, irrelevant, unsuitable.

permission, *n.* SYN.-approval, authority, authorization, consent, grace, grant, leave, liberty, license, permit, sanction. ANT.-denial, opposition, prohibition, refusal.

permit, *v.* SYN.-allow, authorize, give, grant, indulge, let, sanction, suffer, tolerate, yield. ANT.-forbid, object, protest, refuse, resist.

permitted, *a.* SYN.-allowed, authorized, granted, legalized, licensed, sanctioned.

perpetrate, *v.* SYN.-commit, do, execute, perform. ANT.-fail, miscarry, neglect.

perpetual, *a.* SYN.-ceaseless, continual, endless, eternal, everlasting, infinite, timeless, undying. ANT.-ephemeral, finite, mortal, temporal, transient.

perpetually, *adv.* SYN.-always, constantly, continually, eternally, ever, evermore, forever, incessantly, unceasingly. ANT.-fitfully, never, occasionally, rarely, sometimes.

perplex, *v.* SYN.-bewilder, confound, confuse, dumfound, mystify, nonplus, puzzle. ANT.-clarify, explain, illumine, instruct, solve.

perplexed, *a.* SYN.-bewildered, confused, deranged, disconcerted, disordered, disorganized, indistinct, mixed, muddled. ANT.-clear, lucid, obvious, organized, plain.

perplexing, *a.* SYN.-complex, complicated, intricate, involved. ANT.-plain, simple, uncompounded.

persecute, *v.* SYN.-afflict, annoy, badger, harass, harry, hound, oppress, pester, plague, torment, torture, vex, worry. ANT.-aid, assist, comfort, encourage, support.

persevere, *v.* SYN.-abide, continue, endure, last, press, persist, strive. ANT.-desist, discontinue, vacillate, waver.

perseverance, *n.* SYN.-constancy, determination, fortitude, industry, persistence, persistency, pertinacity, resolution, steadfastness, tenacity. ANT.-cessation, idleness, laziness, rest, sloth.

persist, *v.* SYN.-abide, continue, endure, last, persevere, remain. ANT.-cease, desist, discontinue, vacillate, waver.

persistence, *n.* SYN.-constancy, endurance, grit, perseverance, pluck, resolve, tenacity,

persistent, a, SYN.-constant, dogged, enduring, fixed, immovable, indefatigable, lasting, obstinate, persevering, perverse, steady, stubborn. ANT.-hesitant, unsure, vacillating, wavering.

persuade, *v.* SYN.-allure, coax, convince, entice, exhort, incite, induce, influence, prevail upon, urge, win over. ANT.-coerce, compel, deter, dissuade, restrain.

persuasion, *n.* SYN.-belief, conviction, decision, feeling, idea, impression, judgment, notion, opinion, sentiment, view. ANT.-fact, skepticism, misgiving, knowledge.

pertain, *v.* SYN.-apply, bear, concern, include, involve, refer, relate.

pertinent, *a.* SYN.-applicable, apposite, appropriate, apropos, apt, fit, germane, material, related, relating, relevant. ANT.-alien, extraneous, foreign, unrelated.

perturb, *v.* SYN.-annoy, agitate, bewilder, bother, confound, disturb, irritate, perplex, pester, worry.

pervade, *v.* SYN.-diffuse, fill, infiltrate, penetrate, permeate, run through, saturate.

perverse, *a.* SYN.-contrary, disobedient, forward, fractious, intractable, obstinate, peevish, perverted, petulant, sinful, stubborn, ungovernable, untoward,

wicked. ANT.-agreeable, docile, obliging, tractable.

perverted, *a.* SYN.-corrupt, degenerate, depraved, deviated, distorted, kinky, lascivious, sick, twisted, unnatural, warped.

pessimistic, *a.* SYN.-cynical, despairing, fatalistic, foreboding, gloomy, hopeless, morbid, morose, sullen, troubled.

pester, *v.* SYN.-annoy, bother, chafe, disturb, irk, irritate, tease, trouble, vex. ANT.-accommodate, console, gratify, soothe.

petition, *n.* SYN.-appeal, entreaty, invocation, plea, prayer, request, suit, supplication.

petty, *a.* SYN.-frivolous, insignificant, paltry, small, trifling, trivial, unimportant. ANT.-important, momentous, serious, weighty.

petulant, *a.* SYN.-fretful, irritable, peevish, testy, touchy. ANT.-affable, genial, good-natured, good-tempered, pleasant.

philanthropy, *n.* SYN.-altruism, beneficence, benevolence, charity, generosity, humanity, kindness, liberality, magnanimity. ANT.-malevolence, selfishness, unkindness.

philosophic, *a.* SYN.-pensive, profound, rational, reflective, thoughtful.

phlegmatic, *a.* SYN.-cold, cool, frigid, passionless, stoical, unfeeling. ANT.-hot, torrid; ardent, passionate.

phony, *a.* SYN.-affected, artificial, assumed, bogus, counterfeit, ersatz, fake, feigned, fictitious, sham, spurious, synthetic, unreal. ANT.-genuine, natural, real, true.

phrase, *n.* SYN.-clause, excerpt, expression, idiom, maxim, slogan, term, word.

physical, *a.* SYN.-bodily, carnal, corporal, corporeal, material, natural, somatic, tangible, visible. ANT.-mental, spiritual.

pick, *v.* SYN.-accumulate, acquire, choose, collect, criticize, cull, get, elect, opt, pluck, reap, select. ANT.-refuse, reject.

picture, *n.* SYN.-appearance, cinema, drawing, effigy, engraving, etching, film, illustration, image, landscape, likeness, painting, panorama, photograph, portrait, portrayal, print, rendering, representation, resemblance, scene, sketch, view.

piece, *n.* SYN.-amount, bit, fraction, fragment, morsel, part, portion, scrap, section, share. ANT.-all, entirety, sum, total, whole.

pigment, *n.* SYN.-color, dye, hue, paint, shade, stain, tincture, tinge, tint. ANT.-achromatism, paleness, transparency.

pinnacle, *n.* SYN.-apex, crest, crown, head, summit, top, zenith; ornament, steeple, turret. ANT.-base, bottom, foot, foundation.

pious, *a.* SYN.-blessed, consecrated, devout, divine, hallowed, holy, religious, sacred, saintly, spiritual. ANT.-evil, profane, sacrilegious, secular, worldly.

pitch, *v.* SYN.-cast, fling, hurl, propel, throw, thrust, toss. ANT.-draw, haul, hold, pull, retain.

pitfall, *n.* SYN.-ambush, snare, stratagem, trap, trick, wile.

pitiable, *a.* SYN.-contemptible, insignificant, pathetic, piteous, poignant, sad. ANT.-comical, funny, ludicrous.

pitiful, *a.* SYN.-afflicted, depressing, dismal, distressed, miserable, mournful, pathetic, sorrowful, suffering, tearful, touching.

pity, *n.* SYN.-charity, commiseration, compassion, condolence, mercy, understanding, sympathy. ANT.-brutality, cruelty, hardness, inhumanity, ruthlessness.

place, *v.* SYN.-arrange, deposit, dispose, lay, locate, put, set. ANT.-disarrange, disturb, mislay, misplace, remove.

placid, *a.* SYN.-calm, composed, dispassionate, imperturbable, pacific, peaceful, quiet, serene, still, tranquil, undisturbed, unruffled. ANT.-excited, frantic, stormy, turbulent, wild.

plain, *a.* SYN.-even, flat, level, smooth; apparent, clear, distinct, evident, manifest, obvious, palpable, visible; candid, frank, modest, open, simple, sincere, unpretentious; absolute, unqualified. ANT.-abrupt, broken, rough, undulatory, uneven; abstruse, ambiguous, enigmatical, obscure; adorned, embellished, feigned, insincere.

plan, *n.* SYN.-delineation, design, draft, drawing, method, outline, plat, plot, scheme, sketch; intent, intention, objective, purpose, system. ANT.-result; accident, chance, confusion, disorder.

plan, *v.* SYN.-contrive, delineate, design, devise, intend, outline, plot, prepare, project, scheme, sketch.

plausible, *a.* SYN.-believable, credible, feasible, possible, practicable, probable, reasonable. ANT.-impossible, impracticable, visionary.

play, *n.* SYN.-amusement, diversion, entertainment, fun, game, pastime, recreation, romp, sport. ANT.-boredom, labor, toil, work.

play, *v.* SYN.-caper, frolic, gamble, gambol, revel, romp, sport, stake, toy, wager; execute, perform; act, impersonate, pretend.

plea, *n.* SYN.-appeal, entreaty, invocation, overture, petition, prayer, request, suit, supplication.

plead, *v.* SYN.-appeal, ask, beg, beseech, entreat, implore, petition, supplicate; argue, defend, discuss, rejoin. ANT.-deny, deprecate, refuse.

pleasant, *a.* SYN.-acceptable, agreeable, amiable, charming, gratifying, pleasing, pleasurable, suitable, welcome. ANT.-disagreeable, obnoxious, offensive, unpleasant.

please, *v.* SYN.-appease, gratify, satisfy, suffice. ANT.-annoy, displease, dissatisfy.

pleasing, *a.* SYN.-agreeable, delightful, engaging, gentle, honeyed, luscious, mellifluous, melodious, saccharine, sugary, sweet, winning. ANT.-acrid, bitter, offensive, repulsive, sour.

pleasure, *n.* SYN.-amusement, comfort, delight, enjoyment, felicity, gladness, gratification, happiness, joy. ANT.-affliction, pain, suffering, trouble, vexation.

pledge, *n.* SYN.-agreement, assurance, assuredness, certainty, contract. con-

viction, guarantee, oath, pact, security, surety, promise, word, vow; assertion, declaration, statement.

pledge, *v.* SYN.-consign, entrust, relegate, trust; bind, commit, guarantee, obligate, promise, swear, vouch, vow. ANT.-fail, miscarry, neglect; mistrust, release, renounce; free, loose.

plentiful, *a.* SYN.-abundant, ample, bounteous, bountiful, copious, luxurious, plenteous, profuse, replete. ANT.-deficient, insufficient, rare, scanty, scarce.

pliable, *a.* SYN.-compliant, ductile, elastic, flexible, limber, lithe, pliant, resilient, supple, tractable. ANT.-brittle, hard, rigid, stiff, unbending.

plight, *n.* SYN.-danger, difficulty, dilemma, fix, peril, predicament, scrape, situation, strait. ANT.-calmness, comfort, ease, satisfaction.

plot, *n.* SYN.-cabal, conspiracy, design, intrigue, machination, plan, scheme, stratagem; chart, diagram, graph, sketch.

plotting, *n.* SYN.-artfulness, contrivance, cunning, design, planning, scheming. ANT.-candor, sincerity.

ploy, *n.* SYN.-antic, artifice, deception, device, fraud, guile, hoax, imposture, ruse, stratagem, stunt, subterfuge, trick, wile. ANT.-candor, exposure, honesty, openness, sincerity.

plump, *a.* SYN.-chubby, corpulent, fat, obese, paunchy, portly, pudgy, rotund, stocky, stout, thickset. ANT.-gaunt, lean, slender, slim, thin.

poignant, *a.* SYN.-affecting, heart-rending, impressive, moving, pitiable, sad, tender, touching. ANT.-animated, enlivening, exhilarating, removed.

point, *v.* SYN.-aim, direct, indicate, level, train. ANT.-deceive, distract, misdirect, misguide.

pointed, *a.* SYN.-acute, cutting, keen, sharp; acrid, biting, bitter, pungent; penetrating, piercing, severe, shrill. ANT.-bland, blunt, gentle.

poise, *n.* SYN.-balance, calmness, carriage, composure, equanimity, equilibrium, self-possession. ANT.-agitation, anger, excitement, rage, turbulence.

poise, *v.* SYN.-balance, dangle, hang, hover, ready, suspend.

poison, *v.* SYN.-contaminate, corrupt, infect, pollute, taint. ANT.-disinfect, purify.

polished, *a.* SYN.-courtly, cultivated, cultured, diplomatic, genteel, glib, polite, refined, suave, urbane, well-bred; glossy, shiny, sleek, slick, smooth. ANT.-boorish, bluff, coarse, crude, rude, vulgar; harsh, rough, rugged.

polite, *a.* SYN.-accomplished, civil, considerate, courteous, cultivated, genteel, refined, urbane, well-bred, well-mannered. ANT.-boorish, impertinent, rude, uncivil, uncouth.

pollute, *v.* SYN.-befoul, contaminate, corrupt, defile, infect, poison, sully, taint. ANT.-disinfect, purify.

pomp, *n.* SYN.-affectation, display, flourish, ostentation, pageantry, parade, show, splendor, vaunting, vanity. ANT.-humility, modesty, reserve, unobtru-

siveness.

pompous, *a.* SYN.-arrogant, condescending, contemptuous, haughty, proud, superior.

ponder, *v.* SYN.-cogitate, contemplate, deliberate, meditate, muse, reflect, study, think, weigh.

poor, *a.* SYN.-destitute, impecunious, indigent, needy, penniless, poverty-stricken; bad, deficient, inferior, scanty, shabby, unfavorable, wrong. ANT.-affluent, opulent, rich, wealthy; ample, good, right, sufficient.

popular, *a.* SYN.-common, familiar, favorite, general, prevailing, prevalent. ANT.-esoteric, exclusive, restricted, unpopular.

portal, *n.* SYN.-doorway, entrance, entry, gate, inlet, opening. ANT.-departure, exit.

portion, *n.* SYN.-bit, division, fragment, parcel, part, piece, section, segment, share. ANT.-bulk, whole.

portray, *v.* SYN.-delineate, depict, describe, draw, paint, picture, represent, sketch. ANT.-caricature, misrepresent, suggest.

position, *n.* SYN.-locality, place, site, situation, station; caste, condition, place, rank, standing, status; berth, incumbency, job, office, post, situation; attitude, bearing, pose, posture.

positive, *a.* SYN.-assured, certain, definite, fixed, indubitable, inevitable, secure, sure, undeniable, unquestionable. ANT.-doubtful, probable, questionable, uncertain.

possess, *v.* SYN.-control, have, hold, occupy, own; affect, obtain, seize. ANT.-abandon, lose, renounce, surrender.

possessions, *n.* SYN.-belongings, effects, estate, goods, property, stock, wares, wealth. ANT.-deprivation, destitution, poverty, privation, want.

possible, *a.* SYN.-credible, feasible, likely, plausible, practicable, practical, probable. ANT.-impossible, impracticable, visionary.

possibility, *n.* SYN.-chance, contingency, opening, opportunity. ANT.-disadvantage, hindrance, obstacle.

post, *n.* SYN.-locality, place, site, situation, station; berth, incumbency, job, office, position, situation.

postpone, *v.* SYN.-defer, delay, interrupt, pause, stay, suspend. ANT.-continue, maintain, persist, proceed.

postulate, *n.* SYN.-adage, aphorism, apothegm, axiom, byword, fundamental, maxim, principle, proverb, saw, saying, theorem, truism.

posture, *n.* SYN.-attitude, carriage, demeanor, presence, pose, stance.

potency, *n.* SYN.-ability, capability, competency, effectiveness, efficacy, efficiency, power, strength. ANT.-inability, ineptitude, wastefulness.

pound, *v.* SYN.-beat, belabor, buffet, conquer, dash, defeat, hit, knock, overpower, overthrow, pummel, punch, rout, smite, strike, subdue, thrash, thump, vanquish; palpitate, pulsate, pulse, throb. ANT.-defend, shield, stroke, fail, surrender.

poverty, *n.* SYN.-destitution, indigence,

necessity, need, penury, privation, want. ANT.-abundance, affluence, plenty, riches, wealth.

power, *n.* SYN.-ability, authority, capability, cogency, command, competency, control, dominion, energy, faculty, force, influence, might, predominance, potency, sovereignty, strength, sway, talent, validity, vigor. ANT.-debility, disablement, fatigue, impotence, incapacity, inaptitude, weakness.

powerful, *a.* SYN.-athletic, cogent, concentrated, firm, forceful, forcible, fortified, hale, hardy, impregnable, mighty, potent, robust, sinewy, strong, sturdy, tough. ANT.-brittle, delicate, feeble, fragile, insipid.

practical, *a.* SYN.-aware, cognizant, discreet, intelligent, judicious, prudent, reasonable, sagacious, sage, sensible, sober, sound, wise. ANT.-absurd, impalpable, imperceptible, stupid, unaware.

practice, *n.* SYN.-custom, drill, exercise, habit, manner, training, usage, use, wont. ANT.-disuse, idleness, inexperience, speculation, theory.

pragmatic, *a.* SYN.-intelligent, logical, practical, rational, realistic, sensible, utilitarian.

praise, *n.* SYN.-acclaim, adulation, applause, approval, commendation, compliment, eulogy, flattery, laudation. ANT.-abuse, censure, condemnation, disapproval.

praise, *v.* SYN.-acclaim, applaud, commend, compliment, eulogize, extol, flatter, glorify, laud. ANT.-censure, condemn, criticize, disparage, reprove.

prayer, *n.* SYN.-appeal, entreaty, invocation, petition, plea, request, suit, supplication.

preach, *v.* SYN.-discourse, exhort, harangue, lecture, moralize, sermonize, teach.

preamble, *n.* SYN.-beginning, forward, introduction, preface, prelude, prologue, start. ANT.-completion, conclusion, end, epilogue, finale.

precarious, *a.* SYN.-critical, dangerous, hazardous, insecure, menacing, perilous, risky, threatening, unsafe. ANT.-firm, protected, safe, secure.

precept, *n.* SYN.-belief, creed, doctrine, dogma, teaching, tenet. ANT.-conduct, deed, performance, practice.

precious, *a.* SYN.-costly, expensive, valuable; dear, esteemed; profitable. ANT.-cheap, mean, poor; trashy, worthless.

precise, *a.* SYN.-accurate, ceremonious, correct, definite, distinct, exact, formal, prim, rigid, stiff, strict, unequivocal. ANT.-careless, easy, erroneous, informal, loose, rough, vague.

preclude, *v.* SYN.-bar, ban eliminate, forestall, hinder, impede, obstruct, obviate, omit, prevent, thwart. ANT.-aid, encourage, expedite, permit, promote.

preclusion, *n.* SYN.-exception, exclusion, omission. ANT.-inclusion.

predicament, *n.* SYN.-condition, difficulty, dilemma, fix, impasse, plight, scrape, situation, strait. ANT.-calmness, comfort, ease, satisfaction.

predilection, *n.* SYN.-affection, attach-ment, bent, bias, desire, disposition, inclination, leaning, penchant, preference. ANT.-apathy, aversion, distaste, nonchalance, repugnance.

predominant, *a.* SYN.-cardinal, chief, foremost, highest, leading, main, overwhelming, paramount, principal, supreme. ANT.-auxiliary, minor, subordinate, subsidiary, supplemental.

preference, *n.* SYN.-alternative, choice, disposition, election, favorite, fondness, liking, option, partiality, predilection, selection.

prejudice, *n.* SYN.-bias, bigotry, disposition, partiality, preconception, predisposition, slant. ANT.-fairness, impartiality, proof, reason.

prejudiced, *a.* SYN.-bigoted, disposed, dogmatic, fanatical, illiberal, intolerant, narrow-minded. ANT.-liberal, progressive, radical, tolerant.

premeditated, *a.* SYN.-contemplated, deliberate, designed, intended, intentional, studied. ANT.-accidental, fortuitous.

premeditation, *n.* SYN.-deliberation, forecast, forethought, intention. ANT.-accident, extemporization, hazard, impromptu.

premise, *n.* SYN.-assumption, base, basis, foundation, ground, groundwork, postulate, presumption, presupposition, principle, support, underpinning. ANT.-derivative, implication, superstructure, trimming.

preoccupied, *a.* SYN.-abroad, absent, absent-minded, abstracted, away, departed, distracted, inattentive. ANT.-attending, present; attentive, watchful.

prepare, *v.* SYN.-concoct, condition, contrive, equip, fit, furnish, get ready, make ready, predispose, provide, qualify, ready.

preposterous, *a.* SYN.-absurd, foolish, inconsistent, irrational, nonsensical, ridiculous, self-contradictory, silly, unreasonable. ANT.-consistent, rational, reasonable, sensible, sound.

prerogative, *n.* SYN.-authority, grant, liberty, license, privilege, right. ANT.-encroachment, injustice, violation, wrong.

present, *n.* SYN.-boon, donation, gift, grant, gratuity, largess; instant, moment, now, today.

present, *v.* SYN.-advance, exhibit, extend, introduce, offer, proffer, propose, sacrifice, submit, tender, volunteer. ANT.-accept, receive, reject, retain, spurn.

presentation, *n.* SYN.-award. contribution, donation, gift, grant, present, remembrance; demonstration, display, exhibition, exposition, performance, show, unveiling.

presented, *a.* SYN.-bestowed, conferred, given.

preserve, *v.* SYN.-conserve, defend, guard, keep, maintain, protect, rescue, safeguard, save, secure, spare, uphold. ANT.-abandon, abolish, destroy, impair, injure.

preside, *v.* SYN.-arbitrate, chair, control, direct, lead, moderate, referee, regulate, umpire.

press, *v.* SYN.-crowd, drive, force, impel, propel, push, shove; hasten, pressure, promote, urge. ANT.-drag, falter, halt, pull, retreat; ignore, oppose.

pressing, *a.* SYN.-cogent, compelling, critical, crucial, exigent, impelling, imperative, important, importunate, insistent, instant, necessary, serious, urgent. ANT.-insignificant, petty, trifling, trivial, unimportant.

pressure, *n.* SYN.-compression, force; constraint, influence; compulsion, exigency, hurry, press, stress, urgency. ANT.-ease, lenience, recreation, relaxation.

prestige, *n.* SYN.-fame, name, renown, reputation, standing, status.

presume, *v.* SYN.-apprehend, assume, believe, conjecture, deduce, guess, imagine, speculate, suppose, surmise, think. ANT.-ascertain, conclude, demonstrate, know, prove.

presumption, *n.* SYN.-audacity, boldness, effrontery, impertinence, impudence, insolence, rudeness, sauciness. ANT.-diffidence, politeness, subserviency, truckling.

pretend, *v.* SYN.-act, affect, assume, feign, imitate, profess, sham, simulate. ANT.-display, exhibit, expose, reveal.

pretense, *n.* SYN.-affectation, cloak, disguise, excuse, garb, mask, pretension, pretext, semblance, show, simulation, subterfuge. ANT.-actuality, fact, reality, sincerity, truth.

pretty, *a.* SYN.-attractive, beauteous, beautiful, charming, comely, elegant, fair, fine, handsome, lovely. ANT.-foul, hideous, homely, repulsive, unsightly.

prevalent, *a.* SYN.-common, customary, efficacious, familiar, frequent, general, ordinary, popular, regular, superior, universal, usual. ANT.-exceptional, extraordinary, odd, rare, scarce, singular.

prevent, *v.* SYN.-arrest, block, forestall, frustrate, hinder, impede, obstruct, obviate, preclude, stop, thwart. ANT.-aid, encourage, expedite, permit, promote.

previous, *a.* SYN.-aforesaid, antecedent, anterior, foregoing, former, preceding, prior. ANT.-consequent, following, later, subsequent, succeeding.

price, *n.* SYN.-charge, cost, expenditure, expense, payment, value, worth.

pride, *n.* SYN.-arrogance, conceit, haughtiness, self-esteem, self-respect, superciliousness, vainglory, vanity. ANT.-humility, lowliness, meekness, modesty, shame.

prim, *a.* SYN.-decorous, demur, formal, orderly, precise, stiff, tidy, trim.

primary, *a.* SYN.-beginning, earliest, first, initial, original, prime, primeval, primitive, pristine; chief, foremost. ANT.-hindmost, last, latest; least, subordinate.

prime, *a.* SYN.-beginning, best, chief, choice, earliest, first, fundamental, original, primary, principal, top.

primitive, *a.* SYN.-aboriginal, ancient, antiquated, crude, early, old, primary, primeval, primordial, pristine, raw, rough, simple, undeveloped. ANT.-civilized, late, modern, modish, sophisticated.

princely, *a.* SYN.-abundant, ample, generous, grand, lavish, liberal, luxurious, noble, profuse, regal, stately, sumptuous.

principal, *a.* SYN.-cardinal, chief, essential, first, foremost, highest, leading, main, paramount, predominant, supreme. ANT.-auxiliary, minor, subordinate, subsidiary, supplemental.

principal, *n.* SYN.-chief, commander, dean, director, head, leader, master; asset, capital, equipment, property. ANT.-follower, subordinate, underling; base, bottom, foot.

principle, *n.* SYN.-axiom, canon, formula, guide, law, maxim, method, order, precept, regulation, rule, standard, statute, system. ANT.-chance, deviation, exception, hazard, irregularity.

prior, *a.* SYN.-aforesaid, foregoing, former, past, preceding, previous. ANT.-consequent, following, later, subsequent, succeeding.

privacy, *n.* SYN.-isolation, retreat, seclusion, solitude, withdrawal.

private, *a.* SYN.-clandestine, concealed, confidential, covert, exclusive, hidden, isolated, latent, masked, personal, remote, secret, separate, special, surreptitious, unknown. ANT.-conspicuous, disclosed, exposed, known, obvious.

privilege, *n.* SYN.-advantage, exemption, favor, immunity, liberty, license, prerogative, right, sanction. ANT.-disallowance, inhibition, prohibition, restriction.

prize, *n.* SYN.-accolade, award, bonus, booty, bounty, compensation, honor, plunder, premium, recompense, remuneration, reward. ANT.-assessment, charge, earnings, punishment, wages.

prize, *v.* SYN.-appreciate, cherish, esteem, treasure, value.

probable, *a.* SYN.-conceivable, feasible, inclined, liable, likely, possible, prone.

probe, *v.* SYN-ask, explore, extend, inquire, investigate, penetrate, query, question, reach, search, seek, stretch.

problem, *n.* SYN.-difficulty, dilemma, enigma, issue, obstacle, predicament, puzzle, riddle.

procedure, *n.* SYN.-course, deed, fashion, form, habit, maneuver, manner, method, mode, operation, plan, practice, process, style, system, way.

proceed, *v.* SYN.-advance, arise, continue, emanate, further, improve, issue, progress, rise, thrive. ANT.-hinder, oppose, retard, retreat, withhold.

proceeding, *n.* SYN.-affair, business, deal, deed, gathering, meeting, negotiation, occurrence, transaction.

procession, *n.* SYN.-cavalcade, cortege, file, parade, retinue, sequence, succession, train.

proclaim, *v.* SYN.-affirm, announce, assert, aver, broadcast, declare, express, make known, profess, promulgate, protest, state, tell. ANT.-conceal, repress, suppress, withhold.

procure, *v.* SYN.-acquire, attain, buy, earn, gain, get, obtain, purchase, secure. ANT.-dispose of, sell, vend.

prodigal, *a.* SYN.-abundant, bountiful, copious, extravagant, lavish, plentiful, profligate, profuse, reckless, wasteful.

prodigal, *n.* SYN.-carouser, playboy, spendthrift, wastrel

prodigious, *a.* SYN.-amazing, astonishing, astounding, enormous, huge, immense, marvelous, monstrous, monumental, remarkable, stupendous, vast. ANT.-commonplace, insignificant, small.

prodigy, *n.* SYN.-curiosity, marvel, spectacle, wonder.

produce, *n.* SYN.-crop, fruit, harvest, proceeds, product, reaping, result, store, vegetables, yield.

produce, *v.* SYN.-bear, breed, conceive, exhibit, fabricate, fashion, generate, hatch, make, manufacture, procreate, show, supply, yield; accomplish, cause, effect, occasion, originate. ANT.-consume, destroy, reduce, waste; conceal, hide.

productive, *a.* SYN.-bountiful, fecund, fertile, fruitful, luxuriant, plenteous, prolific, rich, teeming. ANT.-barren, impotent, sterile, unproductive.

profane, *v.* SYN.-debauch, defile, deflower, desecrate, dishonor, infringe, invade, pollute, ravish, transgress, violate.

profess, *v.* SYN.-affirm, announce, assert, aver, broadcast, declare, express, make known, proclaim, promulgate, protest, state, tell. ANT.-conceal, repress, suppress, withhold.

profession, *n.* SYN.-avocation, business, calling, career, employment, occupation, vocation, work; allegation, assertion, claim, contention, declaration, statement, vow.

professional, *a.* SYN.-adept, competent, efficient, expert, learned, licensed, proficient, skilled, trained.

proficient, *a.* SYN.-able, accomplished, adept, clever, competent, cunning, expert, ingenious, practiced, skilled, skillful, versed. ANT.-awkward, bungling, clumsy, inexpert, untrained.

profit, *n.* SYN.-advantage, avail, benefit, emolument, gain, improvement, service, use. ANT.-damage, detriment, loss, ruin, waste.

profitable, *a.* SYN.-advantageous, beneficial, favorable, lucrative, productive, remunerative, valuable.

profligate, *a.* SYN.-contaminated, corrupt, corrupted, crooked, debased, depraved, dishonest, impure, putrid, spoiled, tainted, unsound, venal, vitiated.

profound, *a.* SYN.-abstruse, deep, intellectual, intense, penetrating, recondite, solemn, wise. ANT.-shallow, slight, superficial, trivial.

profuse, *a.* SYN.-abundant, copious, excessive, extravagant, exuberant, immoderate, improvident, lavish, luxuriant, overflowing, plentiful, prodigal, wasteful. ANT.-economical, meager, poor, skimpy, sparse.

profusion, *n.* SYN.-abundance, excess, extravagance, immoderation, intemperance, superabundance, superfluity, surplus. ANT.-dearth, deficiency, lack, paucity, want.

program, *n.* SYN.-agenda, bulletin, calendar, curriculum, plan, presentation, schedule,

progress, *n.* SYN.-advance, advancement, betterment, course, development, growth, improvement, proceeding, progression. ANT.-decline, delay, regression, relapse, retrogression.

progress, *v.* SYN.-advance, augment, elevate, enlarge, further, improve, increase, proceed, promote, rise, thrive. ANT.-hinder, oppose, retard, retreat, withhold.

progression, *n.* SYN.-arrangement, chain, following, gradation, order, sequence, series, string, succession.

prohibit, *v.* SYN.-ban, debar, enjoin, forbid, halt, hinder, impede, inhibit, interdict, obstruct, prevent, restrain. ANT.-allow, permit, sanction, tolerate.

project, *n.* SYN.-aim, contrivance, design, device, intention, plan, proposal, proposition, scheme. ANT.-accomplishment, performance, production.

project, *v.* SYN.-brew, concoct, contemplate, contrive, devise, forecast, frame, plan.

prolific, *a.* SYN.-bountiful, fecund, fertile, fruitful, luxuriant, plenteous, productive, rich, teeming. ANT.-barren, impotent, sterile, unproductive.

prolong, *v.* SYN.-drag, draw, extend, lengthen, protract, stretch. ANT.-abbreviate, contract, curtail, shorten.

prominent, *a.* SYN.-celebrated, conspicuous, distinguished, eminent, famous, illustrious, influential, noteworthy, outstanding, remarkable, renowned. ANT.-common, humble, low, ordinary, vulgar.

promiscuous, *a.* SYN.-careless, confused, garbled, immoral, indiscriminate, licentious, loose, mixed,

promise, *n.* SYN.-agreement, assurance, bestowal, contract, covenant, engagement, fulfillment, guarantee, oath, pledge, undertaking, vow.

promote, *v.* SYN.-advance, advocate, aid, assist, back, champion, encourage, facilitate, forward, foster, patronize, support, urge. ANT.-demote, discourage, hinder, impede, obstruct.

prompt, *a.* SYN.-exact, precise, punctual, timely. ANT.-dilatory, late, slow, tardy.

prompt, *v.* SYN.-arouse, cause, coach, create, cue, effect, evoke, help, incite, induce, inspire, instigate, make, occasion, originate, provoke, remind, suggest.

promptly, *adv.* SYN.-directly, forthwith, immediately, instantaneously, instantly, now, quickly, presently, rapidly, straight-away. ANT.-distantly, hereafter, later, shortly, sometime.

promulgate, *v.* SYN.-affirm, announce, assert, aver, broadcast, declare, express, make known, proclaim, profess, state, tell. ANT.-conceal, repress, suppress, withhold.

proof, *n.* SYN.-confirmation, corroboration, demonstration, evidence, experiment, test, testimony, trial, verification. ANT.-failure, fallacy, invalidity.

propaganda, *n.* SYN.-advertising, broadcasting, inducement, influence, notice, persuasion, promotion, publicity.

propagate, *v.* SYN.-bear, beget, breed,

conceive, engender, generate, procreate.

propel, v. SYN.-actuate, agitate, drive, impel, induce, instigate, move, persuade, push, shift, stir, transfer. ANT.-deter. halt, rest, stay, stop.

propensity, n. SYN.-bent, bias, capacity, drift, inclination, leaning, predisposition, proclivity, proneness, talent, tendency, trend. ANT.-aversion, deviation, disinclination.

proper, a. SYN.-appropriate, befitting, conventional, correct, decent, fit, formal, legitimate, meet, respectable, right, seemly, suitable.

property, n. SYN.-belongings, commodities, effects, estate, goods, merchandise, possessions, stock, wares, wealth; attribute, characteristic, peculiarity, quality, trait. ANT.-deprivation, destitution, poverty, privation, want.

prophesy, v. SYN.-anticipate, augur, divine, envision, forecast, foresee, predict.

prophet, n. SYN.-astrologer, clairvoyant, economist, forecaster, fortuneteller, medium, meteorologist, oracle, palmist, seer, soothsayer, sorcerer, wizard.

proponent, n. SYN.-advocate, champion, defender, patron, promoter, supporter.

proportion, n. SYN.-balance, dimensions, distribution, equilibrium, extent, part, percentage, piece, portion, ratio, share, size, symmetry.

proposal, n. SYN.-bid, motion, offer, overture, plan, proposition, suggestion, tender. ANT.-acceptance, denial, rejection, withdrawal.

propose, v. SYN.-design, intend, move, offer, present, proffer, propound, purpose, suggest, tender. ANT.-effect, fulfill, perform.

propound, v. SYN.-adduce, advance, advise, allege, elevate, forward, further, offer, promote, propose, submit, suggest. ANT.-hinder, oppose, retard, retreat, withhold.

proprietor, n. SYN.-employer, head, leader, master, manager, overseer, owner. ANT.-employee. helper, laborer, servant, slave, worker.

propriety, n. SYN.-aptness, congruity, decency, decorum, dignity, etiquette, fitness, modesty, protocol, seemliness.

prosper, v. SYN.-achieve, burgeon, flourish, flower, gain, grow, increase, prevail, succeed, thrive, win. ANT.-fail, miscarry, miss.

prosperous, a. SYN.-affluent, ample, bountiful, copious, exorbitant, luxurious, opulent, plentiful, rich, sumptuous, wealthy, well-to-do. ANT.-beggarly, destitute, indigent, needy, poor.

protect, v. SYN.-defend, guard, keep, maintain, preserve, safeguard, save, secure, uphold. ANT.-abandon, abolish, destroy, impair, injure.

protection, n. SYN.-bulwark, defense, fence, guard, refuge, safeguard, security, shelter, shield.

protest, n. SYN.-challenge, demonstration, disagreement, dissent, dissentience, objection, remonstrance, revolt, riot. ANT.-acceptance, agreement, assent, compliance.

protest, v. SYN.-complain, demonstrate, demur, disagree, disapprove, object, oppose, rebel, reject, remonstrate, riot. ANT.-acquiesce, approve, assent, comply, concur.

prototype, n. SYN.-archetype, example, illustration, instance. model, pattern, sample, specimen. ANT.-concept, precept, principle, rule.

protract, v. SYN.-distend, distort, elongate, expand, extend, lengthen, spread, strain, stretch. ANT.-contract, loosen, shrink, slacken, tighten.

proud, a. SYN.-arrogant, conceited, disdainful, egotistical, haughty, imposing, lofty, magnificent, majestic, overbearing, stately, supercilious, vain, vainglorious. ANT.-ashamed, humble, lowly, meek.

prove, v. SYN.-affirm, confirm, corroborate, demonstrate, document, establish, justify, manifest, substantiate, test, try, validate, verify. ANT.-contradict, disprove, refute.

proverb, n. SYN.-adage, aphorism, apothegm, axiom, byword, maxim, motto, platitude, saw, saying.

provide, v. SYN.-accommodate, afford, assist, endow, equip, fit, furnish, give, help, oblige, outfit, produce, supply, yield. ANT.-denude, despoil, divest, strip.

provident, a. SYN.-careful, economical, frugal, niggardly, saving, sparing, thrifty. ANT.-extravagant, improvident, lavish, prodigal, wasteful.

provincial, a. SYN.-awkward, boorish, bucolic, callow, coarse, crude, ignorant, rough, rustic, simple, unpolished, unrefined, unsophisticated

provision, n. SYN.-accumulation, arrangement, fund, hoard, plan, preparation, reserve, stock, store, supply; condition, requirement, stipulation.

provoke, v. SYN.-agitate, arouse, awaken, cause, disquiet, disturb, encourage, excite, foment, goad, incite, induce, instigate, irritate, rouse, stimulate, stir up, urge. ANT.-allay, calm, pacify, quell, quiet.

prowess, n. SYN.-boldness, bravery, chivalry, courage, fearlessness, fortitude, intrepidity, mettle, resolution. ANT.-cowardice, fear, pusillanimity, timidity.

proxy, n. SYN.-agent, alternate, deputy, lieutenant, representative, substitute, understudy. ANT.-head, master, principal, sovereign.

prudence, n. SYN.-care, caution, heed, vigilance, wariness, watchfulness. ANT.-abandon, carelessness, recklessness.

prudent, a. SYN.-aware, cognizant, comprehending, conscious, discreet, intelligent, judicious, perceiving, practical, reasonable, sagacious, sage, sensible, sentient, sober, sound, wise. ANT.-absurd, impalpable, imperceptible, stupid, unaware.

prying, a. SYN.-curious, inquiring, inquisitive, interrogative, meddling, nosy, peeping, peering, searching, snoopy. ANT.-incurious, indifferent, unconcerned, uninterested.

psychic, a. SYN.-extrasensory, mental, mystic, telepathic, supernatural.

psychosis, n. SYN.-delirium, dementia, derangement, frenzy, insanity, lunacy, madness, mania. ANT.-rationality, sanity, stability.

publication, n. SYN.-advertisement, airing, announcement, broadcast, disclosure, dissemination, notification, statement.

publish, v. SYN.-advertise, air, announce, broadcast, declare, disclose, disseminate, divulge, issue, proclaim.

pull, v. SYN.-allure, attract, drag, draw, entice, haul, induce, lure, persuade, tow, tug. ANT.-drive, propel, push, repel.

pulsate, v. SYN.-beat, buffet, palpitate, pound, pulse, throb, thump, vibrate.

punctual, a. SYN.-exact, nice, precise, prompt, ready, timely. ANT.-dilatory, late, slow, tardy.

punish, v. SYN.-castigate, chastise, correct, discipline, pummel, reprove, strike. ANT.-acquit, exonerate, free, pardon, release.

punishment, n. SYN.-chastisement, correction, discipline, fine, forfeiture, penalty, retribution. ANT.-chaos, confusion, turbulence.

puny, a. SYN.-decrepit, delicate, enervated, exhausted, faint, feeble, forceless, impaired, infirm, languid, powerless, weak. ANT.-forceful, lusty, stout, strong, vigorous.

purchase, v. SYN.-acquire, buy. get, obtain, procure. ANT.-dispose of, sell, vend.

pure, a. SYN.-chaste, clean, clear, genuine, guiltless, immaculate, innocent, modest, sincere, spotless, unadulterated, undefiled, untainted; virginal; absolute, bare, sheer, utter. ANT.-foul, polluted, sullied, tainted, tarnished; corrupt, defiled.

purified, a. SYN.-clarified, clean, cleansed, distilled, pure, purged, refined, sweet. ANT.-boorish, coarse, crude, rude, vulgar.

purify, v. SYN.-clean, cleanse, disinfect, filter, mop, refine, rinse, scrub, sweep, wash. ANT.-dirty, pollute, soil, stain, sully.

purpose, n. SYN.-aim, aspiration, design, drift, end, expectation, goal, intent, intention, object, objective. ANT.-accident, fate, hazard.

pursue, v. SYN.-chase, endeavor, follow, hunt, maintain, persist, proceed, seek, track, trail. ANT.-abandon, elude, escape, evade, flee.

push, v. SYN.-crowd, drive, force, impel, jostle, press, propel, shove; hasten, promote, urge. ANT.-drag, falter, halt, pull, retreat; ignore, oppose.

put, v. SYN.-deposit, establish, install, lay, plant, set, situate.

puzzle, n. SYN.-conundrum, enigma, mystery, problem, riddle. ANT.-answer, clue, key, resolution, solution.

puzzle, v. SYN.-bewilder, confound, confuse, dumfound, mystify, nonplus, perplex. ANT.-clarify, explain, illumine, instruct, solve.

Q

quack, *n.* SYN.-charlatan, fake, impostor, phony, pretender, rogue, swindler.

quaint, *a.* SYN.-curious, cute, eccentric, odd, peculiar, queer, strange, unusual, whimsical. ANT.-common, familiar, normal, ordinary, usual.

qualified, *a.* SYN.-able, capable, clever, competent, efficient, fitted, skillful. ANT.-inadequate, incapable, incompetent, unfitted.

quality, *n.* SYN.-attribute, characteristic, distinction, feature, peculiarity, property, trait; caliber, grade, value. ANT.-being, essence, nature, substance.

quantity, *n.* SYN.-aggregate, amount, content, extent, measure, number, portion, sum, volume. ANT.-nothing, nothingness, zero.

quarrel, *n.* SYN.-affray, altercation, argument, bickering, contention, disagreement, dispute, feud, spat, squabble, wrangle. ANT.-agreement, friendliness, harmony, peace, reconciliation.

queer, *a.* SYN.-curious, droll, eccentric, odd, peculiar, quaint, singular, strange, unusual, whimsical. ANT.-common, familiar, normal, ordinary, usual.

quest, *n.* SYN.-examination, exploration, inquiry, interrogation, investigation, query, question, research, scrutiny, search. ANT.-disregard, inactivity, inattention, negligence.

question, *v.* SYN.-ask, challenge, dispute, doubt, examine, inquire, interrogate, pump, query, quiz. ANT.-accept, answer, reply, respond, state.

quick, *a.* SYN.-active, brisk, excitable, fast, hasty, impatient, irascible, lively, nimble, precipitate, rapid, sharp, speedy, swift, testy, touchy; acute, clever, discerning, keen, sensitive, shrewd. ANT.-slow, sluggish; dull, inattentive, unaware.

quicken, *v.* SYN.-accelerate, dispatch, expedite, facilitate, forward, hasten, hurry, push, rush, speed. ANT.-block, hinder, impede, retard, slow.

quiet, *a.* SYN.-calm, gentle, hushed, meek, mild, modest, motionless, passive, patient, peaceful, placid, quiescent, silent, still, tranquil, undisturbed. ANT.-agitated, disturbed, loud, perturbed, strident.

quiet, *n.* SYN.-calm, calmness, hush, peace, quiescence, quietude, repose, rest, serenity, silence, stillness, tranquility. ANT.-agitation, disturbance, excitement, noise, tumult.

quiet, *v.* SYN.-allay, alleviate, appease, assuage, calm, compose, lull, pacify, placate, quell, relieve, satisfy, soothe, still, tranquilize. ANT.-arouse, excite, incense, inflame.

quirk, *n.* SYN.-caprice, characteristic, flavor, idiosyncrasy, irregularity, oddity, peculiarity, style, temperament, whim.

quit, *v.* SYN.-abandon, cease, depart, desist, discontinue, leave, relinquish, resign, stop, surrender, withdraw. ANT.-continue, endure, occupy, persist, stay.

quiver, *v.* SYN.-quake, shake, shiver, shudder, tremble, tremor.

quiz, *v.* SYN.-ask, examine, inquire, interrogate, pump, query, question. ANT.-answer, reply, respond, state.

quote, *v.* SYN.-adduce, cite, extract, paraphrase, plagiarize, recite, repeat. ANT.-contradict, misquote, refute, retort.

R

rabble, *n.* SYN.-crowd, masses, mob, people, populace, proletariat.

race, *n.* SYN.-ancestry, clan, culture, family, folk, lineage, nation, people, stock, strain, tribe.

racket, *n.* SYN.-cacophony, clamor, clatter, din, noise, pandemonium, row, rumpus, sound, tumult, uproar. ANT.-hush, quiet, silence, stillness.

racy, *a.* SYN.-erotic, indecent, lewd, risqué, suggestive.

radiance, *n.* SYN.-brightness, brilliance, brilliancy, effulgence, luster, splendor. ANT.-darkness, dullness, gloom, obscurity.

radiant, *a.* SYN.-brilliant, bright, dazzling, effulgent, glorious, gorgeous, grand, illustrious, magnificent, resplendent, shining, showy, splendid, sumptuous, superb. ANT.-dull, mediocre, modest, ordinary, unimpressive.

radical, *a.* SYN.-basic, complete, constitutional, extreme, fundamental, inherent, innate, insurgent, intrinsic, natural, organic, original, total, thorough, ultra, uncompromising. ANT.-conservative, moderate, superficial; extraneous.

rage, *n.* SYN.-anger, animosity, choler, fury, indignation, ire, passion, resentment, temper, wrath. ANT.-conciliation, forbearance, patience, peace, self-control.

raging, *a.* SYN.-acute, boisterous, extreme, fierce, forceful, furious, impetuous; intense, passionate, powerful, raving, severe, turbulent, vehement, violent, wild. ANT.-calm, feeble, gentle, quiet, soft.

raid, *n.* SYN.-assault, attack, foray, incursion, invasion.

rain, *v.* SYN.-deluge, drench, drizzle, drop, fall, mist, patter, pour, shower, storm.

raise, *v.* SYN.-elevate, erect, exalt, heave, heighten, hoist, lift, uplift; breed, cultivate, grow, produce; gather, levy, muster. ANT.-abase, depreciate, depress, destroy, lower.

ram, *v.* SYN.-bump, butt, collide, crash, cram, hit, jam, pound, stuff.

ramble, *v.* SYN.-deviate, digress, err, range, roam, rove, saunter, stray, stroll, traipse, wander. ANT.-halt, linger, settle, stay, stop.

rampant, *a.* SYN.-frantic, furious, raging, tumultuous, turbulent, uncontrolled, violent, widespread, wild.

rancor, *n.* SYN.-animosity, enmity, grudge, ill-will, malevolence, malice, malignity, spite. ANT.-affection, kindness, love, toleration.

random, *a.* SYN.-accidental, aimless, casual, chance, haphazard, indiscriminate, unplanned, unpredictable.

rank, *n.* SYN.-blood, class, degree, dignity, distinction, eminence, estate, grade, quality, standing, station, status; fetid, foul, gamy, malodorous, nasty, putrid, rancid, reeking, smelly, stinking. ANT.-disrepute, shame, stigma; clean, pleasant, sweet.

rapid, *a.* SYN.-expeditious, fast, fleet, hasty, lively, precipitate, quick, speedy, swift. ANT.-slow, sluggish.

rapture, *n.* SYN.-blessedness, bliss, blissfulness, delight, ecstasy, exaltation, felicity, happiness, joy, pleasure, satisfaction, transport, trance. ANT.-grief, misery, sorrow, woe, wretchedness.

rare, *a.* SYN.-choice, exceptional, incomparable, infrequent, occasional, precious, scarce, singular, strange, uncommon, unique, unusual. ANT.-abundant, commonplace, customary, frequent, numerous, ordinary, usual, worthless.

rascal, *n.* SYN.-beggar, bum, cad, charlatan, knave, rake, reprobate, rogue, scalawag, scamp, sneak, scoundrel, tramp, villain, wastrel, wretch.

rash, *a.* SYN.-blind, careless, hasty, headlong, heedless, impetuous, impulsive, oblivious, passionate, quick, undiscerning, unmindful, unseeing. ANT.-aware, calculated, cautious, discerning, perceiving, reasoning, sensible.

rate, *v.* SYN.-appraise, assess, classify, evaluate, grade, judge, rank, value.

ratify, *v.* SYN.-approve, authorize, confirm, endorse, sanction.

rational, *a.* SYN.-calm, circumspect, cool, discerning, intelligent, judicious, logical, prudent, reasonable, sane, sensible, sober, sound, wise. ANT.-absurd, foolish; irrational, insane.

rationale, *n.* SYN.-aim, argument, basis, design, excuse, explanation, ground, intelligence, justification, motive, purpose, reason, rationalization, sake.

ravage, *v.* SYN.-annihilate, demolish, despoil, destroy, devastate, exterminate, extinguish, pillage, plunder, ransack, ruin, sack, strip, waste. ANT.-accumulate, economize, preserve, save.

ravish, *v.* SYN.-debauch, defile, desecrate, dishonor, pollute, profane, violate.

raw, *a.* SYN.-coarse, crass, crude, green, harsh, ill-prepared, rough, uncouth, unfinished, unpolished, unrefined. ANT.-finished, well-prepared; cultivated, refined.

raze, *v.* SYN.-annihilate, demolish, destroy, devastate, eradicate, exterminate, extinguish, obliterate, ravage, ruin, wreck. ANT.-construct, establish, make, preserve, save.

reach, *v.* SYN.-approach, arrive, attain, extend, overtake, stretch, touch. ANT.-fail, fall short, miss.

react, *v.* SYN.-answer, counter, counteract, experience, feel, rejoin, reply, respond, retort. ANT.-disregard, ignore, overlook.

reaction, *n.* SYN.-answer, backlash, feedback, rejoinder, reply, response, retort.

ready, *a.* SYN.-aged, available, complete, consummate, convenient, finished, full-grown, handy, mature, matured, mellow, prepared, ripe, seasonable, steeled.

ANT.-crude, green, immature, raw, undeveloped.

ready, v. SYN.-condition, equip, fit, furnish, get ready, make ready, predispose, prepare, provide, qualify.

real, a. SYN.-actual, authentic, certain, genuine, positive, substantial, true, veritable. ANT.-apparent, fictitious, imaginary, supposed, unreal.

realize, v. SYN.-appreciate, apprehend, comprehend, conceive, discern, grasp, know, learn, perceive, see, understand. ANT.-ignore, misapprehend, mistake, misunderstand.

realm, n. SYN.-area, circle, domain, kingdom, orbit, province, sphere

reap, v. SYN.-acquire, gain, garner, gather, get, glean, harvest, obtain, pick, receive. ANT.-lose, plant, sow, squander.

reaping, n. SYN.-crop, harvest, proceeds, produce, product, result, yield.

rear, v. SYN.-bear, beget, breed, conceive, engender, foster, generate, nurture, procreate, propagate, raise, train.

reason, n. SYN.-aim, argument, basis, cause, design, ground, motive, purpose, sake; intelligence, mind, rationality, sense, understanding.

reason, v. SYN.-argue, conclude, deduce, deliberate, discuss, infer, judge, reflect. ANT.-bewilder, confuse, guess.

reasonable, a. SYN.-appreciable, apprehensible, perceptible; alive, awake, aware, cognizant, comprehending, conscious, discreet, intelligent, judicious, perceiving, practical, prudent, sagacious, sage, sensible, sentient, sober, sound, wise. ANT.-absurd, impalpable, imperceptible, stupid, unaware.

rebel, v. SYN.-defy, mutiny, oppose, resist, revolt, strike.

rebellion, v. SYN.-coup, insurrection, mutiny, overthrow, revolt, revolution, uprising.

rebellious, a. SYN.-defiant, disobedient, insubordinate, undutiful, unruly. ANT.-compliant, dutiful, obedient, submissive.

rebuild, v. SYN.-reconstruct, reestablish, rehabilitate, renew, renovate, repair, restore.

rebuke, v. SYN.-censure, chide, reprimand, reprove, scold, upbraid.

rebuttal, n. SYN.-answer, defense, rejoinder, reply, response, retort; ANT.-inquiry, questioning, summoning; argument.

recall, v. SYN.-recollect, remember, remind, reminisce. ANT.-disregard, forget, ignore, overlook.

recede, v. SYN.-abate, decline, decrease, drop, ebb, lessen, retreat, subside.

receive, v. SYN.-accept, admit, entertain, gain, get, inherit, shelter, take, welcome. ANT.-bestow, discharge, give, impart, reject, turn away.

recent, a. SYN.-fresh, late, modern, new, newfangled, novel, original. ANT.-ancient, antiquated, archaic, obsolete, old.

recitation, n. SYN.-address, discourse, interpretation, lecture, monologue, narration, reading, soliloquy, speech, recital.

recite, v. SYN.-declaim, deliver, describe, detail, enumerate, mention, narrate, recapitulate, recount, rehearse, relate, repeat, tell.

reckless, a. SYN.-careless, heedless, imprudent, inattentive, inconsiderate, indiscreet, neglectful, negligent, remiss, thoughtless, unconcerned. ANT.-accurate, careful, meticulous, nice.

reckon, v. SYN.-assess, consider, estimate, evaluate, judge, weigh.

recognize, v. SYN.-acknowledge, apprehend, avow, concede, confess, identify, own, perceive, recollect, remember. ANT.-disown, forget, ignore, overlook, renounce, repudiate.

recollection, n. SYN.-memory, remembrance, reminiscence, retrospection. ANT.-forgetfulness, oblivion.

recommend, v. SYN.-advise, allude, counsel, hint, imply, insinuate, intimate, offer, propose, refer, suggest. ANT.-declare, demand, dictate, insist.

recommendation, n. SYN.-advice, caution, counsel, exhortation, instruction, suggestion, warning.

reconsider, v. SYN.-analyze, consider, ponder, review, revise. ANT.-ignore, reject.

record, n. SYN.-account, achievement, archive, career, chronicle, document, history, mark, memorandum, memorial, minute, note, report, register, trace, vestige.

recount, v. SYN.-describe, narrate, recite, relate, report, tell.

recover, v. SYN.-cure, rally, recuperate, restore, revive; recapture, recoup, redeem, regain, repossess, retrieve. ANT.-regress, relapse, revert, weaken; forfeit, lose.

recreation, n. SYN.-amusement, diversion, entertainment, fun, game, pastime, play, sport. ANT.-boredom, labor, toil, work.

rectify, v. SYN.-amend, correct, mend, reform, right. ANT.-aggravate, ignore, spoil.

recuperate, v. SYN.-heal, rally, recover, restore, revive; recapture, recoup, redeem, regain, repossess, retrieve. ANT.-regress, relapse, revert, weaken; forfeit, lose.

redeemer, n. SYN.-deliverer, liberator, protector, rescuer.

reduce, v. SYN.-abate, assuage, curtail, decline, decrease, deduct, diminish, lessen, lower, moderate, shorten, subtract, suppress. ANT.-amplify, enlarge, increase, intensify, revive.

refined, a. SYN.-courtly, cultivated, cultured, genteel, polished, polite, wellbred; clarified, purified. ANT.-boorish, coarse, crude, rude, vulgar.

refinement, n. SYN.-breeding, civilization, cultivation, culture, education, enlightenment. ANT.-boorishness, ignorance, illiteracy, vulgarity.

reflect, v. SYN.-apprehend, cogitate, consider, contemplate, deliberate, imagine, meditate, muse, opine, picture, ponder, reason, recall, recollect, reckon, regard, remember, speculate, suppose, think. ANT.-conjecture, forget, guess.

reflection, n. SYN.-cogitation, conception, consideration, contemplation, deliberation, fancy, idea, imagination, impression, judgment, meditation, memory, notion, opinion, recollection, regard, retrospection, sentiment, thought, view.

reform, v. SYN.-ameliorate, amend, better, change, correct, help, improve, mend, rectify, renew, right. ANT.-aggravate, corrupt, damage, debase, ignore, impair, spoil.

refrain, v. SYN.-abstain, desist, forbear, withhold. ANT.-continue, indulge, persist.

refreshing, a. SYN.-modern, new, novel, recent; artless, brisk, cool, fresh, green, inexperienced, natural, raw. ANT.-decayed, faded, hackneyed, musty, stagnant.

refuge, n. SYN.-asylum, harbor, haven, retreat, sanctuary, shelter. ANT.-danger, exposure, hazard, jeopardy, peril.

refuse, v. SYN.-decline, deny, rebuff, reject, repudiate, spurn, withhold. ANT.-accept, grant, welcome.

refute, v SYN.-confute, controvert, disprove, rebut. ANT.-accept, affirm, confirm, establish, prove.

regain, v. SYN.-recapture, recoup, recover, redeem, repossess, retrieve. ANT.-forfeit, lose.

regal, a. SYN.-courtly, dignified, grand, imperial, kingly, lordly, majestic, monarchal, noble, princely, royal, ruling, sovereign, stately, supreme. ANT.-common, humble, low, plebeian, proletarian, servile, vulgar.

regard, n. SYN.-affection, attention, care, concern, consideration, esteem, liking, notice, observation. ANT.-antipathy, disgust, disaffection, neglect.

regard, v SYN.-esteem, honor, respect, value; behold, contemplate, look, mark, notice, observe, see, view, watch; account, believe, deem, hold, imagine, reckon, suppose, think. ANT.-insult, mock; ignore, neglect, overlook.

region, n. SYN.-area, belt, locale, locality, location, place, sector, site, situation, spot, station, vicinity, zone.

regret, n. SYN.-compunction, contrition, grief, penitence, qualm, remorse, repentance, self-reproach, sorrow. ANT.-complacency, impenitence, obduracy, self-satisfaction.

regular, a. SYN.-customary, methodical, natural, normal, orderly, ordinary, periodical, steady, systematic, uniform, unvaried. ANT.-abnormal, erratic, exceptional, rare, unusual.

regulation, n. SYN.-canon, control, correction, discipline, guide, law, order, principle, punishment, regulation, restraint, rule, self-control, standard, statute. ANT.-chaos, confusion, turbulence.

rehabilitate, v. SYN.-cure, heal, rebuild, reconstruct, recover, reestablish, refresh, rejuvenate, renew, reinstate, renovate, repair, replace, restore, return, revive

reiterate, v. SYN.-cite, copy, duplicate, iterate, quote, recapitulate, recite, relate, repeat, reproduce.

reject, v. SYN.-decline, deny, discard, eliminate, exclude, rebuff, refuse, repudiate, spurn. ANT.-accept, grant, welcome.

rejection, n. SYN.-challenge, disagreement, dissent, dissentience, noncompliance, nonconformity, objection, protest, remonstrance, variance. ANT.-acceptance, agreement, assent, compliance.

relate, v SYN.-describe, narrate, recite, recount, rehearse, repeat, report, tell; ally, associate, connect, correlate, link, pertain, refer.

relation, n. SYN.-alliance, association, coalition, combination, compact, confederacy, connection, covenant, dependence, entente, federation, league, marriage, partnership, treaty, union. ANT.-divorce, schism, separation.

relationship, n. SYN.-affinity, alliance, association, bond, conjunction, connection, link, tie, union. ANT.-disunion, isolation, separation.

relatives, n. SYN.-clan, blood, family, kin, kindred, kinsfolk, people, race, relations, tribe. ANT.-disconnection, foreigners, strangers.

relaxed, a. SYN.-casual, cozy, gratifying, informal, nonchalant, offhand, pleasing, restful, unconcerned, unpremeditated. ANT. formal, planned, pretentious.

release, v. SYN.-deliver, discharge, emancipate, fire, free, lay off, let go, liberate, loose, set free, terminate, unloose, unfetter, untie. ANT.-confine, imprison, oppress, restrict, subjugate.

relent, v. SYN.-abdicate, accede, acquiesce, capitulate, cede, quit, relinquish, resign, submit, succumb, surrender, waive, yield. ANT.-assert, resist, strive, struggle.

relevant, a. SYN.-applicable, apposite, appropriate, apropos, apt, fit, germane, material, pertinent, related, relating, to the point. ANT.-alien, extraneous, foreign, unrelated.

reliable, a. SYN.-certain, dependable, safe, secure, sure, tried, trustworthy, trusty. ANT.-dubious, fallible, questionable, uncertain, unreliable.

reliance, n. SYN.-belief, confidence, constancy, conviction, credence, dependence, faith, fidelity, hope, loyalty, trust. ANT.-doubt, incredulity, mistrust, skepticism; infidelity.

relief, n. SYN.-aid, assistance, backing, furtherance, help, succor, support. ANT.-antagonism, counteraction, defiance, hostility, resistance.

relieve, v. SYN.-abate, allay, alleviate, assuage, comfort, diminish, ease, extenuate, lighten, mitigate, soften, solace, soothe. ANT.-aggravate, agitate, augment, increase, irritate.

religion, n. SYN.-belief, creed, doctrine, dogma, faith, persuasion, tenet; constancy, fidelity, loyalty. ANT.-doubt, incredulity, mistrust, skepticism; infidelity.

religious, a. SYN.-devout, divine, godly, holy, pietistic, pious, reverent, sacred, sanctimonious, spiritual, theological. ANT.-atheistic, impious, profane, secu-

lar, skeptical.

religiousness, n. SYN.-ardor, consecration, dedication, devotion, devoutness, fidelity, loyalty, piety, zeal. ANT.-alienation, apathy, aversion, indifference, unfaithfulness.

relinquish, v. SYN.-abandon, acquiesce, capitulate, cede, renounce, resign, sacrifice, submit, surrender, yield. ANT.-conquer, overcome, resist, rout.

relish, v. SYN.-anticipate, appreciate, enjoy, fancy, like, prefer.

reluctance, n. SYN.-abhorrence, antipathy, aversion, disinclination, distaste, dread, hatred, loathing, repugnance, repulsion. ANT.-affection, attachment, devotion, enthusiasm.

reluctant, a. SYN.-averse, disinclined, hesitant, loath, slow, unwilling. ANT.-disposed, eager, inclined, ready, willing.

remain, v SYN.-abide, continue, dwell, endure, halt, last, rest, stay, survive, tarry, wait. ANT.-depart, go, leave; dissipate, finish, terminate.

remains, n. SYN.-balance, relics, remainder, residue, rest, surplus.

remark, n. SYN.-annotation, assertion, comment, declaration, observation, statement, utterance.

remark, v. SYN.-aver, comment, express, mention, note, observe, state, utter. ANT.-disregard, ignore.

remarkable, a. SYN.-arresting, commanding, exciting, imposing, impressive, majestic, moving, overpowering, splendid, stirring, striking, thrilling, touching. ANT.-commonplace, ordinary, regular, unimpressive.

remedy, n. SYN.-antidote, cure, help, medicant, restorative; redress, relief, reparation.

remedy, v. SYN.-ameliorate, better, correct, cure, fix, heal, improve, mend, patch, rectify, refit, reform, repair, restore. ANT.-deface, destroy, hurt, injure, rend.

remember, v SYN.-mind, recall, recollect, remind, reminisce. ANT.-disregard, forget, ignore, overlook.

remembrance, n. SYN.-commemoration, memento, memorial, monument, recollection, reminiscence, souvenir, token.

remonstrate, v. SYN.-complain, grouch, grumble, lament, murmur, protest, regret, repine, whine. ANT.-applaud, approve, praise, rejoice.

remorse, n. SYN.-contrition, grief, penitence, regret, repentance, self-reproach, sorrow. ANT.-impenitence, obduracy, self-satisfaction.

remote, a. SYN.-distant, far, faraway, removed; aloof, cold, reserved, stiff, unfriendly. ANT.-close, near, nigh; cordial, friendly.

remove, v. SYN.-dislodge, displace, move, shift, transfer, transport; discharge, dismiss, eject, oust, vacate; extract, withdraw. ANT.-leave, remain, stay; retain.

renounce, v. SYN.-abandon, deny, disavow, disclaim, disown, forego, forsake, quit, reject, relinquish, resign, retract, revoke, sacrifice. ANT.-acknowledge, assert, defend, maintain, recognize, up-

hold.

renovate, v. SYN.-rebuild, reconstruct, reestablish, refresh, rehabilitate, renew, repair, restore.

renown, n. SYN.-acclaim, distinction, eminence, fame, honor, luster, notability, reputation. ANT.-disgrace, disrepute, obscurity.

renowned, a. SYN.-celebrated, distinguished, eminent, famous, glorious, illustrious, noted, well-known. ANT.-hidden, ignominious, infamous, obscure, unknown.

repair, v. SYN.-amend, correct, darn, fix, mend, patch, refit, redress, remedy, renew, renovate, restore, retrieve, tinker. ANT.-break, destroy, harm.

repay, v. SYN.-avenge, compensate, indemnify, pay, recompense, refund, reimburse, retaliate, settle.

repeal, v. SYN.-abolish, abrogate, annul, cancel, eliminate, expunge, invalidate, nullify, obliterate, quash, rescind, revoke. ANT.-confirm, enact, enforce, perpetuate

repeat, v SYN.-cite, copy, duplicate, iterate, quote, recapitulate, recite, rehearse, reiterate, relate, reproduce.

repentance, n. SYN.-contrition, grief, penitence, regret, remorse, self-reproach, sorrow. ANT.-impenitence, obduracy, self-satisfaction.

repentant, a. SYN.-contrite, penitent, regretful, remorseful, sorrowful, sorry. ANT.-obdurate, remorseless.

repine, v. SYN.-complain, grouch, grumble, lament, murmur, protest, regret, remonstrate, whine. ANT.-applaud, approve, praise, rejoice.

replace, v. SYN.-displace, reinstate, restore, return, substitute, supplant.

replica, n. SYN.-copy, duplicate, exemplar, facsimile, imitation, Photostat, reproduction, transcript. ANT.-original, prototype.

reply, n. SYN.-answer, defense, rebuttal, rejoinder, response, retort. ANT.-inquiry, questioning, summoning; argument.

reply, v. SYN.-answer, react, rebut, rejoin, respond. ANT.-disregard, ignore, overlook.

report, v. SYN.-advertise, announce, declare, give out, herald, make known, notify, proclaim, promulgate, publish. ANT.-bury, conceal, stifle, suppress, withhold.

repose, n. SYN.-calm, calmness, hush, peace, quiescence, quiet, quietude, rest, serenity, silence, stillness, tranquility. ANT.-agitation, disturbance, excitement, noise, tumult.

represent, v. SYN.-depict, describe, draw, paint, picture, portray, sketch. ANT.-caricature, misrepresent, suggest.

representation, n. SYN.-drawing, effigy, engraving, etching, illustration, image, landscape, likeness, painting, panorama, photograph, picture, portrait, portrayal, print, rendering, resemblance, scene, sketch, view.

representative, n. SYN.-agent, ambassador, delegate, deputy, emissary, envoy, legislator, proxy.

repress, v. SYN.-bridle, check, constrain,

curb, hinder, hold back, inhibit, limit, restrain, stop, suppress. ANT.-aid, encourage, incite, loosen.

reprimand, v. SYN.-admonish, berate, blame, censure, lecture, rate, rebuke, reprehend, scold, upbraid, vituperate. ANT.-approve, commend, praise.

reproduction, n. SYN.-copy, duplicate, exemplar, facsimile, imitation, Photostat, replica, transcript. ANT.-original, prototype.

repugnance, n. SYN.-abhorrence, antipathy, aversion, disgust, disinclination, dislike, distaste, dread, hatred, loathing, repulsion, reluctance. ANT.-affection, attachment, devotion, enthusiasm.

repulsive, a. SYN.-deformed, despicable, disgusting, hideous, homely, horrid, nauseating, offensive, plain, repellent, repugnant, revolting, ugly, uncomely, vile. ANT.-attractive, beautiful, fair, handsome, pretty.

reputation, n. SYN.-character, description, estimation, individuality, kind, nature, repute, sort, standing.

repute, n. SYN.-character, class, disposition, esteem, estimation, fame, honor, name, nature, reputation, sort, standing.

request, v SYN.-appeal, ask, beg, beseech, desire, entreat, implore, importune, petition, pray, seek, sue, supplicate. ANT.-demand, require.

require, v SYN.-ask, claim, command, demand, exact, lack, necessitate, need, order, prescribe, want.

requisite, a. SYN.-basic, essential, fundamental, important, indispensable, intrinsic, necessary, needed, vital. ANT.-expendable, extrinsic, optional, peripheral.

rescind, v. SYN.-abolish, abrogate, annul, cancel, delete, eliminate, expunge, invalidate, nullify, quash, repeal, revoke. ANT.-confirm, enact, enforce, perpetuate

rescue, v. SYN.-deliver, free, liberate, recover, retrieve, save,

research, n. SYN.-exploration, interrogation, inquiry, investigation, query, quest, question, scrutiny. ANT.-disregard, inactivity, inattention, negligence.

resemblance, n. SYN.-analogy, correspondence, likeness, parity, similarity, similitude. ANT.-difference, distinction, variance.

reserve, n. SYN.-accumulation, fund, hoard, provision, stock, store, supply.

reserved, a. SYN.-aloof, cautious, cold, demure, diffident, distant, modest, remote, reserved, retiring, stiff, unfriendly. ANT.-audacious, close, cordial, friendly.

residence, n. SYN.-abode, base, castle, domicile, dwelling, estate, habitat, hearth, home, house, hovel, manor, palace, quarters, seat, shack.

resign, v. SYN.-abandon, depart, discontinue, give up, leave, quit, relinquish, stop, surrender, withdraw. ANT.-continue, endure, occupy, persist, stay.

resignation, n. SYN.-composure, endurance, forbearance, fortitude, long-suffering, patience, perseverance. ANT.-

impatience, nervousness, restlessness, unquiet.

resigned, a. SYN.-composed, forbearing, indulgent, long-suffering, passive, patient, stoical, uncomplaining. ANT.-chafing, clamorous, high-strung, hysterical, turbulent.

resist, v. SYN.-attack, confront, defy, hinder, impede, obstruct, oppose, repel, repulse, thwart, withstand. ANT.-accede, allow, cooperate, relent, yield.

resolution, n. SYN.-courage, decision, determination, firmness, fortitude, persistence, resolve, steadfastness. ANT.-inconstancy, indecision, vacillation.

resolve, n. See **resolution.**

resolve, v. SYN.-adjudicate, conclude, decide, determine, end, fix, settle, terminate. ANT.-doubt, hesitate, suspend, vacillate, waver.

respect, v. SYN.-admire, consider, heed, honor, regard, revere, reverence, value, venerate. ANT.-abuse, despise, disdain, neglect, scorn.

respectable, a. SYN.-adequate, befitting, decent, decorous, fit, fitting, proper, seemly, suitable, tolerable. ANT.-coarse, gross, indecent, reprehensible, vulgar.

respond, v. SYN.-answer, react, rejoin, reply. ANT.-disregard, ignore, overlook.

response, n. SYN.-answer, defense, rebuttal, rejoinder, reply, retort. ANT.-inquiry, questioning, summoning; argument.

responsibility, n. SYN.-accountability, amenability, burden, capability, duty, liability, obligation, reliability, trust, trustworthiness.

responsible, a. SYN.-accountable, amenable, answerable, bound, capable, dependable, liable, obligated, reliable, stable, trusty, trustworthy. ANT.-exempt, free, immune; careless, negligent.

rest, n. SYN.-calm, ease, leisure, peace, quiet, relaxation, repose, sleep, slumber, tranquility; cessation, intermission, pause, respite; balance, remainder, remains, residue, surplus. ANT.-agitation, commotion, disturbance, motion, tumult.

restless, a SYN.-active, agitated, disquieted, disturbed, irresolute, roving, sleepless, transient, uneasy, unquiet, wandering. ANT.-at ease, peaceable, quiet, tractable.

restore, v. SYN.-cure, heal, rebuild, reconstruct, recover, reestablish, refresh, rehabilitate, reinstate, rejuvenate, renew, renovate, repair, replace, return, revive.

restrain, v. SYN.-bridle, check, constrain, curb, hinder, hold back, inhibit, limit, repress, stop, suppress. ANT.-aid, encourage, incite, loosen.

restraint, n. SYN.-control, discipline, order, regulation, self-control; correction, punishment. ANT.-chaos, confusion, turbulence.

restrict, v. SYN.-circumscribe, confine, contain, control, hamper, impede, inhibit, limit, regulate, restrain, suppress, tether.

result, n. SYN.-conclusion, consequence,

determination, effect, end, eventuality, issue, resolution, resolve.

retain, v. SYN.-hold, keep, maintain, preserve, save.

retaliation, n. SYN.-reprisal, requital, retribution, revenge, vengeance, vindictiveness. ANT.-mercy, pardon, reconciliation, remission, forgiveness.

retard, v. SYN.-arrest, delay, detain, hamper, hinder, impede, slow, stay. ANT.-expedite, hasten, precipitate, quicken.

retort, n. SYN.-answer, defense, rebuttal, rejoinder, reply, response. ANT.-inquiry, questioning, summoning; argument.

retribution, n. SYN.-punishment, reparation, reprisal, retaliation, reward, revenge. ANT.-mercy, pardon, forgiveness.

return, v. SYN.-go back, recur, retreat, revert; repay, replace, requite, restore. ANT.-appropriate, keep, retain, take.

reveal, v. SYN.-betray, disclose, discover, divulge, expose, impart, show, uncover. ANT.-cloak, conceal, cover, hide, obscure.

revelation, n. SYN.-apparition, dream, ghost, hallucination, mirage, phantasm, phantom, prophecy, specter, vision. ANT.-reality, substance, verity.

revenge, n. SYN.-reparation, reprisal, requital, retaliation, retribution, vengeance, vindictiveness. ANT.-mercy, pardon, reconciliation, remission, forgiveness.

revenge, v. SYN.-avenge, requite, retaliate, vindicate. ANT.-forgive, pardon, pity, reconcile.

revere, v. SYN.-adore, esteem, honor, venerate, worship. ANT.-despise, hate, ignore.

reverence, n. SYN.-adoration, deference, dignity, esteem, homage, honor, praise, respect, worship. ANT.-contempt, derision, disgrace, dishonor, reproach.

reverse, v. SYN.-annul, countermand, invert, overthrow, overturn, repeal, rescind, revoke, subvert, transpose, turn about, unmake, upset. ANT.-affirm, confirm, endorse, maintain, stabilize, vouch.

revert, v. SYN.-go back, repay, replace, restore, retreat, return. ANT.-keep, retain.

review, n. SYN.-commentary, criticism, critique, examination, inspection, reconsideration, retrospect, retrospection, revision, survey, synopsis; digest, journal, periodical.

review, v. SYN.-analyze, consider, criticize, discuss, edit, examine, inspect, reconsider, revise, survey. ANT.-ignore, reject.

revision, n. SYN.-amendment, change, correction, remedy.

revoke, v. SYN.-abolish, abrogate, annul, cancel, delete, eliminate, erase, expunge, invalidate, nullify, obliterate, quash, repeal, rescind. ANT.-confirm, enact, enforce, perpetuate

revolting, a. SYN.-abominable, detestable, execrable, foul, hateful, loathsome, odious, vile. ANT.-agreeable, commendable, delightful, pleasant.

revolution, n. SYN.-coup, insurrection, mutiny, overthrow, rebellion, revolt, uprising.

revolve, *v.* SYN.-circle, gyrate, rotate, spin, turn, twirl, wheel, whirl. ANT.-proceed, stop, stray, travel, wander.

reward, *n.* SYN.-award, bonus, bounty, compensation, premium, prize, recompense, remuneration, requital. ANT.-assessment, charge, earnings, punishment, wages.

rich, *a.* SYN.-abundant, affluent, ample, bountiful, copious, costly, exorbitant, luxurious, opulent, plentiful, prosperous, sumptuous, wealthy, well-to-do; fecund, fertile, fruitful, luxuriant, prolific. ANT.-beggarly, destitute, indigent, needy, poor; barren, sterile, unfruitful, unproductive.

riddle, *n.* SYN.-conundrum, enigma, mystery, problem, puzzle. ANT.-answer, clue, key, resolution, solution.

ridicule, *n.* SYN.-banter, derision, gibe, irony, jeering, mockery, raillery, sarcasm, satire, sneering.

right, *a.* SYN.-accurate, appropriate, correct, direct, erect, ethical, fair, fit, just, lawful, legitimate, proper, real, seemly, straight, suitable, true, upright. ANT.-bad, false, improper, wrong.

right, *n.* SYN.-authority, grant, liberty, license, prerogative, privilege; equity, honor, justice, propriety, virtue. ANT.-encroachment, injustice, violation, wrong.

righteous, *a.* SYN.-chaste, decent, ethical, good, honorable, just, moral, pure, right, scrupulous, virtuous. ANT.-amoral, libertine, licentious, sinful, unethical.

rigid, *a.* SYN.-austere, harsh, inflexible, rigorous, severe, stern, stiff, strict, stringent, unbending, unyielding. ANT.-compassionate, lax, lenient, mild, yielding; elastic, flexible, resilient, supple.

rigorous, *a.* SYN.-arduous, burdensome, cruel, difficult, hard, harsh, jarring, onerous, rough, rugged, severe, stern, strict, stringent, tough, unfeeling. ANT.-easy, effortless, facile; simple; gentle, lenient, tender.

rim, *n.* SYN.-border, boundary, brim, brink, edge, fringe, frontier, limit, margin, outskirts, termination, verge. ANT.-center, core, interior, mainland.

ring, *v.* SYN.-circle, confine, encircle, encompass, loop, surround; chime, clap, clang, peal, resound, strike, toll.

rinse, *v.* SYN.-bathe, clean, dip, soak, wash.

rip, *v.* SYN.-disunite, lacerate, rend, rive, sever, split, sunder, tear. ANT.-join, mend, repair, sew, unite.

ripe, *a.* SYN.-aged, complete, consummate, finished, full-grown, mature, matured, mellow, ready, seasonable. ANT.-crude, green, immature, raw, undeveloped.

rise, *v.* SYN.-adduce, advance, climb, elevate, further, improve, mount, proceed, progress, promote, scale, soar, thrive. ANT.-descend, fall, hinder, retard, retreat, sink.

risk, *n.* SYN.-danger, hazard, jeopardy, peril. ANT.-defense, immunity, protection, safety.

risk, *v.* SYN.-endanger, expose, hazard, jeopardize, peril; speculate, venture. ANT.-insure, protect, secure.

risky, *a.* SYN.-critical, dangerous, hazardous, insecure, menacing, ominous, perilous, precarious, threatening, unsafe. ANT.-firm, protected, safe, secure.

rite, *n.* SYN.-act, ceremony, custom, formality, liturgy, practice, protocol, ritual, system.

ritual, *n.* SYN.-ceremony, form, formality, observance, parade, pomp, protocol, rite, solemnity.

rival, *n.* SYN.-adversary, antagonist, competitor, contestant, enemy, foe, opponent. ANT.-ally, comrade, confederate, teammate.

rivalry, *n.* SYN.-adversary, antagonist, competition, contention, dispute, opposition, struggle.

road, *n.* SYN.-boulevard, drive, highway, parkway, roadway, street, thoroughfare, turnpike.

roam, *v.* SYN.-drift, meander, ramble, range, rove, stray, wander. ANT.-halt, linger, settle, stay, stop.

rob, *v.* SYN.-burglarize, cheat, defraud, despoil, fleece, loot, pilfer, pillage, plunder, sack, steal, strip.

robber, *n.* SYN.-burglar, cheat, pirate, plunderer, raider, swindler, thief, thug.

robbery, *n.* SYN.-burglary, depredation, larceny, pillage, plunder, theft.

robust, *a.* SYN.-hale, healthy, hearty, sound, strong, well. ANT.-delicate, diseased, frail, infirm.

rock, *n.* SYN.-boulder, gravel, jewel, pebble, stone.

rogue, *n.* SYN.-cheat, criminal, knave, outlaw, rascal, scamp, scoundrel.

role, *n.* SYN.-character, function, lines, impersonation, part, performance.

romantic, *a.* SYN.-dreamy, extravagant, fanciful, fantastic, fictitious, ideal, idealistic, imaginative, maudlin, mawkish, picturesque, poetic, sentimental. ANT.-factual, literal, matter-of-fact, practical, prosaic.

room, *n.* SYN.-abode, apartment, chamber, cubicle, dormitory, flat, garret, hotel, inn, motel, niche, office; latitude, leeway, scope, space, vastness.

roomy, *a.* SYN.-ample, broad, capacious, extensive, large, spacious, vast, wide. ANT.-confined, cramped, limited, narrow.

root, *n.* SYN.-ancestor, base, basis, bottom, foundation, ground, groundwork, substructure, support, underpinning.

roster, *n.* SYN.-catalogue, document, index, list, register, roll, scroll.

rot, *v.* SYN.-decay, decompose, disintegrate, putrefy, spoil, waste. ANT.-flourish, grow, increase, luxuriate, rise.

rotten, *a.* SYN.-bad, decayed, defective, depraved, disgusting, filthy, offensive, putrid, putrefied, rancid, rank, spoiled.

rotate, *v.* SYN.-circle, circulate, invert, revolve, spin, turn, twirl, twist, wheel, whirl. ANT.-arrest, fix, stand, stop.

rotund, *a.* SYN.-bulbous, chubby, plump, round.

rough, *a.* SYN.-blunt, brusque, churlish, coarse, craggy, crude, cursory, gruff, harsh, imperfect, incomplete, irregular, jagged, rude, rugged, scabrous, scratchy, severe, stormy, tempestuous, turbulent, uncivil, uneven, unfinished, unpolished, violent; approximate, imprecise, inexact. ANT.-calm, civil, courteous, even, fine, finished, gentle, level, mild, placid, polished, refined, sleek, slippery, smooth, tranquil, unruffled.

round, *a.* SYN.-bulbous, chubby, circular, complete, curved, cylindrical, entire, globular, plump, rotund, spherical.

roundabout, *a.* SYN.-circuitous, crooked, cunning, devious, distorted, indirect, tortuous, tricky, wandering, winding. ANT.-direct, honest, straight, straightforward.

rouse, *v.* SYN.-anger, aggravate, annoy, animate, awaken, excite, incite, irk, provoke, startle, stimulate, urge.

rout, *v.* SYN.-beat, conquer, crush, defeat, humble, master, overcome, quell, subdue, subjugate, surmount, vanquish. ANT.-capitulate, cede, lose, retreat, surrender.

route, *n.* SYN.-avenue, channel, course, passage, path, road, street, thoroughfare, track, trail, walk, way.

routine, *n.* SYN.-act, custom, fashion, habit, norm, practice, procedure, system, usage, use, wont.

rove, *v.* SYN.-explore, meander, range, roam, wander.

rowdy, *n.* SYN.-bully, rascal, ruffian, thug.

royal, *a.* SYN.-courtly, dignified, grand, imperial, kingly, lordly, majestic, monarchal, noble, princely, regal, ruling, sovereign, stately, supreme. ANT.-common, humble, low, plebeian, proletarian, servile, vulgar.

rub, *v.* SYN.-brush, burnish, chafe, clean, massage, polish, scour, scrub, shine,

rude, *a.* SYN.-blunt, boorish, coarse, crude, discourteous, fierce, gruff, harsh, ignorant, illiterate, impolite, impudent, inclement, insolent, primitive, raw, rough, saucy, savage, surly, tumultuous, uncivil, unpolished, untaught, violent, vulgar. ANT.-calm, civil, courtly, dignified, genteel, mild, noble, peaceful, polished, stately.

ruffle, *v.* SYN.-agitate, anger, annoy, bother, disturb, fret, harass, irritate, rumple, torment, tousle, upset.

rugged, *a.* SYN.-craggy, harsh, irregular, jagged, rough, scabrous, severe, stormy, tempestuous, turbulent, uneven, violent. ANT.-even, fine, finished, level, polished, refined, sleek, slippery, smooth.

ruin, *v.* SYN.-annihilate, bankrupt, demolish, destroy, devastate, drain, fleece, obliterate, ravage, raze, sabotage, vandalize, wreck. ANT.-construct, establish, make, preserve, save.

ruinous, *a.* SYN.-baneful, deadly, deleterious, destructive, detrimental, devastating, fatal, injurious, noxious, pernicious. ANT.-beneficial, constructive, creative, profitable, salutary.

rule, *n.* SYN.-axiom, canon, formula, guide, law, maxim, method, order, precept, principle, propriety, regulation, standard, statute, system; authority, control, direction, dominion, government, jurisdiction, mastery, reign, sovereignty, sway. ANT.-chance, deviation, exception, hazard, irregularity; anarchy, chaos, misrule.

rule, v. SYN.-command, control, direct, dominate, govern, manage, regulate, superintend. ANT.-abandon, follow, forsake, ignore, submit.

rumor, n. SYN.-chatter, fabrication, gossip, hearsay, news, scandal, slander.

run, v. SYN.-bound, dart, dash, escape, go, hurry, jog, move, race, rush, scramble, scurry, sprint, trot,

rupture, v. SYN.-break, burst, crack, crush, demolish, destroy, fracture, rack, rend, shatter, smash. ANT.-join, mend, renovate, repair, restore.

rural, a. SYN.-agrarian, agricultural, bucolic, pastoral, rustic, suburban.

ruse, n. SYN.-artifice, deception, device, fraud, guile, hoax, imposture, ploy, stratagem, stunt, subterfuge, trick, wile. ANT.-candor, exposure, honesty, openness, sincerity.

rush, v. SYN.-accelerate, expedite, hasten, hurry, precipitate, quicken, speed. ANT.-delay, detain, hinder, retard, tarry.

rustic, a. SYN.-boorish, bucolic, coarse, country, homely, pastoral, plain, rural, simple, uncouth, unsophisticated. ANT.-cultured, elegant, polished, refined, urbane.

ruthless, a. SYN.-barbarous, bestial, brutal, brute, brutish, carnal, coarse, cruel, ferocious, fierce, gross, inhuman, merciless, remorseless, rough, rude, savage, sensual. ANT.-civilized, courteous, gentle, humane, kind.

S

sabotage, v. SYN.-attack, damage, destroy, subvert, undermine, vandalize.

sacrament, n. SYN.-association, ceremony, communion, covenant, fellowship, intercourse, observance, participation, pledge, rite, union. ANT.-alienation, non participation.

sacred, a. SYN.-blessed, consecrated, devout, divine, hallowed, holy, pious, religious, saintly, scriptural, spiritual. ANT.-evil, profane, sacrilegious, secular, worldly.

sacrifice, n. SYN.-atonement, forfeiture, offering, penance, reparation, tribute.

sacrifice, v. SYN.-forfeit, forgo, relinquish, renounce, surrender.

sad, a. SYN.-cheerless, dejected, depressed, despondent, disconsolate, dismal, doleful, downcast, gloomy, lugubrious, melancholy, mournful, somber, sorrowful. ANT.-cheerful, glad, happy, joyous, merry.

sadness, n. SYN.-blues, dejection, depression, despondency, gloom, grief, melancholy, sorrow,

safe, a. SYN.-certain, dependable, harmless, protected, reliable, secure, snug, trustworthy. ANT.-dangerous, hazardous, insecure, perilous, unsafe.

safeguard, n. SYN.-bulwark, defense, guard, protection, refuge, security, shelter, shield.

safety, n. SYN.-asylum, protection, refuge, sanctuary, security, shelter.

sagacity, n. SYN.-discretion, erudition, foresight, information, insight, intelligence, judgment, knowledge, learning, prudence, reason, sageness, sense, wisdom. ANT.-foolishness, ignorance, imprudence, nonsense, stupidity.

sage, n. SYN.-disciple, intellectual, learner, philosopher, pupil, savant, scholar, student. ANT. dolt, dunce, fool, idiot, ignoramus.

saint, n. SYN.-altruist, believer, example, ideal, martyr, paragon.

salary, n. SYN.-compensation, earnings, fee, pay, payment, recompense, stipend, wages. ANT.-gift, gratuity, present.

sale, n. SYN.-barter, commerce, deal, marketing, selling, trade, transaction,

salient, a. SYN.-clear, conspicuous, distinguished, manifest, noticeable, obvious, projecting, prominent, protruding, striking, visible. ANT.-common, hidden, inconspicuous, obscure.

salutary, a. SYN.-advantageous, beneficial, good, helpful, profitable, serviceable, useful, wholesome. ANT.-deleterious, destructive, detrimental, harmful, injurious.

salve, n. SYN.-balm, cream, emollient, lubricant, ointment, unguent.

same, a. SYN.-coincident, equal, equivalent, identical, indistinguishable, like, similar. ANT.-contrary, disparate, dissimilar, distinct, opposed.

sample, n. SYN.-case, example, illustration, instance, model, pattern, prototype, specimen.

sanction, n. SYN.-approbation, approval, assent, commendation, consent, endorsement, praise, support. ANT.-censure, reprimand, reproach, stricture.

sanction, v. SYN.-allow, authorize, give, grant, let, permit, suffer, tolerate, yield. ANT.-forbid, object, protest, refuse, resist.

sanctuary, n. SYN.-asylum, church, cover, harbor, haven, protection, refuge, retreat, safety, security, shelter, shrine, temple. ANT.-danger, exposure, hazard, jeopardy, peril.

sane, a. SYN.-intelligent, logical, lucid, normal, rational, reasonable, sensible, sound.

sarcasm, n. SYN.-asperity, banter, bitterness, contempt, derision, irony, lampooning, mockery, ridicule, satire,

sarcastic, a. SYN.-acrimonious, biting, caustic, cutting, derisive, ironic, sardonic, satirical, sneering, taunting. ANT.-affable, agreeable, amiable, pleasant.

sardonic, a. SYN.-acrimonious, bitter, caustic, cruel, fierce, harsh, relentless, ruthless, severe. ANT.-delicious, mellow, pleasant, sweet.

satiate, v. SYN.-accomplish, cloy, deluge, fulfill, glut, gratify, inundate, meet, oversupply, satisfy.

satire, n. SYN.-banter, cleverness, fun, humor, irony, mockery, ridicule, sarcasm, wit, witticism. ANT.-commonplace, platitude, sobriety, solemnity, stupidity.

satirical, a. SYN.-acrimonious, biting,

caustic, cutting, derisive, ironic, sarcastic, sardonic, sneering, taunting. ANT.-affable, agreeable, amiable, pleasant.

satisfactory, a. SYN.-adequate, ample, commensurate, enough, fitting, sufficient, suitable. ANT.-deficient, lacking, scant.

satisfy, v. SYN.-appease, compensate, content, fulfill, gratify, please, remunerate, satiate, suffice. ANT.-annoy, displease, dissatisfy, frustrate, tantalize.

saturate, v. SYN.-fill, impregnate, overfill, penetrate, permeate, pervade, soak.

sauciness, n. SYN.-audacity, boldness, effrontery, impertinence, impudence, insolence, presumption, rudeness. ANT.-diffidence, politeness, subserviency, truckling.

savage, a. SYN.-barbarous, bestial, brutal, brute, brutish, carnal, coarse, cruel, ferocious, gross, inhuman, merciless, remorseless, rough, rude, ruthless, sensual. ANT-civilized, courteous, gentle, humane, kind.

save, v. SYN.-conserve, defend, guard, keep, maintain, preserve, protect, rescue, safeguard, secure, spare, uphold. ANT.-abandon, abolish, destroy, impair, injure.

savings, n. SYN.-accumulation, assets, cache, hoard, investment, property, reserve, resources, security.

savor, v. SYN.-appreciate, enjoy, like, relish, sample, sip, taste.

savory, a. SYN.-appetizing, aromatic, agreeable, delectable, delicious, delightful, luscious, hearty, palatable, tasty. ANT.-acrid, distasteful, nauseous, unpalatable, unsavory

say, v. SYN.-articulate, converse, declare, discourse, express, harangue, speak, talk, tell, utter. ANT.-be silent, hush, refrain.

saying, n. SYN.-adage, aphorism, apothegm, byword, maxim, motto, proverb, saw.

scamper, v. SYN.-dash, hasten, hurry, run, speed, sprint.

scan, v. SYN.-browse, consider, examine, inspect, peruse, scrutinize, skim, study, survey.

scandal, n. SYN.-abasement, chagrin, disgrace, dishonor, disrepute, humiliation, ignominy, mortification, odium, opprobrium, shame. ANT.-dignity, glory, honor, praise, renown.

scandalize, v. SYN.-abuse, asperse, defame, disparage, ill-use, malign, revile, traduce, vilify. ANT.-cherish, honor, praise, protect, respect.

scandalous, a. SYN.-abusive, damning, discreditable, disgraceful, dishonorable, disreputable, false, ignominious, infamous, gossiping, libelous, malicious, outrageous, shameful, slanderous, sordid. ANT. teemed, honorable, renowned, respectable.

scanty, a. SYN.-inadequate, insufficient, lean, little, meager, paltry, scarce, sparse.

scar, n. SYN.-blemish, defect, disfigurement, flaw, mark.

scarce, a. SYN.-choice, exceptional, incomparable, infrequent, occasional, precious, rare, singular, uncommon, unique, unusual. ANT.-abundant, commonplace, customary, frequent, numerous, ordinary, usual, worthless.

scare, v. SYN.-affright, alarm, appall, daunt, dismay, frighten, horrify, intimidate, startle, terrify, terrorize. ANT.-allay, compose, embolden, reassure, soothe.

scared, a. SYN.-afraid, apprehensive, fainthearted, fearful, frightened, terrified, timid, timorous. ANT.-assured, bold, composed, courageous, sanguine.

scatter, v. SYN.-broadcast, diffuse, dispel, disperse, disseminate, dissipate, separate, sprinkle, strew, throw. ANT.-accumulate, amass, assemble, collect, gather.

scenery, n. SYN.-countryside, landscape, panorama, spectacle, view, vista.

scenic, a. SYN.-beautiful, breathtaking, dramatic, picturesque, pretty, spectacular, unspoiled.

scent, n, SYN.-aroma, fetidness, fragrance, fume, incense, odor, perfume, redolence, smell, stench, stink.

schedule, n. SYN.-agenda, calendar, catalogue, inventory, plan, program, record, register, roll, timetable.

scheme, v. SYN.-contrive, design, devise, outline, plan, plot, prepare, project, sketch.

scheme, n. SYN.-arrangement, artfulness, cabal, conspiracy, contrivance, cunning, design, diagram, intrigue, machination, outline, pattern, plan, planning, plotting, program, project, sketch, stratagem, system. ANT.-candor, result, sincerity.

scheming, a. SYN.-crafty, crooked, deceitful, devious, dishonest, foxy, perverse, planning, plotting, sly, treacherous, underhanded, unfaithful.

scholar, n. SYN.-disciple, intellectual, learner, pupil, sage, savant, student. ANT. dolt, dunce, fool, idiot, ignoramus.

scholarly, a. SYN.-academic, bookish, erudite, formal, learned, pedantic, scholastic, theoretical. ANT.-commonsense, ignorant, practical, simple.

scholarship, n. SYN.-cognizance, comprehension, erudition, information, knowledge, learning, lore, understanding, wisdom. ANT.-ignorance, illiteracy, misunderstanding, stupidity.

school, n. SYN.-academy, conservatory, institution.

science, n. SYN.-discipline, enlightenment, knowledge, learning, scholarship. ANT.-ignorance, nascence, superstition.

scold, v. SYN.-admonish, berate, blame, censure, chide, lecture, rate, rebuke, reprehend, reprimand, upbraid, vituperate. ANT.-approve, commend, praise.

scoot, v. SYN.-bustle, dart, hasten, hurry, rush, speed.

scope, n. SYN.-amount, area, compass, degree, expanse, extent, length, magnitude, measure, range, reach, size, stretch.

scorch, v. SYN.-blister, burn, char, scald, sear, singe. ANT.-extinguish, put out,

quench.

scorn, n. SYN.-contempt, contumely, derision, detestation, disdain, hatred, loathing. ANT.-awe, esteem, regard, respect, reverence.

scoundrel, n. SYN.-blackguard, cad, knave, rascal, rogue, scamp, villain.

scrap, v. SYN.-discard, dismiss, eliminate, exclude, reject; bicker, clash, conflict, fight, feud, quarrel, squabble.

scream, v. SYN.-cry, howl, shout, shriek, yell.

screen, v. SYN.-cloak, conceal, cover, hide, protect, shelter, shield, shroud, veil; choose, eliminate, select, sift.

scrimp, v. SYN.- conserve, curtail, economize, limit, pinch, save, skimp, squeeze, tighten.

scrub, v. SYN.-brush, clean, cleanse, mop, rub, scour, wash. ANT.-dirty, pollute, soil, stain, sully.

scruple, n. SYN.-compunction, doubt, hesitation, misgiving, reluctance, uncertainty, uneasiness.

scrupulous, a. SYN.-accurate, careful, cautious, conscientious, exact, particular, precise, strict.

scrutinize, v. SYN.-analyze, appraise, assess, audit check, contemplate, criticize, dissect, evaluate, examine, inspect, notice, question, review, scan, survey, view, watch. ANT.-approve, disregard, neglect, overlook.

search, n. SYN.-examination, exploration, inquiry, investigation, pursuit, quest. ANT.-abandonment, cession, resignation.

search, v. SYN. examine, explore, ferret, hunt, investigate, look, probe, ransack, rummage, scour, scrutinize, seek.

searching, a. SYN.-curious, inquiring, inquisitive, nosy, peeping, peering, prying, seeking, snoopy. ANT.-incurious, indifferent, unconcerned, uninterested.

seasoned, a. SYN.-experienced, established, mature, practiced, settled, skilled, versed.

secede, v. SYN.-depart, leave, retire, retreat, withdraw.

secluded, a. SYN.-alone, deserted, desolate, isolated, lone, lonely, only, single, sole, solitary, unaided. ANT.-accompanied, attended, surrounded.

seclusion, n. SYN.-isolation, insulation, loneliness, quarantine, retirement, segregation, separation, solitude, withdrawal. ANT.-association, communion, connection, fellowship, union.

secondary, a. SYN.-dependent, derived, indirect, inferior, lesser, lower, poorer, subordinate, subsequent, subsidiary. ANT.-better, greater, higher, superior.

secrecy, n. SYN.-concealment, confidence, hiding, mystery, privacy, seclusion, stealth, solitude.

secret, a. SYN.-clandestine, concealed, covert, hidden, latent, mystical, private, secluded, secretive, shrouded, surreptitious, unknown, veiled. ANT.-conspicuous, disclosed, exposed, known, obvious.

secrete, v. SYN.-cloak, conceal, cover, curtain, disguise, envelop, hide, mask, protect, screen, shield, shroud, veil. ANT.-bare, divulge, expose, reveal, un-

veil.

section, n. SYN.-district, division, domain, dominion, land, place, province, quarter, region, territory.

secular, a. SYN.-earthly, laic, lay, mundane, profane, temporal, worldly. ANT.-ecclesiastical, religious, spiritual, unworldly.

secure, a. SYN.-assured, certain, definite, fixed, indubitable, inevitable, positive, sure, undeniable, unquestionable. ANT.-doubtful, probable, questionable, uncertain.

secure, v. SYN.-achieve, acquire, attain, earn, gain, get, obtain, procure, receive. ANT.-forfeit, leave, lose, renounce, surrender.

security, n. SYN.-assurance, bail, bond, earnest, guarantee, guaranty, pawn, pledge, surety, token, warrant.

seduce, v. SYN.-allure, attract, bait, beguile, deceive, delude, dupe, entice, induce, lure, pervert, stimulate, tempt, trick, violate.

see, v. SYN.-behold, contemplate, descry, discern, distinguish, espy, glimpse, inspect, look at, notice, observe, perceive, scan, scrutinize, view, watch, witness.

seek, v. SYN.-ask, attempt, endeavor, ferret, hunt, investigate, look, probe, pursue, rummage, scour, scrutinize, search, try.

seem, v. SYN.- appear, look, resemble, suggest. ANT.-be, exist.

segment, n. SYN.-allotment, apportionment, division, fragment, moiety, part, piece, portion, scrap, section, share. ANT.-entirety, whole.

segregate, v. SYN.-detach, divide, insulate, isolate, separate, sever, split.

seize, v. SYN.-apprehend, arrest, capture, catch, check, clutch, confiscate, detain, grab, grasp, grip, hinder, hold, interrupt, obstruct, restrain, retain snatch, stop, take, withhold. ANT.-activate, discharge, free, liberate, release.

seldom, a. SYN.-hardly, infrequently, occasionally, rarely.

select, a. SYN.-best, choice, chosen, cream, elite, exceptional, pick, picked, preferred.

select, v. SYN.-choose, cull, elect, opt, pick, prefer, winnow. ANT.-refuse, reject.

selection, n. SYN.-alternative, choice, decision, election, option, preference.

selfish, a. SYN. egoistic, illiberal, mercenary, narrow, parsimonious, self-centered, self-seeking, stingy, ungenerous. ANT.-altruistic, charitable, liberal, magnanimous.

sell, v. SYN.-barter, liquidate, market, merchandise, peddle, trade, vend.

send, v. SYN.-cast, discharge, dispatch, emit, impel, propel, ship, throw, transmit. ANT.-bring, get, hold, receive, retain.

senior, a. SYN.-elder, older, superior.

seniority, n. SYN.-age, dotage, precedence, priority, senescence, senility, senior, rank. ANT.-childhood, infancy, junior, youth.

sensation, n. SYN.-apprehension, feeling, image, impression, perception, sense, sensibility. ANT.-apathy, insensibility, stupor, torpor.

sense, *n.* SYN.-connotation, drift, explanation, gist, implication, import, intent, interpretation, meaning, purport, purpose, significance, signification.

senseless, *a.* SYN.-brainless, crass, dense, dull, dumb, foolish, obtuse, stupid, witless. ANT.-alert, bright, clever, discerning, intelligent.

sensible, *v.* SYN.-alive, appreciable, apprehensible, awake, aware, cognizant, comprehending, conscious, perceiving, perceptible, sentient; discreet, intelligent, judicious, practical, prudent, reasonable, sagacious, sage, sober, sound, wise. ANT.-absurd, impalpable, imperceptible, stupid, unaware.

sensitive, *a.* SYN.-delicate, impressionable, nervous, perceptive, prone, responsive, sentient, susceptible, sympathetic, tender, tense, touchy. ANT.-callous, dull, hard, indifferent, insensitive.

sensitivity, *n.* SYN.-awareness, consciousness, sensibility, sympathy.

sensual, *a.* SYN.-carnal, earthy, lascivious, lecherous, lewd, licentious, moving, pleasing, sensory, sensuous, sexual, stimulating, stirring, voluptuous, wanton. ANT.-abstemious, ascetic, chaste, continent, virtuous.

sentence, *n.* SYN.-decree, decision, dictum, edict, judgment, order, pronouncement.

sentence, *v.* SYN.-blame, censure, confine, convict, condemn, damn, denounce, incarcerate, imprison, judge, punish. ANT.-absolve, acquit, exonerate, pardon.

sentiment, *n.* SYN.-affection, emotion, feeling, impression, opinion, passion, sensibility, tenderness. ANT.-coldness, imperturbability, insensibility.

sentimental, *a.* SYN.-dreamy, extravagant, fanciful, ideal, idealistic, imaginative, maudlin, mawkish, picturesque, poetic, romantic. ANT.-factual, literal, matter-of-fact, practical, prosaic.

separate, *v.* SYN.-disconnect, divide, isolate, part, sever, split, sunder. ANT.-combine, gather, join unite.

separation, *n.* SYN.-alienation, insulation, isolation, quarantine, seclusion, segregation, solitude, withdrawal. ANT.-association, communion, connection, fellowship, union.

sequence, *n.* SYN.-arrangement, chain, classification, continuity, distribution, flow, following, gradation, order, placement, progression, series, string, succession, train.

serene, *a.* SYN.-calm, composed, dispassionate, imperturbable, pacific, peaceful, placid, quiet, still, tranquil, undisturbed, unruffled. ANT.-excited, frantic, stormy, turbulent, wild.

serenity, *n.* SYN.-calm, calmness, hush, peace, quiescence, quiet, quietude, repose, rest, silence, stillness, tranquility. ANT.-agitation, disturbance, excitement, noise, tumult.

series, *n.* SYN.-arrangement, chain, following, gradation, order, progression, sequence, string, succession, train.

serious, *a.* SYN.-alarming, critical, dangerous, earnest, grave, great, impor-

tant, momentous, risky, sedate, sober, solemn, staid, weighty. ANT.-informal, relaxed, small, trifling, trivial.

sermon, *n.* SYN.-discourse, guide, homily, lesson, lecture, message, oration, speech, talk.

servant, *n.* SYN.-aid, aide, attendant, domestic, helper, hireling, menial, orderly, retainer.

serve, *v.* SYN.-administer, aid, assist, attend, benefit, cater, contribute, distribute, enlist, follow, forward, help, obey, oblige, promote, purvey, succor, work; provide, satisfy, suffice, supply. ANT.-command, dictate, direct, rule.

service, *n.* SYN.-aid, assistance, attendance, co-operation, duty, help, ministration, use, value; ceremony, rite, sermon, worship.

servile, *a.* SYN.-abject, base, contemptible, despicable, dishonorable, groveling, ignoble, ignominious, low, lowly, mean, menial, sordid, vile, vulgar. ANT.-teemed, exalted, honored, lofty, noble, righteous.

servitude, *n.* SYN.-apprenticeship, bondage, captivity, confinement, imprisonment, serfdom, slavery, subjugation, thralldom, vassalage. ANT.-freedom, liberation.

session, *n.* SYN.-assembly, conference, confrontation, congress, council, encounter, gathering, meeting, parley, rally.

set, *v.* SYN.-arrange, deposit, lay, place, put. ANT.-disarrange, disturb, mislay, misplace, remove.

setback, *n.* SYN.-blow, calamity, check, delay, difficulty, hindrance, misfortune, mishap, reversal, shock.

setting, *n.* SYN.-arena, atmosphere, backdrop, circumstances, context, environment, milieu, perspective, position, scene, stage, surroundings, viewpoint.

settle, *v.* SYN.-adjudicate, conclude, confirm, decide, determine, end, judge, resolve, terminate. ANT.-doubt, hesitate, suspend, vacillate, waver.

settlement, *n.* SYN.-agreement, close, completion, conclusion, decision, deduction, end, finale, issue, judgment, termination. ANT.-beginning, commencement, inception, prelude, start.

sever, *v.* SYN.-chop, cut, divide, part, separate, split, sunder. ANT.-combine, convene, gather, join unite.

severe, *a.* SYN.-acute, arduous, distressing, exacting, extreme, hard, harsh, intense, relentless, rigid, rigorous, sharp, stern, stringent, unmitigated, unyielding, violent. ANT.-considerate, genial, indulgent, merciful, yielding.

shabby, *a.* SYN.-deficient, inferior, mean, paltry, poor, ragged, scanty, seedy, threadbare, worn. ANT.-ample, good, new, opulent.

shack, *n.* SYN.-hovel, hut, shanty, shed.

shade, *n.* SYN.-amount, cast, color, complexion, hint, hue, obscurity, pigment, shadow, stain, tinge, tint, trace, variation. ANT.-achromatism, paleness, transparency.

shadowy, *a.* SYN.-dark, dim, dismal, gloomy, mournful, murky, obscure,

somber, sorrowful, unilluminated; evil, sinister, sullen, wicked; hidden, mystic, occult, secret. ANT.-bright, clear, light, lucid, pleasant.

shake, *v.* SYN.-agitate, flutter, jar, jolt, quake, quaver, quiver, rock, shiver, shudder, sway, totter, tremble, vibrate, waver.

shaky, *a.* SYN.-dubious, faltering, insecure, loose, precarious, questionable, rickety, tentative, tenuous, uncertain, unreliable, unsteady, unsound, unstable, vacillating.

shallow, *a.* SYN.-cursory, exterior, flimsy, frivolous, imperfect, inconsequential, slight, superficial, trite. ANT.-abstruse, complete, deep, profound, thorough.

sham, *n.* SYN.-counterfeit, cover, fabrication, fake, forgery, fraud, imitation, pretense.

shame, *n.* SYN.-abasement, chagrin, disgrace, dishonor, disrepute, humiliation, ignominy, mortification, odium, opprobrium, scandal. ANT.-dignity, glory, honor, praise, renown.

shameful, *a.* SYN.-discreditable, disgraceful, dishonorable, disreputable, humiliating, immoral, ignominious, indecent, lewd, mortifying, obscene, odious, outrageous, scandalous, vulgar. ANT.-teemed, honorable, renowned, respectable.

shameless, *a.* SYN.-audacious, blatant, bold, brazen, corrupt, depraved, forward, immodest, incorrigible, insolent, unabashed, unashamed. ANT.-modest, principled, proper.

shape, *n.* SYN.-appearance, build, cast, configuration, contour, cut, figure, form, frame, guise, image, mold, outline, pattern. ANT.-contortion, deformity, distortion, mutilation.

shape, *v.* SYN.-arrange, combine, compose, constitute, construct, create, devise, fashion, forge, form, frame, invent, make, mold, organize, produce. ANT.-destroy, disfigure, dismantle, misshape, wreck.

share, *n.* SYN.-allotment, allowance, bit, division, fragment, parcel, part, piece, portion, section, segment. ANT.-bulk, whole.

share, *v.* SYN.-accord, allot, apportion, appropriate, assign, bestow, cooperate, dispense, distribute, divide, give, parcel, partake, participate, partition, portion. ANT.-aggregate, amass, combine, condense.

shared, *a.* SYN.-common, communal, correlative, interchangeable, joint, mutual, reciprocal. ANT.-dissociated, separate, unrequited, unshared.

sharp, *a.* SYN.-acrid, acute, biting, bitter, cutting, keen, penetrating, piercing, pointed, pungent, severe, shrill; astute, clever, cunning, quick, shrewd, wily, witty. ANT.-bland, blunt, gentle, shallow, stupid.

shatter, *v.* SYN.-break, burst, crack, demolish, destroy, fracture, pound, rack, rend, rupture, smash. ANT.-join, mend, renovate, repair, restore.

shattered, *a.* SYN.-broken, crushed, destroyed, flattened, fractured, reduced, rent, ruptured, smashed, wrecked.

ANT.-integral, repaired, united, whole.

shed, *v.* SYN.-cast, discard, drop, emit, molt, radiate, scatter, spread.

sheer, *a.* SYN.-delicate, fine, flimsy, gossamer, thin, transparent; absolute, downright, pure, simple, utter; abrupt, precipitous, steep.

shelter, *n.* SYN.-asylum, cover, harbor, haven, protection, refuge, retreat, safety, sanctuary, security. ANT.-danger, exposure, hazard, jeopardy, peril.

shelter, *v.* SYN.-clothe, cover, defend, envelop, fortify, guard, protect, safeguard, shield. ANT.-bare, expose, reveal.

shield, *v.* SYN.-cloak, clothe, conceal, cover, curtain, disguise, envelop, guard, hide, mask, protect, screen, shroud, veil. ANT.-bare, divulge, expose, reveal, unveil.

shift, *v.* SYN.-alter, change, convert, modify, transfigure, transform, vary, veer. ANT.-continue, establish, preserve, settle, stabilize.

shifting, *a.* SYN.-changeable, fickle, fitful, inconstant, unstable, vacillating, variable, wavering. ANT.-constant, stable, steady, unchanging, uniform.

shine, *v.* SYN.-beam, blaze, flash, flicker, glare, gleam, glimmer, glisten, glitter, glow, radiate, scintillate, shimmer, sparkle, twinkle; brush, buff, burnish, clean, polish, wax.

shining, *a.* SYN.-brilliant, bright, dazzling, effulgent, glorious, gorgeous, grand, illustrious, magnificent, radiant, resplendent, showy, splendid, sumptuous, superb. ANT.-dull, mediocre, modest, ordinary, unimpressive.

shirk, *v.* SYN.-avoid, evade, malinger, neglect, slack.

shock, *v.* SYN.-alarm, amaze, astonish, astound, disconcert, dumbfound, flabbergast, startle, stun, surprise, take aback. ANT.-admonish, caution, forewarn, prepare.

shocked, *a.* SYN.-aghast, appalled, astonished, astounded, awed, bewildered, dumbfounded, offended, overwhelmed, startled, stunned, upset.

shocking, *a.* SYN.-appalling, dreadful, fearful, frightful, gruesome, hideous, horrible, horrid, severe, terrible. ANT.-happy, joyous, pleasing, safe, secure.

short, *a.* SYN.-dumpy, dwarfed, little, low, pudgy, small, squat, undersized; abrupt, brief, compendious, concise, curt, laconic, succinct, summary, terse; deficient, inadequate, insufficient, lacking, limited. ANT.-abundant, ample, big, extended, protracted.

shorten, *v.* SYN.-abbreviate, abridge, condense, contract, curtail, diminish, lessen, limit, reduce, restrict. ANT.-elongate, extend, lengthen.

shortsighted, *a.* SYN.- expedient, improvident, impulsive, incautious, heedless, mindless, rash, reckless, thoughtless, unmindful, unthinking.

shout, *v.* SYN.-bellow, call, call out, cry, cry out, holler, scream, vociferate, yell. ANT.-intimate, whisper, write.

show, *n.* SYN.-array, display, exhibition, exposition; demonstration, flourish, ostentation, parade, spectacle, splurge; entertainment, movie, performance,

production.

show, *v.* SYN.-demonstrate, disclose, display, evidence, exhibit, expose, indicate, manifest, parade, present, prove, reveal, unfold, verify; conduct, direct, guide, inform, instruct, teach, usher. ANT.-conceal, confuse, hide.

showy, *a.* SYN.-affected, artificial, ceremonious, dramatic, flashy, gaudy, histrionic, melodramatic, ostentatious, pretentious, stagy, superficial, tawdry, theatrical. ANT.-modest, subdued, unaffected, unemotional.

shred, *n.* SYN.-bit, crumb, fragment, ort, particle, piece, scrap, snip, tatter.

shred, *v.* SYN.-lacerate, rend, rip, rive, sever, slit, split, sunder, tear. ANT.-join, mend, repair, sew, unite.

shrewd, *a.* SYN.-artful, astute, calculating, clever, crafty, cunning, foxy, furtive, guileful, insidious, intelligent, keen, perceptive, quick, sharp, sly, stealthy, subtle, surreptitious, tricky, underhanded, wily. ANT.-candid, frank, ingenuous, open, sincere.

shrill, *a.* SYN.-acute, cutting; biting, penetrating, piercing, sharp. ANT.-bland, blunt, gentle.

shrine, *n.* SYN.-column, crypt, mausoleum, memorial, monolith, monument, obelisk, statue.

shrink, *v.* SYN.-cringe, flinch, recoil, wince, withdraw; decrease, diminish, dwindle, lessen, reduce, shrivel.

shrivel, *v.* SYN.-abate, contract, decline, dry, parch, shrink, wilt, wither, wizen. ANT.-refresh, rejuvenate, renew.

shun, *v.* SYN.-avert, avoid, disregard, dodge, eschew, elude, evade, forbear, forestall, ignore, reject, scorn, slight, snub, spurn. ANT.-confront, encounter, face, meet, oppose.

shut, *v.* SYN.-close, conclude, fasten, lock, secure, seal. ANT.-open.

shy, *a.* SYN.-bashful, cautious, chary, demure, diffident, fearful, modest, reserved, retiring, sheepish, shrinking, timorous, wary. ANT.-audacious, bold, brazen, forward, immodest.

sick, *a.* SYN.-ailing, diseased, ill, indisposed, infirm, morbid, unhealthy, unwell. ANT.-healthy, robust, sound, strong, well.

sickness, *n.* SYN.-ailment, complaint, disease, disorder, illness, infirmity, malady. ANT.-health, healthiness, soundness, vigor.

siege, *n.* SYN.-assault, attack, blockade, invasion, offensive, onslaught, raid, strike.

sight, *n.* SYN.-display, scene, spectacle, view, vision.

sign, *n.* SYN.-beacon, clue, emblem, foreboding, gesture, hint, indication, mark, note, omen, premonition, portent, proof, signal, suggestion, symbol, symptom, token.

signal, *n.* SYN.-alarm, beacon, call, flag, impulse, warning, wave. ANT.-calm, inactivity, quiet, security, tranquillity.

significance, *n.* SYN.-connotation, drift, explanation, gist, implication, import, intent, interpretation, meaning, purport, purpose, sense, signification.

significant, *a.* SYN.-critical, grave, impor-

tant, indicative, material, momentous, telling, weighty. ANT.-insignificant, irrelevant, meaningless, negligible, unimportant.

signify, *v.* SYN.-denote, designate, disclose, imply, indicate, intimate, manifest, reveal, show, specify. ANT.-conceal, distract, divert, falsify, mislead.

silence, *n.* SYN.-hush, quiet, quietude, serenity, stillness, tranquility. ANT.-noise, tumult.

silent, *a.* SYN.-calm, dumb, hushed, mute, noiseless, peaceful, quiet, still, taciturn, tranquil. ANT.-clamorous, loud, noisy, raucous.

silly, *a.* SYN.-absurd, asinine, brainless, crazy, foolish, idiotic, irrational, nonsensical, preposterous, ridiculous, senseless, simple, witless. ANT.-judicious, prudent, sagacious, sane, wise.

similar, *a.* SYN.-akin, alike, allied, analogous, comparable, correlative, correspondent, corresponding, like, parallel. ANT.-different, dissimilar, divergent, incongruous, opposed.

similarity, *n.* SYN.-analogy, correspondence, likeness, parity, resemblance, similitude. ANT.-difference, distinction, variance.

simple, *a.* SYN. easy, effortless, elementary, facile, mere, pure, single, uncompounded, unmixed; artless, frank, homely, humble, naive, natural, open, plain, unsophisticated; asinine, credulous, foolish, silly. ANT.-adorned, artful, complex, intricate, wise.

simply, *a.* SYN.-absolutely, directly, easily, frankly, honestly, merely, openly, plainly, purely, sincerely, utterly.

simulate, *v.* SYN.-ape, copy, counterfeit, duplicate, feign, imitate, impersonate, mimic, mock. ANT.-alter, distort, diverge, invent.

sin, *n.* SYN.-crime, evil, guilt, iniquity, offense, transgression, ungodliness, vice, wickedness, wrong. ANT.-goodness, innocence, purity, righteousness, virtue.

sincere, *a.* SYN.-candid, earnest, frank, genuine, heartfelt, honest, open, straightforward, true, truthful, unfeigned, upright. ANT.-affected, dishonest, hypocritical, insincere, untruthful.

sincerity, *n.* SYN.-candor, fairness, frankness, honesty, integrity, justice, openness, rectitude, responsibility, trustworthiness, uprightness. ANT.-cheating, deceit, dishonesty, fraud, trickery.

sinful, *a.* SYN.-bad, corrupt, dissolute, immoral, indecent, licentious, profligate, unprincipled, vicious, wicked. ANT.-chaste, high-minded, noble, pure, virtuous.

sing, *v.* SYN.-carol, chant, croon, hum, intone, lilt, warble.

singe, *v.* SYN.-burn, char, scorch, sear. ANT.-extinguish, put out, quench.

single, *a.* SYN.-alone, distinct, distinctive, exclusive, individual, lone, only, particular, separate, singular, sole, solitary, special, specific, unattached, unwed, unique. ANT.-common, general, ordinary, universal.

singly, *a.* SYN.-apart, independently, individually, separately.

singular, *a.* SYN.-choice, curious, distinctive, exceptional, extraordinary, individual, matchless, odd, particular, peculiar, rare, remarkable, special, strange, striking, uncommon, unequaled, unique, unusual. ANT.-common, general, normal, ordinary.

sinister, *a.* SYN.-bad, base, dire, evil, foreboding, malevolent, menacing, ominous, perverse, threatening, unlucky, wicked. ANT.-beneficent, desirable, encouraging, favorable, fortunate, good, lucky.

sire, *v.* SYN.-beget, breed, create, engender, father, generate, originate, procreate, produce, propagate. ANT.-abort, destroy, extinguish, kill, murder.

site, *n.* SYN.-locale, locality, location, place, plat, plot, position, section, spot, station.

situated, *a.* SYN.-entrenched, established, fixed, located, placed, placement, positioned.

situation, *n.* SYN.-case, circumstance, condition, employment, job, plight, predicament, post, rank, standing, state, station, status.

size, *n.* SYN.-amount, amplitude, area, bigness, bulk, dimensions, expanse, extent, greatness, largeness, magnitude, mass, proportions, scope, stature, volume.

skeptic, *n.* SYN.-agnostic, cynic, deist, doubter, freethinker, infidel, questioner, unbeliever. ANT.-adorer, believer, follower, worshiper.

skepticism, *n.* SYN.-ambiguity, distrust, doubt, incredulity, scruple, suspicion, unbelief, uncertainty. ANT.-belief, certainty, conviction, determination. faith.

sketch, *n.* SYN.-blueprint, chart, contour, delineation, description, draft, drawing, illustration, image, likeness, outline, plan, portrayal, profile, rendering, representation, scene, silhouette, view.

sketch, *v.* SYN.-chart, compose, delineate, depict, draft, draw, formulate, outline, picture, portray, represent, trace, write.

skill, *n.* SYN.-ability, adroitness, cleverness, cunning, deftness, dexterity, facility, ingenuity, knack, readiness, skillfulness, ANT.-awkwardness, clumsiness, inability, ineptitude.

skilled, *a.* See **skillful.**

skillful, *a.* SYN.-able, accomplished, adept, clever, competent, cunning, expert, ingenious, practiced, proficient, skilled, versed. ANT.-awkward, bungling, clumsy, inexpert, untrained.

skimpy, *a.* SYN.-deficient, lacking, inadequate, insufficient, scant, scarce, short.

skinflint, *n.* SYN.-cheapskate, hoarder, miser, piker, tightwad.

skirmish, *n.* SYN.-assault, attack, battle, clash, conflict, encounter, engagement, fight, offensive.

slack, *a.* SYN.-baggy, disorderly, limp, loose, negligent, relaxed, remiss, slovenly, unbound, unfastened, unkempt, untied. ANT.-tight, restrained.

slander, *n.* SYN.-aspersion, backbiting, calumny, defamation, libel, scandal, vilification. ANT.-applause, commendation, defense, flattery, praise.

slaughter, *n.* SYN.-bloodshed, butchery, carnage, massacre, murder, pogrom, slaying.

slaughter, *v.* SYN.-assassinate, butcher, devastate, execute, kill, massacre, murder, slay. ANT.-animate, protect, resuscitate, save, vivify.

slavery, *n.* SYN.-bondage, captivity, confinement, imprisonment, serfdom, servitude, thralldom, vassalage. ANT.-freedom, liberation.

sleazy, *a.* SYN.-base, cheap, flimsy, shoddy, tacky, trashy.

sleek, *a.* SYN.-glossy, polished, silky, slick, smooth. ANT.-harsh, rough, rugged.

sleep, *n.* SYN.-catnap, doze, drowse, nap, nod, repose, rest, slumber, snooze, trance.

slender, *a.* SYN.-lean, skinny, slight, slim, spare, thin. ANT.-broad, bulky, fat, thick, wide.

slight, *a.* SYN.-delicate, emaciated, flimsy, frail, insignificant, lean, paltry, petty, scrawny, skinny, slender, slim, spare, superficial, thin, trifling, unimportant. ANT.-broad, bulky, fat, thick, wide.

slight, *n.* SYN.-affront, disdain, contempt, disregard, insult, neglect, scorn.

slightly, *a.* SYN.-barely, hardly, inconsiderably, lightly, little, scarcely.

slink, *v.* SYN.-cower, lurk, prowl, skulk, sneak, steal.

slip, *n.* SYN.-blunder, error, fallacy, fault, inaccuracy, indiscretion, lapse, mistake, misstatement. ANT.-accuracy, precision, truth.

slogan, *n.* SYN.-axiom, device, legend, motto, trademark.

slope, *n.* SYN.-bank, bending, grade, inclination. incline, leaning, ramp

slothful, *a.* SYN.-idle, inactive, indolent, inert, lazy, slow, sluggish, supine, torpid. ANT.-active, alert, assiduous, diligent.

slow, *a.* SYN.-dawdling, delaying, deliberate, dull, gradual, laggard, leisurely, sluggish, tired. ANT.-fast, quick, rapid, speedy, swift.

sluggish, *a.* See **slow, slothful.**

slumber, *n.* SYN.-inactivity, quiescence, repose, rest, sleep.

slumber, *v.* SYN.-catnap, doze, drowse, nap, nod, repose, rest, sleep, snooze.

sly, *a.* SYN.-artful, astute, clandestine, covert, crafty, cunning, foxy, furtive, guileful, insidious, shrewd, stealthy, subtle, surreptitious, tricky, underhanded, wily. ANT.-candid, frank, ingenuous, open, sincere.

small, *a.* SYN.-diminutive, insignificant, little, miniature, minute, petty, puny, slight, tiny, trivial, wee. ANT.-big, enormous, huge, immense, large.

smart, *a.* SYN.-adroit, adept, alert, astute, bright, clever, discerning, enlightened, ingenious, intellectual, intelligent, knowledgeable, quick, quick-witted, sharp, talented, well-informed, witty. ANT.-awkward, bungling, clumsy, dull, foolish, slow, stupid.

smart, *n.* SYN.-affront, bite, burn, hurt, insult, prick, sting, wound.

smash, *v.* SYN.-break, burst, crack, crush, demolish, destroy, fracture, pound, rack, rend, rupture, shatter. ANT.-join, mend, renovate, repair, restore.

smell, *n.* SYN.-aroma, fetidness, fragrance, fume, incense, odor, perfume, redolence, scent, stench, stink.

smolder, *v.* SYN.-burn, fester, fret, fume, stew, seethe, smoke.

smooth, *a.* SYN.-diplomatic, even, flat, glib, level, plain, polished, sleek, slick, suave, urbane. ANT.-bluff, blunt, harsh, rough, rugged.

smother, *v.* SYN.-choke, drench, gag, quench, stifle, throttle.

smug, *a.* SYN.-complacent, conceited, egotistical, satisfied, self-righteous, snobbish.

snag, *n.* SYN.-adversity, complication, barrier, difficulty, hindrance, obstacle, pitfall, problem.

snare, *v.* SYN.-capture, catch, enmesh, entangle, grasp, grip, seize, trap. ANT.-liberate, lose, release.

snatch, *v.* SYN.-grab, grasp, nab, pluck, seize, steal, swipe.

sneak, *v.* SYN.-creep, lurk, prowl, skulk, slink.

sneer, *v.* SYN.-deride, flout, gibe, jeer, mock, scoff, scorn, taunt. ANT.-compliment, flatter, laud, praise.

sneering, *n.* SYN.-derision, gibe, jeering, mockery, raillery, ridicule, sarcasm.

snob, *n.* SYN.- elitist, egotist, pretender, showoff, upstart

snoopy, *a.* SYN.-curious, inquiring, inquisitive, interrogative, meddling, nosy, peeping, peering, prying, searching. ANT.-incurious, indifferent, unconcerned, uninterested.

snub, *v.* SYN.-disdain, disregard, humiliate, ignore, neglect, slight.

snug, *a.* SYN.-close, comfortable, compact, cozy, constricted, homey, intimate, secure, tight. ANT.-lax, loose, open.

soar, *v.* SYN.-flit, float, flutter, fly, glide, hover, mount, sail. ANT.-descend, fall, plummet, sink.

sober, *a.* SYN.-calm, composed, controlled, earnest, grave, rational, restrained, sedate, serious, solemn, somber, sound, staid, steady, subdued, temperate. ANT.-boisterous, informal, joyful.

sobriety, *n.* SYN.-abstention, abstinence, continence, forbearance, moderation, self-denial, temperance. ANT.-excess, gluttony, greed, intoxication, self-indulgence.

social, *a.* SYN.-affable, civil, communicative, congenial, friendly, gregarious, hospitable, outgoing, pleasant, sociable. ANT.-antisocial, disagreeable, hermitic, inhospitable.

soft, *a.* SYN.-compassionate, flexible, gentle, lenient, malleable, meek, mellow, mild, subdued, supple, tender, yielding. ANT.-hard, rigid, rough, tough, unyielding.

soil, *n.* SYN.-dirt, earth, ground, land, loam.

soil, *v.* SYN.-befoul, blemish, spot, stain, sully, tarnish. ANT.-clean, cleanse.

solace, n. SYN.-alleviate, comfort, consolation, contentment, ease, relief, soothe, succor. ANT.-affliction, discomfort, misery, suffering, torment, torture.

sole, a. SYN.-alone, deserted, desolate, isolated, lonely, secluded, unaided, lone, only, single, solitary. ANT.-accompanied, attended, surrounded.

solemn, a. SYN.-august, awe-inspiring, ceremonious, earnest, formal, grave, imposing, impressive, majestic, reverential, ritualistic, sedate, serious, sober, staid. ANT.-boisterous, informal, joyful, ordinary.

solicitude, n. SYN.-anxiety, care, caution, circumspection, compassion, concern, consideration, thoughtfulness, regard, wariness, worry. ANT.-disregard, indifference, neglect.

solid, a. SYN.-compact, dependable, firm, fixed, genuine, hard, reliable, sound, stable, substantial, unbroken, whole. ANT.-counterfeit, divided, elastic, flimsy, frail.

solitary, a. SYN.-alone, deserted, desolate, isolated, lone, lonely, only, secluded, single, sole, unaided. ANT.-accompanied, attended, surrounded.

solitude, n. SYN.-alienation, asylum, concealment, isolation, loneliness, privacy, refuge, retirement, retreat, seclusion. ANT.-exposure, notoriety, publicity.

somber, a. SYN.-bleak, cheerless, dark, dismal, doleful, dreary, dull, funereal, gloomy, melancholy, morose, sad, sullen. ANT.-cheerful, gay, joyous, lively.

song, n. SYN.-air, aria, lyric, melody, music, strain, tune.

soon, adv. SYN.-beforehand, betimes, early, easily, readily, shortly, speedily. ANT.-belated, late, over-due, tardy.

soothe, v. SYN.-cheer, comfort, console, encourage, gladden, mitigate, relieve, soften, solace, sympathize. ANT.-antagonize, aggravate, depress, dishearten.

soothing, a. SYN.-benign, calm, comforting, docile, gentle, mild, peaceful, placid, relaxed, serene, soft, tame, tractable. ANT.-fierce, harsh, rough, savage, violent.

sophisticated, a. SYN.-artificial, blasé, complex, cultivated, cultured, mature, practical, precious, refined, worldly, worldly-wise. ANT.-crude, ingenuous, naive, simple, uncouth.

sorcery, n. SYN.-alchemy, black art, conjuring, enchantment, legerdemain, magic, necromancy, voodoo, witchcraft, wizardry.

sordid, a. SYN.-abject, base, debased, depraved, despicable, foul, ignoble, loathsome, low, mean, obscene, odious, revolting, vicious, vile, vulgar, wicked, worthless, wretched. ANT.-attractive, decent, honorable, laudable, upright.

sorrow, n. SYN.-affliction, anguish, distress, grief, heartache, lamentation, misery, mourning, sadness, tribulation, woe. ANT.-comfort, consolation, happiness, joy, solace.

sorry, a. SYN.-afflicted, beggarly, contemptible, grieved, hurt, mean, pained, paltry, pitiable, pitiful, poor, sad, shabby, sorrowful, vexed, vile, worthless, wretched; contrite, penitent, remorseful, repentant. ANT.-cheerful, delighted, impenitent, splendid; unrepentant.

sort, n. SYN.-category, character, class, description, kind, nature, type. ANT.-deviation, eccentricity, monstrosity, peculiarity.

sound, a. SYN.-binding, dependable, healthy, hearty, legal, orthodox, powerful, proper, prudent, rational, reasonable, reliable, robust, sane, stable, strong, valid, vigorous, weighty. ANT.-counterfeit, null, spurious, void, weak.

sound, n. SYN.-din, intonation, noise, note, resonance, timbre, tone, vibration. ANT.-hush, quiet, silence, stillness.

sound, v. SYN.-articulate, echo, enunciate, pronounce, reverberate, say, shout, utter.

sour, a. SYN.-acid, acrimonious, bitter, glum, morose, peevish, rancid, sharp, sullen, tart. ANT.-genial, kindly, sweet, wholesome.

source, n. SYN.-agent, beginning, cause, determinant, incentive, inducement, motive, origin, principle, reason. ANT.-consequence, effect, end, result.

sovereignty, n. SYN.-authority, command, control, dominion, influence, power, predominance, sway.

spacious, a. SYN.-ample, broad, capacious, extensive, large, roomy, vast, wide. ANT.-confined, cramped, limited, narrow.

sparkle, v. SYN.-flicker, gleam, glimmer, glisten, glitter, glow, radiate, shimmer, shine, twinkle.

sparse, a. SYN.-barren, deficient, lean, meager, scanty.

speak, v. SYN.-articulate, converse, declare, discourse, express, harangue, lecture, say, talk, tell, utter. ANT.-be silent, hush, refrain.

special, a. SYN.-distinctive, exceptional, extraordinary, individual, particular, peculiar, uncommon, unusual. ANT.-broad, comprehensive, general, prevailing, widespread.

specific, a. SYN.-definite, explicit, limited, precise; categorical, characteristic, especial, peculiar. ANT.-general, generic, vague.

species, n. SYN.-class, division, family, genus, kind, order, variety, sort.

specify, v. SYN.-appoint, call, categorize, choose, classify, denominate, differentiate, distinguish, entitle, identify, mention, name, stipulate. ANT.-hint, miscall, misname.

specimen, n. SYN.-example, illustration, model, pattern, prototype, sample.

spectacle, n. SYN.-array, display, exhibition, exposition; demonstration, flourish, ostentation, parade, show, splurge.

speculate, v. SYN.-apprehend, assume, believe, conjecture, deduce, guess, imagine, presume, suppose, surmise, think. ANT.-ascertain, conclude, demonstrate, know, prove.

speech, n. SYN.-conversation, dialogue, discourse, discussion, lecture, report, talk. ANT.-correspondence, meditation, silence, writing.

speed, v. SYN.-accelerate, dispatch, expedite, facilitate, forward, hasten, hurry, push, quicken, rush. ANT.-block, hinder, impede, retard, slow.

spend, v. SYN.-circulate, consume, deplete, disburse, dispense, pass, pay, squander

spherical, a. SYN.-bulbous, circular, curved, cylindrical, globular, plump, rotund, round.

spirit, n. SYN.-apparition, ghost, phantom, soul, specter; courage, enthusiasm, fortitude, liveliness, temper, verve, vigor, vitality, zeal. ANT.-body, flesh, substance; languor, listlessness.

spirited, a. SYN.-active, alive, animated, blithe, lively, sprightly, vivacious.

spiritual, a. SYN.-divine, ethereal, ghostly, holy, immaterial, incorporeal, religious, sacred, supernatural, unearthly, unworldly. ANT.-carnal, corporeal, material, mundane, physical.

spiteful, a. SYN.-disagreeable, ill-natured, malicious, surly, vengeful, vicious. ANT.-peaceful, placid.

splendid, a. SYN.-brilliant, bright, dazzling, effulgent, glorious, gorgeous, grand, illustrious, magnificent, radiant, resplendent, shining, showy, sumptuous, superb. ANT.-dull, mediocre, modest, ordinary, unimpressive.

splendor, n. SYN.-brightness, brilliance, brilliancy, effulgence, grandeur, luster, magnificence, radiance. ANT.-darkness, dullness, gloom, obscurity.

split, v. SYN.-cleave, rend, rip, rive, sever, shred, slit, sunder, tear. ANT.-join, mend, repair, sew, unite.

spoil, v. SYN.-decay, decompose, disintegrate, putrefy, rot, ruin, waste. ANT.-flourish, grow, rise.

spoken, a. SYN.-literal, oral, phonetic, told, uttered, verbal, vocal. ANT.-documentary, recorded, written.

spontaneous, a. SYN.-automatic, extemporaneous, impulsive, instinctive, offhand, voluntary, willing. ANT.-compulsory, forced, planned, prepared, rehearsed.

sport, n. SYN.-amusement, contest, diversion, fun, game, match, merriment, pastime, play, recreation. ANT.-business drudgery, hardship, labor, work.

sport, v. SYN.-caper, frolic, gamble, gambol, play, revel, romp, stake, wager

spread, v. SYN.-air, broadcast, distribute, exhibit, expand, extend, open, scatter, smear, unfold, unfurl. ANT.-close, conceal, shut.

sprightly, a. SYN.-animated, blithe, buoyant, cheerful, effervescent, elated, gay, light, lively, resilient, spirited, vivacious. ANT.-dejected, depressed, despondent, hopeless, sullen.

spur, n. SYN.-cause, impulse, incentive, incitement, inducement, motive, principle, purpose, reason, stimulus. ANT.-action, attempt, deed, effort, result.

squabble, v. SYN.-altercate, argue, bicker, contend, contest, debate, disagree, discuss, dispute, quarrel, wrangle. ANT.-agree, allow, assent, concede.

squalid, a. SYN.-dirty, filthy, foul, grimy,

mean, muddy, nasty, pitiful, shabby, soiled, wretched. ANT.-clean, neat, presentable; pure, wholesome.

squander, *v.* SYN.-dissipate, lavish, misuse, waste, wear out. ANT.-accumulate, economize, preserve, save.

stable, *a.* SYN.-constant, durable, enduring, established, firm, fixed, immovable, immutable, lasting, permanent, secure, staunch, steadfast, steady, unwavering. ANT.-changeable, erratic, irresolute, vacillating, variable.

staff, *n.* SYN.-assistants, cadre, crew, employees, force, help, helpers, organization, personnel.

staid, *a.* SYN.-demure, grave, modest, sedate, serious, sober, solemn. ANT.-boisterous, informal, joyful, ordinary.

stain, *v.* SYN.-befoul, blemish, blight, defile, discolor, disgrace, soil, spot, sully, tarnish; color, dye, tinge, tint. ANT.-bleach, cleanse, decorate, honor, purify.

stale, *a.* SYN.-banal, common, dry, dull, flat, insipid, musty, old, trite.

stand, *v.* SYN.-abide, bear, continue, endure, suffer, sustain, tolerate; halt, pause, remain, rest, stay, stop. ANT.-advance, progress, run, submit, yield.

standard, *n.* SYN.-criterion, gauge, law, measure, norm, rule, test, touchstone. ANT.-chance, fancy, guess, supposition.

start, *n.* SYN.-beginning, commencement, genesis, inception, opening, origin, outset, source. ANT.-close, completion, consummation, end, termination.

start, *v.* SYN.-arise, begin, commence, establish, found, inaugurate, initiate, institute, organize, originate. ANT.-complete, end, finish, terminate.

startle, *v.* SYN.-alarm, amaze, astonish, astound, disconcert, dumbfound, flabbergast, frighten, panic, scare, shock, stun, surprise, terrify. ANT.-admonish, caution, forewarn, prepare.

starved, *a.* SYN.-craving, famished, hungry, ravenous, voracious. ANT.-full, gorged, sated, satiated, satisfied.

state, *n.* SYN.-case, circumstance, condition, plight, predicament, situation; commonwealth, community, kingdom, nationality, people, realm.

state, *v.* SYN.-affirm, assert, avow, claim, declare, explain, express, propound, recite, recount, say, specify, tell, utter. ANT.-conceal, deny, imply, retract.

stately, *a.* SYN.-courtly, dignified, grand, imperial, kingly, lordly, majestic, monarchal, noble, princely, regal, royal, ruling, sovereign, supreme. ANT.-common, humble, low, plebeian, proletarian, servile, vulgar.

statement, *n.* SYN.-allegation, announcement, assertion, communication, declaration, mention, proposition, report, thesis.

station, *n.* SYN.-level, location, occupation, office, order, place, position, post, rank, spot, standing.

statuesque, *a.* SYN.-august, beautiful, dazzling, divine, elegant, exquisite, gorgeous, graceful, grand, impressive, radiant, stately, venerable.

status, *n.* SYN.-caste, class, condition, estate, grade, incumbency, job, office,

place, position, post, quality, rank, situation, standing, station.

statute, *n.* SYN.-act, decree, edict, law, ordinance.

stay, *v.* SYN.-abide, arrest, check, delay, halt, hinder, linger, obstruct, remain, sojourn, stand, tarry, wait. ANT.-advance, expedite, hasten, leave, progress.

steadfast, *a.* SYN.-authoritative, constant, dependable, dogmatic, fast, firm, fixed, inflexible, reliable, secure, solid, stable, steady, unswerving, unyielding. ANT.-insecure, loose, unstable, unsteady.

steal, *v.* SYN.-burglarize, embezzle, loot, pilfer, pillage, plagiarize, plunder, purloin, rob, snatch, swipe. ANT.-buy, refund, repay, restore, return.

steep, *a.* SYN.-abrupt, hilly, precipitous, sharp, sheer, sudden. ANT.-flat, gradual, level.

steer, *v.* SYN.-direct, conduct, control, escort, guide, lead, manage, regulate.

stench, *n.* SYN.-aroma, fetidness, fragrance, fume, incense, odor, perfume, redolence, scent, smell, stink.

stern, *a.* SYN.-absolute, austere, dogmatic, exacting, hard, harsh, intense, relentless, rigid, rigorous, severe, sharp, stringent, unmitigated, unyielding. ANT.-considerate, genial, indulgent, merciful, yielding.

stiff, *a.* SYN.-constrained, formal, inflexible, obstinate, prim, resolved, rigid, severe, stern, stilted, strict, stringent, unbending, unyielding; abrupt, awkward, clumsy, crude. ANT.-compassionate, lax, lenient, mild, yielding; elastic, flexible, resilient, supple.

stigma, *n.* SYN.-brand, mark, scar, stain, stigmata, trace, vestige.

still, *a.* SYN.-hushed, motionless, noiseless, peaceful, placid, quiescent, quiet, silent, tranquil, undisturbed; calm, silent. ANT.-loud, strident.

stimulate, *v.* SYN.-agitate, arouse, disquiet, excite, incite, irritate, provoke, rouse, stir up. ANT.-allay, calm, pacify, quell, quiet.

stimulus, *n.* SYN.-arousal, encouragement, goad, incentive, instigation, motive, provocation, spur, stimulant. ANT.-depressant, discouragement, dissuasion, response.

stingy, *a.* SYN.-acquisitive, avaricious, greedy, miserly, niggardly, parsimonious, penurious, tight. ANT.-altruistic, bountiful, extravagant, generous, munificent.

stock, *n.* SYN.-accumulation, fund, goods, hoard, inventory, merchandise, provision, reserve, store, supplies, supply.

stock, *v.* SYN.-equip, fill, furnish, have, replenish, retain, save, store, supply. ANT.-deplete, drain, empty, exhaust.

stoical, *a.* SYN.-calm, composed, forbearing, impassive, passive, patient, resigned, serene, uncomplaining. ANT.-chafing, clamorous, hysterical, turbulent.

stone, *n.* SYN.-boulder, gravel, jewel, pebble, rock.

stop, *v.* SYN.-abstain, arrest, bar, cease,

check, close, cork, desist, discontinue, end, halt, hinder, impede, interrupt, obstruct, plug, seal, terminate. ANT.-begin, proceed, promote, speed, start.

storm, *n.* SYN.-blizzard, cloudburst, cyclone, downpour, hurricane, squall, tempest, tornado.

stormy, *a.* SYN.-blustery, gusty, inclement, roaring, rough, tempestuous, turbulent, windy. ANT.-calm, clear, peaceful, quiet, tranquil.

story, *n.* SYN.-account, anecdote, chronicle, fable, fabrication, falsehood, fiction, history, narration, narrative, novel, report, tale, yarn.

stout, *a.* SYN.-chubby, corpulent, fat, obese, paunchy, plump, portly, pudgy, rotund, stocky, thickset. ANT.-gaunt, lean, slender, slim, thin.

straight, *a.* SYN.-direct, erect, fair, honest, honorable, just, right, square, unbent, undeviating, unswerving, upright, vertical. ANT.-bent, circuitous, crooked; dishonest, winding.

strain, *n.* SYN.-ancestry, breed, extraction, kind, sort, species, stock, subspecies, variety; effort, exertion, force, pressure; bruise, injury, sprain, twist, wrench; anxiety, pressure, stress, tension.

strange, *a.* SYN.-abnormal, bizarre, curious, eccentric, extraordinary, foreign, grotesque, irregular, odd, mysterious, peculiar, queer, singular, surprising, uncommon, unusual. ANT.-common, conventional, familiar, ordinary, regular.

stranger, *n.* SYN.-alien, foreigner, immigrant, interloper, intruder, newcomer, outsider. ANT.-acquaintance, associate, countryman, friend, neighbor.

strategy, *n.* SYN.-approach, method, plan, procedure, scheme, system, tactics.

stray, *v.* SYN.-deviate, digress, err, ramble, range, roam, rove, saunter, stroll, traipse, wander. ANT.-halt, linger, settle, stay, stop.

stream, *v.* SYN.-abound, come, emanate, flow, gush, issue, run, spout, spurt; abound.

street, *n.* SYN.-avenue, boulevard, court, lane, passage, path.

strength, *n.* SYN.-durability, force, fortitude, intensity, lustiness, might, potency, power, stamina, stoutness, sturdiness, toughness, vigor. ANT.-feebleness, frailty, infirmity, weakness.

strengthen, *v.* SYN.-approve, confirm, encourage, fix, fortify, hearten, intensify, ratify, reinforce, sanction, temper, toughen.

stress, *n.* SYN.-accent, compulsion, constraint, distress, exigency, force, hurry, importance, influence, press, pressure, significance, strain, tension, urgency. ANT. ease, lenience, recreation, relaxation.

stretch, *v.* SYN.-distend, distort, elongate, expand, extend, lengthen, protract, spread, strain. ANT.-contract, loosen, shrink, slacken, tighten.

strict, *a.* SYN.-austere, critical, demanding, exacting, harsh, rigorous, rough, rugged, severe, stringent. ANT.-gentle, melodious, mild, smooth, soft.

strife, *n.* SYN.-battle, clash, combat, conflict, fight, struggle.

strike, *v.* SYN.-beat, clout, cuff, hit, knock, pound, pummel, punch, slap, smite; boycott, picket, quit, stop.

striking, *a.* SYN.-affecting, arresting, august, commanding, exciting, forceful, grandiose, imposing, impressive, majestic, moving, overpowering, remarkable, splendid, stirring, thrilling, touching. ANT.-commonplace, ordinary, regular, unimpressive.

stringent, *a.* SYN.-forcible, harsh, rigorous, rough, rugged, severe, strict. ANT.-gentle, melodious, mild, smooth, soft.

strive, *v.* SYN.-aim, attempt, endeavor, try, struggle, undertake. ANT.-abandon, neglect.

stroll, *v.* SYN.-amble, meander, ramble, roam, saunter, walk.

strong, *a.* SYN.-athletic, cogent, concentrated, enduring, firm, forceful, forcible, fortified, hale, hardy, impregnable, mighty, potent, powerful, robust, sinewy, sturdy, tough. ANT.-brittle, delicate, feeble, fragile, insipid.

struggle, *n.* SYN.-battle, combat, conflict, contest, encounter, fight, fray, skirmish, strife. ANT.-agreement, concord, peace, truce.

struggle, *v.* SYN.-battle, brawl, combat, conflict, contend, dispute, encounter, fight, scuffle, skirmish.

stubborn, *a.* SYN.-contumacious, determined, dogged, firm, headstrong, immovable, inflexible, intractable, obdurate, obstinate, pertinacious, uncompromising, unyielding. ANT.-amenable, compliant, docile, submissive, yielding.

student, *n.* SYN.-disciple, learner, observer, pupil, scholar.

study, *v.* SYN.-cogitate, contemplate, examine, investigate, learn, master, meditate, muse, ponder, reflect, scrutinize, weigh.

stuff, *n.* SYN.-items, material, matter, substance, thing. ANT.-immateriality, phantom, spirit.

stuff, *v.* SYN.-cram, fill, glut, gorge, occupy, pervade, sate, satiate, satisfy. ANT.-deplete, drain, empty, exhaust, void.

stumble, *v.* SYN.-blunder, drop, fall, falter, hesitate, sink, topple, trip, tumble. ANT.-arise, ascend, climb, mount, soar.

stun, *v.* SYN.-amaze, astound, dumbfound, flabbergast, shock, startle, surprise, take aback. ANT.-admonish, caution, forewarn, prepare.

stunning, *a.* SYN.-astonishing, astounding, beautiful, charming, dazzling, exquisite, gorgeous, marvelous, remarkable, shocking, staggering, striking.

stupid, *a.* SYN.-addled, brainless, crass, dense, dull, dumb, foolish, obtuse, senseless, witless. ANT.-alert, bright, clever, discerning, intelligent.

stupor, *n.* SYN.-daze, drowsiness, insensibility, languor, lethargy, numbness, stupefaction, torpor. ANT.-activity, alertness, liveliness, readiness, wakefulness.

sturdy, *a.* SYN.-enduring, firm, formidable, fortified, hard, hardy, impregnable,

mighty, potent, powerful, robust, sinewy, stout, strong, tough. ANT.-brittle, delicate, feeble, fragile, insipid.

suave, *a.* SYN.-courtly, cultured, elegant, genteel, glib, polished, refined, smooth, sophisticated, urbane.

subdue, *v.* SYN.-beat, conquer, crush, defeat, humble, master, overcome, quell, rout, subjugate, surmount, vanquish. ANT.-capitulate, cede, lose, retreat, surrender.

subject, *n.* SYN.-citizen, dependent, inferior, liegeman, subordinate, vassal; argument, case, matter, object, patient, point, theme, thesis, topic.

sublime, *a.* SYN.-elevated, exalted, glorious, grand, high, lofty, majestic, noble, raised, splendid, supreme. ANT.-base, ignoble, low, ordinary, ridiculous.

submerge, *v.* SYN.-absorb, bury, dip, dunk, engage, engross, immerse, plunge, sink. ANT.-elevate, recover, uplift.

submissive, *a.* SYN.-compliant, deferential, dutiful, obedient, tractable, yielding. ANT.-insubordinate, intractable, obstinate, rebellious.

submit, *v.* SYN.-abdicate, accede, acquiesce, capitulate, cede, quit, relent, relinquish, resign, succumb, surrender, waive, yield. ANT.-assert, resist, strive, struggle.

subordinate, *a.* SYN.-following, inferior, lesser, lower, minor, poorer, secondary. ANT.-better, greater, higher, superior.

subordinate, *n.* SYN.-aide, assistant, citizen, dependent, helper, inferior, liegeman, subject, underling, vassal.

substantial, *a.* SYN.-abundant, ample, considerable, plentiful; actual, concrete, corporeal, material, physical, tangible, visible; firm, large, sound, strong; affluent, important, influential, rich, wealthy.

substantiate, *v.* SYN.-attest, authenticate, confirm, corroborate, validate, verify.

substitute, *n.* SYN.-agent, alternate, deputy, double, lieutenant, proxy, representative, stand-in, surrogate, understudy; equivalent, expedient, makeshift. ANT.-head, master, principal, sovereign.

substitution, *n.* SYN.-alteration, alternation, change, modification, variation, variety, vicissitude. ANT.-monotony, stability, uniformity.

subterfuge, *n.* SYN.-alibi, disguise, evasion, excuse, pretense, pretext. ANT.-actuality, fact, reality, sincerity, truth.

subtract, *v.* SYN.-decline, decrease, deduct, diminish, lessen, reduce, remove, shorten, wane. ANT.-amplify, enlarge, expand, grow, increase.

succeed, *v.* SYN.-achieve, flourish, gain, prevail, prosper, thrive, win; ensue, follow, inherit, supersede, supplant. ANT.-fail, miscarry, miss; anticipate, precede.

successful, *a.* SYN.-auspicious, flourishing, fortunate, lucky, prosperous, triumphant.

succession, *n.* SYN.-arrangement, chain, following, gradation, order, progression, sequence, series, string, train.

succinct, *a.* SYN.-brief, compendious, concise, curt, fleeting, laconic, momentary, passing, pithy, short, terse, transient. ANT.-extended, lengthy, long, prolonged, protracted.

succor, *n.* SYN.-aid, assistance, comfort, consolation, relief, solace, support. ANT.-affliction, discomfort, misery, suffering, torment, torture.

sudden, *a.* SYN.-abrupt, hasty, immediate, instantaneous, rapid, unexpected. ANT.-anticipated, gradual, slowly.

sue, *v.* SYN.-appeal, beg, claim, demand, entreat, indict, litigate, petition, plead, pray, prosecute, solicit.

suffer, *v.* SYN.-bear, endure, feel, stand, sustain, tolerate, undergo; allow, indulge, let, permit, tolerate. ANT.-banish, discard, exclude, overcome.

suffering, *n.* SYN.-ache, agony, anguish, distress, misery, pain, throe, torment, torture, woe. ANT.-comfort, ease, mitigation, relief.

sufficient, *a.* SYN.-adequate, ample, commensurate, enough, fitting, satisfactory, suitable. ANT.-deficient, lacking, scant.

suggest, *v.* SYN.-advise, allude, counsel, hint, imply, insinuate, intimate, offer, propose, recommend, refer. ANT.-declare, demand, dictate, insist.

suggestion, *n.* SYN.-admonition, advice, caution, counsel, exhortation, hint, information, instruction, intelligence, notification, recommendation, warning.

suitable, *a.* SYN.-acceptable, agreeable, amiable, gratifying, pleasant, pleasing, pleasurable, welcome. ANT.-disagreeable, obnoxious, offensive, unpleasant.

sullen, *a.* SYN.-dour, fretful, gloomy, glum, moody, morose, sulky, surly. ANT.-amiable, gay, joyous, merry, pleasant.

sum, *n.* SYN.-aggregate, entirety, total, whole. ANT.-fraction, ingredient, part, sample.

sum, *v.* SYN.-add, affix, append, attach, augment, increase, total. ANT.-deduct, detach, reduce, remove, subtract.

summarize, *v.* SYN.-abridge, abstract, outline, part, recap. ANT.-add, replace, restore, return, unite.

summit, *n.* SYN.-apex, crest, crown, head, pinnacle, top, zenith. ANT.-base, bottom, foot, foundation.

sundry, *a.* SYN.-different, divers, few, miscellaneous, several, unlike, various. ANT.-alike, congruous, identical, same, similar.

sunny, *a.* SYN.-bright, clear, cloudless, fair. ANT.-cloudy, foul, overcast.

superb, *a.* SYN.-beautiful, elegant, excellent, impressive, grand, magnificent, marvelous, splendid.

superficial, *a.* SYN.-cursory, exterior, flimsy, frivolous, imperfect, shallow, slight. ANT.-abstruse, complete, deep, profound, thorough.

superintend, *v.* SYN.-command, control, direct, dominate, govern, manage, regulate, rule. ANT.-abandon, follow, forsake, ignore.

superiority, *n.* SYN.-advantage, edge, lead, mastery, supremacy. ANT.-handicap, weakness.

supernatural, *a.* SYN.-marvelous, metaphysical, miraculous, other-worldly, preternatural, spiritual, superhuman, unearthly. ANT.-common, human, natural, physical, plain.

supervise, *v.* SYN.-boss, command, control, direct, dominate, govern, manage, oversee, regulate, rule, superintend. ANT.-abandon, forsake, ignore.

supervision, *n.* SYN.-charge, control, direction, inspection, instruction, management, oversight, superintendence, surveillance. ANT.-attention, care, observation, scrutiny .

supplant, *v.* SYN.-overcome, overthrow, overturn, remove, replace, rout, ruin, uproot, upset, vanquish. ANT.-build, conserve, construct, preserve, uphold.

supple, *a.* SYN.-compliant, ductile, elastic, flexible, lithe, pliable, pliant, resilient, tractable. ANT.-brittle, hard, rigid, stiff, unbending.

supply, *n.* SYN.-accumulation, fund, hoard, provision, reserve, stock, store.

supply, *v.* SYN.-endow, equip, fit, fit out furnish, provide. ANT.-denude, despoil, divest, strip.

support, *n.* SYN.-base, basis, brace, buttress, foundation, groundwork, prop, stay; aid, assistance, backing, comfort, encouragement, favor, help, patronage, succor; livelihood, living, maintenance, subsistence; confirmation, evidence. ANT.-attack, enmity, opposition.

support, *v.* SYN.-advocate, assist, back, bear, brace, encourage, foster, further, help, keep, maintain, preserve, prop, sustain, uphold, ANT.-abandon, betray, destroy, discourage, oppose.

supporter, *n.* SYN.-adherent, apologist, apostle, attendant, devotee, disciple, follower, henchman, partisan, successor, votary. ANT.-chief, head, leader, master.

suppose, *v.* SYN.-apprehend, assume, believe, conjecture, deduce, guess, imagine, presume, speculate, surmise, think. ANT.-ascertain, conclude, demonstrate, know, prove.

supremacy, *n.* SYN.-ascendancy, domination, mastery, predominance, sovereignty, sway, transcendence. ANT.-inferiority.

supreme, *a.* SYN.-cardinal, chief, foremost, highest, leading, main, paramount, predominant, principal. ANT.-auxiliary, minor, subordinate, subsidiary, supplemental.

sure, *a.* SYN.-assured, certain, definite, fixed, indubitable, inevitable, positive, secure, undeniable, unquestionable. ANT.-doubtful, probable, questionable, uncertain.

surly, *a.* SYN.-disagreeable, dour, ill-natured, quarrelsome, rude, spiteful, sullen, vicious. ANT.-friendly, pleasant.

surplus, *n.* SYN. abundance, excess, extra, extravagance, overs, profusion, remains, superabundance, superfluity, . ANT.-dearth, deficiency, lack, paucity, want.

surprise, *n.* SYN.-amazement, astonishment, awe, bewilderment, wonder, wonderment. ANT.-apathy, expectation, indifference.

surprise, *v.* SYN.-alarm, amaze, astonish, astound, disconcert, dumbfound, flabbergast, shock, startle, stun, take aback. ANT.-admonish, caution, forewarn, prepare.

surrender, *v.* SYN.-abandon, acquiesce, capitulate, cede, relinquish, renounce, resign, sacrifice, submit, yield. ANT.-conquer, overcome, resist, rout.

surround, *v.* SYN.-bound, circumscribe, confine, enclose, encompass, envelop, fence, limit. ANT.-develop, distend, enlarge, expand, expose, open.

survey, *n.* SYN.-critique, examination, inspection, outline, poll, review, study.

survey, *v.* SYN.-examine, inspect, observe, scan, scrutinize, view, watch.

survive, *v.* SYN.-endure, last, persevere, persist, outlast, outlive, remain, weather.

suspect, *v.* SYN.-distrust, doubt, hesitate, mistrust, question, waver, wonder. ANT.-believe, confide, decide, rely on, trust.

suspend, *v.* SYN.-adjourn, defer, delay, discontinue, interrupt, postpone, stay; balance, dangle, hang, poise, swing. ANT.-continue, maintain, persist, proceed, prolong.

suspense, *n.* SYN.-apprehension, doubt, hesitation, indecision, irresolution, uncertainty, vacillation, wavering.

suspicion, *n.* SYN.-distrust, doubt, hesitation, incredulity, misgiving, mistrust, skepticism, unbelief, uncertainty. ANT.-belief, certainty, conviction, determination. faith.

suspicious, *a.* SYN.-distrustful, doubtful, dubious, peculiar, questionable, shady, skeptical, strange, suspect, untrustworthy, unusual, wary.

sustain, *v.* SYN.-advocate, back, encourage, foster, further, help, keep, maintain, preserve, prop, support, uphold, ANT.-abandon, betray, destroy, discourage, oppose.

sustenance, *n.* SYN.-diet, edibles, fare, feed, food, meal, nutriment, provisions, rations, repast, subsistence, viands, victuals. ANT.-drink, hunger, starvation, want.

swap, *v.* SYN.-barter, exchange, interchange, switch, trade.

swarm, *n.* SYN.-bevy, crowd, flock, horde, host, mass, multitude, pack, throng.

sway, *n.* SYN.-authority, control, dominion, influence, mastery, power.

sway, *v.* SYN.-actuate, affect, bias, control, direct, dominate, govern, impel, incite, influence, prevail, rule; fluctuate, oscillate, swing, wave.

swear, *v.* SYN.-affirm, assert, aver, declare, maintain, promise, protest, state, testify. ANT.-contradict, demur, deny, dispute, oppose.

sweeping, *a.* SYN.-broad, exaggerated, extravagant, expanded, extensive, large, vast, wide; liberal, tolerant. ANT.-confined, narrow, restricted.

sweet, *a.* SYN.-agreeable, delightful, engaging, gentle, honeyed, luscious, mellifluous, melodious, pleasing, saccharine, sugary, winning, ANT.-acrid, bitter, offensive, repulsive, sour.

swell, *v.* SYN.-balloon, bloat, bulge, di-late, enlarge, expand, grow, increase, inflate.

swift, *a.* SYN.-abrupt, expeditious, fast, fleet, quick, rapid, speedy, sudden, unexpected. ANT.-slow, sluggish.

swindle, *n.* SYN.-cheat, chicanery, deceit, deception, duplicity, fraud, guile, imposition, imposture, trick. ANT.-fairness, honesty, integrity, sincerity.

swindle, *v.* SYN.-bilk, cheat, circumvent, deceive, defraud, dupe, fool, gull, hoax, hoodwink, outwit, trick, victimize.

switch, *v.* SYN.-alter, exchange, rearrange, replace, shift, substitute.

syllabus, *n.* SYN.-abridgement, brief, condensation, digest, outline, summary, synopsis.

symbol, *n.* SYN.-character, emblem, mark, representation, sign, token.

symbolic, *a.* SYN.-characteristic, illustrative, indicative, representative, typical.

sympathetic, *a.* SYN.-affable, benevolent, benign, compassionate, forbearing, gentle, good, humane, indulgent, kind, kindly, merciful, tender, thoughtful. ANT.-cruel, inhuman, merciless, severe, unkind.

sympathize, *v.* SYN.-cheer, comfort, commiserate, console, empathize, encourage, gladden, solace, soothe. ANT.-antagonize, aggravate, depress, dishearten.

sympathy, *n.* SYN.-affinity, agreement, commiseration, compassion, concord, condolence, congeniality, empathy, harmony, pity, tenderness, warmth. ANT.-antipathy, harshness, indifference, malevolence, unconcern.

synonymous, *a.* SYN.-corresponding, equivalent, identical, like, same.

synopsis, *n.* SYN.-See **syllabus.**

synthetic, *a.* SYN.-artificial, bogus, counterfeit, ersatz, fake, feigned, fictitious, phony, sham, spurious, unreal. ANT.-genuine, natural, real, true.

system, *n.* SYN.-arrangement, method, mode, order, organization, plan, process, regularity, rule, scheme. ANT.-chance, chaos, confusion, disarrangement, disorder, irregularity.

T

tact, *n.* SYN.-acumen, address, adroitness, dexterity, diplomacy, discrimination, finesse, knack, perception, poise, prudence, refinement, savoir faire, skill. ANT.-awkwardness, blunder, incompetence, rudeness, vulgarity.

tactful, *a.* SYN.-adroit, attentive, careful, concerned, delicate, diplomatic, discreet, discriminating, gentle, judicious, politic. ANT.-boorish, churlish, coarse, gruff, rude.

tactless, *a.* SYN.-clumsy, crude, discourteous, gruff, hasty, impolite, imprudent, rough, stupid.

tainted, *a.* SYN.-contaminated, corrupt, corrupted, debased, depraved, impure, poisoned, profligate, putrid, spoiled, unsound, venal, vitiated.

take, *v.* SYN.-accept, adopt, appropriate, assume, capture, catch, choose, claim, clasp, clutch, confiscate, demand, ensnare, espouse, gain, get, grasp, grip, obtain, purloin, receive, remove, require, seize, select steal; bear, endure, stand, tolerate; bring, carry, convey, escort; attract, captivate, charm, delight, interest.

tale, *n.* SYN.-account, anecdote, chronicle, exaggeration, fable, fabrication, fiction, narration, narrative, novel, story, yarn.

talent, *n.* SYN.-ability, aptitude, capability, cleverness, endowment, faculty, genius, gift, knack, skill. ANT.-incompetence, ineptitude, stupidity.

talented, *a.* SYN.-able, adroit, apt, bright, clever, dexterous, ingenious, quick, quick-witted, sharp, skillful, smart, witty. ANT.-awkward, bungling, clumsy, dull, foolish, slow, stupid, unskilled.

talk, *n.* SYN.-chatter, conference, conversation, dialogue, discourse, discussion, gossip, lecture, report, rumor, speech. ANT.-correspondence, meditation, silence, writing.

talk, *v.* SYN.-argue, blab, chat, comment, confer, consult, converse, declaim, deliberate, discourse, discuss, gossip, harangue, jabber, lecture, mutter, plead, prattle, preach, rant, reason. speak, spout, tattle.

talkative, *a.* SYN.-chattering, chatty, communicative, garrulous, glib, loquacious, verbose, voluble. ANT.-laconic, reticent, silent, taciturn, uncommunicative.

tall, *a.* SYN.-elevated, high, lofty, towering; exaggerated, outlandish, unbelievable. ANT.-small, stunted, tiny; actual, honest, true.

tame, *a.* SYN.-docile, domestic, domesticated, gentle, meek, subdued, submissive; dull, flat, insipid, tedious. ANT.-fierce, savage, spirited, wild; animated, exciting, lively, spirited.

tangible, *a.* SYN.-corporeal, manifest, material, palpable, perceptible, physical, real, sensible, substantial. ANT.-mental, metaphysical, spiritual.

tarnish, *v.* SYN.-blemish, blight, defile, discolor, disgrace, soil, spot, sully, stain. ANT.-cleanse, honor, purify.

tart, *a.* SYN.-acrid, acrimonious, biting, bitter, caustic, distasteful, galling, grievous, harsh, painful, poignant, pungent, sardonic, severe, sour. ANT.-delicious, mellow, pleasant, sweet.

taste, *n.* SYN.-flavor, relish, savor, tang; discernment, disposition, inclination, judgment, liking, predilection, sensibility, zest. ANT.-antipathy, disinclination, indelicacy, insipidity.

taught, *a.* SYN.-directed, educated, instructed, trained.

taunt, *v.* SYN.-badger, deride, flout, gibe, harass, harry, jeer, mock, sneer, torment, worry. ANT.-compliment, flatter, laud, praise.

taunting, *a.* SYN.-biting, caustic, contemptuous, cutting, derisive, insulting, rude, sarcastic, scornful, sneering. ANT.-affable, agreeable, amiable, pleasant.

taut, *a.* SYN.-contracted, firm, stretched, tense, tight. ANT.-lax, loose, open, relaxed, slack.

tax, *n.* SYN.-assessment, custom, duty, exaction, excise, impost, levy, rate, toll, tribute; burden, encumber, strain. ANT.-gift, remuneration, reward, wages.

tax, *v.* SYN.-appraise, assess, calculate, compute, evaluate, levy, reckon; burden, demand, encumber.

teach, *v.* SYN.-educate, inculcate, inform, instill, instruct, school, train, tutor. ANT.-misguide, misinform.

tear, *v.* SYN.-cleave, disunite, lacerate, rend, rip, rive, sever, shred, slit, split, sunder, wound. ANT.-join, mend, repair, sew, unite.

tease, *v.* SYN.-aggravate, annoy, badger, bother, disturb, harass, harry, irritate, molest, nag, pester, plague, provoke, tantalize, taunt, torment, vex, worry. ANT.-comfort, delight, gratify, please, soothe.

tedious, *a.* SYN.-boring, burdensome, dilatory, dreary, dull, humdrum, irksome, monotonous, slow, sluggish, tardy, tiresome, uninteresting, wearisome. ANT.-amusing, entertaining, exciting, interesting, quick.

tedium, *n.* SYN.-boredom, doldrums, dullness, ennui, monotony, weariness. ANT.-activity, excitement, motive, stimulus.

telepathy, *n.* SYN.- insight, premonition, prescience.

tell, *v.* SYN.-acquaint, announce, apprise, betray, communicate, confess, describe, direct, disclose, divulge, express, inform, instruct, mention, narrate, notify, order, publish, recount, rehearse, relate, report, request, reveal, speak, state, utter; discern, discover, distinguish, recognize.

temerity, *n.* SYN.-audacity, boldness, foolhardiness, precipitance, rashness, recklessness. ANT.-caution, hesitation, prudence, timidity, wariness.

temper, *n.* SYN.-anger, choler, fury, ire, irritation, passion, petulance, rage, resentment, wrath. ANT.-conciliation, forbearance, patience, peace, self-control.

temperament, *n.* SYN.-character, constitution, disposition, humor, mood, nature, temper.

temperance, *n.* SYN.-abstention, abstinence, continence, fasting, forbearance, moderation, self-denial, sobriety. ANT.-excess, gluttony, greed, intoxication, self-indulgence.

tempest, *n.* SYN.-blast, gale, gust, hurricane, squall, storm, wind.

temporal, *a.* SYN.-earthly, laic, lay, mundane, profane, secular, worldly. ANT.-ecclesiastical, religious, spiritual, unworldly.

temporary, *a.* SYN.-brief, ephemeral, evanescent, fleeting, momentary, short-lived, transient. ANT.-abiding, immortal, lasting, permanent, timeless.

temptation, *n.* SYN.-appeal, enticement, fascination, inducement, lure, stimulus.

tenacity, *n.* SYN.-cohesion, obstinance, perseverance, persistence, persistency, pertinacity, steadfastness. ANT.-cessation, idleness, laziness, rest, sloth.

tend, *v.* SYN.-accompany, attend, escort, follow, guard, protect, serve, watch.

tendency, *n.* SYN.-aim, bent, bias, drift, inclination, leaning, predisposition, proclivity, proneness, propensity, trend. ANT.-aversion, deviation, disinclination.

tender, *a.* SYN.-affectionate, compassionate, considerate, delicate, gentle, kind, mild, moderate, soft, soothing, sympathetic, sweet. ANT.-bitter, fierce, harsh, rough, severe.

tenderness, *n.* SYN.-commiseration, compassion, condolence, empathy, endearment, fondness, kindness, love, pity, sweetness, sympathy, warmth. ANT.-hatred, indifference, repugnance.

tenet, *n.* SYN.-belief, concept, creed, doctrine, dogma, opinion, precept, principle, teaching. ANT.-conduct, deed, performance, practice.

tense, *a.* SYN.-agitated, excited, nervous, strained. ANT.- calm, composed, relaxed.

term, *n.* SYN.-boundary, duration, interval, limit, period, time; condition, expression, name, phrase, word.

terminal, *a.* SYN.-concluding, conclusive, decisive, ending, eventual, extremity, final, last, latest, limit, terminus, ultimate. ANT.-first, inaugural, incipient, original, rudimentary.

terminate, *v.* SYN.-abolish, cease, close, complete, conclude, end, expire, finish, stop. ANT.-begin, commence, establish, initiate, start.

terms, *n.* SYN.-agreement, conditions, details, particulars, settlement, understanding.

terrible, *a.* SYN.-appalling, awful, dire, dreadful, fearful, frightful, gruesome, hideous, horrible, horrid, severe, shocking. ANT.-happy, joyous, pleasing, safe, secure.

terrify, *v.* SYN.-affright, alarm, daunt, frighten, horrify, intimidate, scare, startle, terrorize. ANT.-allay, compose, embolden, reassure, soothe.

territory, *n.* SYN.-country, district, division, domain, dominion, land, place, province, quarter, region, section.

terror, *n.* SYN.-alarm, consternation, dismay, dread, fear, fright, horror, panic. ANT.-assurance, calm, peace, security.

terse, *a.* SYN.-brief, compact, concise, condensed, incisive, neat, pithy, succinct, summary. ANT.-lengthy, prolix, verbose, wordy.

test, *v.* SYN.-analyze, assay, examine, experiment, inspect, prove, try, verify.

testimony, *n.* SYN.-attestation, confirmation, declaration, evidence, proof, witness. ANT.-argument, contradiction, disproof, refutation.

testy, *a.* SYN.-choleric, churlish, fractious, ill-natured, ill-tempered, irritable, peevish, petulant, snappish, touchy, waspish. ANT.-affable, genial, good-natured, good-tempered, pleasant.

theatrical, *a.* SYN.-affected, artificial, ceremonious, dramatic, histrionic, melodramatic, showy, stagy. ANT.-modest, subdued, unaffected, unemotional.

theft, *n.* SYN.-burglary, depredation, larceny, pillage, plunder, robbery.

theme, *n.* SYN.-composition, essay, motive, subject, text, thesis, topic.

theory, *n.* SYN.-conjecture, doctrine, hypothesis, opinion, postulate, presupposition, speculation. ANT.-fact, practice, proof, verity.

therefore, *adv.* SYN.-accordingly, consequently, hence, so, then, thence.

thick, *a.* SYN.-abundant, close, compact, compressed, concentrated, crowded, heavy; dull, dense, obtuse, slow, stupid; guttural, husky, indistinct, muffled. ANT.-dispersed, dissipated, sparse, thin; clever, quick; clear, distinct.

thin, *a.* SYN.-attenuated, diaphanous, diluted, emaciated, fine, flimsy, gaunt, gauzy, gossamer, lank, lean, meager, narrow, rare, scanty, scrawny, skinny, slender, slight, slim, spare, tenuous. ANT.-broad, bulky, fat, thick, wide.

think, *v.* SYN.-apprehend, believe, cogitate, conceive, consider, contemplate, deem, deliberate, esteem, imagine, judge, meditate, muse, opine, picture, ponder, reason, recall, reckon, recollect, reflect, regard, remember, speculate, suppose; devise, intend, mean, plan, purpose. ANT.-conjecture, forget, guess.

thorough, *a.* SYN.-accurate, attentive, complete, careful, detailed, painstaking, perfect, persevering, thoroughgoing, total, unbroken, uncompromising, undivided. ANT.-imperfect, lacking, superficial, unfinished.

thought, *n.* SYN.-cogitation, conception, consideration, contemplation, deliberation, fancy, idea, imagination, impression, judgment, meditation, memory, notion, opinion, recollection, reflection, regard, retrospection, sentiment, view.

thoughtful *a.* SYN.-attentive, careful, cautious, concerned, considerate, heedful, provident, prudent: contemplative, dreamy, introspective, meditative, pensive, reflective. ANT.-heedless, inconsiderate, precipitous, rash, thoughtless.

thoughtless, *a.* SYN.-careless, desultory, heedless, imprudent, inaccurate, inattentive, inconsiderate, indiscreet, lax, neglectful, negligent, reckless, remiss, unconcerned. ANT.-accurate, careful, meticulous, nice.

threatening, *a.* SYN.-approaching, dangerous, grave, imminent, impending, menacing, nigh, ominous, serious, troublesome. ANT.-afar, distant, improbable, remote, retreating.

thrifty, *a.* SYN.-economical, frugal, parsimonious, provident, saving, sparing, stingy, temperate. ANT.-extravagant, intemperate, self-indulgent, wasteful.

throb, *v.* SYN.-beat, palpitate, pound, pulsate, pulse, thump, vibrate. ANT.-defend, shield, stroke, fail, surrender.

throng, *n.* SYN.-bevy, crowd, crush, horde, host, masses, mob, multitude, populace, press, rabble, swarm.

throw, *v.* SYN.-cast, fling, hurl, pitch, propel, thrust, toss. ANT.-draw, haul, hold, pull, retain.

thrust, *v.* SYN.-drive, force, impel, propel. ANT.-drag, falter, halt, pull, retreat.

thwart, *v.* SYN.-baffle, block, check, circumvent, defeat, disappoint, foil, frustrate, hinder, impede, obstruct, outwit,

prevent, restrain, stop. ANT.-accomplish, fulfill, further, promote.

tidings, *n.* SYN.-greetings, information, intelligence, message, news, report.

tidy, *a.* SYN.-neat, orderly, precise, spruce, trim. ANT.-dirty, disheveled, sloppy, slovenly, unkempt.

tie, *n.* SYN.-accord, agreement, alliance, association, bond, conjunction, connection, connective, juncture, link, pact, relationship, union. ANT.-disunion, isolation, separation.

tie, *v.* SYN.-attach, bind, connect, engage, fasten, fetter, join, link, oblige, restrain, restrict. ANT.-free, loose, unfasten, untie.

tight, *a.* SYN.-close, compact, constricted, contracted, firm, narrow, snug, stretched, taut, tense; closefisted, niggardly, parsimonious, penny-pinching, stingy. ANT.-lax, loose, open, relaxed, slack.

time, *n.* SYN.-age, date, duration, epoch, era, interim, period, season, span, spell, tempo, term.

timid, *a.* SYN.-afraid, apprehensive, bashful, coy, diffident, fainthearted, fearful, frightened, humble, recoiling, scared, sheepish, shy, timorous. ANT.-adventurous, assured, bold, composed, courageous, daring, fearless, gregarious, outgoing, sanguine.

tiny, *a.* SYN.-diminutive, insignificant, little, miniature, minute, petty, puny, slight, small, trivial, wee. ANT.-big, enormous, huge, immense, large.

tire, *v.* SYN.-bore, exhaust, fatigue, jade, tucker, wear out, weary. ANT.-amuse, invigorate, refresh, restore, revive.

tired, *a.* SYN.-exhausted, fatigued, spent, wearied, weary, worn. ANT.-fresh, hearty, invigorated, rested.

title, *n.* SYN.-appellation, denomination, designation, epithet, name; claim, due, privilege, right.

toil, *n.* SYN.-drudgery, effort, labor, slave, travail, work. ANT.-ease, leisure, play, recreation, vacation.

tolerant, *a.* SYN.-broad, compassionate, forbearing, forgiving, humane, kind, lenient, liberal, long-suffering, merciful, patient, understanding. ANT.-confined, narrow, restricted.

tolerate, *v.* SYN.-abide, allow, bear, brook, endure, permit, stand. ANT.-forbid, prohibit; protest.

toll, *n.* SYN.-assessment, exaction, excise, impost, levy, tax, tribute; burden, damage, destruction, losses, sacrifice, strain. ANT.-gift, remuneration, reward, wages.

too, *adv.* SYN.-also, besides, furthermore, in addition, likewise, moreover, similarly.

tool, *n.* SYN.-agent, apparatus, device, instrument, means, medium, utensil. ANT.-hindrance, impediment, obstruction, preventive.

top, *n.* SYN.-apex, chief, crest, crown, head, pinnacle, summit, zenith. ANT.-base, bottom, foot, foundation.

topic, *n.* SYN.-discourse, issue, matter, point, subject, theme, thesis.

torment, *n.* SYN.-ache, agony, anguish, distress, misery, pain, suffering, throe,

torture, woe. ANT.-comfort, ease, mitigation, relief.

torment, *v.* SYN.-aggravate, annoy, badger, bother, disturb, harass, harry, haze, irritate, molest, nag, pain, persecute, pester, plague, provoke, tantalize, taunt, tease, trouble, vex, worry. ANT.-comfort, delight, gratify, please, soothe.

torpor, *n.* SYN.-apathy, daze, insensibility, languor, lethargy, numbness, stupefaction, stupor. ANT.-activity, alertness, liveliness, readiness, wakefulness.

torrid, *a.* SYN.-burning, hot, scalding, scorching, steaming, sweltering, tropical,; ardent, fervent, fiery, hot-blooded, impetuous, intense, passionate. ANT.-cold, cool, freezing, frigid; apathetic, impassive, indifferent, passionless, phlegmatic.

torture, *n.* SYN.-ache, anguish, agony, distress, misery, pain, suffering, throe, torment, woe. ANT.-comfort, ease, mitigation, relief.

torture, *v.* SYN.-badger, harass, harry, hound, oppress, persecute, plague, torment. ANT.-aid, assist, comfort, encourage, support.

toss, *v.* SYN.-cast, fling, hurl, pitch, propel, throw, thrust. ANT.-draw, haul, hold, pull, retain.

total, *a.* SYN.-all, complete, concluded, consummated, detailed, ended, entire, finished, full, perfect, thorough, unbroken, undivided, whole. ANT.-imperfect, lacking, unfinished.

total, *n.* SYN.-aggregate, amount, collection, conglomeration, entirety, sum, whole. ANT.-element, ingredient, part, particular, unit.

total, *v.* SYN.-add, calculate, count, figure, sum.

touching, *a.* SYN.-affecting, heart-rending, impressive, moving, pitiable, poignant, sad, tender; adjacent, adjunct, bordering, tangent. ANT.-animated, enlivening, exhilarating, removed.

touchy, *a.* SYN.-choleric, excitable, fiery, hasty, hot, irascible, irritable, peevish, petulant, snappish, testy. ANT.-agreeable, calm, composed, tranquil.

tough, *a.* SYN.-cohesive, firm, hardy, stout, strong, sturdy, tenacious; difficult, formidable, hard, laborious, troublesome, trying; callous, incorrigible, obdurate, stubborn, vicious. ANT.-brittle, fragile, frail; easy, facile; compliant, forbearing, submissive.

toughness, *n.* SYN.-durability, fortitude, might, potency, power, stamina, stoutness, strength, sturdiness. ANT.-feebleness, frailty, infirmity, weakness.

tour, *v.* SYN.-go, journey, ramble, roam, rove, travel, trek, visit. ANT.-stay, stop.

tow, *v.* SYN.-drag, draw, haul, pull, tow, tug.

train, *v.* SYN.-direct, educate, inform, instill, instruct, school, teach, tutor; aim, level, point. ANT.-misdirect, misguide.

training, *n.* SYN.-cultivation, development, drill, education, exercise, instruction, knowledge, learning, lesson, operation, schooling, study, tutoring.

trait, *n.* SYN.-attribute, characteristic,

feature, mark, peculiarity, property, quality.

traitorous, *a.* SYN.-apostate, disloyal, faithless, false, perfidious, recreant, treacherous, treasonable. ANT.-constant, devoted, loyal, true.

tramp, *n.* SYN.-beggar, bum, hobo, rover, vagabond, vagrant, wanderer. ANT.-gentleman, laborer, worker.

tranquil, *a.* SYN.-appease, calm, collected, composed, dispassionate, imperturbable, pacific, peaceful, placid, quiet, sedate, serene, still, undisturbed, unmoved, unruffled. ANT.-excited, frantic, stormy, turbulent, wild.

tranquility, *n.* SYN.-calm, calmness, hush, peace, quiescence, quiet, quietude, repose, rest, serenity, silence, stillness. ANT.-agitation, disturbance, excitement, noise, tumult.

transact, *v.* SYN.-carry on, conduct, execute, manage, negotiate, perform, treat.

transaction, *n.* SYN.-affair, business, deal, deed, negotiation, occurrence, proceeding.

transfer, *v.* SYN.-assign, consign, convey, dispatch, relegate, remove, send, transmit, transplant, transport.

transform, *v.* SYN.-alter, change, convert, modify, remodel, shift, transfigure, vary, veer. ANT.-retain; continue, establish, preserve, settle, stabilize.

transient, *a.* SYN.-brief, ephemeral, evanescent, fleeting, momentary, short-lived, temporary. ANT.-abiding, immortal, lasting, permanent, timeless.

translate, *v.* SYN.-decipher, decode, elucidate, explain, explicate, interpret, render. ANT.-confuse, distort, falsify, misconstrue, misinterpret.

transmit, *v.* SYN.-convey, disclose, divulge, impart, inform, notify, relate, reveal, send, tell. ANT.-conceal, hide, withhold.

transparent, *a.* SYN.-clear, crystalline, limpid, lucid, thin, translucent; evident, explicit, manifest, obvious, open. ANT.-muddy, opaque, thick, turbid; ambiguous, questionable.

transpire, *v.* SYN.-bechance, befall, betide, chance, happen, occur, take place.

transport, *v.* SYN.-bear, carry, convey, move, remove, shift, transfer; enrapture, entrance, lift, ravish, stimulate.

trap, *n.* SYN.-ambush, artifice, bait, intrigue, lure, net, pitfall, ruse, snare, stratagem, trick, wile.

travel, *v.* SYN.-go, journey, ramble, roam, rove, tour. ANT.-stay, stop.

treachery, *n.* SYN.-collusion, conspiracy, deception, dishonesty, disloyalty, intrigue, machination, perfidy, plot, subversion, treason, violation.

treason, *n.* SYN.-betrayal, cabal, collusion, combination, conspiracy, intrigue, machination, plot, subversion, treachery.

treasure, *v.* SYN.-adore, appreciate, cherish, hold dear, prize, protect, value. ANT.-dislike, disregard, neglect.

treat, *v.* SYN.-apply, conduct, employ, handle, manage, manipulate, use. ANT.-ignore, neglect.

treaty, *n.* SYN.-alliance, association, coalition, compact, confederacy, covenant,

entente, federation, league, marriage, partnership, union. ANT.-divorce, schism, separation.

tremble, *v.* SYN.-agitate, flutter, quake, quaver, quiver, shake, shiver, shudder, vibrate, waver.

trespass, *v.* SYN.-encroach, infringe, intrude, invade, penetrate, violate. ANT.-abandon, evacuate, relinquish, vacate.

trial, *n.* SYN.-examination, experiment, proof, test; attempt, effort, endeavor, essay; affliction, hardship, misery, misfortune, ordeal, suffering, tribulation, trouble. ANT.-alleviation, consolation.

trick, *n.* SYN.-antic, artifice, cheat, deception, device, fraud, guile, hoax, imposture, ploy, ruse, stratagem, stunt, subterfuge, wile. ANT.-candor, exposure, honesty, openness, sincerity.

tricky, *a.* SYN.-artful, covert, crafty, cunning, foxy, furtive, guileful, shrewd, sly, stealthy, subtle, surreptitious, underhanded, wily. ANT.-candid, frank, ingenuous, open, sincere.

trifling, *a.* SYN.-frivolous, immaterial, insignificant, paltry, petty, slight, small, trivial, unimportant, worthless. ANT.-important, momentous, serious, weighty.

trim, *v.* SYN.-adorn, beautify, bedeck, decorate, embellish, garnish, gild, ornament. ANT.-deface, deform, disfigure, mar, spoil.

trip, *n.* SYN.-cruise, expedition, jaunt, journey, passage, pilgrimage, safari, tour, travel, vacation, voyage.

trite, *a.* SYN.-banal, common, hackneyed, ordinary, stale, stereotyped. ANT.-fresh, modern, momentous, novel, stimulating.

triumph, *n.* SYN.-achievement, conquest, jubilation, ovation, victory. ANT.-defeat, failure.

trivial, *a.* SYN.-frivolous, insignificant, paltry, petty, small, trifling, unimportant. ANT.-important, momentous, serious, weighty.

trouble, *n.* SYN.-affliction, annoyance, anxiety, bother, calamity, care, disorder, distress, disturbance, embarrassment, grief, hardship, irritation, misery, pain, problem, sorrow, torment, woe, worry; effort, exertion, labor, toil.

trouble, *v.* SYN.-agitate, annoy, bother, chafe, disturb, inconvenience, interrupt, irk, irritate, molest, pester, tease, vex, worry. ANT.-accommodate, console, gratify, pacify, settle, soothe.

troublesome, *a.* SYN.-annoying, arduous, bothersome, burdensome, difficult, distressing, disturbing, irksome, laborious, tedious, trying, vexatious. ANT.-accommodating, amusing, easy, gratifying, pleasant.

true, *a.* SYN.-accurate, actual, authentic, correct, exact, genuine, real, veracious, veritable; constant, faithful, honest, loyal, reliable, sincere, steadfast, trustworthy. ANT.-counterfeit, erroneous, false, fictitious, spurious; faithless, false, fickle, inconstant.

trust, *n.* SYN.-confidence, constancy, credence, dependence, faith, fidelity, loyalty, reliance. ANT.-doubt, incredulity, infidelity, mistrust, skepticism.

trust, *v.* SYN.-believe, commit, confide, credit, depend on, entrust, esteem, hope, reckon on, rely on. ANT.-doubt, impugn, question, suspect.

trustworthy, *a.* SYN.-dependable, honest, honorable, reliable, safe, secure, sure, tried, trusty. ANT.-dubious, fallible, questionable, uncertain, unreliable.

truth, *n.* SYN.-accuracy, actuality, authenticity, correctness, exactness, fact, honesty, rightness, truthfulness, veracity, verisimilitude, verity. ANT.-falsehood, falsity, fiction, lie, untruth.

truthful, *a.* SYN.-accurate, candid, correct, exact, frank, honest, open, reliable, sincere, true, veracious. ANT.-deceitful, misleading, sly.

try, *v.* SYN.-aim, aspire, attempt, design, endeavor, intend, mean, strive, struggle, undertake; afflict, prove, test, torment, trouble. ANT.-abandon, decline, ignore, neglect, omit; comfort, console.

trying, *a.* SYN.-annoying, bothersome, distressing, disturbing, irksome, troublesome, vexatious. ANT.-accommodating, amusing, easy, gratifying, pleasant.

tumult, *n.* SYN.-chaos, clamor, commotion, confusion, din, disarray, disorder, jumble, noise, racket, row, stir, turmoil, uproar. ANT.-certainty, order, peace, tranquility.

tune, *n.* SYN.-air, harmony, melody, strain.

turbulent, *a.* SYN.-blustery, gusty, roaring, rough, stormy, tempestuous, windy. ANT.-calm, clear, peaceful, quiet, tranquil.

turmoil, *n.* SYN.-agitation, chaos, commotion, confusion, disarrangement, disarray, disorder, ferment, jumble, stir, tumult. ANT.-certainty, order, peace, tranquility.

turn, *v.* SYN.-circle, circulate, invert, revolve, rotate, spin, twirl, twist, wheel, whirl; avert, deflect, deviate, divert, swerve; alter, change, transmute. ANT.-arrest, fix, stand, stop; continue, proceed; endure, perpetuate.

twist, *v.* SYN.-bend, bow, crook, curve, deflect, lean, revolve, rotate, spin, turn, twirl, whirl; influence, mold. ANT.-break, resist, stiffen, straighten.

type, *n.* SYN.-emblem, mark, sign, symbol; category, character, class, description, exemplar, kind, model, nature, pattern, sort, stamp. ANT.-deviation, eccentricity, monstrosity, peculiarity.

typical, *a.* SYN.-common, customary, familiar, habitual, normal, ordinary, plain, regular, usual. ANT.-extraordinary, marvelous, remarkable, strange, uncommon.

tyrant, *n.* SYN.-autocrat, despot, dictator, oppressor, persecutor.

U

ugly, *a.* SYN.-deformed, hideous, homely, plain, repellent, repulsive, uncomely; disagreeable, ill-natured, spiteful, surly, vicious. ANT.-attractive, beautiful, fair, handsome, pretty.

ultimate, *a.* SYN.-extreme, final, last, latest, terminal, utmost. ANT.-beginning, first, foremost, initial, opening.

unadulterated, *a.* SYN.-clean, clear, genuine, immaculate, pure, spotless, undefiled, untainted. ANT.-foul, polluted, sullied, tainted, tarnished.

unassuming, *a.* SYN.-compliant, humble, lowly, meek, modest, plain, simple, submissive, unostentatious, unpretentious. ANT.-arrogant, boastful, haughty, proud, vain.

uncertain, *a.* SYN.-ambiguous, dim, hazy, indefinite, indistinct, obscure, unclear, undetermined, unsettled, vague. ANT.-clear, explicit, lucid, precise, specific.

uncertainty, *n.* SYN.-ambiguity, distrust, doubt, hesitation, incredulity, scruple, skepticism, suspense, suspicion, unbelief, uncertainty. ANT.-belief, certainty, conviction, determination, faith.

uncompromising, *a.* SYN.-dogged, firm, headstrong, immovable, inflexible, intractable, obdurate, obstinate, pertinacious, stubborn, unyielding. ANT.-amenable, compliant, docile, submissive, yielding.

unconcern, *n.* SYN.-apathy, disinterestedness, impartiality, indifference, insensibility, neutrality. ANT.-affection, ardor, fervor, passion.

unconditional, *a.* SYN.-absolute, actual, complete, entire, perfect, pure, ultimate, unqualified, unrestricted. ANT.-accountable, conditional, contingent, dependent, qualified.

uncouth, *a.* SYN.-awkward, clumsy, coarse, crass, crude, discourteous, harsh, ill-mannered, rough, rude, unfinished, unpolished, unrefined, vulgar. ANT.-cultivated, refined.

uncover, *v.* SYN.-disclose, discover, divulge, expose, impart, reveal, show. ANT.-cloak, conceal, cover, hide, obscure.

under, *prep.* SYN.-below, beneath, under, underneath. ANT.-above, over.

undergo, *v.* SYN.-bear, brave, encounter, endure, experience, stand, suffer, sustain, tolerate. ANT.-banish, discard, exclude, overcome.

understand, *v.* SYN.-appreciate, apprehend, comprehend, conceive, discern, grasp, know, learn, perceive, realize, see. ANT.-ignore, misapprehend, mistake, misunderstand.

understanding, *n.* SYN.-accordance, agreement, bargain, coincidence, compact, concord, concurrence, contract, covenant, harmony, pact, stipulation, unison. ANT.-difference, disagreement, discord, dissension, variance.

understudy, *n.* SYN.-alternate, proxy, representative, substitute. ANT.-principal.

undertaking, *n.* SYN.-attempt, effort, endeavor, essay, experiment, trial. ANT.-inaction, laziness, neglect.

undivided, *a.* SYN.-all, complete, entire, intact, integral, perfect, total, whole. ANT.-deficient, incomplete, partial.

undying, *a.* SYN.-ceaseless, deathless, endless, eternal, everlasting, immortal, infinite, perpetual, timeless. ANT.-ephemeral, finite, mortal, temporal, transient.

unearthly, *a.* SYN.-metaphysical, otherworldly, preternatural, spiritual, supernatural. ANT.-common, human, natural, physical, plain.

uneducated, *a.* SYN.-ignorant, illiterate, uncultured, uninformed, unlearned, unlettered, untaught. ANT.-cultured, educated, erudite, informed, literate.

unemployed, *a.* SYN.-dormant, idle, inactive, indolent, inert, lazy, slothful, unoccupied. ANT.-active, employed, industrious, occupied, working.

unexpected, *a.* SYN.-abrupt, sudden, unforeseen. ANT.-anticipated, gradual, slowly.

unfasten, *v.* SYN.-free, loosen, open, unbar, unlock, untie. ANT.-bar, close, fasten, lock, shut.

unfavorable, *a.* SYN.-adverse, antagonistic, contrary, counteractive, disastrous, hostile, opposed, opposite, unlucky. ANT.-benign, favorable, fortunate, lucky, propitious.

unfold, *v.* SYN.-amplify, develop, elaborate, enlarge, evolve, expand, open. ANT.-compress, contract, restrict.

uniform, *a.* SYN.-methodical, orderly, periodical, regular, steady, systematic, unvaried. ANT.-abnormal, erratic.

uninteresting, *a.* SYN.-boring, burdensome, dreary, dull, humdrum, monotonous, tedious, tiresome. ANT.-amusing, entertaining, exciting, interesting, quick.

union, *n.* SYN.-agreement, alliance, amalgamation, coalition, combination, concert, concord, concurrence, confederacy, fusion, harmony, incorporation, joining, league, marriage, solidarity, unanimity, unification. ANT.-disagreement, discord, division, schism, separation.

unique, *a.* SYN.-choice, distinctive, exceptional, matchless, peculiar, rare, singular, sole, solitary, uncommon, unequaled. ANT.-common, commonplace, frequent, ordinary, typical.

unison, *n.* SYN.-accordance, agreement, coincidence, concord, concurrence, harmony, understanding. ANT.-difference, disagreement, discord, dissension, variance.

unite, *v.* SYN.-amalgamate, associate, attach, blend, combine, conjoin, connect, consolidate, embody, fuse, join, link, merge, unify. ANT.-disconnect, disrupt, divide, separate, sever.

universal, *a.* SYN.-broad, common, familiar, frequent, general, omnipotent, omnipresent, ordinary, popular, prevalent, ubiquitous, usual, vast. ANT.-exceptional, extraordinary, odd, scarce.

unlawful, *a.* SYN.-criminal, illegal, illegitimate, illicit, outlawed, prohibited. ANT.-honest, lawful, legal, permitted.

unlike, *a.* SYN.-different, dissimilar, distinct, divergent, diverse, incongruous, opposite, variant; divers, miscellaneous, sundry, various. ANT.-alike, congruous, identical, same, similar.

unlimited, *a.* SYN.-boundless, endless, eternal, illimitable, immeasurable, immense, infinite, interminable, unbounded, vast. ANT.-bounded, circumscribed, confined, finite, limited.

unobstructed, *a.* SYN.-clear, free, immune loose, open, unconfined, unfastened, unrestricted. ANT.-blocked, clogged, confined, impeded, restrained, restricted.

unsafe, *a.* SYN.-chancy, critical, dangerous, hazardous, insecure, menacing, perilous, precarious, risky, threatening. ANT.-firm, protected, safe, secure.

unselfish, *a.* SYN.-beneficent, bountiful, generous, giving, liberal, magnanimous, munificent, openhanded. ANT.-covetous, greedy, miserly, selfish, stingy.

unsophisticated, *a.* SYN.-artless, candid, frank, ingenuous, innocent, naive, natural, open, simple. unlearned, untutored. ANT.-crafty, cunning, sophisticated, worldly.

unstable, *a.* SYN.-capricious, changeable, fickle, fitful, inconstant, restless, unreliable, variable. ANT.-constant, reliable, stable, steady, trustworthy.

untainted, *a.* SYN.-clean, clear, genuine, immaculate, spotless, pure, unadulterated. ANT.-foul, polluted, sullied, tainted, tarnished.

untamed, *a.* SYN.-barbarous, boisterous, extravagant, fierce, foolish, frenzied, giddy, impetuous, irregular, mad, outlandish, rash, reckless, rough, rude, savage, stormy, tempestuous, turbulent, uncivilized, uncultivated, undomesticated, wanton, wayward, wild. ANT.-calm, civilized, gentle, placid, quiet.

unusual, *a.* SYN.-aberrant, abnormal, capricious, devious, eccentric, irregular, unnatural, variable. ANT.-fixed, methodical, ordinary, regular, usual.

unyielding, *a.* SYN.-constant, fast, firm, inflexible, secure, solid, stable, steadfast, steady, unswerving. ANT.-slow, sluggish; insecure, loose, unstable, unsteady.

upbraid, *v.* SYN.-admonish, berate, blame, censure, lecture, rebuke, reprehend, reprimand, scold, vituperate. ANT.-approve, commend, praise.

uphold, *v.* SYN.-advocate, bolster, defend, endorse, help, maintain, protect, safeguard, screen, shield, support, sustain. ANT.-assault, attack, deny, submit.

upright, *a.* SYN.-erect, straight, unbent, vertical; direct, fair, honest, honorable, just, right, square, undeviating, unswerving. ANT.-bent, crooked; circuitous, devious, dishonest, fraudulent, winding.

upset, *v.* SYN.-annoy, bother, disturb, harass, haunt, inconvenience, molest, perplex, pester, plague, tease, trouble, worry. ANT.-gratify, please, relieve, soothe.

urge, *n.* SYN.-appetite, aspiration, craving, desire, hunger, hungering, longing, lust, wish, yearning. ANT.-abomination, aversion, distaste, hate, loathing.

urge, *v.* SYN.-allure, coax, entice, exhort, incite, induce, influence, persuade, prevail upon. ANT.-coerce, compel, deter, dissuade, restrain.

urgency, *n.* SYN.-compulsion, crisis, emergency, exigency, press, pressure, stress.

urgent, a. SYN.-cogent, compelling, critical, crucial, exigent, impelling, imperative, important, importunate, insistent, instant, necessary, pressing, serious. ANT.-insignificant, petty, trifling, trivial, unimportant.

use, n. SYN.-custom, habit, manner, practice, training, usage, wont. ANT.-disuse, idleness, inexperience, speculation, theory.

use, v. SYN.-apply, avail, consume, employ, exercise, exert, exhaust, expend, exploit, handle, manage, manipulate, operate, practice, treat, utilize; accustom, familiarize, inure, train. ANT.-ignore, neglect, overlook, waste.

useful, a. SYN.-advantageous, beneficial, good, helpful, serviceable. ANT.-deleterious, destructive, detrimental, harmful, injurious.

usefulness, n. SYN.-advantage, application, edge, gain, merit, utility, value, worthiness. ANT.-cheapness, uselessness, valueless.

useless, a. SYN.-abortive, empty, fruitless, futile, idle, ineffectual, pointless, unavailing, valueless, vain, vapid, worthless. ANT.-effective, potent, profitable.

usual, a. SYN.-accustomed, common, customary, every-day, familiar, general, habitual, normal, ordinary. ANT.-abnormal, exceptional, extraordinary, irregular, rare.

utensil, n. SYN.-apparatus, appliance, device, gadget, instrument, tool.

utilize, v. SYN.-apply, avail, employ, occupy, use. ANT.-banish, discard, discharge, reject.

V

vacant, a. SYN.-bare, barren, blank, empty, unoccupied, vacuous, void. ANT.-busy, employed, engaged, full, replete.

vacate, v. SYN.-abandon, abdicate, abjure, desert, forsake, leave, quit, relinquish, renounce, resign, surrender, waive. ANT.-defend, maintain, uphold; stay, support.

vacillate, v. SYN.-change, fluctuate, hesitate, oscillate, totter, undulate, vary, waver. ANT.-adhere, decide, persist, resolve, stick.

vacillating, a. SYN.-fluctuating, inconsistent, irreconcilable, irresolute, unsteady, wavering. ANT.-consistent, sure.

vagabond, n. SYN.-beggar, mendicant, nomad, pauper, ragamuffin, rascal, scrub, starveling, tatterdemalion, tramp, wanderer, wretch.

vagrant, n. SYN.-beggar, bum, hobo, rover, tramp, vagabond, wanderer. ANT.-gentleman, laborer, worker.

vague, a. SYN.-ambiguous, dim, hazy, indefinite, indistinct, obscure, uncertain, unclear, undetermined, unsettled. ANT.-clear, explicit, lucid, precise, specific.

vain, a. SYN.-abortive, bootless, empty, fruitless, futile, idle, ineffectual, pointless, unavailing, useless, valueless, vapid, worthless; conceited, proud, vainglorious. ANT.-effective, potent,

---

profitable; meek, modest.

vainglory, n. SYN.-boastfulness, conceit, haughtiness, pomp, pride, self-esteem, self-respect, vainglory, vanity. ANT.-humility, lowliness, meekness, modesty, shame.

valiant, a. SYN.-adventurous, audacious, brave, bold, chivalrous, courageous, daring, dauntless, fearless, gallant, heroic, intrepid, valorous. ANT.-cowardly, cringing, fearful, timid, weak.

valid, a. SYN.-binding, cogent, conclusive, convincing, effective, efficacious, legal, logical, powerful, sound, strong, telling, weighty. ANT.-counterfeit, null, spurious, void, weak.

valuable, a. SYN.-costly, dear, esteemed, expensive, precious, profitable, use. ANT.-cheap, mean, poor, trashy, worthless.

value, n. SYN.-excellence, merit, price, usefulness, utility, worth, worthiness. ANT.-cheapness, uselessness, valueless.

value, v. SYN.-appraise, appreciate, cherish, esteem, hold dear, prize, treasure. ANT.-dislike, disregard, neglect.

vanity, n. SYN.-conceit, egotism, haughtiness, pride, self-esteem, vainglory, vanity. ANT.-diffidence, humility, meekness, modesty.

vanquish, v. SYN.-beat, conquer, crush, defeat, humble, master, overcome, quell, rout, subdue, subjugate, surmount. ANT.-capitulate, cede, lose, retreat, surrender.

variable, a. SYN.-changeable, fickle, fitful, inconstant, shifting, unstable, vacillating, wavering. ANT.-constant, stable, steady, unchanging, uniform.

variant, a. SYN.-changing, contrary, different, differing, dissimilar, divergent, diverse, fickle, incongruous, inconstant, restless, unlike. ANT.-alike, congruous, identical, same, similar; constant.

variation, n. SYN.-alteration, alternation, change, modification, mutation, substitution, variety, vicissitude. ANT.-monotony, stability, uniformity.

variety, n. SYN.-assortment, change, difference, dissimilarity, diversity, heterogeneity, medley, miscellany, mixture, multifariousness, variety; breed, kind, sort, stock, strain, subspecies. ANT.-homogeneity, likeness, monotony, sameness, uniformity.

various, a. SYN.-divers, miscellaneous, several, sundry. ANT.-same, singular.

vary, v. SYN.-alter, change, convert, modify, remodel, shift, transfigure, transform. ANT.-retain; continue, establish, preserve, settle, stabilize.

vassalage, n. SYN.-bondage, serfdom, servitude, slavery, thralldom. ANT.-freedom, liberation.

vast, a. SYN.-big, capacious, colossal, extensive, great, huge, immense, large, wide. ANT.-little, mean, short, small, tiny.

vehement, a. SYN.-ardent, burning, fervent, fervid, fiery, impetuous, passionate. ANT.-apathetic, calm, cool, deliberate, quiet.

veil, v. SYN.-cloak, conceal, cover, cur-

---

tain, disguise, envelop, guard, hide, mask, protect, screen, shield, shroud. ANT.-bare, divulge, expose, reveal, unveil.

venerate, v. SYN.-admire, adore, appreciate, approve, esteem, respect, revere, worship. ANT.-abhor, despise, dislike.

vengeance, n. SYN.-reprisal, requital, retaliation, retribution, revenge, vindictiveness. ANT.-mercy, pardon, reconciliation, remission, forgiveness.

vent, v. SYN.-breathe, discharge, eject, emanate, emit, expel, hurl, shed, shoot, spurt.

venture, v. SYN.-brave, dare, hazard, jeopardy, peril, risk. ANT.-defense, immunity, protection, safety.

verbal, a. SYN.-literal, oral, spoken, vocal. ANT.-documentary, recorded, written.

verbose, a. SYN.-chattering, chatty, garrulous, glib, loquacious, talkative, voluble. ANT.-laconic, reticent, silent, taciturn, uncommunicative.

verbosity, n. SYN.-long-windedness, redundancy, talkativeness, verboseness, wordiness. ANT.-conciseness, laconism, terseness.

verification, n. SYN.-confirmation, corroboration, demonstration, proof, testimony. ANT.-failure, fallacy, invalidity.

verify, v. SYN.-ascertain, conclude, confirm, corroborate, define, determine, substantiate; acknowledge, assure, establish, settle.

veritable, a. SYN.-accurate, actual, authentic, correct, exact, genuine, real, true, veracious. ANT.-counterfeit, erroneous, false, fictitious, spurious.

vertical, a. SYN.-erect, perpendicular, plumb, straight, upright. ANT.-horizontal, inclined, level, oblique, prone.

vex, v. SYN.-aggravate, anger, annoy, bother, chafe, disturb, embitter, exasperate, harass, inflame, irritate, nettle, pester, plague, provoke. ANT.-appease, palliate soften, soothe.

vexation, n. SYN.-annoyance, chagrin, exasperation, irritation, mortification, pique. ANT.-appeasement, comfort, gratification, pleasure.

vibrate, v. SYN.-agitate, flutter, quake, quaver, quiver, shake, shiver, shudder, sway, tremble, waver.

vice, n. SYN.-corruption, crime, depravity, evil, immorality, iniquity, offense, sin, transgression, ungodliness, wickedness, wrong. ANT.-goodness, innocence, purity, righteousness, virtue.

vicinity, n. SYN.-area, district, environs, locality, neighborhood; adjacency, nearness, proximity. ANT.-distance, remoteness.

victory, n. SYN.-achievement, conquest, mastery, success, triumph. ANT.-defeat, failure.

view, n. SYN.-observation, outlook, panorama, perspective, prospect, range, scene, regard, review, sight, survey, vista; belief, conception, impression, judgment, opinion, sentiment.

view, v. SYN.-behold, discern, examine, eye, gaze, glance, inspect, look, observe, regard, scan, see, stare, survey, watch, witness. ANT.-avert, hide, miss, overlook.

viewpoint, *n.* SYN.-angle, aspect, attitude, outlook, perspective, pose, position, posture, slant, stand, standpoint.

vigilant, *a.* SYN.-alert, anxious, attentive, careful, cautious, circumspect, observant, wakeful, wary, watchful. ANT.-careless, inattentive, lax, neglectful, oblivious.

vigor, *n.* SYN.-endurance, energy, enthusiasm, health, liveliness, potency, power, spirit, stamina, strength, temper, verve, vitality, zeal. ANT.-languor, listlessness.

vigorous, *a.* SYN.-active, alert, animated, blithe, bright, brisk, clear, effective, energetic, forceful, fresh, frolicsome, glowing, lively, spirited, sprightly, striking, strong, supple, vivacious, vivid. ANT.-dull, insipid, listless, stale, vapid.

vile, *a.* SYN.-abject, base, debased, depraved, despicable, foul, ignoble, loathsome, low, mean, obscene, odious, revolting, sordid, vicious, vulgar, wicked, worthless, wretched. ANT.-attractive, decent, laudable; honorable, upright.

vilify, *v.* SYN.-abuse, asperse, assail, criticize, defame, denounce, disparage, ill-use, impugn, malign, revile, scandalize, traduce. ANT.-cherish, honor, praise, protect, respect.

villainous, *a.* SYN.-bad, baleful, base, deleterious, evil, immoral, iniquitous, noxious, pernicious, sinful, unsound, unwholesome, wicked. ANT.-excellent, good, honorable, moral, reputable.

vindicate, *v.* SYN.-absolve, acquit, assert, clear, defend, excuse, exonerate, justify, support, uphold. ANT.-abandon, accuse, blame, convict.

violate, *v.* SYN.-break, defile, debauch, deflower, desecrate, dishonor, disobey, infringe, invade, pollute, profane, ravish, transgress.

violence, *n.* SYN.-brutality, clash, coercion, compulsion, commotion, disorder, disturbance, energy, force, fury, injury, intensity, might, outrage, passion, potency, power, severity, strength, vehemence, vigor. ANT.-feebleness, frailty, gentleness, impotence, mildness, persuasion, respect, weakness.

violent, *a.* SYN.-boisterous, fierce, forceful, furious, impetuous, passionate, powerful, raging, raving, turbulent, vehement, wild; acute, extreme, intense, severe. ANT.-calm, feeble, gentle, quiet, soft.

virgin, *a.* SYN.-chaste, guiltless, innocent, pure, undefiled. ANT.-defiled, sullied, tainted.

virtue, *n.* SYN.-chastity, goodness, integrity, morality, probity, purity, rectitude, virginity; effectiveness, efficacy, excellence, force, merit, power, strength, worth. ANT.-corruption, lewdness, sin, vice; fault.

virtuous, *a.* SYN.-chaste, decent, ethical, good, honorable, just, moral, pure, right, righteous, scrupulous. ANT.-amoral, libertine, licentious, sinful, unethical.

visible, *a.* SYN.-apparent, clear, distinct, evident, intelligible, lucid, manifest,

obvious, open, plain, unobstructed. ANT.-ambiguous, obscure, unclear, vague.

vision, *n.* SYN.-apparition, daydream, dream, ghost, hallucination, mirage, phantasm, phantom, prophecy, revelation, specter. ANT.-reality, substance, verity.

visionary, *a.* SYN.-exemplary, fancied, faultless, ideal, imaginary, perfect, supreme, unreal, utopian. ANT.-actual, faulty, imperfect, material, real.

vital, *a.* SYN.-alive, animate, living; basic, cardinal, essential, indispensable, necessary, paramount, urgent. ANT.-inanimate, inert, lifeless; nonessential, unimportant.

vitality, *n.* SYN.-animation, buoyancy, life, liveliness, spirit, vigor, vivacity. ANT.-death, demise, dullness, languor, lethargy.

vitiate, *v.* SYN.-abase, adulterate, alloy, corrupt, debase, defile, degrade, deprave, depress, pervert. ANT.-enhance, improve, raise, restore, vitalize.

vitiated, *a.* SYN.-contaminated, corrupted, crooked, debased, depraved, dishonest, impure, profligate, putrid, spoiled, tainted, venal, vitiated.

vivid, *a.* SYN.-animated, bright, brilliant, clear, expressive, fresh, graphic, intense, lively, lucid, striking. ANT.-dull, dim, dreary, dusky, vague.

vocation, *n.* SYN.-business, employment, engagement, enterprise, job, occupation, profession, trade, work. ANT.-avocation, hobby, pastime.

void, *a.* SYN.-bare, barren, blank, empty, unoccupied, vacant, vacuous. ANT.-busy, employed, engaged, full, replete.

volatile, *a.* SYN.-animated, blithe, cheerful, effervescent, elated, hopeful, jocund, light, lively, resilient, spirited, sprightly, vivacious; changeable, ephemeral, transient. ANT.-dejected, depressed, despondent, hopeless, sullen; constant, sure, unchanging.

volition, *n.* SYN.-choice, decision, desire, determination, intention, preference, resolution, taste, testament, will, wish. ANT.-coercion, compulsion, disinterest, indifference.

volume, *n.* SYN.-amount, bulk, capacity, cube, extent, magnitude, mass, measure, quantity, size; book, edition, encyclopedia, manuscript, tome; amplification, loudness, intensity.

voluntary, *a.* SYN.-automatic, extemporaneous, impulsive, instinctive, offhand, spontaneous, willing. ANT.-compulsory, forced, planned, prepared, rehearsed.

volunteer, *v.* SYN.-donate, enlist, offer, proffer, suggest, tender. ANT.-rejection, withdrawal.

vulgar, *a.* SYN.-common, familiar, general, ordinary, plebeian, popular; base, coarse, gross, impolite, indecent, low, nasty, obscene, odious, ribald, rude, tasteless, unrefined. ANT.-esoteric, select; aristocratic, polite, refined.

W

wages, *n.* SYN.-compensation, earnings,

pay, payment, recompense, salary, stipend. ANT.-gift, gratuity, present.

wait, *v.* SYN.-abide, bide, delay, linger, remain, rest, stay, tarry; await, expect, watch; attend, minister, serve. ANT.-act, expedite, hasten, leave.

wander, *v.* SYN.-deviate, digress, err, ramble, range, roam, rove, saunter, stray, stroll, traipse. ANT.-halt, linger, settle, stay, stop.

want, *v.* SYN.-covet, crave, desire, lack, long for, need, require, wish.

wariness, *n.* SYN.-care, caution, heed, prudence, vigilance, watchfulness. ANT.-abandon, carelessness, recklessness.

warm, *a.* SYN.-ardent, cordial, eager, earnest, enthusiastic, gracious, hearty, sincere, sociable. ANT.-aloof, cool, reserved, taciturn.

warn, *v.* SYN.-admonish, advise, alert, apprise, caution, counsel, inform, notify.

warning, *n.* SYN.-admonition, advice, caution, indication, information, notice, portent, sign.

wary, *a.* SYN.-alert, alive, awake, aware, careful, heedful, mindful, observant, thoughtful, vigilant, watchful. ANT.-apathetic, indifferent, oblivious, unaware.

wash, *v.* SYN.-bathe, clean, cleanse, launder, rinse, scrub, wet. ANT.-dirty, foul, soil, stain.

waste, *a.* SYN.-abandoned, bare, barren, bleak, deserted, desolate, devastated, extra, forlorn, forsaken, lonely, ravaged, ruined, solitary, uninhabited, useless, wild. ANT.-attended, cultivated, fertile.

waste, *v.* SYN.-consume, corrode, decay, despoil, destroy, devastate, diminish, dissipate, dwindle, lavish, misuse, pillage, plunder, ravage, ruin, sack, scatter, spend, squander, strip, wear out, wither. ANT.-accumulate, economize, preserve, save.

watch, *v.* SYN.-behold, discern, distinguish, espy, inspect, look at, observe, perceive, scan, scrutinize, view, witness.

waver, *v.* SYN.-distrust, doubt, falter, flicker, hesitate, mistrust, quiver, question, suspect, sway, tremble, vacillate. ANT.-believe, confide, decide, rely on, trust.

wavering, *a.* SYN.-changeable, fickle, fitful, inconstant, shifting, unstable, vacillating, variable. ANT.-constant, stable, steady, unchanging, uniform.

wax, *v.* SYN.-accrue, amplify, augment, enhance, enlarge, expand, extend, grow, heighten, increase, intensify, magnify, multiply, raise. ANT.-atrophy, contract, decrease, diminish, reduce.

way, *n.* SYN.-avenue, channel, course, passage, path, road, route, street, thoroughfare, track, trail, walk; fashion, form, habit, manner, method, mode, plan, practice, procedure, process, style, system.

weak, *a.* SYN.-bending, debilitated, decrepit, delicate, feeble, fragile, frail, impotent, infirm, illogical , inadequate, ineffective, irresolute, lame, pliable, pliant, poor, tender, vacillating, vague, wavering, yielding; assailable, defenseless, exposed, vulnerable. ANT.-potent, powerful, robust, strong, sturdy.

weakness, *n.* SYN.-disability, handicap, impotence; inability, incapacity. ANT.-ability, capability, power, strength.

wealth, *n.* SYN.-abundance, affluence, fortune, luxury, money, opulence, plenty, possessions, riches. ANT.-indigence, need, poverty, want.

wealthy, *a.* SYN.-affluent, luxurious, opulent, plentiful, prosperous, rich, sumptuous, well-to-do. ANT.-beggarly, destitute, indigent, needy, poor.

wearied, *a.* SYN.-bored, dim, drained, faded, faint, feeble, languid, pale. ANT.-conspicuous, glaring; strong, vigorous; brave, forceful.

weary, *a.* SYN.-bored, exhausted, faint, fatigued, jaded, spent, tired, wearied, worn. ANT.-fresh, hearty, invigorated, rested.

weary, *v.* SYN.-annoy, distress, exhaust, fatigue, harass, irk, jade, tire, tucker, vex, wear out. ANT.-amuse, invigorate, refresh, restore, revive.

wedlock, *n.* SYN.-espousal, marriage, matrimony, nuptials, union. ANT.-celibacy, divorce, virginity.

weigh, *v.* SYN.-consider, contemplate, deliberate, examine, meditate, ponder, reflect, study. ANT.-ignore, neglect, overlook.

weight, *n.* SYN.-burden, gravity, heaviness, load, pressure; emphasis, import, importance, influence, significance, stress, value. ANT.-buoyancy, levity, lightness; insignificance, triviality.

well, *a.* SYN.-hale, happy, healthy, hearty, sound; beneficial, convenient, expedient, good, profitable. ANT.-depressed, feeble, infirm, weak.

whim, *n.* SYN.-caprice, fancy, humor, impulse, inclination, notion, quirk, thought, urge, vagary, whimsy.

whole, *a.* SYN.-all, complete, entire, intact, integral, perfect, total, undivided, unimpaired; hale, healed, healthy, sound, well. ANT.-defective, deficient, imperfect, incomplete, partial.

wholesome, *a.* SYN.-hale, healthy, hearty, robust, sound, strong, well; hygienic, salubrious, salutary. ANT.-delicate, diseased, frail, infirm; injurious, noxious.

wicked, *a.* SYN.-bad, baleful, base, deleterious, evil, immoral, iniquitous, malevolent, malicious, noxious, pernicious, sinful, unsound, unwholesome, villainous, virulent. ANT.-benevolent, excellent, good, honorable, kind, moral, reputable.

wide, *a,* SYN.-broad, expanded, extensive, large, sweeping, vast. ANT.-confined, narrow, restricted.

wild, *a.* SYN.-barbarous, boisterous, fierce, outlandish, rude, savage, stormy, tempestuous, uncivilized, undomesticated, untamed; deserted, desolate, rough, uncultivated, waste; extravagant, foolish, frantic, frenzied, giddy, impetuous, irregular, mad, rash, reckless, turbulent, wanton, wayward. ANT.-civilized, gentle; calm, placid, quiet.

willful, *a.* SYN.-contemplated, deliberate, designed, intended, intentional, premeditated, studied, voluntary. ANT.-accidental, fortuitous.

will, *n.* SYN.-choice, decision, desire, determination, intention, pleasure, preference, resolution, testament, volition, wish. ANT.-coercion, compulsion, disinterest, indifference.

win, *v.* SYN.-achieve, gain, prevail, prosper, succeed, thrive. ANT.-fail, miscarry, miss.

wind, *n.* SYN.-blast, breeze, draft, gale, gust, hurricane, squall, storm, tempest, zephyr.

wisdom, *n.* SYN.-discretion, erudition,. foresight, information, insight, intelligence, judgment, knowledge, learning, prudence, reason, sagacity, saneness, sense. ANT.-foolishness, ignorance, imprudence, nonsense, stupidity.

wise, a, SYN.-deep, discerning, enlightened, erudite, informed, intelligent, knowing, learned, penetrating, profound, sagacious, scholarly, sound; advisable, expedient, prudent. ANT.-foolish, shallow, simple.

wish, *n.* SYN.-aspiration, craving, desire, hungering, longing, yearning. ANT.-abomination, aversion, distaste, hate, loathing.

wish, *v.* SYN.-covet, crave, desire, hanker, hunger, long, thirst, want, yearn. ANT.-decline, despise, reject, repudiate, scorn.

wit, *n.* SYN.-comprehension, intellect, intelligence, mind, perspicacity, reason, sagacity, sense, understanding; banter, cleverness, fun, humor, irony, pleasantry, raillery, sarcasm, satire, witticism. ANT.-commonplace, platitude, sobriety, solemnity, stupidity.

witchcraft, *n.* SYN.-black art, conjuring, enchantment, legerdemain, magic, necromancy, sorcery, voodoo, wizardry.

withdraw, *v.* SYN.-depart, give up, go, leave, quit, relinquish, renounce, retire, vacate. ANT.-abide, remain, stay, tarry.

wither, *v.* SYN.-decline, droop, dry, fail, languish, sear, shrink, shrivel, sink, waste, weaken, wilt, wizen. ANT.-refresh, rejuvenate, renew, revive.

withhold, *v.* SYN.-abstain, desist, forbear, refrain, restrain. ANT.-continue, indulge, persist.

witness, *n.* SYN.-attestation, confirmation, declaration, evidence, proof, testimony. ANT.-argument, contradiction, disproof, refutation.

witty, *a.* SYN.-amusing, bright, clever, comical, droll, funny, humorous, ingenious, quick, quick-witted, sharp, smart. ANT.-dull, foolish, melancholy, sad, serious, sober, solemn, stupid.

wonder, *n.* SYN.-curiosity, marvel, miracle, phenomenon, prodigy, rarity, spectacle; admiration, amazement, astonishment, awe, bewilderment, curiosity, surprise, wonderment. ANT.-familiarity, triviality; apathy, expectation, indifference.

word, *n.* SYN.-account, assertion, assurance, commitment, declaration, expression, guarantee, name, news, phrase, pledge, promise, report, statement, tidings, utterance.

work, *n.* SYN.-achievement, business, drudgery, effort, employment, labor, occupation, opus, performance, production; task, toil, travail. ANT.-ease, leisure, play, recreation, vacation.

worldly, *a.* SYN.-base, carnal, corporeal, fleshly, gross, lustful, sensual; cultured, discriminating, sophisticated, urbane. ANT.-exalted, spiritual, temperate.

worn, *a.* SYN.-exhausted, fatigued, jaded, spent, tired, wearied; frayed, tattered, threadbare, shabby. ANT.-fresh, hearty, invigorated, rested; new, unused.

worry, *n.* SYN.-anxiety, apprehension, concern, disquiet, fear, misgiving, trouble, uneasiness. ANT.-contentment, equanimity, peace, satisfaction.

worry, *v.* SYN.-annoy, bother, disturb, gall, harass, harry, haze, irritate, pain, persecute, tease, torment, trouble, vex; care, chafe, fidget, fret, fume, fuss. ANT.-comfort, console, solace.

worship, *v.* SYN.-adore, deify, honor, idolize, respect, revere, reverence, venerate. ANT.-blaspheme, curse, despise, loathe, scorn.

worth, *n.* SYN.-excellence, merit, price, usefulness, utility, value, virtue, worthiness. ANT.-cheapness, uselessness, valueless.

worthless, *a.* SYN.-abortive, empty, fruitless, futile, ineffectual, irrelevant, pointless, unavailing, unnecessary, useless, vain, valueless, vapid. ANT.-effective, potent, profitable.

wound, *v.* SYN.-abuse, cut, damage, disfigure, harm, hurt, injure, maim; affront, dishonor, insult, wrong. ANT.-benefit, help, preserve; compliment, praise.

wrap, *v.* SYN.-cloak, clothe, cover, envelop, shield, shroud, veil. ANT.-bare, expose, reveal.

wrath, *n.* SYN.-anger, choler, fury, indignation, ire, passion, rage, resentment, temper. ANT.-conciliation, forbearance, patience, peace, self-control.

wreck, *v.* SYN.-annihilate, demolish, destroy, devastate, eradicate, exterminate, extinguish, obliterate, ravage, raze, ruin. ANT.-construct, establish, make, preserve, save.

wretched, *a.* SYN.-comfortless, disconsolate, distressed, forlorn, heartbroken, miserable, pitiable; abject, beggarly, contemptible, despicable, low, mean, paltry, pitiful, poor, shabby, sorry, vile, worthless. ANT.-contented, fortunate, happy; noble, significant.

writer, *n.* SYN.-author, artist, composer, essayist, reporter.

wrong, *a.* SYN.-amiss, askew, awry, erroneous, fallacious, false, faulty, inaccurate, incorrect, mistaken, imprecise, untrue; improper, inappropriate, unsuitable; aberrant, bad, criminal, evil, immoral, iniquitous, reprehensible. ANT.-correct, right, true; suitable; proper.

Y

yearning, *n.* SYN.-appetite, aspiration, craving, desire, hungering, longing, lust, urge. ANT.-abomination, aversion, distaste, hate, loathing.

yield, *n.* SYN.-crop, fruit, harvest, proceeds, produce, product, profit, reaping, result.

yield, *v.* SYN.-afford, bear, bestow, breed, generate, impart, pay, produce, supply; accord, allow, concede, grant, permit; abdicate, accede, acquiesce, capitulate, cede, quit, relent, relinquish, resign, submit, succumb, surrender, waive.

ANT.-deny, dissent, oppose, refuse; assert, resist, strive, struggle.

yielding, *a.* SYN.-compliant, deferential, dutiful, obedient, submissive, tractable. ANT.-insubordinate, intractable, obstinate, rebellious.

young, *a.* See **youthful**.

youthful, *a.* SYN.-boyish, callow, childish, childlike, girlish, immature, juvenile, puerile, young. ANT.-aged, elderly, mature, old, senile.

Z

zeal, *n.* SYN.-ardor, devotion, earnestness, enthusiasm, excitement, fanaticism, fervency, fervor, intensity, vehemence. ANT.-apathy, detachment, ennui, indifference, unconcern.

zealous, *a.* SYN.-ardent, eager, enthusiastic, fervent, fervid, fiery, impassioned, intense, keen, passionate, vehement. ANT.-apathetic, cool, indifferent, nonchalant.

zenith, *n.* SYN.-acme, apex, climax, consummation, culmination, height, peak, summit. ANT.-anticlimax, base, depth, floor.

zone, *n.* SYN.-belt, climate, locality, region, sector, tract.